# PEARS
## CYCLOPAEDIA
### 1969–70

A BOOK OF BACKGROUND INFORMATION
AND REFERENCE FOR EVERYDAY USE

EDITOR
## L. MARY BARKER
B.Sc.Lond.

*Seventy-eighth edition*

The Editor desires to express her gratitude to readers for their criticisms and suggestions and to all those who in one way or another have contributed to the making of this edition.   Correspondence should be addressed to the Editor at 'Middlemarch', Halstead, Sevenoaks, Kent.

*First published 1897*

S.B.N.  7207 0298 4

*Printed and Bound in Great Britain by Richard Clay (The Chaucer Press), Ltd., Bungay, Suffolk*

© *Pelham Books Ltd. 1969*

# CONTENTS

# INDEX

Some of the sections are alphabetically arranged and index themselves. Their contents are not included here except where it is anticipated some special difficulty in reference may arise. Each section has a letter and, where appropriate, the column is given in brackets after the page number, *e.g.*, F8(1), G26(2). The sections " Greek Myths and Legends ", " Medical Matters " and " The World of Music " have each a separate index and glossary.

# HISTORICAL EVENTS

Chronicle of events from the earliest times to the present day. For events in pre-history the reader may also like to consult the Geological Time Scale in Part IV and the subsection "The Earliest Men and their Dates" in Part V of the Science Section.

# CHRONICLE OF EVENTS

*Note.—For classical history and for the past millennium most dates are well established. For other periods there is sometimes considerable uncertainty. Many of the dates in ancient history are either dubious or approximate, sometimes both.*

B.C. **PREHISTORY**

| | |
|---|---|
| 5,000,000,000 | Age of Earth. |
| 3,300,000,000 | Earliest known rocks (found in Rhodesia and Manitoba). |
| 2,000,000,000 | Life appears. |
| 600,000,000 | First large-scale occurrence of fossils. |
| 30,000,000 | Earliest ape fossils (Oligovene period—Fayum, Egypt). |
| 20,000,000 | Early ape fossils (Miocene period—*Proconsul*, E. Africa). |
| 1,700,000 | Earliest known hominids (Lower Pleistocene—*Australopithecus*, and *Homo habilis* S. Africa, E. Africa.) Oldowan culture—first stage of Palaeolithic or Old Stone Age (hunting and food-gathering) which persisted until end of Ice Age, *c.* 8,000 B.C. |
| 400,000 | *Homo erectus* stage (Java, China, Africa) with crude chopping tools and early hand-axes. Heidelberg jaw, Vertezöllös remains (Europe). |
| 180,000 | Ancestors of Neandertalers and *Homo sapiens*, with advanced hand-axes (Europe: Steinheim and Swanscombe). |
| 70,000 | Neandertalers (Europe, Asia, N. Africa). Rhodesian Man (S. Africa). Solo Man (Java). Flake tools. |
| 40,000 | First cold phase ends. Neandertal race becoming extinct. |
| 30,000 | Second cold phase. *Homo sapiens* (modern man). Implements show significant advances: small knife-blades, engraving tools. Paintings and sculpture; magic rites and ceremonies. Cro-Magnons with Aurignacian culture. |
| 18,000 | Final culmination of last ice age. Aurignacian culture dying out to be replaced by Solutrean and then by the Magdalenian cultures. Great flowering of Palaeolithic art. |
| 15,000 | First immigrants from Asia to cross Behring Straits? |
| 8,000 | Last glaciers in Britain disappeared. Proto-Neolithic in Middle East. Agricultural settlements (*e.g.*, Jericho). Settled way of life leading eventually to such skills as weaving, metallurgy; inventions as ox-drawn plough, wheeled cart. |
| 5,000 | Britain becomes an island (land connection with continent severed by melting ice-sheets). |

B.C. **CIVILISATION IN THE MIDDLE EAST**

| | |
|---|---|
| 4000 | Susa founded. |
| 3500 | Sumerian civilisation flourishes. Cuneiform writing. |
| 3000 | First Egyptian Dynasty. Hieratic writing already perfected. Early Minoan Age (Crete). Pictorial writing, copper, silver, gold in use. Early Mycenean civilisation begins. |
| 2980 | Memphis capital of Egypt. |

B.C.

| | |
|---|---|
| 2870 | First settlements at Troy. |
| 2850 | Golden Age of China begins (legendary). |
| 2700 | Great Pyramid age in Egypt begins. |
| 2400 | Aryan migrations. Sargon founds Agade: Semitic empire. |
| 2205 | Hsia Dynasty begins in China (legendary). |
| 2200 | Middle Minoan Age; pottery, linear writing in pen and ink. |
| 1900 | Bronze Age begins in Britain. Stonehenge (1860–1560 B.C.). |
| 1760 | Shang Dynasty begins in China (dated traditionally 1760–1122 B.C.). |
| 1750 | Aryan invasion of Mesopotamia. |
| 1720 | Hyksos conquest of Egypt. War chariots introduced. |
| 1700 | Code of Hammurabi at Babylon. |
| 1600 | Late Minoan Age: bronze in use. |
| 1550 | Sack of Babylon by Hittites. |
| 1546 | 18th Dynasty in Egypt commences. Civilisation at peak (under Thotmes III, 1490). Chronology more certain. |
| 1500 | Powerful Mitanni (Aryan) kingdom in Asia Minor. Phoenicia thriving—trade with Egypt and Babylonia. Vedic literature in India. |
| 1450 | Zenith of Minoan civilisation. |
| 1400 | Ugarit (N. Syria) culture at its zenith. Cretan civilisation ends: Knossos burnt. Temple at Luxor built. |
| 1377 | Amenhotep IV (Ikhnaton), the "heretic" Pharaoh. |
| 1350 | Zenith of Hittite civilisation. |
| 1300 | Israelite oppression (Rameses II). Phoenician settlements—Hellas and Spain (Cadiz). Tyre flourishing. |
| 1250 | Assyrian conquest in Babylon: dominant in Western Asia. |
| 1230 | Exodus of Israelites from Egypt. |
| 1200 | Attacks on Egypt by "Peoples of the Sea". Downfall of Hittite kingdom. Siege of Troy (Homeric). Beginning of sea-power of independent Phoenician cities. Probably all these are connected with Achaean and other migrations in Aegean area. |
| 1122 | Chou Dynasty begins in China (870 years). |
| 1115 | Magnetic needle reputed in China. |
| 1028 | Establishment of kingship in Israel (Saul). |
| 1000 | Jerusalem capital of Israel. David king. *Rig Veda* (India). |
| 961 | Solomon begins temple at Jerusalem. |
| 900 | Probably period of writing of Homer's epics. |
| 893 | Assyrian chronological records begin. |
| 850 | Foundation of Carthage (traditional). |
| 781 | Chinese record of an eclipse. |
| 776 | First Olympiad to be used for chronological purposes. |
| 753 | Foundation of Rome (traditional). |
| 750 | Greek colonists settling in Southern Italy. |
| 745 | Accession of Tiglath-Pileser III; Assyrian Power at its height. Deportation of subject peoples (Israel 722). |
| 683 | Kingship abolished in Athens. |
| 625 | Neo-Babylonian (Chaldean) Empire (Nineveh destroyed 612). |

B.C.

621   Publication of Athenian laws by Draco.

610   Spartan constitution, made rigid after Messenian Wars: later attributed to Lycurgus.

594   Athenian constitution reformed by Solon.

586   Jerusalem taken by Babylonians. Inhabitants exiled till 538.

561   Pisistratus tyrant of Athens.

560   Accession of Croesus—great prosperity of Lydia.

538   Babylon taken by Persians: Empire founded by Cyrus, soon covers almost all of civilised Middle East.

509   Foundation of Roman Republic (traditional).

508   Democratic constitution proclaimed in Athens.

500   Etruscans at height of their power in Northern Italy. Iron age beginning in Britain.

### GREAT AGE OF GREECE

499   Revolt of Ionian Greek cities against Persian king Darius.

494   Secession of Plebeians from Rome. Tribunes established.

490   Battle of Marathon: Athenian repulse of Persian attack.

480   Death of Buddha. Battle of Thermopylae: Spartans under Leonidas wiped out by Persians. Battle of Salamis: Persian fleet defeated by Athenians under Themistocles; Persian invasion of Greece halted.

479   Battles of Plataea and Mycale: Greek victories by land and sea respectively destroy Persian invasion force. Death of Confucius.

477   League of Delos founded by Athens for defence against Persia; soon becomes Athenian Empire. (467 Naxos kept in by force.)

461   Pericles comes to power in Athens.

458   Cincinnatus saves Rome (traditional).

456   Death of Aeschylus.

447   Building of Parthenon begun.

431   Death of Phidias. Outbreak of Great Peloponnesian War between Athens and Sparta. Pericles "Funeral Oration" (according to Thucydides).

425   Death of Herodotus.

416   Massacre of Melos by Athenians.

415   Sicilian Expedition: flight of Alcibiades from Athens to Sparta.

413   Loss of entire Athenian expeditionary force at Syracuse.

406   Death of Euripides and Sophocles.

405   Battle of Aegospotami: Athenian navy destroyed by Sparta.

404   Athenian surrender to Sparta: beginning of Spartan hegemony in Greece.

403   Beginning of epoch of Warring States in China.

400   Death of Thucydides, Greek historian (?).

399   Execution of Socrates.

390   Occupation of Rome by Gauls under Brennus.

371   Battle of Leuctra: Spartans defeated by Thebans: beginning of Theban hegemony in Greece.

370   Death of Hippocrates of Cos (?).

347   Death of Plato.

338   Battle of Chaeronea: Greek city-states defeated by Philip II of Macedon, who becomes supreme in Greece.

336   Assassination of Philip of Macedon: accession of Alexander.

334   Alexander's invasion of Persian Empire. Battle of Granicus, first victory.

333   Battle of Issus: Alexander defeats Darius of Persia.

332   Alexander's siege and capture of Tyre, occupation of Egypt.

B.C.

331   Battle of Arbela (Gaugamela)—final defeat of Darius.

330   Death of Darius and end of Persian Empire. Alexander heir to civilisations of Middle East.

326   Battle of Hydaspes: Alexander conquers the Punjab.

323   Death of Alexander at Babylon. Beginning of Hellenistic Age in Middle East and Eastern Mediterranean. Ptolemy I founds dynasty in Egypt. Alexandria becomes intellectual centre of Hellenic world.

322   Death of Demosthenes.

321   Death of Aristotle. Maurya dynasty unites N. India.

312   Seleucus I founds dynasty in Asia.

300   Zeno the Stoic, Epicurus and Euclid flourishing.

### ROME: CONQUESTS AND DECAY OF REPUBLICAN INSTITUTIONS

290   End of Third Samnite War. Rome dominates Central Italy.

275   Battle of Beneventum: Rome finally defeats Pyrrhus and the Greek cities of Southern Italy. Rome dominates all Italy.

274   Asoka becomes ruler of two-thirds of Indian sub-continent.

264   Beginning of First Punic War (Rome v. Carthage).

260   Battle of Mylae: first great Roman naval victory.

255   Defeat and capture of Regulus by Carthaginians.

250   "La Tène" Iron Age people invade Britain.

241   End of First Punic War. Sicily becomes first Province of Rome.

221   Kingdom of Ch'in completes conquest of all Chinese states, under Shih Huang Tih.

218   Outbreak of Second Punic War: Hannibal crosses Alps.

216   Battle of Cannae: Hannibal wipes out great Roman army.

214   Great Wall of China constructed (by linking existing walls).

213   Burning of Chinese classics.

212   Capture of Syracuse by Romans and death of Archimedes.

207   Battle of Metaurus: defeat and death of Hasdrubal. End of Hannibal's hopes of overcoming Rome.

205   Roman provinces organised in Spain.

202   Former or Eastern Han Dynasty in China. Battle of Zama: Hannibal defeated by Scipio Africanus.

201   End of Second Punic War. Rome dominates Western Mediterranean.

196   After defeating Macedon, Rome proclaims independence of Greek city-states. Death of Eratosthenes the geographer (?).

160   Death in battle of Judas Maccabaeus: Jewish revolt against Seleucids continues successfully.

149   Outbreak of Third Punic War.

146   Carthage destroyed. Roman province of Africa formed. Roman provinces of Macedonia and Achaea formed, and most of remainder of Greece reduced to vassal status.

134   First Servile War: Revolt of slaves in Sicily under Eunus. Suppressed 132.

133   Siege and destruction of Numantia by Romans. Tiberius Gracchus Tribune. Attempted land reforms. Murdered 132.

129   Roman province of Asia formed from lands bequeathed by Attalus of Pergamum.

124   Chinese Grand College to train Civil Service officials.

123   Caius Gracchus Tribune. Attempted land reforms. Murdered 121.

110   Chinese expansion to include most of south-east of modern China, under Emperor Wu Ti. Commercial activity in Indian Ocean.

**B.C.**

106  Jugurtha captured by Marius and Sulla.

104  Second Servile War: revolt of slaves in Sicily under Tryphon and Athenion. Suppressed 101.

102  Chinese expedition to Ferghana and possible knowledge of West.

101  Battle of Vercellae: Marius ends threat of Cimbri to Rome.

91  Social War: revolt of Italian cities against Rome. Suppressed 88. Roman franchise granted to most Italians.

88  Civil Wars of Marius and Sulla begin.

87  Massacre in Rome by Marius.

82  Proscriptions in Rome by Sulla.

75  Belgic invasion of south-eastern Britain.

73  Third Servile War: revolt of slaves in southern Italy under Spartacus the gladiator. Suppressed 71.

63  Conspiracy of Catiline exposed by Cicero.

60  First Triumvirate: Pompey, Caesar, Crassus.

58  Beginning of Caesar's conquest of Gaul.

55  Caesar's first British expedition: second, 54.

53  Battle of Carrhae: destruction of Roman army under Crassus by Persians.

52  Revolt of Vercingetorix against Caesar.

50  Migration to Britain of Commius and his followers.

49  Caesar crosses the Rubicon. Beginning of war against Pompey and the Senate.

48  Battle of Pharsalus: defeat of Pompey by Caesar.

46  Caesar's calendar reforms.

44  Murder of Caesar.

43  Second Triumvirate: Antony, Octavian, Lepidus.

42  Battle of Philippi: defeat and death of Brutus and his associates.

31  Battle of Actium: naval victory of Octavian over Antony and Cleopatra. Octavian unchallenged master of the Roman world.

**THE ROMAN EMPIRE**

27  Octavian given the title of Augustus by the Senate.

19  Death of Virgil.

8  Death of Horace.

6  Birth of Jesus Christ. (?)

**A.D.**

6  Civil Service Examination system in China.

9  Radical reforms by Emperor Wang Mang. Annihilation of Roman army under Varus by Teutonic tribesmen under Arminius.

10  Cunobelinus reigning over much of south-east Britain from Colchester.

14  Death of Augustus.

17  Death of Livy.

18  Death of Ovid.

25  Beginning of Later or Eastern Han Dynasty in China.

29  Crucifixion of Christ (?).

43  Roman invasion of Britain under Aulus Plautius.

51  Caractacus taken to Rome as prisoner.

60  Revolt of Boudicca.

63  Death of St. Paul.

64  Great Fire of Rome.

65  Death of Seneca.

66  Jews of Palestine rebelled against Roman rule.

68  Death of Nero—end of Julio-Claudian line of Roman Emperors.

70  Jerusalem taken and Jewish revolt suppressed by Titus.

79  Destruction of Pompeii and Herculaneum by eruption of Vesuvius.

**A.D.**

80  Completion of Colosseum (Flavian Amphitheatre).

83  Battle of Mons Graupius: Agricola crushes Caledonians.

96  Accession of Nerva: first of the "Five Good Emperors."

97  Chinese expedition under Kang Yin (lieutenant of Pan Ch'ao) penetrates to Persian Gulf.

117  Death of Trajan, accession of Hadrian. Roman Empire at its greatest extent.

122  Beginning of Hadrian's Wall (Tyne–Solway) by Aulus Platorius Nepos.

135  Suppression of Bar-Cochba's revolt and Dispersion of Jews.

142  Construction of Antonine Wall (Forth–Clyde) by Quintus Lollius Urbicus.

180  Death of Marcus Aurelius, last of the "Five Good Emperors." Beginning of the "Decline" of the Roman Empire (Gibbon).

193  Praetorian guards murder Emperor Pertinax, sell Empire to highest bidder (Didius Julianus).

196  Clodius Albinus, governor, withdraws forces from Britain to support his attempt to become Emperor. Northern Britain overrun by barbarians.

208  Septimius Severus visits Britain to punish Caledonians (death at York 211).

212  Edict of Caracalla. Roman citizenship conferred on all free inhabitants of Empire.

220  End of Han Dynasty: China divided and frequently invaded for next three centuries.

227  Sassanid Empire in Persia.

230  Emperor Sujin—Japanese history emerging from legendary stage.

251  Goths defeat and kill Emperor Decius.

259  Break-away "Gallic Empire" set up: suppressed 273.

273  Defeat of Zenobia and destruction of Palmyra by Emperor Aurelian.

284  Accession of Diocletian, who reorganises Roman Empire (293) with rigid social laws and heavy taxation.

287  Carausius attempts to found independent "Empire of Britain": suppressed 297.

306  Constantine proclaimed Emperor at York.

313  Edict of Milan. Christianity tolerated in Roman Empire.

320  Gupta dynasty reunites India.

325  Council of Nicaea: first general Council of the Church.

367  Successful attack on Britain by Picts, Scots, Saxons.

369  Restoration of Roman authority in Britain by Theodosius.

378  Battle of Adrianople: Goths defeat and kill Eastern Roman Emperor Valens.

383  Magnus Maximus withdraws forces from Britain to support his attempt to conquer north-western part of Empire.

388  Magnus Maximus defeated and killed in Italy.

395  Death of Emperor Theodosius the Great: the division of the Empire into East and West at his death proves eventually to be the final one.

406  Usurper Constantine III withdraws forces from Britain to support his claims: probable end of Roman military occupation of Britain.

410  Sack of Rome by Alaric the Goth. Emperor Honorius tells Britons to arrange for their own defence.

**THE BARBARIAN INVASIONS**

415  Visigoths begin conquest of Spain.

419  Visigothic kingdom of Toulouse recognised by Roman government.

429  Vandals begin conquest of North Africa.

432  St. Patrick begins mission in Ireland.

A.D.

**446** " Groans of the Britons "—last appeal to Rome (traditional).

**451** Châlons: Attila the Hun repelled from Gaul by mixed Roman–Barbarian forces.

**452** Attila's raid into Italy: destruction of Aquilea and foundation of Venice by refugees.

**455** Rome pillaged by Vandals.

**476** Romulus Augustulus, last Western Roman Emperor, deposed by Odovacar: conventionally the end of the Western Roman Empire.

**481** Clovis becomes King of the Franks, who eventually conquer Gaul (d. 511).

**493** Theodoric founds Ostrogothic Kingdom in Italy (d. 526).

**515** Battle of Mount Badon: West Saxon advance halted by Britons, perhaps led by Arthur (?).

### BYZANTIUM AND ISLAM

**527** Accession of Justinian I (d. 565).

**529** Code of Civil Law published by Justinian. Rule of St. Benedict put into practice at Monte Cassino (traditional).

**534** Byzantines under Belisarius reconquer North Africa from Vandals.

**552** Byzantine reconquest of Italy complete.

**563** St. Columba founds mission in Iona.

**568** Lombard Kingdom founded in Italy.

**570** Birth of Mohammed.

**577** Battle of Deorham: West Saxon advance resumed.

**589** Reunion of China under Southern Ch'en dynasty

**590** Gregory the Great becomes Pope.

**597** St. Augustine lands in Kent.

**605** Grand Canal of China constructed.

**618** T'ang Dynasty in China: their administrative system lasts in essentials for 1,300 years.

**622** Hejira or flight from Mecca to Medina of Mohammed: beginning of Mohammedan era.

**627** Battle of Nineveh: Persians crushed by Byzantines under Heraclius.

**632** Death of Mohammed: all Arabia now Moslem. Accession of Abu Bakr, the first Caliph.

**634** Battle of Heavenfield: Oswald becomes king of Northumbria, brings in Celtic Christianity.

**638** Jerusalem captured by Moslems.

**641** Battle of Mehawand: Persia conquered by Moslems.

**643** Alexandria taken by Moslems.

**645** Downfall of Soga clan in Japan, after establishing Buddhism: beginning of period of imitation of Chinese culture.

**650** Slav occupation of Balkans now complete.

**663** Synod of Whitby: Roman Christianity triumphs over Celtic Christianity in England.

**685** Nectansmere: end of Northumbrian dominance in England.

**698** Carthage taken by Moslems.

**711** Tarik leads successful Moslem invasion of Spain.

**718** Failure of second and greatest Moslem attack on Constantinople. Pelayo founds Christian kingdom of Asturias in Northern Spain.

**726** Byzantine Emperor Leo III begins Iconoclast movement: opposed by Pope Gregory II, and an important cause of difference between Roman and Byzantine churches.

### THE HOLY ROMAN EMPIRE AND THE TRIUMPH OF CHRISTIANITY IN EUROPE: NORSEMEN AND NORMANS

**732** Tours: Moslem western advance halted by Charles Martel.

**735** Death of Bede.

**750** Beginning of Abbasid Caliphate (replacing Omayyads).

A.D.

**751** Pepin King of the Franks: founds Carolingian dynasty. Ravenna taken by Lombards: end of Byzantine power in the West.

**754** Pepin promises central Italy to Pope: beginning of temporal power of the Papacy.

**778** Roncesvalles: defeat and death of Roland.

**786** Accession of Haroun-al-Rashid in Baghdad.

**793** Sack of Lindisfarne: Viking attacks on Britain begin.

**795** Death of Offa: end of Mercian dominance in England.

**800** Coronation of Charlemagne as Holy Roman Emperor.

**814** Death of Charlemagne: division of his empire.

**825** Ellandun: Egbert defeats Mercians and Wessex becomes leading kingdom in England.

**827** Moslem invasion of Sicily.

**840** Moslems capture Bari and occupy much of Southern Italy.

**843** Treaty of Verdun: final division of Carolingian Empire, and beginning of France and Germany as separate states.

**844** Kenneth MacAlpin becomes king of Picts as well as Scots: the kingdom of Alban.

**862** Rurik founds Viking state in Russia: first at Novgorod, later at Kiev.

**866** Fujiwara period begins in Japan. Viking " Great Army " in England: Northumbria, East Anglia and Mercia subsequently overwhelmed.

**868** Earliest dated printed book in China.

**872** Harold Fairhair King of Norway.

**874** Iceland settled by Norsemen.

**885-6** Viking attack on Paris.

**893** Simeon founds first Bulgar Empire in Balkans.

**896** Arpad and the Magyars in Hungary.

**899** Death of Alfred the Great.

**900** Ghana at the height of its power in North West Africa.

**910** Abbey of Cluny founded: monastic reforms spread from here.

**911** Rolf (or Rollo) becomes ruler of Normandy.

**912** Accession of Abderrahman III: the most splendid period of the Omayyad Caliphate of Cordova (d. 961).

**923** Brandenburg taken from the Slavs by Henry the Fowler, first of the Saxon Holy Roman Emperors.

**929** Death of Wenceslas, Christian King of Bohemia.

**937** Battle of Brunanburh: crowning victory of Athelstan. West Saxon kings now masters of England.

**955** Battle of Lechfeld: Magyars finally defeated by Otto the Great and settle in Hungary.

**960** Beginning of Sung Dynasty in China.

**965** Harold Bluetooth, king of Denmark, accepts Christianity.

**966** Mieszko I, king of Poland, accepts Christianity.

**968** Fatimids begin their rule in Egypt.

**982** Discovery of Greenland by Norsemen.

**987** Hugh Capet king of France: founder of Capetian dynasty.

**988** Vladimir of Kiev accepts Christianity.

**991** Battle of Maldon: defeat of Byrhtnoth of Essex by Vikings—renewed Viking raids on England.

**993** Olof Skutkonung, king of Sweden, accepts Christianity.

**1000** Leif Ericsson discovers North America.

**1001** Coronation of St. Stephen of Hungary with crown sent by the Pope.

**1002** Massacre of St. Brice's Day: attempt by Ethelred to exterminate Danes in England.

A.D.
1014  Battle of Clontarf: victory of Irish under Brian Boru over Vikings.

1016  Canute becomes king of England; builds short-lived Danish "empire."

1018  Byzantines under Basil II complete subjection of Bulgars.

1040  Attempts to implement Truce of God from about this time.

1046  Normans under Robert Guiscard in southern Italy.

1054  Beginning of Almoravid (Moslem) conquests in West Africa.

1060  Normans invade Sicily.

1066  Norman conquest of England under William I.

1069  Reforms of Wang An-Shih in China.

### THE CRUSADES

1071  Manzikert: Seljuk Turks destroy Byzantine army and overrun Anatolia.

1073  Hildebrand (Gregory VII) becomes Pope. Church discipline and Papal authority enforced.

1075  Seljuk Turks capture Jerusalem.

1076  Kumbi, capital of Ghana, sacked by Almoravids: subsequent break-up of Ghana Empire.

1084  Carthusians founded by St. Bruno at Chartreuse.

1086  Compilation of Domesday Book.

1094  El Cid takes Valencia.

1095  Council of Clermont: Urban II preaches First Crusade.

1098  Cistercians founded by St. Robert at Cîteaux.

1099  First Crusade under Godfrey of Bouillon takes Jerusalem.

1100  Death of William Rufus in the New Forest. Baldwin I: Latin Kingdom of Jerusalem founded.

1106  Tinchebrai: Henry I of England acquires Normandy, captures his brother Robert.

1115  Abelard teaching at Paris. St. Bernard founds monastery at Clairvaux.

1119  Order of Knights Templars founded.

1120  Loss of the White Ship and heir to English throne.

1122  Concordat of Worms: Pope and Emperor compromise on the Investiture Controversy, but continue to quarrel over other matters (Guelfs and Ghibellines).

1135  Stephen takes English crown: civil wars with Matilda and anarchy ensue.

1143  Alfonso Henriques proclaimed first king of Portugal.

1144  Moslems take Christian stronghold of Edessa.

1148  Second Crusade fails to capture Damascus.

1150  Carmelites founded about this time by Berthold.

1152  Accession of Emperor Frederick Barbarossa.

1154  Henry of Anjou succeeds Stephen: first of Plantagenet kings of England.

1161  Explosives used in warfare in China.

1169  Strongbow invades Ireland: beginning of Anglo-Norman rule. Saladin ruling in Egypt.

1170  Murder of Thomas Becket in Canterbury cathedral.

1171  Spanish knightly Order of Santiago founded.

1176  Battle of Legnano: Frederick Barbarossa defeated by the Lombard League. Italian autonomy established.

1185  Kamakura Period in Japan: epoch of feudalism: until 1333.

1187  Hattin: destruction of Latin kingdom of Jerusalem by Saladin.

A.D.
1189  Third Crusade launched: leaders—Frederick Barbarossa, Philip Augustus of France, Richard Lionheart of England.

1191  Capture of Acre by Crusaders.

1192  End of Third Crusade without regaining Jerusalem. Richard I seized and held to ransom in Austria on return journey.

1198  Innocent III becomes Pope.

1202  Fourth Crusade, diverted by Venetians, takes Zara from Byzantines.

1204  Fourth Crusade captures Constantinople, founds Latin Empire. King John of England loses Normandy to France.

1206  Temujin proclaimed Gengiz Khan (Very Mighty King) of all the Mongols: soon controls all of Central Asia.

1208  Albigensian Crusade launched: the first against Christians.

1212  Battle of Las Navas de Tolosa: decisive victory of Spaniards over Moors. The Children's Crusade.

### THE CULMINATION OF THE MIDDLE AGES

1215  Fourth Lateran Council: the authority of the mediaeval Church and Papacy at its zenith. Dominicans recognised by the Pope. Magna Carta extorted by barons from John.

1223  Franciscans recognised by the Pope.

1229  Emperor Frederick II, through diplomacy, recognised by Moslems as King of Jerusalem.

1230  Teutonic Knights established in Prussia.

1237  Golden Horde (Mongols) begin subjugation of Russia.

1241  Mongol incursions into Central Europe.

1250  St. Louis of France captured on his Crusade in Egypt. Mamelukes become rulers of Egypt. Mandingo king declares his independence of Ghana and embraces Islam.

1256  Conference of Baltic ports; the first form of the Hanseatic League.

1258  Provisions of Oxford: barons under Simon de Montfort force reforms on Henry III of England. Baghdad destroyed by Mongols.

1260  Kublai Khan ruling in China.

1264  Battle of Lewes: Montfort's party become rulers of England.

1265  Simon de Montfort's Parliament. Battle of Evesham: defeat and death of de Montfort.

1274  Death of Thomas Aquinas.

1281  Repulse of Mongol attack on Japan.

1282  Sicilian Vespers: rising of Sicilians against French ruler.

1284  Completion of Edward I of England's conquest of Wales.

1290  Expulsion of Jews from England. Death of Maid of Norway: Edward I begins attempts to rule Scotland.

1291  Fall of Acre: end of Crusading in Holy Land. Everlasting League of Uri: beginnings of Swiss Confederation.

1294  Death of Roger Bacon, the founder of experimental science. Death of Kublai Khan: unity of Mongol Empire now only nominal.

1295  " Model Parliament " of Edward I (anticipated in 1275).

1308  Death of Duns Scotus.

### THE DECLINE OF THE MIDDLE AGES

1309  Papacy moves to Avignon: beginning of the Babylonish Captivity.

1312  Suppression of Templars by king of France and Pope.

1314  Battle of Bannockburn: victory of Robert Bruce secures Scottish independence.

1321  Death of Dante.

1325  Zenith of Mandingo Empire of Mali (North West Africa) under Mansa Musa; superseded at end of 15th century by Songhai empire.

1327  Deposition of Edward II; subsequently murdered.

A.D.

**1336** Ashikaga Period in Japan: great feudal lords semi-independent of authority of Shogun.

**1337** Death of Giotto.

**1338** Beginning of Hundred Years' War between England and France.

**1340** Battle of Sluys: English capture French fleet.

**1344** Swabian League: weakness of Imperial authority in Germany obliges towns to form leagues for mutual protection.

**1346** Battles of Crecy and Neville's Cross: spectacular English victories over French and Scots.

**1347** Calais taken by Edward III of England. Cola di Rienzi attempts to reform government of Rome: killed 1354.

**1348** Black Death reaches Europe (England 1349, Scotland 1350).

**1351** Statute of Labourers: attempt by English Parliament to freeze wages.

**1353** Statute of Praemunire: restraints placed on Papal intervention in England.

**1354** Ottoman Turks make first settlement in Europe, at Gallipoli.

**1355** Death of Stephen Dushan: collapse of Serbian Empire which he had built.

**1356** Battle of Poitiers: capture of King John of France by Black Prince. "Golden Bull" regulates Imperial elections in such a way as to place power in the hands of the German princes: valid until 1806.

**1358** The Jacquerie: rising of French peasants.

**1360** Peace of Bretigny: Edward III makes great territorial gains in France.

**1362** English becomes the official language in Parliament and the Law Courts.

**1363** Timur (Tamerlane) begins his career of conquest in Asia.

**1368** Ming Dynasty in China.

**1370** Bertrand du Guesclin Constable of France: regains much territory from the English. Peace of Stralsund: Hansa in complete control of Baltic Sea.

**1377** Pope returns to Rome: End of Babylonish Captivity.

**1378** Disputed Papal Election; Beginning of Great Schism.

**1380** Battle of Chioggia: decisive victory of Venice over Genoa. Battle of Kulikovo: Dmitri Donskoi of Moscow wins first major Russian victory over Golden Horde.

**1381** Peasants' Revolt in England under Wat Tyler.

**1384** Death of John Wyclif.

**1385** Battle of Aljubarotta: Portugal safeguards independence from Castile.

**1386** Battle of Sempach: Swiss safeguard independence from Habsburgs. Jagiello (Vladislav V) unites Lithuania and Poland.

**1389** Battle of Kossovo: crushing defeat of Serbs and neighbouring nations by Turks.

**1396** Battle of Nicopolis: "the last crusade" annihilated by Turks.

**1397** Union of Kalmar: Denmark, Norway and Sweden united under one crown: dissolved 1448.

**1398** Timur invades and pillages Northern India.

**1399** Richard II deposed by Henry IV: first of the Lancastrian kings of England.

**1400** Owen Glendower revolts in Wales. Death of Chaucer.

**1401** De Haeretico Comburendo: the burning of heretics made legal in England.

**1410** Battle of Tannenberg: Poles and Lithuanians break power of Teutonic Knights.

**1415** Battle of Agincourt: great success of Henry V of England in France. Council of Constance ends Great Schism, burns John Hus.

**1420** Treaty of Troyes: English claims to French throne recognised. Hussite Wars begin: Bohemian heretics defend themselves successfully.

A.D.

**1429** Relief of Orleans by Joan of Arc.

**1431** Burning of Joan of Arc.

**1433** Rounding of Cape Bojador: first great achievement in exploration ordered by Henry the Navigator.

**1434** Cosimo dei Medici begins his family's control of Florence.

**1435** Congress of Arras: Burgundians withdraw support from England, in favour of France.

**1438** Albert I becomes Emperor—the first Habsburg Emperor.

**1440** Death of Jan van Eyck.

**1450** Rebellion of Jack Cade against government of Henry VI of England.

**1453** Battle of Castillon: final English defeat and end of Hundred Years' War. Constantinople taken by Turks: end of Byzantine or Eastern Roman Empire.

## RENAISSANCE, DISCOVERIES, "NEW MONARCHIES"

**1454** First dated printing from movable types in Europe: Papal indulgence printed at Mainz.

**1455** First battle of St. Albans: beginning of Wars of the Roses.

**1458** Mathias Corvinus becomes king of Hungary. George of Podiebrad becomes king of Bohemia.

**1461** Battle of Towton: Yorkist victory in a particularly bloody battle. Louis XI becomes king of France.

**1467** Charles the Bold becomes Duke of Burgundy.

**1469** Marriage of Ferdinand of Aragon with Isabella of Castile: union of the main kingdoms of Spain. Lorenzo the Magnificent becomes ruler of Florence.

**1470** Warwick ("The Kingmaker") turns Lancastrian, dethrones Edward IV.

**1471** Return of Edward IV: Lancastrians crushed at Barnet and Tewkesbury. Ivan III of Moscow takes Novgorod: Muscovy rising to supremacy in Russia.

**1476** Caxton sets up his press at Westminster.

**1477** Battle of Nancy: defeat and death of Charles the Bold: end of the greatness of Burgundy.

**1479** Pazzi conspiracy against the Medici in Florence.

**1481** Inquisition becomes active in Castile (1484 in Aragon).

**1485** Battle of Bosworth Field: beginning of Tudor period in England.

**1487** Lambert Simnel's rising fails.

**1488** Bartholomew Diaz rounds Cape of Good Hope.

**1491** Brittany acquired by King of France (by marriage).

**1492** Rodrigo Borgia becomes Pope Alexander VI. Granada, last Moorish foothold in Western Europe, conquered by Spain. Christopher Columbus discovers the West Indies.

**1493** Sonni Ali brings Songhai Empire to height of its prestige: Timbuktu renowned centre of literary culture.

**1494** Italy invaded by French led by Charles VIII: beginning of Italian Wars and "modern" European diplomacy and international relations. Treaty of Tordesillas: Spain and Portugal agree to divide unexplored part of world; subsequently approved by Pope.

**1496** Hapsburg-Spanish marriages: foundation of later empires.

**1497** Perkin Warbeck captured by Henry VII (hanged 1499). John Cabot discovers Newfoundland.

**1498** Savonarola burned. Vasco da Gama at Calicut: the sea route to India found.

**1499** Amerigo Vespucci charts part of the South American coast.

A.D.
1500   Brazil discovered by Pedro Cabral.

1503   Casa de Contratación established at Seville: beginnings of Spanish colonial government. Fall of Caesar Borgia.

1507   Affonso de Albuquerque becomes Viceroy of Portuguese Empire in the East.

1513   Accession of Pope Leo X, zenith of Renaissance Papacy. Machiavelli writes *The Prince*. Balboa discovers the Pacific (South Sea). Battle of Flodden: James IV of Scotland defeated and killed by English.

1514   Battle of Chaldiran: Turkish victory begins long series of wars between Turkish and Persian Empires.


REFORMATION, HAPSBURG-VALOIS WARS

1515   Francis I becomes king of France: victory of Marignano ends legend of Swiss invincibility. Thomas Wolsey becomes Lord Chancellor of England and Cardinal.

1516   Algiers taken by Barbarossa: beginning of the Corsairs.

1517   Martin Luther nails up his Ninety-five Theses: beginning of the Reformation. Turks conquer Egypt.

1519   Charles V inherits Hapsburg lands and elected emperor. Magellan begins first circumnavigation of the world. Death of Leonardo da Vinci.

1520   Suleiman the Magnificent becomes Sultan; Turkish power at its height. Field of Cloth of Gold; celebrated diplomatic meeting, spectacular but with no results.

1521   Mexico conquered by Hernando Cortes. Belgrade taken by the Turks. Diet of Worms: Luther commits himself irrevocably. Charles V divides his dominions: Austrian and Spanish Hapsburgs.

1522   Rhodes taken by the Turks; Knights of St. John move to Malta. Election of Adrian VI, last non-Italian Pope.

1523   Swedes expel Danish overlords, elect Gustavus Vasa King.     (1525).

1524   Peasants' War in Germany (suppressed

1525   Battle of Pavia: defeat and capture of Francis I by Imperialists.

1526   Battle of Mohács: Turkish victory ends Hungarian independence. Foundation of Danubian Hapsburg Monarchy (Hungarian and Bohemian crowns united with Austrian patrimony of Hapsburgs): Holy Roman Empire prolonged for 300 years. Battle of Panipat: Babar begins Moslem conquest of India, founds Mogul Empire.

1527   Sack of Rome by Imperialists. Italy under control of Charles V.

1529   Siege of Vienna by the Turks. Peace of Cambrai; pause in Hapsburg-Valois struggle, end of serious French intervention in Italy. Diet of Speyer: origin of the name Protestant.

1532   Peru conquered by Francisco Pizarro.

1533   Ivan IV (the Terrible) becomes Tsar. Marriage of Henry VIII and Catherine of Aragon declared null.

1534   Act of Supremacy: Henry VIII asserts control over English Church.

1535   Coverdale's English Bible printed. Execution of Thomas More and John Fisher.

1536   Execution of Anne Boleyn. Dissolution of smaller Monasteries by Henry VIII and Thomas Cromwell (remainder dissolved 1539). Pilgrimage of Grace: Northern rising because of religious grievances.     de Quesada.

1538   Chibchas of Bogota conquered by Gonzalo

1540   Francisco de Coronado begins explorations in North America. Society of Jesus recognised by Pope.

1541   John Calvin regains authority in Geneva.

1542   First Portuguese reach Japan. New Laws of the Indies: first attempt to legislate for welfare of colonial natives, by Spanish government.

1543   Death of Copernicus.     [Reformation.

1545   Opening of Council of Trent: the Counter-

A.D.
1547   Death of Henry VIII: Somerset Protector in the name of the boy king, Edward VI.

1549   First English Book of Common Prayer. Kett's Rebellion in Norfolk, because of economic grievances.

1550   Deposition of Protector Somerset: Northumberland rules England.

1553   Lady Jane Grey proclaimed Queen by Northumberland on death of Edward VI: Mary I succeeds. Servetus burned by Calvin.

1555   Latimer and Ridley burned by Mary. Religious Peace of Augsburg: policy of *cuius regio, eius religio* accepted in Germany.

1556   Charles V abdicates imperial powers in favour of brother Ferdinand. Cranmer burned. Akbar becomes Mogul Emperor (d. 1605).

1557   Macao becomes permanent Portuguese port in China.

1558   Calais lost by English to French. Elizabeth I becomes Queen of England.

1559   Peace of Cateau-Cambrésis: end of Hapsburg-Valois duel.


RELIGIOUS WARS

1561   Mary, Queen of Scots, returns to Scotland.

1562   First War of Religion in France: wars continue intermittently until 1598.

1563   Thirty-nine Articles define Elizabethan Church settlement.

1564   Birth of Shakespeare; death of Michelangelo.

1565   Malta beats off Turks.

1567   Deposition of Mary, Queen of Scots. Alva in the Netherlands: severe rule.

1568   Flight of Mary, Queen of Scots, to England: imprisonment. San Juan de Ulua: defeat of Hawkins, and end of his slave-trading voyages. Beginning of Anglo-Spanish maritime feud. Revolt of Moriscos of Granada (suppressed 1570).     England.

1569   Rebellion of Northern Earls (Catholic) in

1570   Elizabeth I anathematised by Pope.

1571   Battle of Lepanto: spectacular defeat of Turkish sea-power by Don John of Austria. Bornu (or Kanem) in Central Sudan at its zenith under Idris III.

1572   Dutch "Sea Beggars" take Brill. Massacre of St. Bartholomew in France. Polish Crown elective again, on death of Sigismund II.

1576   Catholic League formed in France, led by Guise family.     [1580).

1577   Drake begins voyage round world (returns

1578   Battle of Alcazar-Quivir: death of King Sebastian of Portugal. Parma re-establishes Spanish rule in Southern Netherlands.

1579   Union of Utrecht: seven northern provinces of Netherlands form what becomes Dutch Republic. Death of Grand Vizier Sokolli: decline of Turkish power begins.

1580   Philip II of Spain becomes king of Portugal.

1582   Gregorian Calendar (or New Style) introduced by Pope Gregory XIII.

1584   Assassination of William the Silent.

1585   Hidéyoshi Dictator of Japan: unification of the country. English intervention in Spanish-Dutch War.

1587   Execution of Mary, Queen of Scots. Drake " singes King of Spain's beard." Shah Abbas I (the Great) becomes ruler of Persia (d. 1629).

1588   Spanish Armada defeated.

1589   Death of Catherine de' Medici, Queen-Mother of France.

1591   Songhai Empire destroyed by troops from Morocco.

1593   Henry IV of France becomes Catholic.

1598   Edict of Nantes: French Protestants guaranteed liberty of worship. End of French Wars of Religion.

1600   English East India Company founded. Tokugawa Period begins in Japan (Ieyasu takes title of Shogun, 1603): lasts until 1868.

A.D.

**1601** Rebellion and execution of Earl of Essex. Elizabethan Poor Law.

**1602** Dutch East India Company founded.

**1603** Irish revolts finally suppressed by Mountjoy. Accession of James VI of Scotland as James I of England: Union of English and Scottish Crowns.

**1604** Hampton Court Conference: James I disappoints Puritans.

**1605** Gunpowder Plot.

**1607** Virginia colonised by London company: Jamestown founded.

**1608** Quebec founded by Champlain.

**1609** Twelve Years' Truce between Spain and United Provinces: Dutch independence in fact secured. Expulsion of Moriscos from Spain.

**1610** Assassination of Henry IV of France.

**1611** Plantation of Ulster with English and Scottish colonists. Authorised Version of the Bible in England.

**1613** Michael Romanov becomes Czar: the first of the dynasty.

**1614** Napier publishes his explanation of logarithms.

**1616** Death of Shakespeare and Cervantes. Edict of Inquisition against Galileo's astronomy.

**1618** "Defenestration of Prague": Bohemian assertion of independence begins Thirty Years' War.

**1620** Pilgrim Fathers settle in New England.

**1624** "Massacre of Amboina": English driven out of spice islands by Dutch. Richelieu becomes Chief Minister in France.

**1628** Murder of Duke of Buckingham. Petition of Right by Commons to Charles I. Fall of La Rochelle: French Protestants lose political power. Harvey publishes his work on the circulation of blood.

**1629** Charles I begins Personal Rule.

**1630** Gustavus Adolphus of Sweden enters Thirty Years' War, turns tide against Imperialists.

**1631** Sack of Magdeburg, one of the worst incidents of the Thirty Years' War.

**1632** Battle of Lützen: death of Gustavus Adolphus.

**1633** William Laud appointed Archbishop of Canterbury. Thomas Wentworth takes up his post as Lord Deputy of Ireland.

**1634** Dismissal and murder of Imperialist general Wallenstein.

**1635** John Hampden refuses to pay Ship Money.

**1636** Japanese forbidden to go abroad.

**1637** Russian pioneers reach shores of Pacific.

**1638** Covenant widely signed in Scotland.

**1639** First Bishops' War: Charles I comes to terms with Scots.

**1640** Second Bishops' War: Charles I defeated by Scots. Long Parliament begins: abolition of Royal prerogatives. Great Elector (Frederick William) becomes ruler of Brandenburg. Revolt of Catalonia (finally suppressed 1659). Revolt of Portugal: Duke of Braganza proclaimed king.

**1641** Japanese exclude all foreigners (except for small Dutch trading fleet). Massacre of Protestants in Ireland. Wentworth (Earl of Strafford) executed. Grand Remonstrance of Commons to Charles I.

**1642** Charles I attempts to arrest the Five Members. Outbreak of English Civil War: first general engagement, Edgehill. Death of Richelieu.

**1643** Mazarin becomes Chief Minister of France. Battle of Rocroi: French victory, end of Spanish reputation for invincibility. English Parliament agrees to Solemn League and Covenant, secures services of Scots army.

**1644** Marston Moor: decisive battle of English Civil War. North lost to Charles I. Tippemuir: Montrose begins victorious Royalist

A.D.

campaign in Scotland. Ch'ing Dynasty (Manchu) in China.

**1645** Formation of New Model Army. Naseby: main Royalist army crushed. Battle of Philiphaugh: Montrose's army destroyed.

**1646** Charles I surrenders to Scots.

**1647** Charles I handed over to Parliament. Charles I seized by Army. Charles I flees to Carisbrooke Castle.

**1648** Second Civil War: New Model Army defeats Scots and Royalists. "Pride's Purge": Parliament refashioned by Army. Peace of Westphalia ends Thirty Years' War.

## ASCENDANCY OF FRANCE

**1649** Charles I executed. England governed as Commonwealth. Cromwell in Ireland. New Code of Laws in Russia completes establishment of serfdom.

**1651** Battle of Worcester: Cromwell's final victory, now master of all Britain. First English Navigation Act. Hobbes' *Leviathan* published.

**1652** Foundation of Cape Colony by Dutch under Van Riebeek. First Anglo-Dutch War begins (ends 1654).

**1653** Cromwell dissolves Rump, becomes Protector.

**1655** Major-Generals appointed to supervise districts of England. Jamaica seized by English.

**1656** Grand Vizier Kiuprili: revival of Turkish government.

**1658** Death of Cromwell.

**1659** Peace of the Pyrenees: France replaces Spain as greatest power in Western Europe.

**1660** Restoration of monarchy in Britain: Charles II. Royal Society founded.

**1661** Death of Mazarin: Louis XIV now rules in person. "Clarendon Code": beginning of persecution of Non-conformists in England.

**1664** New York taken by English: Second Anglo-Dutch War ensues (ends 1667).

**1665** Great Plague of London.

**1666** Great Fire of London. Newton's discovery of law of gravitation.

**1667** Dutch fleet in the Medway. War of Devolution begins: first of Louis XIV's aggressions.

**1668** Portuguese Independence recognised by Spain.

**1669** Death of Rembrandt.

**1670** Secret Treaty of Dover between Charles II and Louis XIV. Revolt of peasants and Don Cossacks under Stenka Razin (suppressed 1671).

**1672** Third Anglo-Dutch War begins (ends 1674). Murder of De Witt brothers: William of Orange becomes leader of Dutch against French invasion.

**1673** Test Act deprives English Catholics and Non-conformists of public offices. Death of Molière.

**1675** Battle of Fehrbellin: Swedes defeated by Great Elector: rise of Prussian military power.

**1678** "Popish Plot" of Titus Oates utilised by Shaftesbury and the Whigs to bring pressure on Charles II.

**1679** Bothwell Brig: suppression of Scottish Covenanters. Habeas Corpus Act passed.

**1680** Chambers of Reunion: Louis XIV uses legal arguments to complete annexation of Alsace.

**1681** Oxford Parliament: Charles II overcomes his opponents, begins to rule without Parliament.

**1683** Rye House Plot. Siege of Vienna by the Turks: last major Turkish attack on Europe.

**1685** Sedgemoor: Monmouth's rebellion crushed by James II. Revocation of Edict of Nantes: persecution of French Protestants by Louis XIV.

A.D.
**1675** Greenwich Royal Observatory founded.

**1688** Seven Bishops protest against James II's policy of toleration, and are acquitted. William of Orange lands in England: flight of James II. "The Glorious Revolution."

**1689** Derry relieved: failure of James II to subdue Irish Protestants. Killiecrankie: death of Dundee and collapse of Highland rising. Bill of Rights defines liberties established by "Glorious Revolution."

**1690** Locke's *Two Treatises on Government* published. Beachy Head: French victory over Anglo-Dutch fleet. Boyne: defeat of James II by William III.

**1691** Capitulation of Limerick: surrender of Irish supporters of James II on conditions which are not fulfilled.

**1692** Massacre of Glencoe: Government's "lesson" to Highlanders. La Hogue: Anglo-Dutch fleet regains command of the sea.

**1693** National Debt of England begun.

**1694** Bank of England founded.

**1695** Press licensing abandoned: freedom of the press in England.

**1696** Peter the Great sole Czar.

**1697** Peace of Ryswyck between Louis XIV and William III. Peter journeys "incognito" to the West.

**1699** Treaty of Karlowitz: great Turkish concessions to Austrians. Death of Racine.

**1700** Great Northern War, involving all Baltic powers, begins (ends 1721). Battle of Narva: Russians defeated by Charles XII of Sweden. Death of Charles II of Spain: under French influence Louis XIV's grandson Philip of Anjou named successor.

**1701** War of the Spanish Succession begins. Hungarian revolt led by Francis Rakoczi against Austrians. Elector of Brandenburg receives title of King of Prussia. Act of Settlement establishes Protestant Hanoverian Succession in England.

**1703** Methuen Treaty between England and Portugal. St. Petersburg founded.

**1704** Gibraltar taken by Rooke. Blenheim: Marlborough stops France from winning war.

**1706** Ramillies: Marlborough's second great victory. Turin: Eugene defeats French in Italy.

**1707** Almanza: Anglo-Austrian forces in Spain defeated by French under Berwick. Act of Union: English and Scottish Parliaments united. Death of Aurungzib, last powerful Mogul.

**1708** Oudenarde: Marlborough's third great victory.

**1709** Pultava: Charles XII's invasion of Russia smashed by Peter the Great. Malplaquet: Marlborough's fourth great victory—at great cost in lives.

**1710** Tory government in England.

**1711** Dismissal of Marlborough.

**1713** Peace of Utrecht: England makes advantageous peace with Louis XIV. Bourbon king of Spain grants Asiento (monopoly of Spanish American slave trade) to England.

**1714** Peace of Rastatt between France and Austria. Death of Queen Anne: accession of George I. Beginning of Hanoverian Dynasty in Britain. Whig oligarchy rules.

**1715** Jacobite Rising defeated at Preston and Sheriffmuir. Death of Louis XIV. France under Regent Orleans.

**ENLIGHTENED DESPOTS: FIRST BRITISH EMPIRE**

**1716** Septennial Act: English Parliament prolongs its life from three to seven years.

**1717** Belgrade taken by Austrians under Eugene.

**1720** Collapse of Law's system of banking ("Mississippi Bubble") in France. "South Sea Bubble" in England.

A.D.
**1721** Robert Walpole becomes first Prime Minister. Peace of Nystad: Sweden no longer a major power at end of Great Northern War. Russian gains.

**1723** Death of Christopher Wren.

**1727** First Indemnity Act for Non-conformists.

**1729** Methodists begin at Oxford.

**1730** Resignation from government of Townshend, who becomes agricultural pioneer.

**1733** First Family Compact between Bourbon kings of France and Spain. Withdrawal of Walpole's Excise Bill. John Kay invents flying shuttle, first of the great textile inventions. Jethro Tell publishes *The Horse-Hoing Husbandry*, advocating new agricultural methods.

**1738** Lorraine ceded to France.

**1739** Nadir Shah with Persian army sacks Delhi, ruins Mogul power. War of Jenkins' Ear begins between Spain and Britain.

**1740** Frederick II (the Great) becomes king of Prussia. Maria Theresa succeeds to Austrian dominions. Frederick siezes Silesia, begins War of the Austrian Succession.

**1742** Fall of Walpole.

**1743** Dettingen: George II, last British king to command his army in the field, defeats French.

**1745** Fontenoy: Duke of Cumberland defeated by Marshal Saxe. Jacobite Rebellion under Prince Charles Edward: initial success, victory of Prestonpans, march to Derby.

**1746** Culloden: Jacobites destroyed by Cumberland.

**1748** Treaty of Aix-la-Chapelle: Frederick retains Silesia, elsewhere status quo.

**1750** Death of J. S. Bach.

**1751** First volume of the *Encyclopédie* published in France. Clive takes and holds Arcot: checks plans of Dupleix in Southern India. Chinese conquest of Tibet.

**1752** Britain adopts New Style calendar.

**1753** British Museum begun by government purchase of Sloane's collection.

**1755** Lisbon earthquake. Braddock's defeat and death at the hands of French and Indians.

**1756** Diplomatic Revolution (alliance of Austria with France) achieved by Kaunitz; Britain and Prussia perforce became allies. Seven Years' War begins. Minorca taken from British by French (Byng executed 1757). Black Hole of Calcutta: suffocation of many British prisoners.

**1757** Pitt Secretary of State, main influence in British government. Rossbach: one of Frederick II's numerous victories against heavy odds. Plassey: Clive conquers Bengal.

**1759** "Year of Victories" for Britain: Quebec, Minden, Lagos, Quiberon Bay. James Brindley designs Worsley-Manchester Canal: the beginning of this form of transport in Britain. Voltaire publishes *Candide*. Death of Handel.

**1760** Wandewash: decisive defeat of French in India, by Coote.

**1761** Panipat: Mahrattas heavily defeated by Afghans. Fall of Pitt.

**1762** Catherine II (the Great) becomes Czarina. Rousseau's *Social Contract* and *Émile* published.

**1763** Peace of Paris: British colonial gains, First British Empire at its height. Peace of Hubertusburg: Frederick II retains his gains. Pontiac's Conspiracy: failure of Red Indian attempt to destroy British power.

**1764** John Wilkes expelled from Commons. James Hargreaves invents spinning jenny.

**1766** Henry Cavendish proves hydrogen to be an element.

**1768** Royal Academy of Arts founded.

**1769** Richard Arkwright erects spinning mill (invention of water frame).

**1770** Struensee comes to power in Denmark (executed 1772). "Boston Massacre." James Cook discovers New South Wales.

**1772** First Partition of Poland between Russia, Prussia, and Austria.

A.D.

**1773** Society of Jesus suppressed by Pope (restored 1814). Revolt led by Pugachov in Russia (suppressed 1775). " Boston Tea Party."

**1774** Warren Hastings appointed first Governor-General of India. Treaty of Kutchuk Kainarji: great Turkish concessions to Russia. Karl Scheele discovers chlorine. Joseph Priestley's discovery of oxygen.

**1775** Watt and Boulton in partnership at Soho Engineering Works, Birmingham. Lexington: first action in American War of Independence.

**1776** American Declaration of Independence. Adam Smith's *Wealth of Nations* published.

**1777** Saratoga: surrender of British army under Burgoyne to Americans.

**1779** Beginning of great Franco-Spanish siege of Gibraltar (raised finally, 1783). Samuel Crompton invents spinning mule.

**1780** Joseph II assumes sole power in Austria. Armed neutrality of maritime nations to restrain British interference with shipping.

**1781** Joseph II introduces religious toleration, abolishes serfdom in Austria. Yorktown: surrender of British under Cornwallis to American and French forces.

**1782** Battle of the Saints: Rodney's victory saves British West Indies.

**1783** Treaty of Versailles: American independence recognised. Pitt the Younger becomes Prime Minister of Britain. First flights in hot-air (Montgolfier) and hydrogen (Charles) balloons.

**1784** Death of Dr. Samuel Johnson.

**1785** Edmund Cartwright invents the power loom.

**1787** American Constitution drafted.

**1788** Impeachment of Warren Hastings begins (ends 1795).

## FRENCH REVOLUTION AND NAPOLEON

**1789** Washington first President of U.S.A. French Revolution begins. Storming of the Bastille (July 14).

**1790** Civil constitution of the Clergy in France.

**1791** Flight of Louis XVI and Marie Antoinette to Varennes.

**1792** Battle of Valmy: French Revolution saved from intervention of European kings. Denmark becomes first country to prohibit slave trade. France becomes a Republic.

**1793** Louis XVI beheaded. Second partition of Poland.

**1794** " Glorious First of June." Fall of Robespierre and end of Jacobin Republic. Negro revolt in Haiti led by Toussaint L'Ouverture.

**1795** The Directory established. " Whiff of Grapeshot": Napoleon Bonaparte disperses Paris mob, Oct. 5. Batavian Republic set up by France.

**1796** First Italian campaign of Bonaparte: victories of Lodi, Arcola.

**1797** Treaty of Campo Formio: Bonaparte compels Austria to make peace. Britain left to fight France alone.

**1798** Bonaparte goes to Egypt. Battle of the Nile. Vinegar Hill rebellion in Ireland suppressed.

**1799** New coalition against France: Suvorov and Russians victorious in Italy. Bonaparte returns to France. *Coup d'état* of Brumaire, Nov. 9. Consulate set up.

**1800** Parliamentary Union of Great Britain and Ireland.

**1801** Treaty of Lunéville: Austria makes peace; great French gains in Germany.

**1802** Peace of Amiens between Britain and France. *Charlotte Dundas*, first practical steamship, on Clyde.

**1803** Insurrection in Ireland under Robert Emmet. Britain again at war with France.

A.D.

**1804** Bonaparte becomes Emperor. Spain declares war against Great Britain. Serbian revolt against Turks under Kara George.

**1805** Battle of Trafalgar, Nelson's great victory and death, Oct. 21. Battle of Austerlitz, Dec. 2.

**1806** Death of Pitt, Jan. 23. Confederation of the Rhine: Napoleon's reorganisation of Germany, July 12. End of Holy Roman Empire, Aug. 6. Prussia overthrown at Jena. Napoleon declares Great Britain in a state of blockade—" Continental System."

**1807** Slave trade abolished in British Empire. Treaty of Tilsit: with Alexander of Russia his friend, Napoleon controls all of Europe. Occupation of Portugal by French, to enforce Continental Blockade.

**1808** Occupation of Spain by French. Spanish rising: guerrilla warfare. Peninsular War begins. Battle of Vimeiro (defeat of French by Wellington), Aug. 21.

**1809** Battle of Corunna and death of Sir John Moore, Jan. 16. Attempted risings in Germany against Napoleon: Austria renews war. Treaty of Schönbrunn, Oct. 14.

**1810** Self-government established in Argentina: first South American state to become independent of Spain.

**1811** Massacre of Mamelukes at Cairo. Luddite riots.

**1812** Retreat from Moscow: destruction of Napoleon's Grand Army.

**1813** War of Liberation starts in Germany. Defeat of French by Wellington at Vitoria, June 21.

**1814** Soult defeated by Wellington at Toulouse, April 10. Abdication of Napoleon, April 11; Louis XVIII king of France. Congress of Vienna (concluded June 1815) under guidance of Metternich. Resettlement of Europe, usually by restoration of kings. Germanic Confederation under Austrian supervision. Poland ruled by Czar. Kingdom of Netherlands to include Belgium.

## THE OLD ORDER RESTORED

**1815** Escape of Napoleon from Elba. Battle of Waterloo, June 18. Corn Law in Britain to safeguard agricultural interests by keeping up prices. Quadruple Alliance (Austria, Russia, Prussia, Britain) to maintain Vienna settlement and hold regular meetings (" Congress System ") —frequently confused with Holy Alliance, which was simply a declaration of Christian principles. Napoleon sent to St. Helena, Oct. 16.

**1818** Bernadotte made king of Sweden (Charles XIV), Feb. 6.

**1819** Singapore founded by Stamford Raffles. Beginnings of Zollverein (Customs Union) in Germany under Prussian influence. Parliamentary reform meeting at Manchester dispersed by military (" Peterloo "), Aug. 16.

**1820** Death of George III, Jan. 29.

**1821** Death of Napoleon at St. Helena, May 5.

**1822** Congress of Verona: congress system breaks down with refusal of Britain (Canning) to intervene against revolutions.

**1823** " Monroe Doctrine " announced by U.S.A. President, Dec. 2.

**1824** Repeal of Combination Acts in Britain which had forbidden Trades Unions. Charles X king of France.

**1825** Independence of all Spanish American mainland now achieved. Nicholas I Czar of Russia. First railway, Stockton to Darlington, opened.

**1826** First crossing of Atlantic under steam by Dutch ship *Curaçao*. Menai suspension bridge opened.

**1827** Battle of Navarino, Turkish and Egyptian fleet destroyed. Death of Beethoven.

**1828** Death of Chaka, great Zulu conqueror.

**1829** Greece independent. Catholic Emancipation Act in Britain. Metropolitan Police established.

A.D.

**1830** Death of George IV, June 26. Louis Philippe ousts Charles X. Belgium breaks away from Holland. Russian Poland revolts ineffectually.

**1831** First Reform Bill introduced by Lord John Russell. Leopold of Saxe-Coburg becomes king of independent Belgium. British Association founded. Faraday discovers electromagnetic induction.

**1832** Reform Bill passed, June 7. Walter Scott, Jeremy Bentham, and Goethe die. Electric telegraph invented by Morse.

**1833** Beginning of " Oxford Movement " in English Church. First government grant made to English schools. First British Factory Act.

**1834** Poor Law Amendment Act: tightening up of relief in Britain. "Tolpuddle Martyrs " victimised to discourage British working-class movement. Carlist wars begin in Spain.

**1835** Municipal Reform Act revises British local government. The word "socialism " first used. " Tamworth Manifesto " of Peel defines aims of Conservative Party.

**1836** People's Charter states programme of Chartists. Great Trek of Boers from British South African territory. Texas achieves independence of Mexico.

**1837** Queen Victoria succeeds to the throne.

**1838** National Gallery opened.

**1839** First Afghan war begins. Chartist riots at Birmingham and Newport. Anti-Corn Law League founded. Aden annexed by Britain.

**1840** Penny postage instituted. Queen Victoria marries Prince Albert of Saxe-Coburg-Gotha. " Opium War " with China begins. Union Act gives Canada responsible government. Last convicts landed in New South Wales.

**1841** Hong Kong acquired by Britain.

**1842** Chartists present second national petition and put themselves at the head of strikes.

**1846** Repeal of the Corn Laws. Peel resigns.

**1847** British Museum opened.

## REVOLUTIONS AND NEW NATIONS

**1848** Monster meeting of Chartists on Kennington Common, procession abandoned, Apr. 10. General revolutionary movement throughout the Continent. Louis Philippe abdicates: French Republic proclaimed. Swiss Federal Constitution established after defeat of Sonderbund (Catholic secession movement). Rising in Vienna: flight of Metternich, accession of Francis Joseph. Nationalist risings in Bohemia and Hungary. Frankfurt Parliament: attempt to unite Germany on liberal principles. Communist Manifesto produced by Marx and Engels. U.S.A. makes great territorial gains from Mexico. Gold discovered in California.

**1849** Collapse of revolutionary movements. Rome republic besieged by French (June 3), defended by Garibaldi, holds out until July 2. Austrians take Venice, Aug. 22. Repeal of old Navigation Laws. Punjab annexed by Britain.

**1850** Cavour becomes Prime Minister of Piedmont. Don Pacifico affair; privileges of British citizenship at their highest defended by Palmerston.

**1851** Great Exhibition in Hyde Park. First satisfactory submarine telegraph cable between Dover and Calais laid. Gold discovered in Australia.

**1852** Independence of Transvaal recognised by Britain. Napoleon III Emperor of the French.

**1853** Perry lands in Japan: beginning of Western influence. Russia and Turkey at war.

**1854** War declared against Russia by France and Britain. Allied armies land in Crimea, Sept. 14 (Alma, Siege of Sevastopol, Balaklava, Inkerman). Orange Free State set up.

**1855** Sardinia joins Britain and France against Russia. Fall of Sevastopol and end of Crimean War. Alexander II Czar of Russia.

A.D.

**1856** Peace Treaty signed at Paris. Bessemer invents process for large-scale production of steel. Livingstone completes journey across Africa.

**1857** Indian Mutiny. Relief of Lucknow. Canton captured by English and French.

**1858** *Great Eastern* launched. Crown assumes government of India. Treaty of Aigun, by which China cedes Amur region to Russia.

**1859** Darwin publishes *Origin of Species*. French support for Piedmont in war with Austria (Magenta, Solferino). Piedmont receives Lombardy. Harper's Ferry raid: John Brown hanged, Dec. 2.

**1860** Garibaldi and the Thousand Redshirts in Sicily and Naples; most of Italy united to Piedmont. Vladivostok founded; Russia strongly established on N.W. Pacific.

**1861** Abraham Lincoln takes office as Pres. of U.S. American Civil War commences with 11 states breaking away to form Southern Confederacy. Bull Run (July 21) Confederate success ends Federal hopes of easy victory. Victor Emmanuel proclaimed by first Italian Parliament as king of Italy. Emancipation of Serfs in Russia. Death of Prince Albert, Dec. 14.

**1862** Bismarck becomes leading minister in Prussia. Garibaldi attempts to seize Rome but wounded at Aspromonte, Aug. 29. Cotton famine in Lancashire.

**1863** Polish rising against Russia (suppressed 1864). French in Mexico. Battle of Gettysburg, July 1–3. Maximilian of Austria made emperor of Mexico.

**1864** Cession of Schleswig-Holstein to Prussia and Austria. First Socialist International formed. Taiping rebellion in China ended. Federal army enters Atlanta, Sept. 2: General Sherman captures Savannah (" From Atlanta to the sea "), Dec. 22. Geneva Convention originated.

**1865** Death of Cobden, Apr. 2. General Lee surrenders to Grant, Apr. 9. Lincoln assassinated, Apr. 14. Thirteenth Amendment to Constitution: slavery abolished in U.S. Death of Palmerston, Oct. 18. Lister introduces antiseptic surgery in Glasgow. Tashkent becomes centre of Russian expansion in Central Asia. Mendel experiments on heredity. William Booth founds Salvation Army.

**1866** Austro-Prussian War over Schleswig-Holstein (" Seven Weeks War "). Prussian victory at Sadowa (July 3). Venice secured for Italy, who had, however, been defeated by Austrians at Custozza (June 24) and Lissa (July 20). Treaty of Prague, Aug. 23.

**1867** North German Confederation founded. Emperor Maximilian of Mexico shot. Dominion of Canada established. Russia sells Alaska to America for $7 million. Garibaldi makes second attempt to seize Rome, but defeated by Pope with French support at Mentana, Nov. 3. Second Parliamentary Reform Bill passed (Disraeli " dished the Whigs ").

**1868** Shogunate abolished in Japan: Meiji period of rapid Westernisation under Imperial leadership begins. Ten Years' War (1868–78): struggle for Cuban independence from Spain. Disraeli succeeds Derby as Prime Minister but defeated in general election by Gladstone, Nov.

**1869** General Grant, Pres. of U.S. Irish Church disestablished. Suez Canal formally opened.

**1870** Napoleon III declares war against Prussia. French defeated at Woerth, Gravelotte, and Sedan. Paris besieged. Rome and Papal states annexed to kingdom of Italy. Irish Land Act passed. Forster's Education Act puts elementary education within reach of all British children. Papal Infallibility announced.

**1871** William I of Prussia proclaimed emperor of Germany at Versailles, Jan. 18. Paris capitulates, Jan. 28. Commune of Paris proclaimed, Mar. 28. Peace signed at Frankfurt-on-Main, May 10. Government troops enter Paris and

A.D.

crush Communards, May 28. Thiers President of the Republic, Aug. 31. Mont Cenis tunnel opened. Trade Unions in Britain legalised.

## RIVAL IMPERIAL POWERS

**1872** Ballot introduced in Britain. Death of Mazzini, Mar. 10.

**1873** Death of Livingstone, May 4. Ashanti war.

**1874** Disraeli succeeds Gladstone as Prime Minister.

**1875** England purchases Khedive's shares in Suez Canal, Nov.

**1876** Bulgarian massacres. Serbo-Turkish war. Bell invents the telephone. Custer defeated and killed in last large-scale Red Indian success. Porfirio Diaz in power in Mexico (until 1911).

**1877** Victoria declared Empress of India. Transvaal annexed to British Empire. War between Russia and Turkey. Satsuma rebellion in Japan: final unsuccessful attempt to halt new ideas.

**1878** Congress of Berlin: general Balkan settlement. Cyprus ceded to Britain. Second war with Afghanistan (ended 1880). Edison and Swan produce first successful incandescent electric light.

**1879** Dual control (Britain and France) in Egypt. Zulu War. Gladstone's Midlothian Campaign. Tay Bridge destroyed, Dec. 28.

**1880** Beaconsfield ministry succeeded by second Gladstone ministry. Transvaal declared a republic.

**1881** British defeat at Majuba: independence of Transvaal recognised. France occupies Tunis. Gambetta becomes Prime Minister of France. Revolt of the Mahdi in the Sudan. Pasteur's famous immunisation experiment to show that inoculated animals can survive anthrax.

**1882** Lord Frederick Cavendish, Irish Secretary, assassinated in Phoenix Park, Dublin, May 6. Triple Alliance (Germany, Austria, Italy) first formed. Alexandria bombarded, July 11. Cairo occupied by British troops, Sept. 14.

**1883** National Insurance begun in Germany. Death of Wagner.

**1884** Wolseley heads expedition to Khartoum to rescue Gordon. French establish complete protectorate in Indo-China. Evelyn Baring takes over administration of Egypt. Russians capture Merv. Berlin Conference defines rights of European Powers in Africa. Third Parliamentary Reform Bill. Parsons invents his turbine. Greenwich meridian internationally recognised as prime meridian. Fabian Society founded.

**1885** Khartoum captured; Gordon slain, Jan. 26.

**1886** Upper Burma annexed by Britain. Home Rule Bill defeated in Commons. All Indians in U.S.A. now in Reservations. Daimler produces his first motor car. Completion of Canadian Pacific Railway. Gold discovered in the Transvaal.

**1887** Queen Victoria's Jubilee celebration, June 21.

**1888** William II German Emperor. County Councils set up in Britain.

**1889** Mayerling: tragic death of Prince Rudolf of Austria, Jan. 30. Flight of General Boulanger, after attempting to become master of France. Second Socialist International set up. Great London dock strike, Aug. 15–Sept. 16. Parnell Commission concludes sittings, Nov. 23 (129th day).

**1890** Parnell ruined by divorce case: Irish politicians split. Sherman Anti-Trust Law: first attempt in U.S.A. to break cartels. Opening of Forth Bridge, Mar. 4. Bismarck resigns, Mar. 17. Caprivi succeeds. Heligoland ceded to Germany.

**1891** The United States of Brazil formed.

**1892** Panama Canal financial scandals in France.

**1893** Home Rule Bill passes third reading in Commons, Sept. 1: Lords reject Bill, Sept. 8.

**1894** Opening of Manchester Ship Canal, Jan. 1.

A.D.

Gladstone resigns, Mar. 3, Lord Rosebery succeeds. Armenian massacres by Turks: repeated at intervals for next quarter of century. Japan declares war against China. Dreyfus convicted of treason.

**1895** Opening of Kiel canal, June 21. Rosebery resigns, June 22; Salisbury Ministry succeeds. Treaty of Shimonoseki: Japan gets Formosa, free hand in Korea. New Cuban revolution breaks out against Spanish. Marconi sends message over a mile by wireless. Röntgen discovers X-rays. Freud publishes his first work on psycho-analysis. Jameson Raid, Dec. 29.

**1896** Jameson raiders defeated by Boers, Jan. 1. Adowa: Italian disaster at hands of Abyssinians, the first major defeat of a white colonising power by " natives."

**1897** Cretan revolt leads to Greek–Turkish War. Hawaii annexed by U.S.A. Queen Victoria's Diamond Jubilee, June 22.

**1898** Port Arthur ceded to Russia. Spanish–American War. *Maine*, U.S. warship, blown up in Havana harbour. Treaty of Paris, Dec. 10: Cuba freed, Puerto Rico and Guam ceded to U.S.A., Philippines surrendered for $20 million. Death of Gladstone, May 19. Battle of Omdurman, decisive defeat of Mahdists, Sept. 2. Empress of Austria assassinated, Sept. 10. The Curies discover Radium.

**1899** Boer War begins, Oct. 10. Gold discovered in the Klondike.

**1900** Boers attack Ladysmith, Jan. 6. Battle of Spion Kop, Buller repulsed with severe losses, Jan. 24. Relief of Kimberley, Feb. 15. Ladysmith relieved, Feb. 28. Mafeking relieved May 17. Boxer outbreak in China, May. Annexation of Orange Free State, May 26. Roberts occupies Johannesburg, May 31. " Khaki Election." Annexation of the Transvaal, Oct. 25. Australian Commonwealth proclaimed, Dec. 30.

**1901** Queen Victoria dies, Jan. 22. Trans-Siberian Railway opened for single-track traffic.

**1902** Anglo-Japanese Alliance, Jan. 30. Death of Cecil Rhodes, Mar. 26. Treaty of Vereeniging ends Boer War, May 31.

**1903** Congo scandal: celebrated case of misrule and exploitation. Royal family of Serbia assassinated, June 11. First controlled flight in heavier-than-air machine—Orville and Wilbur Wright at Kitty Hawk, U.S.A., Dec. 17.

**1904** Russo-Japanese War begins, Feb. 8. Japanese victory at Yalu River, May 1. British forces under Younghusband reach Lhasa, Aug. 3. Treaty with Tibet signed at Lhasa, Sept. 7.

**1905** Port Arthur falls to Japanese, Jan. 3. " Bloody Sunday " massacre at St. Petersburg, Jan. 22. Destruction of Russian fleet under Rozhdestvenski at Tsushima by Admiral Togo (May). Treaty of Portsmouth (U.S.A.) ends Russo-Japanese war. Separation of Church and State in France. Norway separates itself from Sweden.

**1906** General strike in Russia. San Francisco destroyed by earthquake and fire, Apr. 18. Simplon tunnel opened for railway traffic, June 1. First Duma (Parliament with limited powers) in Russia. Liberal " landslide " majority in Britain: Labour M.P.s appear. Movement for Women's Suffrage becomes active in Britain. Algeciras Conference: Franco-German crisis resolved in favour of France. Death of Ibsen. Vitamins discovered by F. G. Hopkins.

**1907** New Zealand becomes a dominion.

**1908** Annexation of Congo by Belgium. Young Turk revolution. Annexation of Bosnia and Herzegovina by Austria: severe rebuff for Russia. Asquith becomes Prime Minister of Britain.

**1909** Old Age Pensions in Britain. Peary reaches North Pole. Blériot makes first cross-Channel flight. House of Lords rejects Lloyd George's budget. Union of South Africa formed. Henry Ford concentrates on producing Model T chassis: beginnings of cheap motors.

A.D.

**1910** Accession of George V on death of Edward VII, May 6. Liberals win two General Elections. Labour Exchanges established in Britain. Death of Tolstoy and Florence Nightingale.

**1911** Parliament Act: power of Lords decisively reduced. British M.P.s paid for first time. National Insurance in Britain. Great British rail strike. Tripoli taken from Turkey by Italy. Chinese Revolution. Amundsen reaches South Pole, Dec. 14.

**1912** China becomes a Republic under Sun Yat Sen. *Titanic* disaster off Cape Race, Apr. 14–15. Great British coal strike. Scott's last expedition. Outbreak of Balkan Wars.

**1913** Treaty of Bucharest: most of Turkey-in-Europe divided among Balkan states.

## FIRST WORLD WAR

**1914** Archduke Francis Ferdinand, heir to the Hapsburg thrones, assassinated at Sarajevo, June 28. Austria–Hungary declares war against Serbia, July 28. Germany declares war against Russia, Aug. 1. Germany declares war against France, Aug. 3. German invasion of Belgium: Great Britain declares war against Germany, Aug. 4. Great Britain declares war on Austria–Hungary, Aug. 12. British Expeditionary Force concentrated before Mauberge, Aug. 20. Battle of Mons: Japan declared war on Germany, Aug. 23. Battle of the Marne, Sept. 5–9. Trench warfare began on Aisne salient, Sept. 16. Three British cruisers (*Aboukir, Hogue,* and *Cressy*) sunk by one U-boat, Sept. 22. First Battle of Ypres, Oct. 12–Nov. 11. Raiding of German cruiser *Emden* until destroyed, Nov. 9. Battle of Coronel: German cruisers *Scharnhorst* and *Gneisenau* sink British cruisers *Good Hope* and *Monmouth*, Nov. 1. Great Britain declares war against Turkey, Nov. 5. Destruction of German squadron off Falkland Is., Dec. 8. British protectorate over Egypt proclaimed, Dec. 17. First Zeppelin appeared over British coast, Dec. 29.

**1915** Turkish army defeated in Caucasus, Jan 5. Great Britain declared blockade of Germany, Mar. 1. Battle of Neuve Chapelle, Mar. 10–13. Naval attack on Dardanelles called off, Mar. 22. First landing of British, Australian, New Zealand troops on Gallipoli Peninsula, Apr. 25. Second Battle of Ypres, Apr. 22–May 25: Germans first used gas. Sinking of *Lusitania*, May 7. Battle of Aubers Ridge, May 9–25. Italy declares war on Austria, May 22. British Coalition Government formed, May 26. Italian army crosses Isonzo, June 2. Zeppelin destroyed by R. A. J. Warneford, June 7. Second landing of Allied troops at Suvla Bay. Italy declares war on Turkey, Aug. 20. Turks defeated at Kut-el-Amara, Sept 28. Serbia conquered by Austria and Bulgaria, Nov. 23. French and British troops occupy Salonika, Dec. 13. British troops withdraw from Anzac and Suvla, Dec. 20.

**1916** Evacuation of Gallipoli completed, Jan 8. Opening of Battle of Verdun, Feb. 21. Sinn Fein rising in Ireland, Apr. 24. First Daylight Saving Bill passed. Fall of Kut, Apr. 29. Battle of Jutland, May 31. Brusilov's offensive in Galicia begins, June 4. Kitchener drowned when *Hampshire* struck mine, June 5. Battle of the Somme, July 1–Nov. 13: British losses: 420,000. Italians capture Gorizia, Aug. 10. Hindenburg and Ludendorff chiefs of German staff, Aug. 27. Rumania declares war against Austria and Germany, Aug. 27. Tanks first used by British, Sept. 15. Death of Francis Joseph of Austria, Nov. 21. Lloyd George forms War Cabinet, Dec. 6. Joffre replaced by Nivelle, early Dec.

**1917** Unrestricted submarine warfare begins, Feb. 1. British troops occupy Baghdad, Mar. 11. Revolution in Russia, Mar. 12. U.S.A. declares war on Germany, April 6. Battle of Arras, Apr. 9–14: Vimy Ridge taken by Canadians, Apr. 10. Pétain replaced Nivelle, May 15. Messines Ridge taken by British, June 7. First American contingents arrive in France, June 26. · Allenby assumes Palestine

A.D.

command, June 29. Third Battle of Ypres opened, July 31. Russia proclaimed a Republic, Sept. 15. British victory on Passchendaele Ridge, Oct. 4. French victory on the Aisne, Oct. 23. Caporetto: Italians severely defeated by Austrians, Oct. 24. Bolshevik Revolution, Nov. 7 (Oct. 25 O.S.). Passchendaele captured by British, Nov. 6. Balfour declaration recognised Palestine as " a national home " for the Jews, Nov. 8. Hindenburg Lines smashed on 10-mile front, Nov. 20. Fall of Jerusalem, Dec. 9. Russo-German armistice signed, Dec. 15.

**1918** Treaty of Bresh-Litovsk, Mar. 3. German offensive against British opened on Somme, Mar. 21. Battle of Arras, Mar. 21–Apr. 4. Second German offensive against British, Apr. 9–25. British naval raid on Zeebrugge and Ostend, Apr. 23. Foch appointed C.-in-C. Allied armies, Apr. 14. Peace signed between Rumania and Central Powers, May 7. *Vindictive* sunk in Ostend harbour, May 9. Last German offensive against French, July 15. British, Canadians, and Australians attack in front of Amiens, Aug. 8. Allenby destroyed last Turkish army at Megiddo, Sept. 19. Bulgarians signed armistice, Sept. 29. General Allied offensive in West began, Sept. 26. Germans accepted Wilson's Fourteen Points, Oct. 23. Great Italian advance, Oct. 24. Turkey surrenders, Oct 30. Austria accepts imposed terms, Nov. 3. Popular government in Poland (Lubin), Nov. 7. Revolutionary movement begins in Germany, Nov. 8. Kaiser abdicates and escapes to Holland, Nov. 9. Armistice signed by Germans, Nov. 11.

## THE TWENTIES AND THIRTIES

**1919** Peace Conference in Paris, Jan. 18. First direct flight across Atlantic by Sir J. Alcock and Sir A. W. Brown, June 15. Interned German fleet scuttled at Scapa Flow, June 19. Treaty of Peace with Germany signed at Versailles, June 28. Treaty of St. Germain: break-up of Austrian Empire, Sept. 10.

**1920** Peace Treaty ratified in Paris. First meeting of League of Nations, from which Germany, Austria, Russia, and Turkey are excluded, and at which the U.S.A. is not represented. Prohibition in U.S.A. Peace Treaty with Turkey signed at Sèvres: Ottoman Empire broken up, Aug. 10. Degrees first open to women at Oxford Univ., Oct. 14.

**1921** Riots in Egypt, May 23. In complete disregard of the League of Nations, Greece makes war on Turkey. Heligoland fortresses demolished, Oct. 14. Irish Free State set up by Peace Treaty with Britain, Dec. 6.

**1922** Four-Power Pacific Treaty ratified by U.S. Senate, Mar. 24. Heavy fighting in Dublin, the Four Courts blown up, July 2. Defeat of Greek armies by the Turks, Aug.–Sept. Mussolini's Fascist " March on Rome," Oct. 28. Great find of treasures in Tutankhamen's tomb, Nov. 29.

**1923** French troops despatched to Ruhr, Jan. 11. Treaty of Lausanne, July 24. Earthquake in Japan, Tokio and Yokohama in ruins, Sept. 1. Rhine Republic proclaimed, Bavaria defies the Reich, Oct. 20. Turkish Republic proclaimed: Kemal Pasha, first President, Oct. 29.

**1924** Lenin dies, Jan. 21. First Labour Ministry in Britain under MacDonald, Jan. 22; lasts 9 months. George II of Greece deposed and a Republic declared, Mar. 25. Dawes Plan accepted by London conference; Ruhr evacuation agreed to, Aug. 16.

**1925** Hindenburg elected German President, Mar. 26. Treaty of Locarno signed in London, Dec. 1. Summer Time Act made permanent.

**1926** Ibn Saud proclaimed king of the Hedjaz in Jeddah, Jan. 11. Evacuation of Cologne by British forces, Jan. 31. General strike in Britain.

**1927** Canberra, the new capital of Australian Commonwealth, inaugurated, May 9. Lindbergh flies Atlantic alone, May 21.

**1928** Earthquake in Greece, Corinth destroyed, Apr. 23. Capt. Kingsford-Smith flies the

A.D.

Pacific, June 9. General Nobile rescued by aeroplane from Arctic one month after disaster. June 24. Kellogg Pact accepted by Gt. Britain, July 18. German airship with 60 persons crosses Atlantic, Oct. 15. Women in Britain enfranchised.

1929 King Amanullah of Afghanistan abdicates, Jan. 14. Second Labour Ministry under Mac-Donald. Graf Zeppelin makes numerous successful inter-continental flights. Commander Byrd flies over South Pole, Nov. 30. American slump and Wall Street crash.

1930 *R.101* destroyed in France on first flight to India, 48 lives lost, Oct. 5—end of British interest in airships.

1931 Great floods in China. Resignation of Labour Government and formation of Coalition under MacDonald.

1932 Manchuria erected into Japanese puppet state of Manchukuo, Feb. 18. Sydney Harbour Bridge opened, Mar. 19. Ottawa Imperial Conference.

1933 Hitler appointed Chancellor by Hindenburg, Jan. 30, and step by step gains supreme control. German Reichstag set on fire, Feb. 27.

1934 Dollfuss, Austrian Chancellor, murdered by Austrian Nazis, July 25. Death of Hindenburg, Aug. 2. Hitler becomes Dictator.

1935 Saar plebiscite for return to Germany, Jan. 13. Baldwin succeeds MacDonald as Prime Minister, June 7. War begins between Italy and Abyssinia, Oct. 3. Ineffectual economic "sanctions" by League of Nations against Italy, Nov. 18.

1936 Accession of King Edward VIII, Jan. 20. Repudiation of Locarno Treaty by Germany, Mar. 7. Remilitarisation of Rhineland, Mar. 8. Italian troops occupy Addis Ababa, May 5. Civil War breaks out in Spain, July 18. King Edward VIII abdicates after a reign of 325 days, Dec. 10. The Duke of York succeeds his brother as King George VI, Dec. 12.

1937 Coalition Ministry under Chamberlain, May 28. Japanese begin attempted conquest of China—" China incident," July 7.

1938 Singapore naval base opened, Feb. 14. Austria annexed by Germany, Mar. 13. British navy mobilised, Sept. 28. Munich Agreement between Chamberlain, Daladier, Hitler, and Mussolini, Sept. 29.

1939

February 27 Great Britain recognises General Franco's Government.

March 16 Bohemia and Moravia annexed by Hitler and proclaimed a German Protectorate. 22 Memel ceded to Germany by Lithuania. 28 Anti-Polish press campaign begun by Germany.

April 1 Spanish War ends. 7 Italy seizes Albania. 14 First British talks with Russia. 27 Conscription introduced in Great Britain. 28 Hitler denounces Anglo-German Naval agreement and the Polish Non-Aggression Treaty.

May 12 Great Britain signs defensive agreement with Turkey. 22 Italy and Germany sign pact. 23 France and Turkey sign defensive agreement. 25 Anglo-Polish treaty signed in London.

July 10 Chamberlain re-affirms British pledge to Poland.

August 23 German-Soviet Pact signed by von Ribbentrop. 25 Japan breaks away from the Anti-Comintern Pact. 28 Holland mobilises. 31 British fleet mobilised.

SECOND WORLD WAR

September 1 Poland invaded by German forces. Great Britain and France mobilise. 1–4 Evacuation schemes put in motion in England and Wales: 1,200,000 persons moved. 2 Compulsory military service for all men in Britain aged 18 to 41. 3 War declared (11 a.m.) between Britain and Germany as from 5 p.m. 4 British liner *Athenia* sunk by submarine. R.A.F. raid the Kiel Canal entrance and bomb German warships. 6 First enemy air raid on Britain. 8 Russia mobilises. Russian troops on Polish border. 11 British troops on French soil. 17

A.D.

Russian troops cross the Polish frontier along its entire length. Russian and German troops meet near Brest Litovsk. 27 Capitulation of Warsaw. 29 Nazi-Soviet pact signed in Moscow approving partition of Poland.

October 14 *Royal Oak* sunk in Scapa Flow with a loss of 810 lives.

November 8 Bomb explosion in the Bürgerbräukeller at Munich after Hitler's speech. Germans using magnetic mines. 29 Diplomatic relations between Russia and Finland severed. 30 Finland attacked by Russia.

December 11 Italy leaves the League of Nations. 13 Battle of the River Plate: engagement of German warship *Admiral Graf Spee* by H.M. cruisers *Exeter, Ajax,* and *Achilles.* 14 Rejection by Russia of the League of Nations' offer of mediation in the Russo-Finnish war. Russia expelled from the League of Nations. 18 *Admiral Graf Spee* scuttles herself in the entrance of Montevideo harbour.

1940

February 14 Finnish advanced posts captured by Russians. 16 299 British prisoners taken off the German Naval Auxiliary *Altmark* in Norwegian waters. 26 Finns lose the island fortress of Koivisto. Finns retreat from Petsamo.

March 12 British ships to be fitted with a protective device against magnetic mines. Finland concludes a peace treaty whereby she cedes to Russia the Karelian Isthmus, the town of Vipuri and a military base on Hango Peninsula.

April 9 Invasion of Denmark and Norway by Germany. 15 British troops arrive in Norway. 19 British soldiers land in the Faroes.

May 2 British troops withdrawn from Norway. 10 Holland, Belgium and Luxembourg invaded by German forces. Parachute troops landed near Rotterdam. British troops cross the Belgian border. British troops land in Iceland. Rotterdam bombed. 11 National Government formed under Churchill. 13 Queen Wilhelmina arrives in London. 14 Rotterdam captured. Holland ceases fighting. Allied troops land near Narvik. 17 Belgian Government moves to Ostend. 24 German forces enter Boulogne. 27 Belgian army capitulates on the order of King Leopold. British forces to be withdrawn from Flanders. Narvik captured by Allied forces. 29 Ostend, Ypres, Lille and other Belgian and French towns lost to the Germans.

June Evacuation of British army from Dunkirk (May 27–June 4): 299 British warships and 420 other vessels under constant attack evacuate 335,490 officers and men. 5 Hitler proclaims a war of total annihilation against his enemies. 8 German armoured forces penetrate French defences in the West near Rouen. 10 Italy declares war on Great Britain and France. 14 Paris captured by German forces. 15 Soviet troops occupy Lithuania, Latvia and Estonia. 22 French delegates accept terms for an Armistice. 25 Hostilities in France cease at 12.35 a.m.

July 1 Channel Islands occupied by Germany. 3 French naval squadron at Oran immobilised. 10 Battle of Britain began.

August 19 British withdrew from British Somaliland. 25 British began night bombing of Germany.

September 6 King Carol of Rumania abdicates in favour of his son Michael. 7 London sustains severe damage in the largest aerial attack since war commenced. 15 Battle of Britain ends with British victory: German aeroplanes destroyed, 1,733; R.A.F. losses, 915. 23 Japanese troops enter Indo-China.

October 7 German troops enter Rumania. 28 Greece rejects an Italian ultimatum.

November 1 Greeks repel Italian attacks. 5 H.M.S. *Jervis Bay* lost defending Atlantic convoy from German warship *Admiral Scheer.* 11 Italian fleet at Taranto crippled by Fleet Air Arm. 14 Coventry heavily attacked, the Cathedral destroyed. 22 Albanian town of Koritza captured by the Greeks.

December 2 Bristol heavily bombed. 11 Sidi Barrani captured by British forces: beginning

A.D.

of Wavell's destruction of Italian forces in Cyrenaica. 29 City of London severely burned by incendiary bombs: Guildhall and eight Wren Churches destroyed.

**1941**

**January 5** Bardia captured. 22 Tobruk captured by Australian troops.

**February 7** Benghazi captured. 26 Mogadishu, capital of Italian Somaliland, occupied by Imperial troops. German mechanised troops in Libya.

**March 4** British raid Lofoten Islands. 11 U.S. Lease and Lend Bill signed by Roosevelt. 27 Keren—main battle in British conquest of Abyssinia and Somaliland. 28 Cape Matapan: Italian fleet routed by British. 30 Rommel opens attack in N. Africa.

**April 4** Addis Ababa entered by Imperial troops. 6 Greece and Yugoslavia invaded by German troops. 8 Massawa capitulates. 11 Belgrade occupied by German forces. 13 Bardia given up by British. Tobruk holds out. 24 Empire forces withdrawing from Greece. 27 Athens captured by the Germans.

**May 2** Evacuation from Greece completed. 10 Rudolf Hess descends by parachute in Scotland. 20 Crete invaded by German air-borne troops. 24 H.M.S. *Hood* sunk. 27 German battleship *Bismarck* sunk; British forces withdraw from Crete.

**June 2** Clothes rationing commences. 4 William II (ex-Kaiser of Germany) dies. 18 Treaty of friendship between Turkey and Germany signed. 22 Germany attacks Russia. 24 Russia loses Brest Litovsk.

**July 3** Palmyra (Syria) surrenders to Allied forces. 7 U.S. forces arrive in Iceland. 9 General Dentz, the French High Commissioner in Syria, asks for Armistice terms. 25 Fighting round Smolensk.

**August 25** British and Russian troops enter Persia. 27 The Dnepropetrovsk dam blown up by the Russians.

**September 18** Crimea cut off from mainland. 19 Kiev entered by Germans.

**October 6** German attack on Moscow. 16 Soviet Government leaves Moscow. Odessa occupied by German and Rumanian troops. 19 Taganrog on Sea of Azov captured by Germans. 26 Kharkov captured by the Germans.

**November 14** *Ark Royal* sunk. 18 Libyan battle opens: Eighth Army's first offensive. 23 Bardia and Fort Capuzzo captured by British. 24 H.M.S. *Dunedin* torpedoed. 25 H.M.S. *Barham* sunk. 30 Russians re-take Rostov.

**December 1** Points rationing scheme in force in Britain. 4 German attack on Moscow halted. 6 Japanese attack on Pearl Harbour. 8 Japanese forces land in Malaya. 9 British forces in Tobruk relieved. 10 H.M.S. *Repulse* and *Prince of Wales* sunk off Malaya by Japanese. Phillipines invaded by Japanese. 26 Hongkong surrenders to Japanese.

**1942**

**January 2** Manila and Cavite taken by Japanese. 23 Japanese forces land in New Guinea and the Solomon Islands.

**February 9** Soap rationed. 12 Escape through English Channel of German ships *Scharnhorst*, *Gneisenau*, and *Prinz Eugen*. 15 Singapore surrenders to Japanese. 27 Battle of Java Seas.

**March 9** Surrender of Java to Japanese.

**April 15** George Cross awarded to the island of Malta.

**May 4–8** Battle of Coral Sea. 7 Madagascar invaded by British forces. 7 U.S. forces sink 11 Japanese warships off the Solomon Islands. 30 Over 1,000 bombers raid Cologne. Canterbury bombed.

**June 3–7** Midway Island: U.S. naval victory turns tide in Pacific. 20 Tobruk captured by the Germans.

**July 16** R.A.F. make first daylight raid on the Ruhr.

**August 6** Germans advancing towards the Caucasus. 10 American forces land in the Solomon

A.D.

Islands. 11 Malta convoy action (loss of H.M.S. *Eagle*, *Manchester*, *Cairo*, and one destroyer). 19 Raid on Dieppe. 23–25 Battle of Solomons.

**September 6** Germans halted at Stalingrad.

**October 23** El Alamein: Allied offensive opens in Egypt.

**November 4** Rommel's army in full retreat. 5 Red Army holding firm at Stalingrad. 7 Allied invasion of N. Africa. 27 German forces enter Toulon. French Fleet scuttled.

**December 2** First self-sustained, controlled nuclear chain reaction in uranium took place on a Chicago tennis court. 24 Admiral Darlan assassinated.

**1943**

**January 6** German armies in the Caucasus and the Don elbow in retreat. 18 Leningrad 16-month siege ended. 23 Tripoli occupied by the Eighth Army. 27 American bombers make their first attack on Germany. 31 Remnants of the German army outside Stalingrad surrender.

**February 9** Guadalcanal Island cleared of Japanese troops. 16 Kharkov retaken by the Russians.

**March 1–3** Battle of Bismarck Sea. 23 8th Army penetrates the Mareth Line.

**May 7** Tunis and Bizerta captured by Allies. 12 All organised German resistance in Tunisia ceases. 16 Dams in the Ruhr breached by the R.A.F. 22 Moscow dissolves the Comintern.

**June 3** French Committee for National Liberation formed in Algiers.

**July 10** Allied invasion of Sicily. 25 Mussolini overthrown. 28 Fascist Party in Italy dissolved.

**August 17** Sicily in Allied hands.

**September 3** Italian mainland invaded. 7 Italy surrenders. 9 British and American troops land near Naples. 10 Rome seized by the Germans. 14 Salamaua captured from the Japanese. 23 *Tirpitz* severely damaged (sunk Nov. 12, 1944). 25 Smolensk taken by the Russians.

**October 1** Naples taken. 25 Russians capture Dnepropetrovsk and Dneprodzerzhinck.

**November 6** Kiev taken by the Russians. 26 Second Battle of Solomons. 28 Churchill, Roosevelt, and Stalin meet in Teheran.

**December 2** Men between 18 and 25 to be directed to the mining industry by ballot in Britain. 26 Sinking of German battleship *Scharnhorst*.

**1944**

**January 22** Allied landings at Anzio. 28 Argentina breaks with the Axis Powers.

**February 1** American forces land on the Marshall Islands. 2 Russians penetrate Estonia.

**March 15** Cassino (Italy) destroyed by Allied bombers.

**May 9** Sevastopol captured by Russians. 18 Capture of Cassino and Abbey by Allies. 19 50 Allied officers shot after escaping from a German prison camp. 30 Battle for Rome commences.

**June 4** Allied forces enter Rome. King of Italy signs decree transferring his powers to Prince Umberto, his son. 6 *D-Day*: invasion of Europe (over 4,000 ships in invasion fleet). 7 Defeat of Japanese thrust at India, outside Imphal. 9 Heavy fighting near Caen. 12 First V-1 falls on England. 18 Cherbourg peninsula cut by the Americans. Russians break through the Mannerheim Line.

**July 3** Minsk captured by Russians. 9 Caen captured by Allies. 20 " Bomb plot " on Hitler' life. 21 Guam captured by Americans.

**August 1** Uprising in Warsaw. 4 Myitkyina falls to Allied forces. 15 Allied forces land in southern France. 23 Paris liberated. Marseilles taken. Rumania surrenders. 25 Rumania declares war on Germany.

**September 3** Allies in Belgium. 4 Antwerp and Brussels taken by Allies. Holland entered. Finland " ceases fire." 6 Bulgaria asks for an armistice. 7 Boulogne entered by Allies. Bulgaria declares war on Germany. 8 First V-2 falls on England. 11 Allied forces fighting on

A.D.

Reich territory. 17 Allied air-borne troops land near Arnhem. 22 First Battle of Philippines.

October 3 Warsaw rising crushed by the Germans. 5 British troops land on the mainland of Greece. 14 Athens occupied by Allies. 15 Hungary asks for armistice terms. 20 Aachen captured by the Americans. 25 Battle of Leyte Gulf: end of Japanese sea-power. 28 Second Battle of Philippines.

December 6 Civil war breaks out in Athens. 16 German forces counter-attack in the Ardennes: last German offensive in the West. 26 Budapest encircled by Russians.

**1945**

January 5 Organized fighting in Athens ceases. 11 U.S. forces land on Island of Luzon. 17 Warsaw captured by the Russians. 21 Russian troops in Silesia. 23 Burma road to China re-opened.

February 4 Yalta conference. 14 Bombing of Dresden. 19 Americans land on Iwojima Island.

March 6 Cologne captured by Allies.

April 1 U.S. Invasion of Okinawa. 5 Russian Government denounces the Soviet-Japan neutrality pact. Japanese Cabinet resigns. 11 Russian Army enters Vienna after 7-day battle. 12 Death of President Roosevelt. 25 Berlin surrounded by Russian troops. 27 Russians and Americans link up in Germany. 28 Mussolini and his mistress shot by Italian partisans. 30 Hitler killed himself and his mistress.

May 2 German armies in Italy surrender. Berlin captured by the Russians. 3 Rangoon captured by British. 4 German forces in N.W. Germany, Holland and Denmark surrender. 8 End of World War II against Germany officially declared to be one minute past midnight (Tuesday). 28 Naval air attacks on Japan.

June 26 United Nations Charter signed at San Francisco.

July 5 Polish Government in Warsaw recognised by Allies. 26 Labour Party remarkably successful in General Election.

August 6 Atomic bomb first used against Japan: Hiroshima laid waste. 8 Russia declares war against Japan. 9 Russia advances into Manchuria. Nagasaki target for atomic bomb No. 2. 14 Japan surrenders unconditionally to the Allies. 17 Lend-Lease terminated.

September 2 Victory over Japan celebrated: end of Second World War.

## " COLD WAR ": AFRO-ASIAN INDEPENDENCE

October 9 U.S.A. to keep secret of manufacture of atomic bomb. 15 Laval executed.

November 20 Trial of major war criminals opens at Nuremberg.

**1946**

February 1 Mr. Trygve Lie elected Secretary-General of UNO.

April 19 League of Nations formally wound up.

June 5 Italy votes for Republic. 30 United States atom bomb tests at Bikini.

July 13 United States House of Representatives approves loan to Britain. 22 Bread rationing in Britain. British H.Q. in Jerusalem blown up. 24 Underwater atom bomb test at Bikini.

August 1 Peace Conference opens in Paris.

September 6 United Nations F.A.O. considers establishment of World Food Board.

October 16 Nuremberg sentences on Nazis carried out, Goering commits suicide. 23 General Assembly of the United Nations opens in New York.

November 10 Communists head poll in French General Elections.

December 2 Agreement signed for economic fusion of British and American zones in Germany.

A.D.

**1947**

January 1 British coal industry nationalised. 14 M. Vincent-Auriol elected first President of Fourth Republic.

March 15 Floods in England worst recorded. 24 Netherlands Government and Indonesian Cabinet sign agreement in Batavia for a United States of Indonesia.

April 1 School leaving age raised to 15 in Great Britain.

June 5 Inauguration of " Marshall Aid ".

August 3 Dutch military action in Indonesia ends. 15 India and Pakistan assume Dominion Status. Viscount Mountbatten appointed Governor-General of India and Mr. Jinnah Governor-General of Pakistan. 29 Palestine Committee agrees British Mandate should end, majority report recommends partition.

September 22 First Atlantic automatic flight by U.S. pilotless aircraft.

October 6 Cominform, new international Communist organization, set up in Belgrade.

November 20 Marriage of Princess Elizabeth. 29 Palestine Committee of U.N. Assembly votes in favour of partition of Palestine into Jewish and Arab States.

December 15 Breakdown of 4-Power Conference on Germany. 30 King Michael of Rumania abdicates; Rumania becomes a People's Republic.

**1948**

January 1 British Railways nationalised. 4 Burma becomes independent Republic. 30 Mahatma Gandhi assassinated in New Delhi.

February 1 New Malayan federal constitution comes into force. 4 Ceylon Independence Act. 25 New Czechoslovak Government formed under Communist leadership.

March 10 Death of Jan Masaryk.

April 1 British electricity industry nationalised. 5 First European Aid shipments sail from America. 16 O.E.E.C. established.

May 3 Mr. Rajagopalachari appointed Gov.-Gen. of India in succession to Earl Mountbatten. 14 British Mandate for Palestine ended at midnight. Jews proclaim new State of Israel.

June 28 Yugoslavia expelled from Cominform; " Titoism " denounced.

July 1 " Berlin Airlift ": American, British and French zones of Berlin supplied by air. 21 Malayan Communist party outlawed. 29 Bread rationing in Great Britain ends.

August 15 Republic of Korea proclaimed.

September 3 Death of Dr. Benes. 11 Death of Mohammed Ali Jinnah. 17 Count Bernadotte, U.N. Mediator for Palestine, assassinated.

October 30 Chinese Communist forces capture Mukden.

November 3 Mr. Truman elected U.S. President. 14 Birth of a son to Princess Elizabeth.

December 21 Republic of Ireland Bill signed in Dublin.

**1949**

March 15 Clothes rationing ends in Great Britain. 31 Russia protests against Atlantic Pact.

April 1 Newfoundland becomes part of Canada.

May 1 Gas Industry nationalised. 3 Ten-power conference in London establishes Council of Europe. 12 Berlin blockade lifted.

August 24 North Atlantic Treaty comes into force.

September 12 Professor Theodor Heuss elected first President of West German Republic. 21 General Mao Tse-Tung proclaims People's Republic of China.

October 2 Russia recognises newly-established Chinese People's Republic. 11 Herr Wilhelm Pieck elected first President of East German Republic.

December 8 Chinese Nationalist Government leaves mainland and sets up H.Q. in Formosa. 27 United States of Indonesia come into being.

**1950**

January 6 Britain recognizes Communist Government of China ; 24 Dr. Rajendra Prasad elected

A.D.

first President of Indian Republic; 26 New Constitution of Indian Republic comes into force.

**February 14** 30-year treaty of alliance between Russia and China signed in Moscow; 23 Labour Party wins General Election with narrow majority.

**March 5** Lord Boyd Orr warns world that communism spreads where hunger prevails; 22 First of U.S. super-fortresses arrives in Norfolk.

**April 1** Italy takes over from Britain administration of Somaliland; 13 First shipment of military aid to France under N.A. Pact unloaded at Cherbourg.

**May 1** New Chinese marriage law abolishes polygamy and child marriages and gives both sexes equal rights; 19 Points rationing ends in Britain after 8 years; 25 Middle East Tripartite Declaration by Britain, France, and U.S.A.; 26 Petrol rationing ends in Britain.

**June 25** N. Korean troops advance into S. Korea; Security Council calls for cease fire; 27 Pres. Truman orders U.S. air, and sea forces to support S. Korea and protect Formosa; U.N. Commission in Korea proposes neutral mediator; military assistance to S. Korea endorsed by Security Council; 30 Pres. Truman authorizes use of American ground troops in Korea.

**July 2** American troops land in S. Korea; 8 Gen. MacArthur designated C.-in-C. of U.N. forces in Korea.

**August 1** Security Council meets under chairmanship of M. Malik, the Soviet delegate; 7 American forces in Korea open offensive and halt drive on Pusan; 15 Princess Elizabeth gives birth to a daughter; severe earthquake in Assam; 17 Independence Day in Indonesia.

**September 6** British troops in action in Korea; 9 Soap rationing ends in Britain.

**October 9** U.N. forces across the 38th parallel in strength; 19 Sir Stafford Cripps retires from public life on account of illness; Pyongyang, N. Korean capital, captured by U.N. forces; 21 Princess Anne Elizabeth Alice Louise christened; 26 New Chamber of House of Commons opened at Westminster; 29 King Gustav V of Sweden dies.

**November 2** Death of George Bernard Shaw aged 94; 6 Chinese forces from Manchuria reported fighting in Korea.

**December 3** Mr. Attlee flies to Washington for talks with Pres. Truman; 4 Pyongyang occupied by Chinese; 19 Gen. Eisenhower appointed Supreme Commander of West European Defence Forces set up by Atlantic Powers; 25 Stone of Scone stolen from Westminster Abbey.

**1951**

**January 30** U.N. Assembly rejects resolution of 12 Asian and Arab nations calling for 7-nation conference for peaceful settlement of Korean question; 31 Decree confiscating property of Alfred Krupp cancelled.

**February 15** Vesting date for Iron and Steel.

**April 11** Gen. MacArthur relieved of all his commands by Pres. Truman and replaced by Lt.-Gen. Ridgway; 13 Coronation Stone returned to Westminster Abbey.

**May 2** Persian oil industry nationalized; Germany admitted to Council of Europe; 3 H.M. the King opens Festival of Britain from steps of St. Paul's.

**June 23** M. Malik, Russian delegate to the U.N., appeals for settlement of Korean war.

**July 1** Colombo plan comes into force; 9 State of war between Britain and Germany officially ended; 10 Armistice negotiations open at Kaesong; 17 King Leopold abdicates in favour of his son Baudouin, who becomes fifth King of the Belgians; 20 King Abdullah of Jordan assassinated.

**September 1** Tripartite Security Treaty between U.S.A., Australia, and New Zealand signed in San Francisco; 8 Japanese Peace Treaty—to which Russia, China, and India are not

A.D.

parties—signed at San Francisco; Security Pact between Japan and U.S.A., providing for retention of American forces in Japan, also signed; 23 H.M. the King undergoes successful operation; 30 Festival of Britain ends.

**October 8** Princess Elizabeth and Duke of Edinburgh leave for Canadian tour; 15 Egyptian Parliament passes unanimously Bills abrogating Anglo-Egyptian treaty of 1936 and 1899 Sudan Condominion Agreement; 16 Assassination of Liaquat Ali Khan; 25 General Election won by Conservatives with small majority.

**November 5** Mr. Attlee receives the Order of Merit.

**December 17** London foreign-exchange market reopens after 12 years; 24 Libya becomes independent state; 31 I.R.O. closes down.

**1952**

**January 2** Mutual Security Agency replaces Economic Co-operation Administration; 31 Princess Elizabeth and Duke of Edinburgh leave London on first stage of Commonwealth tour.

**February 6** King George VI died at Sandringham aged 56; 7 Queen Elizabeth II and the Duke of Edinburgh arrive home by air from Kenya; 15 Funeral of King George VI at Windsor; 21 Identity cards abolished.

**March 20** South African Supreme Court rules invalid Dr. Malan's Act which places Cape coloured voters on separate electoral register.

**April 11** H.M. the Queen declares that she wishes her children and descendants to bear the name of Windsor; 21 Death of Sir Stafford Cripps in Switzerland; 28 Japan regains status as sovereign and independent power.

**May 5** H.M. the Queen takes up residence at Buckingham Palace; 27 Treaty setting up European Defence Community signed in Paris.

**June 23** Power plants along Yalu River attacked by U.S. aircraft in biggest raid of Korean war.

**July 7** American ship *United States* wins Atlantic Blue Riband; 19 Fifteenth Olympic Games held in Helsinki; 23 Military *coup d'état* takes place in Cairo.

**August 1** Ratification of Bonn Agreement, by which W. Germany again becomes independent nation, and Treaty of Paris, which sets up the European Defence Community, approved by Government against Labour opposition; 16 Severe thunderstorms in Somerset and N. Devon cause rivers to flood; W. Lyn changes course bringing devastation to Lynmouth; 26 Passive resistance campaign against racial laws in S. Africa gains momentum.

**September 2** Sir William Slim appointed Gov.-Gen. of Australia (from 1953); 8 New Egyptian Cabinet appoints Gen. Neguib military Gov.-Gen. of Egypt and approves land reforms.

**October 3** Britain's first atomic weapon exploded in Monte Bello Islands, off N.W. Australia; 5 Tea derationed and decontrolled; 20 State of emergency declared in Kenya as a result of Mau Mau activities.

**November 1** Reported explosion of U.S. hydrogen bomb at Eniwetok atoll in mid-Pacific; 4 Gen. Eisenhower, Republican Candidate, wins sweeping victory in American Presidential election.

**December 29** Fish recently caught off Madagascar confirmed as species of the prehistoric Ocelacanth.

**1953**

**January 20** Inauguration of General Eisenhower as 34th President of the United States; 31 Violent N.E. gales combined with surging high tides caused extensive flooding with loss of life along coasts of eastern England, the Netherlands, and Belgium.

**February 4** Sweet rationing ended; 23 War-time deserters in Britain granted amnesty.

**March 6** Marshal Stalin died, aged 74; 24 Death of Queen Mary at Marlborough House, aged 85; 31 Mr. Dag Hammarskjöld elected U.N. Sec.-Gen. in succession to Mr. Trygve Lie.

**April 15** Dr. Malan's National Party again returned to power in S. Africa with increased

A.D.

majority; 24 Mr. Churchill created a Knight of the Garter by the Queen.

May 4 Duke of Edinburgh received his pilot's "wings"; 29 E. P. Hillary and Sherpa Tenzing of the Everest Expedition led by Colonel John Hunt reached summit of Everest (29,002 ft.).

June 2 Coronation of H.M. Elizabeth II in Westminster Abbey amid scenes of magnificent pageantry; ceremony televised; 26 Republic of Egypt accorded *de facto* recognition by Britain.

July 4 German–Austrian Expedition reached summit of Nanga Parbat in the Himalayas; 13 De-nationalisation of British steel industry; 14 Royal Assent given to Central African Federation Bill; 27 Korean Armistice signed at Panmunjom.

August 9–12 Disastrous earthquakes in Greek Ionian Islands; 12 Explosion of Russian hydrogen bomb reported.

September 17 Bank rate reduced from 4 to 3½ per cent; 23 Royal Commission on Capital Punishment recommended that juries should decide whether death sentence or life imprisonment should be imposed on prisoners found guilty of murder, and that the M'Naghten Rules on insanity should be abrogated or amended; 26 Sugar rationing ended after nearly 14 years; 30 Professor Piccard in his bathyscaphe dived 10,000 ft. off Italian coast.

October 15 Sir Winston Churchill awarded 1953 Nobel Prize for Literature.

November 11 Great bell at Notre Dame rung by electricity for first time; 21 Piltdown skull, discovered in Sussex in 1911, found by anthropologists to be partial hoax; 23 The Queen and Duke of Edinburgh left in stratocruiser *Canopus* on first stage of 6-months' tour of Commonwealth.

December 1 Agreement signed for laying first transatlantic telephone cable; 23 M. René Coty elected Pres. of France at the 13th ballot; L. P. Beria, former chief of Soviet Secret Police, and six associates sentenced to death and shot; 25 The Queen gave her Christmas broadcast from Auckland; 31 Mildest December for 20 years, and before that for over 200 years.

1954

January 9 Self-government began in the Sudan; 12 M. Le Trouquer (Socialist) elected President of French National Assembly on retirement of M. Herriot; 16 M. René Coty became President of France in succession to M. Vincent Auriol; 31 Intense cold covered most of Europe.

February 3 The Queen and the Duke of Edinburgh arrived in Australia; First Parliament of newly formed Federation of Rhodesia and Nyasaland opened in Salisbury; 5 Britain's first "breeder" pile in operation at Harwell.

March 1 American hydrogen bomb exploded at Bikini; 22 London gold market reopened after 15 years.

April 1 The Queen and the Duke of Edinburgh left Australia; 3 Oxford won 100th Boat Race; 21 Russia joined UNESCO; 26 Conference on Far East opened in Palais des Nations, Geneva, Mr. Chou En-lai representing China; Russia joined I.L.O.

May 6 Roger Bannister ran the mile in under 4 min., the first man in the world to do so; 7 Fortress of Dien Bien Phu fell to Viet-Minh after siege of 8 weeks and final battle of 20 hours; 11 Bank rate reduced from 3½ to 3 per cent; 15 The Queen and the Duke of Edinburgh returned from their six-months' tour of the Commonwealth; 18 Liverpool Cotton Exchange re-opened

June 1 Television licence fee raised from £2 to £3 a year; 2 Mr. John A. Costello (Fine Gael) elected Prime Minister of Ireland; 17 Indo-Chinese crisis brought M. Mendès-France to power in France; 22 First all-African Cabinet in British Africa appointed in the Gold Coast; 27 First electric power station using atomic energy began working in Soviet Union; 30 Eclipse of the sun.

July 3 All food rationing ended in Britain; 8 Mr. Nehru opened the world's longest canal

A.D.

(Bhakra–Nangal hydro-electric project); 27 Agreement reached in Cairo for withdrawal of British troops from Suez Canal Zone; 31 K2 (Mount Godwin Austen), second highest peak in the world, climbed by Italian team led by Prof. Ardito Desio of Milan Univ.

August 5 Persian oil dispute settled; 11 Cessation of hostilities in Indo-China after 8 years of fighting.

September 14 Sheffield–Manchester electrified railway opened.

October 14 Mr. Anthony Eden created a Knight of the Garter by the Queen; 19 Anglo-Egyptian Suez Canal Agreement.

November 1 French settlements in India passed under Indian control; 22 Death of Andrei Vyshinsky; 30 Sir Winston Churchill celebrated his 80th birthday and was presented by both Houses of Parliament with a portrait of himself by Graham Sutherland.

1955

January 27 Bank rate increased from 3 to 3½ per cent; 31 Princess Margaret left for tour of W. Indies.

February 8 Marshal Bulganin succeeded Mr. Malenkov as chairman of the Soviet Council of Ministers; 15 Plans to build 12 atomic power stations in Britain during next 10 years announced; 17 Britain to proceed with manufacture of hydrogen bombs; 24 Bank rate raised to 4½ per cent and restrictions on hire purchase announced; Dr. Albert Schweitzer appointed honorary member of the Order of Merit; Turco-Iraqi pact signed at Baghdad (Britain, Pakistan, and Persia acceded later).

April 5 Sir Winston Churchill resigned as Prime Minister; 6 Sir Anthony Eden succeeded as Prime Minister; 18 Afro-Asian conference (29 nations) opened at Bandung; Death of Dr. Albert Einstein; 29 Signor Gronchi elected President of Italy.

May 5 Ratification of London and Paris agreements completed; Germany attained full sovereignty and Western European Union came into being; 26 British general election resulted in Conservative majority of 59.

June 15 U.S. and Britain agreed to co-operate on atomic energy; 16 Revolt against the Perón government in Argentina.

July 9 Leading world scientists issued appeal for renunciation of war because of possible effects of hydrogen bomb; 18 Four-Power conference opened in Geneva (Pres. Eisenhower, Sir Anthony Eden, M. Faure, Marshal Bulganin), the first meeting between heads of Government since Potsdam, 1945; 27 Austrian State Treaty came into force.

August 8 International conference on peaceful uses of atomic energy opened in Geneva (1200 scientists from 72 countries attended).

September 16 Universal Copyright convention came into force, bringing U.S. into agreement with European countries; 19 General Perón resigned after rebels threatened to bombard Buenos Aires; 22 Independent television service began.

October 2 City of London became a "smokeless zone"; 12 British and Soviet warships exchanged courtesy visits; 20 Syria and Egypt signed mutual defence treaty; 23 Referendum on Saar European Statute gave victory to pro-German parties.

November 5 Vienna State Opera House re-opened; 23 *Hamlet* played on Russian stage by British company, the first since Tsarist times.

December 7 Mr. Attlee announced his retirement and was created an earl; 12 Completion of 830-mile pipeline through Urals, crossing 6 rivers; 14 Mr. Hugh Gaitskell elected leader of the Parl. Labour Party; 18 Anglo-American offer of financial assistance to Egypt in building Aswan High Dam; 24 In Christmas broadcast the Pope spoke of need to suspend nuclear test explosions.

1956

January 1 Sudan proclaimed an independent republic; 27 The Queen and the Duke of Edin-

A.D.
burgh left by air for 3 weeks' tour of Nigeria;
200th anniversary of birth of Mozart celebrated;
Terrorist activity in Cyprus increasing.

February 1 Britain had coldest day since 1895;
13 Referendum in Malta resulted in vote in
favour of integration with Britain; 16 House
of Commons rejected by majority of 31 Government motion to retain death penalty; Bank
rate increased from 4½ to 5½ per cent. (highest
since 1932); 23 Remarkable sunflare caused
increased cosmic radiation and long-wave radio
disturbances; 25 M. Khrushchev in speech to
Congress of Russian Communist Party denounced Stalin.

March 2 King Hussein of Jordan discharged
Lieut.-Gen. J. B. Glubb; 5 Telephone weather
forecast began; 9 Archbishop Makarios with
leaders of Enosis movement in Cyprus deported
to the Seychelles; 23 The Queen laid foundation stone of new Coventry Cathedral; Pakistan
proclaimed an Islamic Republic within the
Commonwealth.

April 6 Earl Attlee created Knight of the Garter;
11 Five-day week for Civil Servants announced;
18 Cease-fire between Israel and Egypt came
into force; 29 French occupation of Indo-China
ended after 80 years.

May 23 First atomic power station in Britain
started working at Calder Hall; 24 2,500th
anniversary of the death of Buddha celebrated
in India; 31 May was the sunniest month at
Kew since 1922 and the driest since 1896.

June 3 Third-class travel abolished on British
Railways to conform to continental practice;
13 Last British troops left Suez; 24 Col. Nasser
elected Pres. of Egypt.

July 20 Britain joined U.S.A. in withdrawing offer
to help Egypt finance Aswan High Dam; 26
Pres. Nasser announced nationalisation of Suez
Canal Company.

August 30 French troops arrived in Cyprus.

September 25 Newly-laid submarine telephone
cable linking Britain and America opened to
public service.

October 3 Bolshoi Ballet danced at Covent Garden;
15 Duke of Edinburgh left on world tour; 16
Prime Minister left with For. Sec. for Paris
meeting; 17 The Queen opened Calder Hall, the
world's first nuclear power station for commercial use; 19–21 New liberalised policy adopted
by Central Committee of Polish United Workers'
Party; M. Gomulka elected first secretary; 23
Insurrection broke out in Budapest and spread
throughout country; 28 Pres. Eisenhower
called upon Israel not to " endanger the peace ";
29 Israeli forces invaded Egypt and after 5 days'
fighting had control of Sinai peninsula, heavy
fighting at Abu Aweigila; 30 Britain and France
issued 12-hour ultimatum to Israel and Egypt
to cease fighting; Britain and France vetoed
US resolution in Security Council calling upon
Israel to withdraw behind armistice line; 31
Anglo-French offensive launched against
military targets in Egypt.

November 2 UN Gen. Assembly called for
immediate cease fire in Egypt; 4 Canadian
resolution calling for international UN force
for Middle East adopted; Soviet forces launched
attack on Budapest to crush uprising; 5
Anglo-French airborne troops landed at Port
Said; 6 Seaborne troops landed at Port Said;
Pres. Eisenhower re-elected President with
Congress controlled by Democrats; Anglo-
French forces ceased fire at midnight; 7 Egypt
accepted cease fire on UN conditions; 15
UN Emergency Force left Naples for Suez;
16 Suez Canal blocked by 49 ships; 17 First
refugees from Hungary arrived in Britain; 22
Duke of Edinburgh opened 16th Olympic
Games in Melbourne; 23 Sir Anthony Eden
flew to Jamaica for rest cure; 24 UN for third
time called upon Britain, France, and Israel to
withdraw troops from Egypt.

December 5 140 people arrested in S. Africa for
alleged treason; Anglo-French forces began to
leave Port Said; 19 Lord Radcliffe's proposals
for a constitution for Cyprus published; 29
Suez Canal clearing operation by UN salvage
fleet began.

A.D.
1957
January 1 Anglo-Egyptian treaty of 1954 abro-
gated by Pres. Nasser as from October 31, 1956;
Saar became tenth *Land* of German Federal
Republic; Road Traffic Act came into force; 5
Eisenhower Doctrine for Middle East an-
nounced; 9 Resignation of Sir Anthony Eden
as Prime Minister; 10 Mr. Harold Macmillan
appointed Prime Minister; 16 Sadlers Wells
Ballet group combined to form The Royal
Ballet; Death of Signor Toscanini; 20 Mr.
Gomulka's National Unity Front overwhelm-
ingly returned in Polish general election;
India's first atomic reactor, *Apsara*, inaugu-
rated; 31 Trans-Iranian oil pipeline from
Abadan to Teheran (600 m.) completed.

February 7 Bank Rate reduced from 5½ to 5 per
cent; 15 Mr. Gromyko replaced Mr. Shepilov
as Soviet Foreign Minister; 16 The Queen flew
to Portugal on State visit and joined Duke of
Edinburgh there who had just completed
World tour; 22 Duke of Edinburgh granted
title of Prince of the United Kingdom; 26
Indian resolution adopted by UN for " peaceful, democratic, and just solution " of Cyprus
problem.

March 1 Mass protest in Tokio against nuclear
weapon tests in Pacific; 5 Fianna Fail party
under Mr. de Valera secured absolute majority
in general election; 6 Ghana celebrated independence; Israeli withdrawal from Sinai
completed; 11 Warning by WHO of genetic
effects of radiation; 13 Anglo-Jordanian treaty
of 1948 ended; 21 Homicide Act in force
(death penalty retained only for five categories
of " capital murder "); 25 European Common
Market and Euratom treaties signed by France,
Germany, Italy, and Benelux countries.

April 3 British Labour Party called for abolition
of H-bomb tests; 4 No further call-ups for
National Service after 1960; 8 The Queen and
Prince Philip arrived in France on State visit;
9 Suez Canal cleared and opened to all shipping;
11 Agreement signed in London granting full
internal self-government to Singapore from Jan.
1, 1958; 17 Archbishop Makarios arrived in
Athens from exile; During the month appeals
were made by the Pope, Dr. Schweitzer and
Mr. Nehru for the banning of nuclear tests and
weapons.

May 14 Petrol rationing (imposed 17.12.56)
ended; 15 First British H-bomb exploded in
Central Pacific near Christmas I.; 16 M. Spaak
succeeded Lord Ismay as NATO Sec. Gen.;
18 The Queen and Prince Philip left for State
visit to Denmark; 20 Death of Dr. Gilbert
Murray.

June 1 New Copyright Act came into force; First
drawing of Premium Bond prizes; 17 Historic
decisions taken by US Supreme Court on
matters relating to civil liberties; 19 Completion of British H-bomb tests in Pacific; 30
The IGY opened at midnight.

July 1 Women voted for the first time in Egypt's
first general election since revolution of 1952;
17 Electricity Bill enacted appointing new Central Electricity Generating Board and Electricity Council in place of Central Electricity
Authority; 18 President Mao Tse-tung's
famous " Let 100 flowers blossom and 100
schools of thought contend " speech published;
25 Tunisia declared a republic; 31 Federation
of Malaya Independence Act received Royal
Assent.

August 1 Sir Christopher Hinton appointed chairman of new C.E.G.B., responsible for new
nuclear power stations; 31 Royal Charter
granted to Tangier by King of Morocco.

September 6 Disarmament discussions in London
ended without agreement; 15 German general
election (Dr. Adenauer re-elected Chancellor
Oct. 22); 19 Bank Rate raised from 5 to 7 per
cent.; 20 Death of Jean Sibelius, the Finnish
composer; 30 Network Three introduced by
B.B.C.

October 4 First earth satellite launched by Russia
(180 lb. sphere, 23 in. diameter); 10 U.S.A.
abolished fingerprinting for foreign visitors
staying less than a year; 11 Largest radio tele-

A.D.

scope in world went into operation at Jodrell Bank for Manchester University; **14** The Queen opened Canadian Parliament in Ottawa; New road-rail double-decker bridge over Yangtse, one of largest in world, opened to traffic; **17** Endorsement of cheques no longer necessary save when negotiated.

**November 3** Second earth satellite weighing half a ton launched into space by Russia with dog on board; **16** Russia announced construction of " scientific city " of 12 research institutes in Siberia; **20** Britain's first export order for nuclear power station for Northern Italy announced.

**December 1** Latin 26-letter alphabet to be adopted in China; **4** Ninety people killed in railway accident in fog at Lewisham; **6** Attempt to launch earth satellite in the U.S.A. failed; *Sputnik I* completed its thousandth circuit of the Earth; **25** The Queen's Christmas broadcast televised for the first time; **31** The *Sputniks* were still circling the Earth, the first being expected to fall in the first days of January.

**1958**

**January 1** Treaties establishing EEC (Common Market) and EAEC (Euratom) came into force; Metric system of weights and measures adopted throughout Japan; **3** Inauguration of West Indian Federation; Sir Edmund Hillary and New Zealand party reached South Pole; **4** *Sputnik I* disintegrated after completing 1,367 circuits of the Earth and travelling 43 million miles; **6** First non-stop flight across Antarctica by single-engine British aircraft (1,600 miles in 10 hr. 57 min.); Mr. Thorneycroft resigned from Government after disagreement in Cabinet over pruning Budget estimates; **7** Mr. Macmillan left for six-week tour of Commonwealth; **8** Summit talks proposed by Marshal Bulganin and Notes sent to 19 States; **13** Over 9,000 scientists from 44 countries petition UN Sec. Gen. to end nuclear weapons tests; **20** Dr. Vivian Fuchs, leader of Commonwealth expedition, reached South Pole; **24** Announcement that Harwell scientists working with ZETA had passed first milestone on road towards power from nuclear fusion; **28** Abolition of licensed prostitution in Italy; **31** First American earth satellite *Explorer I* (30·8 lb.) successfully launched.

**February 1** Union of Egypt and Syria in the United Arab Republic; **5** Continuation of Antarctic research for at least 5 years after end of IGY announced; **8** French aircraft bombed Tunisian frontier village of Sakhiet; **14** Merger of Iraq and Jordan under name of Arab Federation; **19** Worst colliery disaster in Indian history in West Bengal; **25** Restoration plans for Stonehenge announced; Campaign for Nuclear Disarmament launched under presidency of Lord Russell.

**March 2** IGY Commonwealth Trans-Antarctic Expedition, led by Dr. Vivian Fuchs, completed first crossing of Antarctic (2,200 miles in 99 days); **8** Federal union between UAR and Yemen established; **14** Birth of Prince Albert of Monaco; Small test satellite, *Beta 1958*, successfully launched by US Navy; **20** Bank rate reduced from 7 to 6 per cent; **21** Opening of London planetarium, the first of its kind in Britain; **26** Third US earth satellite, *Explorer III*, successfully launched; **27** M. Khrushchev elected Prime Minister in succession to M. Bulganin; **31** Russian resolution to suspend nuclear tests: other powers invited to follow suit.

**April 1** Abolition of legalised prostitution in Japan; **4** Campaign for Nuclear Disarmament organised 50-mile protest march from London to Atomic Weapons Research Establishment at Aldermaston, Berkshire; **14** *Sputnik II* disintegrated over Caribbean, having completed 2,370 circuits of the Earth and travelled 62 million miles; **17** Nationalist Party of S. Africa returned with increased majority; Sir Grantley Adams elected first Prime Minister of the new West Indian Federation; **22** Princess Margaret opened the new Federal Parliament in Trinidad.

A.D.

**May 1** Intense radiation belt in outer space discovered by US *Explorer* earth satellite; **10** Anti-government disturbances in Lebanon; **13** Military and colonist insurrection in Algeria; President of Italy paid state visit to Britain; **15** *Sputnik III* launched under IGY programme; New college to be built at Cambridge University (Churchill College); **22** Further reduction in Bank Rate to 5½ per cent.; **24** Nuclear reactor at Dounreay began working; **29** General de Gaulle accepted invitation to form a " Government of national safety."

**June 1** General de Gaulle became Prime Minister of France; Clean Air Act banning emission of dark smoke came into force; **9** Gatwick Airport opened by the Queen; **19** Further cut in Bank Rate from 5½ to 5 per cent.; New British plan for Cyprus announced; **20** London bus strike ended after 7 weeks; **21** Greek Government rejected British plan for Cyprus; **23** Ghana to be declared a republic.

**July 1** Conference of scientists, including Russian delegation, met at Geneva to discuss ways of detecting nuclear tests; **14** Iraq monarchy overthrown, King Faisal assassinated; establishment of Republic announced; **15** US marines landed in Lebanon; **17** British troops flown to Amman in response to King Hussein's appeal; **24** First life barons and baronesses under Life Peerages Act named; **26** H.M. the Queen created her son, Charles, Prince of Wales; **31** British Prime Minister sent appeal to all Cypriots to end violence.

**August 1** British Government recognised Republic of Iraq; **5** U.S. nuclear submarine *Nautilus* surfaced after having passed under North Pole; **7** Litter Act came into force in Britain; **14** Bank Rate reduced from 5 to 4½ per cent.; **17** First attempt by America to launch moon rocket failed; Britain to resume nuclear tests on Christmas Island; **23** Bombardment by Chinese of Quemoy (Formosa Strait); **29** More American warships join Seventh Fleet in Formosa Strait.

**September 1** International conference on peaceful uses of atomic energy opened in Geneva; **7** Britain successfully fired its first ballistic rocket (Black Knight) from Woomera; **15** Ambassadors of America and China met in Warsaw for discussions on Formosa crisis; **16** Relaxations in hire-purchase; **29** Referendum resulted in overwhelming victory for General de Gaulle; Lord Goddard retired as Lord Chief Justice; succeeded by Lord Justice Parker; Gen. Sir Francis Festing succeeded Field-Marshal Sir Gerald Templer as Chief of the Imperial General Staff.

**October 1** India began change to metric system; **2** French Guinea proclaimed Republic of Guinea after overwhelming vote for independence in French referendum; **8** Martial law in Pakistan; **9** Death of Pope Pius XII at age of 82; **11** The London weeklies *John Bull* and *Illustrated* merged; US *Pioneer* space-rocket successfully launched (but failed to reach moon); **21** First women peers introduced to House of Lords; **28** State opening of Parliament and Queen's Speech televised; Cardinal Roncalli, Patriarch of Venice, elected as Pope John XXIII at age of 76; **31** Conference opened in Geneva (Russia, Britain, and the United States) on suspension of nuclear tests.

**November 20** Bank Rate reduced from 4½ to 4 per cent.; **21** Work started on Forth road bridge, the largest suspension bridge in Europe; **27** Russian plan for withdrawal of troops and demilitarised free Berlin.

**December 8** Last of four nuclear reactors at Calder Hall brought into operation; **17** Chinese leader, Mao Tse-tung, to resign as chairman of Republic but to retain party office; **18** US 4-ton missile fired into orbit; Empire Day to be known in future as Commonwealth Day; **21** General de Gaulle elected President of France; **27** Partial convertibility between £ and $ announced; UAR and Russia signed agreement on Russian co-operation in Aswan high dam project; **28** General de Gaulle announced devaluation of the franc; **31** IGY officially came to an end.

A.D.
**1959**

**January 1** Batista Government in Cuba overthrown by revolutionary movement under Dr. Fidel Castro; **2** Russia launched planet round the sun (*Lunik I*); **3** Alaska became 49th state of American Union; **4** Mr. Mikoyan, Soviet Dep. Prime Min., arrived in Washington on 16-day visit; Rioting in Leopoldville; **7** Britain recognised new Cuban Government; **8** Gen. de Gaulle installed as first Pres. of Fifth French Republic; **10** Russian proposal for conference of 28 nations to draw up German Peace Treaty; **25** Oecumenical Council, the first since 1870, convened by Pope John XXIII.

**February 1** Votes for women rejected by Swiss national poll; **9** New research reactor to be built at Windscale, Cumberland; **11** M. Vincent Auriol resigned from French Socialist Party; **21** Mr. Macmillan arrived in Moscow on official visit; **23** Archbishop Makarios returned to Cyprus after 3-year exile; Cyprus to become a republic with Greek Pres. and Turkish Vice-Pres.; **26** State of emergency declared in Southern Rhodesia; **27** Riots in Malta dockyard due to dismissal of workers.

**March 3** American *Pioneer IV* went into planetary orbit round sun; State of emergency declared in Nyasaland; British scientists isolated basic molecule of penicillin; **17** Uprising in Lhasa against Chinese rule; Flight of Dalai Lama to India; **24** Iraq withdrew from Baghdad Pact.

**April 5** Panchen Lama arrived in Lhasa to take over local government of Tibet; **8** Chair of Criminology founded at Cambridge; **14–16** Worst flood disaster of century in S. America; **23** British heart specialists in Moscow to demonstrate heart surgery; **27** Liu Shao-ch'i succeeded Mao Tse-tung as Chairman (President) of Chinese People's Republic.

**May 1** Opening of Rajendra Bridge (6,074 ft.) over Ganges at Hathidah (Bihar); **2** First Scottish nuclear power-station opened at Chapelcross; **15** Jodrell Bank radioed message to United States via moon; **28** Opening of Mermaid Theatre in City of London; **30** Auckland Harbour Bridge officially opened; **31** World's population (2,800 millions) increasing at rate of 45 millions a year.

**June 8** U.S. Post Office made first successful delivery of mail by guided missile; **17** Mr. de Valera elected Pres. of Rep. of Ireland; Serious riots in African townships in Durban; **18** Five-year plan for Scottish Highlands announced; **24** World record price (£275,000) paid at Sotheby's for Rubens' *The Adoration of the Magi*; **26** St. Lawrence Seaway formally opened by the Queen and Pres. Eisenhower; **29** Norwegian Halden nuclear reactor in operation;

**July 2** Italy to build nuclear submarine *Guglielmo Marconi*; Tancarville road bridge near Le Havre, longest suspension bridge in Europe, opened; **4** Transatlantic record flight set up by Vickers *Vanguard* turbo-prop airliner (2,500 m. in 5½ hrs.); **5** Recovery in good condition of 3 animals from outer space; **7** Litter Act passed making it an offence to drop litter (fine up to £10); **21** Launching of first nuclear merchant ship *Savannah* by Mrs. Eisenhower; **28** £100 tax-free annuity for V.C. holders.

**August 16** The Street Offences Act came into force; **21** Baghdad Pact renamed Central Treaty Organisation; **22** First round-the-world service by British airliners inaugurated; **23** Announcement of plan for oil-pipeline network between Soviet Union and East European countries (completion 1963).

**September 11** British loan made available for Malta dockyard; **13** Russia launched *Lunik II* which landed on moon; **15** Soviet atomic icebreaker *Lenin* made maiden voyage into Baltic; **25** Mr. Bandaranaike, Prime Min. of Ceylon, assassinated; **27** Typhoon in W. Japan (5,000 killed and missing, 1,000,000 homeless).

**October 4** Russia fired *Lunik III*, which took photographs of back of moon; **8** General Election returned Conservatives with 100 overall majority; **10** End of one of longest droughts ever recorded in Britain; **24** Opening of new

A.D.
airport for Wellington, N.Z.; **29** Dublin's famous Abbey Theatre to be rebuilt (destroyed by fire 1951).

**November 1** Basic travel allowance for British tourists ended (foreign currency up to £250 a year and further amounts on application to Bank of England); **2** First section of London-Yorkshire motorway (M1) opened to traffic; **5** Philip Noel-Baker awarded Nobel Peace Prize; **8** Sudan and U.A.R. signed agreement on distribution of Nile waters; **17** Announcement of discovery by American scientists of submarine plateau in Arctic Ocean; **19** Bank of England announced introduction of new series of bank notes (10s., £1, £5, £10); **14** Dounreay fast breeder reactor went into operation; **21** British book exhibition opened in Moscow; **24** CERN's proton synchrotron at Geneva went into full operation generating 24,000 million electron volts (24 GeV.); **27** Duke of Edinburgh opened Ghana's Academy of Learning in Accra; **28** Naval dockyard at Hong Kong closed after 80 years; **30** Inauguration of Italy's first nuclear research reactor; Pink Zone traffic plan went into operation in London.

**December 1** Anglo-Russian cultural agreement signed in London; **12**-power treaty on Antarctica signed in Washington; State of emergency in Cyprus ended; Bursting of dam at Fréjus killed 384 people; Pres. Eisenhower began tour of Europe, Asia, and Middle East; **5** Opening of 400-mile Sahara pipeline by French Prime Minister; **6** Inauguration of Panchet Hill Dam on Damodar R., Bihar; **10** Raising of school-leaving age to 16 recommended by Crowther Report; **14** Archbishop Makarios elected first Pres. of Cyprus; **15** New world speed record of 1,520 m.p.h. set up by U.S. Air Force pilot; **21** Marriage of Shah of Persia to Miss Farah Diba; **26** Soviet Antarctic expedition reached South Pole; **28** Jugoslavia's first nuclear reactor went into operation; Tokyo reported that in 1959 38 people died in hospital from 1945 Hiroshima atomic bomb attack.

**1960**

**January 1** Republic of Cameroun (formerly French Cameroons) became independent state. **4** Albert Camus, French writer, killed in car crash. **7** Hirfanli Dam in Turkey opened, largest in Europe. **9** Work begun on Aswan High Dam. **12** State of emergency ended in Kenya after 8 years; **13** Mr. Aleksander Soldatov appointed to succeed Mr. J. Malik as Soviet Ambassador to Britain. **21** Bank rate increased to 5%. **23** M. Jacques Piccard and an American naval officer descended 7 miles under Pacific in Marianas Trench. **24** Army rising in Algeria. **29** Broadcast of Pres. de Gaulle to nation contributed to collapse of military revolt.

**February 3** Mr. Macmillan addressed S. African Parliament (famous "wind of change" speech). **4** Announcement that American university had made radar contact with Sun. **13** First French atomic test in Sahara. **17** British agreement to U.S. ballistic missile early-warning system at Fylingdales Moor, Yorkshire. **19** Prince Andrew born. **29** Agadir destroyed by earthquake.

**March 17** New £1 notes issued in Britain. **18** Last steam locomotive of British Railways named. **21** Sharpeville shooting in S. Africa when police fired on African gathering. **23** Mr. Khrushchev in Paris. **30** State of emergency in S. Africa.

**April 1** U.N. Security Council adopted resolution deploring shootings in S. Africa. Dr. Hastings Banda, Pres. of proscribed Nyasaland African Congress, released from detention in S. Rhodesia. **5** Pres. de Gaulle on state visit to Britain. **9** Attempt on life of Dr. Verwoerd. **13** *Blue Streak* as military weapon abandoned. **27** Rep. of Togo (former Togoland) came into being as independent state.

**May 1** U.S. aircraft engaged in military reconnaissance flight over Soviet territory shot down. **6** Wedding of Princess Margaret and Mr. A. Armstrong-Jones in Westminster Abbey. **7** U.S. to resume underground nuclear tests; Tal beat Botvinnik in world chess championship; Mr.

A.D.

Leonid Brezhnev succeeded Marshal Voroshilov as Pres. of Soviet Union. 16 Opening and breakdown of Summit conference in Paris. 17 Queen Elizabeth The Queen Mother officially opened Kariba Dam. 21 Earthquake disaster in Chile. 25 Everest climbed by 3 Chinese by northern slope. Army seized control in Turkey. End of U.S. foreign aid to Cuba. 30 Death of Boris Pasternak.

June 10 Britain's first guided-missile destroyer *Devonshire* launched. Britain's nuclear power programme to be slowed down. 23 Bank rate raised to 6%. 25 Completion of second Saharan oil pipe-line (Edjelé to La Skirra on Tunisian coast). 26 British rule in Somaliland ended; Madagascar became independent state within French Community. 29 House of Commons rejected Wolfenden Committee's recommendations on homosexuality. 30 Belgian Congo became independent as the Congo Republic (Pres. M. Kasavubu, Prime Min. M. Lumumba).

July 1 Ghana proclaimed a Republic; Somali Republic came into being (merging of former British Somaliland and Italian Somaliland). 6 Army mutiny in Congo. Death of Aneurin Bevan. 11 Ivory Coast, Dahomey, Niger, and Upper Volta became independent. M. Tshombe, Congolese privincial leader, declared Katanga independent. M. Lumumba asked for U.N. help in reorganising mutinous *Force publique*. 12 Congo (French), Chad and Central African Rep. became independent. 14 Sec. Council called for withdrawal of Belgian troops from Congo. 19–26 Royal Society Tercentenary celebrations.

August 2 Rawalpindi capital of Pakistan instead of Karachi. 8 Military *coup d'état* in Laos. 9 Sec. Council called on Belgium to withdraw troops from Katanga and authorised U.N. troops to replace them. 16 End of British rule in Cyprus which becomes independent Republic. 25 Olympic Games opened in Rome. 29 Prime Minister of Jordan assassinated.

September 5 Announcement by Pres. Kasavubu that he had dismissed M. Lumumba as Prime Minister of Congo. 14 M. Lumumba appealed to U.N. for protection. 19 India and Pakistan signed Indus Waters Treaty. 23 Mr. Khrushchev led Soviet delegation to U.N. General Assembly in New York and criticised U.N. operations in Congo.

October 1 Federation of Nigeria became independent state and a Member of the Commonwealth. 5 Labour Party Conference voted against Party's official defence policy. 14 Turkish trials of members of Menderes régime began. 21 Royal Navy's first nuclear submarine *Dreadnought* launched at Barrow-in-Furness by the Queen. 27 Bank rate reduced to 5½%

November 1 U.S. *Polaris* missile-firing submarines to have base on Clyde. 3 Mr. Gaitskell re-elected leader of Parliamentary Labour Party. 9 Senator John Kennedy elected Pres. of United States. 28 Islamic Republic of Mauritania proclaimed its independence.

December 1 Capture of M. Lumumba by Col. Mobutu's forces. 2 Archbishop of Canterbury visited the Pope at the Vatican. 3 Bank rate reduced to 5%. 14 Fighting in Vientiane, cap. of Laos, between right-wing and left-wing forces. 15 Marriage of King Baudouin of Belgium. 17 Revolt in Ethiopia crushed. 24 Strikes in Belgium. 27 Union of Ghana, Guinea, and Mali. 31 Farthing ceased to be legal tender.

1961

January 18 M. Lumumba, first Prime Min. of the independent Congo, sent to Katanga for imprisonment. 20 The Queen and the Duke of Edinburgh left for tour of India, Pakistan, Nepal and Iran; Mr. John Kennedy took office as 35th Pres. of the United States. 23 Portuguese liner *Santa Maria* seized in Caribbean by armed insurgents under Captain Henrique Galvão as protest against Salazar dictatorship. 26 Full diplomatic relations resumed between Britain and United Arab Republic. 31 M. Spaak resigned as Sec.-Gen. of Nato.

A.D.

February 1 Increased National Health Service prescription charges announced. 3 Capt. Galvão hands over *Santa Maria* to Commander of Brazilian Navy in Recife. 5 Riots in Angola. 13 Death of M. Lumumba announced (violent demonstrations in many countries). 15 Total eclipse of the sun visible from Europe. 21 U.N. authorised the use of force " if necessary, in the last resort " to prevent civil war in Congo: measures also to be taken for withdrawal of all foreign military personnel and mercenaries. 26 Death of King Mohammed V of Morocco; succeeded by elder son who becomes King Hassan II.

March 3 First of American nuclear-powered submarines carrying Polaris missiles arrived at Holy Loch; Death of Sir Thomas Beecham. 12 First winter ascent of the Eiger. 14 The New English Bible (New Testament) published. 15 Uprising of tribal groups in Angola, Portuguese murdered; brutal retaliation of Portuguese by burning and bombing. 25 Russian satellite with dog aboard launched and brought safely back to earth. 29 Four-year South African treason trial ended with acquittal of accused. 31 The Nore Command ceased to exist.

April 9 Death of former King Zog of Albania. 11 Opening of trial of Adolf Eichmann in Jerusalem. 12 Major Yuri Gagarin made first flight into space and back. 17 Unsuccessful invasion of Cuba by rebel forces. 22 Insurrection of part of French army in Algeria: State of emergency declared in France. 23 Census held in Great Britain. 24 Gen. de Gaulle ordered blockade of Algeria. 25 Both sides in Laos agreed to cease-fire. 26 Collapse of mutiny in Algeria. 27 Independence of Sierra Leone.

May 1 Betting and Gaming Act came into force in Britain: betting shops opened. 5 Commander Alan Shepard made first American flight into space; The Queen and the Duke of Edinburgh visited Pope John XXIII at the Vatican. 12 Botvinnik regained world chess championship from Tal. 16 International conference on Laos opened in Geneva; Army in South Korea seized power. 17 Guildford Cathedral consecrated. 19 British Trade Fair in Moscow opened (M. Khrushchev present). 20 Talks opened at Evian between French government and Algerian provincial government (broke down July 18). 31 Gen. Trujillo, dictator of Dominican Republic, assassinated; South Africa became a Republic and withdrew from British Commonwealth.

June 1 N. Cameroons became part of Nigeria. 3 Meeting of Pres. Kennedy and M. Khrushchev in Vienna. 9 Security Council voted for Afro-Asian resolution calling upon Portugal to end repressive measures in Angola. 24 Promulgation by Pope John XXIII of new constitution for the Knights of Malta. 27 Enthronement of Dr. Ramsey as Archbishop of Canterbury in Canterbury Cathedral. 30 Portuguese refused to stop repressive measures in Angola.

July 1 British forces landed in Kuwait following appeal from ruler. 2 Death of Ernest Hemingway. 7 Soviet Trade Exhibition opened in London. 11 Major Yuri Gagarin, Russian pioneer of space travel, welcomed in London. 18 Over £9 million raised in Britain for 1960 World Refugee Year. 19 Fighting began between French and Tunisian forces over Bizerta naval base; Announcement of U.K.–U.S. agreement to establish Missile Defence Alarm (Midas) Station at Kirkbride, Cumberland. 21 U.S. launched its second space traveller (Capt. V. Grissom) 118 m. high, flight time 16 mins.; New Runcorn-Widnes Bridge opened over Mersey and Manchester Ship Canal (third largest span of its kind in the world and the largest span arch in Europe). 24 Bank rate rose from 5 to 7%. 30 Israel began construction of deep-sea port at Asdod.

August 4 International Monetary Fund placed £714 million at Britain's disposal. 6 Major Titov, Russia's second space man, circled earth 17 times before landing back near Moscow 25 hours later. 13 Soviet sector of Berlin sealed off from Western sectors. 14 Jomo Kenyatta

A.D.

became a free man again. 15 U.N. recognised M. Adoula's government as the central government of the Congo. 16 Dr. Hastings Banda's Malawi Congress Party won control in the Nyasaland Legislative Assembly. 30 No agreement reached at Geneva on banning of nuclear tests. 31 Soviet announcement of resumption of nuclear weapons tests.

September 5 International conference on preservation of wild life opened at Arusha, Tanganyika; U.S. to resume underground nuclear tests. 18 Mr. Hammarskjöld killed in plane crash when flying from Leopoldville, Congo, to Ndola, N. Rhodesia, to meet M. Tshombe in effort to arrange cease-fire between U.N. and Katanga forces. 28 Syria seceded from the United Arab Republic (the latter name to continue to be used by Egypt).

October 1 S. Cameroons gained independence as part of Cameroun. 3 Mr. A. Armstrong-Jones created Earl of Snowdon. 4 Labour Party Conference voted against Polaris bases and German troops in Britain. 5 Bank rate reduced to 6½%. 10 Volcanic eruption on Tristan da Cunha; whole population evacuated to Britain. 21 U.S. put into space, amid world-wide protest, 350 million copper needles for reflecting radio signals (they failed to disperse into orbit). 23 Nobel Peace Prize for 1960 awarded to South African, Albert Luthuli, former Zulu chief; that for 1961 posthumously to Dag Hammarskjöld. 30 Russia tested a bomb of over 60 megatons amid world-wide protest. 31 Hurricane struck British Honduras, Belize devastated; Stalin's body removed from the Lenin Mausoleum in Red Square; Australia's new radio telescope at Parkes, N.S.W. officially commissioned by Gov.-Gen.

November 1 Boy scouts permitted to wear long trousers. 2 Bank rate reduced to 6%. 3 U Thant, Burma's chief representative at U.N., elected Acting Sec.-Gen. of U.N.; Birth of son to Princess Margaret and Lord Snowdon; Government refused to save Doric arch at Euston station. 7 Dr. Adenauer re-elected Chancellor of Fed. German Rep. for fourth time. 8 Official negotiations for entry of Britain into Common Market opened in Brussels; Wales votes for Sunday opening. 9 The Queen and the Duke of Edinburgh left for tour of Ghana, Liberia, and Sierra Leone. 20 Admission of Russian Orthodox Church to World Council of Churches meeting at New Delhi. 28 South Africa's apartheid policy condemned by U.N.

December 8 Cross-Channel submarine cable linking electricity systems of England and France officially inaugurated. 9 Tanganyika became independent sovereign state within British Commonwealth; Russia broke off diplomatic relations with Albania. 15 Adolf Eichmann sentenced to death by Israeli court for crimes against the Jewish people and against humanity; Mr. Macmillan and Pres. Kennedy met in Bermuda. 17 Indian troops took over Portuguese colony of Goa. 19 Decimal coinage accepted in principle by British government. 20 Mr. Adoula and Mr. Tshombe agreed on Katanga's subordinate status. 27 Belgium and the Congo resumed diplomatic relations.

1962

January 1 Western Samoa became independent. 10 Avalanche disaster in Peru. 11 Smallpox outbreak in Britain. 15 Centigrade first used in weather forecasts. 16 Death of R. H. Tawney. 24 T.U.C. decided to join "Neddy". 27 New world record for mile by New Zealander Peter Snell (3 min. 54·4 secs.). 30 Birth of son to King Hussein of Jordan.

February 11 Death of Lord Birkett. 20 American first manned orbital flight.

March 7 Franco-Algerian negotiations began at Evian; Publication of Royal College of Physician's Report on dangers to health from cigarette smoking. 8 Bank rate reduced from 6 to 5½%. 14 Opening of 17-nation disarmament conference at Geneva. 19 End of Algerian war. 28 Inauguration of Marlborough

A.D.

House, built by Wren, as Commonwealth Centre.

April 1 Government's "pay pause" ended. 2 "Panda" crossings in operation in number of British towns. 5 Completion of Gt. St. Bernard road tunnel. 7 Strike in Asturias—first of many throughout Spain. 8 French people voted in referendum approving Algerian peace settlement. 11 Pres. Kennedy condemned U.S. steel industry for raising prices. 13 International agreement (40 countries) to stop oil pollution of seas and beaches. 20 Gen. Salan, O.A.S. leader, arrested by French in Algiers. 25 U.S. began new series of atmospheric nuclear tests in Pacific. 26 Britain's first satellite, Ariel, launched from Cape Canaveral; Bank rate down from 5 to 4½%. 30 Norway applied to join Common Market.

May 6 Signor Segni elected Pres. of Italy; Canonisation of St. Martin de Porres of Lima (d. 1639), first mulatto saint of the R.C. church. 8 Trolleybuses ran for last time in London. 13 Dr. Radhakrishnan elected Pres. of India. 25 Consecration of new Coventry Cathedral. 29 Dawley, Shropshire, designated new town. 31 Eichmann executed in Israel; Dissolution of The West Indies Federation.

June 5 Creation of University of Lagos, Nigeria. 14 Creation of European Space Research Organisation (ESRO). 15 Nuclear power station at Berkeley, Glos., began electricity supply to national grid. 18 The Flying Scotsman made centenary journey; Conservatives (Mr. Diefenbaker) won Canadian general election by small majority. 23 Cease-fire in Laos. 24 Opening of Punjabi University, India. 28 U.N. called for more liberal constitution for S. Rhodesia.

July 1 Burundi and Rwanda became independent; After 132 years French colonial rule in Algeria ended; Commonwealth Immigrants Act came into force. 3 Plan for British national theatre and opera house accepted by L.C.C. and Government. 5 Independence celebrated in Algeria. 8 Pres. de Gaulle and Chan. Adenauer attended Mass in Rheims cathedral. 10 Telstar, first experimental satellite in space communication, launched—first live television between U.S. and Europe. 20 Death of G. M. Trevelyan, the historian. 25 Opening of new civic centre at Plymouth. 26 Government announce setting up of "Nicky". 30 Archbishop of Canterbury visited Moscow. 31 Rendezvous of U.S. nuclear submarines at North Pole.

August 5 Russia began series of atmospheric nuclear tests; Death of Marilyn Monroe, at age 36. 5 Jamaica became independent. 10 Abandonment of Blue Water missile. 11 British mountaineers scaled Russia's highest peak (Mt. Communism). 11 and 12 Russia launched two men into orbit (64 orbits and 48 orbits). 13 British travel allowances further eased from £250 a year to £250 a journey. 14 Completion of Mont Blanc tunnel (7½ m.). 17 Pres. Kennedy's, Bill on medical care rejected by Senate. 20 Government approval for construction of new underground railway between Victoria and Walthamstow. 21 Maiden voyage of Savannah, world's first nuclear-powered merchant ship. 27 U.S. Mariner II launched towards Venus. 31 Trinidad and Tobago became independent.

September 3 Opening of Trans-Canada highway (4,800 m. from St. John's, Newfoundland, to Victoria, B.C.). 7 Life presidency for Dr. Nkrumah. 15 In exchange of Notes Iran assured Russia that no foreign rocket bases would be permitted. 20 Zimbabwe African People's Union banned in S. Rhodesia; Fighting between Chinese and Indian troops on disputed N.E. frontier. 27 Overthrow of Imamate and republic proclaimed in Yemen. 29 Canada launched her first satellite, the Alouette, into orbit. 30 U.S. troops enforced Fed. Government's order that Negro student should enrol at Mississippi State University.

October 3 6-orbit flight of U.S. astronaut. 9 Uganda became independent. 11 21st Oecumenical Council opened at St. Peter's, Rome.

A.D.

17 Opening of Hyde Park Corner underpass; Electricity for national grid generated at Dounreay reactor. 24 Commencement of U.S. naval quarantine of Cuba. 28 Dismantling of missile base in Cuba agreed upon by Russia; Gen. de Gaulle won referendum for his proposal for direct election of President.

November 1 Russia sent spacecraft on 7-month journey to Mars. 6 Admiralty announced record ocean depth by H.M.S. *Cook* in Mindanao trench (37,782 ft); Opening of Commonwealth Institute (replaces Imperial Institute, S. Kensington). 18 Death of Niels Bohr. 20 Cuba blockade ended. 21 Cease-fire declaration by China on Sino-Indian border dispute (no further hostilities occurred after this date). 29 Announcement of new Indo-Pakistan negotiations on Kashmir. 30 U Thant unanimously elected Sec.-Gen. of U.N.

December 5 Soviet-American space research co-operation agreement; Uprising in British prot. of Brunei in protest to joining Fed. of Malaysia; British nuclear device exploded underground in Nevada. 9 Tanganyika became republic and Dr. Julius Nyerere its first president. 12 British troops in control of Brunei uprising. 14 Signals from *Mariner II* as it passed within 21,000 miles of Venus; Eritrea became province of Ethiopia; N. Rhodesia's first African dominated government formed. 15 Sir Edgar Whitehead's party lost to right-wing party in S. Rhodesian general election. 17 Mr. Macmillan left for meeting with Pres. Kennedy at Nassau, Bahamas. 21 U.S. decision to abandon *Skybolt*; offer of *Polaris* missiles for British submarines to form part of multilateral Nato nuclear force. 23 M. Fedorenko succeeded M. Zorin as Soviet perm. rep. at U.N. 25 Europe snowbound with freezing temperatures. 28 Agreement in principle reached between China and Pakistan defining mutual boundary. 29 Southern England swept by blizzard. 30 Worst snowstorms in England since 1881. 31 British Transport Commission replaced by British Railways Board (created by Transport Act, 1962), with Dr. Beeching as chairman.

**1963**

January 2 Gen. Lemnitzer succeeded Gen. Norstad as Supreme Allied Commander, Europe. 3 Bank rate reduced from 4½ to 4 per cent. 14 Gen. de Gaulle's press conference repulsing Britain's entry to EEC and rejecting U.S. Polaris offer. 15 Official ending of Katanga secession. 18 Death of Hugh Gaitskell; Aden acceded to Fed. of S. Arabia. 29 Britain was refused entry to EEC; Death of Robert Frost, the American poet.

February 1 Nyasaland became self-governing protectorate. 5 Death of Lord Samuel. 6 Shipping restrictions on Cuba announced by U.S. Government. 8 Overthrow of Iraq government and execution of Gen. Kassim. 12 Seventeen-nation disarmament conference resumed in Geneva. 14 Harold Wilson elected leader of Labour Party. 19 Bali volcano disaster (others followed March 19, May 19). 22 Unemployment figures showed 878,356, highest since 1947.

March 5–6 First frost-free night in Britain since Dec. 22. 8 Syrian government overthrown by military coup. 17 Typhoid broke out in Zermatt; First of Tristan de Cunha islanders returned home. 27 Publication of Beeching Report on British Railways.

April 5 Opening of Berkley and Bradwell civil nuclear power stations. 6 Polaris missile agreement signed between U.S. and Britain. 8 Mr. Diefenbaker's Conservative Party defeated by Liberals in Canadian general election. 9 Honorary American citizenship conferred on Sir Winston Churchill. 10 Pope John XXIII published his encyclical *Pacem in Terris*; New Zealand to change to decimal coinage in 1967; Loss of U.S. nuclear submarine *Thresher* with 129 lives. 17 Commissioning of Royal Navy's first nuclear-powered submarine, H.M.S. *Dreadnought*. 20 Execution of Julian Griman, Spanish communist leader.

A.D.

May 1 End of Dutch East Indies: New Guinea (West Irian) handed to Indonesia. 15 Twenty-two-orbit flight of Major Cooper of U.S. Air Force. 16 Radio contact lost with Soviet *Mars I* launched Nov. 1962. 20 Petrosian won world chess title from Botvinnik; Life presidency for Pres. Sukarno of Indonesia.

June 1 Death of Pope John XXIII; new internal self-government constitution for Kenya came into force with Jomo Kenyatta as Kenya's first Prime Minister. 11 Iraq resumed war against Kurds. 12 Rioting on big scale in Georgetown, British Guiana. 14–19 Bykovsky-Tereshkova space flights (first woman astronaut). 16 Resignation of Mr. Ben-Gurion announced. 20 House of Commons censure on Mr. John Profumo, former Sec. of State for War. 24 Zanzibar achieved internal self-government. 28 Inauguration in Nairobi of Univ. of East Africa. 30 Pope Paul VI crowned.

July 2 Franco-German Treaty of Co-operation came into force. 5 Sino-Soviet ideological talks began. 9 State visit of King and Queen of Greece to Britain. 26 Skopje destroyed by earthquake. 29 Pres. de Gaulle rejected Moscow test-ban treaty. 31 The Peerage Bill received the Royal Assent; Security Council called on member states to impose partial arms embargo on Portugal.

August 1 Under Criminal Justice Act, 1961 minimum prison age raised to 17. 3 First successful solo climb on north wall of Eiger by Michel Darbellay, a Swiss mountain guide. 5 Partial nuclear-test-ban treaty signed in Moscow by America, Russia, and Britain. 7 Security Council resolution to stop sale and shipment of arms to S. Africa. 8 Glasgow-London mail train robbery (£2·5 million). 9 Caernarvon declared royal borough (first in Wales). 16 Announcement of American-Soviet weather-and communications-satellite programme. 20 Mr. Khrushchev visited Yugoslavia. 21 Buddhists arrested and martial law imposed in South Vietnam. 28 Great Negro "freedom march" on Washington. 31 Death of George Braque, the French painter; The "hot line" linking Kremlin with White House went into service.

September 5 Soviet-American co-operation in cosmic ray research in Antarctica announced. 15 Ben Bella elected first President of Algeria. 16 New state of Malaysia (Malaya, Singapore, North Borneo (now Sabah), and Sarawak) came into being. 17 Malaysia broke off diplomatic relations with Indonesia; Fylingdales ballistic missile early warning station came into operation. 18 New Australian decimal currency to be introduced Feb. 1966 (unit to be called the dollar). 19 Anglo-French report recommended rail tunnel as Channel link. 21 Reform of Roman Catholic Curia announced by Pope Paul VI. 23 Report on decimal currency advocated division of £1 into 100 units. 25 Denning report on Profumo affair published. 29 Reopening of Vatican Council; First buildings of University of East Anglia opened at Norwich.

October 1 Nigeria became a republic within the Commonwealth with Dr. Azikiwe its first President; Algeria nationalised French-owned land 3 Honduras government overthrown by Army. 4 Hurricane Flora struck the Caribbean. 9 Viaont dam disaster (N. Italy); the Kubaka of Buganda became first President of Uganda. 15 Dr. Adenauer retired after 14 years as Chancellor of Fed. German Republic; succeeded by Prof. Ludwig Erhard. 18 Mr. Macmillan resigned as Prime Minister; succeeded by the Earl of Home; French sent cat into space and brought it safely back. 23 Robbins report on higher education published.

November 1 Diem oligarchy of S. Vietnam overthrown by military coup; First executions in S. Africa under the Sabotage Act of 1963. 7 Eleven German miners rescued after a fortnight underground; Sir Alec Douglas-Home elected at Kinross and W. Perthshire. 9 Train and mine disasters in Japan. 13 Death of Dr. Margaret Murray, the archaeologist, at age 100. 16 Greece began to release Communist prisoners

A.D.
taken during last war. 17 Temples of Abu Simbel to be removed and re-sited. 18 Opening of Dartford–Purfleet tunnel, linking Kent and Essex under Thames. 22 Assassination of President Kennedy in Dallas, Texas; Vice-President Lyndon Johnson sworn in as new President. 27 Publication of Buchanan report.

December 3 Britain's second nuclear submarine, the *Valiant*, launched. 4 Second session of Vatican Council ended; Closure of Woolwich Arsenal announced. 10 Zanzibar became an independent state within the Commonwealth. 12 Kenya became an independent state within the Commonwealth. 22 Greek liner *Lakonia* caught fire and sank on Christmas cruise, 250 miles W. of Gibraltar. 31 Dissolution of Federation of Rhodesia and Nyasaland.

**1964**

January 4–6 Pope Paul made pilgrimage to Holy Land: first meeting between Pope and Patriarch of Constantinople since 1439. 9 Rioting in Panama. 12 Republican régime in Zanzibar. 20 Army mutiny in Tanganyika. 27 France recognized China; School-leaving age to be raised to 16 in 1970–71. 28 Riots in Salisbury, S. Rhodesia, after trial of Joshua Nkomo.

February 6 Anglo-French agreement on rail Channel tunnel announced. 11 Fighting between Greeks and Turks at Limassol, Cyprus. 27 Bank rate raised from 4 to 5%.

March 4 August Bank holiday in 1965 and 1966 to be moved to last Monday in month. 6 Death of King Paul of the Hellenes; son proclaimed King Constantine XIII. 10 Birth of Prince Edward. 11 S. Africa withdrew from I.L.O. 19 Opening of Great St. Bernard tunnel. 24 Stansted, Essex, provisionally chosen as site of London's third airport. 25 Plinth at Runnymede and scholarship fund for study in U.S. to be memorials to President Kennedy. 27 U.N. peacekeeping force in Cyprus operational; Britain's second space satellite, *Ariel* 2, launched in Virginia; Severe earthquake and tidal wave in Alaska.

April 4 Dr. Leakey confirmed discovery in Tanganyika of *Homo habilis*; heavy fighting in Cyprus between Greek and Turkish communities. 5 Death of General MacArthur. 8 Shaikh Abdullah, former Prime Minister of Kashmir, released by Indian Government. 9 First Greater London Council election: Labour 64, Conservatives 36. 10 Mr. Macmillan declined earldom and Order of the Garter. 13 Mr. Ian Smith became Prime Minister of S. Rhodesia on resignation of Mr. Winston Field. 16 Sentences totalling 307 years passed on 12 men found guilty in mail train robbery trial (two subsequently escaped from prison). 21 Opening of BBC-2. 23 Shakespeare quatercentenary celebrations. 27 Tanganyika and Zanzibar united (United Republic of Tanzania).

May 1 Birth of a daughter to Princess Margaret and Lord Snowdon. 9 Mr. Khrushchev's first visit to Egypt (completion of first stage Aswan High Dam). 22 State of emergency declared in British Guiana. 26 Typhoid outbreak in Aberdeen. 27 Death of Jawaharlal Nehru.

June 2 Mr. Lal Bahadur Shastri elected Prime Minister of India. 3 Senator Barry Goldwater of Arizona defeated Mr. Nelson Rockefeller, Governor of New York, in Republican Party's primary election in California. 5 First flight into space of Britain's *Blue Streak* rocket (fired from Woomera). 9 Death of Lord Beaverbrook. 12 Life imprisonment imposed on Nelson Mandela and others in Rivonia trial, Pretoria; 20-year treaty of friendship signed between Soviet Union and E. Germany. 24 Picturephone, whereby speakers can see as well as hear each other, in operation in U.S. 30 Last U.N. troops left Congo.

July 2 Enactment of U.S. Civil Rights Bill. 6 Nyasaland became independent state of Malawi. 8 Opening of Commonwealth Prime Ministers'

A.D.
Conference in London. 10 M. Tshombe succeeded M. Adoula as Prime Minister of the Congo. 12 Death of Maurice Thorez, French communist leader. 15 Mr. Mikoyan succeeded Mr. Brezhnev as President of the Soviet Union. 17 Court of Session, Edinburgh, ruled that Harris Tweed must be wholly made in Outer Hebrides; Mr. Donald Campbell broke land-speed record on Lake Eyre with 403·1 m.p.h. 27 Last appearance of Sir Winston Churchill in House of Commons. 31 American *Ranger* 7 hit moon after sending back over 4,000 pictures of surface.

August 2 U.S. destroyer attacked by N. Vietnam torpedo boats off coast of N. Vietnam. 4 Nine French miners rescued after being trapped underground at Champagnole for 8 days; Bodies of three murdered civil rights workers found near Philadelphia, Mississippi. 5 Congolese rebels captured Stanleyville; U.S. air raid on N. Vietnam. 13 General Grivas, former EOKA leader, took over supreme command of Cypriot National Guard. 13 Common Market set up by Arab League (Iraq, Jordan, Kuwait, Syria and U.A.R.) to come into force Jan. 1965. 21 Death of Togliatti, Italian Communist leader.

September 2 Indonesian landings in Malaya. 4 Opening of new Forth bridge (largest suspension bridge in Europe). 7 People's Republic of the Congo declared by Congolese rebels. 14 Third session of Vatican Council opened (closed 21 Nov.). 20 Gen. de Gaulle began his tour of S. America. 21 Malta became independent state within the British Commonwealth after 164 years of British rule. 22 Hunterston nuclear power station opened. 28 Maiden flight of supersonic TSR 2; Death of Harpo Marx, the great film comedian.

October 5 The Queen and the Duke of Edinburgh arrived in Canada on week's visit. 10 Opening of Olympic Games in Tokyo. 12 Soviet 3-man spaceship launched on 24-hour flight; First shipment of liquid methane from Saharan oilfield to Britain. 14 1964 Nobel Peace Prize awarded to Dr. Martin Luther King. 15 Mr. Khruschev replaced in posts of First Secretary of the CPSU and Prime Minister by Mr. Brezhnev and Mr. Kosygin respectively; General election in Britain: Labour won with overall majority of five. 16 Mr. Harold Wilson became Prime Minister; China exploded an atomic device. 22 M. Jean-Paul Sartre declined Nobel Prize for Literature which had been awarded him. 24 Northern Rhodesia achieved independence as Republic of Zambia with Kenneth Kaunda as its first President; S. Rhodesia became officially known as Rhodesia. 26 Government proposed 15% import surcharge and export tax rebate to deal with balance of payments crisis. 29 Nobel Prize for Chemistry awarded to Prof. Dorothy Hodgkin.

November 2 Deposition of King Saud of Saudi Arabia and accession of his brother Faisal. 3 U.S. Presidential election: sweeping victory for President Johnson over Senator Goldwater. 5 Mr. Chou En-lai in Moscow for 47th anniversary of October revolution; Cease-fire in Yemen after two years of civil strife. 10 Australia to introduce selective compulsory service for military service overseas. 12 Grand Duchess Charlotte of Luxembourg abdicated after 45 years' rule in favour of her son. 17 Government to ban export of arms to S. Africa. 23 Bank rate rose from 5 to 7%. 21 Opening of Verrazano-Narrows bridge spanning mouth of New York harbour, the world's longest bridge. 24 Belgian paratroops landed at Stanleyville to rescue rebel-held hostages.

December 1 Death of J. B. S. Haldane. 2 The Pope welcomed in Bombay. 5 Bishopsgate railway goods depot destroyed by fire, two customs officers dying in blaze. 12 Kenya became Republic within Commonwealth with Mr. Kenyatta as first President. 16 Statement of Intent on productivity, prices and incomes signed by Government, T.U.C. and Employers' organisations. 17 Free prescriptions from 1 February 1965. 28 Signor Saragat elected

A.D.

President of Italy. **31** Mr. Donald Campbell broke world water-speed record with speed of 276·33 m.p.h. on Lake Dumbleyung in W. Australia.

**1965**

**January 7** Indonesia withdrew from U.N. **15** Child's body found (Dec. 11, 1964) in coffin in Stepney identified as that of Lady Anne Mowbray (1472–81), child wife of Richard, Duke of York (one of Princes in the Tower); remains reinterred in Westminster Abbey; Prime Minister of Burundi assassinated. **20** Lyndon Baines Johnson inaugurated as 36th President of U.S. **21** Prime Minister of Iran assassinated. **24** Death of Sir Winston Churchill. **26** Hindi became official language of India with English an additional official tongue. **31** National Health prescription charges ended.

**February 1** The Queen and Duke of Edinburgh in Ethiopia on state visit. **4** Lysenko dismissed as Director of Institute of Genetics. **7** First U.S. retaliatory raids against N. Vietnam. **17** Pres. Johnson announced U.S. would continue " actions that are justified as necessary for defence of S. Vietnam." **18** Gambia became independent as 21st member of the Br. Commonwealth. **24** U.S. piloted jets bombed Vietcong in S. Vietnam. **25** Dr. Heenan, Archbishop of Westminster, created a cardinal.

**March 3** Remains of Roger Casement, from Pentonville Prison, reburied in Dublin; Seretse Khama became Bechuanaland's first Prime Minister. **7** First of 3,500 American marines landed in S. Vietnam. **18** Alexei Leonov became first man to leave a spaceship and float in space. **19** Record price of 760,000 guineas paid at Christie's for Rembrandt's *Titus*. **23** First successful two-man manœuvrable flight by Grissom and Young in *Gemini III*; Dr. Dorothy Hodgkin awarded Order of Merit. **24** Successful completion of U.S. *Ranger* moon shot programme. **25** Defeat of Mrs. Bandaranaike in Ceylon elections; Mr. Senanayake became Prime Minister. **28** Death of the Princess Royal; Earthquake in Chile.

**April 1** Younger brother of King Hussein made heir to Jordan throne in place of his 3-year-old son. **6** Launching of *Early Bird* commercial communication satellite; Cancellation of TSR 2. **9** Fighting broke out between Indian and Pakistan forces in Rann of Kutch. **11** Tornadoes in mid-western U.S. killed 278 people. **23** Opening of 250-mile Pennine Way, Britain's first long-distance footpath from Edale in Derbyshire to Kirk Yetholm in Roxburghshire. **24** Outbreak of civil war in Dominican Republic. **27** Import surcharge of 15 per cent reduced to 10 per cent. **28** Landing of American troops in Dominican Republic. **29** Australian troops to be sent to S. Vietnam.

**May 8** Arrest of Sheik Abdullah on return to India from tour abroad; Spanish confirmation that one of bodies found near Portuguese border in Feb. was that of General Delgado, Portuguese opposition leader. **11** Cyclone and tidal wave disaster in E. Pakistan killing 16,000 people. **13** Conservatives made big gains in U.K. local government elections. **14** Inauguration of Kennedy memorial at Runnymede; China exploded second atomic bomb. **15** Completion of Benmore power station and Cook Strait cable—part of New Zealand's 10-year power development scheme. **17** Britain and France to co-operate in developing two military aircraft; **31** miners killed in Welsh colliery disaster. **18** The Queen and the Duke of Edinburgh on 10-day state visit to Fed. German Republic. **20–29** Indian ascents of Everest. **28** 267 miners killed in Indian colliery disaster.

**June 1** 237 miners killed in Japanese colliery explosion. **3** Bank rate reduced to 6 per cent; Launching of U.S. *Gemini IV* with McDivitt and White; the latter walked in space for 20 min. **4–7** Visit of Mr. Chou En-lai to Tanzania. **7** 128 miners killed in Jugoslav mine disaster. **9** World record for mile broken by M. Jazy of France (3 min. 53·6 sec.). **17** Opening of Commonwealth Prime Ministers' Conference

A.D.

in London. **19** Pres. Ben Bella of Algeria deposed by Revolutionary Council under Col. Boumedienne. **22** 700th anniversary of Parliament celebrated. **28** *Early Bird* went into commerical service (poised 23,000 miles above Atlantic between Brazil and Africa). **30** Cease-fire agreement in Rann of Kutch signed.

**July 8** Another mail train robber escaped from prison. **6** Inauguration of SRC radiotelescope at Lord's Bridge, Cambridge. **11** Mme. Furtseva, Soviet Minister of Culture, visited Britain. **14** Adlai Stevenson died in London, suddenly. **14** Mme. Vaucher climbed north wall of Matterhorn, the first woman to do so. **15** First close-up pictures of Mars successfully transmitted to earth by U.S. *Mariner IV* across 134 million miles; King Constantine of Greece dismissed his Prime Minister, Mr. Papandreou. **16** Opening of Mont Blanc tunnel. **19** Death of Syngman Rhee, former Pres. of S. Korea. **20** Malawi to become a republic on July 6, 1966. **22** Sir Alec Douglas-Home resigned as leader of the Conservative Party; succeeded by Mr. Edward Heath (July 28). **26** Maldive Islands became independent. **29** Rebuilding of London Bridge planned; Appointment of Lord Casey as Governor-General of Australia. **30** U.S. Medical Care for the Aged Bill passed.

**August 1** Radio and television licence fees increased; Television ban on cigarette advertising. **3** Creation of a new award " The Queen's Award to Industry " for export and technological achievement; M. Malraux, French Minister of Culture, met Mao Tse-tung in Peking. **5** Clashes on Kashmir border. **6** U.S. Voting Rights Bill passed. **9** Singapore seceded from Malaysia; Marriage between Moslems and Communists forbidden in U.A.R. **11** Negro riots in Los Angeles. **12** Appointment of first woman High Court judge. **21** U.S. *Gemini V* (Cooper and Conrad) launched (landed Aug. 29 after 120 orbits). **24** Pres. Nasser and King Faisal signed cease-fire agreement in Yemen.

**September 1** Pakistan forces crossed Kashmir cease-fire line. **2** Death of Sir Harry Hylton-Foster, Speaker of the House of Commons. **5** Death of Dr. Albert Schweitzer. **6** Indian forces invaded W. Pakistan and bombed Lahore. **12** American division 20,000 strong landed in S. Vietnam; General election in Norway: Labour Government defeated. **14** Second Vatican Council reconvened for 4th session. **16** Publication of Government's White Paper, *The National Plan*, covering Britain's economic development 1964–70. **21** British Petroleum oil rig *Sea Gem* struck oil in North Sea. **22** Cease-fire in Indo-Pakistan war.

**October 1** Attempt to overthrow Pres. Sukarno of Indonesia; reprisals against communists. **3** First international symposium on water desalination met in Washington. **4** The Pope flew to New York and addressed the U.N. Assembly; First Commonwealth Medical Conference met in Edinburgh. **6** Sir Robert Menzies appointed Lord Warden of the Cinque Ports. **8** Talks in London on Rhodesian independence ended without agreement. **11** Publication of Vinland Map, the only known example of mediæval Norse cartography. **13** Pres. Kasavubu of Congo dismissed Mr. Tshombe. **17** Demonstrations throughout U.S. and in London against war in Vietnam. **19** Dr. Erhard re-elected Chancellor of Fed. Rep. of Germany. **22** Pakistan and India accept cease-fire call of Security Council. **26** Dr. Horace King elected Speaker of House of Commons—the first Labour Speaker. **28** Parliament passed Bill abolishing death penalty for murder.

**November 1** Severe gales swept Britain. **8** New British colony of British Indian Ocean Territory set up. **11** Mr. Ian Smith of Rhodesia signed unilateral declaration of independence; Britain declared rebel regime illegal and introduced economic sanctions. **15** New land speed record of 600·6 m.p.h. set up in Utah by jet-powered car. **20** Security Council called on all states to sever economic relations with Rhodesia, and urged oil embargo. **25** General Mobuto

A.D.
deposed Pres. Kasavubu. **25** France launched her first earth satellite. **27** Pres. Kaunda of Zambia asked Britain to send troops to Kariba.

**December 1** R.A.F. Javelins arrived in Zambia. **4** *Gemini VII* (Borman and Lovell) launched. **6** Russia increased her defence expenditure. **8** The Second Vatican Council closed. **9** Mr. Mikoyan retired as President of the Soviet Union; replaced by Mr. Nikolai Podgorny. **15** Rendezvous in orbit between *Geminis VI* and *VII*; Tanzania and Guinea broke off diplomatic relations with Britain over Rhodesia. **16** Mr. Wilson addressed the U.N. Assembly; Dead Sea Scrolls exhibited at British Museum. **17** Britain imposed oil embargo on Rhodesia; New forms of service for Anglican Church published. **19** General de Gaulle re-elected French President. **22** Christmas truce in Vietnam; Death of Richard Dimbleby, the B.B.C. commentator; 70 m.p.h. speed limit on British roads came into force. **27** Oil rig *Sea Gem* collapsed in North Sea; 5 killed, 8 missing. **28** 900th anniversary of Westminster Abbey celebrated.

## 1966

**January 3** Indo-Pakistani summit talks in Tashkent with Mr. Kosygin as host. **9** Violent rioting in Nigeria. **10** Sudden death of Mr. Shastri in Tashkent. **11** Opening of Lagos Commonwealth Conference under chairmanship of Fed. Prime Min. of Nigeria. **12** Death of Alberto Giacometti, sculptor and painter. **15** Army coup in Nigeria: Fed. Prime Min. killed. **16** General Ironsi, C.-in-C. of Nigerian army, took over command to restore law and order; Death of Sergei Korolyov, Russian space scientist. **18** Arrival in London of Sir Hugh Beadle, Chief Justice of Rhodesia, for talks with British Government. **21** Smith regime in Rhodesia rejected Royal Prerogative commuting death sentences on two Africans. **22** Opening of Volta River project in Ghana. **24** Air India *Boeing* crashed into Mont Blanc: 177 killed, including Homi Bhabha, the Indian nuclear physicist. **31** U.S. bombing of N. Vietnam resumed after 37 days; British Government banned all trade with Rhodesia; Russia launched *Luna* 9.

**February 3** Successful soft landing on moon by *Luna* 9: tracked by Jodrell Bank radio telescope. **5** Pres. Johnson went to Honolulu to review Vietnam with other American leaders. **9** Britain to build prototype fast reactor (PFR) at Dounreay in Caithness. **17** Britain protested to S. Africa over petrol supplies to Rhodesia. **23** Military coup in Damascus (ninth in Syria in 17 years). Death of Vicky (Victor Weisz), political cartoonist. **24** Army coup in Ghana while Dr. Nkrumah absent in Far East.

**March 1** Britain to adopt decimal currency in 1971; Russian rocket landed on Venus. **2** Dr. Nkrumah arrived in Guinea from Moscow; Britain protested to Portugal over oil storage tanks being built in Mozambique to pump oil to Rhodesia. **3** Pres. Sékou Touré of Guinea appointed Dr. Nkrumah executive head of state. **4** Britain recognised new régime in Ghana; Canadian *DC 9* crashed near Tokyo: 64 killed. **5** BOAC *Boeing* crashed near Tokyo: 124 killed; Nelson pillar in O'Connell Street, Dublin, blown up. **8** Severe earthquake in Hopeh, N. China. **9** U Thant called for cessation of bombing in N. Vietnam and for participation of Vietcong in any peaceful settlement. **10** Marriage of Princess Beatrix of the Netherlands and Herr Claus von Amsberg; U.S. to establish world-wide satellite communications system by 1968, based on *Early Bird*. **11** Chi-Chi, the London Zoo's giant panda, flew to Moscow for union with An-An of the Moscow Zoo. **23** Historic meeting in Rome of Archbishop of Canterbury and the Pope. **25** Two of the team climbing north face of the Eiger reached summit. **31** British General Election: Labour victory with overall majority of 97.

**April 3** Soviet *Luna 10* became the first lunar orbiter (orbital period: 2 hr., 58 min., 15 sec.). **5** Britain warned Portugal of consequences of

allowing oil to be pumped from port of Beira to Rhodesia. **6** Greek Government withdrew registration from oil-tanker *Joanna V* off Beira. **7** Recovery of U.S. hydrogen bomb lost off coast of Spain. **9** U.N. Security Council passed resolution authorising British Government " to prevent by the use of force if necessary the arrival at Beira of vessels reasonably believed to be carrying oil destined for Rhodesia." **10** C.-in-C., instructed to stop any ship going to Beira with oil for Rhodesia: *Manuela* intercepted and boarded by British naval party and escorted away from Beira; Death of Evelyn Waugh, the novelist. **11** Students and militant Buddhists intensified campaign for return to civilian rule in S. Vietnam. **21** Opening of Parliament televised for first time. **30** Official support from Chou En-lai for " cultural revolution " to wipe out " bourgeois ideology " in all fields of culture.

**May 9** China exploded third nuclear device. **14** Death of Lady Megan Lloyd George. **16** Seamen's strike began (ended 1 July—biggest strike in England since the war and the first of its kind since 1911). **18** Talks between Britain and Spain opened over Gibraltar. **26** British Guiana became independent state of Guyana.

**June 1** Peace talks between Malaysia and Indonesia: restoration of friendly relations. **2** American *Surveyor I* made soft landing on Moon; De Valera re-elected President of Irish Republic. **6** *Gemini* 9, manned by 2 astronauts, recovered after 45 orbits, making most accurate return to earth yet: 2 hour space walk. **11** Commonwealth Day (the Queen's official birthday) to be observed on this date in future. **27** Death of Arthur Waley, translater from Chinese and Japanese.

**July 3** Resignation of Mr. Frank Cousins as Minister of Technology over prices and incomes policy. **5** Indonesian People's Consultative Assembly deprived Dr. Sukarno of life-presidency. **6** Malawi became a Republic within Commonwealth with Dr. Banda as its first President. **7** Sino-Tanzanian co-operation in joint shipping line; Inauguration of Eurochemic plant at Mol in Belgium. **8** British industrial exhibition opened in Moscow. **14** Bank rate raised from 6 to 7 per cent; In first by-election since General Election, Labour lost seat in Carmarthen to Welsh Nationalist. **16** Prime Minister in Moscow for talks with Mr. Kosygin and for British industrial exhibition. **18** International Court of Justice at the Hague ruled in favour of S. Africa: no violation of mandate of S.W. Africa. **20** Prime Minister announced 6-month freeze on wages, salaries, and prices. **21** Successful landing of *Gemini 10*: docking manoeuvre and space walk. **24** Common Market completed its agricultural policy: free trade by 1 July 1968. **25** Report that Mao Tse-tung had swum 9 miles in Yangtze R. in 65 minutes. **27** Retirement of M. Spaak from political life. **29** Mutiny by section of Nigerian army; General Ironsi later reported to have been killed; U.S. aircraft attacked oil depots near Hanoi and Haiphong. **30** World Cup won by England: West Germany defeated 4–2.

**August 1–2** Plenary session of Central Committee of Chinese Communist Party: Marshal Lin Piao officially recognised as Mao Tse-tung's successor. **3** Post Office to become public corporation in 1969. **4** Sir Edmund Compton named Britain's first Parliamentary Commissioner (Ombudsman). New plan for rebuilding Piccadilly Circus published. **7** Opening of Salazar Bridge spanning Tagus River (longest suspension bridge in Europe). **10** American *Orbiter I* launched—first U.S. moon satellite; Public inspection of Cabinet and other official documents to be allowed after 30 years instead of present 50; Cabinet reshuffle: Mr. George Brown became Foreign Secretary. **11** Indonesian-Malaysian peace agreement signed in Djakarta. **17** New world mile record: J. Ryun of Kansas Univ. (3 min. 15·3 sec.). **18** Mass rally of Chinese Red Guards in Peking celebrating the " cultural revolution," attended by Mao Tse-tung, Lin Piao, and Chou En-lai; Tay road bridge opened (longest road bridge in Britain: 7,356 feet between anchorages); Earthquake in E. Turkey:

over 2,000 killed. 27 Francis Chichester set sail round world: arrived Sydney 12 Dec. 31 Decree restoring federal system of government to Nigeria announced.

September 1 Britannia airliner crashed at Ljubljana in Yugoslavia: 95 killed. 4 President de Gaulle's suggestion that U.S. should withdraw from Vietnam prior to peace negotiations rejected. 5 Selective Employment Tax came into force. 6 Dr. Verwoerd assassinated in Parliament, Cape Town. 8 Opening of new Severn road bridge (centre span 3,230 ft., side spans 1,000 ft.). Pakistan and Malaysia agreed to resume diplomatic relations (broken off 1965). 11 Dr. Immanuel Jakobovits elected Chief Rabbi of Commonwealth in succession to Dr. Jacob Brodie; Fourth French nuclear device exploded over Mururoa testing site in S. Pacific. 13 Mr. John Vorster chosen as S. Africa's new Prime Minister. 15 German submarine *Hai* sank off Dogger Bank. 16 Opening of new Metropolitan Opera House at Lincoln Centre. New York; Launching at Barrow of H.M.S. *Resolution*, Britain's first Polaris submarine. 17 Red Guards warned by Chou En-lai not to interfere with the economy. 19 Inauguration of Paris–Shanghai air service: Civil Rights Bill providing housing integration defeated in U.S. Senate. 25 Congolese Government troops regained control of Kisangani. 28 Indonesia resumed U.N. membership. 30 Sir Seretse Khama became first President of Republic of Botswana.

October 1 Release of Speer and von Schirach from Spandau, leaving only Rudolf Hess there. 2 Heavy casualties after cyclone and tidal wave struck E. Pakistan; Many deaths in path of hurricane Inez in Caribbean. 4 Basutoland became independent kingdom of Lesotho. 5 Part 4 of 1966 Prices and Incomes Act came into effect, giving Government power to freeze wages and prices. 21 Aberfan disaster: avalanche of sludge from coal tip slid down upon South Wales mining village killing 144, including 116 children in school. 26 Brussels chosen as new headquarters of NATO Council. 27 China's fourth nuclear test. 28 Channel Tunnel to be built and opened to traffic by 1975 (subject to satisfactory solution of problems involved); Indonesia readmitted to U.N.

November 4 Italian floods: torrential rain caused Arno to burst its banks into city of Florence; Venice flooded after highest tide for 200 years. 9 " Hot line " between Paris and Moscow. 22 Organic Law of Spanish State provided for appointment of Prime Minister. 25 Security Council censured Israel for military attack on border villages of S.W. Jordan on 13 Nov. 23 Red Guards demanded dismissal of Liu Shao-Ch'i, China's Head of State. 26 Opening of the Rance barrage; Australian General Election: Liberal–County Party Coalition Government led by Mr. Harold Holt returned; New Zealand General Election: Mr. Keith Holyoake's National Party returned. 29 King Ntare of Burundi overthrown while in Congo: republic proclaimed. 30 Resignation of Dr. Erhard, Western German Chancellor; Barbados (British dependency since 1627) became independent.

December 1 Mr. Kosygin in France for 8-day visit: Dr. Kiesinger (Christian Democratic Union) took office as Chancellor of German Federal Republic with Herr Willi Brandt (Social Democratic Union) as Foreign Sec. 2 Meeting of Prime Minister and Mr. Ian Smith of Rhodesia on board H.M.S. *Tiger* off Gibraltar: working document prepared; U Thant re-elected U.N. Sec.-Gen. for further 5 years. 5 Mr. Ian Smith and colleagues rejected working document. 10 Opening of first stage of Roseires dam on Blue Nile, Sudan. 16 U.N. Security Council voted for British resolution for mandatory sanctions (including oil) against Rhodesia. 28 China exploded her fifth nuclear bomb. 29 Death of Lord Brain, authority on nervous diseases. 31 Death of Mr. Christian Herter, former U.S. Sec. of State.

1967

January 4 Turkish oil pipeline opened, from Batman to Iskenderun on Black Sea coast; Donald Campbell killed at Coniston while trying to break own water speed record. 10 General Election in Bahamas (first all-Negro Cabinet took office Jan. 16 under Mr. Lynden O. Pindling). 11 Last detachment of British troops left Sarawak. 13 Army took over power without bloodshed in Togo. 15 Prime Minister and Foreign Secretary in Rome for first round of Common Market talks. 16 Britain and France agreed to go ahead with swing-wing military aircraft (French withdrew on 5 July) and to collaborate in building helicopters. 18 Mr. Jeremy Thorpe, M.P. for North Devon, elected Leader of Liberal Party following resignation of Mr. Grimond. 20 Agreement on Soviet–Japanese air service between Moscow and Tokyo via Siberia. 26 Bank rate reduced from 7 to 6½ per cent. 27 Death of Marshal Juin; Three American astronauts killed in fire in cabin during ground test at Cape Kennedy.

February 2 Direct peace talks between U.S. and N. Vietnam proposed by Pres. Johnson in letter to Pres. Ho Chi Minh. 5 Launching of *Vittorio Veneto*, Italy's first guided missile cruiser. 6 Mr. Kosygin arrived in London for 8-day visit. 7 Bush fire in Tasmania: 62 lives lost and heavy damage to homes and farms. 8 Inauguration of Bhutan's first hydroelectric station at Thimpu. 9 Historic meeting between H.M. the Queen and Mr. Kosygin at Buckingham Palace. 13 Agreement on establishment of a " hot line " between Kremlin and 10 Downing Street. 15 President Ho Chi Minh replies to Pres. Johnson: stipulated cessation of U.S. bombing raids against N. Vietnam prior to talks; Chinese authorities ordered dissolution of all " revolutionary organisations " and return of their members to their own provinces. 19 Death of Robert Oppenheimer, the American physicist, " father of the atom bomb." 22 Mr. Sangster succeeded Sir Alexander Bustamente as Prime Minister of Jamaica; Pres. Sukarno of Indonesia surrendered rule to Gen. Suharto. 23 Trinidad and Tobago first Commonwealth member to join OAS (Organisation of American States). 25 Launching at Birkenhead of Britain's second Polaris submarine, H.M.S. *Renown*. 26 Congress Party returned to power in Indian elections but lost 8 states. 27 International treaty banning nuclear weapons from outer space and prohibiting use of Moon and other celestial bodies signed in London, Moscow, and Washington.

March 1 Opening of London's new concert hall: Queen Elizabeth Hall adjoining Royal Festival Hall. 6 Death of Zoltán Kodály, the Hungarian composer. 9 Confirmation that American planes based on Thailand were bombing N. Vietnam. 12 Mrs. Indira Gandhi re-elected Prime Minister of India; Launching of Italy's first submarine since the war, the *Enrico Toti*. 13 In French general elections Gaullists gained bare majority in National Assembly: Death of Sir Frank Worrell the West Indies cricketer; £ sterling reached strongest position for year on foreign exchange markets. 14 U Thant proposed plan for bringing peace to Vietnam. 15 Announcement that American bombing of N. Vietnam would continue. 16 Bank rate reduced to 6 per cent. 18 *Torrey Canyon* (American owned, flying Liberian flag) ran aground on Seven Stones reef off Land's End with 120,000 tons of crude oil aboard. 20 Sir Francis Chichester in *Gipsy Moth IV* rounded Cape Horn. 22 Army in Sierra Leone siezed power. 28 High explosives dropped on *Torrey Canyon* by Royal Navy Buccaneer aircraft successful in releasing oil from wreck and setting fire to it; U Thant made public his revised peace proposals: (1) general standstill truce; (2) preliminary talks between those concerned; (3) reconvening of 1954 Geneva conference; Pope Paul issued encyclical *Populorum Progressio* on duties of rich nations towards poor nations. 29 Launching of France's first nuclear submarine, *Le Redoutable*; Last link of South-East Asia Commonwealth cable system (SEACOM) inaugurated by the Queen. 31 Death of Marshal Malinovsky, defender of Stalingrad, at age of 68.

**April** 5 Oil from *Torrey Canyon* reached Cherbourg peninsula. 13 Conservatives gained landslide victory in GLC elections. 19 Death of Konrad Adenauer. 21 Army coup in Greece (suspension of parliamentary democracy); Stalin's daughter arrived in New York. 23 Colonel Vladimir Komarov, the Soviet cosmonaut, killed (parachute failure after completion of test flight). 27 Crown Princess Beatrix of the Netherlands gave birth to a son; Opening in Montreal of Expo 67—Canada's 100th birthday international fair.

**May** 2 Prime Minister's statement to Commons: Britain to apply to join the Common Market. 4 Bank rate reduced to 5½ per cent. 6 Disturbances in Hong Kong. 8 Dr. Zakir Hussain elected President of India, the first Muslim to hold that office. 11 Britain presented application to join Common Market. 14 Opening of Liverpool's new Roman Catholic cathedral. 15 First day of new Spanish restrictions on air space around Gibraltar. 19 U Thant complied with Pres. Nasser's request to remove U.N. peace force from Egypt–Israel border. 22 Egypt closed Straits of Tiran to Israeli shipping; Japan joined European Nuclear Energy Agency's Reactor programme at Halden in Norway. 23 J. Ryun (U.S.A.) broke his own world mile record, 3 min. 51·1 sec. 28 Francis Chichester arrived in Plymouth. 30 Secession of Eastern Nigeria (Biafra) from Federation of Nigeria; Jordan and Egypt concluded 5-year defence agreement similar to that signed by Egypt and Syria in 1966.

**June** 1 General Moshe Dayan appointed Defence Minister of Israel. 3 160 people killed in two British air crashes: at Perpignan in France and at Stockport the following day. 5 Outbreak of 6-day war in Middle East: lightning attack by Israel caused severe Arab losses and capture of Gaza strip, Sinai, Jordanian territory west of R. Jordan and small area of Syria. 6 East African Economic Community Treaty signed (Kenya, Tanzania, Uganda). 8 U.N. called for immediate cease-fire in the Middle East. 8–9 More riots in Hong Kong. 9 Pres. Nasser offered his resignation, but later withdrew it; France extended fishing limit around French coasts to 12 miles. 10 Fighting in Middle East ceased following U.N. Security Council's cease-fire resolutions; Soviet Union broke off diplomatic relations with Israel. 11 Israeli cargo ship sailed through Strait of Tiran. 12 Soviet Union launched Venus spacecraft. 14 Security Council rejected Soviet motion condemning Israel for aggression. 17 China exploded her first hydrogen bomb. 19 Pres. Nasser took over as Prime Minister; Mr. Kosygin addressed U.N. General Assembly. 20 Mutiny of South Arabian troops. 23 Meetings between Pres. Johnson and Mr. Kosygin in Glassboro, New Jersey. 23–24 More violent outbreaks in Hong Kong. 26 Council of Ministers of E.E.C. decided to refer British application for membership to Commission of the Communities; Mr. Kosygin visited Cuba; U.S.A. and Panama agreed on new treaties concerning Panama Canal and possible new sea-level canal. 27 Ron Clarke of Australia set world 2-mile record of 8 min. 19·8 sec. at Vaesteras, Sweden. 28 Israel took over control of Old City of Jerusalem. 29 Queen Elizabeth and Duke of Edinburgh arrived in Ottawa on week's visit to Canada. 30 End of period of severe economic restraint in Britain.

**July** 1 Mr. Tshombe arrested in Algeria after having been kidnapped in mid-flight; Colour television (first in Europe) began on B.B.C. 2. 2 Third French nuclear test at Mururoa atoll in Pacific (previous ones, 6 and 27 June). 3 Coronation of King Taufa'ahau Tupou IV of Tonga. 4 Emergency Special Session of U.N. General Assembly (convened at request of Soviet Union on 17 June) called on Israel to rescind measures taken to change status of Jerusalem and to alleviate suffering resulting from Arab–Israel hostilities. 7 Francis Chichester knighted by the Queen at Greenwich. 8 Police post at Sha

Tay Kok, Hong Kong, attacked by demonstrators from China. 10 New fast passenger service fully operative on completion of electrification between Waterloo, Southampton, and Bournemouth: use of steam traction eliminated in Southern Region of British Rail; New Zealand changed over to decimal currency. 12 Negro riot in Newark, N.J.; Motorway speed limit in Britain to remain at 70 m.p.h. 13 Public Records Act, 1967, reduced from 50 to 30 years the period for which public records are closed to public inspection (Act came into operation Jan. 1968). 14 The Decimal Currency Act, 1967, came into operation, providing for the introduction of decimal currency in Britain in 1971. 15 *Lake Palourde*, sister ship of *Torrey Canyon*, arrested at Singapore as surety for oil pollution damage. 17 U.N. observers began operating on Arab–Israeli cease-fire line; London's first supersonic boom tests. 18 Government announcement of cuts in defence commitments: planned withdrawal East of Suez by mid-1970s. 20 Recommendation by Latey Committee that legal age of majority should be 18. 21 Albert Luthuli killed in railway accident in South Africa. 22 Earthquake in N.W. Turkey. 23 Urban Negro riot in Detroit. 24 Pres. de Gaulle rebuked by Mr. Pearson for using Quebec separatist slogan, *Vive Quebec libre*, in speech in Montreal; visit cut short. 25 Pope Paul visited Istanbul, Izmir, and Ephesus (first papal visit since A.D. 711). 28 Vesting day of the National Steel Corporation.

**August** 3 National Coal Board blamed in Aberfan tribunal report for the disaster; Lord Roben's offer of resignation not accepted by Minister of Power. 13 U.S. bombed N. Vietnam 10 miles from Chinese border. 17 U Thant asked U.S. to suspend bombing of N. Vietnam for 3 or 4 weeks. 21 Britain began phased withdrawal of British forces from Aden and S. Arabia.

**September** 1 Death of Ilya Ehrenburg, the Soviet writer. 3 Chinese Red Guards ordered to cease violence; Sweden's traffic changed from left to right. 10 Gibraltar referendum result: overwhelming vote to stay with Britain. 18 Merseyside and London dockers went on strike with the ending of the casual work system; U.S. announced its decision to deploy an anti-ballistic missile system against China. 20 Launching on Clydebank of Cunard liner *Queen Elizabeth II*, largest passenger liner built in Britain since the war. 26 Agreement for construction of European airbus signed in Bonn by Britain, France, and Fed. Rep. of Germany. 27 *Queen Mary* arrived at Southampton at end of her last transatlantic voyage (sold for £1·2 million to the city of Long Beach, California).

**October** 2 H.M.S. *Resolution*, Britain's first Polaris submarine, commissioned. London Bridge put up for sale (work began on new bridge, Nov. 6). 8 Death of Lord Attlee. 9 Provisions of Road Safety Act dealing with drink and driving came into force: it is an offence to drive after drinking if the amount of alcohol in the bloodstream exceeds the prescribed limit of 80 milligrams per 100 millilitres of blood; Che Guevara, Cuban revolutionary leader, killed in guerrilla fighting in Bolivian jungle. 10 Outer Space Treaty ratified by 93 countries. 13 Tyne toll tunnel opened by the Queen: crosses lower Tyne at Jarrow, linking motorways in Northumberland and Durham. 16 Opening of new NATO H.Q. at Evère, Brussels. 18 Russian craft (*Venus* 4) made first soft-landing on Venus. 19 American space probe *Mariner 5* passed within 2,000 miles of Venus; Bank rate increased from 5½ to 6 per cent. 21 Israeli destroyer *Eilat* sunk off Sinai coast by missile boats of Egyptian Navy. 22 Big demonstrations against Vietnam war in Washington, London, and other capitals. 24 Israeli bombardment of Egypt's Suez oil refineries. 25 Foot-and-mouth epidemic began at Oswestry. 26 Coronation of Shah of Iran; Government decision not to build national library on proposed Bloomsbury site; Anglo-French agreement on joint production of helicopters. 30 Canadian Expo 67 closed: total attendance for the 6 months—50,360,648; Old age pensions and other benefits increased in Britain; First automatic link-up and separation of unmanned spacecraft by Russian *Cosmos 186* and *Cosmos 188*.

**November 9** Bank rate increased from 6 to 6½ per cent; Successful launching of U.S. giant *Saturn 5* rocket. **14** The Queen paid state visit to Malta. **17** Régis Debray, French Marxist writer, sentenced to 30 years' imprisonment for guerrilla activities in Bolivia. **18** Devaluation of £ sterling by 14·3 per cent ($2.80 to $2.40 to the £); Bank rate increased from 6½ to 8 per cent. **20** Professor Blackett and Sir William Walton appointed to the Order of Merit. **22** House of Lords ruled that barristers could not be sued for professional negligence; Security Council unanimously adopted British resolution requiring withdrawal of Israeli forces from occupied Arab territories and an end to all belligerency; Britain abandoned plan to build staging post on island of Aldabra (unique wild life sanctuary). **23** Indus water project inaugurated with opening of Mangla Dam on the Jhelum R., W. Pakistan, one of biggest in world. **26** Lisbon and suburbs flooded: death roll 464. **27** Gen. de Gaulle in press conference ruled out early Common Market negotiations with Britain; 8-week unofficial London dock strike ended. **29** Aden became independent as the Republic of South Yemen. **30** Greece, Turkey, and Cyprus agreed on peace plan for settlement of Cyprus issue.

**December 1** Inauguration by Queen of Isaac Newton telescope at Royal Observatory, Herstmonceux, the biggest in Europe; world record price of 560,000 guineas paid for Monet's impressionist painting *La Terrasse à Sainte-Adresse* at Christie's. **3** First human heart transplant operation took place at Cape Town. **13** King Constantine attempted unsuccessfully to overthrow the Greek military junta. **14** Ban on arms to S. Africa reaffirmed by Prime Minister. **17** Mr. Harold Holt, Australian Prime Minister, drowned in swimming accident. **19** France voted against negotiations for Britain's entry to Common Market: Britain stated application would not be withdrawn. **20** Diplomatic relations resumed between Britain and Egypt. **29** Statement by N. Vietnam Foreign Minister that N. Vietnam ready to hold talks with U.S. once bombing of N. Vietnam ceased.

**1968**

**January 9** U.S. *Surveyor* spacecraft soft-landed on moon; Departure of Cardinal Ottaviani from Roman Curia; Senator John G. Gorton elected Prime Minister of Australia. **14-15** Violent earthquake tremors in W. Sicily. **16** Prime Minister's announcement of cuts in public expenditure to release resources from home to export. **19** Anglo-Soviet agreement for scientific and technological cooperation signed in London. **23** Seizure by N. Korea of USS *Pueblo* on intelligence mission off N. Korean coast.

**February 11-12** U Thant in Moscow and London for talks on Vietnam. **13** U.S. planes bombed outskirts of Saigon: 10,500 more American troops to be sent to Vietnam. **18** Second Communist offensive in Vietnam; U.S. "San Antonio formula" rejected by N. Vietnam (Pres. Johnson's offer of 19 Sept. 1967 to halt bombing of N. Vietnam on condition that peace talks would follow and no military advantage would be taken of the pause); Introduction of British Standard Time. **19** Rann of Kutch tribunal decision: nine-tenths to India; one-tenth to Pakistan. **24** Battle of Hué: end of 25-day defence by Vietcong guerrillas.

**March 2** The Queen exercised royal prerogative of mercy in respect of 3 Africans under sentence of death in Rhodesia. **3** Government White Paper on foot-and-mouth epidemic: 2,339 farms affected; 422,900 animals slaughtered; circumstantial evidence that virus came from lamb imported from Argentina. **6** Africans in Rhodesia hanged in defiance of the Queen's reprieve. **12** Mauritius became independent. **14** Speculative rush for gold in leading financial centres: U.S. Bank rate raised from 4½ to 5 per cent. **15** Stock Exchange closed and Bank Holiday declared in Britain; Resignation of

Mr. George Brown as Foreign Secretary. **17-18** Summit meeting in Washington of Western central bankers: two-tier system for gold agreed (deals between central banks at $35 an ounce, commercial deals at free price); London gold pool dissolved. **20** Mr. Roy Jenkins's first Budget. **21** Bank rate reduced to 7½ per cent. **22** Resignation of Pres. Novotny of Czechoslovakia; American battle deaths in Vietnam since 1961: 20,000 (3,000 since Tet (lunar new year) offensive); General Westmoreland, American field commander in Vietnam, recalled to Washington to become U.S. Army Chief of Staff at Pentagon. **27** Yuri Gagarin killed in air crash. **30** Money Conference in Stockholm: agreement to launch special drawing rights scheme in face of French non-cooperation. **31** Pres. Johnson announced his decision to abdicate presidency in January, to limit bombing of Vietnam, and to initiate peace moves.

**April 1** Death of Russian physicist, Prof. Lev Laudau, Nobel Prize winner. **4** Assassination of Martin Luther King at Memphis, Tennessee. **8** N. Vietnam agreed to direct talks with U.S. **13** Tanzania first country to recognise Biafra–Nigeria's secessionist eastern region. **16** Britain decided to withdraw from ELDO. **17** Lake Havasu City in Arizona to be site for London Bridge. **20** Pierre Trudeau became Canada's new Liberal Prime Minister. **28** Extreme right-wing N.P.D. Party won 12 seats in state parliament of Baden-Württemberg.

**May 3** Pres. Johnson accepted a N. Vietnam proposal to meet in Paris on 10 May for preliminary talks; Student riots in Latin quarter of Paris. **10** Violent clashes between students and police: 500 security police led charge through barricades. **13** Vietnam peace talks began in Paris. **17** French workers occupied factories. **18** Pres. de Gaulle cut short Rumanian tour to return to Paris. **19** Parliamentary elections in Italy: Christian Democrats and Communists largest parties in both Chamber of Deputies and Senate. **22** French National Assembly adopted amnesty law after trade unions had declared their readiness to negotiate with employers and Government. **29** UN Security Council adopted resolution imposing comprehensive mandatory sanctions on Rhodesia. **31** Dissolution of French National Assembly.

**June 5** Senator Robert Kennedy shot in Los Angeles; he died the next day. **10** National Health prescription charge of 2/6d introduced. **12** Death of Sir Herbert Read. **14** Restrictions on entry into Britain by anyone connected with illegal régime in Rhodesia. **15** Warsaw Pact manoeuvres in Czechoslovakia. **26** Liberal Party, led by Mr. Pierre Trudeau, won Canadian general election. **30** In French general election Gaullists won increased majority.

**July 1** All tariffs on industrial goods traded between EEC members abolished and a common external tariff came into effect. **4** Fourth assembly of World Council of Churches opened at Uppsala; Mr. Alec Rose landed at Portsmouth after sailing single-handed round the world in *Lively Lady*; he was knighted the next day. **10** M. Couve de Murville replaced M. Pompidou as Prime Minister of France. **22** New 1,058-mile oil pipeline from Dar es Salaam, Tanzania, to Ndola, Zambia, in operation. **26** Government decision to remove Aberfan tips. **28** Death of Otto Hahn, the German physicist; serious student riots in Mexico City. **29** The Pope issued encyclical *Humanae vitae* condemning all forms of artificial birth control; Four-day summit conference opened between Czech and Soviet leaders at Cierna.

**August 3** Meeting in Bratislava between Czech leaders and leading personalities from Bulgaria, East Germany, Hungary, Poland and the Soviet Union; Death of Marshal Rokossovsky, Russian military hero of Second World War. **5** Talks between both sides in Nigerian civil war at Addis Ababa (adjourned 9 Sept. without agreement). **20** Soviet forces with contingents from Bulgaria, East Germany, Hungary and Poland entered Czechoslovakia. **22** The Pope visited Bogota, Colombia, the first papal visit to Latin America in its 450 years of connection with Roman Catholic Church.    27 End of four-day talks in Moscow between Soviet and Czech leaders: Czech leaders gave certain undertakings to Moscow in order to secure withdrawal of Soviet troops;    Death of Princess Marina, Duchess of Kent.    28 Tear gas and clubs used by Chicago police against demonstrators at Democratic National Convention.    31 Major earthquake in Khorassan province NE Iran.

September 6 Swaziland became independent.    11 Departure of Russian troops from Prague.    13 From 1 July 1969 banks in England and Wales to close on Saturdays;    the Appellate Division of the High Court of Rhodesia ruled that the 1965 constitution was legal.    15 Worst flooding in England since 1953 (rain caused by warm air from S. France meeting cold air from Scandinavia over SE England).    16 Two-tier postal system began in Britain.    19 Bank rate reduced from 7¼ to 7 per cent.    21–22 Clashes between students and police in Mexico City.    22 Successful recovery of Soviet spacecraft *Zond 5* in Indian Ocean, after research voyage round moon;    Inauguration of reconstructed Abu Simbel temple on new site above Lake Nasser.    26 The Theatres Act, abolishing censorship, came into force;    Professor Marcello Caetano appointed Prime Minister of Portugal because of illness of Dr. Salazar.    27 French again vetoed British entry into Common Market.

October 1 Federal Nigerian troops captured Okigwi, having taken Aba and Owerri in Sept.    5 Clashes between police and crowds in London-derry.    9 British Prime Minister and Mr. Ian Smith discussed proposals for settlement of Rhodesian question on HMS *Fearless* off Gibraltar (talks ended in disagreement).    11 U.S. 3-man moon rocket *Apollo 7* successfully launched on 10-day orbital test manoeuvres.    12 Olympic Games opened in Mexico City;    Fernando Po and Rio Muni, dependencies of Spain, became independent as Rep. of Equatorial Guinea.    14 The Queen opened new Euston station.    16 Visit of Soviet Prime Minister, Mr. Kosygin, to Prague: treaty signed providing for stationing of Soviet troops in Czechoslovakia.    27 Czechoslovakia became a two-state federation;    Massive demonstration march in London against Vietnam war.    31 President Johnson ordered halt to bombing of N. Vietnam.

November 1 Pres. Liu Shao-chi expelled from Chinese Communist Party.    4 NLF delegation arrived in Paris.    5 Presidential elections in U.S. gave victory to Mr. Richard Nixon, Republican.    12 Credit restrictions in France:    Bank rate raised from 5 to 6 per cent;    Major policy statement by Mr. Brezhnev at Polish Party Congress —"a threat to a Socialist country is a threat to all Socialist countries."    11 Maldive Islands became a republic.    15 New Greek Constitution came into force with increased power for Prime Minister, Mr. Papadopoulos.    19 Germany refused to revalue the Deutsche Mark.    20 Meeting of Group of Ten countries in Bonn to deal with speculative movements.    22 Standby credit of 2,000 million dollars arranged for support of franc: higher taxation in Britain, totalling £250 million;    France did not devalue but introduced stringent measures of exchange control and economies;    Mexican students ended their four-months strike.    26 Death of Upton Sinclair, the American novelist.    29 Serious rioting in Rawalpindi.    30 Civil rights disturbances in Armagh.

December 1 Pres. Ayub Khan agreed to students' educational demands;    Bishop of Cadiz condemned wage and working conditions in southern Spain in pastoral letter;    Civil rights demonstrations in Armagh.    2 Two pipelines blown up carrying water over Welsh border.    8 Royal naval dockyard in Singapore formally handed over to authorities there.    10 Mandate of UN Force in Cyprus extended to June 1969.    20 Launching of HMS *Churchill*, Britain's eighth nuclear submarine.    21–27 *Apollo 8* moon mission (Borman, Lovell and Anders made first lunar orbits).    27 China tested thermonuclear weapon.    28 Following attack (26th) by Arabs

on two Israeli airliners at Athens, Israeli commandos retaliated by wrecking 13 Arab aircraft at Beirut airport.    31 Successful maiden flight of Soviet TU-144 supersonic airliner (rival to Anglo-French Concorde).

**1969**

January 4 Spanish enclave of Ifni ceded to Morocco.    5 Soviet Venus probe launched.    7 Opening of Commonwealth Prime Ministers Conference in London.    16 First manned docking operation in orbiting flight by Soviet *Soyuz 4* and *Soyuz 5*.    16 Vietnam peace talks in Paris resumed after 2 months.    20 Spain extended her territorial waters from 6 to 12 miles.    20 State of emergency throughout Spain;    UN Sec. Council decided to add Russian and Spanish to its working languages (hitherto English and French).

February 3 Assassination of Dr. Edourdo Mondlane, Mozambique nationalist leader.    12–13 Visit of Mr. Wilson to Bonn and W. Berlin.    16 Inauguration of Kainji Dam on Niger River, Nigeria.    18 Attack by Arabs on Israeli airliner at Zurich airport;    Opening of submarine cable between Cape Town and Lisbon.    19 Death of Lady Asquith.    20 Kilimanjaro climbed by 8 blind Africans.    22 Vietnam Tet offensive began.    23–March 2 Visit of President Nixon to European capitals;    Death of former King Saud of Saudi-Arabia.    24 U.S. *Mariner* Mars spacecraft launched.    26 Death of Mr. Eshkal, Prime Minister of Israel.    27 India's first nuclear power station at Tarapur (near Bombay) went into operation.    28 Bank rate raised to 8 per cent.

March 2 Successful maiden flight of French-built Concorde at Toulouse.    Mrs. Golda Meir chosen as Israel's Prime Minister.    Sino-Soviet border clash on Ussuri river.    3 *Apollo 9* launched on 10-day earth orbital test mission.    5 Dr. Gustav Heinemann elected W. Germany's first Social Democratic President by Federal Assembly meeting in W. Berlin.    7 Opening of Victoria line (first underground railway to be built in London for over 60 years).    9 General Riad, Egyptian Chief of Staff, killed during 3-hour artillery battle with Israel along Suez canal.    11 Milton Keynes to be site for Britain's Open University.    13 Alaskan oil deposit found by British Petroleum.    14 Mortgage rate in Britain increased to 8½ per cent.    16 Mrs. Martin Luther King preached at St. Paul's, the first woman to do so.    18 U.S. offensive in S. Vietnam;    1969 Geneva Conference opened;    Longhope lifeboat disaster.    19 British troops landed with no opposition on Anguilla.    25 Resignation of Pres. Ayub Khan: Gen. Yahya Khan, C.-in-C. Pakistan Army took over power.    27 Mr. Wilson in Lagos on fact-finding mission.    28 Death of General Eisenhower;    Visit of Lord Caradon to Anguilla.

April 1 Opening of China's ninth Communist Party congress in Peking.    9 Successful maiden flight of British-built Concorde.    14 Lin Piao declared Mao's successor.    17 Mr. Dubcek replaced as First Secretary of Czechoslovak Communist Party by Dr. Husak (Mr. Dubcek later elected Chairman of the Federal Assembly).    21 British army units to guard key points in Northern Ireland.    23 President Saragat of Italy on 8-day state visit to Britain;    Biafran capital of Umuahia captured by Federal forces.    25 Owerri recaptured by Biafrans.    28 General de Gaulle resigned as President of France after vote defeat in referendum;    Anglo-Italian declaration of policy on Europe signed in London;    Mr. Terence O'Neill resigned as Prime Minister of Northern Ireland.

May 1 Secrecy oath taken by new cardinals in final consistory ceremony not to reveal any instructions given to them by the Pope;    Major James Chichester-Clark became Prime Minister of Northern Ireland;    Talks between United States and Soviet Union on limitation of strategic armaments expected to begin in July.

# PROMINENT PEOPLE

Glimpses of some of the famous people in the history of the world. See also Section E for composers; Section I for contemporary dramatists; Section M for novelists and poets of the twentieth century.

# PROMINENT PEOPLE

## A

**Abbot, George** (1562–1633), Archbishop of Canterbury in 1611, and one of the translators of the authorised version of the Bible.

**Abdullah ibn Husein** (1882–1951); King of Jordan; made ruler under the British mandate in 1921 and proclaimed King in 1946 when Transjordan (renamed Hashimite Kingdom of the Jordan in 1949) was created an independent state by treaty with Britain. Assassinated.

**Abelard, Peter** (1079–1142), one of the most influential thinkers of the mediaeval world, b. near Nantes, pupil of Roscelin and William of Champeaux. Living in age of great theological controversy he applied his creative and versatile mind to the problem of Christian faith and held that goodness depends upon intention and free choice. Unrivalled as a dialectician, he acquired great popularity as a teacher and attained great scholastic glory. His romance with Heloïse, niece of Canon Fulbert, has been much written about. The Canon had Abelard castrated and they retired from the world, he to the monastery at St. Denis and she to a nunnery at Argenteuil. Their bodies lie in one tomb at Père la Chaise.

**Abercrombie, Lascelles** (1881–1938), English poet and critic. Professor of English Literature at London University, 1929–35; Lecturer in Poetry at Queen's University, Belfast, 1931–32.

**Abercrombie, Sir (Leslie) Patrick, M.A., F.S.A. F.R.I.B.A.** (1879–1957), architect and town-planner. Brother of the above. Lever Prof. of Civic Design at Liverpool, 1915–35; Prof. of Town Planning at University College, London, 1935–46. Consulted on the replanning of Plymouth, Hull, Bath, the Clyde Valley, Dublin, Addis Ababa, Colombo, and Cyprus. Produced the famous plan for Greater London, 1943.

**Acheson, Dean Gooderham, A.B., LL.B.** (b. 1893), U.S. Secretary of State in the Truman Administration, 1949–52.

**Acton, John Emerich Edward Dalberg, 1st Baron, K.C.V.O., D.C.L., LL.D.** (1834–1902), English historian and brilliant scholar: Professor of Modern History at Cambridge, 1895–1902.

**Adam, Robert** (1728–1792), one of four Scottish brothers, all distinguished architects. Developed a characteristic style in planning and decoration and designed many important public and private buildings and interiors. His achievements include the great aristocratic houses of Harewood, Yorks; Osterley, Middlesex; Syon, Middlesex; Kedleston, Derbyshire.

**Adams, John** (1735–1826), succeeded Washington as President of the United States, and was the first of the Republic's ambassadors to England.

**Adams, John Couch, F.R.S.** (1819–92), English mathematician and astronomer. Shared credit for discovery of the planet Neptune, 1846, with the French astronomer, Leverrier (1811–77).

**Adams, Samuel** (1722–1803), American statesman, known as the " American Cato," who worked all his life for American Independence and signed the Declaration (1776). He organised the " Boston Tea Party."

**Adams, William** (c. 1564–1620), first Englishman to visit Japan; b. Gillingham, Kent. His knowledge of shipbuilding, navigation and European affairs proved of great value to the Japanese emperor Ieyasu at a time when he was interested in developing foreign trade.

**Addams, Jane, B.A., M.A.** (1860–1935), famous American sociologist who founded Hull House, Chicago, in 1889.

**Addison, Christopher, 1st Viscount, K.G. P.C. M.D., F.R.C.S.** (1869–1951). After joining the Labour Party held successive Ministerial offices in 3 Labour Governments and became leader of the House of Lords. Forsook his profession as professor of anatomy at Sheffield Univ. for a political career because of his great interest in public health and social reform.

**Addison, Joseph** (1672–1719), achieved fame both as a writer and a politician. Held many offices under various governments; contributed to the *Tatler* started by his friend Steele and with him founded the *Spectator*.

**Adenauer, Dr. Konrad** (1876–1967), Chancellor of the West German Federal Republic, 1949–63. Founder and Chairman of the Christian Democratic Party, 1945–66. To a defeated Germany he gave stable constitutional government, a place in the Western alliance, and provided strong, consistent leadership. He brought about reconciliation with France but resisted all attempts at accommodation with Russia. *See also* Section C, Part I.

**Adler, Alfred** (1870–1937), Austrian physician and psychiatrist and founder of the school of individual psychology. An earlier pupil of Freud, he broke away in 1911, rejecting the emphasis on sex, and regarding man's main problem as a struggle for power to compensate for feelings of inferiority. (*See* Section J.)

**Adrian IV, Nicholas Breakspear** (d. 1159), pope (1154–59), the only English pope, b. near St. Albans. Crowned Frederick Barbarossa as German emperor. Granted overlordship of Ireland to Henry II which started a dispute which raged for 800 years.

**Adrian, Edgar Douglas, 1st Baron, O.M., M.A., M.D., F.R.S., F.R.C.P.** (b. 1889), Prof. of Physiology, Cambridge Univ. 1937–51; Master of Trinity Coll., Cambridge, 1951–65, Pres. of the Royal Society 1950–55; Pres. of the British Association, 1954. Trustee of Rockefeller Institute, 1962. Chanc. Leicester Univ., 1957, Cambridge Univ., 1967. Nobel Prize for Medicine, 1932.

**Æschylus** (525–456 B.C.), father of Greek tragic drama. Composed seventy plays and gained the prize for dramatic excellence thirteen times.

**Æsop**, name famous for the fables preserved principally through Babrius (2nd century A.D.). About him nothing is known; according to legend he was a Greek slave in the 6th century B.C. who had a number of wild adventures.

**Agassiz, (Jean) Louis (Rodolphe)** (1807–73), Swiss-American zoologist and geologist. Author of *Researches on Fossil Fishes* (1833–43), and *Studies on Glaciers* (1840). He was an opponent of Darwin.

**Agricola, Gnæus Julius** (A.D. 37–93), became Roman Consul of Britain A.D. 78. Strengthened the power of the Romans in this country, corrected many abuses, and did much to encourage trade and industry. Remained in Britain 7 years.

**Agrippa, Marcus Vipsanius** (63–12 B.C.), the greatest military commander of Rome after Julius Cæsar.

**Ahmad Khan, Sir Syed** (1817–98), great Indian educationist and social reformer who founded what is now the Aligarh Muslim University.

**Aird, Sir John, Bart.** (1833–1911), contracting engineer of eminence, associated with many great undertakings in different parts of the world, the Aswan Dam on the Nile, completed in 1902, being one of his achievements.

**Airy, Sir George Biddell, K.C.B., F.R.S.** (1801–1892), Astronomer Royal (1835–1881) at Greenwich Observatory, where his brilliance and industry led to many important researches.

**Akbar, Jalal-ud-din Mohammed** (1542–1605), the greatest and wisest of the Mogul emperors and one of the great figures of history. He initiated economic and social reforms and succeeded in unifying his vast empire. His courts at Delhi and Agra were centres of culture and learning.

**Alanbrooke, Field-Marshal Viscount, K.G., G.C.B.,**

O.M., G.C.V.O., D.S.O. (1883–1963), one of the greatest soldiers of modern times; Chief of Imperial General Staff, 1941–46. Sir Arthur Bryant's *The Turn of the Tide* (1957), and *Triumph in the West* (1959), are based on the war diaries of Lord Alanbrooke.

**Alaric I** (376–410), the famous chief who after the death of Theodosus I led the Visigoths against the Romans, and afterwards invaded both Greece and Italy. He took Rome in 410, and died soon afterwards.

**Alarcón, Pedro Antonio de** (1883–91), Spanish novelist. His short story, *El Sombrero de tres picos* (*The Three-Cornered Hat*) became the subject of Falla's ballet and of Hugo Wolf's opera, *Der Corregidor*.

**Alban, St.**, who flourished in the latter part of the 3rd century, was born at Verulamium (where St. Albans now stands) and served as a soldier under Diocletian at Rome. Later he was converted to Christianity, and was for a time a renowned preacher of that religion, finally suffering martyrdom. Offa, king of the Mercians, built a monastery to his memory near Verulamium, four or five hundred years later. St. Alban's Day: Roman Catholic Church, June 22nd; Anglican Church, June 17th.

**Albani, Madame** (1852–1930), stage name of Marie Louise Emma Lajeunesse, Canadian operatic soprano. Made her first appearance in England at Covent Garden in 1872 and was for many years a leading prima donna, achieving great celebrity as Elsa in *Lohengrin*.

**Albert, Prince Francis Augustus Charles Emmanuel**, Consort of Queen Victoria (1819–1861). On his marriage with the Queen in 1840 Parliament granted him an income of £30,000 a year. The prince adapted himself with considerable success to the difficulties of his position, and gradually secured the confidence and esteem of statesmen and public alike. The great Exhibition of 1851 owed much of its success to his efforts. He died of typhoid fever in December, 1861. The Albert Memorial forms a national tribute to his memory.

**Albertus Magnus, St.** (1206–80), Dominican scholastic philosopher, b. Bavaria, one of the great mediaeval university teachers and the most learned man of his time. St. Thomas Aquinas was his favourite pupil. Took scientific interest in nature and made notable botanical observations.

**Alcibiades** (*c.* 450–404 B.C.), treacherously killed in battle at Melissa, Phrygia, was the celebrated Athenian statesman and general, pupil and friend of Socrates.

**Alcock, Sir Walter Galpin, M.V.O., Mus. Doc., F.R.C.O.** (1861–1947), English musician, eminent both as organist and composer of church music. He played at the Coronations of Edward VII, George V and George VI. Organist to Salisbury Cathedral, 1916–47, and Prof. of Organ Royal College of Music, 1893–1939.

**Alcott, Louisa May** (1832–88), American authoress; the charm and naturalness of her writings made her a favourite among children's authors, and her books are still read on both sides of the Atlantic. Her most famous book, *Little Women*, appeared in 1868.

**Alcuin** (735–804), scholar and ecclesiastic, a leader of the Carolingian Renaissance. His works include poems and historical and theological writings. (*See also* J30(1)).

**Aldred** (d. 1069), a powerful ecclesiastic of the 11th century in great favour with the Conqueror, whom he crowned. Bishop of Worcester (1044–60), and Archbishop of York (1060–1069).

**Alekhine, Dr. (Aljechin) Alexander** (1892–1946), world chess champion, 1927–35, 1937–46.

**Alembert, Jean le Rond d'** (1717–1783), a Parisian mathematician and philosopher who achieved great eminence by his numerous scientific works, including the *Theory of the Winds* and the *Precession of the Equinoxes*.

**Alexander of Hillsborough, Earl, K.G., P.C., C.H.** (1885–1965). Leader of the Labour peers in House of Lords, 1955–65; Min. of Defence, 1946–50; First Lord of the Admiralty, 1929–31, 1940–45, 1945–56.

**Alexander of Tunis, Field-Marshal Earl, P.C., K.G., G.C.B., O.M., G.C.M.G., D.S.O.** (b. 1891). Comm. 1st Div. at Dunkirk; C.-in-C. Southern Command, 1940–42; G.O.C. in Burma, 1942,

when he conducted a masterly retreat; C.-in-C. Middle East, 1942–43, when he was largely responsible for driving the enemy out of North Africa; C.-in-C. Allied Armies in Italy, 1944; and Supreme Allied Commander, Mediterranean, 1944–45, when he successfully led a force drawn from many different nations. Gov.-Gen. of Canada, 1946–52; Min. of Defence, 1952–54.

**Alexander II. of Russia** (1818–1881), succeeded his father, the Emperor Nicholas, in 1855. In 1861 he emancipated 23 millions of serfs. On March 13, 1881, was assassinated by bombs thrown beneath his carriage in St. Petersburg by Nihilists.

**Alexander the Great** (356–323 B.C.). King of Macedon, succeeded his father Philip in 336 B.C., and from the first showed himself fitted for mighty military exploits. He conquered in turn the Thebans, the Persian Satraps, overthrew Darius, overran Syria and Phœnicia, possessed himself of all the cities along the Mediterranean, conquered Egypt, founded Alexandria, and finally retired upon Babylon, where he died eleven days later.

**Alexandra, Queen** (1844–1925), d. of Christian IX. of Denmark, married to the Prince of Wales (afterwards Edward VII.) on March 10, 1863. Queen from Jan. 22, 1901, to May 6, 1910.

**Alfieri, Count Vittorio** (1749–1803), the Italian poet, was the author of twenty-one tragedies and six comedies.

**Alfonso the Wise** (1221–1284), a celebrated King of León and Castile, founder of the legal code which became the basis of Spanish jurisprudence, a liberal patron of literature and science, particularly of astronomy; dethroned by his son Sancho in 1282.

**Alfred the Great** (849–99), king of Wessex, son of Aethelwulf; succeeded his brother as king in 871 and found himself in conflict with the Danes from the outset. After years of effort he won decisive battle of Ethandun (Edington), 878. He prepared for further attacks by the Danes by building ships, fortifications, and by reorganising the militia or *fyrd*, defensive measures which eventually withstood the invading forces. Besides being a great warrior, a very able legislator and administrator, he was also a man of letters and responsible in great measure for the revival of English scholarship.

**Allenby, Field-Marshal Viscount, G.C.B., G.C.M.G., G.C.V.O.** (1861–1936), brilliant cavalry soldier. Served on Western front, 1914–16; commanded in Palestine, 1917–18, capturing Jerusalem on December 9th, 1917. High Commissioner for Egypt, 1919–25.

**Alleyne, Edward** (1566–1626), a famous actor, contemporary of Shakespeare and founder of Dulwich College.

**Alma-Tadema, Sir Lawrence, O.M., R.A.** (1836–1912), the son of a Netherlands notary, he came to England in 1869, where he soon made a name for himself as a painter of classical pictures of great beauty of colour and delicate design.

**Ampère, André Marie** (1775–1836), French mathematician who devoted himself to the study of electricity and magnetism, and was the first to propound the electro-dynamic theory.

**Amundsen, Captain Roald** (1872–1928), Norwegian explorer, the first to navigate the North-west Passage and the first to reach the South Pole. Sailing in the fishing smack *Gjöa*, he negotiated the North-west Passage in the 3 years, 1903–6. In 1911 he sailed south in the *Fram* and reached the Pole on December 14th, 1911, a month before his English rival Scott. He failed to complete a flight across the North Pole in 1925, but succeeded the next year. He lost his life in the Arctic while attempting to rescue Nobile, who had crashed in the *Italia*.

**Anacreon** (*c.* 560–475 B.C.), the celebrated Greek poet whose Odes hold a high place in poetic literature.

**Anaxagoras** (488–428 B.C.), Greek philosopher of Ionia who came to Athens 464 B.C. He inspired Pericles and the poet Euripides with his great love of science, and is said to have been the teacher of Socrates, who, however, differed from him. His rational theories outraged religious opinion and he retired to his native Asia Minor.

**Anaximander** (611–547 B.C.), Greek philosopher of Miletus in Asia Minor, pupil of Thales. He was the first among the Greeks to make geographical maps, and to speculate on the origin of the heavenly bodies; he introduced the sun-dial from Babylon or Egypt.

Anaximenes (b. c. 570 B.C.), the last of the Milesian school founded by Thales. For him the primal substance was air and he was the first to see the differences between substances in quantitative terms.

Andersen, Hans Christian (1805–1875), perhaps the most gifted writer of fairy tales the world has known. *Mit Livs Eventyr* (The Story of My Life) is as interesting as his fairy tales, which include *The Ugly Duckling, The Little Mermaid, The Emperor's New Clothes, The Little Matchseller.* Born and died in Denmark.

Anderson, Elizabeth Garrett, M.D. (1836–1917), one of the first English women to enter the medical profession. Practised in London for many years. In 1908–9 was Mayor of Aldeburgh, her native town, the first woman to be a mayor.

Andrea del Sarto (1487–1531). This celebrated son of a Florentine tailor was one of the great Italian artists of his time, known as the " faultless painter." Most of the famous galleries of the world contain examples of his magnificent fresco and other painting, mainly dealing with religious subjects.

Andrée, Salomon August (1854–1897), a Swedish explorer who attempted in 1897 to reach the North Pole by balloon, but, except for a message by pigeon despatched two days after his ascent, was not heard of again until in August 1930 a Norwegian scientific expedition led by Dr. Gunnar Horn discovered the remains of the Andrée expedition on White Island. The discovery included a log-book, sketch maps and the diaries kept by Andrée.

Andrew, Saint, one of the apostles of Jesus, brother of Simon Peter, whose festival is observed on November 30th. He became the patron saint of Scotland in the eighth century.

Angelico, Fra (1887–1455). Italian painter of religious subjects, mostly in the form of frescoes, of which the best examples are at Florence.

Angell, Sir Norman (1872–1967), political commentator. author of *The Great Illusion* (1910), in which he argued that war could no longer pay, and *The Money Game* 1918. Nobel Prize for Peace, 1933.

Ångström, Anders Jöns (1814–74), Swedish physicist, whose life was devoted to the study of heat, magnetism and spectroscopy, and in all three he contributed greatly to scientific knowledge. The unit used for measuring the wavelength of light was named *Angstrom* in his honour.

Anne, Queen (1665–1714), Queen of Great Britain and Ireland from 1702 to the time of her death, was a daughter of James II., and succeeded William III., her cousin. During her reign England, in alliance with Austria, Holland, Prussia, Savoy, and Portugal, entered upon the War of the Spanish Succession. Anne's reign has been called the Augustan Age of Britain because of the many eminent men of letters who flourished during that period. She was the last of the Stuarts to occupy the British throne. The most important domestic event of her reign was the passing of the Act of Union with Scotland in 1707.

Anouilh, Jean (b. 1910), French playwright, several of whose plays have been translated into English, including *Roméo et Jeannette* (Fading Mansion), *Eurydice* (Point of Departure), *L'Invitation au Château* (Ring Round the Moon), and he has made a number of films. (*See also* Section I.)

Anselm St. (1033–1109), Archbishop of Canterbury, was a native of Aosta, and succeeded Lanfranc as English Primate. He was in serious conflict with William Rufus on the question of ecclesiastical rights, and for a time suffered exile. Under Henry I., he regained power, making a compromise with that monarch which enabled him to carry on his theological work in comparative harmony. He died at Canterbury, and was canonised in 1494, his day being celebrated in the Roman Church on April 21st.

Anson, George, 1st Baron (1697–1762), a navigator of great eminence, whose *Voyage round the World* is still a popular book of adventure. He won many victories, obtained a peerage, rose to full Admiral's rank in the Navy, and served two terms as First Lord of the Admiralty.

Antoninus Pius (86–161), Emperor of Rome from A.D. 138 to 161, the successor of Hadrian. He governed with ability and his reign brought peace and prosperity to the empire. It was during his reign that the wall between the Forth and Clyde was built.

Antonius Marcus or Mark Antony (c. 83–30 B.C.), celebrated Roman Triumvir and General; a warm supporter of Cæsar; but engaged in intrigues after the latter's death, and was opposed by Brutus and Cassius. His association with the Egyptian Queen Cleopatra is the subject of Shakespeare's play. Committed suicide after defeat by Octavian.

Antony, St. (or Anthony) (c. 251–356), was a native of Upper Egypt, and according to his own account spent much time in conflict with the devil. He is one of the best-known saints of the Roman calendar, and his festival is on January 17th. He was believed to give relief to those who appealed to him when suffering from erysipelas, from which tradition the name St. Anthony's Fire is given to the disease.

Apelles, Greek painter, the most celebrated of antiquity, who flourished in the 4th century B.C. at the time of Alexander the Great. His most famous pictures, which have not survived, are of Alexander wielding the thunderbolts of Zeus and of Aphrodite rising from the sea.

Apollinaire, Guillaume (Wilhelm Apollinaris Kostrowitzi) (1880–1918), French poet representative of the restless and experimental period in the arts before the First World War. He invented the term *surrealism.* Born in Rome of Polish extraction.

Appert, Nicholas (1752–1841), sometimes known as François Appert, invented the method of preserving animal and vegetable foods by means of hermetically sealed cans or tins. He had no scientific training, but his painstaking work and countless experiments bore the mark of a true scientist. His revolutionary methods paved the way for the creation of a vast world industry which cans millions of tons of food a year.

Appleton, Sir Edward Victor, G.B.E., K.C.B., D.Sc., F.R.S. (1892–1965), English physicist; worked under Rutherford at Cavendish Lab. (1920–24); Prof. of Physics, London Univ. (1924–36); Prof. of Natural Philosophy at Cambridge (1936–39), Sec. of D.S.I.R. (1939–49). Best known as the discoverer of the ionised region of the upper atmosphere which became known as the Appleton Layer. His researches led to the development of radar. Nobel Prize for Physics, 1947; Pres. Brit. Ass., 1953.

Apollonius of Perga (fl. 220 B.C.), Greek mathematician of the Alexandrian school, remembered for his conic sections; introduced the terms *ellipse, parabola,* and *hyperbola.*

Apollonius Rhodius (fl. 250 B.C.), scholar and poet of Alexandria and Rhodes, librarian at Alexandria. He wrote on the text of Homer and is remembered for his epic *Argonautica* about the Argonaut heroes.

Aquinas, Thomas, Saint (c. 1225–74), chief scholastic philosopher whose system was ruled by Leo XIII in 1879 to be the official Catholic philosophy. He was greatly influenced by Aristotle. The most important of his works are *Summa contra Gentiles* and *Summa theologica.*

Arago, Dominique François Jean (1786–1853), French astronomer and physicist, remembered for his discoveries in electromagnetism and optics.

Archimedes (287–212 B.C.), Greek mathematician, physicist, and inventor, to whom we are indebted for his discoveries in mechanics (notably the lever), hydrostatics (floating bodies), and for the invention of the famous Archimedean screw. He lived most of his life in Syracuse, and was killed there during the siege by the Romans under Marcellus.

Argand, Aimé (1755–1803), Swiss physician, inventor of the lamp bearing his name, which was the first to admit a current of air to increase the power of the flame, by use of a chimney glass and circular wick.

Ariosto, Ludovico (1474–1533), one of the most celebrated of the Italian poets, author of *Orlando Furioso.* Besides this famous epic he wrote many comedies, satires, and poems.

Aristides (530–467 B.C.) Athenian statesman and

general who achieved fame at the battle of Marathon, 490 B.C.

**Aristippus** (c. 435–356 B.C.), founded the Cyrenaic school of philosophy, which taught that sensual pleasure was the only happiness. He was a native of Cyrene, in Africa, but became a pupil of Socrates, and settled in Athens.

**Aristophanes** (c. 444–c. 385 B.C.) was one of the foremost Athenian play-writers and the greatest of the Greek comic poets. His plays are full of satire, and deal unsparingly with the people and institutions of his time.

**Aristotle** (384–322 B.C.), Greek philosopher, pupil of Plato, after whose death in 347 he left Athens to become tutor to the young prince Alexander of Macedon. Subsequently at Athens he established his famous school in the garden known as the *Lyceum*, where he lectured in the *peripatos* (cloister) which gave it its name *Peripatetic*. He took the whole field of knowledge as his subject, giving it unity, and providing a philosophy which held its own for 2,000 years.

**Arkwright, Sir Richard** (1732–1792), was a native of Preston, and in early life a barber and travelling hairdealer. Becoming interested in mechanical problems, he set himself the task of inventing an improved cotton-spinning machine. Hargreaves' spinning-jenny was then the leading machine, but the yarn it produced could only be used for weft; it was not compact enough for warp threads. Arkwright therefore experimented until, by adopting an arrangement of rollers that moved with different velocities, he succeeded in perfecting his " spinning-frame," which successfully produced a yarn that could be used for warp as well as for weft. He took out his first patent in 1769, and entering into partnership with Mr. Jedediah Strutt, of Derby, became a manufacturer on a large scale, in 1771 establishing the first spinning-mill worked by water-power.

**Arne, Dr. Thomas Augustine** (1710–1778), English composer of considerable merit and of great popularity in his day. He composed numerous ballad operas, and at Drury Lane, Covent Garden, and Vauxhall organised the chief performances for long periods. His best-known opera was *Artaxerxes*, and his most popular songs were *Rule, Britannia!* and *Where the Bee Sucks.*

**Arnold, Matthew** (1822–1888), son of Dr. Thomas Arnold, achieved a high reputation as poet and critic. As the propounder of the principles of " sweetness and light," as well as by his graceful verse, he secured a high place amongst the literary men of the Victorian era.

**Arnold, Thomas, D.D.** (1795–1842), headmaster of Rugby from 1828 to his death. His influence at Rugby was such as to give that institution a supreme position among English public schools. A man of intense spiritual feeling, of a sympathetic and lovable nature, yet possessed of all the necessary attributes of scholarship, he was greatly esteemed and venerated.

**Arrhenius, Svante August** (1859–1927), Swedish chemist, one of the founders of modern physical chemistry. Received 1903 Nobel Prize for originating the theory of electrolytic dissociation (ionisation). Director of the Nobel Institute, 1905–27.

**Arrol, Sir William** (1839–1913), well-known contractor and engineer, whose firm built the Tay, Forth, and London Tower Bridges as well as the Manchester Ship Canal. Originally a piecer in a cotton-mill, and later a working blacksmith.

**Artaxerxes** was the name borne by several ancient Persian kings, some of whom achieved great distinction. The first Artaxerxes was the son of Xerxes, and reigned from 464 B.C. for 40 years; he was succeeded by Darius II. (424–404 B.C.), who in turn was followed by Artaxerxes II., who reigned until 358. Artaxerxes III, the last to bear the name, was a cruel and treacherous man and was poisoned in 338.

**Arthur**, fabled Celtic warrior of c. A.D. 600, the first reference to whom is in the 9th-cent. chronicle of Nennius, who speaks of his 12 victorious battles against the invading Saxons. His legend developed into a vast literature in mediaeval times, which was welded together by Sir Thomas Mallory in his great work *Morte d'Arthur*, printed by Caxton in 1485.

**Arundel, Thomas, Archbishop of Canterbury** (1353–1414), in the reigns of Richard II, and Henry IV.

previously Bishop of Ely and Archbishop of York, and for a time Lord Chancellor. An active politician and bitter enemy of heresy.

**Ashfield, Lord, P.C.** (1874–1948), President Board of Trade, 1916–19; M.P. Ashton-under-Lyne, 1916–20; first Chairman of the London Passenger Transport Board created in 1933.

**Aske, Robert**, the leader of the Pilgrimage of Grace, directed against the Reformation; executed 1537.

**Asoka** (273–232 B.C.), Emperor of India (c. 255–c. 237 B.C.), and the most powerful ruler of his time, his Empire extending from the Himalayas to what is now Madras. He was the first ruler to embrace Buddhism and accord it recognition. Becoming a Buddhist (c. 257 B.C.) he turned aside in disgust from the thought of his earlier military conquests, and attempted by missionary propaganda to spread Buddhism throughout his lands. Many rocks and pillars are inscribed with his moral exhortations. He gave great impetus to Buddhism by organising it as the state religion.

**Asquith, Herbert Henry, 1st Earl of Oxford and Asquith** (1852–1928), Liberal statesman who led a great peacetime administration from 1908 until the outbreak of the First World War and the wartime coalition with the Conservatives from 1915–16 when he was displaced by Lloyd George. Home Sec. (1892–95) in Gladstone's last ministry; Chan. of the Exchequer (1904–8) under Campbell-Bannermann whom he succeeded as Prime Minister. His government enacted important social reforms including old-age pensions (1908) and unemployment insurance (1911). The death of Edward VII in 1910, the struggle over the Irish Home Rule Bill, the declaration of war on Germany, and the Easter Rising in Dublin in 1916 were among the events of his premiership. He resigned the leadership of the Liberal Party in 1926. Earldom of Oxford and Asquith conferred, 1925. His daughter Violet, Lady Asquith (1887–1969), was an eloquent speaker. She entered the Lords as a life peeress in 1964.

**Asser**, a Welsh monk of the tenth century, author of a remarkable life of King Alfred.

**Astor, John Jacob** (1763–1848), the founder of the Astor family of millionaires, was a native of Heidelberg, and emigrating to America, went out to the North-West and began trading in furs, soon building up a large fortune, which he invested in New York real estate.

**Astor, Nancy Witcher, Viscountess, C.H.** (1879–1964), the first woman M.P. to take her seat in the House of Commons, an American by birth, wife of the 2nd Viscount Astor (1879–1952).

**Atatürk, Kemal** (1881–1938), builder of modern Turkey. A fine soldier, he defended the Dardanelles against the British in 1915 and drove the Greeks out of Turkey in 1922. President of the Turkish Republic, 1923–38.

**Athanasius, St.** (296–373), was Bishop of Alexandria. He spent much of his time in bitter theological controversy, and was driven from Alexandria; taking refuge in the desert, he wrote numerous letters in support of Christian doctrine, and under Julian was recalled to Alexandria. The Athanasian creed is supposed to reflect his belief.

**Athelstan** (895–940), grandson of Alfred the Great, was crowned King of England in 925, and was the first ruler of all England.

**Atherstone, William Guybon** (1813–98), South African geologist and an originator of the South African diamond industry. He drew attention to the possibility of diamonds near Kimberley and in 1867 identified a crystal found near the Vaal River, thus helping to start mining development.

**Attila** (406–453), King of the Huns, was a warlike leader, who achieved many conquests over the Roman forces, committing great ravages and laying large tracts of country waste. He marched through Germany and Gaul, and died as he was preparing for another invasion of Italy.

**Attlee, Clement Richard, 1st Earl, O.M., K.G., P.C., C.H.** (1883–1967), Prime Minister in two successive Labour Governments, 1945–51; served as Deputy Prime Minister to Churchill, 1942–45. He was educated at Haileybury and University Coll., Oxford. Called to the Bar in 1905; tutor and lecturer in social science at the London School of Economics, 1913–23.

**B6**

Became Mayor of Stepney in 1919, Labour M.P. for Limehouse in 1922, and Parliamentary Leader of the Labour Party, 1935-55. During his Premiership the welfare society was established and the freedom and independence of India granted. Retired in 1955; earldom conferred. His writings include an autobiography, *As it Happened* (1954), and *Empire into Commonwealth* (1960). *See also* Section C, Part I.

**Auchinleck**, Field-Marshal Sir Claude J. E., G.C.B., G.C.I.E., D.S.O. (b. 1884), Indian Army officer who was C.-in-C. Middle East, 1941-42, and the last British C.-in-C. in India, 1943-46.

**Auden**, Wystan Hugh (b. 1907), influential poet and dramatist, b. in England, naturalised American. Succeeded C. Day Lewis as Prof. of Poetry, Oxford Univ., 1956-61. *See* Section M.

**Auer**, Leopold (1845-1930), the famous Hungarian violinist and teacher of the violin, among his pupils being Mischa Elman and Jascha Heifetz.

**Augustine, Saint** (354-430), the greatest of the Latin fathers, bishop of Hippo, b. at Tagaste in N. Africa of a pagan father and Christian mother (Saint Monica). He ranks high as a philosopher and his influence on Christianity has been second only to that of St. Paul. He was a voluminous writer, the most important works being his *Confessions*, the *City of God*, *On the Trinity*, and *On the Work of Monks*.

**Augustine of Canterbury, Saint** (d. c. 605), the Roman Benedictine missionary monk who was sent to Britain by Gregory the Great in 597 to convert the English peoples to Christianity. He became the first archbishop of Canterbury.

**Augustus**, Caius Octavianus (63 B.C.-A.D. 14), Roman emperor, succeeded Julius Cæsar. After a triumvirate of twelve years, in which he was associated with Mark Antony and Lepidus, he became supreme ruler and for forty-five years exercised a beneficent and powerful sway. He was a devoted patron of Horace and Virgil.

**Aurelius**, Marcus Antoninus. *See* Marcus Aurelius Antoninus.

**Auriol**, Vincent (1884-1966), French politician. Voted against surrender in 1940, was interned and escaped to London in 1943. President of the French National Assembly, 1946, and of the Fourth Republic, 1947-54.

**Aurangzeb** (1618-1707), Mogul emperor of India, 1659-1707, son of Shah Jehan. He was a ruler of ability, and greatly extended his empire by conquest, but his zeal for Mohammedanism aroused the hatred of the Hindus and his persecution of the Sikhs transformed them from a pacifist sect into a militant brotherhood. When he died the disruption of the vast Mogul territory rapidly followed.

**Austen**, Jane (1775-1817), author of *Emma, Mansfield Park, Northanger Abbey, Persuasion, Pride and Prejudice*, and *Sense and Sensibility*. Though confining herself to the personal relations of the English middle classes, she combined artistry, accuracy, imaginative power, satiric humour, sense, and genuine feeling with the ability to create a vast range of living characters, and is often considered the most perfect English novelist.

**Austin**, 1st Baron, K.B.E. (1866-1941), was the well-known English motor manufacturer. He was the pioneer of the small car—the 7-horse-power car—which he put on the market in 1921.

**Avenzoar** (Ibn Zuhr) (c. 1090-1162), a Moslem physician, born in Seville, the greatest of his time. His chief work was the *Tasir*.

**Averroës** (Ibn Rushd) (1126-98), Arab philosopher and medical writer, born in Córdova, last and most famous thinker of Moslem Spain. He studied philosophy, theology, mathematics, medicine, and jurisprudence. His greatest works are his commentaries on Aristotle. He was a friend of Avenzoar.

**Avicenna** (980-1037) of Bokhara, Arab philosopher and physician whose *Canon of Medicine* had an enormous influence on mediaeval Europe.

**Avogadro**, Amedeo (1776-1856), Italian physicist, remembered for his hypothesis, since known as Avogadro's Law, that equal volumes of gases under identical conditions of temperature and pressure contain the same number of molecules.

**Avon**, Earl of. (*See* Eden, R. Anthony.)

**Ayrton**, William Edward, F.R.S. (1847-1908), English electrical engineer, inventor of a number of electrical measuring instruments. His first

wife, Matilda Chaplin Ayrton (1846-83), was one of the first woman doctors and his second wife, Hertha Ayrton (1854-1923), became known for her scientific work on the electric arc and sand ripples and for her work for woman suffrage.

**Ayub Khan, Mohammad**, Field Marshal (b. 1907), military leader and President of Pakistan since 1958; educated at Aligarh Moslem Univ. and Sandhurst. In 1969 he announced his decision to withdraw from political life.

**Azikiwe**, Rt. Hon. Nnamdi, LL.D. (b. 1904), Nigerian statesman. His office as Pres. of Fed. of Nigeria, held since 1963, was suspended by military coup (Jan. 1966).

# B

**Baber or Babar** (Zahir ud-din-Mahomet) (1483-1530), founder of the Mogul dynasty which ruled Northern India for three centuries, and a descendant of Tamerlane.

**Bach, Johann Sebastian** (1685-1750). Born at Eisenach, Germany, he became one of the greatest composers in history and has been called the father of modern music. During his appointment as organist at the Thomaskirche, Leipzig, he composed all his great devotional music, including the wonderful St. Matthew and the St. John Passion and the B minor Mass. His incessant labour affected his eyes, and in 1749 he became totally blind. His family was connected with music for seven generations, of which his was the fifth. *See* Section E.

**Bach, Carl Philipp Emanuel** (1714-88), third son of Johann Sebastian Bach. He is important in the history of music as one of the first experimenters in the symphonic and sonata form.

**Backhaus**, Wilhelm (b. 1884), German pianist, recognised as one of the most gifted, especially in the interpretation of the great classical and romantic concertos. Professor of the Piano at the Royal College of Music, Manchester, 1905.

**Bacon, Francis, Lord Verulam, and Viscount St. Albans** (1561-1626), one of the greatest of English philosophers and statesmen; Attorney-General to Elizabeth; Lord Chancellor under James I. His political career was tarnished by certain acts of corruption, for which he paid the penalty, but his writings were marked by keen insight, brilliancy of language, and a depth of thought which place them in the first rank of philosophical literature. His *Novum Organum* and his *Essays* are splendid monuments of learning and wisdom.

**Bacon, Roger** (1214-1294), the Franciscan friar, was a man of remarkable gifts, of great learning and inventive power. In an age of darkness he was the first to insist on the importance of experiment and can claim the title of founder of experimental science. Optics, explosives, engines, mechanical flight came within the range of his researches. The invention of gunpowder has been attributed to him, but without adequate evidence. For a long time he was looked upon as an alchemist and sorcerer, though of late his discoveries have been more truly appreciated.

**Baden-Powell**, Lt.-Gen. Lord, O.M., G.C.M.G., G.C.V.O., K.C.B. (1857-1941), brilliant cavalry soldier, famous for his defence of Mafeking in the South African War. Founded the organisation of Boy Scouts (1908) and Girl Guides (1910) to promote good citizenship in the rising generation. Chief Scout of the World, 1921-41.

**Baer**, Karl Ernst von (1792-1876), Estonian biologist, founder of the science of embryology, and discoverer of the mammalian ovum.

**Baffin**, William (1584-1622), navigator and explorer who in 1616 discovered the bay which separates the north-east coast of British North America from Greenland, which bears his name.

**Bagehot**, Walter (1826-77), English economist and journalist. Editor of *The Economist*, 1861-77. Wrote three books of lasting importance. *The English Constitution*, 1867, *Physics and Politics*, 1872, and *Lombard Street*, a description of the Money Market, 1873. He was among the first to advocate the creation of Life Peers to strengthen the House of Lords.

**Baird, John Logie** (1888-1946), Scottish television pioneer; inventor of the televisor and the noctovisor.

**Baker, Sir Benjamin**, K.C.B., K.C.M.G., F.R.S.

(1840–1907), an eminent engineer. He was consulting engineer to the Egyptian Government for the Aswan Dam, joint engineer with Sir John Fowler of the Forth Bridge, and engineer of the Central London Tube Railway.

**Baker, Sir Herbert,** K.C.I.E., R.A. (1862–1946) was an eminent architect who designed the Bank of England, Rhodes House, Oxford, and, with the late Sir E. Lutyens, New Delhi.

**Bakst, Léon** (1868–1924), Russian painter who designed scenery and costumes for the Russian Ballet of Serge Diaghilev.

**Balboa, Vasco Nuñez de** (1475–1517), Spanish explorer, who was the first European to set eyes upon the Pacific Ocean.

**Baldwin of Bewdley, 1st Earl,** K.G., P.C. (1867–1947), the leading Conservative politician between the two world wars and Prime Minister, 1923–24, 1924–29, and 1935–37.

**Baldwin, James** (b. 1924), American Negro writer, regarded as the most significant of his time. Novels include *Go Tell It to the Mountain* (1953) and *Another Country* (1962). *See* Section M

**Balewa, Sir Abubakar Tafawa,** K.B.E. (1912–1966), Federal Prime Minister of Nigeria, 1960–66; murdered during the crisis of January 1966.

**Balfour, Arthur James, Earl of,** K.G., O.M., P.C. (1848–1930), statesman, scholar, and philosopher. Entered Parliament as a Conservative in 1874. Prime Minister, 1902–5. He also served as First Lord of the Admiralty under Asquith and as Foreign Secretary under Lloyd George. His most notable action was issuing the Balfour Declaration on Palestine.

**Balliol, John de,** English baron whose widow in 1269 founded the college at Oxford which bears his name. Fought for Henry III, against Simon de Montfort. Died in exile in 1269.

**Baliol, John** (1249–1315), son of the above, competed with Robert Bruce for the Scottish throne, and Edward I. decided in his favour. Only reigned four years, when Edward deposed him, committing him to the Tower, and finally banished him from the country. He retired to Normandy. His son, Edward Baliol, recovered his father's kingdom in 1332, and was upheld by Edward III. whilst very unpopular by reason of his having given up the south of Scotland to the English. He renounced his title and throne in 1356, and retired to England on an annuity.

**Ball, John** (d. 1381), English priest and a leader of the Peasants' Revolt, after which he was executed. Author of the couplet *When Adam delved, and Eve span, Who was then the gentleman?*

**Balzac, Honoré de** (1799–1850), one of the greatest of French novelists, and the author of over eighty novels to which he gave the covering title of *La Comédie Humaine,* depicting the appetites and passions of the new social class born of the revolution and Napoleon.

**Bampton, John** (1689–1751), an eminent divine, who founded the Oxford Bampton Divinity lectures.

**Bancroft, Sir Squire** (1841–1926), one of the best-known Victorian actor-managers.

**Bandaranaike, Hon. Solomon West Ridgway Dias,** B.A. (1899–1959). Socialist Prime Min. of Ceylon from 1956 until his assassination in 1959. His widow, Mrs. Sirimawo Bandaranaike, became the world's first woman Prime Minister, 1960–65.

**Banks, Sir Joseph,** Bt., F.R.S. (1743–1820), was president of the Royal Society for upwards of forty years. As a naturalist he was one of the most eminent men of his time, and encouraged science in every form. When Captain Cook made his voyage to the South Seas in 1768, Sir Joseph accompanied him for the purpose of observing the transit of Venus. He left very valuable botanical collections to the British Museum.

**Banting, Sir Frederick Grant,** K.B.E., M.C., D.Sc., M.D., F.R.S. (1891–1941). Canadian physician and discoverer of insulin. Prof. of Medical Research, Toronto University, 1923–41.

**Bantock, Sir Granville,** Mus. Doc. (1868–1946), Professor of Music at Birmingham University 1908–34; Chairman of Trinity Coll. of Music, London. He wrote songs, orchestral and choral music.

**Barbirolli, Sir John,** F.R.A.M. (b. 1899), English conductor; succeeded Toscanini as conductor of the New York Philharmonic Symphony Orchestra, 1937–42; conductor of the Hallé Orchestra since 1943.

**Barbarossa** (Red Beard), name given to Frederick I

(c. 1122–90), greatest of the mediæval Holy Roman emperors who struggled (1159–77) to free the Empire from the domination of the Pope. The two brothers who were Barbary pirates also had this name: Uruj (c. 1482–1518) was killed by the Spaniards, and Khaireddin (c. 1482–1546) conquered Tunis for the Turks in 1534 and died in Constantinople.

**Barbusse, Henri** (1874–1935), noted French author and writer of the famous war novel *Le Feu,* which is one of the most remarkable and realistic of all war books, and portrays in a starkly vivid way the experience of the common soldier.

**Barker, Dame Lilian,** D.B.E. (1874–1955), governor of the Borstal Institution for Girls at Aylesbury. 1923–35; Ass. Comm. of Prisons, 1936–43.

**Barnardo, Dr. Thomas John** (1845–1905), the founder of the well-known homes for orphanwaifs, for some forty years devoted himself to the protection, education and advancement of destitute children.

**Barrie, Sir James Matthew,** Bt, O.M. (1860–1937). popular Scottish author and playwright. Among his novels are *A Window in Thrums* and *The Little Minister,* while his plays include *Quality Street, The Admirable Crichton, Dear Brutus, Mary Rose, Shall We join the Ladies?* and the children's classic, *Peter Pan.* His work is clever and entertaining and is tinged with mysticism.

**Barrow, Isaac** (1630–1677), a famous divine, mathematician, Greek scholar, and tutor of Sir Isaac Newton. His "Sermons" are amongst the finest in the language.

**Barry, Sir Charles,** R.A. (1795–1860), architect of the Houses of Parliament at Westminster which took twenty years to build. Knighted in 1852, and buried in Westminster Abbey. His son:

**Barry, Sir John Wolfe Wolfe-,** K.C.B., F.R.S. (1836–1918), an eminent engineer, designed and carried out some of the most prominent undertakings of the time, including Barry Dock and Tower Bridge.

**Barth, Karl** (b. 1886), Swiss theologian, one of the leading Protestant thinkers of the 20th century, described by the late Pope John as a Protestant St. Thomas Aquinas.

**Bartók, Bela** (1881–1945), Hungarian composer, one of the great figures in the music of his century. From an early age deeply interested in folk-song which inspired him in his researches into Hungarian and Rumanian peasant music. His compositions include string quartets, violin sonatas, concertos, orchestral music, a ballet and an opera, and a collection of over 7,000 melodies. Professor at Budapest Conservatory, 1907–12, when he retired into private life as a result of the opposition his compositions aroused. *See* Section E.

**Bartolommeo, Fra** (1469–1517), the distinguished Florentine painter and friend of Savonarola, at whose death he became a monk.

**Bartolozzi, Francesco,** R.A. (1727–1815), a Florentine engraver who came to London in 1764 where he became one of the original members of the Royal Academy. He produced an enormous number of engravings and was responsible for the stipple technique.

**Baruch, Bernard Mannes** (1870–1965). American economist. Assisted U.S. Government in both world wars, and in 1946 was chairman of the United Nations Atomic Energy Commission.

**Bashkirtseff, Marie** (1860–84), Russian painter and writer of a famous autobiographical diary.

**Bassi, Agostino** (1773–1856), Italian amateur microscopist who first suggested that infectious diseases might be caused by the invasion of the body by micro-organisms.

**Batten, Jean Gardner,** C.B.E. (b. 1909) the famous New Zealand airwoman who made aviation history by her record solo flight from England to Australia in 1934.

**Baudelaire, Charles Pierre** (1821–67), French poet of startling originality and great sensitivity, best known for his book of verse *Les Fleurs du Mal,* also a brilliant critic. He was inordinately attached to his mother and allowed his life to be ruined by poverty, despair, and ill-health.

**Bax, Sir Arnold Edward Trevor,** K.C.V.O., F.R.C.M., F.R.A.M. (1883–1953), Master of the King's Musick, 1942–52; Master of the Queen's Musick, 1952–53. His work includes seven symphonies and several tone-poems for orchestra.

Baxter, Richard (1615–91), a great Nonconformist divine, remarkable for the ability and boldness of his writings.

Bayard, Pierre du Terrail, Chevalier de (1475–1524), a French knight of exemplary conduct and remarkable for his chivalry. Fell at the Battle of Sesia, and was named " Le Chevalier sans peur et sans reproche."

Baylis, Lilian Mary, C.H. (d. 1937), manager of the Old Vic theatre from 1898 and of Sadler's Wells from 1931. Did great work for the British stage.

Beaconsfield, Benjamin Disraeli, Earl of, K.G., P.C. (1804–81). Son of Isaac D'Israeli (q.v.). Statesman and novelist; with Burke (q.v.) exercised most influence on Conservative political theories. His first novel, Vivien Grey, published when he was only twenty-one, was a brilliant success and the author was able to enter Society. Coningsby and Sibyl, published twenty years later, helped to rouse the social conscience to the evils of industrial life and of the deplorable relations existing between rich and poor (the " two nations "). Disraeli entered Parliament in 1837, but had only short periods of office before his terms as Prime Minister in 1868 and 1874–80. The second period was marked by the purchase of the Suez Canal shares, by the conferment on the Queen of the title, Empress of India, and by a diplomatic triumph at the Congress of Berlin, abroad, and by a continuation of measures for social reform, at home. He was a gifted orator, the rival and antithesis of Gladstone and the friend of Queen Victoria, who favoured his policies, honoured his wife, and called him " Dizzy."

Beardsley, Aubrey Vincent (1872–98), black-and-white artist, whose illustrations in the Yellow Book aroused much controversy.

Beatty, 1st Earl, Admiral of the Fleet, P.C., G.C.B., O.M., G.C.V.O., D.S.O. (1871–1936). First Sea Lord, 1919–27. From 1912 to 1916 Commander of Battle Cruiser Squadron. From Nov. 1916 to 1919 succeeded Lord Jellicoe as Admiral of the main British Fleet. On Aug. 28, 1914, fought the German fleet in the Heligoland Bight. On May 31, 1916, Lord Beatty with his battle cruisers was engaged in a great sea fight with the Germans off Jutland, for which he was granted £100,000 and an Earldom in 1919.

Beaumont, Francis (1584–1616), and Fletcher, John (1579–1625), joint authors of many plays, including The Maid's Tragedy and Philaster. Beaumont was buried in Westminster Abbey, and Fletcher interred in St. Saviour's, Southwark.

Beaverbrook, 1st Baron (William Maxwell Aitken) (1879–1964), British newspaper owner and politician, a Canadian by birth. A man of tremendous energy and will-power, he rendered great service as Minister of Aircraft Production in the crucial years, 1940–1. He controlled the Daily Express, Sunday Express, and Evening Standard which sponsored his various political campaigns, notably the Empire Free Trade Movement. Known affectionately as " Max " or " The Beaver."

Becket, Thomas (1118?–70), saint and martyr, Archbishop of Canterbury under Henry II. A powerful and ambitious prelate who boldly supported the authority of the Pope against the dictates of the King, and was assassinated in Canterbury Cathedral December 29th, 1170, being canonised two years later.

Beckett, Samuel (b. 1906), Anglo-Irish dramatist and novelist. See Sections I and M.

Becquerel, Antoine Henri (1852–1908), French physicist who in 1896 discovered radioactivity in uranium. Shared with the Curies the 1903 Nobel Prize in Physics.

Bede, " The Venerable " (673–735), a monk of great influence and ability whose historical works cover a great range and are valuable in the outline they give of the early history of this country.

Beecham, Sir Thomas, Bt., C.H. (1879–1961), conductor and impresario. Founded the London Philharmonic Orchestra in 1931; introduced into England the operas of Richard Strauss, Russian operas, and the Diaghilev ballet; championed the music of Delius. Recognised as one of the world's greatest conductors, especially in the interpretation of Mozart and Wagner. Conductor of the Royal Philharmonic Orchestra (1946). Pub. Frederick Delius

biography (1959); Memoirs: A Mingled Chime.

Beecher, Henry Ward (1813–1887), an eminent American preacher and lecturer, whose church at Brooklyn was for many years the most popular in the United States. Brother of Mrs. H. B. Stowe.

Beerbohm, Sir Max (1872–1956), brilliant critic and caricaturist who contributed to the Saturday Review during his " twelve years' bondage to dramatic criticism " (1898–1910).

Beethoven, Ludwig van (1770–1827), one of the world's greatest musicians and composers, born at Bonn of a poor but musical family, his father being a tenor singer in the service of the electoral prince at Bonn. As a child he was already remarkable for his playing of the harpsichord and violin and for his power of extemporization. Some of his compositions, sonatas, songs and pianoforte variations were published when he was only 13. At 17 he visited Vienna and played before Mozart who promptly recognised his genius. When he was about 30 he began to suffer from the worst malady that could possibly have befallen him: he became deaf. He faced his fate with indomitable courage and perhaps more than any other artist continued to develop until he reached the loftiest pinnacle of musical fame. Between the years 1805 and 1808, Beethoven composed some of his greatest works: the oratorio Mount of Olives, the opera Fidelio, and the Pastorale and Eroica symphonies besides a number of concertos, sonatas and songs. He composed four overtures to Fidelio at different periods: Leonore No. 2 (1805), Leonore No. 3 (1806), Leonore No. 1 (1807) and Fidelio (1814). The Mass in C was first performed in 1810 and the Mass in D was written between the years 1819 and 1822. The symphonies, nine in number, rank as the greatest ever written and the pianoforte sonatas and string quartets are unequalled in beauty. He died at Vienna at the age of 56. See Section E.

Behring, Emil von (1854–1917), German bacteriologist and father of the science of immunology. Awarded Nobel Prize in 1901.

Behring, Vitus (1680–1741), Danish navigator who entered the Russian service and in 1728 discovered Behring's Strait, afterwards being wrecked on Behring's Island, where he died.

Belisarius (505–565), brilliant Roman general under Justinian, famed for his campaigns against the Vandals, Ostrogoths, and Persians.

Bell, Alexander Graham, (1847–1922), born in Edinburgh, emigrated to Canada in 1870 and in 1871 lectured in Boston, mainly to teachers of the deaf, later becoming an American citizen. In 1876 exhibited an invention which was developed into the telephone. Invented the photophone, and devoted much attention to the education of deaf-mutes.

Bell, Gertrude Margaret Lowthian, C.B.E. (1868–1926), the " uncrowned Queen of Arabia," was a famous traveller in the East, especially in Arabia.

Bellamy, Edward (1850–1898), American journalist and author of Looking Backward, a utopian novel in which he foretells of many changes that have since come to pass.

Bellini, a celebrated family of Venetian painters of the Early Renaissance: Jacopo (c. 1400–70) and his two sons Gentile (1429–1507), whose works include the Adoration of the Magi (National Gallery), and Giovanni (c. 1429–1516), brother-in-law of Mantegna, and teacher of Giorgione and Titian.

Bellini, Vincenzo (1801–35), Italian operatic composer; born in Sicily, the son of an organist. His graceful vocal melodies were much admired by his friend Chopin and he enjoyed successes in Paris and London. His best-known operas are I Capuleti ed i Montecchi, La Sonnambula, Norma, and I Puritani. See also E10(1).

Belloc, (Joseph) Hilaire (Pierre) (1870–1953), a writer of great versatility whose works include The Bad Child's Book of Beasts, The Path to Rome, Hills and the Sea, Cautionary Tales, and historical studies of Danton, Robespierre and Richelieu.

Belzoni, Giovanni Battista (1778–1823), Italian archæologist who settled in England at the beginning of the 19th century. He turned his attention to hydraulic experiments, and went to Egypt with a view to getting the Government to sanction a scheme for raising the water of the Nile. He was then attracted to the study of Egyptian antiquities.

**Benedict, St.** (*c.*480 – *c.*543), b. at Nursia near Spoleto, in Umbria; founded twelve monasteries, and the Order of Benedictine Monks, at Monte Cassino, near Naples. Here he wrote his celebrated Rule, a unique document of wide application. (*See* Monasticism, J30).

**Benes, Dr.** Eduard (1884–1948), Czechoslovak statesman; co-founder with Thomas Masaryk of the Czech Republic; Foreign Minister, 1918–35, and President 1935–38 and 1940–48. An all-party ministry was overthrown by a communist *coup d'état* in February 1948, and Benes, in failing health, resigned the Presidency in June, dying in September.

**Benavente y Martinez, Jacinto** (1866–1954), one of the greatest of Spanish dramatists. Author of *Los Intereses Creados* and other famous plays. Nobel Prizewinner, 1922.

**Ben-Gurion, David** (b. 1886), Zionist leader, prominently connected with the Labour movement in Palestine in between the world wars. Prime Minister of Israel, 1948–63.

**Bennett, Enoch Arnold** (1867–1931), author and journalist. His stories of the Pottery Towns, where he was brought up, are of high merit. *The Old Wives' Tales, Clayhanger,* and *Hilda Lessways* are among his most successful novels. He also wrote plays, including *Milestones, The Great Adventure,* and *Mr. Prohack.*

**Bennett, James Gordon** (1841–1918), proprietor of the *New York Herald,* and a famous yachtsman and motorist. He sent out Stanley on the expedition which resulted in the finding of Livingstone.

**Bennett, Sir William Sterndale** (1816–1875), English composer best known for his oratorio *The Woman of Samaria.* Schumann pronounced him to be " a thorough Englishman, a glorious artist, and a beautiful and poetic soul."

**Bentham, Jeremy** (1748–1832), the founder of the school of political philosophy, the tenets of which were extended by John Stuart Mill. His works on *Government, Usury,* and *The Principles of Morals and Politics,* expound the Utilitarian system with great lucidity.

**Bentley, Richard** (1662–1742), an eminent classical scholar and critic, for long Master of Trinity College, Cambridge. He was a formidable controversialist and did pioneer work in textual criticism.

**Benz, Karl** (1844–1929), German engineer whose motor car produced in 1885 was one of the first to be driven by an internal-combustion engine.

**Béranger, Jean Pierre de** (1780–1857), was the most popular song writer that France has produced. His songs were often written to serve some passing political purpose, and were invariably in harmony with popular sentiment.

**Beresford, William Carr Beresford, Viscount** (1768–1854), British General. Participated in capture of Cape Colony and of Buenos Aires. Reorganised Portuguese Army. Master-General of Ordnance in Wellington administration.

**Berg, Alban** (1885–1935), Austrian composer whose best known work is the three-act opera *Wozzeck,* based upon a drama by Büchner (*q.v.*), which has become a modern classic. (E16(2).

**Bergson, Henri Louis** (1859–1941), French philosopher, exponent of the theory of vitalism and the life force. Member of French Academy, 1941; Nobel Prize for Literature, 1927. Author of *Matter and Memory* (1896) and *Creative Evolution* (1907).

**Bériot, Charles Auguste de** (1802–70), Belgian violinist, whose first wife was the great operatic contralto Malibran. His son Charles Wilfrid de Bériot (1833–1914) was a fine pianist and the teacher of Ravel.

**Berkeley, George, D.D.,** Bishop of Cloyne (1685–1753), the propounder of the philosophy that the only things that are real are our ideas of what is presented to our senses. In support of this philosophy he wrote several works of great ingenuity of argument, chief amongst them being his *Alciphron, or the Minute Philosopher.*

**Berlin, Irving** (b. 1888), American composer of popular songs, and the pioneer of both ragtime and jazz music; his songs including *Alex-ander's Rag-time Band, Always, What'll I Do?* were the beginning of popular jazz.

**Berlin, Sir Isaiah, C.B.E., M.A.** (b. 1909), British University teacher, b. Riga; Chichele Professor of Social and Political Theory at Oxford since 1957. His works include *Karl Marx* (1948), *The Hedgehog and the Fox* (1953), *The Age of Enlightenment* (1956). His series of lectures on *Some Sources of Romanticism,* broadcast 1966–7 were much enjoyed.

**Berlioz, (Louis) Hector** (1803–69), composer, born in S.E. France, the son of a country doctor; eccentric, highly-endowed, he was the greatest figure in the French romantic movement. His outstanding dramatic works are *La Damnation de Faust* and the *Roméo et Juliette* symphony. His first wife was an Irish actress, Harriet Smithson, for whom he formed a romantic attachment while she was appearing in Shakespearean parts in Rome.

**Bernadotte, Count Folke** (1895–1948), nephew of King Gustav V. of Sweden; active in Swedish Red Cross; intermediary through whom Himmler attempted to capitulate in 1945; U.N. mediator in Palestine in 1947; assassinated by Jewish terrorists.

**Bernadotte, Jean Baptiste** (1764–1844), was a French commander of great distinction who served under Napoleon, and in 1810 was chosen heir to the throne of Sweden. In 1818 he succeeded as Charles XIV., and was a capable ruler.

**Bernal, John Desmond, M.A., F.R.S.** (b. 1901). Professor of Physics, Birkbeck College since 1938. Author of *Science in History, The Physical Basis of Life, The Origin of Life,* and of many other works on scientific and social subjects, notably crystallography, poison gases, and post-war housing.

**Bernard of Menthon** (923–1008), patron saint of mountaineers. Founded the alpine hospices of Saint Bernard on the famous Great Saint Bernard Pass between Switzerland and Italy.

**Bernard, Saint,** of Clairvaux (*c.* 1090–1153), famous French abbot of the monastery of Clairvaux whose sermons and letters had very great influence in Western Europe.

**Bernhardt, Sarah** (1845–1923), the most renowned tragedienne of her time. Became a member of the Comédie Française after the Siege of Paris, and thereafter occupied a specially prominent position as an actress. Her first performance in London was in 1879. Among her most conspicuous successes are *Théodora, Fédora,* and *La Tosca,* while she also appeared as Hamlet with distinction.

**Berthelot, Marcellin Pierre Eugène** (1827–1907), French chemist and politician, and the first to produce organic compounds synthetically.

**Berzelius, Jöns Jakob** (1779–1848), Swedish chemist, whose researches laid the foundations for modern chemical science. He devised the system of chemical symbols in use today and discovered several elements.

**Bessemer, Sir Henry, F.R.S.** (1813–1898), famous for his invention of the well-known process of converting cast-iron direct into steel. His invention entirely revolutionised steel manufacture, greatly reducing the cost of production and making it possible to utilise steel in many directions where previously iron only had been used.

**Bevan, Rt. Hon. Aneurin, M.P.** (1897–1960). British socialist politician of remarkable genius; architect of the National Health Service which came into operation in 1948. M.P. for Ebbw Vale, 1929–60; Min. of Health, 1945–51; Min. of Labour, Jan.–Apr. 1951.

**Beveridge, Lord, K.C.B.** (1879–1963), British economist. Director of the London School of Economics, 1919–37, and Master of University College, Oxford, 1937–44. Drew up the Beveridge Plan, published in 1942, which formed the basis of the present Health and Insurance Schemes.

**Bevin, Rt. Hon. Ernest, M.P.** (1881–1951), Secy. of State for Foreign Affairs 1945–51; Minister of Labour and National Service, 1940–45. A British Trade Union Leader who became prominently associated with the Dockers Union, of which he was Assistant General Secretary and of the Transport and General Workers Union of which he was still General Secretary when he entered the Coalition Government as Minister of Labour. He was Chairman of the General Council of Trades Union Congress, 1937.

**Bichat, Marie François Xavier** (1771–1802), French physiologist and anatomist whose study of tissues founded modern histology. His theory was that life is " the sum of the forces that restrict death."

**Biddle, John** (1615–62), the first English Unitarian. He was fined, imprisoned and banished for his publications attacking the Holy Trinity. Under a general Act of Oblivion in 1652 he resumed his teachings, which led to further imprisonment, and as a result he died of fever.

**Binyon, (Robert) Laurence, C.H.** (1869–1943), English poet, art critic, and authority on Oriental art, keeper of prints and drawings at the British Museum.

**Birch, (Samuel John) Lamorna, R.A.** (1869–1955), English landscape painter in oils and watercolours, well known for his charming Cornish landscapes and sea studies. His pictures are hung in all the principal galleries of England.

**Birkbeck, George** (1776–1841), physician, philanthropist, and philosopher. A Yorkshireman who settled in London in 1804, and became the chief founder of Mechanics' Institutes.

**Birkenhead, 1st Earl of, P.C., G.C.S.I.** (1872–1930), Sec. for India, 1924–1928. Lord Chancellor, 1919–1922, Attorney-General 1915 to 1919. M.P. for the Walton Divn. of Liverpool from 1906 to 1918, and West Derby Divn. thereof from Dec. 1918 to Jan. 1, 1919.

**Birkett, 1st Baron (William) Norman, Q.C.** (1883–1962), great English advocate; Lord Justice of Appeal, 1950–7; Judge King's Bench Div. 1941–50; British Mem. (Deputy) Int. Mil. Tribunal at Nuremberg 1945–46; M.P. (L.) for East Nottingham, 1923–24 and 1920–31.

**Bishop, Sir Henry Rowley** (1786–1855), composer of many popular ballad operas and songs. *Maid Marian, Guy Mannering* and *The Miller and his Men,* are his best-known operas. He was also a very successful glee-writer, and was the composer of *Home, Sweet Home.* Was the first musician to be knighted in 1842.

**Bismarck, Otto Eduard Leopold von, Prince Bismarck, Duke of Lauenburg** (1815–98), Prusso-German statesman, chief architect of the German empire. Of Junker family he began his diplomatic career in 1851 when he was appointed Prussian member of the revived German Diet of Frankfurt. Prussian ambassador at St. Petersburg (1859–62), where he gained the confidence of the new Tsar (Alexander II), and at Paris (1862), where he had the opportunity of studying Napoleon III. Recalled to Germany by William I to head his government, from which time dates the autocratic rule which was ultimately to prove so disastrous for Germany and the world. There followed the events which led to the victory over Austria in 1866, the humiliation of France in 1871 culminating in William I being proclaimed emperor of Germany at Versailles. From 1871 until the death of William I in 1888 the rule of the " iron chancellor " dominated Europe and German domestic affairs. A struggle for supremacy developed between Bismarck and William II which ended (1890) in the " old pilot " being dropped, to use a figure of speech made memorable by one of Tenniel's cartoons. Bismarck retired to his country estates to spend the rest of his life in criticism of the emperor.

**Bizet, Georges** (1838–75), properly Alexandre César Léopold, French composer who gave the operatic stage several operas full of charming melody and whose immortal *Carmen* from the story by Mérimée was his greatest achievement. He died too young to enjoy popularity.

**Björnson, Björnstjerne** (1832–1910), the Norwegian poet, dramatist, and novelist is one of the great names in modern European literature. his poems, plays, and stories being marked by a strong intellectuality and a rich imagination,

**Black, Joseph** (1728–99), Scottish chemist. Prof. of anatomy at Glasgow (1756–60) and of medicine and chemistry at Edinburgh (1760). Specially known for discoveries of carbon dioxide (he called it " fixed air ") and latent heat. His original work earned him the title father of quantitative chemistry.

**Blackett, Patrick Maynard Stuart, Baron, O.M., C.H., F.R.S., M.A.** (b. 1897), British physicist;

Professor Emeritus and Senior Research Fellow of Imperial College, London; one of Labour Government's senior scientific advisers. Worked with Rutherford at Cavendish Laboratory and his work on nuclear and cosmic ray physics gained him a Nobel Prize in 1948. His studies also include operational research and magnetism. Author of *Military and Political Consequences of Atomic Energy* (1948). Pres. British Association, 1957; Pres. Royal Society, 1966.

**Blackmore, Richard Doddridge** (1825–1900), a novelist who in 1869 made a great reputation with his romantic story of *Lorna Doone.*

**Blackstone, Sir William** (1723–1780), was a Justice of the Court of Common Pleas. His great work, *Commentaries on the Laws of England,* became one of the British classics.

**Blackwood, Algernon, C.B.E.** (1869–1951), British author. As a young man, farmed in Canada and worked on New York newspapers. Then, from 1906, produced a steady flow of books, plays, and short stories of high quality.

**Blair, Robert** (1699–1746), a noted Scottish poet, whose poem, *The Grave,* entitles him to a place in all collections of British poetry.

**Blake, Robert** (1599–1657), Parliamentary general and an admiral in the Cromwellian navy in the Dutch and Spanish wars.

**Blake, William** (1757–1827), painter, poet, and mystic, whose *Songs of Innocence* and scriptural drawings reveal an intense spirituality. He was a highly independent and original thinker and has been called " the great teacher of the modern western world."

**Blanqui, Louis Auguste** (1805–81), French revolutionary leader, master of the technique of insurrection; believed in direct action and was prominent in the revolutionary struggles of 1830, 1848, and 1871. He invented the phrase " dictatorship of the proletariat " and his social theories, stressing the class struggle, influenced Marx. Much of his life was spent in prison.

**Blériot, Louis** (1872–1936), French airman; the first to fly the English Channel from Calais to Dover, July 25, 1909.

**Bligh, William** (1754–1817), British sailor who had a noted career as a brave and able officer but who is chiefly remembered for the mutiny in 1789 on his ship *The Bounty* on a breadfruit expedition from Tahiti to the West Indies. In 1776 he had sailed with Cook as master of the *Resolution.* As Governor of New South Wales (1806) he fought to suppress the rum traffic. Promoted vice-admiral in 1814.

**Blind, Karl** (1826–1907), was a native of Mannheim, and in 1847 associated himself with the German revolutionary movement, but was arrested and imprisoned. Gaining his liberty, he resided in Brussels for a time, and afterwards settled in London, remaining in close touch with men like Mazzini and Louis Blanc, and by pen and speech constantly advocating political freedom.

**Bliss, Sir Arthur** (b. 1891), English composer, succeeded Sir Arnold Bax as Master of the Queen's Musick in 1953. His best known works are the *Colour Symphony* (1922), *Morning Heroes* (1930) and his ballet *Checkmate* (1937). Mus. Dir. B.B.C., 1941–44.

**Bloch, Ernest** (1880–1959), composer, whose music is characterised by its Jewish and oriental themes. He was born in Geneva, Switzerland, and became a naturalised American citizen.

**Blomfield, Sir Reginald, R.A., M.A., F.S.A.** (1856–1942); was a prominent architect, designer of gardens and country houses.

**Blondin, Charles (Jean François Gravelet)** (1824–1897), a famous French rope performer, who crossed Niagara Falls on a tight-rope.

**Blücher, Field-Marshal Gebhard Leberecht von** (1742–1819), was the famous Prussian commander who, after a long and brilliant military career, joined forces with Wellington in the final campaign against Napoleon, and materially helped to win the great victory of Waterloo by advancing to Wellington's support.

**Blum, Léon** (1872–1950), statesman and architect of French socialism. Led a " popular front " government in 1936 and a " caretaker " government for a brief period 1946–47. Served as vice-premier 1937–38. During 1940–45 was interned in Germany.

**Blunden, Edmund Charles** (b. 1896), English poet and critic; Prof. of Eng. Lit. at Tokyo Univ., 1924–27; Fellow and Tutor Eng. Lit., Merton College, Oxford, 1931–43; Prof. of English, Hong Kong Univ., 1953–64. Prof. of Poetry at Oxford, 1966–68.

**Blunt, Wilfred Scawen** (1840–1922), English poet and political writer who after retiring from the diplomatic service (1858–70) championed Egyptian, Indian, and Irish independence; imprisoned in 1888 for activities in the Irish Land League. His *Secret History of the English Occupation of Egypt* (1907) aroused much controversy. He married a granddaughter of Lord Byron.

**Boadicea**, queen of the Iceni (of Norfolk), also called **Boudicca**. She raised an army against and defeated the Roman invaders, but was afterwards vanquished by Suetonius and committed suicide in 62.

**Boccaccio, Giovanni** (1313–1375), an Italian author who has often been called the father of the novel. He had a lively imagination and a graceful style, and his famous *Decameron*—condemned by two Popes and by the Council of Trent—has been a fount of inspiration to poets and story-tellers from Shakespeare to Keats.

**Boccherini, Luigi** (1743–1805), Italian composer, contemporary of Haydn, who first gained fame as a 'cellist. Settled in Madrid in 1769 as composer to the Chapel of the Infante, which position he held until 1785. Was appointed composer to the Court of Frederick William II. of Prussia, but returned to Spain in 1797, and died in poverty in Madrid.

**Bode, Johann Elert** (1747–1826), German astronomer remembered mainly for his law (known as Bode's Law) for the calculation of the relative distances of the planets from the sun.

**Boehm, Sir Joseph Edgar, Bt., R.A.** (1834–90), British sculptor. Executed several famous monuments and statues including that of Carlyle on the Chelsea Embankment, the monument to Dean Stanley in Westminster Abbey, Darwin in the Natural History Museum, Kensington, and the equestrian statue of the Duke of Wellington at Hyde Park Corner.

**Bohr, Niels Henrik David** (1885–1962), Danish nuclear physicist whose researches into the structure of the atom gave him great authority in the world of theoretical physics. With Rutherford he applied the quantum theory to the study of atomic processes. Awarded Nobel Prize for Physics, 1922.

**Boïeldieu, François Adrien** (1775–1834), French composer whose masterpiece, *La Dame Blanche*, was published in 1825. Composed many works in collaboration with Cherubini and Mehul. Succeeded Mehul as Professor of Composition at the Conservatoire, Paris, in 1817.

**Boileau-Despréaux, Nicolas** (1636–1711), literary critic and French poet who was contemporary with Molière, Racine, and La Fontaine. He wrote many classical imitations and is famous for his *Satires*.

**Boïto, Arrigo** (1842–1918), Italian poet and composer. He wrote the libretti of *Otello* and *Falstaff* for Verdi, and for his own operas of *Mefistofele* and many others.

**Boleyn, Anne** (1507–36), queen of Henry VIII and mother of Queen Elizabeth. Originally maid-in-waiting to Catharine of Aragon and her successor when Catharine's marriage was annulled. She failed to produce a male heir and was beheaded on a charge of adultery.

**Bolívar, Simón** (1783–1830), South American revolutionist, b. Caracas, called the Liberator; today revered as the greatest of Latin American heroes; with some British aid freed N.W. South America from Spain, founding Grand Colombia (now Venezuela, Colombia, Panama, Ecuador); died poor, of tuberculosis, in Colombia, after Venezuela had left the Union.

**Bonaventura, St.** (1221–1274), a Franciscan monk of great learning and piety, and a leading Schoolman. He was called the "Seraphic Doctor."

**Bondfield, Rt. Hon. Margaret Grace, C.H.** (1873–1953), Min. of Labour, 1929–31. Represented Northampton, 1923–24. Wallsend, 1926–31. First woman member of a British Cabinet.

**Bone, Sir Muirhead** (1876–1953), Scottish artist, famous for his drawings and etchings of architectural subjects. Excelled in dry-point and drawings of intricate scaffolding. His son Stephen Bone, painter and critic, died in 1958 at the age of 53.

**Bonheur, Rosa** (1822–1899), a native of Bordeaux, and one of the most noted animal painters of the 19th century.

**Boniface, St.** (*c.* 675–754), a Benedictine monk, native of Devon, original name Wynfrith. Sent by Pope Gregory II. on missionary work in Germany; appointed archbishop of Mainz, 746. Attacked and killed with over 50 companions by pagans in Friesland

**Bonnard, Pierre** (1867–1947), French painter of landscapes, still-lifes, and nudes, a great colourist and skilled draughtsman, acclaimed as one of the greatest painters of the century. Exhibition at the Royal Academy, 1966.

**Booth, Edwin** (1833–93), American Shakespearean actor, son of Junius Brutus Booth, the English tragedian, and brother of John Wilkes Booth, who assassinated President Lincoln.

**Booth, William** (1829–1912), founder and first general of the Salvation Army, b. Nottingham. He entered the Methodist New Connexion and was from the first interested in evangelical work. In 1865, with the help of his wife, Catherine Booth, he began mission work in the East End of London which led to the creation in 1878 of the Salvation Army on military lines. His zeal and organising ability developed it into a great religious military organisation with branches in many parts of the world. His son Bramwell (*d.* 1929) and his daughter Evangeline were among his successors. *See also* J39.

**Borgia, Cæsar** (1476–1507), the masterful and unscrupulous son of Pope Alexander VI., who paved his way to power by the murder of those who stood in his way, and aided by Louis XII. of France, became ruler of Romagna, the Marches, and Umbria. Pope Julius II. banished him from Rome, and he was imprisoned in Spain, but escaped to find a soldier's death in the Army of Navarre in the invasion of Castile.

**Borodin, Alexander Porfyrievich** (1834–87), Russian composer who was a professor of chemistry and founded a school of medicine for women. In a busy professional life he wrote two symphonies, three string quartets, the symphonic sketch *In the Steppes of Central Asia*, some beautiful songs, piano music, and the opera *Prince Igor*, left unfinished at his death but completed by his friends Rimsky-Korsakov and Glazunov.

**Borrow, George Henry** (1803–81), English author, for many years agent for the British and Foreign Bible Society; in the course of his wanderings studied gypsy life and wrote of his experiences in *Lavengro*, *Romany Rye*, *Bible in Spain*.

**Bose, Subhas Chandra** (1897–1945), Indian nationalist leader; killed in aeroplane crash.

**Boswell, James** (1740–1795), made himself famous by writing *The Life of Dr. Johnson*, spending some years in close intimacy with the great lexicographer, and producing what is probably the finest biography in the language. His own journals and letters, collected together by Yale University and published in 1949 as *The Boswell Papers*, are among the greatest literary collections ever assembled.

**Botha, General the Rt. Hon. Louis** (1862–1919), the Boer general who succeeded Joubert in command of the Transvaal forces in the Boer War 1899–1902. On parliamentary government being granted to the Transvaal in 1907 he became the first Prime Minister, and attended the Imperial Conference in England the same year. In 1910 made first Premier of the South African Union. After the outbreak of war with Germany took the field at the head of a Union force and, in addition to putting down a rebel movement engineered by Germany, conquered a large portion of German African Territory.

**Bottesini, Giovanni** (1821–89), Italian double-bass player, also famous as an opera conductor and composer.

**Botticelli, Sandro** (*c.* 1444–1510), Italian painter and disciple of Savonarola, the democrat. Produced many notable pictures, and assisted in the decoration of the Sistine Chapel. His illustrations to Dante's *Divine Comedy* are world-famous.

**Bottomley, Horatio** (1860–1933), politician, journalist, financier, and for many years one of the most notorious characters in England.

A brilliant speaker, he was twice M.P. for South Hackney. Altogether 260 petitions in bankruptcy were presented against him, mostly without effect; he was constantly in the law courts, defending himself with skilful audacity against famous K.C.s. Millions of pounds passed through his hands, much of it obtained from small investors, but he died in poverty after serving seven years' penal servitude for fraud.

Botvinnik, Mikhail (b. 1911), Russian chess player; world champion 1948–57, 1958–60, 1961–63. Retired 1965.

Boughton, Rutland (1878–1960), English composer who has also written on the history and philosophy of music. His opera *The Immortal Hour* has enjoyed great success.

Boult, Sir Adrian C., Kt., C.H., M.A., D.Mus., F.R.C.M. (b. 1889). President London Philharmonic Orchestra, 1965; and its chief conductor, 1950–57; conductor of the B.B.C. Symphony Orchestra, 1930–50, and Musical Director B.B.C., 1930–42.

Bowdler, Thomas (1754–1825), a pious English physician, who issued expurgated editions of Shakespeare and Gibbon, eliminating all expressions offensive to good taste. Hence the term "bowdlerise."

Boyce, William (1710–79), famous London organist, composer of church music, songs and cantatas, and master of the orchestra of George III.

Boyd Orr, John, 1st Baron, C.H., F.R.S., M.D., D.Sc. (b. 1880), scientist, farmer and nutritional expert. Prof. of Agriculture, Aberdeen University, 1942–45; Director-General, World Food and Agricultural Organisation, 1945–48. Chancellor of Glasgow Univ, 1946. Nobel Peace Prize, 1949.

Boyle, Hon. Robert, F.R.S. (1627–1691), English scientist who with Robert Hooke laid the foundations of the modern sciences of chemistry and physics. He established "Boyle's law," which states that the volume of a gas varies *inversely* as the pressure upon it, provided temperature be constant.

Bradley, General of the Army Omar N. (b. 1893), distinguished American soldier who was appointed chairman of the Joint Chiefs of Staff in succession to Gen. Eisenhower in 1949. Commanded 2nd U.S. Army Corps in Tunis and Sicily, the American Assault Forces in Normandy in 1944, and later the 12th U.S. Army Group. Retired 1953.

Bradman, Sir Donald George (b. 1908), Australian cricketer and one of the world's best batsmen. Captained Australia in Test matches against England, 1936–48.

Bragg, Sir Wm. (Henry), O.M., K.B.E., F.R.S., M.A., D.Sc. (1862–1942), was a brilliant scientist. Nobel Physics Prize, 1915. Was Director of the Royal Institution of Great Britain; Fullerian Prof. of Chemistry, Royal Institution, and Director of Davy-Faraday Research Laboratory, 1923–42; President of British Association, 1928. President of the Royal Society, 1936–40.

Bragg, Sir (William) Lawrence, C.H., O.B.E., M.C., F.R.S. (b. 1890), succeeded Lord Rutherford as Cavendish Prof. of Experimental Physics, Cambridge Univ., 1938–53. Dir. Royal Institution, 1954–66. Shared with his father (Sir Wm. H. Bragg) the 1915 Nobel Prize for research work on X-rays and crystal structures.

Brahe, Tycho (1546–1601), a celebrated Danish astronomer, and fellow-worker of Kepler. With large sums of money put at his disposal by Frederick II. of Denmark, he built an observatory called Uraniborg on the island of Hveen, near Copenhagen, where for over 20 years he carried out a vast programme of accurate and systematic observations of the heavenly bodies and compiled tables of their motions.

Brahms, Johannes (1833–97), composer, regarded as outstanding figure of German classic-romantic school; born in Hamburg, the son of a double-bass player. His compositions are classical in form yet possess deep intensity of expression and poetic significance. He composed four symphonies which rank amongst the greatest ever written, two piano concertos, a violin concerto, a double concerto for violin and 'cello, much fine chamber music, numerous songs of great lyrical beauty, and choral work, notable among which is his *German Requiem*. Lifelong

friend of the Schumanns. His life was devoted to music; he never married.

Braille, Louis (1809–52), French educationist, who, as teacher of the blind, perfected his system of reading and writing for the blind. As the result of an accident when he was three years old he was himself blind.

Bramah, Joseph (1749–1814), a Yorkshireman who devoted himself to invention, introduced numerous mechanical improvements, including the hydrostatic press, a liquid-pumping apparatus, a most ingenious series of safety locks, and bank-note printing machines.

Brampton, Lord, P.C. (1817–1907), long known to the public as Sir Henry Hawkins. Was famous as an advocate, and took part in many celebrated cases, including the Tichborne trial. His *Reminiscences*, published in 1904, was one of the books of the year.

Brandes, Georg Morris Cohen (1842–1927), Danish literary critic who exerted a vitalising influence on literature and art.

Brangwyn, Sir Frank, R.A., R.P.E. (1867–1956), artist of Welsh extraction born at Bruges; first worked for William Morris making cartoons for textiles. He was regarded as the greatest mural artist and etcher of his day.

Breakspear, Nicholas. *See* Adrian IV.

Brecht, Bertolt (1898–1959), German dramatist and poet, whose cynical and satirical works are characteristic of the period between the two world wars. He left Germany in 1933 for Russia, went to the United States in 1941, and returned to E. Germany after the war. His plays include *Die Dreigroschenoper* (with music by Kurt Weill). *See also* Section I.

Brennan, Louis, C.B. (1853–1932), successful inventor, born in Ireland. Paid £120,000 by the British Government for his gyro-directed torpedo; also the inventor of a mono-rail locomotive on the gyroscope principle.

Breton, Andrée (1896–1966), French poet, founder of the surrealist literary movement in France and a close friend of Apollinaire.

Brewster, Sir David, LL.D., F.R.S. (1781–1868), Scottish physicist, a great experimenter and a prolific writer. Noted for his researches into the polarisation of light; invented the kaleidoscope Helped to found the British Association for the Advancement of Science.

Brezhnev, Leonid Ilyich (b. 1906), succeeded Nikita Khrushchev as First Secretary of the Soviet Communist Party in Oct. 1964; formerly President of the Supreme Soviet of the U.S.S.R.

Bridges, Edward, 1st Baron, K.G., G.C.B., G.C.V.O., P.C., M.C. (b. 1892), son of Robert Bridges. Permanent Secretary to the Treasury and Head of Civil Service, 1945–56. Secretary to the Cabinet, 1938–46. Chanc. Reading Univ., 1959. Chairman British Council, 1959–.

Bridges, Robert, O.M., M.A. (1844–1930), was Poet Laureate 1913–30. Practised medicine up to 1882, thenceforward devoting himself mainly to literature. He published several volumes of poems and plays, displaying refined fancy and a broad philosophic spirit. His *Testament of Beauty* was published in 1930.

Bridgewater, Francis Egerton, 3rd (and last) Duke of (1736–1803). The projector of the famous Bridgewater Canal, which was the beginning of the great English canal system, and yielded his family enormous wealth; it was absorbed in 1887 by the Manchester Ship Canal Company, who paid £1,710,000 for it.

Bridgewater, Francis Henry Egerton, 8th (and last) Earl of, F.R.S. (1756–1829), grand-nephew of the last-named, and founder of the famous *Bridgewater Treatises*, written by the most celebrated divines and scientists of the day.

Bridie, James, (pseudonym of Osborne Henry Mavor), C.B.E., LL.D., M.D. (1888–1951). Scottish author and dramatist. Educated at Glasgow Academy and University. The first of his many successful plays was *The Anatomist*, produced in 1931. Others include *Tobias and the Angel, Jonah and the Whale, Mr. Bolfrey, Dr. Angelus.*

Brieux, Eugène (1858–1932), French dramatist, whose moral and realistic plays deal with social evils, such as venereal disease in *Les Avariés* ("Damaged Goods"). Elected a member of the French Academy in 1909.

Bright, Sir Charles Tilstone (1832–88), English

telegraph engineer, who after superintending the laying of telegraph lines in many parts of Great Britain organised the Atlantic Telegraph-Company (1856), and as Engineer-in-chief supervised the laying of the first Atlantic Cable (1858).

**Bright, Rt. Hon. John** (1811–1889), a famous Radical Quaker statesman and orator, one of the chief promoters of the Reform movement which led to the introduction of Free Trade.

**Britten, Edward Benjamin,** O.M., C.H. (b. 1913), English composer of a variety of music, including song cycles, chamber music, choral works, and the operas *The Rape of Lucrezia, Peter Grimes, Albert Herring, Billy Budd, The Turn of the Screw* and *A Midsummer Night's Dream.* His great *War Requiem* was first heard at the consecration of the new Coventry cathedral in 1962. Closely associated with the Aldeburgh Festival. *See* Section E.

**Broca, Pierre Paul** (1824–80), French pathologist, anthropologist, and a pioneer in neuro-surgery. He localised the seat of speech in the brain in the convolution named after him and originated methods for measuring brain and skull ratios.

**Broch, Hermann** (1886–1951), Austrian novelist, author of *Die Schlafwandler* (Eng. tr. *The Sleepwalkers,* 1932). Lived in U.S.A. after 1938.

**Brock, Sir Thomas,** K.C.B., R.A. (1847–1922), pupil of Foley, achieved a high reputation as a sculptor. The Queen Victoria Memorial in front of Buckingham Palace is his work.

**Brogan, Denis William,** M.A. (b. 1900), Prof. of Political Science at Cambridge. An authority on France, America, and Britain, and his works include *The Development of Modern France, Politics and Law in the United States,* and *The English People.*

**Broglie,** French noble family of Piedmontese origin who settled in France in the 17th cent. **Victor Maurice, comte de Broglie** (1671–1745) was marshal of France and fought in the wars of Louis XIV. **Louis Victor, prince de Broglie** (b. 1892) and **Maurice, duc de Broglie** (1875–1960) the eminent French physicists are grandsons.

**Brontë, Charlotte** (1816–1855), one of the most gifted novelists of the 19th century. Her *Jane Eyre,* published in 1847, attracted universal notice, and her other novels, *Shirley, Villette,* and *The Professor,* are all marked by the force of strong genius. Her sisters, **Emily** (1818–48) and **Anne** (1820–49), also wrote novels and poems, Emily's *Wuthering Heights* and some of her verse showing exceptional power.

**Brooke, Rupert** (1887–1915), a British poet who died during the first world war, whose works, though few, showed great promise and include the poems *Grantchester* and *If I Should Die.*

**Brougham, Lord,** P.C., F.R.S. (1778–1868), one of the chief legal luminaries of the 19th century, who made a great name by defending Queen Caroline against George IV.

**Brown, Sir Arthur Whitten,** K.B.E. (1886–1948), together with Sir John Alcock (d. 1919) in 1919 made the first transatlantic flight, crossing from Newfoundland to Ireland in 16 hr. 12 min.

**Brown, John,** " of Ossawatomie " (1800–1859), the hero of Harper's Ferry, whose action in inciting certain negro slaves to rebel in 1859 struck the note of alarm which resulted in the Civil War. His attempt to take the Arsenal at Harper's Ferry was defeated, and he was hanged, being afterwards regarded as a martyr by the Abolitionists.

**Browne, Charles Farrer** (Artemus Ward) (1834–1867), was one of the most whimsical and entertaining humorists America has produced. In addition to his books he wrote and delivered exceedingly funny lectures, and was making an English tour with them when he was seized with a fatal illness, dying at Southampton.

**Browne, Hablot Knight** (1815–1882), best known as " Phiz," the illustrator of Dickens's novels, from the *Pickwick* period down to *Little Dorrit.*

**Browne, Sir Thomas** (1605–82), author of *Religio Medici,* was a London physician and antiquary.

**Browning, Elizabeth Barrett** (1806–1861), English poet, wife of Robert Browning. She was an astonishingly brilliant child, reading Homer at the age of eight. While saddling her pony she injured herself and on her father's orders spent her youth lying on her back in her room, studying and writing. Her meeting with Browning brought a remarkable recovery. In the autumn

of 1846 they were secretly married and went to live in Florence. Although now regarded as a comparatively minor poet she was more read than her husband in their lifetime. Best known poems are " Cry of the Children ", *Sonnets from the Portuguese* (her own love story) and *Aurora Leigh,* a novel in verse.

**Browning, Robert** (1812–1889), English poet, son of artistic and cultured parents, whose money enabled him to travel and write poetry. His earlier poems and plays, though marked by singular insight and power, were far from popular, mainly because of a somewhat obscure and involved style. His *Strafford* and *The Blot on the 'Scutcheon* were both produced by Macready, and attained some measure of stage success. After the death of his wife he returned to England and wrote some of his finest work including *Dramtis Personae* and *The Ring and the Book.* He died in Venice.

**Bruce, Robert** (1274–1329), took part with Sir William Wallace, (*q.v.*) in the revolt against Edward I., later leading the popular cause. Achieved one victory after another, until at Bannockburn he overthrew the English army and ultimately secured Scottish independence. He reigned twenty-two years as King Robert I.

**Bruch, Max** (1838–1920), German composer, best known for his G minor violin concerto.

**Bruckner, Anton** (1824–96), Austrian composer and organist. He wrote nine symphonies, much religious music, including a *Te Deum* for chorus and orchestra, and a string quintet. *See* Section E.

**Brummell, George Bryan** (1778–1840), " Beau Brummell," the fashion leader in English Society when George IV. was Prince of Wales; was a *bon vivant* and gamester whose excesses involved him in imprisonment and ultimate imbecility.

**Brunel, Isambard Kingdom** (1806–1859), a prominent engineer who constructed the more difficult portions of the Great Western Railways, and many other important works. He also achieved eminence as a designer of steamships.

**Brunel, Sir Mark Isambard** (1769–1849), father of the last-named, and constructor of the Thames tunnel, finished in 1843.

**Brunelleschi, Filippo** (1377–1446), Italian architect, born in Florence, pioneer of Renaissance architecture, adapting the ideals of the Roman or classic period to the conditions of his own day. Many examples of his work are to be seen in Florence—in the Pitti Palace, the Churches of San Lorenzo and San Spirito, the great cupola of the cathedral of Santa Maria del Fiore and the beautiful carved crucifix in the Church of Santa Maria Novella.

**Bruno, Giordano** (*c.* 1548–1600), Italian philosopher and martyr; entered the Dominican Order at Naples in his 15th year. Accused of heresy he fled from his convent and roamed over Europe. In 1592 he returned to Italy and was arrested by the Inquisition. After 7 years in prison was burned at the stake, Feb. 17, 1600. A statue to him was erected in the Campo dei Fiori, 1889.

**Brutus, Marcus Jonius** (85–42 B.C.), Roman Governor and one of the founders of Roman civil law.

**Bryant, Arthur Wynne Morgan** (b. 1899), English historian and pageant producer. Among his works are *English Saga, 1840–1940,* a life of *George V., The Story of England,* and several books on the Napoleonic war years and the Restoration period, including a balanced and informative biography of Pepys.

**Buchanan, George** (1506–82), Scottish humanist who spent most of his life in France lecturing and writing Latin poems, plays, and treatises. Montaigne, Mary Queen of Scots, and James VI of Scotland were his pupils at various times. He was the best Latin scholar of his age, and his most important works are *De jure regni apud Scotos* and *Rerum Scoticarum historia.*

**Buchman, Rev. Frank Nathan David** (1878–1961). American evangelist. founder of the movement known as Moral Re-Armament. Initiated in 1920 the religious fellowship known as the Oxford Group Movement. *See* J30.

**Buchner, Eduard** (1860–1917), German chemist and professor, famous for his discovery of the enzymes within yeast cells and for his work in the chemistry of fermentation. For this he was awarded the 1907 Nobel Prize for Chemistry.

**Büchner, Georg** (1813–37), German dramatist

whose career was terminated by his early death at the age of twenty-four, but whose limited output (principally *Dantons Tod* and the fragment *Wozzeck*) is marked by extraordinary power and maturity.

**Buckle, Henry Thomas** (1821–1862), the author of *The History of Civilisation in England*, one of the most vigorous productions of the 19th century.

**Budge, Sir Ernest Alfred Wallis,** Litt. D., D. Litt., F.S.A. (1857–1934), a distinguished archæologist who conducted many excavations in Mesopotamia and Egypt. Was Keeper of Egyptian and Assyrian Antiquities at the British Museum, 1893–1924.

**Buffon, Georges-Louis Leclerc, Comte de** (1707–88), French author and naturalist who devoted his life to the study of natural history and whose great work *Histoire Naturelle* in 36 volumes appeared between 1749 and 1789.

**Bulganin, Marshal Nikolai Alexandrovitch** (b. 1895), Prime Minister of Soviet Russia, 1955–58. Formerly Soviet Defence Minister. Retired 1960.

**Bull, John** (c. 1562–1628), was organist to James I. and composed much acceptable music, including, it is supposed, our National Anthem *God save the Queen.*

**Bülow, Hans Guido von** (1830–94), German pianist and conductor, an outstanding figure among the musicians of his day. He married Liszt's daughter Cosima, who later left him to marry Wagner.

**Bunsen, Robert Wilhelm** (1811–1899), German chemist, discoverer of the metals cæsium and rubidium, and inventor of the Bunsen burner, battery, and pump. Made many important observations in spectrum analysis.

**Bunyan, John** (1628–1688), was originally a travelling tinker and is believed to have served in the Parliamentary army. He joined an Independent church in Bedford in 1655 and became a popular preacher. After the Restoration he was thrown into prison, and there wrote *Pilgrim's Progress*, the finest allegorical work in this or any language. Of his other works the *Holy War, Grace Abounding*, and *Mr. Badman* are the best known.

**Burckhardt, Jacob Christoph** (1818–97), Swiss historian whose *The Civilisation of the Renaissance in Italy* is one of the great classics on the subject.

**Burghley, William Cecil, Lord** (1520–1598), Secretary to Lord Protector Somerset, an influential statesman under Edward VI, and Queen Mary, and subsequently Queen Elizabeth's favourite Minister for forty years.

**Burke, Edmund** (1729–1797), the acknowledged philosopher of conservatism; son of a Dublin attorney, went to London in 1756, and made his mark in literature by his famous work on the *Sublime and Beautiful*. Later on was private secretary to the Marquis of Rockingham, then Premier, and entered Parliament, where he quickly made a name. An able and earnest debater, he took part in all the great movements of his time, and in 1795, after his retirement, was awarded a handsome pension from the Civil List.

**Burnet, Bishop Gilbert** (1643–1715), wrote a *History of His Own Times*, which deals with many events of which he had personal knowledge, and is a valuable legacy to historical scholars.

**Burnet, Sir John James,** R.A. (1859–1938), was a leading British architect, whose most important work was the King Edward VII Galleries of the British Museum, opened in May 1914. Among his many large buildings in London are Adelaide House, and the extension to Selfridge's.

**Burney, Fanny** (*See* D' Arblay, Madame.)

**Burns, Robert** (1759–1796), Scotland's greatest poet. Startled the world with a little book of poems in 1786 which proclaimed him a true son of the muses. With the £500 that his book yielded him he bought a farm, obtained an appointment with the Excise in 1789, and for the last five years of his life lived at Dumfries. In his career he poured forth song after song of emotional tenderness, and made his name immortal.

**Burton, Sir Richard Francis,** K.C.M.G. (1821–1890), explorer, orientalist, and diplomatist, who became famous after making a pilgrimage to Mecca in 1853 disguised as a Mohammedan. Later he did much exploring in Central Africa, wrote several books and made a remarkable literal translation of the *Arabian Nights* (16 vols.).

**Burton, Robert** (1577–1640), English clergyman and scholar, author of *The Anatomy of Melancholy.*

**Busoni, Ferruccio Benvenuto** (1866–1920), the greatest pianist of his age, and composer of 3 operas (the last, *Dr. Faust*, unfinished at his death), much orchestral and chamber music, and works for the piano. He was born in Empoli near Florence but spent much of his life in Germany. *See* E17(1).

**Butler, Joseph** (1692–1752), an English divine who occupied an important place among 18th cent. thinkers. He declined the Archbishopric of Canterbury in 1747, but in 1750 became Bishop of Durham. In 1736 he published his *Analogy of Religion*, a reply to the deistic attacks on revealed religion.

**Butler, Nicholas Murray** (1862–1947), American educationist; Pres. Columbia Univ., 1902–45. Shared with Jane Addams (*q.v.*), American sociologist, the Nobel Prize for Peace, 1931.

**Butler, Richard Austen, Baron,** C.H., P.C. (b. 1902), British statesman; Foreign Sec., 1963–4; First Min. of State, 1962–3; Dep. Prime Min., 1961–3; Home Sec., 1957–62; Chair. Cons. Party, 1959–61; Leader of the House of Commons, 1955–61; Chan. of the Exchequer, 1951–55; Min. of Education, 1941–45; and responsible for the Education Act, 1944. A member of the distinguished Cambridge family, son of Sir Montague Butler, Master of Pembroke. Took leading part in drafting various political charters setting out Conservative policy. Chancellor of Univ. of Sheffield (1959), of Essex (1964); Master of Trinity College, Cambridge (1965). Life barony conferred 1965.

**Butler, Samuel** (1612–1680), renowned as the author of *Hudibras*, one of the wittiest poems in the language and one of the most quoted. His last years were spent in poverty, and he was buried in the churchyard of St. Paul's, Covent Garden, and given a memorial in Westminster Abbey, " that he who was destitute of all things when alive might not want a monument when dead."

**Butler, Samuel** (1835–1902), author of the satirical novel *Erewhon* and its sequel *Erewhon Revisited*. Other works include *The Fair Haven* (1873), *Life and Habit* (1877). *Evolution Old and New* (1879), in which he attacked Darwinism. *The Way of All Flesh* and his famous *Notebooks* were published posthumously. Butler was a man of great originality and scholarship. He studied painting and exhibited regularly in the Academy and was also a musician.

**Butt, Dame Clara,** D.B.E. (1872–1936), the famous English contralto, made her début in London in 1892. She married Kennerly Rumford in 1900.

**Buxton, Sir Thomas Fowell, 1st Bart.** (1786–1845), a philanthropist and zealous advocate of the abolition of slavery.

**Buys Ballot, Christoph Heinrich Diedrich** (1877–90), Dutch meteorologist; formulated law named after him (an observer with back to wind in northern hemisphere has lower pressure to left; in southern hemisphere to right).

**Byrd, Rear-Admiral Richard Evelyn** (1888–1957), American aviator and Polar explorer; commanded Macmillan Arctic Expedition, 1925; flew over the North Pole, 1926; across the Atlantic, 1927, and in 1929 made the first flight over the South Pole. He made a second expedition in 1933–5, a third in 1939, and a fourth in December 1946.

**Byrd, William** (1543–1623), English writer of keyboard music and the greatest musician of the 16th century. He wrote church music, sacred choral music, string music, vocal and instrumental music, and founded the school of English madrigalists. He was organist of Lincoln Cathedral at 20 and later of Queen Elizabeth's Chapel Royal. *See* Section E.

**Byron, George Gordon, 6th Baron** (1788–1824), English Romantic poet who exercised far-reaching influence on European literature and thought. Educated at Harrow and Cambridge, he published his *Hours of Idleness* at twenty, a volume which was violently attacked by the *Edinburgh Review* which provoked his retaliatory *English Bards and Scotch Reviewers*, which caused a great sensation because of its unsparing criticisms of the writers of the day. His *Childe Harold's Pilgrimage*, the first two cantos of which were published in 1812, at once placed him in the front rank of poets, and, thenceforward to the time of his death he continued to produce poems, most of which were marked by an intense Republican sentiment, yet full of passion and charm and beauty. He made an unhappy marriage in 1815 with the daughter of Sir Ralph Milbanke, from whom he parted after a twelvemonth. He lived abroad for the rest of his life and died at Missolonghi, whither he had proceeded with a view to aiding the Greeks in their battle for national independence. *See also* Romantic Movement, J39.

## C

Cable, George Washington (1844–1925), a well-known American author, born in New Orleans, the scene of many of his best works. Among his writings were *Ole Creole Days* (1879), *Strange Stories of Louisiana* (1889), and serious sociological studies such as *The Negro Question* (1890).

Cabot, John (c. 1455–c. 1498), Genoese explorer who settled in Bristol and sailed westwards under letters-patent from Henry VII of England in 1497. Discovered Newfoundland and Nova Scotia, believing them to be part of Asia, and may have reached the mainland of America before Columbus did. His son:—

Cabot, Sebastian (c.1483–1557) was born in Venice, and in 1509 sailed in search of a north-west passage to Asia. Sailed as far as the entrance of Hudson Bay. Entered Spanish service in 1512, and in 1518 was appointed chief pilot. Spent several years exploring the Plate and Parana rivers. Re-entered English service in 1548 and organised expedition to seek a north-east passage to open up trade with India, which resulted in trade with Russia. English claim to North America is founded on the voyages of the Cabots.

Cabral, Pedro Alvarez (c. 1467–c. 1520). Portuguese navigator, friend of Vasco da Gama, and discoverer of Brazil, which he named " Terra da Santa Cruz."

Cadbury, George (1839–1922), was a prominent member of the Society of Friends, a well-known Philanthropist, and ardent Liberal, and head of the firm of Cadbury Bros., Bourneville. He took the lead in the Garden City project, and the village of Bourneville may be regarded as the first enterprise of the character to be practically completed; it has an endowment of over £200,000.

Cadogan, Rt. Hon. Sir Alexander, O.M., G.C.M.G., K.C.B. (1884–1968), English diplomat. Helped to draft the Charter of the United Nations Organisation, and became Great Britain's first permanent representative on the Security Council. Chairman of the B.B.C., 1952–7.

Caedmon, the first English Christian poet, lived in the seventh century and, according to Bede, was first a cowherd and later a monk at Whitby. His poetry was based on the Scriptures.

Caesar, Caius Julius (c. 101–44 B.C.), Roman general. Was appointed successively military tribune, quaestor in 68, aedile in 65, and pontifex maximus in 63. A year later he was praetor, and later formed one of the first triumvirate. He invaded Gaul and Britain, in the Civil War defeated Pompey, and in the Alexandrine war met Cleopatra, and established her firmly on the throne of Egypt. On his return to Rome in 44 the crown was offered to him, a circumstance which caused the aristocratic party to compass his assassination.

Caine, Sir Thomas Henry Hall, C.H., K.B.E. (1853–1931), author of numerous novels, including *The Deemster*, *The Manxman*, *The Christian*, *The Prodigal Son*, *The Woman Thou Gavest Me*, the latter being one of the fiction sensations of 1913.

Calderón de la Barca, Pedro (1600–1681), a Spanish dramatist of great eminence whose plays number nearly 200. He was writer of court spectacles for Philip IV.

Calvin, John (1509–1564), one of the leading Reformers of the 16th century. Was born in Picardy and attained great popularity as a preacher in Paris, but was expelled, and subsequently lived at Geneva, where he continued to preach the new doctrine, giving it that special shape which resulted in the formation of the Calvinist body, distinguished by its greater austerity from that of the Lutherans. *See* J7.

Camden, William (1551–1623), an antiquary, historian, and master of Westminster School, whose researches, especially in the field of topography, have been of the greatest value. He became Clarencieux King-at-Arms, and was buried in Westminster Abbey. The Camden Society is named after him.

Cameron, Sir David Young, R.A. (1865–1945), was one of the best known of British etchers as well as an excellent landscape-painter. King's Painter and Limner in Scotland, 1933–45.

Cameron, Richard (c. 1648–1680), one of the Scottish 17th-century preachers who raised the standard of revolt in defence of the Solemn League and Covenant; he was, after many vicissitudes, slain in combat near Aird's Moss, Ayrshire, in 1680. The members of the Reformed Presbyterian Church were afterwards called Cameronians.

Cameron, Verney Lovett, C.B. (1844–1894), a noted African explorer who was the first to cross the African continent from east to west. Explored Lake Tanganyika, and made many valuable geographical discoveries. In 1872 went out to find Livingstone, and in 1873 met a party of natives bearing the dead body to the coast.

Camillus, Marcus Furius (446–365 B.C.), was five times Dictator of the Roman Republic, a supporter of the patrician order, and one of the most successful of the Roman generals. He died of the pestilence, 365 B.C.

Camm, Sir Sydney, C.B.E. (1893–1966), designer of the Hawker Hurricane Fighter aeroplane.

Cammaerts, Emile, C.B.E. (1878–1953), Belgian poet, critic, historian and dramatist. Born in Brussels, he settled in England in 1908, and became Professor of Belgian Studies and Institutions in the University of London. He became widely known during the war of 1914–18 for a series of Belgian poems.

Camões or Camoëns, Luis Vaz de (1524–1580), the author of *Os Lusiadas*, the great epic poem of Portugal, which sets forth the adventures of the discoverers of India, and celebrates the achievements of the principal personages in Portuguese history.

Campbell, Sir Colin. *See* Clyde, Baron.

Campbell, Sir Malcolm (1885–1948), the racing driver who held the land-speed record of 301 m.p.h. (1935) and water-speed record 141·7 m.p.h. (1939). His son Donald held the world water-speed record of 276·33 m.p.h. (1964). He was killed in 1967 at Coniston while attempting to set up a new speed record on water.

Campbell, Mrs. Patrick (1865–1940), English actress of great beauty and wit. Remembered also for her friendship with G. B. Shaw. Her maiden name was Beatrice Stella Tanner.

Campbell, Thomas (1777–1844), Scottish poet who at 22 published *The Pleasures of Hope*. He was one of the founders of University College, London, and is chiefly remembered for his war songs and the poems *Ye Mariners of England*, *The Battle of the Baltic*.

Campbell-Bannerman, Rt. Hon. Sir Henry, G.C.B. (1836–1908), Prime Minister in the Liberal Ministry from December 1905 until shortly before his death in April 1908. His Government at once faced a General Election and obtained a very large majority. Notable events of his period of office were the Trades Disputes Act, 1906, the Deceased Wife's Sister Act, 1907, and the simmering quarrel between the Liberals and the House of Lords, while the settlement of the South African problem was to a great extent due to his efforts. His Ministry contained a galaxy of talent—Grey, Haldane, Lloyd George, Asquith, Morley, Churchill—and was mainly held together by his personal popularity.

Camus, Albert (1913–60), important French writer.

native of Algiers, whose works show the influence of existentialism. The Nobel Prize was awarded him in 1957 for " his important literary work, which has with penetrating seriousness thrown light on the problems of human conscience in our times." His most well-known novels are *l'Etranger* (1942), *La Peste* (1947), *l'Homme Révolté* (1952). Killed in car crash.

Canaletto (1697–1768), Venetian artist who excelled in the art of architectural painting. Some of his work is in the National Gallery, and there is a fine collection at Windsor. His real name was Antonio Canale.

Canning, Rt. Hon. George (1770–1827), entered Parliament in 1793 and became a great orator and a devoted adherent of Pitt, under whom he served first as Under-Secretary of State and later as Treasurer to the Navy. He was Secretary for Foreign Affairs under the Duke of Portland, and in 1827 became Prime Minister, but died four months later.

Cannizzaro, Stanislao (1826–1910), Italian chemist who carried forward the work of Avogadro in distinguishing between molecular and atomic weights. He was professor of chemistry at Alexandria, Geneva, Palermo, and Rome, became a member of the Italian senate, and did much to develop scientific education.

Canova, Antonio (1757–1822), an Italian sculptor, leader of the classical revival in Italy, whose works achieved the first eminence.

Canton, John (1718–72), English physicist and schoolmaster, the first to verify in England Franklin's experiments on the identity of lightning with electricity. He was the first to demonstrate that water is compressible and produced a new phosphorescent body (Canton's phosphorus) by calcining oyster shells with sulphur.

Canute the Great (995–1035), invaded England with a Danish force, and in 1013 succeeded in dethroning Ethelred the Unready, and setting up his own father, Sweyn, in Ethelred's stead. Sweyn dying in 1014, Canute claimed the crown, but it took him some years to establish himself firmly.

Capablanca, José Raoul (1888–1942), world's chess champion, 1921–27; defeated by Alekhine.

Caractacus was the name by which a Prince of ancient Britain became famed for his resistance to the Romans in the 1st century. He was ultimately captured and taken prisoner to Rome where the Emperor Claudius was so moved by his dignity of bearing that he pardoned him.

Carey, William, D.D. (1761–1834), the first Baptist missionary to proceed to India, and from 1800 to 1830 Professor of Oriental Languages at Port William College, Calcutta. Became famed as an Oriental scholar, and published twenty-four different translations of the Scriptures.

Carissimi, Giacomo (1604–74), an Italian composer who is historically important for his development of the sacred cantata and the oratorio. Was maestro at Assisi, and later at Rome. The best collections of his works are in the National Library in Paris, and the Library of Christ Church, Oxford.

Carlyle, Thomas (1795–1881), was educated at Edinburgh University, and, after passing through some years of teaching drudgery, settled in London in 1824 and began the career of a serious man of letters; but, marrying Jane Welsh in 1826, he returned to Scotland and spent the next few years on a farm at Craigenputtoch, coming to London again in 1834. His *Sartor Resartus* was published in 1833. In 1837 he gave lectures in London, and in 1839 his *Chartism* appeared. His *French Revolution, Past and Present, Life and Letters of Oliver Cromwell, Latter-Day Pamphlets,* and *Frederick the Great* were works of noble conception.

Carnegie, Andrew (1835–1919), **b. in** Dunfermline, emigrated to America **with** his father in 1848, and after passing through much menial employment became connected with the Pennsylvania Railroad as Divisional Superintendent at Pittsburg, and ultimately established the Carnegie iron works, from which he retired in 1901 with a fortune of many millions. His munificent gifts for Free Libraries, educational work, and charitable objects are well known.

Carnot, General Lazare Nicolas Marguerite (1753–

1823), a military engineer, prominent in the French revolution and responsible for the success of the French in the French revolutionary wars, 1792–1802. His son, Nicolas Léonard Sadi Carnot (1796–1832) was a physicist and engineer, famous for his work on the motive power of heat (see F17).

Caroline, Queen, wife of George IV. (1768–1821), was married to her husband in 1795 while he was Prince of Wales. The royal couple lived together only a very short time. When George succeeded to the throne in 1820 the Queen took steps to assert her position, and the King retaliated by having a Bill introduced to dissolve the marriage; the result was the famous trial before the House of Lords, when Lord Brougham distinguished himself by a most eloquent defence of the Queen. The Bill was passed by a narrow majority, but public feeling was too strong on the side of the Queen to admit of its being enforced.

Carrel, Dr. Alexis (1873–1944), American surgeon who won the Nobel Prize in 1912 for his remarkable achievements in suturing blood vessels and in the transplantation of organs. Member of the Rockefeller Institute for Medical Research 1906–44. A Frenchman by birth.

Carroll, Lewis. (*See* Dodgson, Charles Lutwidge.)

Carson of Duncairn, Lord, P.C. (1854–1935), had a highly successful career first at the Irish and then at the English Bar. Solicitor General for Ireland 1892; and for England 1900–6; Attorney General 1915; First Lord of the Admiralty 1917; Lord of Appeal 1921–29. Led a semi-militant organisation against the Home Rule Bill 1912–14.

Carter, Howard (1873–1939), Egyptologist and archaeologist who was associated with the 5th Earl of Carnarvon in discovering in 1922 the tomb of Tut-Ankh-Amen in the Valley of Kings, Egypt.

Cartier, Jacques (1494–1557), 16th-century navigator, born at St. Malo, whose exploration of Canada, and especially of the gulf and river of St. Lawrence, proved of great geographical importance.

Cartwright, Edmund, D.D. (1743–1823), invented the power loom, and also a wool-combing machine. Although these inventions were developed into fortune-making instruments, they benefited their inventor but little, and in 1809 Parliament made him a grant of £10,000. In 1904 a Cartwright Memorial Hall was opened at Bradford, the gift of Lord Masham.

Caruso, Enrico (1873–1921), a celebrated tenor, was born in Naples, and made his first operatic appearance in his native city. His success was unbounded.

Carver, George Washington (1864–1943), American negro agricultural chemist of world repute.

Casabianca, Louis de (c. 1754–1798), captain of the French flagship *L'Orient* at the Battle of the Nile. He and his ten-year-old son died together in the burning ship, refusing to quit the vessel.

Casals, Pablo (b. 1876), the famous Spanish violoncellist and conductor, who made his first appearance in Paris and London in 1898. He exiled himself from Spain in 1938 as a protest against dictatorship.

Cassatt, Mary (1845–1926), American painter and etcher. Spent most of her life in France, greatly influenced by the Impressionists and enjoyed friendship of Degas and Manet. Motherhood was her favourite subject.

Cassini, the name of a French family of Italian origin, distinguished for their services to astronomy and geography, who through four generations (1671–1793) were heads of the Paris Observatory.

Cassius, Caius Longinus, a distinguished Roman general who opposed the Dictatorship of Julius Cæsar, and took part in his murder. He died in 42 B.C., after being defeated by Mark Antony.

Castlereagh, Viscount, K.G., P.C. (1769–1822), British Minister of War and Foreign Secretary during the Napoleonic wars, who incurred much unpopularity because of the disastrous condition of home affairs. Succeeded to the Marquessate of Londonderry in 1821, and ended his life by suicide the following year.

Castro, Fidel (b. 1927), popular revolutionary hero of Cuba who came to power in 1959 with two main aims: (a) to end dictatorship, injustice and poverty, and (b) to end dependence on America. Far-reaching agrarian reforms are in progress, but in fulfilling the second aim he has come into conflict with American interests.

**Catherine, St.,** was the name borne by a celebrated virgin of Alexandria, who was put to death in 307 for professing Christianity, being, according to some accounts, tortured on a spiked wheel before execution, though other authorities aver that the intended torture was miraculously prevented. From this we get the term "St. Catherine's wheel." Festival 25 Nov.

**Catherine of Aragon** (1485–1536), first wife of Henry VIII., was previously the wife of Arthur, Henry's elder brother, who died shortly after the marriage. She was the daughter of Ferdinand and Isabella of Spain, aunt of the Emperor, Charles V, and mother of Mary Tudor. Henry's failure to obtain papal consent to the dissolution of their marriage precipitated the Reformation crisis in England.

**Catherine the Great** (1729–96), Empress Catherine II of Russia. Daughter of a Prussian general, she married in 1745 the future Peter III, a weakling, later deposed and murdered. Intelligent, cultivated, autocratic, she proved herself a capable ruler for a time but was hampered and opposed by the landed interests and, despite plans for reform, her reign was marked by imperialist expansion and extension of serfdom.

**Catherine de' Medici** (1519–1589), wife of Henry II. of France, and a woman of commanding power and influence, especially during her Regency, which continued while her son Charles IX. was in his minority. Her antagonism to the Protestants may have led to the Massacre of St. Bartholomew. In spite of her cruelty, she was an able woman, and showed a great appreciation of art and literature.

**Cato, Marcus Porcius** (234–149 B.C.) a Roman statesman, soldier, and writer, of strict virtue, simplicity and wisdom, who strongly condemned the luxury of his time and carried out his duties as Censor so rigorously that he became known as " Censorius."

**Catullus, Caius Valerius** (87–54 B.C.), an elegant Roman poet, whose lyrics to Lesbia are amongst the finest compositions of the kind in literature.

**Cavell, Edith Louisa** (1865–1915), a British nurse who assisted wounded British soldiers to escape over the Dutch frontier from Belgium during the Great War. She was shot by the Germans.

**Cavendish, Hon. Henry,** F.R.S. (1731–1810), English chemist and physicist who made researches into the nature of gases. Is chiefly remembered for his discovery of the chemical composition of water. He also discovered hydrogen (1766).

**Cavour, Count Camillo Benso** (1810–1861), a distinguished Italian statesman, who, as Premier to Victor Emmanuel, did much for the unification of Italy.

**Caxton, William** (1422–1491), was born in Kent and employed in commerce for a time. While visiting Flanders he obtained an insight into the then new invention of printing, and afterwards set up a printing-press of his own at Westminster.

**Cecil of Chelwood, 1st Viscount,** P.C., Q.C., C.H. (1864–1958), third son of the third Marquess of Salisbury. Took part in the Peace Conference, 1919, and helped to draft the Charter of the League of Nations. Awarded Nobel Prize for Peace, 1937.

**Cecilia, Saint,** the patron saint of music, martyred in Sicily under Marcus Aurelius (c. 176). She became patroness of music only about the beginning of the 15th century when painters showed her with harp, organ, or other musical instruments. Her festal day is Nov. 22.

**Cellini, Benvenuto** (1500–71), Italian sculptor and goldsmith of the later Renaissance. Possessed remarkable talent and skill, and produced innumerable works of great accomplishment, decorative and exquisite in detail, most of which have perished. Some examples are to be found in the Vienna Museum, the Louvre, and in the Metropolitan Museum. His famous bronze statue *Perseus with the Head of Medusa* can be seen in the Loggia dei Lanzi, Florence. His fame, however, rests more on his *Autobiography*, which gives a vivid account of the period and of his own craft.

**Celsius, Anders** (1701–44), Swedish physicist and astronomer who became professor of astronomy at Uppsala in 1730 and worked at the new Uppsala observatory, 1740–44. He invented the Centigrade or Celsius thermometer with freezing point of water at the zero-degree and boiling point at the 100-degree point.

**Cervantes Saavedra Miguel de** (1547–1616), Spanish novelist, dramatist, and poet, b. at Alcalá de Henares, famous throughout the world as the author of *Don Quixote*, a wonderful study of feudalism in decay in which is to be found much social science. He had a most adventurous career, taking part in many military expeditions, and not turning to literature until his retirement from the profession of arms. In spite of the great success of his work he died in poverty and two centuries went by before he was honoured.

**Cézanne, Paul** (1839–1906), an outstanding figure in the world of art; b. in Aix-en-Provence, the son of a wealthy banker and tradesman. He developed a highly original style, using colour and tone in such a way as to increase the impression of depth. He said that he wanted " to make of Impressionism something solid and durable, like the art of the Museums." Like Giotto, six hundred years before, he more than any other artist determined the course European painting was to take. *La Vielle au Chapelet* and *Les Grandes Baigneuses* may be seen at the National Gallery. He was a friend of Zola.

**Chadwick, Sir James,** F.R.S. (b. 1891), physicist, one of Rutherford's most brilliant collaborators in the field of atomic research. Discovered the neutron in 1932, one of the main steps in the discovery of the fission process which led to the production of the atom bomb.

**Chagall, Marc** (b. 1889), Russian painter, born at Vitebsk of Jewish parents, the forerunner of surrealism.

**Chaliapin, Fedor Ivanovich** (1873–1938), a worldfamous Russian opera singer, a bass with great dramatic gifts.

**Chamberlain, Rt. Hon. (Arthur) Neville** (1869–1940), son of Joseph Chamberlain by his second wife. Prime Minister, 1937–40. His appeasement policy, which culminated in the Munich Agreement of 1938, has been the subject of much criticism.

**Chamberlain, Rt. Hon. Joseph** (1836–1914), did much active municipal work at Birmingham. In 1876 he entered Parliament, and at first was an enthusiastic Liberal with Republican tendencies and served in various offices under Mr. Gladstone. When the Home Rule split occurred, he became the most active member of the Liberal-Unionist party. In 1895 he accepted office as Secretary of State for the Colonies under Lord Salisbury, and in that post won a great reputation, notwithstanding the fact that during his term of office he had the Boer War to contend with. In May, 1903, he caused great sensation by suddenly advocating a scheme of fiscal reform, involving a partial return to Protection. This policy was afterwards adopted as one of the leading planks of the Unionist platform.

**Chambers, Sir William,** R.A. (1726–1796), a British architect, who rebuilt Somerset House in 1775. He also laid out Kew Gardens and designed the Pagoda there.

**Chaminade, Cécile** (1857–1944), French pianist and composer of orchestral music, ballets, songs, and charming piano pieces.

**Champlain, Samuel de** (1567–1635), a French navigator who founded Quebec in 1608, and in the following year discovered the lake known by his name.

**Chantrey, Sir Francis Legatt,** R.A. (1781–1841), a renowned English sculptor who contributed many fine statues to Westminster Abbey and St. Paul's. His famous " Sleeping Children " tomb is in Lichfield Cathedral. He left a considerable fortune to the Royal Academy for the purchase of works of art executed in Gt. Britain. The collection is in the Tate Gallery.

**Chaplin, Charles Spencer** (b. 1889), the first international screen star and one of the world's greatest artists, b. in South London. His mother was a music-hall singer and he made his stage début at the age of five. In 1910 he went to the United States and there attracted the attention of Mack Sennett. It was with the Keystone Company in Los Angeles (1914–15) that he created the unforgettable figure with the minute moustache and the baggy trousers.

His most famous films include *The Tramp, Shoulder Arms, The Kid, The Gold Rush, The Circus, City Lights, The Great Dictator, Modern Times, Monsieur Verdoux,* and *Limelight.* In 1953 he decided to leave America and live in Switzerland. He is an English citizen. *My Autobiography* was published in 1964.

**Chapman, George** (1559–1634), an Elizabethan scholar-poet, writer of poems and lyrics, comedies and tragedies, and translator of the *Iliad* and the *Odyssey.* Prof. MacLure's critical study of the poet was publ. in 1967.

**Chapman, Sydney,** M.A., D.Sc., F.R.S. (b. 1888), mathematician and geophysicist; Chief Prof. of Mathematics, Imperial College of Science, 1924–46; Pres. Int. Comm. which organised the International Geophysical Year, 1957–8.

**Charcot, Dr. Jean Baptiste Etienne Auguste** (1867–1936), a famous French explorer, who in 1903-05 and 1908–10 commanded expeditions which carried out important work in mapping, sounding, etc., in the South Polar regions. Charcot Island in the Antarctic Ocean, which he discovered in 1905, is named after him.

**Chares** (*c.* 300 B.C.), sculptor of the Colossus of Rhodes, a gigantic bronze statue of the sun-god, and one of the seven wonders of the world, destroyed in the earthquake of 224 B.C.

**Charlemagne** (" Charles the Great ") (742–814), a wise and powerful ruler, general and statesman, who from being King of the Franks became Emperor of the Romans, and governed an empire comprising Gaul, Italy, and large parts of Spain and Germany.

**Charles, Jacques Alexandre César** (1746–1823), French physicist, the first to use hydrogen gas in balloons and who anticipated Gay-Lussac's law of the expansion of gases on heating.

**Charles Edward** (Stuart) (1720–1788), the " Young Pretender " as he came to be called, grandson of James II., and the hero of 1745, lived in exile after Culloden, and his later career was mainly one of dissipation.

**Charles I.** (1600–1649), King of England, Scotland, and Ireland (1625–49), succeeded his father James I. in 1625. His marriage to the Catholic princess, Henrietta Maria, sister of Louis XIII. of France, displeased the English public. He was in continual trouble with his ministers and parliament; Cromwell's career began in his reign. He was beheaded in front of the Banqueting House at Whitehall, Jan. 30, 1649.

**Charles II.** (1630–1685), King of England, Scotland, and Ireland (1660–85), eldest surviving son of Charles I. After defeat by Cromwell at Worcester (1651) escaped to France; restored to throne 1660. During his reign Pepys was recording the great London plague of 1665, and the fire of 1666, Wren was building St. Paul's, John Bunyan was writing *Pilgrim's Progress* and Milton *Paradise Lost,* Newton was a fellow of the Royal Society (founded by Charles) and England was becoming a great sea power. Famed as the " Merry Monarch " because of his pleasure-loving ways. Dabbled in chemistry and probably died of mercury poisoning.

**Charles V.** (1500–1558), Hapsburg ruler, succeeded his grandfather, Maximilian I, as emperor of the Holy Roman Empire, and as heir to Ferdinand and Isabella succeeded to Spanish Crown. Administering such vast dominions involved him in many struggles: rivalry with Francis I of France led to four wars. Crushed revolt of peasants (1525). Augsburg settlement (1553) brought Lutherans religious equality with Roman Catholics. Retired to a monastery in Spain (1557).

**Charles XII of Sweden** (1682–1718), a brave but impulsive monarch whose reign was distinguished by the great Nordic War against Denmark, Poland, and Russia. Peter the Great decisively defeated him at Poltava in 1709. In 1718 he invaded Norway and was killed while besieging the fortress of Fredrikshald.

**Chateaubriand, François René, Vicomte de** (1768–1848), French writer and diplomat who in the midst of an adventurous and somewhat eccentric political career wrote a number of stories, poems, and essays which reflect the richness of his personality and give him a unique place in French literature. He was the friend of Mme Récamier for many years. His last years were spent in writing *Mémoires d'outre-tombe* (memoirs from beyond the tomb).

**Chatham, William Pitt, Earl of** (1708–1778), had a long and distinguished career as a statesman, and was the most eloquent Parliamentarian of his time. In the long conflict with France that preceded the American War of Independence, Chatham showed great resourcefulness and vigour, but his patriotic efforts were of little avail against the obstinacy of the King and his party, and he ultimately retired from contention, only making a last appearance in the House of Lords to urge a greater resistance to the war with the American Colonists, and, after a powerful speech, fell back in an apoplectic fit and died a few weeks later, being buried in Westminster Abbey.

**Chatterton, Thomas** (1752–1770), young English poet of remarkable talent, unappreciated until after his death. Unsuccessfully tried to pass off his writings as newly discovered ancient manuscripts and killed himself at the age of 17.

**Chaucer, Geoffrey** (*c.* 1343–1400). Achieved immortality by his *Canterbury Tales,* giving a most graphic description of the life and characters of his time. He was buried in Westminster Abbey.

**Chekhov, Anton** (1860–1904), Russian dramatist and short-story writer, whose plays *The Cherry Orchard, Uncle Vanya,* and *The Three Sisters* continue to delight modern audiences.

**Cherubini, Maria Luigi Carlo Zenobia Salvatore** (1760–1842), a Florentine musician, for many years director of the Paris Conservatoire and composer of operas and church music. Admired by Beethoven and Mendelssohn.

**Chesterfield, Earl of,** K.G. (1694–1773), English statesman whose fame rests upon the letters to his natural son, Philip Stanhope, under the title *Letters to his Son,* which are full of grace, wit, and worldly wisdom.

**Chesterton, Gilbert Keith** (1874–1936), English essayist and novelist; contributed to the *Illustrated London News,* etc., and kept himself in evidence in many literary and journalistic quarters; handled social questions, art, politics, and criticism with dexterity and audacity. Published studies of Robert Browning and Charles Dickens. Completed his autobiography shortly before he died.

**Chevalier Albert** (1861–1923), English music-hall comedian of great originality; celebrated for his coster sketches and songs.

**Chevalier, Maurice** (b. 1888), French stage and film actor.

**Chiang Kai-shek, Generalissimo** (b. 1887), former President of China and member of the Kuomintang Party. Emerged from the welter of events succeeding the death of Sun Yat Sen in 1925 as the leading man in China, a position he maintained for a quarter of a century of trouble and bloodshed until the collapse of the Kuomintang régime in 1949. *See also* Section C, Part I.

**Chichester, Sir Francis,** K.B.E. (b. 1902), English seaman, who after a long career of feats at the helm and in the air sailed his *Gipsy Moth IV* into Sydney Harbour in Dec. 1966 after a 107-day voyage from Plymouth. He was knighted on the eve of his return round the Horn.

**Chippendale, Thomas** (*c.* 1717–1779), a celebrated designer of furniture, born in Otley, Yorkshire. His *The Gentleman and Cabinet Maker's Director* (1752) shows the wide variety of domestic furniture made in England at that time.

**Chirico, Giorgio de** (b. 1888), painter associated with surrealism, born in Greece of Italian parents.

**Chopin, Frédéric François** (1810–1849), Polish pianist and composer, son of a French father and Polish mother. He has been called " the poet of the piano " because of the originality and delicacy of his playing. His music, composed mostly for the piano, includes preludes, mazurkas, impromptus, nocturnes, études, sonatas, and a barcarolle and a berceuse. He enjoyed Paris intellectual and musical society, and played in numerous concerts all over Europe. He died of consumption and was buried in Père-Lachaise, next to his friend Bellini.

**Chou-En-lai, General** (b. 1898), Prime Minister of the Chinese People's Republic since 1949; Foreign Min. 1949–58. Took important part in Geneva Conference of 1954, where his talents for negotiation helped to bring to an end the 8 years' war in Indo-China and the new China into world diplomacy.

**Chrysostom, St. John** (347–407), a father and

saint of the Greek Church who was made Archbishop of Constantinople and was famous for his eloquent preaching and persuasive writing.

**Churchill, Rt. Hon. Lord Randolph (Henry Spencer), P.C.** (1849–1895), was the third son of the seventh Duke of Marlborough. Entered Parliament in 1874, and four years later became prominent on the Conservative side for his scathing attacks on what he called the " Old Gang " of his own Party, and was one of Mr. Gladstone's most severe critics. In 1885 he became Secretary for India, and in the following year was Chancellor of the Exchequer and Leader of the House of Commons, but after a few months of brilliant work resigned on a difference of opinion with his colleagues.

**Churchill, Rt. Hon. Sir Winston (Leonard Spencer), K.G., O.M., C.H., C.L.,** (1874–1965), British statesman, soldier, and author, son of the last-named. He entered Parliament in 1900 and represented Oldham, 1900–06; N.W. Manchester, 1906–08; Dundee, 1908–22; Epping, 1924–45; Woodford, 1945–64. He served as a junior officer with the British force during the Indian frontier troubles of 1897–98 and in the Sudan Campaign, and during the Boer War as a war correspondent he had many dramatic adventures. He held the following ministerial posts: Under-Secretary for the Colonies, 1905–08; President of the Board of Trade, 1908–10; Home Secretary 1910–11. First Lord of the Admiralty, 1911–15 and 1939–40. Chancellor of the Duchy of Lancaster, 1915. Minister of Munitions, 1917; Minister of War, 1918–21; Minister of Air, 1919–21. Sec. of State for the Colonies, 1921–22. Chancellor of the Exchequer 1924–29; Prime Min. and Min. of Defence, 1940–45; Prime Min. 1951–55. Lord Rector of Aberdeen University, 1914–18; Lord Rector of Edinburgh University, 1929–32; Chancellor of Bristol University, 1930; Lord Warden of the Cinque Ports. A man of action, cast in the heroic mould, he lived a full and adventurous life, and will be remembered as the inspired war leader who expressed the determination of the British people to defeat Hitler. His numerous writings include a biography of his famous ancestor, Marlborough, and stories of the First and Second World Wars. He exhibited at the Royal Academy and was elected Academician Extraordinary in 1948. Hon. American citizenship conferred, 1963. Awarded Nobel Prize for Literature in 1953.

**Chulalongkorn, Phra Paramindr Maha** (1853–1910), great Siamese monarch whose appreciation of foreign institutions inspired him to carry out many reforms in his country.

**Cibber, Colley** (1671–1757), a London actor and dramatist of great repute in his day. *The Careless Husband*, and *Love's Last Shift* are the best of his comedies. Poet Laureate 1730–57.

**Cicero, Marcus Tullius** (106–43 B.C.), a Roman Republican orator and philosopher. His younger brother, Quintus Tullius Cicero (102–43 B.C.), was a Roman soldier of some note. Both were slain.

**Cid (El Campeador)** (c. 1035–1099), the name given to the famous Spanish knight, Rodrigo Diaz, Count of Vivar, whose exploits in battle and adventure made him the national hero. He drove the Moors out of Spain before he had completed his twentieth year.

**Cierva, Juan de la** (1895–1936), the Spanish engineer who invented the autogiro.

**Cimabue, Giovanni** (1240–1302), a Florentine painter whose real name was Cenni di Pepo, master of Giotto, and the leader of the movement which led to the formation of what is called the Florentine school.

**Cimarosa, Domenico** (1749–1801). One of the earliest Italian composers whose works in his time were as popular as they were numerous. Was composer to the Russian Court from 1789 to 1792. His most popular opera during his lifetime was *Il Matrimonio Segreto*, and it is still to-day the most frequently heard of his works.

**Cimon** (c. 507–449 B.C.), Athenian statesman and general, son of the great Miltiades who commanded at Marathon. He worked for friendship with Sparta to unite forces against Persia. Decisively defeated Persian land and sea forces at the mouth of the Eurymedon in 468 B.C. Died at the siege of Citium, in Cyprus.

**Cipriani, Giovanni Battista** (1727–85), Florentine painter and engraver who worked in London and was one of the foundation members of the Royal Academy. Collections of his pen-and-ink drawings are in the British Museum and Victoria and Albert Museum.

**Clair, René,** (b. 1898), French film producer, whose early films, full of wit and satire, included *Sous les Toits de Paris* and *A Nous la Liberté*.

**Clarendon, Edward Hyde, 1st Earl of** (1609–1674), a statesman of great ability who filled the office of Lord High Chancellor under Charles II., and for a time was in high favour but, refusing to pander to Charles's whims, was dismissed and went to live in retirement. His *History of the Rebellion* is a valuable work, having the advantage of being written by one who was a witness of, and often an important figure in, the events described. His daughter Anne was the wife of the Duke of York, afterwards James II., and it was her daughter who became Queen Anne. Clarendon died in exile at Rouen.

**Clark, Sir Kenneth McKenzie, C.H., K.C.B.** (b. 1903), British art critic. Director, National Gallery, 1934–45; Chairman Arts Council of Great Britain, 1953–60; Chairman, Independent Television Authority, 1954–57. His broadcasts on art and architecture are much enjoyed.

**Clark, Sir Wilfred Edward le Gros, M.A., M.D., D.Sc., F.R.C.S., F.R.S.** (b. 1895), anatomist and anthropologist; Prof. of Anatomy, Oxford Univ., 1934–62; one of the scientists to expose the forgery of the Piltdown skull. Pres. British Association, 1961.

**Clarke, Marcus Andrew Hislop** (1846–81), Australian novelist, born in London. Emigrated to Australia in 1863, where he became a journalist. During his stay in Tasmania he wrote *For the Term of his Natural Life*, which has become a minor classic.

**Clarkson, Thomas** (1760–1846), was one of the leaders of the Negro Emancipation movement, to which he devoted the main part of his life.

**Claude Lorrain** (1600–1682), the most famous landscape painter of his century. His real name was Claude Gelée, and he was born at Chamange in the Vosges, going from France to Rome as a lad and there laying the foundation of his worldwide celebrity. He lived in Rome most of his life.

**Claudius I.** (10 B.C.–A.D. 54), Emperor of Rome, who succeeded his nephew Caligula when he was murdered. He was the grandson of Tiberius Claudius Nero, erected many imposing buildings in Rome, and visited Britain. In his later years he became the tool of favourites, and was poisoned by his wife Agrippina.

**Clausewitz, Gen. Carl von** (1780–1831), Germany's greatest military expert. His classic book *Vom Kriege*, which expounds his theories on war, dominated Prussia in the nineteenth century, and is still studied in military schools throughout the world.

**Clemenceau, Georges Eugène** (1841–1929), a prominent French statesman and editor of strong Radical tendencies who supported General Boulanger for a time and then bitterly opposed him. Was still a leading exponent of French Radicalism, though he sacrificed his independent position to become Premier and Minister of the Interior in October, 1906–1909, Prime Minister and Minister for War, France, 1917–20. Was a great orator, and a sturdy defender of Dreyfus.

**Clemens, Samuel Langhorne** (" Mark Twain ") (1835–1910). After the Civil War drifted into journalism, making himself popular as a humorist in 1869 by his *Innocents Abroad*, the result of a trip to Europe. His other works include *A Tramp Abroad, Tom Sawyer, Huckleberry Finn,* and *Pudd'nhead Wilson*.

**Cleopatra** (69–30 B.C.), daughter of Ptolemy XI, the sixth queen of Egypt by that name, a brilliant, ambitious woman of captivating charm. On the death of her father in 51 she became joint sovereign with her younger brother Ptolemy XII, whom she married in accordance with Egyptian custom. She was banished to Syria, but obtaining the help of Cæsar, led a revolt and won the kingdom for herself. Cleopatra and Cæsar became lovers. In 47 she bore him a son Cæsarion (later Ptolemy XIV) and followed him to Rome. After the murder of

Cæsar she returned to Egypt, where in 41 she was summoned to meet the triumvir Mark Antony. He fell in love with her and became enslaved. She bore him twins Alexander Helios and Cleopatra Selene. He deserted Octavia his wife and broke with Octavian (later Augustus), his brother-in-law, in an attempt to re-establish the power of Egypt. Antony and Cleopatra were, however, defeated at Actium in 31 B.C. and at Alexandria. Antony fell upon his sword, and Cleopatra, unable to influence Octavian, killed herself by allowing an asp to bite her. The drama of her life has been described by Shakespeare in *Antony and Cleopatra* and by Shaw in *Cæsar and Cleopatra*.

Clive, Robert, Lord (1725–1774), went out to India as a clerk in the service of the East India Company when 17, and during the diplomatic difficulties which arose between England and France attracted the attention of his superiors by some able suggestions for the curbing of the French influence. In the war that followed he was given a command and displayed such remarkable military genius that he virtually became Commander-in-Chief. In the troubles that followed with the native rulers, he was equally resourceful, and succeeded in laying the foundation of the British empire in India on a secure basis.

Clovis (c. 465–511) was the founder of the Merovingian-line of Frankish kings, and a convert to Christianity. He defeated the Burgundians and West Goths, and fixed his court at Paris.

Clyde, 1st Baron, Colin Campbell, K.C.B. (1792–1863), a British Field-Marshal who served in the Peninsular and Crimean wars and made a great reputation as Commander-in-Chief in India during the Mutiny.

Cobbett, William (1763–1835), a politician and controversialist, who, through the medium of his *Political Register*, attacked both Radical and Tory in turn. Entered Parliament in 1832. In 1830 his *Rural Rides* were published in book form.

Cobbold, 1st Baron, Cameron Fromanteel, P.C., G.C.V.O. (b. 1904), Governor of the Bank of England, 1948–61; Lord Chamberlain, 1962–.

Cobden, Richard (1804–1865), the son of a Sussex farmer, who during the Corn Law Agitation came into great prominence as an advocate of Free Trade. He devoted himself so completely to this cause, that for some years he entirely neglected his business affairs and in recognition of his services a subscription of £80,000 was raised for him in 1845, and in 1860 a further sum of £40,000. He entered Parliament in 1841, and except for an interval of two years remained a member till his death. Titles and other honours were offered to him but declined.

Cochran, Sir Charles Blake (1872–1951), a prominent English theatrical manager and producer who began as an actor in America. Among his many successes were *Bitter Sweet*, *Cavalcade*, and a number of brilliant revues.

Cochrane, Thomas, 10th Earl of Dundonald (1775–1860), able and daring British naval hero who had a singularly brilliant yet chequered career. He succeeded in crippling a French fleet in Biscay (1809), aided the liberation of Chile and Peru from Spanish rule (1819–22), of Brazil from Portuguese rule (1823–25), and assisted the Greeks in their struggle to throw off the Turkish yoke (1827).

Cockcroft, Sir John Douglas, K.C.B., O.M., C.B.E., M.A., Ph.D., F.R.S. (1897–1967), Cambridge nuclear physicist who shared with Dr. E. T. S. Walton the 1951 Nobel Prize. They had worked together at Cambridge in the historic "atom-splitting" experiments beginning with the transmutation of lithium into boron. Dir. Atomic Energy Research Estab. at Harwell, 1946–58. As Member (Research) U.K. Atomic Energy Authority, 1958–59, he was directly involved in Britain's first nuclear power programmes. Master of Churchill College, Cambridge.

Cockerell, Christopher, C.B.E., M.A. (b. 1910), British inventor of the hovercraft. *See* Hovercraft, Section L.

Cocteau, Jean (1891–1963), French writer and artist whose achievements in widely varied forms of art were prodigious. Elected to the Académie Française in 1955.

Cody, Samuel Franklin (1861–1913), American

aviator whose name is associated with flights at Farnborough, Hampshire, England. He was the first man to fly in Britain (1,390 feet on 16 Oct. 1908). He became a British subject in 1909. Killed while flying.

Cody, William Frederick (1846–1917), American showman, known as "Buffalo Bill," who in 1883 founded his great Wild West Show with which he toured America and Europe for many years.

Cohn, Ferdinand Julius (1828–98), German botanist, founder of the science of bacteriology.

Coke, Sir Edward (1552–1634), Attorney-General under Elizabeth and Chief Justice under James I; great rival of Francis Bacon. His extensive legal erudition added many new interpretations to the Common Law system. Among his publications are his four *Institutes*, the first of which (*Coke upon Littleton*) is very famous.

Colbert, Jean Baptiste (1619–83), French statesman, who fostered new industries and encouraged commerce, endeavoured to reform the finances, and established the French Navy on a sound basis. A patron of literature, science, and art.

Cole, George Douglas Howard, M.A., (1889–1959), British economist, sociologist, and writer; Chichele Professor of Social and Political Theory at Oxford, 1944–57; Chairman Fabian Society, 1939–46; Pres. Int. Society for the Study of Socialism from 1956 until his death. Among his numerous writings on social and economic problems are *The Intelligent Man's Guide through World Chaos* (1932), *The Post-War Condition of Britain* (1956), *The Case for Industrial Partnership* (1957), *A History of Socialist Thought* (5 vols.).

Coleridge, 1st Baron (1820–94), Lord Chief Justice of England from 1880 until his death. Was a distinguished scholar, orator and barrister, his most famous case being the Tichborne trial in 1871, when his speech for the defence lasted 23 days.

Coleridge, Samuel Taylor (1772–1834), one of the great poets of the early part of the 19th century, whose *Ancient Mariner* and a few other poems stand unsurpassed for poetic beauty and originality.

Coleridge-Taylor, Samuel, A.R.C.M. (1875–1912), British composer, the son of a West African negro doctor practising in London, and an Englishwoman. He studied at the Royal College of Music where his *Hiawatha's Wedding Feast* was performed in 1898.

Colet, John (c. 1467–1519), humanist and divine, founded St. Paul's School, 1512. As scholar and friend of Erasmus he helped to bring the New Learning to England.

Colette (Sidonie Gabrielle Claudine Colette) (1873–1954), author of a number of highly successful novels including the famous *Claudine* stories, *Chéri* and *La Fin de Chéri*. Grand Officier de la Légion d'Honneur (1953).

Collier, Hon. John (1850–1934), English painter who became highly popular for his "problem" pictures. He is best remembered, however, as a distinguished portraitist.

Collingwood, Lord (1750–1810), British admiral whose ship the *Royal Sovereign* led the fleet to battle at Trafalgar and who on Nelson's death assumed the command.

Collins, Michael (1890–1922), brilliant and daring Irishman, leading spirit of the Sinn Fein political movement. Took part in the Easter Rebellion and organised the guerilla warfare which eventually led to the breakdown of British government and to the Anglo-Irish Peace of Dec. 6, 1921. Killed in ambush by Republicans after his return from England.

Collins, William, R.A. (1788–1847), a noted landscape and figure painter, and father of Wilkie Collins.

Collins, William Wilkie (1824–1889), the novelist, was for many years associated with Charles Dickens, and wrote *The Dead Secret*, *The Woman in White*, and *No Name*.

Colt, Samuel (1814–1862), of Hartford, Connecticut, invented the revolver and patented it in 1835. It was some time before its utility was recognised, but after being used with great effect in the war with Mexico it was universally adopted.

Columba, St. (521–597), the founder of the monastery of Iona, was a native of Ireland. From his lonely island shrine he made frequent missionary journeys to the Highlands of Scotland where he made many converts and was greatly revered.

**Columbus, Christopher** (c. 1446–1506), the famous Italian navigator, who, prevailing upon Ferdinand and Isabella of Spain to bear the expense of an expedition of discovery, set out on his first voyage in 1492. He first discovered the Bahamas, Cuba, and other West Indian islands, and, on his third voyage, in 1498, landed on the lowlands of South America.

**Comenius, Johann Amos** (1592–1670), famous Czech educationist. Was the first advocate of the " direct " method of teaching languages, of the use of pictures in education, and of the teaching of science.

**Compton, Arthur Holly** (1892–1962), American physicist whose work on X-rays led to the discovery of the so-called " Compton Effect," for which he shared with C. T. R. Wilson the 1927 Nobel Prize for Physics. He also made important cosmic-ray investigations and helped to develop the atomic bomb. His brother Karl Taylor Compton (1887–1954) was also a physicist who did important research on radar and the ionisation of gases.

**Compton-Burnett, Ivy**, D.B.E., British novelist, whose books deal with family relationships and include *Men and Wives, A House and its Head, Man Servant and Maid Servant, The Present and the Past, A Heritage and its History. See Contemporary Novel, Section M.*

**Comte Auguste** (1798–1857), French philosopher; founder of positivism, and father of social philosophy. *See Positivism, Section J.*

**Condé, Louis II.**, de Bourbon, Prince de, " The Great Condé " (1621–1686), was a distinguished military commander. Victor of Rocroi, 1643.

**Confucius** (c. 551–479 B.C.), Chinese philosopher and sage, founder of the great world religion of Confucianism. He was not concerned with the supernatural but appealed to reason and taught love and respect of one's fellows, superiority to ambition, charity, forgiveness, and repentance. (*See Confucianism, Section J.*)

**Congreve, William** (1670–1729), was a famous Restoration dramatist, whose comedies of manners reflect the grossness of his age only too closely, but are redeemed by the brilliancy of his wit. He was buried in Westminster Abbey.

**Conrad, Joseph** (1857–1924), English novelist of Polish birth whose parents were exiled to France for political reasons. He became master mariner in the British merchant service and began to write novels after he left the sea in 1884. He has a beautiful prose style and is acknowledged to be a significant figure in English literature. His novels include: *Almayer's Folly* (1895), *Lord Jim* (1900), *Nostromo* (1904).

**Conscience, Hendrik (Henri)** (1812–83), the famous Flemish novelist whose historical romance, *The Lion of Flanders*, earned him a distinguished place in the world of literature.

**Constable, John**, R.A. (1776–1887), was a native of East Bergholt, Suffolk, and became one of the greatest of English landscape painters. He had long to wait for recognition, but ultimately attained high honour and exerted a strong influence in the development of landscape art.

**Constant, Jean Joseph Benjamin** (1845–1902), French portrait and subject painter; *Prisoners in Morocco, The Harem*, and *The Emir's Favourite* are among his celebrated Oriental pictures.

**Constantine the Great** (c. 272–337). Emperor of Rome from 306 to his death. Transferred the Capital of the Empire from Rome to Byzantium, thence called Constantinople after his name.

**Constantine I.** (1868–1923). King of Greece, 1913–17, and 1920; married Princess Sophia of Prussia, sister of the Kaiser.

**Cook, James** (1728–79), celebrated English navigator, son of an agricultural labourer. He entered the Royal Navy and gained a high reputation for his scientific skill. He made successful voyages of discovery in the ships under his command, *Endeavour, Resolution* and *Adventure*, adding greatly to our knowledge of the Pacific and the Antarctic. He also made an attempt to find the North-West Passage. He was murdered on the island of Hawaii.

**Cooper, Sir Astley Paston**, Bt., F.R.S. (1768–1841), one of the greatest surgeons of his time, and the author of several important medical textbooks.

**Cooper, James Fenimore** (1789–1851), was a very popular American novelist, who from about 1820 to the time of his death produced a succession of stirring stories of adventure, which enjoyed much popularity, among them *The Spy, The Last of the Mohicans, The Pathfinder*, and *The Deer Slayer*.

**Cope, Sir Arthur Stockdale**, K.C.V.O., R.A. (1857–1940), was a well-known portrait painter.

**Copernicus, Nicholas** (1473–1543), founder of modern astronomy, was born at Thorn on the Vistula, then under Polish suzerainty. Studied at Cracow and in Italy, lectured on astronomy and mathematics at Rome and in 1512 settled at Frauenburg, where he was canon of the cathedral. He also practised medicine. His beliefs concerning the universe were set forth in his great book *De revolutionibus orbium coelestium*, which was not published until his death for fear of the storm his revolutionary theories would raise. In it he proved that the planets, including the earth, revolve round the sun.

**Coppée, François Joachim** (1842–1908), French poet, dramatist and novelist.

**Coquelin, Benoît Constant** (1841–1909), eminent French actor (" Coquelin aîné "), and Coquelin, Ernest (" Coquelin cadet "), his youngest brother (1848–1909), were leading lights of the Théâtre Français.

**Corelli, Arcangelo** (1653–1713), Italian composer and the first great violinist to enjoy universal fame; founded the present art of violin playing and gave definitive form to the *concerto grosso.*

**Corneille, Pierre** (1606–1684) the French tragic dramatist, whose *Cid, Polyeucte, Le Menteur*, and other plays marked a new era in French dramatic production.

**Cornwallis, 1st Marquess** (1738–1805), commander of the British forces which surrendered to the Americans, at Yorktown in 1781, thus ending the War of Independence; was twice Governor-General of India.

**Corot, Jean Baptiste** (1796–1875), a French landscape painter of great repute.

**Correggio, Antonio Allegri da** (1494–1534), the great Italian painter of the Lombard School, whose " Ecce Homo " is in the British National Gallery.

**Cortes (or Cortez), Hernando** (1488–1547), a Spanish adventurer who earned great renown by capturing Mexico for Spain, and held that country in subjection for ten years.

**Cortot, Alfred** (1877–1962), French pianist and conductor, best known for his playing of Chopin, Liszt, and Schumann; chorus director at Bayreuth; conducted first complete performance in Peris of Wagner's *Ring.*

**Cosgrave, William Thomas** (b. 1880), President of Executive Council, Irish Free State, 1922–32; Finance Min., 1923; Defence Min., 1924; Parl. Chairman Fine Gael, 1933–44.

**Costello, John A.**, S.C. (b. 1891), Prime Minister of Irish Republic 1948–51 and 1954–57. When Attorney General, Irish Free State, 1926–32, helped to draft the Statute of Westminster.

**Coulton, George Gordon**, Litt. D., LL.D. (1858–1947), scholar and historian of the Middle Ages, whose main claim to fame rests upon *Five Centuries of Religion*, works in which he set forth his interpretation of monastic history in England from the Conquest to the Reformation.

**Couperin.** A notable family of French musicians who were organists at St. Gervais, Paris, from about 1650 until 1826. François Couperin (1668–1733), called " Couperin the Great," is the best known today for his harpsichord music.

**Cousin, Victor** (1792–1867), French educationist and philosopher, founder of the eclectic school. He was a remarkable lecturer and his writings cover nearly the whole field of philosophy.

**Cousins, Samuel**, R.A. (1801–1887), the greatest mezzoprint engraver of his day, whose plates after Reynolds, Millais, Landseer, and Hogarth reach the highest point of this kind of art work.

**Cousteau, Jacques-Yves** (b. 1910), French underwater explorer, pioneer of aqualung diving, whose research into the feasibility of humans living in undersea " villages " has aroused wide interest.

**Couve de Murville, Maurice** (b. 1900), French diplomat; General de Gaulle's Foreign Minister, 1958–68; appointed Prime Minister after the Gaullist victory which followed the French crisis of May 1968.

**Coverdale, Miles** (1488–1568), one of the early English Reformers, was born in Yorkshire, and afterwards became a monk of Norwich and later Bishop of Exeter. He collaborated with Tyndale in translating the Bible; the Psalms still used in the Prayer Book are taken from their translation.

Coward, Noel (b. 1899), a successful English playwright and actor. His works include *Hay Fever*, *Private Lives*, *Blithe Spirit*, the operetta *Bitter Sweet* and the films *In Which We Serve*, *This Happy Breed*, and *Brief Encounter*.

Cowper, William (1731–1800), an English poet imbued with much piety of sentiment and a remarkable poetic talent. His *Task* is one of the great poems of the 18th century.

Cox, David (1783–1859), an eminent landscape painter—son of a Birmingham blacksmith—whose pictures are thoroughly English in spirit and treatment.

Crabbe, Rev. George (1754–1832), a poet of rural life and scenes, noted for his faithful pictures, characterisation and soundness of his sentiments.

Craig, Edward Gordon, C.H. (1872–1966), the son of Ellen Terry, author of several books on stagecraft. He produced many plays in England and on the Continent.

Cranmer, Thomas (1489–1556), Archbishop of Canterbury under Henry VIII, and Edward VI.; an ardent promoter of the Reformation. On Mary's accession at first consented to return to the old faith, but when called upon to make public avowal of his recantation, refused, and was burnt at the stake. His great contributions were the English Bible and Book of Common Prayer.

Crichton, James (1560–1582). Scottish adventurer who earned considerable renown for his scholarly accomplishments and charm and was called "The Admirable Crichton." He was assassinated when only twenty-two years of age in Mantua.

Cripps, Rt. Hon. Sir (Richard) Stafford, C.H., Q.C. (1889–1952), British statesman and barrister, younger son of Lord Parmoor and nephew of Beatrice Webb. In charge of postwar Britain's economic affairs. His programme was one of purposeful austerity, but his outstanding ability and masterly exposition of the economic situation won him support from all sides. He showed that liberty and planning can be reconciled in the modern world. Labour M.P. for S.E. Bristol, 1931–50. Gave up a brilliant career at the bar to enter politics. Ambassador to Moscow, 1940–42, and Min. of Aircraft Production, 1942–45. Went on missions to India in 1942 and 1946. Resigned his seat in Parliament and as Chancellor of the Exchequer in 1950 because of broken health; was taken to Switzerland for a cure, but he did not recover.

Crispi, Francesco (1819–1901), noted Italian statesman, who aided Garibaldi and was his supporter throughout. Premier 1887–91 and 1893–96. Achieved many reforms for his country.

Crispin, St., a saint of the Roman Church and patron of shoemakers. In the 3rd century he and his brother, natives of Rome, settled in Soissons, France, and there preached Christianity, supporting themselves by shoemaking. Suffered martyrdom under Diocletian in 289, by being thrown into a cauldron of molten lead; commemorated on Oct. 25.

Croce, Benedetto (1866–1952), Italian philosopher and critic and one of the great figures of the 20th century. Devoted his long life to studying and writing, and his philosophy is expounded in the four volumes of *Filosofia dello Spirito* (which has been translated into English). He founded and edited *La Critica* in 1903, a review of literature, history, and philosophy. Strongly opposed to fascism, he was described during the war as "the grand old man who kept a torch burning in Naples which even Mussolini did not dare to extinguish."

Crœsus (died c. 546 B.C.) the last King of Lydia (560–546 B.C.), who reigned fourteen years, and acquired such immense wealth that his name has ever since been proverbial. He was a wise king, whose memory still survives in his wise sayings. Solon was his friend, and it was Solon's name that he uttered thrice while standing before the pyre on which Cyrus had condemned him to be burnt. This touched Cyrus, who spared his life and made

him his companion. He succeeded his father Alyattes on the Lydian throne, 560 B.C.

Crome, John (1769–1821), known as "Old Crome," from being a humble house-painter became eminent as a painter of landscape.

Cromer, 1st Earl of, P.C., G.C.B., O.M., G.C.M.G., K.C.S.I., C.I.E., F.R.S. (1841–1917), a diplomatist who won celebrity in the post of British Comptroller-General in Egypt from 1883 to 1907. It was a stupendous task that he had imposed upon him, but he resolutely devoted himself to it, with the result that Egypt was lifted from financial difficulty and internal disorder to a condition of prosperity. Pubs. *Modern Egypt* (1908) and *Abbas II* (1915).

Crompton, Samuel (1753–1827), was a poor cotton worker at Bolton who invented the spinning mule, which greatly increased the power of cotton production. Received little recognition.

Cromwell, Oliver (1599–1658), Lord Protector of the commonwealth of England, Scotland and Ireland. 1653–58. Born at Huntingdon, educated at Sidney Sussex College, Cambridge, and entered parliament as member for Huntingdon in 1628. With outbreak of civil war served with the parliamentary army under Essex and won renown at Edgehill (1642). Celebrated as a great general, leader of his Ironsides, for his religious toleration, and strong foreign policy. His victories include Marston Moor (1644), Naseby (1645), Dunbar (1650), Worcester (1651).

Cromwell, Richard (1626–1712), son of the foregoing, and his successor in the Protectorate.

Cromwell, Thomas (1485–1540), originally a protégé of Wolsey, rose to high office under Henry VIII, and began the suppression of the monasteries. Executed after the failure of the Anne of Cleves marriage, which was part of his policy of alliance with the Protestant princes of Germany.

Crookes, Sir William, O.M., F.R.S. (1832–1919) eminent British scientist whose researches in chemistry and physics led to many important discoveries and inventions. He discovered the metal thallium in 1861, invented the radiometer and the Crookes' tube, which was used by J. J. Thomson and others in their researches on conduction of electricity in gases. He was also an authority on sanitation. President of the Royal Society, 1913–16.

Cruikshank, George (1792–1878), a celebrated book illustrator who was for a time associated with Charles Dickens, and later on illustrated numerous works of other novelists of his day, showing great humour and power of characterdelineation.

Cummings, Bruce Frederick (1889–1917), English zoologist and man of letters. Won fame with his *Journal of a Disappointed Man*.

Cunard, Sir Samuel, Bt. (1787–1865), shipowner and co-founder of the British and N. American Royal Mail Steam Packet Co. which later became the Cunard Line and as a result of a merger in 1934, the Cunard-White Star Line, owners of the great passenger ships, *Queen Mary* (1936–67), *Queen Elizabeth* (1940–68) and *Queen Elizabeth II* (launched 1967).

Cunningham of Hyndhope, Admiral of the Fleet, Viscount, K.T., G.C.B., O.M., D.S.O. (1883–1963), won the D.S.O. and two bars in the first world war, C.-in-C., Mediterranean, 1939–42 Allied Naval C.-in-C., North African campaign. First Sea Lord, 1943–46.

Cunningham, General Sir Alan Gordon, G.C.M.G., K.C.B., D.S.O., M.C. (b. 1887), brother of Viscount Cunningham. Directed Abyssinian campaign and commanded 8th Army, 1941. From 1945 served as the last British High Commissioner in Palestine.

Cunningham, Admiral of the Fleet, Sir John Henry Dacres, G.C.B., M.V.O. (1885–1962), C.-in-C., Mediterranean, 1943–46. First Sea Lord 1946–48.

Curie, Prof. Pierre (1859–1906) and Madame Marie (1867–1934) are names that have become famous as the discoverers of radium. M. Curie was a Frenchman, Mme. Curie a Pole; they were both indefatigable scientific investigators. Shared the Nobel Prize for Physics 1903, while their daughter, the late Mme. Irène Joliot-Curie, shared with her husband the 1935 Nobel Prize for Chemistry, awarded for their researches in radioactivity.

**Curzon** of Kedleston, Marquess, K.G., P.C., G.C.S.I., G.C.I.E. (1859–1925), statesman and administrator. As a young man gained distinction as traveller and author. From 1899 to 1905 was a vigorous and outstanding Viceroy of India. Foreign Secretary, 1919–23, when he played a dominant part in the reconstruction of the Middle East and was prominent at many conferences after the first world war.

**Cuthbert, St.** (635–687), a famous monk who became prior of Melrose, and afterwards of Lindisfarne. For a time he lived in seclusion on one of the Farne Islands, but from 684 was Bishop of Hexham.

**Cuvier, Georges Léopold, Baron** (1769–1832),† a French naturalist who founded a system of classification in zoology, and originated the science of comparative anatomy.

**Cuyp, Albert** (1620–1691), a famous Dutch landscape painter, several of whose works are in our National Gallery.

**Cyprian, St.**, was an eminent ecclesiastic of the 3rd century, who wrote several notable treatises on matters of Christian doctrine. He was beheaded in 258, at an advanced age, and the present English calendar commemorates him on Sept. 26.

**Cyrus the Great** (d. 529 B.C.), the founder of the Persian Empire who by his conquests of Media, Lydia, and Babylonia, made himself master of Asia Minor. He was a great warrior and a wise ruler and figures prominently in the Bible. He was slain in battle on the river Jaxartes.

# D

**Daguerre, Louis Jacques Mandé** (1789–1851), a French artist, who acquired fame as the inventor of the earliest photographic process, and then devoted himself to scene-painting and became part-proprietor of the Diorama in Paris.

**Daimler, Gottlieb** (1834–1890), German inventor with N. A. Otto of Cologne of the Otto gas engine, and in his later years eminent as the inventor of the motor-car that is named after him.

**Dale, Sir Henry Hallett,** O.M., G.B.E., F.R.S., M.D., D.Sc. (1875–1968), leader of medical research in Britain; Pres. British Association, 1947, of Royal Society, 1940–5. Chair. Lister Institute of Preventive Medicine, 1942. Nobel Prize for Medicine, 1936.

**Dalhousie, 1st Marquess of,** P.C., K.T. (1812–1860). The tenth Earl and first Marquess of Dalhousie was one of the most famous of India's Governors-General. He controlled the affairs of India during a period of great difficulty, and annexed the Punjab after the second Sikh War; later on also annexing Nagpur Jhansi, Pegu and other States. He left India in 1856, the year before the Mutiny.

**Dali, Salvador** (b. 1904), Spanish painter whose *Persistence of Memory* with its bleak landscape and drooping watches is typical of surrealist art. In 1940 he went to live in America.

**Dalton, John** (1766–1844), famous chemist and mathematician, renowned for his work on the construction of matter. In 1810 published his classic *A New System of Chemical Philosophy*, in which the modern chemical atomic theory was first propounded. According to this theory the atoms of the chemical elements are qualitatively different from one another.

**Damien, Father** (Joseph de Veuster) (1840–1889), a Belgian missionary who, going out to Honolulu in 1864, and witnessing the terrible sufferings of the lepers confined on the Island of Molokai, obtained permission to take spiritual charge of the Government settlement, and remained there working nobly for this wretched community, until in 1889 he himself was stricken with leprosy and died.

**Damocles**, a Syracusan of the 5th cent. B.C., member of the court of Dionysius I. The legend related by Cicero concerning him is that he flattered his master by expressing his envy of the tyrant's riches and power, whereupon Dionysius, to demonstrate the precariousness of high estate, invited him to a banquet where he found himself sitting beneath a naked sword suspended by a hair. Hence the phrase "the sword of Damocles"—to hang by a thread.

**Damrosch, Walter Johannes** (1862–1950), American musician, active in the musical develop-ment of the United States. Conductor of the New York Symphony Society, 1885–1927, and composer of three operas and of incidental music to Greek plays.

**D'Annunzio, Gabriele** (1863–1938), Italian poet, soldier and airman. In Sept. 1919 he led an unofficial raid on Fiume and seized the port and town; when the Treaty of Rapallo was signed in 1920, he refused to recognise it, and declared war against Italy but was forced to surrender. His bodyguard wore the blackshirt which was to become the uniform of the Fascists.

**Dante Alighieri** (1265–1321), the greatest Italian poet and one of the great figures of world literature, was born in Florence in a period of political upheaval caused by the strife between Guelph and Ghibelline, which had divided mediaeval Italy for over a century. Though he saw her but once or twice, he conceived an abiding love for a Florentine lady, Bice Portinari (called by Dante Beatrice), wife of Simone di Bardi, whom he first met in 1274. She died in 1290. Some of his finest work was written after he was driven from his native city in 1301. His works include the *Vita Nuova* (written 1292–93 in memory of Beatrice), his supreme masterpiece the *Divine Comedy*, begun 1308–9 and completed shortly before his death, many beautiful lyrics, and some Latin treatises.

**Danton, Georges Jacques** (1759–1794), a famous member of the National Convention at the period of the first French Revolution. Was made President of the Committee of Public Safety, but Robespierre attacked and supplanted him. Danton was consigned to the guillotine shortly afterwards.

**D'Arblay, Madame** (1752–1840), better known as Frances (Fanny) Burney, daughter of the organist Dr. Charles Burney, made a great sensation while quite young and unmarried by her novel *Evelina*, which opened the doors of Society to her and gained her the friendship of Dr. Johnson.

**Darius** was the name borne by three Persian kings. The first reigned from 521 to 485 B.C., and was defeated by the Greeks at Marathon. The second was a natural son of Artaxerxes Longimanus, and having obtained the crown by the murder of his brother, reigned from 424 to 405 B.C. The third Darius was the last of the Persian kings, reigning only from 336 to 331 B.C. when Alexander the Great invaded his kingdom and defeated him in two great battles. Soon after he was assassinated.

**Darling, Grace Horsley** (1815–1842), English heroine who by putting off in a small boat from the lighthouse on one of the Farne Islands, of which her father was keeper, saved the shipwrecked crew of the *Forfarshire*.

**Darnley, Earl of** (1545–1567), was married to Mary Queen of Scots—as her second husband—in 1565. Two years later, after Mary had entered into an intrigue with Bothwell, he was murdered.

**Darwin, Charles Robert,** F.R.S. (1809–1882), the distinguished scientist, whose *Origin of Species* first clearly formulated and elaborated the theory of evolution. His first work (1837) described a five years' cruise in the *Beagle*, which the Government had sent out for scientific purposes. His *Origin of Species* appeared in 1859, and, though defended and supported by the scientific thought of the time generally, was much attacked by theologians. In 1871 Darwin issued his *Descent of Man*, a still further elaboration of the evolution theory. His other principal works were *The Expression Of Emotion in Man and Animals* (1872), *Insectivorous Plants* (1875), *Different Forms of Flowers* (1877), and *Worms* (1881).

**Daudet, Alphonse** (1840–1897), the celebrated French humorist and novelist, all of whose works have been translated into English.

**Davenant, Sir William** (1606–1668), a dramatist and poet of much note in his time, who filled the office of Poet Laureate in succession to Ben Jonson.

**David I.** (1084–1153) was King of Scotland and uncle of Matilda, daughter of Henry I.; he took up arms against Stephen on his repudiation of Matilda's claims to the English crown.

**David II.** (1324–1371), King of Scotland from 1330 to 1370. He was the son of Robert Bruce, and in conflict with the English Army at Neville's Cross, in 1346, was defeated and made prisoner by Queen Philippa.

**David, Sir (Tannatt William) Edgeworth, K.B.E., C.M.G., D.S.O., F.R.S.** (1858–1934), an Australian geologist of the first rank, who was Professor of Geology at Sydney University 1891–1924. Spent much of his time in exploration, and accompanied as geologist Shackleton's Antarctic Expedition, 1907–9, leading the party that ascended Mt. Erebus, and discovering with Sir Douglas Mawson the South Magnetic Pole.

**David, Jacques-Louis** (1748–1825), a celebrated French painter of classic subjects, who put his art at the service of the New Republic.

**David, St.,** patron saint of Wales, whose festival falls on March 1st, lived in the 6th century in Wales, and founded various monasteries.

**Davidson, Randall Thomas Davidson, 1st and only Baron, P.C., G.C.V.O.** (1848–1930), Archbishop of Canterbury, 1903–1928. Dean of Windsor, 1883–1891; Bishop of Rochester, 1891–1895; and Bishop of Winchester, 1895–1903. Was for a long period Domestic Chaplain and Clerk of the Closet to Queen Victoria, and married in 1878 the daughter of Archbishop Tait.

**Davies, Rt. Hon. Clement, Q.C., M.P.** (1884–1962), lawyer and politician. Called to the Bar, 1909, took silk, 1926. He led the Liberal Party from 1945 until 1956, and represented his native Montgomery from 1929 until his death.

**Davies, Sir (Henry) Walford, K.C.V.O., O.B.E., Mus.D., D.Mus.** (1869–1941), Master of the King's Music, 1934–41; Director of Music and Chairman of the National Council of Music, University of Wales, 1919–41, the Gresham Prof. of Music, 1924–41.

**Davies, William Henry** (1871–1940), was a Welsh poet who spent his early life as a tramp and odd-job man. For six years he wandered about America, where he lost a foot " train-jumping," and for eight years followed a similar life in England, tramping, peddling and stopping in common lodging-houses. His poems reveal an intimate knowledge of and love for Nature. An account of his life is given in his *Autobiography of a Super Tramp.*

**Da Vinci.** *See* Leonardo.

**Davis, Jefferson** (1808–1889), an American statesman, who on the breaking out of Civil War, was made President of the Confederate States. After the war he was a prisoner in the hands of the Federals, put on his trial for treason, and subjected to much indignity, but was ultimately discharged and wrote (1881) *The Rise and Fall of the Confederate Government.*

**Davis, John** (c. 1550–1605), one of the great Elizabethan explorers and discoverer of Davis's Strait, the channel between the Atlantic and Arctic Oceans on the west of Greenland. Invented the backstaff, or Davis's quadrant.

**Davitt, Michael** (1846–1906), after a hard-working and precarious bringing up this ardent Irish Nationalist attracted much notice by the bitter speeches he made on behalf of the Fenian Brotherhood, and in 1870 was sentenced to fifteen years' penal servitude for treason-felony, but was released on ticket of leave in 1877. Was one of the founders of the Irish Land League 1879. In 1881 was sent back to penal servitude, but released again in the following year. Was elected to Parliament while a prisoner at Portland but disqualified. Succeeded in entering Parliament in 1892, and resigned in 1899.

**Davy, Sir Humphry, Bt., F.R.S.** (1778–1829), the inventor of the safety-lamp. Was an eminent chemist whose researches and discoveries were of great scientific importance. Was the first to employ the electric current in chemical decomposition and discovered that nitrous oxide was perfectly respirable.

**Dawber, Sir (Edward) Guy, R.A.** (1861–1938), English architect. As Chairman of the Council for the Preservation of Rural England, he did much to bring about the restoration of buildings throughout the country.

**Dawkins, Sir William Boyd** (1837–1929), British geologist, noted for his research on fossil mammals. Made Channel Tunnel survey in 1882.

**Dawson, (George) Geoffrey** (1874–1944), editor of *The Times*, 1912–19, and 1923–41.

**Deakin, Rt. Hon. Arthur, C.H., C.B.E., J.P.** (1890–1955), Trade Union leader; succeeded Ernest Bevin as general secretary of the Transport and General Workers' Union in 1949 and like him was a master negotiator.

**Debussy, Claude Achille** (1862–1918), French composer and founder of the Impressionist school in music, whose harmonies have a vague " atmospheric " effect. Among his works are *Suite bergamasque*, containing the popular *Clair de lune, L'après-midi d'un Faune*, inspired by the poem of Mallarmé, and *La Mer*. He also wrote an opera *Pelléas et Mélisande* based on Maeterlinck's drama and many piano compositions and songs. *See* Section E.

**Defoe, Daniel** (1660–1731), the son of a London butcher. He became a political writer and novelist, obtaining world-wide fame by his *Robinson Crusoe*, written when he was nearly sixty years of age.

**De Forest, Lee** (1873–1961), American inventor who was the first to use alternating-current transmission, improved the thermionic valve detector and amplifier, which revolutionised wireless and by which modern wireless and sound films (Talkies) were made possible. He designed the first high-power station for the United States Navy and was granted over three hundred patents.

**Degas, (Hilaire Germain) Edgar** (1834–1917), French painter and sculptor, son of a banker, an important figure in the impressionist movement and a great experimenter. The subjects which interested him were those of everyday life—dancers, café life, the racecourse.

**De Gasperi, Alcide** (1881–1954), Italian catholic politician. Founded the Christian Democrat Party and worked for European federation. Died on eve of breakdown of Brussels Conference on E.D.C. Prime Min. 1945–53.

**De Gaulle, General.** *(See* Gaulle, Charles de.)

**De Havilland, Sir Geoffrey, O.M., C.B.E., F.R.Ae.A.** (1882–1965), a pioneer of civil and military aviation. Began flying in 1908 and was the founder of the Stag Lane Aerodrome at Hendon and the designer of the famous Moth machines. Contributed in great measure to the advance of civil aviation since the first world war. Awarded the Guggenheim Medal in 1952. His son was killed in 1946 while testing a plane in preparation for breaking world speed record.

**Delacroix, Ferdinand Victor Eugène** (1798–1863), French painter of great imaginative and dramatic force, of the romantic school.

**De la Mare, Walter John, O.M., C.H.** (1873–1956), English poet and novelist whose work has a characteristic charm. Much of it was written for children.

**Delane, John Thadeus** (1817–1879), the famous editor of *The Times*, who, though he did not write himself, made his paper the greatest journal in the world. He occupied the editorial chair from 1841 to 1877.

**Delaroche, Paul (Hippolyte)** (1797–1856), an eminent French historical painter.

**Delibes, Clément Philibert Léo** (1836–91), French composer of much graceful music, including several operas, of which *Lakmé* is the most famous, and ballets, among them *Coppélia*.

**Delius, Frederick, C. H.** (1862–1934), English composer of German parentage. Highly idiosyncratic in idiom, his music was more readily received in Germany than England until Sir Thomas Beecham's inspired performances won popularity for him in his native land. *See* Section E.

**Democritus** (c. 470–c. 400 B.C.), one of the first scientific thinkers, pupil of Leucippus (fl. c. 475 B.C.), also probably of Miletus. He took an atomic view of matter, denied the existence of mind as a separate entity, and counted happiness and inner tranquillity as important moral principles. His attitude was not shared by his contemporary Socrates, nor by Plato and Aristotle. The atomic theory thus passed into the background for many centuries. His followers were known as Epicureans, after the most distinguished of them, Epicurus of Samos (342–270 B.C.).

**Demosthenes** (385–322 B.C.), the famous Greek orator, statesman and warrior who, by his *Philippics*, roused the Athenians to resist the growing power of Philip of Macedon. Sixty-one of his orations were preserved, and are regarded as the finest examples of their kind.

**De Quincey, Thomas** (1785–1859), an eminent essayist and critic, the friend of Coleridge, Wordsworth, and Southey. His *Confessions of an Opium-eater* is a British classic.

**De Reszke, Jean** (1853–1925) and **De Reszke, Edouard** (1856–1917), Polish operatic singers, the first a tenor, the second a baritone, who achieved fame and fortune by their singing.

**Derwentwater, 3rd Earl of** (1689–1716), the leader of the English Jacobite movement for placing the Pretender on the English throne. The rising took place in 1715, but was completely crushed by the Battle of Preston, and Derwentwater was beheaded.

**Descartes, René** (1596–1650), the famous French philosopher, mathematician, and author. Unconvinced by scholastic tradition and theological dogma, he sought to get back to primary truth, to the very definition of knowledge or the reason why anything can be said to be true. The basis of his Cartesian philosophy is summed up in his own words *cogito, ergo sum* (I am thinking so I exist).

**Desmoulins, Lucie Simplice Camille Benoist** (1760–1794), was one of the fiercest of the French Revolutionary leaders, and from the destruction of the Bastille to the early days of the Terror was unflagging in his onslaughts upon the aristocrats and the priesthood. He fell under the displeasure of Robespierre, however, and was sent to the guillotine along with Danton.

**De Valera, Eamon, LL.D.** (b. New York, 1882), Pres. Rep. of Ireland, 1959– ; leader of the Fianna Fail Party; Prime Minister 1938–48, 1951–54, and 1957–59; Minister for External Affairs 1932–48. Pres. of Executive Council of Irish Free State, 1932–38; Pres. of Sinn Fein 1917–26 when Fianna Fail was founded; Delegate to Assembly and Council of League of Nations, 1932, and President thereof 1932 and 1938.

**De Valois, Dame, Ninette, D.B.E.** (b. 1898). Irish-born ballet dancer and choreographer. Between world wars had many triumphs as a dancer with the British National Opera company and with the Diaghilev Russian ballet. Director of the Royal Ballet School (formerly the Sadler's Wells School).

**Dewar, Sir James, F.R.S.** (1842–1923), physicist and chemist, a native of Kincardine. From 1875 until his death Jacksonian Prof. of Natural Philosophy at Cambridge and from 1877 Fullerian Prof. of Chemistry at the Royal Institution. Famous for his work on the liquefaction of gases and his invention of the Thermos flask. Invented, with Sir F. Abel, the explosive cordite.

**Dewey, Prof. John** (1859–1952), the eminent American philosopher, psychologist and educationist, who, after holding professorships at the Universities of Minnesota, Michigan, and Chicago, where he was also Director of the School of Education until 1904, was Prof. of Philosophy at Columbia University, New York, 1904–32. A follower of William James, he became well known in America as an adherent of pragmatism.

**De Witt, Jan** (1625–72), Dutch republican statesman, who carried on war with England and later negotiated the Triple Alliance, but was overthrown by the Orange Party and murdered.

**Diaghilev, Sergei Pavlovich** (1872–1929), Russian ballet impresario and founder of the Russian ballet, who selected the best dancers, musicians, and artists in his productions. Among those associated with him were Anna Pavlova, Vaslav Nijinsky, Tamara Karsavina, Leonide Massine, Michel Fokine, the choreographer, L. N. Bakst, the painter, and Igor Stravinsky, the composer.

**Dick, Sir William Reid, K.C.V.O., R.A., F.R.B.S.** (1879–1961), British sculptor whose works include the Livingstone statue (Victoria Falls, Africa), memorial statue of King George V. at Westminster, and the statue of Pres. Roosevelt in Grosvenor Square.

**Dickens, Charles (John Huffam)** (1812–1870), the most popular novelist of the 19th century, who from very humble beginnings worked himself up to the highest position in the world of letters. His literary output was enormous. From the time of the publication of the *Pickwick Papers* down to his death in 1870, covering a period of

33 years, he produced novel after novel, all possessing the original Dickensian characteristics, yet each wonderfully different from the rest and his popularity continues undiminished. He did so much for the cultivation of the true sentiment of Christmas that, whenever that season comes round, his name is recalled with honour and homage. As a public reader of his own works Dickens evinced a marvellous dramatic gift. He was buried in Westminster Abbey.

**Dickinson, Goldsworthy Lowes** (1863–1932). English scholar, author and philosopher; an interpreter and upholder of the Greek view of life, which is the subject of many of his books.

**Dicksee, Sir Francis Bernard, R.A.** (1853–1928), well known as the painter of numerous pictures, including "Harmony," "Romeo and Juliet," and "The Funeral of a Viking."

**Diderot, Denis** (1713–1784), the famous French philosopher and editor of the *Dictionnaire Encyclopédique*, which occupied him thirty years.

**Diefenbaker, Rt. Hon. John George, M.A., Q.C.** (b. 1895), Canadian lawyer and leader of the Canadian Progressive Conservative Party; Prime Min., 1957–63.

**Diemen, Anthony van** (1593–1645). Dutch Admiral who was Governor-General of the East Indian Colonies, 1636–45. He extended Dutch influence and trade throughout the Far East, promoted explorations to Australia, 1636–42, and on one of such explorations, Abel Tasman discovered New Zealand and named the island which we now know as Tasmania, Van Diemen's Land.

**Diesel, Rudolf** (1858–1913), German engineer, inventor of an internal-combustion engine which he patented in 1893. The modern so-called Diesel engine represents the improvements achieved by many men and has evolved mainly from the invention of Herbert Akroyd-Stuart, patented in 1890.

**Diocletian (Caius Aurelius Valerius [Diocletianus)** (245–313), Roman Emperor (284–305). Inaugurated the system of partnership emperors, whereby the Empire was divided into four sections (the famous tetrarchy), administered by himself in the East, Maximian in Italy and Africa, Constantius in Britain, Gaul, etc., and Galerius in Illyricum. Ruthlessly persecuted the Christians.

**Diogenes** (412–322 B.C.), the celebrated Greek cynic philosopher who is said to have lived in a tub wearing the coarsest clothing and living on the plainest food. Many of his sayings have been preserved.

**Dionysius.** Two of the tyrants of Syracuse bore this name. The first was a great soldier and statesman as well as a poet and philosopher, and lived from *c.* 430–367 B.C. The second Dionysius was his son and successor, but was of such a cruel disposition that he was driven from the throne and died in obscurity in 343.

**Disney, Walter Elias ("Walt")** (1901–66). American film cartoonist; creator of Mickey Mouse. His *Silly Symphonies, Snow White and the Seven Dwarfs, Pinocchio,* and *Fantasia* brought him world-wide fame.

**Disraeli, Benjamin.** (*See* Beaconsfield).

**D'Israeli, Isaac** (1766–1848), father of Benjamin Disraeli, worked in a special literary field, and produced some interesting volumes dealing with authors and their writings. His best-known work is *Curiosities of Literature.*

**Dixon, Harold Bailey** (1852–1930). Professor of Chemistry at Manchester University, 1887–1922, whose work on gaseous explosions opened a new era in combustion research.

**Dobson, Frank, C.B.E., A.R.A., A.R.B.S.** (1888–1963). English sculptor. President of the London Group, 1923–27.

**Dobson, Henry Austin, LL.D.** (1840–1921), a Civil Servant from 1860 to 1901, he was the author of several volumes of Society verse and prose works, dealing chiefly with the 18th century.

**Dodd, Francis, R.A., R.W.S.** (1874–1949), painter, engraver and draughtsman. He was one of the official artists during the War of 1914–18, and executed a valuable series of portraits of British Admirals and Generals on active service. Appointed one of the official artists for the second world war, 1939–45.

**Dodgson, Charles Lutwidge** (1832–1898), a writer and mathematical lecturer at Christ Church, Oxford, who, under the pseudonym of Lewis Carroll, achieved lasting fame by his *Alice's*

**B26**

*Adventures in Wonderland*, one of the most delightful books for children ever written.

**Dolci, Carlo** (1616–1686), the famous Florentine painter, examples of whose Madonnas and Saints are to be found in most National collections.

**Dolci, Danilo** (b. 1925), Italian architect who since 1952 has dedicated himself to the rehabilitation of the people of Sicily in their desperate poverty. He began with no resources but his own humanity, but now his work—agricultural, educational, and social—is inspiring world-wide interest.

**Dominic, St.** (1170–1221), founder of the Order of Dominicans, or Black Friars, who devoted much energy to the conversion of the Albigenses, but meeting with small success, instituted a policy of persecution after the manner of the later Inquisition.

**Domitian (Titus Flavius Domitianus)** (A.D. 51–96), Roman Emperor, son of Vespasian, who after many cruel and tyrannical acts aroused the enmity of the people and was assassinated.

**Donatello (Donato di Niccolò di Betto Bardi)** (1386–1466) the famous Italian sculptor, whose works are to be seen chiefly at Florence, though several examples are at South Kensington.

**Donizetti, Gaetano** (1797–1848), Italian operatic composer. Most popular of his sixty operas are *Lucrezia Borgia*, *Lucia di Lammermoor*, *La Fille du régiment*, *La Favorita*, and *Don Pasquale*.

**Donne, John** (1573–1631), an English poet and divine. As a preacher he was celebrated in his lifetime but few of his poems were printed and it was not until the 20th century that he was universally recognised as one of the most original of English poets. His writings include *Songs and Sonnets*, *Satyres*, *Elegies*, *Problems and Paradoxes*, and the *Holy Sonnets*. He took orders in 1615 and was made dean of St. Paul's in 1621. Sir Edmund Gosse's *Life and Letters* appeared in 1899 and Sir Herbert Grierson's monumental edition of Donne's poetry in 1912.

**Donoghue, Stephen ("Steve")** (1884–1945), in his day a famous jockey. Rode the Derby Race winner six times, and established a new record by winning this classic event in three successive years, 1921–22–23.

**Doré, Gustave** (1833–1883), the well-known French artist, famous for his colossal scriptural paintings and his powerful illustrations to the works of Dante, Milton, and Tennyson.

**Dostoyevsky, Feodor Mikhailovitch** (1821–1881), one of Russia's greatest novelists. Author of *Crime and Punishment*, *Brothers Karamazov*, *The Idiot*, *The Possessed*, etc. Dostoyevsky's novels are quite exceptional for their deep psychological insight, vision and marvellous tragic and analytic power, and have had a profound influence on modern European writers.

**Douglas, Marshal of the R.A.F. Lord**, G.C.B., M.C., D.F.C. (b. 1893), commanded Fighter Command, 1940–42, R.A.F. Middle East, 1943–44, and Coastal Command, 1944–45. C.-in-C. and Military Governor of British Zone of Germany, 1946–47. A Labour peer.

**Douglas, Norman** (1868–1952), novelist and writer of witty and elegant prose. A Scot, born in Austria, he made his home on the Mediterranean and was buried on Capri. Travel books include *Siren Land* (1910). *Fountains in the Sand* (1912), *Old Calabria* (1915), *Alone* (1921), *Together* (1923); his highly entertaining novel *South Wind* was published in 1917.

**Douglas-Home, Rt. Hon. Sir Alexander Frederick**, M.P. (b. 1903), British statesman; Prime Minister, 1963–64; Leader of the Conservative Party, 1963–; M.P. for Kinross and W. Perthshire, 1963–; Foreign Sec., 1960–63; Sec. of State for Commonwealth Relations, 1955–60. Formerly the 14th Earl of Home; renounced title in 1963 to stand as candidate for House of Commons. Chancellor, Heriot-Watt Univ.

**Doulton, Sir Henry** (1820–1897), famous potter and the inventor of Doulton ware.

**Dowden, Edward**, M.A., LL.D., D.C.L., Litt.D. (1843–1913). Well known for his critical and other writings, mainly dealing with the lives and works of the poets. Was Professor of Literature at Trinity College, Dublin, for 37 years

**Dowding, Air Chief Marshal Lord**, G.C.B., G.C.V.O., C.M.G. (b. 1882), Chief of Fighter Command in Battle of Britain, 1940.

**Dowland, John** (c. 1563–1626), English composer whose songs with lute accompaniment estab-

lished him as the foremost lutanist of his day. His son Robert succeeded him as Court lutanist to Charles I.

**Doyle, Sir Arthur Conan**, M.D. (1859–1930), masterly writer of detective stories, the creator of Sherlock Holmes, the archetype of detectives, who shared a flat in Baker Street with his friend and chronicler, Dr. Watson, and conducted a long series of investigations. The immensely popular stories appeared in the *Strand Magazine* and include the *Hound of the Baskervilles* and the *Speckled Band*.

**Doyle, Richard** (1824–1883), an artist of much humour and fancy, who was exceedingly popular while on the staff of *Punch* from 1841 to 1850. The familiar cover of *Punch* is his work.

**D'Oyly Carte, Richard** (1844–1901), English theatrical manager, associated with the production of the Gilbert and Sullivan comic operas. The D'Oyly Carte Opera Companies played Gilbert and Sullivan all over the world.

**Drake, Sir Francis** (c. 1540–1596), the great admiral of Queen Elizabeth's time, who made many adventurous voyages, bent partly on discovery and partly on plunder. He was a leading figure—under Lord Howard—in the attack on and destruction of the Spanish Armada in 1588.

**Draper, John William** (1811–82), American chemist, b. near Liverpool, aided in the organisation of the medical school of New York university and became its professor of chemistry and physiology. He was the first to take a satisfactory photograph of the human face (1840).

**Dreiser, Theodore** (1871–1945), an American author whose novels of American life are written in vigorous native prose.

**Dreyfus, Lt.-Col. Alfred** (1859–1935), a French officer, condemned by a military secret tribunal on a charge of divulging secrets in 1894 to a foreign power, and condemned to imprisonment for life on Devil's Island in French Guiana. At a sensational new trial in 1899 he was again found guilty, and sentenced to a mitigated term of incarceration for ten years; but strenuous efforts on his behalf secured a pardon later. In 1906 he was entirely exonerated and reinstated in the army, with the rank of Major, and made a Chevalier of the Legion of Honour.

**Drinkwater, John** (1882–1937), was a well-known dramatist and poet. His plays *Abraham Lincoln* and *Oliver Cromwell* have had great praise and success.

**Driver, Samuel Rolles** (1846–1914) a distinguished Hebrew and Old Testament scholar who was Regius Prof. of Hebrew at Oxford, 1883–1914.

**Drummond, William** (1585–1649), a Scottish poet —laird of Hawthornden—whose works dealt largely with political matters, but revealed considerable poetic power. Ben Jonson walked from London to Scotland to pay him his respects.

**Drury, (Edward) Alfred (Briscoe)**, R.A. (1857–1944), English sculptor, responsible for many public monuments, including the colossal statues of Queen Victoria at Bradford and Portsmouth (1903), the decorations for the exterior of the War Office (1905) and of the Victoria and Albert Museum (1909).

**Dryden, John** (1631–1700), one of the most vigorous and prolific of English poets and writers, and a popular dramatist. He excelled in satire, and drew some powerful pictures of the statesmen of his day. His translation of Virgil ranks with Pope's translation of the *Iliad*. He was buried in Westminster Abbey. Originally a Parliamentarian he went over to the Royalists and was laureate and historiographer-royal, 1670–88.

**Du Barry, Marie Jeanne Bécu, Comtesse** (1746–1793), succeeded Mme de Pompadour as mistress of Louis XV of France. Guillotined by the Revolutionary Tribunal.

**Du Chaillu, Paul Belloni** (1835–1903), a noted African traveller who was chief of General Gordon's staff in 1874, and wrote many valuable books of travels, his studies of the gorilla being especially interesting.

**Dufferin and Ava, 1st Marquess of**, P.C., K.P., G.C.B., G.C.S.I., G.C.M.G., G.C.I.E., F.R.S. (1826–1902), was a diplomatist of great experience, a writer of brilliance, and filled many high offices with distinction and success, including those of Governor-General of Canada and Viceroy of India.

Dulles, John Foster, (1888–1959), U.S. Secretary of State in the Republican Administration, 1953–59. In his foreign policy he encountered widespread criticism for his inflexible opposition to negotiation with Russia and U.S. recognition of China.

Dumas, Alexandre (1802–1870), French novelist and dramatist, who published more volumes than any man of his time. In the field of historical romance he showed wonderful power and resource and his thrilling story *Monte Cristo* is one of the great novels of the nineteenth century. He also wrote *The Three Musketeers.*

Dumas, Alexandre, Fils (1824–1895), French dramatist and novelist, son of the last-named, author of *La Dame aux Camélias.*

Du Maurier, George Louis Palmella Busson (1834–1896), one of the best known of the *Punch* artists during a long period and author of the novels of *Peter Ibbetson, Trilby,* and *The Martian.*

Dundee, John Graham of Claverhouse, 1st Viscount (1648–89), known as "Bonnie Dundee," royalist leader employed in the suppression of the Covenanters, taking part in the defeat at Drumclog and the victory of Bothwell Brig under the Duke of Monmouth in 1679. Defeated Mackay in the pass of Killiecrankie but was killed in the moment of victory.

Duns Scotus, John (c. 1265–c. 1308), famous scholastic, born at Maxton, in the county of Roxburgh; joined the Franciscan Order at Dumfries in 1281; ordained priest at Lincoln in 1291; student and teacher at Oxford and Paris; died at Cologne. He was the great doctrinal opponent of Thomas Aquinas and has been named the Subtle Doctor.

Dunstable, John (c. 1380–1453), the earliest great English composer known by name. He was a contemporary of the Netherlands composers Dufay and Binchois. *See Section E.*

Dunstan, Saint (909–988), the famous Abbot of Glastonbury and Archbishop of Canterbury, who lived through seven reigns from Ethelstan to Ethelred and exercised great political influence.

Dupleix, Joseph François (1697–1763), was governor of the French East Indian possessions at the time when Clive was guiding the fortunes of the East India Company, and after Clive's victory at Plassey Dupleix's day was over. He returned to France, and fell into disgrace and poverty.

Dürer, Albrecht (1471–1528), the great German painter and engraver of Nuremberg, friend of Luther and Melancthon. Like his great Italian contemporary, Leonardo, he was not only a superb artist but a man of boundless intellectual curiosity and scientific insight, a true son of the Renaissance. His copper engravings include his three great masterpieces, *The Knight, Melancholia,* and *St. Jerome in His Study.* Many of his engravings are in the British Museum. He may be regarded as the founder of the German school and the inventor of etching.

Durham, John George Lambton, Earl of (1792–1840), served as Governor-General of Canada after the disturbances of 1837, and in 1839 presented the famous *Durham Report* to Parliament. This laid down the principle of colonial self-government and marks a turning-point in the affairs of the Empire.

Duse, Elenora (1861–1924), an Italian tragedienne of world-wide reputation.

Duval, Claude (1643–1670), a notorious highwayman who, coming to England from Normandy in the Duchess of Richmond's service, took to "the road," and for a few years successfully evaded capture. He was hanged at Tyburn.

Duveen, 1st and only Baron, of Millbank (1869–1939), was head of a firm of noted art dealers, and a generous benefactor to British Art.

Dvořák, Antonin (1844–1904), Czech composer whose music is rich in the folk-song melodies of his native Bohemia and has a characteristic lilt and harmony. In 1884 he conducted his *Stabat Mater* in London, where this cantata and his *Slavonic Dances* were very popular. Composed his *From the New World* symphony in New York where he was head of the National Conservatoire (1892–94). He wrote 9 symphonies besides much orchestral and chamber work. *See Section E.*

Dyson, Sir Frank (Watson), K.B.E., F.R.S. (1868–1939), Astronomer Royal (1910–33). Was previously (1905–10) Astronomer Royal for Scot-

land. Was the author of a number of works on astronomy, and widely celebrated for his interesting public lectures.

Dyson, Sir George, K.C.V.O., M.A., Mus.D., LL.D., F.R.C.M. (1883–1964), Director of the Royal College of Music 1938–53. Author of *The New Music,* in which he analyses the technique of modern schools of composition. Composed a symphony, a violin concerto, and several choral works such as *The Canterbury Pilgrims* and *Nebuchadnezzar.*

# E

Eastlake, Sir Charles Lock (1793–1865), English painter of historical and religious works. Pres. of R.A. 1850.

Eastman, George (1854–1932), American inventor who invented the roll photographic film and the famous Kodak camera. He amassed a vast fortune and his philanthropies were estimated at over £60 million. After a long illness he committed suicide.

Eck, Johann von (1486–1543), one of the most vigorous opponents of the Reformation in Germany.

Eddington, Sir Arthur Stanley, O.M., F.R.S. (1882–1944), Plumian Professor of Astronomy, Cambridge, 1913; Director of the Cambridge Observatory, 1914–44. Author of *The Nature of the Physical World* (1928) and many scientific works.

Eddy, Mrs. Mary Baker (1821–1910), founder of the religion (theology and practice) which she named Christian Science, and of the Church of Christ, Scientist. Author of the Christian Science textbook, *Science and Health with Key to the Scriptures,* published in 1875. *See also J9.*

Edelinck, Gerard (1640–1707), French engraver, b. in Antwerp, the first to reproduce in print the colour, as well as the form, of a picture. Patronized by Louis XIV.

Eden, (Robert) Anthony, 1st Earl of Avon, K.G., M.C., (b. 1897), succeeded Sir Winston Churchill as Prime Minister in April 1955. He had been Deputy Prime Minister and Foreign Secretary since 1951. First appointed Foreign Secretary in 1935 (the youngest to hold that office for over a century), but resigned in 1938 on a difference of policy with Mr. Neville Chamberlain about relations with Italy. Entered Parliament as a member for Leamington in 1923. He has many diplomatic achievements to his credit, though his Suez policy in 1956 divided the country. Resigned because of ill-health in Jan. 1957. Memoirs, *Facing the Dictators; The Reckoning;* and *Full Circle.* Earldom conferred 1961.

Edgar (943–75), King of England 959–75, who under the influence of Dunstan was able to carry out many useful reforms.

Edgar Atheling (c. 1060–c. 1130), as grandson of Edmund Ironside, was the lawful heir of Edward the Confessor, but in the confusion of the Norman invasion he was unable to maintain his claim.

Edgeworth, Maria (1767–1849), Irish novelist, whose stories included *Castle Rackrent, The Absentee,* and *Belinda.*

Edinburgh, H.R.H. Prince Philip, Duke of, K.G., P.C., K.T., G.B.E. (b. 1921), consort of H.M. Queen Elizabeth II. Relinquished his title of Prince Philip of Greece and of Denmark on his naturalisation in 1947, taking the name of Mountbatten. He is the great-great-grandson of Queen Victoria, grandson of Admiral Prince Louis of Battenberg, and nephew of Earl Mountbatten of Burma. Educated in England and Germany and at the Royal Naval College. Served in the Royal Navy throughout the war. Pres. of the National Playing Fields Association; Pres. of the British Association, 1951–52. Chanc. Univs. Wales, Edinburgh and Salford.

Edison, Thomas Alva (1847–1931), an American inventor, who after an adventurous boyhood became a telegraph operator and interested in electrical problems. Established himself in New York in 1869, and invented an improved printing telegraph. In 1867 set up an elaborate laboratory and factory at Menlo Park, New Jersey, from which place he sent out many clever and some startling inventions, including a system of duplex telegraphy, afterwards improved into quadruplex and sextuplex transmission, the phonograph, and a method of preparing carbon filaments for the electric lamp; patented over 1300 inventions.

Edmund II. (Ironside) (980–1016), the son of Ethelred, after years of contention with the Danes, made a compact with Canute to divide England between them, but dying shortly afterwards the kingdom was settled on Canute.

Edward the Confessor (c. 1004–1066), the Anglo-Saxon king who immediately preceded—save for the brief reign of Harold of less than a year—the Norman Conquest, and founded Westminster Abbey, where a smaller church, then dilapidated, had previously for a period had a precarious existence. He was a religious-minded mystic, and was canonised in 1161, and given the shrine in the Abbey of his origination, which yet remains fairly intact, despite the ravages of time and disturbing hands.

Edward the Elder was the son of Alfred, and succeeded him as King of the West Saxons in 899. He was successful in overcoming the Danes, and became overlord of the Northern counties.

Edward the Martyr (963–979) became king in succession to Edgar, but, although supported by Dunstan, was not able to prevail against his stepmother Elfrida, who had him murdered.

Edward I. (1239–1307) was king of England from 1272 to 1307. Took part in the Crusades, completed the conquest of Wales, overcame Scottish opposition—executing Wallace and receiving the submission of Bruce, and promulgated many wise laws. He was nicknamed " Longshanks."

Edward II. (1284–1327), the son of Edward I. succeeded his father when the latter died at Burgh-over-Sands in 1307. Suffered defeat at the hands of the Scots at Bannockburn, and on account of his arbitrary disposition, cruelty and lavish concessions to favourites, was deposed in 1327, and afterwards murdered at Berkeley Castle.

Edward III. (1312–1377) was one of the ablest of English monarchs who, although much taken up with long and bitter wars with France and Scotland, did much for the commercial interests of the nation, and was the means of introducing large numbers of Flemings into the country, who laid the foundation of the English textile manufacturers. He married Philippa of Hainault, and was the father of Edward the Black Prince.

Edward IV. (1442–1483) Yorkist leader whose reign brought about a revival in the power of the monarchy, in English sea power, and in foreign trade. Spent 1470–71 in exile. He died of dissolute living after having made a fortune in trade. Patron of Caxton. Began rebuilding of St. George's Chapel, Windsor.

Edward V. (1470–1483)—elder son of Edward IV. and Elizabeth Woodville. Succeeding his father at the age of 12, he was a pawn in the quarrels of his maternal relatives and his paternal uncle, Richard, Duke of Gloucester. He and his younger brother, Richard, Duke of York, were shut up in the Tower by Richard, declared bastards, and there probably murdered, though conclusive proof of their exact fate has never been established. Thus Richard, who had had himself made Protector, became the legitimate heir to the Crown.

Edward VI. (1537–1553), succeeded his father, Henry VIII., when in his tenth year and died in his sixteenth year. The Reformation under the Regency of Somerset first, and then of Northumberland, made considerable progress during his brief reign. He was induced during his last illness to name Lady Jane Grey his successor, with results disastrous to that unfortunate personage and many others concerned.

Edward VII. (1841–1910). Was married to Princess Alexandra of Denmark in 1863. Visited India in 1875, and from that time onward was constantly in the public eye, taking part in all kinds of functions. Succeeded to the throne on the death of Queen Victoria, Jan. 22, 1901. The Coronation, which had been planned for June 26, 1902, had to be postponed in consequence of the King's sudden illness, but eventually took place on August 9 in the same year. His Majesty was a powerful factor in the preservation of the peace of Europe, his friendly intercourse with the heads of the French, Ger-man, and other nations earning for him the title of " Edward the Peacemaker."

Edward VIII. (b. 1894), succeeded to the throne on the death of his father, George V., Jan. 20, 1936; Prince of Wales 1911–36. Abdicated in favour of his brother H.R.H. the Duke of York Dec. 10, 1936, and was created Duke of Windsor. Governor of the Bahamas 1940–45.

Edwin (585–633), King of Northumbria, killed in battle at Hatfield Chase, Yorkshire, in 633. He was baptised into the Christian faith at York in 627, and built a church there.

Egbert was a descendant of Cerdic, king of the West Saxons, and reigned from 802 to 839 in Wessex; in his later years became the first king of all England. In 835 he had to drive the Northmen away from Cornwall.

Ehrlich, Paul (1854–1915), a noted German scientist who was Director of the Royal Institute for Experimental Therapeutics at Frankfurt-on-Main, which he made famous by his experimental laboratory work in connection with cancer. His prolonged experimental researches brought him world-wide renown, his greatest triumphs being the discovery of salvarsan and neo-salvarsan. He received the Nobel Prize in 1908.

Eiffel, Alexandre Gustave (1832–1923), French engineer, one of the first to employ compressed-air caissons in bridge building. Among his notable works are the great Eiffel Tower, Paris (1887–89) and the Panama Canal Locks.

Einstein, Albert (1879–1955), one of the greatest men of science of all time, whose chief claim to fame rests upon his theories of relativity. He was born in Ulm of Jewish parents and lived for many years in Switzerland. Awarded the Nobel Prize in 1921 for his work in quantum theory. In 1933 he was driven by the Nazis to seek asylum in America and became a professor at the Institute for Advanced Study at Princeton, 1933–45. His works include *Relativity* (1920), *Zur Einheitlichen Feldtheorie* (1929), *About Zionism* (1930), *The Evolution of Physics* (1938), *The Meaning of Relativity* (1950).

Eisenhower, Gen.Dwight David,G.C.B.,O.M.(1890–1969), Republican President of the United States, 1953–61. Supreme Commander Atlantic Forces in Europe 1950–52. U.S. Chief of Staff, 1945–48. C.-in-C. Allied Forces, European theatre of operations, 1943–45, and Allied Forces, N. Africa, 1942–43. Pres. Columbia Univ., 1948–50.

Eisenstein, Sergei Mikhailovich (1898–1948), Russian film director, whose silent film classic *The Battleship Potemkin* brought him world-wide fame. He also produced *Alexander Nevsky* and *Ivan the Terrible.*

Eleanor, Queen of Edward I. (d. 1290), was a woman of great piety and devotion. After her death the king had memorial crosses erected at the twelve places where her body rested on its way from Grantham to Westminster.

Elgar, Sir Edward, Bart., O.M., G.C.V.O. (1857–1934), English composer and Master of the King's Musick, 1924–34. Starting as a violinist and a teacher, he composed many choral-orchestral works for various festivals and sprang to fame with the *Enigma Variations*, musical portraits of his friends. Other compositions include the oratorios, *The Kingdom*, *The Apostles* and *The Dream of Gerontius* and the tone-poem *Falstaff*. *See Section E.*

Elgin, Thomas Bruce, 7th Earl of, P.C. (1766–1841), a British diplomatist who brought to England from Athens the famous " Elgin marbles," now in the British Museum.

Eliot, George (1819–1880), the pen name of Marian Evans, who produced some of the most memorable novels of the 19th century, including *Adam Bede*, *The Mill on the Floss*, *Silas Marner*, *Middlemarch* and *Daniel Deronda.*

Eliot, Thomas Stearns, O.M. (1888–1965), poet and critic, one of the foremost literary figures of the 20th century. He was born in St. Louis, Missouri, came to London during the First World War, and became a British subject in 1927. His poems include *Prufrock and Other Observations*, *The Waste Land*, *The Hollow Men*, *Ash Wednesday*, *Four Quartets*, his verse dramas *Murder in the Cathedral*, and *The Family Reunion*. He described himself as " classicist in literature, royalist in politics, and

Anglo-Catholic in religion." Awarded 1948 Nobel Prize for Literature. *See* Sections I and M.

**Elizabeth** (b. 1900), Queen Consort of George VI., daughter of the 14th Earl of Strathmore. Before her marriage in 1923 she was Lady Elizabeth Angela Marguerite Bowes-Lyon. Chancellor, Univ. of London, Univ. of Dundee.

**Elizabeth I.** (1533–1603) came to the throne in 1558 at the age of twenty-five, and reigned forty-five years. Was a fervid Protestant, a sincere lover of her country, a masterful and enlightened ruler—fickle as far as her favourites were concerned—and added distinction to a distinguished period. The defeat of the Spanish Armada, the execution of Mary Stuart, the naval supremacy of England, the extension of her colonies, and the glory of a great new literature of which Shakespeare was the brightest ornament are features associated with her reign.

**Elizabeth II.** (Elizabeth Alexandra Mary of Windsor) (b. 1926), ascended the throne in February 1952 at the age of twenty-five on the death of her father George VI. Her Consort, Prince Philip, Duke of Edinburgh, is the son of Prince Andrew of Greece and a descendant of the Danish royal family. They have four children, Charles, Prince of Wales (b. 1948), Princess Anne (b. 1950), Prince Andrew. (b. 1960), and Prince Edward (b. 1964).

**Ellis, (Henry) Havelock** (1859–1939), literary and scientific writer and an authority on sex.

**Emerson, Ralph Waldo** (1803–1882), the American essayist and philosopher. His *Conduct of Life, Representative Men*, and *Essays*, are among the most brilliant literary productions of America.

**Emin Pasha**, the name adopted by Eduard Schnitzer (1840–92), a German explorer associated with Gen. Charles Gordon in the pacification of the Sudan. He joined Gordon's forces as a medical officer and showing marked administrative ability was made governor of the Equatorial Province in 1878. He was menaced by the Mahdi and rescued by Stanley in 1889. While engaged in exploration for Germany in the region of Lake Tanganyika he was murdered by Arabs.

**Emmet, Robert** (1778–1803), the enthusiastic youth who led the rebellion in Ireland in 1803 and was tried and executed in the same year for high treason. He is one of Ireland's patriot heroes.

**Empedocles** (c. 500–c. 430 B.C.), Greek philosopher, b. Agrigentum in Sicily, founder of a school of medicine which regarded the heart as the seat of life, an idea which passed to Aristotle, as did his idea that all matter was composed of four elements: earth, air, fire, and water. He was also a poet.

**Engels, Friedrich** (1820–1895), Socialist writer and lifelong friend of Karl Marx with whom he collaborated in producing the Communist Manifesto of 1848. *See also* Marxism, J27.

**Epictetus of Hierapolis**, the Stoic philosopher, who lived in the 1st century, and was a moral teacher of great repute and influence.

**Epicurus** (342–270 B.C.), the founder of the Epicurean philosophy, which taught that virtue should be followed because it leads to happiness.

**Epstein, Sir Jacob**, K.B.E. (1880–1959), sculptor, born in New York of Russian-Polish parents. His work includes *Rima*, the Hudson memorial in Hyde Park; *Day* and *Night* on the building of the Underground Headquarters at St. James' Park; *Genesis*, exhibited in 1931; *Lazarus*, which has a fine setting in New College, Oxford; the *Madonna and Child* group for the restored 18th cent. buildings in Cavendish Square; the figure of *Christ in Majesty*, cast in aluminium, in Llandaff Cathedral; a monumental sculpture for the T.U.C. headquarters in London, and a bronze group depicting St. Michael triumphing over the Devil for Coventry Cathedral, his last major work.

**Erasmus Desiderius** (1466–1536), the great Dutch philosopher and scholar, of whom it was said that he " laid the egg which Luther hatched."

**Erhard, Dr. Ludwig** (b. 1897), German economist and politician; succeeded Adenauer as Chanc. of the West German Federal Republic, 1963–7.

**Ericsson, John** (1803–1889), Swedish engineer who entered into competition with George Stephenson in the first famous trial of locomotives.

**Ervine, St. John Greer** (b. 1883), author, dramatist and critic, noted as an able controversialist.

**Essex, Robert Devereux, 2nd Earl of** (1566–1601), the favourite of Queen Elizabeth in her old age, son of Walter Devereux (1541–76) and stepson of Leicester. Proved an incapable governor-general of Ireland, returning to England against the Queen's express wish. He was imprisoned and executed for organising a rebellion in London.

**Ethelbert, King of Kent** at the close of the 6th century and commencement of the 7th. Famous for having accepted Christianity on the entreaty of St. Augustine. Published the first code of written laws in English. Canonised later.

**Ethelred II.** (c. 968–1016), became king of England on the murder of his half-brother, Edward the Martyr (978). He was an incompetent ruler and unable to organise resistance against the Danish raids. Called " the Unready " (from Old Eng. uræd = without counsel).

**Ethelwulf** was the Anglo-Saxon sovereign who succeeded his father Egbert in 837. Died in 857. and was buried at Winchester.

**Etty, William** (1787–1848), a famous English R.A., who contributed to the Royal Academy some of its most admired pictures between 1820 and 1849.

**Eucken, Rudolf Christoph** (1846–1926), a famous German philosopher and theologian.

**Euclid** (c. 330–c. 260 B.C.), illustrious Greek mathematician whose *Elements of Geometry* remained a standard text-book until the present century.

**Euler, Leonhard** (1707–83), Swiss mathematician, regarded as the founder of pure mathematics. He was called by Catherine I. to St. Petersburg, where he became Professor, 1730–41.

**Euripides** (480–406 B.C.), the greatest of Greek tragic poets. He wrote 92 plays, 18 of which have been preserved, the most famous being *Alcestis, Medea, Iphigenia*, and *Orestes*.

**Eusebius** (264–340), an ecclesiastical historian whose *Chronicon* is a history of the world down to his own time, while his *Ecclesiastical History* traces the chief events of the Christian Church.

**Evans, Sir Arthur John** (1851–1941), distinguished archæologist, chiefly famed for his excavations at Knossos in Crete and his discovery of the pre-Phœnician script.

**Evans, Dame Edith Mary**, D.B.E. (b. 1888), the versatile and brilliant English actress who made her first appearance as Cressida in *Troilus and Cressida* in 1912. She has played many leading roles and has also appeared in films.

**Evatt, Rt. Hon. Herbert Vere**, M.A., LL.D. (1894–1965), Australian lawyer and politician; Min. for External Affairs 1941–49; leader of the Federal Labour opposition, 1951–60; Chief Justice, New South Wales, 1960–2.

**Evelyn, John** (1620–1706), was one of the founders of the Royal Society and wrote several scientific works, but is best remembered for his *Diary* which covers the period 1640–1706.

**Eyck, Hubert van** (c. 1366–1426), and **Eyck, Jan van** (c. 1386–1440), two of the greatest masters of the early Flemish School of Painters.

# F

**Fabius Maximus (Cunctator)** (d. 203 B.C.), the Roman Consul and Dictator, saved Rome from conquest by Hannibal by deliberate and well-planned strategic evasion of battle. The term " Fabian Policy " is derived from Fabian's tactics.

**Fabre, Jean Henri Casimir** (1823–1915), French naturalist whose lifelong interest was the study of the habits of insects and whose observations were delightfully recorded in his *Souvenirs entomologiques*, a work of many volumes.

**Faed, Thomas**, R.A. (1826–1900), one of the most successful of Victorian painters, won a great reputation for his Scottish subjects.

**Fahrenheit, Gabriel Daniel** (1686–1736), German physicist, born in Danzig, improved construction of thermometers, notably in using quicksilver for alcohol. Devised the scale with freezing-point at 32° boiling-point at 212°.

**Fairbairn, Sir William, 1st Bt.**, F.R.S. (1789–1874), mechanical engineer and inventor. By the first utilisation of iron in shipbuilding, became eminent and wealthy.

**Fairfax, Thomas, 3rd Lord** (1612–1671), a promi-

**nent** leader of the Parliamentary army during the Civil War, who greatly distinguished himself at Marston Moor and Naseby.

**Falla, Manuel** (1876–1946), Spanish composer whose music is highly individual with a strong folk-song element. His compositions include operas, ballets (*The Three-Cornered Hat* was one of Diaghilev's greatest successes), piano music, pieces for piano and orchestra, songs, harpsichord concerto, and guitar solo in memory of his friend Debussy. *See* Section E.

**Faraday, Michael, F.R.S.** (1791–1867), great experimental physicist, founder of the science of electromagnetism. He was the son of a Yorkshire blacksmith and at 13 became apprenticed to a bookseller in London. In 1813 he became laboratory assistant to Sir Humphry Davy at the Royal Institution, becoming professor of chemistry there in 1833. He was one of the world's most brilliant experimenters and set himself the problem of finding the connections between the forces of light, heat, electricity, and magnetism. The epoch-making discoveries he made form the basis of the modern electrical industry. He lectured superbly well and inaugurated the Christmas lectures for juvenile audiences at the Royal Institution. Standard biography by L. Pearce Williams (1965).

**Farman, Henri** (1874–1958), French aviator, one of the pioneers of aviation and a famous designer and builder of aeroplanes.

**Farouk I** (1920–65), King of Egypt, 1936–52. Forced to abdicate as a result of a military *coup d'état* in July 1952.

**Farrar, Very Rev. Frederic William, D.D., F.R.S.** (1831–1903), Dean of Canterbury, 1895–1903; a divine and author, some of whose writings attained a large circulation and exercised a considerable influence. His most popular publications were *The Life of Christ*, *The Life and Works of St. Paul*, and *Early Days of Christianity*. Author of the schoolboy story *Eric*.

**Faulkner, William** (1897–1962), American novelist, recognised as one of the great writers of the century, whose series of novels *The Sound and the Fury*, *As I Lay Dying*, *Light in August*, *Sanctuary* (which brought a Nobel Prize) give a vivid picture of the American South. *See* Contemporary Novel, Section M.

**Fauré, Gabriel Urbain** (1845–1924), French composer and teacher; pupil of Saint-Saëns. He was much revered by his pupils at the Paris Conservatoire, among whom was Ravel. His works include chamber music, nocturnes and barcarolles for piano, an opera, *Pénélope*, some exquisite songs, and *Requiem*. *See* Section E.

**Fawcett, Rt. Hon. Henry** (1833–84), blind Liberal statesman and economist; Prof. of Political Economy at Cambridge. Author of *Manual of Political Economy* (1863).

**Fawcett, Dame Millicent Garrett, G.B.E.** (1847–1929), widow of the above; educational reformer and leader of the movement for women's suffrage; a very able writer on political economy and one of the founders of Newnham College, Cambridge.

**Fawkes, Guy** (1570–1606), a Yorkshire Catholic, who with Catesby and other conspirators planned the Gunpowder Plot. Although warned of the discovery of the plot, Fawkes persisted and was captured in the cellar of the Parliament House and hanged. (*See* Gunpowder Plot, General Information section.)

**Fénelon, François de Salignac de la Mothe** (1651–1715), Archbishop of Cambrai and a writer of distinction. His *Telemachus* is a French classic.

**Ferdinand V.** of Aragon (1452–1516), who married Isabella of Castile, and with her reigned over Spain during a period of great events. He saw the Moors expelled from Spain, equipped Columbus for the discoveries which led to Spain's vast colonial possessions, and instituted the Inquisition.

**Ferguson, James, F.R.S.** (1710–1776), a Banffshire man of great ability and inventiveness, who, from being a shepherd-boy, educated himself in astronomy, mathematics, and portrait painting, so that he was able to support his parents, and became eminent as a scientific lecturer. He was made a Fellow of the Royal Society.

**Fermi, Enrico** (1901–54), Italian nuclear physicist whose research contributed to the harnessing of atomic energy and the development of the atomic bomb. Prof. of Physics at Rome, Columbia Univ., New York, and Univ. of Chicago. He postulated the existence of the neutrino and discovered the element Neptunium. Awarded the 1938 Nobel Prize in Physics.

**Festing, Field Marshal Sir Francis Wogan, G.C.B., K.B.E., D.S.O.** (b. 1902), Chief of Imperial General Staff, 1958–61. During the war he commanded the 36th Division in Burma; known to his troops as the "front line general."

**Feuchtwanger, Dr. Lion** (1884–1958), German-Jewish author famous for his historical novels, such as *Jew Süss* and *'Tis Folly to be Wise*.

**Fichte, Johann Gottlieb** (1762–1814); was Professor of Philosophy, first at Jena and then at Erlangen, and later Rector of the University of Berlin. His works had great influence upon the thought of his time and prepared the way for the later Hegelian dialectic.

**Field, John** (1782–1837), composer and pianist, born in Dublin; pupil of Clementi and teacher of Glinka. At early age travelled Europe as virtuoso pianist. Composed seven concertos, three sonatas, and numerous piano pieces. Chopin's nocturnes were modelled on those of Field. The later part of his life was spent in Moscow, where he died.

**Fielding, Henry** (1707–1754), a celebrated English novelist, author of *Tom Jones*, *Joseph Andrews*, and *Amelia*, as well as many plays.

**Fields, Gracie, C.B.E.** (b. 1898), an inimitable Lancashire comedienne, and a great popular favourite with the British public. Made her first London appearance in 1915. Equally successful on the films as on the stage, she gained the affections of her music hall audiences through her abundant vitality, her Lancashire humour and her remarkably flexible voice.

**Fildes, Sir Luke, K.C.V.O., R.A.** (1844–1927), first attracted notice as a black-and-white artist, and illustrated Dickens' *Edwin Drood*. Exhibited at the Royal Academy in 1872, and at successive exhibitions was represented by many important works.

**Finsen, Prof. Niels Ryberg** (1860–1904), a Danish physician whose light-ray treatment of *lupus vulgaris* won the approval of Queen Alexandra and the aid of many philanthropists. He established in Copenhagen an institute for light therapy. Inventor of the Finsen ultra-violet lamp. Awarded 1903 Nobel Prize for Medicine.

**Firdousi,** *nom de plume* of Abdul Kasim Mansur (c. 930–1020), Persian poet whose great epic *Shahnama*, or *Book of Kings*, relates the history of Persia in 60,000 verses.

**Fisher of Lambeth, Baron** (Most Rev. Geoffrey Francis) P.C., G.C.V.O., M.A., Hon. D.D. (b. 1887). Archbishop of Canterbury, 1945–61, the 99th holder of the office; Bishop of London, 1939–45; Bishop of Chester, 1932–39; Headmaster Repton School, 1914–32.

**Fisher, Rt. Hon. Herbert Albert Laurens, O.M., F.R.S.** (1865–1940), English historian and educational reformer; author of *A History of Europe*.

**Fisher, Professor Sir Ronald Aylmer, Sc.D., F.R.S.** (1890–1962), one of the greatest of British scientists who revolutionised both genetics and the philosophy of experimentation by founding the modern corpus of mathematical statistics.

**FitzGerald, Edward** (1809–1883). English poet who gained world-wide fame by his translation of the *Rubaiyát* of Omar Khayyam (1859).

**Fitzroy, Vice-Admiral Robert, F.R.S.** (1805–1865). Attained celebrity as a meteorologist, and in 1854 was made superintendent of the Meteorological Department, and was the introducer of the system of storm warnings which were the beginning of weather forecasts.

**Flammarion, Camille** (1842–1925), French astronomer, famous for his observations on double stars, star-drift and popular lectures and books on astronomy. Founded the Astronomical Society of France in 1887. His best-known work is *L'Astronomie Populaire*.

**Flamsteed, John, F.R.S.** (1646–1719), was the first English Astronomer Royal, and a close friend of Sir Isaac Newton, whom he aided in many of his experiments.

**Flaubert, Gustave** (1821–80), one of the greatest of French novelists and creator of *Madame Bovary* which took five years to write. His perfection of style was attained only through unremitting effort. Other works were *Salammbo*, *L'Education sentimentale* and *Bouvard et Pécuchet*.

**Flaxman, John** R.A., (1755–1826), a great English sculptor who was born at York, and at 20 was employed as modeller by Josiah Wedgwood. In 1787 he went to Rome, where he stayed 7 years. In 1800 he was elected R.A. and in 1810 became professor of sculpture to the Royal Academy.

**Flecker, James Elroy** (1884–1915), English poet whose works include *Golden Journey to Samarkand*, *Hassan* (staged in London, 1923) and *Don Juan*, as well as many lyrics.

**Fleming, Sir Alexander,** F.R.S. (1881–1955), as a bacteriologist he made many original contributions, including the discovery of the antibacterial enzyme lysozyme in 1922 and penicillin in 1928. Full recognition of his discovery came only during the war, when Florey separated the drug now used for treatment from the original penicillin. Awarded Nobel Prize for Medicine jointly with Florey and Chain, 1945.

**Fleming, Sir (John) Ambrose,** F.R.S. (1849–1945), British scientist whose invention of the radio valve in 1904 was destined not only to revolutionise radio telegraphy but also to solve the problems which had so far prevented the successful development of radio-telephony, and eventually to make possible the transmission of high-quality speech, music, and even vision signals, and thus lead to broadcasting and television.

**Fletcher, John** (1579–1625), the famous collaborator with Beaumont in numerous plays which were popular in their day and take high position in the dramatic literature of the country.

**Flinders, Matthew** (1774–1814), an explorer and navigator, who made important discoveries in and around Australia. He sailed through Bass Strait, so called in honour of his surgeon. Sir William Matthew Flinders Petrie (*q.v.*), the archaeologist was his grandson.

**Florey, Baron, Howard Walter,** O.M. (1898–1968), British pathologist, b. Australia; co-discoverer of penicillin. Shared 1945 Nobel Prize with Fleming and Chain. Pres. Royal Society, 1965.

**Foch, Marshal Ferdinand,** O.M. (1851–1929), Generalissimo commanding the Allied Forces in France from April 1918 until after the Armistice was signed, Nov. 11, 1918. Under his direction the great German offensive was checked and turned at the Marne in July 1918. He followed up this success with a series of rapid attacks culminating in the German surrender, Nov. 11, 1918, when he imposed the conditions of the Armistice.

**Fokine, Michel** (1880–1944), famous Russian dancer who became choreographer to Diaghilev's company. Creator of *Les Sylphides*, *Prince Igor*, *Scheherazade*, *Firebird*, and *The Spectre of the Rose*.

**Fokker, Anton Hermann Gerard** (1890–1939), Dutch (naturalised American) airman and aeronautical engineer, designer and builder of the well-known Fokker triplanes and biplanes employed by the German army.

**Fonteyn, Dame Margot** (Mme. Roberto de Arias), D.B.E. (b. 1919), Prima ballerina of the Royal Ballet (formerly Sadler's Wells Ballet) and acclaimed foremost English dancer of to-day.

**Ford, Henry** (1863–1947), founder of Ford Motor Co., 1903, of which he was President until 1919, when he was succeeded by his son, Edsel B. Ford (1893–1943). Henry Ford became the world's leading industrialist and its second richest man. Was the pioneer of the cheap motor-car, of which, since 1920, more than a million have been produced annually.

**Forester, Cecil Scott** (b. 1899), British novelist, author of the *Captain Hornblower* series.

**Forster, Edward Morgan,** O.M., C.H., LL.D., C.L. (b. 1879), English novelist whose novels *A Room with a View*, *Howards End*, *A Passage to India*, have given him great authority in the world of literature. *See also* Contemporary Novel, Section M.

**Foscari, Francesco** (*c.* 1372–1457), Doge of Venice from 1423 to 1457. A great historical character, who governed Venice with a firm hand and increased her renown.

**Fosdick, Rev. Harry Emerson** (b. 1878), American Baptist preacher. Professor of Theology, Union Theological Seminary, New York, and Pastor,

Riverside, formerly Park Avenue, Baptist Church, New York, 1926–46.

**Fourier, François Charles Marie** (1772–1837), the famous French socialist, who propounded a system of associated enterprise for giving everyone ample means on a system of communal industry. He made some attempts to carry out his Utopian ideas, but they did not succeed. He is best known by his *Traité de l'Association Domestique Agricole*.

**Fowler, Sir John,** Bart., K.C.M.G. (1817–1898), an eminent civil engineer, son of a Sheffield land surveyor. With Sir Benjamin Baker he was the engineer of the Forth Bridge and of the Metropolitan Railway.

**Fox, Rt. Hon. Charles James** (1749–1806) was the second son of the first Lord Holland. Entered Parliament at nineteen, and became a Lord of the Admiralty in 1770. His opposition to the Royal Marriage Bill drew down upon him the displeasure of George III. Through the whole of Pitt's Premiership he was that statesman's most formidable opponent. He favoured American Independence; opposed the war with France; was one of the impeachers of Warren Hastings; denounced the Slave Trade and advocated Parliamentary Reform. After the death of Pitt in 1806 he was made Foreign Secretary, but died a few months later, and was buried in Westminster Abbey.

**Fox, George** (1624–1691), was the founder of the Society of Friends.

**Foxe, John** (1516–1587), the English martyrologist, whose *Acts and Monuments* (*Book of Martyrs*) is one of the best-known books in the language. Born at Boston in Lincolnshire, he became a clergyman of the Anglican Church and died in London.

**Frampton, Sir George James,** R.A., F.S.A. (1860–1928). English sculptor, best remembered by his Peter Pan statue in Kensington Gardens, and the Edith Cavell Memorial in St. Martin's Place, London.

**France, Anatole** (Jacques Thibault) (1844–1924), one of France's notable writers of fiction, showing a great mastery of character portrayal and satire. Most of his works are translated into English.

**Francis I.** (1494–1547), King of France (1515–47). Recovered Milan from Swiss at Marignano (1515). Tried to gain support of Henry VIII (Field of the Cloth of Gold, 1520). Contested supremacy in Europe of Hapsburg emperor, Charles V; defeated and captured at Pavia (1525). French renaissance flourished during his reign.

**Francis of Assisi, Saint** (1181/82–1226), one of the great Christian saints, founder of the Franciscan Order. Son of a wealthy cloth-merchant of Assisi, he underwent a conversion in 1208 and turned from a life of pleasure to follow the life of the gospel, committing himself to poverty and to the complete observance of Christ's teaching. He and his friars went about preaching the gospel by word and example and the brotherhood increased rapidly in numbers. He received the stigmata (the marks of the five wounds of Christ) on Monte La Verna in Tuscany on 14 Sept. 1224. The last years were spent in illness; he was canonized by his friend Gregory IX two years after his death.

**Francis, Sir Philip,** K.B. (1740–1818), an English statesman, the reputed author of the famous *Letters of Junius*.

**Franck, César Auguste** (1822–90), composer and organist, born at Liége in Belgium. From 1872 until his death was professor of organ at the Paris Conservatoire. His music is romantic, mystical, and personal in idiom. Much of his finest composition is for the organ, and his *Symphonic Variations for Piano and Orchestra*, *Sonata for Violin* and the *Symphony in D* rank him, with his younger contemporary Debussy, among the great 19th-cent. musicians.

**Franco, General Francisco** (b. 1892), Spanish soldier and Dictator who served with the Spanish Forces in the Moroccan campaign of 1920–25 and was later Head of the Military Academy at Saragossa. Chief of the General Staff 1935–36. Was Commander-in-Chief of the Nationalist Forces during the Spanish Civil War, 1936–39. President of Spain since Aug. 1939.

**Franklin, Benjamin,** F.R.S. (1706–1790), the

famous American statesman and philosopher, who after serving an apprenticeship as a printer attracted public attention by publishing his *Poor Richard's Almanac*. He then began a series of scientific experiments, inventing among other things the lightning conductor. He was for ten years a member of the General Assembly; then lived in Britain as agent for his State for eighteen years; returning to America he took part in framing the Constitution of the United States.

**Franklin, Rear-Admiral Sir John**, F.R.S. (1786–1847), the famous Arctic explorer, whose final expedition in command of the *Erebus* and *Terror* ended disastrously, all the members of the expedition perishing. Many attempts were made to discover Franklin, but without obtaining anything save very fragmentary knowledge concerning his fate. He was born at Spilsby.

**Franks, Rt. Hon. Sir Oliver Shewell**, G.C.M.G., K.C.B., C.B.E., M.A. (b. 1905), British Ambassador to U.S.A. 1948–52; Provost of Worcester College, Oxford, 1962. Chanc. Univ. of East Anglia, 1965.

**Fraser of the North Cape, Admiral of the Fleet, Lord**, G.C.B., K.B.E. (b. 1888), commanded Home Fleet, Eastern Fleet, and British Pacific Fleet successively, 1943–46. First Sea Lord, 1948–51.

**Fraser of Lonsdale, Ian, Baron**, C.H., C.B.E. (b. 1897). Chair. St. Dunstan's since 1921; Pres. British Legion, 1947–58.

**Fraunhofer, Joseph von** (1787–1826), famous optical instrument maker of Munich, the first to map the dark lines of the solar spectrum named after him.

**Frazer, Sir James George**, O.M., LL.D., F.R.S. (1854–1941), was an eminent British anthropologist; author of *The Golden Bough* and numerous other works on his subject.

**Frederick I.** (c. 1123–90), Holy Roman emperor from 1152. Nicknamed Barbarossa. A commanding personality, he won for the empire prestige unknown since Otto the Great. Though failing to subjugate his Italian territories, for his armies suffered from the Italian climate, he dominated his German subjects, expelled the semi-independent Duke of Saxony, Henry the Lion, from his duchy, encouraged the German cities, and was a national hero. Though not an ascetic, he was remarkable for an impeccable private life, distinguished himself on the second Crusade, and was drowned in Asia Minor on his way to the third.

**Frederick II.** (1194–1250), Holy Roman Emperor, an enlightened ruler whose court in Sicily was a centre of culture and learning, attracting Jewish, Mohammedan, and Christian scholars. Forced by illness to return from crusade in 1227, he was excommunicated by Pope Gregory IX.; still excommunicated, he again set sail for Palestine and by skilful diplomacy gained possession of Jerusalem, Bethlehem, and Nazareth. Frederick was a philosopher and man of science and delighted in exploding superstition. He founded the university of Naples, was a patron of the medical school at Salerno, wrote a treatise on falconry, and gave Sicily a code of laws.

**Frederick II. or Frederick the Great** (1712–86), King of Prussia (1740–86). By his masterful government and military successes he raised Prussia to the rank of a great power. He was a scholarly potentate, composed music and played the flute.

**French, Field-Marshal Sir John.** (*See* Ypres, 1st Earl of.)

**Freud, Sigmund**, M.D. (1856–1939), psychiatrist and founder of psychoanalysis; b. Moravia, studied medicine in Vienna where he lived until 1938 when the Nazi invasion of Austria sent him into exile in London where he died. His theories of the mind, based on years of unremitting scientific investigation of individual cases, illuminated the way we think about ourselves, and had immense influence upon modern thought. *See* **Q7** for Unconscious Mechanisms.

**Freyberg, 1st Baron, Lieut.-Gen. Bernard Cyril**, V.C., G.C.M.G., K.C.B., K.B.E., D.S.O. (1889–1963), Gov.-Gen. of New Zealand, 1946–52. Served with distinction in both world wars.

**Friese-Greene, William** (1855–1921), inventor of the cinematograph. His pioneer work in commercial photography brought him no profit, and for many years he lived in poverty.

**Frobisher, Sir Martin** (1535–1594), was the earliest of British navigators to attempt to find the North-West passage from the Atlantic to the Pacific through the Arctic seas, and his name is commemorated in Frobisher's Strait, to the south of Baffin Land. For his services in connection with the defeat of the Spanish Armada he was knighted.

**Froebel, Friedrich Wilhelm August** (1782–1852), was the founder of the Kindergarten system of education, the object of which is "to give children employment in harmony with their nature, to strengthen their bodies, to exercise their senses and lead them up to the original ground of all life, to the idea of unity with themselves." *See also* **J14(2)**.

**Froissart, Jean** (1337–1410), a celebrated French writer who visited England and Scotland, and was the author of the famous *Chronicles*, which tell us so much of the achievements of the barons of old.

**Frost, Robert** (1874–1963), best loved of American poets. "Stopping by Woods on a Snowy Evening"; "Birches"; "The Death of the Hired Man"; "After Apple-Picking". Awarded Pulitzer Prize for poetry in 1924, 1931, 1937, and 1943.

**Froude, James Anthony** (1818–1894), the celebrated historian and biographer of Carlyle.

**Fry, Christopher** (b. 1907), English poet and dramatist of Quaker family. Author of *The Lady's Not for Burning, Venus Observed*, and *The Dark is Light Enough. See also* **Modern Drama.**

**Fry, Elizabeth** (1780–1845), a Norwich lady who devoted much of her life to the promotion of prison reform, and achieved considerable reputation as a preacher. She belonged to the Society of Friends.

**Fry, Roger** (1866–1934), English art critic and painter. Introduced the work of Cézanne and the post-impressionists into England. His most important book is *Vision and Design*. Biography by Virginia Woolf (1940).

**Fuchs, Sir Vivian Ernest**, M.A., Ph.D. (b. 1908), British geologist and explorer. Dir. of the Falkland Islands Dependencies Scientific Bureau since 1951; leader of the British Commonwealth Trans-Antarctic Expedition 1957–58, the first to cross the Antarctic continent.

**Fuller, Thomas** (1608–1661), the author of *Worthies of England* and a *Church History of Britain*, two well-known and valuable works.

**Fulton, Robert** (1765–1815), an inventive American engineer who distinguished himself by experiments in the application of steam to navigation, and finally in 1807, launched the *Clermont* on the Hudson.

**Furniss, Harry** (1854–1925), British caricaturist, was born in Wexford and came to London as a young man. He was a famous cartoonist and served on the staff of *Punch* from 1878–94. Illustrated the works of Dickens and Thackeray.

**Furtwängler, Wilhelm** (1886–1954), famous German conductor, and popular in Great Britain for his visits with the Berlin Philharmonic Orchestra, of which he succeeded Herr Nikisch as conductor.

# G

**Gade, Niels Vilhelm** (1817–90), Danish composer. While studying at Leipzig he met Mendelssohn, whom he succeeded as conductor of the Gewandhaus orchestra. He wrote eight symphonies, chamber music, and choral works. Though characteristically Scandinavian, his work shows the influence of German romanticism.

**Gagarin, Yuri Alexeyevich** (1934–68), Soviet airman who stirred the imagination of the world on 12 April 1961 by being the first man to be launched into space and brought safely back. His flight was made in the front portion of a Soviet multi-stage rocket which made a single circuit of the earth, the whole adventure taking 108 minutes. Killed in air crash.

**Gainsborough, Thomas**, R.A. (1727–1788), English landscape and portrait painter, whose works are remarkable for their grace and refinement. He was born in Sudbury in Suffolk, the youngest of nine children of a cloth-merchant.

**Gaiseric** or **Genseric** (c. 390–477), king of the Vandals, the ablest of the barbarian invaders of the Roman empire. He led his people from Spain into Africa, took Carthage, gained control of the Mediterranean by his pirate fleets, and sacked Rome in 455, thereby bringing about the fall of the western empire.

**Gaitskell, Rt. Hon. Hugh Todd Naylor, C.B.E.** (1906–63), statesman and economist; leader of the Labour Opposition, 1955–63; M.P. (Labour) for South Leeds, 1945–63. He was succeeded as leader of the Labour Party by Harold Wilson. See also Section C, Part I.

**Galdós, Benito Pérez** (1843–1920), considered greatest Spanish novelist since Cervantes; has been compared to Balzac for his close study and portrayal of all social classes and people. Most prolific writer. In 1873 commenced long series of historical novels (Episodias Nacionales), written in addition to some 30 novels of contemporary life and over 20 plays.

**Galen, Claudius** (A.D. 131–201), physician, b. Pergamum (Asia Minor) of Greek parents. He systematised medical knowledge in accordance with his idea of purposive creation by the will of God. This unscientific attitude, by discouraging original investigation, hampered medical progress for a thousand years. Many of his treatises still survive.

**Galileo** (1564–1642), great Italian scientist whose experimental-mathematical methods in the pursuit of scientific truth laid the foundations of modern science. He became professor of mathematics at Pisa university when he was 25 and lectured at Padua university for 18 years. He made a number of fundamental discoveries, e.g., in regard to the hydrostatic balance, thermometer, magnet, telescope, and foreshadowed Newton's laws of motion. He detected the four major satellites of Jupiter, the ring of Saturn, and the spots of the sun. He proved the superiority of the Copernican over the Ptolemaic theory, and was imprisoned for so doing. He died the year Newton was born.

**Galsworthy, John, O.M.** (1867–1933), an English novelist and dramatist of force and originality who wrote a great series of novels dealing with the history of an upper middle class family. Awarded Nobel Prize for Literature in 1932.

**Galton, Sir Francis, F.R.S.** (1822–1911), founder of eugenics, cousin of Darwin. His early work, Meteorographica (1863), contains the basis of the modern weather chart. He is also remembered for his device of finger-print identification and for being one of the first to apply mathematics to biological problems.

**Galvani, Luigi** (1737–1798), Italian physician and physiologist, whose experiments at Bologna university demonstrated the principle of animal electricity.

**Gama, Vasco da** (c. 1460–1524), the adventurous Portuguese navigator who discovered the sea route to India in 1498 by doubling the Cape of Good Hope.

**Gandhi, Indira** (b. 1917), daughter of Nehru, succeeded Shastri in 1966 to become India's first woman Prime Minister.

**Gandhi, Mohandas Karamchand** (1869–1948), great Indian patriot, social reformer, and moral teacher. Believed in the doctrine of non-violence. In the tense situation following the granting of independence to India, he strove to promote the co-operation of all Indians but was assassinated on his way to a prayer meeting.

**Garbo, Greta** (b. 1905), Swedish film actress. The most arresting and poetical actress on the screen of her day.

**Garcia, Manuel de Popolo Vicente** (1775–1832), Spanish tenor, composer, and singing master. His son Manuel Patricio Rodriguez (1805–1906) was tutor to many celebrities including Jenny Lind. Both his daughters (Mme Malibran and Mme Viardot) were celebrated operatic singers.

**Gardiner, Samuel Rawson** (1829–1902), an English historian, whose works deal mainly with the period from the accession of James I. to the end of the Commonwealth. Many of his books remain the standard authorities on their subjects.

**Garibaldi, Guiseppe** (1807–82), Italian soldier and patriot, who with Mazzini and Cavour created a united Italy. In 1834 he was condemned to death for participating in a republican plot

to seize Genoa but escaped to S. America. He returned in 1848 to fight for Mazzini but was again forced to flee. In 1851 he returned and gave his support to Cavour, taking part in the Austrian war of 1859. In 1860 with a thousand volunteers he freed Sicily, took Naples and handed over the Two Sicilies to Victor Emmanuel who was proclaimed King.

**Garrick, David** (1717–1779), the leading tragic actor of his time and a highly successful manager. Was buried in Westminster Abbey.

**Garrison, William Lloyd** (1805–1879), an eminent anti-slavery leader of America.

**Gaskell, Mrs. Elizabeth Cleghorn** (1810–1865), English novelist, author of Mary Barton, Ruth Cranford, and Life of Charlotte Brontë.

**Gaudi i Cornet, Antonio** (1852–1926), Spanish architect of great inventiveness, noted for the fantastic shape and decoration of his buildings which have many qualities in common with Art Nouveau (Spanish modernismo). He worked mainly in Barcelona.

**Gauguin, Paul** (1848–1903), influential French artist whose rejection of Western values led to his departure in 1891 for Tahiti where his greatest paintings were done.

**Gaulle, Charles André Joseph Marie de** (b. 1890), French general and statesman, chosen President of the Fifth Republic, Dec. 1958. On collapse of France in 1940 refused to surrender, but raised and led the Free French fighting forces, with headquarters in England. Took no part in parliamentary life from 1953 until June 1958, when a rebellion of colonists in Algeria brought him to supreme power. His system of government, based on personal prestige and skill in manoeuvre, has carried his country through many crises; the most serious were the army revolt in Algeria in April 1961, and the students' and workers' uprising of May 1968. Repulsed Britain's attempts to enter the Common Market. See also Section C.

**Gauss, Johann Karl Friedrich** (1777–1855), great German mathematician and astronomer. The unit of magnetic induction is named after him.

**Gautier, Théophile** (1811–1872), French critic, novelist, and poet, at one time secretary to Balzac. His romance, Mademoiselle de Maupin, caused a great sensation.

**Gay, John** (1685–1732), English poet and playwright, famous for The Beggar's Opera. He was a writer of great wit and fancy, and much patronised by Society.

**Gay-Lussac, Joseph Louis** (1778–1850), a French chemist, whose experiments with gases were of much scientific importance.

**Ged, William** (1690–1749), was one of the inventors of the process of stereotyping. He was a goldsmith and a native of Edinburgh.

**Geddes, Sir Patrick** (1854–1932), Scottish scientist, professor of biology at Dundee for 30 years and a pioneer in town and regional planning. Invented the term "conurbation".

**Geikie, Sir Archibald, O.M., K.C.B., F.R.S.** (1835–1924), noted geologist; President of the Royal Society 1908–13. His brother James Geikie (1839–1915) was a specialist in glacial geology.

**Geoffrey of Anjou, Duke of Brittany** (1113–51), founder of the Angevin dynasty of England, was son-in-law of Henry I. and father of Henry II., the first Angevin or Plantagenet king.

**Geoffrey of Monmouth** (1100–1154), was the author of the famous Old English chronicle which bears his name. He was born at Monmouth, and became Bishop of St. Asaph in 1152. His Chronicon is a compilation from older authors, and is notable for having contained the stories of King Arthur, King Lear, and Cymbeline.

**George I.** (1660–1727) was King of Great Britain from 1714 to his death, ascending the throne as direct descendant of James I. His reign saw many memorable events, including the Jacobite Rebellion, the South Sea Bubble, and the beginning of Walpole's great ministry.

**George II.** (1683–1760), son of the last-named, was King of Great Britain from 1727 to 1760. His reign covered a prosperous period in spite of wars and rebellions, and saw the Empire extended in India and North America, though he himself was a man of limited powers.

**George III.** (1738–1820), grandson of George II., reigned 1760–1820. In this period came the King's clash with John Wilkes over foreign policy, the loss of the American colonies, the prolonged war with France, England's agrarian and industrial revolutions, the spread of Methodism. In 1966 two British psychiatrists published convincing evidence that the King's long mental illness was due not to insanity but to acute intermittent porphyria, an inborn error of metabolism.

**George IV.** (1762–1830) eldest son of George III, reigned 1820–30, having become Prince Regent in 1812. The monarchy remained at a low ebb and was not to recover until after the accession of Victoria. Though styled " the first gentleman of Europe ", his personal conduct, especially in marital affairs, showed a want of dignity. But he is now remembered for his interest in art and architecture.

**George V.** (1865–1936), was the second son of Edward VII. and Queen Alexandra. Entered the Navy as a cadet in 1877 and became second in the line of succession to the throne on the death of the Duke of Clarence in 1892. Married to Princess Mary of Teck in 1893. Succeeded to the throne May 6th, 1910, and celebrated his Silver Jubilee in 1935. Maintained the royal tradition of strenuous public engagements combined with unfailing attention to business of State.

**George VI.** (1895–1952), (Albert Frederick Arthur George of Windsor), second son of George V., was called to the throne in December 1936 on the abdication of his elder brother, Edward VIII. His reign was marked by the ordeal of war, by world revolution and social change and at the same time by a remarkable degree of constitutional harmony which his fine example and personal qualities did much to achieve.

**George, Henry** (1839–1897), American political economist whose " single tax " on land values as a means of solving economic problems is expounded in his *Progress and Poverty*, pub. 1879.

**George, Saint,** the tutelary saint of England, adopted by Edward III. He is believed to have been a native of Cappadocia and a vigorous champion of Christianity in the days of Diocletian, and to have suffered martyrdom at Nicomedia 303 A.D. The dragon which he is said to have slain symbolises the powers of evil over which he triumphed.

**German, Sir Edward** (1862–1936), English composer, best known for his incidental music and light opera *Merrie England*. (His name was originally Edward German Jones.)

**Gershwin, George** (1898–1937), American jazz pianist and song-writer, composer of the famous *Rhapsody in Blue* and other works including the negro " folk-opera " *Porgy and Bess*.

**Gesner, Konrad von** (1516–1565), a scholarly Swiss naturalist, and father of the science of zoology.

**Ghiberti, Lorenzo** (1378–1455), Florentine sculptor whose bronze doors, beautifying the baptistery in Florence, were described by Michaelangelo as fit for the gates of paradise.

**Giacometti, Alberto** (1901–66), Swiss sculptor and painter. He settled in Paris in 1922 and is considered one of the most important artists of modern times.

**Gibbon, Edward** (1737–1794), celebrated historian of the *Decline and Fall of the Roman Empire*.

**Gibbons, Grinling** (1648–1720), the celebrated wood-carver and sculptor, was born at Rotterdam and was brought to the notice of Charles II. by Evelyn, the diarist. The choir stalls of St. Paul's and the carving in the Wren library at Trinity College, Cambridge, are his work.

**Gibbons, Orlando** (1583–1625), a noted English composer of Church music who was organist of the Chapel Royal.

**Gide, André Paul Guillaume** (1869–1951) French man of letters, novelist, dramatist and poet. Awarded the Nobel Prize for Literature in 1947.

**Gielgud, Sir (Arthur) John** (b. 1904), English actor, member of the Terry family. Began by walking on at the Old Vic, and, later, became a Shakespearian actor, making a marked success as Hamlet, Richard II., and Prospero.

**Gigli, Beniamino** (1890–1957), the great Italian operatic tenor of the Metropolitan Opera House New York. The possessor of a voice of great natural beauty, and one of the finest exponents of the music of Puccini and Verdi.

**Gilbert, Sir Alfred,** M.V.O., R.A., (1854–1934), sculptor and designer of gold and silver objects.

Among his best-known sculptures are *Perseus Arming, Icarus, Eros* in Piccadilly Circus, the Shaftesbury Memorial and the Duke of Clarence Memorial at Windsor.

**Gilbert, Sir Humphrey** (1539–1583), knighted by Queen Elizabeth for his bravery in Ireland, later made voyages of discovery, and added Newfoundland to the British possessions.

**Gilbert, Sir John,** R.A. (1817–1897), English painter, one of the chief artists on the *Illustrated London News*, and noted for his illustrations to Staunton's edition of Shakespeare.

**Gilbert, William** (1543–1603), physician to Queen Elizabeth I., has been called the father of electric and magnetic science. Published his great book on the magnet in 1600.

**Gilbert, Sir William Schwenck** (1836–1911), English humorist and playwright, is best remembered for the " Bab Ballads " and for the famous Savoy series of operas in which he collaborated with Sir Arthur Sullivan. Among the operas are *H.M.S. Pinafore, Patience, Iolanthe, The Mikado, The Gondoliers*, and *The Yeomen of the Guard*. The Gilbertian humour of plot and paradox, the kindly satire and the delightful metres combine with Sullivan's music to make the operas unforgettable and ever popular.

**Gill, Arthur Eric Rowton,** A.R.A. (1881–1940), English sculptor and engraver, whose works include the *Stations of the Cross* (Westminster Cathedral), *Prospero and Ariel* (Broadcasting House), *Christ Driving the Money-changers from the Temple* (Leeds University). He also worked as a designer for printing (Gill Sans type) and the George VI stamps were his designs.

**Gillray, James** (1757–1815), the eminent caricaturist of the time of George III., who produced upwards of a thousand political cartoons.

**Giotto di Bondone** (c. 1266–c. 1337), great Florentine artist, the first to break away from byzantine tradition and paint in a naturalistic way. Much of his work has perished but still surviving are the great frescoes in the churches of Assisi, Padua, and Florence. He designed the western front of the cathedral at Florence and the campanile, the lower part of which was completed from his designs before his death.

**Gissing, George Robert** (1857–1903), English author whose novels deal with poverty and the sociological problems of his day. *New Grub Street, The Unclassed, Charles Dickens, A Critical Study, The Private Papers of Henry Ryecroft* are among his best-known works.

**Giulio Romano** or **Giulio Pippi** (c. 1492–1546) was a pupil of Raphael, and himself a distinguished painter and architect.

**Gladstone, Rt. Hon. William Ewart** (1809–98), the great Liberal statesman of the latter part of the nineteenth century, popularly known as the Grand Old Man. Entered Parliament in 1832 as a Tory, held various offices under Peel, and joined the Aberdeen coalition in 1852. From that time he served several terms as Chancellor of the Exchequer and was Liberal Prime Minister, 1868–74, 1880–85, 1886, and 1892–94. His financial policy was able, accurate, lucidly exposed, and very successful. His first ministry was active, its legislative achievements including the Disestablishment of the Church of Ireland, the Education Act of 1870, the Ballot Act of 1872, and the Irish Land Act, but in 1873 they were aptly described by Gladstone's great rival, Disraeli, as " exhausted volcanoes." His second ministry, returned to power after the astonishing Midlothian campaign, witnessed the defeat by the Boers at Majuba, the bombardment of Alexandria, and the disaster of General Gordon at Khartoum. His last two ministries were marked by the adoption of the policy of Home Rule for Ireland, which he was unable to carry. Gladstone was a good classical scholar and an earnest high churchman, who in 1838 published the *State in its Relations with the Church*, a work of considerable interest.

**Glazunov, Alexander Constantinovich** (1865–1936), Russian composer, pupil of Rimsky-Korsakov. He was an accomplished and prolific composer, the first of his eight symphonies being composed when he was only 16.

**Glendower, Owen** (1359–1415), a famous Welsh chieftain who proved a formidable opponent to Henry IV., and gathered around him a great following of Welshmen, whom he led with much bravery, though finally defeated in 1405.

**Glinka, Mikhail Ivanovich** (1804–57), Russian composer whose music has a strong folk-song element. Notable among his works are his two operas, *A Life of the Tsar* and *Russlan and Ludmilla*, based on a poem by Pushkin. He is recognised as the first of the Russian national school. *See Section E*.

**Gluck, Christoph Willibald** (1714–87), German composer, a figure of great historical importance in the development of the opera. He was the son of a Bohemian forester and studied in Prague, Vienna, and Italy. His first operas were in the Italian tradition, but with *Orfeo ed Euridice* (1762), inspired by classical Greek drama, he began his reform of the opera. Then followed the great operas *Alceste, Armide,* and *Iphigénie en Tauride* (1779), which is considered his masterpiece. *See Section E*.

**Godfrey of Bouillon** (c. 1061–1100) was the leader of the First Crusade, and after the conquest of Jerusalem, exchanged the title of King for that of "Protector of the Holy Sepulchre." He liberated the Holy Land, and was buried on Mount Calvary.

**Godiva, Lady** (1040–1080), was the pious and beautiful wife of Leofric, Earl of Chester and Lord of Coventry. Having appealed to her lord to remit certain impositions from the inhabitants, he promised to grant her request if she would ride naked through the town. This she did, says the legend, having first passed the word to have blinds and shutters drawn at the appointed hour, and so obtained the people's ransom.

**Godwin, Earl of the West Saxons** (990–1053), was one of the most influential noblemen of his time and gave his daughter in marriage to Edward the Confessor, against whom he was afterwards in rebellion. Godwin's son, Harold, claimed the throne after Edward's death, but was killed at Hastings.

**Godwin, William** (1756–1836), English Radical philosopher, author of *Political Justice* and a novel, *Caleb Williams*. Married Mary Wollstonecraft (1759–97), author of *A Vindication of the Rights of Women*, in which she pleaded for the equality of the sexes, particularly in education. Their daughter, Mary Wollstonecraft Godwin (1797–1851), married the poet, Shelley, and was the author of *Frankenstein*.

**Goethe, Johann Wolfgang von** (1749–1832), German poet of great gifts and versatility. Born at Frankfurt-on-Maine of a cultivated and well-to-do family, he was able to integrate all the powers with which nature had endowed him in one harmonious personality. Before he went to Weimar at the age of 25 he had written *Götz von Berlichingen* and *Werthers Leiden* and many beautiful lyrics. He settled at Weimar in 1775, received a Ministerial appointment and actively interested himself in the welfare of the state. *Faust*, the great dramatic poem which accompanied him from early manhood to the end, epitomises his whole life and was his crowning achievement. Not only was he a great poet, but scientist and philosopher besides.

**Gogol, Nikolai Vasilievich** (1809–52), one of the greatest of Russian novelists whose stories of provincial life are in the same setting as his *Dead Souls* (1842), a masterpiece of humour. Another masterpiece is his play *The Government Inspector* (1836), a satire on provincial bureaucracy. An artist of supreme originality.

**Goldsmith, Oliver** (1728–1774), the celebrated author of *The Vicar of Wakefield, The Deserted Village*, and *She Stoops to Conquer*. The son of a poor Irish curate, he found his way to London in 1756, subsequently devoting himself entirely to literature, being befriended by Dr. Johnson and held in great esteem by Reynolds, Burke and other eminent men of the time. He was buried in the churchyard of the Temple.

**Góngora y Argote, Luis de** (1561–1627), Spanish poet, b. Cordova, considered to be Spain's greatest sonnet writer. In his two great poems *Polifemo* and *Soledades* he attempted to express the core of poetry in new experimental forms.

**Goodyear, Charles** (1800–1860), American inventor who discovered the art of vulcanising rubber.

**Goossens, Sir Eugène** (1893–1962), English composer and conductor of Belgian parentage. He was associated with many famous orchestras, and his compositions include the operas *Judith* and *Don Juan de Mañara*. His brother Léon is a celebrated oboe virtuoso, both his sisters are gifted harpists, and his father and grandfather, who also bore the name Eugène, were conductors.

**Gordon, Adam Lindsay** (1833–1870), an Australian poet who wrote many stirring ballads and poems, his *Bush Ballads and Galloping Rhymes* being a great success.

**Gordon, Major-General Charles George, C.B.** (1833–1885), a distinguished soldier, administrator, and earnest Christian, who had a most adventurous, useful, and self-sacrificing career. He saw active service in the Crimea, China, and India, and in 1873 was made Governor of the Equatorial provinces of Egypt. In 1877 he went out to the Sudan for the Egyptian Government, and in 1884 again proceeded thither on behalf of the English Government to deal once more with the difficulties which had arisen consequent on the Mahdi's Rebellion. While defending Khartoum he was murdered by the Mahdi's forces on the palace staircase.

**Gordon, Lord George** (1751–1793), was tried for treason as the instigator of the Anti-Popery riots of 1780, but acquitted on the ground that he had no treasonable intention. Some years later he was committed to Newgate for libelling Marie Antoinette and died there of fever.

**Gorky, Maxim** (pseudonym of Alexey Maximovich Peshkov) (1868–1936), great Russian writer and playwright. Worked in a variety of trades from the age of ten—shoemaker's apprentice, scullion on a Volga steamboat, birdwatcher, baker, fisherman, railway guard—during which time he learned to write. His early years are described in *My Childhood* (1913). His first story was published in 1892. His works are noted for their vividly drawn characters and social realism.

**Gorton, Rt. Hon. John Grey** (b. 1912), leader of Australian Liberal Party and Prime Minister since 1968.

**Gosse, Sir Edmund, C.B., LL.D., Litt.D.** (1849–1928), a distinguished poet and critic who wrote lives of Gray, Congreve and Dr. Donne, and his *History of 18th Century Literature* and *History of Modern English Literature* show great critical power and appreciation. Was librarian to the House of Lords 1904–14, and wrote a book on French literary men and a life of Sir Thomas Browne. In 1907 he published *Father and Son*, being recollections of his father.

**Gounod, Charles François** (1818–93), French composer whose fame rests chiefly on his operas *Faust* and *Roméo et Juliette*, though his lyrical gifts are best shown in some of his earlier works, such as *Le Médicin maloré lui* and *Mireille*.

**Gower, John** (1325–1408), an English poet of the time of Chaucer, who wrote many elegant ballads and devotional poems. His *Confessio Amantis* was his outstanding work.

**Goya y Lucientes, Francisco José** (1746–1828), a famous Spanish painter and etcher, and one of the greatest artists of all time, renowned for his wonderful series of etchings and satirical drawings. His portraits can only be described as ruthless in their realism, and his etchings in the *Horrors of War* tell of his hatred of the cruelty and reaction in his own country. In addition to portraits and genre he painted frescoes in the Cathedral at Saragossa. England's first exhibition of his art was held in 1963.

**Grace, Dr. William Gilbert** (1848–1915), renowned and almost legendary cricketer who dominated English cricket for over forty years, and was probably the best-known man in England. Altogether in first-class cricket he scored 54,896 runs, including 126 centuries, and took 2876 wickets. Scored 1000 runs in May 1895; and three times made over 300 runs in an innings.

**Graham, John**, of Claverhouse, Viscount Dundee (1643–1689). Renowned for his sturdy adherence to the Stuarts, and headed a rebellion in Scotland against William and Mary, but was killed at the Battle of Killiecrankie.

**Grahame, Kenneth** (1859–1932), as a writer of books for children ranks almost with Lewis Carroll. *The Golden Age, Dream Days*, and *Wind in the Willows*, all achieved great popularity.

**Grahame-White, Claude** (1879–1959), aviator and engineer, the first Englishman to gain an aviator's certificate, 1909; won the Gordon Bennett Cup with the then record speed of 60½ miles per hour in 1910, founded the first British Flying School and published many works on aircraft.

**Grant, General Ulysses Simpson** (1822–1885), the most distinguished American general of the Civil War. President of the United States from 1869 to 1877.

**Granville-Barker, Harley, D. Litt., LL.D., F.R.S.L.** (1877–1946), distinguished English dramatist, producer, and actor. Introduced plays of Ibsen and Shaw to British public. His own plays reflect influence of Shaw, and are particularly notable for their realistic dialogue.

**Grattan, Henry** (1746–1820), an Irish orator and statesman who, first in the Irish Parliament and afterwards in the Imperial Parliament, did memorable work for the cause of his country.

**Graves, Robert Ranke** (b. 1895), English poet and writer. His most famous work, apart from his poems, is *Goodbye to All That*, written after the first great war. Succeeded Auden as Prof. of Poetry at Oxford, 1961–66.

**Gray, Thomas** (1716–1771), the English poet, whose *Elegy written in a Country Churchyard* is one of the most beautiful in the language. His other poems were not numerous but included a fine *Ode on a Distant Prospect of Eton College* and a notable *Ode to Adversity*.

**Greeley, Horace** (1811–1872), founder of the *New York Tribune* and a political writer of great power and influence. Was an unsuccessful candidate for the United States Presidency in 1872.

**Green John Richard** (1837–1883), an eminent English historian. Published a *Short History of the English People* in 1874.

**Greenway, Kate** (1846–1901), a gifted book illustrator and water-colour artist, whose drawings of children won her great popularity and the warm approval of no less a critic than Ruskin.

**Greene, Graham, C.H.** (b. 1904), English novelist and journalist whose novels (*The Heart of the Matter, Brighton Rock, The Quiet American, Our Man in Havana, A Burnt-out Case*), like his plays (*The Complaisant Lover*), and films (*Fallen Idol, The Third Man*), deal with moral problems in a modern setting from a Catholic standpoint.

**Gregory, St.** (257–336), was founder of the Armenian Church, and spent his last years in a cave at the foot of Mount Sebuh.

**Gregory the Great, St.** (c. 540–604), Pope 590–604. The last great Latin Father and the forerunner of scholasticism. The real founder of the temporal power and the political influence of the papacy, he also maintained the spiritual claims of Rome, enforcing discipline, encouraging monasticism, defining doctrine, and adding to the music, liturgy, and canons of the Church. Thus he exerted enormous influence on the life and thought of the Middle Ages.

**Gregory VII** (c. 1020–85), Pope from 1073. Originally called Hildebrand. Battled for papal omnipotence within the Church, stamping on simony and the marriage of priests. His victory in the conflict of empire and papacy came when the emperor, Henry IV, did penance for three days in the snow at Canossa, but had the unfortunate result of leading to further internal dissensions in Germany and to papal absorption with power politics rather than to Gregory's aim of an ideal theocracy embracing all States.

**Gregory XIII** (1502–85), Pope, 1572–85; introduced the Gregorian calendar.

**Gregory, James** (1638–1675), Scottish mathematician, invented a reflecting telescope and was the first to show how the distance of the sun could be deduced by observations of the passage of Venus across the disc of the sun. In many successive generations his family reached distinction in the academic world.

**Grenville, Sir Richard** (1541–1591), the Elizabethan sea-captain, who with his one ship engaged a fleet of Spanish war-vessels off Flores, in 1591, was captured and shortly after died on the Spanish flagship *San Pablo*, an exploit celebrated in Tennyson's noble ballad, *The Revenge*.

**Gresham, Sir Thomas** (1519–1579), was the wealthiest London merchant and financier of his time. He built the first Royal Exchange and founded Gresham College. The son of

Sir Richard Gresham (Lord Mayor of London), he succeeded his father as King's Agent at Antwerp, and proved an astute money-finder for the Court in four successive reigns, ending as Queen Elizabeth's " Royal Merchant."

**Greuze, Jean Baptiste** (1725–1805), French painter, whose works, especially his studies of girls, display much delicacy and beauty of handling.

**Grey, Charles, 2nd Earl, K.G.** (1764–1845), a great English Whig statesman under whose Premiership were passed the Reform Bill of 1832, the Bill abolishing slavery throughout the British Empire (1833), and the Poor Law Amendment Act, 1834.

**Grey, Lady Jane** (1537–1554), was the daughter of the Duke of Suffolk and great-granddaughter of Henry VII. On the death of Edward VI, she was proclaimed Queen, but only reigned for nine days, Queen Mary ousting her and maintaining the Tudor succession. Six months later Lady Jane and her husband, Lord Guildford Dudley, were executed.

**Grey of Fallodon, 1st and only Viscount, K.G.,** P.C. (1862–1933). Under-Secretary for Foreign Affairs, 1892. Foreign Secy., 1905–16. He won high approval for his handling of the Balkan difficulties of 1912–13, and all through the difficult strain which preceded Germany's rush into war acquitted himself with force and dignity. Leader of Liberal Party in House of Lords until Aug. 1924. Chancellor of Oxford Univ., 1928–33.

**Grieg, Edvard Hagerup** (1843–1907), a Norwegian musical composer, who presented the characteristics of his country's music in numerous compositions of great melodic beauty.

**Griffin, His Eminence Cardinal Bernard William** (1899–1956), Roman Catholic Archbishop of Westminster from 1944 until his death.

**Griffith, Arthur** (1872–1922), was the first President of the Irish Free State 1921; founder and first editor of *Sinn Fein* 1906–15, and founder of the *Sinn Fein* movement.

**Griffith, David Wark** (1880–1948), pioneer American film producer. Noted especially for his remarkable films *Broken Blossoms* and *The Birth of a Nation*. Invented much of the technique of the modern cinema.

**Grimm,** the brothers **Jakob Ludwig Karl** (1785–1863) and **Wilhelm Karl** (1786–1859), German philologists and folk-lorists who wrote the world-famous *Fairy Tales*. They planned a gigantic etymological dictionary of the German language. which was completed by German scholars in 1961.

**Grimond, Rt. Hon. Joseph** (b. 1913), Leader of the Liberal Parliamentary Party 1957–67; Liberal M.P. for Orkney and Shetlands since 1950; Liberal Chief Whip, 1951–57.

**Grimthorpe, 1st Baron, LL.D.** (1816–1905), long known as Sir Edmund Beckett, Bt., K.C., was a great authority on horology, and, with Professor Sir George Airy (*q.v.*), designed " Big Ben." He restored St. Albans Cathedral at his own cost.

**Gromyko, Andrei A.** (b. 1908), Russian diplomat; Foreign Minister, 1957–. Ambassador to Britain, 1952–3, and to the U.S.A., 1943–46. Representative of the Soviet Union on the U.N. Security Council, 1946–49.

**Grossmith, George** (1847–1912), the well-known actor and entertainer. His father, George Grossmith the elder, was also a popular entertainer and lecturer, his brother, Weedon Grossmith, was an actor and artist of considerable attainments, and his son, George Grossmith (1874–1935), was a successful comedian, and the first to introduce revue and also cabaret entertainment into England.

**Grote, George** (1794–1871), English historian famous for his *History of Greece*, 1846–56, an epoch-making and standard work.

**Groot, Hugo de (or Grotius)** (1583–1645), Dutch jurist, the founder of international law. He was condemned to life imprisonment for supporting religious toleration but made a daring escape and found refuge in Paris, where he wrote his masterpiece *De Jure Belli et Pacis*.

**Grouchy, Marshal Emmanuel, Marquis de** (1766–1847), a famous Napoleonic general who, at Hohenlinden, Wagram, and in the Moscow retreat rendered signal service. After Waterloo he led the defeated army back to Paris.

**Grove, Sir George** (1820–1900) was a distinguished engineer and bridge and lighthouse builder, but better known as an enthusiastic lover of music, the study and performance of which in England he did much to promote. His *Dictionary of Music and Musicians* is a standard work.

Guedalla, Philip, M.A. (1889–1944), was an English historian and essayist. Author of *The Partition of Europe* (1914), *The Second Empire* (1922), *Palmerston* (1926), *The Missing Muse* (1929), *The Duke* (1931), and other works.

Guido Reni (1575–1642), Italian painter of the Bolognese school whose works are characteristic of the Italian baroque art of his period and include the famous *Aurora* fresco in the Rospigliosi palace at Rome, and *Crucifixion of St. Peter* (Vatican).

Gustavus Adolphus, King of Sweden (1594–1632), the "Lion of the North," after a lengthy campaign in Poland, entered the Thirty Years' War in support of Swedish interests and Protestant distress, won the Battle of Breitenfeld in 1631, and was killed in action the next year.

Gutenberg, Johann (c. 1400–68), German printer, b. Mainz, the first European to print with movable types cast in moulds. The earliest book printed by Gutenberg was the Mazarin Bible (L76).

Guy, Thomas (1644–1724), founder of Guy's Hospital, was a dealer in Bibles, speculator and money-lender, who after making a large fortune, bequeathed £300,000 for the erection and endowment of the famous hospital.

Gwynne, Nell (1650–1687) English actress; as a girl, orange-seller near Drury Lane Theatre; favourite mistress of Charles II. Her eldest son was made Duke of St. Albans.

# H

Haakon VII. (1872–1957), King of Norway. Formerly Prince Carl of Denmark, second son of Frederick VIII.; elected to the throne on the separation of Norway from Sweden in 1905. Married Princess Maud, youngest daughter of King Edward VII. in 1896.

Hadfield, Sir Robert Abbott, Bt., F.R.S. (1858–1940), English metallurgist whose discovery of manganese steel in 1882 brought him recognition from every steel-producing country.

Hadrian (76–138) was Emperor of Rome in succession to his uncle Trajan, and one of the greatest of Roman rulers. He visited Britain, and in A.D. 121 built the wall between Newcastle and Carlisle for protection of his dominions against the Picts and Scots.

Hafiz, pseudonym of Shams ad-Din Mohammed (1320–1389), great Persian lyrical poet. His principal work is the *Divan*, a collection of short sonnets called *ghazals*. The sobriquet *Hafiz*, meaning one who remembers, is applied to any one who has learned the Koran by heart.

Hahn, Otto (1879–1968), German chemist and physicist, chief discoverer of uranium fission, the phenomenon on which nuclear power and the atom bomb are based.

Hahnemann, Samuel Christian Friedrich (1755–1843), the German physician who founded the system of homoeopathy. Dissatisfied with the state of medicine at the time, he set himself the task of formulating general principles governing the restoration of health.

Haig, Field-Marshal, 1st Earl of Bemersyde, K.T., G.C.B., O.M., G.C.V.O., K.C.I.E. (1861–1928), C.-in-C. of the British Expeditionary Forces in France and Flanders, 1915–19.

Haile Selassie I., G.C.B., G.C.M.G., G.C.V.O. (b. 1891), Emperor of Ethiopia, April 1930 to May 1936, and since May 1941.

Hakluyt, Richard (1553–1616), the first of English naval historians. By his *Divers Voyages touching the Discovery of America*, and *Principal Navigations, Voyages, and Discoveries of the English Nation*, did much to help forward the colonising spirit.

Haldane, John Burdon Sanderson (1892–1964), biologist and geneticist, noted not only for his influence in his special field of mathematical evolutionary theory but for the use he made of his great gifts in explaining science to the layman. He held the Chair of Biometry at University College, London, from 1937 until 1956. Emigrated to India in 1957. He was the son of John Scott Haldane (1860–1936) whose researches led to improvements in public health and industrial safety.

Haldane, Viscount, P.C., K T., O.M., F.R.S. (1856–1928), sat for Haddingtonshire, 1885–1911. In 1901 was Vice-President of the Liberal Imperialist League, and at the close of 1905 was made War Minister and organised the Territorial Force. Lord Chancellor, 1912–15, and again in first Labour Government, 1924.

Halévy, Ludovic (1834–1903), a brilliant French writer who supplied Offenbach with libretti for some of his most famous comic operas: among them *La Belle Hélène*, *La Grande Duchesse*, and *Barbe Bleue*. In conjunction with Meilhac he wrote several notable plays of which *Frou-frou* was perhaps the most successful.

Halifax, Charles Montague, Earl of (1661–1715), seventeenth century financier who was responsible for the National Debt, the window tax, the revaluation of the currency, and the foundation of the Bank of England.

Halifax, 1st Earl of, Edward Frederick Lindley Wood, K.G., P.C., O.M., G.C.S.I., G.C.I.E., T.D. (1881–1959), filled many difficult positions with distinction and success and was especially notable as Viceroy of India, 1926–31. Foreign Secretary, 1938–40, and British Ambassador in Washington, 1940–45. He wrote a life of John Keble and was prominent in the life of the Church of England. Chancellor of Oxford University 1933–59.

Halifax, George Savile, Marquess of (1633–95), author of *Advice to a Daughter* and *Character of a Trimmer*, was a gifted and independent politician, pamphleteerist, and orator.

Hallam, Henry (1777–1859), a graceful and scholarly historian who contributed several important works. His *View of the State of Europe during the Middle Ages*, *Constitutional History of England*, and *Introduction to the Literature of Europe* are distinguished for their clearness of style and correctness of judgment.

Hallé, Sir Charles (1819–1895), a distinguished pianist and conductor who was born in Westphalia. Went to Paris to study music in 1836, and in 1848 settled in London, where he soon became known as a piano-player of the first rank. He organised an orchestra of high-class talent, and for many years conducted it in London and the provinces. He married Madam Norman Neruda (d. 1911), the celebrated violinist in 1888, and was knighted the same year.

Halley, Edmund, F.R.S. (1656–1742), English Astronomer Royal from 1720 to his death and ranked next to Newton among the scientific Englishmen of his time. Made first magnetic survey of the oceans from the naval vessel *Paramour*, 1698–1700. Discovered what is known as Halley's comet.

Hals, Franz (1584–1666), a famous painter of the Dutch School, who is represented in the leading galleries of Europe. The Wallace Collection has his world-famous picture, the *Laughing Cavalier*.

Hamilton, Alexander (1757–1804), American statesman and economist, opponent of Thomas Jefferson, served as Secretary of the Treasury in Washington's cabinet, 1789–95. Though a monarchist by predilection, he urged the adoption of the Constitution, and in conjunction with Maddison and Jay wrote the *Federalist*.

Hamilton, Emma Lyon, Lady (1761–1815), was a woman of humble birth and great personal beauty who attained prominent notice by her association with Sir William Hamilton, British Ambassador at Naples, who married her, and afterwards with Lord Nelson, who conceived an infatuation for her.

Hammarskjöld, Dag Hjalmar Agne Carl (1905–1961), Sec.-Gen. of the United Nations, 1953–61. Killed in air crash on way to the Congo to end dispute between central government in Leopoldville and M. Tshombe of Katanga province. Posthumously awarded 1961 Nobel Peace Prize.

Hammond, John Lawrence Le Breton (1872–1949), English journalist and historian whose works on social and industrial history, written mainly in collaboration with his wife, Barbara Hammond, include *The Village Labourer*, 1911; *The Town Labourer*, 1917; *The Skilled Labourer*, 1919; and *The Age of the Chartists*, 1930.

Hampden, John (1594–1643), English patriot who opposed Charles I.'s "Ship Money" tax, and by his resistance and eloquent advocacy of the wish of the people helped the Parliamentary cause.

**Hamsun, Knut,** pen-name of Knut Pedersen (1859–1952), Norwegian author and farmer, who in his youth struggled for existence, visited America twice and earned his living by casual labour. His monumental work, *Markens Gröde* (*Growth of the Soil*), gained him the Nobel Prize in 1920.

**Handel, George Frederick** (1685–1759), German composer, son of a barber-surgeon to the Duke of Saxony; born the same year as Bach. He spent much of his life in England composing operas and achieving world-wide fame by his magnificent series of oratorios. His operas, of which there are over forty, include *Atalanta, Berenice,* and *Serse,* and his oratorios, of which there are thirty-two, include *Saul, Israel in Egypt, Samson, Messiah, Judas Maccabaeus,* and *Jeptha.* He also composed chamber music, *concerti grossi,* music for chorus and orchestra, solo cantatas, harpsichord suites, and much other beautiful and noble music. Beethoven said of Handel, " Go and learn of him how to achieve great effects with simple means." Eight years before he died he became totally blind and relied upon his old friend and copyist John Christopher Smith to commit his music to paper. He was buried in Westminster Abbey. *See* Section E.

**Hannibal** (247–183 B.C.), the renowned Carthaginian general, who led an army against Rome, and achieved many notable victories over superior numbers. Was defeated by Scipio at the Battle of Zama, and afterwards suffered exile, and poisoned himself.

**Harcourt, Rt. Hon. Sir William Vernon, F.R.S.** (1827–1904), barrister, author, Liberal statesman, an enthusiastic supporter of Mr. Gladstone.

**Hardicanute** (1019–1042), son of Canute the Great, was King of England from 1040 to 1042, and imposed the tax called Danegeld. He was the last Danish sovereign of this country.

**Hardie, James Keir** (1856–1915), a Socialist politician and Labour representative who acted as editor of the *Miner* and the *Labour Leader* from 1887 to 1904. He is regarded as the founder of the Labour Party. During his early life he worked in a Scottish coal pit, but in 1882 became a journalist, and entered Parliament as member for West Ham (South) in 1892–95, being the first Socialist to be elected to the House of Commons. First Chairman of the Parliamentary Labour Party, 1906–8, M.P. for Merthyr Tydvil from 1900 till his death.

**Hardy, Thomas, O.M.** (1840–1928), was educated as an architect and practised for some time, but became known as a promising novelist in 1871 with his story *Desperate Remedies.* In 1874 his *Far from the Madding Crowd* was published, which at once made him a name. Following that, at short intervals, came a long series of powerful novels from his pen. Perhaps the most notable of his stories are *The Trumpet Major, The Mayor of Casterbridge, Tess of the D'Urbervilles,* and *Jude the Obscure.* In 1908 he completed a dramatic poem entitled *The Dynasts,* whose central figure is Napoleon.

**Hargreaves, James** (1720–1778), was a poor Lancashire-born mechanic who invented the spinning jenny, one of the revolutionising labour-saving contrivances of the latter half of the 18th century. It met with much opposition, however, and kept him poor, though the community afterwards reaped the advantage in a greatly improved industry.

**Harkness, Edward Stephen, B.A., M.A., LL.D.** (1874–1940) was a banker and one of America's greatest philanthropists. Donor of the Pilgrim's Prize of £2,000,000 to Great Britain; founded in 1930 the Pilgrim Trust in appreciation of Great Britain's acceptance of financial burdens in the Great War of 1914–18.

**Harley, Robert, 1st Earl of Oxford, K.G., P.C.** (1661–1724), a distinguished Tory statesman—originally, however, a Whig—of the Queen Anne period, who fell into disgrace after that Sovereign's death in consequence of being suspected of intriguing with the Stuarts. He served at different times as Speaker of the House of Commons, Chancellor of the Exchequer, and Lord Treasurer. " The Harleian Collection " in the British Museum is a reminder of his cultured literary tastes.

**Harold II.** (1022–1066), the last of the Saxon Sovereigns of England, and the son of Earl Godwin, was crowned King in succession to Edward the Confessor in 1066. The coming of William the Conqueror, with his great army, soon, however, put an end to the hopes of Harold and his followers; and the Battle of Hastings terminated at once his life and Saxon sway in this country.

**Haroun-Al-Raschid** (763–809), the famous Caliph of Bagdad, familiar to all by the references to him in the *Arabian Nights.*

**Harriman, William Averell** (b. 1891), American public official; under-secretary of state for political affairs, 1963; Pres. Kennedy's roving ambassador, 1961; special U.S. representative in Europe for Marshall Aid, 1948–52.

**Harris, Joel Chandler** (1848–1908), American journalist and author, famous as the creator of " Uncle Remus." The negro humour of his stories brought him world-wide popularity among adults and children alike. His Brer Rabbit in the Uncle Remus negro folk-tales was the forerunner of Mickey Mouse, impudently victorious in every contest against fearful adversaries.

**Harrison, Frederic** (1831–1923), as leader of the English Positivists, filled a prominent part in philosophical discussions during the last quarter of the 19th century. In 1907 he published *The Creed of a Layman* and *The Philosophy of Common Sense,* and in 1908 *Realities and Ideals.*

**Harrison, John** (1693–1776), the inventor of the chronometer, for which he received the Government grant of £20,000, was a mechanician of great ingenuity, who effected many important improvements in clocks, watches, and other instruments. In 1715 he made an 8-day clock with wooden wheels, which is still working in the Science Museum, South Kensington.

**Harte, Francis Bret** (1839–1902), the American poet and author, who leapt into popularity in the late 'sixties by his clever sketches and stories of Californian mining life.

**Harty, Sir (Herbert) Hamilton, Mus. Doc.** (1880–1941), was a well-known British composer and conductor. Conductor of Hallé Orchestra 1920–33; Musical Adviser and Conductor-in-Chief of London Symphony Orchestra 1932–41.

**Harvey, William** (1578–1657), an English physician who rose to great eminence both as anatomist and physiologist. He spent five years at Padua where Galileo was a teacher at the University. He immortalised himself by discovering the circulation of the blood in 1616. He was physician to both James I and Charles I.

**Hastings, Sir Patrick, Q.C.** (1880–1952), lawyer, politician, and playwright. Attorney-General in first Labour Government, 1924. Author of *The Blind Goddess.*

**Hastings, Warren** (1732–1818), the first Governor-General of India. On his return to England 12 years later he was impeached on charges of excessive cruelty and corruption. The trial lasted seven years, and cost Hastings £76,000. He was ultimately acquitted, and the East India Company settled an annuity of £4,000 upon him, and he lived to see his plans for the security of British rule in the Orient publicly applauded.

**Hauptmann, Gerhart** (1862–1946), one of the leading dramatic poets of Europe. Born in Silesia, he devoted himself first to agriculture, then to art, and subsequently to the drama, and lived in Rome, Berlin, Switzerland, and the United States. Produced many plays, including *The Weavers.* Winner of the Nobel Prize for Literature, 1912.

**Havelock, Major-Gen. Sir Henry, K.C.B.** (1795–1857), one of the heroes of the Indian Mutiny, who led the troops to the relief of Cawnpore and Lucknow.

**Hawke, Edward, 1st Baron, K.C.B.** (1705–1781), one of the great admirals of the 18th century. He won a brilliant victory over the French fleet at Quiberon in 1759 in a tremendous storm.

**Hawkins, Sir John** (1532–1595), a brilliant naval officer of the Elizabethan period, who did much sea fighting in many climes, and served as vice-admiral in the expedition against the Spanish Armada, for which he was knighted.

**Hawthorne, Nathaniel** (1804–1864), American novelist, author of *The Scarlet Letter* and *The Blithedale Romance.*

**Haydn, Franz Joseph** (1732–1809), Austrian composer, who belongs to the great classical period of Bach, Handel, and Mozart and whose style also influenced Beethoven. He has been given the title "father of the symphony." Much of his life was spent as musical director to the princely Hungarian house of Esterhazy. In 1791 and again in 1794 he visited London, where he conducted his Salomon symphonies. He composed many operatic works, string quartets, symphonies (104 in all), sonatas, songs, Masses, and chamber music. His two great oratorios, *The Creation* and *The Seasons*, were written in his old age. *See* Section E.

**Hazlitt, William** (1778–1830), English essayist and critic. His *Characters of Shakespeare's Plays* and his published lectures on the poets and dramatists, besides his *Table Talks*, are still widely read. His son William (1811–1893) was also of literary tastes, though he became Senior Registrar in the Bankruptcy Court; and the son of the latter, William Carew Hazlitt (1834–1913), though originally a civil engineer, acquired celebrity as a bibliographer and numismatist.

**Hearst, William Randolph** (1863–1951), American newspaper proprietor who established his supremacy in sensational journalism, and built up the biggest newspaper empire in the world.

**Heath, Rt. Hon. Edward Richard George,** M.P. (b. 1916), Leader of the Conservative Party, 1965–; began his political career in 1950 when he entered Parliament as member for Bexley.

**Hedin, Dr. Sven Anders,** Hon. K.C.I.E. (1865–1952), a Swedish traveller who made discoveries in Central Asia, and wrote extensively thereon.

**Heenan, His Eminence Cardinal John Carmel** (b. 1905), Archbishop of Westminster (1963); member of Sacred College (1965).

**Hegel, Georg Wilhelm Friedrich** (1770–1831), a famous German philosopher and professor who taught that truth or reality has three aspects revealing itself in dialectical development (thesis, antithesis, synthesis) and identified reality with rationalism. Among his important works are *The Phenomenology of the Spirit, The Science of Logic, Philosophy of Right. See also* Dialectical Materialism, J12.

**Heidenstam, Carl Gustaf Werner von** (1859–1940), Swedish author and one of the most brilliant and outstanding figures in Swedish literature. Received Nobel Prize for Literature, 1916.

**Heifetz, Jascha** (b. 1901), Russian-born violinist who became a naturalised American. He was the first musician to win a reputation in England by gramophone records before his first personal appearance there.

**Heine, Heinrich** (c. 1797–1856), the German lyric poet, who lived for the best part of his life in Paris, and produced from time to time poems of profound beauty and subtlety of thought. Cynical, satirical, and often bitter, many of his writings excited great conflict of opinion.

**Helmholtz, Hermann Ludwig Ferdinand von** (1821–94), German physiologist, physicist, and mathematician who made many important contributions to the knowledge of thermodynamics, electrodynamics, and optics. His pupil Heinrich Hertz discovered electromagnetic radiation.

**Helmont, Jan Baptista van** (1577–1644), Belgian chemist who devoted himself to the study of gases. His chief work is *Ortus medicinae* (1648).

**Héloïse** (c. 1101–64), niece of Canon Fulbert of Notre Dame. Famed for her romantic attachment to Abelard. (*See* Abelard.)

**Hemingway, Ernest** (1899–1961), American author of some celebrated novels: *A Farewell to Arms, Death in the Afternoon, For Whom the Bell Tolls, The Snows of Kilimanjaro, The Old Man of the Sea.* He suffered from persecution mania in his last days and committed suicide. Considered one of the most influential writers of his generation. Nobel Prize 1954.

**Henderson, Rt. Hon. Arthur** (1863–1935), President of World Disarmament Conference, 1932–35; Leader of the Labour Party, 1931–32; Foreign Secretary, 1929–31; Home Secretary, 1924. Awarded the 1934 Nobel Peace Prize.

**Henrietta Maria** (1609–1669), the daughter of Henry IV. of France and wife of Charles I.

**Henry, Joseph** (1797–1875), American physicist who invented and operated the first electro-magnetic telegraph. The unit of inductance is named after him.

**Henry I.** (1068–1135), king of England, 1100–35; youngest son of William the Conqueror, ascended the throne during the absence on crusade of his elder brother Robert of Normandy. His long reign brought order and progress, not entirely destroyed by the anarchy under his successor Stephen.

**Henry II.** (1133–1189), first Angevin king of England, 1154–89, son of Matilda, daughter of Henry I, and her second husband, Geoffrey Plantagenet, count of Anjou; his lands stretched from the Solway Firth to the Pyrenees. He was a strong ruler to whom we owe the establishment of the Common law system (see D4(1)) and many permanent administrative reforms. His conflict with the Church brought about the murder of his archbishop Becket, a man of equally resolute character.

**Henry III.** (1207–1272), king of England, 1216–72; at war with his barons for the greater part of his reign; incurred unpopularity by his patronage of French favourites. Though an inept ruler his reign showed progress in many fields.

**Henry IV.** (1367–1413), king of England, 1399–1413, son of John of Gaunt, grandson of Edward III; called Henry Bolingbroke, first of the Lancastrian kings. He was a lover of music and poetry.

**Henry IV. of France** (Henry of Navarre) (1553–1610), prior to becoming king was the leader of the French Huguenots, and although going over to the Catholics on being crowned, remained in sympathy with the Protestants and protected them by the famous Edict of Nantes. Ravaillac, a religious fanatic, assassinated Henry.

**Henry V.** (1387–1422), king of England, 1413–22, succeeded his father Henry IV; distinguished himself in the wars with France, his victory at Agincourt (25 Oct. 1415) being his greatest triumph. Though masterful and hard, he was devout and just and made an able and energetic monarch.

**Henry VI.** (1421–1471), king of England, 1422–61, only son of Henry V., by nature gentle and retiring. Succeeding to the throne under a protectorship as a baby nine months old, he had a troubled reign, including a long war with France and loss of French possessions, the Jack Cade insurrection, and the beginning of the Wars of the Roses, which led to his deposition and the enthronement of Edward IV by the triumphant Yorkists. He was imprisoned in the Tower and there probably murdered. Founded Eton College (1440) and King's College, Cambridge (1441).

**Henry VII.** (1457–1509), the first of the Tudor line, reigned 1485–1509; succeeded Richard III, after defeating and killing him on Bosworth Field. Conspiracies and rebellions marked his reign, but he reasserted the power of the state over feudal indiscipline.

**Henry VIII.** (1491–1547), king of England, 1509–47, ascended the throne at the age of 18, a prince of the Renaissance, handsome, skilled in music and sports, with a love of the sea and a deep interest in theology. His marriages, the judicial murders, his quarrel with Rome and the rejection of papal supremacy, the suppression of the monasteries, the rise and fall of Wolsey, the last of England's great ecclesiastical statesmen, made his reign one of the most crucial in history. He built the royal dockyards at Woolwich and Deptford, founded Trinity House, and was the first English monarch to have a navy.

**Henry "the Navigator"** (1395–1460), a Portuguese Prince, son of John I. He discovered Madeira and the Azores, and was the chief instrument of the national impetus for navigation.

**Henschel, Sir George,** Mus.D. (1850–1934), English baritone singer, composer and conductor; born in Breslau, he became a naturalised Englishman in 1890. Founder and part conductor of London Symphony Concerts, 1886.

**Hepplewhite, George** (d. 1786). One of the four great English 18th-century cabinet-makers. He was a contemporary of Chippendale, Robert Adam and Sheraton. His name is identified with the style of furniture which followed the Chippendale period.

**Heraclitus of Ephesus** (c. 540–475 B.C.), a Greek philosopher. His discovery of a *changing* world (he lived in an age of social revolution when the ancient Greek tribal aristocracy was beginning to give way to democracy) influenced the philosophies of Parmenides, Democritus, Plato, and Aristotle.

**Herbert, George** (1593–1633), the most purely devotional of English poets.

**Hereward the Wake**, the last of the Saxon nobles to hold out against the Normans. Taking refuge in the Fen country, he long defied the Conqueror's forces, but was at last betrayed into the enemy's hands by monks. William afterwards honoured him with a place at Court.

**Herod the Great** (c. 73–4 B.C.), the tyrannical king of Judæa who secured the title from Marc Antony in 37 B.C. This was the Herod who was ruling when Christ was born and who ordered the massacre of the Innocents.

**Herodotus** (c. 485–425 B.C.), the great Greek historian, called by Cicero the father of history. Has also been called the father of anthropology.

**Herrick, Robert** (1591–1674), an English lyric poet, unrivalled in his own field. Author of *Gather ye Rose Buds, Cherry Ripe, Oberon's Feast*, etc.

**Herriot, Edouard** (1872–1957), French statesman; Pres. of the National Assembly, 1947–54. Mayor of Lyons for more than a generation, three times Prime Minister, the recognised spokesman of the Left-Centre party, which was for so long dominant in French politics.

**Herschel, Sir John Frederick William, Bt., F.R.S.** (1792–1871), a celebrated astronomer who did much to extend the power of the telescope.

**Herschel, Sir William, F.R.S.** (1738–1822), great astronomer, father of the last-named, discovered the planet Uranus. His sister, Caroline Lucretia (1750–1848), was the author of *Index to Flamsteed's Observations of the Fixed Stars* and *Errata*.

**Hertz, Heinrich** (1857–1894), German physicist whose laboratory experiments confirmed Maxwell's electromagnetic theory of waves and yielded useful information about their behaviour.

**Herzl, Theodor** (1860–1904), founded modern political Zionism.

**Hesiod** (*floruit* c. 735 B.C.), ancient Greek nature poet, author of the poems *Work and Days*, which tells of life in the country.

**Hill, Octavia** (1838–1912), a noted pioneer English social reformer who took a practical interest in the housing conditions of the poor, and a pioneer in slum clearance in London. Helped to institute the Charity Organisation Society, and was one of the first women to sit on a Royal Commission.

**Hill, Sir Rowland, K.C.B., F.R.S.** (1795–1879), the first propounder of the idea of the penny postal system, was secretary to the Postmaster-General from 1846 to 1854, after which he was Chief Secretary to the Post Office until 1864.

**Hindemith, Paul** (1895–1963), German composer and violinist. Much of his work is *Gebrauchsmusik* (workaday music written with the aim of establishing closer contact between composer and public). His works are numerous and strikingly varied, and include sonatas and chamber works, songs, operas, ballet music, symphonies, and the oratorio *Das Unaufhörliche*.

**Hindenburg, Field-Marshal Paul von** (1847–1934). President of the German Reich, 1925–34; Chief of the General Staff, 1916–18.

**Hinshelwood, Sir Cyril Norman, O.M., F.R.S.** (1897–1967),Pres. of the Royal Society,1955–60; Dr. Lee's Prof. of Chemistry, Univ. of Oxford, 1937. Shared with Prof. Semenov of Russia the 1956 Nobel Prize for Chemistry for researches into the mechanism of chemical reactions.

**Hinton, Christopher, Baron, K.B.E., M.A., D.Eng., D.Sc(Eng.), F.R.S.** (b. 1901), as Man. Dir. of the Industrial Group of the U.K. Atomic Energy Authority played important part in the building of Calder Hall. Chairman (1957–64) Central Electricity Generating Board (which owns and operates Britain's nuclear power stations). Chanc. Univ. of Bath.

**Hippocrates of Chios** (fl. c. 430 B.C.), a Greek business-man who specialised in mathematics and was the first to compile a work on the elements of geometry.

**Hippocrates of Cos** (c. 460–c. 370 B.C.), Greek physician, the father of medicine, b. on the island of Cos off the coast of Asia Minor. He established medical schools in Athens and elsewhere and separated medicine from superstition and so placed it on a scientific basis.

**Hirohito, Emperor of Japan** (b. 1901), acceded to the throne Dec. 1926.

**Hitler, Adolf** (1889–1945), German dictator, founder of National Socialism, b. in Austria, son of customs official. Worked in Vienna as artisan; already held anti-semitic views. Came to Munich in 1912; enlisted in Bavarian Infantry at outbreak of first world war. At the end of the war conditions in Germany favoured the growth of a fascist movement and under his leadership the National Socialist (Nazi) Party climbed to power. Appointed Reich Chancellor, 1933. On death of Hindenburg in 1934 became Führer. Commander-in-Chief Wehrmacht, 1935. Under the Hitler regime working class movements were ruthlessly destroyed; all opponents—communists, socialists, Jews—were persecuted and murdered. By terrorism and propaganda the German state was welded into a powerful machine for aggression. There followed the occupation of the Rhineland (1936), the annexation of Austria and Czechoslovakia (1938–39), the invasion of Poland and declaration of war by Great Britain and France (1939), the invasion of Soviet Russia (1941). Final defeat came in 1945 and on April 30 Hitler committed suicide in the Chancellery as the Russians closed in on Berlin.

**Hobbes, Thomas** (1588–1679), English philosopher who published his most famous work, *Leviathan*, in 1651. He favoured strong Government and therefore supported the supremacy of the State even in religion, but his arguments aroused great antagonism even among the Royalists. He was a child of his age in his enthusiasm for scientific enquiry, and his works provoked fresh thought.

**Hobbs, Sir John Berry (" Jack ")** (1882–1963), first played for Surrey 1905; retired from first-class cricket Feb. 1935. Scored 61,221 runs including 197 centuries.

**Hobhouse, Leonard Trelawney** (1864–1929), English sociologist; Prof. of Sociology, London Univ., 1907–29; editor of the *Sociological Review*, 1908–10, and writer for the *Manchester Guardian*, 1897–1902. His books include *The Theory of Knowledge, Morals in Evolution*, and *Development and Purpose*.

**Ho Chi-minh** (b. 1892), leader of the Vietnam revolutionary nationalist party of Indo-China. Successfully led the struggle for independence during and after the second world war. President of North Vietnam. *See* **Section C, Part I**.

**Hodgkin, Dorothy Crowfoot, O.M., Hon. D.Sc.** (b. 1910), Wolfson Research Professor of the Royal Society at Oxford since 1960; the third woman to receive the Nobel Prize for Chemistry, awarded in 1964 for her X-ray analysis to elucidate the structure of complex molecules, notably penicillin and vitamin B-12.

**Hogarth, William** (1697–1764), the celebrated engraver and painter who satirised the follies of his time in a series of engravings instinct with character, humour and power. His *Harlot's Progress*, of six engravings, was published in 1734, and gained him immediate fame. In 1735 he produced his equally celebrated *Rake's Progress*, a series of eight engravings. These were followed by *Marriage à la Mode, Industry and Idleness*, and *The March to Finchley*.

**Hogben, Lancelot, M.A., D.Sc., F.R.S.** (b. 1895), physiologist; Prof. Medical Statistics, 1947–61, Prof. of Zoology, 1941–47, Birmingham Univ.; Prof. Natural History, Univ. of Aberdeen, 1937–41; Prof. Social Biology in London Univ., 1930–37. Author of the great popular works *Mathematics for the Million, Science for the Citizen*, and *Mathematics in the Making*.

**Hogg, Quintin** (1845–1903), was an educationist and philanthropist who, purchasing the old Polytechnic Institution in 1882, turned it into a popular college, providing instruction in every department of education at moderate rates.

**Hokusai, Katsushika** (1760–1849), Japanese artist of the Ukiyo-e (popular school), whose work is highly original and of singular beauty and delicacy. He excelled in landscapes.

**Holbein, The Elder** (c. 1460–1524), a famous German painter, father of Hans Holbein.

**Holbein, Hans—The Younger** (1497–1543), was born at Augsburg, and settled in London in 1530, where he won the favour of Henry VIII.

**Holden, Charles, F.R.I.B.A.** (1875–1960), British architect, designer of modern public buildings, including British Medical Assen. Building, Strand, London Underground Railway Head

Offices, Piccadilly Circus, University of London buildings (Senate House), Bloomsbury.

**Holden, Sir Isaac, Bt.** (1807–1897), an inventor and manufacturer who achieved fame and fortune in connection with wool-combing inventions.

**Hölderlin, Johann Christian Friedrich** (1770–1843), friend of Hegel and contemporary of Goethe and Schiller, now considered among the very greatest of German poets. His mind became unhinged in his middle years.

**Holford, William Graham, Baron, M.A., F.R.I.B.A.** (b. 1907), British architect and town-planner. Prof. of Civic Design, Univ. of Liverpool, 1936–47; Prof. of Town Planning, London Univ., 1949–; planned post-war redevelopment of City of London, including precincts of St. Paul's Cathedral; architect of proposed Piccadilly Circus rebuilding scheme; Member Transport Advisory Council, 1965–.

**Holmes, Oliver Wendell** (1809–1894), an American doctor and author of great humour and geniality. His writings include *Autocrat of the Breakfast Table*, *The Professor at the Breakfast Table* and *The Poet at the Breakfast Table*.

**Holst, Gustav Theodore** (1874–1934), a British composer of Swedish descent whose compositions include *The Planets* suite, *The Hymn of Jesus*, an opera *The Perfect Fool*, and a choral symphony. His long career as a teacher of outstanding gifts included the appointment of musical director at St. Paul's Girls' School, London (1905–34) and at Morley College (1907–24). *See* Section E.

**Holt, Rt. Hon. Harold Edward** (1908–1967), Australian politician; succeeded Sir Robert Menzies as Prime Minister and leader of the Liberal Party in January 1966. Drowned in swimming accident.

**Holyoake, George Jacob** (1817–1906), an eminent secularist lecturer and author, who was identified with many popular movements, especially Co-operation, of which he was the historian.

**Holyoake, Rt. Hon. Keith Jacka** (b. 1904), New Zealand politician and farmer; Prime Minister since 1960.

**Homer** (c. 700 B.C.), the most famous of all epic poets. Is supposed to have been a Greek who lived probably at Chios or Smyrna, and has generally been regarded as the author of the *Iliad* and the *Odyssey*, though tradition rather than ascertained fact connects his name with those great poems. *See* H3.

**Hood, Samuel, 1st Viscount Hood** of Whitley, G.C.B. (1724–1816), a successful British admiral, who in 1793 was in command of the Mediterranean fleet, and showed great capacity in that post, taking and occupying Toulon, and capturing Corsica among other exploits.

**Hood, Thomas** (1799–1845), an English poet, who, as a prolific writer of serious as well as humorous poems, stands in his own line unique. Of his serious verse, *The Song of the Shirt*, *The Dream of Eugene Aram* and *The Bridge of Sighs* may be cited as the best examples, while his comic poems, notably those of the punning order, are unequalled.

**Hooke, Robert** (1635–1703), English physicist, a great experimenter and inventor. He was also an architect and drew up a plan for rebuilding London after the Great Fire.

**Hooker, Richard** (1554–1600), Master of the Temple from 1585–91, and afterwards Rector of Boscome. Famed for his book on *Ecclesiastical Polity*, and for his exquisite choice of words, was known as "Judicious Hooker."

**Hopkins, Sir Frederick Gowland, O.M., F.R.S.** (1861–1947), an eminent English bio-chemist, noted for his important work on proteins and vitamins. In 1929 was awarded the Nobel Prize in Medicine for his discovery of Vitamin D. Pres. of the Royal Society 1931–36, and of the British Association, 1933.

**Hopkins, Harry** (1890–1946). Franklin Roosevelt's personal assistant. Particularly assisted the President at the important war-time foreign conferences, as his personal representative abroad, in working out the New Deal, and in the administration of Lend-Lease.

**Hopkinson, John, D.Sc., F.R.S.** (1849–98), English engineer and physicist. Senior Wrangler and Fellow at Cambridge. Studied engineering in his father's works, and set up as a consultative engineer. Specialised in electrical work, and by developing the theory of alternating current and of the magnetic current in dynamos he paved the way to the common use of electricity in daily life. Was Professor of Electrical Engineering at King's College, London, 1890–98.

**Hoppner, John, R.A.** (1758–1810), English portrait painter born in Whitechapel of German parents; studied at the Academy Schools, winning great distinction and painted portraits of many members of the Royal Family.

**Horace,** or more properly Flaccus Quintus Horatius (65–8 B.C.), the famous Roman satirist and poet, who was the friend of Virgil, and attained immortal fame by his *Satires*, *Epodes*, and *Odes*.

**Horniman, Annie Elizabeth Fredericka, C.H.** (1830–1937). English theatre manager and founder of the repertory system in England. She was the daughter of F. J. Horniman, the traveller and collector, who founded the Horniman Museum in Forest Hill and presented it to the L.C.C. in 1901.

**Houdini, Harry** (1874–1926), American magician, son of a Hungarian rabbi, world-famed for his escapes from handcuffs, locked chambers, sealed cases under water, etc. His real name was Erich Weiss, and he took his stage name from the French conjuror Houdin. He was a keen student of psychic phenomena and exposed fraudulent mediums.

**Housman, Laurence** (1865–1959). English playwright, poet, and novelist, younger brother of Alfred Edward (1859–1936) also a poet of distinction, a professor of Latin at Cambridge and an eminent classical scholar, author of *A Shropshire Lad*.

**Howard, John** (1726–1790), earned celebrity for his philanthropic efforts on behalf of prison reform, the pursuit of which eventually exposed him to a fatal fever attack in Russia.

**Howard of Effingham, Lord** (1536–1624), commander of the fleet which defeated the Spanish Armada, 1588, and took part in the capture of Cadiz, 1596.

**Howe, Elias** (1819–1867), an ingenious American who was the inventor of the first sewing machine, by which he made a great fortune.

**Howe, Julia Ward** (1819–1910), American philanthropist and poetess, famous as the authoress of the *Battle Hymn of the Republic* (1861), a leader of the American Suffragette movement, and the first woman to be elected to the American Academy of Arts and Letters.

**Howe, Richard, 1st (and last) Earl** (of first creation), K.G. (1726–1799), the British admiral who in 1758 destroyed Cherbourg and in 1794 won the famous victory over the French off Brest.

**Howells, William Dean** (1837–1920), American critic and novelist.

**Hubble, Edwin Powell, B.Sc., Ph.D.** (1889–1953), U.S. astronomer at Mount Wilson Observatory from 1919 until his death. Noted for his work on extragalactic nebulæ and with the aid of the 200-in. telescope at Mount Palomar made important discoveries.

**Hudson, Henry** (c. 1550–1611), was a famous English navigator who discovered the Hudson River, Hudson Strait and Bay, and his two books describing his voyages are of the greatest interest.

**Hudson, William Henry** (1841–1922), English author and naturalist, who spent his early years in South America, memories of which influenced much of his work. His books include *The Purple Land* (1885), *Green Mansions* (1904), *Afoot in England* (1909) and *British Birds* (1895). The Hyde Park Bird Sanctuary (opened in 1925) was established in his memory, and contains the famous figure of *Rima* by Epstein.

**Huggins, Sir William, O.M., K.C.B., F.R.S.** (1824–1910), British astronomer who pioneered in spectroscopic photography. Collaborated with his wife, Margaret Lindsay Murray (1848–1915), who was also an able astronomer.

**Hughes, Thomas** (1822–1896), educated at Rugby and at Oxford; practised at the Bar, and became a County Court Judge in 1882. His best-known work is *Tom Brown's Schooldays*.

**Hugo, Victor Marie** (1802–1885), the great poet, dramatist and novelist who headed the Romantic movement in France in the early part of the 19th century. He was a man of abounding energy and creative ability. His dramas include *Hernani*, *Ruy Blas*, and *Le Roi s'amuse*. Of his novels, *Notre Dame* belongs to his early period, *Les Misérables* and *The Toilers of the Sea*, to his later life, written while he was living in exile in Guernsey. Less well known is his astonishing skill as a graphic artist, evident even in his boyhood.

Hull, Field Marshal Sir Richard Amyatt, K.C.B., D.S.O., B.A. (b. 1907), British Army cavalry officer, succeeded Sir Francis Festing as C.I.G.S. in 1961, and Lord Mountbatten as Chief of the Defence Staff in 1965.

Humboldt, Baron Friedrich Heinrich Alexander von (1769–1859), German naturalist and explorer whose researches are recorded in his two great books *Voyage de Humboldt et Bonpland* (23 vols., 1805–34) and *Cosmos* (5 vols., 1845–62).

Hume, David (1711–1776), the celebrated historian and philosopher whose *History of England* long held chief place in English historical literature. But Hume's enduring fame rests upon his philosophical writings. He developed the empiricism of Locke into the scepticism inherent in it. His main works are *Treatise of Human Nature* and *Dialogues Concerning Natural Religion*.

Hunt, Brig. (Henry Cecil) John, Baron, C.B.E., D.S.O. (b. 1910), leader of the successful 1953 British Everest Expedition, and director of the Duke of Edinburgh's Award Scheme for Youth. Life peerage conferred, 1966.

Hunt, (James Henry) Leigh (1784–1859), an English poet, politician and essayist. In 1813 he was fined £500, and sentenced to two years' imprisonment for libelling the Prince Regent, and while in prison wrote his poem, *The Story of Rimini*, and other works. In later life he was a constant contributor to literature and from 1847 enjoyed a pension of £200 a year from the Civil List.

Hunt, Wm. Holman, O.M. (1827–1910), one of the three founders of the Pre-Raphaelite movement, and an artist who achieved distinction by several remarkable paintings, the chief of which is, perhaps, *The Light of the World*, an allegorical work.

Hunter, the brothers William, F.R.S. (1718–83) and John, F.R.S. (1728–93), were both famous Scottish physicians. William had remarkable success as a lecturer and obstetrician. His valuable anatomical collection was bequeathed to the Univ. of Glasgow. John showed real genius for anatomy, became one of the greatest surgeons of his day and made many discoveries. His surgical museum forms part of the Museum of the Royal College of Surgeons.

Huss, or Hus, John (1369–1415), the Bohemian religious reformer, was strongly influenced by Wyclif and himself urged reform both of abuses in the church and of doctrine. Sentenced to death or recantation he suffered martyrdom on July 6, 1415. His death caused a civil war which lasted for many years.

Hussein ibn Talal (b. 1934), grandson of King Abdullah, succeeded his father Talal as King of Jordan, Aug. 11, 1952.

Hutton, James, M.D. (1726–97), an Edinburgh doctor whose geological researches established the fundamental principles of modern geology. Before his time geology did not exist as a science, all was speculation. He drew his evidence from the rocks themselves, and his *Theory of the Earth* is one of the great classics of science.

Huxley, Aldous (Leonard), C.L. (1894–1963), noted modern writer, grandson of T. H. Huxley and brother of Julian; author of *Crome Yellow*, *Jesting Pilate*, *Brave New World*, *Point Counter Point*, *Ends and Means*, *Grey Eminence*, *The Perennial Philosophy*, etc. *See also* M5.

Huxley, Sir Julian Sorrell, M.A., F.R.S. (b. 1887), biologist and writer, grandson of T. H. Huxley. Director-General of Unesco, 1946–48. Secy. of Zoological Soc. of London 1935–42.

Huxley, Thomas Henry, F.R.S. (1825–1895), an eminent scientist and author of numerous works covering a great range of research. After the publication of Darwin's *Origin of Species*, Huxley became an ardent evolutionist. His biological work, *Man's Place in Nature*, and his numerous essays were marked by great vigour and clearness of thought, and gave him a leading position. He held numerous important appointments was President of the Royal Society in 1883, and belonged to many learned societies.

Huygens, Christiaan (1629–1695), Dutch mathematician, physicist, and astronomer, son of the poet Constantijn Huygens (1596–1687); discovered the rings of Saturn, invented the pendulum clock, and developed the wave theory of light in opposition to the corpuscular theory of Newton.

Hyde, Dr, Douglas (1860–1949), the distinguished Irish scholar, historian, poet and folk-lorist. President of Eire, 1938–45.

Hypatia of Alexandria, the only woman mathematician of antiquity. She excited the enmity of Christian fanatics, who raised an agitation against her, and she was put to death in A.D. 415.

# I

Ibrahim Pasha (1789–1848), an able Egyptian statesman, general, and Viceroy, who, adopted by Mohammed Ali as his son, contributed largely to the success of Egyptian policy during the quarter of a century or more of his influence. His conquest of Syria was a notable feat of generalship. He died a few months after being appointed Viceroy.

Ibsen, Henrik Johan (1828–1906), the Norwegian playwright and poet, moralist, and humanist, whose plays, though arousing considerable opposition at the time, are acknowledged as the work of one of the world's greatest dramatists. A master of technique, charging every detail with significance, fusing the comic with the tragic, Ibsen revolutionised the European theatre. His chief works are *Ghosts*, *The Master Builder*, *The Wild Duck*, *A Doll's House*, *Hedda Gabler* and the poetic drama *Peer Gynt*.

Inge, Very Rev. William Ralph, K.C.V.O., D.D. (1860–1954), English divine; Dean of St. Paul's, 1911–34; Assistant Master at Eton, 1884–88; Lady Margaret Prof. Camb., 1907–11. Earned the sobriquet "the gloomy Dean" for his incisive and somewhat pessimistic comments on contemporary affairs.

Ingersoll, Robert Green (1833–99), American lawyer, writer, and lecturer, became known by reason of his lectures directed principally against Christianity.

Ingres, Jean Auguste Dominique (1780–1867), a great French historical painter who was elected to the Institute in 1824, and at his death was a Senator of France.

Innocent III. (1160–1216), Pope from 1198, successfully asserted the power of the papacy over such secular princes as the emperor, Philip II. of France, and John of England. He promoted the 4th Crusade, initiated the crusade against the Albigensian heretics, and held the 4th Lateran Council. His pontificate marks the zenith of the medieval papacy.

Inönü, General Ismet (b. 1884), Prime Min. of Turkey; leader of the Republican People's Party founded by Kemal Atatürk whom he succeeded as Pres., 1938–50, after serving as Prime Min. from 1923 to Atatürk's death in 1938.

Iqbal, Dr. Sir Muhammad (1875–1938), poet-philosopher of the East, b. Sialkot, W. Pakistan, acknowledged as a great authority in the world of literature, both in prose and poetry. He wrote in Urdu, Persian, and English.

Ireland, John (1879–1962), English composer, best known for his settings of the poems of Thomas Hardy, A. E. Housman, and Masefield's *Sea Fever*. He also wrote chamber music, orchestral work and piano pieces.

Irving, Sir Henry (1838–1905), a great English actor who made his first appearance in London in 1866 and whose first distinct success was as Digby Grant in *Two Roses*. His record at the Lyceum Theatre from 1871 onwards covered a brilliant series of productions, including *The Bells*, his first triumph, *Charles I.*, *Eugene Aram*, and a number of Shakespearean impersonations, in some of which, notably Shylock and Hamlet, Irving gave memorable performances.

Irving, Washington (1783–1859), a writer of charming stories and miscellaneous works which won wide favour on both sides of the Atlantic.

Isabella of Castile (1451–1504), reigned jointly with Ferdinand V., her husband. During their thirty years' sway Spain was united as a single monarchy, and achieved the height of its greatness, the discovery of America, the conquest of Granada, and the expulsion of the Moors from Spain being among the events of her reign.

Ismail Pasha (1830–95), grandson of Mohammed

**B43**

Ali was a man of modern ideas and great public spirit, whose policy rendered Egypt practically independent of Turkey, the Sultan confirming him in the position and title of Khedive in 1873. It was his adoption of the idea of the Suez Canal that enabled that work to be successfully carried out. By reckless extravagance he involved himself in difficulties, entailing the sale of his Suez Canal shares to England, the establishment of the dual control of England and France, and his own abdication in 1879, when his son Tewfik succeeded.

**Israels, Joseph** (1824–1911), outstanding Dutch genre painter of the 19th century.

**Ito, Hirobumi, Prince** (1841–1909), one of the most enlightened statesmen of Japan. The unparalleled social metamorphosis which Japan underwent in the latter half of the nineteenth century owed much to his guidance and influence. Was four times Premier.

**Ivan the Great** (1440–1505), succeeded in bringing the scattered provinces of Muscovy under one supreme governmental control, and put an end to Tartar rule.

**Ivan the Terrible** (1530–84), crowned as first Czar of Russia in 1547, was a strong and autocratic ruler. He furthered internal consolidation and Russian eastward expansion and entered into trading relations with Queen Elizabeth.

# J

**Jacks, Lawrence Pearsall** (1860–1955), Principal of Manchester College, Oxford, 1915–31, and Professor of Philosophy in that College, 1903–31. Entered ministry in 1887 as assistant to the Rev. Stopford Brooke. Editor of the *Hibbert Journal*, 1902–47, and author of several books of religious studies.

**Jackson, Andrew** (1767–1845), American general who was twice President of the United States.

**Jackson, Thomas Jonathan** (1824–1863), popularly known as " Stonewall Jackson," was the most brilliant general on the Southern side in the American Civil War. Was accidentally killed at the Battle of Chancellorsville. The term " Stonewall " refers to his dogged resistance at the first Battle of Bull Run.

**Jacobs, William Wymark** (1863–1943), novelist of quaint and peculiar humour, whose stories and sketches of East End riverside life are inimitable.

**Jacquard, Joseph Marie** (1752–1834), a French mechanic whose Jacquard loom provided a new and effective method of weaving designs in textile fabrics, and was an invention of the very first rank.

**Jagellons, Lithuanian-Polish** dynasty, ruled in Poland 1386–1572.

**James I.** (1566–1625), King of England (1603–25) and, as James VI., King of Scotland (1567–1625). He was the son of Mary Stuart and succeeded to the English throne on the death of Elizabeth. Numerous plots were formed against him, including the Gunpowder Plot of 1605. He persecuted the Puritans, granted many monopolies, and saw the Authorised Version of the Bible published. Described by Henry IV of France as " the wisest fool in Christendom."

**James II.** (1633–1701) King of England and, as James VII., of Scotland (1685–88), younger son of Charles I. As Duke of York he was Lord High Admiral in the Second and Third Dutch Wars, during which New Amsterdam fell to England and was renamed New York. As a Roman Catholic he resigned his office after the Test Act of 1673, was nearly excluded from the Succession, and, when he came to the throne in 1685, aroused and united strong opposition by his attempts to obtain better conditions for his co-religionists. The unsuccessful Monmouth Rebellion, the Bloody Assize, the Declaration of Indulgence, and the Seven Bishops' Trial marked a reign which ended in the flight of the King and the Revolution Settlement of 1689.

**James, Henry, O.M.** (1843–1916), an Anglo-American novelist and younger brother of William James. He wrote over 100 tales and short stories (many of them foremost examples of their kind) and was one of the most sensitive critics of his day. For the last thirty years of his life he resided mostly in London. His best-

known novels are *The Europeans* (1878), *Daisy Miller* (1878), *The Portrait of a Lady* (1881), *The Bostonians* (1886), *What Maisie Knew* (1897), and *The Wings of the Dove* (1902). Became a British subject 1915.

**James, William** (1842–1910), the great American psychologist and philosopher, brother of Henry James, the novelist. He became Prof. of Philosophy at Harvard University, 1882, and was the founder of the philosophical system known as pragmatism. His first important work, *Principles of Psychology*, 1890, stamped him as one of the most lucid, penetrating and engaging writers of his day.

**Janáček, Leoš** (1854–1928), Czech composer, conductor, teacher, and student of folk music, b. in Moravia, son of a village schoolmaster, creator of a national style. He wrote much choral, orchestral, and instrumental music and his best known opera is *Jenufa*. *See* Section E.

**Jeans, Sir James Hopwood, O.M., F.R.S.** (1877–1946), mathematician and astronomer, author of *The Universe Around Us*, *The Mysterious Universe*.

**Jefferies, Richard** (1848–1887), an English naturalist, who, between 1873 and the time of his death, wrote some of the most beautiful descriptions of natural scenery and the customs and habits of the rural world that we possess. His *Gamekeeper at Home* and *The Life of the Fields* are books of great power and sympathy.

**Jefferson, President Thomas** (1743–1826), took part in the American Revolution, and drew up the Declaration of Independence. Twice U.S. Pres.

**Jeffreys, George, 1st Baron of Wem** (1645–1689), Lord Chief Justice of Charles II and Lord Chancellor of James II, won for himself unenviable notoriety by his harsh and cruel judgments at the Bloody Assize. He died in the Tower shortly after the flight of James II. It is now thought that the traditional view of Jeffreys is probably untrue as local records give a rather different picture of an able and conscientious judge.

**Jellicoe, Adml. of the Fleet, Earl, G.C.B., O.M., G.C.V.O.** (1859–1935), Commander-in-Chief of British Fleet, August 1914 to Nov. 1916; and First Sea Lord, Nov. 1916 to Dec. 1917; Gov.-Gen. of New Zealand, 1920–24.

**Jenghiz Khan** (1162–1227), the famous Mogul ruler who twice conquered China, and forced the Turks within European confines.

**Jenner, Edward, M.D., F.R.S.** (1749–1823), an English physician who became celebrated by his discovery of the vaccination system of alleviating smallpox, which has been of such incalculable benefit to mankind. Parliament made him grants amounting to £30,000 which left him still out of pocket.

**Jerome, Jerome Klapka** (1859–1927), a clever journalist and writer, who made his first success with his humorous book, *Three Men in a Boat*. He founded *The Idler*.

**Jerome, St.** (340–420), a noted theologian of the 5th century, whose Latin translation of the Scriptures (*The Vulgate*) made him famous. He died at Bethlehem.

**Jesus Christ** (c. 6 B.C.–c. A.D. 29), the founder of Christianity and the greatest figure of human history. The main source of information on His life and work is the New Testament. Jesus was born at Bethlehem in Judæa, and was the first-born of His mother Mary. According to Matthew. He was miraculously conceived and Joseph was His foster-father. The family home was at Nazareth in Galilee. Jesus lived at a critical period in Jewish history. His teaching is summarised in the Sermon on the Mount. So far as scholars can tell Jesus was born some six years earlier than the date which Christian tradition has chosen to fix the first year of its era.

**Jiménez, Juan Ramón** (b. 1881), Spanish lyric poet who was awarded the Nobel Prize for Literature in 1956.

**Jinnah, Mohammed Ali** (1876–1948), Indian statesman. The emergence of a separate Moslem state of Pakistan when the British left India was mainly due to his efforts. He was for many years the active President of the Moslem League, and in 1947 became the first Gov.-Gen. of Pakistan.

**Joachim, Joseph** (1831–1907), Hungarian violinist and composer of the classical-romantic school of

Mendelssohn, Schumann, and Brahms. He ranks as the greatest solo violinist the world has ever known.

**Joan of Arc, St.** (1412–1431), the girl whose heroism inspired the French to drive the English out of Orleans, and enabled Charles to be proclaimed King at Rheims. She was burned as a heretic at Rouen. Canonised at St. Peter's, Rome, 1920.

**Joffre, Marshal Joseph Jacques Césaire,** G.C.B., Hon. O.M. (1852–1931), Commander-in-Chief of the French Armies 1911–16. With Gen. Gallieni deserves credit for the French counter-attack at the Battle of the Marne. Entered the Army in 1870, and commanded a battery during the siege of Paris.

**John XXIII.** (1881–1963), elected Pope in 1958 on the death of Pius XII; formerly Cardinal Angelo Giuseppe Roncalli, patriarch of Venice. The Ecumenical Council which opened in Rome in 1962 was one of the great achievements of his short reign. He sought to reform the Church to meet the needs and conditions of the times and set in train movements towards Christian unity. The principal sources of his teaching are the two enlightened encyclicals, *Mater et Magistra* (1961) and *Pacem in Terris* (1963).

**John, St.,** the Baptist (executed A.D. 28), the forerunner of Christ.

**John, St.,** the Evangelist, one of the twelve apostles of Jesus, a Galilean fisherman, son of Zebedee and brother of James, traditionally the author of the fourth Gospel.

**John,** surnamed "Lackland" (1167–1216), King of England from 1199 to his death at Newark after deposition by the Barons in 1216. One of the most detested of English monarchs, but whose reign stands out large in history because of his having granted, under compulsion, the Magna Carta, England's great bulwark of liberty.

**John of Gaunt** (1340–1399), Duke of Lancaster, son of Edward III, and father of Henry IV., one of the most powerful English nobles of his day. In Wat Tyler's rebellion his palace in the Savoy was destroyed.

**John Augustus Edwin,** O.M., R.A. (1878–1961), British painter and etcher, b. in Wales; a noted portrait painter whose sitters included Lloyd George, Bernard Shaw, T. E. Lawrence.

**Johnson, Amy,** C.B.E. (1903–1941), was the first woman aviator to fly solo from England to Australia, when she made a record flight to India (6 days to Karachi). Lost her life when flying as a pilot of the Air Transport Auxiliary over the Thames Estuary.

**Johnson, Lyndon Baines** (b. 1908), Democratic President of the United States, 1963–9; Vice-Pres., 1961–3. Automatically became Pres. on death by assassination of Kennedy; won decisive victory over Goldwater in 1964. He steered many progressive Bills into the Statute book, but the achievements of his regime were clouded by the war in Vietnam and the urban riots. He did not stand for a further term of office.

**Johnson, Dr. Samuel** (1709–1784), the great lexicographer and writer, who for a number of years was the most prominent literary man in England. His *Dictionary* was published in 1755, before which he had attained eminence by several works including the *Vanity of Human Wishes*. His *Rasselas* appeared in 1759, and for two years he published *The Idler*, a collection of essays after the style of the *Spectator*. His *Lives of the Poets* appeared in 1781. He was greatly honoured during his life, enjoyed a pension of £300 a year from 1762, at his death was buried in Westminster Abbey, and had the best biography in the language written upon him by James Boswell.

**Johnston, Sir Harry (Hamilton),** G.C.M.G., K.C.B. (1858–1927), was a daring and successful explorer, who led scientific expeditions into the interior of Africa. Helped to crush the Arab slave trade in East Africa and to add Nyasaland and part of N. Rhodesia to the British empire.

**Joliot-Curie, Jean Frédéric** (1900–58), French physicist. His wife Irène (1896–1956), daughter of Pierre and Marie Curie, was also a distinguished scientist. Their discovery of artificial radioactivity brought them a Nobel Prize in 1935. Both were dismissed from the French Atomic Energy Commission because of their sympathy for communism.

**Jones, Ernest Charles** (1819–69), one of the best-known leaders of the Chartist movement, was sentenced in 1848 to two years' imprisonment for his revolutionary speeches.

**Jones, Sir Harold Spencer,** K.B.E., F.R.S. (1890–1960), Astronomer Royal, 1933–55; H.M. Astronomer Cape of Good Hope, 1923–33. His major research was to determine the mean distance of the earth from the sun, 93,004,000 miles.

**Jones, Inigo** (1573–1652), a noted architect, who became known as "the English Palladio," and built, among other famous structures, the Banqueting Hall at Whitehall and the gateway of St. Mary's at Oxford. He was a Royalist, and suffered severely in the Civil War.

**Jonson, Ben** (1573–1637), a friend of Shakespeare and one of the great poets and dramatists of his age. Was Poet Laureate from 1619. His best plays are *Every Man in his Humour* and *The Alchemist.* Buried in Westminster Abbey.

**Josephine, Empress** (1763–1814), was the wife of Napoleon I. until he divorced her in 1809 and married Marie Louise. Josephine had previously been married to Vicomte Alexandre Beauharnais, by whom she had two children.

**Josephus, Flavius** (A.D. 38–c. 100), Jewish historian whose *History of the Jewish War* and *Antiquities of the Jews* contained much valuable historical evidence bearing upon Biblical history.

**Joule, James Prescott,** F.R.S. (1818–1889), one of the greatest of English physicists, famous for his researches on electro-magnetism and for his determination of the mechanical equivalent of heat.

**Jowett, Benjamin** (1817–93), English scholar remembered as the greatest Master of Balliol College, winning a great reputation for his sympathy and erudition. His outstanding works include translations of the *Dialogues of Plato* and *History of Thucydides.* His Mastership raised Balliol to a proud pre-eminence among the Colleges.

**Jowitt, William Allen,** Earl, P.C. (1885–1957), Lord High Chancellor in the Labour Governments, 1945–51. Pub. *The Strange Case of Alger Hiss* (1953).

**Joyce, James** (1882–1941), Irish author who because of the originality, daring, and range of his work exercised a great influence on the younger school of novelists, critics, and poets. Notable among his works are *Portrait of the Artist as a Young Man*, *Ulysses*, and *Finnegans Wake.*

**Juin, Alphonse,** Marshal of France (1888–1967), C.-in-C. of French troops in N. Africa, 1942; Res.-Gen. in Morocco, 1947–51; C.-in-C. Allied Forces, Central Europe (NATO), 1951–56.

**Julian the Apostate (Flavius Claudius Julianus)** (331–363) was Roman Emperor for the last two years of his life, during which period he was an avowed pagan, though previously he had professedly been a Christian. He was slain by an arrow during an expedition against Persia.

**Julius Cæsar.** (See Cæsar Caius Julius.)

**Jung, Carl Gustav** (1875–1961), Swiss psychiatrist, founder of the Zür School, and a former pupil of Freud (*q.v.*) until 1911, when he formulated a system of analytical psychology. (See Section J.)

**Junot, Andoche, Duc d'Abrantès** (1771–1813), one of Napoleon's great generals, brilliantly successful until defeated by Wellington at Vimeiro.

**Jusserand, Jean Adrien Antoine Jules** (1855–1932), French author and diplomat; Ambassador to U.S.A., 1902–25. A well-known authority on English literature, his works include *The English Theatre from the Conquest to Shakespeare* (1878), *The English Novel* (1886), *The Literary History of the English up to the Renaissance* (1894).

**Justinian I. (Flavius Anicius Justinianus)** (483–565) was the Roman Emperor of the East whose fame rests chiefly on his laws. His *Corpus Juris Civilis* remained the accepted text-book of Roman Law to the end of the 9th century, and is still the most important of all monuments of jurisprudence. He reigned from 527 to 565.

**Juvenal (Decimus Junius Juvenalis)** (60–140), the famous Roman poet and rhetorician of the age of Trajan. His sixteen celebrated *Satires* are the finest in classical literature.

# K

**Kafka, Franz** (1883–1924), Jewish writer, born in Prague, whose introspective work, the bulk of which was not published till after his early death from tuberculosis, has been widely acclaimed and discussed, and has had a notable influence on later schools, including the Surrealists. *See also* M6.

**Kálidāsa** (c. A.D. 400), the most illustrious figure in classic Sanskrit literature and one of the greatest Oriental poets. No facts are known about his life and date, but certain evidence places him in the 5th cent. Seven of his works survive: two lyrics, *Ritu-samhara* (The Seasons), and *Megha-dūta* (Cloud Messenger); two epics, *Raghu-vamśa* (Dynasty of Raghu) and *Kumāra-sambhava* (Birth of the War-God); and three dramas, *Śakūntalā*, *Mālavikāgnimitra*, and *Vikramorvaśīya*.

**Kant, Immanuel** (1724–1804), great German philosopher, author of three great *Critiques*: *Critique of Pure Reason* (1781), *Critique of Practical Reason* (1788), and *Critique of Judgement* (1790). He came from a Pietist family of Königsberg and was influenced by the writings of his neighbour Hamann (*see* Romanticism, J39) and by Rousseau and Hume. His own works were of immense influence in shaping the liberal thought of the 18th and 19th centuries. He was a man of humanitarian ideas and believed passionately in the freedom of man to make his own decisions and considered the exploitation of man as the worst evil.

**Kapitsa, Pyotr** (b. 1894), one of Russia's greatest physicists; worked with Rutherford on atomic research at the Cavendish Laboratory, Cambridge; returned to Russia in 1935. Dir. Inst. for Physical Problems, Academy of Sciences of the U.S.S.R.

**Kauffmann, Angelica**, R.A. (1741–1807), Anglo-Swiss painter, one of the foundation members of the Royal Academy.

**Kaulbach, Wilhelm von** (1805–1874), an eminent German painter who illustrated books by Goethe and Schiller.

**Kean, Charles John** (1811–1868), an English actor-manager, son of the tragedian, Edmund Kean. Charles Kean married Ellen Tree, and in the 'fifties played with her in a series of spectacular revivals at the Princess's Theatre in London.

**Kean, Edmund** (1787–1833), one of the greatest tragic actors in the history of the British stage.

**Keats, John** (1795–1821), the great English poet who, though dying at the early age of twenty-five, produced a number of poems which in richness of imagination and beauty of thought are not excelled by anything in the language. His *Odes*, his two poems, *Isabella* and *The Eve of St. Agnes*, are exquisite in form and expression.

**Keble, John** (1792–1866), an English clergyman and poet, whose *Christian Year* is one of the most notable works of its class.

**Keller, Helen Adams**, B.A. (1880–1968), American author and lecturer who overcame great physical handicaps (blind and deaf before the age of two) to live an active and useful life.

**Kelvin, William Thompson, Lord**, P.C., O.M., G.C.V.O., F.R.S. (1824–1907), British mathematician and physicist, famed for his work on heat and thermodynamics, and for his contributions to electrical science and submarine telegraphy. In the domain of heat he stands to Joule as Maxwell stands to Faraday in the history of electrical science, both bringing pre-eminently mathematical minds to bear on the results of experimental discoveries. He introduced the Kelvin or Absolute Scale of temperature and was one of the original members of the Order of Merit.

**Kemble, Frances Anne ("Fanny")** (1809–1893), was a noted actress in the early part of the 19th century. She was the daughter of Charles Kemble (1775–1854), who was also a celebrated actor, associated in many appearances with his brother, John Philip Kemble and their talented sister, Mrs. Siddons (*q.v.*).

**Kempenfelt, Admiral Richard** (1718–1782), an English naval officer who saw distinguished service, and sank with his ship the *Royal George* off Spithead, through a shifting of the guns when refitting which caused the vessel to capsize.

**Kempis, Thomas à** (1380–1471), name by which the German mystic and writer Thomas Hammerken was known, was a monk of the St. Augustine order, whose life was mainly spent at a monastery near Zwolle. He was the author of *The Imitation of Christ*, a work which has been translated into all languages.

**Kennedy, John Fitzgerald** (1917–63), President of the United States, 1961–63, the youngest and the first Roman Catholic ever to be elected, son of a wealthy financier. He enjoyed a world-wide personal pre-eminence and gave to the American people a new sense of purpose to meet the changes and challenges of a scientific age. He fought to end racial discrimination and though he had small success in getting his legislation through Congress, he made his mark in foreign affairs, initiating a new era in East-West relations. Assassinated during a motor-cade drive through Dallas, Texas, on 22 November 1963. His brother, Senator Robert Kennedy, was shot dead in Los Angeles in 1968 while campaigning in the presidential election of that year. *See also* Section C, Part I.

**Kent, William** (1684–1748), a leading figure in British art, 1725 until middle of eighteenth century—architecture, landscape gardening, interior decoration, furniture, and painting. Strong Italianate influence. Surviving works: The Great Hall at Holkham, Norfolk, and lay-out at Rousham, Oxfordshire.

**Kenyatta, Jomo** (b. 1893), African national leader who became Kenya's first Prime Minister (1962) and first President (1964) when Kenya became a Republic within the Commonwealth.

**Kepler, Johann** (1571–1630), renowned German astronomer, assistant to Tycho Brahe (1546–1601), whose measurements he used in working out his laws of planetary motion, which are: 1. The planets describe elliptic orbits, of which the sun is one focus. 2. The line joining a planet to the sun sweeps out equal areas in equal times. 3. The square of the period of revolution of a planet is proportional to the cube of its average distance from the sun. The explanation of these laws was given by Newton.

**Keyes, Admiral of the Fleet, Lord**, G.C.B., K.C.V.O., C.M.G., D.S.O. (1872–1945). Commodore of the submarine service during war of 1914–18, and commanded operations against Zeebrugge in 1918.

**Keynes, John Maynard, 1st Baron**, C.B., M.A., F.B.A. (1883–1946), British economist of international reputation. Bursar and Fellow of King's College, Cambridge. His *Treatise on Money* (1930) and *The General Theory of Employment, Interest and Money* (1936) profoundly influenced economic thought and government policy all over the world. Led the British delegation to Bretton Woods and negotiated the American loan agreement of 1945.

**Khrushchev, Nikita Sergeyevich** (b. 1894), Russian statesman who became leader of the Soviet Union soon after the death of Stalin; First Secretary of the Soviet Communist Party, 1953–64; Prime Minister, 1958–64. After the harsh years of the Stalinist régime radical changes became essential and he pursued a policy of relaxation both in home and foreign affairs. Relations with America improved but relations with China became strained. Great advances were made in scientific achievement, notably in the field of space research. In Oct. 1964 his posts were taken over by Leonid Brezhnev (First Secretary) and Alexei Kosygin (Prime Minister). *See also* Section C, Part I.

**Kierkegaard, Sören** (1813–55), Danish philosopher and religious thinker whose views have had great influence on contemporary existentialism. His main work is *Either—Or*.

**King, Martin Luther** (1929–68), American clergyman and Negro integration leader; awarded 1964 Nobel Peace Prize for his consistent support of the principle of non-violence in the coloured people's campaign for civil rights. Assassinated at Memphis, Tennessee.

**King, Rt. Hon. (William Lyon) Mackenzie**, O.M., C.M.G. (1874–1950), Prime Minister of Canada, 1921–25, 1926–30 and 1935–48.

**Kingsley, Charles** (1819–1875), English clergyman and novelist, best known for his historical novels *Hypatia*, *Westward Ho!*, *Hereward the Wake* and children's book *The Water Babies*.

**Kipling, Rudyard** (1865–1936), poet, novelist, and miscellaneous writer. Made himself celebrated while yet a youth by some exceedingly clever and characteristic sketches of Indian life written for the most part while performing journalistic duties in India. He subsequently settled in London and produced a remarkable succession of stories, sketches, ballads, and poems, all marked by intense vigour. In 1907 was awarded the Nobel Prize.

Kirchhoff, Gustav Robert (1824–87). German physicist. He did important work in electricity and thermodynamics and put spectrum analysis on a firm basis. Published, among other scientific works, *Researches on the Solar Spectrum*.

Kitchener, of Khartoum, Field Marshal Earl, K.G., K.P., G.C.B., O.M. (1850–1916), British soldier. By his victory at Omdurman in 1898 he crushed the Sudanese dervishes and avenged General Gordon. In the early stages of the South African War he assisted Lord Roberts and took over command himself in 1900. C.-in-C. India, 1902–9; Secretary of War, 1914–16. Drowned while on his way to Russia.

Klee, Paul (1879–1940), Swiss artist, studied at Munich, Paris and Rome and later became Professor at Düsseldorf Academy. He lived in a restless, experimental period. His paintings are small-scale, delicate dream-world fantasies, full of poetical content.

Kneller, Sir Godfrey, Bt. (1646–1723), the most celebrated portrait painter of his day in England, who enjoyed the patronage in succession of Charles II., James II., William III., Anne, and George I.

Knox, John (1505–1572), the famous divine and Reformer, who stirred Scotland to mighty religious impulses in the reign of Mary Queen of Scots.

Knox, Rt. Rev. Mgr. Ronald Arbuthnot (1888–1957), Catholic Chaplain at the University of Oxford,1926–39, and a well-known author. His works include detective stories, among which are *The Viaduct Murder* and *Footsteps at the Lock*.

Koch, Robert (1843–1910), the most noted bacteriologist of the time, whose discoveries in connection with the bacillus of tuberculosis have greatly benefited mankind. He also closely studied the causes of Asiatic cholera and bubonic plague.

Kodály, Zoltán (1882–1967), Hungarian composer and teacher. He worked with Bartók in the collection of folk-tunes and his compositions include chamber music, sonatas, songs, the great choral work *Psalmus Hungaricus*, the orchestral suite *Háry János*, and the symphony in C, written in 1961. *See* Section E.

Kokoschka, Oskar (b. 1886), Austrian portrait and landscape painter, ranking as one of the world's great interpretative artists. Taught (1920–24) at the Dresden academy of art, lived for a time in Prague before settling (1938) in England.

Koniev, Marshal of Soviet Union, Ivan Stepanovich (b. 1898), one of Russia's outstanding military leaders in the war against Germany, 1941–45.

Korolyov, Sergei (1907–1966), Russian space scientist who designed the world's first earth satellite, the first manned spaceship and the first moon rocket.

Kosciuzko, Tadeusz Andrzoj Bonawentura (1746–1817), a Polish general and patriot who achieved great distinction in 1794 by his gallant leading of the Polish revolutionary forces against Russia. From 1776 to 1783 took part in the American War of Independence.

Kossuth, Louis (1802–1894), a Hungarian patriot and leader, who in the struggle for his country's freedom in 1849 was for a time successful, but ultimately had to acknowledge defeat, and fled first to Turkey and afterwards to England, where he lived for some years.

Kosygin, Alexei Nikolayevich (b. 1904), succeeded Nikita Khrushchev as chairman of the Council of Ministers of the U.S.S.R. (Prime Minister) in Oct. 1964; formerly a deputy chairman of the State Economic Planning Commission, Gosplan.

Kreisler, Fritz (1875–1962), world-famed Austrian violinist, studied in Paris under Massart. First played in United States in 1888. He composed numerous violin pieces, a quartet, and some operettas. Became an American citizen in 1943.

Krenek, Ernst (b. 1900), Austrian composer of partly Czech descent. He first composed in a neo-classic or anti-romantic style, later the influence of jazz was prominent in his compositions, which include the jazz opera *Jonny spielt auf* and many instrumental works and songs. In 1938 he emigrated to the United States.

Kropotkin, Peter Alexeivich, Prince (1842–1921),

anarchist, geographer and explorer, who, after a distinguished career in Russia, his native country, was imprisoned for favouring the political action of a working men's association, but escaped to England. He wrote many important books on socialistic and geographical subjects. Returned to Russia in 1917.

Kruger, Stephanus Johannes Paulus (1825–1904), Boer leader, active in Transvaal politics, serving as President, 1883–1900. His attitude towards the Uitlanders (English and other non-Boer white inhabitants of the Transvaal) produced much of the tension which led to the South African War. During the war he made unsuccessful attempts to secure help for the Boers from various European powers.

Krupp, Alfred (1812–1887), founder of the famous German gun factories at Essen. He installed in a disused factory left him by his father a new steam-engine from England, began to make cast steel, and from 1844 specialised in armaments, building his firm into a vast concern, employing 21,000 workmen at his death. The Emperor William I attended his funeral. The firm continued to expand under his descendants. The Big Bertha guns that shelled Paris in 1918 came from the Krupp works. The founder's great grandson Alfried Krupp von Bohlen und Halbach (b. 1907) was tried as a war criminal in 1948. The Krupp corporation is no longer under one-man control.

Kubelik, Jan (1880–1940), Czech violinist—son of a gardener at Michle, near Prague—who at the age of twelve played in public, and was one of the most renowned instrumentalists of his day. His son Rafael (b. 1914), a conductor of international repute, became musical director of the Royal Opera House, Covent Garden, in 1955.

Kublai Khan (1216–1294), a famous Mogul emperor and grandson of Jenghiz Khan. He greatly extended the Mogul empire by conquest, and lived in unparalleled splendour.

# L

Lablache, Luigi (1794–1858), a famous bass singer and actor, especially popular in London. He held the position of singing tutor to Queen Victoria.

La Fayette, Marie Joseph Paul Roch Yves Gilbert du Motier, Marquis de (1757–1834), French soldier and humanitarian politician who fought on the side of the Colonists in the American War of Independence and on returning to France became C.-in-C. of National Guard of Paris. By signing the demand that the king summon the States-General he became the first leader of the French Revolution, but stood out against its later excesses. In 1830 he was instrumental in setting Louis Philippe on the French throne.

La Fontaine, Jean de (1621–1695), the celebrated French poet and fabulist. His fables have been translated into all languages, and are unique.

Lagerlöf, Selma, Ph.D. (1858–1940), the famous Swedish novelist who was awarded in 1909 the Nobel Prize for literature. In 1914 was elected the first woman member of the Swedish Academy.

Lagrange, Joseph Louis, Comte (1736–1813), noted French astronomer and mathematician.

Lalande, Joseph Jerome Lefrançais de (1732–1807), a famous French astronomer and director of the Paris Observatory. He founded the Lalande yearly prize for the best astronomical work or observation and wrote a well-known treatise on astronomy.

Lamarck, Jean Baptiste Pierre Antoine de Monnet, Chevalier de (1744–1829), the prominent French zoologist who occupied important scientific posts in Paris. A precursor of Darwin, his name rests mainly on his theory of the evolution of animals, known as Lamarckism. His chief work was the *Histoire Naturelle des Animaux sans Vertèbres*.

Lamb, Charles (1775–1834), one of the most delightful of our essayists. His *Essays of Elia* are characterised by great felicity of expression, much genial humour and an ardent love both of rural life and London life. He was a clerk in the office of the East India Company for thirty-five years. In some of his writings he was assisted by his sister, Mary Lamb, to whom he was greatly devoted.

Lamb, Sir Horace, F.R.S. (1849–1934), a British

scientist, was the leading authority on hydro-dynamics, and did valuable research work on wave motions and electricity.

**Lambert, Constant** (1905–51), English composer, conductor and critic; musical director of the Sadler's Wells Ballet. His *Rio Grande* for chorus, piano, and orchestra, shows some jazz influence.

**Landor, Walter Savage** (1775–1864), English poet and writer, best known for his *Imaginary Conversations*.

**Landseer, Sir Edwin Henry**, R.A. (1802–1873), the most celebrated English animal painter of his time. He designed the lions for the base of the Nelson Monument in Trafalgar Square.

**Lane, Edward William** (1801–1876), English Arabic scholar, translator of the *Arabian Nights*.

**Lanfranc** (c. 1005–89), Italian churchman, b. at Pavia; Archbishop of Canterbury, 1070. Closely associated with Duke William of Normandy (William I. of England); carried out Church reforms and preserved its independence.

**Lang, Andrew** (1844–1912), Scottish scholar and writer of great versatility, his numerous works including poetry, fiction, history, fairy tales, folk-lore, and translations from the classics.

**Lang of Lambeth, Most Rev. Cosmo Gordon Lang,** 1st Baron, P.C., G.C.V.O., D.D. (1864–1945), Archbishop of Canterbury, 1928–42; and of York, 1908–28; Bishop of Stepney, 1901–08.

**Langland, William** (c. 1330–1400), author of the alliterative poem *The Vision of Piers the Plowman*.

**Langton, Stephen** (1151–1228), was Archbishop of Canterbury from 1213, and one of the chief instruments in forcing the Magna Carta from John.

**Lansbury, Rt. Hon. George** (1859–1940). British Labour politician; Chairman of Parliamentary Labour Party, 1931–35, Leader of the Labour Party, 1932–35. M.P. Bow and Bromley, 1910–12, and 1922–40.

**Lao-Tzŭ**, one of the ancient philosophers of China, who flourished about 600 B.C. The classic upon which his fame rests, *Tao-té-ching*, was written many years later. (*See* Taoism. Section J.)

**Laplace, Pierre Simon, Marquis de** (1749–1827), French mathematician and astronomer whose researches on the motions of the solar system and the theory of probability earned him the title of "the Newton of France."

**La Rochefoucauld, François, Duc de** (1613–1680), a renowned French statesman and writer of the Louis XIV. period. His *Reflections and Moral Maxims* is a classic.

**Lasker, Emanuel**, Ph.D. (1868–1941), world's chess champion, 1894–1921—defeated by Capablanca (q.v.).

**Lassalle, Ferdinand** (1825–64), founder of the German Socialist movement, and as such exerted deep influence throughout Europe. His life story forms the basis of George Meredith's novel *The Tragic Comedians*.

**Lasso, Orlando di** (c. 1532–94), Flemish composer and choirmaster, contemporary of Palestrina, and the writer of over 2,000 compositions, including *chansons*, madrigals, and sacred music.

**Latimer, Hugh** (circa 1485–1555), the English Reformer who became Bishop of Worcester under Henry VIII., but when Mary came to the throne was condemned as a heretic and burned at the stake.

**Laud, William** (1573–1645), an eminent ecclesiastic, who, after filling three minor bishoprics, was made Archbishop of Canterbury in 1633. He did much to direct the policy of Charles I., and when trouble followed, he was impeached by the Long Parliament and committed to the Tower. Was tried for treason and beheaded.

**Lauder, Sir Harry (MacLennan)** (1870–1950), famous singer of Scottish songs and ballads. Composed own songs and wrote own music. Knighted 1919 for services in raising money for war purposes.

**Laval, Pierre** (1883–1945), French politician, won notoriety over the Hoare–Laval pact in 1935. During the German occupation he was the arch French collaborator, and was afterwards tried for treason and shot.

**Lavery, Sir John**, R.A. (1856–1941), an eminent portrait painter; Pres. of the Royal Society of Portrait Painters, 1932–41.

**Lavoisier, Antoine Laurent** (1743–1794), often called the "father of chemistry," was born in Paris, and was the first to establish the fact that combustion is a form of chemical action.

**Law, Rt. Hon. Andrew Bonar** (1858–1923), Conservative politician. He became leader of the Opposition in 1911, joined the Coalition in 1915, and served as Prime Minister from 1922 until shortly before his death in 1923.

**Lawrence, David Herbert** (1885–1930), English poet and novelist, one of the most powerful and original of modern writers; author of *The White Peacock, Sons and Lovers, The Rainbow, Women in Love, Lady Chatterley's Lover.* He also wrote a number of plays. *See* Sections I and M.

**Lawrence, Sir Thomas**, P.R.A. (1769–1830), one of the fashionable portrait painters of his day.

**Lawrence, Col. Thomas Edward** (1888–1935), known as "Lawrence of Arabia," British soldier who led the Arabs against the Turks in the war of 1914–18. Author of *The Seven Pillars of Wisdom* (1926).

**Leacock, Stephen Butler** (1869–1944), Head of Dept. of Economics, McGill University, Montreal, 1908–36; but best known throughout the world as a humorous writer.

**Leavis, Frank Raymond** (b. 1895), outstanding literary critic, university teacher at Downing College, Cambridge, 1930–62. Edited the influential quarterly magazine *Scrutiny* from 1932 until its demise in 1963. His critical works include *The Great Tradition* (1948), *D. H. Lawrence, Novelist* (1955), and *Anna Karenina and Other Essays* (1967).

**Lecky, Rt. Hon. William Edward Hartpole**, O.M. (1838–1903), an eminent historian. His best-known works are *The History of England in the Eighteenth Century* and *The History of European Morals*.

**Leclerc (de Hauteclocque), General Jacques Philippe**, Marshal of France (1902–1947), French soldier of considerable personal popularity. Was Governor of the Cameroons in 1940, declared for the Free French and later led a Free French force from Lake Chad across the Sahara desert to join the Allied Forces in North Africa. Liberated Paris in 1944; commanded French troops in Indo-China, 1946. Killed in air crash in Algeria.

**Le Corbusier**, pseudonym of Charles-Edouard Jeanneret-Gris (1887–1965), Swiss-born French architect and town-planner whose works and theories with their emphasis on organic planning have profoundly influenced contemporary architecture. Famous for his *ville radieuse* conception of a city and architect of *L'Unité d'Habitation* at Marseilles and of Chandigarh, the joint capital of Punjabi Suba and Hariana.

**Lee of Fareham, Viscount**, P.C., G.C.B., G.C.S.I., G.B.E. (1868–1947). First Lord of the Admiralty, 1921–22. Minister of Agriculture, 1919–21. Presented Chequers Court to the nation as a residence for British Premiers, 1917.

**Lee, Robert Edward** (1807–70), was one of the ablest Confederate generals in the American Civil War, and C.-in-C. when the final surrender was made at Appomattox in 1865.

**Lee, Sir Sidney** (1859–1926), the great authority on Shakespeare, and joint editor with Sir Leslie Stephen of the *Dictionary of National Biography*, exercising undivided control over the completion of that monumental work during the last ten years of its publication.

**Leech, John** (1817–1864), perhaps the most popular of all the *Punch* artists, whose sketches and cartoons were the life and soul of the paper for many years.

**Lehar, Franz** (1870–1948), Hungarian composer, chiefly of light operas, which include *The Merry Widow, The Count of Luxembourg, Frederica, The Land of Smiles*.

**Leibnitz, Gottfried Wilhelm, Freiherr von** (1646–1716), German writer and philosopher and one of the world's supreme intellects. Invented the infinitesimal calculus which he published in 1684, independently of Newton whose previous work on the same subject was published in 1687.

**Leicester, Robert Dudley, Earl of** (1531–88), son of John, Duke of Northumberland (q.v.), was a favourite of Queen Elizabeth. He commanded the English troops in the Netherlands, 1585–87, and in England before the Armada. Married to Amy Robsart (q.v.).

**Leif Ericsson** (fl. A.D. 1000), discoverer of Vinland on the north-east coast of America; born in Iceland, the son of the Norse explorer, Eric the Red, who first colonised Greenland.

**Leighton, Frederick, Baron, P.R.A.** (1830–96), English painter whose popular pictures dealt with classical subjects, characterised by delicacy of finish and splendour of colour.

**Lely, Sir Peter** (1618–80), the famous painter to whom we owe so many of the portraits of the beauties of the Court of Charles II. He was born at Soest and his proper name was Van der Faes.

**Lenin, Vladimir Ilyich Ulyanov** (1870–1924). Russian revolutionary and statesman, architect of the Russian revolution for which cause he worked both " underground " in Russia and abroad during the years 1893–1917. It was in this period that the revolutionary Social-Democratic party was formed. An uncompromising revolutionary group, known as the Bolsheviks, developed within this party and Lenin was its leading spirit. In April 1917 Lenin and his fellow exiles returned to Russia. After the 1917 November revolution Lenin headed the new government and with intense energy consolidated the revolution, applying Marxist principles without dogmatism to the planning of Soviet social and industrial development.

**Leonardo da Vinci** (1452–1519), Italian artist and man of science, natural son of a Florentine lawyer and a peasant girl. He was a painter, an architect, a philosopher, a poet and composer, a sculptor, an athlete, a mathematician and inventor, and an anatomist. These are the qualifications he gave when applying to Lodovico Sforza, Duke of Milan, who was seeking a city planner and civil engineer. Perhaps because he was so many-sided, his artistic output was small, and he is best known for his *Last Supper* painted on the wall of the refectory of Sta. Maria delle Grazie in Milan, and his famous *Mona Lisa* in the Louvre. The extraordinary thing is that, although Leonardo was much admired, few people in his time had any notion of his universal genius. The main reason for this was that much of his work was relegated to the Notebooks which he did not publish and which were written from right to left in what is known as " mirror writing." The anatomy of the body (he himself carried out dissections), the growth of the child in the womb, the laws of waves and currents, the laws of flight, all were studied by this astonishing man, who believed nothing but had to see for himself. He was said to have been exceptionally handsome.

**Leoncavallo, Ruggiero** (1858–1919), Italian composer of the opera *Pagliacci*.

**Leonidas** was king of Sparta at the time of the invasion of Greece by Xerxes, 480 B.C., and led the defence of the Pass of Thermopylæ, where he fell.

**Lermontov, Mikhail Yurevich** (1814–41), great Russian poet and novelist, exiled to the Caucasus for the passionate, revolutionary poem addressed to Czar Nicholas I. written on the death of Pushkin. He has often been called the poet of the Caucasus, for the stern, mountainous country of his youth and exile had a great influence on his poetry. His novel *A Hero of Our Time* was written while he was at St. Petersburg in 1839. Lost his life in a duel.

**Le Sage, Alain René** (1668–1747), author of the famous stories *Gil Blas* and *Le Diable Boiteux*, also a dramatist of note.

**Lesseps, Vicomte Ferdinand de** (1805–94), an engineer of large ideas who, while Vice-Consul at Alexandria, conceived the plan of the Suez Canal, which work was completed in 1869. He afterwards projected the original Panama Canal, which failed.

**Lessing, Gotthold Ephraim** (1729–81), a noted German critic and dramatic poet, whose most celebrated work was his *Laokoon*.

**Leverhulme of the Western Isles, 1st Viscount** (1851–1925). Chairman and founder of the soapmaking firm of Lever Brothers, Port Sunlight, which later, by purchase and amalgamation, increased in size and importance to become Unilever Ltd.

**Leverrier, Urbain Jean Joseph** (1811–77), the French astronomer, co-discoverer with John Couch Adams of the planet Neptune.

**Levi-Strauss, Claude** (b. 1908), eminent French anthropologist and philosopher, leading exponent of the theory of symbolic structures. His works include *Les Structures élémentaires de la parenté*, *Tristes tropiques*, and *Mythologiques*, vols. 1–3.

**Lewis, Cecil Day, C.B.E., M.A., D.Litt.** (b. 1904), poet and critic. Prof. of Poetry, Oxford Univ., 1951–6. Compton Lecturer in Poetry at Hull Univ. 1967–. Besides poetical works he has published translations of Virgil's *The Georgics* and *The Aeneid*; also detective novels under pseudonym of Nicholas Blake. Succeeded John Masefield as Poet Laureate in 1967.

**Lewis, Sinclair** (1885–1951), an American author who secured his first great success in 1920 with his novel of provincial American life, *Main Street*. *Babbitt*, published two years later, ruthlessly satirised the 100 per cent. disciple of American *Big Business*, and added a new term, " Babbitry," to the American language. Awarded the Nobel Prize for literature, 1930.

**Liaquat Ali Khan** (1895–1951), leader of the Moslem League (1946) and first Prime Minister of Pakistan after independence in 1947. Assassinated at Rawalpindi.

**Lie, Trygve** (1896–1968), Sec.-Gen. of the United Nations 1946–52. Formerly a leading Norwegian politician and Foreign Minister, 1941–46.

**Li Hung Chang** (1823–1901), an enlightened Chinese statesman and general, who by sheer ability rose from a humble position to be Chief Minister, and exercised almost supreme control for a number of years.

**Lilburne, John** (1614–57), an English political agitator and pamphleteer, who became the leader of the Levellers, the democratic party in the English Revolution.

**Linacre, Thomas** (c. 1460–1524), humanist scholar and physician, founder of the College of Physicians. Published translations of Galen's works.

**Lincoln, Abraham** (1809–65), was a native of Kentucky; in early life he became a lawyer, and was returned to Congress in 1846 from Springfield, Illinois, and in 1861 was elected 16th President of the United States, when he delivered his famous anti-slavery pronouncement, which led to the Civil War of 1861–65. In 1864 he was re-elected, and in the following year was assassinated by John Wilkes Booth.

**Lind, Jenny** (1820–87), a famous prima donna, " the Swedish nightingale " as she was called, who made a great sensation by her wonderful voice for some seasons in Europe, London and in America, from 1837 onward.

**Linnæus, Carl von Linné** (1707–78), a tireless Swedish doctor and scientist who became one of the most distinguished of naturalists, and the founder of modern botany. His *Systema Naturae* was published in 1735, and other monumental works followed. First to expound the true principles for defining genera and species.

**Lippi, Fra Filippo** (1406–69), one of the great artists of the Italian quatrocento, whose frescoes can be seen in Prato Cathedral. His son Filippino (1457–1504) was equally gifted and executed many great works, including frescoes in the Carmine, Florence, and the altar-piece *Virgin and Saints* in the Uffizi Gallery.

**Lippmann, Gabriel** (1845–1921) French physicist, whose more important work was in the field of colour photography. His numerous inventions include the capillary-electrometer, which bears his name, and many other delicate instruments. Nobel Prize for Physics, 1908.

**Lippmann, Walter** (b. 1889), American journalist, who began writing for the New York *Herald Tribune* in 1931 an influential column which moved to the Washington *Post* in 1962.

**Lipton, Sir Thomas Johnstone, Bt., K.C.V.O.** (1850–1931), Scottish merchant and yachtsman; after several years in the United States he returned to his native Glasgow and opened a grocery store. A pioneer in publicity, he became within a few years the world's biggest shopkeeper. He made five attempts to win the America's Cup.

**Lister, Lord, P.C., O.M., F.R.S.** (1827–1912), achieved renown for his discovery of the antiseptic treatment which has accomplished so much on behalf of surgery. Pres. of Royal Socy. 1895–1900; and of British Assn. 1896.

**Liszt, Franz** (1811–86). Hungarian pianist and composer, whose brilliant playing astonished and delighted Europe and rather overshadowed his importance as a composer. He originated the symphonic poem. His daughter Cosima married Wagner.

**Litvinov, Maxim Maximovich** (1876–1952), Russian diplomat and statesman; Soviet Diplomatic Agent to Great Britain, 1917, Commissar for Foreign Affairs, 1929–39; Soviet Ambassador to United States, 1941–43.

**Liu Shao-ch'i** (b. 1898), Chinese Communist leader; succeeded Mao Tse-tung as Head of State in 1959 and until the "cultural revolution" of 1966–67 considered to be his heir-apparent. Expelled from party and state posts, 1968.

**Livingstone, Dr. David** (1813–73), the great Scottish explorer and missionary, whose discoveries in Africa included the course of the Zambesi, the Victoria Falls, and Lake Nyasa. He opened up Central Africa to the influences of Christianity, and stirred the public conscience to the horrors of the Slave Trade. In 1871 considerable apprehension was felt in regard to his fate, but he was discovered by H. M. Stanley at Ujiji near Lake Tanganyika.

**Lloyd, Marie** (1870–1922), English music-hall artist and genius of Cockney comedy.

**Lloyd George of Dwyfor, Earl, O.M.** (1863–1945), Chairman of the Liberal Party, 1924–31. Prime Minister, 1916–22. M.P. for Caernarvon, 1890–1944. As a War Premier he displayed activity, resourcefulness, and driving power, which proved a tremendous influence in bringing about the defeat of Germany; and at the Peace Conference, in conjunction with Clemenceau and President Wilson, he was a master spirit. His daughter Lady Megan Lloyd George (d. 1966) who was Liberal M.P. for Anglesey, 1929–51, joined the Labour Party in 1955.

**Locke, John** (1632–1704), one of the great English liberal philosophers and founder of empiricism, the doctrine that all knowledge is derived from experience. His chief work in theoretical philosophy, *Essay Concerning Human Understanding*, was written just before the revolution of 1688 and published in 1690. Other writings include: *Letters on Toleration, Treatises on Government,* and *Education.*

**Lombroso, Cesare, M.D.** (1836–1909), famous Italian criminologist; in 1889 published his monumental work *L'uomo delinquente*, in which he put forward the theory that there was a definite criminal type which could be distinguished from the normal type, both anatomically and psychologically. He did much by his writings to hasten prison reform.

**Lomonosov, Mikhail Vasilyevich** (1711–65), Russian poet, philosopher, and scientist, associated with the foundation of Moscow University in the reign of the Empress Elizabeth.

**London, John Griffith ("Jack")** (1876–1916), an American novelist who led an adventurous life and wrote many popular novels and stirring books of adventure.

**Longfellow, Henry Wadsworth** (1807–82), an American poet who produced a number of volumes of poetry of great purity of thought and beauty of language. Author of *Hiawatha.*

**Lonsdale, Dame Kathleen D.B.E., F.R.S.** (b. 1903), Professor of Chemistry and head of the Dept. of Crystallography, Univ. College, Univ. of London. Pres. British Association, 1968.

**Lonsdale, 5th Earl of, K.G., G.C.V.O.** (1857–1944), was a well-known sportsman whose special interests were horse-racing, hunting and boxing, the Lonsdale belts having been founded by him.

**Lope de Vega Carpio, Félix** (1562–1635), founder of the Spanish drama, and one of the great figures of Spanish literature. He was one of the most prolific of writers, his dramatic productions alone numbering 1500 plays, of which some 450 survive.

**Louis IX.** (1214–70), St. Louis, king of France, crusader, and peace-maker, fulfilled the medieval ideal of the knightly king. Memoirs by the Sire de Joinville.

**Louis XIV.** (1638–1715), ruled France as absolute monarch after Mazarin's death in 1661, having come to the throne at the age of 5. Asserted French supremacy through an efficient and all-powerful monarchy, but had to face coalition of European powers (League of Ausburg and the Grand Alliance). Revoked Edict of Nantes (1685). The magnificent palace at Versailles is a fitting monument to one who considered himself the most powerful monarch in Christendom.

**Louis XV.** (1710–74), French king during whose reign France was involved in the war of the Austrian succession, and the Seven Years war which resulted in the loss of Canada, India, and Senegal to England. Among his mistresses were the celebrated Mme de Pompadour and Mme du Barry.

**Louis XVI.** (1754–93), king of France whose history is the history of the French Revolution. Dominated by his queen, Marie Antoinette, faced with court intrigue, the cost of French intervention in the war of American Independence and the ruin of France's credit, the French Revolution began with the calling of the States-General in 1789. Executed 21 Jan. 1793.

**Louis, Joe** (b. 1914), American world heavyweight boxing champion, son of a Negro sharecropper. Established a record by successfully defending his title 24 times in the years 1937–48. Retired from the ring in 1949.

**Low, Archibald Montgomery, D.Sc.** (1888–1956), a distinguished British scientist who had many inventions to his credit connected with wireless, television, coal and petrol engines, anti-aircraft and anti-tank rocket apparatus.

**Low, Sir David Alexander Cecil** (1891–1963), celebrated political cartoonist who interpreted events for the British reader for over 30 years; invented a number of stock characters, including Colonel Blimp and the T.U.C. carthorse. Born in New Zealand, he came to Britain in 1919 and joined *The Star.* Subsequently his cartoons appeared in the *Evening Standard,* the *Daily Herald,* and the *Guardian.*

**Lowell, James Russell** (1819–91), an American writer and poet of singular power and humour.

**Lowell, Robert** (b. 1917), American poet, expert on European poetry, author of the verse play *The Old Glory* and *Life Studies* (1959), an autobiographical volume in verse and prose.

**Loyola, St. Ignatius** (1491–1556), was the founder of the order of Jesuits.

**Lucretius (Titus Lucretius Carus)** (99–55 B.C.), great Roman poet of antiquity, whose life-work was the poem *On Nature (De rerum natura).*

**Ludendorff, General Erich** (1865–1937), German soldier; Chief of the General Staff to Hindenburg with whom he shared the military leadership of Germany during the Great War. Largely responsible for the victory of Tannenberg and the successes of 1915.

**Lugard, Frederick, Lord** (1858–1945), British colonial administrator, a man of abounding energy, initiative, tact and firmness, and possessing considerable military abilities. Helped to build up the British dominions in tropical Africa (Nyasaland, Uganda, Nigeria) and to establish the principles of British African administration, notably the system of "indirect rule" through native rulers.

**Luther, Martin** (1483–1546), leader of the Protestant Reformation in Germany; entered the order of Austin Friars in 1505, ordained priest in 1507, taught at Wittenberg university and preached in the town church. Until 1517 he was an orthodox Roman Catholic. His first idea of revolt occurred when he saw indulgences being sold, a practice which he openly condemned. For this he was excommunicated, and summoned before the Diet at Worms, where he made a memorable defence. He lived to see the principles of the Reformation widely established. *(See Lutheranism, Section J.)*

**Luthuli, Albert** (1899–1967), ex-Zulu chief, former Pres. of the now banned African National Congress, who upheld non-violence in face of cruel laws against his people in S. Africa. Killed in train accident. Nobel Peace Prize, 1960; Rector Glasgow Univ., 1962.

**Lutyens, Sir Edwin Landseer, O.M.** (1869–1944), English architect; designed and restored many country houses and castles (e.g., Lindisfarne), architect Hampstead garden suburb, 1908. Other works include the Cenotaph in London, city plan and viceroy's house, New Delhi, British Embassy, Washington, Liverpool R.C. cathedral. Pres. Royal Academy 1938–43.

**Lyell, Sir Charles** (1797–1875), British geologist whose great *Principles of Geology* (1830–33) profoundly influenced 19th-century scientific thought and helped to shape Darwin's ideas.

Lyell was responsible for the division of the Tertiary period into Pliocene (*Greek* = more recent), Miocene (less recent) and Eocene (dawn of recent).

Lysenko, Trofim (b. 1898), Russian biologist whose concept of genetics, that environmental experiences can change heredity, though discredited in scientific circles outside the U.S.S.R., was accepted there as dogma until 1953.

Lytton, Edward George Earle Bulwer, 1st Baron, P.C., G.C.M.G. (1803–73), a prolific novelist and dramatist, whose romantic stories included *The Last Days of Pompeii*.

# M

Macadam, John Loudon (1756–1836), Scottish engineer who invented the process of road-repairing which bears his name.

MacArthur, General Douglas, Hon. G.C.B., D.S.C., D.C.M. (1880–1964), American soldier famous for his gallant defence of the Philippines against the Japanese, 1941–42. Relieved of his commands in the Far East during the Korean campaign by President Truman in April 1951.

Macaulay, Rose, D.B.E. (1881–1958), an English authoress and literary critic. Among her literary successes are *Potterism*, *Dangerous Ages*, *Told by an Idiot*, *Orphan Island* and other novels noted for their keen satirical wit.

Macaulay, Thomas Babington, Lord (1800–59), the most brilliant historian of the Victorian era. His fame was assured by his *Essays* and *Lays of Ancient Rome*, and his *History* did more than confirm it. He was a son of Zachary Macaulay (1768–1838), the anti-slavery agitator, and sat in Parliament as member for Calne for some years, also serving for five years as a member of the Supreme Council of Calcutta. On his homecoming, he again entered Parliament as member for Edinburgh, and gained a new celebrity by his speeches. He served as Paymaster-General and Secretary for War.

Macbeth, immortalised by Shakespeare, was maormor of Moray and succeeded Duncan as king of Scotland in 1040, having slain him in fair fight. He appears to have governed the kingdom with great ability and equity. Defeated and slain by Malcolm Canmore, eldest son of Duncan in 1057. Shakespeare's Macbeth is based on the story in Holinshed and is not true to the historic figure.

McCormack, (Count) John (1884–1945), was the world famous Irish tenor who became a naturalised American citizen in 1919; received a Papal peerage as Count from Pius XI in 1928.

MacDiarmid, Hugh (pseudonym of Christopher Murray Grieve) (b. 1892), Scottish poet, the greatest since Burns. He stood as a Communist candidate against Sir Alec Douglas Home at Kinross in 1964.

Macdonald, Flora (1722–90), Scottish Jacobite heroine who saved the life of Prince Charles Edward after the defeat at Culloden Moor in 1746.

Macdonald, Sir John Alexander (1815–91), Canadian statesman of great vigour and imagination who became the first Prime Minister of the Dominion of Canada.

MacDonald, Rt. Hon. James Ramsay (1866–1937), Prime Minister in the first two Labour Governments, 1924, 1929–31, and in a Coalition Government dominated by Conservatives, 1931–35. His son, Malcolm (b. 1901), has held a number of diplomatic posts and in 1965 was appointed Special Representative of the British Government in Kenya, Tanzania, Malawi, and Zambia.

McDougall, William, F.R.S. (1871–1938), British psychologist. Professor of Psychology at Harvard University 1920–27, and Duke University, North Carolina 1927–38. His *Introduction to Social Psychology* (1908) achieved international reputation.

Machiavelli, Niccolo (1469–1527), Florentine diplomat, the first social scientist and theorist of the modern state, whose famous book *The Prince*, written in 1513, is concerned with the reality of politics. He believed that the end justifies the means.

Mackail, Prof. John William, O.M. (1859–1945), British classical scholar, Prof. of Poetry at Oxford, 1906–11, and translator of the *Odyssey*.

McKell, Sir William John, G.C.M.G., K.C. (b. 1891), Gov.-Gen. of Australia 1947–52.

Mackenzie, Sir (Edward Montague) Compton, O.B.E. (b. 1883), British novelist; literary critic to the *Daily Mail*, 1931–35; Rector of Glasgow Univ., 1931–34.

McLuhan, Herbert Marshall (b. 1911), a Canadian, former professor of English at Toronto Univ., author of a number of books on contemporary communications, inc. *The Medium is the Massage*, *The Gutenberg Galaxy*. *See* J26.

Macmillan, Rt. Hon. Harold, M.C. (b. 1894), British statesman; Prime Min., 1957–63. First entered Parliament in 1924 as Conservative M.P. for Stockton-on-Tees; represented Bromley, Kent, 1945–64; served as Minister of Housing and Local Government, Min. of Defence, Foreign Sec., Chancellor of the Exchequer. He is a member of the well-known publishing family. Chanc. Oxford University, 1960. The first volume of his autobiography was published in 1966, the second in 1969. *See also* Section C, Part I.

McMillan, Margaret, C.H., C.B.E. (d. 1931), Scotswoman, born in America who with her sister Rachel was a pioneer of child welfare work. Founder of open-air nursery schools. The Rachel McMillan nursery school at Deptford is a memorial to her work.

McNaughton, Gen. Hon. Andrew George Latta, C.H., D.S.O. (b. 1887), Canadian soldier, politician, electrical engineer, and representative on the U.N. Atomic Energy Commission.

Macneice, Louis (1907–63), English poet, B.B.C. script writer, and producer and director of many radio plays.

Macready, William Charles (1793–1873), English actor and manager who established himself as a tragedian of the first rank.

Maeterlinck, Count Maurice (1862–1949), Belgian man of letters whose plays include *La Princesse Maleine*, *Pelléas et Mélisande*, and *L'Oiseau Bleu*. Well known for his work on bees and ants.

Magellan, Ferdinand (c. 1480–1521), a famous Portuguese navigator, and commander of the first expedition (1519) to sail round the world.

Mahler, Gustav (1860–1911), Austrian composer and conductor; a writer of symphonies and songs, a classical romantic, much influenced by Anton Bruckner and Wagner. He completed nine symphonies (some with voices), and examples of his work in song-cycle form are *Das klagende Lied*, *Kindertotenlieder*, and *Das Lied von der Erde* (for solo voices and orchestra). *See* Section E.

Maintenon, Françoise d'Aubigné, Marquise de (1635–1719), after being the wife of the poet Scarron, drifted into Court circles, and so fascinated Louis XIV. that he ultimately married her. At his death she retired to a convent.

Makarios III, Archbishop (b. 1913), Cypriot ecclesiastic and national leader. Deported by British to Seychelles, 1956–57. Pres. of Rep. of Cyprus since independence, Aug. 16, 1960.

Malibran, Marie Félivité (1808–36), was one of the most famous operatic singers of her time.

Malik, Yakov Alexandrovich (b. 1906), Soviet diplomat who has been Deputy Min. of Foreign Affairs, Permanent Rep. of U.S.S.R. to U.N., 1948–52, and Soviet Ambassador to Great Britain, 1953–60.

Malory, Sir Thomas (c. 1430–70), compiled the *Morte d'Arthur*, which was printed by Caxton in 1485, and relates the story of King Arthur and the Knights of the Round Table.

Malraux, André (b. 1895), French novelist whose works include *La Condition humaine* (*Man's Fate*), *L'Espoir* (*Man's Hope*), and *Psychologie de l'art* (translated into 2 vols., *Museum without Walls* and *The Creative Act*).

Malthus, Thomas Robert, F.R.S. (1766–1834), an English clergyman and economist who in his essay *The Principle of Population* contended that population growth could only be checked by war and disease and by moral restraint.

Malvern, 1st Viscount, Godfrey Martin Huggins, C.H., K.C.M.G., F.R.C.S. (b. 1893), Prime Min. of S. Rhodesia, 1933–53 and of the Federation of Rhodesia and Nyasaland, 1953–56.

Manet, Edouard (1832–83), French Impressionist painter, whose pictures *Olympia* and *Lola de Valence* have been acclaimed masterpieces.

Mann, Thomas (1875–1955), German writer who won immediate world recognition at the age of 25 with his novel *Buddenbrooks*. His liberal humanistic outlook had developed sufficiently by 1930 for him unerringly to expose the nature of National Socialism. He left Germany in 1933 to live in Switzerland and then settled in the United States. Awarded the Nobel Prize for Literature in 1929; E. and W. Germany combined to honour him with the Goethe Prize in 1948. His best-known works, apart from many volumes of essays, stories, and shorter novels, are *The Magic Mountain* (1924), the *Joseph* tetralogy (1935–43), *Dr. Faustus* (1947) and *Felix Krull* (1954).

**Mann, Tom** (1856–1941), was a prominent British Labour leader for more than 50 years.

**Manning, Henry Edward, Cardinal** (1808–92), Cardinal Archbishop of Westminster 1875–92, was a prominent Anglican Churchman up to 1851, when he joined the Church of Rome.

**Mansfield, Katherine** (1890–1923), short-story writer, born in Wellington, New Zealand, whose work was strongly influenced by the short stories of Chekov. Her second husband was John Middleton Murry, author and literary critic.

**Manson, Sir Patrick, G.C.M.G., M.D., F.R.S.** (1844–1922), an eminent physician who specialised in parasitology and became physician and medical adviser to the Colonial Office. He was the first to formulate the hypothesis that the malarial parasite was transmitted by the mosquito. The joint work of Sir Patrick Manson and Sir Ronald Ross rendered habitable vast areas of the earth hitherto closed.

**Manuzio, Aldo Pio** (1450?–1515), Italian printer, founder of the Aldine press in Venice, which for just over a century issued books famed for their beautiful type and bindings.

**Manzoni, Alessandro Francesco Tomaso Antonio** (1785–1873), Italian writer, whose romantic novel *I Promessi Sposi* (" The Betrothed ") is generally regarded as the most important work in Italian literature after "The Divine Comedy."

**Mao Tse-tung** (b. 1893), great leader of the Chinese people. Chairman of the Central Committee of the Chinese Communist Party since 1936 and Chairman (equivalent to President) of the People's Republic of China from 1949 (when it was first established following the military defeat of the Nationalist forces) until the end of 1958 when his policy of collectivism ended in the great leap forward. He came to the fore again in 1966–8 leading the cultural revolution. *See also* Section C, Part I.

**Marat, Jean Paul** (1743–93), one of the leading actors in the French Reign of Terror. Killed by Charlotte Corday.

**Marconi, Guglielmo Marchese** (1874–1937), Italian electrical engineer celebrated for his development of wireless telegraphy. With a home-made apparatus he sent long-wave signals over a distance of 1 mile in 1895. He came to England in 1896 and established the Marconi Company in 1897. Succeeded on Dec. 12, 1901 in transmitting and receiving transatlantic signals. Awarded Nobel Prize for Physics, 1909.

**Marco Polo.** (*See* Polo, Marco.)

**Marcus Aurelius Antoninus** (121–180), the greatest of Roman emperors and a disciple of the stoics.

**Marcuse, Herbert** (b. 1898), Professor of Political Thought at Univ. of California; b. Berlin; emigrated to U.S.A. during Nazi regime. Foremost contemporary critic of Western industrial society. Whereas Marx regarded the working classes as the agent of revolutionary change today Marcuse sees the international student protest movement as the catalyst.

**Maria Theresa** (1717–80), Archduchess of Austria, Queen of Bohemia and Hungary; a woman of remarkable strength of character and ability, succeeded her father Charles VI., as monarch of the Hapsburg dominions. She was an enlightened ruler and has been called a "benevolent despot."

**Marie Antoinette Josephe Jeanne** (1755–93) was daughter of the Empress Maria Theresa and the Emperor Francis I. of Austria, and became wife of Louis XVI. of France. She entered with spirit into the gaiety of French Court life, and drew down upon herself much popular hatred in consequence. In the terrible events which followed the outbreak of the Revolution she was one of the chief sufferers, but bore her fate with dignity and resignation, and met her death on the scaffold with unflinching courage.

**Marie Louise** (1791–1847), daughter of Francis I.

of Austria, became wife of Napoleon in 1810, and bore him a son. (*See* Napoleon II.)

**Marius, Caius** (c. 155–86 B.C.), the famous Roman general of humble birth who became tribune (119 B.C.), praetor (115 B.C.), propraetor in Spain (114 B.C.) and was seven times consul. Married an aunt of Julius Caesar.

**Mark Antony.** (*See* Antonius, Marcus.)

**Marlborough, John Churchill, 1st Duke of** (1650–1722), brilliant soldier, the victor of Blenheim, Ramillies, Oudenarde, and Malplaquet. Married to Queen Anne's favourite, Sarah Jennings.

**Marlowe, Christopher** (1564–93), one of the greatest of the Elizabethan dramatists. His principal plays are *Dr. Faustus, Tamburlaine the Great, Edward II.*, and *The Jew of Malta*. He was killed in a tavern brawl at Deptford.

**Marryat, Captain Frederick** (1792–1848), an exceedingly popular writer of sea stories. Author of *Peter Simple, The King's Own, Jacob Faithful*, and *The Children of the New Forest*.

**Marshall, General George Catlett** (1880–1959), American soldier and statesman; Chief of Staff of U.S. Army, 1939–45. Initiated the American offer of aid to Europe, which led to the European Recovery Programme. Nobel Peace Prize, 1953.

**Martial (Marcus Valerius Martialis)** (A.D. c. 40–A.D. c. 104) was born at Bilbilis in Spain, but spent the greater part of his life in Rome, where he acquired much fame as a poet and epigrammatist.

**Marvell, Andrew** (1620–78), English poet, satirist and diplomatist, friend of Milton, who was best known for his many prose satires and lampoons.

**Marx, Heinrich Karl** (1818–83), German philosopher and socialist and lifelong partner and friend of Engels with whom he collaborated in writing many important works on socialism and in developing his theories of dialectical materialism. After being expelled from the continent he settled in London where he wrote his monumental work *Das Kapital*. Communism is based on the teachings of Marx. During the 1850s he lived at 28 Dean Street, Soho. Buried at Highgate Cemetary. *See* Marxism, J27. *also* Q14(2).

**Mary I.** (1516–58), daughter of Henry VIII. and Catherine of Aragon. Was Queen of England from 1553 to her death. She was a strenuous Roman Catholic, and entirely reversed the religious order of things during her brief reign, persecuting, imprisoning, and burning at the stake many of the Protestant reformers, nearly three hundred persons being put to death as heretics. She married Philip of Spain in 1554.

**Mary II.** (1662–94), daughter of James II; came to the English throne in 1689, having married her cousin, William of Orange, in 1677. After assenting to the "Declaration of Rights," they reigned jointly until her death.

**Mary, H.M. Queen, K.G., K.T., G.C.V.O.** (1867–1953), Queen Consort of George V.

**Mary, Queen of Scots** (1542–87), daughter of James V. of Scotland, married to the Dauphin of France at sixteen years of age. On the death of her husband in 1560 she returned to Scotland, and for a time was the acknowledged Queen of the Scots. In 1565 she married Lord Darnley, who a year later was murdered and Mary married Bothwell. The Scottish nobles rebelled against Mary, and she was made prisoner and confined in Loch Leven Castle, compelled to abandon Bothwell and to sign an Act of Abdication in favour of her son. She escaped to England, sought the protection of Elizabeth, and was imprisoned for nineteen years in various castles, and ultimately beheaded on a charge of conspiracy. She was buried in Peterborough Cathedral but after her son James I. of England ascended the throne her remains were removed to Westminster Abbey.

**Masaryk, Jan Garrigue** (1886–1948), son of Thomas Masaryk. Served as Czech Minister in London, 1925–38 and as Foreign Secretary, 1940–48.

**Masaryk, Thomas Garrigue** (1850–1937), Czech philosopher and statesman, one of the greatest fighters for a democratic society; founder and first President of Czechoslovakia, 1918–35.

**Mascagni, Pietro** (1863–1945), Italian composer, whose brilliant one-act opera *Cavalleria Rusticana* produced in 1890 brought him sudden celebrity. None of his later operas was as successful.

**Masefield, John Edward, O.M., C.L.** (1878–1967), English poet laureate, 1930–67. Most popular among his poems are the *Salt-Water Ballads*, *Reynard the Fox*, and *Right Royal*.

**Maskelyne, John Nevil** (1839–1917), famous illusionist who exposed the mysteries of the Davenport spiritualistic quacks.

**Massenet, Jules Emile Frédéric** (1842–1912), French composer whose melodious compositions include songs, orchestral suites, oratorios, and 23 operas, among them *Manon* and *Thaïs*.

**Massine, Léonide** (b. 1896), a famous Russian dancer who was for some years Ballet Master at the Roxy Theatre, New York. Among his more famous ballets are *The Good Humoured Ladies*, *Boutique Fantasque*, *Pas d'Acier*, *Les Matelots*, *Le Beau Danube* and *Les Présages*.

**Matisse, Henri** (1869–1954), French painter, the foremost member of a group known as *les Fauves*. His work is remarkable for its use of pure and brilliant colour and its reliance on colour variations to express form and relief.

**Matsys or Metzys, Quintin** (1466–1530), a distinguished Flemish painter, who was originally a blacksmith. He excelled in Scriptural subjects.

**Maugham, (William) Somerset, C.H., C.L.** (1874–1965), British novelist, playwright, and short-story writer. Born in Paris, he qualified as a doctor, but soon abandoned medicine for literature, achieving a great success with his first novel in 1897, *Liza of Lambeth*, a study of slum life. He travelled widely which gave him a deep insight into human nature.

**Maupassant, Henri René Albert Guy de** (1850–93), the famous French author and writer of short stories, was a friend of Flaubert, Zola, and Daudet. He was the greatest of all European short-story writers, standing alone in grace, wit and epigram.

**Mauriac, François** (b. 1885), French novelist whose works are regarded as among the chief literary productions of to-day. In addition to a long series of novels he has written many critical works and essays. Leader-writer for *Figaro*; Nobel Prizewinner. 1952.

**Maurois, André, Hon., K.B E.** (1885–1967), French biographer, novelist and essayist who has written ten lives of Shelley, Disraeli, Byron, Voltaire, Fleming, Dickens, and Balzac.

**Maxim, Sir Hiram Stevens** (1840–1916), the inventor of the famous automatic quick-firing gun.

**Maxton, James** (1885–1946), was a prominent Socialist politician; M.P. for the Bridgeton Divn. of Glasgow, 1926–46. Chairman of I.L.P. 1926–31 and 1934–39.

**Maxwell, James Clerk** (1831–79), Scottish physicist who wrote his first scientific paper at the age of 15. He was Professor of Natural Philosophy at Aberdeen, 1856, and at King's College, London, 1860–68. In 1871 he became the first Cavendish Professor of Experimental Physics at Cambridge. He brought his pre-eminently mathematical mind to bear on the results of the experimental discoveries of Faraday and others and gave to physics a celebrated set of equations which account for the basic laws of electricity and of magnetism. His work revolutionised the whole aspect of fundamental physics and led to great practical results. *See Section F, Part I.*

**Mazarin, Jules** (1602–61), an Italian Cardinal who became chief Minister of State under Louis XIV., and was for a number of years the practical ruler 'of France. He succeeded Richelieu.

**Mazeppa-Koledinsky, Ivan Stepanovich** (1644–1709), the hero of Byron's poem, was a real personage, and a Pole, and was tied naked on the back of a wild horse, and so sent out across the Russian desert, for an intrigue with a noble's wife. He was liberated by Cossacks and afterwards attained an honourable position.

**Mazzini, Giuseppe** (1805–72), an Italian patriot, who, in his endeavours to secure the independence of Italy, incurred the disfavour of the authorities, and was compelled to leave the country. He started a newspaper called *Young Italy* at Marseilles, and in 1837 came to London, and kept up his attacks upon existing governments. In 1848 he was back in Rome and was elected dictator of the Roman Republic. He was not allowed to hold this position long, however, for the French occupied Rome and Mazzini was driven to England again. The unification of Italy was accomplished in other ways than

those advocated by Mazzini, but he lived to see Victor Emmanuel King of United Italy.

**Medawar, Sir Peter Brien, F.R.S.** (b. 1915), British zoologist, author of *The Art of the Soluble* and *The Future of Man*. Nobel Prize for Medicine, 1960, Pres. British Association, 1969.

**Medici**, the famous Florentine family who combined the career of merchants and bankers with the exercise of political power and patronage of the arts. Cosimo the Elder (1389–1464) was for over thirty years the virtual ruler of Florence. He was wealthy, cultivated, liberal, and a consummate statesman. His illustrious grandson, Lorenzo the Magnificent (1449–92), poet, friend of artists and scholars, governed the state in great munificence. His grandson, Lorenzo, was the father of Catherine de' Medici, Queen of France (*q.v.*). Then the family had some reverses until Cosimo (1519–74), one of the most able rulers of the 16th cent., became Duke of Florence and then Grand-Duke of Tuscany, which title the Medicis held until 1737.

**Méhul, Etienne Nicolas** (1763–1817), French operatic composer. *Joseph* being considered his masterpiece.

**Melanchthon, Philip** (1497–1560), German scholar and humanist who assisted Luther and wrote *Loci communes*, the first great Protestant work on the principles of the Reformation.

**Melba, Dame Nellie, G.B.E.** (1861–1931), the celebrated Australian soprano, b. in Richmond (Victoria), who made her operatic début in Brussels in 1887.

**Melbourne, 2nd Viscount** (1779–1848), Queen Victoria's first premier, holding office over six years, and identified with many important Liberal measures.

**Mendel, Gregor Johann** (1822–84), Austrian botanist. After joining the Augustinian order, he moved to the monastery at Brünn where he afterwards became Abbot and taught natural history in the school there. His main interest, however, was the study of inheritance, and his elaborate observations of the common garden pea resulted in the famous law of heredity which to-day bears his name. His hypothesis was published in 1866 but no attention was given to it until 1900. *See Section F, Part II.*

**Mendeleyev, Dmitry Ivanovich** (1834–1907), Russian chemist who made important contributions to physical chemistry and general chemical theory. First to discover the critical temperatures and formulated the Periodic Law of atomic weights.

**Mendelssohn-Bartholdy, (Jacob Ludwig) Felix** (1809–47), German composer, grandson of Moses Mendelssohn, the philosopher. He belongs with Chopin and Schumann to the early 19th century classic-romantic school, and his music has a delightful delicacy and melodic beauty. He was conductor of the famous Gewandhaus concerts at Leipzig for a time and often visited England. Frequently performed are his overtures *A Midsummer Night's Dream* and *The Hebrides* (or *Fingal's Cave*), written in his youth, two oratorios *St. Paul* and *Elijah*, the violin concerto in E minor, the piano works *Variations Sérieuses* and *Songs without Words*, and the *Scotch* and *Italian* symphonies. The name Bartholdy was added to the surname when his father abandoned Jewry. *See Section E.*

**Mendès-France, Pierre, LL.D.** (b. 1907), French statesman. His skilful diplomacy and energy helped to solve the many problems that faced his country when he took office as Prime Minister in June 1954. His government was overthrown on his Algerian policy in Feb. 1955.

**Menuhin, Yehudi** (b. 1916), violin virtuoso, one of the greatest musical prodigies of the 20th century. Born in New York of Jewish parentage; made his first London appearance in the San Francisco Orchestra, 1929.

**Menzies, Rt. Hon. Sir Robert Gordon, K.T., C.H., Q.C.** (b. 1894), Australian Liberal leader; Prime Minister, 1939–41, 1949–66. Lord Warden of the Cinque Ports, 1966.

**Mercator, Gerhardus** (1512–94), the Flemish geographer who invented a celestial and a terrestrial globe, by which he introduced his famous projection, in which meridians and parallels of latitude cross each other at right angles, both being indicated by straight lines.

**Meredith, George, O.M.** (1828–1909), novelist and

poet, "the Grand old Man of English letters." His works are rich in imagery, poetry, wit, and characterisation, and as a delineator of womanhood he is unsurpassed. Among his great novels are *Ordeal of Richard Feverel, Evan Harrington, Rhoda Fleming, The Egoist, Diana of the Crossways,* and *The Amazing Marriage.*

Mesmer, Friedrich Anton (1733–1815), was a German doctor who founded the system of mesmerism or animal magnetism.

Mestrovic, Ivan (1883–1962), a Dalmatian sculptor, recognised as one of the leading European sculptors of his day. The Tate Gallery and the Victoria and Albert Museum have examples of his work.

Metastasio, Pietro (1698–1782), the celebrated Italian librettist who provided texts for such composers as Gluck, Handel, Haydn, and Mozart. He lived in Vienna as court poet and his real name was Pietro Bonaventura Trapassi.

Metchnikov, Ilya (1845–1916), an eminent Russian biologist; Nobel Prize for Medicine, 1908.

Michelangelo (1475–1564), the name given to Michelagniolo Buonarroti, the great painter and the last great Italian sculptor, who was also a poet. Born of a poor but genteel family in Tuscany, he was as an infant sent out to a wetnurse, the wife of a stone-cutter, and this he was accustomed to say gave him his passion for sculpture. His apprenticeship began in Florence in the workshop of one of the leading Quattrocento masters, Domenico Ghirlandaio. Like Leonardo, he studied anatomy, but instead of spreading his talents over a wide field as Leonardo had done, he became obsessed with the problem of how to represent the human body. In Michelangelo classical idealism, mediaeval religious belief, and renaissance energy met to produce some of the finest art ever known. The paintings on the ceiling of the Sistine Chapel—a surface of about 6,000 square feet—are perhaps the most impressive of Michelangelo's works, but the finest is the painting of the *Last Judgement* behind the altar of the same building. Michelangelo always thought of himself primarily as a sculptor; his marble *Pietà* (St. Peter's) and the statue of *David* (Academy, Florence) are famous, as are the great figure of *Moses* in the church of San Pietro in Vincoli, Rome (originally intended for the tomb of Julius in St. Peter's), and the four allegorical figures, Day and Night, Dawn and Twilight (intended for the tombs of the Medici family at San Lorenzo in Florence).

Michelet, Jules (1798–1874), a noted French historian and author.

Michelson, Albert Abraham (1852–1931), American physicist, born in Poland. Collaborated with E. W. Morley in the *Michelson-Morley* experiment to measure the velocity of the earth through the "ether" which led to the conclusion that the ether is non-existent, a finding which had great value for Einstein's theory of relativity. The first American scientist to win the Nobel prize for Physics, 1907.

Mickiewicz, Adam (1798–1855), greatest Polish poet and revolutionary. Chief works *The Ancestors, Pan Tadeusz.*

Mill, John Stuart (1806–73), achieved high reputation by his numerous works on philosophical questions. He was an ardent liberal and leader of the utilitarian school of philosophy. Radical M.P. for Westminster, 1865–68, died in Avignon. His chief works are *Principles of Political Economy, System of Logic, On Liberty.*

Millais, Sir John Everett, Bt. P.R.A. (1829–96), English painter, b. in Southampton; with Holman Hunt and Rossetti formed the "preRaphaelite brotherhood." Of his numerous paintings we have room to mention only the *Blind Girl, Autumn Leaves,* and *Bubbles.* He married Effie Grey, previously married to Ruskin.

Millet, Jean François (1814–75), French painter of pastoral subjects; *The Angelus* and *The Gleaners* can be seen in The Louvre.

Millikan, Robert Andrews (1868–1953), American physicist who is world famous for his researches on electrons, and for discovering the cosmic rays. Awarded Nobel Prize for Physics, 1923.

Milne, Alan Alexander (1882–1956), English humorist, poet, and playwright who wrote much delightful verse and stories for children.

Milner, Alfred, Viscount (1854–1925), imperial statesman, who served in South Africa from 1897 to 1905 and had great influence on the history of that country. Was Secretary for War in 1918 and for the Colonies, 1919–21.

Miltiades (d. 489 B.C.), one of the leaders of the Athenian army against the Persians at Marathon.

Milton, John (1608–74), England's greatest epic poet, whose *Paradise Lost* is the greatest poem of the kind in the language. The best known of his other poems are probably the *Ode on the Morning of Christ's Nativity, L'Allegro, Il Penseroso, Lycidas,* and the sonnet *On his Blindness.* In 1652 he became totally blind, and at his death was buried in St. Giles's Church, Cripplegate, London, a monument being erected to his memory in Westminster Abbey.

Minot, George Richards, M.D. (1885–1950), an eminent American doctor who became Prof. of Medicine at Harvard in 1928, and famous for his researches in the pathology of the blood, and for his discovery of the curative properties of liver in pernicious anæmia. Shared the Nobel Prize for Medicine, 1934.

Mirabeau, Gabriel, Comte de (1749–91), one of the prominent figures of the French Revolution, and a famous orator.

Mistral, Frédéric (1830–1914), French poet who spent his whole life in Provence and wrote many works of great lyrical beauty, founded the Félibrige society (*q.v.* Gen. Inf.); completed *Lou Trésor dòu Félibrige* in 1886, a Provençal dictionary and encyclopædia of Provence. Nobel Literary Prize, 1904.

Mithridates (*circa* 132–63 B.C.), was King of Pontus from 120–63 B.C., and showed great capacity as a commander conquering a great part of Asia Minor and Greece.

Modigliani, Amedeo (1884–1920), Italian painter, b. Livorno, whose portraits and figure studies show a highly individual style. He spent most of his short life in Paris which was one of poverty, illness, and disillusionment.

Moffatt, James (1870–1944), Scottish divine who translated the Bible into modern English.

Mohammed (570–632), the founder of Islam, the religion of the Moslems, fled from Mecca to Medina in 622, from which date the Mohammedan era opens. By his constant preaching and proclaiming of the one and only Deity Allah he gathered round him a small and loyal, hard, fighting band of followers and was able to return to Mecca eight years later, an acknowledged conqueror. The Sacred Book of Islam, the *Koran*—though presented by him as an original revelation from the Angel Gabriel—may in the main be traced to Biblical and Rabbinical sources. (*See* Islam, Section J.)

Molière (Jean Baptiste Poquelin) (1622–73), the greatest of French comic dramatists, who, from being a poor strolling player, became the leading dramatist of his time. His greatest comedies were *Le Tartuffe, Le Misanthrope, Le Malade imaginaire* and *Le Médecin malgré lui.*

Molotov, Vyacheslav Mikhailovitch (Skryabin) (b. 1890), Russian diplomat; succeeded Litvinov as Commissar for Foreign Affairs, 1939–49. Chief representative of the Soviet Union at numerous post-war conferences. Expelled from Communist Party, 1964.

Moltke, Field-Marshal Count Helmuth von (1800–91), was responsible for the Prussian strategy in the Danish, Austrian, and Franco-Prussian wars, in all of which he was outstandingly successful.

Mond, Ludwig, Ph.D., F.R.S. (1839–1909), German chemist who in 1867 settled in England as an alkali manufacturer and in partnership with John Brunner successfully manufactured soda by the Solvay process.

Monet, Claude (1840–1926), the most representative of the French Impressionists. Exhibited in 1874 his landscape *Impression Soleil levant,* from which the word *Impressionism* was derived.

Monier-Williams, Sir Monier, K.C.I.E., LL.D., Ph.D. (1819–99), a great Sanskrit scholar who laboured with distinction in bringing westward the wisdom of the Orient.

Monk, George, 1st Duke of Albemarle (1608–69), served with distinction as general and admiral, particularly in the Anglo-Dutch wars, and in 1660 effected the Restoration of Charles II.

Monroe, James (1758–1831), Fifth President of the U.S. Was appointed Governor of Virginia in 1799, and in 1803 went to France and carried through the purchase of Louisiana. Best known as the author of the Monroe Doctrine, which he outlined in his Presidential message of 1823.

**Montagu, Lady Mary Wortley** (1689–1762), the greatest of English woman letter writers. The three volumes of her *Complete Letters* were published in 1965–67. *See also* **P16(1).**

**Montaigne, Michel de** (1533–92), a French essayist of world-wide celebrity, who may be regarded as the inventor of the essay form, and had a great influence on English writers.

**Montcalm, General Louis Joseph, Marquis de** (1712–59), commander of French Army against British in Canada in final struggle for possession. Defeated by Wolfe in 1759 and mortally wounded.

**Montesquieu, Charles Louis de Secondat, Baron de La Brède et de** (1689–1755), French philosopher and author. His works include *Les Lettres Persanes*, a witty satire on contemporary life, and *L'Esprit des Lois*, setting out his ideas on politics and law. Greatly admired England and her constitution, which he misunderstood, and his influence on the authors of the American constitution consequently led to the impractical separation of the executive (the President) from the law-making power (Congress).

**Montessori, Maria** (1869–1952), educationist, whose methods for infant teaching have wide recognition. *See* **J14(2).**

**Monteverdi, Claudio** (1567–1643), an Italian composer of importance by reason of his pioneer work in the operatic form. His most important dramatic work was *Orfeo* (1608). *See* Section E.

**Montezuma II.** (1466–1520) was Emperor of Mexico when Cortes invaded that country, and the last Aztec ruler of Mexico.

**Montfort, Simon de, Earl of Leicester** (1206–65), was a powerful baron, with liberal views, and a hatred of kingly tyranny. It was his bold action that forced Henry III., his brother-in-law, to grant the first English Parliament. He met his death at the Battle of Evesham.

**Montgolfier, Joseph Michel** (1740–1810) and Jacques Etienne (1745–1799), two French brothers who invented the first practical balloon.

**Montgomery, Field-Marshal Viscount, K.G., G.C.B., D.S.O.** (b. 1887), rose to military fame as Commander of the 8th Army in the North African and Italian campaigns, 1942–44. C.-in-C. British Forces in France and Germany, 1944–46; C.I.G.S., 1946–48. Permanent Military Chairman of the Western Union Defence Committee, 1948–51; Deputy Supreme Allied Commander Europe (NATO), 1951–58. Retired 1958. His *Memoirs* were published in 1958.

**Montrose, James Graham, Marquess of** (1612–50), brave and inspiring Scottish general who raised the Highland clansmen for Charles I. and again for Charles II. His lyric poetry included *My dear and only love.*

**Moody, Dwight Lyman** (1837–99), the American revivalist preacher, associated for many years in mission work on both sides of the Atlantic with Ira D. Sankey, the " American Singing Pilgrim."

**Moore, George** (1852–1933), a well-known Irish novelist; author of *Confessions of a Young Man, Esther Waters, Evelyn Innes,* etc.

**Moore, Henry, O.M., C.H.** (b. 1898), greatest living sculptor in semi-abstract style, son of a Yorkshire coalminer. Examples of his work are to be seen in the Tate Gallery, St. Matthew's Church, Northampton, the Unesco Building in Paris, and on an outside site opposite the House of Lords.

**Moore, Sir John** (1761–1809), British general, who trained the infantry for the Spanish Peninsular campaigns and conducted a brilliant retreat to Corunna, where he was mortally wounded after defeating the French under Soult.

**Moore, Thomas** (1779–1852), Ireland's greatest poet, the author of *Irish Melodies, Lalla Rookh, The Epicurean,* and many other works. He enjoyed immense popularity both in England and Ireland. Friend and biographer of Byron.

**More, Sir Thomas** (1478–1535), succeeded Wolsey as Lord Chancellor under Henry VIII., but fell into disgrace by refusing to take the oath of Supremacy, and was ultimately executed. His *Utopia* (*see* **J43**) is one of the world's most noted books. Canonised in 1935 along with John Fisher, Bishop of Rochester, who was similarly martyred by Henry VIII.

**Morgan, Sir Henry** (*c.* 1635–88), Welsh buccaneer of great skill and daring; operated in the Caribbean against the Spaniards, capturing and plundering Panama in 1671. Knighted by Charles II. and made Deputy-governor of Jamaica.

**Morgan, John Pierpont** (1837–1913), one of the great financiers of his time who built the family fortunes into a vast industrial empire.

**Morland, George** (1763–1804), a painter of English rural life.

**Morley, John, Viscount, O.M.** (1838–1923). Liberal statesman and author, served as Secretary for Ireland in 1886 and 1892–95, and for India, 1905–10. Biographer of Gladstone, Voltaire, Rousseau, Burke, Walpole, Cromwell, and Cobden.

**Morley, Thomas** (*c.* 1557–1603), English Elizabethan composer of madrigals, noted also for his settings of some of Shakespeare's songs. He was a pupil of Byrd, organist of St. Paul's Cathedral, and wrote an important theoretical work *Plaine and Easie Introduction to Practicall Music* (1597).

**Morris, William** (1834–96), poet and craftsman. His hatred of 19th-cent. ugliness, his belief in human equality, and in freedom and happiness for all, conspired to make him a socialist, and he accomplished much for the improvement of domestic decoration. He was a popular lecturer, founded the Socialist League and the Kelmscott Press.

**Morrison of Lambeth, Herbert Stanley, Baron, P.C. C.H,** (1888–1965), entered Parliament as Labour M.P. for S. Hackney in 1923. Leader of the L.C.C. 1933–40. Dep. Prime Min. and Leader of the House of Commons in the Labour administration, 1945–51. Life peerage conferred, 1959.

**Morse, Samuel Finley Breese** (1791–1872), an American artist and designer, who became the inventor of the Morse system of electric telegraphs, and of the Morse code of signals.

**Moseley, Henry Gwyn-Jeffreys** (1887–1915). lecturer in physics under Rutherford at Manchester Univ., 1910–12. Made great contributions to the theory of the structure of the atom. Killed at Gallipoli.

**Mountbatten of Burma, 1st Earl, Admiral of the Fleet, P.C. K.G., G.C.B., G.C.V.O., D.S.O.** (b. 1900), naval officer and statesman. Chief of Combined Operations, 1942–43; Supreme Allied Commdr. S.E. Asia, 1943–46; Viceroy of India, Mar.–Aug. 1947 and first Gov. Gen. of Dominion of India, Aug. 1947–June 1948. Resuming his naval career in 1948 he has served successively as Flag Officer Commanding the 1st Cruiser Squadron, Mediterranean, Fourth Sea Lord, C.-in-C. Mediterranean, C.-in-C. Allied Forces, Mediterranean, and First Sea Lord and Chief of Naval Staff, 1955–59, Chief of the Defence Staff, 1959–65.

**Mountevans, Admiral Lord, K.C.B., D.S.O.** (1881–1957), " Evans of the Broke," British sailor and explorer. Author of *South with Scott.*

**Mozart, Wolfgang Amadeus** (1756–91). The composer who bears this immortal name is universally acknowledged as the world's greatest musical genius. He was born at Salzburg, began his musical career at the age of four, toured the European courts as an infant prodigy, left the service of the Archbishop of Salzburg in his twenty-sixth year to live in Vienna, where his friendship with Haydn began and where his greatest music was written. Mozart's genius lies in the effortless outpouring of all forms of music, in the ever-flowing melodies, in the consistent beauty and symmetry of his compositions, and in the exactness of his method. Among the loveliest and grandest works in instrumental music are his three great symphonies in E flat, in G minor, and in C (called the " Jupiter "), all written in six weeks in 1788. Three of the greatest operas in musical history are his *Marriage of Figaro* (1786), *Don Giovanni* (1787), and *The Magic Flute* (1791). His last composition, written under the shadow of death, was the Requiem Mass, a work of tragic beauty. *See* Section E.

**Müller, Ferdinand von, Baron** (1825–96), German botanist and explorer. Director of the Botanical Gardens at Melbourne, 1857–73. Introduced the eucalyptus into the south of Europe and other regions, and took leading part in promoting Australian exploration.

**Mumford, Lewis** (b. 1895), American social historian and authority on town planning and urban culture. His works include the trilogy *Techniques and Civilization* (1934), *The Culture of Cities* (1938), *The Condition of Man* (1944), *The Myth of the Machine* (1967), and *The Urban Prospect* (1969)

**Munkacsy, Michael von** (1844–1900), a celebrated Hungarian painter of historical subjects.

**Munnings, Sir Alfred James, K.C.V.O.** (1878–1959), British painter whose country scenes and pictures of horses have gained him world-wide fame. P.R.A., 1944–49.

**Murdock, William** (1754–1839), engineer and inventor, first to make practical use of coal gas as an illuminating agent.

**Murillo, Bartolomé Esteban** (1617–82), one of the greatest Spanish painters. His chief works are altar-pieces and religious subjects.

**Murray, (George) Gilbert (Aimé), O.M., D.Litt., D.C.L., LL.D.** (1866–1957), classical scholar and humanist whose verse translations of Euripides are known throughout the world. Became Professor of Greek at Glasgow at early age of 23; Regius Professor of Greek at Oxford, 1908–36.

**Mussolini, Benito** (1883–1945), Fascist dictator of Italy, 1922–43. From 1935 an aggressive foreign policy in Abyssinia, Spain, etc., was at first successful, and in June 1940, he entered the second world war on the side of Germany. The defeat of Italian arms in North Africa and the invasion of Sicily caused the collapse of his Government, but he was rescued from imprisonment by parachutists. Shot dead by Italian partisans while attempting to escape to Switzerland.

**Mussorgsky, Modest Petrovich** (1839–81), Russian composer whose masterpiece is the opera *Boris Godunov* after the play by Pushkin. His piano suite *Pictures at an Exhibition* was orchestrated by Ravel. *See* Section E.

# N

**Nansen, Fridtjof, G.C.V.O., D.Sc., F.R.G.S.** (1861–1930), the Norwegian explorer who, after two or three expeditions across Greenland, in 1893 started out on his famous North Polar expedition when he reached the highest latitude until then attained—86° 14′—a feat later eclipsed by the Duke of the Abruzzi and by Peary, as well as by airship or aeroplane. He published a fascinating narrative of his exploration under the title of *Farthest North*. Active in Russian famine relief, 1921. Awarded Nobel Prize for Peace, 1922.

**Napier, John** (1550–1617), mathematician, who made important contribution to the advance of astronomy and other branches of science by his invention of logarithms (published 1614).

**Napoleon I. (Bonaparte)** (1769–1821) was born at Ajaccio in Corsica. Sent to France to receive a military education and was a captain at the age of twenty. In 1794 served in Italy with such distinction that he won a generalship, and next year was appointed Commander-in-Chief. A series of most brilliant successes followed. He defeated the Austrian forces in 1797, conducted an expedition to Syria and Egypt in 1798, returned in 1799 to find himself the most popular man in France, and in November of that year he proclaimed himself First Consul. In 1800 he was again in Italy and once more victorious. In 1804 he was made Emperor, and the following year was in the field against England, Russia, and Austria, achieving a splendid series of victories at Austerlitz and elsewhere, and practically became Dictator of Europe, distributing kingships amongst his brothers in the most profuse manner, Joseph becoming King of Naples, Louis King of Holland, and Jerome King of Westphalia. His invasion of Russia was disastrous, the Peninsular War went against him, and in 1814 the Allies entered Paris and forced him to abdicate. He was sent to Elba, but made his escape in the following year, gathered his old army about him and went forth to meet the English and Prussian armies. He was finally defeated at Waterloo on 18 June 1815, and held in captivity on the lonely island of St. Helena, where he died of a stomach cancer. His remains were removed to Paris in 1840, and rest in a magnificent tomb.

**Napoleon II.** (1811–32) was the son of Napoleon I. and Maria Louisa. Was born in Paris and proclaimed King of Rome, but died of consumption when only twenty-one, being known at the time of his demise as the Duke of Reichstadt.

**Napoleon III.** (1808–73) was the son of Louis Bonaparte, King of Holland, and of Hortense, daughter of the Empress Josephine. After unsuccessful attempts to secure the French throne and years of imprisonment he took advantage of the revolution of 1848 to return to France and, following the famous *coup d'état* of December 2, 1851, emerged as master of France and was proclaimed Emperor the following year. Married Eugénie de Montijo in 1853. Dictatorial and discredited at home, unsuccessful in his foreign adventures, his surrender at Sedan in the Franco-Prussian war of 1870 brought ruin to the Second Empire, and France once again became a republic. Louis Napoleon took refuge in England and died at Chislehurst in Kent.

**Nash, John** (1752–1835), architect. Planned Regent Street, laid out Regent's Park, enlarged Buckingham Palace, and designed Marble Arch and the Brighton Pavilion.

**Nash, Paul** (1889–1946), distinguished English painter and designer. Official war artist in both world wars. Best known pictures *The Menin Road* of 1918 and *Totes Meer* of 1941.

**Nash, Rt. Hon. Sir Walter** (1882–1968), New Zealand Labour politician; Prime Min., 1957–60. Resigned party leadership 1963.

**Nasmyth, James** (1808–90), the inventor of the steam-hammer, which became indispensable in all large iron and engineering works.

**Nasser, Gamal Abdal** (b. 1918), first President of the first Egyptian Republic and influential leader of the Arab world. Fought in Palestine War of 1948–49 and organised the military coup of July 23, 1952, which brought the abdication of King Farouk. The most important events of his presidency have been the nationalisation of the Suez Canal, the building, with Russian help and finance, of the Aswan High Dam, and the Middle East war of June 1967.

**Needham, Joseph, M.A., Ph.D., Sc.D., F.R.S.** (b 1900), British biochemist, historian of science, orientalist; Master of Gonville and Caius, Cambridge, since 1966. Author of the great historical work *Science and Civilisation in China* (7 vols., 1954–).

**Nehru, Pandit Jawaharlal** (1889–1964), Indian statesman and one of the world's great leaders; Prime Min. and Min. of Foreign Affairs, 1947–64. Educated at Harrow and Cambridge where he studied science and law. A leading member of the Congress Party for many years, during which he was frequently imprisoned for his political activities. Played distinguished part in the final negotiations for the independence of India. Under his enlightened leadership India made dramatic technical, industrial, and social advances. *See also* Section C, Part I.

**Nelson, Horatio, Viscount, K.C.B.** (1758–1805), the great English naval commander; son of a Norfolk clergyman. Went to sea at twelve years of age, and was post-captain at twenty-one. In 1793 he was captain of the *Agamemnon* and proved his capacity and daring against the French. He lost his right eye at the siege of Calvi in 1794, and his right arm at the siege of Santa Cruz in 1797. In 1798 he achieved a great victory over the French in Aboukir Bay, in recognition of which he was created a Baron and granted a pension of £2,000 a year. Victorious at Copenhagen in 1801, he was promoted to the rank of Viscount. In 1805 the French fleet was destroyed at Trafalgar and Nelson was killed. Buried in St. Paul's Cathedral.

**Nenni, Pietro** (b. 1883), Italian politician and Secretary-General of the Italian Socialist Party since 1944. Minister of Foreign Affairs, 1946–47.

**Nernst, Walther Hermann** (1864–1941), German scientist who established the third law of thermodynamics. Nobel Prizeman, 1920.

**Nero, Claudius Cæsar** (A.D. 37–68), the Roman Emperor whose reign of fourteen years was rendered infamous by his cruelty and licentiousness.

**Newcomen, Thomas** (1663–1729), was one of the first to put a steam-engine into practical operation, and in 1705 patented his invention, which was the pumping-engine used in Cornish mines until the adoption of Watt's engine.

Newman, Ernest (1868–1959), English music critic successively of *The Manchester Guardian*, *The Birmingham Post*, *The Observer*, and of *The Sunday Times*, 1920–58. Outstanding among his numerous writings is the *Life of Richard Wagner*.

Newman, John Henry, Cardinal (1801–90). Educated at Oxford, he was incumbent of St. Mary's there from 1828 to 1843, taking an active part in the religious discussions of the time, gradually showing a tendency to adopt Roman Catholic views, and ultimately allying himself with the Romanists, resigning his living and settling at Edgbaston, Birmingham, as the head of a community of the Order of St. Philip Neri. In his *Apologia pro Vita Sua* he described the development of his religious thought. The hymn *Lead, kindly Light*, and the *Dream of Gerontius* were written by him.

Newton, Sir Isaac, F.R.S. (1642–1727), generally acknowledged as the world's greatest man of science. Achieved immortal fame for his work on the nature of white light, the calculus and gravitation Greatest published work, the *Principia*, was produced in 1687, revolutionizing the scientific thought of his time. Was Member of Parliament for Cambridge in 1688, Master of the Mint in 1699, and President of the Royal Society from 1703 till his death. Honoured with knighthood in 1705.

Ney, Marshal Michel (1769–1815), was one of Napoleon's most noteworthy generals.

Nicholas II., Ex-Czar of Russia (1868–1918), son of the Emperor Alexander III. Came to the throne in 1894, and had a reign full of trouble, being unable to handle the difficulties by which he was beset. He avowed full harmony with the British and French in the war which opened in 1914, but the acts of the Empress and Court belied these pretensions, and a Revolution resulted in March, 1917, which overthrew the Romanoffs. Nicholas was detained a prisoner together with the Czarina and his children; all were probably shot on July 16, 1918.

Nicholas, St., Bishop of Myra and patron saint of Russia, flourished in the 4th century, and is popularly associated with Christmas under the corrupted name of Santa Claus.

Nicholson, Sir William (1872–1949), English painter, well known for his portraits, engravings and woodcuts as well as for his illustrations in the *Almanack of Twelve Sports* (with Kipling) and *London Types* (with Henley). His son. Ben Nicholson O.M. (b. 1894), also an artist, is noted for his abstract paintings.

Nicolson, Hon. Sir Harold, K.C.V.O., C.M.G. (1886–1968), diarist, author, and critic, whose publications include *King George V: His Life and Reign* (1952), *Good Behaviour* (1955), and *Diaries and Letters, 1945–62* (1968).

Niemöller, Martin (b. 1892), German religious leader. A pastor in the Evangelical (Protestant) Church. Actively opposed the Nazification of the German Church and was incarcerated in a concentration camp throughout the second world war.

Nietzsche, Friedrich Wilhelm (1844–1900), German philosopher, in his younger years greatly influenced by the work of Wagner and Schopenhauer. His "superman" philosophy is eloquently expressed in his many writings, *i.e.*, *Thus spake Zarathustra*, *Beyond Good and Evil*, *The Will to Power*.

Nightingale, Florence, O.M. (1820–1910), English nurse and pioneer of hospital reform whose genius for administration was shown during the Crimean War, when she organised in face of considerable official opposition a nursing service to relieve the sufferings of the British soldiers who called her "The Lady with the Lamp." Her system was adopted and developed in all parts of the world, and she was honoured with a testimonial of £50,000, which she applied to the founding of the Nightingale Training School for Nurses, attached to St. Thomas's Hospital, London.

Nijinsky, Vaslav (1892–1950), Russian dancer, who was one of the famous company of dancers, which included Pavlova, Karsavina and Fokine, brought by Diaghilev to Paris and London just before the War of 1914–18, and was in some respects the most remarkable of them all. His sensational dancing in such Ballets as *Les Sylphides*, *Spectre de la Rose* and *Après-Midi*

*d'un Faune* won him the supreme place among male dancers.

Nikisch, Arthur (1855–1922), Hungarian musician and one of the first virtuoso conductors. His early and later years were connected with Leipzig. Famed also as piano-accompanist to the Lieder singer, Elena Gerhardt.

Nimitz, Admiral of the Fleet Chester William 1885–1966), commanded the American fleet in the Pacific, 1941–45, together with army and marine forces. Chief of Naval Operations, 1945–47.

Nixon, Richard Milhous, LL.B. (b. 1913), Republican President of the U.S.A., 1969–; elected to Congress, 1946; to Senate, 1951; Vice-President, 1952, re-elected, 1956; received Republican presidential nomination in 1960 when Kennedy won with narrow majority.

Nkrumah, Kwame (b. 1909), African leader whose country (Gold Coast) achieved independence in 1957, and in 1960 became the Republic of Ghana. Prime Min. (1957) and Pres. (1960). Deposed (1966) by military coup while absent in Far East.

Nobel, Dr. Alfred Bernhard (1833–96), the inventor of dynamite, was a Swedish engineer and chemist who amassed a large fortune from the manufacture of explosives, a great portion of which at his death in 1896 he set apart as a fund for annual prizes to such persons as during each year shall have contributed most materially to the benefit of mankind. *See* list of Nobel Prizemen, Section L.

Northcliffe, 1st Viscount, Alfred Charles William Harmsworth (1865–1922), British journalist and newspaper proprietor, b. near Dublin. He began *Answers* in 1888 with his brother Harold, later Lord Rothermere. In 1894 they bought the *Evening News*, and in 1896 the *Daily Mail*. In 1908 Northcliffe took over *The Times*.

Northumberland, John Dudley, Duke of (1502–53), an expert intriguer who dominated the Government of Edward VI. from 1549 onwards and attempted to maintain his influence when the king died by proclaiming as Queen his daughter-in-law, Lady Jane Grey, but failed and was executed.

Nostradamus or Michel de Notre Dame (1503–66), French astrologer who acquired great distinction by his labours during the plague. Publ. in 1555 *Centuries*, a book of rhymed prophecies, the fulfilment of some of which greatly added to his reputation. *Centuries* was condemned by the papal court of 1781.

Novalis, the pseudonym of Baron Friedrich von Hardenberg (1772–1801), German poet and novelist, representative of German romanticism. His chief work was the novel *Heinrich von Ofterdingen*, unfinished at his death.

Nuffield, 1st Viscount, William Richard Morris, G.B.E., C.H. (1877–1963), industrialist and philanthropist and until he retired in 1952 Chairman of Morris Motors, Ltd. Established the Nuffield Foundation, endowing it with £10 million, and provided large sums for the advancement of medicine in the University of Oxford.

Numa Pompilius, legendary king of Rome, to whom is ascribed Roman ceremonial law.

Nyerere, Julius (b. 1922), African statesman; President of the United Republic of Tanzania, 1964–.

# O

Oaksey, Geoffrey Lawrence, 1st Baron, P.C., Q.C., D.S.O. (b. 1880), presided over the International Military Tribunal which tried the major war criminals at Nuremberg, 1945–46. A Lord of Appeal in Ordinary since 1947.

Oates, Captain Lawrence Edward Grace (1880–1912), a British explorer who, having seen active service in the South African War, joined Capt. Scott's Antarctic Expedition in 1910. He was one of the sledge party who accompanied Scott in his final dash for the South Pole. On returning, the party became stormbound, and on March 17, 1912, Oates, crippled by frost-bite, went out in the blizzard to die rather than be a burden to his starving comrades. Described in Scott's diary as a very gallant gentleman.

Oates, Titus (1649–1705), a notorious informer against Roman Catholics in reign of Charles II.

O'Casey, Sean (1883–1964), Irish dramatist of remarkable powers whose plays include *Juno and* the Paycock, The Silver Tassie, Red Roses for Me, and Oak Leaves and Lavender.

**Occam (Ockham), William of** (c. 1270–1349), English scholar and philosopher and one of the most interesting, independent and original thinkers of all time. He belonged to the Order of Franciscans, violently opposed the temporal power of the Pope, espoused the cause of nominalism and laid the foundations of modern theories of government and theological scepticism. (See Occam's Razor, Section J.)

**O'Connell, Daniel** (1775–1847), the Irish " Liberator," as he was called, was a famous orator and politician and a highly successful barrister. In Parliament he advocated the cause of Ireland with courage and audacity.

**O'Connor, Feargus** (1796–1855), was an Irish lawyer who became the most influential figure in the Chartist movement.

**O'Connor, Rt. Hon. Thomas Power** (1848–1929), sat in Parliament from 1880 until 1929, being for many years father of the house, and was one of the most successful journalists and editors of his time. He founded several publications including the Star.

**Oersted, Hans Christian** (1777–1851), the Danish physicist and chemist, whose discoveries in electrical research did much to help forward the invention of the electric telegraph.

**Offa** was King of Mercia from circa 757 to 796, and had a war-like career; he built an embankment from the Dee to the Wye, 100 miles long, which was called Offa's Dyke. He imposed " Peter's Pence " as a gift to the Pope for absolution.

**Offenbach, Jacques** (1819–80), French composer, born of a Jewish family at Cologne. Was the composer of many light operas, including the posthumous Les Contes d'Hoffmann (Tales of Hoffmann), the most popular of all his works.

**Ohm, Georg Simon** (1787–1854), was the discoverer of a law of electric current now known universally as Ohm's law. He was a native of Bavaria, professor at Munich from 1852, and gained much fame as a physicist and mathematician.

**Olivier, Sir Laurence Kerr** (b. 1907), British actor and director whose performances in Shakespearean and other roles have brought wide acclaim. He has also produced, directed, and played in many films, including Henry V., Hamlet, and Richard III. Director of the National Theatre.

**Oman, Sir Charles (William Chadwick), K.B.E.** (1860–1946), English historian who was Chichele Professor of Modern History at Oxford, 1905–46 and M.P. for the University from 1919 to 1935. His works include a popular History of Greece, A Short History of England, which is a familiar school book, and a History of the Art of War in the Middle Ages.

**Omar Khayyám** (c. 1050–1123), Persian poet and mathematician, called Khayyám (tent-maker) because of his father's occupation. His fame as a scientist has been eclipsed by his Rubaiyat, made known to English readers by Edward Fitz-Gerald in 1859.

**O'Neill, Eugene Gladstone** (1888–1953), an American playwright who, after spending his adventurous youth in such activities as sailing, gold-prospecting, and journalism, first won success in 1914 with the one-act play, Thirst. His later plays include Anna Christie, Strange Interlude, Mourning Becomes Electra, The Iceman Cometh. See also Section I.

**Orchardson, Sir William Quiller** (1835–1910), an eminent R.A.; among his best-known works are Napoleon I. on board H.M.S. Bellerophon and Ophelia.

**Origen** (c. 185–c. 254), Christian philosopher and biblical scholar, famed for his teaching at Alexandria and Cæsarea. He attempted to synthesise Greek philosophy and Hebrew scriptures so as to prove the Christian view of the universe was compatible with Greek thought. In the persecution of Decius in 250 he was imprisoned, tortured, and pilloried.

**Orpen, Sir William, K.B.E., R.A.** (1878–1931), British portrait-painter; many of his celebrated war pictures were presented to the nation.

**Ortega y Gasset, José** (1883–1955), Spanish philosopher and essayist, one of the most eloquent men of our times. His The Revolt of the Masses (1932) brought him international fame.

**Orwell, George** (1903–50), English satirist, author of Animal Farm (1946) and Nineteen Eighty-Four (1949). His real name was Eric Blair; b. in India.

**Osler, Sir William, Bt., M.D., F.R.S.** (1849–1919). Canadian physician and medical historian; an authority on diseases of the blood and spleen.

**Ossietzky, Carl von** (1889–1938), German pacifist, leader of the peace movement in Germany after the First World War. Sent to a concentration camp by Hitler. Awarded the 1935 Nobel Peace Prize.

**Oswald, St.**, King of Northumbria from 625 to 642, established Christianity amongst his subjects.

**Ouida**, pseudonym of Louise de la Ramée (1839–1908), English novelist of flamboyant personality whose many romantic stories were very popular and included Under Two Flags, A Dog of Flanders, and Moths. Born at Bury St. Edmunds and buried at Bagni di Lucca in Tuscany. Her father was French.

**Otto, Nikolaus August** (1832–91). German inventor of the four-stroke cycle that bears his name.

**Otto the Great** (912–973), son of Henry the Fowler, crowned King of the Germans at Aachen in 936 and Emperor at Rome in 962. Overawed the papacy, checked the barbarian invasions, founded the East Mark (Austria), and considerably consolidated Germany.

**Ovid** (43 B.C.–A.D. 18), the famous Latin poet (Publius Ovidius Naso) whose Metamorphoses and Art of Love are among the best-known examples of Roman literature of the lighter kind.

**Owen, Robert** (1771–1858), socialist and philanthropist, devoted his life and fortune to the carrying out of his theories, and established socialistic colonies in Lanarkshire, Hampshire and America.

# P

**Pachmann, Vladimir de** (1848–1923), Russian pianist, an unrivalled interpreter of the works of Chopin.

**Paderewski, Ignace Jan** (1860–1941), achieved unrivalled fame as a pianist and for half a century worked for the freedom of his native Poland. He represented his country at Versailles and became her first Prime Minister.

**Paganini, Niccolo** (1782–1840), Italian violinist and composer whose playing became a legend and brought him much fame and wealth. He ranks as first among virtuosi of the violin.

**Paine, Thomas** (1737–1809), English revolutionary writer, b. Thetford, Norfolk, son of a Quaker; emigrated to America (1774), becoming famous with the publication of his pamphlet Common Sense in favour of American independence. On return to England (1787) wrote The Rights of Man in reply to Burke's Reflections on the Revolution in France. This was extensively read but his attack on English institutions procured him a trial for sedition and he fled to France. There he wrote The Age of Reason, an attack on Christianity which excited great indignation in England. Returned to America where he lived his last years in solitude and ill-health.

**Palestrina, Giovanni Pierluigi da** (c. 1525–94), great Italian composer of unaccompanied church music and madrigals, among whose works are the Missa Papae Marcelli and the Stabat Mater for 8 voices, which is among the greatest musical glories of all time. See Section E.

**Palgrave, Sir Francis** (1788–1861), English historian, best known for his A History of Normandy and England. His son, Francis Turner Palgrave (1824–97), was Professor of Poetry at Oxford, and edited the famous anthology, The Golden Treasury. Another son, William Gifford Palgrave (1826–88), was a diplomat and prose writer of ability.

**Palissy, Bernard** (c. 1510–89), French potter who discovered the art of producing white enamel.

**Palladio, Andrea** (1518–80), the great Italian architect, who introduced the style of architecture known as Palladian.

**Palmer, John** (1742–1818), originator of the mail-coach postal service in 1784.

**Palmerston, Henry John Temple, 3rd Viscount** (1784–1865). English statesman, was long dominant in European affairs because of his vigorous and popular policy. He spent many years of his life in office, serving as Tory Secretary for War from 1808 till 1828 as Foreign Secretary in all the Whig cabinets between 1830 and 1851, and as Prime Minister in 1855 and from 1859 until his death. He had a lofty conception of the strength and duties of England and was the irreconcilable foe of oppression and injustice.

**Pancras, St.,** the patron saint of children, was the son of a Roman noble, was baptised in Rome in the reign of Diocletian, where he was put to death at the age of fourteen for refusing to renounce Christianity.

**Pandit, Vijaya Lakshmi** (b. 1900), India's first Ambassador to the Soviet Union (1947–9) and to the United States (1949–51), the first woman to be elected Pres. of the U.N. General Assembly (1953–4). Sister of Jawaharlal Nehru.

**Panizzi, Sir Anthony,** K.C.B. (1797–1879), an Italian political exile, who in 1831 was appointed to the Assistant Librarianship and Keepership of the Printed Books of the British Museum. In 1856 he became Principal Librarian, retiring in 1866. The great Reading Room was constructed from his designs.

**Pankhurst, Emmeline** (1858–1928) was a prominent and indefatigable worker for women's suffrage, together with her daughters Dame Christabel and Sylvia.

**Papin, Denis** (1647–1712?), French physicist and inventor. After working in Venice, London, Marburg and Cassel he settled in London where he died. He invented a steam digestor (forerunner of the autoclave), a condensing pump, and was a pioneer in the development of the steam engine. Not being a mechanic, he made all his experiments by means of models.

**Paracelsus, Philippus Aureolus** (1493–1541), a famous Swiss mystic and alchemist. He made numerous important discoveries, being the first to employ laudanum and antimony in pharmacy. The English translation of his *One Hundred and Fourteen Experiments and Cures* appeared in 1596. His real name was Theophrastus Bombastus von Hohenheim.

**Park, Mungo** (1771–1806), famous British traveller who in 1799 published an arresting account of his *Travels in the Interior of Africa.*

**Parker, Rev. Joseph** (1830–1902), a popular Nonconformist preacher and author who built the City Temple, and ministered there up to the time of his death.

**Parnell, Charles Stewart** (1846–91), the Irish politician, who as leader of the Nationalist Party made it more powerful than it had ever been and successfully enlisted the support of Gladstone for the policy of Home Rule. Accused by *The Times* of complicity in the crimes of the Land League on the basis of letters forged by Richard Pigott, he was completely vindicated by a Royal Commission and awarded heavy damages. Was dropped from the leadership of his party following the O'Shea divorce proceedings and died soon afterwards.

**Parry, Rear-Admiral Sir William Edward** (1790–1855), an Arctic explorer and naval commander of great distinction, who undertook several expeditions to the Polar regions and made numerous important discoveries.

**Parsons, Hon. Sir Charles Algernon,** O.M., K.C.B., F.R.S. (1854–1931), was head of the electrical and engineering works of C. A. Parsons and Co., and of the Parsons Marine Steam Turbine Co., Ltd., Newcastle-on-Tyne, and inventor of the steam turbine which has effected a remarkable improvement in the propulsion of war and mercantile vessels.

**Pascal, Blaise** (1623–62), celebrated French mathematical genius and religious philosopher whose *Provincial Letters* are one of the world's literary masterpieces. At the age of nineteen he invented an ingenious adding machine and was the first to demonstrate the barometric effects of altitude.

**Pasternak, Boris Leonidovich** (1890–1960), Russian poet and writer. Translations of his great novel *Dr. Zhivago* appeared in 1958, though it was forbidden in the Soviet Union. In that year he was awarded—though he declined it—the Nobel Prize for Literature " for his important contributions both to contemporary lyric poetry and to the great Russian narrative tradition."

**Pasteur, Louis** (1822–95), French chemist, whose work was inspired by an interest in the chemistry of life which abided with him until his death. His researches on fermentation led to the science

of bacteriology and his investigations into infectious diseases and their prevention to the science of immunology. The pathological bacteriological import of Pasteur's researches came about mainly through his disciples (Lister, Roux, and others) and not directly, though all founded on his early non-medical investigations on organisms of fermentation, etc., which were of great importance in industry, and fundamentally. He spent most of his life as director of scientific studies at the Ecole Normale at Paris, where he was appointed in 1857. The Institut Pasteur was founded in 1888.

**Patmore, Coventry** (1823–96), poet of the Victorian era, and author of *The Angel in the House.*

**Patrick, St.** (c. 387–c. 463), the patron saint and Apostle of Ireland, was for many years a great and successful Christian missionary in that country. Few authentic facts about his life are known, but many miraculous stories, such as his alleged extermination of serpents in the island, have been associated with him.

**Patti, Adelina Juana Maria (Baroness Cederström)** (1843–1919), coloratura soprano, b. in Madrid of Italian parents, unsurpassed for purity of tone and style.

**Pattison, Dorothy Wyndlow** (1832–78), a sister of Mark Pattison, who devoted a great part of her life to hospital work in Walsall, where, as "Sister Dora," she is revered for her saintly life and devotion to the sick poor.

**Pattison, Mark** (1813–84), scholar and critic, rector of Lincoln College, Oxford. His wife, Emilia Francis Strong (afterwards Lady Dilke), was well known as a French art historian.

**Paul, Saint** (A.D. 10–c. 67), Greek Jew, a Pharisee, b. Tarsus (southern Turkey); converted to Christianity A.D. 37. His missionary journeys took him to the Roman provinces of Asia, Macedonia, and Greece. His epistles form nearly half the New Testament and were written in the following order: 1 and 2 Thessalonians; 1 and 2 Corinthians; Galatians; Romans; Philippians; Ephesians; Colossians; Philemon; 1 Timothy; Titus; 2 Timothy. The Epistle to the Hebrews was not written by him. The four Gospels were written after his death. His Hebrew name was Saul. It is not known how he spent his last years but tradition says he was beheaded in Rome.

**Paul VI, Pope** (Giovanni Battista Montini) (b. 1897), elected pope in 1963 on the death of John XXIII. Formerly Archbishop of Milan. Made pilgrimage to Holy Land in Jan. 1964.

**Pavlov, Prof. Ivan Petrovich** (1849–1936), an eminent Russian physiologist: Director of the Physiological Institute. Foreign member of the Royal Society and Nobel Prize-winner.

**Pavlova, Anna** (1885–1931), one of the greatest exponents of the Russian school of dancing.

**Peabody, George** (1795–1869), an American merchant who lived for the greater part of his life in London, and, acquiring a large fortune, bequeathed immense sums for philanthropic purposes in England and the United States.

**Peacock, Thomas Love** (1785–1866), English satirist, whose novels include *Headlong Hall* and *Nightmare Abbey,* and who ranks high in English literature for the wit and grace of his style.

**Pearson, Lester Bowles,** O.B.E., M.A. (b. 1897), Prime Min. of Canada, 1963–; Min. for External Affairs, 1948–57.

**Peary, Rear-Admiral Robert Edwin** (1856–1920), an American Arctic explorer who, in 1891–92, conducted a sledging expedition towards the Pole. In 1893, 1895, and 1898 was again in the Arctic regions; and in 1900–02 reached the highest latitude hitherto attained. In the spring of 1906 he touched 87 degs. 6 min. N. latitude. On April 6, 1909, making the journey by sledge over sea-ice and accompanied by only his native servant, he succeeded in reaching the Pole.

**Peel, Rt. Hon. Sir Robert,** 2nd Bt. (1788–1850), a prominent British statesman who entered Parliament at twenty-one years of age, and immediately exhibited great capacity, being appointed Under-Secretary for the Colonies in the following year. From 1812 to 1818 he was Secretary for Ireland; and in 1822 he became Home Secretary, introducing, whilst fulfilling that office, the new police service associated with his name. In 1834, Peel was for four months Prime Minister. and in 1841 formed a second ministry. It was

**B59**

then that the Anti-Corn Law agitation became formidable, and Peel abandoned his former Protectionist attitude, and carried his Repeal measure in 1846. He was thrown from his horse in Hyde Park and died from injuries.

**Penfield, Wilder Graves,** O.M., M.D., M.A., D.Sc., F.R.S. (b. 1891), Canadian brain surgeon; Dir. Montreal Neurological Institute; Prof. of Neurosurgery McGill Univ.; Pub. *The Cerebral Cortex of Man* (1950), *Epilepsy and the Functional Anatomy of the Human Brain* (1954).

**Penn, William** (1644–1718), became a Quaker, and wrote some powerful pamphlets supporting his new faith. He devoted himself to good works, and in 1682, having obtained a special grant from King Charles II., went to America and founded Pennsylvania.

**Penney, William George, Baron,** K.B.E., M.A., Ph.D., D.Sc., F.R.S. (b. 1909), British scientist; Chair. U.K. Atomic Energy Authority, 1964–7. After 23 years in atomic research and development, returned to academic life in 1967 to become Rector of Imperial College. His nuclear research team at AEA developed the advanced gas-cooled reactor (AGR) chosen for the new power stations at Dungeness and Hinkley Point.

**Pepys, Samuel,** F.R.S. (1633–1703), naval administrator, sometimes called the "Father of the British Civil Service." The *Diary* was written while he was a comparatively young man and is a unique revelation of a man and his age, besides including eye-witness descriptions of the Great Plague and Fire of London.

**Pereda, José María de** (1833–1906), Spanish regional novelist (around his native Santander).

**Pergolesi, Giovanni Battista** (1710–36), Italian composer, best known for his humorous opera *La Serva Padrona* and his *Stabat Mater.*

**Pericles** (c. 490–429 B.C.), the distinguished Athenian statesman, general, and orator, who raised Athens to the point of its fullest prosperity.

**Perkin, Sir William Henry,** F.R.S., D.Sc. (1838–1907), great organic chemist and famous for his discovery of mauve, the first synthetic dye.

**Perkin, William Henry** (junior) (1860–1929), foremost organic chemist of his day; Professor of Organic Chemistry at Manchester University, 1892–1912 and later at Oxford. His researches led to important industrial results.

**Perrin, Francis** (b. 1901), French scientist and socialist; succeeded Joliot-Curie as High Commr. for Atomic Energy in 1951. Prof. Atomic Physics, Collège de France, 1946–.

**Persius Flaccus, Aulus** (A.D. 34–62), a famous Stoic philosopher.

**Perugino, Pietro** (1446–1524), Italian artist who excelled in religious subjects and painted many fine frescoes including some in the Sistine Chapel at Rome. Raphael was his pupil.

**Pestalozzi, Johann Heinrich** (1746–1827). Swiss educational reformer whose theories laid the foundation of modern primary education. His teaching methods were far in advance of his time, but are now employed with outstanding success in schools in many parts of the world.

**Pétain, Marshal Henri Phillipe** (1856–1951), became a French national hero after the successful defence of Verdun in 1916 and was made C.-in-C. of all the French armies. In 1940 he became Prime Minister, signed an armistice with Germany, and set up a quasi-independent administration at Vichy. In 1945 he was sentenced to death for treason, the sentence being commuted to life imprisonment.

**Peter I, called The Great** (1672–1725). Czar of Russia, showed great ability and energy of character, devoting himself largely to the reorganisation of his army and navy. He spent some months at Deptford studying shipbuilding. He founded St. Petersburg (1703), which was his "window on to Europe," and gained control in the war with Sweden of Karelia, Ingermanland, and Livonia. Among the prisoners taken by him at the Battle of Poltava (1709) was Catherine Skavronsky, daughter of a Lithuanian peasant, whom he later married. By her care and understanding she did much to strengthen his power. Peter died without naming an heir, and Catherine became Empress of Russia (1725–27).

**Peter, the Hermit** (c. 1050–1115), was the main instrument of the agitation which brought about the first Crusade. He was a French monk, of great eloquence and earnestness, and lived to see Jerusalem in the hands of the Christians.

**Petrarch, Francesco** (1304–74), Italian poet and scholar, whose odes and sonnets *To Laura* are unmatched for their lyrical beauty and passion.

**Petrie, Sir** (William Matthew) **Flinders,** F.R.S. (1853–1942), British egyptologist; carried out excavations in Britain (1875–90), Egypt (1880–1924), and Palestine (1927–38); Prof. of Egyptology at University College, London, 1893–1935.

**Phidias,** the greatest of Greek sculptors, flourished from about 500 to 432 B.C., was specially famous for his work in gold, ivory and bronze. Nothing now remains to attest his genius although the sculptures in the British Museum, widely known as the Elgin Marbles, may have been from his designs.

**Philip II. of France** (1180–1223), was a prominent figure in the third Crusade, in which for a time he associated himself with our Richard I. Victor over a strong coalition at the momentous battle of Bouvines in 1214.

**Philip II. of Macedonia** (382–336 B.C.), trained in military arts in Greece, when he came to the throne instilled martial ideas into his subjects, and entered upon a career of conquest that did not end until he had become master of Greece. Father of Alexander the Great.

**Philip II. of Spain** (1527–98), succeeded his father the Emperor Charles V. in half his dominions. The Revolt of the Netherlands, the annexation of Portugal in 1580, and the unsuccessful attempt to subdue England by the Armada, were outstanding events of his troubled reign. He was a devout Roman Catholic, strongly supported the Counter-Reformation, built the strange Escorial, and was four times married, his second wife being Mary Tudor.

**Philip V. of Spain** (1683–1746), founded the Bourbon dynasty in Spain, and was the son of the Dauphin of Louis XIV. and Maria Theresa of Spain. His uncle, Charles II. of Spain, bequeathed the kingdom to him, and this led to the war of the Spanish Succession, which ultimately confirmed him in his kingship.

**Phillip, Arthur** (1738–1814), first governor of New South Wales. Under his command the first fleet of 717 convicts set sail from Britain to Australia, and with the founding of Sydney in 1788 colonisation of the whole country began.

**Phillips, Stephen** (1868–1915), dramatist and poet of distinction. Wrote popular verse dramas, including *Paolo and Francesca, Herod,* and *Ulysses.*

**Piasts,** first Polish dynasty in Poland until 14th century and until 17th century in Silesia.

**Piazzi, Giuseppe** (1746–1826), an Italian astronomer. He was the discoverer of the planet Ceres, the first known of the asteroids.

**Picasso, Pablo Ruiz** (b. 1881), Spanish painter; received his early training in Catalonia and settled in Paris in 1903. He and Braque were the originators of Cubism (c. 1909). His influence over contemporary art is comparable with that exercised by Cézanne (q.v.) over the artists of his time. Perhaps the best known single work is his mural *Guernica,* painted at the time of the Spanish civil war, expressing the artist's loathing of fascism and the horrors of war. His genius has also found scope in sculpture, ceramics, and the graphic arts, and he has designed décor costumes for the ballet.

**Piccard, Auguste** (1884–1962), Swiss physicist, noted for his balloon ascents in the stratosphere, and his submarine research. In 1960 his son, Jacques Piccard, made a descent of over 7 miles in the Marianas trench in the western Pacific in a bathyscaphe designed and built by him.

**Pilsudski, Joseph** (1867–1935), Polish soldier and statesman. Led unsuccessful Polish attack on Russia in 1920 seeking the restoration of 1772 frontiers. Exercised military dictatorship from 1926 until his death.

**Pindar** (522–443 B.C.), the eminent lyric poet of ancient Greece.

**Pinero, Sir Arthur Wing** (1855–1934), was an able English dramatist and former actor, of Portuguese descent. *Dandy Dick, The Second Mrs. Tanqueray* and *Mid-Channel* are among his plays.

**Pirandello, Luigi** (1867–1936), Italian dramatist and novelist. Awarded Nobel Prize for Literature, 1934.

**Pissarro, Camille** (1830–1903), French Impressionist painter of landscapes; studied under Corot,

**Pitman, Sir Isaac** (1813–97), founded the Pitman system of phonographic shorthand.

**Pitt, William** (1759–1806), was the second son of the Earl of Chatham. Entered Parliament at twenty-one, and by his brilliant oratory captivated the House of Commons. In 1782, when only twenty-three, he became Chancellor of the Exchequer, and in the following year was made Premier, and held that office for seventeen years, through the trying period of the French Revolution, when war with France was almost continuous. He was undoubtedly one of the most brilliant statesmen that England has produced, and his death at the early age of forty-six was a great loss to the country. He was buried in Westminster Abbey.

**Pius XII.** (1876–1958), elected Pope, March 2, 1939. As Cardinal Eugenio Pacelli, he was Papal Secretary of State, 1930–39, and was outspoken in his condemnation of communism. Before he became a Cardinal he was for many years Papal Nuncio in Germany. He was a brilliant diplomat but has been criticised for his failure to protest publicly against the crimes of the Nazi regime.

**Pizarro, Francisco** (c. 1478–1541), was an adventurous Spaniard who, after Columbus's discoveries in the New World, set out for South America, overthrowing the Inca empire and conquering Peru for the Emperor Charles V.

**Planck, Prof. Dr. Max** (1858–1947), German physicist, whose investigations into radiation of energy culminated in 1901 in his law of radiation, which laid the foundation of the quantum theory. Awarded Nobel Prize for Physics, 1918.

**Plato** (427–347 B.C.), great Athenian philosopher, pupil of Socrates, teacher of Aristotle. He founded a school at Athens under the name of the Academy, where he taught philosophy and mathematics. His great work is his *Dialogues*, which includes the *Republic*, the longest and most celebrated of them all. All Plato's known writings have come down to us, and they constitute one of the most influential bodies of work in history.

**Playfair, Lyon** (1818–98), a far-sighted Victorian who stood for the greater recognition of science in national life. He forsook his profession as professor of chemistry at Edinburgh to enter Parliament. Pres. of the British Association in 1885.

**Plimsoll, Samuel** (1824–98), was a native of Bristol, and while M.P. for Derby got up an agitation on behalf of merchant sailors, procuring the passing of the Merchant Shipping Act of 1876, which by defining a line above which no ship must sink in the water when loaded has ever since made the overloading of ships illegal. The line is known as the Plimsoll Mark.

**Pliny the Elder** (A.D. 23–79), Roman naturalist who dedicated his great work *Natural History* to the Emperor Titus. He died of fumes and exhaustion while investigating the eruption of Vesuvius. His nephew, Pliny the Younger (A.D. 62–113), achieved renown with his series of historical *Letters*.

**Plotinus** (c. 204–270), Greek philosopher, was the founder of Neoplatonism, which had considerable influence on early Christian thought.

**Plutarch** (c. 46–120), a pagan Hellenic writer, a contemporary of the authors of the two gospels according to St. Matthew and St. Luke. His *Lives of Agis and Cleomenes* form one of the world's most famous literary productions.

**Poe, Edgar Allan** (1809–49), was an American poet of unique genius, author of " The Raven," " The Bells," " Annabel Lee," and other poems of haunting melody and dainty fancy. Poe's *Tales of Mystery* are thrilling examples of their class.

**Poincaré, Raymond Nicolas Landry** (1860–1934), was President of France from 1913 to 1920 and won the confidence and admiration of the French people and their Allies by his services during the first world war. He was Prime Minister in 1912, 1922–24, and 1926–29.

**Pole, Reginald** (1550–58), archbishop of Canterbury (1556–58), cardinal of the Roman Church, antagonist of the English reformation, whose mother was Margaret Plantagenet, half-sister of Henry VII's mother. His difference with Henry VIII over the divorce of Catherine evoked his famous treatise *De Unitate Ecclesiastica*, a defence of papal supremacy and a denunciation of the king. His activity brought about his own attainder, and the execution of his brother and mother as participators in his treasonable designs.

**Pollard, Professor Albert Frederick**, F.B.A. (1869–1948), English historian and first director of the Institute of Historical Research; author of many authoritative works on the Tudor period.

**Polo, Marco** (1256–1323), the famous Venetian traveller and explorer, who made journeys through China, India, and other eastern countries, and published the record of his various wanderings, recounting the many wonders and marvels he had seen—a record which seemed for the most part beyond credence to his contemporaries, but now largely confirmed.

**Pompadour, Jeanne Antoine Poisson, Marquise de,** (1721–64), was for a long time the favourite of Louis XV. of France, over whom she exercised great influence.

**Pompey the Great** (106–48 B.C.), distinguished himself as a general while young, clearing the Mediterranean of pirates, and ultimately became, with Caesar and Crassus, triumvir.

**Pope, Alexander** (1688–1744), the celebrated 18th century poet and translator of *Homer*. Author of *The Rape of the Lock*, *Essay on Criticism*, and *Essay on Man*.

**Pound, Ezra Loomis** (b. 1885). American poet and scholar, famous both for the beauty of his individual verse and for his excellent translations of Provencal, Latin, Chinese, French and Italian poets.

**Poussin, Nicolas** (1593–1665), an eminent French painter patronised by Louis XIII.

**Powys, John Cowper** (1872–1963), English writer, best known for his novel *Wolf Solent* (1929) and his essays *The Meaning of Culture* (1929) and *A Philosophy of Solitude* (1933). His brothers, **Theodore Francis Powys** (1875–1953) and **Llewelyn Powys** (1884–1939), were also writers of originality.

**Prasad, Dr. Rajendra** (1884–1963), first President of the Indian Union, 1950–62.

**Praxiteles**, a great Greek sculptor who lived in the 4th century B.C.

**Preece, Sir William Henry**, K.C.B., F.R.S. (1834–1913), a Welsh electrician, connected with the Electric Telegraph Service from 1853, and conspicuously successful in his experiments which led to the later developments in telegraphy. He was associated with Marconi in his wireless-telegraphic schemes and introduced the block system into England.

**Prescott, William Hickling** (1796–1859), one of the best known of American historians.

**Prichard, James Cowles, M.D.,** F.R.S. (1786–1848), British ethnologist and physician, whose knowledge of anatomy, psychology, and languages enabled him to pave the way for anthropological research in England.

**Priestley, John Boynton, M.A.** (b. 1894), critic, novelist, essayist, playwright and broadcaster, whose work has received great praise and includes the novels *The Good Companions*, *Angel Pavement*, the plays *Dangerous Corner*, *Time and the Conways*, *The Linden Tree*, and a literary history, *Literature and Western Man* (1960).

**Priestley, Joseph,** F.R.S. (1733–1804), English chemist, famous for his work on gases; shares with Scheele credit for discovery of oxygen. He was also a great advocate of freedom and progress. Biography: *Adventurer in Science and Champion of Truth* by F. W. Gibbs (1965).

**Prior, Matthew** (1664–1721), a well-known poet and wit who acquired celebrity by writing *The City Mouse and Country Mouse*.

**Prokofiev, Sergey Sergeyevich** (1891–1953), celebrated Russian composer, whose music has a strong folk-song element, rich in melody and invention. He has written operas: *The Love of Three Oranges*, *The Betrothal in a Nunnery*, *War and Peace*, ballets: *Romeo and Juliet*, *Cinderella*, symphonies, chamber music and the music for Eisenstein's films *Alexander Nevsky*, *Ivan the Terrible*, etc. See Section E.

**Protagoras** (c. 480–411 B.C.), a Greek philosopher, chief of the Sophists, famous for his scepticism and disbelief in objective truth.

**Proudhon, Pierre Joseph** (1809–65), a French political economist.

**Proust, Marcel** (1871–1922), French psychological novelist; author of a series of 15 novels known under the title of *A la recherche du temps* *perdu.* Proust's works have been admirably translated into English by C. K. Scott Moncrieff. Biography by George D. Painter. *See* M5.

**Prudhon, Pierre Paul** (1758–1823), a French historical and portrait painter.

**Ptolemy, Claudius Ptolemæus,** a famous astronomer and geographer of Alexandria, who flourished from *c.* A.D. 90–168. He founded the Ptolemaic system, which taught that the earth was stationary and the heavenly bodies revolved around it. His great works are the *Almagest* and his *Geographical Outline.*

**Puccini, Giacomo** (1858–1924), Italian composer whose operas met with great success and include *Manon Lescaut, La Bohème, La Tosca, Madam Butterfly,* and *Turandot* (finished after his death).

**Purcell, Henry** (1658–95), one of the great figures in English music; organist of the Chapel Royal and composer to Charles II. Anthems form the greater part of his sacred music, and he wrote not only for the Court but for the stage. *See* Section E.

**Pusey, Edward Bouverie** (1800–82), a famous Anglican cleric; he published *Tracts for the Times,* which inaugurated the Tractarian movement that developed into what became known as Puseyism.

**Pushkin, Alexander** (1799–1837), the national poet of Russia, several times exiled for his liberal views and held in high honour by contemporary Russia. Died of wounds received in a duel. His poetical tales are full of dramatic power. *Eugene Onegin* and *Boris Godunov* are considered masterpieces.

**Pym, John** (1584–1643), a prominent statesman in the reign of Charles I. A leader of the Puritan opposition in Parliament.

**Pythagoras** (*c.* 582–*c.* 507 B.C.), most influential of the early Greek scientists. He was born on the island of Samos, off the Turkish mainland, which he left *c.* 530 to settle at Croton, a Greek city in southern Italy. He was a mystic and mathematician and believed in the transmigration of souls. He died in exile.

## Q

**Quaritch, Bernard** (1819–99), a famous dealer in rare books, who was a native of Germany but settled in London, and became naturalised in 1847. His knowledge of scarce and valuable books was unique. His shop in Piccadilly was a storehouse of literary treasures.

**Quasimodo, Salvatore** (1901–68), Italian poet and author, whose greatness lies in his humanity and his rejection of the Fascist influence. He won the Nobel Prize for Literature in 1959.

**Quiller-Couch, Sir Arthur Thomas** (1863–1944), was a well-known novelist and essayist, who as "Q" published many delightful stories. Edited the *Oxford Book of English Verse.* Professor of English Literature, Cambridge University, 1912–44.

## R

**Rabelais, François** (*c.* 1495–1553), the great French satirist, first adopted the career of a monk, then studied medicine, and settled at Lyons as a doctor, and it was there that he published his *Gargantua and Pantagruel,* among the wittiest though coarsest books in any language.

**Rachel, Mlle** (stage name of Elizabeth Félix) (1821–58), acknowledged as the greatest tragic actress of her time and reached the height of her fame in Racine's *Phèdre* in 1843.

**Rachmaninov, Sergey Vasilyevich** (1873–1943), Russian pianist, composer, and conductor. He wrote operas, symphonies, piano concertos, piano pieces, and songs, and was one of the greatest pianists of his age. *See* Section E.

**Racine, Jean** (1639–99), French tragic poet whose great dramas include *Andromaque, Iphigenie* and *Phèdre.* Left an orphan at an early age he was brought up by his paternal grandparents who sent him to the famous school of Port-Royal where he acquired his love of the classics. He enjoyed favour at the court of Louis XIV and along with his friend Boileau was joint historiographer to the king. Mme de Maintenon

persuaded him to write *Esther* and *Athalie* two other masterpieces of French literature.

**Rackham, Arthur, R. W. S.** (1867–1939), a noted English artist who excelled in the illustration of books such as *Peter Pan, Alice in Wonderland,* Wagner's *Ring Librettos, Mother Goose,* Grimm's and Andersen's *Fairy Tales.*

**Radhakrishnan, Sir Sarvepalli,** O.M., M.A., D.Litt. (b. 1888). Pres. Indian Union, 1962–7; Vice-Pres., 1952–62; formerly Spalding Professor of Eastern Religions and Ethics at Oxford.

**Raeburn, Sir Henry, R.A.** (1756–1823), was a famous Scottish portrait painter, and friend and pupil of Sir Joshua Reynolds.

**Raffles, Sir Thomas Stamford** (1781–1826), an eminent naturalist. He was the founder and first President of the Zoological Society of London. Founded Singapore, 1819.

**Raikes, Robert** (1735–1811), a practical propounder of the Sunday School system.

**Raleigh, Sir Walter** (1552–1618), courtier, writer, adventurer, stepbrother of Sir Humphrey Gilbert: entered Elizabeth's court where he found favour, distinguished himself in the Irish rebellion of 1580, began colonisation of Virginia in 1584, introduced potatoes and tobacco to British Isles, served in defence against Spain, found gold in Guiana. He lost favour on accession of James I, sentenced to death for treason, reprieved and sent to the Tower where he found solace in scientific and literary pursuits and wrote his *History of the World.* Released in 1615, after 12 years, to make another voyage in search of gold. He failed and was put to death on his return to England to conciliate the Spanish court.

**Raman, Sir (Chandrasekhara) Venkata,** F.R.S. (b. 1888), Indian physicist whose main work has been in spectroscopy. For his research on the diffusion of light and for the discovery of the "Raman Effect" he was awarded the 1930 Nobel Prize in Physics.

**Rameau, Jean Philippe** (1683–1764), French composer and church organist whose works on musical theory profoundly influenced musical development in the 18th century.

**Ramón y Cajal, Santiago** (1852–1934), Spanish histologist who made many discoveries in the structure of the nervous system. Nobel Prize-man, 1906.

**Ramsay, Sir William,** K.C.B., F.R.S. (1852–1916), chemist and discoverer with Lord Rayleigh of argon. Later he discovered helium and detected other inert gases, which he called neon, krypton, and xenon. With F. Soddy carried out research on radium emanation. Awarded Nobel Prize in Chemistry, 1904. President of the British Association, 1911.

**Ramsey, Most Rev. Arthur Michael,** D.D. (b. 1904), Archbishop of Canterbury, 1961. Archbishop of York, 1956–61; Prof. of Divinity at Cambridge, 1950–52; Lord Bishop of Durham, 1952–56.

**Ranke, Leopold von** (1795–1886), the painstaking and thorough German historian who laid the basis of modern historical research and demonstrated many of its methods.

**Raphael** (1483–1520) of Urbino was the youngest of the three great artists of the High Renaissance. He had been taught at Perugia by Perugino, and it was only when he came to Florence that he came under the influence of Leonardo and Michelangelo. Raphael's Madonnas, which have gained him popularity with all ages for their simplicity and grace, include the *Madonna of the Grand Duke* (Palazzo Pitti, Florence), the *Sistine Madonna* (Dresden), the *Madonna with the Goldfinch* (Uffizi, Florence), and the *Ansidei Madonna* (National Gallery, London). He painted the frescoes on the walls of the *Stanza della Segnatura* in the Vatican, those in the adjoining rooms and elsewhere, and his finest portrait is that of Castiglione. After the death of Bramante he was appointed architect in charge of the rebuilding of St. Peter's.

**Rasputin, Grigori Yefimovich** (1871–1916), a "holy man" of the old Russia who lived quietly in his native village until 1904, when he became notorious for his extravagant teachings, which gave him a Messianic-like position. He was a debauchee and advocated sin in order to obtain repentance and salvation. In 1907 he was presented to the Court where he soon became all-powerful. A seeming miracle which improved the health of the Tsarevich Alexis increased his influence with the Tsar and Tsaritsa. Assassinated by a group of conspirators from the nobility.

**Rathbone, Eleanor** (1872–1946), social reformer, humanitarian, and independent politician. Championed widows' pensions and family allowances and laboured for political refugees, particularly children.

**Ravel, Maurice** (1875–1937), French composer, pupil of Fauré, one of the leaders of the impressionist movement. He wrote chiefly chamber music, piano pieces, songs, and ballet music, including *Daphnis et Chloé*, specially commissioned by Diaghilev. *See Section E.*

**Raven-Hill, Leonard** (1867–1942), English artist and cartoonist, was well known for his drawings and cartoons in *Punch*, 1896–1935.

**Rawlinson, Sir Henry Creswicke, Bt.**, G.C.B., F.R.S. (1810–95), diplomat, soldier and orientalist. For a number of years he superintended explorations in Assyria and Babylon, accumulating a valuable collection of antiquities now in the British Museum.

**Ray, John** (1627–1705), an English naturalist, famous for his contributions to the science of botany. He has been called the "father" of English natural history.

**Rayleigh, 3rd Baron**, O.M., F.R.S. (1842–1919), one of the most eminent of British physicists; an authority on sound vibrations, and the co-discoverer with Sir William Ramsay of argon. In 1904 was awarded the Nobel Prize for physics.

**Read, Sir Herbert**, Kt., D.S.O., M.C. (1893–1968), English poet, literary critic, art historian, and interpreter of art. He was assistant keeper at the Victoria and Albert Museum (1922–31), professor of fine art at Edinburgh (1931–33), and edited the Burlington Magazine (1933–39). His writings include *Poems 1914–1934*, *In Retreat, Reason and Romanticism, Education through Art, The Meaning of Art.*

**Reade, Charles** (1814–84), holds high rank amongst the Victorian novelists. His first story, *Peg Woffington*, was published in 1852. *It's Never too Late to Mend, Griffith Gaunt*, and *The Cloister and the Hearth* are his best-known novels.

**Réaumur, René Antoine Ferchault de** (1683–1757), an eminent French chemist, who invented the temperature scale which bears his name.

**Récamier, Madame Jeanne Françoise Julie Adélaïde Bernard** (1777–1849), a noted society woman of the days of Napoleon.

**Reeves, (John) Sims** (1818–1900), was the most celebrated English tenor of his time.

**Regnault, Henri Victor** (1810–78), a French scientist who made highly successful experiments in regard to the physical properties of bodies and their relation to heat.

**Regnault, Jean Baptiste, Baron** (1754–1829), a talented French genre painter.

**Reith, John Charles Walsham, 1st Baron, Kt**, (b. 1889), British civil engineer, first Director-General of British Broadcasting Corporation, 1927–38. Recognised as a man of great organising ability, he has served successively as Chairman of Imperial Airways (1938–39), Chairman of B.O.A.C. (1939–40), Min. of Information (Jan–May 1940), Min. of Transport (May–Oct. 1940), Min. of Works and Buildings (Oct. 1940–Feb. 1942), Dir. of the Admiralty's Combined Operations Material Dept. (1943–45), Chairman Commonwealth Telecommunications Conference (1945), Chairman Commonwealth Communications Council (1946), and Chairman Colonial Development Corporation, 1950–59.

**Rembrandt, Harmens van Rijn** (1606–69), Dutch painter and engraver, one of the greatest painters who ever lived. His paintings were portraits, landscapes, and large groups, many on religious themes. He began as a fashionable painter, but his realism offended many of his sitters. The path from relative wealth to lonely old age is depicted in his series of self-portraits, which with his other paintings and etchings (*Jan Six, an Amsterdam Patrician, St. Simeon in the Temple, Lesson in Anatomy, The Night Watch, Christ Preaching*) reveal his immense genius. He was masterly in his treatment of light and shade. Even in his religious pictures, he took his figures from life;

the Jews in the etching *Christ Preaching* are from the Jewish quarter of Amsterdam where he lived for many years.

**Renan, Ernest** (1823–92), a noted French author who wrote upon religious subjects, and won special fame by his *Life of Jesus*, published 1863.

**Reni, Guido.** (*See* Guido Reni.)

**Rennie, John**, F.R.S. (1761–1821), a Scottish civil engineer. He was the constructor of the Waterloo and Southwark and new London bridges over the Thames, the London Docks, the East and West India Docks, the Plymouth breakwater, and many other works at Liverpool, Leith, Dublin, Hull, and elsewhere.

**Renoir, Auguste** (1841–1919), great French artist of the Impressionist school, whose vision was carefree and romantic. Some of his greatest achievements were in still-life and landscape. *La Loge, Les Parapluies, La Première Sortie* are famous pictures.

**Reuter, Baron Paul Julius de** (1821–99), was the pioneer of telegraphic press services.

**Reymont, Vladislav Stanislav** (1868–1925), Polish novelist; Nobel Prize 1924 (*The Peasants*).

**Reynolds, Sir Joshua**, P.R.A. (1723–92), was the first President of the R.A. from 1768 till his death, and the most fashionable portrait painter of his time. He was born at Plympton in Devon, son of the master of the grammar school there.

**Rhodes, Rt. Hon. Cecil John** (1853–1902), born at Bishop's Stortford. Went to South Africa in 1871, entered upon a diamond-mining enterprise at Kimberley, and acquired a considerable fortune. Was a member of the Cape Legislature in 1881, and became Premier in 1890. He was at the head of the British South Africa Chartered Company, for which a vast amount of territory was annexed, the holding obtaining the name of Rhodesia. Mr. Rhodes was Cape Premier again in 1896; then followed the Jameson Raid and his retirement from political life. During the Boer War he was detained in Kimberley and did not live to see the campaign closed. He left the bulk of his fortune for the founding of scholarships at Oxford.

**Ricardo, David** (1772–1823), a celebrated English political economist of Hebrew descent, whose *Principles of Political Economy* gained him a high place among the exponents of the science.

**Richard I.** (1157–99) was King of England from 1189 to his death. He laid heavy burdens upon the people in order to equip an army for the third Crusade. At first he was victorious and did such valiant deeds that he received the name of "Cœur de Lion." Being ultimately defeated, he signed a truce with Saladin, and on his way back to England was shipwrecked. Disguised as a pilgrim, he was identified in Austria, and handed over to the Emperor of Germany, who imprisoned him in a remote castle. A large sum was demanded and paid for his ransom, and after over a year of durance he returned to England, and was crowned at Winchester. Later he was engaged in a war with France, and was mortally wounded by a bolt from a crossbow while besieging the castle of Chaluz in the province of Limousin.

**Richard II.** (1367–1400), son of the "Black Prince," succeeded his grandfather, Edward III., in 1377, when but ten years old, a Regency being appointed during his minority. In the Wat Tyler rising of 1381 the King confronted the rioters and promised them redress, an undertaking which he did not fulfil. For a time he was greatly under the influence of his uncle, Thomas, Duke of Gloucester, but on coming of age dismissed him, and ruled with some approach to dignity for the next seven years. After 1396 he developed a highly tyrannical disposition and banished or put to death many of the leading statesmen. The opposition against him came to a head in 1399, when Bolingbroke defeated him, and he was made prisoner and died —probably by starvation—in Pontefract Castle.

**Richard III.** (1452–85), last Plantagenet king of England who took the throne on the death of his brother Edward IV. in 1483, probably murdering his two younger nephews in the Tower. This led to a rebellion in favour of the Earl of Richmond (later Henry VII.) and he was slain on Bosworth Field. His character has been the subject of dissension among historians but there is no doubt that despite his unscrupulousness (not uncommon in those days) he was a brave soldier and able administrator.

**Richards, Sir Gordon** (b. 1904), British jockey who had one of the most successful riding records in the history of the British Turf: 21,834 mounts, 4870 winners, including the Derby (1953). Retired, 1954.

**Richardson, Sir Albert Edward,** K.C.V.O., P.R.A., F.S.A., F.R.I.B.A. (1890–1964), British architect and Pres. of the Royal Academy, 1954–56.

**Richardson, Henry Handel,** pseudonym of Henrietta Richardson Robertson (1870–1946), Australian novelist whose major work, outstanding in Australian fiction, is the trilogy *The Fortunes of Richard Mahony.*

**Richardson, Sir Owen Williams,** D.Sc., F.R.S. (1879–1959), distinguished English physicist. Awarded Nobel Prize in 1928 for his researches on the emission of electricity from hot bodies.

**Richardson, Sir Ralph David** (b. 1902), actor who has made many appearances on stage, screen, and radio.

**Richardson, Samuel** (1689–1761), author of *Pamela, Clarissa,* and *The History of Sir Charles Grandison,* exercised considerable influence on the development of the novel in England.

**Richelieu, Armand Jean du Plessis, Cardinal Duc de** (1585–1642), the eminent French ecclesiast and statesman, who was Minister to Louis XIII for eighteen years. He was practically Master of France during the best part of this Cardinalate.

**Ridley, Nicholas** (1500–55), was Bishop of Rochester in 1547 and Bishop of London in 1550. He took an active part in the Reformation. He was burned at the stake along with Latimer.

**Rienzi, Cola di** (1313–54), a Roman patriot of humble birth who inflamed the people against their rulers, and aroused such enthusiasm that they proclaimed him " Tribune." During the seven months that he was permitted to exercise supreme power, he proved himself the true friend of the poor. Later murdered in a popular uprising.

**Rilke, Rainer Maria** (1872–1926), German lyric poet, born in Prague. His work, marked by great beauty of style, culminated in the *Duineser Elegien* and *Sonette an Orpheus.*

**Rimbaud, Jean Nicolas Arthur** (1854–91), French poet of great originality and friend of Paul Verlaine. All his poems were written between his sixteenth and nineteenth years.

**Rimsky-Korsakov, Nikolai Andreyevich** (1844–1908), Russian composer whose works include the operas *The Maid of Pskov* (also known as *Ivan the Terrible*), *The Snow Maiden, Le Coq d'Or,* and the symphonic suite *Scheherezade.* He was a brilliant orchestrator and rescored many works, including Borodin's *Prince Igor.*

**Rizzio, David** (c. 1540–66), was the Italian secretary of Mary Queen of Scots and an accomplished musician. Suspected of a too great attachment to Mary, he was murdered by Darnley and his friends in the Queen's presence in the Palace of Holyrood.

**Robbia, Luca Della** (1400–1482), a famous Florentine sculptor. He was the introducer of enamelled terra-cotta work.

**Robens, Rt. Hon. Alfred, Baron** (b. 1910), Chairman, National Coal Board, 1961–  ; Parl. Sec. Min. of Fuel and Power, 1947–51; Min. of Labour and National Service, 1951.

**Roberts, Field-Marshal Earl,** V.C., K.G., P.C., K.P., G.C.B., O.M., G.C.S.I., G.C.I.E. (1832–1914), the distinguished soldier, first saw service in the Indian Mutiny, when he won the V.C. In 1880 during the Afghanistan campaign made his historic march from Kabul to Kandahar where he won a complete victory. After serving as C.-in-C., India, 1885–93, and as C.-in-C., Ireland, 1895–99, took over in South Africa in December, 1899, and entirely reversed the unhappy military situation before handing over to Kitchener a year later. C.-in-C. from 1901 until the office was abolished in 1904, and was latterly an ardent advocate of conscription.

**Robertson, Sir Charles Grant,** C.V.O. (1869–1948), English historian who was Vice-Chancellor of Birmingham University, 1927–38, and Principal 1920–38. His works include *The Rise of the English Nation,* 1895, *England under the Hanoverians,* 1911, and *Bismarck,* 1918.

**Robertson, Field-Marshal Sir William, Bt.,** G.C.B., G.C.M.G., G.C.V.O., D.S.O. (1860–1933), the only British soldier to rise from Private to Field-Marshal, served as C.I.G.S., 1915–18. His son, Brian Hubert, Lord Robertson, G.C.B. (b. 1892), has had a distinguished military career and was Chairman of the British Transport Commission, 1953–61.

**Robeson, Paul Le Roy** (b. 1898), the famous Negro singer and actor, who through his singing of spirituals has increased our knowledge and understanding of the Negro. Was a great success in London in 1930 playing *Othello.*

**Robespierre, Maximilien François Marie Isidore de** (1758–94), was a country advocate until the outbreak of the French Revolution, when he went to Paris, became an enthusiastic leader of the Jacobin Party, and was made a Member of the Assembly. In the Reign of Terror as President of the Committee of Public Safety he sent vast numbers to the guillotine. Then a countermovement was set on foot and he was denounced in the Assembly, and, trying to escape, was shot and subsequently guillotined.

**Robey, Sir George,** C.B.E. (George Edward Wade), (1869–1954), famous British comedian of the music-hall.

**Robinson, William Heath** (1872–1944), English book illustrator, but especially known for the fantastically comic designs of his cartoons and stage scenery.

**Rob Roy** (the traditional nickname of Robert McGregor) (1671–1734), a noted Highland outlaw who levied blackmail on the farmers and rich people of the country-side in return for certain protective services. He belonged to the clan McGregor.

**Robsart, Amy** (1532–1560), daughter of Sir John Robsart, and wife of Robert Dudley, afterwards Earl of Leicester. While living in seclusion at Cumnor Place under the charge of Anthony Forster, she met her death either by accident or foul play, by the latter according to common belief, Elizabeth's favourite having reason to wish her out of the way. She was discovered dead at the bottom of an old staircase.

**Rockefeller, John Davison** (1839–1937), American capitalist and philanthropist, b. Richford, N.Y., settled in Cleveland, Ohio, 1853. With his brother William founded Standard Oil Company and acquired a fabulous fortune. His philanthropic enterprises are carried on by the Rockefeller Foundation. Governor Nelson Rockefeller of New York is his grandson.

**Rodin, Auguste** (1841–1917), the most celebrated French sculptor of recent days, who possessed a bold and original genius. His numerous statues and his fine historic monuments, especially that for Calais commemorating the bravery of Eustache de Saint-Pierre, brought Rodin well-deserved fame.

**Rodney, 1st Baron,** K.B. (1719–92), a famous English admiral who, having gained numerous victories routed the French fleet under the Comte de Grasse, whom he took prisoner, the result of this crowning success being the Peace of Versailles, 1783.

**Rogers, William Penn Adair ("Will")** (1879–1935) was America's foremost humorist and a famous stage and film star; was killed with Wiley Post on a holiday flight to Alaska Aug. 15, 1935.

**Roland de la Platière, Madame Manou Jeanne** (1754–93), was one of the leading figures of the French Revolution. Her husband, Jean Marie Roland de la Platière (1734–93), who was one of the Ministers during the Girondist period, escaped from Paris on the disruption of his Party, but his wife remained behind, and was sent to the guillotine. During her incarceration she wrote an *Appeal to Posterity,* remarkable for its beauty of sentiment and patriotic enthusiasm. Her husband committed suicide on receiving the news of her execution.

**Rolland, Romain** (1866–1944), an eminent French author whose finest work, *Jean-Christophe,* in ten vols., gained him the Nobel Prize for Literature, 1915.

**Romilly, Sir Samuel,** K.C. (1757–1818), a famous English lawyer who was Solicitor-General in 1806 and for many years had a distinguished career both in Parliament and at the Bar. He effected many improvements in the Criminal Law.

**Rommel, Field-Marshal Erwin** (1891–1944), was probably the ablest German general engaged in the second world war. His conduct of the war during the North African campaign won high praise and brought the redoubtable Afrika Corps nearly to Alexandria. He was also engaged in the campaigns in Western Europe in 1940 and 1944.

Romney, George (1734–1802), was born in North Lancashire, studied portrait painting with a Kendal artist, and for a few years obtained a living by local portrait painting. Going to London in 1762, his talent gained him speedy recognition; and after studying for a couple of years in Rome, he set up as a portrait-painter in Cavendish Square, and became highly successful. His portraits are among the finest examples of that kind of art that England has produced, and to-day realise large prices.

Röntgen, Professor Wilhelm Konrad (1845–1923), the eminent German scientist who discovered the Röntgen rays in 1895. He made other important laboratory investigations, resulting in the solution of difficult chemical problems.

Roosevelt, President Franklin Delano (1882–1945), great American statesman. Was Assistant Secretary to the Navy under Wilson and unsuccessful Democratic candidate for the vice-presidency in 1920. In 1921 was stricken with infantile paralysis, but recovered sufficiently to re-enter public life and become Governor of New York in 1929. From 1933 until his death served as President of the U.S.A., being the first American to be elected for more than two terms. His New Deal programme (see Gen. Information Section) was outstanding in his domestic policy. His " good neighbor " attitude towards the other American countries, his hamstrung efforts to restrain Axis aggression in the 1930s, his inspired and generous adoption of Lend-Lease, his war-time meetings with Churchill and Stalin, and his energetic prosecution of the war after Pearl Harbour, were the more important features of his foreign policy. His " fireside " talks on the radio brought him into close contact with the American people and his passing in the hour of victory was mourned all over the world. In 1905 married his distant cousin, Eleanor Roosevelt (1884–1962), who became known on her own account as a sociologist and newspaper columnist. She became Chairman of the U.N. Human Rights Commission in 1947.

Roosevelt, Theodore (1858–1919), Republican President of the U.S.A., 1901–9, and unsuccessful third party candidate in 1912 following a dispute with Taft. His daring exploits in the Spanish-American war won him wide popularity and he was elected vice-president in 1900 becoming president on McKinley's assassination. For his efforts in promoting peace, notably between Russia and Japan, was awarded the Nobel Prize in 1906. The great struggle with the Trusts marked his years of office.

Rops, Félicien (1833–98), Belgian artist, famous for drawings, etchings, and illustrations. His work is highly original, spirited, humorous and a valued commentary on the life at the time. Was an engraver of magnificent technical skill and a painter of merit.

Ross, Sir James Clark, F.R.S. (1800–62), most experienced polar explorer of the century. He accompanied his uncle, Sir John Ross, and Captain Parry on their expeditions. In the *Victory* commanded by his uncle he located the north magnetic pole in 1831. He commanded the expedition of the *Erebus* and the *Terror* to the antarctic (1839–43), discovering Victoria Land, Mounts Erebus and Terror, and the Ross ice barrier.

Ross, Rear Admiral Sir John, K.C.B. (1777–1856), the eminent explorer who made several voyages to the arctic and searched for the North-west Passage. He discovered Boothnia peninsula, and his nephew reached the magnetic pole.

Ross, Colonel Sir Ronald, K.C.B., K.C.M.G., F.R.S. (1857–1932), professor of tropical sanitation and a leading authority on tropical diseases generally, was for many years in the Indian Medical Service, and was awarded the Nobel Prize for Medicine in 1902. Discovered the malaria parasite.

Rossetti, Dante Gabriel (1828–82), was the son of Gabriele Rossetti (1783–1852), an exiled Italian author who settled in London in 1824. Dante

showed great talent as a painter from boyhood, and became one of the Pre-Raphaelite Brotherhood, formed in 1848. He also distinguished himself as a poet. His sister, Christina Georgina Rossetti (1830–94) was also noted as a poet.

Rossini, Gioacchino Antonio (1792–1868), Italian operatic composer. His first opera *Tancredi* was produced at Venice when he was 21, and between 1816 and 1823 he wrote 21 operas, including *Il Barbiere di Seviglia*, *La Cenerentola*, *Otello*, *La Donna del Lago*, and *Semiramide*. After writing *Guillaume Tell* in 1829, which was hailed as his masterpiece, he gave up composing, producing only a *Stabat Mater* (1832–41) and a mass (1864). *See* Section E.

Rostand, Edmond Eugene Alexis (1868–1918), French dramatist whose *Cyrano de Bergerac* created a sensation in 1898.

Rothenstein, Sir William (1872–1945), English painter and writer. Prof. of Civic Art in Sheffield University, 1917–26; Principal of Royal College of Art, 1920–35; Trustee, Tate Gallery, 1927–33. His son, Sir John Rothenstein (b. 1901), was until 1964 Director of the Tate Gallery and is now Rector of St. Andrews University.

Rothschild, Anselm Meyer (1743–1812), the founder of the famous financial family was born at Frankfurt-on-Main. After some experience in a bank as clerk, set up for himself first as a moneylender, then as a banker and displaying a genius for finance acquired a large fortune. His son, Nathan Meyer Rothschild (1777–1836), took charge of the London house, and conducted its affairs with great success, and was made an Austrian Baron in 1822. He was succeeded by his eldest son, Baron Lionel de Rothschild (1808–1879), who was the first Jewish member of the House of Commons.

Roubillac, Louis François (1695–1762), a French sculptor who contributed many monuments to Westminster Abbey.

Rouget de Lisle, Claude Joseph (1760–1836), a French poet who was the author of the words and the music of the *Marseillaise*, the revolutionary song and national anthem of France.

Rousseau, Jean-Jacques (1712–78), French philosopher, political writer, and composer. He was born at Geneva, and after a hard and wandering life made the acquaintance of Madame de Warens, who became his patroness and with whom he resided during the years 1731–41. He then proceeded to Paris, where he made the acquaintance of Diderot, to whose *Encyclopédie* he contributed the musical section. With the production of his pastoral melodrama *Le Devin du village* in 1722 he appeared as a successful composer. Meanwhile he had been studying social questions with great ardour, and in 1761 published his novel *Julie, ou la Nouvelle Héloïse*, which was followed in 1762 by *Emile*, a treatise on education in novel form. These two works contained so much that was at variance with convention, and so opposed to all ideas of moral restraint, that they called forth the condemnation of the orthodox, and Rousseau was obliged to leave France for a time. It was while in England that he wrote his remarkable *Confessions*, and his celebrated *Le Contrat Social*. He laid down principles of government and conduct which bore fruit in the French Revolution. (*See also* Education, Section J.)

Rubens, Sir Peter Paul (1577–1640), one of the most notable of Flemish painters. In 1629 he painted for Charles I., who knighted him. His *Adoration of the Magi* was sold in 1959 for the record price of £275,000.

Rubinstein, Anton Grigorovich (1829–94), a famous Russian pianist and composer and founder of the Conservatory St. Petersburg (now Leningrad). His brother Nicholas (1835–81), also a pianist. founded the Conservatory of Moscow.

Rupert, Prince (1619–82), the brilliant Royalist cavalry general opposing Cromwell and a distinguished admiral in the Dutch wars. He was also an early mezzotinter, an experimental scientist, and the first governor of Hudson's Bay Company.

Rusk, Dean, M.A., LL.D. (b. 1909), U.S. Secretary of State in the Democratic Administrations of Kennedy and Johnson, 1961–9; Pres. The Rockefeller Foundation, 1952–60. Former Rhodes scholar at St. John's Coll., Oxford.

**Ruskin, John** (1819–1900), writer and art critic, the son of a wealthy London wine merchant. His *Modern Painters* exhibited a masterly perception of the principles of art and a boundless gift of literary expression. Other volumes appeared at intervals including *The Seven Lamps of Architecture* and *The Stones of Venice*, two memorable works which considerably enhanced the author's fame. His writings undoubtedly hastened the recognition of Turner and the Pre-Raphaelite painters. Always taking a deep interest in economic questions, Ruskin delivered and published numerous lectures on a wide range of subjects—art, pleasure, religion, war, work, and so forth; and he was acknowledged to be one of the greatest thinkers of the time. Often his views were impracticable and even eccentric, but behind them there was always evident a sincere desire to promote the well-being of the people.

**Russell, Bertrand (Arthur William) 3rd Earl, O.M., F.R.S., M.A.** (b. 1872), great English rationalist philosopher, whose vigorous and sceptical writings have profoundly influenced present-day thought. He writes and speaks in a clear, witty, and elegant style and regards the task of the philosopher as one of clarification rather than speculation. In recent years Lord Russell has been actively engaged in the campaign against nuclear warfare. His numerous writings include books on mathematics, philosophy, and ethics, besides works on political and sociological subjects: *The Principles of Mathematics* (1903), *Principia Mathematica* (1910), written in collaboration with A. N. Whitehead, *Problems of Philosophy* (1911), *Marriage and Morals* (1929), *History of Western Philosophy* (1945), *Human Knowledge* (1948), *Commonsense and Nuclear Warfare* (1959). His *Autobiography*, in two volumes,' was published 1967–8. Nobel Prize for Literature, 1950.

**Russell, George William** (1867–1935), Irish poet generally known by his pen name of A.E. or Æ. Widely known as a leader in co-operative enterprise and a pioneer of Abbey Theatre, Dublin.

**Russell, John, 1st Earl, K.G., P.C.** (1792–1878), third son of the 6th Duke of Bedford. Entered Parliament as Lord John Russell on attaining his majority, and, ranging himself on the Liberal side, showed great capacity for affairs. Introduced first great measure of Reform, which was passed in 1832. Held several offices before succeeding Peel as Prime Minister in 1846. Remained in power until 1852, and was again Prime Minister from 1865 to 1866, resigning when he failed to carry a further reform bill. He also wrote lives of Thomas Moore and Charles James Fox.

**Russell of Killowen, Baron, P.C., G.C.M.G.** (1832–1900), Lord Chief Justice of England 1894–98. Was one of the greatest British judges and advocates of the 19th century.

**Rutherford, Lord, O.M., F.R.S.** (1871–1937), British physicist, b. in New Zealand, preeminent in the field of atomic research. Conducted his experiments at Montreal, Manchester, and at the famous Cavendish Laboratory at Cambridge, which attracted brilliant young scientists from all over the world. In 1911 announced his nuclear theory of the atom, and in 1918 succeeded in splitting the atom for the first time. His work paved the way for future nuclear research.

**Ruysdael, Jacob van** (c. 1628–82), great Dutch landscape painter, some of whose pictures are in the National Gallery.

**Ruyter, Admiral Michiel Adriaanzoon de** (1607–76), the Dutch admiral who in 1667 invaded England with a fleet of Dutch war vessels, advancing up the Thames and Medway and setting fire to considerable shipping. He soon saw fit to retreat, and more serious trouble was averted.

# S

**Sachs, Hans** (1494–1576), the German shoemaker-poet of Reformation times, was an earnest worker in the Protestant cause, and wrote over 5,000 different pieces, poetry and prose.

**Sadi, or Saadi (Muslih-Uddin)** (c. 1184–1292), the Persian poet who flourished in the 13th century, and won national fame by his poems *The Garden of Roses* and *The Orchard*.

**Sainte-Beuve, Charles Augustin** (1804–69), French critic, and one of the most accomplished men of letters under the Second Empire. Author of *Causeries du lundi* and *Histoire de Port Royal*.

**Saint-Just, Antoine** (1767–94), one of the later leaders of the French Revolution closely associated with Robespierre.

**St.-Laurent, Rt. Hon. Louis Stephen, Q.C.** (b. 1882). Prime Minister of Canada, 1948–57.

**Saint-Saëns, Charles Camille** (1835–1921), French composer. His compositions have a classical style and elegance and include symphonic and chamber music and the opera *Samson et Dalila*, which was produced by Liszt at Weimar in 1877.

**Saint-Simon, Claude, Comte de** (1760–1825), a French scientist and socialist who had great influence upon the thought of his time.

**Saintsbury, George Edward Bateman** (1845–1933). Professor of Rhetoric and English Literature, Edinburgh University, 1895–1915. Author of numerous critical works on literary subjects, on which he was a leading authority.

**Sala, George Augustus Henry** (1828–95), journalist of high literary merit who contributed to *Household Words*, the *Illustrated London News*, and the London *Daily Telegraph* (foreign correspondent in all parts of the world).

**Saladin** (1137–93), the great Sultan of Egypt and Syria who led the Moslems against the Christians in the Third Crusade. In 1187 he had driven the Christians from Jerusalem after a brilliant victory at Hattin near Tiberias. This gave rise to the Third Crusade led by the Emperor Frederick I., Philip II. of France, and Richard I. of England, which achieved little. Besides being a great warrior, Saladin was a wise and cultured man, renowned for his chivalry.

**Salazar, Antonio d'Oliveira** (b. 1889), Prime Minister and virtual dictator of Portugal since 1932 and responsible for drafting the Portuguese constitution of 1933. Foreign Minister, 1936–47.

**Salda, Frantíšek** (1867–1937), Czech critic, essayist, and poet whose influence on Czech thought has been profound.

**Salimbene de Adamo** (1221–c. 1288), mediæval chronicler whose vivid description of life in the 13th century is embodied in his *Cronica*.

**Salisbury, Robert Arthur Talbot Gascoyne Cecil, 3rd Marquess of, K.G.** (1830–1903), led the Conservative Governments of 1885–86, 1886–92, and 1895–1902. Has been considered one of the best Foreign Secretaries England has ever had, holding the office from 1878 to 1880, when he attended the Congress of Berlin, and for much of his premiership. Retired from political life after peace was declared in South Africa. His grandson, **Robert Arthur James Gascoyne-Cecil, 5th Marquess of Salisbury, K.G.** (b. 1893), was Leader of the House of Lords, 1942–45 and again 1951–57 when he resigned from the Government over its Cyprus policy.

**Samuel, 1st Viscount, P.C., O.M., G.C.B., G.B.E.** (1870–1963). Liberal statesman, High Commissioner for Palestine, 1920–22; Postmaster-General, 1910–14, and again May to Dec. 1915; Home Secretary, 1916, and again 1931–32. M.P. for Cleveland Division (N. Riding, Yorks), 1902–18, and Darwen Div. of Lancs., 1929–35. Chancellor of the Duchy of Lancaster, 1909–10 and 1915–16. Leader of the Liberal Party in the Commons, 1931–35, in the Lords, 1941–55.

**Sand, George** (1804–76) the leading French authoress of her time—proper name, Armandine Lucile Aurore Dupin, baronne Dudevant—who, both as novelist and dramatist, achieved the highest success. A friend of men of such singular power as Alfred de Musset, Chopin and Sandeau.

**Sandow, (Frederick William) Eugene** (1867–1925), German "strong man"; overcame his early physical weakness to become a powerfully built man; adviser on physical culture to King George V.

**Sanger, Frederick, B.A., Ph.D., F.R.S.** (b. 1918). British scientist; Prof. of Biochemistry, Cambridge. Awarded 1958 Nobel Prize for Chemistry for his work in determining the chemical structure of the protein insulin.

**Sankey, Ira David** (1840–1908), the celebrated American evangelist, singer, and composer, associated with Dwight L. Moody, the revivalist (1837–1899) in mission-work.

**San Martin, General José de** (1778–1850), the

principal figure in the liberation from Spanish rule of three countries: his native Argentina, Chile, and Peru.

**Santayana, George** (1863–1952), philosopher and poet, born in Madrid of Spanish parentage. He was Professor of Philosophy at Harvard University (where he graduated in 1886) from 1907–12. His books include *The Life of Reason* (1905–6), the four volumes of *Realms of Being* (1923–40), *Persons and Places* (1945), and *The Middle Span* (1948).

**Santos-Dumont, Alberto** (1873–1932), Brazilian aeronaut, his most notable flights being made in Paris, and at Monte Carlo. He visited London in 1903.

**Sappho of Lesbos** (fl. early 6th cent. B.C.), famous lyric poetess of ancient Greece, of whose love poems only a few fragments remain.

**Sardou, Victorien** (1831–1908), French dramatist who had a long series of successes—*Nos Intimes*, *Séraphine*, *Rabagas*, *Divorçons*, *Fédora*, *Théodora*, *Patrie*, *La Tosca*, *Madame Sans-Gêne*, *Robespierre*, and *Dante*, the last-named written specially for Sir Henry Irving. He was elected to the French Academy in 1877.

**Sargent, Sir Malcolm**, Mus.D., A.R.C.O. (1895–1967), British conductor, renowned for his conductorship of the Promenade Concerts from 1950 until his death; succeeded Sir Adrian Boult as conductor of the B.B.C. Symphony Orchestra, 1950–57.

**Sargent, John Singer**, R.A. (1856–1922), American painter, born in Florence, educated in Germany and Italy, noted for his portraits of celebrities.

**Sartre, Jean-Paul** (b. 1905), French existentialist philosopher, left-wing intellectual, dramatist, essayist and novelist. His major philosophical work is *L'Etre et le Néant* and his plays include *Les Mouches*, *Huis Clos*, *Crime passionnel*, *La Putain respectueuse*, and *Les Séquestrés d'Altona*. The first volume of his autobiography, *Les Mots*, was published in 1964. He was awarded (though he declined it) the 1964 Nobel Prize for Literature. *See* Section I.

**Sassoon, Siegfried** (Lorraine), C.B.E. 1886–1967 English poet and writer who received the Hawthornden Prize, 1929, for *The Memoirs of a Fox-hunting Man*.

**Savonarola, Girolamo** (1452–98), Florentine preacher and reformer, a Dominican friar, who denounced vice and corruption not only in society but also in the Church itself, especially attacking Pope Alexander VI. He was excommunicated, imprisoned, and with two of his companions hanged in public. His passion for reform made him impatient of opposition and incapable of compromise. He understood men's hearts but not their limitations. Yet he was a noble figure rightly commanding the respect of later ages. George Eliot's historical romance *Romola* gives a fine portrait of Savonarola.

**Sayce, Prof. Archibald Henry**, D.Litt., LL.D., D.D. (1845–1933), a distinguished Assyriologist and philologist who was Prof. of Assyriology at Oxford University, 1891–1919.

**Scarlatti, Alessandro** (1659–1725), Italian musician whose influence on the history of opera has been great, founded the Neapolitan school. He composed over 100 operas, 200 masses, and over 700 cantatas and oratorios. His son Domenico (1685–1757) was a harpsichord virtuoso and his work has had an important influence in the evolution of the sonata. The chief years of his life were spent at the Spanish Court in Madrid.

**Scheele, Carl Wilhelm** (1742–86), Swedish chemist, discoverer of many chemical substances, including oxygen (c. 1773 but published in 1777 after the publication of Priestley's studies).

**Schiaparelli, Giovanni Virginio** (1835–1910), famous Italian astronomer who was Director of the Milan Observatory, 1862–1900, and did valuable work on meteors and double stars, but is best known for his discovery of so-called canals on Mars.

**Schiller, Johan Christolph Friedrich** (1759–1805), the famous German dramatist and poet. Was born at Marbach in Württemberg. Educated at the military Academy at Stuttgart, and intended for a soldier, he evinced an irresistible desire for literary fame, and in 1782 had his first play, *The Robbers*, successfully produced at the Mannheim Theatre, to which he was subsequently appointed dramatic composer. Later he went to Dresden, where he completed his *Don Carlos*; from 1789 to 1793 he held the chair of history at Jena Univ. when he wrote his *History of the Thirty Years' War*, and gained the friendship of Goethe, at whose suggestion he removed to Weimar, and during the next ten years produced his greatest works—*Wallenstein*, *Mary Stuart*, *The Maid of Orleans*, and *William Tell*.

**Schlegel, Karl Wilhelm Friedrich von** (1772–1829), German poet, critic, and scholar. As founder of the Romantic School (J39) we owe to him and his followers the revolutionary and germinating ideas which so influenced thought at the beginning of the 19th century. His brother August Wilhelm (1767–1845) also has a permanent place in the history of German literature. He is best known for his translations of Shakespeare (which established Shakespeare in Germany), Dante, Calderón, and Camões.

**Schliemann, Heinrich** (1822–90), German archæologist who made many notable excavations, discovered Troy and other Homeric sites.

**Schnabel, Artur** (1882–1951), American pianist of Austrian birth, regarded as the greatest exponent of Beethoven's pianoforte sonatas.

**Schoenberg, Arnold** (1874–1951), Austrian composer who in 1933 was dismissed from his post as head of the Prussian Academy of Fine Arts because of his Jewish ancestry. He went to the United States, teaching first at Boston and then at Los Angeles. Among his works are the choral orchestral *Gurre-Lieder* and *Pierrot Lunaire*, a cycle of 21 poems for voice and chamber music. *See* Section E.

**Schopenhauer, Arthur** (1788–1860), German philosopher of a pessimistic cast of mind, a great admirer of Plato and Heraclitus. Regarded his contemporary Hegel as a charlatan. His chief works are *The World Considered as Will and Idea* and *The Two Fundamental Problems of Ethics*.

**Schreiner, Olive**, pen name of Mrs. Cronwright Schreiner (1855–1920), a noted South African novelist, born in Basutoland. She first attracted attention with her *Story of an African Farm* (1883). She excelled in depicting veldt scenery and Dutch character.

**Schubert, Franz Peter** (1797–1828), Austrian composer, born in Vienna, the son of a schoolmaster. He was a contemporary of Beethoven and wrote not only symphonies, sonatas, string quartets, choral music, and Masses but also over 600 songs of unsurpassed lyrical beauty. It is as creator of the German *Lied* that his name is immortal. He died in Vienna at the age of 31, in poverty, before the full flowering of his musical genius.

**Schumann, Robert Alexander** (1810–56), composer of the early 19th-century German Romantic school. He wrote much chamber music, four symphonies, a piano concerto, and choral music, but it is his early piano pieces and songs that give constant delight. His wife Clara (1819–96) was one of the outstanding pianists of her time, especially as interpreter of Chopin.

**Schweitzer, Albert**, D.Theol., Dr. Phil., Dr. Med. (1875–1965), famous medical missionary in Lambaréné, remembered for his reverence for life. A musical critic and authority on Bach's music, a famous organist, and a noted biblical critic he became a Doctor of Medicine in order to devote his life to missionary work in Equatorial Africa. Awarded 1952 Nobel Prize for Peace and Hon. O.M. in 1955.

**Scipio, Publius Cornelius** (*circa* 232–183 B.C.), the greatest of the Scipios known as Scipio Africanus the elder. A distinguished Roman general in the 2nd Punic War.

**Scott, Charles Prestwich** (1846–1931), English journalist who was editor of the *Manchester Guardian*, 1872–1929, which under his editorship became one of the leading journals of the country.

**Scott, Sir George Gilbert**, R.A. (1811–78), architect who gained special fame for his restorations of Gothic churches and cathedrals, incl. Westminster Abbey, designer of the Albert Memorial, St. Pancras Station, the Martyrs' Memorial at Oxford, and St. Anne's Church in Alderney.

**Scott, Sir Giles Gilbert**, O.M., R.A., F.R.I.B.A. (1880–1960), architect whose work includes the great modern Gothic Liverpool Cathedral, the Bodleian Library, Oxford, and the Forth Road Bridge (opened 1964). Grandson of the above.

**Scott, Peter Markham**, M.B.E., D.S.C. (b. 1909), son of Captain Scott, is known as yachtsman, broadcaster, and bird-artist.

**Scott, Captain Robert Falcon,** C.V.O. (1868–1912), commanded the National Antarctic Expeditions in 1901–4 and in 1910. His ship, the *Terra Nova*, left England on June 1, 1910. In Jan. 1911, winter quarters were established at Cape Evans, and in the following November Scott and a select party left Hut Point for the South Pole, which they reached on Jan. 18, 1912, finding there the Amundsen records. On the return journey every member of the party perished. Leading-seaman Edgar Evans died from concussion of the brain on Feb. 17; Capt. Oates from exposure on March 17; and on March 29 the rest of the party (Scott, Wilson and Bowers) died from starvation and exposure in a blizzard when only 11 miles from One Ton Depot.

**Scott, Sir Walter,** Bart. (1771–1832), one of the greatest of British novelists and a distinguished poet. He was educated for the Bar. His *Minstrelsy of the Scottish Border* was published in 1802. This was followed in 1805 by *The Lay of the Last Minstrel,* in 1808 by *Marmion; The Lady of the Lake, Rokeby* and *The Lord of the Isles* coming afterwards in quick succession. In 1814 he published *Waverley* anonymously, which obtained instant success. Other stories followed and the Waverley novels and their author, "The great Unknown," were everywhere the subject of discussion. *Guy Mannering, The Antiquary, Old Mortality, Rob Roy,* and the *Heart of Midlothian* were all published before the secret of their authorship was disclosed. The chief works of his last years were *Woodstock, Life of Napoleon,* and *Tales of a Grandfather.* He died at Abbotsford. Created a baronet in 1820.

**Scott-Paine, Hubert** (1891–1954), pioneer in the design and construction of aircraft and sea craft.

**Scriabin, Alexander** (1872–1915), Russian composer and pianist. He studied at the Moscow conservatoire, where he was later professor of the pianoforte, 1898–1904. He was deeply interested in theosophy, and in such works as *The Divine Poem,* and *Prometheus: a Poem of Fire* he attempted to unite music and philosophy

**Seeley, Sir John Robert,** K.C.M.G. (1834–95), English historian and author of *Ecce Homo.*

**Segovia, Andrés** (b. 1894), Spanish concert-guitarist. He has adapted works by Bach, Haydn, Mozart, and other classical composers to the guitar.

**Selfridge, Harry Gordon** (1858–1947), the American who revolutionised the British department store when he opened the famous shop of Selfridges in Oxford Street in 1909.

**Semmelweis, Ignaz Philipp** (1818–65), Hungarian physician, a pioneer in employing antiseptic methods in obstetric cases, having discovered that puerperal fever is an infection caused by germs. It was then the practice of doctors in maternity wards to examine expectant mothers with unwashed hands.

**Seneca, Lucius Annaeus** (*circa* 4 B.C.–A.D. 56), the famous stoic philosopher, who was tutor to Nero, and one of that emperor's most influential advisers; he was sentenced to end his own life, a sentence which he courageously carried out.

**Senefelder, Alois** (1772–1834), was the son of an actor at Munich, and himself engaged in dramatic composition. Being too poor to bear the cost of having his works printed, he turned his attention to inventing lithography, the main feature of the invention being discovered by accident.

**Severus, Lucius Septimius** (146–211), was Roman Emperor from 193 to his death. After many victories in the East he passed over to Britain with an army, subjugated the Caledonians, and repaired and partly rebuilt the famous Hadrian's wall from the Solway Firth to the mouth of the Tyne. He died at York.

**Sévigné, Marie de Rabutin-Chantal, Marquise de** (1626–96), French woman of letters. Her letters to her daughter Françoise written in an unaffected elegance of style give a moving picture of fashionable society in 17th-century France.

**Sgambati, Giovanni** (1841–1914), Italian pianist and composer who revived interest in classical instrumental music in an age of opera. Well known is his quartet in D flat.

**Shackleton, Sir Ernest (Henry),** C.V.O., O.B.E. (1874–1922), commander of the Nimrod Farthest South expedition of 1907–9, reached within 100 miles of the South Pole, and embarked on a new expedition in 1914. He died whilst on a scientific voyage to the Antarctic.

**Shaftesbury, Anthony Ashley Cooper, 7th Earl of** (1801–85), great social reformer, largely responsible for the legislation reducing the misery of the industrial revolution. He agitated for the abolition of slavery and was connected with the Ragged School Union, reformatories, refuges, and Christian associations of many kinds.

**Shakespeare, William** (1564–1616), England's greatest poet and dramatist, was born at Stratford-on-Avon, and was the son of a tradesman of that town who must have been at one time fairly well-off, seeing that he was made an alderman, and afterwards served as High Bailiff. Later on, however, he appears to have been unfortunate and fallen into straitened circumstances. William was the eldest son, and was probably educated at the Stratford Grammar School, but very little is known of his career up to his eighteenth year, when we have it on record that he married Anne Hathaway, who was eight years his senior. Five years after his marriage he went to London, and the next we hear of him is that he was connected with the Globe Theatre and appeared in sundry small parts. He first appeared before the public as a poet in 1593, with his *Venus and Adonis,* following this in 1594 with *The Rape of Lucrece.* Shortly afterwards he was proprietor of the Globe Theatre, and also had an interest in the Blackfriars Theatre. Then he began that remarkable career of play-writing which has since been the wonder of the world. Thirty-eight plays comprise the Shakespeare canon. Thirty-six were printed in the First Folio of 1623 (the first collected edition of his dramatic works), of which eighteen had been published during his lifetime in the so-called Quartos. *Love's Labour's Lost* and *The Comedy of Errors* seem to have been among the earliest, being followed by *The Two Gentlemen of Verona,* and *Romeo and Juliet.* Then followed *Henry VI, Richard III, Richard II, Titus Andronicus, The Taming of the Shrew, King John, The Merchant of Venice, A Midsummer Night's Dream, All's Well that Ends Well, Henry IV, The Merry Wives of Windsor, Henry V, Much Ado about Nothing, As You Like It, Twelfth Night.* Then came some of his greatest plays, *Julius Cæsar, Hamlet, Troilus and Cressida, Othello, Measure for Measure, Macbeth, King Lear, Timon of Athens, Pericles, Antony and Cleopatra, Coriolanus, Cymbeline, A Winter's Tale, The Tempest, Henry VIII,* and *The Two Noble Kinsmen.* He was able to purchase property at Stratford, and when he retired from his profession (about 1610 or 1612) he returned to his native town to live in a house which he had himself built. He was buried in Stratford Church.

**Sharp, Granville** (1735–1813), slavery abolitionist and founder of the colony of Sierra Leone.

**Shastri, Shri Lal Bahadur** (1904–66), Indian politician who became Prime Minister of India after the death of Nehru in 1964. He died of a heart attack at the end of the Soviet-sponsored Tashkent talks. *See also* Section C. Part I.

**Shaw, George Bernard** (1856–1950), brilliant Irish dramatist who conquered England by his pungent wit and devastating exposure of hypocrisy, cant and national weaknesses, and persistently expressed a highly individual opinion whether in his musical criticisms, socialist pamphlets or plays. He wrote many plays including *Man and Superman, Heartbreak House, Back to Methuselah, Saint Joan, The Apple Cart, Buoyant Billions,* most of which have important prefaces, sometimes equalling the play in length. Was music critic (1888–94) successively to the London *Star* and *World* and during this period wrote *The Quintessence of Ibsenism* and *The Perfect Wagnerite.* Joined the Fabian Society in 1884 and was awarded Nobel Prize for Literature in 1925. He was greatly interested in the reform of the alphabet.

**Shelley, Percy Bysshe** (1792–1822), one of the most brilliant poetic geniuses of the 19th century, renowned for the daring and unorthodox opinions which he held. His *Queen Mab* (written when he was nineteen), his *Alastor, The Revolt of Islam, The Witch of Atlas,* and *Adonais* all breathe the true spirit of poetry, securing him a place in the first rank of British poets. He showed fine dramatic gifts in the *Cenci* and *Prometheus Unbound*, almost reaching sublimity in the latter masterpiece. His *Adonais* was a splendid tribute to the genius of Keats. His first wife, whom he married while very young, committed suicide. He afterwards married Mary Wollstonecraft Godwin, and formed other attachments of a complicating nature. Was always at war with his family, and finally, after spending some time with Byron and Leigh Hunt and other friends in various parts of Italy, was drowned in the Gulf of Spezia by the capsizing of his boat in a storm.

Sheppard, Very Rev. Hugh Richard Lawrie (Dick), C.H., D.D. (1880–1937), Vicar of St. Martin-in-the-Fields, London, 1914–27, where he established a reputation by his broadcast sermons and attracted large crowds of listeners. Dean of Canterbury, 1929–31; Canon of St. Paul's, 1934–37. Buried in Canterbury Cathedral.

Sheraton, Thomas (1751–1806), was the last of the great English furniture designers of the 18th cent. There is no evidence that he was a maker of furniture; his reputation rests solely on his published works which helped to create a certain trend or style, notably the *Cabinet-Makers' and Upholsterers' Drawing Book* (1791–94).

Sheridan, Rt. Hon. Richard Brinsley Butler (1751–1816), one of the greatest of English playwrights, whose comedies are frequently revived. Was born in Dublin, and educated partly at Harrow. Showing considerable capacity for dramatic composition he obtained an introduction to the Covent Garden management, and it was at the Covent Garden Theatre in 1775 that his first comedy, *The Rivals*, was produced, with such a gratifying result that Garrick, who was then at Drury Lane, opened up negotiations with the dramatist which ended in Sheridan becoming part (and ultimately sole) proprietor of Drury Lane. *The Duenna*, a musical comedy, was produced in 1775, and ran through the winter. From 1777 Sheridan managed Drury Lane, opening with an adaptation of Vanbrugh's *Relapse*. This was followed by the production of the greatest of his comedies, *The School for Scandal*, which had a wonderful success. In 1779 *The Critic* was given, and after that Sheridan wrote no more plays until 1789, when *Pizarro* was produced. In 1780 he obtained a seat in Parliament.

Sherman, General William Tecumseh (1820–91), a famous American soldier who, after taking part in the War with Mexico (1846–48), volunteered at the outbreak of the Civil War (1861). He took part in the battles of Bull Run and Shiloh, and was placed in command of the Army of the Tennessee (1863) and of the military division of the Mississippi with a force of 100,000. In 1864 there occurred the famous 300-mile march across Georgia to the sea. In 1865 his second march, through the Carolinas, culminated in the defeat of Johnston, which led directly to the termination of the war.

Sherrington, Sir Charles Scott, O.M., G.B.E., F.R.S., M.D., D.Sc. (1857–1952), one of the greatest of British scientists, and a leading authority on the physiology of the nervous system, whose research work over many years led to great advances in the surgery of the brain. Pres. of the British Association 1920, and of the Royal Society, 1920–25. Awarded Nobel Prize for Medicine, 1932.

Shirley, James (1596–1666), was an eminent dramatist and poet, imbued with the Elizabethan traditions.

Sholokhov, Mikhail Aleksandrovich (b. 1905), great Russian novelist who won international fame with his novel *And Quiet Flows the Don*. Nobel Prize for Literature, 1965.

Shostakovich, Dmitri (b. 1906), one of the most celebrated of present-day Russian composers. His music is complex, profound, and deeply significant of the Soviet age in which he lives. His works include operas, ballets, symphonies, chamber music, and music for films. Hero of Soviet Labour (1966). *See* Section E.

Sibelius, Jean Julian Christian (1865–1957), Finnish composer, generally acknowledged as the greatest of the century. Works include seven symphonies, violin concerto, several tone poems,

about 200 pianoforte compositions and songs. *See* Section E.

Sickert, (Walter) Richard (1860–1942), British painter and etcher; became President of Royal Society of British Artists, 1928.

Siddons, Sarah (1755–1831), the greatest of the English tragic actresses, b. at Brecon, South Wales, eldest of the famous Kemble family. She made her first appearance in London at Drury Lane in 1775 in the part of Portia.

Sidgwick, Henry (1838–1900), Professor of Moral Philosophy at Cambridge, and besides being an eminent educationist in the broader sense, devoted himself with special success to the cause of women's education, Newnham and Girton being largely the outcome of his efforts.

Sidney, Sir Philip (1554–86), statesman, poet and soldier; was one of Queen Elizabeth's favourites, and a man of singular ability and bravery. While living in temporary retirement he composed his famous *Arcadia*, but did not allow it to be published in his lifetime. He did not lack for literary fame, however, his *Apology for Poetry* and *Defence of Poesy*, as well as numerous miscellaneous pieces all distinguished for their beauty of expression and tender sentiment, having won much favour, especially in the circle of the Court. In 1586 he was given a command in the Netherlands and was killed at Zutphen.

Siemens, Sir William, F.R.S. (1823–83), a German-born scientist and inventor, chiefly in the field of heat and electricity. Constructed many overland and submarine telegraphs. Brother of Werner v. Siemens, founder of the famous firm of Siemens-Halske.

Sienkiewicz, Henryk (1846–1916), famous Polish novelist; Nobel prizewinner, 1905 (*Quo Vadis*).

Sikorski, Wladyslaw (1881–1943), Polish general and statesman; Prime Minister in exile during second world war. Killed in airplane crash near Gibraltar.

Simpson, Sir James Young, Bt., F.R.S. (1811–70), the discoverer of the utility of chloroform as an anæsthetic, was a native of Scotland, and was a most accomplished experimental surgeon.

Sinclair, Upton (1878–1968), American novelist whose documentary novel *The Jungle* about the Chicago slaughter yards caused a sensation in 1906.

Singer, Isaac Meritt (1811–75), American mechanical engineer who devoted himself to the improvement of the early forms of the sewing-machine and patented a single-thread and chain-stitch machine.

Sisley, Alfred (1839–1899), French Impressionist painter of English origin. Painted with great delicacy and sensitivity, landscapes, villages, trees, and rivers. Influenced by Corot and Manet.

Sitwell, Edith (Louisa), D.B.E. (1887–1964),English poet whose works include *Bucolic Comedies*, *Gold Coast Customs* and *Collected Poems*. Her two brothers are Osbert (b. 1892), a well-known poet and novelist, and Sacheverell (b. 1900), a poet and critic. *See also* Section M.

Slim, Field-Marshal Viscount, K.G., G.C.B., G.C.M.G., G.C.V.O., G.B.E., D.S.O., M.C. (b. 1891), Gov.-Gen. of Australia 1953–59. In 1943 took command of the 14th Army in Burma, later becoming commander of the Allied Land Forces, S.E.A.C., and then Commandant of the Imperial Defence College. Succeeded Lord Montgomery as C.I.G.S., 1948–52.

Sloane, Sir Hans, Bt., F.R.S. (1660–1753), was born in County Down, Ireland, but settled in London, and became famed as a physician and naturalist. For some years he held the office of President of the Royal College of Physicians, and was elected President of the Royal Society in succession to Sir Isaac Newton. His Library of 50,000 vols., and treasures in natural history and MSS., worth £50,000 to £80,000, were offered by his will to the nation and bought for £20,000; with that nucleus the British Museum was founded.

Slowacki, Julius (1809–49), Polish romantic poet. He was a revolutionary, lived in exile and died in Paris. His tragedies include *Kordian*, *Belladyna* and *Lilli Weneda*.

Smeaton, John (1724–92), English engineer; rebuilt Eddystone lighthouse (1756–59), improved Newcomen's steam-engine, and did important work on bridges, harbours, and canals. He was also the inventor of an improved blowing apparatus for iron-smelting.

**Smetana, Bedřich** (1824–84), Czech composer, creator of a national style. He was principal conductor of the Prague National Theatre, for which he wrote most of his operas, including *The Bartered Bride* and *The Kiss*. Best known of his other compositions are the cycle of symphonic poems *My Country* and the string quartets *From My Life*. He became totally deaf in 1874, suffered a mental breakdown, and died in an asylum. *See Section E*.

**Smiles, Dr. Samuel** (1812–1904), was in early life a medical practitioner; achieved wide popularity by his *Self Help*, a book that has had an enormous sale.

**Smith, Adam, F.R.S.** (1723–90), the father of the science of political economy. Author of *Theory of Moral Sentiments* and *Wealth of Nations*, which immediately obtained the admiration of the leading men of the day, and secured him the friendship of Gibbons, Hume, Burke, Reynolds, and Dugald Stewart.

**Smith, Sir Grafton Elliot, M.A., Litt.D., D.Sc., F.R.S.** (1871–1937), Australian anatomist and archaeologist who was professor of anatomy at Manchester and London Universities. His works include *The Royal Mummies* (1912), *Tutankhamen* (1923), *The Evolution of Man* (1924), and the *Diffusion of Culture* (1933).

**Smith, Captain John** (1580–1631), the noted seafarer and adventurer who in 1605 was the leading spirit of an expedition to Virginia, and founded Jamestown.

**Smith, Joseph** (1805–44), founder of Mormonism, son of a Vermont farmer. Claimed to have been granted revelation of the *Book of Mormon*, which came to be held as equal in authority and as a necessary supplement to the Scriptures. Smith, who was murdered, was not a polygamist; Brigham Young, who succeeded him, was. (*See* Mormonism, Section J.)

**Smith, Sydney** (1771–1845), an Anglican divine, who enjoyed a great reputation as a wit and writer. Founder of and contributor to the *Edinburgh Review* and author of *Peter Plymley's Letters*, supporting Catholic Emancipation.

**Smith, William** (1769–1839), English surveyor and geologist, the first to map the rock strata of England and to identify the fossils peculiar to each layer.

**Smith, Sir William Alexander** (1854–1914), b. in Glasgow; founder of the Boys' Brigade (1883), the oldest of the national organisations for boys in Britain.

**Smith, William Robertson** (1846–94), Scottish biblical scholar whose contributions to the 9th edition of *The Encyclopaedia Britannica* resulted in an unsuccessful prosecution for heresy and led to the modernisation of Scottish theology.

**Smollett, Tobias George** (1721–71), a famous novelist and humorist, b. in Scotland, whose *Roderick Random*, *Peregrine Pickle*, *Count Fathom* and *Humphry Clinker* abound in fun and genial characterisation, while their pictures of sea-life are inimitable.

**Smuts, Field-Marshal Rt. Hon. Jan Christian, O.M. C.H., K.C.** (1870–1950), South African soldier and statesman, one of the dominating political figures of our century. Born in Cape Colony, studied at Cambridge University, and called to the Bar. Was an outstanding Boer commando leader during the South African War, but afterwards worked for friendship with the British and took office in Botha's Government when the Union was set up in 1910. In the first world war joined the Imperial War Cabinet. As Prime Minister, 1919–24, helped to launch the League of Nations, and later was associated with the United Nations. Prime Minister, Foreign Minister and Minister of Defence from 1939 to 1948 when he was defeated at the General Election by the Nationalists under Dr. Malan. He was a keen botanist; Pres. of British Association, 1931. Published *Holism and Evolution* in 1926.

**Smyth, Dame Ethel Mary** (1858–1944), English composer, the daughter of a general, and a militant suffragette. She studied in Germany, where her most important opera *The Wreckers* was first produced. She also wrote chamber music, a comic opera *The Boatswain's Mate*, and a *Mass in D*.

**Snow, Charles Percy, Baron, C.B.E.** (b. 1905), English scientist and novelist whose ideas on the "two cultures" are expressed in *The Two Cultures of the Scientific Revolution* (1959) and in his novels (*see* M13). Life peerage conferred, 1964.

**Snyders, Frans** (1597–1657), a great Flemish still-life and animal painter who studied under Breughel.

**Soane, Sir John, R.A.** (1753–1837), an eminent architect who designed numerous public buildings. By his will he left his museum, library, pictures, etc., for the use of the public, and the house in which he lived at Lincoln's Inn Fields still constitutes the Sir John Soane Museum.

**Sobieski, John III.** (1624–96), King of Poland from 1674, and heroic defender of his country from Cossacks, Tartars, and Turks.

**Socinus, Lælius** (1525–62), an Italian Protestant thinker and anti-Trinitarian, founder with his nephew Faustus Socinus (1539–1604), of the Socinian system of theology.

**Socrates** (470–399 B.C.), Greek philosopher and great intellectual leader, was the son of a sculptor and for some time followed that calling himself, but, having other ambitions, joined the army, and was present at the battle of Potidæa, and also at the battle of Delium, saving the life of Alcibiades in the first, and of Xenophon in the second. Returning to Athens he devoted himself to study and began to exhort the people on public questions and the conduct of life. Socrates wrote nothing himself, but we know of his teachings through the writings of his pupils Xenophon and Plato. In 399 B.C. he was charged with impiety and with corrupting the morals of the young, found guilty, and sentenced to death, events immortalised in Plato's *Apology*, *Crito*, and *Phaedo*.

**Soddy, Frederick, M.A., LL.D., F.R.S.** (1877–1956), Prof. of Inorganic and Physical Chemistry, Univ. of Oxford, 1919–36. Nobel Laureate in Chemistry 1921. The foundation of the isotope theory was laid by him in Glasgow about 1912 before the physicists became prominent in that field.

**Soldatov, Alexander** (b. 1917), Soviet diplomat, succeeded J. Malik as ambassador to Britain, 1960.

**Solon** (638–558 B.C.), was one of the Seven Sages of Greece, and became an eminent legislator, after having made a reputation as a poet. Solon's Laws were so highly esteemed that they were adopted by the Romans in the Twelve Tables.

**Solyman** (1490–1566), the celebrated Ottoman Sultan known as "the Magnificent," who won fame as a conqueror, law-giver, administrator, and patron of learning.

**Somerset, 1st Duke of** (1506–52), was Protector of England in the early part of the reign of Edward VI., but was deposed from power, tried for felony, and executed. A liberal and tolerant ruler who opposed enclosures and pursued a moderate religious policy.

**Sophocles** (495–406 B.C.), the famous Athenian dramatist who enjoyed the highest popularity at Athens, and in a contest with Æschylus was crowned the victor. Of the 100-odd plays of Sophocles only seven have survived: *Antigone*, *Electra*, *Œdipus*, *Ajax*, *Trachiniae*, *Philoctetes*, and *Œdipus at Colonus*.

**Soult, Marshal Nicolas Jean de Dieu, Duke of Dalmatia** (1769–1851), was one of Napoleon's favourite and most capable generals, distinguishing himself in the Swiss and Italian campaigns, and also in the Peninsular War, where he was Wellington's bravest opponent.

**Sousa, John Philip** (1854–1932), American bandmaster and composer of numerous stirring marches. His father was Portuguese and his mother German.

**Southey, Robert** (1774–1843), English poet and historian. In 1803 he settled near Keswick to be near Coleridge and became one of the Lake poets. He was made poet Laureate in 1813. His best work was in prose: histories of Brazil and of the Peninsular War; life of Nelson, and biographies of Wesley and others.

**Southwell, Robert** (1561–95), a famous Jesuit and religious poet of Elizabethan times. Beatified in 1929.

**Spaak, Paul-Henri** (b. 1899), Belgian statesman; first President of the U.N. General Assembly in 1946 and of the Assembly of the Council of Europe during its first session in 1949. Sec. Gen. of NATO, 1957–61.

B70

**Spantz, General Carl Andrew** (b. 1891), American soldier who held high commands in Europe, North Africa, and the Pacific, 1942–46.

**Spartacus,** a Thracian who became a Roman slave and gladiator in Capua, and headed an insurrection in Italy in 73 B.C. The slaves he raised routed several Roman armies, but he was eventually defeated by Crassus in 71 B.C. and slain.

**Speke, Capt. John Hanning** (1827–64), was the discoverer, along with Lt.-Col. J. A. Grant, of the Kagera, the main source of the White Nile, in 1862. In 1856 he discovered Lake Tanganyika and in 1858 Victoria Nyanza.

**Spence, Sir Basil, O.M.** (b. 1907), architect of the new Coventry cathedral, the university of Sussex, Glasgow air terminal, Hampstead civic centre, and the new British embassy in Rome. Prof. of Architecture, Royal Academy.

**Spencer, Herbert** (1820–1903), was the son of a Derby schoolmaster. For some time followed the profession of civil engineer. His first book was published in 1851, under the title of *Social Statics*, when he was filling the position of sub-editor of the *Economist*. In 1855 his *Principles of Psychology* appeared, in which he seems to have anticipated Darwin's theory of Evolution. The *System of Synthetic Philosophy* began to appear in 1860, and the last of its ten volumes was issued in 1896.

**Spencer, Sir Stanley, C.B.E., R.A.** (1891–1959), British artist whose work shows great visionary and spiritual power. His paintings include the Resurrection pictures and the Cookham Regatta series.

**Spenser, Edmund** (1552–99), was born in London, educated at Cambridge, and early attracted notice by his poetic writings. After the publication of his *Shepheardes Calendar*, he was made known to Queen Elizabeth, and in 1580 received the appointment of Secretary to the Lord Deputy of Ireland, and in the division of confiscated lands that afterwards took place, Spenser received Kilcolman Castle and 3,000 acres of land. Here he wrote his *Faerie Queene*. In 1598 a rebellion broke out, and Spenser's castle was burned to the ground. He then returned to London, and there died.

**Spinoza, Baruch or Benedict** (1632–77), one of the greatest of modern philosophers, was born at Amsterdam, the son of a Portuguese Jew who had settled there as a merchant. He had a sceptical turn of mind and having expounded philosophical doctrines antagonistic to Judaism, was excommunicated by the rabbis as a heretic. He owed much to Descartes and in 1663 published his work on the Cartesian philosophy. The attainment of truth was his one object in life. Indifferent to money, he spent his life in study and earned his living as a lens grinder. His writings have had an extensive and enduring influence though during his lifetime some of his works, including his *Ethics*, were not allowed to be published. *See also* J20(1).

**Spofforth, Reginald** (1770–1827), a writer of glees, including *Hail, Smiling Morn.*

**Spurgeon, Rev. Charles Haddon** (1834–92), a renowned Baptist who preached at The Tabernacle, near the Elephant and Castle, London, from 1861 until his death.

**Staël, Madame de (Anne Louise Germaine Necker, Baronne de Staël-Holstein)** (1766–1817), the daughter of Necker, the famous Finance Minister under Louis XVI., was married to Baron de Staël (Swedish Minister) at twenty. She was a brilliant woman, deeply imbued with philosophical sentiments. Two years after her marriage she made a considerable impression by her *Letters on Rousseau*, and was regarded as in sympathy with the Revolution. Later on, however, she was in disfavour, first with the Revolutionary leaders, and then with Napoleon, and was in turn exiled by both and during this time wrote *Corinne* and other able works.

**Stalin, Generalissimo Joseph Vissarionovich (Djugashvili)** (1879–1953), Soviet statesman who for nearly thirty years was leader of the Russian people. Studied for the priesthood at the Tiflis theological seminary. From the age of 17 was an active revolutionary and took important part in the civil war after 1917. After the death of Lenin became the outstanding figure in Russia and his aim to make Russia a great industrial power was carried into effect by

modernizing agriculture on socialist lines and by a series of five-year plans, the first of which was introduced in 1929. Assumed military leadership against the German invasion, June 1941. Attended the Allied war conferences at Teheran, Yalta, and Potsdam. The denunciation of Stalin and the "personality cult" by M. Khrushchev at the Soviet Communist Party Congress in Feb. 1956 led to profound and far-reaching political consequences in Communist countries.

**Stanford, Sir Charles Villiers, Mus. D.** (1852–1924), Professor of Music at Cambridge University, and Professor of Composition and Orchestral Playing in the Royal College of Music. An organist and conductor of remarkable ability, and a composer of much fine instrumental choral, operatic, and other music.

**Stanley, Sir Henry Morton, G.C.B.,** (1841–1904), British explorer, after an adventurous early career during which he fought for the Confederates in the American Civil War, joined the *New York Herald* as a correspondent in 1867 and was commissioned by Gordon Bennett to search for Livingstone. In 1871 he discovered the great missionary at Ujiji and with him explored the northern end of Lake Tanganyika. After further exploration he founded the Congo Free State in 1879. Among his books were *How I found Livingstone*, *Through the Dark Continent*, *In Darkest Africa*, and an *Autobiography*.

**Steele, Sir Richard** (1672–1729), b. in Dublin, founder of *The Tatler*, which made a great hit, his friend Addison contributing many papers. Two years later he and Addison were associated in *The Spectator*, Addison, however, being the leading contributor; the *Guardian* was another of Steele's ventures. He sat in Parliament for some time, and was knighted by George I.

**Steer, Philip Wilson, O. M.** (1860–1942), was the most distinguished of British landscape painters, and a fine portraitist.

**Stefansson, Vilhjalmur** (b. 1879), a famous Arctic explorer, born in Manitoba of Icelandic parents. Took part in the Anglo-American (1908–12) and Canadian (1913–18) Arctic expeditions.

**Stein, Sir Aurel, K.C.I.E.** (1862–1943), was a famous British archæologist who conducted expeditions, chiefly to Chinese Turkestan, resulting in priceless additions to the British Museum and the Delhi Central Indian Museum. Explored Baluchistan, 1926–28, and South Iran, 1932–33. Was Superintendent of Archæological Survey, North-West Frontier Circle, India, 1910–29.

**Stendhal,** *nom de plume* of the French novelist, Marie Henri Beyle (1783–1842), who has been an important influence in the development of the French novel and whose books show searching psychological insight. Best known for his two novels, *Le Rouge et le Noir*, and *La Chartreuse de Parme.*

**Stephen** (1105–54) was King of England from 1135 to his death, usurping the crown that belonged to Matilda, the daughter of Henry I.

**Stephen Sir Leslie, K.C.B.** (1832–1904), an eminent writer, critic and biographer. Edited the *Cornhill Magazine* (1871–82), and the *Dictionary of National Biography* (1882–91). He was the father of Mrs. Virginia Woolf.

**Stephenson, George** (1781–1848), was born at Wylam, near Newcastle, and up to 1804 was mainly engaged in ordinary colliery occupations. In 1804, however, an engagement as brakesman at Killingworth colliery brought him in touch with the working of Watt's steam engine, and his first efforts in invention were in improving one of those engines, showing so much ability that he was offered an engine-wright's position at Killingham, which he held for some time. Then it was that he began to think seriously of producing a locomotive engine, and managed to construct an engine that would draw coal trucks at the rate of four miles an hour. In 1821, when the Stockton and Darlington Railway was undertaken, he was appointed engineer, and when the railway was opened in 1825, as a line for the transport of coal only, Stephenson won his first great triumph, by putting a locomotive on the line that was able to draw a train of thirty-eight carriages, laden with goods and passengers, at a rate of twelve miles an hour. George Stephenson, subsequently assisted by his son Robert, constructed the Liverpool and Manchester line, and after that the railway era commenced. His only son Robert (1803–59) attained eminence as a civil engineer and constructed many railway lines and bridges, notably the high level bridge at Newcastle, the Menai and Conway tubular bridges, the Victoria bridge across the St. Lawrence at Montreal, and two bridges over the Nile at Damietta.

**Sterne, Laurence** (1713–68), British humourist whose *Tristam Shandy* (1759–67) brought him fame. He also wrote *The Sentimental Journey* and published some volumes of sermons.

**Stevenson, Adlai Ewing** (1900–65), American lawyer and politician; Ambassador to U.N., 1960–65; Gov. of Illinois, 1949–53; Democratic candidate for Presidency, 1952 and 1956.

**Stevenson, Robert,** F.R.S.E. (1772–1850), a native of Glasgow, famed as a builder of lighthouses, including that on Bell Rock. He invented the "flashing" system of throwing light at sea.

**Stevenson, Robert Louis** (1850–94), was the Scottish author of a remarkable series of essays, stories, and poems, including *Travels with a Donkey*, *Virginibus Puerisque*, *Treasure Island*, *Kidnapped*, *Dr. Jekyll and Mr. Hyde*, and *A Child's Garden of Verses*. He always suffered from delicate health and travelled extensively, finally settling in Samoa with his Californian wife, formerly Mrs. Osbourne. His literary influence was considerable, particularly on the generation which followed him.

**Stewart, Robert Michael Maitland,** C.H., M.P. (b. 1906), British socialist politician; M.P. for Fulham East, 1945–55, and for Fulham since 1955; Sec. of State for Foreign and Commonwealth Affairs, 1968–.

**Stinnes, Hugo** (1870–1924), German industrialist who built up a huge coal-mining, iron and steel, and transport business, and also developed a large shipping concern. His group controlled the greater part of Germany's coal, iron and steel supply. In 1920 he entered the Reichstag, and later became a newspaper proprietor.

**Stirling, Elizabeth** (1819–95), English organist whose recitals in London exercised much influence and made Bach's music more widely known. She wrote the part-song " All among the barley."

**Stoker Bram** (Abraham) (1847–1912), b. in Ireland, author of *Dracula* and *Personal Reminiscences Of Henry Irving*, which records his association with the actor in managing the Lyceum Theatre.

**Stokes, Sir George Gabriel,** LL.D., F.R.S. (1819–1903), Irish mathematician and physicist; Prof. of Mathematics at Cambridge from 1849; served as Sec. (1854–85) and as Pres. (1885–92) Royal Society, and as Pres. British Association (1869). Renowned for his researches in hydrodynamics and the theory of light.

**Stopes, Marie Carmichael,** D.Sc., Ph.D., F.L.S., F.R.S. (1880–1958), woman scientist who published many influential works on birth control and eugenics, and pioneered birth-control clinics.

**Stowe, Harriet Elizabeth Beecher** (1811–96), authoress of *Uncle Tom's Cabin* which exposed the horrors of slavery and did much to advance the cause of abolition.

**Strachey, Rt. Hon. Evelyn John St. Loe** (1901–63), English writer and politician; served in Attlee's cabinet, 1945–51. Author of lucid and vigorous books on the principles of democratic socialism. Son of the journalist John St. Loe Strachey and cousin of Giles Lytton Strachey, the biographer.

**Stradivari, Antonio** (1644–1737), an Italian maker of violins, b. Cremona, first in his art.

**Strafford, Thomas Wentworth, Earl of** (1593–1641), the distinguished statesman, sent by Charles I. to Ireland as Lord Deputy in 1631. Was the founder of the Irish linen manufacture. He obtained the name of "Thorough" by his sweeping measures for asserting the King's authority, but was ultimately impeached on a variety of charges, found guilty, and executed.

**Strauss, David Friedrich** (1808–74), German theological writer, who made a great stir in the religious world by his *Life of Jesus*, published in 1835, which attempted to prove that the evangelical history rested on a series of myths.

**Strauss.** Family of Viennese musicians. Johann Strauss (1804–49), "the elder," was a composer of dance music who with Joseph Lanner established the Viennese waltz tradition. His son, Johann Strauss (1825–99), " the younger," although not so good a violinist or conductor as his father, is the more famous as the composer of over 400 waltzes, which include *The Blue Danube* and *Tales from the Vienna Woods*. Two of his brothers Joseph Strauss (1827–70) and Eduard Strauss (1835–1916) were also composers and conductors.

**Strauss, Richard** (1864–1949), German composer and conductor, the son of a horn player in the opera orchestra at Munich. He succeeded von Bülow as court musical director at Meiningen. Among his compositions which are widely acclaimed are the operas *Salome*, *Elektra*, and *Der Rosenkavalier*, the symphonic poems *Don Juan*, *Till Eulenspiegel*, and *Don Quixote*, and many songs of great lyrical beauty. *See Section E.*

**Stravinsky, Igor** (b. 1882), Russian composer and conductor, pupil of Rimsky-Korsakov. His ballets, *The Fire Bird* (1910), *Petruska* (1911), representative of his early romantic style, and the revolutionary *The Rite of Spring*, which caused a furore when it first appeared in 1913, were written for the ballet impresario Diaghilev. He adopted a neo-classical style in later works, for example, in the ballets *Pulcinella* and *Apollo Musagetes*, and the opera-oratorio *Oedipus Rex*. Younger composers have been much influenced by his music. He became a French citizen in 1934, and a U.S. citizen in 1945. *See Section E.*

**Strindberg, Johan August** (1849–1912), Swedish writer of intense creative energy. His work is subjective and reflects his personal conflicts. He married three times but never happily. He produced some fifty-five plays as well as novels, stories, poems, and critical essays. *Lucky Peter*, *Gustav Adolf*, *Till Damascus*, *The Father*, *Miss Julie* are some of his plays.

**Stuart, Arabella** (1575–1615), daughter of the Earl of Lennox and cousin of James I., whose next heir she was both to the English and Scottish thrones. In 1610 she married William Seymour, afterwards Earl of Hertford and Duke of Somerset, and thereby incurring the king's displeasure, she was incarcerated in the Tower of London, where she died insane.

**Suckling, Sir John** (1609–42), wit, courtier, and poet; served under Gustavus Adolphus and in Charles I's first Scottish war (1639). Being concerned in a plot to rescue the Earl of Strafford from the Tower, he fled to France, where he may have killed himself. He wrote poems, ballads, songs, and prose work and is said to have invented cribbage.

**Sudermann, Hermann** (1857–1928), German dramatist, poet and novelist. His brilliant novel, *Frau Sorge* (1887), translated into English as *Dame Care* (1892), reached its 125th edition in 1912. From 1890 he produced a succession of realistic plays and novels.

**Sullivan, Sir Arthur Seymour,** C.V.O. (1842–1900), gifted composer, gained his first musical experiences as choir-boy at the Chapel Royal, and later studied at Leipzig. He composed oratorios but at the same time cultivated a lighter vein with pronounced success. Became famous for the light operas written in collaboration with W. S. Gilbert, which include *Trial by Jury*, *The Sorcerer*, *H.M.S. Pinafore*, *Pirates of Penzance*, *Patience*, *The Mikado*, *The Yeomen of the Guard*, *The Gondoliers*.

**Sully, Maximilien de Béthune, Duc de** (1560–1641), a French Protestant statesman, a friend and companion of Henry of Navarre. His *Memoirs* made notable reading.

**Sun Yat Sen, Dr.** (1867–1925), Chinese revolutionary, founder and first President of the Chinese Republic, 1912, resigning almost immediately in favour of Yuan Shih-kai. Was the first graduate of medicine at Hongkong, 1891. Founded in 1905 the China Revolutionary League in Europe and Japan, and played a large part in the revolution of 1911, which overthrew the Manchu Dynasty. *See also Section C, Part I.*

**Sutherland, Graham Vivien,** O.M. (b. 1903), British artist; he painted the 80th birthday portrait of Sir Winston Churchill commissioned by Parliament and designed the vast tapestry for Coventry Cathedral.

Sutro, Alfred (1863–1933), author and dramatist. His most successful plays were *The Walls of Jericho* (1904) and *John Glayde's Honour* (1907).

Swedenborg, Emanuel (1689–1772), Swedish philosopher, scientist, mystic. In later life he announced that Divine authority had been given him to explain natural and spiritual evidences. He published in quick succession *Arcana Coelestia, The Apocalypse Revealed, Four Preliminary Doctrines*, and *The True Christian Religion*. He also claimed that his soul had been permitted to travel into hell, purgatory and heaven. His works became the scriptures of the sect named Swedenborgians.

Sweelinck, Jan Pieterszoon (1562–1621), famous Dutch organist and composer of sacred music. In his fugues he was the first to make independent use of the pedals, and thus prepared the way for Bach.

Swift, Jonathan (1667–1745), the greatest English satirist, b. in Dublin of English parents, author of *A Tale of a Tub* and *The Battle of the Books* (1704) and *Gulliver's Travels* (1726), works unmatched in satirical power. He crossed to England in 1688 to become secretary to Sir William Temple, took orders in the Church of England when he was 27, but the promotion he hoped for did not come. He was active in Whig politics but changed to Tory in 1710, writing powerful political tracts, notably *The Conduct of the Allies* (1711). He retired to Ireland in 1714 as Dean of St. Patrick's. Both his devoted women friends followed him there—Hester Johnson (d. 1728), the Stella of his famous *Journal*, and Esther Vanhomrigh (d. 1723), the Vanessa of his poetry. It was during the last 30 years of his life that his greatest work was written. *The Drapier's Letters*, in which he exposed the misery of the Irish people under English rule and articulated their feelings for them, made Irishmen worship him. He was buried at St. Patrick's beside Stella.

Swinburne, Algernon Charles (1837–1909), was educated at Oxford, and in the early 'sixties of last century gave to the world a number of poems of singular poetic beauty and musical charm, which procured him a high rank among English poets. Swinburne's most famous productions include *Atalanta in Calydon, Songs before Sunrise, Bothwell*, and *Mary Stuart*. Perhaps the best of his writings is his essay on William Blake.

Swithin, St. (*circa* 800–862), Bishop of Winchester in 852, and on the translation of his remains to a shrine in the interior of the cathedral from the graveyard, fixed for July 15th, 971, violent rain intervened, and, it is said, continued for forty days; hence the superstition as to rain upon St. Swithin's Day.

Symonds, John Addington (1840–93), acquired fame as a poet and writer on *The Renaissance Period in Italy*.

Synge, John Millington (1871–1909), Irish poet and playwright. His best known work, *The Playboy of The Western World*, met with a hostile reception when first produced in Dublin in 1907, but English audiences were at once enthusiastic.

Szymanowski, Karol (1883–1937), Polish composer and director of the Conservatoire at Warsaw.

## T

Tacitus, Caius Cornelius (55–*circa* 120). His chief claim to remembrance is that he was one of the ablest of Roman historians, and left behind him a number of works; among them a life of *Agricola* and his *Annales*, which have formed the ground-work of much that has since been written on the period he covered.

Tacitus, Marcus Claudius (205–276), the Roman Emperor who succeeded Aurelian in A.D. 275. His short reign was wise and marked by moderation.

Taft, Wm. Howard (1857–1930), Chief Justice United States 1921–30. President of the United States 1908–13.

Tagore, Rabindranath (1861–1941), a Bengal poet who won the Nobel Literature Prize in 1913.

Talbot, William Henry Fox, F.R.S. (1800–1877), English scientist who first discovered the principles of photography in 1833. Inventor of the calotype or Talbot-type process of which modern photography is a development.

Talleyrand-Périgord, Charles Maurice de (1754–1838), French politician and diplomat, led a mission to England in 1792 and was Foreign Minister from 1797 until 1807. He represented France at the Congress of Vienna.

Tallis, Thomas (c. 1510–85), a distinguished musician, who was, as organist, attached to the Chapel Royal under Henry VIII., Edward VI., Mary, and Elizabeth, and was the composer of some of the finest of our Church music.

Tamerlane or Timur Lenk (= Timur the Lame) (1336–1405), Mongol conqueror who turned his energies from deliverance of his people from barbarism to military conquest for its own sake. He made himself ruler of Samarkand in 1369 and in a series of campaigns conquered Iran, Transcaucasia, Iraq, Armenia and Georgia, invaded India and Syria, and defeated the Ottoman Turks at Angora. While preparing for the invasion of China death overtook him. His reputation is that of a ruthless and cruel conqueror who showed no mercy even to his fellow Moslems, but he was also a patron of literature and the arts. The Timurids are the line of rulers descended from him.

Tannhäuser, a mythical German minnesinger of the 13th century, who belonged, according to the legend handled so romantically in Wagner's opera, to the Salzburg family of Tanhusen, and was the beloved of Lisaura.

Tarkington, (Newton) Booth (1869–1946), American novelist whose best-known book is *Monsieur Beaucaire*, a sentimental romance which he successfully dramatised.

Tarquin Superbus (or "the Proud"), the last King of Rome. Was banished 510 B.C. After his deposition came the Consuls.

Tarquin the Elder, 5th King of Rome, succeeded Ancius Mastius 615 B.C., reformed the laws, embellished the city, and was assassinated.

Tartini, Giuseppe (1692–1770), great violinist and anticipator of romanticism in Italian music. In practising double stops he discovered a differential tone which modified the intonation—becoming known as Tartini's or "the third" tone—a scientific explanation of which was later given by Helmholtz. His best-known sonata is *The Devil's Trill* written after a dream in which the devil played to him.

Tasman, Abel Janszoon (*circa* 1602–59), a famous Dutch navigator; in 1642 he discovered Tasmania and New Zealand shortly thereafter.

Tassigny, Jean de Lattre de, Marshal of France, Hon. G.C.B. (1890–1952), outstanding commander of the Free French Movement in Second World War; High Commissioner and C.-in-C. Indo-China, 1950–52. C.-in-C. Land Forces, Western Europe, 1948–50.

Tasso, Torquato (1544–95), one of the great Italian epic poets, author of *Jerusalem Delivered* (Ital. *Gerusalemme liberata*) which celebrates the First Crusade.

Tawney, Richard Henry, B.A. (1880–1962), great historian, pioneer of adult education, leader of socialist thought, the first critic of the affluent society; Prof. Emeritus Economic History, Univ. of London, 1931–49. Among his standard works are *The Acquisitive Society, Equality, Religion and the Rise of Capitalism*.

Taylor, Jeremy (1613–67), an English divine of great influence. The most famous of his works was his *Holy Living and Holy Dying*.

Tchaikovsky, Peter Ilich (1840–93), Russian composer. His music is melodious and intensely emotional and he excelled in several branches of composition. Amongst his works are ten operas, including *Eugene Onegin* and *The Queen of Spades* (both from stories by Pushkin), seven symphonies, including *Manfred*, the *Little Russian* and the *Pathétique*, his last completed work, ballets, including *Swan Lake, The Sleeping Beauty*, and *The Nutcracker*, the fantasies *Romeo and Juliet* and *Francesca da Rimini*, the piano concerto in B flat minor, the violin concerto in D, and numerous songs. *See* Section E.

Tedder, Marshal of the R.A.F., Arthur William, 1st Baron, G.C.B. (1890–1967), was Deputy Supreme Commander under Eisenhower for the invasion of Europe, Chief of the Air Staff, 1946–48; Chairman, Western Europe Chiefs of

Staff committee, 1948–50; Vice-Chairman of the Governors of the B.B.C., 1952–54; Chancellor Univ. of Cambridge, 1950–67.

**Telemann, Georg Philipp** (1681–1767), composer of great facility and output in all fields of music. Founded Collegium Musicum at Leipzig Univ. and held appointments in many other German towns, including Hamburg. His music has vitality and originality of form and is appreciated today after long period of neglect.

**Telford, Thomas** (1757–1834), was a Scottish working stone-mason who became a great engineer and attained special fame as a builder of bridges, the Menai Suspension Bridge being, perhaps, his greatest work. He constructed the Ellesmere Canal, made many hundreds of miles of difficult mountain roads, was chief engineer of the Caledonian Canal, and altogether did an immense amount of public work.

**Tell, William**, a legendary figure in Swiss folk-lore. The story of his having been compelled by order of the imperial governor, Gessler, to shoot an apple from the head of his own son and his dramatic revenge is regarded as a legendary feat which has its origins in Teutonic myth. The Swiss hero of the Uri, however, played a great part in freeing his country from the Austrian yoke in the early part of the 14th century.

**Temple, Most Rev. Frederick** (1821–1902), a famous Anglican Churchman who became Headmaster of Rugby in 1858; in 1860 attained notoriety as the author of the first of the much-controverted *Essays and Reviews*, advocated the disestablishment of the Irish Church in 1868, was appointed Bishop of Exeter in 1869, translated to London in 1885, and in 1896 was raised to the Primacy. He made a strong Archbishop, and dominated the Church with his vigorous personality.

**Temple, Most Rev. William**, P.C., D.Litt., D.D. (1881–1944), one of the outstanding Christian leaders of his time and the son of Frederick Temple, was Archbishop of Canterbury, 1942–44, after being Headmaster of Repton, 1910–14, Bishop of Manchester, 1921–29, and Archbishop of York, 1929–42. His influence was felt among Christians of all denominations, and he strove for the unity of the Churches.

**Temple, Rt. Hon. Sir William**, Bt. (1628–99), English statesman and author; Ambassador to The Hague in Charles II.'s time, and instrumental in bringing about the marriage between William of Orange and the Princess Mary. William III. twice offered him the position of Secretary of State, but he declined the honour, spending the years of his retirement at Moor Park (where Swift served him for a time as private secretary). Married Dorothy Osborne (1627–95), the letter-writer.

**Templewood, Samuel John Gurney Hoare, 1st Viscount**, P.C., G.C.S.I., G.B.E., C.M.G. (1880–1959), Conservative politician; Sec. of State for Air, 1922–29; Sec. of State for India, 1931–35; Foreign Sec., June–Dec. 1935; Home Sec., 1937–39; Special Ambassador to Spain, 1940–44.

**Teniers, David** (the younger) (1610–94), was born at Antwerp, and his paintings of the old rustic Flemish life are unsurpassed in their humour and fidelity. He died at Brussels. His father, **David Teniers the elder** (1582–1649), was also one of the leading landscape painters of the time.

**Tenniel, Sir John** (1820–1914), for over fifty years leading artist of *Punch*, illustrated numerous books, including *Alice in Wonderland*.

**Tennyson, Alfred Lord** (1809–92), was Poet Laureate from 1850 to his death. Born at Somersby, in Lincolnshire, he showed poetic gifts while quite young, and in 1827, joined his brother Charles in the publication of *Poems by Two Brothers*. In 1847 he published *The Princess*; in 1850 *In Memoriam*, a poem of great beauty and depth of thought, in which he enshrined his affection for the memory of his dead friend Arthur Hallam; and in 1855 *Maud* appeared. His other works include *The Idylls of the Kings*, *Enoch Arden*, *Queen Mary*, *Harold*, and *Becket*.

**Terence, Publius Terentius Afer** (c. 184–159 B.C.), a Latin poet and dramatist, an African (Berber), who rose from the position of a slave to that of one of the most honoured men in Rome.

**Teresa, St.**, or **Theresa** (1515–82), a Spanish saint

and author, born at Avila, entered the Carmelite order in 1534, established a reformed order in 1562, became famous for her ascetic life and mystic visions, and died at Alba de Liste. Her religious writings include *The Way of Perfection* and *The Castle of the Soul*. She was canonised by Pope Gregory XV.

**Terry, Dame Ellen**, G.B.E. (Mrs. James Carew) (1847–1928), one of the most distinguished of English actresses. Played Shakespeare with Sir Henry Irving at the Lyceum and later appeared in plays of Bernard Shaw.

**Tertullian, Quintus** (circa 150–230), a Father and writer of the Latin Church. His chief work was his *Apologeticus*, a defence of Christianity.

**Tetrazzini, Luisa** (1871–1940), an Italian prima donna who sprang into prominence in 1907 by her wonderful singing at Covent Garden and hailed as a second Patti.

**Tetzel, John** (c. 1460–1519), the German Dominican monk and Inquisitor, the scandal of whose sale of indulgences roused Luther to publish his ninety-five theses at Wittenberg in 1517.

**Thackeray, William Makepeace** (1811–63), English novelist, author of *Vanity Fair*, *Pendennis*, *Esmond*, *The Newcomes*, *The Virginians*, *Philip* and *Lovel the Widower*. He edited the *Cornhill Magazine* from the first number, January, 1860, for a few years his most notable contributions being his *Roundabout Papers*. His *Yellowplush Papers* and *The Book of Snobs* (republished from *Punch*) were widely read and admired; and the lectures he delivered in America on *The Four Georges* were pungently powerful.

**Thales of Miletus** (c. 624–565 B.C.), earliest of the Greek scientists, he created a sensation by his prediction of an eclipse of the sun, which was visible at Miletus in 585 B.C. He looked upon water as the basis of all material things and in his mathematical work was the first to enunciate natural laws.

**Thant, Sithu U** (b. 1909), Secretary-General of the United Nations, 1962–   ; Acting Sec.-Gen. after Dr. Hammarskjöld's death in 1961; Burmese Perm. Rep. to U.N. 1957–61.

**Themistocles** (c. 514–449 B.C.), Athenian soldier and statesman. By fortifying the harbour of Piraeus as the port of Athens, by the remission of taxes on aliens, and by the creation of the Athenian navy, he established Athenian prosperity and made possible the later Athenian empire. Defeated the Persian fleet at Salamis in 480 B.C.

**Theocritus** (285–247 B.C.), one of the great Greek poets. Thirty *Idylls* have come down to us and a number of *Epigrams*.

**Theodoric the Great** (455–526), a celebrated King of the East Goths, born at Pannonia. In mediæval German romance he is known as "Dietrich von Bern," and had a reputation for good government, akin to that ascribed in England to King Alfred. He was the founder of the Gothic Kingdom of Italy.

**Theodosius the Great** (346–95) was Roman Emperor of the East for nearly twenty years. He gained victories over the Goths, and the year before his death became sole Emperor. Noted in ecclesiastical history for his conversion to Christianity, and for his submission to the penance imposed by St. Ambrose.

**Theophrastus** (c. 372–287 B.C.), succeeded Aristotle as President of the Lyceum at Athens. His *History of Plants* and his *Moral Characters* are the best known of his writings.

**Thibaud, Jacques** (1880–1953) famous French violinist. Killed in aeroplane crash.

**Thierry, Jacques Nicolas Augustin** (1795–1856), a distinguished French historian, known by his *History of the Norman Conquest*.

**Thiers, Louis Adolphe** (1797–1877), a French statesman and man of letters, author of *History of the French Revolution*.

**Thomas, Dylan** (1914–53), Welsh poet whose *Eighteen Poems* (1934) brought him instant recognition as an original and gifted artist. Other works include *Twenty-five Poems* (1936), *Deaths and Entrances* (1945), *Under Milk Wood*, a play for voices. *See Section M*.

**Thomson, James** (1834–82), a Scottish poet who wrote *The City of Dreadful Night*.

**Thomson, Sir (John) Arthur** (1861–1933), was a well-known biologist.

**Thomson, Sir Joseph (John)**, O.M., D.Sc., F.R.S.

**B74**

(1856–1940), physicist and mathematician; Master of Trinity College, Cambridge, 1918–40; Cavendish Prof. of Experimental Physics, Cambridge, 1884–1919. Awarded Nobel Prize in 1906 for his work on conduction of electricity through gases; also discovered the electron. Pres. of the Royal Society, 1913–15. His son, Sir George Paget Thomson, (b. 1892) F.R.S., is also a physicist and Nobel Prizeman; former Master of Corpus Christi College, Cambridge.

**Thoreau, Henry David** (1817–62), American essayist and nature-worshipper. He was the friend of, and for a time lived with, Emerson. Best known for his classic *Walden, or Life in the Woods.*

**Thorez Maurice** (1900–64), French communist, under whose leadership the Communists became the largest single party in the French elections of 1945 and 1946; Sec.-Gen. of French Communist Party, 1930–64.

**Thorndike, Dame Sybil,** D.B.E., LL.D. (b. 1882), celebrated British actress who made her début with the Ben Greet players in 1904 and worked with the Old Vic from 1914–18. She won great success in the Greek tragedies, Shakespeare, Shaw, and in Grand Guignol. Both she and her husband, Sir Lewis Casson, received the honorary degree of D. Litt. at Oxford University in 1966 in commemoration of their long and splendid partnership.

**Thornycroft, Sir William Hamo,** R.A. (1850–1925), English sculptor whose works include the Gladstone Memorial, the statue of General Gordon in Trafalgar Square, of Queen Alexandra in the Royal Exchange, Lord Granville in the Houses of Parliament, Cromwell at Westminster, and John Bright in Rochdale.

**Thorpe, Sir (Thomas) Edward,** C.B., Ph.D., D.Sc., F.R.S. (1845–1925), a noted English chemist. His chief research work was done on paraffin hydrocarbons, and the derivatives of fluorine and phosphorus. Author of a standard *Dictionary of Applied Chemistry* and a *History of Chemistry.*

**Thorwaldsen, Bertel** (1770–1844), a famous Danish sculptor.

**Thucydides** (*c.* 460–399 B.C.), the first scientific historian, was an Athenian and took part in the Peloponnesian War, about which he wrote his *History.* Attempted an impartial account, weighing the testimony of eye-witnesses and keeping to carefully verified facts. The *History* is a graphic narrative, but Thucydides was not merely a chronicler; he saw the general significance of particular events and wished to pass on the political lessons of the past to the future. The speeches which he put into the mouths of the various actors reveal the political ideas and climate of opinion of contemporary Greece, and include the famous Funeral Oration of Pericles.

**Tiberius, Claudius** (42 B.C.–A.D. 37), the second Emperor of Rome, had an evil reputation but was an able ruler and successful soldier. Spent his later years in Capri.

**Tillett, Benjamin** (1860–1943), M.P. for North Salford 1917–24 and again 1929–31, came into prominence in the great dock strike of 1889. He was the organiser and secretary of the Dockers' Union; for several years alderman of the L.C.C.; and an active labour leader. Chairman of the General Council T.U.C. 1928–29.

**Tillotson, John** (1630–94), a celebrated preacher at Lincoln's Inn, " Popery " and " Atheism " being the main objects of his attacks: in 1691 became Archbishop of Canterbury.

**Tindal, Matthew** (*c.*1653–1733), noted English Deist.

**Tintoretto** (1518–94), Venetian painter whose aim it was to unite the colouring of Titian with the drawing of Michelangelo. He is among the most original and decorative of artists whose numerous paintings, mostly of religious subjects, were executed with great speed, some of them on enormous canvasses. His real name was Jacopo Robusti, and he was called Il Tintoretto (little dyer) after his father's trade. Three of his six children were painters.

**Tippett, Sir, Michael Kemp,** Kt., (b. 1905), English composer whose works include Concerto for Orchestra, *Midsummer Marriage, King Priam,* the cantata *Boyhood's End,* and the song-cycle *The Heart's Assurance. See* Section E.

**Titian, or Tiziano Vecelli** (1477–1576), one of the greatest of painters. He studied under the

Bellinis, and made his first essays in painting for the public in conjunction with Giorgione, whom he soon surpassed. In 1511 he was at Padua, where he painted some notable frescoes; in 1512 he was back in Venice, with a studio on the Grand Canal, employed on important commissions. From this time forward he was in great demand, and exercised his marvellous powers almost to the end of his life, dying of the plague at ninety-nine.

**Titiens (or Tietjens), Teresa** (1831–77), a famous German operatic prima donna and concert-room singer.

**Tito, Marshal (Josif Broz)** (b. 1892), Prime Minister of the Federal People's Republic of Yugoslavia since 1945. Leader of the partisan forces which successfully fought against German occupation. President National Liberation Committee, 1943.

**Titus** (40–81), the Roman Emperor, and son of Vespasian. Attained great renown by his successful part in the Jewish war which terminated in the capture and destruction of Jerusalem; he was deemed a profligate and a tyrant, but no sooner was he in sole power than he exerted himself to the utmost to please the people, completed the Colosseum, built splendid baths, and otherwise made himself popular.

**Tizard, Sir Henry Thomas,** G.C.B., F.R.S. (1885–1959), scientist and administrator; Pres. British Association, 1948. Played important part in the higher scientific direction of the second world war and as Chair. Advisory Council on Scientific Policy, 1947–52.

**Tocqueville, Alexis, Comte de** (1805–59), author of *De La Démocratie en Amérique* and *De L'Ancien Régime,* which set out nineteenth-century liberal ideas.

**Todd, Alexander Robertus, 1st Baron,** D.Sc., F.R.S. (b. 1907), British biochemist; Prof. of Organic Chemistry at Cambridge, 1944– . For his work on the structures of nucleic acids he received the 1957 Nobel Prize for Chemistry.

**Tolstoy, Count Leo Nikolayevitch** (1828–1910), was the most distinguished personality in modern Russian literature. Born of a good family, he was for a time in the army, but was so greatly moved by the trials and sufferings of the people that, out of pure sympathy of heart, he was impelled " to take up his pen and write." At twenty-four he published his *Childhood,* and in 1854, while in camp in the Crimea, wrote his *Tales from Sebastopol,* which procured him considerable literary fame. Later on he was a persistent advocate of progressive ideas, and, before the Emancipation Act for freeing all Russian serfs was enforced, he himself had given the serfs on his own estate their freedom. In 1862 he married, and settled down to a quiet country life, shortly afterwards publishing his *War and Peace* and *Anna Karenina.* In his latter years Tolstoy developed a sort of religious mysticism. Among his later works are *The Power of Darkness, The Kreutzer Sonata, The Cossacks, Resurrection,* and *The End of the Age.*

**Tooke, John Horne** (1736–1812), English politician and pamphleteer, was a supporter of Wilkes and later Pitt. His tracts advocated reform. After the French Revolution was tried for high treason, but was acquitted.

**Toole, John Lawrence** (1832–1906), for half a century a popular English comedian.

**Torquemada, Tomás de** (1420–98), the chief officer of the Spanish Inquisition.

**Torricelli, Evangelista** (1608–47), Galileo's pupil. He invented the barometer and improved both the microscope and the telescope.

**Toscanini, Arturo** (1867–1957), famous Italian conductor, La Scala Theatre, Milan, 1898–1908, and 1920–29; at the Metropolitan Opera House, New York, 1908–15; and of the Philharmonic Symphony Society of New York, 1926–36. Returned to Milan in 1946 after a ten-year exile.

**Toulouse-Lautrec, Henry de** (1864–1901), French painter, whose pictures portray with stark realism certain aspects of Parisian life in the nineties.

**Tovey, Sir Donald Francis** (1875–1940), pianist and composer who for 25 years held the chair of music at the University of Edinburgh. Outstanding among his many writings is *Essays in Musical Analysis,* and his compositions include chamber music, a piano concerto, and an opera *The Bride of Dionysus.*

**Toynbee, Arnold** (1852–83), after graduating at Oxford, devoted himself to practical philanthropy and social reform. From his self-denying efforts sprang the settlement in East London —Toynbee Hall.

**Toynbee, Arnold Joseph,** C.H., Hon.D.Litt. (Oxford, Cambridge, and Birmingham) (b. 1889), eminent scholar and historian, nephew of above. Dir. of Studies Royal Inst. of Int. Affairs, 1925–55. Major work *A Study of History.*

**Trajan** (*circa* 52–117) was Roman Emperor from 98 to his death. His rule was enlightened, and he was esteemed by his people.

**Tree, Sir Herbert Beerbohm** (1852–1917), the London actor-manager who scored successes at the Haymarket and His Majesty's Theatre.

**Trenchard, Marshal of the R.A.F., Viscount,** G.C.B., O.M., G.C.V.O., D.S.O. (1873–1956), Chief of Air Staff, 1918–29; Commissioner of Police of the Metropolis, 1931–35; often known as father of the Air Force.

**Trent, 1st Baron, of Nottingham (Jesse Boot)** (1850–1931), founder of Boots Cash Chemists, Ltd.; a great benefactor of Nottingham, especially of the University of Nottingham.

**Trevelyan, George Macaulay,** O.M., C.B.E. (1876–1962). English historian, son of Sir George Otto Trevelyan and great nephew of Thomas Babbington Macaulay. Regius Professor of Modern History at Cambridge 1927–40; Master of Trinity College, 1940. Chancellor of Durham University, 1949. His chief works are: *History of England*; a trilogy of books on *Garibaldi*; *England under the Stuarts*; *England under Queen Anne*; *Grey of Falloden*; *English Social History*; *An Autobiography and other Essays.*

**Trevelyan, Rt. Hon. Sir George Otto, 1st Bt.,** O.M. (1838–1928), Liberal statesman and historian. Became Chief Secretary for Ireland in 1882, and was later Secretary of State for Scotland. Wrote a biography of his uncle, Lord Macaulay, which was highly praised. Father of Professor G. M. Trevelyan.

**Trevithick, Richard** (1771–1833), a Cornish mine-manager's son, who invented the road-locomotive, putting upon the highway on Christmas Eve, 1801, the first steam-propelled vehicle for passengers.

**Trollope, Anthony** (1815–82), author of many novels. His Barchester series depicts a number of scenes of higher clerical life with great fidelity and success.

**Trotsky, Leon,** name assumed by Lev Davidovich Bronstein (1879–1940), one of the leaders of the Bolshevist revolution. War Minister of the Bolshevist Government and its leading representative at the Brest-Litovsk conference of 1917–18. He differed from the Communist Party on policy and was dismissed from office in 1925. In 1929 took up exile in Mexico where he was assassinated.

**Trudeau, Rt. Hon. Pierre Elliott** (b. 1919), Federal leader of the Canadian Liberal Party and Prime Minister since 1968.

**Truman, Harry S.** (b. 1884), President of the United States, 1945–53. Inherited the Presidency on the death of Roosevelt in 1945 and won the Pres. election in 1948. He took the historic decision to enter Korea in 1950, dismissed Gen. MacArthur in 1951, and will perhaps best be remembered for his "Point Four" programme of raising levels of living in backward, and underdeveloped countries.

**Tulsi Das** (1532–1623), mediæval poet of India whose great masterpiece *Rām-Charit-Mānas* (popularly known as the *Rāmayana* and based on the Sanskrit epic of Vālmiki) is venerated by all Hindus just as the Bible is in the West.

**Turenne, Henri de la Tour d'Auvergne, Vicomte de** (1611–75), a famous French commander and Marshal of France, who was highly successful in the Thirty Years' War.

**Turgenev, Ivan Serveyvich** (1818–83), was a friend of Gogol and Tolstoy, and a famous Russian novelist and short-story writer. His works were frequently satirical and directed against the oppression of the peasants by the nobles. Was the inventor of the term "nihilist" to describe the Russian anarchist movement.

**Turner, Joseph Mallord William,** R.A. (1775–1851), was the son of a London barber, but while quite a child showed the possession of artistic genius. In 1789, after some miscellaneous schooling, he entered the Royal Academy classes, and soon began to make headway. Of his larger pictures may be mentioned *The Sun Rising through Vapour, Crossing the Brook, Dido Building Carthage, The Fighting Téméraire,* and *Calais Pier.* Ruskin, in his *Modern Painters,* wrote with great eloquence and critical insight regarding Turner's work, and brought about a fuller appreciation of his genius. Turner never married, and took little interest in anything outside his art. He left the oil paintings and drawings he had preserved to the National Gallery.

**Tussaud, Madame Marie** (1760–1850), a Swiss who while practising the art of modelling wax in Paris at the time of the French Revolution, made her escape to England and set up a small exhibition of wax figures in the Strand, later carried on by her son, grandson and great-grandson at Baker Street and in 1884 transferred to Marylebone Road.

**Tut-ankh-amen** (*circa* 1350 B.C.), an Egyptian Pharaoh of the 18th dynasty, whose tomb was discovered by Howard Carter in 1922, with the mummy and gold sarcophagus intact. The magnificence of the objects found aroused world-wide interest.

**Twain Mark.** (*See* Clemens, Samuel L.)

**Tweedsmuir, John Buchan, 1st Baron,** C.H. (1875–1940), Gov.-Gen. of Canada 1935–40, journalist, politician, and author, wrote numerous biographies, historical novels, and adventure stories, including *Montrose, The Path of the King, Greenmantle,* and *Sick-Heart River,* and an autobiography *Memory Hold the Door.*

**Tyler, Wat** (d. 1381), the leader of the peasants' revolt of Richard II.'s time against the iniquitous poll-tax. Over 100,000 peasants followed Tyler into London in June 1381, and the king met them in Smithfield and made promises of redress that were never fulfilled. It was at this meeting that Sir William Walworth, Lord Mayor of London, stabbed Tyler to death.

**Tyndale, William** (c. 1492–1536), was educated at Oxford, and conceived a strong desire to be the medium of presenting the Bible to his countrymen in their own language. He completed the translation of the New Testament at Wittenburg, where he was associated with Luther. This version was first published at Antwerp, and then found its way to England, where it was publicly burnt at St. Paul's Cross. Tyndale afterwards was associated with Miles Coverdale in a translation of the Old Testament, but only completed the Pentateuch and the book of Jonah. Antwerp was Tyndale's retreat during this later period, and in 1535 he was arrested for heresy and put to death by strangling and burning.

**Tyndall, Prof. John,** F.R.S. (1820–93), was an eminent scientist. His books on light, sound, and heat are well-known text-books.

# U

**Unamuno, Miguel de** (1864–1936), Spanish philosopher, poet, essayist, and novelist, author of *El Sentimiento Trágico de la Vida* (The Tragic Sense of Life).

**Ulanova, Galina** (b. 1910), Russian ballet dancer, made her début in 1928 and is the world's greatest living exponent of the art. She danced in Florence in 1951 and in London in 1956.

**Undset, Sigrid** (1882–1949), Norwegian novelist, daughter of a distinguished Norwegian antiquary, from whom she derived her knowledge of life in ancient and mediæval Norway. Her first success came with *Jenny* (1911), and the great works based on mediæval history, *Kristin Lavransdatter* (1920–22) and *Olav Audunnson* (1925–27), won for her the 1928 Nobel Prize for Literature.

**Unwin, Sir Raymond** (1863–1940), English architect and expert on Town Planning, who became known as the architect of the first garden city at Letchworth, and of the Hampstead Garden Suburb.

**Ursula, St.,** is said to have been an English princess, who with 11,000 virgins set out on a pilgrimage, but compelled by a fierce storm to take refuge in Cologne, was there put to death with her following by an army of Huns.

**Usher or Ussher, James** (1581–1656), Irish prelate and scholar, one of the most distinguished theologians of his day. He worked out a system of dates setting the creation at 4004 B.C.

# V

**Valentine, St.,** was a Christian martyr of the reign of the Emperor Claudius II (d. 270 A.D.). His festival was commemorated on February 14 before Gregory the Great's time. The custom of sending valentines had its origin in a heathen practice associated with the worship of Juno about this date in the calendar, and had no connection with the saint.

**Vanbrugh, Sir John** (1664–1726), was a prominent architect as well as a successful dramatist.

**Vancouver, George** (1758–98), a British navigator who served under Captain Cook and later explored the Gulf of Georgia and the Straits of San Juan de Fuca, as also the shores of Vancouver Island.

**Vanderbilt, Cornelius** (1794–1877), a noted American merchant and railway speculator who accumulated a fortune of twenty millions sterling. His son **William Henry Vanderbilt** (1821–85) inherited and added to it.

**Van Dyck (or Vandyke), Sir Anthony** (1599–1641), was born at Antwerp, and after studying under Rubens went to Italy and there made a name as a portrait painter. In 1629 he came to England on the invitation of Charles I., but remained only a short time; in 1631 Charles prevailed upon him to return, made him a knight, granted him an annuity, and he became the Society painter of the day.

**Vane, Sir Henry** (1613–62), was a prominent statesman and diplomatist. At the Restoration he was arrested as an enemy of the State and ultimately beheaded on Tower Hill.

**Van Gogh, Vincent** (1853–1890), Dutch painter of some of the most colourful pictures ever created. With passionate intensity of feeling he painted without pause whatever he found around him—landscapes, still-lifes, portraits; his was a truly personal art. His life was one of pain, sorrow and often despair and in the end he committed suicide.

**Van Loon, Hendrik Willem** (1882–1944), Dutch-American historian, born in Rotterdam, who became famous in 1922 with the publication of *The Story of Mankind*, a picture history-book originally intended for children.

**Vauban, Marshal Sebastien le Prestre de** (1633–1707), a renowned French military engineer who introduced great improvements in methods of fortification, conducted fifty-three sieges, and took part in 140 battles.

**Vaughan Williams, Ralph,** O.M., M.A., D. Mus. (1872–1958), English composer. After Charterhouse and Cambridge he studied music in Berlin under Max Bruch and, later in Paris, under Ravel. He wrote nine symphonies besides a number of choral and orchestral works including *Sancta Civitas* and *Benedicite, Magnificat, Five Tudor Portraits, Dona Nobis Pacem,* operas including *Hugh the Drover, Riders to the Sea,* ballets, chamber music and songs. *See* Section E. He showed great interest in folk tunes. *See* Section E.

**Velasquez, Diego** (1465–1523), a Spanish soldier and companion of Columbus, sent to conquer Cuba. Velasquez founded Santiago and Havana.

**Velazquez, Diego Rodriguez de Silvay** (1599–1660), a famous Spanish painter, whose pictures rank among the finest in Spanish art.

**Venizelos, Eleutherios** (1864–1936), the Greek patriot and statesman, suffered many vicissitudes of fortune during his career. A Cretan by birth, he became Prime Minister of Greece for the first time in 1910, and again on several subsequent occasions, but died in exile. Best known probably for his activity during the Balkan wars, his finally successful attempts to bring his country into the first world war on the side of the Entente Powers, and his ambitions in Asia Minor. At the post-war conferences in 1919 he exercised more influence than anyone else outside the "Big Four."

**Verdi, Giuseppe** (1813–1901), Italian composer, foremost figure in 19th-century opera. Early works include *Nabucco, Ernani, I Due Foscari,* and *Macbeth.* A middle period is represented by *Rigoletto, Il Trovatore, La Traviata, Un Ballo in Maschera,* and *Don Carlo.* To the last and greatest period of his life belong *Aida, Otello,* and his last opera *Falstaff,* produced when he was 80. *See* Section E.

**Verlaine, Paul** (1844–1896), French poet, also well known for his memoirs and confessions; died in great poverty and degradation in Paris.

**Vermeer, Jan** (1632–75), Dutch painter and the greatest of all the "Little Masters." Jan Vermeer of Delft, as he was frequently referred to, was born in Delft, and obtained considerable recognition in his lifetime, but strangely his existence was entirely overlooked after his death, and until 1860 his paintings were attributed to other Dutch painters. *Lady at the Virginals* is in the National Gallery.

**Verne, Jules** (1828–1905), was one of the most popular authors of wonder-stories in Europe. The best-known of his numerous works are *Five Weeks in a Balloon, Twenty Thousand Leagues Under the Sea, Round the World in Eighty Days.*

**Vernier, Pierre** (1580–1637), inventor of the small sliding scale which enables readings on a graduated scale to be taken to a fraction of a division.

**Veronese, Paul, or Paolo Cagliari** (1528–88), a celebrated Italian painter of religious subjects. His *Marriage Feast at Cana in Galilee, The Feast in the House of Simon,* and *The Presentation of the Family of Darius to Alexander,* are paintings of world-wide celebrity, while his *Adoration of the Magi,* in our National Gallery is a grand work.

**Veronica, St.,** a legendary woman of Jerusalem, who was said to have handed to Christ her kerchief on His way to Calvary. The old belief was that the Redeemer wiped His brow therewith, leaving on the handkerchief a miraculous impression of His face, the so-called "Veronicon." The Saint is commemorated on February 4th.

**Verwoerd, Dr. Hendrik Frensch** (1901–66), succeeded J. G. Strydom as Prime Minister of South Africa in 1958. Prof. of Psychology at Stellenbosch Univ., 1928–50. Assassinated in Parliament, Cape Town, 6 Sept. 1966. *See also* Section C.

**Vespasian (Titus Flavius Vespasinus)** (9–79 A.D.) was Roman Emperor during the last nine years of his life. At one time he commanded the Roman army of occupation in Britain.

**Vespucci, Amerigo** (1451–1512), Florentine merchant and navigator, who settled in Spain as commercial agent of the house of Medici. He made several voyages across the Atlantic and, according to his own accounts, which are disputed by many authorities, reached the American continent on June 16, 1497. A German geographer paid him the tribute of giving the name America to what is now known as South America in a map he published in 1507.

**Victor Emmanuel II.** (1820–78) was King of Sardinia from 1849 to 1861, became King of Italy, according the the Proclamation of the Sardinian Senate; but it was not until 1870, when the unification of Italy was fully secured, that the title came to have its true significance.

**Victoria** (1819–1901), Queen of Great Britain and Ireland and Empress of India, was daughter of the Duke of Kent, and came to the throne in 1837 on the death of her uncle, William IV. In 1840 she married Prince Albert of Saxe-Coburg-Gotha, who died in 1861. Lord Melbourne was Prime Minister at the date of the Queen's accession, and for a number of years the country lived through troublesome times, the Corn Law and Chartist agitations being at times very threatening, but a more settled condition of things supervened, and for the remainder of the long and illustrious Victorian reign there was no serious home unrest. The Jubilee of Queen Victoria's accession was celebrated in 1887, and the Diamond Jubilee 10 years later.

**Villeneuve, Pierre Charles Baptiste Silvestre** (1763–1806), the French naval commander who was opposed to Nelson at Trafalgar and captured along with his ship, the *Bucentaure.*

**Villon, François** (1431–c. 1485), French poet who lived at a turbulent time in French history at the close of the Hundred Years War. His extant works consist of *Le Lais* (or *Petit Testament*) and *Grand Testament,* masterpieces of French mediæval verse.

**Virgil (Publius Vergilius Maro)** (70–19 B.C.), the great Roman epic poet, was born near Mantua, and cultivated a farm in the adjacent village of Andes. He proceeded to Rome in his thirtieth year to obtain redress for the occupation of his lands by the military. Became known to Octavian and Mæcenas, and, having had his demand satisfied, began the writing of his *Eclogues*. The *Georgics* followed: his most famous work, the *Æneid*, comprised twelve books dealing with the story of the wanderings of Æneas after the destruction of Troy.

**Vitus, St.,** Roman Catholic saint and martyr, who lived in the 4th century. It used to be the custom to dance before his shrine on this festival day, June 15th, in the belief that good health was thereby ensured for the next twelvemonth. The nervous ailment, St. Vitus' dance, derives its name from this practice.

**Vivaldi, Antonio** (*c.* 1675–1743), Venetian composer. For many years violin master at the Ospedal della Pieta there. His output of orchestral works was prolific, and their reassessment in recent years has immensely added to his reputation, long disparaged by English writers. Bach indeed arranged some of his violin pieces for the harpsichord. *See* Section E.

**Volta, Alessandro** (1745–1827), Italian physicist, professor at Como and Pavia. Working on the results of Galvani, he found that the essential thing in producing an electric current was contact of dissimilar metals. He invented the voltaic pile, the first instrument for producing an electric current, and thereby laid the foundation of electrochemistry.

**Voltaire, François-Marie Arouet de** (1694—1778), one of the greatest of French philosophers and writers. His first essays offended the authorities, and he spent the years 1726–9 in England where he wrote some of his dramas. Returning to France he published his *Philosophical Letters*, which aroused the enmity of the priesthood. At this juncture, the Marquise du Châtelet offered him the asylum of her castle of Cirey, and for the next fifteen years he made this his home, writing there his *Discourses on Man*, *Essay on the Morals and Spirit of Nations, Age of Louis XIV.*, &c. The Marquise was a mathematician and taught him some science, thus helping him in his interpretation of Newton's *Principia*. To Voltaire we owe the story of the falling apple. He spent the years 1750–3 in Berlin, at the invitation of Frederick the Great.

**Vondel, Joost van den** (1587–1679), the greatest of the Dutch poets. Most of his dramas are on biblical subjects, and the two most famous are *Jephtha* and *Lucifer*.

**Voroshilov, Marshal of the Soviet Union, Klimentiy Efremovich** (b. 1881), President of the Supreme Soviet of the U.S.S.R., 1953–60; commander of the Leningrad defences in 1941.

**Vyshinsky, Andrei Yanuarievich** (1883–1954), Russian jurist and diplomat; conducted the prosecution of the Moscow treason trials, 1936–38; represented Russian interests at U.N.

# W

**Wade, George** (1668–1748), military engineer who after the Jacobite rebellion of 1715 commanded the royal forces in Scotland and constructed the great military roads through the Highlands, some of which have continued to be the main lines of communication. Promoted to Field-Marshal in 1743 and in 1744 George II made him Commander-in-Chief in England. In the last Jacobite rising of 1745 his army was the first to be evaded by the Young Pretender, Charles Edward, on his famous march south.

**Wagner, Richard** (1813–83), German composer, born at Leipzig. He achieved a new type of musical expression in his operas by the complete union of music and drama, and his influence on later composers was immense. He made use of the *leitmotif* principle and was his own librettist. His originality and modernism aroused a good deal of opposition, and he was exiled for some years. But he was supported by many loyal friends, including Liszt, the young King Ludwig of Bavaria, and the philosopher Nietzsche. He began the music of the *Ring des Nibelungen* in 1853, finishing it a quarter of a century later. It was not until 1876 that the whole of this great drama (Rheingold, Valkyrie, Siegfried, Götterdämmerung) was performed at Bayreuth under the conductor Hans Richter. Other

operas include *The Flying Dutchman, Rienzi, Tannhäuser, Lohengrin, Tristan und Isolde, Die Meistersinger von Nürnberg, Parsifal* a religious drama. He married Liszt's daughter Cosima, formerly wife of his friend Hans von Bülow. *See* Section E.

**Waley, Arthur, C.H., C.B.E., M.A.** (1889–1966), orientalist, well known for his translations of Chinese and Japanese poetry and prose, being the first to bring the literature of those countries to the western world.

**Walker, George** (1618–90), the hero of the siege of Londonderry, in 1688, who kept the besiegers at bay for 105 days.

**Wallace, Alfred Russel, O.M., F.R.S.** (1823–1913), British naturalist and joint author with Darwin of the theory of natural selection, b. at Usk, Monmouth. In 1858, while down with illness in the Moluccas, he sent a draft of his theory to Darwin in England who was amazed to find that it closely agreed with his own theory of evolution which he was on the point of publishing. The result was a reading of a joint paper to the Linnean Society.

**Wallace, Edgar** (1875–1932), English novelist and playwright, famous for his detective thrillers.

**Wallace, Sir Richard, Bt.** (1818–90), son of the Marquis of Hertford, and inheritor from him of a famous collection of pictures and other works of art to which he himself added largely. This was bequeathed to the nation by his widow along with Hertford House and now forms one of the most important exhibitions in London.

**Wallace, Sir William** (*circa* 1270–1305), the great Scottish patriot and chieftain who led the Scottish armies against Edward I., and for a time the English were kept completely in check. Later, Edward defeated him at Falkirk, and finally in 1304 he was captured, taken to London, condemned for treason, executed at Smithfield.

**Wallenstein, Albrecht von** (1583–1634), German soldier and statesman during the Thirty Years' War. An able administrator of his own estates, he sought the unity of Germany, but was distrusted and eventually assassinated.

**Waller, Edmund** (1606–87), was one of the most graceful of English poets, who tuned his lyre to suit both the Cromwellians when they were a power, and Charles II, when his turn came.

**Wallis, Sir Barnes Neville, Kt. C.B.E., F.R.S.** (b. 1887), British scientist and inventor whose many designs include the R100 airship, the Wellington bomber, the swing-wing aircraft, and the " bouncing bomb " that breached the Ruhr Dams in 1943.

**Walpole Horace, 4th Earl of Orford** (1717–97), younger son of Sir Robert Walpole. He was a member of Parliament from 1741 to 1768, when he retired to his favourite house at Strawberry Hill (" a little Gothic castle ") and devoted himself to the writing of books and the accumulation of works of art. His letters give a graphic picture of Georgian England.

**Walpole, Sir Hugh Seymour, C.B.E.,** (1884–1941), a well-known British novelist, whose novels include *Mr. Perrin and Mr. Traill* (1911), *The Dark Forest* (1916), and *The Herries Chronicle*, a work in four volumes (1939).

**Walpole, Sir Robert, K.G.(1st Earl of Orford)** (1676–1745), great 18th-century Whig statesman. He sat in the House of Commons for over forty years, and was Prime Minister for the record period of twenty-one years. Although he enriched himself at the public expense, he was a great financial statesman, and his management of the national debt, encouragement of trade and industry, and his mercantilist colonial policy made England materially very prosperous.

**Walter, Bruno** (1876–1962), a noted conductor of German birth and American citizenship, associated especially with the opera in many different cities.

**Walter, John** (1776–1847), son of the founder of *The Times* and known as the second John Walter. Was the leading spirit of *The Times* from 1803 to 1847, and it was his efforts that made the journal the greatest newspaper in the world.

**Walton, Izaak** (1593–1683), one of the most lovable of English writers, the famous author of *The Compleat Angler, or the Contemplative Man's Recreation*. Also published lives of Donne, Hooker and George Herbert.

**Walton, Sir William Turner,** O.M. (b. 1902) English composer, whose works include concertos for string instruments, two symphonies, two coronation marches, *Façade* (a setting to music of poems by Edith Sitwell), and an oratorio, *Belshazzar's Feast.*

**Warbeck, Perkin** (1474–99), a Pretender to the English Crown. The son of a Tournai Jew, he claimed to be Richard, Duke of York, supposed to have been murdered in the Tower, and therefore entitled to the throne of England in preference to its then occupant, Henry VII. The Duchess of Burgundy and Charles VIII. of France and James IV. of Scotland gave him their countenance. Warbeck was enabled in 1497 to appear in England at the head of a force of 7,000 men, but was easily defeated, tried for treason and hanged at Tyburn.

**Warwick, Richard Neville, Earl of** (*circa* 1428–71). "The King Maker," was the leader of the York party in the Wars of the Roses. At the battle of Northampton he made Henry VI. captive, and afterwards proclaimed Edward, Earl of March, king under the title of Edward IV. Then, when Edward showed a disposition to resent Warwick's protection, the latter drove Edward from the country and once more placed Henry VI. on the throne.

**Washington, Booker Taliaferro** (1856–1915), a famous Negro educationist who made his way to become principal of Tuskegee Institute, Alabama, which under his direction (1881–1915) became a leading centre for Negro education. He was a tireless worker for a better understanding between black and white Americans. Wrote several books, including his autobiography, *Up from Slavery.*

**Washington, George** (1732–99), was of English descent, and was living on his American estate at Mount Vernon when the dispute between the British home government and the colonists broke out. He became one of the leaders of the local opposition, and later was elected to the first Congress at Philadelphia. The following year, 1775, saw him Commander-in-Chief of the American army, and from that time to the end of the struggle in 1783 he was trusted and adored by the people, and on the founding of the Republic became its first President in 1789. He served a second term of office from 1793 onwards, and refused election for a third time.

**Watson, John Broadus** (1878–1958), American psychologist of international fame who formulated the theory known as Behaviourism, in which behaviour is described in terms of physiological response to stimuli. It substantiates the work of Pavlov. *See* J6.

**Watson-Watt, Sir Robert,** F.R.S. (b. 1892), British physicist and engineer, chief of team of scientists engaged in radio location research which resulted in every aircraft and ship being equipped with radar aids enabling them to detect, locate, and shadow enemy craft with great accuracy during the Second World War. *See* Radar, Section L.

**Watt, James,** F.R.S., F.R.S.E. (1736–1819). Born at Greenock, this genius was originally a mathematical instrument maker, and being brought into touch with mechanical problems, conceived the idea of the modern, that is, high-pressure steam-engine. Watt took out his first patent in 1769; the engine, however, was used only for mining operations until 1785, when it was applied to a cotton factory, Watt being greatly aided in his developments of the engine by the business ability of his partner, Matthew Boulton.

**Watteau, Jean Antoine** (1684–1721), a French landscape painter of transcendent ability, and especially great in *genre*. His shepherds and shepherdesses, rustic dance and fête scenes were wonderful for their harmonious brilliancy of coloration. His *chef-d'œuvre* is the *Embarkation for the Isle of Cytherus,* in the Louvre.

**Watts, George Frederick,** O.M., R.A. (1817–1904), English painter, among whose works may be mentioned *Hope,* which enjoyed great popularity, *Love and Death* and a number of portraits, including Swinburne, Carlyle, Cardinal Manning, Browning, Matthew Arnold, and Tennyson.

**Watts, Isaac** (1674–1748), a great English hymn-writer; author of *O God, our help in ages past.*

**Watts-Dunton, Walter Theordore** (1836–1914), a prominent critic and close friend of Swinburne; author of *The Coming of Love* and *Aylwin.*

**Waugh, Evelyn Arthur St. John** (1903–66), English satirical writer, one of the foremost of his generation; author of *Vile Bodies, The Loved One, Brideshead Revisited, Life of Edmund Champion, The Ordeal of Gilbert Pinfold,* and an autobiography, *A Little Learning. See* M12. His brother, Alec Waugh (b. 1898), also a successful writer, is the author of *The Loom of Youth.*

**Wavell, Field Marshal Earl,** P.C., G.C.B., G.C.S.I., G.C.I.E., C.M.G., M.C. (1883–1950), Viceroy of India 1943–47; Com.-in-Chief India 1941–43; Com.-in-Chief British Forces in Middle East 1939–41; previously Southern Command 1938–39 and of troops in Palestine 1937–39. Described as one of the cleverest generals in the British Army; his strategy against the Italians in the winter campaign of 1940–41 was brilliantly successful.

**Webb, Sir Aston,** G.C.V.O., C.B., R.A. (1849–1930), President of the Royal Academy, 1919–24, one of our foremost architects, and the designer of the general scheme of the Victoria Memorial in front of Buckingham Palace, the new Birmingham University, the Britannia Naval College at Dartmouth and other fine structures.

**Webb, Matthew** (1848–83), in 1875 swam the English Channel in twenty-two hours, and was drowned eight years later in an attempt to swim through the Niagara rapids.

**Webb, Rt. Hon. Sidney James,** O.M. (1859–1947), eminent Socialist, one of the founders of the Fabian Society in 1884. Sec. of State for the Colonies 1929–31, and for the Dominions, 1929–30. Pres. of Board of Trade in first Labour Government, 1924. His wife Beatrice, equally with himself, was a great investigator and writer on political and economic affairs. Among their books were *History of Trade Unionism, English Local Government* and *Soviet Communism.* He founded (1913) and edited (till 1922) the *New Statesman.* Raised to the Peerage, 1929, as Lord Passfield.

**Weber, Carl Maria Friedrich Ernst von** (1786–1826), German composer, who is usually looked upon as the founder of the German national opera and of the German romantic movement, which found its complete musical expression in Wagner. His fame rests principally on his three great operas *Der Freischütz, Euryanthe,* and *Oberon,* the last being written for Covent Garden. He was an able pianist, conductor, and musical director as well as composer. He died in London after the performance of *Oberon,* and his body was taken back to Dresden in 1844.

**Webster, Daniel** (1782–1852), an American, who, as statesman, lawyer, and orator, exerted enormous influence on American constitutional ideas and practice. Served twice as Secretary of State and in 1842 negotiated the Ashburton Treaty which settled the Maine–Canada boundary.

**Webster, Noah** (1758–1843), American lexicographer and grammarian, author of the *Dictionary of the English Language.*

**Wedgwood, Josiah,** F.R.S. (1730–95), was the most famous of English potters. He was born at Burslem, served an apprenticeship, and in 1759 was able to set up in business for himself. He engaged Flaxman to make classical designs for him, and his pottery became the fashion, and led to a great extension of the Staffordshire earthenware industry.

**Weill, Kurt** (1900–50), German composer of satirical, surrealist operas, including *Die Dreigroschenoper* (librettist Bert Brecht), and musical comedies, including *Lady in the Dark,* and *One Touch of Venus.* He left Germany in 1933 for France and went to the United States in 1935. *See* Section E.

**Weingartner, Paul Felix von** (1863–1942), Austrian conductor and composer, studied at Leipzig and with Liszt. Established himself as a brilliant conductor, held several appointments in Germany, succeeded Mahler at the Vienna State Opera, and became head of the Conservatory of Music at Basle. His compositions include six symphonies, several operas, and some chamber music.

**Weismann, August** (1834–1914), a distinguished German biologist who was Prof. of Zoology at

Freiburg, 1866–1912. He is remembered for his theory that heredity is a question of the continuity of the germ-plasm and that acquired characteristics cannot be transmitted to descendants.

**Weizmann, Chaim, D.Sc., LL.D., Ph.D.** (1874–1952), Zionist leader, became provisional President of Israel in May 1948, and was elected first President in 1949. Distinguished microbiologist and organic chemist.

**Wellesley, Richard Colley Wellesley, Marquess, K.G., P.C., K.P.** (1760–1842) was Pitt's famous governor general of India, the son of the Earl of Mornington, the first professor of music at Trinity College, Dublin, and elder brother of the Duke of Wellington.

**Wellington, Arthur Wellesley, 1st Duke of, K.G., P.C., G.C.B.** (1769–1852), was the most famous British general of the 19th century. He distinguished himself in India and conducted successfully the Peninsular War. In 1814 he was British Ambassador at Paris. Then came Napoleon's escape from Elba, the short and sharp campaign which terminated at Waterloo, and the final overthrow of Napoleon. Wellington became the most prominent man in the Empire. From 1828 to 1830 he was Prime Minister. From 1842 to his death he was Commander-in-Chief. His funeral at St. Paul's was one of the great pageants of last century.

**Wells, Herbert George** (1866–1946), English novelist, sociologist and reformer, one of the most creative and influential writers of his time, a man with a passionate faith in progress through science. His long series of books included romances of the Jules Verne variety (*The Time Machine, The Island of Dr. Moreau, The Invisible Man*), sociological autobiography (*Love and Mr. Lewisham, Kipps, Tono-Bungay, The History of Mr. Polly, Mr. Britling Sees it Through*), and popular education (*Outline of History, The Science of Life, The Work, Wealth, and Happiness of Mankind, The Shape of Things to Come, The Fate of Homo Sapiens*). His great attempt at educating the common man proved so successful that his imitators have been legion. He was a founder member of the Fabian Society.

**Wesley, Charles** (1708–88), brother of John Wesley, and the poet of Methodism. Wrote a large number of hymns of enduring merit.

**Wesley, John** (1703–91), the founder of the great religious communion of the people called "Methodists," and the son of a clergyman of the Anglican church. Taking orders himself, in 1735, he went to Georgia as a missioner and allied himself with the Moravians, but later he abandoned all ecclesiastical traditions, and established, on a wonderfully well-devised basis, the connexion called by his name. His own open-air preaching was powerful in the extreme, his energy and depth of purpose inspiring, and his organising ability exceptional. He accomplished a great work of religious revivification, taking the world as his parish; and profound as was his conviction of his high calling as an Evangelist, John Wesley " builded better than he knew " in rearing the denominational edifice which is the monument of his faith and vigour. *See also* Methodism, Section J.

**West, Rebecca, D.B.E. (Mrs. Cicily I. Andrews)** (b. 1892) novelist, critic and journalist. Among her books are *Black Lamb and Grey Falcon* (a travel book and commentary on Yugoslavia, 1942), *The Fountain Overflows*, 1957, and *The Birds Fall Down*, 1967.

**Westermarck, Edward Alexander, Ph.D.** (1862–1939), a distinguished Finnish scientist who was Professor of Sociology at the University of London, 1907–30. Born at Helsingfors, he made an international reputation with the monumental *History of Human Marriage*, written in English and published in 1891. His many other works include *Origin and Development of the Moral Ideas*, 1906–8, *A Short History of Marriage*, 1926, and *The Oedipus Complex*.

**Westinghouse, George** (1846–1914), American engineer who built the dynamos for Niagara Falls, and in 1865 invented the compressed air brake known by his name and developed a compressed air system of railway signalling.

**Westmacott, Sir Richard, R.A.** (1775–1856), a great English sculptor who studied under Canova at Rome, and succeeded Flaxman as Professor at the Royal Academy. He executed many fine monuments in Westminster Abbey, at St. Paul's Cathedral, and elsewhere, including the statue of Achilles in Hyde Park and the pediment of the British Museum.

**Wharton, Edith (Jones)** (1862–1937), American novelist whose *House of Mirth* (1905) brought her fame as a social satirist. Her work was greatly influenced by her friend Henry James, and most of her fifty-four volumes were written after she was thirty-five.

**Whately, Archbishop Richard** (1787–1863), was for over thirty years Archbishop of Dublin, and achieved a high reputation as a writer on theology and philosophy. His treatises on *Rhetoric* and *Logic* are among the most notable books of their class.

**Wheatstone, Sir Charles, F.R.S.** (1802–75), was an eminent English electrician and scientist, whose experiments in association with Mr. W. F. Cooke resulted in the first application in this country of the principle of the electric telegraph. The stereoscope was also one of his inventions. He was Professor of Natural Philosophy to King's College, London, for many years.

**Wheeler, Sir Charles, K.C.V.O., C.B.E., P.R.A., F.R.B.S.** (b. 1892), British sculptor; P.R.A., 1956–66.

**Whistler, James Abbott McNeill** (1834–1903), was an original artist, writer, and wit, who first came to Europe from America in 1857, and made a name as an etcher both in Paris and in London. His studies of Thames scenery are especially fine. When he began to exhibit pictures in oils he greatly puzzled the critics, some of whom discovered in his " nocturnes " and other studies an impressionist of surpassing genius, while others, including Mr. Ruskin, who described one of the " nocturnes " at the Grosvenor Gallery as a " pot of paint flung in the public face," looked upon them as mere audacious eccentricities. The finest of his oil paintings are the portrait of his mother, and that of Carlyle. He brought an action against Ruskin for the criticism referred to, but only obtained a verdict of one farthing damages without costs.

**White, Field-Marshal Sir George Stuart, V.C., G.C.B., O.M., G.C.M.G., G.C.I.E., G.C.V.O.** (1835–1912), the heroic defender of Ladysmith in the South African War and a soldier who achieved renown at many points of a long military career.

**Whitefield, George** (1714–70), was for a time associated with John Wesley at Oxford in the propagation of Methodism and attracted great attention by his gifts as a preacher. He was Wesley's most powerful champion; but in 1741, differing from Wesley on a point of doctrine he left the Methodists, and thenceforward simply preached as an evangelist, allying himself with no sect, but expounding Calvinistic doctrines with fervour and eloquence.

**Whitgift, John** (1530–1604), a gifted Anglican prelate. Persecuted the Puritans, and was one of the authors of the famous *Lambeth Articles*. Was Archbishop of Canterbury 1583–1604.

**Whitman, Walt** (1819–92) was an original figure in the world of American authorship, and produced many works of striking poetic merit. He served in the Civil War, and his vigorous humanity, as expressed in his writings, made him a distinguished personality. His works include *Leaves of Grass, Drum Taps*, and *Democratic Views*.

**Whittier, John Greenleaf** (1807–92), America's Quaker poet, was the son of a New England farmer, and for a time followed the trade of a shoemaker. After some experience in journalism, he published his first book of poems, *Legends of New England* (1831). His best-known volumes are: *Lays of My Home* (1843), *Voices of Freedom* (1846), *Songs of Labour* (1850), and *National Lyrics* (1865).

**Whittington, Richard** (c. 1358–1423), the son of a Gloucestershire knight, Richard became a wealthy London mercer and was three times mayor of London, 1397–98, 1406–7, 1419–20. His wealth enabled him to supply large loans to Henry IV and Henry V. He was well styled " the model merchant of the Middle Ages ". His fortune he bequeathed to charitable institutions. The famous legend about him lacks historical evidence, the " cat " story being a familiar theme in the folklore of almost all the nations of Europe.

**Whittle**, Air Commodore Sir Frank, K.B.E., C.B. (b. 1907), pioneer in the field of jet propulsion. The first flights of Gloster jet-propelled aeroplanes with Whittle engine took place in May 1941.

**Whymper, Edward**, F.R.S.E. (1840–1911), a wood-engraver and artist; also one of the best-known Alpine climbers, and the first to reach the summit of the Matterhorn. Author of books on mountaineering in various countries.

**Wiggin, Kate Douglas (Mrs. George C. Riggs)** (1856–1923), an American novelist of quaint charm and humour. Author of *Rebecca of Sunnybrook Farm*.

**Wilberforce, William** (1759–1833), was the son of a Hull merchant. He was educated at Cambridge, and entered Parliament in 1780. In 1789 made the first of his many proposals in the House of Commons for the abolition of the slave trade, but it was not until 1807 that the Act embodying these proposals was carried.

**Wilcox, Mrs. Ella Wheeler**, a popular American poetess (1855–1919). Writer of sentimental verse.

**Wilde, Oscar Fingall O'Flahertie Wills** (1854–1900), Irish author and dramatist, son of Sir William Wilde, a Dublin surgeon; leader of the cult art for art's sake. His works include poems, fairy-tales, short stories, and brilliantly witty comedies, *Lady Windermere's Fan*, *A Woman of No Importance*, *The Ideal Husband* and *The Importance of Being Earnest*. In 1895 he brought an action for libel against the Marquess of Queensberry, the father of his friend, Lord Alfred Douglas, but he himself was convicted of homosexual practices and sentenced to prison for two years where he wrote his famous poem, *The Ballad of Reading Gaol*.

**Wilder, Thornton Niven** (b. 1897), American author and playwright. Among his books are *The Bridge of San Luis Rey* and the *Ides of March*.

**Wilkes, John** (1727–97), a forceful and daring Whig politician who championed the cause of the people with great vigour. For a violent attack on George III's Government in his paper *The North Briton*, he was committed to the Tower, but obtained release on the ground that he was a member of Parliament. He was later expelled from the House and fled to France. He returned in 1768 and was repeatedly elected M.P. for Middlesex and as often denied his seat. A great agitation ensued, and so high was he in favour among the people, that he was made alderman, then sheriff, then Lord Mayor of London. In the end his opponents gave way, the orders against him were withdrawn, and from 1779 he was Chamberlain of the City of London.

**Willcocks, Sir William**, K.C.M.G. (1852–1932), a British engineer, born in India, who in 1898 planned the great Aswan Dam, which he completed in 1902. In 1911 he undertook for Turkey a vast scheme for irrigating some 31 million acres in Mesopotamia.

**Willett, William** (1856–1915), an English builder, noted for his long and tireless advocacy of the Daylight Saving scheme, which, however, he did not live to see put into effect. It was adopted as a war-time measure in the year following his death. (*See* Summer Time, Section L).

**William I.** (1027–87), the "Conqueror," Duke of Normandy, claimed the English throne as legally appointed successor to Edward the Confessor and, at the Battle of Hastings in 1066, defeated Harold II. who was killed. The new king crushed Saxon resistance in the North and West, transferred most of the land to his Norman followers, and drew England into closer relations with the Continent. Maintaining many old institutions such as the shire-court and the fyrd (a non-feudal army), William governed firmly, and was supported by the Church, especially by Lanfranc, Abp. of Canterbury. In 1085 he ordered the Domesday Survey (*q.v.*).

**William I. of Prussia** (1797–1888), the maker of modern Germany, succeeded to the throne of Prussia in 1861. It fell to him to have the control of his country during a period of mighty transition and development, with Bis-

marck as his chief minister. The war with Austria rendered him highly popular, and when in 1870 the war with France was entered upon the whole German people rallied round him, and after a series of brilliant achievements by his army he was proclaimed German Emperor on the 18th of January, 1871.

**William II.** (1056–1100), the Conqueror's son, surnamed "Rufus," King of England from 1087 to his death. Was in constant conflict with his barons, lived a life of wanton pleasure, was oppressive to his subjects, and was shot (by accident or design) while hunting in the New Forest.

**William II., the Kaiser** (1859–1941), King of Prussia and German Emperor 1888 until he abdicated Nov. 9, 1918, and fled to Holland, where he was subsequently interned in the castle of Doorn, living there in complete retirement until his death in June, 1941. Educated at Cassel and Bonn, afterwards entered the army and took a keen interest in military affairs. Succeeded his father, the Emperor Frederick, in 1888. His reign was marked by a strong militarism and an intense ambition to secure the dominance of Germany in the Councils of Europe —an ambition which contributed to the outbreak of the first great war in 1914.

**William III** (1650–1702), King of England, Scotland, and Ireland (1689–1702), son of William II of Orange (1626–50) and Mary (1631–60), daughter of Charles I. He married Mary, eldest daughter of the Duke of York (later James II) while Stadtholder of Holland. As captain-general of the Dutch forces he was successful against the French, and in 1688, when James had abdicated and fled the country, William was invited to succeed him and he and Mary afterwards became joint King and Queen. Later he was at war with France, and suffered defeats, but ultimately effected an honourable peace by the Treaty of Ryswick in 1697.

**William IV of England** (1765–1837) was the third son of George III., and ascended the throne in 1830 in succession to his brother, George IV. He had seen some sea service, and was flatteringly styled the "Sailor King." He was genial and pleasure-loving, but placed no obstacles in the way of government. In the early part of his reign (1832) the first great Reform Bill was passed.

**William the Silent** (1533–84), Prince of Orange, made many attempts to secure a peaceful settlement of Netherlands' disputes with Philip II, but became the leader of the ensuing Revolt and was assassinated. He established the independence and Protestant character of the Northern Netherlands, where literary, artistic, colonising, and commercial activity flourished in the following century.

**Williams, Sir George** (1821–1905), the founder of The Young Men's Christian Association.

**Williams, (George) Emlyn** (b. 1905), Welsh actor-playwright, and producer, who has had great success in numerous plays and films, and latterly in his readings from Dickens and Dylan Thomas. Author of *Night Must Fall*, *The Corn is Green*, and *The Light of Heart*.

**Wilson, Rt. Hon. (James) Harold**, O.B.E., M.P., M.A. (b. 1916), British statesman and economist; Prime Minister 1964–; elected Leader of the Labour Party after the death of Gaitskell in 1963; Labour M.P. for Ormskirk, 1945–50; for Huyton, 1950–; Pres. of the Board of Trade, 1947–51; Chair. Public Accounts Committee, 1959–63. Chancellor, Univ. of Bradford. *See also* Section C, Part II.

**Wilson, Richard**, R.A. (1714–82), a landscape and portrait painter.

**Wilson, (Thomas) Woodrow** (1856–1924), President of the United States 1913–21. Was Governor of New Jersey, 1912–13. In 1916 secured from the Kaiser a promise to abandon the more inhuman forms of submarine warfare, and, on their resumption in 1917, broke off official relations with Germany and proclaimed a state of war. Entered into the conflict with the utmost vigour, bringing the full military and financial resources of the Republic into play against Germany. Was a great factor in the winning of victory and in the concluding of a just peace. Largely responsible for the setting up of the League of Nations, which was foreshadowed in his famous Fourteen Points.

**Wingate, Major-Gen. Orde Charles**, D.S.O. (1903–44), the leader of the Chindit forces engaged behind the Japanese lines in Burma during the second world war. Killed in an air crash.

**Winifred, St.**, patron saint of virgins, a Welsh maiden, who was beheaded by Prince Caradoc for treating him with scorn.

**Wiseman, Nicholas Patrick Stephen, Cardinal** (1802–65), the first R.C. Archbishop of Westminster, created Cardinal. Much of his life was spent in the reorganisation and development of the Roman Catholic Church in Great Britain. He was one of the three great R.C. prelates of the nineteenth century, the other two being Manning and Newman.

**Wodehouse, Pelham Grenville** (b. 1881), English humorist, creator of the inimitable Jeeves in the Bertie Wooster stories. American citizen (1955).

**Wolf, Friedrich August** (1759–1824), a great German scholar, regarded by some as the founder of scientific classical philology.

**Wolf, Hugo** (1860–1903), Austrian song-writer. In his settings of over 300 German lyrics, including many of Mörike and Goethe, he achieved complete union of poetry and music.

**Wolfe, General James** (1727–59), commanded the British forces in Canada at the siege of Quebec, where he won a brilliant victory, which cost him his own life.

**Wolsey, Cardinal Thomas** (c. 1473–1530), was the son of an Ipswich butcher. Showing ability, he was sent to Oxford to be educated, later on entering the Church, where he gradually rose to a position of eminence, and was entrusted with several diplomatic missions. He was especially favoured by the King, Henry VIII., and secured rapid preferment under that monarch, being in turn Bishop of Lincoln, and Archbishop of York. He was subsequently made Cardinal and became Henry's Chancellor. For a number of years he was supreme, and by his diplomacy did much to strengthen the kingly power. But when Wolsey was unable, though willing enough, to obtain the papal sanction for Henry's divorce of Catherine, he fell into disfavour, and his decline was rapid indeed. From being a great personage, with a princely entourage, he was humbled, persecuted, and harried, and died at Leicester Abbey a broken, dejected man.

**Wood, Sir Henry Joseph, C.H.** (1869–1944), the most popular English musical conductor of his day. He introduced many works and composers previously unknown to the British public and greatly stimulated and encouraged interest in classical music. His long association with the Promenade Concerts began in 1895 at the Queen's Hall, and after it was destroyed in an air raid in 1941 the concerts continued at the Albert Hall and are now named after him. He composed songs and cantatas, and his arrangement of sea shanties ends every series of Promenade Concerts.

**Woodcock, George, Rt. Hon.** (b. 1904), Trade Union leader who was general secretary of the T.U.C. from 1960 to 1969 when he was appointed Chairman of the Commission on Industrial Relations set up by the Government to supervise the reform of industrial relations.

**Woodville, Elizabeth** (1437–91), wife of Sir John Grey. After her first husband's death she made a secret marriage with Edward IV., and became the mother of Edward V., and his brother Prince, both of whom were put to death in the Tower by order of Richard III. She was also mother to Elizabeth, Queen of Henry VII.

**Woolf, Mrs. (Adeline) Virginia** (1882–1941), English novelist and essayist, daughter of Sir Leslie Stephen and wife of Leonard Woolf, writer and publisher. Together they formed the Hogarth Press. Among her best known works are *To the Lighthouse, Mrs. Dalloway, The Waves, The Years, A Room of One's Own, Orlando.* *See also* M4(1).

**Woolley, Richard van der Riet, Sc.D., F.R.S.** (b. 1906), succeeded Sir Harold Spencer Jones as Astronomer Royal at the Royal Greenwich Observatory in 1956; formerly Commonwealth Astronomer at the Observatory at Canberra.

**Wootton, Barbara Frances, Baroness, M.A., L.H.D., J.P.** (b. 1897), Prof. of Social Studies, Univ. of London, 1948–52. Chair. Metropolitan Juvenile Courts. Her book *Social Science and Social Pathology* (1959) examines the state of our knowledge about social pathology, with particular emphasis on criminology and social work. Her *Autobiography* was published in 1967. Created a life peeress in 1958.

**Wordsworth, William** (1770–1850), the chief of the " Lake Poets," and one of the most inspired of all British bards, was a native of Cockermouth, and was educated at Hawkshead and St. John's College, Cambridge. In association with Coleridge he issued a volume of *Lyrical Ballads* in 1793. The following year saw him settled at Grasmere, and there and at Rydal Mount he passed the rest of his days. In 1802 he married Mary Hutchinson, his cousin, and the two, with the poet's sister Dorothy, formed an ideally poetic household. Here he carried out his creed of " plain living and high thinking," and produced at intervals some of the purest and noblest poetry in the language. As an interpreter of Nature in her many moods he stands unrivalled. Succeeded to the Poet Laureateship on the death of Southey in 1843.

**Wren, Sir Christopher, F.R.S.** (1632–1723), the most famous English architect of his time. He did not quite have all his own way with the tremendous thirty-five years' task he accepted in undertaking the reconstruction of St. Paul's after the Fire, but he produced a masterpiece of which Britain may well be proud. Chelsea and Greenwich Hospitals, and a number of London's finest churches were also his work.

**Wright, Sir Almroth (Edward), K.C.B., C.B., M.D., F.R.S.** (1861–1947), discovered the system of anti-typhoid inoculation, the method of therapeutic inoculation for bacterial infections (vaccinotherapy), and methods of measuring the protective substances in human blood.

**Wright, Frank Lloyd** (1869–1959), American architect who, with others, brought into fashion the present-day horizontal strip and all-glass design. His imaginative ideas, both as to structure and look, have influenced architecture all over the world. Early buildings were the Larkin office building, Buffalo, N.Y., and the Imperial Hotel, Tokio, which withstood the 1923 earthquake. His last building was the Guggenheim Museum in New York, based on a spiral.

**Wright, Orville** (1871–1948), American airman who, with his brother Wilbur (1867–1912), began gliding experiments on the sand dunes at Kitty Hawk, North Carolina. To the glider they built they added a petrol engine, and on 17th Dec., 1903, they made four flights, the longest being 852 ft. These flights were the first in which a man had been carried from the ground in sustained, controlled flight in a powered heavier-than-air machine.

**Wyatt, James, R.A.** (1746–1813), a celebrated architect in his day. He built Fonthill Abbey for Beckford and the Royal Military Academy at Woolwich. Pres. of R.A. 1805–6.

**Wyatt, Sir Thomas** (1503–42), was the first writer of English sonnets, and a poet who did much to develop the earlier forms of verse.

**Wyatt, Sir Thomas (" The Younger ")** (c. 1520–54); joined with the Duke of Suffolk in favour of Lady Jane Grey and against Queen Mary, son of the last-mentioned. Led the men of Kent in rebellion on London in 1554, but was captured and executed.

**Wycherley, William** (1640–1715), English Restoration dramatist, a master of satiric comedy. His plays include *Love in a Wood*, which won him the favour of the Duchess of Cleveland, mistress of Charles II, *The Plain Dealer*, and his masterpiece *The Country Wife*. His marriage to the Countess of Drogheda lost him court favour.

**Wyclif, John** (c. 1324–84), born in Yorkshire, educated at Oxford, and one of the most eminent ecclesiastics of his time. He adopted principles many of which became general at the Reformation, and brought down upon himself the bitter enmity of the Roman Catholic leaders, and would probably have been put to death but for the protection of John of Gaunt. While in comparative retirement as Rector of Lutterworth, in Leicestershire, he finished his translation of the Bible.

**Wykeham, William of** (1324–1404), was Bishop of Winchester from 1366 to his death, and from 1367 to 1371 Lord Chancellor. He was a man of great learning and an excellent preacher, and wielded great influence. He founded New

College, Oxford, in 1379 and Winchester College in 1382.

Wyllie, William Lionel, R.A. (1851–1931), English marine painter whose *The Thames Below London Bridge* was bought by the Chantrey Bequest.

Wyspianski, Stanislav (1869–1907), great Polish poet, dramatist and painter.

# X

Xavier, St. Francis (1506–1552), the apostle of the Indies, was the follower of Ignatius de Loyola, and devoted his life to missionary work in the East. He was canonised in 1622.

Xenophon (444–359 B.C.), the Athenian general and historian of Socrates. His chief works are *Anabasis Hellenica*, and *Cyropædia*.

Xerxes (*circa* 519–465 B.C.), King of Persia, was the son of the first Darius and a great commander. In 481 B.C. he started on his famous expedition against Greece when, according to Herodotus, he had a combined army and navy of over two and a half million men. He defeated the Spartans at Thermopylæ, but his fleet was overcome at Salamis. He reigned from 485 to 465 B.C. and met his death by assassination.

Ximenes de Cismeros, Francisco (1436–1517), Spanish statesman and Cardinal who reformed the Franciscan Order to a great extent, and in 1502 began to direct the preparation of a polyglot bible, the *Complutensian*, which greatly influenced subsequent versions. In 1506 was made Regent for Queen Juana, and raised to the cardinalate in 1507. Personally conducted a military campaign in Africa in 1509, and afterwards became Inquisitor-General, and in 1516, Regent of Castile, but in the following year was dismissed by the Emperor Charles V.

# Y

Yeats, William Butler (1865–1939), Irish lyric poet and dramatist and major figure in the Irish literary revival of the 20th century. With Lady Gregory and others founded the Abbey Theatre in Dublin, for which he wrote many plays. Interested in mysticism and the occult. Member of the Irish Senate, 1922–28; awarded Nobel Prize in Literature in 1923. Some of his best work was written in his later years in *The Tower* (1928) and *Last Poems* (1940). Plays include *Cathleen Ni Houlihan* (1902), *The Hour Glass* (1904), *Deirdre* (1907). *See Section M.*

Yonge, Charlotte Mary (1823–1901), author of over 120 novels, school books, and other works, including *The Heir of Redclyffe*, *The Daisy Chain*, *The Dove in the Eagle's Nest*, and *The History of Christian Names*.

Young, Brigham (1801–77), Mormon leader, and head of the Latter Day Saints of Salt Lake City. At his death he had seventeen wives.

Young, Francis Brett (1884–1954), British novelist. His books include *My Brother Jonathan* and *Doctor Bradley Remembers*.

Young, James, F.R.S. (1811–83), a Glasgow chemist who discovered the method of distilling oil from shale, and founded the mineral oil industry of Scotland, which led to the development of petroleum concerns.

Young, Thomas (1773–1829), one of the most versatile geniuses in history, descended from a Quaker family of Somerset. Studied languages, medicine, and held the Professorship of Physics at the Royal Institution. In 1804 elected Foreign Secretary of the Royal Society. He was very successful in deciphering Egyptian hieroglyphics and was the first to translate the inscription on the Rosetta Stone. Famous for his share in establishing the undulatory theory of light and for his work on physiological optics.

Younghusband, Lt.-Col. Sir Francis Edward, K.C.S.I., K.C.I.E. (1863–1942), soldier, explorer and writer. Wrote many works on the East. Headed the British Mission to Tibet, 1903–04. Was *Times* correspondent with the Chitral expedition. Pres. of Royal Geographical Soc., 1919–22.

Ypres, 1st Earl of, P.C., K.P., G.C.B., O.M., G.C.V.O., K.C.M.G. (1852–1925), entered Navy in 1866, afterwards passing into Army in 1874, making his mark as a Cavalry officer in the

Egyptian campaign of 1884; served in South African War with brilliant success. C.-in-C. British Forces in France, 1914–15; C.-in-C. Home Forces, 1915–18; Lord Lieut. of Ireland, 1918–21.

Ysaÿe, Eugène (1858–1929), Belgian violinist and conductor, noted chiefly for his playing of the works of Bach and César Franck.

Yukawa, Hideki (b. 1907), Japanese physicist, who received the 1949 Nobel Prize for predicting the existence of the meson.

# Z

Zadkiel (the angel of Jupiter in Jewish rabbinical lore) was the name assumed by Lilly (1602–81) the astrologer, and also by Richard James Morrison (1794–1874), Hebrew scholar and amateur astronomer, in the almanack known as Zadkiel's Almanack and first issued in 1831.

Zadkine, Ossip (b. 1890), French sculptor, one of the greatest of our time, whose works include *Orpheus*, *The Return of the Prodigal Son*, *The Birth of Forms*, *Poet*, *Harlequin*. Exhibition at Tate Gallery, 1961.

Zaharoff, Sir Basil, G.C.B., G.B.E. (1849–1936), was an influential Greek banker and financier who became an armaments magnate, supplying the Allies in the first world war.

Zamenhof, Ludwig Lazarus (1859–1917), Polish linguist who was by profession an oculist, but gained fame as the inventor of Esperanto.

Zeno of Citium (*c.* 340–264 B.C.) was a Greek philosopher who founded the Stoic system.

Zeppelin, Ferdinand, Count von (1838–1917), inventor of the huge dirigible airship bearing his name. His first ascent was in 1900. He organised a Zeppelin service for the German army in the war of 1914–18, but their extreme vulnerability militated severely against their usefulness.

Zeromski, Stefan (1864–1925), great Polish novelist, poet and playwright.

Zhukov, Marshal of the Soviet Union Grigory Konstantinovich (b. 1895), led the defence of Moscow and Leningrad during second world war; served on Allied Control Commission in Germany; C.-in-C. Land Forces and Deputy Minister of Armed Forces of Soviet Union, 1946–55; succeeded Marshal Bulganin as Defence Minister, 1955–57.

Zhukovsky, Vasily Andreyevich (1783–1852), Russian poet whose original work had very important influence on Russian literature.

Zola, Emile Edouard Charles Antoine (1840–1902), was the son of an Italian engineer, and came before the public as a novelist in 1867 with *Thérèse Raquin*. He then conceived the idea of a series of novels which should depict the history of a Second Empire family in various realistic phases, and began the series with *La Fortune des Rougons*, in 1871. In 1877 he made a higher success by *L'Assommoir*. From that time every novel he published had an immense sale.

Zorn, Anders Leonhard (1860–1920), was a noted Swedish painter, etcher and sculptor.

Zoroaster, the Greek form of the name of the Persian prophet, Zarathustra, who lived about the seventh century B.C. He was a monotheist, believing in a good and holy God whom he called Ahura Mazda. Many of his teachings were absorbed by the ancient Persian religion which survives today among the Parsees in India.

Zoshchenko, Mikhail (1895–1958), Russian writer whose humorous short stories, satirising the Soviet way of life, were wildly popular throughout Russia in the 1920s. Several have been translated and published in England.

Zosimus (fl. c. A.D. 300), the first known alchemist. He lived in Alexandria.

Zuccarelli, Francesco (1702–88), a very celebrated Italian artist, who came to England, succeeded, made a handsome fortune, and was one of the first members of the Royal Academy.

Zuckermann, Sir Solly, O.M., C.B., M.A., M.D., D.Sc., F.R.S. (b. 1904), British biologist; Prof. of Anatomy, Birmingham Univ., 1939–; chief scientific adviser to the Government and head of the Government's scientific service.

Zwingli, Ulrich (1484–1531), was one of the ablest of the Swiss Reformation leaders.

Zwirner, Ernst Friedrich (1802–61), an eminent Silesian architect. Restored Cologne Cathedral.

# BACKGROUND TO PUBLIC AFFAIRS

This section is in two parts. The first is a narrative of political events in Britain since the war and of some significant events around the world. The second part explains the structure of our own political institutions and the main international ones.

# TABLE OF CONTENTS

# BACKGROUND TO PUBLIC AFFAIRS

This section is in two parts. The first describes some major events since the war and carries the story to 1969. The second part describes our own political institutions, the Commonwealth, the United Nations, Western and other International Organisations.

## I. NARRATIVE OF POLITICAL EVENTS

### 1. BRITAIN: POLITICAL BACKGROUND.

**The End of Another War.**—The way the British people greeted the end of the Second World War was markedly different from their feelings in 1918. The First World War had ended almost as suddenly as it had begun; and there was then an explosion of relief and rejoicing of a kind which has not been seen since. After all, that was a "war to end war." It could never happen again. England was to be a land "fit for heroes to live in." The outbreak of the war in 1914 had been a sudden shock to a world confident of peaceful evolution. The British people, having seen it through, were again confident that nothing like it could recur. The instant reaction when the end came was therefore one of delirious relief. The mood at the end of the last war, however, was very different. That war came gradually but relentlessly all through the 'thirties and it ended gradually too. We were in a sense at war long before it formally started; and at the end there was no clear emergence into a cloudless era of assured peace and progress. To maintain peace a continuous effort was seen to be necessary. Ideas had played a much greater part in sustaining men and women in the second great war than in the first; their sense of responsibility had grown so that the mood when the end came on 8 May 1945 was more questioning and cautious than in November 1918. Further, the second great war had touched everyone more directly—the bombing of cities, the imminence of invasion, the food shortages, the evacuation of school children, all this had spread the impact; and, when it was over, the mood was one of sober resolve.

**The Age of Bewilderment.**—Before we continue our narrative let us take a backward glance at the years between the wars, not to describe the events, which included the emergence of authoritarian tyrannies and a world-wide economic crisis, but to mark some of the moral characteristics. It was said to be a period of disillusionment, of moral and intellectual decay. There was the loss of faith in democracy; a sense of aimlessness reflected in the arts, a good deal of confusion and uncertainty about values, and, above all, insecurity. That there was this political apathy and bewilderment is true; but much to the contrary is true also. This was, after all, the nation which had won the war and, by resolution and will, was to win the next. The nation faces difficulties again. We shall see later that these difficulties seem hard to diagnose but we shall try to disentangle in this story the elements in what has been called our social malaise.

**The First Atomic Explosion.**—Momentous events were to come. The war with Japan was not yet over. Although the secret was kept at the time, the first full-scale atomic bomb explosion was made in the Mexican desert in July 1945 through the concerted efforts of a team of scientists working in America. The bomb was detonated at the top of a pylon 100 feet high and a space of ten miles cleared. Devastation inside a one-mile circle was absolute. It offered a means to a speedy end of the war with Japan. It has proved to be the first of a series of tests of increasingly powerful bombs which pose the greatest threat which has ever faced mankind and may yet destroy civilisation. A few days later the United States and Great Britain called for unconditional surrender by Japan and upon its rejection a bomb was dropped on August 6 on Hiroshima and a second on Nagasaki on August 9. The surrender terms were then accepted. Churchill in his account of the war describes his own view that there should have been no rigid insistence on "unconditional surrender." "It would be a mistake", he writes, "to suppose that the fate of Japan was settled by the atomic bomb. Her defeat was certain before the first bomb fell."

**The Face of the Post-war World.**—Far-reaching changes mark the decade which ended with the Suez affair of 1956. Asian countries, driving towards independence, reached their objectives, and a similar drive in African countries was gathering momentum. The war had impoverished Britain and France, which could no longer be powers great enough to follow an independent course; and they both played rôles, although different ones, in launching Western Europe towards unity. The victors of the war quarrelled and this vitiated the working of the United Nations, which had been founded on the hope that the victors would not quarrel—not, at any rate, so profoundly that we should no longer have a state of peace but a condition given the frank but dispiriting title of "the cold war." The direct confrontation of the two great Power blocs—the United States and the Soviet Union—was therefore a cardinal feature of the decade, with the development of atomic weapons. The competition in armaments was matched by another competition in economic power. Both sides made a bid for the support of the new Afro-Asian countries; and it was seen that what attracted those countries was naturally the technical means to satisfy hunger and to secure clothing, shelter, and the materials with which to live. Russia, therefore, turned increasingly to the training of scientists and technologists in the drive towards industrialisation and economic growth, likely to comfort the peasantries of the new continents.

**Estrangement between West and East.**—The war had engendered friendship between Western Powers and Russia. Why did they so quickly fall apart with the defeat of the enemy—a fact which was to transform the history of the world? The fact was that relations were reverting to their pre-war state of hostility. Nazi Germany had divided the West from Russia; Russia had been suspicious of our appeasement of Germany which might liberate her for attack eastwards. And when, eventually, Russia and Germany signed a non-aggression pact in 1939, which freed Germany to turn west instead of east and to attack us, our hostility towards Russia naturally deepened. Popular feeling changed when Hitler invaded Russia in 1941 but co-operation between Western and Soviet leaders was not so close as to prevent ill-feeling—one cause of mistrust being the Russian belief that our invasion of Europe was being unjustifiably delayed. When the war ended there was still an abundance of goodwill towards Russia. But a number of political facts worked the other way. The Russians had taken a hold over a number of countries in the eastern half of Europe; and this led to the establishment in those countries of communist régimes. Were the ideas of

Russia necessarily antagonistic to the West? They were certainly incompatible. In Stalin's view, especially after his experience of Germany's invasion, there could not but be hostility from the West. This sense of suspicious defensiveness made Soviet foreign policy complex and enigmatic. Whatever the reason might be, Russia's policy followed a course which could not be easily understood; and the goodwill towards her was allowed to evaporate.

**The Bomb.**—In the first years of the decade the Red Army was supreme on the ground in Europe and Asia and the U.S. Air Force supreme in the air. It was the Red Army versus the atomic bomb. But in September 1949 the Soviets exploded an atomic bomb and the four years of American monopoly was over. The race for bigger bombs intensified. The United States exploded a hydrogen bomb in November 1952 and Russia followed in August 1953. The new weapon was different not only in degree but in kind. The killing effects were incalculable; and the after-effects on future generations unpredictable. Eisenhower said there was no alternative to peace; but no solution was reached on practical issues—on the two Germanys, on the status of the satellite countries in Eastern Europe, on the future of the Middle East. The post-war world disintegrated. Neutralism was seen as the only hope of survival by those countries where pent-up forces of nationalism were being released.

**The Technological Race.**—The race between Russia and the West was not a new one; Professor Toynbee has pointed out that it began in 1700 when Peter the Great created a strong country against invaders who had deprived her earlier of so much. Russia, defeated in the first great war, made a new start in 1917 when she threw communism (a creed borrowed from the West) into the scale. She drew ahead and after a long and bitter struggle beat the Germans in 1945 as Peter the Great had driven Russia ahead, eventually beating the French in 1812. With the American success with the atomic bomb Russia fell behind again; but she resumed the race with the West and was first with an earth satellite (1957) and a manned satellite (1961). In their technological breakthrough in 1957 the Russians developed the first inter-continental ballistic missile. The see-saw continued and, in 1961, the Americans perfected the cheap, quickfiring ICBM, the Minute-man.

**The Creation of the " Satellite " States.**—The satellite states, as they are known, were set up by Russia in the countries of Eastern Europe which had been occupied by Russia in the final stages of the war. This occupation had been made militarily easier when the Americans, in August 1944, had withdrawn 100,000 men from the Italian campaign for a seemingly needless invasion of the south of France. The states were Czechoslovakia, Poland, Roumania, Albania, Hungary, Bulgaria, and Yugoslavia—all, except Hungary, inhabited by peoples mainly of Slav race. Yugoslavia, however, eventually broke away under its national leader, Marshal Tito, though the country remained communist. At the Yalta conference of February 1945 attended by Roosevelt, Churchill, and Stalin, Russia had agreed that democratic governments should be set up in Eastern Europe. But the transformation of the countries to Communist régimes began very shortly afterwards and by 1948 was complete.

**The Cold War and the West.**—The failure of the nations to make treaties of peace or arrangements for general disarmament, and the continuing loss of confidence between Russia and the West led to an increase of armaments and defensive pacts by both sides. In the West rearmament was carried out by the U.S.A. and Western Europe on the lines of an agreement made in 1949 and known as the North Atlantic Pact. They formed the North Atlantic Treaty Organisation (NATO), the first supreme commander being Eisenhower who afterwards became, for two

terms, President of the United States (being succeeded by Kennedy in 1961). The Russians, on their side, organised the Communist countries by a " Warsaw Pact." It is refreshing to note that Austria, by agreement in 1956, established a democratic republic, to be permanently neutral like Switzerland. In Asia a number of countries which met at Bandung in Indonesia in 1955 with some African countries decided to keep neutral. Four Asian countries, however (Turkey, Iraq, Iran and Pakistan), neighbours of Russia, formed a defensive pact with Britain—the Baghdad Pact (later to become the Central Treaty Organisation or CENTO). Some countries bordering the East and South Pacific, including Australia and New Zealand, formed the South East Asia Treaty Organisation or SEATO for mutual defence against the Communists.

**The General Election of 1945.**—This election was quiet, conducted on an out-of-date register but with a postal vote for the Forces. A lively issue had been introduced by Churchill, who declared that if the Labour Party won the election Attlee, as Prime Minister, would be under the control of Harold Laski who was then chairman of the national executive of the Labour Party. This declaration stemmed from a statement which had been made by Laski that the Labour Party would not be bound by any commitments entered into by Attlee when, as leader of the Labour Party, he accompanied Churchill to the Potsdam conference with Stalin and Truman in June. A correspondence of increasing bitterness followed between Churchill and Attlee who asserted " The Chairman has not the power to give me instructions." Attlee seemed on surer ground in the interpretation of the constitution of his own party. The popular impression was that the matter was an election scare devised by Churchill's campaign advisers. The Labour Party had a dramatic victory, 393 Labour M.P.s being returned, with a clear majority over all other parties. They did not have a clear majority among the voters, the Liberals holding a balance. But the bias present in the constituency system worked in favour of the Labour Party.

**The Resignation of Churchill.**—Ordinarily Churchill might have been expected to take a few days to wind up the affairs of the Government. This would have enabled him to present the unconditional surrender of Japan to the nation. But two factors led him to resign at once and advise the King to send for Mr. Attlee. These factors were the need for Britain to be represented with proper authority at the Potsdam conference where great issues were coming to a head; and the overwhelming nature of the verdict of the electors. He thanked the nation that day for the " unflinching, unswerving support " which they had given him in his task in the war and " for the many expressions of kindness which they have shown towards their servant."

**Churchill's Premonition.**—There is a moving story in the last volume of Churchill's work *The Second World War* of his sudden premonition of electoral defeat. On 25 July 1945 he flew home from Potsdam and went to bed, accepting the view of the Conservative Party managers that the British people would wish him to continue his work and that it would be possible to reconstitute the National Coalition Government in the proportions of the new House of Commons. On that belief he slumbered. " However, just before dawn," he writes, " I woke suddenly with a sharp stab of almost physical pain. A hitherto subconscious conviction that we were beaten broke forth and dominated my mind. . . . The power to shape the future would be denied me. . . . I was discontented at the prospect, and turned over at once to sleep again." When he awoke the first results had begun to come in and they were, as he now expected, unfavourable. By noon it was clear that the Socialists would have a majority. His wife said to him, " It may well be a blessing in disguise," to which he replied, " At the moment it seems quite effectively disguised."

The Causes of the Conservative Defeat, 1945.—Looking back over twenty years later it must seem puzzling that the country could have been so ungrateful to the man who had pulled the nation through tragedy to triumph. But the people were not ungrateful. Their verdict was registered, rightly or wrongly, against the Party which had excluded Churchill from office during the pre-war years. The verdict was directed against the Conservatives despite the admiration for Churchill. It was they, not he, who were condemned for the Munich Agreement and for the pre-war unemployment. There was also an undercurrent of concern that events might follow the pattern of the First World War when the war leader, Lloyd George, was re-elected on generous promises which were not fulfilled.

**Labour Faces a Financial Crisis.**—On coming to office in 1945 the Labour Government was faced with the end of the financial assistance given to Britain during the war by the United States under the system known as Lend-Lease (*see* L70). The Government accepted a dollar loan but the money ran out by 1947. Stafford Cripps was appointed Minister of Economic Affairs to deal with the crisis and, in the autumn, when Dr. Hugh Dalton resigned as Chancellor of the Exchequer after an indiscreet Budget disclosure to a journalist, he combined both posts. Cripps had been a brilliant lawyer before entering politics. He was now master of the economic affairs of the nation. He introduced a programme of austerity in order to reduce the demand for foreign currency; and the trade unions co-operated by accepting a policy of " wage restraint." This co-operation was willingly accorded because Cripps controlled prices, maintained an equitable taxation system and because of the social services which the Government had introduced.

**The Marshall Plan.**—Assistance to Britain came in a new way. In 1947 George Marshall, U.S. Secretary of State, proposed a scheme whereby his country would assist in a programme for putting Europe on a sounder economic basis. The programme would need to be a joint one, agreed to by a number, if not all European nations; and the initiative must come from Europe, the United States giving friendly aid and support. Ernest Bevin, Foreign Secretary, jumped at the offer and with fifteen other nations drew up what became known as the European Recovery Programme. The Organisation for European Economic Co-operation which, of course, is still in being, came into existence to administer the programme.

**Bevin and America.**—Bevin worked increasingly for effective collaboration with America and he was a prime mover in creating the North Atlantic Treaty Organisation (1949). This was the first treaty in which the U.S.A. had ever undertaken European commitments in peace time. It grew out of fear of Russian power. Bevin's policy was criticised by some members in his own party. Criticisms varied. One was that Bevin had abandoned a specifically socialist foreign policy and that he should have attempted to retain independence between the two worlds—the capitalist and communist worlds—and tried to build a bridge between them. This view was crystallised in the advocacy of a " third force " of powers standing between America and Russia and led by Britain. The group expressing this view were known as the " Keep Left " group, and it was about this group that Bevin made the often quoted remark that he had been " stabbed in the back." The members of this group of " Labour Independents " were defeated in the 1950 election.

**The Work of the Labour Government, 1945–50.**—The first measure was the nationalisation of the Bank of England which Churchill said did not raise any question of principle and there was little opposition. The National Coal Board, established as a public but semi-independent body, took over a very inefficient industry. The British Transport Commission was created in 1947 and took over railways, canals, and road haulage. Cable and wireless companies were nationalised and public corporations created to run airlines; in these measures the new Government were following the lines of policy accepted by earlier governments. The creation of the British Electricity Authority (1948) and the Gas Council (1949) enabled management to be taken of industries which were already under some public control. Beyond all this the Government built a " welfare state " in which the social services were no longer regarded as a form of poor relief but as a co-operative system of mutual aid and self-help provided by the whole nation and designed to ward off distress and strain wherever they may fall. At the centre of the system were the social insurance scheme and the national health service.

**The Controversy over Iron and Steel.**—The question of the nationalisation of this industry proved controversial and difficult. It was left to the last by the Government. The industry, which was profitable and fairly efficient, was also very complex, ownership penetrating into industries other than engineering. The nationalisation of iron and steel took effect in February 1951 (by the administration formed after the general election of 1950 when the overall Commons majority of the Labour Party was reduced to only six); but the Conservatives, returned to power in 1951, denationalised the industry. It was re-nationalised in 1967. *See* G14(1).

**The National Health Service.**—This welfare service was created by the Labour Government's National Health Service Act of 1946 and became operative in 1948. It provided all those who take advantage of it with free medical and hospital treatment. The cost is met partly by contributions from general taxation and partly by compulsory contributions from all citizens (except certain exempted persons) and these contributions are payable whether or not advantage is taken of the service. Aneurin Bevan who as Minister of Health had piloted this great scheme through all its stages, resigned when the Labour Government imposed charges on spectacles and teeth in 1951 although this was intended only as a temporary measure. Since then, however, governments have continued to increase general charges —on contributions, on spectacles, dentures, welfare foods, and amenity beds. The charge on prescriptions has been removed and reimposed. *See also* G24(1).

**The Continuing Needs of a Welfare Society.**—Writing nearly two decades later we can see that social services can never be finished articles. A school of writers led by Professor Richard Titmuss have recently shown that some groups have benefited far less than others from the recent increase in production and that behind the façade of affluence there are " submerged groups." Serious social problems remain like the adequate care of the aged, housing and unemployment caused by economic and technical changes. The subject of the care of the aged becomes more urgent every year since the number of people above working age in the United Kingdom is steadily increasing.

**Labour and Asia.**—The granting of independence by the Attlee Government to India, Pakistan, Ceylon and Burma was of the greatest importance. Seen at the time as a historic achievement, the passage of time has confirmed its momentous nature. It is difficult to contemplate into what tragic paths we might have fallen had independence for India been further delayed. Independence to countries is very rarely given too soon. How easy it is to see now that Britain would have benefited enormously—and the wider world too—had a settlement between her and Ireland not been tragically delayed. The clock of progress was put back fatally. We were spared further conflict with our Asian dependencies by the decisive action of Attlee in sending Lord Mountbatten to India as the last Viceroy in order to transfer power to the Indians. Of the four new states in Asia only Burma elected to sever its links with the Commonwealth.

**The Changing Commonwealth.**—At this point we may glance ahead at the further evolution of the Commonwealth which followed the grant of independence to the Asian countries—a step criticised vehemently at the time but now seen to have been wise. As other countries in the Commonwealth reached sovereign status most of them sought full membership, so that there were welcomed to membership Ghana and Malaya in 1957, the Federation of Nigeria in 1960, Cyprus, Sierra Leone and Tanganyika in 1961, Jamaica, Trinidad and Tobago, and Uganda in 1962, Kenya and Zanzibar in 1963, Malta, Malawi, and Zambia in 1964, Gambia and Singapore in 1965, Botswana, Guyana, Barbados and Lesotho in 1966, Mauritius and Swaziland in 1968. Thus we have a system which bears no resemblance to the empires of the past, a partnership based upon friendship between nations with a diversity of race, religion, and language. This evolution we are now beginning to take for granted; but it must not be forgotten for it is one of the most heartening features of our time. *See also* Part II.

**Labour Faces the Country, 1950.**—During the whole of its term of office, 1945-50, the Labour Government had not lost a single by-election. But the general election of 1950 gave the Labour Party only a very slight majority. They secured only 315 seats, against 298 Conservatives, 9 Liberals, and 2 Irish Nationalists. A considerable defection of middle-class voters resulted in suburban seats in London and the Home Counties returning to Conservative allegiance. Dissatisfaction with continued shortages and with rationing no doubt played a part. The redistribution of seats due to population movement had resulted, in 1950, in an electoral system with a slight bias against the Labour Party since support in working-class areas was so strong as to bank up enormous Labour majorities there, whereas the Conservative vote was more diffused and thus more effective in electoral figures. The result ended Labour's effective control of Commons. Government was scarcely possible with a majority of six and the parties renewed their fight at another election which Attlee called in October 1951.

**The Conservatives Regain Power, 1951.**—The Labour Party secured the highest total poll that it or any other party had received in a general election—fourteen million votes. The Conservatives received a quarter of a million less; but they secured a majority of seats. This anomaly was due to the character of the electoral system described above. The composition of the new House was 321 Conservatives, 295 Labour, 6 Liberals and 3 Irish Independents. In the atmosphere of relaxed responsibility the controversy which had begun within the Labour Party while they were in power was renewed.

**Churchill at Eighty.**—No Prime Minister had been so honoured as when members of both Houses assembled in 1954 in Westminster Hall to present to him a book signed by them and a portrait of him by Graham Sutherland. A memorable description of the scene is reprinted from *The Guardian* in " The Glory of Parliament " by Harry Boardman—the throng of several thousand, the drums of the Guards' band beating the opening bar of the Fifth Symphony, which Churchill had so memorably converted into a victory sign ten years earlier. He disclaimed having inspired the nation in the war. He had had only to appeal, he said, to the remorseless, unconquerable will of the people. " It was the British race that had the lion's heart. I had the luck to give the roar."

**Eden Succeeds Churchill.**—The new Prime Minister, Anthony Eden, who succeeded Churchill in April 1955 decided upon a general election, thus taking advantage of two factors, the controversy within the Labour Party and the economic recovery at that time. There were also, at the time, a number of strikes or threats of strikes which affected a wide public and these disputes were unfortunately due in part to inter-

union rivalries. The Conservatives increased their majority from 17 in 1951 to 58.

**The Election of 1955.**—The Conservatives had a total of 345 M.P.s, Labour 277, Liberal 6 and Sinn Fein 2. Both the Conservative and Labour votes fell—the first by some 400,000 and the latter by over 1·5 million. When Parliament assembled four older members, including Dalton, resigned because of their age from the Labour Shadow Cabinet; and when at the end of the year Attlee resigned the leadership, Hugh Gaitskell was elected leader of the party by a substantial majority. The Labour Party was more solidified as a result of the Government's Suez adventure and Bevan was brought back as " Shadow Foreign Secretary."

**Attlee's Achievement.**—Attlee, who thus retired from the leadership of the Labour Party, went to the House of Lords as Earl Attlee. If Churchill stood for the " finest hour " in our history, Attlee stood for the social revolution which followed it. He was the most modest man ever to engage in politics. As a young man he had gone to the East End of London to take up social work and had become Mayor of Stepney. Nobody then could possibly have imagined that he would one day become Prime Minister and Churchill's Deputy Prime Minister for five years of war. " The difference between the two," wrote Harry Boardman (who described the Parliamentary scene so brilliantly for many years for *The Guardian*), " is between genius and extraordinary ordinariness." " True there is no colour, no magnetism, but there is great concentration of purpose, a mind with a razor edge and something of harsh resolution." This simple man of few words transformed the social and economic fabric of the country and changed the face of the Commonwealth into the beneficent world-wide system it has become. He was widely mourned when he died in 1967.

**Conservatives' Third Consecutive Victory, 1959.**—During the 'fifties the Labour Party had to endure the loss of three consecutive elections and a loss of increasing margins. In 1959 after eight years in office the Conservative Party secured the return of 365 Conservative members, with 258 Labour and 6 Liberal members and one Independent. It was at this election that the Liberals doubled their share of the vote partly by running more candidates and partly by the increase of votes in many of the contests in which they took a part.

**Hugh Gaitskell.**—In the three years preceding the death of Hugh Gaitskell Labour had lost its best orator in Aneurin Bevan and its best organiser in Morgan Phillips. It was to lose Hugh Gaitskell when, after ten years, it seemed he had won public confidence as the head of a possible alternative government. Educated at Winchester College and New College, Oxford he achieved the highest academic distinction as an economist. It was under the inspiration of Professor G. D. H. Cole at Oxford that he chose to work for the underdog; and on graduation when he became a university lecturer in economics he gave all his spare time in the service of the Workers' Educational Association, teaching economics to Nottingham miners. During the war, serving in the Civil Service, he came under the notice of Hugh Dalton. At the end of the war he chose politics as a career and won the confidence of Stafford Cripps. Upon Cripps' death, Gaitskell succeeded him as Chancellor of the Exchequer, making the spectacular rise from member to Chancellor in six years. This rapid rise was due to his intellectual powers, his gift of exposition, his industry and his character; the whole of these qualities being informed by his humanity and hatred of injustice. Disappointed by Labour's third defeat in 1959 he initiated discussion as to how the Labour Party could be modernised. In the words of a colleague, he was able to show that the Party's " socialist idealism, which is essential to it, is not static, not something writ on tablets but a constantly developing attitude of heart and mind capable of embracing and giving a new meaning to twentieth century society." At Brighton in 1962 he clearly had a united Conference behind him when he delivered a searching speech on the Common Market, setting out the criteria which needed to be satisfied before entry could be regarded as a benefit to country and Commonwealth. When struck by illness at the end of that year, Gaitskell had been acclaimed as a potential prime minister; but the greatest opportunities were lost to him. He was succeeded as leader of the Party by Harold Wilson who became Prime Minister in 1964 and for the second time in 1966.

**The Macmillan Years.**—Harold Macmillan succeeded Eden in January 1957 at the age of 62, in the aftermath of Suez, and he devoted himself to re-establishing the friendly relations with the United States which had been strained by the Suez affair. Early in 1959 he went to Russia for preliminary soundings for a Summit Conference, which, through no fault of his, was to collapse immediately it opened in Paris in May of the following year. In February 1960 he had shown great courage in a speech before both Houses of the Union Parliament in South Africa when he referred to " the wind of change " in the relations between Black and White in the continent of Africa. It was in July 1961 that Macmillan announced that Britain would apply for full membership of the Common Market, negotiations continuing till their breakdown in January 1963. Among other important events of his premiership were: the explosion of the first British hydrogen bomb; the settlement of the Cyprus dispute; the winning of the General Election of October 1959 with an increased majority of 100 seats; the cancellation of the *Blue Streak* missile programme, and the agreement for U.S. *Polaris* submarines to use Holy Loch; the failure in 1958 to secure free trade with the Common Market and the consequent setting up in 1960 of a European Free Trade Area with countries outside the Market; the setting up of the National Economic Development Council; the legalisation of betting shops; the winding up of the Central African Federation; the nuclear test ban treaty; and the establishment of a Federation of Malaysia.

**The Resignation of Macmillan.**—From the middle of 1962 the Government seemed dogged by misfortune which, it was doubtless hoped, would be changed by Britain's entry into the Common Market. Quickly following Britain's exclusion came the hardships of a severe winter and of a sudden increase in unemployment. When the spring came the Government were caught in another misfortune, the Profumo affair, involving the resignation of its War Minister. This did nothing to still the feeling in the Conservative Party that the Prime Minister should make way for a younger man, although there was a natural reluctance to press the Profumo affair as a suitable occasion for his departure. Mr. Macmillan indicated that he hoped to lead the Party at the next election. This discordant position was suddenly cut by Mr. Macmillan's illness, which compelled him to resign. By a coincidence his announcement came (10 October 1963) the day after the annual Party Conference had opened. The resignation would in any event have caused a great debate in the Party; but dropped suddenly into the excited atmosphere of a conference it caused a tumult. Many analyses have been made of the history of those days.

**Lord Home Becomes Prime Minister.**—Mr. Macmillan's sick-bed became the centre of the vortex in the following week. The Cabinet approved a memorandum by him as to how soundings should be taken in the Cabinet, the two Houses, and the Party Organisations. Soundings were taken and two days later they were said to show a continuing deadlock between Hailsham and Butler but a small lead for a third; and this third man was not Maudling but Lord Home, then Foreign Secretary, who had been widely regarded as a non-starter. Mr. Macmillan recommended Home to the Queen. How confused the situation was is illustrated by the fact that on the very morning when the Queen sent for Lord Home the first headline in *The Times* was "The Queen may send for Mr. Butler today."

There was an acute debate within the Party as to the way in which the leadership had been decided; and this debate resulted in a method (described below) of electing the leader of the party.

**Election Year 1964.**—Parliament's legal term expired in the autumn of 1964 but there remained the question whether Sir Alec Douglas-Home would go to the country in the spring or in the autumn. Concealing his hand till the last moment Sir Alec decided to wait till the autumn. For many months, therefore, the country discussed the issues involved and thus went through much of the emotions of an election, which, when it came, seemed belated, the people being a little weary of worked up turmoil by politicians, press, and pollsters. Some of the fire of an election had thus been drawn prematurely from it, but no General Election can lack drama. The Government's majority dissolved and Mr. Wilson kept the lead to a photo-finish. The resultant position is examined in Part II with an outline of some of the far-reaching consequences. Before, however, leaving this point in our story we must note the coincidence by which, within the very two days on which the results came in, there occurred two events of world-wide importance—the fall of Khrushchev and the explosion by China of an atomic bomb. If the latter was expected, the former was certainly not. These events, which are discussed later, were more than could be assimilated and their significance will take a long time to digest.

**Problems Facing the New Government at Home.** —Let us take a glance at the sea of troubles which immediately advanced upon the Wilson administration. The general nature of these troubles had, of course, been foreseen; but they were none the less formidable for that and their exact nature when revealed (like the Treasury's forecast of the payments deficiency) showed they were even more severe than supposed. Production needed to be raised and steadily expanded. For this a number of fundamental steps were necessary. To expand without inflation, an incomes policy (coupling incomes and wages with production) needed to be introduced; and this called for fresh attitudes by both sides of industry. Industry needed to be reinvigorated by science and technology and fresh educational foundations required to be laid. Planning, detailed in character and comprehensive in scope, required both regional, as well as national, planning. " They've given me a bed of nails," said the new Minister of Labour. The metaphor could have been aptly used by the whole of the new team.

**Problems Abroad.**—The problem of our security posed the question of what kind of co-operation with our allies was desirable and what, then, was possible, an enigmatic France being antagonistic to a Western alliance. How could the long deadlock on disarmament be broken? What rescue could be raced to an overstrained and threatened United Nations? The most ominous troubles seethed in Africa, in the Congo, in Rhodesia, in South Africa. In Asia, the sub-continent of India was developing all too slowly. China, estranged (through no fault of Britain) remained unpredictable as estranged people are apt to be. There was an ugly confrontation between Malaysia and Indonesia. And beyond all these questions and many more remained perhaps the gravest of the lot— half the world underfed, ill-housed, underdeveloped, with insufficient hope. One of the mysteries which will baffle future historians is why so little popular concern was expended on a plight fraught with so much danger for all of us.

**The Passing of Winston Churchill.**—When Churchill died, not long after his ninetieth birthday, on 24 January 1965 his countrymen and the whole world paid their tributes to the greatest Englishman of his time and recalled the facts of a truly astonishing career. In his *Study of History*, Arnold Toynbee traces a common pattern in the lives of certain great creative figures like Moses, Saint Benedict, Peter the Great, and Lenin. They had all left the scenes of their youth, spent an interval in solitude or in entirely strange surroundings, and then returned to rise to some occasion of social crisis, to meet the challenge confronting the society to which they belonged. Churchill falls into that pattern, being for so many years, in the prime of his life, ostracised by his own Party and politically frustrated; and never more so than during the appeasement years prior to the Second World War which he so clearly foresaw and during which he returned from neglect to dominate the field at home and abroad. He is thus the most recent example in history of Toynbee's " Withdrawal-and-Return " theory.

### Election Results 1900 to 1966.

|  | Cons. & supporters. | Lib. | Lab. | Irish | Others |
|---|---|---|---|---|---|
| 1900 | 402 | 184 | 2 | 82 | — |
| 1906 | 157 | 379 | 51 | 83 | — |
| 1910 (Jan.) | 273 | 275 | 40 | 82 | — |
| 1910 (Dec.) | 272 | 272 | 42 | 84 | — |
| 1918 | 526 | 28 | 63 | 73 | 17 |
| 1922 | 347 | 118 | 142 | — | 8 |
| 1923 | 261 | 155 | 191 | — | 8 |
| 1924 | 413 | 40 | 151 | — | 11 |
| 1929 | 260 | 59 | 287 | — | 9 |
| 1931 | 521 | 37 | 52 | — | 5 |
| 1935 | 431 | 21 | 158 | — | 5 |
| 1945 | 212 | 12 | 398 | — | 18 |
| 1950 | 298 | 9 | 315 | — | 3 |
| 1951 | 321 | 6 | 295 | — | 3 |
| 1955 | 345 | 6 | 277 | — | 2 |
| 1959 | 365 | 6 | 258 | — | 1 |
| 1964 | 303 | 9 | 317 | — | 1 |
| 1966 | 253 | 12 | 363 | — | 2 |

(b) approved prospective candidates; and
(c) the executive of the National Union of Conservative and Unionist Associations.

This body totalled in 1965 about one thousand. That the Conservatives in the Commons should have first say in the choice of leader is based on the fact that the leader depends on their support. In theory the meeting of the party might reject the M.P.s' choice; and in that event the M.P.s would have to ballot again.

**The Effect of the New Procedure on the System of Government.**—Mr. Edward Heath was elected leader of the party in July 1965. The new method of selecting Conservative leaders was a great change in our system of government. It marked the end of a secret ritual whereby a leader was lifted up above his colleagues by a Royal summons in which they themselves played no open part. There is thus a crucial constitutional change—power being conferred by the Parliamentary party instead of by Royal prerogative. The change from Mr. Macmillan and Sir Alec Douglas-Home to Mr. Heath marked a change from the amateur to the professional. It would be wrong to regard Mr. Macmillan as other than a professional; but he generated the Victorian view that it was best to have a well-educated gentleman at the head of affairs; and this view was realised in the image and promotion of Sir Alec. This pattern was broken in 1965. The Party seemed to be facing the view that to regain power they must narrow the social and financial gap between those who lead the Party and those who support it in the country. The traditional method of choice by " the customary processes " which had lasted for so many decades has been finally abandoned.

**The General Election, 1966.**—Against all the odds and expectations, Labour had governed for seventeen months with a majority over Conservatives and Liberals fluctuating between five and only one. Not only that, but when Parliament

| Party | 1950 (Electorate 34,269,764) | | 1951 (Electorate 34,622,891) | | 1955 (Electorate 34,852,179) | | 1959 (Electorate 35,397,304) | | 1964 (Electorate 35,894,054) | |
|---|---|---|---|---|---|---|---|---|---|---|
|  | Votes | Seats | Votes | Seats | Votes | Seats | Votes | Seats | Votes | Seats |
| Conservatives (and allies) | 12,501,953 | 298 | 13,724,418 | 321 | 13,311,938 | 345 | 13,750,935 | 365 | 11,981,047 | 303 |
| Labour | 13,295,736 | 315 | 13,948,885 | 295 | 12,405,246 | 277 | 12,216,166 | 258 | 12,205,812 | 317 |
| Liberal | 2,621,489 | 9 | 730,551 | 6 | 722,395 | 6 | 1,640,761 | 6 | 3,101,106 | 9 |
| Communist | 91,815 | — | 21,640 | — | 33,144 | — | 30,897 | — | 45,086 | — |
| Others | 258,454 | 3 | 177,329 | 3 | 288,031 | 2 | 223,949 | 1 | 324,097 | 1 |
|  | 28,769,447 | 625 | 28,602,323 | 625 | 26,760,754 | 630 | 27,862,708 | 630 | 27,657,148 | 630 |

| Party | 1966 (Electorate 35,964,684) | |
|---|---|---|
|  | Votes | Seats |
| Conservative | 11,418,433 | 253 |
| Labour | 13,064,951 | 363 |
| Liberal | 2,327,533 | 12 |
| Communist | 62,040 | — |
| Others | 390,649 | 2 |
|  | 27,263,606 | 630 |

was dissolved it was entirely at the Prime Minister's own choosing. Such is the unexpected course of political events. It might reasonably have been held, and was indeed maintained by very many, that no government, short of a coalition could exist with a majority of less, say, than a dozen. But Mr. Wilson governed with the air of one commanding a secure majority, for he neither trimmed his controversial programme nor made the slightest gesture towards a coalition with Liberals. And he maintained this course against the particularly severe economic circumstances we have described; and against adverse changes in his Party's popularity. Mr. Wilson chose to appeal to the country on 31 March 1966 and Labour's recovery was complete.

**Election of Conservative Party Leader.**—A new procedure for choosing the leader of the Conservative Party was announced in February 1965 and it was first used in July of that year when Sir Alec Douglas-Home resigned. The following are the chief features of the new procedure. Ballots will be held among members of the House of Commons who receive the Conservative and National Liberal Whips; and the successful candidate will be presented to a meeting of the party for election as leader. This meeting of the party consists of:

(a) members of both Houses who take the Conservative Whip;

**The July '66 Crisis: some political implications.**—As explained in the Economics section the Government, to save a further run on the £, declared in July 1966 drastic measures to deflate the economy; unemployment rose; and confidence in future expansion declined, causing business to cut back investment plans. Were there inherent reasons for the crisis or was it caused by external causes? The crisis seemed a recurrence of similar previous crises—the last being that before October 1964 when the Conservatives were in power. As this crisis was one of a series it did not seem convincing that it was due to Socialist measures and policies, as some Tories said; nor, on the other hand, was the Labour claim convincing that the Government had been " blown off course " by an unlucky chain of events outside their control like the seamen's strike or the rise in copper prices. We had not seemed able to steer a sensitive middle course between a runaway expansion and a crude and wasteful recession. The Government in 1966 initiated a number of steps to be better able to chart a smoother course. These were to secure better information on which to base decisions; to strengthen planning machinery to carry them out; to stimulate modernisation; and to promote mobility and retraining of labour. But three major political questions remained to be solved to turn deficits into gold. Could we afford to continue to be the world's banker; and a world supplier of capital; and a world military power? These questions were to be answered in 1967.

**Devaluation of the £, 1967.**—In November 1967 the Government reduced the exchange rate of the £ against the $ from 2·80 to 2·40. The main object was to force the pace of exports in order to take advantage of the lower value of the £ abroad. In other words, the price of our exports to the foreign purchaser would be cut and we should therefore stand to capture a bigger slice of the market abroad. This devaluation in the exchange rate of the £ was accompanied by measures to deflate the economy at home. The next stage was the series of cuts in public spending announced in January 1968, and the taxation increases in the March Budget, followed by further measures to curb private consumption. The 1967 devaluation marked a change in political attitudes. We elected to make our domestic expansion more important than our world role as banker or policeman.

**Reduction in Public Spending.**—Economies were most drastic in the defence field with the cancellation of the order for 50 F-111 bombers and a complete withdrawal of forces from Singapore, Malaysia, and the Persian Gulf by the end of 1971. At home the raising of the school leaving age was deferred for two years, from 1971 to 1973; and National Health prescription charges were reintroduced with exemptions. These two sets of changes, introduced primarily for financial reasons, marked two new principles. The withdrawal from the east of Suez by 1971 marked a momentous change, and represented the third great recognition in recent years of the trend of history —the other two being the decision of the Attlee Government to give India independence and Mr. Macmillan's recognition of the wind of change in Africa to steer a number of Commonwealth countries towards independence. The alterations in the policy on prescription charges and recovery, from those who did not need them, of family allowances exemplified the other change, namely the idea of selectivity in social benefits.

**The Decision to Impose an Incomes Policy.**—In his Budget speech in March 1968 the Chancellor, Mr. Roy Jenkins, announced that the Government had decided to impose a much firmer policy for prices, incomes and dividends backed by extended statutory powers, at least until the end of 1969. There would be a ceiling of 3½ per cent on increases in all forms of remuneration, but excluding increases directly related to the amount of work done. The Minister of Employment and Productivity, Mrs. Barbara Castle, responsible for carrying through Parliament the controversial prices and incomes legislation and of reconciling the unions to the new compulsory provisions, emphasised the possibilities of higher earnings in return for higher productivity. The Prices and Incomes Bill, as outlined by Mr. Jenkins in his Budget speech, became law in July 1968. The 1968 Trades Union Congress criticised the legislation for its compulsory powers and called for its repeal, though accepting the need for a prices and incomes policy.

**Unpopular Measures in National Interest.**— Speaking at the Labour Party Conference at Blackpool in October 1968, the Prime Minister said: " There is no party political strategy. There is only the strategy for Britain. And that means continuing to pursue the economic policies that are necessary, regardless of popularity, whatever the pressures, until we are paying our way, and have achieved independence. At the end of the road Britain will reap all the dividends from the industrial change which at such pain and cost we are forcing through."

**Reform of the Civil Service.**—*See* C24.

**Reform of Industrial Relations.**—*See* C26.

**The Herculean Task of Government Today.**— Of all the comments made in the public discussions on the Government's general record two cardinal inferences remained unstated. One was that in recent years the sphere of Government has widened and this necessary extension of Government involves a responsibility which is different not only in degree but in kind. For example, the need to work closely with industry and, of course, both sides of industry, at a most critical juncture makes demands on Government of an unprecedented nature and imposes strains which earlier Governments did not know. This is only one example of the wholly novel responsibilities before Government, to be shouldered on top of all their traditional tasks. But worse. The very sequence of political problems is rapidly quickening and incurs bewildering and novel repercussions. Account must now be taken of events which may occur anywhere in the wide world, bringing instant reactions by telephone, television and other means which earlier Prime Ministers like Gladstone, Campbell-Bannerman, Asquith or Baldwin could hardly have imagined or perhaps sustained.

## 2. WORLD PROBLEMS AND EVENTS.

**The Doubling of Population: the 1968 statistics and forecast.**—Based upon figures supplied by the United Nations, the Population Reference Bureau at Washington announced in March 1968 that the world's population was increasing by almost 200,000 people a day and was expected to reach 7,000 million or more by the year 2000. World population on 1 January 1968 was estimated at 3,443 million. The 3,500 million mark was expected to be reached by 1969, the 4,500 million mark by 1983. The most rapid growth rate was in North and Central America. The Bureau found that nearly one-third of the world's population was under 15 years of age. India, the Soviet Union, the United States, Pakistan, Indonesia, Japan and China accounted for 58 per cent of the world's population. About one-third only of the world's population live in " have " countries.

**Population and the Supply of Food and Natural Resources.**

The future relation between population and food and resources is an obviously vital aspect of the world's currently high rate of population growth. Broadly speaking, there are two opposed schools of thought, the one contends that with scientifically directed exploitation the earth's resources are large enough to solve the food and population problem, the other that there is a real and early danger of the demand from increased population outstripping the supply from resources. If a much greater degree of political compatibility and fluidity of trade between nations could be achieved, the world could probably support the existing growth rate of population of 2 per cent per annum for a century or so without making too many speculative assumptions about scientific and technical developments. National boundaries and international rivalries cannot however be ignored, and serious analyses indicate that the population of some of the more crowded countries of Asia, such as India, already face the grim possibility of being condemned to a lasting state of undernourishment and malnutrition, unless successful and simultaneous action is taken both to reduce the rate of population increase and to improve agricultural and industrial productivity.

**The Needs of Underdeveloped Countries.**—*See* Section G, Part III.

## WESTERN EUROPE.

**France and de Gaulle.**—One of the biggest changes in France after the war was the wiping out, as a serious factor, of the Radical Socialist party so powerful before the war. The newspaper reader must not be misled by the titles of foreign political parties—the Radical Socialist party was not radical and it was not socialist, giving those terms the meanings they have in England. They never regained their place in the Fourth Republic which spanned the years 1946–58. There was one hopeful spell when Pierre Mendès-France made a vigorous attempt to reform the party. In 1958 General de Gaulle, who had had a brief period of power in 1945–46, established a semi-presidential system with himself as President, taking certain powers away from Parliament and thus opening France's Fifth Republic next year. The President's seven-year term ended in December 1965 and although he had then reached the age of seventy-five he submitted himself for re-election and won with 55·2 per cent of the votes. During his first term of office he steadily brought the war in Algeria to an end, despite all the hopes reposed in him that he would suppress the independence movement. This was a tremendously courageous achievement; and what was equally courageous he brought France through the threat of civil war precipitated by those who were for continuing force upon Algeria. The drive to economic recovery had, it is true, commenced before he came to power. But on the political side he reassembled French spirit and struck out upon a lonely path, building his nuclear force without receiving technical knowledge from America (as we had).

**De Gaulle's Reckoning with the "Anglo-Saxons."**—The key to de Gaulle's foreign policy is his conflict with the Anglo-Saxon allies, against whom he had fought all through the war itself. A narrative and an analysis of his "hour of reckoning with the Anglo Saxons" will be found in an unusually compelling and revealing biography *The Three Lives of Charles de Gaulle* by David Schoenbrun (Hamish Hamilton). (The three lives, very different ones, are de Gaulle as a soldier in the Third Republic, as the liberator in the Fourth Republic, and as the creator of the Fifth Republic.) Mr. Schoenbrun's thesis is that de Gaulle, from June 1940 to May 1945, had fought a war within a war, an uncivil war with the Anglo-Saxons behind their united front against the Axis powers. De Gaulle alleged in his memoirs that the war-time allies, freed of the necessity of union against the common enemy, set themselves "to relegate us to a secondary place among the nations responsible for conducting the peace." He added, "I have no intention of letting this happen." Thus the first uncivil war lasted five years, from 1940 to 1945; the second uncivil war broke out in 1958 and is now—in 1969 in its eleventh year. It has grown more uncivil each year. The boiling point of the first was the intervention of British troops against the French in Syria in 1945. It was never forgotten, and the uncivil war broke out again in 1958 when de Gaulle returned to power. The conflict was the more open because by that time the fear of Russia and of China, which might have bound the Anglo-Saxons and France more closely, had diminished.

**The Right to Participate in Decisions.**—Recovery by France having been accomplished by 1958, de Gaulle was determined that France should "assume its historic rôle in world affairs." She could therefore no longer assent to delegating to the U.S. exclusive authority to make the vital decisions for the defence of the free world everywhere in the world. He wanted not only the right to participate but the official and public recognition of that right by the creation of a three-power organisation to take joint decisions on global problems. The United States declined. Next year came de Gaulle's next step—the withdrawal of naval units from NATO's Mediterranean Command. The following year, 1959, de Gaulle announced that France would proceed to build an independent national atomic force. In 1962 when Kennedy proposed Atlantic partnership with Europe, de Gaulle replied with a plan to group the Western European nations into "an organisation

that would be one of the three powers of the planet." In January 1963 de Gaulle rejected an offer by Kennedy to make American *Polaris* missiles available to them but to be assigned to a multilateral Atlantic force. Macmillan accepted a similar offer at the Nassau Conference. The division between de Gaulle and Macmillan was thereupon wide open. At the beginning of 1963 the General slammed the door to the Common Market in Macmillan's face and refused to sign the atomic test-ban treaty. Exactly a year later de Gaulle recognised Communist China which must have angered the United States deeply. In 1965 de Gaulle left SEATO, the South-east Asia Treaty Organisation; and next year NATO was asked to remove its headquarters from France. The agreement in 1967 between Britain and France to collaborate in building military helicopters, and the signing of an agreement on the Concorde, the supersonic airliner, were hailed as a hopeful augury.

**De Gaulle's Continuing Antipathy to the Anglo-Saxons.**—De Gaulle's antagonism to America and to countries who he thought were unduly influenced by that country, so far from abating, was lifted to what was described as all-out "war" during 1967—on the monetary front, in the Common Market, on Quebec, Vietnam, the Middle East, and other aspects. At his press conference in November 1967 he asserted that membership of the Common Market was incompatible with the economy of Britain. Britain must undergo a fundamental and radical transformation before she could hope to become a member of the Community. He discussed prospects of technological co-operation with Britain. He maintained his intransigent support of French Canada and declared that it would be necessary to change all the institutions of Canada to wipe out "the Anglo-Saxon dominance" and bring about, perforce, a sovereign Quebec. While disclaiming responsibility for the speculative pressure against the dollar, which was mounting to an intense pitch in the days before he spoke, it was clear that he was not displeased by it. In fact "the squalls which are breaking out at the moment" might end up, he said, with the reestablishment of "a monetary system based on the universality, immutability, and impartiality which are the privileges of gold." He complained that the massive outflow of dollars had enabled the U.S. to take over control of many French concerns—due not, he said, "to the superiority of the U.S. but to the inflation which it is exporting to other nations under cover of the gold exchange system." He analysed Britain's political place in the changing world: he thought we were "in jeopardy"; and he did not conceal that this did not disturb him. "The English people no doubt can see more and more clearly that its structures, activities, and even its nationality are from now on put in jeopardy in the great movement which is sweeping the world—in face of the enormous power of the U.S., the growing power of the Soviet Union, the renascent power of the continental nations, the new power of China, and the growing centrifugal movement apparent within the Commonwealth."

**A Crisis of Government, May–June 1968.**—The student rising of May 1968 touched off a nation-wide wave of unrest. The most violent battles raged in the Latin Quarter between students and riot police. An eye-witness said it might have been in the days of the Commune. Universities were occupied by militant students and factories by workers. Mass strikes, involving more than 2 million workers, paralysed the French economy for much of May and part of June.

The immediate aim of the French students had been to force changes in the running of their universities and their grievances were very real. But this discontent in the academic field overlapped with political and ideological discontents and gave expression to the dissatisfaction felt by thousands of young people whether at universities or not. They are discontented with present-day Western civilisation, with paternalism, and demand the right to question and dissent.

**Sweeping Gaullist Victory.**—On May 24 President de Gaulle announced his intention of holding a referendum asking the people for a mandate to reform the nation's economic, social, and educational institutions, the reforms to include participation by workers in the running of the factories and by students in the running of the universities. However, after a visit to the French forces in Western Germany on May 29 (kept secret at the time) and a Cabinet meeting the next day, the President dissolved the National Assembly and the referendum was dropped. Instead a general election was held on May 31 and a new government under the premiership of M. Pompidou was formed. There was a gradual return to work after demands for higher wages had been met and by mid-June the student occupation of the universities ended. The revolutionary students' organisations that had taken part in the revolution—anarchist, Trotskyite, Maoist, Castroist, and Daniel Cohn Bendit's " Movement of March 22 " were dissolved under a law of 1936.

It is ironic that the elections resulted in a sweeping victory for the Gaullists. The Federation of the Left and the Communist Party lost half their seats in the Assembly. M. Mendès-France was rejected by his parliamentary constituency of Grenoble. A new " Union of the Defence of the Republic " was set up as the official Gaullist organisation. Why after the events of May and June did the Gaullists return to power with the biggest majority they had ever had? It may be that the French people saw that a defeat of de Gaulle in 1968, as nearly happened in 1958, could lead to something worse—a dictatorship of the extreme right with power in the hands of the colonels. In July 1968 M. Pompidou was asked to relinquish the premiership in favour of M. Couve de Murville. De Gaulle's term of office as President ends in 1972. He will then be eighty-two. Adenauer was eighty-seven when he retired, Churchill eighty.

**French Monetary Crisis.**—President de Gaulle in a broadcast on 24 November 1968 explained why the French Government had decided not to devalue the franc. The monetary crisis which France had undergone was, he said, the consequence of the economic and social crisis following the events of May and June. Considerable international credits had been made available to France which she accepted (there had been rumours that she would refuse) and the Government had considered that recovery of the economy could be continued without resorting to devaluation. The next day stringent measures of exchange control were introduced and the Prime Minister, M. Couve de Murville, gave further details of the reductions in Government spending which included cancellation of the 1969 nuclear weapons testing programme in the Pacific and a reduction in credits for the *Concorde* supersonic airliner project.

**Adenauer and Western Germany.**—A notable personal achievement of the last two decades was Dr. Konrad Adenauer's Chancellorship of the West German Federal Republic for fourteen years until his retirement in October 1963 at the age of 86. He gave to a people who had not known democratic government for 15 years a new confidence and self respect. He committed himself to constitutional government despite the fact that he was a natural autocrat. Under him Germany enjoyed the first period of stable government since the First World War. As a consequence of this new confidence Germany rebuilt prosperity from decay. His work in building a special relationship with France, culminating in a treaty of friendship, was a dramatic contrast to the long tradition of enmity with France through which he had lived. But while he succeeded in building his country into the Western community he remained intransigent over East Germany; and since a solution must be found it remained for a more imaginative successor to grapple with it.

**Erhard and Kiesinger.**—In September 1966, when financial troubles were developing, Dr. Erhard, Chancellor, tried to amend the constitution so as to curb the financial powers of the Länder. For this he needed a two-thirds majority in the Bundestag, which he could not secure. His place was taken by Dr. Kurt Kiesinger, Germany's

third post-war Chancellor who was able to take office only by the fact that the Social Democrats agreed to join the Christian Democrats. Dr. Erhard had become Chancellor in 1963 as the most popular politician in the country; he left when Germany's rôle in world affairs was undecided and its internal political future dangerously uncertain. Erhard was a determined opponent of hysterical nationalism and was a loyal supporter of the Atlantic Alliance—indeed it was held that he encouraged ties with the United States at the expense of the Franco-German friendship treaty, which had not lived up to the hopes reposed in it. It was this factor which accounted for the enmity of the Bavarian wing of the Christian Democrats, called the Christian Social Union, the party of Herr Strauss. The C.S.U. put its weight behind Dr. Kiesinger's nomination for the Federal Chancellorship and Herr Strauss was suitably rewarded with a Cabinet post.

**The Right-wing in Germany.**—When the third annual conference of the National Democratic Party was held at Hanover at the end of 1967 it was claimed that membership had nearly doubled in a year—from 18,300 to 33,511. It had 48 seats in six State Parliaments and the party was organised in 466 urban and rural areas out of a possible 500. It expressed confidence in being able to secure between 40 and 50 seats in the next Federal Parliament, in 1969. The undisputed leader of N.P.D. was Adolf von Thadden who for nearly twenty years had been leading Right-wing movements. Despite his attempts to check those even more extreme than himself, for fear of scaring potential supporters, he failed to dissuade the party from accepting a proposal to reintroduce the death penalty and castration for sexual offences. The N.P.D. aims to defend by its own nuclear force a Germany which will embrace, if possible, not only Sudetenland but Austria and S. Tirol.

The Soviet Government in December 1967 sent notes to the U.S., British, French, and Federal German Governments giving warning of the revival of neo-Nazism in Western Germany, describing the N.P.D. as " the direct successor to Hitler's National Socialist Party." The Berlin branch of the N.P.D. went into voluntary dissolution in October 1968. It is thought that the chances of a ban being imposed on the party throughout Germany are slim.

**Spain.**—A new Law—called an Organic Law—raised hopes in 1966 of some change in Franco's anachronistic and authoritarian rule in Spain. But in the following year Franco postponed the new trade union law and imposed fresh curbs on the freedom of the press. In October 1967 a " week of struggle " ended with over a thousand workers in detention. In January 1969, to deal with the wave of unrest among students, workers, and intellectuals, Franco decreed a state of emergency depriving the Spanish people still further of their civil rights. The decree was to last for 3 months. More freedom of worship has had to be conceded to religious minorities—a symbolic defeat for Church authoritarians holding Spain's educational system back. But the main questions remain: How has the Generalissimo been able to remain in power for so long? Is it the American acceptance of him? Have the balances from the tourist trade made him safe? Is it the fear of revolution after a desperate civil war? Is it the effective prohibition of the discussion of alternatives to him? What price has Spain paid for his régime?

**Greece.**—Fearing the confidently expected victory at the elections of 28 May 1967 of the Centre Union, dictatorial power was seized by the Right in the preceding month. Many politicians, journalists, and others were arrested, no charges in many cases being preferred. A rigid press censorship was imposed. The 26-year-old King was confronted with an immensely difficult task, the colonels of the Right junta not wishing for his abdication although they would have pressed forward with their policy even if he had. The new régime was naturally susceptible to foreign opinion. But a very important key was held by the U.S. since Greece has been described as an American protectorate. But the Council of

Europe gave the Greek generals a warning. Four member countries complained that the new Greek régime had violated eight articles of the European Convention on Human Rights. The Council warned Greece that unless the Generals ceased to repudiate the values which the council exists to uphold Greece will be suspended or expelled.

The critical position of the King came to a head in December 1967 when after an abortive attempt to free himself of the military junta he went into exile at Rome. The sequel to the warning given to the junta by the Council of Europe is dealt with in some detail in the passage on Human Rights in Part II.

### EASTERN EUROPE.

A Turning Point in Soviet History.—In 1961 Khrushchev publicly and dramatically completed the process which he had begun in 1956, of drawing a line under the Stalin régime and finally rejecting the cult of Stalin. This change was symbolised by the removal of Stalin's body from the mausoleum at the Kremlin. At the same time Khrushchev was confronted by an external challenge to his leadership of the Communist world—by China who believed that Russia was moving steadily away from classical communist doctrine.

Stalin had made the Soviet Union a modern industrial society and a great armed power. But the arbitrary bureaucracy through which this had been achieved had, in Khrushchev's view, overrun itself. Radical changes became essential and Khrushchev attempted various steps—the scaling down of the secret police; the rebuilding of the administrative apparatus; the opening up of virgin lands; and a new theory that war was not inevitable. The legacy of the Stalinist era had been the concept of the " monolithic " party, that is to say, a party which, however torn by internal conflict, must never allow any open division of opinion and free debate, much less the formation of any groups expounding distinctive views. In the light of the trials of authors in 1966–7 the view was bound to be taken outside Russia that the process of deStalinisation had not gone quickly enough. In 1968, 220 dons at British Universities publicly protested against the treatment by the Soviet Union of her Jewish population.

Khrushchev Leaves the Political Scene.—The career of Nikita Khrushchev as Soviet Prime Minister and Leader of the Communist Party came to an end—to the surprise of the world—in October 1964. Stalin had died in 1953 and the struggle for succession then continued for five years, when Khrushchev emerged with supreme authority. Upon Stalin's death a triumvirate of successors, Malenkov, Molotov, and Beria had decided to give the post of party chief—First Secretary—to Khrushchev, then a relatively harmless outsider, or so he was deemed by them. Beria, the all powerful police chief, was executed as a spy in 1953, Malenkov was forced to give up the premiership in 1954 and three years later both he and Molotov were expelled from the Central Committee. Khrushchev thereupon emerged with supreme powers, and became the talkative and jocular leader whom the world knew.

The Pattern of Change in Leadership.—The student of affairs may be puzzled by the strains and dislocations which occur upon a change of leadership in Russia. But this is less surprising when it is remembered that there is no constitutional manner of embodying a change of opinion or policy in an alternative party or group of men. It will be seen from the diagram of events that after Lenin's death control was divided between the Secretary of the Party and the Premier for seventeen years, until Stalin combined both posts. After Stalin's death in 1953 control was again split (except for ten days) for another five years until, in 1953, Khrushchev who had been Secretary for five years combined the two posts again until 1964. The pattern repeated itself in 1964 Kosygin becoming Premier and Brezhnev Secretary. A meeting of the Supreme Soviet in 1965 confirmed the principle of collective leadership. At the 23rd Soviet Party Congress held in April 1966 it was decided that the Praesidium of the Central Committee

should go back to being the Politburo and the First Secretary should revert to General Secretary. The 11-man Politburo has an inner cabinet of four members: Brezhnev, General Secretary, Kosygin, Prime Minister, Suslov, the Party's theoretician, and Podgorny, the President of the Soviet Union.

Lenin 1917–24

> *Premier:* Rykov 1924–30
> *Premier:* Molotov 1930–41
> *Secretary:* Stalin 1922–53

*Premier and Secretary*
Stalin 1941–53

Malenkov      Beria      Molotov
(*Triumvirate*)
1953

*Premier and Secretary*
Malenkov (10 days in 1953)

*Premier:* Malenkov 1953–55
*Premier:* Bulganin 1955–58
*Secretary:* Khrushchev 1953–64

*Premier and Secretary*
Khrushchev 1958–64

*Premier:* Kosygin 1964
*Secretary:* Brezhnev 1964

Recent events suggest a split in Soviet leadership, a struggle between the conservatives (hawks) and radicals (doves). On the decision to invade Czechoslovakia, Victor Zorza, one of the best of the analysts of Russian affairs, says what evidence there is puts Mr. Kosygin with the doves, as he has been on other issues, and Mr. Brezhnev with the hawks. But once a majority decision is taken in the Politburo the minority accepts it and carries it out.

Russia and Conventional War.—In 1967–8 a basic change appeared in Russia's attitude to war, the Soviet High Command accepting, from all appearances, the possibility of large-scale conventional fighting in Europe. In Krushchev's time the assumption seemed that fighting in Europe would immediately burst into nuclear warfare. The new policy became known as "graduated deterrent" or "flexible response." Krushchev did not accept this wider strategy because of the cost beyond what he was prepared to spend. In 1968, however, the Soviet's defence budget was increased by 8 per cent to £6,200 million. This was the figure given to western correspondents. Industrial growth in Russia is rising more rapidly than in the West and it seemed that there was a debate at the highest levels as to the division of the national product between military and civilian. In 1967–68 it seemed that both wings, military and civilian, received some of the increased money available. In the words of Victor Zorza, Russia opted for guns *and* butter.

Russian Military Intervention in Czechoslovakia.—In March 1968, when public pressure had secured the removal of President Novotny of Czechoslovakia, it was thought that a genuinely democratic form of communism could be evolved in a communist country and that the Czech example would encourage other Communist countries to reform themselves. But the Soviet Union did not see the new liberalisation policy like that, but rather as preparation for a counter-revolution leading Czechoslovakia back to capitalism. In July, Mr. Brezhnev said that the Soviet Union could not be indifferent to the building of socialism in other socialist countries, and referred to the Hungarian 1956 uprising. Leaders of the Warsaw Pact countries sent a letter to the Czechoslovak party saying that they were deeply disturbed by recent events in Czechoslovakia. The allegations were refuted by the Czechoslovak Presidium and Mr. Dubcek broadcast to the nation reaffirming that "we have no alternative but to complete the profound democratic and socialist changes in our life, together with the people." Talks between the Czechoslovak Presidium and the Soviet Politburo opened at Cierna at the end of July 1968 and at the beginning of August another meeting was held at Bratislava. Afterwards Mr. Dubcek, in a television broadcast, said that the meetings had opened up new scope for the revival process in Czechoslovakia. Then, without the knowledge of the President of the Republic, Russian forces, with contingents from East Germany, Poland, Hungary, and Bulgaria, entered Czechoslovakia on the night 20–21 August. The Czech Presidium appealed to all citizens to maintain calm and not to put up resistance to the invading troops.

The Soviet Union justified the military intervention on the grounds that a departure from Marxism-Leninism by a communist country affects all others. This view has been challenged by those who argue that Marx and Lenin accepted the theory of different paths towards socialism.

**Implications of Czechoslovak Crisis.**—The invasion of Czechoslovakia necessitated a reappraisal of the political and military situation by the countries of the North Atlantic Alliance. In an address to the British Atlantic Committee in November 1968, Mr. Denis Healey, British Secretary of State for Defence, said: " In historical terms the real importance of the crisis is that the Czech people have demonstrated, as the Hungarians demonstrated before them, that the human spirit demands national independence and political freedom in Eastern Europe no less than in Africa or Asia, and that this demand is incompatible with the survival of an empire based on force. Colonialism is as out of date in Europe as it is elsewhere."

**Federal State Structure.**—Czechoslovakia became a Federal State on 1 January 1969. It consists of the Czech Socialist Republic and the Slovak Socialist Republic. The former Prime Minister, Mr. Oldrich Cernik, who is a Czech, is Prime Minister of the Federal Government. The Federal Parliament consists of the Chamber of the Nations, comprising 75 Czech and 75 Slovak representatives; and the Chamber of the People, whose 200 elected members are divided in proportion to the number of Czechs and Slovaks in the country.

## THE MIDDLE EAST.

**Nasser and the New Egypt.**—A new factor in the Middle East was introduced when the Egyptian Army revolted in 1952, overthrowing the monarchy, leading two years later to the emergence of Nasser as Prime Minister. In that year Nasser secured the agreement whereby all British forces were to leave the Suez Canal Zone by 1956. Egypt did not become a democracy in any Western sense but the government runs all the basic enterprises of the country. In 1956 Nasser internationalised the Suez Canal Company as a reply to the withdrawal by the United States of its offer to finance the High Dam at Aswan. The attack by the British and French on Egypt followed, causing serious disagreement with the United States, which inspired international action to rescue Egypt. (It was while we were bombing Egypt that Russia suppressed a revolt in the satellite of Hungary.) It was in obedience to a demand by the UN Assembly that Britain, France, and Israel withdrew from the attack on Egypt and an international force of about 6,000 men was organised to help avert further conflict. When, in April 1957, the canal was cleared and in use Egypt not only insisted on full control of the canal but on the right to bar Israeli trade from the canal. Egypt and Saudi Arabia said they would resume blockading the Gulf of Aqaba (a N.E. arm of the Red Sea), but in fact Israeli ships subsequently got through to their previously blockaded port of Eilat. A small UN force remained on the Gaza–Eilat armistice line.

The closure of the canal in the summer of 1967 cost Britain's balance of payments about £20 million a month, since oil had to be brought more expensively from non-Middle East areas. " The growth of big tankers," said Mr. Wilson, " may very soon make the Suez Canal a rather pathetic irrelevance." But all the same he declared it as intolerable that any nation should keep the canal closed to international shipping.

**The Middle East War of 1967.**—The third Arab-Israeli war began on 5 June 1967. In the words of *The Times*: " What began as the usual spring exercises of the Syrian army, shelling Israeli settlements in Galilee, ended with the complete overthrow of the Middle Eastern balance of power." Israel destroyed the air forces of Egypt, Jordan, and Syria in a few hours, destroyed their three armies in six days, occupying all Sinai to the banks of the Suez Canal (which was therefore closed), the west bank of the Jordan, and the Syrian hills above Galilee. The war was a disaster for Britain, who, with America, was blamed for a catastrophe which, in the view of *The Times*, the Arabs had " brought on their own heads." Among other results, the Russians moved permanently into the Middle East, backing the Arabs. The toll of human misery was, and remains, too immense to imagine: at least 300,000 new and old refugees fleeing the occupied territories. And despite the cost of this human and material loss and distress the problem of Israeli–Arab hostility remains unresolved, liable to flare up again one day. Will this be one of those tragic, intractable problems like the Alsace–Lorraine problem or that of divided Germany, which drag their bitter way for decades with terrible consequences? One can only hope that by the time these lines appear the deadlock will seem, at least, less difficult to resolve. The benefits of co-operation could be immense; the consequences of continued enmity are incalculable.

**The Problem of the Palestine Refugees.**—When the Israeli state was created, most of the Arab population left and were not permitted to return. Some 900,000 fled to Jordan, Lebanon, Syria, and the Gaza strip. In the twenty years since then, very few have been assimilated in the countries of refuge or found homes elsewhere. The Arab states have tended to oppose schemes for resettlement, claiming that such action would condone Jewish occupation of Israel. The tragedy of a million Arab refugees was thus deepened by the reluctance of Arab states who could have made plans for absorption, if they had so wished, instead of using the refugees to strengthen their political attitudes. International aid continues to do what it can; but only real co-operation between Jew and Arab can begin to remedy the disaster. The present number of refugees is in the neighbourhood of one and a half million.

**UN Appoints Envoy to the Middle East.**—Thanks to the efforts of Lord Caradon, British Ambassador to the UN, the members of the Security Council in November 1967 reached agreement, and unanimously, to send a special emissary to the Middle East, Mr. Gunnar Jarring, a Swedish diplomat, whose mastery of twelve languages includes Arabic. An active Arab scholar, he was not known to have sympathies one way or the other in the Middle East. Nasser criticised the Security Council's resolution to send Jarring as inadequate and Syria rejected it. Nasser repeated the formula he had declared at the Arab summit conference in September of " no peace, no recognition and no negotiations." The chief obstacle faced by the UN mediator was the mistrust by each side of the other's motives and ultimate intentions.

**Aden.**—The Government decided to evacuate the Crown Colony of Aden in November 1967. By that time the political differences between the NLF (National Liberation Front) and Flosy (Front for the Liberation of Occupied South Yemen) had become slender and Flosy duly received its *coup de grace*. Flosy, an amalgamation of nationalist parties, had been inspired by Egypt with whose support it was formed in January 1966. NLF was an indigenous reaction against a foreign directed force and it was as much opposed to Nasser as to Britain. After the Israeli–Arab war of 1967 Egypt's interest in Aden waned. The NLF wanted Aden as the keystone to its growing ascendancy in the shaikdoms. Britain's calculation that her withdrawal from Aden would bring the rivals together went astray. The independent Peoples Republic of South Yemen came into existence and the last British troops left on 29 November 1967.

## ASIA.

The independence and unity of India on the one hand and the emergence in China of the Central People's Republic on the other form, with the Vietnam war, the three important political features of Asia. India and China have lived, historically speaking, in different worlds; their experiences at the hands of the West have been different; their recent developments and their present political systems are entirely dissimilar—the one a democracy and the other authoritarian.

**Indian Changes under British Rule.**—The pattern of her development after independence had been set during British rule. The main features were: the concept of law and the rule of law; a civil service superior to any known before in Asia; a system of education introduced as far back as 1835; English as a common language; and the growth of an intelligentsia (to use a word with a Russian origin) with a humanistic outlook and responsive to Western ideals and traditions. Important consequences followed from these changes. They enabled Hindu society to reform itself on the basis of modern ideas; to create an educated leadership; to modernise Indian languages; and to introduce modern science to India.

**Leadership Since Independence.**—That the dissolution of British rule was made so peacefully, a miracle of modern times, was due principally to Gandhi who associated nationalism with ethical concepts, summed up in the term " Gandhism " and denoting pacifism, the value of the individual soul and humane ideas. He made India conscious of the social reforms which needed to be made and created the discipline to make a democracy able to carry them through. Gandhi's ideal of religious unity, though disrupted by the partition into the two states, Pakistan and India, made it possible for the new India to be a secular state, in which all religions and minorities had equal rights.

Nehru, India's first prime minister, symbolised India's highest aspirations. As a disciple of Gandhi he revered him; but his political outlook had been different. He was an enlightened liberal working towards a modernised, rational, democratic, secular state enjoying both the benefits of large-scale scientific organisation and the spiritual good of individual liberty. Under great strains this way and that he maintained neutrality in the face of world power blocs and embodied in his politics characteristics from differing régimes. He overtowered everybody in Indian public life and was one of the few great figures on the world scene.

Shastri succeeded Nehru. Lal Bahadur was born in 1903 into a caste lower than the Brahmins but equally dedicated to learning; " Shastri " is in fact the title of the degree he received. His air of gentleness was enhanced by his small size; and even by his adversaries in India he was regarded as a good, kind, and tolerant man. He faced problems as complex as any statesman, in the world's biggest, hungriest, and restless democracy. One of his biggest decisions was not to follow China in the nuclear weapons race.

Mrs. Indira Gandhi became Prime Minister of India in January 1966 upon Mr. Shastri's death at the Tashkent conference. Her father was Nehru and she must be regarded as the only daughter in history to have succeeded her father. She is not a relation of Mahatma Gandhi. In Indian families women have always been very highly regarded and India is one of the very few countries where nothing stands in the way of a woman going to the very top. Mahatma Gandhi so far back as 1929 had been uncompromising on women's rights and after Indian independence Hindu law was changed to satisfy his requirements on the status of women. Thus it was Gandhi who took women into politics and paved the way for the election in 1966 of Mrs. Gandhi, the world's most powerful woman. (Mrs. Bandaranaike of Ceylon holds the distinction of being the first woman Prime Minister in history.) Mrs. Gandhi is more radical than both her father Nehru and Mr. Shastri but clings to no " Ism " and will confront each problem individually. Among those round Shastri who helped to guide India, she was by far the most cosmopolitan. Educated in Switzerland and at Oxford, she travelled widely with her father and as his hostess met many world leaders.

Her family is Hindu and there is no doubt that she shares her father's devotion to the ideal of a secular state. She faced, on election, many difficulties; she promised to honour the agreement with Pakistan reached only a few days earlier at Tashkent where Mr. Shastri died, and she announced her willingness to negotiate with China if favourable conditions are created.

**The Indian Elections, 1967.**—The monopoly of power enjoyed by the Congress Party of Gandhi and Nehru over India for twenty years was dramatically broken in March 1967. Between 60 and 70 per cent of the Indian electorate of 240 million used their vote. Half Mrs. Indira Gandhi's Congress Cabinet lost their seats, as well as three of the most powerful Congress Party leaders. Several State Governments were overturned. The result represented therefore an emphatic protest vote against continued Congress rule rather than a positive choice of a clear alternative vote. The protest vote went to whichever party seemed locally most capable of turning Congress out. The Congress Party was left with a very thin majority, but it remains the largest single party in the country. The right-wing parties are the Swantantra Party (the main Opposition party in Parliament), and the Jan Sangh. Mrs. Indira Gandhi was unanimously re-elected Prime Minister of India for a five-year term.

**India and Pakistan.**—The strained relations between these two countries have formed a sorrowful chapter. The concrete problems which have recently arisen between the two countries are not, in themselves, the cause of the strain but are the result of earlier deterioration of feeling. This deterioration was most severe in the year before actual partition, when tension between Hindus and Muslims exploded into communal warfare in Calcutta and in certain provinces including the Punjab. This strife had roots which struck deep into history for the Muslims had, between the eleventh and sixteenth centuries, conquered by stages almost the whole of India. The Muslims had forestalled the British Westerners in bringing almost the whole of India under a single government. Therefore in the territories now in the Indian Union, the Hindus are masters in their own house for the first time since the beginning of the Muslim conquest of India so long ago. The partition of the sub-continent inevitably left large pockets of minorities of Muslims in India and of Hindus in Pakistan. The long history of conquest, of difference of religion and culture and the bitterness of partition itself—all this background accentuated problems which would not in themselves have been so difficult to solve. We must recall that Gandhi, Nehru and other Indian leaders did their best to heal communal strife.

**India's Problems.**—Since independence India has gone through critical times. She has endured several bad years of harvest, two years of disastrous drought, economic recession, acute inflation, and a sharp decline in foreign aid. She has been involved in two wars. She has lost two great Prime Ministers—Nehru and Shastri. Her currency has been devalued. India can take pride in her hydroelectric dams and irrigation schemes, her oil refineries, steel plants, airlines, nuclear power projects, and so on. Schools have been trebled and the literary rate of 15% at independence is now 30%. But observers note first a feeling of disappointment in the country and a lack of faith in planning; and second, a feeling of hurt national pride. Taking these two streams of feeling in turn: the first, it is said, springs from a lack of will and resources in making effective new farming methods and methods of family planning, health and hygiene and this becomes increasingly critical as the population climbs to 500 million. The second element in national feeling is equally tragic, the feeling of hurt national pride, the loss of confidence in some countries which India had relied upon for friendship. The shock of the conflict with China in 1962 brought understandably a sense of disillusion and this was intensified when she became convinced—in her difficulties with Pakistan—of partisanship with that country of certain countries from whom she had expected sympathy. This general disillusion has forced her back upon the domestic problems which need attention; and this explains, it is said, India's apparent apathy to external problems like Vietnam. There is thus no strong interest in Afro-Asian co-operation or even in the Commonwealth. She is dependent upon the United States for food and aid, and her main concern is the threat from China and Pakistan and this concern fosters a demand for an Indian bomb. Economic planning was one of the two main personal contributions by Nehru to India's political thought, the other being the concept of non-alignment in foreign policy.

**China.**—It is only in the last fifty years that the people of China have emerged from centuries of exploitation. It is very difficult for a Western observer to appreciate the dramatic changes which followed the overthrow of the repressive dynasty in 1911 and the advent of the Republic next year. The new leader, Sun Yat Sen, a great idealist and humanitarian, pitted himself against the age-long combination of landlords, military men, and reactionary scholars. For all his achievements Sun failed; or rather Sun's party, the Kuomintang, failed him. Power passed to the military remnants of the old Imperial army and Sun did not succeed in giving his party teeth for militant action for reform. Unfortunately, two years after Sun's death in 1925 his successor General Chiang Kai-shek opened an anti-Communist drive.

Sun's exhortations had been taken to heart by a poet and a scholar, Mao Tse-tung, son of a yeoman farmer from Hunan in the heart of China. Mao's success in raising peasant armies established his pre-eminence as a leader. The countryside helped the Communists to develop honest government. The peasants were ready to work in field and forge. They created a people's army superior to all other armies in Chinese history.

**Mao-Tse-tung and Other Leaders.**—Mao's reputation is based upon his ability first as a military theorist (of guerrilla warfare); second as a political philosopher (adapting Marxism to Chinese needs); and, third, as a more ardent champion of world revolution than the Russian leaders. Chou En-lai, the premier of the State Council, is the best known of Chinese leaders in the outside world and also knows the outside world better than his colleagues. Until the recent upheavals Mr. Liu Shao-ch'i was Mao's right-hand man and his heir-apparent. But now the Defence Minister, Marshal Lin Piao, or Vice-chairman Lin, as he is now called, is Mao's chosen successor. This has been formally stated in the new constitution that comes before the Ninth Party congress in 1969. His devotion to Maoism is beyond doubt.

**China's Cultural Revolution.**—What were the features of China's cultural revolution, as it was called, of which so much was heard in 1966 and 1967? We first briefly indicate the main elements: (1) it was an organised demonstration of the young; (2) it was in favour of Mao-Tse-tung; (3) it disseminated Mao's essential teaching; (4) it was intended to keep alive revolutionary fervour; (5) it thus engendered a sense of China's special path of development; and (6) it emphasised opposition to " revisionism " leading to " bourgeois decay " as, it was said, had occurred in Russia. When Mao himself in December 1965 gave the first hint of a coming purge he styled it a "cultural revolution" against bourgeois and revisionist elements. Let us amplify the main elements in the movement.

**Youth Emergent.**—The organisation was directed to the under-25s who joined in mammoth demonstrations. Slogans and portraits of Mao appeared everywhere. Huge crowds of young people with red armbands thronged the streets in general excitement. Red Guards took a prominent part. This tremendous emotional support for Papa Mao gave that leader (then 73) the assurance that his choice of successor would be accepted with confidence. Mao's essential teaching was disseminated by millions of copies of a little 300-page book of his selected writings, in a red plastic cover, carried by almost everyone and

universally quoted, discussed, and preached. An objective of the movement was to stimulate the young who might otherwise take for granted the achievements of their elders made possible only by their past suffering and hunger. The revolution must be uninterrupted; the class struggle continued. This revolution was set upon a special path, being opposed to the super-Japan western-type technological society. At the same time the cultural revolution emphasised opposition to bourgeois attitudes and encouragement of revolutionary fervour. Beyond all this the young were urged to show initiative, to make suggestions for improvements, not to be afraid to criticise. The upheaval was described as a militant and not a militarist movement; the weapons being the tongue, the pen and the brush justified, it was argued, the description of the revolution as a cultural one. But it developed into violent struggles between revolutionaries and reactionaries and then between the revolutionaries themselves. Mr. Chou En-lai warned that industrial production was being seriously affected. The situation remained very confused until 1968 when there was a gradual return to moderation. Of the 17 surviving members of the Politburo elected at the eighth Communist Party congress of 1956, 13 were declared "bourgeois reactionaries" during the cultural revolution. President Liu Shao-chi was among those expelled from the party. In September 1967 a Yugoslav journalist in Peking told his readers: "In this struggle are involved contradictions and problems which took shape long before the beginning of the cultural revolution, long before Mao proclaimed the People's Republic on Oct. 1, 1949. There are contradictions between the permanent separatist tendencies of the provinces and the permanent centralising tendencies of Peking, contradictions between the developed and the underdeveloped regions, between the " aristocratic " North and the " plebeian " South, between the soldiers and the civilians, between the Chinese and the 40 or so national minorities living especially in the frontier regions. It is no accident that the gravest incidents and the strongest demonstrations of anti-Maoism occur in regions where separatist tendencies are most open. . . ."

That era of turmoil is now over and Mao has to unite the country once again.

**Signs of a Change in China's Foreign Policy.**—Writing in *The Times* in January 1969 Mr. Richard Harris, suggested that the China of 1969 might be ready to come out of its shell and consider some of the alternatives in world affairs to those that she had so consistently preached for years past. Not that Mao's view of world revolution had been abandoned, but that she might be ready, in China's national interest, to explore a change in her foreign relations. The key, says Mr. Harris, is Vietnam. "It is worth repeating the view that this was a revolutionary war that China never wanted; still less could a cautious man like Mao Tse-tung relish the thought of 500,000 American troops almost on China's doorstep." Although at first China scorned the peace talks as a trap she now appears to have accepted the possibility of a settlement. If peace were to come and if the Americans withdrew it would be foolish for the settlement to be reached over China's head. But a change in China's attitude would also depend on a shift in American policy towards China which has remained deadlocked for so many years.

**Sino-Soviet Border Incidents.**—Serious clashes took place in March 1969 between Chinese and Russian troops on the Ussuri river boundary for control of the river islands. The region was once Chinese, ceded to Russia in 1858. From this far eastern extremity the frontier with the Soviet Union runs for 4,000 miles to the great mountain chains of the Pamirs. China has wanted to renegotiate her borders ever since 1949 and amicable boundary settlements have been made with Afghanistan, Burma, Pakistan, Nepal, and Outer Mongolia. China entered into negotiations with the Soviet Union in 1964, being willing to take the Treaties of 1858 and 1860 as the basis for a settlement, but without success.

**China Tests Nuclear Missiles.**—In October 1966 without giving details of the weapon, China announced she had tested a guided missile with a nuclear warhead, thus conforming roughly to the timetable for the development of her missile-nuclear capability anticipated by U.S. Intelligence studies. The Chinese announcement reiterated the assurance that China would never be the first to use nuclear weapons. According to American sources, China exploded her eighth nuclear device in December 1968. The projected American anti-ballistic (ABM) system is designed as defence against a Soviet or a Chinese attack. *See* C19.

**Vietnam.**—In 1941 the Vichy Government in France gave Japan, who was our fighting enemy in the Second World War, permission to use French Indo-China as a base against us. Resistance groups were formed to win back independence and to overthrow both French and Japanese fascists. Japan collapsed in 1945, when the only organised troops were controlled by Ho Chi-minh, a Communist, who set up a Democratic Republic in the northern part of Vietnam. France was bent upon restoring her colonial empire in the south and next year war broke out between the French and Ho Chi-minh. Readers will remember the dramatic seige and capture by Ho's forces of the fort of Dien Bien Phu in 1954. As a result of a 14-nation conference on Indo-China at Geneva in the same year Vietnam was partitioned after a cease-fire, the country to be united after free elections. Laos and Cambodia became independent.

A declaration taking note of the agreement was signed by the following nations who took part: U.K., France, China, Russia, Cambodia, Laos, and North Vietnam. Unfortunately the United States refused to sign the agreement and South Vietnam refused to hold elections, but both affirmed that they would not use force to upset the agreement. There was thus a crystallisation into two Vietnams—Ho Chi-minh's Hanoi régime in the North and that of the Catholic nationalist Ngo Dinh Diem at Saigon in the South. The Diem régime was corrupt but John Foster Dulles sent in men and materials to prop it up. By 1960 the Communist guerrillas in the South, known as the Vietcong, had set up a National Liberation Front. For eight or nine years a civil war was waged in South Vietnam against a very unpopular dictatorship. All that time it has received United States military support and phrases like " the defence of freedom " in Vietnam are to be construed in the light of that fact. It is true, of course, that the North has been helping the rebels in the South. The position became increasingly untenable, and in 1963 the Buddhists rioted against the ruling Roman Catholic minority. The Diem régime which had savagely persecuted the Buddhists was overthrown by the military, the first of a number of military coups. In August 1964 a vessel of the U.S. fleet was attacked in the Gulf of Tonkin (off the North Vietnam coast) and American planes bombed North Vietnam installations as retaliation. This was the first of a series of bombing raids. At first the U.S. Government said that these were tit-for-tat raids but this specific basis was superseded by unrelated attacks. In March 1965 the American Ambassador in South Vietnam said that pressure against Hanoi would continue "until the enemy gives in." In June 1965 the State Department gave authority to the American military commander to use troops in offensive operations against the Vietcong.

There have been many attempts to bring about peace negotiations. In December 1967 N. Vietnam said peace talks would follow if the U.S. stopped their bombing unconditionally. In January 1968 President Johnson reaffirmed his San Antonio speech of September 1967 to halt bombing of N. Vietnam on condition that peace talks would follow and no military advantage would be taken of the pause. The San Antonio formula was dismissed by N. Vietnam as being a delaying tactic. N. Vietnam again stressed the necessity for the withdrawal of U.S. forces and said peace talks would begin as soon as the U.S. " has proved that it has really stopped unconditionally the bombings and all other acts of war against N. Vietnam." Meanwhile the Tet (lunar new year) Vietcong offensive developed into a major campaign, covering practically the whole of S. Vietnam.

Mr. Robert McNamara left as Defence Secretary in 1968. He had become a counsellor of coolness and restraint; he rationed General Westmoreland in the supply of troops; and he opposed some escalations, which happened, like the bombing of Hanoi and Haiphong. General Westmoreland, who took over as field commander in Vietnam in 1964, was recalled to Washington in March 1968 to become U.S. Army Chief of Staff at the Pentagon. A major review of the Vietnam situation took place in Washington made necessary by the military, political and psychological impact of the Vietcong Tet offensive.

In March 1968 President Johnson announced his partial bombing pause, peace talks began in Paris in May, and now at long last (January 1969) with all four sides (U.S., S. Vietnam, N. Vietnam, and the National Liberation Front (NLF) round a table there are hopes of a settlement.

A Sketch of Ho Chi Minh.—Relatively little has been written about Ho Chi Minh and this is remarkable of the President of the Democratic Republic of Vietnam which has figured so dramatically and tragically in post-war history. Let us therefore take a brief look at him; first, by recalling some of the external facts about him and, second, by a word of interpretation of his achievements and efforts. He is 78 and has been President of Vietnam since 1945, and this innings must be in the running for a world record. In 1911, as a young man of 21, he went abroad and for thirty years remained an exile from his native land. In France, in England, and elsewhere he studied the world-wide struggle against colonialism and saw the problem he was particularly interested in—the oppression in Vietnam—as part of the widespread colonial exploitation. Thus the Russian Revolution must have made a great impression upon him, illustrating that great changes were possible. Though for this reason he was sympathetic to Communism his first concern was the anti-colonial revolution in Vietnam. His main purpose therefore from 1945 was to weld together the two elements in Vietnam of nationalism and Communism. By unusual powers of organisation and ruthlessness he was successful in this. The evidence is that he did make a genuine and protracted attempt to negotiate independence with the French in 1945–46 and was prepared to make many concessions. The determination of the French to regain control of Indo-China after the Second World War must be regarded as one of the most tragic mistakes of the period. Austere, ruthless, advocating violence to achieve independence but not indiscriminately, being capable, as we have said, of making concessions, Ho remains a mysterious figure. The special character of his achievement is the dovetailing of the national and communistic elements in Vietnam, as we have noted; and the balance between the two has been skilfully maintained, however uneasy it may seem. Flowing from this is Ho's refusal to take sides in the Sino-Soviet conflict. His attempt to bind together nationalistic and communistic elements has been the more remarkable when it is seen that Vietnam is the only country in South-east Asia where this has been possible, the Communists having been checked in Malaya, in Burma, in Cambodia, and in the Philippines.

Steps in Vietnam History.

| | |
|---|---|
| 1940 | Japanese invasion. France withdrew. |
| 1942–5 | Vietnamese engage in guerrilla war on invaders, Nationalists and Communists joining forces. |
| 1945 | Japan withdrew and Nationalists declare Vietnam independent. |
| | Potsdam agreement makes Britain and China responsible for administration of Vietnam. |
| 1946 | Britain invites French to help and then withdraws leaving French in charge. Terrorist attacks on French who made massive reprisals against civilians. |
| 1949 | French instal Bao Dai as national leader. |
| 1954 | French defeated at Dien Bien Phu by the Viet Minh. Geneva Agreements. |
| 1955 | Boa Dai persuaded by U.S. to replace his prime minister by Hgo Dinh Diem |

(American educated Catholic) who in 1956 refutes Geneva Agreements and refuses elections.

1960-3 Three years of increasing conflict between Diem and the National Liberation Front formed to oppose the Diem regime.

1963     Neutral Buddhists appeal to Government for elections. Diem attacks Buddhists. Diem assassinated.

1964     August 2. Gulf of Tongking incident: US destroyer *Maddox* attacked by North Vietnam torpedo boats. Prompted Congress to give Pres. Johnson authority to step up American military intervention in S.E. Asia.

1965     February. Large-scale air raids on N. Vietnam opened.

1966     January. Major military operations by U.S. in the south.

1966     March 18. Hanoi bombed for the first time.

1967     February. Bombing of N. Vietnam increased.
May. Fighting in the demilitarised zone running between N. and S. Vietnam.
August. Bombing near Chinese Border.

1968     January-February. Tet offensive: co-ordinated Vietcong attack on cities in S. Vietnam, including Saigon.
March 31. Pres. Johnson announced partial bombing pause.
May. Beginning of peace talks in Paris between U.S. and N. Vietnam.

1969     January 25. Full-scale peace talks open (U.S., S. Vietnam, N. Vietnam, NLF).

**Basic Facts about Vietnam.**—The population is 32 million (N. 15·5, S. 16·5). Racially they are cousins of the Chinese and their culture is largely derived from China. Nevertheless they are ancient enemies of the Chinese. They are Confucians in their social attitudes. The main religion is Buddhism 70–80 per cent, Roman Catholic 7 per cent (mostly in S.). The land area is 129,000 square miles (N. 63,000, S. 66,000). The President of N. Vietnam is Ho Chi Minh and the Prime Minister Pham van Dong. The Government of S. Vietnam had been formed by military coup and as result of a limited election in 1967 the President is Lt.-General Nguyen Van Thien and the Vice-President Air Vice-Marshal Nguyen Cao Ky.

## AFRICA.

**Africa's Faltering Steps to Unity.**—President Nyerere has confessed sadly that "Africa is in a mess." The disunity extends beyond Africa to the whole of the non-aligned world which appeared to have so much cohesion at the Bandung Conference of 1955. What is the cause? Is it the disappearance of forceful leaders like Sukarno, Nkrumah, and Nehru, and the fact that men like Tito and Nasser are not in the mainstream of Asia and Africa? Does the disunity support Nkrumah's contention that without his form of militancy Africans can only be pawns of the neo-colonialists? Has the leap to statehood been too quick? We must hope that the potentially rich countries of Nigeria, Zambia, Ghana, Guinea, the Ivory Coast, and the Congo will plan development with poorer neighbours. But a little perspective will be salutary for European observers. After many centuries Europe has not yet completed by a very long way the evolution of nationalism, industrialisation, and supranationalism; the process in Africa has been at work only for about a couple of decades. We have insufficient reason to be self-satisfied; and future wellbeing both of ourselves and other peoples calls for understanding.

**The Congo.**—At the beginning of 1967 President Mobutu took over the entire Congolese operations of the Belgian Union Minière Company which for 60 years had mined copper and cobalt in Katanga. This "congolisation" was described by the company as "the largest grab in history". During 1966 there were two interesting declarations from the capital, Kinshasa (the new name for Leopold-

ville—Kisangani being the new name for Stanley-ville): (1) In June 1966, the 6th anniversary of Congolese independence, Patrice Lumumba, assassinated in 1961 was declared a national hero and (2) that presidential elections would be held in 1970 by universal adult suffrage, including women. Tshombe made an abortive attempt to return in 1967 but was captured in Algeria. The problem of the mercenaries was finally settled in November 1967 when President Mobutu had them repatriated from Rwanda where they had fled after the fall of Bukavu. On Congo's relations with Belgium President Mobutu said one should look not backwards but towards the future. Belgium is sending a number of teachers and doctors to the Congo.

**The Civil War in Nigeria.**—The civil war began in July 1967 after the secession of the Eastern Region under its Ibo leader, Colonel Ojuku. This region became known as Biafra. Federal troops, under the head of the Federal Military Government, General Gowon, advanced into Biafra and cut the secessionists off from the sea and confined them to the Ibo heartland. Margery Perham, writing in *The Listener* (19 September 1968) explained that there was a very wide difference between the Ibo way of life and that of the other major tribes in Nigeria—the Hausa and the Yoruba. " This difference had seemed to matter less when all the tribes were held together within the overarching structure of the British government. But with independence, with the full tribal competition for power and economic advance, certain deep rivalries began to appear." The Hausa (Muslim) and the Yoruba (Muslim and Christian) both belong to old civilisations and are grouped in large city states, the Ibos (mostly Roman Catholic) are poorer, thirsty for education and eager for change. The tension between the main tribal groups led to the assassination in 1966 by Ibo officers of the Hausa Prime Minister, Anubakar Tafewa Balewa. General Ironi, an Ibo soldier, tried to impose a unitary system of government, but was murdered by non-Ibo soldiers. This tragic civil war, seen by millions on their television screens, evoked a response for practical action and Lord Hunt and his mission have been successful in organising help.

The Federal Military Government has said that the military operations could cease immediately if Colonel Ojukwu and his associates would agree to renounce secession, remain part of Nigeria and accept the new structure of the Federation based on the 12 states, including the South Eastern and Rivers States.

Biafra, as an independent state, has been recognised by Tanzania, Ivory Coast, Senegal, Uganda, Zambia and Gabon as they thought there was no longer a basis for unity between the Ibo people and the remaining people of Nigeria.

As regards the supply of arms to the Nigerian Federal Government, Mr. Stewart, the Foreign and Commonwealth Secretary, re-stated the British Government's position in the House of Commons on 18 November 1968 as follows: " We believe that this rebellion was a disastrous and tragic error and that it would not have been right for us to cut off arms to a Commonwealth country whose traditional supplier we were because it was faced with a rebellion. To have done so would have amounted to giving support to rebellion and thereby all the suffering for which it is responsible." A similar view was taken by the United States Under-Secretary of State when he said on 3 December 1968 that if the British Government stopped British arms sales to Nigeria " they would, in fact, be helping to support the diememberment of a fellow Commonwealth country," and added, " Unfortunately, however, other nations have covertly provided arms to Biafra, a fact which, perhaps more than any other, has prolonged the fighting."

**The Assassination of Verwoerd.**—Dr. Verwoerd, who was murdered in September 1966, while the members of the Commonwealth were assembled in Conference in London, was the man who gave form and substance to the idea of apartheid, led South Africa into a republic and took her out of the Commonwealth. He studied applied psychology in Germany and on return took an interest in politics, organising in 1936 a protest against the admission to South Africa of a shipload of Jews fleeing from Germany. He became a power behind the scenes in the Nationalist Party which, in 1948, ousted the Smuts régime on the slogan of apartheid. He succeeded J. G. Strydom as Premier in 1959, a year after being elected to the House of Assembly. The Bantu Self Government Act of 1960 provided for the division of the non-white population into tribal units, the abolition of their existing representation in Parliament and the creation of self-governing " native states." But the aim of apartheid, the physical separation of races is, apart from other objections, a dishonest myth, as the economy cannot be run without black labour. The call by The Pan-African Organisation for a nationwide campaign against the law requiring all African men to carry passes for identification led to the massacre by the police at Sharpeville. Verwoerd banned the two major African political movements, the African National Congress and the Pan-African Congress and most African leaders were sent to prison, proscribed or fled. Verwoerd was born in Holland, a land noted for its enlightened policy of racial integration; but after his return to South Africa from Germany he held the separation of races to be blessed by scriptural authority and, as a follower of the Dutch Reformed Church, carried his philosophy into politics.

**Violence and Southern Africa.**—Violence has begun to erupt over southern Africa. The indecisiveness over Rhodesia, the absence of serious economic pressure on South Africa and on the Portuguese, whatever the reasons for this policy, have encouraged those ready to use violence. And this applies to the advocates of violence on both sides, black and white. The guerrilla has suddenly become a reckonable factor, said Colin Legum, in a part of the world where, until a few years ago, black violence was unknown. Guerrillas are operating in South West Africa, in Angola, in Mozambique, and in Rhodesia. Until 1966 President Kaunda of Zambia—opposed to violence—was successful in denying guerrillas even passage through Zambia. But he has been unable to resist pressures. In this new and menacing situation Dr. Banda, President of Malawi, is in an anomalous position. He has ranged himself with the White Supremacists against the guerrillas by opening diplomatic relations with South Africa. He has become a Black ally of the White Front.

**Rhodesia.**—*See* Part II.

## THE UNITED STATES.

**The Assassination of President Kennedy** in November 1963 at Dallas, Texas, shocked the entire world. The world recognised the growing mastery which this young man had shown during his three years of office in leadership and commitment to policies which promised increasing conciliation among nations. His youthfulness had galvanised hope in a world in which political decisions were so widely in the hands of leaders past their prime. He was the youngest elected American President (43) when he succeeded Eisenhower at the White House in January 1961, Eisenhower being then America's oldest President. Kennedy had had difficulties with Congress; and it was reassuring, therefore, that Lyndon B. Johnson, who as Vice-President automatically succeeded Kennedy, should have had the reputation of being a skilful negotiator in Congressional matters.

**Cuba and the United States.**—In 1961 the United States broke off diplomatic relations with Cuba with whom relations had been strained since the Castro revolution of 1959. Shortly afterwards two U.S. aeroplanes, but manned by Cubans, attacked the principal military bases near Havana, the capital. Two days later 1,500 invaders, Cuban exiles—armed, trained and largely controlled by U.S. agencies—landed on the island but were driven back. The United States intelligence service had assumed that the Cuban people would rise against Dr. Castro directly they heard of the landing. Controversy broke out in the States. Confidence in the new Kennedy administration was shaken for the affair was fundamentally alien to the American character. Relations were more bitter than ever, and, by the

end of 1961, Cuba became a Communist state in the full sense.

**The Crisis of the Autumn of 1962.**—The world came to the brink of war during the last week of October 1962. President Kennedy had pledged the United States to take measures to oppose the creation of offensive military power in Cuba. On 22 October, upon alleged evidence of offensive Soviet missile sites there, he announced a blockade of ships (or more precisely a quarantine of ships) carrying weapons to Cuba. Some Soviet ships altered course thus avoiding a direct confrontation. The United Nations made proposals to both sides in preparation for talks; and shortly afterwards Khrushchev decided to dismantle Soviet missile bases in Cuba and ship " offensive weapons " back to the Soviet Union, the United States agreeing to give assurances against an invasion of Cuba which had been threatened.

**The Presidential Election, 1968.**—The midterm Congressional elections of 1966 rehabilitated the Republican Party which had been so sundered by the rout of Goldwater in 1964. It chose as its Presidential candidate Richard Nixon (who had once been Vice-President and a Presidential candidate). On the Democratic side the candidature of Lyndon Johnson was first challenged by Senator Eugene McCarthy, who took his stand upon the criticism of America's war in Vietnam, and by Senator Robert Kennedy who was later assassinated. The President announced to the nation on 31 March that he would initiate peace moves in Vietnam and lay down the presidency in January. This dramatic turn of events threw the presidential race into confusion. Vice-President Humphrey then entered the lists to become the chosen candidate for the Democratic Party. It was one of the most closely contested presidential elections in American history, Nixon, the Republican candidate, having a majority of only 499,704 over Humphrey in a total poll of 72 million. Although securing only a small majority of the popular vote Nixon obtained 301 votes in the Electoral College against Humphrey's 191. In January 1969 he became the 37th President of the United States.

**The New Administration, 1969.**—

| | |
|---|---|
| President | Mr. Richard M. Nixon |
| Secretary of State | Mr. William Rogers |
| Secretary of Defence | Mr. Melvin Laird |
| Secretary of the Treasury | Mr. David Kennedy |
| Attorney General | Mr. John Mitchell |
| Postmaster General | Mr. Winton Blount |
| Secretary to the Interior | Mr. Walter Hickel |
| Secretary of Agriculture | Mr. Clifford Hardin |
| Secretary of Commerce | Mr. Maurice Stans |
| Secretary of Labour | Mr. George Shultz |
| Secretary of Health, Education and Welfare | Mr. Robert Finch |
| Secretary of Housing and Urban Development | Mr. George Romney |
| Secretary of Transportation | Mr. John Volpe |

## 3. THE THREAT OF NUCLEAR CONFLICT.

**Terms Used.**—

A **deterrent** is a weapons system capable of causing such a degree of destruction to an attacker that it would be too high a price for him to pay for any advantages sought. Of course, the attacker may not know what destruction the deterrent could cause, so that what is important is not the owner's estimate of his deterrent but the potential aggressor's estimate of it. Furthermore, deterrent forces must be able to strike back after an aggressor's missile attack. So there is a distinction between first and second strike weapons. The nuclear deterrent is said to be the ultimate deterrent, because nuclear weapons are the most advanced form of weapon.

The **nuclear or thermonuclear bomb** means a bomb or a missile with an explosive power measured in megatons, *i.e.*, one million times more powerful than bombs used during the Second World War. A ten megaton bomb contains the equivalent of a train of railway wagons filled with high explosive stretching from London to New York—and of course fall-out with its genetic effects.

The independent bomb. Independence, in this context, means the right and ability to launch a force alone against an aggressor. For this it is necessary to own and control thermo-nuclear weapons and be able to deliver them. The ability to deliver weapons, without which they are useless as a deterrent, raises crucial difficulties.

It is argued that the bomb, like earlier types of armament, is the ultimate guarantee of the nation's security; that without it we should not reach the conference table with other great powers; that it gives us freedom of action and, as such, is a safeguard against the possibility of a change in American policies which might leave us unprotected. The facts and policy of an independent nuclear deterrent have been seriously challenged.

ABM is the anti-ballistics missile defence system, whereby missiles are launched to destroy the missiles of the enemy—anti-missile missiles. Both the U.S.S.R. and U.S.A. are developing an ABM system.

Other terms. *Escalation* is a term used for the belief that once a conflict begins which involves nuclear powers, the contesting parties are riding on an escalator from which there is no escape and rising to an all-out thermonuclear war. A weapon is said to be *credible* when it is trustworthy and it can be believed in for its purpose: thus it is sometimes said that the U.K. manned bomber force is credible only for a first strike. *Conventional* weapons and forces are other than nuclear. Atomic devices are described as *tactical* when they are in support of ground forces and *strategic* when they are part of an all-out major strike force.

The Partial Nuclear Test-Ban Treaty was signed in Moscow in August 1963 between Britain, the U.S.A., and the U.S.S.R. who undertook not to conduct nuclear tests in three out of four possible spheres—in the atmosphere, in outer space and under water. The fourth possibility—underground tests—was not touched by the Treaty, but it declares that agreement on such tests remains a desirable aim. There has been little hope of extending the test-ban treaty to underground explosions, despite the appeal of the United States to Russia to agree. The U.S. and Britain still disagree with Russia over the question of identifying the nature of all underground explosions. The Western Powers insist that no foolproof method has yet been devised and they cannot therefore accept a ban on nuclear underground explosions without a limited number of on the spot inspections. But this is just what Russia is opposed to, on the grounds that this would amount to espionage.

Treaty to Prevent Spread of Nuclear Weapons.— Ever since 1960 there had been talks on how to prevent the proliferation of the bomb and the round of talks, which ended in August 1966, finished without any substantial new progress. The stumbling block was Russia's suspicions that despite declarations by America the arrangements to be made for the future of NATO would give Germany a finger on the nuclear trigger. Talks were resumed at the 18-power Conference at Geneva in February, 1967, where a draft treaty was tabled by the U.S. and U.S.S.R. By March 1968 a single text, sponsored by both the U.S.S.R. and U.S. emerged, containing a number of additions to meet at least some of the demands that had been put forward by the non-nuclear Powers. This joint U.S.-Soviet draft treaty was sent to the UN General Assembly where it was adopted in June by 95 votes to 4, with 21 abstentions. One of the countries that voted against was India—the American-Soviet joint offer of guarantees did not appear to provide the cast-iron protection that India might like against China.

The Nuclear Non-Proliferation Treaty flowing from this agreed draft was signed in London, Moscow, and Washington on 1 July 1968. But it will not enter force until it has been ratified by the three depositary Powers—Britain, the Soviet Union and the United States—and by 40 other states. Britain was the first nuclear weapon power to ratify the treaty on 27 November 1968.

UN Warning on Nuclear Power.—There are now enough nuclear warheads in existence to "eliminate all mankind." This was the view of twelve international experts expressed in a report to the United Nations in October 1967. Security would not be ensured by the acquisition of further development of nuclear weapons. In fact greater tension and greater instability in the world was the highest probable consequence of a further increase in the number of nuclear weapon States or of existing nuclear arsenals. There is no active defence system in sight, they said, which would prevent all nuclear weapons from reaching their selected targets. (Both the Soviet Union and the United States were preparing anti-ballistic missile systems.) The cost of producing weapons is so great that only six states, besides the existing five nuclear powers, could consider building "a modest nuclear armament" without reallocating a major part of their resources from constructive activities. These were West Germany, India, Canada, Italy, Poland, and Sweden. And only these could find the resources to expend the £200 million needed to develop "a small, high quality" force of nuclear weapons. (Israel and Japan are countries which might be regarded as having advanced nuclear technologies; and other powers which might obtain a nuclear capacity with external assistance include Pakistan and the United Arab Republic.)

American ABM Programme.—The estimated cost of the original Sentinel or so-called "thin" ABM screen, ostensibly designed as a protection against a Chinese missile attack in the mid-1970s was about 5,000 million dollars; that of a heavy or "thick" Soviet-orientated ABM system upwards of 50,000 million dollars (or nearly twice the total national income of India). This programme has since been modified and a limited Safeguard ABM system was under consideration in Washington in the spring of 1969.

America's decision to enter the anti-ballistic missile defence system was announced in September 1967 after the Russians had already begun work on their ABM system around Moscow. Under the old plan there were to be ABM sites around some 15 to 20 cities including Boston, Chicago, Seattle, and San Francisco. But there was strong protest from American civilians who were against spending money on more weapons when so much needed to be done in urban development. The modified system provides for local defence of selected Minuteman sites and an area defence of the country's bomber bases, command and communication centres. It was described as essentially a "safeguard" programme to strengthen the American deterrent. The only way to protect America's cities, said President Nixon, was to prevent war.

Hopes of a detente and of cooperation between the two great powers came when the Soviet Foreign Ministry at one of its rare Press conferences, on the day of Mr. Nixon's inauguration, emphasised that it was prepared for negotiations with the U.S. on the question of offensive and defensive missiles.

Outer Space for Peaceful Developments.—An international treaty to preserve outer space for peaceful purposes was completed in December 1966. It was described by President Johnson as "the most important arms control development since the limited test-ban treaty of 1963." Mr. Johnson first proposed such a treaty in May 1966 since when there had been extensive talks between the U.S. and Russia, the only two powers which are seriously involved in space research. The drafting of the treaty was prepared by the United Nations. It provides for rights of exploration in space for all countries; no claims of sovereignty over celestial bodies; no orbiting of weapons of mass destruction (already provided for in an earlier UN resolution); the preservation of space and all celestial bodies for peaceful purposes; and other procedures for peaceful co-operation among nations in space and in the exploration of space.

# II. POLITICAL STRUCTURES AND INSTITUTIONS

## HOW BRITAIN GOVERNS HERSELF.

### CENTRAL GOVERNMENT.

We devote most of our available space to recent changes in the structure of Government, but we recapitulate first a few basic facts. The skeleton of our democratic system, the way Government works (Parliament, the Civil Service, Local Government, the Judiciary) can be fairly simply described. Our constitution is not a written one so that we cannot refer to chapter and verse of an actual text. It is the actual working of the constitution that matters and this changes over the years in subtle, complex and often disguised ways. Thus the reader will find that books on this subject fall into two main groups. In the first are those which give the current outline or anatomy of Government. In the other group are a considerable number of books (all the way from Bagehot and Dicey) on how the constitution has evolved, what it needs to do, the dangers and efficacy of changes and so on. We thus have a whole range of treatises by jurists, historians, political scientists, and politicians analysing concepts, history, actual working of parts of the constitution, and comparisons with Government in other countries.

We are unique in having an unwritten constitution. Democracy is preserved by the ordinary law, by the political organisation of the people, by custom, and by rights which depend upon the capacity of the people to preserve them. The supreme law-making body is Parliament (a word which originally meant a talk). Parliament has grown from the original principle that in important matters such as making the laws the monarch ought not to act without counsel and consent, and it now consists of two Houses, the House of Lords, composed of lords spiritual and temporal, and the House of Commons representing the commoners. The principal share of parliamentary business is conducted in the Commons. Its business is divided into three branches: legislative, financial, and critical. The life of a Parliament is limited to five years, although, on the advice of the Prime Minister, the Queen may dissolve Parliament and issue a proclamation calling for election of a new Parliament. Parliament is adjourned from day to day while in session. At the end of the session it is prorogued. At the expiry of its life it is dissolved.

**The Queen.**—The Central Government is vested in the High Court of Parliament or The Queen in Parliament, consisting of the Queen and the two Houses. The Queen's tenure of the Crown holds for life (unless she abdicates), it is hereditary, and it is held by statutory right. The Queen is a constitutional monarch; she takes an oath at her Coronation to rule according to the laws and customs of the people. The Queen is the head of the Forces, which are governed by "Queen's Regulations." She is also head of the Executive, that is, all the work of the State is enacted in the name and under the authority of the Crown. Her assent is necessary before a Bill becomes an Act of Parliament. Member countries of the Commonwealth (except Malaysia, Lesotho, Swaziland and the Republics) owe allegiance to the Queen and she is represented by a resident Governor-General.

**The Parties.**—The right of a minority to oppose is an essential of democracy, and this idea means that political parties are allowed to function. The party system implies a government party (which has the largest number of candidates) and an opposition known as Her Majesty's Opposition. The system emerged in the latter half of the seventeenth century as Parliament gained the right to be the law-making body.

**The Executive.**—The work of applying the law and securing obedience is called the exutive work of the Government. The Executive comprises five bodies; the Queen, the Privy Council, the Cabinet, the Government Departments or Departments of State and the Civil Service.

The Cabinet was originally a committee of the Privy Council. It consists of the principal Ministers of the Crown, and is responsible for deciding the policy of the Government on all matters affecting the country, whether on foreign or home affairs. It has also complete control of the Government Departments. It is thus the central link in the whole machine of government. The Cabinet is responsible for the individual actions of its members. This follows from the requirement that a Minister's policy must be in agreement with Cabinet policy. Thus the Government have a common policy and act as one man. This is the meaning of the phrase "Ministerial responsibility."

**The Prime Minister.**—The Office of Prime Minister, like the existence of the Cabinet, was not formally mentioned in law until recent times. He is the link between Cabinet and Queen. It is he who decides when to advise the Queen to dissolve Parliament. He is leader of the Government party in the House of Commons and gives a lead on policy. A recent writer has pointed out how the Constitution has, after long evolution, divided the functions of leadership and vested them in two personages—a Prime Minister who is temporary and removable by the will of the electorate, and the Queen, who, by contrast, embodies the principle of continuity.

**Legislation.**—The law of this country consists of common law, statute law, and equity. One may describe the common law as that based on custom and usage as declared and expounded by judges. Statute law is the law made by Parliament, enshrined in Acts of Parliament or statutes of the realm. Parliament is thus concerned with the making of statute law. The subdivisions of English law are given on D3.

**How Laws are Made.**—Any member of the House of Commons may present a Bill after giving formal notice, but the principal Bills are those introduced by the Government based upon its programme outlined in the Queen's Speech.

The Bill has to pass three Readings before it can become law. The First Reading is a formality. The House gets down to discussion at the Second Reading when general principles as distinct from details are discussed. If the principles are approved, the Bill passes its Second Reading. It is then referred for detailed examination either to a standing committee or to the whole House sitting in committee. After the committee stage comes the report stage when the House considers the Bill as reported to it by the committee and decides whether further changes should be made. The final stage is the Third Reading when the House considers the Bill as a whole and whether it should or should not become law. If passed, it is sent to the Lords, where it enters on the same course. When Bills have passed through their various parliamentary stages they are sent to the Sovereign for Royal Assent.

The Lords cannot require the Commons to agree to amendments; nor can they delay a Bill indefinitely. They have no power in respect of Money Bills; and since the passing of the Parliament Act 1949 any other Public Bill which has been passed by the Commons in two successive sessions may be presented for Royal Assent without the consent of the Lords provided that a year has elapsed between the date of the Second Reading of the Bill in the Commons and the date on which it is finally passed in that House.

Bills may originate in either House, unless they deal with finance or representation when they are always introduced in the Commons. The procedure is basically the same.

Money Functions of the Commons.—The second function of the Commons (and one of its earliest in history) is to provide the State with money. The Government cannot raise money by taxation (or in any other way) or spend money without the authority of Parliament; and this power of authority belongs exclusively to the Commons. The House can vote money only on the demand and on the responsibility of a minister of the Crown.

Critical Functions of the Commons.—Parliament itself does not govern. The Queen's ministers are responsible for government and parliamentary government means that Parliament ensures that those ministers represent and have the confidence of the party which possesses a majority in the House; and further, that it controls the action of ministers by questions and criticisms. Any member may propose a motion of condemnation of any member or department of the Government, and such a motion would become a vote of want of confidence if it were made by the Leader of the Opposition.

The House of Lords is the oldest second chamber in the world and the most hereditary in its character. The House of Lords has two sets of functions, legislative and judicial. It is a party to legislation within the limits imposed by the Parliament Acts of 1911 and 1949. These limits are based on the fundamental principle that the function of the Lords, which is a non-representative assembly, is not to thwart the will of the people, but to ensure that that will is precisely and reasonably interpreted. The Conservative Party retains an overwhelming majority in the Lords and their powers of delay can limit the effective term of the life of a Labour Government. The right to run a full term of office ought not to be the privilege of the party which commands a majority in the Lords. The reform of the Lords came to the fore again in 1968 and is dealt with under Parliamentary Reform. The judicial functions of the House of Lords sprang from the fact that it is the highest Court of Appeal for the United Kingdom.

Constitutional Commission.—In the Queen's Speech (Oct. 1968), outlining the Government's legislative programme for the new session, the setting up of a constitutional commission was announced. It would look at the whole sphere of central and local government reform in relation to Scotland, Wales, the regions of England, N. Ireland, Channel Islands, and Isle of Man. When he spoke in the debate on the Address, the Prime Minister tentatively suggested that the Commission should: (1) examine the present functions of the central Legislature and Government in relation to the various parts of the United Kingdom; (2) consider, in the light of developments in local government organisation and the administrative relationship between the various parts of the United Kingdom, what changes are desirable in those functions; and (3) consider whether any changes are desirable in the constitutional and economic relations between the United Kingdom, the Channel Islands, and the Isle of Man.

## CHANGES IN THE MACHINERY OF GOVERNMENT.

The administrative changes introduced by the Wilson Government and the Parliamentary reforms contemplated are described in the following paragraphs.

### 1. The Cabinet.

The Strengthening of the Cabinet.—One of the major changes made by the Labour Government was the strengthening of the position of the Prime Minister and the Cabinet by giving the Cabinet a much stronger Secretariat. The primary object of this is to ensure that the Premier and Cabinet are briefed at every significant stage of a political objective. A number of other benefits flow from this earlier briefing of the Cabinet. It is easier by this means to ensure that there is co-ordination between departments, which does not always

operate between strong departmental chiefs. Further, such strengthening of the Cabinet secretariat ensures that someone is looking all the time at government as a whole and that the Prime Minister is as well briefed, as he should be, as any of his colleagues, when a subject comes up for final decision for which the whole Cabinet is responsible.

In reconstructing his Government in April 1968 Mr. Wilson set up a new committee of the Cabinet, called the parliamentary committee, to co-ordinate work in Parliament and consider the broader political aspects of the Government's business. It consisted of ten members and the intention was that this non-departmental Cabinet, or inner Cabinet, should meet more often and regularly than the full Cabinet and be the chief policy making body. But it proved too big for intensive discussion and in April 1969 the Prime Minister decided to replace it by a committee of six senior Ministers under his chairmanship. It will be concerned with the general strategy of the Government in legislative and party senses.

The Need to Look Ahead.—The whole scope and complexity of the problems of Government have become increasingly greater. That is a change which needs a novel solution. But great as that change is there is a further new factor, the need to look ahead; the pattern of our life and institutions and of the world is changing so fast that we need ministers sufficiently free to visualise what things will be like one decade or two decades ahead and the character of the problems for which we need to prepare now. An important step in this direction was taken in 1968 with the appointment of Mr. Richard Crossman as co-ordinator of the social services. In his new rôle he will help to prepare the ground for the social advance expected after the " two years' slog "—promised by the tough 1968 Budget and the Incomes and Prices legislation—has brought success to the Government's economic policy.

A list of Cabinet Ministers will be found at the end of the section.

### 2. The Government Departments.

Revision of the Machinery of Government.—Some of the changes in the Departments of the Civil Service made by the Labour Government on taking office in 1964 had been fully anticipated, but some were a surprise. A change fully expected was the appointment of a Minister for Economic Affairs, whose new office was designed, it was claimed, " to put new heart and drive into the economy." The new Ministry was responsible for framing and supervising the plan for economic development; for the general co-ordination of action to implement that plan; and for all the economic policy related to industrial expansion, allocation of physical resources and regional implications of the expansion programme. Another new ministry of great importance was that of Technology described below.

Division of Responsibility between the Department of Economic Affairs and the Treasury.—While the former is concerned with physical resources, the Chancellor of the Exchequer at the Treasury is concerned with financial questions. The Treasury retains the traditional functions of government expenditure, accounting for Government expenditure, budgetary policy, taxation policy, and all aspects, including international ones, of monetary policy. The two Ministries work closely together: programmes for capital expenditure must be related to the industrial development plan. The relation of monetary policy to the rate of expansion links the two Departments. In the previous Conservative Government the Chancellor of the Exchequer presided over the National Economic Development Council; in the Labour Government the chair is now taken by the Prime Minister.

The Prime Minister and DEA.—In August 1967 Mr. Wilson temporarily took over direct responsibility for the DEA, appointing Mr. Peter Shore to run the day-to-day affairs. (Mr. Shore was given a place in the Cabinet.) Mr. Wilson's step was an extension of the powers of the Cabinet in a field that mattered more than any other, the harnessing of the country's resources. This special responsibility was given up by the Prime Minister in April 1968 but he retains the responsibility he has had from the beginning for co-ordination, not only of industrial matters but of economic matters generally.

The Economic Network is illustrated below:

A fundamental innovation was the creation of a Council of Scientific Policy (CSP) to advise the Minister on the financial priorities of Science policy. It replaced the old Advisory Council on Scientific Policy; and the deletion of "Advisory" from its title denoted the basic change from an ineffective to an effective body, a change advocated by Lord Blackett, O.M.

Scientific Research and Development.—Since January 1967 scientific research and development

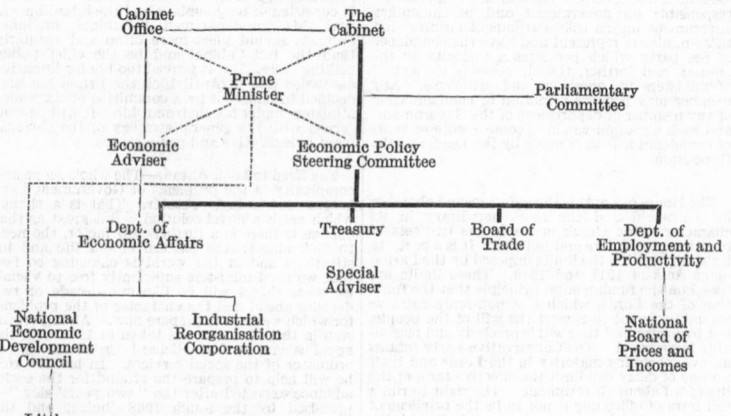

The Direction of Incomes Policy and Productivity.—A further change in the scope of the DEA was made in April 1968, when direct responsibility for the incomes policy and its implementation was transferred to a Secretary of State for Employment and Productivity, at the head of a newly constructed Ministry of Labour. The DEA was thus shorn of its day-to-day executive function in administering the incomes policy and left to concentrate on long-term economic planning—its original objective.

Ministry of Technology.—By the absorption of the Ministry of Aviation in 1966, the Ministry of Technology (Mintech) has become the biggest State-directed complex of scientific and industrial power in Europe. It was already responsible for the Atomic Energy Authority; grants to the National Research Development Corporation and fifty industrial research associations; and ten civil research establishments. The acquisition of Aviation brought in (1) the purchase of aircraft and electronics; (2) research and development contracts with industry; and (3) seven research and development establishments.

The problems before the Minister (Mr. Anthony Wedgwood Benn) are not only technological but how to design an effectual partnership between academic Science, Industry, and Government. This is a totally new task. It requires the same order of boldness and skill as the Government needs in their attempt to link Unions, Industry, and Public in the refashioning of the economy.

The Department of Education and Science.—To this Department have been added Ministers of State with special responsibility for higher education and science, for schools, and for the arts. Within the scope of the Department fall the "pure science" research bodies:

Medical Research Council (MRC)
Agricultural Research Council (ARC)
Natural Environment Research Council (NERC)
(for geology, hydrology, and oceanography)
Science Research Council (SRC) (for astronomy space, university nuclear research, etc.).

has been co-ordinated under the Central Advisory Council for Science and Technology, responsible to the Cabinet and working under Sir Solly Zuckerman, O.M. Its function is to advise the Government on the most effective national strategy for the use and development of our scientific and technological resources.

Reorganisation of Government Departments.— A number of changes were made in 1968, covering overseas affairs, the social services, and the management of the Civil Service.

The Foreign Office and the Commonwealth Office were merged into a single department, known as the Foreign and Commonwealth Office.

A new office of Secretary of State for Social Services was created with the amalgamation of the Ministries of Health and Social Security into a single Department of Health and Social Security.

The Government accepted the recommendation of the Fulton Committee, which reported in 1968, that responsibility for the management of the Civil Service should be transferred from the Treasury to a new Civil Service Department under the direction of the Prime Minister as Minister for the Civil Service. The new Civil Service Department will assume the Treasury's functions in respect of the pay and management of the Civil Service and the co-ordination of government policy in relation to pay and pensions throughout the public sector. The Civil Service Commission is to form part of the new department, though it will continue to act with independence and political impartiality in the selection of individuals for appointment to the Civil Service. See Civil Service.

Integration of the Social Services.—The problem of integration cannot be solved until the ideas of the Seebohm Committee on local authority social services, the Maud report on local government, expected in July 1969, and the Government's revised Green Paper on the health service are considered together. In speaking of the health service, Mr. Richard Crossman said what was wrong with the Green Paper of July 1968 was that it seemed to concentrate authority at the centre and to exclude the possibility of a second tier of district level executive committees in which both the local people who used the service and doctors and others who worked in it could have effective voices. There had been criticism of a centralised structure but support for a unified service and the concensus seemed to be emerging for a two-tier solution. A revised Green Paper was expected in July 1969.

**The Land Commission.**—The Land Commission Act, 1967, created the Land Commission which from 6 April 1967 has the power to acquire, manage, and dispose of land and to impose " a betterment levy " in respect of all land transactions. Its purpose is to ensure that the right land is available at the right time for the implementation of national, regional, and local plans; and that a substantial part of the development value created by the community returns to the community. Its purpose further is to reduce the cost of land needed for essential purposes. The Land Commission is enabled to buy land compulsorily when it is suitable for development, although it may not be needed at the moment for development. Thus the Act creates a land bank; and by halting speculation in land likely to be needed for building it attempts to reduce the cost of land for housing.

The Act provides for some exemptions from the betterment levy and gives the Commission power to postpone collection and to allow payments by instalments. The Land Commission is an independent body substantially exercising its own discretion and judgement.

It its first annual report since the passing into law of the Land Commission Act, 1967, the Commission stated that its research had shown that there was little land available for development, especially around London and in the Midlands, where need was greatest. Accordingly, local planning authorities in the south-east of England had been asked to allocate more land for development in their plans so that this land could be acquired by the Commission and developed as required. In Scotland the Commission found that much of the land suitable for housing development was owned by a small number of building firms which had accumulated large stocks. Action had been taken by the Commission to bring some of this land on to the market so that it might be developed more quickly.

Despite the fact that many people started developments before the appointed day, and thus escaped the levy, the Commission's achievements so far have been impressive and it has been estimated that by 1970–1 the yield from the levy will be about £20 million a year, and by 1972–3, £80 million.

### 3. Parliamentary Reform.

**The Reform of Parliament.**—So far back as 1963 Mr. Crossman had written: " More time is wasted and more energy and talent frustrated in the British Parliament than in any other organisation of which I have any experience. Under the Attlee Government and in the first years of Opposition it was difficult to raise the faintest interest either in the National Executive at Transport House or at Westminster for reforms which were dismissed as purely academic. Since the 1959 Election the mood has changed. . . . Collectively as members of Parliament they resent both the rapid decline in its prestige and the process by which it is being stripped of any real rôle in the great decisions of State." In the following year Mr. Harold Wilson spoke out strongly on the need of House of Commons reform. His proposals included:

(a) relaxation of the parliamentary voting system to allow more " free votes " and to eliminate the rigid doctrine of each vote involving an issue of confidence; and

(b) development of all-party committees on the lines of the existing Estimates Committee and Public Accounts Committee, not only to make investigations but to draft more controversial legislation.

The whole subject was examined by the Select Committee on Procedure in the Session 1964–5.

The aspect in their reports which attracted most attention was how the extension of the Committee system might be used to provide greater information for M.P.s and improve the efficiency of Parliament.

**Committees of the House.**—It may be helpful if we classify the existing Committee system. Committees fall into four groups: (1) Standing Committees; (2) Select Committees; (3) Joint Committees; and (4) Private Bill Committees.

A Standing Committee is a miniature of the House itself and the function of these Committees is to take over Bills for their Committee stage and thus to save time which would be spent on them if they were taken on the floor of the House. A Select Committee is a body of special powers and privileges to which the House has delegated its authority in a special way, for example, the finding out of facts, the examination of witnesses, the sifting of evidence, and the drawing up of conclusions which are reported to the House. Apart from ad hoc Select Committees there are a number of Sessional Select Committees which are almost permanent bodies (like the Committee of Public Accounts, the Estimates Committee, and the Committee of Privileges). Joint Committees consist of members of Lords and Commons. They are really a Select Committee of the Commons deliberating with a Select Committee of the Lords; and are used to save duplication of Committee work in each House, generally on uncontentious Bills. Private Bill Committees deal, as the name connotes, with the Committee stage of Private Bills.

Committees are, of course, portions of the House; but in addition to these true Committees there are " Committees of the whole House." Such Committees consider Bills at the Committee stage and at them members may speak more than once to the same question, a valuable concession when discussing details of legislation. Committees of the whole House also include the Committees on Supply and the Committees of Ways and Means. The former consider details of money to be spent on the Services, including the Civil Service; and the latter discuss ways and means of raising the money to be thus spent.

**The Voting Age.**—The Government has decided to adopt the recommendation of the Latey Committee (see D7(2)). The voting age did not come within the terms of reference of the Committee, but the Home Secretary said it would be illogical to accept the view that, for all other purposes except voting, the adult status should begin at 18; it would be better to have consistency between the age of majority and the age of voting. At the time of writing (January 1969) a Bill was before Parliament to reduce the age of majority and the voting age to 18.

**Reform of the Lords.**—An undertaking to curtail the delaying powers of the Lords was included in the manifestos of the Labour Party both in 1964 and 1966. The Government's promise, which appeared in the Queen's Speech, when she opened Parliament on 31 October 1967, was " to reduce the powers of the House of Lords and to eliminate its present hereditary basis "; and this would be supported by measures to ensure that the Government of the day always has a working majority in the Upper House over all other political parties. No serious argument between the parties seemed likely on the underlying principle of abolition of the hereditary basis of the Lords. Out of 1,062 present members, 736 are lords because their fathers were, 122 are there because past Prime Ministers have made them hereditary peers and 26 are there because they are bishops in the Church of England. Their presence has nothing to do with democratic government. But while there would be general agreement that the hereditary principle was indefensible, there would be differences of view upon how to abolish the principle, over what period to complete the process, how to select hereditary peers who are to continue to sit in the new Chamber, and the working of the system of appointing life peers. As regards reform of the powers of the Lords, criticism springs from two facts:

    (1) the power of the Lords to reject Statutory Instruments, exercised regardless of the wishes of the Commons; and

    (2) their power to delay legislation, which the Commons has approved, by wrecking amendments.

The result of the second power can be the delay of a Bill for 13 months from the time of second reading in the Commons, and a considerable waste of the Commons' time.

After inter-party talks, the Government proposals to reform the House of Lords, reducing its total membership to 230 and curbing its delaying powers, were published in a White Paper in Nov. 1968. It was proposed that the reformed House should have a two-tier structure comprising voting peers (peers of first creation or life peers), with the right to speak and vote, and non-voting peers (mainly hereditary peers) with the right to speak but not to vote.

The Commons " Watchdog ".—By the Parliamentary Commissioner Act of 1966 a functionary new to the British constitution arrived—a commissioner who resembled the Ombudsman who had been the pride of Sweden for a hundred years. His office was designed to protect the citizen from bureaucratic maladministration. The Government recognised that there was a deficiency in the present method of investigating by questions and by letters to Ministers.

### 4. The Civil Service.

Ministers and Civil Servants.—The relationship between the political head of a Department and his senior officials is a subject hitherto insufficiently analysed. Ministers are often appointed because they have a special knowledge or interest in the office to which they go. But very often this is not so at all. It could scarcely be otherwise under our practice by which a Minister can be switched from Economic Affairs to Foreign Office overnight or from Transport to Employment and Productivity, both recent examples. They were not unusual; the practice is as old as ministerial government. The new Minister, whether he knows nothing or much of his new duties, must assume instant responsibility. His advisers are steeped in the subject; they have known the subject inside out for many years and they cannot but have formed their own views. The Minister is dependent on them for the whole body of relevant facts. It is their duty to put all the facts to the Minister and for him to decide on policy. It sounds much more simple than it can possibly be. The civil servants are doubtless men of integrity and impartiality; they are devoted and loyal. But the actual situation must often be complex and subtle between a Minister who comes with a new broom of a changing policy and a group of officials who for years have been setting their compass on a different course. Every student of politics must have concluded by changes of attitude that Mr. X, so enthusiastic about a policy before his appointment, had yielded to the subtle pressure of his permanent staff; and on the other hand he can discern when a new Minister has clearly had the force of character to lead his civil servants and not be subservient to them.

The Labour Party's Proposals for Reform of Civil Service.—These proposals were contained in a testimony given by the Party to the Fulton Committee set up by the Prime Minister in February 1966 to examine the structure, recruitment, and management, including training, of the Home Civil Service. The testimony made proposals which would revolutionise the whole Government machine. The importance of the proposals lay in the fact that they were endorsed by the National Executive Committee of the Labour Party and that the Committee contained eight Cabinet Ministers including the Prime Minister. (The principal members of the Cabinet also testified privately to the Fulton Committee.) The proposals dealt with:

    (1) the relations between administrators and politicians;

    (2) those between administrators and specialists; and

    (3) relations between the Civil Service and the public.

On the first the complaint was made of the excessive secrecy and of the amount of information which, in some departments at least, is kept from the Minister. " An enormous amount of work goes on in a department," said the document, " which the Minister knows nothing of—some of it research work which produces important results which are never shown to the Minister . . . some of it planning work which may be deliberately concealed from him. . . . It is this secrecy which makes some Ministers tools of their departments a good deal of the time. . . . Inter-departmental committees are a particularly effective way of undermining the authority of Ministers." On the second head the document argued that the separation of administrator from the specialist was running against the whole trend of modern management. Most scientists produce their best work when they are still young; scientific creativity tends to dry up as middle age approaches; at this stage a scientific officer will probably be glad of the chance to move on to the management side of the service; and his scientific background will give him something special to offer as an administrator. This mobility should help to avoid the moribundity which sometimes afflicts research establishments twenty years or so after their initiation. Thus scientists, engineers, and other " professionals " should be groomed as potential administrators from the very early days in the Service. The complaint of secrecy reappeared in the passage on the third aspect, the relations between the Civil Service and the public, which it was said " sometimes make it appear that the whole structure of British Government is designed to protect the policy-making functions of Government from public scrutiny."

The Fulton Committee reported in June 1968 and the Government has accepted its main recommendations for the reshaping of the Civil Service.

Fulton Committee Report, 1968.—In spite of its many strengths, the Civil Service was found to be inadequate in six main respects:

    (a) It was still too much based on the philosophy of the amateur (or " generalist " or " all-rounder "). This was most evident in the administrative class, which holds the dominant position in the service.

    (b) The present system of classes in the service (there are over 1,400, each for the most part with its own separate pay and career structure) seriously impeded its work.

    (c) Scientists, engineers, and members of other specialist classes were frequently given neither the full responsibilities and opportunities nor the corresponding authority they ought to have.

    (d) Too few civil servants were skilled managers.

    (e) There was not enough contact between the service and the community it is there to serve.

    (f) Personnel management and career planning were inadequate.

Fulton Recommendations for Reform of Civil Service.—The Committee's principal recommendations aimed at equipping the Civil Service for the most efficient discharge of the responsibilities of government included:

    (1) The establishment of a new Civil Service Department to absorb the recruitment and selection functions of the present Civil Service Commission, and to take over the responsibilities for central management of the Service at present

carried by the Treasury, but on an expanded scale. The new Department to be accountable to the Prime Minister with day-to-day responsibility delegated to a non-departmental Minister of Cabinet rank. The official head of the new Department (the Permanent Secretary) to be designated Head of the Home Civil Service.

(2) The abolition of the class system in the Civil Service. All classes to be abolished and replaced by a single managerial class of civil servant combining the present adminstrative and executive classes. A unified grading structure to cover the entire Civil Service, each post graded by the technique of job evaluation.

(3) The development of greater professionalism in the Service. Professional and technical officers (i.e., specialists) to be given more training in management and opportunities for greater responsibility and wider careers. Administrators to develop a fuller professionalism by specialising, especially in their early years, in particular areas of government, e.g., in economic and financial affairs or social policy.

(4) The establishment of a Civil Service College to provide training courses in management and organisation, and in research. Not restricted to civil servants.

(5) In addition to the Permanent Secretary, who has overall responsibility, under the Minister, for the running of a Department, the Minister should also have a Senior Policy Adviser who would normally be head of the planning and research unit to be set up within departments for major long-term policy planning. The main task of the new adviser would be to look to and prepare for the future and to ensure that current policy decisions were taken with as full recognition as possible of likely future developments.

(6) The delegation to departments of a larger rôle in recruitment and the speeding up of recruitment procedures.

(7) The devotion of more resources to the career management of all civil servants so that they have the opportunity of advancing on their merits.

(8) The encouragement of greater mobility between the Civil Service and other employments through a reform of the restrictions on the transfer of pensions. The Committee recommend an expanded " late entry," temporary appointments, short-term exchanges of staff, freer movement out of the Service.

The Prime Minister told the House of Commons in June 1968 that arrangements would be made to ensure the continued independence and political impartiality, within the new Civil Service Department, of the Civil Service Commission in the selection of individuals for appointment in the Civil Service. He also said that the Government had accepted the recommendation to set up a Civil Service College to develop the training of civil servants broadly on the lines advocated in the report, and that consultations with the staff associations would at once begin for the implementation of the proposed unified grading structure of the Civil Service.

## LEGISLATION.

The volume of legislation can be gauged from the fact that during 1968 over seventy Public Acts were passed. A feature of the Labour Government's legislation has been the number of consolidating Acts, i.e., Acts which bring together in one document several enactments on a specific subject. Among the Acts passed in 1968 were:—

*Prices and Incomes Act, 1968*, to provide support for the productivity, prices, and incomes policy.

*Transport Act, 1968*, to provide for a better integration of road and rail transport and promote higher standards in the road transport industry. The Act also enables improvements to be made in traffic management and the financial and other arrangements for the railways and nationalised inland waterways.

*Industrial Expansion Act, 1968*, to promote industrial expansion by enabling the Government to assist projects likely to benefit the economy.

*Trade Descriptions Act, 1968*, to strengthen the law prohibiting inaccurate or misleading descriptions of goods, services, and facilities provided or offered in the course of trade, and false or misleading indications of the prices of goods. *See* D42.

*The Race Relations Act, 1968*, to make discrimination on racial grounds unlawful in employment, housing, and the provision of goods, facilities, and services, and to encourage the development of harmonious community relations. *See* D41.

*Countryside Act, 1968*, to enlarge the functions of the National Parks Commission (now called the Countryside Commission), confer new powers on local authorities and other bodies for the management of rural areas in England and Wales, and to provide greater opportunities for leisure and recreational activities in the countryside. It obliges every government department and public authority to have due concern for amenity. The Act provides for the appointment of a Welsh committee of the Commission.

The Queen's Speech (Oct. 1968) foreshadowed the introduction in 1969 of legislation to implement the report of the Royal Commission on Trade Unions and Employers' Associations; to reform the House of Lords; to reduce to 18 the age for voting and to make other reforms in electoral law; to reduce the age of majority to 18; to reform the law in England and Wales relating to children and young persons; to make reforms in the administration of justice; to convert the Post Office from a department of state to a public corporation; and to transfer London Transport to the Greater London Council.

A Private Member's Bill on Divorce Reform was before Parliament at the time of going to press.

## GOVERNMENT and INDUSTRY.

**Economic Planning.**—The National Plan, the incomes policy, and the strengthened pound were the three lines of advance in the Labour Government's attempt to put Britain in a position to earn its living and pay its debts. The National Plan set out to expand output, exports, and earnings over the five years to 1970. It was knocked sideways by the July 1966 emergency measures and abandoned. In February 1969 the Government issued a Green Paper entitled *The Task Ahead*. It provides a guide to the likely development of the economy in the next four years and is based upon an immense amount of knowledge. This assessment to 1972 is not a national plan with planned targets but is seen by the Government as a basis for consultation and discussion so that Government and both sides of industry can work towards a better-managed economy and better-managed individual industries. Industry wants to see that Government policy helps it to perform effectively; Government needs all the information available from industry. Mr. Fred Catherwood, the Director-General of the National Economic Development Council, said: " It is said that the communications problem of the next few years will be to enable computer to talk to computer. But the overwhelming problem, to my mind, is to enable Government and industry to communicate in terms which both understand, in order to solve the vast number of problems where a joint solution is essential and unilateral action could be disastrous. This is what the current consultative process is all about."

Special detailed consultations will take place with key industries, in the private sector through seven Economic Development Committees, or " Little Neddies " (chemicals, electrical engineering, mechanical engineering, electronics, motor vehicles, machine tools, and paper and board), and separately where industries are not covered by EDCs (shipbuilding, aircraft, and iron and steel castings). Industries in the public sector selected for discussions include energy and steel. Feedback of information and views will determine what changes are necessary. *See* Section G, Part IV for National Plan, National Economic Development Council, Department of Economic Affairs, National Board for Prices and Incomes.

**Industrial Relations Reform.**—A Royal Commission was appointed in 1965 under the chairmanship of Lord Donovan " to consider relations between management and employees and the rôle of trade unions and employers' associations in promoting the interests of their members and in accelerating the social and economic advance of the nation, with particular reference to the law affecting the activities of these bodies." The Commission reported in June 1968 and recommended a change in Britain's system of collective bargaining, involving the replacement of industry-wide agreements by company or factory agreements. It proposed that an Industrial Relations Act should be passed under which an Industrial Relations Commission would be set up. In January 1969 Mrs. Barbara Castle, Secretary for Employment and Productivity, presented to Parliament the Government White Paper " In Place of Strife—A Policy for Industrial Relations " (Cmnd 3888), containing the Government's plans for modernising labour relations based on the Donovan Report. The White Paper began: " There are necessarily conflicts of interest in industry. The objective of our industrial relations system should be to direct the forces producing conflict towards constructive ends. This can be done by the right kind of action by management, unions and the government itself." Its main legislative proposals may be summarised as follows:

(1) A Commission on Industrial Relations (CIR) to be set up immediately as a Royal Commission. (Mr. George Woodcock, due to retire as general secretary of the TUC in 1969, agreed to act as full-time chairman.

(2) The Secretary of State for Employment and Productivity to have a discretionary power to require a 28-day " conciliation pause " in unconstitutional strikes and strikes where adequate joint discussions have not taken place. The Secretary of State to have also a discretionary power, where a major official strike is threatened, to require a union to hold a strike ballot among its members. (Neither of these proposals was in the Donovan Report.)

(3) A Register of agreements to be set up covering, at first, companies employing more than 5,000 people.

(4) Trade unions to be given the right to obtain from employers certain sorts of information needed for negotiation.

(5) The right to belong to a trade union to be made part of all contracts of employment.

(6) The CIR to be able to look into trade union recognition problems, including inter-union disputes, if the TUC is not first able to resolve the problem.

(7) A Trade Union Development Scheme to be introduced under which grants and loans will be available by the CIR to promote reforms.

(8) Statutory machinery to be established to safeguard employees against unfair dismissal.

(9) A new Industrial Board to have power to impose financial penalties for breach of Orders issued by the Department for Employment and Productivity. But there is to be no imprisonment for default.

(10) The Industrial Board to hear complaints by individuals against unfair or arbitrary action by trade unions resulting in substantial injustice.

(11) Trade unions to be required to register with a new Registrar of Trade Unions and Employers' Associations.

The White Paper was seen as a challenge to both sides of industry to work towards a co-opera-

tive solution and make it unnecessary for legal sanctions to be involved. The Commission on Industrial Relations will be the major body supervising the Government's planned reform of industrial relations and though it was to be established initially as a royal commission, to enable it to begin work without delay, provisions to put it on a statutory basis were to be included in the Industrial Relations Bill to be put before Parliament.

**Introduction of New Machinery.**—The Commission on Industrial Relations will work on references by the Secretary of State for Employment and Productivity, to whom it will report. Its primary concern will be with ways of improving and extending procedural arrangements, for example, how to promote suitable company-wide procedures, how to develop acceptable rules governing disciplinary practices and dismissals, how to encourage effective and fair redundancy procedures, and how to bring shop stewards within a proper framework of agreed rules in their firms and ensure that they are provided with the right kind of facilities to do their job.

The CIR will also tackle other problems not now the direct responsibility of any public agency, such as investigation of trade union demands for recognition, encouragement of reforms in trade union structures and services, and examination of cases in which companies report failure to negotiate satisfactory agreements, and it will report on other questions related to its responsibilities such as the effectiveness of existing procedures. It will also be asked to give advice to the Secretary of State from time to time on the reform of the industrial relations system, and report periodically to Parliament. The Government look on the new Commission as a disseminator of good practices and a focus for reform by example. It would not be appropriate, the White Paper says, for the CIR to be asked to adjudicate or award any kind of penalties. For these functions the Government proposes a new Industrial Board.

**New Forms of Government Enterprise.**—A revolutionary new Government agency (the Industrial Reorganisation Corporation) to act as a holding company for new forms of Government commercial and industrial enterprise was announced in 1966. Armed with massive sums of capital it is intended to have almost unlimited powers to buy up privately-owned enterprises, found new ones, and create the circumstances for big mergers between existing industrial institutions. This formed a dramatic new method of taking over—short of public ownership—firms which are falling down on their task, coupled with plans for new incentives to industry and special incentives to regions. The Government is thus able to step into a lagging section of the economy.

The Industrial Act, 1968, is designed to promote industrial expansion by enabling the Government to assist projects likely to benefit the economy. It extends the powers of the National Research Development Corporation and the Industrial Reorganisation Corporation. The Bill was attacked by the Confederation of British Industry as " backdoor nationalisation."

**Industrial Research and Development.**—New arrangements were announced in January 1969 for linking the work of the major industrial research establishments of the Ministry of Technology more closely to the needs of industry. A basic objective of the Ministry is to strengthen the competitive ability of industry by accelerating the rate of application of innovation. Its establishments are not only engaged on research and development for industry but on the application of techniques and discoveries to design, production, quality control, distribution, marketing and sales. To achieve this objective, industry, said the Minister, Mr. Wedgwood Benn, will be associated as closely as possible with research planning. Direct links between establishments and both industrial organisations and universities are being fostered. The Atomic Energy Authority has already been authorised to undertake research and development outside the atomic field, and the results of research at Ministry of Technology defence establishments are being made increasingly available for civil exploitation, so far as this is compatible with security.

**Retraining.**—Industrial retraining was launched on an extended basis at the end of 1966 by a number of measures, including a Government contribution of up to £2 million in 1967 to help employers to provide additional places in their own training centres for retraining adults for semi-skilled jobs. Among the Government's measures were a move for new Government centres; more intensive use of space in Government centres; and apprenticeship training classes in technical colleges. The new factor in the retraining campaign was the recognition that training facilities can be expanded quickly only by making use of the resources available within industry and the training establishments of the armed services. These arrangements were aimed mainly at training semi-skilled workers but the main shortages were among more advanced skills.

**Regional Planning and Organisation.**— *See* Section G, Part IV.

## LOCAL GOVERNMENT.

Local Government is concerned with the domestic duties of a community as distinct from national questions like defence or taxes which must be decided by Central Government. England and Wales (exclusive of London) are divided into Administrative Counties, County Boroughs,

abundance of facts. It was expected that a reformed Local Government would reduce the demand for elective Regional Government. But one supreme thing was expected: that the result would be a root-and-branch reform. In the meantime, reform has already been effected in London.

### Local Government in Greater London.

The London Government Act, 1963, involved the abolition of the London County Council and the Middlesex County Council, and parts of Essex, Surrey, Kent, and Hertfordshire have been incorporated in Greater London, which now covers the whole of the continuously developed area within the green belt. The system came fully into effect on 1 April 1965.

The London Boroughs.—There are 32 London boroughs and the population of each is between 170,000 and 340,000. Broadly speaking the new boroughs are responsible for all the important personal services such as housing, health, and welfare. Each council has a maximum of 60 directly elected councillors, plus aldermen up to one-sixth, making a maximum of 70. The councillors retire together every three years. The independent position of the City of London remains unchanged and it has the powers of a borough.

The Greater London Council, a directly elected body, carries out functions which need to be planned and administered over Greater London as a whole and consists of 100 councillors and 16

*Local Government in England and Wales*

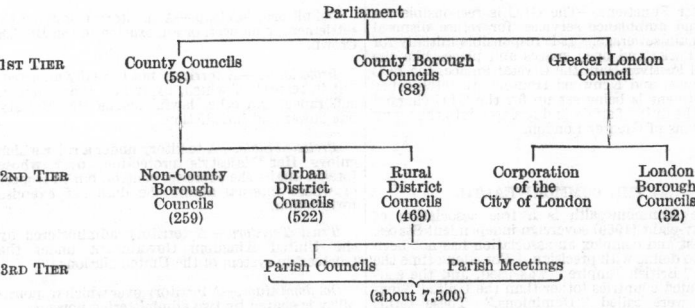

(about 7,500)

Boroughs, Urban Districts, Rural Districts, and Parishes. The structure, as the chart shows, is split vertically: on the one side stand the county boroughs (all local government therein being in the hands of one authority—the county borough council); and on the other the organisation governing the administrative county (where there is a division of function). In Scotland there are County Councils, Burgh Councils, and District Councils; and in Northern Ireland there are County Councils, County Borough Councils, and Borough. Urban, and Rural District Councils.

. Two New Royal Commissions.—In 1966 the Government decided to be bold and appointed two Royal Commissions to review and to revise Local Government in England and in Scotland respectively. They were expected to take two years to produce a finished plan and not just a set of principles. A third year will be needed to debate legislation so that by 1970 there should be the new structure essential for a modern Britain. The Local Government Commission, set up under the Local Government Act, 1958, has been disbanded. The evidence which that Commission gathered, together with the reports of the Maud and Mallaby Committees on the management and staffing of Local Government will provide an

aldermen. The new Councils in Greater London came into existence as local authorities when they were elected—the GLC on 9 April 1964, and the London Borough Councils on 7 May 1964—and from then until 1 April 1965 the new authorities and the old continued side by side. On 1 April 1965 the new councils took over their full functions and the older authorities ceased to exist.

Elections for the Greater London Council.—For the first election of the Council, held on 9 April 1964, each of the 32 London Boroughs was also the electoral area and returned two, three, or four councillors, according to the size of the electorate in each area. These electoral arrangements may, however, be changed for future elections and it is possible that the number of electoral areas will be increased and will probably return one councillor only. Elections will be held every third year on a day which is fixed by the Home Secretary.

The Powers of London Boroughs.—Each London borough is a housing authority although the Greater London Authority is the "overspill" authority. Local development plans are drawn up by the boroughs (within the framework of the overall development plan of the GLC) and the boroughs are responsible for dealing with applications for planning permission. They are wholly responsible for a wide range of personal health services and welfare services for the elderly, the sick and the handicapped, and children's services. The GLC will complete the LCC housing programme and, for the time being, inherits the LCC stock of houses (about 230,000) and will eventually transfer them to the boroughs.

**Education in Greater London.**—In Inner London, virtually the ex-LCC area, education is the responsibility of a special committee of the Greater London Council, consisting of members of the GLC elected from the central area together with a representative of each London Borough Council, and of the City of London. The ILEA maintains the education service and decides the amount of money needed to be raised by precepts on Inner London Borough Councils and by borrowing. The education committee established by the ILEA consists of the members of the Authority together with 16 other persons chosen from people experienced in education. The unique arrangements for Education in Inner London preserve the continuity of the service which has developed since 1870 as a unity without regard to local boundary divisions. In the Outer London Area education is the responsibility of the borough council.

**Highways and Traffic.**—The GLC is the traffic authority for the whole of Greater London. Thus " metropolitan roads " come under the GLC and the new boroughs take the remaining roads except trunk roads which the Ministry of Transport continues to look after.

**Other Functions.**—The GLC is responsible for fire and ambulance services, for refuse disposal and main sewerage. It is responsible initially for LCC Parks and open spaces and places like the Royal Festival Hall, the Crystal Palace, the LCC museums, and Kenwood House. An intelligence department is being set up for the GLC charged with the duty of study and research into the many problems of Greater London.

## THE COMMONWEALTH.

The Commonwealth is a free association of twenty-eight (1969) sovereign independent States. So vast and complex an association has not been easy to define with precision. For a long time the term " British Empire " was used, and the self-governing countries (other than the United Kingdom) were called " Dominions." These terms have now given place to " Commonwealth " or " Commonwealth of Nations " and " Members of the Commonwealth." The last term describes the sovereign countries named on **K189.** Other parts of the Commonwealth, such as Colonies, while they may be described as " Commonwealth countries " are not *Members* of the Commonwealth.

**The Nature of the Commonwealth.**—The Commonwealth is not a federation, for there is no central government, defence force, or judiciary, and there are no rigid obligations or commitments between them. Nor is it a contractual association as the United Nations is. Like the United Kingdom itself the Commonwealth of Nations has no written constitution. But all its members have a broad community of interests, and they are bound together by a common sense of ideals and by a common interest in the maintenance of peace, freedom, and security. Although the Commonwealth includes about a quarter of the total population of the world about three-quarters of the Commonwealth's people live in India. The white population of the Commonwealth is only a small fraction of the whole. The diversity is further illustrated in religion, for the Commonwealth includes over 200 million Hindus, 100 million Moslems, and 80 million Christians. The

same variety appears in climate and natural resources. But in spite of diversities of race, religion, language, and tradition, members share a common political heritage which has given rise to a broadly common pattern of institutions.

**The Sovereign and the Commonwealth.**—The Queen's legislative power in the parliaments of the Commonwealth is a formality—she reigns, though she does not rule; but she provides the element of continuity in the administration. The Queen is, therefore, Queen of the United Kingdom, Canada, Australia, New Zealand, Ceylon, Jamaica, Trinidad and Tobago, Sierra Leone, Malta, Gambia, Guyana Barbados and Mauritius, all of whom owe her allegiance, and she is the symbol of their free association in the Commonwealth. Those countries which are Republics (India, Pakistan, Ghana, Cyprus, Nigeria, Tanzania, Zambia, Malawi, Botswana, Uganda, Singapore, and Kenya) with Presidents as Head of State; Malaysia, which has one of the Malay Rulers as Head of State; Lesotho and Swaziland, which have their own monarchs, do not owe allegiance to the Queen. All members accept her as the symbol of the free association of member nations of the Commonwealth and as such Head of the Commonwealth.

**The Colonies.**—As stated in the opening passage of this outline, the United Kingdom, in common with other members of the Commonwealth, has certain dependencies which are described as " The Colonies." But this is a loose term, for " the Colonies " are not really all Colonies in the strict sense. What are loosely spoken of as Colonies are properly divided into Colonies, Protectorates, Protected States, Trust Territories etc.

**Definitions.**—*Colony.*—A territory belonging by settlement, conquest, or annexation to the British Crown.

*Protectorate.*—A territory not formally annexed, but in respect of which, by treaty, grant, usage, sufferance, and other lawful means Her Majesty has power and jurisdiction.

*Protected State.*—A territory under a ruler which enjoys Her Majesty's protection, over whose foreign affairs she exercises control, but in respect of whose internal affairs she does not exercise jurisdiction.

*Trust Territory.*—A territory administered by the United Kingdom Government under the trusteeship system of the United Nations.

*Condominium.*—A territory over which responsibility is shared by two administering powers.

*Leased Territories.*—This term applies only to that part of the mainland of China which was in 1898 leased to Great Britain for ninety-nine years and is administered by the Government of Hong Kong.

*Associated State.*—A former colonial territory which has entered into a free and voluntary association with Britain to become self-governing in all matters except for external affairs and defence. The term applies to six of the East Caribbean islands—Antigua, St. Kitts–Nevis–Anguilla, and the four Windward islands of Dominica, St. Lucia, St. Vincent, and Grenada.

**Responsibility of the British Government.**—The British Government is responsible for the affairs of Colonies (properly called Crown Colonies) both internal and external, and for their defence, and their peoples are British subjects. Protectorates are governed in the same way as Colonies, but have not been annexed. The peoples of Protectorates are not British subjects but British-protected persons. In the case of an Associated State the British Government is responsible for defence and external relations, though it may confer upon the Associated State's government authority to deal with specific matters of foreign affairs.

**The Countries of the Commonwealth.**—At the end of the Gazetteer is a list of all the countries of the Commonwealth showing their land area and recent estimates of population. The list distinguishes between the sovereign members and the British dependent territories, and classifies the latter according to the kind of dependency. Not all the British dependencies come exactly within the definition either of Colony or Protectorate, since, for historical reasons, many come partly under one heading, partly under another. Mauritius, Nauru, Swaziland, and Aden (as part of the People's Republic of Southern Yemen) became independent in 1968. Nauru, the world's smallest independent state, was previously a UN trust territory, administered jointly by Australia, New Zealand, and the United Kingdom. The next countries which seemed, at the opening of 1969, to be coming up for independence were Fiji and British Honduras.

**Rebellion in Rhodesia.**—The dissolution in December 1963 of the Federation of Rhodesia and Nyasaland led to the independence of Northern Rhodesia (as Zambia) and of Nyasaland (as Malawi) and left Southern Rhodesia, renamed Rhodesia, as a self-governing colony. Rhodesia's white, minority Government pressed for complete independence. The Rhodesian Front, under the Prime Ministership of both Mr. Winston Field and Mr. Ian Smith, had insisted that Rhodesia had an immediate right to independence based on (a) the fact that it has been self-governing for forty years, and (b) that this was morally, if not indeed explicitly but privately, promised by British Ministers when the Rhodesian Federation was broken up. The British Government, both under Conservative and Labour rule, specified only that while Rhodesia should move to independence like any other self-governing dependency, it should be under a constitution broadly acceptable to the people as a whole and should provide for a peaceful transition to majority rule. This principle was elaborated in a statement of five conditions set out in the following paragraph. It was not said by either party that independence could not be granted to Rhodesia until a government elected on a franchise wide enough to be described as a government " of the majority " is actually in power. But that majority rule must be the precondition was asserted by the two Rhodesian African leaders (divided, but both in prison), by the African States, by the United Nations, and by some Commonwealth countries.

**Five Conditions for Independence of Rhodesia.**— In the protracted negotiations between Mr. Smith and Mr. Wilson to reach a settlement in 1965 the latter took his stand on the following five conditions:—

1. a guarantee of unimpeded progress towards the majority rule already envisaged in the 1961 Constitution;

2. a guarantee of no retrogressive amendments of the 1961 Constitution;

3. an immediate improvement in the political status of the African population;

4. progress towards the elimination of racial discrimination; and

5. the overriding requirement that Britain must be satisfied that any proposed basis for independence would be acceptable to the Rhodesian population as a whole.

The British Government offered to co-operate in a crash programme of education for Africans to fit them to take an effective share in the economic and political life of the country within the span of, possibly, a decade.

The 1961 Constitution, which has been the subject of so much dispute, provided (for the first time) fifteen African members (in a Parliament of sixty-five) elected on a virtually all-African roll. The other fifty are elected on a common roll with residential and property qualifications, which were said to be low enough to enable enough Africans to become the voting majority in due course. But, even if this outcome were to be practicable, this period might be as high as twenty years. The African nationalists have largely boycotted registration on either roll; and the acceptance of the 1961 Constitution is tantamount to the indefinite continuance of minority—i.e., white—government.

**Unilateral Declaration of Independence.**—The long pressure for independence from 1963 to 1965 reached its climax on 11 November 1965, when Mr. Ian Smith declared the independence of Rhodesia; and the British Government were confronted by an act of rebellion. (U.D.I. became known as I.D.I., the illegal Declaration). The rebels protested their loyalty to the Sovereign, whose commands, however, they were repudiating. African opinion was outraged, and among the countries which broke off relations with Britain were two Commonwealth countries (Ghana and Tanzania), Mauritania, Guinea, Mali, the Sudan, Algeria, and the Congo (Brazzaville). Britain ruled out, from the start, the use of force; but Mr. Wilson embarked on a policy of graduated economic sanctions, including an oil embargo; the objective being the emergence, under economic hardship, of a liberal alternative to the Smith régime. The United Nations took the view that the 1961 constitution had broken down and that the decrees signed upon I.D.I. amounted to the destruction of all safeguards for the rule of law and for human rights in the 1961 constitution and earlier legislation.

There are many aspects of the complex position in Rhodesia, and several interpretations can be given. But one central fact must be stated simply: four million Africans remain subordinate to 220,000 whites. The implications of the rebellion go far beyond Rhodesia. It has exacerbated the whole problem of race division in Africa. As such it has aroused strong feelings in black African countries and has strained the Commonwealth (on the multi-racial character of which Britain has set such store). The rebellion exacerbates in particular the threatening confrontation between black African countries and South Africa and Portugal.

**Commonwealth Conference 1966 and Rhodesia.** —At the Conference of September 1966 it was decided to give the Rhodesian Front régime a final chance of a negotiated settlement with Britain. If the offer were rejected Britain undertook to sponsor jointly mandatory sanctions at the UN, withdraw all previous proposals for a constitutional settlement, and not grant independence before majority rule was achieved. The final offers by Britain had to be accepted before a fixed date.

It was agreed that the British Government would not recommend to Parliament any constitutional settlement which did not conform with six principles. These six principles were the five conditions for independence set out in an earlier paragraph together with a sixth, namely: no oppression of the majority by the minority or of the minority by the majority.

**The Ride on the " Tiger."**—After secret " talks about talks " between officials during the summer of 1966 Mr. Wilson and Mr. Smith had talks on 2 December on board H.M.S. *Tiger* off Gibraltar and prepared a working document which the Rhodesian Cabinet rejected three days later; and on the 16th the UN Security Council voted on a British resolution for mandatory sanctions, including oil. Mr. Smith said that in his view Rhodesia had become a Republic, a statement which he later modified.

**The " Fearless " Talks.**—Mr. Wilson and Mr. Smith met on H.M.S. *Fearless* in Gibraltar harbour on 9 October 1968 in yet another attempt to settle the dispute. But the talks ended on the 13th with disagreement on the fundamental issues still remaining. On 18 November the proposals based on the *Fearless* talks were rejected by

Rhodesia. The white majority in the crisis affecting their country had found themselves unready to give the Africans reasonable prospects of education, jobs, political and civil rights.

In the House of Commons debate of 22 October 1968 the Prime Minister emphasised that the limit of what Britain could offer to reach a settlement with the illegal regime in Rhodesia had been reached.

**Commonwealth Conference 1969.**—During the discussions at the Commonwealth Prime Ministers' Conference held in London in January 1969, Britain was criticised for abandoning the principle of no independence before majority rule (NIBMR) in putting forward to Mr. Smith the *Fearless* proposals. The majority view was that these proposals should be withdrawn. But Mr. Wilson could not accept that view. The *Fearless* terms were still on offer to Rhodesia. He considered that it would be right, if it proved possible, to give the people of Rhodesia as a whole an opportunity to decide for themselves whether or not they wished for a settlement which would be fully consistent with the Six Principles laid down by successive British Governments. Any such settlement would need to be clearly shown to be the wish of the Rhodesian people as a whole. If that took place, he would consult his Commonwealth colleagues about the NIBMR commitment. He emphasised, however, that a settlement based on the Six Principles would not be possible if it were shown that there could be no genuine test of its acceptability in present circumstances in Rhodesia.

The Commonwealth Secretariat was established in 1965. This body acts as a central source of information and preparation, independent of Britain's Foreign and Commonwealth Office. Thus the Commonwealth has its own staff with no ties to any single member.

Arnold Smith, Canadian diplomatist, was appointed to the new post of Commonwealth Secretary General. The quality of paramount importance in a Secretary General of a family of 730 million is his ability to get along with people regardless of race. It was said that his indifference to the colour of skin was nothing theoretic—he just did not notice, a colour blindness of attitude. But of course his views on racial equality are strong. Just before becoming Secretary General of the Commonwealth he said: " The division of humanity between the white and other races, which coincides too closely for comfort with the division between the affluent industrialised peoples and the poor underdeveloped peoples, is, I think, the most difficult and potentially dangerous problem in the world." The Secretariat were no doubt concerned to examine ways in which the rest of the Commonwealth might help to heal the tragic war in Nigeria.

**Britain's Special Representative in Africa.**—A Special Representative dealing with Britain's relations with Kenya, Tanzania, Malawi, and Zambia was appointed in 1965. He was Mr. Malcolm MacDonald, then British High Commissioner in Kenya. He became a roving ambassador to Commonwealth countries in Eastern and Southern Africa. The British high commissioners in those countries continued their functions in the three capitals now concerned—Nairobi, Lilongwe, and Lusaka; and Mr. MacDonald's responsibilities are to co-ordinate major policy problems in which some or all of these four countries are involved. Uganda preferred not to enter the co-ordination arrangement for the present.

## THE UNITED NATIONS.

**Charter of the United Nations.**—The Charter of the United Nations was signed on June 26, 1945. The purposes of the United Nations can be divided into four groups (security, justice, welfare, and human rights) and the nations undertook to carry out four main duties (to settle disputes peacefully, to refrain from treating or using force, to assist in carrying out the Charter, and not to assist an aggressor). The UN affirms faith in the human rights of all without distinction of race, language, sex, or religion.

**Membership of the United Nations.**—The UN had one hundred and twenty-six member countries in 1969. They were:

| | |
|---|---|
| Afghanistan | Laos |
| Albania | Lebanon |
| Algeria | Lesotho |
| Argentina | Liberia |
| Australia | Libya |
| Austria | Luxembourg |
| Barbados | Malagasy Republic |
| Belgium | Malta |
| Bolivia | Malawi |
| Botswana | Malaysia |
| Brazil | Maldive Islands |
| Bulgaria | Mali |
| Burma | Mauritania |
| Burundi | Mauritius |
| Byelorussian S.S.R. | Mexico |
| Cambodia | Mongolia |
| Cameroun | Morocco |
| Canada | Nepal |
| Central African Republic | Netherlands |
| | New Zealand |
| Ceylon | Nicaragua |
| Chad | Niger |
| Chile | Nigeria |
| China (Taiwan) | Norway |
| Colombia | Pakistan |
| Congo (Brazzaville) | Panama |
| Congo (Kinshasa) | Paraguay |
| Costa Rica | Peru |
| Cuba | Philippines |
| Cyprus | Poland |
| Czechoslovakia | Portugal |
| Dahomey | Roumania |
| Denmark | Rwanda |
| Dominican Republic | Saudi Arabia |
| Ecuador | Senegal |
| El Salvador | Sierra Leone |
| Equatorial Guinea | Singapore |
| Ethiopia | Somalia |
| Finland | South Africa |
| France | Spain |
| Gabon | Sudan |
| Gambia | Swaziland |
| Ghana | Sweden |
| Greece | Syria |
| Guatemala | Tanzania |
| Guinea | Thailand |
| Guyana | Togo |
| Haiti | Trinidad and Tobago |
| Honduras | Tunisia |
| Hungary | Turkey |
| Iceland | Uganda |
| India | Ukrainian S.S.R. |
| Indonesia | United Arab Republic |
| Iran | U.S.S.R. |
| Iraq | United Kingdom |
| Ireland | United States |
| Israel | Uruguay |
| Italy | Venezuela |
| Ivory Coast | Voltaic Republic |
| Jamaica | Yemen |
| Japan | Yemen, Southern |
| Jordan | Yugoslavia |
| Kenya | Zambia |
| Kuwait | |

Botswana was formerly Bechuanaland, Lesotho was Basutoland, Guyana was British Guiana, and Southern Yemen was the Prot. of Southern Arabia (Aden). Thus there are now two Yemens like two Congos.

The membership includes 27 members of Commonwealth countries, representing one quarter of the world's population. The African group is numerically the strongest, with a membership of 39 (excluding S. Africa). Twelve member states are communist. Switzerland is not a member of the UN because of her tradition of strict neutrality.

**Major Organs of the United Nations.**—The UN have six major organs: (1) a General

Assembly, (2) a Security Council, (3) an Economic and Social Council, (4) a Trusteeship Council, (5) an International Court of Justice, and (6) a Secretariat. It is especially the inclusion of the third body on this list (with all the Commissions and specialised agencies which stem from it) which makes the UN more broad and balanced than the League of Nations.

**General Assembly.**—The General Assembly occupies a central position in the structure of the UN. But its business is quite distinct from the Security Council. It meets once a year. The Assembly can consider the general principles of co-operation for peace and security and disarmament and regulation of armaments. It can discuss any question concerning peace and security brought before it. It makes recommendations, but any question upon which action is necessary must be referred to the Security Council. The carrying out of its humanitarian work is the function of the Economic and Social Council (dealt with below) which it elects and supervises. Further, the Assembly controls the purse.

**Principal Organs of the United Nations.**

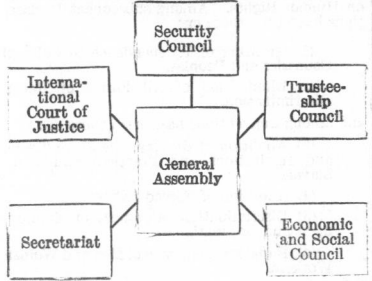

**The Security Council.**—The aims of the UN are wide—from feeding starving peoples to encouraging self-government in backward areas —but it cannot advance towards the noble objectives set out in the Preambles unless peace is maintained. The principal organ to preserve peace and security is the Security Council. The size of the Security Council was enlarged from 11 to 15 with effect from January 1966. Five seats are permanently occupied by Great Britain, the U.S.A., the U.S.S.R., China, and France. The China which is represented in the UN and on the Security Council is not, however, the Republic of China (or Communist China). It is the régime of Chiang-kai-Shek, who occupies Formosa. The other seats are normally elected for two years by the General Assembly. The ten temporary members are: Colombia, Finland, Nepal, Spain, and Zambia (retiring at end of 1970), and Paraguay, Hungary, Pakistan, Senegal, and Algeria (retiring at the end of 1969). The Security Council sits continuously. It has two functions: (1) to promote the peaceful settlement of disputes and (2) to stop aggression. Under the Charter, parties to a dispute have already promised not to use force, to settle their quarrels peaceably, and to refer their dispute to the Security Council if they really cannot reach a peaceful settlement. On its side the Council can call on the parties to settle disputes peacefully, it can investigate any situation likely to cause a breach of the peace, and at any stage it can recommend a solution.

**The Veto.**—At this point we must deal with the veto, which applies to substantive questions. The number of affirmative votes required for adopting decisions on substantive matters is 9, including the votes of the five permanent members. In other words if any one of the permanent members says " No " to the use of force, even after a full investigation, the Council cannot use force to

settle the dispute. Thus when it comes to imposing sanctions for a breach of the peace the assent is required of the Great Powers, and one of them may of course be a party to the dispute. If the Great Powers imposed sanctions on each other it would mean a major war in which the present UN would disappear. Partly in order to overcome the difficulty of the veto the Assembly set up a Committee to remain in permanent session consisting of one representative of each member. It is known as the Little Assembly, its formal title being the Interim Committee.

**The Uniting for Peace Resolution, 1950.**—The General Assembly had always been able to discuss matters of peace and security, although it could not make recommendations about them if they were being considered by the Security Council. But in 1950, after the Korean crisis, a new decision was taken by the General Assembly whereby if there were some threat or breach of the peace on which the Security Council was in deadlock, the Assembly, on a vote of seven members of the Security Council, could consider it immediately and make a recommendation about it. This decision, to which Russia and four other countries were opposed, was called the " Uniting for Peace " resolution. By this resolution, too, the Assembly can be called together within twenty-four hours. It was the standing Interim Assembly which considered the Israeli–Egyptian dispute in November 1956.

**The Economic and Social Council.**—The UN pledged themselves to a broad humanitarian policy of which the following are salient points: to promote higher standards of living; full employment; the conditions of economic and social progress; solutions of international economic, social, health, and other related problems; educational co-operation; universal respect for human rights; and the fundamental freedoms for all. The main business of the Economic and Social Council is to carry out this broad policy. The size of the Council was increased from 18 to 27 with effect from January 1966. To tackle these huge problems the Council established a number of important commissions and bodies, the principal being the following:—

*Regional Economic Commissions*

Economic Commission for Europe (ECE)

Economic Commission for Asia and the Far East (ECAFE)

Economic Commission for Latin America (ECLA)

Economic Commission for Africa (ECA)

*Functional Commissions*

Disarmament
Statistics
Population
Social
Human Rights
Status of Women
Narcotic Drugs

*Special Bodies*

UN Children's Fund (UNICEF)

Commissioner for Refugees

Conference on Trade and Development (UNCTAD)

Industrial Development Organisation (UNIDO)

*Intergovernment Agencies (previously called Specialised Agencies).*—The agencies are organisations established by intergovernmental agreements, and their activities as a rule are co-ordinated by the Economic and Social Council. The list of the fifteen Agencies are given below.

International Atomic Energy Agency (IAEA)

International Labour Organisation (ILO)

Food and Agriculture Organisation (FAO)

UN Educational, Scientific and Cultural Organisation (UNESCO)

World Health Organisation (WHO)

World Bank (Bank)

International Finance Corporation (IFC)

International Monetary Fund (FUND)

International Development Association (IDA)

International Civil Aviation Organisation (ICAO)

Universal Postal Union (UPU)

International Telecommunication Union (ITU)

World Meteorological Organisation (WMO)

Inter-Governmental Maritime Consultative Committee (IMCO)

General Agreement on Tariffs and Trade (GATT)

Several of these organisations were at work before the UN was set up. One such body is the ILO.

**A Peace Force.**—In the twenty-four years since its inception the UN has been called on only four times for military action—in Korea (1950), in the Congo (1960) and in Cyprus (1964). Korea was really an American "containment" action under the covering of the UN. In the other operations, the number of troops ranged from 6,000 to 20,000. Apart from military action, the UN has sent observers or "presences" to various parts of the world, mainly to the Middle and Far East, to facilitate settlement of disputes. Thus to maintain a standby force of 20,000 men, when it might be needed so rarely, would be a waste, apart from problems of bases, control, and equipment. Two ideas about the best kind of peace force hold the field. They are:—

(1) the earmarking of national military units; and

(2) a permanent multiracial force.

The cogent arguments for a permanent UN Military Force can be studied in *United Nations Forces* by D. W. Bowett, pub. by Stevens in 1967.

**A United Nations Success: Technical Assistance.**
—That the United Nations is something more than a place of talk is proved by a glance at the history of its programme of Technical Assistance. The object of this aid is to help countries to develop their economic and political independence; and, since this must be a truly co-operative venture, receiving countries must not only invite the experts but actively participate in projects they undertake both with money and with local personnel—even the poorest being encouraged to make a contribution. A major reform was made in 1966 by the simplification of the existing systems of capital and technical aid by the United Nations. The two main channels of aid were fused—the UN Special Fund and the UN Technical Assistance Board—to become a single Council for a UN Development Programme (UNDP). *See also* Underdeveloped Economies, Section G, Part III.

**Unicef.**—Of all the United Nations agencies Unicef has most caught public imagination. In the early years of the war the attempt began to make amends to children whose early years had been shattered by war; and during the quarter century since Unicef has been bringing aid to millions all over Africa and Asia. Unicef does not draw directly on United Nations funds but voluntary help from Governments and individuals. There have been two developments of policy:

(1) a change in 1950 from post-war relief work to programmes of help for mothers and children in developing countries; and

(2) from 1960, an emphasis on education and vocational training rather than pure survival projects.

**Human Rights.**—The 20th anniversary of the adoption and proclamation of the Universal Declaration of Human Rights by the General Assembly on 10 December 1948 was marked by the observance of the year 1968 as International Year for Human Rights. There seemed, however, in 1968, a good deal to deplore as well as to celebrate. There had been a good deal of thinking on the subject and over two decades numerous conventions had been drawn up. But there had, unfortunately, been a good deal of obstruction and non-co-operation; and in 1968 the situation of slaves, political prisoners, and minorities of all kind was distressing. Let us take these two parts of the problem in turn—the resolution for improvement and the actuality.

**Declarations and Conventions on Human Rights.**
—Every member of the UN endorsed the Universal Declaration of Human Rights. It marked the determination to prevent the recurrence of the genocide and brutality which occurred in the Second World War. Out of it sprang a Commission on Human Rights and numerous other Declarations and Conventions. Thus the European Convention on Human Rights prescribed that "no one shall be subjected to torture or to inhuman or degrading treatment or punishment" and there has been established a European Court on Human Rights. Among subsequent Declarations have been those on:

(1) Granting of Independence to Colonial Countries and Peoples.

(2) Elimination of All Forms of Racial Discrimination.

and among Conventions have been those on:

(3) Abolition of Slavery, the Slave Trade, and Institutions and Practices Similar to Slavery.

(4) Abolition of Forced Labour.

(5) Discrimination in respect of Employment and Occupation.

(6) Equal remuneration of Men and Women Workers.

(7) Freedom of Association and Protection of the Right to Organise.

(8) Descrimination in Education.

(9) Prevention and Punishment of the Crime of Genocide.

(10) Political Rights of Women.

Drafts were being prepared for Covenants or Conventions on:

(11) Civil and Political Rights; Economic, Social, and Cultural Rights.

(12) Elimination of All Forms of Religious Intolerance.

(13) Freedom of Information.

But after conventions are adopted at UNO they need to be ratified; thereafter signed; thereafter nations need to take the necessary action to enable the provisions to be put into force; and finally to put them into force. These are the stages between declaration of intent and fulfilment. As U Thant has said: "The mere adoption of various covenants and international agreements is not enough by itself." We need, therefore, to temper enthusiasm for intentions with critical regard for what is actually happening.

**Why Nations Refuse to Ratify.**—All kinds of political reasons are offered for failure to ratify and sign by big countries and small. America has signed three of the 19 International Conventions on Human Rights. It has ratified the Slavery Convention. The Russians have ratified nine and signed one. Britain has ratified ten and signed one. American reluctance to ratify is said to be fear of conferring on outsiders the right to interfere in their treatment of Negroes. Russia and other Communist countries oppose allowing individuals the right to petition against the State. Broadly Governments dislike minorities and about a tenth of the world's population are minorities; and that tenth comes to something like 300 million. Ironically the growth of independent countries has sometimes led to injustices for minorities, and an extension of the minority problem.

**The Persistence of Slavery.**—Slavery persists today in five forms defined in the UN Supplementary Convention on the Abolition of Slavery (1956), namely chattel slavery, serfdom, debt bondage, sham adoption, and servile forms of marriage. The Anti-Slavery Society (for the Protection of Human Rights) stated in 1967 that it has recent information of the existence of one or more of these forms of slavery in thirty countries in the " free world." Apart from servile marriage the other forms probably embrace between one or two million people. This exploitation can only be fought when governments legislate against it and their officials and people uphold the law. To encourage them to do so is the main function of the Anti-Slavery Society. Founded so far back as 1823 it is the principal organisation in the world working to end slavery; and it has consultative status at the Economic and Social Council at UNO. It supports the setting up of machinery to implement the slavery conventions called for in October 1967 by the Int. Commission on Prevention of discrimination and Protection of Minorities. Besides the eradication of slavery in all its forms the Society's aims include the abolition of labour systems resembling slavery and the protection and advancement of aboriginal and primitive peoples. The address of the Anti-Slavery Society is Denison House, Vauxhall Bridge Road, S.W.1.

**The Anatomy of the United Nations** has undergone ironical changes since its inception. At the outset the Security Council was built as the organ through which the Great Powers would together discharge their collective responsibility as policemen. They were the superior powers. They had the authority and the means to act as the big policemen to keep others in order. But this assumed that the big five permanent members would agree and act in concert. This is just what they did not do. As a result, in 1950, by Anglo-Saxon device, the General Assembly was mobilised to ensure action when action was vetoed in the Security Council. But over the last decade the Assembly has grown both in numbers and in the independence of its views. It is not at all as interested in the conflict with Communism as those assumed who vested it with additional power: it is more interested in colonialism. So those who gave the Assembly this additional strength would like to reverse the position. But here we confront another difficulty. China, one must expect (and hope), will join the Security Council. That will make the unity in that body which is vitally necessary for peacekeeping even more difficult. But in 1967 the General Assembly again barred Communist China from membership and upheld Nationalist China's right to a seat.

**The General Assembly's 23rd Annual Session** met in the autumn of 1968. We give some extracts from the Secretary-General's report covering 1967–8.

On East–West relations: " In the final analysis there can be no solid foundation for peace in the world so long as the super-Powers insist on taking unilateral military action whenever they claim to see a threat to their security. Why should they also not bring their fears and complaints about threats to their security to the Security Council, as they regularly demand that less powerful States do? In the Cuban missile crisis this course proved helpful, and it could prove equally useful in other cases where big-Power interests and peace are both directly involved."

On Disarmament: " During the 23 years of the existence of the United Nations, there has never been a thorough discussion in any UN organ of the problems posed by chemical and biological weapons, nor has there been a detailed study of them. Recently the matter has been receiving more attention and it is felt that the time has come to deal more fully with the problem."

On the Arab–Israeli conflict in the Middle East: " It must be borne in mind, in considering the background for the many and regrettable breaches of the cease-fire, that on one side the cease-fire sectors in the Middle East are almost entirely areas under military occupation. History shows that such situations tend to give rise to a more than ordinary incidence of acts of violence."

On problems in Southern Africa: " The situation resulting from the unresolved question of the policies of *apartheid* of the Government of the Republic of South Africa has in the past year become more serious than ever, for the South African Government has not only continued to enforce its policies with more determination in South Africa but has also been attempting to consolidate and extend the influence of its racial philosophy in neighbouring territories, notably Namibia (South-West Africa) and Southern Rhodesia." Referring to Rhodesia, he said: " Not content with flouting the authority of the U.K. Government by proceeding with the execution of a number of African nationlists, the illegal régime has, with South Africa's assistance, resorted to suppressive military operations and has pursued the application of policies of separate racial development, including plans for creating a façade of African participation in its activities."

## WESTERN EUROPE.

### 1. Introduction.

This outline is an attempt to explain the various organisations through which European countries are trying to co-operate. It is hoped that the reader, with the help of the chart will find the pattern less bewildering than at first appears. The destruction in Europe in the Second World War emphasised the need for greater union, both for recovery and for defence. A bewildering array of organisations has sprung up. They differ in form, in function, and in membership. Some overlap in function. Some are much less effective than others. The edifice is not, moreover, built on a single harmonious plan. Beneath the edifice are two different kinds of foundations, that is to say, two rival theories. These two theories (the federalist and the functionalist) are explained as the story unfolds. The story traces four main streams—the military, the political, the economic, and the scientific and technological—and describes the bodies which evolved in each stream.

**Historic Origin of European Unity.**—Sully, the famous Minister of Henry IV, King of France, outlined, in 1638, a proposal for achieving European unity and putting an end to war in Europe. He called it the " Grand Design." It was revived in modern dress by Monsieur Briand, the French Prime Minister, in 1929. During the War (1943) the concept of a United Europe which should be created after victory was won was outlined by Sir Winston Churchill: and he returned to the subject in his famous speech at Zurich University in 1946.

**Two Starting Points: ERP and the Brussels Treaty.**—There were two main sources of the present numerous European bodies. The first was the European Recovery Programme in 1947 (ERP), and the second was the Brussels Treaty of 1948.

The **European Recovery Plan** was popularly known as the Marshall Plan, as it was the result of the invitation made in 1947 by Mr. Marshall (then U.S. Secretary of State) to the European countries to draft a programme to put Europe on her feet economically. The U.S.A. was ready to give this aid if the countries concerned would agree on co-operation and plan their needs. In March 1948 the countries concerned created the Organisation for European Economic Co-operation (OEEC) to administer the programme of aid. This body was replaced by the Organisation for European Co-operation and Development in 1961.

The Brussels Treaty, 1948, was the other main source of the West European organisations. In March 1948 Britain, France, and the Benelux countries (Belgium, Holland, and Luxembourg), agreed at Brussels to pursue a common policy on economic, political, and military collaboration, and to promote a better understanding of the principles which form the basis of the common civilisation of Western Europe. It also provided for the creation of a Consultative Council. This Council, when formed, was the Council of Europe, and it is described below, together with an account of all the organisations which stemmed from the Treaty. Italy and the German Federal Republic joined the Brussels Treaty Organisation in May 1955, which then became the Western European Union.

## 2. Military Organisations.

The Brussels Treaty and the Western Union Defence Organisation.—As we have seen, under the Brussels Treaty, so far back as 1948, the five Western Powers concerned pledged themselves to military collaboration; and in the same year they formed the Western Union Defence Organisation. At that time policy was being framed by a fear of a revival of German aggression. But in time this fear was replaced by distrust of the Soviet Union. There were two developments. In the course of seven years the Western Union Defence Organisation was transformed by the inclusion of the German Federal Republic itself and of Italy into a larger body called the Western European Union. How this change came about is described in the following paragraphs, which tell the story of the creation of the new Federal Republic of Germany, the proposal for a European Defence Community (which did not materialise), and the eventual emergence of Western European Union (in 1955). The second sequel of a military character of the Brussels Treaty was the creation of the North Atlantic Treaty Organisation (NATO). Whereas WEU is a regional organisation, NATO has an even larger range, as its members include Canada and the U.S.A. An account of NATO follows the story, to which we now turn, of the emergence of the new German Republic and its eventual incorporation in WEU.

Government of Germany after the War.—As a result of Germany's unconditional surrender on June 5, 1945, all power in Germany was transferred to the Governments of the four principal Allies. By decisions at Potsdam in 1945 that power was exercised by the Commanders-in-Chief of the U.S.A., the United Kingdom, the Soviet Union, and France, each being responsible in his own zone of occupation. On matters affecting Germany as a whole, the four would be jointly responsible as members of the Control Council. Berlin was divided into four sectors of occupation.

The London Conference 1947 of the four Foreign Ministers concerned failed to agree on a joint German settlement. Unfortunately, the effect was to set in motion political and economic developments which were speedily to make Germany the battleground of the conflict of ideas between Soviet Russia and the Western Powers. The Allied Control Council could no longer function efficiently; and by the end of 1948 four-Power rule had virtually collapsed and the partition of Germany was complete. A federal Parliament and Government were formed in Western Germany. The Soviet zone prepared a rival form of Government for East Germany.

Western Germany's New Status.—In May 1952 the German problem acquired a new complexion, when the so-called " Contractual Agreements " were signed by the three Allied Powers and Western Germany at Bonn. These Agreements did not form a Peace Treaty, but they attempted to define how W. Germany and the three Allied Governments should work together. Sovereignty was to be restored to Germany and she was to enter a military alliance with France. Indeed, a Treaty called the European Defence Treaty was drawn up between the four Powers, with Italy and the Benelux countries, which was to fit German Armed Forces into a Western European system. But this system, called the European Defence Community, never came to fruition as such, owing to the refusal of France to ratify the Treaty in 1954.

Collapse of EDC.—With the collapse of EDC there was a halt to the idea of a Political Community designed to embrace both the proposed EDC and the existing European Coal and Steel Community. It was logical that these two Communities formed by the same countries should not have separate institutions but should take their place within a single political community.

The London Nine Power Conference and the Paris Agreements, 1954.—Nine Powers met in London to devise a substitute for EDC. They were Belgium, Canada, France the German Federal Republic, Italy, Luxembourg, Netherlands, United Kingdom, and the U.S.A. The Conference considered how to assure full association of the German Federal Republic with the West and the German defence contribution. All the decisions which were reached formed part of one general settlement and these were embodied in agreements signed shortly afterwards in Paris. These decisions included the following:—

1. The occupation of W. Germany by Great Britain, the U.S.A., and France should end.

2. The German Federal Republic and Italy should join the Brussels Treaty Organisation.

3. The W. German Republic was admitted to the North Atlantic Treaty Organisation (NATO).

Western European Union.—These agreements took effect on May 5, 1955, when the occupation régime in Western Germany ended and the Republic attained full sovereignty and independence. At the same time the Republic became a member of the Western European Union (the expanded Brussels Treaty Organisation), which came into formal being on May 5, 1955, and also of NATO, to which we now turn. The WEU includes the EEC countries *and* Britain and is therefore a useful forum for consultation and discussion.

The North Atlantic Treaty, 1949.—The founder members of this Pact (which widened the scope of the Brussels Treaty) were Great Britain, the U.S.A., Canada, France, Holland, Belgium, and Luxembourg. The parties agreed that an armed attack against one or more of them in Europe or North America shall be considered an attack against them all and consequently they agreed that if such an armed attack occurs, each of them, in exercise of the right of individual or collective self-defence recognised by the Charter of the UN, will assist the party so attacked.

Changing Problems in NATO.—How can the North Atlantic Alliance be kept together? As time goes on the problems of cohesion become greater. Circumstances have been against finding a solution. First, for some years there has been no avowed threat from the Soviet Union to Western Europe. Of course NATO comprises much more than that; but this brings us to the second great change. At the beginning of NATO there were only two substantial powers in the organisation—Britain and the United States. But now two more members have become substantial powers—France and Germany. So externally the threat has diminished and internally the difficulties of cohesion have increased. The key question has been the control of nuclear weapons. The United States is clearly not going to let control over its destiny leave its own hands. Nor will other powers leave ultimate control of their own destinies to an American President. The problem is not only how to create unity; but how unity is to be made effective for, and in, a crisis.

A Crisis in NATO.—In 1966 it seemed that NATO was facing its gravest crisis since its inception in 1949. De Gaulle demanded that all foreign forces and military establishments in France should pass under French control or be withdrawn. He asked that SHAPE (NATO's military headquarters) and all other integrated headquarters then in France should be removed. In the words of *Punch* he was not only knocking SHAPE out of Europe but knocking Europe out of shape. The general reason for de Gaulle's action was that the position in 1966 was fundamentally changed: (1) the threat of Russian aggression in Europe had receded for several reasons, including Russia's preoccupation with China; (2) the United States' guarantee of Europe, so important in 1949, was becoming less credible since, with the development of inter-continental missiles, America was now herself threatened with instantaneous nuclear retaliation against her own territory. It was not alliance with the United States which de Gaulle appeared to be rejecting but he was questioning the further need for integrated command and American domination of the alliance. So it was that France withdrew from NATO in 1966 and all NATO's installations were moved from French soil. The new headquarters of SHAPE, near Mons in southern Belgium, were officially opened by the Supreme Allied Commander Europe in March 1967.

Future Tasks of NATO.—At the first ministerial meeting of the North Atlantic Council held at its new Brussels headquarters in December 1967, a report, the Harmel Report (named after the Belgian Foreign Minister), was approved. The report called attention to the two main functions of NATO: (1) to maintain adequate military strength and political solidarity to deter aggression and pressure and to defend its members; (2) to search for progress towards a more stable relationship in which the underlying political issues could be solved. Military security and a policy of *détente* were not antagonistic but complementary. The participation of the U.S.S.R. and the U.S.A. would be necessary to achieve a settlement of the political problems of Europe.

Britain's Rôle.—In an address to the British Atlantic Committee on 6 November 1968, Mr. Denis Healey, Secretary of State for Defence, said that as British forces were withdrawn from South-East Asia and the Persian Gulf, Britain would be able to increase its contribution to NATO. He believed that as a European military power Britain would be able to derive military, political and economic advantages from a more intimate co-operation with the other European military powers of the alliance than is open to members like the United States which retain major military responsibilities in other parts of the world as well. But the military security of Western Europe was likely to depend for as far as he could foresee on America's commitment to collective defence through NATO. "Anything which weakened that commitment or even seemed likely to weaken it would be disastrous." But there are areas, he said, of military co-operation open to the European members of NATO which may not always be open to the same degree for the United States: the geographical unity of Europe itself creates certain common interests which can only be fully exploited in common policies. "To give expression to the natural unity of Europe by closer defence co-operation within NATO is not to weaken Europe's links with North America. On the contrary . . . American leaders of both parties have for years been asking the European countries to express their unity more fully. . . . After all, it is Europe's freedom, Europe's security, and the peace of Europe which is at stake." Mr. Healey said the role of NATO, and of Europe inside NATO, in a possible *détente* is a matter of vital importance.

## 3. Political Organisations.

Federal Union.—The development of greater political unity among the European countries may be best introduced by a word about the federalists. The Federal Union had, before the War, urged a federation of Europe as a first step in a progression towards a world federation. The Federalists advocated the surrender of absolute national sovereignty, a part of that sovereignty being vested in a federal authority. This authority, it was urged, should possess a government responsible to peoples and not to the States. It should have a Supreme Court to settle disputes between States which are members of the federation; and have an armed police force to uphold its decisions.

The Hague Congress, 1948.—Several schools of thought were represented at the Congress, one main difference being between the federalists, who want to create a real federation in Europe, and those, like the United Europe Movement, who were not committed to a federation in so far-reaching a sense. The Congress declared that the European nations must transfer some part of their sovereign rights so as to secure common action, and it demanded an early convening of a European Assembly chosen by the Parliaments of the participating nations. But in the event the political reality has not become so radical as the surrender of any sovereign rights to the Council of Europe.

The Creation of a Council of Europe.—In May 1949 the Foreign Ministers of the ten countries consisting of the five Brussels Treaty Powers and Denmark, Eire, Italy, Norway, and Sweden, concluded a formal Agreement called "The Statute of the Council of Europe." It set up a Committee of Ministers and a Consultative Assembly, forming together a Council of Europe. The Council was established twelve months after the Hague Congress, almost to a day. The Committee of Ministers provides for the development of co-operation between governments, while the Consultative Assembly provides a means through which the aspirations of the European peoples may be expressed. The seat of the Council was fixed at Strasbourg.

Council of Europe.—The Council came into existence in August 1949, and the Assembly opened at Strasbourg when M. Spaak was elected President. Mr. Churchill (as he then was) sat as an ordinary member. Procedure is a combination of British and Continental systems, but the design of the chamber follows the Continental pattern, delegates sitting at tables arranged to form a semi-circle. In November 1949 the Council of Ministers agreed to meet the wishes of the Assembly that it would not in practice exercise its right of control to fix the agenda of the Assembly.

The Consultative Assembly.—This, the deliberative organ of the Council, is empowered to debate and make recommendations upon any matter which: (i) is referred to it by the Committee of Ministers with a request for its opinion, or (ii) has been approved by the Committee. The Assembly consists of representatives of each member state appointed by national parliaments. All resolutions of the Assembly require a two-thirds majority of the representatives casting a vote. The Assembly meets annually.

The Responsibility of Members of Assembly.—The Assembly comprises over two hundred individual members of Parliament from fifteen different countries. Although they are entitled to group themselves on any particular issue if they choose, a member is in particular relationship to his country and his party or even to his constituency. There is therefore a position of some confusion and subtlety. Originally the Deputies in the Strasbourg house were seated in alphabetical order of their names: today they sit grouped in political parties.

Relations with National Parliaments.—The attempt made by the Joint Committee between Ministers and the Assembly to act as an organ of co-ordination between the two sides of the Council did not satisfy the Assembly. It therefore set up a Working Party to analyse the relations between the Assembly and national parliaments. This Party tries to see what steps can be taken in each national parliament to secure consideration of recommendations and ratification of Conventions which have been approved at Strasbourg. They have gone so far as to appoint a spokesman for each country.

**What Has the Council of Europe Achieved?**—The Council plays an important part in law-making. It has itself framed and launched important Conventions like that on Human Rights, and it also frames general principles and gives opinions on texts of laws. On the diplomatic side it prepared the way for a solution of the Saar problem, which had divided France and Germany since the War. It is working on the simplification of frontier formalities, and it is concerned (in common with several other international bodies) with refugees. Among other actions, it has encouraged the growth in reciprocity between countries of their social services, and established a European Court of Human Rights.

### 4. Economic Organisations.

The Organisation for European Economic Co-operation (OEEC).—We now turn to the third stream, the economic. We have seen that OEEC was created to administer American (Marshall) aid. But it needed also to re-create a sound European economy. The allocation of aid continued until 1952; but the practice of mutual consultation on economic matters continued in order to carry out long-term programmes. Owing to the nature of its original task of distributing Marshall Aid, the U.S.A. and Canada became associate members of the Organisation. In 1961 these two countries formed with members of OEEC the Organisation for Economic Co-operation which replaced OEEC and is described below.

**European Coal and Steel Community.**—A further economic development came in 1950 with the proposal for the co-ordination of coal and steel production in Germany, Belgium, France, Italy, Luxembourg, and the Netherlands. The organisation of the Community is an example of co-operation on a supra-national basis, since the governing authority is not responsible to the individual governments of member countries but only to the Community. The High Authority has the right to deal directly with the coal and steel enterprises of the Community without passing through national governments. In 1954 Great Britain formed a Standing Council of Association with the High Authority for consultations on coal and steel and for co-ordination where necessary.

**The European Economic Community (EEC), or Euromarket.**—In 1955 " the Six " (namely the countries in ECSC) decided to drive towards further economic integration. This decision was taken at Messina, and the six are sometimes referred to as the Messina Powers. The EEC was established by a Treaty of Rome in 1958 and is an extension to the whole economic field of the institutional method of co-operation already adopted in the European Coal and Steel Community of the Six. The principal institutions are the Parliamentary Assembly (which is common to EEC, ECSC, and Euratom), a Council of Ministers, and an executive Commission of nine members. The common Parliamentary Assembly is now called the European Parliament. The Community is merging the Six into a single economic unit by harmonising economic, social, and investment policies and establishing a common market in trade.

**What is a Common Market?**—A common market is a trading area with no internal tariffs (import duties) or quotas (which are quantitative restrictions on imports) and a single external tariff and quota structure. The first tariff reductions on

manufactured goods inside the Six (10 per cent.) took place on January 1, 1959. By January 1962 there had been cuts totalling 40 per cent. in internal tariffs. During 1960 the Council of the Community speeded up the process of further reductions which, on original intentions, would have taken from twelve to fifteen years, so as to aim at complete liberalisation of internal tariffs by 1966.

**A European Free Trade Area.**—When the Six were discussing the Common Market the British Government declared (1956) that they would consider joining a free-trade area in Europe. Although she would not join the Common Market scheme itself, she would consider sharing in the stage-by-stage reduction of inter-European tariffs on all non-agricultural goods. They would not attempt (unlike the Six) to standardise their own tariff walls in relation to the world outside the European free-trade area. Such a free-trade area would be independently controlled with permanent co-ordination with EEC. In November 1958 France rejected the British proposals for linking the six European common-market nations with the eleven other OEEC countries in a free-trade area. It appeared to the French impossible to establish a free-trade area between the six treaty powers and the other eleven OEEC countries without a single customs tariff between all of them and the outside world and without measures of harmonisation in the economic and social sphere.

**The European Free Trade Association.**—Thereupon seven countries outside the area of the Six formed a European Free Trade Association. They were Great Britain, Austria, Denmark, Norway, Portugal, Sweden, and Switzerland, and they agreed upon a plan at Stockholm in November 1959. Inside the free-trade area comprising these seven countries it was contemplated that there would eventually be no internal tariffs or quotas, but member states would retain separate external systems. The Seven, upon the foundation of their Association, immediately offered friendly co-operation to the existing Common Market. But the problem of finding a political link—called by the diplomatists the problem of the three half-crowns (seven and six)—remained a difficult one.

**Britain and the Common Market.**—Reference to the negotiations for British entry to the EEC (1961–3) and to the second application for membership (1967) will be found in Section G. The political aspects of the Common Market are discussed below.

**Organisation for Economic Co-operation and Development.**—This new body has taken the place of OEEC. Canada and the United States, who were associated members of OEEC, joined with the eighteen members countries of that body to set up OECD. The convention was signed in Paris in December 1960, and the new body came into existence in the autumn of 1961. Thus Canada and the U.S.A. join in facing the broader objectives and the new tasks of today, namely to achieve in Europe the highest sustainable economic growth, employment, and standard of living; to contribute to economic development; and to expand world trade on a multilateral and non-discriminatory basis, in accordance with international obligations. The scope of OECD has been further widened by the accession to membership of Japan.

**Economic Commission of Europe.**—As explained in the preceding outline of the UN, ECE was the first of the great regional commissions to be set up by UNO. It was created in 1947 to concert action for the economic reconstruction of Europe, and it was hoped to strengthen economic co-operation between all European members of UNO. Russia and some of the Communist Eastern European countries are members of ECE, and it is the only European organisation where the Western bloc and Soviet powers can meet for discussion and action.

## 5. The Political Aspects of Membership of the Common Market.

The Treaty of Rome, 1958, which had established the European Economic Community defined (in Articles 2 and 3) the principles and objects for which the Community is to work. Those articles specify in detail the steps for creating a Common Market, for approximating the economic policies of member States, the promotion of harmonious development of economic activities, and raising the standard of living. But the aim of " closer relations between its member States " is stated without elaboration. It is into this gap that speculation is poured. No limit is set in the Treaty to the process of integration; on the other hand there is no commitment to join a Federation of Europe. While member States commit themselves to a common policy on a number of economic issues there will be co-ordination of national policies designed to take account of the needs of the rest of the Community.

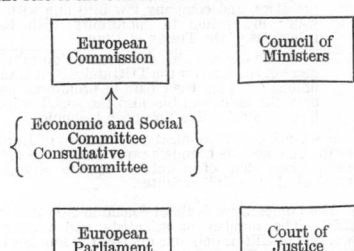

**Two Kinds of Political Aspects.**—We need to distinguish between two things. First, the machinery by which the aims of the Common Market are to be achieved—the Commission, the Council of Ministers, the European Assembly, Court of Justice, and so on. This may be described as the political machinery of the Common Market. Second, we have to think of the kind of political relationship which will grow up, either by deliberate design or practical development, between member countries. We may think of the first set of facts as the engine or locomotive of the Common Market train; and we can regard the second as what sort of journey the train will take —will it take a direct run to federation or follow some other line?

**The Organs of EEC.**—The machinery of government of the European Economic Community (into which is now integrated the machinery for ECSC and Euratom) consists of:

1. The Council
2. The Commission
3. The Court
4. The Parliament or Assembly
5. The Economic and Social Committee (for the Common Market and Euratom): and
6. The Consultative Committee (for ECSC).
7. The Ambassadors of the member Governments.

The meetings of Ambassadors form unofficial permanent liaison between Council and Commission. Let us examine the chief official organs.

**The Council** issues regulations and decisions which are, upon issue, binding in law on all member States. It consists of one member from each member State (normally a Cabinet Minister). They have votes as follows:—

| France | 4 votes |
| Germany | ,, |
| Italy | ,, |
| Belgium | 2 votes |
| Holland | ,, |
| Luxembourg | 1 vote |

**The Commission.**—Whereas the Council consists of politicians the Commission consists of permanent officials. There are nine members appointed by Governments, for a minimum term of four years and not more than two members may come from any one country. Its business is to further the general purposes of the Treaty and decisions are by majority vote. From the Commission flow two streams:—

(a) Proposals, which it sends to the Council.

(b) Under powers of its own:—

1. Decisions to named countries and binding on them.

2. Directives to named countries to achieve certain results, without specifying the means.

3. Recommendations and Opinions, which are not binding.

4. Authorisations without which many things are forbidden.

**The Court**, whose procedure is wholly Continental, consists of seven Judges appointed by Governments for a maximum of six years. Its word is final on the interpretation of the Treaty, on the rules made under the Treaty, and on the legality of all the actions of the organs of the Community.

**The Parliament** or Assembly consists of representatives of the national Parliaments. There are 142 representatives in all—36 from each of the three bigger powers, 14 from the two medium ones, and 6 from Luxembourg. It meets once a year as of right and its only power is to pass (by a two-thirds majority) a vote of censure on the Commission (the permanent officials) which must then resign. If Britain were to join its quota of members to the Assembly would presumably be 36. It is generally held that one day the Assembly will consist of representatives elected by direct universal suffrage but this will not occur until everybody is willing. In the meantime the Assembly can only consist of nominated parliamentarians.

**The Working of the Organs: the Commission.**—We look first at the Commission (of officials) as this is held to be by far the most powerful of the organs. Broadly speaking, it is the only body with a right of initiative, sending, as we have explained, proposals to the Council which cannot prepare its own proposals for consideration. The Commission can thus prevent the Council considering anything it does not want to be considered. Its proposals to the Council can normally be amended by the Council only by unanimous or qualified majority vote.

The Commission prepares the budget, takes member Governments into Court, runs the agricultural market and is the Monopoly and Restrictive Practices Court.

In addition to all this the Commission has its own powers as we have explained under heading (b) in the earlier paragraph about the Commission. By its *decisions* it can give orders to member States over a wide field. For example, it can give orders on the details of applying rules of free competition to nationalised industries or to industries with special rights. Its *directives* order the result to be achieved (for example the framework within which agricultural prices are to be negotiated). It gives (or refuses) *authorisations* over a wide range of subjects, like the postponement of the raising or lowering of a tariff in certain circumstances. The powers of the Commission are thus seen to be extensive and important and they affect, among many other matters, the running of nationalised industries and the uses of Government aid.

**The Powers of the Commission contrasted with the Council.**—That the Commission (of officials or " Eurocrats " as they have been called) are the real rulers of the Community is more clearly seen when that body is contrasted with the Council (of politicians), quite apart from the range and importance of the powers given to the Commission. The Commission decides by simple majority and can easily reach a decision: but the Council, which requires either unanimity or qualified majority, is often unable to make a decision. The Commission has almost all the right of initiative. It sits for a minimum of four years, while Council members come and go. The Commission meets as often as it wishes, the Council once a month. The Commission thus acquires a real personality but not the Council. It is furthermore the Commission which controls the Community Civil Service.

**The Bureaucratic Commission.**—During Britain's first application for membership of the Common Market (1961–3) an important discussion took place in this country on the constitutional nature of the Commission and on the relative powers of Commission and Council. A most trenchant analysis of the Commission was made by Mr. William Pickles of the London School of Economics. He described the Commission as a bureaucracy of a kind which it would be impossible to contemplate in this country, for, in his view, it was entirely undemocratic. Mr. Pickles resumed the debate in 1967 and analysed the major developments within the Community in the past six years (see *The Listener*, 16 Feb. 1967). He found that, instead of a single Commission bureaucracy which he had originally complained of, there was now, alongside that, and very much enmeshed with it, a six-nation bureaucracy (a Committee of Permanent Representatives where the six understudies, as it were, of the Council members sit permanently—with technical staffs of their own—in Brussels). There had now developed, therefore, two closely interlocked bureaucracies, both without any kind of democratic control. Add to that de Gaulle's determination to fight for his national interests. We have not therefore discovered, argues Mr. Pickles, whether the Community can work without supranational powers (which British Ministers say they do not believe in).

### 6. Scientific and Technological Organisations.

Euratom is the short title of the European Atomic Energy Community (EAEC) formed in 1957 to further the use of nuclear energy in Europe for peaceful purposes and to ensure that Europe does not lag behind in the atomic revolution. The negotiation for this Community opened at the same time, in 1956, as that for the Common Market and the Treaty for it was signed at Rome on 25 March 1957, when the Treaty for the Common Market was signed. Prior to the merger of the three Executives in July 1967 of the three executive bodies (the Common Market and Euratom Commissions and the ECSC High Authority) into a single Commission and of the three Councils into a single Council, Euratom was supervised by its own Commission. Euratom's rôle is to ensure that the Community undertakes the research necessary for the development of nuclear energy not only for power, but also, through the use of radioisotopes and radioactive sources, for agricultural, industrial, and medical purposes. It has joined international projects such as the European Nuclear Energy Agency (ENEA) *Dragon* project at Winfrith, Dorset, which is sponsored by OECD.

**The Six Co-ordinate on Scientific and Technological Policies.**—The Council of Ministers in 1967 reached agreement on a procedure for such co-ordination. Existing co-operation in international organisations included ELDO (European Rocket Launcher Development Organisation), ESRO (European Space Research Organisation), and CERN (European Nuclear Research Centre) in all of which the Six are associated with Britain. (But in 1968 Britain announced its withdrawal from ELDO when the present development programme ends in 1972.) The urgency of the general problem of co-operation has been sharpened by growing anxiety in Europe generally about the consequences of a technological gap, the difficulties actually encountered in *ad hoc* co-operation—in the aero-space sector, for example —and the extensive overlapping of effort and expenditure.

**Britain's 7-Point Technology Plan.**—Mr. Wilson's seven-point plan for European technology was outlined at the Lord Mayor's banquet in London in November 1967. The points were:

(1) Bilateral projects for technological co-operation in any field.

(2) Multilateral discussions to create a new dynamic in European technology.

(3) Discussions between the Confederation of British Industries and sister industrial organisations in Europe on a basis for integrated industrial and technological advance.

(4) To sponsor a multilateral European Institute of Technology.

(5) To organise " European Companies " on a basis which transcends national frontiers.

(6) To bring British arrangements in the field of patents, monopolies, and restrictive practices, and company law into line with a wider integration in conformity with the principles of the Treaty of Rome.

(7) To discuss with the trade union movement of the Six how the TUC and EFTA trade unions can play their part in promoting not only the industrial but also the social objectives of a collective European technology.

The scientific and technical development of European countries has been less rapid during the past years than that of countries outside Europe, particularly the United States.

**The Comparative Scale of Scientific Research in EEC.**—The number of scientists and research workers in EEC is only one quarter the number in the U.S.A. The U.S.A. spends seven times as much on research as the EEC countries. In the opinion of Professor Brzezinski (in the Faculty of Political Science at Columbia University), to whom we owe these figures, it is likely that the gap will widen, given the fact that scientific development is a dynamic process.

### 7. Recent Attitudes in Europe.

**Merger of the Three European Communities.**—The Common Market complex advanced a further step by an agreement in 1965 for the merging of the executives of the Economic Commission, the Coal and Steel Pool, and Euratom. This meant that in 1967 there was a single Commission of 14 members instead of three Commissions of 23 members. By July 1968 the Six had constructed a customs union whereby:

(1) all customs duties and restrictions on trade in industrial goods within the Community were abolished; and

(2) a common external tariff came into effect.

A common farm policy was also completed by that date.

What kind of political system will be built to control the European Community with a unified executive? France was asking in 1965 for revision or interpretation of the Rome Treaty on two important points: (1) the powers of the Commission; and (2) whether a majority voting system should replace unanimous voting in the Council of Ministers in January 1966 as laid down in the Treaty. On the second point it should be explained that the Treaty provides for a transition from unanimous agreement of the Council to weighted majority to be achieved by stages, the first stage from 1958–61, the second to the end of 1965, and the third stage ending 1970. It was the step due on 1 January 1966 which caused objection by France. France had absented herself for some time from the Council of the Six, causing a serious break between her and the other five member countries.

**France and the Five Agree to Disagree.**—France, which had withdrawn from the Council of Ministers in July 1965, in violation of the Treaty of Rome, returned at a critical meeting at Luxembourg in January 1966. Neither France nor the Five were prepared for their differences to lead to a total breakdown. The Treaty of Rome's provision for majority voting remained unaltered; but France's insistence on a right of veto was met by the Five agreeing that every effort should be made for a reasonable period to secure unanimity on issues of importance. The Common Market thus survived but continued in a state of nervous tension. Everything turned on de Gaulle's actions and intentions. The four-point face-saving agreement may be summarised as follows:

(1) When very important issues of one or more partners are at stake the members of the Council will try, within a reasonable time, to reach solutions which can be adopted by all the members of the Council, while respecting their mutual interests and those of the Community.

(2) The French delegation considers that where very important issues are at stake, the discussion must be continued until unanimous agreement is reached.

(3) The six delegations note that there is a divergence of views on what should be done in the event of a failure to reach complete agreement.

(4) This divergence does not prevent the community's work being resumed by normal procedure.

**Britain and the Common Market: New negotiations.**—After the General Election of 1966 the Government made a thorough re-examination of all the arguments for and against British entry. This was the first fundamental reappraisal of the position since the Whitehall exercise in 1960 which preceded the application for membership in August 1961. The Government decided to open talks first with the EFTA countries and then with EEC countries to find out if the conditions did, or did not, exist for fruitful negotiations for Britain's entry into the EEC. The purpose of the conference with EFTA was to demonstrate solidarity with Britain's partners there and to help them to consider their own plans, either to apply for membership of the Common Market or to seek some form of association with it. As things then stood Sweden, Norway, and Denmark were expected to seek full membership with Britain. The Irish Republic which was outside EFTA was also expected to apply. Mr. Wilson said he would approach the discussions " with the clear intention and determination to enter the Community, if, as we hope, our essential British and Commonwealth interests can be safeguarded." Among the stiff obstacles hindering Britain's entry was of course President de Gaulle's attitude to Britain's defence arrangements with the United States. (It was the Nassau agreement that led de Gaulle to veto Britain's entry into EEC.) In his declaration of intent in November 1966—or, more accurately, of desire—Mr. Wilson said that matters of defence or of foreign policy are not directly involved in negotiations on the Common Market. It is true that there is nothing in the Rome Treaty that requires us to hand over power to a European authority or Parliament on subjects which are not related to an economic union. But economic union needs political direction and this corollary needs to be faced, although the Common Market countries themselves have not yet decided on the precise forms of its political institutions.

**De Gaulle Again Bars Door to British Entry, 1967.**—At his press conference of 27 November 1967 de Gaulle argued that the report of the Brussels Commission of 29 September 1967 demonstrated that the present Common Market was incompatible with the economy " as it is " of Britain. The incompatible features, were said to be Britain's chronic balance of payments deficit; her sources of supply; her working conditions; " the way the English get their food "—partly by subsidising their own production and partly by food bought cheaply all over the world and particularly in the Commonwealth; and other features. He said we were watching the fifth act of a play in which England had taken up " very different and apparently inconsistent attitudes towards the

Common Market." The British Government quickly published a detailed rejoinder. They made it clear that they expected a reply from the Six. Their announcement, after the General's press conference, was to be interpreted as meaning that de Gaulle was speaking for himself, but the decision rested not with France solely but also with the other five members. " We have made an application in full accord with the terms of Art. 237 [of the Treaty of Rome] and we expect a reply from the Community." When the Council of Ministers of the Community met again in December 1967, France voted against negotiations for British membership and this was in effect a French veto. The application by Britain remained on the table and any member state could raise the matter again before the Council. The action of France raised a question mark upon the future good functioning of the Community itself.

**Anglo-French Policy Differences.**—Opinions differ as to the Anglo-French dispute over the disclosure by Britain to her partners in Western European Union (and to the United States) of President de Gaulle's proposals for British entry to Europe made to our Ambassador to Paris, Mr. Christopher Soames, at an interview granted to him by the President, on 4 February 1969. In his explanation to the Commons, Mr. Michael Stewart, the Foreign Secretary, made it clear that (1) Britain rejected the French view on NATO—which was that, since President de Gaulle wanted to see a Europe completely independent of the United States, NATO must disappear; (2) Britain was still seeking full membership of the European Economic Community, whereas the President had proposed that it should be changed into a looser form of free trade area with arrangements by each country to exchange agricultural produce, with a smaller inner council of a European political association consisting of France, Britain, Germany and Italy. " We felt it right," said Mr. Stewart, "to tell our other allies in Western European Union what was proposed. These are major problems which cannot be settled between France and Britain alone. We therefore made it clear in our reply to the French Government that we rejected their views on NATO and maintained our position on entry into the European Economic Community. It was on these understandings that we were prepared to have discussions with them provided our partners were fully in the picture."

Sir Con O'Neill, former Ambassador to the European Communities, writing in *The Times* of 24 February 1969, expressed the view:

" British perseverance has had limited objectives. There is no immediate prospect of reopening the application for membership or getting round the French veto. But there remained important activities, either wholly or largely outside the scope of the Treaty of Rome (foreign policy, defence and technology are examples), which it has seemed worth while to try to pursue in common with the Six. Not to overcome the veto, but to create a habit of cooperation, common interests, policies and attitudes which would, admittedly, help to smooth our path for entry into the Community of Europe if things should change. There has been no lack of such proposals: the Harmel plan, the Fanfani plan, the Nenni memorandum. France has done her best to frustrate them all."

" This activity and pressure has irritated and apparently even alarmed, the French Government. French official spokesmen accused the British Government five months ago of ' diplomatic terrorism,' and now of ' diplomatic activism and sensationalism.' The French have appeared rather rattled, although it is hard to see why as their defences against our actual entry into the Community are impregnable so long as they choose to man them. Their over-reaction last week to the possible use of WEU for consultation on foreign policy (which is one of its purposes) seemed to be based on irritation and apprehension; and perhaps the same motives underlie the General's latest effort to divert us from our objective."

## OTHER GROUPINGS OF STATES.

### 1. The Organisations of the Communist World.

There have been two organisations of Communist Parties. The Comintern (or the Third Communist International) was founded in 1919 by Lenin, but was dissolved in 1943. It was followed by the Cominform in 1947, comprising the Communist Parties of Bulgaria, Czechoslovakia, France, Hungary, Italy, Poland, Roumania, the Soviet Union, and Yugoslavia. Yugoslavia was expelled in 1948 for " deviation " and in 1956 the Cominform was dissolved by the agreement of the remaining eight national parties that the organisation had exhausted its functions.

The Warsaw Pact, formed in 1955, is the equivalent in Eastern Europe of NATO. Its full title is the Eastern European Mutual Assistance Treaty. The 20-year treaty is between Albania, Bulgaria, Czechoslovakia, Eastern Germany, Hungary, Poland, Roumania, and the Soviet Union. (Albania has not taken part since the severance of relations with the Soviet Union in 1961.)

The Comecon, a Council for Mutual Economic Assistance, was established in 1949, the founder members being Bulgaria, Czechoslovakia, Hungary, Poland, Roumania, and the Soviet Union.

The Eastern Joint Institute for Nuclear Research is the fourth international Communist organisation, founded in 1956 the members being Albania, Bulgaria, Czechoslovakia, Eastern Germany, Hungary, North Korea, the Mongolian People's Republic, Poland, Roumania, the Soviet Union, and the Democratic Republic of Vietnam. The Republic of China withdrew in 1966.

### 2. Organisations of the Third World.

The Third World is the name given to those countries representing the less privileged part of the world, most of them forming part of neither the Western (Capitalist) bloc nor the Eastern (Communist) bloc. They are sometimes called " non-aligned " or " uncommitted nations."

They have three permanent organisations:

    (a) The Afro-Asian People's Solidarity Council (1957);

    (b) The Afro-Asian Organisation for Economic Co-operation (1958); and

    (c) The Three Continents Solidarity Organisation (1966).

The Bandung Conference of 1955 in Indonesia was the first inter-continental conference of the so-called coloured peoples in the history of the world. It adopted a Declaration on Problems of Dependent Peoples that colonialism was an evil and should be brought to an end. It also adopted a Declaration on World Peace and Co-operation, involving five principles of peaceful coexistence.

Other conferences of the Third World have been:

    The Belgrade Conference of 1961 was attended by 25 countries and adopted a 27-point declaration containing their common views on international problems and an " Appeal for Peace " addressed particularly to the U.S.A. and the U.S.S.R.

    The Cairo Conference of 1964 at which 47 countries attended. Neo-colonialism and imperialism in all forms were condemned particularly in South Africa.

### 3. Organisation of the Americas.

The Organisation of American States (OAS) was formed in 1948 as a regional alliance under the United Nations to foster mutual understanding and co-operation among the nations of the Western Hemisphere. The Charter of the OAS gave permanent legal form to the hitherto loosely and indefinitely organised Pan-American system.

Members: Argentina, Barbados, Bolivia, Brazil, Chile, Colombia, Costa Rica, Dominican Republic, Ecuador, El Salvador, Guatemala, Haiti, Honduras, Mexico, Nicaragua, Panama, Paraguay, Peru, Trinidad and Tobago, U.S.A., Uruguay, Venezuela.

The Organisation of Central American States (OCAS) was set up in 1951.

Members: Costa Rica, El Salvador, Guatemala, Honduras, Nicaragua.

Latin American Free Trade Association (LAFTA) was formed in 1960 and now comprises 11 nations —Argentina, Bolivia, Brazil, Chile, Colombia, Ecuador, Mexico, Paraguay, Peru, Uruguay, Venezuela.

### 4. Organisations of the Middle East.

The Arab League with its seat at Cairo comprises Algeria, Iraq, Jordan, Kuwait, Lebanon, Libya, Morocco, Saudi Arabia, Sudan, Syrian Arab Republic, Tunisia, United Arab Republic and Yemen. A " Pact of the Union of Arab States " was signed in 1945 by representatives of Egypt, Iraq, Lebanon, Saudi Arabia, Syria, Transjordan, and Yemen. Later adherents were Libya, Sudan, Tunisia, Morocco, Kuwait, and Algeria.

The Central Treaty Organisation (CENTO), comprising Britain, Iran, Pakistan, and Turkey (with U.S.A. as an associate member) is both a defence organisation and an organisation for regional co-operation in the economic, cultural, and technical fields.

### 5. Organisations of Africa.

The Organisation of African Unity (OAU) was constituted at Addis Ababa in 1963. All independent countries in Africa, except South Africa, are members of the OAU.

There are a number of regional organisations in Africa such as: (1) the East African Common Services Organisation (1962) for Kenya, Tanzania, and Uganda, and (2) the West African Common Market (1967) comprising twelve countries—Dahomey, Ghana, Ivory Coast, Liberia, Mali, Mauritania, Niger, Nigeria, Senegal, Sierra Leone, Togo, and Upper Volta.

### 6. Organisations of South and East Asia and the Pacific Area.

1. The Anzus Pact is a tripartite security treaty between Australia, New Zealand, and the United States (1952).

Also known as the Pacific Security Treaty.

2. The S.E. Asia Treaty Organisation (SEATO) is a defence organisation between Australia, Britain, France, New Zealand, Pakistan, Philippines, Thailand, and the U.S.A.

3. The 1954 Geneva Agreements on Indo-China (Vietnam, Cambodia, and Laos).

This concluded the eight-year war in Indo-China from 1946 to 1954 between the Vietminh and France. There was an eight-nation declaration on the problem of restoring peace in Indo-China; declarations by the French, Cambodian, and Laotian Governments; and a unilateral American declaration defining the position of the U.S. Government.

The Colombo Plan, owing its inception in 1951 to the Commonwealth Consultative Committee, is a plan for the economic development of South and South East Asia. It was originally adopted for development programmes in India, Pakistan, Ceylon, Malaya, Singapore, North Borneo, and Sarawak, but the scheme has been widened to include non-Commonwealth countries, and the U.S.A. has agreed to join Australia, Britain, Canada, and New Zealand in making available aid within the framework of the Colombo Plan.

# GROWTH OF WESTERN INTERNATIONAL ORGANISATIONS

## WILSON'S SECOND LABOUR CABINET
### (1969)

*Prime Minister and First Lord of the Treasury*—Harold Wilson.
*Secretary of State for Foreign and Commonwealth Affairs*—Michael Stewart.
*Chancellor of the Exchequer*—Roy Jenkins.
*Lord Chancellor*—Lord Gardiner.
*Secretary of State for the Social Services*—Richard Crossman.
*First Secretary of State and Secretary of State for Employment and Productivity*—
Barbara Castle.
*Home Secretary*—James Callaghan.
*Secretary of State for Defence*—Denis Healey.
*Lord President of the Council and Leader of the House of Commons*—Frederick Peart.
*Secretary of State for Economic Affairs*—Peter Shore.
*President of the Board of Trade*—Anthony Crosland.
*Secretary of State for Education and Science*—Edward Short.
*Minister without Portfolio*—George Thomson.
*Secretary of State for Scotland*—William Ross.
*Secretary of State for Wales*—George Thomas.
*Minister of Technology*—Anthony Wedgwood Benn.
*Minister of Agriculture, Fisheries, and Food*—Cledwyn Hughes.
*Minister of Power*—Roy Mason.
*Minister of Transport*—Richard Marsh.
*Minister of Housing and Local Government*—Anthony Greenwood.
*Paymaster-General*—Judith Hart.
*Lord Privy Seal*—Lord Shackleton.
*Chief Secretary to the Treasury*—John Diamond.

> *SPEAKER TO THE HOUSE OF COMMONS*—Dr. Horace M. King.
> *LEADER OF THE OPPOSITION*—Edward Heath.
> *GOVERNMENT CHIEF WHIP AND DEPUTY LEADER OF THE HOUSE OF COMMONS*—Robert Mellish.

---

## MINISTERS NOT IN THE CABINET

*Chancellor of the Duchy of Lancaster*—Frederick Lee.
*Minister for Planning and Land (Housing and Local Government)*—Kenneth Robinson.
*Postmaster-General*—John Stonehouse.
*Minister of State, Treasury*—Dick Taverne.
*Minister of Defence (Administration)*—Gerald Reynolds.
*Minister of Defence (Equipment)*—John Morris.
*Minister of State, Department of Economic Affairs*—Thomas Urwin.
*Ministers of State, Department of Education and Science*—Shirley Williams, Jennie Lee, Alice Bacon.
*Ministers of State, Foreign and Commonwealth Office*—Frederick Mulley, Goronwy Roberts, Lord Shepherd, Lord Caradon (United Nations), Lord Chalfont (Western Europe and the Americas).
*Minister of State, Home Office*—Lord Stonham.
*Ministers of State, Board of Trade*—Edmund Dell, William Rodgers, Lord Brown.
*Ministers of State, Health, and Social Security*—David Ennals, Lady Serota.
*Minister of State, Technology (Aviation)*—J. P. W. Mallalieu.
*Minister of Overseas Development*—Reginald Prentice.
*Minister of Public Building and Works*—John Silkin.
*Minister of State, Scottish Office*—J. Dickson Mabon.
*Minister of State, Welsh Office*—Eirene White.
*Attorney-General*—Sir Elwyn Jones.
*Solicitor-General*—Sir Arthur Irvine.
*Lord Advocate*—Lord Wilson.
*Solicitor-General for Scotland*—E. G. F. Stewart.

# THE LAW OF ENGLAND

A concise survey of the English legal system, its history and development from early times, with further detail of some particular branches of the law which are of practical interest to the ordinary citizen.

# TABLE OF CONTENTS

# THE LAW OF ENGLAND

**A.—The Sources**

Comprising

| COMMON LAW | CASE LAW | EQUITY* | STATUTE LAW |
| --- | --- | --- | --- |

**B.—The Sub-divisions**

| COMMON LAW | CASE LAW | EQUITY* | STATUTE LAW |
| --- | --- | --- | --- |
| **I. CONSTITUTIONAL LAW.**<br>Main Principles:<br>1. The Supremacy of Parliament.<br>2. The Rule of Law.<br>(a) *The Legislature:* The franchise, elections, Parliamentary procedure, relations between Lords and Commons, Bills and Acts.<br>(b) *The Executive:* The Crown, the Ministry, Government Departments and their powers.<br>(c) *The Judiciary:* The Courts and their functions, the Judges, means of controlling the Executive and inferior courts.<br>(d) *Local Government:* County, Borough, Urban and Rural District and Parish Councils and their powers. | | | |
| **II. CRIMINAL LAW.** dealing with the relations between the individual and the State.<br>A, Grave offences against—<br>1. *Public Order:* Treason, sedition, riot, blasphemy, obscenity, forgery, bigamy, perjury.<br>2. *Persons:* Homicide, assault, sexual offences.<br>3. *Property:* Theft, burglary, dishonestly obtaining property by deception, blackmail.<br>Subsidiary matters:<br>(a) Criminal responsibility.<br>(b) Unconsummated Crimes.<br>(c) Joint Crimes.<br>(d) Punishment and its purpose.<br>B, *Petty Offences, e.g.,* Road Traffic, Factories and Shops, Sale of Food, etc. (dealt with by J.P.s) | | | |
| | **III. STATUS.**<br>1. Nationality.<br>2. Domicil.<br>3. Marriage and Divorce.<br>4. Infancy.<br>5. Lunacy.<br>6. Bankruptcy.<br>7. Corporations.<br>8. Adoption. | | |
| | **IV. LAW OF PERSONS,*** dealing with the relations between one individual citizen and another, established—<br>1. *By act of parties (Law of Contract):*<br>(1) Simple Contracts.<br>(2) Deeds:<br>*(a) Capacity of parties.*<br>*(b) When writing necessary.*<br>*(c) Mistake.*<br>*(d) Misrepresentation.*<br>*(e) Duress and undue influence.*<br>*(f) Illegality.*<br>*(g) Breach.* | 2. *By Law (Law of Tort):* Civil Wrongs committed against—<br>(1) *The Person:* Trespass, assault, malicious prosecution, and false imprisonment.<br>(2) *Land:* Trespass. Nuisance.<br>(3) *Other Property:* Trespass, Conversion.<br>(4) *Persons towards whom there is a duty to take care:* Negligence.<br>(5) *Reputation (libel or slander):* Defamation.<br>(6) *Personal and Trade Relationships:* Seduction, trade molestation and—<br>(a) *Liability.*<br>(b) *Immunity.*<br>(c) *Effect of Death.*<br>(d) *Remedies.* | |
| | | | **V. LAW OF PROPERTY.***<br>IN GENERAL:<br>1. *Living Persons:* (Effect of Status on Ownership).<br>2. *Deceased Persons:* (Wills and Intestacies, Probate and Administration).<br><br>IN LAND (Immoveable Property):<br>1. Freeholds (Settlements).<br>2. Leaseholds.<br>3. Mortgages.<br>4. Title.<br>5. Joint Ownership.<br><br>IN OTHER PROPERTY (Moveable Property):<br>1. Chattels.<br>2. Things in action. |

\* *Note:* Equity is applied only in matters of civil law relating to persons and property. It has no application to constitutional or criminal law.

# THE LAW OF ENGLAND

THE Table set out on **D3** shows in concise form—

A—the sources, and

B—the subdivisions

of the Law of England. The intention is to give a general picture of the whole system in tabular form, to explain briefly what the Table represents, and finally to deal, in slightly more detail, with a few selected subjects which may be of particular interest to the ordinary reader.

A word of warning is necessary. Learned text-books have been written on every one of the many subjects referred to in the Table, and the application of the law in any particular case is a matter for the professional expert. The following pages do not claim to do more than to make a brief survey of the whole field of English Law, for the general guidance and interest of the ordinary citizen. The system of English Courts is set out in tabular form at the end of the section.

## A. THE SOURCES OF ENGLISH LAW

The citizen who desires to make some acquaintance with the English Legal System must begin by disabusing himself of several popular fallacies: for example, that it is a fixed and unalterable code, that it is strictly logical, that it is coldly impersonal and uninfluenced by human factors. The history and practice of the law display precisely the opposite characteristics.

### 1. COMMON LAW AND CASE LAW

The English Legal System is a *living organism,* not a dead, static code. The system as we know it began to develop in the twelfth century, when Henry II extended the practice of sending the royal judges about the country " on circuit," to deal with crimes and disputes, and to adapt and give official authority to the best of the local customs, some of which had been in force since Anglo-Saxon days. The judges did this by *empirical methods*—that is, by practical, common-sense decisions on the actual cases brought before them, and by setting out their reasoning in detail. Simple records of the most important decisions were kept from the earliest times; as the centuries passed, the gradual elaboration of a system of *law-reporting* ensured that the *facts* of significant cases, the *reasoned judgments* delivered on those facts, and the *principles* those judgments enshrined, should be recorded and preserved; at the same time the doctrine of *precedent*—the rule that those principles, enunciated by a superior court, should be followed by all courts inferior to it—ensured consistency throughout the country. Thus there was gradually developed a body of principles—living, growing, and adaptable to new sets of facts as they arose; principles, moreover, which rose above local differences of custom and became *common* to the whole Realm. Hence the expression *common law.*

*Case Law.* The system we have described is by no means a thing of the past: it is still in force today. New circumstances are continually arising; cases come before the judges for decision, and it frequently happens that the principles laid down in the past do not apply precisely, in all respects, to the particular facts in point. When this occurs it is the judge's right and duty to *interpret* and *adapt the principle to the new facts* before him; his judgment is reported, and his reasoning made clear. The adapted principle of that judgment becomes part of the law of England; it must be followed by all inferior courts; and it will not be ignored or abandoned by courts of the same rank, or any superior court, without reasoned argument and careful consideration. Thus the practising lawyer can never sit back with the comfortable assurance that he has " completed " his studies; he must continually keep his knowledge up to date. The practice of law is not a science, based on rigid rules, but an art—the art of *applying the known principles to the facts of new cases* as they arise.

In July 1966 the House of Lords (the Supreme Court of Appeal) announced that it would hence-forth regard itself as free to depart from its own previous decisions when it appeared right to do so, though this power would be sparingly used.

### 2. EQUITY

But the English genius for practical improvisation has never excluded spiritual and *ethical motives* of conduct. For hundreds of years the Church was a great power in the land, extending its influence far beyond the strictly ecclesiastical sphere. The great church-leaders of the past took an important part in the secular activities of government and administration; from an early date the King's Chancellor was an ecclesiastic. The Chancellor was not only the King's Secretary of State and Keeper of the royal seal; as royal chaplain he was " the Keeper of the King's conscience." It was to him, therefore, that the King turned for advice on matters of state where *ethical and moral considerations* were involved.

All human institutions are fallible, and the rough-and-ready methods of the early common law sometimes fell short of those ideals of abstract justice that inspire men's minds. Despite, or perhaps because of, its practical outlook, the common law tended to become circumscribed by its own precedents. As the machinery of justice became more elaborately organised, the idealistic doctrine—" Where there is a right there is a remedy "—was apt to degenerate, in practice, into the realistic but soulless form—" Where there is a legal remedy, there is a legal right." Too close an adherence to legal formalities led sometimes to a denial of justice. This was particularly so for the weak, who could not help themselves—feeble-minded persons, tricked or cajoled into " legally " signing away their property; infants unconscionably treated by guardians who, having got legal custody (under a will or otherwise) of the infants' inheritance, refused to honour their solemn trust; borrowers who, having delayed beyond the date fixed for the repayment of a loan, found themselves deprived, under the strict terms of the mortgage deed, of property many times more valuable which they had pledged only as security. For such cases as these the common-law courts provided no remedy, since the victims had suffered *no actual illegality.* Petitions were therefore sent to the King, "the father of his people," begging him to right such wrongs; and the question of redress was delegated by the King to his Chancellor. The Chancellor had no power directly to revoke or interfere with the decisions of the royal judges by depriving the oppressive party of the property he had " legally " acquired, but he could, and did, insist that that party should not enjoy such acquisition, *unconscionably*, for his own sole advantage. The defaulting guardian, though he continued legally to hold the infant's property was compelled to use it for the infant's benefit; the oppressive creditor, who had legally got possession of or sold the debtor's estate, was permitted to take out of the proceeds the amount of his loan, with reasonable interest and expenses, but must hand back the balance to the debtor. Thus the Chancellor administered a kind of *abstract justice*, based upon the promptings of conscience, and not on legalistic rules. He dealt with these cases in his own court—the Chancellery or *Chancery*—where the yardstick was *equity*—that which was right or fair. And over the centuries the principles on which the Court of Chancery acted became crystallised into a set of rules which followed their own precedents and made *conscientious conduct* their guiding star.

Naturally enough, the activities of the Court of Chancery were viewed with jealousy and misgiving by the royal judges of the Common Law Courts, and many were the clashes between the two. Equity, however, had come to stay, and the two systems were administered independently until as late as 1873. In that year Parliament passed the Supreme Court of Judicature Act, which (in effect) fused the two systems into one. By means of that and subsequent legislation there was constituted *one High Court of Justice*, of which the *Queen's Bench Division*, the *Chancery Division*, and the *Probate, Divorce* and *Admiralty Division* are component parts. The first-named is concerned primarily with common-law suits, the second with equitable matters; but both these Divisions must have regard to *both common law and equitable principles*. In case of a conflict of principles, those of equity are to prevail. The last-named Division (for historical reasons) deals with the diverse subjects of wills and intestacies, matrimonial suits, and disputes relating to ships at sea. Criminal cases fall within the jurisdiction of the Queen's Bench Division, but are dealt with in special courts. The criminal law (in strict fairness to accused persons) must be absolutely certain and clearly defined; it is administered on strict legalistic principles, from which the doctrines of equity are excluded.

### 3. STATUTE LAW

While, as we have shown, the Courts have the function of *interpreting and adapting* the principles of law laid down in earlier times, they cannot legislate—*i.e., the Judge cannot make new laws*, or repeal or amend old laws, even when changes are rendered desirable by developing social conditions. The law-making body, or *Legislature*, is Parliament. *A Statute* or *Act of Parliament* is the joint act of the Queen, the House of Lords, and the House of Commons; while each of these three "Estates of the Realm" has its own functions, new law can be made, and old law repealed, only by these three Estates acting together, *i.e.*, by *Parliament*, or by some person or body of persons to whom Parliament has *delegated authority* to make *rules having the force of law*. Parliament is free of control by any written constitution or any person or body of persons whatsoever; an Act of Parliament must be enforced by all courts as the law of the land, unless and until it is repealed or amended by Parliament itself. Parliament is not bound by the Acts of a previous parliament, which it is free to repeal or amend as occasion may require. It is equally free to modify the rules of the common law and the rules of equity, however firmly entrenched; but those rules, unless and until modified by parliamentary legislation, continue to guide the Judges both in their interpretation and enforcement of *Statute Law—i.e.*, the body of Acts of Parliament still in force for the time being—and in their decisions on those common-law and equitable rules which the Statute Law has left untouched. For example, the Peerage Act, 1963, enables a peer to renounce his title and to become a commoner for all purposes, including voting for, and standing as, a candidate for the House of Commons. (At the time of writing (Jan. 1969), the Government was proposing to reform the composition and powers of the House of Lords). By the Law Commission Act, 1965, a body of Commissioners was appointed: (1) to consider various branches of the law; (2) to consolidate and codify the law wherever possible; (3) to draft reforms on certain subjects. The Commission's Third Report, issued in July 1968, reviews recommendations for the first three years of its activities and is referred to under various headings in the text that follows.

### THE ENGLISH LEGAL SYSTEM

These three main streams—*common law* (and *case law*), *equity*, and *statute law*—have flowed throughout the centuries, sometimes independently and sometimes in conjunction, to feed the waters of that great river which is the *English Legal System*.

# B. THE SUBDIVISIONS OF ENGLISH LAW

### I. CONSTITUTIONAL LAW

This is that part of the English Legal System which relates to four main branches of national administration:—

(a) *The Legislature—i.e.*, the *law-making* body known as Parliament.

(b) *The Executive—i.e.*, the *Government* and the functions of its various components.

(c) *The Judiciary—i.e.*, the *Judges*, their *Courts* and powers.

(d) *Local Government—i.e.*, the *Local Authorities* and their powers.

The two main principles of the Constitution are:—

1. **The Supremacy of Parliament.**—*I.e.*, there is nothing that Parliament cannot lawfully do, and there is no person or body of persons above Parliament. Its Acts cannot be unconstitutional, since it can itself modify the Constitution at will. Its Acts for the time being in force are the law of the land, and nobody can question their validity.

2. **The Rule of Law.**—This means that no person or body of persons is above the law of the land, and that there is one system of law, and one system alone, for everybody. This principle was reaffirmed by the Court of Appeal in the Enfield schools cases in August 1967—ministries and local councils must obey the law like everybody else. There is not in England, as there is in some other states, a special system of law and special courts for scrutinising the acts of ministers, civil servants, or other functionaries; such persons are bound by the same rules of conduct as other citizens. A complaint by a private citizen against a Secretary of State or a Commissioner of Police is investigated by the same courts, and under the same legal rules, as a complaint against another private citizen. Any apparent exception will be found to result from some special provision in an Act of Parliament itself. For example, the Army Act sets up a code of conduct for officers and soldiers, and does not apply to civilians; but that code is part of the Law of England because it is contained in an Act of Parliament—a code which (incidentally) remains valid only if it is confirmed by Parliament in every successive year. Again, the Emergency Powers (Defence) Act, 1939, conferred upon the Crown and its Ministers extensive powers, during the last War, to make Defence Regulations which should have the force of law; but the Act itself had to be passed by Parliament with the proper formalities. Such Regulations derive their legal and binding effect solely from the *powers delegated by Parliament*; and the High Court of Justice is competent to scrutinise, and frequently does scrutinise, the wording of the Regulations and the manner in which those powers are exercised, and to satisfy itself that the Minister concerned is not attempting to exceed the authority which Parliament has vested in him—in other words, to protect the citizen against the *arbitrary abuse of lawful powers* and against their *unlawful enlargement*. *Delegated legislation* is always subject to such control; parliamentary legislation is not, since *nobody can question the*

*validity of an Act of Parliament.* But the *interpretation* of any Act of Parliament—the ascertainment of its legal meaning and effect—is one of the proper functions of the Courts. By an Act of Parliament in 1966 an office new to the British Constitution was set up—that of Parliamentary Commissioner or Ombudsman (a name borrowed from a Scandinavian institution) to whom complaints of injustice by Government departments may be made.

## II. CRIMINAL LAW

This is that part of the English Legal System which deals with the relations between the individual citizen and society as a whole. Thus, if A murders or robs B, the question of redress is not one merely for B or his family; the victim cannot, in a civilised community, be permitted " to take the law into his own hands," nor can it be left to him to decide what action should be taken against the offender—otherwise blood-feuds and public disorder would result. For that reason it has been the law for centuries past that, in the case of offences (1) against public order, (2) against the person and (3) against property, *the State (representing society as a whole) itself intervenes* and *prosecutes* the offender, for the purpose of upholding public order and vindicating the rule of law by inflicting *punishment* upon him—*not* for the purpose of *compensating* the injured party (which, as will be seen below, is the contrasting function of *Civil Law*). But recent legislation includes power to make payment of compensation for personal injuries to victims of violent crime. For offences against public order, *see* D39–41.

The two main categories of Crime (as the Tables (D3, 44) show) are:—

(a) *Grave, Indictable,* or *Arrestable Offences,* which are dealt with at Assizes, the Central Criminal Court, and Quarter Sessions, and which carry severe penalties—death or lengthy sentences of imprisonment (death only for treason in time of war); and

(b) *Petty* or (now) *Non-arrestable Offences,* which are dealt with in *Magistrates' Courts,* and are punishable by light sentences of imprisonment or by fines (with short sentences in the alternative). Examples of this latter class are (*e.g.,* under the Road Traffic Acts) driving without due care and attention, exceeding the speed-limit, causing an obstruction, etc. (*See also* Justices of the Peace, D37–9.)

Examples of (a) *Grave, Indictable,* or *Arrestable Offences* are set out in the Table (D3) under the three main headings of:

(1) *Offences against Public Order;*

(2) *Offences against the Person;* and

(3) *Offences against Property.*

In connection with all these categories of offences the *Criminal Law* is concerned with the following general considerations:—

(a) **Criminal Responsibility.**—*I.e.,* the primary principle that every person is presumed (until the contrary is proved) to be sane, provided that his acts are *voluntary* (*i.e., intentional*). It would, for example, be absurd for a man, accused of wounding another person by shooting, to plead that he did not intend, when he discharged the firearm at the other person, to do him any bodily harm. On the other hand, it would be outrageous to convict and punish a child of four who, without understanding the wrongfulness of his behaviour, picked up and took away some attractive and valuable object from a shop-counter; a lunatic who killed somebody under an insane delusion that the victim was a wild beast; a boy (like Oliver Twist) who was compelled, by force or violent threats, to break into a house, or a man who took an overcoat from a public cloak-room, honestly but mistakenly believing it to be his own. In none of these last illustrations is the act a *voluntary* one in the sense that there was the *intention to do something wrong.* To the rule that an act is not a crime unless it is intentional in this sense there are a few rare exceptions—cases

where an Act of Parliament has expressly and clearly made some form of *conduct punishable in itself,* whether it was intentional or not; for example, during the War, permitting a light to be visible in black-out hours was punishable, even if it was unintentional and involuntary on the part of the accused. And see Criminal Justice Act, 1967, below.

*Intention* must not be confused with *motive.* For example, in what has become known as " mercy-killing "—*i.e.,* taking the life of a person suffering from a painful and incurable disease—the killer is often actuated by a good *motive*—the desire to relieve hopeless suffering; but the *intention* is to kill, and the act is therefore a crime. (It is not necessary for the prosecution to prove any motive.)

The *burden of proof* in criminal cases is on the prosecution, *i.e.,* it is the duty of the prosecution to prove the accused guilty; not the duty of the accused to prove his innocence. The accused is presumed to be innocent unless and until his guilt is proved to the reasonable satisfaction of a jury. The jury are the sole judges of the true facts of the case, and their verdict had to be unanimous until recently; but by the Criminal Justice Act, 1967, it may now be by a majority of 10 to 2. The Act also contains a clause for major changes in committal proceedings by magistrates. See below, D7(2).

(b) **Unconsummated Crimes.**—*I.e., attempts* to commit crimes which are frustrated by some outside event or by some person's intervention. For obvious reasons the *attempt* to commit a grave crime is *itself an offence* for which the offender can be prosecuted and, if convicted of the attempt, punished by fine or imprisonment. *Incitement,* by one person, of another to commit a crime, and *conspiracy* between two or more persons to commit a crime, are usually offences in themselves, whether the incitement or the conspiracy proves successful or not.

(c) **Joint Crimes** are those in which two or more persons take part. Such participation may arise in different ways. A *principal in the first degree* is the man who commits the actual offence with *guilty intention* (see (a) above), or who induces its commission by some other person who himself does not understand what he is doing. A *principal in the second degree* is one who *aids and abets* the guilty perpetrator at the time when the crime is committed. An *accessory before the fact* is one who *instigates* or *helps to prepare* the commission of the crime by another person, though not himself present when that other person commits it. In most cases all these *three classes of participants* in a crime are *equally guilty,* and liable to the same punishment, provided that all of them shared the same *common criminal purpose.* (Thus, if two armed burglars break into a house, with their weapons drawn, and one of them shoots and kills the householder, both will be guilty of murder; while the accomplice who helped to plan the burglary will be equally guilty if the plan included the carrying of loaded weapons.)

(d) **Punishment and its Purpose.**—The purpose of punishment is fourfold:—

    (i) *Retribution*—to demonstrate to the community in general that crime " does not pay " and thus to uphold the rule of law and to prevent the deterioration of public morals;

    (ii) *Prevention*—to restrain offenders, so far as possible, from repeating their crimes by keeping them in custody;

    (iii) *Reformation*—to make them, so far as possible, better citizens by means of moral and ethical training—teaching them to "go straight "; and

    (iv) *Deterrence*—to inspire among offenders and would-be offenders a fear of and a healthy respect for the law and the strength of society as a whole, which it protects.

There has been much controversy on the relative importance of these four functions of punishment. During the past half-century, *reformation* of the offender, whenever possible, has become a paramount aim.

**(e) Insanity.—**

If a person does an act which, if *voluntary or intentional*, would constitute a *crime* (see *Criminal Responsibility*, D6), and his legal advisers put forward a defence of insanity, he can still be convicted unless he can prove, to the satisfaction of a jury, that he was " suffering from such a *defect of reason*, due to *disease of the mind*, as not to know the *nature and quality of the act* he was doing, or (if he *did* know this) not to know that what he was doing was *wrong*." Medical men, psychologists, and social reformers have long regarded this rule (which has been in force since 1843) as too severe. It was a rule applicable to *all* crimes; but the controversy became associated in the public mind chiefly with *murder*. The rule was amended by section 2 of the Homicide Act, 1957; but *only in its application to murder cases*. It is now provided that " a person who kills (or is a party to the killing of) another shall *not* be convicted of *murder* if he was suffering from such *abnormality of mind* as substantially *impaired his mental responsibility* for his acts and omissions in doing, or being a party to the killing." (It does not matter whether the " abnormality of mind " arises from " a condition of arrested or retarded development of mind," or from " any inherent causes," or is " induced by disease or injury.") The Act goes on to provide that a person who, under the old law, would have been convicted of murder shall instead be liable to conviction of *manslaughter*.

In other crimes, where the accused person is clearly proved to have been insane at the time the crime was committed, the verdict is now " Not guilty by reason of insanity."

The Murder (Abolition of Death Penalty) Act, 1965, provides that no person shall suffer death for murder; a person convicted of murder shall be sentenced to imprisonment for life. In passing sentence the Court may declare the minimum period which it recommends the Home Secretary to allow to elapse before he orders the murderer's release on license. The new Act is to continue in force until 31 July 1970, and then expire unless both Houses of Parliament pass contrary resolutions; if the new Act does expire, the law as it existed before the passing of the new Act shall again come into operation.

The Criminal Justice Act, 1967 revolutionises many provisions of criminal law and procedure:

Magistrates or J.P.s conducting a preliminary inquiry to determine whether there is a *prima facie* case for Quarter Sessions, Assizes or the Central Criminal Court (D44) may commit an accused for trial on written evidence, signed by the witness(es) who made the statement, and declared by them to be true, provided that a copy is handed to the defendant(s), solicitor, or counsel, none of whom objects; but only if the accused is represented by counsel or solicitor. (The statement must be read over to any person who cannot read it.) If the witness is under the age of majority, it must state his age. (The purpose is to save time.) In any case the Court may require such witness to give evidence by word of mouth, either on its own initiative or on the request of any party. The same applies to the trial itself, and admissions are to be good evidence.

Although the examining justices must sit in open Court, no report of the proceedings may be published, unless (*a*) one of the accused so requests, or (*b*) the magistrates discharge the accused, or (*c*) a brief summary of matters excluding evidence is printed. Penalty for unauthorised publication is £500. (*Note:* The purpose of these provisions is to avoid prejudice to the accused at the main trial.) Notice of discharge or committal must be displayed after the preliminary hearing. Any permitted publication is privileged.

A Court shall not be bound to infer intention or foresight of the results of the accused's actions, but in every case shall decide whether that particular accused did intend or foresee them

on the whole of the evidence. (This reverses a decision in 1962, *Director of Public Prosecutions* v. *Smith*, where the House of Lords inferred an intent to kill from the mere fact that the accused accelerated a car and drove with a policeman clinging to the bonnet.)

Notice of the defence of *alibi* must be given to the prosecutor at least 7 days before the end of the committal proceedings, except with leave of the Court. (This is intended to avoid an alibi being " sprung " on the prosecutor at the last moment, when he cannot disprove it.)

Verdicts of juries need no longer be unanimous. If there are not less than 11 jurors, 10 may return a verdict; if there are 10, 9 may do so. But the jury must be allowed at least 2 hours for deliberation. Persons who have served a term of at least 3 months imprisonment (or in a borstal), summarily, or who have been sentenced to at least 5 years or for life (which usually means about 12 years), are disqualified from serving on a jury— penalty £25; but a verdict is not to be held void because of such disqualification.

Magistrates hearing an offence carrying not more than six months imprisonment may no longer refuse bail to an accused over seventeen, on remand or committal, or in certain other cases. No J.P. may take part in the trial if he knows of previous convictions (to avoid prejudice). A constable may arrest without warrant any person who he believes is likely to break his bail. If the J.P.s refuse bail, the accused may apply for bail to the High Court. A Magistrates' Court shall not sentence an accused to imprisonment in his absence. Magistrates may now impose fines up to £400 (instead of £100). Imprisonment in default of payment is abolished, except when the accused has means to pay but will not. Instead, enforcement shall be by seizing his goods, or by deduction from his earnings.

Preventive detention and corrective training are abolished as is also corporal punishment in prisons. Suspended sentences may be passed; if the accused commits a further offence, he may have to serve the suspended sentence. The Home Secretary may make rules requiring a " Social inquiry report " before sentence. Deportation of a Commonwealth immigrant may be substituted for imprisonment for life.

There is now power to release prisoners on licence, to revoke such licence, to remand or release young offenders to or from detention or approved schools.

The Criminal Law Act, 1967. The old distinction into felonies and misdemeanours is abolished: the expressions " indictable " and " summary " offences are retained, but for some purposes offences are divided into " arrestable " and " non-arrestable " offences. Arrestable offences are those for which (i) the sentence is fixed by law; those for which (ii) the offender is liable to five years imprisonment, and those which (iii) there has been an attempt (D6(2)–(b)) to commit. Arrestable offences, therefore, now include practically every variety of grave crime. Others are known as non-arrestable offences.

The old offence of being an accessory after the fact (except in treason) is abolished: instead, a new offence of " assisting offenders " is created by the Criminal Law Act providing that " where a person has committed an arrestable offence, any other person who, knowing or believing him to be guilty, does, without lawful authority or reasonable excuse, any act with intent to impede his apprehension or prosecution " shall be liable to periods of imprisonment proportionate to the sentence for the main offence. Where the arrestable offence is itself triable summarily (*i.e.*, by a Magistrates' Court) with the defendant's consent, then the offence of " assisting " is also so triable. But the proceedings may be brought only by or with the consent of the Director of Public Prosecutions. A husband or wife has no special exemption.

A new crime of " concealing arrestable offences " is created. In effect the new offence amounts to the prohibition of accepting a bribe in consideration of such concealment, and the consent of the Director of Public Prosecutions must be obtained beforehand, if a prosecution is contemplated. The defendant must know or believe that his information might be of material assistance in securing the conviction of an offender. But the common law rule that " you may show mercy but shall not sell mercy " is modified, so that it is not unlawful to agree not to prosecute or give information on condition that the offender makes good any loss or injury caused by his offence, or makes reasonable compensation for it. It remains unlawful to help to conceal any act of treason.

A new summary offence is created under the Act—the making of false reports to cause wasteful employment of the time of the police in regard to any kind of alleged offence.

Power is given to award compensation to the injured party, in case of any indictable offence, up to the sum of £400 (but compensation for damage due to an accident arising out of the presence of a motor vehicle on a road is excluded; such claims are covered by compulsory insurance). Such compensation may be awarded by the Court trying the offence.

Powers of arrest: Any person may now arrest (i) anyone who is in the act, or whom he suspects to be in the act, of committing an arrestable offence, and (ii) where an arrestable offence has been committed, anyone who is guilty, or whom he suspects to be guilty, of the offence. A constable may without warrant arrest (i) where he suspects with reasonable cause that an arrestable offence has been committed, anyone whom he, with reasonable cause, suspects to be guilty, and (ii) anyone who is about to commit, or whom the constable, with reasonable cause, suspects to be about to commit an arrestable offence. Common law powers of arrest, such as to prevent violence or breach of the peace (D39), are unaffected by the new Act. A constable may enter (if necessary by force) and search any place where anyone (whom he has the right to arrest) is or where, with reasonable cause, he suspects him to be. A person may use such force as is reasonable in the circumstances in the prevention of crime or in effecting or assisting in the lawful arrest of offenders or suspected offenders or of persons unlawfully at large. (This power is not restricted to constables, nor in actual terms to indictable offences; but the words " such force as is reasonable in the circumstances " prevent or, by implication, forbid the use of force for arrest in the case of trivial offences.)

The common law offence of receiving is defined as follows: " A person shall be treated as receiving property if he dishonestly undertakes or assists in its detention, removal, or realisation by or for the benefit of another or if he arranges so to do." The common law crimes of theft, and similar offences, codified in the Larceny Act, 1916, have now been recodified, expanded, and more clearly defined by the Theft Act, 1968.

## III. STATUS

A person's *Status*—*i.e.*, his legal position in society—affects his legal rights and duties in most civil matters and, in some few cases, in criminal matters too (see *Criminal Responsibility*, D6).

1. **Nationality**, in this connection, means British Nationality under the British Nationality Acts, the latest of which was passed in 1965. By the 1948 Act the term " Commonwealth Citizen " was created which can be used as an alternative to British Subject. A person may be a British subject by birth, by naturalisation, by marriage, or by registration, though under the Act of 1948 a woman who was not a British subject before marriage does not automatically acquire British nationality merely by reason of her marriage to a British subject. The law and the courts of this country can determine whether a person is a *British subject* or an *alien*; they cannot determine whether or not he is a citizen of some particular *foreign state*, since that is a matter for the law of

the foreign state concerned. Generally speaking, in times of peace, an *alien* in this country has the same rights and duties as a British subject, except that an *alien* has *no right to vote* in parliamentary or municipal elections, and that some professions (*e.g.*, that of a solicitor) are closed to him. By the Act of 1964, a person who is *stateless* may apply to be registered as a citizen of the U.K. and Colonies if either parent was such a citizen when he was born, or if the place of his birth is within the U.K. and Colonies at the time of his application. By the Act of 1965 *alien wives* of those British subjects who are *not citizens of any Commonwealth country* may be *registered* as British subjects.

2. **Domicil** means the country where a person has his *permanent home* without any present intention of changing it. His *domicil of origin* is that of his parents while he is an infant; at the age of majority he is free to acquire a new domicil by making his permanent home elsewhere. Domicil is of particular importance in matters of—

3. **Marriage and Divorce.**—English law generally regards as valid a *marriage ceremony* carried out in this country after the proper preliminaries and with the proper formalities, whatever the nationality or domicil of the parties. English law also accepts the validity of a *marriage ceremony* which has been carried out abroad according to the law of the country where it took place. But if one party or the other has an *English domicil*, the *status of the marriage as an institution* must depend on English law, whether the *ceremony* was in proper form or not. For example, a man who has his permanent home in England cannot evade the English rule against consanguinity by going through a *ceremony* of marriage, in Ruritania, with his mother's sister—even if such a marriage is lawful by Ruritanian law, and even if the ceremony has been carried out with the usual Ruritanian formalities, it is still *null and void* by the law of England. The English court will *not*, generally speaking, grant a *divorce* to a man who is *domiciled abroad*, since the law of the country which is his permanent home may not recognise this divorce, or perhaps any divorce, as valid; and it is improper that he should be regarded as a single man in England and a married man in his homeland. Similarly, English law *will* generally recognise the validity of a divorce granted by the proper court of his domicil (*i.e.*, of the state where he had his permanent home at the time) or of a divorce which the law of his domicil regards as valid, even if it was granted by a court elsewhere—and that whether he is a British subject or not. Under recent court decisions, English law may also recognise a divorce granted by the court of a country with which he has some *genuine connection*. But a person, whatever his nationality, whose permanent home is in England will not be regarded here as validly divorced merely because he has spent a few weeks in Angria, where divorce procedure is simple, and has been granted a decreee there. His *status*—married or single—generally *depends on the law of his domicil*—*i.e.*, the law of the country which is his permanent home. (*See also* D30–1.)

4. **Infancy** is the status of a person under the age of majority (now eighteen). An *infant cannot vote at elections*; he *cannot hold freehold or leasehold property*, and *he cannot be made bankrupt*. (In exceptional cases where the debt is for " necessaries " (D11(1), a bankruptcy notice may be issued against an infant.) If he enters into certain kinds of *contracts* during his infancy he *can repudiate* them, if he so desires, up to a reasonable time after his majority. He *cannot make a valid will*, and his rights under another person's will or settlement cannot be compromised or altered without the leave of the High Court. An infant *cannot make a valid marriage without consent* of his parent or guardian, or of the appropriate court. His rights are at all times the special care of the Chancery Division of the High Court, which will protect those rights according to the Rules of Equity (*see* D5). (The Latey Committee in 1967 recommended reducing the age of majority to eighteen and the Government has adopted this

recommendation for all purposes, including the parliamentary vote and marriage without parental consent.)

5. Lunacy, in the broad legal sense, is the status of a person who is "incapable, by reason of unsoundness of mind, of managing his affairs." "Lunacy" in this sense is not necessarily identical with any of the mental conditions to which such psychological terms as "insanity," "imbecility," "idiocy," and the like are applied; there need be no actual mental *disease*. When a person becomes incapable, for this reason, of managing his affairs, the law, in order to protect both him and society at large, *changes his status* by putting the custody of his person, or the control of his property, or both, into reliable hands. Such matters come under the supervision of the Chancery Division, since one of the functions of Equity (see above) is to protect those who cannot help themselves. Certification of "insanity" (in the psychological sense) is not necessary; but with the proper medical certificate and legal safeguards the *patient* (as he must be called) may be removed to a mental hospital. Some reliable person (usually a near relative) may be appointed, by an Order of the *Court of Protection* (a branch of the Chancery Division), as *Receiver* of his property. The Receiver's duties are to look after the property and income of the patient, pay his debts and defray the expenses of his maintenance and medical care, and generally to deal with the patient's property on the patient's behalf. Periodical accounts must be submitted to the Court, which will scrutinise them strictly and at once intervene if there appears to be any irregularity on the part of the Receiver. If there is no relative to take the responsibility, the *Official Solicitor* at the Royal Courts of Justice will be appointed as Receiver, with the same duties and liabilities.

Apart from these matters of administration, a person of unsound mind is regarded as incapable of making a valid will, of entering into a legal agreement, or of dealing with his property. None of these transactions is valid unless the person concerned *understood the nature and effect* of what he was doing; and whether he did understand or not is a question of *evidence* in every individual case: medical and other witnesses must testify to his conduct and demeanour at the time when he entered into the transaction in question. If the Court comes to the conclusion that he was unable to understand the nature and effect of the transaction, the Court will *rescind*—*i.e.*, set aside or cancel—the transaction, even though it was in proper legal form.

6. Bankruptcy is the creation of Statute Law—there was no common law of bankruptcy. It is the status of a person (the "debtor") who is *insolvent*—*i.e.*, who is unable to pay his debts (exceeding £50) as they fall due. By the appropriate procedure the State takes the management of the debtor's property out of his hands and places it in the hands of the *Official Receiver*, whose duty it is to realise it and (subject to certain privileged claims) to distribute it *proportionately among his creditors*. The procedure is that one of the creditors files at the Bankruptcy Court a *bankruptcy petition*, on which the Court may make a *receiving order*, which has the effect of *transferring the legal management* of the debtor's property to the Official Receiver. That official investigates the debtor's finances and draws up an account, called a *statement of affairs*, showing the debtor's liabilities and assets. There is a *meeting of creditors* and a *public examination* of the debtor in Court, as a result of which the Court may either *discharge* the *receiving order* (on the debtor's showing that he can pay his debts, if he is given time, or persuade the general body of creditors to accept his proposals for a *composition* of so much in the £), or the Court may *adjudicate* the debtor a bankrupt. In the latter case it is open to the creditors either to leave the management of the debtor's property in the Official Receiver's hands or themselves to appoint a *trustee in bankruptcy* (usually an accountant) nominated by some or all of them, and that trustee takes over the management of the debtor's affairs. The

debtor is bound, under penalty, to give *full information* about his affairs to the Official Receiver and the trustee in bankruptcy; he cannot, while he is a bankrupt, sit or vote in Parliament or act as a Justice of the Peace or in certain other offices. He will be committing an *offence* if he conceals any property or debt or falsifies his books of account, if he obtains property on credit or secures credit of £10 or more without disclosing his status, if he trades without such disclosure or fails to keep proper books of account, or if he leaves or attempts to leave the country taking with him property, worth £20 or more, which ought to be divided among his creditors. It is also an offence for him to transfer property with intent to defraud any creditor, and any such transaction may be set aside by the Court.

7. A Corporation or Incorporated Body is an association of persons recognised by *Act of Parliament*, or by its *Charter*, as *one single legal entity*. It may be a *chartered* or a *statutory corporation* (*e.g.*, the British Broadcasting Corporation or the London Transport Board), a *local authority* (*e.g.*, the Greater London Council or the Westminster City Council), or a *company* incorporated under the Companies Act, 1948, or one of the earlier Companies Acts. Generally speaking, a corporation of any kind has power only to do such things as it is given power to do by its Charter or by the Act of Parliament under which it was constituted; if it goes beyond that power it is behaving *ultra vires* —"beyond its powers"—and such acts on its part will be regarded by the Courts as null and void. The Court may also restrain the corporation by *injunction*—an Order forbidding it to act in such a manner.

Every corporation, being a single legal entity, is a legal *person* distinct from the individuals who are its members. Thus the *corporation itself* can take *proceedings*, or have proceedings brought against it, in the Civil Courts, and it may itself be *prosecuted* in the Criminal Courts, if it commits an offence, and be liable to a fine. No personal liability rests upon its individual members, directors, or officers unless they have personally done something unlawful or aided and abetted the corporation in its wrongdoing. The corporation itself can *enter into a legal agreement* with one or more of its members or a member of the public, and any person injured by its acts can enforce his legal rights against the property or assets of the corporation, which are distinct from the property or assets of the individuals who compose it.

A *company* is usually a commercial concern and generally takes advantage of the principle of *limited liability*, in which case the last word in its name must be the word "Limited." The principle is that, in the event of the company's becoming *insolvent*, none of its members can be compelled to contribute to its funds a larger sum than the sum which he agreed to pay for his *shares*, however large the indebtedness of the company itself. Every company must file at the Companies Registry a *Memorandum of Association*, setting out its *name*, the situation of its *registered office*, its *objects* (beyond which it has no power to act), its *capital*, and whether or not it is a *limited*. It should also file its *Articles of Association*, setting out its *rules of management*, the method of issuing, allotting, and transferring its *shares*, the procedure for *meetings*, the powers and duties of its *directors* and other officers, and similar matters. If and when its objects have been *fully achieved*, or if it is desired to discontinue its activities, or if it becomes *insolvent*, it will be *wound up* and *dissolved*. The winding-up is undertaken by a *Liquidator* whose duties are similar to those of the trustee in bankruptcy. The liquidator may be nominated by the members of the company or, in case of the company's insolvency, by some or all of the creditors, and the liquidator's appointment must be confirmed at a special meeting. If the winding-up of an insolvent company takes more than a year the liquidator must report annually to the *Board of Trade*, the Government Department which watches the interests of the persons concerned.

8. Adoption. *See* D34–7.

## IV. The CIVIL LAW or LAW OF PERSONS

This deals with the relations between *one individual citizen and another*, and their mutual rights and duties. If A makes a business agreement with B, and breaks it, or if A walks without permission across B's field of new-mown hay, B will be able to secure *redress* against A by proceedings in a court of law. But in neither case is it necessary for the State to intervene, by way of prosecution, to punish A for what he has done, since no offence against society at large, and no violation of public order, or the rule of law, has arisen. The issue is one merely between A and B; B may choose to ignore the wrong done to him, or he may negotiate amicably with A for the payment of compensation or, if this fails, he may *as plaintiff sue A as defendant* in a *civil action* for *damages*. Unlike a criminal prosecution, undertaken by the State for the preservation of public order and vindication of the rule of law, with a view to punishing the offender, the *civil action* will be brought, if B so chooses, *by B himself* for the purpose of recovering *compensation* in money for the harm he has suffered and (in some cases) of obtaining an *injunction*—a Court Order prohibiting A from continuing his wrongful conduct. Again, a criminal prosecution will not be discontinued even at the request of the injured party, since the State itself is interested to see justice done; but a *civil action* can be *discontinued* by B at whatever stage he desires, with or without an agreement for the payment of *damages* in compensation.

These *relations between one individual and another*, interference with which may give rise to a *civil action for damages or injunction*, may arise in two alternative ways:—from the acts of the parties themselves, or from the operation of law. Hitherto *evidence of a criminal conviction* has *not been admitted in Civil cases*, but this rule is abolished by the Civil Evidence Act, 1968. *The onus* of proving that the conviction was wrong lies on the accused.

### 1. Law of Contract

The relations between individuals which arise from the acts of the parties themselves are usually brought about by a *contract*—i.e., by an agreement between them. A contract may be (a) *expressed in words*, as where A agrees to buy B's motor-car for £400, on certain stated conditions, or (b) *implied by conduct*, as where A calls a taxi and tells the driver to take him to a certain address. (a) In the former case, particularly if the contract is put into writing, the parties will normally have *expressed* all the necessary terms and conditions. (b) In the latter case it is *implied* by A's conduct, and understood by law and custom, that A will be expected to pay, at the end of the journey, the amount of the fare recorded by the taximeter; it is not necessary for the driver to stipulate those terms in advance. Everybody, several times in the course of each day, enters into an *implied contract* of this kind—when he steps on an omnibus to go to his work, when he orders a meal in a restaurant, when he tells the grocer to deliver goods to his house, and so on.

### Simple Contracts and Deeds

(1) A Simple Contract is a contract *expressed in words* (whether in writing or not) without the formalities of a *deed* (see below), or a contract *implied by conduct*. There is no legal contract (a) unless there is *complete certainty* on the terms; (b) unless the basis of the agreement is lawful; and (c) unless both parties are *legally capable* of entering into it (see above, *Status*), and (d) in *complete agreement* on their intentions. And the agreement is not enforceable (e) unless there is some *consideration*, i.e., some *quid pro quo*, expressed or implied, on either side. (The Law Commission, however, is considering the abolition of *consideration* as essential to every contract). Thus (a) a promise by A that he will buy B's motor-car cannot be enforced by either side unless the price is mentioned, nor (b) if the car has been stolen by B, nor (c) if A is of unsound mind, nor (d) if B owns two cars, and A is thinking of the Ford, while B intends to sell the Austin.

Again (e) a promise by C, during the course of the year's work, that he will give his employee, D, a Christmas box of £5 is not enforceable by D unless he has made a promise, or done something in return. If C tells D that he will give D the £5 at Christmas *on condition that* D puts in certain *extra time* over and above his normal working-hours, and D complies or promises to comply, that compliance, or promise of compliance, will be sufficient *consideration* to turn A's promise into an enforceable contract. There need be nothing at all in writing, except in a few cases laid down by law; in all other cases the only *value of a written agreement*, signed by both parties, is that it provides clear *evidence* of the terms that were agreed. A written contract requires a sixpenny revenue stamp if it is to be produced as evidence in a court of law. (The Law Commission is recommending a code to cover the whole law of contract).

(2) A Deed (broadly speaking) is a contract or other written document, *signed, sealed,* and *delivered* by the parties. The formalities of *affixing one's seal* to a legal document, and pronouncing the formula, "I deliver this as my act and deed," have emphasised the significance and solemnity of certain important transactions for many centuries past; and even persons who were unable to write their names were capable of carrying out the formalities of *sealing* and *delivery*. The legal requirement that deeds should also be *signed* was imposed only in 1925, by section 73 (1) of the Law of Property Act. The chief practical distinction between a simple contract and a deed is that a *deed requires no consideration* to make it enforceable. The special formalities which constitute the *execution* of a deed (i.e., signing, sealing, and delivery) take the place of that moral obligation which (in a simple contract) the common law required to be satisfied by consideration on the part of the person to whom the promise was made. For this reason a *deed* is required in a case where A makes a promise to B which he desires to render enforceable without any corresponding promise by B to A, and also in a case where A desires to make to B a *gift of property* of such a nature that it cannot be physically handed over. This second case arises particularly where the subject of the gift is *land or buildings*; in fact, by a provision of the Law of Property Act, 1925, a *deed* is always necessary to *transfer the ownership* of any *freehold or leasehold* property, and also to grant a *tenancy* for a term of *more than three years*. The transfer of a *legal right* of some kind (e.g., a share in a company or the claim to moneys under an insurance policy) is generally effected *by deed*.

In connection with the Law of Contract the following subsidiary matters must be considered:—

### Subsidiary Matters

(a) **Capacity of Parties.**—The question whether a party to a contract is *legally capable* of entering into it usually depends on that party's *status* (see above):—

(1) *Nationality.*—Nothing turns on this, except that *no commercial contract* can be made with an *alien enemy* in time of war.

(2) *Domicil.*—Where the two or more parties to a contract have their *permanent homes in different countries* it is a wise precaution for them to state, in the contract, under which country's law and by which country's courts, in case of a dispute, its terms are to be construed. If they omit to do so, and some dispute is brought before the English Court, it will endeavour to decide, by considering the wording of the contract, the language in which it is written, the domicil of the parties, and the general circumstances in which the contract was made, what legal system the parties intended to apply and by what court they intended is to be judged. Sometimes it will decide the dispute according to the rules of the foreign law.

(3) *Marriage and Divorce.*—There is now no practical difference in contractual capacity between single persons, married persons, and divorcees.

(4) *Infancy.*—It is not (generally speaking) impossible for a minor to enter into a valid contract, but he will be entitled to repudiate it at any time

up to the date of his majority (or a reasonable period after that) *unless* the contract is (a) clearly for the *infant's benefit* on the whole (*e.g.*, professional articles or an agreement for apprenticeship), or (b) for the provision of *necessaries*—*i.e.*, food, drink, clothing, or services which are necessary to the infant in his particular station in life. (The origin of this latter rule is probably the practical consideration that, in earlier times, few people would have taken the risk of providing an infant, on credit, with the bare necessities of life if they had been precluded from suing him for reasonable payment.)

(5) *Lunacy.*—A party to a " contract " who knows that the other party is of unsound mind will not be permitted to hold the latter to his bargain.

(6) *Bankruptcy.*—A bankrupt cannot make a valid agreement to deal with his property in a manner which contravenes the law of Bankruptcy.

(7) *Corporations.*—Whether a corporation is capable of entering into a particular contract depends upon the legal powers conferred by the Charter or Act of Parliament under which it was constituted, or (if a company) by its Memorandum of Association. If the matter to which the contract relates is of grave importance it will usually signify its adherence to the contract by *affixing its seal* with the formalities laid down by its Rules or Articles of Association. If it is an everyday or trivial matter the corporation will normally enter into a contract through some agent (*e.g.*, its Town Clerk, Director, or Secretary, as the case may be) who is empowered to sign or speak on its behalf.

(b) **When Writing is Necessary.**—There are certain exceptions, laid down by Act of Parliament, to the rule that a contract is enforceable even if made only by word of mouth or implied by conduct. The Statute of Frauds, 1677, provided that contracts of these exceptional kinds cannot be enforced by action in the Courts " unless the agreement upon which such action shall be brought, or some memorandum or note thereof, shall be in writing, and signed by the party to be charged therewith, or some other person thereunto by him lawfully authorised "—these last words mean an *agent*. It is *not necessary* that the *whole of the agreement* shall be formally set down in *writing*; but there must be a *written and signed record* of all the *essential terms*.

(i) *A Guarantee.*—*I.e.*, a promise by A to B in the form—" Please lend money (or supply goods) to C, and if C does not pay you I will." A's promise by word of mouth cannot be enforced against him.

The provision of the Statute of Frauds still holds good.

(ii) An *agreement* for the *sale or disposition of land* (*or buildings*) or of any interest in land (or buildings). We have already stated that the actual *transfer* of a *freehold* or *leasehold* interest must be effected by *deed*. This is not the same as an *agreement to sell or dispose of* land or buildings; a *transfer* effects an *immediate change of ownership*, while an *agreement to sell* binds the party who signs it to make a transfer of ownership at some *future time*. Such an agreement need not be in the form of a deed, but its *essential terms* must be *in writing*.

Some other parts of the Statute of Frauds have been repealed: that contained in (ii) above has been replaced by a similar provision set out in section 40 of the Law of Property Act, 1925.

(iii) A *bill of exchange* or *promissory note* must be in writing, by virtue of section 3 of the Bills of Exchange Act, 1882.

(iv) A contract of *Marine Insurance* is inadmissible in evidence unless it is embodied in a marine policy as laid down in the Marine Insurance Act, 1906, sections 22–24, with all relevant conditions fully specified, and duly signed by or on behalf of the insurer.

(v) By the Contracts of Employment Act, 1963 (in force since July 1964), it is the *duty of an employer* (not later than 13 weeks after the employment commenced) to hand his employee a *written statement of particulars of the employment* (period, wage, working hours, and what length of notice is required for termination).

(c) **Mistake.**—Suppose that John Brown wants his portrait painted by a famous artist called William Brush, of whom he has heard but whom he has never met. He looks up " William Brush " in the directory and writes to him, at the address shown, offering him 100 guineas to paint the portrait. Suppose that particular " William Brush " is not the artist at all but a stockbroker of the same name. Even if that William Brush accepts Brown's offer, their apparent agreement will not constitute a valid contract, since Brown's *mistake* as to Brush's identity is so *fundamental* that it *destroys the very basis* of the agreement. Where there is a mistake of this kind, " going to the very root of the agreement," no valid contract has, in the eyes of the law, been made. In other special cases *equity* may, on the ground of *conscience*, *relieve* one or both parties from liability under a concluded contract by *rectification* (*i.e.*, by correcting the terms they have inadvertently recorded) or by *rescission* (*i.e.*, by cancellation of the contract). It is not every mistake that will lead to these results; either the mistake must have been *fundamental* or the circumstances must have been such that it would be *unconscientious* for one party or the other to try to enforce his apparent rights.

(d) **Misrepresentation.**—Equity, on similar grounds, has often relieved a party from liability under a contract into which he has been induced to enter through a *representation* by the other party which is *substantially false*—*i.e.*, a statement which is misleading on some essential point. Whether the misrepresentation was *deliberate or innocent*, the deceived party will usually be able to have the contract *set aside*—*i.e.*, cancelled.

Suppose, for example, Jones wants to insure his life with the Markshire Insurance Company. Before issuing the policy, which is the contract between them, the Company will ask Jones— " Have you ever suffered from any serious illness?" Suppose Jones says " No," though he did in fact suffer from tuberculosis five years ago. Even if the policy contains a promise by the Company to pay Jones's widow £5000 upon Jones's death, the Company will be entitled to refuse to pay when that event happens; it has been induced to enter into the contract through Jones's misrepresentation.

By the Misrepresentation Act, 1967, if a person enters into a contract (later than April, 1967, when the Act became law) after a misrepresentation has been made by the other party, and (a) the misrepresentation has become a term of the contract, or (b) the contract has been carried out, or both, then, if under the old law he would have been entitled to rescind (*i.e.*, cancel) the contract without alleging fraud, he shall be entitled to do so, in spite of (a) and (b). (Under the old law, once the contract had been carried out, his only remedy was damages, if he had suffered loss.) It is now provided that where such misrepresentation has been made to a person as a result of which he has suffered loss, then the other party shall be liable to damages even if there was no fraud (*i.e.*, deliberate deceit), unless he proves that he believed, on reasonable grounds, up to the date of the contract, that his representations were true. In any case the Court may award damages instead of, or in addition to, rescission, if the Court thinks it equitable to do so, whether the misrepresentation was innocent or fraudulent.

If an agreement is made containing a clause excluding or restricting liability for misrepresentation, that clause shall be ineffective unless the Court thinks it fair and reasonable.  In sales of goods rescision and/or damages are to be available to the buyer even after he has become the owner of the goods.  And he is not deemed to have accepted them until he has been afforded and has had a reasonable opportunity of inspecting them to ascertain whether they conform to the contract or not.

(*Note:* This Act is expected to remove abuses, particularly at some auction sales, where the sellers, in their catalogues, have been reckless in attributing a work of art to a particular artist, and have excluded liability for misdescription in the contract.)

(*e*) **Duress** means compulsion by *threats or force*. If a man has been compelled in this manner to put his name to a contract it is *voidable by him* at any time—*i.e., he may repudiate* it on the ground of duress, and will be upheld by law in doing so. *Undue influence* means influence exerted by A upon B to such an extent that B could not have exercised any free and independent will in doing a particular act.  Equity has always been jealous to protect certain classes of persons from this kind of influence: it goes so far as to *presume* that there has been undue influence where a guardian has got some benefit out of his ward, a parent from his child who is under (or only just over) majority, a doctor from his patient, a solicitor from his client, or a priest from his parishioner. In most of such cases the onus is upon the person in the influential position, who has obtained the benefit, to prove that there was no undue influence; it is not for the other person to prove that his mind was wrongfully influenced by the former.

(*f*) **Illegality** of contract arises where the parties have agreed to do an act (i) forbidden by law or (ii) contrary to " public policy."  (i) The former includes not only an agreement to commit a crime, but also an agreement to do an act which might be harmful to a third party and give him a right of action for breach of contract or tort. The courts will obviously not lend their assistance to a plaintiff who complains that the defendant has refused to honour his agreement to do something unlawful, whether (for example) the agreement was to burgle a house or merely to write a libellous article about another person.  (ii) Even if the act agreed upon was not actually unlawful, the courts will refuse to enforce the agreement if it was to do something which is regarded as harmful to the community.  It is not, for example, a crime for a man and a woman to live together without being married, nor is it even " unlawful " in the civil sense that such a way of life gives the one a right of action against the other; but no court would enforce an agreement by a woman to become a man's mistress, nor an agreement by the man to maintain her in return.

(*g*) **Breach of Contract** occurs when one of the parties breaks his promise and neglects or refuses to perform his duty under the contract.  Breach by one party entitles the other party to sue for *damages,* the amount of which is usually assessed so as to compensate the latter for the *actual loss* he has suffered (" special damage ").  In certain cases the court may award *general damages* in addition—*e.g.,* in an action for breach of promise of marriage the jilted woman may be awarded *general damages* for the distress she has suffered, her loss of reputation, etc., as well as *special damages* to cover the amount by which she is *out-of-pocket* by reason of giving up her employment, buying a trousseau, etc.

(1) *Damages* have always been the *common-law remedy* for breach of contract.  In special cases, however, equity may grant two other remedies in addition to, or in substitution for, damages; but only where equity regards damages as an insufficient compensation.  These additional remedies are:—

(2) *Specific Performance.*—*I.e.,* an order, to the party in breach, *actually to carry out* what he contracted to do.  In practice this remedy is

confined to: (i) contracts for the sale or letting of *land or buildings,* and (ii) contracts for the sale of some *article of a special nature* which cannot be replaced by spending money in the open market —for example, the sale of an original painting by Rembrandt.  The remedy of *specific performance* is *never* granted to enforce a contract for *personal services,* since it would be impossible for the court to supervise the carrying out of such a contract.

(3) *Injunction.*—*I.e.,* an order by the court to the party in default *prohibiting him* from carrying out some positive act which would constitute a breach of contract.  For example, where a singer has entered into a contract to work, for a certain period, only under the management of one particular impresario and no other, the court may order the singer not to offer or engage her services elsewhere during that period.  Disobedience to an injunction constitutes *contempt of court,* and is punishable by fine or imprisonment.

## 2. Law of Tort

This branch of the law deals with the relations between one individual citizen and another, which arise from the operation of the law itself, without the necessity for the parties to do any act to put them into legal relations with one another.  As was pointed out above (**D10**(1)), if A and B are to be linked in a contractual relationship, each of them must take some step to bring that relationship about.  No such step, however, is necessary in connection with the matters dealt with by the Law of Tort.  Everybody has a right to expect that his person and his property shall be inviolable by other private citizens; he also has a right to expect others to refrain from attacks upon his character and his business reputation.  These rights do not arise from any agreement or other act on his part, but from the general principles of the law.

A *tort* is the violation of such a right, which entitles the injured party to bring a *civil action* for damages to *compensate* for the injury he has suffered.  The word *tort* (in French " wrong ") is derived from the Latin *tortus* meaning " twisted " or " distorted."

It will be seen from the Table (**D3**) that some torts (*e.g.,* assault) may also be crimes—that is, they may entitle the injured party *either* to bring a *civil action* for *damages* or to *prosecute* the offending party and have him *punished* by a *criminal* court in cases where the offending party's action is liable to harm the community at large; a personal assault, for example, may lead in some circumstances to general disorder, and in that event it will become a matter for intervention by the State through the criminal courts (*see* **D44**). This section, however, deals only with the *civil remedies* which, as in breaches of contract, are primarily *damages* and sometimes *injunction.*

*Trespass* is a wrongful act committed by one citizen, against the will of another citizen, either against the latter's person or in disturbance of his possession of land or other property.

(1) **Trespass against the Person** may be by way of *assault, battery,* or *false imprisonment.*  An *assault* is an attempt to do violence to the person of another; if the act is fully consummated it becomes a *battery.*  Thus it is an *assault* for one man to shake his fist in the face of another, or to adopt a threatening attitude towards another, or deliberately to set his dog on another person.  If the first person actually strikes the other person, or if the dog, encouraged by the first person, actually bites or harms the other person, that is a *battery.*  In order to constitute an assault or battery, and to render the trespasser liable to an action for damages, his act must be *deliberate.*  It is not assault and battery if A *accidentally* knocks against B in a crowd, with the result that B falls and is injured.  The act by the trespasser must also be *against the will* of the person injured.  Thus an operation performed by a surgeon, though it may seriously affect the body of the other person, is not an assault or battery if the other person has

consented to the operation; but such an operation, performed without the other person's consent, may amount to an assault or battery.

Certain acts which would in the ordinary way constitute assault or battery are excusable; it is recognised, for example, by the common law, that a parent or a teacher has the right to inflict reasonable chastisement upon a child or pupil in his care, and provided that the chastisement is not excessive the child or pupil has no right of action. If, however, the chastisement results in serious injury or amounts to brutal violence, then the person inflicting it will be liable to an action for damages. (The present Government is considering abolition of corporal punishment in schools.)

*False imprisonment* means the *unlawful restraint* of one person by another. It need not amount to actually locking up a person in a room; it is sufficient if his freedom of movement is *totally restrained* either by confinement or by the use of force or threat of force. It should be noted that the restraint must be unlawful; it is not, for example, unlawful for a police officer to arrest a person engaged in committing a crime, or a person whom the officer has reasonable grounds for suspecting of committing, or being about to commit, a violent crime. Even a private citizen may lawfully arrest a person who has actually committed a violent crime or whose behaviour has led to a breach of the peace (*see* D8(1), 39(1)).

The tort of *malicious prosecution* is committed by a person who makes a *criminal charge* against another person where the proceedings terminate in the acquittal of the latter, where the first person was actuated by spite or ill-will, where there was no reasonable or proper cause for the proceedings, and where the second person has suffered damage as a result. The essence of the tort is *malice* on the part of the person who brought the criminal charge; it is not sufficient that he was honestly mistaken.

(2) Trespass to Land arises whenever one person *enters unlawfully* upon land or a building in the possession of another person. Two important points should be noted, as several popular fallacies exist about this tort. First, trespass to land is *not* in the ordinary case a *crime*, unless there is some Act of Parliament which makes the trespass a criminal offence (for example, under certain statutes it is a criminal offence for an unauthorised person to cross a railway-line or to enter a Government airfield from which considerations of security require unauthorised persons to be excluded). Secondly, it is not necessary, to constitute a trespass, that *actual damage* should be done to the land or building on which the trespasser has set foot. The essence of the tort is interference with the possession of the other party, and this may arise by merely walking across his field, or throwing refuse upon it, or placing or erecting anything on the land without the other party's consent; any act of *physical interference* suffices.

(3) Nuisance.—The *tort of nuisance* arises when an occupier of land or premises does something there which substantially interferes with the enjoyment by a neighbouring occupier of his land or premises. In *trespass* (see above) the interference must be *physical*; this is not so in cases of nuisance. For example, it is a nuisance if A allows his factory chimney to emit volumes of thick smoke which drifts continually into B's house or garden, or for A to carry on, in a building belonging to him, a trade or process which causes noxious smells or disturbing vibrations liable to interfere with B's enjoyment of his property. It is not, however, every such act that gives rise to an action for nuisance; there must be a certain amount of "give and take," particularly in urban areas, but people must not use their premises in an unreasonable or wilfully annoying manner. Thus it has been held that a teacher of music who had pupils singing in her house for several hours a day and on several days a week, which caused considerable disturbance to the person next door, was not committing a nuisance, since it was not unreasonable for her to use her house in this manner. On the other hand, when the person next door retaliated by clashing domestic implements and deliberately making as much noise as possible while the lessons were going on, he was held to have committed a nuisance because his conduct was unreasonable and wilfully annoying. But every case depends upon its own special facts. A building contractor who keeps a pneumatic drill going outside a private house, in connection with building operations, is not liable to an action for nuisance, provided that the use of the drill is necessary to the work, that it is confined to reasonable working hours and limited to a temporary period; but if the owner of a motor-cycle were to keep its engine running, merely to demonstrate its power, outside his own garage for several hours a day, and on several days a week, his neighbours could claim that that was (in law) a nuisance. The Noise Abatement Act, 1960, gives rights to local councils (on their own initiative or on complaint by three householders) to order reduction of unnecessary noise (including loudspeakers) in streets, parks and gardens, and to prosecute offenders.

All the above examples may be classed as *private nuisances*, and they are torts but not crimes. There is, however, another class, known as *public nuisances*, which become criminal offences if they are liable to injure the public in general. Examples of these are leaving an unlighted obstruction on a public road, blocking a public footpath, or allowing a building to get into such a state of disrepair that it causes a danger to users of the public highway. In such cases the person causing the public nuisance may be prosecuted and punished and, moreover, any individual citizen injured by such conduct may have a right to bring a civil action for damages.

(4) Trespass to Goods is an unlawful disturbance by A of B's lawful possession of his goods. Such disturbance may arise by seizure or removal of the goods without the owner's consent or by conduct causing damage to the goods. It follows that every theft of goods is also a trespass; but for the preservation of public morality it is laid down that, if there is a criminal element in the conduct of the wrongdoer which makes his trespass theft, the injured party cannot bring a civil action for damages unless the thief has first been prosecuted in a criminal court.

The *tort of detinue* consists in the wrongful detention by one person of another's goods and his failure or refusal to deliver them up when demanded.

The *tort of conversion* or *trover* arises when A wrongfully appropriates the goods of B to his own use or to the use of another person, depriving the owner of them permanently or for a substantial time, or destroying them. These torts of *detinue* and *conversion* can be committed only against goods or articles of property; they cannot arise from interference with fixtures permanently attached to a building, growing crops or trees; but these torts may be committed if, after such things have been removed or cut down, the wrongdoer detains or converts them to his own use.

(5) Negligence in law has a very specialised meaning; it is not " neglect " or " carelessness " in the ordinary sense, but failure to take such care as the circumstances of the particular case demand. In the *tort of negligence* there are two essential elements—first, a *legal duty* to exercise proper care and, secondly, a *failure* to take such care. No action for negligence can be brought by A against B, even if B has been grossly careless, unless the relations between the parties were such that B was under that legal duty towards A. Moreover, the *degree of care* which A is entitled to expect from B will vary according to the nature of those relations.

One obvious example where the legal duty of care arises is among persons using the roads. All of us have the right to use the roads for the purpose of travelling, on foot or in some vehicle, and the manner in which each of us exercises that right will obviously affect the safety and comfort of other road-users. There is therefore a *legal duty of care* upon every road-user (under the common law, and quite apart from the provisions of Acts of Parliament relating to motor-cars) to exercise his right to walk or drive with due regard to the similar rights of other road-users. And, equally obviously, the *standard or degree of care* which it is reasonable to expect from the driver of a powerful car is higher than that which is expected from a pedestrian, since the amount of damage which will be caused by carelessness on the part of the driver is very much greater than that which the pedestrian is capable of inflicting.

We are *not* here referring to *offences* under the Road Traffic Acts, for which drivers or pedestrians may be *prosecuted and punished* under the *criminal law.* Dangerous or reckless driving or walking may be a criminal offence under those Acts, even if it has caused no injury to any person or property. In cases where such injury *has* been caused the *test* to be applied, in determining whether the injured person can *sue and recover damages* against the other party, is whether that other party has fallen short of the *standard of care* reasonably to be expected from him. It is true that disobedience to a provision of the Road Traffic Acts, or neglect of the Highway Code, may constitute *evidence* helping to prove that the latter party was lacking in the proper standard of care required of him; but there may be other circumstances which show that he was *negligent* in law, and liable to an action by the injured party for *damages*, even though he committed *no criminal offence.*

There are many other relationships where the *duty to take care* arises. One of these is the relation between *the occupier of premises* and persons *coming on to the premises*, whether they have a right to be there or not. Towards *trespassers* (see above) the duty of the occupier is merely a negative one—he must not "set a trap"—*i.e.*, he must not deliberately do anything calculated to cause injury, nor must he do any act which, if done carelessly, is reasonably likely to cause injury. If he knows a trespasser is on the premises he must *warn* him before he *does any dangerous act*; the fact that the trespasser has no lawful right to be there does not entitle the occupier (for example) to weaken the supports of a bridge or set off an explosion without warning. If the occupier does so, he will be liable to be sued for damages, in an action for negligence, even by a trespasser who is injured as a result. (The Law Commission has recommended that ownership or use of dangerous things, dangerous activities, and damage by animals be penalised by civil action. Damages are to be assessed on a broader basis.)

The other rules, relating to the duty of care owed by an occupier to persons coming on to his premises are now contained in the Occupiers' Liability Act, 1957.

The occupier's duty towards a *trespasser* remains *unchanged.* The Act, however, abolishes the former distinction between an *invitee* and a *licensee*, both of whom it describes by the new term, *visitor.* The principal rules are:—

1. The occupier owes the *same duty* (" the common duty of care ") *to all his visitors*, except in so far as he is free to, and does, extend, restrict, modify, or exclude his duty, to any visitor, by agreement or otherwise.

2. The " common duty of care " means a duty to take such care as in all the circumstances is *reasonable*, to see that the visitor will be *reasonably safe* in using the premises for the purpose for which he is invited or permitted to be there.

There are *subsidiary rules—e.g.*, that an occupier must expect *children* to be *less careful than adults*, and that a person " in the exercise of his calling " (*e.g.*, a window-cleaner) can be expected to appreciate and guard against special risks incidental to that calling. And a *landlord* of premises, if he is under a *legal obligation towards his tenant* to keep the premises in repair, is to owe *to visitors the same duty* as if the landlord were the occupier, so far as concerns dangers arising from his default in carrying out that obligation. One of the matters recommended by the Law Commission is the creation of a right of redress, for purchasers and visitors injured by defects in a building, against vendors and landlords.

Among the classes of persons upon whom the law imposes a *duty to take care* are those who practise a *profession or calling* which, from its nature, demands some special skill, ability, and experience. A man who is advised or treated by a physician, surgeon, or dentist, or who consults a lawyer or an architect, is entitled to expect him both to possess and to exercise a reasonable degree of such skill, ability, and experience. If the professional man falls short of the *proper standard*, the patient or client may bring against him an action for damages on account of his negligence. But a mere error of judgment on a difficult point does not amount to negligence, provided that the professional man possesses the proper standard of knowledge and skill and has used them carefully and conscientiously to the best of his ability. And he is not liable, by virtue of his professional status, to an action of negligence for something he has done while acting otherwise than in his professional capacity—*e.g.*, a solicitor who is asked to express an opinion on the value of a house (which is no part of his professional duty). (But a barrister cannot be sued for negligence in the conduct of a case in court.)

(6) Defamation.—The tort of *defamation* is committed by a person who *attacks the reputation* of another by " *publishing* " *a false and defamatory* statement concerning him to a third party. If the defamatory statement is *in writing* or some other *permanent* form (*e.g.*, a picture, a film, or a gramophone record), then the action will be for *libel.* If the defamatory statement is in *spoken words* or some other *non-permanent* form (*e.g.*, by signs or gestures) it will be *slander.*

Another important distinction must be observed at the outset. In cases of *libel* the person whose reputation has been attacked may sue for damages *without proof of " special damage "—i.e.*, proof that he has *suffered actual harm* from the libellous statement; while in *slander no action* can normally be brought *unless special damage* can be proved. There are, however, five exceptional cases where such proof is unnecessary, *viz.*, in slanders:—

(a) *disparaging* a person in the way of his *business, profession*, or *office of profit* (*e.g.*, saying of a doctor that " he is ignorant of the first principles of medicine ");

(b) imputing *dishonesty* to a person holding an *office of honour* (*e.g.*, saying of a Councillor that " he gives contracts to his friends ");

(c) imputing that a person has committed a *crime punishable by imprisonment* (*e.g.*, saying of a man " he is no better than a thief ");

(d) imputing that a person is suffering from a *contagious disease* of a disgraceful kind (especially a venereal disease);

(e) imputing *unchastity* to a *woman or girl.*

In these five cases " publication " of the slander alone is sufficient to give rise to an action, without proof of special damage; for slanders of other kinds no action can be brought unless special damage can be proved.

Note also that no action can succeed, either in libel or slander, unless the statement complained of is (1) *false*, and (2) *defamatory* and unless (3) there has been *publication* to a *third party*. (1) The statement must be false "in substance and in fact "; if it is substantially true the person complaining has suffered no injury, recognised by law, to his right to the inviolacy of his reputation. (2) The statement must be *defamatory—i.e.*, it must be one which " tends to lower him in the estimation of right-thinking members of the community," or which is " calculated to expose him to hatred, ridicule, or contempt." (3) *Publication*, in this context, means simply *making known* the defamatory statement to at least one *third party*. If the defamatory statement is conveyed *only to the person defamed*, and to no one else, there is no "publication," and the person defamed has *no civil remedy*.

In one exceptional case—where a defamatory statement, *in writing*, is likely to lead to a *breach of the peace*—the person making it may be *prosecuted* for the offence of *criminal libel*, for the purpose not of compensating the injured party, but of upholding law and order (**D6(1)**). In this exceptional case the *truth* of the statement (see above) is *no defence*, and *publication* to a third party is not necessary to secure a conviction. But there is no such offence as "criminal slander."

If a defamatory statement is made reflecting on a *class of persons* generally (*e.g.*, an attack on "Methodists" or "coloured people" or "money-lenders") that will not entitle a person who happens to belong to that class to bring an action unless he can show that *he personally* was aimed at and defamed. (**But see D41(1) — Race Relations Acts, 1965 and 1968.**) The family of a *deceased person* cannot bring an action for a libel or slander upon the reputation of the deceased.

If the person sued puts forward the defence that the words he used were " not published of and concerning " the person bringing the action, the question must be decided whether those to whom the statement was published could *reasonably understand* it to refer to him. If such understanding is reasonable, then it is no defence for the person who made the statement to show that he *did not in fact intend* to refer to the other person, or even that the latter's existence was unknown to him.

Some statements are defamatory in their *natural and primary sense* (*e.g.*, " John Brief is a thoroughly dishonest lawyer "); others may appear unexceptionable if looked at literally, but may have a defamatory meaning in a particular context, or in particular circumstances known to the persons to whom they are published (*e.g.*, " I hear Mrs. B has left her doctor a lot of money. A fine kind of doctor *he* is! "). In cases of the latter kind the person who claims that the published words are defamatory of him must plead an *innuendo*—*i.e.*, he must set out, in his statement of claim, the meaning in which he alleges the words complained of were used. It will be the duty of the judge to decide, as a matter of *law*, whether the words are *capable* of bearing that meaning; the jury will have to decide, as a question of *fact*, whether the words complained of did actually convey that meaning to those who heard or read them. There are several recognised defences to actions of libel or slander:—

(1) *Justification.*—A plea that the words complained of were *substantially true*. Once the words have been shown to be defamatory, it is for the person who used them to prove their truth—not for the party injured to prove them false.

(2) *Absolute Privilege.*—By common law, or by Act of Parliament, defamatory words used on certain particular occasions, though published to third parties, cannot give rise to any right of action. The occasion is " absolutely privileged." No party to any *legal proceedings*, nor any witness, counsel, or member of the jury, nor of course the judge, can be called upon to answer for any words he has used *during the proceedings*, however spiteful, and however harmful they may have been to the reputation of any other person. The rule applies to *pleadings* (*i.e.*, allegations in writing, filed at the court) as well as to statements made in court by word of mouth.

Similar protection applies to words spoken *in Parliament* by a member of either House (though words spoken outside either House are not protected). And under the Parliamentary Papers Act, 1840, those who publish (in the ordinary sense of the word) the proceedings of either House, by its authority, are protected in the same way; so are official communications, on *affairs of State*, made by a minister to the Monarch, or by one officer of State to another in the course of his official duty. To all these *absolute privilege* applies.

(3) *Qualified Privilege.*—Apart from the cases just mentioned, there are other *occasions* which are *privileged*, not absolutely, but in a *qualified* sense. The *nature of the qualification* will be explained below; meanwhile it may be said that a *privileged occasion* of this latter kind arises whenever the person making a communication has an *interest*, or a legal, social, or moral *duty* to *make it*, and the person to whom it is made has a corresponding interest or duty to *receive it*. A common example is a reference given, about the character of a servant, by a former to a prospective employer; another is a report made, on the commercial credit of a trader, by one person who has dealt with him to another who intends to do so. Other occasions of *qualified privilege* are *reports* of *judicial proceedings*, of *public meetings*, and of the *proceedings* of municipal or other *public bodies*.

Such occasions are *privileged* to this extent and with this qualification—that there was no *malice* (*i.e.*, spite or other *improper motive*) in the mind of the person when he made the communication. If there was malice, then the fact that the occasion was one of qualified privilege will not protect him from an action for damages at the suit of the person defamed. In any such action it is the duty of judge to decide, as a question of *law*, whether the occasion was one of qualified privilege; it is for the jury to decide, as a matter of *fact*, whether the defendant was malicious in what he wrote or spoke. (Contrast occasions of *absolute privilege*, where the presence or absence of *malice* is *immaterial*.)

(4) *Fair Comment* " on a matter of public interest."—This form of defence is most commonly employed by newspapermen, reviewers, and critics. If this defence is to succeed, the words to which it relates must be really *comment* (*i.e.*, expressions of opinion, not statements of fact): the comment must be concerned with *a matter of public interest* (*e.g.*, a book, a play, a musical performance, a political speech, or the public actions of men in the public eye—but not their private lives). Lastly, the comment must be *fair*—and it cannot be fair if it is actuated by *malice* in the mind of the commentator. If he has mingled with his comment some statement of *fact*, and that statement is inaccurate or misleading, that in itself will prevent the comment from being regarded as fair. The *onus is on the defendant* who is pleading fair comment to establish that what he is seeking to defend is really *comment*, that the matter on which he commented was one of *public interest* (not, for example, private scandal), and that the comment is *not based on any misstatement* of facts or *otherwise unfair*. Dishonest or insincere comment cannot be fair; but, on the other hand, an honest belief in the commentator's mind that his comment was fair is not enough for a successful defence. The comment must be fair *in fact*.

The usual *remedy* in actions of *libel* and *slander* is damages—a sum of money sufficient (in the jury's view) to compensate a man for the harm his reputation has suffered. In certain rare cases the Court may, in its discretion, grant an *injunction* ordering the defendant not to publish or not to repeat the publication of a libel.

The Defamation Act, 1952, reduces the risk of legal proceedings against anyone who *innocently* " published " a libel. The " publisher " may make an *offer of amends, i.e.*, an offer to " publish " a *correction and apology*, and to take practicable steps to *notify* those who have received copies of any defamatory document. (*a*) If the offer is *accepted* and the promise performed, the party defamed cannot bring, or continue, an action for libel or slander. (*b*) If the offer is *rejected*, then the " publisher," in any action taken against him, may plead, *in defence*, that the words were " published " innocently, and that the offer of amends was made as soon as practicable. *Innocent* publication means: (1) that the " publisher " did not intend the defamatory words to refer to the other party, and knew of no reason why they might be understood to refer to him; or (2) that the words were not in themselves defamatory, and that the " publisher " knew of no reason why they might be understood to defame the other party; also that, in either case, the " publisher " exercised all reasonable care in regard to the " publication."

## V. THE LAW OF PROPERTY

### I. In General

(1) **Living Persons.**—The special rights and disabilities which affect the ownership and disposal of property by certain classes of persons have been already dealt with under the heading of *Status* (D8–9). It is unnecessary to add anything here on the law of property *in general*, so far as living persons are concerned; but different rules are applicable (as will be seen below) to the ownership and disposal of *land and buildings* as compared with *property of other kinds*. The reason for this main distinction is that the former are, in their nature, *immoveable* and *cannot be physically transferred*, as can money and " chattels " (*i.e.*, animals and *tangible objects* which are capable of being owned). In addition, there is a third class—certain *intangible things* which can be owned and dealt with—for example, the right to be paid a debt, a share or stock in a company, an insurance policy, or a patent; these are known as *things in action*, and they can be transferred only in certain formal ways, which will be described below.

(2) **Deceased Persons.**—It is obvious that the law of any civilised community must make provision, not only for the *transfer by a living person of his property*, but also for the *transmission of that property* (*his " estate "*) *upon his death*. English Law permits every person who is *not disqualified by infancy or lunacy* (D8, 9) to *give directions, during his lifetime, as to the disposal of his estate upon his death*; he can do this by means of a *will*. If he leaves *no valid will* he is said to die *intestate*, and in that event *the law itself* lays down how his estate is to be distributed. A concise survey of the law governing the estates of deceased persons is given below. (Some of these rules have been modified, so far as *domicil* is concerned, by the Wills Act, 1963.)

**Wills and Intestacies.**—The law of wills is highly technical; much trouble can be caused by a " home-made " will, and it is wise to seek a solicitor's advice. It is only possible here to outline the *formalities* necessary to make a valid will, and the *procedure* to be adopted after a death. The rules stated are those under English law—applicable to England and Wales, but not Scotland or Northern Ireland.

(1) **The Nature of a Will.**—The person making a will—the *testator*—sets down how he wishes his property to be disposed of after his death, and states the names of the persons (the *executors*) who are to attend to its disposal.

The executors may be, but need not be, some or all of the persons whom the testator desires to benefit under his will. One executor alone is sufficient in law; but if that one dies before he (or she) has completed his duties, delay and difficulty may arise. It is therefore better to appoint *at least two* executors: if one dies, the other has full powers to continue the work. If the testator's *estate* (that is, his property) is large, it may be best to appoint a bank as executor; all banks have trustee departments which are experienced in such matters. They have scales of charges for executorship work, which will be supplied on request. An executor is not permitted to charge for his work, unless the will authorises him to do so—a thoughtful provision for a complicated estate. Nor is the executor bound to accept the executorship when the death occurs.

A will " speaks from death "—that is, it has no legal effect until the testator dies; it can be *revoked* (that is, cancelled) in various ways, or alterations can be made by *codicils*, which is really a supplementary will. Further, the property to which it relates is that of the testator *at the date of his death*, which may be more or less than what he owns at the date when the will is made. The will can be revoked or varied as often as desired to suit changing circumstances; its provisions are not final until death.

Generally speaking, a testator may make whatever provisions, in regard to his or her property and the persons to be benefited, he or she thinks fit. He or she may even direct that his or her wife, husband, or children are to be deprived of all benefit from the estate; but, if he or she does so, it will be well to give the reasons, either in the will itself, or in a signed, witnessed, and dated document, which should be left with the will.

Under Acts of 1938, 1952, 1965, and 1966 a husband or wife, an *unmarried daughter or son* under majority, or a son or daughter, either natural or adopted, " under disability " (that is, one who for some reason is incapable of looking after himself or herself), who is not adequately provided for under the will, may apply to the Court for " reasonable provision for maintenance " out of the estate; the Court has power either to refuse the application or to grant the applicant whatever maintenance it thinks fit. In making its decision the Court will take note of the testator's reasons for his failure to provide for the applicant in question. Similar rules now apply to former husbands and wives.

If a person dies without leaving a valid will, he is said to die *intestate*. In that case somebody (usually the husband or wife or next of kin) must apply to the Probate Registry (at Somerset House in London or in the nearest District Registry elsewhere) to be appointed *administrator*. An administrator has the same rights and duties as an executor. If there are children under majority, and in certain other cases, there must be at least two administrators, and the procedure on death is more involved and troublesome than where executors have been appointed by will. Further, as the testator has not directed what is to happen to his property, the law has laid down an *order of succession*, which the administrators must observe. The intestate's husband or wife is then entitled first to the *personal effects* (furniture, household goods, motor-cars, books, etc.); next, to the whole of the estate, if there are no children or near relatives, or £8,750 if there are, and, after that, the husband or wife and children have certain rights in the remainder of the estate, if any; details of which can be found in the Intestates' Estates Act, 1952, and the Family Provision Act, 1966. If there is no husband or wife, or no children, or neither, the next of kin of the intestate will benefit in order of nearness of their relationship to the deceased.

It is always prudent to make a will, however simple, since by doing so the testator exercises control over the disposal of his property and saves considerable trouble for his family.

(2) **The Execution of a Will.**—The formalities must be strictly observed, except in the case of soldiers, sailors, and airmen on active service (including members of the Women's Services and nurses), for whom informal directions, even in a letter or by word of mouth, are sufficient. For all other testators, inattention to the formalities may render the will invalid, and will in any case cause considerable trouble and expense.

The will must be *in writing*—i.e., not by word of mouth—handwritten, typewritten, or printed, but the wording need not be in legal or formal language, so long as it clearly identifies the testator, the executors, the various kinds of property dealt with, and the persons to be benefited. It should also state that the following formalities have been carried out when it was executed—that is, signed by the testator and *attested*—i.e., witnessed by two competent persons:

(a) *The will must be signed* by the testator, or by some other person in his presence and by his direction. If the testator can write, his *usual* signature will suffice; if he is illiterate or too unwell to sign in full, he may make his " mark " or his initials alone. If he is incapable of holding a pen, someone else may sign for the testator, provided he is present at the time and authorises the signature. If the testator is blind or otherwise incapable of reading the will, it should be read over to him before his signature or mark is placed on it, and the fact of his blindness should be mentioned in the final clause.

(b) *The signature or mark must be at the foot or end* of the will. This means (i) nothing added *below* the testator's signature, and (ii) nothing written anywhere on the document *after the testator himself has finished signing*, will be valid, except the signatures, addresses, and descriptions of the witnesses. If, therefore, at the last minute the testator desires some addition, alteration, or deletion to be made, he and the same witnesses must sign or put their initials against the addition, alteration, or deletion, which otherwise will be ignored.

(c) *The testator's signature* must be made or (if he cannot sign) acknowledged *in the presence of two witnesses*, who must both be *present at the same time*. Any persons may be witnesses, so long as they are capable of understanding what is going on. They need not read the will or know its contents; but if either of them is a *person who is to take a benefit* under the will, or the husband or wife of such a person, he or she will *lose that benefit*. It is therefore safest to call in witnesses who are strangers to the testator. Both witnesses must be *present together* when the testator signs (or acknowledges) his signature; it will not be a valid attestation if first one witness, and then the other, is called into the room.

(d) *The witnesses must sign* the will *in the presence of the testator*. Either witness may, if necessary, sign by mark or initial, but no other person may sign on his behalf. For identification purposes it is usual and desirable for the witnesses to add their addresses and occupations, in case of a subsequent dispute which may necessitate their being found to give evidence.

If the will consists of several pages, they should be fastened together before execution, and the signatures of the testator and witnesses should appear at the end of every page, not to satisfy the rules set out above, but as evidence that every page formed part of the will when it was executed.

It is desirable (though not legally essential) that the will should bear, just above the signatures of the witnesses, an *attestation clause*—that is, a formal statement that these formalities have been carried out. The usual wording of this clause will be found in the example shown below.

All these rules apply in exactly the same way to a *codicil*, which is a *supplementary* document, *amending* the will in part, *e.g.*, by adding a new legacy.

(3) **The Contents of a Will.**—The opening words should clearly identify the testator by his full names, occupation or description, present address and (if possible) other recent addresses, and declare that this is his *Last Will*. It is sometimes found at death that a testator has a banking account or stocks and shares registered in his name at some past address, and in such cases the bank or company concerned, wishing to be sure that his identity is clear, may insist upon a sworn statement to the effect that he is the same person as the person they knew as customer or shareholder. (See the example below.)

Next follows the *revocation clause*—a declaration that the will now being made *revokes* (that is, cancels) all previous wills and codicils. If this is not inserted, doubts may arise after death as to whether the new provisions are intended to be substituted for, or merely to supplement, provisions in an older will. If it is intended that the older will is to remain valid in part, that should be clearly stated. If the document now being executed is a *codicil*, it should be described as such, and the date of the original will to which it is a codicil should be mentioned, and also which parts of the original will are being *confirmed*, to stand good, and which *revoked*.

The next clause should appoint the executors, who must be identified by their full names and descriptions or addresses. "My brother John," "my son Charles," or "my mother" will suffice, since only one person could possibly answer to any of these descriptions; but "my wife" is not enough without giving her names in full, since it does not follow that the person who is the testator's wife at the time of his death was necessarily his wife when the will was made.

Next follow the directions for disposal of the testator's property. *Bequests or legacies* of particular articles ("my pearl necklace," "my oak bedroom suite") or of particular investments ("my 3% War Stock")—these are *specific legacies*—must clearly identify exactly what is being bequeathed. In the case of land or a house, the full description should be given—"my leasehold house and grounds at 31, Acacia Road, Redhill in the County of Surrey," or "my freehold farm known as ' Newlands ' at Northgate in the County of Derby." The words "I devise" are the technical words appropriate to freeholds: "I bequeath" to all other kinds of property: the effect is the same. (Bequests or legacies of *sums of money—pecuniary legacies*—should preferably be stated in words rather than figures; if figures are used the accidental omission of a nought may be disastrous.)

Finally, there is the clause that deals with the *residue* of the Estate—that is to say, whatever will remain after the executors have paid the funeral expenses, death duties (if any), legal and other fees, the testator's debts, and the pecuniary legacies he has bequeathed, and after the specific bequests have been handed over to those entitled. Such a clause is necessary because no testator can be sure, when he makes his will, that he has disposed exactly of everything of which he may die possessed, or that all the persons to whom he has made bequests will necessarily be alive, when he dies. In general, the death of such a person—a *legatee*—before the testator causes that person's legacy to *lapse*; but if there is a bequest of the *residue* for division among a number of persons, no harm is done: the *lapsed legacy*, being left over and undisposed of, leaves the residue to be divided among the surviving *residuary legatees*. The expression " such of the following persons who may survive me " may be properly used.

(4) **Revocation and Revival.**—A will or codicil may be *revoked* (*i.e.*, cancelled) by " burning, tearing, or otherwise destroying " it with the intention of revoking. Destruction by accident, or without the testator's desire to revoke it, is ineffective, and if a copy exists, its provisions may be put forward as still valid. The revocation clause in a later will (see above) will be equally effective to revoke an earlier will; or some part of the earlier will may be revoked by a later codicil clearly referring to that part.

A will is also *revoked*—generally speaking—by *subsequent marriage*, since the law assumes that, if the testator who is newly married had had time for or given thought to the matter, he would have altered his will. If he did not do so after marriage, he will die intestate.

If a testator makes *Will A*, and later on *Will B* containing a revocation clause, *Will A* is revoked —*i.e.*, cancelled. But if *Will B* is in turn revoked by *Will C*, that does *not revive*—*i.e.*, revalidate— *Will A*, unless *Will C* says, in so many words, that " *Will A* is hereby revived."

## SPECIMEN WILL

I JOHN SMITH of 31 Acacia Road Redhill in the County of Surrey Company Director [1] HEREBY REVOKE [2] all wills and testamentary documents [3] heretofore made by me AND DECLARE this to be my LAST WILL.

1. I APPOINT my wife JANE SMITH [4] and my Solicitor EDWARD JONES to be jointly the Executors of this my Will.

2. I DEVISE my freehold farm known as " Newlands " situate at Northgate in the County of Derby unto my son JAMES SMITH in fee simple. [5]

3. I BEQUEATH the following specific legacies: [6]

(1) To my son THOMAS SMITH any motor-car of which I may be the owner [7] at the date of my death.

(2) To my said son JAMES SMITH all my shares in the Company known as John Smith & Sons Limited.

(3) To my said wife all my personal chattels [8] not hereby or by any codicil hereto otherwise bequeathed [9] for her own absolute use and benefit.[10]

4. I BEQUEATH the following pecuniary[11] legacies:

(1) To my daughter JULIA SMITH the sum of TWO THOUSAND POUNDS.

(2) To my secretary EVELYN ROBINSON the sum of ONE HUNDRED POUNDS.

5. I DEVISE AND BEQUEATH all the residue [12] of my real and personal estate whatsoever and wheresoever not hereby or by any codicil hereto otherwise expressly disposed of as to my freeholds in fee simple [5] and as to my personal estate absolutely unto my said wife JANE SMITH for her own absolute use and benefit.[10]

6. I DIRECT that any executor of this my Will being a Solicitor or a person engaged in any profession or business may be so employed and act and shall be entitled to make all proper professional charges [13] for any work done by him or his firm in connection with my Estate including work which an executor not being a Solicitor or a person engaged as aforesaid could have done personally.

IN WITNESS whereof I the said JOHN SMITH the Testator have to this my LAST WILL set my hand this twelfth day of April One Thousand Nine Hundred and Sixty-Five.

[14] SIGNED AND ACKNOWLEDGED by the above-named JOHN SMITH the Testator as and for his LAST WILL in the presence of us both present at the same time who at his request in his presence and in the presence of each other have hereunto subscribed our names as witnesses:     }John Smith

George Matthews,
6, Elm Road,
Redhill, Surrey.

Chauffeur.

Ida Gray,
10, Oaktree Road,
Redhill, Surrey.

Children's Nurse.

[1] Profession is usually inserted for identification purposes.

[2] Revocation Clause—cancels all *previous* wills and codicils.

[3] " Testamentary documents "—includes both wills and codicils.

[4] Wife's *name* should be mentioned—he may have a different wife by the time he dies.

[5] " In fee simple "—technical words showing that the entire freehold interest is disposed of.

[6] " Specific legacies "—*i.e.*, legacies of actually specified things.

[7] Not " my motor-car "; he may sell his present car before he dies and perhaps buy a new one, in which case there might be a dispute as to whether he meant only the car he owned at the date of his will.

[8] This expression is defined in the Administration of Estates Act, 1925. It includes furniture plate, china, wines, cigars, books, and other *personal effects*. It is better to use a word clearly *defined* by Act of Parliament than a vague word like " possessions."

[9] *i.e.*, all personal effects which the Testator has not left or will not leave to anybody else.

[10] These words show clearly that, although the wife is one of the Executors, with the duty of clearing up the estate for the benefit of *all* the persons to be benefited, these particular bequests are for *her own personal benefit*.

[11] " Pecuniary "—*i.e.*, money.

[12] " Residue "—everything left after all the other gifts have been disposed of, and debts paid.

[13] Charging Clause, without which the Executor who is a Solicitor would not be able to charge for his work on the Estate.

[14] This is the proper form of *attestation clause*—*i.e.*, the clause showing that the proper formalities for signing and witnessing were observed.

**Probate and Letters of Administration.**—It is a peculiarity of the English system that a deceased person's estate, upon his death, does not " vest in " (*i.e.*, fall into the possession of) the persons to whom he has left it by will, or among whom it has by law to be distributed (the " beneficiaries "); the estate vests, in the first instance, in his executor or executors, if he has appointed any such. (If he has made no such appointment, then, pending the appointment of administrator or administrators (see above), the estate vests (for the time being) in the Presiding Judge of the Probate Division of the High Court of Justice; that Judge has no duties in relation to the estate, but any notices that would, if there were executors, have to be served upon them, must be served for the time being upon him.) The generic name that applies both to executors and administrators, when their title has been lawfully recognised, is *legal personal representatives*; that is to say, they are *recognised by law as representing the deceased person*, for all purposes under the law of property, and for most purposes under the law of contract and the law of tort. Generally speaking, the deceased person's rights and liabilities are transmitted to his legal personal representatives, and can be enforced by or against them as soon as they have taken out a *grant of probate* or of *letters of administration*. (Small estates—less than £1,000 net or £3,000 gross—are dealt with more simply.)

The " grant," in either case, is a document issued by one of the Registries and bearing the seal of the Probate Division of the High Court and the signature of one of its Registrars. It states the deceased's name and address, the date and place of his death, and *either* (1) that his *last will* has been *proved and registered* in the Registry concerned, or (2) that he died *intestate* (as the case may be); that (in the former case) the *executors*, or (in the latter case) the *administrators*, whose names, addresses, and descriptions are given, are *entitled to administer* (*i.e.*, to deal with) all the estate which " vests in " them by law; and the document concludes by certifying that an *Inland Revenue Affidavit* has been delivered, showing the *gross and net values* of the estate and the amount of *estate duty and interest* (if any) paid. Where a will has been " proved," a photostat copy of the will is bound up inside the " grant "; if no will has been " proved " the " grant " consists of a single sheet bearing the above-mentioned particulars. It is important to note that, in either case, the *title* of the *legal personal representatives* (*i.e.*, their legal right to deal with the estate) is evidenced by the " grant "—*i.e.*, the document by which the Court's authority is conferred upon them—and not directly by the terms of the will or by their relationship (if any) to the deceased. Anybody, for example, who is *purchasing property of the deceased* from the legal personal representatives is required only to *satisfy himself that probate or letters of administration have been granted to them*; such a purchaser is not in the least concerned with the terms of the will.

Whenever any *formal transaction* has to be carried out in connection with the deceased person's estate the " grant " must be produced; this applies in particular to dealings with land or buildings, " things in action " (*see* D23(2)), the initiation, defence, or continuation of legal proceedings for the benefit of the estate, and the transfer of the deceased's contractual rights. There are, however, a number of *informal acts* which the persons (if any) appointed by the will to be executors, or the nearest relatives who intend to apply for letters of administration, may properly do before the issue of the " grant "; these include such common-sense matters as arranging the funeral, safeguarding and insuring documents and valuables, feeding livestock, locking up premises, and preserving property which would deteriorate if neglected. All persons should, however, take care *not to sell or dispose of any part of the estate before the " grant "* is issued; a person who, without lawful authority, meddles with the estate may find himself regarded as *executor de son tort*—*i.e.*, placed in the position of an executor by his own wrongdoing—and thereby bound to meet the liabilities of the deceased person, and pay the death duties (if any), for which he ought to have provided. Even a person named in the will as executor takes a risk if he does more than the most urgently necessary acts before probate, since it may turn out that that will is, for some technical reason, invalid, or some later will may come to light in which he is not named.

*Not more than four* persons can apply for a grant of probate or letters of administration. If therefore the will names more than four executors, the persons named will have to decide among themselves which of them are to apply. Even if there are no more than four, *none of them is compelled* to apply, unless he has already meddled with the estate; he can renounce his right by signing a form of renunciation. If the deceased has appointed no executor by will, one or more (not exceeding four) of the next-of-kin can apply for letters of administration. Apart from the special cases (D16(2)) in which there must be at least two administrators, no grant will be made to any more distant relative of the deceased unless and until all nearer relatives have renounced their rights or been " cleared off "; this last expression means that it must be clearly shown that they are dead or for some other reason are incapable of acting as administrators. (The order of priority among the relatives entitled to take out a grant is: (1) husband or wife; (2) children and their " remoter issue " (*i.e.*, grandchildren, great-grandchildren, etc.); (3) parents; (4) brothers and sisters and issue of deceased brothers and sisters; (5) half-brothers and half-sisters and issue of deceased half-brothers and half-sisters; (6) grandparents, and so forth.)

It has been said above that the property of a deceased person " vests " on his death in his executor or executors, if any; if there are no executors it " vests " in his administrators as soon as they have been duly constituted as such by the " grant." *In law* these *legal personal representatives* (executors or administrators) have the same *powers* of disposing of the deceased's property as if they were the owners of that property in the fullest sense; but in accordance with the rules of *equity* (*see* D4) they must exercise their powers of disposal strictly in accordance with what is *just and conscionable*—*i.e.*, they must distribute the property itself, or sell it and distribute the net proceeds, as laid down by the terms of the *will* (if any); in case of an intestacy, as laid down by the *law of succession*, as set out in the Intestates' Estates Act, 1952, and the Family Provision Act, 1966. That strict exercise

of their powers which conscience demands will be enforced, in case of need, by the Chancery Division of the High Court of Justice (*see* D5), *at the suit of any beneficiary* under the will or intestacy. But *purchasers* and persons other than the beneficiaries can safely deal with the legal personal representatives as though they were legal owners of the deceased's property, provided the " grant " is produced as evidence of their powers.

The *procedure* in applying for a *grant of probate* or *letters of administration* is that the applicants must make a *valuation* of the various kinds of property of which the estate consists; the value of each item is to be the value on the date of death. (It is not usually necessary to employ a licensed valuer, though this may be helpful if the estate includes valuable jewellery, antiques, or works of art.) An *Inland Revenue Affidavit*, for death-duty purposes, must be *completed* and *sworn before a Commissioner for Oaths*. This document is one of a number of printed forms (varying according to the nature and composition of the estate, and obtainable from Somerset House, the Estate Duty Office, and certain principal post offices). It is divided into headed columns showing (*a*) the descriptions and the values of the various parts of the estate (*e.g.*, cash at bank, Government securities, stocks and shares, furniture and effects, and so forth); a separate section shows (*b*) the funeral expenses and the debts which the deceased left owing. The *gross estate* consist of the items under (*a*); the *net estate* is calculated by deducting those under (*b*) from the gross total (the cost of a tombstone cannot be deducted).

In the simplest cases *estate duty* is payable on the *net estate*, according to a sliding scale; but no duty is payable on an estate of £5000 or less. (In all but the simplest cases it would be wise to consult a solicitor, as the law relating to estate duty is excessively complicated.)

Another part of the document sets out particulars of the deceased and of the applicants, and the kind of grant required. The document, when sworn, must be forwarded to the Estate Duty Office, who will *assess the duty payable* (if any) and interest on such duty from the date of death. This must be *paid in full* before proceeding further, *except* the part of the duty that relates to *freehold property*, which may be paid by instalments. (The deceased's bank will usually grant a loan or overdraft for the purpose of such payment.) When the duty has been paid the Inland Revenue Affidavit will be returned to the applicants receipted.

The second document required is the *Form of Oath for Executors or Administrators*. This gives particulars of the deceased and of the applicants, as before, and declares *either* (*a*) that they believe the " paper writing " before them to be the deceased's *last will*, or (*b*) that the deceased died *intestate*; in either case they declare their *relationship* (if any) to the deceased, and the *capacity* in which they apply (*e.g.*, " the executors named in the will," or " the lawful widow of the deceased," or as the case may be); and they swear *to administer* the estate (the gross amount of which they mention) *according to law*, and to produce proper accounts whenever called upon to do so. This Oath must also be sworn before a Commissioner.

If there is a will it must now be signed (for identification purposes) by the applicants and the Commissioner for Oaths. If there is no will a third document is required, known as an *Administration Bond*. This is a printed form which must be completed and signed, sealed, and delivered (*see* D10(2)) by the applicants and two *sureties*—*i.e.*, independent persons who are willing to *guarantee* that the applicants will carry out their duties according to law, under the *penalty* of forfeiting double the value of the estate if there is any default. (In practice, an *insurance company* will usually undertake *the duty of surety* for a reasonable premium, and in that event no other surety is required.) The Bond must be executed (*i.e.*, signed, sealed, and delivered by the individual sureties, or sealed by the insurance company, and also signed, sealed, and delivered by the applicants) before a Commissioner for Oaths.

Finally, the applicants must take to the Principal Probate Registry at Somerset House, or to one of the District Registries outside London, (a) the receipted Inland Revenue Affidavit; (b) the duly sworn Oath for Executors or Administrators; (c) either the will (if any), duly marked with the signatures of the applicants and the Commissioner, or the Administration Bond, duly executed. If there is no hitch, the grant of probate or letters of administration will usually be posted to the applicants (or their solicitor) within about fourteen days.

(For the convenience of persons who have no legal adviser, there is a Personal Applications Department, situated in Bush House, Aldwych, W.C.2, where the officials are extremely helpful in answering questions and showing applicants how to complete the forms. But in most cases trouble and delay will be avoided by employing a solicitor.)

## II. Property in Land (Immoveable Property)

Although the logical distinction preserved in the legal systems of other countries is between property in land and buildings and property of other kinds ("immoveables" and "moveables"), English law has from an early date made the more artificial distinction between real property or realty (i.e., freeholds) and personal property or personalty (i.e., leasehold land and property of all other kinds). The reason is historical. In early times, if the possession of freehold land was withheld from its rightful owner, his remedy was an action for recovery of the actual thing withheld—i.e., the freehold land itself—and that very thing (in Latin, res) would be restored to the owner under an order of the Court. On the other hand, when property of other kinds (including leaseholds) was withheld from its rightful owner, his remedy was an action against the wrongdoer, in which the remedy would be the award of damages against the wrongdoer personally (in personam)—not an order for the restoration of the actual goods or other property withheld. Although that distinction in the remedies is no longer generally applicable, the terms (realty and personalty) have been retained.

**1. Realty or Freehold Property.**—The difficulties of this branch of the law are due principally to historical reasons which go back to the Feudal System. In a very practical sense that System recognised only the Monarch as the owner of land; those who held it from him were tenants (in French, "holders"). If the tenancy was one which was not limited to expire at the end of a fixed period it was known as "an estate in fee simple"—i.e., a freehold; a tenancy which was for a fixed period only was known as "a term of years absolute," or a leasehold.

When the Feudal System came to an end this distinction remained. A freehold estate in land is still an interest which has no fixed expiry date; and the freeholder, out of that unlimited interest, can "carve," as it were, fixed leasehold terms, during which tenants will hold the land of him.

The property legislation of 1925 has profoundly changed and simplified the law. Until the end of 1925 one important characteristic of the freehold estate was that of primogeniture—the rule that, on the death of the freeholder intestate, the freehold passed intact to his eldest son or (if he left no son) to his eldest male heir. This was abolished by the Administration of Estates Act, 1925, which enacted that, in the event of a person's dying intestate after December 31st, 1925, the whole of his property (realty as well as personalty) should devolve upon his legal personal representatives (see D18); and that it should, as one whole, be sold and converted into money so far as necessary for the payment of the deceased's funeral expenses and debts, death duties, administration expenses, and for distribution among his next of kin. The eldest son, or heir, has no longer any special privilege.

Settlements.—On the other hand, a freeholder (whom we will call Charles), having a freehold estate in land—i.e., an interest which has no expiry date—can during his lifetime create successive interests to take effect one by one. Charles can, if he so desires, settle his freehold estate to be enjoyed by himself during his lifetime; after his own death, by his eldest son George during that son's lifetime; then by his second son John, during John's lifetime, and finally by George's son Peter "in fee simple." The successive interests of Charles, George, and John are called life interests; the ultimate, future freehold interest, reserved for Peter to enjoy after the deaths of his grandfather, his father, and his uncle, is called a remainder. Both the life interests and the remainder are rights of property to which Charles, George, John, and Peter become entitled immediately the settlement is made—that is, they are present rights to the future enjoyment of the property, and those rights can be dealt with at any time, even before they "fall into possession." Since Charles, George, and John must some time die, Peter knows now that his freehold remainder must come, some time, to him or his personal representatives and, through them, to his next of kin (see above); for even if he dies young, while George and John are still alive, his right will not be "defeated" but will be preserved for those to whom his property may eventually pass under his will or intestacy. Therefore that present right to future enjoyment is a piece of property which Peter can deal with now, unless he is a minor, or unless he is restricted by the terms of the settlement from doing so. George and John can, if they are so minded, do the same with their life interests—that is, they can now sell to another person, for hard cash, their present rights of future enjoyment, or they can mortgage (i.e., pledge) those rights against a loan, on the understanding that they will get back those rights when the loan is repaid.

To watch over these successive interests, and to preserve the rights of the ultimate successor, Charles appoints trustees of the settlement, whose duty it is to act impartially by all the beneficiaries. A trust corporation (usually one of the bank trustee companies), which never dies, or at least two individuals, may act as trustees. The Trustee Act, 1925, provides for the appointment, by a simple procedure, of new trustees to take the place of those who die, become unfit, or unwilling to go on acting, etc. In the last resort the Chancery Division of the High Court (the guardian of equity) has power to make such an appointment; for "equity never lacks a trustee."

In order to enable landed property to be freely disposed of, it is provided by the Settled Land Act, 1925, that the person who is for the time being enjoying the current life interest (see above) has power to sell the entire freehold estate if he so desires. Nevertheless, the scheme of interests under the settlement is not defeated, for the purchaser from the tenant for life must pay the purchase-money not to him but to the trustees; they must invest the money in safe investments, and carry out the provisions of the trust with the necessary modifications. Each tenant for life will then receive the interest or dividends on the investments during his lifetime, just as formerly he would have received the rents and profits of the land during his lifetime; while the remainder-man (Peter) will ultimately come into the capital of the trust fund (i.e., the investments themselves) in lieu of the freehold interest. (By the terms of a recent Act, half the investments may consist of stocks or shares in commercial concerns recommended by a stockbroker or other competent adviser.)

**2. Leaseholds.**—We have seen above that the freeholder, out of his estate which is unlimited in time, can "carve" fixed terms of years absolute or leasehold estates. These terms may be of any length; the most common are terms of 999 and 99 years. The document by which such a term is granted is called a lease; the person granting the term is the landlord or lessor; the person to whom it is granted is the tenant or lessee. But the lessor, by the grant of a lease, has not given up all interest in the land. The lessor's freehold estate is unlimited in time; when, therefore, the leasehold term (however long) comes to an end, the right to possession and enjoyment of the land will *revert* to the freeholder. That right, known as a *reversion*, is again a *present right to future enjoyment* and, as such, a piece of property which the freeholder can, if he wishes, dispose of *now*. The "sale of a reversion" is, in fact, equivalent to the sale of the freehold subject to an existing lease; it confers upon the purchaser the lessor's right to receive rent from the lessee throughout the leasehold term, and at the expiration of that term to *repossess and enjoy* the land without limit of time.

The *lessee* has a *legal estate* in the land for a *fixed term* of years, and he in turn (unless prohibited by the provisions of his lease) can grant *sub-terms* to expire at any time before his own *head-term*. This is a process which can be repeated, in turn, by each lessee, underlessee, subunderlessee, and so forth, who will become respectively the underlessor, sub-underlessor, and so forth, of the person to whom the next subordinate interest is granted. Thus Michael, the freeholder, by granting to James a term of 999 years, leaves himself with a *freehold reversion* which will revert, at the expiration of the 999 years, into the possession of the then freeholder. James, by the grant of an underlease, can carve (out of his leasehold term of 999 years) a sub-term of 99 years in favour of William, whose underlessor or landlord he becomes, leaving himself with a *leasehold reversion* of 900 years. William, in his turn, can grant to Anne a sub-underlease for 21 years, leaving himself a *leasehold reversion* of 78 years, and so forth. The relationship of lessor and lessee, or landlord and tenant, subsists between William and Anne, James and William, Michael and James; this relationship is one of *privity of estate* as well as *privity of contract*. The former phrase means that each of these pairs of individuals is linked by their *mutual interest in the same term of years* as above described. The latter phrase, *privity of contract*, means that the *link is contractual*—it arises from the agreement between Michael and James contained in the headlease, the agreement in the underlease between James and William, and that in the sub-underlease between William and Anne. But between Anne and James, between William and Michael, there is no relationship of any kind, neither of contract nor of estate; Michael can look only to James, James to William, and William to Anne, to carry out the terms of the respective tenancies.

In certain circumstances, however, there may be *privity of estate* between two parties without *privity of contract*. Suppose Michael *conveys* (*i.e.*, transfers) his freehold reversion, *during the subsistence of James's lease*, to Robert. Thereby Robert will take over all Michael's rights: *i.e.*, he will become lessor, in place of Michael, to James as lessee, as well as being entitled to possession of the freehold when James's lease expires. Between Robert and James there will be *privity of estate*, arising from their mutual interest in the term of 999 years (as lessor and lessee respectively); but there is between them no *privity of contract*, for Robert and James have made *no agreement* with one another. The distinction may in certain circumstances be important.

*The Form and Contents of a Lease.*—A lease for a term of more than three years must be made by deed (D10(2)) between the lessor and the lessee. It names and describes the parties, and sets forth that, in return for an annual *rent* (and sometimes on payment, in addition, of a lump sum called a *premium*), the lessor demises (*i.e.*, lets) to the lessee, for a term of so many years from such and such a date, the land in question with the buildings erected thereon. (In the law of property the buildings go with the land on which they stand.) Then follow the *lessee's covenants*—the promises which he is to perform: to pay the rent by stipulated instalments, on certain dates; to pay rates, taxes, and other outgoings on the property; to put and keep the property in full repair; to paint the inside and the outside of the buildings at stated times; to keep the property insured, to its full value, in the names of the lessor and himself; to permit the lessor periodically to inspect the condition of the property; to carry out repairs which the lessor, as a result of such inspections, may call upon him to carry out. These are some of the stock clauses; but every individual lease must be carefully studied in order to ascertain what the lessee's obligations are.

Next come the *lessor's covenants*—the promises which the lessor is to perform; the chief of these is that, if the lessee carries out his part of the bargain, the lessor will permit him "quiet enjoyment" of the property without disturbance during the term. Some leases also contain *stipulations* binding on both parties; for example, a *stipulation* that the rent shall be reduced or suspended if the property is damaged or destroyed by fire, and sometimes an arbitration clause. At the end of most leases comes a *proviso*, for the protection of the lessor, to the effect that he shall be entitled to expel the lessee, and to re-enter and repossess the property, if the lessee ceases to pay his rent or to perform his covenants as required, or in the event of the lessee's bankruptcy.

One copy of the lease (the *original*) is signed, sealed, and delivered (D10(2)) by the lessor, and handed over to the lessee as evidence of his *title* to the leasehold interest. The other copy (the *counterpart*) is signed, sealed, and delivered by the lessee, and handed over to the lessor as evidence of his entitlement to the rent and to the performance of the covenants by the lessee. The counterpart requires a stamp (impressed by the Stamp Duty Branch of the Inland Revenue) of only five shillings; but the original must be stamped at the rate of 5s. for every £50 of the rent in leases not exceeding 7 years (and at higher rates in longer leases) if rent is £300 or more, besides 10s. per £50 of any premium from £5,500 upwards. No stamp duty is payable on rents up to £100 in short leases, or on a premium below £5,500.

*Statutory Reforms in Law of Landlord and Tenant.*—The above text on Leaseholds and Leases sets out the common law rules. But, at various times since 1920, Parliament has considerably amended and added to those rules—particularly to protect (1) tenants of trade, business and professional premises, and (2) tenants of dwellings of comparatively low rateable value.

*Business Tenancies.*—The Landlord and Tenant Act, 1954, Part II gives security of tenure to the tenant of most business premises. Fuller details are given on D33.

*Residential Tenancies.*—The Rent Act, 1965 restores the security of tenure which had been undermined by the 1957 Rent Act; full security of tenure, accompanied by rent regulation, is given to tenants of low and moderate-rented properties (*i.e.*, of rateable value up to £400 in London and £200 elsewhere). It is now an offence for a landlord to evict a tenant from premises of any value whatever without a court order. This is now a permanent part of the law of Landlord and Tenant, and replaces the temporary provisions of the Protection from Eviction Act, 1964. The 1957 Rent Act allowed controlled rents to become decontrolled when the premises were re-let. The new Act stipulates that the vacation of a controlled property will result not in decontrol but in conversion on re-letting to a regulated tenancy under the new Act. For fuller details *see* D34.

3. **Mortgages.**—The word *mortgage* is Norman-French; its literal meaning is "dead pledge." The process of mortgaging land and buildings is roughly analogous to that of pawning a piece of jewellery as security for a loan of money—with the important difference that the land cannot, of course, be physically handed over to the lender (as can the jewellery) to be kept in his custody until the loan is repaid. But a pledge and a mortgage have this in common—that the parties intend no change of *ownership*; the borrower (the *mortgagor*) is and remains *owner* of the property *after*, as well *as before, the transaction*. In exchange for a loan of a certain sum, the lender (the mortgagee) temporarily enjoys a *charge* upon property worth (it may be) much more than that sum, as *security* for the repayment of the loan, with the stipulated interest, at the stipulated time. The borrower is still the property-*owner*.

Because of the essential immoveability of land, the mortgage transaction is effected by a *mortgage deed*, which sets out the terms on which the loan is granted. Generally speaking, the borrower (the mortgagor) is permitted to remain in *possession* of the mortgaged property unless and until he fails to pay an instalment of interest or to repay the capital when called upon, or unless and until he breaks some condition of the mortgage deed. In early times such failure was often the signal for the lender (the mortgagee) to oust him *permanently* from possession, and even to deprive him of *ownership* of the property. But the courts of equity, as we have seen (**D4(2)**), gradually evolved the rule that it was unconscionable for the lender to enrich himself, at a low cost to himself, from a transaction in which the intention of the parties was to *pledge the property temporarily* as a *security*, not to sell it permanently for a small sum. Hence was evolved the concept known as the *equity of redemption*—the rule that, even *after the legal date* fixed by the deed for repayment of the loan and for freeing the property from the mortgage, the borrower should still remain entitled to *redeem* the property (*i.e.*, to free it from the charge) by tendering to the lender the balance of the loan, with all interest and costs to date; and that the lender should thereupon be *bound* to give the borrower full and unfettered rights over the property, free from all the conditions of the mortgage, and in the same state as it was in originally. The lender (the mortgagee) must get no collateral (or additional) advantage of a permanent kind once the loan, interest, and costs were paid off; and this is still the law today.

The law, as stated above, has established the principle that the borrower who mortgages his freehold or leasehold interest, as security for a loan of money, shall not be deprived of his ownership, but shall retain such ownership after the execution of the mortgage deed. That deed is, in the first place, a *contract or agreement* under which the borrower promises to repay the loan to the lender, with interest at a certain rate, in one sum or by instalments, and meanwhile, for the lender's protection, to keep the property insured, in proper repair, and so forth. But that is not all; it is clearly important that the lender (the mortgagee) should, in addition, be granted an interest *in the property itself*—an interest which will enable him to take actual *possession* of the property, if need be, to enforce his rights, much as the pawnbroker has the right to *possession* (though not *ownership*) of the pledged article until the loan is repaid.

The Law of Property Act, 1925, devised a method of giving the lender (the mortgagee) a legal estate in the property while still preserving the rights of ownership of the borrower (the mortgagor). That Act provides that the grant of a mortgage of land, in *whatever form* it is effected, shall confer upon the lender (the mortgagee) *a term of years absolute—i.e., a legal estate* in the *land itself*, which the mortgagee can deal with by sale, and which will be transmitted, as an interest in land, to his legal personal representatives upon his death. It is further provided that, on the final discharge of the mortgage (*i.e.*, the repayment of the loan, with all interest and expenses due to the mortgagee), that term of years shall *cease and be extinguished*, the mortgagor thereafter continuing to hold his freehold or leasehold estate *free from the mortgage term of years*, and free also from all the conditions of the mortgage deed.

In such a scheme it was necessary to distinguish the term of years conferred by the mortgage from any term of years absolute which might be or might have been conferred upon a lessee or underlessee by way of a lease or tenancy (see above, *Leaseholds*). For the purpose of such distinction the Act provides that, if the mortgagor's legal estate is a *freehold*, the mortgage deed confers upon the mortgagee a *term of 3000 years*, thus leaving to the mortgagor a legal *reversion* to commence after the expiration of that term (since the freehold estate is not limited to expire at any particular time). And if the mortgagor's legal estate is a *leasehold*, due to expire at the end of a fixed period, the mortgage deed confers upon the mortgagee a *term of years to expire ten days before* the leasehold term, thus again leaving the mortgagor with a legal reversion (in this case of ten days only).

In this way each party has a legal estate in the *land itself*, quite apart from the *contractual* rights and obligations in regard to the loan, which can be enforced by and against him *personally*. The mortgagor can sell his freehold *subject to the mortgage term* and the obligations of the mortgage deed; the mortgagee can *sell his mortgage term* with the benefit of the rights that go with it. The sale of a freehold (whether subject to a mortgage or not) is effected by a deed called a *conveyance*; the sale of a leasehold is effected by a deed called an *assignment*. The mortgage term can be dealt with in a deed called a *transfer of mortgage*. In every case the purchaser takes over the vendor's legal estate in the land, subject to, or with the benefit of, the personal obligations or rights in the original deed. In case of the death of the mortgagee or mortgagor, the legal estate in question, and the rights or obligations, are transmitted to his personal representatives.

Finally, it should be mentioned that, as an additional safeguard, the *title deeds* (evidencing the mortgagor's freehold or leasehold title) must be handed over to the mortgagee when the mortgage deed is executed, as part of the latter's security. The mortgagor must take care to get them back when he *redeems* the property by paying off the loan, interest, and expenses.

4. **Title.**—(a) *Evidence of title.*—Before freehold or leasehold property changes hands, it is the duty of the purchaser's solicitor to *investigate title—i.e.*, to satisfy himself that the vendor has a proper title himself and a proper right to convey or assign. Generally speaking, the purchaser's solicitor must go through the deeds (evidencing sales, transmissions on death, grants of leases, grants and redemptions of mortgages) for at least *thirty years back*; he must check every step in the *devolution of title* (*i.e.*, every change in ownership) and make *requisitions* (*i.e.*, demand explanations) on any point which is doubtful. This is still the system over the greater part of the country. No stamp duty is payable on conveyances up to £4,500; from £4,500 to £6,000 it is 10s. per cent; after that it rises to £1 per cent.

(b) *Registration of Title.*—With a view, however, to simplifying such procedure the Land Registration Acts have provided for a different system. In areas to which an Order in Council has made the system applicable, *registration of title* is *compulsory* upon any sale of freeholds, or of leaseholds having more than forty years to run. Under the Land Registration Act, 1966, this system is gradually being extended over the whole country. Registration is effected in the following way: one of a number of District Registries investigates the title of every freehold or leasehold sold after the appropriate date, *once and for all*. If they are satisfied that it is in order, they register the owner as *registered proprietor* of the land with *absolute title* to his freehold or *good leasehold title* to his leasehold. (These kinds of titles indicate that the title is unexceptionable, but if there is a slight doubt the proprietor may be granted a *qualified title*: and if he is in possession of the land he may be granted a *possessory title*, which signifies little more than the fact of possession. The Chief Land Registrar is empowered, however, to convert both qualified and possessory titles into absolute or good leasehold titles, after fifteen years in the case of freeholds, and after ten years in the case of leaseholds.)

The Land Registry issues to the registered proprietor a *land certificate*, certifying (on behalf of the Government) that a registered title of the appropriate kind has been granted. In any further transactions relating to that particular land the purchaser's solicitor need not concern himself with the original deeds save in exceptional cases; he can generally rely upon the certified statements made in the *land certificate*, on which the name of the new registered proprietor is entered by the Land Registry officials when a *transfer* in his favour, or the grant of a lease to him, is lodged at the Registry. There are appropriate sections in the land certificate for registration of a mortgage and the particulars of the mortgagee for the time being.

**5. Joint Ownership.**—If two or more persons are the owners of freehold or leasehold property, that does not mean that A owns one part of the land and buildings, and B and C other parts; the effect is that all of them *jointly own the whole*. (The analogy will be clear if the reader considers the case of a motor-car owned jointly by A, B, and C; clearly *all three own the entire car* between them; it cannot be said that A owns the engine, B the chassis, and C the body.) The Law of Property Act, 1925, recognises such joint ownership of land by means of a device known as a *trust for sale*. The respective rights of A, B, and C (equal or unequal) can be fully enforced only if and when the property is *sold* and the net proceeds of sale, in money, divided up in the proper proportions; and any or all of the joint owners can insist upon such sale or division for the purpose of obtaining their *proper shares*. But, while the property remains unsold, all the joint owners have rights according to the proportions of their shares; if, for example, the property is let, the net rents, after paying for repairs and other expenses, must be divided between them in those proportions. Up to four persons can jointly own a freehold or leasehold legal estate in land; if more than four are entitled to the *beneficial interest*, then four of their number only must hold the *legal* estate, and *equity* will enforce the *beneficial rights* of all against the legal owners. A purchaser from joint owners of the legal estate is concerned only with the latters' *legal title*: provided he hands over the purchase-money to them (not being less than two), or somebody authorised by them, *the purchaser is not responsible* for what they may do with that money. If those legal owners, from whom the purchaser buys, fail to pay over the proper shares to those *beneficially interested*, it is for the latter to enforce their rights against the vendors, who have sold the legal estate, by action in the Chancery Division, the guardian of equity. The purchaser's title to the land itself is not affected by the vendors' failure properly to carry out the terms of the trust for sale, so long as the *legal estate* has been properly transferred to him and he has paid the purchase-money to *not less than two* legal owners.

## III. Property Other than Land (Moveables)

**1. Chattels.**—Chattels are *concrete things* which can be the subject of ownership, other than land or buildings, and other than objects so closely affixed to land or buildings that they are regarded as part thereof (*e.g.*, growing crops and trees, or " landlord's fixtures " built into some structure or so closely attached that they cannot be removed without serious damage to the structure).

In the ordinary way chattels can be *sold* or *given away* without any special legal formalities—merely by *physical transfer*—*i.e.*, by the owner handing them over to somebody else. If a chattel is to be *mortgaged* as security for a loan, the procedure differs according to whether the person pledging it (the borrower) is or is not to retain *possession* of the chattel. (His *ownership*, in either case is not disturbed.)

(*a*) If, as happens when an article is *pawned*, the borrower is not to keep the article in his possession, he hands it over to the pawnbroker, who hands him in exchange the agreed loan and a *pawn-ticket*. On production of the pawn-ticket, and repayment of the loan with the stipulated interest, the borrower is entitled to receive the article back. (Provision is made by law for cases where the borrower defaults in payment, or where an un-

reasonable time elapses before he seeks to *redeem* what he has pledged.)

(*b*) If, however, the arrangement is that the *borrower* is to *retain possession* of the mortgaged article (as may happen if he borrows from a *moneylender* on the security of his furniture), then the borrower must execute and hand to the lender a document called a *bill of sale*. The law relating to such a document is extremely complex; but the most important provision is that the lender cannot enforce his rights unless he *registers* the bill of sale, at the Bankruptcy Court, in a register which any member of the public can inspect for a small charge. If then some member of the public desires to purchase the article from the person in whose possession it remains, but has reason to suspect that that person, though he may be the owner, has mortgaged it to a money-lender, it is open to the proposing purchaser to inspect the *register of bills of sale* to satisfy himself on the point. If he finds an entry against the owner's name, he will be wise not to proceed with the transaction. If he finds no such entry, and has no reason to believe the owner to be bankrupt, he can usually assume that there is nothing to prevent the person in possession from passing a good title to him. The proposed purchaser can also inspect the register of bankruptcies in order to see whether the vendor has the right to sell (*see* **D9(1)**).

**2. Things in Action.**—These (*see* **D16(1)**) are *intangible rights* which can be owned and dealt with but, because of their abstract nature, cannot be *physically* transferred. If Brown owes Jones £50, Jones (the creditor) can transfer to Robinson the right to collect the £50 from Brown. Jones does this by a document called an *assignment* of the debt and (most important) by giving *written notice* to Brown (the debtor) that Robinson is now the creditor instead of Jones.

Similarly, if Jones owns ten shares in Brown & Co., Ltd., Jones will hold a *share certificate*—*i.e.*, a document certifying the amount of his share-holding. He has certain rights in the company, but these depend upon the company's *memorandum and articles* (**D9(2)**) and upon the *registration* of his name in the company's register of shareholders. The share certificate is only *evidence* of his rights—it is not in itself a piece of property, and the physical handing over of the certificate will effect nothing unless Jones executes a *share transfer* in Robinson's favour and Robinson sends it to the company for registration, together with the old share certificate in Jones's name. After *registration* of Robinson's name, the company will destroy the old certificate and issue a fresh one to him.

Again, if Jones has insured his life with the Brown Life Assurance Society, he will have received a *policy* which is *evidence* of the right of his legal personal representatives to be paid £1000 on Jones' death. If Jones wishes, during his lifetime, to transfer that benefit to Robinson, he can do so, but it will not suffice for him merely to hand Robinson the policy. To transfer the *rights* under the policy he must execute an *assignment* in which it is stated that Jones, being the policy-holder and entitled to certain rights thereunder, now *assigns* those rights to Robinson. But no transfer of those rights will have been effected until Robinson has *notified* the Assurance Society of what has been done and sent it the policy and the assignment for *registration* in its books.

These examples illustrate the principle, set out in the Law of Property Act, 1925, that an *unconditional assignment*, in writing, by a person (the assignor) entitled to any debt or other thing in action, in favour of another person (the assignee), if *notice in writing* is given *to the debtor* or other person on whom the obligation rests (in the above examples, to Brown, the Company, and the Assurance Society), shall entitle the assignee to all the assignor's rights, including the right to enforce those rights by action in the Courts, without calling upon the co-operation of the assignor in whom the right to the debt, or other thing in action, was originally vested.

# C. FURTHER DETAIL ON SOME BRANCHES OF THE LAW

## DIVORCE AND OTHER MATRIMONIAL CAUSES

### 1. HISTORICAL SKETCH

The anomalies in this branch of the Law of England, and the legalistic attitude of the Courts to the subject, are principally due to historical reasons. For centuries the Church of Rome was the supreme ecclesiastical authority, and the law of that Church (Canon Law) applied to *matrimonial causes*—that is to say, disputes relating to any marriage and the mutual rights and duties of the spouses. Marriage was *indissoluble*—that is, there was no such thing as divorce in the modern sense of *breaking the legal tie*. But the Ecclesiastical Courts, which alone administered the matrimonial law before 1858, might for certain reasons grant a *decree of nullity* (a declaration that a particular "marriage" was null and void). In other cases they might grant what is now called a *legal separation* (known, in those days, as a "divorce *a mensa et thoro*," *i.e.* banishment from bed and board); this latter decree, however, *did not dissolve* the marriage bond, but merely gave judicial sanction to the spouses' living apart from each other, and regulated the terms of the separation. After the Reformation the Ecclesiastical Courts continued to deal with matrimonial causes on the same legal principles as before.

As a result of the Acts of Supremacy passed in the reigns of Henry VIII and Elizabeth I, the Sovereign was declared to be the supreme governor of the Realm in all spiritual and ecclesiastical, as well as temporal, causes. This royal supremacy, exercised constitutionally through Parliament, was part of the law of the land; since there was no limitation upon the power of Parliament (*see* D5), special Acts were passed, from time to time, to effect that which neither the Ecclesiastical nor the Civil Courts then had jurisdiction to do, *viz.*, to break the marriage tie itself. A divorce of this kind, known as " divorce *a vinculo matrimonii* " (a divorce from the marriage bond) was rare, for the procedure was cumbersome and expensive. Except by the passing of a special Act of Parliament, there was no means of getting a marriage dissolved before the year 1858.

The Matrimonial Causes Act, 1857, transferred the jurisdiction in matrimonial matters from the Ecclesiastical Courts to the new Civil " Court for Divorce and Matrimonial Causes "; but perpetuated the old ecclesiastical practice with regard to nullity suits and judicial separation (formerly known as " divorce *a mensa et thoro* "). Apart from this rearrangement, the Act took the revolutionary step of conferring upon this Court a new judicial power—that of granting a *divorce in the modern sense* of a complete *dissolution of marriage*. As we have seen (D5) the Supreme Court of Judicature Act, 1873, and subsequent legislation, set up one single High Court of Justice, of which the Probate, Divorce, and Admiralty Division formed part, taking over (with other work) the jurisdiction which had been conferred in 1857 upon the " Court for Divorce and Matrimonial Causes." This jurisdiction remains in the hands of the Probate, Divorce, and Admiralty Division to-day. Great changes have been effected *by statute* (notably in 1923, 1925, 1937, 1950, 1963, 1965, and 1967) extending the grounds for divorce and the jurisdiction of the Court; but in the interpretation and adaptation of principles the great body of *case law* (*see* D4), which enshrined the principles and practice of the old Ecclesiastical Courts, is not without its influence to-day. The principles of equity (*see* D4), however, have not modified the strict legalism of this branch of the law; *equity has no application to the law of matrimonial causes* (except for resort to *injunction* (*see* D12) and for the protection of the wife's person or property).

### 2. POWERS OF INFERIOR COURTS— SUMMARY JURISDICTION

Concurrently with the jurisdiction of the Divorce Division of the High Court, Magistrates' Courts now have power (Matrimonial Proceedings (Magistrates' Courts) Act, 1960, and Rules made thereunder) to grant relief (by a *matrimonial order*) to *either spouse* (the *complainant*) in certain cases of misconduct on the part of the other spouse (the *defendant*). The procedure is simpler, quicker, and cheaper than in the High Court. A Magistrates' Court may grant a matrimonial order; if such order provides (*a*) that the complainant shall be no longer bound to cohabit with the defendant that has the same effect as a High Court decree of judicial separation (*see* D28). A Magistrates' Court may also provide (*b*) that the husband shall pay the wife (or (*c*) where the husband's earning capacity is impaired by age, illness, mental or physical disablement, that the wife shall pay the husband) such weekly maintenance as the Court thinks reasonable *plus* (*h*) weekly payments for each dependent child; (*d*) the child's custody (up to 16 years of age) may be granted to the complainant or (*e*) to a county council or county borough council or (in special circumstances) (*f*) such child may be ordered to be placed under the supervision of an independent person (such as a probation officer) and (*g*) access to the child may be granted to either spouse or to any parent. (There are special provisions relating to (*d*), (*e*) and (*f*).) The former limits of £7. 10*s*. for wife or husband and of £2. 10*s*. for a child were repealed by the Maintenance Orders Act, 1968.

*Either spouse may apply for relief* on the ground that the defendant—

    (1) has *deserted* the complainant;

    (2) has been guilty of *persistent cruelty* to the complainant or an infant child of the family;

    (3) has been convicted (i) on indictment (*i.e.*, by a jury) of any *assault* on the complainant, or (ii) by a Magistrates' Court of certain offences (involving imprisonment for not less than one month) *against the person* of the complainant, or (iii) of a *sexual offence* (or an attempt threat) against an infant child of either spouse who is a child of the family;

    (4) has committed *adultery*;

    (5) while knowingly suffering from *venereal disease*, has insisted upon sexual intercourse with the complainant, or permitted such intercourse without the complainant being aware of such disease;

    (6) is a *habitual drunkard* or a *drug addict*;

    (7) being the *husband*, has compelled the *wife*, or led her, *to submit to prostitution*;

    (8) being the *husband*, has wilfully *neglected to provide reasonable maintenance* for the wife or any dependant child of the family;

    (9) being the *wife* (in case (*c*) above) has *wilfully neglected to provide*, or make a reasonable contribution to, *reasonable maintenance* for the husband or any dependant child of the family, having regard to any resources of the spouses.

A Magistrates' Court has jurisdiction to hear any such complaint *if either spouse ordinarily resides in the Court district,* or (except in (3) above) *if the cause of complaint arose in that district,* or (in case (3)) if the offence or attempt arose in that district. Jurisdiction is also exercisable *if the complainant resides in England* and the parties last resided together in England (even if the defendant now resides in Scotland or Northern Ireland), or *if the defendant resides in England* though the complainant resides in Scotland or Northern Ireland. The Court may order the *costs* of the application to be paid by either party.

The general rule is that a complaint under (4) above must be made *within six months* of the date when the act of adultery first became known to the complainant. A complaint on any other grounds must generally be made within six months of the ground of the complaint arising, unless the complainant was abroad at the time; but this time limit does not apply to such continuing offences as desertion (see below) or wilful neglect to maintain.

These " domestic proceedings," as they are termed, may be heard before one stipendiary (legally qualified) magistrate) or not more than three justices of the peace, including, so far as practicable, both a man and a woman. The *hearing* is *in private,* the public being excluded, and newspapers are prohibited from publishing details; " domestic proceedings " must be dealt with separately from other matters, and reports from probation officers may be received on the subject of any attempted reconciliation or on the means of the parties. In general, the magistrates should apply the same general principles as are applied in the Divorce Division; lay justices of the peace are advised on the law by their legally qualified clerk.

A *Magistrates' Court,* however, has *no power to grant a divorce* or *to annul a marriage;* the jurisdiction to make such a decree is in the hands of the Divorce Division of the High Court of Justice and, since 1967, of certain County Courts in undefended cases.

A maintenance order may be enforced by committing the defendant to prison if his failure to comply with the order is shown to be due to wilful refusal or culpable neglect, and if he has fallen into arrears. *See also* **D32.**

*No order is enforceable* while a wife is *residing with her husband,* and *no order* may be made on the application of a complainant where it is proved that he or she was *guilty of adultery,* unless the defendant condoned or connived at (see below), or by his wilful neglect or misconduct conduced to (*i.e.,* tended to lead to), the adultery. An order *already granted* will be *discharged* (i.e., its effect will be terminated) on *proof of the complainant's adultery,* or *on* proof that the spouses *voluntarily resumed cohabitation.*

If a matrimonial cause is pending in the Divorce Division of the High Court, no application for a separation or maintenance order ought to be dealt with by a Magistrates' Court. And a Magistrates' Court may refuse to make any order when the suit in question would, in its opinion, be more conveniently dealt with by the Divorce Division.

Appeals. A Magistrates' Court has power " to state a case," upon *a point of law* (not a question of *fact*) arising on the application, for decision by a Divisional Court consisting of two or more judges of the Divorce Division. And an appeal from a Divisional Court lies to the Court of Appeal, by leave of either the former or the latter.

## 3. MATRIMONIAL CAUSES in the HIGH COURT and UNDEFENDED DIVORCE CASES in DESIGNATED COUNTY COURTS

### (1) Constitution of the Courts

The President of the Probate, Divorce, and Admiralty Division and not less than three other High Court Judges attached to that Division are the permanent judges for Matrimonial Causes. They sit both at the Royal Courts of Justice in London and at Assizes. Certain subsidiary duties are performed by the seven Registrars of the Principal Registry of the Division at Somerset House, and by District Registrars in the principal cities of England and Wales. The Matrimonial Causes Act, 1967, permits designated County Courts to grant divorces in undefended cases.

### (2) Practice and Procedure

In contrast to " domestic proceedings " in Magistrates' Courts, the *Judges* of the Divorce Division sit normally in *open court,* though they have power to sit *in camera* (in private) where the ends of justice so require. In *nullity proceedings,* however, it is provided by statute that evidence on the question of *sexual incapacity* must be heard *in camera* unless the Judge is satisfied that the ends of justice require such evidence to be heard in open court. Press publicity is limited by statute to certain matters, and the publication of indecent matter may give rise to prosecution, in *any* matrimonial proceedings.

In general, practice and procedure in the Divorce Division and designated County Courts are governed by statute, by rules of Court framed by a judicial committee under statutory authority, and by the principles and practice of the old Ecclesiastical Courts—except in proceedings for dissolution of marriage, which the old Courts could not entertain (*see* D24(1).

### (3) Relief and Grounds for Relief

(a)—Nullity of Marriage. The High Court has power to declare a " marriage " null and void in two main classes of case:

    (i) " *Marriages* " *Void from their Inception* —*i.e.,* where one of the parties had *another husband or wife living* at the time of the ceremony; where there was a *mistake* as to the *nature* of the ceremony, or the *identity* of the other party; where one party had been declared of *unsound mind* and was detained as a lunatic at the time of the ceremony; where the parties were within the *prohibited degrees* of relationship (*e.g.,* brother and sister, or uncle and niece); or where the *ceremony was not in due form,* or was a mock " marriage."

    (ii) *Marriages which are Voidable—i.e.,* which stand good unless and until one party or the other (" the Petitioner ") successfully petitions the Court for annulment—*i.e.,* where either party was sexually *impotent at the date of the ceremony;* where either party has wilfully *refused to consummate* the marriage; where the marriage was *induced by threats* or fear or duress (*i.e.,* force), or where one spouse was *intoxicated* at the time of the ceremony.

The Act of 1965 added certain other grounds: (*a*) where either party was, at the time of the ceremony, in fact of *unsound mind* but had not been declared so, or was then a *mental defective,* or then subject to recurrent fits of *insanity or epilepsy;* (*b*) where the other spouse was, at the time of the marriage, suffering from *venereal disease* in a communicable form; and (*c*) where the wife was, at the time of the marriage, *pregnant by some person* other than the petitioning husband. But in those last cases (*a*), (*b*), and (*c*) the Court must not grant a decree unless it is satisfied that the petitioner was, at the time of the marriage, ignorant of the facts alleged; that the proceedings were instituted within a year of the marriage, and that there has been no sexual intercourse between the parties, with the consent of the petitioner, since he or she discovered that there were grounds for a decree of nullity.

Where a " marriage " is *void* (see above) the law regards it as *never having taken place* at all. Where it is *voidable*, the decree *annuls the marriage retrospectively* from its inception; but certain transactions between the parties while they actually remained married are validated, and the Court has power to order maintenance for the woman; and *any child* who would in the normal way have been the legitimate child of the parties *remains legitimate*, notwithstanding the annulment.

*Sterility—i.e.,* inability to produce children—is not, in itself, a ground for annulment of the marriage. If the *impotence* of one spouse appears to be *curable* without danger the Court may, before pronouncing a decree, require that opportunity for cure be first given. If he or she *refuses to undergo examination or treatment* the Court may infer, after hearing the other party's evidence, that impotence exists. The petitioning husband or wife may ask for a nullity decree on the ground of *his or her own impotence*, provided he or she did not know of it at the time of the marriage. And there have been recent cases in which *both partners* have been granted decrees.

Apart from the one-year rule (mentioned in the last paragraph but two) in certain cases, delay (however long) in petitioning for nullity is no bar to the grant of a decree.

(3) (b) Divorce —(i) *Its Nature and Purpose.*— Divorce means the *breaking of the legal tie* of marriage by a decree of the Court. There is much controversy on the subject.

We have to start by facing the unpalatable truth that *some marriages do break down* in fact. The symptoms of break-down may be continual strife, and sometimes violence, between the spouses, so long as they continue to live together; or there may be an actual breaking-up of the home because one or the other finds the situation intolerable and leaves. The function of the law should be to deal with this state of affairs as best it can, paying due regard: (a) to the interests of the children (if any), who are innocent parties to the dispute; (b) to the interests of the spouses and of any third party involved; (c) to the interests of public decency and the safeguarding of family life generally.

Divorce is the drastic *remedy* provided by the civil law in the case of a marriage which has already *broken down in fact;* the availability of divorce does not bring about the break-down, any more than the availability of surgical treatment can be said to bring about ill-health. A marriage may break down—that is to say, the " kernel " of the marriage, the mutual respect and affection between the spouses, has withered away; only an empty shell—the legal tie—continues to subsist between them. How should this situation be dealt with by law?

It is common ground, among both the upholders of the orthodox view and those who advocate reform, first that every possible effort should be made, by private individuals and public institutions, to effect a reconciliation, if at all possible. Such efforts are favoured by the law, and excellent work is done to this end by religious organisations, medical men, probation officers, lawyers, and such institutions as the Marriage Guidance Council.

Secondly, it is common ground that, if such efforts are unsuccessful and the *breach proves irreparable* in fact, the interest of the children (if any)

should be paramount, and no pains should be spared to secure their proper care and maintenance. This is laid down by law; the Judge in a matrimonial cause may take the initiative in providing for the custody, maintenance, and education of the children, or for placing them under the care of the Chancery Division (*see* D5); whether the initiative is taken by the Judge or by one of the parents, the welfare of the children is the *paramount consideration*, irrespective of the rights and wrongs as between the parents. Nobody will deny that, once the marriage has broken down *in fact*, the children will suffer to some extent; but it does not follow that they would suffer less if the legal tie between the parents were preserved, or if the home, with its atmosphere of strife, and perhaps of violence, were kept together at all costs—even assuming such a thing were possible. A divorce may not be granted unless the Judge is satisfied that all possible arrangements have been made for the care and upbringing of the children (D29, 31).

It is at this point that the main controversy begins. Where the " kernel " of the marriage has withered away, should the " shell "—the legal tie —be preserved or discarded? And if discarded, then in what circumstances and on what conditions?

The Christian Churches declare that marriage is not merely a civil institution but a religious sacrament, and the Roman Church regards it as indissoluble. This last is a matter of religious dogma and belief; not a question for rational argument. It is a view as deserving of respect as any other; but, as we have seen, it was abandoned by Parliament a century ago, and is unlikely to be reinstated in the civil law of England. Many churchmen regard this view as binding on their consciences, but it is no longer the law of the land. For better or worse, a marriage can now be legally dissolved, leaving each party free to contract another union if he or she so desires. On what basis, then, ought such dissolution to be granted?

This is the second stage of the controversy. The conventional view, the attitude of the present law, is that a decree of divorce can, and ought to, be granted solely as a result of some *matrimonial misconduct* by the " guilty " party, entitling the " innocent " party—and only the " innocent " party—to go to the Court for relief. According to this view, the decree of divorce (though in law a merely civil remedy) is regarded virtually as in the nature of a *penalty* upon the " guilty " party for his or her wrongdoing—a view that has survived from biblical times. The reformers consider this an anachronism and an anomaly, pointing out: (a) that in those times (as is the case under Islamic law to-day) it was only the husband who could divorce his wife (not *vice versa*)—a step which was then a very severe punishment, since divorce meant, for the woman, disgrace, degradation, and poverty; whereas it is to-day little or no economic penalty or social stigma upon the " guilty " spouse, who is frequently no less— and often more—desirous than the " innocent " spouse of obtaining his or her freedom. The reformers further emphasise: (b) that the matrimonial law has never pretended to identify itself wholly with the doctrines of the Church; for example, the Book of Common Prayer declares, of marriage, that " first, it was ordained for the procreation of children "; yet not even the Ecclesiastical Courts went so far as to annul a deliberately childless marriage, and under the present law a refusal to have children is not a matrimonial offence and involves no penalty. Finally, (c) the reformist view is that the essence of the married state—the " kernel "—is the mutual respect and affection between the spouses; once that " kernel " has withered away and the marriage has *irretrievably broken down in fact*, the preservation of the legal tie is a mere pretence; the breaking of that legal tie, from the point of view of public decency, should be regarded as the necessary and proper result of the break-down of the essence of the marriage, or the break-up of the marital home. Under the present system, a refusal by the " innocent " party to take proceedings for divorce, however malicious his or her motive for such refusal, cannot be questioned, and this makes for irregular unions and illegitimate births; on the other hand, the law's insistence that there must be an "innocent" and a "guilty" party inevitably induces two spouses, who find their union intolerable, to resort to unworthy subterfuges; under a more rational system (such as obtains, for example, in the Scandinavian states) both parties might amicably join forces to have the marriage dissolved, once it was quite clear that reconciliation was out of the question.

The reformist view has gradually gained ground. Following recommendations by the Archbishop of Canterbury's Committee and the Law Commission (D5(2)), a Divorce Reform Bill was before Parliament at the time of writing (January 1969) but has not yet passed into law. It recommends that adultery, cruelty, and desertion, and even consensual separation, be regarded as *symptoms* and *evidence* of breakdown. The Lord Chancellor is also in favour of these changes, and also several Nonconformist Church bodies. Meanwhile, in this edition, we can only state the *present law*. But the Courts have already begun to avoid keeping hopeless marriages in being, subject to *reconciliation efforts* before decree.

(ii) *Grounds for Divorce.* The *Petitioner* (i.e., the husband or wife who is *asking the Court for a divorce* against the other spouse) may present a petition on the ground that the *Respondent* (the other spouse):

(a) has since the celebration of the marriage *committed adultery*;

(b) has *deserted* the Petitioner *without cause* for at least *three years* preceding the presentation of the petition; but, by the Act of 1965, the 3 years' period is not to take account of any one period of 3 months during which the spouses came together again with a view to reconciliation.

(c) has since the celebration of the marriage treated the Petitioner with *cruelty*; or

(d) is *incurably of unsound mind* and has been *continuously under care and treatment for at least five years* immediately preceding the presentation of the petition. (*See also* D31(2).)

Further, a *wife* may petition for divorce on the grounds that:

(e) her husband has, since the celebration of the marriage, been guilty of *rape, sodomy, or bestiality.*

Finally, to cover those cases where one of the spouses has disappeared and not been heard of for many years:

(f) any married person who alleges that reasonable grounds exist for *supposing the other party to be dead* may petition the Court *to have it presumed* that the other party is dead and *to have the marriage dissolved.*

*No petition for divorce* on any ground may be presented *until the expiration of three years* from the date of the marriage, unless a Judge is satisfied that there is a case of *exceptional hardship* upon the Petitioner or *exceptional depravity* on the part of the Respondent. Whether there is such a case is a question for the Judge's discretion upon the evidence brought before him.

As to the above-mentioned grounds for divorce:

(a) *Adultery* means *voluntary sexual intercourse* between a husband and a woman who is not his wife, or between a wife and a man who is not her husband. (A woman who has been raped—*i.e.*, forced to have intercourse with another man against her will—is not guilty of adultery.) For obvious reasons, *direct evidence* of the act of adultery is rare, and the Court may infer from circumstantial evidence that adultery has taken place.

(b) *Desertion* means, primarily, the *intentional permanent abandonment*, by one spouse of the other, *without that other's consent*, and *without reasonable cause.* Therefore there is *no desertion* in such cases (for example) as: (i) where a husband *cannot* live with his wife because he is serving a sentence of imprisonment; (ii) where a husband leaves his wife for a *short time* for necessary business or family reasons, *intending to return to her*; (iii) while a *separation continues with the consent of both parties*; (iv) where the spouse who abandoned the other had *just cause* to do so; (v) any one period of 3 months cohabitation with a view to reconciliation does not break the period of desertion.

Indeed, in certain cases under (iv) the doctrine known as constructive desertion may apply *against the other spouse*, if he or she has (figuratively speaking) *driven the first spouse away.* Constructive desertion means, not "desertion" in the literal sense of walking out of the matrimonial home, but conduct on the part of a husband which is intended to force, and virtually forces, his wife to leave him, or *vice versa.* Thus, if a husband brings his mistress to live with him in the matrimonial home and, as a result, his wife leaves him, not only is the wife innocent of desertion in the legal sense, but the husband is himself guilty of constructive desertion; it will be presumed against him that he intended to terminate his marital association, and he has in fact *carried out that intention.* Such a case illustrates the principle that there are *two elements* in the legal meaning of desertion—the *act* of physical separation and the *intention* to bring normal married life to an end.

In order to bring about desertion it is not necessary that the spouses should cease to live under the same roof; "desertion is not withdrawal from a place, but from a state of things." It is sufficient that the Respondent (the "guilty" spouse) has withdrawn from, or forced the other to withdraw from, *cohabitation*—*i.e.*, from sharing a common "home" in the full sense of the word. A wife "deserts" her husband if she refuses (against his will) to share his room, to take her meals with him, and to perform the usual duties of a wife. On the other hand, the mere refusal of sexual intercourse, in itself alone, does not amount to desertion, though it *may amount to cruelty* (D28) if it has broken or is likely to break the health or spirit of the Petitioner.

It should also be noted that desertion is not a single act but a continuous state of affairs. The Petitioner must prove *that desertion without cause continued* during the entire period of *three years* required by law as the basis of a divorce petition. Although (see above) desertion in the legal sense must be *without the consent* of the petitioning spouse, recent judicial decisions have tended to dispense with the requirement that the deserted party must prove a *continuing desire* for the deserting party to return, and a *continuing willingness* to receive and reinstate the deserting party, during the *entire period of three years* preceding the commencement of proceedings; in other words, once the latter party's *original act and intention of deserting* has been proved, that intention is *presumed to have continued*, unless there is evidence to the contrary. (But see above (b)(v).) But any kind of *agreed separation* is fatal to the case, whether the agreement be in writing, by word of mouth, or implied by conduct. An agreement, however, by a husband, who is *already living apart* from his wife, to *maintain* her and the children does not constitute a separation by agreement, unless there is evidence that the *wife actually consented* to his leaving her. A *matrimonial order* made by a Magistrates' Court (*see* (D24(2)) does not necessarily prevent the period of desertion from running, unless the order contains a clause, deliberately inserted, to the effect that "the parties shall no onger be bound to cohabit." And the insertion of such a clause is rare.

If the deserting party makes an *offer to return* to the matrimonial home it is the duty of the other party to receive him (or her) back and to resume normal married life together, *if the offer to return is genuine* and if no other matrimonial offence (such as adultery or cruelty) has been committed by the deserting party. Whether such an offer is "genuine" is a question of fact, to be decided on all the evidence: it will generally be a wise safeguard for a deserted party who receives such an offer to *take legal advice* before accepting or rejecting it; for if rejection of the offer subsequently proves to have been unjustified, he (or she) may become the deserting party. This situation, again, arises from the legal view that " desertion " consists of two elements—the *act* and the *intention* of deserting. (*See also* (b) (v), above).

An *honest and reasonable belief*, by one spouse, that the other spouse has committed, or is committing, adultery, if such a belief is induced by the other spouse's conduct, may be " just cause " for the first spouse to refuse cohabitation, and prevent him (or her) from being regarded as the deserting party.

(c) *Cruelty* is not defined by statute, but has been decided, in reported cases, to mean conduct causing danger to life, limb, or bodily or mental health, or giving rise to a reasonable apprehension of such danger. (The term "Mental Cruelty" is unknown to English law; but there may be *cruelty* in the legal sense *without physical violence*.) The Courts have refused to commit themselves to a comprehensive definition; *every* case must be considered on its *own facts* in the light of the whole history of the marriage. One single act, even of violence, can seldom be regarded as " cruelty "; but the conduct complained of must be of a *grievous nature*—not mere conduct which (however reprehensible) may be regarded as " part of the wear and tear of married life." In order to constitute cruelty, the conduct must be understood to be likely to break the latter's *health or spirit*. An *insane person*, who does not understand the nature and quality of his acts, and so cannot form the necessary " intention " (D9(1)), *can be guilty of cruelty* if he was warned of the probable result; for it is no longer necessary for the petitioner to prove that the respondent *intended* to be cruel or was aiming or directing his conduct against the petitioner.

*Drunkenness, in itself*, is *not* cruelty; but if it is so *persistent*, or its effects so inevitably *distressing* to the other spouse, as to *threaten his or her health*, it may amount to cruelty. Similar considerations apply to persistent refusal of sexual intercourse, excessive sexual demands, or sexual malpractices either forced upon the other spouse or committed with third parties.

A *divorce petition* based wholly or partly on cruelty must *set out specifically the acts* complained of, evidence of which is to be given at the trial. (This ensures that the Respondent knows the details of the case he has to meet.)

(3) (c) **Restitution of Conjugal Rights.**—Either spouse may petition the Court for such a decree where the other spouse has " wrongfully withdrawn from cohabitation " (see above). *Willingness to return* to cohabitation, *if genuine*, or *proof of just cause* (see above) for refusal are good defences. If the petition succeeds, and the Court orders the erring spouse to return, his or her *noncompliance* with the order *will not lead to enforcement* by arrest or otherwise; but it will (so to speak) fix upon him or her responsibility for the separation, and *establish* his or her status as the deserting party (see above). And *non-compliance* with a restitution decree is in itself *a ground* for the other party to petition for a decree of *judicial separation* (see below).

(3( (d) **Judicial Separation.**—A petition for this form of relief may be presented by either spouse

on the ground last mentioned in the foregoing paragraph, or on any of the grounds for which a divorce petition (see above) might have been presented. The *effect of the decree* (as in the case of a similar order made by a Magistrates' Court) is that the Petitioner is *no longer bound to cohabit* with the Respondent, and cannot therefore be regarded as a deserting party. (The *legal bond* of marriage *remains in force*; the procedure is therefore often employed by a spouse who does not desire divorce, perhaps for reasons of conscience, perhaps merely so as not to allow the other party freedom to marry somebody else.) It is, however, open to a Petitioner, who has obtained a decree of judicial separation, to petition for divorce, on the same facts, at a later date—*provided that three years have elapsed* since the date of the marriage (see D27(1)).

**Bars to Relief.**—(1) *Absolute Bars*.—It is, by statute, the duty of the Court to investigate, so far as it reasonably can, the facts alleged in any petition for divorce or judicial separation, and to inquire whether there has been any *connivance* or *condonation* on the part of the Petitioner, and whether any *collusion* exists between the parties. *The Court must dismiss* the petition, and *refuse a decree, even in an undefended suit, unless* it is satisfied: (a) that the *Petitioner has proved his or her case*; (b) that the Petitioner has not been *accessory to or connived at* the adultery (if any) of the other party; (c) that the Petitioner has not *condoned* the adultery (if any) or the cruelty (if any) of the other party.

(a) *The Petitioner must prove the case*—that is to say, satisfy the Court that there are *proper grounds* for a decree *according to law*; there is no such thing, in suits for divorce and judicial separation, as judgment by consent, by admission, or in default of defence (as is possible, for example, in actions for breach of contract and tort (D10(1)). *In matrimonial suits the State*, and not merely the parties themselves, must see that the provisions of the law are *strictly observed*.

(b) *There must be no connivance*—that is to say, the Petitioner must not have intended *to promote or encourage or provide opportunity for* the commencement or the continuance of the Respondent's adultery. Merely *keeping watch upon a suspected spouse*, for the purpose of obtaining evidence, is not necessarily connivance; there must be active *encouragement or acquiescence*—wilfully " shutting one's eyes " to what is going on or likely to take place. (But, if a spouse who has connived at his partner's adultery repents and withdraws his acquiescence, the connivance may be regarded as " spent," and no longer be a bar to divorce.)

(c) *There must be no condonation* of adultery or cruelty—that is to say, *forgiveness* of all such acts as are known to, or suspected by, the injured spouse, and the restoration of normal marital relations with the offending spouse. (" Forgiveness " means forgiveness *on condition* that there shall be *no further matrimonial offence*.) Condonation may be by words or conduct. The Petitioner *cannot obtain a decree* on the ground of any offence or offences which he or she has *condoned*, except in case of *revival*. But adultery or cruelty shall not (now) be deemed to have been condoned merely because of a resumption of cohabitation (for not more than three months) with a view to reconciliation.

*Revival*—If, subsequent to the condonation, the offending spouse again commits some matrimonial offence or offences, the former offence or offences, other than adultery, are *revived—i.e.*, the effect of the forgiveness and restoration are thereby is cancelled, and the former offence or offences will again afford a ground for divorce or judicial separation. It does not matter whether or not the new offence is of the same nature as the old; condoned cruelty will be revived by new acts of cruelty or desertion; condoned cruelty will be revived by a new act of adultery, and so forth. But, by the Act of 1965, adultery, once condoned, cannot be revived.

(2) *Discretionary Bars*—(a) *There may be an agreement or bargain* between the parties (whether for financial consideration or otherwise) that the Petitioner will commence or conduct a suit for divorce or judicial separation, or that the Respondent will not defend such a suit. There is *collusion* if one party *requests or suggests* that the other *should commit adultery* in order to provide evidence for a divorce, and the other party *accedes* to the request or suggestion. But it is not necessarily collusion for the Petitioner, knowing that *adultery has already been committed*, to ask the other party *for details or for evidence* on which the Petitioner can act. The Court regards financial arrangements between the parties with suspicion, if they are entered into *before the suit is commenced*, and it will carefully investigate such arrangements, and it has a discretion, under the 1965 Act, to permit such financial arrangements if they are fully disclosed. Once the petition has been filed, there is no objection to discussion, between the parties or their advisers, of necessary financial arrangements as to alimony or maintenance (*see* **D30**(1)) or the disposal of the matrimonial home.

(b) Apart from connivance and condonation, either of which (as we have seen) is a *bar* to the granting of a decree, the *Court has a discretion either to refuse or to grant* a decree of divorce or judicial separation, according to circumstances, if it finds that the *Petitioner* has himself (or herself): (i) been *guilty of adultery* during the marriage; (ii) *shown unreasonable delay* in presenting or prosecuting the petition; or (iii) been guilty of cruelty, or desertion without reasonable cause, *before* the Respondent's acts of adultery or cruelty on which the petition is based. The Court has a similar *discretion*, where the ground for the petition is *adultery, desertion,* or *unsoundness of mind*, either to refuse or to grant a decree to a *Petitioner* who has (iv) been guilty of such *wilful neglect or misconduct* as has conduced to (*i.e.*, helped to bring about) the Respondent's adultery, desertion, or unsoundness of mind; and (v), by the 1965 Act, it has a discretion to grant a divorce where there has been an agreement between the parties, if full disclosure is made (*see* (2) (a) above).

In a case where each party is asking for a divorce against the other, each admitting his (and her) own misconduct and asking the Court to exercise its discretion in his (and her) favour, the *Court may exercise its discretion in favour of both* and dissolve the marriage. The same applies to *nullity*.

In case (i) above, where the *Petitioner* has himself (or herself) been *guilty of adultery*, it is the Petitioner's duty to lodge in the Divorce Registry a *discretion statement*—*i.e.*, a written statement in a sealed envelope (to be opened by the Judge at the hearing) admitting the facts and explaining the circumstances of his (or her) adultery. The *petition* in such a case must *contain a clause praying the Court* " to exercise its discretion in the Petitioner's favour." The Petitioner's *own* adultery, admitted in open Court, may be the only such evidence available.

**Decree Nisi and Decree Absolute.**—When the case comes on for trial the Judge will hear the *evidence of the Petitioner* and his or her witnesses, *and legal argument* on his or her behalf; *if the case is defended* by the Respondent spouse, or by the Co-respondent (*i.e.*, any *man* accused, in the petition, of adultery with a Respondent *wife*), or by any *woman named* in the petition as having committed adultery with a Respondent *husband*, the Judge will hear their evidence and legal argument on their behalf. The Judge, if not satisfied on the points (a), (b), and (c), (**D28**) in a case of divorce or judicial separation, must *dismiss the petition*, in which event the married status of the parties will remain unchanged. (But see **D26**(1).) If the Judge *is* satisfied on the points mentioned he will, in a suit for *judicial separation*, pronounce a *final decree*; in a *suit for restitution of conjugal rights* he will *order* the deserting spouse *to return*

to cohabitation (the effect of the decree and the order is described above, **D28**(1)).

In a suit for *nullity* or *divorce*, the Judge will pronounce a decree *nisi*—*i.e.*, an order that the marriage is to be *annulled* or *dissolved* unless (*nisi*), before that event takes place, *some cause* is shown to the Court *why final annulment or dissolution ought not to be permitted*. Intervention for this purpose may be made by an official known as the *Queen's Proctor*, or by any member of the public. Such interventions after decree *nisi* are rare, but may be made on the ground, for example, that there was a collusive arrangement (see above) which was not disclosed, or some other material fact, which was concealed from the Court at the hearing.

If such intervention succeeds, the decree *nisi* will be *rescinded* (*i.e.*, cancelled) and the parties will retain their former status. If there is *no such intervention*, or if such intervention is *dismissed*, then the marriage will be *finally annulled or dissolved* on application (on a special form), at the Divorce Registry concerned (not in open court), by or on behalf of the *Petitioner*, not earlier than *three months* after the decree *nisi* (unless the Court fixes a shorter time by special order). If the Petitioner does not make such an application, then the Respondent may do so after the lapse of a *further three months* (*i.e.*, six months after the date of the decree *nisi*), and the Court has power to grant or refuse such application or to deal with the case as it thinks fit.

The decree which *finally annuls or dissolves* the marriage is called a *decree absolute*. Unless and until it is granted, the marriage tie still subsists; the decree *nisi* does *not* terminate the status of husband and wife. But the *decree absolute* does terminate that status, leaving both parties free to marry again.

### Incidental Matters

(1) **Custody and Maintenance of Children.**—Apart from the general power of the Chancery Division, as guardian of equity (**D5**), *to protect the person and the property of any infant* (**D8**) and of the Local Authority under the Children and Young Persons Act, 1963, (even though there may be no matrimonial proceedings between its parents), and apart from the additional powers of that Division and of Magistrates' Courts, under the Guardianship of Infants Act, 1925, *to appoint a guardian or guardians for any infant*, and to make orders for either parent to have *access* to the infant (*i.e.*, to see it periodically) and for the infant's *maintenance*, the Divorce Division itself may make orders for the *custody, maintenance, and education* of the *children of the family* (*see* **D31**(2)) in any matrimonial proceedings, and give directions for placing them under the protection of the Court, and for access to them by either or both of the parents. The expression " children of the family " includes children lawfully adopted by both husband and wife, children of a bigamous " marriage " which has given rise to nullity proceedings (**D25**), and also children born before the marriage of their parents and legitimated by that (subsequent) marriage. The Court may make such orders and give such directions at any time after proceedings have been commenced for nullity, divorce, judicial separation, or restitution of conjugal rights; it may make interim orders, and give interim directions, from time to time *during the proceedings*. It is, however, *unusual* for the Divorce Division to make orders for custody or access to any child *over the age of sixteen* (since such orders would be difficult to enforce). (*See also* **D31**(1) for recent changes in the law.)

In all such proceedings, in *whatever court* they may be taken, the *paramount consideration* is the *welfare of the children*—*not the punishment of the " guilty " parent, nor any privilege* of the father as against the mother, or *vice versa*. (It is, for example, unusual for the Court to deprive the mother of the custody of a very young child, even though she has committed, or is living in, adultery —unless, or course, she is neglecting the child or is a " bad mother " in the widest sense.) In some cases, for good reason, both parents may be passed over, and the custody of the child may be given to some third party.

(2) **Financial Provision.**—(a) *Alimony Pending Suit.*—On any petition for nullity, divorce, judicial separation, or restitution of conjugal rights, the Divorce Division may make such order for *payment by the husband to the wife* of alimony pending suit (*i.e.,* a periodical sum for or towards her support *during the proceedings*) as the Court thinks just. The Court may also *order a wife Petitioner,* in a suit for divorce or judicial separation on the ground of the *husband's insanity,* to pay *alimony pending suit* for or towards the *support of the husband during the proceedings.*

(b) *Permanent Alimony* is the term used for similar payments which the Court may order the husband to make to the wife *after* the pronouncement of a *decree of judicial separation* on any ground, and such an order *in favour of the wife* may be made even where a decree has been pronounced *against her.* An order for *permanent alimony* may also be made *in favour of the husband* in a case where the *wife petitioned* for judicial separation on the ground of *his insanity.* *Permanent alimony* may also be ordered in favour of the wife where an order for *restitution of conjugal rights* has been made in her favour.

(It will be observed that, in all the above cases, the period during which the payment of *alimony* may be ordered is *while the status of marriage remains in being.*)

(c) *Permanent Maintenance* is the provision which the Court may order the husband to make in favour of the wife *after a decree absolute of divorce or nullity—i.e.,* for the period *after the married status has been terminated.* (The Court may, *in exceptional cases,* make an order for *permanent maintenance* in favour of a " guilty " wife.) In *one case permanent maintenance* may be ordered *against a wife* and *in favour of a husband*—where the *wife petitioned* for divorce on the ground of *his insanity.* The order may be for payment of a *monthly or weekly sum* during the *joint lives of the parties* (*i.e.,* so long as they shall *both* live), or for a capital sum to be invested so as " to secure to the wife such lump or annual sum of money, for any term not exceeding her life," as the Court thinks reasonable, in both cases having regard to " *her fortune* (if any), to the *ability of the husband,* and to the *conduct of the parties.*" The amount of the order is therefore left to the *discretion of the Court*; and it may be varied by the Court from time to time as the circumstances of the parties change. (The words " conduct of the parties " show that, in fixing the payments, the Court does not necessarily regard the question of " guilt " or " innocence " as clear-cut on the one side or the other; it may take into consideration the *whole history of the marriage.* The Court also takes into account the *property and income of both parties.*) (*See also* D32(1)). The Court may also order the husband to pay a reasonable lump sum to the wife.

(d) *Periodical Payments* may be ordered to be made, *by the husband to the wife,* on or after the making of a *decree for restitution of conjugal rights,* for the joint lives of the parties. The Court may order the husband to " secure " such payments as in the case of permanent maintenance. Where the *husband successfully applied* for the decree, the Court may order the wife, if she is " in receipt of any *profits of trade or earnings,*" to pay to the husband, or for the benefit of the children, such part of those profits or earnings as it thinks reasonable. *See also* D32 (D *and* E).

Where a husband has been guilty of *wilful neglect to provide reasonable maintenance* for his wife or infant children, then, in any case where the wife might have petitioned for judicial separation,

the Court may (on the wife's application) order the husband to make to her such *periodical payments* as may be just, and it may order the husband to " secure " such payments (as described above). (Thus, where there has been wilful neglect to maintain, on the part of the husband, the wife may apply for financial relief in the Divorce Division (or in a designated County Court) instead of in the Magistrates' Court. And the wife may make such an application even if she does not wish to petition for a decree of nullity, divorce, judicial separation, or restitution of conjugal rights.)

(e) In any case where the Court has power to make a *permanent* order, it may now order the payment of a *lump sum* (1965 Act).

(f) *Settlements.*—In any case in which the Court pronounces a decree for divorce or judicial separation by reason of the *wife's adultery, cruelty, or desertion,* the Court has power to order the wife's property, or any part of it, to be *settled* (D20) for the benefit of the innocent party, or of the children of the marriage, or both.

The Court also has power, after a decree for nullity or divorce, to vary the terms of any settlement which may have been made on the parties before or after their marriage; the variation may be made to benefit the children, or the parties or either of them, as the Court thinks fit.

(g) *Damages against Co-respondent.*—A husband who is petitioning for a decree of *divorce or judicial separation,* on the ground of his *wife's adultery,* may ask for an award of *damages against the Co-respondent* (*i.e.,* the man with whom she has committed adultery). Such a claim, which is comparatively rare nowadays, is usually tried before a judge and jury; the damages should be assessed so as to *compensate the husband,* so far as possible, for the loss of his wife where she has been seduced from his side by the adulterer.

(h) *Costs.*—The costs of the proceedings are *always in the discretion of the Court,* each case depending on its own facts. Generally speaking, however, the costs " follow the event "—*i.e.,* when a decree or order is made against a husband, he will usually be ordered to pay the costs incurred; costs, however, are rarely awarded against a " guilty " wife, but are not infrequently ordered to be paid by the Co-respondent (if any). An order for costs may be made, but rarely is, against the " woman named " in a petition as having committed adultery with the husband.

*Note on Domicil.*—It has been explained above (*see* D8) why the English Court will *not, generally speaking,* grant a *divorce* to a man who is *domiciled abroad.* Since the *domicil of a wife* is the same as *that of her husband* (even if she has not lived with him for many years), the refusal of the English court to accept jurisdiction has caused hardship in many cases. To mitigate this hardship the Matrimonial Causes Act, 1965, confers upon the Divorce Division an additional statutory jurisdiction in the following cases, *in favour of a wife,* even if her husband is *not domiciled in England*:

(a) In *any* matrimonial proceedings, *other than* for a " decree of presumption of death and dissolution of marriage " (see below), if: (i) the wife has been deserted by her husband, or the husband has been deported from the United Kingdom as an alien; and (ii) immediately *before the desertion or deportation* the husband *was* domiciled in England.

(b) In proceedings for *divorce or nullity,* if: (i) the wife is *resident* (*i.e.,* actually living for the time being) in England; and (ii) has been *ordinarily resident* there for a period of *three years* immediately preceding the commencement of the proceedings; and (iii) the husband is *not* domiciled *in any other part of the United Kingdom*, or in the Channel Islands or the Isle of Man. (The two last-named territories have their own separate systems of law.)

(c) In proceedings for a decree of " presumption of death and dissolution of marriage ": the husband is presumed by law (*for the purpose of ascertaining the wife's domicil*) to have died " immediately after the last occasion when she knew, or had reason to believe him, to be living." (Thus the wife can acquire an English domicil of her own as from that date.)

(d) Recent cases have decided that the English courts shall have the right to recognise a divorce granted by the court of a foreign country with which the petitioner has some " genuine connection " (*e.g.*, that he or she was born or is resident there, even if not domiciled there (*see* D8(2)) at the time of the foreign divorce.

And, under the Matrimonial Causes (War Marriages) Act, 1944:

(e) In the special case of *marriages celebrated during the Second World War*, where: (i) the *husband* was, at the time of the marriage, domiciled *outside the United Kingdom*; (ii) the *wife* was, immediately before the marriage, *domiciled in England*; and (iii) the parties *never resided together* in the country which was the husband's domicil at the time of the marriage, the Divorce Division may deal with proceedings for divorce or nullity *as if both parties* were at all material times *domiciled in England*. (This provision was to cover the special cases of soldiers from the Dominions or Colonies, the United States or other foreign countries who, while stationed here during the War, married English girls and had to go back to their own countries, *leaving their wives behind*—in some instances without communicating with them again.)

## RECENT CHANGES IN THE LAW

Important changes in the law have been effected by Acts of Parliament in 1958, 1965, and 1967:

**A.1.** In any agreement for maintenance made between spouses, without recourse to a Court, any restriction against applying to a Court for changes in financial arrangements is void, but the other provisions are valid and enforceable. " Financial arrangements " mean provisions governing rights and liabilities towards each of the spouses while living apart, including cases where the marriage may be dissolved or annulled, and rights and duties regarding the maintenance of a child of the family.

2. Where there has been a change of circumstances since the agreement was made, causing provisions to have been included or omitted, or where the agreement does not make proper provision for the children, the High Court or a Magistrates' Court may vary or revoke those clauses and insert others which appear to the Court to be just.

3. Neither 1 nor 2 (above) precludes the right of either spouse to apply for an order containing " financial arrangements " under some other Act.

4. Where a maintenance agreement provides for continuing payments after the death of a party who dies after 16 August 1957, the surviving party may, within six months from probate or letters of administration (D18(2)) or, with the Court's leave, at any time before the estate is fully administered, apply to the High Court for an order under 2 above. The legal personal representatives (D18(2)) are not liable for distributing the estate after the expiration of the six months without taking these provisions into account; but the surviving spouse is not precluded from claiming from the beneficiary.

5. These provisions do not apply to any sum payable under a maintenance agreement made before 17 August 1957; and 1 (above) does not apply unless at least four-fifths of the estate is left after providing for funeral and legal expenses and debts, and no liability falls upon the legal personal representatives.

**B.1.** The powers of the Divorce Division and of Magistrates' Courts to provide for the *custody, maintenance, and education of the children* of the family (D29(2)) are enlarged to apply also to a *child of one of the parties* (including an *illegitimate* or *adopted* child) " who has been accepted as one of the family by the other party," as they apply to a child (whether legitimate or illegitimate) of *both parties*. All such children are referred to as " children of the family ", or " relevant children ".

2. Where a husband has been *guilty of wilful neglect to provide reasonable maintenance* for his wife or infant children (D30(2)), enabling the Divorce Division to order the husband to make *periodical payments* to the wife, the words " infant children " are to include any *illegitimate* or *adopted child* of both parties, and the Court may make orders for *custody of and access to* (D29(2)) any such children. If the Court considers it in the *child's best interests*, it may order the periodical payments for the child's benefit to be made *to the child* itself, or *to some other person* on the child's behalf, instead of to the wife (D30(1)).

3. The 1965 Act contains further enlightened and much-needed reforms for the *protection of the relevant children* in matrimonial proceedings (whether defended or undefended). The Court, generally speaking, is *not* to pronounce a decree of *judicial separation* (D29(1)), or make *absolute* any decree for *divorce or nullity* (D29(2)), unless and until the Court is satisfied *either*—

(a) that arrangements have been made for the *care and upbringing* of every such child under 16, and that such arrangements are satisfactory or the best that can be devised in the circumstances, *or*

(b) that it is impracticable for the party or parties appearing before the Court to make any such arrangements

But the Court *may* proceed without observing these requirements if: (i) there are *special reasons* against delay, and (ii) either or both of the parties have given to the Court a *satisfactory undertaking* to bring the question of such arrangements for the children before the Court within a specified time. The Report of the Committee set up by the Archbishop of Canterbury (D29(1)) would refuse a decree *nisi* (D28(2)) until satisfactory arrangements for the children are made.

4. On any application to the Court for *special leave* to present a divorce petition *within three years from the date of marriage* (D27(1)), the Judge must consider, not only the *possibility of a reconciliation* between the parties and the *interests of the children of the family* (which was his duty under the Act of 1950), but also the interests of any child referred to in para. B.1 above.

5. Even if proceedings for divorce, nullity, or judicial separation are *dismissed*, the Court may still make provision for the custody, maintenance and education of any child referred to in para. B.1 above, and may vary such orders from time to time.

6. Finally, the Court is given power, in exceptional circumstances, to commit the care of any such child *either*: (i) to a *county council* or *county borough council, or* (ii) to an *independent person* under the *supervision* (if the Court think fit) of a *welfare officer* or of a county council or county borough council. Further powers are conferred on *Local Authorities* by the Children and Young Persons Act, 1963.

C.1. The words " continuously under care and treatment " (in relation to a spouse of unsound mind) (D27(1)) are to be interpreted *more liberally and more broadly* (in various ways) then has been the practice of the Court in the past.

2. A person who has *deserted* his or her spouse and is now of *unsound mind* may be regarded (for the purpose of divorce or judicial spearation) as *capable of forming the intention of continuing* the desertion, if the Court takes the view that the " deserting " party would in any event have stayed away (even if no unsoundness of mind had supervened). (*Note.* Hitherto the Petitioner has faced almost insuperable difficulties in such cases, since it is not normally possible to attribute to a person of unsound mind the capability of forming any " intention " whatsoever (D9(1)). *See also* Cruelty—D27(ii) (c), and D28 (c).

3. Where the Petitioner is seeking *divorce* on the ground of the Respondent's *desertion* without cause for at least *three years* preceding the presentation of the petition (D27(1)), any *agreement for separation* (whether in writing or not), entered into before *1st January 1938*, shall be *disregarded* by the Court if either: (*a*) the Respondent *had already deserted* the Petitioner, or (*b*) the Court is satisfied that the *circumstances* in which the agreement was made would have amounted to desertion (*without cause*) by the Respondent but for the Petitioner's apparent consent, in the agreement, to a separation.

(*Note.* Desertion did not become a ground for divorce until *1st January 1938*. Some deserted spouses may have entered into separation agreements, inadvertently, *before* that date, and this provision is intended to mitigate hardship where there was (at that time) a genuine case of desertion but the case was ruined by the signature of a written agreement to live apart, or by some form of spoken words or conduct, on the part of the deserted party, appearing to signify consent to the separation.)

D.1. Maintenance Orders *made by the High Court* (or a County Court) may be *registered in a Magistrate's Court*, which is given power to *vary* and to *enforce* such Orders. Maintenance Orders *made by a Magistrates' Court* may be *registered in the High Court*, which is given power to *enforce* such Orders. (The purpose of such registration is to make enforcement more easily effective; in some cases it may be more convenient for the wife to resort to High Court procedure; in others to proceed in the Magistrates' Courts.)

2. If the spouse (usually the husband) liable for payments under a Maintenance Order is a person *in employment*, and if his maintenance payments are at least four weeks *in arrear*, then the Court may make an *Attachment of Earnings Order.* This Order will *authorise and direct his employer to deduct from his earnings* certain sums (which the Court will specify), to be handed over *by the employer* to an official of the Court, who will pass them on to the wife as instalments towards the payment of: (*a*) the arrears, and (*b*) the amounts currently falling due under the original Maint~nance Order. (*Note.* Hitherto the Courts have had no power to compel employers to collect such payments out of the defaulting husband's earnings; the wife's only remedy has been to ask for an order committing the defaulting husband to prison—a procedure which gave her *no financial redress or assistance.*)

The *Attachment of Earnings Order* will also specify the " protected earnings rate "—*i.e.*, the rate below which the Court thinks the defaulting husband's earnings should *not* be reduced by virtue of the authorised deductions. (*Note.* In other words, the Court will see that the defaulter is left with a reasonable part of his earnings to live on.)

E.1. The Court is given power to make an order against the Respondent (D27(1)) for financial pro-

vision (D30 (1)) in favour of the Petitioner (D27(1)) or the children, *either* at the time of the decree *nisi* (D29(2)) *or* at any subsequent date; but the Court is not to disregard any delay on the part of the Petitioner in applying for such financial provision.

2. The Court is given power to set aside (*i.e.*, cancel the effect of) any disposition of property by a Respondent husband (or former husband) in favour of some third party, if that disposition of property has been made within the past three years (preceding the Petitioner's application for financial provision), and seems to have been made with the intention of defeating or frustrating the Petitioner's application. But no such disposition of property is to be set aside if it was made *for valuable consideration* in favour of a *person who acted in good faith* and without knowing of the Respondent's intention to defeat or frustrate the Petitioner's application. (*Note.* This will enable the Court to protect a wife, in certain circumstances, if the Respondent husband (or former husband) has (for example) transferred part of his property to his mistress, with the intention of defeating his wife's claim to maintenance, alimony, *etc.* Up to now the Court has had no power to remedy such action by a husband who has made a transfer of the kind *prior to* a Court Order for maintenance, *etc.*) *See also* Lump Sum orders, D30 (e), and Matrimonial Homes Act, 1967 (H below).

3. The power of the Court to order " reasonable provision for maintenance " out of the estate of a deceased person (D16(2)), in a case where his will or intestacy does not leave his wife " reasonably " provided for, is now extended to benefit a *former wife* (*i.e.*, " a woman whose marriage with him was during his lifetime dissolved or annulled.") (*Note.* This definition is not limited to a former wife who was the " innocent " party in divorce proceedings; but the Court has a discretion to make or refuse the order, taking all the circumstances into account.) Such an order may be discharged, varied, suspended or revised at the suit of various interested parties.

4. The Court's powers under paras. 2 and 3 (above) are extended to protect: (*a*) a *former husband* whose former wife has divorced him, or obtained a judicial separation against him, on the ground of *his insanity* (D27(1)), or (*b*) where the Court has ordered a settlement of the wife's property, or " periodical payments " out of her income, where there has been a decree for restitution of conjugal rights (D28(1)).

5. The executors or administrators (D18(2)) of the deceased spouse are not to be liable if, when a claim under para. 3 is made, they have already distributed the deceased's estate (provided they waited for 6 month after the Grant of Probate or Letters of Administration (D18(2)); but the claimant under para. 3 can follow the property into the hands of a beneficiary and recover it (if it is still available) by means of an order under para. 3 (above).

6. Under the Married Women's Property Act, 1882, the Court was given power to decide in a *summary manner* (*i.e.*, by a rapid and simple procedure) disputes between any husband and wife about the *ownership of any property.* That power is now extended to cases where the respondent spouse *has been, but no longer is,* in control of the property, or the *claimant does not know* whether it is still in the respondent's control or not. The Court may order the necessary enquiries to be made; in appropriate cases it may also order property in the hands of the respondent, or of a third party, *to be sold,* so that the claimant may have his or her share paid out of the proceeds.

F. The Court is given power to grant an injunction against any person who appears likely to dispose of property so as to defeat any of the provisions of E (above) or to transfer such property abroad.

G. If any question arises as to the right of a husband or wife to money derived from any allowance made by the husband for housekeeping, or any similar expenses, or to any property acquired out of such money, the money or property (in the absence of agreement to the contrary) shall be treated as belonging to them both in equal shares. (The old rule was that the wife's savings out of housekeeping allowances belonged to the husband.)

H.1. Following certain Court decisions, on equitable grounds (D4–5), the Matrimonial Homes Act, 1967, *protects* the rights of either spouse to *remain in occupation of the matrimonial home, even if it belongs to the other spouse.* If already in occupation, he or she is *not to be evicted* except with leave of the Court; if not in occupation, he or she *may enter and occupy the home.* The Court has power to enforce, restrict or terminate these rights, *having regard to the conduct of both* spouses, *their needs and financial resources,* those of the *children,* and all the *circumstances.* The Court's powers include the right to *except part of the home* from a spouse's occupation, to order one spouse in occupation to make *periodical* payments in respect of such occupation, and to *impose on either* obligations for *repairing, maintaining* or *discharging liabilities* on the home. Any payment made by the occupying spouse towards satisfaction of the other *spouse's* liabilities for *rent, rates, mortgage payments,* etc., shall count as if it were made by the other spouse. Occupation of the home by one spouse shall be *treated as possession by the other spouse* if he or she is *protected by the Rent Control* provisions (D34(1)); but this shall not affect any right of the occupying spouse against the other under any Act or Order. These rights are to *last only so long* as the marriage subsists, unless provision is made ((2) below) for such rights to be a *charge* on the other spouse's ownership or lease.

2. If one spouse is *entitled in law* to *occupy* the house as *owner* or *lessee,* the *other spouse's rights* of occupation shall be a *charge* on the first spouse's *title* (D22(2)), from the date of acquisition of the right, the marriage, and the coming into force of the Act. The right shall be *terminated* (a) *by death of the second spouse,* or (b) *by the termination of the marriage (unless the Court otherwise orders).* Any *surrender* of ownership or tenancy shall be *subject to these rights;* so also shall *bankruptcy* of the owner or lessee. The rights on *any one home* may be *registered* at the Land Registry for the second spouse's protection; only a *mortgagee* (D22) *can enforce his rights* against both spouses.

3. If the owner or lessee *contracts to sell or let* his *legal estate* (D22(2)) in the home, such *registered charge must be cancelled before* vacant possession can be promised. The Chief Land Registrar shall cancel the charge if either spouse is dead, or on a divorce or nullity decree (D25(2), D29(2)), or under a Court Order. A spouse entitled to such protection may release his or her rights in writing.

4. If the Rent Control Acts (D34(1)) apply, and there is a *decree absolute* (D29(2)) of *divorce or nullity,* the *Court may direct* that the ownership or lease be *transferred to the former spouse* if he or she was not already owner or lessee, and the originally protected spouse shall no longer be protected. Or the *Court may direct that both spouses,* together or separately, shall be *liable for any obligations* in respect of the home; but the *landlord* must have an opportunity of being *heard by the Court.* (This paragraph does not affect the rights in paragraph (1) above.)

(*Note:* Broadly, these provisions *prevent* a husband or wife who is owner or lessee of the matrimonial home from turning out the other spouse after the marriage has been broken up).

# STATUTORY REFORMS IN LAW OF LANDLORD AND TENANT

## (1) Business Tenancies

Under the *Landlord and Tenant Act, 1954, Part II* (and cases decided under it) *security of tenure* is granted (under certain conditions) to a lessee or under-lessee who *occupies premises for the purpose of a trade, business, profession or employment* carried on by him on the premises. (We shall refer to such premises as " *the holding* ".) The holding may not be used as business premises, and there is no security, if the lease or tenancy agreement prohibits their use as such, unless permission has been given by the lessee's (or under-lessee's) landlord to that effect. *Tenancies excluded* from protection include agricultural holdings, mining leases, on-licensed premises (except certain hotels and restaurants) and tenancies not exceeding three months, unless the tenant and the person who carried on the same business there before him have occupied the premises for more than six months altogether.

A holding is protected by the Act by the provision that the *tenancy does not automatically come to an end* on the date specified in the original lease, but only (i) *if the landlord gives to the tenant not less than six nor more than twelve months notice* in writing to terminate the tenancy; (ii) *if the tenant gives to the landlord, within a similar period, a request for a new tenancy;* (iii) where the tenancy is for a *fixed period,* if the *tenant gives at least three months notice* (expiring at the end of the period or on any quarter day afterwards) *that he does not want the tenancy continued;* (iv) if it is a *periodic tenancy* (from month to month or year to year), the *tenant gives the landlord notice to quit,* of the full legal length; (v) if the tenancy is *surrendered* or (vi) if the tenancy is *forfeited* (which can be done by the landlord only on a Court application). In cases *(i) and (ii),* the *parties may agree* to fresh terms for a new tenancy. It is *vital* in such cases that the *time-table* laid down in the Act shall be adhered to, and the *advice of a solicitor* should be sought *at least twelve months before the end of the lease;* if any request or application is out of time,

the Court cannot help the party in question. The twelve months or six months *notice of termination* (see above) *must not expire* earlier than the date of expiry of the original lease.

Where (i) the landlord serves the notice of termination: (a) it must require the *tenant, within two months of the notice being given, to notify the landlord whether or not he is willing to give up possession* on the specified date; (b) it must state *whether or not the landlord will oppose an application to the Court* for a new tenancy, and if so on what grounds. Four of the grounds are that the tenant has neglected repairs or payment of rent for which he is liable or committed some other breach of his lease, or that the landlord has offered reasonable alternative accommodation. Three further grounds are: (e) that the existing tenancy is an underlease of part of premises held under the head lease, and the separate lettings would produce a lower total rent than if the whole were let together; (f) that on the termination of the current tenancy the *landlord intends to demolish or reconstruct* the holding or a substantial part, and could not reasonably do so without obtaining possession of the whole; (g) finally, that on the termination of the current tenancy, the *landlord intends to occupy the holding* for the purposes of a business to be carried on by him, or as his residence. (But the landlord *may not oppose* the grant of a *new lease on this final ground* if his interest was purchased or created within *five years* immediately preceding the termination of the lease.)

If the *tenant* prefers to *request a new tenancy,* he must propose to the landlord that it shall commence not more than twelve nor less than six months from the date of request; but the commencement must *not be earlier than the date of expiry* of his existing lease. The tenant must also propose the period of the new lease, the rent he is willing to pay and the other particulars of the proposed new tenancy. The tenant cannot make such request (a) if the landlord has already served a termination notice, or (b) if the tenant has served notice to quit; nor can either (a) or (b) take place after the tenant's request for a new tenancy.

*Within two months after the tenant's request*, the landlord must serve on the tenant notice stating on which of the above grounds (if any) he will oppose the Court's grant of a new tenancy. The parties cannot make any agreement to the effect that the Act shall not apply.

The next step is for the *tenant, not less than two months nor more than four months after the landlord's termination notice or the tenant's request* for a new tenancy, *to apply to the County Court*, which *must grant him a new tenancy* on such terms as the parties may agree on or the Court thinks fit, unless the landlord establishes any of the above grounds of objection. If the *landlord's objections are false*, the Court will grant the tenant *damages*.

*If the landlord establishes any of grounds* (e), (f) or (g), so that the Court cannot grant a new tenancy, the Court orders the *landlord to pay to the tenant compensation for disturbance*. If the tenant has carried on *business* on the holding *for the whole of fourteen years* preceding the termination, the compensation is *twice the net rateable value;* if for a *lesser period, a sum equal to the rateable value*.

If the above procedure is carried out, the *old tenancy continues* in effect *until the final disposal of the case*, even if the lease has expired meanwhile. "*Final disposal*" includes any necessary *time for appeal*.

### (2) Residential Tenancies

*Under the Rent Act, 1965, security of tenure* is provided for *tenants of dwellings* with *rateable value* (a) *up to £400 a year in the Metropolitan Police District* and *£200 elsewhere* (including (b) those still controlled by the old Rent Restriction Acts 1920 to 1939, which now apply only to very small and low-rated dwellings.) The Act imposes a *standstill on present rents* (except variations of rents including rates, cost of services and owner's improvements). *Rent officers or assessment committees* can *revise rents* in category (a). The protected tenancies under (a) are called "*regulated tenancies*" Certain *statutory tenancies* of *formerly requisitioned dwellings* (which would have *expired on March 31, 1966*) are continued after that date as regulated tenancies. *Occupiers who are not tenants* (i.e. those in occupation *necessarily because of their employment*, such as caretakers) *are included* under the term "tenants". A tenancy of which a non-profit-making Housing Association is landlord is exempt from regulation).

The task of the *rent officers and rent assessment committees* is to *fix fair rents* on application of landlord or tenant, or both, in counties, county boroughs, London boroughs and the City of London. They are *to take into account all the* circumstances, age, character, locality and state of repair of the dwelling; but *disrepair due to the*

*tenant's neglect* and *improvements by the tenant* are to be *disregarded*, as is *also any great demand (exceeding supply) of dwellings in the district*. The fixed rents are to be registered, and must *include payments for furniture and services (if any)*. *If the landlord pays rates*, that fact is to be noted, and the *registered rent plus the rates may be recovered from the tenant*. If the cost of services, or of repairs to be done by the landlord, is a variable sum, the registered terms must say so. The landlord cannot lawfully recover more than the registered rent, taking the above variations into account.

It is *unlawful for any person* (with intent to *cause the residential occupier to give up occupation* or to refrain from pursuing his rights or remedies) to do anything calculated *to interfere with his peace or comfort* or *persistently to withdraw or withhold services* reasonably required for occupation. "Residential occupier" means a person occupying the premises as a residence, either by contract or by any Act of Parliament. The penalty is a fine up to £100 or imprisonment up to six months or both, before the magistrates, for a first offence, and a fine up to £500 or the imprisonment, or both, for a subsequent conviction. The *occupier*, even if the premises are not "protected" (i.e., not subject to the Rent Restrictions Acts or certain other statutes) *cannot lawfully be evicted even when* the tenancy has terminated and the occupier continues to reside there, *without leave of the Court*. *In default*, the owner is liable, on conviction before the magistrates, to a *fine up to £100 or six months' imprisonment or both*—unless he can prove that he reasonably believed that the occupier had ceased to reside in the premises. *Occupiers protected* are the tenant or *former tenant*, a lawful *subtenant*, and the widow or widower, or any member of the family of either, residing with the occupier at his death.

The demand for or taking of a premium as a condition of the grant, renewal, continuance or transfer of a *protected tenancy* (in addition to the rent) *is forbidden* (except in case of expenses, paid by the outgoing tenant, for a period after the transfer, or improvements he has paid for, or as a refund to the outgoing tenant of any reasonable premium which he himself paid on taking possession, or (if part of the premises are business premises) for goodwill transferred to the incoming tenant.) There are also *restrictions on the demand for, or taking of, a premium in relation to a "regulated tenancy*"; broadly speaking, a premium is lawful only if the tenancy or its continuance is for more *than seven years*—and then only if the registered rent is higher than the rent payable under the tenancy.

There are wide provisions regarding the protection of occupiers of furnished dwellings and regarding mortgages.

(*Note:* Parliament has recently passed legislation to reform the leasehold system for residential property (D21)).

# ADOPTION OF CHILDREN

Adoption is the act of a person who takes upon himself the position of parent to a child who is not in law his own legitimate child. It has been for centuries very common in India and most Continental countries, and for over a hundred years in most parts of the United States. It was recognised by the laws of Greece and Rome from early times. Julius Caesar adopted his grand-nephew Octavian (afterwards the Emperor Augustus) in 46 B.C. But there was no provision for adoption under the Common Law of England (D4); the transfer of parental rights and duties in respect of a child to another person was unknown to our law until 1926, when the first of a series of Adoption Acts was passed. There have been a number of amendments since then. The present law is mainly contained in the Adoption Acts 1958 and 1968. "Informal adoption," outside the Acts, is invalid. (But under the Adoption Act, 1968, adoptions effected under the law of certain foreign

countries may be recognised by the English courts.)

The procedure for adoption is as follows:

(1) Approach by would-be adopters to a registered Adoption Society or Local Authority for help in adopting a child, and explanations of their qualifications.

(2) Investigations of suitability of persons and home, including medical matters, and notification to parent(s) of eventual need for formal consent and effects of Order when made.

(3) Informal consent of parents or guardian to handing over of child to would-be adopters "on trial."

(4) Actual handing over of child to would-be adopters "on trial."

(5) Formal application by would-be adopters to a Court.

(6) Formal consent of parents to adoption.

(7) Hearing by the Court. If an Order is refused, and there is no appeal, the child must be returned to its parent(s), or to the Local Authority if the parents are unsuitable. There may be an appeal, while the child is still in the hands of the Applicants, to the Court of Appeal and the House of Lords. If the original application, or appeal, succeeds, an Order is made. *Then, and only then is the child adopted.*

We shall now explain the sequence in more detail.

**Applications for Adoption.**—The would-be adopters (the "Applicants") normally approach a registered Adoption Society, a County Council or County Borough Council to make and participate in adoption arrangements, which must eventually be confirmed by an Order of the High Court, a County Court, or a Magistrates' Court hearing juvenile cases. The Adoption Society or Local Authority carefully investigates the suitability of the Applicants, interviews them and sees their home, and ascertains the religion in which the parents wish the child to be brought up. The Applicants must produce a certificate from a registered medical practitioner to the effect that they are in good health, as must the parents of the child to certify that its health is good. The Society or Local Authority must hand the parents a memorandum, in ordinary language, explaining the effects of an Adoption Order if made by the Court, and calling attention to the parents' formal consent being eventually required. Such consent may be withdrawn at any time before the Order is actually made, but may be dispensed with by the Court on special grounds (see below, D35(2)).

If all these preliminary matters are satisfactory the Society or Council may hand the child over provisionally to the Applicants for a "trial period" of not less than three consecutive months preceding the Order, if made; but no period is counted before the child is six weeks old. No maximum period is laid down by law within which the Applicants must apply to the Court. This is regarded by reformers as a serious defect in procedure. In a recent case (December 1965) nearly two years had elapsed between the handing over of the child "on trial" to the would-be adopters in their home, and the Court hearing. The parents of the child were F, a married man, and his mistress M, a single woman, both Roman Catholics. Without the knowledge of F, M arranged to hand over the child to the would-be adopters (X and Y, also Roman Catholics but "strangers" of good repute), whose home was eminently suitable and who would have made excellent adopters. (A "stranger" is anyone who is not a "parent" or "relative".) The child remained in their care and possession from the age of six weeks to two years. Meanwhile F had left M and had become reconciled with his wife. He complained, shortly before the Court heard the case, that his formal consent had not been obtained, and claimed the right for himself to have access to and custody of the child under the Legitimacy Act 1959; his wife supported his application. The result of the delay was that the High Court Judge, having seen and heard all parties, decided reluctantly that there was little to choose between F and his wife, on the one hand, and the Applicants X and Y; but felt that the "blood-tie" between father and child justified refusing an Order to the "strangers," and ordered the child to be handed over to F and his wife (who in due course applied for an Adoption Order). X and Y appealed to the Court of Appeal, but two out of three Judges upheld the original Judge's decision, and a further appeal to the House of Lords failed. Thus the child, two years old, was taken away from the only "parents" it had ever known and handed over to F and his wife whom the child did not know at all. This is an unusual case, but a very sad one, and reformers consider that there should be a maximum period of (say) six months, within which the Applicants must apply to the Court for an Order,

and the parents should be compelled to decide within that period whether or not they are prepared to give formal written consent to the proposed adoption. (The Chancery Division of the High Court has recently issued directions to speed up administrative work on adoptions.)

Formal consent may be dispensed with by the Court if a parent, or his or her wife or husband, cannot be found, is incapable of consenting, or is living apart in what seems likely to be a permanent separation. A parent's consent may also be dispensed with if he or she has abandoned, neglected, or ill-treated the child, or is "unreasonably" refusing consent. If the parent does not attend the Court hearing, that consent must be given in writing, witnessed by a J.P., County Court officer, or Magistrate's Clerk; or outside England by a British Consul or Vice-Consul or foreign Notary.

None of the provisions relating to consent applies to the proposed adoption of an infant who is not a U.K. national; but such adoption must conform to the internal law of the country of which he is a national (Act of 1968).

As soon as an application to the Court is filed by the Applicants, the Official Solicitor (or, in Magistrates' Court cases, the Children's Officer of the Local Authority) is appointed the child's guardian *ad litem* (*i.e.*, guardian for the purpose of the proceedings, who looks after the interests of the child without regard to those of anybody else). If no appointment for the Court hearing is made within 15 days from the application to the Court, the guardian *ad litem* must apply for the Court's directions. (This is a new rule, to avoid executive delay). The Court then hears the case *in camera* (*i.e.*, in private, the public not being admitted) and has a complete discretion either to make or to refuse an Adoption Order. If refused, and there is no appeal, the child must be returned to its parent(s) or, if they are unsuitable, placed in the care of the Local Authority. If an Order is made or the Applicant(s) successfully appeal, the child remains with the Applicant(s): only on the making of an *Adoption Order* by the Court is the child legally adopted.

**Adoption Orders.**—The High Court, a County Court, or a Magistrates' Juvenile Court may make an Adoption Order authorising an Applicant, in the prescribed manner, to adopt a child. An Order may be made on the application of two spouses jointly, or by one spouse with the consent of the other spouse; but in no other case may an Order be made in favour of more than one person. (Dispensing with consent—*see Applications for Adoption*, para 3). An Order may be made authorising the adoption of an illegitimate or legitimated child, or the re-adoption of an already adopted child (*e.g.*, in case of the death of the Adopter(s)), by his or her mother or natural father, either alone or jointly with his or her spouse: this facilitates the adoption of illegitimate or legitimated children and puts them (for record purposes) on a par with legitimate children who have been adopted. (A legitimated child is one born out of wedlock, but whose parents have subsequently married).

An adoption Order may not generally be made in England unless the Applicant and the child are living in England. (But see Act of 1968, above.) Nor may an Order be made unless the Applicant (or one of two Applicants) is: (a) the mother or father of the illegitimate or legitimated child (with the other parent's consent); or (b) a "relative," *i.e.*, a grandparent, brother, sister, uncle, or aunt of the child, or a person who would be such relative if the child were the legitimate child of its mother or father, or of former adopters, and such relative is aged 21 or over; or (c) in any other case, is 25 years old or more. On the application of a sole male Applicant to adopt a female child, no Order may be made unless the Court is satisfied that there are "special circumstances" justifying an Adoption Order "as an exceptional measure."

No Adoption Order may be made unless the child has been continuously in the care and possession of the Applicant for at least three consecutive months immediately preceding the Order (not counting any time before the infant is six weeks old); this is subject to the safeguards detailed below as to supervision of a " protected child." (But in the case of Applicants domiciled (D8) outside Great Britain, who desire to adopt an infant under the law of the country of domicil, and to obtain a provisional Adoption Order in England, the child may be taken or sent abroad for the purpose first mentioned and the period of three consecutive months is extended to six). Except where one of the Applicants is a parent of the child, no Order is to be made in respect of that child who, at the hearing, is below the upper limit of the compulsory school age, unless the Applicant has given notice, in writing, to the Local Authority of his intention, at least three months (in cases of provisional adoption, six months) before the Court Hearing.

**Formal Consents Required.**—No Order may be ordinarily made without the consent of every person who is a parent or guardian of the child (which may be given either unconditionally or subject to conditions as to the religion in which the parent or guardian requires the child to be brought up). Even so, the consent of the parent or guardian may be dispensed with (*see Applications*, para 3). Where a parent or guardian has given informal consent without knowing the identity of the Applicant(s), and subsequently withdraws his or her consent solely on this ground, he or she is deemed to be witholding consent " unreasonably." (*See also* Act of 1968, above.)

**Matters on which the Court must be satisfied.**—Before making the Order the Court must be satisfied:

(a) that every person whose consent is necessary, and has not been dispensed with, has consented to and understands the nature and effect of the proposed Adoption Order; in particular that every parent understands that the effect will be to deprive him or her permanently of his or her parental rights;

(b) that the proposed Order will be for the child's welfare;

(c) that the Applicant has not received or agreed to receive, and that no person has made or given, or agreed to make or give, any payment or other reward, in consideration of the adoption, except such as the Court may sanction (if any).

As to (a), the Court must have regard to the Applicant's health, to be evidenced by the certificate of a fully registered medical practitioner; the Court shall also give due consideration to the wishes of the child, having regard to his or her age and understanding. The Court may impose such terms and conditions as it thinks fit, including a requirement that the adopter shall make such financial provision for the child as is just and expedient. It may postpone a decision on the application and make an interim order giving the Applicant *custody* of the child for a probationary period not exceeding two years, upon such terms as it may think fit, for the maintenance, education, and supervision of the child's welfare. The same rules apply to an interim order for custody, as to consent and dispensing with consent, as for a final Adoption Order; but the Court may not make an interim order without the three months' care and possession and notice to the Local Authority as are provided above. An interim custody order for less than two years may be extended to the full two years, but no longer. An interim order for custody is not an Adoption Order.

**Procedure and Appeals.**—To safeguard the child's interests during the hearing the Court has to appoint a guardian *ad litem* (*see Applications for Adoption*, para 5).

**Effects of Adoption Orders.**—Upon an Order being made, all rights, duties, obligations, and liabilities of the parents or guardians in relation to custody, maintenance, and education of the child, including rights to appoint a guardian by will, to consent or refuse consent to its marriage, shall be extinguished; and all such rights, etc., shall be exercisable by, and enforceable against, the Adopter(s) as if the child were his, her, or their legitimate child, and the child shall stand to the Adopter(s) in the same position. If two spouses are the Adopters, they shall stand to each other and to the child (for the purpose of court orders (D29(2), 31(2)) as if they were his lawful father and mother, and the child shall stand to them in the same relation.

For the purpose of the marriage laws, an Adopter and Adoptee shall be regarded as if they were within the prohibited degrees of blood relationship—even if a later Adoption Order is made in favour of another person (*i.e.*, an Adopter may not in any circumstances marry the Adoptee).

**Succession to Property.**—If, after an Adoption Order, the Adopter or Adoptee dies without a will in respect of any property, the property shall devolve as if the Adoptee were the lawful child of the Adopter (D18–20) and not the child of any other person. In any disposition of property made by will, codicil or settlement (D16, 20) after an Adoption Order, a reference to the " child or children " of the Adopter shall include a reference to the Adoptee (unless the contrary intention appears). The will or codicil is treated as having been made at the Adopter's death. But any reference to the " child or children " of the natural parents (or either of them) shall not include a reference to the Adoptee. And any reference to a " relative " of the Adopter shall (unless the contrary intention appears) be regarded as a reference to the person who would be such a relative if the Adopter were his lawful parent. (But these provisions do not apply to any dignity or title of honour—*e.g.*, a hereditary peerage).

For the purposes of the Administration of Estates Act, 1925 (D18–19), an Adoptee shall be regarded as a brother or sister of any child or adopted child of the Adopter. Executors and administrators (D18–19) are not liable if they distribute the estate of the Adopter without ascertaining that no Adoption Order has been made; but the Adoptee may sue the beneficiary for the Adoptee's share of the property; if there has been more than one Adoption Order, the earlier adoption shall be disregarded.

**Citizenship.**—If the Adoptee was not a citizen of the United Kingdom and Colonies (D8) but the Adopter or male Adopter is, the Adoptee shall be such a citizen as from the date of the Adoption Order.

**Registration.**—The Registrar-General is to keep an Adopted Children's Register, to contain authorised entries but no others. A certified copy of the entries counts as evidence; the index may be searched by anybody, who may obtain a certified copy of any entry. No other record may be seen by the public without a Court Order. Every entry shows only its number, date, and country of birth of the child, the name and adopted surname of the child and of the Adopters, the date of the Adoption Order and of the Court, the date of entry, and signature of the Registrar. The word " adopted " or " re-adoption " is written against the name of the child in the Register of Births; but this shall be cancelled if an Adoption Order is refused or an appeal against adoption succeeds.

If a child adopted by its mother or natural father is subsequently legitimated by their marriage, the Court of Adoption may, on their application, revoke the Adoption Order and the entries in the register and any certificate shall be cancelled (and the parents' names substituted).

Local Authorities and Adoption Societies.—Except for the Local Authorities or registered Adoption Societies mentioned at the commencement of *Applications for Adoption*, para 1, no other body may make adoption arrangements; and even the authorised bodies may not place the child in the care and possession of a would-be adopter if the last-named person could not lawfully adopt him, under the penalty of a fine of £100 or six months' imprisonment; and the Court may order the child to be returned to his parent(s) or guardian(s) or to the Local Authority or registered Adoption Society. There are strict provisions as to which Adoption Societies may be registered or struck off the register, and as to appeals.

Care and Possession of Infants awaiting Adoption.—While an application is pending, a parent or guardian who has assented may not, without the court's leave, remove the infant from the care and possession of the Applicant; the Court will not give leave without considering the infant's welfare. The parent(s) or guardian(s) may not take back an infant, in the care and possession of any Applicant, before the actual Adoption Order, and must give written notice to the Authority or Society (before an Adoption Order is made) of the parent's or guardian's intention to part with the child, in which case the child must be handed to the Applicant(s) through the Authority or the Society. Only in cases where the adoption application is refused by the Court or on appeal, may the child be returned to or retained by the parent or guardian.

Supervision.—Where arrangements have been made for placing a child, below the upper limit of compulsory school age, in the care and possession of a " stranger," or where notice of intention to apply for an Adoption Order is given, then the child is known as a " protected child " while it is in the care and possession of a " stranger "; but not if it is in an Approved School or some other home under the Children's Acts. The child ceases to be a " protected child " at the age of 18, or on the making of an Adoption Order. It is the duty of every Local Authority to see that every " protected child " is periodically visited by its officers, who shall satisfy themselves of the child's well-being and give such advice as may be needed. The officers must produce a document of authority, and may then inspect any premises where the child is kept or to be kept. It is the duty of any " stranger " to give notice of all arrangements with regard to " protected children," including any change of address, and particulars of the name, sex, date and place of birth, and name and address of the parent(s) or guardian(s) or person(s) from whom the child is received. In the event of a " protected child's " death, the person(s) having care and possession must give written notice to the Authority. If neither the Local Authority nor a registered Adoption Society took part in the arrangements, and it appears to the Authority that such arrangements would be detrimental to the child, the Authority may in writing prohibit the proposed Adopters from keeping the child in any premises, subject to appeal to a Juvenile Court. If the Court is satisfied that a " protected child " is received or about to be received by an unfit person, or in non-approved premises, the Court may order his removal to a place of safety until he can be restored to his parent(s) or guardian(s) or relative(s). On proof that there is imminent danger to the child's health or well-being, this power may be exercised by a J.P. A Local Authority may receive any child so removed (even if not a " protected child " and even if he is over 17) informing the parent(s) or guardian(s) of what has been done. There are heavy penalties for any contravention by a " stranger " of these provisions.

A warrant may be issued, in the event of refusal to allow a visit, or the inspection of premises by an authorised person.

General.—It is generally unlawful to give any payment in consideration of the adoption of a child, any grant of consent (*i.e.*, formal or informal) in connection therewith, the transfer of care and possession, the making of arrangements for adoption—penalty, fine £100 and/or six months' imprisonment; but this does not apply to payment of a registered Adoption Society's expenses, or any payment authorised by a Court. No advertisement may be published indicating the desire of the parent(s) or guardian(s) to have his, her, or their child adopted, that a person desires to adopt a child, or that any person (except a Local Authority or registered Adoption Society) can make such arrangements—penalty, fine £50.

Detailed Court Rules have been made for the carrying out of these arrangements.

There are five Schedules to the 1958 Act. Schedule III, the most important, sets out the nature and purposes of the Regulations which every Adoption Society must have.

Every Adoption Society must set up a " case committee " of not less than three, to consider each individual case.

No child shall be delivered to the proposed Adopter until the latter has been interviewed by the case committee, who must inspect the premises where the child is to live permanently after all the reports have been considered.

Every Society must furnish a report on its activities and the prescribed accounts.

Provision must be made for the care and supervision of any child placed with a Society with a view to adoption.

There is a prohibition of or restriction upon disclosure of records kept by the Society, and provision for their safe keeping.

*Note:* The Law Commission has recommended a new branch of law called " Family Law " to include *all* matters relating to infants (including adoption, legitimation, care, custody, and control, as well as matters of marriage, divorce, and separation), to be supervised by one Division of the High Court, instead of sharing them (as at present) between the Chancery and Divorce Divisions.

# JUSTICES OF THE PEACE

Sentencing Policy.—The arrangements, announced at the end of May 1964, by the Lord Chief Justice, " for the purpose of achieving greater uniformity of sentencing policy and a deeper understanding of the many social factors involved," comprise the organisation of more and longer conferences of all holders of judicial office, including justices of the peace, chairmen of quarter sessions, recorders and High Court judges. Working parties, in groups, are to consider case histories of " offenders," and later meet to discuss the sentences which each group would have passed if these cases had come before them in court. On the same day it was announced from Downing Street that a Royal Commission was being appointed (under the chairmanship of Lord Amory (former Chancellor of the Exchequer)),

" to conduct a fundamental review of penal methods, the concepts and purposes which should underlie the punishment and treatment of offenders in England and Wales; to report how far they are realized by the penalties and methods of treatment available, and whether any changes are desirable in these, or in the arrangements and responsibility for selecting the sentences to be imposed on particular offenders; and to review the work of the services and institutions dealing with offenders and the responsibility for their administration, and to make recommendations."

Some of the Commission's recommendations are incorporated in the Criminal Justice Act, 1967 (D7).

**Compulsory Training of New J.P.s.**—Early in June 1964 the Lord Chancellor announced new arrangements for the *compulsory* training and instruction of newly-appointed justices of the peace, and fresh attempts to stop " glaring instances of inadequate, excessive or inconsistent sentences." An advisory council has re-organised the present scheme for *voluntary* training (which started in 1950), and every newly-appointed justice is to give an undertaking not to try cases, without the Lord Chancellor's authority, until he or she has been through a *compulsory* course. The course includes attending as observers in their own and other courts and at quarter sessions, and visits to prisons, borstals, and similar institutions.

**General Duties of J.P.s**—All these announcements have focused attention upon the work of justices of the peace—the unpaid, lay magistrates throughout the country who deal with the largest proportion of criminal offences, in various courts. Other manifold duties fall upon them—the appointment of special constables, certain matters relating to highways, the grant and renewal of licences for the sale of intoxicating liquors, " domestic proceedings " (matrimonial orders between husband and wife), custody of children and affiliation and adoption orders. Certain magistrates—both laymen and lawyers—with special qualifications sit in juvenile courts to deal with offences by and against young people, and with the committing of young people to the care of approved persons or authorities, whenever the young people are in need of care and protection.

Although, therefore, the criminal jurisdiction of J.P.s (as they are generally known) is by no means the full extent of their duties, it is this criminal jurisdiction which has been most frequently in the public eye; and the three announcements mentioned above relate only to that aspect of the J.P.s' duties. Neither historically nor currently are J.P.s expected to be lawyers; the clerk of the court, who advises them on points of law, is always a solicitor; and at quarter sessions the chairman and deputy chairman are usually barristers or solicitors of not less than ten years' standing, with special qualifications for the task.

**Procedure and Powers.**—For " domestic proceedings " and in juvenile courts (outside the City of London and the metropolitan stipendiary court area, where full-time, legally-qualified, paid magistrates preside), not more than three J.P.s should sit, including both a man and a woman, whenever practicable. For other duties not more than seven J.P.s (and, preferably, not more than five, and an odd, not even, number) should sit. The election of a chairman and a number of deputy-chairmen is held by the J.P.s in October; those elected hold office for one year from January 1, and are eligible for re-election. All sittings are held in public, except in " domestic proceedings," custody and adoption cases; and in these and in juvenile courts the press, though not usually excluded, are not permitted to identify the parties by name or address, or to publish evidence of an indecent character.

The powers of one single J.P., sitting alone, are restricted to adjourning a trial, remanding a prisoner in custody or on bail, and taking recognisances. An information charging an offence may be laid before him; if it is in writing, and substantiated on oath, he may issue a warrant; in a civil matter, in similar circumstances, he may issue a summons. Search warrants may, in most cases, be issued by a single J.P., and so may a summons or warrant requiring the attendance of a witness. A stipendiary (legally-qualified, paid, full-time istrate) is not so limited; he has all the

powers of a court of summary jurisdiction (*i.e.* two or more J.P.s sitting together).

**Criminal Jurisdiction.**—Except in those instances in which a special limit of time is prescribed by a particular Act of Parliament, no information may be laid (in regard to a criminal offence), nor complaint (in a civil case) after the lapse of six months from the date when the offence was committed or the matter of complaint arose. The J.P.s' criminal jurisdiction covers (1) the trial of " summary offences " (minor offences triable by a magistrates' court other than under (2) below) punishable by a maximum of six months imprisonment for one offence, or a fine (in general) not exceeding £100. The jurisdiction also extends to (2) certain "indictable" (or "arrestable") offences which may be tried summarily if the accused consents; in such cases the maximum punishments are 6 months imprisonment or a fine not exceeding £400, or both, for one such offence, or 12 months imprisonment for two or more such offences. There are also (3) certain petty offences which the accused or the prosecution may elect to be tried on indictment, before a jury at quarter sessions. No offender under the age of 17 may be sentenced to imprisonment by a court of summary jurisdiction; but such young offender may be sent to a detention centre. Alternatively, he may be committed, in custody, to quarter sessions for sentence to a period of borstal training. First offenders should not be sent to prison; they are frequently placed on probation.

One J.P. or more may sit as a court of preliminary enquiry to determine whether there is a *prima facie* case (*i.e.* one that calls for a defence) against an accused which will require his being indicted before a jury. For this purpose the J.P.s take depositions (that is, evidence given (*see* D6–7) under oath, by prosecution witnesses, and reduced to writing and signed by each witness who has given it). If the J.P.s decide, at the end of the hearing, that the prosecution has disclosed no *prima facie* case, the accused is discharged; if there is such a case, then after due warning to the accused that he is not obliged to say anything but that, if he does answer the charge, anything he says will be written down and may be used in evidence at his trial, he is committed for trial, on bail or in custody (according to the gravity of the charge), at quarter sessions or assizes. (For restrictions on newspaper reports of such proceedings, see Criminal Justice Act, 1967 (D7)).

**History of the Office of J.P.**—The above is by no means an exhaustive account of the duties of J.P.s and of the procedure before them; but sufficient has been said to indicate the vital importance of their work. The office is both honorary and honourable; as early as 1327, in the reign of Edward III, the King appointed " conservators " of the peace within his Kingdom; and the Justices of the Peace Act, 1361, in the same reign, determined " what sort of persons should be Justices of the Peace and what authority they should have." From that day to this their duties have gradually become more difficult and extensive, as society has grown more complex. It would seem that, while there are many advantages in leaving the trial of the less grave offences to lay magistrates (as J.P.s are), the system, which for over six centuries has prominently figured in our penal practice, will be brought up to date and made more efficient by the proposed compulsory training. The only doubts have arisen on the ground that persons " of the best of reputation in the counties " (Act of 1344), who are prepared to give their time, without remuneration, to these public-spirited duties, may find it difficult, or in some cases impossible, to attend courses of training, in their spare time, in addition.

**Recruitment of J.P.s.**—The Lord Chancellor in his 1965 presidential address to the Magistrates' Association at Guildhall, London, said he would like to see the J.P.s recruited from more varied walks of life, a new system of training for the Bench and the abolition of the *ex officio* justices (e.g., Mayors during their term of office). "The strength of the lay magistracy," he said, "is dependent on the ordinary man and woman realising that the Benches reflect all shades of opinion and are not representative of one section only." He said he would also like to see more coloured magistrates appointed. "There are now two coloured justices serving on the Bench and these appointments have both been tremendously successful."

Justices of the Peace Act, 1968. By this Act *ex officio* J.P.s (see previous paragraph) are abolished, except for the Lord Mayor and aldermen of the City of London, who may still sit together with lay justices appointed by the Lord Chancellor.

# FREE SPEECH AND PUBLIC ORDER

In the constitution of our parliamentary democracy (*see* D5) certain unwritten rules have been recognised for about three centuries past. These rules, which are not always easy to reconcile, may be summarised as follows:

(1) **Free Speech.**—Free and open discussion, *within the law*, ought to be permitted, both in private and in public, of all political, social, moral and religious questions.

(2) **Unpopular Opinions.**—Unpopular or minority opinions, *lawfully expressed*, privately or publicly, by act or word, *do not become unlawful* merely because their expression may induce *other people* to commit *unlawful* acts.

(3) **Provocation.**—Every man is presumed to *intend* the *natural consequences* of his acts; hence, the use of *threatening, abusive or insulting* language or behaviour, if it is *naturally* provocative of disorder, is *unlawful*.

(4) **Public Order.**—The *preservation of public order* is of paramount importance; a magistrate or police officer, or any person (*see* D8(1)) has a *right and duty* to take *any steps* necessary to *stop a breach of the peace* taking place, or to prevent a breach which he reasonably apprehends.

These rules have recently been widely discussed, as a result of the activities of political extremists who make a special feature of propaganda against racial or religious minorities. Some of their meetings and marches have been accompanied by grave public disorder.

Until comparatively recent times the whole subject depended upon common law decisions (D4), not statute law (D5). For example:

**Unlawful Assembly** is a common law offence, constituted by an assembly of three or more persons, intending either *to commit a crime* by open force, or to carry out any *common purpose, whether lawful or unlawful*, in such manner as to give *firm and courageous persons* in the neighbourhood *reasonable grounds* to apprehend a *breach of the peace* in consequence of the assembly. (The words " any *common* purpose, *whether lawful or unlawful*," should be noted.)

**Sedition** is a common law crime, which includes the doing of *acts* or the speaking of *words* with the *intention* of promoting feelings of *ill-will or hostility* between different classes of the Queen's subjects. If the words or acts (whatever the intention) have a *direct tendency* to cause *unlawful meetings or disturbances*, they are seditious, since "a man is *presumed to intend* the *natural* consequences of his acts" (see (3), above). This does not mean that there must be no full and free discussion, nor that there is any prohibition upon criticism, or even censure; but there must be *no malignity*, nor any imputation of *corrupt or malicious motives*, such as to incite people *to take the law into their own hands* and to provoke them to *tumult and disorder*.

With these principles in mind, let us consider some actual cases (decided during the past eighty years) in which these rules have been applied.

**Beatty v. Gillbanks** (1882) arose from the activities of the newly-founded Salvation Army,

which was "an association for carrying out religious exercises among themselves, and for a religious revival among certain classes of the community." Its leaders formed their followers into *processions* which marched through the streets of Weston-super-Mare, with *bands and banners*, collecting people as they marched back to their hall, where *prayer-meetings* were held. They were opposed on several occasions by an organisation calling itself the "Skeleton Army," which objected to these religious exercises. In consequence, disorders frequently arose, and the Salvation Army leaders were charged with "unlawfully and tumultuously assembling to the disturbance of the peace." The Magistrates bound them over to be of good behaviour; the Salvation Army appealed to the High Court.

The Judges decided that *the Magistrates were wrong.* "Everyone must be taken to intend the *natural* consequences of his acts" ((3), above) "and *if* this disturbance of the peace was the *natural consequence* of the Salvation Army's activities, they would have been liable, and the Magistrates would have been right to bind them over. But the evidence does not support this contention. ... There was nothing in their conduct which was either tumultuous or against the peace; on the contrary, the evidence shows the disturbances were caused by other people, antagonistic to them. What has happened here is that an *unlawful organisation* has assumed to itself the right *to prevent* the Salvation Army from *lawfully assembling*, and the *decision of the Magistrates* amounts to this—that a man may be *convicted for doing a lawful act if he knows that his doing it may cause another to do an unlawful act.* There is *no authority* for such a proposition."

**Wise v. Dunning** (1902) is a contrasting case. A fanatical *Protestant clergyman* had, on several occasions, held meetings in parts of Liverpool containing a *strong Roman Catholic population*. At these meetings he had used *offensive, violent, and provocative language*, attacking the Pope and the Roman Catholic Church. In consequence, breaches of the peace had occurred, and the Liverpool Magistrate had bound him over to be of good behaviour. The Protestant clergyman appealed to the High Court, protesting that there was no evidence that he had committed or intended to commit a breach of the peace, and that the Magistrate's decision (as in the earlier case) was wrong. But the Judges *upheld the Magistrate's decision and dismissed the appeal.* The Lord Chief Justice said " there was abundant evidence that, in the public streets, he had used *language which was abusive*, which had *caused an obstruction*, and that he intended to do *similar acts* in another place." The two other Judges said that every case depends upon its own *facts* and *evidence*:

> " The law does not as a rule regard an illegal act as being the natural consequence of a temptation held out to commit it; but ... the cases show that *the law regards the infirmity of human temper* to the extent of considering that a breach of the peace, although an illegal act, may be the *natural consequence of insulting or abusive* language or conduct ".

The clergyman's behaviour (unlike that of the Salvation Army leaders in the earlier case) was *in itself violently provocative;* therefore the Magistrate was justified in binding him over, " under preventive power " to stop breaches of the peace, which were the " natural result " of his behaviour.

Both the above cases, as it happened, dealt with religious controversies. But the same rules apply in controversies of other kinds.

Duncan v. Jones (1936) was concerned with provocation on a *political and social* question. There was grave unemployment at the time, and feelings between the unemployed, and their supporters, against the Government, and its policies, ran high. Mrs. Jones had held a *meeting of unemployed* men right *opposite an unemployed training-centre*; she had made a speech strongly attacking the Government's policy, and a *disturbance had followed*. Fourteen months later, when she appeared at the *same place* for the *same purpose*, the Police Superintendent forbade her to hold the meeting there. She insisted on doing so, stepped on her box, and began to address the bystanders. It was not, at that stage, suggested that she was obstructing the highway, or inciting anybody to commit a breach of the peace. Nevertheless she was *convicted of obstructing* the Superintendent *in the execution of his duty*, and her conviction was upheld by the High Court. " She must have known (from earlier experience) the *natural consequence* of holding such a meeting at that place; the Superintendent *reasonably apprehended a breach of the peace;* it therefore became *his duty to prevent it*, and she was guilty of *obstructing him in carrying out that duty.*"

**The Public Order Act, 1936.**—In the period preceding the Second World War, extremist political organisations held meetings at which they wore political uniforms and used " strongarm " tactics similar to those in vogue among the Italian Fascists and German Nazis. They also indulged, like the Nazis, in virulent propaganda calculated to stir up racial hatred. As a result of the exasperation of public feelings, in the existing state of international tension, grave disorders took place in London and other cities. The situation was discussed in both Houses of Parliament and it was generally agreed that the law required to be *clarified and strengthened*. On December 18, 1936, the *Public Order Act* received the Royal Assent, and came into force on January 1, 1937.

**Prohibition of Political Uniforms.**—Section 1 of the Act (subject to certain exceptions) *forbids the wearing*, in a *public place* or at a *public meeting*, of *uniform* signifying the wearer's association with a *political organisation*, or with the promotion of a *political object*. (The exceptions are " ceremonial, anniversary or other special occasions " on which the Chief Officer of Police may permit a relaxation of the prohibition (with the Home Secretary's consent) only if he is satisfied that no risk of public disorder is likely to be involved.)

**Prohibition of Quasi-Military Organisations.**—Section 2 makes it an *offence* to participate in the *control or management* of an *association* whose members are (a) *organised* or *trained* or *equipped* to enable them to be employed " in usurping the functions of the police or of the armed forces of the Crown," or (b) *organised and trained*, or *organised and equipped* as follows: either (i) for the purpose of the use or display of *physical force* in promoting a *political object*, or (ii) in such manner as to arouse *reasonable apprehension* that they are *organised*, and either *trained or equipped*, for the purpose described in (i). (It was under (b) (ii) that two of the leaders of a present-day extremist political organisation were convicted and sentenced to imprisonment in October, 1962, at the Central Criminal Court; their appeals were dismissed.) The consent of the Attorney-General (the Senior Law Officer of the Crown) is required before a prosecution under Section 2 can be instituted. In certain circumstances a High Court Order may be made to search the premises of the organisation and to impound its property.

**Preservation of Public Order on the Occasion of Processions.**—Section 3 confers powers for this purpose, as follows:

(1) On a *Chief Officer of Police*, if he has *reasonable grounds* for *apprehending* that a *procession* may occasion *serious public disorder* (having regard to time, place and circumstances), power *to impose* such *conditions* as appear *necessary for preserving public order* (including the route of the procession and power to prohibit it from entering any "public place "); but no conditions restricting the display of *flags, banners or emblems* are to be imposed unless they are *reasonably necessary to prevent risk of a breach of the peace.*

(2) On a *Borough or Urban District Council* (if the Chief Officer of Police believes that his powers under (1) (above) will not suffice to prevent serious public disorder, and on application by him) power to *make an Order* (with the consent of the Home Secretary) *prohibiting* all *public processions*, or certain classes of public processions in the area for a period *not exceeding three months*. (This power does not apply within the City of London or the Metropolitan Police Area, as to which see (3) (below).)

(3) On the *Commissioner of the City of London Police*, and the *Commissioner of Metropolitan Police*, a power similar to that described in (2) (above), and on similar conditions. Thus, within the *London Area* the *Police Authorities*, and in *urban areas outside London* the *Local Authorities*, are given *power to prohibit processions* (or " marches ") on the conditions described in (2) above.

It is an *offence* for anybody *knowingly to fail to comply* with any *Order* or *condition* imposed, or *to organise* or *assist in organising* a public procession *in contravention* of the Section.

**Prohibition of Offensive Weapons.**—By Section 4, anybody is guilty of an *offence* if he has with him any *offensive weapon* at a *public meeting* or *on the occasion of a public procession*, without lawful authority. (Note the words " *on the occasion of* a public procession "; it is *not only those taking part* in the procession, *but also bystanders*, who may commit this offence.) " Lawful authority " extends to servants of the Crown, Members of Parliament or of a Local Authority (acting as such), police officers, members of Fire Brigades or Cadet Corps, and so forth.

**Prohibition of Offensive Conduct Conducive to Breaches of the Peace.**—Section 5 (as now amended by the Race Relations Act, 1965) reads—" Any person who in any public place or at any public meeting (a) uses threatening, abusive or insulting words or behaviour, or (b) distributes or displays any writing, sign or visible representation which is threatening, abusive or insulting with intent to provoke a breach of the peace, or whereby a breach of the peace is likely to be occasioned, shall be guilty of an offence."

**Disorderly Conduct at a Public Meeting.**—Section 6 refers to the Public Meeting Act, 1908. Section 1 of the 1908 Act makes it an offence for a person to *act in a disorderly manner* at a *lawful* public meeting for the purpose of *preventing the transaction of the meeting's business*. Section 6 of the 1936 Act gives power to a constable, if he *reasonably suspects* an offence under the 1908 Act, *to demand* of the suspected offender his *name and address* (provided that the chairman of the meeting requests him to do so). If the suspected offender *refuses* or fails to give his name and address, or gives a *false name and address*, he *commits an offence*, and the constable may arrest him without warrant. (Note that, to qualify for protection, the public meeting must, in the first place, be *lawful*.) Section 6 of the 1936 Act has been considerably extended and strengthened by Section 6 of the Race Relations Act, 1965, for stirring up hatred on grounds of race or colour. The Public Order Act, 1963, has greatly increased the penalties under Section 5 of the Act of 1936 and Section 1 of the Act of 1908; but an undertaking has been given by the Home Office that the new Act will not be used to suppress mere "heckling" at a public meeting. *See also* Race Relations Act, 1968, below.

**Jordan v. Burgoyne** (1963) was similar to *Wise v. Dunning* (1902), except that the 1963 case was concerned with section 5 of the Public Order Act, 1936. At a *public meeting* in Trafalgar Square, to an audience of 5,000, *which included many Jews*, Colin Jordan used the words—"Hitler was right. Our real enemies—the people we should have fought—were not the National Socialists of Germany, but World Jewry and its associates." There was *complete disorder* and a general surge towards the speaker by the crowd, but they were restrained by the police, under Superintendent Burgoyne; and 20 arrests were made while the crowd was being dispersed.

Before the Bow Street Magistrate Jordan was convicted and sentenced to imprisonment, for " *using at a public meeting insulting words whereby a breach of the peace was likely to be occasioned*." He appealed to Quarter Sessions, who found as a fact that, though *the words were highly insulting*, they were *not likely to lead ordinary responsible persons to commit breaches of the peace*; they

therefore allowed Jordan's appeal against conviction. The prosecution then asked for " a case to be stated " for the High Court on the question whether the words in section 5 could properly be interpreted to mean " likely to lead to a breach of the peace by ordinary citizens."

The Lord Chief Justice, with two other Judges, decided that *Quarter Sessions were wrong*. *The test was not* whether the insulting words were likely to cause a breach of the peace by a *hypothetical audience*, whatever their creed, faith, race, or political views; in any case the Judges imagined that any *reasonable citizen would be provoked* beyond endurance. But this was an *Act to keep order in public places*, and " a speaker must *take his audience as he finds it*. If those words to that audience are likely to provoke a breach of the peace, the *speaker is guilty of an offence*. The right of *free speech is not in question*; he *may express his views as strongly* as he likes, *but he must not threaten, abuse or insult that audience*." The case was sent back to Quarter Sessions with a direction to find the offence proved, and to dismiss Jordan's appeal from the Magistrate's conviction. *See* **D44**.

# D. LAW REFORM

The Lord Chancellor, among his many duties, acts as a sort of Minister of Justice. The present Lord Chancellor is an enthusiastic reformer; the setting up of the Law Commission **(D5(2))** was on his initiative. Many recommendations of the Law Commission, and fresh legislation resulting from them, have been noted under their various headings in the main text of the section, *e.g.*, Criminal Justice Act, 1967; Criminal Law Act, 1967 **(D7-8)**.

The **Race Relations Act, 1968** came into force on 25 November 1968. The Act of 1965 made certain forms of discrimination a civil wrong **D12(2)** and also strengthened the Public Order Act, 1936 **(D40)** by making it a criminal offence to stir up hatred on grounds of race or colour. The 1968 Act is not penal in its remedies, but makes " discrimination " a civil wrong, giving rise (in the first place) to conciliation (see below) by regional committees, and (if these fail) to damages **(D12–1)** or injunction **(D12(2))** or both. A person who feels there has been discrimination against him can complain, in writing or by word of mouth, or someone else, authorised by him in writing, can complain on his behalf, within two months of the discriminating act, to the local conciliation committee or to the Race Relations Board direct. The Act applies to discrimination on grounds of race, colour, or ethnic or national origins. Unlawful discrimination means treating a person less favourably than others, on any of the above grounds; " separate but equal " treatment (*e.g.*, segregation) counts as less favourable treatment.

It is unlawful for anyone providing the public with goods, facilities, or services to discriminate by refusing, or deliberately omitting to provide, anybody with goods, *etc.*, of the like quality, in the like manner, or on the like terms as are normally made available to others. Examples are—access to and use of any place which the public may enter; facilities for entertainment, recreation or refreshment; accommodation in a hotel, boarding-house, *etc.*; facilities for banking, insurancegrants, loans, credit, or finance; for education, instruction, or training, or the services of any trade, profession, business, local or other authority. But hotels, *etc.*, are exempted if the landlord or some of his immediate family live on the premises; or where there is not normally accommodation for more than twelve persons in the first two years of the Act, or six persons thereafter, besides the landlord and some of his family.

It is also unlawful to discriminate in employment—terms, recruitment, training, promotion,

dismissal, or conditions of work; also to refuse to employ a person, on grounds of race, *etc.*, on work of any description which is available and for which he is qualified (though employers *may* treat employees differently by reason of seniority, ability, or educational standards). During the first two years of the Act employers of less than twenty-five employees are exempted; for the following two years the number is ten. And if an employer " discriminates " in good faith for the purpose of preserving " a reasonable balance " of different groups, the discrimination is not unlawful; but " reasonable balance " must be between (1) those who (of whatever race, colour, *etc.*) were born, or wholly or partly educated, in Britain, and (2) others, whatever their race, *etc.* Other exemptions are *inside* employees in a private household (*e.g., au pair* girls) but not *outside* employees (*e.g., builders*); employment wholly or mainly outside Britain, in any country, ship, or aircraft; in a British ship if persons of different races, *etc.*, would otherwise have to share sleeping, mess, or sanitary accommodation; or where race, *etc.*, is a *bona fide* qualification (*e.g.*, waiters in a Chinese restaurant).

It is unlawful for any organisation of employers or workers to discriminate in admitting members, benefits of membership, or expulsion; in selling or letting all types of premises (including furnished or unfurnished living accommodation, business premises, or land). The prohibition applies equally to property-owners (including companies), estate-agents, developers, and local authorities (*e.g.*, borough councils)—unless (1) the person offering accommodation (" the landlord ") lives in the premises and shares facilities with others, *and* (2) there is accommodation for not more than two households besides the landlord; *or* (3) the landlord, wholly occupying the premises, sells without any advertisement or estate-agent. It is also unlawful to publish or display any discriminatory advertisement or notice.

Anybody who deliberately aids, induces, or incites another unlawfully to discriminate will be equally liable—*e.g.*, neighbours who put pressure on a vendor to prevent sale of his house to a coloured, *etc.*, person. (But incitement to *racial hatred* is still a crime **(D40(2))**.

If a regional committee or the Race Relations Board thinks, on investigation of a complaint, there has been unlawful discrimination, it will try by private conciliation to settle the complaint and to get the discriminator to give a satisfactory written assurance for the future. Only if such assurance is refused will court proceedings arise.

The Board will proceed in one of the special county courts (D43), where the judge will be assisted by two assessors. The court may grant an injunction to restrain future unlawful discrimination, or damages for actual or potential loss suffered by the victim, or both. Disobedience will mean a penalty for contempt of court. Employment complaints are an exception; they will be first referred to the Department of Employment and Productivity, which will try to settle by conciliation if there is suitable machinery. If the complainant is dissatisfied, he can appeal to the Board, which can then apply for injunction or damages for actual loss and loss of opportunity (compensation for lost benefit which the complainant might have expected).

**The Trade Descriptions Act, 1968** came into force on 1 December 1968. It strengthens the law prohibiting inaccurate and misleading descriptions of goods, services (*e.g.*, in garages), accommodation (*e.g.*, in hotels) and facilities provided or offered in the course of trade, and false or misleading indications of the prices of goods. It gives power to the Board of Trade to require information or instructions, relating to goods, to be marked on or accompany the goods or to be included in advertisements; it forbids the unauthorised use of devices signifying royal appointment or awards. The general penalty for infringement is—on conviction before justices (D38(2)) a fine not exceeding £400; on indictment a fine or imprisonment not exceeding two years, or both; but no prosecution is to take place for an offence committed more than three years earlier or one year after its discovery, whichever is earlier. It is a defence to prove that the infringement was due to a mistake, or to reliance on information supplied to the offender, or the act or default of another person, an accident or some cause beyond the offender's control; *and* that he took all reasonable precautions and exercised due diligence to avoid commission of the offence by himself or anyone under his control; also if he proves that he did not know, and could not with reasonable diligence have ascertained, that the goods, *etc.*, did not conform to the description or that the description had been applied to them.

(The Misrepresentation Act, 1967, already gives a person injured by a misrepresentation certain civil remedies (D11(2)); the new Act adds criminal penalties to deter or punish contraventions (D38(2)).)

The expression " trade description " is closely defined—quantity, quality, size, method of manufacture or processing, composition, fitness for purpose, results of any tests, place or date of manufacture, *etc.* A " false " description must be false or misleading to a material degree. A word-of-mouth statement, as well as a written indication, may amount to a " description ". In advertisements (including catalogues, circulars and price-lists) the description refers to all goods of the class advertised, whether existing or not when the advertisement appears; not only its form and content, but also its time, manner, place, and frequency of publication, are to be regarded. " Offer " includes exposing goods, or having them in one's possession, for supply. Goods manufactured or produced wholly or partly abroad are included, unless the Board of Trade is satisfied that the interests of U.K. buyers are sufficiently protected already. And goods produced abroad bearing foreign false descriptions (*e.g.*, " champagne " for a wine of different origin) may be prohibited from being imported. Anybody who, in the U.K., assists in or induces the commission of an offence, is equally guilty if the false or misleading description indicates that the goods were manufactured in the U.K., or if they contravene an order of the Board of Trade. Importation of goods bearing infringing trademarks is restricted.

It is an offence falsely to pretend that goods have been reduced in price, or are being sold at a price less than that at which they are in fact being offered; so is a false indication that the offered price is equal to or less than a price recommended (*i*) by the manufacture or producer, and (*ii*)

generally in the area where they are offered for retail.

A false indication that goods or services are supplied to or approved by any member of the Royal Family or any other person (*e.g.*, the phrase " by appointment "), or have been granted the Queen's Award to Industry, is an offence. In regard to services it is an offence to make a statement known to be false, or recklessly to make a statement which is in fact false, on the provision, nature, time, manner, examination, or approval of such services.

If an offence is committed by a corporation (D9(2)) with the consent or connivance, or due to the neglect, of a director, manager, secretary, or other officer, he as well as the corporation shall be guilty of the offence and punished accordingly.

If an offence is committed both under the new Act and the Weights and Measures Acts, the notices required by the latter Acts must be served on the offender; and if the Food and Drugs laws are contravened, the relevant provisions of those laws must be complied with. Enforcement is in the hands of the local weights and measures authority and its officers and inspectors, who may make test purchases and secure the provision of services to which the new Act applies. Inspectors, on production of their credentials, have power to enter premises, inspect and seize goods and documents; if admission is likely to be prevented or refused, they may obtain a warrant from the justices (D38) for the purpose. Wilful obstruction of an inspector or other authorised officer is an offence punishable by a fine not exceeding £50. The officer must give notice to the supplier about any test to be applied and its result.

**Sexual Offences Act, 1967.** Male homosexual practices are no longer an offence if committed in private between consenting adults, except on merchant ships; but living on the earnings of a male prostitute is still liable to punishment from 6 months to 3 years imprisonment. (Female homosexual practices have never been an offence.) If an adult commits a homosexual act with a minor over 16, imprisonment is for 10 years, unless the minor consented, in which case it is 5 years (instead of life imprisonment). If the minor is under 16, the penalty is 10 years. No proceedings may be brought more than 12 months after the act was committed, nor without the consent of the Attorney-General. (This is to avoid blackmail.)

**The Abortion Act, 1967,** provides for an abortion to be performed by a registered medical practitioner if two registered medical practitioners are of the opinion:

> (1) that the continuance of the pregnancy would involve risk to the life of the pregnant woman, or of injury to the physical or mental health of the pregnant woman or any existing children of her family, greater than if the pregnancy were terminated; or

> (2) that there is substantial risk that if the child were born it would suffer from such physical or mental abnormalities as to be seriously handicapped.

The Act states that in determining whether the continuance of a pregnancy would involve risk of injury to health as is mentioned in (1) above, account may be taken of the pregnant woman's actual or reasonably foreseeable environment. (The provision under (1) for a termination on the grounds of injury to the health of other children in the family became known as the " social " clause during the course of the debate on the Bill).

The Act provides for abortions to be carried out in National Health Service hospitals or in premises approved by the Minister of Health or the Secretary of State for Scotland, unless a termination is immediately necessary. Notification must be made of all abortions carried out.

# THE SYSTEM OF ENGLISH COURTS
## I. CIVIL COURTS

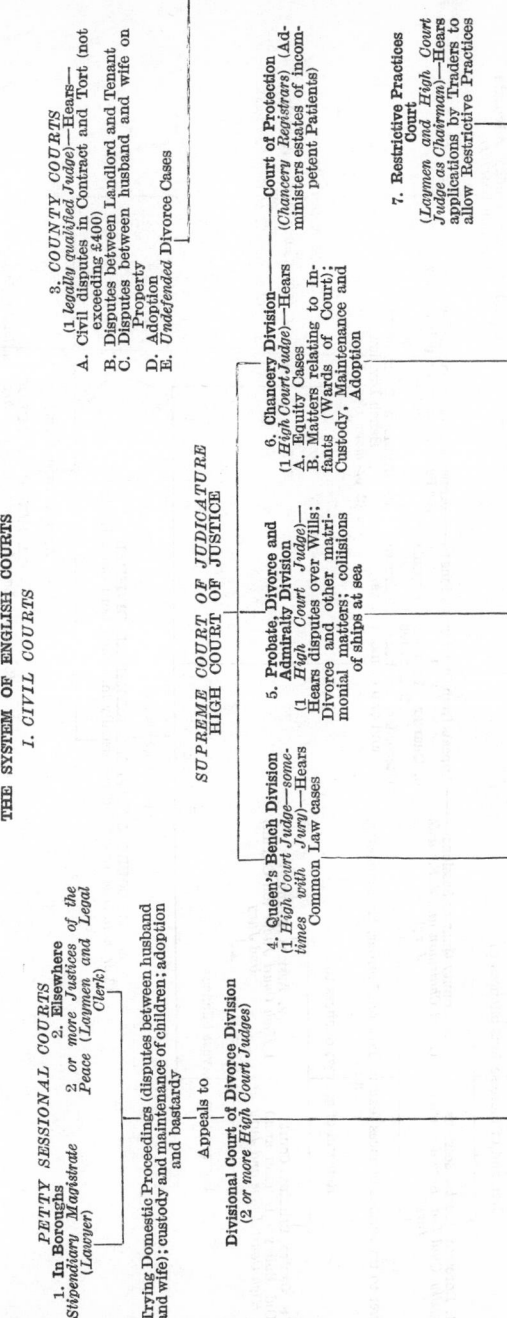

*PETTY SESSIONAL COURTS*
1. In Boroughs
1 Stipendiary Magistrate (*Lawyer*)
2. Elsewhere
2 or more Justices of the Peace (*Laymen and Legal Clerk*)

Trying Domestic Proceedings (disputes between husband and wife); custody and maintenance of children; adoption and bastardy

Appeals to

Divisional Court of Divorce Division
(2 or more High Court Judges)

*3. COUNTY COURTS*
(1 *legally qualified Judge*)—Hears—
Civil disputes in Contract and Tort (not exceeding £400)
A. Disputes between Landlord and Tenant
B. Disputes between husband and wife on Property
C. Adoption
D. *Undefended* Divorce Cases

*SUPREME COURT OF JUDICATURE*
HIGH COURT OF JUSTICE

4. Queen's Bench Division
(1 *High Court Judge*—sometimes with *Jury*)—Hears Common Law cases

5. Probate, Divorce and Admiralty Division
(1 *High Court Judge*)—Hears disputes over Wills; Divorce and other matrimonial matters; collisions of ships at sea

6. Chancery Division
(1 *High Court Judge*)—Hears
A. Equity Cases
B. Matters relating to Infants (Wards of Court); Custody, Maintenance and Adoption

Court of Protection
(*Chancery Registrars*) (Administers estates of incompetent Patients)

7. Restrictive Practices Court
(*Laymen and High Court Judge as Chairman*)—Hears applications by Traders to allow Restrictive Practices

Appeals to

8. COURT OF APPEAL (CIVIL DIVISION)
(2 or more High Court Judges—usually including Master of the Rolls)

Appeal (with leave) to

9. HOUSE OF LORDS
(3 or more Law Lords who have held high Judicial Office)

*APPEALS ON CIVIL MATTERS FROM*
10. Ecclesiastical Courts
11. Commonwealth Courts

12. JUDICIAL COMMITTEE OF THE PRIVY COUNCIL
(3 or more Law Lords with Privy Councillors)

*Note:* Proposals were before Parliament (January 1969) to permit appeals, in certain cases, *direct* from the High Court to the House of Lords, to save expense.

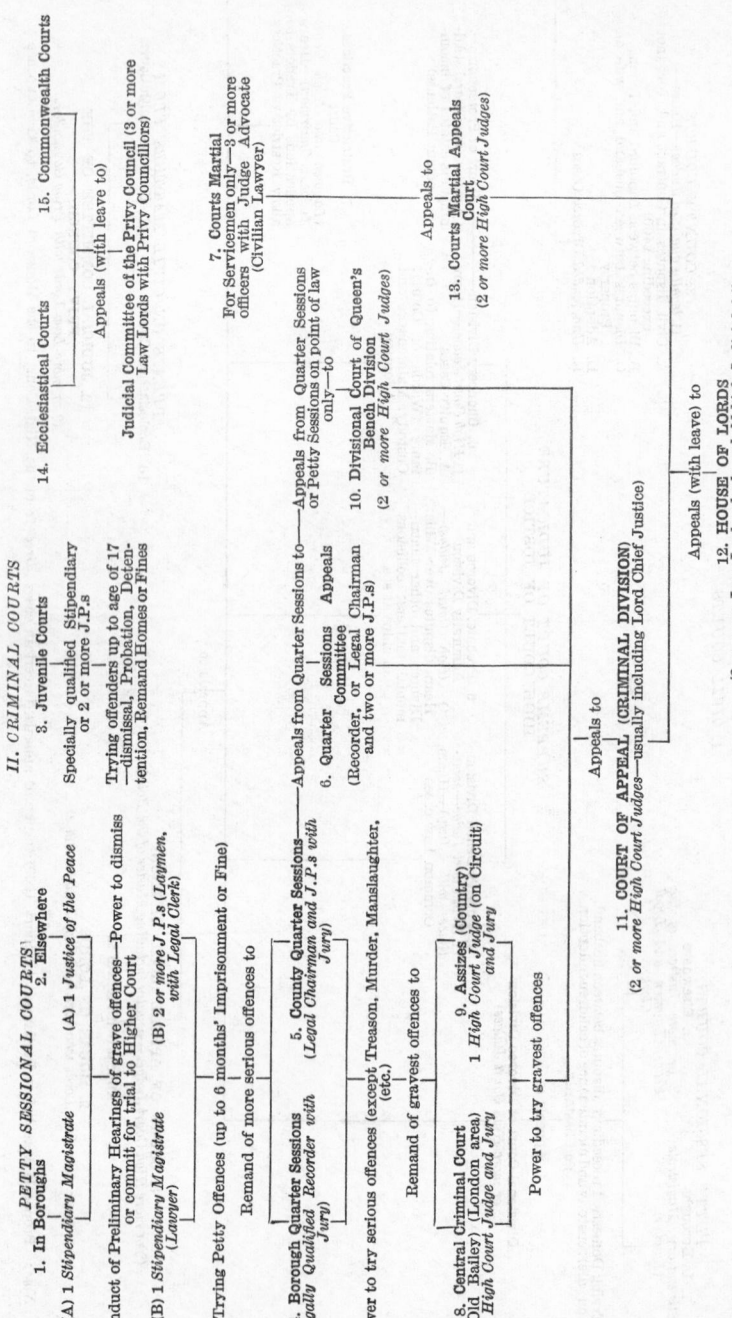

## II. CRIMINAL COURTS

*PETTY SESSIONAL COURTS*

**1. In Boroughs**

(A) 1 *Stipendiary Magistrate*

(B) 1 *Stipendiary Magistrate (Lawyer)*

**2. Elsewhere**

(A) 1 *Justice of the Peace*

(B) 2 or more *J.P.s (Laymen, with Legal Clerk)*

Conduct of Preliminary Hearings of grave offences—Power to dismiss or commit for trial to Higher Court

Trying Petty Offences (up to 6 months' Imprisonment or Fine)

Remand of more serious offences to

**3. Juvenile Courts**

Specially qualified Stipendiary or 2 or more J.P.s

Trying offenders up to age of 17 —dismissal, Probation, Detention, Remand Homes or Fines

**4. Borough Quarter Sessions** *(Legally Qualified Recorder with Jury)*

Power to try serious offences (except Treason, Murder, Manslaughter, (etc.)

Remand of gravest offences to

**5. County Quarter Sessions** *(Legal Chairman and J.P.s with Jury)*

Appeals from Quarter Sessions to

**6. Quarter Sessions Appeals Committee** *(Recorder, or Legal Chairman and two or more J.P.s)*

**7. Courts Martial** For Servicemen only—3 or more officers with Judge Advocate *(Civilian Lawyer)*

**14. Ecclesiastical Courts**     **15. Commonwealth Courts**

Appeals (with leave to)

Judicial Committee of the Privy Council (3 or more Law Lords with Privy Councillors)

Appeals from Quarter Sessions or Petty Sessions on point of law only—to

**10. Divisional Court of Queen's Bench Division** *(2 or more High Court Judges)*

**8. Central Criminal Court** (Old Bailey) (London area) 1 High Court Judge and Jury

**9. Assizes** (Country) (on Circuit) 1 High Court Judge and Jury

Power to try gravest offences

Appeals to

**11. COURT OF APPEAL (CRIMINAL DIVISION)** *(2 or more High Court Judges—usually including Lord Chief Justice)*

Appeals to

**13. Courts Martial Appeals Court** *(2 or more High Court Judges)*

Appeals to

Appeals (with leave) to

**12. HOUSE OF LORDS** *(3 or more Law Lords who have held high Judicial Office)*

# THE WORLD OF MUSIC

The art of music as it has developed in the Western world, with a glossary of musical terms and an index to composers.

# TABLE OF CONTENTS

# THE WORLD OF MUSIC

In writing this section no special knowledge on the part of the reader is assumed; it is for those who want to know about the history of music, how different styles evolved, and how one composer influenced another. It is a background to music as the science section is a background to science, and just as the latter cannot show the reader the colours of the spectrum but only tell of Newton's experiments and of the relationship between colour and wavelength, so in this section we can only describe man's achievements in the world of sound. But knowing something about a composer, his work, and when he lived can help to bring fuller understanding and enjoyment when listening to his music.

The section is in three parts:

I. Historical Narrative and Discussion

II. Glossary of Musical Terms

III. Index to Composers

## I. HISTORICAL NARRATIVE AND DISCUSSION

The history of music, like that of any people or art, is not one of uninterrupted progress towards some ideal perfection. For five centuries or more music in the West has achieved peaks of accomplishment in one style or another before society has dictated or composers have felt the need for something new and different. Thus Wagner's music-drama *Parsifal*, lasting five hours, is not necessarily a more rewarding work than what Monteverdi achieved in *Orfeo* 250 years earlier. More complex yes, more rewarding—well, that is for the listener to judge.

We must keep this in mind when considering the development of music from a starting point of, say, Gregorian chant down to the complicated structures of a Schoenberg in our own day. In this development there is no true dividing line between one period and another, nor must simplifying terms such as "classical" or "romantic" be taken too literally.

The earliest history of Western music as we know it today is closely bound up with the Church, for music had to be provided for services. The earliest Christian music was influenced by Greek songs, few of which unfortunately have survived, and by the music of synagogues, where the art of chanting originated. The modal system of the ancient Greeks was highly organised. The earliest Greek scale was from A to A and the four descending notes A,G,F,E became the basis of their musical theory, and it is from them that Western music learned to call notes after the letters of the alphabet. A scale can begin on any note and always includes two semitones upon which much of the character of a melody depends.

The Greek modes were based on the white notes only; the Dorian, Phrygian, Lydian, and Mixolydian began respectively on E,D,C, and B. Their character was thus decided by the position of the semitones, and they formed the basis, often corrupted, of the mediaeval modes. This system was transmitted through Latin writers such as Boethius and Cassiodorus, and through Arabic writers. The eight Church modes were not established until the 8th or 9th cent. These plagal modes, as they are called, started in each case, for technical reasons, a fourth below the authentic modes.

By the end of the 6th cent. Gregorian chant had developed so far that some sort of permanent record was required. *Neumes*, signs placed over the Latin text, were the earliest attempt at musical notation. Gradually lines came into use until a four-line stave was established, probably in the 11th and 12th cent., and with them clef signs, although the treble clef as we know it today did not appear until the 13th cent.

And what is this music—plainchant—like? It is an unaccompanied, single line of melody, which, when we have become used to its "antique" flavour is heard to have a wide range of spiritual and emotional expression, not excluding word painting. The texts used came from the Liturgy. These beautiful, extended lines of flowing, flexible melody can still be heard on Sundays in Roman Catholic cathedrals and churches.

### Polyphony is Born.

The 10th cent. saw the appearance of a book called *Musica Enchiriadis* (whose authorship is disputed) which introduced theories about unison singing in which the melody is doubled at the fourth or fifth. Organum, or diaphony, is used to describe this method of writing, a term which confusingly could also be used for a kind of singing where melismatic melody was heard over a drone note on the organ. Rules came into fashion defining which intervals were allowed and which parts of the church services could be sung in more than one part. By the time of Guido d'Arezzo (c. 990–1050), a Benedictine monk who helped advance notation, contrary motion was permitted as the cadence was approached, another technical advance. Gradually the voices became more and more independent, and the third, so long considered a discord, came into use. Pérotin, of Notre Dame, was the first composer to write for three and four voices, and he and his great predecessor Léonin were the great masters of early polyphony. The proximity and spikiness of Pérotin's harmony is almost modern-sounding, and as with Gregorian chant, once we have adjusted ourselves to the sound, this music can be a rewarding experience.

### Early Secular Music.

In mediaeval France, towards the end of the 11th cent., there developed what has become known as the age of the troubadours, poet-musicians. They were the successors to the *jongleurs*, or jugglers, and minstrels about whom we know little as practically none of their music has survived. The troubadours hymned the beauty of spring and of ladies. Contemporary with them in Germany were the Minnesingers. Their songs were mostly set in three modes. Adam de la Halle (d. 1287), because so much of his music survives, is perhaps the best-known of the troubadours. He was a notable composer of *rondels*, an early form of round, of which the English *Sumer is icumen in*, written by a monk of Reading c. 1226, is a fine example.

## Ars Nova.

The term *ars nova* derives partly from writings of Philippe de Vitry (1291–1361) who codified the rules of the old and the new music in a valuable treatise. This *new art* represented a freeing of music from organum and rhythmic modes, and an increase in the shape and form of melodic line. France was the centre of music during the 14th cent. and apart from Philippe de Vitry the leading composer was Guillaume de Machaut (1300–77), who wrote many secular works as well as a polyphonic setting of the Mass. His music is notable for its vigour and tenderness as well as for its technical expertise. Meanwhile in 14th-cent. Italy a quite separate branch of *ars nova* was developing. Imitation and canon were to be noted in the music of Italian composers, and choral forms such as the Ballata, Madrigal (which often included instrumental accompaniment) and Caccia (a two-voice hunting song in canon) were common. The greatest Italian composer of this period was the blind organist and lutenist Francesco di Landini (c. 1325–97).

England was less affected by *ars nova* and tended to remain loyal to older forms. Not until the 15th cent. did she begin to make a significant contribution to the history of music. Both John Dunstable (c. 1380–1453), who was no less eminent as a mathematician and an astronomer than as a musician, and his contemporary Lionel Power advanced the technique of music by their method of composition (use of the triad, for instance) and mellifluous style. Their musicianship was much appreciated on the Continent. Dunstable did away with the use of *cantus firmus*—a fixed melody—and increased the use of free composition.

After Dunstable the next great figure in European music was Guillaume Dufay (c. 1400–74), the most celebrated composer of the Burgundian school. His music is distinguished for its blend of flowing melody, cleverly wrought counterpoint and tender expressiveness. Much travelled, Dufay was a man of catholic outlook. Together with Dunstable and the Burgundian Gilles Binchois he bridged the gap between 14th cent. *ars nova* and the fully developed polyphony of the 15th cent.

*Ars nova* composers also showed an interest in secular music and many of their *rondeaux* and *chansons* (those of Binchois particularly) have been preserved. Personality began to play a distinguishing part in composition.

The results of Dufay's good work can be heard in the flowering of the Franco-Netherland school later in the 15th cent. Its two most notable representatives are Ockeghem (c. 1420–95) and his pupil Josquin des Prés (c. 1450–1521), who carried musical expressiveness even further than Dufay; their work can also be grand and majestic. Indeed Josquin's wide range, from the humorous to the dignified, partially accounts for his justly deserved high reputation. He was a master of counterpoint but tempered his mechanical ingenuity with imaginative insight.

Throughout the Renaissance choral music was breaking away, as we have seen, from its earlier bonds. The mediaeval tradition of having the *cantus firmus* in the tenor went by the board; the use of dissonance, when only two voices were used in mediaeval times, was abandoned in favour of euphony; and all the voices, democratically, came to share the musical lines. Composers also began to respect their texts; where words were previously fitted to the music, the reverse was now the case. In Josquin's music, indeed, we have the first attempts at symbolism: matching verbal ideas with musical ones. The importance of this musical renaissance has been realised only over the past twenty years. At last the Renaissance composers are coming to be seen not merely as historical figures relevant only in so far as their work culminated in the great classical composers, but as masters in their own right, whose music should be nearly as familiar to us as is that of a Mozart or a Beethoven.

With the exception of Dufay, little is known of the lives of the musicians so far mentioned. Most of them were in the service of royal or ducal households where they were in charge of the chapel choir, or else they worked in or around the great cathedrals, teaching at choir-schools. They were well rewarded for their services and their social position was probably high.

## The Sixteenth Century.

By the 16th cent. music in England was a steadily expanding art and much encouraged. Music-making in the home was becoming quite the fashion in social circles. The Chapels Royal remained the chief musical centres but the music was changing with the development of new secular forms so that it was not so much religious as a part of life. Composers began their lives as choirboys and received a thoroughgoing education, both theoretical and practical.

Carrying on from where Josquin and his contemporaries left off, Palestrina in Italy, Victoria in Spain, Lassus in the Netherlands, and Byrd in England brought the polyphonic style to its zenith. At the same time came the rise of the madrigalists, first in Italy, then in the Netherlands; and then the beginnings of instrumental music as it came to be known in the succeeding centuries.

The vocal composers began to use chordal (homophonic) as well as contrapuntal (polyphonic) methods of writing—examples are Victoria's *Ave Verum Corpus* and Palestrina's *Stabat Mater*—but polyphony was still the fullest most magnificent instrument of composition, as for instance in Byrd's *O Quam Gloriosum* which shows an eager response to the mood and to the inflection of the words in a kind of vocal orchestration. A feature of all these composers' music, but more especially that of Victoria (c. 1535–1611) and Palestrina (1525–94), is its serene simplicity and fervour of utterance. Palestrina was perhaps more spacious in his effects, Victoria the more passionate. How well we can imagine—and sometimes hear—their music resounding down the naves of the great cathedrals of Europe.

The music of Lassus (c. 1530–94) is distinguished both in sheer amount and in vitality. His mastery in the field of motets was unrivalled, encompassing a wide range of subject and mood. He and his fellow Flemish composers, Willaert, de Monte and Arcadelt, were also expert in the Madrigal, a form popular in Italy and England as well. The Madrigal was a contrapuntal setting of a poem, usually not longer than twelve lines, in five or six parts. The subject (of the poetry) was usually amorous or pastoral. It was a short-lived, but highly prolific vogue. Orlando Gibbons (1583–1625), Thomas Weelkes (c. 1575–1623), and John Wilbye (1574–1638) were the most prominent English exponents.

## Instrumental Music.

By the end of the 14th cent. instrumental music began to become something more than mere anonymous dance tunes or primitive organ music. Instruments often accompanied voices, or even replaced them, so that the recorder, lute, viol, and spinet indoors, and sackbuts and shawms outdoors, had already been developed by the time instrumental music came to be written down. Gradually a distinction grew up between what was appropriate to the voice and what was suitable for instruments. Byrd, Gibbons, and Giles Farnaby in England, the great blind keyboard player, Cabezón (1510–66) in Spain, and Frescobaldi (1583–1643) in Italy produced valuable instrumental works. Perhaps the *Parthenia* and the *Fitzwilliam Virginal Book*, collections of Early English Keyboard music, give as fair a representative idea as any of the development of instrumental form at this time.

In chamber music musicians often played collections of dance tunes strung together to make a whole; or they chose fantasies (or " fancies "), where a composer altered a tune as he wished. Then there were sets of variations on a ground, that is a simple tune played over and over again on a bass viol.

As far as brass instruments are concerned, they were often used on festive occasions in spacious halls or in cathedrals. The Venetian composer Andrea Gabrieli (c. 1510–86) was the first to combine voice and instruments and his son Giovanni Gabrieli (1557–1612) carried the process further to produce sacred symphonies, often using antiphonal effects.

### Drama in Music.

Not until the end of the 16th cent. did anyone begin to think about combining drama and music, and so " invent " the new art we know today as opera. A group of artistic intelligentsia met together in Florence and conceived the idea of reviving the ancient declamation of Greek tragedy. They took Greek mythological subjects, cast them in dramatic form, and set them to music, not in the choral polyphonic style of the Madrigal, but with single voices declaiming dialogue in music. The earliest examples of what was called *Dramma per Musica* were Peri's *Daphne* in 1597 (now lost) and his *Eurydice*, in which he co-operated with Caccini. The new style came to its full flowering with the appearance of Monteverdi (1567–1643), whose genius would surely have shone in any age.

Monteverdi's first opera, *Orfeo*, produced in 1607, is a landmark of dramatic expression, and it is nothing less than a catastrophe that so many of his later operas have been lost. His *Orfeo* provides the basic ground work for the operas of the next two centuries: recitative, accompanied recitative, and aria. His last opera *L'Incoronazione di Poppaea*, written when he was at the great age (for those days) of 75, succeeds in its aim of creating a free, fluid form, slipping easily from recitative to arioso and even aria without the strict, closed forms that were to be used in the 17th and 18th cent. He focusses attention to an almost unbelievable extent on character rather than situation. He creates real people with all their faults and foibles—the kittenish, sexually attractive Poppaea, the power-drunk, infatuated Nero, the noble Seneca, and the dignified, rejected empress Octavia. As recent productions have shown these characters leap from the musical page as if they had just been created, each unerringly delineated in musical terms. Only the vocal line, the continuo, and the very incomplete instrumental ritornelli parts have been preserved, but in sensitive, knowledgeable hands tonal variety in the shape of wind and string parts can be added, as we know certain instruments were available to the composer.

Monteverdi's successors were Cavalli (1602–76), Cesti (1623–69) and Stradella (1642–82), who gave the solo voice more and more prominence encouraged by the advent of the castrati's brilliant voices. These artificially created singers had a vogue and popularity similar to " pop " singers of today, fêted wherever they appeared. The aria became more extended and ornate, and dramatic verisimilitude gradually but inexorably took second place to vocal display. An aria was nearly always in *da capo* form, the first section being repeated after a contrasting middle one.

### Sixteenth- and Seventeenth-century Church Music.

Of course, the invention of a new dramatic style affected church music too. The concentration on the vertical aspect of music (homophony) as opposed to the horizontal (polyphony) led to the increasing importance of the voice in religious music. In Italy, it is true, there was the late-flowering, great madrigalist Carlo Gesualdo (1560–1614), whose harmonic daring still astonishes us today, but by 1600 the cantata was coming to replace older forms in church music. In its simplest form this was a story told in accompanied recitative. Giacomo Carissimi (c. 1604–74) was one of the first significant composers of this new form. He too was in on the birth of the oratorio, whose forerunner was the *sacra rappresentazione* (mystery or miracle play) of early 16th-cent

Florence. Then in the mid-16th cent. St. Philip Neri brought in elements from popular plays on sacred subjects in his services in Rome, designed to hold the attention of youth—rather as certain parsons have tried with " pop " services today. Emilio di Cavalieri (c. 1550–1662) and Carissimi developed the form adding arias and choral movements, omitting actual representation. Alessandro Scarlatti (1660–1725), whose oratorios bear a close resemblance to his operas, brought oratorio to its zenith in Italy.

Heinrich Schütz (1585–1672), Bach's great predecessor, was the founder of German church music. His historical place has never been called into question but only in recent times have the intrinsic merits of his own music come to be recognised. He studied with Giovanni Gabrieli in his youth and later came under the influence of Monteverdi, so it was not surprising that he brought Italian ideas across the Alps to Germany and wrote the first German opera *Daphne*, now sadly lost. He also introduced his country to the Italian declamatory style and to the new kind of concertato instrumental writing. But his dramatic religious works were his greatest contribution to musical development. He wrote with a devout intensity, bringing to life the scriptural texts by closely allying his urgent music to the words. His three settings of the Passions—Matthew, Luke, and John—paved the way for Bach's even more remarkable works in this genre. Two contemporaries of Schütz, Johann Hermann Schein (1586–1630) and Samuel Scheidt (1587–1654), were both important figures in German Reformation music.

### Lully, Purcell, and Seventeenth-century Opera.

France resisted the tide of Italian opera, although paradoxically it was an Italian, Jean-Baptiste Lully (c. 1632–87), who charted the different course of French opera which was from the beginning associated with the court ballet. His musical monopoly during the reign of Louis XIV was put to good use. In his thirteen operas the libretto, usually on classical, allegorical themes, plays a vital part in the composition, which is therefore less clearly divided between recitative and aria than in Italian opera. The orchestration and the ballets assume greater importance than in the traditional Italian form. It was, in short, a more realistic, less stylised art.

In England, opera developed out of the entertainment known as the Masque, a succession of dances, accompanied by voices and instruments and often incorporated in a drama or spectacle. Henry Lawes's (1596–1662) setting of Milton's *Comus* is probably the most famous of these entertainments. The *Venus and Adonis* of John Blow (1649–1708) can be called the first English opera because here the music is gradually gaining the ascendancy over the spoken word. However, it was Purcell (1658–95), Blow's pupil, with *Dido and Aeneas*, who really gave dramatic life to the new medium by giving his characters a true musical personality that was subtler than anything the mere spoken word could achieve. The grief-laden lament of the dying Dido " When I am laid in earth " has an expressive power, achieved by extraordinarily bold harmonic effects, never before and seldom since achieved. The opera was in fact written for a young ladies' boarding school. Purcell followed it with several outstanding semi-operas—such as *The Fairy Queen* (to Dryden's text). His untimely death at the age of 36 probably robbed us of several full-length operas—and perhaps a consequence of this was that English music after him did not develop as it should have done.

His verse anthems and much of his instrumental music, especially the Fantasias, are also rich in imaginative mastery through his original use of harmony and counterpoint. However, a great deal of his pieces were written for a specific occasion and many of the odes are set to impossibly trite texts. At least his genius was partly acknowledged in his own day, and he was appointed organist in Westminster Abbey where he was buried with due pomp. He is said to have died through catching cold when locked out of his own house at night.

## Vivaldi and the Rise of Instrumental Music.

Out of the dance suites popular in the 16th cent. and the beginning of the 17th (known in Italy as the *Sonata da Camera*) developed the concerto. This began as two groups of instrumentalists compared and contrasted with each other as in Giovanni Gabrieli's *Sonata piano e forte*. With Arcangelo Corelli (1653–1713) the concerto grosso took a more definite shape, alternating a solo group of instruments with the main body of strings in three or more contrasting movements. Guiseppe Torelli (1658–1709), Francesco Geminiani (1687–1762) and Tommaso Albinoni (1671–1750) were other notable contributors to the form, but none of the composers so far mentioned has today achieved the popularity of the priest Antonio Vivaldi (c. 1678–1741), himself a violinist, who had at his disposal the orchestra at the Ospedale della Pieta in Venice. The young women at this music school also contributed the vocal side of the concerts there of which there are many descriptions. One says: " They sing like angels, play the violin, flute, organ, oboe, cello, bassoon—in short no instrument is large enough to frighten them . . . I swear nothing is so charming than to see a young and pretty nun, dressed in white, a sprig of pomegranate blossom behind one ear, leading the orchestra, and beating time with all the grace and precision imaginable." For this body, Vivaldi wrote about 500 concertos which maintain a remarkably even quality, of which " The Four Seasons" are perhaps the most felicitous.

Meanwhile organ music was advancing rapidly in technique. Girolamo Frescobaldi (1583–1643) and Jan Pieterszoon Sweelinck (1562–1621) wrote works that provided the foundation of the Italian and Northern German schools of organ music. Their ricercares gradually developed into the fugue, a vein so richly mined by Bach. Among their successors the most notable figure before Bach was Johann Pachelbel (1653–1706).

Other keyboard music, especially for the harpsichord, was the particular province of France and Jean-Philippe Rameau (1683–1764) and François Couperin (1668–1733) were both masters of keyboard style and harmonic invention.

## Bach (1685–1750).

The two giant figures of Bach and Handel bestride the first half of the 18th cent. Their differences are perhaps greater than their similarities. Bach wrote essentially for himself (although of course, he had to satisfy his employers at Cöthen and Leipzig) while Handel was composing to please his wide public. Bach was a provincial, always remaining in central Germany; Handel was widely travelled. Bach was devoutly religious, almost ascetic; Handel was more a man of the world. They never met.

To summarise Bach's vast output in a short space is virtually impossible. One can only try to distil the flavour of his music. He brought the art of polyphony to the highest pitch of mastery that has ever been achieved or is ever likely to be achieved. In his famous " Forty-Eight " and " the Art of the Fugue " he explored all the fugal permutations of the major and minor keys. At the same time his music rose above technical brilliance to achieve, especially in his organ music, the two Passions, many of the church cantatas, and the B minor Mass, intense emotional and expressive power. The cantatas, from his Leipzig appointment (1723) onwards, were integrated into the services. They consisted usually of a chorus based on a Lutheran hymn tune, recitatives, several extended arias, and a concluding chorus usually a straightforward version of the hymn tune in which the congregation joined. There are some two hundred of these works and they contain a wealth of comparatively unknown and sometimes even unrecognised beauties. The St. John and the St. Matthew Passion extend these procedures to a grand scale, an Evangelist telling the new Testament story in vivid recitative, the chorus taking the part of the crowd, soloists pondering in arias on the meaning of the Gospel, and Jesus's words being sung by a bass. Anyone who has heard either of these works well performed cannot help but dismiss from his mind any idea of Bach as a mere dry-as-dust musical mathematician. In the St. Matthew Passion, every suggestion in the text that can possibly be illustrated by a musical equivalent is so illustrated. The Old Testament Pharasaic law is represented by strict musical forms such as the canon; Christ's sayings are given noble arioso life; and the arias reflect truly the New Testament's compassionate message. Technically the work is a marvel; expressively it is eloquent. The B minor Mass, although it contains borrowings from many of his own works, still stands as a satisfying monumental whole in which Bach's choral writing achieved a new richness, the adaptations being in accord with their new setting.

Bach's instrumental music, especially the violin concertos and the unaccompanied works for violin and cello, not only show the immense range of his powers but also contain many of his deeper thoughts, whereas the orchestral suites and the Brandenburg concertos are more extrovert, particularly the rhythmically exuberant fast movements.

Bach closes an era—that of the later contrapuntalists—by achieving the *ne plus ultra* in fugal composition; his last, incomplete work, the Art of the Fugue, is evidence of this.

## Handel (1685–1759).

During his lifetime Handel was far more widely recognised as a great composer than Bach, and his music, unlike Bach's, maintained its place in popular esteem until the re-discovery of Bach and the dominance of the symphony placed Handel somewhat in the background.

During the latter part of the 19th cent. Handel's name was mainly associated with mammoth, anachronistic performances of a small sample of his oratorios at the Crystal Palace and elsewhere in England. In his lifetime these works, and all his other works in the genre, were sung by a small choir who were outnumbered by the instrumental players. Over the past few years authentic-sized performances of his oratorios and a revival of interest in his operas have revealed the real Handel, unknown to our grandparents.

The operas were neglected partly because the vocal prowess they required—and which the castrati so brilliantly supplied—was no longer available and because their dramatic life, at least according to 19th- and early 20th-cent. tenets, hardly existed. Now it is realised that this neglect has deprived us of an unending stream of glorious melody and of much daring harmony. But perhaps it is in the hitherto disregarded oratorios, such as *Semele*, that Handel's innate dramatic sense and musical range are to be heard gloriously fulfilled, and the pastoral serenade *Acis and Galatea* is surely one of the most delightful scores ever composed.

Handel was a colourful, imaginative orchestrator, and this can be heard both in his accompaniment to vocal music and in his concerti grossi, op. 3 and 6, the earlier set exploiting a diversity of interesting string and wind combination. In his writing he was at home in a polyphonic or homophonic style as his superb choruses show. His organ concertos, of which he was the "Inventor" (to quote a contemporary source), were often played between the acts of his oratorios. They are alternately expressive and exuberant pieces calling for some virtuosity from the player. His occasional works, such as the Water Music and Fireworks Music show his ingenuity in extending the range of the typical 17th cent. suite to serve a particular occasion.

Handel's working life was mostly spent in England where his Italian operas were acclaimed. In the years between his arrival here in 1711 and 1729 he wrote nearly thirty operas. It was only when the public tired of these and his reputation slumped that he turned to oratorio with equal success.

Bach and Handel between them crowned the age of polyphony that had lasted for two hundred years or more. After them, it is hardly surprising that composers began looking for a new style, already anticipated in the music of Rameau and particularly Dominico Scarlatti (1685–1737), whose harpsichord sonatas foreshadowed the classical sonata form that was to dominate music for the next two hundred years. The change in musical style about 1750 was partly the result of a change in musical patronage. Bach was the last great composer to earn his living through being employed by the church. The new patrons were the nobility who liked to have a composer on hand to write for the various evening entertainments of the time. For this purpose the princes and dukes had their own orchestras and their own small opera houses. The music required had to be elegant, formal, galant. Haydn was exceptionally fortunate in having an employer, Prince Nicholas of Esterhazy, who allowed him to write more of less as he wished so that he was able to develop symphonic form into something more than a pleasing way of passing an evening.

The early symphonists, culminating in Haydn, broke away from Bach's contrapuntal treatment of the orchestra. Instruments now came to be treated in a more colourful manner according to their particular timbre. The court of Mannheim had an orchestra of a standard unheard hitherto, and Johann Stamitz (1717–57) and his son Karl (1745–1801) influenced the great composers who were to follow in their footsteps. The composition of their orchestra was flexible, oboes, flutes, and horns often being added to the standard string section. Bach's son Carl Philipp Emanuel (1714–88) added to and developed symphonic and sonata form, especially as regards keys and subjects.

### Haydn and Mozart.

These two figures dominate the second half of the 18th cent. as Bach and Handel did the first. In a brief space only a general picture can be presented of their huge output and influence. Of Haydn's 104 symphonies (there may even be others) more than half are worthy of study and hearing. The craftsmanship is always remarkable, the invention ever new. Indeed without Haydn's harmonic daring or his melodic ingenuity, the even greater symphonic thought of Beethoven would have been impossible: Haydn laid the groundwork on which his successor built towering edifices. A work such as the 93rd symphony in D is typical of his mature style with its searching introduction, powerfully wrought, earnestly argued first movement, beautiful Largo and resourceful bustling finale. Haydn did not fight shy of contrapuntal writing: the development section of this symphony's first movement and the finale are evidence of that, but it was only as an integral part of a predominantly homophonic technique.

Mozart's symphonies are not so different in form from Haydn's and—this must be a subjective judgment—he put more emotional feeling into his. Nobody could listen to the heart-searching first movement of his 40th symphony without being deeply moved. It was in his final three works in the medium that Mozart brought his symphonic art to perfection, and these obviously had an effect on Haydn's later symphonies written after them. For passion and tenderness contained within a classical form these late symphonies, and many other of Mozart's works, have yet to be surpassed.

Haydn, who has been rightly termed "the Father of the Symphony" was also the founder of the string quartet—perhaps the most perfect, because the most exactly balanced, form of musical expression. The four instruments—two violins, viola, and cello—discuss, argue, commune with each other over the whole gamut of feeling. In his quartets Haydn's mastery of structure is even more amazing than in his symphonies. Mozart's quartets (especially the six devoted to Haydn) and even more his quintets achieve miracles of beauty in sound, nowhere more so than in the first movement of the G minor (his most personal key)

quintet. The two late piano quartets show how the piano can be ideally combined with strings. His clarinet quintet is also a masterly work.

Haydn did not leave any concertos of consequence. Mozart's, especially those for piano, are among his greatest works. As a brilliant clavier player himself, he showed a consummate skill in writing for the keyboard. Although the instrument he knew was slightly less advanced than the piano today, his concertos call for virtuosity in execution, yet they are as searching in emotional content as the late symphonies and quartets. Indeed the C major concerto (K. 467) and the C minor (K. 491) may be said to hold the quintessential Mozart. As well as twenty (mature) piano concertos, Mozart wrote six for the violin, four for the horn, and eighteen others, but none of these delightful as they are, can be placed in quite the same class.

Of their church music, Haydn's sixteen masses and his oratorios—The Creation and the Seasons (both late works)—are perhaps more worthy of attention than Mozart's various masses, but we must not forget Mozart's final work—the Requiem or the serene late Motet Ave Verum Corpus.

### Eighteenth-century Opera.

Mozart—for many the first great opera composer—did not, of course, create his masterpieces out of nothing. In France, Lully was followed by Rameau (1683–1764), who carried on his tradition of using classical themes but developed a more flexible style of recitative and greatly increased vividness of expression. But it was Gluck (1714–87) who more than anyone broke out of the straitjacket of the now ossified Italian form of opera—dominated by the singer—and showed just what could be achieved in moving human terms. Drama in music really came of age with his Orfeo e Eurydice (1762), Alceste (1767) and Iphigénie en Tauride (1779). His simplicity and poignancy of expression were not lost on Mozart.

Meanwhile in Germany a kind of opera called Singspiel appeared during the 18th cent. Breaking away from classical themes, mundane stories were told in dialogue and music.

Until quite recently Haydn's operas were dismissed as unworthy representations of his genuis but, chiefly through the enlightening efforts of the Haydn scholar, H. C. Robins Landon, some of his fifteen surviving works in the medium have been successfully revived. They have proved to be perfectly viable for the stage and, especially in the ensembles, full of that delightful invention to be found in the rest of his opus, if on a less fully developed scale. Still as musical drama they inevitably fall far short of Mozart's achievements, for the younger composer seems to have had an instinctive feeling for the stage. Into his operas he poured his most intense, personal music. He vividly portrays the foibles, desires, loves, and aspirations of mankind.

The earlier, immature stage pieces of his youth led to such works as Lucio Silla (1772) and La Finta Giardiniera (1775) with their first glimpses of the glories to come. His first indubitably great opera is Idomeneo (1781). Despite its unpromisingly static plot, Idomeneo reveals Mozart's stature through its ability to breathe new life into a conventional opera seria form. Though influenced by Gluck it is yet more human and touching in its musical expression. To succeed this Mozart wrote a much more frivolous piece Die Entführung aus dem Serail. Stemming from the Singspiel tradition, it none the less creates real-life characters who have much charming music to sing.

After three lesser pieces Mozart embarked on his four masterpieces—Le Nozze di Figaro (1786), Don Giovanni (1787), Così fan tutte (1790), and Die Zauberflöte (1791).

Figaro, as well as being a delightful comedy, explores more fully than any previous opera situation and character, which find expression in beautiful arias and in two finales of symphonic proportion. In *Don Giovanni*, less satisfactory as a dramatic structure, the range of musical characterisation and insight into human motives is widened still further. *Così* lyrically but humorously expresses the follies of love. Mozart could not help but love his characters and his music for them is at one and the same time amusing and heartfelt. *Die Zauberflöte*—The Magic Flute—displays Mozart's deep-felt love of his fellow men and of truth in an opera of great spiritual strength. Nor has opera any more loveable personality than the birdcatcher Papageno. Mozart's final opera *La Clemenza di Tito*, extolling imperial magnanimity, has never achieved the success or popularity of his other maturer stage works, though it contains much excellent music.

### Beethoven.

Mozart was the last major composer to depend, to any large extent, on private patronage for his living, and even he left the service of the Archbishop of Salzburg because he could not stand the restrictions imposed on his freedom. Henceforth composers would have to stand on their own two feet with all the advantages (liberty) and disadvantages (lack of security) that implied. Beethoven (1770–1827) was the first such composer of importance.

Although his work is usually divided into three periods, this division is somewhat too arbitrary, for no other composer in history, with the possible exception of Wagner, has shown such a continual development of his genius. Coming at just the right moment in musical history, he crowned the achievements of Haydn and Mozart with music of the utmost profundity of thought and feeling that looks back to its classical heritage and forward to the romantic movement of the 19th cent. His influence on musical thinking and writing is incalculable.

His first period shows his strong melodic gifts and the beginning of his individuality in developing form and structure to suit his own ends and match his particular genius. Unusual keys are explored, unusual harmonic procedures employed. With the "Eroica" (his third symphony) he established his position as a great composer. The unity of purpose he here achieved within a long and diverse structure is truly staggering, even today. In the first movement alone the structural invention and cogency went far beyond what even Mozart had achieved in his "Jupiter" symphony, and the second movement—a vast funeral March—has an overwhelmingly tragic emotional content. But the "Eroica" was followed by six equally great symphonies, each one as varied, as inventive, as unified as the others. The ninth symphony is significant in both its length and finale. Here Beethoven crowns three superb instrumental movements with a choral movement that, as well as summing up all that has gone before, expresses in music the joy in existence more ecstatically than any other work.

The burning intensity of Beethoven's genius is just as evident in his chamber music. His quartets are the product of a revolutionary age in which the social graces and formal restraint of the 18th cent. were thrown off in a search for a more personal mode of expression. The early op. 18 set, and the Razoumovsky quartets, op. 59, go even beyond the range of Haydn's and Mozart's works in the medium but it was in his late quartets, his final musical testament, that Beethoven refined and distilled his art for posterity. No words can possibly describe their unique quality, but any and every chance should be taken to make their acquaintance: the effort required will be more than amply rewarded.

The early piano concertos do not reach quite this level of attainment, but the last three, together with the violin concerto, are on a par with the finest of the symphonies and quartets, as well as being considerable tests of the performers' technique. The Triple Concerto for piano, violin, and cello is an unusual and rewarding work.

Beethoven's grandest choral work—and one of the most noble in existence—is the Mass in D (*Missa Solemnis*). Its vast scale and sublime utterance often defeat performers, but when it is successfully done there is no more spiritually uplifting experience for the listener. Except perhaps Beethoven's only opera, *Fidelio*. This simple escape story was transformed by Beethoven's creative fire into a universal symbol of liberty, the composer identifying himself with the struggle for freedom from tyranny and release from darkness.

Beethoven lived in a period of war and revolution. A passionate belief in the brotherhood of man and in liberty, he was shocked to find his ideals thrown over by revolutionaries-turned-dictators. His own tragedy of deafness, which came upon him at the moment of his triumph, nearly submerged him, but in the end he won through and produced the string of masterpieces from the "Eroica" onwards. Hope springing from despair, love from hatred, victory over defeat, these are the unquenchable legacies left by Beethoven.

### The Romantic Movement.

Inevitably, the Romantic movement in literature that burst forth about 1800 was bound to have its counterpart in music. And so it was. Breaking the classical bonds, composers such as Schubert, Schumann, Liszt, and Berlioz sought a new freedom in musical expression. Form became of less importance than content; and that content often had literary connections. For their purposes a larger orchestra was needed and supplied, but the miniature, the song especially, because of its very personal connotation, was also a favourite form.

Schubert (1797–1828)—described by Liszt as "the most poetic of musicians"—is perhaps the greatest lyrical genius in musical history. In him the Viennese tradition and influence of Haydn, Mozart, and Beethoven reached its zenith. The song was always Schubert's starting point, so it is hardly surprising that his reputation as a song writer has never been impaired but in his symphonic and instrumental works too it is always his inexhaustible fund of melody that first calls for attention. Nobody could listen to his "Trout" quintet, for piano and strings, his octet, his fifth symphony, or his song cycle *Die Schöne Müllerin* without being enchanted and invigorated by the sheer tunefulness of the music. But there is much more to Schubert than this: his understanding of the possibilities of harmonic change, his grasp of orchestral coloration (in the great C major symphony, for instance), his free use of sonata structure.

Although Mozart, Haydn, and Beethoven had all contributed to the song as an art form, it was with Schubert that it achieved its first full flowering. If he had written nothing but his songs, his place in the musical firmament would be assured. With his *Erlkönig* in 1815 the German *Lied* came of age and from then until the end of his life he wrote more than six hundred songs, hardly a dud among them. Whether it is the charm of *Heidenröslein*, the drama of *Der Doppelgänger* or the numbed intensity of the *Winterreise* cycle Schubert unerringly went to the heart of a poet's meaning; indeed he often raised poor verses to an inspired level by his settings. And for the first time the pianist shares a place of equal importance with the singer.

There is only room to mention one or two other composers, some of them wrongly neglected, who were roughly contemporaries of Beethoven and Schubert: the Czech Dussek (1760–1812), who like Beethoven bridges the classical-romantic gulf, Boccherini (1743–1805), the two Italian opera composers Cimarosa (1749–1801) and Paisiello (1740–1816), the Frenchman Méhul (1763–1817) and the German Hummel (1778–1836).

Weber (1784–1826) lacked Beethoven's energy and constructive powers and Schubert's sheer lyrical profundity, but he is an important figure, especially in the field of opera, where his *Der*

*Freischütz* and *Oberon* led the way to a more flexible, dramatically realistic form of opera. His vivid imagination exactly fitted the new romantic mood abroad. The sheer beauty in the melodic shape of his music is also not to be denied.

## Mendelssohn and Schumann.

Mendelssohn (1809–47) was the civilised craftsman among the Romantic composers. A boy genius—many of his finest works were written before he was twenty—he maintained the importance of classical form while imbuing it with his own affectionate brand of poetic sensibility. His third and fourth symphonies—the " Scottish " and " The Italian "—(and possibly the fifth " The Reformation "), his string quartets (some of which go deeper than most of his music), violin concerto, first piano concerto, and of course, the incidental music to " A Midsummer Night's Dream " represent his tidy yet effervescent style at its most winning.

Schumann (1810–1856) is less easy to categorise. His early romantic flame was burnt out by some flaw in his intellectual and/or emotional make-up, and his inspiration seems to have declined in later years. No matter, by then he had given us the marvellous song cycles of 1840, an ever fresh piano concerto, many fine piano solos, including the mercurial, popular *Carnaval* and several symphonies, which, if not structurally perfect, contain much lovely music. The joys and sorrows of love and the feeling for natural beauty are all perfectly mirrored in these charming, lyrical works.

## Romantic Giants.

Berlioz (1803–69) and Liszt (1811–86) are the two most typical representative figures of the Romantic era. Both have always been controversial figures, with ardent advocates and opponents either unduly enthusiastic or unfairly derogatory. Berlioz might be termed the perfect painter in music. With an uncanny mastery of orchestral sound he could conjure up the countryside, the supernatural and the historical with the utmost ease. He based his music on the " direct reaction to feeling " and a desire to illustrate literature by musical means. That his technical expertise was not always the equal of his undoubted genius, can be heard in many of his larger works such as the dramatic cantata *The Damnation of Faust* and the dramatic symphony *Romeo and Juliet*, yet most people are willing to overlook the occasional vulgarity for the ineffable beauty of his many fine pages, but brutal cuts in his music, such as are often made in, for instance, his epic opera *The Trojans* only have the effect of reducing the stature of his works. We must accept him, warts and all. Anyone who has seen the two parts of *The Trojans*, presented complete in one evening at Covent Garden, will realise that Berlioz knew what he was about.

His output is not quantitatively large but includes several monumental works, as well as *The Trojans*. The *Requiem* (" Grand Messe des Morts ") requires a tenor solo, huge chorus and orchestra, and brass bands, although Berlioz uses these forces fastidiously. The *Symphonie funèbre et Triomphale*, calls in its original form, for choir, brass, and strings. But Berlioz was just as happy writing on a smaller scale as his exquisite song cycle, to words of Théophile Gautier, *Nuits d'Été*, shows. Gautier perhaps summed up better than anyone Berlioz's singular talent: " In that renaissance of the 1830s Berlioz represents the romantic musical idea, the breaking up of old moulds, the substitution of new forms for unvaried square rhythms, a complex and competent richness of orchestration, truth of local colour, unexpected effects in sound, tumultuous and Shakespearian depth of passion, amorous or melancholy dreaminess, longings and questionings of the soul, infinite and mysterious sentiments not to be rendered in words, and that something more than all which escapes language but may be divined in music."

During his lifetime Liszt was fêted and honoured not only by his musical colleagues but by the world at large, which idolised him and his piano. Then his reputation took a plunge from which it has only recently recovered. To be sure much of his early music is glitter and gloss, but his symphonies and tone poems—especially the Faust Symphony, the Dante Symphony (both, of course, inspired by literature), and *Orpheus* and *Prometheus*—and his late piano works show that he was an extraordinary harmonic innovator. The piano sonata in B minor brings his romantic, wilful temperament within a reasonably stable, pianistic form, and as such is a landmark in the repertory of the instrument. Liszt's output was prodigious, but the inquiring listener should explore the more original of his compositions already mentioned to form a true picture of his fertile genius.

## Chopin.

Chopin (1810–49) was the master of the keyboard, par excellence. His development of the technical and expressive capabilities of the piano is unique in musical history. His inventive powers were poured out with nervous passionate energy and in a highly individual style through twenty astonishing, possibly agonised years of creative activity before his early death. A Chopin melody, limpid, transparent, singing, can be recognised easily by anyone, but his style gradually developed into something more subtle, more satisfying than pure melody. He took the greatest care of every detail so that any alteration, however small, upsets the perfect balance of his work. His poetic sensibility can be found in any of his works; for his constructive ability we must turn to the Ballades, the B minor Sonata, and the Barcarolle, while the Preludes and Studies blend technical powers and emotional expressiveness in ideal proportions.

## Nineteenth-century Opera.

After Mozart's operas and Beethoven's *Fidelio*, the medium might have been expected to decline. Instead it took on a new, if different, lease of life that culminated in Verdi's extraordinary output.

Rossini (1792–1868) created a world of exuberant high spirits in his operatic works that are as cheerful and heart-warming today as they were a hundred or more years ago.

He always worked in and around the lyric theatres of Italy and between 1810 and 1830 poured out a stream of works, not all of which can be expected to be masterpieces. However, *Il Barbiere di Siviglia*, *L'Italiana in Algieri*, *La Cenerentola* and *Le Comte Ory* will always delight audiences as long as opera houses exist. Although these works are difficult to sing really well, their vitality and charm can never be submerged even by poor voices or indifferent staging.

His German contemporaries were critical of his confidence and frivolity, but his works show a consistency of invention and an irresistible tunefulness that anyone might envy. In recent years, there has also been a renewed interest in his more serious operas—*Otello* (1816), *La Gazza Ladra* (1817), *Semiramide* (1823), *La Siège de Corinthe* (1820), and *Guillaume Tell* (1829)—which were certainly surpassed in dramatic power by his successors but which nevertheless are not to be despised or neglected.

*William Tell*, to give it its more popular title, was his last work for the stage although he lived on for nearly forty years in retirement in Paris, scene of many of his greatest successes. There he enjoyed good living, dispensing *bons mots*, and occasionally composing trifles. An exception is the unpretentious *Petite Messe Solennelle*, written originally for soloists, chorus, a harmonium, and two pianos. Rossini later orchestrated it, but he would not allow it to be performed during his lifetime. The first public performance was on 28 February 1869, as near as possible to the 78th anniversary of the composer's birth on Leap Year Day 1792.

In contrast to the mercurial Rossini, Vincenzo Bellini (1801–1835) was an exquisite, romantic figure dealing with exquisite, romantic stories, an operatic equivalent to Chopin, who much admired him. His delicate, sinuous vocal line (in the arias) and brilliant acrobatics in the final sections (cabalettas) require singers of the utmost accomplishment to do them justice, although his music is never as florid as Rossini's. His most typical and popular works are probably *La Sonnambula* (1831), *Norma* (1831) and *I Puritani* (1835). The first is a tender, homely country story, the second an almost heroic lyrical drama of sacrifice, and the third a rather unsatisfactory historical story redeemed by its appealing music. In the past few years singers of the calibre of Maria Callas, Joan Sutherland, Guiletta Simionato, and Marilyn Horne have brought Bellini's operas a popularity almost equal to that they enjoyed at the time they were written.

Gaetano Donizetti (1797–1848) was an even more prolific operatic composer than Rossini. He wrote at least 75 works, mostly for the Italian stage, several of which, such as *Alfredo il Grande* or *Emilia di Liverpool*, are never likely to be revived, but during the past few years, with the renewed interest in what are called the *Ottocento* operas, many of his serious operas have been resuscitated and found as enjoyable in performance as his more frequently heard comedies.

He was a well-grounded musician and although his invention is often criticised for being too tied to the conventions of his day performances often belie this reputation, his dramatic instinct proving sure. *Lucia di Lammermoor*, because of the chances it offers to a coloratura soprano with tragic pretensions, has always held the stage and of late *Lucrezia Borgia*, *Anna Bolena*, *La Favorita*, and *Poliuto* have all been successfully revived. Of his lighter works, the comedies *L'Elisir d'Amore* and *Don Pasquale* have never declined in popularity. One of his last works was *Linda di Chamounix* (1842) which he wrote for Vienna where it aroused such enthusiasm that the Emperor appointed him Court Composer and Master of the Imperial Chapel.

### French Opera.

The taste in Paris was for more and more lavish productions. Following Spontini (1774–1851), whose works were comparatively austere, came Halévy (1799–1862) and Giacomo Meyerbeer (1791–1864) whose operas contain all the ingredients that came to be expected of "Grand Opera"—spectacle, huge ensembles, showpieces for the soloists, and extended, if superfluous ballet. Drawing from Italian, German, and French traditions Meyerbeer's music contained everything the public wanted, yet today they are seldom revived, perhaps because his creative powers were essentially derivative, yet when they *are* given, operas like *Les Huguenots*, *Le Prophète*, and *L'Africaine* still have the power to fascinate and his influence on his successors, notably Wagner, was considerable.

### Verdi.

Italian opera in the 19th cent. culminated in the works of Giuseppe Verdi (1813–1901), who rose from a peasant background to become his country's most noted composer, as well as something of a natural hero during the period of the Risorgimento. His earliest works, indeed, often roused his hearers to patriotic fervour. For instance, *Nabucco* (1842), with its theme of an oppressed people seeking deliverance, was treated as a symbol of the Italians' fight for freedom.

Musically, Verdi developed out of all recognition during the course of his long career. The continuously flowing structure of his last two operas *Otello* and *Falstaff* is very far removed from the start-stop formulas, inherited from his predecessors, of his first works, yet even they are touched, in harmonic subtleties, orchestral felicities, and a sense of drama, by a spark of genius, a burning inspiration that sets him apart from all other operatic composers. *Ernani* (1844), *I due Foscari* (1844), and *Luisa Miller* (1849) all have foretastes of glories to come even if as a whole they are flawed dramas, and these "gallery years", as Verdi himself later described them, gave him the essential know-how to produce his later, greater operas, as well as establishing him incontrovertibly as the most popular Italian composer of the time.

However, it was with *Rigoletto* (1851), *Il Trovatore* (1853), and *La Traviata* (1853) that Verdi first really staked his claim to immortality. In these pieces his increasing dramatic mastery are married to a wonderful flow of lyrical melody, at the same time controlled by a fine musical sensibility. They were followed by four operas—*Simon Boccanegra* (1857), *Un Ballo in Maschera* (1858), *La Forza del Destino* (1862), and *Macbeth* (revised version, 1865)—in which Verdi overcame complexities of story line by his continually developing musical powers. This period is crowned by *Don Carlos* (written for the Paris Opéra, 1867) a masterly exercise in combining private and public situations in a single, grand, and characterful work. In some respects Verdi never surpassed the subtlety of his writing in this opera. *Aïda* (1871) carried on the process but the characterisation in this ever-popular piece is less refined than in *Don Carlos*, if the grandeur of the design is more spectacular.

The success of *Otello* (1887) owes nearly as much to the skill of Boito whose literary ability combined with musical knowledge (he was himself a composer) presented Verdi with an ideal libretto for his seamless music in which the drama moves inevitably to its tragic end. Recitative, aria, ensemble are fused in a single, swiftly moving music-drama, which in its very different way equals that of Wagner. *Falstaff* (1893) achieves the same success in the field of comic opera, a brilliant, mercurial ending to a distinguished career. If Verdi had written only these two final masterpieces his place in musical history would be assured.

### Brahms.

Brahms (1833–1897) has justly been described as "a romantic spirit controlled by a classical intellect," for while complying with most of the formal regulations of sonata form he imbued them with an emotional content that accorded with his time. Indeed Schumann declared that he was the "one man who would be singled out to make articulate in an ideal way the highest expression of our time."

Perhaps in his chamber music will be found the quintessence of his art. The piano and clarinet quintets, the two string sextets, the horn trio, and the violin sonatas all are designed on a large scale yet the expression remains intimate, the design and structure clear.

The symphonies and concertos, though, remain his most popular works; they are part of the solid repertory of every orchestra and most piano and violin players in the world. Their high seriousness, constant lyrical beauty, and control of form are deeply satisfying. They do not provide the extremes of passion and excitement provided by his contemporaries, but their study provides continuous absorption and delight. The double concerto for violin and cello deserves a mention as a unique work in music.

Brahms wrote more than two hundred songs in which the desire for melodic beauty takes precedence over the words and meaning. Many are set to poor poetry, but hidden away are still some unexplored treasures, and the Four Serious Songs, at least, are tragic masterpieces. In a lighter vein the two sets of *Liebeslieder Walzer* for four voices are irresistible. The choral Requiem, too, is a fine work.

### Bruckner.

In recent years Bruckner's reputation *vis-à-vis* his great contemporary Brahms has been enhanced in England. The old conception of him as a naïve Austrian unable to grasp the fundamentals of symphonic architecture has died hard, and the prevailing popularity of his grandest works is at last gaining him his rightful place in the 19th-cent. firmament. The nine symphonies and the masses are his chief claim to immortality. They contain melodies of unforgettable beauty, symphonic paragraphs of unparalleled grandeur, and an appreciation of formal development that, though different, is as equally valid as that of Brahms. The movements of his symphonies are long and he often pauses, as if for breath and to admire the scenery, before he reaches the climactic peak of his musical journey. His idiom is best approached by a newcomer to his work through the fourth and seventh symphonies as they are perhaps the easiest to understand, but the fifth, sixth, eighth, and ninth (unfinished) are just as beautiful—and cogently argued—once one has acquired the knack, so to speak, of listening to his music. Most of these works are now to be heard in their original form, stripped of the veneer of "improvements" suggested to the diffident composer by his friends.

As well as the masses, which translate Bruckner's symphonic ideas to the choral plain, Bruckner's delightful string quintet is worth investigating.

## Wagner.

Praised only this side of idolatry by his admirers, unmercifully criticised by his detractors, Richard Wagner (1813–83) is perhaps the most controversial composer in musical history. And so it was bound to be with such a revolutionary figure, whose writings, other than his music, contain, to say the least, dubious theories and whose operas, composed to his own libretti, broke the bonds of the form as known until his time. He regarded music-drama as a fusion of all the arts—music, literature, painting—in one unity. With *The Ring of the Nibelungs* he achieved his purpose: no other work of art has ever tried to encompass the whole of existence. Today, and surely forever, musicians, philosophers, and writers will argue over its meaning, and each age will reinterpret it according to its own lights.

But before he reached this pinnacle of achievement, Wagner gradually transformed opera—through *Rienzi, The Flying Dutchman, Tannhäuser*, and *Lohengrin*—so that a new mould was fashioned to take what he wanted to pour into it. He introduced the *Leitmotiv*, a musical theme that could be associated with a particular person, situation, or idea, each time it occurred. Slowly he developed the musical form so that the drama could unfold continuously without breaks for arias. By the time he began to write *Tristan and Isolde* and *Die Meistersinger*, he had perfected his methods and had he never undertaken *The Ring* that tragedy and that comedy would have assured him his place in the musical firmament. Indeed, *Die Meistersinger* is considered a masterpiece even by those who are not willing or prepared to accept the rest of the Wagnerian ethos.

The length and complexity of these operas, and of *Parsifal*, a work of unique beauty in spite of certain *longueurs*, means that it is almost essential to prepare oneself by homework, with libretti and records, before attempting to assimilate them in the opera house. The added effort is well worth while for the ultimate musical satisfaction they bring because Wagner was more than an operatic reformer: he opened up a new harmonic language (especially in the use of chromaticism) that was logically to develop into the atonality of the 20th cent.

## Wolf.

As Wagner was the culmination of the 19th cent. symphonic and operatic tradition, so Hugo Wolf (1860–1903) summed up, if he did not surpass, the achievements in song-writing of Schubert Schumann, and Loewe (1796–1869).

Wolf was a lonely pathetic man. He lived much of his life in poverty, and eventually lost his reason and died of an incurable disease. These circumstances account perhaps for his almost feverish bursts of creative activity, which were also the outward sign of his burning genius. His greatest contributions to the art of *Lieder* were his extraordinary insight into the poet's meaning and the harmonic means by which he heightened the expression of the words. He raised the importance of the piano part even higher than had Schumann, and in some of his songs the vocal part takes the form of a free declamation over a repeated idea in the piano. However, in the main the vocal and piano parts are interweaved with great subtlety, and he unerringly matched the very varied moods of the poems he chose to set. His greatest creative period was between early 1888 and early 1890 when songs poured from his pen daily—more than 50 settings of the German poet Mörike, 20 of Eichendorff, more than 50 of Goethe, and more than 40 of Heyse and Geibel (the Spanish Song-book). Later he composed songs from Heyse's Italian Song-book and the three Michelangelo sonnets. And the range of his creative understanding was wide, taking in the almost wild passion of the Spanish songs, the humanity and humour of the Italian love-songs, the titanic power of *Prometheus* (Goethe), the varying moods of the Mörike book, and the intangible power of the Michelangelo sonnets. There are almost inexhaustible riches here for the inquiring mind to discover. Outside Lieder, Wolf's output is small, but it includes a sadly neglected opera, *Der Corregidor*, the Italian Serenade for string quartet (alternatively for small orchestra) and a tone poem *Penthesilea*.

Ernest Newman, his greatest champion, summed up his work most aptly: "Wolf practically never repeats himself in the songs; every character is drawn from the living model. It is a positively Shakespearian imagination that is at work—Protean in its creativeness, inexhaustibly fecund and always functioning from the inside of the character or the scene, not merely making an inventory from the outside."

## National Movements.

During the course of the 19th cent., alongside the emergence of national political identity, came the rise of nationalism in music, fertilising traditional Western—that is basically German—musical forms with folk material. Of these groups the Russian is certainly the most important, if not the most vital.

Glinka (1804–57) was the first important Russian composer of the national school and, although his two operas *A Life for the Tsar* (sometimes called *Ivan Susanin*) and *Russlan and Ludmilla* are strongly influenced by Italian models, they do introduce Russian song and harmony into the texture. He undoubtedly influenced Borodin (1833–87), Cui (1835–1918), Balakireff (1837–1910), Mussorgsky (1839–81) and Rimsky-Korsakov (1844–1908)—the so-called "Five" of 19th-cent. Russian music. However, each was very much of an individualist too. Borodin was a lecturer in chemistry who wrote in his spare time. His two symphonies, two string quartets led up to his most notable work, the opera *Prince Igor*, left incomplete at his death. Balakireff, friend and adviser to the rest of the group, wrote little himself, but his orchestral works and the piano fantasia, *Islamey*, are worthy of investigation.

Modest Mussorgsky (1839–81) is today seen as the most important and inspired of "The Five." More than the others he used Russian song and Russian speech as the basis of his operas in which he portrayed the lives and destinies of his own people. Although his capacities were seriously impaired by an uncongenial job, poverty, and drinking, he produced two great operas, *Boris Godunov* and *Khovanshchina*, and another *Sorochintsy Fair* that is immensely enjoyable. *Boris* should be given in its original, with spare orchestration, but more often than not it is heard in Rimsky-Korsakov's more elaborate revision. In any case the opera exists in various versions, none of them necessarily the right one: what is important is to hear it in one or the other because of its great portrayal of Boris's personality set against the background of the Russian people, unforgettably presented in choral outbursts. *Khovanshchina* was completed by Rimsky-Korsakov, *Sorochintsy Fair* by Tcherepnin (although other versions also exist). Mussorgsky's songs explore a new vein of naturalistic vocal declamation. Each of the four *Songs and Dances of Death* is a miniature drama worthy of Wolf, although of course in a quite other idiom. The *Nursery* songs miraculously conjure up a child's world as seen from a child's point of view. Many of the individual songs, the *Sunless* cycle too, should be investigated.

Rimsky-Korsakov (1844–1908) is perhaps a less attractive figure because so much of his music seems heartless or merely decorative, but this judgment is probably made on the strength of hearing *Shéhérazade* and the *Capriccio Espagnol* a few too many times. Such of his 15 operas that are played evince a (literally) fantastic mind and lyrical vein, and it is a pity that *Sadko*, *The Snow Maiden*, and *The Tsar's Bride*, at least, are not heard more often.

## Tchaikovsky.

Peter Ilyich Tchaikovsky (1840–93) is a more universally admired figure than any of "The Five" and his music is indubitably closer to the mainstream than theirs in that it adheres more nearly to Western European forms. His popularity is due to his unhesitating appeal to the emotions and to his tender, often pathetic melodic expression. His lyrical gift is stronger than his sense of architecture, as he himself admitted. Yet his later symphonies—the fourth, fifth, and sixth (the *Pathétique*)—are all cogently enough argued and invigorating, as can be heard in the hands of a conductor willing to emphasise their formal power rather than their tendency towards sentimentality; the orchestral craftsmanship is also superb. The three piano concertos and the violin concerto offer rare opportunities for virtuoso display within a reasonably dramatic structure and his various overtures are always exciting to hear.

The three ballets—*The Sleeping Beauty*, *Swan Lake*, and *Nutcracker* show Tchaikovsky's skill on a smaller and perhaps more congenial scale, but only two of his operas—*Eugene Onegin* and *The Queen of Spades*—survive in regular performance. They demonstrate his ability to delineate character and his always eloquent melodic invention. His songs often felicitously capture a passing mood or emotion.

## Bohemia (Czechoslovakia).

The Czech national school is dominated by two composers—Smetana (1824–84) and Dvořák (1841–1904). In his own country Smetana holds a unique position as the father of his country's music—which is remarkable when you consider that he lived in a country that was then under Austrian rule and never spoke the Czech language perfectly. Yet his music is filled with the spirit of Czech history and national life, and many of his operas, his most important contribution, deal purely with national subjects. The reawakening of interest in things national, after Austria's defeat by Italy in 1859, led to the establishment of a Provisional Theatre in 1862 and Smetana's first opera *The Brandenburgers in Bohemia* was produced there in 1866, but its success was eclipsed by the enormous popularity of *The Bartered Bride*, which appeared the same year. Its melodic charm, lively characterisation and cosy humour have carried it round the world and it is the one Smetana opera to be in the repertory of most opera houses. However, his next opera *Dalibor* (1868) is considered by some authorities as his masterpiece. It is conceived on a heroic scale, and frequently rises to great dramatic heights. His later operas include *Libuše* (1872) a solemn festival tableau, *The Two Widows* (1874), a delightful comedy, *The Kiss* (1876), *The Secret* (1878), and *The Devil's Wall* (1882).

His main orchestral work *Má Vlast* (My Country), written between 1874 and 1879, is a cycle of six symphonic poems nobly depicting the life and legends of his country. He wrote only three mature chamber works—an elegiac piano trio, written in 1855 in memory of the death of his eldest daughter, and two string quartets, both autobiographical. The first in E minor (1876)—" From My Life "—tells of his youth and aspirations until a terrible, screeching E in *altissimo* describes the onset of deafness; the second in D minor, sadly neglected, was described by the composer as an attempt to explain the " whirlwind of music in the head of one, who has lost his hearing," and was probably influenced by Beethoven's later music.

Dvořák combined a fecund melodic gift with an intelligent grasp of structure. His symphonies and chamber music are mostly written in classical form, yet the works are imbued with a spontaneity and freshness that have not lost one whit of their charm over the years.

He wrote nine symphonies and, although only the last three or four are regularly performed, they are mostly mature works, several of which, for instance No. 7 in D minor (formerly known as No. 2) reach a tragic grandeur at times. They are all orchestrated in a masterly way and are full of delightful detail. Dvořák wanted to show that a Brahms could come out of Bohemia—and he succeeded in doing so while maintaining a definitely individual flavour, strongly influenced by natural rhythms.

He wrote three concertos, one each for piano, violin, and cello. The earlier ones are interesting without being quite in the first flight of the composer's output, but the cello concerto of 1895 is perhaps the composer's crowning achievement—warm, mellifluous, romantic.

He wrote chamber music throughout his long creative life. Some of the early works are weak and derivative, but the later string quartets, the " Dumky " trio, and the piano quartet and quintet are expressive and full of unforced invention. Dvořák felt himself somewhat hampered when setting words, nevertheless his *Stabat Mater* and *Te Deum* are both deeply felt choral works and he wrote songs throughout his career, many of them very fine indeed. He wrote ten operas, but only *Rusalka* (1901) has gained a foothold outside Czechoslavakia.

## Janáček.

The Moravian composer Leoš Janáček (1858–1928) spent most of his life in Brno as a working musician. His music has recently come to be recognised as some of the most original written in the past hundred years. His operas, in which he closely followed the inflection of the speech of his native land, are his finest works. Over the score of his last opera, *From the House of the Dead*, he wrote the words "In every human being there is a divine spark" and it is this deep love of humanity that permeates all his works. Of his operas *Kátya Kabanová* (1921) and *The Cunning Little Vixen* (1924), the *Makropoulos Affair* (1926), and *From the House of the Dead* (adapted from a Dostoyevsky novel, 1928) are the most important and they have all been produced in Britain in recent years. His original genius is self-evident in all of them.

Among his orchestral works *Taras Bulba* and *Sinfonietta* should be noted, and his two string quartets, very difficult to play, should be better known. The song cycle, *Diary of one who has disappeared*, for tenor, contralto, and three female voices with piano, and the Glagolithic Mass contain music of much expressive beauty.

## Hungary.

The Hungarian musical outburst came somewhat later than that in other countries. Its great figure is Bela Bartók (1881–1945) who, as well as being a national figure, has proved an influential composer in the whole of 20th-cent. music. His mind was full of folk music, but it was transmuted by his strongly personal style and powerful intellect into something highly original. His music is tense and volatile but this restlessness is sometimes relieved by a kind of other-wordly, ethereal lyricism, as in the lovely slow movements of his quartets.

Bartók was affected as much by the musical innovations of Debussy and Stravinsky (see below) as by East European, notably Magyar, folk music and many of his works are an attempt to meld the two.

The most important part of his output is undoubtedly his string quartets which cover most of his creative life. To this intimate form he confided his personal innermost thoughts and in it conducted his most far-reaching musical experiments, thereby extending its boundaries beyond anything previously known. As with Beethoven's late quartets many of Bartók's rely on organic or cyclic development while remaining just within the laws of classical form. As Mosco Carner puts it, "For profundity of thought, imaginative power, logic of structure, diversity of formal details, and enlargement of the technical scope, they stand unrivalled in the field of modern chamber music."

The most important of his orchestral works are the three piano concertos, of which the first two are harsh and uncompromising, and fiendishly difficult to play, while the third, written in 1945, is mellower and more diatonic. The second violin concerto (1937–8) shows the various elements of Bartók's style in full flower, by turns exhuberant, passionate, and brilliant. The *Music for Strings, Percussion and Celesta* (1937) is remarkable for its strange sonorities and its fascinating texture. The *Concerto for Orchestra* (1944) is more immediately appealing and again shows the composer in complete command of a large canvas. Of the piano works *Mikrokosmos* (1935) and the sonata for two pianos and percussion (1937) are especially to be noted.

His chief stage pieces are *The Miraculous Mandarin* (1919), a harsh, cruel ballet which drew appropriately dramatic music from the composer, and the opera *Duke Bluebeard's Castle* (1911), a luscious, original score that makes one regret that he wrote no more operas later in his career.

Kodály (1882–1967) was from early years closely associated with Bartók and with him collected Hungarian folk melodies using many of them in his music. He worked in many forms and the more important of his works are the Peacock Variations for orchestra, the choral *Psalmus Hungaricus* and *Te Deum*, The *Dances of Galánta*, and the opera *Háry János*, and the sonatas for cello and for unaccompanied cello.

### Sibelius, Nielsen and Grieg.

Among Scandinavian composers the Finn Jean Sibelius (1865–1957) and the Dane Carl Nielsen (1865–1931) are outstanding. Sibelius is a lone northern figure ploughing his own furrow, oblivious or, at any rate, ignoring the unusual developments that were taking place in Central Europe, yet his seven symphonies are strong as granite, honest, rugged works that will undoubtedly stand the test of time. They are not by any means all similar in mood, or even form. The first is very much influenced by Tchaikovsky and Borodin, the second and third show a more personal style developing, the fourth is terse and tragic, the fifth lyrical, bright, and lucid; the sixth is perhaps most typically Sibelian in its evocation of primeval nature, and the seventh—in one continuous movement—is a more purely abstract piece, notable for its structural logic and the grandness of its themes. The violin concerto is the most easily understood of the composer's main works and has a grateful part for the soloist.

The tone poems *The Swan of Tuonela, Pohjola's Daughter, En Saga, Night Ride and Sunrise, The Bard,* and *Tapiola* uncannily evoke the icy words of the legends of the far north, and the primeval

forces of nature. Sibelius's one string quartet *Voces Intimae* and many of his songs are worth hearing too. The quality of this enigmatic composer's music has recently been the subject of much argument, but his musical personality is probably strong enough to survive the quirks of fashion.

Carl Nielsen (1865–1931) is another individualist. His six symphonies, like Sibelius's seven, are the most important part of his output, but whereas Sibelius was dealing with a huge, uninhabited northern landscape, Nielsen is more friendly and serene in his music, which is seldom forbidding, always inventive, throwing a new light, through unusual ideas about harmony, structure and tonality, on traditional forms. He also wrote highly individual concertos for the flute and clarinet, four string quartets and two operas—the dramatic, rather Brahmsian *Saul and David* (1902) and a delightful comedy, *Maskarade* (1906), full of lyrical music.

The Norwegian composer Edvard Grieg (1843–1907) was essentially a miniaturist whose range of feeling was not wide but whose music is always gentle and appealing. His most notable works are the romantic piano concerto, the atmospheric incidental music to Ibsen's play *Peer Gynt*, the charming Lyric Suite, and the small piano pieces. Not an important composer, then, but always an attractive one.

### Elgar and the English Revival.

After the death of Purcell there is hardly a name in English music worth speaking of until the 19th cent. when Hubert Parry (1848–1918) and Charles Villiers Stanford (1852–1924), actually an Irishman, led a revival. Their music is seldom heard today, but their pioneer work paved the way for Edward Elgar (1857–1934). Although all were influenced by Brahms they nevertheless managed to establish a new English tradition that has been carried on in our own day. Elgar's symphonies are laid out on a grand, leisurely scale and they are both eloquent and exhilarating. His violin concerto has an elegiac slow movement as has the glorious cello concerto and both contain many fine opportunities for the soloist. The cello concerto is as appealing a work as any by Elgar expressing his innermost thoughts. His *Enigma* variations are a series of portraits in sound of his friends, but there is another overall theme to go with them that has never been identified. This has not prevented the work from becoming Elgar's most popular, not surprisingly when one considers its charm and melodiousness. Three other orchestral pieces that should not be neglected are his symphonic study *Falstaff*, a many-sided musical picture of the Fat Knight, and the overtures *Cockaigne*, a happy evocation of London, and *In the South*, inspired by a visit to Italy. His three late chamber works, written when he was 61, are reticent, economic pieces that remove any misconception of Elgar as a bombastic composer. His songs are mostly feeble, but the oratorios, notably *The Dream of Gerontius*, show the composer's ability to control a large canvas. The composer himself wrote over the score of *Gerontius*, "This is the best of me"—a verdict with which we can readily agree.

### The French Impressionists.

César Franck (1822–90) was the main figure in mid-19th-cent. musical France and his influence spread even wider than his music of which only the D minor Symphony, the Symphonic Variations for piano and orchestra, the piano quintet, and the violin sonata are likely to be encountered today. The leading French opera composers of that time were Massenet (1842–1912) and Gounod (1818–93).

Concurrently with similar movements in French painting and poetry came the French Impressionist composers at the end of the 19th cent. Their leader—and one of the great seminal forces of modern music—was Claude Debussy (1862–1918). His aim was to capture a mood or sensation and he did that by more or less inventing a fresh system of harmony using a whole-tone scale, unusual chords, and creating in the orchestra new, highly personal textures—there is no mistaking the Debussy idiom once you have heard at least one piece by him. His impressionistic style did not lead him, however, to abandon form as some have suggested, and his main works are just as closely organised as those by classical German composers. His music is sensuous and poetic yet nearly always formally satisfying as well.

His reputation, at least with the general musical public, rests largely on his orchestral music, a few piano pieces and his only opera *Pelléas et Mélisande.* *La Mer* is a scintillating evocation of the sea in all its moods; *Nocturnes*, *Images*, and *Prélude à l'Après midi d'un Faune* exactly suggest different places, times, moods—the " Iberia " and " Gigues " sections of *Images*, calling to mind respectively the spirit of Spain and the flickering light of a rainy English night. *Pelléas*, based on a Symbolist drama by Maeterlinck, tells a story of love, jealousy, and murder in predominantly restrained yet emotionally loaded terms. It is an elusive original work that has no predecessor or successor. Intensely atmospheric, rivetingly beautiful, it weaves an irresistible spell over the listener.

Debussy's chamber music is unjustly neglected. His string quartet (1893) was one of the first works in which he displayed his new and strange world of sound, and the three late sonatas, one for violin, one for cello, and the third for flute, viola, and harp are elliptical, compressed pieces which seem to be questing disjointedly into new regions of sound. His songs too, are worthy of investigation, and his piano music, especially the twenty-four Preludes and some of the shorter pieces, contain some of his most imaginative and original ideas and thoughts.

Gabriel Fauré (1845–1924) is a difficult figure to place. He lived through all kinds of musical revolutions yet they seemed to affect the character of his work very little. He has never been, and is never likely to be, a widely known or popular composer, yet his music has a reticence and delicacy that is very appealing. Despite his dreamy, retiring art he was not a recluse, but a very sociable man.

He was content with forms as he found them, but he imbued them with a very personal, human style. Perhaps his art is best heard in his songs. They are not overtly passionate or dramatic but the long, sinuous melodies and subtle harmonies are exquisitely wrought. Of the song-cycles, *La Bonne Chanson, Cinq Mélodies* (Verlaine), *Le Chanson d'Eve*, and *L'Horizon Chimérique* are best known. The last written in 1922, when the composer was seventy-seven, is a beautiful setting of words by a soldier killed in the first World War. There are also many remarkable single songs, many of them settings of poems by Verlaine.

He wrote few orchestral pieces, but the *Ballade* for piano and orchestra and the *Pavane* are among his most typical, and delicate compositions, and his outstanding piano music, modelled on Chopin's, includes Nocturnes, Impromptus, and Barcarolles. His chamber music covers more than half a century from the violin sonata of 1876 to the string quartet written the year he died. In that period he composed two piano quartets, two piano quintets, another violin sonata and two cello sonatas, the later works failing to show quite the unforced lyrical grace of the earlier ones. Perhaps Fauré is best approached with the first piano quartet, a charming, easily assimilated work, and the beautiful choral *Requiem.*

Saint-Saëns (1835–1921), an accomplished, cultivated musician, has had a " bad press " but his craftsmanship, as displayed in his symphonies, concertos, and *Samson et Dalila* (one among his 12 operas) is not to be despised.

Henri Duparc (1844–1933), despite a very long life, is known today only for a group of songs he wrote before he was forty. They are among the most emotionally direct yet tasteful melodies ever written. Paul Dukas (1865–1935) is another

figure off the beaten track, as it were. He, too, is known only for a handful of compositions. He was strongly influenced by Vincent d'Indy (1851–1931) and the school who strongly opposed Debussy's new ideas, yet he could not help but come under Debussy's spell. Dukas's one great work is his opera *Ariane et Barbe-Bleue*, the text adapted from a Maeterlinck play written with the composer in mind.

Maurice Ravel (1875–1937), a pupil of Fauré, followed in Debussy's footsteps, although his later pieces were more ascetic. Indeed, he was one of the most fastidious of composers, always seeking, and often finding, artistic perfection. The works he wrote before 1918 are definitely of the Impressionist School and it would be difficult to imagine more beautiful sounds than are to be found in the ballet *Daphnis et Chloé*, in the song-cycle *Shéhérazade*, and the piano fantasy *Gaspard de la Nuit.* His first style was summed up in the A minor piano trio (1915). In his later music Ravel was struggling, not always successfully, to keep up with new developments such as jazz and atonality. The piano concerto, for instance, shows very strongly the influence of jazz.

Outstanding orchestral works of his, other than *Daphnis* are *Rapsodie espagnole* (1907), *La Valse* (1920), a sumptuous evocation of the Vienna waltz, and the ever-popular *Boléro.* Two chamber works, besides the trio, are masterpieces—the string quartet (1902–3) and the Introduction and Allegro for Harp, String Quartet, Flute, and Clarinet. This Septet composed in 1906, ravishes the senses with magical sound.

Ravel's piano pieces are perhaps his most notable contribution to music, combining an extraordinary feeling for the instrument's technical possibilities with the sensibility of a Chopin, and in this field *Jeux d'eau, Miroirs,* and *Ma Mère l'Oye*, all written just after the turn of the century, come very close to the perfection of *Gaspard de la Nuit.* His songs show his unusual appreciation of the need to fuse poetic and musical values, and he set exotic poems for preference. The song-cycle *Histoires naturelles* (1906) is an acutely observed setting of five poems about birds and animals; *Cinq Mélodies populaires Grecques* (1907) are charming settings of Greek folk songs; *Trois Poèmes de Mallarmé* (1913), *Chansons Mendécasses* (1926), are suitably exotic settings of three poems by an 18th-cent. Creole poet called Parny. Finally in 1932 came *Don Quichotte à Dulcinée*, three poems by Paul Morand, Ravel's last composition.

Ravel wrote two operas—the slight but moderately amusing *L'Heure espagnole* (1907), nicely orchestrated in a faintly and appropriately Spanish style and *L'Enfant et les Sortilèges* (1925) to a story by Colette, a delicious fantasy about a naughty child who gets his due punishment for tormenting animals and destroying furniture.

### Spain.

Felipe Pedrell (1841–1922) has been aptly described as the midwife of Spanish nationalist music. As a musicologist and teacher he strongly influenced the two main composers of the school, Manuel Falla (1876–1946) and Enrique Granados (1867–1916). Falla's output was not large and most of it was written about the time of the first World War. He had spent the years before the war in Paris and there he naturally came under the influence of Debussy. Debussy wrote Spanish music without ever having been to Spain but so true was it that even to Falla, born and bred in Andalusia, it had new things to say. He was able to take something from Debussy and blend it with his own highly individual style, evoking in his music all the passion and gaiety of his native land. Perhaps his most typical works are the two ballets *Love the Magician* (1915) full of Spanish atmosphere, and *The Three-Cornered Hat* (1919). The opera *La Vida Breve* (1905), despite its weak libretto, has much appeal, especially when the leading rôle is sung by such a vibrant artist as Victoria de los Angeles. The Seven Popular Spanish Songs (1914) conjure up the vivacity and smouldering passion at the heart of the country's character, as does *Nights in the Garden of Spain* (1916), an evocative piece for piano and orchestra. His later works, especially the harpsichord concerto of 1926, show Falla tending towards a less ebullient, more neo-classical style. His second opera *Master Peter's Puppet Show* (1923) is a miniaturist work, refined and intense. His third opera *Atlántida*, left unfinished at his death, was completed by his pupil Ernesto Halffter and first staged in 1962. It is a long work, more a dramatic cantata than an opera, and as such a rather unwieldy epic.

Granados, who was drowned when his ship was torpedoed by the Germans in 1916, was perhaps a more restrictedly Spanish composer than Falla, but his music is unfailingly attractive, and surely others of his seven operas, besides *Goyescas* (which is heard occasionally), deserve to be rescued from oblivion. *Goyescas* itself is especially famous for the second interlude and opening of Act III—*La Maja y el Ruiseñor* (The lover and the nightingale), a haunting, sinuous melody for soprano, sometimes heard in its original form as a piano solo. He wrote a set of *Tonadillas*. A tonadilla is a type of Spanish song popular in the 18th cent., and Granados's set ably and enchantingly recaptures a lost age of grace and character. His exciting Spanish Dances are heard in both their piano and orchestral form.

The chief claim to fame of Albéniz (1860–1909) is *Ibéria*, masterly descriptive pieces for piano. Turina (1882–1949), not altogether successfully, attempted a more cosmopolitan style, but his most often heard music, especially that for guitar, is typically Spanish.

### The Late German Romantics.

While composers such as Debussy, Sibelius, Stravinsky, and Schoenberg (see below for the latter pair) were striking out along new paths, Richard Strauss (1864–1949) continued in the trend of 19th-cent. German composers; he was the tradition's last great figure. At least two of his operas—*Salome* and *Elektra*—were considered shocking at the time, but today we can hear that they are essentially big-scale, romantic works—natural successors to Wagner's—however startling the harmonies may once have seemed.

If Strauss did not achieve the granite intellectual greatness of Beethoven or Wagner, there is no denying his melodic genius and powers of fertile invention which overlaid the streak of vulgarity and inflation in his musical make-up. His first outstanding achievement was in the field of the symphonic poem, where he carried the work of composers such as Liszt and Berlioz to its logical conclusion. Starting with *Don Juan* in 1888 and ending with *Sinfonia Domestica* in 1903 he wrote a series of kaleidoscopic works, full of enormous vitality, endless melody, and fascinating orchestration. The most easily assimilated—and the most popular—are *Don Juan* and *Till Eulenspiegel* but some of the longer works, notably *Also Sprach Zarathustra* (based on Nietzsche's prose poem) and *Don Quixote* (based, of course, on Cervantes's great work) will reward the persistent, inquiring mind with long hours of enthralled listening. Other works sound somewhat dated in their bombastic over-confidence, though Strauss's skill in composition seldom flagged at this stage of his long creative career. The symphonic poems all tell something of a story usually based on a literary source, but it is not essential to the enjoyment of the music to know what this is, although it may be helpful.

Strauss's reputation is even more solidly based on his fifteen operas, the earliest of which *Guntram* was first performed in 1894, the last, *Capriccio*, in 1942. During these years the essentials of Strauss's style changed little, though it became very much more refined as the years passed. His first operatic period ended with the violent, sensuous tragedies *Salome* (1905) and *Elektra* (1909), the latter being his first collaboration with his chief librettist Hugo von Hofmannsthal. Then came their unique *Der Rosenkavalier* (1911), which

filters the charm and the decadence of 18th-cent. Vienna through early 20th-cent. eyes. This was followed by *Ariadne auf Naxos* (1912). Originally intended to be given after Molière's *Le Bourgeois Gentilhomme*, it was later presented (1916) without the play but with a preceding scene, written by von Hofmannsthal. *Die Frau ohne Schatten* is the most grandiose result of the Strauss-Hofmannsthal partnership. It is a complex psychological allegory, but Strauss's contribution is not on as consistently lofty a level as is his librettist's. *Intermezzo* (1924), which has a libretto by Strauss himself, is a largely autobiographical domestic comedy, which has lately gained in reputation as a compact, charming piece. With *Die Aegyptische Helena* (1928), an opera on a mythical theme, and *Arabella* (1933), another charming Viennese comedy, the Strauss-Hofmannsthal collaboration ended on account of the librettist's death. Strauss then wrote *Die Schweigsame Frau* (1935) to a libretto by Stefan Zweig, based on a play by Ben Jonson, and *Friedenstag* (1938), *Daphne* (1938)—a beautiful opera—and *Die Liebe der Danae* (written 1938–40) with Josef Gregor as librettist. His swan-song was *Capriccio*, a dramatisation of the old argument about the relative importance of words and music in opera. The libretto is by the conductor Clemens Krauss and the opera, a serene, melodious work, was a fit end to a great operatic career.

However, Strauss went on composing till nearly the end of his life, adding a group of late orchestral pieces to his already large catalogue of works. The *Metamorphoses* for 23 solo string instruments, is probably the best of these. During his long creative career he wrote numerous songs, many of them, such as *Morgen*, *Wiegenlied* and *Ruhe, meine Seele* of surpassing beauty.

Other notable figures in German music at this time were Max Reger (1873–1916), a somewhat ponderous but highly accomplished composer who, in a quarter of a century of creative life, wrote more than 150 works, of which his sets of variations, his piano concerto, and chamber music are probably the most impressive. Hans Pfitzner (1869–1949), another German traditionalist, is chiefly remembered today for his opera *Palestrina*, about events, now known to be spurious, in the life of the 16th-cent. Italian composer.

### Mahler.

Gustav Mahler (1860–1911), the Austrian Jewish composer, is one of the most important figures in 20th-cent. music. In a sense he bridges the gulf between the late Romantics, who were tending more and more towards chromaticism and away from established key relationships, and the atonalists, who abandoned key signatures entirely. His detractors maintain that his inflation of allegedly banal Viennese beer-house music to unheard-of lengths rules him out of court as a serious writer. His admirers would claim that his music encompasses the whole of life in enormous, valid structures. The truth, if truth there be, perhaps lies somewhere in between: that if his material does not always justify the length of his symphonies, if there are occasional imperfections and *longueurs*, these shortcomings are worth putting up with for the sake of the depth of utterance, the humanity and the poetry of the great pages. He admitted himself that "I cannot do without trivialities," but it is out of these impurities that he forged his titanic victories.

His music is undoubtedly best approached through his songs, where the words force him to discipline his wide-ranging vision. *Lieder eines fahrenden Gesellen* (1884), to his own words, *Kindertotenlieder* (1901–4), to poems by Rückert, and some individual songs perfectly relate words to music, and are all of a poignant loveliness. Similarly *Das Lied von der Erde* (1908), especially the last of the six songs, is a touching farewell to the world, nobly expressed.

The ten symphonies, however, are Mahler's most impressive legacy to posterity. They are almost impossible to characterise briefly so vast are they in terms of both length and variety. The first, fourth and ninth are probably the easiest to grasp but the fifth, sixth and seventh, despite flaws, contain some of his most awe-inspiring conceptions. The second and third, both of which use soloists and chorus, are revolutionary in layout and concept; they both try, inevitably without complete success, to carry out the composer's dictum, " a symphony should be like the world—it must contain everything." The eighth is even more gargantuan, but as in all Mahler's work size does not mean loss of clarity or an overloading of the structure. Part one—a mighty choral invocation—is a visionary setting of the mediæval hymn *Veni Creator Spiritus.* Part two, which incorporates adagio, scherzo, and finale in one, is a setting of the final scene of Goethe's *Faust.* Until recently all of Mahler's unfinished tenth symphony has ever performed was the the Adagio, but the musicologist and Mahler scholar, Deryck Cooke, has recently completed the symphony to critical and popular acclaim and thus added a noble, and also optimistic epilogue to the Mahler opus. The debate over the quality of Mahler's music is likely to continue: one fact, however, that cannot be gain-said is his popularity with an ever-increasing audience, many of them young people. There must be something in his uncertainty and intense self-inquiry that accords with the mood of today.

### Schoenberg and the Second Viennese School.

Arnold Schoenberg (1874–1951) revolutionised Western music by his twelve-note theory—a system which uses all the notes of the chromatic scale " and denies the supremacy of a tonal centre," as Schoenberg himself puts it. This serial technique of composition, as it is commonly called, naturally sounds strange to an ear acclimatised to music written, as it were, with a home base, but Schoenberg and his disciples Berg and Webern showed that the system could produce works that were something more than mere intellectual exercises. None of the more recent advances in music would have been possible, even thinkable, without Schoenberg's pioneer work.

Schoenberg always regarded himself as much as a composer as a theorist or teacher, and his works are supposed to appeal as much to the emotions as to the intellect, although to be understood they do, of course, require the listener's concentrated attention. To appreciate how his ideas developed it is necessary to hear first his pre-atonal music, such as the *Gurrelieder* (1900–1) and *Verklärte Nacht* (1899), in which he carried Wagnerian chromaticism to extreme lengths. The *Gurrelieder,* in particular, is a luxuriant, overblown work that shows the Wagnerian idiom in an advanced stage of decay, in spite of many beautiful pages of music. In his succeeding works the feeling of tonality began to disappear until in the Three Piano Pieces (opus 11), of 1909, he finally rejected tonality, although the new 12-note scheme is not yet evident; traces of the old order can still be heard. The succeeding works were mostly short, highly compressed, and very expressive. Schoenberg was reaching out for a new system, which would " justify the dissonant character of these harmonies and determine their successions." By 1923 he had formulated his 12-note system and the Five Piano Pieces (opus 23), and the Serenade (opus 24) of that year, can thus be considered the first works that used a note-row as the fundamental basis of their composition. Between 1910 and 1915, however, the Russian composer Alexander Scriabin (1872–1915) had attempted to define a new method of composition of his own employing the " mystic chord " of ascending fourths, but his scheme proved comparatively abortive when compared with Schoenberg's. Josef Hauer (1883–1959) also developed a 12-note system which he propounded in 1919 and he always considered himself, rather than Schoenberg, as the true founder of the system. He later worked out a system of tropes (*i.e.,* half-series of six notes).

To return to Schoenberg, in later works he shows much more freedom and assurance in the use of his system. The wind quintet (1924), the variations for orchestra, opus 31 (1927–8), the third (1926), and fourth (1936) string quartets, and the

string trio (1946) are modern classics of their kind: they require concentrated listening and a degree of understanding of the unfamiliar style of composition. The set of songs with piano *Das Buch der hängenden Gärten* (opus 15), written in 1908, *Pierrot Lunaire,* opus 21 (1912) and the Four Songs, opus 22 (1913–14) provide a kind of bridge between tonality and atonality that the adventurous mind should cross. The monodrama *Erwartung* (1909) is another fascinating work, but perhaps the unfinished *Moses and Aaron* (1932) is Schoenberg's masterpiece as its production at Covent Garden in 1965 showed. Here, for certain, the composer matched his obvious intellectual capacities with an evident emotional content and managed to combine *Sprechgesang* (speech-song) and singing with a real degree of success.

It is only in recent years that Schoenberg's music has had a real chance to make its mark through the essential prerequisite of frequent performance. If his idiom now seems approachable, and a reasonably natural outcome of late 19th-cent. developments, it is perhaps because other, more recent composers have extended the boundaries of sound much further.

Schoenberg's two most respected disciples were Anton Webern (1883–1945) and Alban Berg (1885–1935). Webern's output is small, reaching only to opus 31, and many of his works are very brief. They are exquisitely precise, and delicate almost to a fault. He was trying to distil the essence of each note and in so doing carried the 12-note system to its most extreme and cerebral limit. His music has often been described as pointillist in the sense that one note is entirely separated from the next, there being little discernible melody. Beyond Webern's music, there is indeed the sound of nothingness, and he was rightly described during his lifetime as the " composer of the *pianissimo espressivo*". In his later works, Webern tended towards a strict, and often ingenious use of form and the Variations for Orchestra of 1940 are a good example of this and of his delicacy of orchestration. Webern's influence has perhaps been greater than the impact of his own music, even though he has had no direct successor.

Berg's music is much more accessible. Like Webern his total output was not large but nearly all his works are substantial additions to the repertory. He is also the directest link between Mahler and the second Viennese School, as Mahler's music influenced him strongly. He studied with Schoenberg from 1904 to 1910. His music is more intense, more lyrical, and less attenuated in sound than Schoenberg's or Webern's. His humanity and abiding compassion can be heard most strongly in his finest opera *Wozzeck* (1925) and his violin concerto (1935), written as an elegy on the death of Manon Gropius, a beautiful 18-year-old girl. Both works are very carefully designed yet formal considerations are never allowed to submerge feeling, and the note-row is fully integrated into the structure.

Both *Wozzeck* and the unfinished but rewarding *Lulu* are concerned with society's outcasts who are treated with great tenderness in both operas. The later work is entirely dodecaphonic, all the opera's episodes being based on a theme associated with Lulu. Between these operas Berg wrote the highly complex Chamber Concerto for piano, violin, and thirteen wind instruments (1925) and the expressive Lyric Suite (1926). Among his early works the Seven Early Songs (1908–9) and the concert aria *Der Wein* (1929) are notable.

### Stravinsky.

Igor Stravinsky (b. 1882) is another vital figure in 20th-cent. music. If his influence has been in quite another and perhaps less drastic direction than Schoenberg's it is hardly less important. Indeed, future musical historians may consider his achievement the more significant. He has been compared with the painter Picasso in his almost hectic desire to keep up with the times, yet, although he has written in a number of very different styles during the past fifty years, every work of his is stamped with his own definitive musical personality. His most revolutionary and seminal work is undoubtedly *The Rite of Spring* (written for the ballet impresario Diaghilev), which caused a furore when it first appeared in 1913, and although it no longer shocks, the rhythmical energy, the fierce angular thematic material, and the sheer virtuosity of the orchestration will always have the power to excite new audiences. Before *The Rite* Stravinsky had written two ballets for Diaghilev—*The Firebird* and *Petrushka*—that are no less filled with vitality and new, albeit not so violent, sounds. During the next thirty years Stravinsky wrote a series of ballet works, gradually becoming more austere and refined in composition. *Apollo* (1928) and *Orpheus* (1947) belong among his most attractive scores.

Stravinsky has not confined himself in stage works to the ballet. *The Nightingale* (1914) is a charming, early opera; *The Soldiers Tale* (1918) is a witty combination of narration, mime, and dance; *Les Noces* (1923) is a concise, original choreographic cantata for soloists and chorus; *Oedipus Rex* (1927) is a dignified version of the Sophocles play, which can be staged or given on the concert platform; either way it is a moving experience. *Perséphone* (1934), a melodrama for reciter, tenor, chorus, and orchestra is an appealing, lucid score. Since the war his most important stage work by far has been *The Rake's Progress* (1951), with a libretto by W. H. Auden and Chester Kallman. This fascinating opera is deliberately based on 18th-cent. forms and the music itself is neo-classical, always attractive, sometimes haunting.

Stravinsky has been no laggard in writing for the concert-platform either. The finest of these works are probably the fervent impressive choral *Symphony of Psalms* (1930), the Violin Concerto (1931) and the aggressive compact Symphony in three movements (1945). Of his chamber music the Octet (1923), a Duo Concertant (1932), and Septet (1952) are probably the most important, but no piece, even the dryest and most pedantic, is without redeeming features.

Stravinsky is often thought of as an aloof, detached figure. He has been castigated for his lack of lyrical warmth. But in spite of his own professed desire to drain his music of specific emotion, craftsmanship and originality, often with a strange other-worldly beauty added, are unmistakeably there throughout his many scores. Quirky and annoying he may be, dull never.

## Busoni and Puccini.

Italian music in the early part of the century was dominated by two very different composers—Ferruccio Busoni (1866–1924) and Giacomo Puccini (1858–1924). Busoni is a difficult figure to place. His austere, intellectual power is never called in question, but he seldom, if ever, succeeded in translating his technical prowess into altogether successful compositions. We can admire the strength, honesty, and often beauty of such works as his huge piano concerto (1903–4), *Fantasia Contrappuntisca* (1912)—for piano solo—and his unfinished opera *Doktor Faust* without ever capitulating to them entirely. None the less, it has to be admitted that those who have studied his music closely have always fallen completely under his spell. In style his music is anti-Romantic and often neo-Classical yet he was an ardent admirer of Liszt and more especially of Liszt's realisation of the possibilities of the pianoforte. Busoni, himself a great pianist, carried on where Liszt had left off in his own piano music, in which form and expression often find their perfect balance. *Doktor Faust* is undoubtedly his most important opera but *Die Brautwahl* (1908–10) and *Turandot* (1917) have many points of interest too.

Puccini's *Turandot*—his last opera—is a much grander version of the same Gozzi fable and the culmination of this great opera composer's work. His achievement is at an almost directly opposite pole to Busoni's. Not for him the severity or intellectuality of his contemporary. He sought and found an almost ideal fusion of straight-forward lyricism and dramatic truth. His music

unerringly follows the pathos and passion of the stories he sets and all his characters "live" as human beings. That, and his abundant flow of easy, soaring melody, are the reasons for his immense popular success, unequalled by any other 20th-cent. composer. Whether it is the pathetic Mimi (*La Bohème*—1896) and Cio-Cio-San, (*Madama Butterfly*—1904), the evil Scarpia, (*Tosca* —1900), the cunning Schicchi (*Gianni Schicchi*— 1918), the ardent Rudolfo (*La Bohème*) and Cavaradossi (*Tosca*), or the ice-cold Turandot (*Turandot*—1926), Puccini's musical characterisation is unfailing. And he backs his *verismo* vocal writing with an orchestral tissue that faithfully reflects the milieu of each opera, for instance, Japanese for *Butterfly*, Chinese for *Turandot*, while never losing his particular brand of Italian warmth. His orchestration is always subtle and luminous.

Other Italian composers who wrote operas in the *verismo* style of Puccini were Leoncavallo (1858– 1919), Mascagni (1863–1945), and Giordano (1867– 1948).

## Prokofiev, Shostakovich, and Rachmaninov.

Sergey Prokofiev (1891–1953) spent part of hi creative life in his native Russia, part of it (1918– 34) abroad, mostly in Paris. His early music, apart from the popular Classical Symphony (1916– 17) tended to be acid and harsh, but on his return to Russia his style, though still frequently satirical, became warmer, more Romantic. The third piano concerto (1917) and the second symphony (1924) are good examples of the former period, the ballets *Romeo and Juliet* (1935) and *Cinderella* (1941–44) and the fifth (1944) and sixth (1949) symphonies of the latter. His music gives the impression of immense rhythmical energy, as in the outer movements of several of his nine piano sonatas, but this fierce drive is often leavened by the soft, wistful lights of his slow movements. His second string quartet (1941), perhaps, presents all the elements of his music in the kindest light.

His strong leaning towards fantasy and mordant parody is felt in his earlier operas *The Love of the Three Oranges* (1921) and *The Fiery Angel* (1922–25). *War and Peace* (1941–42) was written in the face of strong pressure from the Soviet authorities.

Dmitri Shostakovich (b. 1906) has also suffered from attacks of "formalism". He had to conform to Stalin's requirements for writing music, but he has survived and continues to produce music of universal appeal, as, for example, his most recent string quartets. Like Prokofiev, his music falls into two very distinct styles: one humorous and spiky, the other intense, very personal and often large-scale in its implications. Not all his twelve symphonies reach the expressive depths of numbers one, five, six, and eight, but they all have rewarding passages and his recent violin and cello concertos are of high quality. He has so far written eleven string quartets, a piano quintet (an attractive piece) and two operas: the satirical *The Nose* (1930) and *Katerina Ismailova* (1934, revised 1959), originally known as "Lady Macbeth of Mstensk." It is much too early to " place " Shostakovich in musical history, but his original genius cannot be doubted.

Although Sergey Rachmaninov (1873–1943) was born in Russia, he left his home country in 1918, disliking the Soviet régime, and lived mostly in Switzerland and the United States. His music is chiefly notable for its Romanticism, nostalgic melody, nervous energy and, in the piano works, its opportunities for displays of virtuosity. The first three piano concertos, the third symphony, the piano preludes, and the Rhapsody on a theme of Paganini, are his most typical and attractive works, and many of his songs are touching and beautiful. He wrote three operas.

## Modern French Music.

French music after Debussy and Ravel was dominated by the slighter composers known as *Les Six*, the most important of whom were Arthur

Honegger (1892–1955, Swiss born), Darius Milhaud (b. 1892) and Francis Poulenc (1899–1963). Each has contributed music of some wit and charm to the repertory. They were influenced by Erik Satie (1866–1925), an eccentric but interesting figure, who wrote works with odd titles such as *Three Pear-Shaped Pieces*. His music is entirely unsentimental, often ironic.

Much more revolutionary has been the work of Olivier Messiaen (b. 1908), who has turned to Indian music and, above all, to bird-song for inspiration. He first came to notice as a composer of organ music. Then his *Quatuor pour la fin de temps*, written in captivity between 1940 and 1942, his long piano pieces, based on bird-song (often literally) and his gigantic *Turangalîla* symphony show him experimenting with complex rhythms, strange sonorities (using unusual instruments such as the Ondes Martenot in the symphony), and considerably widening music's horizons. Edgar Varèse (1885–1965) cultivated an even broader spectrum of sound, employing electronic instruments to complement and contrast with traditional ones. Pierre Boulez (b. 1925), a pupil of Messiaen, bases his extremely complex works on mathematical relationships. His music, other than that for the piano, mostly calls for a variety of percussion instruments often combined with the soprano voice in evocations of of French poetry (Mallarmé in particular). The resulting timbre and sonorities are intriguing even when the intellectual basis of the music is but dimly perceived.

### Modern German Music.

Kurt Weill (1900–50) is chiefly known for his socio-politically pointed operas, such as *Die Dreigroschenoper* (1929), *Mahagonny* (1929), *Der Jasager* (1930), and *Happy End* (1929), all effective works on the stage, and for his particular brand of brittle, yet fundamentally romantic music. His influence on later composers has been considerable.

Carl Orff (b. 1895) has written chiefly for the stage. His music is rhythmically insistent, avoids counterpoint, and is deliberately, even self-consciously straightforward. Most frequently heard is his *Carmina Burana*, lively, rumbustious choral settings of mediæval poems.

Paul Hindemith (1895–1964) in his later years wrote in a strictly tonal, often neo-classical idiom, after being one of the most advanced intellectuals of his time. As well as many chamber and orchestral works, he wrote three formidable operas: *Die Harmonie der Welt*, *Cardillac* and *Mathis der Maler*.

Karlheinz Stockhausen (b. 1928), a pupil of Messiaen, is another extreme innovator. He more than anyone puts electronics to musical use. His scores are a maze of diagrams and instructions, which really need the composer's presence for their true interpretation. It is too early to say whether his music is evidence of a passing vogue or a real step forward in musical ideas.

Hans Werner Henze (b. 1926) has rebelled against the musical climate in Germany, and now lives in Italy, yet his music combines the intellectuality of the modern German schools with the lyricism of Italian music. He has written five symphonies, though none follow the traditional form, and nine operas, among them two impressive large-scale works, *König Hirsch* (1952–55) and *The Bassarids* (1966), to an Auden-Kallman libretto.

### American Music.

It was not until the 20th cent. that American music really got under way and an American school came into being. With the possible exception of MacDowell (1861–1908) no earlier composers are remembered or played today. Many composers of the American school have, of course, taken their cue from Europe but the influence of American jazz and folk-song is also recognisable in some of their music. Aaron Copland (b. 1900) is probably the most important figure on the

current scene, and such works as *Appalachian Spring*, *Billy the Kid*, and his third symphony have gained a certain amount of international recognition and popularity. Samuel Barber (b. 1910) works along traditional lines and his music, like Copland's, is essentially diatonic. He has contributed to all the usual forms (symphony, concerto, sonata), most recently to opera with *Vanessa* (1958) and *Antony and Cleopatra* (1966), which opened the new Metropolitan Opera House in New York's Lincoln Centre. Roy Harris (b. 1898) has written seven symphonies and several concertos, which include folk elements.

Charles Ives (1874–1954) has recently been recognised as the most original American composer. While carrying on a highly successful career in insurance, Ives yet managed to anticipate in his works, all written before 1920, many of the innovations which were later " invented " in Europe. His orchestral music is much influenced by the sounds, such as brass bands, which he heard in his native New England as a boy. His *Three Places in New England* and *The Unanswered Question* have a beautiful, elusive quality about them. In his five symphonies and *Concord* sonata we notice the working of an original mind employing polytonality and polyrhythms in larger and more complex works. An element of improvisation is sometimes introduced, another anticipation of latter-day technique. Ives is unlikely ever to become a popular composer—his music is too complicated and eclectic for that—but his importance as a prophet is surely established.

### Modern English School.

The amazing 20th cent. revival of music in England owes much to Ralph Vaughan Williams (1872–1958) and Gustav Holst (1874–1934). Vaughan Williams's music is today suffering a decline in reputation, but the best of his symphonies (one, four, five, and six), his Fantasia on a theme by Tallis, his ballet *Job*, and the best of his choral music have a sturdiness about them that will no doubt weather the whim of passing fashion. His music alternates between the forceful and the contemplative and both moods are expressed in a distinctive musical vocabulary, based on modalism and 16th-cent. polyphony.

Holst was a more enigmatic figure, but his influence has undoubtedly been greater. Only his suite *The Planets* and the choral *The Hymn of Jesus* have established themselves as repertory works, but his bold harmonic experiments and the austerity, even mysticism, of his style as heard in the orchestral pieces *Egdon Heath*, *Beni Mora*, and the opera *Savitri* are perhaps more typical of this contemplative original composer. His daughter Imogen, a conductor, has done much to promote understanding of her father's music. Contemporaries who deserve a bare mention are John Ireland (1879–1962) and Sir Arnold Bax (1883–1953).

Frederick Delius (1862–1934) was the only important English disciple of the French impressionist school. He lived in France from 1888 onwards. His most important works are the atmospheric tone-poems for orchestra, such as *Brigg Fair*; the vocal and orchestral *A Mass of Life*, *Sea Drift* and *Appalachia*, and the opera *A Village Romeo and Juliet*.

Of the more recent generation of English composers the most important are undoubtedly Benjamin Britten (b. 1913) Sir Michael Tippett (b. 1905), Alan Rawsthorne (b. 1905), and Sir William Walton (b. 1902). Britten has done more than anyone to establish English music on the forefront of the international stage. Much of his music seems to have an immediate appeal to large audiences and certainly his many stage works have earned him a quite exceptional prestige both at home and abroad. *Peter Grimes* (1945), *Billy Budd* (1951), *Gloriana* (1953), *A Midsummer Night's Dream* (1960) all, in their very different ways, show his consummate mastery of stage technique and the first two are also moving human documents. On a smaller scale he has achieved as much with his chamber operas—*The Rape of Lucretia* (1946), *Albert Herring* (1947), and *The Turn of the Screw* (1954, based on a Henry James novel)—and with the two recent Parables for Church Performance—*Curlew River* (1964) and *The Burning Fiery Furnace* (1966). If he had written nothing else, those dramatic works would have marked him out as a composer of outstanding imaginative gifts.

But there is more—the choral works culminating in the *War Requiem* (1962), his various song cycles written for the tenor Peter Pears, the Serenade for tenor, horn, and string, *Nocturne* for tenor and orchestra, the three Canticles, and the Spring Symphony are further evidence—in very different media—of both his intense emotional commitment and his technical skill. While being strongly influenced by such composers as Schubert, Verdi, Mahler, and Berg, his style is entirely his own: it is a musical personality that manages to combine, as it has been said, " a deep nostalgia for the innocence of childhood, a mercurial sense of humour and a passionate sympathy with the victims of prejudice and misunderstanding."

This last quality is particularly evident also in Tippett's emotional makeup as expressed in his music, especially in one of his earliest successes, the choral work *A Child of Our Time* (1941), which shows both his compassion and his ability to write on a large scale. But Tippett is as much a mystic and searcher as a composer and he is constantly seeking new and different ways of widening his listeners' horizons, as may be heard in the exceedingly complex *Vision of St. Augustine* (1965), which tellingly sets to music the striving to understand the " beyond " of Augustine's words.

Tippett has also sought new means of musical expression as he has shown in his second opera *King Priam* (1962), very spare and pointed in idiom, and in the concerto for orchestra (1962). These works, as well as his piano concerto (1956) and second symphony—a luminous work—and his three string quartets, are very difficult to perform —and to get to know—but the effort to understand the composer's wide-spanning mind is always richly rewarded. However, perhaps a newcomer to his music does better to approach him through the more straightforward earlier works, the concerto for double string orchestra (1939), the Fantasia Concertante on a theme of Corelli (1953) —a lyrically poetic piece—or the song cycles *Boyhood's End* (1943) and *Heart's Assurance* (1957). The quality of his allegorical opera *The Midsummer Marriage* (1952), in spite of its involved libretto (by the composer), may be better appreciated since its revival at Covent Garden in 1968. Tippett is an uncompromising individualist, writing without fear or favour, perhaps considerably in advance of his time in thought and achievement.

Rawsthorne's style is admirably direct and honest. Eschewing the latest fashions in music he has ploughed his own furrow of deeply felt writing. His ideas are argued out with considerable lyrical force, and his astute regard for form does not hide the underlying emotional content of his music nor the touch of wit that pervades some of his more lively movements. Among his most important accomplishments to date are his three string quartets, violin concerto, two piano concertos, and the quintet for piano and wind instruments.

Walton's outstanding contribution was made before the second World War in music that was alternately gay and romantic. The irreverent *Façade* (1923) for speaker and chamber orchestra falls into the former category, the poetic viola concerto (1930) into the second. His first symphony (1934-5) is an arresting, dramatic score, and the oratorio *Belshazzar's Feast* (1931) is a landmark in choral music. Since the war his works have never quite recaptured the same urgency of expression.

Elisabeth Lutyens (b. 1906) is Britain's leading twelve-note composer. For long shunned by the musical establishment, she has now been accepted as an important and seminal figure in the history of 20th-cent. music. Her output has been large and includes numerous works for unusual, small groups of instruments, often combined with a solo voice. Benjamin Frankel (b. 1906), Edmund Rubbra (b. 1901), Sir Arthur Bliss (b. 1891), and Lennox Berkeley (b. 1903) are other composers of note among the senior school of living British composers. Egon Wellesz (b. 1885), Austrian born, settled in this country in 1939. He has written operas, choral works, symphonies, and chamber music, and is still active. There is a thriving junior school of British composers who have already made their mark, among them Alexander Goehr, Richard Rodney Bennett, Malcolm Williamson, and Nicholas Maw, each of whom has written one or more operas.

### Where Does the Future Lie?

It is anybody's guess which way music will develop during the next few decades. Are older forms quite outmoded, as some recent innovators suggest, and does the future therefore lie with the electronic music and/or percussive sounds—of Boulez, Stockhausen, Luigi Nono (b. 1924), and their disciples? Or will what has been recognised as musical sound for several generations adapt itself to the new mood abroad? Has atonalism still something to offer or was it a passing phase, already dated and out of fashion? Perhaps the only answer that can be given with certainty is that, as with other centuries, a dozen or so composers' music will survive to delight later generations and that these geniuses will be found among composers who do and say what they must in music without regard to fashion, patronage, or fear of what anyone writes about them. May they be worthy of their rich heritage.

# II. GLOSSARY OF MUSICAL TERMS

*A.* Note of scale, commonly used for tuning instruments.

*Absolute Music.* Music without any literary descriptive or other kind of reference.

*A Capella.* Literally " in the church style." Unaccompanied.

*Accelerando.* Quickening of the pace.

*Accidental.* The sign which alters a note by a semitone, *i.e.*, ♯ (sharp) raises it; ♭ (flat) lowers it; ♮ restores a note to its original position.

*Accompaniment.* Instrumental or piano part forming background to a solo voice or instrument that has the melody.

*Ad. lib.* (L. *ad libitum*). Direction on music that strict time need not be observed.

*Adagio.* A slow movement or piece.

*Aeolian mode.* One of the scales in mediæval music, represented by the white keys of the piano from A to A.

*Air.* A simple tune for voice or instrument.

*Alberti bass.* Rhythmical accompanying figure made up by splitting a chord. Used extensively in 18th-cent. music and associated with the Italian composer Alberti.

*Allegretto.* Not quite so fast as *Allegro*.

*Allegro.* Fast, but not too fast.

*Alto.* An unusually high type of male voice; also the vocal part sung by women and boys with a low range.

*Ambrosian Chant.* Plainsong introduced into church music by St. Ambrose, bishop of Milan (d. 397), and differing from Gregorian chant.

*Andante.* At a walking pace, not so slow as *Adagio* nor as fast as *Allegretto*.

*Animato.* Lively.

*Answer.* Second entry in a fugue, usually in the dominant.

**Anthem.** Composition for use in church during a service by a choir with or without soloists.

**Antiphonal.** Using groups of instruments or singers placed apart.

**Appoggiatura.** An ornament consisting of a short note just above or below a note forming part of a chord.

**Arabesque.** Usually a short piece, highly decorated.

**Arco.** Direction for string instruments to play with bow.

**Aria.** Vocal solo, usually in opera or oratorio, often in three sections with the third part being a repeat of the first. An *Arietta* is a shorter, lighter kind of aria.

**Arioso.** In the style of an aria; halfway between aria and recitative.

**Arpeggio.** Notes of a chord played in a broken, spread-out manner, as on a harp.

**Ars antiqua.** The old mediæval music, based on organum and plainsong, before the introduction of *Ars nova* in 14th cent.

**Ars nova.** Musical style current from 14th cent., more independent than the old style in the part-writing and harmony.

**Atonal.** Not in any key; hence *Atonality.*

**Aubade.** Morning song.

**Augmentation.** The enlargement of a melody by lengthening the musical value of its notes.

**Ayre.** Old spelling of *air.*

**B.** Note of scale, represented in Germany by *H.*

**Bagatelle.** A short, generally light piece of music. Beethoven wrote 26 Bagatelles.

**Ballad.** Either a narrative song or an 18th-cent. drawing-room song.

**Ballade.** Instrumental piece in story-telling manner. Chopin wrote 4.

**Ballet.** Stage entertainment requiring instrumental accompaniment; originated at French court in 16th and 17th cent.

**Bar.** A metrical division of music; the perpendicular line in musical notation to indicate this.

**Barcarolle.** A boating-song, in particular one associated with Venetian gondoliers.

**Baritone.** A male voice, between tenor and bass.

**Baroque.** A term applied, loosely, to music written in the 17th and 18th cent., roughly corresponding to baroque in architecture.

**Bass.** The lowest male voice; lowest part of a composition.

**Bass Drum.** Largest of the drum family, placed upright and struck on the side.

**Bassoon.** The lowest of the woodwind instruments, uses double reed.

**Beat.** Music's rhythmic pulse.

**Bel canto.** Literally " beautiful singing "—in the old Italian style with pure tone and exact phrasing.

**Berceuse.** Cradle song.

**Binary.** A piece in two sections is said to be binary in form. The balance is obtained by a second phrase (or section) answering the first.

**Bitonality.** Use of two keys at once.

**Bow.** Stick with horsehair stretched across it for playing string instruments.

**Brass.** Used as a collective noun for all brass or metal instruments.

**Breve.** Note, rarely used nowadays, with tone value of two semibreves.

**Bridge.** Wood support over which strings are stretched on a violin, cello, guitar, etc.

**Buffo(a).** Comic, as in *buffo bass* or *opera buffa.*

**C.** Note of scale.

**Cabaletta.** Final, quick section of an aria or duet.

**Cadence.** A closing phrase of a composition or a passage, coming to rest on tonic (key note).

**Cadenza.** Solo vocal or instrumental passage, either written or improvised, giving soloist chance to display technical skill to audience.

**Calando.** Becoming quieter and slower.

**Canon.** Device in contrapuntal composition whereby a melody is introduced by one voice or instrument then repeated by one or more voices or instruments, either at the same pitch (canon at the unison) or at different intervals (canon at the fifth, for example).

**Cantabile.** Song-like, therefore flowing and expressive.

**Cantata.** Vocal work for chorus and/or choir.

**Cantilena.** Sustained, smooth melodic line.

**Cantus firmus.** Literally " fixed song." Basic melody from 14th to 17th cent., around which other voices wove contrapuntal parts.

**Canzonet.** Light songs written in England *c.* 1600.

**Carillon.** A set of bells in tower of church, played from a keyboard below.

**Carol.** Christmas song.

**Castrato.** Artificially-created male soprano and alto, fashionable in 17th and 18th cent. (The castration of vocally gifted boys prevailed in Italy until the 19th cent.)

**Catch.** A part-song like a round, in vogue in England from 16th to 19th cent.

**Cavatina.** An operatic song in one section, or a slow song-like instrumental movement.

**Celesta.** Keyboard instrument with metal bars struck by hammers.

**Cello.** Four-stringed instrument, played with bow, with a bass range. Comes between viola and double bass in string family.

**Cembalo.** Originally the Italian name for the dulcimer, but sometimes applied to the harpsichord.

**Chaconne.** Vocal or instrumental piece with unvaried bass.

**Chamber Music.** Music originally intended to be played in a room for three or more players.

**Chanson.** Type of part-song current in France from 14th to 16th cent.

**Chant.** Singing of psalms, masses, etc., in plainsong to Latin words in church.

**Choir.** Body of singers, used either in church or at concerts.

**Chorales.** German hymn tunes, often made use of by Bach.

**Chord.** Sounding together of several notes, always more than three.

**Chording.** Spacing of intervals in a chord.

**Chorus.** Substantial body of singers, usually singing in four parts.

**Chromatic.** Using a scale of nothing but semitones.

**Clarinet.** Woodwind instrument with single reed in use since mid-18th cent.

**Clavichord.** Keyboard instrument having strings struck by metal tangents, much in use during 17th and 18th cent. as solo instrument.

**Clavier.** Used in German (*Klavier*) for piano, in England for any stringed keyboard instrument.

**Clef.** Sign in stave that fixes place of each note.

**Coda.** Closing section of movement in Sonata form.

**Coloratura.** Term to denote florid singing.

**Common chord.** *See* Triad.

**Common Time.** Four crotchets to the bar, 4/4 time.

**Compass.** Range of notes covered by voice or instruments.

**Composition.** Piece of music, originated by a composer's own imagination; act of writing such a piece.

**Compound time.** Any musical metric not in simple time.

**Con Brio.** With dash.

**Concert.** Public performance of any music.

*Concertato.* Writing for several solo instruments to be played together.

*Concerto.* Work for one or more solo instruments and orchestra.

*Concerto grosso.* Orchestral work common in 17th and 18th cent. with prominent parts for small groups of instruments.

*Concord.* Opposite of discord, *i.e.*, notes that when sounded together satisfy the ear. (Conventional term in that its application varies according to the age in which one lives.)

*Conduct.* To direct a concert with a baton.

*Consecutive.* Progression of harmonic intervals of like kind.

*Consonance.* Like Concord.

*Continuo.* Bass line, used in 17th- and 18th-cent. music, for a keyboard instrument, requiring special skill from performer.

*Contralto.* A woman's voice with a low range.

*Counterpoint.* Simultaneous combination of two or more melodies to create a satisfying musical texture. Where one melody is added to another, one is called the other's counterpoint. The adjective of counterpoint is contrapuntal.

*Counter-tenor.* Another name for male alto.

*Courante.* A dance in triple time.

*Crescendo.* Getting louder.

*Crook.* Detachable section of tubing on brass instruments that change the tuning.

*Crotchet.* Note that equals two quavers in time value.

*Cycle.* Set of works, especially songs, intended to be sung as group.

*Cyclic form.* Form of work in two or more movements in which the same musical themes recur.

*Cymbal.* Percussion instrument; two plates struck against each other.

*D.* Note of scale.

*Da Capo* (abbr. D.C.). A *Da Capo* aria is one in which the whole first section is repeated after a contrasting middle section.

*Descant.* Additional part (sometimes improvised) sung against a melody.

*Development.* Working-out section of movement in sonata form. *See* Sonata.

*Diatonic.* Opposite of chromatic; using proper notes of a major or minor scale.

*Diminished.* Lessened version of perfect interval, e.g., semitone less than a perfect fifth is a diminished fifth.

*Diminuendo.* Lessening.

*Diminution.* Reducing a phrase of melody by shortening time value of notes.

*Discord.* Opposite of concord, *i.e.* notes that sounded together produce a clash of harmonies.

*Dissonance.* Like discord.

*Divertimento.* A piece, usually orchestral, in several movements; like a suite.

*Dodecaphonic.* Pertaining to 12-note method of composition.

*Dominant.* Fifth note of major or minor scale above tonic (key) note.

*Dorian Mode.* One of the scales in mediæval music, represented by the white keys on the piano from D to D.

*Dot.* Placed over note indicates staccato; placed after note indicates time value to be increased by half.

*Double bar.* Two upright lines marking the end of a composition or a section of it.

*Double bass.* Largest and lowest instrument of violin family; played with bow.

*Drone bass.* Unvarying sustained bass, similar to the permanent bass note of a bagpipe.

*Drum.* Variety of percussion instruments on which sound is produced by hitting a skin stretched tightly over a hollow cylinder or hemisphere.

*Duet.* Combination of two performers; composition for such a combination.

*Duple time.* Time in which main division is two or four.

*Dynamics.* Gradations of loudness or softness in music.

*E.* Note of scale.

*Electronic.* Term used to describe use of electronic sounds in music.

*Encore.* Request from audience for repeat of work, or extra item in a programme.

*English horn* (Cor anglais). Woodwind instrument with double reed of oboe family.

*Enharmonic.* Modulation made by means of change of note between sharps and flats, although note remains the same (E flat becomes D sharp, for example).

*Ensemble.* Teamwork in performance; item in opera for several singers with or without chorus; a group of performers of no fixed number.

*Episode.* Section in composition usually divorced from main argument.

*Exposition.* Setting out of thematic material in a sonata-form composition.

*Expression marks.* Indication by composer of how he wants his music performed.

*F.* Note of scale.

*False relation.* A clash of harmony produced when two notes, such as A natural and A flat, are played simultaneously or immediately following one another.

*Falsetto.* The kind of singing by male voices above normal register and sounding like an unbroken voice.

*Fanfare.* Flourish of trumpets.

*Fantasy.* A piece suggesting free play of composer's imagination, or a piece based on known tunes (folk, operatic, etc.).

*Fermata.* Pause indicated by sign ⌒ prolonging note beyond its normal length.

*Fifth.* Interval taking five steps in the scale. A perfect fifth (say, C to G) includes three whole tones and a semitone; a diminished fifth is a semitone less, an augmented fifth a semitone more.

*Figure.* A short phrase, especially one that is repeated.

*Fingering.* Use of fingers to play instrument, or the indication above notes to show what fingers should be used.

*Flat.* Term indicating a lowering of pitch by a semitone, or to describe a performer playing under the note.

*Florid.* Term used to describe decorative passages.

*Flute.* Woodwind instrument, blown sideways. It is played through a hole, not a reed. Nowadays, sometimes made of metal.

*Folksong.* Traditional tune, often in different versions, handed down aurally from generation to generation.

*Form.* Course or layout of a composition, especially when in various sections.

*Fourth.* Interval taking four steps in scale. A perfect fourth (say, C to F) includes two whole tones and a semitone. If either note is sharpened or flattened the result is an augmented or a diminished fourth.

*Fugato.* In the manner of a fugue.

*Fugue.* Contrapuntal composition for various parts based on one or more subjects treated imitatively but not strictly.

*G.* Note of scale.

*Galant.* Used to designate elegant style of 18th-cent. music.

*Galliard.* Lively dance dating back to 15th cent. or before.

*Gavotte.* Dance in 4/4 time, beginning on third beat in bar.

*Giusto.* Strict, proper.

*Glee.* Short part-song.

*Glissando.* Rapid sliding scales up and down piano or other instruments.

*Glockenspiel.* Percussion instrument consisting of tuned steel bars and played with two hammers or keyboard.

*Grace note. See* Ornament.

*Grave.* In slow tempo.

*Grazioso.* Gracefully.

*Gregorian Chant.* Plainsong collected and supervised mainly by Pope Gregory (d. 604).

*Ground bass.* Figure on theme used as bass in a composition and constantly repeated without change.

*Guitar.* Plucked string instrument of Spanish origin, having six strings of three-octave compass.

*H.* German note-symbol for *B.*

*Harmony.* Simultaneous sounding of notes so as to make musical sense.

*Harp.* Plucked string instrument of ancient origin, the strings stretched parallel across its frame. The basic scale of C flat major is altered by a set of pedals.

*Harpsichord.* Keyboard stringed instrument played by means of keyboard similar to a piano but producing its notes by a plucking, rather than a striking action.

*Homophonic.* Opposite of polyphonic, *i.e.,* indicated parts move together in a composition, a single melody being accompanied by block chords, as distinct from the contrapuntal movement of different melodies.

*Horn.* Brass instrument with coiled tubes. Valves introduced in 19th cent. made full chromatic use of instrument possible.

*Hymn.* Song of praise, especially in church.

*Imitation.* Repetition, exactly, or at least recognisably, of a previously heard figure.

*Impromptu.* A short, seemingly improvised piece of music, especially by Schubert or Chopin.

*Improvise.* To perform according to fancy or imagination, sometimes on a given theme.

*In alt.* The octave above the treble clef; *in altissimo,* octave above that.

*Instrumentation.* Writing music for particular instruments, using the composer's knowledge of what sounds well on different instruments.

*Interlude.* Piece played between two sections of a composition.

*Intermezzo.* Formerly meant interlude, now often used for pieces played between acts of operas.

*Interval.* Distance in pitch between notes.

*Ionian mode.* One of the scales in mediæval music, represented on piano by white keys between C and C. identical therefore to modern C major scale.

*Isorhythmic.* Term applied to motets of 14th and 15th cent. where rhythm remains strict although melody changes.

*Jig.* Old dance usually in 6/8 or 12/8 time.

*Kettledrum* (It. pl. *Timpani*). Drum with skin drawn over a cauldron-shaped receptacle, can be tuned to definite pitch by turning handles on rim, thus tightening or relaxing skin.

*Key.* Lever by means of which piano, organ, etc., produces note; classification, in relatively modern times, of notes of a scale. Any piece of music in major or minor is in the *key* of its tonic or keynote.

*Keyboard.* Term used to describe instruments with a continuous row of keys.

*Key-signature.* Indication on written music, usually at the beginning of each line, of the number of flats or sharps in the key of a composition.

*Kitchen Department.* Humorous term for percussion section of an orchestra.

*Lament.* Musical piece of sad or deathly significance.

*Largamente.* Spaciously.

*Largo.* Slow.

*Leading-motive* (Ger. *Leitmotiv*). Short theme, suggesting person, idea, or image, quoted throughout composition to indicate that person, etc.

*Legato.* In a smooth style (of performance, etc.)

*Lento.* Slow.

*Libretto.* Text of an opera.

*Lied.* (pl. *Lieder*). Song, with special reference to songs by Schubert, Schumann, Brahms, and Wolf.

*Lute.* String instrument plucked with fingers, used in 15th- and 16th cent. music especially.

*Lydian mode.* One of the scales in mediæval music, represented by white keys of piano between F and F.

*Lyre.* Ancient Greek plucked string instrument.

*Madrigal.* Contrapuntal composition for several voices, especially prominent from 15th to 17th cent.

*Maestoso.* Stately.

*Major.* One of the two main scales of the tonal system with semitones between the third and fourth, and the seventh and eighth notes, identical with 16th-cent. Ionian mode.

*Mandolin(e).* Plucked string instrument of Italian origin.

*Manual.* A keyboard for the hands, used mostly in connection with the organ.

*Master of the King's* (or *Queen's*) *Musick.* Title of British court appointment, with no precise duties.

*Melisma.* Group of notes sung to a single syllable.

*Mélodie.* Literally a melody or tune; has come to mean a French song (cf. German *Lied*).

*Metronome.* Small machine in use since the beginning of the 18th cent., to determine the pace of any composition by the beats of the music, *e.g.,* ♩ = 60 at the head of the music indicates sixty crotchets to the minute.

*Mezzo, Mezza.* (It. = " half ") *Mezza voce* means using the half voice (a tone between normal singing and whispering). *Mezzo-soprano,* voice between soprano and contralto.

*Minim.* Note that equals two crotchets in time value.

*Minor.* One of the two main scales of the tonal system (cf. major), identical with 16th-cent. Aeolian mode. It has two forms—the harmonic and melodic, the former having a sharpened seventh note, the latter having the sixth and seventh note sharpened.

*Minuet.* Originally French 18th-cent. dance in triple time, then the usual third movement in symphonic form (with a contrasting trio section) until succeeded by scherzo.

*Mixolydian mode.* One of the mediaeval scales represented by the white keys on the piano from G to G.

*Modes.* Scales prevalent in the Middle Ages. *See* Aeolian, Dorian, Ionian, Lydian, Mixolydian, Phrygian.

*Modulate.* Changing from key to key in a composition, not directly but according to musical " grammar ".

*Molto.* Much, very; thus *allegro molto.*

*Motet.* Sacred, polyphonic vocal composition. More loosely, any choral composition for use in church but not set to words of the liturgy.

*Motive, motif.* Short, easily recognised melodic figure.

*Motto.* Short, well-defined theme recurring throughout a composition, cf. *Idée fixe* in Berlioz's *Symphonie Fantastique.*

*Movement.* Separate sections of a large-scale composition, each in its own form.

*Music drama.* Term used to describe Wagner's, and sometimes other large-scale operas.

*Mutes.* Devices used to damp the sound of various instruments.

*Natural* (of a note or key). Not sharp or flat.

*Neo-classical.* Term used to describe music written mostly during the 1920s and 30s in the style of Bach or Mozart.

*Ninth.* Interval taking nine steps, *e.g.,* from C upwards an octave and a whole tone to D.

*Nocturne.* Literally a " night-piece ", hence usually of lyrical character.

*Nonet.* Composition for nine instruments.

*Notation.* Act of writing down music.

*Note.* Single sound of specified pitch and duration; symbol to represent this.

*Obbligato.* Instrumental part having a special or essential rôle in a piece.

*Oboe.* Woodwind instrument with double reed, descended from hautboy; as such, in use since 16th cent., in modern form since 18th cent.

*Octave.* Interval taking eight steps of scale, with top and bottom notes having same " name ": C to C is an octave.

*Octet.* Composition for eight instruments or voices.

*Ondes Martenot.* Belongs to a class of melodic instruments in which the tone is produced by electrical vibrations controlled by the movement of the hands not touching the instrument.

*Opera.* Musical work for the stage with singing characters, originated in early years of 17th cent.

*Opera seria.* Chief operatic form of 17th and 18th cent., usually set to very formal librettos, concerning gods or heroes of ancient history.

*Operetta.* Lighter type of opera.

*Opus.* (abbr. *Op.*) With number following *opus* indicates order of a composer's composition.

*Oratorio.* Vocal work, usually for soloists and choir with instrumental accompaniment, generally with setting of a religious text.

*Orchestra.* Term to designate large, or largish, body of instrumentalists, originated in 17th cent.

*Orchestration.* Art of setting out work for instruments of an orchestra. To be distinguished from *Instrumentation (q.v.).*

*Organ.* Elaborate keyboard instrument in which air is blown through pipes by bellows to sound notes. Tone is altered by selection of various stops and, since the 16th cent., a pedal keyboard has also been incorporated.

*Organum.* In mediæval music a part sung as an accompaniment below or above the melody or plainsong, usually at the interval of a fourth or fifth; also, loosely, this method of singing in parts.

*Ornament.* Notes that are added to a given melody by composer or performer as an embellishment.

*Overture.* Instrumental introduction or prelude to larger work, usually opera. Concert overtures are simply that: *i.e.,* work to be played at start of a concert.

*Part.* Music of one performer in an ensemble; single strand in a composition.

*Part-song.* Vocal composition in several parts.

*Passacaglia.* Composition in which a tune is constantly repeated, usually in the bass.

*Passage.* Section of a composition.

*Passion.* Musical setting of the New Testament story of Christ's trial and crucifixion.

*Pastiche.* Piece deliberately written in another composer's style.

*Pavan(e).* Moderately paced dance dating from 16th cent. or earlier.

*Pedal.* Held note in bass of composition.

*Pentatonic Scale.* Scale of five notes—usually piano's five black keys or other notes in the same relation to each other.

*Percussion.* Collective title for instruments of the orchestra that are sounded by being struck by hand or stick.

*Phrygian Mode.* One of the scales of mediæval music, represented by the white keys on piano from E to E.

*Piano.* Soft, abbr. *p*; *pp* = *pianissimo,* very soft; instrument, invented in 18th cent., having strings struck by hammer, as opposed to the earlier harpsichord where they are plucked. The modern piano has 88 keys and can be either " upright " (vertical) or " grand " (horizontal).

*Pianoforte.* Almost obsolete full Italian name for the piano.

*Pitch.* Exact height or depth of a particular musical sound or note.

*Pizzicato.* Direction for stringed instruments, that the strings should be plucked instead of bowed.

*Plainchant, Plainsong.* Mediæval church music consisting of single line of melody without harmony or definite rhythm.

*Polka.* Dance in 2/4 time originating in 19th cent. Bohemia.

*Polonaise.* Polish dance in 5/4 time.

*Polyphony.* Combination of two or more musical lines as in *counterpoint.*

*Polytonality.* Simultaneous use of several keys.

*Postlude.* Closing piece, opposite of Prelude.

*Prelude.* Introductory piece.

*Presto.* Very fast. *Prestissimo.* Still faster.

*Progression.* Movement from one chord to next to make musical sense.

*Quartet.* Work written for four instruments or voices; group to play or sing such a work.

*Quaver.* Note that equals two semiquavers or half a crotchet.

*Quintet.* Work written for five instruments or voices; group to play or sing such a work.

*Rallentando.* Slowing down.

*Recapitulation.* Section of composition that repeats original material in something like its original form.

*Recitative.* Term used for declamation in singing written in ordinary notation but allowing rhythmical licence.

*Recorder.* Woodwind instrument, forerunner of flute.

*Reed.* Vibrating tongue of woodwind instruments.

*Register.* Set of organ pipes controlled by a particular stop; used in reference to different ranges of instrument or voice (*e.g.,* chest register).

*Relative.* Term used to indicate common key signature of a major and minor key.

*Répétiteur.* Member of opera house's musical staff who coaches singers in their parts.

*Rest.* Notation of pauses for instrument in composition, having a definite length like a note.

*Retrograde.* Term used to describe a melody played backwards.

*Rhapsody.* Work of no definite kind with a degree of romantic content.

*Rhythm.* Everything concerned with the time of music (*i.e.,* beats, accent, metre, etc.) as opposed to the pitch side.

*Ritornello.* Passage, usually instrumental, that recurs in a piece.

*Romance, Romanza.* Title for piece of vague song-like character.

*Romantic.* Term used vaguely to describe music of 19th cent. that has other than purely musical source of inspiration.

*Rondo.* Form in which one section keeps on recurring.

*Rubato.* Manner of performing a piece without keeping strictly to time.

*Sackbut.* Early English name for trombone.

*Saxophone.* Classified as wind instrument, although made of brass, because it uses a reed.

*Scale.* Progression of adjoining notes upwards or downwards.

*Scherzo.* One of two middle movements, usually third, in four-movement sonata form. Displaced minuet in this form at beginning of 19th cent.

*Score.* Copy of any music written in several parts.

*Second.* Interval taking two steps in scale. *e.g.,* C to D flat, or to D.

*Semibreve.* Note that equals two minims or half a breve.

*Semiquaver.* Note that equals half a quaver.

*Semitone.* Smallest interval commonly used in Western music.

*Septet.* Composition for seven instruments or voices.

*Sequence.* Repetition of phrase at a higher or lower pitch.

*Serenade.* Usually an evening song or instrumental work.

*Seventh.* Interval taking seven steps in the scale.

*Sextet.* Composition for six instruments or voices.

*Sharp.* Term indicating a raising of pitch by a semitone.

*Shawm.* Primitive woodwind instrument, forerunner of oboe.

*Simple time.* Division of music into two or four beats.

*Sinfonietta.* Small symphony.

*Sixth.* Interval taking six steps in the scale.

*Solo.* Piece or part of a piece for one performer playing or singing alone.

*Sonata.* Term to denote a musical form and a type of composition. In *sonata form* a composition is divided into exposition, development and recapitulation. A *sonata* is a piece, usually, for one or more players following that form.

*Song.* Any short vocal composition.

*Soprano.* Highest female voice.

*Sostenuto.* Sustained, broadly.

*Sotto voce.* Whispered, scarcely audible, applied to vocal as well as instrumental music.

*Sprechgesang.* (Ger. Speech-song.) Vocal utterance somewhere between speech and song.

*Staccato.* Perform music in short, detached manner.

*Staff.* Horizontal lines on which music is usually written.

*Stop.* Lever by which organ registration can be altered.

*String(s).* Strands of gut or metal set in vibration to produce musical sounds on string or keyboard instruments. Plural refers to violins, violas, cellos, and basses of orchestra.

*Study.* Instrumental piece, usually one used for technical exercise or to display technical skill, but often having artistic merits as well (*e.g.* Chopin's).

*Subject(s).* Theme or group of notes that forms principal idea or ideas in composition.

*Suite.* Common name for piece in several movements.

*Symphony.* Orchestral work of serious purpose usually in four movements, occasionally given name (*e.g.,* Beethoven's "Choral" symphony).

*Syncopation.* Displacement of musical accent.

*Tempo.* Pace, speed of music.

*Tenor.* Highest normal male voice.

*Ternary.* A piece in three sections is said to be in ternary form. The balance is obtained by repeating the first phrase or section (though it need not be exact or complete) after a second of equal importance.

*Tessitura.* Compass into which voice or instrument comfortably falls.

*Theme.* Same as *subject* but can also be used for a whole musical statement as in "theme and variations."

*Third.* Interval taking three steps in scale.

*Time.* Rhythmical division of music.

*Timpani. See* Kettledrum.

*Toccata.* Instrumental piece usually needing rapid, brilliant execution.

*Tonality.* Key, or feeling for a definite key.

*Tone.* Quality of musical sound; interval of two semitones.

*Tonic Sol-fa.* System of musical notation to simplify sight-reading.

*Transcribe.* Arrange piece for different medium, instrument, or voice than that originally intended.

*Transition.* Passage that joins two themes of sections of a composition.

*Transpose.* Perform a piece at different pitch from that originally intended.

*Treble.* Highest part in vocal composition; high boy's voice.

*Triad.* A chord consisting of a note with the third and fifth above it, *e.g.,* C-E-G. A common chord is a triad of which the 5th is perfect, e.g., C-E-G or C-E flat-G. Thus major and minor triads are common chords.

*Trio.* Work written for three instruments or voices; group to play or sing such a work.

*Trombone.* Brass instrument with slide adjusting length of tube.

*Trumpet.* Metal instrument of considerable antiquity; modern version has three valves to make it into a chromatic instrument.

*Tuba.* Deepest-toned brass instrument with three or four valves.

*Twelve-note.* Technique of composition using full chromatic scale with each note having equal importance. Notes are placed in particular order as the thematic basis of works.

*Unison.* Two notes sung or played together at same pitch.

*Valve.* Mechanism, invented in early 19th cent. to add to brass instruments allowing them to play full chromatic scale.

*Variation.* Varied passage of original theme. Such variations may be closely allied to or depart widely from the theme.

*Verismo.* Term to describe Italian operas written in "realist" style at the turn of this century.

*Vibrato.* Rapid fluctuation in pitch of voice or instrument. Exaggerated it is referred to as a "wobble" (of singers) or tremolo.

*Viol.* String instrument of various sizes in vogue until end of 17th cent.

*Viola.* Tenor instrument of violin family.

*Violin.* Musical four-string instrument, played with bow, of violin family, which superseded viol at beginning of 18th cent.

*Virginals.* English keyboard instrument, similar to harpsichord of 17th and 18th cent.

*Vivace.* Lively.

*Voluntary.* Organ piece for church use, but not during service.

*Waltz.* Dance in triple time, fashionable in 19th cent.

*Whole-tone scale.* Scale progressing by whole tones. Only two are possible, one beginning on C, the other on C sharp.

*Xylophone.* Percussion instrument with series of wood bars tuned in a chromatic scale and played with sticks.

*Zither.* String instrument laid on knees and plucked. Common in Central-European folk music.

# III. INDEX TO COMPOSERS

Adam de la Halle (d. 1287) . . . . 3(2)

Albéniz, Isaac (1860–1909) . . . . . 15(1)

Albinoni, Tommaso (1671–1750) . . . 6(1)

Arcadelt (*c.* 1514–*c.* 1570) . . . . . 4(2)

Bach, Carl Philipp Emanuel (1714–88) . 7(1)

Bach, Johann Sebastian (1685–1750) . . 6

Balakireff, Mily (1837–1910) . . . . 11(2)

Barber, Samuel (b. 1910) . . . . . 18(2)

Bartók, Bela (1881–1945) . . . . . 12(2)

Bax, Sir Arnold (1883–1953) . . . . 18(2)

Beethoven, Ludwig van (1770–1827) . . 8

Bellini, Vincenzo (1801–35) . . . . 10(1)

Bennett, Richard Rodney . . . . . 19(2)

Berg, Alban (1885–1935) . . . . . 16(2)

Berkeley, Lennox (b. 1903) . . . . . 19(2)

Berlioz, Hector (1803–69) . . . . . 9(1)

Binchois, Gilles (*c.* 1400–60). . . . . 4(1)

Bliss, Sir Arthur (b. 1891) . . . . . 19(2)

Blow, John (1649–1708) . . . . . 5(2)

Boccherini, Luigi (1743–1805) . . . . 8(2)

Boito, Arrigo (1842–1918) . . . . . 10(2)

Borodin, Alexander (1834–87) . . . 11(2)

Boulez, Pierre (b. 1925) . . . . . 18(1)

Brahms, Johannes (1833–97) . . . . 10(2)

Britten, Benjamin (b. 1913) . . . . . 18(2)

Bruckner, Anton (1824–96) . . . . 10(2)

Busoni, Ferruccio (1866–1924) . . . 17(1)

Byrd, William (*c.* 1542–1623) . . . . 4(2)

Cabezón, Antonio de (1510–66) . . . 4(2)

Caccini, Giulio (*c.* 1558–1615) . . . . 5(1)

Carissimi, Giacomo (*c.* 1604–74) . . . 5(1)

Cavalieri, Emilio di (*c.* 1550–1600) . . . 5(2)

Cavalli, Pietro Francesco (1602–76) . . 5(1)

Cesti, Marc'Antonio (1623–69) . . . 5(1)

Chopin, Frédéric François (1810–49) . 9(2)

Cimarosa, Domenico (1749–1801) . . . 8(2)

Copland, Aaron (b. 1900) . . . . . 18(1)

Corelli, Arcangelo (1653–1713) . . . 6(1)

Couperin, François (1668–1733) . . . 6(1)

Cui, César (1835–1918) . . . . . . 11(2)

Debussy, Claude (1862–1918) . . . 13(2)

Delius, Frederick (1862–1934) . . . . 18(2)

d'Indy, Vincent (1851–1931). . . . . 14(2)

Donizetti, Gaetano (1797–1848) . . . 10(1)

Dufay (*c.* 1400–74) . . . . . . . 4(1)

Dukas, Paul (1865–1935) . . . . . 14(1)

Dunstable, John (*c* 1380–1453) . . . 4(1)

Duparc, Henri (1844–1933) . . . . 14(1)

Dussek, Jan Ladislav (1760–1812) . . 8(2)

Dvořák, Antonín (1844–1904) . . . . 12(1)

Elgar, Sir Edward (1857–1934) . . . 13(2)

Falla, Manuel (1876–1946) . . . . 14(2)

Farnaby, Giles (latter half 16th cent.) . . 4(2)

Fauré, Gabriel (1845–1924) . . . . 14(1)

Franck, César (1822–90) . . . . . 13(2)

Frankel, Benjamin (b. 1906) . . . . 19(2)

Frescobaldi, Girolamo (1583–1643)      4(2), 6(1)

Gabrieli, Andrea (*c.* 1510–86) . . . . 5(1)

Gabrieli, Giovanni (1557–1612) . . . . 5(1)

Geminiani, Francesco (1687–1762) . . . 6(1)

Gesualdo, Carlo (1560–1614) . . . . 5(1)

Gibbons, Orlando (1583–1625) . . . 4(2)

Giordano, Umberto (1867–1948) . . . 17(2)

Glinka, Mikhail (1804–57) . . . . . 11(2)

Goehr, Alexander . . . . . . . 19(2)

Gounod, Charles (1818–93) . . . . . 13(2)

Granados, Enrique (1867–1916)      14(2), 15(1)

Grieg, Edvard (1843–1907) . . . . . 13(2)

Guido d'Arezzo (*c.* 990–1050) . . . . 3(2)

Guillaume de Machaut (1300–77) . . . 4(1)

Halévy, Jacques François (1799–1862) . 10(1)

Handel, George Frederic (1685–1759) . . 6(2)

Hauer, Josef (1883–1959) . . . . . 16(1)

Haydn, Franz Joseph (1732–1809) . . 7

Henze, Hans Werner (b. 1926) . . . . 18(1)

Hindemith, Paul (1895–1963) . . . . 18(1)

Holst, Gustav (1874–1934) . . . . 18(2)

Honegger, Arthur (1892–1955) . . . 18(1)

Hummel, Johann Nepomuk (1778–1837) . 8(2)

Ireland, John (1879–1962) . . . . . 18(2)

Ives, Charles (1874–1954) . . . . . 18(2)

# THE WORLD OF SCIENCE

Designed to explain some of the most important ideas in modern physics, chemistry, biology, and anthropology, and to give some account of recent research in science and technology.

# TABLE OF CONTENTS

# THE WORLD OF SCIENCE

In Parts I, II, and III the inanimate universe is described. This is the domain of cosmology, astronomy, geology, physics, and chemistry. There are already many interesting links which join this realm to that of the living and make it difficult to say where the boundary lies. Nevertheless it is still convenient to accord to the biological and social sciences two separate chapters, Parts IV and V. In Part VI our intention is to give some short accounts of recent developments in both science and technology. They are usually contributed by scientists actively engaged in these, their own special fields.

## I. ASTRONOMY AND COSMOLOGY—THE NATURE OF THE UNIVERSE

The universe includes everything from the smallest sub-atomic particle to the mightiest system of stars. The scientific view of the universe (not the only view but the one we are concerned with here) is a remarkable achievement of the human mind, and it is worth considering at the outset what a " scientific view " is, and what is remarkable about it.

A scientific view of something is always an intimate mixture of theories and observed facts, and not an inert mixture but a seething and growing one. The theories are broad general ideas together with arguments based on them. The arguments are designed to show that, if the general ideas are accepted, then this, that, or the other thing ought to be observed. If this, that, or the other actually are observed, then the theory is a good one; if not, then the theoreticians have to think again. Thus theoretical ideas and arguments are continually subjected to the severe test of comparison with the facts, and scientists are proud of the rigour with which this is done. On the other hand, theories often suggest new things to look for, i.e., theories lead to predictions. These predictions are frequently successful, and scientists are entitled to be proud of that too. But it follows that no theory is immutable; any scientific view of any subject may, in principle, be invalidated at any time by the discovery of new facts, though some theories are so soundly based that their overthrow does not seem imminent.

A remarkable aspect of the scientific view of the universe is that same principles are supposed to operate throughout the whole vastness of space. Thus the matter and radiation in stars are not different from the matter and radiation on earth, and their laws of behaviour are the same. Therefore theories hard won by studies in terrestrial physics and chemistry laboratories are applied at once to the whole cosmos. Astronomy and cosmology are spectacular extensions of ordinary mechanics and physics.

### LOOKING AT THE UNIVERSE.

The universe is observable because signals from it reach us and some manage to penetrate our atmosphere.

First, there are waves of visible light together with invisible rays of somewhat longer (infra-red) and somewhat shorter (ultra-violet) wavelengths. These waves show us the bright astronomical objects and, to make use of them, astronomers have constructed telescopes of great power and precision backed up with cameras, spectroscopes, and numerous auxiliaries. The most powerful telescope, at Mt. Palomar, California, has a 200-inch-diameter mirror. The next major advance in optical telescope performance probably awaits the erection of telescopes on satellites outside the earth's atmosphere, which at present acts as a distorting and only partially transparent curtain.

Secondly, there are radio waves of much longer wavelength than light. These can be detected by sensitive radio receivers with special aerial systems. These are the radio telescopes. The most well known British one is at Jodrell Bank and it started working in 1957.

Other types of radiation from outer space impinge on the atmosphere. Cosmic radiation consists of very fast-moving fundamental particles, including protons (**F14**). Cosmic rays are detected by Geiger counters, by the minute tracks they leave on photographic plates, and by other means. The origin of cosmic rays is still uncertain, but many people think they must have an intimate connection with the nature and evolution of the universe itself.

X-rays and neutrinos (**F14**) from outer space can also be detected, the former especially by satellite-borne detectors and the latter by apparatus buried in deep mines. X-ray astronomy and neutrino astronomy are being born.

By interpreting the signals that reach us by these various routes, astronomers have formed a remarkably detailed picture of its structure. The merest outline of this will now be given.

### Great Distances and Large Numbers.

Let us start with nearby objects. This raises at once the question of what " nearness " and " distance " are in astronomy and how they are to be expressed. A convenient unit of distance is the *light-year*, i.e., the distance that light, travelling at 186,000 miles per second, traverses in one year. Since vast numbers as well as vast distances will enter the question, we need a shorthand for large numbers. Ten times ten times ten will be represented by $10^3$; six tens multiplied together (i.e., one million) will be written $10^6$, and so on. $10^{14}$ would mean a hundred million million. One divided by a million (i.e., one-millionth) will be written $10^{-6}$; the very small number obtained by dividing one by the product of fourteen tens will be written $10^{-14}$. A light-year is $5 \cdot 88 \times 10^{12}$ miles; the radius of an atom is about $10^{-8}$ cm.

## PLANETS, STARS, AND GALAXIES.

### The Solar System.

The earth is the third, counting outwards, of nine planets revolving in nearly circular orbits round the sun. Their names and some other particulars are given in the table (**F7**). The sun and its planets are the main bodies of the solar system. Between Mars and Jupiter revolve numerous chunks of rock called the asteroids; the largest of these, Ceres, is 480 miles across. Apart from these, the solar system is tenuously populated with gas, dust, and small particles of stone and iron. Dust continuously settles on the earth, and frequently small fragments enter the atmosphere, glow, and evaporate; these are meteors or shooting stars. Sometimes larger rocks, called meteorites, hit the earth. Comets are relatively compact swarms of particles—containing ice according to one theory—which travel in elongated orbits round the sun. Their spectacular tails form under the sun's influence when they approach it. Not all comets stay indefinitely in the solar system; some visit us and go off into space for ever.

The sun itself is a dense, roughly spherical mass of glowing matter, 865,000 miles across. Its heat is so intense that the atoms are split into separated electrons and nuclei (see F10) and matter in such a state is called plasma. At the sun's centre the temperature has the unimaginable value of about 13 million degrees Centigrade (a coal fire is about 800° C). Under such conditions the atomic nuclei frequently collide with one another at great speeds and reactions occur between them. The sun consists largely of hydrogen and, in the very hot plasma, the nuclei of hydrogen atoms interact by a series of reactions whose net result is to turn hydrogen into helium. This is a process which releases energy just as burning does, only these nuclear processes are incomparably more energetic than ordinary burning. In fact, the energy released is great enough to be the source of all the light and heat which the sun has been pouring into space for thousands of millions of years.

Emerging from the sun and streaming past the earth is a " solar wind " of fast-moving electrons and protons (see F10) whose motion is closely linked with the behaviour of an extensive magnetic field based on the sun. In fact, the region round the sun and extending far into space past the earth is full of complex, fluctuating particle streams and magnetic fields which interact with planetary atmospheres causing, among other things, auroras and magnetic storms.

### Stars.

In colour, brightness, age, and size the sun is typical of vast numbers of other stars. Only from the human point of view is there anything special about the sun—it is near enough to give us life. Even the possession of a system of revolving planets is not, according to some modern views, very unusual.

No star can radiate energy at the rate the sun does without undergoing internal changes in the course of time. Consequently stars evolve and old processes in them give rise to new. The exact nature of stellar evolution—so far as it is at present understood—would be too complex to describe here in any detail. It involves expansion and contraction, changes of temperature, changes of colour, and changes in chemical composition as the nuclear processes gradually generate new chemical elements by reactions such as the conversion of hydrogen to helium, helium to neon, neon to magnesium, and so on. The speed of evolution changes from time to time, but is in any case very slow compared with the pace of terrestrial life; nothing very dramatic may occur for hundreds of millions of years. Evidence for the various phases of evolution is therefore obtained by studying many stars, each at a different stage of its life. Thus astronomers recognise many types with charmingly descriptive names, such as blue giants, sub-giants, red and white dwarfs, supergiants.

The path of stellar evolution may be marked by various explosive events. One of these, which occurs in sufficiently large stars, is an enormous explosion in which a substantial amount of the star is blown away into space in the form of high-speed streams of gas. For about a fortnight, such an exploding star will radiate energy 200 million times as fast as the sun. Japanese and Chinese (but not Western) astronomers recorded such an occurrence in A.D. 1054, and the exploding gases, now called the Crab nebula, can still be seen in powerful telescopes and form a cloud six or seven light-years across. While it lasts, the explosion shows up as an abnormally bright star and is called a supernova.

### Groups of Stars.

It is not surprising that ancient peoples saw pictures in the sky. The constellations, however, are not physically connected groups of stars but just happen to be patterns visible from earth. A conspicuous exception to this is the Milky Way, which a telescope resolves into many millions of separate stars. If we could view the Milky Way from a vast distance and see it as a whole we should observe a rather flat wheel of stars with spiral arms something like the sparks of a rotating Catherine wheel. This system of stars is physically connected by gravitational forces and moves through space as a whole; it is called a galaxy.

The galaxy is about $10^5$ light-years across and contains roughly $10^{11}$ stars. An inconspicuous one of these stars near the edge of the wheel is our sun; the prominent stars in our night sky are members of the galaxy that happen to be rather near us. Sirius, the brightest, is only 8·6 light-years away, a trivial distance, astronomically speaking.

The galaxy does not contain stars only, there are also clouds of gas and dust, particularly in the plane of the galaxy. Much of the gas is hydrogen, and its detection is difficult. However, gaseous hydrogen gives out radio waves with a wavelength of 21 cm. Radio telescopes are just the instruments to receive these, and workers in Holland, America, and Australia detected the gas clouds by this means. In 1952 they found that the hydrogen clouds lie in the spiral arms of the galaxy, and this is some of the strongest evidence for the spiral form.

Another important feature of the galactic scene is the weak but enormously extensive magnetic field. This is believed to have an intimate connection with the spiral structure.

Around the spiral arms, and forming part of the galaxy, are numerous globular clusters of stars. These are roughly spherical, abnormally densely packed, collections of stars with many thousands of members. Because of its form and density, a globular cluster may be assumed to have been formed in one process, not star by star. Thus all its stars are the same age. This is of great interest to astronomers, because they can study differences between stars of similar age but different sizes.

### Galaxies.

One might be forgiven for assuming that such a vast system as the galaxy is in fact the universe; but this is not so. In the constellation of Andromeda is a famous object which, on close examination, turns out to be another galaxy of size and structure similar to our own. Its distance is given in the table (F7). The Milky Way, the Andromeda Nebula, and a few other smaller galaxies form a cluster of galaxies called the Local Group. Obviously it would not be so named except to distinguish it from other distinct groups, and it is indeed a fact that the universe is populated with groups, or clusters, of galaxies. A cluster may contain two or three galaxies, but some contain thousands. So far as the eye of the telescope and camera can see, there are clusters of galaxies.

On a photograph a galaxy is a nebulous blob without the hard outline that a single star produces. Such nebulæ were formerly thought to be inside the Milky Way, but, after controversy, it was established that many of them were separate distant galaxies. By about 1920 it was known that there were at least half a million galaxies, and with the advent of the 100-in. Mt. Wilson telescope this number rose to $10^8$ and is being increased further by the 200-in. telescope which can see out to a distance of $7 \times 10^9$ light-years. Through the powerful telescopes the nearer galaxies reveal their inner structures. Photographs of galaxies are among the most beautiful and fascinating photographs ever taken, and readers who have never seen one should hasten to the nearest illustrated astronomy book. Recent careful co-operation between optical and radio-astronomers has revealed that some very remote galaxies are strong sources of radio waves. Sometimes these radio galaxies have unusual structures suggestive of violent disturbance.

### The Expanding Universe.

Two discoveries about galaxies are of the utmost importance. One is that, by and large, clusters of galaxies are uniformly distributed through the universe. The other is that the distant galaxies are receding from us.

How is this known? Many readers may be familiar with the Doppler effect first discovered in 1842. Suppose a stationary body emits waves of any kind and we measure their wavelength, finding it to be $L$ ins. Now suppose the body approaches us; the waves are thereby crowded together in the intervening space and the wavelength appears less than $L$; if the body recedes the wavelength appears greater than $L$. The Austrian physicist, J. Doppler (1803–53), discovered this behaviour in sound waves, and it explains the well-known change of pitch of a train whistle as it approaches and passes us. The same principle applies to the light. Every atom emits light of definite wavelengths which appear in a spectroscope as a series of coloured lines—a different series for each atom. If the atom is in a receding body all the lines have slightly longer wavelengths than usual, and the amount of the change depends uniquely on the speed. Longer wavelengths mean that the light is redder than usual, so that a light from a receding body shows what is called a "red shift." The speed of recession can be calculated from the amount of red shift.

It was the American astronomer, V. M. Slipher, who first showed (in 1914) that some galaxies emitted light with a red shift. In the 1920s and 1930s the famous astronomer E. Hubble (1889–1953) measured both the distances and red shift of many galaxies and proved what is now known as Hubble's Law. This states that the speed of recession of galaxies is proportional to their distance from us. This does not apply to our neighbours in the Local Group, we and they are keeping together. Hubble's Law has been tested and found to hold for the farthest detectable galaxies; they are about $7 \times 10^9$ light-years away and are receding with a speed $\frac{2}{3}$ of that of light.

Does this mean that the Local Group is the centre of the universe and that everything else is rushing away from us? No; Hubble's Law would appear just the same from any other cluster of galaxies. Imagine you are in a square on some fabulous chess board which is steadily doubling its size every hour; all other squares double their distances from you in an hour. Therefore the farther squares from you must travel faster than the nearer ones; in fact, Hubble's Law must be obeyed. But anyone standing in any other square would get the same impression.

This extraordinary behaviour of the universe is one of the most exciting discoveries of science. Let us envisage one possible implication. If the galaxies have always been receding, then in the past they must have been closer together. Following this to its conclusion, it seems that all the matter in the universe must have been packed densely together about $10^{10}$ years ago. Was this really so? The lack of any definite answer to this question is one of the things that makes cosmology so interesting.

## Quasars and Pulsars.

In November 1962 Australian radio-astronomers located a strong radio emitter with sufficient precision for the Mt. Palomar optical astronomers to identify it on photographs and examine the nature of its light. The red shift was so great that the object must be exceedingly distant; on the other hand it looked star-like, much smaller than a galaxy. By the beginning of 1967 over a hundred of these objects had been discovered and other characteristics established, such as strong ultra-violet radiation and inconstancy, in some cases, of the rate at which radiation is emitted. Not all of these so-called quasars are strong radio emitters; some show all the other characteristics except radio emission. It has been estimated that the "quiet" kind are about a hundred times more numerous than the radio kind. One great problem here is: how can such relatively small objects generate such inconceivably great amounts of energy that they appear bright at such huge distances? So far this is unanswered; these quasi-stellar objects are a great mystery, though they are generally held to be an important pointer towards a deeper understanding of cosmology.

Late in 1967, while investigating quasars, Cambridge radio-astronomers discovered pulsars, a new type of heavenly body. Their characteristic is the emission of pulses of radio waves every second or so with a repetition rate that is regular to at least 1 part in $10^8$. At present they are believed to be peculiar stars hardly bigger than the Earth and situated inside our galaxy.

# THE ORIGIN AND DEVELOPMENT OF THE UNIVERSE.

Errors of observation and interpretation occur of course. But there are many checks and repetitions made, so that, on the whole, the descriptive account of the universe would be generally agreed among astronomers. When it comes to inventing theoretical explanations, however, science is on less sure ground, and indeed the theory of the universe is an arena of controversy at present. In most other sciences experiments can be repeated and the same phenomena observed under differing but controlled conditions. This is very helpful. But, by definition, there is only one universe: one cannot repeat it or do experiments with it. On the other hand, it must be remembered that the light from distant galaxies has taken perhaps $10^9$ years to reach us, so it tells us what the galaxies were like that number of years ago. Therefore we are not confined simply to describing the present state of the universe; by looking farther into space we are looking farther into the past as well. How, then, does the state of the universe vary with time?

## Evolutionary Theories.

One answer to this can be obtained from Einstein's general theory of relativity. Some slight indication of what this theory is about is given on page F15, and its logical development is, of course, a matter for mathematical specialists. It turns out that, if we assume that matter is distributed uniformly throughout space (as observation strongly suggests), then the solutions of Einstein's equations show how the state of the universe may vary with time. Unfortunately there are many possible solutions corresponding to expanding, static, or contracting universes. As we have already seen, the actual universe is expanding, therefore the static and contracting solutions can be ruled out. There is still a multiplicity of expanding possibilities; some correspond to indefinite expansion from an initially very dense state, others to expansion followed by contraction to a dense state followed by expansion and so on repeatedly, i.e., a pulsating universe. The "dense state" is presumably to be identified with the time when the receding galaxies were all concentrated near one another, possibly in some dense conglomeration of atoms. This initial state is thought by some to be the origin of the universe; they would say it has been expanding and evolving ever since. If the universe is pulsating, then sooner or later, gravitational attractions between galaxies will slow the observed recession down and turn it into a mutual approach and so back to the dense state. A straightforward application of the mathematics makes this dense state infinitely dense, and presumably something must happen before this inconceivable situation arises. For example, forces between atomic nuclei may play an important part and determine what the dense state (if any) is actually like.

## The Steady-State Theory.

A rival theory was proposed in 1948 by Bondi, Gold, and Hoyle. They suggested that the universe is not changing with time: there was no initial dense state and no pulsations; the universe always has been, and always will be, like it is now. This does not mean that no local changes can be observed—this would clearly be contrary to the facts. But it does mean that, on the large scale, the clusters of galaxies have a distribution which is uniform in space and unchanging in time. If the numbers of clusters of galaxies in a large volume of space were counted every few thousand million years the answer would always be the same.

At first sight this appears to contradict outright the observed expansion of the universe. For if the galaxies are receding from one another how can the number in a given volume remain constant? The situation is saved by a bold proposal. It is that matter, in the form of hydrogen atoms, is being continuously created throughout space. This gas accumulates in due course into new galaxies, so that as the old ones move apart the young ones appear to keep the numbers up. The necessary amount of continuous creation can be calculated and is equivalent to the appearance of one atom in an average-sized room every 20 million years. If this seems absurdly small, try calculating the rate of creation in tons per second in a sphere of radius $10^9$ light-years.

The rate of creation is, however, much too small to have affected any of the laws of ordinary physics. The famous law of the conservation of matter (" matter can neither be created nor destroyed ") is violated, but on such a small scale that physicists, it is said, should not complain. Nevertheless, some do complain and see in this violation a strong point against this theory.

## The Formation of Galaxies and Stars.

On any theory of the universe, some explanation has to be found for the existence of clusters of galaxies. In all theories galaxies condense out from dispersed masses of gas, principally hydrogen.

Once a huge gas cloud becomes sufficiently condensed to be separately identifiable as a galaxy, further condensation goes on inside it. It is believed on theoretical grounds that it could not condense into one enormous star but must form many fragments which shrink separately into clusters of stars. In these clusters many stars, perhaps hundreds or thousands or even millions, are born at once. A small cluster, visible to the naked eye, is the Pleaides. The Orion nebula, visible as a hazy blob of glowing gas in the sword of Orion, is the scene of much star-forming activity at present.

According to the evolutionary theory, the " initial dense state " consisted of very hot plasma in a state of overall expansion. The expanding plasma was both cooling and swirling about. The random swirling produces irregularities in the distribution of the hot gas—here it would be rather denser, there rather less dense. If a sufficiently large mass of denser gas happened to occur, then the gravitational attraction between its own particles would hold it together and maintain its permanent identity, even though the rest of the gas continued to swirl and expand. Such a large mass would gradually condense into fragments to become galaxies, the whole mass turning into a cluster of galaxies.

The steady-state view is interestingly and significantly different, for, on this theory, galaxies have always been present, and the problem is one of finding how existing galaxies can generate new ones out of the hydrogen gas which is supposed to be continuously created everywhere. Moreover, this has to be done at just the right rate to maintain the galactic population density constant —otherwise it would not be a *steady-state* theory.

A theoretical proposal allowing for galaxy creation was in fact provided by steady-state cosmologists but will not be outlined here because it now seems that the steady-state theory is losing ground.

## The Changing Scene.

The 1960s are seeing revolutionary developments in both observational and theoretical astronomy. By 1966 the attractive simplicity of the original steady-state theory had been obscured by modifications forced upon its protagonists by new evidence or theoretical objections. It is an interesting and significant fact that the apparent demise of the steady-state theory has resulted from a welcome injection into cosmology of the characteristic activity of the other sciences, namely, the comparison of theory with observation. For example, it now seems agreed after some years of uncertainty that remote sources of radio waves are more abundant the weaker their intensity. This strongly suggests that they are more abundant at greater distances. Thus the universe is not *uniform* as the original steady-state theory prescribed. Since greater distances correspond to earlier times, any extra abundance of objects observed at the greater distance means that the universe was denser in its younger days than now. This favours an evolutionary theory of the universe.

The same theory requires that the initial dense state of the universe—aptly christened " the primaeval fireball "—should contain intense electromagnetic radiation with a distribution of wavelengths characteristic of the high temperature. As the fireball, *i.e.*, the universe, expanded over a period of about $10^{10}$ years it cooled, and one feature of this process is that the wavelengths of the radiation increase and their distribution becomes characteristic of a much lower temperature. In fact, the wavelengths should now be concentrated round about 1 mm to 1 cm (corresponding to about −270° C) and the radiation should approach the earth uniformly from all directions. Radiation just like this has recently been detected in several laboratories, first by Penzias and Wilson in America during 1965. They used very sensitive radio receivers originally designed to detect signals from artificial satellites. No plausible terrestrial or galactic origin for the radiation has yet been conceived; the waves appear to have something to do with the universe itself. Neither is there a rational basis for the radiation within the steady-state theory which probably receives here its *coup de grâce*. The evolutionary theory survives so far.

## The Formation of the Chemical Elements.

A stable nucleus is one that lasts indefinitely because it is not radioactive. There are 274 known kinds of stable atomic nuclei and little likelihood of any more being found. These nuclei are the isotopes (*see* F10) of 81 different chemical elements; the other elements, including, for example, uranium and radium are always radioactive. Some elements are rare, others abundant. The most common ones on earth are oxygen, silicon, aluminium, and iron. However, the earth is rather atypical. It is especially deficient in hydrogen, because the gravitational attraction of our small planet was not strong enough to prevent this very light gas from escaping into space.

It is possible to examine the chemical constituents of meteorites and to infer the composition of the sun and other stars from the spectrum of the light they emit. By such means, the conclusion has been reached that 93% of the atoms in our galaxy are hydrogen, 7% are helium; all the other elements together account for about one in a thousand atoms. A glance at the Table of Elements (Section N) will show that hydrogen and helium are two of the lightest elements; they are in fact the two simplest.

According to the steady-state theory, hydrogen atoms are constantly being created. The evolutionary theory supposes that the dense initial state was a system of very hot protons and electrons, *i.e.*, split-up hydrogen atoms. In either case, therefore, the problem is to explain how the heavier chemical elements appear in the universe at all. It is here that a fascinating combination of astronomy and nuclear physics is required.

We have already referred to the fact that the energy radiated from the sun originates in nuclear reactions which turn hydrogen into helium. Why is energy given out? To answer this question we note that nuclei are made up of protons and neutrons (*see* F10). These particles attract one another strongly—that is why a nucleus holds together. To separate the particles, energy would have to be supplied to overcome the attractive forces. This amount of energy is called *binding energy* and is a definite quantity for every kind of nucleus. Conversely, when the particles are brought together to form a nucleus the binding energy is *released* in the form of radiations and heat. Different nuclei consist of different numbers of particles, therefore the relevant quantity to consider is the *binding energy per particle*. Let us call this B. Then if elements of *high* B are formed out of those of *low* B there is a *release* of energy.

Now B is small (relatively) for light elements like lithium, helium, and carbon; it rises to a maximum for elements of middling atomic weight like iron; it falls again for really heavy elements like lead, bismuth, and uranium. Consequently, energy is released by forming middleweight elements either by splitting up heavy nuclei (" nuclear fission ") or by joining up light ones (" nuclear fusion ").

It is the latter process, fusion, that is going on in stars. The fusion processes can be studied in physics laboratories by using large accelerating machines to hurl nuclei at one another to make them coalesce. In stars the necessary high velocity of impact occurs because the plasma is so hot. Gradually the hydrogen is turned into helium, and helium into heavier and heavier elements. This supplies the energy that the stars radiate and simultaneously generates the chemical elements.

The very heavy elements present a problem. To form them from middleweight elements, energy has to be *supplied*. Since there is plenty of energy inside a star, a certain small number of heavy nuclei will indeed form, but they will continually undergo fission again under the prevailing intense conditions. How do they ever get away to form cool ordinary elements, like lead and bismuth, in the earth? One view links them with the highly explosive supernovæ, to which we have already referred (F4 (1)). If the heavy elements occur in these stars the force of the explosion disperses them into cool outer space before they have time to undergo the fission that would otherwise have been their fate. The heavy elements are thus seen as the dust and debris of stellar catastrophes. This view is in line with the steady-state theory, because supernovæ are always occurring and keeping up the supply of heavy elements. In the evolutionary theory some of the generation of elements is supposed to go on in the very early stages of the initial dense state and to continue in the stars that evolve in the fullness of time. It cannot be claimed that the origin of the chemical elements is completely known, but we have said enough to show that there are plausible theories. Time and more facts will choose between them.

### The Formation of the Planets.

Did the sun collect its family of planets one by one as a result of chance encounters in the depths of space? Or was the solar system formed all at once in some generative process? To this fundamental question at least there is a fairly definite answer. The planetary orbits all lie in about the same plane and the planets all revolve the same way round the sun. This could hardly have happened by chance; indeed, it provides almost conclusive evidence for the alternative view. But what was the generative process?

Many ideas have been proposed, and the problem is very intricate. One view is that the sun and its planets formed in a stellar condensation, a feature of which was the pushing outwards from the central sun of a disc of matter which subsequently became the planets. Such a process would be regarded as normal in stars, and not exceptional.

On the other hand, the planets have been attributed to the effect of a passing star whose gravitational attraction drew out from the sun a jet of gaseous matter which condensed into the planets. Such an encounter between stars is very rare and, on this theory, the formation of planets must be an outside chance. This theory is not widely held now.

The connection between stellar and planetary theory is brought out again by the existence on the planets of the heavier chemical elements. How did they get there? If it be true that heavy elements are hurled into space by exploding supernovæ (see above), then at least one such explosion must have mingled its products with the widespread interstellar hydrogen before the planets condensed. At one time Hoyle put forward the view that the sun was once accompanied by another star (there are many such binary systems known to astronomers) and that the sun's partner exploded. Some of the ejected gases, captured by the sun's gravitational attraction, later condensed into planets, while the remnant of the star recoiled from the explosion and got away into space. This explanation was later modified in that the exploding star and the sun need not be a close pair but merely two of a cluster of stars formed at the same time.

Before leaving this subject, where theories are more numerous than firm conclusions, one more question may be raised: was the earth formed hot or cold? There are adherents to both opinions. One side would say that the planets condensed from hot gases, became liquid, and subsequently cooled and solidified, at the surface if not throughout. Others would say that dust, ice, and small particles formed in space first and subsequently accumulated into large bodies, whose temperature rose somewhat later on. With space exploration beginning in earnest, considerable future progress in understanding planetary formation can be anticipated. (See also Section L: Mars, Venus, Planets.)

### THE SOLAR SYSTEM.

| Name. | Distance from Sun (millions of miles). | Diameter (thousands of miles). | Average density (water = 1). | Number of Satellites. |
|---|---|---|---|---|
| Sun | — | 865 | 1·41 | — |
| Mercury | 36 | 3·1 | 3·73 | 0 |
| Venus | 67 | 7·6 | 5·23 | 0 |
| Earth | 93 | 7·9 | 5·52 | 1 |
| Mars | 142 | 4·2 | 3·94 | 2 |
| Jupiter | 484 | 85·0 | 1·34 | 12 |
| Saturn | 887 | 70·0 | 0·69 | 9 |
| Uranus | 1785 | 30·9 | 1·36 | 5 |
| Neptune | 2797 | 33·0 | 1·32 | 2 |
| Pluto | 3670 | ? | ? | 0 |

### SOME ASTRONOMICAL DISTANCES.

(1 light-year = $5·88 \times 10^{12}$ miles).

| Object. | Distance from Earth (light-years). | Velocity of recession (miles per second). | Object. | Distance from Earth (light-years). | Velocity of recession (miles per second). |
|---|---|---|---|---|---|
| Sun | $1·6 \times 10^{-5}$ | — | Andromeda Galaxy | $1·5 \times 10^{6}$ | — |
| Nearest star (Proxima Centauri) | 4·2 | — | Galaxy in Virgo | $7·5 \times 10^{7}$ | 750 |
| Brightest star (Sirius) | 8·6 | — | Galaxy in Gt. Bear | $10^{9}$ | 9,300 |
| Pleiades | 340 | — | Galaxy in Corona Borealis | $1·3 \times 10^{9}$ | 13,400 |
| Centre of Milky Way | $2·6 \times 10^{4}$ | — | Galaxy in Bootes | $4·5 \times 10^{9}$ | 24,400 |
| Magellanic clouds (the nearest galaxies) | $1·6 \times 10^{5}$ | — | Very remote quasi-stellar object | $\sim 1·5 \times 10^{10}$ | $\sim 150,000$ |

## THE EARTH.

### Shape and Size.

The earth has the form of a slightly flattened sphere, the polar radius being 6,357 km (3,950·4 miles) and the equatorial radius 6,378 km (3,963·5 miles). Its mass is $5·97 \times 10^{27}$ g and its volume is $1·083 \times 10^{27}$ cc; hence its average density is about 5·5 grams per cubic centimetre. This is about twice the average density of the surface material, so it is inferred that there exists a large volume of high density material within the earth.

### Structure.

From a study of the passage of earthquake waves through the earth and observations of such properties as magnetism, moment of inertia, temperature increase with depth, etc. it is deduced that the earth has a structure consisting of a series of shells. The central *core* has a radius of some 3,600 km (2,250 miles); it is probably in part liquid, and is almost certainly composed of an alloy of nickel and iron. Separated from the core by a fairly sharp boundary is the *mantle*; this has a thickness of about 2,800 km (1,750 miles) and is solid. It is probably composed of silicates of iron and magnesium with some metallic iron in the inner region. The outer 100 km (62·5 miles) is the *crust*, which is solid under ordinary conditions but which may partially liquefy during periods of igneous activity. Under the continents it is possible to distinguish two layers in the crust; an upper, less dense one, probably granitic in character, known as the sial, and a lower, denser one, the sima, probably basaltic in character. The sial appears to be absent under the Pacific Ocean and very thin or absent under the Atlantic and Indian Oceans. The concept of the sial blocks "floating" in the sima provides an explanation for the observed vertical movements of continents and leads to the theory that they may have "drifted" to their present positions. The junction between the sima and the mantle is quite sharp, the break being known as the Mohorovičić Discontinuity.

### Composition.

Direct observation of the crust is confined to the surface and mines or boreholes, the deepest of which reach only to about 5 miles. From analyses of the crustal rocks, the abundance of the elements in the crust can be estimated. The commonest is oxygen (46·6%), followed by silicon (27·7%), aluminium (8·13%) and iron (5%). The next four are calcium, sodium, potassium, and magnesium, ranging between 3·6 and 2%. These 8 elements total 97·57% of the whole crust. Most of the other 84 elements are present in amounts to be measured in parts per million; *e.g.*, copper occurs to the extent of 45 p.p.m., tin, 3 p.p.m. These are average proportions over the whole crust; to be workable as ores, concentrations need to be much higher—*e.g.*, both copper and tin ores have to contain a minimum of 1% metal to be economic. Locating the rare occurrences of such concentrations is the job of the prospecting geologist. Taking the earth as a whole, *i.e.*, core, mantle and crust, most authorities agree that the commonest element is iron, followed by oxygen, silicon, and magnesium in that order; after this, there is only partial agreement.

### The Age of the Earth.

It is possible to make an estimate of the age of the earth's crust by considering the rate at which radioactive elements break down into inert elements. A number of methods are now available, the most important being those based on the study of the abundances of isotopes of lead and other elements. From the data obtained, estimates can be made of the following points on the time scale: Age of earth's crust about $5·0 \times 10^9$ years (as a planet the earth has existed for several thousand million years); life emerged about $2 \times 10^9$ years ago; first large-scale occurrence of fossils, $600 \times 10^6$ years ago. Other points on the scale

are given in the table in Part IV ($10^9$ = thousand million; $10^6$ = million).

### The Materials of the Earth's Crust.

Geologists recognise three main classes of rocks making up the crust—Igneous, Sedimentary, and Metamorphic. Rocks are aggregates of minerals, which may be regarded as simpler, homogeneous compounds, in contrast to the complex, inhomogeneous mixture which is a rock. The bases of rock classification are minerals present, shape and size of the individual grains, and the mode of origin of the material.

*Igneous rocks* are usually regarded as having crystallised from a molten state, although certain types may have arisen in other ways, *e.g.*, by reaction between high-temperature fluids, of the right composition, and pre-existing rocks. Typical igneous rocks are granite and basalt; granite is coarse-grained, intrusive into other rocks, and contains the minerals quartz, potash or soda felspar, and usually a mica. Basalt is fine-grained, flows out as lava at the surface and contains the minerals augite, calcium felspar, and usually olivine. Between these extreme types are some thousands of intermediates, but together granite and basalt constitute 90–95% of all igneous rocks seen at the surface.

*Sedimentary rocks* are derived from pre-existing rocks by the processes of weathering and erosion, followed by transport to the point of ultimate deposition of the material, which is then converted from unconsolidated sediment to rock by the process of lithifaction. Typical sedimentary rocks are sandstone, limestone, and shale. Sandstone consists of particles of quartz and occasional other minerals, whereas shales may become slate if compressed clays, which may become slate if compressed very strongly during mountain building. Limestones may be chemical precipitates, but are commonly formed by the aggregation of skeletal material of animals. Some other sedimentary types of interest are conglomerates—lithified pebble beds—and evaporites, such as rock salt and gypsum beds. The bulk of the sedimentary rocks were formed under marine conditions.

*Metamorphic rocks* are produced by the action of heat and/or pressure upon pre-existing rocks, producing considerable changes in mineralogy and texture. Rocks subjected to heat alone are termed hornfelses (marbles if the original rock was a limestone). Pressure alone may produce slates, but often pressure results in shearing forces which crush and break up rocks to a fine powder (subsequently lithified), known as mylonite. Heat and pressure together produce the type of metamorphism known as regional, because it occurs over large areas (*e.g.*, the Scottish Highlands), where it can be seen to have been associated with mountain-building processes. Typical rocks of this kind are schist and gneiss; the former is a foliated rock, usually with much mica, while the latter is a banded rock, with dark and light bands of quartz and/or felspar and mica and/or hornblende. Some gneisses, called migmatites, were produced by the injection of granitic material along the foliation planes of schists.

### Mountain Building.

There is no general agreement among geologists about the origin of mountains, despite many years of argument. It is a matter of observation that the great mountain ranges are built of sedimentary rocks—usually much metamorphosed in the deeper levels—and occur in relatively narrow belts of great length. The idea has developed that long, narrow depressions known as *Geosynclines* develop in the crust, into which vast quantities of sediments are poured. The floor is slowly depressed by the weight of material, and ultimately the two sides of the geosyncline move together, folding the sediments both upwards and downwards, producing the complex structures seen in such regions as the Alps and Himalayas. It has been suggested that convection currents in crust, core, or mantle may provide the forces required, but some geologists believe that the earth is contracting and causing the skin to "wrinkle." Another possibility is that the sial blocks move about in the sima, and the Alps, for example, were formed when Africa drove northwards towards Europe. It is suggested that radioactive heating of the sima layers may make them sufficiently mobile to allow movement to take place, and this seems to be an essential feature of most theories of mountain building.

### Glaciation.

Within the last million years much of the northern part of the Northern Hemisphere was covered by ice-sheets, now reduced to the Arctic ice-cap. This has profoundly modified the landscape, especially in mountainous regions such as the Alps, North Wales, and the Scottish Highlands. The ice, moving first as valley glaciers and later as sheets over wide areas, scraped off all loose surface material, which was then available to abrade the bare rocks to give the characteristic scenery. In Britain the maximum advance of the ice-sheets brought them to the line Bristol Channel–Thames Estuary, passing just north of London. The great heaps of débris transported by the glaciers are known as moraines. The cause of the ice age is not fully understood, but it is worth noting that in the Permo-Carboniferous period in the Southern Hemisphere there was a widespread glaciation at the same time as the coal measures and desert sediments were being laid down in the Northern Hemisphere. Other glaciations are known from several other epochs as far back as $2 \times 10^9$ years.

### The Oceans.

The oceans cover $75\%$ of the earth's surface. They may be divided into three main types of environment—the *shelf seas*, bordering the continents, the *continental slopes*, transitional between the shelves and the *abyssal region*. Each region has its own type of sedimentation, fauna, and flora. Because of the virtual absence of a sial layer under the oceans, the study of the ocean floor yields special information about the sima and mantle, and may provide data leading to a solution of current problems relating to geosynclines and mountain building. Study of sedimentation in the oceans is important for understanding the ancient sedimentary rocks.

### The Atmosphere.

The atmosphere at sea-level contains about $78 \cdot 1\%$ nitrogen and $21\%$ oxygen, the remainder being carbon dioxide ($0 \cdot 03\%$) and the inert gases. It is thought that in the early stages of the earth's history much more carbon dioxide existed and less oxygen. When plants developed, the carbon dioxide was utilised in the building up of food substances with the release of oxygen in the process of photosynthesis (F23). *See also* Air, Atmosphere, Section L.

# II. PHYSICS—THE FUNDAMENTAL SCIENCE OF MATTER

### WHAT PHYSICS IS ABOUT

Anyone compelled by curiosity or professional interest to look into contemporary journals of pure physics research is soon struck by the fact that the old text-book division of physics into "heat, light, sound, electricity, and magnetism" has become very blurred. The indispensable periodical of research summaries, *Physics Abstracts*, contains about 3,000 entries a month, under many separate headings. This is very daunting even to the experienced physicist and, as a token of the human effort devoted to one single branch of science, it is impressive for variety, for degree of specialisation, and for sheer volume. How can the main features of this great work be presented to the non-specialist?

Two different, though complementary, sections can be distinguished. First, there is the physics concerned with the properties of matter in bulk, with solids, liquids, and gases, and with those odd but very important substances, such as paints, plastic solutions, and jelly-like material, which are neither properly solid nor liquid. In this vast domain of physics questions like this are asked: Why is iron magnetic, copper not? What happens when solids melt? Why do some liquids flow more easily than others? Why do some things conduct electricity well, others badly, some not at all? During the last century, particularly the last few decades, it has become clear that such questions can be answered only by raising and solving others first. In particular, we must ask: (i) Of what nature are the invisible particles of which matter is composed? and (ii) How are those particles arranged in bulk matter?

The first of these two questions has generated the second major category of modern physics: this is the physics of particles and of the forces that particles exert on each other. In this field, which represents science at its most fundamental, questions like this are asked: If matter is composed of small units or particles, what are they like? How many kinds of particle are there? Do the particles possess mass? electric charge? magnetism? How do the particles influence each other? How can their motion be described and predicted?

Once scientists became convinced that matter did indeed consist of particles, the *arrangement* of the particles in matter became an important question. This is the problem of *structure*. It was discovered, by von Laue in Germany and by W. H. and W. L. Bragg in England, that the structure of solids could be inferred from the way X-rays are reflected. It is well known that X-rays can penetrate solids. In doing so, they encounter successive layers of particles and are reflected from them. The reflections reveal how far apart the layers are and how the particles are arranged in space. This is the technique of X-ray crystallography. By now it has shown that most solid matter is *crystalline, i.e.*, it consists of a regular pattern of particles repeated over and over again to fill the volume of the solid—just as a wallpaper is covered by repeated units of design. The units in a crystal are very small, often about $10^{-8}$ cm across, and the particles in them are very close together.

Liquids, on the other hand, have no repeated pattern, but consist of particles which are jumbled up, though still very closely packed—lik marbles in a bag. In gases, the particles are widely separated and moving rapidly about; the average distance between particles in air is about 10 times that in ordinary solids, and air particles have an average speed of $5 \times 10^4$ cm per sec. (1,000 m.p.h.).

In general, therefore, the structure of matter is fairly well understood. This does not mean that structure studies are out of date, but only that now they are devoted to elucidating the structure of particular substances, often extremely complex ones such as are found in living matter. We shall therefore say no more about structure, but turn to the major divisions of physics introduced above: (i) particles and their forces; (ii) the properties of matter in bulk.

### PARTICLES AND FORCES.

The idea that matter is composed of small particles, or atoms, originated, it is true, in classical times. Nevertheless, the modern views need be traced back no farther than the beginning of the nineteenth century, when Dalton and his contemporaries were studying the laws of chemical combination. By that time the distinctions between elements, compounds, and mixtures were already made. Compounds and mixtures are substances which can be separated into smaller amounts of chemically distinguishable constituents. Elements (see N34) cannot be so divided. In a mixture the components may be mixed in any proportion and sorted out again by non-chemical means. In a compound the elements are combined in fixed proportions by weight. This last fact gives the clue to atomic theory.

## Dalton and Atomic Theory.

Dalton pointed out that the fixed combining weights of elements could easily be explained if the elements consisted of atoms which combined in simple numerical ratios, e.g., 1 atom of element A with one of B, or one of B with two of C, and so on. For instance, 35·5 g of chlorine combine with 23·0 g of sodium to make 58·5 g of ordinary salt. If we assume one atom of chlorine links with one of sodium, then the atoms themselves must have weights in the ratio 35·5 to 23·0. This turns out to be consistent with the combining weights of chlorine and sodium in all other compounds in which they both take part. Sometimes two elements combine in several different proportions by weight. But this is easily explained by assuming that the atoms link up in different numbers, e.g., one iron atom with one oxygen, or two irons with three oxygens, or three irons with four oxygens. Then the three different combining proportions arise from the three different numbers of atoms, using in each case the same ratio of oxygen atom weight to iron atom weight.

## Atomic Weight.

Over the century and a half since Dalton, these ideas have been repeatedly tested by chemical experiments. No one now doubts that every chemical element has atoms of characteristic weight. By convention the number 12·0000 is ascribed to carbon and called its "atomic weight." The atomic weights of other atoms are expressed by giving their ratio to that of carbon, e.g., hydrogen, 1·008; iron, 55·85. These numbers are only ratios; the real weight of one single oxygen atom is $2·7 \times 10^{-23}$ g.

## J. J. Thomson and the Electron.

Matter is electrically uncharged in its normal state, but there exist many well-known ways of producing electric charges and currents—rubbing amber, or rotating dynamos, for example. It is therefore necessary to have some theory of electricity linked to the theory of matter. The fundamental experiment in this field was made by J. J. Thomson when, in 1897, he discovered the electron.

If you take two metal electrodes sealed inside a glass vessel, and if the air is suitably pumped out and a high voltage applied to the electrodes, then the negative one emits a radiation which causes the walls of the tube to glow. The rays are called cathode rays. The discovery of the electron was essentially a clarification of the nature of cathode rays. Thomson showed that they were streams of particles with mass and negative electric charge and a general behaviour unlike any other atomic particle known at that time. The importance of this discovery for the world of science cannot be overestimated, and its technical progeny are in every home and factory in radio valves, television tubes, and other devices.

## Rutherford–Bohr Atom.

Since the electrons emerge from matter, they are presumably parts of atoms. The relation between the negative electrons and the positively charged constituents of matter was elucidated by the great experimenter Rutherford and the great theoretician Bohr. Their work, just before the First World War, showed that the positive charge, together with almost all the mass, is concentrated in the central core or nucleus of the atom about which the very light-weight electrons revolve. The diameter of an atom is about $10^{-8}$ cm, roughly one three-hundred-millionth part of an inch. The

central nucleus has a diameter about 10,000 times smaller still. The nucleus and the electrons hold together because of the electric attraction between them.

At this stage work could, and did, go on separately along several different lines:

(i) Electrons could be studied on their own. Nowadays the handling of beams of electrons of all sizes and intensities has become a major industry.

(ii) The nucleus could be treated as a special problem, and this led to the mid-century flowering of nuclear physics, to the atomic bomb, and to nuclear power.

(iii) The behaviour of electrons in the atom could be analysed; this is the great domain of atomic physics which spreads into many other sciences as well.

Volumes have been written about each of these three fields, but we can spare only a few lines for each.

## The Electron.

Electrons are expelled from solids by light, heat, electric fields, and other influences. It has therefore been possible to study beams of electrons on their own in vacuo. Electrons inside matter, either as constituents, or temporarily in transit, can also be observed by their innumerable effects. These observations all show the particles to be indistinguishable one from another; all electrons are the same wherever they come from. They have a definite mass] ($9·11 \times 10^{-28}$ g), a negative electric charge, a magnetic moment, and a "spin" (intrinsic rotatory motion). No one has ever subdivided an electron or obtained an electric charge smaller than that on one electron. The electronic charge is therefore used as a basic unit of charge in atomic physics. The electron has come to be the best known of all the "fundamental particles."

## The Nucleus.

The early research programmes in nuclear physics were greatly facilitated by the occurrence in nature of certain unstable (radioactive) nuclei which emit fast-moving fragments. The latter can be used as projectiles to aim at other nuclei as targets; the resulting impacts yield much valuable information. This technique still dominates nuclear physics, though nowadays the projectiles are artificially accelerated by one or other of the large costly machines designed for the purpose.

The most important early discovery was that the nucleus consists of two types of fundamental particle—the positively charged proton and the electrically neutral neutron. These two are of nearly equal mass (about 1,800 times that of the electron), and like electrons, have a magnetic moment and spin. The proton charge is equal to the electron charge, though opposite in sign. Consider a moderately complex nucleus like that of iron. This usually has 30 neutrons and 26 protons. Its atomic weight therefore depends on the total number of neutrons plus protons, but the total charge depends only on the number of protons—called the atomic number. The latter is denoted by $Z$ while the total number of neutrons plus protons is called mass number and denoted by $M$. A species of nucleus with given values of $Z$ and $M$ is called a nuclide. $Z$ is also the number of electrons in the atom, since the atom as a whole is electrically neutral. The atomic number determines the chemical nature of the atom (see below), so that by altering the number of neutrons in a nucleus we do not change the chemical species. It is therefore possible to find—and nowadays to make—nuclei of the same element which nevertheless differ slightly in weight because they have different numbers of neutrons. These are called isotopes. Iron isotopes are known with 26, 27, 28, 29, 30, 31, 32, and 33 neutrons, but all have 26 protons. Thus a set of isotopes consists of the various nuclides that have the same $Z$ but different $M$'s.

## Stable Nuclides.

The protons and neutrons in a nucleus are bound together by strong forces called *nuclear forces*. In many cases, the forces are so strong that no particles ever escape and the nucleus preserves its identity. There are two hundred and seventy-four different combinations of neutrons and protons of this kind, and they are called the *stable nuclides*. The earth is largely composed of such stable nuclides, because any unstable ones have, in the course of time, spontaneously broken up into stable residues.

Nevertheless, there are some unstable nuclei left on earth. They give rise to the phenomenon of radioactivity which was discovered by Becquerel in 1893.

## Unstable Nuclides: Radioactivity.

Becquerel found that certain chemicals containing uranium gave off rays capable of blackening a photographic plate, and shortly afterwards Marie and Pierre Curie discovered more substances, including radium, which produce similar but stronger effects. By now, about fifty chemical elements having radioactive properties are known to exist on earth, some, like radium, being strongly radioactive, others, like potassium, being so weak that the radiations are difficult to detect. These are called the *natural radioactive nuclides*.

The main facts about radioactivity are as follows: it is a *nuclear* phenomenon and (with minor exceptions) proceeds quite independently of whatever the electrons in the atom may be doing. Thus, the radioactivity of an atom is not affected by the chemical combination of the atom with other atoms, nor by ordinary physical influences like temperature and pressure. The radioactivity consists of the emission by the substance of certain kinds of rays. The early workers, Rutherford being the giant among them, distinguished three kinds of rays labelled $\alpha$, $\beta$, and $\gamma$. These are described below. Whatever kind of ray is examined, it is found that the radiation from a given sample decreases gradually with time according to a definite law which states that the intensity of radiation decreases by half every $T$ seconds. The number $T$, called the half-life, is constant for each radioactive material, but varies enormously from substance to substance. For instance, radium decreases its activity by a half every 1,622 years, whereas the half-life of one of the polonium isotopes is about $0·3 \times 10^{-6}$ sec.

## $\alpha$-, $\beta$-, and $\gamma$-rays.

The three most well-known types of radioactive emission are quite distinct from one another.

(i) $\alpha$-rays or $\alpha$-particles consist of two protons and two neutrons bound together. They are ejected from the radioactive nucleus with one of several well-defined speeds. These speeds are high, often of the order $10^9$ cm per sec. Two protons and two neutrons are the constituents of the nucleus of helium, and $\alpha$-particles are thus fast-moving helium nuclei.

(ii) $\beta$-rays are moving electrons. They may emerge from their parent nucleus with any speed from zero to a definite maximum. The maximum speed often approaches that of light, and is different for each isotope. The electron has a positively charged counterpart, the positron (see below), and $\beta$-rays are sometimes positrons. To distinguish the two cases, the symbols $\beta^-$ and $\beta+$ are used. The naturally occurring $\beta$-radiations are almost all $\beta^-$.

(iii) $\gamma$-rays travel with the speed of light because they are in fact electromagnetic waves differing from light only in the extreme shortness of their wavelength. They have no electric charge.

It is unusual, though not unheard of, for the same radioactive substance to emit both $\alpha$- and $\beta$-rays. On the other hand, $\gamma$-rays frequently accompany either $\alpha$- or $\beta$-rays.

$\gamma$-rays pass through matter easily; in fact, they are extra penetrating X-rays. $\alpha$-rays can be stopped by thin sheets of tissue paper. $\alpha$-rays brought to rest pick up a pair of electrons from

the surrounding matter and become neutral helium atoms, and helium gas from this source is consequently found imprisoned in certain radioactive rocks. $\beta$-rays are intermediate in penetrating power between $\alpha$- and $\gamma$-rays.

We must now try to interpret these observations.

## Radioactive Disintegration.

A nucleus is a collection of neutrons and protons interacting with each other and possessing collectively a certain amount of energy. Just as some human organisations lose their coherence if they accept too many members, so nuclei can remain stable only if (i) the total number of particles is not too great, and (ii) neutrons and protons are there in suitable proportions. Radioactive nuclei are the ones for which either or both these conditions do not hold. Sooner or later such nuclei eject a fragment, thus getting rid of some energy they cannot contain. This is called a *radioactive disintegration*, and the fragments are the $\alpha$-, $\beta$-, and $\gamma$-rays. $\alpha$-emission relieves a nucleus of two neutrons and two protons and some energy; $\gamma$-emission simply carries off excess energy without altering the number or kind of particles left behind. $\beta$-emission is more complicated. There are no electrons normally present in a nucleus, but they are suddenly created and explosively emitted if a neutron changes into a proton; positive electrons are similarly generated if a proton changes into a neutron. $\beta$-emission is therefore a mechanism for changing the ratio of protons to neutrons without altering the total number of particles.

Both $\alpha$- and $\beta$-emission change the $Z$ of a nucleus, and the product, or daughter nucleus, is a different chemical element. $\alpha$-emission also changes the $M$. It might happen that the daughter nucleus is unstable, in which case it too will disintegrate. Successive generations are produced until a stable one is reached. Part of such a family tree is shown below. The symbols above the arrows show the kind of rays emitted at each stage, the figures are the mass numbers, $M$, and the names and symbols of chemical elements can be found in Section N.

$$U^{238} \xrightarrow{\alpha} Th^{234} \xrightarrow{\beta} Pa^{234} \xrightarrow{\beta} U^{234} \xrightarrow{\alpha} Th^{230} \xrightarrow{\alpha}$$
$$Ra^{226} \xrightarrow{\alpha} Rn^{222} \xrightarrow{\alpha} Po^{218} \xrightarrow{\alpha} Pb^{214} \xrightarrow{\beta} Bi^{214} \xrightarrow{\beta}$$
$$Po^{214} \xrightarrow{\alpha} Pb^{210} \xrightarrow{\beta} Bi^{210} \xrightarrow{\beta} Po^{210} \xrightarrow{\alpha} Pb^{206}$$
$(Pb^{206}$ is stable lead).

This family exists naturally on earth, because the head of the family, $U^{238}$, has so long a half-life $(4·5 \times 10^9$ years) that there has not yet been time enough since its formation for it to have disappeared.

## Artificial Radioactivity.

Nowadays many new radioactive isotopes can be man-made. All that is required is to alter the $M$ or $Z$ (or both) of a stable isotope to a value which is incompatible with stability. The means for doing this is *bombardment*, *i.e.*, stable nuclei are exposed to the impacts of atomic particles such as streams of protons from an accelerator, or neutrons in an atomic reactor, or simply the $\alpha$-particles from another radioactive substance. The new material is called an *artificially radioactive isotope*. Artificial radioactivity is not different in kind from that of the naturally radioactive substances, but the half-lives are usually on the short side. Indeed, the isotopes in question would exist in nature but for the fact that their short half-lives ensured their disappearance from the earth long ago.

Suppose a piece of copper is exposed to the intense neutron radiation in an atomic reactor at Harwell.

The more abundant of the two stable isotopes of ordinary copper has thirty-four neutrons and twenty-nine protons (*i.e.*, $Z = 29$, $M = 63$). In the reactor many (not all) of these nuclei absorb a neutron, giving an unstable copper nucleus with $Z = 29$, $M = 64$. When removed from the reactor the specimen is observed to be radioactive with a half-life of 12·8 hours. It is somewhat unusual in that it gives out both $\beta^-$ and $\beta^+$ rays. Some nuclei emit electrons, leaving a daughter nucleus with one more positive charge than copper, i.e., a zinc nucleus ($Z = 30$, $M = 64$). One neutron has become a proton, and the resulting zinc nucleus is stable. The others emit positrons, leaving behind a nucleus in which a proton has been turned into a neutron ($Z = 28$, $M = 64$); this is a stable nickel nucleus. The overall process is one example of the artificial transmutation of the chemical elements which is now a commonplace of nuclear physics. It was first discovered by Irene and Frederick Joliot-Curie in 1934.

### Lack of a Complete Theory.

Consider now a collection of, say, one million radioactive nuclei of the same kind. It is impossible to tell exactly when any one of them will disintegrate; it is a matter of chance which ones break up first. All we know is that, after a time equal to the half-life, only a half a million will survive unchanged. In general, the more excess energy a nucleus has, the more likely it is to break up, and therefore the shorter the half-life of that particular nuclear species. In principle, to calculate the half-life theoretically, one would have to have a reliable theory of nuclear forces and energies. This is still being sought after, so it is probably fair to say that while the laws of behaviour of radioactive isotopes are well and accurately known, the *explanation* of this behaviour in terms of the properties of protons and neutrons is by no means complete.

### Nuclear Fission—Chain Reaction.

A discovery important not just for nuclear physics but for the whole of mankind was made by Hahn and Strassman in 1939. This was the discovery of nuclear fission in uranium. One of the natural isotopes of uranium is an unstable one, $U^{235}$, with 143 neutrons and 92 protons. It normally shows its instability by emitting $\alpha$- and $\gamma$-rays. If uranium is bombarded with neutrons, some $U^{235}$ nuclei temporarily gain an extra neutron, which makes them even less stable. This they show by splitting into two roughly equal parts, called fission fragments, together with two or three neutrons. There are two highly important things about this disintegration. One is that the two or three neutrons can promote further disintegrations in other uranium nuclei, and the process can therefore be self-propagating: it is then called a *chain reaction*. The other is that the total mass of the fission products is less than that of the original nucleus. This mass difference does not disappear without trace; it turns into energy according to a formula referred to in a paragraph below (F15(1).

### Application of these New Forces.

The world has found two uses for the energy liberated in nuclear chain reactions: the atomic bomb and nuclear power plants. In the first, conditions are arranged to promote and encourage a tremendous and rapid chain reaction leading to an explosion; in the second, the steady liberation of energy in the form of heat is controlled for use in turbines which can generate electricity or provide propulsion. Both uses represent epoch-making technical achievements, but mankind has yet to show itself capable of bearing sanely the burden of responsibility which nuclear physicists have laid upon it. One thing is certain: the discoveries will not cease. Already, other fissionable elements have been created; new chemical elements have been made and used; nuclear plants ("atomic piles") have stimulated great demands for new materials that will stand the heat and radiation inside the reactor, and this promotes research in other fields of science; irradiation inside an atomic pile gives new and potentially useful properties to old materials; nuclear power drives ships and aircraft. It is difficult to write even briefly about contemporary nuclear physics without feeling keenly the ambiguity of its powerful promises.

Although so much is known about the behaviour of nuclei, the theory of the nucleus leaves much to be desired. What holds the neutrons and protons together? Why are some nuclei more stable than others? It is certain that the forces between neutrons and protons in a nucleus are unlike the electrical attractions between the nucleus as a whole and its surrounding electrons. Nor have they anything to do with gravitation. Indeed, the best description and explanation of nuclear forces is the objective of much of the contemporary research effort in nuclear physics.

### Atoms.

A nucleus surrounded by its full complement of electrons is an electrically neutral system called an atom. Neither the atom as a whole, nor its nucleus, counts as a "fundamental particle" because either can be subdivided into more elementary parts, thus:

$$atom \longrightarrow electrons + nucleus \longrightarrow electrons + neutrons + protons$$

The chemical identity of the atoms of a given element, which was Dalton's key idea, depends entirely on the number and motion of the electrons. For example, the simplest element, hydrogen, has one proton for a nucleus, and one electron. The latter is comparatively easily detached or disturbed by the electric forces exerted by neighbouring atoms, consequently hydrogen is reactive chemically, i.e., it readily lends its electron to build chemical structures with other equally co-operative elements. The second element, helium, has a nucleus of two protons and two neutrons; outside are two electrons in a particularly stable arrangement. Indeed, this pair of electrons is so difficult to disarrange that a special name has been coined to cover such cases—*closed shells*. Helium, with its closed shell, will not react chemically with anything. As the nuclear charge increases, different electron arrangements of greater or lesser stability succeed one another, with every so often a closed shell corresponding to one of the chemically inert gases neon, argon, xenon, krypton. *See* F20 (1).

Such considerations, pursued in sufficient detail, enable atomic physics to account for all the differences and similarities among the chemical elements and, in principle at least, for the other facts of chemistry as well.

### Ions.

It is possible to remove one or more electrons from an atom, leaving it positively charged. The atom is then said to be *ionised* and is called a *positive ion*. Alternatively, some atoms are capable of accepting electrons above their normal complement, thus becoming negative ions. The behaviour of ions is very important in many fields of physics and chemistry, and some of these will be referred to later.

### Molecules.

Electrical attractions of various kinds cause atoms and ions to form compound groups. This is the basis of chemical combination, and the smallest conceivable fragment of compound which still preserves the chemical identity of that compound is called a molecule. Molecules have a wide range of complexity, from simple pairs of atoms to highly intricate spirals and chains composed of thousands of atoms. *See* Part III.

### Excited Atoms.

Like the nuclei described above, atoms can be given excess energy and will then return to their ground state with the emission of radiation. The excess energy usually resides in one of the electrons which is executing unusually violent motion. The electron returns to normal by releasing its excess energy in the form of light whose colour is characteristic of the atom involved.

Herein lies the explanation of innumerable natural and technical phenomena, such as the colours of glowing gases whether they exist in the sun and stars, in aurorae, or in street-lamps and neon signs. Herein also lies the reason for the importance of spectroscopy, which is the study of the characteristic radiation from excited atoms: for spectroscopy is not only a useful tool for the chemical identification of elements (" spectroscopic analysis ") but was one of the main routes along which twentieth-century physicists broke through to a knowledge of the inner nature of the atom.

## Maxwell and Electromagnetic Waves.

Atoms are held together by the electric attraction of the nucleus for the electrons. Finer details of atomic behaviour depend on the magnetic moments of the particles. Any region of space subject to electric and magnetic influences is called an *electromagnetic field*. Before the discovery of the electron, Maxwell had perfected a general theory of the electromagnetic field, giving to physics a celebrated set of equations which describe satisfactorily almost all electric and magnetic phenomena. *Inter alia*, he proved that disturbances in the electric and magnetic conditions at one place could be propagated to another place through empty space, with a definite velocity, just as sound waves are propagated through air. Such electromagnetic disturbances in transit are called *electromagnetic waves*, and their velocity turned out experimentally to be the same as that of light and radio waves—which was a decisive argument to show that both of these phenomena are themselves electromagnetic waves.

## Einstein and Photons.

In the years between about 1900 and 1920 this view was upset by Planck, Einstein, Millikan, and others, who focused attention on phenomena (radiant heat, photoelectricity) in which light behaves like a stream of particles and not at all like waves. A wave and a particle are two quite different things, as anyone will admit after a moment's contemplation of, say, the ripples on a pond and a floating tennis ball. The acute question was: is light like waves or particles? This celebrated dilemma soon multiplied its horns. In 1927 electrons were shown to be quite capable of behaving as waves instead of particles, and this is now known to be true of protons, neutrons, and all other fundamental particles as well.

Theoretical physicists have devised means of having it both ways. To say that light behaves as particles means that the waves of the electromagnetic field cannot have their energy subdivided indefinitely. For waves of a given frequency, there is a certain irreducible quantity of energy that must be involved whenever light interacts with anything. This quantity is the product $h\nu$, where $\nu$ is the frequency and $h$ is a constant named after Planck. Each such unit is called a *quantum of the electromagnetic field* or a *photon* and is counted as one of the fundamental particles. Frequencies and wavelengths vary widely; typical wavelengths are: radio—hundreds or thousands of metres; radar—a few centimetres; visible light—$5 \times 10^{-5}$ cm; X-rays—$10^{-8}$ cm.

## Elementary Particles.

Nature seems to use four different kinds of force to make one particle interact with another. The weakest force is gravity; while this dominates celestial mechanics its effect inside atoms is negligible compared with the other three. The binding forces inside atoms are *electromagnetic*, *e.g.*, the attraction of nuclei for electrons. Considerably stronger still is the nuclear force which holds the nuclei together and this is called the *strong interaction*. The fourth force is called the *weak interaction* and is intermediate in strength between electromagnetic and gravitational forces. It is responsible for a number of phenomena of which the best known is $\beta$-radioactivity.

Particles may respond to some or all of the forces. Protons are involved with all of them but electrons respond to all except the " strong " interaction." When new particles are discovered physicists try to find out their fundamental properties and among these is their response (if any) to each kind of force. Some other basic properties are: electric charge (if any), mass (if any), and the speed with which the particle splits up spontaneously into other types.

So many so-called elementary particles have been discovered (about a hundred) that the whole conception of " elementary-ness " has been in question. Are all the particles equally " elementary "? Are some of them excited states or combinations of others? When a family reaches a hundred it becomes difficult to believe they are *all* grandparents. One current trend is away from setting up a hierarchy in which some particles are elementary and some composite and towards treating them all as mutually dependent for their existence. This, however, is a very difficult problem, not yet solved.

A few particles are stable but most decay into products. The lifetimes of unstable particles are extraordinarily short by everyday standards but, even so, some (of about $10^{-17}$ sec. or upwards) are much longer than others (of about $10^{-22}$ sec.). The Table on page F14 contains the stable particles and a *selection* of the moderately unstable ones with brief comments on their properties.

The Table shows a rudimentary classification into four groups: (i) the photon; (ii) leptons—which are particles, lighter than protons, which do not react to the " strong " type of force; (iii) mesons—which are particles, lighter than protons, which are subject to all the kinds of force; (iv) baryons—which include protons, neutrons, and heavier particles, all of which react to the " strong " force. Many of these particles have been produced for the first time in recent years by bombarding matter with beams of high energy particles. Much of this work is done in the large accelerating machines at Brookhaven, New York, and the European Organisation for Nuclear Research, Geneva.

Forming particles into groups is an important matter. It is comparable with arranging chemical elements into the Periodic Table. The pattern does not of itself explain anything but it strongly suggests where to look for explanations. The classification of particles currently favoured is based on the very sophisticated mathematical ideas known as *group theory*. Group theory is a branch of mathematics which is finding increasing application in physics and it had a resounding success recently which illustrates the value of grouping. It turned out that there was no known particle to occupy a vacant position in one of the family groups required by the theory. This particle, the omega minus, was sought and found with exactly the right properties in February 1964. This is reminiscent of finding the missing elements in the Periodic Table. The discovery of omega minus generated much excitement in the scientific world and many physicists believe that a new and deeper understanding of fundamental physics is just round the corner. The corner may be turned if three much sought after but as yet undiscovered particles called the quarks are found. Some theoreticians believe that the properties of all other particles could be explained by the behaviour of the three really fundamental quarks. The latter are hypothetical but are being taken very seriously by those who are trying to detect them experimentally.

It is now accepted that every fundamental particle is a manifestation of the waves of one or other kind of field. Physicists speak of waves, particles, and fields in the same breath or rather the same equation. Little is to be gained by asking if electrons or photons are " really " particles or waves. All one can say is that they are things whose behaviour is predicted and described by certain equations. Those who must visualise can imagine particles in some phenomena and waves in others: neither conception contains the whole truth. Why should the ultimate invisible constituents of matter be forced into one or other category derived from everyday experience? For convenience, however, we shall continue to call these things " elementary particles."

## SOME MEMBERS OF THE ATOMIC FAMILY

The numbers in brackets after the name denote first the electric charge and second, the mass. The charge on an electron is counted as $-1$ unit and the electron mass as $+1$ unit. Thus $(+1, 207)$ means the particle has a positive charge of 1 unit and a mass 207 times that of the electron.

| | |
|---|---|
| Photon (0, 0) | A quantum of electromagnetic radiation, *e.g.*, light, X-rays, $\gamma$-rays. The concept was introduced by M. Planck in 1900 when he described the emission of light as taking place in "packets" rather than in a steady stream. The energy of a photon is proportional to the frequency of the radiation and inversely proportional to the wavelength. |

*Leptons*

| | |
|---|---|
| Electron ($-1$, 1) | Discovered by J. J. Thomson in 1897. The number of orbital electrons in an atom determines its chemical properties. Actual rest mass = $9 \cdot 1 \times 10^{-28}$ g. Emitted as $\beta$-rays by some radioactive nuclei. A stable particle. |
| Positron ($+1$, 1) | Positive counterpart or, "anti-particle," to the electron. Predicted theoretically by P. A. M. Dirac in 1928 and first discovered in cosmic rays by C. D. Anderson in 1932. Emitted as $\beta$-rays by some radioactive nuclei. When positrons and electrons collide they usually annihilate each other and turn into $\gamma$-rays; consequently, positrons only last about $10^{-10}$ sec. within ordinary matter, but are stable in isolation. |
| Neutrino (0, 0) and Anti-neutrino (0, 0) | These particles travel with the speed of light and are distinguished from one another by the relation of their spin to their direction of motion. A neutrino is emitted with the positron during positive $\beta$-decay; and an anti-neutrino with the electron during negative $\beta$-decay. Their interaction with matter is extremely slight. First postulated by Pauli in 1933 and detected in 1956. $\pi$-meson decay also produces neutrinos and anti-neutrinos but in 1962 it was proved experimentally that these are a different species. Thus there are two kinds of neutrino each with an anti-neutrino. All these particles are distinguished from photons by having different spin. |
| Muon ($\pm 1$, 207) | Similar to, but heavier than, the electron and positron; disintegrates into electron (or positron if positive) + neutrino + anti-neutrino. |

*Mesons*

| | |
|---|---|
| Pion ($\pm 1$, 273) or (0, 264) | The $\pi$-meson. Charged pions decay either into muons and neutrinos or into electrons and neutrinos. Neutral pions decay into $\gamma$-rays, into "positron-electron pairs," or both. Pions are intimately connected with nuclear forces, *i.e.*, with the "strong" interaction. |
| Kaon ($\pm 1$, 967) or (0, 974) | The K-mesons. These decay in many different ways producing other mesons, electrons, and neutrinos. |

*Baryons*

| | |
|---|---|
| Proton ($+1$, 1836·1) | The positively-charged constituent of nuclei; the hydrogen nucleus is one proton. Fast-moving protons occur in cosmic rays. Does not spontaneously disintegrate. |
| Anti-proton ($-1$, 1836·1) | Negative anti-particle of the proton. Its existence was long suspected. Artificially produced and detected for the first time in 1955. Will react with the proton to produce pions or kaons. |
| Neutron (0, 1838·6) | Discovered by J. Chadwick in 1932. The neutral constituent of nuclei. When free it spontaneously disintegrates into a proton, an electron, and an anti-neutrino, after an average lifetime of about 18 minutes. Passes through matter much more easily than charged particles. |
| Anti-neutron (0, 1838·6) | The anti-particle of the neutron from which it is distinguished by properties connected with its magnetic moment and spin. Will react with neutron to produce pions or kaons. |
| Lambda Particle (0, 2183) | Discovered in 1947. Decays into proton plus pion. |
| Sigma Particle (0 or $\pm 1$; about 2330) | Various modes of disintegration, producing neutrons, protons, mesons and lambda particles. |
| Omega Minus ($-1$, 3270) | Predicted by recent theory and discovered at Brookhaven, New York, in 1964. Still under intensive study. |

## QUANTUM THEORY AND RELATIVITY.

### Quantum Theory.

The point of view of the last paragraph is characteristic of quantum theory, which is the currently accepted fundamental theory of matter and motion. One can reasonably ask at what position in space, exactly, is a particle? Or, what, exactly, is the wavelength of a wave? But the first question cannot be reasonably asked of a wave, nor the second of a particle. Since electrons have something in common with both, one question cannot be answered precisely for electrons without ignoring the other; alternatively, both questions can be given an imprecise answer. As the wavelength of electrons is intimately connected with their speed, one has to accept an accurate knowledge of the speed (wavelength) and ignorance of position, or the converse, or *inaccurate* knowledge of both. This is the famous Heisenberg Uncertainty Principle. Quantum theory is a set of mathematical rules for calculating the behaviour of fundamental particles in accordance with the Uncertainty Principle. In spite of its equivocal-sounding name, the principle has led to an enormous increase in the accuracy with which physical phenomena can be described and predicted. Quantum theory includes all that previous theories did and more.

Quantum theory grew up in the same epoch as the Theory of Relativity. Heroic attempts have been made to combine the two, but with only partial success so far. Relativity is concerned with all motion and all physical laws, but its characteristic manifestations occur only when something is moving with nearly the velocity of light. Quantum theory is likewise all-embracing, but its typical phenomena almost always occur when something on the minute atomic scale is in question. Consequently, the vast majority of everyday mechanics needs no more than the classical theory laid down by Newton, which is neither relativistic nor quantum.

### Relativity.

Historically, relativity grew out of attempts to measure the speed with which the earth moved through that hypothetical medium, called the ether, which was supposed at that time to be the bearer of light waves. To take a simple analogy: sound waves travel through still air with a certain definite speed. $v$. If you move through the air with speed $v'$ towards oncoming sound waves, they will pass you at the speed $v + v'$. Michelson and Morley, in their celebrated experiment of 1887, failed to find the corresponding behaviour on the part of light. This is so important an experiment that it has been repeated, and repeatedly discussed, ever since. In October 1958 the latest and most accurate confirmation of the Michelson-Morley result was announced. It seems as if light always travels with the same speed relative to an observer, however fast he moves relative to anything else. Einstein put it this way: two observers moving with any constant velocity relative to each other will always agree that light travels past them at the same speed; this speed is denoted by $c$, and is approximately 186,000 miles per second.

This postulate, logically developed, leads to remarkable conclusions. For instance: if you walk from tail to nose of an aircraft at 4 m.p.h. and the plane is receding from me at 300 m.p.h., then you recede from me at 304 m.p.h. "Common sense," Newton, and Einstein would all agree on this. But if you could walk at $0 \cdot 25c$ and the plane moved at $0 \cdot 5c$, the Newtonian mechanics would give your recession speed as $0 \cdot 75c$, whereas Einsteinian relativity would give about $0 \cdot 71c$. Although at the everyday speed of 300 m.p.h., the disagreement, though present in principle, is absolutely negligible, at speeds near that of light it becomes very pronounced. Many experiments show that the relativity answer is right.

### Equivalence of mass and energy.

Another famous consequence of relativity is the equation $E = mc^2$, connecting energy, $E$, with mass, $m$. $c$ is so great that when mass is converted to energy a small mass gives a large energy. The grim demonstration of this was given to the world at Hiroshima; a more hopeful one at Calder Hall, the world's first nuclear power station. The life-giving energy of the sun is derived from nuclear processes which consume mass and deliver energy according to this equation.

### Mass and rest mass.

"Mass" is far from being a simple notion. The only complication we shall note here is that the mass of a body is not necessarily constant. A stationary body can be observed to have a mass called its *rest mass*. If the body moves, it has energy of motion and therefore, according to Einstein's mass–energy equation, it increases its mass. Mass thus depends on speed, but in such

a way that there is very little change unless the speed approaches that of light. Many experiments on atomic particles demonstrate this. The interesting question now arises: do all fundamental particles have rest mass? or do some have mass derived solely from their energy? The answer appears to be that photons and neutrinos have no rest mass; all other particles have. The Table on F14 gives their rest masses.

### Special theory of relativity.

The mathematical development of Einstein's ideas, leading to the conclusions just referred to, constitutes the Special Theory of Relativity. Stated more generally, the theory raises the question whether two observers in uniform relative motion could ever detect, as a result of their relative speed, any difference in the physical laws governing matter, motion, and light. To this, Special Relativity answers: No. The detailed theory involves special consideration of the results the two observers would obtain when measuring (i) the spatial distance, and (ii) the time interval, between the same two events. It turns out that they would not agree on these two points. They would agree, however, on the value of a certain quantity made up jointly of the spatial distance and the time interval in a somewhat complex combination. The intimate mixture of space and time in this quantity has led to the treatment of the three space dimensions and time on an equivalent footing. Hence the frequent references to time as the "fourth dimension." Minkowski devised an extremely elegant presentation of relativity theory by using an extension of ordinary geometry to four dimensions. A line drawn in his four-dimensional space represents the path of a particle in space and time, *i.e.*, the whole history of the particle. Thus the movement of particles in the ordinary world is turned into the geometry of lines in Minkowski's four-dimensional world of "space-time."

### Relativity and Gravitation.

The apparently innocuous extension of the preceding ideas to include observers in accelerated relative motion opened up new fields of mathematical complexity, but enabled Einstein to bring gravitation into the argument. In speaking of atoms and particles we have not yet mentioned gravity. This is because the electrical and magnetic forces acting between the particles constituting matter are much stronger than the gravitational; gravity need not enter atomic theory at all. But in the discussion of astronomical problems and the movements of large-scale, electrically uncharged bodies, it has been usual, ever since Newton, to say that two bodies of mass $m_1$ and $m_2$, separated by a distance $r$, attract one another with a force proportional to $m_1 m_2 / r^2$. This is Newton's inverse square law of gravitation. With this, Newton explained the movements of planets and comets and the falling to earth of the apple from his tree.

The apple's fall is accelerated, and we observe this by noting its position relative to certain marks fixed with respect to us, and by timing it with some sort of clock. This system of location in space and time may be called our "frame of reference." We therefore assert that, in our frame of reference, the apple falls down with an acceleration which Newton saw no alternative but to attribute to a thing called gravitational attraction. Galileo had shown that *all* bodies fall with the same acceleration at all points, and we can now rephrase this by saying that in our frame of reference there is a constant gravitational attraction or *uniform gravitational field*. (This last statement and Galileo's demonstration only refer strictly to points fairly near the earth's surface; at greater distances the gravitational field decreases and is therefore not uniform.)

Now suppose a collection of falling bodies is observed by an intelligent creature, designated $C$, who inhabits one of them. $C$ has his own frame of reference fixed relative to him. In $C$'s frame neither his own body, nor any of the others, is accelerated, and therefore he has no reason to suppose a gravitational force is acting on them. We have, therefore, the following situation:

(i) in our frame, fixed relative to us, we find all the bodies falling subject to a gravitational pull;

(ii) in C's frame, undergoing accelerated fall relative to us, no gravitational field is apparent.

It looks, therefore, as if one has only to choose the correct frame of reference for the measurements in order to remove the need for any assumptions about the existence of gravitational fields. This is a simple illustration of the connection between gravitation and frames of reference for the measurement of space and time. Einstein's General Theory of Relativity extends this to cover non-uniform gravitational fields and shows that what Newton taught us to call the gravitational field of material bodies is better thought of as a peculiarity of the space and time in the neighbourhood of such bodies. Since space-time, as we mentioned above, can be expressed in geometrical terms, Einstein has transformed the theory of gravitation into an exercise (a difficult one) in the geometry of space-time. Other physicists, in Einstein's tradition, are trying to turn all physics into geometry, but no one knows whether this is really feasible.

All this abstruse work is much more than a demonstration of mathematical power and elegance. Observable phenomena which fall outside the scope of Newton's theory of gravitation are accounted for by relativity. One is the small but definite discrepancy between the actual orbit of the planet Mercury and the predictions of Newton's theory. Another is the bending of stellar light rays as they pass close to the sun, an effect which results in the apparent displacement of the position of the star. A third is the effect of a gravitational field on the wave-length of light emitted by atoms. Similar atoms in different places in a gravitational field emit radiations with slightly different wavelengths. For example, the light from an atom in the intense field of a star should have slightly longer wave-length than the corresponding light from an atom on earth. This effect has always proved very difficult to detect with certainty. However, Einstein's prediction was verified with moderate accuracy in 1960 by a very subtle method which was purely terrestrial in its operation. The atoms being compared were placed at the top and bottom of a water tower and the difference in their emission was detected by means that belong rather to nuclear physics than to astronomy.

### Quantum Theory and Relativity Combined.

The atomic family table refers to "antiparticles." The theory which first introduced such things in 1934 is due to the Cambridge physicist Dirac and was epoch-making. Dirac conceived an equation to describe the motion of electrons subject to the laws of both quantum theory and relativity. His achievement was thus to synthesise these two great ideas. The spin of the electron was originally a supposition that helped to make sense of spectroscopic observations of light emitted from atoms. Dirac's equation made spin a logical consequence of the union of relativity and quantum theory. Perhaps even more important was the brilliant inference that the equation for the electron implied the existence of another particle having the same mass and spin but with a positive instead of a negative electric charge. This object is called the electron's anti-particle and is now well known as a positron.

A positron and electron can be created simultaneously (" pair production ") and can annihilate each other when they collide.

Every particle is now believed to imply an anti-particle, so it is conceivable that the universe could have been (but isn't) an anti-universe, i.e., all the electrons and protons might have been positrons and antiprotons and so on. The laws of physics would still have been applicable, however.

Not all particles are charged electrically but, when they are, their antiparticles have equal charges of the opposite sign. Whenever charged particles interact the total amount of electric charge is the same before and after whatever events occur. This is called the law of conservation of charge.

### Conservation Laws.

Parity. Charge conservation and the conservation of energy (F 17(2)) are only two of a considerable number of conservation laws. Readers who have studied mechanics will also be aware of the conservation of momentum and of angular momentum. A conservation law is the proposition that in the course of physical happenings such and such a quantity is " conserved," i.e., maintains a constant value.

The establishment of conservation laws is playing a great part in our growing understanding of elementary particles although the things that are conserved are somewhat abstruse. One of them is called parity.

Any reader who looks in a mirror knows that the left- and right-hand sides of his face are interchanged in the image. Fortunately mirrors do not also turn the image upside down, but, if they did, the face would then have undergone what is called " a parity transformation." A screwdriver driving a right-handed screw downwards becomes, on parity transformation, a screwdriver driving a left-handed screw upwards. The law of conservation of parity is a way of asserting that any physical process that goes on in the world could equally well go on—obeying the same laws—in a parity transformed world. There is nothing left-handed that does not in principle have a right-handed counterpart.

For many years this belief was strongly held. It came as something of a shock when, in 1957, after theoretical proposals by Lee and Yang in America, Wu and his team proved that parity was not always conserved. To understand Wu's experiment, we must recall that nuclei can have intrinsic spin. Suppose the axis of spin were downwards into the page and the rotation were suitable for driving an ordinary screw into the page. Then Wu showed that beta-rays from such a nucleus are emitted preferentially upwards, i.e., against the direction of travel of the screw. The parity transformed version of this would have the beta-rays preferentially emitted in the same direction as the travel of the screw and, if parity is conserved, this process would happen too. But it does not. If the beta-rays in the experiment had been emitted in equal numbers up and down, then the parity transformed version would have had this feature too, and thus parity would have been conserved.

Of the four types of force referred to on F 13(1), only the weak interaction does not conserve parity. The whole matter is bound up with the anti-neutrino which is emitted simultaneously with the negative beta-ray. It appears that antineutrinos are always " right-handed " which means that if one could look at an antineutrino receding from us it would be seen to be spinning clockwise.

Modern research on elementary particles is greatly concerned to find out which types of process obey which conservation laws. The parity surprise is only one of the stimulating shocks that this type of work is heir to. It is very much in the tradition of Einstein, part of whose monumental contribution to physics was his demonstration of the need to analyse conservation laws.

### Conclusion.

Over a century's development of the atomic ideas has brought a progressive, if jerky, increase in the mathematical precision of the theories. In some fields of particle physics, observations to one part in a million, or even better, can be explained, to that level of accuracy, by the existing theories. At the same time, however, the theories have lost visual definition. An atom as an invisible but none the less solid billiard ball was easy enough; so was a light wave conceived like a sound wave in air. Even after Rutherford, an atom consisting of a miniature solar system merely exchanged the solid billiard ball for a system of revolving billiard balls and was no great obstacle to visualisation. But since quantum theory and the Uncertainty Principle, every unambiguous visualisation of fundamental wave-particles leaves out half the picture, and although the electrons are in the atom, we can no longer represent them in definite orbits. The moral seems to be that visualisation is unnecessary, or at best a partial aid to thought. All the theoretical knowledge is in the equations, and these are very precise. Hence the non-physicists' grumble—that physics is too mathematical these days—has some justification, and hence also the growing distinction in physics between the theoreticians, who are usually mathematically trained, and the experimenters, who can rarely read the papers their theoretical colleagues write, but provide the results for them to write about.

### THE PROPERTIES OF MATTER IN BULK.

One of the most obvious and at the same time most wonderful things about the properties of matter is their great variety. Think of air, diamond, mercury, rubber, snow, gold, pitch, asbestos. . . . Even the differences of state of the same chemical substance are remarkable enough, ice, water, and steam, for example. One of the aims of physics is to reach an understanding of all these different properties by explaining them in terms of the behaviour of the particles discussed in the previous section (F9–17). The widespread success with which this imposing programme has been carried out indicates the maturity of physics. It is difficult to think of any major property of matter in bulk for which there is not some attempted theoretical explanation, though future physicists will no doubt regard some present-day theories as rudimentary or incorrect.

### Physics, Statistics, and Thermodynamics.

Take a number equal to the population of London, multiply it by itself, and multiply the product by another million. The answer is about the number of molecules in 1 cubic centimetre of ordinary air. They are constantly moving about and colliding with one another. Even if the nature of the molecules and their laws of motion were perfectly understood, it would clearly be impracticable to calculate the exact paths described by each particle of so vast an assembly. This difficulty brought into being a whole branch of physics concerned with calculating the overall or average properties of large numbers of particles. Just as statisticians will provide the average height, income, expectation of life, and so on, of the population of London, without knowing everything about every individual, so statistical physicists can work out average properties of molecules or atoms in large groups. This important branch of physics is called *Statistical Mechanics*. It was founded in the nineteenth century by Maxwell, Boltzmann, and Gibbs and is still being actively developed.

Consider now all the molecules in 1 cubic centimetre of air contained in a small box. They are continually bombarding the walls of the box and bouncing off. This hail of impacts (it is actually about $10^{23}$ impacts per square centimetre per second) is the cause of the pressure which the gas exerts against the walls of the box. Now suppose we pump air in until there is twice as much as before, though the box is still the same size and at the same temperature. This means that the density of the gas (*i.e.*, the mass of 1 unit of volume) has doubled. We should now expect twice as many impacts per second on the walls as before, and consequently twice the pressure. We therefore arrive at a conclusion that, if the volume and temperature are constant, the pressure of a gas is proportional to its density. This is one of the simplest statistical arguments that can be checked against observation; in fact, it stands the test very well.

### Heat, temperature, and energy.

The proviso about the temperature remaining the same is an important one for the following reason. In the nineteenth century there was

much discussion about the nature of heat. To Joule we owe the now well-established view that heat is equivalent to mechanical work. In one of his experiments, in the 1840s, the work necessary to rotate paddle wheels against the resistance of water in a tank generated heat that caused a slight rise in the temperature of the water. Joule found out exactly how much work was equivalent to a given quantity of heat. However, one can do other things with work besides generate heat; in particular, work creates motion, as when one pushes a car. Bodies in motion possess a special form of energy, called kinetic energy, which is equal to the work done in accelerating them from a state of rest. We have, then, three closely connected ideas: work, heat, and kinetic energy. Now according to the views of the nineteenth century, which are still accepted, any heat given to a gas simply increases the kinetic energy of its molecules; the hotter the gas, the faster its molecules are moving. If, therefore, the gas in our box is allowed to get hotter, there is an increase in molecular speed, and the impacts on the walls become correspondingly more violent. But this means the pressure increases, so we have another law: if the density remains the same, the pressure increases if the temperature does.

### Laws of Thermodynamics.

Such considerations as these have been pursued with great elaboration and subtlety. The notions of heat, temperature, energy, and work—familiar but vague in everyday life—have been given precise definitions, and the relations between them have been enshrined in the Laws of Thermodynamics. Enshrined is perhaps a suitable word, because these laws are so soundly and widely based on experimental results that they have greater prestige than any others in physics. If any proposed physical law comes in conflict with thermodynamics, then so much the worse for that law—it has to be revised. It is sometimes asserted that no one is properly educated who does not understand the Second Law of thermodynamics. We cannot, therefore, leave this section without at least stating the two best known thermodynamic laws:

First Law: *If any physical system is given a quantity of heat, and if the system performs some work, then the energy of the system increases by an amount equal to the excess of heat given over work done.* This law asserts that heat, energy, and work are convertible one into the other, and that all such transactions balance exactly. This is one form of a principle accepted as fundamental in all science, viz., the Principle of the Conservation of Energy, according to which energy can never be created or destroyed, but only changed from one form to another.

Second Law: *It is impossible to make an engine which will continuously take heat from a heat source and, by itself, turn it all into an equivalent amount of mechanical work.* In fact, all engines which produce work from heat—steam engines for example—always use only a fraction of the heat they take in and give up the rest to some relatively cool part of the machine. The Second Law makes this obligatory on all work-from-heat devices. This statement of the Second Law has an engineering ring about it and, indeed, it arose from the work of the nineteenth-century French engineer Carnot. Nevertheless, it can be re-phrased in very abstract terms, and has been applied with unbroken success to all fields of science involving the transfer of heat and allied matters. It sets a definite limit to the kinds of physical process that can be conceived to take place. Nothing has been known to contravene it.

### The States of Matter.

The molecular motion in gases has been referred to in the previous section. Tacitly it was assumed that each molecule acted independently of all others, except that collisions occurred between them. In reality, molecules exert attractive forces on one another and, if a gas is cooled so that molecular movements become relatively sluggish, a time comes when the attractive forces succeed in drawing the molecules close together to form a liquid. This process is called condensation.

The molecules in a liquid are packed tightly together and they impede each others' movements. On the other hand, movement still persists, and the molecules struggle about like people in a milling crowd. Besides wandering about, the molecules vibrate. These motions represent the energy contained in the liquid.

The fact that the molecules, though irregularly packed, can still slip past one another and move from place to place, explains the essential property of liquids that distinguishes them from solids—ability to flow. As a matter of fact, although the rather vague assertion that in a liquid molecules are irregularly packed would be generally accepted, there is no agreed opinion on what the irregularity is actually like. Indeed, not only the precise structure of liquids, but the theory of liquids in general, is fraught with such considerable mathematical difficulties that the liquid state is much less well understood than the solid or gaseous.

Most solids are crystals. The popular idea of a crystal is of something which has a more or less regular geometrical form with faces that glint in the light—like snowflakes or gems. However, crystallinity really depends on a regular inner pattern of the atoms, and may or may not show itself on the visible surface. A lump of lead, for example, is crystalline, though it may not look it.

The actual arrangement of the atoms in a crystal can be extremely complex. Some are quite simple, however. The largest model of a crystal structure must surely be the 400-ft. "Atomium" building in the 1958 Brussels Exhibition. This consisted of eight balls, representing atoms, situated at the corners of a cube, and one more ball exactly in the middle. Imagine this repeated in all directions so that every ball is the centre of a cube whose corners are the eight neighbouring balls. This is known to crystallographers and physicists as the "body-centred cubic structure"; it is the actual arrangement of atoms in iron, sodium, chromium, and some other metals. If every ball, instead of being the centre of a cube, were the centre of a regular tetrahedron (a solid figure with four equal triangular faces), and had its four neighbours at the corners of the tetrahedron, then we should have the "diamond structure." This is how the carbon atoms are arranged in diamonds.

In crystals the atoms are locked into a regular ordered structure by attractive forces which give the solid its rigidity and prevent it from flowing. The atoms are so close together that any attempt to press them closer involves crushing or distorting the atoms—a process they resist strongly. This explains why solids (and liquids too) are so difficult to compress. Gases can easily be compressed because there is so much space between the molecules.

The distinction between solid and liquid is not so sharp as is commonly supposed. A lump of dough will not bounce, but is plastic; a steel ball-bearing is very elastic and bounces excellently, but one cannot mould it in the fingers. Neither dough nor steel qualifies for description as a liquid. There are, however, substances which can be moulded like plasticine into a ball that will then bounce very well on the floor like an elastic solid, and finally, if left on a flat table, will spread into a pool and drip off the edge like a liquid. There is no point in trying to force such things into rigid categories. One may say instead that for short, sharp impacts the material behaves like an elastic solid, but under long-sustained forces it flows like a liquid. The properties of these, and many other anomalous materials, are increasingly engaging the attention of those who study the science of flow—*rheology*. It is interesting to see how many familiar and important materials exhibit peculiar rheological behaviour—paint, dough, ball-pen ink, cheese, unset cement, and solutions of nylon and other plastics are only a few examples.

### Inside a Crystalline Solid.

We now return to our wallpaper analogy of crystal structure and give some free play to our visual imagination.

Suppose we have walls papered with a regular pattern of, say, roses, fuchsias, and green leaves. These represent the different kinds of atoms in the solid. Careful observation shows that the whole pattern is shimmering. The flowers and leaves are not stationary, but are undergoing slight random oscillations about their proper positions. In a crystal these movements are called thermal vibrations, and are never absent. The hotter the crystal, the more the vibration, and at a high enough temperature the vibrations become so great that the atoms get right out of position and the pattern disappears altogether, *i.e.*, the crystal melts. Thermal vibrations are essential to the theory of solids, and are responsible for numerous physical properties.

Next we note something extraordinary about some of the papered walls. On these the paper has been hung in irregular patches fitted together like a not very well-made jig-saw puzzle. Lines of roses which should be vertical are horizontal in some patches, oblique in others. This represents the situation in most ordinary solids, for they consist of many small pieces of crystal irregularly packed together. Such material is called *polycrystalline*, and the small pieces are *crystal grains*. Crystal grains may be almost any size, sometimes visible to the naked eye, as often on galvanised iron.

However, on one wall we see excellent regularity and no obvious patches at all. The physicist would call this a *single crystal*, and several techniques exist for preparing them. Natural single crystals can be found, and there are some beautiful large single crystals of rock salt. But on examining the single crystal wall closely, we find a number of places where the paperhanger has failed to make adjacent pieces register perfectly—there is a slight disjointedness. This occurs in real single crystals, and the line along which the structure fails to register is called a *dislocation*. These are much studied by physicists because of their bearing on the mechanical properties of solids, on the yielding of metals under strong stress, for instance.

This by no means exhausts the possibilities of the wallpaper analogy; several other phenomena can be found. For example, in a place where there should be a fuchsia there is actually a daffodil—something completely foreign to the pattern. Or perhaps a small wrongly shaped leaf is jammed between the proper leaves in a place that should really be blank. These represent chemical impurity atoms. The first is called *substitutional*, because it occupies the position of an atom that should be there, the second is called *interstitial*, because it does not. Substitutional impurities of indium metal, deliberately added to the semi-conductor germanium, make possible the manufacture of transistors (*see* Section L). Some steels derive their valuable properties from interstitial carbon atoms within the iron pattern.

What physicists call a vacancy would occur if a flower or leaf were simply missing. Remembering that all the atoms are vibrating, we should not be surprised if occasionally an atom jumps into a neighbouring vacancy if there happens to be one, *i.e.*, the atom and the vacancy change places. Later this may occur again. In the course of time, a rose which was near the ceiling may make its way to the floor by jumping into vacant rose positions when they occur near enough. This process, which the physicist calls *diffusion*, is also analogous to the game in which numbers or letters can be moved about in a flat box because there is one vacant space to permit adjustment. The more vacancies there are in a crystal, the faster diffusion occurs. It is, in fact, very slow in solids, but is nevertheless evidence that apparently quiescent materials are really internally active.

### Metals, Electricity, and Heat.

There is ample evidence that inside metals there are large numbers of free electrons. To illuminate this statement let us take sodium metal as an example. One single sodium atom has a nucleus with eleven protons; there are therefore eleven electrons in the atom. The outermost one is easily detached, leaving a positively charged sodium ion behind. We may think of these ions arranged in the three-dimensional pattern characteristic of sodium crystals. It is the same as the iron structure previously described. The detached electrons, one per atom, occupy the spaces in between. The usual metaphor is that the structure of ions is permeated by a " gas " of electrons. Like all visualisations of fundamental particles, this must be taken as a rough approximation. The important point is that the electrons in the gas are not bound to individual atoms but may wander freely about the crystal, hindered only by the collisions they make with the vibrating ions.

This is the picture as it appeared to physicists of the first decade of this century, and we can explain many properties of metals with it. Naturally the theory has developed greatly since then, thanks to the great work of Lorentz, Sommerfeld, and Bloch; it now relies heavily on quantum theory, but it is surprising how little violence is done to modern ideas by the simple picture we are using.

The free electrons move randomly in all directions at thousands of miles per hour. If the metal is connected across a battery it experiences an electric field. Electrons are negatively charged particles, and are therefore attracted to the electrically positive end of the metal. They can move through the metal because they are free; this flow is not possible to those electrons which remain bound to the ions. The function of the battery is to keep the flow going and, for as long as it is going, it is the electric current.

The flow of electrons is not unimpeded. They constantly collide with the ions and are deflected from the path of flow. This hindrance is what the electrician calls *electrical resistance*. The electric force, due to the battery or a dynamo, accelerates the electrons, thus giving them extra energy; but they lose this to the ions at collisions because the ions recoil and vibrate more than before. The net effect of innumerable collisions is to increase the thermal vibrations of the ions, *i.e.*, to make the metal hotter. This is the explanation of the fact well known to every user of electric irons; that electric current heats the conductor. If a strong current is passed through a wire, the heating is so great the wire glows, as in electric-light bulbs, or melts and breaks, as in blown fuses.

If one end of a metal rod is heated we soon feel the heat at the other end; metals are excellent thermal conductors. This is because the mobile free electrons carry the heat energy down the rod, passing it on to the ions by colliding with them. Substances without free electrons cannot do this, nor can they conduct electricity well; so we have, in the free electrons, an explanation of the fact that the good electrical conductors are the good heat conductors. For technical purposes, it would be useful to have electrical insulators that would conduct heat well, and *vice versa*; but this is almost a contradiction in terms, and one can only compromise.

## Non-conductors and Semi-conductors.

There are some elements, and numerous compounds, in which all the electrons are so tightly bound to their parent atoms that free electron flow is impossible. These materials are electrical and thermal insulators.

Let us return to our sodium atom. It readily loses its outer electron, forming a positive ion. The ion is very stable; indeed, its electron arrangement resembles the "closed shell" belonging to the inert gas neon. The chlorine atom, on the other hand, would have a very stable structure, resembling the inert gas argon, if only it could be given one extra electron to complete the closed shell. If the outer sodium electron were given to a chlorine atom we should have two stable ions, one positive and one negative. These would then attract each other and form a compound. This is just how common salt, sodium chloride, is formed, and its crystals consist of a regular network of alternate sodium and chlorine ions. As all the electrons are bound to ions, it is not surprising that salt will not conduct electricity or heat to any appreciable extent. Not all insulating compounds are built on this pattern, but all have structures which bind the electrons tightly.

We have seen (F18) that Nature does not permit a hard-and-fast distinction between solids and liquids; nor does she between conductors and insulators. Over a hundred years ago, Faraday knew of substances which would conduct electricity, but rather badly. A common one is the graphite in pencils. Others are the elements selenium, germanium, and silicon, and a considerable number of compounds. Such substances are called semi-conductors.

Semi-conductors conduct badly because they have so few free electrons, many thousands of times fewer than metals. In very cold germanium—say, 200 degrees below freezing—all the electrons are tightly bound to atoms and the substance is an insulator. It differs from normal insulators in that, on warming it, the gradually increasing thermal vibration of the crystal detaches some of the electrons, for they are only moderately tightly bound. The warmer the crystal becomes, the more of its electrons become detached and the better it conducts electricity. By about the temperature of boiling water, there are so many freed electrons that conduction is moderately good, though less good than in metals. This is basic semi-conductor behaviour. Because transistors can be made of germanium, and because they are of such great technical importance, more knowledge has accumulated about germanium than about any other material. *See also* Transistor, Section L.

## Magnetism.

The most important thing about magnetism is that it is inseparably connected with electricity. Oersted showed this in July 1820, when he deflected a magnetic compass needle by passing an electric current through a wire near it. Since then, many experiments have shown that wherever a current flows there will certainly be a magnetic field in the surrounding space. The laws of this are very well known now—they are the Maxwell equations previously referred to (F13). However, most people first meet magnetism when, as children, they pick up pins with a magnet. Where is the electricity here? and what is a magnet?

The explanation of magnetism exemplifies beautifully the technique of explaining the bulk properties of matter in terms of fundamental particles. In the atoms the electrons are moving, and a moving electric charge constitutes an electric current. Therefore each moving electron is a tiny source of magnetism. It does not immediately follow that every atom is a source of magnetism because it might—and often does—happen that the magnetic effect of different electrons in the atom cancel out. In helium atoms, for example, the two electrons have equal but opposed magnetic effects. Nevertheless, some atoms and ions have a net effect called their *magnetic moment*. This simply means they behave like tiny magnets. Crystals containing such atoms will be magnetic, though the magnetism is much weaker than in ordinary magnets because the different atoms largely annul one another's effects. In a very limited number of crystals, however, the magnetic ions act on one another in a special way which forces all the atomic magnets to point in the same direction. The total effect of many co-operating atoms is very strong and the crystal becomes what we normally call a magnet. Iron acts like this, so do cobalt and nickel, the rarer elements gadolinium and dysprosium, and a fair number of alloys. On the whole, this behaviour, which is called *ferromagnetism*, is very rare. The reason for the co-operation of all the atomic magnets is not explained to everyone's satisfaction yet, though the key idea was given by Heisenberg in 1928.

In the section dealing with the electron it was pointed out that every electron has an *intrinsic* magnetic moment. This is in addition to any effect simply due to the electron's motion round a nucleus. The net effects of ions are therefore partly due to the intrinsic magnetism of electrons. In the ferromagnetic metals the latter is by far the most important contribution. Thus we pick up pins, and benefit from magnets in other ways, because innumerable fundamental particles act in co-operation for reasons that are still somewhat obscure. It is interesting to ask whether the electrons responsible for magnetism are the same free electrons that allow the metals to conduct electricity. It is thought not.

We are accustomed to think of magnets as metallic. Actually the magnet originally discovered by the Chinese was the mineral lodestone, which is a non-metallic oxide of iron. Nowadays a number of non-metallic magnets are made. They are called *ferrites*, and some are insulators and some are semi-conductors. The combination of magnetism and insulation is technically very valuable in radio, radar, and other applications. The explanation of ferrite behaviour is related to that of metallic ferromagnetism, but is not the same.

Conclusion.

The aim of the second part of this account of physics is to show how our conception of fundamental particles allows us to build theories of the properties of matter. This very aim shows that the two " major divisions " of physics referred to at the beginning (F9) are divided only in the way that labour is divided by co-operating workers to lighten the task. For the task of physics is a very great one—no less than to explain the behaviour of matter; and since the universe, living and inanimate, is made of matter, physics must necessarily underlie all the other sciences.

# III. THE WORLD OF THE CHEMISTS

## WHAT CHEMISTRY IS ABOUT.

The science of chemistry is concerned with the properties of atoms, the laws governing their combination to form molecules, and, more generally, with the behaviour of materials composed of large numbers of molecules. Thus chemistry borders on or, rather, interpenetrates physics—a fact illustrated by the existence of professional journals devoted to " chemical physics " and " physical chemistry." Physics is more concerned with the fundamental nature of matter and radiation; chemistry concentrates on the ways in which atoms combine, or can be made to combine, with each other to form innumerable compounds. Chemistry also merges with the life sciences where it deals, as in biochemistry, with the properties of the complex molecular building blocks of living organisms, e.g., proteins, carbohydrates, nucleic acids. Because of its comprehensiveness, the science of chemistry has been subdivided into what were at one time convenient sub-sciences, e.g., organic chemistry, electrochemistry, but here too the borderlines are becoming progressively blurred. Our task here will be to outline some of the ideas in use by present-day chemists.

## ELEMENTS AND COMPOUNDS.

### Electron Shells and Stability.

The reader will find in Part II a brief description of the atom and definitions of atomic number, atomic weight, isotope, and other terms. The simplest atom is hydrogen (H) with atomic number 1. Some common elements with their chemical symbols and atomic numbers are:—carbon (C) 6; oxygen (O) 8; sodium (Na) 11; chlorine (Cl) 17; calcium (Ca) 20; silver (Ag) 47; and uranium (U) 92. Let us now consider atoms in more detail.

The electrons in atoms move in well-defined *orbits* and the orbits fall into well-defined groups called *shells*. If all the orbits in a shell have electrons actually present in them the shell is *filled* or *closed* and this confers on the shell an unusual stability or inertness. Conversely, unfilled shells lead to activity and the electrons in the incompletely filled shells largely determine the chemical and physical properties of the element and are responsible for the combination of atoms to form molecules. The inner shell, i.e., the one nearest the nucleus, can accommodate only two electrons (the element helium has just that number) and the next two shells can hold eight each. Large atoms, e.g., lead, radium, have many filled shells and, subject to special exceptions, the general rule is that the inner shells are the filled ones and the outer shell may be incomplete. Elements which have equal numbers of electrons in their outer shell resemble each other. Thus the elements with complete electronic shells are chemically unreactive gases, e.g., argon and neon (minor constituents of the atmosphere). Elements with just one electron in the outer shell are highly reactive metals, e.g., sodium and potassium, whereas those with just one electron too few are also reactive but are not metals, e.g., chlorine, bromine, iodine.

### Molecules, Ions, and Bonds.

The general tendency of matter is for those changes that are possible to go on happening until a lasting arrangement or *stable state* is reached. Atoms with closed shells are stable but atoms with unfilled shells can achieve stability in several ways, of which two are as follows:

#### (i) Electron sharing.

When atoms share electrons, the resulting structure, composed of several atoms, is known as a molecule. The simplest case is the molecule of hydrogen, composed of two atoms each contributing one electron. Thus each atom will have a share of two electrons which is the number required to fill completely the inner shell. The shared electrons constitute a *chemical bond* and confer stability on the resulting hydrogen molecule.

A more complex molecule is carbon tetrachloride, $CCl_4$. Here the carbon atom with four electrons in its outer shell is bonded to four chlorine atoms each of which needs one electron to complete a set of eight. Thus by sharing the electrons each of the five atoms can form a complete shell of eight electrons. The properties of the resulting molecular species do not usually bear any resemblance to the constituent atoms. Whereas molecular chlorine is a gas and carbon is a solid, carbon tetrachloride is a liquid which finds application as a dry cleaning fluid.

#### (ii) Electron transfer.

Another method of completing electron shells is by transfer of one or more electrons from an atom with one or two electrons in its outer shell to one with that number too few. Thus sodium, with one electron in its outer shell, will combine with chlorine, deficient in one electron. This results in two electronically stable species (ions), both of which carry electric charges. Thus the sodium will now have a net positive charge of 1 unit (11 protons, 10 electrons), whereas the chlorine has an excess negative charge (17 protons, 18 electrons). Because of these electric charges, solutions of ionic substances conduct electricity and this property is utilised in industrial processes such as electroplating and in the extraction of metals from their ores.

Thus the electrons which participate in the formation of chemical bonds are those in partly-filled shells (valence electrons), and the simplest and most stable type of bonds are those in which two electrons are shared (a covalent bond) and those in which there is a net transfer of electrons (an ionic bond). Sometimes, in order to attain a complete electronic shell, a chemical bond will require the sharing of four or even six electrons. The resulting molecules are highly reactive and will readily, and sometimes violently, combine with other molecules or atoms to achieve the greater stability associated with the two-electron covalent bond.

Molecules must not be envisaged as rigid assemblies of atoms with electrons uniformly distributed around the various nuclei. The properties of molecules are best acccounted for by imagining the atomic nuclei to be vibrating about mean positions the bonds acting like spiral springs, holding the nuclei together. The electrons form a mobile cloud of negative charge which sorrounds the nuclei. The valence electrons, constituting the bond between pairs of atoms, also have no fixed location but fluctuate about mean positions, more or less along the line joining the atoms. Although the electrons are shared, their mean position is not usually halfway between the two

and 46 g of alcohol, both quantities will contain the same number of molecules. Similarly, 1 litre of water with 342 g of sugar dissolved in it, and 1 litre with 58·5 g of salt, will again contain the same number of dissolved molecules because the molecular weights of sugar ($C_{12}H_{22}O_{11}$) and salt (NaCl) are 342 and 58·5 respectively. In each case the number of grams taken is numerically equal to the molecular weight and this amount is called 1 *mole* of a substance or the *gram molecular weight*.

Fig. 1. The arrangement in space of molecules $CCl_4$, $NH_3$, and $H_2O$.

atoms but depends on the relative atomic sizes and charges. In the carbon-chlorine bond of carbon tetrachloride the valence electrons are subjected to electrical attractions due to 17 positive charges on the chlorine nucleus and 6 positive charges on the carbon nucleus. Although the forces due to the chlorine nucleus are partially compensated by the intervening negative charges of the complete electronic shells, they are stronger than the forces from the carbon nucleus, and the valence electrons are therefore pulled towards the chlorine atom which thus attains a net negative charge, leaving the carbon with a corresponding positive charge. The magnitude of this charge is less than that of an ion, and the carbon–chlorine bond should be symbolised $\overset{+}{C} - \overset{-}{Cl}$ to emphasise that separate positive and negative charges of equal magnitude are embodied in the structure, and are attracting each other as well as causing an electric field outside the molecule.

A pair of equal and opposite charges like this is called a *dipole* and is the electrical analogue of the ordinary magnet which has north and south *poles* instead of charges. Chemical bonds made with dipoles are called *polar bonds*. Most molecules, both simple and complex, are bound with polar bonds, but in the case of $CCl_4$ the four bonds are symmetrically arranged in space so that the electric effects of the dipoles cancel each other outside the molecule which therefore does not, as a whole, act like a dipole. On the other hand, the bond dipoles in a molecule may not cancel in this way (Fig. 1) in which case the whole molecule will possess the properties of a dipole *e.g.*, when subjected to an electric field it will rotate to align itself with the field just as a compass needle will line up with a magnetic field.

### Atomic and Molecular Weights.

The masses of the electron and proton were determined early in the 20th century by ingenious experiments. The electronic mass is extremely small, about $9 \times 10^{-28}$g and the mass of a hydrogen atom is $1·7 \times 10^{-24}$g, which indicates that the proton is 1,837 times heavier than the electron and that the mass of the atom is almost completely confined to the nucleus.

The molecular weight of a compound is the sum of the atomic weights (F10) of all the constituent atoms, *e.g.*, water ($H_2O$) and ethyl alcohol ($C_2H_5OH$) have molecular weights 18 and 46 respectively. This means that the alcohol molecule weighs more than the water molecule in the ratio 46 to 18. If therefore we take 18 g of water

The word mole may also be used for atoms or ions and means, in general, that amount of molecules (or atoms or ions, as the case may be) such that the total number of them is equal to the number of atoms in 12 g of carbon (F10). This number, called Avogadro's number, is approximately $6 \times 10^{23}$. Thus one mole of any substance contains $6 \times 10^{23}$ molecules of that substance and this fact makes the mole a very useful unit both in theory and practice.

### Forces between Molecules.

Something has already been said (F17, 18) about the differences between solids, liquids, and gases and we may now put the question: what forces are responsible for the organisation of molecules in liquids or solids and their disorganisation in the gaseous state? Questions of this kind are of profound interest to chemists, physicists, and biologists.

unpolarized

polarized

Fig. 2. Mutual polarisation of molecules by distortion of their electron clouds.

The forces which act between molecules depend mainly on the fact that the electrons orbiting a molecule form a mobile cloud of negative charge. If a polar molecule is brought up to another molecule, then the latter will become polarised, *i.e.*, its electronic cloud will be displaced with respect to the nucleus. This is shown in Fig. 2 and it is apparent that the formerly non-polar molecule has acquired a temporary polar character. In this state it will be able to polarise other nearby molecules, and the ease with which molecules are polarised depends on how strongly the electrons are held in position by the nuclear charge, and this in turn depends on the mean distance between the nucleus and the electronic cloud. Thus, the larger the molecule, the more easily the electron cloud can be distorted by a nearby dipole and hence the stronger are the intermolecular forces. These forces are attractions or *binding forces*. They can be disrupted by violent vibratory or other motions whose source is heat, as when a solid is first melted and then boiled and its molecules fly off in all directions to form a gas. Since strong attractions are due to ease of polarisation, the latter must influence the melting and boiling points of substances.

As a general rule substances composed of small molecules have low boiling points and are gaseous at room temperature and atmospheric pressure, because when they approach each other during a collision, the forces they exert upon one another are not strong enough to produce cohesion and condensation. Examples of this type of behaviour are hydrogen and helium which boil at −253°C and −269°C respectively. Larger molecules are likely to be liquid at ordinary temperature, and if the forces between them are even stronger, they may be solid. Thus carbon tetrachloride, which contains five atoms, boils at 77°C, whereas glucose, with 24 atoms ($C_6H_{12}O_6$) is a solid, melting at 146°C. Chemical compounds which are ionic in character are usually crystalline solids with high melting points (*e.g.*, common salt, quicklime) because ions, possessing permanent charges, exert stronger forces on one another than do molecules.

## Metals and Salts.

It has already been explained that chemical elements are conveniently classified according to the number of electrons in the outer shell, because it is mainly those electrons which participate in chemical reactions and make bonds. Thus elements with 1, 2, or at most 3 electrons in the outer shell (*e.g.*, sodium, calcium, aluminium respectively) will undergo reactions which enable them to lose those electrons, *i.e.*, they will attempt to form ionic compounds. These elements are metallic, and when solid or liquid, conduct heat and electricity. On the other hand, elements which need 1 or 2 electrons to form a complete shell (*e.g.*, chlorine, oxygen respectively) can also form ionic compounds by reacting with a metal, though these elements are themselves classed as non-metals and can be gases, liquids, or solids at room temperature. When a metal atom combines with one or more atoms of non-metal, the resulting ionic compound is termed a salt. Common salts of the metal sodium are the chloride, carbonate, and sulphate. Other examples of industrially important salts are silver bromide (used in photographic films), calcium sulphate (plaster of paris), and magnesium sulphate (epsom salts.)

Metals do not normally occur in the pure state in nature but are found as compounds (ores), sometimes of a complex structure. The science of metallurgy is concerned with the extraction of metals from their ores, and with their properties and uses. Since many metals possess useful mechanical and electrical properties, they find use as materials of construction, and hence the knowledge of their properties and behaviour under different conditions is of great importance. One need only remember the imperfectly understood phenomenon of metal fatigue which led to the crashes of the early Comet aircraft to appreciate how vital is the contribution of metallurgy to the process of engineering.

Although metals can be mixed with other metals to form alloys, the large majority of metallic compounds are the salts in which the metal is present as positive ion (*cation*), and the negative ion (*anion*) is composed of one or several non-metallic elements. Common anions are the chloride, bromide, iodide, nitrate, sulphate, phosphate, and carbonate. Metals with simple electron structures can form only one type of ion. Thus sodium, with one outer shell electron forms $Na^+$ and 1 electron; calcium with two outershell electrons forms $Ca^{++}$ and 2 electrons. There are, however, a number of metals with more complex electronic structures, involving partially filled inner electronic shells and these can exist in a variety of ionic forms. They include many metals which find application as structural materials, *e.g.*, iron, copper, gold, platinum, nickel, chromium. For instance, iron can exist as $Fe^{++}$ or $Fe^{+++}$ and the process of removing a further electron from $Fe^{++}$ is termed *oxidation*, and any chemical reagent which is capable of bringing about such a process is an *oxidising agent*. Conversely the addition of an electron is called *reduction* and the reagent which can give up an electron is a *reducing agent*. Thus the conversion of $Fe^{++}$ to $Fe^{+++}$ is achieved by an oxidising agent which is itself reduced in the process. Processes involving the transfer of one or several electrons are called Redox (reduction-oxidation) reactions and are of great importance in many branches of chemical technology and biochemical processes.

The non-metals which feature in the anions of salts include the well-known and industrially important elements, sulphur, phosphorus, iodine, bromine, and the common gases oxygen, nitrogen, and chlorine. Table 1 (F23) provides a summary of the classification of a few of the more common elements according to the number of electrons in their outer shell. Although some of these elements, *e.g.*, aluminium, undoubtedly possess metallic properties and others, *e.g.*, nitrogen, are non-metals, the dividing lines are not always so clearly defined and most of the compounds formed by elements near the centre of Table 1 are of the covalent type.

## ACIDS AND BASES.

### pH Values.

Hydrogen occupies a unique position in Table 1. According to its electronic structure it can be classified with sodium and potassium, as having one electron in its outer shell. It therefore readily forms cations, $H^+$, but it can hardly be called a metal. Having lost its electron, what remains is a proton (F10), a single positive charge. Thus we can compare sodium chloride, $Na^+$ $Cl^-$, with $H^+$ $Cl^-$, but whereas sodium chloride exists in the ionic form in the solid and liquid states and in solution, HCl is a covalent gas in the pure state, but readily ionises in solution, because the $H^+$ does not exist on its own, but attaches itself to a solvent molecule. Thus when HCl is dissolved in water, it ionises and the $H^+$ combines with the water: $HCl + H_2O \rightarrow (H^+ H_2O) + Cl^-$. This is a typical example of what is known as an *acid-base reaction*, an acid being defined as a substance which in solution can produce one or several protons (hydrogen ions), and the base as being a substance which can accept protons from an acid. In the above reaction HCl is the acid and $H_2O$ the base, and the reaction consists of the transfer of the proton from acid to base. Other common acids include sulphuric acid ($2H^+ + SO_4^{--}$) and nitric acid ($H^+ + NO_3^-$). When ammonia ($NH_3$), a covalent gas, is dissolved in water, an acid base reaction also occurs: $NH_3 + HOH \rightarrow (NH_3.H^+) + OH^-$. Here water acts as acid, since it donates a proton to the ammonia, forming $NH_4^+$, the ammonium ion. When a proton is removed from water, the remainder, a negatively charged ion, is called the hydroxyl ion, $OH^-$. It has now been established that water can act either as an acid or a base, and in pure water two molecules of water can react: $H_2O + H_2O = (H^+ H_2O) + OH^-$, so that one molecule behaves as an acid and the other as a base. This phenomenon is called self-ionisation and also occurs in other solvents.

The extent to which water ionises is very small, thus 1 litre of "pure" water contains $10^{-7}$ moles each of $H^+$ and $OH^-$ ions. However, when a stronger acid, *i.e.*, one that can produce more hydrogen ions than water, is added, the concentration of hydrogen ions increases and that of $OH^-$ ions decreases correspondingly, so that the product of the amounts of $H^+$ and $OH^-$ ions will always be constant and equal to $10^{-14}$ (see law of chemical equilibrium). It is important to be able to compare the strengths of acid solutions and this is done by reference to the concentration of hydrogen ions. The numerical measure is obtained by taking minus the logarithm of the hydrogen ion concentration and this number is called the $pH$ *value* of the solution. Thus in pure water, the hydrogen ion concentration is $10^{-7}$ moles per litre and the $pH$ value is therefore 7.

Vinegar, which is a dilute solution of acetic acid in water, has a hydrogen ion concentration of about $10^{-4}$ moles per litre; its $pH$ is 4. Thus, solutions with a $pH$ value below 7 are acidic (they contain an excess of hydrogen ions) and those with a $pH$ value greater than 7 are basic (they contain an excess of $OH^-$ ions). Many chemical and most biological reactions are extremely sensitive to small changes in the $pH$ and steps must frequently be taken to adjust the $pH$ to an optimum value for a given reaction. This is achieved by means of substances known as buffers, which have the capacity of mopping up or producing hydrogen ions and to maintain a constant $pH$. An example of this buffering action is the prevention of stomach acidity by the use of bicarbonates.

## THE HYDROGEN BOND AND WATER.

Where hydrogen is covalently bonded to a small, fairly strongly electronegative atom, *i.e.*, one which requires 1, 2, or 3 electrons to fill its outer shell, the one electron which can be supplied by hydrogen is not shared equally by the two atoms but is pulled closer to the electronegative atom. The most common examples of this phenomenon are liquid water and ice. Here the electronegative atom is oxygen, as shown in Fig. 3. The dots represent the outer shell electrons of oxygen and the crosses the electrons contributed by hydrogen. The oxygen atom 1 exerts a strong pull on the lone electron supplied by the hydrogen, so that at the position of the oxygen atom 2 it appears as though the hydrogen is in fact an ion ($H^+$), devoid of electrons, and since a pair of electrons of oxygen atom 2 are already pointing in the direction of this hydrogen atom, a weak bond will be formed. Thus the "hydrogen bond" consists of one hydrogen atom

between two oxygen atoms. The actual strength of such a bond is only about 10 per cent of that of an ordinary covalent bond, and not very much energy is required to disrupt it. In terms of most chemical reactions the hydrogen bond is therefore not of great significance, but it is vital in reactions which occur with small changes in energy, *i.e.*, biochemical reactions, where the making and breaking of hydrogen bonds is frequently of supreme importance. It must also be

Fig. 3. Formation of a hydrogen bond between neighbouring water molecules.

borne in mind that all biological reactions take place in an aqueous medium which is highly hydrogen-bonded and it is well known that water is the essential substrate for all life processes, although it is not always appreciated that water is also the most anomalous of chemical compounds. It is one of very few substances that are denser in the liquid than in the solid state (ice floats on water) and it is unique in that upon heating the liquid from its melting point to 4°C, a further contraction takes place. From our discussion on intermolecular forces it is apparent that a chemical compound made up of small molecules, being not very easily polarised, should exist in the gas state at ordinary temperature, and this is the case for other substances whose molecules have approximately the same dimensions as those of

TABLE 1.

ELECTRONS IN OUTER SHELL (VALENCE ELECTRONS)

| 1 | 2 | 3 | 4 | 5 | 6 | 7 | 8 |
|---|---|---|---|---|---|---|---|
| Hydrogen | | | | | | | |
| Sodium Potassium | Magnesium Calcium | Aluminium | Carbon Silicon | Nitrogen Phosphorus | Oxygen Sulphur | Chlorine Bromine | Neon Argon |
| Silver | Radium | | | | | Iodine | |

| Metals Positive ions | | Non-metals Negative ions or covalent |
|---|---|---|
| | Covalent → | |

TABLE 2

| Class of Compound | Elements | Example | Origin or Use |
|---|---|---|---|
| Hydrocarbon | C,H | Octane Benzene | Nat. oil deposit, fuel Coal tar, solvent, and raw material |
| Alcohols | C,H,O | Ethyl alcohol | Formed by fermentation of sugar |
| Amides | C,H,O,N | Acetamide | Constituents of synthetic polymers, *e.g.*, nylon |
| Lipids | C,H,O | Olive oil | Found in plant seeds, used as food energy |
| Carbohydrates | C,H,O | Sugar, starch, cellulose | Occur in Nature—sources of energy and plant structural materials |
| Amino acids | C,H,N,O,(S) | Glycine, alanine | Building blocks of proteins |
| Steroids | C,H,O | Cholesterol | Hormone substances |
| Terpenes | C,H,O | Geraniol | Occur in Nature—perfumes |

water, viz., $CO_2$ (carbon dioxide), $NH_3$, and HCl. The abnormal physical properties of water are due to the extensive hydrogen bonding which exists in its liquid and solid forms. Indeed, ice is the most perfectly hydrogen-bonded structure, and liquid water appears to retain some of this regular crystalline order, the main difference being that such crystalline regions are short-lived, forming and melting many million times every second. Nevertheless a snapshot of short enough exposure would no doubt reveal ice-like regions in liquid water.

### ORGANIC CHEMISTRY—THE CHEMISTRY OF CARBON COMPOUNDS.

Of all the hundred-odd elements which are now known and whose properties have been studied in detail, carbon is unique in the manner in which it can combine with itself to give rise to very large molecules (polymers) which can have molecular weights of several millions. Carbon compounds form the basis of the substances which make up living organisms, and thus the chemistry of carbon compounds is known as organic chemistry. Reference to Table 1 (F23) shows that carbon is capable of forming 4 covalent bonds, and the simplest organic compound is methane, $CH_4$ (the main constituent of North Sea gas). The hydrogen atoms are capable of being replaced by other atoms or groups of atoms, including carbon. Thus by replacing one of the C—H bonds by a C—C bond, $CH_3.CH_3$ (or $C_2H_6$) can be obtained. This process can continue and result in long chains of carbon atoms and the compounds so obtained form a series whose general formula is $C_nH_{2n+2}$, where $n$ is any whole number. The compound $C_8H_{18}$ is known as octane and forms the basis of petrol. The larger members of the series are the paraffin waxes. Starting again from methane and replacing one hydrogen atom by oxygen + hydrogen so that the carbon is covalently bonded to the oxygen, methyl alcohol, $CH_3OH$ is obtained. Once again this is the first member of a series, the alcohols, whose second member, $C_2H_5OH$ (ethyl alcohol), forms the basis of all alcoholic drinks.

In addition to ordinary 2-electron covalent bonds carbon also forms bonds involving 4 and 6 shared electrons. These bonds are much less stable than the ordinary covalent bonds so that compounds possessing them are extremely reactive. Carbon atom chains can also form side branches or closed rings, usually containing 5 or 6 carbon atoms. Furthermore, the important group of aromatic compounds are based on benzene, $C_6H_6$, in which the 6 carbon atoms form a planar ring and each has one hydrogen atom bonded to it. The remaining electrons form a mobile pool, so that the whole molecule is easily polarised and can be made to react with many other substances. It follows that a large variety of compounds can be obtained using only the elements carbon, hydrogen, and oxygen. If the elements nitrogen, phosphorus, sulphur are included, as well as chlorine, bromine, and iodine, the number of possible compounds becomes even larger. Table 2 provides some examples of classes of organic compounds and their occurrence in nature or their industrial application.

To achieve the growth of molecules by the elongation of the carbon chains is not usually feasible technically, although in nature this is a common process, brought about by enzymes (F25(1)). However, some molecules, especially those with four or six electron bonds, can react with one another to form polymers. In addition many molecules can be made to react (condense) to form more complex molecules with the elimination of a simple molecule, such as water or ammonia. Examples of the latter type of polymer are the proteins which are composed of amino-acid units (Table 2), the polysaccharides (carbohydrates), such as starch and cellulose, made up of condensed sugar molecules (Table 2), and synthetic condensation polymers of acids and alcohols known as polyesters, e.g., Terylene Additional polymers also figure largely in chemical technology, examples being polyvinyl chloride (PVC), polyolefines (e.g., polythene) and polystyrene.

### CHEMICAL REACTIONS.

#### Laws Governing Chemical Reactions.

Large amounts of energy are locked up within molecules and some of this energy is used up in chemical reaction. Like other forms of energy (e.g., electrical and mechanical) it is subject to certain laws, such as the law of conservation of energy which states that energy cannot be created or destroyed, but can be converted from one form to another. Thus, part of the chemical energy during the reaction may be converted into heat, and this is frequently the case (F17).

Another very important law deals with the extent to which a chemical reaction will proceed. The reaction of nitrogen with hydrogen, which combine to give ammonia, forms the basis of the fixation of atmospheric nitrogen in the manufacture of fertilisers. The two gases combine in the molecular ratio of 1:3, two molecules of ammonia being produced, i.e., $N_2 + 3H_2 = 2NH_3$. However, ammonia also decomposes to form nitrogen and hydrogen, and at a certain stage the rates of the two opposing reactions will be equal and the mixture is then said to be at equilibrium. The position of the equilibrium, i.e., the amount of ammonia formed, can be influenced by changes in temperature, pressure, or the amounts of the reacting substances, and the law of chemical equilibrium states that, if any factor governing an equilibrium is altered, then the equilibrium will shift in an attempt to counter the imposed alteration. Thus, in the ammonia synthesis, if ammonia is removed then more nitrogen and hydrogen will react in trying to re-establish the equilibrium. Furthermore, the reaction between hydrogen and nitrogen proceeds with the evolution of heat, so, if the temperature of the gas mixture is raised (i.e., heat is added) then the equilibrium will readjust itself in an attempt to nullify the imposed change, and accordingly some ammonia will decompose into hydrogen and nitrogen, because this process absorbs heat.

The laws governing the influence of temperature, pressure, and chemical composition on reactions are termed chemical thermodynamics and the effects described can be calculated in quantitative terms. Some of the problems of chemical engineering are concerned with maximising yields of chemical reactions, while at the same time reconciling the necessary conditions with the economics of the process, e.g., cost of plant, materials, and fuel.

One other important consideration is the speed with which chemical reactions proceed, and the time taken to reach equilibrium (chemical kinetics). This cannot be predicted by the laws of chemical thermodynamics. According to thermodynamic calculations, gaseous hydrogen and oxygen will react to form liquid water, but this reaction is so slow that even in a million years not very much water would be formed.

#### Catalysts.

Molecules react as a result of collisions, during which the energy due to the collision must be channelled into the chemical bond which is to be broken or to be made. Although at ordinary pressure and temperature molecules collide many million times every second, if all these collisions were to result in chemical reaction, then all reactions would occur with explosive violence. In fact, only a very small number of collisions are of a high enough energy for reaction to take place. This energy, termed the energy of activation, is therefore an important factor controlling the rate of a chemical reaction. The combination of hydrogen and oxygen normally has a large energy of activation and the two gases do not react to form water, although thermodynamics predicts that the reaction is feasible. Reaction rates can be increased, i.e., the activation energy lowered, if certain solids are added, on which one or several of the reacting species are adsorbed. The bond formed between the added solid (e.g., platinum) and the reacting gas is strong enough to weaken other bonds in the molecules, so that, on collision with another molecule, reaction takes place more readily. The solid which itself does not participate in the chemical reaction, is called a catalyst. Its function is to promote chemical reactions between substances which, because of the high activation energy, would not react in its absence. Catalysts find applications not only in many industrial processes but are also extensively used by living organisms, where they are called *enzymes*. Current theories hold that the reacting molecule fits into a hole or groove, like a key into a lock, on the enzyme protein where it is held while the reaction takes place; an example of an enzyme catalysed reaction is the breakdown of starch by the body. This consists of several steps, each of which is controlled by its own specific enzyme. These biological catalysts are much more efficient than those used in synthetic reactions, both in their specificity and in the lowering of the energy of activation (*i.e.*, the increase in the reaction rate). Sometimes a foreign molecule which bears a similarity to the molecule whose reaction is to be catalysed, will combine with a catalyst. If this foreign molecule is very strongly held by the catalyst then the latter can no longer perform its function and is said to be poisoned. This is also true for enzymes: *e.g.*, carbon monoxide and cyanides act as poisons by combining with certain important enzymes and thus inhibit the biochemical reactions on which the functioning of organs depends.

## SOME USEFUL APPLICATIONS OF CHEMISTRY.

The application of basic chemical and physical principles to the manufacturing industries has led to the technological revolution which began at the turn of the century and is still gathering momentum. Although it is impossible to cover fully the areas in which the chemical sciences find application, a few of the more important fields are noted below:

### Electrochemistry.

Electrochemistry deals with processes in which chemical energy is converted into electrical energy or *vice versa*. The most common examples are the dry battery and the lead storage battery (L13), although the generation of electricity by fuel cells (L43) is fast becoming of industrial importance. Conversely, if a current is passed through an ionic solution, a chemical reaction will take place, and this principle is employed in the electrolytic refining of metal ores and in metal plating processes.

### Surface Chemistry.

Surface chemistry is based on the fact that solid and liquid surfaces have properties which are different from those of matter in the bulk state. A molecule A situated in the bulk interacts with its neighbours, but the various forces will cancel, as shown in Fig. 4. For a molecule B in the

SURFACE

FIG. 4—Surface Forces: molecules within the solid (or liquid) are subject to balanced forces, but for molecules in the surface there is a resultant downward force.

surface there is a net inward pull. The surface is therefore a high energy state and thermodynamics predicts that substances will try to minimise their total surface area. In a liquid this leads to the formation of spherical drops. The solid, on the other hand, will attract vapours and liquids which deposit surface films and thus reduce its surface energy. One application o adsorbed films, catalysis, has already been discussed.

Surface effects become significant in processes where the ratio of surface area to bulk volume is large, for instance, where matter is finely dispersed. This is the case in the technology of paints, printing inks, detergency, dairy products, air and water pollution, and solutions of polymers. The above-mentioned properties are also utilised in processes which involve the deposition of substances on surfaces, *e.g.*, textile finishing (water- and crease-proofing), metal coating, herbicides, cosmetics, and adhesives. Perhaps the most important field in which surface behaviour is one of the determining factors is biology. All living cells are separated from each other by membranes, and nutrients and other chemicals are adsorbed on, and diffuse through, these membranes, the nature and action of which are as yet very imperfectly understood (F27(1)).

### Photochemistry.

Like other forms of energy, light, both visible and ultraviolet, can cause chemical changes to take place and, conversely, some reactions will give rise to the emission of radiation, *e.g.*, fluorescence. The ultimate source of most of the energy on each is the radiation from the sun which, by the process of photosynthesis (F28(1)), can be converted by green plants into the chemical energy stored in coal, oil, and carbohydrates. The mechanism of photosynthesis is one of the most baffling problems in chemical kinetics.

In photography a film of gelatin, in which are embedded small grains of silver bromide, is exposed to light, when a " latent image " is formed. This is believed to consist of submicroscopic specks of silver in some of the grains, but the mechanism of its formation is still uncertain. The latent image can be " developed " into a negative image (silver) which is then " fixed " by dissolving away the unreduced silver bromide.

### Analytical Chemistry.

This is an important branch of Chemistry and deals with the identification and quantitative estimation of substances, often in complex mixtures. Where a quantitative analysis is to be achieved, the component under study has first to be separated in the pure state and then a suitable method must be found to determine its concentration in the mixture. In earlier days most analytical techniques were based on chemical reactions which were specific for the compound to be separated. Thus, sodium chloride and sodium sulphate can be separated by making use of the fact that many metal sulphates are insoluble in water, so that if a solution of, say, barium chloride is added to the mixture, barium sulphate will precipitate as solid and can be removed from the sodium chloride by filtration. If the amount of mixture initially used and the amount of precipitated barium sulphate are known, then, from the chemical formulae for barium and sodium sulphates, $BaSO_4$ and $Na_2SO_4$, it is easy to calculate the percentage of sodium sulphate in the original mixture.

During the last 25 years chemical analytical techniques have gradually been superseded by much more refined physical methods. Most important among these are the spectroscopic methods which can distinguish between small differences in energies associated with the vibrational motions of different chemical bonds. Some of these techniques not only measure energy differences but can detect minute amounts of energy, such as the energy liberated by a burning candle at a distance of 1 mile.

The detection, identification, and sometimes the quantitative estimation of very minor constituents of mixtures is frequently of great importance in industrial processes and products. For instance the presence of 1 g of iron in a ton of edible oil will rapidly cause the oil to turn rancid. Another example of the importance of traces of chemical compounds is provided by flavour and aroma of foodstuffs and perfumes. Frequently the characteristic, agreeable odour of a product is due to minute concentrations of one or several fairly simple organic compounds which at higher concentrations possess a quite unpleasant odour. The isolation of these compounds from natural products such as fruit or flowers and their identification provides a continous challenge to the ingenuity of the analytical chemist.

## Conclusion.

It will now be readily seen that the science of chemistry covers a large field which extends from the very simple molecules, such as $H_2O$, to the complex naturally occurring molecules with molecular weights of several millions. It involves very fundamental studies, ranging from the nature of the forces between atoms and the how and why of apparently simple chemical reactions, to the very applied problems encountered in the manufacture of high-strength construction materials. Among new fields which have developed rapidly during recent years petroleum chemicals rank high. This industry, which is centered on the oil companies, produces a large variety of substances, such as detergents, polymer raw materials, solvents, dyestuffs, fats and waxes, from by-products obtained during oil refining. Pharmaceutical chemistry, too, is rapidly developing and attempts

are being made not only to synthesise new drugs but to gain a better understanding of the mechanism of drug action.

Probably the most significant developments during the next twenty years will occur in the field of biochemistry. The elucidation of the structure and genetic functions of nucleic acids and some proteins has provided the impetus for further investigation into the chemistry and physics of these and other biologically active molecules. Other outstanding problems which may well be solved in the not too distant future include the mechanism of membrane action, muscle contraction and nerve impulse propagation in molecular terms. Where a hundred years ago the sciences of physics, chemistry, and biology parted ways to follow their own separate paths, they are now seen to be converging and the areas of overlap are gradually increasing, as the molecular concepts of chemistry are providing a means of studying biological processes in terms of established physical laws and mechanisms. This part of the story will now be taken up in the section that follows.

# IV.  BIOLOGY—THE SCIENCE OF LIFE

## WHAT BIOLOGY IS ABOUT.

Biology embraces the study of all living things which exist on earth at the present time and also the recognisable remains of those that are extinct. Living things or organisms range from the apparently simple micro-organisms such as viruses and bacteria to the largest animals and plants.

## Living Processes.

The enormous variation and complexity of living processes make the task of understanding and defining life a very difficult one. Every living organism undergoes continual physical and chemical changes which, in spite of their diversity, are referred to as the metabolism of the organism. Metabolism involves the processing of food materials, the production of waste products, and all the intermediate stages between these whereby energy and matter are provided for the operation, maintenance, and growth of the organism. These reactions are under very exact chemical or nervous control at every stage and can be slowed down or speeded up as the need arises. Thus the organism can react to changes in the environment in which it lives, adjusting its activities in relation to the external changes. Finally, organisms can reproduce either in an identical or very slightly modified form. In this process new individuals are produced and the species continues to survive. Differences between offspring and parents can, under certain circumstances, act cumulatively over many generations and so form the basis of evolutionary change in which new species of organism are ultimately formed.

## Molecular Biology.

It has been evident for many years that the most fundamental aspects of these living processes occur in basic structural units known as cells. We shall examine this level of organisation first before we attempt to look at the larger questions of the organisation of multicellular animals and plants and their interactions in groups or populations. The study of living processes at the molecular and cell level has been given a tremendous impetus in recent years by the advent of new techniques which enable microscopic and submicroscopic parts of cell to be examined. Physicists, chemists, and mathematicians have found themselves working alongside biologists in this field and several of the very notable advances have been made by physical scientists. At this level of organisation the traditional division of Biology into Botany, the study of plants, and Zoology, the study of animals, has little meaning. Even the more recent Genetics, the study of inheritance, Biophysics and Bio-

chemistry, concerned with the physics and chemistry of organisms, and Cytology, the study of cell structure, are losing such identity as they may once have had. Molecular biology is a term frequently used in describing this rapidly expanding and fascinating field of research.

## THE CELL.

Cells were first seen in 1665 by Robert Hooke when he looked at a piece of cork under his primitive microscope. It was not until 1839, however, that Schlieden and Schwann produced the cell doctrine which visualised the cell as both the structural and functional unit of living organisation. Exceptions may be found to the cell doctrine. For example, some protozoa, algae, and fungi show very complex internal organisation but are not divided into cells; they are usually called acellular organisms. The viruses also constitute a difficulty since in many ways they are intermediate between living and dead matter. They are absolutely dependent on cells of other organisms for their continued existence. Outside living cells they are inert molecules which may take a crystalline form. Inside a host cell, however, they become disease-producing parasites which multiply and show many of the other properties of living organisms. They are minute and lack the complex organisation usually associated with cells. Notwithstanding their somewhat ambiguous position, the viruses are often treated as though they were single cells or parts of cells and their extreme simplicity has made them ideal material for many types of research at this level. The bacteria also lack some of the properties of cells but the differences are not so clearly defined as they are in the case of viruses.

## Structure and Function of Cells.

Though the constituent cells of a multicellular organism are usually specialised to perform particular functions, they have a great many features in common. The cell is often said to be made up of a substance called protoplasm, a term for the fundamental material of life which dates from the 19th cent. Protoplasm has two main constituents, the cytoplasm and the nucleus, and is bounded on the outside by a cell or plasma membrane. Plant cells generally have an additional wall composed primarily of cellulose and used for support. The nucleus is the controlling centre of the cell and has rather limited metabolic capabilities. The cytoplasm contains various subunits which operate to produce energy and new cell structure during the normal metabolism of the cell.

Cells take up the raw materials for metabolism

through the cell membrane from extracellular fluid which surrounds them. The nutrients include carbohydrates, fats, proteins, minerals, vitamins, and water. Fats and carbohydrates are important principally as sources of energy, though both types of compound are found in permanent cell structure. Proteins are complex substances of high molecular weight which contain nitrogen in addition to the carbon, hydrogen, and oxygen found in the other compounds. They are of fundamental importance in the structure and function of the cell and are built up of a number of simple nitrogen-containing organic molecules called amino acids. There are twenty amino acids occurring commonly in nature so that the number of possible combinations in large protein molecules is quite clearly enormous. A group of proteins whose significance is well established are the enzymes which are the catalysts of chemical reactions in living cells. Each enzyme will control and speed up a specific reaction even though it is present in very small amounts and is usually unchanged at the end of the process. A large number of inorganic mineral salts are essential for cells to function normally. Some, such as sodium, potassium, and calcium salts, are needed in considerable quantity; others are required only in trace amounts and these include iron, copper, and manganese. The trace elements are usually important constituents of enzyme systems. Vitamins are also necessary in very small amounts and it seems reasonable to conclude that their function is also a catalytic one in parts of some enzyme systems.

## I. CYTOPLASM.

For a long time cytoplasm was thought to be a homogenous and structureless substrate in which enzymes occurred as part of a general colloidal system. With the refinement of techniques such as electron microscopy and ultracentrifugation, more and more identifiable components have been found within the cytoplasm. It now seems certain that the material other than these recognisable particles is not a structureless matrix but a highly organised and variable complex at the molecular level.

### Identification of Components: recent techniques.
#### Ultracentrifuge.

When soft tissues such as liver are ground up in a homogeniser, which usually takes the form of a plunger fitting fairly tightly into a glass tube, the cells are broken up but the smaller particles escape destruction. The particles remain in a highly active biochemical state if the salt concentration of the liquid into which they are released by homogenisation is more or less the same as that within the cell from which they came. Early failures to isolate cell fractions were almost all attributable to osmotic difficulties in which differences of salt concentration led to the movement of water into or out of the particles and to their subsequent destruction. The homogenate can be treated in a centrifuge at a higher speed rotation subjects the particles to forces many thousands times greater than gravity. As a result the heaviest particles, such as the nuclei, are deposited first on the bottom of the centrifuge tube. The liquid is then transferred to another tube and the process repeated at a higher speed which brings down slightly lighter particles called mitochondria. The next collection of particles which can be obtained is called the microsomal fraction. By careful use of this technique, biochemists can produce a variety of cell constituents which can be studied in the absence of all the other reacting systems of the cell.

#### Radioactive Isotopes.

In many of the studies of cell chemistry which have been made on whole cells, on cell fractions, or on isolated enzyme systems, progress has been due in a large part to the availability of isotopes. With the aid of compounds prepared in the laboratory and labelled with the radioactive isotopes of elements such as carbon, hydrogen, nitrogen, oxygen, sulphur, and phosphorus, biochemists can now follow the metabolic fate of these substances in living organisms. The presence of a radioactive " labelled " element in any of the products of metabolism can be determined by means of Geiger and scintillation counters. The studies involving radioactive isotopes have shown more clearly than any others that living material is never static but is in a state of dynamic equilibrium. Substances are constantly broken down and replaced by other substances so that an organism may appear to be more or less unchanging but its components are always turning over.

#### Light Microscopy.

Many of the particles which can be isolated and studied have been identified within the living cell by means of the light microscope. Especially useful in this respect have been the phase contrast and interference modifications which make structures of different refractive index visible and do not depend on differences in light absorption as does the ordinary instrument.

#### Electron Microscope.

In light microscopy true images of particles smaller than the wavelength of light cannot be formed. Great difficulty is experienced in resolving particles much smaller than 0·5 microns (0·0005 millimetre) in size. The electron microscope, which uses a beam of electrons instead of light, is capable of much greater resolution because electrons behave as rays of extremely short wavelengths. Details as fine as 20 Angstroms (0·002 microns) have been resolved and a tremendous amount of structure has been revealed by this instrument. However, many of the objects which are well known from electron microscope studies have not been isolated nor their functions been ascribed to them. Conversely, much of the biochemistry of cells cannot be linked to known structures. One of the great limitations of the electron microscope is that it can only be used to examine very thin slices of dead material.

#### X-ray Diffraction.

A method which can reveal a great deal of information about the arrangement of constituent parts in very complex biological molecules is that of X-ray diffraction. In this method X-rays are reflected from regularities in the molecular structure so as to form a pattern characteristic of the structure. Studies of X-ray diffraction patterns can be made on living material so that the internal shape of biological molecules can be worked out and the changes, if any, followed during phases of activity. In many ways X-ray diffraction has been useful in filling the gaps between biochemical studies of molecular behaviour and the essentially static view of cell structure obtained from the electron microscope.

#### Constituents of Cytoplasm.

The following are some of the particulate and membranous constituents of cytoplasm which have been identified and analysed with varying degrees of success by these and many other techniques:

#### 1. Mitochondria and Oxidation.

Mitochondria vary in shape from cylindrical rods to spheres and in size from 0·2 to 3·0 microns. When seen in the living cell they are in constant motion. The whole structure is enclosed within a thin double membrane, the inner layer of which is thrown into folds extending across the central cavity of the mitochondrion and dividing it into small chambers. The function of mitochondria is to provide energy for the reactions of the rest of the cell. Almost the whole machinery for the oxidation of foodstuffs is to be found in the mitochondria and, as might be expected, is related in some way to the complex structure. Slight damage to the mitochondrion will render it unable to carry out a complete cycle of oxidative processes. Destruction of parts of the double membrane system prevents the production of energy-rich phosphate bonds in adenosine triphosphate (ATP) in which energy is stored and transported about the cell.

*The Krebs Cycle.*

The oxidative reactions which produce the energy are quite unlike those in which hydrocarbons are burnt in the laboratory. They proceed through a large number of controlled steps during which the energy is slowly evolved. The basic fuel substances, carbohydrates, fats, and proteins, are broken down outside the mitochondria to four major intermediate products which are pyruvic acid, oxalacetic acid, acetic acid and ketoglutaric acid. These acids diffuse into the mitochondria and are oxidised in a cyclical system of reactions called the Krebs or citric acid cycle which ultimately leads to the production of carbon dioxide and water. The actual oxidation of the various compounds participating in the cycle is brought about by a series of enzymes described as an electron transport chain. Oxidation in these cases is essentially a removal of electrons from the substrate, invariably accompanied by an equal number of hydrogen nuclei. The electrons, sometimes with and sometimes without the hydrogen nuclei, are passed from one compound to another until eventually they combine with oxygen to form water. One of the best known electron transport systems is that involving iron-containing substances called cytochromes.

An example of a typical stage in the Krebs cycle is the conversion of succinic acid to fumaric acid under the control of the enzyme succinic dehydrogenase. Both acids are compounds containing four carbon atoms but the latter has two electrons and two hydrogen nuclei fewer than the former which is therefore said to be oxidised during the conversion. The electrons are accepted by the first member of a chain of cytochromes which is thus reduced and the hydrogen is set free as hydrogen ions. The electrons are passed down the chain of cytochromes which are reduced in turn and re-oxidise the earlier members of the chain. In the final stage the reduced cytochrome is oxidised by oxygen which accepts the electrons and combines with the hydrogen ions to form water. These steps produce energy, but this does not all appear as heat because some is used to drive a reaction which consumes energy. The first law of thermodynamics states that such a coupling is necessary if a high energy compound is to be produced. The energy consuming reaction is the conversion of adenosine diphosphate (ADP) to adenosine triphosphate (ATP) with its energy-rich phosphate bond. The whole process is known as oxidative phosphorylation. The mitochondria produce far more energy than they require and the ATP passes into the cytoplasm for use in the rest of the cell.

## 2. Chloroplasts and Photosynthesis.

Chloroplasts are particles found in cells in the green parts of plants, in fact they contain the green pigment which is called chlorophyll. They are involved in the extremely important process known as photosynthesis in which energy absorbed from light is used to synthesise carbohydrates from carbon dioxide and water, oxygen being formed as a by-product.

Chloroplasts are disc-shaped or flat ellipsoids from 2 to 20 microns across, possessing a complex structure which in many ways is reminiscent of that found in mitochondria. A typical double membrane surrounds the structure and the inside is made up very largely of a stack of discs consisting of paired membranes connected at their ends to form closed systems. This seems to be a further development of the type of lamellated structure seen dividing the central cavity of a mitochondrion. The chlorophylls and other pigments, such as the orange yellow carotenoids, seem to be arranged in layers a single molecule thick in the chloroplast discs so that they are maximally exposed to light.

*Photosynthesis.*

In photosynthesis there are two somewhat independent sets of reactions, one needing light and the other going on in the dark. The primary process is the absorption of light quanta by the chlorophyll which causes some of the electrons of its molecule to pass from one orbital to another and thus enter an excited state. It is thought that chlorophyll then loses electrons which pass either to a recently discovered protein called ferrodoxin or to another oxidising agent, plastoquinone. The electrons from plastoquinone are transferred via a complex series of steps involving a cytochrome chain back to the chlorophyll. During these sequences oxygen is liberated from water molecules and energy-rich phosphate bonds are produced. The production of ATP in this reaction, which can only take place in the light, is called photosynthetic phosphorylation and, in this respect, makes plants independent of stored carbohydrate as their primary energy source.

The reactions so far described have not involved carbon dioxide and though it is possible to make the system operate solely in this way it is not usual for it to do so. Normally the electrons from ferrodoxin are passed to another electron accepting system together with hydrogen ions from water. At the same time, as recent isotope studies have revealed, carbon dioxide is combined with a 5-carbon sugar and the resulting compound immediately splits into two molecules of a 3-carbon, phosphoglyceric acid. The reduced electron system which has oxidised ferrodoxin now comes into operation and, together with energy from ATP, is used to synthesise sugar and starch from the 3-carbon compounds. The reactions in which carbon dioxide is taken up or "fixed" and then reduced during the formation of sugar, can go on in the dark unlike those of photosynthetic phosphorylation described earlier.

The importance of this process whereby plants can make use of the energy in sunlight to fix carbon dioxide and produce carbohydrates is quite clear. The whole animal population of the world, including man, is dependent on plants for food since even the meat-eating carnivores prey upon herbivores. Although scientists continue to make efforts to produce adequate food materials from simple compounds, there is still no better machinery known for doing this than the plant cell. Man is dependent on photosynthesis not only for his supplies of food but also for much of

FIG. 1. *Nucleic Acids.* A portion of a DNA molecule showing how it is made up of two strands of nucleotides. Each nucleotide consists of a base, which may be Adenine (A), Thymine (T), Guanine (G), or Cytosine (C), united to the Pentose Sugar, Desoxyribose (S), in turn joined to Phosphoric Acid (P). The nucleotides are linked through the phosphoric acid groups. The two strands are held together by hydrogen bonds between bases, adenine linking only with thymine, and guanine only with cytosine.

his fuel, since much of the combustible material removed from the earth is of plant origin. In this respect atomic energy may eventually prove to be an adequate alternative.

### 3. Endoplasmic reticulum, Ribosomes, and Protein Synthesis.

A network of elaborate and oriented double membranes existing within parts of the cytoplasm can be seen in the electron microscope. In the space between the pairs of double membranes small granules are visible, either free in the space or attached to a membrane. The whole system is called the endoplasmic reticulum or ergastoplasm. When the cell is homogenised and centrifuged the endoplasmic reticulum appears as the microsomal fraction. Biochemical analysis after separation of the membranous from the granular components reveals that the former is composed largely of phospholipids and cholesterol, which are compounds closely related to fats, and the latter of ribonucleic acid (RNA).

### Nucleic Acids.

The term nucleic acid covers a class of substances, usually of great complexity, built up from smaller units called nucleotides. Each nucleotide consists of a base, united to a sugar, in turn united to phosphoric acid. Nucleotides are joined together in a linear fashion by means of the phosphoric acid residues to form a chain from which the bases project at right angles (Fig. 1). Two types of sugar are found in naturally occurring nucleic acids and these are the ribose of RNA and the desoxyribose of desoxyribonucleic acids (DNA). We shall return to the latter when the nucleus is considered. Four nitrogen-containing bases occur in nucleic acids and in RNA—adenine, cytosine, guanine, and uracil. In DNA the uracil is replaced by thymine.

### Protein Synthesis.

There is good evidence that RNA is manufactured exclusively within the nucleus and subsequently moves out into the cytoplasm. Some of it, called ribosomal RNA, unites with protein to form the granules, or ribosomes, of the endoplasmic reticulum. Another form, called messenger RNA, also migrates from the nucleus to associate with ribosomes but does not become incorporated into their permanent structure. It is also well established that the ribosomes are closely linked with protein synthesis in the cell because radioactive amino acids, when fed to an animal, are always found first in the ribosomes before any other cell structure. The specification for a particular protein is not carried on the ribosome which is merely the factory for making these complex molecules. It is thought that messenger RNA carries instructions from the nucleus which specify exactly the protein to be synthesised at a ribosome. This is done by means of a code in which a "triplet" of three nucleotide bases codes one amino acid (Fig. 2). Thus on a long molecule of RNA, three adjacent uracil bases would specify an amino acid called phenylalanine. If these were followed by one uracil and two guanines then the amino acid tryptophan would be specified and this would be

FIG. 2. A portion of a molecule of messenger RNA, associated with a ribosome and synthesising a protein. The base sequence on the messenger RNA has been determined by the helix labelled with the downward pointing arrow in Fig. 3. Adenine specifies Uracil (U), Cytosine specifies Guanine (G), Thymine specifies Adenine (A), and Guanine specifies Cytosine (C). The ribosome is moving down the messenger RNA strand "reading" the triplet code. Amino acid 4, which is phenylalanine specified by UUU, has just been joined to three other amino acids and its carrier RNA released to the cytoplasm. Amino acid 5, tryptophan specified by UGG, is attached to its carrier RNA and in position ready to be joined to the protein chain by the ribosome. Amino acid 6, methionine specified by UAG, is attached to its carrier RNA but has not been brought into position on the messenger RNA strand. Other amino acids and carrier RNA molecules exist free in the cytoplasm and have not yet associated.

joined to the phenylalanine. In this way complex protein molecules can be built up according to instructions emanating from the nucleus for each of the 20 different amino acids. It is far from clear how the amino acids in the cytoplasm are brought into position on the RNA "template" and how they are activated so as to combine and form protein. It is thought that they are first attached, by appropriate enzymes, to small molecules of so-called carrier RNA in the cytoplasm before associating on the template of messenger RNA. The association is then accomplished by a ribosome which moves along the messenger RNA chain, as it were "reading" the code, and taking appropriate carrier RNA-amino acid complexes from the surrounding medium. There are still many gaps in our knowledge of the exact sequence of events.

This system is responsible for building and maintaining much of the organisation of the cytoplasm. All the enzymes, for example, catalysing every reaction within the cell will be specified and built up on the appropriate RNA template. The understanding of protein synthesis is of fundamental importance to the whole of biology and has particular significance in studies on cancer where cell growth becomes abnormal.

## 4. The Golgi Apparatus.

The characteristic features of the Golgi apparatus are numbers of large vacuoles or spaces, bordered by closely packed layers of double membranes. The latter look very much like the membranes of the endoplasmic reticulum but do not have the ribosome particles along their edge. They are therefore known as "smooth" membranes in contrast to the "rough" membranes of endoplasmic reticulum. The function of the Golgi apparatus is not established though it may be associated with secretory activity of the cell.

The Golgi apparatus has been the subject of controversy for many years and illustrates one of the major difficulties in working at the molecular cell level. The Golgi structure can only be seen through the light and electron microscopes after the cell has been through a number of preparative stages. Many biologists thought that the preparation itself was responsible for creating the Golgi apparatus and that nothing like the objects seen would really exist in the living cell. Though there is now little doubt that the Golgi apparatus is a real constituent of the cytoplasm, the general problem of creating artefacts by the involved treatment in many investigations remains a very real one.

## 5. Cell Membrane.

Though the cell membrane plays a most vital part in regulating what can enter and leave the cell, it remains rather poorly understood. It is thought to consist of a double layer of lipid molecules with a layer of protein probably outside the lipid. Fairly large molecules seem to be able to penetrate the membrane in relation to their fat solubility, which would support the hypothesis of its lipid framework. Small molecules and ions appear to penetrate in relation to their size, the smaller ones getting through more readily than the larger. This suggests that pores of a certain size exist in the membrane.

The cell membrane has mechanisms which can move ions and other substances against concentration differences either into or out of the cell. A fine microelectrode can be pushed into a cell and the electrical potential of the inside determined with respect to the outside. In all the cells studied so far there is a potential difference across the membrane which is produced by the non-uniform distribution on either side of ions, particularly those of sodium, potassium, and chloride. Though these potentials have been studied in animal and plant cells generally, they are best known from the work on nerve cells where sudden changes in the membrane potential are the basis of nerve impulses. A great deal is now known about the mechanism whereby the potential change, and thus the nerve impulse, is propagated from one end of a nerve to the other. The basic process which produces the nerve impulse in any

region of the nerve fibre has been shown to be a sudden increase in permeability of the membrane to sodium ions in that region. A problem of much interest is how such activity can be passed from one nerve to the next, that is to say how a change of potential in one cell membrane can be made to affect an adjacent cell membrane. Such a process is fundamental to the large collections of nerve cells which form the nervous systems of animals. Transmission takes place at a special region called a synapse and when an impulse reaches this region it causes the release of a small amount of chemical transmitter substance which diffuse to the membrane of the adjacent cell. There it combines with the membrane in such a way as to change its permeability to ions and so produce a nerve impulse in the second cell. A number of transmitter substances have now been identified and many of them are related chemically to tranquillisers and other drugs affecting the nervous system.

## II. NUCLEUS.

The main regions of the nucleus are the surrounding nuclear membrane, a mass of material known as chromatin, and a small sphere called the nucleolus. The nuclear membrane is a double structure very much like the membranes of the cell surface and endoplasmic reticulum. Suggestions have been made that these membranes are continuous at some regions within the cell. The status of chromatin was in doubt for many years. Light microscope studies reveal very little structure in the nucleus until the time when the cell is preparing for, and undergoing, division or mitosis. At this time a number of discrete double strands, the chromosomes, are revealed by virtue of their chromatin content—the material stains heavily with basic dyes.

## Cell Division.

During division the chromosomes behave in regular and recognisable sequence. In the first stage called prophase they appear and at the same time the nuclear membrane breaks down. Next, in metaphase, the chromosomes become arranged across the equator of a spindle-shaped collection of fibrils which appears in the area formerly outlined by the nucleus. Then follows anaphase in which the two threads of each chromosome, the chromatids, move to opposite poles of the spindle. Finally in the last stage, telophase, nuclear membranes are formed round the two separate collections of chromosome material and the cytoplasm itself divides into two. Thus two cells are formed each containing the same number of chromosomes as the parent and the cells enter a period of rest, or interphase, between divisions. During interphase the chromatin material disappears and the possibility was considered of the chromosomes being assembled as a prelude to every cell division and then being dispersed in the nuclear sap afterwards.

This suggestion is in direct conflict with the view that chromosomes are the carriers of genes.

## Genes.

These are the elements which contain all hereditary information and the medium whereby hereditary features are transmitted from one cell to the next, either in the same organism or from parents to offspring via the fertilised egg. Experiments indicated that the same genes always occupy the same position on chromosomes and this really demands a structural continuity through the life of the cell. The chromosomes undoubtedly persist, but it is still not certain why or how they change so as to become visible during division. One suggestion has been that the nucleic acids of which they are very largely made up condense during the period of prophase. In the resting nucleus the chromosomes may be much more swollen and occupy much of the nucleus.

The problem that has attracted the most attention and is possibly the most fundamental that biology has to offer is that of the nature of the genes. The important material of the genes is known to be desoxyribosenucleic acid (DNA), made up of nucleotides as is RNA, though in this case the bases are adenine, cytosine, guanine, and thymine. The DNA molecule is large and complex. Two long chains of nucleotides are known to coil round in a double helix with the pairs of bases on each helix directed towards one another and linked by means of hydrogen bonds (Fig. 3).

FIG. 3. The actual arrangement of the two nucleotide strands in a double helix, with the bases projecting and linking the two helices as shown.

Furthermore, if adenine is the base on one chain, thymine must be its partner on the other and similarly guanine can link only with cytosine. Because of this pairing off of bases there is sufficient information in a single chain of nucleotides to resynthesise the double helix once more. Thus if we examine a section of a single strand of the helix and find bases in the order adenine, thymine, guanine, adenine, cytosine, we can predict that in similar positions on the other strand we shall find thymine, adenine, cytosine, thymine, guanine. The capacity of one half of a DNA molecule to specify the other half exactly, enables the system to be self-replicating in a way that is essential in a hereditary transmitter and fits in well with what is known of chromosome behaviour during cell division.

Transmission of Genetic Information.

Accepting that DNA is the material of the gene it remains now to examine the nature of the information which it passes from cell to cell and organism to organism. Long before the structure and significance of the DNA molecule was known, geneticists were finding that alterations in a gene, known as a mutation, usually affected a particular chemical reaction and this in turn caused the changes seen in the organism as a whole. The effect was due to the failure to synthesise a necessary enzyme and so the hypothesis "one gene = one enzyme" gathered currency. This view has now been extended to include proteins other than enzymes and it is now certain that specific genes control the synthesis of specific proteins. The DNA of the genes transmits the instructions about protein synthesis to the ribosomes via messenger RNA. In the nucleus, messenger RNA is made with specific base sequences in its molecule by using DNA as the template; thus a group of three adjacent adenine bases in DNA would produce a group of three adjacent urocil bases in the synthesised RNA and this would lead to the specification of phenylalanine at the ribosome as we have seen. Only one of the two strands in the DNA double helix participates in the production of RNA.

Within the nucleus, the nucleolus is believed to play an important part in the synthesis of RNA since its turnover of this material is very rapid. It has been suggested that the nucleolus supplements the RNA produced by chromosomes and acts as the channel through which this material is released to the cytoplasm. There is now some good evidence which points to the nucleolus as the source of ribosomal RNA since cells which lose the nucleolus have no ribosomes.

The processes involved in nuclear control and the transmission of information from cell to cell is summarised in the aphorism "DNA makes RNA and RNA makes protein." The system of carrying that information in the base sequences of DNA molecules has become known as the "genetic code." A remarkable landmark in the study of DNA occurred when, towards the end of 1967, Kornberg and his colleagues managed to synthesise a virus DNA in a test tube. The synthesised molecules proved to be capable of infecting bacteria in the same way that the naturally occurring virus would. The DNA was synthesised using an extracted virus DNA molecule as template and attaching nucleotides by means of appropriate enzymes. The newly made molecules were then separated from the template. It can hardly be claimed that this is the creation of life in a test tube since the template was extracted from a living virus. The experiment suggests many possibilities in experimental modification of the genetic constitution of an organism with all the far reaching ethical consequences.

## MULTICELLULAR ORGANISATION.

It is axiomatic, if evolutionary theory is accepted, that in the course of very long periods of time there has been a general change in multicellular organisation from the simple aggregation of cells with little individual differentiation, to the highly specialised and differentiated cells and tissues seen in complex animals and plants. It is fascinating to speculate on the environmental variations and internal mechanisms which together produced this result. The problem is so vast, however, that a complete analysis is impossible and even a statement of the sequence of changes is in many cases highly controversial.

Another aspect of becoming multicellular, where the problems offer more hope of analysis, is that the complex organisation must be built up in the lifetime of each animal or plant from the single-celled stage of the fertilised egg. We have already seen how cells can divide repeatedly, handing on self-replicating chromosomes so that each cell is apparently identical. If this were really so then division of the fertilised egg would result in an unorganised mass of cells showing no differentiation. The essential problems in development are: (1) how is the smooth succession of shape changes produced during cell division so that an appropriate and recognisable end product is reached?; (2) how do the cells differentiate during this temporal sequence so that those which form part of the eye, say, are different from those of liver and blood?

Method of Development.

There are some important differences in the method of development in animals and plants. In animals there tends to be a relatively short period during which the basic structure is produced and after which growth, repair, and replacement may cause adjustment rather than major change. In higher plants, on the other hand, the apical regions of both roots and shoots remain in a permanently embryonic state and add material, which then differentiates, in a continuous process throughout the life of the plant. In spite of these differences—and in any case there are many exceptions—the two main problems in development are essentially similar in both animals and plants.

A great deal of work has been done on animal development since this takes place in a fairly stereotyped way during a short period of time. The fertilised egg of an animal divides in such a way as to form a hollow ball of cells, the blastula, which folds in on itself to produce a two-layered sac, the gastrula. A third layer, the mesoderm, is now added between the two layers, known as ectoderm on the outside, and endoderm on the inside. At this stage much of the animal's basic structure is established. Many aspects of this orderly sequence can be explained in terms of specific adhesive properties of cells, so that a cell will stick to others of the same type but not to unrelated types. Other mechanical properties such as elasticity, particularly in surface layers, are important in maintaining shape and producing appropriate changes during processes when one layer is folded in on another. Why cells should have the different physical properties necessary to produce an integrated whole embryo s not known, but certainly it cannot be thought that every cell has an absolutely fixed constitution and therefore a predetermined role in development. Large parts of developing embryos can be removed in early stages and their places taken by remaining cells so that intact organisms are still produced. One is led to conclude that the surroundings of a cell have a great deal of influence on the way it reacts and that there is a great deal of adaptability in the developing system, especially in its early stages.

### Formation of Specialised Tissues.

These points lead us on to the second major question concerning the differences which appear progressively in cells during development so that specialised tissues are ultimately formed. This is essentially a problem in the regulation of gene activity since we know that each cell division produces daughter cells which are genetically identical. It seems likely therefore that instructions are carried on the chromosomes to cope with all requirements of the organism, but that in specialised cells only a small fraction of this full potential is realised. For a long time embryologists have known that egg cytoplasm shows regional differences which make identical nuclei behave differently, and it is thought that regional cytoplasm can in some way control gene activity. Techniques for the transplantation of nuclei in developing frog embryos have been perfected and it has been possible to put a nucleus from an intestinal cell of a tadpole into an enucleate egg. The egg will go on to develop normally even though its nucleus came from a fully specialised cell derived from endoderm. The embryo will form blood and muscle from the mesodermal layer and all the other components of an organism, under the influence of a nucleus which normally would have produced none of these things. One can conclude that all the genes are present, even in the nuclei of specialised cells, but that they have to be placed in a suitable cytoplasmic environment in order to be activated. Similar nuclear transplantation experiments indicate that genes can be " turned off " as well as " turned on " by an appropriate cytoplasmic environment, even though the nuclei come from cells which are so specialised as to stop dividing. The components of cytoplasm which control gene activity are still quite unknown.

A study of cell differentiation and the development of multicellular organisation leads us to the view that, important though the nucleus and its genes are in controlling cell activity, an integrated organism is the result of complex interactions between its constituent cells and between the cytoplasm of those cells and their nuclei.

## THE CLASSIFICATION OF ORGANISMS.

It was clear to the biologists of the 17th cent. that animals and plants could be fitted into different groups or species. John Ray, a leading biologist of the day, defined a species as a group of individuals capable of interbreeding within the group. This criterion, with its corollary that a species is reproductively isolated from organisms outside the group, has survived more or less unchanged to the present day. The early workers also saw that some species were very similar to one another while others were obviously dissimilar. Systems of classification based on the similarities and differences were drawn up so that all organisms could be fitted into an orderly scheme and species could be given names in accordance with the scheme. The most famous collector and classifier was the Swede, Linnaeus, who established his reputation in the 1730s. A very large number of animals and plants are known by the names given to them by Linnaeus.

Systematics, as the study of species and of higher groups of classification is called, acquired a new significance after Darwin and the Theory of Evolution. From the biological point of view the most satisfactory classification became one which reflected the evolution of the organisms classified. Such a system, based on the phylogeny or evolutionary history of a group, is called a natural classification. It is not always easy to produce because ancestral types tend to become extinct and the problem then becomes one of reconstructing a whole branching system when only the ends of the branches are known. A great deal of the work on systematics has, of necessity, to be done on museum specimens which may be fossils or material preserved in some way by the collectors. The biological criterion of reproductive isolation cannot be used to define a species when the only available representatives are in a preserved state. In this case the scientist must resort to an assessment of structural differences in an attempt to decide whether two organisms are of different or the same species. It has often been said, unfairly, that such species are subjective concepts which exist only in the mind of the systematist. In recent years computer techniques have been used to compare large numbers of structural differences between groups of animals or plants. Physiological and biochemical characteristics are also becoming part of the armoury of the 20th cent. systematist. All these techniques have led to the realisation that even the species cannot be regarded as a static point in an evolutionary pattern. Some species die out and others arise as conditions in the environment slowly change. This essentially dynamic view of a continually shifting equilibrium between animals, plants and their environment has given rise to what Huxley has aptly called " The New Systematics " in his book of that title.

When the systematist shifts his attention to the higher levels of classification the problems are just as great as at the species level. Different species having features in common can be grouped together into genera, genera into families, families into orders, orders into classes, and classes into phyla. The dividing lines between different groups at all levels is always difficult and in the final analysis somewhat arbitrary since at these levels we do not have any biological criterion such as exists for the species. The evolutionary status of the larger groups is also poorly defined. Many are now recognised to be polyphyletic, which is to say that there are several main evolutionary lines running right through the group.

## THE ANIMAL KINGDOM.

The animal kingdom is divided into about 24 large groups or phyla though the number varies between different classifications. Ten of the more important phyla are listed below.

1. **Protozoa.**—Microscopic, unicellular forms of great variety. Some may have more than one nucleus and others form colonies. Many are able to swim by waving hair like flagella or cilia.

Others move by putting out extensions of the body or pseudopodia into which the rest of the body then flows. Protozoa are found in the sea, in fresh water and in the soil. Some are parasitic and cause important diseases in animals and man such as sleeping sickness and malaria.

**2. Porifera.**—Sponges. Very primitive multicellular animals whose cells display considerable independence of one another. Largely marine. The body which may become branched and plantlike is supported by a framework of spicules and fibres. The bath sponge is the fibrous skeleton of certain species.

**3. Coelenterates.**—Hydra, jellyfish, sea anemones, corals. Simple animals which have a body only two cells thick surrounding a gut cavity with a single opening to the outside. Largely marine. Many are colonial. Coral reefs are formed from the calcareous skeletons of these animals.

**4. Platyhelminths.**—Flatworms, which are free living in water, and liver flukes and tapeworms, which are parasitic. A third, solid block of cells, the mesoderm, has been developed between the two layers of cells seen in the coelenterates. A simple gut may be developed and the reproductive system is complex especially in the parasitic forms.

**5. Nematodes.**—Roundworms. The body is smooth and pointed at each end. Some of the most numerous and widespread of all animals. Free living in all environments and parasitic in practically all groups of plants and animals. At the same level of complexity as the Platyhelminths.

**6. Annelids.**—Segmented worms such as earthworms, marine worms and leeches. A system of spaces, the body cavity, is developed in the mesoderm so that movements of the main body of the animal and movements of the gut become more or less independent. Digestive, excretory, circulatory, nervous and reproductive systems are all well developed.

**7. Arthropods.**—A very large, diverse and important group of animals which includes crustaceans such as crabs, shrimps and water fleas; myriapods, such as centipedes and millepedes; insects; and arachnids, such as spiders and scorpions. The arthropods show many of the developments seen in annelids and in addition they possess a jointed, hard exoskeleton. Paired appendages grow out from the segments of the body and form antennae, mouth parts, walking legs, etc. The muscles within the skeleton are able to exert a fine control over the movement of the appendage. In order to grow these animals have to shed the exoskeleton periodically.

**8. Molluscs.**—Mussels, clams, oysters, squids, octopods and snails. Complex body form but somewhat different from annelid-arthropod type. Unsegmented body protected by shell which is variously developed in different types. It forms two valves in mussels and oysters, a spiral structure in snails, is reduced and internal in squids and completely lost in octopods.

**9. Echinoderms.**—Starfish, brittle stars, sea cucumbers, sea urchins, and sea lilies. All marine and all radially symmetrical, usually with five radii. Completely unlike the other advanced, major groups. Circulatory, excretory and nervous systems differently developed. Locomotion and feeding by means of hundreds of tube feet projecting from under surface.

**10. Chordates.**—Sea squirts, Amphioxus, fish, amphibia, reptiles, birds and mammals. Segmented animals which at some stage in their life have gill slits leading from pharynx to the outside and a supporting notochord from which, in all chordates except sea squirts and Amphioxus, is developed a vertebral column or backbone. Those animals with a backbone are commonly referred to as vertebrates, all those without as invertebrates. These are obviously names of convenience having no phylogenetic significance since they lump together totally unrelated phyla in one case and align these with a part of a single

phylum in the other. The vertebrates have been investigated more completely than any other animals because of their direct structural and functional relationship with man himself. There are five well defined classes which are listed below. The first vertebrates were the fish and from them came the amphibia. The amphibia gave rise to the reptiles and both birds and mammals evolved from different reptilian stock.

**(a) Fish**

Cold blooded, aquatic animals breathing by means of gills. Sharks, rays and dogfish belong to a group known as the elasmobranchs characterised by a skeleton made of cartilage. Bony fish, or teleosts, include almost all the fresh water fish and the common marine fish such as cod, mackerel, plaice, herring, etc.

**(b) Amphibia**

Cold blooded, more or less terrestrial animals which have to return to water to breed. Five fingered limbs are developed in place of the fins of fish. The egg hatches into a tadpole larva which is aquatic and breathes by gills. At metamorphosis the larva changes into the terrestrial adult which possesses lungs. Some amphibia such as the axolotl may become sexually mature as a larva and so never metamorphose into the adult. The class includes newts, salamanders, frogs and toads.

**(c) Reptiles**

Cold blooded and terrestrial. These animals do not return to water to breed because they have an egg with a relatively impermeable shell containing the food and water requirements of the developing embryo. There is no larval stage. Present day reptiles such as lizards, snakes and crocodiles are all that remains of a tremendous radiation of dinosaur-like creatures which occurred in the Mesozoic (F41).

**(d) Birds**

Warm blooded and adapted for aerial life. The characteristic feathers act both to insulate the body against heat loss and to provide the airfoil surfaces necessary for flight. The birds are an astonishingly uniform group and show less diversity of structure than much lower classification categories (e.g., the teleosts) in other classes. The relationships of the 19,000 or more species of bird are difficult to establish because of this uniformity. It is clear that the flightless forms such as the ostrich are primitive and that the penguins are also in a separate category but the typical modern birds are classified in a large number of rather arbitrary orders. About half of all the known species are placed in one enormous order called the Passeriformes or perching birds.

**(e) Mammals**

Warm blooded animals which have been successful in a tremendous variety of habitats. Mammals are insulated from the environment by the characteristically hairy and waterproofed skin. They are, with two exceptions, viviporous which means that their young are born alive and in typical mammals at an advanced stage of development. In the marsupials of Australia the young are born at an early stage and transferred to a pouch where they develop further. The two exceptions referred to are primitive monotreme mammals known as the duck-billed platypus and spiny ant-eater and these animals lay eggs. The young of mammals are suckled by means of the milk producing mammary glands. The mammals include aquatic whales and dolphins, hoofed ungulates, flesh eating carnivores, rodents and insectivores, the aerial bats, and the tree climbing primates to which man himself belongs.

## THE PHYSIOLOGY OF ANIMALS.

Some basic features of cell organisation have already been dealt with, and in unicellular animals all life processes, such as respiration, movement, growth and reproduction, proceed in the single cell. However in multicellular animals cells are of various types, constituting distinct tissues and organs which perform special functions in the body. Although each cell has its own complex metabolism there must be co-ordination between cells forming special tissues and between the tissues which form the whole organism in order for the body to function efficiently. The study of these functional interrelationships at the tissue and organism level of organisation is the province of the physiologist.

## 1. Movement, Fibrils and Skeletons.

(a) Muscles.—The prime movers in almost all animal movement are large protein molecules in the form of microscopic fibrillar threads. In some way not yet fully understood these fibrils can convert the chemical energy stored in the high energy phosphate bonds of ATP into mechanical energy. In the long, thin cells forming the muscles of animals, it has been discovered that there are two sets of fibrils, one formed of a protein called myosin, the other of actin, arranged in a regular, interdigitating fashion. When the muscle contracts the fibrils slide into one another so that, although the fibrils themselves do not change in length, the muscle as a whole develops tension and shortens. This, the Sliding Filament Theory of Muscle Contraction, was formulated in 1953 by A. F. Huxley, H. E. Huxley and J. Hanson. Fine bridges extend from the myosin fibrils to attach on to the actin and it is here that the conversion of chemical to mechanical energy goes on.

(b) Skeletons.—In order for muscles to work effectively it is necessary for them to operate in some sort of skeletal system. Contraction but not relaxation is an active process; muscles must be arranged in antagonistic pairs so that one muscle can extend the other. A skeleton also provides a system of levers so that the muscles can do work against the environment in an efficient manner. A simple type of skeleton found in fairly primitive animals is the hydrostatic system of coelenterates and worms. Here the animal can be thought of as a fluid filled bag or tube which can change shape but whose volume remains constant. By contraction of circular muscles the tube will become long and thin and conversely contraction of longitudinal muscles makes the tube short and fat. Examination of an earthworm will demonstrate how alternating waves of activity of this type passing from head to tail can move the animal over the ground. The earthworm shows an advance over the simplest systems because the hydrostatic tube is broken up into small units by the segmentation of the body. This makes local responses possible. The next advance to be seen is the development in animals such as arthropods and vertebrates of a firm skeleton to which muscles are directly attached. The skeleton can then be used to support the body and to engage the environment. It seems to matter little whether an endoskeleton (vertebrates) or exoskeleton (arthropods) is developed since in both cases a tremendous radiation of fins for swimming, legs for walking and wings for flying can be seen. However in other respects these two types of skeleton show significant differences. The exoskeleton for example offers more protection than the endoskeleton while apparently setting an upper size limit. All the really big animals have endoskeletons.

(c) Cilia.—Fibrillar systems are also seen in the fine hair-like cilia which project from the surface of some cells. Cilia are important in a number of ways. They are the organelles of movement in many Protozoa, they are used to produce water currents past the bodies of some aquatic animals, and they are of great importance in moving fluid within the body of almost all animals. They beat in a regular fashion, the effective stroke being accomplished with the cilium held straight out from the surface and the recovery stroke with the cilium flexed at the base. Cilia possess the same structure no matter

where they come from. In transverse section eleven fibrils can be seen which run the whole length of the organelle. Two of the fibrils are single and situated centrally while the other nine are double fibrils arranged in a circle around the periphery of the cilium. Work is still going on in this field, but it has been suggested that the peripheral fibrils are contractile and cause the cilium to bend. The function of the central fibrils is unknown.

## 2. Nutrition and the Alimentary Canal.

All animals must take in and digest food materials. As well as water they require complex organic substances, proteins, fats and carbohydrates, together with small amounts of salts and vitamins. These materials are obtained by eating the dead bodies of plants and other animals. They are taken into the alimentary canal and there broken down or digested by enzymes into simpler, soluble amino acids, sugars and fatty acids. These substances are absorbed and distributed to various parts of the body where they are used in cell metabolism (F26, 27) or stored for future use.

(a) The Size of Food—Microphagy and Macrophagy.

Many animals, called macrophagous feeders, take in relatively large masses of food. Some such as frogs and snakes swallow their food whole, but many break it up first. Arthropods have modified appendages arranged round the mouth for cutting, some molluscs have a rasp-like radula with which to scrape off particles, and many mammals break up their food with jaws and teeth. The teeth are usually well adapted to the type of food. Carnivores have large, sharp canines, premolars and molars with which to tear the flesh of the prey, fish eating seals have small peg-like teeth to grip the fish and herbivorous ungulates have flat grinding teeth with which they break up hard plant material.

In contrast, microphagous feeders collect small particles of food material from the environment by continuous filtration. In bivalve molluscs and many marine worms water currents are produced by beating cilia. Food is trapped within the confined space through which the water flows by means of a plentiful supply of sticky mucus in the filtering region. Some crustacea use fine hairs to sieve off food material, often from water currents created by the swimming movements. The most startling of filter feeders is the whalebone whale. As the whale swims forward a stream of water flows in at the front of the mouth and out at the sides via sheets of whalebone which filter off the organisms on which the animal feeds. Though macrophagy seems to favour the attainment of larger size there are exceptions! Another type of particulate feeding is seen in those animals which eat deposits of detritus as do many worms. Finally some animals take in only soluble food materials. These fluid feeders include internal parasites like the tapeworm which absorb substances over the surface of the body, and insects such as the aphid with sucking mouth parts.

(b) Reception and Storage.

The food now passes into the alimentary canal which may be fairly simple, straight tube but more usually becomes long and coiled. The gut tube may be divided into several functional components though the divisions must not be regarded as absolute. The first section is usually involved in the selection, by taste, smell and texture, and the reception of food. A lubricating mucus, together with some digestive enzymes, may be added at this stage from glands such as salivary glands. A large crop for food storage occurs in animals as diverse as insects and birds but in mammals this region remains as a simple tube called the oesophagus.

(c) Mixing, Grinding and Early Digestion.

Waves of contraction in the muscles of the gut move the food onwards. This peristaltic action delivers the food to a region known variously in different animals as the stomach, gizzard or gastric mill. Here the further disintegration and mixing with enzymes is accomplished in many forms simply by contraction of the muscle of the stomach wall. Stones may assist the action in the gizzard of birds for example, and more bizarre modifications are seen in some crustaceans and molluscs. In the former there is a complicated gastric mill with grinding surfaces, teeth and a filter, and in the latter a long rod, called the crystalline style, is rotated by ciliary action against a hard pad on the opposite wall of the stomach. In the ruminating mammals such as sheep and cattle the stomach is divided into four chambers. The function of the first two of these is to mix food with a bacterial culture which exists in this region and to regurgitate the cud for further grinding. The bacteria break down plant cell walls and so benefit the host which cannot deal unaided with the main component known as cellulose. The final two chambers of the ruminant stomach are more typical in function.

A variety of digestive enzymes are released into the stomach region. Carbohydrates, fats and proteins are all broken down to some extent. The main enzyme in the stomach of vertebrate animals is a proteinase which works under acid conditions.

#### (d) Final Digestion and Absorption.

The finely divided food now passes on to the intestine where digestion continues, using enzymes liberated in the preceding region, or under the action of new enzymes released from intestinal glands. In the vertebrates the pancreas secretes a number of enzymes acting on all types of food material, one of the most important being the protein-breaking trypsin. The pancreatic secretion is liberated into the anterior end of the intestine known as the duodenum and operates in an alkaline medium.

Soluble products of the process of digestion are absorbed through the wall of the intestine into the blood stream. Blood vessels carry the food material to the liver where it is put to use in the animal's metabolism or stored as liver glycogen. The surface for absorption is increased by tremendous folding of the intestine interior, seen as finger-like villi in higher vertebrates or as the so called spiral valve in some fish.

#### (e) Processing of Waste Material.

The undigested remains of the food now pass through the most posterior regions of the alimentary canal known simply as the hindgut in many forms or as the colon and rectum in others. A major function of this region, particularly in terrestrial animals, is the removal of water so as to conserve this vital material. In the rectum the faeces are formed and stored before being eliminated from the body.

### 3. Respiration. Gills, Lungs and Tracheae.

The oxidations which consume oxygen and produce carbon dioxide go on at the cellular level as explained earlier (F20). All living cells respire and remain alive only if supplied with oxygen. In a multicellular body, however, many cells are remote from the oxygen of the environment and the need arises for an efficient respiratory system by which oxygen can be taken up and carbon dioxide released. In addition a circulatory system is necessary to transport the oxygen to and from the respiring cells.

#### (a) Simple Gas Exchange Systems.

Animals such as protozoa which because of their size have a high surface area to volume ratio do not need special structures for gas exchange. Diffusion over the whole body surface ensures an adequate supply of oxygen. Much larger animals such as earthworms also find it possible to rely on diffusion alone, partly because their consumption of oxygen is fairly low, and partly because their bodies are permeable all over. For various reasons most animals restrict the permeability of the outer layers of the body and under these conditions special respiratory areas have to be developed.

#### (b) Gas Exchange in Water.

Aquatic animals, except those such as whales breathing at the surface, have to obtain their oxygen from the supplies which are dissolved in the water. This presents several problems because water is a dense medium, there is not a lot of oxygen in solution, and its diffusion rate is low. For these reasons there is a surprising functional uniformity in gill systems and they are very different from lungs. Gills are fine, finger-like processes with a good blood supply which are held out in a water stream. The water current is brought very close to the gill filaments so that the length of diffusion pathway for oxygen is minimal. There is a " counter current " flow of water and blood so that the water containing most oxygen comes into contact with the blood just leaving the gill. This ensures that most of the oxygen can be transferred from water to blood through the thin gill cells. The efficiency of " counter current " systems is well known to the engineer but they were invented by aquatic animals long before they were by man. These features can be seen in the gills of molluscs, crustacea and fish. The pumping devices which maintain the water currents also operate economically. Flow is maintained in crustacea by appendages modified to form beating paddles, in many molluscs by ciliary movement, and in fish by the operation of a double pump in mouth and opercular cavities. In almost all cases there is a continuous current over the gills, the water coming in one way and going out another. Thus the animal avoids reversing the flow with the consequent waste of energy in accelerating and decelerating a large mass of water. Fish, for example, take water in at the mouth and force it out through the gill slits (sharks) or operculum (teleosts).

#### (c) Gas Exchange in Air.

Air breathing animals do not encounter these problems since the medium is less dense, contains a great deal (20%) of oxygen and diffusion rates are high. Lungs are therefore in the form of sacs whose walls are well supplied with blood. The area of the walls may be increased by folding so that the lung becomes spongy and full of minute air spaces called alveoli where the gas exchanges goes on. Only the main airways receive fresh air as the lung expands; oxygen is renewed in the alveoli by diffusion. Ventilation of the lung is accomplished by a tidal flow of air in and out of the same tubular opening known as the trachea. The actual ventilating mechanism varies in different animals. In the amphibia for example air is forced into the lungs when the floor of the mouth is raised with the mouth and nostrils shut. The lungs are emptied by elastic recoil and by lowering the floor of the mouth. Higher vertebrates use a costal pump which changes the volume of chest and lungs by movements of the ribs. This change in volume is further assisted in mammals by the diaphragm, a sheet of muscle which lies beneath the lungs and separates thorax and abdomen. In many animals sound producing organs are associated with the lungs and trachea. The larynx is a vocal organ in frogs, some lizards, and most notably mammals. In birds voice production takes place in the syrinx situated further down at the base of the trachea.

A completely different gas exchanging system is seen in insects. Branching tubes, known as tracheae, run throughout the body and carry oxygen directly to the cells without the intervention of a blood system. The tracheae communicate with the outside world via a series of holes called spiracles. Although the main tubes may be actively ventilated, diffusion in the system accounts for a large part of the movement of oxygen between the outside world and cells.

### 4. Circulation.

In simple, small animals there is no blood system and dissolved oxygen, nutrients and other materials move about the body solely by diffusion, assisted to a certain extent by streaming movements of protoplasm within the cells. In larger animals a transport system is necessary to convey materials about the body and in many, but not all, it is in the form of a blood system. Blood systems are of two types, closed and open.

## (a) Open Systems.

In an open circulatory system blood is pumped from the heart into a few major arteries but these very quickly give way to large tissue spaces or sinuses so that the tissues and organs of the body are directly bathed in blood. Blood flows slowly from the sinuses back to the heart. Both molluscs and arthropods possess an open system. The heart in most arthropods is a long, thin tube in the dorsal part of the body, pumping blood towards the head. Auxiliary muscles may be attached to the heart to pull it out and refill it after the pumping cycle. Mollusc hearts on the other hand are of the chambered type, with thin walled auricles receiving blood from the gills and pumping it to a more muscular ventricle. The ventricle in turn contracts to pump blood to the body. In squids and octopods two auxiliary hearts are seen, receiving blood at low pressure from the body and pumping it through the gills and thence to the main heart.

## (b) Closed Systems.

In a closed system blood is pumped round the body in a branching network of arteries, and comes into contact with tissues and cells via very thin walled vessels called capillaries. Substances diffuse into and out of the blood through capillary walls. From capillaries, blood enters the veins and so returns to the heart. Blood flow in the tubes of a closed system is much more brisk and blood pressures tend to be higher than in an open system. In annelids the closed system is fairly simple with a vessel above the gut in which blood moves forward connecting to one below in which blood moves backwards. The blood is pumped by peristaltic contraction of the vessels and this system must be regarded as the precursor of a localised pump. Simple hearts are in fact seen in some annelids.

In vertebrates a well defined heart is always present, situated ventrally at the level of the forelimbs. In fish there is a single auricle and ventricle and the latter pumps blood directly to the gills. From the gills the blood is collected into a dorsal aorta which then branches to serve the rest of the body. Associated with the development of lungs and loss of gills in the tetrapods, we see a progressive modification of this simple pattern. The most posterior gill vessel is taken over as the lung or pulmonary artery and slowly a completely separate circuit evolves. This involves the division of the single heart into right and left sides, the former pumping blood to the lungs and the latter to the body. In the birds and mammals where the division is complete the system can be seen to be functionally satisfactory. Blood flows along the following route: left auricle to left ventricle, to body, to right auricle, to right ventricle, to lungs, to left auricle, and so on. Thus blood charged with oxygen in the lungs returns to the heart before being pumped to the body. In the lower tetrapods, division of the heart is incomplete and considerable interest centres on the function of these apparently imperfect systems. Amphibian hearts have two auricles but only a single ventricle. In spite of this, evidence is accumulating to show that blood from the lungs and body is not mixed as it passes through the ventricle. A further complication in amphibia is due to the moist skin also being used for gas exchange. Some oxygen is thus contained in blood returning from the body. Reptiles show a further advance in that the ventricle is almost completely divided into two. The system appears still to be functionally inadequate because one of the major arteries to the body leaves from the deoxygenated side along with lung vessels.

## (c) Function of the Blood.

Most of the materials transported by the blood such as nutrients, waste materials and hormones are carried in solution in the plasma. The respiratory gases, oxygen and carbon dioxide, are present in greater quantity than would be possible if they were in simple solution. Carbon dioxide is carried in the form of bicarbonate and oxygen combines with blood pigment. The best known blood pigment is haemoglobin which is found in a variety of animals and gives the red colour to blood. When oxygen is present in high concentration, as it is in the lungs, combination occurs to give oxyhaemoglobin. If the concentration of oxygen is low, as in the tissues, dissociation occurs and oxygen is given off leaving reduced haemoglobin. Carbon monoxide will combine more readily than oxygen with haemoglobin so that in carbon monoxide poisoning the blood cannot transport oxygen. The haemoglobin of vertebrates is contained in high concentration in red blood corpuscles. The amount of haemoglobin and, hence, oxygen carried is greater than if the pigment is not in corpuscles. In mammals the oxygen carrying capacity of blood is thirty times that of a similar quantity of water. Other blood pigments are the blue haemocyanin found in crustacea and molluscs, and the violet haemerythrin found in some worms. Also present in the blood are various types of white corpuscle which are part of the defence mechanism of the body and ingest invading bacteria. Special blood proteins such as fibrinogen, causing clot formation, and antibodies effective against foreign substances occur in the plasma.

## 5. Excretion, Ionic Regulation and Kidney Tubules.

As the chemical reactions included under the term metabolism proceed, so numerous waste products accumulate. The most important of these are compounds containing nitrogen, such as ammonia, urea and uric acid, arising from the use of protein as an energy source. In terrestrial animals they are removed from the blood by the kidney. The basic unit of a kidney is the tubule; in worms these tubules are not concentrated into a solid kidney but occur, a pair in every segment, right down the body. The kidney tubule begins with an end sac, corpuscle or funnel which is closely associated with the body cavity or the blood system. Fluid is filtered from the body cavity or blood into the corpuscle whence it passes to the tubule proper. During passage down the tubule, useful materials are reabsorbed through the tubule cells into the blood whereas unwanted materials remain and pass to the outside world.

Although it is usual to think of kidney function being primarily one of nitrogenous excretion, it is quite common to find that in aquatic animals the kidneys are hardly used for this purpose. In these animals the tubules are primarily concerned in regulating the salt and water levels in the body, nitrogenous wastes being eliminated by diffusion through any permeable surface. In fresh water for example all animals have osmotic problems since the body fluids have a much greater osmotic pressure than the environment. Water tends to enter the body and salts tend to leave. Fresh water animals produce large quantities of very dilute urine, filtering off a lot of blood plasma into the tubules but reabsorbing all wanted materials including the invaluable salts. Fresh water crustacea, molluscs and fish all possess tubules of different morphology which show very similar functional properties.

Different environmental conditions impose different demands on the osmotic and ionic regulating machinery. In very dry conditions, such as in deserts, it is obviously of advantage to reabsorb as much water from the tubule as possible. All animals do this but it is interesting that only birds and mammals have discovered the secret of so concentrating the urine that its salt concentration is higher than that in the blood. This is done by means of a hairpin-like loop in the tubule called the Loop of Henle, another example of a counter current device.

## 6. Co-ordinating Systems.

Overall co-ordination of the animal's body, so that it functions as a whole and reacts appropriately to environmental changes, is largely the province of two systems, one chemical or hormonal, the other nervous. In one respect these are systems for homeostasis, that is for preserving the *status quo*, in spite of considerable environmental fluctuation. Paradoxically they can also initiate change as, for example, one can see in the daily repertoire of complicated behaviour patterns produced by almost any animal.

## (a) Nervous Systems.

### (i) Sensory Information.

Before appropriate reactions can be produced to any stimulus it is necessary to measure its intensity, position, duration and, most important, character. This is done by sense organs which are usually specialised to receive stimuli of a single modality or character. Thus photoreceptors detect light, mechanoreceptors detect mechanical disturbance and chemoreceptors detect specific chemicals. In all cases the sense organs produce a message about the stimulus in the form of nerve impulses (see F30–Cell Membrane) which travel up the nerve from the sense organ to the rest of the nervous system. Change of stimulus intensity is usually signalled as a change in frequency of nerve impulses. The position of the sense organ which is active indicates the position of the stimulus within or without the body. The duration of the repeated discharge of nerve impulses indicates the duration of the stimulus.

### (ii) Simple Networks.

The simplest type of nervous system is the network of interconnected nerve cells (neurones) found in the coelenterates. Branching processes of the nerve cells communicate with neighbouring processes at special regions called synapses (F30). Quite complicated behaviour is possible even with this relatively simple system. If a sea anemone is prodded violently it will close up equally violently, showing that activity has spread throughout the network. If it is tickled gently it will respond with local contractions around the site of stimulation. The movements of feeding and locomotion are very delicately performed at appropriate times.

### (iii) Central Nervous Systems.

In the majority of animals all the nerve cells tend to become collected into a solid mass of tissue referred to as a central nervous system (C.N.S.). Within the mass the nerve cells are interconnected via synapses in the same way as in a nerve net. The connexions with sense organs and muscles are made via long processes called axons. Numbers of axons are usually bound together with connective tissue to form a nerve trunk. In annelids and arthropods the C.N.S. is seen as a ventral cord lying beneath the gut with a swelling or ganglion in each segment of the body. In molluscs, the ganglia are usually more closely grouped around the oesophagus, with the possible provision of a pair of ganglia further back in the viscera. Vertebrates possess a dorsal nerve cord which is uniform in diameter and not ganglionated, though nerves emerge from it in a segmental fashion. The segmental nerves arise in two separate bundles or roots. The dorsal root is made up entirely of sensory nerves conveying information to the C.N.S. The ventral root consists of motor nerves which convey nerve impulses to the muscles of limbs and alimentary canal together with other effector organs such as glands.

### (iv) Reflexes.

A reflex, in which stimulation of a sense organ or sensory nerve results in the almost immediate contraction of a muscle, is the simplest type of C.N.S. activity. Reflexes have been studied in all animals but the best known ones can be seen in frogs, cats, dogs, and sometimes humans. The very simplest is the stretch reflex, in which a stretched muscle is made to contract by activity coming into the C.N.S. from stretch receptors in the muscle. The activity is relayed directly to the motor neurones of the muscle concerned, making them active and thus causing the muscle to contract. This reflex is monosynaptic, i.e. there is only the single synaptic connexion between sensory nerve and motor neurone. The knee jerk in humans is a stretch reflex, the stretch being caused by hitting the muscle tendon as it passes over the knee. Much of the recent work on reflexes has been done on this simple system, notably by Eccles. The flexor reflex, which is seen as the sudden withdrawal of a limb from any painful stimulus, is more complicated. Although the stimuli may vary, the withdrawal response is always accomplished by contraction of flexor muscles which bring the limb in towards the body. The reflex is polysynaptic, i.e. several intermediate neurones connect the sensory nerves through to the motor neurones. More complicated still is the scratch reflex in which an animal is made to scratch its flank in response to an irritation or tickling in that region. This reflex demonstrates some of the more involved properties of the C.N.S. For example a dog will continue to scratch for a time after the tickling has stopped, so that the C.N.S. must continue to be active in the absence of sensory stimulation. This has been called after-discharge.

### (v) The Brain.

The C.N.S. functions in a more complicated way than is suggested by study of the reflexes and most of these higher activities are co-ordinated by the brain. A greater condensation of neurones is seen at the front end of the C.N.S. of all animals because of the larger numbers of sense organs in that region. Brains, which become the dominant part of the C.N.S., can be seen in arthropods, molluscs and vertebrates. The close association with sense organs is illustrated by the vertebrate brain which is divided into three regions: (a) forebrain (nose), (b) midbrain (eye) and (c) hindbrain (ear and taste). However, the brain is much more than a relay station for these stimulus modalities and it receives information from other parts of the body via the spinal cord. All this information is correlated and activity patterns initiated and transmitted to appropriate regions. In lower vertebrates, the roof of the midbrain (the optic tectum) is the important correlation centre and its effectiveness has been well established in studies on instinct and learning in fish. Another region of the brain of importance in all vertebrates is a dorsal upgrowth of the hindbrain called the cerebellum. This is a motor co-ordinating centre which ensures that all activities are performed in a smooth and well balanced way by the muscles and limbs of the body. In reptiles, the forebrain begins to take over the correlation role and in mammals this development reaches its peak in the cerebral cortex. In man the cortex overshadows the rest of the brain and contains some 1000,000,000 neurones. It is easy to see the magnitude of the problem of understanding a system of this complexity. The bee's brain with far, far fewer cells can initiate complicated behaviour such as the hive dances. The possibilities offered by the human cortex seem vastly greater, though they are often realised in ways which give cause for concern. At the moment it would be quite impossible to build a computer with the properties of the human brain. To do this in the future would depend on major advances in computer technology and even greater advances in the knowledge of central nervous systems.

## (b) Hormonal Regulation.

Many aspects of an animal's metabolism are regulated, not by the nervous system, but by specific chemical signals known as hormones which are circulated in the blood stream. Growth, carbohydrate metabolism, salt balance, activity of ovaries and testes and their associated structures, and colour change are all regulated in some way by hormones. The substances are secreted by endocrine glands or ductless glands as they are often called. The important endocrine glands in vertebrates are the thyroid, parathyroid, adrenal, pancreas, the sex glands, and the pituitary.

In the past the endocrine and nervous systems were regarded as exerting an independent control in slightly different functional areas of the body. It is clear now that the integration of the two systems is much greater than was formerly envisaged and in vertebrates is accomplished through the pituitary gland. Secretions of this gland regulate almost all other endocrine glands and the secretions of the pituitary are either produced in the C.N.S. with which it is directly connected or are controlled by C.N.S. secretions. An astonishing, parallel development of other neurosecretory systems, such as those of the pituitary, has been found in a variety of animals and in all types the neurosecretory organ complex is the dominant endocrine gland of the body. In crustacea the so called X organ complex found within the eyestalk, and in insects neurosecretory cells connecting to the corpora cardiaca glands, occupy the functional position of the vertebrate pituitary. They all regulate growth, metabolism and reproductive physiology, either directly or through the mediation of other endocrine glands.

## 7. Animal Behaviour.

In discussing the nervous system we have already dealt with simple mechanisms such as the reflex. Very much more complicated are the instinctive and learned patterns of behaviour which are studied by animal psychologists and ethologists such as Lorenz and Tinbergen.

### (a) Instinct.

Instinct is inborn behaviour which does not have to be learnt and is usually performed in a stereotyped way. For example a gull will retrieve an egg taken out of its nest by shovelling it back with the underside of its beak. The gull will never replace an egg in its nest in any other way, for example by using a wing or leg, and once it has begun a retrieval it will usually continue the movements back to the nest even though the egg is taken away. An instinctive behaviour pattern is triggered off by a particular stimulus or " releaser " which may be a very small part of the total environment. A male stickleback will attack a very crude model with a red belly but will not attack an exact model without it. The red underside appears to be a much more important stimulus than general shape. A particular instinctive pattern cannot always be elicited and the reaction of an animal very largely depends on when the behaviour was last produced. The longer the time that elapses, the easier it is to trigger off the instinctive pattern until eventually it may appear in the absence of an appropriate set of environmental circumstances.

### (b) Learning.

Learning is that behaviour acquired during the organism's lifetime as a result of experience. Evidence of learning has been seen in many animals from worms upwards though, as might be expected, the more complicated types of learning are found only in those animals with elaborate nervous systems. A simple type of learning is seen when an animal, upon repeated exposure to a stimulus, gradually decreases the normal response which is usually one of flight, until eventually the response may disappear completely. This process is called habituation. More complex are the conditioned reflexes, which were first discovered by Pavlov. In these an animal can in some way connect a conditioned stimulus such as a bell, with an unconditioned stimulus such as meat, so that eventually it salivates when the bell is rung. Trial and error learning of the type needed to be successful in running a maze is more complicated still. In this there is a retrospective element because the reward at the end of the maze comes after all the responses. Many animals can run mazes but the white rat has been extensively used in experiments of this nature and there is a huge literature on this one animal. A final category of learning can be called insight learning; in this an animal shows evidence of resolving a new problem without trial and error. This type of learning involves the perception of relations between different parts of the environment and though there may be examples in arthropods and molluscs the clearest evidence of it is seen in the behaviour of birds and mammals.

## 8. Reproduction.

A single animal may live for a short or long time, but eventually it dies, and the continuance of the species is dependent upon reproduction. Some protozoa, such as *Amoeba*, reproduce asexually by the simple division of the cell to produce two new individuals. Asexual reproduction also occurs in some coelenterates, such as jelly-fish, in which there is an alternation of sexual and asexual generations. However, the vast majority of animals only reproduce sexually.

This involves the fusion of two cells, the gametes, produced by adult individuals, and each zygote thus formed develops into an individual of the next generation. The gametes are of two kinds, the large, spherical, immobile ova produced by the female gonad or ovary and the much smaller motile sperms produced by the male gonad or testis. The motility of the sperms helps them to reach the passive ovum, which contains food reserves to support the early development of the embryo.

*Worms.*—The flat worms, particularly parasitic forms, have complicated life cycles, and many are hermaphrodite, *i.e.*, each individual has both male and female organs. Cross-fertilisation usually occurs, the sperms from one worm being introduced into the female duct of another. The round worms are unisexual, and internal fertilisation also occurs. Of the annelids the polychaete worms are unisexual, but the ova and sperms are shed into the sea, where fertilisation takes place. However, *Lumbricus* and the leeches are hermaphrodite, cross-fertilisation takes place and the eggs are laid in cocoons.

*Arthropods.*—Many crustacea are unisexual, though the sedentary barnacles are hermaphrodite. Internal fertilisation may occur, but in the crabs and crayfish pairing takes place and the sperms are deposited on the tail of the female. When the eggs are shed they become fertilised and remain attached to the abdominal appendages. Most crustacea have motile larval stages into which the eggs first develop. In *Daphnia*, the water-flea, parthenogenesis sometimes occurs, *i.e.*, the eggs develop without being fertilised. The sexes are separate in the arachnida and there are usually no larval stages except in the primitive king-crabs. The insects are also unisexual, and the fertilised eggs are laid after copulation. In some, *e.g.*, dragon-flies, an immature nymph similar to the adult is formed, but in flies, beetles, moths, and many others the egg hatches into a larval form. This then develops into a pupa, from which the final adult or imago is produced. In the social ant's nest the workers are sterile females with large heads, reduced eyes, and no wings. The males and queens are winged, and insemination of the latter occurs during the " nuptial " flight.

*Molluscs and Echinoderms.*—Most lamellibranchs are unisexual, although some species of scallops and oysters are hermaphrodite. There are motile larval forms, and in the swan mussel, *Anodonta*, the larvae develop in the mantle cavity of the parent and when liberated become attached to the gills or fins of fish, where they remain parasitic for some time. Some gasteropods are unisexual, but the slugs and snails are hermaphrodite. In the latter cross-fertilisation occurs, the two approaching snails being stimulated to copulate by firing small sharp darts of calcium carbonate into each other. The echinoderms are unisexual, and fertilisation takes place in the sea. The egg first develops into a ciliated larval form.

*Vertebrates.*—The sexes are always separate in the vertebrates. In some cartilaginous fish, *e.g.*, dogfish, internal fertilisation occurs and the eggs are laid in protective sacs. In contrast, the bony fish shed ova and sperms into the water, where fertilisation takes place. Although pairing may take place in the amphibia, fertilisation occurs in water, and there is usually an aquatic larval stage. The reptiles, birds, and mammals are independent of water for fertilisation, as copulation takes place and the sperms from the male are introduced directly into the female. Most reptiles and all birds lay eggs with hard shells. Development of the embryo in marsupial mammals begins in the female uterus, but is continued in a ventral pouch which surrounds the teat of the mammary gland. In the two living species of monotreme mammals the eggs are incubated in a similar pouch. Finally, in the eutherian mammals the embryo develops in the female uterus and is born at an advanced stage.

*Diversity of Sexual Reproduction.*— This brief survey will give some idea of the diversity of sexual reproduction in animals. External fertilisation is very much a matter of chance, and large numbers of gametes are produced which offset the great losses of gametes and embryos that this method involves. Internal fertilisation is more certain, and is also independent of external water—an important factor in land animals. In vertebrates particularly there is increase in the care of the young by the parents, involving the development of characters of behaviour as well as those of structure. Some fish lay their eggs in holes or nests which are protected by the male. Similarly, a few frogs build nests, while others carry the eggs about. The eggs of birds require a constant high temperature for their development, and they are usually incubated by the parents. After hatching the young are fed and guarded by the parents until they can leave the nest and fend for themselves. In the eutherian mammals the embryos are attached to the uterus wall by the placenta, *via* which food materials pass from the mother. The period of gestation is long, and after birth the young are supplied with milk from the mother until they are weaned and can feed themselves. Another feature in mammals is the period of " childhood " during which they play and learn and are protected and fed by their parents. The internal fertilisation, internal development, and care and protection of the young after birth which is so conspicuous in the higher vertebrates results in the reduction of losses dur'ng the vulnerable embryonic and young stages, and in consequence relatively few progeny are produced by a pair of individuals.

## CLASSIFICATION OF PLANTS.

There are various ways in which the main classes of the plant kingdom can be grouped, but a simple, up-to-date arrangement is given in the chart. Vascular plants are often known as the *Tracheophyta* because they all possess woody conducting elements. These are absent in non-vascular plants, and the bacteria, fungi, and algæ are often called *Thallophyta, i.e.,* they have a relatively simple plant body or thallus. Many of the bryophytes also possess a thallus, but in some there is a stem bearing leaves, although a true vascular system is absent. Many thallophytes are aquatic, whereas the tracheophytes are mostly land plants in which the development of woody tissues can be related to the attainment of the land habit as the plant kingdom evolved. However, the chart should not be taken as indicating the evolutionary relationships of the various groups. It is more a convenient arrangement which reflects the relative complexity of the plant body.

Bacteria.—This is a vast group of minute organisms of very simple structure. They are spherical or rod shaped and may exist as separate cells, some species being motile, or as long chains or irregular masses. Their minute size makes the elucidation of their structure very difficult. There is a wall of complex composition, and cytoplasm which contains glycogen and fat. Electron-microscope studies have revealed the presence of structures which appear to consist of nuclear material. Multiplication is by simple division, which may take place very rapidly. For example, *Bacillus subtilis* can divide every 20 minutes, so that in 8 hours a single cell may give rise to 16 millions. Recent research indicates that a sexual process may also occur. Bacteria can survive unfavourable conditions by producing a resistant spore within the cell. They do not possess chlorophyll, though a few are pigmented. Most obtain their food already formed, and are thus either saprophytes or parasites. The saprophytic bacteria occupy a vital position in the living world. They are responsible for most of the decay of dead organic matter, and it has been truly said that without them the surface of the earth would soon become completely covered with the dead bodies of animals and plants. Bacteria also play a vital part in the circulation of nitrogen in nature. By breaking down organic material, ammonia is released and ammonium carbonate is formed in the soil. This is oxidised by other bacteria to form nitrates, which can be absorbed by plants again. Yet other bacteria can "fix" atmospheric nitrogen, and one species, *Rhizobium leguminosum*, occurs in the root nodules of plants such as clover and lupins. These plants are often grown on poor soils and ploughed in, thus improving the fertility of the soil. The parasitic bacteria are also of great importance, as they are responsible for many diseases of plants, animals, and man. (*See* **P7(1)**.)

Fungi.—This is a large group of plants, none of which contain chlorophyll. Hence, like the bacteria, they are either parasites on other living plants and animals or saprophytes which live on dead organic matter. Some are unicellular aquatic plants, but many have a body called a mycelium composed of many branched threads or hyphæ. In the higher fungi (*e.g.,* toadstools, bracket fungi, and puff-balls) complex reproductive structures are formed. All fungi produce spores. In the aquatic species these may be motile, but the majority form minute, airborne spores. The spore output is often very great, and a single mushroom may produce 1,800 million spores. Some fungi are serious diseases of crop plants, such as potato blight and wheat rust.

Algæ.—These are essentially aquatic plants which contain chlorophyll. They range from microscopic forms to the large seaweeds. The green algæ (*Chlorophyceæ*) live mostly in fresh water and may be unicellular, motile or non-motile, or filamentous, though a few found in tropical seas are more complex. The brown algæ (*Phæophyceæ*) are mostly seaweeds which possess a brown pigment, fucoxanthin, which masks the green chlorophyll. They include the bladder-wracks (*Fucus*) and kelps (*Laminaria*) of our coasts and the seaweeds which form dense floating masses over hundreds of square miles of the Sargasso Sea. Other groups are the red algæ (*Rhodophyceæ*), mostly seaweeds of delicate form, the unicellular motile diatoms (*Bacillariophyceæ*), and the blue-green algæ (*Cyanophyceæ*). All algæ possess unicellular reproductive organs. Various types of life cycle occur, the most complex being found in the red algæ.

Bryophyta.—These are the liverworts (*Hepaticæ*) and the mosses (*Musci*). They are all small plants characterised by a sharply defined life-cycle. This consists of an alternation of generations, the " plant " being a gametophyte bearing sex organs. The latter are multicellular, the female archegonium containing a single stationary ovum and the male antheridium producing many motile sperms. The latter are released and swim in water to the archegonium, where fertilisation takes place. After this a sporophyte is formed which is always dependent on the gametophyte and never becomes free living. The sporophyte usually consists of an absorbing foot buried in the tissue of the gametophyte and a stalk or seta bearing at the top a single sporangium. In many mosses this is a complex structure with hygroscopic teeth which move apart only when dry, thus releasing the minute spores only when conditions are suitable for their dissemination in the air. The bryophytes are of little economic importance, and may be looked upon as an evolutionary sideline. However, they occupy suitable " niches " in many plant communities, and species of the bog-moss *Sphagnum* cover large areas where rainfall is high.

**Psilopsida.**—This is a small group of primitive, vascular, spore-bearing plants. Its only living representatives are two rare genera of the Southern Hemisphere. However, a number of fossil forms are known from the Devonian period. The best known are those found in the chert at Rhynie in Scotland. The plants are excellently preserved, and their internal structure can be easily seen. They were probably marsh plants with prostrate and erect leafless stems, although *Asteroxylon* had simple leaves.

**Sphenopsida.**—The only living members of this group are about twenty-five species of horsetails (*Equisetum*). In the Carboniferous period many tree forms existed (e.g., *Calamites*), the remains of which are very common in coal deposits.

**Lycopsida.**—In the Carboniferous period the tree clubmosses were also prominent members of the forests (e.g., *Lepidodendron*). They often reached 100 ft. in height, were branched or unbranched, and had large simple leaves. They also had extensive root systems. The only living members belong to a few genera of small herbaceous clubmosses, such as *Lycopodium* and *Selaginella*. Like the true mosses, they have an alternation of generations, but the elaborate plant with stem, leaves, and roots is the sporophyte, and the gametophyte is very small. In *Lycopodium* only one kind of spore is produced, and the resultant gametophyte is bisexual. *Selaginella* produces numerous small microspores which give rise to the very reduced male gametophytes and motile sperms and the few large megaspores which produce the female gametophytes. The latter are formed within the megaspore wall, which splits to allow the sperms to reach the small archegonia.

**Filicinæ.**—These are the true ferns, which in some classifications are put with the horsetails and clubmosses in the Pteridophyta or vascular cryptogams (i.e., vascular plants without seeds). The ferns have a long fossil history, and remains very similar to the living Royal ferns (*Osmunda*) are known from the Carboniferous. The ferns are widespread and particularly abundant in tropical forests. The majority are herbaceous perennial plants, but a few are aquatic, and there are some tree ferns, which may reach 20 ft. in height. Most ferns possess a stem bearing roots and large leaves or fronds. The plant is the sporophyte and produces numerous spores in sporangia borne on the fronds. Each spore gives rise to a minute green free-living gametophyte known as the prothallus, which bears the archegonia and antheridia. After fertilisation a young sporophyte develops, which at first draws nourishment from the prothallus. Thus, as in the *Bryophyta*, external water is essential for the motile sperms to swim in, and there is a clearly defined alternation of generations, but the sporophyte is a complex independent plant, and the gametophyte is reduced though free-living.

**Gymnospermæ.**—These were the dominant land plants in the Mesozoic era, although fossil remains are found as far back as the Devonian. The living members still form large forests in the North Temperate regions. They are mostly tall evergreen trees with roots, stems, and small leaves. The conifers include the pines (*Pinus*),

larches (*Larix*), and yews (*Taxus*). The cycads are a relic group of tropical plants with thick, unbranched trunks and large fern-like leaves. The maiden-hair tree of Japan (*Ginkgo biloba*) has also had a long geological history. Another interesting Gymnosperm is *Metasequoia*, a genus well known to palæobotanists. In 1948 a few living specimens were found in a remote area of China. Seeds were collected and plants are now being grown in botanical gardens all over the world. The Gymnosperms are characterised by the production of " naked " seeds, which are usually borne on cones. The male pollen grains, which are equivalent to the microspores of *Selaginella*, are carried by wind to the ovule of the female cone. The pollen germinates and the pollen tube carries the male gametes to the reduced archegonia borne on the female prothallus, which, unlike those of the ferns, is retained within the ovule on the parent plant. After fertilisation an embryo is formed, the prothallus becomes the food store or endosperm, and the outer part of the ovule becomes the seed coat. The cycads and *Ginkgo* retain a primitive feature in that the male gametes are motile and they swim to the archegonia from the pollen tube.

**Angiospermæ.**—The apparent sudden rise of the Angiosperms in the Cretaceous period is still the " abominable mystery " it was to Darwin. Various suggestions have been put forward, but nothing definite is known about the origin of the group. The Angiosperms or flowering plants are now the dominant group over most of the land surface of the earth, and at least 250,000 species are known. Apart from the natural vegetation, the majority of our crop and garden plants are Angiosperms. They occur in every type of habitat and range in form from gigantic trees to minute plants, such as the duck-weeds. Some are climbers, others succulents, and a number have reverted to the aquatic habit. Although most possess chlorophyll, a few are partial (e.g., Mistletoe) or complete parasites (e.g., Dodder).

*Flower, Fruit and Seeds.*—The diagnostic feature of the group is the production of seeds, which are completely enclosed within the female part of the flower, the ovary. Basically a flower is a short reproductive shoot which bears several whorls of lateral organs. At the base are several, often green, protective sepals forming the calyx, and above this are the often brightly coloured petals of the corolla. Within this are the stamens of the androecium or male part of the flower. Centrally is the female gynoecium of one or more carpels containing the ovules. The parts of the flower may be free, as in the buttercup, or fused together. In many species the petals are fused (sympetalous), the stamens are borne on the corolla (epipetalous), and the carpels are fused to form a compound gynoecium (syncarpous). The stamens possess anthers, which produce pollen grains. These are shed and carried by insects or wind to the receptive stigmas of the carpels. Each produces a tube which grows down the style to the ovary and enters an ovule. The ovule is a complex structure containing an ovum and a primary endosperm nucleus. Two male nuclei are discharged from the pollen tube, one fuses with the ovum and the other fuses with the primary endosperm nucleus. After this " double fertilisation " an embryo is formed which is embedded in the nutritive endosperm and the outer tissues of the ovule form the seed coat or testa. The ovary of the carpel develops into the fruit containing the seeds. Fruits are of various kinds, being either dehiscent and opening when mature to release the seeds or indehiscent, with a succulent or dry wall. The indehiscent fruits are shed as a whole, and often contain only a single seed. Seeds and fruits show great variation in structure, and often have adaptations assisting dispersal. Some have hairs or wings which aid wind dispersal, whereas others have hooks or are sticky and are transported by animals. Some have flotation devices and may be carried a great distance from the parent plant by water. Seeds vary in size from the microscopic seeds of orchids to those of the double coconut, which may weigh 40 lb. Only about 10% of the weight of a seed is water, and the embryo, although alive, is dormant. The bulk of a seed consists of stored food material, commonly fats or starch and proteins, which may be contained in the endosperm surrounding the embryo, although in some species the endosperm is absorbed during seed development and the food is stored in the one or two swollen seed leaves or cotyledons of the embryo.

*Classification of Flowering Plants.*— John Ray (1627–1705) was the first botanist to recognise the two great divisions of the Angiosperms—the dicotyledons with two seed leaves and the monocotyledons with only one. This primary division of the flowering plants has stood the test of time and is still recognised. Other differences are also found between the two groups. The dicotyledons usually have net-veined leaves and the floral parts are in fours or fives, whereas the monocotyledons usually have leaves with parallel veins and the floral parts are in threes.

## THE GEOLOGICAL RECORD.

The various stages in the history of the earth can be read by the geologists in the strata or layers of rock laid down since the planet began to solidify, and it is in these rocks, too, that the record of life upon earth may be traced.

**No Life Rocks.**—The earliest rocks in the record are known as the Azoic (no life) rocks, because they show no trace of living things, and these layers are of such thickness that they occupy more than half of the whole record. That is to say, for more than half of the earth's history nothing living existed upon any part of the globe. For millions of years the surface of our planet was nothing but bare rock without soil or sand, swept by hot winds exceeding in violence the wildest tornadoes of today, and drenched by torrential downpours of tropical rain, which, as we have seen elsewhere, gradually tore away the surface to form sandy sediments at the bottom of the seas. In such ancient rocks pushed above the surface by later upheavals we can still trace the marks of primeval oceans as they rippled upon the barren shores or of raindrops which left their imprint perhaps 1,500 million years ago.

**Primitive Sea-life.**—As we move upwards through the strata, however, traces of life begin to appear and steadily increase as we come to the more recent levels. The earliest signs appear in what is known as the Early Paleozoic Age (or by some writers as the Proterozoic Age), when we find the fossilised remains of small shellfish, sea-weeds, and trilobites—the latter were creatures

somewhat like the plant-lice of modern times. All these primitive animals and plants lived in the shallow tidal waters of ancient seas; for as yet life had not invaded either the dry land or the deep oceans. It is, of course, clear that these creatures of Early Paleozoic times were not the first living things: they were merely the first creatures capable of leaving fossilised remains, and without doubt must have had more primitive ancestors—amœbic-like forms, jellyfish, bacteria, and so on whose bodies were too soft to leave any traces in the record of the rocks.

**The Age of Fishes.**—Towards the end of the Early Paleozoic Era, in what we now know as the Silurian period, there arose a new form of life: the first backboned animals, primitive fishes somewhat similar to the sharks of today; and in the division of the Upper Paleozoic Era known as the Devonian, they had come to multiply so greatly that this is frequently described as the Age of Fishes.

**First Land Animals and Plants.**—It is about this time, too, that we begin to find traces of animal and plant life upon the dry land. Both animals and plants had acute problems to solve before it became possible for them to live out of water; for both animals and plants had hitherto been supported by the surrounding water and respired by removing oxygen dissolved in the water. In land animals this problem was solved by a long series of adaptations from gills to lungs. Plants were able to invade the land because of the evolution of an impermeable outer cuticle which prevented water loss and also the development of woody tissues which provided support and a water-conducting system for the whole plant body.

**Amphibia and Spore-bearing Trees.**—The first type of vertebrates (backboned animals) to live upon dry land was the group of amphibia in the Carboniferous Age, which is today represented by the newts, frogs, toads, and salamanders. In all these forms the eggs give rise to a tadpole stage with gills which lives for some time entirely in water. Later the gills give place to a primitive form of lung which enables the animal to live upon land. Even so, amphibia are restricted more or less to swampy or marshy land, and without a damp environment they would dry up and shrivel to death. The most abundant forms of plant life in the Carboniferous period were the tree-like horsetails, clubmosses, and ferns, the fossilised tissues of which are found in the coal measures and are burned as household coal. But these plants also, as in the case of the amphibia,

### THE GEOLOGICAL TIME SCALE.

| ERAS | PERIODS | AGE (millions of years) | LIFE |
|---|---|---|---|
| CAENOZOIC | Pleistocene | 1 | Man |
| | Pliocene | | |
| | Miocene | 25 | Birds, Mammals and modern plants |
| | Oligocene | | Molluscs |
| | Eocene | 70 | |
| MESOZOIC | Cretaceous | 135 | Dinosaurs, Cycads; Earliest Birds; |
| | Jurassic | 180 | Ammonites and Sea-urchins |
| | Triassic | 225 | |
| PALAEOZOIC | Permian | 270 | First mammals; Early reptiles |
| | Carboniferous | 350 | Amphibians, tree-ferns, first insects |
| | Devonian | 400 | Fishes, first land plants |
| | Silurian | 440 | Mainly invertebrate animals; no |
| | Ordovician | 500 | life on land. Trilobites and |
| | Cambrian | 600 | graptolites |

PRE-CAMBRIAN (also PROTEROZOIC, ARCHAEOZOIC)    2,000   Life emerges
                                                                       5,000   Age of Earth

could exist only amongst the swamps and marshes, and life, although it had freed itself from the necessity of existence in the waters of the earth, still had to return to the water in order to reproduce itself. The highlands and the deeper waters of the planet were still empty of living things. Although the Carboniferous period had been a period of warmth and abundance, the Paleozoic Era came to an end with a long cycle of dry and bitterly cold ages. Such long-term climatic changes were due, it is now supposed, to such factors as changes in the earth's orbit, the shifting of its axis of rotation, changes in the shape of the land masses, and so on. Long before the Ice Ages of more recent times, there are records in the rocks of alternating periods of warmth and cold as far back as the Azoic and Early Paleozoic Eras. This long cold spell at the close of the Paleozoic era came to an end about 220 million years ago, and was succeeded by a long era of widely spread warm conditions—the Mesozoic Era, the so-called Age of Reptiles.

**The Mesozoic Era.**—The reptiles first appeared in the Permian, but it was during the Mesozoic era that they became the dominant group of animals. The giant reptiles included the stegosaurus, the gigantosaurus, the diplodocus, and many other kinds which were far larger than any land animals living today. Some, for example the diplodocus, were 100 ft. long, although they were vegetarian in habit and were preyed upon by other almost equally huge flesh-eating reptiles. Some species, such as the plesiosaurs and ichthyosaurs, became secondarily aquatic, while the pterodactyl possessed wings with which it could glide and perhaps fly short distances. However, they all differed from the amphibia in that they had hard, dry skins, their lungs were more efficient, fertilisation was internal due to the development of copulatory organs, and they laid eggs with hard, protective shells.

It was also during the Mesozoic era that the warm-blooded birds arose. The birds, like the reptiles, lay eggs with hard shells, and they have several internal features found in the reptiles. The fossil bird Archæopteryx, three specimens of which have been found in Germany, lived in the Jurassic period. Although it was obviously a bird, it retained many reptilian features. Earliest mammals are recognised in rocks of the late Palæozoic but in the Mesozoic considerable evolution of the group took place. The fossil Trituberculata which are also found in the Jurassic, are believed to be related to forms from which both the marsupial and placental mammals arose. Although insects were present as far back as the Carboniferous, it was in the Mesozoic that many of the groups we know today first appeared.

Great changes also took place in the plant cover of the land during this era. The spore-bearing giant horsetails and tree clubmosses declined and were replaced by gymnosperms—trees bearing naked seeds. One large group of these, the cycadeoids, has become extinct, but the conifers and a few of the once abundant cycads still remain. The flowering plants or angiosperms also made their appearance, and towards the end of the Cretaceous their evolution was extremely rapid. In fact, many of the fossil leaves found in rocks of Cretaceous age are indistinguishable from those of some present-day flowering plants.

**A New Era.**—But, perhaps 150 million years later, all this seemingly everlasting warmth and sunshine, the lush tropical life, the giant reptiles who had ruled the world, were wiped out by a new period of bitter cold which only the hardy species could survive. A new Era known as the Caenozoic was beginning, ushered in by a period of upheaval and volcanic activity, following which the map of the world came to resemble more closely the picture we know today. The cold period may have lasted several million years, and the main species to survive it were those which had come into existence towards the end of the Mesozoic Era, the seed-bearing flowering plants, the birds, and the mammals. The once all-powerful reptiles from this time onwards are represented only by the comparatively few and relatively small reptilian species of today: the snakes,

lizards, crocodiles, and alligators. It was at this time, too, that, long after the creation of the mountains of Scotland and Norway (the so-called Caledonian revolution), or even of the Appalachian mountains (the Appalachian revolution), there arose the great masses of the Alps, the Himalayas, the Rocky Mountains, and the Andes. These are the mountain chains of the most recent, the Caenozoic revolution. Initially, as we have seen, the climate of the Caenozoic Era was cold, but the weather grew generally warmer until a new period of abundance was reached, only to be followed at the end of the Pliocene by a period of glacial ages generally known as the First, Second, Third, and Fourth Ice Ages.

## THE EVOLUTION OF ORGANISMS.

**Introduction.**—It is commonly thought that the great 19th cent. naturalist Charles Darwin was the first person to suggest that life had continually evolved. However, the idea that species of living organisms could change over long periods of time was considered by some Greek writers and, much later, by the Frenchmen Buffon and Lamarck at the end of the 18th cent. Further, the work of the 18th cent. geologists such as James Hutton and William Smith provided a basis without which Darwin's contribution would have been impossible. Hutton showed that the earth's surface had undergone prolonged upheavals and volcanic eruptions with consequent changes in sea level. This implied that the earth was much older than had previously been supposed. Smith developed a method of dating the geological strata by means of the fossils found in them and demonstrated that widely different types of animals and plants existed at different periods of the earth's history. As described in the previous section a general picture is presented of the evolution of organisms from the simple to the complex and from the aquatic to the terrestrial environment. These discoveries were in conflict with the Biblical account in the book of Genesis and, although various attempts were made to explain them away or discredit them, it became abundantly clear that through millions of years life has been continually changing, with new species constantly arising and many dying out. Before considering Darwin's major contribution to the theory of evolution it will be appropriate to outline briefly the various lines of evidence which indicate that, in fact, evolution has taken place.

### The Evidence for Evolution.—

1. *The Geological Record.*—It has already been pointed out that successively younger rocks contain fossil remains of different and relatively more complex organisms. The spore-bearing plants preceded the gymnosperms and the angiosperms arose much later. Similarly in the vertebrate series the fish appeared before the amphibia which were followed by the reptiles and later by the air breathing, warm-blooded birds and mammals. On a more restricted level the rocks provide even greater support for the occurrence of evolution. For example, the evolution of the horse has been worked out in great detail from the small Eohippus which was about a foot high and had four digits on the forefeet and three on the hind feet to the large one-toed animal living today. However, such complete series are rare and the geological record is very incomplete. There are a number of gaps, particularly between the major groups of organisms. No satisfactory fossil evidence is known of the ancestors of the angiosperms (F40) and although some may be discovered it could be that they did not grow in conditions which favoured their preservation as fossils. On the other hand, Archæopteryx provides an indisputable link between the reptiles and the birds.

Another important point should also be made about the geological record. Although we talk about the age of fishes, the age of reptiles and so on it must be emphasised that these are the periods during which particular groups were abundant or even dominant. Each group probably originated many millions of years before it became widespread. Further, some groups, such as the giant reptiles and the seed-ferns, died out completely whereas others, the fishes and true ferns for example, are still common today. However, even in the latter groups there is evidence that they have continued to evolve so that many fishes and ferns that exist today are very different from those of the Devonian and Carboniferous periods (F41). On the other hand, the geological record also shows that some species, for example the Maiden-hair tree, have remained unaltered for many millions of years.

2. *Geographical Distribution.*—Nearly all the marsupials or pouched mammals are found in the Australian continent which was cut off from the mainland about 60 million years ago. All the fossil evidence indicates that at that time the eutherian or placental mammals did not yet exist. The marsupials are the only naturally occurring mammals in Australia (F33(2)) but since the isolation of the continent the group has given rise to a large number of species very similar in appearance to those which evolved elsewhere in the world among the eutherian mammals. There are marsupials which look like wolves, dogs, cats and squirrels; yet they have no close biological relationships to these animals. Further, some marsupials such as the kangaroos have evolved which are unlike any other creatures in the rest of the world. Quite clearly the isolation of Australia so long ago has resulted in the evolution of these distinct types. A similar small-scale effect of isolation was studied by Darwin in the Galapagos islands where each has its own distinct flora and fauna which differ also from those of the S. American mainland.

3. *Anatomy.*—The comparative study of the development and mature structure of the mammalian body provides much evidence that all the species have evolved from a single ancestral stock. Although the arm of an ape, the leg of a dog, the flipper of a whale and the wing of a bat appear very different externally they are all built on the same skeletal plan. It would be difficult to explain such similarities unless they had all evolved from a common type. There is also evidence that the early development of an animal recapitulates its biological history to a certain extent. For example, the gill slits found in fish are formed during the early stages in the development of a mammal although later they disappear. Finally, apparently useless vestigial structures sometimes occur which would be inexplicable unless regarded in the light of an evolutionary history. In man a small appendix and vestiges of a third eyelid occur but these are functionless although in other animals such structures are well developed and functional, *e.g.*, the appendix in the rabbit.

4. *Human Selection.*—During his brief history on earth modern man has continually selected and bred animals and plants for his own use. We have only to look at the various breeds of dogs which have been developed from a single wild type to see that under certain circumstances great structural divergence can occur in a species even in a relatively short time.

**The Darwinian Theory of Evolution.**—Darwin amassed a great deal of information such as that outlined above which convinced him that evolution of life had taken place over millions of years. His was the first real attempt to collect all the evidence scientifically and no other satisfactory alternative explanation of all the facts he presented has been proposed. Perhaps even more important was his attempt to explain *how* evolution had actually occurred. He published his theory after many years of work in his book *The Origin of Species by Means of Natural Selection* in 1859. Some of his ideas have since been modified owing to our increased knowledge of genetics but they are so important that it is worth while recounting the main points of his theory.

1. *The Struggle for Existence.*—It is clear that in nature there is a severe struggle for existence in all animals and plants. Over a period of time the number of individuals of a species in a given community does not vary greatly. This implies that the number of progeny which survive to become mature breeding individuals more or less replaces the number of mature ones that die. Generally speaking the reproductive output of a species is much greater than this. For example, a single large foxglove plant may produce half a million seeds each one of which is potentially capable of giving rise to a new individual. Obviously nearly all the progeny die before reaching maturity and the chance of any single one surviving is very remote.

2. *Variation.*—The individuals of any generation of human beings obviously differ from one another and such differences are found in other organisms. No two animals of the same species (except perhaps for identical twins) are exactly alike and when a large number of individuals are examined it is clear that they vary considerably in structure, colour, activity and so on. Darwin also pointed out that generally these variations were passed on from one generation to the next, for example, the children of tall parents tend to grow tall.

3. *Survival of the Fittest.*—If there is an intense struggle for existence in their natural environment among individuals of a species having different characteristics, those which are best "fitted" to a given set of conditions are most likely to survive to maturity. These will reproduce and the features which enabled them to survive will be passed on to their offspring. This process is liable to continue and a species will become better adapted to its environment.

4. *Natural Selection.*—Over a long period of time the environment of a given species is never stable but will change in various ways. As it does so the characters which best fit the individuals to the changed environment will be selected (not consciously of course) and the species will change. The environment may change only in part of the range of the species and thus lead to divergence and the production of a new species alongside the old one.

**Darwin and Lamarck.**—Darwin pictured evolution as a slow continuous process with natural selection operating on the small inheritable variations found between the individuals of a species which are undergoing intense competition. This neglects the important effect of the environment on the growth and structure of the individual. It is obvious that external conditions will affect the development of an organism, for example the effect of various soil conditions on the growth of a plant or the amount of food material available to an animal. Lamarck maintained that the characters acquired by an individual owing to the effect of its environment could be passed on to its offspring. Undoubtedly characters are acquired by the individual during its growth but in spite of many attempts to prove otherwise no experiments have been done which prove conclusively that these are inherited by the offspring. Thus Lamarck's theory that evolution has occurred by the inheritance of acquired characters is not generally acceptable today.

**Mutation Theory.**—The data accumulated by Darwin showed that the variations between individuals of a species are small and graded into one another. If a particular character in a group of individuals is measured it is found that it varies symmetrically about a mean or average, with most values clustered about the mean and with few extreme ones. Darwin himself was worried about this fact because, although selection over a long period of time might shift the position of the mean, he did not see how it could bring about the discontinuity necessary for the establishment of a distinct new species. De Vries in his *Mutation Theory* published in 1901 put forward the view that evolution depends, not on the accumulation of continuous minute variations, but primarily upon large discontinuous variations or mutations. The importance of such spontaneous "sports" was considered by Darwin but he rejected the idea because when they appear they are usually "monstrous". Such individuals are less "fitted" to their environment and therefore they will not survive to reproduce and give rise to a new species. That mutations are important factors in evolution is undoubtedly true but modern work has shown that the whole problem is far more complex than either Darwin or De Vries supposed.

**Mendelism.**—It is remarkable that in spite of carrying out many careful experiments on inheritance in plants Darwin did not discover the simple laws which are the basis of modern genetics. Mendel investigated inheritance in the garden pea

The importance of Mendel's work in relation to evolution is that it showed that there was no blending of the characters in the offspring. Mutations can be hidden as recessive characters in a population and are not diluted or lost. Although they may not be of importance when they first appear they may be so if the selection pressure changes and they become of survival value. Thus specific characters may change or diverge and evolution will take place. His investigations also

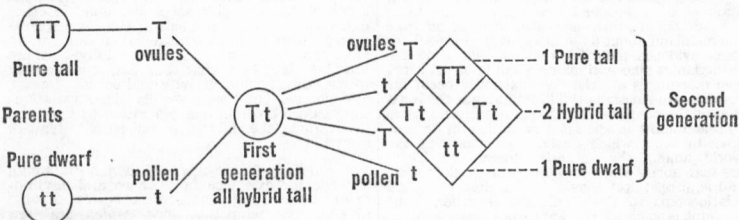

and published his results in 1865, i.e., at the time that Darwin's work was being widely discussed. However, Mendel's important discoveries were not generally known until 1900. When he crossed a pure breeding tall plant with a pure breeding dwarf plant all the progeny were tall. When these plants were self-pollinated the next generation consisted of approximately one quarter dwarf plants and three quarters tall. From this and similar experiments Mendel deduced that the "factors" passed from parents to offspring were paired, only one of the pair came from each parent and that one could be dominant over the other. When he dealt with two pairs of characters, e.g., tall or dwarf plants and round or wrinkled seeds, he found that they segregated and recombined independently and in predictable ratios.

showed that recombination of factors could give rise to plants with new characteristics. By crossing a pure bred tall plant having round seeds with a dwarf plant having wrinkled seeds he produced in the second generation some tall plants with wrinkled seeds and dwarf plants with round seeds. When a large number of characters are involved it is obvious that considerable variation and recombination occurs upon which natural selection can work.

Mendel was fortunate in his choice of experimental material with its easily recognisable contrasting characters. It is now known that his "factors" are the genes carried by the chromosomes in the nucleus of the cell. At the present time the biochemical basis of heredity is being vigorously investigated. *See* F31.

# V. SCIENCES OF MAN

A biologist's interest in classification might supplement the account of the animal kingdom in Part IV with the following further description of Man:

"Man is a member of the order of Primates which is sub-divided into two sub-orders: Prosimii and Anthropoidea. The Prosimii include the lemurs and the Tarsier; the Anthropoidea include the monkeys, the apes and man. The anthropoid apes form a family called Pongidae and the extinct and living forms of man together constitute the family Hominidae. Although these two families constitute one superfamily, the Hominoidea, there are many differences between them in both body form and function. Apes progress by over-arm swinging in trees and they are usually quadrupedal on the ground; hominids habitually stand and walk upright."

But human beings have many remarkable attributes and it is not surprising therefore that besides biologists, scientists of many kinds contribute to the study of man. Even anthropology, which literally means "the study of man" is not a single well-defined science but has become diversified into a number of parts which have complicated connections with biology, archaeology, sociology, history, psychology, and many other studies. Physical anthropology, with which we shall deal first, is much concerned with the description of those physical characteristics of man which distinguish race from race, and man from animals. Such a study is important if we are to learn how man evolved. To describe physical characteristics quantitatively, suitable measurements must be made, i.e., we must have techniques of anthropometry (man measurement). Physical measurement of the body cannot however exhaust the study of man, and therefore we shall also look at some of the current ideas of social anthropology which is one of a number of disciplines concerned

with the study of man in society. There we shall stop, not, of course, because there are no further aspects to consider. Psychology, with its many different approaches, is the study of mind, and something of the nature of mind and mental development will be found in Section Q.

### PHYSICAL ANTHROPOLOGY

#### The Earliest Men and Their Dates

Fossil Primates.

Some fossil forms are known both in the Eocene and the Oligocene periods (F41). However, during the Miocene period in East Africa many varieties of Primates appeared, probably as a direct result of major climatic fluctuations in the area. These Miocene primates possessed attributes later to be more fully developed either among the Pongids or among the Hominids. Thus Proconsul, a common form in Miocene East Africa, was less specialised in locomotion and in cranial detail than are the apes of today. During the Miocene some of these East African primates left the trees and learned to walk upright, gradually adapting their pelvic and leg bones to an erect posture. By freeing the arms and hand this opened the way to tool-using and eventually to tool-making also.

#### Man's Distinctive Attributes.

Man has been variously defined as a large-brained hominid, as a bipedal hominid and also as a maker of tools to a set and regular pattern. These criteria imply both morphological and functional attributes. In tracing man's ancestry we do not find all of these characteristics appearing simultaneously. The further back in time we proceed, the fewer of these attributes are recognisable. Bipedalism is an early feature; the other attributes were to follow later.

### The Australopithecinae.

These creatures probably lived during the Pliocene and Lower Pleistocene periods. For many years controversy raged as to whether they were to be classified as Pongid or as Hominid. Many dental features, for example, indicate their hominid affinities and they were, moreover, bipedal. However, their brains were very small and fall within the Pongid range. They might well have used tools, a widespread propensity among many Primates, but it is far less likely that the South African forms were capable of making tools in the manner described. It may well be that the use of bones, teeth and wood as tools might long have predated the use of more durable stone artifacts. On balance, however, the Australopithecinae might be described as the earliest Hominids.

Many fossil remains of the Australopithecinae have been found and they have been given a variety of names. It appears, however, that in South Africa a single genus existed probably with two species. Of these, one is small, generalised and lightly built, and is termed *Australopithecus* or *A. africanus*, while the other is larger, more specialised and robust, and is termed *Paranthropus* or *A. robustus*. It is improbable that either of these South African forms constituted a major source of the later, more advanced hominids.

In the Lower Pleistocene Bed I in the Olduvai Gorge, Tanzania, a fossil rather similar to the more rugged Australopithecines of South Africa was found. *Zinjanthropus boisei*, as it was named, is now frequently referred to as *Australopithecus boisei*. Estimated to be some 1,700,000 years old, this creature was perhaps the earliest tool-maker, but it is likely that *Homo habilis*, a more advanced hominid contemporaneously existing at Olduvai, was the maker of the numerous Oldowan stone tools found in Bed I. Oldowan tools, widely distributed in Africa, represent the first tool-making tradition, and with this culture the Palaeolithic Age begins.

### Homo erectus.

Remains are very widespread in the Old World and they represent the next major stage in the evolution of the Hominids. Most finds are dated to the Middle Pleistocene period. The brain is now much larger than in the Australopithecines, though smaller than in modern man. The skull bones are very thick and the skull exhibits massive bony ridges. There is neither a chin nor a forehead present. The first finds were made in Middle Pleistocene deposits in Java by Dr. E. Dubois. This creature, *Pithecanthropus erectus* (*Homo erectus javanensis*) was indisputably erect and bipedal in locomotion. Dr. G. H. R. von Koenigswald discovered more specimens of the same general type in Java and he also found the remains of a Lower Pleistocene more rugged form which he named *P. robustus*. A massive jaw which he found—*Meganthropus palaeojavanicus*—probably represents the Australopithecine stage in Java and has also been named *Paranthropus* (*Australopithecus*) *palaeojavanicus*.

In 1927 and 1929 the first remains of Pekin Man (*Sinanthropus pekinensis*; *Homo erectus pekinensis*) were found in Chou Kou Tien cave near Pekin. These remains were Middle Pleistocene contemporaries of Java Man whom they closely resembled.

Until certain finds were made in East Africa in the nineteen fifties and sixties, particularly at Olduvai, *Homo erectus* remains were only known from the Far East. It had been widely accepted that man originated in Asia and not in Africa, an interpretation that is little supported today. A skull found in the Middle Pleistocene Bed II at Olduvai, as well as certain mandibles found at Ternifine, Algeria, are also without doubt representatives of *Homo erectus*. The Ternifine (*Atlanthropus*) jaws as well as very similar mandibles found at Sidi Abderrahman, near Casablanca, Morocco, are accompanied by hand axes of the so-called Acheulean culture. The Olduvai *Homo erectus* skull dated at approximately 490,000 years was also associated with hand axes.

European fossil remains approximately contemporaneous with Pekin Man include the massive Mauer Jaw found without associated artifacts in 1907 near Heidelberg in Germany. In 1964 and 1965 equally ancient remains were found at Vertezöllös, Hungary, and these are also of the *Homo erectus* type.

### Absolute and Relative Dating.

In tracing the emergence of man it is desirable that the various finds should be dated as accurately as possible, both in relative terms and also, if possible, in absolute terms. Various methods have been devised and the results are often expressed by giving the date as so many years B.P. The initials B.P. stand for " before present " and the present conventionally means the year A.D. 1950.

The potassium-argon method, depending on the rate of radioactive decay of potassium to argon is useful for dating material from 230,000 to 26 million years old. For more recent finds up to about 50,000 years old, the Carbon-14 method is appropriate. Dating with this method depends on establishing the ratio of Carbon-14 (the radioactive isotope of Carbon) to Carbon-12—ordinary Carbon. One method of relative dating is called the fluorine method depending as it does on the fact that fossil bones contain fluorine in proportion to their antiquity. Relative dating may also be deduced from the depths at which fossil bones are found in undisturbed strata. Relative dating is also possible from the known sequence of glacial events during the Pleistocene. During this period much of northern Eurasia witnessed four major glacial advances, the so-called Ice ages, Günz, Mindel, Riss, and Würm. Milder periods or Interglacials separated the Ice Ages and geological deposits of the glacial and interglacial periods, easily characterised by the remains of the distinctive flora and fauna which they contain, provide a framework for dating fossil man. Thus two human skulls from the second, Mindel–Riss Interglacial (130–180,000 B.P.) are known in Europe, those of Steinheim, Germany, and Swanscombe, Kent. The latter was associated with the Mid-Acheulean hand-axe culture. No artifacts were found with Steinheim man. The Steinheim cranium is much more complete than the Swanscombe remains and in size it approximates to modern man. Some of its morphological features are similar to modern man; others to Neanderthal man. Steinheim could in fact be a generalised ancestor for both these major human types. The Swanscombe bones are sometimes similarly interpreted though they have on occasion been classed as an early form of *Homo sapiens*, pre-dating the Neanderthalians.

### Neanderthal Man.

Neanderthaloids are found in Upper Pleistocene times during the early part of the Würm glaciation, particularly in Europe, West and Central Asia, and North Africa. Early discoveries included those in the Neander valley in Germany, Gibraltar, Spy (Belgium), and Krapina (Jugoslavia). Subsequently many other finds were made including, for example, La Chapelle (France), Teshik-Tash (Uzbekistan) Hauna Fteah (Cyrenaica), and Rabat (Morocco).

Early proto-Neanderthalers, such as Steinheim, were followed by the " classic " Neanderthal forms, conventionalised as of brutish appearance, with massive eyebrow ridges, sloping foreheads, long, large, crania and receding chins. The cave of Tabun on Mt. Carmel, Israel, yielded remains of these " classic " forms, while the nearby Skhull cave contained remains of men much more similar to those of today. The remains may represent variation normal within a group or else may indicate that the Neanderthalers interbred with people of modern type, thus producing the Skhull hybrids. Rhodesian Man, found in 1921, in Broken Hill, Zambia, is clearly neither a Neanderthaler nor a modern type of man. The skull was for long thought to be unique, if not highly aberrant. However, in 1951 a similar skull was found at Saldanha Bay in the Cape Province of South Africa. These are early Upper Pleistocene remains, approximately 40,000 years B.P. Solo Man, in Java, is a not altogether dissimilar and may be the direct descendant of *Homo erectus* in South East Asia. Both Rhodesian and Solo Man are sometimes regarded as variants of the basic Neanderthal type.

## Homo Sapiens.

*Homo sapiens* emerged during the fourth, Würm, glaciation, a process precisely dated by the radiocarbon technique among others. Neanderthal Man seems to have been replaced by *Homo sapiens*, of completely modern appearance, certainly by some 30,000 years B.P.

Neanderthal Man's stone tools were made on flakes, and in Europe constituted the so-called Mousterian industry. Post-Neanderthal men were technically more advanced, their stone tools including small knife blades and engraving tools specialised for different purposes. This is the typical Upper Palaeolithic tool assemblage, of the Aurignacian, Solutrean and Magdalenian, and other tool-making cultures. It was during this Upper Palaeolithic period that man, though still everywhere a hunter and gatherer of foodstuffs, first showed artistic tendencies.

Combe Capelle in southern Central France yielded the earliest known skull (approximately 34,000 years B.P.) of completely modern type in western Eurasia and Africa. The Cromagnon people were somewhat later (20–30,000 years B.P.). Physically, the Cromagnon people were tall, with long heads, very large brain cases and short, broad faces. Approximately similar humans have been found elsewhere, as in the Upper Cave at Chou Kou Tien, and a skull from the Niah Cave in Sarawak dated at about 40,000 years B.P. is the earliest known representative of *Homo sapiens* in Asia. In Java, the descendants of Solo Man may well be the Wadjak people of about 10,000 years B.P. These are similar to the Australian Aborigines and they may be roughly contemporary with a skull from Keilor near Melbourne which indicates that Australia was populated in late Pleistocene or early post-Pleistocene times. Again in Upper Pleistocene Southern Africa there were people with very large brain cases and with features rather like the present-day Bushmen and Hottentots. The Boskop skull is of this type. No skeletons showing characteristic Negro features have been found in Africa before post-Pleistocene times. This suggests a late evolutionary emergence for the Negroes. The Americas were peopled by immigrants from North East Asia some 15–20,000 years ago, and subsequently. Some of the early groups of immigrants have been described as " Archaic White ", as have the Ainu of Northern Japan, but it is more generally accepted that successive waves of Mongoloids moved into the Americas from Asia, the Eskimo being the last group to arrive.

Even today the total number of known fossil human remains is small for the long time span of human evolution and it is very difficult if not impossible as yet to trace the precise ancestry of each of the races of man.

## The Races of Man.

The species *Homo sapiens* to which all living men belong is differentiated into local variant populations which are interfertile and not always sharply distinguished from one another. Many attempts have been made to classify mankind into races, usually on the basis of readily visible external features such as head shape, stature, and skin colour. Such formal classifications express real features of human variation but in somewhat artificial not misleading manner, since the impression is created that the species is naturally partitioned into discrete, discontinuous groups, whereas changes from one region to another are often gradual rather than abrupt transitions. Again all human groups are variable within themselves and populations frequently overlap considerably in quantitative characters, in which case, the distinction between them is best expressed in statistical terms as differences in average values. Discrete variables such as blood groups are usually found in most populations but with different frequencies of occurrence.

A race is best considered as a Mendelian population, that is, as a reproductive community of individuals who share in a common gene pool. Again a race has been defined as a group of people who have the majority of their physical attributes in common. It is manifestly improper to refer to religious or linguistic groupings as races since cultural attributes obviously vary quite independently of the physical features used in race definition.

Three types of Mendelian populations or races are sometimes distinguished: (1) Geographical, (2) Local and (3) Microgeographical or Microraces.

### (1) *Geographical Race.*

This is a collection of Mendelian populations such as occupy whole continents or large islands and separated by major barriers such as mountains and deserts. The Australian Aborigines and the African Negroes provide examples.

### (2) *Local Races.*

These are sub-populations within the Geographical Races, frequently corresponding with distinct or isolated breeding populations. They are adapted to local environmental pressures and are maintained by social and physical barriers which prevent gene flow between them. Examples include the tribes within the Amerindian Geographical Race, the Basques, Ainu and Gypsies.

### (3) *Micro-races.*

These are the numerous distinct populations which are not clearly bounded breeding populations or isolates other than in a statistical sense. Their existence is demonstrated by variations in the frequencies of genes within a densely populated country. Many of man's physical attributes, including hair and skin pigmentation, head shape, etc. vary from group to group and since these traits have a genetic component, then they also are characteristic of micro-races.

## Anthropometry.

This constitutes a system of techniques for the measurement of the skeleton and of the body. From the early 19th cent. onwards anthropometry was an important means of giving quantitative expression to the variation in physical traits among human beings. In fact until fairly recently, anthropometry has been the mainstay of physical anthropology, preoccupied as it was with the problems of evolutionary descent. The measurement of the skeleton was stressed since skeletal remains constitute the most direct evidence of earlier populations. The shape of the living body and of the skeleton can precisely be expressed metrically, but it is usual to use relatively few measurements, and these normally represent the major features, including, for example, stature, shoulder width, head length, and head breadth. The latter two were especially favoured and the cephalic index was obtained by expressing the breadth as a percentage of the length. Long heads, with low cephalic indices (below 75) were termed dolichocephalic, while round heads, with high indices (above 81) were termed brachycephalic.

Anthropometric features are known to vary widely among the world's populations. Thus while the Nilotes of the Sudan have an average stature of 1·78 m the African pygmies average 1·36 m. Dolichocephalic heads are prevalent among Australian Aborigines while brachycephaly is extremely prevalent among the Mongoloid peoples of Asia.

Anthropometric characteristics such as these are not immutable and it has been shown in studies in the United States, Hawaii, and elsewhere that immigrants' offspring rapidly develop bodily changes when compared with their parents or when compared with groups in their homelands. It is impossible to say whether the races of man are becoming more or less heterogeneous as a result of such processes.

## Pigmentation.

Hair, skin, and eye colour were traditionally described either in subjective terms or else by reference to matching standards. Both procedures presented serious limitations in reliability and in comparability of results. Recent years have witnessed the use of much more satisfactory objective procedures, involving spectrophotometers in hair and skin colour studies. These instruments record the percentage of light of a number of known specified wavelengths reflected from a surface relative to the reflectance from a pure white surface. In general the darker the specimen, say of hair, the lower the percentage of light which it reflects. Using such instruments precise and reliable quantitative estimations of hair and skin colour are possible; the genetic basis of the traits may be clarified and comprehended and the selective advantages of skin and hair colour may be examined quantitatively. Dark skins confer advantages in hot, sunny areas since they protect the body against the harmful effects of ultraviolet radiation minimising the incidence of skin cancer for example. Light skins are advantageous in cloudy areas with low insolation since they facilitate the body's synthesis of Vitamin D, thus reducing the incidence of rickets. The correlation between dark pigmentation and high levels of solar radiation is high, but it is impossible to state how much of the geographical distribution of skin colour mirrors the spread of dark- and light-skinned peoples from one or two sources and how much of the patterning is due to independent adaptations in many human groups in the past.

Physiometric Observations.

These cover a range of phenomena including handedness, the ability to taste phenylthiocarbamide (P.T.C.), colour-blindness, and fingerprints. The genetic basis for many of these attributes are well known. Thus red-green colour blindness is a sex-linked character, males being far more frequently affected than females. Within Britain percentages of colour-blind males range from 5·4 in N.E. Scotland to 9·5 in S.W. European populations. Non-European populations generally exhibit much lower frequencies.

The tasting of P.T.C. is controlled by two genes, T and t, the former being dominant. TT and Tt individuals normally experience a bitter taste sensation when they sip P.T.C. solutions; tt individuals either cannot taste the substance at all or else only in very strong concentrations. The tt individuals are termed Non-tasters; TT and Tt individuals are termed Tasters. High frequencies of Non-tasters (exceeding 38 per cent) occur in parts of Wales and in Orkney, while low values (approximately 24 per cent) occur in North Lancashire and Northumberland. A clue to the selective significance of this trait is provided by the excess of Non-tasters among individuals with nodular goitres (thyroid abnormalities). Non-European populations usually have lower percentages of Non-tasters than the British figures quoted.

Attributes of the Blood.

1. *Blood Groups.*

Many blood group systems (*see* Index to Section P) are known today in addition to the ABO system which was the first discovered and which matters so much in blood transfusion. The mode of inheritance of the numerous blood-group substances is known. Blood grouping is relatively simple depending as it does on reactions between antigens on the red blood cells [and specified antibodies derived from the blood serum.

The ABO system basically involves three genes, A, B, and O. Every individual inherits two of these genes from parents and so the genotype (genetic constitution) must be one of the following: AA, AO, BB, BO, AB, or OO. O is recessive to both A and B and thus there are four possible phenotypes (genetic constitutions detectable by blood grouping): A, B, AB, and O.

The ABO genes constitute a polymorphic system, that is several genes occur with frequencies such that the least frequent of them occurs with a frequency exceeding that due to mutation alone. Certain selective advantages and disadvantages of the ABO genes in human populations are known. Thus stomach cancers are more frequent among individuals of group A than they are in the population at large. Again, duodenal ulcers are almost 40 per cent more common among persons of blood group O than in individuals of the other ABO groups.

Both on a global and on a local scale, the ABO genes display marked racial variation. Within Britain A varies from 31 per cent to 53 per cent, increasing in frequency from North to South; O

varies from 38–54 per cent, increasing in frequency from South to North. B shows less variation, though it is most prevalent in the Celtic areas. The regional fluctuations are not random but systematic and statistically highly significant despite the enormous migrations within Britain during the last few hundred years, which might well have masked or minimised the underlying variability.

Globally the ABO variation is also striking. Thus the percentage of the blood group B exceeds 30 among the Mongoloids of Central and East Asia but the B gene is virtually absent in the Australian Aborigines, the American Indians and in the Basques. Many Amerindian tribes are 100 per cent O; some others have very high A frequencies.

In the Rhesus blood group system all humans are either Rh+ (DD or Dd) or Rh− (dd) (*see* Index to Section P). All the Amerindians and Australian Aborigines, and most of the East Asians are Rh+. Rh− individuals are more frequent in western Asia, in parts of Africa and especially in north west Europe where the Rh− percentage is approximately 15. The Basques are distinctive in having a 40 per cent Rh− frequency. Racial variation is partly explained by selection via haemolytic disease of the newborn (*erythroblastosis foetalis*), whereby Rh+ offspring of Rh− women (possible if the father is Rh+) may die before birth owing to their Rh blood group incompatibility with their mother (*See* Section P for more details).

2. *Haemoglobins.*

Haemoglobin exists in alternative forms in man and these are genetically controlled. The frequencies of some of the genes which control haemoglobins vary markedly among human populations. The principal technique used to show variant haemoglobins is electrophoresis—the movement of charged particles in an electric field. Normal human haemoglobin comprises two different haemoglobins (A and A2). An interesting variant is haemoglobin S. This may be indicated by electrophoresis and also by a sickling test. Red cells containing haemoglobin S placed in an oxygen-free atmosphere assume sickle shapes. Individuals who have inherited one S gene (AS heterozygotes) have a mild, non-fatal anaemia—the sickle cell trait. Homozygous SS individuals suffer from the severe sickle cell anaemia which is usually fatal before maturity. Some abnormal haemoglobins including S, E, and C have high frequencies and their existence, since all of them are deleterious to some extent, provides opportunities for viewing the action of natural selection and gene flow in human populations. Haemoglobin S reaches very high frequencies among some populations in southern Asia and particularly in much of tropical Africa (10–40 per cent), despite its severe effect on individual viability and fertility. Haemoglobin C is most prevalent in northern Ghana and contiguous areas while Haemoglobin E is found principally in South East Asia, with frequencies as high as 27 per cent in Cambodia.

Homozygous SS individuals hardly ever live to transmit the S gene and without a compensatory effect the gene would be totally lost except for certain cases possibly occurring as mutations. Compensation is through positive selection in favour of AS individuals who are more resistant to and so protected from falciparum malaria. Again AS females might be more fertile than AA females in certain populations, and this again would help to maintain the high S frequencies.

Other polymorphisms include the haptoglobins (proteins that bind the haemoglobin of old and broken-down red blood cells), serum transferrins (proteins in the blood sera used in transporting iron within the body) and the enzyme Glucose-6-phosphate Dehydrogenase (G6PD) and selective agencies are operative on these also.

The non-uniform distribution of blood group, haemoglobin, and other gene frequencies in the races of man may be explained in terms of natural selection, gene flow between populations, random genetic drift, the founder principle and the development of geographical and socio-cultural isolation. As a principal agency only natural selection can account for the magnitude of the population differences and for the maintenance of the observed balanced genetic polymorphisms in man. Known frequency distributions suggest that there is some relationship between the environment and the incidence of, for example, the blood group genes. Both the variability and also the geographical gradients for the A and B genes are consistent with the hypothesis that these genes are influenced by environmental selection and it seems unlikely that such a phenomenal relationship is confined to the ABO system. Human populations or races are defined in terms of traits, only some of which have here been indicated, which are brought into being and maintained primarily by natural selection—by the incidence of disease, blood group incompatibilities, diseases of the new born, and by differential fertility.

## THE STUDY OF SOCIAL ANTHROPOLOGY.

### What the Subject is About.

Social anthropology is concerned with the way men live as members of ordered societies. It has been described as a branch of sociology, or as the sociology of the simpler peoples. Neither description is wholly correct. A social anthropologist seeks to identify the *structure* of the society he studies and the *processes* of social interaction within it. His method is direct contact—what has been called "participant observation." Therefore he must deal with a unit small enough to be manageable with this technique. Nation-states, such as sociologists commonly work among, are too large. Most social anthropologists have done their work in what we call "small-scale" societies; that is, peoples who lacked such media of communication as writing or money, let alone mechanical means of transport, until these were brought to them from Europe. A social anthropologist may choose to work in some section of a society that possesses those techniques—in the ancient countries of the East or in Europe or America. In that case he confines himself to a microcosm such as a village or a factory. When he is writing of societies alien to his own and that of most of his readers he is obliged to describe their *culture* as well as their social relationships, since without such a description his readers would not be able to picture, or even understand, the social rules that are his main subject of study; this would be superfluous for a sociologist taking modern machine society for granted. Culture has been called the raw material out of which the anthropologist makes his analysis of social structure. It is the sum total of standardised ways of behaving, of lore and technique, of belief and symbolism, characteristic of any given society.

### The Notion of Roles.

All the world, as Shakespeare said, is a stage, and this is a key metaphor for social anthropologists. Every individual does indeed play many parts, not consecutively but all together; for every social relationship carries with it the expectation of society that the parties to it will behave in approved ways. Father and children, ruler and subjects, buyers and sellers, husband and wife; every one of these words is the name of a *role* to be played by the person it describes. The playing of roles involves the recognition of claims and obligations as well as appropriate modes of behaviour in personal contacts. All these rules are called *norms*; when they are concerned with rights and obligations they are *jural norms*. A social norm is what people think ought to happen; unlike a statistical norm, it may or may not be what happens in the majority of cases.

### Kinship and Marriage.

In societies of simple technology most roles are *ascribed*; that is, the parts people will play in life are given them at birth by the fact of their parentage and of the group in which this makes them members. In other words, the most important principle of organisation is *kinship*. W. H. R. Rivers called this "the social recognition of biological ties." The ties in question can be called genealogical; they all derive from the recognition of common ancestry. Such ties may be fictitious, as when a child is adopted. But in the vast majority of cases the relationships that are recognised are actually biological.

No man can recognise for social purposes all the individuals with whom he has a common ancestor somewhere in the past, or even know of their existence; their number increases with every generation. In every society a selection is made, from the whole universe of genealogically related persons, of certain categories towards which an individual recognises specific obligations and on whom he can make specific claims. Such *corporate groups* of kin have a permanent existence; they recruit new members in each generation in accordance with recognised rules. Kin groups are concerned largely with the transmission of property, and for this and other purposes they recognise the common authority of a senior man; they are also religious groups, performing together rituals directed to their common ancestors.

The common patrimony of a kin group normally consists in land or livestock; in societies of more advanced technology it may be a boat, as in Hong Kong, or even, as in Japan, a family business. It may have non-material resources too, such as the right to supply chiefs or priests for the society as a whole; this may be put conversely as the right to hold political or religious office. Those who share a common patrimony have a common interest in preserving and increasing it. Wrongs done by their members to outsiders are compensated from their collective resources, and they have joint responsibility for seeking compensation if one of their own members is injured, particularly in the case of homicide.

### Descent.

Kin groups may be recruited according to a number of principles. A principle widely followed in small-scale societies is that of *unilineal descent*; that is, group membership is derived from one parent only, either the father (*patrilineal* or *agnatic*) or the mother (*matrilineal*). Property is *administered* by men in either system, but in the matrilineal system it is *inherited* from the mother; hence its control passes from a man to the sons of his sisters. In a unilineal system every individual recognises kin linked to him through the parent from whom he does not trace his descent; this is the principle of *complementary filiation*. The complementary kin are *matrilateral* where the descent rule is patrilineal, *patrilateral* where it is matrilineal. A unilineal descent group is called a *lineage*.

Descent can also be traced *cognatically*; that is, all descendants of a common ancestral pair may be recognised as forming one *kindred*. In such a system there is no permanent group patrimony; people inherit a share of the property of both their parents, and this is often conferred upon them when they marry, while their parents are still living. Or all the inhabitants of a village may share rights in its rice-fields or fishing ponds; a man chooses among what kin he will live, but he can have rights in one village only. In such a system there are no continuing groups defined by descent; the permanent group is territorial, consisting in the inhabitants of the village.

### Marriage.

Kinship status is defined by legitimate birth, and this in its turn by legal marriage. There are always rules against marriage with specified categories of kin, though these are not necessarily near kin. Some societies consider that the ideal marriage is that between the children of a brother and a sister; if such marriages are repeated through the generations they create a permanent link between two lineages. Marriage between members of the same lineage is nearly always forbidden; this is expressed in the term *lineage exogamy*. The general effect of the prohibitions is to spread widely through a society the links created by marriage; links that impose an obligation of friendship on groups that without them would be mutually hostile.

In a matrilineal system women bear children for their own lineage; it is expected that they should be fathered by a man who has married their mother according to the approved procedure, but a child's lineage membership is not affected by the marriage of its mother. But in a patrilineal society wives must be brought from outside to bear children for the group. Associated with this fact is the payment of *bridewealth*, which used to be mistakenly interpreted as the purchase of wives.

This payment is what fixes the status of a woman's children; all those she bears while the bridewealth is with her lineage are reckoned as the children of the man on whose behalf it was paid, even if he is dead and she is living with another partner. In a matrilineal society the making of gifts is part of the marriage procedure, but they are of slight economic value in comparison with bridewealth. The difference is correlated with the difference in what the husband acquires by the marriage; in both cases he gains the right to his wife's domestic services and sexual fidelity, but where bridewealth is paid he can also count her children as his descendants and call on their labour when he needs it.

In societies where most roles are ascribed by the fact of birth, marriage is the most important field in which there is freedom of choice. But the choice is commonly exercised not by the couple but by their lineage seniors, who are more concerned with alliances between lineages than with the personal feelings of the pair. *Polygamy*, or the simultaneous marriage of a man to more than one woman, is permitted in lineage-based societies; indeed it is the ideal, though only a minority of men attain it. One reason why it is valued is that it enables a man who has the resources necessary for successive bridewealth payments to build up a network of alliances.

## Authority Systems.

Every society has some arrangements for the maintenance of order, in the sense that force may be used against those who infringe legitimate rights. In every society theft, adultery, and homicide are treated as offences. Where no individual has authority to punish these on behalf of the community, *self-help* is the approved course. Lineage membership is significant here; a man who is wronged will go with his kin to seek redress (for a theft or adultery) or vengeance (for the homicide of a kinsman). Vengeance can be bought off by the payment of compensation; but because the taking of life is a serious matter in the most turbulent of societies, there must also be a solemn reconciliation, with a sacrifice to the ancestral spirits, between the lineages of killer and victim. The recognition of an appropriate method of dealing with injuries has been described as " the rule of law " in its simplest form.

Within a lineage the senior man is expected to settle quarrels, and the ancestral spirits are believed to punish with sickness juniors who do not listen to him. When quarrels break out between members of different lineages, their elders may meet and seek a solution. Where there is no hereditary authority individuals may attain positions of leadership in virtue of their powers of mediation by persuasion.

In addition to the maintenance of rights, most societies require at some time arrangements for the organisation of collective activities. It is possible for there to be no ascribed role of organiser; in such a case leadership is a matter of competition. Competitive leadership in economic activities is characteristic particularly of the very small societies of New Guinea. What is needed here is not only powers of persuasion but resources to reward the participants. The very important principle, to be discussed later, that every gift ought at some time to be returned, is the basis of their position. A man who can put others in his debt can call upon their labour. It may take a long time to build up the necessary resources for acknowledged leadership, and leadership may be lost to a rival and is not necessarily passed to an heir.

Responsibility both for law and order and for collective activities may be shared on recognised principles among the whole adult male population. This is done where society is organised on the basis of *age*, a system widely found in east and west Africa. In such a system all adult men pass through a series of stages at each of which appropriate tasks are allotted to them. In its simplest form the division is made into ' warriors ' and ' elders '. This principle may be complicated in various ways, but the essence of it is that men in their prime are responsible for activities requiring physical strength, impetuosity, and courage, while their elders have the task of mediating in disputes, discussing public affairs, and performing sacrifices to the ancestors. Men in the warrior grade are the fighting force, and may also have the police functions of summoning disputants and witnesses before the elders, and seizing property from a man who has been adjudged to pay compensation and does not do so voluntarily. Sometimes specific public works are allotted to them, such as rounding up stray cattle or clearing weeds from paths or springs. It is also possible for community responsibilities to be shared in more complicated ways, as for example among the Yakö of Nigeria, where the adherents of particular religious cults are believed to call on the spirit which they worship to punish persons guilty of particular offences.

Where there are hereditary chiefs, both public works and the maintenance of law and order are the responsibility of the chief and his subordinate officials. Resources are accumulated for public purposes by the collection of tribute, and labour is obtained for public works by the recognition of the principle that persons in authority can claim the labour of those subject to them. Expectations are attached to the role of chief as to any other. Chiefs are expected to dispense justice fairly, to be generous to the poor, to reward loyalty, and to be successful in war, and they are reminded of these expectations in the course of the elaborate rituals performed at their accession. The prosperity of the whole land is commonly held to be bound up with the health of the chief and the favourable attitude towards him of supernatural beings. He may be obliged to obey all kinds of ritual restrictions to this end; for example it was believed of the ruler of Ruanda, in east Africa, that he must not bend his knee lest the country be conquered. Chiefs are either themselves responsible for the performance of ritual on behalf of the whole populace or must maintain priests to do this.

Social anthropologists have recently turned their attention to the process of competition for the commanding roles which any society offers. Some would claim to have discarded the idea of structure altogether in favour of that of process; yet the structure must be taken into account as the set of rules in accordance with which the game is played. There are societies where it is the rule that on the death of a chief his sons must fight for the succession to test who is the strongest and has the largest following. There are others where the rule of succession may seem to be clear, and yet there can always be dispute as to who fits it best. Sometimes people pursue the struggle for power by accusing their rivals of witchcraft; sometimes by massing their followers behind them in a show of strength before which their adversaries retire; the first is the method of the Ndembu in western Zambia, the second that of the Pathans in the Swat Valley in Pakistan. Such confrontations occur at moments of crisis, but the process of building up support is going on all the time. The study of these processes is among the most interesting new developments in social anthropology.

## Economic Systems.

In societies where money provides a common standard for measuring the relative value of different kinds of goods, people who exchange goods can make very exact calculations of profit and loss. It is often assumed that where there is no such common medium of exchange people do not make any economic calculations, and dispose of their property in ways that are the reverse of businesslike. The principal reason why this assumption is made is the great importance attached in societies of simple technology to the making of gifts. The essential difference between a gift and a commercial exchange is that no return is stipulated. In the commercial world goods are sold, services hired, at a price, and anyone who fails to pay has broken a contract and is liable to be punished. The obligation to return a gift is a moral one. Moreover, to compete in the giving of gifts seems at first sight the very opposite of competition in the acquisition of wealth. But in most societies people who have a surplus of wealth like to have a reputation for generosity; only in the affluent world of machine production people feel the need to have many more material possessions before they begin to think in terms of surplus.

The exchange of gifts plays a particularly large part in the societies of Melanesia, where men form partnerships for the express purpose of giving and receiving valuable objects, and earn prestige at least as much by giving as by receiving. This exchange of valuables, mostly shell ornaments, is so important that it has a name in the language of each society. The first such exchange system to be described by an anthropologist was the *kula* of the Trobriand Islands, observed by Malinowski. An important man had a partner in an island on either side of his own home: from one he received armbands and returned necklaces, from the other he received necklaces and returned armbands. These objects did not become part of a store of wealth for any man; nobody could hold one long before it was time to pass it on to his partner. To receive his gift a man sailed by canoe to his partner's home; he was there welcomed peaceably, and while he was making his formal visit the crew were bartering their goods on the shore with the local populace. Thus the *kula* partnership had the nature of a political alliance; it was a means of maintaining peaceful relations between populations which would otherwise have been hostile.

In the highland area of New Guinea identical objects are exchanged, so that the relative value of amounts given and received can be calculated. In some parts the ideal is that a return gift should be twice the original one. Naturally it is no small achievement to carry on a prolonged series of exchanges at such a rate. Very few men manage it, and those who do are the acknowledged leaders of their community. For each large gift he has made a man wears a little bamboo stick hung round his neck; thus his munificence is publicly proclaimed. A new partnership is initiated by making the minimum gift. Men make these partnerships with others not bound to them by kinship, notably with their relatives by marriage. Each partnership extends the range within which a man can count on friendly treatment. So widespread is the idea that gifts should be repaid, and services rewarded, after some delay, and at the discretion of the man making the return, that where the highland people have taken to growing coffee for sale, the large-scale planters do not pay wages but employ young men for planting who get their return by coming to them later for help in difficulties. Of course the young men would stop giving their work if they judged that the return was not adequate.

Gift-giving, then, is an investment, but not one that produces a direct material return. One anthropologist, R. F. Salisbury, has called it an investment in power. The extreme case of such an uneconomic use of goods was found—before it was forbidden—in the *potlach* of some Indians of the north-west coast of America. There a man who was insulted would challenge the offender to a competition in destruction. Great quantities of fish-oil would be poured on the fire, and sheets of copper thrown into the sea. The challenger was demonstrating how much wealth he could afford to destroy.

Certainly this is not turning resources to material advantage. No more is the giving of a very expensive dinner-party in London or New York. But equally certainly, it is not done without calculation. In the affluent society people display their superior affluence because this demonstrates their prestige rating, just as in the *potlach*; and they keep on good terms, through the hospitality they offer, with people from whom they may later seek a return in professional dealings, rather as in the Melanesian gift-exchanges. The difference between the uses to which resources are put in societies of simple and of complex technology is one only of degree. The proportion that is devoted to securing non-material advantages is higher in the small-scale societies, and so is the proportion of gift-giving to commercial exchange. In gift-giving there is no bargaining, but there is a clear expectation of return. The initiation of new social relationships by the making of gifts is not by any means confined to New Guinea. Bride-wealth which legitimises children is the most widespread example. Pastoral peoples in East Africa also make gifts of stock to selected friends in distant parts. The friend on his home ground is a sponsor for his partner, and he is expected to make return gifts from time to time, and may be asked for a beast if his partner is in difficulties. One could think of such an arrangement as a type of insurance.

A small number of social anthropologists have specialised in the study of the economic systems of small-scale societies, and have asked whether the concepts devised for the analysis of monetary economies—such notions, for example, as capital and credit—can be applied to people who gain their livelihood directly from the resources of their immediate environment. Starting from the assumption that there is always some choice in the allocation of resources, they have observed how these choices are actually made in the societies where they have worked. They have asked how the value of such goods as are obtained by barter is measured; how labour is obtained, how directed and how rewarded for such enterprises as the building of a canoe or a temple, which call for the co-operation of large numbers. They have examined the use of media of exchange, asking how far any of these fulfil the functions that we associate with money.

The general conclusion of these studies is that peoples of simple technology are perfectly capable of rational calculation in the allocation of their resources, even though their calculations are rough by comparison with those of the entrepreneur in an industrial society. They know what to regard as an adequate return when they are bartering goods. They withhold goods from consumption when they are planning an enterprise; that is to say, a man who proposes to initiate such an activity as canoe-building arranges to be able to feed his labour force.

Religion.

At a time when people questioned whether " primitive " societies could be said to have religion, E. B. Tylor offered as a " minimum " definition of religion " the belief in spiritual beings." All societies of simple technology have such beliefs, and think that unseen personalised beings influence the course of nature by direct intervention, causing rain to fall if they are pleased with the actions of men and withholding it if they are angry, sending sickness as a punishment and so forth. In the great majority of such societies the most important spirits to be worshipped are those of dead ancestors. But there may also be a belief in gods responsible for particular aspects of the world, to whom offerings are made for protection or success in their special fields. Many pre-literate peoples believe in a 'high god' from whom all other spirits derive their power, and one school of anthropology sees this as evidence of an original state of higher religious consciousness from which man has declined; but this view is not widely held.

Rituals involving groups of people are commonly performed on occasions when changes of status are to be signalised. A child becomes a member of society not by being born, but at a naming or showing ceremony. A youth or girl becomes adult at initiation. Marriage, which makes a couple into potential parents and links their kin groups, is another such ritual.

In funerary rites the dead person is made into an ancestor, and his heir adopts his social personality and his responsibilities. The accession of a man to political office is surrounded by ritual, and chiefs frequently observe annual rites at the time of harvest, when it is the season, not the person, that is changing. These are *confirmatory* rituals, designed to keep society and the world on an even course. When something goes wrong, a drought or epidemic or an individual sickness, *piacular* rituals are performed to make peace with the spirits responsible for the disaster.

An essential aspect of many of these religions is the belief in witchcraft—that is that it is possible for humans to harm one another merely by hating them. Witchcraft supplies an explanation of undeserved misfortune. Diviners employ a multitude of techniques (which anthropologists rather inaccurately call oracles) to detect whether a disaster is a merited punishment or is due to witchcraft.

Every small-scale society has its myths—stories which tell how the world as people know it came to be. Sometimes their ritual re-enacts the myth; often the myth tells how the ritual was first performed and thereby gives a reason for its continuance. Then there are myths telling how death and evil came into the world. Some myths lend authority to the existing social order, and particularly to the claims of ruling groups, by telling how the social structure was divinely ordained. Under the influence of the French anthropologist Lévi-Strauss, many anthropologists are beginning to see both myths and the symbolism of ritual as man's earliest attempt to order intellectually the world of his experience.

### Social Change.

No doubt all the societies that anthropologists have studied have been gradually changing throughout the centuries when their history was not recorded. But they experienced nothing like the rapidity of the changes that came to them when they were brought under the rule of European nations and introduced to mass production and a money economy. The effect of this has been in essence to widen the range of choice in the relationships that people can form. A man may choose to be dependent on an employer rather than on work in co-operation with his kin or village mates. He is more likely to rise in the world by going to school and getting a city job than by earning the respect of the villagers or the approval of a chief. Small-scale societies are now becoming merged in larger ones, and the close ties of the isolated village are loosened. In the newly created industrial areas new specialised associations are formed to pursue professional and other interests. The social insurance that kinship provided is lacking, and it has not as yet been replaced by what the state offers in the highly industrialised societies. The minority that has whole-heartedly adopted the values of the industrialised world now produces the political rulers of new states. They are impatient to carry the majority along the same road, but there are profound conflicts of value between them and the still largely illiterate masses.

# PART VI.   SPECIAL TOPICS

## THE PLANET VENUS.

Venus, the second innermost planet of the solar system, and the evening or morning star of our sky, revolves round the Sun in 224·71 days in an almost circular orbit inclined but little to the ecliptic. This brings it at inferior conjunction (when nearest to the Earth) to within 40·7 million km. At such times it becomes our nearest planetary neighbour (Mars comes no nearer than 55·5 million km), appearing almost as a twin of our Earth, having 0·8150 of the terrestrial mass within a globe of 6,056 km radius. But this seeming likeness conceals physical properties that are very different from those of the Earth. How unlike the two planets are is only now being revealed by the modern methods of space research.

Before the advent of space astronomy our knowledge of the physical as well as the dynamical properties of Venus had remained remarkably meagre. Much more was known about Mars. There were two reasons for this: Venus has no natural satellite, and, as befits the goddess of love, she protects herself from inquisitive terrestrial onlookers by hiding her face behind an impenetrable "veil of chastity" in the form of a cloud layer. Little was known about the composition of this cloud until it could be penetrated in the microwave domain of the spectrum.

One of the milestones in Cytherean observation (and they have been few and far between) was when Galileo in 1611 recognised (rather late, to tell the truth) that "Mater Amorum aemulatur Cynthiae formas"—meaning that the telescopic image of Venus simulates the phases of the Moon. This observation had important cosmological consequences, for according to Ptolemaic astronomy (which supposed both the Sun and Venus to revolve round the Earth) Venus could never show us more than half its illuminated surface, since, according to Ptolemy, the planet was always between us and the supposed orbit of the Sun. Therefore, when Galileo observed with his newly invented telescope that Venus exhibited gibbous phase as well as the crescent, it proved that the planet revolved round the Sun rather than round the Earth. This sounded the deathknell of the Ptolemaic system, though not yet the enthronement of the Copernican, for Galileo's observation could be made consistent with either the heliocentric (Copernican) or the Tychonic system.

### Size, Distance, and Brightness.

From telescopic observations carried out since Galileo's day the apparent diameter of the planet ranges from 64" at inferior conjunction to only 10" at superior conjunction (when farthest from the Earth). The big disparity is due to the large variation in the planet's distance from the Earth which ranges from 41 to 258 million km at the two positions. At these distances the apparent angular diameters of Venus correspond to a globe of a little less than 6,100 km diameter of a shape differing insignificantly from a sphere. Accordingly, compared with the Earth the surface of Venus is 0·906 and its volume 0·862. On the other hand, from the orbital perturbations which Venus produces on Earth (or, more recently, on fly-by spacecraft), the mass of the planet was found to be 1/408523 that of the Sun, or 0·8150 that of the Earth. As a result, compared with the Earth the mean density of the Cytherean globe is 0·945 or 5·23 g/cm³ and the surface gravity 0·900 or 882 cm/sec². Thus a man who weighs 160 lb on Earth would weigh only 144 lb on Venus.

Whenever visible from the Earth, Venus appears brighter than any other planet, ranging from −3·3 to −4·2 in stellar magnitudes. As it moves from superior to inferior conjunction, the increase in apparent diameter at first more than makes up for the diminution of the illuminated portion of the disc, and the planet grows brighter. As, however, the crescent begins to narrow, the area of the illuminated portion of the disc begins eventually to diminish, and with it the apparent brightness. As a result the planet reaches its maximum brightness, not when it is nearest to us, but about 36 days before or after inferior conjunction—at an elongation of 39° from the Sun (i.e., less than the maximum elongation of 47·5°) when the phase of Venus is like that of the Moon about five days old (i.e., two days before "first quarter"). At that time Venus is bright enough for shadows to be cast in its light at night and to be visible to the naked eye in full daylight.

The observed brightness of the planet discloses that its surface must act as a pretty efficient reflector—approximately 59 per cent of sunlight incident upon it is scattered in all directions (as compared with a mere 7 per cent scattered by the Moon). Moreover, compared with the Moon, the rate at which the brightness of Venus waxes and wanes with the phase (when the effects of varying distances are allowed for) is much slower. From this we conclude that the visible surface of Venus is much smoother than that of the Moon (or Mercury). Moreover, the colour of Venus is only slightly yellower than the illuminating sunlight. Therefore, the actual process of light scattering must be almost independent of frequency. In other words, the visible disc of Venus appears to be monotonously "white"—as might be expected of a surface completely covered with clouds. That this is probably the case is suggested also by the fact that—unlike the Moon, or Mars—Venus does not exhibit any noticeable surface markings that could be recognised for any length of time; the usual telescopic appearance of the disc of the planet shows uniform distribution of brightness, shading off smoothly towards the terminator (i.e., line of Sunrise) without much trace of detail.

If, therefore, the surface of Venus is covered perpetually by clouds, such a cloud layer would presuppose the existence of a sufficiently dense atmosphere surrounding the whole planet; and other observations indicate that this is indeed the case. In point of fact, conclusive evidence that Venus does possess an atmosphere has been known for a long time. Thus, near the time of inferior conjunction, the horns of the Cytherean crescent are seen to extend notably beyond the terminator; and when the planet is very close to the Sun the cusps of the crescent have been observed actually to run together—forming a complete aureola around the disc. This phenomenon is due to diffuse reflection of sunlight in the planetary atmosphere (like that which causes our twilight). From the observed amount of prolongation of the cusps of the crescent it is possible to estimate the total amount of gas necessary to produce it; and that would be equivalent to a layer of about 1 km in thickness at our atmospheric air pressure. This is, however, the amount of gas extending above the top of the visible cloud layer; below this layer the atmosphere can be many times that dense.

## The Atmosphere of Venus.

What does this atmosphere consist of? As usual, we have to turn to the spectroscope for the answer, and the latter will not disappoint us. In 1932, Adams and Dunham of Mt. Wilson Observatory detected in the deep red spectrum of Venus three complex bands (with heads at wavelengths 7,820, 7,883 and 8,689 Å; $1 Å = 10^{-10}$ metres) due obviously to molecular absorption, which have no counterpart in the spectrum of illuminating sunlight; and these were subsequently identified with the absorption spectrum of carbon dioxide ($CO_2$). Moreover, from the intensity of these bands it has been inferred that the amount of $CO_2$ above the visible cloud surface must be equivalent to a layer not less than 400 metres thick at standard (atmospheric) pressure, which is about 250 times the quantity of $CO_2$ present in the Earth's entire atmosphere.

Oxygen, or water vapour, could be detected, in principle, in the same manner, for (unlike nitrogen, or argon) the absorption of their molecules produces imprints in the visible part of the spectrum. However, all spectroscopic tests for oxygen have so far proved entirely negative—indicating a well-nigh complete absence of the gas in the Cytherean atmosphere accessible to observation. As regards water vapour, it was not until recently (1966) that the first traces of it were detected in the deep red part of the spectrum of Venus by Spinrad and Shawl from Berkeley; and independently by Belton and Hunten at Kitt Peak; in amounts corresponding to not more than 10–20 microns of precipitable water. This is in agreement with measurements of the infrared $H_2O$ absorption at 11,300 Å, performed in 1964 by Strong from unmanned balloons flying at a height of 80,000 feet. The atmosphere of Venus above the visible surface appears, therefore, to be very dry—about as dry as in our own terrestrial stratosphere above the high-flying cirrus clouds—and the reasons for it will transpire when we turn to inquire into the temperature prevalent over the visible parts of the Cytherean surface.

## Temperature.

As is well known, the absolute temperature (L2) of any cosmic body can be deduced from the measured intensity of its thermal emission; and, for solid planetary bodies, the bulk of this emission can be expected (in accordance with Planck's Law) to occur in the near infrared. When the first reliable measurements of infrared emission from Venus between wavelengths of $8–12\mu$ ($1\mu = 10^{-6}$m) were performed in 1955 by Pettit and Nicholson, it transpired that while the mean temperature of the "daylight" hemisphere of Venus appeared to be about 235° K (i.e., −38° C), that of the "night" hemisphere came out as 240° K (−33° C)—i.e., actually higher than in daytime. The difference between the two is scarcely significant, and the ensemble of all measurements indicates that the temperature prevalent above the visible surface of Venus remains virtually constant regardless of day or night.

How to explain this perplexing phenomenon? The correct clue was probably found by Strong, who pointed out that these measured temperatures are virtually identical with the "Schaefer point," below which saturated water vapour cannot cool without spontaneous crystallisation. Therefore, the clouds on Venus are probably nothing else than high cirrus clouds as in our own atmosphere—i.e., frozen ice crystals—and the failure of their outer surface to cool at night is probably due to the liberation of the latent heat of water vapour (about 600 cal/g) as the vapour condenses to form clouds.

How high are these clouds above the actual surface of the planet? This question obviously cannot be decided by observations made in the visible, or near infrared, light; for the cloud cover appears to be totally opaque to this light at all times. In order to penetrate deeper, light of much longer wavelength must be employed, which is no longer absorbed by water vapour. This will, in general, obtain only at wavelengths in excess of one millimeter. Observations of thermal emission from Venus in the mm- and cm-domain of the planet's radio spectrum began in 1959–60. The results were dramatic. The intensity of thermal emission at wavelengths between 8–8·6 mm (Gibson, 1959; Kuzmin and Salomonovich, 1960) corresponded to absolute temperatures between 300°–400° K; and in the centimetre range (3–10 cm) attained the tremendous level of 580°–600° K—i.e., over 320° C (Mayer et al., 1959–60)!

This latter temperature undoubtedly prevails at the solid surface of the planet; but if it is due to the storage of sunlight—i.e., to the "greenhouse effect" of the Cytherean atmosphere which traps so much of the heat received from the Sun through absorption by its gaseous constituents—the amount of gas involved in this process below the cloud layer must be enormous. In fact, theoretical calculations of the Cytherean model atmospheres disclose that, for a temperature difference of 350° between the solid ground and the top of the clouds, an atmosphere consisting predominantly of $CO_2$ would have to attain a ground pressure close to 20 terrestrial atmospheres; with the top of the cloud layer located at an altitude of some 40–50 km above solid ground.

Thus it is not until at altitudes which on Earth would take us well into the midst of the ozone layer that anyone emerging from the Cytherean atmosphere could see the starry sky. Far below the deceptive calm of these rarefied heights, the cloud layer which is totally impenetrable at optical frequencies conceals a veritable inferno of pitch-black darkness, filled with carbon dioxide of increasing density and temperature, which attains on the ground a pressure believed to approach 20 atmospheres and a temperature of 350° C. Such a medium would act as an ideal steriliser for any living matter, and as good surroundings for the appropriate treatment of most obdurate sinners as could be found anywhere in the solar system within convenient reach of the Earth. And yet, even this inferno has already been penetrated—not by any Dante (provided with a suitable kind of spacesuit), but by inanimate Hermes messengers in the form of spacecraft, sent out by human hand several times since 1962 to reconnoitre the environment of our nearest planetary neighbour. This story represents one of the most interesting developments in recent experimental astronomy, and has disclosed many new facets of Venus which could not have been obtained by any means available to Earth-bound astronomy. Therefore, in what follows, we shall give a brief account of its principal results.

## Visits to Venus by Spacecraft.

The first terrestrial messenger to Venus sent out by human hand from the Earth was the Russian probe, *Venera 1*, launched from Baikonur in Central Asia on 12 February 1961. Although this spacecraft failed to attain its goal (radio contact having been lost after 4·7 million miles in space), it proved to be a harbinger of greater things to come; and the first close call on Venus was paid by the American spacecraft *Mariner 2* before the end of 1962. *Mariner 2* carried aboard six scientific experiments directed to a study of the planet: a microwave radiometer capable of scanning the image of Venus at wavelengths of 13·5 and 19 mm (i.e., radiation which penetrates the Cytherean cloud veil); and an infrared radiometer scanning at wavelengths between 8 and 11μ, the radiation emitted by the top of the cloud layer. In addition, a magnetometer was carried aboard to measure the strength and direction of any Cytherean as well as interplanetary magnetic field.

The results obtained with the aid of this equipment in the course of the spacecraft's 130 days of experimental lifetime covered an impressive range of diverse phenomena. During its rendezvous with Venus accurate two-way Doppler tracking of the spacecraft's motion furnished a much-improved value for the mass of the planet. The latter was notoriously difficult to obtain otherwise, as Venus possesses no natural satellite. However, the measured reflection of the spacecraft's trajectory in the proximity of Venus, caused by the latter's gravitational attraction, disclosed the mass of Venus to be equal to $0\cdot81485\pm0\cdot00015$ times that of the Earth.

The results obtained with the aid of the two radiometers aboard were no less valuable. At the time of the closest approach (between 2 hr 59 min and 3 hr 34 min p.m. EST, 14 December 1962) both instruments scanned Venus (then visible from the spacecraft as an apparent disc of $21\cdot4°$ angular diameter illuminated at " first quarter ") three times—first on the dark side, then along the terminator line and finally on the illuminated side; and a total of eighteen data readings were made during the scans. Microwave scans at $13\cdot5$ mm wavelengths included atmospheric as well as surface radiation (though predominantly the former if the atmosphere were a strong microwave absorber—such as it would be if it contained an appreciable amount of water). On the other hand, the 19 mm wavelength is not affected by water vapour; and radiation received at it probably refers to the planet's surface. Thus the larger the brightness temperatures recorded by the two channels of the microwave radiometer, the greater the amount of water vapour in the atmosphere of the planet.

The effective temperatures obtained by the microwave radiometer were close to $450°$ K $(180°$ C) on the night side, $550°$ K $(280°$ C) near the terminator and only $390°$ K $(110°$ C) in daylight. These figures disclosed strong effects of limb-darkening; but no evidence was obtained for the presence of any water vapour.

The infrared radiometers operated at two wavelength ranges of $8$–$9\,\mu$ and $10$–$11\,\mu$, selected so because the absorption by carbon dioxide could strongly affect the latter but not the former. Any marked difference in signal intensity would indicate a break in the cloud layer surrounding the veiled planet, as it would allow the shorter but not the longer wavelength band to penetrate more deeply towards the surface. In actual fact, both channels indicated virtually the same temperature (close to $235°$ K or $-39°$ C) which clearly refers to the top of the cloud layer visible from the Earth. No breaks in the clouds were seen from the vantage-point of the spacecraft; and a scan carried out at the same time with the 200-inch reflector of Palomar Mountain, using a radiometer operating in the atmospheric transmission window between 8 and $12\,\mu$, gave results in good agreement with the measurements carried out in space.

In addition, the magnetometer aboard *Mariner 2* could find no evidence of any Cytherean magnetic field at any point along the spacecraft's trajectory. Comparisons of *Mariner 2* magnetic observations in the vicinity of Venus with the *Pioneer 5* measurements near the Earth indicate that the strength of the magnetic dipole moment of Venus, if any, is less than $0\cdot05$–$0\cdot10$ of that of the Earth.

Owing to low resolution generally attainable in the infrared and microwave domain, the contributions of *Mariner 2* to optical astronomy were, perhaps, not too extensive; and neither were those of the Russian space probes *Venus 2* and *3* which followed *Mariner 2* on the same journey three years later. *Venus 2*, launched on 12 November 1965, missed the planet on 27 February 1966, by only 24,000 km—*i.e.*, approached it by 9,600 km more closely than *Mariner 2* did in 1962. Two days later *Venus 3* actually crashed on the Cytherean surface and thus became the first man-made spacecraft to land on another planet. Throughout the entire flight regular radio communications were maintained with the spacecraft, and scientific information on interplanetary environment received en route. However, communications failed in the last twenty-four hours before approach; and whether or not *Venus 3* did anything else than crash-land on the planet is not known.

The 1967 conjunction between the Earth and Venus attracted to the latter two other spacecraft sent out to carry out further exploration of the veiled planet: namely, the U.S.S.R. *Venus 4*, and the American *Mariner 5*; and both rendez-

vous met with a large measure of success. *Venus 4*—a 2,438-lb. spacecraft launched on 12 June 1967 —successfully reached its destination on 18 October after a journey of $128\cdot4$ days through interplanetary space; and released an egg-shell capsule about 1 m in size, coated with an ablative heat shield that burned away as the capsule entered the Cytherean atmosphere and plunged into the clouds. Once it had been sufficiently slowed down by air drag, the capsule released a parachute and, with its aid, completed its descent in 94 minutes—thus accomplishing the first soft landing on any planet.

The measurement carried out by the instrumental package en route indicated that the atmosphere of Venus consists of about 92 per cent of carbon dioxide ($CO_2$); the rest being water vapour and molecular oxygen or nitrogen. The temperature prevailing at some 16 miles (25 km) above the surface was reported to be about $313°$ K $(+40°$ C), but rose to $553°$ K $(+280°$ C) at the end, where air pressure became 15–22 terrestrial atmospheres. It is not certain, however, whether these final readings were made of the planet's actual surface, for intense heat may have destroyed the electronic recording equipment in the capsule before it reached the ground.

The American *Mariner 5*—a substantially lighter spacecraft (540 lb)—began its four-month voyage to Venus on 14 June 1967; and on 19 October—$1\cdot5$ days after the Russian touchdown, *Mariner 5* by-passed Venus at a minimum distance of 2,480 miles (3,970 km) from the surface, while its instruments viewed the planet and sampled its environment. *Mariner 5* sent also radio-signals (at 10 cm wavelength) through the Cytherean atmosphere, as it was occulted by the planet, and reappeared 21 minutes later to bid farewell to Venus and depart along a heliocentric orbit to become a new asteroid of the Sun. The telemetry of all data back to the Earth across 49 million miles (78 million km) with the available power of 10 watts took 34 hours of real time.

A preliminary analysis of these data led to a number of significant results. Thus *Mariner 5* detected no belt of charged particles (similar to the terrestrial van Allen belts (L120) girdling Venus. The data are not consistent with any planetary magnetic field of strength not more than about $0\cdot01$ gauss (the Russian probes likewise failed to detect any Cytherean magnetic field at all); and the upper limit to a possible magnetic dipole moment of Venus is estimated to not more than about $0\cdot002$ of that of the Earth. According to *Mariner 5*, the atmosphere of Venus at the height of its closest approach consists of 75–85 per cent carbon dioxide, with some traces of hydrogen (but not oxygen).

### Exploring Venus by Radar.

The foregoing brief account exhausts the principal recent contributions of space astronomy to the exploration of Venus. However, in a real sense such an exploration had already begun on 10 March 1961 when the first contact with Venus was established by means of radar. On that day, a radio signal beamed at Venus from the Jet Propulsion Laboratory of the California Institute of Technology at a wavelength of $12\cdot5$ cm produced a detectable echo within a few minutes of double transit time; and since that time further important contributions have been made by the Lincoln and Arecibo Observatories in the United States, as well as by the Radiophysics Institute of the U.S.S.R. Academy of Sciences in Russia.

The contributions of radar astronomy to the study of Venus since 1961 have been both extensive and important, and some of them entirely unique. By the determination of the time-lag between the outgoing and returning signal, the distance separating us from Venus could be obtained with a precision far surpassing that of any other astronomical measurements; and radar measurements at different times (*i.e.*, when the planet occupies different positions in its relative orbit round the Sun) led to a determination of the orbital elements of the planet so precise as to mark an entirely new epoch in celestial astronautics. For instance, the semi-major axis of the Cytherean orbit ($0\cdot723,329,860 \pm 0\cdot000,000,002$ astronomical units) is now known to us within an error of two parts in $10^9$ and the length of the astronomical unit (*i.e.*, the semi-major axis of the terrestrial orbit round the Sun) was deduced by the same method to be 149,597,892 km in length (or 499·004786 light seconds), with an error of only ±5 km (or 5 microseconds of light). This value is more than two thousand times as precise as the best previous "astronomical" determinations of the astronomical unit by celestial triangulation.

The strength of the radar echoes from Venus received back on the Earth furnishes valuable information on reflecting properties (*i.e.*, the dielectric constant) of the Cytherean solid surface. The average dielectric constant of Venus so obtained turns out to be about 4–7 times as large as that of a vacuum—in contrast with the ratio of 2 for the lunar surface, or about 15 (average) for the Earth. The Cytherean value of the dielectric constant is definitely smaller than it is for the Earth (indicating a smaller proportion of solid rocks), and comparable with that of dry, sandy desert ground; but, on the other hand, it is indicative of a more compact surface than that exposed by the Moon.

### The Rotation.

The greatest contribution of radar astronomy to the study of Venus has, however, been the determination of the axial rotation of the planet.

Observations of Venus at the Jet Propulsion Laboratory of the California Institute of Technology, extending over several years, led Goldstein and Carpenter to a conclusion that Venus rotates in a retrograde direction (*i.e.*, one opposite to the orbital motion), in a period of 243·06 ± 0·05 days, about an axis that is virtually perpendicular to the ecliptic (and, therefore, inclined by 87° to the orbital plane of the planet). This case of a retrograde rotation is unique in the inner precincts of the solar system. But even more noteworthy is the fact that a period of axial rotation of 243·16 days—*i.e.*, very close to that deduced from the radar data—would allow Venus to complete exactly four axial rotations between successive inferior conjunctions of the planet as seen by a terrestrial observer. The duration of a Cytherean "day"—*i.e.*, its rotation period with respect to the Sun—would then correspond to 177 terrestrial days. This remarkably close coincidence (which would imply that at each inferior conjunction Venus shows us the same face) strongly suggests the existence of tidal coupling between the two neighbouring sister planets, but the details of the processes by which it could have come into being are as yet largely obscure.

The range-Doppler radar tracking of our sister planet in recent years led to another unique contribution—in the form of "radar maps" of the Cytherean surface. Such maps previously obtained for the Moon were comparable in accuracy with direct photography; and an extension of the same technique to Venus led to a first glimpse of what its surface looks like underneath the clouds. Radar signals sent out at a frequency of 420 Mc/sec by the Arecibo Ionospheric Observatory in Puerto Rico during 1967–68 attained a resolution about equivalent to that which could be obtained with the 200-inch telescope on Palomar Mountain if that instrument could observe the surface of the planet. A synthesis of the images obtainable from the anatomy of the returning echoes disclosed that although the surface of Venus is less rough than that of the Moon, it is by no means smooth. In fact, several rough regions of enhanced radar reflectivity have been detected which appear to be mountains. To be sure, the nature of the backscattering of radar signals is largely determined by surface slopes, the dimensions of which are of the same order of magnitude as the radar wavelength or larger. Consequently, radar echoes cannot enable us to decipher the characteristics of the reflecting ground without ambiguity. Rough regions of considerable size have been identified on the surface of Venus, and their positions determined, but whether these are jumbled rock-strewn fields or real mountain chains we cannot as yet say.

### Conclusion.

And with this we come to the end of the story of the exploration of Venus in so far as it can be written up to the beginning of 1969. The reader of this brief account will undoubtedly notice that most of what we know today has been

obtained in the past ten years. The application of modern methods of space research since 1961 has deprived our nearest planetary neighbour of many secrets hidden jealously below its veil of white clouds; and a man-made spacecraft has already effected a soft landing on its solid surface. Yet each new fact we learn has given rise to many more problems and questions which remain so far unanswered—hopefully not for long. And the story could not have been unfolded without the close collaboration of many branches of astronomy, physics, radio communications, and space engineering, thus demonstrating once more that—in scientific progress as in any other aspect of human endeavour—in unity there is strength.

### NORTH SEA GAS—ITS ORIGIN, DISCOVERY, AND EXTRACTION.

Introduction.

The North Sea has long been regarded by geologists as part of the province represented by Britain on the one hand and Holland and Germany on the other, and the rock strata (Fig. 1) that dip

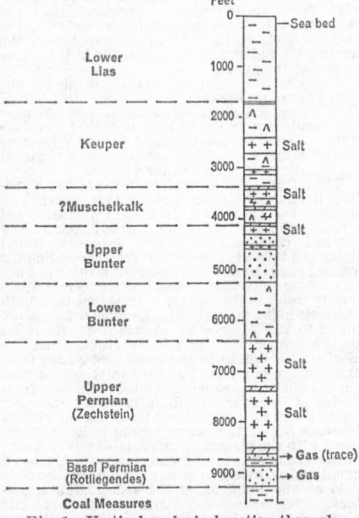

Fig. 1—Vertical geological section through British Petroleum's North Sea discovery well.

downwards towards the sea along the east coast of England appear again, rising up from the sea, in the Low Countries. Geological reconstructions indicate that the North Sea was for much of its history the central portion of a shallow sea basin, where the sediments brought down by rivers flowing northwards from the mountainous parts of Europe were deposited (Figs. 2 and 3). Although the North Sea is today again covered by water, it is, geologically speaking, similar to the land that borders it.

The continents, together with their shallow-water continental shelves, rise up from the deep ocean bed as if they were giant icebergs, with a great root of lighter material stretching down into the mantle rock. In the course of geological history, these continental blocks were subjected to tilting and warping, since they form part of only a comparatively thin skin on the earth, and are therefore affected by small readjustments in its body. A relatively slight tilting or warping of the European block could change the North Sea to dry land again and flood the present-day land areas. All the continental blocks have frequently alternated between shallow seas and dry land in the past.

Oil is normally formed due to the decay of marine animals in shallow sea water conditions, the sort of conditions that exist in the North Sea today. Rivers bring down loads of silt and sand that are deposited in shallow water to form layers of sedimentary rocks. These sedimentary rocks trap within them the decayed marine animals,

**Upper Palaeozoic (Carboniferous)**

Prospective Carboniferous basin

Gas field ○

Oilfield ◉

Fig. 2—A reconstruction of the North Sea area in Carboniferous times (about 300 million years ago)

which, in the course of millions of years, change into the peculiar series of hydrocarbons ranging from methane with one carbon atom and four hydrogens attached together at the one end of the scale, to heavy bitumens used for road making which may have a molecule with two or three hundred carbon atoms. *See* **F24(1)**.

It is not just enough to have sedimentary rocks; the rock must be porous to house the oil in a reservoir so that there is petroleum in sufficient concentrations for economic production. Two kinds of sedimentary rock that are porous are limestones and sandstones. The petroleum is not contained in a vast underground cavern; it is held in very

finding oil under the sea will be as good or as poor as that for the land that surrounds it. In Britain small oilfields have been found in the Carboniferous rocks, and gas has been produced at Eskdale on the Yorkshire coast and at Cousland near Edinburgh. A similar picture appears in Holland and in Germany. Although German production is about 7 million tons a year, it all comes from small, barely economic oilfields. Such small fields would certainly no longer be economic propositions were they covered with water, because they require closely spaced wells for their production, and drilling at sea is many times more costly than on land. This pessimistic view of the North Sea was apparently confirmed by explorations from 1946 on in Denmark, where no oilfields at all have been found.

The estimate of the profitability of North Sea drilling changed almost overnight when one of the world's largest gas fields was discovered in 1959 at Groningen in North Holland. The gas was at a depth of about 9,000 feet in a porous sandstone rock, whose thickness was much more reminiscent of the large oil-bearing structures of the Middle East than of the thin sands that had been found previously on land. The reservoir rock was a desert sand, laid down and drifted by the wind some 270 million years ago, when what is now Holland was experiencing a tropical climate.

The gas that was discovered shows one peculiarity; it consists mostly of methane, with a small percentage of ethane and very little of the heavier hydrocarbons. This, with other evidence discussed below, suggests that it is derived from the Coal Measures that were laid down in Carboniferous times before the Permian period. This has an important bearing on North Sea exploration, since it means that there is little hope of finding valuable quantities of oil associated with the gas. The ratio of the isotopes carbon-12 to carbon-13 in the methane has been measured, and the results confirmed the belief that the gas originated in coal. The argument starts from the fact that coal is formed from decayed plant life in fresh-water swamp conditions. The plants collect their carbon dioxide in the atmosphere, and this has a $^{12}C{:}^{13}C$ ratio different from that of carbon dioxide dissolved in sea water and assimilated by marine animals and plants to make their hydrocarbons. The methane from oil of marine origin is therefore distinguishable from that of coal. An added curiosity of the Groningen gas is that it contains 15 per cent nitrogen. This is presumably the end

Fig. 3—Section across the North Sea.

fine pores of this limestone or sandstone, pores that may be half a millimetre in diameter or less.

In addition to porous rock some form of trap is needed. The commonest type of trap is produced by a gentle folding of the porous layer of rock; petroleum, which is lighter than water, can then be trapped in the top of a fold with water sealing it and pushing it up from underneath. An impervious layer of rock, called 'cap-rock', must rest on the reservoir rock to hold the petroleum in place.

With all these various conditions it is not surprising that commercially exploitable reservoirs of oil or gas are not continuous over a very large area, but are in fact the exception rather than the rule. The North Sea, which has an area of about 200,000 square miles, probably contains only a few hundred square miles' worth of porous reservoir gas-containing rock, which is only about 1/1,000th of the area of the sedimentary basin.

### Geology.

Since the North Sea is part of the geological province of north-west Europe, the likelihood of

product of trapped air, the oxygen having been removed either chemically or biologically. The gas from the first successful North Sea well sunk by British Petroleum shows a $^{12}C{:}^{13}C$ ratio similar to that from Groningen, but in this case the nitrogen content is only 1 per cent. In addition to 94 per cent of methane, the gas contains 3 per cent ethane, 0·5 per cent propane, (L95) and about 0·1 per cent each of butanes (L19) and pentanes, with a little carbon dioxide. The sulphur content is less than one part in a million and the helium content is low (0·03 per cent). However, some hydrogen sulphide has been found associated with the North Sea gas from subsequent discoveries. The lack of higher hydrocarbons means that the gas is not in general very attractive as a raw material for the chemical industry, but the fact that it can be supplied at a pressure of more than 1,000 lb/in² may make it an economical starting point for fertiliser manufacture.

The cap-rock at Groningen consists of several thousand feet of rock salt and other similar rocks formed when rapid evaporation of shallow salt seas took place some 250 million years ago.

The main geological characteristics of the Groningen field are (i) the Coal Measures which form the source of the gas, (ii) the porous Basal Permian sandstone which is the reservoir rock, and (iii) the cap-rock of rock salt and other evaporites. The knowledge that existed from examination of the geology of the countries surrounding the North Sea suggested that similar conditions might occur under the water-covered part of the North West Europe sedimentary basin. Although the prospect of finding oil derived from decay of marine animals was poor, the hopes of finding further gas accumulations originating in the Coal Measures were high, and have since been justified by the discovery of at least four major gas fields. Although there is always a possibility of finding oil beneath the North Sea, it is the large gas fields which are of prime importance; this is disappointing in one respect, in that in many parts of the world gas is found associated with oil, and the oil production helps to pay for the production of gas, and to keep the price of gas down.

## Geophysics.

On land, especially in places where there is sparse vegetation and little surface cover of soil, it is often possible to locate the rock folds which form underground oil reservoirs by visual examination supplemented by aerial photography. When the prospective territory is covered by opaque sea water, such examination is almost impossible (although some new tools have been devised to probe the water and the sea-floor mud, and some useful observations have been made by diving). To locate underground structures that could be potential oil or gas reservoirs, geophysics must be employed. Even with the most modern geophysical techniques there is still a statistical chance of ten to one against finding oil deposits of economic value. This figure is for exploration on land; at sea, since oil fields must be larger than on land to be economic in face of increased production costs, the chance is probably 20 to 30 to one against.

Three main geophysical tools are used in the oil industry, and all have been adapted for use in offshore prospecting.

### Magnetic measurements.

Measurements of the Earth's magnetic field in different places give an empirical measure of the thickness of the sedimentary rocks. This is because the field changes are caused by the intrusion of volcanic material into ancient basement rock, and these changes are blurred if the material is distant and covered by thick layers of sedimentary rock. Magnetic measurements can now be made rapidly from an aircraft, and in the North Sea they confirmed geological opinion that there was a sedimentary layer several miles thick.

### Gravitational measurements.

Surveys of the Earth's gravitational field, made to an accuracy of one part in a hundred million, have been most effective on land in pinpointing oilfields associated with salt-plugs, and similar methods can be used for gas fields. Salt behaves geologically as a fluid substance such as pitch, and thick layers of salt, when compressed by the weight of the overlying rock, burst out into vertical moving plugs of salt. The upward pressure of the salt plug causes the overlying rock strata to bend into structures that form traps for oil or gas. As salt is less dense than the surrounding rock, the presence of these salt plugs can be located by an accurate gravity survey.

At sea, the movement of the waves precludes any measurements of gravity to better than a few parts in a million. Although this is not good enough to locate such salt plugs as exist under the North Sea, it does provide some regional information which indicates interesting areas. In the late Permian times, the desert continental surface suffered transgressions of shallow seas which evaporated rapidly in the heat, leaving thousands of feet of rock salt and other evaporites, such as anhydrite. These form the impermeable cap-rock that contains the Groningen gas, which is at a pressure of 4,000 lb/in$^2$. This large thickness of evaporites shows up as an area of low gravity, and

a similar low area is known to exist to the south of the Dogger Bank.

### Seismic measurement.

Although these approaches can indicate promising areas, at sea it is the seismic reflection method that points the way for the driller. Something better than random drilling is needed to find even as large a target as the Groningen field, which has an area of a few hundred square miles. The seismic " probe " uses sound waves from an explosion to plot the sub-surface profiles of the layers of rock. The sound echoes back from discontinuities in the underground strata, and the travel times of the waves is less when reflected from a hump in the rock layer than when reflected from a valley. The technique is relatively easy to use—so much so that in spite of the inherent expense of any operation associated with ships, it is cheaper to survey a given sea area than a similar one on land. This is because on land the explosive charges must be put 50–100 ft below surface in order to give a strong wave in the ground. Furthermore, at each shot the instruments must be precisely laid out and moved again for the next. At sea, the instruments are trailed behind the ship with fixed relative positions, and the location of the recording is automatically plotted. The explosive, as charges of about ten pounds of " Geophex " or " Ammonal," is thrown overboard and fired in the water.

The speed of the method at sea has required rapid advances in automatic processing of the records, and today most recording is made on magnetic tape. In many cases, it is recorded in digital form so that it can be fed directly to a computer. This corrects for such factors as depth of the water, and it also allows many empirical calculations that would be too tedious to do in any other way.

One of the difficulties experienced in areas covered by water is caused by multiple sound reflections between the sea surface and the sea bed. These were especially troublesome in the North Sea, and very broad spreads of instruments were found to be necessary to obtain good results. The increase in the spread brought with it a new source of error, as the long streamer with its detecting instruments is carried away from the line of the ship's course by transverse currents. With a cable 2,400 m in length, cross currents of one and a half knots can move the end of the cable 1 km off course. However, the computer was able to make the appropriate correction.

### Drilling.

There have been many attempts to devise a combination of geophysical and geochemical methods that would specifically select the structures actually containing economic quantities of petroleum from the others—approximately ten times as numerous—that are merely promising. However, none of these has yet been proved reliable, and the expensive method of drilling is still the only one that can eliminate those structures indicated as promising by seismic reflection that in the event either contain water or consist of non-porous rock.

Drilling is by far the most expensive operation in looking for oil, and a " wildcat " well at sea may cost as much as half a million pounds. The heavy drilling equipment must be held in position above the sea surface either by a platform supported on legs which rest on the sea floor, or as a floating structure. The most popular technique in the North Sea has been the use of the " jack-up " type of platform, where an artificial island is erected by raising the drilling equipment above the sea surface well out of reach of the highest waves. In water depths of more than about 150 ft ships' hulls, fitted with a drilling derrick, are anchored in position, but these are not suitable in very rough weather. The latest type of exploration drilling rig is the " semi-submersible," which is a floating platform which takes its buoyancy from chambers 70 ft below the sea surface. This makes the platform stable even in bad weather, since the up and down water movement diminishes rapidly with depth.

## Weather Difficulties.

Although offshore oil production is a comparatively new venture, knowledge and experience have been gained gradually over the past twenty years; offshore drilling rigs are now familiar sights not only in the Gulf of Mexico but also in the Middle East and Nigeria. However, the North Sea is by comparison very inhospitable. For example, gales reaching nearly to hurricane force occur over much more of the year than they do in the more regular climatic conditions of the Gulf of Mexico. The rise and fall of the tide is large in many parts of the North Sea, and the associated currents make diving operations hazardous, and cause scouring round anchors and the legs of drilling platforms. Fogs are frequent, and the ambient temperature is often very low. Thus, for most of the year, working conditions are much worse than in offshore oil production areas in more southerly latitudes.

The hazards of the North Sea have been demonstrated by several accidents to drilling rigs, and the expense of operating in this area has been greatly increased by delays caused by bad weather. Improvements are continually being made, and a better understanding of the fatigue of metal caused by the pounding of waves, and measurements of movement of sand on the sea bed are two aspects of research which is being carried out to further offshore work in the future.

## Production.

The economic way to produce from a comparatively shallow area, such as that of the North Sea gas fields, is to construct a permanent platform on piles driven into the sea bed. This type of structure is cheaper than the " jack-up " platforms used for exploration and it is also available for valves and other production controls when drilling is completed. A further saving results from the possibility of drilling at large angles from the vertical when working from a fixed platform. In this way half a dozen wells may be drilled from one platform, and gas can be extracted from points within a radius of a few miles. The gas reservoir is two miles below surface, so that the bending of the drill pipe needed to make these divergent holes is well within the elastic limit of steel. The deviation is achieved by edging the drill sideways by means of a steel wedge lowered down the borehole or, more easily, by the use of a turbo-drill, in which the driving force for the cutting bit is at the bottom of the hole, and so is susceptible to steering by an angle joint placed above the turbine motor. Although turbo-drills have been much used in Russia, they are comparatively new to the Western world, and one of the advantages of the North Sea activity is that it provides an incentive for the European development of drilling equipment.

A steel pipeline, which may be anything from 16 to 36 inches diameter, and which is protected and weighted by a reinforced concrete coating, carries the gas to the shore, flow being maintained by the pressure of the gas which is well over 1,000 p.s.i. at the production platform. The pipeline is normally laid from a special craft, where 40-ft lengths are welded together and fed in a continuous line down a sloping ramp at the after part of the pipe-laying vessel. The pipe is buried in a subsequent operation, using a vessel equipped with powerful jets and suction devices.

## Reserves of Gas.

Four fields with commercial capabilities have been located in the North Sea after the drilling of more than 180 wells. These are BP's West Sole, the Amoco/Gas Council Indefatigable, Shell-Esso's large Leman Bank reservoir and the shallow Phillips/Arpet Hewett field. The latter is of geological interest in that the gas reservoir is higher up the geological scale than the Basal Permian (270 million years old) sandstone, since the gas has seeped upwards into the Bunter sandstone before being trapped.

It is probable that the proved reserves of gas are between $25–30 \times 10^{12}$ standard cubic feet. This is approximately 50 per cent of the Dutch Groningen gas field and in terms of oil equivalent is about 700 million tons of fuel oil. The quantity is such that a production of 2,500 to 3,000 million cubic feet a day could be sustained for 25 years

(by which time, no doubt, cheap nuclear electric power will have made North Sea gas redundant). Some new discoveries are almost certain to bring the available production up to 4,000 million cubic feet a day, and it is probable that a higher production rate could be operated for a shorter time than 25 years if it was required. One unknown in relation to the total reserves is concerned with the movement of the water seal at the underside of the porous rock reservoirs. If the water moves upwards to replace the produced gas there will be an advantage in that the gas pressure is maintained but the ultimate volume of gas recovered will be diminished by gas trapped in large blocks of rock by the invading water.

Of the 180 holes drilled in the British sector of the North Sea, about 120 have been exploratory, the remainder being drilled for production purposes in fields already discovered. Although in the early days of North Sea exploration the success ratio was about one hole in 4 or 5, the worldwide statistics were matched once sufficient wells were bored, and the offshore ratio of 20 or 30 to 1 now holds.

Some borings have been made in other parts of the North Sea with limited success. Oil has been observed in holes in Norwegian and Danish territory, but as might be forecast from experience on land around the North Sea it is present in quantities too small to be of economic value. A gas discovery in Netherlands offshore waters appears to be a discovery of standard North Sea size, but with only one well drilled caution about prospects is advisable.

It is unfortunate that arguments about price of gas have slowed down progress in the North Sea. However, sufficient drilling has taken place to prove a large reserve of indigenous hydrocarbon fuel, and other discoveries may be made in the future. It is possible but not likely that oil in large quantities will be discovered. Now that both geophysics and drilling ability have been improved to probe deeper into the earth, new territory is available for the prospector. During the past 20 years oil has been found in many parts of the world which were regarded as of little potential before the war. On the other hand, there is no large oil reservoir on neighbouring land to suggest that a big oil field lies under the North Sea.

# THE DEVELOPMENT OF A NATURAL GAS INDUSTRY IN THE UNITED KINGDOM.

## Discovery of Natural Gas under the North Sea.

Natural gas has been discovered under the bed of the North Sea at a rate unprecedented in most other parts of the world. The first commercial strike of gas was made in October 1965 about 40 miles off the Humber, and by January 1966 it was clear that the first major British natural gas field had been found—the West Sole Field. Over the next eighteen months three further fields, much larger in size, were discovered off the coast of Norfolk, and were christened Hewett, Leman Bank, and Indefatigable. In all four fields the gas is contained in the minute pores of a layer of rock known as Rotliegendes Sandstone at a depth of about 8,000 to 10,000 ft, except in one part of the Hewett Field, where it is located in the pores of the Upper Bunter Sandstone at about half that depth. The gas has originated from the effects of very high pressure and temperature on the coal in the Carboniferous rocks lying beneath the Rotliegendes sandstone, the coal itself being formed from vegetation that grew in the North Sea basin some 350 million years ago.

The present estimate of the reserves of gas in these four fields alone is that there is sufficient to maintain an average daily flow rate some $3\frac{1}{2}$ times the present average flow rate in the whole United Kingdom for 20 to 30 years. Such reserves of natural gas are more than sufficient to replace manufactured town gas completely in Britain. They do not take account of any future fields and significant discoveries have already been made in other areas of the North Sea which may well be capable of exploitation.

## The Present Gas Industry and Natural Gas

If the rate of discovery of natural gas under the North Sea has been unprecedented, the speed of development of the fields has been even more remarkable. The full commercial potential of the West Sole field had been assessed by January 1966. Under a special agreement with British Petroleum, the first test quantities of natural gas came ashore at Easington in Yorkshire on 21 March 1967, and the contract quantity of 100 million cubic feet per day was flowing into the Gas Council's transmission system on 20 July 1967. As will be seen, development of the Leman Bank field has been equally rapid.

This speedy development was very largely due to a technological revolution that had been taking place in the industry over the previous six years or so. Traditionally, town gas had always been manufactured from coal. In the 1950s it was becoming increasingly clear that if the gas industry was not to be priced out of the energy market, some cheaper method of manufacturing town gas had to be found. A research programme was therefore instituted in the industry's own research stations to devise means of manufacturing gas from oil. These researches were completely successful, and three novel processes making town gas at high pressure from oil were designed. These were brought to the full commercial scale

in the industry's works, and they are now operating widely throughout the industry. In 1960 90 per cent of the United Kingdom's gas was still made from coal: today less than 30 per cent is made from coal. The new processes achieved substantial savings in capital costs of building the plants, in running, and transmission costs. They are processes of complete gasification, all the feedstock going to gas with no by-products, solid or liquid.

As the new processes came into operation, it was felt desirable to find an alternative feedstock to the light distillate oil for which they were designed. One obvious alternative is natural gas itself. Natural gas consists almost entirely of one single chemical, the hydrocarbon methane. Oil is a mixture of a very large number of liquid hydrocarbons. In one of the new processes, natural gas can replace oil and be transformed in the process to town gas of the same characteristics as any other town gas, whether made from coal or oil. At this stage the possibility of natural gas under the North Sea seemed remote, and the nearest large source of natural gas was in the Sahara Desert in Algeria.

A project was therefore developed to bring

Fig. 4—Transmission system for natural gas imported from Algeria. Pipelines operational in 1964.

natural gas in bulk in liquid form from Algeria in specially designed ships. A 200-mile pipeline brings the gas from the desert field to the port of Arzew on the Mediterranean. A huge liquefaction plant here turns the gas into a liquid at the very low temperature of −160° C. This installation with its storage and loading facilities is, after the Aswan Dam, the largest single industrial project in the whole of Africa. Two ships each bring a cargo of 12,000 tons of the very cold liquid natural gas to Canvey Island, where a special terminal was built to store the liquid and to re-gasify it back to natural gas. A new trunk transmission pipeline was built, 200 miles in length, from Canvey to Leeds, with 120 miles of branches and spurs, to feed bulk supplies of this Algerian natural gas (in gaseous form) to eight out of the twelve Area Boards that supply gas in the United Kingdom. These Boards use it in place of oil to make ordinary town gas. The total quantity of natural gas imported from Algeria is not far short of 10 per cent of the total U.K. output of gas. This whole scheme went into operation in October 1964 and the pipeline system illustrated in Fig. 4 formed a splendid framework into which the North Sea project could be grafted.

## Development of the North Sea Project.

Fig. 5 shows the location of the four natural gas fields so far discovered, and the various pipelines built, under construction and proposed to bring the full potential of the North Sea fields into operation.

## Fixed Platforms over the Fields.

One fixed platform is built and operating on the West Sole field, four on the Leman Bank field, and two are built and will shortly be operating on the Hewett field. At a later stage, platforms will be built on the Indefatigable field. It is intended to bring the gas from all three of these fields ashore at a single shore station at Bacton in Norfolk. The platforms act as the well-head installation and have radio contact with the shore station.

## Undersea Pipelines.

As stated earlier, the single undersea pipeline from West Sole is complete and operational. Two pipelines from Leman Bank are also complete, and contract supplies are already flowing along one of them. Test quantities are expected through the

Fig. 5—The Gas Council natural gas transmission system.

second very early in 1969. A pipeline from the Hewett field is nearing completion (January 1969).

## Shore Stations.

There are two sides to a shore terminal, one operated by the producers, the other by the Gas Council. On the producers' side condensate is removed from the gas, it is dried, the pressure is regulated, and the gas is metered. Reduction of pressure from the 3,000–4,000 p.s.i. at the well-head to about 1,000 p.s.i. results in a sharp fall in gas temperature which could lead to freezing of the regulator valves, and this is counteracted by passing the gas through heaters immediately before the pressure reducing point. The natural gas enters the Gas Council side at a pressure of about 1,000 p.s.i. and is passed through filters into a manifold which serves two metering streams, one in operation, the other a stand-by. This second metering is a check against the pay meters installed on the producers' side, and after this the gas flows into the outlet main which has facilities to inject an odorant to give the odourless natural gas the familiar smell of town gas required by the Gas Acts.

A control room contains all the essential instruments and controls and is manned throughout 24 hours a day. Adjustments to flow and pressure are carried out automatically through a small computer operated from the control desk. Calorific value, specific gravity, and other important properties of the natural gas are continuously recorded.

The Easington terminal, serving the West Sole field, has been dealing with an average of 100 million cubic feet of natural gas per day for well over 1½ years. Phase One of the much larger terminal at Bacton is already complete and operational. When the full contract quantities from Leman Bank, Hewett, and Indefatigable come ashore the Bacton terminal will have a maximum capacity of 4,000 million cu. ft of natural gas a day. This compares with 1,100 million cu. ft a day which is the natural gas equivalent of the present average daily demand of the 13 million consumers of gas in the whole United Kingdom. Phase Two of the station, already under construction, will be completed by the autumn of 1969, which will give a total capacity at that stage of 1,500 million cu. ft per day.

## Natural Gas Transmission System.

From the shore station at Easington a 24-in diameter high pressure pipeline, 80 miles long and known as the No. 1 Feeder, was laid under the Humber and across country to tee into the existing Canvey–Leeds system at Totley, near Sheffield, and contract supplies of natural gas from the West Sole field have been flowing through this pipeline since the middle of 1967. The average contract quantity is approximately the same as that supplied from Algeria.

From the Bacton terminal there will ultimately be four very large pipelines. The No. 2 Feeder, shown by a solid line in Fig. 5, was completed in January 1968, and is now operational. It is a 36-inch-diameter pipeline, 125 miles long, routed so as to avoid interference as far as possible with built-up areas, but it passes near to King's Lynn, Wisbech, Peterborough, Stamford, Corby, and Market Harborough, to feed into the Canvey–Leeds system at Churchover, near Rugby. The pipeline will be capable of delivering up to 1,000 million cu. ft of natural gas per day, roughly equivalent to the average demand for gas in the whole of Britain at the present time.

The other three pipelines from Bacton will be of similar size and capacity. All are tested to a pressure of 1,000 p.s.i. The No. 3 Feeder main, shown as under construction in Fig. 5 comes 106 miles across country, passing close to Cambridge to tee into the existing system at Whitwell, near Cambridge. An extension from here (part of which has already been completed) to North Surrey will provide additional supplies to the North Thames, South-Eastern, and Southern Gas Boards. The whole of the No. 3 Feeder and its extension is (January 1969) nearing completion. Preliminary work has already started on the other two pipelines from Bacton: one to tee in to the system at Alrewas, near Burton-on-Trent, should by completed by the end of 1969; and finally, in

1970, one to the Essex end of the Canvey–Leeds system with an extension to link up with the other extension from Whitwell.

Concurrently, the system is being extended to feed natural gas to the four Gas Boards not yet connected to the Canvey–Leeds system. A 90-mile, 30-inch-diameter pipeline from Westgate Hill, between Leeds and Bradford, will extend the existing system northward to Blaydon, near Newcastle-upon-Tyne where it will feed into the Northern Gas Board's transmission and distribution system. The pipeline will cross the rivers Aire, Warfe, Nidd, Skell, Laver, Swale, Tees, and Wear, as well as the Leeds–Liverpool canal, while among the many road crossings is the A1 north of Northallerton. This pipeline is scheduled for completion in the spring of 1969. From Blaydon, a pipeline to Glasgow to feed natural gas into the Scottish Board's system will be built during 1969–70.

Construction is nearing completion of a pipeline which will take natural gas from the grid at Churchover to Wormington, north of Cheltenham, and on to Pucklechurch, near Bristol. This 85-mile pipeline will be 24 inches in diameter and a further 17-mile extension of 18 inch diameter will bring natural gas to the Seabank gasworks of the South Western Board at Hallen, near Avonmouth, where the Board will use it initially in the manufacture of town gas. A branch from Wormington to Swansea to feed into the southern part of the Wales Board's system at Swansea will be completed in 1969–70.

Farther north, another new pipeline is nearing completion to take natural gas from the grid near Alrewas to the Maelor gasworks at Wrexham to supply the North Wales distribution grid, with a branch to Partington (Manchester) for additional supplies to the North Western Gas Board.

By the early 1970s, therefore, there will be a 2,500-mile network for a national transmission system for natural gas, capable of taking between three and four times as much gas as is made in Britain today, and delivering it in bulk to the transmission and distribution grids of all twelve Area Boards.

## Control of the Gas Council Natural Gas Transmission System.

A national control centre for the whole of the Gas Council's transmission system for natural gas is to be established at Hinckley, Leicestershire, and it is expected that this will be operational by the summer of 1969. The system is best controlled from its centre, since access to all parts of the pipeline is facilitated and the highest reliability is achieved in the communications system. Hinckley has been selected as the geographical centre of the network, and it will provide a system of control which will be among the most advanced in the world. It will control and monitor the flow of natural gas through the national transmission network and into the Area Boards' local systems. It will help to ensure that gas is available to meet sudden shifts in demand for peak gas usage in different parts of the country and that the demand is satisfied in the most economical manner from the available sources of gas. A single-storey building will house the control room and its associated equipment such as computer, telemetry, and communications equipment and support functions. It is expected that thirty people will be employed at the control centre, with a further forty working in the pipelines department and concerned with construction and maintenance of the pipeline system.

Such a control system requires sophisticated communications, and microwave radio has been selected for this, mainly because it is less vulnerable to physical disturbance than a landline system. There will be about 60 major relay grids on towers about 150 ft high sited along the routes of the pipes at about 30-mile intervals. A second type of aerial, erected to provide contact with the governing stations and off-take points will be needed, and between 300 and 400 are planned for the whole gas industry. Around 50 ft high or less, they will be attached either to existing buildings or to slender poles, and are no bigger than a domestic television aerial.

The completed control system, taking advantage

of all the latest techniques will provide fully automatic computerised control and monitoring with a very high degree of reliability and efficiency.

## Peak Load Storage of Natural Gas.

For seasonal peak load purposes it is necessary to have strategic storage of large quantities of gas readily available. The North Sea fields themselves could only be used as strategic storages if a large number of extra wells were sunk to provide extra gas in the winter, and these would only be in operation for a relatively short part of the year. Because of the high cost of drilling these wells such a mode of operation of the fields would be uneconomic. The Gas Council has therefore decided to store natural gas in liquid form. There is already a large storage of Algerian liquid natural gas at Canvey, but the first strategic storage has been constructed at Ambergate in Derbyshire. In a special tank, 70 ft high and 100 ft in diameter, 5,000 tons of the very cold liquid, equivalent to a quarter of the average daily demand for the whole of Britain, is stored. Liquefied natural gas is taken to Ambergate by road tanker from the Canvey Island terminal.

A second strategic storage is planned to store liquid natural gas in Scotland at Glenmavis, near Coatbridge, Lanarkshire. The tank here will be 130 ft high and 150 ft in diameter, and the 20,000 tons of liquid gas it will hold is enough to supply the whole of Britain with gas for one day. About 400 average-sized gasholders would be needed to store this quantity of gas by traditional methods. At this site, a liquefaction plant will be built, and gas will be taken from the new transmission grid to Scotland and liquefied on the spot before being stored. The liquefaction plant will be capable of liquefying 5 million cu. ft. of natural gas a day.

## The Conversion of a Town Gas System to Natural Gas.

Natural gas has a quite different composition from town gas, whether that town gas is made from coal, from oil or, indeed, from natural gas. The composition of a typical town gas and of natural gas from the North Sea are given below in percentages by volume:

| Constituent | Town Gas | Natural Gas |
| --- | --- | --- |
| Hydrogen | 48·2 | Nil |
| Carbon monoxide | 15·5 | Nil |
| Methane | 18·2 | 95·0 |
| Other Hydrocarbons | 6·6 | 3·8 |
| Carbon Dioxide | 3·8 | Nil |
| Nitrogen | 7·7 | 1·2 |

These differences have important consequences when the gases are burnt in appliances. First, natural gas has twice the calorific value of town gas—a cubic foot of natural gas produces 1,000 units of heat, whereas a cubic foot of town gas produces only 500 units of heat. This also means that a given volume of natural gas requires twice as much air to burn it completely in an appliance as does the same volume of town gas. Second, natural gas has a low flame speed, while town gas has a high flame speed. These two effects together mean that if natural gas is burnt in an existing appliance designed to town gas, the resulting flame is under-aerated (giving incomplete combustion) and also tends to lift away from the burner, so giving an unstable flame. Every existing town gas appliance must therefore be converted before natural gas can be fed directly into it.

The conversion of whole towns and cities, with their inter-connecting complex of distribution networks, to natural gas is unparalleled in size. Large-scale conversions have, of course, been carried out in the United States, Canada, and Europe, but this is the first time that a programme for a conversion covering nearly 13 million consumers has been faced. It is obvious that this cannot be achieved at once, but must be carried out piecemeal over a period, and it is estimated that conversion of the country as a whole may take as long as seven to ten years. A start has already been made, and by the end of March 1969 over half a million consumers will already be receiving the new gas direct on converted appliances. However, the natural gas from the North Sea will continue to be used in increasing quantities as it becomes available, in the same way as the Algerian natural gas has been used, i.e., it will be processed instead of oil in the new plants to make present-type town gas, but sector by sector the new gas will progressively be supplied direct to the consumer as conversion proceeds.

The cost of this huge conversion will be about £400 million, and this cost will be met by the gas industry and not by the consumer. It is reasonable to ask why this costly conversion is necessary since, as has been seen, natural gas can be processed to town gas and can thus be used in existing appliances without conversion being needed. There are three reasons why the Gas Council believes this to be the wrong way of using natural gas:

(1) The processing of natural gas to town gas costs money in building and running the plants, so the price of gas to the consumer must be higher than it would have been without processing to town gas.

(2) The thermal efficiency of the town gas process is only 90 per cent, so that 10 out of every 100 therms of natural gas are lost in the process, which are not lost if natural gas is supplied direct.

(3) Because the calorific value of natural gas is double that of town gas, a given volume in a pipe contains twice as many therms as would the same volume of town gas. In other words, the passage of natural gas through a distribution system automatically doubles the capacity of the system. Without this doubling, a further programme of extra main laying within a very short time, and costing many times the cost of conversion of appliances, would be required to keep pace with the expansion of the industry's business, with consequent rises in the price of gas to the consumer.

The saving in building, running, and maintaining town gas production plants, and in constructing these extra distribution mains, by supplying natural gas direct to all consumers through a pipeline without any intervening processing, could well be £1,400 million over the next 20 years.

## Conclusion.

The potential advantages of this indigenous, non-toxic, natural gas to the country's economy, and not least to the balance of payments, are enormous. By 1971 some £50 million a year will be saved on oil imports, and by 1980 the saving could well average £100 million a year. The discovery of natural gas under the North Sea could well change the fortunes of the nation.

## SOME SPECULATIONS CONCERNING THE CHARACTERISTICS AND ORIGINS OF LIFE.

Few biologists are dogmatic about the characteristics by which they recognise organisms. In the past, systems were thought to be alive which we should not consider living today. The Romans thought ores were alive, believing they could replace themselves like oysters. Oysters are now accepted organisms, ingots are not. Oysters are considered alive because their soft parts undergo a number of intricate transformations definable in terms of gross morphology, biochemistry and biophysics. These transformations are also characteristic of other obviously living systems. In borderline systems, where only a few vital characteristics are found, the use of the term "living" is usually avoided. A consideration of borderline systems is nevertheless central to the study of the characteristics and origins of life. In this article, the term "biopoesis" will be used in place of the phrase "origins of life." Biopoesis is defined by N. W. Pirie, who coined it, as "the creation of something that some people might wish to call living from non-living material."

## Milestones in the Scientific Theory of Biopoesis.

Life has only been interpreted in terms of the stock-in-trade of the rest of science for a century. Until then, vitalist concepts vied with mechanist views of life. Vitalists held that life is an indefinable essence separable from the base matter which it activates. Charles Darwin indulged in vitalist terminology in the more rhetorical passages of *The Origin of Species*, published in 1859. His concluding lines describe life being " breathed by the Creator into a few forms or into one, and that from so simple beginning, forms most wonderful have been and are being evolved." Darwin's vitalist turn of phrase was roundly disapproved of by T. H. Huxley. " This is the very passage of Darwin's book to which, as he knows right well, I have always objected," Huxley wrote to Charles Kingsley in 1863. In the same year, Darwin confided to Hooker: " I have long regretted that I truckled to public opinion and used the Pentateuchal term of " creation " by which I really mean (life) appeared by some wholly unknown process."

During the period 1860–80, Huxley and a number of other eminent evolutionists, theoreticians like Herbert Spencer, and experimentalists like John Tyndall, indulged in a great deal of intense private and public discussion of possible forms of biopoesis. These discussions were considerably clarified by the rapid development that was in progress in the study of the life cycles and heat resistance of micro-organisms, and of the composition of chemicals of biological origin. The first recognisably modern lecture on biopoesis was delivered to the British Association in 1870 by T. H. Huxley. Lucid and garrulous, orthodox and controversial, papers originating in the specialised fields of almost every branch of science have followed it. An expansion of international interest in the field of biopoesis after the Second World War has resulted in a number of international symposia on the subject, one in Moscow in 1957, for example, and another at Wakulla Springs, Florida, in 1963. As the phase of research draws near when it will be possible to test samples of extra-terrestrial matter for signs of life, an increasing volume of the literature is concerned with the so far hypothetical subject of exobiology.

In *The Origin of Species* Darwin concerned himself with the evolution of present-day morphological complexity. He argued that this had been built up by the gradual and opportunist mechanism of natural selection. Projecting the idea backwards into Pre-Cambrian times, Darwin inferred that the whole process of morphological evolution was initiated by a few, morphologically simple species. Although biopoesis did not seem to Darwin a fruitful field for scientific speculation, he did believe that natural selection must have operated from the very earliest times. He wrote in 1859: " As we have no facts to guide us, speculation (on the first dawn of life) is almost useless. It is, however, an error to suppose that there would be no struggle for existence, and consequently no natural selection, until many forms had been produced." The notion that a form of natural selection could have operated on very primitive biological systems is in line with current biopoeic theory.

The evolutionary aspect of biopoesis has been emphasised by A. I. Oparin of the U.S.S.R., and his co-workers, for the last forty years. Oparin's first contribution on the subject was presented to the Moscow Botanical Society in 1922 and together with the early contributions of J. B. S. Haldane provides a cornerstone to present theories. Oparin's experimental work is largely concerned with liquid concentrates rich in colloids, such as enzyme extracts of biological origin. He calls these systems " coacervate droplets." He points out that such fissile, macromolecular concentrates show somewhat life-like characteristics. In his original paper, unfortunately not read outside Russia at the time, since it was not translated, Oparin wrote: " Selection of the better-organised bits of gel was always going on. It is true that the less-organised could grow alongside the more efficient, but they must have soon stopped growing. The leading part was always played by the qualitatively better-organised entities." Further work, not with liquid concentrates but with spontaneously formed amino-acids, heated together in the absence of water, has been carried out by Sidney Fox and his co-workers in the U.S. Named " microspheres," these systems, often of bacterial dimensions, have been shown to retain mixtures of internal polymers within a double-walled containing layer. They can also catalyse

reactions in a quasi-enzymic manner, and show phenomena analogous to replication. Systems like Oparin's coacervate droplets and Fox's microspheres have the life-like property of developing an organisation that uses a readily available source of energy in order to persist. But neither the synthetic droplets nor the spheroids satisfy most people's minimum vital requirements for an organism. Oparin reminded delegates at the Wakulla Springs conference that a thousand million years were needed before life could be produced by such mixtures of organic and inorganic materials with structured phase boundaries and inclusions. How much time was in fact required for such a transition? The experimentalists will continue to try to circumvent the time problem, in the hope of discovering chemical systems which integrate themselves after prolonged laboratory incubation, into still more life-like systems.

## Experiments with Spontaneous Syntheses.

The energy changes and molecular segregations characteristic of complex emulsions do not carry us back far enough. How did the material that composed these emulsions originate in probiotic times (*i.e.*, before life began)? This problem was treated in J. B. S. Haldane's classic paper in the *Rationalist Annual* of 1928. He suggested that a plausible mechanism for the initial stages of biopoesis might be the synthetic action of ultra-violet light on various gases present in the probiotic atmosphere. He wrote: " Now when ultra-violet light acts on a mixture of water, carbon dioxide " (he later substituted methane for $CO_2$ " and ammonia, a vast variety of organic substances are made. . . . In this present world such substances, if left about, decay, that is to say, they are destroyed by micro-organisms " (a point also emphasised by Darwin in a private letter in 1871) " but before the origin of life they must have accumulated till the primitive oceans reached the consistency of hot dilute soup." Becquerel and others had already suggested that ultra-violet light could have provided the synthetic energy required for biopoesis. What was crucial to Haldane's suggestion was that if there had been no oxygen in the probiotic atmosphere, the amount of ultra-violet solar radiation reaching the Earth would have been far greater than it is today. It would have been more on the level of the lethal intensities reaching the surface of the planet Venus today (F52), which would be sufficient to burn up any unprotected present-day form of terrestrial life. Haldane suggested that, unlike conditions prevailing in the Earth's atmosphere today, in probiotic times there was no stratospheric filtering layer of ozone. This layer was only built up later as primitive biological systems developed metabolic processes akin to fermentation and photosynthesis, thus releasing carbon dioxide and oxygen for the first time into the atmosphere. Haldane's suggestion that ultra-violet solar radiation, at a much higher intensity than it is experienced today, could have built up, from the probiotic atmosphere and sea, a metastable system of macromolecules has been verified by experimental work in laboratories all over the world.

Simulated biopoeic syntheses use as their starting point those ratios of reducing gases most strongly suggested by the geochemical evidence. They may also include carefully selected matrices such as crystals or powdered rocks and lava for the products of synthesis to settle on and possibly interact with. Successful investigations are taken to be those where complex molecules of present-day biological importance are identified among the products of synthesis. Using, for example, ultra-violet light between wavelengths 2,400–2,900 Å as energy flux, and suitable concentrations of hydrogen, ammonia, methane and water vapour, H. C. Urey, S. L. Miller, Carl Sagan and others have produced sludges containing such chemicals as glycine, alanine, ATP, and traces of porphyrins. Although palaeo-biochemistry is a highly speculative subject, this evidence is of interest. How much light it sheds on the exact biochemical pathways that were followed for original biopoeses is an open question. The difficulty is that most living species, with the exception of some micro-organisms and a few rare and apparently relict groups, are characterised by a very high degree of biochemical uniformity. Is it justifiable to project this uniformity directly backwards to probiotic times?

It has been suggested, for example, that the emergence, at a given point in time, of a single group of macromolecules of present-day importance, such as the nucleic acids, can explain away the problem of biopoesis. This is a gross over-simplification, which has been labelled "bio-chemical monotheism" by Pirie. J. D. Bernal also uses a theological metaphor. He writes: "The picture of a solitary molecule of DNA on a primitive sea-shore generating the rest of life has been put forward with slightly less plausibility than that of Adam and Eve in the garden." As more research is carried out into possible probiotic syntheses using different raw materials, more possible routes for biopoesis can be mapped. This route-mapping is slow and intricate, and as with the biopoeic studies of the previous century, often awaits the elucidation of biochemical processes such as protein synthesis which are still under active investigation today, for any adequate assessment.

### Geochemical Evidence for the Oxygenless Atmosphere.

Huxley and Haldane, and a number of others concerned with the problem of biopoesis, assumed that early life forms depended on some anaerobic form of metabolism. An example of an anaerobic mechanism is glycolysis in yeast, whereby the mildly metastable molecule of glucose is fragmented to produce energy, ethyl alcohol and carbon dioxide. Glycolysis provides a rather inefficient system for releasing energy, a system that is held to be more primitive than that used in aerobic respiration. The geochemical evidence, too, seems to suggest that the probiotic Earth was without oxygen. Very large amounts of oxygen and carbon dioxide are thought to have passed through the atmosphere since the Cambrian Period (F41), but most of the Earth's oldest sedimentary and plutonic rocks contain unoxidised minerals such as sulphur and iron-containing minerals. Later rocks, deposited during the actively oxidising and weathering climate of more recent times, are found in an oxidised state. Thus, relatively recent iron-bearing sediments contain ferric iron ($Fe^{+++}$) if they have been laid down in contact with the atmosphere. Their salts are rust-red or dark brown in colour. In the oldest rocks the picture is different. There is a preponderance of the greenish grey salts of un-oxidised iron ($Fe^{++}$) (see F 22(2)).

The evidence for a reducing atmosphere in probiotic times has to be viewed with caution. Oxidising and reducing conditions are found closely juxtaposed in biologically-active areas of sedimentation, such as freshwater swamps or basins of marine deposition. Deposits dating as far back as the Pre-Cambrian have probably been subjected to extensive alteration because reducing and oxidising solutions can percolate through ancient strata after deposition. This diminishes the value of the iron-bearing minerals as indicators of the original environmental conditions. Nevertheless, a complete lack of unoxidised iron throughout a deposit suggests that reducing conditions prevailed exclusively at the time of deposition, and this seems to be borne out by most of the Pre-Cambrian geological evidence.

### The Pre-Cambrian Fossil Evidence.

The balance of opinion about the age of the Earth seems to be that it originated in the accretion of small cold particles about $5 \times 10^9$ years ago (see F8). Pre-Cambrian rocks are not exposed in many parts of the Earth. They are overlain by later rocks or, more frequently, they have been eroded away millions of years ago. Two areas in which valuable evidence has been found for the existence of ancient forms of cellular life are the Middle Pre-Cambrian deposits of the Gunflint cherts of Ontario, Canada, and the early Pre-Cambrian cherts of the Fig Tree series of the Transvaal, South Africa. Micro-fossils embedded in stratified cherts from both these Pre-Cambrian formations have been described by E. S. Barghoorn. A number of Pre-Cambrian species have

been named. They have been dated by various methods. The oldest named species is a group of unicellular rods measuring $0.56 \times 0.24 \mu$ ($1 \mu = 10^{-6}$ metre), a length-to-width ratio which is comparable with that most common in present-day bacteria. This ratio is clearly of a very ancient one. So is the apparent width of the containing membrane. One of these micro-fossils is called *Eobacterium isolatum*. It has been dated to $3.1 \times 10^9$ years ago. Barghoorn concludes: "Life must have originated during the preceding 30 per cent of the Earth's history."

It is not easy from the fossil evidence to speculate with any accuracy on the paleo-biochemistry of a group as ancient as this, although recent chromatographic work suggests that 22 different amino-acids, including glycine and $\alpha$-alanine may have been present. One possible line of investigation has been suggested by some comparative work that has been done in connection with a curious Gunflint organism named *Kakabekia umbellata*. This micro-fossil is identified by its remarkable morphology, which includes a bulbous stipe, ending in a spoked circular tip. A previously unknown, modern micro-organism of identical morphology and size has been isolated in urine-soaked soil from the moat of Harlech Castle. Spores from this contemporary micro-organism were successfully cultivated on agar in a highly reducing atmosphere. Their growth was inhibited by oxygen. Can we assume from this evidence that the assemblage of micro-organisms found in the Gunflint cherts lived at a time when the terrestrial atmosphere was still without oxygen?

Any such interpretation must be set against the conflicting evidence provided by the isotope segregations revealed in the fossil organisms. (see F 10(2) for isotope.) Living systems, and non-living ones characterised by a series of stages of absorption, diffusion, and phase equilibrium, are able to differentiate between isotopes of many biologically important elements, such as carbon and sulphur. They pack into a small compass the capacity for isotope fractionation that would demand a long separating column in an isotope factory. The two stable isotopes of carbon have atomic weights 12 and 13. Living organisms that are capable of carbon assimilation or photosynthesis contain a larger proportion of C-12 than the average non-living substance. The proportion of C-12 isotope segregated in some of the algal micro-fossils accompanying *Kakabekia* is almost identical with that found in much later carbonaceous deposits of biological origin. This suggests that photosynthesis may already have been established in some areas in the Middle Pre-Cambrian. The Gunflint chert assemblages most probably survived by modes of nutrition very little different from those we should expect to find in any contemporary micro-environment in which aerobic and anaerobic conditions are closely juxtaposed. (One further line of research into the Gunflint cherts is concerned with their optical activity.)

### Anomalous Biochemical Systems Today.

An approach to the problem of the origins of life which has been receiving some attention recently is that of the study of present-day biochemical systems that are in some way anomalous. Such studies suggest that the biochemical systems dominant today may not be the only possible ones. Present-day systems were evidently sufficiently amenable to evolutionary integration to resist competition from rival groups of molecules in probiotic times. They have also apparently blocked possibly equally feasible alternatives, as successful morphological evolution closed the door to further biochemical innovation. Gross biochemical differences are not found between present-day organisms. All we can do in the search for present-day anomalies is to look for minor differences. Two instances of these will be considered here. Both suggest that an initially more catholic approach to biochemistry is possible.

The group of animals to which the sea-squirts belong (F33), the Tunicates, are sedentary animals with greater powers to concentrate rare trace elements from sea-water between the tide lines then any other known creature. These trace elements are scavenged opportunistically from sea-water and are found associated with tissues forming the tunic of the animal. This tunic is built up of a chemical closely related to cellulose, which is not found in any other group. From morphological and palaeontological considerations, the tunicates seem to be a group of respectable antiquity. In place of the usual iron-content in their blood corpuscles, some species contain the oxides of elements such as vanadium, titanium, rare bio-elements like chromium, manganese, niobium, tantalum, and other metals. The cell vacuoles of these tunicates are also atypical. They contain concentrated solutions of sulphuric acid in a concentration twenty times that found in mammals. Curious biochemical details like this leave no fossil record. If the tunicates became extinct, we could not recognise from their morphological record that vanadium and sulphuric acid played an important part in their metabolism.

At a molecular level, we can consider an apparently primitive protein, ferredoxin. Ferredoxin is an iron-based catalyst. The iron shifts from ferrous to ferric during catalysis, and is loosely bound to hydrogen sulphide. This small and atypical protein only contains about two-thirds of the twenty amino-acids found in all normal proteins (F 27(1)). (The peptide chain in ferredoxin is made up of fifty amino-acids altogether, but they are selected from a smaller group than those of most other present-day proteins).

It appears possible that most changes in the course of biochemical evolution have been simplifications from an initially more catholic approach, as exemplified perhaps by the greater biochemical expertise of a few relict forms, like the Tunicates today. The only exception to this rule appears to be the proteins, which offer a potentiality for specificity greatly in excess of anything organisms at present use.

### The Smallest Free-living Organism.

Studies in apparently relict biochemical structures help to broaden our approach to the problem of biopoesis. It is also useful to consider some equally fundamental problems posed by the characteristics of the smallest organisms known today. One of these is an organism *Mycoplasma gallisepticum*, belonging to the group of Pleuropneumonia-like organisms (PPLO). Each PPLO cell is surrounded by a double mucopeptide membrane separated by a layer of lipid. This membrane encloses in suspension in the cell fluids random segregations of ribosomes, each one 20 nm (1 nm = $10^{-9}$ m; see N14) in diameter. At least 20 ribosomes are thought necessary to the existence of a free-living cell. There is thought to be room on each ribosome for about 14 average-size protein molecules and the ribosomes are thought to be responsible for protein synthesis, without which growth and replication would be impossible. A PPLO cell can be as small as 100 nm in diameter. (The minimum diameter compatible with replication in PPLO seems to be about 1000 nm). Organisms smaller than this have not yet been identified. Many viruses are smaller, but they merely transmit information to a living host for their own replication, without having any metabolism of their own. They are not therefore included among the organisms.

### Optical Activity and the Origins of Life.

Pasteur studied the effect of plane-polarised light on various optically-active solutions such as tartaric acid (from grape juice), egg white, and quinidine. Ever since, the ability of solutions of biological origin to rotate plane-polarised light in one of two possible directions has been accepted as one of the most characteristic diagnostic features of life. Optical activity will be described in this article by the term " chiral selectivity." This term describes the selection in biochemical systems of one of two possible forms of chemical structure each of which is the mirror-image of the other. D- and L- (dextro = right, laevo = left) are prefixes given to molecules depending on which of the two types of arrangement they have round one chiral centre. At present, all known proteins are built up from the left-handed (L-) isomers of amino-acids. The only organisms that use right-

handed amino-acids are a few bacteria and fungi, like Penicillin. These more versatile groups are further down the evolutionary scale. Why is it that no proteins are built up of the right-handed isomer of an amino-acid? It is generally accepted that the answer to this question must be that a dominant preference will be perpetuated by the close metabolic relationships that exist between organisms. Very few organisms synthesise their own metabolites. The rest live on the residues of the few (F34(2)). This forces all mutually dependent organisms to conform in their chiral preferences. If they did not, their metabolism would break down.

This structural determinism has been studied experimentally in two groups of complex chemicals. In the first group, crystals of a single chiral form have been separated from an unbiased mother liquor in the presence of suitable unbiased " adducts " in a few laboratories. The second group, which is thoroughly authenticated, is the process of polymerisation, the building up of biased polymers like the well-known $\alpha$-helix characteristic of many biological structures. Chain polymers are built up more effectively in the presence of polymer components of a single chiral form. The " wrong " isomer not only inhibits chain building, but it is actually obstructive. Mixed polymers are less stable than pure ones and do not last. If phenomena like this operated during biopoesis, it looks as though organisms are perpetuating a structural necessity that preceded them.

The chiral uniformity of biological systems has also been thought by a number of scientists to have originated in external organising forces like circularly-polarised light, or absorption on optically orientated mineral surfaces. V. M. Goldschmidt was a pioneering proponent of the view that organic life was constructionally adapted to the edges and corners of mineral crystals. The idea provides a number of interesting biopoeic possibilities. Thus hydrated silica, alumina, cyanides, phosphates, and carbonates absorb molecules and hold them in an orientated array in a manner comparable to that in which they are held by proteins. Some experimental work has been done in the U.S.S.R. using model catalysts with left- or right-handed quartz as a base. This base, coated with catalytically active materials (F 24(2)) has in some instances successfully transmitted a marked chiral bias in various solutions.

### Chirality at the Atomic Level?

An interesting suggestion put forward by Pasteur and after him by J. B. S. Haldane, was that chirality may be characteristic of matter at a subatomic level. Pasteur noted in 1874: " What is the nature of the disymmetry (chirality) of vital actions? I personally believe they are of a cosmic order." This statement seemed nebulous at the time. Experiments publicised in 1960, and still under investigation, suggest that while we should expect the properties of fundamental particles to have no bias, the emission of certain products from low-energy nuclear reactions consistently indicates that there may be a built-in " screw " in atoms themselves. This could suggest that the preferred chiral selectivity of biological material today is a consequence of nuclear preferences inherent in the atom.

Haldane suggested that the only way this thesis could be invalidated would be if the D-isomer of an amino-acid (biased opposite in form to that characteristic of the terrestrial environment) were returned from an extra-terrestrial environment, such as that of Mars. The discovery of an alien, mirror-image chiral form would invalidate the Pasteur–Haldane hypothesis. If the terrestrial form were found on Mars, we could draw two inferences. First that there had been a coincidence during Martian and terrestrial biopoesis. Secondly, that our life and that on Mars could have emanated from the same source. The possibility of the built-in screw at atomic level would remain.

Speculation such as this serves to remind us that rather than drawing up any prematurely detailed scheme for biopoesis, the best we can do is to keep in mind a number of possibilities from as many directions as possible.

# BACKGROUND TO ECONOMIC EVENTS

The aim of this section is to help the ordinary reader to follow economic events as they happen, and to understand the controversies that accompany them.

# TABLE OF CONTENTS

# BACKGROUND TO ECONOMIC EVENTS

This section is divided into four parts. Part I gives a brief description of the most important problems of economic policy. Part II is concerned with a more detailed survey of the British economy and the way in which it operates. In the course of this survey, the specialised terms used by economists are explained, and the attempt is made to present an intelligible summary of the information, facts, and figures relevant to an understanding of economic events. There are five main sub-sections: International Trade and Payments; Production, Employment, and Industry; Incomes, Wages, and Prices; Money, Banking, and Finance; and Economic Aspects of the Public Services. Part III outlines the main economic problems faced by the underdeveloped countries, and the economic policies of Britain and other developed countries towards the underdeveloped world. Some suggestions for further reading are given at the end of Parts II and III. Part IV is written as shortly before publication as possible, and contains a survey of developments in the British economy since 1960.

## I. CENTRAL PROBLEMS OF ECONOMIC POLICY

### Unemployment.

Between the wars, unemployment was Britain's most urgent economic problem. The level of unemployment varied with the ups and downs of the trade cycle. Quite the worst slump was that of the early 1930s: in 1932, nearly 3 million workers were without a job. But unemployment remained high even in the best years, and in no year between 1919 and 1939 were there fewer than a million workers unemployed. Economists make a distinction between *structural* unemployment and *cyclical* unemployment. Structural unemployment appears when the structure of industry gets out of line with the pattern of demand for industrial products. In Britain, unemployment was particularly severe and persistent in areas which were dependent on the coal, textile, and shipbuilding industries, and some sections of the engineering industry. These industries had been in the forefront of Britain's industrial growth in the 19th cent., and had contributed greatly to the expansion of exports. In areas like South Wales, Tyneside, Clydeside, and Northern Ireland there was little alternative work for those no longer needed in the " staple " industries: new industries were being built up in the inter-war period, but they tended to be located in the relatively prosperous Midlands and South-East England. Cyclical unemployment appears when there is a general decline in the level of demand for goods and services, which leads to a decline in the employment of workers producing those goods and services. In the slump years unemployment was so high because of a combination of structural and cyclical unemployment; in the best years, unemployment was largely structural.

Unemployment means waste. Men willing to work, who could produce valuable goods and services, are idle; the economy produces fewer goods and services than it is capable of producing. Unemployment also means hardship and low standards of living for those out of work, and for their families.

The avoidance of mass unemployment has been accepted as a primary objective of economic policy by all political parties, and there is a wide measure of agreement on the policies which must be applied to ensure that unemployment on the scale of the 1930s never occurs again. Cyclical unemployment has to be tackled by measures to increase total demand and total spending by consumers, by investors, and by the Government. Structural unemployment has to be tackled by inducing new industries to move into areas where other employment is declining, or by inducing labour to move from those areas to areas where there is a demand for its services.

There have been ups and downs in unemployment in the post-war years, but these have been very slight compared to those of the pre-war years. In most post-war years, less than 2 per cent of the working population was unemployed —a sharp contrast with the 11 per cent for 1937 and the 22 per cent for 1932. But there are still areas of the country where structural unemployment is serious. In Northern Ireland, for example, despite the efforts which have been made to attract new industries, unemployment ranged between 6 and 10 per cent in the last decade.

### Inflation.

A characteristic of the British economy in post-war years has been a persistent rise in prices and money incomes. For example, between 1954 and 1964, retail prices went up by about 35 per cent, or—expressed as an annual rate—by 3·1 per cent per annum, export prices rose by 18 per cent (or 1·6 per cent per annum), and weekly wage rates by about 55 per cent (4·4 per cent per annum). However, these rates of increase were considerably slower than the corresponding rates in the immediately post-war decade. This inflation of prices and money incomes is considered undesirable for two main reasons. Firstly, it is associated with an arbitrary redistribution of purchasing power. Prices rise for everyone, but some members of the community are better placed than others to secure increases in their money incomes which offset, or more than offset, the rise in the price of the goods and services they buy. The feeling that particular groups are falling behind, in that their money incomes have not risen as fast as those of other groups, is a source of much unrest and discontent. Secondly, and crucially for the British economy, an inflation of prices makes it more difficult to achieve a satisfactory balance of payments. As prices of our exports rise, it becomes harder to sell them in foreign markets; and as imports become cheap in comparison with goods produced at home there is a tendency to buy more of them.

Two main explanations have been advanced to account for the inflation which has occurred. The first stresses the role of an excess of demand or spending power in the economy—of too much money chasing too few goods, and so leading to a rise in prices. The inflationary problem is seen as the obverse of the cyclical unemployment problem: the latter involves a deficiency of spending, and the former an excess. Those who consider an excess of demand (*demand-pull*) to be an important factor in the inflationary situation favour policies designed to reduce purchasing power: for example, the reduction of spendable income by levying higher taxes, or the reduction of spending financed through borrowing by making credit more expensive or more difficult to get. The second stresses the role of an excessive increase in incomes: it is argued that prices have risen mainly because costs have increased faster than productivity (*cost-push*). Those who take this view favour measures to restrain or control increases in wages, profits, rents, and other forms of income. Neither explanation excludes the other. Many would agree that both demand-pull and cost-push factors have contributed—with different strengths at different times—to the inflationary spiral in prices and incomes, and that measures both to control demand and to restrain or control incomes may be necessary.

But it is easier to specify in general terms the measures needed to combat inflation than it is to apply policies which are successful in practice. In particular, policy measures to restrain or control wage increases are difficult to reconcile with widely-accepted procedures of collective bargaining.

## The Balance of Payments.

Britain is heavily dependent on imports. This country must import food: it cannot produce enough food within its borders to feed its population. Many of the raw materials necessary for its industry have to be purchased from abroad. Furthermore, some manufactured goods produced in other countries will be purchased because they are cheaper or more attractive than similar goods produced at home. All these goods, and our imports of services, have to be paid for in foreign currency. Foreign currency is earned by exporting goods and services to other countries. It is not, however, considered sufficient to earn enough foreign currency from our exports to pay for our imports. The objective is to earn considerably more than that, so that we have a surplus of foreign currency available to pay off external debts, to build up our external assets by investing abroad, to enable us to lend and give aid to underdeveloped countries, and to increase our foreign exchange resources.

Since the war, our balance of payments position has been precarious. Exports have increased considerably, but so have imports; and the margin of safety has been so narrow that unfavourable turns of events have led to crises in the balance of payments. In several years, our earnings from the export of goods and services have not even been sufficient to cover our payments for imports, and in no year has the surplus been as large as is considered necessary. With the balance of payments delicately poised even in favourable years, and with corrective action necessary in crisis years, economic policies have been much influenced by our foreign trade problems. It is easy to say that most of the problems would disappear, or would become less urgent, if we could achieve a major expansion of our exports. But most export markets are highly competitive, and we cannot expect to sell more unless the price, quality, and terms of delivery of our goods and services are at least as attractive as those of our rivals in export markets.

## Economic Growth.

Taking a longer view, the most important objective of internal economic policy must be to raise the standard of living. The standard of living can increase only if more goods and services are produced per head of population. In a fully-employed economy, the main source of increased output is a higher productivity—output per person—of the working population.

Standards of living in this country have been rising: the output of goods and services per head of population increased by about 24 per cent between 1954 and 1964. Nevertheless, many economists are of the opinion that the rate of growth of output and productivity can be, and

should be, increased. In particular, they point out that our rate of growth compares unfavourably with that achieved by some other countries. The potentialities for higher productivity are enormous. The U.S.A. has the highest standard of living in the world: in many industries, output per person employed is twice or more that yet attained in this country. In order to achieve a higher level of productivity in this country, more and better machinery and capital equipment will have to be installed; and also, work will have to be planned, organised, and controlled in such a way as to make more effective use of labour and machinery.

## Underdeveloped Countries.

Britain and the other developed countries of the world have important responsibilities towards the underdeveloped countries. The poorest two-thirds of the world's population account for only a sixth of total world income and output, while two-thirds of world income accrue to the richest sixth of world population, a category which includes Britain. The poorest two-thirds suffer from poverty, hunger, malnutrition, debilitating diseases, and widespread illiteracy. To make matters worse, most of the poor countries are experiencing a rapid growth of population. Output has to rise as fast as population just to prevent standards of living from falling, and an increase in standards of living requires an even faster growth of output.

Few underdeveloped countries can hope to solve the increasing problems they face without active and generous help from developed countries. This help must take many forms. Financial aid in the form of grants or loans, in order to place resources at the disposal of underdeveloped countries which they would otherwise not be able to obtain; technical aid to assist in the solution of the many technical problems which have to be solved; trading policies which do not hinder underdeveloped countries from getting the imports they need or from selling their exports—these are all activities in which Britain must play her part. In particular, of course, Britain must contribute to the development of the underdeveloped countries of the Commonwealth.

## The Inter-relationship of Economic Problems.

Each of the problems briefly described above is extremely complex. The difficulties of achieving successful solutions are further aggravated by the fact that the problems are inter-related in such a way that measures which are helpful for one problem can make others more difficult to solve. For example, a reduction of purchasing power might be considered helpful in the control of inflation, and might ease balance of payments problems by reducing—or slowing down the increase of—imports. But it could also lead to an increase in unemployment, and to a slowing down in the rate of growth of the economy. Or again, a reduction in aid to underdeveloped countries could make it easier to balance our external accounts, but such action could hardly be reconciled with our responsibilities towards underdeveloped countries. In the next section, particular aspects of the British economy are considered in some detail; the final section discusses the main features of the development of the economy since 1960.

# II.  SURVEY OF THE BRITISH ECONOMY

## 1. INTERNATIONAL TRADE AND PAYMENTS

### Imports and Exports.

In 1964 the United Kingdom bought from abroad goods to the value of £5,514 million, or just over £100 per head. Food is a large item in this bill, accounting for 32 per cent of the total. Fuel, largely oil, costs about 11 per cent, basic materials for industry 31 per cent, and manufactured goods (a category that includes a large number of semi-manufactured goods bought for

further processing) 36 per cent. This last category of imports has increased sharply in recent years. In 1954 they represented only 20 per cent in an import bill of only £3,359 million. All this can be seen in the table.

There are three main determinants of the level of British imports. One is the competitiveness of British with foreign producers. Britain imports those commodities which—at the current exchange rate between the pound and foreign currencies—can be bought more cheaply from foreign than from home producers. Secondly, the level of imports depends on the extent to which free trade is prevented by tariffs on imported goods or by other devices. Thirdly, as total incomes in the economy expand, there is a general increase in the demand for goods and services, including imports. Therefore imports can be expected to vary directly with the total of incomes in the economy, known as the *national income*.

One would expect that the liberalisation of trade since the early 1950s, together with a decline in the competitiveness of British producers, would have produced an expansion of imports relative to national income. In fact imports as a proportion of national income fell from 23 to 21 per cent between 1954 and 1964. The observed decrease must be explained by the sluggish demand for *primary products* such as food and raw materials. The British spend little of their additional income on imported food, and the development of synthetic substitutes and new products has slowed down the growth in demand for raw materials. Moreover, since the demand for primary products of this sort has been sluggish on a world scale, while supply has increased, their price has fallen in relative terms, and this too has reduced the total cost of British imports.

—fell or stagnated in world markets over the decade.

### The Volume of Trade.

Superficially it would appear that any improvement in the terms of trade raises the value of British exports relative to imports. However, this is not always true: faster inflation in this country, leading to a more rapid increase in export prices, would harm rather than help the balance of payments. If the prices of our export goods rise faster than the prices of our competitors in overseas markets, it will become progressively more difficult to sell our exports. Conversely, an inflation in Britain will make it progressively more attractive to buy goods produced abroad. Thus between 1954 and 1964 the value of imports grew slightly faster than the value of exports despite the slower growth of import prices than of export prices. This was because the volume of imports increased by 61 per cent and the volume of exports by only 40 per cent. The trade balance may well be helped by a fall in the price of imported primary products; but the balance of trade

### UNITED KINGDOM IMPORTS AND EXPORTS

| Imports of goods (c.i.f.) | | £ million. | | Percentage of total. | |
|---|---|---|---|---|---|
| | | 1954. | 1964. | 1954. | 1964. |
| Food, drink, and tobacco | | 1,314 | 1,773 | 39 | 32 |
| Basic materials | | 1,015 | 1,119 | 30 | 20 |
| Fuels and lubricants | | 329 | 585 | 10 | 11 |
| Semi-manufactures | | 513 | 1,173 | 15 | 21 |
| Finished manufactures | | 174 | 838 | 5 | 15 |
| TOTAL* | | 3,359 | 5,514 | 100 | 100 |
| Exports of goods (f.o.b.) | | | | | |
| Food, drink, and tobacco | | 154 | 283 | 6 | 7 |
| Basic materials | | 101 | 158 | 4 | 4 |
| Fuels and lubricants | | 151 | 138 | 6 | 3 |
| Metals | | 338 | 500 | 13 | 12 |
| Engineering products | | 1,007 | 1,915 | 38 | 45 |
| Textiles | | 324 | 275 | 12 | 6 |
| Other manufactured goods | | 490 | 847 | 18 | 20 |
| TOTAL* | | 2,650 | 4,254 | 100 | 100 |
| Re-exports of imports | | 98 | 154 | — | — |

\* The column figures do not add up to the totals because the former exclude postal packages.

Since the exports of one country must be the imports of another, the same factors in reverse, foreign competitiveness, access to foreign markets, and the level of foreign incomes determine the level of British exports. In 1964 these amounted to £4,254 million, of which no less than 83 per cent were manufactures, mainly of engineering products. Thus Britain gains from trade by exporting manufactures, in which she has a *comparative advantage*, in return for food and raw materials, which she is not suited to produce.

### The Terms of Trade.

Between 1954 and 1964 the value of British imports rose by 64 per cent and the value of exports by 61 per cent. These changes can be separated into two components, volume and price. Imports rose in price by only 4 per cent, whereas export prices rose by 19 per cent. The ratio of the average price of exports to that of imports is known as the *terms of trade*; and a rise in the price of exports relative to imports indicates an improvement in the terms of trade. Thus when we note in the table that the terms of trade improved by 15 per cent between 1954 and 1964, we mean that in 1964 15 per cent less exports by volume would have been needed to buy the same amount of imports as in 1954. This improvement in the terms of trade reflects the fact that the prices of many primary products—food and raw materials such as wheat, cocoa, rubber, or copper

in manufactures will be worsened by an improvement in their terms of trade.

### VISIBLE TRADE: VOLUME AND PRICES

| | 1961 = 100. | | Percentage increase 1954–64. |
|---|---|---|---|
| | 1954. | 1964. | |
| *Value* | | | |
| Imports | 76 | 125 | 64 |
| Exports | 72 | 116 | 61 |
| *Volume* | | | |
| Imports | 74 | 119 | 61 |
| Exports | 80 | 112 | 40 |
| *Price* | | | |
| Imports | 103 | 107 | 4 |
| Exports | 89 | 106 | 19 |
| Terms of trade | 116 | 99 | 15 |

Over the decade there was a persistent fall in Britain's share of world exports, from 20·0 per cent of exports of manufactures in 1954 to 13·6 per cent in 1964. Her competitors in export markets—and particularly Germany and Japan—were more successful in expanding their exports. Had the prices of British exports risen less rapidly over this period, Britain's share of world exports would have been higher in 1964.

### The Balance of Visible Trade.

*The balance of (visible) trade* is the difference between exports and imports of goods. It is said to be in *surplus* if exports exceed imports and in *deficit* if imports exceed exports. In estimating the balance of trade it is important that imports and exports be valued on the same basis. The normal method in the trade returns is to measure imports *c.i.f.* (cost, insurance, and freight) and exports *f.o.b.* (free on board). In other words import prices are shown to include the costs of transporting them to Britain, and exports are valued at the prices when loaded in British ports. Our table shows both imports and exports *f.o.b.*

In no year except 1958 was there a surplus in the British balance of trade. Moreover, the deficit was particularly big in certain years, 1951, 1955, 1960, and 1964. The deficit of 1951 was largely due to the Korean war which led to a stockpiling of primary products and a startling increase in their prices. The other three years coincided with booms in the British economy. These were periods of very full employment and high demand which could be met only by increased imports. Moreover, there was a building up of raw material stocks which had been depleted during the preceding upswings of the economy.

### Invisible Trade, and the Current Balance of Payments.

The chronic deficit in the balance of visible trade has in normal years been offset by a surplus in the *balance of invisible trade.* This surplus derives from four main groups of transactions. The first covers receipts from non-residents *less* payments to non-residents, for services such as shipping and insurance. The second covers receipts from foreign governments in respect of

together. A deficit with non-sterling area countries persisted throughout the 1950s and into the 1960s.

### The Long-term Capital Account.

We have seen that Britain earned a surplus on its current balance of payments in most recent years. Yet it is not sufficient for this country to avoid deficits on its current account. The objective is to earn a substantial surplus in order to finance investment in and lending to other countries—particularly the underdeveloped countries of the Commonwealth; to repay debts to foreign countries which have been incurred; and to build up reserves of gold, dollars, and other currencies which can help to tide us over difficult periods. In fact the objective of the Government was to earn current account surpluses of more than £200 million in normal years; and a surplus of this magnitude was only achieved in the exceptionally favourable year 1958.

Between 1954 and 1964 there was a persistent and growing amount of British private investment abroad. Since private foreign investment in Britain also rose, the *balance of long-term capital transactions* did not show a clear trend. Nevertheless it was generally in deficit to the extent of £100–£200 million. As with current transactions there were considerable regional differences. Usually there was a heavy deficit in long-term capital transactions with the sterling area and only minor imbalance with the rest of the world. Thus in 1965 Britain had a deficit with the sterling area of £307 million and a surplus with the rest of the world of £92 million, giving an overall deficit on long-term capital account of £215 million. The net flow of long-term capital to the sterling area neutralised the current account surplus with the sterling area, equal to £313 million; and this was also the tendency in other years.

## CURRENT BALANCE OF PAYMENTS
### (£ million)

|  | 1951. | 1952–54. | 1955. | 1956–59. | 1960. | 1961–63. | 1964. |
|---|---|---|---|---|---|---|---|
| Imports (f.o.b.) . . | 3,501 | 2,958 | 3,432 | 3,497 | 4,137 | 4,166 | 5,005 |
| Exports (f.o.b.) . . | 2,752 | 2,778 | 3,076 | 3,366 | 3,733 | 4,058 | 4,471 |
| Balance of visible trade. | −749 | −180 | −356 | −131 | −404 | −108 | −534 |
| Balance of invisible trade | 330 | 386 | 283 | 255 | 131 | 170 | 122 |
| Current balance of payments . . | −419 | 206 | −73 | 124 | −273 | 62 | −412 |

military bases in the country *less* payments by this country in respect of military bases abroad. The third covers receipts of gifts and grants made to this country, *less* gifts and grants made by this country. The fourth includes all receipts of interest, dividends, and profits earned on overseas investment *less* interest, dividends and profits paid out on foreign investment in this country.

The table shows that in most years the surplus on invisibles exceeded the deficit on visibles, so that Britain earned a surplus on the *current balance of payments.* However, there was a long-run tendency for the surplus on invisibles to decline: net earnings from shipping services fell and Government military expenditure abroad and grants to other countries increased.

### The Current Balance of Payments by Regions.

All the figures presented so far refer to Britain's trade with the external world as a whole. These hide a marked pattern of trade. In 1964 just over a third of visible imports and exports came from and went to the countries of the overseas sterling area—comprising the Colonial territories, independent Commonwealth countries other than Canada, British protected states in the Persian Gulf and a few countries such as Burma and South Africa. One reason for Britain's declining share of world trade is that trade within the sterling area has been growing less rapidly than world trade as a whole. Almost 35 per cent of our visible trade was done with Western Europe, and rather less than 17 per cent with North America. The current balance of payments surplus found in normal years is generally made up of a large surplus with sterling area currencies, partially offset by a deficit with all other countries taken

### Monetary Movements.

In 1965 Britain had a current account deficit of £104 million and a deficit on long term capital account of £215 million; implying a deficit in the *balance of current and long-term capital transactions* of £319 million. This balance had to be financed either through an increase in liabilities (for example, an increase in the sterling liabilities held by foreigners, or in short-term loans from the International Monetary Fund) or by a reduction in assets (for example a reduction in the gold and dollar reserves). In fact, the gold and foreign currency reserves actually rose in 1965 by £246 million, but the sterling balances increased by £55 million and our debts to the International Monetary Fund by no less than £499 million. Total recorded net monetary movements to meet the deficit amounted to only £232 million, so that there must have been an unrecorded increase in credit equal to £87 million, known as the *balancing item.* Let us consider each of these " financing " transactions in turn.

### The Sterling Balances.

Sterling is an international currency, and governments and individuals may hold balances in sterling (*e.g.*, Treasury bills, Government stocks and bank accounts) for many reasons. Sterling area countries reckon to keep a high proportion of their international trade reserves in the form of sterling balances. It is convenient to hold sterling to finance trading transactions because sterling is widely acceptable in settlement of trading debts. Sterling balances will also be held to the extent that they are considered a profitable and safe way of holding liquid assets. It may be profitable to hold sterling if the rate of interest paid on balances in London is higher than that paid in other financial centres. And it may be considered safe to hold sterling if the chances of sterling devaluation (which would automatically reduce the value of the balances in terms of any currency which did not devalue) are thought to be remote.

An increase in the sterling balances enables Britain to finance an adverse balance on current plus long-term capital account without reducing the gold and foreign exchange reserves. Conversely, a reduction in sterling balances can impose a drain on reserves even if there is no adverse balance on current plus long-term capital account.

At the end of 1965 sterling balances held by non-residents (excluding the International Monetary Fund) amounted to £3,470 million; far in excess of Britain's reserves of gold and convertible currencies, equal to £1,070 million. Nearly three-quarters of this amount was held by the rest of the sterling area. However, it is unlikely that Britain would be able to finance a persistent deficit in her balance of payments through a progressive increase in the sterling balances: in the long run the sterling balances will probably be reduced—as indeed they were between 1955 and 1965, by some £200 million. Many underdeveloped countries of the sterling area will want to run down their sterling balances in order to help finance the imports required for their development programmes.

Sterling holdings outside the sterling area, and particularly the unofficial (*i.e.*, private) holdings, are highly volatile, in that they may be withdrawn very rapidly if for any reason it is thought less profitable or less safe to hold sterling than some other currency or gold. Since confidence in sterling is weakest (*i.e.* fear that it will be devalued is greatest) when the balance of payments is in deficit, sterling balances tend to move perversely, so accentuating movement in the reserves. Such was the case in the sterling crisis at the end of 1964. It is ironical that Britain's position as an international currency country makes it more and not less difficult to rely on a running down of reserves to meet a temporary deficit in the balance of payments.

### Foreign Exchange Reserves.

The gold and convertible currency reserves are used to finance payments abroad which cannot be financed in any other way: they are a last line of defence in international trade. The reserves held in London belong to the sterling area as a whole, and not just to this country. Members of the sterling area are willing to pay into these central reserves some or all of their net earnings of gold and convertible currencies, in exchange for sterling balances. They do this on the understanding that they can, should they wish to do so, call upon the central reserves by exchanging sterling balances for gold and convertible currencies.

The central reserves of gold and foreign currencies amounted to £1,070 million at the end of 1965; a level which, though higher than in many previous post-war years, was felt to be quite inadequate. There are bound to be imbalances in international trade and payments, and the function of these reserves is to tide over temporary imbalances by increasing reserves in favourable periods and running down reserves in unfavourable periods. If reserves are not sufficient to withstand temporary pressures, measures to protect the reserves will have to be taken—*e.g.*, raising Bank Rate and tightening up monetary policies generally— and these measures may create unemployment and recession, and restrict the growth of the economy.

### The International Monetary Fund.

The *International Monetary Fund* (IMF) was set up after the war with the objective of working towards free trade at stable exchange rates. Under the original agreement setting up the Fund, members agreed to make their currencies convertible into other currencies and gold at fixed rates of exchange, and agreed not to impose exchange or import controls without the permission of the Fund. Any alteration in the rates of exchange by more than 10 per cent also requires the per-

mission of the Fund. For many years after the war, the imbalances in world trade—and particularly the acute shortage of dollars—were such that many countries had to invoke the clauses in the agreement which permitted them to impose restrictions during a "transitional" period. Although there is still a long way to go before the Fund reaches its objectives, considerable progress towards them was made during the 1950s. The progressive relaxation of exchange and import controls by this country was paralleled in some other countries, and most of the currencies important in world trade and payments were declared convertible.

The function of the Fund is to make foreign exchange resources available to members who run into balance of payments difficulties. Each member country makes a deposit (called its quota) partly in gold and partly in its own currencies, with the Fund. The size of the deposit is fixed in relation to the country's share in world trade. In return, it is granted certain automatic drawing rights, which entitle it to borrow foreign currencies from the Fund. Furthermore, the Fund has power to make larger loans, and to grant stand-by credits to be drawn on if required. Before the Fund will make such loans and credits available, it has to be satisfied that the borrowing country is taking appropriate action to correct the balance of payments disequilibrium.

In 1956, at the time of the Suez crisis, there was a running down of sterling balances, and Britain negotiated a loan of £202 million from the Fund and an even larger stand-by credit. Again in 1964 and 1965, when there was a severe deficit on current and long-term capital account and heavy speculation against sterling, the Government borrowed from the I.M.F. £369 million in 1964 and £499 million in 1965. In this way the country could ride out crises of confidence in sterling without a severe loss of reserves.

### Correcting a Deficit.

If an imbalance in the current plus long-term capital account persists, the deficit cannot be met indefinitely from monetary movements. At some stage the Government must take action to remove the deficit. What action can it take? There are a number of alternatives available, each with its advantages and disadvantages, and economic opinion is by no means unanimous on the choice of policy. Let us consider each of these alternatives in turn.

### Variation of the Exchange Rate.

The *exchange rate* is the ruling official rate of exchange of pounds for gold and other currencies. It determines the value of British goods in relation to foreign goods. If the pound is devalued in terms of gold and other currencies, British exports (which are paid for in pounds) become cheaper to foreigners and British imports (paid for by purchasing foreign currency) become more expensive to holders of pounds. In this way *devaluation* can improve the British balance of payments position by encouraging exports and discouraging imports.

But there are certain disadvantages attached to devaluation. The prospect of devaluation results in a speculative outflow of foreign funds: and one devaluation may be taken as a sign that there will be further devaluation in the future. Secondly, the sterling area countries—many of them underdeveloped—will suffer a capital loss, because they hold their international reserves largely in the form of sterling rather than gold. Thirdly, the rise in the price of imports of raw materials and consumption goods results in higher costs and prices and then in wage demands to maintain the British standard of living. It is possible that inflation will in this way neutralise the beneficial effects of devaluation.

The pound was devalued in 1949, when an official exchange rate of £1 = $2·8 was established, and again in 1967, to a rate of £1 = $2·4.

### Exchange Controls and Convertibility.

A currency is fully *convertible* if it can be freely exchanged for any other currency, or for gold, at the ruling official rates of exchange. Exchange controls impose restrictions on convertibility by limiting the powers of holders of a currency to exchange their holdings for other currencies or gold at the official rate of exchange. For many years after the war, for example, there was a world-wide shortage of dollars: if sterling had been convertible, there would have been a rush to convert sterling into dollars, with the consequence that the dollar reserves of the sterling area would soon have been exhausted. In fact, a premature attempt to establish sterling convertibility in 1947 led to such a drain on reserves that strict exchange controls had to be re-imposed.

Exchange controls on residents can be enforced by requiring that earnings of foreign currencies (e.g., the proceeds from the sale of exports) be handed over to the exchange control authority—the Bank of England acts as the Government's agent—in exchange for sterling; and by permitting the exchange of sterling for foreign currencies (e.g., to enable the purchase of imports) only for transactions approved by the exchange control authority. There was a move towards convertibility of sterling during the 1950s, and the sterling held by non-residents was made fully convertible in 1958. Residents, however, continued to be subject to exchange controls.

By restricting convertibility the Government can make it more difficult for funds to move into or out of sterling. In this way the Government can impede capital movements, e.g., British private investment abroad, or flows of short-term capital; or it can restrict current spending abroad, e.g., on foreign holidays.

### Import Controls and Tariffs.

Import controls impose limitations on the quantity or value of goods which are permitted to enter a country: tariffs are duties levied on imported goods so that the price of those goods to consumers in a country is higher than the price received by the foreigners supplying the goods. In the early post-war years, this country maintained strict import controls over a wide range of goods. These were gradually dismantled, until in 1959 the last remaining import controls on goods were abandoned, except on habit-forming drugs and some agricultural products and textiles from the Far East—to give a measure of protection to British producers.

All countries impose tariffs. Some tariffs are primarily intended to raise revenue for the Government, and others are primarily intended to protect home industries by raising the price of competing goods from abroad. The rights of countries to raise tariffs, or to operate tariffs in a discriminatory way (i.e., to offer lower tariffs on goods from some sources than on similar goods from other sources), are closely circumscribed by the rules of the *General Agreement on Tariffs and Trade* (GATT). The object of the GATT is to work towards free trade, especially through a reduction in tariffs. In the post-war period GATT held several major conferences, at which bargaining to reduce tariffs was attended by modest success. The most significant moves towards free trade in this period were on a regional basis.

The disadvantage of introducing import controls or tariffs to correct a deficit in the balance of payments is that the benefits of free trade are lost. Moreover, there is always the possibility of retaliation by Britain's trading partners. Nevertheless, import controls or tariffs may well be preferable to another measure which has been used to correct a deficit, deflation.

### Deflation.

Throughout the post-war period the U.K. balance of payments was far from secure. As a result, domestic economic policies were much influenced by balance of payments considerations. Devaluation was turned to only as a last resort. The movement in the 1950s and 1960s was towards greater freedom of trade. By ruling out devaluation and trade restrictions, the authorities had to fall back on *deflation* of the economy to correct periodic deficits. In other words, the Government took measures to discourage demand and so cut back incomes and employment. By reducing demand in general, the authorities secured a fall in demand for imports. However, it was necessary to cut back national income by many times

the ensuing fall in imports. Deflation is a painful method of correcting a deficit. Not only does it have a direct effect on the level of incomes and employment, but it is also liable to slow down the rate of growth of the economy. This can happen because deflation can weaken the incentive to expand productive capacity by investing in new plant, machinery, and other capital goods.

The problem which faced British policy-makers attempting to raise the rate of economic growth was this: as total demand for goods and services expands, it is difficult to prevent growth in the demand for imports and diversion of exports to the home market, particularly when home industries reach the limit of their productive capacity. Yet if consequent balance of payments difficulties are met by restrictions on total demand, it is difficult to maintain the investment necessary for growth in the productive capacity of the economy. The main need in the mid-1960s was the same as that at the start of the 1950s: to achieve an expansion of exports relative to imports so as to secure economic growth without running into balance of payments difficulties.

The international monetary system is partly to blame for the British decisions to resort to periodic deflation of the economy. The use of sterling as a reserve currency has subjected the balance of payments to violent swings in short-term capital flows. Moreover, a world-wide shortage of *international liquidity*, i.e., gold and foreign exchange reserves, means that countries have an incentive to maintain a surplus in their balance of payments and so increase their reserves. In this situation surplus countries do not help to correct an imbalance in foreign transactions: the burden of correcting the imbalance is placed on the deficit country. If the Government of the deficit country feels itself unable to devalue its currency or to impose trade restrictions, it has to deflate the economy. The existing international monetary system contains a " deflationary bias," which the IMF has at most only ameliorated.

### The European Common Market and the European Free Trade Area.

By the end of the 1950s, Europe was divided into two major trading groups: the Common Market, or *European Economic Community* (EEC) comprising: Belgium, France, Holland, Italy, Luxembourg, and West Germany, and the *European Free Trade Association* (EFTA) comprising: Austria, Denmark, Norway, Portugal, Sweden, Switzerland, and the United Kingdom. An account of the negotiations for British entry to the EEC in the 1960s is given in Part IV.

## 2. EMPLOYMENT, PRODUCTION AND INVESTMENT

### Population.

In June 1965 the population of the United Kingdom was estimated to be 54·4 million—47·8 million in England and Wales, 5·2 million in Scotland, and 1·5 million in Northern Ireland. The total was still rising slowly, at a rate of about 0·7 per cent per annum. Prediction of future trends is difficult. Before the war it was common to predict that Britain's population would fall later in the century; but these predictions were made at a time when the birth-rate was very low. Since then the birth-rate has risen sharply, and the *net reproduction rate* (the ratio of the birth-rate of girls less their infant mortality to the population of women of child-bearing age) has been above one in most years since the war. In the near future population will certainly continue to rise slowly as improving medical services raise the average length of life and as the gap between generations shortens.

### The Population of Working Age.

Of the total population only some are of working age. Working age is defined as the period between the minimum school leaving age of 15 and retiring age—65 for men and 60 for women. Of course, not all those of working age do work and not all those above working age have retired; nevertheless the ratio between population not of working age and the total is a useful statistic, as it does provide a rough guide to the numbers who have to be supported out of the current national income, but who do not contribute to it. This ratio is rising and will continue to rise. In 1965, 23·3 per cent of the UK population was below working age and 15·0 per cent above. By 1980 it is fairly certain that 16 per cent of the population will be above working age; and much more speculatively, it is guessed that 26 per cent will be below. So the population not of working age will rise from 38·3 to 42 per cent. The expected growth in the proportion of the old explains why the proportion on pensions (see G24(2) is going to grow steadily. More generally, it is clear that some growth in output per worker will be needed to meet the needs of the increasing proportion of dependants.

## The Working Population.

Not all persons of working age actually work, although the vast majority do; but only a part are gainfully employed, i.e., work for wages, salaries, and profits. And it is only those who are gainfully employed who are counted in the working population. Housewives, mothers, and those who give their services gratis to good causes are excluded, unless they also do some work for cash. In 1965, when the total population of Great Britain was 53 million, of whom 32·7 million were of working age, the total working population (including the unemployed who are seeking employment) was only 25·5 million. Of the 17·5 million women of working age only 8·8 million were gainfully employed. So for every person gainfully occupied there was just over one other person to be supported out of the goods and services they provided. One feature of the postwar years was a steady increase in the proportion of persons going out to work. Whereas in 1965, 78 per cent of the working-age population was gainfully employed, in 1955 the figure was only 66 per cent.

or less inevitable. Some seasonal rise in unemployment in the winter must be expected, e.g., in seaside towns, and for this reason unemployment in January is half a per cent or so higher than in June. Moreover, some unemployment is bound to be involved in job-changing and as the demands of industries change. " Full employment " means that there should be about as many jobs vacant as there are workers looking for jobs. A large excess of vacancies is evidence of inflationary pressure in the labour market, for it means that the employers needing workers to meet the demands for their products will have to compete with each other by bidding up wages.

To some extent unemployment figures are misleading, as not all unemployed workers are eligible for unemployment benefit under the National Insurance Scheme. Most married women who go out to work normally opt not to pay the full National Insurance contributions, so that, when they become unemployed, they just drop out of the " working population ". Unemployment figures definitely understate the seriousness of recessions, as they do not count all the persons who would like to work, but cannot find, jobs.

Of the 317,000 persons unemployed in mid-1964, 240,000 were men and 77,000 women. Of the men, over half, 147,000, had been unemployed for over eight weeks. Thus long-term unemployment was nearly 1 per cent of the labour force, serious enough for those affected but not the kind of unemployment to be cured easily by reflationary measures.

## Regional Unemployment.

A peculiarly dreadful feature of the inter-war years was the emergence of the depressed areas—the regions of the country where a third of the men had not had a job for a year or more. Such extreme regional unemployment has not recurred since 1945: only in Northern Ireland was unemployment very high. Between 1954 and 1964

## DISTRIBUTION OF WORKING POPULATION, JUNE 1965.
(Thousands)

| Basic Industries. | | Manufacturing Industries. | | Services. | |
|---|---|---|---|---|---|
| Agriculture and fishing | 486 | Food, drink, and tobacco | 810 | Distribution trades | 2,961 |
| Mining and quarrying | 624 | Chemicals and allied | | Financial, professional, | |
| Construction | 1,656 | industries | 515 | and scientific services | 3,045 |
| Gas, electricity, and water | 411 | Metal manufacture | 632 | Catering, hotels, etc. | 612 |
| | | Vehicles | 862 | Public administration: | |
| Transport and communication | 1,628 | Engineering and other metal goods | 2,848 | National | 545 |
| | | Textiles | 767 | Local | 758 |
| | | Paper printing and publishing | 633 | Miscellaneous | 1,574 |
| | | Other manufacturing | 1,779 | | |
| Total | 4,805 | Total | 8,846 | Total | 9,495 |
| Percentage of working population | 20·8 | | 38·2 | | 41·0 |

Most of the working population work for wages or salaries as employees. Of the total for Great Britain in June 1965 of 25·5 million, 1·7 million were employers or self-employed, 0·4 million were in the Forces, and 23·4 million were either employees or unemployed persons looking for work. The table shows the industries in which people work. Some 38 per cent of the total work in manufacturing industry, 2·8 million of these in engineering and allied industries, 21 per cent work in the basic industries, and the remaining 41 per cent are in the so-called service industries.

## Employment and Unemployment.

In 1965 an average of 329,000 persons—1·4 per cent of the working population—were unemployed. Even in January 1959, the worst month of the 1950s, the rate rose only to 2·8 per cent, and in February 1963—an exceptional month—to 3·9 per cent. In most post-war years the average was lower than 1·5 per cent. This contrasts with an average figure in 1937, the best year of the 1930s, of 11 per cent, and with a figure of 22 per cent at the bottom of the slump in 1932. Probably 1–1·5 per cent is somewhere near the practicable minimum; for some unemployment is more

unemployment there ranged between 6 and 10 per cent. Nevertheless, regional inequalities exist, and much attention has been paid to this problem in recent years.

## UNEMPLOYMENT AND VACANCIES
(Great Britain, thousands)

| | Unemployment. (Annual average.) | Vacancies. (End of period.) | Unemployment as percentage of total employees. |
|---|---|---|---|
| 1932* | 2,829 | n.a. | 22·1 |
| 1937* | 1,482 | n.a. | 10·9 |
| 1954 | 285 | 338 | 1·3 |
| 1956 | 257 | 279 | 1·2 |
| 1958 | 457 | 163 | 2·1 |
| 1960 | 360 | 294 | 1·6 |
| 1962 | 463 | 157 | 2·0 |
| 1964 | 381 | 311 | 1·6 |

* Figures relate only to population insured against unemployment.

## PERCENTAGE OF WORKERS UNEMPLOYED, BY REGIONS

| | February 1963. | February 1965. |
|---|---|---|
| London and South-eastern . . . | 2·3 | 1·0 |
| Eastern and Southern . | 3·6 | 1·2 |
| South-western . . | 3·8 | 1·8 |
| Midlands . . . | 3·4 | 0·8 |
| Yorkshire and Lincolnshire . . . | 3·3 | 1·2 |
| North-western . . | 4·1 | 1·8 |
| Northern . . . | 7·1 | 3·1 |
| Scotland . . . | 6·2 | 3·6 |
| Wales . . . | 6·0 | 2·8 |
| North Ireland . . | 11·2 | 6·9 |
| *Great Britain* . . | *3·9* | *1·6* |

## DECREASE IN EMPLOYMENT IN SELECTED INDUSTRIES, 1945–65.

| | Thousands. | Per cent. |
|---|---|---|
| Textiles . . . | 224 | 23 |
| Mining and quarrying | 242 | 28 |
| Shipbuilding . . | 77 | 27 |
| Agriculture, forestry, and fishing . . | 221 | 21 |

In February 1963—during a period of recession and also cold weather—the percentage of all workers unemployed in Great Britain was 3·9. But the table shows a lower proportion of the labour force was unemployed in the Midlands and the South, and that there was a much higher percentage of unemployment in the North, in Scotland, and in Northern Ireland. Moreover, the labour shortage of early 1965 was not shared equally: unemployment remained significant in these areas. In this situation checks have to be placed on the economy before full employment is reached, because in the booming areas vacancies far exceed unemployment.

One of the main reasons for the regional pattern of unemployment is that certain industries and services, in which big changes have been taking place, tend to be grouped in specific regions. Most of our early industrial centres had to be established close to coal, iron ore, and adequate water supplies. But employment in many long-established industries has recently been declining. The scale of this contraction can be seen from the table. On the other hand new and growing industries, and their related offices, have been concentrated in Greater London, the South East, and the Midlands. The growth of services, too, has centred on the areas where industry is booming and population is increasing. In the absence of Government intervention, the process would tend to become cumulative, and regional inequalities would grow rather than diminish.

### National Income.

Gross domestic income (GDY) is the sum total of incomes received for the services of labour, land, or capital in a country. Gross domestic product (GDP) is the money value of all the goods and services produced in the country. So as to avoid double-counting, only the *value added* at each stage of production is included: firms' purchases are excluded. The revenue from selling the GDP is either paid out to the hired factors of production—labour, land, and capital—or retained in the form of profits. Therefore, provided it is calculated net of taxes on goods produced, GDP must equal GDY. To estimate gross national income from GDY it is necessary to add the net income—such as profits and interest—received from abroad. If an allowance is made for wear and tear of the nation's capital equipment, *i.e.*, for *capital consumption*, we arrive at net national income, better known as the *national income*.

In 1965 the national income of the United King-

dom was £28,280 million, implying a national income per head of £518. In 1955 the corresponding figures had been £15,514 million and £303 per head. However, only part of this increase in value was due to an increase in the quantity of goods and services produced: some of the increase simply reflected a rise in prices. It is important to calculate changes in the volume of output—known as *real output*—as well as changes in its value. Real output is calculated by the statistical device of constructing an index number. This is done by calculating the volume of goods and services provided in each year and then valuing these goods and services at the prices found in one particular year. Thus between 1955 and 1965 the money value of national income rose by 82 per cent; whereas real output increased by only 33 per cent, and the difference represented a rise in prices.

In real terms national income per head rose by 24 per cent between 1955 and 1965, or by 2·2 per cent per annum. National income per head is the most useful indicator of the standard of living. However, this measure is necessarily a crude one. For instance, it cannot take account of new products, *e.g.*, television or the plastic bucket; nor of changes in the distribution of income between rich and the poor; nor of the "quality of life," affected by such things as traffic jams and smokeless zones; nor of the length of the working week.

### Industrial Production.

It is fairly easy to measure output in the main manufacturing industries, and in many of the basic industries. It is much more difficult to do so for the service industries: the output of a doctor or a teacher is not easily measured. So each month the Central Statistical Office calculates the *index of industrial production* covering the main "productive" industries. However, this tends to give a false impression of the rate of growth of output, since the industrial sector is the one best placed to raise its output per head and for which demand expands most rapidly. Roughly a 5 per cent increase in industrial output is likely to be accompanied by a 3 per cent increase in GDP, on which the average standard of living depends.

Manufacturing industry accounts for more than three-quarters of industrial production. Within manufacturing industry two industries have expanded most rapidly—chemicals, which includes drugs, plastics, cosmetics, detergents, and oil refining; and vehicles, which includes cars, tractors, commercial vehicles, and aircraft. The slowest growing manufacturing industries are textiles and shipbuilding, which are losing their markets to cheaper competitors. Those industries in which demand has stagnated are also the industries in which output per employee, *i.e.*, productivity, has stagnated.

### International Comparisons.

Between 1955 and 1964 Britain's GDP grew less rapidly than that of any other country listed in the table, except the U.S.A. The British economy was also characterised by a relatively slow growth of output per head, *i.e.*, productivity. Many explanations of Britain's poor performance have been suggested, and there is by no means agreement on this matter among economists. It has been argued that the U.K.—like the U.S.A.—has a highly advanced economy, in which there is a relatively high demand for services; and that it is difficult to raise productivity in the large services sector. Another argument is that Britain has been hampered by its slowly growing labour force, which has restricted growth not only in output but also in output per man. The reason given is that an expanding labour force needs to be equipped with additional plant and machinery; so that its capital equipment tends to be newer on average than that used by a static labour force, and thus more up-to-date and efficient.

Some commentators have put the blame on the inefficiency of our business management; some on our educational system, biased towards the humanities; some on the social milieu which looks down on money-making as a career; some on over-manning and other restrictive practices of trade unions. A good deal of attention has

## AN INTERNATIONAL GROWTH LEAGUE TABLE

| | Percentage change per annum, 1955–1964. | | | Investment as percentage of G.N.P. | |
|---|---|---|---|---|---|
| | Output. | Employment. | Output per head. | Including dwellings. | Excluding dwellings. |
| Japan . . | 10·4 | 1·4 | 8·8 | 28·8 | 21·5 |
| W. Germany . | 6·3 | 1·3 | 5·0 | 23·7 | 18·4 |
| Italy . . . | 5·7 | 0·1 | 5·6 | 21·6 | 15·6 |
| Sweden . . | 5·4 | 1·5 | 3·9 | 22·8 | 17·4 |
| France . . | 5·2 | 0·3 | 4·9 | 19·2 | 14·3 |
| Denmark . . | 5·0 | 1·2 | 3·8 | 18·7 | 15·4 |
| Belgium . . | 3·6 | 0·6 | 3·0 | 18·4 | 13·7 |
| U.S.A. . . | 3·1 | 1·1 | 2·0 | 17·1 | 12·2 |
| U.K. . . . | 3·1 | 0·5 | 2·6 | 15·8 | 12·7 |

also been paid to the proportion of output which different countries devote to *investment, i.e.,* expenditure on commodities—such as plant and machinery—for use in future production. These investment ratios are shown in the table. With the exception of the U.S.A., all countries have investment ratios considerably higher than in the U.K., with correspondingly higher growth rates of output and productivity. Since investment in dwellings contributes very little to growth, it is appropriate to exclude this investment: however, the same results are obtained. This leads to the hypothesis that Britain's growth rate could be raised if a higher proportion of output were devoted to investment, particularly in plant and machinery. There is probably some truth in many of these explanations, and it is unlikely that any one remedy will be sufficient to raise the British growth rate.

### Capital and Automation.

Many of the growing industries are capital-intensive; they use much machinery and equipment per unit of output produced. In chemicals, steel, and, above all, electricity, the plant is extremely expensive. Most of the innovations since the war—nylon, atomic power, electronics, polythene, etc.—require a high capital investment, and cannot pay unless they are worked nearly full-out. One way to achieve this is by shift work, and it may be that a full exploitation of the potentialities of these new industries will require a greater extension of this system of work. And the future holds out prospects of still more intensive requirements for capital as automation spreads. With automation, much of the manual semi-skilled work should come to an end. The new electronic computers will be able to control the machines that actually do the manufacturing operations. " Transfer " machines can read details of the work to be done off a piece of tape; they can adjust themselves to correct mistakes or to adjust for faulty materials.

So far the impact of automation has been small. The main use has been in the office, where electronic computers can carry out far more efficiently much of the routine calculating, recording, and checking operations previously done by clerks. But it will continue to spread, and must do so if the growth in output is to continue. The change will come only gradually. But ultimately one can envisage that both in manufacturing industry and in office work the machine will have replaced much of the human effort in work, and even more of its drudgery. The typical manual job will become that of the skilled maintenance man.

This revolution will take many decades to effect. It raises no spectre of widespread redundancy; but it does mean that over the years more and more emphasis will need to be laid on the training of workers for skilled work, and indeed on raising the general level of education. Also over the years the average size of factory is likely to grow as these new methods, if they are to be profitable, have to be used on a large scale. Finally, the prospect is for ever-increasing requirements of capital—and of course for the savings to finance it.

### Investment.

In 1965 gross investment in capital assets amounted to £6,252 million. This is about 20 per cent of the gross national product (GNP). In other words, about one part in five of total production was used to replace old assets or to add to the nation's stock of capital equipment. The addition to the stock of capital assets (net investment) accounts for 60 per cent of gross investment; the remainder is needed to offset the wastage of assets already in use. We have seen (above) that the proportion of total output invested in Britain is lower than in countries with faster growth rates of output and productivity; and there is reason to believe that a higher proportion would improve the growth rate. But a rise in the investment ratio would involve a fall in other forms of expenditure, notably private and public consumption; and this would have to be brought about by increasing taxation or encouraging people to save. In other words, a faster rate of growth—which was achieved by this method would involve a sacrifice in current consumption. A choice must be made between the loss in current consumption and the ensuing gain in future consumption. Of course not all consumption expenditure is equally important to the standard of living: some would argue that if defence expenditure was pruned to permit more investment, there would be no loss to set against the future gain.

### Types of Investment.

There are four main kinds of investment: plant and machinery; vehicles; dwellings and other construction. In 1965 the four categories accounted for 37, 10, 21, and 32 per cent respectively of total gross investment. Investment may also be analysed by the purpose for which it is used. It is clear from the table that some sectors are more capital-intensive than others. Manufacturing and social services (such as education and health) take a surprisingly small proportion of total investment; distribution (retail, wholesale, banking, and finance) and public utilities and services take a large proportion. Investment in electricity alone accounts for 10 per cent of the total. Investment in real terms rose most rapidly for social services and for distribution over the decade; manufacturing, other production industries, and transport fared badly.

### GROSS INVESTMENT BY PURPOSE, 1965.

| | Percentage of total 1965. | Percentage increase 1955–65. |
|---|---|---|
| Manufacturing . . | 21 | 48 |
| Other production industries . | 7 | 36 |
| Transport. . | 9 | 46 |
| Distribution . | 17 | 127 |
| Public utilities and services. . | 20 | 121 |
| Housing . . | 20 | 62 |
| Other social services . | 6 | 155 |
| Total . . | 100 | 76 |

### The Finance of Investment.

Any business is allowed to charge as a cost the depreciation of its assets. Normal depreciation allowances are based on the original cost of the asset and on its expected useful life. In a time of price inflation depreciation allowances will not provide sufficient finance to permit the replacement of assets at higher prices, and there are many supporters of depreciation allowances being based on replacement costs. Many firms do set aside extra funds specifically to cover these extra replacement costs. However, an official committee of enquiry recommended against a change in practice, and with prices rising less rapidly the issue became less important.

Governments have, however, adopted certain fiscal devices to encourage replacement and investment. Soon after the war initial allowances were introduced. Under this system firms were permitted to charge against profits in the first year of its life 20, or at times 40, per cent of the cost of any new equipment, and the system amounted to a loan of the tax saved in the first year, repaid over the life of the asset. In 1954 initial allowances for machinery were replaced by a system of investment allowances, under which a firm could charge against profits 20 per cent of the cost of any new machine, with the difference that all ordinary depreciation allowances were still chargeable. So the investment allowance was a grant, not a loan, of the saved tax. In 1966 it was announced that initial and investment allowances on new plant and machinery in the key sectors—manufacturing, mining, and shipping—would be replaced by cash grants. Other plant and machinery and industrial building would receive higher initial allowances.

Depreciation allowances and government allowances and grants for investment are sufficient to cover the majority of investment (excluding dwellings) by the private sector, and to cover a minor part of public (non-housing) investment. The residue of investment, and housebuilding, has to be provided from savings. Companies rely mainly on retained profits, which are often larger, taking companies as a whole, than their net investment; and so too do the profit-making nationalised industries. Much public investment must be financed by the Treasury.

### Monopoly and Competition.

This trend to increasing size and increasing capitalisation has been going on now for many decades, and in the process it has changed the face of British industry. In the early 19th cent. the typical firm was the owner-managed textile mill. Then in the 1860s and 1870s came the discovery of cheap methods of making steel, with the consequential immense growth in the engineering industries. Most of the chemical industry is still newer—some very new—and in these capital-intensive industries the big firm predominates. In some it has become almost a monopoly; no small firm can easily challenge industrial giants like Imperial Chemical Industries, the Dunlop Rubber Company, or Unilever. In others the pattern is of a few firms, all large, as in motor cars, detergents, and steel. Competition goes on, but it has changed its form. In the old days competition was largely by price. Now it is largely by advertising and by variations in the quality and other features of the product—detergents and motor cars being good examples. And in many industries groups of firms producing similar products entered into agreements which had the effect of restricting competition, for example through schemes for price-fixing.

### Legislation against Restrictive Practices.

The Restrictive Practices Act of 1956 outlawed many of the main forms of restrictive agreements to prevent competition. Collective price fixing was declared to be illegal unless the industry could show that the practice brought substantial benefit to the public. Collective price-fixing was the the system under which a central association for the industry lays down minimum prices at which members may sell. Usually such a system was backed by arrangements for collective boycotts, under which members of the association would refuse to sell goods to wholesalers or retailers who broke the rules. Often the wholesalers too were in the scheme, and they would collectively refuse to buy from manufacturers who broke the rules. Collective boycotts were also found in industries without collective price-fixing, one common purpose being to make sure that retailers did not sell a manufacturer's products below his recommended price. This form of collective resale price maintenance was also outlawed by the Act. Under the Act any restrictive agreements of several specified kinds had to be registered with the Registrar of Restrictive Practices. He then had to decide whether there was a *prima facie* case for the discontinuation of the agreement, and, if he thought there was, the case was referred to a new Restrictive Practices Court, containing both judicial and lay members.

The Act of 1956 permitted individual manufacturers to enforce *resale price maintenance* (r.p.m.) for their own products. Few suppliers would want the publicity of enforcing r.p.m. through the courts, but individual suppliers could still put some commercial pressure on price-cutters, *e.g.*, by offering less favourable terms or by refusing them supplies. The Resale Prices Act of 1964 prohibited all methods of enforcing minimum resale prices. However, goods which had been registered in due time with the Registrar of restrictive trading agreements or have been approved by the Restrictive Practices Court, were exempted, temporarily in the former case and permanently in the latter. For r.p.m. to be approved by the Court, it must be shown that some ensuing benefit to consumers (*e.g.*, of increased quality or more retail outlets) outweighed any detriment. It is also lawful to withhold supplies to retailers selling goods at a loss to attract customers. The list of applications for exemption is a long one, but the effect of the Act should be lower prices in the shops. It will also mean a more rapid decline of small retailers.

The Restrictive Practices Acts leave untouched the industries where one firm is dominant: these remain the responsibility of the Monopolies Commission, who report on industries referred to them by the Board of Trade, and make recommendations after investigation. The Monopolies and Mergers Act of 1965 strengthened control over monopolies and mergers. With regard to monopolies, the Government wished to provide itself with legal powers of enforcement: previously monopolies had been expected to comply voluntarily with the findings of the Monopolies Commission. The Act also permits the Government to refer a merger or a proposed merger to the Monopolies Commission in cases where the merger would lead to monopoly (defined as control of at least one third of the market) or would increase the power of an existing monopoly, or where the value of the assets taken over exceeds £5 million. But it would be wrong to presume that mergers are always bad: it is possible that mergers—by facilitating research and other economies of large-scale operation—will increase industrial efficiency. For this reason the Government proposed in 1966 to establish an Industrial Reorganisation Corporation to promote the grouping of firms in cases where such grouping would be beneficial to their industry.

Restrictive labour practices—which result in the "over-manning" of plant or the "under-employment" of men—are common in British industry. These stem from such causes as the fear of redundancy and unemployment, anxiety to preserve a craft skill threatened by technical progress, the desire to work at overtime rates, and sometimes just inertia. In the fully-employed economy of the 1960s, redundancy should not be a problem, and under-employed labour is urgently needed elsewhere. The elimination of these restrictive practices requires more enlightened management, more union co-operation, and more Government measures to promote the mobility of labour between occupations.

### Nationalised Industries.

Nationalised industry accounts for about 20 per cent of British industry. Local authorities also run some services—largely in bus transport and water provision. With the exception of coal-mining, all these industries are natural monopolies in which the provision of competing services would be obviously wasteful. They are thus obvious candidates for nationalisation. With the exception of steel—nationalised 1951–53 and re-nationalised in 1967—nationalisation has not been extended into manufacturing industry, not even where the existence of a private monopoly might suggest that there was a strong case. But nationalised industries are not free from competition. The railways face competition from road transport, some publicly and some privately owned: the fuel industries compete with each other, and with the privately owned oil industry.

Nationalised industries are supposed to earn enough to cover their costs. In the first ten years the two airways corporations were granted subsidies; but these have now ceased. Costs for a nationalised industry include interest payments on capital—both on the compensation paid to the previous owners and on the rather larger amounts of capital raised since nationalisation. The electricity boards, and to a lesser extent the gas boards, earn something above their costs to finance expansion, but not even then on the scale which is normal practice in private industries. The National Coal Board has accumulated a deficit by not increasing coal prices sufficiently to meet the increasing costs of production. The British railways have been in chronic deficit which it was the object of the Beeching Report to reduce.

The nationalised industries are voracious users of capital, as they are nearly all highly capitalised industries. Until 1956 they raised new capital, when they wanted it, by floating an issue on the Stock Exchange, the issue being guaranteed by the Government. Since then the nationalised industries have drawn directly on the Exchequer for their capital. This system has been attacked on both sides. The advocates of private enterprise have pointed to the strain this puts on the Exchequer, and to the unfairness whereby the nationalised industries get their capital cheaper or more easily than private industry. From the other side, it has been pointed out that the nationalised industries have suffered from their dependence on the Exchequer. In times of balance of payments crises the nationalised industries have been forced by the Government to cut back their planned programmes, sometimes at serious cost in disorganisation.

### 3. INCOMES, WAGES, AND PRICES

Personal Income, Spending, and Saving.

National income is a measure of the total income accruing to residents in return for services rendered. It therefore consists of the sum of wages, salaries, profits, and rents. Not all this income accrues to persons. Thus, companies do not distribute all their profits to shareholders: in 1965 undistributed profits amounted to £4,040 million. This is part of national income but not of personal income. On the other hand, some personal incomes are not payments for services rendered. Such incomes are called " transfer incomes " to emphasise that their payment does not add to the national income, but only transfers income from one recipient to another. Included in this category are retirement pensions, children's allowances, National Assistance payments, etc., amounting in 1965 to £2,724 million; and the interest on the National Debt paid out to persons. Total personal income in 1965 was £29,736 million.

The table shows what happened to this income. Direct taxation—income tax and surtax—took about 11 per cent of total personal income, and National Insurance contributions, which being compulsory are in effect a form of tax took a further 6 per cent. The remainder of personal income—called disposable income—was available for spending or saving. In 1965 total personal savings amounted to 6 per cent of personal income and 8 per cent of personal disposable income.

The other 92 per cent of disposable income was spent on consumption goods and services. Consumption expenditure in turn was broken down in the following way: a quarter on food; an eighth on drink and tobacco; 16 per cent on housing, fuel, and light; 9 per cent on clothing; 8 per cent on durable goods (motor cars, television

sets, refrigerators, etc.); 7 per cent on travel; leaving just over a fifth for other goods and services. Almost as much was spent on drink and tobacco as on housing, fuel, and light. This is partly because drink and tobacco is subject to heavy indirect taxation, which is the name given to taxes which are levied on particular goods and services. Thus nearly three-quarters of expenditure on tobacco goes to the Government. Total indirect taxation on consumers' expenditure amounted to £4,196 million in 1965, though this was offset by subsidies—payments by the Government towards the cost of particular goods and services, mainly some foods and housing—amounting to £508 million.

### DISPOSAL OF PERSONAL INCOME, 1965

| | £ million. | Percentage. |
|---|---|---|
| Total Personal Income . | 29,700 | 100 |
| less: | | |
| Direct Taxes . . | 3,390 | 11 |
| National Insurance contributions. . . | 1,690 | 6 |
| gives: | | |
| Disposable Income . . | 24,620 | 83 |
| Available for: | | |
| Consumption . . | 22,710 | 77 |
| Saving . . . | 1,910 | 6 |

Types of Personal Income.

Compare the sources of personal income in 1938 and in 1963. We see in the table that income from employment increased considerably, largely owing to a rise in the salary bill. The reason is not that salaries have increased faster than wages, but rather that the number of salaried workers has increased much faster than the number of wage-earners. There has also been an increase in the proportion of incomes derived from public grants—old age pensions, war pensions, sickness benefits, student grants, etc.

### SOURCES OF PERSONAL INCOME, 1938 AND 1963
(As percentage of total)

| | 1938. | 1963. |
|---|---|---|
| Income from employment of which: | 59·5 | 71 |
| wages . . . | 38 | 39 |
| salaries . . . | 18 | 25 |
| Forces' pay . . | 1·5 | 1·5 |
| employers' contributions* . | 2·5 | 5·5 |
| Income from self-employment of which: | 12·5 | 9 |
| professional persons . | 2 | 1·5 |
| farmers . . . | 1·5 | 2 |
| others . . . | 9 | 5 |
| Income from property . | 22·5 | 11·5 |
| Grants from public authorities . | 5·5 | 8·5 |
| Total . . . . | 100 | 100 |

\* To National Insurance and other superannuation schemes.

The types of income which have fallen as a proportion of the total are incomes of self-employed persons and incomes from property. During the war and for several years afterwards property incomes changed little—the effects of rent control, excess profits tax, and low interest rates were such that these incomes did not rise, while other incomes increased sharply. In more recent years there was a rise, as rent control on some property was lifted and as interest rates increased; but nevertheless the share of property incomes in 1963 was only about half of what it had been in 1938. Over this quarter of a century there was a fundamental redistribution of income away from property-owners towards employees.

## Incomes by Size.

In 1964 over 70 per cent of income-receivers had incomes under £1,000 and over 90 per cent under £1,500. The remaining 9 per cent with incomes over £1,500 received 27 per cent of the total income, and the top 1 per cent received 8 per cent of the total. Thus Britain is far from being an egalitarian society; income is still very unevenly distributed, but not so unevenly as before the war,

allowance now adds substantially to spending power. As tax rates have risen, it has become increasingly profitable for such classes to claim every expense to which they are conceivably entitled. Particularly important are cars required for business and also used for pleasure.

Second, only in 1965 did capital gains become taxable. If one buys an asset which then rises in value, one has clearly gained extra spending power. Not only have people in Britain been exempt from tax on capital gains, a considerable advantage in periods of boom in ordinary share prices, but also they have been able by a number

### BRITISH INCOMES BY SIZE, 1964

| Range of incomes before tax. | As percentage of total. | | | |
| --- | --- | --- | --- | --- |
| | Number of incomes. | Incomes before tax. | Incomes after tax. | Rates of tax as percentage. |
| £50–£250 | 14 | 3 | 4 | 0 |
| £250–£500 | 22 | 10 | 11 | 2 |
| £500–£1,000 | 35 | 31 | 33 | 6 |
| £1,000–£1,500 | 20 | 29 | 30 | 9 |
| £1,500–£2,000 | 5 | 11 | 10 | 14 |
| £2,000–£3,000 | 2 | 6 | 5 | 20 |
| £3,000–£5,000 | 1 | 4 | 3 | 27 |
| £5,000– | 0·5 | 6 | 4 | 46 |
| Total | 27.5m. | £22,885 m. | £20,268 m. | 11 |

when the top 1 per cent received 16 per cent of total income.

Taxes on income are of course highly progressive, rising sharply as income increases. Those with low incomes pay no income tax, and in so far as they are pensioners, no compulsory contributions either. We see from the table that the proportion of income paid in direct taxes rises from 2 per cent in the income bracket £250–£500 to 9 per cent in the bracket £1,000–£1,500 to 46 per cent for incomes exceeding £5,000 per annum.

This tax burden somewhat changes the distribution of incomes. After tax the top 9 per cent received only 23 per cent, and the top 1 per cent only 5·5 per cent of total incomes. But the redistributive effect of taxation must not be overstressed; the levelling-up of incomes before tax has been very much more important in making Britain rather more egalitarian than has been any taxation policy.

### Income and Spending Power.

In many ways figures for incomes alone substantially over-estimate the degree of equality found in Britain. First, incomes are incomes as defined for income-tax purposes. Any allowed

of devices to convert income into capital gains, and thus avoid paying income tax. Before 1965 various Chancellors of the Exchequer merely tried to close loopholes by making illegal various transactions aimed at tax avoidance.

### Distribution of Capital.

Spending power depends not only on income and capital gains but also on the sheer amount of capital owned; and in respect of capital Britain is still far from egalitarian. The only figures are those that arise in connection with the payment of death duties. In 1964/5 those who at death left estates of more than £5,000—just over a fifth of the total numbers dying—owned 77 per cent of the total, and the richest 1 per cent owned 24 per cent of the total. And this in spite of a growing tendency for the rich to pass on their money before death to avoid death duties. Compared with 1938, the main change appears to be that the fairly rich are more numerous and the extremely rich are somewhat less numerous. The vast majority still own very little, and Britain is far from being a property-owning democracy.

### Wages and Salaries.

In 1965 two thirds of personal income was paid in the form either of wages, salaries, or Forces' pay. The distinction between the first two is

### DISTRIBUTION OF WEALTH: VALUE OF ESTATES FOR DEATH DUTIES, 1964/5.

| Size of estate. £,000. | As percentage of total. | |
| --- | --- | --- |
| | Number of estates. | Value of estates. |
| −1 | 38 | 3 |
| 1–2 | 17 | 5 |
| 2–3 | 11 | 5 |
| 3–5 | 13 | 10 |
| 5–10 | 11 | 14 |
| 10–25 | 6 | 19 |
| 25–50 | 2 | 15 |
| 50–100 | 1 | 13 |
| 100– | 0·4 | 16 |
| Total | 295,798 | £1,531 m. |

expenses are excluded; and for the self-employed and the higher ranks of management the expense

### WAGE AND SALARY LEVELS IN MANUFACTURING INDUSTRY
(Earnings per week, October 1965.)

| | Administrative, Clerical, and Technical Staff. | | Wage earners. (Adults only.) |
| --- | --- | --- | --- |
| | Monthly paid. | Weekly paid. | |
| Men | £30 3s. | £19 9s. | £20 3s. |
| Women | £12 17s. | £9 10s. | £9 12s. |

very much a matter of convention; many salary-earners now earn less than wage earners, and the main division is between those salary-earners who are paid monthly and the rest. This we see in the table. Even though weekly-paid staff do not now earn more than wage-earners, they may still in effect be better off: for they generally work shorter hours; are more likely to be covered by private superannuation schemes; and usually work in better conditions.

No regular statistics are collected about salary levels; but every half-year the Ministry of Labour publishes detailed figures of the actual earnings in one week of wage-earners in a wide range of industries. There is a considerable variation in earnings between industries. Manufacturing industries pay well; and within manufacturing industries, vehicles and paper, printing and publishing pay the highest weekly wages. Public administration (including local government roadmen and the like) is a low-wage sector, particularly for men. For women the best paying industry is the buses where there is equal pay for male and female conductors. It should be borne in mind, however, that the average earnings for an industry may disguise a wide dispersion of earnings among firms of the industry and also within firms.

### AVERAGE WEEKLY EARNINGS OF MANUAL WORKERS IN CERTAIN INDUSTRIES
(April 1968)

| | Men. | Women. |
|---|---|---|
| Vehicles | £26 0s. | £13 0s. |
| Paper, printing, and publishing. | £26 2s. | £11 11s. |
| Chemicals | £23 8s. | £10 14s. |
| Food, drink, and tobacco | £21 3s. | £10 9s. |
| Textiles | £20 7s. | £10 13s. |
| All manufacturing industries* | £22 17s. | £10 19s. |
| Transport and communication (except railways) | £22 19s. | £14 11s. |
| Construction | £22 6s. | £10 4s. |
| Public administration | £17 7s. | £11 4s. |
| All industries* | £22 5s. | £10 19s. |

\* Including industries not listed.

### Differentials.

Women earn on average much less than men, and juveniles usually much less than adults. Before the war the gap was relatively greater. Men, for instance, earned 5·6 times as much in October 1965 as they did in October 1938; but for women the ratio was 6·2 times. Nearly all this narrowing occurred during the war, when it was the common practice for wage advances to take the form of a flat-rate increase to all employees regardless of sex. Since 1950 the practice has altered. The usual thing has been to grant roughly similar percentage increases to all grades, and there has in fact been a slight widening of the gap.

The same narrowing occurred in other differentials. Skilled workers, for instance, were during the war granted the same flat-rate advances as unskilled and there was then and, to some extent, also in the years immediately after the war, a sharp narrowing of the reward for skill in many industries. As for the sex differential, the narrowing has now come to a halt; but it has not been reversed, and wages within the working-class are much less widely spread than they used to be. Some would say the rewards for skill were insufficient; but, on the other hand, the upgrading of the lowest-paid has, together with the reduction in long-term unemployment, been the main means by which the grinding poverty of the worst-off members of society—with all its undesirable consequences, such as malnutrition of children—has been eliminated. Today the really numerous poor are the old, the sick, and the handicapped—and not, as before the war, families with a working head who was earning too little to make ends meet.

Differentials have been a major source of industrial strife in some industries. In engineering there has been continued conflict between unions with membership largely among the skilled and those with membership largely among the semi-skilled over what form demands for wage increases should take. On the railways the strife has been even more open.

### Overtime and Short-time.

The earnings of any individual worker depend on many factors, and are usually far above the minimum wage-rates payable for a week. They include overtime earnings; and overtime working is common for men. In most weeks 1·5 to 2 million workers in manufacturing will be working overtime to the extent of 8 to 9 hours. So the average-week in April 1966 was 45 hours, which is at least 4 hours above the average standard working week without overtime. In the cement industry the average working-week for men was as much as 55 hours. Indeed the average working-week in 1960 was higher than before the war, even though the standard working-week had been reduced. In most industries it was cut by 4 hours soon after the war from 48 to 44 hours, a 42-hour week was introduced between 1960 and 1962, and there was a movement towards a 40-hour standard working-week between 1964 and 1966.

Short-time, the working of less than the standard week, has not been common since the war. It has been important in particular industries at particular times; but even in February 1963, at the bottom of the recession, it was far smaller than overtime. Then 165,000 workers were on an average short-time of 12·5 hours—a total of 2·0 million hours lost, as against 12·3 million hours of overtime in the same week.

### Earnings and Rates.

Overtime is not, however, the main reason why earnings exceed minimum wage-rates; for most workers earn very much more than the minimum in the standard working-week. One reason is payment by results, the system of payment under which the worker's wage depends partly on output. The commonest form is still the piecework system, under which pieceworkers are paid a fixed low rate per hour for each hour worked plus a fixed piecework price for each operation performed; but increasingly employers tend to prefer as a more effective incentive some scheme under which the bonus payment is related to the output of a larger group or to that of a whole factory. With payment by results systems—these cover about 40 per cent of the workers in manufacturing industry—earnings rise as productivity rises, and, as usually such workers also participate in advances in wage-rates negotiated between employers and unions, the gap between earnings and wage-rates tends to widen for them. So workers not paid by results press for similar advances for themselves, and in times of booming trade get them under a wide variety of names and forms—merit payments, lieu rates, compensation bonuses, etc. Between 1955 and 1965 wage-rates rose by 51 per cent and earnings by 75 per cent. The advance in rates was little more than the rise in retail prices—only 15 per cent—so that anyone who actually earned the minimum rate throughout was not much better off. But earnings rose by 40 per cent more than prices, so that the main source of the extra real income of the working-class is to be found in the widening gap between earnings and rates.

### Wage Negotiation.

In Britain there were 10·1 million trade union members in 590 unions in 1964. Most of these unions are very small, over 500 having less than 2,500 members, but 18 have a membership of over 100,000. The main job of unions is collective bargaining with employers, and in most industries most employers also belong to associations which bargain collectively on their behalf. Some big firms, however, prefer to remain outside the associations, and strike their own bargain with the unions. Before the war many firms tried to encourage the formation of Company Unions, i.e., of unions confined to employees of a single firm; but this is now uncommon. In some lowly paid trades—catering, baking, dressmaking, and others—minimum wages are fixed by Wages Boards or Councils set up by the Ministry of Labour; and representatives of the workers and employers, and independent members, meet together to reach agreement on the settlement to be recommended to the Minister. But over most of industry the aim of collective bargaining is to reach voluntary agreement, and the Ministry of Labour intervenes only when no agreement is reached. Even in the nationalised industries, the Government does not usually intervene unless negotiations between the Boards and the unions break down.

The usual pattern of negotiation is like this. First, the union puts in a claim for an all-round increase, usually much larger than it expects to get. Then after a time the employers reply, often offering a much smaller increase, and sometimes none at all. They then argue round a table until either they reach agreement or they definitely fail to reach agreement. If the latter happens the next step varies considerably from industry to industry. Many industries have their own "conciliation" machinery, in which outsiders try to help the two sides to reach agreement. Some, though not many, also have their own "arbitration" machinery, in which outsiders can recommend a solution of the dispute, which is sometimes binding and sometimes not. It depends on what the two sides have agreed on in advance. Many industries have no machinery of their own and depend on the general facilities the Minister of Labour can offer. He may appoint an impartial conciliator; or he may, with the agreement of both parties, refer the matter to the Industrial Court, which arbitrates between the parties; or he may set up a Court of Enquiry which enquires into the dispute and makes recommendations, which are not binding on the parties; or he may decide to do nothing at all, if he judges intervention to be useless. Nor need either unions or employers call him in; the former may opt to put pressure on the employers immediately either by strike action, or by banning overtime or piecework, or by other action.

Thus the British Government traditionally has little power to control wages directly or to impose agreements The recent attempts to introduce compulsion in wage-determination are described in Part IV.

## Important Negotiations.

A few negotiations are particularly important in determining how wages rise in a year; for the pattern of later settlements tends roughly to follow those of earlier settlements. Probably the most important of all are those between the Confederation of Engineering and Shipbuilding Unions—an organisation representing 3 million workers—and the Engineering Employers' Federation, as this single negotiation directly affects the wages of 3¼ million workers, and indirectly many more. On several occasions since the war negotiations between these two have broken down, and only finally been settled after a Court of Enquiry had recommended a compromise wage-advance. The Confederation is a special negotiating body comprising all the unions who have members working in the engineering and shipbuilding industries. These include many small, skilled workers' unions, such as the Patternmakers' Union, but they also include, besides the 1 million-strong Amalgamated Engineering Union, the two large general unions, the Transport and General Workers' Union, with about 1½ million members, and the General and Municipal Workers' Union, with not far short of a million. These last two represent the semi-skilled and unskilled workers, and conflict between them and the skilled unions concerning differentials is common.

The other really important negotiation is that between the British Transport Commission and the three railway unions—the large National Union of Railwaymen, representing most grades, the Amalgamated Society of Locomotive Engineers and Firemen, representing the drivers and the firemen, and the Transport Salaried Staffs' Association, representing the ticket collectors, railway clerks, etc. The importance of this negotiation lies in the fact that railwaymen are comparatively badly paid; but, as the Transport Commission runs a deficit, any wage advance has effectively to be paid for by the Government. Time and time again—for example the rise in early 1960 arising out of the Guillebaud Report on railway pay—wage advances have been given to railwaymen with the purpose of trying to narrow the gap between them and other workers; but the advance given to railwaymen then acts as a guide to other settlements, so that the railwaymen remain relatively as badly paid as before.

## Strikes.

The strike is the unions' weapon of last resort. Most unions maintain strike funds in order to support their members when they call them out on strike; but these funds are small, and strike pay is usually very much below normal wages. So unions cannot afford to call strikes irresponsibly, and major official strikes are uncommon. In most years there will be one or two, but not more, and the total number of working-days lost is usually negligible—less than one day per head. Even in the industry affected the lost working-days are usually made up in the following weeks by overtime.

Nevertheless, the big strikes are important; for the success or failure of one big strike can affect the results of all the other collective bargaining under way at the time. They can also affect the awards of arbitration tribunals since, in the main, arbitration awards tend to follow the pattern of settlements already made in other industries. There is no purpose in a tribunal trying to be fair if it cannot get its awards accepted. So the settlement reached as a result of a strike often determines the amount by which wage-rates will rise on average over all industries.

Most strikes are neither large nor official, nor about wages. An official strike is one called by a union, usually by decision of the national executive, and is usually the result of a breakdown in collective bargaining about wages. But unofficial strikes called by local leaders with the authorisation of unions are usually about other matters. None of the big unofficial strikes which have plagued the London Docks since the war was about wages, but usually about some relative triviality that only bore witness to the thoroughly poor state of labour relations in that industry. Much the same may be said about the continual strikes in shipbuilding, many of them caused by demarcation disputes concerning which jobs should be done by which type of skilled worker. These sort of strikes are really a form of industrial protest, and the employers have to bear their share of the blame.

In 1965 there were in all 2,350 strikes in the United Kingdom; 869,000 workers were directly or indirectly involved, and 2,932,000 working days were lost. This means that the average strike involved about 370 workers and lasted over 3 days.

In most industries there are very few strikes. The main strike-prone industries, apart from the mines, are vehicles, shipbuilding, and docks; but even in these the extent of strikes must not be exaggerated. In shipbuilding with the worst record of disputes, losses are only just over one day a year and, if that were all, could safely be ignored. But, of course, strikes are also a symptom of industrial trouble; and it is no accident that in shipbuilding productivity has scarcely improved at all since the war.

## Prices and Real Incomes.

The aim of a trade union is to get for its members a higher standard of living, and its success depends on the extent to which wage advances exceed the rise in the cost-of-living. Prices rose very rapidly

### WAGES AND PRICES
(1955 = 100)

|      | Weekly wage-rates. | Weekly earnings. | Index of retail prices. | Real wage-rates. | Real earnings. |
|------|------|------|------|------|------|
| 1950 | 73   | 68   | 77   | 96   | 91   |
| 1955 | 100  | 100  | 100  | 100  | 100  |
| 1960 | 124  | 126  | 114  | 110  | 112  |
| 1965 | 151  | 163  | 136  | 115  | 127  |

(by over 30 per cent) between 1949 and 1953, and earnings only just kept ahead in this period. But since then real earnings (i.e., command over goods and services of money earnings) have risen steadily. Thus, between 1955 and 1965, the real earnings of a wage-earner rose by 27 per cent.

Real incomes of pensioners and those on National Assistance have gone up too, after the serious erosion of their value in the late 1940s. The retirement pension is still inadequate for a decent life; but that is because when the National Insurance scheme was set up in 1948 it was believed that the nation could not afford anything better, and not because inflation has eroded the value of the pension. Inflation can no longer be deplored on the main ground that it leads to much hardship. The main danger is that British exports become uncompetitive, and that the balance of payments position deteriorates and puts a brake on the growth of the economy.

### Price Changes.

In the calculation or real wages it is usual to make use of the *index of retail prices*, commonly called the cost-of-living index. This index is calculated monthly by the Ministry of Labour, and in a few industries with sliding-scale agreements, wages are adjusted to take account of the index. In other industries the index has naturally had an influence on the course of negotiations. Indeed, up to 1958 it was probably the dominant influence. In no year before then had the annual rise in prices been less than 2 per cent.

in 1951. Since then, however, the dominant trend of import prices has been downwards, and changes in prices of imports cannot be directly blamed for the continuing rise in prices since 1951. The source has to be looked for in the tendency of wages, salaries, profits, and other incomes to rise faster than real output, and this they have done in almost every year since the war.

### Wages and Prices.

Wage increases are probably the most important. When a trade union negotiates a wage advance for all or most of the employees in an industry, firms will immediately consider whether they should increase their prices to cover their increased wage-costs. As it is common practice for firms to fix the selling prices of their products by first calculating the direct cost of labour and of materials, and then adding on a percentage to cover overhead costs and profits, they will tend to want to raise their prices not only to cover the cost of the wage advance but also to cover their percentage addition. Moreover, in deciding whether or not their customers will stand for such increases, firms will be influenced by the knowledge that their competitors have to pay the

### INDEX OF RETAIL PRICES
(January 1956 = 100)

|  | 1965 Weight.* | Monthly average index. | | | |
|---|---|---|---|---|---|
|  |  | 1950. | 1955. | 1960. | 1965. |
| Food . . . . . | 311 | 65 | 98 | 107 | 124 |
| Drink . . . . | 65 | }94 | 100 | 98 | 127 |
| Tobacco . . . | 76 |  | 98 | 112 | 146 |
| Housing . . . | 109 | 83 | 98 | 132 | 169 |
| Fuel and light . . | 65 | 65 | 92 | 117 | 150 |
| Durable household goods . | 59 | 80 | 94 | 98 | 107 |
| Clothing and footwear . . | 92 | 83 | 98 | 104 | 114 |
| Transport and vehicles . . | 105 | — | — | 118 | 135 |
| Services . . . . | 63 | 73 | 97 | 115 | 147 |
| Other goods . . . | 55 | 77 | 96 | 120 | 140 |
| *All items . . . .* | *1000* | *74* | *97* | *111* | *132* |

\* *I.e.*, proportionate importance of item in total expenditure in 1965.

Price changes have not been the same for all types of goods. For instance, between 1956 and 1965, when the total index rose by 32 per cent, housing went up by 69 per cent and fuel and light by 50 per cent; but the prices of food, clothing, drink, and especially durable household goods rose less than the average. Since rent, fuel, and food form a much higher proportion of total expenditure for the poor, and particularly for pensioners, than for most households, it is possible that prices rose more for the poor than for the rich over these years.

### The Causes of Price Inflation.

Prices charged in the shops are determined by a great many factors, over many of which the Government has little or no control. First among these is the price of imports. Prices of imported food and raw materials are determined in the world markets, in which Britain is only one of many purchasers. In the raw material markets the U.S.A. is usually the dominant purchaser, and prices depend greatly on the level of economic activity there. In the food markets British purchases are much more important, since the U.S.A. grows most of its own food, and is a large exporter of some foods. Prices in raw material markets are continually changing, and can fluctuate wildly. For instance, the average price of copper rose 40 per cent between 1954 and 1955, and then fell back in 1957 to 10 per cent below its 1954 level. Fluctuations at the time of the Korean War were even more fantastic. The price of wool rose over four times, and then came down just as abruptly to only a quarter above its earlier level; the price of rubber behaved similarly. The large rise in import prices, coming on top of the rise that had been brought about by devaluation, caused the cost-of-living index to shoot up sharply

increased wages too, and will probably therefore be raising their prices. So industry-wide wage advances—and changes in costs of materials—are particularly likely to be passed on to the consumer; and, as wage-earners are also consumers, to generate further demands for wage advances to cover the increased prices. Profits per unit also go up under this tendency to set prices on a *cost-plus* basis; but it is the wage advance which tends to set the spiral off, by providing the opportunity for price increases.

Once this spiral gets going, it is very hard to stop it. In general, the requirement is that wage earnings should not rise faster than productivity (output per man). But, as in some industries productivity is very slow to rise, and as it would be unfair and impracticable to exclude their workers from participating in any general rise in the standard of living, this requirement means that in industries with a rapid growth of productivity wage advances should be kept well below the rate of rise of productivity. For two reasons this is rather difficult. First, rising productivity often raises the wages of some workers in these industries automatically, because they are paid by results or through some incentive scheme. The rise of wages from this source takes the form of a tendency on the part of earnings in these industries to rise faster than wage-rates; but that does not mean that all employees benefit, or that there is any likelihood that the unions in these industries will not press for the same rate of increase in wage-rates as is achieved in the slowly-growing industries. Second, employers in the rapidly-growing industries have far less reason to resist demands for wage increases than those in slowly-growing industries. Indeed, they are quite likely to bid up wages in order to get the labour they need, rather than to try to hold down wages.

There are therefore major problems in preventing a faster rise in wages than in productivity, with its consequence of rising prices. And once a wage-price spiral has started, the problems become more acute because unions and employers become accustomed to substantial annual advances in money wages. A main source of continuing price inflation has been the tendency of money wages to continue to advance at a rate that was appropriate when the cost-of-living was going up sharply, but ceased to be appropriate in later years.

## The Stopping of Price Inflation.

There are several possible methods of attack on the inflationary spiral of wages and prices. Perhaps the most fundamental, and certainly the most helpful to other objectives of economic policy, is to achieve a faster rate of productivity growth. The faster the growth of average productivity, the faster can average incomes rise without an increase in average prices. But if wages and other incomes rise more rapidly than productivity, it will be difficult to maintain price stability.

Comprehensive and detailed Government control of wages must probably be ruled out for political and institutional reasons, and so must comprehensive and detailed control of prices. Either would involve a much more " controlled " economy than we have at present, and experience suggests that such detailed control would involve a major loss of flexibility in the economy. At the other extreme, general exhortations to unions to exercise restraint on wages, and to manufacturers to exercise restraint on prices, have probably had little effect.

Various intermediate lines of approach have been or could be tried. In 1948–50, the Government secured the co-operation of the T.U.C. in the wages " freeze ". For a time this was successful, but the increases in prices which followed the devaluation in 1949 made substantial increases in wages unavoidable, and the freeze was abandoned. By setting an example in the nationalised industries over which it has a more direct influence, the Government can encourage employers to take a tougher attitude towards wage claims. This was one strand of policy in the later 1950s. Its disadvantage is the obvious unfairness of a policy which is most likely to be effective in nationalised industries, many of whose workers are relatively badly-paid. Another approach is to lower tariffs or remove quotas on imports, thus exposing some manufacturers at home to tougher competition from abroad. Manufacturers would be less able to raise prices without losing markets, and unions would be less willing to press wage claims if there was a real danger that some of their members would lose their jobs as a consequence. But the gains from a policy which depends for its success on higher imports have to be weighed against its effects on the balance of payments. Or again, many prices in the economy are directly influenced by Government indirect taxation which raises the price of some goods, and Government subsidies which lower the prices of other goods. By manipulating its tax and subsidy policies, the Government can exercise a powerful influence on the price level: though of course any reduction in indirect taxation or increase in subsidies would probably have to be financed by increases in direct taxation, which may in turn have undesirable effects on incentives to harder **work** and greater effort.

More indirectly, the Government can attempt to control the wage-price spiral by controlling purchasing power through its monetary and fiscal policies. If purchasing power is curbed, manufacturers find it more difficult to raise **prices**, and the bargaining power of unions may be reduced. In the 1950s, the Government relied heavily on fiscal and more especially monetary policies, the nature of which will be examined in later sections. The main danger is that curbing purchasing power is likely to curb the rise in output and productivity, so that attempts to control the wage-price spiral in this way could result in the stagnation of the economy. Furthermore, there is a danger that some wage increases will continue in periods of stagnation so that inflation cannot be entirely avoided.

It is clear that there is no easy solution—there are difficulties and disadvantages attaching to every possible measure for controlling price inflation. In Part III we shall discuss the solutions which have been attempted in the 1960s.

## 4. MONEY, BANKING, AND FINANCE

### The Radcliffe Report.

In September 1957 the Chancellor set up the Radcliffe Committee to report on the working of Britain's monetary institutions. The report of the committee, published in 1959, contains a detailed description of the monetary institutions of this country, and a systematic appraisal of monetary policies in the 1950s. It is complicated, because the monetary system is complicated; but it is written in terms which can be understood by the layman. Any reader who finds the following account inadequate should consult it.

### Money.

In Britain money consists of bank-notes, coinage, and banks' debt. Bank-notes—mainly in denominations of £5, £1, and 10s.—are issued by the Bank of England, which has been publicly owned since 1946, and which acts in effect as an agent of the Government. We shall see below (G21(1)) how commercial banks can also create money.

The total size of the bank-note issue is not a good guide to the amount of purchasing power in the economy. The Bank of England stated in its evidence to the Radcliffe Committee that it was now its policy to issue bank-notes in accordance with the convenience of the public, and not to use this means of controlling the amount of purchasing power. As a result, the various checks on the size of the note issue—in particular the Parliamentary control over the fiduciary issue, *i.e.*, the permitted maximum level of the note issue—have become functionless and may be ignored. An increase in the value of the note issue is now only a symptom and not a cause of inflation.

### Determination of Income and Employment.

What matters is the amount of purchasing power available to the public. Most private expenditure is financed out of income—after paying taxes—and most government expenditure out of taxes; but most investment, public and private, and a growing amount of purchases of durable goods by consumers, is not financed out of income, but out of borrowing of one kind or another. And the primary purpose of monetary policy must be to keep the total of this kind of expenditure out of credit in line with the amount of savings private individuals and profit-making companies are prepared to make out of their incomes. For if such investment expenditure exceeds the amount which the community wishes to save out of its current level of income, it means that the total demand for goods and services exceeds total current output. If output cannot be increased because men and machines are already fully-employed, prices and wages and also imports are forced up in response to the demand. If, on the other hand, investment expenditure falls short of saving out of full-employment income, production and employment are reduced below the full-employment level.

There is no automatic mechanism in our economic system which ensures full-employment of resources, and it is the task of Government to balance savings and investment at the right level of employment. This important fact was first established by the great economist J. M. (later Lord) Keynes. Prior to the Great Depression, economists believed that any divergence from full-employment was a temporary phenomenon, which would right itself. However, in the 1930s Keynes produced a new explanation of how income and employment are determined; and so brought about what has come to be known as the *Keynesian Revolution* in economics.

### Government Control of Income and Employment.

The Government can control the level of income and employment in various ways. First, in many fields the Government has only very restricted powers to influence behaviour. It cannot compel persons or companies to save; it can only offer them inducements to do so in the form of higher interest rates or of tax concessions on receipts from interest, and their effectiveness is limited. Nor in general has it very much direct power over expenditure out of credit. It can and does control the conditions under which hire-purchase agreements are made—and this does, temporarily at any rate, make a great deal of difference to the amount of goods bought on hire-purchase. It can to a certain extent influence private companies in their investment policies by granting and withdrawing incentives to invest ment (see G13(1)); but it is doubtful quite how much influence these changes have. And it can, if it chooses, exercise direct control over building, by allowing building only on licence. This power, however, is not now used in order to control the level of investment, but only in order to encourage it in depressed areas and discourage it elsewhere. The only authorities over whose investment the Government does have real control are the nationalised industries; and, as the Radcliffe Committee pointed out, there are obvious dis advantages in any system whereby investment in public utilities is determined, not by the need for such investment, but by the need to balance savings and investment.

The two main means remaining are fiscal and monetary control. If the Government thinks there is going to be a shortage of private savings it raises more in taxation or reduces its current expenditure and so increases the Budget surplus (see G24(2)). The second form of control is much more complex; in principle, the aims are twofold. One is to keep the amount of credit-creation down (or up) to the required extent; the second is to ensure that the Government gets the share of savings it needs to cover its investment pro grammes. The complexity arises from the inter relations between these two tasks.

### The Government as Borrower.

The Government is a heavy borrower from the rest of the economy. In 1965 total public borrow ing—by government, nationalised industries, and local authorities—stood at £38,000 million, equiva lent to 1·4 times the annual national income. Most of this immense National Debt was built up during the war, when government expenditure far ex ceeded taxation; but the total continues to advance year by year, owing to the heavy capital requirements of the nationalised industries.

The Government borrows in six main ways. First, the issue of bank-notes is in effect a form of government borrowing. Second, it borrows from foreign governments. Third, it borrows from companies through tax reserve certificates, which are a means by which companies let the Govern ment have the taxes they would have to pay on profits as the latter are earned, rather than when the taxes legally become due. Fourth, it borrows direct from private individuals through the various forms of national savings. In all forms of national savings the Government pays interest—or in the case of premium bonds prizes in lieu of interest to the winners of the monthly draw—to the holders, who have the right either on demand or at short notice to the repayment of their loans.

### Gilt-edged Securities and Treasury Bills.

The fifth and sixth methods of borrowing are through the market. The main method is through the Stock Exchange by the issue of fixed-interest securities, called gilt-edged securities. In 1965 the net amount owing to the public on all such securi ties was nearly £13,000 million—a third of total public debt. Most gilt-edged securities are pro mises to repay at a specified date in the future the amount originally borrowed; and in the mean time to pay a fixed amount of interest each half-year. Some gilt-edged securities are irredeem able, and consist therefore simply of a promise to pay the interest in perpetuity.

Most gilt-edged securities are held by institu tions: the banks, discount houses, and other major financial institutions of the country, and foreign governments (whose holdings represent their sterling balances, (see G7(2)); only a fifth of the total being held by private individuals. Gilt-edged securities, unlike national savings, are not liquid assets. Until they become due for replace ment they can only be sold on the Stock Exchange for what they will fetch, and variations in their market value are quite considerable. Dealings in second-hand securities can have important effects on the economy. Variation in the market price of securities implies an inverse variation in the effective rate of interest which they earn. This in turn can influence the general level of interest rates, hence the amount of investment which it is profitable to carry out, and hence the general level of economic activity.

The sixth form of borrowing is by means of Treasury Bills, of which £2,100 million were out standing in 1965. A Treasury Bill is an extremely short-term loan to the Government—usually for three months. Each week the Treasury offers for sale some £300 million of these, and a number of specialised institutions bid for them. The difference between their bids and the value of these bonds on repayment is called discount, and is a substitute for interest. These bills play a crucial role in the monetary system, for it is by affecting the rate of discount on Treasury Bills that Bank Rate influences monetary conditions in the economy; but more of that a little later.

### Government Borrowing and Liquidity.

Monetary policy consists largely in varying the way in which the Government borrows to finance its expenditure. This is because the form of borrowing affects the amount of liquidity in the economy. All financial institutions have some policy regarding liquidity. In general they try to maintain sufficient reserves either of cash or of assets which can be immediately converted into cash to meet any foreseeable sudden increase in their commitments. But they do not hold all their assets in liquid form. The chance that all their creditors simultaneously demand their money back can be ruled out, and therefore most of them act on the principle that they should maintain cash or other liquid assets to cover some percentage of their total outstanding commit ments. Whereas currency and Treasury Bills are regarded as liquid assets, government securities and most other forms of government borrowing are illiquid.

If therefore the Government borrows more by issuing currency or Treasury Bills and less by other means, this action increases the amount of liquid assets about and therefore the total lending which financial institutions think it safe to make. And, conversely, if the Government borrows less by issuing currency or Treasury Bills and more by other means, this tends to decrease the total amount of loans which financial institutions are prepared to make. However, government con trol over the way in which it borrows is circum scribed. The public can be persuaded to hold more government securities only if the rate of interest earned on securities is increased. In the 1950s the British Government was unable to pre vent a rapid accumulation of short-term debt, even though it allowed the rate of interest earned by irredeemable government securities to rise from less than 4 per cent in 1950 to over 5 per cent in 1960.

### The Commercial Banks.

In the centre of the financial world stand the commercial banks. In England these are known as the London clearing banks. In this country, unlike the United States, the banking system is highly concentrated; there being five main banks with branches in every town. The commercial banks are important because their debts are used by the public as money. Anyone who has a bank current account can sign cheques or withdraw cash on demand up the limit of his account. Because they can be used as a means of payment just as readily as bank-notes, bank deposits are money.

Commercial banks earn a profit by borrowing funds and then lending part of these funds at higher rates of interest. Because it is unlikely that all deposits will be withdrawn at once, the banks hold only a small proportion of their de posits in the form of cash. The Bank of England requires them to hold 8 per cent; and we see in the table that in 1965 the average cash ratio was

LONDON CLEARING BANKS, 1965.
(£ million)

| Liabilities. | | Assets. | | Percentage of deposits. |
|---|---|---|---|---|
| Capital and reserves . . | 513 | Cash . . . | 739 | 8·2 |
| Deposits . . . . | 8,989 | Other liquid assets . | 2,042 | 22·5 |
| Other. . . . . | 542 | " Special deposits " . | 56 | 0·6 |
| | | Investments . . | 1,087 | 12·1 |
| | | Advances . . | 4,653 | 51·8 |
| | | Other . . . | 1,467 | |
| Total . . . . | 10,044 | Total . . . | 10,044 | |

8·2 per cent. In addition they hold by conventional liquid assets (Treasury bills and money at call and short notice) equal to at least 30 per cent of their deposits; the ratio being 30·7 per cent in 1965. These liquid assets are easily transferable into cash. Their remaining assets are more remunerative; the majority being advances made to the public and earning a rate of interest higher than Bank Rate. In 1965 cash held by the commercial banks amounted to £739 million, whereas the public had deposits with the banks totalling £8,989 million. Thus the banking system can create money: it does so by accepting bank deposits far in excess of the cash held to meet demands for these deposits.

### The Control of Commercial Banks.

The first step in any credit squeeze is to put pressure on the commercial banks by reducing their liquidity; so causing them to restrict their advances to would-be investors. This can be done in two main ways. The first is by *open-market operations*, in which the Bank deliberately sells more government stock than it otherwise would. The purchasers pay by cheque, and thus create a debt from the commercial banks to the Bank of England. Such debts have to be settled in cash, and so pressure is put on the banks' liquidity. The second is *Bank Rate*. If Bank Rate is raised it has the immediate effect of raising the rate of discount on Treasury Bills. A high rate of discount on these makes them appear attractive investments to those who do not normally buy them, and the commercial banks find it difficult to get as many of them as they would like. So again there is pressure on the banks' liquidity.

Faced by such pressure, the banks have to take steps to restore their liquidity either by selling securities or by calling in advances. Neither method brings in much cash directly; for since the banks will be paid by cheque rather than in cash, they have to go on until the depletion of deposits caused by the paying of these cheques cuts down the total of deposits to the level where liquid assets once again represent 30 per cent of the total. To this there is one major exception; if the Bank of England buys the securities the banks sell—and the need to ensure an orderly market may force it to do so—then selling securities brings more cash into the banks, and thus enables them to replenish their liquidity.

Since 1958, the monetary authorities have had the power to call upon the banks to make *special deposits* in cash with the Bank of England. Unlike other deposits of the banks with the Bank of England, special deposits cannot be treated as forming part of the liquid assets of commercial banks. This is in effect another way of putting pressure on the liquidity position of banks: the necessity of making such deposits could force them to sell securities or reduce advances. " Special deposits " amounted to 0·6 per cent of the banks' total deposits in 1965.

### Bank Advances and Other Credit.

Bank advances are the simplest of all forms of credit; the customer is just given the right to sign cheques beyond his credit account, and interest is charged on the overdraft. In the late 1950s, a new form of advance—the personal loan—was introduced by some banks. These are granted to customers who would not earlier have been regarded as credit-worthy. A higher rate of interest is charged than on ordinary overdrafts, and more specific rules about repayment are laid down.

Most advances, however, are made to business, particularly to small business, and to farmers. In business the common practice is to finance working capital—stocks and work-in-progress—out of bank advances, and to depend on more permanent forms of borrowing for the purchase of fixed capital. But there are no fixed rules; business gets its finance wherever it can, and in fact there is such a variety of ways in which it can get capital that a squeeze on bank advances alone is not as effective as might be expected. Big businesses, in practice, scarcely suffer at all; for they are in the best position to tap other sources of credit. Quite a good example is provided by the hire-purchase finance companies. During the credit squeeze of 1956–58 the banks were asked by the Chancellor of the Exchequer not to hold down advances, and in particular not to increase advances to hire-purchase finance companies. They did so; but the companies had no difficulty in getting the money they needed by borrowing direct from the public at high rates of interest. The real sufferers tend to be small businesses and professional people, who do find it hard to obtain credit elsewhere; but even they may be able to do so; for instance, by taking out a mortgage on their property or by buying their equipment on hire-purchase where previously they had paid cash, or by cashing some national savings.

The Radcliffe Committee discussed at length how effective a squeeze on the banks was likely to be, and in general their conclusion was that it was not likely to be very effective, because most borrowers would usually find other sources of credit. The other sources would usually be more expensive; but they thought this mattered very little, as interest payments form only a small part of most business costs, except in very highly capitalised industries, most of which are now publicly owned. Interest does matter in housing; the monthly interest payments due on a mortgage to a building society can go up substantially when the rate of interest goes up, although usually for existing, as opposed to new, mortgages no more money is asked for; instead the term of the mortgage in years is extended. But in hire-purchase, where service charges far exceed the interest element in any loan, interest is of trivial importance.

### The Stock Exchange.

The banks through their advances are the main providers of short-term credit; but most long-term credit is provided through the Stock Exchange. In 1965 the total market value of all securities traded on the Stock Exchange was £75,000 million, of which £57,000 million represented stocks or shares in public companies. There are three main types. *Debenture Stock* is simply a fixed-interest loan. *Preference Stock* is a fixed-interest loan, with provisions for waiving the interest if the company fails to earn profits. Preference shareholders cannot get a company declared bankrupt if it does not pay them a dividend; but Debenture holders can. The third type—and much the most important—is *Ordinary Shares*. Nominally the owner of an Ordinary Share is a part-owner of the company concerned, with most of the rights of ownership. He has no right to any particular dividend or interest payment, but only the right to participate in net profits if there are any. In addition to stocks or shares in public companies, British Government gilt-edged securities worth £15,000 million were quoted on the Stock Exchange.

### The Return on Financial Assets.

Each type of holding has obvious advantages. The fixed-interest security brings in a guaranteed income; the Ordinary Shareholder has no such guarantee, though in practice during the post-war period the risk of a decline in dividend was small. In a time of inflation the risks attached to holding fixed-interest securities are in some ways greater than those attached to holding Ordinary Shares; for, while Ordinary Shares appreciate in market value when there is inflation, fixed-interest securities tend to fall in market value, because the Government is forced to increase interest rates as an anti-inflationary measure. Furthermore, in the long run the growth of the economy tends, even without inflation, to raise the value of Ordinary Shares by increasing the value of companies. And, lastly, for investors who pay tax at heavy rates on their incomes—and most large personal investors in the Stock Exchange are rich people—capital gains are worth more than income in dividends. So for private investors, the Ordinary Share was a much better bet in the 1950s; and because Ordinary Shares were so popular, the yield on such shares—the ratio of dividends to market value—fell below the yield obtainable on Government securities (see table).

and manipulated in an attempt to control demand. This policy was adhered to by both Governments in the 1960s. We see in the table that the rate on Treasury Bills has kept in line with Bank Rate.

In addition to influencing the cost of credit by manipulating interest rates, the Government influenced the availability of certain sorts of credit through the credit-squeeze. At times it made it more difficult for the banks to extend their lending by operating on the banks' liquidity position, and it also issued more or less strongly-worded " requests " that banks should restrict growth of, or secure a reduction in, their advances.

A form of monetary control which was particularly important after 1950 was the control of hire-purchase. By increasing or lowering the proportion of the price which has to be paid as a down-payment, and by reducing or lengthening the time over which repayments can be made, the Government was able greatly to influence the volume of hire-purchase transactions, and therefore the use of this particular form of credit. These controls, of course, only affect the rather narrow class of goods—cars, furniture, washing-machines, television sets, etc.—for which a substantial proportion of sales are on hire-purchase terms. In consequence, the output of those industries concerned with the manufacture of these goods fluctuated widely.

### The Effectiveness of Monetary Controls.

Running through the Radcliffe Report is a scepticism concerning the likely general effective-

PERCENTAGE YIELD ON FINANCIAL ASSETS

| | Bank Rate.* | Treasury bill rate.† | Irredeemable government bond rate. | Ordinary Share rate. |
|---|---|---|---|---|
| 1950 . . | 2 | 0·5 | 3·5 | 5·3 |
| 1955 . . | 3–4·5 | 3·6 | 4·2 | 5·4 |
| 1960 . . | 4–6 | 4·9 | 5·4 | 4·6 |
| 1965 . . | 6–7 | 5·9 | 6·4 | 5·5 |

\* Range during year.                            † Annual average.

Most Ordinary Shares are held by private individuals; but increasingly in recent years holdings by insurance companies and pension funds have become more important, because of the growth of private superannuation schemes. Insurance companies and pension funds cannot afford to take risks, so the main bulk of their funds is still invested in fixed-interest securities; but they have shown a growing tendency to increase the proportion of their funds invested in Ordinary Shares. This switch, by lowering the demand for gilt-edged securities relative to Ordinary Shares, contributed to the downward pressure on the prices of gilt-edged securities. Legislation was introduced in 1960 to permit trusts to invest up to 50 per cent of their funds in the Ordinary Shares of large companies. In the same way, this has depressed the yield on Ordinary Shares and raised the yield on gilt-edged.

Historically, the greater security of gilt-edged holdings has normally been reflected in lower yields. If inflation is controlled, or if the prospect of industrial expansion becomes less bright, the demand for gilt-edged may increase and that for Ordinary Shares decrease; and the " normal " pattern of yields may then return.

### Survey of Monetary Controls.

The post-war Labour Government pursued a *cheap money* policy. There was no major use of monetary policy as an economic regulator; Bank Rate for instance was kept at 2 per cent throughout, and the rate on Treasury Bills was only ½ per cent. Instead the Government relied on controls and on fiscal measures to keep inflation in check. For this neglect of money controls there was, in fact, a very good case: the pent-up demand for goods was so strong, and the funds available to companies and individuals so large, that monetary restrictions would not have made very much difference. The Conservative Government reintroduced monetary policy in 1951. Bank Rate was raised—reaching a peak in 1957—

ness of monetary policy, both as an anti-deflationary and an anti-inflationary weapon of control. In the former case, it is clearly difficult to encourage spending by making credit more easily available, if business prospects are so poor that no investment looks profitable. In the latter case, the Committee concluded on the use of monetary policy to counter inflation in the 1950s (para. 469):

> " The obstructions to particular channels of finance have had no effect on the pressure of total demand, but have made for much inefficiency in financial organisation."

They went on to add (para 472):

> " We are driven to the conclusion that the more conventional instruments (*e.g.*, Bank rate) have failed to keep the system in smooth balance, but that every now and again the mounting pressure of demand has in one way or another (generally *via* the exchange situation) driven the Government to take action, and that the quick results then required have been mainly concentrated on the hire-purchase front and on investment in the public sector which could be cut by administrative decision. The light engineering industries have been frustrated in their planning, and the public corporations have had almost equally disheartening experience. That these two should be the ' residuary legatees ' for real resources when sharp adjustments were called for is not a comforting thought. It is far removed from the smooth and widespread adjustment sometimes claimed as the virtue of monetary action; this is no gentle hand on the steering wheel that keeps a well-driven car in its right place on the road."

However, the Radcliffe Committee did recognise that monetary measures have influenced " confidence " in sterling. A rise in interest rates increased the attractiveness of holding sterling balances, and stern monetary measures were taken as indicative of the Government's intention to solve its problems without recourse to devaluation. In these ways, monetary policy has helped to stem speculative outflows of sterling balances which threatened to impose heavy strains on our reserves. Many commentators feel that these effects provide an important justification for the use of certain forms of monetary controls.

## 5. ECONOMIC ASPECTS OF THE PUBLIC SERVICES

The Cost of Public Services.

In 1965 total public expenditure was no less than £14,055 million, about £260 per head. Of this total, the central government spent over 60 per cent, the local authorities under 30 per cent, and the nationalised industries' investment programme was responsible for 10 per cent. Total public expenditure almost doubled between 1955 and 1965; and rose as a proportion of the national income from 46 to 50 per cent.

ing expenditure consists of two quite different items. The first, housing subsidies, is a recurrent cost, and represents the difference between the cost of housing, including the cost of borrowing, and rents received on council housing. In 1965 costs exceeded the rents of £324 million by £149 million, so that the average council-house tenant was paying just under 14s. in the £ of the cost of accommodation. Up to 1957 the Government contracted to pay a flat subsidy per year on every council house built. From 1957, Government subsidies were no longer paid on ordinary new council houses, but in 1961 were reintroduced, in a form intended to encourage councils to charge higher rents on their existing houses. The Labour Government substantially increased the subsidy in 1967; it being calculated as the difference between interest payable on new housing at current interest rates and at 4 per cent.

The other part consists of the capital cost of building new houses, £628 million in 1965. This is financed out of borrowing by local authorities. In the early 1950s local authorities were able to borrow from the Government, but they have been

### THE COST OF PUBLIC SERVICES
(£ million.)

| | 1955. | 1965. | Percentage increase. 1955–65. | Percentage of total. 1965. |
|---|---|---|---|---|
| *Expenditure:* | | | | |
| Defence | 1,567 | 2,121 | 35 | 15·1 |
| Housing | 532 | 934 | 76 | 6·6 |
| Environmental services | 240 | 556 | 132 | 4·0 |
| Roads, transport, and communication | 352 | 1,005 | 186 | 7·2 |
| Education | 549 | 1,567 | 185 | 11·1 |
| Child care, school meals, milk, and welfare foods | 103 | 173 | 68 | 1·2 |
| National Health Service | 579 | 1,269 | 119 | 9·0 |
| National Insurance, pensions, and assistance | 993 | 2,413 | 143 | 17·2 |
| Agriculture | 188 | 336 | 79 | 2·4 |
| External relations | 135 | 428 | 217 | 3·0 |
| Police and prisons | 101 | 247 | 145 | 1·8 |
| Debt interest | 907 | 1,457 | 61 | 10·4 |
| Other expenditure | 842 | 1,549 | 84 | 11·0 |
| Total expenditure | 7,088 | 14,055 | 98 | 100·0 |
| *Revenue:* | | | | |
| Income taxes | 2,287 | 4,016 | 76 | 28·6 |
| Indirect taxes | 2,177 | 3,766 | 73 | 26·8 |
| *of which:* drink | 389 | 588 | 51 | 4·4 |
| tobacco | 656 | 994 | 52 | 7·1 |
| Local rates | 475 | 1,230 | 159 | 8·8 |
| National Insurance and health contributions | 594 | 1,685 | 184 | 12·0 |
| Other revenue | 1,472 | 2,124 | 44 | 15·1 |
| Total revenue | 7,005 | 12,821 | 83 | 91·2 |
| Net borrowing | 83 | 1,234 | — | 8·8 |
| Total expenditure | 7,088 | 14,055 | 98 | 100·0 |

The Government collects in revenue considerably more than it spends itself, but transfers funds to the local authorities, to the National Insurance Fund, and to the nationalised industries. The expenditure of the public sector as a whole generally exceeds its revenue, and the difference is met by net borrowing.

A breakdown of public expenditure is shown in the table. Not all categories of expenditure expanded at the same rate: expenditure on roads, transport and communication, education, external relations, and National Insurance, pensions and assistance increased faster than the total; and expenditure on defence, debt interest, child care, the agricultural subsidy, and housing fell behind the total. Nevertheless, defence expenditure accounted for 15 per cent of the total (*i.e.*, 7·5 per cent of national income) in 1965.

### Public Housing.

Expenditure on public housing amounted to 6·6 per cent of public expenditure in 1965; this percentage having fallen over the decade. Hous-

increasingly forced to borrow from the market. The two policies of freezing subsidies and making borrowing more difficult have slowed down the expansion of council housing. In 1953, the peak year, councils built 245,000 houses, in 1960 only 128,000 and in 1965, 165,000. Private building has exceeded council building since 1959, and in 1965 council building represented only 40 per cent of the total.

### Education.

Educational expenditure rose by no less than 185 per cent between 1955 and 1965; and accounted for just over 11 per cent of public expenditure in 1965. A small part of the increase is explained by the expansion of enrolment; total school enrolment in Britain increased by only 7 per cent over the decade. In addition, expenditure rose because the more expensive types of education—secondary schools and universities—expanded more rapidly. University enrolment increased by 60 per cent over the decade; but the enrolment of 157,000 students in 1965 still did not meet the demand for higher education. Secondary school enrolment also shot up: pupils of school-leaving age (15 or over) as a percentage of the age-group 15–19 nearly doubled in England and Wales. Nevertheless, this proportion was only 19 per cent in 1965. Therefore it is to be expected that expenditure will continue to increase rapidly in the future.

However, quantitative expansion is not enough: there is general recognition that qualitative reform is also needed. It is important to reduce the size of classes—there were on average 29 pupils per teacher in primary schools and 18 in secondary schools in 1965, but these averages cover a wide dispersion; to raise the school-leaving age to 16—scheduled for 1970; to get rid of the gaunt Board Schools inherited from the Victorian era; and to raise teaching standards by improving the conditions for recruitment of teachers.

It is increasingly recognised that education can be an economic investment for the future just as much as capital formation in, say, machinery or roads. There is a " private return " on " investment in education ", which takes the form of higher earnings over the lifetime of the person educated; and there is a " social return " on public resources devoted to education, being the greater contribution to the national product which trained and educated people can make.

## Social Security.

Social security benefits come from two sources. The larger part (£1,780 million in 1965) is paid out of the National Insurance and Industrial Injury Funds. These funds are built up largely out of the compulsory weekly National Insurance contributions which most of the adult population have to pay. For employees, both employer and employee pay a contribution, in return for which employees receive rights to pensions, sickness-, unemployment-, and other benefits. The self-employed also pay contributions of smaller size than the sum of the employer's and employee's contribution, and are not entitled to unemployment and one or two other benefits. And most non-employed persons, other than married women and the retired, have to pay still lower contributions and are entitled to even fewer benefits. Weekly contributions include a contribution to the cost of the National Health Service.

The most costly benefit is the retirement pension. The pension is paid as of right on retirement. Individuals may increase their rate of pension by staying on at work after the minimum retiring age of 65 for men or 60 for women; but the number who do so for more than a year is small—partly, but probably not mainly, because most private superannuation schemes lay down a fixed retiring age. Assistance grants, on the other hand, are given only on proof of need after a test of means. The high number of supplementary grants shows that the statutory pension remained below what the National Assistance Board regards as the minimum acceptable standard, and it was partly to improve the pensions of those able to afford higher contributions that the scheme for graduated pensions was introduced.

## The Finance of Social Security.

The National Insurance Scheme is an odd mixture of insurance and tax. The levels of contributions, when the scheme started in 1948, were fixed on the actuarial principle that contributions by or on behalf of an individual plus a specified State contribution should on average suffice to pay for the benefits to which he was entitled. But the scheme did not allow for inflation, and a succession of increases granted in the rate of pensions has put an end to this actuarial probity. Whenever a bill is introduced to increase pensions the Government Actuary calculates by how much contributions should be raised in order that those who contribute throughout their working lives at the new rates would just earn their right to the new benefits; but the new rates of pensions are granted to all, including those who have already retired. It was always expected that as the number of retired persons grew the fund would move into deficit; but with each rise in pensions the estimated size of the future deficit has risen. The scheme for graduated pensions also had the objective of reducing this deficit.

## Graduated Pensions.

Under this scheme, which affects only employees, there are two kinds of workers—*ordinary* and *contracted-out*. In the case of the contracted-out workers, their employer (on whom the decision whether to contract out rests) must institute a private superannuation scheme that gives at least as favourable terms as the new State scheme, including the provision that rights under the scheme should be transferable up to the limits of the State scheme. Transferability is the guarantee that the individual does not lose his pension rights when he changes his job; but one unsatisfactory feature of the private schemes that have existed has been their use to tie employees to their jobs. For ordinary workers the contribution now depends on earnings. Those earning less than £9 a week pay a flat-rate contribution, which is lower than that paid by contracted-out workers. Those earning more than £9 pay in addition a percentage of the amount by which earnings exceed £9 up to a limit of £18 and in return receive the right to an increased pension on retirement.

The scheme is devised partly to encourage private superannuation, which is still largely confined to salaried employees and employees of the State. But one purpose is clear: in return for a promise of higher pensions when they retire, most workers who are contracted-in pay more now, and thus contribute now to the cost of the pensions of the retired. The estimated deficit is eliminated, and indeed the principle is established that the basic rates of contributions should not be fixed on actuarial principles but on the principle that on balance benefits paid in a year should roughly balance receipts. No provision was made for automatically increasing pensions as the cost of living goes up or indeed as the average standard-of-living rises; all changes in rates of benefit still require a new Act of Parliament. (*But see* G38.)

## Public Revenue.

We see from the table that, of the sources of revenue, local rates and National Insurance contributions were the most buoyant over the decade. Over 28 per cent of the total public revenue in 1965 came from income tax, which was levied both on individuals and on the undistributed profits of companies. Indirect taxes on goods and services accounted for a further 27 per cent. It is interesting to note that direct and indirect taxation actually fell as a proportion of national income between 1955 and 1965.

Two commodities in particular were heavily taxed: drink and tobacco. Together they accounted for 12 per cent of public revenue. These commodities are singled out partly for social reasons and partly because—in economists' jargon—the demand for them is *inelastic*; *i.e.*, the public reduces its consumption of drink and tobacco only slightly in response to a rise in their price. In 1965 taxation increased the price of cigarettes by 2·3 times; drink by 0·7 times; consumer durables, such as cars and washing machines, by 0·2 times; and food hardly at all. For goods and services in general, tax raised the price by roughly a quarter.

## The Budget.

Each year in April the Chancellor of the Exchequer announces his Budget for the coming fiscal year. The most important and most difficult task in drawing up the Budget is to decide on the size of deficit to aim for. The deficit is the excess of public expenditure over public revenue; and it has to be financed by borrowing from the private sector. A large deficit is inflationary: sometimes that may be required to get the economy out of recession. A small deficit—and even more, a surplus—is deflationary, and is a means of holding an inflation in check.

The calculation of the precise deficit or surplus needed is a chancy business; for the level that is required depends on the amount of saving and on the amount of spending out of credit that people intend to do—and this is not easily predictable. It also depends on the change in the foreign balance. Nor can the Chancellor be sure his figures are right: estimating next year's revenue, and even next year's expenditure, by the Government is difficult enough, but he needs to estimate also the likely trends of private income and expenditure, without really reliable information as to what they were in the past year. So it cannot be expected that fiscal policy alone can prevent inflation and deflation.

Nevertheless, fiscal policy—running large deficits when economic activity is low, and small ones when it seems to be excessively high—is the most important action through which the economy can be kept on an even keel. Monetary policy may help; but the decision of the Chancellor on the size of his Budget surplus is the key one.

## 6. SOURCES OF STATISTICS, AND SOME SUGGESTIONS FOR FURTHER READING

The non-specialist will find that most of the statistics he needs are given in the *Annual Abstract of Statistics*, published every year by Her Majesty's Stationery Office. This comprehensive document includes figures on population, social conditions, education, labour, production, trade and balance of payments, national income and expenditure, wages and prices, and many other topics. For more up-to-date information, reference should be made to the *Monthly Digest of Statistics* which has a similar coverage and give month-by-month figures. A selection of the more important series, presented in a manner which can more easily be understood by the layman, is given in another Stationery Office publication, *Economic Trends*, also issued monthly.

Even greater detail is given in various other Government publications. The most important of these are the Blue Book on *National Income and Expenditure*, published annually; and the *Balance of Payments* White Paper, published twice a year. Both these are extremely valuable sources of information for the economist, but are difficult for the layman. Fuller information on labour problems is given in the *Ministry of Labour Gazette*, on trade in the *Board of Trade Journal*, and on financial matters in the *Bank of England Quarterly Bulletin*. These three periodicals include discussions on the statistics presented.

For an analysis of developments in the economy the reader is recommended to the official *Economic Report*, published just before the Budget by the Treasury. It contains a survey of the economic events of the previous year. Rather more technical is the *Economic Review*, a private publication issued by the National Institute for Economic and Social Research. To explain economic events and policy the Department of Economic Affairs publishes a monthly *Progress Report*, available free of charge to the public.

For a scholarly critique of Government economic policy see J. C. R. Dow, *Management of the British Economy 1945–60* (Cambridge University Press). An excellent, North American, survey of the British economy is found in the Brookings Institution Report, *Britain's Economic Prospects*, edited by Richard E. Caves (George Allen and Unwin). An entertaining account of economic ideas and their application is found in Michael Stewart, *Keynes and After* (Penguin Books). Other Pelicans include Joan Robinson, *Economic Philosophy*, and J. Pen, *Modern Economics*. A thorough explanation of international monetary affairs is given in Fred Hirsch. *Money International* (Allen Lane).

# III.   THE UNDERDEVELOPED ECONOMIES

**Income Levels.**

Two-thirds of the world's population live in dire poverty—a poverty which can scarcely be imagined by those accustomed to the standards of living attained in the relatively few developed countries of the world. The orders of world inequality may be seen from the table comparing annual income per capita by region, converted into pounds sterling at official exchange rates.

NATIONAL INCOME PER CAPITA
BY REGION, 1963.

|  | (£ p. a.) |
|---|---|
| North America | 882 |
| Oceania | 443 |
| Europe | 350 |
| Latin America | 107 |
| Middle East | 93 |
| Africa | 43 |
| Asia (excl. Japan) | 36 |

These figures are only very approximate because exchange rates are misleading indicators of purchasing power and because the averages conceal considerable income inequalities within some regions and countries. Nevertheless, it is clear that poverty is widespread in the world. The alleviation of this poverty is widely recognised as the most important economic—and indeed political—task of the second half of the twentieth century.

**Peasant Agriculture.**

" Underdeveloped " (or " developing " or " less developed " or " poor ") countries have predominantly agricultural economies, and peasant *subsistence agriculture* is widespread. In subsistence agriculture the primary object is to produce the food for your own family. Primitive tools and techniques of cultivation are used, and the margin between what can be produced and what is required to support life is narrow: the failure of crops because of drought, or the destruction of crops by floods or pests, can lead to famine unless food is quickly supplied from outside the area affected.

Agricultural production may be kept down by a shortage of land, or by a lack of farming knowledge and skills, or by a lack of funds for investment in land improvements or machinery, or by an unjust system of land tenure which deprives the farmer of incentive to raise his production. In many underdeveloped countries there is considerable potential for increasing agricultural output; but before such increases can be achieved new skills have to be mastered and different techniques of production introduced, investment funds have to be provided, and—in some countries—there must be land reform. If power lies in the hands of landlords and money-lenders who favour the *status quo*, political change must come first.

**The Population Problem.**

In many underdeveloped countries there is population pressure on the land and much underemployment in the sense that people have insufficient work to keep them occupied for more than part of the day or year. With the application of modern methods of disease control—*e.g.*, the eradication of malaria through DDT spraying —death rates have tended to fall, while birth rates have remained high. Birth rates are kept up by such factors as tradition, social prestige, religion, the need for security in old age, and a lack of facilities for family planning. In consequence, many underdeveloped countries are experiencing an unprecedented population explosion: annual rates of increase of between 2 and 3 per cent, which double population in as little as 35 and 24 years respectively, have been recorded.

The table indicates that over half of the world's population lives in Asia, and that the developed regions account for under a third of the total. Apart from Australasia (into which immigration is high) the developed regions show slower rates of population growth than Africa, Latin America, and Asia. The figures of population density may easily be misinterpreted, since they take no account of the nature of the area, *e.g.*, deserts and lakes are included. But it is clear that Asia is more densely populated than Africa or Latin America. Population density is a hindrance only in agricultural economies: because it is industrialised and has accumulated much capital, Europe can support at a high standard of living a population more concentrated even than that of Asia.

## POPULATION SIZE, GROWTH AND DENSITY BY REGION

| | Popula-tion 1966 (m). | Growth rate 1960–66 (% p. a.) | Density 1966 (per sq.km). |
|---|---|---|---|
| North America | 217 | 1·5 | 10 |
| Europe | 449 | 0·9 | 91 |
| USSR | 233 | 1·4 | 10 |
| Oceania | 18 | 2·1 | 2 |
| Africa | 318 | 2·3 | 11 |
| Latin America | 251 | 2·9 | 12 |
| Asia | 1867 | 2·0 | 63 |
| World Total | 3353 | 1·9 | 25 |

As a result of rapid population growth the pressure of population on the land has increased, particularly in Asia. Less productive land has been brought into cultivation, and erosion and loss of fertility have become major problems. A substantial increase in output is required to prevent a fall in per capita income as population grows, and an even greater increase is required if living standards are to be improved. Between 1957–59 and 1966 food production in the developing countries as a group increased by 18 per cent, but per capita food production fell by 3 per cent. Even in those countries with plenty of land a rapid increase in population diverts scarce investment resources away from directly productive investments such as factories and irrigation projects so as to meet the needs of the expanding population for more schools, hospitals, housing, cities, and other public services.

### International Trade.

Almost all underdeveloped countries export primary products (foodstuffs, industrial raw materials, and minerals) and import manufactured goods, especially the capital goods (plant, machinery, and vehicles) required for development. This international division of labour has recently operated to the disadvantage of the underdeveloped countries. The world demand for their primary products has increased only very slowly. This is because people spend just a small part of their additional income on food (e.g., tea, coffee, cocoa), because synthetic substitutes have been developed for many raw materials (e.g., rubber, cotton, jute), because developed countries protect their own agriculture (e.g., sugar) and because demand in the developed countries has moved towards commodities with low raw material content (e.g., from heavy industries to services). In consequence, the general trend has been for the prices of primary products to fall. This was an important cause of the improvement in Britain's terms of trade (see G6). The reverse of the coin was a deterioration in the terms of trade of many underdeveloped countries, i.e., they could now buy fewer imports for a given quantity of exports. Primary commodities exported by developing countries decreased in price on average by 16 per cent over the period 1957–62, and increased by only 6 per cent between 1962 and 1966. Over the period 1957–66 their terms of trade worsened by 14 per cent. This contributed to the shortage of foreign exchange which restricts investment expenditures in many underdeveloped countries.

The prices of various primary products tend to fluctuate violently from one year to another. Many underdeveloped economies depend heavily on the exports of one or two commodities. For instance, coffee is the most important product in Brazil, cotton in Egypt, copper in Zambia, sugar in Cuba, cocoa in Ghana, and rice in Burma. Fluctuations in the world price of its main export cause instability in the export revenues of a country, and this in turn can produce fluctuations in income throughout its domestic economy.

### Industrialisation.

In those underdeveloped countries where there is population pressure on the land, alternative employment has to be created in industry or services. Even in countries with a surplus of land, if there is heavy dependence on one or two primary products, industrialisation provides a means of diversifying the economy.

But industrialisation is not an easy course. Because the margin between agricultural production and food consumption is narrow, the surplus from the agricultural sector exchangeable for the products of other sectors—e.g., industry and services— is small; i.e., the demand for the goods and services produced by other sectors is low. A second constraint on industrialisation is imposed by competition from abroad; new industries in an underdeveloped country have to compete with established industries in developed countries, which have the advantage of experience, a trained labour force, and markets big enough for them to reap all the potential economies of large-scale production. On the other hand, underdeveloped countries with their relatively cheap labour may have an advantage in the production of simple labour-intensive products: witness the success of Hong Kong in exporting textiles and plastic products to the developed countries.

Underdeveloped countries can of course take advantage of the technical advances made in the developed countries. But this is not without its drawbacks. Even in countries with cheap labour the most profitable techniques of production in industry are normally highly capital-intensive, so that the amount of investment funds required to equip a worker is often enormous and the amount of employment provided in meeting the local demand for a manufactured product is often small. Hence the argument for developing an *intermediate technology* which is both profitable and suited to the needs of the underdeveloped countries.

### Educated Manpower.

Many underdeveloped countries are faced with the dual problem of unskilled labour surpluses and scarcities of skilled and educated manpower. The problem is particularly acute in some of the recently independent countries of Africa. To give an extreme example: at the time of its independence in 1964, Zambia had only 100 Zambian university graduates and 1,200 secondary school graduates in a population of 3·5 million. In such countries the great shortage of educated and skilled people enables them to earn high incomes—with the result that there is a very unequal distribution of income. And even in countries where surpluses have developed, the existence of an international market for professional people like doctors and engineers helps to keep up their earnings: these countries suffer from a " brain drain " to the developed world.

Because teachers are educated people, education in underdeveloped countries can be very expensive. In Uganda in 1965 only 45 per cent of the children in the relevant age-group were at primary school and only 2 per cent were at secondary school. Yet the salary bill paid to their teachers exceeded 2 per cent of the gross domestic product. In such circumstances it is difficult to meet the demands for universal primary education; especially if the sort of primary education provided does not enable children to become better farmers.

Economic development is not just a matter of capital accumulation: it requires also an increase in educated manpower. Not only more knowledge but also new habits and attitudes—e.g., attitudes towards risk-taking, hard work, and thrift. Education—of the right sort and with suitable content—is generally acknowledged to be important for development, although the benefits of education cannot be quantified at all satisfactorily.

### Economic Aid.

The gap between living standards in the underdeveloped areas of the world and in the areas already developed has tended to widen in recent years. In the 1950s real income per capita rose in the developed countries by 2·7 per cent per annum on average, and in the underdeveloped countries by 2·3 per cent per annum. It was through a growing world recognition of this situation that the 1960s were designated " The United Nations Development Decade." But between 1960 and 1965 these rates of growth widened to 3·7 and 2·2 per cent per annum respectively. World inequalities increased despite a larger flow of economic assistance from the richer to the poorer nations. The total net flow of economic assistance from Western industrial countries to the developing world was over £3,500 million in 1966. Roughly £1,200 million of this was net private investment, and £2,300 million official Government aid. But whereas total aid increased rapidly in the 1950s, the increase was not continued in the 1960s: total aid in 1966 was no higher than the estimate for 1961. More than half of the official Government aid in 1966 was contributed by the United States; the other principal donors were France, Britain, and West Germany, in that order.

Aid to underdeveloped countries takes many forms, it serves many purposes, and it is given for many reasons. Underdeveloped countries need aid to provide finance for development projects; to provide foreign exchange with which imports for development purposes can be bought; and to provide the trained manpower and technical knowledge which they lack. The motives of the donor are not always humanitarian. " Aid " can take a military form; it can be used to prop up an incompetent or unjust government, or to buy support in the cold war. Nor is aid always beneficial to the recipient country. It may be wasted on ill-conceived or prestige projects, or cause the Government simply to relax its own efforts. Sometimes schools or hospitals are built with aid but there is a lack of local revenues with which to staff and run these institutions. Concern over donors' motives and instances of waste has led some people to react against aid-giving. However, the correct remedy is not to cut off aid but rather to prevent its misuse.

One form of aid is private investment by firms and individuals from developed countries. These investments—setting up branch factories, for example—are concentrated in those projects which appear profitable to the investor. However, it is a characteristic of underdevelopment that there are few openings for profitable investment. Most of the U.K. private investment overseas, for example, has been concentrated in relatively highly developed countries of the sterling area. Private investment cannot be relied upon to provide an adequate flow of aid.

Donor governments may finance specific projects, or they may contribute to the general pool of funds available for expenditure by the governments of underdeveloped countries. But financial aid is not always enough. Most underdeveloped countries need help and advice in planning their development, to ensure that development possibilities are exploited and that scarce resources are used to best advantage. Hence the many schemes for providing experts by individual countries and by the technical agencies of the United Nations, such as the Food and Agriculture Organisation (FAO), the World Health Organisation (WHO), the International Labour Organization (ILO), the United Nations Educational, Scientific, and Cultural Organisation (UNESCO), the Technical Assistance Board (UNTAB) and so on. Hence also the schemes for educating and training people from the developing countries in universities and colleges in the developed countries.

## The International Bank.

The International Bank for Reconstruction and Development (IBRD), known as the *International Bank* or as the *World Bank*, is an agency of the United Nations established in 1945. It has the primary function of making funds available to assist underdeveloped countries. Member nations agree to subscribe quotas—fixed in much the same way as the quotas for the IMF—to the Bank. In fact, only a small proportion of the quotas has been called up by the Bank; the major part of the Fund's resources are borrowed—on the security of the remainder of the quotas—in financial centres: particularly in New York, but also in London and elsewhere.

Usually, loans are made to finance specific projects of investment in underdeveloped countries; and the Bank will normally make a loan only if it is satisfied that the investment will yield a revenue sufficient to enable the payment of interest on the loan, and the repayment of the sum lent. In 1964–5 the Bank made loans to the value of about £350 million. Thus a sizeable amount of lending is channelled through the Bank, but it is clear that some projects of great value to underdeveloped countries cannot be financed in this way, because they would not yield returns quickly or large enough to meet the Bank's stringent requirements for interest and repayment. Accordingly a new institution, the *International Development Association*, was set up in 1960 with the power to make loans at low rates of interest and with more generous repayment conditions. The IDA contributes (but only on a limited scale) towards the development of education and agriculture.

## Unctad.

In 1964 the United Nations Conference on Trade and Development (UNCTAD) was held. For the first time the poorer nations of the world—77 were represented—came together to act as a pressure group on trading matters. The Conference made the following recommendations. Developing countries should be given freer access to world markets for their manufactures and semi-manufactures by the elimination of quotas and tariffs. International commodity agreements should be made for each major primary commodity in world trade, to stabilise commodity prices. Compensation schemes—whereby countries are compensated for the declining prices of their primary products—were recommended for consideration. The conference also resolved that the developed countries should aim to provide at least 1 per cent of their national income as aid for the underdeveloped countries.

Nothing concrete resulted from the 1964 Session: no significant trade measures in favour of the developing countries were taken, and the international transfer of financial resources diminished in relation to the income of the developed countries. A second Session of the Conference was held in 1968. Again, no action resulted from the Session; but the developed countries did accept more firmly the principle of discrimination in favour of developing countries in trade and shipping, and the 1 per cent target for aid.

## British Aid.

The table shows how British Government aid to underdeveloped countries has increased in

### BRITISH GOVERNMENT AID, 1957/8 TO 1967/8.

| Fiscal year | Total aid | | | Multi-lateral aid £m. | Bilateral Aid | | |
|---|---|---|---|---|---|---|---|
| | £m. | per capita £ | as percentage of GNP | | Total £m. | Grants £m. | Loans £m. |
| 1957/8 | 65 | 1·3 | 0·33 | 3 | 62 | 50 | 12 |
| 1960/1 | 147 | 2·8 | 0·65 | 17 | 130 | 60 | 70 |
| 1961/2 | 170 | 3·2 | 0·69 | 14 | 155 | 81 | 74 |
| 1962/3 | 156 | 2·9 | 0·61 | 14 | 142 | 74 | 68 |
| 1963/4 | 173 | 3·2 | 0·64 | 15 | 158 | 72 | 87 |
| 1964/5 | 191 | 3·5 | 0·65 | 16 | 175 | 92 | 83 |
| 1965/6 | 205 | 3·8 | 0·66 | 19 | 186 | 93 | 94 |
| 1966/7 | 211 | 3·8 | 0·65 | 19 | 192 | 88 | 104 |
| 1967/8 | 208 | 3·8 | 0·61 | 24 | 183 | 83 | 100 |

recent years. It was fairly constant before 1957/8 but more than tripled to £208 million in the decade following 1957/8. Aid per capita of the British population nearly tripled, and amounted to £3. 16s. 0d per head in 1967/8. However, when aid is expressed as a percentage of the gross national product (GNP), we see that the percentage increased from 0·33 of 1 per cent in 1957/8 to 0·65 of 1 per cent in 1960/1 and has since remained at that level. To be just 1 per cent of GNP, aid would have to be raised by about £100 million. Aid may be divided into multilateral aid and bilateral aid. Multilateral aid is given through the medium of the international institutions, such as the IBRD and the IDA; bilateral aid is given directly to the developing countries. Multilateral aid was still only £24 million in 1967/8. The increase in aid since 1957/8 has taken place in bilateral aid. Whereas loans were fairly negligible in 1957/8, they increased rapidly, and exceeded grants from 1964/5.

It must be remembered in deciding the terms on which Government aid is provided, that the foreign indebtedness of the developing countries is increasing sharply. About four-fifths of British loans is made available for 20 years or more. Normally the rate of interest on these loans is the rate at which the British Government can borrow on the capital market. However, the Government decided in 1965 to make development loans free of interest in appropriate cases. About a third of expenditure on aid is formally tied to the purchase of British goods and services. Other aid is not tied formally, and may be used directly to finance local expenditure; but when it is used to finance imports directly, it has to be spent on British goods if these are available on competitive terms. Multilateral aid is untied. The tying of aid tends to raise the costs to developing countries; but it also enables countries with precarious foreign balances—such as Britain—to be more generous.

Aid takes the form not only of financial but also of technical assistance. To co-ordinate and pro-mote technical assistance the Department of Technical Co-operation (DTC) was set up in 1961. British Government expenditure on technical assistance amounted to £38 million in 1967. At the end of 1967 British technical assistance personnel overseas totalled altogether 15,000 (excluding volunteers recruited by voluntary societies); over 2,000 administrators, 4,700 teachers, 1,400 agricultural advisers, 3,000 industrial and technological advisers, and 1,200 doctors and medical workers.

In the past decisions on aid were made separately by a number of Government bodies—the Treasury, the DTC, the Colonial Office, Commonwealth Relations Office, Foreign Office, and so on. In 1964 the Government established an Overseas Development Ministry (ODM), through which all British aid is now channelled and co-ordinated. The amount of aid which ought to be provided has become a political issue in some countries such as the United States: thankfully this has not occurred in Britain.

Some Suggestions for Further Reading.

For an introduction to the subject the reader is referred to Jagdish Bhagwati, *The Economics of Underdeveloped Countries* (World University Library). An interesting account of life in rural India is found in Kusum Nair, *Blossoms in the Dust* (Duckworth). On Asia the reader may wish to dip into the three volumes of Gunnar Myrdal entitled *Asian Drama: An Enquiry into the Poverty of Nations* (Alan Lane, The Penguin Press). A helpful introduction to African problems is found in Andrew M. Kamarck, *The Economics of African Development* (Praeger). The Overseas Development Institute has published a number of pamphlets on aid topics, including *The Less Developed Countries in World Trade*, *British Development Policies*, and *Volunteers in Development*. The Ministry of Overseas Development compiles a handbook of *British Aid Statistics* (HMSO).

# IV. DEVELOPMENTS IN THE BRITISH ECONOMY SINCE 1960

## 1. INTERNATIONAL DEVELOPMENTS

The Balance of Payments.

The balance of payments has dominated events in the British economy in the 1960s. It is therefore important to analyse the balance of payments in some detail, and to understand the circum-stances which led to the devaluation of the pound in 1967.

(i) The Current Account.

The deterioration in the current balance of payments of well over £400 million between 1959 and

BALANCE OF PAYMENTS, 1960–68.

(£ million)

|  | 1960 | 1961 | 1962 | 1963 | 1964 | 1965 | 1966 | 1967 | 1968 |
|---|---|---|---|---|---|---|---|---|---|
| Visible imports (f.o.b.). | 4,141 | 4,045 | 4,098 | 4,370 | 5,014 | 5,053 | 5,222 | 5,661 | 6,899 |
| Visible exports (f.o.b.). | 3,733 | 3,892 | 3,994 | 4,287 | 4,471 | 4,784 | 5,116 | 5,026 | 6,103 |
| Balance on visible trade | −408 | −153 | −104 | −83 | −543 | −269 | −106 | −635 | −796 |
| Balance on invisible trade . | +133 | +148 | +205 | +190 | +150 | +160 | +75 | +236 | +377 |
| Current balance of payments . | −275 | −5 | +101 | +107 | −393 | −109 | −31 | −399 | −419 |
| Balance on long-term capital transactions . | −192 | +68 | −98 | −170 | −368 | −239 | −102 | −116 | −39 |
| Balance on current account *plus* long-term capital transactions . | −467 | +63 | +3 | −63 | −761 | −348 | −133 | −515 | −458 |
| Balance of monetary movements* . | +158 | −39 | −89 | +116 | +734 | +248 | +146 | +300 | +545 |
| *Of which:* change in foreign exchange reserves . | −177 | −31 | +183 | +53 | +122 | −246 | −34 | −16 | +114 |
| change in account with IMF . | −151 | +374 | −379 | +5 | +359 | +499 | −2 | −318 | +525 |

* A plus sign denotes a rise in liabilities or a fall in assets, and a minus sign a fall in liabilities or a rise in assets.

1960 was mainly attributable to an increase of nearly £500 million in imports: exports also increased but not by enough to pay for the increased imports. The main cause was the upsurge in demand in 1959–60. During the upsurge, productive capacity at home became strained, and some goods were imported to supplement home supplies. Stocks of imported goods were run down in 1959 and replenished in 1960. And higher incomes meant higher demands for imported goods. These developments might be interpreted as indicating the adverse effects on the balance of payments of internal expansion. No doubt imports will increase as the economy expands; but it can be argued that sudden and very rapid bursts of expansion, as in 1959–60, will have a much greater effect on imports than would a steadier and more sustained growth.

In the following two years, imports were steady at about the 1960 level: the internal economy was relatively stagnant, partly because restrictive measures had been adopted to curb demand at home and protect the balance of payments. Imports were sharply up by over £250 million in 1963 with the rapid expansion of national expenditure, but there was a slightly larger increase in the value of exports.

The surplus on invisible trade, which had exceeded £300 million in the early and middle fifties, ranged between £100 and £200 million in the early sixties (see G7).

### (ii) Flows of Long-term Capital.

The deficit on long-term capital—representing the excess of the amounts we lend, invest and re-invest abroad over the corresponding amounts lent, invested and re-invested by foreigners in Britain—is subject to abnormal fluctuations. Thus the deficit in 1959 was abnormally large because it included the British subscription to the IMF (see G8), and became a small surplus in 1961 owing to receipts of a special nature. Allowing for such abnormal factors, however, the capital outflow was fairly stable over the period 1959–63 at £100–200 million per annum.

### (iii) Monetary Movements.

Any deficit in long-term capital transactions, together with any deficit on current account, has to be financed either by increasing our short-term liabilities to foreigners, or by reductions in our assets. In 1960, over £450 million had to be financed, but the imbalance on current plus capital account was very small in the following years until the crisis year of 1964. Oddly enough, the financing of the huge 1960 deficit did not raise any immediate problems, owing to a substantial inflow of short-term funds (i.e., additions to our short-term liabilities). The sterling balances (see G8) rose by the unprecedented amount of over £400 million. This was largely due to speculation against the dollar, based on fears that it might be devalued. So great was the inflow that there was a curious combination of a very large deficit on current plus long-term capital account and a substantial rise in our reserves of gold and convertible currencies.

The dangers inherent in the financing of deficits through additions to short-term liabilities were vividly demonstrated the following year. Much of the funds which moved in during 1960 was moved out again before July 1961 in a wave of speculation against sterling. The outflow was financed partly by running down reserves of gold and convertible currencies by £280 million between end-1960 and July 1961, and partly through the Basle agreement under which European central banks undertook to build up short-term holdings in centres (London in this case) from which funds were being withdrawn. The rapid drain on the reserves had to be stopped; and the European central banks were not prepared to see their sterling holdings rise much higher. So in July 1961 a series of crisis measures—including the raising of Bank Rate to 7 per cent—were taken, primarily to protect sterling. In addition, arrangements were made to withdraw over £500 million from the IMF with provision for further credits if necessary. In 1962, speculative movements of funds were much less violent. Aided by a substantial improvement in the current

balance of payments, Britain was able to complete repayments of its IMF drawing. These repayments did, however, involve a drain on the reserves; and this explains the substantial fall in the reserves over the year.

### The 1964 Crisis.

Imports in 1964 were some £640 million higher than in 1963, whereas exports were up by less than £200 million. The remarkable increase in the value of imports cannot be explained simply as a rise in import prices: imports increased by 15 per cent in value and by 11 per cent in volume. Nor can it be seen merely as a response to the expansion of the economy: if imports had done no more than rise in line with output, they would have increased in volume only by about 4 per cent. Part of the explanation lies in the fact that importers were stockbuilding after the depletion of raw material stocks during the boom of 1963. More important, however, is the fact that imports of manufactured goods rose by 28 per cent, or two-thirds of the total rise in import value. This leads us to the conclusion that home producers were losing ground in the British market to foreign competitors. In the same way, the disappointing performance of exports was due, not to lack of overseas demand—world trade in manufactures rose by about 15 per cent in 1964—but to the diminishing competitiveness of British products.

### (i) Remedial Measures.

The timing of Government action on the balance of payments position was influenced by the General Election of mid-October. The out-going Government had been concerned with the impending Election, and argued that the deficit was abnormal and could be expected to improve without remedial action. On taking office, the new Government decided that immediate remedial action was necessary. Three courses were possible. It could devalue the pound and so improve the competitive position of British exports and import-substitutes (see G8). But a devaluation was seen to have disadvantages. The price of necessary imports would be increased and this would lower the British standard of living; the ensuing wage demands would make it more difficult to implement an Incomes Policy—which is an alternative method of improving the British competitive position in world markets (see G35). Furthermore, the devaluation of the pound might have necessitated the devaluation of other currencies including the dollar: this would have defeated the purpose of the devaluation. These real arguments against devaluation are not to be confused with the spurious argument that devaluation is somehow morally wrong. A second possible course of action was to reduce imports to a satisfactory level by the deflation of the economy. However, national income would have to fall by a multiple of the required cut in imports. Deflation was rejected because it would cause unemployment and because it was considered to provide only a short-term solution to Britain's economic problems: somehow the foreign imbalance had to be corrected without impeding the growth of output and productivity. A third course of action was to impose import controls or tariffs and export subsidies. Import controls were rejected: for one reason, it would take time to set up the necessary administrative machinery. So it was that the Government decided upon an additional import tariff and an export subsidy.

Within two weeks of coming to power, the Government announced its measures (which had in fact been investigated by the previous Chancellor). There was to be an immediate but temporary surcharge of 15 per cent on all imports of manufactures and semi-manufactures: the more necessary imports such as foodstuffs and basic raw materials were excluded. A new system of export rebates was introduced, representing the indirect taxes paid in Britain by British exporters, mainly duties on oil, petrol, and vehicle licenses. The value of the rebate averaged 1½ per cent of the value of exports. The import surcharge was critically received by the other EFTA members: it clashed with their objective of eliminating all tariffs by the end of 1966.

Some commentators have argued that Britain should direct its policies towards removing restraints on trade, by cutting tariffs within EFTA or GATT or even unilaterally: lowering tariff barriers will contribute to efficiency by subjecting British industries to stiffer competition. By contrast, it is also possible to argue that we should at times impose greater restraints on imports, so that economic growth can occur without being hampered by balance of payments difficulties. The Government defended its action to the GATT Council in terms of an article in the Treaty which allows parties in balance of payments difficulties to resort to tariff restriction (see G9). Regrettably, the GATT Council declared the import surcharge a violation of the Treaty

### (ii) Speculation Against Sterling.

The long-term capital outflow in 1964 of £400 million was as remarkable as the deficit on current account. The outflow was due to an increase in private investment abroad; there was no increase in net Government lending. Part of the net private capital outflow in the first half of the year may have been abnormal and part in the second half of 1964 may have been related to the growing current account deficit: portfolio investment in this country was not an attractive proposition, and foreign firms tended to repatriate any funds available.

There was a net short-term capital inflow in the first half of 1964, which financed the growing overall deficit. The crisis arose in the second half of the year, when an outflow of short-term capital —a " flight of hot money "—took place in expectation that a British devaluation would be necessary to cure the worsening imbalance. To protect the reserves, the IMF granted Britain a stand-by credit of £330 million. However, once the feeling developed that the pound would have to be devalued, the process became cumulative: the greater the outflow the more likely it seemed that Britain would be forced to devalue. A great deal of sterling was offered for sale by speculators holding pounds—the " Gnomes of Zurich "—and by British and foreign importers and exporters. In order to prevent the price of sterling from falling below the official minimum limit to the exchange rate of £1 = 2·78 (i.e., to " support sterling ") the Bank of England was itself forced to buy pounds. To do this the Bank had to draw on the country's reserves of gold and foreign exchange. The vast drain on the reserves could not be allowed to continue, and in late November, Bank Rate was raised by 2 per cent to 7 per cent. The aim of this measure was to lure back short-term capital funds with the high rate of interest, and also to convince speculators that the pound would not be devalued. Speculators were not convinced, however, and the crisis continued. Two days later it was announced that an enormous loan totalling £1,070 million would be made available to Britain from all the leading Western central banks. This news was sufficient to slow down the speculative outflow, and by the close of 1964 the selling had come to an end.

### Events Leading to Devaluation.

Imports increased a good deal more slowly than output in 1965; rising by only 1 per cent. This was partly because the stockbuilding of 1964 had come to an end, and partly because the import surcharge held back imports of manufactured consumer goods. The value of exports was 7 per cent higher in 1965 than in 1964, and their volume 5 per cent higher. Thus the current deficit was more than halved, from the record of £400 million in 1964 to just over £100 million in 1965. The deficit on long-term capital was also cut considerably. Nevertheless, an overall deficit amounting to £350 million in 1965 had to be financed by monetary movements.

The trade balance showed little improvement by mid-1965, and in the third quarter fear of devaluation led to yet another run on sterling, probably as severe as that of November 1964. The Government was again forced to draw on the IMF and to borrow from the United States Federal Reserve Bank. This time, however, the extent of speculation against the pound was successfully concealed. When the trade balance improved rapidly in the second half of 1965, the speculation died away.

However, this progress did not continue into 1966, and confidence in the pound was further upset by the seamen's strike in May and June. Yet another flight of short-term capital occurred; and this led the Government in panic to introduce a policy of deflation, in a package-deal known as the " July measures " (see G38). Only two measures improved the balance of payments directly: a reduction of the personal travel allowance outside the sterling area to £50 per annum and a proposed cut in Government overseas spending. The fall in demand resulting from the deflationary policy, together with a wage-freeze introduced at the same time (see G36), improved the trade balance and actually turned it into a surplus at the end of 1966. But it should be remembered that this improvement was achieved only at the cost of some unemployment of men and machinery and a slower rate of economic growth.

Imports rose in value by over 6 per cent and exports fell in value by nearly 2 per cent between 1966 and 1967. Thus the trade gap which had almost closed in 1966 widened to a record level in 1967. The rise in imports cannot be explained simply by the rise in demand, as incomes rose by only 1 per cent between the two years: the " July measures" were taking effect. One reason for the surge in imports was the removal of the temporary import surcharge in the preceding November, which caused a postponement of purchases until 1967, and reduced the price of imported goods competing with British products. Other reasons were the building up of imported stocks which had been depleted, and the Middle East war in June, which raised the price of essential oil imports. The main reason for the fall in exports was the exceptionally slow growth of world production in 1967: demand in the countries importing British goods was fairly stagnant. Exports were also hit by the dock strikes in September. The long-term capital account remained the same in 1967. Nevertheless, the deficit on current plus long-term capital account in that year exceeded £500 million. With the trade returns deteriorating, sterling came under almost unremitting speculative pressure from the end of May onwards, reaching a climax in November.

### Devaluation of the Pound.

The Government recognised that action would have to be taken to improve the balance of payments, and to obtain further foreign loans to protect the depleted reserves. The same alternatives were open as in 1964: deflation, import controls, tariffs and devaluation (see G29). Simple deflation to reduce imports was ruled out politically as the economy was now already in recession. Import controls and tariffs would meet with resistance from Britain's competitors and the GATT, and tariffs had been tried in 1964 without success. The Government decided to devalue the pound.

The case for devaluation is a mixed one (see G8 and 29). It makes imports more expensive relative to home-produced goods, and so demand for manufactured goods shifts away from imports; but in the case of food and raw materials, Britain must continue to import these essentials at the higher price because there are no domestic substitutes. It is possible, therefore, that devaluation will actually raise the import bill. However, export receipts should be increased by a greater amount: Britain exports its products in a highly competitive market, so that the reduced price of British goods in terms of foreign currencies should lead to a considerable increase in the amount of exports.

This improvement in the trade balance depends on Britain being able to retain at least part of the price advantage gained by devaluation. However, since devaluation raises the price of imported goods, it raises the cost of living both directly and indirectly, e.g., imported raw materials rise in price, so increasing production costs, which are passed on as higher prices. The trade unions react to this cut in the standard of living by demanding wage increases. In this way a spiralling inflation can occur which entirely neutralises the gain from devaluation. Devaluation makes an incomes policy both more difficult and more important (see G36).

On November 18, 1967, the pound was devalued

by 14·3 per cent, from $2.8 to $2.4 to the £. Devaluation was anticipated by speculators, and on the day before, there was a run on the pound said to be greater than any previously experienced. The devaluation was unfortunately delayed by the need to achieve international co-operation so as to prevent a flurry of competitive devaluations. As it was, only a few minor currencies—including those of Denmark, Hong Kong, Ireland, Jamaica, New Zealand, and Spain—were devalued with sterling. It was also agreed among central bankers that Britain should be given credits of up to $3,000 million, including $1,400 million standby credit from the IMF (see G8). This credit protects the reserves against speculation; but it will have to be paid back out of balance of payments surpluses over the next few years.

Devaluation increases the demand for domestically produced goods and services: imports are replaced by local substitutes and foreign demand for British goods increases. This switch in demand requires also a switch in scarce resources—labour and capital—into the exporting and import substituting industries, if the new demand is to be met. To release resources for these industries it is necessary to reduce the demand for resources elsewhere in the economy. Accordingly, the devaluation was accompanied by a series of deflationary measures (see G38).

### After Devaluation.

In his Letter of Intent to the IMF immediately after devaluation the Chancellor stated the Government's aim to improve the balance of payments by at least £500 million a year. However, progress after devaluation was disappointing and fell far short of official expectations. The current plus long-term capital account showed a deficit for 1968 of £460 million: no great improvement on the deficit for 1967 of £515 million. Moreover, this improvement came on the invisible and long-term capital accounts: the trade gap actually widened. The value of exports rose by 20 per cent between 1967 and 1968, 8 per cent in price and 12 per cent in volume. But less than half of the increase in volume was due to devaluation, since world trade was growing rapidly. Despite the devaluation the volume of imports rose by no less than 7 per cent, outstripping the growth of output, and largely because of devaluation import prices rose by 11 per cent; so that imports increased in value by 18 per cent.

Devaluation takes time to have its effect, and it is reassuring to note that the accounts for the second half of 1968 were in balance. The efficacy of devaluation can only be judged after a number of years, and even then with difficulty, since we need to know what would have happened in the absence of devaluation. But by 1969 it had already become obvious that sufficient surpluses would not be generated for the Government to repay its debts according to the repayment schedule.

In November 1968, to speed up the improvement in the balance of payments, the Government introduced a temporary import deposit scheme, by which importers were required to deposit with H.M. Customs for a period of six months, money equal to half the value of certain imports.

### The International Monetary System.

#### (i) International Liquidity.

Imbalance in payments between countries is financed by transfers of gold or foreign exchange (see G8). These reserves of gold and foreign exchange are known as international liquidity. Their basic characteristic is general acceptability: they can perform their function only if they retain the confidence of those engaged in international transactions. Unless it is ultimately convertible into goods and services, gold has merely an industrial and ornamental value. But since most central banks are prepared to buy and sell gold at a fixed price in terms of their local currency, confidence in gold is maintained.

Two international reserve currencies have emerged to supplement gold: the pound and the dollar. The pound has performed this function since World War I, but the dollar has become the main reserve currency since World War II. Sur-

plus countries are prepared to hold short-term debt in pounds or dollars—so earning a rate of interest—confident that their future trading deficits can be financed by payment of these currencies or by their conversion into gold. These holdings are the dollar and sterling balances (see G7–8). Like gold, they can perform their function as international reserves only if there is confidence that they can be converted into other currencies and hence into goods and services at current exchange rates. There is one other form of international liquidity—drawing rights on the IMF (see G8). At the end of 1967 gold accounted for 56 per cent of total international liquidity, foreign exchange reserves for 36 per cent, and the IMF for 8 per cent.

In recent years two developments have undermined the present international monetary system. First, the growth of international trade has outstripped the growth of reserves with which to finance imbalances in this trade. Between 1952 and 1966 world trade, measured in dollars, rose by 140 per cent, whereas international liquidity, measured in dollars, rose by only 30 per cent. Gold reserves have been a declining proportion of international liquidity, partly because gold production has been hampered by the fixed price in the face of rising costs of gold production, and also because an increasing proportion of newly-mined gold has found its way into private speculative hoards and not into official stocks. The other main source of new international liquidity was an increase in dollar balances. By 1967 dollar balances actually exceeded the United States gold reserves.

The second problem to have emerged is the weakness in the balance of payments of the reserve currency countries. Both Britain and the United States have had persistent deficits in recent years. As a result there have been periodic fears that the dollar or the pound would be devalued in terms of gold and other currencies; and this has resulted in speculation against the dollar and the pound (see G29). The inadequacy of international liquidity and the weakness of the reserve currencies produces a dangerous " deflationary bias " in the world economy (see G9).

#### (ii) The Gold Crisis 1968.

The United States has run a large and persistent payments deficit in the 1950s and 1960s. This was initially financed through the willingness of foreigners to run up dollar balances. However, distrust of the dollar has grown, and between 1960 and 1967 U.S. gold reserves were run down, from $19,500 million to $12,100 million. After the devaluation of sterling in November 1967, the interest of speculators transferred from the pound to the dollar. Since many speculators expected the devaluation of the dollar in terms of gold to be followed by a corresponding devaluation of other currencies, there was a growing demand for gold.

After 1961 the central banks of the major trading nations operated a gold pool in the London market, whereby they agreed to exchange gold for currencies at existing official exchange rates. But with the growing speculation against the dollar, the system could not be continued without endangering the U.S. gold reserves. The central bankers gathered for a crisis meeting in Washington on 17 March, and decided to terminate the gold pool. They introduced two markets for gold, with private transactions taking place in the free market at a price determined by supply and demand, and transactions among central banks taking place in the official market at the official gold price. The United States was now prepared to convert dollars into gold only for central banks, i.e., to finance a deficit only on its current plus long-term capital account. In this way speculation against the dollar could be controlled; but the problem of the U.S. deficit on current and long-term capital account was still to be solved.

The further monetary crisis of November 1968, produced by speculation against the franc and towards the mark, the possibility that the incoming Nixon Administration would raise the dollar price of gold, and the limited sales on the free market by gold producers all helped to keep up the speculative demand for gold and its price in the free market. In the first year after the gold-crisis the free market price averaged about $40 compared with the official price of $35 a fine ounce.

### (iii) Reform of the International Monetary System.

There is an increasing shortage of international liquidity, which gives a deflationary twist to the world economy and threatens the continuation of free trade. What means are available to increase international liquidity? There are two main alternatives: a rise in the price of gold in terms of all currencies or the creation of an international paper money.

A rise in the gold price would increase international liquidity; first, by increasing the money value of existing and future gold reserves, and second, by encouraging gold production. However, there are certain disadvantages. It helps those countries most which need help least—those with large gold reserves; it represents a victory for the gold speculators and so acts as a stimulus to further hoarding and speculation in the future; it helps in particular the gold-producing countries Russia and South Africa; and finally, it represents a sheer waste of economic resources: gold has little value except as a means of international payment. The most likely method of securing a general rise in the price of gold would be a devaluation of the dollar. since most other currencies would be devalued simultaneously. Therefore, devaluation could not cure the U.S. deficit. For these reasons the United States Government decided against devaluation of the dollar at the time of the gold crisis.

The domestic currency of the United Kingdom is not backed by gold: on a one pound note the Governor of the Bank of England promises to pay the bearer on demand the sum of one pound—another pound note! Yet, within Britain, there is complete confidence in the currency, because it is generally acceptable and so convertible into goods and services. Just as gold no longer backs the domestic currency, there is no need for gold in settlement of international payments. All we need is a generally acceptable international currency, *i.e.*, one in which all countries have confidence.

Such a currency could be created by an international authority constituted for this purpose: and it could be made available to deficit countries, which could then pay their creditors in the new currency. In this way the current shortage of international liquidity could be made good, and indeed gold—Keynes' " barbarous relic "—could be supplanted. There are various difficulties in such a scheme. It would involve some loss of national autonomy and the vesting of considerable power in the international authority issuing the paper currency. Decisions would have to be made as to which countries should receive the new currency, and in what quantities. And there is a fear that it would enable reckless governments to pursue inflationary policies without the discipline imposed by shortage of reserves, and that their inflation would be infectious. Many variations on this basic scheme have been devised in an attempt to surmount these—largely political—objections.

### (iv) Special Drawing Rights.

In the past the IMF has merely provided deficit countries with loans, to be repaid over a certain period (*see* G8). However, the amount of these credit facilities has been increased over time. In 1959 the quotas paid by members to the IMF were raised by 50 per cent, and in 1964 by a further 25 per cent. Moreover, in order to increase the resources available to neutralise the massive movements of short-term funds which had so disrupted balance of payments in 1960 and 1961, the IMF initiated a scheme for a " lenders' club ". In December 1961 the main trading countries— the *Group of Ten*—undertook (subject to some control by lending countries over the use of the funds) to make available loans totalling over £2,000 million to the IMF for relending to countries of the Group suffering an outflow of short-term funds.

In September 1967 the members of the IMF agreed in principle to a scheme according *special drawing rights* (SDRs) to member countries. SDRs

will be distributed annually to all members in proportion to their quotas with the IMF. They will have a fixed value in terms of gold, and like gold, will be generally accepted as a means of payment. Thus a deficit country can use its SDRs to buy the currency of the countries with which it has a deficit, and the surplus countries, in accumulating SDRs, earn a rate of interest on them. This is a movement towards an international paper currency, since the SDRs, unlike IMF loans, do not have to be repaid: they will be a permanent addition to international reserves. The amount of SDRs which has been proposed is small in relation to the size of the problem, and the scheme has yet to be put into practice; but it is a step in the right direction.

### (v) Sterling as a Reserve Currency.

The sterling balances (*see* G7 and 31) came under pressure from a new quarter in 1968. There were many sterling area holders of sterling balances, including most governments, who did not speculate against the pound in 1967 and suffered a capital loss when the pound was devalued. Anticipating further capital loss at the time of the gold crisis in 1968, they ran down their sterling balances, so endangering the British gold reserves. In September the central banks of the major industrial countries agreed at Basle to grant the United Kingdom new credit facilities of up to £800 million for ten years with which to finance such sales of sterling. Also the British Government guaranteed the value, in terms of US dollars, of most of the official sterling reserves held by these countries, in return for their holding at least a certain proportion of their reserves in sterling. These arrangements should help to protect sterling against the dangers of being a reserve currency.

## Trading Arrangements.

### (i) First Application for Membership of the Common Market.

In mid-1961 it was announced that Britain would apply for full membership of the *European Economic Community*, otherwise known as the Common Market, set up by the Treaty of Rome which was ratified in 1958. The European Economic Community (EEC) consists of six full members —Belgium, France, Holland, Italy, Luxembourg, and Western Germany (*see* G9). Britain had participated in the negotiations which led up to its formation, and had argued in favour of a looser " free trade area " without a common external tariff, and excluding trade in agricultural products. No compromise acceptable to the Six was found, and Britain joined with six other European countries—Austria, Denmark, Norway, Portugal, Sweden, and Switzerland—in forming the *European Free Trade Area* (EFTA).

Later, however, when the Common Market proved to be highly successful in terms of the growth of production and trade, the British Government decided to apply for membership. There were three main problems to be solved in the negotiations. The first two—the trading links with Commonwealth countries, and the position of British agriculture—were those which had influenced the British attitude in the earlier negotiations. Now Britain also had obligations to her trading partners in EFTA. The Common Market countries welcomed the British application, but made it clear that renewed negotiations must take place within the framework of the Treaty.

### (ii) The British Proposals.

The British delegation made the following proposals for the solution of Britain's special problems. For British *agriculture* there was to be a long " transition period "—that is to say, a period for adjustment before British agriculture became fully integrated into the Common Market agricultural arrangements—possibly 12 to 15 years from the date of joining the Common Market. By contrast, it was not proposed to negotiate for favourable conditions for British *industry*: on joining the Common Market, Britain was prepared to make a reduction in her tariffs equivalent to the reductions which had already been made by the Six.

Two lines of approach were suggested for protecting the trading positions of the under-developed countries of the Commonwealth. One involved granting those countries the status of " associated territories " which would give their products access to European markets on pre-ferential terms. There was a precedent for this sort of arrangement, in that France had already negotiated associated status for some of her former colonies in Africa. But it was recognised that the Six might not be prepared to offer associated status to some of the larger under-developed countries of the Commonwealth—e.g., India, and that some countries might wish to reject an offer of associated status for political reasons. As an alternative, therefore, it was suggested that the Common Market external tariff on some of the more important agricultural exports from these countries—e.g., Indian tea—should be reduced or eliminated; and that arrangements should be made to ensure that the external tariff on manufactured goods exported from these countries—e.g., textiles from Hong Kong—did not lead to a reduction of such exports. For the more developed countries of the Common-wealth, there were proposals that the Common Market external tariff on raw material imports should be reduced or eliminated for certain Commonwealth produced materials, such as aluminium, zinc, and woodpulp. It was also proposed that certain arrangements should be made with respect to foodstuffs—chiefly wheat, meat, and dairy products—produced by developed members of the Commonwealth. The principle underlying these arrangements, it was suggested, should be that Commonwealth producers " be given in the future the opportunity for outlets for their products comparable to those they now enjoy."

#### (iii) The Negotiations.

In the course of prolonged negotiations, con-siderable progress towards a final agreement was gradually made: progress in reducing tariffs important in Commonwealth trade, in agreeing that Commonwealth countries in Africa and the West Indies should be offered associated status on the same terms as the ex-French territories, and in agreeing that the problems of India, Pakistan, and Ceylon could best be solved by trade treaties negotiated between the Common Market and these countries. The problem of temperate foodstuffs proved the most intractable. Britain wanted specific arrangements to ensure that Commonwealth-produced temperate foods would be able to find markets in Europe, at least in the short term. France made it clear that she envisaged a reduction of food imports into Common Market countries, to permit an expansion of her agricultural output: this point of view was clearly incompatible with the British proposal for " comparable outlets " for Commonwealth pro-ducers. Nor was there agreement on the transi-tional arrangements for British agriculture.

Nevertheless, it was the opinion of many observers that by January 1963 the stage had been set for a round of bargaining, and that given goodwill on both sides Britain's entry could have been assured. It therefore came as a surprise when France decided that the negotiations should be broken off. Despite opposition from

the other five, a French veto was imposed on the British application. Perhaps the fundamental reason for the breakdown can be inferred from a statement attributed to General de Gaulle: " The Europe I prefer is the Europe of the Six."

#### (iv) Britain's Second Application.

In 1967 the British Government again began discussing with the EEC countries the possibility of British membership. This move had the sup-port of most British industrialists: a Confederation of British Industry Survey in March showed that 90 per cent of replying companies believe EEC membership would be to their advantage. Confi-dential discussions went on; but in December, France vetoed the opening of negotiations on Britain's entry.

Economists are by no means agreed on the economic value to Britain of joining the Common Market: a lot depends on the precise terms of entry and on unmeasurable factors. Moreover, entry to the EEC is as much a political decision as an economic one. See C36–9.

### 2. INTERNAL DEVELOPMENTS

Industrial Output and Employment.

In the fourth quarter of 1968, industrial pro-duction was 42 per cent higher than it had been in 1958. This expansion occurred largely in two spurts: during the twelve months between March 1959 and March 1960 industrial output increased by 11 per cent, and between March 1963 and March 1964 it rose by 14 per cent. The three years before March 1959, the three years between the booms and the three years after March 1964 were periods of industrial stagnation. Industrial production picked up again in 1967 and 1968, but not as rapidly as before. The table also indicates that the numbers employed in industry were only 1per cent higher near the end of 1968 (allowing for seasonal variation) than in 1958, so that producti-vity—output per person employed—rose by about 41 per cent over the period. Here again, a very high proportion of the increase was secured in the boom periods.

Restriction and De-restriction.

The 1960s have witnessed several changes in the emphasis of Government monetary and fiscal policies. In the first half of 1960 the emphasis was on restrictive policies, both because of the deterioration in the balance of payments position, and because it was apparent that the very rapid expansion of output had created shortages and inflation in the economy at home. No doubt there would have been a slowing down in the rate of growth of output even if restrictive measures had not been taken: an increase as rapid as that in 1959 was possible only because a substantial excess capacity had developed over the preceding years. But the measures taken to restrict demand reinforced this tendency, and growth in industrial output was halted.

A relaxation of restraints did help to stimulate some increase in output in the early months of 1961. But from July 1961—again primarily for balance of payments reasons—there was a phase

INDUSTRIAL PRODUCTION, EMPLOYMENT, AND PRODUCTIVITY, 1959–68
(Quarterly averages of seasonally adjusted index numbers, 1958 = 100)

| Year | | | Quarter | Industrial production (1) | Employment in industry (2) | Productivity in industry $100 \times (1) \div (2)$ |
|------|---|---|---------|---------------------------|----------------------------|----------------------------------------------------|
| 1959 | . | . | I | 102 | 100 | 102 |
| 1960 | . | . | I | 112 | 102 | 110 |
| 1961 | . | . | I | 114 | 104 | 109 |
| 1962 | . | . | I | 114 | 104 | 110 |
| 1963 | . | . | I | 113 | 101 | 112 |
| 1964 | . | . | I | 127 | 103 | 123 |
| 1965 | . | . | I | 132 | 105 | 125 |
| 1966 | . | . | I | 134 | 106 | 126 |
| 1967 | . | . | I | 132 | 103 | 128 |
| 1968 | . | . | I | 137 | 101 | 136 |
| 1968 | . | . | IV | 142 | 101 | 141 |

of even sterner restrictions. The progressive relaxation of restrictions during the summer of 1962, coupled with measures designed to stimulate industrial output, had not had any major effect by the end of the year.

In some ways, the situation early in 1963 was analogous to that of early 1959. There was a substantial under-utilisation of capacity in many branches of industry, since some new investment had continued in 1960–62. Labour resources for expansion were available, in that unemployment —at over 3 per cent—was higher than in any period since the war. Consequently the expansionist policies of 1963 helped to produce a year of boom which saw a spurt of industrial output, and a substantial increase in productivity. This progress could not be maintained in 1964, when industrial production and productivity flattened out, and the balance of payments deteriorated. However, the 1960 remedy of deflation was not immediately repeated; it was now realised that "stop-go" policies were harmful to the growth of the economy, and that the balance of payments problem would have to be solved by other measures. Full employment was maintained between 1964 I and 1966 I, but industrial production per man rose by only 1·5 per cent per annum. Two reasons have been suggested for this slow growth of productivity: a decline in the average working week (output per man-hour increased more rapidly), and the tendency of employers to adjust their labour force to the level of production only with a considerable delay.

Balance of payments difficulties eventually led the Government to deflate the economy; and there was a fall in industrial production in the second half of 1966 as the July measures took effect. Employers now began to lay off workers, and unemployment rose from 1·2 per cent of the labour force in early 1966 to average 2·2 per cent in 1967 and 2·3 per cent in 1968. Industrial production rose by 8 per cent between 1966 I and 1968 IV, but because productivity increased, industrial employment actually fell by 5 percentage points.

### Regional Planning.

Much publicity has been given in the 1960s to the varying degrees of prosperity and levels of unemployment in the United Kingdom (see G13). Government measures are necessary to reduce disparities and probably even to prevent them from growing.

There are essentially two ways of tackling the problem of regional imbalances: taking jobs to the people or bringing people to the jobs. In so far as the latter alternative is chosen, the Government should encourage the mobility of labour, e.g., through retraining schemes or a housing subsidy. However, the migration of population may damage community life in the denuded areas, and cause congestion, housing shortages, and overcrowding in the booming regions. The Government can create employment opportunities in the relatively depressed regions in various ways. It can try to induce expanding industries to set up new plants in these regions by offering tax incentives; it can authorise additional expenditure on public works —e.g., by accelerating road-building programmes —to provide additional employment; it can place orders for the goods it needs—e.g. defence contracts—where work is required.

On taking office in October 1964, the Labour Government made regional planning the responsibility of its Department of Economic Affairs. Britain was divided into eight regions, with the intention of producing a plan for each region. The Government also established two kinds of planning body: regional economic planning Councils and Boards to advise on and co-ordinate the planning of each region.

Recent Government policy to cure regional unemployment has taken the following forms. Various measures to defer public construction programmes have excluded the "Development Areas." Fiscal incentives to locate industry in the depressed regions have been given, e.g., the cash grants provided since 1966 for new plants and machinery in manufacturing are at twice the national rate in the Development Areas. By contrast, office building in the main conurbations,

London and Birmingham, was strictly limited. To encourage the mobility of labour, the Government introduced redundancy compensation and achieved some expansion in both public and private training facilities. In 1967 regional differentials in the selective employment tax were introduced (see G37). Under this scheme manufacturers in Development Areas are paid 30s. per week for each full-time adult male employee and lower amounts in respect of other workers; so giving the Development Areas a wage cost advantage in manufacturing of 5–10 per cent.

### Planning for Faster Growth.

There has been an increasing dissatisfaction with the rate of growth achieved in this economy over the past decade or so. The economies of most Common Market countries have increased their industrial output at a much faster rate. Furthermore, there has been dissatisfaction with the way in which the economy has grown: the characteristic pattern has been one of sharp bursts of expansion interrupted by rather lengthy periods of stagnation.

### (i) The National Economic Development Council.

To stimulate a more systematic study of the problems involved in securing a faster and more even rate of growth in the British economy, the Conservative Government established the *National Economic Development Council* (NEDC or "Neddy"). The two-tier organisation was similar to that of the corresponding planning council in France. The Council itself consisted of representatives from the T.U.C. and employers' organisations, Government ministers and independent members, and it was served by a group of experts. This group undertook research into the problems of securing a faster rate of growth, into the means of overcoming obstacles to growth, and into the economic policies which could be most conducive to faster growth.

In its first report, in 1963, the Council made a projection for the economy. It adopted a target rate of growth of output over the period 1961–66, equal to 4 per cent per annum, which was substantially faster than the rate of growth actually achieved in previous years. It attempted to predict how investment, exports, imports, consumption, and the output of each industry would have to grow if the target rate of growth was to be achieved. The merit of this exercise was twofold: it helped to focus Government attention on the long-term, by showing that policies designed to solve short-term difficulties might intensify the problem of raising long-term economic growth; and, by bolstering expectations, it encouraged firms to invest.

A particularly interesting feature of the work of the NEDC is its study of individual industries. Seventeen major industries were surveyed in detail to assess the changes in output, employment, productivity, investment, and exports which were feasible in each industry. Economic Development Committees (EDCs)—which have come to be known as "little Neddies"—were established as part of the NEDC machinery to report on the problems of individual industries. It is impossible for an individual firm or industry to make correct decisions on future expansion without knowing how the rest of the economy will behave; by relating planning at the national level and planning at the level of individual industries the NEDC did valuable work.

### (ii) The Department of Economic Affairs.

In October 1964 the Labour Government established a new *Department of Economic Affairs* (DEA). While short-term measures to regulate the economy or the balance of payments remained the responsibility of the Treasury, the DEA took over from the Treasury the responsibility for long-term economic policy. The DEA was charged with the task of preparing and implementing a realistic plan for economic expansion, a prices and incomes policy and an industrial and regional policy. The NEDC, now reconstituted, became a consultative and advisory body; a link between the Government and the economic community.

However, the EDC's continue to function and have produced a great many reports.

### (iii) The National Plan.

The National Plan for the British economy over the period 1964–70 was published by the Government in 1965. The Plan was based on the assumption that output would rise by 3·8 per cent per annum over the period. Since the labour force was expected to grow at 0·4 per cent per annum, this meant an annual growth in productivity of 3·5 per cent—considerably higher than the 2·7 per cent average over the period 1960–64. The Plan specified the changes in investment, consumption, and public expenditure required to achieve this target.

In many ways, the crucial assumptions were those concerned with the balance of payments. The Plan supposed that imports would increase by 4·0 per cent per annum, and that to achieve a " satisfactory " surplus of £250 million on the overall balance of payments in 1970, exports would have to rise by 5·6 per cent per annum. If such a rapid expansion of exports were not achieved—and in the period 1960–64 the annual increase averaged only 3·1 per cent—the whole Plan could be jeopardised, in that the balance of payments difficulties might, as in the past, appear to justify policies to restrict the growth in domestic output.

Indeed, this is precisely what happened. The tardy improvement in the balance of payments led the Government eventually in July 1966 to deflate the economy. The ensuing stagnation meant that the Plan's targets for 1970 could no longer be achieved. However, it should not be concluded that planning is necessarily an academic exercise; planning has a valuable sight-setting function; it can bolster firms' expectations and hence their investment; and it can help to co-ordinate their decisions. Rather, we should recognise that planning is worthless unless combined with Government policies which enable the planned targets to be reached.

### (iv) " The Task Ahead ".

In the uncertain economic climate after the July measures there was little point in long-range planning. However, early in 1969 the Government published as a Green Paper a new planning document *The Task Ahead: an Economic Assessment to 1972*. It was neither a plan nor a forecast but " part of the consultative planning process ". Implementation was to take the form of consultation with the EDC or other representatives of each industry. The document was flexible in that new developments could be accommodated without requiring the whole assessment to be rewritten. There are three sets of projections—lower, " basic " and higher—on the assumptions of a growth rate in real output of 3, 3½ and 4 per cent per annum respectively. These projections compare with an actual growth rate of 3·3 per cent per annum between 1960 and 1966.

The actual outcome will again depend crucially on the balance of payments. A large surplus is needed in future years to pay off the foreign debts, amounting to more than £2,000 million, incurred between 1963 and 1968. On the " basic " projection, to achieve an overall balance of payments surplus of £550 million in 1972, exports must rise by 6 per cent per annum and growth in private consumption must be restricted to 2·4 per cent per annum. *See also* C25.

### Wages and Prices.

Retail prices have continued to edge upwards in the early years of the 1960s: in 1967 they were 29 per cent higher than in 1958. Hardly any of this increase can be attributed to an increase in import prices. To explain the inflation we must look to the behaviour of labour costs. Between 1958 and 1967 the nationally negotiated weekly wage rates rose by 40 per cent, and weekly earnings—including overtime payments and payments negotiated on the factory-floor—by 61 per cent. Since the increase in productivity over this period was slow, income from employment per unit of output (indicating labour costs per unit of output) rose by 32 per cent.

One of the main dangers of this inflation of costs and prices is that exporters will find it more difficult to compete in foreign markets. Export prices in fact increased slowly. But this may well imply that producers were having to accept lower profit margins on exports than on sales in the home market; and this would not encourage producers to push their sales in overseas markets.

### Incomes Policy.

Britain's competitive position in world trade has deteriorated relative to that of her main rivals the United States, West Germany, and France; hence her balance of payments difficulties. The British share in total world exports of manufactures fell from 17·7 per cent to 11·9 per cent between 1959 and 1967. There are essentially two methods of remedying this situation. We must secure either a relative fall in the external value of the pound, or a relative rise in its internal value. In other words, either there must be a devaluation of the pound in terms of other currencies, or we must have a policy to limit the increase in the British price-level. Up to 1967 the Government concentrated on the latter alternative; and attempts were made to introduce some form of *incomes policy*. In 1967 the Government opted for devaluation; but incomes policy was still necessary if the devaluation was to be successful.

### (i) The Pay Pause.

In July 1961 the Chancellor of the Exchequer called for a " pause " in wages, salaries, and dividend payments. Exhortations for restraint have been a familiar feature of ministerial statements for many years, but on this occasion the Government soon made it clear that it intended to use such power as it has to influence the amount and timing of wage and salary awards. It has power to decide when the pay awards recommended by the Wages Councils—which fix minimum wages for 3½ million workers—shall be implemented. The Government's power is strongest over workers which it directly or indirectly employs, e.g., civil servants, teachers, and Post Office workers. Their pay awards were cut back. The Government also had a limited influence on awards made in nationalised industries.

The " pay pause " came to an end in April 1962. It was envisaged as a temporary policy, and its effects are difficult to assess. It certainly postponed some wage awards which would otherwise have been made in that period, and it may have contributed to a stiffening of resistance to wage claims. But because the pause affected some groups of people more severely than others, this form of incomes policy was seen to be discriminatory.

### (ii) The National Incomes Commission.

In February 1962 the Government issued a White Paper which outlined its incomes policy for the period after the pause. It stated that " the objective must be to keep the rate of increase in incomes within the long-term rate of growth of national production. . . . In recent years national production has risen by about 2 to 2½ per cent a year. . . . It is accordingly necessary that the increase of wages and salaries, as of other incomes, should be kept within this figure during the next phase." The Government stressed that most of the arguments which had in the past been advanced in justification of wage and salary claims— *e.g.*, increases in the cost of living, trends in productivity or profits in particular industries, and comparisons with levels or trends in other employments—should be given less weight; and that " general economic considerations "—*i.e.*, the increases which the economy can afford given the prospective rate of increase in national production —should be given more weight.

Late in 1962 the Government set up the *National Incomes Commission* (NIC). However, the powers of this body were limited. It could not participate in, nor comment upon, wage claims while negotiations were in progress unless the parties involved consented; and as the T.U.C. did not intend to co-operate with the Commission, such consent was unlikely. It could be asked to report on inflationary settlements which had been reached (unless the settlement was reached by arbitration); but it had no power to cancel or modify an agreement. NIC produced only 4 reports, and was wound up after the change in Government.

### (iii) The National Board for Prices and Incomes.

In October 1964 the Labour Government's new Department of Economic Affairs was made responsible for achieving an incomes policy. The lessons of the past had been learned; the Government recognised that a successful incomes policy would require the support of both sides of industry. Its first objective was to achieve a "Joint Statement of Intent on Productivity, Prices and Incomes"; this was signed in December 1964. In this document the T.U.C. and the employers' organisations undertook to co-operate with the Government in producing an effective machinery for the implementing of an incomes policy.

It was Government policy that growth in earnings per employee should equal the planned growth in national output per employee of 3-3½ per cent per annum. Thus, in those industries (e.g., engineering) in which productivity growth exceeds this "norm", earnings should rise less rapidly than productivity, and in those industries (e.g., railways) in which productivity growth falls short of the norm, earnings could rise more rapidly than productivity. Moreover, prices would be expected to fall in industries such as engineering, and permitted to rise in industries such as railways. Growth in earnings per employee should exceed the norm only in exceptional cases; i.e., as a reward for increasing productivity by eliminating restrictive working practices; if necessary to transfer labour from one industry to another; if earnings are too low to maintain a reasonable standard of living; or if a group of workers have fallen seriously out of line with earnings for similar work.

To make specific recommendations on the basis of this policy, the Government set up a National Board for Prices and Incomes. It consists of an independent Chairman, a number of independent experts, a businessman and a trade unionist. The Prices Review Division of the Board can investigate the price of any goods in the economy, and the Incomes Review Division has power to investigate all claims and settlements relating to wages, salaries, and other incomes. In less than 4 years of operation the Board had produced over 100 reports on prices and earnings.

There was no statutory authority to enforce the recommendations of the Board: reliance was placed on voluntary methods and the power of persuasion and public opinion. However, in late 1965 the Government introduced a compulsory "Early Warning" system, whereby it is notified in advance of any intended increase in incomes or in certain prices. As a result, the Government and the Board now have enough time to consider increases before they are put into effect.

### (iv) The Prices and Incomes Standstill.

A voluntary incomes policy is very difficult to implement, since it depends on co-operation among Government, workers, and employers; moreover, co-operation among representatives at the top may be undermined by "wage-drift" at the factory level. Thus the annual average of weekly wage-rates rose by no less than 6 percentage points between 1965 and 1966. In fact all of this increase took place in the period before July 1966. Clearly the voluntary incomes policy was meeting with little success.

Therefore, as part of the July measures taken to deal with the balance of payments problem, the Government introduced a "prices and incomes standstill." Increases in prices and incomes were as far as possible avoided altogether until the end of 1966. The only exceptions in the case of incomes were pay increases resulting directly from increases in output (e.g., piece-work or over-time earnings) and from genuine promotion or regular increments on a predetermined scale. Increases already negotiated but not yet implemented were deferred for 6 months. The first

half of 1967 was a period of "severe restraint." Any price increases were carefully examined, and the norm for income increases was zero. Any increase in earnings had to be justified by one of the four conditions for exception, referred to above. To enforce its "freeze" the Government took the unprecedented step of asking Parliament for reserve powers, which were to be used only if the need should arise. These powers—including penalties for offenders—were contained in the new Part IV of the Prices and Incomes Act. For the most part, there was a voluntary observation of the standstill; but from October 1966 the Government found it necessary to exercise its power of compulsion in a few cases, e.g., laundry and dry cleaning charges, and a wage agreement in the electrical engineering industry. The power of compulsion lapsed in August 1967.

The period of compulsion was followed by a year in which there was to be a "nil norm" except where increases in incomes could be justified by one of the four criteria listed above. The Government could no longer legally enforce its policy, but it did retain the power to delay price and pay increases, through reference to the Board, by up to 7 months. Whereas the Government succeeded in almost stabilising wages and prices during the year in which it took compulsory powers, in the second half of 1967 weekly wage rates rose by 6 per cent. The advantage gained from the previous restraint was reduced but not entirely lost.

### (v) Incomes Policy after Devaluation.

Incomes policy was made both more difficult and more important by the devaluation of the pound: more difficult in that devaluation involved a cut in the standard of living, and more important in that the trading benefit from devaluation should not be neutralised by inflation.

In April 1968 the Government published a White Paper outlining its policy for the period until the end of 1969. Wage increases must still be justified by the four criteria, and there is a "ceiling" to increases in income of 3½ per cent per annum except for "productivity agreements" and low-paid workers in certain cases. Price increases are permitted only as a result of unavoidable increases in cost per unit of output, and price reductions are required when costs fall. Dividend increases are also subject to the ceiling of 3½ per cent per annum, and home rent increases restricted. The Government intended to rely on the voluntary co-operation of unions and employers over pay; but it decided to lengthen its delaying powers for pay and price increases up to 12 months, and take powers to enforce price reductions recommended by the Board.

Between November 1967 and November 1968 the retail price index rose by 5·2 per cent, mainly due to the effect of devaluation on import prices. In the face of this rise in the cost of living the incomes policy met with firm resistance. In practice the nominal ceiling of 3½ per cent per annum rapidly became the normal increase. In the first year after devaluation basic wage rates rose by 6·0 per cent and average earnings by 7·5 per cent. Workers were able to protect themselves against the inflation and to increase slightly their real incomes.

### Monetary and Fiscal Policies since 1960.

There is probably no country in the world which has made fuller use than Britain of budgetary policy as a means of stabilising the economy. Since 1941, almost all adjustments to the total level of taxation have been made with the object of reducing an excess in total demand or of repairing a deficit. Whereas in the United States there is still a public clamour for "balanced budgets," British Governments have accepted Keynesian principles—first laid down by Lord Keynes—for managing the economy by adjusting the level of taxation and private saving relative to public expenditure and private investment. This does not mean to say that British policies have always been successful. Apart from the difficulty of deciding when demand is excessive or deficient, there are the difficulties that data are available only with a serious time-lag, and may be inaccurate; that economic events cannot be predicted with any certainty; and that the quantitative effects of Government measures are not easy to estimate.

**1960.**

In the first half of 1960 there were a series of restrictive measures designed to curb the increase in home demand and to improve the balance of payments position. Bank Rate was raised to 6 per cent. To exert pressure on the banks' liquidity positions, and so help to curb bank advances, the banks were called upon to place special deposits (*see* G21) with the Bank of England. Restrictions on hire purchase transactions were also imposed. Furthermore, the Budget was restrictive: the Chancellor estimated an overall deficit (*see* G24) for 1960–61 of only £320 million.

**1961.**

The Budget was sternly anti-inflationary: profits tax and some indirect taxes were increased; but there was a major reduction in surtax. In addition, the Chancellor was granted powers to introduce, if he considered it necessary, an economic "regulator": a surcharge on, or rebate of, indirect taxes by up to 10 per cent. This power provides greater scope for using fiscal measures to influence the economy in the periods between Budgets. In July 1961 the Chancellor introduced a collection of restrictive measures. These measures were primarily intended to ease the critical foreign exchange situation but they were not without effect on the domestic economy. Bank Rate was raised to 7 per cent. To restrict the growth in demand, the Chancellor imposed a 10 per cent surcharge in indirect taxation and called the banks to increase their special deposits at the Bank of England. Furthermore, the Chancellor announced that he aimed to restrict the increase in government spending. Not only was the outflow of funds stopped, but it was actually reversed. These measures were all too successful in restricting demand at home: there was a fall in industrial production in the second half of 1961.

**1962.**

The 1962 Budget was, however, no less restrictive in intention than the 1961 Budget. The estimated overall deficit, at £70 million, was virtually unchanged. There was a move towards uniformity of purchase tax rates. The main novelty of the 1962 Budget was a tax on certain speculative gains. From the summer of 1962 onwards, monetary and fiscal policies were designed to stimulate economic activity. Bank Rate was reduced to 4 per cent, all special deposits held by the Bank of England were released, qualitative restraints on bank lending were abolished, some post-war credits were released, investment allowances for industry were increased, and the purchase tax on cars reduced.

**1963.**

January 1963 saw further reduction in purchase taxes, and a very considerable increase in social payments. The estimated overall Budget deficit for 1963–64 was more than £600 million greater than that of the previous year. Tax reliefs were announced: the most important benefits to individuals were derived from increases in the allowances which can be charged against income before income tax is levied; in addition, Schedule A taxes were abolished for owner-occupiers. Other changes in taxation were designed to stimulate investment spending by companies: depreciation allowances were increased for tax purposes, and companies investing in areas of high unemployment were permitted to charge depreciation on their assets at a rate of their own choosing. The Budget was designed to provide a fiscal boost to the economy, and in this it succeeded: national output rose by more than 5 per cent over the year.

**1964.**

By 1964 the economy was beginning to show signs of strain, and the trade figures revealed a rapid deterioration in the balance of visible trade. The Chancellor's objective in his April budget was to slow down the rate of growth without producing deflation. He planned an overall deficit of £790 million, but provided for additional taxation by increasing the duties on tobacco and alcoholic drinks by about 10 per cent.

Both consumption expenditure and industrial production jumped sharply towards the end of 1964, and there were reports of a growing labour shortage. The balance of payments was heavily in deficit throughout the year. Nothing was done about it, however, until after the General Election in October. In November the Chancellor of the Exchequer presented a "little budget." An additional 6d. in the £ was placed on the standard rate of income tax, and there were increases in petrol duties, in National Insurance contributions and payments. But old-age pensions were increased. During the sterling crisis of November (*see* G30) Bank Rate was raised to 7 per cent to stem the outflow of funds, but this was not accompanied by a "credit squeeze" to restrict productive investments, as in the crisis of 1961. Unlike some of his predecessors, the Chancellor had not opted for deflation as the cure for the balance of payments deficit. Instead, reliance was placed on an import surcharge and an export rebate. However, the British policy came under fire from some European Governments, who called for a deflation of the British economy.

**1965.**

The Budget contained two major fiscal innovations. A *corporation tax* was introduced to replace the existing company income tax and profits tax. This tax at a rate of 40 per cent, was imposed on distributed as well as undistributed profits, so as to encourage the retention of profits for the financing of business expansion. A further innovation was the introduction of a *capital gains tax*, far more comprehensive than the first move in this direction taken in 1962. This tax is levied on the gain realised on an asset between its purchase and sale, provided this does not exceed the gain between 6 April 1965 and sale. It applies to all assets, with limited exceptions: the most important being owner-occupied houses, and goods and chattels realised for less than £1,000. Gains realised within a period of one year are treated as ordinary income and taxed accordingly. Gains on assets held for more than a year are taxed at a flat rate of 30 per cent in the case of individuals. However, gains realised by companies over any period are taxed at corporation tax rates. There are many administrative difficulties in implementing such a tax. Nevertheless, it is an important attempt to remedy the inequality in the taxation of earned and unearned incomes.

Full employment was maintained in 1965. The April Budget was not deflationary: the Government's overall deficit for 1965–66 was estimated at £720 million. In July, because the balance of payments had shown no sign of rapid improvement, the Chancellor found it necessary to introduce further measures: tighter controls on foreign exchange and on the terms of hire-purchase, and a postponement of public expenditure programmes. But this action was not sufficient to produce deflation, and at the end of the year unemployment was still very low.

**1966.**

The 1966 Budget was somewhat deflationary; but its impact was delayed until September when the new *selective employment tax* (SET) came into force. All employers were required to pay this tax at the weekly rate of 25s. for men, 12s. 6d. for women and boys and 8s. for girls. However, manufacturing industries received a refund of 130 per cent, the public sector 100 per cent, while other industries—*e.g.*, services and construction—receive no refund. The tax discriminates against those industries which are labour-intensive, export little, and whose output bears little indirect taxation. The SET is therefore a rough and ready means of forcing employers to release hoarded labour, of subsidizing exports, and of evening up the incidence of indirect taxation.

Up to mid-1966 the Labour Government's

policy can be summarised as follows: to restrict the growth of demand somewhat but not as drastically as in the past, to take direct action on the immediate balance of payments, and to strengthen the long-run balance by means of productivity policy and incomes policy. However, in July, during yet another run on sterling, the Government embarked on a policy of deflation. In its "July measures" the Government raised indirect taxation 10 per cent by means of its "regulator," placed a 10 per cent surcharge on surtax, tightened building controls, cut public investment for 1967/8, increased hire-purchase restrictions, and raised Bank Rate to 7 per cent. As a result of these measures, the economy went into recession in the second half of 1966.

#### 1967.

Despite unemployment of 2·4 per cent and predictions of a further rise during the year, the Chancellor produced a "no-change" April Budget, with an estimated surplus of £640 million. The balance of payments prevented him from taking reflationary measures. In mid-year the Government gave some stimulus to consumers' expenditure by relaxing hire purchase terms and increasing family allowances. But the balance of payments deteriorated, and, since further deflation was politically unacceptable, the Government devalued the pound. Devaluation was itself strongly reflationary—increasing demand for exports and for import-substitute goods—and had to be accompanied by measures to release resources for these industries. Bank Rate was raised to the unprecedented height of 8 per cent, bank advances were limited to all but priority borrowers, e.g., exporters, hire purchase on cars was tightened, corporation tax was raised to 42½ per cent, and the SET premium was to be withdrawn except for Development Areas.

There were also to be cuts in defence, other public spending and nationalised industries' investment. Further cuts in government spending were announced in December, and again in January, when future defence spending was considerably reduced because of the decision to withdraw forces from East of Suez, and the planned rise in the school-leaving age from 15 to 16 was put off until 1972. Despite these several blows of the axe, public expenditure was still likely to rise in 1968/9 by nearly 4 per cent in real terms; but the rise in 1969/70 was estimated to be no more than 1 per cent.

#### 1968.

The April budget was highly deflationary. The Chancellor increased taxation to yield an additional £920 million per annum. Most of this came from indirect taxation, with purchase tax and taxes on spirits, wines, and tobacco all raised. Motorists were particularly hit by the increased vehicle and petrol taxes—perhaps not unfairly in view of the heavy social costs caused by road congestion. SET was to be raised 50 per cent, and betting duties were put up. Partly to gain support for the incomes policy, the Chancellor raised family allowances and placed a heavy "special levy" for one year on unearned income above £3,000 per annum. In deflating the economy the Chancellor was attempting to reduce private consumer demand so as to free resources for the export market and for replacing imports. Without such a transfer of resources the advantage gained from devaluation would be lost. His strategy was to produce an overall balance of payments surplus of the order of £500 million before resuming growth, and in this way to break the vicious circle of "stop-go".

There was a stronger recovery of consumer demand and output and a weaker improvement in the balance of payments in 1968 than the Chancellor had expected, and further restrictive measures were taken during the year. In May bank lending restrictions were tightened selectively, and in November hire purchase terms were tightened and the "regulator" used to raise indirect taxes by 10 per cent.

#### 1969.

In February Bank Rate was raised to the record height of 8 per cent, partly to help reduce bank

lending and partly to retain short-term funds in London: owing to the shortage of international liquidity (see G31) central banks compete for short-term capital by raising their discount rates.

The April Budget was somewhat restrictive; an additional £350 million per annum being raised in taxation. This was achieved mainly by increasing corporation tax to 45 per cent, and SET to 48 shillings a week for adult males. In an attempt to encourage saving the Chancellor introduced a contractual savings scheme offering attractive tax-free interest payments after a five-or seven-year period. Perhaps as a result of pressures from Britain's creditor, the IMF, the Chancellor emphasised the importance he would give to monetary policy (see G22). The Budget continued the strategy of improving the balance of payments at the expense of consumption.

#### Decimalisation 1971.

The decimalisation of the currency has been a recurrent theme in public debate for about 150 years. But in 1966 the Government announced its decision to adopt a decimal currency system in February 1971. The advantage of this change is that it will be easier for the public and also commerce and industry to reckon in decimal units than in terms of £. s. d.

Two main alternative forms of decimalisation were considered: either to make 10s. the major unit, with division into 100 cents, or to retain the £ as the major unit to be subdivided. The Government decided on the latter course: the £ will remain the main unit of the British currency, but it will be divided into 100 new pennies, instead of into twenty shillings each of twelve pence. Since the new penny will be worth 2·4d., it will be necessary to have a new halfpenny as well. In making its choice the Government took the long view: the process of transition would be easier with the 10s. unit, and there would be no need for half-cents; but as incomes and prices rose over the years, 10s. would eventually be too small a unit.

After the new currency is introduced we shall have the following coins: ½ new penny (worth 1·2d.), 1 new penny (2·4d.), 2 new pence (4·8d.), 5 new pence (1s.), 10 new pence (2s.), 50 new pence (10s.). For a year or two both currencies will be used. The costs of decimalisation—the replacement of business machines, and administration—will be more than £100 million, but the benefits—in time and effort saved—will exceed this figure many times over in the long run.

#### Earnings-related Social Security.

In January 1969 the Government published a White Paper on its proposals to replace the national insurance scheme (see G24) by a new scheme of national superannuation and social insurance, in which both contributions and benefits will be related to the earnings of the individual employee. It argued that the existing national insurance scheme fails to provide security in old age: nearly a third of all pensioners are dependent in some degree on supplementary benefit.

According to the proposals, the new earnings-related contributions will be mostly higher than contributions under the existing scheme, especially among higher earners. In return, those who pay the new contributions will earn higher pensions and other benefits. Twenty years of new-scheme contributions will be required before the first pensions at the full rates are paid, to people reaching pension age then. Contributors reaching pension age within the next 20 years will be paid at intermediate rates, and existing pensioners are not eligible for the new earnings-related pensions.

An important feature of the proposed scheme is that, unlike the existing graduated pensions scheme, benefits are to take into account changes both in price levels and in general living standards. Thus, for instance, a contributor who has received earnings equal to the national average throughout his working life will receive a pension calculated on the national average earnings at the time he reaches pension age, not on the money he received over his working life. Moreover, the Government will be bound by statute to review every two years the main rates of pensions and other benefits (including existing flat-rate pensions) so as to make the necessary adjustments.

# GREEK MYTHS & LEGENDS

The ancient stories of Greece, woven into the fabric of our European culture by playwrights, artists and psychologists, are retold in the light of recent research. An index to the narratives ensures easy reference.

# TABLE OF CONTENTS

## Part I.   Introduction.

(a) The significance of the myths and legends.

(b) The historical background in which they developed.

(c) Bibliography.

(d) Guide to Pronunciation and Spelling.


## Part II.   Narrative Outlines.

The main cycles of myth and legend told in continuous narrative.

## Part III.   Index and Glossary.

An alphabetical index of names already mentioned referring the reader to the appropriate paragraph in the narrative, together with a glossary of names not appearing in the narrative.

# GREEK MYTHS AND LEGENDS

## PART I. INTRODUCTION

### (a) The Significance of the Myths and Legends.

We all know how the stories and books that we knew in our youth have coloured our thought. So it is with the myths and legends of the earliest civilisation of Europe, that of the Greeks. Their stories have entered the stream of consciousness of European men and women through the ages, affecting their literature and art, and even their ways of thinking.

The **Origin of Myths.** True myth has been defined by Robert Graves as "the reduction to narrative shorthand of ritual mime performed on public festivals, and in many cases recorded pictorially." These rituals were, says Graves, "archaic magic-makings that promoted the fertility or stability of a sacred queendom or kingdom—queendoms having, it seems, preceded kingdoms throughout the Greek-speaking area."

The immense diversity of these myths is partly due to geographical causes, for, in the widely differing districts of Greece, different conceptions of the divinity and varying rituals of propitiation were evolved. There are also historical causes, for the Mediterranean peoples worshipping an earth goddess were conquered by successive waves of Hellenes bringing with them some form of tribal sky god.

**Legends.** Interwoven with the religious myths were a host of legends, traditional stories, which though not authentic had, like the tales of Troy, a substratum of fact. There were, also, all kinds of fables and anecdotes, folk-tales such as that of Perseus, and allegories and romances, which fused with the myths and legends to make a fascinating complex of stories.

**Their Preservation in Literary Form.** These have been preserved for us largely by the Greek poets, especially by Homer in his *Iliad* and *Odyssey*, and by Hesiod in his *Theogony*, works which probably date from about the eighth century B.C. The Greek dramatists of the fifth century B.C.—Aeschylus, Sophocles, and Euripides—who relied on myth and legend for most of their plots, also handed on the ancient tales, though often in slightly altered form. Then about five centuries later Roman writers, such as Virgil, Ovid and Horace, modelling themselves on the Greeks, refashioned and embroidered their themes. It is not surprising that we have so many variants of the same tale.

This rich and complex treasure of Greek myth and legend has become increasingly familiar in Western Europe, at first in Latin versions, then after the Renaissance in the original Greek, and today in excellent modern translations.

**Their Significance Today.** Because of their extraordinary vitality and pervasiveness, some familiarity with Greek myth and legend is almost indispensable to a full appreciation of our European culture.

**In Art and Literature.** Great painters like Botticelli, Veronese and Rubens made the ancient stories the subject of their pictures, and writers from Shakespeare to James Joyce have enriched their work by constant reference. The French dramatists from Racine to Giraudoux are notable for relying on them for the basic plot of their dramas. Today when good and inexpensive translations enable us to go direct to Homer's *Iliad*, or to see Euripides' *Medea* on the stage, it is especially useful to have some general knowledge of the mythical background to the particular epic or play.

**Psychology.** Not only to those who love art and literature is the knowledge of Greek mythology rewarding. Psychologists have found here suggestive symbols for the profound mental processes they are endeavouring to elucidate. Through Freud the term "Œdipus complex" is now a commonplace, and Jung has found in the myths symbolic archetypes of human response.

**Philosophy and Religion.** Philosophers also have found it profitable to return to the myths. Bertrand Russell emphasises the influence of Greek religion on Greek philosophy, and, through such philosophers as Pythagoras and Plato, on Christianity itself.

**Anthropology.** Of recent years anthropologists scrutinising the myths have been able to discern something of the way of life of primitive societies. The two-volume Penguin *The Greek Myths*, by Robert Graves, incorporates some of their interpretations.

**Archæology.** Perhaps the most exciting of all recent investigations are those of the archæologists working on sites once considered only legendary. The German Schliemann, trusting to the fidelity of his Homer, actually unearthed the foundations of Priam's Troy and Agamemnon's Mycenæ, finding fabulous treasure and proving to the astonished world that these antique tales were indeed rooted in fact. Through Schliemann's trust in Homer we have added an early chapter to History, that of the Mycenæan culture of pre-classical Greek which flourished from about 1550 to 1200 B.C.

Another centre of ancient story, the island of Crete, was the field of Sir Arthur Evans' enquiries, and his excavation of the magnificent Palace of Cnossos not only pushed back the frontiers of history yet further to about 3000 B.C., but also showed how many Cretan legends had some factual basis.

More recent excavations at legendary Mycenæan sites on the mainland have led to the discovery of the Palace of Nestor at Pylos, and the House of Cadmus at Thebes.

Tablets found at Mycenæan towns and in Cnossos inscribed in an entirely unknown script, "Linear B," have challenged scholars with a fascinating puzzle. After years of study Michael Ventris and others have at last been able to decipher the script. Although so far only inventories are available, it is significant that the language used is archaic Greek. We now know therefore that the Greeks of the Mycenæan age could write, and that Homer's single reference to writing is once more a faithful record of fact. (See Book VI of the *Iliad* and the reference to Bellerophon's " folded tablet.")

### (b) The Historical Background to the Myths and Legends.

Our knowledge of the earliest periods of Greek history is very recent. The great historian Grote, writing in 1846, said that we must consider the First Olympiad of 776 B.C. as the starting point. Anything earlier was matter for conjecture. It is largely due to the discoveries of archæologists that scholars are now able to push back the frontiers of history. From archæological evidence they can now reconstruct the probable course of events from as early a date as 3000 B.C.

**3000 B.C. Early Bronze Age.** It was about 3000 B.C., when the Neolithic Age was succeeded in the Eastern Mediterranean by the Early Bronze Age, that a bronze-using people, akin to those of early Crete and the Cyclades, entered Greece and fused with the Neolithic folk already there. These invaders were not Aryans, but of Mediterranean stock, and they worshipped the Great Goddess, a fertility goddess who appeared in many guises. She was unmarried, and in many instances her lover appeared to her in the form of a bird.

**2000 B.C. Coming of Hellenes.** A thousand years later, in the Middle Bronze Age a very different kind of people began to enter Greece. These were the Hellenes or Greeks, an Aryan people from the North, for whom transport and conquest were easy by reason of their horses and wheeled vehicles. Unlike their predecessors, they were patriarchal, and their chief divinity was a tribal sky-god, but as they fused with the pre-Hellenic stock already in the country, so their patriarchal worship mingled with the matriarchal and the sky-god married the earth-goddess.

**Minyans and Ionians.** Successive waves of these Hellenes invaded the country in three main groups beginning in about 2000 B.C. with Minyans and Ionians.

**Minoan Culture.** Penetrating far south to the islands, and to Sicily, Southern Italy, and Asia Minor, they became expert navigators. They were much influenced by a brilliant and sophisticated Minoan culture already flourishing in Cnossos in Crete, and this began to have considerable effect on the mainland of Greece from about 1580 B.C. onwards.

**1400 B.C. Achæans.** In about 1400 B.C., however, Cnossos fell, destroyed either by earthquakes or by invaders, for the Achæans, the second wave of Hellenes, had now begun to enter Greece, and from about 1400 to 1100 B.C. Mycenæ on the mainland was probably the centre of civilisation in the Ægean world.

**Mycenæan Culture.** It is this Mycenæan culture of the Late Bronze Age which, seen through legend, is depicted in Homer's *Iliad* and *Odyssey*. Mycenæ is Agamemnon's own citadel, and other cities where archæological remains are now being found are named in the *Iliad's* " Catalogue of Ships." The Achæans as Homer shows them were a conquering feudal aristocracy and a concerted attempt probably made by them in the beginning of the twelfth century B.C. to seize the Black Sea trade may be reflected in the epic of the siege of Troy.

**1200 B.C. Dorians.** But the Achæans themselves were soon to be defeated, for at the end of the twelfth century B.C. the last influx of invading Hellenes, the Dorians, ancestors of the classical Greeks, entered the country. They practically destroyed the Mycenæan civilisation, and the Late Bronze Age now gave way to the Iron Age.

**The Olympian Divinities.** The close fusion between the early non-Aryan Mediterranean people, with their matriarchal culture, and the successive waves of patriarchal Hellenes was reflected in the Greek worship of Olympians. The ancient earth-goddess of fertility lived on in such guises as Aphrodite or Hera, and Zeus, sky-god of the Hellenes, appropriately took Hera to wife. Indeed, many deities, such as Demeter or Athene, combined, in the single divinity, both Mediterranean and Hellenic traits.

A third element in Greek Olympian religion derived from a Hittite culture flourishing in Asia Minor in about 1300 B.C. which had developed from a Hurrian culture of about 1500 B.C. Hesiod writing in about 750 B.C., incorporated some violent Hurrian myths of the cannibalism of the gods, in his *Theogony* or *Birth of the Gods.*

**The " Epic Cycle."** By the eighth century B.C. there was in existence a rich store of myth and legend known as the " Epic Cycle," which was drawn on by Homer and also by later poets and dramatists.

**Homer's Picture.** Homer, whose epics were probably completed at the end of the eighth or in the seventh century B.C. presents the composite myth and legend of Greece in highly civilised form, as the beliefs of a successful war-like aristocracy. The twelve deities dwelling on Olympus acknowledged the supremacy of Zeus, and Dionysus the god of wine and ecstasy who entered from Thrace in the eighth century B.C. was still an outsider, a god of the lower orders.

**The Coming of Dionysus.** But by the fifth century B.C. Dionysus had been accepted as an Olympian, taking the place of Hestia. The growing popularity of his worship which induced an ecstatic union with the god in a frenzy partly stimulated by wine, partly mystical, shows the need of the recently civilised Greeks for an impulsive religious expression which was not always satisfied by the prudent cults of the serene Olympians.

**Orpheus.** From the worship of Dionysus developed that of Orpheus, which aimed at mystic union with the god through enthusiasm wholly mystic, and through purification. The Orphics, believing in the transmigration of souls and an after life, had much influence on the Greek philosopher Pythagoras, and this influence was transmitted through Plato into Christianity itself.

The great influence of Greek religion on philosophy has only recently been recognised, and Bertrand Russell commends especially the study of John Burnet's *Early Greek Philosophy*, especially its second chapter, " Science and Religion."

### (c) Bibliography.

There is no one book or Bible of Greek myths. Many versions exist, and in a short account it is not possible to record all variations. The reader is advised to consult the masterpieces of Greek literature now available in translation.

*The Iliad*. Homer, transl. E. V. Rieu. Penguin L14.
*The Odyssey*. Homer, transl. E. V. Rieu. Penguin L1.
*The Theban Plays*. Sophocles, transl. E. F. Watling. Penguin L3.
*Electra* and other plays. Sophocles, transl. E. F. Watling. Penguin L28.
*Alcestis* and other plays. Euripides, transl. P. Vellacott. Penguin L31.
*Bacchae* and other plays. Euripides, transl. P. Vellacott. Penguin L44.
Plays. Aeschylus, transl. G. M. Cookson. Everyman 62.
Dramas. Sophocles, transl. Sir George Young. Everyman 114.
Plays, 2 vols. Euripides, transl. A. S. Way. Everyman 63 and 271.
*Greek Drama for Everyman*. F. L. Lucas. J. M. Dent & Sons.

*Men and Gods* (Myths of Ovid).  Rex Warner. Penguin 885.
*Greeks and Trojans* (Siege of Troy).  Rex Warner. Penguin 942.
*The Greek Myths*, 2 vols.  Robert Graves.  Penguin.
*The Golden Ass.*  Apuleius, transl. Robert Graves. Penguin L11.
*The Greeks.*  H. D. F. Kitto.  Pelican.
*The Twelve Olympians.*  Charles Seltman.  Pan.
*Women in Antiquity.*  Charles Seltman.  Pan.
*The Bull of Minos.*  Leonard Cottrell.  Pan.
*Dr. Smith's Classical Dictionary.*  William Smith. John Murray.

*A Smaller Classical Dictionary.*  Ed. Blakeney. J. M. Dent & Sons.

**(d) Guide to Pronunciation and Spelling.**

This Cyclopædia uses the long-established convention of spelling Greek names which is also used by such modern scholars as Robert Graves and E. V. Rieu.

It is helpful to remember that :—
" ch " and " c " are pronounced " k."
" œ " and " æ " are pronounced " ē," as in " see."
" eus " rhymes with " juice."

# Part II.  NARRATIVE OUTLINES

## THE OLYMPIAN CREATION MYTHS, 1–22.

**1. Uranus and Ge.**  The infinite and empty space which existed before creation was known as Chaos.  The Earth, or Ge, sprang from Chaos, and herself gave birth to Uranus, the Heavens, and Pontus, the Sea.  Ge then became, by Uranus, the mother of the hundred-handed giants, the Hecatoncheires or Centimani (Cottus, Briareus, also called Ægæon, and Gyes or Gyges) ; of the one-eyed Cyclopes (Brontes, Steropes and Arges) ; and of the twelve Titans.  Greek writers give inconsistent lists of these Titans, but those most frequently mentioned are Cronus, Oceanus, Hyperion, and Iapetus, and the Titanesses Rhea, Themis, Tethys, and Mnemosyne.

**2.** Barbarous stories follow of Uranus' dealings with his descendants, and these have been influenced by myths from the Hittite culture which flourished in 1300 B.C. in Anatolia, or Asia Minor, and which probably embodied still earlier Babylonian material.  These Hittite legends reached Greece through the Phœnicians, and Hesiod (eighth century B.C.), a poet whose family had recently come from Asia Minor incorporated them in his *Theogony*.

**3. Revolt of Cronus.**  Uranus had thrown his rebellious sons the Cyclopes into Tartarus, in the Underworld, and Ge persuaded the Titans, with the exception of Oceanus, to rise against their father.  She gave Cronus, the youngest, a flint sickle, and with this he unmanned Uranus.  Drops from the wound falling upon Mother Earth, she bore the three Erinnyes or Eumenides, the furies Alecto, Tisiphone, and Megaera, and from drops that fell into the sea Aphrodite was born.

**4.** Uranus deposed, the Titans freed the Cyclopes, but Cronus, now supreme, consigned them again to Tartarus along with the Hundred-handed giants.

**5.** Cronus then married his sister Rhea, and mindful of the curse of Uranus and Ge, that he also would be deposed by his own son, he swallowed each of his children at birth.

**6. Birth of Zeus.**  But when Zeus the youngest was born, Rhea gave Cronus a stone to swallow and saved Zeus, who, according to Minoan tradition, was brought up in the Dictæan cave in Crete.  In 1900 the reputed " birth-cave " was explored by archæologists—probably the first men to enter for two thousand years, and there they found votive offerings to the god which may have been left there in the second millennium B.C.  It was here that the Curetes, Rhea's priests, clashed their weapons to drown the cries of infant Zeus, while a goat, Amalthea, acted as his nurse, and was rewarded by being placed among the stars as Capricorn, while one of her horns became the Cornucopia or horn of plenty.

**7.** Zeus when of age was counselled by Metis, the daughter of Oceanus, and with Rhea's help gave to Cronus a potion which obliged him to disgorge first the stone and then his other children, Hestia, Demeter, Hera, Hades, and Poseidon. These now joined with Zeus in a contest against their father and the other Titans, who were led by Atlas.

**8. War between Zeus and Titans.**  The war, known as the Titanomachia, was waged in Thessaly, and lasted ten years, until Ge promised Zeus victory if he would free the Cyclopes and the Hundred-handed giants from Tartarus.

**9.** The Cyclopes gave to Zeus a thunderbolt, to Hades a helmet of darkness, and to Poseidon a trident.  Thus aided, the three brothers overcame Cronus, and the Hundred-handed giants stoned the other Titans, who were defeated and consigned either to an island in the West or to Tartarus, guarded by the Hundred-handed.  Atlas was punished by being made to carry the sky on his shoulders, but the Titanesses were spared.  The supersession of the old dynasty of Titans by the new order of gods is the theme of Keats' fine poem, *Hyperion.*

**10. The Olympians.**  Zeus and his brothers now divided the government by lot.  To Hades fell the Underworld, to Poseidon the sea, and to Zeus the sky, while the earth was common to all. Zeus, the greatest of the gods, lived on the lofty summit of Mt. Olympus between Macedonia and Thessaly, along with Poseidon and their sisters, Hestia, goddess of the hearth-fire, Demeter, goddess of agriculture, and Hera, who became the wife of Zeus.  Seven other divinities, Aphrodite, Pallas Athene, Apollo, Artemis, Hephæstus, Ares, and Hermes were also numbered among the twelve great Olympians, and at a later date a new-comer, Dionysus, took the place of Hestia.

**11. The Giants' Revolt.**  But the troubles of Zeus were not over.  A post-Homeric story tells of the giants' revolt.  Twenty-four giants with serpents' tails, sons of Ge, tried to avenge the imprisonment of their brothers the Titans by attacking Olympus.  Led by Alcyoneus, they included Porphyrion, Ephialtes, Mimas, Pallas, Enceladus, and Polybutes.  Only after terrible struggles in Olympus and on earth, were the giants defeated by the gods, who were helped by a magic herb of invulnerability found by Heracles, who always dealt the giants the final blow.

**12.** The story offered some explanation of huge bones found at Trapezus and volcanic fires at neighbouring Bathos and Cumæ, the reputed sites of the battles.  The burial of Enceladus under Mt. Etna in Sicily, and of Polybutes under Nisyrus, likewise accounted for their volcanic nature.  The inclusion of Heracles before his apotheosis indicates the late origin of the legend.

**13. Ephialtes and Otus.**  Another version of the giants' revolt ascribes it to the gigantic Alceidæ, Ephialtes, and Otus, sons of Iphimedeia by Poseidon, but named after Alœus, whom their mother later married.  At the age of nine Ephialtes and Otus first captured and imprisoned Ares, god of war, and then, vowing to outrage Hera and Artemis, they piled Mount Pelion on

Ossa in their attack on Heaven. Artemis induced them to go to the island of Naxos in the hope of meeting her, but disguised as a doe she leapt between them and they killed each other in error. Hermes then released Ares, and the spirits of the Alœidæ were tied with vipers back to back to a pillar in Tartarus.

**14. Typhon.** After the destruction of the giants, Ge in revenge brought forth the gigantic monster Typhon, fathered on her by her own son Tartarus. His huge limbs ended in serpents' heads and his eyes breathed fire. When he approached Olympus the gods in terror fled to Egypt disguised as animals, Zeus as a ram, Apollo a crow, Dionysus a goat, Hera a white cow, Artemis a cat, Aphrodite a fish, Ares a boar and Hermes an ibis. Athene alone was undaunted and persuaded Zeus to attack Typhon. After a fearful struggle, in which Zeus was temporarily incapacitated and only rescued by Hermes and Pan, he destroyed Typhon with his thunderbolts and buried him under Mt. Ætna, which still breathes fire.

**15.** The flight of the gods to Egypt serves to explain the Egyptian worship of them in animal form.

**16. Prometheus and Epimetheus.** The creation of mankind is often ascribed to Prometheus, whose name signifies "forethought," as that of his brother, Epimetheus, means "afterthought." These two, unlike their brother Atlas, had supported Zeus during the war with the Titans. But Prometheus, the clever benefactor of mankind, by stealing fire from Olympus and giving it to humans, brought upon himself divine vengeance.

**17.** The infuriated Zeus ordered Hephæstus to make a lovely woman, Pandora, the Eve of Greek myth, who was endowed by the gods with baleful powers and taken by Hermes to Epimetheus. When he had married her, she opened a box from which escaped all ills which plague mankind.

**18.** Zeus punished Prometheus by chaining him to a crag in the Caucasus, where all day long an eagle tore at his liver, which grew whole again during the night. Only after many generations did Heracles, with the consent of Zeus, shoot the eagle and free the heroic rebel.

**19.** The agony of Prometheus is the theme of Æschylus' tragedy *Prometheus Bound*; the liberator is depicted in his lost drama, *Prometheus Unbound*. Shelley's dramatic poem of the same name takes Prometheus as a symbol of those who challenge tyranny for the sake of mankind.

**20. Deucalion and Pyrrha.** Deucalion, the son of Prometheus, is the Noah of Greek myth. When Zeus decided to wipe out mankind by releasing a great flood on earth, Deucalion, warned by his father, made an ark which saved both himself and his wife Pyrrha, daughter of Epimetheus. After nine days the flood subsided and the ark came to rest on Mt. Parnassus.

**21.** Deucalion and Pyrrha then earnestly prayed at the shrine of Themis that the earth might be re-peopled. Themis appeared and commanded them to throw the bones of their mother behind them. They interpreted this as meaning the rocks of mother earth and those flung by Deucalion became men, those thrown by Pyrrha women.

**22.** Their son, Hellen, was the mythical ancestor of all the Hellenes.

## THE OLYMPIAN DEITIES, 23–128.

### ZEUS, 23–28.

**23.** Zeus, identified with Jupiter by the Romans, was the greatest of the Olympian divinities, omnipotent king of gods, father of men, and possibly master even of fate. Legends of his origin and supremacy are told in para. 6–20.

**24.** Zeus was the bright god of the sky, whom the invading Achæans introduced into Greece in about 1200 B.C., together with his consort Dione. Her worship, however, did not penetrate south of Zeus' shrine at Dodona in Epirus, where the rustling of oak leaves was interpreted as the voice of the god, and Zeus found other wives. His Olympian consort was Hera, who was in origin the Great Goddess of the pre-Hellenic matriarchal society. This marriage symbolises the fusion of the Achæans with their predecessors.

**25.** He first married Metis, daughter of Oceanus and Tethys, but when she was pregnant with Athene he swallowed her and brought forth Athene from his head. His second wife was Themis, daughter of Uranus and Ge, a divinity representing order, and their children were the Horæ and the Mœræ, or Fates, though some say that the Fates were daughters of Erebus and Night, and that even Zeus was subject to them. To Zeus and Hera were born the deities Ares, Hebe, and Hephæstus, unless the latter was the parthenogenous son of Hera. Zeus was also the father of Persephone by his sister Demeter, of the Charities, or Graces, by Eurynome, and of the Muses by Mnemosyne.

**26.** By mortal women four Olympian deities were children of Zeus; Hermes the son of Maia, Apollo and Artemis the children of Leto, and Dionysus the son of Semele. Zeus loved many mortal women, and Hera was intensely jealous and revengeful towards them and their children.

**27.** Although Zeus' earliest oracle was at Dodona, he was said to dwell with his fellow divinities on the summit of Olympus in Thessaly, and was also worshipped at Olympia in Elis. The Greeks dated their era from the first festival of the Olympiad in 776 B.C.

**28.** Zeus alone used the thunderbolt and was called the thunderer. The oak, the eagle, and mountain summits were sacred to him, and his sacrifices were usually bulls, cows, and goats. His attributes were the sceptre thunderbolt, eagle, and a figure of Victory held in his hand. The Dodonean Zeus sometimes wore a wreath of oak leaves, the Olympian Zeus one of olive.

### HERA, 29–35.

**29.** Hera, identified by the Romans with Juno, was the Great Goddess of the pre-Hellenic matriarchal society, whom Zeus, supreme god of the Achæans, appropriately took to wife.

**30.** She was said to be a daughter of Cronus and Rhea and reluctantly married her brother Zeus, who in the form of a cuckoo sought her out at Cnossos in Crete, or perhaps in Argos, and their wedding night was spent on Samos. Ge gave Hera the tree with the golden apples later guarded by the Hesperides.

**31.** Though Hera was treated with reverence by the gods, she was greatly inferior in power to Zeus and must obey him, her subordination reflecting the attitude of the Achæans towards women. Only in her power to bestow the gift of prophecy was Hera equal to her husband.

**32.** She was often rebellious and jealous of Zeus' intrigues and persecuted his children by mortal women. At one time, with Poseidon and Apollo, she led a conspiracy of all the Olympians save Hestia to put Zeus in chains. He was freed by Thetis and Briareus, and punished Hera by hanging her with wrists chained to the sky and an anvil on each ankle.

**33.** Hera bore Zeus Ares and Hebe and annually renewed her virginity by bathing in a spring near Argos. As properly speaking, the only married goddess among the Olympians, she was worshipped as goddess of marriage and the birth of children, the Ilithyiæ being her daughters.

**34.** Hera was of majestic stature, and her attributes were a diadem, veil, sceptre, and peacock. Samos and Argos were seats of her worship.

**35.** Because of the judgment of Paris she was relentlessly hostile to the Trojans.

## HESTIA, 36–37.

**36.** Hestia, called Vesta by the Romans, and the eldest sister of Zeus, was a divinity brought to Greece by the invading Achæans. Though Poseidon and Apollo both sought her love, she swore by Zeus always to remain a virgin.

**37.** She was goddess of the fire on the hearth, supremely important in those days because so difficult to rekindle, and was naturally thought of as goddess of home life. Each town or city had its sacred hearth, which, like that of the home, was an asylum for suppliants. The first part of all sacrifices offered to the gods was due to Hestia, the most peaceable and kindly of all the Olympians, but at a later date Dionysus took her place among the twelve Olympian gods.

## ATHENE, 38–45.

**38.** Athene, whom the Romans identified with Minerva, was the embodiment of wisdom and power.

**39.** The Achæans brought with them a young warrior goddess, who bore the titles, Kore, Parthenos, Pallas, meaning girl, virgin, maiden, and she was in about 1700 B.C. identified with an older pre-Hellenic " Palace Goddess," worshipped in Crete. The " Palace Goddess " was one aspect of the Great Goddess, revered not for motherhood but for feminine intuition, and from pre-Hellenic times comes the name Athene.

**40.** The complex Pallas Athene was thus not only the patroness of women's arts such as weaving, protectress of agriculture, inventor of plough, rake, and ox-yoke, but also a warrior, a wise tactician, appearing in armour and wearing on her ægis or shield the head of Medusa, during the Trojan War the great protagonist of the Greeks. Legends of the birth of Pallas Athene reveal how the patriarchal Hellenes took over, and made their own a matriarchal divinity.

**41.** She was said to be a daughter of Zeus and Metis, but before her birth an oracle had foretold that she would be a girl, and that if Metis had another child it would be a son who would depose his father. Zeus therefore swallowed Metis, and later, suffered an agonising headache as he walked by Lake Triton. Hermes realising the cause, persuaded Hephæstus, or, according to some, Prometheus, to cleave open Zeus' skull, from which Athene sprang completely armed.

**42.** The centre of her cult was Attica and Athens, and legend said that when Athene and Poseidon contended for the possession of the city, the gods judged it should belong to Athene, who in planting the olive-tree had conferred the better gift.

**43.** Preferring to settle quarrels peaceably, Athene established here the court of the Areopagus, where if votes were equal, she herself gave a casting vote to free the accused, as in the trial of Orestes.

**44.** In 566 B.C. Pesistratus founded the great Panathenaic festival, celebrated every fourth year, and its magnificent procession was represented on the frieze of the Parthenon now in the British Museum, while the birth of Athene was represented in the gable at the east end of the Parthenon, and the contest with Poseidon at the west. Pesistratus also introduced a new coinage, with the head of Athene on one side, and the owl, her bird, upon the other.

**45.** Other pre-Hellenic acropolipses were sacred to Athene, and her worship flourished in Sparta, Corinth, Argos, and Thebes.

## HEPHÆSTUS, 46–56.

**46.** Hephæstus, identified with Vulcan by the Romans, was the smith-god, a superb artist in metals.

**47.** He probably originated as a pre-Hellenic fire-god near the Mt. Olympus of Lycia in Asia Minor, where gaseous vapour, seeping through the soil, ignited. The Lycians emigrated to Lemnos, where they became known as Pelasgians, and again found fire issuing from the earth, and this fire became the symbol of their god Hephæstus.

**48.** The cult of Hephæstus spread to Athens, where his artistic genius was so venerated that in the frieze of the Parthenon where two pairs of gods are given positions of honour, Zeus appears with Hera, and Hephæstus with Athene.

**49.** In Homer's time Hephæstus was one of the twelve Olympians, his exalted position reflecting the importance of the smith in a Bronze Age society when weapons and tools had magical properties. He is, like other smith-gods, represented as lame, possibly because the tribe deliberately lamed their smith to prevent his running away, possibly because work at the forge developed muscular arms but feeble legs.

**50.** According to Homer, Hephæstus was the son of Zeus and Hera, though later tradition says that he was son of the goddess alone, just as his fire sprang mysteriously from the earth.

**51.** Born lame and weak, Hephæstus was so much disliked by Hera that she threw him from Olympus, when he fell into the sea and was cared for by the sea-goddesses Thetis and Eurynome in a grotto under the sea.

**52.** After nine years Hera took him back to Olympus, where he had a fire smithy, but on one occasion he enraged Zeus by taking Hera's part, so that he was again flung from Olympus, this time by Zeus. He was a day falling, and alighted in the evening on the island of Lemnos, as described in *Paradise Lost*, Book I, lines 740–746. Later writers diverge from Homer in making this second fall the cause of Hephæstus' lameness.

**53.** He again returned to Olympus and acted as mediator between Zeus and Hera, though the gods laughed at him as he hobbled about.

**54.** His workshop in Olympus was in his own palace, and all the palaces of the gods were made by him. He also made the magnificent armour of Achilles, as is described in the eighteenth book of the *Iliad*, the necklace of Harmonia, and the bulls of Æëtes. Later accounts place his workshop on the volcanic island of Sicily, where the Cyclopes served him.

**55.** In the *Iliad*, Hephæstus' wife was Charis, but in the *Odyssey* she was Aphrodite, who was unfaithful to him with Ares. How Hephæstus caught the two together in an invisible net he had made, and exposed them to the ridicule of the gods, is told in a poem known as the " Lay of Demodocus," incorporated in the eighth book of the *Odyssey*.

**56.** Hephæstus' favourite spots on earth were Lemnos, and volcanic islands like Lipara, Hiera, Imbros, and Sicily. In Greek art he is represented as a vigorous man with a beard, carrying a hammer or similar instrument, and wearing an oval cap or chiton.

## APHRODITE, 57–63.

**57.** Aphrodite, goddess of desire, identified by the Romans with Venus, was derived from the Great Goddess of pre-Hellenic times, her counterparts being the orgiastic Ishtar of Babylon and Astarte of Syria.

**58.** She was worshipped as a fertility goddess at Paphos in Cyprus, whence Phœnicians took her worship to Cythera, an island off Southern Peloponnesus. Probably as late as the eighth century B.C. her fertility cult was established on Acrocorinthus above Corinth. There was a similar sanctuary on Mt. Eryx in Western Sicily. In these places the goddess was served by young girls, but in other Greek states her worship was more that of protectress of the city.

**59.** According to Hesiod, Aphrodite sprang from the seed of Uranus and rose naked from the sea, as in Botticelli's picture "The Birth of Venus." Rising near the island of Cythera, she passed to Paphos in Cyprus.

**60.** Homer makes Aphrodite the daughter of Zeus and Dione, and represents her as wife to Hephæstus. She was, however, unfaithful to him and in love with Ares. The amusing situation when they were caught together is described in para. 55. Harmonia was one of their children.

**61.** Aphrodite also bore sons to Poseidon, and Priapus to Dionysus, and later stories tell that she bore Hermaphroditus to Hermes, and Eros to either Hermes, Ares, or Zeus.

**62.** Her love for the mortal Adonis is the theme of Shakespeare's *Venus and Adonis*, and one of the Homeric hymns tells of her passion for Anchises, cousin of Priam, to whom she bore Æneas, the hero of Virgil's *Epic*. Unfortunately Anchises, boasting of Aphrodite's love, was struck by Zeus with a thunderbolt.

**63.** Aphrodite possessed a magic girdle which made the wearer irresistibly lovely and desirable. Doves and sparrows were sacred to her. Her most beautiful statue was that of Praxitiles in the fourth century B.C., a copy of which is preserved in the Vatican. The Venus de Milo may be seen in the Louvre.

### ARES, 64–67.

**64.** Ares, god of war, who was identified by the Romans with Mars, was a divinity of Thracian origin, whose worship spread through Macedonia to Thebes, Athens, and cities of the Peloponnesus, especially Sparta. Ares was, however, not popular with the Greeks, who disliked purposeless war and despised the Thracians for enjoying it, and their attitude is reflected in the myths of Ares.

**65.** He was the son of Zeus and Hera, and as he delighted in battle for its own sake he was hated by the other gods, except Eris, Hades, and Aphrodite, who was in love with Ares and he with her. The two were once trapped together in a net which Hephæstus had engineered, as is described in para. 55.

**66.** Ares was not always successful in battle. The Alœidæ conquered him and left him imprisoned in a brazen vessel for thirteen months, until he was released by Hermes. Athene twice vanquished him, and Heracles also defeated him and forced him to return to Olympus.

**67.** According to a late tradition, Ares once defended himself before the gods in a trial where he was accused of murdering Halirrhothius, son of Poseidon. Since he pleaded that he had saved his daughter, Alcippe, from being violated, Ares was acquitted, and the place of the trial became known as the Areopagus.

### APOLLO, 68–80.

**68.** Apollo's worship probably derived from two sources, from the Dorians, who in about 1100 B.C. entered Greece and reached as far south as Crete, and from Ionians, living in the islands and mainland of Anatolia, or Asia Minor, who became acquainted with a Hittite divinity worshipped in Lycia, and hence called Lycius.

**69.** Apollo's Dorian shrine was at Delphi, near the Castalian spring on Mt. Parnassus, where he was called the Pythian, or Loxias, the Ambiguous. His Ionian shrine was at Delos, where he was called Lycius, and Phæbus, or Shining, and where he was more closely associated with his twin-sister, Artemis.

**70.** Legends said that Apollo and Artemis were the children of Zeus and Leto, but before their birth, jealous Hera caused Leto to wander from place to place till she gave birth to Artemis under a palm-tree at Ortygia, and to Apollo beside a palm in the isle of Delos.

**71.** This story is told in the Delian Homeric Hymn of 700 B.C., while the Delphic Hymn tells how Apollo, soon after his birth, sought out the she-dragon Python, on Mt. Parnassus, and there killed her, taking over the Oracle of Earth at Delphi, where his priestess the Pythoness became the mouthpiece of his oracles, which were imparted in hexameter verse. Apollo was commanded by Zeus to visit the Vale of Tempe for purification, and to preside over the Pythian games held in Python's honour.

**72.** Hera, still implacable, sent the giant Tityus to violate Leto, as she came with Artemis to Delphi, though some say that it was Artemis who was attacked, but the giant was killed by the arrows of Apollo and Artemis.

**73.** Apollo was not always subservient to Zeus. He once, with Hera, Poseidon, and other Olympians, bound Zeus with chains and was punished by being sent with Poseidon as bondman to King Laomedan, where by playing the lyre and tending the flocks he helped Poseidon to build the walls of Troy. On another occasion, furious that Zeus had slain his son Asclepius, Apollo retaliated by killing the Cyclopes. Zeus now sent him to serve King Admetus of Pheræ in Thessaly, and again he kept flocks. He also helped Admetus to win his bride Alcestis and even ensured that the king should be restored to life if one of his family would die in his stead.

**74.** Apollo loved many mortal women, including Cyrene, mother of Aristæus, Coronis, mother of Asclepius, the healer, and Aria, mother of Miletus. The nymph Dryope was also seduced by Apollo, but when he pursued the nymph Daphne she cried for help and was turned into a laurel, henceforth Apollo's tree; and the nymph Marpessa preferred his rival, Idas. Apollo loved Cassandra, daughter of Priam, and conferred on her the gift of prophecy, but, when she disappointed him, decreed that she should never be believed. Hyacinthus, a Spartan prince, in origin an earth deity, was beloved by Apollo, and when he was killed by the god's jealous rival, Zephyrus, the hyacinth flower sprang from his blood.

**75.** Apollo had varied characteristics. He was destroyer, as his arrows indicated, and sudden deaths were ascribed to him. It was he who sent plagues among the Greeks besieging Troy. But he was also protector, warding off evil, as his fatherhood of Asclepius indicated. He protected flocks and cattle, as his service to Laomedan and Admetus showed, and later writers particularly stressed this aspect.

**76.** As god of prophecy, Apollo could communicate the gift to gods and mortals, and of all the centres of his worship Delphi was the most famous. The shrine had probably been established by pre-Hellenic people, worshipping Mother Earth, and had been seized by invading Hellenes who killed Python the oracular serpent, took over the oracles in the name of their own Apollo, and held funeral games in honour of Python to placate the original inhabitants. The shrine was supposed to contain the Omphalos, or navel stone of earth, and a chasm which occasionally gave out intoxicating vapours. Over this Apollo's priestess, Pythia, sat on a tripod, and uttered his oracle after chewing intoxicating laurel leaf. She was regarded as the mystical bride of the god.

77. As god of song and music Apollo appears in the *Iliad* delighting immortals. He was said to have received the lyre from Hermes, and its seven strings were connected with the seven Greek vowels. In music none surpassed Apollo, not even Pan, nor Marsyas, the satyr who had found Athene's discarded flute which played by itself. Defeated in a contest, Marsyas was flayed alive by the victorious god. Apollo, as leader of the Muses, was called Musagetes. He valued order and moderation in all things, his favourite maxims being " Nothing in Excess," and " Know thyself."

78. Apollo also delighted in the foundation of towns, and his oracle was always consulted before a town was founded.

79. In later writers he was identified with the sun god, the result of Egyptian influence, for in Homer, Helios, god of the sun, is completely distinct from Apollo.

80. The worship of Apollo, typical of all that is most radiant in the Greek mind, has no counterpart in the religion of Rome. Not till the end of the third century B.C. did the Romans adopt his religion from the Greeks.

## ARTEMIS, 81–89.

81. Artemis, whose Roman counterpart was Diana, had two chief aspects. One was as " Mistress of Animals," a goddess of the chase, worshipped in primitive matriarchal society, and probably owing something to the Britomartis and Dictynna, worshipped as huntresses in Crete. The other, originating in Asia Minor, was of the age-old mother-goddess, and is most clearly seen in Artemis Ephesia, who was worshipped as an orgiastic goddess.

82. Legends of the birth of Artemis are told in the story of Apollo, and as his sister she shared many of his characteristics. She carried bow and arrows, made for her by Hephæstus, and had power to send plague and sudden death, as when she and Apollo killed the children of Niobe. She was also protectress of children and young animals and goddess of the chase.

83. Like Apollo, Artemis was unmarried, and later writers stressed that she was a maiden goddess and severely punished any lapses. She changed Actæon to a stag to be torn to pieces by his own hounds, only because he had seen her bathing, and some traditions say that she killed Orion because of his unchastity. The nymph Callisto, who had been seduced by Zeus, was in the form of a bear hunted down by the hounds of Artemis.

84. When Apollo was identified with the Sun, Artemis was identified with Selene, the Moon.

85. The Arcadian Artemis, early worshipped in Arcadia as a huntress among the nymphs, was unconnected with Apollo.

86. Another aspect of the goddess was as the fierce Artemis of Tauris, to whom all strangers were sacrificed. Iphigeneia was once her priestess, and she and Orestes took her image to Brauron in Attica, whence the goddess was called Brauronia. This Brauronian Artemis was worshipped in Athens, and also in Sparta, where boys were scourged at her altar until they sprinkled it with their blood.

87. Artemis as an orgiastic goddess had her chief centre in Ephesus, with its immensely wealthy temple, and it was this Artemis that St. Paul encountered. (See Acts of the Apostles, Ch. XIX.)

88. Though usually regarded as a rural divinity, Artemis was supreme in three great cities, in Ephesus, in Marseilles, to which Ionian Greeks from Asia Minor took her cult between 600 and 540 B.C., and in Syracuse, where she was known as Artemis Arethusa.

89. The goddess was often portrayed as a huntress, as in the so-called Diana of Versailles, now in the Louvre. As huntress her chlamys reached only to the knees, and she carried a bow, quiver, and arrows, or a spear, and was accompanied with stags or dogs. As Selene, she wore a long robe and veil, and a crescent moon on her forehead.

## HERMES, 90–98.

90. Hermes, whom the Romans called Mercurius, was originally one of the gods of the pre-Hellenic people, the divinity dwelling in the cairn, or " herma," set up by shepherds as a landmark in wild country, and so developing as a protector against predatory animals and a guide to travellers. This Hermes was identified with a similar divinity worshipped in Minoan Crete, a " Master of Animals," a son or lover of the Great Goddess, and therefore a god of fertility.

91. Legends said that Hermes was the son of Zeus and Maia, an embodiment of the Great Goddess, and a daughter of Atlas, whence Hermes' name Atlantiades.

92. The " Hymn to Hermes " of 600 B.C. tells that he was born in a cavern on Mt. Cyllene in Arcadia (from which he was sometimes called Cyllenius), and that he grew with amazing rapidity. When only a few hours old he went to Pieria and stole some of the oxen of Apollo, which he drove to Pylos, and then, returning to Cyllene, he invented the lyre by stringing a tortoise-shell with cow-gut. Apollo, on discovering the thief, accused him to Zeus, who ordered Hermes to restore the oxen. But when Apollo heard the lyre he was delighted, took it in exchange for the oxen, and became the friend of Hermes, leading him back to Zeus.

93. Zeus gave to Hermes supreme power over animals and appointed him his herald, Hermes also acted as herald to Hades, conducting shades to the underworld. (See Virgil's *Æneid*, Bk. IV, ll. 242 *sqq*.) As herald he was regarded as god of eloquence, whence St. Paul, " the chief speaker," was mistaken for him in Lystra of Asia Minor. (See Acts of the Apostles, Ch. XIV.) Heralds promote peace and therefore trade. Thus Hermes came to be looked on as god of peaceable commerce.

94. He was also god of prudence and cunning, and even of theft, and was said to have helped the Fates in composing the alphabet. Many inventions ascribed to Hermes, such as weights and measures, the musical scale, astronomy, olive-culture, and the arts of boxing and gymnastics, were pre-Hellenic, and the stories of his childhood may indicate how the Hellenes took over these arts in the name of their god Apollo. As a god of fertility and luck, Hermes presided over games of dice.

95. He played a part in such incidents as the rescue of Dionysus, the punishment of Ixion, the selling of Heracles to Omphale, the judgment of Paris, and the leading of Priam to Achilles, but his most famous exploit was perhaps the slaying of Argus, the hundred-eyed giant sent by Hera to watch Io.

96. Hermes had several sons, including Echion, herald to the Argonauts, Autolycus the thief, his son by Chione, and Daphnis.

97. His worship flourished in Arcadia, where he was to be found with Pan and the muses. It spread to Athens, and he became one of the best loved of the Olympians.

98. Hermes' attributes were the Petasus, a travelling-hat, in later time adorned with wings, the Alipes, or winged-sandals, and the Caduceus, or heralds' staff, whose white ribbons were later mistaken for serpents because he was herald to Hades. Sacred to Hermes were the tortoise, the palm-tree, the number four, and some kinds of fish, and his sacrifices were incense, honey, cakes, pigs, lambs, and kids.

## POSEIDON, 99–109.

**99.** Poseidon, identified by the Romans with Neptune, derived from a god worshipped by the earliest Aryan invaders of Greece, the Minyans and Ionians, who entered the country in about 2000 B.C. It was with the aid of horses and wheeled vehicles that they quickly overcame any resistance, and their god Poseidon was often thought of as the horse whose hooves thunder on the earth. He is constantly spoken of in Homer as "earth-shaker," while many legends show him in equine guise. It is possible that he was originally thought of as a sky-god, a thunderer, and the mate of an earth-goddess who later developed as Demeter.

**100.** But when in about 1450 B.C., another wave of invading Aryans, the Achæans, entered Greece, they also brought their sky-god, a thunderer called Zeus, possibly in origin identical with Poseidon, and the latter, recognised as an older brother of Zeus, came to be revered as a sea-divinity, for the Minyans were, by now, expert in navigation.

**101.** According to legend, Poseidon was the eldest son of Cronus and Rhea, and when, after the deposition of Cronus, he and his brothers Zeus and Hades cast lots for sovereignty, the sea became Poseidon's share. He dwelt in an under-water palace near Ægæ in Eubœa, which is described in the beginning of the 13th book of the *Iliad*, and here he kept his horses with brazen hooves and golden manes, and when they drew his chariot over the sea it became tranquil.

**102.** He was said to have created the horse when disputing with Athene for the possession of Athens, and he taught men how to bridle horses. He was the protector of horse-races, and horse and chariot races were held in his honour on the Corinthian isthmus.

**103.** In the form of a horse he raped his sister Demeter, when she was disguised as a mare. Their offspring were the horse Arion and the nymph Despœna, and some say Persephone also, though according to another version Demeter was searching for Persephone, her daughter by Zeus, at the time of the rape.

**104.** Poseidon, though equal to Zeus in dignity, was less powerful and resented the pride of his younger brother. He once joined with Hera, Apollo, and other Olympians, to put Zeus in chains, and he and Apollo were punished by being sent as bondsmen to Laomedan. Here Poseidon built the walls of Troy, hence called Neptunia Pergama. When Laomedan refused the wages due, Poseidon sent a sea-monster, which would have devoured the king's daughter Hesione if she had not been rescued by Heracles. In the Trojan War, Poseidon naturally sided with the Greeks, though he became hostile to Odysseus after he had blinded Polyphemus, son of the god.

**105.** Poseidon desired earthly kingdoms, his attempts to take control possibly being political myths. He disputed with Athene for the possession of Athens, but she was awarded the city because her planting of the olive was judged the better gift. When these divinities, however, disputed the possession of Trœzen, Zeus judged they should share it equally. In his claim for Corinth, Poseidon received only the isthmus, where the quadrennial Isthmian games were held in his honour, while the Areopagus was awarded to Helios.

**106.** Poseidon first intended to marry Thetis, but when it was prophesied that her son would be greater than his father he paid court to Amphitrite, daughter of Nereus. Only after Delphinos had most eloquently pleaded his suit did Amphitrite accept Poseidon, who in gratitude placed Delphinos' image among the stars, as the Dolphin. Amphitrites' reluctance, paralleled by Hera's shrinking from Zeus, and Persephone's from Hades, probably represents the resistance of an early matriarchal society to a patriarchal system.

**107.** Poseidon's son by Amphitrite was Triton, but he had many more children by other divinities and mortals.

**108.** One of them, Scylla, was particularly hateful to Amphitrite, who is said to have turned her into a monster with six barking heads and twelve feet. Poseidon also loved the nymph Tyro, mother of his children Pelias and Neleus, and Æthra, the mother of Theseus. His offspring by Medusa were Chrysaor and Pegasus.

**109.** Sacrifices to Poseidon were usually black-and-white bulls. His symbol of power was the trident, possibly in origin a thunderbolt, by means of which he could shake the earth or subdue the waves, and which became in Hellenistic and Roman times a symbol of sea-power, as it is today. Poseidon's other attributes were the horse and the dolphin, and he was usually represented as accompanied by Amphitrite, Triton, Nereids, and dolphins.

## DEMETER, 110–116.

**110.** Demeter, counterpart of the Roman Ceres, was probably in origin a divinity of the Minyans, who entered Greece in about 200 B.C., and who revered her as an earth-goddess, a mate to their sky-god, who later developed as Poseidon. Both these divinities could take the form of a horse. The worship of this earth-goddess then merged with that of the Great Goddess of the pre-Hellenic matriarchal society, and Demeter was worshipped as the corn-goddess.

**111.** She was daughter to Cronus and Rhea, and sister to Zeus, by whom she became the mother of Persephone, or Core, the maiden, herself another aspect of the goddess. According to the Homeric Hymn of the seventh century B.C., Hades asked Zeus' permission to marry Persephone, and as he received no downright refusal was emboldened to carry off the maiden as she was gathering flowers. Demeter wandered the earth searching for her daughter until Helios told her what Hades had done. She then shunned Olympus and wandered still on earth, which she forbad to bring forth fruit. Zeus finally told Demeter that her daughter might return, provided she had eaten nothing in the Underworld, and he sent Hermes to escort her back. Hades agreed to let Persephone go, but gave her a pomegranate to eat, and it was at last agreed that she should spend a third of the year with him in Hades, as Queen of the Underworld, and the rest of the year with Demeter, who once more allowed the earth to bear its fruit.

**112.** Inconsistent accounts are given of the place of the rape. Demeter's priests said it was Eleusis, about twelve miles from Athens, the Latin poets Enna in Sicily, where, according to Ovid, Persephone was gathering poppies. Some say it was Ascalaphus who saw Persephone take food in the Underworld and that because he revealed this, he was turned by Demeter into an owl.

**113.** It is said that during her wanderings, Demeter punished those, like Abas, son of Celeus, who were unkind to her, but showered blessings on those like Celeus himself and his son Triptolemus who received her hospitably in Eleusis and whom she taught the art of agriculture.

**114.** The Eleusinian Festival in honour of Demeter and Persephone was probably fully established in Athens by Pesistratus at the end of the sixth century B.C., probably about the time when the cult of Dionysus was instituted. There was an annual procession from Eleusis to Athens, and those who spoke Greek could be initiated into the final rite of the mysteries. The Thesmophoria, celebrating the foundation of laws, was also held in the goddesses' honour, in Athens and in other parts of Greece.

**115.** The myth originated in the most primitive rites of seed time and harvest at a time when only women practised the arts of agriculture. Persephone, representing the vegetation which dies down during the winter, had her counterpart in the primitive corn-puppet which was buried in winter to be dug up again sprouting in spring, and later writers saw the story as an expression of the death of the body and the immortality of the soul.

116. In art Demeter was represented with a garland of corn or a ribbon, and holding a sceptre, corn ears, or a poppy, and sometimes a torch and basket. Pigs were sacred to her. There is in the British Museum a fine statue of Demeter of about 330 B.C., which was found at Cnidos in Asia Minor.

## DIONYSUS, 117–128.

117. Dionysus, god of wine, also called Bacchus by both Greeks and Romans, was not in Homer's time one of the aristocratic Olympian deities, but a god worshipped by humble folk whom wandering bands of ecstatic worshippers brought into Greece from Thrace in the eighth century B.C. The cult, which spread through Macedonia and Thessaly, to Bœotia, Delphi, Athens, and beyond, was characterised by a mystic frenzy when the worshippers, intoxicated with wine, believed themselves to be at one with Dionysus or Bacchus, sometimes called Bromius "the Boisterous." The men who followed him were known as Bacchoi, the women Bacchæ, or Bacchantes or Mænads, or in Athens and Delphi, Thyiads.

118. The immense popularity of the Dionysian cult, especially with women, indicates that among the recently civilised Greeks there was a longing for a more instinctive and impulsive life, valuing enthusiasm rather than prudence, and during the sixth century certain wise statesmen introduced the new cult among the other state religions. Dyonisiac festivals were established in Corinth, Sicyon, Delphi, and Athens. In Delphi the sepulchre of Bacchus was placed near the very tripod of Pythia, and his temple, a theatre, was at the highest point of the sacred precinct. In Athens Pesistratus founded the Dionysia and the Panathenaic Games at about the same time, and a theatre was set up where the worshippers of Bacchus enacted the first primitive drama. In the fifth century, when the Parthenon was finished, the new god had been accepted among the twelve Olympians taking the place of Hestia. This change incidentally secured a majority of gods over goddesses on Mt. Olympus, and is perhaps evidence of a society becoming increasingly patriarchal.

119. Legends said that Dionysus was the son of Semele by Zeus, who visited his beloved disguised as a mortal. When Semele was six months with child, jealous Hera, disguised as an old woman, persuaded her to ask her mysterious lover to appear in his true form. Unwillingly Zeus consented, " hapless Semele " was consumed by fire, and her unborn child sewn up in Zeus' thigh to be delivered three months later as Dionysus.

120. The child was first entrusted to Athamas and Ino of Bœotia, and reared in the women's quarters disguised as a girl, until Hera undeceived punished Athamas with madness so that he killed his own son. Hermes then took Dionysus to Mt. Nysa, where the nymphs cared for him, feeding him with honey, and where he first invented wine. Zeus later placed the images of the nymphs among the stars as Hyades.

121. When Dionysus had grown to manhood Hera drove him mad and he wandered through the world with his old tutor Silenus and a wild rout of Satyrs and Mænads. He went through Egypt, Syria, and Asia to India, overcoming military opposition, teaching the culture of the vine, founding cities and laws. He returned to Europe through Phrygia and then invaded Thrace.

122. Here Lycurgus, King of the Edones, opposed his worship, but, maddened by Rhea, he killed and mutilated his own son, and the Edones caused him to be torn to death by horses.

123. Dionysus now proceeded to Bœotia, and in Thebes was resisted by King Pentheus. But Pentheus was also driven mad and torn to pieces by the Mænads or Bacchæ, among whom were his own mother Agave and her two sisters, for in their frenzy they believed him to be a wild beast. This is the legend used by Euripides in his play, *The Bacchæ.*

124. Dionysus also visited the islands of the Adriatic. At Icaria he hired a ship bound for Naxos, but the sailors were Tyrrhenian pirates and steered towards Asia, intending to sell Dionysus into slavery. The god, however, turned himself into a lion and the oars into serpents. Ivy grew round the ship and flutes were heard. The terrified pirates, leaping overboard, were transformed to dolphins. Arrived at Naxos, Dionysus found Ariadne deserted by Theseus and at once married her. A Renaissance conception of this incident can be seen in Titian's picture " Bacchus and Ariadne " in the National Gallery, or in Tintoretto's picture in the Doge's Palace in Venice.

125. At Argos people refused at first to accept Dionysus, but when the women had been maddened by him, they admitted he was a god.

126. His worship established throughout the world, Dionysus was received into Olympus as one of the twelve great divinities, taking the place of Hestia. He brought Semele there from the Underworld, and she was henceforth known as Thyone.

127. Dionysus was worshipped as god of the vital and intoxicating powers of nature, and also, because of his close connection with tillage and early civilisation, as a law-giver. He was also god of tragic art. In art he was represented as young, handsome, and athletic, but later as slightly effeminate. He was accompanied with a wild crowd of Satyrs, and Mænads, the latter frenzied with wine and mystic exaltation, and carrying cymbals, swords, serpents, or the Thyrsus, a wand wreathed with ivy and crowned with a fir-cone. The worship of Dionysus appealed strongly to women, and many would spend the whole night on the mountain in ecstatic dancing and tearing wild animals to pieces. Sacred to the god were the ivy, laurel, and asphodel, and the dolphin, serpent, tiger, lynx, panther, and ass. His sacrifice was usually a goat or ass.

128. The myths of Dionysus are evidence that there was at first much opposition to the ritual use of wine, and the frenzy it engendered. The earlier drink of the Greeks had been a kind of beer flavoured with ivy and mead, and mead was the drink of Homer's Olympians. Wine was not invented by the Greeks, but probably first imported by them from Crete, whither vine culture had probably spread from Mt. Nysa in Libya. The use of wine spread from Thrace to Athens and other civilised cities. The story of Dionysus' wanderings in India represents the spread of vine culture there.

## PERSEUS, 129–144.

129. The ancient folk-tale of Perseus, grandson of Acrisius, has been told by Kingsley in *The Heroes.*

130. Acrisius and Prœtus, the twin sons of Abas, King of Argos, eventually agreed, after much discussion, to divide their inheritance. Prœtus became ruler of Tiryns, whose massive walls he built by the aid of the Cyclopes, while Acrisius ruled uneasily in Argos, for an oracle had declared that he would be killed by a son born to his daughter Danaë.

131. To prevent this disaster, Acrisius had Danaë immured in a brazen dungeon or tower, with doors of brass, but all in vain, for Zeus visited her in a shower of gold, and she became the mother of Perseus.

132. Not daring to kill Danaë, Acrisius set mother and son adrift on the sea in a chest, which floated to the isle of Seriphos, one of the Cyclades. Here it was found by the sailor Dictys, and he took Danaë and her son to the king Polydectes, who received them hospitably.

133. When Perseus was grown to manhood, however, Polydectes sought to marry Danaë and

seized a pretext to send Perseus off to fetch the head of the Gorgon Medusa.

134. Medusa and her sister Gorgons, Stheno and Euryale, who were the daughters of Phorcys and Ceto, and dwelt in Libya, had once been beautiful. But Medusa lay with Poseidon in one of the temples of Athene, and the enraged goddess turned her into a winged monster with brazen claws and serpent hair, so hideous that she turned to stone all who looked upon her.

135. Athene, eager to help Perseus, against her enemy, gave him a polished shield whereby he might see Medusa only in reflection. Hermes provided him with a sickle, and told him how to procure winged sandals, a magic wallet in which to carry the decapitated head, and Hades' helmet of invisibility.

136. On Hermes' advice Perseus visited the Gorgons' sisters, the Grææ, three old women grey from birth who had only one eye and one tooth between them, and these they passed from one to another. Perseus found them on Mt. Atlas and, by snatching the eye and tooth, forced the Grææ to tell him where he could find the sandals, wallet, and helmet. They directed him to the Stygian nymphs, who gave him what he needed.

137. Flying westward to the land of the Hyperboreans, Perseus found the Gorgons asleep. He successfully beheaded Medusa and was astonished to see, springing fully grown from her body, the winged horse Pegasus and the warrior Chrysaor, both of whom had been begotten on her by Poseidon.

138. Though pursued by Stheno and Euryale, Perseus in Hades' helmet escaped to the south. Some say that he petrified the Titan Atlas by showing him the Gorgon's head and then flew over Æthiopia.

139. Here he saw, chained naked to a rock on the sea coast, the lovely Andromeda, and at once fell in love with her. He learned the cause of her plight from her parents, Cepheus, King of Æthiopia, and his wife Cassiopeia. The latter had rashly boasted that Andromeda was more beautiful than the Nereids, and when they had complained of this to Poseidon, the sea god had sent a monster to lay waste the country. Only by the sacrifice of Andromeda, said the oracle of Ammon, could the land be delivered.

140. Perseus promptly offered to rescue the maiden, provided she would become his wife, but, after he had slain the monster, Cepheus and Cassiopeia were reluctant to keep their promise, for they said Andromeda had already been contracted to another. Their protégé and his followers, arriving at the wedding, attempted to seize the bride, but were easily circumvented by Perseus, who showed them Medusa's head and turned them all to stone. Poseidon set the images of Cepheus and Cassiopeia among the stars, the latter in a humiliating position.

141. Perseus, with Andromeda, now hastened to Seriphos, where he found that Danaë and Dictys had been obliged to take refuge in a temple, but going to Polydectes' palace, he exposed the Gorgon's head and turned the king and all his followers to stone. He then gave the head to Athene, who set it in her ægis, and Hermes restored Perseus' accoutrements to the Stygian nymphs.

142. After making Dictys King of Seriphos, Perseus, taking with him Danaë and Andromeda, returned to Argos, and Acrisius, mindful of the oracle, fled to Larissa, in vain, however, for Perseus, visiting Larissa and taking part in public games, accidentally killed his grandfather by a throw of the discus.

143. Grieved by this mishap, Perseus arranged to exchange kingdoms with his cousin Megapenthes, the son of Prœtus, who now moved to Argos while Perseus became King of Tiryns. He also founded Mycenæ, which, like Tiryns itself had mighty fortifications built by the Cyclopes.

144. The massive remains of both cities have been investigated by Schliemann and other archæologists, and remain as some of the most interesting antiquities in all Greece.

## BELLEROPHON, 145–150.

145. The story of Bellerophon is told by William Morris in *The Earthly Paradise.*

146. Bellerophon, the son of Glaucus, King of Corinth, having killed one Bellerus, fled to Prœtus, King of Tiryns. Unfortunately Prœtus' wife, Anteia, fell in love with the young man, and when he refused her advances falsely accused him to her husband of trying to seduce her. Prœtus, reluctant to kill a guest, sent him instead to Anteia's father, Iobates, King of Lycia, carrying a letter which requested that the bearer be put to death.

147. Iobates also shrank from killing a guest and decided to send Bellerophon against the Chimæra, a fire-breathing monster with a lion's head, goat's body, and serpent's tail, said to be the offspring of Echidne and Typhon, which was now ravaging Lycia.

148. Bellerophon was advised to catch the winged horse Pegasus, sprung from Medusa. Pegasus, by striking his hoof on the earth of Mt. Helicon, had created the spring of Hippocrene, sacred to the Muses, and he was found by Bellerophon at another of his fountains, that of Pirene in the Acropolis of Corinth. The hero flung over the horse's head a golden bridle, which Athene had given him, and astride his flying steed he easily shot the Chimæra with his arrows.

149. The frustrated Iobates now sent Bellerophon against the Amazons, and, when the hero again returned victorious, planted an ambush of guards against his arrival. Bellerophon slew them all, and Iobates, convinced at last that there had been some mistake, produced Prœtus' letter and learned the truth. He gave his guest his daughter in marriage and made him his heir.

150. Later tradition records that Bellerophon presumptuously tried to soar to Olympus mounted on Pegasus, but that Zeus sent a gadfly which stung the horse and caused him to throw his rider to earth. Bellerophon ended his days in wretchedness, but Pegasus gained Olympus.

## JASON AND THE ARGONAUTS, 151–163.

151. The story of Jason and the Argonauts was already popular in Homer's day, and has more recently been told by Kingsley in *The Heroes,* and by William Morris in *The Life and Death of Jason.*

152. Jason's father Æson, the rightful King of Iolcus, had been deprived of his kingdom by his two half-brothers, Pelias and Neleus. The mother of all three was Tyro, who, seduced by Poseidon, bore him the twins Pelias and Neleus. She exposed the twins, but they were reared by a horse-herd, and when Tyro later married Cretheus, founder and King of Iolcus, they were adopted by him.

153. Tyro's son by Cretheus was Æson, but on Cretheus' death Pelias imprisoned Æson, expelled Neleus, and made himself supreme. The life of Æson's infant son Jason was saved only because he was smuggled out of Iolcus and entrusted to the care of Cheiron, the Centaur.

154. When a young man, Jason returned to Iolcus, fearlessly demanding his kingdom, and

Pelias, to be rid of him, asked him to go to Colchis to fetch the golden fleece. This, the fleece of the ram on which Phrixus had escaped, and which he had given to King Æëtes of Colchis, was now hanging on an oak-tree in the grove of Ares, guarded night and day by a sleepless dragon.

155. Jason welcomed the enterprise and commanded Argus, the Thespian to build him a fifty-oared ship called the *Argo*, into whose prow Athene herself fitted an oracular beam. Most of the heroes of the day flocked to join Jason, and his crew included the Dioscuri, Castor and Polydeuces, Heracles, and Orpheus the musician.

156. They met many adventures on the way. After lingering too long with the women of Lemnos, they slipped through the Hellespont and reached Mysia. Here Hylas, the squire of Heracles, while fetching water was stolen away by the Naiads, leaving nothing but an empty pitcher, and Heracles left the *Argo* in a vain search for him.

157. On the island of Bebrycos the Argonauts were met by its king, Amycus, son of Poseidon, and a renowned boxer, who contrived to kill all strangers by challenging them to a boxing match, but Polydeuces met the challenge and killed the bully. In Thrace they freed the blind king and prophet Phineus from a plague of Harpies, and in gratitude he advised Jason how to navigate the Bosphorus. At its entrance were the perilous floating islands, the Symplegades. It is possible that rumours of icebergs gave rise to the fable of these islands, which clashed together and crushed any ship which attempted to pass between them. But Jason, following the advice of Phineus, released a dove, and the *Argo* slipped between the islands as they recoiled. Henceforth they remained fixed. After overcoming other dangers, the Argonauts at last reached the River Phasis and Colchis.

158. Here Æëtes promised that he would give Jason the fleece if he could yoke together two fire-breathing bulls with brazen feet, the work of Hephæstus, plough the field of Ares, and sow it with the dragon's teeth left over by Cadmus at Thebes. It was Medea who enabled Jason to perform this terrible task. This sorceress princess, the daughter of Æëtes by his first wife, fell instantly in love with Jason and promised to help him if he would swear by all the gods to marry her and be faithful. She gave him a fire-resisting lotion and he completed the task. Then when Æëtes failed to keep his promise Medea charmed the dragon to sleep while Jason took down the fleece and they fled together in the *Argo*.

159. The furious Æëtes pursued them, but Medea ruthlessly murdered the young half-brother Absyrtus she had brought with her, and cut him into pieces which she dropped one by one over the side of the boat, Æëtes, stopping to collect the fragments for burial, soon lost sight of the fugitives.

160. There are many conflicting accounts of the *Argo*'s return journey, but none of them is feasible, for the Greek knowledge of geography was at that time very limited. Tradition said that the ship reached the Western Mediterranean and visited the island of Circe, who purified Jason and Medea of murder.

161. On their return to Iolcus they found that Pelias had forced Æson to take his life, though one tradition mentioned by Ovid and by Shakespeare in *The Merchant of Venice*, says that he was renewed to youthful vigour by Medea. All agree that Medea took a terrible revenge on Pelias. She persuaded his daughters, with the exception of Alcestis, to cut their father up and boil him in a cauldron, promising falsely that this would rejuvenate him. Pelias' son Acastus, horrified at the murder, then expelled Jason and Medea and they repaired to Corinth.

162. For many years they lived happily until they were involved in the final tragedy, dramatised by Euripides in his *Medea*. Jason deserted

Medea for Glauce, also called Creusa, daughter of Creon, and the sorceress sent the young bride a garment which consumed her in flames, set fire to the palace, and involved Creon also in death. Some say that Medea also killed her own children by Jason.

163. Medea then escaped in a chariot drawn by winged serpents and took refuge with Ægeus of Athens, who married her. But on Theseus' arrival in the city, Medea departed and after many wanderings became an immortal. Some say that Jason took his own life; others that he was mercifully killed when the poop of his own ship *Argo* fell upon him.

## HERACLES, 164–202.

164. Heracles, the most famous of the Greek heroes, was the son of Alcmene by Zeus.

165. Alcmene's brothers having been killed by the Taphians, she would not consummate her marriage with her husband Amphitrion, son of Alcæus, until he had avenged their death. While Amphitrion was away from Thebes fighting the Taphians, Zeus visited Alcmene in her husband's likeness and told her how he had been victorious. The true Amphitrion returned the following day, and the ensuing confusion is the theme of comedies by Plautus, Molière, and Dryden.

166. Nine months later Zeus boasted that he was about to become the father of a son who would be called Heracles, or glory of Hera, and who would be ruler of the house of Perseus. The jealous Hera exacted from him a promise that any son born that day to the house of Perseus should be king. She then hastened the birth of Eurystheus, who was a grandson of Perseus, and delayed that of Heracles. Alcmene bore two children, Heracles, son of Zeus, and Iphicles, Amphitrion's son who was a night younger. Alcmene, fearing Hera, exposed Heracles, but Hera in error nursed him, thus conferring on him immortality.

167. Returned to Alcmene, Heracles prospered, and when still in his cradle, strangled with either hand two terrible snakes which Hera had sent to destroy him. In his youth he was taught how to drive the chariot by Amphitrion, fighting by Castor, how to sing and play the lyre by Eumolpus, wrestling by Autolycus, and archery by Eurytus. Linus, who was once teaching him to play the lyre, censured him, and Heracles then promptly killed his teacher with his own lyre, so Amphitrion sent him away to keep cattle.

168. In his eighteenth year he set out to attack the lion of Mt. Cithæron which was destroying the herds of both Amphitrion and his neighbour Thespius. The chase lasted fifty days, and Thespius, who was Heracles' host all this time; rewarded him by giving up his fifty daughters to him. Heracles killed the lion with a wild-olive club and made himself a garment of the pelt, with the head as helmet, though some say that he wore the skin of the Nemean lion.

169. On his return to Thebes, Heracles challenged the Minyan heralds from Orchomenus, who had come to collect tribute of cattle, and then led a victorious campaign against the Minyans in which his foster-father Amphitrion was killed.

170. Heracles was rewarded by Creon King of Thebes, who gave him his eldest daughter, Megara or Megera, in marriage, and Heracles became by her the father of several children. Creon's youngest daughter was married to Iphicles.

171. But Hera now visited Heracles with madness, so that he killed his own children and two of Iphicles'. When he recovered his reason he went, after purification, to consult the oracle at Delphi. The Pythia, calling him, for the first time, Heracles, advised him to go to Tiryns and there serve Eurystheus King of Argos for twelve years, doing whatever he was commanded. At the end of that time immortality would be conferred on him.

172. Most reluctantly Heracles set out. The gods gave him gifts of armour, but he relied on his bow and arrows and on the olive clubs which he cut for himself. His nephew Iolaus, oldest son of Iphicles, accompanied him as his faithful charioteer and companion. Thus supported, Heracles embarked on the twelve gigantic tasks imposed on him by Eurystheus.

### The Twelve Labours of Heracles.

173. The First Labour was to bring back the skin of the Nemean or Cleonæan lion, an enormous creature, said to be the offspring of Typhon and Echidne, which was devastating the valley of Nemea near Cleonæ. As the pelt could not be pierced by any weapon, Heracles strangled the lion with his hands. He rededicated the Nemean games to Zeus and took the lion's carcase back to Tiryns, where he flayed it with its own claws. Some say that he wore the pelt as his armour. Eurystheus was so terrified that he now took refuge in a brazen urn below the earth whenever Heracles approached.

174. The Second Labour was to kill the Lernean Hydra, another monster which was said to be the offspring of Echidne by Typhon, and which Hera brought up. It lived at the sevenfold source of the River Amymone and haunted the neighbouring swamp of Lerna. It had a dog-like body and nine snaky heads, one of them immortal. As soon as Heracles struck off one head with his club, two grew in its place, whilst an enormous crab seized the hero's foot. He crushed the crab and called on Iolaus to burn the necks of the eight heads as he crushed them. The immortal head was buried and Heracles poisoned his arrows in the monster's gall, so that henceforth any wound they caused was fatal. Hera placed the image of the crab among the signs of the zodiac.

175. The Third Labour was to capture alive the Ceryneian Hind. This creature had brazen feet and golden antlers, and was therefore often called a stag. Heracles pursued it tirelessly for a year, and eventually shot an arrow which pinned the forelegs together without causing bloodshed. He then carried the creature back on his shoulders.

176. The Fourth Labour was to capture alive the Erymanthian boar, which had come down from Mt. Erymanthus to ravage Psophis. During his journey Heracles was entertained by the Centaur Pholus, who had a cask of wine given by Dionysus. When this was opened, other Centaurs besieged the cave. Repulsed by Heracles, some of them fled to the Centaur Cheiron. Heracles accidentally wounded Cheiron, who was an old friend, with one of his poisoned arrows. Cheiron, an immortal, could not die, although he now longed to do so, and was relieved from pain only when he later surrendered his immortality to Prometheus. Heracles continued his pursuit of the boar, drove it into a snow-drift, bound it with chains, and carried it to Eurystheus, but when he heard that the Argonauts were gathering for Colchis he hastened to join them, accompanied by Hylas.

177. The Fifth Labour was to cleanse in one day the stables of Augeias, King of Elis, who had more cattle and sheep than any man on earth. The dung had not been cleared away for years. Heracles swore a bargain with Augeias that he would cleanse the stalls in one day in return for a tenth of the cattle, and Phyleus, son of Augeias, was a witness to their mutual oaths. Heracles then diverted the Rivers Peneius and Alphaeus through the stalls, which were thus cleansed in a day. But Augeias now learned that Heracles had been under Eurystheus' orders, and therefore refused the reward and even denied the bargain. When Phyleus was loyal to the truth Augeias banished him. Heracles later avenged himself on Augeias.

178. The Sixth Labour was to free the marshy lake of Stymphalia in Arcadia of the Stymphalian birds which were sacred to Ares. These man-eating creatures had brazen beaks, claws, and wings, and used their feathers as arrows.

Heracles, helped by Athene, frightened the birds with a rattle and then shot them down, though some say that they flew off to the island of Aretius in the Black Sea, where they were found later by the Argonauts.

179. The Seventh Labour was to capture the Cretan bull. Poseidon had sent the bull to Minos for a sacrifice, but he had substituted another, and it was now raging over the island. Heracles did not avail himself of Minos' offers of help, but captured the bull single-handed and took it to Eurystheus, who set it free again. It roamed through Greece to Marathon, where Theseus captured it and took it to Athens for sacrifice to Athene.

180. The Eighth Labour was to bring back the mares of Diomedes, a savage King of the Bistones in Thrace, who fed his horses on human flesh. On his way Heracles visited Admetus and freed Alcestis from death. Then with a few companions he drove the mares down to the sea, and turning to repel the attacking Bistones, he left them in the charge of his friend Abderus, who was soon eaten by them. Heracles, however, killed Diomedes and threw his body to the mares. He then founded the city of Abdera in honour of his friend and drove the mares back to Eurystheus, who set them free on Mt. Olympus, where they were eaten by wild beasts.

181. The Ninth Labour was to fetch for Admete, daughter of Eurystheus, the golden girdle that Hippolyte, Queen of the Amazons, had received from Ares. After an eventful journey through Europe and Asia, Heracles and his companions reached the land of the Amazons, where Hippolyte, sister of Antiope, received him kindly and promised him the girdle. But Hera roused the Amazons, and they attacked Heracles. In the fight he killed their leaders and Hippolyte herself, from whom he took the girdle. On his way home Heracles came to Troy, where he rescued Laomedan's daughter Hesione from a sea monster sent by Poseidon.

182 The Tenth Labour was to fetch the oxen of Geryon without either demand or payment. Geryon, a powerful monster with three bodies, lived on the island of Erythia. Its site was disputed. Some said it was beyond the ocean stream. Others identified it with Gades. Heracles travelled to the frontiers of Libya and Europe, where he set up two pillars, Calpe and Abyla, on the two sides of the Straits of Gibraltar, hence called the " Pillars of Hercules." When Helios shone too brightly, Heracles shot at him with an arrow, and Helios, admiring such boldness, gave him a golden cup or boat in which he sailed to Erythia. Geryon's cattle were guarded by the two-headed dog Orthrus, said to be the offspring of Typhon and Echidne, and the herdsmen Eurytion, son of Ares. Heracles felled both of these with his club, and, after overcoming Geryon, he sailed with the cattle to Tartessus in Spain, where he returned the golden boat to Helios. On his adventurous journey back through Gaul, Italy, Illyricum, and Thrace, he resisted many attempts, such as that of Cacus, to steal the cattle and eventually handed them over to Eurystheus, who sacrificed them to Hera.

183. The Eleventh Labour was to fetch the golden apples of the Hesperides. These grew on the tree which Hera had received from Ge at her wedding and which she had planted in a garden on Mt. Atlas. It was guarded by the Hesperides and the dragon Ladon, another offspring of Typhon and Echidne. Heracles first consulted Proteus, or as some say Prometheus, and, following the advice he received, he persuaded Atlas to fetch the apples, while he himself upheld the celestial globe. According to some, he also shot Ladon. Atlas, returning with three apples, tried to avoid taking back the burden of the globe, but Heracles, by a ruse, transferred the globe back to the giant's shoulders, took the apples, and hastened away. On his return journey he killed the giant Antæus, and also persuaded Zeus to free Prometheus, the arrow with which Apollo shot the vulture being placed among the stars as

Sagitta. Eurystheus made Heracles a gift of the apples, but the hero dedicated them to Athene, who returned them to their rightful place.

**184.** The Twelfth Labour was to bring back the dog Cerberus from Tartarus, the most difficult task of all. Heracles descended from Tænarum in Laconia and was guided by Athene and Hermes. After he had crossed the Styx and freed his friend Theseus and Ascalaphus, he obtained Hades' permission to carry away Cerberus, provided he could do so without using any weapon. Heracles seized Cerberus by the throat and dragged him up to show Eurystheus. He then carried the monster back to Tartarus.

**185.** According to most writers Heracles now returned to Thebes and gave his wife Megara to his nephew Iolaus, but Euripides, in his play *Heracles*, uses a different version. He represents the hero first killing the tyrant of Thebes, who had attempted to kill Megara and her children, and then, driven insane by Hera, himself killing his wife and family.

**186.** Heracles now desired to marry Iole, daughter of his friend Eurytus, King of Œchalia. Eurytus had promised her to the man who could surpass him and his sons in shooting with the bow. Though Heracles surpassed them all, Eurytus still refused to give him Iole because he had murdered his own children, and in this Eurytus was supported by all his sons except Iphitus. Later when Iphitus appeared suspicious of him, Heracles in a frenzy of rage slew him. Though purified from this murder, he was still troubled in mind, and consulted the Delphic Oracle. He was advised to serve as a slave and to give the proceeds to the family of Iphitus.

**187.** Heracles was purchased by Omphale, Queen of Lydia, and widow of Tmolus, and he served her either for one or for three years. Later writers say that he lived effeminately at this time, and that he used to change garments with Omphale, but others say that he continued to perform heroic deeds.

**188.** His period of servitude to Omphale completed, Heracles sailed against Troy. On a previous occasion, probably when returning from the land of the Amazons, Heracles and his friend Telamon had come to Troy, where they had found Laomedan's daughter, Hesione, exposed naked to a sea-monster, sent by Poseidon (*see para.* 104). Heracles had freed Hesione and killed the monster, but Laomedan had refused to give him the reward he had promised, the white horses given by Zeus in exchange for Ganymede.

**189.** Heracles and Telamon therefore now sailed to Troy to take their revenge. How they sacked the city is described in para. 275. Hesione was given to Telamon and bore him the son Teucer. On his return, Heracles faced a terrible storm raised by Hera and perils on the island of Cos. He was then led by Athene to Phlegra, where he helped the gods in their battle with the giants.

**190.** Heracles now took his revenge on Augeias, who had refused him payment for cleansing the stables. He invaded Elis and eventually killed Augeias, his sons, and their allies, the Moliones, though some say that he spared Augeias. He then founded the Olympic Games, and fetched from the source of the Danube the wild-olive tree whose leaves should crown the victor. Heracles then destroyed the city of Pylus, which had helped Elis. He killed Neleus the king and all his sons except Nestor.

**191.** Heracles next marched against Hippocoon who had fought against him under Neleus. Hippocoon had driven out his brother Tyndareus and seized the kingdom of Sparta. Heracles killed him and all his sons, and restored Tyndareus. He was helped in this enterprise by Cepheus and his twenty sons, but Cepheus and seventeen sons were killed. It was about this time that Heracles seduced the priestess Auge, daughter of Aleus,

King of Tegea, and became by her the father of Telephus.

**192.** After four years in Arcadia, Heracles left for Ætolia, where Œneus was King of Calydonia and Pleuron. Heracles wished to marry Œneus' daughter Deianeira and won her by defeating Achelous, the mighty river-god, son of Oceanus and Tethys. He now sent Iolaus as leader of his sons by the daughters of Thespius to settle in Sardinia.

**193.** Three years later, while at a feast, Heracles accidentally killed the boy Eunomus, and went into voluntary exile, taking Deianeira and their son Hyllus.

**194.** They reached the River Evenus, across which the centaur Nessus carried travellers for a small fee. Heracles let Nessus carry Deianeira, while he himself swam, but the centaur galloped off with her and would have violated her if Heracles had not shot him through the breast. The dying centaur then told Deianeira to take his blood as a charm to keep Heracles' love.

**195.** Heracles now resided at Trachis, and from there invaded Œchalia with an army in order to avenge himself on Eurytus, who had refused to surrender his daughter Iole, even though Heracles had won her in the archery contest. The hero killed Eurytus and all his family, and sent Iole to Deianeira in Trachis while he visited Cenæum in Eubœa and prepared a thanksgiving sacrifice to Zeus.

**196.** He had sent Lichas to Deianeira to fetch a white shirt to wear at the ceremony. Deianeira, fearful that Iole might win Heracles' love, rubbed the shirt in Nessus' blood, not knowing that Heracles' arrow, steeped in the Hydra's blood, had poisoned it. When Heracles put the shirt on, it burned with excruciating agony into his body, and attempts to tear it off took his flesh with it. Heracles seized Lichas and flung him into the sea and then commanded his son Hyllus to take him to Trachis. Deianeira, aghast at what she had unintentionally done, hanged herself. Heracles asked Hyllus to promise to marry Iole and to build him a funeral pyre on Mt. Œta.

**197.** This tragic climax to Heracles' career has been dramatised by Sophocles in the *Women of Trachis*, or *Trachiniæ*, where Deianeiras' distress at Ioles' arrival and her ill-fated ruse to keep her husband's love are touchingly represented.

**198.** Heracles finally ascended his funeral pyre to be burned alive. To Philoctetes, who kindled the flame, he gratefully bequeathed his quiver, bow, and arrows. Thunderbolts demolished the pyre, and Heracles was carried by a cloud to Olympus. There he became immortal, Hera was persuaded by Zeus to adopt him as her son, and reconciled to her at last, he married her daughter Hebe.

### The Children of Heracles, or Heracleidæ.

**199.** Eurystheus now determined to expel from Greece Alcmene and all the children of Heracles. Only in Athens did they find protection, and when Eurystheus attacked the city he was resisted by Theseus (or by his son Demophon), Iolaus, and Hyllus. As an oracle had demanded the sacrifice of one of Heracles' children, his daughter Macaria killed herself. Eurystheus was then defeated, by either Iolaus or Hyllus, and despatched by Alcmene.

**200.** These events are the theme of Euripides' play, *The Children of Heracles* or *Heracleidæ*.

**201.** Hyllus later, endeavouring to enter Peloponnesus, was slain in single combat by Echemus, King of Tegea. Only Tleopolemus settled in Argos.

**202.** Some generations later, the descendants of of Heracles conquered Peloponnesus in conjunction with the Dorians. This legend indicates the conquest of the Achæans by the later invaders.

## THESEUS, 203–218.

203. Theseus, the great hero of Attica, was the son of Æthra by Ægeus, King of Athens, though he was also reputed to be the son of Poseidon. Æthra was the daughter of Pittheus, King of Troezen and here she secretly brought up her young son.

204. When he was of age, Æthra showed him the sandals, and a sword which was an heirloom of Cecrops, that Ægeus had left for him under a great rock. Theseus was able to lift the rock, recover the tokens, and proceed to Athens.

205. He insisted on going not by sea, but by the dangerous land route, and, like Heracles, he freed the country of many terrors. He killed Periphetes, whose club he afterwards carried, Sinis, the the wild sow of Crommyum, Sciron, Cercyon, and Sinis' father Polypemon, who was surnamed Procrustes.

206. Meanwhile in Athens Ægeus had married Medea, who had fled for safety from Corinth. Medea recognised Theseus, and jealous for Medus, her son by Ægeus, she attempted to poison him. But Ægeus recognised Cecrops' sword in time and welcomed his son with great rejoicing. Medea fled, taking Medus, and Theseus then scattered other rivals, the fifty sons of Pallas, nephews of Ægeus, who had hoped to succeed him to the throne.

207. Theseus next captured and sacrificed to Athene, the Marathonian bull which Heracles had brought from Crete and which had been driven to Marathon.

208. He now, of his own free will, went as one of the seven youths who with seven maidens were chosen by lot to be sent to Crete as yearly tribute, to be devoured there by the Minotaur. But Ariadne, daughter of Minos, King of Crete, fell in love with Theseus, and gave him a sword and a clue of thread by which he might find his way out of the labyrinth where the Minotaur lived. Theseus slew the monster, released his fellow Athenians, and fled with them and Ariadne, but at Naxos he deserted her and she was consoled by Dionysus, to whom the island was sacred.

209. Theseus forgot on his return to hoist the white sail which was to have been a sign of victory, and Ægeus, seeing the black sail, threw himself in despair into the sea now called Ægean. Theseus then became the King of Athens.

210. He is said to have invaded the country of the Amazons either with Heracles or later, and here he carried off Antiope, who became his wife, though according to another tradition, Theseus took not Antiope but her sister Hippolyte. It is "Hippolyta" who appears as his bride in *The Midsummer Night's Dream*. In revenge the Amazons invaded Attica, and were eventually defeated by Theseus in the midst of Athens itself.

211. Later Theseus married Ariadne's sister Phædra, another daughter of Minos, who bore him the sons Acamas and Demophon. But Phædra fell desperately in love with her step-son Hippolytus (Theseus' son by either Antiope, or Hippolyte), and when the young man rejected her advances she killed herself, after leaving a letter falsely accusing him to Theseus. The enraged Theseus prayed to Poseidon that Hippolytus might die that very day, and the god sent a sea-monster which so terrified the chariot horses of Hippolytus that they dragged him to death. The story is the theme of Euripides' tragedy *Hippolytus*, and the *Phèdre* of Racine.

212. Theseus was a close friend of Pirithous, King of the Lapithæ, and attended his wedding to Hippodameia, and when a drunken Centaur attempted to carry off the bride, Theseus joined with the Lapithæ in the famous fight against the Centaurs.

213. After Hippodameia's death, Pirithous and Theseus together carried off the girl Helen of Sparta, and she fell by lot to Theseus. As she was too young to marry, he concealed her in the village of Aphidnæ, where she was cared for by his mother Æthra.

214. Theseus then, full of misgiving, fulfilled his promise to Pirithous to help carry off another daughter of Zeus, by accompanying him to the Underworld to take away Persephone. But Hades chained them both to a rock, where they languished till Heracles came to the Underworld and released Theseus only (*see para.* 184).

215. Meanwhile Helen's brothers, the Dioscuri Castor and Polydeuces, invaded Attica, and being told by Academus where Helen was hidden, they rescued her, taking Æthra as her slave.

216. When Theseus returned from Tartarus he was unable to keep order among his people, who were being stirred up against him by Menestheus. He retired to the island of Scyros, where he was treacherously killed by King Lycomedes. He nevertheless returned in spirit to help the Athenians at the Battle of Marathon, and though Menestheus succeeded Theseus as king, the sons of Theseus were afterwards restored to the throne.

217. Theseus, like Heracles, took part in the heroic enterprises of his age. He joined in the Calydonian hunt and helped Adrastus at Thebes, and he may have been one of the Argonauts.

218. Although Athenians in later times looked on Theseus as an historical figure, ascribing political institutions to him, he was in fact a legendary hero.

## CRETAN MYTHS, 219–239.

219. Recent archæological discoveries have indicated that many of the ancient legends concerned with Crete have a factual basis, and a very readable book on the subject is the "Pan" Book *Bull of Minos*, by Leonard Cottrell.

220. In 1899 Sir Arthur Evans began his excavations at Cnossos and soon unearthed the remains of the magnificent, unfortified and labyrinthine so-called "Palace of Minos" with its indications of an elegant and highly artistic civilisation.

221. From the architectural evidence available, scholars now consider that there existed in Crete between 2500 and 1400 B.C., a "Minoan" pre-Hellenic culture which had affinities with that of Egypt. This maritime, commercial culture, its sea-power making fortification unnecessary, spread to the mainland of Greece, where it became known as Mycenæan. It is in fact possible that Crete may have exercised some kind of suzerainty over the mainland. The Cretans probably worshipped a goddess who was served by priestesses. The favourite sport was bull-fighting, in which men and women toreadors showed amazing skill. Cretan architects and engineers were exceptionally ingenious.

222. Discoveries such as these give special significance to such legends as that of Minos' sea power, and of Crete's exaction from Athens of a tribute of men and maidens for the Minotaur. Again the constant appearance of the bull in Cretan legend and Dædalus' building of the labyrinth appear to have foundation in historical fact.

223. It was to Crete that Zeus, in the form of a bull, brought Europa, said to be the daughter of Agenor, son of Poseidon and King of Phœnicia, and of his wife Telephassa.

224. As the lovely Europa was playing on the sea-shore with her maidens, Zeus appeared as a white bull and she dared to climb on his back, an incident depicted in the masterly painting by

Paul Veronese in the Palace of the Doges in Venice. Suddenly Zeus, plunging into the sea, carried off Europa to Crete, where he fathered on her the three sons, Minos, Rhadamanthus, and Sarpedon. When the reigning king later married Europa he adopted her three sons as his heirs.

**225.** The brothers quarrelled, however, over the boy Miletus, son of Apollo. As Miletus preferred Sarpedon, they both fled from Minos to Asia Minor. Here Miletus founded the kingdom that bore his name, and Sarpedon, after aiding Cilix, King of Cilicia, against the Lycians, became king of the latter and was permitted by Zeus to live for three generations.

**226.** Rhadamanthus, though at first ruler of part of Crete, also found it wise to flee. He went to Bœotia, and on Amphitrion's death married Alcmene. So just a ruler did he prove, that he became one of the judges of the Underworld.

**227.** Minos, now sole ruler of Crete, was confirmed in his power by Poseidon, who sent him a magnificent white bull. This so delighted the king that he withheld it from sacrifice, and when it later ran savage it was captured by Heracles as his Seventh Labour, and eventually slain by Theseus.

**228.** Minos was the law-giver to Crete and was helped in the defence of the island by Talos, a bull-headed, brazen giant and by his powerful fleet.

**229.** Curious legends are told of Minos' loves. One was Procris, another Britomartis, a Cretan nymph whom he pursued for nine months, until she leaped into the sea and was deified by Artemis, sharing with her the epithet Dictynna.

**230.** Once when Minos was besieging Nisa, the port of Megara, which belonged to King Nisus, Scylla, Nisus' daughter, fell in love with him, and killed her father by cutting off the hair on which his life depended. Although Scylla let him into the city, Minos was so horrified at her parricide that he left her, and she swam after his ship until her father's soul, changed to a sea-eagle, pounced on her, and she was turned to the bird Ciris. Others say that Minos drowned Scylla, and she was turned into the fish Ciris. She has sometimes been confused with Scylla the daughter of Phorcys.

**231.** The wife of Minos was Pasiphaë daughter of Helios and Persë and several of their children, as Glaucus, Androgeos, Ariadne, and Phædra were the subject of legend.

**232.** Glaucus when a boy was drowned in a cask of honey, and his body found by the seer Polyeidus. Unable to resuscitate Glaucus, Polyeidus was entombed with him, but here a serpent revealed a herb which restored Glaucus to life, and the seer and the boy were released.

**233.** Androgeos won every contest in the Pan-athenaic games and was slain at the instigation of Ægeus. Minos in revenge exacted from Athens a yearly tribute of seven youths and maidens to be devoured by the Minotaur.

**234.** This monster with bull's head and man's body, was the offspring of Pasiphaë and the white bull. Dædalus the craftsman that enabled her to satisfy her desire, and afterwards built the labyrinth in which her shameful offspring was housed.

**235.** When Ægeus' son Theseus voluntarily joined the youths destined for the Minotaur, Ariadne fell in love with him, and enabled him to kill the monster by giving him a sword and a clue of thread by means of which he found his way out of the labyrinth. Ariadne then escaped with Theseus, but was deserted by him on Naxos, where she was found by Dionysus, as depicted in Titian's "Bacchus and Ariadne" in the National Gallery. Tintoretto's picture in the Doge's Palace in Venice shows the marriage of Ariadne to the god.

**236.** Her sister Phædra was later married to Theseus, and her unrequited passion for her step-son Hippolytus and its tragic outcome has been described in para. 211.

**237.** The cunning Dædalus, whose craftsmanship was symbolic of the latest development in sculpture and architecture, had been welcomed by Minos after his flight from Athens. The legend runs that he had been so bitterly jealous of his nephew Talos, or Perdix, inventor of the saw, chisel, and compasses, that he threw him headlong from Athene's temple on the Acropolis. Athene changed Talos into the bird "perdix" or partridge, and the Areopagus banished Dædalus.

**238.** Welcomed to Crete, he found his skill greatly valued by Minos, until the king discovered how he had aided Pasiphaë. Minos then imprisoned Dædalus with his son Icarus in his own labyrinth. They were released by Pasiphaë, and Dædalus made wings fastened to the shoulders with wax on which they flew away. Icarus mounted too high, the sun melted the wax and he was drowned in the Icarian Sea, but Dædalus reached Cumæ near Naples, and fled thence to Sicily. Here Cocalus welcomed him, and when Minos pursued the craftsman, Cocalus' daughters enabled him ingeniously to kill the king.

**239.** After Minos' death, although his son succeeded him, Cretan civilisation collapsed. Minos himself became a judge in the Underworld.

## THEBAN MYTHS, 240-271.

**240.** The legend concerning the origin of Thebes is that of Cadmus, who according to common tradition was the son of Agenor, son of Poseidon and the King of Phœnicia, and of his wife Telephassa.

**241.** The sister of Cadmus, Europa, was one day carried off by Zeus, who appeared to her in the form of a bull (as is described in para. 224) and Agenor sent Cadmus in search of his sister.

**242.** Unable to find her, Cadmus consulted the Delphic oracle, who advised him to relinquish his search but to follow a cow and build a town where she should sink down with fatigue. Cadmus followed the cow from Phocis to Bœotia, and where she rested he built Cadmea, later the citadel of Thebes.

**243.** Making sacrifice to Athene, he sent his men for water from a spring of Ares not knowing that it was guarded by a dragon which killed most of his men. When Cadmus had killed the dragon Athene advised him to sow its teeth, and immediately there sprang up, fully armed, the Sparti, or "Sown Men," who fought with each other till only five survived—Echion, Udæus, Chthonius, Hyperenor, and Pelorus. These five were the ancestors of Thebes, and with their help the Cadmea was built.

**244.** Zeus gave to Cadmus as wife Harmonia, daughter of Ares and Aphrodite, and the Olympian deities attended the wedding. Harmonia received as a gift from Aphrodite the famous necklace made by Hephæstus, which Zeus had originally given Europa, and which conferred irresistible loveliness upon its wearer. From Athene she received a magic robe which conferred divine dignity. The children of Cadmus and Harmonia were Autonoe, Ino, Semele the mother of Dionysus, Agave, Polydorus, and later Illyrius.

**245.** It is said that Cadmus introduced to Thebes from Phœnicia the use of letters.

**246.** In old age Cadmus resigned the throne to Pentheus, his grandson, the son of Agave and Echion. But Pentheus, resisting the worship of Dionysus, was destroyed by Agave and her sisters Autonoe and Ino, as is depicted in *The Bacchæ* of Euripides.

**247.** Cadmus and Harmonia then left Thebes and were later, in the form of serpents, received in the Islands of the Blessed.

248. Another legend concerning Thebes is that of Amphion and Zethus the twin sons of Antiope by Zeus.

249. Antiope was divorced by her husband Lycus of Thebes, and cruelly treated by his second wife, Dirce. Meanwhile Amphion and Zethus were brought up by cattle men on Mt. Cithæron. When they were old enough to know what had happened they took their revenge. They killed Lycus and Dirce, who was tied to the horns of a wild bull and her body thrown into a fountain which henceforth bore her name, and then took possession of Thebes.

250. Amphion and Zethus now built the lower fortifications below the Cadmea, and so skilfully did Amphion play on the lyre given him by Hermes that the stones moved into place of their own accord. The brothers ruled jointly, Zethus married Thebe, who gave her name to the city, and Niobe became the wife of Amphion.

251. Niobe, the proud daughter of Tantalus and sister of Pelops, had seven sons and seven daughters, and boasted that she was superior to Leto, who had only two children. As punishment to her, Apollo killed the boys with his arrows, and Artemis the girls, and Niobe "all tears" was turned by Zeus into a stone on Mt. Sipylus. The crag of Niobe, being snow-capped, appears to weep when the sun strikes the snow. It is said the Amphion also was either killed by Apollo or that he took his own life.

252. Most famous of Theban kings was Œdipus, who claimed direct descent from Cadmus through Polydorus, Labdacus, and Laius, and all three of the great Greek tragic dramatists were inspired by the fateful story of Œdipus and his children.

253. Œdipus the son of Laius, King of Thebes, and of his wife Jocasta, was as a new-born child exposed on Mt. Cithæron, his feet tied together and pierced with a nail, for Laius had learned from the oracle at Delphi that he would be killed by his own son. Found by a shepherd of Polybus, King of Corinth, the child was called from his swollen feet Œdipus, and was reared by Polybus as his own son.

254. When Œdipus grew to manhood, he was told by the Delphic oracle that he was destined to kill his own father and marry his mother, and he resolved never to return to Corinth. But going from Delphi, he met Laius riding in a chariot, and in a quarrel killed him.

255. Laius had been on his way to ask the Delphic oracle how he could rid Thebes of the Sphinx, a winged lion with the head and breast of a woman. This monster was said to be the offspring of Typhon and Echidne, or of Orthrus and the Chimæra. Seated on a rock, she challenged each wayfarer with her riddle and strangled him when he failed to solve it.

256. Œdipus, arriving in Thebes, heard the Sphinx's riddle. "Which being, having only one voice, has sometimes two feet, sometimes three, and sometimes four and is weakest when it has most." Œdipus answered rightly that the being was man, who crawls in infancy and supports himself with a staff in old age, and the Sphinx thereupon flung herself to death.

257. As the Thebans had promised that whoever should vanquish the Sphinx should become king and marry Jocasta, Œdipus became King of Thebes and had four children by his own mother, Eteocles, Polyneices, Antigone, and Ismene.

258. Thebes, thus defiled by murder and incest, was visited by plague and the blind seer Teiresias said that the city would be saved when one of the "Sparti" (a title given also to descendants of the "Sown Men") should give his life. When he learned this, Menœceus, father of Jocasta, leapt from the walls to his death.

259. The plague still raging, Œdipus consulted Teiresias, and it is at this point that the famous

*Œdipus Tyrannus* of Sophocles begins. Œdipus was horrified when at last convinced of his unconscious guilt and, after Jocasta had hanged herself, he blinded himself with a pin taken from her garment and prayed her brother Creon to banish him.

260. Eventually Œdipus went into exile accompanied by Antigone, and followed later by Ismene. At Colonos in Attica he found refuge in a grove of the Eumenides and, protected by Theseus, was received at last by the gods. These last hours of Œdipus are most touchingly presented by Sophocles in his *Œdipus at Colonos*.

261. Angered by his sons' neglect, Œdipus had cursed them, saying that they should divide their inherited land by the sword. They therefore agreed to rule in turn, but when Eteocles' term had expired he refused to abdicate. Polyneices then sought the help of Adrastus, son of Talaus and King of Argos, whose daughter Argia he married, while her sister Deipyle married Tydeus (son of Œneus of Calydon), who, on account of some murder he had committed, was also a fugitive.

262. When Adrastus prepared to restore Polyneices, his brother-in-law, the seer Amphiaraus, prophesied death for all the leaders save Adrastus. Amphiaraus had married Adrastus' sister Eriphyle, and Polyneices, following the advice of Tydeus, bribed Eriphyle, giving her the famous necklace of Harmonia on the condition that she would persuade her husband to join the expedition.

263. Adrastus, Amphiaraus, Polyneices, and Tydeus were joined by Capaneus, Hippomedon, and Parthenopaeus, the son of Meleager and Atalanta, and these seven marched against Thebes. The war that followed was dramatised by both Æschylus, in his *Seven against Thebes*, and by Euripides, in *The Phœnician Maidens*.

264. After Thebes had suffered initial reverses, Teiresias prophesied that a royal prince must sacrifice himself, and a second Menœceus, the son of Creon, now took his own life.

265. The attackers were soon repelled. Capaneus, scaling the walls, was struck by Zeus with lightning. Tydeus, wounded by Melanippus, might have been saved by Athene with an elixir given her by Zeus, but Amphiaraus, who bore him a grudge, persuaded him to drink the brains of the dead Melanippus. This so disgusted Athene that she left him to his fate. Hippomedon and Parthenopæus also having been killed, offered to settle the dispute in single combat with Eteocles, but both were mortally wounded. Amphiaraus fled in his chariot and the earth opened and swallowed him. As the seer had prophesied, Adrastus was the only one of the seven left alive.

266. Thebes was not unscathed. The *Antigone* of Sophocles opens at the point where Creon refused to allow burial to Polyneices. The courageous Antigone dared to disobey him and he ordered that she should be imprisoned alive in a cave. Here she hanged herself, and Creon's son Hæmon, to whom she was betrothed, took his own life in despair.

267. Euripides, in *The Suppliants*, dramatises the next phase of the story. Since the Thebans had refused burial to their fallen enemies, Adrastus and the mothers of the slain went to Eleusis and secured the help of Theseus. He defeated the Thebans, and the bodies of the Argives received burial rites, but Evadne, daughter of Iphis and wife of Capaneus threw herself on to the flaming pyre and perished.

268. Thebes was again attacked ten years later, when Adrastus assembled the "Epigoni," the descendants of the "Seven." His own son Ægialeus made one, and also Diomedes, son of Tydeus, with his faithful companion Sthenelus, son of Capaneus and Evadne.

269. Since Alcmæon, like his father Amphiaraus, was unwilling to join the Epigoni, Thersander followed the example of his father Polyneices in

once more bribing Eriphyle, this time with the magic robe of Harmonia. She then persuaded Alcmæon to join the expedition along with his brother the seer Amphilochus.

270. Ægialeus was killed before the walls of Thebes, and Teiresias then advised the Thebans to evacuate the city and himself accompanied them, though he died next dawn on drinking from the well of Tilphussa. That day Adrastus, hearing of Ægialeus' death, also died of grief, and in accordance with Teiresias' prophecy the Argives took the empty city.

271. Alcmæon, on return, slew his mother Eriphyle, in revenge for her vanity and deceit towards his father and himself. Pursued by the Erinnyes, he fled to Phlegeus, King of Psophis, who purified him and gave him his daughter Arsinoë in marriage. Alcmæon gave his wife Harmonia's necklace and robe, but was soon forced by the Erinnyes to flee once more. He was next purified by the river-god Achelous and married his daughter Callirrhoë, who soon demanded the necklace and robe. Alcmæon, daring to revisit Psophis, obtained them from Phlegeus on the pretext of taking them to Delphi, but when Phlegeus discovered that they were destined for Callirrhoë he ordered his sons to slay Alcmæon. Finally, Phlegeus himself sent the ill-fated treasures to Delphi.

## LEGENDS OF TROY, 272–352.

272. One of the most romantic discoveries of modern times is that of the German Schliemann, who, trusting the descriptions of Homer, excavated a site on the coast of Asia Minor, near the entrance to the Dardanelles. Between 1871 and 1873 he unearthed the foundations not of one Troy but of seven, his most spectacular find being a hoard of exquisite gold ornaments. His work proved that Troy belonged not only to legend but also to history.

273. It is now considered that in the Bronze Age Troy was an important centre for trade. Frequently attacked, it was many times rebuilt, and Greeks, Cretans, and Phrygians all claimed to have had a hand in establishing it. In Homer's time, when the sixth Troy was standing, it had probably absorbed three small towns, Dardania, Tros or Troy, and Ilium, and was probably inhabited by three tribes, Dardanians, Trojans, and Ilians, whose names are all represented in the early legends of Troy's foundation.

274. One of these tells how Scamander of Crete founded a colony in Phrygia, and how, jumping into the River Xanthus, he changed its name to his own. The nymph Idæa bore him a son Teucer (whence the Trojans are called Teucri), and Teucer gave a piece of land to Dardanus, the son of Zeus by the Pleiad Electra, who built there the town of Dardania. The grandson of Dardanus was Tros, who became the father of Ilus and also of Ganymede, whom he relinquished to Zeus for a gift of horses. The son of Ilus was Laomedan.

275. It was to Laomedan that Zeus assigned Apollo and Poseidon as labourers. They built for him the walls of Troy, and when Laomedan refused payment, Poseidon sent the sea-monster, which would have devoured his daughter Hesione had not she been rescued by Heracles. But again Laomedan refused the agreed reward—the white horses given by Zeus in exchange for Ganymede—and Heracles returned later to sack Troy. He gave Hesione to his fellow-warrior Telamon, and killed Laomedan and all his sons save Podarces, who was ransomed by his sister Hesione, and his name was changed to Priam, which means " redeemed."

276. After a few years Priam sent Antenor to demand that Telamon should send back Hesione, and the Greeks' scornful refusal was one of the causes of the Trojan War.

277. Priam had fifty sons, nineteen of them by his second wife Hecabe, or Hecuba, who bore him many famous children, including Hector, Paris, Deïphobus and the prophetic twins Helenus and Cassandra. Troilus may have been her son by Apollo.

278. Before the birth of her second son, Hecuba dreamed that she had brought forth a blazing firebrand, and the new-born child was therefore exposed on Mt. Ida. Brought up by a shepherd, he was called Paris, and later, by his courage earned the name Alexander or " defender of men." Paris was beloved by the nymph Œnone, but he deserted her as the result of a tempting suggestion of Aphrodite's.

279. The occasion of this was the famous " Judgment of Paris," of which a Renaissance version can be seen in Rubens' picture in the National Gallery.

280. The story goes that alone of all the gods, Eris was not invited to the marriage of Peleus and Thetis, and in revenge she flung in the golden apple of discord with " to the fairest " inscribed upon it. Immediately Hera, Athene, and Aphrodite disputed its possession, and Zeus commanded Hermes to lead the goddesses to Mt. Ida for Paris to judge the dispute.

281. Although Hera promised him rule in Asia, and Athene fame in war, Paris gave the apple to Aphrodite, who promised him as his wife the loveliest of all women.

282. Paris now discovered his parentage and was joyfully welcomed by Priam, and under Aphrodite's protection sailed to Sparta.

283. His sister Cassandra foretold doom, but was as usual unregarded. In her youth she had been loved by Apollo, who had taught her the art of prophecy on condition that she became his lover. But she had disappointed him, and Apollo had then ordained that her prophecy should never be believed.

284. Welcomed to Sparta by King Menelaus, Paris fell in love with his beautiful queen, Helen, and in Menelaus' absence he succeeded in carrying her off to Troy with much treasure, thus precipitating the Trojan War, now inevitable by reason of an oath sworn by the leading chieftains of Greece to defend Helen's husband.

285. Helen, the daughter of Leda by Zeus, had been brought up in the Court of Leda's husband, Tyndareus of Sparta. So lovely was she that even as a young girl she had been carried off by Theseus and Pirithous, to be rescued and brought back by her brothers, the Dioscuri. All the noblest in Greece then became rivals for her hand, and at the instigation of Tyndareus swore an oath to defend her chosen husband.

286. Helen married Menelaus, and when the Dioscuri were immortalised, he succeeded Tyndareus as King of Sparta.

287. After Helen had fled with Paris, leaving her husband and daughter Hermione, Menelaus summoned the chieftains to war. His powerful brother Agamemnon, King of Mycenæ, who had married Helen's half-sister, Clytemnestra, was leader, and from the Peloponnese came also old Nestor of Pylus, whose Palace has only recently been discovered. Nestor was the only one of Neleus' twelve sons spared by Heracles. Renowned for wisdom and eloquence, he had been a courageous fighter. He had defeated the Arcadians and Eleans and had taken part in the Calydonian hunt and the fight between Centaurs and Lapithæ. Although he had ruled over three generations, he gladly joined the expedition to Troy.

288. The courageous Diomedes, son of Tydeus, and King of Argos, also came from the Peloponnese with eighty ships. He had been one of the Epigoni who had taken Thebes, and two fellow Epigoni came with him—Sthenelus, son of Capa-

neus, and Euryalus, the Argonaut. Tleopolemus, son of Heracles, the Argive who had settled in Rhodes, brought nine ships, and Palamedes, son of Nauplius, joined the muster from Eubœa.

289. But Agamemnon needed more distant allies, and together with Menelaus and Palamedes, he went to Ithaca to persuade Odysseus to join them.

290. Odysseus was the son of Anticleia, a daughter of the wily thief Autolycus, and of Lærtes, King of Ithaca, though some say that his father was really Sisyphus. He had won his wife Penelope, daughter of King Icarius of Sparta, in a foot race, and when Icarius had tried to persuade Penelope to remain with him, Odysseus had told her she might do as she wished. Penelope had veiled her face to hide her blushes and had followed her husband to Ithaca.

291. An oracle had warned Odysseus not to join the expedition to Troy, and when the envoys arrived they found him ploughing and sowing salt. But the far-sighted Palmedes placed Odysseus' infant son Telemachus in front of the plough, and Odysseus was tricked into revealing his sanity and joining the expedition.

292. Agamemnon also welcomed allies from Salamis and Locris. From Salamis, bringing twelve ships, came Great Ajax, son of King Telamon, a courageous fighter, who boasted that he needed not the help of the gods. His half-brother, Teucer, son of Telamon by Hesione and the best archer in Greece, fought behind Great Ajax' shield. Little Ajax also fought with them. Son of Oileus, King of the Locrians, he was small in stature but swift of foot, and skilled in throwing the spear. He brought forty ships.

293. An important contingent from Southern Thessaly also sailed to Troy, for Calchas, a renegade prophet from Troy, foretold that the city could not be taken without the help of Achilles, son of Peleus, King of the Myrmidones at Phthia in Thessaly, and of the Nereid, Thetis.

294. By dipping her son into the Styx, Thetis had made him invulnerable, except for the heel which she was holding. Achilles had been taught by Cheiron and by his tutor Phœnix, and was renowned for strength, speed, and high courage.

295. Thetis, knowing that if Achilles went to Troy he would never return alive, sent him disguised as a girl to the Court of Lycomedes, King of Scyros, and here Lycomedes' daughter Deidamia bore him the son Neoptolemus, or Pyrrhus. When Odysseus, accompanied by Nestor and Ajax, visited Scyros, he left a spear and shield among a pile of gifts for the maidens, and Achilles, seizing these, revealed his identity.

296. Achilles joined the Greeks together with his tutor Phœnix and Patroclus, his cousin, who had come as a boy to Peleus' Court after an accidental murder and had become the inseparable friend of Achilles.

297. The Greeks were further strengthened by Idomeneus, King of Crete, who brought 100 ships and shared the command with Agamemnon. Meriones accompanied Idomeneus.

298. The fleet was fortunate in being abundantly supplied with provisions, by Anius, son and priest of Apollo in Delos, for his three daughters who had been dedicated to Dionysus received from the god power to produce at will corn, oil, and wine.

299. The expedition set out from Aulis, but first made a false landing and ravaged the country of Telephus, son of Heracles and Auge, and now King of Mysia. When he repelled the Greeks, Dionysus caused him to stumble over a vine, and he was wounded by Achilles. Told by an oracle that his wound could be cured only by him who had inflicted it, he visited the Greeks, who likewise knew through an oracle that they could not take

Troy without the aid of Telephus. Achilles therefore gladly cured him with rust from the spear which had injured him, and Telephus showed the Greeks the route they should take.

300. Assembled a second time at Aulis, the Greeks were delayed by unfavourable winds, for Agamemnon, by killing a hart, had vexed Artemis. Calchas foretold that only the sacrifice of Agamemnon's daughter Iphigeneia would appease the goddess, and Agamemnon reluctantly gave his consent, though some say that Artemis snatched Iphigeneia from the altar and bore her off to Tauris (see para. 396). Certainly the winds changed and the fleet set sail.

301. When they landed on the island of Tenedos, in sight of Troy, Achilles killed King Tenes and his father Cycnus, and here Philoctetes, son of Poeas suffered misfortune. Most famous of the Greek archers, he had been the friend of Heracles, and had received from him the famous bow and poisoned arrows when he set fire to the hero's funeral pyre on Mt. Œta. He was now injured in the foot by one of these arrows or, as some say, by the bite of a snake, and the smell of the wound became so offensive that, on the advice of Odysseus, Philoctetes was left behind on the island of Lemnos.

302. It was probably from Tenedos that the envoys Menelaus, Odysseus and Palamedes were sent to Priam to request the return of Helen. They were courteously entertained by Antenor, the wisest of the Trojans, who advised that Helen should be sent back, but the Trojans were obdurate.

303. The Greeks then attacked the mainland, and Protesilaus of Thessaly, who was an uncle of Philoctetes, was the first to leap ashore, though he knew through an oracle that it meant death. Wordsworth, in his poem Laodamia, tells how Laodamia his wife, the daughter of Acastus, desolate with grief, begged the gods to let her husband return for only three hours. Hermes led Protesilaus to her, and when he died the second time she died with him.

304. Achilles, the second to land on Trojan soil, soon distinguished himself as the most courageous and formidable of all the Greeks.

305. It was through Achilles that Æneas entered the war. At first he took no part, although he was the son of Priam's cousin Anchises. But when Achilles raided his herds on Mt. Ida, he led his Dadanians against the Greeks, and distinguished himself in battle. His mother, Aphrodite, frequently helped him, and once carried him away when wounded by Diomedes, while the god Poseidon, though hostile to Troy, saved him from Achilles.

306. Many cities allied to Troy were raided by Achilles. In Thebes in Cilicia he killed King Eëtion, father of Hector's wife Andromache, and Great Ajax raided the Thracian Chersonesus and in Teuthrania killed the King Teuthras and took his daughter Tecmessa.

307. In the tenth year of the war the Greeks at last concentrated their armies before Troy itself, which was defended by the mighty Hector, by Æneas, and by many allies, including Sarpedon, a son of Zeus, who was in command of the Lycians.

308. The Greeks were hampered by rivalries between the chiefs. Odysseus took a cruel revenge on Palamedes, who had tricked him into joining the forces. He bribed one of Palamedes' servants to hide under his master's bed a letter written in the name of Priam, and then accused Palamedes of treachery. Palamedes' tent was searched, the letter was found, and he was stoned to death by the whole army. Thus perished the sage, who was said to have invented lighthouses, scales, measures, the discus, certain letters of the alphabet, and dice.

309. Then in the tenth year there broke out the notorious quarrel between Achilles and Agamem-

non with which the *Iliad* opens. Chryseis, the daughter of the Trojan priest, Chryses had been taken prisoner and assigned to Agamemnon, and when Chryses came to ransom her, Agamemnon roughly repulsed him. Apollo, in revenge, sent a plague among the Greeks, and on Calchas' advice, Agamemnon unwillingly sent Chryseis back. He recompensed himself, however, by seizing Briseis, who had been given to Achilles, and Achilles then stubbornly refused to take any further part in the fighting, though some say that his motive in this was to curry favour with Priam, for he had fallen deeply in love with Priam's daughter Polyxena.

310. The Trojans quickly seized this opportunity to attack, and Agamemnon was glad to grant a truce so that Paris and Menelaus might settle the quarrel by a duel. But when Paris was losing, Aphrodite carried him away and fighting broke out again.

311. Diomedes wounded Æneas and Aphrodite and then strove with Glaucus, a Lycian prince second in command to Sarpedon, but when they remembered the friendship between their forefathers they desisted and exchanged gifts. Hector and Ajax fought in single combat till nightfall, when they also exchanged gifts, Hector giving Ajax a sword and receiving a purple baldric.

312. The Greeks, hard-pushed, were now forced to build a wall and trench, and when they were driven back even farther, Agamemnon in alarm offered to return Briseis to Achilles, but he courteously and firmly refused.

313. Diomedes and Odysseus then made a night-raid on the Trojan lines. After killing the spy, Dolon, they slew Rhesus the Thracian and drove off his snow-white horses, for an oracle had declared that once they had drunk of Scamander, and eaten the grass of the Trojan plain, the city would not be taken. The play *Rhesus*, attributed to Euripides, dramatises these incidents from the *Iliad*.

314. Next day, however, the Trojans victoriously set fire to the very ships, and Achilles went so far as to lend Patroclus his own armour and let him lead the Myrmidones. After killing Sarpedon, Patroclus drove the Trojans back to their very walls, until he was at last himself wounded by Euphorbus, son of Panthous, and slain by Hector, who at once stripped him of his borrowed armour, though Menelaus, who had killed Euphorbus, now joined with Ajax in rescuing the body.

315. Achilles was prostrate with grief, but Thetis visited him with new armour made by Hephæstus, and he made peace with Agamemnon, who at last sent Briseis back. Achilles then drove the terrified Trojans back to the city. The noble Hector alone withstood him, though Priam and Hecuba, implored him to come in. Thrice did Achilles chase Hector round the walls of Troy, and then finally killed him, stripped him of his armour, and, tying him by the ankles to his chariot, dragged him ignominiously back to the ship, though some say that Achilles dragged Hector three times round the walls of Troy by the purple baldric that Great Ajax had given him.

316. Each day at dawn Achilles, crazed with grief, pulled the corpse three times round the tomb of Patroclus until at last, in one of the most touching scenes of the *Iliad*, Priam, led by Hermes, went to Achilles' tent and begged to ransom his son's body for burial.

317. The lovely Penthesilea now came to the Trojans' aid. She was the daughter of Otrere and Ares, and Queen of the Amazons. But Achilles killed her, and as he mourned over her, he was ridiculed by Thersites, the ugliest and most scurrilous of the Greeks, and Achilles felled him with a blow. This angered Diomedes, a kinsman of Thersites, and he flung the body of Penthesilea into the Scamander, but it was rescued and honourably buried, some say by Achilles himself.

318. Memnon the black-skinned, handsome son of Eos and Priam's half-brother Tithonus, and King of Ethiopia, now reinforced the Trojans. He killed several Greeks, including Antilochus, the gallant son of Nestor, who, too young to sail from Aulis, joined his father later.

319. The vengeful Achilles then engaged Memnon in fierce single combat while Zeus weighed their fates in the balance. Memnon was slain and, at the request of Eos, Zeus honoured him by causing birds, called Memnonides, to rise from his funeral pyre and fight above it till they fell as a sacrifice. They were said to visit yearly the hero's tomb on the Hellespont.

320. Many great monuments, called Memnonia, were supposed by the Greeks to have been erected in Memnon's honour, the most famous being the colossal statue behind the temple of Egyptian Thebes, which gave forth each sunrise a sound like the breaking of a lyre-string.

321. Achilles' own course was now run, and in a battle near the Scæan gate Paris, aided by Apollo, shot him through the vulnerable ankle.

322. Great Ajax then killed Glaucus, and he and Odysseus rescued the body of Achilles. But they quarrelled violently over the possession of the armour. Homer, in the *Odyssey*, says that Odysseus killed Ajax, and that when he summoned the spirits of the dead, Ajax held sullenly aloof. Sophocles, however, in his tragedy *Ajax*, represents Ajax thrown into madness by defeat and slaying the sheep of the Greeks, believing them to be his rivals, and finally falling on the very sword that Hector had given him.

323. So many heroes dead, the Greeks lost heart, and Calchas said they must fetch the bow and arrows of Heracles. Odysseus and Diomedes therefore sailed to the island of Lemnos, where Philoctetes had been left to languish, and Sophocles, in his play *Philoctetes*, shows how he was persuaded to return.

324. Cured of his wound by one of the sons of Asclepius, either Machaon or Podalirius, Philoctetes challenged Paris to an archery contest. Mortally wounded, Paris besought his former lover Œnone to cure him, but she refused, and then in remorse at his death took her own life, events described by Tennyson in his *Death of Œnone*.

325. Helenus and Deiphobus now quarrelled for the possession of Helen, now homesick for Sparta, and when Deiphobus forcibly married her, Helenus, as some say, fled to Mt. Ida, where either he freely joined the Greeks, or was captured or ensnared by Odysseus, for Calchas had said that only Helenus knew the secret oracles which protected Troy. Helenus said it would fall that summer, if a bone of Pelops were brought to the Greeks, if Achilles' son Neoptolemus, or Pyrrhus, joined them, and if Athene's Palladium were stolen from the citadel.

326. Agamemnon at once sent for the shoulderblade of Pelops, while Odysseus, Phœnix, and Diomedes went to Scyros and persuaded Lycomedes to let Neoptolemus join them. Odysseus then gave Neoptolemus his father's armour.

327. It is said that Priam now sent Antenor to Agamemnon to sue for peace, but Antenor, out of hatred for Deiphobus, conspired with the Greek leader as to how they might secure the Palladium. They arranged that Odysseus, disguised as a filthy runaway slave, should gain entrance to Troy. Recognised by Helen alone, he gained much useful information, including the confession that she longed to return home. It was either on this occasion that he stole the Palladium, or later when he was accompanied by Diomedes.

328. Odysseus is said to have devised the stratagem of the wooden horse. This was built by the cowardly Epeius, son of Panopeus, under the supervision of Athene, and it bore an inscription

saying that it was dedicated to the goddess. Then twenty-three or more of the bravest Greeks, including Neoptolemus, Odysseus, Sthenelus, and Thoas of Calydon, climbed into the hollow belly.

329. At nightfall, Agamemnon and the remaining Greeks burnt their camp and sailed to the island of Tenedos, leaving behind only Sinon, a cousin of Odysseus and grandson of the cunning Autolycus.

330. At dawn Priam and his sons found the wooden horse on the shore, and believing it to be sacred to Athene, had it hauled in spite of opposition up to the citadel. Cassandra declared that warriors were within it, and she was supported by Laocoön, son of Antenor, and priest to both Apollo and Poseidon, who flung a spear at the horse's flank and caused a clatter of arms. Their warning was, however, neglected, partly because Sinon, who had let himself be taken prisoner, said that the horse was the Greeks' atonement for stealing the Palladium, partly because the fate which now befell Laocoön was misinterpreted.

331. Laocoön had offended Apollo by marrying in spite of vows of celibacy, and the god now punished him by sending two enormous serpents, which crushed to death both the priest and his two sons—a disaster represented in the magnificent sculpture probably dating from the first century B.C. and now in the Vatican. Priam wrongly supposed this to be a punishment for smiting the horse, and it was now welcomed with feasting and revelry.

332. In the evening Helen with Deiphobus strolled round the horse and, imitating in turn the voice of each man's wife, she called to the heroes, who stifled their replies.

333. At night Agamemnon, warned by a beacon lit by Sinon, sailed to the shore, and as Antenor gave the word the warriors within the horse leapt down to slaughter and pillage.

334. Priam had been persuaded by Hecuba to take refuge with her and her daughters before an altar to Zeus, but their son Polites was slain before their very eyes by Neoptolemus, and when the old king feebly tried to attack the slayer, Neoptolemus butchered him also. Odysseus and Menelaus meanwhile killed and mangled Deiphobus, but Menelaus pardoned Helen, and led her safely to the ships.

335. Cassandra fled to the sanctuary of Athene, but Little Ajax roughly dragged her away, and she was claimed as booty by Agamemnon. Her sister Laodice, the wife of Helicaon, was mercifully swallowed up by the earth.

336. Hector's widow Andromache was given to Neoptolemus, and the Greeks, eager to exterminate the whole family of Priam, even killed her infant son Astyanax, by hurling him to death from the city walls, fearful lest he should one day avenge his parents.

337. At the demand of Achilles' ghost Polyxena was sacrificed to him by Neoptolemus, to ensure favourable winds. Some say this happened at Troy, others only when the Greek fleet had reached Thrace.

338. Hecuba fell to the share of Odysseus, who took her to the Thracian Chersonesus, and there she avenged the death of one of her sons. Polydorus, the youngest of Priam's sons, had, according to Homer, been slain by Achilles, but later accounts speak of another son of the same name. Just before the fall of Troy Priam had entrusted him, together with much gold, to Polymester, King of the Thracian Chersonesus, and when Troy fell Polymester murdered Polydorus for his gold and cast him into the sea. Hecuba discovered the body. She contrived to kill Polymester and his two sons, and she then evaded the angry Thracians by turning herself into a bitch named Mæra.

339. Euripides combined this story of Hecuba's revenge with that of the sacrifice of her daughter Polyxena in his tragedy Hecuba.

340. Few of the inhabitants of Troy escaped death or slavery. The wise Antenor, his wife Theano, and their children were all spared, and were said to have sailed to the West Coast of the Adriatic and there to have founded Venice and Padua.

341. Æneas' carried on his back his blind father Anchises through the Dardanian gate and so to safety. The Romans said that he took with him the Palladium, that stolen by Odysseus being only a replica, and, after seven years' wandering, reached Latium, where he founded Lavinia, and became their ancestral hero.

342. Æthra, the mother of Theseus, who had served Helen as a slave, was rescued by her grandsons, Acamas and Demophon, the sons of Theseus and Phædra.

## THE RETURNS FROM TROY.

343. Part of the ancient "Epic Cycle" of the Greeks was the cycle known as "The Returns," which was used both by Homer and Æschylus. It told of the adventures of the Greeks on their way home. Most suffered misfortune.

344. The fate of Agamemnon is described in para. 386–388, and that of Odysseus in para. 353–369.

345. Menelaus, who failed to sacrifice to Athene, took eight years, and only by seizing Proteus learned how to reach Sparta, where he married Hermione to Neoptolemus.

346. Neoptolemus had been accompanied by Andromache and by Helenus, who prophesied a safe route. He had abandoned his kingdom in Thessaly and settled in Epirus, part of which he gave to Helenus, who married Andromache. Neoptolemus then claimed Hermione, although her grandfather, Tyndareus, had betrothed her to Orestes, and as a result he was murdered, either by Orestes himself or at his instigation.

347. Many Greeks settled in Italy. Diomedes, hated by Aphrodite, finding on his return to Argos that his wife had been unfaithful, left for Ætolia to help his grandfather Œneus, and later settled in Daunia in Italy, where he married Euippe, daughter of King Daunus. He was buried in one of the islands since called Diomedans, and his companions were turned into gentle birds. Philoctetes also settled in Italy.

348. Idomeneus, caught by tempest on his return to Crete, vowed to sacrifice to Poseidon the first person he met on return. As this was his own son, Crete was punished by pestilence, and Idomeneus exiled. He settled in Calabria in Italy.

349. Demophon, son of Theseus visited Thrace and gained the love of the king's daughter, Phyllis, but when he left her to visit Athens, she killed herself in despair of his return and was turned into a tree.

350. Many sailors were ship-wrecked on the dangerous promontory of Capharcus, where Nauplius, King of Eubœa, eager to avenge the death of his son Palamedes, lighted misleading fires.

351. The seer, Calchas, like Amphilochus, went safely overland to Colophon. Here he contended in prophecy with Mopsus, a son of Apollo and Manto, the daughter of Teiresias, and being surpassed, he died of grief. Amphilochus joined with Mopsus in founding the city of Mallus, but they killed each other in a fight for its possession.

352. Nestor alone returned home without mishap and enjoyed a happy old age.

## THE WANDERINGS OF ODYSSEUS
### 353-369.

353. Odysseus' journey home, lasting ten years, and his final arrival in Ithaca are the theme of Homer's epic the *Odyssey*. E. V. Rieu says that this may be thought of as a novel, and Samuel Butler argued that it might well have been written by a woman! The incidents of the *Odyssey* form the background of reference to the *Ulysses* of James Joyce.

354. After leaving Troy, Odysseus and his men visited the Cicones, where he obtained several jars of sweet wine, and then they landed on the Libyan promontory of the Lotophagi. Here lived the Lotus-eaters, who gave his men some of the fruit, inducing the enervating dreaminess described by Tennyson in *The Lotus-eaters*.

355. Next, landing on the west coast of Sicily, Odysseus, with twelve companions, entered the cave of a giant, but when the owner, the one-eyed Cyclops, Polyphemus, son of Poseidon, came in with his flocks, he blocked the entrance with a gigantic stone, and devoured two of Odysseus' companions. Next evening, by which time only six of his men survived, Odysseus made Polyphemus drunk with his sweet wine and then blinded him. At dawn the Greeks escaped by clinging under the bodies of the sheep as they went out to graze, and so reached their ship, but henceforth they had to reckon with the vengeful hostility of Poseidon.

356. Odysseus was next entertained by Æolus, who gave him a bag of winds, but when his foolish crew untied this, they were blown back to Æolus, who now refused further help.

357. In Telepylos, city of Lamus, King of the cannibal Læstrygones, Odysseus lost all his ships except one, but in this he reached Ææa, the island of the enchantress Circe, daughter of Helios and Perse. Men sent by Odysseus to explore were turned by her to swine, and only Eurylochus returned to tell the news. Odysseus, hastening to their rescue, was given, by Hermes, the plant Moly, which vanquished Circe's charms. She restored his companions and lavishly entertained them all for a year.

358. Then, on Circe's advice, Odysseus sought the counsel of the dead seer Teiresias. He sailed to the River Oceanus, and in the land of the Cimmerians summoned the spirits of the dead, who thronged to lap the blood of a libation he had prepared. First appeared Elpenor, one of his crew, who while drunk had fallen to death from Circe's roof. Later came Teiresias, who gave him prophetic advice, and then Anticleia, the mother of Odysseus, the men and women of antiquity, and his former comrades.

359. He again visited Circe, who advised him how to circumvent the Sirens and Scylla and Charybdis. Odysseus nullified the Sirens' spell by having himself lashed to the mast, and by filling the sailors' ears with wax, and he just avoided the whirlpool Charybdis, though Scylla's six mouths snatched and devoured as many of his seamen.

360. At the island of Thrinacia, against the warnings both of Teiresias and Circe, Odysseus' companions slaughtered the cattle of Helios, and when they put to sea Zeus destroyed all save Odysseus himself.

361. Clinging to wreckage, he drifted ten days until he reached the island of Ogygia. Here the nymph Calypso lovingly kept him for eight years, until at Athene's request Zeus sent Hermes to command his release.

362. On a raft that Calypso had taught him to make, Odysseus sailed for eighteen days, till it was wrecked by vengeful Poseidon. Then helped by Leucothea and Athene, Odysseus landed on the island of Scheria. Here he was led by the beautiful Nausicaa to the Court of her father Alcinous, who was the prosperous ruler of the Phæacians. Alcinous gave Odysseus a ship, and after an absence of ten years he at last landed on Ithaca. Athene disguised him as a beggar and he was hospitably welcomed by his swineherd Eumæus.

363. Odysseus' mother Anticleia had died of grief, Laertes his father had withdrawn to the country, and his wife Penelope had been keeping at bay a crowd of unruly suitors led by Antinous. She had promised to wed one of them when she had finished a robe for Laertes, but each night she unpicked the work of the day, until her servants betrayed her ruse, and she was now hard-pressed. Her son Telemachus had gone in search of Odysseus, and after visiting Nestor and Menelaus, he now returned to Ithaca and also visited the hut of Eumæus.

364. Here Odysseus made himself known to Telemachus and they planned revenge. First the son set out for home, followed later by Odysseus still in beggar's disguise. He was recognised only by his aged hound Argus, which at once expired, and by his nurse Eurycleia.

365. Next day Penelope announced that she would accept the suitor who could shoot with the great bow of Eurytus which only Odysseus had been able to wield. No one could bend it till Odysseus seized it and shot Antinous. Supported by Telemachus, he killed the suitors, and at last made himself known to Penelope. He then visited Laertes, but the kinsmen of the suitors rose against him and battle ensued until Athene, disguised as Mentor effected a reconciliation.

366. At this point the *Odyssey* ends, though Teiresias had prophesied that Odysseus must again set out on a journey and propitiate Poseidon and then return to an honourable old age till death came to him from the sea.

367. Tennyson, in his poem *Ulysses*, imagines him, even in age, hungry still for travel.

368. Another tradition says that Telegonus, son of Odysseus by Circe, while searching for his father, landed on Ithaca and began to plunder for food. When opposed by Odysseus and Telemachus, all unknowing he killed his father. He then took Telemachus and Penelope back to Ææa, and there married Penelope, while Telemachus married Circe.

369. Although Homer represents Penelope as a faithful wife, other writers say that she became the mother of Pan, either by Hermes or by all the suitors. It is a tradition such as this that Joyce evidently follows in his *Ulysses*.

## LEGENDS OF THE HOUSE OF PELOPS,
### 370-398.

370. Some of the most dramatic of all Greek stories have their setting in Mycenæ, city of the legendary hero Agamemnon. In 1876 Schliemann began excavation on this ancient site, and here he unearthed the famous shaft-graves with their precious treasures, which probably date from 1600 B.C., four centuries before the era of Agamemnon and the siege of Troy. Schliemann thus proved to the learned world that the city at all events was historical, and scholars now believe that it was the centre of a Late Bronze Age culture.

371. According to legend, Agamemnon was a descendant of Tantalus, son of Zeus and the nymph Pluto and father of Pelops, Broteas, and Niobe. Tantalus was said to be a wealthy king, but whether of Lydia, Argos or Corinth, is uncertain.

372. Highly favoured by his father Zeus, Tantalus was even invited to Olympian banquets, but he proved unworthy of such honours, divulging Zeus' secrets and stealing nectar and ambrosia from Olympus.

373. Tantalus was also said to have received from Pandareus a dog made of gold, and then to have sworn by Zeus that he had never seen or heard of it. As this dog was the one which Hephæstus had made for Rhea, and which she had set to watch the cradle of the infant Zeus, the gods were naturally incensed. Pandareus perished miserably, and his orphan daughters were carried off by Harpies, and Tantalus suffered agonising punishment for this and other crimes, the most ghastly of which was his murder of his son Pelops. Having invited the gods to a banquet, he cut Pelops into pieces and served them in a stew. Demeter, still grieving for Persephone, was the only divinity who did not notice what she was eating, and she consumed the shoulder.

374. Tantalus' punishment became proverbial. Tortured with thirst, he was placed in a lake whose waters receded whenever he attempted to drink, while above his head were laden fruit boughs which flew upwards as soon as he reached for them. Thus " tantalised," he also saw suspended above his head a huge rock which threatened to fall and crush him.

375. After punishing Tantalus, Zeus ordered Hermes to put the limbs of Pelops into a cauldron and boil them. Clotho took him from the cauldron, Demeter gave him an ivory shoulder, which became a kind of birthmark for his descendants, and Pelops was restored to life.

376. Pelops was later expelled from his kingdom of Phrygia and came with his followers to Pisa in Elis. Here Œnomaus, son of Ares, was king, and as an oracle had said that he would be killed by his son-in-law, he challenged to a chariot race all who came to woo his daughter, Hippodameia. If the young man won, he would marry Hippodameia, if not he would be killed by the spear of Œnomaus, which, like his wind-begotten horses, was a gift of his father Ares.

377. Many suitors had lost their lives when Pelops arrived in Pisa. He was already possessed of a winged golden chariot, the gift of Poseidon, but he also bribed Œnomaus' charioteer Myrtilus, the son of Hermes, with the promise of half the kingdom, to remove the lynch-pin from the chariot of his master and substitute one of wax. Œnomaus was flung out and killed, and Pelops married Hippodameia.

378. Pelops refused to keep faith with Myrtilus and flung him into the sea. Myrtilus, as he died, cursed the whole race of Pelops, and his image was set among the stars as the charioteer by his father Hermes. Pelops soon became master of Olympia and revived the Olympic Games. His wealth and power in the peninsula were so great that it was called the Peloponnesus, or " Island of Pelops."

379. The eldest sons of Pelops, Atreus and Thyestes, with the connivance of their mother, killed Chrysippus, their half-brother, and were obliged to flee their home.

380. They were kindly received at Mycenæ, and after the death of King Eurystheus, Atreus seized the kingdom in spite of the bitter rivalry of Thyestes, whom he forthwith banished.

381. Thyestes, however, who had already succeeded in seducing Atreus' second wife Ærope, now tricked his brother into killing Pleisthenes, his own son by his first wife. Atreus, planning grisly reprisals, lured Thyestes to Mycenæ by promising him half the kingdom. He then killed the sons of Thyestes and served him their flesh at a banquet. When the horror-stricken father realised what he had eaten, he laid a curse on the house of Atreus and fled once more.

382. Thyestes, seeking revenge, was advised by the Delphic Oracle to beget a son by his own daughter, and going to King Thesprotus at Sicyon, where his daughter Pelopia was a priestess, he ravished her and fled.

383. Atreus now visited Sicyon, and, believing Pelopia to be a daughter of Thesprotus, married

her as his third wife. When she gave birth to Thyestes' son, Ægisthus, she exposed the baby, but Atreus, believing Ægisthus to be his own child, took him in and reared him.

384. When later Thyestes was seized and brought back to Mycenæ, Atreus commanded Ægisthus to slay him, but Thyestes disarmed the boy, and recognising him as his own son, ordered him to kill Atreus. Then, at last, Thyestes ruled in Mycenæ.

385. According to Homer, Atreus had two sons by Ærope, Agamemnon and Menelaus, and these two now took refuge with King Tyndareus of Sparta. Here Menelaus married Helen, daughter by Zeus of Tyndareus' wife, Leda, and some say that Agamemnon was helped by Tyndareus to expel Thyestes and gain his father's throne.

386. Agamemnon's wife was Clytemnestra (the daughter of Tyndareus and Leda), whom he forcibly married after killing her first husband in battle. But when his brother's wife, Helen, was stolen away by Paris, and the Trojan War broke out, Agamemnon was away fighting for ten years, and it was not difficult then for Ægisthus to seduce Clytemnestra.

387. Not only had Agamemnon forcibly married Clytemnestra, but he had also agreed to the sacrifice of their daughter, Iphigeneia at Aulis, and her cup of bitterness was full when she learned that he was returning from Troy, bringing with him Priam's daughter, the prophetess Cassandra, as his mistress.

388. It is at this point that Æschylus' great trilogy of the Oresteia begins. Clytemnestra conspired with Ægisthus to kill both Agamemnon and Cassandra. She welcomed her husband royally on his return, but while he was in his bath entangled him in a net, and after Ægisthus had twice struck him, she beheaded him with an axe. She then went out to kill Cassandra, who had refused to enter the palace because, in visionary trance, she was horrified to smell the ancient shedding of blood and the curse of Thyestes (see para. 381).

389. It was not difficult now for Clytemnestra to seize power, for Orestes, her young son, had been smuggled out of Mycenæ by his sister Electra, and for many years Clytemnestra and her paramour ruled in Mycenæ.

390. Ægisthus, however, lived in constant fear of vengeance. He would have killed Electra had Clytemnestra allowed, so he married her to a peasant, who was fearful of consummating their union. Orestes meanwhile had taken refuge with Strophius, King of Phocis, who had married Agamemnon's sister, and here he formed that friendship with the king's son, Pylades, which became proverbial.

391. The intensely dramatic situation at this point has inspired all three of the great Greek tragedians, and it is most interesting to compare the various interpretations given by Æschylus, in The Libation Bearers, the second play of his trilogy, by Sophocles, in Electra, and by Euripides, in Electra.

392. Electra, burning for revenge, sent constant messages to Orestes, and when he and Pylades were of age they came secretly to Mycenæ, and with Electra's help killed both Ægisthus and Clytemnestra.

393. The agonising punishment that Orestes now endured is portrayed in the Eumenides, the last play of Æschylus' trilogy, and in the Orestes of Euripides. Although the Delphic Oracle had encouraged Orestes to avenge his father, she was powerless to prevent his being pursued by the Erinnyes, the avengers of matricide, who drove him mad and hounded him from land to land. At length, on the further advice of the Pythian Priestess, he reached Athens and embraced the image of Athene in her temple on the Acropolis. The goddess then summoned the Areopagus to

judge his case. Apollo defended him against the Erinnyes on the grounds that motherhood is less important than fatherhood, and he was acquitted by the casting vote of Athene, the verdict being a triumph for the patriarchal principle.

394. The furious Erinnyes were then pacified by Athene, who persuaded them to accept a grotto in Athens, where they would be offered sacrifices, libations, and first fruits. Their name henceforward was Eumenides, or the " well-meaning."

395. According to another tradition, followed by Euripides, in his *Iphigeneia Among the Taurians*, Orestes was told by Apollo that he would be freed from madness by fetching the statue of Artemis from the Tauric Chersonese.

396. When Orestes and Pylades reached Tauris they were seized by the barbarous natives, who sacrificed all strangers to Artemis, but they found to their amazement that the priestess was none other than Orestes' own sister Iphigeneia. Orestes believed that she had lost her life when sacrificed to Artemis at Aulis (as is described in para. 300), but she had in fact been rescued by the goddess and brought to Tauris as her priestess.

397. Iphigeneia, by her ready wit, rescued Orestes and Pylades from sacrifice, and all three returned to Greece, carrying with them the image of the goddess. Here they were reunited with Electra, and returned to Mycenæ, where Orestes, by killing Ægisthus' son and becoming king, finally ended the strife between the sons of Atreus.

398. Orestes, after killing his rival Neoptolemus, married his cousin Hermione, and Electra was married to Pylades.

## THE UNDERWORLD, 399–409.

399. The Greeks expected to enter after death into the cheerless nether world, the domain of Hades, known to the Romans as Orcus, or Dis, but as Hades was possessor of all the rich metals and gems of the earth, the ancients usually preferred the euphemism " Pluto," " the wealth," when speaking of one so dreaded.

400. The word " Hades " was used too of his actual domain, which was also called Tartarus, although in the *Iliad*, the word " Tartarus " had been reserved for the very lowest region of the Underworld, where the rebel Titans had been thrust.

401. Hades, son of Cronus and Rhea, won the lordship of the nether world when his brother Zeus won the sky, and Poseidon the sea. His most treasured possessions were the helmet of darkness, given him by the Cyclopes, and the staff with which he drove the ghosts.

402. He ruled with his queen, Persephone, whom he had forcibly abducted from the upper world, but he was not always faithful to her, and she once changed the nymph Minthe, whom he was pursuing into the plant mint, and the nymph Leuce, whom he loved, was afterwards changed into the white poplar.

403. The companion to Persephone was Hecate, who had once aided Demeter in her search for the lost maiden. Hecate was a mysterious divinity, a triple goddess, mighty in heaven, on earth, and in the Underworld, honoured by Zeus and all the immortal gods. She came to be regarded by the Hellenes as primarily a dread divinity of the Underworld, as one who kept company with the dead and who fostered sorcery and witchcraft. She figures as such in *Macbeth*. Worshipped where three roads met, she was represented with three bodies and three heads.

404. Also dwelling in the Underworld were the Erinnyes, winged daughters of earth or of night, with serpent hair, who punished unnatural crime. They were later known euphemistically, as the " Eumenides," or " well-meaning," and this name was said to have been given them after the acquittal of Orestes, as is portrayed in the *Eumenides* of Æschylus. Late writers named three Erinnyes, Alecto, Megera, and Tisiphone.

405. Ghosts conducted to Hades' realm by Hermes had first to cross the Styx, the " hated " river, and supplied by relatives with a coin laid under the tongue of the corpse, they paid the surly ferryman Charon. Without this coin they were unable to cross the Styx. Arrived on the farther bank, they propitiated Cerberus, represented by later writers as a fierce dog with three heads, said to be another of the monsters born to Echidne.

406. Styx was not the only river ghosts encountered. There was also Acheron, river of woe, Phlegethon, river of flames, Cocytus, river of wailing, and Lethe, the river of forgetfulness, where ghosts drank and forgot their past.

407. The three judges of the Underworld were Æacus, Rhadamanthus, and Minos. Wicked spirits were sent by them to the place of punishment, those who had led an indifferent life to the cheerless asphodel fields, and the virtuous to Elysium.

408. Although Elysium was said to be near the Underworld, it formed no part of Hades' dominion, and Homer placed it far away to the west of the earth, near Oceanus. It was a blessed abode, without cold or snow. Later writers also spoke of the " Fortunate Isles," located by Greek geographers as beyond the pillars of Heracles, and eventually identified with the Canary and Madeira islands.

409. In their picture of life after death the Greeks combined contradictory ideas. Broadly speaking, the figures of Persephone and Hecate represent the hopes of pre-Hellenic people for an after-life, while Hades personifies the Hellenic fear of the finality of death.

# PART III. INDEX AND GLOSSARY

*Note :* The numbers in this part refer to the numbered paragraphs in Part II.

Apollo, 10, 14, 26, 32, 36, 68–80, 82–85, 92, 94, 104, 183, 251, 277 283, 298, 309, 321, 330, 331, 351, 393, 395.

Apple of Discord, 280.

Arachne, a Lydian maiden who challenged Athene to compete with her in weaving. When Athene found Arachne's work faultless, she angrily tore it up, and the terrified maiden hanged herself. Athene then turned her into a spider and the rope into a cobweb.

Arcadia, 85, 92, 97.

Arcas, son of Zeus and Callisto, who was supposed to have given his name to Arcadia.

Arctos, see Callisto.

Areopagus, 43, 67, 105.

Ares, see especially 64–67 and also 10, 13, 14, 25, 33, 55, 60, 61, 154, 158, 178, 243, 317, 376.

Arethusa, 88.

Arges, 1.

Argia, 261.

Argo, The, 155–160, 162.

Argonauts, 154–160.

Argos, 30, 33, 34, 45, 125, 130, 142, 143.

Argus. (1) The hound of Odysseus, 364.
(2) The hundred-eyed, 95.
(3) The builder of Argo, 155.

Aria, the mother of Miletus by Apollo.

Ariadne, 231, 235.

Arion. (1) An actual historical character was a lyric poet and player on the lyre, who lived at the Court of Periander of Corinth at about 625 B.C. The following curious fable is told of him. On one occasion Arion visited Sicily and won the prize in a musical contest. Laden with gifts, he took ship for Corinth, and the captain and crew decided to murder him for his treasure. They gave him permission to sing one last song. Arion then invoked the gods, and leapt into the sea. Here he was rescued by one of the music-loving dolphins that had gathered to hear his song, and taken on its back to Corinth, where he told Periander of his adventures. Later, when the ship arrived, the captain and crew swore that Arion had been detained in Sicily. Periander then confronted them with Arion himself and had them executed. The images of Arion and his lyre were set among the stars.
(2) A fabulous horse, 103.

Aristæus was the son of Apollo and Cyrene, born in Libya. He went to Thrace and fell in love with Eurydice, who, fleeing from him, perished by a snake bite. As a punishment Aristæus lost his bees, and how he raised a new swarm is told in Virgil's fourth Georgics. After death was worshipped as a god.

Arsinoë, 271.

Artemis, 10, 13, 14, 26, 69, 70, 72, 81–89, 251, 229, 300.

Ascalaphus, 112, 184.

Asclepius or Æsculapius was a son of Apollo by Coronis. He was brought up by Cheiron, who taught him healing. He once recalled a dead man to life and was killed by Zeus with a thunderbolt. At Apollo's request, however, he was placed among the stars. Another tradition says that Asclepius was a native of Epidaurus. In Homer he was not a god, but the "blameless physician," father of Machaon and Podalirius, physicians to the Greek Army. His supposed descendants were the Asclepiadæ, a caste of priests who transmitted from father to son the knowledge of medicine as a sacred secret. Epidaurus was the centre of Asclepius' worship. Cocks were sacrificed to him and serpents sacred.

Asopus, a river god, son of Oceanus and Tethys, and father of Evadne, Euboea, and Ægina.

Astarte, 57.

Astræus, a Titan, was father, by Eos, of the beneficent winds and, some say, of the stars also.

Astyanax, 336.

Atalanta. (1) The Arcadian Atalanta, daughter of Iasus and Clymene, was exposed by her father and suckled by a bear. She always carried arms. She joined the Calydonian hunt and bore a son, Parthenopæus, to Meleager. Reconciled to her father, she refused to marry unless a suitor should conquer her in a foot race, those who failed in the attempt being killed by her. Eventually Milanion outstripped Atalanta by dropping in her way one after the other, three golden apples given him by Aphrodite. Atalanta stopped to gather these and lost the race. See also 263.
(2) The Bœotian Atalanta was said to be daughter of Schoeneus and to have married Hippomenes, but the same tales are told of her. See Swinburne's play Atalanta in Calydon and the poem Atalanta's Race, by William Morris.

Athamas, was the son of Æolus and King of Orchomenus in Bœotia. At Hera's command he married Nephele, and had children Phrixus and Helle. But Athamas secretly loved Ino, daughter of Cadmus and Harmonia, who bore him Learchus and Melicertes. Deceived by Ino's intrigues, Athamas would have sacrificed Phrixus, had not a ram with a golden fleece, sent by Hermes, rescued the boy and flown through the air with him and his sister Helle. Between Europe and Asia, Helle fell into the straits since called Hellespont, but Phrixus reached Colchis, where he sacrificed the ram to Zeus and gave the fleece to Æëtes, from whom it was later carried off by Jason. Meanwhile Athamas, driven mad by Hera because he had sheltered Dionysus, killed his son Learchus, and Ino flung herself into the sea with Melicertes, where both were transformed into marine deities. Ino became Leucothea, and Melicertes changed to Palæmon. Athamas, forced to flee, settled in Thessaly. See also 120.

Athene, see especially 38–45 and also 14, 15, 48, 66, 77, 102, 105, 134, 135, 141, 148, 155, 178, 184, 189, 243, 244, 265, 280, 281, 325, 328, 330, 335, 345, 361, 362, 393, 394.

Athens, 42, 48, 86, 97, 102, 105, 112, 114, 117, 118, 128.

Atlantiades, 91.

Atlantis was a legendary island, west of the Pillars of Hercules. Its virtuous and powerful inhabitants, becoming degenerate, were defeated by the Athenians, and the island was swallowed up by the ocean in a day and night. See the Timæus of Plato.

Atlas, the son of Iapetus and Clymene, was father of the Pleiades, Hyades, and Hesperides. See also 7, 9, 16, 91, 138, 183.

Atlas, Mt., 136, 183.

Atreus, 379, 380, 381, 383, 384, 385, 397.

Atropos, one of the Fates.

Auge, 191.

Augeias, stables of, 177, 190.

Aulis, 299, 300, 318, 387.

Autolycus, 96, 167, 290, 329.

Autonoe, 244, 246.

Bacchæ, 117, 123. Also called Bacchantes, Mænads, or Thyiads.

"Bacchæ, The," 123, 246.

Bacchoi, 117.

Bacchus, a name for Dionysus, 117–128.

Bassareus was an epithet of Dionysus. "Bassaris" was a fox-skin which was worn by the god and also the Mænads in Thrace. Hence Bassaris means Mænad or Bacchante.

Bathos, 12.

Baucis, see Philemon.

Bebrycos, 157.

Bellerophon, 145–150.

Bellerus, 146.

Belus, son of Poseidon and father of Ægyptus, Danaus, and Cepheus.

Bias, brother of Melampus.

Biton and Cleobis, sons of a priestess of Hera at Argos, in their filial devotion once dragged their mother's chariot to the temple. Their mother prayed Hera to grant them the best gift for mortals, and they both died while asleep in the temple.

Bœotia, 117, 120, 123.

Boreas, the North wind, was the son of Astræus and Eos, and brother to the other beneficent winds—Notus, Eurus, and Zephyrus. He carried off Oreithyia, daughter of Erectheus, who bore him twin sons, Zetes and Calais, and the daughters Chione and Cleopatra (the wife of Phineus). Boreas was friendly to the Athenians and destroyed the ships of Xerxes.

Bosphorus, 157.

Brauron, 86.

Briareus, one of the Hecatoncheires, 1, 32.

Briseis, 309, 312, 315.

Britomartis, 81, 229.

Bromius, 117.

Brontes, 1.

Broteas, 371.

Butes, son of Pandion, King of Athens, was a priest of Pallas Athene.


Cacus, 182.

Cadmea, 242, 243, 250.

Cadmus, 158, 240, 241, 242, 243, 244, 245, 246, 247, 252.

Caduceus, 98.

Cæneus, offspring of Elatus, was originally the nymph Cænis, beloved by Poseidon, who had consented to change her to a man. Cæneus accompanied the Argonauts and helped to hunt the Calydonian Boar. Although invulnerable, he was killed by the Centaurs in the battle with the Lapithæ, for they buried him under a mass of trees. His soul flew out as a bird, and in the Underworld he regained female form.

Calais, see Zetes.

Calchas, 293, 300, 309, 323, 325, 351.

Calipe, one of the pillars of Heracles, 182.

Calliope, the Muse of epic poetry, is represented with a tablet and stylus and sometimes with a roll of paper or a book.

Callirrhoë, 271.

Callisto, daughter of Lycaon, was one of Artemis' huntresses. She was seduced by Zeus, who tried to deceive Hera by turning her into a bear. Hera, discovering the ruse, contrived that Artemis should hunt Callisto down, but Zeus caught her up and set her image among the stars as Arctos. Some say that Artemis herself in anger turned Callisto into a bear; others that she was pursued by her own son Arcas and that Zeus snatched both to heaven, Callisto becoming the Great Bear and Arcas the Little Bear.

Calypso, 361, 362.

Capaneus, 263, 265, 267, 268.

Capricorn, 6.

Cassandra, 277, 283, 330, 335, 387, 388.

Cassiopeia, 139, 140.

Castalian Spring, 69.

Castalides, the Muses.

Castor, one of Dioscuri, 155, 167, 215, 285, 286.

Caucasus, 17.

Cecrops was said to be the first king of Attica, and to have founded Athens. See also 204, 206.

Celeus, 113.

Centaurs in Homer appear as savage creatures, but in later accounts are described as having the upper part of the body human, the lower part equine. They were said to be the offspring of Ixion and a cloud. They lived on Mt. Pelion in Thessaly, a district famous for hunting the bull on horseback. On one occasion they fought with Heracles (see 176), but their most celebrated fight was that with the Lapithæ (see 212). Wisest of the Centaurs was Cheiron.

Centimani, 1.

Cephalus had married Procris, but Eos, who fell in love with him, revealed that Procris was easily seduced by gold. Procris then fled in shame to Crete, where she was seduced by Minos. She later returned to Athens, disguised as a youth and bringing a hound and spear, the gifts of Artemis, that never missed their quarry. Cephalus so coveted these, that husband and wife became reconciled. Procris, however, suspected him of loving Eos, and jealously watched him while hunting. One day

Cephalus accidentally killed her with the unerring spear.

Cepheus. (1) Son of Aleus, and one of the Argonauts, was King of Tegea in Arcadia, but he and most of his sons were killed while helping Heracles against Hippocoon. See also 191.
(2) King of Æthiopia, 139, 140.

Cerberus (and Heracles), 184, 405.

Cercyon was the son of Poseidon or Hephæstus. He lived near Eleusis, where he killed all travellers by challenging them to a wrestling-match, but was himself overcome and killed by Theseus. See also 205.

Ceres, Roman counterpart of Demeter, 110–116.

Ceryneian Hind, 175.

Ceto, 134.

Ceyx, see Alcyone.

Chaos, 1.

Charis, 55.

Charities or Graces, were called Gratiæ by the Romans. At first the Greeks personified one Grace only—Charis, who in the Iliad appears as the wife of Hephæstus. Later the Greeks spoke of three Graces, Euphrosyne, Aglaia, and Thalia, daughters of Zeus. They were especially the friends of the Muses, living with them on Mt. Olympus.

Charon, 405.

Charybdis, see Scylla and 359.

Cheiron or Chiron was the wisest and best of all the Centaurs. He was the son of Cronus and Philyra, and was hence called Philyrides, and lived on Mt. Pelion. Taught by Apollo and Artemis, he was skilled in music, medicine, prophecy, hunting, and gymnastics, and taught many of the heroes of antiquity, such as Jason, Castor and Pollux, Peleus, and Achilles. Heracles accidentally caused his death (see 176), and Zeus placed his image among the stars as Sagittarius.

Chimæra, 147, 148, 255.

Chione. (1) The daughter of Oreithyia and Boreas and mother by Poseidon of Eumolpus, hence called Chionides.
(2) Mother of Autolycus by Hermes. She was killed by Artemis.

Chiron, see Cheiron.

Chrysaor, 108, 137.

Chryseis, 309.

Chrysippus, 379.

Chthonius, one of Sparti, 243.

Cicones, 354.

Cilix, 225.

Cimmerians, 358.

Circe, 160, 357, 358, 359, 360, 368.

Ciris, 230.

Cithæron was a lofty range of mountains between Bœotia and Attica, sacred to Dionysus and the Muses. Pentheus and Actæon were killed there. See also 168.

Cleobis, see Biton.

Cleonæan (or Nemean) Lion, 173.

Clio, the Muse of History, represented with a roll of paper or a chest of books.

Clotho, one of the Fates, 375.

Clymene. (1) Mother of Phæton by Helios.
(2) Wife of Iapetus.

Clytemnestra, 287, 386, 387, 388, 389, 390, 392.

Cnidos, 116.

Cnossos, 30, 220.

Cocalus, 238.

Cocytus, 406.

Colchis, 154, 157.

Colonos, 260.

Core, the Maiden, 39, 111.

Corinth, 45, 58, 102, 105, 118, 146, 148, 161.

Cornucopia, 6.

Coronis, 74.

Corybantes, priests of Rhea in Phrygia noted for their dances to drums and cymbals.

Cottus, one of the Hecatoncheires.

Horæ, goddesses of the order of nature and the seasons (*see* 25). It is said that Zeus' fatherhood of the Horæ on Themis indicates that the Hellenes took over control of the calendar.

Hyacinthus, 74.

Hyades, 120.

Hydra of Lerna, 174, 196.

Hygeia, the goddess of health, was either the daughter or the wife of Asclepius. She is represented as dressed in a long robe and feeding a serpent from a cup.

Hylas, 156.

Hyllus, 193, 196, 199, 201.

Hyperboreans, 137.

Hyperenor, one of Sparti, 243.

Hyperion, a Titan and father of Helios, Selene, and Eos. 1, 9.

Hypermnestra, *see* Danaides.

Hypnus, the god of sleep.

Hypseus was the father of Cyrene beloved by Apollo.

Hypsipyle was the daughter of Thoas, King of Lemnos. When the women killed all the men in the island she saved her father. She welcomed Jason on the Argonauts' landing in Lemnos and bore him twins. Later the women of Lemnos discovered that she had spared Thoas and sold her as a slave to King Lycurgus of Nemea, who entrusted his son Opheltes to her care.

Iacchus, the name of Dionysus in the Eleusinian mysteries, where the god was regarded as the son of Zeus and Demeter.

Iapetus, a Titan and father of Atlas, Prometheus, and Epimetheus, 1.

Iasion, Iasius, or Iasus was the son of Zeus and Electra. Demeter loved him and bore him a son Pluton or Plutus, and Zeus, in anger, slew Iasion with a thunderbolt.

Icaria, 124.

Icarius. (1) Was an Athenian who received Dionysus hospitably and learned from him the cultivation of the vine. He gave some wine he had made to shepherds who, seeing double, believed they had been bewitched and killed Icarius. His daughter Erigone was led to his grave by his dog Mæra, and she hanged herself in despair from the tree under which her father had been buried.

(2) Of Sparta, 290.

Icarus, 238.

Ida, Mt., near Troy, 278, 280, 305, 325.

Idæa, 274.

Idas, the twin brother of Lynceus, was said to be son of Aphareus. He was in love with Marpessa, whom he carried off in a chariot given him by Poseidon, who was really his father. Idas' rival Apollo fought with him for Marpessa, but Zeus separated the combatants, and she chose Idas. With his devoted twin he took part in the Calydonian hunt, and the Argonauts' expedition, and both were finally killed in a battle with their rivals, the Dioscuri.

Idomeneus, 297, 348.

"Iliad," 77, 101, 309, 313, 316, 400.

Ilithyiæ, daughters of Hera, who in the *Iliad* and early poets are represented as helping women in childbirth. In the *Odyssey* and later poets only one goddess, Ilithyia, is represented. *See also* 33.

Illyrius, son of Cadmus, 244.

Ilus, 274.

Imbros, 56.

Inachus, son of Oceanus and Tethys, was first King of Argos, and gave his name to the river.

Ino, 120, 244, 246.

Io, daughter of Inachus was beloved by Zeus, who turned her into a white heifer through fear of Hera. The goddess Hera set Argus of the hundred eyes to watch the heifer, but Hermes, at Zeus' bidding, charmed Argus to sleep and cut off his head. Hera placed Argus' eyes in the

tail of her favourite bird, the peacock, and sent a gadfly to torment Io, who fled from land to land till she came to the Nile. Here she recovered her human form and bore Zeus a son Epaphus. The Ionian Sea and the Bosphorus, (or cow's ford) were said to have derived their name from Io.

Iobates, 146–149.

Iolaus, 172, 174, 185, 192, 199.

Iolcus, 152, 153, 154, 161.

Iole, 186, 195, 196, 197.

Ion, *see* Xuthus.

Ionians, 68, 88, 99.

Iphicles. (1) Son of Amphitrion, 166, 170, 171, 172.

(2) One of the Argonauts.

Iphigeneia, 86, 300, 387, 395, 396, 397.

" Iphigeneia Among the Taurians " of Euripides, 395.

Iphimedeia, wife of Alœus, 13.

Iphis, 267.

Iphitus, 186.

Irene, called Pax by the Romans, was goddess of peace and according to Hesiod one of the Horæ, daughters of Zeus and Themis. She was worshipped in Athens.

Iris, in the *Iliad* she appears as messenger of the gods, but in the *Odyssey* she is never mentioned. She was originally a personification of the rainbow.

Ishtar, 57.

Ismene, 257, 260.

Issa, daughter of Macareus, was loved by Apollo

Isthmian Games, 105.

Ithaca, 289, 290, 353, 362, 363, 368.

Itys was the son of Tereus and Procne.

Ixion, the son of Phlegyas, King of the Lapithæ, treacherously murdered his father-in-law. Though pardoned by Zeus, Ixion now tried to seduce Hera, but was deceived by a phantom, Nephele, who bore him a Centaur. Ixion was punished by being chained to a fiery wheel which rolled ceaselessly through the sky. His son was Pirithous. See Browning's *Ixion*.

Jason, 151–163.

Jocasta, 253, 257, 258, 259.

Juno, Roman counterpart of Hera, 29–35.

Jupiter, Roman counterpart of Zeus, 23–28.

Juventas, *see* Hebe.

Labdacus, 252.

Lachesis, one of the Fates.

Ladon, 183.

Lælaps, the swift dog which Procris gave to Cephalus.

Læres, 290, 363, 365.

Læstrygones, 357.

Laius, 252, 253, 254, 255, 258.

Lamia, daughter of Belus, loved by Zeus. She became one of the Empusæ.

Lamus, 357.

Laocoön, 330, 331.

Laodameia, wife of Protesilaus, 303.

Laodice. (1) Daughter of Priam, 335.

(2) Homeric name for Electra, daughter of Agamemnon.

Laomedan, 274, 275.

Lapithæ were a mythical people living in Thessaly and governed by Pirithous, who, being a son of Ixion, was half-brother to the Centaurs. Rivalry between the Centaurs and Lapithæ reached its climax at the celebrated struggle at the wedding of Pirithous. *See also* 212.

Larissa, 142.

Leander, a youth of Abydos, swam across the Hellespont every night to visit Hero, priestess of Aphrodite in Sestos. One night he was drowned, and Hero then flung herself into the

Mimas, 11.

Minerva, Roman counterpart of Athene.

Minoan Tradition, 6.

Minos, 220, 222, 224, 225, 227, 228, 229, 230, 231, 233, 237, 238, 239, 407.

Minotaur, 222, 233, 234, 235.

Minthe, 402.

Minyans, 99, 100, 110, 169.

Mnemosyne or " Memory " daughter of Uranus, 25.

Mœræ or Moiræ, see Fates and 25.

Moly, 357.

Mopsus, 351.

Musæ or Musagetes. The Muses were divinities presiding over the arts and sciences. They were daughters of Zeus and Mnemosyne, and were born at Pieria near Mt. Olympus. Their worship spread from Thracia and Pieria into Bœotia, where they dwelt on Mt. Helicon, with its sacred fountains of Aganippe and Hippocrene. Mt. Parnassus and its Castalian Spring were also sacred to them. Libations of water or milk and honey were offered to the Muses. Originally three in number, they were afterwards spoken of as nine, Clio of history, Euterpe of lyric poetry (or of music), Thalia of comedy, Melpomene of tragedy, Terpsichore of choral dance and song, Erato of erotic poetry and mime, Polymnia, or Polyhymnia, of the sublime hymn, Calliope of epic poetry, and Urania of astronomy.

Mycenæ, 143, 144, 370, 380, 381, 384, 389, 392, 397.

Myrmidones, 293, 314.

Myrtilus, 377, 378.

Mysia, 156.


Naiades or Naiads, the nymphs of fresh water, 156.

Narcissus, see Echo.

Nauplius, 350.

Nausicaa, 362.

Naxos, 13, 124.

Neleus was twin brother of Pelias (see 108, 152, 153). Driven from Iolcus by Pelias, he went with Melampus and Bias to Pylus, where he became king. He had twelve sons. See also 190, 191.

Nemean Lion, 173.

Nemean Games, 173.

Nemesis, who was said to be a daughter of Oceanus, was a goddess who originally measured out to men happiness and misery, chastening those who were over-fortunate. Later she came to be thought of as one who punished crime. She had a shrine at Rhamnus in Attica. The wheel which she habitually carried was probably in origin a symbol of the solar year, according to whose seasons the sacred king was fated to rise to the height of his fortune or to die.

Neoptolemus or Pyrrhus, 295, 325, 326, 328, 334, 336, 337, 345, 346, 398.

Nephele, a phantom created by Zeus to deceive Ixion, became the wife of Athamas.

Neptune, see Poseidon.

Nereides or Nereids, daughters of Nereus, nymphs of the Mediterranean, 109, 139.

Nereus, 106.

Nessus, 194, 196.

Nestor, 190, 287, 295, 318, 352, 363.

Niobe, 82, 250, 251, 371.

Nisus, 230.

Nisyrus, 12.

Nomius, the Pasturer, a name given to gods, such as Apollo, Hermes, Pan, who protect pastures.

Notus, called Auster by the Romans, was the South-west wind. He was a son of Astræus and Eos.

Nymphæ were lesser deities which peopled all parts of nature.

Nysa, Mt., 120, 128.


Oceanides, nymphs of the ocean, daughters of Oceanus.

Oceanus, 1, 3, 7, 25, 358.

" Odyssey," 60, 322, 353–366.

Odysseus, 289, 290, 291, 295, 301, 302, 308, 313, 322, 323, 325, 326, 327, 328, 329, 334, 338, 344, 353–369.

Œbalus. (1) King of Sparta and father of Tyndareus, Hippocoon, and Icarius.

Œdipus, 252–261.

" Œdipus at Colonos," 260.

" Œdipus Tyrannus," 260.

Œneus, King of Pleuron and Calydon in Ætolia, married Althæa and was father of Tydeus, Meleager, Gorge, and Deianeira. His realm was ravaged by the Calydonian Boar, and was later seized by his nephews, but his grandson Diomedes, son of Tydeus, avenged him and put Gorge's husband Andræmon on the throne. Œneus accompanied Diomedes to the Peloponnesus, where he was eventually killed by two nephews who had escaped Diomedes' vengeance. See also 192, 261.

Œnomaus, 376, 377.

Œnone, 278, 324.

Ogygia, 361.

Oileus, King of the Locrians, was one of the Argonauts, 292.

Olympia, 27.

Olympic Games, founded by Heracles, 190, 378.

Olympius, a name for the Muses and all the gods who were supposed to live in Olympus and not in the lower world.

The twelve great Olympian gods in some places worshipped as a body were Zeus, Poseidon, Apollo, Ares, Hermes, Hephæstus, Hestia, Demeter, Hera, Athene, Aphrodite, and Artemis. At a later date Dionysus became one of the great twelve, in place of Hestia.

Olympus, Mt., 14, 27, 47, 51, 52, 53, 54, 66, 118, 150, 372.

Omphale, 95, 187, 188.

Omphalos, 76.

Opheltes was the son of King Lycurgus of Nemea. The Nemean games were founded in his honour, but Heracles re-dedicated them to Zeus.

Orchomenus was the capital of the Minyans of Bœotia, 169.

Orcus, 399.

Oreades were the nymphs of mountains and grottoes.

" Oresteia " of Æschylus, 388.

Orestes, 346, 389, 390, 392, 393, 395, 396, 397, 398, 404.

" Orestes " of Euripides, 393.

Orion, a son of Poseidon was a giant hunter and exceedingly handsome. He fell in love with Merope, the daughter of Œnopion of Chios. Œnopion promised Merope to Orion if he would free the island of wild beasts. When he failed to keep his promise Orion seduced Merope, and was blinded by Œnopion, who was helped by his father Dionysus. An oracle told Orion that he would regain his sight if he travelled East and exposed his eyeballs to the rising sun. He went to Lemnos, where Hephæstus lent him a guide to the East. There Eos fell in love with him, and her brother Helios restored his sight. Orion later joined Artemis as a hunter, boasting that he would kill all the wild animals. Apollo, hearing this and fearing that Artemis also might fall in love with Orion, cunningly contrived that the goddess should accidentally kill him. After his death Orion's image was set among the stars, where he appears as a giant with " belt and sworded hip." The story of his blindness cured in the East is a myth of the sun, on whose rising the animals retire to their dens.

Oreithyia, daughter of Erectheus, carried away by Boreas.

Orpheus, the son of King Œagrus and Calliope, received a lyre from Apollo and was taught to play by the Muses, so that he was able to enchant beasts, trees, and rocks to follow his music. On returning from his voyage with the Argonauts (see 155), he married Eurydice, and when she died from a snake bite, he followed her

Pheræ was an ancient town in Thessaly, the home of Admetus.

Pheres, son of Cretheus and Tyro, was the father of Admetus and Lycurgus and the founder of Pheræ in Thessaly.

Philemon, an old man of Phrygia who, with his wife Baucis, hospitably received Zeus and Hermes.

Philoctetes, 198, 301, 303, 323, 324, 347.

" Philoctetes " of Sophocles, 323.

Philomela, see Tereus.

Phineus was the son of Agenor and ruled in Salmydessus in Thrace. He imprisoned his sons, by his first wife, Cleopatra, because of a false accusation made by their stepmother, Idæa. For this, or some other fault, he was punished with blindness, and two Harpies tormented him. When the Argonauts reached Thrace, Zetes and Calais, brothers of Cleopatra, killed the Harpies and were also said to have vindicated and freed their nephews, the sons of Phineus. In return, he advised Jason what course to take (see 157). Milton compares himself to Phineus (Paradise Lost, Book III, lines 35, 36).

Phlegethon, 406.

Phlegeus, 271.

Phocis, a country in Northern Greece, its chief mountain Parnassus and its chief river Cephissus, 390.

Phocus, son of Æacus, killed by his half-brothers Telamon and Peleus.

Phœbe, a name of Artemis as goddess of the moon.

Phœbus, 69.

"Phœnician Maidens, The," 263.

Phœnix, 294, 296, 361.

Pholus, a Centaur, 176.

Phorcys, a sea-deity, was, by Ceto, the father of Ladon, Echidne, the three Gorgons, and the three Greæ.

Phoroneus, son of Inachus and the nymph Melia, was an early mythical King of Argos.

Phrixus, son of Athamas and Nephele.

Phrygia, 121.

Phylachus, father of Iphiclus.

Phyleus, son of Augeias, 177.

Phyllis, beloved by Demophon, 349.

Pieria, on the south-east coast of Macedonia, was inhabited by Thracian people, who in early times worshipped the Muses, hence called Pierides. See also 92.

Pierides. (1) The Muses.
(2) The nine daughters of Pierus, a king in Macedonia, named after the Muses. They were conquered in a contest with the Muses and turned into birds.

Pirene, 148.

Pirithous, the son of Ixion and Dia, was King of the Lapithæ in Thessaly. He became a close friend of Theseus. See also 212, 213, 214.

Pisa, in Elis, 376, 377.

Pittheus, King of Troezen, was son to Pelops and father of Æthra, 203.

Pleiades, daughters of Atlas and Pleione were companions of Artemis. They were changed into doves and placed among the stars.

Pleione, mother by Atlas of the Pleiades.

Pleisthenes, 381.

Pluto. (1) A name for Hades, 399.
(2) The nymph, 371.

Podalirius, 324.

Podarces. (1) Original name of Priam, 275.
(2) Son of Iphiclus, who led the Thessalians against Troy.

Pœas, 301.

Polites, 334.

Pollux, Roman name for Polydeuces.

Polybus, 253.

Polybutes, 11, 12.

Polydectes, 132, 133, 141.

Polydeuces, one of Dioscuri, 155, 157, 215, 285, 286.

Polydorus. (1) Son of Cadmus and Harmonia, 244, 252.
(2) Son of Priam, 338.

Polyeidus, 232.

Polymester, 338.

Polymnia or Polyhymnia, the Muse of the sublime hymn.

Polyneices, 257, 261, 262, 263, 265, 266, 269.

Polypemon, see Procrustes and 205.

Polyphemus, 355.

Polyxena, 309, 337, 339.

Pontus, 1.

Porphyrion, 11.

Poseidon, see especially 99-109 and also 7, 9, 10, 13, 32, 36, 42, 44, 60, 67, 73, 110, 134, 137, 139, 140, 152, 157, 211, 223, 227, 305, 330, 348, 362, 366, 377.

Praxiteles, 63.

Priam, 275, 276, 277, 282, 302, 309, 315, 316, 318, 327, 330, 331, 334, 336, 338.

Priapus, son of Dionysus and Aphrodite, a god of fruitfulness.

Procne, see Tereus.

Procris was the daughter of the second Erectheus to be King of Athens. She married Cephalus. See also 229.

Procrustes or the " Stretcher " was the surname given to the robber Polypemon. He used to tie travellers to a bed, and if they were too short he would rack them, and if too tall, he would hack off their legs. He was served in the same way by Theseus. See also 205.

Prœtus, son of Abas, King of Argolis, inherited the kingdom jointly with his twin brother Acrisius. Soon expelled, he fled to Iobates, King of Lydia, whose daughter Anteia, also called Stheneboea, he married. Returning to Argolis, he forced his brother to divide the kingdom and became ruler of Tiryns, whose massive walls he built by aid of the Cyclopes. See also Melampus, Bellerophon.

Prometheus, 16-20, 41, 176, 183.

Protesilaus, 303.

Proteus was the prophetic old man of the sea, subject to Poseidon, whose flocks of seals he tended. By assuming any shape he chose, he could avoid the need of prophesying, unless gripped fast, when he would at last resume his usual shape and tell the truth. He could be found at midday in the island of Pharos. See also 183, 345.

Psamathe, see Linus (1).

Psyche appears in late Greek literature as a personification of the soul, purified by suffering to enjoy true love. The beauty of the maiden Psyche excited the envy of Aphrodite who sent Eros to persecute her, but he fell in love with her and secretly visited her nightly. When Psyche, urged by her two sisters, sought to discover his identity, he left her. Searching for Eros, she endured further persecution, but he secretly helped her, and she finally overcame Aphrodite's hatred, to become immortal and united with Eros for ever. The story is told in The Golden Ass of Apuleius.

Pygmalion of Cyprus is said to have fallen in love with the ivory image of a maiden that he himself had made, and to have prayed Aphrodite to breathe life into it. When she consented, Pygmalion married the maiden, whom he called Galatea. By her he became the father of Paphus and Metharme. It is probable that the story concerns a priest of Aphrodite at Paphus who kept the image of the goddess in order to retain power. See William Morris's version in The Earthly Paradise.

Pylades, 390, 392, 396, 397, 398.

Pylos, 92.

Pyrrha, 20, 21.

Pyrrhus, see Neoptolemus.

Pythia, 76, 118, 171.

Pythian or Pythius, 69.

Python, 71, 76.

# THE CONTEMPORARY THEATRE

In recent years a new kind of theatre
has been created under the influence of writers able to break
with convention and experiment for
themselves, making more imaginative use of stage and language. This
section concerns the English theatre
since 1950.

# TABLE OF CONTENTS

# THE CONTEMPORARY THEATRE

This section concerns the English theatre since 1950 and is confined to plays produced before a live audience. It consists of four sections:

I. Introduction
II. Eminent Theatrical Groups
III. Glossary of Dramatic Terms
IV. Directory of Dramatists

## I. INTRODUCTION

What significance can the modern audience be expected to find in such spectacles as squalid garrets and basements, characters most unrealistically bursting into song, old tramps changing hats, a young man trying to teach a set of weighing-machines to sing the Hallelujah Chorus, or three children continuously re-enacting the ritual murder of their parents?

These are some of the questions that trouble the playgoer, and since they are not always easy to answer it may be helpful first to consider what is the function of dramatic art, what are its constituents and background, and how to judge a play.

### The Function of Dramatic Art.

It is not the function of art to make a statement but to induce an imaginative response, and the spectator receives not an answer to a question but an experience.

Drama, like the other arts, gives expression to that subtle and elusive life of feeling that defies logical definition. By feeling is to be understood the whole experience of what it feels like to be alive—physical sensations, emotions, and even what it feels like to think.

This flux of sensibility cannot be netted down in logical discourse, but can find expression in what Clive Bell, when discussing the visual arts, called " significant form."

The contemporary philosopher, Susanne Langer, in her book, *Feeling and Form*, has developed Clive Bell's concept, arguing that all artistic form is an indirect expression of feeling. The artist, be he painter, poet, or dramatist, creates an image, a form that gives shape to his feeling, and it is for the sensitive recipient to interpret its significance.

The especial province of drama, as was pointed out by Aristotle, is to create an image, an illusion of action, that action " which springs from the past but is directed towards the future and is always great with things to come." Both tragedy and comedy depict such action and the conflict which it normally entails.

### The Therapeutic Effect of Drama.

One of the achievements of serious drama is to create an image that will objectify and help to resolve deep human conflicts.

Most people have at some time or another come away from a fine play feeling in some inexplicable way exhilarated and released, and it has long been recognised that drama can have a beneficial, even a therapeutic effect.

It is not difficult to understand the exhilarating effect of comedy, but more difficult to understand that of tragedy. In the 4th century B.C. Aristotle claimed that tragedy accomplishes a beneficial purgation of pity and terror and very recently Miss Bradbrook has attempted a psychological explanation of the effect of serious drama on the audience. She suggests that in watching a mature play we are encouraged to sympathise with many different characters at one and the same time, and it may be that the imaginative effort entailed has a corresponding movement in the unconscious mind. There, at the most primitive level, is an " internal society," the petrified infantile images of father, mother, and siblings, to which we are linked by inflexible attitudes. It may be that the sympathetic response to the playwright's images of these figures helps us to relax our rigid attitudes towards them so that the internal pattern of relationships shifts, and we experience a sense of release and a new access of energy.

It is noteworthy also that drama can be fully appreciated only in a public performance, a social event demanding the co-operation and understanding between author, players, and audience. Because it can flourish only in a community, normally a city, it has been called the metropolitan art.

### The Constituents of Drama.

Drama is a complex art in that it uses two very different kinds of ingredient or material, one speech, the literary constituent, the other the gesture, movement, and confrontation of actors on an actual stage. Speech is man's most precise, subtle, and mature means of expression. Gesture and confrontation, which he shares to some degree with animals, is more primitive and some of the power of drama as an art form is its fusion of civilised speech and primitive gesture into one organic whole.

It is just possible to conduct brief scenes using only one of these media. The chorus in Shakespeare's *Henry V* is virtually confined to speech and there is in Galsworthy's *Justice*, revived in 1968, a remarkable wordless scene, showing a criminal in solitary confinement in his cell, that proved so moving that it is reputed to have led to an amendment of the penal code.

Perhaps the more primitive gesture has the greater emotional force, but it is the words made permanent in the literary script that up till now have constituted the commanding form of drama. Even the wordless mime is given permanence by the printed script.

### The Ritual Element.

While speech and the confrontation of actors are essential to full drama, there is an element that has sometimes been neglected and that is ritual, perhaps the most primitive and evocative of all. The early tragedy of Greece was probably organically connected with the religious ritual of Dionysus and the matrix was song and dance. Similarly in England the origins of drama are to be found in church liturgy and ritual and civic occasion, both of which used procession, pageantry, costume, and symbolic insignia to great effect and also clowning which served as comic relief to the solemnity.

There have naturally been few dramatists who have been able to combine literary ability, a sense of stage situation and also skill in the use of ritual process. The enduring power of Shakespeare is due to his manifold genius in that he could deploy inimitable poetry, swift action, and such ritual enrichments as royal processions, crowning and dethroning, duelling and wrestling, masque and pageantry, song and dance.

## The Background of Modern Drama.

The happy fusion of both literary and theatrical excellence which is to be found in Shakespeare's plays is extremely rare, for it demands not only a versatile genius but also a receptive audience and a suitable building. By the Restoration the delicate balance was already disturbed and by the middle decades of the 19th century popular taste had all but banished literature from the stage. The disorderly audiences of the time demanded only spectacular and sensational theatrical and musical effects, and in the vast monopoly theatres of Drury Lane and Covent Garden they could hardly have heard, let alone appreciated, good dialogue. The managers discouraged men of genius, so that poets like Browning, who had no practical knowledge of the theatre, produced wordy " closet dramas," which were virtually unactable, while the popular theatrical melodramas like *Maria Marten* or *Murder in the Red Barn*, are today unreadable.

With the gradual establishment of smaller theatres, catering for a sober middle-class audience, men of talent again began to write for the stage. It was the turn of literature to take command, and more popular and traditional techniques such as music and clowning were now banished to the music-hall and pantomime.

T. W. Robertson, Henry Arthur Jones and Pinero all furthered the trend towards realism but it was the genius of Ibsen, especially in such works as *Ghosts* and *The Wild Duck*, that set a high standard of excellence for the literary and realistic play of middle-class life. He expressed his profound insight into personal and social problems in finely constructed plays, written in naturalistic prose, the overtones of poetic universality being conveyed in symbolism that was usually verbal.

Able writers, like Granville Barker and Galsworthy, although they lacked the poetic power of Ibsen, firmly established in England a similar type of literary play, realistic, well-constructed, serious-minded, concerned with the middle class and almost exclusively verbal.

Some of the few exceptions to this preoccupation with the realistic and literary are to be found in Shaw. Like Shakespeare, he was not only a literary genius. He was also well acquainted with stage-production and although much too wordy in old age, in his best comedies he combined some of the wittiest dialogue to be found in English drama along with the delightful shocks and surprises of total theatre. Androcles' engaging Lion belongs to the same family as Titania's Ass and Whittington's Cat.

But Shaw in his prime was unique, and between the wars the verbal, realistic play was perpetuated by such writers as Maugham and Coward. Not over-concerned with psychological or social issues, they used it to portray the leisured classes.

By the 'forties the conventional West End play had with a few exceptions come to imitate not life but photography. Confined to the proscenium arch and realistic to the last trivial detail, it presented a prosaic picture of middle- and upper-class life, with stereotyped situation, demanding only stock responses and lacking interest in ideas, poetic intensity, and genuine wit. With the star cast and the long commercial run, theatregoing had become not an artistic experience but a social occasion.

Apart from the novel comedies of such writers as Ustinov and Rattigan and the verse plays of T. S. Eliot and Fry, it was the revivals of the classics, English and European, that were bringing

genuine drama to the stage. Shakespeare could be enjoyed not only at Stratford and the Old Vic, but in the West End. It was largely due to Gielgud that Shakespeare was now a box-office draw.

Gielgud's fine histrionic sense, and his highly sensitive and poetic interpretation had earned him that rare distinction of being the Hamlet of his generation and as early as 1934 his production and performance at the New Theatre had broken all records since Irving.

As actor and producer, working with other fine artists, such as Edith Evans, Peggy Ashcroft, Olivier, Guinness and Scofield, Gielgud later confirmed his success. Enthralling interpretations of plays by Shakespeare, Webster, Otway, Congreve, Sheridan, Wilde and Chekhov demonstrated that the classics could have a wide popular appeal.

Other artists followed and in a successful season at the New Theatre, Sybil Thorndike, Olivier and Richardson played to crowded houses in *Oedipus*, *Henry IV*, *The Critic* and *Peer Gynt*.

Such achievements have reminded audience and aspiring playright that there are many other dramatic styles than that of fashionable realism and so may even have helped to further the dramatic revival that began in the 'fifties.

## The Modern Revival.

It is not easy to identify the causes of this revival, but undoubtedly one reason is that young playwrights like Wesker and Delaney have injected new vigour into the jaded realistic mode by using it to express the vital stresses and conflicts of the working people whom they know. Hence the settings in basement and attic. *See* Neo-realism.

More far-reaching is the general awareness among *avant-garde* playwrights that verbalism is not enough and their readiness to experiment with the resources of " total theatre." Here the way has been shown by scholarly research into the history of the theatre which has given men confidence to revive valid techniques such as song, music and clowning that the early 20th century had exiled to the music-hall.

The most vital stimulus has been the challenge of genius. Brecht's Epic Theatre (q.v.) has offered a more free and fluid form than that of the "well-made play," and his novel uses of traditional theatrical devices (such as song, masks, extravagant costume and settings, direct address to the audience) have been quickly adapted by dramatists like Arden, Bolt, and Osborne.

Meanwhile Ionesco, whole-hearted devotee of the Theatre of the Absurd (q.v.), has introduced monsters like the rhinoceros and has exploited stage properties like empty chairs to satirise man's empty existence. He has soon been followed by Saunders and by Simpson, whose weighingmachines symbolise the dominance of imagination by machinery. Monsters and machinery recently restricted to pantomime are returning to the stage.

A most pervasive influence has been that of Artaud's demand for a Theatre of Cruelty (q.v.). This is both the most novel and the most atavistic type of theatre, for it attempts to re-create in modern terms that primitive, even barbaric ritual from which drama evolved. In England it is best known still in translation of Genet, Weiss, and Triana.

Another interesting aspect of theatre today is a new and highly topical interpretation of Shakespeare, for some critics and producers have traced in his plays the bleak disenchantment that is typical of post-war Europe.

Peter Brook has said that his fine production in 1963 of *King Lear*, with Paul Scofield as protagonist, owed much to the critic Jan Kott, a Polish Professor of Literature, whose book *Shakespeare our Contemporary*, was published here in the following year.

Kott, who lived through the Nazi tyranny and the Stalinist occupation of Poland, urges that the power-politics, chicanery and violence of twentieth century Europe have their counterpart in the Wars of the Roses and the Tudor disturbances. He finds in Shakespeare's Histories and in the Tragedies, especially *Macbeth*, what he terms the " Grand Mechanism " of history, the blood-stained struggle for power with its terrible consequences, and he claims that Shakespeare " condemns war by showing up the Feudal butchery."

The series, " The Wars of the Roses," which was produced for the B.B.C. during 1965–6 by Peter Hall and John Barton with the Royal Shakespeare Company, vividly demonstrated the crime-ridden lust for power and the Feudal butchery. Meanwhile at Stratford and the Aldwych, the production of *Henry V* neglected the traditional, royal splendour and showed the king, grimy and battle-scarred, leading a tattered army, plagued by corrupt camp-followers. Played on a bare, gaunt stage, grey, metallic and cavernous, it was strikingly similar in tone and significance to Brecht's *Mother Courage*, running concurrently at the Old Vic.

A Shakespearean comedy has also been freshly interpreted in Clifford Williams's enchanting production for the National Theatre in 1967 of *As You Like It*, with an all-male cast, the women's parts not being taken as in Shakespeare's time by boys with unbroken voices but by young men. Clifford Williams was aware of the unorthodox theories expressed by Kott in his *The Bitter Arcadia*. Kott observing the almost identical appearance of modern youths and girls was reminded of those Shakespearean comedies where the girl appears disguised as a youth. He argues that their theme is that of the sonnets—" the impossibility of choice between the youth and the woman, the fragile boundary between friendship and love . . . the universality of desire which cannot be contained or limited to one sex."

*New Perspectives.*

Since 1965 there have been further attempts at new kinds of drama. One of the most discussed innovations has been the " theatre of fact " or " living theatre " or " documentary." *The Investigation* of Peter Weiss set an example for plays of this kind, which constitute a sort of documentary of the stage, the dramatist endeavouring to present, usually in an objective way, a selection and concentration of the actual events of contemporary history. But however detached he may be, the dramatist must by the very act of selection betray a certain bias, as indeed must the professional historian himself.

One of the most sober and objective of such factual plays, Kipphardt's *In the Matter of J. Robert Oppenheimer*, follows Weiss in presenting a judicial enquiry, this kind of trial scene being ripe with possibilities of conflict, suspense, and surprise. Hastings's *Lee Harvey Oswald* follows the same pattern. Both were shown in 1966 during the Hampstead " living theatre " season, the Director stressing its preoccupation with ethical problems demanding the live concern of the audience.

The R.S.C. has also carried out an experiment in a new genre, that of " Director's Theatre," and the involvement of the audience was certainly the purpose of *US*, directed by Peter Brook as a direct assault on our apathy concerning the war in Vietnam.

Several recent plays involve biting criticism of the military mentality and recourse to war, notably McGrath's *Bofors Gun*, Vian's *The Generals' Tea Party*, and Charles Wood's *Dingo* and " *H.*"

Meanwhile the pressing international problem of relations between black and white has been illuminated in plays by Fugard, Saunders, Robert Lowell and the Negro Le Roi Jones.

There are indications of a new candour, a more enquiring spirit, about other social problems,

including illness, both physical and mental. Peter Nichols has used remarkable skill in revealing the effects on the parents of the incurable illness of a spastic child, and it is now no longer unusual to see a play, often in the mood of ironic comedy, depicting the distressed mind. David Storey's first play had as protagonist a young husband struggling through a nervous breakdown; Mercer is especially concerned with the malaise of the youth educated beyond his parents; and playwrights as dissimilar as Mortimer and Triana have depicted the disturbed personality.

There is now a much more frank and sympathetic attitude towards sexual deviation. In 1965 *A Patriot for Me*, Osborne's uncompromising record of a homosexual, could be performed only privately, while Frank Marcus' *The Killing of Sister George* indicated a lesbian relationship only under cover of some obvious comic satire of B.B.C. serials and their credulous public. But by 1966 Charles Dyer's *The Staircase*, although serio-comic in tone, could give a direct and uncluttered picture of a homosexual partnership, and in 1968 Christopher Hampton's *Total Eclipse* was completely devoted to a sober, searching, and candid exploration of the historic relationship between Verlaine and Rimbaud.

Very different was the light comedy, Spencer's *Spitting Image*, 1968. This represented a homosexual couple producing a baby, the prelude to a nation-wide vogue for such births.

The abolition in September 1968 of the Lord Chamberlain's powers of theatre censorship removed official taboos on the dramatist's freedom of expression, which will in future be conditioned by the public's response.

In these days of theatrical candour and experiment there are two major pitfalls which can trip up critics. One is the over-rating of technical standards, the way a play expresses itself, and neglecting what is expressed, its inherent values. To encourage a divorce of form and content is to induce dis-association in the response of the audience. The human being is a whole and should so respond to a work of art, which is a whole. However exquisite the artistry by which murder is depicted and condoned it is still murder. One hall-mark of the good play is insight into and affirmation, however obliquely, of the life enhancing values.

Another mistake is to underestimate a play because it is not avant-garde. A case in point is Miller's *The Price* (*q.v.*) criticised because its subject was, unlike the series of the R.S.C., irrelevant to America's current crisis. How can the play's themes, human integrity and resilience, ever be irrelevant? H. G. Wells's warning, " Adapt or perish," has never been more urgent. The play was also criticised for not using modern techniques of " audience participation " and of being a " conversation piece." Yet the audience was spellbound, participating imaginatively as in Shakespeare, and is not Ibsen's *Ghosts* a " conversation piece "?

There is perhaps some danger that in the rediscovery of the resources of total theatre the literary aspect of drama may be neglected. Excellent revivals of the English and European classics of the stage, especially of Shakespeare, many-sided genius, help to restore the balance. Here we are especially indebted to the exquisite ensemble playing of the National Theatre and the Royal Shakespeare Companies.

*Criteria of Judgment.*

How can the value of novel and experimental plays be estimated? The ultimate test of time is obviously impossible and some of the critical principles by which traditional drama has been interpreted are no longer relevant to the revolutionary plays of Brecht and Ionesco.

The first canon of criticism is to remember that every art form determines the criteria by which it is judged, and the good dramatic critic does not approach any play with a pontifical set of rules but endeavours to keep an open mind, and so to discover its unique significance and value.

Since artistic form is an expression of human feeling, the first encounter with a work of art should be in a mood of extreme receptivity, so that by shedding preconceived notions, the recipient may be aware of the feeling implicit in the work, however novel or even bizarre the expression may be. The initial reaction to drama should be intuitive.

The nature and quality of the implicit feeling can then be considered. Is it an original and genuine response to experience, or perfunctory and stereotyped, is it intense or diffuse, profound or shallow, subtle or commonplace, reasoned or irrational?

Questioning its inherent feeling often reveals that a commercially successful piece, although " well-made," is valueless, while an unconventional work, like Pinter's *Dumb Waiter*, explores and reveals deep-seated anxieties and fears.

Drama is an especially complicated art, in that part of its material being words, it may also involve discussion of ideas. This discussion, however, should not be mistaken for a statement of the author's convictions. In a good play it is an expression of his characters' *feeling* about ideas, a very different thing.

Another enquiry concerns the appropriateness and beauty of the form in which the feeling is conveyed. Many consider that Beckett's *Waiting for Godot* conveys the same mood implicit in *King Lear*, and that each play is an image of man, disillusioned, adrift, assailed by despair in an alien universe. This recognised, the critic's task is to explore the form of the two plays. Apart from the fact that they both use a most improbable fable, they could hardly be more different. *King Lear* is a Renaissance verse tragedy of the fall of princes, with subtle presentation of character development and contrast, and with a coherent plot skilfully developed through arresting action up to the tragic climax. *Waiting for Godot* is a prose play about an abortive encounter, almost devoid of individual characterisation and story, with a static, circular structure and an ending as ambiguous and inconclusive as its beginning. Yet in either case the form of the play has artistic significance and appropriateness and repays analysis, and here again the critic needs to be a flexible interpreter of the artist's purpose.

The most searching question to be asked of a play is whether it is life-enhancing, whether, like the finest art, it gives delight or deepens understanding.

Most difficult to estimate are those plays like *Lear* or *Godot*, which express a mood of despair. But if man's honesty and endurance are ultimately affirmed, the play is not negative in import. *Lear* begs forgiveness and the tramps still wait. Similarly a biting satire may be positive if it helps to clear away old wood to make room for new growth. A facile optimism may be a betrayal.

Ideally the best way to know a play is first to see it on the stage, when its theatrical qualities can be enjoyed, and later to read it at leisure, when its literary value can be appreciated.

## II. EMINENT THEATRICAL GROUPS

We are greatly indebted to a few enterprising and devoted groups—chiefly repertory companies and theatre clubs—which help to keep drama alive.

Foremost are the Royal Shakespeare Company and the National Theatre, which have earned an international reputation by their superb productions of both classics and new plays. Some groups, such as the English Stage Company and the Traverse Theatre, Edinburgh, have been particularly concerned in introducing new dramatists.

Many repertory theatres are doing exciting work including revivals and premières and the Council of Repertory Theatres has a membership of over forty, including theatres at Birmingham, Bristol, Bromley, Cheltenham, Coventry, Dundee, Edinburgh, Glasgow, Guildford, Ipswich, Leatherhead, Leicester, Liverpool, Nottingham, Pitlochry, Salisbury, Sheffield, Watford, Windsor, and York.

Among commercial promoters H. M. Tennent can be relied on for the high quality of their revivals of period plays.

### The Royal Shakespeare Company.

When Peter Hall was appointed Managing Director in January 1960 his enterprising work revolutionised the R.S.C. He decided to supplement the annual season of Shakespeare at Stratford-on-Avon by a continuous repertory of classical and contemporary plays at the Aldwych, and in 1962 a special experimental season was also held at the Arts Theatre.

Under the Directors, Peter Hall, Peter Brook, and Paul Scofield a brilliant team of over 100 actors was gathered together and the imaginative direction and artistic perfection of the ensemble playing became world famous.

In the Spring of 1968 there was a rearrangement among the artists and executives at the head of the R.S.C. Peter Hall gave up his post as Managing Director to become Director with special responsibilities for R.S.C. films and for the design and building of the Company's new London theatre in the Barbican. His former work was divided between Trevor Nunn, Artistic Director, and Derek Hornby, Administrative Director. Paul Scofield resigned his position and Peggy Ashcroft became the first woman Director. Each year at the Aldwych original Shakes-pearean productions from Stratford alternate with other classics and stimulating modern work. Between 1960 and 1965 there were productions of highly experimental plays by Beckett, Livings, Pinter, Saunders, and Whiting and by foreign writers such as Arrabel, Brecht, Dürrenmatt, Hochhuth, Tardieu, Vitrac, and Weiss.

The years 1966–7 saw new plays by Duras, Mrozek, Dürrenmatt, Triana, Feiffer, Mercer, and Dyer, and Peter Brook's much discussed *US*, as well as revivals of Gogol and Ibsen. A special American season was launched in the period 1968–9, with British premières from Albee, Chayavsky, Feiffer, and Kopit.

The annual World Theatre Season, dating from 1964, gives a unique opportunity for seeing ensembles from other countries, special apparatus for simultaneous translation having been installed. In 1969 five distinguished companies—Planchon's from Paris, Krejca's from Prague, Koun's from Athens, Anna Magnani's from Italy, and the New York Negro Ensemble—all present their work.

An excellent innovation has been the mobile " Theatreground " for young people which since 1966 has worked in collaboration with educational and municipal authorities.

A thriving R.S.C. Theatre Club provides booking facilities and concessions, discussions and a quarterly magazine, *Flourish*.

### The National Theatre.

Sixty years after Granville Barker and William Archer had formulated plans for a National Theatre, the inaugural production of *Hamlet* took place on 22 October 1963 at its temporary home, the Old Vic, pending the building of the permanent theatre on the South Bank, promised by the end of 1971.

Laurence Olivier already appointed Director, the nucleus of a distinguished company was formed and soon established its high reputation for exquisite ensemble playing, guest artists also appearing on occasion.

The intention has been to build up a large repertoire of classical and modern plays from all countries and between 1963 and the end of the season 1968–9 forty major productions will already have been staged.

The wide and varied list includes works by Shakespeare, Ben Jonson, Congreve, Farquhar, Pinero, Brighouse, Shaw, O'Casey, Maugham, Shaffer, Arden, Chekhov, Ostrovsky, Feydeau, Brecht, and Miller.

The imaginative quality of production and acting has been enthusiastically acclaimed by packed houses and the scenery has often been breathtaking, especially in the designs of the Czech, Svoboda, for Ostrovsky's *The Storm* and Chekhov's *The Three Sisters*.

Recently there has been added to the repertory a superb interpretation of Strindberg's *Dance of Death*, produced by Byam Shaw, with Olivier as Edgar. Gielgud has made his welcome début at The National in *Tartuffe* and Seneca's *Oedipus*. Clifford's fascinating production of *As You Like It* with an all-male cast has appeared, and contemporary pieces include Stoppard's *Rosencrantz and Guildenstern Are Dead*, a work of great virtuosity, Charles Wood's "*H*" and *The Advertisement* by Natalia Ginzburg.

A most attractive booklet is issued for each production and is available to the audience at a trifling cost. This supplies authoritative information about the author, the play, its sources and inner references, notable productions and critical estimates, together with photographs, reproductions, and plans.

Productions of the National Theatre have appeared at the Chichester Festival Theatre, and have gone on provincial tours. In September 1965 the company made its first tour abroad, visiting the foremost Soviet theatre, the Kremljovesky, and the Frei Volks Buhne in West Berlin.

In the autumn of 1967 during a six weeks tour of Canada, plays were staged in Vancouver, Edmonton, Winnipeg, Montreal (for World Festival Expo), and Toronto. During the two weeks continental tour of September 1968 the company played in Stockholm, Copenhagen, Belgrade, and Venice.

A recent welcome development has been an experimental workshop season in the Spring of 1969 when three different productions were staged during three weeks at the Jeannetta Cochrane Theatre.

The film version of the fine *Othello*, with Olivier, had its première in 1966, to be followed by the film of *The Dance of Death*, providing a wonderful opportunity for those unable to reach a theatre.

### The English Stage Company.

Since 1956 the English Stage Company at the Royal Court has been tireless in its discovery and support of new talent. Formed to promote contemporary drama, the company acquired in 1956 a long lease of the Royal Court with George Devine (d. 1965) as Director and Tony Richardson as Assistant. Declaring themselves a Writers' Theatre, they were extraordinarily successful in discovering and sponsoring playwrights hitherto unknown, such as Osborne, N. F. Simpson, Ann Jellicoe, and John Arden, and in persuading the novelist Nigel Dennis to write for the stage.

An offshoot of the Company, the English Stage Society, initiated in May 1957 the inexpensive Sunday night "Productions without Decor", which brought to light such successes as Wesker's *The Kitchen* and Owen's *Progress to the Park*.

Writers beginning to make their reputation elsewhere were welcomed. Beckett's *Endgame* and *Krapp's Last Tape* had their première here. Many distinguished foreign plays were seen in Britain for the first time at the Court, including Arthur Miller's *The Crucible*, Tennessee Williams' *Orpheus Descending*, Ionesco's *The Chairs* and *Rhinoceros*, Sartre's *Nekrassov* and *Altona*, Genet's *The Blacks*, and Brecht's *The Good Person of Szechwan*, the first Brecht ever staged in London.

In October 1965 William Gaskill succeeded Devine and the autumn season 1965 saw new plays, by Jellicoe, Simpson, and Bond. There have since been revivals of both classic and modern works and several British premières of unusual plays, including Wesker's *Golden City*, Orton's *Crimes of Passion*, Charles Wood's *Dingo*, and the Nigerian Wole Soyinka's *The Lion and the Jewel*. A most interesting departure has been to stage here plays from the past hitherto ignored, such as Jarry's seminal French play of 1896, *Ubu Roi*, and the Russian Babel's *Marya* of 1933. The establishment of D. H. Lawrence as a dramatist, culminating in the special Lawrence season of 1968, was an event in theatrical history.

Two similar seasons followed, one of three plays by Osborne in 1968, the other of three by Bond in 1969.

The E.S.C. is now doing valuable educational work by including a series of productions of both modern and classical plays specially chosen to meet the needs of schools. Facilities for cheap seats for holders of Student Cards have also been generously extended.

### The Mermaid Theatre.

It was largely due to the efforts of Bernard Miles that in 1959 the City of London's first new theatre since Shakespeare's time was opened at Blackfriars. Commerce, industry, and the general public had generously given money, the City Corporation had granted the site at a peppercorn rent and the four-foot-thick surviving walls of a blitzed warehouse had been used as the shell for a delightful little theatre of 499 seats.

It has an open stage, based on that of Shakespeare's day, while an excellently raked auditorium, all on one tier, like a segment of a Greek amphitheatre, ensures perfect sight lines. The most modern lighting, revolving stage, and sound and film equipment are installed.

The Mermaid is now part of the City's artistic life with foyer exhibitions, films, concerts, and lectures. The enterprising "Molecule Club" for children uses ingenious theatrical means to demonstrate basic scientific principles.

The Mermaid has a fine, varied record of productions, including British premières of works by Brecht, Camus, and O'Casey. There have been revivals of Shakespeare, Ford, Dekker, Beaumont, and Fletcher and Shaw, and of foreign plays by Ibsen, Pirandello, Henry James, and Lessing.

The year 1967 was notable for an imaginatively planned cycle of four dramas by Euripides concerning the Trojan War, and by the English première of the fine verse play *Benito Cereno* by the distinguished poet, Robert Lowell.

In 1968 the theatre's special design was admirably used for the spectacular production of Luke's *Hadrian the Seventh*.

### The National Youth Theatre.

Originating in Alleyn's School and the enterprise of Michael Croft, the N.Y.T. fosters in young people an appreciation of theatre, whether as audience or participants. Since 1959 it has performed annually in the West End. Constantly expanding it now has several companies and in its foreign tours has presented plays at the festivals in Paris and Berlin. Several members have become professional actors, including John Stride and Derek Jakobi of the National Theatre.

In 1967 and 1968 it was admirably served with two plays specially commissioned from Terson, *Zigger Zagger* and *The Apprentices*.

### Theatre Workshop.

Between 1953 and 1961 Joan Littlewood as Director of Theatre Workshop introduced several new playwrights, including Behan and Delaney. Spontaneity and pseudo-Brechtian techniques and not careful construction were the hallmarks of her work which culminated in *Oh What a Lovely War* (M). This paradoxically used a period pierrot piece brilliantly to satirise the tragic futility of the First World War.

In 1967 Joan Littlewood returned and directed *MacBird* and *Mrs. Wilson's Diary*.

*MacBird* (P), by Barbara Garson, is an American parody on *Macbeth* in doggerel blank verse. Described by Brustein as "brutally provocative" and "grimly amusing", it attacks the American "Establishment", under Lyndon Johnson. Unfortunately Joan Littlewood made such alterations to the text that the satirical parallel with Shakespeare was blurred.

*Mrs. Wilson's Diary* (M), in form a jolly pre-war musical, is described by its authors, Ingrams and Wells, as " an affectionate lampoon " on the Wilson administration.

### The Hampstead Theatre.

The Hampstead Theatre Club, now London's first Civic theatre, under the energetic direction of Roose-Evans, has sponsored many aspiring playwrights. It has to its credit world premières by dramatists such as Giles Cooper, Pinter, Milner, Howarth, Bowen, McGrath, and even Tennessee

Williams. In 1966 a valuable season of " living theatre " included plays by Kipphardt and Hastings.

### The International Theatre Club.

Housed at the Mercury Theatre in London, this club under the Directors Jean-Pierre Voos and Arnold Fry, specialises in modern foreign plays in translation and also gives hospitality to overseas experimental groups, such as the La Mama and that of Jerome Savory.

# III. GLOSSARY OF DRAMATIC TERMS

### Absurd Drama.

The Theatre of the Absurd, originating in Paris, was introduced here through the plays of Beckett and translations of Ionesco, Vian, and Vitrac. It has had considerable impact on Pinter, N. F. Simpson, Saunders, Stoppard, and Campton, while American absurdist plays by Albee, Gelber, and Kopit and by the Swiss, Frisch, have also been produced here.

The concept of the Absurd was first formulated by Camus to indicate the discrepancy between human reason and aspiration and an indifferent and hostile universe. But like Sartre he expressed his convictions through the traditional dramatic form.

Not every playwright of the Absurd is an existentialist and many are more concerned with an irrational human society than with the universe. What they have in common is a technique. All have discarded traditional realism and express absurdity through images that are themselves absurd, including bizarre situations and objects, both sad and comic, such as aged parents consigned to dustbins.

There is in the Absurd an element of Surrealism and Miss Bradbrook has suggested that a better term might be Theatre of Dream, for it is the unconscious dream mind that juxtaposes objects and incidents that in the waking state have no connection, such as a rhinoceros in a provincial street. Pinter seems to have an intuitive awareness of the hinterland of dream, while Simpson makes a conscious manipulation of Surrealism.

Frisch has ably demonstrated that the Absurd can be an effective vehicle for satire and many absurdist writers, such as Ionesco and Simpson, have satirised the modern prostitution of language corrupted by salesmen and politicians, and have used conversation of vapid emptiness to reveal its breakdown as a means of communication.

It is partly because of their distrust of language that they have had recourse to ludicrous objects and images, thus extending the range of total theatre.

### The Aristotelian Play.

Brecht and Ionesco have disparagingly referred, somewhat inaccurately, to " Aristotelianism." Strictly speaking, this means the concept of tragedy which Aristotle first analysed in the *Poetics*, basing it primarily on the poetic tragedies of Sophocles, especially the *Oedipus Rex* (P), c. 425 B.C. The Aristotelian concept, revived since the Renaissance, has obviously been much modified, but certain basic principles can still be discerned.

Aristotle claims that poetry in general aims at that rational pleasure which is part of the good life. He defines tragedy as the imitation of an action. By imitation he does not mean the description of an actual happening but of one that is possible. Hence the poetic licence whereby the dramatist may adapt historical material to his own theme.

Aristotle stresses that the action should be complete in itself and have inner coherence. Tragedy must have an intelligible beginning, a middle necessitated by the beginning and which itself necessitates the end. " The story . . . must represent one action, a complete whole, with its several incidents so closely connected that the transposal or withdrawal of any one will disjoint and dislocate the whole."

The action should be of some magnitude, with " incidents arousing pity and fear wherewith to accomplish the purgation of such emotions." Here is Aristotle's celebrated doctrine of purgation or " catharsis " which has been variously interpreted, some considering that something like a ceremonial purification is intended, with an ethical end in view, others that bodily or psychological relief from tension is meant.

Aristotle emphasised the paramount importance of action or plot, the characters being revealed in and through the action. The kind of plot recommended is one where the hero is an eminent man, neither inordinately good nor bad, whose misfortune is brought upon him by some error of judgment.

Here is the germ of the splendid Renaissance tragedy concerned with the fall of princes and also of the modern finely constructed play, such as Ibsen's *Ghosts*. Such a play has classical symmetry, the beginning, middle, and end, becoming in modern parlance the exposition, development, and climax or denouement. It has its own organic unity and inevitability. But although many writers, such as Sartre, still work within the classical disciplines many have discarded the traditional form.

Brecht and his followers have repudiated the whole pattern in favour of a sequence of self-contained episodes strung along a narrative thread, where ironic detachment supersedes the emotional involvement and catharsis of Greek tragedy.

In this day of the common man few are concerned with the fall of princes, and it is interesting to examine some of the more striking modern plays and to ask how far they stand up to the Aristotelian canon. Should a new concept of tragedy be evolved, that of potentiality unrealised, not a fall from greatness but a failure to rise?

### The Brechtian or Epic Play.

Many British dramatists have felt the pervasive influence of the Bavarian Brecht (*q.v.*), who developed a new kind of Epic or narrative play of debate, with a loose sequence of episodic scenes linked by commentary or songs. Discarding realism, Brecht attempted not to arouse the onlooker's emotions but to stimulate him to think about social issues and to take left-wing action. In the event his ambiguous central situation appealed to deeper levels of experience.

There have been several instances of the ambiguous protagonist, but English playwrights have tended to adopt not the political intentions but the style of the Epic genre. Esslin has said that Shaffer in *The Royal Hunt of the Sun* has joined " Bolt, Arden and John Whiting of *The Devils* in the select group of British dramatists who have genuinely benefited from the conception of epic . . . techniques in drama."

### Theatre of Cruelty.

In 1938 Antonin Artaud published *The Theatre and its Double*, a collection of essays and letters, which forms the theoretic basis of the Theatre of Cruelty, his central purpose being a ritual of cruelty to exorcise fantasies.

Professor Brustein has described how Artaud hated industrial civilisation, believing, like Freud and D. H. Lawrence, that it stifled instinctual life. He claimed that the theatre, as the heart of a common culture, should enact a primitive ritual of cruelty, a sacrificial frenzy and exaltation. In this way it would bring to the surface and exorcise the spectator's latent anarchy, violence, and eroticism, serving as an " outlet for repressions."

Artaud envisaged a total theatre, appealing to total man, primarily visual, where the all important Director would deploy "music, dance, plastic art, pantomime, mimicry, gesticulation, intonation, architecture, scenery and lighting" to induce a state of trance. Attacking the inadequacy of a pallid conceptual language, Artaud demanded that dramatic language should have an emotional and incantatory effect.

It is Genet who most closely fulfils Artaud's demands and in England the specific Theatre of Cruelty has been best represented by his plays, the *Marat-Sade* of Weiss, and Triana's *The Criminals*. But the methods of production advocated by Artaud have had a wide and pervasive influence on the movement towards total theatre.

## Expressionism.

One of the most notable contemporary revivals of Expressionism is Wesker's *Chips with Everything*. The genre flourished in Germany after the First World War, where its chief exponents were Kaiser and Toller, and in Czechoslovakia in the plays of Capek. O'Neill and O'Casey have also occasionally experimented with Expressionism.

Reacting from Realism with its insistence on individual psychology and the detailed representation of actual life, Kaiser, Toller, and Capek sought to express rather the general aspirations and fears of humanity, especially man grappling with the advent of machinery. Their characters are symbolic types, as the Nameless One, representing the mob in Toller's *Man and the Masses*. Their decor is stylised, the dialogue staccato, and the brief scenes are characterised by mass movement and swift action.

## Naturalism.

Naturalism in drama may be regarded as a special case of Realism, and it is not easy, nor perhaps always desirable, to make a sharp distinction between the two.

Naturalistic drama attempts to record as faithfully as possible the actual experiences of life, however banal, and to present life, undistorted by the playwright's theories or too much concern for artistic form. The virtues of Naturalism are fidelity and spontaneity. Its danger is that it may keep so close to life as to lose artistic form and tension, becoming the stage version of the tape recorder. *See* Slice-of-Life Play.

It was Zola in the 1870s who propounded the principles of Naturalism. Distrusting both the play of ideas and the well-constructed play as tending to impose on life a falsifying and artificial pattern, he urged that drama should record as objectively as possible the actual course of man's life, especially the way it is conditioned by environment.

Strindberg's *Miss Julie*, 1888, is an essay in Naturalism but the genre is found in its most accomplished form in the Russian theatre, especially in Stanislavsky's production at the Moscow Art Theatre of the plays of Chekhov and in 1902 of Gorky's *The Lower Depths*.

## Neo-Realism.

There is nothing new in dramatic Realism (*q.v.*) as such. What is novel is the realistic presentation of the shabby lodgings and streets of the underprivileged. Gorky in *The Lower Depths* was perhaps the first dramatist to reveal the wretched condition of the destitute and this play influenced O'Neill's *The Iceman Cometh*. Their recent production in London, with a starkly realistic background, had some effect on those contemporary plays where the kitchen-sink and dustbin are as much in vogue as was formerly the fashionable drawing-room.

Any worth-while play has significance far beyond its milieu and modern neo-realistic plays vary greatly in theme and purpose. Wesker, Delaney, Livings, Owen, Osborne, Orton, Bond, Lawler, and Seymour have all used the style in differing ways.

Several of these playwrights have themselves been workers and their plays are an authentic interpretation of their own culture, once inaccessible to the middle-class audience. The fact that their work is occasionally loose in structure may be attributable to the influence of Naturalism

(*q.v.*) or to the author's unacademic background. The advent of this fresh and vigorous drama from a group that has seldom been articulate is one of the most encouraging aspects of modern theatre.

## Realism.

Writers of realistic drama, such as Galsworthy, attempt to create a stage illusion of actual life, usually through the medium of the well-constructed play. It is not always easy to distinguish between Realism and Naturalism—its extreme form—but one salient difference is that the latter tends to discard organised plot as imposing a false pattern on the flux of life.

Bolt, Cooper, Mortimer, Shaffer, and Porter have all written realistic plays, and since the 'fifties there has been a succession of competently constructed realistic plays associated with the novelists, Graham Greene, C. P. Snow, and Muriel Spark.

## The Satirical Play.

Recent years have seen heartening revivals of plays by Shaw, triggered off by Stage Sixty's production of *Widowers' Houses*, with its topical relevance to Rachmanism. There followed a long succession of Shaw revivals, including *Too True to be Good*, from the Edinburgh Festival, *You Never Can Tell*, with Ralph Richardson, and *Heartbreak House* from Chichester.

Shaw has found few successors, for genuine satire is a most demanding art. Subjective hostility and negative criticism are not enough. The motive power in Ibsen and Shaw was rational indignation, a most difficult fusion of strong emotion and objective reasoning, and their satire was constructive in that it implied and indicated positive values. It was also characterised by a precise aim at a specific target. Vague and wholesale denunciation diffuse a disagreeable tone which has a boomerang effect for it becomes associated not with the targets but with the playwright himself.

The graces of satire are detachment, irony, and wit and it flourishes apparently in a stable society such as that of the 18th century, which produced Swift and Voltaire. The European upheavals of the last half century have been unpropitious for satire and it is significant that the best plays in this genre, those of Frisch and Dürrenmatt, have come from neutral Switzerland.

The English playwright nearest to Shaw is Nigel Dennis, and Giles Cooper shared his ironic detachment.

## The "Slice of Life" Play.

Here is an extreme kind of Naturalism, where the author has been so anxious to preserve fidelity to the natural spontaneity of living, that he has all but discarded form, as having a cramping and distorting effect.

One of the most typical examples is Henry Chapman's *You Won't Always Be On Top*, showing the disconnected minor incident and talk of men ostensibly "at work" on a building site. Shelagh Delaney's *The Lion in Love* is also in this vein.

## Verse Drama.

During the 20th century several attempts have been made to revive drama in verse—the normal vehicle for the Renaissance playwright. Although the verse plays of Shakespeare and his contemporaries, kept alive in excellent revivals, still rise like the Himalayas above the contemporary scene, the dramatist today who tries to use verse has not the benefit of an unbroken tradition. Yeats, T. S. Eliot, and Christopher Fry all succeeded for a time in getting their verse plays on to the stage but at the moment the most successful poetic drama achieves its effect through poetic prose and the theatrical poetry of its situation and stage imagery. Dylan Thomas' *Under Milk Wood* successfully used these media. For many contemporary dramatists it is Beckett, Arden, and Pinter who have captured the poetry inherent in drama.

The finest verse play seen on the English stage for many years is Robert Lowell's *Benito Cereno*.

The Well-made Play.

The term " well-made play " is most frequently used in a derogatory sense. Eric Bentley has pointed out that the " well-made play " is a form of classical tragedy, degenerate in that although the plot is ingeniously contrived, with arresting situation, intrigue, and suspense, the play is mechanical and devoid of feeling. The television series, *The World of Wooster*, is an example.

The expression was frequently used disparagingly of the French plays of Scribe and of Sardou, ridiculed by Shaw for his " Sardoodledum."

# IV. DIRECTORY OF DRAMATISTS

This part, alphabetical in arrangement, includes dramatists whose work, whether English or in translation, has had its British première since 1950. Unless otherwise stated the quotation of date and actor refers to the British première.

Inexpensive paperback editions are referred to thus: F: Faber and Faber. M: Methuen. P: Penguin.

## Arthur Adamov (b. 1908).

Adamov first wrote plays such as *Professor Taranne* (P), which translate his own personal neuroses into images of the absurd, until with the propagandist *Paolo Paoli* he adopted a Brechtian technique. His *Spring 1871*, an epic panorama of the Paris Commune, had its world première in London in 1962.

## Edward Albee (b. 1928).

The American Albee is a brilliant satirist. Early plays include the absurdist *Zoo Story* (P) and *The American Dream* (P), and the realistic *The Death of Bessie Smith*.

*Who's Afraid of Virginia Woolf?* 1964. P.

A brilliant and scarifying satire on sterility in an American campus uses a ritual movement. George and Martha, named after the Washingtons, are an unsuccessful and childless middle-aged couple. They cherish a fantasy " son," whom George, to spite Martha, symbolically " murders " during a liquor-ridden night party, when they attack each other and their guests (a young couple also childless) with ferocious mental cruelty.

*A Delicate Balance.* 1969.

An icy surface glasses over treacherous depths in the well-to-do home of Tobias (Hordern) and Agnes (Peggy Ashcroft) and the play begins and ends with her virtual monologue—phrased with the elegance of a Henry James—on how it will be if she goes mad.

Agnes holds the " delicate balance " of polite manners, while tolerant Tobias is now ineffectual and her alcoholic sister Claire persists in her sarcastic utterance of unwelcome truths. The most galling, obliquely hinted at, is that Tobias is more drawn to Claire than to Agnes.

Their son long since dead, and Tobias having then withdrawn from Agnes, their sole offspring is the neurotic Julia, who now returns home at the breakdown of her fourth marriage.

Suddenly their " oldest friends," Harry and Edna, arrive seeking asylum from some inexplicable terror of " nothing." Bewildered, but courteous, the hosts accept their guests, but after Julia has threatened to shoot the " intruders," Agnes forces Tobias to realise that they bring " the plague."

Tobias, unable to discard his last ideal of friendship, begs them to stay, while telling them this truth, but they depart, realising that they demand a sacrifice they themselves could not make.

Here is a microcosm of a society where love and friendship have died, humanism crumbles, and little but polite diplomacy survive, often a vehicle for fear and hostility. In tone it is a bitter inversion of the Apocryphal *Tobit*, with its touching pictures of religious faith, family love and neighbourliness, and the " entertaining of Angels unawares."

The literary provenance in subject and style is Eliot's *Family Reunion*, where another Harry, fleeing the furies, comes to a Wishwood, also dominated by a woman whose husband had loved her sister, like Clair also a visionary. But in Eliot the visionary is healer not destroyer, and Harry departs to " follow the bright angels."

With literary subtlety Albee exposes the " panic and emptiness " in a society losing its confidence and sense of values.

## Jean Anouilh (b. 1910).

Anouilh is a playwright of remarkable theatrical versatility and skill. Following Giraudoux, he has frequently employed classical themes, as in *Eurydice* (M), and *Antigone*, 1949 (M), with Olivier and Vivien Leigh. More recently he has treated historical figures, Saint Joan in *The Lark* (M), and Becket in the play of that name (M). The play within a play is a favourite expedient of his and he used it again in *The Fighting Cock* (M), produced at Chichester, 1966.

Anouilh's outlook is deeply pessimistic. A recurring theme is that purity is incompatible with experience of life and many of his protagonists say, " No." His plays fall into two categories—the fatalistic *pièces noires* and the romantic fantasies, *pièces roses*.

They have been extraordinarily popular on the London stage of the 'fifties and Anouilh's amoral attitude has been reflected in many West End successes.

## Aleksei Arbuzov (b. 1908).

The Russian producer and playwright Arbuzov has been writing since 1930.

*The Promise.* 1966.

In the best tradition of naturalism *The Promise* is a moving and positive work free from both illusion and despair.

During the siege of Leningrad three adolescents, two boys and a girl, contrive to survive in a bombed house, and here in brief episodic scenes their hardship, gaiety, and the slow awakening of love are shown with a delicate and touching naturalism.

Four years later Lika must choose between the two men and although she loves the engineer Marat she chooses the dependent, poetic Leonidik. The decision brings fulfilment to no one and finally Leonidik courageously summons back Marat and leaves him and Lika together, a conclusion analogous to that of *The Caucasian Chalk Circle*.

## John Arden (b. 1930).

Arden is a vigorous and gifted playwright, who has experimented with a variety of subjects and methods, sometimes too original and complex to find quick acceptance.

His characters are full-blooded and rich in human contradictions, and he has sympathetically brought to life even such bogeys as Herod and King John. He loves to dwell on some ambiguous personality, where generosity conflicts with violence, and to consider the problems of directing man's unruly vitality.

His favourite theme is the dispute between instinctual energy and good government and he pleads the case cogently for both sides, giving no facile judgment or direct " message," unless it be " the recognition of the fallibility of man." Thus although, like Brecht, he is deeply concerned with social and political dilemmas, he remains politically " uncommitted." He is above all the dramatist of the dilemma.

There has been a fruitful cross-fertilisation of Arden's interest in current events and his literary studies; and his historical plays, like Brecht's *Mother Courage*, combine a fine sense of period and a sharp relevance to some current issue.

Arden's plays are poetic in structure, depending in part on the recurrent image and metaphor and, like Arthur Miller in *The Crucible*, he has skilfully devised for each an appropriate dialect of time and place. At the same time he has a keen sense of theatre, and has successfully adapted techniques from Miracle plays, Elizabethan drama, music-hall, puppet stage, and Brechtian epic play.

*Live Like Pigs.* 1958. P.

Seventeen realistic scenes full of comic and frightening incident reveal how fatal conflicts develop between households at different social levels in a new housing estate. Street ballads in Brechtian style preface some scenes.

*The Happy Haven.* 1960. P.

Here, in a good-tempered satirical fable, enlivened by a dash of magic, Arden touches on problems of longevity.

Doctor Copperthwaite, the superintendent of the Happy Haven, an old people's home, is, like a mediaeval alchemist, bent on producing an Elixir of Life and Youth, intending to use his five unsuspecting patients as guinea-pigs. But outwitted by them he is himself transformed into a small boy.

The theme is childishness. The egocentric demands of the very old are seen as amusing childish foibles, while Doctor Copperthwaite, so absorbed in his research as to forget ends for means, brings childishness on himself.

In form the play is an extended puppet show. The characters wear masks, the set is formalised, and there is even a dog, Hector, but unlike Dog Toby he is visible only to the dramatis personae.

*Serjeant Musgrave's Dance.* 1959. M.

For a fine play, which explores the ethical dilemma of war, Arden drew on two sources—contemporary events in Cyprus and a journal written by a deeply devout N.C.O. during the Crimean War. He has fused his material into vivid incidents, which he projects against the background of a fictitious colonial war of the 1880s.

In a frost-bound colliery town there arrive three private soldiers, led by the dominating Serjeant Musgrave. They claim to have come recruiting but are in fact deserters from a colonial war.

In spite of his rigid sense of military duty, Musgrave had been horrified by the terrible fivefold reprisals taken by the British for the assassination of a comrade, Billy Hicks. Believing himself to be God's agent, he has now come to Billy's town, obsessed by one purpose, to expose war's horrors.

Exhibiting Billy's skeleton in the market-place, he at first wins sympathy in his denunciation of atrocities. Then bewildered by his own confused " logic," he demands twenty-five deaths in return for the five taken by the British and turns the gatling on the astonished crowd.

Suddenly, with the thaw, the Dragoons arrive and Musgrave finds himself awaiting execution, stunned that no one has learned the lesson he yearned to teach.

Fierce incident and macabre surprise are used for a play of ideas which enunciates no facile answer. It is typical of Arden's fair and non-doctrinaire approach that the dilemma of the religious man in face of war should be embodied in the fanatical and confused Musgrave. This has sometimes misled the audience, but the spirit of compassion implicit throughout the play is clearly revealed in the gentle, pacific Private Attercliffe, who is also to be executed with Musgrave. The women's parts are also significant, especially that of Mrs. Hitchcock, the owner of the inn, who visits Musgrave in prison and shows him how he had erred in trying to use war itself to end war. In his darkest despair she gives him hope, and it is symbolic that he accepts drink from her hand.

The complex play weaves together many tensions; harsh discord between colliery owner and strikers; contention between the three privates, each of whom is strongly individualised; the discrepancy between a woman's love and the careless soldier's life; Musgrave's own bitter inner struggle.

The dialogue has a wonderful period character and the soldiers' ballads and lyrical songs occur with complete naturalness.

*The Workhouse Donkey.* 1963. M.

Styled by Arden as a " vulgar melodrama ", this ample Brechtian play shows jockeying for power in a northern town between the Tory Alderman Sweetman, a wealthy brewer, and Alderman Butterthwaite (Frank Finlay), the Labour ex-mayor. Both attempt to manipulate the police and to enlist the support of the electorate, represented by the shifty turncoat Doctor Blomax, until all these four elements of the community are deeply corrupted.

Butterthwaite, called " the workhouse donkey " because born in the workhouse, is the dominating Rabelaisian character. A Dionysiac figure, he is drunken, lecherous, and amoral, yet devotedly loyal and generous. Finally in an attempt to help the treacherous Blomax he robs the Borough safe and brings disaster on himself and the town.

The personality of the late Mr. Joseph D'Arcy of Dublin inspired much of the play.

*Armstrong's Last Goodnight.* 1964. M.

The old " Ballad of Johnie Armstrang," c. 1603, forms the framework of a play concerning the dilemmas of government. Armstrong of Gilnockie, the Scots Border laird, freebooter and rebel, is invited to a meeting by the young Scottish King James V and then treacherously hanged. Arden has introduced into this stark story the historical character of the king's herald, Sir David Lindsay, poet and politician, and shows him at first striving by devious diplomatic expedients to persuade Armstrong (Albert Finney) to loyalty, before he finally advises force. The play is diversified by minor characters and incidents which overcomplicate the impressive ballad line.

The introduction of Lindsay was suggested to Arden by his reading of Conor Cruise O'Brien's book *To Katanga and Back*, for he was struck by " a basic similarity of moral " between 20th-century Africa and 16th-century Scotland, the rôle of O'Brien being similar to that which he invents for Lindsay.

Arden makes free use of Elizabethan pageantry and of Brechtian ballad-singing and the setting is the mediaeval convention of " simultaneous mansions," Gilnockie, the Border, and the Court all being formally represented on the stage at one and the same time.

Arden " constructed " a dialect to suggest place and period, but it is difficult to follow.

*Left-handed Liberty.* 1965. M.

Commissioned by the Corporation of the City of London to write a play to commemorate the 750th anniversary of Magna Carta, Arden presents the historical facts with very little transposition and addition.

He approaches his theme of liberty from an unusual angle, showing the aftermath of Runnymede in the apparent failure of the Charter, and demonstrating that the agreement had to take place in people's minds before it could become effective.

Arden does not present a clash of black and white. John is a rounded character, a slippery villain, but shrewd and energetic and gifted with the Plantagenet charm, while some of the barons are coarse and unscrupulous fighters.

The use of stylised scene emblems gives mediaeval colour to the simple stageing and Arden has again invented a suitable dialect.

*The Royal Pardon.* 1967. M.

A play for young teenagers, that developed out of bedtime stories for the Arden children, was written in collaboration with Margaretta D'Arcy.

*Squire Jonathan.* 1968.

In a grim Gothic tower, centuries ago, threadbare old Jonathan, descended from kings, gloats over his treasure chest, suspicious of the Dark Men outside and desiring the White Woman. A foolish, clumsy blonde, she appears wearing a chastity belt and eventually refusing his jewels, goes to the Dark Men. The play, a dramatic metaphor, was interpreted on production as an image of Britain's current situation, Jonathan dressed as Wilson and the White Woman like a Britannia or Boadicea.

*The Hero Rises Up.* 1968.

Written with Margaretta d'Arcy, this parody of melodrama is a sardonic enquiry into the motivation of our national hero, Nelson.

## Isaac Babel (1894–1941).

Between 1937 and 1957 the work of Babel, the Russian Jewish short-story writer, was banned in Russia. He died in Siberia. *Sunset*, the first of his two extant plays, produced in Russia under Stanislavsky in 1928, appeared on B.B.C. television in 1964.

### Marya. 1967. P.

Written in 1933 but not yet professionally produced in Russia, *Marya* is set in Petrograd in February 1920. It evokes a precise period in history—the flux and confusion just before the Bolsheviks consolidated their power in March 1920.

The organisation of the play is poetic, the balance and interplay between two social milieus. One is the decayed elegance of the liberal intelligentsia focused in the home of Mukovnin, a former General, where the men are well-disposed but impotent, the women unchaste. The other is the squalid house where Dymschitz, the Jewish merchant turned black-marketeer, lives with his hangers-on and crooks.

As in Chekhov, the characters are studied in psychological depth and the quiet naturalism of the style is sometimes startled by sudden violence as in the shootings after the rape of Ludmilla, Mukovnin's younger daughter, and the link between the two households.

## James Baldwin (b. 1924).

Baldwin is an American Negro novelist and essayist, and a champion of Civil Rights.

### The Amen Corner. 1965.

Acted by a Negro cast including singers of Spirituals, the successful play gently probes the genuine and the self-deluded elements in religious experience.

## Samuel Beckett (b. 1906).

Beckett, an Anglo-Irishman, who has made his home in France, is both novelist and the most distinguished of the English dramatists of the Absurd. His world is drastically limited, peopled chiefly by old men awaiting their death, but it is the profoundly tragic world of Lear in the storm and it is conceived with the intensity and haunting power and suggestiveness of the true poet.

His work is poetic in its verbal imagery, sometimes as searching and macabre as that of Webster, and his dramatic prose has an underlying poetic rhythm often more flexible and effective than that of Eliot's verse. In structure his plays have a poetic symbolism, a latent significance, like that of the novels of James Joyce, Beckett's close friend, and their striking visual imagery has a kind of theatrical poetry, as for instance the two tramps at the foot of a bare tree in *Waiting for Godot*. It is remarkable that so literary a playwright should also have succeeded with the wordless mime play.

Beckett's chief weakness as a dramatist is that the action and visual imagery are frequently too static, as in the motionless dustbins in *End Game*, much less effective theatrically than Ionesco's movable chairs.

### Waiting for Godot. 1955. F.

This tantalising and compelling tragi-comedy, Beckett's masterpiece, originally written in French and produced in Paris in 1953, was later translated and performed in more than twenty countries.

Character and incident are pared to the bone and only a skeleton situation remains. At evening, on a desolate road, bare but for a single tree, two wretched tramps, Vladimir and Estragon, wait for a mysterious Mr. Godot. As they while away the time with desultory talk and clowning, a tragi-farcical diversion is provided by the entry of Pozzo and Lucky, bullying master and wretched slave, and a boy later brings a message that Mr. Godot cannot come but will arrive the next evening. After discussing whether or not they shall hang themselves from the tree, the tramps decide to go away for the night, but remain on the spot.

Act II presents " Next day, same place," the only difference being that the tree has sprouted a few leaves, and the basic pattern of Act I is repeated.

Although by the skilful use of music-hall techniques Beckett presents his tramps in the guise of amusing clowns, they are at the same time pathetically human as they waver between suicide and irrational hope. A fretful affection has kept them together over fifty years, and their dispositions are complementary, possibly even representing different aspects of the one personality. The practical and extrovert Vladimir, nicknamed Gogo, may depict man's intellect, his executive powers, the ego, while the more poetical and introvert Estragon, nicknamed Didi, may represent the body, instinct, the id.

Pozzo and Lucky, another pair of contrasting characters, are portrayed more farcically. The loud, confident Pozzo drives Lucky in as if he were a beast of burden. Lucky carries in his mouth the whip with which he is beaten and humbly obeys every insolent command. He dances for Pozzo and even thinks for him. In their second appearance Pozzo is blind and Lucky deaf.

They may be considered personifications respectively of master and slave, worldly materialism and higher values, the physical and the intellectual, body and soul, or the two aspects of a sado-masochistic relationship.

The play as a whole is most complex dramatic symbol expressing man's anxiety and suffering as to his origin and destination.

The uncertainty is symbolised by the characters' confusion as to even the physical actualities of time and place, but the dominating symbol is the tramps' doubt as to Godot's identity and purpose.

Such an oversimplified interpretation as to equate Godot with God is inadequate, yet the play has undoubted Christian references. A tree is frequently used as an emblem of the Cross. Beckett, questioned about its theme, quoted a wonderful sentence in Saint Augustine, . . . " Do not despair; one of the thieves was saved. Do not presume; one of the thieves was damned."

Beckett neither affirms nor denies Saint Augustine's statement but inverts it into a question, more distressing than direct denial. Can we any longer accept the existence of divine grace and judgment? It is a question such as this that gives to the play its symbolic shape of doubt, and which is cogently expressed in the theatrical image of two outcasts at the foot of a tree, a tree of life which puts forth leaves, a tree of death which they contemplate using as a gallows.

Yet the significance of the play is even deeper than an exploration of religious doubt, its appeal wider and more contemporary. The anguished uncertainty of the 20th century is whether life has any meaning whatsoever and the play shows the suffering of man, lost and anxious in an apparently meaningless universe.

Some have considered it to be written from the point of view of existentialism: continuing vainly to hope for a supernatural revelation, the tramps lack the courage to come to terms with the nothingness of our existence and the need to choose and create our own destiny.

A Jungian psychologist, Eva Metman, has made a similar interpretation, remarking, " Godot's function seems to be to keep his dependents unconscious."

" Habit is a great deadener," says Vladimir. If Beckett's play enables the audience to escape the drug of habit and to face this image of anguish and so find some relief, then it may have the therapeutic value of that inner knowledge advocated by Freud and Jung.

It is not a play for those who cannot bear to suffer. When performed in San Francisco Gaol, the first play there for forty-four years, it held its audience of fourteen hundred convicts spellbound. They realised that each must find his own personal message. All knew that it spoke to those who must suffer and wait.

### Endgame. 1958. F.

Also re-created from the French, this play again depicts a static situation. In a single, claustrophobic room, the selfish, materialistic Hamm, who keeps his senile and legless parents in dustbins, is now paralysed and blind and dependent on his servant Clov, who longs to leave him. But if Clov should leave, both would die, for Hamm owns the only store of food in a devastated and dead world. Finally Clov sees outside what may be a small boy, " a potential procreator," and he prepares for departure but remains immobile.

The play like poetry can be interpreted in several ways. Since Hamm and Clov are mutually dependent, it probably represents tension between complementary aspects of personality, Hamm sensation and emotion, and Clov intellect. As Clov has vision and sees the boy, the situation suggests the struggle of the mystic endeavouring to escape from a deadening materialism to a vital awakening of the spirit. It may also depict a period of traumatic depression when the whole external world seems dead and unreal.   The play's overall impression is that of the dissolution of the personality in death, both personal and global.

*Endgame* lacks the wry humour of *Waiting for Godot*, and is less compelling than Ionesco's *Exit the King*, but is more potent in its latent imagery than is Ionesco's play.

*Krapp's Last Tape.* 1958.  F.

In the briefest sketch, Krapp, a solitary, decrepit, unsuccessful old man listens to his own autobiographical tape-recording of thirty years ago, but the moment of miraculous insight it commemorates is now so meaningless to him that he switches off that section of the recording and broods on a description of his love-making.

Beckett employs a most effective stage device to pose contemporary queries as to the limitations of verbal communication and the continuity of personal identity.

*Happy Days.* 1962.  F.

Here again the paralysis of later life is indicated. A woman talks ceaselessly, although progressively buried in a mound of earth until it reaches her neck.

Beckett's two " Mimeplays without Words " are in striking contrast to the plays in that all is conveyed in symbolic wordless action.

### Brendan Behan (1923–64).

Behan, a Dubliner, and author of the autobiography, *The Borstal Boy*, used his own experiences in the I.R.A. and as political prisoner to give substance to his two unusual plays.

The scripts of both were sent to Joan Littlewood and considerably altered, especially in the deletion of " chunks of terrible sentimentality," while the length of *The Hostage* had to be trebled. Lacking in structure and depth of characterisation, they are vividly impressionistic, lively, and voluble.  As Tynan says, " Language is out on a spree, ribald, dauntless and spoiling for a fight."

Because they are presented in comic terms, Behan's strong social convictions are fully integrated in his plays.  *The Quare Fellow* is an effective plea for the abolition of capital punishment and *The Hostage* makes the business of war seem extremely childish.

*The Quare Fellow.* 1956.  M.

The scene is an Irish gaol during the twenty-four hours immediately preceding the execution at 8 a.m. of " the quare fellow," who has brutally killed his own brother. Farcical and macabre happenings succeed one another, as the unnerving effect of impending death is shown on both prisoners and warders, while a recurring song from the punishment cell sounds a melancholy refrain. The sombre theme is presented obliquely, masked by the harsh irony of prison jests, and although the play has little plot it is remarkably tense, partly because we never see the condemned man. Much is also due to Joan Littlewood's skill in redistributing dialogue and tightening the structure.

The film version completely distorted the disciplined and claustrophobic atmosphere of the play.

*The Hostage.* 1958.  M.

Again the basic situation is the waiting for an execution.  The scene is an old Dublin house, once the refuge of the I.R.A., now a brothel. Irish patriots bring here a captured Cockney private soldier, Leslie Williams, as hostage for an Irish boy, now a political prisoner in Belfast, who is to be executed next morning.

Teresa, the gentle little Irish maid, reared in a convent, tries to save Leslie.  There is touching pathos as these two orphans, neither of them understanding what the strife is about, recall their childhood, and when in a raid on the house Leslie is shot, Teresa utters her lyric lament. But the mood is only held for a moment.  Leslie leaps up and sings " The bells of hell go ting-a-ling-a-ling," and the play ends.

The mood is much less consistent than that of *The Quare Fellow.*  Here the comedy is chiefly a diversion supplied by a host of minor characters. The action is constantly held up for songs more or less satirical and music-hall exchanges between comedian and " feed," some of them genuine Irish inconsequence, others mediocre backchat and malapropism.  All this pseudo-Brechtian trimming detracts from the growing sense of alarm as Leslie gradually realises his fate and is of doubtful value.

### Robert Bolt (b. 1924).

Bolt has recently said, " I do like plays in which the people have ideas as well as predicaments " and he is one of the few dramatists who have scored West End successes with the play of ideas. He holds the balance of discussion so fairly that only in the outcome is it clear that he himself is committed.  His earlier work, represented by *The Flowering Cherry* (1957), with Ralph Richardson, was in the realistic convention, but more recently he has experimented with other dramatic techniques, owing something to Brecht and to the Theatre of Cruelty and of the Absurd.

*The Tiger and the Horse.* 1960.

This play takes its title from Blake's " The Tygers of wrath are wiser than the horses of instruction."  It is concerned with the inadequacy of detachment, the philosophy held by Jack Dean, (Michael Redgrave), the Master of an Oxbridge college, the well-balanced man who represents Blake's " horse," while his wife, Gwen, the " tiger," passionately concerned for the world's suffering, shows signs of neurosis.  The action revolves round her wish to sign a petition for unconditional nuclear disarmament and Dean eventually, to save her from mental breakdown, bravely identifies himself with her and the cause, thereby deserting his philosophy and his career.

In its outcome the play stresses the value of social idealism, stifled as it may be by philosophic detachment and the pressures of conformity.  It is typical of Bolt's dialectic that this value should be upheld by the disturbed Gwen and by Louis, an oddly irresponsible young man.

Bolt departs from the realistic style by trying to make his characters larger than life in being unusually articulate about what they stand for.

*A Man for All Seasons.* 1960.  P.

Here Bolt attempts to give his characters heroic dimensions by striking back into history.

Believing that our need today is a sense of personal individuality or " self hood," he chooses as his hero of " selfhood " Sir Thomas More. Bolt consciously uses the dramatist's privilege to adapt history to his own purpose, for the theory of conscience accepted by More was not subjective and existentialist but identical with that of Thomas Aquinas.  Hence some inconsistency in his portrayal.

More was described by one of his contemporaries as " a man for all seasons " and Bolt presents More (Scofield) as not only flexibly adjusted to Renaissance society but also preserving an inner core of unassailable integrity.  Suspected of a critical attitude to Henry VIII's divorce, he used his skill in " the thickets of the law," yet resolutely refused to swear the oath to the Act of Succession that would have released him from the Tower and the block, because for him perjury meant the loss of the soul, the self.  His constancy is thrown into relief by the growing corruption of Richard Rich, whose final perjury sends More to his death.

Bolt's More challenges comparison with Brecht's Galileo.  He also is a man of supreme intelligence, whose inner certitude of truth is persecuted by an absolute power.  He also skilfully avoids open clash until he must eventually make a final choice between astute temporising and commitment of his life to his belief.  The difference is that More opts unequivocally for constancy.

Bolt uses what he calls a " bastardized version " of Brecht's style.  Episodic scenes are strung along a strong thread of intellectual argument. There is also a commentator in the form of the Common Man, who with the aid of property box takes a swift succession of minor parts, changes of role which throw into relief the steadfast individuality of More.

Bolt, like Brecht, believing that beauty of language is a means of "alienation," matches fine passages from More himself with his own appropriate use of wit and imagery, using images of land to suggest society and its laws and those of water and sea the superhuman context.

The film version has been highly praised.

*Gentle Jack.* 1963.

Bolt depicts the conflict between the natural spontaneity of nature, represented by the magic figure of folk-lore, Jack-of-the-Green (Kenneth Williams) and the inhibitions of society in the person of Miss Lazara, a plutocrat (Edith Evans). Since Bolt believes that the modern doctrine of the return to nature may lead to violence, Jack finally contrives two murders. Bolt in dealing with this conflict could not, like Euripides in *The Bacchae*, draw on a familiar myth, and his allegorical plot proved puzzling, while the setting was too reminiscent of *Dear Brutus*. The play is too cerebral, the characters are more blueprints than flesh and blood.

*The Thwarting of Baron Bolligrew.* 1965.

A play for children over eight was much praised by the critics as inventive and entertaining.

**Edward Bond (b. 1935).**

Most sensitive people share Bond's appalled dismay at contemporary violence and war, the drab monotony of industrialisation and the stifling of individuality, but it is not yet clear whether his obsessive images of violence, including infanticide, are objective or self-indulgent.

He is not yet in control of his material and is apparently animated by intense, subjective hostility to all authority. He attempts to rationalise this by a naïve anarchy, pontificating that " Society . . . makes men animals " unaware that he is tilting at an abstraction. Some statements are so solipsistic and perverse as to make his intellectual groundwork suspect.

*Saved.* 1965. M.

As a result of casual sexual intercourse with the promiscuous Pam, Len gets involved with her morose South London family, with Fred, the putative father of her baby, and with Fred's lewd gang, which murders the baby on the stage.

Since the play is largely in delinquents' argot, and is limited to a photographic study of inarticulate people, it is in itself somewhat inarticulate, but it constitutes a frank and compassionate social document.

*Early Morning.* 1968.

Esslin interprets this play as infantile fantasy. The archetypal authoritarian figures of mother, father, nurse, and grown-ups appear as Queen Victoria and the Consort at deadly enmity, Florence Nightingale, on whom Victoria has a Lesbian crush, and Gladstone and Dizzy waging civil war. The princes, Siamese twins, suggest sibling rivalry, and the final scene is a nightmare eternity of mutual cannibalism, whose psychoanalytic significance is oral eroticism and sadism. Esslin judges the play absurdist, innocuous as satire, but with an underlying substance " of great seriousness and poetic power."

Wardle says Bond is writing like a wrathful, " omnipotent baby " presenting a " solipsistic muddle," meriting case-book study rather than dramatic criticism.

*Narrow Road to the Deep North.* 1968. M.

The setting, visually very beautiful, is 17th-century Japan, where the War Lord, Shogo, is eventually overthrown by the Commodore, and a " bragging mindless savage," representing Western civilisation, with the tambourine-banging Georgina, a somewhat outdated image of missionary zeal supporting imperialism.

Shogo maintains order by sheer atrocity, Georgina by inculcating also a puritan sense of sin, the " message " being that government is *per se* evil and our only hope the naked man, who finally rises from the river (recalling the Romantic myth of the " noble savage ").

Bond's dubious dogma overlays the most moving aspect of the play, its latent plea for individualism.

**John Bowen.**

Bowen first won recognition as a novelist.

*After the Rain.* 1967.

Bowen dramatises his own novel, where after a great deluge ill-assorted survivors drift on a raft and enact a version of history. Meanwhile the dictatorial Arthur imposes on them his authority, first as dictator and ultimately as god.

Bowen dramatises this fantasy by setting it in a conventional framework: a history lecture given in A.D. 2197 on the origins of the new society descended from the party on the raft. Hypnotised criminals, guilty of such crimes as individuality, are used at intervals as teaching aids. They enact the story of the raft, until eventually Arthur (Alec McCowen) rebels, preferring death to his dramatic role.

The lecture serves as a conventional apologia to the enactment, which eschewing scenery and properties, makes use of the experimental techniques of Weiss's *Marat Sade*.

*Little Boxes.* 1968. M.

A double bill of realistic well-made plays again shows little communities in isolation. In this instance both groups have withdrawn deliberately from society.

In *The Coffee Lace* a pathetic vaudeville troupe, elderly and poverty-stricken, have refused to go out since their performance was cruelly ridiculed thirteen years previously. *Trevor* shows a young Lesbian couple. One girl anticipating her parents' visit pays an actor to pose as boy friend. But both sets of parents arrive and lively farce develops as Trevor attempts simultaneously to attend two parties and to cook scones. All the parents depart refusing to admit the girls' relationship and the play ends on a sentimental note.

*The Disorderly Woman.* 1969.

Bowen follows Anouilh in his capable adaptation of a Greek play, Euripides's *The Bacchae*, to a modern idiom.

**Bertolt Brecht (1898–1956).**

Perhaps the most original and vigorous dramatist and producer of the century, the Bavarian Brecht was remarkable in his command of both literary and theatrical genius.

His practice and theory underwent constant modification. Early plays, like *Baal*, written to provide entertainment, reveal a satiric and anarchic attitude, and in 1928 the ironic *The Threepenny Opera* (P), made him famous. From 1930 onward his work became explicitly communistic, marked by the rejection of the individual in favour of a social ideal. But although Brecht always remained " committed " to Marxist ideology, most of his later plays, written after his withdrawal from Nazi Germany, are less didactic than humanist in spirit and it is by these mature works that he is best known in Britain.

After 1949 Brecht consolidated the famous Berliner Ensemble in East Berlin, where he developed his influential techniques of production.

The most permanent feature of Brecht's mature drama are the Epic form and the *Verfremdung*, or " alienation " effect, both developed in reaction to the traditional dramatic form, which he dubbed " Aristotelian." He considered that the closely constructed Aristotelian play, which encourages the audience's emotional participation in the action, syphons off the spectator's emotion, leaving him a passive and acquiescent member of society.

According to Brecht, the drama should be not ritual but debate. The spectator should be a detached observer, calmly investigating the view of the world that confronts him, rationally considering arguments and stimulated to decisive social action. It is taken for granted that he will find the solution to problems in communism.

Brecht therefore developed his " Epic," or narrative play, loosely constructed with a sequence of individual scenes, functioning as independent dramatic illustrations or quotations to the narrative.

He uses a variety of techniques to establish the narrative tone, such as an actual story-teller on the stage, explanatory verses relayed before the scenes, and banner headlines which foretell the events to be portrayed. Although by throwing the action thus into the past tense, he discards the lure of suspense, his dramatic intelligence, vigour, and inventiveness excite lively interest and curiosity.

To break down the traditional identification of the spectator with the action, Brecht developed his celebrated " alienation " effect, devising techniques to keep him at a critical distance. This implies using an image that suddenly makes the familiar appear strange and novel to the onlooker, so that he is shocked into recognising its significance.

His productions were thus avowedly non-realistic and theatrical, sometimes appearing like an inspired charade. He used not only direct narration but direct address to the audience, formalised settings and properties, masks and stylised make-up, sometimes grotesque in character. His text, " scarcely more than a prompter's copy," was freely adapted during rehearsal, so that an acquaintance with the pattern of Brecht's mime and gesture is often necessary to the full understanding of his plays.

Few find in Brecht's mature work the plea for communism that he intended, and many of his protagonists, designed as exponents of capitalist villainy, appeal strongly to the sympathy. The compelling and fascinating central ambiguity can be ascribed, as Esslin has pointed out, to the tension between Brecht's conscious reason and the unconscious emotional experience on which every creative writer must intuitively draw. This profound tension is the major source of Brecht's power.

Brecht's influence has been pervasive, especially on the dramatists Arden, Bolt, Whiting, and Shaffer, and on the producer Joan Littlewood. Above all his iconoclastic attitude and his fertile experiment have been invaluable in encouraging a new and empirical approach to drama.

*Baal.* Written 1918.

The amoral vagabond poet, Baal (O'Toole), driven by instinct and emotion, expresses the subjective experience of the youthful Brecht.

*Galileo.* Written 1938-9. M.

Brecht intended Galileo's recantation as an image of the scientist's allowing the State to assume authority over science. It has also been interpreted as Galileo's cunning expedient, allowing him to continue research.

*Mother Courage.* Written 1939. M.

In his panorama of war's futility, Brecht designed Mother Courage—a camp follower in the Thirty Years' War—as an epitome of the haggling profiteer. But his intuitive understanding of this dynamic, maternal figure, bereaved eventually of all three children, has endowed her with an ambiguous fascination.

*The Good Person of Szechwan.* Written 1938-40. M.

Shen Te (Peggy Ashcroft), the benevolent prostitute, has to disguise herself as Shui Ta, the harsh task-master, in order to survive in an unjust commercial society.

*Puntila.* Written 1940-1.

The drunken generosity of the mean land-owner, Puntila, designed by Brecht to highlight his harshness when sober, has however given him an attractive inconsistency. The chauffeur who rejects Puntila's daughter, is a Schweikian character.

*The Caucasian Chalk Circle.* Written 1944-5. M.

The prologue to this delightful fairy-tale constitutes an overt plea for communism rare in

Brecht's later work. The rascally judge Adzak who takes bribes from the rich and gives judgment in favour of the poor, is one of Brecht's typical contradictory characters.

Peter Brook (b. 1925). Director.

*US* (or ambiguously *U.S.*). 1966.

*US* is a collaboration between director, actors, designers, musicians, and writers. It is their attempt to confront the Vietnam war, though it cannot be fully understood or influenced, and likewise to involve the audience in encounter with the terrible fact.

Brook admits anti-American bias because of the giant disproportion between the adversaries and " our own close involvement with America."

The First Act is a violent theatrical assault on apathy. Brook re-employs techniques from Weiss's *Marat-Sade* and alternates utmost stillness, as in the initial mime of a Buddhist self-immolation, with loud music and noise. In the hideous uproar and confusion of a bombing raid at the climax a giant war-effigy from the proscenium crashes across the stage. Shattering assault is succeeded in Act Two by a penetration in depth, its centre being a dialogue between a white man about to burn himself alive and a girl whose cold, detached criticism gradually gives way to a bitter indictment of English parochial indifference. In an ambiguous poetic finale an actor silently releases butterflies, one of which he burns.

This daring and controversial use of theatre directly to involve the emotion of the audience in confrontation with contemporary political tragedy may mark a new departure.

David Campton (b. 1924).

Campton's brief " glimpses " or playlets use techniques of the Absurd, which he considers as " a weapon against complacency," to expose the actual dangers that threaten society, especially the bomb. His most notable works are the collections of playlets, *The Lunatic View*, 1957, and *A View from the Brink*, 1961.

Albert Camus (1913-60).

It was the French existentialist philosopher and novelist, Camus, who first enunciated the concept of the Absurd, describing it as whatever in human experience is incompatible with man's desire for reason, justice, happiness, and purpose.

Like Sartre, Camus expressed his views through the traditional dramatic form, and the plays most familiar here were those written before he had moved on to a more humanistic philosophy.

*Caligula.* French publication 1945. P.

The Roman Emperor, Caligula, suddenly decides to act in accordance with the absurdity of the universe and by his violent and perverse crimes forces on the Senators his own recognition of the absurd meaninglessness of existence.

*Cross Purposes.* French publication 1945. P.

Man's futile desire for happiness is dramatised in the legend of the mother and daughter who murder for gain the visitor to their inn, only to discover they have killed the son of the house. They then commit suicide.

Paddy Chayevsky (b. 1923).

*The Latent Heterosexual.* 1968.

This American play begins as a hilarious caricature of homosexuality and drug addiction as embodied in the outrageous poet, Morley. His novel has just earned him $72,000 and his accountant advises him to evade taxation by a token marriage and by turning himself into a Corporation.

The marriage, to an expensive prostitute, is a sensational success, but soon the Corporation usurps Morley's personal identity. Almost paralysed, he makes a frantic effort to liberate himself and can find his only resource in suicide.

The remorseless and impressive final scenes change the tone of the play and constitute a serious satire on the atrophy of the human personality by Big Business.

**Giles Cooper (1918–66).**

*Everything in the Garden.* 1962. P.

Cooper deftly uses sophisticated comedy for a sharp satire on the sacrifice of principle to money in an effeminate bourgeois society. Four bored middle-class wives become part-time employees in an exclusive brothel, while their complaisant husbands enjoy the tax-free profits. There is a sudden horrifying change of key when at a party a neighbour realises the position and the four men destroy this outsider in a kind of ritual murder. In Cooper's second version the play returns rather shakily to the comic vein.

*Happy Family.* 1966. P.

Cooper's last play, outwardly a light, witty comedy, is an incisive assured satire on arrested development and snobbish exclusiveness.

For the well-to-do Mark and his two sisters nobody exists outside the family trio, and they employ their leisure with nursery games, jingles, and punishments. When the elder sister introduces a fiancé he at first serves as catalyst, but he also is retarded, a grocer's assistant posing as solicitor, a "nobody" to the sadistic Mark, who soon contrives that he shall be ousted from the family circle and the nursery prattle resumed.

The bizarre situation skilfully dramatises indifference to others and obsession with the clutter of the past that stifles natural growth.

It is illuminating to contrast Triana's use of the same family triangle.

**Shelagh Delany (b. 1939).**

It is now a decade since Shelagh Delaney, the Salford girl from a secondary modern school, attracted attention with *A Taste of Honey*, 1958 (M). It was followed in 1960 by *The Lion in Love* (M), her last play to be presented.

Although both plays were improved on and produced by Joan Littlewood, they are naturalistic and owed some of their popularity to their fresh and artless picture of the poorer workers and drifters. Verisimilitude in the portrayal of seedy localities was then more of a novelty. *A Taste of Honey* still has significance, both in its unconventional subject, the pregnancy of an unmarried adolescent expecting a black baby and her friendship with a homosexual lad, and also in the direct candour of its emotions. *The Lion in Love* although more mature in outlook is artistically unremarkable.

**Nigel Dennis (b. 1912).**

Dennis, also a novelist, is a hard-hitting satirist in the tradition of Voltaire and Shaw, and in a Shavian preface to his first two plays he wittily defines his favourite targets. One is the doctrine of Original Sin as preached by Saint Augustine, the other the assumptions of psychoanalysis. He argues that both of these undermine natural self-reliance, and tend to delegate power over the mind to a hierarchy, clerical or medical, which may threaten personal individuality. The Preface is a lively firework display, but Dennis' arguments are sometimes one-sided and negative, more striking than valid.

One of the few dramatists to write in a Shavian tradition, he shows considerable dramatic talent, especially in his vigorous first acts, with their strikingly novel situation and witty and intelligent dialogue. But in the middle of his plays satire gets the upper hand and discussion diverts interest from the characters and tends to hold up the action and to weaken the structure, as in some of the later plays of Shaw himself.

*Cards of Identity.* 1956.

The play was adapted from Dennis' own novel. The "Mallets," members of a club formed to give people a changed identity, inveigle local people to a country house, where by exploiting psychological techniques they induce them into accepting changed names, memories, and identities and then use them as servants. Only in face of their Bank Manager do the victims rediscover their original personalities.

Dennis uses the adroit situation to illustrate the thesis developed in his Preface. Arguing that the basis of personality is memory, Dennis infers that the psychologist can edit his patient's memories, inject his own viewpoint and so undermine and manipulate personality. This plausible thesis is not verified by any appeal to scientific evidence.

*The Making of Moo.* 1957.

Compton, a colonial civil servant, has weakened the native taboo on murder by unwittingly killing the river god. He decides to invent the new religion, of Moo (the name suggested by the lowing of cattle), complete with mythology, musical ritual, and ethical code. In this daring satire on revealed religion Dennis exposes similarities between pagan trust in the efficacy of ritual blood sacrifice and the Christian doctrine of Atonement for Original Sin. In his Preface he suggests that to conform to a religious sect is to belong to an Identity Club, which threatens the individuality of its members.

*August for the People.* 1961.

A satire on "stately homes" and the tameness of the common man lacks the pungency and inventiveness of Dennis' early work.

**Marguerite Duras (b. 1914).**

The French novelist and script-writer of the film *Hiroshima Mon Amour*, has recently turned to drama. She has the sensitive novelist's flair for dialogue and for exploring the contradictions and the ebb and flow of feeling in intimate relationships, so that her naturalistic plays move subtly and quietly towards their climax, which is often the agony of parting as in the one-act play *La Musica* (1966. P.).

*Days in the Trees.* 1966.

Duras's first full-length play is virtually a trio whose theme is the love-hate relationship between mother and son. The now ageing woman had indulged her own emotion by spoiling him, conniving at his playing truant for "whole days in the trees," and thereby undermining both their lives. "I've never loved anybody else," he tells her on her final visit to Paris, but she can no longer hide from herself his callous egoism and misery, as now a gambler and pimp he lives contemptuously with the girl for whom he procures.

Peggy Ashcroft's performance as the mother was widely acclaimed as the finest of her career.

**Friedrich Dürrenmatt (b. 1921).**

The German-Swiss Dürrenmatt acknowledges the Greek dramatists, Shakespeare, and Swift as major influences. He describes his work as "theatre of paradox," revealing "precisely the paradoxical effects of strict logic." He is an unsparing critic of contemporary society, whose dangerous tendencies he exposes in striking and bizarre fictions, reminiscent of the later Shaw.

*The Marriage of Mr. Mississippi.* 1959.

An extravaganza poses the opposition between two principles carried to their logical and farcical extreme. One is a passion for the law of Moses, interpreted as retributive justice. The other is pure Marxism. The two characters embodying these principles, together with a Quixotic lover, are manipulated and destroyed by an unscrupulous politician.

*The Visit.*

An old multi-millionairess revisits her birthplace and offers the inhabitants £1,000,000 to murder her former lover, who had denied her paternity order. Gradually persuading themselves that they are acting justly they comply.

Dürrenmatt cleverly maintains suspense in his withering satire on love of money, hypocrisy, and the sycophancy of press and radio.

*The Physicists.* 1963.

Dürrenmatt has said that this arresting play is not so much about the hydrogen bomb as about society itself and the impossibility of escaping the consequences of one's thinking.

The central character, attempting to suppress scientific discoveries that may lead to the hydrogen bomb, retires to a private asylum pretending to be in contact with King Solomon. There he is first in danger of two spies, pretending to the delusion that they are Einstein and Newton, and eventually of the mad proprietress whose use of his discoveries will lead to the destruction of the human race.

## The Meteor. 1966.

Another play of paradox has as hero a man who wishes to die but cannot.

Schwitter (Patrick Magee), famous dramatist and Nobel prizewinner, already proclaimed dead in hospital, returns to the garret of his youth to die. In vain. As the old egoist swaggers, drinks, makes love, one by one those who touch his orbit meet their death.

The symbolism is unclear. Is Schwitter the egoistic kind of artist who feeds on the lives of others? The most effective incident—his dialogue with an ancient tart—cynically suggests that his art also has been prostitution, for he too has supplied artificial emotion to meet public demand. The chief weakness of the play is that the surprise wears thin. An original idea adequate to a one-act play has been inflated too far.

## Charles Dyer.

Dyer's first success was *The Rattle of a Simple Man.*

## The Staircase. 1966.

One of the frankest plays concerning homosexuality is a dialogue between the middle-aged Charles Dyer (Scofield) and Harry C. Leeds (Magee) during a wretched Sunday night in their poky barber's shop in Brixton, the cage they have co-habited for twenty years.

Charlie is sardonic, aggressive, cruel; Harry, " a messy talker " is softer, protective. Their endless squabbling in ribald argot, comic, and searing, vents their exacerbated irritation, but underneath is glimpsed the pain of social isolation, the mother fixation, the frustrated hankering for offspring, the fear of exposure.

Although all proper names are anagrams of Charles Dyer and the author suggests that everything may take place in Charles's mind, Peter Hall's production was firmly realistic.

## T. S. Eliot (1888–1965). *See also* M18.

In his attempt to revive poetic drama the distinguished poet, T. S. Eliot, was moved by deeply religious and social aims, modestly regarding his work as experimental, " that of the first generation only." The verse he evolved was of a flowing poetic rhythm, " close to contemporary speech " and based on natural stress. Normally he used a line with three stresses and varying length.

In his two plays of the 'thirties Eliot had adopted the ritualistic themes and patterns of Greek drama and had achieved a certain tragic intensity. But the *Cocktail Party* inaugurated a new style, the theme still being Christian redemption and the plot deriving from Greek drama, but the idiom, that of the fashionable comedy of manners. In spite of subtle organisation the liaison has been an uneasy one.

It is curious that the creator of Prufrock should seem unable fully to animate his dramatis personae. This is partly because their inspiration is literary, partly because they are used to illustrate Anglican doctrine and to convey a message. Nor do they belong to the impeccable background against which they are so carefully placed.

The wealth and subtlety of reference of these plays and the beauty of the language make them a delight to the reader, but they are less compelling on the stage.

## The Cocktail Party. 1949. F.

This play, revived in 1968, has its literary origin in Euripides' tragi-comedy *Alcestis,* the demi-god Hercules being replaced by Reilly, the psychiatrist, whose intervention breaks the back of the play, for it is not easy to sympathise with people who let their actions be so directed.

## The Confidential Clerk. 1953.

Described as " high farce," this play derives from another tragi-comedy of Euripides, the *Ion,* whose theme of parents seeking their lost children reappears in Terence, Plautus, and Shakespeare.

## The Elder Statesman. 1955.

Eliot here returns to a tragedy, the *Oedipus at Colonus* of Sophocles, but the youthful peccadilloes of Lord Claverton appear pallid compared with the patricide and incest of Sophocles' protagonist.

## Jules Feiffer.

Feiffer, the New York strip-cartoonist of international fame, now writes plays.

## Little Murders. 1967.

The blustering Newquist family of New York embody what Feiffer has called the "national paranoia " in face of " random violence," and when the daughter, Patsy, introduces her fiancé, Alfred, who is so strong that he never retaliates, they are incredulous. But Patsy is killed by some stray bullet, Alfred adopts the Newquist ethos, and the family is happily united sniping down harmless passers by.

The main theme is clear. " Man hates war but is fascinated by it. . . . Peace is a Sissy." The play began as a novel, which may account for the plethora of other stimulating ideas which are never fully integrated, and also for some highly entertaining satirical vignettes not entirely relevant.

## God Bless. 1968.

This Shavian satire scintillates with dramatic and verbal paradox, epigram, and ironic understatement, and improves on reading.

It is timed in " the immediate future," with America waging war in three continents, and is set in the library of the Liberal Brackman (Dotrice), America's " oldest elder statesman."

On his 110th birthday he is cynically dictating the record of his shilly-shallying career, used by Feiffer as an image of the American Liberal compromise as a betrayal of principle, a " sell-out." His narrative is punctuated by teletype and television presentations of mounting insurrection off-stage. Then two heavily armed agitators, for Peace and Civil Rights, formerly Brackman's Harvard students, enter, soon to be followed by the President himself.

As forty-six cities go up in flames, the President reveals that the agitators have actually been financed by him as a tactic to shake up Congress! But the " tactic has gotten out of hand " and while Civil War breaks out the four men settle down to effect yet another compromise. The revolutionaries insist on bombing ten cities, but the President is to decide which ten!

The play operates as an urgent warning.

## Brian Friel.

*Philadelphia, Here I Come!* 1967. F.

The most successful of Friel's four plays uses the novel device of two actors playing the same part, one the public, the other the private self of the protagonist. Otherwise the play is naturalistic and episodic and kept afloat by its Irish poetic eloquence and charm.

## Max Frisch (b. 1911).

Frisch, a German-Swiss who has been influenced by Shaw and Brecht, dramatises current issues in ingenuous, apt, and witty parables that have a lucid economy of outline.

## The Fire-Raisers. 1961. M.

A delightful Absurdist satire on bourgeois self-delusion and ineptitude shows Biedermann (Alfred Marks) persuading himself that he can cajole the incendiaries about to set fire to his house by inviting them to a good dinner. The situation is analogous to that of Benes of Czechoslovakia who included communists in his government, and to that of the Germans who connived at Hitler.

## Andorra. 1964. M.

An incisive and moving satire on the vicious pervasiveness of antisemitism shows the Andorrans' betrayal of the lad Andri, reputedly a Jewish foundling, to the invading totalitarian state. Andri is in fact a Gentile and his assumption of

Jewish traits is an example of identity imposed from without by society.

## Christopher Fry (b. 1907).

Fry was widely acclaimed in the 'forties for bringing verse back to the stage. His delightful verse, which plays over the surface of his plays like lambent flame, has been compared by Allardyce Nicol to that of the youthful Shakespeare.

Fry has written highly original comedies and religious plays and his work is informed by an implicit spirit of affirmation and hope, conveyed with gaiety and insouciance. He has a gift for devising ingenious situations in terms of poetic fable and metaphor.

*Venus Observed.* 1950.

Hope Wallace commented on the " dancing, glancing felicity " of this unusual comedy, in which Olivier was protagonist.

*A Sleep of Prisoners.* 1951.

This original religious play was commissioned for performance in churches during the Festival of Britain.

*The Dark is Light Enough.* 1954.

An eccentric and saint-like old countess (Edith Evans) gives asylum to men from both sides in the Hungarian rising of 1848. The theme of non-intervention is presented with a lightness and elegance which completely save the play from didacticism.

*Curtmantle.* 1962.

A historical play concerning Becket and Henry II concentrates on the contradictory nature of Henry. Fry deliberately uses a plainer and rougher verse and some prose.

## Athol Fugard (b. 1932).

After working in the Far East and Europe, Fugard now has his own Theatre Group in his home town, Port Elizabeth.

*The Blood Knot.* 1966. P.

Of two brothers belonging to the mixed race of " Cape Coloureds," one " tries for white." The dialogue between them, both comic and naïve, and fraught with intense love and hate, is a microcosm of the terrible strains imposed by racial segregation.

## Jack Gelber (b. 1931).

Gelber is one of the few Americans to attempt plays of the Absurd.

*The Connection.*

Beckett's theme of waiting is presented through drug addicts waiting for their dope, to the improvisations of a jazz quartet, but the realistic ending is inconsistent with the Absurdist style.

## Jean Genet (b. 1910).

The French Genet, abandoned as a child, has lived as social outcast and criminal and, while politically " uncommitted," has mirrored his bitter repudiation of society in plays of frightening impact.

His dramatis personae have been the rejected murderers (*Deathwatch* (F)), despised servants (*The Maids* (F)), prostitutes (*The Balcony* (F)), Negroes (*The Blacks*), and Algerian peasants (*The Screens*). These have realised their fantasies of sex, power, violence, and revenge only by compulsive ritual acts, so that sequences of arresting ceremonial, sometimes Absurdist, replace character study and coherent plot.

In his destructive scorn of contemporary society, his recourse to rituals of violence, and his incantatory language, Genet satisfies the requirements of Artaud's Theatre of Cruelty.

*The Maids.* 1956. F.

Two sisters, maids to a fine lady, continually take it in turn to enact the rôle of mistress and maid so that each can vent her envy and rancour on the mistress. When their plot to murder the mistress misfires, one of them herself drinks the poisoned cup of tea.

Their compulsive charade, designed originally for a cast of young men, mirrors the obsessive and self-destroying conflict of envious love and hate in the mind of the outsider.

Triana's *The Criminals* has a similar theme and technique.

*The Balcony.* 1957. F.

This censored play had its world première at the Arts Theatre Club. It opens in a brothel, where the frequenters enact their fantasies of power by dressing up as bishop, judge, or general, until after an abortive revolution they are called upon by the Court to impersonate these authorities in actuality. Eventually the defeated revolutionary leader visits the brothel to enact the part of Chief of Police, who is then satisfied that his image also has been established in popular regard. The film gives a softened version of the play.

## Willis Hall (b. 1929).

In 1958 Hall was one of the few playwrights giving a candid realistic picture of the underprivileged, as in his best play *The Long and the Short and the Tall* (P) about soldiers trapped in the Malay jungle in 1942. He later collaborated with Waterhouse in North country comedies.

## David Halliwell.

*Little Malcolm and His Struggle Against the Eunuchs.* 1965. F.

A deliciously funny send-up of the angry young man cult is located in a Huddersfield garrett. Here Malcolm, a beatnik ex-art student, compensates for his inadequacies—professional and sexual —by fantasies of Hitlerian power. He imposes on his three chums his farrago of " Dynamic Insurrection ", which so distorts reality that they all finally beat up the nice girl who wants to help Malcolm.

The sources of disaffection and violence are scrutinised incisively but with sympathy.

## Christopher Hampton.

*Total Eclipse.* 1968. F.

The story of Verlaine's passionate infatuation for the younger poet Rimbaud (prototype of Brecht's Baal) is dispassionately and convincingly presented, almost like a chronicle, the opening and closing scenes being particularly skilful.

## Michael Hastings (b. 1938).

Hastings's *Don't Destroy Me* was produced when he was 18. *Yes and After* (P) appeared in 1957.

*The Silence of Lee Harvey Oswald.* 1966. P.

The play, an example of " living theatre," begins with a straightforward narrative of the assassination of Kennedy, illustrated by film sequences and stills.

Then verbatim passages from the official interrogation briskly alternate with imaginative reconstructions of Oswald's domestic life—a technique which diffuses the sense of authenticity.

## Rolf Hochhuth (b. 1931).

Hochhuth, like his predecessor Schiller, is specially interested in the historical play, using poetic licence to organise and adapt factual material to his own dramatic purpose.

*The Representative.* 1963. M.

Using some dramatis personae who represent historical personages, this play in verse exposes the failure of Pope Pius XII, Christ's " representative," to protest against the massacre of the Jews. Film sequences of the horrors of Auschwitz are used with harrowing effect.

*Soldiers.* 1968.

Hochhuth's inordinately long play had its genesis in his horror and protest at the bombing of non-combatants. It is set symbolically at Coventry Cathedral but contains a realistic play-within-the-play, the only part produced in 1968 and here discussed.

This is timed for the crucial months, May to July, 1943, and historical persons are assigned fictional parts. Hochhuth embodies his theme by presenting Cherwell as the "eminence grise" who advocates to Churchill (John Colicos), the commanding protagonist, a policy of ruthless saturation bombing. The theme is counterpointed by the suggestion that success in modern warfare demands not only barbarity but treachery. This is given personal urgency in Churchill's confrontation with his ally, the Polish General Sikorski, whose intransigent hostility to Russia was proving a threat to our precarious alliance with Stalin.

Hochhuth's sensational insinuation that Churchill connived at Sikorski's death is a striking and poignant dramatic image and is defended by some critics on the grounds that a play is an agreed fiction. Hochhuth himself, however, claims to have seen secret evidence and has by some been sharply criticised for traducing Churchill when he cannot produce this.

In the final Act, Bishop Bell is presented in a fictional impassioned protest to Churchill against civilian atrocities, but the arguments assigned to him do not unfortunately proceed to their logical conclusion that modern warfare is *per se* an atrocity and here the moral pressure of the play is dissipated.

Hochhuth boldly handles his dominant themes while organising the intricate political detail in a gripping and enthralling way. The presentation of historical characters is remarkably convincing and Churchill emerges as an idiosyncratic, massive, and tragic hero, fully aware of his moral dilemmas and ironically prescient of his role as the servant of history in winning a war that destroyed the balance of Europe.


**Eugene Ionesco (b. 1912).**

Ionesco, one of the leading Parisian playwrights of the Absurd, differs from Camus and Sartre in that he expresses his conviction of life's absurdity, not rationally, but through images that are in themselves absurd.

In 1948, while learning English from a primer, Ionesco stumbled on his vocation, his shocked reaction to the platitudes he was memorising being dramatised in *The Bald Prima Donna*. Here he singled out aspects of contemporary life which remain as the chief targets of his ridicule.

One is the empty, myopic existence of the petit bourgeois, his lack of passion and thought, the yielding to conventional pressures, the urge to conform. Another is the desiccation of language which, stereotyped and inadequate, has become "nothing but clichés, empty formulas and slogans."

Ionesco's sense of life's absurdity has deep roots, for he is keenly aware of the anguish of the modern world, of the flight from reason, both tragic and absurd in its potentialities. He believes that by dramatising his own inner hurt he can best reveal a universal experience. In *The Shepherd's Chameleon* he has plainly stated that for him "the theatre is the projection on to the stage of the dark world within," the world of dream, anguish, dark desires, inner contradictions, and obsessions.

It follows naturally that he is little preoccupied with specific social problems. Regarding the human condition as wider and deeper than the social condition, he dislikes any kind of political message or conformism and deliberately repudiates the "committed" and didactic play.

Iconoclastic in both his principles and technique, Ionesco—as he indicated in *Victims of Duty*—has challenged most dramatic assumptions, including realism, the concept of the "Aristotelian play," consistent characterisation, motivation, plot, and the distinction between tragedy and comedy.

Discarding so much, Ionesco has evolved a new technique of shock tactic, using most ingenious theatrical devices to express his convictions. He attempts "to go right down to the very basis of the grotesque, the realm of caricature . . . to push everything to paroxysm, to the point where the sources of the tragic lie. To create a theatre of violence—violently comic, violently tragic."

In his plays, as in those of Pinter, the traditional dividing lines between tragedy and comedy melt away, for his amusing images are at the same time poignant, expressing as they do human disappointment and folly, so that his hilarious comedy may have a tragic import.

A characteristic technique is the use of proliferating material objects, which externalise the anxieties of his characters—an accumulation of chairs or eggs, for instance, or an expanding corpse. He hopes thus "to make the stage settings speak; to translate action into visual terms; to project visible images of fear, regret, remorse, alienation."

The discarding of proved theatrical techniques is risky. Shock tactics are successful only as long as they surprise by their novelty. It is a measure of Ionesco's talent that he continues to invent the novel and arresting.

In two of his most recent plays, *Rhinoceros* and *Exit the King*, the nihilism for which Ionesco has been criticised has been relieved by the assertion of the human value of fortitude.

Ionesco's plays were introduced into England in the 'fifties and they have had a marked and specific impact on English drama, especially on Simpson and Saunders. Although Pinter has a philosophy and style all his own, his work is based on similar presuppositions.

*The Bald Prima Donna.* Written 1948.

Characters from an English language manual come to life and pour out their clichés in a "parody of a play," which Ionesco first considered to be a "tragedy of language," but which proved theatrically very funny. The first dialogue between husband and wife is now a classic.

Thus Ionesco, almost by accident, wrote the first of many satirical exposures of the sterile language of those who live a merely mechanical existence.

*The Lesson.* Written 1950. P.

A nervous old professor coaches an eager young girl. Elaborately "proving" the impossibility of communicating by words, he arbitrarily decides what various words shall mean, until he rapidly gains assurance and eventually rapes and murders his pupil, the fortieth that day.

Ionesco illustrates the prostitution of language as a means to power, the sexual element in power, and the sadism lurking in the teacher–pupil relationship and indeed in all authority.

*Jack.* Written 1950.

Urged by his conventional family to settle down to married life, the Bohemian son, Jack, resists Roberte, the proposed bride, because having only two noses she is not ugly enough. He eventually succumbs to Roberte II with three noses. Ionesco parodies submission to bourgeois conformity.

*The Chairs.* Written 1951. P.

An ancient concierge and his wife prepare for a crowd of guests who are to hear his final message to posterity. As the totally invisible guests arrive the couple fetch more and more chairs for them, until, with the entry of the professional orator who is to pronounce the message, they jump into the sea. But the orator is deaf and dumb and his writing on the blackboard is a meaningless jumble.

The empty chairs constitute a most effective theatrical image for man's failure to communicate, and the dumb orator makes the record of a lifetime seem utterly futile. It may also suggest how meaningless can be the words of author and actor. Ionesco says, "The theme of the play is nothingness made concrete."

*Victims of Duty.* Written 1952.

By transforming a detective into a psychoanalyst, Ionesco argues that there is little difference between the psychological drama and the mere detective play.

*Amédée.* Written 1953. P.

A corpse in the flat of a married couple, constantly growing at a frightening rate, is a gruesome and appropriate image of their dead love.

*Rhinoceros.* Written 1958. P.

More and more rhinoceroses appear in a small provincial town. They are the inhabitants who, one after the other, want to be turned into these thick-skinned, aggressive animals. Finally only Bérenger (Olivier) resists the urge to conform.

The terrifying lure of conformity is here skilfully and movingly illustrated.

*Exit the King.* Written 1963.

In an agnostic counterpart of the 15th-century *Everyman*, Ionesco shows King Bérenger (Alec Guinness), in his disintegrating palace, reluctantly submitting to the process of dying, his final resource being fortitude alone. This dramatic elegy, inspired by the final scenes of Richard II, is designed with bold simplicity, presenting man's mortal dissolution with unflinching honesty and a tenderness new in Ionesco.

### Alfred Jarry (1873–1907).

*Ubu Roi.* 1966. M.

In 1896, Jarry, initiator of the " Pataphysics " movement, scandalised Paris with his startling *Ubu Roi*, precursor of Absurd drama.

The characters appear as grotesque puppets, shocking and comic. The shameless, greedy Ubu caricatures both Macbeth and bourgeois vulgarity and in his brutal conquest of Poland becomes a monstrous prototype of ruthless cruelty.

### Ann Jellicoe (b. 1928).

Ann Jellicoe's initial work as producer has left its mark on her plays. In an interview given soon after her unusual play, *The Sport of My Mad Mother*, she expounded her aims.

Discounting the concept of man as a rational creature and stressing that people are driven by their emotions, fears, and insecurities, she concentrated in her early plays on people in a highly emotional and irrational condition. What is more unusual, she deliberately tried to stir up in the audience the very emotions that were being portrayed on the stage. To do this she employed violent sensory and emotional stimuli—a barrage of visual action, rhythm, sound and sheer noise. Words were reduced to a minimum and these few frequently incantatory and devoid of meaning. Ann Jellicoe wanted the audience to yield unthinkingly to the emotional impact and to refrain from asking " What does this mean? " Needless to say literary values were being sacrificed to theatrical.

While these plays were often intense and exciting, they were severely limited in range and manner and to some degree obscurantist. The emotional is only one aspect of human experience, and it is inextricably entangled with intellectual experience which is just as valid. To dwell almost exclusively on the irrational to the neglect of coherent speech—man's hard-won tool of thought—is partial and misleading.

The function of the artistic image is so to reveal aspects of experience that they can be recognised and harmonised, and to elucidate the significance of the image intelligence is necessary.

It is interesting that in her latest play, *Shelley*, Ann Jellicoe appears to have discarded her theories.

*The Sport of My Mad Mother.* 1957. F.

A gang of teddy boys, living in terror of another gang which never appears, is dominated by the fierce and enigmatic Greta. Exulting in their feelings of violence, they express themselves in inarticulate and disjointed words and phrases, staccato cries and incantatory songs. Flim, a commentator, emphasises these with a set of instruments, including a motor-horn, which make sounds that are often discordant and arhythmic.

All this makes a receptive audience aware of what it may feel like to belong to an adolescent gang, but Greta is not easy to accept. A mother-schoolmistress figure, she finally gives birth to a child and is evidently an embodiment of the Indian goddess, Kali. The epigraph of the play is " All creation is the sport of my Mad Mother, Kali." In 1964 Ann Jellicoe explained that the play is based on myth and uses ritual, bodying forth " fear and rage at being rejected from the womb or tribe." Such symbolism demanding an interpretation of its significance is out of key with a play so deliberately " anti-intellect " and restricted to a direct emotional impact.

*The Knack.* 1961. F.

The knack in question is that of getting girls and three out of the four characters are frankly exposed in the irrational grip of sex. The inhibited Colin struggles with the over-experienced Tolen for the possession of Nancy (Rita Tushingham) and again the action is carried forward as much by improvisation as by coherent speech. The film version, which in 1965 won the Grand Prize at Cannes, captures the spirit of the play.

*Shelley.* 1965.

A lucid, well-documented chronicle play illustrates incidents in Shelley's life. Unfortunately the simple straight-line structure is not suited to the complexity of poetic genius. One would not guess that this is the Shelley capable of writing *Prometheus Unbound*. The personality that emerges is that of the selfless social idealist and pamphleteer and the theme his theory of free love, involving two women—Harriet and Mary—in disaster. The predicament is viewed more from the women's angle and the initial germinal situation, that with Harriet, who is presented as innocently pathetic, is so over-simplified as to be false.

The frequent change of brief scenes, effective in themselves, has a fragmented effect.

### Heiner Kipphardt.

*In the Matter of J. Robert Oppenheimer.* 1966. M.

The play, already performed in 23 capitals, concerns Oppenheimer, " father of the A bomb." The source is documentary, the 3,000 pages of proceedings before the Personnel Security Board of the US Atomic Energy Commission in 1954.

A hearing taking over a month with 40 witnesses has been condensed and shaped so that evidence is represented by only 6 witnesses. Kipphardt's aim was to follow Hegel in stripping away the adventitious circumstances so that the essential situation clearly emerges. He has made a few additions, such as monologues and final statements, and all deviations from the literal documents are based on historical data.

The play therefore has an extraordinary authenticity and grip while the central dilemmas are lucidly presented. As *The New Scientist* pointed out, it is for the audience to answer the searching questions raised. Was Oppenheimer, with his communist connections, a security risk? Can a scientist work with state authorities and keep his integrity? Is he responsible for the use made of his discoveries?

### Arthur L. Kopit (b. 1938).

*Oh Dad, Poor Dad.* 1961.

This play parodies the devouring American " Mom," who emasculates all her menfolk. She travels accompanied by her husband's corpse in a coffin and dresses and treats her son of 17 as a child. A gruesome Freudian fantasy is presented as a comic " tragifarce," but there is little latent content.

*Indians.* 1968.

The career of Buffalo Bill Cody exemplifies the sweeping theme of America's encroachment on the Redskins. It is focused in the spectacular device of Cody's famous Wild West Show, where imprisoned Indian Chiefs had been specially released to re-enact their former resistance. Cody, at the climax, faced by the accusing ghosts of Red Indians, voices America's compunction at their virtual extermination.

### Bernard Kops (b. 1928).

Kops, who was born in Stepney, of Jewish working folk, left school at the age of thirteen.

His plays include *The Hamlet of Stepney Green*, 1958 (P), *Good-bye World*, 1959, *Change for the Angel*, 1960, *The Dream of Peter Mann*, 1960 (P), the one-act, *Stray Cats and Empty Bottles*, and *Enter Solly Gold*, 1962, chosen for performance in the provinces by Centre 42.

Kops is less successful with realism than with fantasy, enlivened with the gaiety of local colour and frequent Jewish folk-song.

Most of his plays are variations on a basic design—that of the idealistic dreamer-hero, with an uneasy relationship with his easy-going mother, who in some cases is courted by a suitor whom he dislikes. Eventually the hero realises that a devoted girl is his true mate. Kops' plays thus draw nourishment from a deep emotional source, that of the Oedipus–Hamlet myth, on to which he grafts the happy ending of the fairy tale.

Social criticism, especially of mass-produced goods is often a secondary theme.

The attraction of the plays is their fairy-tale charm and naïveté, their uninhibited joyousness and the easy way in which the rhythm of dialogue flows into verse, song, and dance. Kops is like a Jewish J. M. Barrie, with the significant difference that most of his heroes renounce their dream for reality.

The artistic tension between spontaneity of feeling and excellence of form has become so relaxed that dramatic intensity is often sacrificed. The plays are loosely constructed, and the dialogue sometimes so naturalistic as to be banal.

**Ray Lawler (b. 1922). An Australian playwright.**

*The Summer of the Seventeenth Doll.*

A vigorous realistic play was directed by John Sumner both in Melbourne, 1955, and in London. The seventeenth annual "lay-off" of two cane-cutters with their girl friends in Melbourne proves a tawdry fiasco. The more local theme—the awakening from the "Australianist" dream of the virile outback hero—carries with it the universal implication of the pain of disenchantment.

*The Piccadilly Bushman.* 1955.

This play proved disappointing.

**D. H. Lawrence (1885–1930).** *See also* M5.

It is remarkable that the plays of Lawrence should have had to wait half a century before coming to the stage.

In 1965, at the Royal Court, Peter Gill directed Lawrence's first play, *A Collier's Friday Night*, written in 1906. He followed it in 1967 with *The Daughter-in-Law* and in 1968 he re-staged these two, together with *The Widowing of Mrs. Holroyd*, in a special Lawrence season acclaimed by the critics.

These plays, written before the First World War, depict Lawrence's Nottinghamshire mining community with faithful realism. The themes are the universals already familiar through the contemporary *Sons and Lovers*—sex antagonism, the wife who feels "superior" to her miner husband, her possessiveness of the gifted son and jealousy of his wife or sweetheart.

Events of hearth and home, with profound emotional implications, move forward with a leisurely naturalism that is undisturbed by a forced plot and that seems extraordinarily modern in its idiom.

**Henry Livings (b. 1929).**

The protagonist of Livings' frank and realistic comedies of working life is normally the little man, whose unforeseen reactions culminate in hilarious disaster which topples down the petty rulers. Farce and near fantasy are lightly used to suggest a plea for the disregarded people who support the social edifice.

*Stop It, Whoever You Are.* 1960. P.

The insignificant Perkin Warbeck, a lavatory attendant in a factory, is involved in a series of ludicrous mishaps, but indirectly gets his own back on his harsh and frigid wife and his mean, pompous landlord. The comedy, which is very funny indeed, culminates in a fantasy-like scene of Warbeck's death, a séance, and a gas explosion.

*Big Soft Nellie or the Sacred Nit.*

A farcical comedy has as protagonist a mother's boy who is the laughing stock of his mates.

*Nil Carborundum.* 1962. P.

The scene is the kitchen of an R.A.F. station and the action culminates in a riotously-funny mock commando raid, which exposes both the pilfering cook and service routines that are now an anachronism.

*Eh?* 1964. M.

In an ultra-modern factory the incompetent young boiler-man, Val (David Warner), need

attend to the boiler for only a few minutes during the 24 hours. Since he brings his bride to sleep in the bottom bunk and gives most of his attention to growing giant mushrooms, he neglects his duties and blows the place to smithereens. Again a light-hearted farcical comedy shows the underdog confounding established authority. A further significance is a fool's lapse starting the "mushroom cloud."

**Robert Lowell (b. 1917).** *See also* M21.

The first dramatic work of the distinguished American poet, Robert Lowell, is *The Old Glory*, a recent trilogy of plays in free verse based on stories of Hawthorne and Melville. Their unifying motif is the flag.

*Benito Cereno.* 1967.

The third and best play of Lowell's trilogy is based on a short story by Herman Melville, which had its origin in actual incident.

About the year 1800, while off Trinidad, Delano, Captain of an American trader, observes that a Spanish trader, the *San Domingo*, is in great difficulties and generously goes to her aid.

Captained ostensibly by Benito Cereno, the *San Domingo* is in fact in the hands of her cargo of revolted slaves who have spared his life only that he may navigate them back to Africa. The effete and exhausted Cereno lives at the knife point at the hands of Babu, the wily and insinuating Negro who is in actual command.

Delano fails to realise this, for Cereno dare not speak plainly, and the American is too opaque and self-assured to interpret ironic hints. Only when Babu openly defies him is he enlightened, but too late. The only safe course now left to him is open violence and without warning his seamen massacre all the Negroes.

In a final ominous incident the last survivor, Babu, cries out "The future is with us" before Delano empties his pistol into the Negro's body, crying, "This is your future."

This is one of the most truly poetic plays to be seen in London for many years, lucid in verse, rich in themes and suggestive power, austere in design, while the theatrical poetry of mimes, rituals, and masques is used with ironic significance. The Director, Jonathan Miller, envisaged it as a kind of inverted *Tempest*, the Spanish ship a black magic island and Cereno a drugged Prospero held captive by Babu, and he produced it in the formal and stylised manner of opera.

The play is also remarkable in its relevance to America's dilemma, domestic and foreign, including her ambiguous attitude to the contemporary Negro. Jonathan Miller points out that Lowell here shows "the penalties of uninformed generosity" and of the trilogy as a whole he says, "These plays are about the big-hearted blindness of the American nation and they show quite clearly how the country's cardinal virtues can . . . harden into the very vices which so disable the American pursuit."

In a world increasingly threatened by discord between white and coloured peoples *Benito Cereno* has an even wider implication.

**Peter Luke.**

*Hadrian the Seventh.* 1967.

The play derives from a novel by Rolfe (alias Corvo), an extraordinary, autobiographical fantasy [of his own wish-fulfilment, where the oft-rejected hero, Rose, becomes Pope. Luke wisely identifies Rose with Rolf and presents the elevation to the Papacy as a dream, astonishing, spectacular, and witty, within the shabby framework of Rolfe's own circumstances.

**John McGrath (b. 1935).**

Of Irish extraction, McGrath, who had wide experience in the army before reading English at Oxford, has now had several plays published.

*Events while Guarding the Bofors Gun.* 1966. M.

In situation, McGrath's masculine and disciplined play is a realistic counterpart of Giles Cooper's radio fantasy *Mathry Beacon*.

The futility of military routine is exposed with steely irony as, on a freezing night in Germany, during the Cold War, seven men guard the obsolete Bofors gun. The frustrating situation also engenders personal conflict. The uncontrollable desperado O'Rourke defies Lance Bombardier Evans. An insecure boy of 18, Evans is so obsessed by the hope that promotion may provide him a way of escape to England that he connives at insubordination. Finally O'Rourke's reckless suicide destroys them both.

*Bakke's Night of Fame.* 1968.

A play, faithfully based on the novel, *A Danish Gambit,* by William Butler, takes as subject the prisoner's last night in the condemned cell of an American prison.

Bakke, condemned for an apparently motiveless murder, enjoys being as provocative as possible. discomforting the well-meaning guard by first requesting then contemptuously rejecting the traditional routine of food and consolation. He entangles the priest with his contention that society is exercising not justice but revenge, his only constant demand being that he shall meet his "buddy," the executioner.

This granted, Bakke so needles and infuriates the executioner that the man is betrayed into a violent outburst, gloating over his imminent task. Bakke, gleeful and triumphant, has proved his point about revenge.

McGrath shows great ingenuity and expertise in manoeuvre and sudden surprise, but he has not quite achieved the tension and suspense nor the progression of the *Bofors Gun.* The significant encounter with the executioner comes too late and is treated too briefly.

## Frank Marcus.

The best-known plays are *The Killing of Sister George,* 1965, and *Mrs. Mouse Are You Within?,* 1968. Both give a humorously sympathetic account of an unusual human relationship, offset by boisterous comedy coming from off-stage.

## David Mercer (b. 1928).

Mercer is author of the play *Ride a Cock Horse,* 1965, and the film-script, *Morgan.* He is concerned with the modern predicament of the able, educated young man of working-folk origin, a reflection of his own situation, and depicts him as estranged from his parents, disorientated, and childless.

*Belcher's Luck.* 1966.

The rickety English class structure is the framework of a complex play.

On his ramshackle country estate, contemptuously served by his former batman, Belcher, Sir Gerald is becoming senile, Helen, his icy, avaricious niece, persuades Belcher to goad her uncle to his death so that they may together inherit the property. She then scornfully dismisses Belcher in favour of Victor, his bastard son.

Victor, expensively educated by Sir Gerald, is mentally unstable and impotent, but this familiar Mercer figure is now on the periphery. The conflict between the chaste and physically timid Sir Gerald and the coarse and drunken Belcher has become the compelling focus.

## Arthur Miller (b. 1915).

Arthur Miller, an admirer of Ibsen, shares his strong sense of moral purpose and of the individual's responsibility to the community. This is balanced by a sympathetic understanding of the insecurity of the individual in modern society.

Miller's characters, deeply felt and realised, are fallible men who suffer through their own errors of character or judgment in social conditions which are incomprehensible, indifferent, or even hostile to them.

A recurrent pattern is that of paternal responsibility within a patriarchal family unit, and the father's distress as he sees his errors hurting wife and sons. But the sense of responsibility flows outwards to society as a whole, of which the family is but the growing point. Significantly—apart from the benign mother-figures—Miller's most balanced characters are lawyers.

His plays are well constructed, the dialogue economic and telling, and he has progressed from the realism of *All My Sons,* published 1947, to

much freer experimental techniques, while the prose style has become more fluid and eloquent.

*Death of a Salesman.* Published 1949. P.

A compassionate and finely-balanced play exposes the impingement of hire-purchase commercialism on the ageing salesman, Willy Loman, a weak, foolish, and deeply affectionate man, and also reveals his overwhelming sense of guilt towards wife and sons. The play is worked out on two planes, the inexorable present and Willy's past which obsessively enacts itself within his mind. The film version with Frederick March, is excellent.

*The Crucible.* Published 1953. P.

In 1949 Marion Starkey's *The Devil in Massachusetts* dealt with a witch-hunt in Salem in 1692, and pointed out its relevance to our own age, also rent by "ideological intensities." In 1952 the activities of McCarthy gave it a special urgency.

In his powerful play Miller uses this historical incident to depict not an indifferent society but one in which positive evil is unleashed. The evils he explores are the persecution of a minority and the interference of the Establishment in the individual conscience.

Characteristically Miller focuses attention on the plain man, John Proctor, and he invents his former adultery with Abigail, so that the play is not a partisan manifesto but a study of the complex contradictions of actual life. The self-righteous fanaticism of the persecutors and Proctor's own growth in self-knowledge and courage are faithfully and poignantly portrayed.

*A View From the Bridge.* 1956. P.

Eddie Carbone, a Brooklyn docker, is so gripped by jealous possessiveness of his wife's niece, that he eventually betrays her two kinsmen, illegal immigrants, to the Authorities.

In a play of repressed sexual passion, with hints of incest and homosexuality, Miller shows mastery of a kind of situation new to him and the heightening tension is realised in taut and disciplined sequences.

A lawyer, Alfieri, acts as a Greek chorus but is powerless to intervene, for Eddie infringes something more primitive than the legal code and it is by the primitive vendetta that he is eventually killed.

*Incident at Vichy.* 1966. P.

Miller here turns to the responsibility of society for the individual in a play which exposes the latent racial hostility which even the best men may unconsciously harbour.

The example he takes is antisemitism, the place and time Vichy in 1942, the scene a bleak anteroom within sound of a railway, where sealed trucks are deporting Jews to the furnaces of Auschwitz. Here a group of men and a boy, Jewish suspects, await investigation. There is an atmosphere of chill horror and suspense as each tries to summon up his own pitiful defence against the premonition of the ghastly journey he must embark on, once he is summoned behind the closed door.

Eventually only two men remain, the two most aware and articulate, Doctor Leduc, a Jewish analyst (Anthony Quayle) and Von Berg (Alec Guinness), the only Gentile of the group, a cultured and humane Viennese Prince, who is horrified by the vulgarity and barbarism of the Nazis.

In their final dialogue Doctor Leduc convinces the Prince of his unconscious antisemitism and the Prince gives his safe-conduct to the doctor.

A subsidiary theme of the play is the way society imposes extrinsically an identity on the individual, in this instance, as in Frisch's *Andorra,* the rôle of victim on the Jewish people. Through Leduc, Miller also criticises the Jews' acceptance of their rôle.

This disturbing play makes the greatest demands on the emotions, intelligence and humanity of the audience, who like the Prince to some degree undergo psycho-analysis. But the play is also characterised by a fine restraint. As in Æschylus' *Agamemnon* the violence takes place behind closed doors, with the significant difference that in Miller's play the chorus and victims are identical.

*The Price.* 1969.

Two brothers confront each other in an attic crowded with the heavy furniture of their dead father, a financier ruined in the Depression. Its imminent sale is the occasion of their first encounter in sixteen years.

Victor Franz, who had given up a scientific career to support his father, is now a policeman at retiring age but too immobilised by his past to begin a new career in spite of the hysterical pressure of his wife. Walter, a surgeon, in his slick pursuit of success has had a prolonged breakdown and a broken marriage. The " price," ostensibly that of the furniture, is the price each has paid for his decision in life and its inexorable results.

The brothers ruthlessly dissect and probe back to the motivation of their choice. Walter is forced to admit calculated callousness but drives Victor to realise that his sense of social responsibility was also flawed, for he had sentimentally sacrificed his potentiality to a disingenuous father too cowardly to work again.

But no reconciliation ensues, Victor angrily refusing the dubious job which Walter offers as a salve to conscience.

Miller describes his play as stripped to the skeletal structure of two lives, the home the dead husk from which they had developed. But the characters are complex and through the Ibsen-like situation runs a thread of delightful and significant comedy. Solomon, an ancient Jew, survivor of wildly differing professions and four marriages, is the furniture appraiser and embodies the resilience lacking in the Franz's. When he falls he bounces. He shrewdly decides to buy all the furniture at a fair price and at curtain fall sits gleefully in the chair of the beaten father, chuckling exuberantly at his decision to begin life afresh.

The play is realistic, but the muted significance of various remnants of bric-a-brac is symbolic in effect. Organised with meticulous artistry, it is lucid and profound, and rich in the wisdom of experience distilled. Acted without a break it holds the audience absorbed.

**John Mortimer (b. 1923).**

Mortimer, a barrister, first won success with his short plays, such as *The Dock Brief,* 1957, and *Lunch Hour,* 1960 (M)., originally written for radio and television.

Here his talents are seen at their best, especially his gift for seizing on an unusual encounter between " the lonely, the neglected, the unsuccessful," whom he envisages in realistic settings of shabby gentility, and he is particularly sympathetic to those who allow their fantasy to overlap or swamp actuality.

But the moment of insight that gives pathos to his short plays is not enough to illuminate those of full length, like *What Shall We Tell Caroline?* and *The Wrong Side of the Park,* which lack substance.

*Two Stars for Comfort* (1960, M.) is also unsatisfactory. In its basic situation it is an inflated version of *Collect Your Hand Baggage* (M), with little beyond sentiment and pseudo Laurentian special pleading to fill the gaps.

*The Judge.* 1967. M.

After 40 years' absence from his native city, the bachelor Mr. Justice Chard returns for his last assize, but his conduct is disturbing, for he seems to expect some unspecified accusation. Suspicion centres on Serena's Bohemian establishment, but when the judge finally confronts Serena there he demands condemnation of himself.

It is revealed that as a youth he had on one occasion had relations with her knowing her to be a minor, and had subsequently paid for an abortion and that his whole life had been slowly undermined by a rankling sense of crime and inconsistency. When Serena tells him that there was no occasion for an abortion and that she got the money from him to go abroad with her lover, the bewildered and frustrated Chard goes berserk.

The plot is thus an inversion of Dürrenmatt's *The Trial.* The commanding themes of guilt and the difficult and exhausting process of judging are boldly focused in the compulsive personality of

Chard, many-sided and realised in depth. Balancing the themes of guilt and retribution is that of permissiveness, represented by Serena. She is unfortunately pictured in a superficial way as a shallow Bohemian, and her ménage is not unlike that satirised by Mrozek in *Tango.* Although she has some charm, she is too patently silly and childish to command respect and much of the potential tension of the play is therefore slackened and relaxed. Is the author too indulgent to his off-beat characters?

In the scenes with the judge Mortimer returns to the milieu of *The Dock Brief* and much of the attraction of the play is in his wry attitude, fascinated, tolerant, and amused, to the ceremonies and quiddities of the legal process.

**Slawomir Mrozek (b. 1930).**

Mrozek, a Pole, who began as journalist and cartoonist, has recently extablished a reputation for satirical short stories and short plays.

*Tango.* 1966.

Mrozek's first full-length play is like a satirical cartoon, an expressionistic exposure of the cultural and political vicissitudes of 20th-century Europe as liberalism, fascism, and communism succeed one another.

A slovenly household of ageing Bohemians sentimentally cherish their memories of youthful rebellion against social convention when just to dance the tango was an act of defiance.

The son, Arthur, detesting their sloppy anarchy of taste and morals, enlists his reactionary great-uncle Eugene in his own counter-revolution to restore the *status quo.* But he soon resorts to fascist rant and force, terrorising the family until he is himself cut down by his own henchman, the tough lout, Eddie. The curtain falls as Eddie forces Eugene to partner him in a tango.

To an English audience especially the flatness of characterisation incidental to the cartoon style may be a little unsatisfying, but the novel satire is exhilarating.

**Peter Nichois.**

Nichols is well known as a successful TV playwright.

*A Day in the Death of Joe Egg.* 1967. F.

Nichols has shown remarkable sensitivity and skill in developing his theme—the especial difficulties of monogamy when the only child, a ten-year-old girl, is a hopelessly retarded spastic. He uses comic techniques of revue as the parents re-enact their frustrating encounters with doctors and clergy. But below the jesting façade grows the realisation that the wife's compulsive maternity blinds her to her husband's needs and that his endurance is crumbling. The climax comes when after attempting to end the child's life by neglect he creeps away from home.

Nichols, who has a spastic child has said, " It's a play about marriage. . . . It's not autobiographical."

**Eugene O'Neill (1888–1953).**

Although O'Neill's work belongs to the first half of the century, three of his later works had their delayed première here in the 'fifties, two of them making a great impression.

Recognised as the greatest and most influential of American playwrights, O'Neill at his best came to close grips with the serious issues of human life, showing man battling with a harsh environment and with his own inner passions. He was deeply involved with his characters, often the flotsam and jetsam of humanity, conceived with disillusioned compassion, and he could create the powerful theatrical situation which rivets the audience. On the stage these gifts went far to compensate for a looseness of structure and a dialogue which is singularly flat, poor in vocabulary, and lacking in rhythm. His plays are better acted than read.

O'Neill, lacking the advantage of an American dramatic tradition, experimented with many European techniques before finding his own most personal style—a faithful realism with suggestive overtones of emotion and reflection.

British playwrights like Wesker and Alun Owen resemble O'Neill. They also are committed to individuals, especially to working people living insecurely. Like him they reveal the subtle and inhibiting ties that bind members of a family or gang, subjects which lend themselves to a similar rather sprawling and diffuse structure and dialect style. So far they have not matched O'Neill's passionate and gripping intensity.

## The Iceman Cometh. Published 1947.

In a naturalistic play, whose prototype is Gorky's *The Lower Depths*, down-and-outs await the arrival of the dionysiac Hickey. But Hickey has just murdered his wife and his abortive attempt to rouse them from "pipe dreams" to reality leaves them sunk even more deeply than before in drink and self-deceit. The pessimistic theme is that of Ibsen's *The Wild Duck* and the situation that of Beckett's *Waiting for Godot*.

## Long Day's Journey Into Night. Published 1955.

An avowed autobiographical play depicts O'Neill's family on the day when his mother (Gwen Francgon Davies) relapses into drug addiction and Eugene learns that he must leave the doomed circle for a sanatorium. As it was there that he chose his vocation, this constitutes the one note of hope in a deeply mournful reverie. The Freudian love–hate relationships are unfolded with tender understanding.

## Joe Orton (1933–67).

Orton was a successful commercial playwright who also won praise from serious critics especially for his dialogue.

His range is narrow and he is preoccupied with crime, perverted sexuality, and violence portrayed without inhibition as hilariously comic, sometimes with satiric effect. The macabre plots give occasion for a flow of deadpan repartee, normally smutty, sometimes merely facetious, often very apt and funny indeed, always a parody of the would-be genteel. Nearly all Orton's characters speak alike and are as undifferentiated in their lingo as in their lack of morality.

The satire is in the form of caricature or parody and apart from its implications it is almost impossible to discover in Orton any expression of human value or aspiration. It is not always easy to discriminate between the unsavoury matter of his plays and the expertise and aplomb with which it is manipulated, and some feel that he defaces the image of life.

## Entertaining Mr. Sloane. 1964. P.

The handsome young wastrel, Sloane, already a murderer, finds a cosy refuge with Kath. A slattern of forty, she smothers him with motherliness and, sexually insatiable, she seduces him from the first night. Her brother, Ed, a homosexual, soon employs Sloan as his "chauffeur." When Sloane tries to escape their possessiveness, his brutal murder of their father puts him into their power and they agree quite literally to share him, each having him for six months at a time.

The play scores by a skilfully handled plot, an ironic "poetic justice" and the sly and genteel euphemisms of the salacious dialogue, and it won the London Critics Variety Award as the best play of 1964.

Basically the plot is that of Pinter's *The Birthday Party*. In both cases a man on the run is sheltered by a slovenly older woman, but here Kath's sexuality vulgarises the situation and as she constantly refers to herself as Sloane's " mamma " and to their unborn child as his " brother " it is highly suggestive of incest. The kindly husband of Pinter's play has been replaced by the homosexual smart-Alec, Ed.

## Loot. 1966. M.

Helped by his accomplice a young criminal secretes the loot from a burglary in his mother's coffin. This is the key situation in a macabre and complicated farce, which is also an exuberant caricature of funeral ritual, of a police which is represented as hamhanded and venal, and of cheap detective fiction. The characters are cardboard puppets manipulated by the plot and the play is notable for the fact that vice is completely triumphant. It won the *Evening Standard Award* for the best play of 1966.

*Crimes of Passion.* 1967. M.

A double bill consists of *The Ruffian on the Stair*, 1966, Orton's first play, and *The Erpingham Camp*, 1967. Frequent and fussy scene changes betray their origin in radio and television respectively.

## The Ruffian on the Stair.

It is illuminating to see how Orton's first play, a grotesque and savage comedy, uses the plot but not the atmosphere of Pinter's first play, *The Room* (q.v.). Orton cuts any aura of mystery and makes all explicit. The occupants of the room are now Mike, a criminal living with an ex-prostitute, Joyce. The intruder is a boy ostensibly seeking revenge for his brother with whom he had lived in homosexual incest, and whom Mike had murdered. He is in fact seeking his own death and provokes Mike to murder him by pretending that he has seduced Joyce.

## The Erpingham Camp.

A satire on holiday camps shows an uprising of the merrymakers who eventually kill Erpingham. The ebullient parody has some highly comic incidents.

It was first projected as a film script, a modern version of Euripides' *The Bacchae*, but was rejected by Lindsay Anderson. Euripides' great play with Freudian foresight shows Pentheus destroyed by revellers because he had repudiated the liberating worship of Dionysus. (*See* H123.) Orton's sketch completely lacks any such insight or complexity and Erpingham meets his fate simply because he is stupid and dictatorial.

## What the Butler Saw. 1969.

A farce in a psychiatric clinic is typically Orton in its discrepancy between decorous speech and indecent behaviour, but pace and invention flag.

## John Osborne (b. 1929).

Osborne has considerable theatrical talent, torrential eloquence and the journalist's flair for seizing the mood of his own generation.

All these gifts were evident in *Look Back in Anger*, 1956 (F), now well filmed and too familiar to need description. It was perfectly timed and its success immediate. The protagonist, Jimmy Porter, voiced the pent-up feelings of contemporary youth, especially of the classes newly educated, now baffled by the complacency of the privileged classes who had muddled through two wars and left them without sense of security or direction. The play's pervasive mood of self-pity and strident denunciation runs, with some variation, through much of Osborne's later work, although with the passing of years is seems increasingly subjective and irrelevant to the current situation.

In his major plays, *A Patriot for Me* excepted, Osborne keeps to the same basic pattern of characterisation and structure. In Jimmy Porter he created an unforgettable character, a myth. But Jimmy with some change of occupation and age is constantly reappearing, disaffected, disorganised by self-pity, articulate, and dominating. Archie Rice and Bill Maitland are older but they also are Narcissus figures driven on by sado-masochistic urges to destroy themselves and their circle, and it is difficult to escape the impression that the typical Osborne protagonist is not presented with complete objectivity but serves in some degree as mouthpiece of the author. Osborne's minor characters are sketched in a perfunctory, rather stagey way, serving chiefly as audience or target to the protagonist, and there is little dramatic confrontation of equals.

Closely linked with the structure of the plays is the nature of the dialogue. Osborne's forte is rhetoric, the thinly disguised monologue, splendidly uninhibited, with some of the inebriation and excitement of the pub, and with the same coarse and bawdy jests. Sometimes it is a tirade of invective, sometimes shrill and hysterical, always commanding, always flowing exclusively from the protagonist. Minor characters are given little opportunity for repartee or discussion, their rôle being for the most part to act as " feed."

Osborne's plays cannot legitimately be defended as satire for in comparison with the masterpieces of Ibsen and Shaw they express merely negative hostility and are not based on any clear concept of the values that should be realised in a good society.

"There aren't any good, brave causes left." says Jimmy Porter. Neither here nor in any other play is there anything to suggest that Osborne does not endorse this destructive statement, one of the silliest of the century.

His invective is moreover too general, indiscriminate, and direct to be effective. His weapon is the bludgeon of sarcasm, seldom the rapier of irony. Some notable exceptions are to be found in *Luther* where the targets are limited and specific and the speech where Tetzel sells indulgences is finely ironic. In this play Osborne has learned from the intelligence of Luther and the process of history. He is too emotional and subjective a writer to excel in an art which demands disciplined thought and detachment.

The sameness in structure and tone in Osborne's work is cleverly mitigated by experiment in theatrical techniques. The realism of the garret scene in *Look Back in Anger* was in 1956 strikingly original. In *The Entertainer* and *Luther* he profited by the example of Brecht, and *Under Plain Cover* was influenced by Genet.

*The Entertainer.* 1957. F.

Osborne here attempts to use the Brechtian device of "endistancing," employing a framework of music-hall scenes, where Archie Rice (Olivier), a seedy comedian, tries to hold the stage with tawdry patter and songs in a dubious show with nudes called "Rock'n Roll New'd Look." These are intended to "endistance" realistic scenes of Archie's shabby home. But the "endistancing" device serves little purpose for the overall mood of unquestioned disillusion "whooped up" by drink and patter is in both planes unrelieved. Querulous complaint that England has lost the glory and glamour of Edwardian days is crystallised on the realistic plane by the report of the death of Archie's son at Suez and in the music-hall by the presentation of a nude Brittania, wearing only her helmet.

Osborne turns to the music-hall because he claims it to be a folk art with an immediate, direct contact. The film version is good.

*Luther.* 1961. F.

*Luther*, based on a recent biography, is a less subjective work, although Osborne again takes for his hero a rebel, the son of an unsympathetic mother, and emphasises the emotional and not the intellectual sources of Luther's protests.

The play is imitative of Brecht's *Galileo* both in its loose "epic" structure and also in the attempt to present the protagonist in an equivocal light. The first two acts give a sympathetic and leisurely portrayal of Luther's early conflicts of conscience and vigorous attack on superstition while in the third act he is hurriedly presented as having treacherously let down the peasants who had been encouraged to rise against the Emperor. But the political reasons for Luther's dilemma are not even hinted at and at we are invited not to think, as in *Galileo*, but to condemn while ignorant of relevant facts. Structurally this sudden *volte face* is most damaging to the play.

The most effective scenes, such as Tetzel's selling of indulgences and Martin's sermon at Wittenberg are splendid rhetoric, without a word of dialogue and directed straight at the audience.

Skilful period production and the acting of Albert Finney as Luther made the play theatrically effective.

*Two Plays for England.* 1962.

Two slight plays make a double bill.

*The Blood of the Bambergs* is a parody of a royal wedding. Monarchy is held up to ridicule along with its trappings of ceremonial and fulsome adulation by press and radio. The bridegroom having just been killed in his racing-car, an Australian press photographer is secretly passed off in his place. The final act is a film with an unctuous running commentary, the film device deriving from the German Expressionist theatre, where it was first used by Ernst Toller.

*Under Plain Cover* is intended as an attack on sensationalism in the press. The first part shows a pretty provincial couple dressing up in rôles symbolic of sex fantasy, their activities accompanied by a thin trickle of dialogue. In the second half dramatic presentation is abandoned in favour of a charade and commentary by a reporter who reveals that the couple were brother and sister, a feeble presentation of the compelling theme of incest. The first scene is a pallid imitation of the brothel scene in Genet's *The Balcony*, where the assuming of symbolic rôles has powerful sexual and political implications lacking in Osborne's play.

These sketches do not profess to offer convincing studies of character in action and unlike intelligent satire they do not imply positive standards nor use the mature techniques of irony and wit, but rely on parody and mimicry.

*Inadmissible Evidence.* 1964. F.

A play, which many have praised highly, has the ingredients of a commercial success. It provides the sensational spectacle of a middle-aged solicitor, Bill Maitland, obsessed with sex, and disintegrating under the influence of drink and drugs, and, thereby, such a rôle for the star actor (Nicol Williamson) as to constitute a stage *tour de force*.

The play opens with a dream sequence as Maitland is tried in the court of his own mind. What follows is his rancid outpouring of self-pity, as during forty-eight hours, he is progressively deserted by staff, clients, and mistress. Some of the minor characters are here reduced to unheard voices on the telephone and one actress serves to impersonate three faceless clients. Maitland's flagellation of himself and his circumstances is unrelieved and monotonous.

*A Patriot for Me.* 1965.

The protagonist of Osborne's best play, produced privately, is Redl, a distinguished army officer of the Austro-Hungarian Empire, who through his homosexuality is blackmailed into becoming a spy for Tsarist Russia.

Osborne is here finely objective and ironic. He uses a series of brief scenes with significant juxtaposition of characters and swift dialogue. The first act, showing Redl's gradual discovery of his nature, is extremely discriminating and adroit and the drag ball which opens Act Two is an astonishing *tour de force*.

Act Three shows a decline of tension as Redl, now a spy, himself declines, his fibre coarsened through a sequence of sordid infidelities by male lovers and prostitutes. His final unmasking and suicide is almost a foregone conclusion.

The play spans the years 1890–1913 and Osborne presents the ethos and atmosphere of the Imperial Army officer élite, undermined by espionage and treachery, in a vast and unforgettable panorama.

*A Bond Honoured.* 1966.

Osborne, in a free translation of *La Fianza Satisfecha*, is said to have distorted Lope de Vega's play and portrays yet another alienated, and narcissistic "hero."

*Time Present.* 1968. F.

The protagonist, Pamela, is a neurotic actress. Emotionally strangled by the familiar "Electra complex," an exaggerated devotion to her father, a once famous actor, now dying off-stage, she is unable to establish any satisfactory human relationship, in spite of love affairs and the friendship of the devoted Constance, a successful Labour M.P., in whose flat she is living.

Pamela's role is static and verbal; reiteration of her shallow scheme of values (a preference for style over vulgarity), sentimental reminiscences of her father and a relentless spate of contemptuous and indiscriminate derision. Phrased in modish argot some gibes have a bitter wit, especially pleasing to the prejudices of the illiberal.

A contrived plot is super-imposed. The exposition is clumsy, the climax, Pamela's decision to have an abortion to end her pregnancy by Constance's own lover.

Pamela's alienation which should arouse compassion, becomes tiresome rather than moving, largely because of the play's apparent assumption that her outpourings have objective value and interest.

*The Hotel in Amsterdam.* 1968. F.

United by fear and dislike of their employer, a film magnate, cryptically referred to as K.L., three couples retreat to a luxury hotel in Amsterdam as a hide-out from his encroachments.

They pass the weekend in denouncing K.L., drinking, and exchanging desultory jokes and complaints about homosexuals, mothers, and "the working class," until the unwelcome arrival of a relative and the news that K.L. has killed himself disturb the tenuous camaraderie.

Such a structure is perfunctory. Only the garrulous and petulant Laurie (Scofield) is individualised and the characters reveal and discover little of value about themselves or each other.

An interesting sidelight is that Laurie fancies himself as an authority on "the creative process," boasting, "What I do, I get out of the air." Is this Osborne's method? Great creative geniuses give a very different account.

Since the play indicates no positive norm, it cannot be defended as satire. Some critics praised it highly for its sense of mood. Others found it tedious.

### Alexander Ostrovsky (1823–86).

The eminent Russian playwright is unfortunately little known in this country.

*The Storm.* 1966.

Written in 1859, Ostrovsky's fine realistic play portrays a social group unfamiliar to us, the petty tradesmen of an isolated township, who are avaricious, ignorant, and bigoted.

The widow, Kabanovna, is a warped and ruthless matriarch, who saps the vitality of her weak son and cruelly tyrannises over his hapless wife, Katerina. The lonely, susceptible girl yields to the love of a young stranger from Moscow. Then sheltering in a church during a violent storm, she is overcome by superstitious dread and remorse. She confesses and later kills herself.

This perceptive tragedy is that of young and sensitive people striving to escape the yoke of rigid elders, but in the last resort succumbing to the harsh creed by which they have been indoctrinated.

### Alun Owen (b. 1926).

Of Welsh stock but with an Irish mother, Alun Owen spent his youth in Liverpool. Most of his writing has been for television.

His most characteristic style is the new naturalism used in a romantic nostalgic way to evoke the local colour of Liverpool. He seizes on the idiomatic dialects and the dramatic conflict implicit in the clash of race and religion between Welsh, Ulster folk, and Irish, while the restless ambition of some of the younger generation to get away to sea or to London gives a wider horizon to a scene otherwise parochial.

*Progress to the Park.* 1959. P.

This, in Owen's favourite idiom, is a leisurely enquiry into the affinities and animosities of Liverpool working folk, especially of a group of four young men and a girl as they eddy about in street, pub, and park. The clash of race and religion is always just below the surface, and what thread of story there is concerns the crossing of young love by parental prejudice. The most lively character is Telfon, the voluble Welshman, originally a kind of commentator, and the mouthpiece of Owen's views.

*The Rough and Ready Lot.* 1959.

A carefully constructed historical play concerns four mercenary officers in a revolutionary army in South America just after the American Civil War. In a different milieu religious strife is again the theme. The convictions of an Irish Catholic clash violently with those of a Welsh militant atheist as to whether they shall shell a Catholic monastery which blocks the pass. Eventually both men are killed, together with the vacillating English colonel, and it is the "simple and ordinary" man, Kelly, who takes command, the conflict of belief still unresolved.

### Harold Pinter (b. 1930).

Pinter, formerly an actor, is now considered as one of the leading playwrights of the "Theatre of the Absurd." He exerts an almost hypnotic power over his audience, for he has an assured theatrical expertise, an uncanny sense of the novel situation and the telling pause; and, as his plays find resolution in some final surprise, they are aesthetically satisfying.

His art has developed swiftly, and two main phases can now be distinguished. The early plays, culminating in *The Caretaker* in 1960, were concerned with the underprivileged and showed a growing sense of compassion and only a passing interest in sex. More recently Pinter has explored new ground. The plays have been much concerned with sexual experience; the background has usually been sophisticated; and the attitude detached, sometimes to the point of apparent indifference.

Whatever the subject, Pinter's plays have a certain poetic resonance, an imaginative absurdity. His power is probably due to his intuitive awareness of man's sub-conscious life and most of his plays present a dream-like sequence of events, half credible, half absurd. In the early plays the dream drifts into a familiar nightmare of the most primitive kind—that of the violent invasion of personal security—a fear that must have assailed man's stone-age ancestor as he lurked in the squalid shelter of his cave, terrified of wild beasts and the inexplicable catastrophes of nature. Many of Pinter's later plays are still dream-like, fantasies of sexual anxiety and gratification, especially as to marital fidelity.

The situation that first fascinated him was that of a room, a door, and two people. He has said, "Obviously they are scared of what is outside the room. Outside ... there is a world bearing upon them which is frightening." The room is normally cosy but sordid, the people insecure, for Pinter is most interested in people when they are "at the extreme end of their living, where they are living pretty much alone." The danger that breaks in on them is both comic and shocking, but bizarre as the predicament may be, the play is anchored in actual experience. "I think it is impossible," he says, "—and certainly for me—to start writing a play from any kind of abstract idea. ... I start writing a play from an image of a situation and a couple of characters involved and these people always remain for me quite real."

But his basic situation is so novel and striking that, like poetry, it can be interpreted on more than one level, both as a revelation of those periods of intense private anxiety when the individual, all but distraught, holds on precariously to some tiny foothold, and also as an image of the predicament of the whole human race whose existence is threatened by ungovernable forces. Like Kafka, whom he admires, Pinter expresses vividly the feeling of inscrutable menace from some vague hinterland invading humdrum human existence. *The Birthday Party*, in particular, has much in common with Kafka's *The Trial*.

In his first three plays the threat is left deliberately unexplained, so that an aura of mystery surrounds the action and violence actually breaks through, but in *The Caretaker* there develops a more subtle menace from within, threatening the mind rather than the body and there is no overt violence.

The theme of uncertainty has persisted throughout. In his first play, *The Room*, 1957, he mystified his audience by contradictory information about insignificant details. This trick served perhaps to heighten the atmosphere of insecurity but some critics found it irritating, and in later plays, *The Collection*, for instance, we find instead a highly significant uncertainty as to people's veracity and motives. Pinter has explicitly stated that imprecision conveys a truer picture of our experience. "The desire for verification is understandable," he says, "but cannot always be satisfied," and he points out that it is particularly difficult to be precise about people's inner life and motives, especially if they are inarticulate. He consistently rejects the rôle of the omniscient playwright, like Ibsen, and looks at his characters through the eyes of the ordinary observer, frequently puzzled by human inconsistencies.

A related theme has been the ambiguous nature of personal identity, treated with increasing insight, from the puzzle as to who Riley may be in *The Room*, to the pathos of maimed personality in *The Caretaker*, and the possibility of divided personality in *The Lover*. Some of the disturbing fascination that Pinter exerts is due to the state of uncertainty in which he leaves his audience.

As a playwright of the Absurd Pinter is closest in feeling to Beckett, and he shares with Ionesco an awareness of the way that comedy interlocks with tragedy. " Everything is funny," says Pinter, " the greatest earnestness is funny; even tragedy is funny. And I think what I try to do in my plays is to get to this recognised reality of the absurdity of what we do and how we behave and how we speak." Occasionally, like Ionesco, he uses stage " furniture " to heighten the absurdity and both playwrights have a quick ear for the absurd clichés and *non-sequiturs* of everyday speech.

Pinter is a stylist in the use of stage dialogue, an expert in cockney dialect. It is talk rather than dialogue that he records, what Martin Buber has described as " monologue disguised as dialogue," for his characters talk at people rather than to them. They rarely listen or respond, each bolstering up his self-confidence in an intermittent " monologue " spiced with empty boasting. This is particularly appropriate to the confused and defeated people he portrays, who even in their defensive jargon shrink from human contact.

Although Pinter's dialogue appears on the surface to be little more than a tape-recording of casual talk, there is beneath the demotic prose a poetic rhythm more compelling than the carefully calculated verse rhythms of T. S. Eliot.

*The Room.* 1957. M.

Pinter's first play, written in four days for the drama department of Bristol University, is already characteristic. Rose, left alone at night, is nervously aware of the door of her dingy room, especially when a blind Negro, Riley, enters with a message from her father. Her husband on his return savagely kills Riley and Rose goes blind.

The murder of Riley, possibly a rather clumsy death symbol, is melodramatic, but the lit room is a vivid dramatic image of man's tiny area of comfort in an indifferent universe.

*The Dumb Waiter*, written 1957, produced 1960. M. and P.

In a one-acter Ben and Gus, hired assassins working for some mysterious " organisation," uneasily await their unknown victim in a basement room in Birmingham. The sudden intrusion of a grotesque Ionesco-like dumb-waiter increases their anxiety, until it is revealed that the victim is Gus himself. Situation and dialogue are both comic and taut with menace. The trite phraseology, as the killers mention " the senior partner," " the job," and " clearing up," ironically uses a business jargon. The tiny play is a microcosm of a treacherous world where violence can suddenly break up man's apparent alliances.

*The Birthday Party.* 1958. M.

In Pinter's first full-length play, the room is in a shabby boarding-house kept by the motherly Meg. Here Stanley, who claims to have been a concert pianist, has taken refuge, until he is suddenly unnerved by the arrival of a sinister pair, the specious Goldberg and the brutal McCann who like Gus and Ben are there " to do a job." They subject Stanley to a fantastic catechism, a parody of brain-washing, and during his phoney and ludicrous birthday party he is blindfolded and his glasses broken—symbolic of destructon of vision. Next morning the pair lead Stanley away, conventionally dressed in black jacket and striped trousers, incapable of speech, his personality disintegrated.

The menace here is economically sustained through indirect means, and the fact that the identity of the three main characters is never revealed adds to the terror. Some see Stanley as the political refugee; some, since he was a pianist, as the artist who is made to conform by the pressure of society. But by its deliberate lack of definiteness, the play has a wide reference to all who seek refuge from a strange and hostile world.

*The Caretaker.* 1960. M.

The play is set in a junk-filled room, where the kindly Aston lives in his brother's derelict house. He brings home an old tramp, Davies, who grudgingly agrees to stay as " caretaker " and

then tries to encroach further by playing off one brother against the other, until finally rejected by both.

In a naturalistic background Pinter has created two unforgettable characters, presented in psychological depth with reference to their past, and has depicted their failure to come to terms with compassion and restraint.

Davies is one who bites the hand that feeds him. His very identity is suspect for he passes under an assumed name, having " left his papers " years ago " at Sidcup." But he never retrieves them, like Beckett's Krapp repressing part of his past. Aston haltingly tells Davies how he once had periods of unique lucidity, now destroyed by a terrifying shock-treatment he was subjected to in mental hospital, but Davies' only reaction is later to threaten him. It is remarkable that when Aston finally rejects Davies' last encroachment the plight of the tramp should seem as pitiful as Aston's own. Pinter having wisely rejected his first intention to end the play with the violent death of Davies.

This mature play shows a man actually opening the door to his fears and mastering them. Aston in his long speech faces the wrong done to him by " people." His unique vision destroyed, his only creative outlet has been tinkering with his hands, but as he tries to break out of his isolation by befriending another crippled human being, he unhappily meets a man so twisted by his own suffering and resentment that he cannot respond. Some find in Aston a moving image of the mystic and artist in man whose creative insight is destroyed by an imperceptive and mechanical society. The film is excellent.

*A Slight Ache.* 1961. M.

A short play, first heard on the Third Programme in 1959, shows an elderly couple haunted by a match-seller, who stands speechless at their gate. Eventually the wife takes him into the home instead of the husband. It is possible that the silent match-seller may represent the unconscious desires of the wife and the anxieties of the husband.

*A Night Out.* 1961. M.

First broadcast and televised in 1960, this compassionate and realistic brief play shows the clerk, Albert, trying one night to escape from the retarding domination of his nagging and self-righteous mother. After threatening her violently he finally finds himself in the room of a prostitute who proves equally peevish and would-be genteel. It is doubtful whether Albert's violent gestures have won him any independence.

*The Collection.* 1962. M.

In an assured, sophisticated comedy of manners, originally presented on television in 1961, Pinter makes authentic use of mystification.

Did Stella in fact sleep with a stranger, Bill, in Leeds? She tells James, her husband, that she did so, but during the course of the friendship that develops between the two men, Bill gives three contradictory accounts of what is supposed to have occurred, while Harry, an older man who has given Bill a home, becomes increasingly jealous of James.

There is irony in that Stella's story, told perhaps to pique her husband, should impel him away from her to male society and the changing of partners has the elegant formality and economy of a dance movement.

Pinterian violence is here only lightly indicated; in James' half playful throwing a knife at Bill and in Harry's ferocious account of him as a " slum slug " that he has picked up.

*The Lover.* 1963. M.

An arresting short play shows the husband (Alan Badel) and the wife (Vivien Merchant) first as affectionate but distant partners, and then with provocative change of clothes as erotic lovers. The performance of symbolic rôles, including dressing up in fetish garments, had already been used by Genet. Pinter cleverly adapts the device to discriminate between the apparently incompatible strands in the marriage relationship, a distinction analogous to that between Aphrodite Urania and Aphrodite Pandēmus, the Love Sacred and Profane of classical mythology.

*The Homecoming.* 1965. M.

Teddy (Michael Bryant), a Doctor of Philosophy in an American University, brings his wife, Ruth (Vivien Merchant), on a surprise visit to his former home in North London, where Max (Paul Rogers), his widowed father, still lives with his two younger sons, Lenny and Joey. It is gradually revealed that Ruth before her marriage had been a " model " and the family decide to keep her as their common mistress, while Lenny, a pimp, arranges that she shall earn her keep as a prostitute. The plot is underlined by Lenny's bragging anecdotes of sexual brutality—a counterpart to the more undifferentiated violence of the earlier plays.

Because this black comedy is played with clinical detachment, the audience is induced to suspend emotion. Only at the last moment is this cool acceptance shattered by an outburst of human feeling when Max, aged 70, crawls sobbing to Ruth asking to be kissed and the audience is shocked into feeling the degradation involved.

On the surface the play is a disillusioned glance at life. " It would be ridiculous to maintain that what we know merits reverence," says Lenny. It may also be interpreted as a fantasy of sexual gratification, which in a dream state escapes the taboo of ethical and humane feeling and can be indulged in without demur. The use of some accepted sex symbols and the slow and trance-like acting, especially that of Ruth, is dream-like in its effect and the final shock of degradation is analogous to waking up and realising what the dream has implied.

It is possible also to see in Teddy an acquiescent Hamlet. He returns home from a foreign university to find marital infidelity, for it is disclosed that his mother had been unfaithful with an uncle figure. Ruth is the counterpart of Ophelia, who was bidden by Hamlet, " Get thee to a nunnery "—(an Elizabethan cant term for brothel). Teddy is like Hamlet also in that he prefers " to operate on things and not in things."

*The Homecoming* is professionally brilliant, but it lacks the depth of reference and emotional power of Pinter's earlier plays.

**Hal Porter.** An Australian playwright.

*The Tower.* P.

Set in Hobart in 1850, a well-constructed traditional play tensely presents violent passion and incident veiled by the steely dialogue of mannered society.

*The Professor.* 1965.

A play set in the Far East, with a Japanese heroine, was less successful.

**Terence Rattigan (b. 1912).**

With a flair for witty farce and social comedy, Rattigan expertly serves up a nourishing morsel in an appetising *vol-au-vent*.

More recently he has attempted to penetrate suffering as in *The Browning Version*, 1948, and *The Deep Blue Sea*, 1952. *Variations on a Theme* was less successful and incidentally provoked Shelagh Delaney into writing her first play.

**David Rudkind.**

*Afore Night Come.* 1962. P.

In a Worcestershire orchard the fruit pickers enact the ritual murder of a freakish old tramp whom they dread as a threat to their virility. A realistic working day world is infused with the primitive terror of *The Golden Bough.*

**Jean-Paul Sartre (b. 1905).**

The plays of the French philosopher, Sartre, can be fully interpreted only in the light of his atheistic existentialist philosophy. Discarding conventional morality, Sartre insists that the individual must evolve his own ethical code through daring freely to choose and act for himself. He must also will this freedom for others, and by seeking to establish an interdependence of freedoms he " engages," or " commits " himself in the political struggle.

Sartre himself is a communist and his best plays, like those of Brecht, are fully " committed " to left-wing ideology. They have sought to vindicate the inevitability of violence in the struggle for freedom and to decry the " bourgeois morality " which shrinks from such crime.

Sartre is also concerned with the " absurdity " of man's predicament as a rational creature in an illogical and indifferent universe, but unlike Ionesco he presents the situation, not through absurd images but through the medium of the traditional well-made play.

Sartre has had a considerable influence on the climate of ideas, encouraging an attitude of harsh disillusion and stimulating the current discussion as to whether or not drama should be a vehicle for social and political convictions. It is interesting to contrast the views of Wesker and Pinter on this issue.

*Lucifer and the Lord.* Published 1951. P.

The dilemma between non-violence and force is here given greater universality by being projected back into the time of the Peasants' Revolt in Germany. The brilliant General Goetz, having failed in a policy of Christian love, unflinchingly embraces a ruthless violence as the only possible " realist " social ethic.

*Nekrassov.* Published 1956.

A satirical farce ridicules the sensational anti-communism of a section of the popular French press.

*Altona.* Published 1956. P.

This play, showing a former Nazi officer going mad in an attempt to justify his own resort to torture, is an attack on " Western morality " in its own recourse to torture, used by French colonials in Algiers. The film version well reproduces the claustrophobic horror.

**James Saunders (b. 1925).**

In Saunders' early work the influence of Ionesco is apparent in the satirical use of a banal dialogue, in which the characters converse without communicating, and in the reference to some concrete symbol which represents their anxieties or predicament. His later work is reminiscent of Pirandello. Nevertheless Saunders' ingenious plays have a freshness and vigour all their own.

*Alas Poor Fred.*

In a one-act play a friend who had some time ago been cut in half is the symbol of a married couple's former passionate love life, long since sundered. The situation is like that of Ionesco's *Amédée.*

*The Ark.* 1959.

In a more direct style this full-length play of ideas re-interprets the Old Testament story.

*Ends and Echoes.* 1960.

This is the general title for three clever one-acters. In *Barnstable*, the most amusing one, a house is gradually collapsing around its unwitting inhabitants, a symbol of the disintegration of their conventional way of life.

*Next Time I'll Sing to You.* 1963.

Based on Raleigh Trevelyan's book on the hermit of Canfield, who died in 1942, this moving play uses the rehearsal style of Pirandello's *Six Characters.* Like an elegiac quintet is explores the theme of solitude.

*A Scent of Flowers.* 1964.

Like the previous play, this is a reconstruction of the past. It is gradually revealed that the character, Zoe, is in fact the spirit of a girl who has just committed suicide, because her love for a married man is incompatible with her religion. The play proceeds by her touching encounters with the circle of relatives and friends to whom she had turned in vain for help.

*Neighbours.* 1967.

*Neighbours* was presented with another short play, *Dutchman* (F), by Leroi Jones. Both use an emotional encounter between a Negro and a white woman to focus the strain between the races.

A Negro invites himself into the flatlet of a young woman on the floor below. With some hesitation she entertains him. He then steadily challenges her enlightened liberalism as merely patronising and finally in what amounts to moral blackmail asks her to come and sleep with him. Confused and compassionate she yields.

The initial meeting is conveyed with much delicacy. Then as the Negro assumes the rôle of counsel for the prosecution, a logical pattern is unconvincingly forced on the naturalistic material.

**Alan Seymour.** An Australian dramatist.

*The One Day of the Year.* P.

Like Lawler's *Summer of the Seventeenth Doll,* this realistic and moving play examines one of Australia's cherished legends—this time the celebrations of Anzac Day. It is set in Sydney in the working class home of the sentimental " digger," Alf Cook, whose son Hughie is at the university. Alf's deep anger and hurt when Hughie publishes his satirical photographs of the Anzac Day celebrations in which Alf had taken part focuses the universal clash between generation, culture, and class.

**Peter Shaffer (b. 1926).**

Shaffer is an assured and ingenious dramatist whose first success was with the realistic well-made play and who has since moved on to freer modes of composition.

His plays operate successfully on two levels: they offer insight into the subtleties of personal relationships, especially into the difficulties of adjustment between people of different cultural background, and they also involve discussion of ideas. The aesthetic problem of distinguishing between genuine love of art and snobbish pretension is a recurring theme, often presented in a triangular situation.

*Five Finger Exercise.* 1958. P.

An alive, realistic play shows Clive, the young Cambridge student, growing away from his stifling mother, with her pretensions to modish culture, but failing to make contact with his honest philistine father. The advent of an enigmatic stranger, Walter, acts as a catalyst. Mother and son are both attracted to Walter, the father's fierce jealousy is aroused and Walter is narrowly saved from suicide.

Shaffer shows some of Ibsen's precision in his probing of a family situation where the members change and develop as they become painfully aware of their hidden drives.

*The Private Ear and the Public Eye.* 1962.

Two short and spare triangular plays both demonstrate the influence of artistic taste on the relationship between the sexes.

*The Private Ear.*

Bob, a shy music-lover, asks Ted to help him entertain a girl whom he has met at a concert. But the ignorant girl is won by the complacent Ted's vulgar patter and Bob, left alone, defaces his gramophone record and forces himself to listen to the broken music of love.

*The Public Eye.*

A witty, ironic comedy shows Charles, a correct and pompous dilettante, unwarrantably jealous, employing a private detective, Louis (Kenneth Williams) to spy on his wife. She becomes attracted to Louis because of their shared joy in things of beauty. With the entry of the iconoclastic Louis, a brilliant, comic invention, farce and tenderness go hand in hand with high comedy

*The Royal Hunt of the Sun.* 1964.

A sweeping " epic " drama of Pizarro's fantastic conquest of Peru skilfully uses, as narrator, " old Martin ", who watches his own boyhood as page to Pizarro. Shaffer deploys " total theatre " in dazzling ceremonial, processions and masks, in ritual dancing, mime and strange, metallic music.

There is rich thematic material in the clash of " two immense and joyless powers ". in the con-

flict of Christianity and Sun worship. Personal tragedy develops in the mutual attraction felt by the grizzled Pizarro (Colin Blakely) and the young Inca, Atahualpa (Robert Stephens). Captor and prisoner, they painfully seek for the god in each other and the Inca accepts death both as a sacrifice to friendship and the final test of his faith.

*Black Comedy.* 1965.

A highly successful brief comedy frankly uses an effective device of Chinese theatre. During a party the lights fail and the stage, although supposed to be in darkness, is still fully illuminated, so that the ludicrous behaviour of the dramatis personae is visible only to the audience.

**Robert Shaw (b. 1927).**

*The Man in the Glass Booth!* 1967.

Donald Pleasance played the chief part with dazzling virtuosity in an arresting and histrionic play based on Shaw's own novel.

The American tycoon, Goldman, is profoundly disturbed by the irony of the Pope's announcement that the Jews have been forgiven for the crucifixion for, German Jew in origin, he had known the agonies of the concentration camp. He acts strangely, and disguises himself as his double, his cousin Dorff. Dorff, a gentile German, had been a colonel in the S.S. in the same camp and notorious for his sadism.

Goldman, now Dorff, contrives that Eichmann-like he shall be kidnapped by Israeli agents. At his trial he justifies Nazism, makes accusation and insinuations against the Jews and gloats over the obscene cruelties which had defiled the victims. When an old woman reveals his true identity, the mystified court point out that his devil's advocacy has harmed his own people.

The heart of the play, Goldman's motivation, remains a confusing puzzle. Is he an anti-semitic Jew? Does he imagine himself as a Christ figure suffering vicariously? Is he demented by past agonies? Or is the author trying to depict sado-masochism, the whole spectrum of man, the light and shadow in the Jungian sense, not only of the individual but also of the race? Or is Shaw not entirely in control of complex material derived from the leisurely form of the novel?

The play certainly suffers structurally from having only one protagonist circled by flat figures so that there is plenty of assertion and rhetoric but little valid confrontation, discussion, or elucidation. It presents not a genuine dramatic conflict but a contrived enigma.

Much time is wasted in the opening sequence in establishing the Hollywood ostentation and sentimentality of Goldman's apartment and the verbal style see-saws between argot and the florid and pretentious.

It is interesting to contrast *The Investigation* of Weiss, whose fidelity and austerity have an overwhelming effect.

**N. F. Simpson (b. 1919).**

N. F. Simpson's plays of the Absurd are in the peculiarly English vein of Lewis Carroll and Edward Lear, a world of surrealist fantasy, *non-sequitur* and nonsense. It is almost a contradiction in terms to organise such material coherently and to do so in a full-length play is a *tour de force* which Simpson brought off in his *One Way Pendulum.* His best work ridicules the mechanical and conventional existence, the attenuation of feeling, of the little suburban home, his usual milieu.

*The Resounding Tinkle.* 1957. P. F.

A most unusual play, which pokes fun at suburban life, discards plot, progress, and characterisation, and the uniform dialogue is one continuous flow of clever verbal paradoxes and *non-sequiturs.* The apologetic " author " appears at intervals and in the final act there is a parody discussion of the play by a panel of " critics "—devices used by Ionesco in *The Shepherd's Chameleon.*

Simpson's verbal agility is exhilarating, but some find the play over-cerebral. It is certainly at the opposite end of the spectrum from Ann Jellicoe's *The Sport of My Mad Mother.*

*One Way Pendulum.* A Farce in a New Dimension. 1959. F.

Here Simpson has devised a framework built of whimsy and yet firm enough to carry its own logic and to be dramatically satisfying. The characters are drawn simply, but consistently, each with his own " humour," in the manner of Ben Jonson and the dialogue is a close parody of banal family interchange.

The play concerns a suburban family, the Groomkirby's, whose son, Kirby, is teaching a collection of weighing-machines to sing the Hallelujah Chorus. His ineffectual father is combining his two favourite hobbies of law and " do it yourself " carpentry, by building an enormous model of the Old Bailey in the living-room, where the phlegmatic mother pays a char-woman to eat up the " left-overs."

Finally a trial takes place in the Old Bailey and Kirby is convicted of murdering forty-three people in order that he may wear black, the weighing-machines being part of a complicated device to cause a holocaust of death.

The main theme of the play is the tyranny of things, which is exemplified by the absurd Ionesco-like objects. These are treated with the respect due to human beings while human beings are treated as things, and father and son are so obsessed by things that they cannot get into touch with one another.

The tyranny of mechanical routine and social custom is also indicated. Kirby will only eat when a cash-register rings and will only wear black when it is sanctioned by funeral convention.

The anxiety and guilt which result from a starved and mechanical existence are finally symbolised in the nightmare parody of a trial scene in the final act.

Although the stage objects are novel and in-triguing and can be assigned a clear meaning they lack the suggestive power of Ionesco's chairs or rhinoceroses. Contrived rather than intuitive, they illustrate more than they illuminate the human condition. But the play is an original and successful experiment and the implied comment on the unconscious assumptions and compulsive habits of the Groomkirbys has a wide reference.

The film version is recommended.

*The Cresta Run.* 1965.

A play about counter-espionage proved dis-appointing, partly because its mockery is directed at a schoolboy dream rather than at a general malaise, partly because it lacks the bold structural outline of *One Way Pendulum.* Even the absurd objects—keys, codes, disguises—are trivial com-pared with the " Old Bailey." Simpson has also lost some of the claustrophobic compulsion of his earlier plays by his constant switching of the action from the home of the suburban couple to the Ministry and back again.

It is unfortunate that a promising latent theme —the compulsion felt by the Security man to divulge his secret information—is swamped by trivia, while the best jest is only a casual aside— the suggestion that in England Intelligence should logically be in the hands of private enterprise!

*The Hole,* 1957, and *The Form* are one-acters in the same style as the full-length plays.

## Wole Soyinka (b. 1934).

Soyinka, a Nigerian and an English graduate, is an admirer of Brecht, Arden, and Dürrenmatt.

*The Road.* 1965.

*The Road,* set in a drivers' haven in Nigeria, successfully produced with a large cast of coloured actors, later won a Dakar award.

*The Lion and the Jewel.* 1966. O.U.P.

In a lively comedy, presented by the Ijinle Company of African actors, the jewel is Sidi, the belle of a Yoruba village. Elated at being photographed for a glossy magazine, she rejects both the native schoolmaster and the old chief-tain, the Lion, until cunning seduced by him she exultantly joins his harem.

Native culture, with vivid ritual dance and music, is presented as more alluring and virile than European, which is mocked both in amusing mimes and in the shabby, ineffective school-master infatuated with Western gadgets.

## Tom Stoppard (b. 1937).

Stoppard has written plays for radio, including the engaging *Albert's Bridge* (F), and for television.

*Rosencrantz and Guildenstern are Dead.* 1966. F.

Stoppard's diverting play is a gloss on *Hamlet* and he dovetails snatches of Shakespeare's tragedy with his own action or rather inaction, for his archtype is Beckett's *Waiting for Godot.*

He humorously chooses as protagonists the two nonentities, Rosencrantz and Guildenstern. Summoned inexplicably to Elsinore, they hang about, always on the fringe of great events they do not understand, passing the time, like Shakes-pearean jesters, in witty word play and fruitless speculation as to their situation and destiny.

Their predicament is a suggestive image of the bewilderment of the ordinary man faced with world events beyond his grasp and, at a deeper level, with the existential problem of man's very being on this earth, and the imminence of death.

The rehearsals of the Players, the counterpart of the enactments of Pozzo and Lucky in *Godot,* create a further film of unreality and illusion.

The play is too long, the second act not suffi-ciently contrasted, but it is remarkable that so derivative a play should be so delightfully fresh and original.

*Enter a Free Man.* 1968. F.

This comedy is an extended version of a tele-vision play of 1963. Reilly (Michael Hordern), a self-styled " inventor " of unworkable Heath Robinson gadgets, " leaves home " regularly every Saturday to spend in the pub the ten shil-lings pocket money allowed him by his working daughter, always to return home when his money has run out. His long-suffering wife (Megs Jenkins) has consoled herself with the hope that if he's to be " a failure anyhow, he might as well fail at something he'd like to succeed at "!

The situation, although genuinely funny and pathetic, is not adequate to a full-length play.

*The Real Inspector Hound.* 1968.

This crisp and intelligent burlesque, like Sheridan's *The Critic,* uses the device of the play-within-the-play. It is a simultaneous parody of jaded theatrical convention and modish theatrical jargon.

Two critics are watching an absurd drawing-room whodunit, with a corpse ignored by all taking the centre of the stage. But the main focus of interest is the critics. Both are obsessed, the introverted Moon, only a " stand-in," by jealous hatred of his professional superior, the absent Higgs, while the eupeptic Birdfoot is always infatuated with the latest actress.

Then at the ringing of a stage telephone absurdity completely takes over. The call is from Birdfoot's suspicious wife! He is drawn on stage where he takes on the part of the fickle lover, soon to be followed by Moon, when told that the stage corpse is that of Higgs! In a few minutes both critics in consequence of their private obsessions have been shot dead, the sharp crack of retribution not unusual in Stoppard.

Beneath the glittering, zany surface of the play lies the concept of drama as the mirror, Hamlet's " mirror up to nature ," wherein we see and identify ourselves with the dramatic personae.

The play formed part of a double bill with Sean Patrick Vincent's musical satire, *The Audition.* It appears that Stoppard's comic genius finds its best vehicle in the short play, which his dazzling virtuoso invention can sustain to the end.

## David Storey.

Storey has written plays and novels, including *This Sporting Life.*

*The Restoration of Arnold Middleton.* 1967.

Arnold is a jesting, eccentric young schoolmaster whose latest acquisition is an outsize suit of armour, but his clowning disguises an inner malaise. He is less attracted to his wife than to his mother-in-law, and he eventually assaults her and becomes plainly unhinged. Only when she departs is he suddenly restored to his wife and sanity.

Here is an interesting first play on a theme reminiscent of Mercer's *Morgan*, with the gorilla suit. Storey however does not offer sufficient interpretation of his protagonist's instability nor of his lightning recovery. The exuberant hilarity of the comedy confounds the issue.

**Cecil P. Taylor.**

Taylor is quizzically interested in left-wing types, especially their inconsistencies and fallacies. He is very successful in a brisk, brief comedy like *Allergy*, 1966 (P). In *Bread and Butter*, 1966 (P) his naturalistic outline biography of two Jewish couples in the Gorbals between 1931 and 1965 is sympathetically done but too slight to sustain the full-length play.

**Peter Terson.**

Terson is best known for his very successful plays for the N.Y.T. Formerly a games master, he writes about youngsters with affectionate zest and exuberant humour, vividly aware of the lack of opportunity offered by modern society to the young school-leaver.

*Zigger Zagger.* 1967.

Dominating the play is a remarkable manipulation of a youthful football crowd which acts as a living backcloth to the scene. Harry, schoolleaver and near-delinquent, is so possessed by its Dionysiac frenzy that he is opaque to all efforts of authoritative figures such as the youth officer and respectable relatives to gear him into a job. Eventually grudgingly accepting life's economic demands, he becomes an apprentice.

*The Apprentices.* 1968.

During mid-day breaks in a factory yard, crowded and animated as a Breughel, overalled apprentices play football, fight, flirt, and wrangle. The flurried foreman and older hands, caustic yet tolerant, act as foil.

The chief personalities are vividly presented in the round. In the centre is the derisive, irrepressible Bagley, priding himself on his "rebel's instinct," kindly at heart, yet an enthusiast for the barbarous "initiation" ritual. But the progress of events leaves him stranded. Led by the studious Geoff, his fellows, including Harry, are gaining qualifications and getting on and out. The factory, modernised, will need brains not muscle and all have lost interest in the "initiation." Bagley, a married man at 18, his wife already pregnant after a brief holiday encounter, ruefully drifts towards the older fitters he had despised.

Several critics, including Irving Wardle, judged this play to be the best of the year.

**Gwyn Thomas (b. 1913).**
*The Keep.* 1962.

A realistic and fluent comedy of character in a South Wales home is strengthened by the sardonic twist of its surprise ending.

*Jackie the Jumper.* 1963.

A period play with music is set in the Chartist era.

**Jose Triana (b. 1931).**

Triana, born in Cuba, spent four years in Madrid but returned to Cuba after Castro's revolution and has now written several plays.

*The Criminals.* 1967.

The first Cuban play staged here depicts three adults, a brother and his two sisters, acting out fantasies of childhood, hatred of thwarting parents, and the tyranny of home, which culminate in a frenzied ritual of their murder of the parents at the end of Act One. The trial of the children in Act Two gradually develops into an enactment of the parents' mutual detestation. As the curtain falls the ritual begins afresh.

This intense play, in the genre of "Theatre of Cruelty" (q.v.), has less wealth of imagery than Weiss's *Marat-Sade* but a greater universality of reference than Genet's world of criminals and

perverts. It may have been influenced by the work of Arrabal, the Spanish playwright working in France, whose characteristic, says Esslin, is the "highly disturbing mixture of innocence and cruelty."

Triana shows great psychological insight: children's play is often a dramatic projection of their inner anxieties and conflicts and at all ages the sterile process of fantasy gives only temporary relief and must be endlessly and exhaustingly repeated. The most significant moment of the play is when the word "love" is timidly offered as an alternative only to be rejected.

An extremely apt parallel to Triana's vision was the contemporary Reith lecture (26 Nov. 1967), when Dr. Leach, the social anthropologist, criticised our unthinking acceptance of the inward turning type of family life, where "parents and children huddled together in their loneliness take too much out of each other. The parents fight: the children rebel." Of such a family Dr. Leach said, "The strain is greater than most of us can bear," and he considered it to be the source of our social discontents. Triana's play effectively shows it as a potent source of man's aggression. Some critics have seen in it implications of Castro's resistance to the dominance of America.

**Peter Ustinov (b. 1921).**

Ustinov's versatile and ingenious comedies have proved more popular than his serious plays. Recent productions include *Photo Finish*, 1962, *Halfway up the Tree*, 1967, *The Unknown Soldier and His Wife*, 1968.

**Boris Vian (1920–59).**

The French Vian was influenced by the Absurdist approach of Ionesco.

*The Empire Builders.* 1962.

Man's futile flight from death is imaged in a family trying to escape from a terrifying noise by moving up to a higher and higher floor and meaner quarters. Eventually the father alone reaches the attic, where he dies.

*The Generals' Tea Party.* 1966. P.

Written in 1951, Vian's biting, absurdist satire on the military mentality represents his general behaving like a small boy, afraid of Mama, and asking his playfellows—other generals—to tea. After deciding that war would be a nice idea, they then select the target—prophetically Algeria.

**Roger Vitrac (1899–1952).**

The French Vitrac, an associate of Artaud, attempted Surrealist plays which anticipate the Theatre of the Absurd.

*Victor.* 1964.

Victor is a boy of 9 but 7 foot tall and with a mature intelligence. He and his outsize girlfriend are the only rational beings in a farcical adult world.

**Peter Weiss (b. 1916).**

The German-speaking Weiss has adopted Swedish nationality and Marxist doctrine.

*The "Marat Sade."* 1964.

The full title of this verse play, one of the most impressive exemplifications of Artaud's Theatre of Cruelty, is *The Persecution and Assassination of Jean-Paul Marat as Performed by the Inmates of the Asylum of Charenton under the Direction of the Marquis de Sade!* As the title indicates this complex work operates on receding planes of cruelty, thus exciting in the audience that vivid experience of violence which is the aim of Artaud.

Artaud's demand for primitive ritual which shall exorcise repressed fantasy is met not only by Corday's threefold visit and murder of Marat but also by the lunatics' frenzied miming of the ceremony of the guillotine—a background motif to the whole play. Meanwhile the use of pantomime and gesticulation on the open stage satisfy

Artaud's demands for spectacle, for "poetry in space."

Peter Brook, the brilliant Director, has pointed out that these elements are not inconsistent with a Brechtian "alienation"—achieved by the device of a play within a play, the protesting comments of the Director of the asylum, the intellectual debates between Sade and Marat and not least by the ribald songs of a grotesque quartet of zanies. The final effect is an inextricable blend of the comic and the violent.

*The Investigation.* 1965.

A documentary of the Frankfurt War Crime Trials, edited by Weiss, had a multiple première in East and West Germany and at the Aldwych. Described by Weiss as an "Oratorio in 11 Cantos," after Dante's *Inferno*, it indicts the millions, including the German monoply capitalists, who tacitly supported the Nazi atrocities.

At the first impact the grisly facts leave an overwhelming impression of horror. It is remarkable that the author's restraint and dignity in presenting them and the formal austerity of his design have in retrospect the effect of catharsis.

Arnold Wesker (b. 1932).

Wesker, son of a Jewish-Hungarian father and a Russian mother, first became a chef, and worked in Norwich, London, and Paris, before taking a six months' course at the London School of Film Technique, where he wrote his first play.

He is known not only as a dramatist but also as a devoted socialist. Since 1962 much of his time has been given to his efforts to bring an enjoyment of good drama and art to people who would otherwise lack opportunity. To this end he has founded—under the aegis of the Trade Unions—the well-known Centre 42.

Wesker's early plays were in the naturalistic idiom, centred on the vivid portrayal of an East End Jewish family and a farm-labourer's family in Norfolk. He evidently found naturalism inadequate and there gradually appeared in his work strains of Expressionism, which in *Chips with Everything* became the dominant style. Wesker's hold on dramatic structure is erratic, but he has an exhilarating sense of movement on the stage.

His most individual characteristic is his passionate concern for his characters. They are presented in the round, living, aspiring, and erring, so that they achieve an independent existence, especially the women. Although male protagonists like Ronnie Kahn and Pip are seen both in their strength and weakness. Wesker does not entirely detach himself from them, somehow conveying his personal reactions to them—a conflict of love and exasperation. He has nevertheless gone much further than Osborne, for instance, in creating a truly objective image, as his more flexible dialogue indicates. He has a keen ear for social and personal idiosyncracies, especially urban Jewish volubility and the fumbling speech of the country labourer.

Like Sartre, Wesker is deeply "committed." He is a convinced socialist but not a propagandist, for his plays explore the moral and practical difficulties of the socialist position and he shows unusual honesty in portraying Ronnie Kahn, the most vocal of socialists, as a weak if not renegade personality.

The Trilogy—The trilogy consists of three naturalistic plays in which a discursive history of the Jewish family, the Kahns, is fused with political debate on the course of socialism

*Chicken Soup with Barley.* 1958. P.

This is the springboard of the trilogy. It opens on October 4, 1936, the morning of Moseley's attempted march through the East End of London, when the curtain rises on the basement flat of the Kahns, a Jewish family dedicated to socialist activities. It is 1957 when the play ends with the disillusion of the son, Ronnie, at the Russian occupation of Hungary.

Each of the Kahns is a live human being, presented not for moral judgment but with sympathy. Especially commanding is the mother

Sarah. What Jung might call an "extraverted feeling type," she is ignorant of events, contemptuous of books, a strenuous mother figure, and yet in her aggressive dynamic the most masculine person of the group, in contrast to her amiable but shiftless husband, Harry, and the vacillating Ronnie.

The central theme of the play is the conflict between attitudes of mind, "caring," or concern for the welfare of others, and indifference to it. The battle is fought on two fronts, in the home and politically, it being taken for granted that socialism is an expression of "caring." The stalwart Sarah is the centre of the two-fold conflict, for she attacks both social inertia and that of her husband and son.

Structurally the play is sprawling, but Wesker already shows his intuitive sense of theatrical movement. At the end of Scene I there is an exhilarating leap forward as the little band of fighters surges from the basement to the light. A more experienced dramatist might have placed such a triumphal movement as the final climax, but the general pattern of the play is of recoil and listlessness, held only by Sarah's unshakeable faith in caring and Ronnie's honesty with himself.

*Roots.* 1959. P.

There is here a skilful shift of scene to Norfolk, where Beatie Bryant (Joan Plowright), a farmlabourer's daughter on holiday from London, revisits her family. Beatie is engaged to Ronnie, who has for three years been trying to educate her, especially in the arts and in the intelligent use of words (the "bridges" of communication). She has ignored his advice but endlessly parrots his sayings to her phlegmatic family.

Preoccupied with the primal necessities of life the Bryants are the coarse "roots" from which Beatie has sprung. In spite of a rough friendliness they are ignorant, prejudiced, stubborn, and above all inarticulate.

When on the day appointed for his visit, Ronnie sends instead a letter saying their marriage would not work, Beatie is at last galvanised by shock into finding thoughts and words of her own. These folk she realises are without spiritual roots or standards. Then comes her ecstatic moment of self-realisation. She is at last thinking and speaking for herself.

Although he does not know it Ronnie has realised his ambition, "to save someone from the fire."

The play is well constructed, the characters and dialogue are convincing, Beatie delightful. The ideas discussed about "roots" and "bridges," develop organically from the situation.

*I'm Talking about Jerusalem.* 1960. P.

In 1946 the Kahns' daughter and her husband, Dave, settle in Norfolk to put into practice the theories of William Morris, but Dave, finding that his hand-made furniture cannot compete economically with the factory product, faces their failure and in 1959 they return to London.

The theme of disillusion is here fully analysed by the voluble Kahns, but the mood escapes despair and Dave's self-respect and sober appraisal of unpalatable facts is contrasted with the embittered cynicism of a friend.

The play is weak structurally. There is insufficient action and Dave is not a sufficiently commanding figure to hold things together. Then the intimate study of tender family relationships, suitable to a novel, is embarrassing, except for brief moments on the public stage.

Two symbolic moments in Act II indicate that Wesker was realising the limitations of realism. One is the miming of a simple ritual of reconciliation, the other a ritual enactment of the story of creation.

The Trilogy as a Whole—Wesker's trilogy throws up vital questions of good and evil, both personal and social, the chief perhaps being that of heredity. Must Ronnie and Beatie inherit their parents' limitations? Is Mrs. Bryant right when she says, "The apple don't fall far from the tree"? Is man foredoomed and his struggle vain? Ironically it is the undependable Harry who suggests that giving people some love may help them to change, while of socialism he says, "It'll purify itself." Who was right and in what degree?

*The Kitchen.* 1959. P.

In a two-acter, Wesker draws on his experience as a chef to give a vivid impression of a day in the kitchen of Marango's restaurant. The play is notable for its skilful contrasts in pace and movement. The quiet morning quickens to a frenzy of anxiety at lunch-time, and the doldrums of the afternoon are succeeded by the sudden outburst of a German who goes beserk.

The swirling vortex is an image of the blind activity of society, and, while avoiding the rigidity of allegory, Wesker clearly indicates that the kitchen is a microcosm of the world, where men with their casual contacts find themselves in a situation beyond their grasp. The play ends with the dramatic irony of Marango's failure to perceive that work and food alone cannot satisfy man's desires.

Although it destroyed the claustrophobic atmosphere the film version caught very well the movement of the play.

*Chips with Everything.* 1962. P.

In *R.U.R.* (*Rossum's Universal Robots*) the Expressionist playwright, Karel Capek, used robots as dramatis personae. In *Chips with Everything* Wesker brilliantly deploys the techniques of Expressionism to illustrate the process whereby military discipline can reduce individuals to a robot-like uniformity, both the complacency of authority and the inertia of the ranks.

A squad of nine R.A.F. conscripts is subjected to a battery of bullying abuse from the corporal and psychological manipulation by the commissioned officers, until, their personal identity submerged, they learn to move as one mechanical unit and pass out to the blaring of a military band playing "God Save the Queen."

Expressionism is particularly appropriate to his purpose. He uses type characters to represent social forces—the best example being Corporal Hill—and the identity of the recruits is, with two exceptions, indicated very lightly. The dialogue is for the most part staccato, while brief, stylised, symbolic scenes, such as the square bashing and bayonet practice, succeed one another rapidly, a triumphant instance of Wesker's innate command of stage movement.

As to the two recruits presented in greater detail: the plight of the gentle Smiler, broken and suffering, is sufficiently generalised to give pathos and depth to the play without disturbing its tone, but the predicament of Thompson is treated with too much psychological detail to be in key, especially as the portrait is not entirely convincing.

The son of a general, Thompson is at first resistant to authority and appears to be trying to assume leadership of the squad. But the habits of a class that can eat "chips with everything" are too distasteful for him, and accused by the recruits of "slumming" and assailed by the blandishments of the officers, he suddenly capitulates and assumes officer's uniform.

The overall effect is tense and powerful, and scenes of moving comedy, such as the breathtaking mime of stealing coke, alternate with those where the audience, facing the same direction as the recruits themselves, cannot escape feeling the obliterating effects of the military machine.

*The Four Seasons.* 1965. P.

The course of love through the four seasons of the year is traced through the shared experience of a man and woman whose previous marriages had foundered. Wesker has unsuccessfully applied an Expressionist style to unsuitable material, a static situation without incident or plot.

*Their Very Own and Golden City.* 1966. P.

The driving power of an unusual play is probably Wesker's own struggle to realise a communal and artistic ideal in Centre 42.

He skilfully integrates a sweeping expressionistic panorama of social trends since 1926 with the creation of rounded, idiosyncratic characters. The inspired architect, Andrew Cobham, has a vision of the ideal city that shall set a pattern of living for the community, but its full achievement is thwarted by obscurantist Trade Unions and by

his accepting the patronage of a Tory Minister and a capitalist industrialist. Andrew's emotional life is split between frustrated friendship with an aristocratic girl and estrangement form Jessie, his homely wife.

A vantage point is offered by recurring dreamlike scenes in Durham Cathedral. Acting as a flash forward they show Andrew the youth with his fellows and Jessie. Ecstatic with joy at the sublimity of the cathedral he envisages his own life-work. But the final scene, in keeping with the disillusion and compromise that have blighted his vision, serves as a sad, ironic flash-back.

## John Whiting (1915–63).

John Whiting was an original playwright who was much preoccupied with the theme of selfdestruction, but was slow to find his own style.

*A Penny for a Song.* 1951.

Written at a time of great personal happiness this is an agreeable whimsy, depicting two eccentric brothers in their Dorsetshire residence preparing to repel the armies of Napoleon. The appearance on the stage of a balloon and a homemade fire-engine give the authentic period touch of gentlemanly interest in scientific invention, and also impart to the farcical idyll a dash of pantomime.

Whiting cleverly gives a comic perspective to the recent fear of foreign invasion and so takes the sting out of terror.

*Saint's Day.* 1951.

This play, written before *A Penny for a Song,* won the award in a Festival of Britain Play Competition.

It concerns self-destruction, its central figure being the octogenarian Paul Southman, once a famous revolutionary poet who had long ago gone into self-imposed exile because of popular outcry against his work.

The plays opens well. Southman is a striking figure, an embodiment of the angry artist at war with society, and like Swift in his aggressive scorn of compromise, his scurrilous style and final madness. His situation is at first sufficiently distanced to be convincing, but when the fashionable young writer Procathren introduces the glossy contemporary world it begins to seem implausible. Later Procathren accidentally kills Paul's grand-daughter, Stella, and then orders three deserting soldiers to hang Paul and Stella's husband, also an artist, and the initially powerful theme is swamped by melodrama.

The play generally is overloaded with halfdeveloped symbolism and allusion.

*Marching Song.* 1954. P.

In a play much concerned with the existentialist stress on the inescapability of choice, Whiting returns to the theme of self-destruction.

The setting is generalised—a wealthy house "above a capital city in Europe." Rupert Forster, formerly a general, who seven years previously had inexplicably lost a decisive battle, here meets his dilemma. He must either face a trial, which might cause political unrest, or commit suicide. The choices are represented by two people.

In Act II Forster encounters Dido, a young woman who revives his sense of humanity and will to live. She represents the female side of personality, the Jungian anima and her name recalls the Dido of the Æneid, who by her love deflected Æneas from the path of military duty enjoined by fate.

In Act III he has a very different meeting with Captain Bruno, the embodiment of military ambition, who represents the male aspect of personality. To him Forster at last confesses the cause of his fatal defeat. He had been so overcome with compassion for children whom he had destroyed while they were impeding his tanks that he had been unable to follow up his advance. Bruno stigmatises the delay as military error and guilt and Forster commits suicide rather than face disgrace and imprisonment.

This is a strongly constructed play, its dominating theme worked out with single-minded austerity. But it lacks thrust and momentum. Forster's reversion to his original decision to commit suicide gives it a circular movement and it is more concerned to clarify judgment of the past than to affect the future. In its acknowledgment of the discrepancy between military code and humane ethic it is highly topical and stimulating.

*The Devils.* 1962. P.

Suggested to Whiting by Peter Brook, this intricate and distinguished play is based on Aldous Huxley's *The Devils of Loudun*, which treats of an actual case of suspected diabolism in France between 1623 and 1634.

Whiting employs two focal points. One is Grandier (Richard Johnson), again a man who invites his own destruction, a worldly and sensual priest who is yet gifted with a rare religious insight and compassion. The other is a hunchback prioress (Dorothy Tutin). Although she has not met Grandier, she becomes obsessed by fantasies of his amorous adventures and her resulting hysteria, which spreads throughout the convent, is suspected as diabolical possession, instigated by Grandier. Richelieu, for political reasons, uses this as a pretext to get rid of him. Grandier, in spite of excruciating torture and degradation, the prelude to his being burnt alive, struggles to retain his faith.

In its subject and theme *The Devils* is strikingly similar to Miller's *The Crucible*. Both plays show *l'homme moyen sensuel* accused of diabolism and beset by a woman's jealousy, fanatical superstition, and malignant spite, yet still keeping his integrity in the face of death.

There are significant differences. Whiting's intricate play is not realistic but Brechtian in style, with a series of brief episodes and a commentary by a sewerman, whose ironic and sceptical remarks counterpoint Grandier's eloquence. It lacks Miller's reference to the contemporary scene and its final note is one of harsh pessimism, as the sewerman tells the prioress that Grandier's bones are being prized by the crowd as superstitious "charms."

The final act presents an almost unbearable spectacle of a barbarous ritual of physical torture as the maimed and twitching Grandier is paraded in public procession through the streets.

**Tennessee Williams (b. 1914).**

The American Tennessee Williams is a playwright of great talent, whose freely flowing naturalistic plays combine violence and melodrama with haunting portrayal of personality, fluent dialogue, and original settings.

Of recent years the following major plays have been produced in Britain: *The Glass Menagerie*, 1948, revived 1965 (P); *A Street Car Named Desire* 1949 (P); *The Rose Tattoo* (P); *Cat on a Hot Tin Roof* (P); *Camino Real*, the least realistic play, 1957 (P); *Suddenly Last Summer* (P), *Period of Adjustment*, 1961, and *The Two-Character Play*, 1967.

Although his plays breathe the atmosphere of the Deep South—often decadent in tone—Williams, unlike the extravert Miller, is preoccupied not with social issues but with the inner life of his characters. Compelled by their own passions and obsessions and caught in the web of family relationships, they break away only at great cost and pain to themselves and others, so that a mood of determinism, sombre but not altogether despairing, broods over much of Williams' work.

He portrays the vulnerability of those who desire or love anything intensely, humanity's sense of guilt, defiant aggression and despair, all of which he claims to find within himself. The violence characterising so much of his work reaches its climax in *Suddenly Last Summer*.

Especially poignant are Williams' penetrating psychological studies of life's pathetic failures; the crippled Laura retreating to her glass menagerie, Blanche Dubois, of *Street Car*, and the alcoholic Brick and his childless wife in the *Cat*.

*The Two Character Play.* 1967.

Like the early *The Glass Menagerie*, the play treats of an ill-omened brother-sister relationship.

Believing them to be mad, the cast of a touring theatrical company have just deserted the two star actors, a brother and sister, Felice and Clare. Alone on the stage, the pair hysterically decide to put on Felice's own work, *The Two Character Play*. This play within the play is also about a brother and sister who stay immured in an overgrown house in their terror of facing the world outside. Their father had killed their mother and then committed suicide and people now suspect the brother-sister relationship. Whether it is the relationship of Felice and Clare or of the dramatic personae is left ambiguous in a Pirandello-like piece hovering on the confines of reality and illusion, sanity, and madness.

**Charles Wood (b. 1932).**

Ever since *Cockade*, 1963, Wood's plays have been chiefly concerned with military life. An exception was *Fill the Stage with Happy Hours*, 1967 (P).

*Dingo.* 1967.

Wood uses some expressionist techniques to present a phantasmagoria of the last War, beginning in the desert and grinding through Stalag to the unconditional surrender of Germany. It is an assault on the emotions and sensations in a passionate attempt to bring home war's physical horror and spiritual attrition, but Wood's specific concern is to expose latent jingoism and political expediency and the futility of the heroism they demand.

The scurrilous words matter less than certain persistent images: the ranker, Dingo, epitome of bitter disillusion; Tanky, rendered simple-minded because he was powerless to release his mate, screaming to death in a flaming tank; an ENSA comedian who serves to parody Churchillian rhetoric, and breezy morale-boosting of High Command; a young subaltern, dressed as a blonde in a bikini for a concert party designed to cover an escape from Stalag, and now, with Tanky, lolling dead from the barbed wire.

The play is powerful but sprawling, cluttered, one-sided. It attacks the idea that Britain played a more disinterested rôle than in previous wars. It was fought, not for others, says Dingo, but " for all the usual reasons," an emotive statement that needs scrutiny.

*"H".* 1969.

Wood's subject is the heroic march of the elderly General Havelock, or "H", during the Mutiny. His column vastly outnumbered and decimated by disease, he yet relieved Cawnpore and won twelve desperate battles before relieving Lucknow where he died of dysentery.

A devoted and chivalrous Christian and a disciplined commander, Havelock yet ordered some of the terrible reprisals then current, hanging mutinous sepoys or shooting them alive from the mouths of cannon. His equivocal behaviour helps to resolve and focus Wood's own conflicting impulses, his fascination with military discipline and his horror at the bestiality of war, so that the play is more unified than *Dingo*.

The core of the play is irony, centred in the action of the protagonist. But the irony proliferates, as in the contrast between the stylised Victorian language and the brutal deed, and in the many brief unconnected episodes, as, for instance, one recalling the mutual love and sacrifice between British and sepoys. These, demanding a constant reorientation of attitude, tend to distract and confuse.

The fact that Havelock's aide-de-camp is his own son suggests the tender perspective of home. Resolute in courage and obedience, the son differs from his father in opinion and faith and his eventual confession of Christianity at Havelock's death gives pathos to the scene.

The Brechtian epic style is well suited to the simple episodic structure. Brechtian devices are also used:—direct address to the audience, map titles and symbolic emblems, such as the simple blood-stained floor and awning, arrestingly conveying the Indian atrocities at Cawnpore. Brechtian in spirit too is the deliberate theatricality of short scenes projected within a little replica of the popular travelling stage.

Although Havelock on the surface resembles the Brechtian ambiguous protagonist, the chief weakness of the play is that he does not attain the commanding stature of a Galileo or a Mother Courage.

# IDEAS & BELIEFS

This section explains many of the ideas and beliefs that have dominated men's minds during the centuries. The arrangement is alphabetical and the subjects fall broadly into three groups: religious, philosophical, and political.

# IDEAS AND BELIEFS

This section explains many of the ideas and beliefs which people have held at different periods in history. Beliefs may be true or false, meaningful or totally meaningless, regardless of the degree of conviction with which they are held. Since man has been moved to action so often by his beliefs they are worth serious study. The section throws a vivid light on human history.

Man has always felt a deep need for emotional security, a sense of " belonging." This need has found expression in the framing of innumerable religious systems, nearly all of which have been concerned with man's relation to a divine ruling power. In the past people have been accustomed to think of their own religion as true and of all others as false. Latterly we have come to realise that in man's religious strivings there is common ground, for our need in the world today is a morality whereby human beings may live together in harmony.

There is also to be found in man an irresistible curiosity which demands an explanation of the world in which he finds himself. This urge to make the world intelligible takes him into the realm of science where the unknown is the constant challenge. Science is a creative process, always in the making, based on experiment and rational argument, and fired by curiosity and imagination. Basic scientific ideas and some of the results of recent scientific activity are to be found in Section F.

In writing of beliefs, especially cherished beliefs, and of how they fit into the modern picture of the world, it is difficult to avoid causing some offence but the reader is assured that the writer has tried to be fair and helpful.

## A

**Abecedarians,** name (derived from A B C) of a small German religious sect, founded by the Anabaptist Storch in 1522, who claimed that, as knowledge of the Scriptures was communicated directly by the Holy Spirit, it was wrong to learn to read. *See* Baptists.

**Activists,** those in a political movement who insist on taking active steps towards their objectives rather than merely putting forward a programme.

**Adoptionism,** in Christianity, a doctrine advanced at various times which holds that Jesus was not born divine but, in virtue of his human spiritual achievements, was designated by God as the Son of God at the moment of his baptism in the Jordan, as told in all the four Gospels. Among the sects who held this " heretical " doctrine were the Paulicians (*q.v.*). The " Adoptionist " view differs from the orthodox " Conceptionist " view only in regard to the moment in the life of Jesus when the incarnation took place.

**Adventists,** a group of American religious sects, the most familiar being the Seventh-Day Adventist Church, which observes Saturday as the true Sabbath. With more than a million members throughout the world, it shares with other Adventists a belief in the imminent second coming of Christ (a doctrine fairly widespread in the U.S.A. during the early decades of the 19th cent. when the end of the world was predicted by William Miller for 1843, then for 1844). Modern Adventists content themselves with the conviction that the " signs " of the Advent are multiplying, the " blessed event " which will solve the world's ills. Believers will be saved, but the sects differ as to whether the unjust will be tortured in hell, annihilated, or merely remain asleep eternally.

**Agnosticism.** *See* God and Man.

**Albigenses,** also known as Cathari. French 12th cent. heretical sect (named after the town of Albi in Provence), who maintained that material things belonged to the realm of Satan and that salvation was to be achieved by crushing all animal instincts, particularly the sexual instinct; universal continence would end the domination of matter by the extinction of the human race. The eating of animal flesh was forbidden and vegetarianism enjoined in order to weaken the desires. Those who rigidly kept to these rules were initiated into the grade of the " Perfect "; those unable fully to comply were known as the " Believers ". Condemned as heretics by Pope Innocent III, the sect was finally exterminated in the Albigensian Crusade led by Simon de Montfort towards the end of the 12th cent. (In his thoroughness, de Montfort also succeeded in destroying the high culture of the Troubadours.) *See* Manichaeism.

**Alchemy,** ancient art associated with magic and astrology in which modern chemistry has its roots. The earliest mention of alchemy comes from ancient Egypt but its later practitioners attributed its origins to such varied sources as the fallen angels of the Bible, to Moses and Aaron, but most commonly to Hermes Trismegistus, often identified with the Egyptian god Thoth, whose knowledge of the divine art was handed down only to the sons of kings (cf. the phrase " hermetically sealed "). Its main object was the transmutation of metals. Egyptian speculation concerning this reached its height during the 6th cent. in the Alexandrian school. Brought to Western Europe by the Moslems, one of its most famous Arab exponents was Jabir (*c.* 760–*c.* 815), known to the Latins as Geber, who had a laboratory at Kufa on the Tigris. One school of early Greek philosophy held that there was ultimately only one elemental matter of which everything was composed. Such men as Albertus Magnus (1206–80) and Roger Bacon (1214–94) assumed that, by removing impurities, this *materia prima* could be obtained. Although Bacon's ideas were in many ways ahead of his time, he firmly believed in the philosopher's stone, which could turn base metals into gold, and in an elixir of life which would give eternal youth. Modern science has, of course, shown in its researches into radioactivity the possibility of transmutation of certain elements, but this phenomenon has little bearing on either the methods of the alchemist or the mysteries with which he surrounded them.

**Anabaptists.** *See* Baptists.

**Analytical Psychology,** the name given by Carl Gustav Jung (1875–1961) of Zürich to his system of psychology which, like Adler's Individual Psychology (*q.v.*), took its origin from Freud's psychoanalysis (*q.v.*) from which both diverged in 1911. Briefly, Jung differed from Freud: (1) in believing that the latter had laid too much emphasis on the sexual drive as the basic one in man and replacing it with the concept of *libido* or life energy of which sex forms a part; (2) in his theory of types: men are either extrovert or introvert (*i.e.* their interest is turned primarily outwards to the world or inwards to the self), and they apprehend experience in four main ways, one or other of which is predominant in any given individual—sensing, feeling, thinking, or intuiting; (3) in his belief that the individual's unconscious mind contains not only repressed material which, as Freud maintained, was too unpleasant to be allowed into awareness, but also faculties which had not been allowed to develop—*e.g.*, the emotional side of the too rational man, the feminine side of the too masculine one; (4) in the importance he attaches to the existence of a collective unconscious at a still deeper level which contains traces of ancient ways of thought which mankind has inherited over the centuries. These are the *archetypes* and include vague primitive notions of magic, spirits and witches, birth and death, gods, virgin mothers, resurrection, etc. In the treatment of neuroses Jung believed in the importance of (a) the present situation which the patient refuses to face; (b) the bringing together of conscious and unconscious and integrating them.

Jung's school of thought is undeniably not popular with scientific psychologists, but his emphasis on the more spiritual side of man's nature has brought him support from those of a religious or philosophical turn of mind, notably in the Roman Catholic Church.

**Anarchism,** a political philosophy which holds, in the words of the American anarchist Josiah Warren (1798–1874), an early follower of Robert Owen, that " every man should be his own government, his own law, his own church." The idea that governmental interference or even the mere existence of authority is inherently bad is as old as Zeno, the Greek Stoic philosopher, who believed that compulsion perverts the normal nature of man. William Godwin's *Enquiry Concerning Political Justice* (1793) was the first systematic exposition of the doctrine. Godwin (father-in-law of Shelley) claimed that man is by nature sociable, co-operative, rational, and good when given the choice to act freely; that under such conditions men will form voluntary groups to work in complete social harmony. Such groups or communities would be based on equality of income, no state control, no property; this state of affairs would be brought about by rational discussion and persuasion rather than by revolution.

The French economist Proudhon (1809–65) was the first to bring anarchism to the status of a mass movement. In his book *What is Property?* he stated bluntly that " property is theft " and " governments are the scourge of God." He urged the formation of co-operative credit banks where money could be had without interest and goods could be exchanged at cost value at a rate representing the hours of work needed to produce each commodity. Like Godwin, he disapproved of violence but, unlike Marx, disapproved of trades unions as representing organised groups.

In communistic anarchism these ideas were combined with a revolutionary philosophy, primarily by the Russians Michael Bakunin (1814–76) and Peter Kropotkin (1842–1921) who favoured training workers in the technique of " direct action " to overthrow the state by all possible means, including political assassination. In 1868 anarchists joined the First International which broke up a few years later after a bitter struggle between Bakuninists and Marxists. Subsequently small anarchist groups murdered such political figures as Tsar Alexander II of Russia, King Humbert of Italy, Presidents Carnot of France and MacKinley of America, and the Empress Elizabeth of Austria.

Anarchism and communism differ in three main ways: (1) anarchism forms no political party, rejects all relationship with established authority, and regards democratic reform as a setback; (2) communism is against capitalism, anarchism against the state as such; (3) both have the final goal of a classless society, but anarchism rejects the idea of an intermediate period of socialist state control accepted by communism. Philosophical anarchists, such as the American writer Henry David Thoreau (1817–62), were primarily individualists who believed in a return to nature, the non-payment of taxes, and passive resistance to state control; in these respects Thoreau strongly influenced Gandhi as did the Christian anarchist Tolstoy. *See also* Syndicalism.

**Anglicanism,** adherence to the doctrine and discipline of the Anglican, as the genuine representative of the Catholic Church. *See* Church of England.

**Anglo-Catholicism.** To Queen Elizabeth I the Church of England was that of the " middle way " in which human reason and commonsense took their place beside Scripture and Church authority. The extent to which these various factors are stressed creates the distinctions between " high " and " low " church. Anglo-Catholics tend to reject the term " Protestant " and stress the term " Catholic " and, although few accept the infallibility of the Pope, some Anglo-Catholic churches have introduced much or all of the Roman ritual and teach Roman dogmas. *See* Catholicism, Tractarianism.

**Animatism,** a stage in primitive religion in which life is attributed to inanimate objects.

**Animism** (see above) is a more advanced stage in which it is believed that natural objects may be the *abodes* of souls or spirits.

**Anthropomorphism,** the ascription of human physical and moral qualities to God or gods (in psychology to gods or animals). Psychologists use the term *Anthropopathy* for the ascription of such qualities specifically to the Deity.

**Anthroposophy,** a school of religious philosophic thought based on the work of Rudolf Steiner (1861–1925), a German theosophist. His best known work is in education and medicine. The centre of the Anthroposophical Society is at Goetheanum, Basel, Switzerland. Schools, curative homes, and clinics are to be found in many parts of the world. Though concerned with reincarnation and destiny, anthroposophy is essentially Christian in outlook.

**Anticlericalism,** resentment of priestly powers and privileges, traceable in England to Wyclif's insistence in the 14th cent. on the right of all men to have access to the Scriptures. The translation of the Bible into the common tongue was a great landmark in the history of the Bible and the English language. Wyclif's principles were condemned by the Roman Church of his time but were readily accepted during the Reformation. Tudor anticlericalism arose from motives ranging from a greedy desire to plunder the riches of the Church to a genuine dislike of the powers of the priesthood whose spiritual courts still had the right to decide on points of doctrine or morals in an age when the layman felt he was well able to decide for himself. In innumerable ways the Church was permitted to extort money from the laity. It is generally agreed, says Trevelyan, that the final submission of church to state in England was motivated quite as much by anticlericalism as by Protestantism. The rise of the Reformed churches in England satisfied the people generally and anticlericalism never became the fixed principle of permanent parties as happened in France and Italy from the time of Voltaire onwards.

**Antisemitism,** a term first applied about the middle of the last century to those who were anti-Jewish in their outlook. Although this attitude was prevalent for religious reasons throughout the Middle Ages, modern antisemitism differed (a) in being largely motivated by economic or political conditions, and (b) in being doctrinaire with a pseudo-scientific rationale presented by such men as Gobineau (1816–82) and Houston Stewart Chamberlain (1855–1927), and later by the Nazi and Fascist " philosophers." Beginning in Russia and Hungary with the pogroms of 1882 it gradually spread south and westwards where, in France, the Dreyfus case provided an unsavoury example in 1894. Thousands of Jews from Eastern Europe fled to Britain and America during this period; for in these countries antisemitism has rarely been more than a personal eccentricity. During the last war the murder of six million Jews by the Nazis and their accomplices led to a further exodus to various parts of the world and finally to the creation of the state of Israel.

The individual Jew-hater makes unconscious use of the psychological processes of projection and displacement: his greed or sexual guilt is projected on to the Jew (or Negro or Catholic) because he cannot bear to accept them as his own emotions, and his sense of failure in life is blamed on his chosen scapegoat rather than on his own inadequacy.

But there are social causes too and politicians in some lands are well versed in the technique of blaming unsatisfactory conditions (which they themselves may have in part produced) upon minority groups and persuading others to do the same. Historically, the Jew is ideally suited for this role of scapegoat: (1) in the Middle Ages when usury was forbidden to Christians but not to Jews, the latter often became moneylenders incurring the opprobrium generally associated with this trade (*e.g.*, to the simple-minded Russian peasant the Jew often represented, not only the " Christ-killer," but also the moneylender or small shopkeeper to whom he owed money); (2) many trades being closed to Jews, it was natural that they concentrated in others, thus arousing suspicions of " influence " (*i.e.* Jews were felt to occupy a place in certain trades and professions which far exceeds their numerical proportion to the population as a whole); (3) even with the ending of ghetto life, Jews often occupy *en masse* some parts of cities rather than others and this may lead to resentment on the part of the original inhabitants who begin to feel themselves dispossessed; (4) Jews tend to form a closed society and incur the suspicions attached to all closed societies within which social contacts are largely limited to members; marriage outside the group is forbidden or strongly disapproved of, and the preservation, among the orthodox, of cultural and religious barriers tends to isolate them from their fellow citizens. Discrimination, hateful as it is, does not come from one side only and it is such barriers as these that help to maintain an old and cruel folly. *See* Racism, Zionism, Judaism.

**Antivivisection,** opposition to scientific experimentation upon live animals based, according to its supporters, both on the moral grounds of the suffering imposed, and on the less secure claim that many doctors and scientists of repute have rejected the value of information gained in this way. It is true that the protagonists of the movement during its early days in the mid-19th cent. included a number of eminent physicians and surgeons, but few today—whatever their moral scruples—would deny the value of the results obtained. Without animal experiments we should be without vaccines, sera, or antitoxins against smallpox, tetanus, typhoid, diphtheria, poliomyelitis, and a multitude of other diseases; we should have no detailed knowledge about vitamins, or about the effects of radioactive fallout; we would be unable to test out new drugs for safety before using them on human beings. There are in Britain two or three large national anti-vivisection societies and several smaller ones. Much of their work is co-ordinated through the British Council of Anti-Vivisection Societies. Animal experimentation is controlled by Act of Parliament which makes obligatory the possession of licences by experimenters, inspection of laboratories by the Home Office, and the issue of annual returns of experiments. A campaign for Government action to improve the conditions under which animals are used in laboratory experiments was launched by the RSPCA in 1968. It aims at bringing public pressure on the Government to implement the recommendations of the Littlewood Committee which reported in 1965.

**Apartheid,** an Afrikaans word meaning " apartness," referred to by South African Government spokesmen as " separate development " or " self-development." To others it means the system of total racial discrimination between Black and White South Africans—the permanent inhabitants of the country—as enforced by the Nationalist Party since it came to power in 1948. Some degree of racial segregation has existed in South Africa since the earliest days of colonialism in the mid-17th cent. and the policy was continued by the United Party under Smuts and Hertzog from 1934 onwards though it was never a political issue. This changed when the Nationalist Party gained power and oppressive measures against the non-White segment of the population have grown steadily under Malan, Strydom, Verwoerd, and Vorster. *Apartheid* involves the beliefs in racial purity and *baaskap*, or white supremacy. It means keeping vast African populations in a condition of helotry. The official policy of the South African Government is to create separate self-governing Black states in which the Africans would be guided to self-government and, it is claimed, eventually to independence. The

first so-called bantu reserve was set up in the Transkei in 1962. But Africans with 70 per cent of the population would have only about 13 per cent of the land; cities and mineral areas would remain the reserve of the Whites. Total *apartheid* or complete separation of the Black and White races in South Africa remains unlikely to be realised since mining, the main industry of the country, is based on relatively low-paid African labour.

*Apartheid* has been condemned by the General Assembly of the United Nations and the Secretary-General, U Thant, has expressed the hope " that, in response to the repeated recommendations and decisions of the United Nations organs the Government of the Republic of South Africa will abandon its policies of *apartheid*, and also implement measures aimed at bringing about racial harmony based on equal rights and fundamental freedoms for all the people of South Africa." *See also* Section C, Part I.

**Apollinarianism,** the heretical belief taught by Apollinaris (*c.* 313–*c.* 390), bishop of Laodicea, near Antioch, that in Jesus the human mind was replaced by the Divine Mind or Logos. The sect was later absorbed by the Monophysites (*q.v.*)

**Arianism,** formed the subject of the first great controversy within the Christian Church over the doctrine of Arius of Alexandria (d. 336) who denied the divinity of Christ. The doctrine, although at first influential, was condemned at the Council of Nicaea (325), called by the Emperor Constantine, at which Arius was opposed by Athanasius, also of Alexandria, who maintained the now orthodox view that the Son is of one substance with the Father. Arius was banished and the heresy had died out by the end of the 4th cent., but disbelief in the divinity of Christ has formed part of the doctrine of many minor sects since, notably in Unitarianism (*q.v.*).

**Arminianism,** the doctrine of Jacobus Arminium or Jakob Harmensen (1560–1609), the Dutch minister of a Protestant church in Amsterdam, who had trained in the universities of Leyden and Geneva where he learned the Calvinistic doctrine of predestination (*See* Calvinism). Later he became deeply convinced of the falsity of this belief which maintained that God had, by an eternal decree, predestined which people were to be saved and which eternally damned. In face of the bitter opposition of his opponent Franz Gomar and his party who held this view, Arminius asserted that God bestows forgiveness and eternal life on all who repent and believe in Christ. In England a modified Arminianism was later to become the theology of Wesleyan Methodism.

**Assassins,** a sect of Moslem Shi'ites, founded by the Persian Hasan i Sabbah (*c.* 1090), which for more than two centuries established a rule of terror all over Persia and Syria. The coming of the Mongols in 1256 destroyed them in Persia and the Syrian branch suffered a similar fate at the hands of the then Mamluk sultan of Egypt, *c.* 1270. It was a secret order, ruled over by a grand master, under whom the members were strictly organised into classes, according to the degree of initiation into the secrets of the order. The devotees, belonging to one of the lower groups, carried out the actual assassinations under strict laws of obedience, and total ignorance of the objects and ritual of the society. It is believed that the latter were given ecstatic visions under the influence of hashish, whence the term *hashshashin*, which became corrupted to " assassin."

**Associationism.** In psychology, the Associationist school of the 19th cent. accepted the association of ideas as the fundamental principle in mental life. It was represented in Britain by the two Mills and Herbert Spencer, in Germany by J. F. Herbart (1776–1841). To these, mental activity was nothing but the association of " ideas " conceived of as units of both thought and feeling—the emotion of anger or the perception of a chair were both " ideas "—and apart from them the self did not exist. Personality was simply a series of these units coming and going, adding to or cancelling each other out, in accordance with rigid and mechanistic scientific laws.

**Assumption of the Virgin.** The Roman Catholic

belief, that the Blessed Virgin ascended bodily to heaven after her death, was proclaimed by Pope Pius XII towards the end of 1950. It is now, therefore, binding on all Catholics under pain of anathema and the guilt of mortal sin. Protestants are liable to make the mistake of supposing that such dogmas are new additions to the faith invented by the pope of the moment. According to Catholic doctrine, no addition can be made to the " faith once delivered to the saints," and every dogma is justified by reference to Bible texts and the traditions of the Church. Both Eastern and Western Churches have been permitted to believe in the Assumption of the Virgin for over a thousand years, and the new dogma merely clarifies the old belief and makes it binding on the faithful.

Astrology, a pseudo-science bearing much the same historical relationship to astronomy as alchemy did to chemistry. Originally it was divided into the two branches of Natural Astrology which dealt with the movements of the heavenly bodies and their calculation, and Judicial Astrology which studied the alleged influence of the stars and planets on human life and fate. It was the former that developed into modern astronomy; the latter was, and remains, sheer superstition.

Astrology owes most to the early Babylonians (or Chaldeans) who, being largely nomadic in an environment which permitted an unobstructed view of the sky, readily accepted the idea that divine energy is manifested in the movements of the sun and planets. Gradually this concept became enlarged and the relative positions of the planets both in relation to each other and to the fixed stars became important together with the idea of omens—that, if a particular event occurred whilst the planets were in a particular position, the recurrence of that position heralded a recurrence of the same sort of event. Soon the planets became associated with almost every aspect of human life. They were bound up with the emotions, with parts of the body, so that astrology played quite a large part in medicine up to late mediaeval times. Not only was the position of the planet to be considered but also the particular sign of the zodiac (or house of heaven) it was occupying, and it was believed possible to foretell the destiny of an individual by calculating which star was in the ascendant (i.e. the sign of the zodiac nearest the eastern horizon and the star which arose at that precise moment) at the time of his birth. Astrology was popular among the Egyptians, the Romans (whose authorities found the Chaldean astrologers a nuisance and expelled them from time to time), and during the Middle Ages when astrologers were often highly respected. Because of people's innate desire to see into the future there are, alas, still astrologers about to exploit ignorance.

Atheism. See God and Man.

Atomism. (1) in philosophy, the atomists were a group of early Greek thinkers, the most important of whom were Leucippus (fl. c. 440 B.C.) and his younger contemporary Democritus (c. 460–370 B.C.). Prior to these men, although it had been agreed that matter must be composed of tiny ultimate particles and that change must be due to the manner in which these mingled or separated from each other, it was supposed that there existed different types of particle for each material—e.g. for flesh, wood, hair, bone. The atomists taught that atoms were all made of a single substance and differed only in the connections (pictured as hooks, grooves, points, etc.) which enabled them to join each other in characteristic ways. Theirs was the first move towards modern atomic theory and a predecessor of the modern concept of chemical linkages. (2) in psychology, atomism refers to any theory which holds that mental states can be analysed without loss into elementary units, e.g. Associationism and Behaviourism (q.v.).

Authoritarianism, a dictatorial form of government as contrasted with a democratic one based on popular sovereignty. Its alleged advantages are the avoidance of the delays and inefficiency said to be characteristic of the latter, but like " Bolshevism " the word is used today mainly as a form of abuse.

# B

Baconian Method, the use in science and philosophy of the inductive (as opposed to the deductive or Aristotelian) method of reasoning as proposed by Francis Bacon (1561–1626). Deduction argues from supposedly certain first principles (such as the existence of God or Descartes's " I think, therefore I am ") what the nature of the universe and its laws must be, whereas Bacon denied the possibility of proving religious or metaphysical doctrines by thought and argument. The only means of obtaining true knowledge of the universe, in his view, was by the amassing of facts and observations so that when enough were obtained the truth would be known in the same way that a child's numbered dots in a playbook joined together by a pencilled line create a picture. This method, known as induction, is essentially the method of modern science, although it is generally agreed today that Bacon underrated the importance of hypothesis and theory since the greatest possible number of observations are of little significance until the scientist's intuition makes sense of them.

Baptists, a Christian denomination whose distinctive doctrines are that members can only be received by baptism " upon the confession of their faith and sins " and that " baptism in no wise appertaineth to infants." Baptism is therefore by total immersion of adults. Modern Baptists base their doctrines upon the teaching of the Apostles and some hold that the Albigenses (q.v.) maintained the true belief through what they regard as the corruption of the Roman Church in mediaeval times. On the other hand any connection with the Anabaptist movement during the Reformation is rejected and the beginning of the modern Church is traced to John Smyth, a minister of the Church of England who in Amsterdam came under the influence of the Arminians (q.v.) and Mennonites. Smyth died in 1612 when the first Baptist church in England was built at Newgate. This, the " General " Baptist Church, rejected Calvinistic beliefs and held the Arminian doctrine of redemption open to all, but some years later a split occurred with the formation of the " Particular " Baptist Church which was Calvinist in doctrine. In 1891 the two bodies were united in the Baptist Union and today the sect is spread throughout the world, notably in the U.S.A.

The Anabaptist movements of Germany, Switzerland, and Holland also practised adult baptism in addition to a primitive communism and demanded social reforms. Persecuted by both Catholics and Protestants, their leader, Thomas Münzer, and many others were burned at the stake (1525). However, this sect was noted for its violence under a religious guise, and its taking over of the state of Münster in 1533 was characterised by wild licentiousness, since, as Antinomians, they believed that the " elect " could do no wrong. A revival begun by Menno Simons (d. 1561), a Dutch religious reformer, led to the formation of the Mennonite sect which, whilst rejecting infant baptism, gave up the objectionable features of the Anabaptists. This reformed sect still exists as small agricultural groups in the original strongholds of the movement and in the United States.

Beat Generation, a term first used by the American writer Jack Kerouac in his novel The Town and the City to define various groups spread across the face of the country, but notably New York and San Francisco, which, belonging to the post-war generation, represented a complex of attitudes. Briefly, these are: rejection of the values of the past and lack of conviction in the possibility of a future for humanity—hence an acceptance of nothing but the immediate present in terms of experience and sensations; rebellion against organised authority, not out of any political conviction (as in the case of anarchism), but rather from lack of any interest or desire to control events, nature, or people; contempt for the " Square "—the orthodox individual who, stuck firmly in his rut, " plays it safe " and remains confident of the rightness and decency of his moral values. The " Beatnik " has contracted out of what one of them describes as " an increasingly meaningless rat-race rigged up by and for Squares " which wastes effort and brutalises feeling. He loathes the pretences without which, he claims, the Square cannot succeed, and throwing off all masks is indifferent to the opinions of others, his dress, or the need to work, thus entering into " the inescapable truth and squalor of his own being." He " digs " (likes) everything, tries everything from drugs to sexual relationships, which have no significance outside the sensations of the moment to the advanced Beatnik or " hipster." All men are addressed as " man," all women as " chick." Of course, the above is an intellectualisation by such Beat writers as Kerouac, Allen Ginsberg, and Carl Solomon or Norman Mailer of a philosophy which for many Beatniks would be meaningless, being satisfied with any excuse for their own exhibitionism, sexual promiscuity, and psychopathic tendencies. Beards (in men), bare feet, sloppy clothes, and unwashed bodies were the familiar Beatnik uniform.

The Beat generation of the 1940s and 50s gave way to the Love generation or Flower people, with their flowers, beads, and cowbells. Their social philosophy is the same—living in the present, unconventionally, seeking personal freedom, believing drugs to be essential, claiming to be acting against the rat race, dissociating themselves from politics, taking a superficial interest in the religions of the East, borrowing much of their language, music, and ideas on dress from the American " hippy "; yet believing in the creation of a new and gentler society based on different forms and values. More recently, the name " drop-outs " has been used for these young non-violent rebels who have turned their backs on modern society.

Behaviourism, a school of psychology founded in 1914 by J. B. Watson (1878–1958), an animal psychologist at Johns Hopkins University, Baltimore. Its main tenet was that the method of introspection and the study of mental states were unscientific and should be replaced by the study of behaviour. When animals or human beings were exposed to specific stimuli and their responses objectively recorded, or when the development of a child, as seen in its changing behaviour, was noted, these alone were methods which were truly scientific. Watson contributed an important idea to psychology and did a great deal towards ridding it of the largely philosophical speculations of the past. But he also went to absurd extremes, as in his view that thought is nothing but subvocal speech, consisting of almost imperceptible movements of the tongue, throat, and larynx (i.e., when we think, we are really talking to ourselves), and his further opinion that heredity is, except in grossly abnormal cases, of no importance. He claimed that by " conditioning," the ordinary individual could be made into any desired type, regardless of his or her inheritance.

The work of Ivan Pavlov had begun about 1901, but was unknown in America until about ten years later, and it was through another Russian, Vladimir Bekhterev, that the concept of " conditioning " was introduced into the country. Bekhterev's book *Objective Psychology*, describing his new science of " reflexology," was translated in 1913 and played a great part in the development of Behaviourist ideas. The conditioned reflex became central to Watson's theory of learning and habit formation (e.g., he showed that a year-old child, at first unafraid of white rats, became afraid of them when they came to be associated with a loud noise behind the head). Finally all behaviour, including abnormal behaviour, came to be explained in terms of conditioned responses; these were built up by association on the infant's three innate emotions of fear, rage, and love, of which the original stimuli were, for the first, loud noises and the fear of falling; for the second, interference with freedom of movement; and for the third, patting and stroking. The Behaviourist method is widely used all over the world as a technique in psychological research, but in the Western world there remain few Behaviourists of the out-and-out Watsonian type. The work of Freud has made it impossible to ignore the importance of introspection in psychology.

Benthamism. *See* Utilitarianism.

Bolshevism, an alternative name for Communism (q.v.), usually used in the West in a derogatory sense. When the Russian Social Democratic Party at a conference held in London in 1903 split over the issue of radicalism or moderation, it was the radical faction headed by Lenin (who subsequently led the 1917 Revolution and became first Head of State of the Soviet Union) which polled the majority of votes. The Russian for majority is *bolshinstvo* and for minority *menshinstvo*; hence the radicals became known as Bolsheviki and the moderates as Mensheviki, anglicised as Bolsheviks and Mensheviks. *See* Communism, Marxism.

British Israelites, a religious group who hold the race-theory that the English-speaking peoples (of the White Race) are the lineal descendants of the " lost Ten Tribes " of Israel (deported by Sargon of Assyria on the fall of Samaria in 721 B.C.). They believe the Anglo-Saxons to be God's " Chosen People " in the literal sense of the term as it is used in the Old Testament, by whom the world will be brought in readiness for the Millennium. The official organisation is the British–Israel World Federation of which the official journal is the *National Message*. Some British Israelites have the notion that the future can be foretold by the measurements of the Great Pyramid.

Buddhism, one of the great Oriental religions. It arose against the background of Hinduism in north India in the 6th cent. B.C., its founder (real or legendary) being the Hindu prince Siddhartha Gautama, known as the Buddha or " Enlightened One." Distressed by the problem of human suffering from which even death allowed no escape—since Buddha accepted the Hindu doctrine of a cycle of lives—he left his palace and his beloved wife and child to become a religious mendicant and ascetic, studying without success for six years the beliefs of Brahmin hermits and self-torturing recluses. After this fruitless search he sat down under a tree (the Bo-tree) and finally came to understand the cause and cure of suffering. The result of his meditations are enshrined in the " four noble truths " which are: (1) that existence is unhappiness; (2) that unhappiness is caused by selfish desire or craving; (3) that desire can be destroyed; (4) that it can be destroyed by following the " noble eightfold path " whose steps are: right views; right desires; right speech, plain and truthful; right conduct, including abstinence not only from immorality but also from taking life, whether human or animal; right livelihood, harming no one; right effort, always pressing on; right awareness of the past, the present, and the future; and lastly, right contemplation or meditation. The more man acquires merit by following these rules in his chain of lives, the sooner is *Nirvana* attained; he loses his individuality, not by annihilation, but " as the dewdrop slips into the shining sea," by merging with the universal life.

Buddhism teaches the way of salvation through ethics and discipline; it preaches the law of *karma*—that a man's actions control his destiny after death as inevitably as cause follows effect, so that his future is solely in his own keeping. A universal God plays no part in this religion, and in many Buddhist nations no word exists for the concept which was neither affirmed nor denied by Buddha himself but simply ignored. Nor did Buddha claim to be other than a man, although much superstition entered the religion at a later date; prayers were made to Buddha, ritual developed, sacred relics preserved under stupas, and the belief in a succession of Buddhas introduced; the sacred writings (*Tripitaka*) are divided into three parts: for the layman, the monks, the philosophers. They were produced by devotees at three councils— the first held immediately after the death of Buddha at the age of 80, the last at the order of King Asoka in 244 B.C. The founder himself wrote nothing.

Buddhism spread to Ceylon, Nepal, Tibet, Mongolia, Indo-China, Burma, Siam, China, and Japan, although on the whole losing influence in India. In Tibet, Buddhism developed into Lamaism (q.v.). In Ceylon and Burma it persisted in its pure form (the Hinayana), while in

China and Japan it developed into the Mahayana with its bodhisattvas and avatars. Sects developed, one of the most important being the Chinese Ch'an (Japanese Zen) Buddhism (q.v.). Outside Asia there are active movements in many Western countries where the serenity and rational humanism of Buddhism appeals to intellectuals as diverse as staid humanists and eccentric beatniks.

Bushido, the traditional code of honour of the Samurai or Japanese military caste corresponding to the European concept of knighthood and chivalry with which it took its separate origin in the 12th cent. Even today it is a potent influence among the upper classes, being based on the principles of simplicity, honesty, courage, and justice which together form a man's idea of personal honour. *Bushido* was strongly influenced by Zen Buddhism (q.v.).

# C

Calvinism, the branch of Protestantism founded basically (although preceded by Zwingli and others) by Jean Chauvin (1509–64), who was born in Noyon in Picardy. John Calvin, as he is usually called, from the Latin form of his name, Calvinius, provided in his *Institutions of the Christian Religion* the first logical definition and justification of Protestantism, thus becoming the intellectual leader of the Reformation as the older Martin Luther was its emotional instigator. The distinctive doctrine of Calvinism is its dogma of predestination which states that God has unalterably destined some souls to salvation to whom " efficacious grace and the gift of perseverance " is granted and others to eternal damnation. Calvinism, as defined in the Westminster Confession, is established in the Reformed or Presbyterian churches of France, Holland, Scotland, etc., as contrasted with the Lutheran churches, and its harsh but logical beliefs inspired the French Huguenots, the Dutch in their fight against Spanish Catholic domination, and the English Puritans. The rule set up under Calvin's influence in Geneva was marred by the burning at the stake of the anatomist Servetus for the heresy of " pantheism," or, as we should say, Unitarianism.

Perhaps its greatest single influence outside the Church was the result of Calvinist belief that to labour industriously was one of God's commands. This changed the mediaeval notions of the blessedness of poverty and the wickedness of usury, proclaimed that men should shun luxury and be thrifty, yet implied that financial success was a mark of God's favour. In this way it was related to the rise of capitalism either as cause or effect. Max Weber, the German sociologist, believed that Calvinism was a powerful incentive to, or even cause of, the rise of capitalism (q.v.); Marx, Sombart, and in England, Tawney, have asserted the reverse view—that Calvinism was a result of developing capitalism, being its ideological justification.

Capitalism is an economic system under which the means of production and distribution are owned by a relatively small section of society which runs them at its own discretion for private profit. There exists, on the other hand, a propertyless class of those who exist by the sale of their labour power. Capitalism arose towards the end of the 18th cent. in England where the early factory owners working with small-scale units naturally approved of free enterprise and free trade. But free enterprise has no necessary connection with capitalism; by the beginning of this century monopolies were developing and state protection against foreign competition was demanded. Capitalism is opposed by those who believe in socialism (q.v.), first, for the moral reasons that it leads to economic inequality and the exploitation of labour and the consuming public, and that public welfare rather than private profit should motivate the economic system; secondly, for the practical reason that capitalism leads to recurrent economic crises. Defenders of the system, however, maintain that it conduces to efficient production by providing the strongest incentive to enterprise and good service.

Catholicism. For those who are not Roman Catholics the term " Catholic " has two separate meanings. The more general refers to the whole body of Christians throughout the world, the more specific refers to a particular view of Christianity. In this latter sense the Church of England, the Orthodox Eastern Churches, and others consider themselves " Catholic " meaning that (a) they belong to Christ's Church as organised on an accepted basis of faith and order; (b) they insist on the necessity of " liturgical " worship through established forms (e.g., baptism, holy communion); (c) they emphasise the continuity of Christian tradition by the use of ancient creeds (e.g., the Apostles' Creed, the Nicene Creed) and regard the ministry as a succession (Apostolic succession) deriving from early practice. In this sense there is thought to be no necessary contradiction between Catholicism and Protestantism regarded as a renewal of the Church in the 16th cent. by an appeal to the Scriptures as interpreted by the early Fathers of the Church. This definition obviously excludes Quakers, Christian Scientists, and many Nonconformist sects.

The Roman Catholic Church is the religious organization of all those who acknowledge the bishop of Rome as head of the Christian Church, recognizing him as the lawful successor of St. Peter, who was the apostle appointed by Christ to be the head of the Church. Whereas in the Protestant Churches prayer and preaching play a central part (each individual soul seeking direct communication with God), in Roman Catholic worship the central service is the Mass, or Holy Eucharist, the seven sacraments (baptism, confirmation, eucharist, penance, extreme unction, orders, and marriage) being administered by a special priesthood. Church discipline and organisation are strong and authoritarian. *See* Papal Infallibility.

Catholic Apostolic Church, a body of Christians which originated in England c. 1831, founded on the teaching of Edward Irving (d. 1834). They disapprove of the term " Irvingites " by which they are sometimes known. The common doctrines of Christianity are accepted; symbolism and mystery characterise the elaborate liturgy, and lights and incense are used.

Characterology, the attempt made over many centuries to classify people into personality types on the basis of physical or psychological characteristics. The first attempt was made by Hippocrates in the 5th cent. B.C. who classified temperaments into the *sanguine* (or optimistic), the *melancholic*, the *choleric* (or aggressive), and the *phlegmatic* (or placid); these were supposed to result from the predominance of the following " humours " in the body: red blood, black bile, yellow bile, or phlegm respectively. Theophrastus, a pupil of Aristotle, described, with examples, thirty extreme types of personality (e.g. the talkative, the boorish, the miserly, etc.); these were basically literary and imaginative but about the same time " physiognomy " arose which attempted to interpret character from the face. Physiognomy became of importance again during the Renaissance and there are still those today who believe in it in spite of the fact that, broadly speaking, there is no connection whatever between facial features and personality (i.e. although it may be possible to tell from the features that a man is an idiot or some extreme abnormal type and some idea of character may be obtained from an individual's characteristic facial expressions, it is not possible to tell (as Johann Lavater, the best-known physiognomist of the late 18th cent. believed) from the shape of the nose, height of the brow, or dominance of the lower jaw, whether anyone is weak, intellectual, or determined). The contention of the 19th cent. Italian criminologist Cesare Lombroso that criminals show typical facial characteristics—prominent cheekbones and jaw, slanting eyes, receding brow, large ears of a particular shape—was disproved by Karl Pearson early this century when he found that 3,000 criminals showed no significant differences of features, carefully measured, from a similar number of students at Oxford and Cambridge.

It has, however, been noted that people in

general tend to be intellectual or emotional, inward- or outward-looking, and this observation is reflected in the classifications of the Scottish psychologist, Alexander Bain (d. 1903), into intellectual, artistic, and practical; Nietzsche's Apollonian and Dionysian types; William James's "tender" and "tough-minded"; and C. G. Jung's introvert and extrovert. Careful experiments have shown that these are not clear-cut and that most individuals fall in between the extremes.

Some connection has been found between temperament and body-build. The German psychiatrist Ernst Kretschmer (b. 1888) showed that manic-depressive patients and normal people who are extroverted and tend to alternate in mood (as do manic-depressives to an exaggerated degree) were usually short and stout or thick-set in build; schizophrenics and normal people, who both show shyness, serious or introverted reactions, were usually tall and slender. The former of "pyknic" body-build are "cyclothyme" in temperament, the latter with "schizothyme" temperament are of two bodily types—the tall and thin or "asthenic" and the muscularly well-proportioned or "athletic." The American Sheldon has confirmed these observations on the whole and gone into further details. According to him the basic body types are: (1) *endomorphic* (rounded build), corresponding to Kretschmer's pyknic, normally associated with the *viscerotonic* temperament (relaxed, sociable); (2) *mesomorphic* (squarish, athletic build), normally associated with the *somatotonic* temperament (energetic, assertive); and (3) *ectomorphic* (linear build) normally associated with the *cerebrotonic* temperament (anxious, submissive, restless). Sheldon may have been over-enthusiastic in his original claims, but there is no doubt that a close relation exists between bodily constitution and temperament. *See also* **Q5(1).**

**Chartism,** a socialistic movement in England (1837–55) which attempted to better the conditions of the working classes. Named after "The People's Charter" of Francis Place (1838), its programme demanded: (1) universal manhood suffrage; (2) vote by ballot; (3) equal electoral districts; (4) annual parliaments; (5) payment of members; (6) abolition of their property qualifications. Chartism was supported by the Christian socialists (*q.v.*), J. F. D. Maurice (1805–72), and Charles Kingsley (1819–75) with certain qualifications.

**Chauvinism,** a term applied to any excessive devotion to a cause, particularly a patriotic or military one. The word is derived from Nicholas Chauvin whose excessive devotion to Napoleon made him a laughing-stock.

**Chirognomy,** the attempt to read character from the lines in the hand (as contrasted with **Chiromancy,** the superstitious attempt to foretell the future in the same way) has few supporters, and not many psychologists would accept that handwriting reveals character in any way that is of practical use. It is highly probable that everything about an individual's acts or productions is *potentially* capable of revealing something about his character; the practical question is whether at present we can interpret them and it is ordinarily agreed that, in the case of the hand and handwriting, we cannot.

**Christadelphians,** a religious denomination formed in the U.S.A. about 1848 at the time of the American Civil War by John Thomas, an Englishman from London. They claim to represent the simple apostolic faith of the 1st cent., and, in common with many other sects, hold that they alone interpret the Scriptures truly. None but those who share their beliefs will rise from the dead and enjoy immortal life when Christ returns after the battle at Armageddon when His kingdom will be established on earth with its capital in Jerusalem. The political events of our time are regarded as fulfilments of biblical prophecies preceding the millennial reign of Christ over the earth. For them heaven and hell do not exist. In social life Christadelphians keep to themselves and hold aloof from organisational activities, though they do take an interest in political events if only from the point of view of their belief in biblical prophecy.

**Christianity,** the religion founded by Jesus Christ whose teaching is found in the New Testament's four Gospels. Simple as His creed may seem it soon became complicated by the various ways in which Christians interpreted it, and the

Early Christian Church
|
(Church of the Roman Empire)
*4th cent.*

*3rd–7th cent. Schisms in the East.*
Controversies concerned with the relation of Jesus Christ to God and to man: Arianism, Nestorianism, Monophysitism. Monotheletism

| Nestorian Church | Armenian Church | Jacobite Church | Coptic Church |

*Great Schism* 1054

Western Christendom
*Latin*
Rome

Eastern Christendom
*Greek*
Constantinople

*Mediaeval Inquisition began c.* 1231

Orthodox Eastern Church

*Spanish Inquisition began* 1481

*Counter Reformation and Inquisition at Rome,* 16*th cent.*          *Reformation,* 16*th*–17*th cent.*          *Renaissance* 15*th cent.*

Roman Catholic Church          Protestantism          Humanism

Moravians     Lutherans     Calvinists     Church of England     (*Henry VIII's break with Rome* 1534. *Excommunication of Elizabeth* 1570)

Presbyterians

*Nonconformism*

Baptists     Congregationalists     Methodists     Evangelicals     Modernists     Anglo-Catholics differences within the early Church are reflected in the numerous Councils held to define truth from heresy. The Eastern Church of the Byzantine Empire from the 5th cent. onwards had differed in various ways from the See of Rome and by 1054 the breach became permanent. The 16th cent. Reformation was the other great break in the unity of the Church and once Protestantism had given in effect the right to each man to interpret the Scriptures in his own way, the tendency to fragmentation increased so that, by 1650, there were no fewer than 180 sects, mostly dogmatic and intolerant towards each other. Today there are many more, some of which are mentioned in this section under the appropriate headings. Nevertheless there are signs today that the trend of disunity is being reversed. The modern ecumenical movement, which has its roots in the great missionary movement of the 19th cent., aims to bring about a reunion of Christendom by uniting Christians throughout the world on the simple basis of the acceptance of Jesus Christ as God and Saviour, i.e., on the basis of Christian fellowship. The movement finds expression in the World Council of Churches (q.v.). The Christian life is expressed in the words of Christ: " Thou shalt love the Lord thy God with all thy heart and thy neighbour as thyself." For many it is the humanitarian side of Christianity that has meaning today: to accept responsibility for others, as well as for oneself.

**Christian Democrats,** a term describing the members of moderate Roman Catholic political parties existing under various names in Belgium, France, the German Federal Republic (most German Protestants are in East Germany), Italy, and the Netherlands. In several of these countries they are the largest parliamentary party, their platform being based on a programme of moderate social reform advocated by members who in many cases have been active in wartime resistant movements. In spite of efforts of Dr. Adenauer of Germany and Sr. Fanfari of Italy in 1955 a Christian Democratic International failed to develop.

**Christian Science,** a religious denomination founded by Mary Baker Eddy (1821–1910), an American lady who sought to organise a church which would reinstate primitive Christianity and its lost element of healing. The sacred book of the movement is *Science and Health with Key to the Scriptures* published by Mrs. Eddy. Its main tenets are that nothing is real save God; that man's essential nature is spiritual and wholly good; that matter, evil, disease, and sickness are unreal—illusions of our mortal minds due to " wrong thinking." Therefore doctors, medicine, surgery and drugs are rejected as irrelevant, spiritual healing being the only cure for what is really mental error. Spiritual healing is claimed to have been brought about in many diseases by Mrs. Eddy herself, by the reading of her book, and, today, by Christian Science practitioners. The name of the movement is misleading since it has nothing to do with any of the natural sciences of which Mrs. Eddy had no first-hand knowledge. Mrs. Eddy was first interested in spiritualism, and afterwards, having been a patient of a faith-healer named Quimby, to whom she was indebted more than she cared to admit, she put herself forward as a mind-healer, claiming that she herself had been divinely healed. The denomination is apparently a wealthy one with widespread membership; its excellent newspaper, the *Christian Science Monitor*, read by many outside the movement, gives well-written accounts of all the world events we imagine to be going on around us.

**Christian Socialism,** a movement launched in 1848, a year of revolutions throughout the continent, by a group in England designed to commit the Church to a programme of social reform. The leaders, notably J. F. D. Maurice, Charles Kingsley (both Anglican clergymen), and John Ludlow were deeply moved by the wretched conditions of the British working class and the two priests had, indeed, given active support to the Chartist movement (q.v.). However, all insisted that socialism in its existing forms ignored the spiritual needs of mankind and must be tempered with Christianity. Tracts were written to expose the sweated industries, the consequences of unrestrained competition, and the evils following the enclosure system; but, more concretely, Christian socialism fostered co-operative workshops and distributive societies based on those of the Rochdale pioneers, organised a working-man's college and set up elementary classes for education, and supported the trade-union movement's right to organise and bargain for its members.

The traditions of Christian socialism have been carried on by the Fabian Society, by adherents of Guild Socialism, and by individuals who reject Marx's teaching of revolutionary change, and seek to bring it about by the methods of action through political parties, education, and encouragement of the unions. They believe that Christ's teachings can only be fully realised in a new society since Christianity implies social responsibility, and material factors are admitted to have an important bearing on the ability to lead a truly religious life. In the U.S.A. the eminent theologians Paul Tillich and Reinhold Niebuhr support these views. The factory-padre in Britain and the Catholic worker-priests of France bear evidence to the continuing influence of the early movement. In England the Christian Socialist Movement (CSM) was revived in 1960 by the coming together of organisations like the Socialist Christian League and the Society for Socialist Clergy and Ministers. *See also* Fabian Society, Guild Socialism.

**Church of England.** There is some evidence of possible continuity with the Christianity of Roman Britain, but in the main the Church derives from the fusion of the ancient Celtic church with the missionary church of St. Augustine, who founded the See of Canterbury in A.D. 597. To archbishop Theodore in 673 is ascribed its organisation in dioceses with settled boundaries, and in parishes. St. Augustine's church was in communion with Rome from the first, but the Church of England was not brought within papal jurisdiction until after the Norman conquest, and was at no time under the complete domination of Rome. It remains the Catholic Church of England without break of continuity, but during the Reformation the royal supremacy was accepted and that of the pope repudiated. It is the Established Church (i.e., the official church of the realm), crowns the sovereign, and its archbishops and bishops in the House of Lords can act as a kind of " conscience of the state " at every stage of legislation. The policy of religious toleration has been accepted since the 16th cent. The Church is organised in two ecclesiastical provinces (Canterbury and York) and 43 dioceses. Its form of worship is embodied in the Book of Common Prayer.

The Anglican Communion comprises the churches in all parts of the world which are in communion with the Church of England. All the bishops of the Anglican Communion meet every ten years in the Lambeth Conference (first held in 1867), over which the Archbishop of Canterbury by custom presides as *primus inter pares*. The theme of the 1968 Conference was " The Renewal of the Church," and for the first time observers and laymen were admitted.

**Church of Scotland,** the established national church of Scotland, presbyterian in constitution, and governed by a hierarchy of courts—the kirk-sessions, the presbyteries, the synods, and the General Assembly. *See* Presbyterianism.

**Clairvoyance.** *See* Telepathy.

**Communism,** ideally refers to the type of society in which all property belongs to the community and social life is based on the principle " from each according to his ability, to each according to his needs." Since no such society as yet exists, the word in practice refers to the Communist Party's attempt to achieve such a society by initially overthrowing the capitalist system and establishing a dictatorship of the proletariat. The modern movement is based on Marxism as further developed by Lenin who applied Marx's analysis to the new conditions which had arisen in 20th cent. capitalist society. Noting the large trusts and combines which (according to the Marxian " theory of concentration ") with their large concentrations of capital were ousting the small producers of an earlier stage. Lenin concluded that the state (representing the ruling class) and these large capital interests were collaborating in imperialist policies which would inevitably lead to recurrent wars; that the skilled worker would become more important and, receiving higher wages, would betray the proletariat by moving to the right; and that the poorer workers would continue to support revolutionary socialism. Communists believe that their first task is the establishment of socialism under which there remain class distinctions, private property to some extent, and differences between manual and brain workers. The state is regulated on the basis "from each according to his ability, to each according to his work." In time this gives place to communism as described above and the state will wither away. Marxism–Leninism develops continuously with practice since failure to apply its basic principles to changed circumstances and times would result in errors of dogmatism. Two fundamental principles of communism are (1) peaceful co-existence between countries of different social systems, and (2) the class struggle between oppressed and oppressing classes and between oppressed and oppressor nations. China, for example, holds that it is a mistake to lay one-sided stress on peaceful transition towards socialism otherwise the revolutionary will of the proletariat becomes passive and unprepared politically and organisationally for the tasks ahead. *See also* Trotskyism.

**Confessional Church,** Lutherans in Germany who, led by Pastor Niemöller (b. 1892), opposed those teachings of the Nazi regime which they found incompatible with Christianity.

**Confucianism.** Confucius (Latinised form of K'ung-Fu-tzu) was born in 551 B.C. in the feudal state of Lu in modern Shantung province. He was thus a contemporary of Buddha, although nobody could have been more dissimilar. Where Buddha was metaphysical in his thought, Confucius was practical; Buddha was original, Confucius had hardly an original idea in his head; Buddha wanted to convert individuals to an other-worldly philosophy, Confucius wanted to reform the feudal governments of his time, believing that in this way their subjects would be made happier. Other religions have, in their time, been revolutionary; Confucius was a conservative who wanted to bring back a golden age from the past. The only respect in which Confucius agreed with the Buddha was that neither was particularly interested in the supernatural, and God or gods played little part in their religions.

Much of his time was spent in going from the court of one feudal lord to another trying to impress them by his example. For he suffered from the curious belief that the example set by the ruler influences his subjects. He made much of etiquette, trembling and speaking in low tones before princes, at ease and polite with his equals, and behaving with "lofty courtesy" to his inferiors. Promoting the idea of "the golden mean," he was not impressed by heroic deeds or unusual people, and was greatly displeased when he heard that a truthful son had reported that his father had stolen a sheep: "Those who are upright," he said, "are different from this; the father conceals the misconduct of the son, and the son conceals the misconduct of the father." One feels that Confucius would have felt not at all out of place in an English public school. Virtue brings its own reward in this world, ceremonial is important, politeness when universal would reduce jealousy and quarrels: "reverence the spirits but keep them far off." Destiny decides to what class a man shall belong, and as destiny is but another name for Nature prayer is unnecessary, for once having received his destiny, a man can demand and obtain from Nature what he chooses—his own will determines all things.

Although not very successful in his lifetime so far as the rulers were concerned, Confucius found numerous disciples before his death at the age of 70 who collected his teachings which are found, together with those of his later follower Mencius (372–289 B.C.), in the *Wu Ching* (five classics), and the *Shih Shu* (four books) which contain the Analects, The Great Learning, The Doctrine of the Mean, and the Book of Mencius. In time Confucianism became with Taoism and Buddhism one of the main religions in China. Unlike Buddhism it had little influence elsewhere.

**Congregationalists,** the oldest sect of Nonconformists who hold that each church should be independent of external ecclesiastical authority. They took their origin from the Brownists of Elizabeth's days. Robert Browne (*c.* 1550–*c.* 1633), an Anglican clergyman, who had come to reject bishops, was forced with his followers to seek refuge, first in Holland and then in Scotland where he was imprisoned by the Kirk. In later life he changed his views and is disowned by Congregationalists because of his reversion to Anglicanism. His former views were spread by Henry Barrow and John Greenwood who, under an Act passed in 1592 "for the punishment of persons obstinately refusing to come to church" (and largely designed for the suppression of this sect), were hanged at Tyburn. They had preached (*a*) that the only head of the church is Jesus Christ; (*b*) that, contrary to Elizabethan doctrine, the church had no relationship to the state; (*c*) that the only statute-book was the Bible whereas the Articles of Religion and the Common Prayer were mere Acts of Parliament; (*d*) that each congregation of believers was independent and had the power of choosing its own ministers. The body fled once more to Holland and were among the Pilgrims who set sail in the *Mayflower* for America in 1620 whilst those who remained were joined by Puritans fleeing from Charles I. They became free once more to live in England under the Commonwealth only to be repressed again under Charles II. Finally full liberty of worship was granted under William III. In 1833 the Congregational Union of England and Wales was formed which has no legislative power. It has issued a Declaration of Faith by which no minster is bound; he is responsible to his own church and to nobody else. The sect is widespread both in Britain and the U.S.A. where it is held in special honour because of its connection with the Pilgrim Fathers.

**Conservatism.** The name "Conservative" came into general use after 1834 in place of the older name of "Tory," although "Tory democracy" is now widely used to describe Conservative social reform policy. Originally the party of the aristocracy and landed gentry, Conservatism has been supported from the end of the 19th cent. by the large business interests, and more recently by lower-income groups in the population. Although originally based upon the teachings of Burke and Disraeli, Conservative doctrine has been considerably modified, especially since 1945 after defeat by the socialists. The Party's industrial policy seeks to reconcile the need for central direction with encouragement of individual enterprise, best described perhaps as "welfare capitalism." The Conservatives increased their parliamentary strength in three successive general elections from 1951–59, but were defeated by Labour in 1964 and 1966. On the continent, Conservatism has generally been identified with fear of social progress, exaggerated respect for authority, and nationalism; such parties have more often than not been extremely reactionary and anti-democratic. *See also* Section C, Part I.

**Coptic Church,** the sect of Egyptian Christians who, holding "Monophysite" opinions (*i.e.*, refusing to grant the two natures, God and Man, of Christ), were declared heretical by the Council of Chalcedon in 451. They practise circumcision and have dietary laws. Their language is a direct descendant of ancient Egyptian. Like the Armenians, they are regarded as a heretical branch of Eastern Christianity. Their religious head is the patriarch of Alexandria.

**Cynics,** a school of philosophy founded in the time of Alexander the Great by Diogenes. Choosing to live like a dog by rejecting all conventions of religion, manners, or decency, and allegedly living in a tub, Diogenes unwittingly brought on his school the title "Cynic," meaning not "cynical," as the word is understood today, but "canine." His teacher, Antisthenes, who had been a disciple of Socrates, decided, after the latter's death, that all philosophy was useless quibbling and man's sole aim should be simple goodness. He believed in a return to nature, despised luxury, wanted no government, no private property, and associated with working men and slaves. Far from being cynics in the modern sense, Diogenes and Antisthenes were virtuous anarchists rather like old Tolstoy (except that in the practice of their beliefs they were more consistent).

# D

**Darwinism.** *See* Section F, Part II. *See also* Vitalism.

**Deism.** *See* God and Man.

**Demonism, Demons, and the Devil.** Demons are ethereal beings of various degrees of significance and power which are believed to be implicated in men's good, but especially evil, fortune. They are common to most cultures. From the anthropological point of view the demon arose as a widespread concept in the following ways: (1) as a psychological projection into the outer world of man's own good or evil emotions and thoughts; (2) as a survival of primitive animism (*q.v.*), thus spirits are believed to haunt places, trees, stones, and other natural objects; (3) when by warlike invasion the gods of the vanquished become the devils of the conquerors (as when the Jews occupied Canaan); (4) as a primitive belief that spirits of the dead continue after death to hover near their former habitation, and not always entirely welcome to the living; (5) the conception of a supreme source of evil (the Devil or Satan) which took shape among the Jews during their sojourn in Babylon under the influence of Zoroastrianism (*q.v.*), a religion in which the struggle between the two spirits, Good and Evil, reached its height in the imagination of the ancient world. The Satan of the Old Testament was first regarded as one of God's servants (in the Book of Job he goes up and down the earth to see whether God's commands are obeyed), but when the Jews returned from their captivity he had become identified with Ahriman, the spirit of evil, who was in continual conflict with Ahura Mazda, the spirit of good. As Dr. Margaret Murray has pointed out, the primitive mind ascribed both good and evil to one power alone: the division into God and the Devil, priest and witch, belongs to a higher stage of civilisation. *See also* Witchcraft, Magic.

**Determinism and Free-will.** The question of whether man is, or is not, free to mould his own destiny is one which has exercised the minds of philosophers since Greek mythology conceived of the Fates as weaving a web of destiny from which no man can free himself. Socrates emphasised that man could through knowledge influence his destiny whilst ignorance made him the plaything of fate; Plato went further in pointing out that man can, and does, defeat the purposes of the universe and its divine Creator. It is our duty to live a good life, but we can live a foolish and wicked one if we choose. Aristotle wrote " Virtue is a disposition or habit involving deliberate purpose or choice." If this were not so morality would be a sham.

*The Problem for Theology.* The last of the great philosophers of antiquity and one of the great influences in moulding Catholic theology was Plotinus (*c.* 204–270). Soul, he taught, is free, but once enmeshed in the body loses its freedom in the life of sense. Nevertheless, man is free to turn away from sensuality and towards God who is perfect freedom; for even when incarnated in matter the soul does not entirely lose the ability to rescue itself. This conception was carried over into the beliefs of the Early Christian Apologists because it appeared to be in line with the teaching of Jesus that He had come to save man from sin. Sin implies guilt, and guilt implies the freedom to act otherwise; furthermore an all-good God cannot be responsible for the sin in the world which must be man's responsibility and this again implies freedom. Pelagius (*c.* 355–*c.* 425), a Welsh priest, not only believed in freewill but, questioning the doctrine of original sin, said that when men act righteously it is through their own moral effort, and God rewards them for their virtues in heaven. This belief became fairly widespread and was declared a heresy by

the Church, being attacked notably by St. Augustine (354–430), a contemporary of Pelagius, who believed in predestination—that, since the sin of Adam, God had chosen who in all future history would be saved and who damned. This represents one tradition in Christianity: the determinism which leads to Calvinism (*q.v.*). St. Thomas Aquinas (1227–74), the greatest figure of scholasticism and one of the principal saints in the Roman Catholic Church, compromised between the two positions in the sense that, believing man to be free, he yet held that Adam's sin was transmitted to all mankind and only divine grace can bring salvation. But even when God wishes to bestow this salvation, the human will must co-operate. God foresees that some will not accept the offer of grace and predestines them to eternal punishment.

*The Problem for Philosophy.* With the Renaissance, thinkers began to free themselves from the domination of the Church and to study the world objectively and freely without preconceptions. But the more man turned to science, the more he discovered that the world was ruled by apparently inexorable laws and, since the scientist must believe that every event has a cause, he was led back to determinism. Man as part of the universe was subject to law too and all that existed was a vast machine. Francis Bacon (1561–1626) separated the fields of religion and science but left man subject completely to the will of God. Thomas Hobbes (1588–1679) was a rigid determinist and materialist although, having had trouble with the church in France whence, as a royalist, he had fled, he took care to announce that the Christian God is the Prime Mover.

Modern philosophy begins with René Descartes (1596–1650), a Frenchman who tried to reconcile the mechanical scientific universe of his time with the spiritual need for freedom. He did this by separating completely mind and body; the former, he said, is free, the latter completely determined. But, by admitting that the will can produce states of body, he was left with the problem of how this could happen—a problem which the so-called Occasionists solved to their own satisfaction by stating that the will is free and God so arranges the universe that what a person wills happens. Baruch Spinoza (1632–77), a Dutch Jew whose independence of thought had led to his excommunication from the Amsterdam Synagogue in 1656, was a complete determinist. He asserted that God and Nature are one, everything that happens is a manifestation of God's inscrutable nature, and it is logically impossible that things could be other than they are. Thus both Hobbes and Spinoza were determinists for entirely opposed reasons. The former as a materialist, the latter because he believed in the absolute perfection and universality of God. Yet the great religious mystic and mathematician Blaise Pascal (1623–62) held that, no matter what reason and cold logic may indicate, we *know* from direct religious experience that we are free. John Calvin (1509–64) and Martin Luther (1483–1546) were both determinists. *See* Calvinism, Lutheranism.

To the more practical British philosophers, John Locke (1632–1704) and David Hume (1711–76), free-will was related to personality. Locke believed that God had implanted in each individual certain desires and these determine the will; the desires are already there, but we use our will to satisfy them. Hume argued that a man's behaviour is the necessary result of his character and if he had a different character he would act otherwise. Accordingly, when a man's actions arise from his own nature and desires he is free. He is not free when external events compel him to act otherwise (*e.g.*, if he strikes another because his own nature is such he is free as he is not if he is compelled to do so against his desire). Leibnitz (1646–1716), although as a German metaphysical philosopher holding very different general views, said much the same thing—that choice is simply selecting the desire that is strongest. But most of the 18th cent. from Voltaire onwards, with the great exceptions of Rousseau and the later German philosophers Kant, Fichte, Schopenhauer, and Hegel, who were initially influenced by him.

accepted determinism. Rousseau (1712–78) began to stem the tide by his declaration that man is a free soul striving to remain free and only prevented from being so by society and the cold science which stifles his feeling heart. Once again the will became important as Kant (1724–1804) asserted that belief in freedom is a moral necessity although it cannot be proved by reason; the moral nature of man shows that there is a " transcendental " world beyond the senses where freedom applies. Fichte and Schelling found freedom in the Absolute ego or God of whom each individual was part and thus also free. Hegel (1770–1831) saw the whole universe as evolving towards self-awareness and freedom in man although this could only be fully realised in a society that makes for freedom. Even God himself only attains full consciousness and self-realisation through the minds of such individuals as are free. This is the goal of the dialectical process. (*See* Dialectical Materialism.)

*The Scientist's View.* For the scientist the law of cause and effect is a useful hypothesis since, by and large, it is necessary for him to assume that all events are caused. Nevertheless the modern tendency is to think in terms of statistical probability rather than relentless mechanistic causality, and, although the free-will problem does not concern the scientist as such, it is clear that freedom and determinism (assuming the terms to have any meaning at all) are not necessarily opposed. In sociology, for example, we *know* that certain actions will produce certain results upon the behaviour of people in general, *e.g.*, that raising the bank rate will discourage business expansion. But this does not mean that Mr. Brown who decides in the circumstances not to add a new wing to his factory is not using his free-will. Even in the case of atoms, as Dr. Bronowski has pointed out, the observed results of allowing gas under pressure in a cylinder to rush out occur because most of the atoms are " obeying " the scientific " law " relating to such situations. But this does not mean that some atoms are not busy rushing across the stream or even against it—they are, but the general tendency is outwards and that is what we note. Lastly, the modern philosophical school of Logical Analysis would probably ask, not whether Free-will or Determinism is the true belief, but whether the question has any meaning. For what scientific experiment could we set up to prove one or the other true? The reader will note that some of the philosophers mentioned above are using the words to mean quite different concepts.

Dialectical Materialism, the combination of Hegel's dialectic method with a materialist philosophy produced by Karl Marx (1818–93) and his friend Friedrich Engels (1820–95). It is the philosophical basis of Marxism (*q.v.*) and Communism (*q.v.*). " Dialectic " to the ancient Greek philosophers meant a kind of dialogue or conversation, as used particularly by Socrates, in which philosophical disputes were resolved by a series of successive contradictions: a thesis is put forward and the opposing side holds its contradiction or antithesis until in the course of argument a synthesis is reached in which the conflicting ideas are resolved.

*From Thesis through Antithesis to Synthesis.* Hegel in the 19th cent. put forward the view that this process applies to the course of nature and history as they strive towards the perfect state. But to him, as to the Greeks, the conflict was in the field of ideas. The " universal reason " behind events works through the ideas held by a particular society until they are challenged by those of another which supersedes them and in turn, usually by war, becomes the agent of universal reason until the arrival of a new challenger. Hegel therefore regarded war as an instrument of progress and his Prussian compatriots found no difficulty in identifying their own state as the new agent of progress by universal conquest. Feuerbach, Lassalle, and other early socialists were impressed by some of Hegel's ideas: *e.g.*, that societies evolved (with the assumption that finally their own ideal society would be achieved) and that truth, morals, and concepts were relative so that a type of society that was

" good " at one time was not necessarily so at another. But Marx and Engels in effect turned Hegel upside-down, accepted his dialectic but rejected his belief that ideas were the motive force. On the contrary, they said, ideas are determined by social and economic change as a result of materialistic forces. (*See* Calvinism, where it is pointed out that the Marxist view is not that Calvin changed men's economic ideas but rather that a developing capitalism unconsciously changed his.) The historical materialism of Marxism purports to show that the inexorable dialectic determines that feudalism is displaced by capitalism and capitalism by creating a proletariat (its antithesis) inevitably leads to socialism and a classless society. The state, as a tool of the dominant class, withers away. Dialectical materialism is applied in all spheres. As a philosophy there is little to be said for it save that it has shown us the close dependence of man's thoughts upon current material and social conditions. But as a battle-cry or a rationalisation of Marxism it wields immense power over the minds of men. *See* Marxism.

Diggers, one of the many sects which flourished under the Commonwealth (others were the Muggletonians, the Levellers, the Millenarians, and the Fifth Monarchy Men), so-called because they attempted to dig (*i.e.* cultivate) untilled land. Gerrard Winstanley, a profoundly religious man, and leader of the Diggers, believed in the economic and social equality of man and castigated the clergy for upholding the class structure of society. In his book *The True Leveller's Standard Advanced* (1649) he wrote: " Every day poor people are forced to work for fourpence a day, though corn is dear. And yet the tithing priest stops their mouth and tells them that ' inward satisfaction of mind ' was meant by the declaration ' the poor shall inherit the earth'. I tell you, the Scripture is to be really and materially fulfilled. You jeer at the name ' Leveller '; I tell you Jesus Christ is the Head Leveller."

Disciples of Christ, a Protestant religious group founded in the United States early in the 19th century by Thomas Campbell, a Scot, his son Alexander, and Barton Warren Stone who had broken away from the Presbyterian church. The basis for faith and conduct is the Bible itself, each individual interpreting it for himself. The group has always had a liberal reputation and stands for racial equality and Christian unity. The Disciples of Christ Church is particularly strong in the central and western states of America.

Docetists, a Gnostic sect (*q.v.*) during the early centuries of Christianity who believed that, since it was unworthy that the Son of God should have died a humiliating death on the cross, the entity that was crucified was a mere phantom. Mohammed, who believed in Jesus as a prophet but not as divine, adopted these views. The heretical Albigenses were influenced by Docetism, Gnosticism, and Manichaeism (*qq.v.*).

Doukhobors, a religious sect of Russian origin, founded by a Prussian sergeant at Kharkov in the middle of the 18th cent., and now mainly settled in Canada. Like many other sects they belong to that type of Christianity which seeks direct communication with God and such bodies tend to have certain traits in common, such as belief in the " inner light," opposition to war and authority in general, and often ecstasies which show themselves in physical ways such as shaking, speaking in strange tongues (glossolalia), and other forms of what to the unbeliever seem mass hysteria. Liturgy, ritual, or ceremony is non-existent. The Doukhobors were persecuted in Tsarist Russia, but in 1898 Tolstoy used his influence to have them removed to Canada where the government granted them uninhabited land in what is now Saskatchewan and seven or eight thousand settled down in peace which they enjoyed for many years. Recently, however, their practices have caused difficulties once more; for even the most tolerant government which is prepared to accept pacifism, total dependence on communally-owned agriculture, refusal to engage in commerce, non-payment of taxes, rejection of the marriage ceremony and separation " when love ceases," finds it difficult to tolerate, as civilisation advances ever closer to Doukhobor communities, their proneness to "put off these troublesome disguises which we wear"—*i.e.*, to walk about naked in the communities of their more orthodox neighbours. What the future of the Doukhobors in their various sects (for even they have their differences) will be it is impossible to say, but it is difficult to believe that these simple people can long resist the pressure of modern civilisation.

**Druidism**, the religion of Celtic Britain and Gaul of which Druids were the priesthood. They were finally wiped out by the Roman general Suetonius Paulinus about A.D. 58 in their last stronghold, the island of Anglesey. There are two sources of our present beliefs in Druidism: (1) the brief and factual records of the Romans, notably Pliny and Julius Caesar, which tell us that they worshipped in sacred oak groves and presumably practised a religion doing reverence to the powers of nature which must have had its roots in early stone age times and had many cruel rites *e.g.*, human sacrifice; (2) the beliefs put forward by William Stukeley, an amateur antiquarian who from 1718 did valuable work by his studies of the stone circles at Stonehenge and Avebury. However, influenced by the Romantic movement, he later put forward the most extravagant theories which unfortunately are those popularly accepted by those without archaelogical knowledge today. Stonehenge and Avebury were depicted as the temples of the "white-haired Druid bard sublime" and an attempt was made to tie up Druidism with early Christianity. above all with the concept of the Trinity. In fact, these circles have no connection with the Druids. They may have made ceremonial use of them but recent evidence suggests that the megalithic stones at Stonehenge (L109) belong to a Bronze Age culture (1860–1560 B.C.). Nor have Druidism and Christianity any relationship. Almost nothing is known of the religion. Yet such were its romantic associations that, even today, one hears of "Druidic" ceremonies practised at the appropriate time of year on Primrose Hill in the heart of London (though whether seriously or with tongue in cheek one does not know).

**Dualism**, any philosophical or theological theory which implies that the universe has a double nature, notably Plato's distinction between appearance and reality, soul and body, ideas and material objects, reason and the evidence of the senses, which infers that behind the world as we perceive it there lies an "ideal" world which is more "real" than that of mere appearance. In religions such as Zoroastrianism or the Gnostic and Manichaeism heresies (*qq.v*), it was believed that the universe was ruled by good and evil "principles"—in effect that there was a good God and a bad one. In psychology, dualism refers to the philosophical theories which believe mind and body to be separate entities. The opposite of dualism is monism which asserts the essential unity of the substance of the universe.

# E

**Ecumenism**, a world movement which springs from the Christian belief that all men are brothers and that the Christian Church should be re-structured to give reality to the belief. Christ's church exists not to serve its own members, but for the service of the whole world. Some see the answer in a united church of a federal type (unity in diversity), others in an organic structure with one set of rules. The period since the convening of the Second Vatican Council by Pope John has been one of fervent discussion among Christian theologians with the aim of promoting Christian unity. *See* **World Council of Churches.**

**Education.** Education was no great problem to primitive man, but as societies became more complex people began to ask themselves such questions as: *What* should young people be taught? *How* should they be taught? Should the aim of their education be to bring out their individual qualities or rather to make them good servants of the state?

The first teachers were priests who knew most

about the traditions, customs, and lore of their societies and thus the first schools were in religious meeting places. This was notably true of the Jews who learned from the rabbis in the synagogue, and throughout the Middle Ages in Christendom as will be seen later.

*The Greeks.* We begin, as always, with the Greeks whose city-states, based on slavery, educated men (not women) for the sort of life described in Plato's *Dialogues*—the leisured life of gentlemen arguing the problems of the universe at their banquets or in the market-place. This made it necessary to learn debate and oratory (or rhetoric) especially for those who proposed to take up politics. The Sophist philosophy taught the need to build up convincing arguments in a persuasive manner, to learn the rules of logic and master the laws and customs of the Athenians, and to know the literature of the past so that illustrations might be drawn from it. These strolling philosophers who taught for a fee were individualists showing the student how to advance himself at all costs within his community.

Socrates had a more ethical approach, believing that education was good in itself, made a man happier and a better citizen, and emphasised his position as a member of a group. His method of teaching, the dialectic or "Socratic" method. involved argument and discussion rather than overwhelming others by rhetoric and is briefly mentioned under **Dialectical Materialism** (*q.v.*). Today this method is increasingly used in adult education where a lecture is followed by a period of discussion in which both lecturer and audience participate; for psychologists have shown that people accept ideas more readily when conviction arises through their own arguments than when they are passively thrust down their throats.

Socrates' pupil Plato produced in his book *The Republic* one of the first comprehensive systems of education and vocational selection. Believing that men are of different and unequal abilities he considered that they should be put into social classes corresponding to these differences, and suggested the following method: (1) For the first 18 years of a boy's life he should be taught gymnastics and sports, playing and singing music, reading and writing, a knowledge of literature, and if he passed this course sent on to the next stage; those who failed were to become tradesmen and merchants. (2) From 18–20 those successful in the first course were to be given two years of cadet training, the ones thought incapable of further education being placed in the military class as soldiers. (3) The remainder, who were to become the leaders of society, proceeded with advanced studies in philosophy, mathematics, science, and art. Such education was to be a state concern, state supported and controlled, selecting men and training them for service in the state according to their abilities.

Plato's pupil Aristotle even suggested that the state should determine shortly after birth which children should be allowed to live and destroy the physically or mentally handicapped; that marriage should be state-controlled to ensure desirable offspring. However, in their time the leisured and individualistic Sophists held the field and few accepted the educational views of Plato or his pupil.

*Rome.* The Romans were not philosophers and most of their culture came from Greece. Administration was their chief aptitude and Quintilian (A.D. *c.* 35–*c.* 95) based his higher education on the earlier classical tuition in public speaking, but he is important for emphasising the training of character and for his humanistic approach to the method of teaching that caused his *Institutio oratoria* to be influential for centuries later—indeed one might almost say up to the time of the great Dr. Arnold of Rugby. Education, he believed, should begin early but one must "take care that the child not old enough to love his studies does not come to hate them" by premature forcing; studies must be made pleasant and interesting and students encouraged by praise rather than discouraged when they sometimes fail; play is to be approved of as a sign of a lively disposition and because gloomy, depressed children are not likely to be good students; corporal punishment should never be used because " it is an insult as you will realise if you imagine it yourself." The world became interested not in *what* he taught but *how* he taught it; he was the pioneer of humanistic education and character-training from Vittorino da Feltre (1378–1446) of Mantua, through Milton and Pope who commended his works, to the modern educationists who have studied their pupils as well as their books.

*The Middle Ages: The Religious View.* With the development of Christianity education once more became a religious problem. The earliest converts had to be taught Christian doctrine and were given instruction in " catechumenal " schools before admission to the group, but as the religion came increasingly into contact with other religions or heresies a more serious training was necessary, and from these newer " catechetical " schools, where the method used was the catechism (*i.e.*, question and answer as known to all Presbyterian children today), the Apologists arose among whom were Clement of Alexandria and the great Origen. From this time education became an instrument of the church and in 529 the Emperor Justinian ordered all pagan schools to be closed.

As typical of the best in mediaeval education whilst the lamp of civilisation burned low during the Dark Ages, after the fall of Roman power, and survived only in the monasteries, we may mention St. Benedict (*c.* 480–*c.* 547) of Monte Cassino. There, in southern Italy, a rule was established which became a part of monastic life in general. Monastic schools were originally intended for the training of would-be monks, but later others were admitted who simply wanted some education; thus two types of school developed, one for the *interni* and the other for *externi* or external pupils. Originally studies were merely reading in order to study the Bible, writing to copy the sacred books, and sufficient calculation to be able to work out the advent of holy days or festivals. But by the end of the 6th cent. the " seven liberal arts " (grammar, rhetoric, dialectic, arithmetic, geometry, music, and astronomy) were added.

*The Renaissance.* The close of the Middle Ages saw the development of two types of secular school. One came with the rise of the new merchant class and the skilled trader whose " guilds " or early trade unions established schools to train young men for their trades but ultimately gave rise to burgher or town schools; the other was the court school founded and supported by the wealthy rulers of the Italian cities—Vittorino da Feltre (mentioned above) presided over the most famous at Mantua.

These Renaissance developments are paralleled in northern Europe by the Protestant reformers who, having with Martin Luther held that everyone should know how to read his Bible in order to interpret it in his own way, were logically committed to popular education, compulsory and universal. In theory this was intended for biblical study, but writing, arithmetic, and other elementary subjects were taught and Luther said that, even if heaven and hell did not exist, education was important. Universal education is a Protestant conception.

*Views of Philosophers.* From this period onwards people were free to put forward any ideas about education, foolish or otherwise, and to create their own types of school. Of English philosophers who theorised about, but did not practise, education we may mention the rationalist Francis Bacon (1561–1626) who saw learning as the dissipation of all prejudices and the collection of concrete facts; the materialist and totalitarian Hobbes (1588–1679) who, as a royalist, believed that the right to determine the kind of education fit for his subjects is one of the absolute rights of the sovereign power or ruler; the gentlemanly Locke (1632–1704) whose ideal was a sound mind in a sound body to be attained by hard physical exercise, wide experience of the world, and enough knowledge to meet the requirements of the pupil's environment. The end result would be one able to get on with his fellows, pious but wise in the ways of the world, independent and able to look after himself, informed but reticent about his

knowledge. Classics and religious study were not to be carried to excess, since Locke held that these subjects had been overrated in the past. Locke's pupil was the well-to-do, civilised young man of the 17th cent. who knew how to behave in society.

Jean-Jacques Rousseau (1712–78) (*q.v.*), a forerunner of the Romantic movement, which despised society and its institutions, put emotion at a higher level than reason. His book *Émile* describes the education of a boy which is natural and spontaneous. Society, he holds, warps the growing mind and therefore the child should be protected from its influences until his development in accordance with his own nature is so complete that he cannot be harmed by it. During the first 4 years the body should be developed by physical training; from 5 to 12 the child would live in a state of nature such that he could develop his powers of observation and his senses; from 13 books would be used and intellectual training introduced, although only in line with the child's own interests, and he would be given instruction only as he came to ask for it. Moral training and contact with his fellows to learn the principles of sympathy, kindness, and helpfulness to mankind would be given between 15 and 20. Girls, however, should be educated to serve men in a spirit of modesty and restraint. His own five children he deposited in a foundling hospital.

*Summary.* Broadly speaking, then, there have been four main attitudes to education: (1) religious, with a view to a life beyond death; (2) state-controlled education, with a view to uniform subservience to authority; (3) " gentlemanly " education, with a view to social graces and easy congress in company; (4) the " child-centred " education, which attempts to follow the pupil's inner nature. It is unnecessary to mention the ordinary method of attempting to instil facts without any considerable degree of co-operation between pupil and teacher in order that the former may, with or without interest, follow some occupation in adult life; for this the philosophers did not consider. Today there remain the two fundamental principles: education for the advantage of the state and its ideology or education for individual development and freedom.

Four educationists of the modern period who have influenced us in the direction of freedom were Johann Pestalozzi of Switzerland (1746–1827) who, by trying to understand children, taught the " natural, progressive, and harmonious development of all the powers and capacities of the human being "; Friedrich Froebel (1782–1852) of Germany, the founder of the Kindergarten who, like Pestalozzi, was influenced by Rousseau but realised the need to combine complete personal development with social adjustment; Maria Montessori (1869–1952) whose free methods have revolutionised infant teaching; John Dewey (1859–1952) who held that the best interests of the group are served when the individual develops his own particular talents and nature.

**Eleatics,** the philosophers of Elea in ancient Greece who, at the time when Heraclitus (*c.* 535–475 B.C.) was teaching that change is all that exists and nothing is permanent, were asserting that change is an illusion. Of the three leaders of this school, Xenophanes asserted that the universe was a solid immovable mass forever the same; Parmenides explained away change as an inconceivable process, its appearance being due to the fact that what we see is unreal; and Zeno (the best-known today) illustrated the same thesis with his famous argument of the arrow which, at any given moment of its flight, must be where it is since it cannot be where it is not. But if it is where it is, it cannot move; this is based, of course, on the delusion that motion is discontinuous. The Eleatics were contemporaries of Socrates.

**Empiricism.** While not a single school of philosophy, empiricism is an approach to knowledge which holds that if a man wants to know what the universe is like the only correct way to do so is to go and look for himself, to collect facts which come to him through his senses. It is, in essence, the method of science as contrasted with rationalism (q.v.) which in philosophy implies that thinking or reasoning without necessarily referring to external observations can arrive at truth. Empiricism is typically an English attitude, for among the greatest empirical philosophers were John Locke, George Berkeley, and David Hume. See Rationalism.

**Epicureanism.** The two great schools of the Hellenistic period (i.e. the late Greek period beginning with the empire of Alexander the Great) were the Stoics and Epicureans, the former founded by Zeno of Citium (not to be confused with Zeno the Eleatic) (q.v.), the latter by Epicurus, born in Samos in 342 B.C. Both schools settled in Athens, where Epicurus taught that " pleasure is the beginning and end of a happy life." However, he was no sensualist and emphasised the importance of moderation in all things because excesses would lead to pain instead of pleasure and the best of all pleasures were mental ones. Pleasures could be active or passive but the former contain an element of pain since they are the process of satisfying desires not yet satiated. The latter involving the absence of desire are the more pleasant. In fact, Epicurus in his personal life was more stoical than many Stoics and wrote " when I live on bread and water I spit on luxurious pleasures." He disapproved of sexual enjoyment and thought friendship one of the highest of all joys. A materialist who accepted the atomic theory of Democritus, he was not a determinist, and if he did not disbelieve in the gods he regarded religion and the fear of death as the two primary sources of unhappiness.

**Epiphenomenalism.** See Mind and Body.

**Erastianism,** the theory that the state has the right to decide the religion of its members, wrongly attributed to Erastus of Switzerland (1524–83) who was believed to have held this doctrine. The term has usually been made use of in a derogatory sense—e.g., by the Scottish churches which held that the " call " of the congregation was the only way to elect ministers at a time when, about the turn of the 17th and 18th cent., they felt that Episcopalianism was being foisted on them. " Episcopalianism " (i.e. Anglicanism) with its state church, ecclesiastical hierarchy, and system of livings presented by patrons was to them " Erastian " in addition to its other " unscriptural practices."

**Essenes,** a Jewish sect which, during the oppressive rule of Herod (d. 4 B.C.), set up monastic communities in the region of the Dead Sea. They refused to be bound by the scriptural interpretations of the Pharisees and adhered rigorously to the letter of Holy Writ, although with additions of their own which cause them by orthodox Jews today to be regarded as a break-away from Judaism. Among their practices and beliefs were purification through baptism, renunciation of sexual pleasures, scrupulous cleanliness, strict observance of the Mosaic law, communal possession, asceticism. Akin in spirit, although not necessarily identical with them, were the writers of Apocalyptic literature preaching that the evils of the present would shortly be terminated by a new supernatural order heralded by a Messiah who would reign over a restored Israel. The casting out of demons and spiritual healing formed part of these general beliefs which were in the air at that time. The sect has an importance far beyond its size or what has been known about it in the past since the discovery from 1947 onwards of the Dead Sea Scrolls (See Section L) of the Qumran community occupying a monastery in the same area as the Essenes and holding the same type of belief. These scrolls with their references to a " Teacher of Righteousness " preceding the Messiah have obvious relevance to the sources of early Christianity and have given rise to speculations as to whether Jesus might have been influenced by views which, like His own, were unacceptable to orthodox Jews but in line with those of the Dead Sea communities. At the very least they seem to show that early Christianity was not a sudden development but a gradual one which had its predecessors.

**Ethical Church,** a movement typical of 19th cent. rationalism which attempted to combine atheism (or at any rate the absence of any belief

in a God which was inconsistent with reason or based on revelation) with the inculcation of moral principles. Prayers were not used and ordinarily the service consisted in the singing of edifying compositions interspersed with readings from poems or prose of a similar nature by great writers holding appropriate views. It terminated in a talk on an ethical or scientific theme. There is an Ethical Church in London and the South Place Institution where Moncure Conway preached from 1864 to 1897 still exists.

**Ethnocentrism,** the exaggerated tendency to think the characteristics of one's own group or race superior to those of any others.

**Evangelicanism,** the belief of those Protestant sects which hold that the essence of the Gospel consists in the doctrine of salvation by faith in the atoning death of Christ and not by good works or the sacraments; that worship should be " free " rather than liturgical through established forms; that ritual is unacceptable and superstitious. Evangelicals are Low Churchmen.

**Evangelism,** the preaching of the Gospel, emphasising the necessity for a new birth or conversion. The evangelistic fervour of John Wesley and George Whitefield (see Methodism) aroused the great missionary spirit of the late 18th and 19th cent. George Fox, founder of the Society of Friends (q.v.), was also an evangelist. Evangelists can be Low, High, or Middle Churchmen.

**Existentialism,** a highly subjective philosophy which many people connect with such names as Jean-Paul Sartre (b. 1905) or Albert Camus (1913–60) and assume to be a post-war movement associated with disillusion and a sordid view of life. However, existentialism stems from Sören Kierkegaard (1813–55), the Danish " religious writer "—his own description of himself—in such works as Either/Or, Fear and Trembling, and Concluding Unscientific Postscript. Between the two wars translations of Kierkegaard into German influenced Martin Heidegger's (b. 1889) great work Being and Time and the other great existentialist Karl Jaspers (b. 1883); it has strongly influenced modern Protestant theology notably in Karl Barth, Reinhold Niebuhr, and Paul Tillich and beyond that field Gabriel Marcel (b. 1887), the Spanish writer Unamuno (1864–1936) in his well-known The Tragic Sense of Life, and Martin Buber of Israel (b. 1878) in his I and Thou. We have it on Heidegger's authority that " Sartre is no philosopher " even if it is to his works that modern existentialists often turn.

Existentialism is extremely difficult for the non-metaphysically-minded to understand; it deals, not with the nature of the universe or what are ordinarily thought of as philosophical problems but describes an attitude to life or God held by the individual. Briefly, its main essentials are: (1) it distinguishes between essence, i.e., that aspect of an entity which can be observed and known—and its existence—the fact of its having a place in a changing and dangerous world which is what really matters; (2) existence being basic, each self-aware individual can grasp his own existence on reflection in his own immediate experience of himself and his situation as a free being in the world; what he finds is not merely a knowing self but a self that fears, hopes, believes, wills, and is aware of its need to find a purpose, plan, and destiny in life; (3) but we cannot grasp our existence by thought alone; thus the fact " all men must die " relates to the essence of man but it is necessary to be involved, to draw the conclusion as a person that " I too must die " and experience its impact on our own individual existence; (4) because of the preceding, it is necessary to abandon our attitude of objectivity and theoretical detachment when faced by the problems relating to the ultimate purpose of our own life and the basis of our own conduct; life remains closed to those who take no part in it because it can have no significance; (5) it follows that the existentialist cannot be rationalist in his outlook for this is merely an escape into thought from the serious problems of existence; none of the important aspects of life—failure, evil, sin, folly—nor (in the view of Kierkegaard) even the existence of God or the truth of Christianity—can be proved by reason.

" God does not exist; He is eternal," was how he expressed it; (6) life is short and limited in space and time, therefore it is foolish to discuss in a leisurely fashion matters of life or death as if there were all eternity to argue them in. It is necessary to make a leap into the unknown, *e.g.*, accepting Christ (in the case of the Christian existentialist) by faith in the sense of giving and risking the self utterly. This means complete commitment, not a dependence on arguments as to whether certain historical events did, or did not, happen.

To summarise: existentialism of whatever type seems to the outsider to be an attitude to life concerning itself with the individual's ultimate problems (mine, not yours); to be anti-rationalist and anti-idealist (in the sense of being, as it seems to the believer, practical)—in effect it seems to say " life is too short to fool about with argument, you must dive in and become committed " to something. Sartre who calls himself an " atheist existentialist " is apparently committed to the belief that " hell is other people," but for most critics the main argument against existentialist philosophy is that it often rests on a highly specialised personal experience and, as such, is incommunicable.

**Extra-sensory Perception.** *See* Telepathy.

# F

**Fabian Society.** In 1848 (the year of *The Communist Manifesto* by Marx and Engels) Europe was in revolt. In most countries the workers and intellectuals started bloody revolutions against the feudal ruling classes which were no less violently suppressed; hence on the continent socialism took on a Marxist tinge which to some extent it still retains. But at the same time England was undergoing a slow but non-violent transition in her political and industrial life which led the workers in general to look forward to progress through evolution. Marxism never became an important movement in England even though it took its origin here. There were many reasons for this: the agitation of the Chartists (*q.v.*); the writings of Mill, Ruskin, and Carlyle; the reforms of Robert Owen; the religious movement led by the Wesleys; the Co-operative societies; the Christian socialists. Furthermore legislation stimulated by these bodies had led to an extension of the franchise to include a considerable number of wage-earners, remedial measures to correct some of the worst abuses of the factory system, recognition of the trade unions, etc.

This was the background against which the Fabian Society was founded in 1884 with the conviction that social change could be brought about by gradual parliamentary means. (The name is derived from Quintus Fabius Maximus, the Roman general nicknamed " Cunctator," the delayer, who achieved his successes in defending Rome against Hannibal by refusing to give direct battle.) It was a movement of brilliant intellectuals, chief among whom were Sidney and Beatrice Webb, H. G. Wells, G. B. Shaw, Graham Wallas, Sidney Olivier, and Edward Pease. The Society itself was basically a research institution which furnished the intellectual information for social reform and supported all contributing to the gradual attainment by parliamentary means of socialism.

The Webbs's analysis of society emphasised that individualist enterprise in capitalism was a hang-over from early days and was bound to defeat itself since socialism is the inevitable accompaniment of modern industrialism; the necessary result of popular government is control of their economic system by the people themselves. Utopian schemes had been doomed to failure because they were based on the fallacy that society is static and that islands of utopias could be formed in the midst of an unchanging and antagonistic environment. On the contrary, it was pointed out, society develops: " The new becomes old, often before it is consciously regarded as new." Social reorganisation cannot usefully be hastened by violent means but only through methods consonant with this natural historical progression—

gradual, peaceful, and democratic. The Fabians were convinced that men are rational enough to accept in their common interest developments which can be demonstrated as necessary; thus public opinion will come to see that socialisation of the land and industries is essential in the same way that they came to accept the already-existing acts in respect of housing, insurance, medical care, and conditions of work. Gradual " permeation " of the power groups—trade unions, political parties, managers, and enlightened employers—would speed the process.

The Society collaborated first in the formation of the Independent Labour Party and then with the more moderate Labour Party and the trade unions and Co-operative movement. But in general it disapproved of independent trade union action since change should come from the government and take political form. The class-war of Marx was rejected and so too was the idea of the exclusive role of the working class —reform must come from the enlightened co-operation of all classes—not from their opposition.

**Faculty Psychology,** a school o psychology, basically belonging to the early 19th cent., which sought to explain mental phenomena by referring them to the activity of certain agencies or faculties such as memory, imagination, will, etc., as if they were entities in their own right rather than merely general terms for various groups of mental phenomena. Its most extreme form was phrenology (*q.v.*) which found no less than thirty-seven so-called faculties.

**Falangists.** The Fascist Party of Spain founded in 1933 by José Antonio Primo de Rivera, son of the man who was dictator of the country from 1923 to 1930; he was shot by the Republicans. In 1937 the falangists who had shown unwelcome signs of social radicalism were merged with the other right-wing political groups to form the *Falange Española Tradicionalista y de las Juntas de Ofensiva Nacional Sindicalistas* which replaced the Cortes (*i.e.* the Government) between 1939 and 1942 when the Cortes was reinstituted. The Falange is the only political party allowed in Spain. *See* Fascism.

**Fascism.** From the end of mediaeval times with the opening up of the world, the liberation of the mind and the release of business enterprise, a new spirit arose in Europe exemplified in such movements as the Renaissance, the Reformation, the struggle for democracy, the rise of capitalism, and the Industrial Revolution. With these movements there developed a certain tradition which, in spite of hindrances and disagreements or failures, was universally held both by right- and left-wing parties however strongly they might fail to agree on the best means of attaining what was felt to be a universal ideal. The hard core of this tradition involved: belief in reason and the possibility of human progress; the essential sanctity and dignity of human life; tolerance of widely different religious and political views; reliance on popular government and the responsibility of the rulers to the ruled; freedom of thought and criticism; the necessity of universal education; impartial justice and the rule of law; the desirability of universal peace. Fascism was the negation of every aspect of this tradition and took pride in being so. Emotion took the place of reason, the " immutable, beneficial, and fruitful inequality of classes " and the right of a self-constituted élite to rule them replaced universal suffrage because absolute authority " quick, sure, unanimous " led to action rather than talk. Contrary opinions are not allowed and justice is in the service of the state; war is desirable to advance the power of the state; and racial inequality made a dogma. Those who belong to the " wrong " religion, political party, or race are outside the law.

The attacks on liberalism and exaltation of the state derive largely from Hegel and his German followers; the mystical irrationalism from such 19th cent. philosophers as Schopenhauer, Nietzsche, and Bergson; from Sorel (*see* Syndicalism) came the idea of the " myth," and an image which would have the power to arouse the emotions of the masses and from Sorel also the rationale of violence and justification of force.

But these philosophical justifications of fascism do not explain why it arose at all and why it arose where it did—in Italy, Germany, and Spain. These countries had one thing in common—disillusionment. Germany had lost the 1914–18 war, Italy had been on the winning side but was resentful about her small gains, Spain had sunk to the level of a third-rate power, and people were becoming increasingly restive under the reactionary powers of the Catholic Church, the landed aristocracy, and the army. In Marxist theory, fascism is the last fling of the ruling class and the bourgeoisie in their attempt to hold down the workers.

*Italian Fascism.* The corporate state set up by Benito Mussolini in Italy claimed to be neither capitalist nor socialist, and after its inception in 1922 the Fascist Party became the only recognised one. Its members wore black shirts, were organised in military formations, used the Roman greeting of the outstretched arm, and adopted as their slogan "Mussolini is always right." Membership of the Party was not allowed to exceed a number thought to be suited to the optimum size of a governing class and new candidates were drawn, after strict examinations, from the youth organisations. The Blackshirts, a fascist militia, existed separately from the army and were ruled by Fascist Headquarters.

At the head of government was Mussolini, "Il Duce" himself, a cabinet of fourteen ministers selected by him and approved by the King to supervise the various functions of government, and the Grand Council or directorate of the Fascist Party, all the members of which were chosen by the Duce. Parliament, which was not allowed to initiate legislation but only to approve decrees from above, consisted of a Senate with life-membership and a Chamber of Fasci and Corporations composed of nominated members of the Party, the National Council of Corporations, and selected representatives of the employers' and employees' confederations. Private enterprise was encouraged and protected but rigidly controlled; strikes were forbidden, but a Charter of Labour enforced the collaboration of workers and employers whose disputes were settled in labour courts presided over by the Party. All decisions relating to industry were government-controlled (*e.g.*, wages, prices, conditions of employment and dismissal, the expansion or limitation of production), and some industries such as mining, shipping, and armaments were largely state-owned.

Italian fascism served as a model in other countries, notably the German National Socialist Party, in Spain and Japan, and most European nations between the wars had their small Fascist parties, the British version led by Sir Oswald Mosley being known as the British Union which advocated the abolition of free speech, greater interest in the Commonwealth, and anti-semitism. Although fascism in all countries has certain recognisable characteristics, it would be wrong to think of it as an international movement taking fixed forms and with a clearly thought-out rationale as in the case of communism. It is doubtful, for example, whether Japanese "fascism" was entitled to be described as such, and the Spanish Falange differs in many respects both in outlook and origins from the German or Italian varieties. In fact the word "fascist," like "bolshevik," is often used as a purely emotive term of abuse. *See* Falange, Nazism.

**Fatalism.** *See* Determinism.

**Fetichism,** originally a practice of the natives of West Africa and elsewhere of attributing magical properties to an object which was used as an amulet, for putting spells on others, or regarded as possessing dangerous powers. In psychology the term refers to a sexual perversion in which objects such as shoes, brassières, hair, etc., arouse sexual excitement.

**Feudalism.** The feudal system took its origins from Saxon times and broadly speaking lasted until the end of the 13th cent. It was a military and political organisation based on land tenure, for, of course, society throughout this period was based almost entirely on agriculture. The activities of men divided them into three classes

or estates. The First Estate was the clergy, responsible for man's spiritual needs; the Second was the nobility, including kings and emperor as well as the lesser nobles; the Third was composed of all those who had to do with the economic and mainly agricultural life of Europe. The praying men, the fighting men and administrators, and the toilers were all held to be dependent on each other in a web of mutual responsibilities.

The theory of feudalism, although it by no means always worked out in practice, was as follows: the earth was God's and therefore no man owned land in the modern sense of the word. God had given the pope spiritual charge of men, and secular power over them to the emperor from whom kings held their kingdoms, and in turn the dukes and counts received the land over which they held sway from the king. Members of the Second Estate held their lands on the condition of fulfilling certain obligations to their overlord and to the people living under them, so when a noble received a fief or piece of land he became the vassal of the man who bestowed it. To him he owed military service for a specified period of the year, attendance at court, and giving his lord counsel. He undertook to ransom his lord when he fell into enemy hands and to contribute to his daughter's dowry and at the knighting of his son. In return the lord offered his vassal protection and justice, received the vassal's sons into his household and educated them for knighthood.

The system was complicated by the fact that large fiefs might be subdivided and abbots often governed church lands held in fief from nobles. The serf or toiling man dwelt on the land of a feudal noble or churchman where he rendered service by tilling the soil or carrying out his craft for his manorial lord in return for protection, justice, and the security of his life and land. He was given a share in the common lands or pastures from which he provided for his own needs. In the modern sense he was not free (although at a later stage he could buy his freedom) since he was attached to the soil and could not leave without the lord's permission. On the other hand he could neither be deprived of his land nor lose his livelihood. Feudal tenures were abolished in England by statute in 1660, although they had for long been inoperative. In Japan a feudal system existed up to 1871, in Russia until 1917, and many relics of it still linger on (*e.g.* the *mezzadria* system of land tenure in parts of Italy).

**Fourierism.** *See* Utopianism.

**Freemasonry,** a secret organisation with different systems in different countries. It shares with other secret societies the characteristics of being secret, having signs by which one fellow-member can recognise another, initiation ceremonies, peculiar regalia, and various grades of enlightenment. In England freemasonry was first organised in 1717 and in France and Germany in 1725 and 1737 respectively. Masons claim to be working for the good of mankind, and carry out various charitable works. Many notable people are in the movement. Whatever their beliefs there can be no doubt that on the continent freemasons have intervened in politics and the organisation is banned by the Roman Catholic Church. Absurd attempts have been made (and quite possibly are part of Masonic belief) to trace the society back to early and even Biblical times. Historically, of course, this is absurd, nor have freemasons any connection with the masons' guilds of the Middle Ages which were intended for masons in the ordinary sense of the word.

**Freudian theory of repressed emotions.** *See* Q7.

**Friends, The Society of,** or Quakers, a religious body founded in England in the 17th cent. by George Fox (1624–91). The essence of their faith is that every individual who believes has the power of direct communication with God who will guide him into the ways of truth. This power comes from the "inner light" of his own heart, the light of Christ. Quakers meet for worship avoiding all ritual, without ordained ministers or prepared sermons; there is complete silence until someone is moved by the Holy Spirit to utter his message.

In the early days Quakers gave vent to

violent outbursts and disturbed church services. Friends had the habit of preaching at anyone who happened to be nearby, their denunciation of " steeple-houses " and references to the " inner light," their addressing everyone as " thee " and " thou," their refusal to go beyond " yea " and " nay " in making an assertion and refusing to go further in taking an oath, must have played some part in bringing about the savage persecutions they were forced to endure. Many emigrated to Pennsylvania, founded by William Penn in 1682, and issionaries were sent to many parts of the world. The former violence gave way to gentleness. Friends not only refused to take part in war but even refused to resist personal violence. They took the lead in abolishing slavery, worked for prison reform and better education. As we know them today Quakers are quiet, sincere, undemonstrative people, given to a somewhat serious turn of mind. The former peculiarities of custom and dress have been dropped and interpretation of the Scriptures is more liberal. Although Quakers refuse to take part in warfare, they are always ready to help the victims of war, by organising relief, helping refugees in distress, or sending their ambulance units into the heat of battle.

# G

Gestalt Psychology. Whilst Behaviourism (q.v.) was emerging in America a new school of thought was arising in Germany which has revolutionised the outlook of psychology in certain fields and is one of the most important schools of today. Basically dealing with problems of perception and learning, it took issue with the old concept of the Associationists (q.v.) that mental life was based on the " association of ideas," and one of the doctrines of the Behaviourists and others that learning is based either on a process of trial and error or conditioning. The three founders of the school were Max Wertheimer, Wolfgang Köhler, and Kurt Koffka who named it the Gestalt school—a German word which is retained because it had no definite English counterpart but may roughly be translated as " pattern " or " configuration." They meant by this that the human mind has a natural tendency to find significant patterns among sensations, contrary to the Associationist view that initially we simply experience atomised elements which we later learn to associate together as an object. The latter was described by the new school as a " brick and mortar " psychology which explained where the bricks came from but failed to explain the mortar which makes the elements a whole. (The whole is not the mere sum of its parts.) Thus a tune is made up from notes in a scale but is not present in them individually, and the tune is still present if we change the key using entirely different notes. Pattern and relationships which have significance are at the basis of mental activity, especially in learning. Thus experiments have shown that if hens are presented with grain laid on both white and grey pieces of paper and are allowed to eat from the grey but are shooed away from the white, they soon learn to go to the grey piece only. This, the Associationists would say, is a perfect example of the association of ideas: white equals punishment, grey equals food, so naturally the paper associated with food wins. But Köhler did a further experiment and substituted black for the white paper. If the theory of association were correct, the hens would still feed at the grey paper which they had learned to associate with food. In fact, they went to the grain on the black paper. The obvious explanation was that the birds were not responding to a simple association, grey equals food, but to the relationship " darker than." They took in the whole situation, not just parts of it.

Similarly the Behaviourist theory of learning was one of conditioning—the dog presented with food preceded by a whistle soon begins to salivate at the whistle alone. Other psychologists emphasised the process of trial and error showing, for example, that a cat placed in a box which could only be opened by a latch or by pulling a wire loop to reach a plate of food outside, at first made completely random movements until by chance the correct one happened to be made. On subsequent occasions the random element grew less and less and thus the cat ultimately learned to go straight for the latch. But Köhler criticised these experiments (without denying that some learning may be by either conditioning or trial and error) by pointing out that in most of the trial and error experiments where mazes or puzzle boxes were used the whole situation was not open to the animal's inspection. An important element in learning, even in animals, is insight. Thus a dog separated from food by a length of fencing will almost immediately run around the fence provided it can see its ends. A chimpanzee with a banana outside its cage and a suitable stick inside within the same field of vision will soon use it to poke the fruit inside. But if the stick is lying at the back of the cage the absence of a compact visual pattern of stick and banana will likely cause it to fail. Gestalt, in short, emphasises the pattern-finding and significance-seeking tendencies of the mind and its ability to learn by insight. It has also criticised the type of personality test which lists individual traits, giving the subject a rating for each trait, on the ground that such tests do not show the function of each trait in the total personality which is an organised whole rather than the sum of its individual characteristics.

Gnosticism. Among the many heresies of early Christianity, especially during its first two centuries, was a group which came under the heading of Gnosticism. This was a system or set of systems which attempted to combine Christian beliefs with others derived from Oriental and Greek sources, especially those which were of a mystical and metaphysical nature, such as the doctrines of Plato and Pythagoras. There were many Gnostic sects, the most celebrated being the Alexandrian school of Valentius (fl. c. 136–c. 160). " Gnosis " was understood not as meaning " knowledge " or " understanding " as we understand these words, but " revelation." As in other mystical religions, the ultimate object was individual salvation; sacraments took the most varied forms. Many who professed themselves Christians accepted Gnostic doctrines and even orthodox Christianity contains some elements of Gnostic mysticism. It was left to the bishops and theologians to decide at what point Gnosticism ceased to be orthodox and a difficult task this proved to be. Two of the greatest, Clement of Alexandria and his pupil Origen, unwittingly slipped into heresy when they tried to show that such men as Socrates and Plato, who were in quest of truth, were Christian in intention, and by their lives and works had prepared the way for Christ. Thus they contradicted Church doctrine which specifically said Extra ecclesiam nulla salus—outside the Church there is no salvation.

God and Man. The idea of gods came before the idea of God and even earlier in the evolution of religious thought there existed belief in spirits (see Animism). It was only as a result of a long period of development that the notion of a universal " God " arose, a development particularly well documented in the Old Testament. Here we are concerned only with the views of philosophers, the views of specific religious bodies being given under the appropriate headings. First, however, some definitions.

Atheism is the positive disbelief in the existence of a God. Agnosticism (a term coined by T. H. Huxley, the 19th cent. biologist and contemporary of Darwin) signifies that one cannot know whether God exists or not. Deism is the acceptance of the existence of God, not through revelation, but as a hypothesis required by reason. Theism also accepts the existence of God, but, unlike Deism, does not reject the evidence of revelation (e.g., in the Bible or in the lives of the saints). Pantheism is the identification of God with all that exists (i.e., with the whole universe). Monotheism is the belief in one God, Polytheism the belief in many (see also Dualism).

Early Greek Views. Among the early Greek philosophers, Thales (c. 624–565 B.C.) of Miletus, in Asia Minor, Anaximander (611–547 B.C.), his pupil, and Anaximenes (b. c. 570 B.C.), another Miletan, were men of scientific curiosity and their speculations about the origin of the universe were untouched by religious thought. They were basically materialist and atheist in thought. Heraclitus of Ephesus (c. 540–475 B.C.), the philosopher of change, and the founder of metaphysics, was scornful of the popular religion of his day. For him fire was the prime element—the *Logos*—the most complete embodiment of the process of Becoming. Empedocles of Agrigentum in Sicily (c. 500–c. 430 B.C.) introduced the idea of opposition and affinity. All matter is composed of the so-called four elements—*earth, water, air,* and *fire*—which are in opposition or alliance with each other. All these were materialist philosophers who sought to explain the working of the universe without recourse to the gods.

*Socrates, Plato, and Aristotle.* Socrates (470–399 B.C.) was primarily concerned with ethical matters and conduct rather than the nature of the universe. For him goodness and virtue come from knowledge. He obeyed an " inner voice " and suffered death rather than give up his philosophy. He believed in the persistence of life after death and was essentially a monotheist. Plato (427–347 B.C.) was chiefly concerned with the nature of reality and thought in terms of absolute truths which were unchanging, logical, and mathematical. (*See* Mind and Matter.) Aristotle (384–322 B.C.) took his view of matter not from Democritus (atomic view) but from Empedocles (doctrine of four elements), a view which came to fit in well with orthodox mediaeval theology. Matter is conceived of as potentially alive and striving to attain its particular form, being moved by divine spirit or mind (*nous*). (An acorn, for example, is matter which contains the form " oak-tree " towards which it strives.) Thus there is a whole series from the simplest level of matter to the perfect living individual. But there must be a supreme source of all movement upon which the whole of Nature depends, a Being that Aristotle describes as the " Unmoved Mover," the ultimate cause of all becoming in the universe. This Being is pure intelligence, a philosopher's God, not a personal one. Unlike Plato, Aristotle did not believe in survival after death, holding that the divine, that is the immortal element in man, is mind.

Among the later Greek thinkers the Epicureans were polytheists whose gods, however, were denied supernatural powers. The Stoics built up a materialist theory of the universe, based on the Aristotelian model. To them God was an all-pervading force, related to the world as the soul is related to the body, but they conceived of it as material. They developed the mystical side of Plato's idealism and were much attracted by the astrology coming from Babylonia. They were pantheists. The Sceptics were agnostics.

*From Pagan to Christian Thought.* Philo, " the Jew of Alexandria," who was about 20 years older than Jesus, tried to show that the Jewish scriptures were in line with the best in Greek thought. He introduced the *Logos* as a bridge between the two systems. Philo's God is remote from the world, above and beyond all thought and being, and as His perfection does not permit direct contact with matter the divine *Logos* acts as intermediary between God and man. Plotinus (204–70), a Roman, and the founder of Neoplatonism, was the last of the great pagan philosophers. Like Philo, he believed that God had created the world indirectly through emanations—beings coming from Him but not of Him. The world needs God but God does not need the world. Creation is a fall from God, especially the human soul when enmeshed in the body and the world of the senses, yet (*see* Determinism) man has the ability to free himself from sense domination and turn towards God. Neoplatonism was the final stage of Greek thought drawing its inspiration from the mystical side of Plato's idealism and its ethics from Stoicism.

*Christianity: The Fathers and the Schoolmen.* It was mainly through St. Augustine (354–430), Bishop of Hippo in North Africa, that certain of the doctrines of Neoplatonism found their way into Christianity. Augustine also emphasised the concept of God as all good, all wise, all knowing, transcendent, the Creator of the universe out of nothing. But, he added, since God knows everything, everything is determined by Him forever. This is the doctrine of predestination and its subsequent history is discussed under Determinism.

In the early centuries of Christianity, as we have seen, some found it difficult to reconcile God's perfection with His creation of the universe and introduced the concept of the *Logos* which many identified with Christ. Further, it came to be held that a power of divine origin permeated the universe, namely the Holy Spirit or Holy Ghost. Some theory had to be worked out to explain the relationships of these three entities whence arose the conception of the Trinity. God is One; but He is also Three: Father, Son (the *Logos* or Christ), and Holy Ghost.

This doctrine was argued by the Apologists and the Modalists. The former maintained that the *Logos* and the Holy Spirit were emanations from God and that Jesus was the *Logos* in the form of a man. The Modalists held that all three Persons of the Trinity were God in three forms or modes: the *Logos* is God creating, the Holy Spirit God reasoning, and God is God being. This led to a long discussion as to whether the *Logos* was an emanation from God or God in another form; was the *Logos* of like *nature* with God or of the same *substance*? This was resolved at the Council of Nicaea (325) when Athanasius formulated the orthodox doctrine against Arius (*q.v.*): that the one Godhead is a Trinity of the same substance, three Persons of the same nature—Father, Son, and Holy Ghost.

St. Thomas Aquinas (1227–74), influenced greatly by Aristotle's doctrines, set the pattern for all subsequent Catholic belief even to the present time. He produced rational arguments for God's existence: *e.g.*, Aristotle's argument that, since movement exists, there must be a prime mover, the Unmoved Mover or God; further, we can see that things in the universe are related in a scale from the less to the more complex, from the less to the more perfect, and this leads us to suppose that at the peak there must be a Being with absolute perfection. God is the first and final cause of the universe, absolutely perfect, the Creator of everything out of nothing. He reveals Himself in his Creation and rules the universe through His perfect will. How Aquinas dealt with the problem of predestination is told under Determinism.

*Break with Mediaeval Thought.* Renaissance thinkers, free to think for themselves, doubted the validity of the arguments of the Schoolmen but most were unwilling to give up the idea of God (nor would it have been safe to do so). Mystics (*see* Mysticism) or near-mystics such as Nicholas of Cusa (c. 1401–64) and Jacob Boehme (1575–1624) taught that God was not to be found by reason but was a fact of the immediate intuition of the mystical experience. Giordano Bruno held that God was immanent in the infinite universe. He is the unity of all opposites, a unity without opposites, which the human mind cannot grasp. Bruno was burned at the stake in 1600 at the instigation of the Inquisition (a body which, so we are told, never caused pain to anyone since it was the civil power, not the Inquisition, that carried out the unpleasant sentences) for his heresy.

Francis Bacon, who died in 1626, separated, as was the tendency of that time, science from religion. The latter he divided into the two categories of natural and revealed theology. The former, through the study of nature, may give convincing proof of the existence of a God but nothing more. Of revealed theology he said: " we must quit the small vessel of human reason . . . as we are obliged to obey the divine law, though our will murmurs against it, so we are obliged to believe in the word of God, though our reason is shocked at it." Hobbes (d. 1679) was a complete materialist and one feels that obeisance to the notion was politic rather than from conviction. However, he does mention God as starting the universe in motion :

infers that God is corporeal but denies that His nature can be known.

*From Descartes Onwards.* Descartes (1596–1650) separated mind and body as different entities but believed that the existence of God could be deduced by the fact that the idea of him existed in the mind. Whatever God puts into man, including his ideas, must be real. God is self-caused, omniscient, omnipotent, eternal, all goodness and truth. But Descartes neglected to explain how mind separate from body can influence body, or God separate from the world can influence matter.

Spinoza (1632–77) declared that all existence is embraced in one substance—God, the all-in-all. He was a pantheist and as such was rejected by his Jewish brethren. But Spinoza's God has neither personality nor consciousness, intelligence nor purpose, although all things follow in strict law from His nature. All the thought of everyone in the world, make up God's thoughts.

Bishop Berkeley (1685–1753) took the view that things exist only when they are perceived, and this naturally implies that a tree, for example, ceases to exist when nobody is looking at it. This problem was solved to his own satisfaction by assuming that God, seeing everything, prevented objects from disappearing when we were not present. The world is a creation of God but it is a spiritual or mental world, not a material one.

Hume (1711–76), who was a sceptic, held that human reason cannot demonstrate the existence of God and all past arguments to show that it could were fallacious. Yet we must believe in God since the basis of all hope, morality, and society is based upon the belief. Kant (1724–1804) held a theory similar to that of Hume. We cannot know by reason that God exists, nor can we prove on the basis of argument anything about God. But we can form an idea of the whole of the universe, the one Absolute Whole, and personify it. We need the idea of God on which to base our moral life, although this idea of God is transcendent, *i.e.*, goes beyond experience.

William James (1842–1910), the American philosopher (*see* Pragmatism), held much the same view: God cannot be proved to exist, but we have a will to believe which must be satisfied, and the idea works in practice. Hegel (1770–1831) thought of God as a developing process, beginning with "the Absolute" or First Cause and finding its highest expression in man's mind, or reason. It is in man that God most clearly becomes aware of Himself. Finally Comte (1798–1857), the positivist, held that religion belongs to a more primitive state of society and, like many modern philosophers, turned the problem over to believers as being none of the business of science.

## Good and Evil.

*Early Philosophers' Views.* The early Greek philosophers were chiefly concerned with the laws of the universe, consequently it was common belief that knowledge of these laws, and living according to them, constituted the supreme good. Heraclitus, for example, who taught that all things carried with them their opposites, held that good and evil were like two notes in a harmony, necessary to each other. "It is the opposite which is good for us." Democritus, like Epicurus (*q.v.*), held that the main goal of life is happiness, but happiness in moderation. The good man is not merely the one who *does* good but who always *wants* to do so: "You can tell the good man not by his deeds alone but by his desires." Such goodness brings happiness, the ultimate goal. On the other hand, many of the wandering Sophist teachers taught that good was merely social convention, that there are no absolute principles of right and wrong, that each man should live according to his desires and make his own moral code. To Socrates knowledge was the highest good because doing wrong is the result of ignorance: "no man is voluntarily bad." Plato and Aristotle, differing in many other respects, drew attention to the fact that man is composed of three parts: his desires and appetites, his will, and his reason. A man whose reason rules his will and appetites is not only a good but a happy man; for happiness is not an aim in itself but a by-product of the good life. Aristotle, however, emphasised the goal of self-realisation, and thought that if the goal of life is (as Plato had said) a rational attitude towards the feelings and desires, it needs to be further defined. Aristotle defined it as the " Golden Mean "—the good man is one who does not go to extremes but balances one extreme against another. Thus courage is a mean between cowardice and foolhardiness. The later philosophers Philo and Plotinus held that evil was in the very nature of the body and its senses. Goodness could only be achieved by giving up the life of the senses and, freed from the domination of the body, turning to God, the source of goodness.

*Christian Views.* St. Augustine taught that everything in the universe is good. Even those things which appear evil are good in that they fit with the harmony of the universe like shadows in a painting. Man should turn his back on the pleasures of the world and turn to the love of God. Peter Abelard (1079–1142) made the more sophisticated distinction when he suggested that the wrongness of an act lies not in the act itself, but in the intention of the doer: " God considers not what is done but in what spirit it is done; and the merit or praise of the agent lies not in the deed but in the intention." If we do what we believe to be right, we may err, but we do not sin. The only sinful man is he who deliberately sets out to do what he knows to be wrong. St. Thomas Aquinas agreed with Aristotle in that he believed the highest good to be realisation of self as God has ordained, and he also agreed with Abelard that intention is important. Even a good act is not good unless the doer intended it to have good consequences. Intention will not make a bad act good, but it is the only thing that will make a good act genuinely good.

In general, Christianity has had difficulties in solving the problem of the existence of evil; for even when one accepts that the evil men do is somehow tied up with the body, it is still difficult to answer the question: how could an all-good God create evil? This is answered in one of two ways: (*a*) that Adam was given free-will and chose to sin (an answer which still does not explain how sin could exist anywhere in the universe of a God who created everything); (*b*) by denying the reality of evil as some Christians have chosen to do (*e.g.*, Christian Science *q.v.*). The Eastern religions, on the other hand (*see* Zoroastrianism), solved the problem in a more realistic way by a dualism which denied that their gods were the creators of the whole universe and allowed the existence of at least two gods, one good and one evil. In Christianity there is, of course, a Devil, but it is not explained whence his evil nature came.

*Later Philosophic Views.* Hobbes equated good with pleasure, evil with pain. They are relative to the individual man in the sense that " one man's meat is another man's poison." Descartes believed that the power to distinguish between good and evil given by God to man is not complete, so that man does evil through ignorance. We act with insufficient knowledge and on inadequate evidence. Locke, believing that at birth the mind is a blank slate, held that men get their opinions of right and wrong from their parents. By and large, happiness is good and pain is evil. But men do not always agree over what is pleasurable and what not. Hence laws exist and these fall into three categories: (1) the divine law; (2) civil laws; (3) matters of opinion or reputation which are enforced by the fact that men do not like to incur the disapproval of their friends. We learn by experience that evil brings pain and good acts bring pleasure, and, basically, one is good because not to be so would bring discomfort.

Kant (*see* God and Man) found moral beliefs to be inherent in man whether or not they can be proved by reason. There is a categorical imperative which makes us realise the validity of two universal laws: (1) " always act in such a way that the maxim determining your conduct might well become a universal law; act so that you can will that everybody shall follow the principle of your action; (2) "always act so as to treat humanity, whether in thine own person or in that of another, in every case as an end and never as a means."

Schopenhauer (1788–1860) was influenced by Buddhism and saw the will as a blind impelling striving, and desire as the cause of all suffering. The remedy is to regard sympathy and pity as the basis of all morality and to deny one's individual will. This is made easier if we realise that everyone is part of the Universal Will and therefore the one against whom we are struggling is part of the same whole as ourselves.

John Stuart Mill and Jeremy Bentham were both representatives of the Utilitarian school, believing that good is the greatest good (happiness) of the greatest number (*see* Utilitarianism). Lastly, there is the view held mostly by political thinkers that good is what is good for the state or society in general (*see* State and Man).

Guild Socialism, a British form of syndicalism (*q.v.*) created in 1906 by an architect, A. J. Penty, who was soon joined by A. R. Orage, S. G. Hobson, and G. D. H. Cole. The background to the movement was the situation that, although at that time the Labour Party had 29 members in the House of Commons, a period of severe economic crisis had shown the government unwilling and the Labourites unable to do anything about it; the workers were resorting again to direct action to secure their demands and the democratic and constitutional methods to which the Fabians had partly persuaded them seemed to have failed. The guild socialists advocated a restoration of the mediaeval guild system as was being recommended by the French syndicalists whose programme involved a return to direct economic action, a functional industrial structure, return of craftsmanship, and distrust of the state. Guild socialists believed that value was created by society as a whole rather than by individuals singly, and that capitalist economists had recommended the acquisition of wealth without emphasising the social responsibilities which wealth should bring. The trade unions were to be organised to take over and run their own industries after nationalisation. Thus guild socialists were not only against capitalism but also against state socialism in which the state took over the control of industry. Political authority was held to be uncongenial to human freedom and therefore nothing was to be gained by the substitution of state bureaucracy for capitalist control. The National Guilds League, formed in 1915, advocated the abolition of the wages system, self-government in industry, control by a system of national guilds acting in conjunction with other functional democratic organisations in the community. This body was dissolved in 1925, but the theories of guild socialism have undoubtedly influenced British socialism.

# H

Heresy, originally meant a sect or school of thought holding views different from others (*e.g.*, Pharisees and Sadducees within Judaism). Later it came to mean beliefs contrary to orthodox teaching (*e.g.*, Arianism, Apollinarianism, Nestorianism).

Hinduism, the religion and social institutions of the great majority of the people of India. Hinduism has no fixed scriptural canon but its doctrines are to be found in certain ancient works, notably the *Veda*, the *Brahmanas*, the *Upanishads*, and the *Bhagavad-gita*. The dark-skinned Dravidians invaded India between about 3250 and 2750 B.C. and established a civilisation in the Indus valley. They were polytheists who worshipped a number of nature-gods; some elements of their beliefs persisted into Hinduism. They were subdued by a light-skinned Nordic people who invaded from Asia Minor and Iran about 1500 B.C. The language of these Aryan people was Vedic, parent of Sanskrit in which their religious literature (the Vedas) came to be written after many centuries of oral transmission.

The *Veda* or Sacred Lore has come down to us in the form of mantras or hymns of which there are four great collections, the best-known being the *Rig-Veda*. These Vedic Aryans worshipped nature-deities, their favourites being Indra (rain), Agni (fire), and Surya (the sun). Their religion contained no idolatry but became contaminated by the more primitive beliefs of the conquered Dravidians. Sacrifice and ritual became predominant in a ceremonial religion.

As a reaction a more philosophic form arose (*c.* 500 B.C.) with its scriptures in the *Upanishads*. At its highest level, known as Brahmanism, belief is in a subtle and sophisticated form of monotheism (*Brahma* is an impersonal, all-embracing spirit), but there is a tolerant acceptance of more primitive beliefs. Thus Vishnu (a conservative principle) and Siva (a destructive principle) grew out of Vedic conceptions. The two great doctrines of Hinduism are *karma* and transmigration. The universal desire to be reunited with the absolute (the *Atman* or *Brahma*) can be satisfied by following the path of knowledge. Life is a cycle of lives (*samsara*) in which man's destiny is determined by his deeds (*karma*) from which he may seek release (*moksa*) through ascetic practices or the discipline of Yoga (*q.v.*). Failure to achieve release means reincarnation—migration to a higher or lower form of life after death—until the ultimate goal of absorption in the absolute is reached.

In the great Sanskrit epic poems *Ramayana* and *Mahabharata* the deity takes three forms, represented by the divine personalities of Brahma, Vishnu, and Siva. There are also lower gods, demi-gods, supernatural beings, and members of the trinity may even become incarnate, as Vishnu became identified with Krishna, one of the heroes of the *Mahabharata* and the well-known *Bhagavad-gita*.

The ritual and legalistic side of Brahmanism is the caste system based on the elaborate codes of the *Law of Manu*, according to which God created distinct orders of men as He created distinct species of animals and plants. Men are born to be Brahmans, soldiers, agriculturists, or servants, but since a Brahman may marry a woman from any of these castes, an endless number of sub-castes arises.

Hinduism has always shown great tolerance for varieties of belief and practice. Ideas pleasant and unpleasant have been assimilated: fetichism, demon-cults, animal-worship, sexual-cults (such as the rites of *Kali* in Calcutta). Today, as would be expected in a country which is in the throes of vast social change, Hinduism itself is changing. Under the impact of modern conditions new ideas are destroying old beliefs and customs. *See also* Jainism, Sikhism.

Humanism, the term applied to (1) a system of education based on the Greek and Latin classics; and (2) the vigorous attitudes that accompanied the end of the Middle Ages and were represented at different periods by the Renaissance, the Reformation, the Industrial Revolution, and the struggle for democracy. These include: release from ecclesiastical authority, the liberation of the intellect, faith in progress, the belief that man himself can improve his own conditions without supernatural help and, indeed, has a duty to do so. " Man is the measure of all things " is the keynote of humanism. The humanist has faith in man's intellectual and spiritual resources not only to bring knowledge and understanding of the world but to solve the moral problems of how to use that knowledge. That man should show respect to man irrespective of class, race or creed is fundamental to the humanist attitude to life. Among the fundamental moral principles he would count those of freedom, justice and happiness.

The British Humanist Association condemns the religious clauses of the 1944 Education Act and wants compulsory religious instruction in schools abolished.

Humanity, Religion of. *See* Positivism.

Hussites, the followers of John Hus, the most famous pupil of John Wyclif. He was the rector of Prague University and, although it is now by no means certain that his beliefs were heretical, he was condemned to death for heresy and burnt at the stake in 1415 at Constance whence he had come with a safe conduct issued by the Emperor Sigismund of Hungary. The latter based his action on the doctrine that no faith need be kept with heretics, but it is obvious that the main objection to Hus was his contempt for authority of any kind. After their leader's death, the Hussites became a formidable body in Bohemia and Moravia. They took up arms on behalf of their faith, their religion being strongly imbued with political feeling (hostility to Germanism and to the supremacy of the Roman Church). Their religious struggles for reform led to the Hussite Wars during which the movement splintered into several groups.

# I

**Iconoclast Heresy.** In 726 the Byzantine Emperor Leo III forbade the use of images in worship by Imperial decree—a decree which was continued intermittently until 843 when the heresy was abandoned. This was the Iconoclast controversy in which Emperor and Papacy were violently opposed. In the end the image-worshippers triumphed and the sacred pictures (icons) have remained to this day. This ecclesiastical conflict between the Iconoclasts and the Papacy over a matter of ritual was the first of the crises which over three centuries were finally to bring about the schism between Orthodox Christendom and Western Christendom. Though temporary, the supremacy of the State over the Church was nevertheless of supreme importance. Although the Iconoclast heresy is often given as the reason for the absence of statues in the Eastern Churches there is no evidence that they existed to any extent even before the movement began.

**Idealism,** in a philosophical sense, the belief that there is no matter in the universe, that all that exists is mind or spirit. *See* Mind and Matter and Realism.

**Immaculate Conception,** one of the important dogmas concerning the Blessed Virgin Mary, as taught by the Roman Catholic Church, is that she was conceived and born without original sin (according to a bull of Pius IX, 1854). Christians in general believe in the immaculate conception of Jesus Christ.

**Immortality.** The belief in a life after death has been widely held since the earliest times. It has certainly not been universal, nor has it always taken a form which everyone would find satisfying. In the early stages of human history or prehistory everything contained a spirit (*see* Animism) and it is obvious from the objects left in early graves that the dead were expected to exist in some form after death. The experience of dreams, too, seemed to suggest to the unsophisticated that there was a part of man which could leave his body and wander elsewhere during sleep. In order to save space, it will be helpful to classify the various types of belief which have existed in philosophical thought regarding this problem: (1) There is the idea that, although *something* survives bodily death, it is not necessarily eternal. Thus most primitive peoples were prepared to believe that man's spirit haunted the place around his grave and that food and drink should be set out for it, but that this spirit did not go on forever and gradually faded away. (2) The ancient Greeks and Hebrews believed for the most part that the souls of the dead went to a place of shades there to pine for the world of men. Their whining ghosts spent eternity in a dark, uninviting region in misery and remorse. (3) Other people, and there were many more of these, believed in the transmigration of souls with the former life of the individual determining whether his next life would be at a higher or lower level. Sometimes this process seems to have been thought of as simply going on and on, by others (*e.g.*, in Hinduism and Buddhism) as terminating in either non-sentience or union with God but in any case in annihilation of the self as self. Believers in this theory were the Greek philosophers Pythagoras, Empedocles, Plato (who believed that soul comes from God and strives to return to God, according to his own rather confused notions of the deity. If it fails to free itself completely from the body it will sink lower and lower from one body to another.) Plotinus held similar views to Plato, and many other religious sects in addition to those mentioned have believed in transmigration. (4)

The belief of Plato and Aristotle that if souls continue to exist after death there is no reason why they should not have existed before birth (this in part is covered by (3)), but some have pointed out that eternity does not mean " from now on," but the whole of time before and after " now "—nobody, however, so far as one knows, held that *individual* souls so exist. (5) The theory that the soul does not exist at all and therefore immortality is meaningless: this was held by Anaximenes in early Greek times; by Leucippus, Democritus, and the other Greek atomists; by the Epicureans from the Greek Epicurus to the Roman Lucretius; by the British Hobbes and Hume; by Comte of France; and William James and John Dewey of America. (6) The thesis, held notably by Locke and Kant, that although we cannot prove the reality of soul and immortality by pure reason, belief in them should be held for moral ends. (For the orthodox Christian view *see* God and Man, Determinism and Free-will.) From this summary we can see that many philosophies and religions (with the important exceptions of Islam and Christianity) without denying a future life do deny the permanence of the individual soul in anything resembling its earthly form (*see* Spiritualism, Psychic research).

**Imperialism,** the practice by a country, which has become a nation and embarked upon commercial and industrial expansion, of acquiring and administering territories, inhabited by peoples usually at a lower stage of development, as colonies or dependencies. Thus the " typical " imperialist powers of the 19th cent. and earlier were Britain, Belgium, Holland, Spain, and Portugal, whilst Germany, Italy, and Japan, which either did not have unity during this period or adequate industrial expansion, tried to make good their lacks in this direction by war in the 20th cent. The term " imperialism " is not easy to define today (although often enough used as a term of abuse). There is economic imperialism exerted, not through armies, but through economic penetration. There is what may be described as ideological imperialism, *e.g.*, the anti-communist crusade that led America (in the name of freedom) into acts of appalling inhumanity in Vietnam; the dogmatism that led the Soviet Union into the invasion of Czechoslovakia. The Afrikaners in South Africa pass laws to permit the exploitation of the Black and Coloured peoples in their midst. Israel, too, whatever one may think of its creation on humanitarian grounds, is surely a piece of land taken from the Arabs who formed 90 per cent of its population, by a people whose only rational claim is that their ancestors lived there two thousand years ago. Imperialism is a dangerous word and, before using it, we would do well to remember the retort of a British statesman who, when lecturing in America prior to Indian independence, was asked by an elderly matron: " What are you going to do about the Indians? " " Which Indians, madam —ours or yours? "

**Individual Psychology.** The term is applied to the psychological system of Alfred Adler of Vienna (1870–1937) who, together with C. G. Jung (*see* Analytical Psychology), broke with Freud in 1911. Adler's system of psychotherapy is based on the idea, not of sex as a driving force as in the case of Freud, but on the concept of " compensation " or a drive for power in an attempt to overcome the " inferiority complex " which he held to be universal in human beings. The child naturally feels inferior to adults, but bullying, making him feel insignificant or guilty or contemptible, even spoiling, which makes him feel important within the family but relatively unimportant outside, increases this feeling. Or the child may have physical defects: he may be small or underweight, have to wear glasses, become lame, be constantly ill, or stupid at school. In these ways he develops a sense of inferiority which for the rest of his life he develops a technique to overcome.

This may be done in several ways: he may try to become capable in the very respects in which he feels incompetent—hence many great orators have originally had speech defects; many painters poor eyesight; many musicians been partially deaf; like Nietzsche, the weakling, he may write about the superman, or like Sandow, the strong man, be born with poor health.

On the other hand he may overdo his attempt and overcompensate. Hence we have the bully who is really a coward, the small man who is self-assertive to an objectionable degree (Hitler, Napoleon, Stalin, and Mussolini were all small men) or the foreigner who like three of these men wanted to be the hero of their adopted country—Hitler the Austrian, Napoleon the Italian, Stalin the Georgian.

But what about the man who can do none of these things, who continues to fail to compensate? He, says Adler, becomes a neurotic because neurosis is an excuse which means " I could have done so-and-so but . . . " It is the unconscious flight into illness—the desire to be ill. Thus a man who used to have a good job lost it through no fault of his own and developed a " nervous break-down," one of the symptoms of which was a fear of crossing streets. Adler would have asked: " What purpose is served by this symptom? " " Why does he unconsciously not want to cross streets? " The answer was that he had only been offered inferior jobs, and although he felt for his family's sake that he ought to take them, something inside said: " No, I have been an important man and I cannot bear to do insignificant work—if I am unable to cross streets I am unable (through no fault of my own) to go out to work." Adler's treatment involves disclosing these subterfuges we play on ourselves so that we can deal with the real situation in a more realistic way. The criticism of Adler's theory is not that it is not true. It is. But it is not the whole truth, for people are much more subtle than Adler gave them credit for; Freud recognised this element of " secondary gain " in neurosis but he knew that there was more to it than that. Nevertheless Adler's method works well in some simpler cases.

**Irrationalism.** An attitude that puts emotion and passion before reason.

**Islam,** the religion of which Mohammed (570–632) was the prophet, the word signifying submission to the will of God. It is one of the most widespread of religions. Its adherents are called Moslems or Muslims. Islam came later than the other great monotheistic religions (Judaism and Christianity) and may be regarded in some respects as a heresy. Mohammed accepted the inspiration of the Old Testament and claimed to be a successor to Moses, and although he did not recognise Jesus as God, he did recognise Him as a prophet (*see* Docetism).

The sacred book of Islam is the Koran, the most influential book in the world next to the Bible. According to Islamic belief the words were revealed to the prophet by God through the angel Gabriel at intervals over a period of 20 years, first at his native Mecca, and then at Medina. The book is divided into 114 *suras* or chapters: all but one begin with the words: " In the name of Allah, the Merciful, the Compassionate." It is written in classical Arabic, and Moslems memorise much or all of it. The Koran superseded the Gospel as Mohammed superseded Christ. Its ethical teachings are high.

The great advantage of Mohammedism is that, like orthodox Judaism, it is a literal-minded religion lived in everyday life. No Moslem is in any doubt as to exactly how he should carry on in the events of his day. He has five duties: (1) Once in his life he must say with absolute conviction: " There is no God but Allah, and Mohammed is His Prophet." (2) Prayer preceded by ablution must be five times daily—on rising, at noon, in mid-afternoon, after sunset, and before retiring. The face of the worshipper is turned in the direction of Mecca. (3) The giving of alms generously, including provisions for the poor. (4) The keeping of the fast of Ramadan, the holy month, during which believers in good health may neither eat nor drink nor indulge in worldly pleasures between sunrise and sunset. (5) Once in his life a Moslem, if he can, must make the pilgrimage to Mecca. In addition, drinking, gambling, and the eating of pork are forbidden and circumcision is practised. Polygamy is permitted,

although decreasing; sexual relations outside marriage are disapproved of; marriage is only with the wife's consent; and divorce may be initiated by either husband or wife. A great advantage in the spread of Islam has been its lack of race prejudice.

Mohammed's main achievements were the destruction of idolatry, the welding of warring tribes into one community, the progress of a conquest which led after his death to the great and cultured empire which spread throughout the Middle East into north Africa, north India, and ultimately to Spain. That it did not spread all over Europe was due to the Muslim defeat by Charles Martel at Tours in 732 A.D.

# J

**Jainism.** The Jains are a small Indian sect, largely in commerce and finance, numbering about 2 million. Their movement founded by Vardhamana, called Mahavira (the great hero), in the 6th cent. B.C. arose rather earlier than Buddhism in revolt against the ritualism and impersonality of Hinduism (*q.v.*). It rejects the authority of the early Hindu Vedas and does away with many of the Hindu deities whose place is largely taken by Jainism's twenty-four immortal saints; it despises caste distinctions and modifies the two great Hindu doctrines of *karma* and transmigration. Jain philosophy is based on *ahimsa*, the sacredness of all life, regarding even plants as the brethren of mankind, refusing to kill even the smallest insect.

**Jansenism,** the name given by the Roman Catholic Church to the heresy of Cornelius Jansen (1585–1638), a Dutch-born professor of theology at Louvain, derived from his work *Augustinus*, published after his death. This book set out to prove, by a study of the works of St. Augustine, that Augustine's teachings on grace, predestination and free-will (which, of course, Augustine denied) were opposed to Jesuit teaching. Already hostile to Jansen for forbidding them entry to Louvain university, the Jesuits were outraged and in 1653 Pope Innocent V condemned five of Jansen's propositions as heretical. This produced one of the most famous controversies in history in which the scholars and divines of the great convent of Port Royal in Paris defended the *Augustinus*, for which they were later expelled from their posts. Meanwhile the great Pascal (1623–62) had taken up his pen in their defence and exposed Jesuit hypocrisy in his *Lettres Provinciales*, one of the masterpieces of world literature for its brilliant phrasing, delicate irony, and deadly quotation from Jesuit writings. The Letters had great influence, filled the Jesuits with rage, but even Pascal could not stop the cruel persecution which followed. Another Jansenist text-book was published late in the century, Quesnel's *Moral Reflections on the New Testament*, which Pope Clement XI in his bull *Unigenitus* condemned as heretical in 1713. The French Church was split from top to bottom, the aged king Louis XIV supported the bull, and in 1720 it was made part of French law. Most Jansenists fled the country. Thus ended Jansenism in France but a small sect still exists in Holland, Catholic in everything except acceptance of the *Unigenitus*.

**Jehovah's Witnesses,** a religious body who consider themselves to be the present-day representatives of a religious movement which has existed since Abel " offered unto God a more excellent sacrifice than Cain, by which he obtained witness that he was righteous." Abel was the first " witness," and amongst others were Enoch, Noah, Abraham, Moses, Jeremiah, and John the Baptist. Pre-eminent among witnesses, of course, was Jesus Christ who is described in the Book of Revelation as " the faithful and true witness." Thus they see themselves as " the Lord's organisation," in the long line of those who through the ages have preserved on earth the true and pure worship of God or, as the Witnesses prefer to call Him, " Jehovah-God."

So far as other people are aware, the movement was founded by Charles Taze Russell (Pastor Russell) of Allegany, Pittsburgh, Pennsylvania, U.S.A. in 1881 under the name, adopted in 1896, of the Watch Tower Bible and

Tract Society, which has continued as the controlling organisation of Jehovah's Witnesses. Its magazine, *The Watch Tower Announcing Jehovah's Kingdom*, first published in 1879, and other publications are distributed by the zealous members who carry out the house-to-house canvassing. The movement has a strong leadership.

Their teaching centres upon the early establishment of God's new world on earth, preceded by the second coming of Christ. Witnesses believe this has already happened, and that Armageddon " will come as soon as the Witness is completed." The millennial period will give sinners a second chance of salvation and " millions now living will never die " (the title of one of their pamphlets).

The dead will progressively be raised to the new earth until all the vacant places left after Armageddon are filled. There is, however, some doubt about the " goatish souls " who have made themselves unpleasant to the Witnesses, those who have accepted (or permitted to be accepted) a blood-transfusion contrary to the Scriptures, and others who have committed grave sins.

Every belief held by the movement, it is claimed, can be upheld, chapter and verse, by reference to the Scriptures. Witnesses regard the doctrine of the Trinity as devised by Satan. In both wars Witnesses have been in trouble for their refusal to take part in war and it is only fair to add that six thousand suffered for the same reason in German concentration camps.

**Judaism,** the religion of the Jews, the oldest of the great monotheist religions, parent of Christianity and Islam, the development of which is presented in the Old Testament. The creed of Judaism is based on the concept of a transcendent and omnipotent One True God, the revelation of His will in the *Torah*, and the special relation between God and His " Chosen People." The idea of Incarnation is rejected, Jesus is not recognised as the Messiah. The *Torah* is the Hebrew name for the Law of Moses (the Pentateuch) which, Judaism holds, was divinely revealed to Moses on Mount Sinai soon after the exodus of the Israelites from Egypt (1230 B.C.). Many critics deny the Mosaic authorship of the first five books of the Bible and believe them to be a compilation from four main sources known as J (Jahvist), E (Elohist), D (Deuteronomist) and P (Priestly Code), distinguished from each other by the name used for God, language, style, and internal evidence. From the historical point of view an important influence on Judaism may have been the monotheism of Ikhnaton, the " heretic " Pharaoh (note, for example, the derivation of Psalm 104 from Ikhnaton's " Hymn to the Sun ").

The Talmud is a book containing the civil and canonical laws of the Jews and includes the Mishna, a compilation from oral tradition written in Hebrew, and the Gemara, a collection of comments and criticisms by the Jewish rabbis, written in Aramaic. There are in fact two Talmuds: the one made in Palestine (the Jerusalem Talmud), finished at the beginning of the 5th cent., and the other made in Babylon, completed at the end of the 6th cent.

Judaism at the beginning of the Christian era had a number of sects: (1) the Pharisees (whose views include the first clear statement of the resurrection of the just to eternal life and the future punishment of the wicked) who held to the *Torah* and the universality of God; (2) the Sadducees, the upper class of priests and wealthy landowners, to whom God was essentially a national God and who placed the interests of the state before the *Torah*; they rejected ideas of resurrection and eternal life; (3) the Essenes (*q.v.*) who were regarded as a puritanical break-away movement by both parties. The views of the Pharisees prevailed.

Jewish writing continued through the years and some books were added to the *Torah*, among them the Three Major Prophets and certain books of the Twelve Minor Prophets. There were also the Apocalyptic writers who were unorthodox in their preaching of a divinely planned catastrophic end to the world with a " new Heaven and a new earth," preceded by a divine Messiah, and a future life—all of which

beliefs influenced early Christianity. Judah Halevi of Toledo (*c.* 1085–*c.* 1140) and Moses Maimonides of Cordova (1135–1204) were the great Jewish philosophers.

Modern movements in Judaism stem from the Enlightenment, notably with Moses Mendelssohn in the 18th cent. who accepted, as was the tendency of the period, only that which could be proved by reason. He translated the Pentateuch into German thus encouraging German Jews to give up Yiddish and Hebrew for the language of the land and thereby preparing them for their vast contribution to Western civilisation. One of his disciples, David Friedländer (d. 1834) instituted "reform" Judaism behind which lay the desire for assimilation. He wanted to eliminate anything that would hamper the relationships of Jews with their neighbours or tend to call in doubt their loyalty to their adopted state. A similar movement in America (1885) called for the rejection of dietary laws, the inauguration of Sunday services, and the repudiation of Jewish nationalism. Between " reform " and orthodoxy there arose the conservative movement which, in England, includes prayers in English in the service, does not segregate men and women in the synagogue, and translates the Law in a more liberal way. (The fact is that it would be almost impossible for a strictly orthodox Jew to live in a modern industrialised community at all.)

Judaism is essentially a social and family religion which, more than almost any other, concerns itself with the observances of every aspect of daily life. As in Islam (*q.v.*) details are laid down in the most minute way for the behaviour of the orthodox.

The home is the main Jewish institution and Jews, like Catholics, cannot surrender their religion. Circumcision takes place eight days after birth, and a boy becomes a man for religious purposes at his Bar Mitzvah at the age of thirteen. Women are spared most of this because their place in the home is considered sufficiently sacred. Among festivals are Passover, recalling the Exodus; Rosh Hashanah (the Jewish New Year), the anniversary of the Creation and the beginning of ten days of penitence ending with Yom Kippur (the Day of Atonement), a day of fasting spent in the synagogue; Purim, celebrating the deliverance of the Jews from Haman; and Chanukah, celebrating their victory against the Syrians under their leader Judas Maccabeus. A new and semi-religious festival is the Yom Haatzmaut the anniversary of the birth of the new Jewish state of Israel.

# K

**Karma.** *See* Buddhism, Hinduism.

**Ku Klux Klan.** After the American Civil War (1861–65) southern conservatives and ex-Confederate leaders began to fear (as they had every reason to do) both Negro and poor White rule. Taxes were rising owing to radical legislation and the tax-burdened and disenfranchised planters finally took to illegal means to achieve their ends by trying to effect an alliance with the poor White and small farmer through appealing to his anti-Negro prejudice.

Hence the Ku Klux Klan was formed in 1866 as a secret society by a small group of Confederate veterans in Tennessee with the intention of frightening Negroes by dressing in ghostly white robes in the guise of the spirits of dead soldiers. But the movement spread like wild-fire throughout the South encouraged by small farmers and planters alike. General Nathan Bedford Forrest was appointed " Grand Wizard " of the Klan " empire " and in every community armed Klansmen riding at night horsewhipped " uppity " Negroes, beat Union soldiers, and threatened carpet-bag politicians (*i.e.*, fortune-hunters from the North). Soon several similar organisations arose, many of which did not stop at torture, burning property, and murder. In fact, although claiming to be a " holy crusade " the Klan was a vicious and contemptible organisation in which former Southern leaders trying to regain control deliberately set poor and middle-class Whites against the Negroes by appeal to race-prejudice. Congress struck back with laws and intervention of Federal troops, and after a large number of convictions in South Carolina much of the violence stopped even if the feelings continued.

After the 1914-18 war the movement, dormant since 1900, revived as a sadistic anti-Negro, anti-Jewish, anti-Catholic society, spreading to the north as well as the south. By 1926, with its white-gowned hooligans and fiery crosses, the Klan began to subside once more. But it rose again after the second world war. After some cruel racial murders in Alabama during 1964-5 President Johnson denounced K-K-K terrorism and promised new criminal legislation to deal with the Klan.

Kuomintang, a Chinese Nationalist party founded in 1891 by Sun Yat Sen. It took part in the first Chinese revolution of 1911 and led the second the following year, dominating south China by 1930 and, under Chiang Kai-shek, who succeeded Sun Yat Sen on his death in 1925, conducted China's defence against Japanese invasion from 1937-45. Sun Yat Sen had attempted to found a democratic republic based on Western parliamentary democracy and in his famous *Testament* laid down the principles upon which the constitution of China should be based. In 1946, Sun Fo, the son of Sun Yat Sen, deplored the party's departure from the principles of social democracy and the welfare of the people in which his father had believed. Beginning as a movement largely inspired by Russia, the Kuomintang under Chiang Kai-shek degenerated into a reactionary and corrupt military oligarchy which, collapsing in 1949, was replaced by the Communist party, leaving Chiang and his followers to rule Formosa with American aid.

# L

Lamaism, the religion of Tibet. Its beliefs and worship derive from the Mahayana form of Buddhism which was introduced into Tibet in 749 A.D. The emphasis laid by its founder on the necessity for self-discipline and conversion through meditation and the study of philosophy deteriorated into formal monasticism and ritualism. The Dalai Lama, as the reincarnated Buddha, was both king and high priest, a sort of pope and emperor rolled into one. Under him was a hierarchy of officials in which the lowest order was that of the monks who became as numerous as one man in every six or seven of the population. The main work carried out by this vast church-state was the collection of taxes to maintain the monasteries and other religious offices. Second in power to the Dalai Lama was the Panchen or Tashi Lama believed to be a reincarnation of Amitabha, another Buddha. The last Dalai Lama fled to India in 1959 when the Chinese entered his country and it remains to be seen what effects Chinese communism will have upon a land for so long secluded from strangers and whether the religion will survive the impact of dialectical materialism.

Latitudinarians, Anglican churchmen of exceedingly broad views (*e.g.*, bishops who would admit dissenters—*i.e.*, those rejecting the views or authority of the Established Church). Although still used today, the term applies especially to such eminent 17th cent. divines as Burnet, Hales, Tillotson, and Chillingworth.

Levellers, an English military-politico-religious party prominent in the Parliamentary Army about 1647 which stood for the rights of the people. See Diggers.

Liberalism. The Liberal Party is the successor to the Whigs (a nickname derived from *whiggamore* used in the 17th cent. for Scottish dissenters) of the 18th and 19th cent. Prior to the victory of the Labour Party in 1922, it was one of the two main British political parties. Liberals are moderately progressive in the sense that most appreciate the humanistic aspects of socialism while strongly disapproving of its policies of state control, and they dislike any form of monopoly, state-run or otherwise. In general, the Party advocates co-ownership in industry, electoral reform (proportional representation), protection of individual liberties, governmental reform, tax reform, strict mea-

sures against any form of monopoly, and separate parliaments for Scotland and Wales.

Logical Positivism, a school of philosophy founded in Vienna in the 1920s by a group known as " the Vienna circle ": their work was based on that of Ernst Mach, but dates in essentials as far back as Hume. Of the leaders of the group, Schlick was murdered by a student, Wittgenstein came to Britain, and Carnap went to America following the entry of the Nazis. Briefly, the philosophy differs from all others in that, while most people have believed that a statement might be (a) true, or (b) false, logical positivists consider there to be a third category; a statement may be meaningless. There are only two types of statement which can be said to have meaning: (1) those which are tautological, *i.e.*, those in which the statement is merely a definition of the subject, such as " a triangle is a three-sided plane figure " (" triangle " and " three-sided plane figure " are the same thing); and (2) those which can be tested by sense experience. This definition of meaningfulness excludes a great deal of what has previously been thought to be the field of philosophy; in particular it excludes the possibility of metaphysics. Thus the question as to whether there is a God or whether free-will exists is strictly meaningless, for it is neither a tautological statement nor can it be tested by sense-experience.

Lollards, a body of Reformers who, under the leadership of Wyclif, were subjected to cruel persecution in the reign of Richard II. Sir John Oldcastle, a prominent Lollard, was burned at the stake.

Lutheranism. The Reformation had a long history before it became, under Luther and Calvin, an accepted fact. The mediaeval Church had held (as the Catholic Church holds today) that the sacraments were the indispensable means of salvation. Since these were exclusively administered by the clergy, any movement which attacked clerical abuses was forced by sheer necessity to deny the Church's exclusive control of the means of salvation, before it could become free from dependence on a corrupt priesthood. Hence the Albigenses and the Waldenses (*q.v.*), the followers of John Hus and Wyclif (*see* Anticlericalism), were bound to deny the authority of the Church and emphasise that of the Bible. Luther began his movement primarily in order to reform the Church from its gross abuses and the famous ninety-five theses nailed to the door of the Church at Wittenberg in 1517 were not primarily theological but moral complaints dealing with the actual behaviour of the clergy rather than Church beliefs. But unlike the earlier reformers, Luther had arrived at the right moment in history when economic individualism and the force of nationalism were bound, sooner or later, to cause the authorities in Germany to line up on his side. Thus he began with the support of the peasants who were genuinely shocked at the abuse of indulgences and other matters, but ended up by being supported by the noblemen who wanted to destroy the power of the pope over the German states and looked forward to confiscating the lands and property of the Church. When the peasants wanted the reform of actual economic abuses relating to the feudal system, Luther took the side of the nobles against them. The contemporary movement in Switzerland led by Ulrich Zwingli had no such secular support, and Zwingli was killed in 1531.

Martin Luther (1483-1546) was the son of a miner in Eisleben in Saxony, entered the order of Austin Friars in 1505, and later taught at the newly founded university of Wittenberg. After the publication of the theses the real issue so far as the Church was concerned was whether he was willing or not to submit to the authority of his superiors; Luther refused to compromise with his conscience in the famous words: " Here I stand; I can do no other." In a further statement Luther recommended the formation of a German national church, the abolition of indulgences and other means whereby Rome obtained money from Germany, and an end to the celibacy of the clergy. For this he was naturally excommunicated. His teaching was based on the German translation of the Bible, but he was by no means a fundamentalist: *e.g.*, he denied that the Book of Hebrews was written by Paul, would have nothing to do with the Apocalypse, and regarded the letter of James as "an epistle of straw." The Scriptures were open to all and could be interpreted by private judgment enlightened by the Spirit of God. Like Calvin, Luther was a predestinarian and determinist, but he was also a conservative and soon became alarmed about the position taken by many extremists once the Reformation was under way. He had really wanted the Church to reform itself, but when he alienated Rome he had perforce to rely more and more on the secular powers which finally resulted in the state-church form which became pronounced in Prussia and later elsewhere. Whereas Calvin wished the Church to be at least the equal of the State and in some respects its superior, Luther's rebellion resulted in the reverse, a state-controlled episcopalianism. See Calvinism, Presbyterianism.

# M

**McLuhanism.** The name of Marshall McLuhan came into wide prominence in Britain about 1967. What is McLuhanism? Or rather, what are the aspects of the unusual explorations of this Canadian professor, whose four books appeared in this country at about the same time to make such an effective impact. The titles of the books are *The Medium is the Message*, *The Mechanical Bride*, *The Gutenberg Galaxy*, and *Understanding Media*. McLuhan pours out his ideas about the whole process of communication as it has extended mankind's horizons, and therefore mankind himself, from the invention of movable type up to and through the mechanical age. We are in the midst of a revolution right now, with vast sociological and technological changes; and we have not yet attained a language to match our need for communication in the new electronic age. It is the *form* of the new media—radio, television, films, and so on—which affect our patterns of human association rather than the *contents*. Hence the phrase "the medium is the message." It is therefore McLuhan's purpose to understand the social changes brought about by all these media which, outside the body and outside the brain, are extensions of oneself—the telephone, photography, record players, radio, T.V., computers, and so on. All these are wielding a power over us beyond our control and McLuhan turns his sardonic, witty, epigrammatic eye and pen on the new, cryptic, changing Electronic Man. McLuhan is a joker all right, but a very original one; and underneath the compelling and allusive wit are seams of sense still to be explored as time goes on. The ideas of *The Gutenberg Galaxy* are in essence that there have been two great turning points in human understanding since man learnt to read and write: the invention of the printed book and now the present electronic revolution. The old linear, logical method of thought and expression affected areas of our activity beyond what are normally associated with printing or even language; now, too, the present transformation is changing civilisation in a way still to be assessed, with profound and unsuspected changes in attitudes and thinking. We are being tightened up into a "global village," information flooding in to us from everywhere in unmanageable quantities, time and space being annihilated. There seems nothing which will not be affected: our personalities, the relations between individuals and between communities, war, crime, race, religion, literature, everything. Like a boxer McLuhan jabs this way and that, with an aphorism here and an epigram there, and allusions all the time. In a whirling attack on so many things about which we have grown comfortable and complacent, we are drawn in to construe the exciting messages from the frontier of a new and exciting age.

**Magic**, a form of belief originating in very early days and based on the primitive's inability to distinguish between similarity and identity. The simplest example would perhaps be the fertility rites in which it is believed that a ceremony involving sexual relations between men and women will bring about fertility in the harvest. Or the idea that sticking pins in an image of an individual will bring about harm or even death to the real person. Magic is regarded by some as a form of early science in that man in his efforts to control Nature had recourse to magical practices when the only methods he knew had failed to bring the desired results. It filled a gap. By others magic is regarded as an elementary stage in the evolution of religion. It can be said to have served a purpose there too. Yet magic differs from religion, however closely at times it may come to be related with it, in this important respect: religion depends upon a power *outside and beyond* human beings, whereas magic depends upon nothing but the casting of a spell or the performance of a ceremony—the result follows automatically. (We do well, as Dr. Margaret Murray reminds us, to keep in mind "that when anything regarded as out of the ordinary course of nature is brought about by human means it is called a miracle if the magician belongs to the beholder's own religion, but it is magic—often black magic—if the wizard belongs to another religion. In Grimm's words, ' Miracle is divine, Magic is devilish.' ")

The idea that "like produces like" is at the roots of imitative magic, and it is interesting to note that in some languages (*e.g.*, Hebrew and Arabic) there is no word for "resembles" or "similar to." Hence one says "All thy garments are myrrh" instead of "are *like* myrrh." It follows that an event can be compelled by imitating it. One engages in swinging, not for pleasure, but to produce a wind as the swing does; ball games are played to get rainy weather because the black ball represents dark rainclouds; other ball games, in which one attempts to catch the ball in a cup or hit it with a stick, represent the sexual act (as some gentlemen at Lords may be distressed to hear) and bring about fertility; in medicine up till a few centuries ago herbs were chosen to cure a disease because in some respects their leaves or other parts looked like the part of the body affected (*e.g.*, the common wildflower still known as "eyebright" was used in bathing the eyes because the flower looks like a tiny eye).

Traces of these beliefs are still found today in children's games and the spells accompanying them have turned into nursery rhymes: dolls are the images of deposed gods or idols; tug-of-war was formerly a sex-conflict with men pulling one end and women the other to bring about fertility; skittles when knocked down by a ball produced the thunder-noise necessary to produce rain. There is reason to believe that the oldest words known in English, relics of our prehistoric language, are " Ena, mena, mina, mo " of the nursery rhyme.

Divination is another aspect of magic and no general of the past would have gone to war without consulting his diviners who referred to animals' livers, how the sacred chickens ate, or the way ceremonially shot arrows fell. Even Cicero wrote a book on divination discussing the significance of dreams, premonitions, and the flight of birds, which revealed the purposes of the gods. If we find it difficult to make any distinction between diviners, priests, medicine-men, rain-makers, shamans, and witch-doctors of early societies, we could perhaps say that they have crystallised out into priests, scientists, and humbugs of our own day. For it would appear that magic, like witchcraft, still exists today—not merely in the form of children's stories and fears, or grown-ups' enjoyment of creepy tales, belief in fortune-telling, omens, and amulets—but as cults attracting many who ought to have more sense. See Witchcraft.

**Malthusianism**, the theory about population growth put forward by the Rev. Thomas Malthus (1766–1834) in *An Essay on Population* (1798). His three main propositions were: (1) "Population is necessarily limited by means of subsistence." (2) "Population invariably increases where means of subsistence increase, unless prevented by some very powerful and obvious checks." (3) "These checks, and the checks which repress the superior power of population, and keep its effects on a level with the means of subsistence, are all resolvable into moral restraint, vice and misery." In other words, no matter how great the food supply may become, human reproductive power will always adjust itself so that food will always be scarce in relation to population; the only means to deal with this is by "moral restraint" (*i.e.*, chastity or not marrying), "vice" (*i.e.*, birth-control methods), or misery (*i.e.*, starvation). More specifically, Malthus claimed that while food increases by arithmetical progression, population increases by geometrical progression.

It is true that these gloomy predictions did not take place in Malthus's time largely owing to the opening up of new areas of land outside Europe, the development of new techniques in agriculture, the growth of international trade to poorer areas, the increased knowledge of birth-control, and developments in medical science which reduced the misery he had predicted. Furthermore, we now know that as a society becomes industrialised its birth-rate tends to fall. Nevertheless there are very few scientists who are not perturbed by the growth in the world's population which has increased from about 465 million in 1650 to over 3,000 million today.

**Manichaeism.** The early Christian apologists who had not yet acquired an adequate knowledge of philosophy had little intellectual trouble in dealing with the heathen: their trouble arose when confronted with religions which had a philosophical basis. Thus Gnosticism (*q.v.*) caused them a good deal of concern, Neoplatonism (*see* God and Man) rather less, since it could never appeal to the masses, and Manichaeism considerable anxiety, because it could appeal both to the philosopher and the masses. Mithraism (*q.v.*), the only other serious contendant, was troublesome for a different reason in that it was the religion of the Roman army and bore a close resemblance to Christianity itself.

Manichaeism was an Asiatic religion which developed from Zoroastrianism (*q.v.*) and shows the influence of Buddhism (*q.v.*) and Gnosticism (*q.v.*) being founded by Mani, a Persian, who was born in Babylonia, *c.* 216 A.D. Mani presented himself to Shapur I as the founder of a new religion which was to be to Babylonia what Buddhism was to India or Christianity to the West. His aspiration was to convert the East and he himself made no attempt to interfere directly with Christianity although he represented himself as the Paraclete (the Holy Ghost or "Comforter"), and, like Jesus, had twelve disciples. His success in Persia aroused the fury of the Zoroastrian priests who objected to his reforming zeal towards their religion and in 276 Mani was taken prisoner and crucified.

Of Mani's complicated system little can be said here, save that it is based on the struggle of two eternal conflicting principles, God and matter, or light and darkness. Like the Albigenses (who followed much of this heresy) Mani divided the faithful into two clases: the "Perfect" who were to practise the most rigid asceticism, and the "Hearers" whose discipline was much less severe. After death the former went to heaven immediately, the latter reached it only through a kind of purgatory, and the unbelievers were doomed to hell. Although its founder had no intention of interfering with the West, after his death his followers soon spread the religion from Persia and Mesopotamia to India and China. (Manichaeism flourished in China until the 11th cent.) It reached as far as Spain and Gaul and influenced many of the bishops in Alexandria and in Carthage where for a time St. Augustine accepted Manichaeism. Soon the toleration accorded it under Constantine ended and it was treated as a heresy and violently suppressed. Yet it later influenced many heresies, including, as we have seen, the Albigenses, and it even had some influence on orthodox Catholicism which had a genius for picking up elements in other religions which had been shown to appeal to worshippers provided they did not conflict unduly with fundamental beliefs.

**Maronites,** a Roman Catholic community of Christians living in the Mount Lebanon region. Their secular clergy marry as in the Greek Church, but their bishops are celibate.

**Marxism.** The sociological theories founded by Karl Marx and Friedrich Engels on which modern communist thought is based. Marx and Engels lived in a period of unrestrained capitalism when exploitation and misery were the lot of the industrial working classes, and it was their humanitarianism and concern for social justice which inspired their work. They co-operated in 1848 in writing the *Communist Manifesto*, and in his great work, *Das Kapital* (1867), Marx worked out a new theory of society. He showed that all social systems are economically motivated and change as a result of technical and economic changes in methods of production. The driving force of social change Marx found to be in the struggle which the oppressed classes wage to secure a better future. Thus in his celebrated theory of historical materialism he interpreted history in terms of economics and explained the evolution of society in terms of class struggle. (*See* Dialectical Materialism). "In the social production of their means of existence," he wrote, "men enter into definite and unavoidable relations which are independent of their will. These productive relationships correspond to the particular stage in the development of their material productive forces." Marx's theory of historical materialism implies that history is propelled by class struggle with communism and the classless society as the final stage when man will have emancipated himself from the productive process. Marx was the first to put socialism on a rational and scientific basis, and he foretold that socialism would inevitably replace capitalism and that in the transition period the revolutionary dictatorship of the proletariat would be necessary. His prophecy, however, came to realisation not in the advanced countries as he had envisaged but in backward Russia and China. *See also* The Social Effects of Technical Change, Section Q, Part II.

**Mennonites.** *See* Baptists.

**Mensheviks.** *See* Bolshevism.

**Methodism,** the religious movement founded by John Wesley in 1738, at a time when the Anglican Church was in one of its periodic phases of spiritual torpor, with the simple aim of spreading "scriptural holiness" throughout the land. Up to that time Wesley had been a High Churchman but on a visit to Georgia in the United States he was much impressed by the group known as Moravians (*q.v.*), and on his return to this country was introduced by his brother Charles, who had already become an adherent, to Peter Böhler, a Moravian minister in England. Passing through a period of spiritual commotion following the meeting, he first saw the light at a small service in Aldersgate in May 1738 "where one was reading Luther's preface to the Epistle to the Romans" and from this time forth all Wesley's energies were devoted to the single object of saving souls. He did this for fifty years and at the end of his life confessed that he had wasted fifteen minutes in that time by reading a worthless book. Even when he was over eighty he still rose at 4 a.m. and toiled all day long.

Soon Whitefield, a follower with Calvinist views, was preaching throughout the country and Charles Wesley was composing his well-known hymns: John's abilities at this time were taken up in organising the movement described as "People called Methodists." They were to be arranged in "societies" which were united into "circuits" under a minister, the circuits into "districts" and all knit together into a single body under a conference of ministers which has met annually since 1744. Local lay preachers were also employed and to maintain interest the ministers were moved from circuit to circuit each year. These chapel services were not originally meant to conflict with the Church of England of which Wesley still considered himself a member. They were purely supplementary, and it used to be the custom (before the Methodists began to count themselves as Nonconformists) for Methodists to attend Church in the morning and Chapel in the evening.

The class-meeting was the unit of the organisation where members met regularly under a chosen leader to tell their "experiences" upon which they were often subjected to severe cross-examination. At the end of every quarter, provided their attendances were regular, they received a ticket of membership which entitled them to come to monthly sacramental services. If attendance was inadequate the name was removed from the list, without appearance on which nobody was deemed a member. The price of the ticket was " a penny a week and a shilling a quarter " but Wesley was not interested in receiving money from anyone who was not utterly devoted to the cause.

John Wesley introduced four other innovations, some of which were regarded by Churchmen who had previously been willing to commend his efforts in bringing religion to the poorer classes as dangerous: (1) He started the Sunday-school scheme and afterwards enthusiastically supported that of John Raikes, often regarded as the founder of the idea; this was of immense importance in the days before the Education Acts. (2) He reintroduced the Agapae or " love feasts " of the early Church which were fellowship meetings deepening the sense of brotherhood of the society. (3) He began to copy the open-air meetings of the eloquent Whitefield and soon unwittingly produced the most extraordinary results, finding that his sermons led to groans, tears, faintingfits, and all sorts of emotional expression. Even his open-air lay speakers produced like results and these came to be associated with Methodism and gave significance to the proud Anglican claim that *their* services would be " without enthusiasm." (4) After some hesitation he ventured to consecrate Dr. Thomas Coke, who was being sent as a missionary to America, as a bishop of his church. In addition to Wesley's religious work he was a great educator of the common man. Thus he introduced the cheap book and the church magazine, publishing books of any sort which he thought would edify and not harm even when the views expressed were different from his own—*e.g.*, Thomas à Kempis's *Imitation of Christ* and works of history, biography, science, and medicine in some cases written by himself. In this way the movement with its cheap books and reading rooms had an influence far beyond its actual membership. Both the Anglican Church and the Evangelical movement of Wilberforce and others profited from Wesley's work. Some social historians, rightly or wrongly, have claimed that it was Wesley's influence among the working classes that spared England the revolutionary activity which characterised most other European countries during the first quarter of the 19th cent.

Methodism, especially after Wesley's death in 1791, began, like other movements, to develop schisms. There were the long-standing differences which the Baptist movement (*q.v.*) had shown too between Arminian and Calvinist sections—*i.e.*, between those who did and those who did not accept the doctrine of predestination. In the case of the Methodists, this led to a complete break in 1811. Then there were differences associated with the status of the laity, or the relationship of the movement with the Anglican Church. The " Methodist New Connection " of 1797 differed only in giving the laity equal representation with the ministers but the more important break of the Primitive Methodists in 1810 gave still more power to the laity and reintroduced the " camp-meeting " type of service. In 1815 the Bryanites or " Bible Christians " were formed, and a further schism which was even brought before the law courts was ostensibly over the foundation of a theological college. The real reason, of course, was that the ministers were becoming more Tory, whilst the laity were becoming more Radical. Finally in 1932, at a conference in the Albert Hall in London, the Wesleyan Methodists, the Primitive Methodists, and the United Methodists became one Church, the Methodist Church. Including America, where Methodism under the original direction of Thomas Coke spread like wildfire, the Methodist is one of the largest Protestant Churches of today.

Mind and Matter.
*Early Greek Views: Idealism and Dualism.* Primitive peoples could see that there is a distinction between those things which move and do things by themselves and others, such as stones, which do not. Following the early state of Animism (*q.v.*), in which spirits were believed to have their abode in everything, they began to differentiate between matter or substance and a force which seems to move it and shape it into objects and things. Thus to the Greek Parmenides (fl. c. 475 B.C.), who was a philosopher of pure reason, thought or mind was the creator of what we observe and in some way not quite clear to himself it seemed that mind was the cause of everything. This is perhaps the first expression of the movement known as Idealism which says, in effect, that the whole universe is mental—a creation either of our own minds or the mind of God. But from Anaxagorus (488-428 B.C.) we have the clearer statement that mind or *nous* causes all movement but is distinct from the substance it moves. He does not, however, think in terms of individual minds but rather of a kind of generalised mind throughout the universe which can be used as an explanation of anything which cannot be explained otherwise. This is the position known as Dualism (*q.v.*) which holds that both mind and matter exist and interact but are separate entities.

Most people in practice are dualists since, rightly or wrongly, mind and body are thought of as two different things: it is the " commonsense " (although not necessarily the true) point of view. Plato in a much more complex way was also a dualist although he held that the world of matter we observe is in some sense not the genuine world. The real world is the world of ideas and the tree we see is not real but simply matter upon which mind or soul has imprinted the idea of a tree. Everything that exists has its corresponding form in the world of ideas and imprints its pattern upon matter. Mind has always existed and, having become entangled with matter, is constantly seeking to free itself and return to God.

Plato's pupil Aristotle had a much more scientific outlook and held that, although it was mind which gave matter its form, mind is not *outside* matter, as Plato had thought, but *inside* it as its formative principle. Therefore there could be no mind without matter and no matter without mind; for even the lowest forms of matter have some degree of mind which increases in quantity and quality as we move up the scale to more complex things.

So far, nobody had explained how two such different substances as matter and mind could influence each other in any way, and this remains, in spite of attempts to be mentioned later, a basic problem in philosophy.

Two later ideas, one of them rather foolish and the other simply refusing to answer the question, are typified by the Stoics and some members of the Sceptic school. The first is that only matter exists and what we call mind is merely a matter of a finer texture, a view which as an explanation is unlikely to satisfy anyone; the other, that of some Sceptics, is that we can know nothing except the fleeting images or thoughts that flicker through our consciousness. Of either mind or matter we know nothing.

*Renaissance Attitude.* Christian doctrines have already been dealt with (see God and Man, Determinism and Free-will), and the past and future of the soul is dealt with under Immortality. Nor need we mention the Renaissance philosophers who were really much more concerned about how to use mind than about its nature. When they did consider the subject they usually dealt with it, as did Francis Bacon, by separating the sphere of science from that of religion and giving the orthodox view of the latter because there were still good reasons for not wishing to annoy the Church.

*17th-cent. Views: Hobbes, Descartes, Guelincx, Spinoza, Locke, Berkeley.* Thomas Hobbes in the 17th cent. was really one of the first to attempt a modern explanation of mind and matter even if his attempt was crude. As a materialist he held that all that exists is matter and hence our thoughts, ideas, images, and actions are really a form of motion taking place within the brain and nerves. This is the materialist theory which states that mind does not exist.

Thus there are three basic theories of the

nature of mind and body: idealism, dualism, and materialism, and we may accept any one of the three. But, if we accept dualism, we shall have to explain precisely the relationship between body and mind. In some of his later writings Hobbes seems to suggest that mental processes are the effects of motion rather than motion itself; *i.e.*, they exist, but only as a result of physical processes just as a flame does on a candle. This theory of the relationship is known as *epiphenomenalism*.

Descartes, the great French contemporary of Hobbes, was a dualist who believed that mind and matter both exist and are entirely different entities; therefore he had to ask himself how, for example, the desire to walk leads to the physical motion of walking. His unsatisfactory answer was that, although animals are pure automatons, man is different in that he has a soul which resides in the pineal gland (a tiny structure in the brain which today we know to be a relic of evolution with no present function whatever). In this gland the mind comes in contact with the "vital spirits" of the body and thus there is interaction between the two. This theory is known as *interactionism*, and since we do not accept its basis in the function of the pineal gland, we are simply left with the notion of interaction but without the explanation of how it takes place.

One of Descartes's successors, Arnold Guelincx, produced the even more improbable theory of *psychophysical parallelism*, sometimes known as the theory of the "two clocks." Imagine you have two clocks, each keeping perfect time, then supposing you saw one and heard the other, every time one points to the hour the other will strike, giving the impression that the first event causes the second, although in fact they are quite unrelated. So it is with the body and mind in Guelincx's view, each is "wound up" by God in the beginning in such a way as to keep time with the other so that when I have the desire to walk purely unrelated physical events in my legs cause them to move at the same time. A variety of this theory is *occasionism*, which says that whenever something happens in the physical world, God affects us so that we *think* we are being affected by the happening.

The trouble about all these theories is (*a*) that they really explain nothing, and (*b*) that they give us a very peculiar view of God as a celestial showman treating us as puppets when it would surely have been easier to create a world in which mind and matter simply interacted by their very nature. Spinoza, too, believed in a sort of psychophysical parallelism in that he did not think that mind and body interacted. But since in his theory everything is God, mind and matter are simply two sides of the same penny.

John Locke, another contemporary, thought of the mind as a blank slate upon which the world writes in the form of sensations, for we have no innate or inborn ideas and mind and matter do interact although he does not tell us how. All we know are sensations—*i.e.*, sense impressions. Bishop Berkeley carried this idea to its logical conclusion: if we know nothing but sensations, we have no reason to suppose that matter exists at all. He was, therefore, an idealist.

*18th cent. Views:* Hume, Kant. David Hume went further still and pointed out that, if all we know are sensations, we cannot prove the existence of matter but we cannot prove the existence of mind either. All we can ever know is that ideas, impressions, thoughts, follow each other. We do not even experience a self or personality because every time we look into our "minds" all we really experience are thoughts and impressions. Hume was quick to point out that this was not the same as saying that the self did not exist; it only proved that we cannot know that it does.

Kant made it clear that, although there is a world outside ourselves, we can never know what it is really like. The mind receives impressions and forms them into patterns which conform not to the thing-in-itself but to the nature of mind. Space and time, for example, are not realities but only the form into which our mind fits its sensations. In other words our mind shapes impressions which are no more like the thing-in-itself than the map of a battlefield with pins showing the position of various army groups at any given moment is like the battlefield. This, of course, is true. From physics and physiology we know that the sounds we hear are "really" waves in the air, the sights we see "really" electromagnetic waves. What guarantee do we have that the source is "really" like the impression received in our brain? Kant was the leader of the great German Idealist movement of the 18th cent. which in effect said: "why bother about matter when all we can ever know is mental?"

*19th and 20th cent. Views.* The Englishman Bradley, and the Frenchman Henri Bergson in the 19th and early 20th cent. both held in one form or another the belief that mind in some way creates matter and were, therefore, idealists, whereas Comte, the positivist (*q.v.*), and the Americans William James and John Dewey, held that mind is a form of behaviour. Certain acts (*e.g.*, reflexes) are "mindless" because they are deliberate; others which are intended may be described for the sake of convenience as "minded" (*i.e.*, purposeful). But like the majority of modern psychologists—insofar as they take any interest in the subject—they regarded mind as a process going on in the living body. Is there any reason, many now ask, why we should think of mind as being any different in nature from digestion? Both are processes going on in the body, the one in the brain, the other in the stomach and intestines. Why should we regard them as "things"?

**Mithraism**, a sun-religion which originated in Persia with the worship of the mythical Mithra, the god of light and of truth. It was for two centuries one of early Christianity's most formidable rivals, particularly in the West since the more philosophical Hellenic Christianity of the East had little to fear from it. (Arnold Toynbee has described Mithraism as "a pre-Zoroastrian Iranian paganism—in a Hellenic dress"; Manichaeism as "Zoroastrianism—in a Christian dress.") Mithraism was a mystery-faith with secret rites known only to devotees. It appealed to the soldiers of the Roman Army which explains its spread to the farthest limits of the Roman empire and its decline as the Romans retreated. The religion resembled Zoroastrianism (*q.v.*) in that it laid stress on the constant struggle between good and evil and there are a number of parallels with Christianity, *e.g.*, a miraculous birth, death, and a glorious resurrection, a belief in heaven and hell and the immortality of the soul, a last judgment. Both religions held Sunday as the holy day of the week, celebrated 25 December (date of the pagan winter solstice festival) as the birthday of the founder; both celebrated Easter, and in their ceremonies made use of bell, holy water, and the candle. Mithraism reached its height about 275 A.D. and afterwards declined both for the reason given above and, perhaps, because it excluded women, was emotional rather than philosophical, and had no general organisation to direct its course. Yet even today, from the Euphrates to the Tyne, traces of the religion remain and antiquarians are familiar with the image of the sun-god and the inscription *Deo Soli Mithrae, Invicto, Seculari* (dedicated to the sun-god of Mithra, the unconquered).

**Mohammedanism.** See Islam.

**Monasticism.** When in the 4th cent. A.D. Constantine in effect united state and church there were naturally many who hastened to become Christians for the worldly benefits they expected it to bring in view of the new situation. But there were others who, in their efforts to escape from worldly involvement, went into the deserts of North Africa and Syria to live as hermits and so in these regions there grew up large communities of monks whose lives of renunciation made a considerable impression on the Christian world. They were men of all types but the two main groups were those who preferred to live alone and those who preferred a community life. Among the first must be included St. Anthony, the earliest of the hermits, who was born in Egypt *c.* 250 and who lived alone in a hut near his home for fifteen years, and then in the desert for a further twenty. As his fame spread Anthony came forth to teach and advocate a life of extreme austerity, until by the end of his life the Thebaid (the desert around Thebes) was full of hermits following his example. (Not unnaturally, he was constantly assailed by lustful visions which he thoughtfully attributed to Satan.) In the Syrian desert St. Simeon Stylites and others were stimulated to even greater austerities and Simeon himself spent many years on the top of a pillar in a space so small that it was only possible to sit or stand. With some of these men it is obvious that ascetic discipline had become perverted into an unpleasant form of exhibitionism.

The first monastery was founded by Pachomius of Egypt c. 315 and here the monks had a common life with communal meals, worship, and work mainly of an agricultural type. In the Eastern part of the Empire St. Basil (c. 360) tried to check the growth of the extreme and spectacular practices of the hermits by organising monasteries in which the ascetic disciplines of fasting, meditation, and prayer, would be balanced by useful and healthy activities. His monasteries had orphanages and schools for boys—not only those who were intended for a monkish life. But the Eastern Church in general continued to favour the hermit life and ascetic extremes. Originally a spontaneous movement, the monastic life was introduced to the West by St. Athanasius in 339 who obtained its recognition from the Church of Rome and St. Augustine introduced it into North Africa beyond Egypt. The movement was promoted also by St. Jerome, St. Martin of Tours, who introduced it into France, and St. Patrick into Ireland. The monastery of Iona was founded by St. Columba in 566. But it must be remembered that the Celtic Church had a life of its own which owed more to the Egyptian tradition than to Rome. Unlike the more elaborate monasteries of the continent those of the early Celtic Church were often little more than a cluster of stone bee-hive huts, an oratory, and a stone cross. It had its own religious ceremonies and its own art (notably its beautifully carved crosses and the illuminated manuscripts such as the Lindisfarne Gospel (c. 700) and the Irish Book of Kells dating from about the same time). The Scottish St. Ninian played a major part in introducing Egyptian texts and art to Britain where, mixed with Byzantine influences and the art of the Vikings, it produced a typical culture of its own. Strangely enough, it was the relatively primitive Celts who played almost as large a part in preserving civilisation in Europe during the Dark Ages as did the Italians since. It was St. Columbanus (c. 540–615) who founded the great monasteries of Annegray, Luxeuil, and Fontaine in the Vosges country, St. Gall in Switzerland, and Bobbio in the Apennines. So, too, it was the Anglo-Saxon Alcuin (c. 735–804) who was called from York by Charlemagne to set up a system of education throughout his empire; the most famous of the monastic schools he founded was at Tours. Among those influenced by him was the philosopher John Scotus Erigena.

Meanwhile from the south, as the disintegrating Roman empire became increasingly corrupt, St. Benedict of Nursia (c. 480–c. 543) fled the pleasures of Rome to lead a hermit's life near Subiaco. Here he founded some small monasteries, but c. 520 made a new settlement, the great monastery of Monte Cassino in southern Italy, where he established a " Rule " for the government of monks. This included both study and work and emphasised that education was necessary for the continuance of Christianity. As his influence spread his Rule was adopted by other monasteries, and schools became part of monastic life. It is not possible to describe the many different orders of monks and nuns formed since, nor the mendicant orders of friars (e.g., Franciscans, Dominicans, Carmelites, Augustinians). In many ways even those outside the Roman Catholic Church owe much to the monastic movement. Monasticism, of course, is not peculiar to Christianity and forms a major aspect of Buddhism, especially in the form of Lamaism in Tibet (q.v.).

**Monophysitism,** a heresy of the 5th cent. which grew out of a reaction against Nestorianism (q.v.). The majority of Egyptian Christians were Monophysites (Mono-physite = one nature)—i.e., they declared Christ's human and divine nature to be one and the same. This view was condemned at the Council of Chalcedon (A.D. 451) which pronounced that Jesus Christ, true God and true man, has two natures, at once perfectly distinct and inseparably joined in one person and partaking of the one divine substance. However, many continued to hold Monophysite opinions, including the Coptic Church (q.v.), declaring the Council to be unoecumenical (i.e., not holding the views of the true and universal Christian Church).

**Monopsychism,** the theory of the intellect held by the Arab philosopher Averroës (1126–98) in his interpretation of Aristotle, maintaining that the individual intelligence has no existence in its own right but is part of the divine mind (nous) from which it emerges at birth and into which it is absorbed at death. He thus denied personal immortality, a view which was opposed by Christian philosophers.

**Monothelites,** a Christian sect of the 7th cent. which attempted to reconcile Monophysitism with orthodoxy. They admitted the orthodox view of Christ's two natures as God and man, but declared that He operated with one will. Monothelitism was condemned as heretical by the Council of Constantinople in 680 A.D.

**Montanism,** a Phrygian form of primitive Puritanism with many peculiar tenets into which the early Christian theologian Tertullian (c. 150–c. 230) was driven by his extremist views that the Christian should keep himself aloof from the world and hold no social intercourse whatever with pagans. The sect had immediate expectation of Christ's second coming and indulged in prophetic utterance which they held to be inspired by the Holy Ghost but which their enemies put down to prompting by the Devil. In seeking persecution and martyrdom they antagonised the Church and were suppressed.

**Moral Re-Armament,** a campaign launched in 1938 by an American evangelist of Lutheran background, Frank N. D. Buchman (1878–1961), founder of the Oxford Group Movement, and at first associated with the First Century Christian Fellowship, a fundamentalist Protestant revivalist movement. On a visit to England in 1920 Buchman preached " world-changing " through life-changing " to undergraduates at Oxford, hence the name Oxford Group. This revivalist movement was based on Buchman's conviction that world civilisation was breaking down and a change had to be effected in the minds of men.

Two of the Group's most typical practices were group confession of sins openly and the " quiet time " set aside during the day to receive messages from the Almighty as to behaviour and current problems. In the eyes of non-Groupers the confession (often of trivial sins) appeared to be exhibitionist and there was felt to be a certain snobbery about the movement which made it strongly conscious of the social status of its converts.

The Oxford Group gave way to Moral Re-Armament, the third phase of Buchmanism. M.R.A. men and women lay stress on the four moral absolutes of honesty, purity, love, and unselfishness. They believe they have the ideas to set the pattern for the changing world and, indeed, claim to have aided in solving many international disputes—political, industrial, and racial. Theologians complained of the Groups that their movement lacked doctrine and intellectual content; M.R.A. is no different in this respect. Conference centres are at Caux, Switzerland, Mackinac Island, Michigan, U.S.A., and Odawara, Japan.

**Moravian Church,** a revival of the Church of the " Bohemian Brethren " which originated (1457) among some of the followers of John Hus. It developed a kind of Quakerism that rejected the use of force, refused to take oaths, and had no hierarchy. It appears to have been sympathetic towards Calvinism but made unsuccessful approaches to Luther. As a Protestant sect it was ruthlessly persecuted by Ferdinand II and barely managed to survive. However, in the 18th cent. the body was re-established by Count

Zinzendorf who offered it a place of safety in Saxony where a town called Herrnhut (God's protection) was built and this became the centre from which Moravian doctrine was spread by missionaries all over the world. Their chief belief (which had a fundamental influence on John Wesley—*see* Methodism) was that faith is a direct illumination from God which assures us beyond all possibility of doubt that we are saved, and that no goodness of behaviour, piety, or orthodoxy is of any use without this " sufficient. sovereign, saving grace."

**Mormons, or Latter-day Saints,** one of the very numerous American religious sects; founded in 1830 by Joseph Smith, the son of a Vermont farmer, who, as a youth, had been influenced by a local religious revival though confused by the conflicting beliefs of the various denominations. He said that while praying for guidance he had been confronted by two heavenly messengers who forbade him to join any existing church but prepare to become the prophet of a new one. Soon, in a series of visions, he was told of a revelation written on golden plates concealed in a nearby hillside. These he unearthed in 1827 and with the help of " Urim and Thummim " translated the " reformed Egyptian " characters into English. Described as the *Book of Mormon*, this was published in 1830 and at the same time a little church of those few who accepted his testimony was founded in Fayette, N.Y. In addition the first of Joseph Smith's " miracles "—the casting out of a devil—was performed. The *Book of Mormon* purports to be a record of early American history and religion, the American Indians being identified as the ten Lost Tribes of Israel, whose fate has never failed to attract the attention of those who prefer myth to fact (cf. British Israelites). Jesus Christ is alleged to have appeared in America after His ascension. Yet Smith's eloquence was able to influence quite educated people, including Sidney Rigdon with whom he went into business for a time. *Doctrine and Covenants* is the title of another book dealing with the revelations Smith claimed to have received. Soon the sect was in trouble with the community both because its members insisted on describing themselves as the Chosen People and others as Gentiles and because they took part in politics, voting as Smith ordered them to. Smith was constantly in trouble with the police. Therefore they were turned out from one city after another until they found themselves a dwelling-place at Nauvoo, Illinois, on the Mississippi.

That would probably have been the end of the story had not Smith been murdered in 1844 and thereby made to appear a martyr, and had there not appeared Brigham Young, a quite extraordinary leader, who stamped out warring factions and drove out the recalcitrant. While persecutions continued Brigham Young announced that it had been revealed that he must lead the faithful to Salt Lake, then outside the area of the United States. There followed the famous trek of more than a thousand miles across desert country in which he led the way, reaching his journey's end in the forbidding valley of the Great Salt Lake on 24 July 1847. By 1851 30,000 Mormons had reached the Promised Land. Here they held their own in a hostile environment and under the practical genius of their leader carried through a vast irrigation scheme and built Salt Lake City which still serves as the headquarters of their sect. In 1850 their pioneer settlement was made Utah Territory, and in 1896 incorporated in the Union. The church was strictly ruled by its leader who also looked after affairs of state for thirty years until his death in 1877.

Polygamy, although opposed by some Mormons, and only sanctioned by Brigham Young when Salt Lake City had been built, is the best-known of Mormon doctrines. It brought the sect into much disrepute and was renounced in 1890. Mormons are millenarians, believing that some time Christ will appear and rule for a thousand years.

There are two orders of priests or leaders: the Melchizedeks, or higher order, include the apostles or ruling elders, and the high priest; the Aaronic priesthood, or lower order, attends to the temporal affairs of the church as the Melchizedeks attend to the spiritual. Members abstain from alcohol, tobacco, coffee, and tea. The church lays stress on the importance of revelation through visions, on education to meet the social, spiritual, and cultural needs of its members, and on community welfare. Members of the Church of Jesus Christ of Latter-day Saints now number over two million in congregations throughout the world.

The Reorganized Church of Jesus Christ of Latter-day Saints with its headquarters at Independence, Missouri, has been separate and distinct since 1852.

**Muggletonians,** one of the many sects which arose during the Commonwealth but, unlike most of the others (Levellers (*q.v.*), Diggers (*q.v.*), Fifth-Monarchy Men, and the Millenarians) which tended to have a strongly political aspect, this was purely religious. Founded by two journeymen tailors, Lodowick Muggleton and John Reeve, who interpreted the Book of Revelation in their own peculiar way, it was decided that Reeve represented Moses, and Muggleton, Aaron. They also believed that the Father, not the Son, had died on the cross (an ancient heresy) but added the strange statement that He left Elijah in control during His period on earth. Rejecting the doctrine of the Trinity, they also asserted that God has a human body. Nevertheless, for a time, they had a large number of followers.

**Mysticism,** a religious attitude which concerns itself with direct relationship with God, " reality " as contrasted with appearance, or the " ultimate " in one form or another. All the higher religions have had their mystics who have not always been regarded without suspicion by their more orthodox members, and, as Bertrand Russell points out, there has been a remarkable unity of opinion among mystics which almost transcends their religious differences. Thus, characteristic of the mystical experience in general, have been the following features: (1) a belief in insight as opposed to analytical knowledge which is accompanied in the actual experience by the sense of a mystery unveiled, a hidden wisdom become certain beyond the possibility of doubt; this is often preceded by a period of utter hopelessness and isolation described as " the dark night of the soul "; (2) a belief in unity and a refusal to admit opposition or division anywhere; this sometimes appears in the form of what seem to be contradictory statements: " the way up and the way down is one and the same " (Heraclitus). There is no distinction between subject and object, the act of perception and the thing perceived; (3) a denial of the reality of time, since if all is one the distinction of past and future must be illusory; (4) a denial of the reality of evil (which does not maintain, *e.g.*, that cruelty is good but that it does not exist in the world of reality as opposed to the world of phantoms from which we are liberated by the insight of the vision). Among the great mystics have been Meister Eckhart and Jakob Boehme, the German religious mystics of the 13th and 16th cent. respectively, Acharya Sankara of India, and St. Theresa and St. John of the Cross of Spain. Mystical movements within the great religions have been: the Zen (*q.v.*) movement within Buddhism; Taoism in China; the Cabalists and Hasidim in Judaism; the Sufis within Islam; some of the Quakers within Christianity.

**Mystery Religions.** *See* Orphism.

# N

**Nancy School of Psychotherapy.** Before Freud, the only satisfactory means of treating neurosis psychologically was hypnosis (used for centuries in one form or another, but rediscovered by Anton Mesmer (1733–1815), hence the name). Also at that time the commonest neurosis was hysteria—a condition in which physical disease is mimicked unconsciously by the production of such symptoms as paralysis, loss of memory, areas of pain, or loss of feeling, even deafness and blindness. This condition was discovered by Ambrose Liébeault of Nancy in Lorraine to be particularly susceptible to treatment by hypnosis (which, unlike Mesmer who was somewhat of a charlatan, he used in a scientific way). Lié-beault (1823–1904) and his colleague Hippolyte Bernheim (1840–1919) believed: (a) that hysteria was produced by suggestion and particularly by autosuggestion on the part of the patient; and (b) that suggestion was a normal trait found in varying degrees in everyone. These conclusions are true, but as Freud showed later, are far from being the whole truth. See Paris School of Psychotherapy.

Natural Law, the specifically Roman Catholic doctrine that there is a natural law irrespective of time and place, which man can know through his own reason. Originally a product of early rational philosophy the Christian form of the doctrine is basically due to St. Thomas Aquinas who defined natural law in relation to eternal law, holding that the eternal law is God's reason which governs the relations of all things in the universe to each other. The natural law is that part of the eternal law which relates to man's behaviour. Catholic natural law assumes that the human reason is capable of deriving ultimate rules for right behaviour since there are in man and his institutions certain stable structures produced by God's reason which man's reason can know to be correct and true. Thus, the basis of marriage, property, the state, and the contents of justice are held to be available to man's natural reason. The rules of positive morality and civil law are held to be valid only insofar as they conform to the natural law, which man is not only capable of knowing but also of obeying.

Protestant theologians criticise this notion. Thus Karl Barth and many others hold that sinful and fallen man cannot have any direct knowledge of God or His reason or will without the aid of revelation. Another theologian Niebuhr points out that the principles of the doctrines are too inflexible and that although they are the product of a particular time and circumstance, they are regarded as if they were absolute and eternal. In fact, as most social scientists would also agree, there is no law which can be regarded as " natural " for all men at all times. Nor does it seem sensible to suppose that all or even many men possess either the reason to discern natural law or the ability to obey it; whether or not we accept man's free-will (and all Protestant sects do not), we know as a fact of science that people are not always fully responsible for their actions and some not at all.

Nazism, the term commonly used for the political and social ideology of the German National Socialist Party inspired and led by Hitler. The term Nazi was an abbreviation of National Socialist. Those in the Federal Republic today sympathetic to National Socialist aims are known as neo-Nazis. See Fascism.

Neoplatonism. See Determinism and Free-will and God and Man.

Nestorian heresy. The 5th cent. of the Christian Church saw a battle of personalities and opinions waged with fanatical fury between St. Cyril, the patriarch of Alexandria, and Nestorius, patriarch of Constantinople. Nestorius maintained that Mary should not be called the mother of God, as she was only the mother of the human and not of the divine nature of Jesus. This view was contradicted by Cyril (one of the most unpleasant saints who ever lived) who held the orthodox view. In addition to his utter destruction of Nestorius by stealthy and unremitting animosity Cyril was also responsible for the lynching of Hypatia, a distinguished mathematician and saintly woman, head of the Neoplatonist school at Alexandria. She was dragged from her chariot, stripped naked, butchered and torn to pieces in the church, and her remains burned. As if this were not enough Cyril took pains to stir up pogroms against the very large Jewish colony of Alexandria. At the Council of Ephesus (A.D. 431) the Western bishops quickly decided for Cyril. This Council (reinforced by the Council of Chalcedon in 451) clarified orthodox Catholic doctrine (see Monophysitism). Nestorius became a heretic, was banished to Antioch where he had a short respite of peace, but later, and in spite of his weakness and age, was dragged about from one place to another on the borders of Egypt. We are assured that his tongue was eaten by worms in punishment for the wicked words he had spoken, but later the Nestorian church flourished in Syria and Persia under the protection of the rulers of Persia and missions were sent to India and China.

Nihilism, the name commonly given to the earliest Russian form of revolutionary anarchism. It originated in the early years of Tsar Alexander II (1818–81), the liberator of the serfs, who, during his attempts to bring about a constitutional monarchy, was killed by a bomb. The term " nihilist," however, was first used in 1862 by Turgenev in his novel Fathers and Children. See Anarchism.

Nominalism. Early mediaeval thinkers were divided into two schools, those who regarded " universals " or abstract concepts as mere names without any corresponding realities (Nominalists), and those who held the opposite doctrine (Realism) that general concepts have an existence independent of individual things. The relation between universals and particulars was a subject of philosophical dispute all through the Middle Ages.

The first person to hold the nominalist doctrine was probably Roscelin or Roscellinus in the late 11th cent., but very little is known of him and none of his works remains except for a single letter to Peter Abelard who was his pupil. Roscelin was born in France, accused twice of heresy but recanted and fled to England where he attacked the views of Anselm, according to whom Roscelin used the phrase that universals were a flatus voci or breath of the voice. The most important nominalist was the Englishman William of Occam in the 13th cent. who, once and for all, separated the two schools by saying in effect that science is about things (the nominalist view), whereas logic, philosophy, and religion are about terms or concepts (the Platonic tradition). Both are justified, but we must distinguish between them. The proposition " man is a species " is not a proposition of logic or philosophy but a scientific statement since we cannot say whether it is true or false without knowing about man. If we fail to realise that words are conventional signs and that it is important to decide whether or not they have a meaning and refer to something, then we shall fall into logical fallacies of the type: " Man is a species, Socrates is a man, therefore Socrates is a species." This, in effect, is the beginning of the modern philosophy of logical analysis which, to oversimplify, tells us that a statement is not just true or untrue, it may also be meaningless. Therefore, in all the philosophical problems we have discussed elsewhere, there is the third possibility that the problem we are discussing has no meaning because the words refer to nothing and we must ask ourselves before going any further " what do we mean by God," has the word " free-will " any definite meaning?

Nonconformism, the attitude of all those Christian bodies which do not conform to the doctrines of the Church of England. Up to the passing of the Act of Uniformity in 1662 they were called " puritans " or " dissenters " and were often persecuted. The oldest bodies of nonconformists are the Baptists, Independents, and (in England) the Presbyterians; the Methodists, although dating from 1738, did not consider themselves nonconformists until some time later. The Presbyterians are, of course, the official Church of Scotland where it is the Anglicans (known as " Episcopalians ") who are the nonconformists, although not generally described as such.

## O

Occam's Razor, the philosophical maxim by which William of Occam, the 13th cent. nominalist (q.v.), has become best-known. This states in the form which is most familiar: " Entities are not to be multiplied without necessity " and as such does not appear in his works. He did, however, say something much to the same effect: " It is vain to do with more what can be done with fewer." In other words, if everything in some science can be interpreted without assuming this or that hypothetical entity, there is no ground for assuming it. This is Bertrand Russell's version, and he adds: " I have myself found this a most fruitful principle in logical analysis."

**Occultism.** *See* Magic, Alchemy, Astrology, and Theosophy.

**Orangemen,** members of an Irish society formed in Ulster in 1795 to uphold Protestantism. Their name is taken from King William III, Prince of Orange, who defeated James II at the Battle of the Boyne (1690), hence the enormous banners depicting " King Billy on the Boyne " and such other subjects or mottoes as appeal to the primitive mind when they are carried in procession on 12 July each year. The society has branches in many English-speaking countries but flourishes chiefly in Ulster.

**Origenists,** a sect of early religionists led by the Christian Father Origen in the 3rd cent., who accepted in general the doctrines of Plotinus (*see* Neoplatonism). They believed that men's souls are created before their bodies and are striving to enter bodies as they are born. When the soul leaves the body it enters another body if it has been sinful since justice requires punishment; but the punishment happens naturally through the driving power of the sinner's own errors. The celestial bodies are believed also to have souls, and it is asserted that Christ was the Son of God by adoption and grace. The Council of Constantinople in 553 condemned Origen's doctrines.

**Orphism.** The Greeks in general thought very little of their gods, regarding them as similar to human beings with human failings and virtues although on a larger scale. But there was another aspect of Greek religion which was passionate, ecstatic, and secret, dealing with the worship of various figures among whom were Bacchus or Dionysus, Orpheus, and Demeter and Persephone of the Eleusinian Mysteries. Dionysus (or Bacchus) was originally a god from Thrace where the people were primitive farmers naturally interested in fertility cults. Dionysus was the god of fertility who only later came to be associated with wine and the divine madness it produces. He assumed the form of a man or a bull and his worship by the time it arrived in Greece became associated with women (as was the case in most of the Mystery Religions) who spent nights on the hills dancing and possibly drinking wine in order to stimulate ecstasy; an unpleasant aspect of the cult was the tearing to pieces of wild animals whose flesh was eaten raw. Although the cult was disapproved of by the orthodox and, needless to say, by husbands, it existed for a long time. This primitive and savage religion in time was modified by that attributed to Orpheus whose cult was more spiritualised, ascetic, and substituted mental for physical intoxication. Orpheus may have been a real person or a legendary hero and he, too, is supposed to have come from Thrace, but his name indicates that he, or the movement associated with him, came from Crete and originally from Egypt, which seems to have been the source of many of its doctrines. Crete, it must be remembered, was the island through which Egypt influenced Greece in other respects. Orpheus is said to have been a reformer who was torn to pieces by the Maenad worshippers of Dionysus. The Orphics believed in the transmigration of souls and that the soul after death might obtain either eternal bliss or temporary or permanent torment according to its way of life upon earth. They held ceremonies of purification and the more orthodox abstained from animal food except on special occasions when it was eaten ritually. Man is partly earthly, partly heavenly, and a good life increases the heavenly part so that, in the end, he may become one with Bacchus and be called a " Bacchus." The religion had an elaborate theology (*see* Section H, 117–128). As the Bacchic rites were reformed by Orpheus, so the Orphic rites were reformed by Pythagoras (*c.* 582–c. 507 B.C.) who introduced the mystical element into Greek philosophy which reached its heights in Plato. Other elements entered Greek life from Orphism. One of these was feminism which was notably lacking in Greek civilisation outside the Mystery Religions. The other was the drama which arose from the rites

of Dionysus. The mysteries of Eleusis formed the most sacred part of the Athenian state religion, and it is clear that they had to do with fertility rites also, for they were in honour of Demeter and Persephone and all the myths speak of them as being associated with the supply of corn to the country (*see* Section H, 110–116). Without being provocative, it is accepted by most anthropologists and many theologians that Christianity, just as it accepted elements of Gnosticism and Mithraism, accepted elements from the Mystery Religions as they in turn must have done from earlier cults. The miraculous birth, the death and resurrection, the sacramental feast of bread and wine, symbolising the eating of the flesh and drinking of the blood of the god, all these are common elements in early religions and not just in one. None of this means that what we are told about Jesus is not true, but it surely does mean: (*a*) that Christianity was not a sudden development but had its predecessors; (*b*) that the early Church absorbed many of the elements of other religions; (*c*) that perhaps Jesus Himself made use of certain symbols which He knew had a timeless significance for man and invested them with new meaning.

**Orthodox Eastern Church.** There are two groups of Eastern churches: (1) those forming the Orthodox Church dealt with here which include the ancient Byzantine patriarchates of Constantinople, Alexandria, Antioch, and Jerusalem, and the national churches of Russia, Greece, Yugoslavia, Bulgaria, Rumania, etc. (although Orthodox communities exist all over the world and are no longer confined to geographical areas); (2) the churches which rejected Byzantine orthodoxy during various controversies from the 5th to the 7th cent., notably the Coptic church (*q.v.*) and the Armenian church. Although all Orthodox churches share the same doctrine and traditions they are arranged as national independent bodies each with its own hierarchy. They do not recognise the pope, and the primacy of the patriarch of Constantinople is largely an honorary one. Although claiming to be the One Holy, Catholic, and Apostolic Church its alleged infallibility rests on universal agreement rather than on any one individual, and agreement over the faith comes from the Scriptures interpreted in the light of the Tradition. The latter includes dogmas relating to the Trinity, Christology, Mariology, and Holy Icons; the testimony of the Fathers (St. Athanasius, St. Basil, St. John Chrysostom, St. Cyril of Alexandria, etc.); the canons or rules as formulated by the Councils and the Fathers. The Orthodox Church did not take part in the great Western controversies about the Bible, nor, of course, in the Reformation. Attempts have recently been made to improve relations between Rome and Constantinople: the two Churches agreed in 1965 to retract the excommunications cast on each other in A.D. 1054, which formalised the Great Schism.

**Oxford Group.** *See* Moral Re-Armament.

**Oxford Movement.** *See* Tractarianism.

# P

**Pantheism.** *See* God and Man.

**Papal Infallibility.** The basis of papal infallibility is (*a*) that every question of morals and faith is not dealt with in the Bible so it is necessary that there should be a sure court of appeal in case of doubt, and this was provided by Christ when he established the Church as His Teaching Authority upon earth; (*b*) ultimately this idea of the teaching function of the Church shapes the idea of papal infallibility which asserts that the pope, when speaking officially on matters of faith or morals, is protected by God against the possibility of error. The doctrine was proclaimed in July 1870.

Infallibility is a strictly limited gift which does not mean that the pope has extraordinary intelligence, that God helps him to find the answer to every conceivable question, or that Catholics have to accept the pope's views on politics. He can make mistakes or fall into sin, his scientific or historical opinions may be quite wrong, he may write books that are full of errors.

Only in two limited spheres is he infallible and in these only when he speaks officially as the supreme teacher and lawgiver of the Church, defining a doctrine that must be accepted by all its members. When, after studying a problem of faith or morals as carefully as possible, and with all available help from expert consultants, he emerges with the Church's answer—on these occasions it is not strictly an answer, it is *the* answer.

Historically speaking, the Roman Catholic Church of the early 19th cent. was at its lowest ebb of power. Pope Pius IX, in fear of Italian nationalism, revealed his reactionary attitude by the feverish declaration of new dogmas, the canonisation of new saints, the denunciation of all modern ideals in the Syllabus of Errors, and the unqualified defence of his temporal power against the threat of Garibaldi. It is not too much to say that everything regarded as important by freedom-loving and democratic people was opposed by the papacy at that time. In 1870, after a long and sordid struggle, the Vatican Council, convened by Pius IX, pronounced the definition of his infallibility. Döllinger, a German priest and famous historian of the Church, was excommunicated because, like many others, he refused to accept the new dogma. It is difficult not to doubt that there was some connection between the pronouncement of the pope's infallibility and his simultaneous loss of temporal power.

After the humanism of the Second Vatican Council (1962–5) the Pope's encyclical *Humanae Vitae* (1968), condemning birth control, came as a great disappointment to the many people (including theologians, priests, and laymen) who had expected there would be a change in the Church's teaching. The Church's moral guidance on this controversial issue, however, does not involve the doctrine of infallibility. (The Roman Catholic Church teaches that papal pronouncements are infallible only when they are specifically defined as such.)

**Paris School of Psychotherapy.** The Paris school is important because it was the school of the famous French neurologist Jean Charcot (1825–93), teacher of Sigmund Freud (1856–1939) and Pierre Janet (1859–1947). At a time when hypnosis and the neurosis known as hysteria were very much " in the air," and Liébeault and his colleagues (*see* Nancy School) were regarding hysteria as a condition which was produced by autosuggestion, Charcot was maintaining the opposite view. Hypnosis, or the ability to be hypnotised, was, in his view, a symptom of a hysterical personality, and hysteria had a physiological basis.

Charcot was a highly controversial figure and his demonstrations were famous, if to some verging on the notorious; he aroused much antagonism among Roman Catholics by stating that faith cures at Lourdes were actually cases of hysteria and not, therefore, miraculous since they could equally well be cured by himself. His supposed words: " You will always find sex at the root of the trouble " and his pupil Janet's evidence that forgotten (or, as we should now say, repressed) traumatic events lay behind the symptoms which would go when the event was allowed expression, had a potent influence on the young Freud who made the uncovering of the past and the importance of sex the foundations of psychoanalysis. Modern belief is that Charcot was wrong about the physical basis of hysteria, wrong about the pathological significance of hypnosis, but right on the whole about the importance of sexual problems in neurosis.

**Parsees.** *See* Zoroastrianism.

**Paulicians,** a Christian heretical sect which derives its name not from Paul the Apostle but from Paul of Samosata who was patriarch of Antioch, 260–72. His followers, the " Pauliani," were condemned for their "Adoptionist " (*q.v.*) attitude by the Council of Nicaea (325). Originally wide-spread in Anatolia, especially in Armenia from the 5th cent. onwards, they were cruelly persecuted by the Byzantine emperors and were deported (*c.* 755) to the Balkans to garrison that part of the East Roman empire. Elsewhere in this section the Albigenses or Cathari are mentioned; the Paulicians form part of their

spiritual ancestry. It is debatable whether the "Adoptionist " doctrines professed by the Albigenses came from the Balkan Bogomils, through the Crusaders, or from the north of Spain, where there was an "Adoptionist " movement in the late part of the 8th cent. The evidence seems to be in favour of the Balkan influence but it should be noted that although the Bogomils were influenced by the Paulicians and the Manichaeans, the Paulicians themselves repudiated Manichaeanism. An authentic liturgical book of the Paulicians—*The Key of Truth*—was discovered in 1891 in Echmiadzin where the Armenian historical archives were kept. This manuscript throws new light on the heresy.

**Pavlovian theory.** *See* Behaviourism.

**Phrenology,** a psychological " school " founded in 1800 by two Germans, Franz Josef Gall and Johann Gaspar Spurzheim. Gall was an anatomist who believed there to be some correspondence between mental faculties and the shape of the head. He tested these ideas in prisons and mental hospitals and began to lecture on his findings, arousing a great deal of interest throughout both Europe and America, where his doctrines were widely accepted. Phrenology became fashionable, and people would go to " have their bumps read " as later men and women of fashion have gone to be psychoanalysed. Roughly speaking, Gall divided the mind into thirty-seven faculties such as destructiveness, suavity, self-esteem, conscientiousness, and so on, and claimed that each of these was located in a definite area of the brain. He further claimed that the areas in the brain corresponded to " bumps " on the skull which could be read by the expert, thus giving a complete account of the character of the subject. In fact, (*a*) no such faculties are located in the brain anywhere for this is simply not the way the brain works; (*b*) the faculties described by Gall are not pure traits which cannot be further analysed and are based on a long outdated psychology; (*c*) the shape of the brain bears no specific relationship to the shape of the skull. Phrenology is a pseudo-science; there is no truth in it whatever. But, even so, like astrology, it still has its practitioners.

**Physiocrats.** A French school of economic thought during the 18th cent., known at the time as *Les Economistes* but in later years named physiocrats by Du Pont de Nemours, a member of the School. Other members were Quesnay, Mirabeau, and the great financier Turgot. The physiocrats held the view, common to the 18th cent., and deriving ultimately from Rousseau, of the goodness and bounty of nature and the goodness of man " as he came from the bosom of nature." The aim of governments, therefore, should be to conform to nature; and so long as men do not interfere with each other's liberty and do not combine among themselves, governments should leave them free to find their own salvation. Criminals, madmen, and monopolists should be eliminated. Otherwise the duty of government is *laissez-faire, laissez passer.* From this follows the doctrine of free trade between nations on grounds of both justice and economy; for the greater the competition, the more will each one strive to economise the cost of his labour to the general advantage. Adam Smith, although not sharing their confidence in human nature, learned much from the physiocrats, eliminated their errors, and greatly developed their teaching.

**Physiognomy.** *See* Characterology.

**Pietism,** a movement in the Lutheran Church at the end of the 17th cent.—the reaction, after the sufferings of the thirty years' war, of a pious and humiliated people against learning, pomp and ceremony, and stressing the importance of man's personal relationship with God. The writings of Johann Georg Hamann (1730–88) who came from a Pietist family of Königsberg influenced Kierkegaard. The Pietist movement was the root of the great Romantic movement of the 18th cent.

**Plymouth Brethren,** a religious sect founded by John Nelson Darby, a minister of the Protestant Church of Ireland, and Edward Cronin, a former Roman Catholic, in 1827. Both were dissatisfied with the lack of spirituality in their own and other churches and joined together in small meetings in Dublin every Sunday for "the breaking of bread." Soon the movement began to spread through Darby's travels and writings and he finally settled in Plymouth, giving the popular name to the "Brethren." Beginning as a movement open to all who felt the need to "keep the unity of the Spirit," it soon exercised the right to exclude all who had unorthodox views and split up into smaller groups. Among these the main ones were the "Exclusives," the Kellyites, the Newtonites, and "Bethesda" whose main differences were over problems of church government or prophetical powers. Some of these are further split among themselves. Readers of *Father and Son* by Sir Edmund Gosse, which describes life with his father, the eminent naturalist Philip Gosse, who belonged to the Brethren, will recall how this basically kind, honest, and learned man was led through their teachings to acts of unkindness (*e.g.*, in refusing to allow his son and other members of his household to celebrate Christmas and throwing out the small tokens they had secretly bought), and intellectual dishonesty (*e.g.*, in refusing for religious reasons alone to accept Darwinism when all his evidence pointed towards it).

The original views of Darby which were perpetuated by the "Exclusive" Brethren were somewhat as follows: Christianity has fallen from New Testament purity and all Christendom and every Church is corrupt and has incurred God's displeasure, notably by establishing ministerial offices which hinder the believer's approach to God. Ministers should not be officials but possess special gifts ("Charismata") granted from above and assigned by the Holy Ghost according to his will; these Charismata have no connection whatever with any official posts although in some cases they may coincide with them. The whole doctrine of the Brethren is based on the need for *direct* access to God and the rejection of any intermediate agency such as priests, ministers or presbyters. The Exclusive Brethren adopted new harsh rules in 1965 designed to prevent "Saints" (members) from having any contact with "Sinners" (non-members). Members sharing homes with non-members were to be expelled; members must declare their bank balances; unmarried members, single or widowed, must marry as soon as possible within the sect.

Today, the majority o] Brethren belong to the "Open Brethren" assemblies and, unlike the "Exclusives," hold that the Lord's Supper (a commemorative act of "breaking the bread" observed once a week) is for all Christians who care to join them. Baptism is required and Brethren believe in the personal premillenial second coming of Christ.

**Poltergeist,** allegedly a noisy type of spirit which specialises in throwing things about, making loud thumpings and bangings, and occasionally bringing in "apports," *i.e.*, objects from elsewhere. Most so-called poltergeist activities are plain frauds, but the others are almost invariably associated with the presence in the house of someone (often, but not always a child) who is suffering from severe mental conflicts usually of a sexual nature. The inference is that those activities which are not simply fraudulent are either due to some unknown influence exuded by such mentally abnormal people, or that they are actually carried out by ordinary physical means by such people when in a state of hysterical dissociation—*i.e.*, unconsciously. The second hypothesis is much the more probable. *See* Psychic Research.

**Polytheism.** *See* God and Man.

**Positivism,** also known as the Religion of Humanity, was founded by Auguste Comte (1798–1857), a famous mathematician and philosopher born in Montpellier, France. His views up to the end of the century attracted many and it would have been impossible throughout that time to read a book on philosophy or sociology that did not mention them, but today his significance is purely of historical interest. In his *Cours de Philosophie Positive* (1830) he put forward the thesis that mankind had seen three great stages in human thought: (1) the theological, during which man seeks for supernatural causes to explain nature and invents gods and devils;

(2) the metaphysical, through which he thinks in terms of philosophical and metaphysical abstractions; (3) the last positive or scientific stage when he will proceed by experiment and objective observation to reach in time "positive truth."

Broadly speaking, there is little to complain of in this analysis; for there does seem to have been some sort of general direction along these lines. However, Comte was not satisfied with having reached this point and felt that his system demanded a religion and, of course, one that was "scientific." This religion was to be the worship of Humanity in place of the personal Deity of earlier times, and for it he supplied not only a Positive Catechism but a treatise on Sociology in which he declared himself the High Priest of the cult. Since, as it stood, the religion was likely to appear somewhat abstract to many, Comte drew up a list of historical characters whom he regarded as worthy of the same sort of adoration as Catholics accord to their saints. The new Church attracted few members, even among those who had a high regard for Comte's scientific work, and its only significant adherents were a small group of Oxford scholars and some in his own country. Frederic Harrison was the best-known English adherent and throughout his life continued to preach Comtist doctrines in London to diminishing audiences.

**Pragmatism,** a typically American school of philosophy which comes under the heading of what Bertrand Russell describes as a "practical" as opposed to a "theoretical" philosophy. Whereas the latter, to which most of the great philosophical systems belong, seeks disinterested knowledge for its own sake, the former (*a*) regards action as the supreme good, (*b*) considers happiness an effect and knowledge a mere instrument of successful activity.

The originator of Pragmatism is usually considered to have been the psychologist William James (1842–1910) although he himself attributed its basic principles to C. S. Peirce. The other famous Pragmatist is Dr. John Dewey, best-known in Europe for his works on education (for although American text-books on philosophy express opinions to the contrary, few educated people in Europe have taken the slightest interest in Pragmatism and generally regard it as an eccentricity peculiar to Americans).

The basic source of Pragmatism is William James's book *The Will to Believe* (1896) in which he points out that we are often compelled to take a decision where no adequate theoretical grounds for a decision exist; for even to do nothing is to decide. Thus in religion we have a right to adopt a believing attitude although not intellectually fully convinced. We should believe truth and shun error, but the failing of the sceptical philosopher is that he adheres only to the latter rule and thus fails to believe various truths which a less cautious man will accept. If believing truth and avoiding error are equally important, then it is a good idea when we are presented with an alternative to believe one of the possibilities at will, since we then have an even chance of being right, whereas we have none if we suspend judgment. The function of philosophy, according to James, is to find out what difference it makes to the individual if a particular philosophy or world-system is true: "An idea is 'true' so long as to believe it is profitable to our lives," and, he adds, "the true is only the expedient in our way of thinking . . . in the long run and on the whole of course." Thus "if the hypothesis of God works satisfactorily in the widest sense of the word, it is true." Bertrand Russell's reply to this assertion is: "I have always found that the hypothesis of Santa Claus 'works satisfactorily in the widest sense of the word'; therefore 'Santa Claus exists' is true, although Santa Claus does not exist." Russell adds that James's concept of truth simply omits as unimportant the question whether God really *is* in His heaven; if He is a useful hypothesis that is enough. "God the Architect of the Cosmos is forgotten; all that is remembered is belief in God, and its effects upon the creatures inhabiting our petty planet. No wonder the Pope condemned the pragmatic defence of religion."

**Predestination.** *See* Calvinism.

**Presbyterianism,** a system of ecclesiastical government of the Protestant churches which look back to John Calvin as their Reformation leader. The ministry consists of presbyters who are all of equal rank. Its doctrinal standards are contained in the *Westminster Confession of Faith* (1647) which is, in general, accepted by English, Scottish, and American Presbyterians as the most thorough and logical statement in existence of the Calvinist creed. The Church of Scotland is the leading Presbyterian church in the British Isles.

The Reformation in Scotland was preceded by the same sort of awareness of the moral corruption of the Roman Church as had happened elsewhere, but for various political and emotional reasons, which need not be discussed here, the majority of the Scottish people (unlike the English who had been satisfied with the mere exchange of Crown for Pope) were determined on a fundamental change of doctrine, discipline, and worship, rather than a reform of manners. The church preachers had learned their Protestantism not from Luther but from Calvin and their leader John Knox had worked in Geneva with Calvin himself and was resolved to introduce the system into Scotland. In 1557 the "Lords of the Congregation" signed the Common Band (*i.e.,* a bond or covenant) to maintain "the blessed Word of God and his congregation" against their enemies, and demanded the right to worship as they had chosen. However, the real date of the Scottish Reformation is August 1560 when Mary of Guise (the regent for Mary Queen of Scots who was not yet of age) died and the Estates met to settle their affairs without foreign pressure; the *Scots Confession* was drawn up and signed by Knox and adopted by the Estates.

The ideas on which the Reformed Kirk was based are found in the *Scots Confession,* the *Book of Discipline,* and the *Book of Common Order,* the so-called Knox's liturgy. Knox's liturgy, the same as that used in Geneva but translated into English, was used until Laud's attempt to force an Anglican liturgy on the Kirk led to an abandonment of both in favour of "free prayers."

The Presbyterian tradition includes uncompromising stress upon the Word of God contained in the Scriptures of the Old and New Testaments as the supreme rule of faith and life, and upon the value of a highly trained ministry, which has given the Church of Scotland a high reputation for scholarship and has in turn influenced the standard of education in Scotland. The unity of the Church is guaranteed by providing for democratic representation in a hierarchy of courts (unlike the Anglican Church, which is a hierarchy of persons). The local kirk-session consists of the minister and popularly elected elders (laymen). Ministers, elected by their flocks, are ordained by presbyters (ministers already ordained). Above the kirk-session is the court of the presbytery which has jurisdiction over a specified area; above that the court of synod which rules over many presbyteries; and finally the General Assembly which is the Supreme Court of the Church with both judicial and legislative powers, and over which the Moderator of the General Assembly presides. The function of the elders is to help the minister in the work and government of the kirk. The episcopacy set up by James VI and I, and maintained by Charles I was brought to an end by the Glasgow Assembly (1638), but General Assemblies were abolished by Oliver Cromwell and at the Restoration Charles II re-established episcopacy. The Covenanters who resisted were hunted down, imprisoned, transported, or executed over a period of nearly thirty years before William of Orange came to the throne and Presbyterianism was re-established (1690). Today Presbyterians no less than other Christian communities are looking at Christianity as a common world religion in the sense that the principles which unite them are greater than those which divide them. *See* Church of Scotland, Calvinism.

**Protestant,** the name first applied to those who favoured the cause of Martin Luther and who protested against the intolerant decisions of the Catholic majority at the second Diet of Speyer (1529), revoking earlier decisions of the first Diet of Speyer tolerating the Reformers in certain cases (1526). In general the name "Protestant" is applied to those Churches which severed connection with Rome at the time of the Reformation. The essence of Protestantism is the acceptance by the individual Christian of his direct responsibility to God rather than to the Church. *See* Lutheranism, Presbyterianism, Calvinism.

**Psychic Research,** the *scientific* study of so-called psychic phenomena as contrasted with spiritualism (*q.v.*) which is the cult of those who already believe in their supernatural nature. It is obviously impossible here to summarise work that has been carried out (in Britain notably by the Society for Psychical Research, founded in 1882) on such subjects as mediumship, apparitions, telepathy and clairvoyance (discussed here separately under the heading of Telepathy), poltergeists (also discussed separately), levitation, and precognition.

But the point at which we must begin is the human mind and the nature of scientific evidence and so far as these are concerned the following points may be made.

(1) There is little use in discussing psychic phenomena until we realise that almost no human being—least of all one with strong convictions—is a completely trustworthy witness. A person may be utterly honest in every other respect except that in which his convictions are involved.

(2) This does not mean that a witness is either telling the whole truth or is simply lying; for the following possibilities exist: (*a*) he may be telling the truth: (*b*) he may be consciously lying for motives of his own; (*c*) his recollections may be incorrect in discussing something that happened in the past; (*d*) he may really believe that he saw or heard what he said he did and may be telling the truth *as he experienced it*—*e.g.*, seeing a ghost—without realising that what he experienced is a product of his own unconscious mind; (*e*) there are various degrees of lying, for the mind has a natural tendency to add coherence and meaning to the only partly coherent events of the day, and it is a normal trait (consciously or unconsciously) to make a "good story" out of what originally were isolated and unconnected happenings; (*f*) even under the most favourable conditions the evidence of scientifically-trained people is not as good as it might be (cf. the psychological experiment in which a class of students is suddenly exposed to a deliberately contrived scene, *e.g.*, two men eccentrically dressed rush into the lecture-room, exchange words, and have a quarrel—and the students are afterwards required to write down what they saw and heard, rarely 10 per cent. being even 70 per cent. correct as to what really happened).

(3) There are many aspects of "psychic" phenomena which are not "psychic" at all, but based on well-known scientific principles. How many people, for example, know: (*a*) that *every* physical illness has its psychological aspect, so that a person with chronic arthritis, let us say, may get up and walk for the first time in years after injection with a new drug which is later proved to be worthless or no better than aspirin (*e.g.,* cortisone), yet if a "spiritual healer" got the same results he would be acclaimed for his psychic powers: (*b*) that it is possible to be completely paralysed, totally blind or deaf, have total loss of sensation in some part of the body, have two or more personalities, *without any physical disease being present,* in the neurosis (cured daily by psychiatrists without mystery) known as hysteria.

(4) It is possible under hypnosis, or self-hypnosis, to produce stigmata—*e.g.*, marks resembling the nail-prints of the Crucifixion on hands and feet, to produce blisters at will, spontaneous bleeding, and many of the phenomena usually described as miraculous, in the consulting room and by scientific means.

(5) We all have more potent senses than we ordinarily realise. We may not consciously know the number of steps leading to our flat but can be made under hypnosis to tell

Furthermore, there are people who are hypersensitive in hearing and vision (often without being aware of it), so that in " thought-transference " experiments where they are sent to another room whilst others decide on some object or idea, they may subconsciously hear what is going on; or in card experiments in telepathy they may be able to read the face of the card reflected in the pupils of the " sender " opposite, or tell in a familiar pack which card is which from almost invisible differences on the backs of the cards.

(6) Most of us have no idea of the mathematical laws of probability and are therefore likely to misinterpret the " mysteriousness " of phenomena. Thus, suppose I have a " premonition " that someone has died and later find my feelings confirmed by the event, then I may not remember or know (a) that on many previous occasions I, in common with most other people, have had " premonitions " the vast majority of which did *not* come true; (b) that, on the last occasion I saw the person, or from things I may have heard, I may have unconsciously noted signs that all was not well and expected the event; (c) that the most " improbable " things happen quite normally (e.g., during the last war a flying bomb fell through the roof of the British Museum and failed to explode, and some time later a second flying bomb fell *through the same hole* and likewise *failed to explode*); (d) that the chance of a pack of cards being dealt so that each of four persons receives a complete suit is exactly the same as the chance that any other combination of cards may come up.

(7) That collective hallucinosis does occur (it would be invidious to mention in detail certain " miraculous happenings " which might hurt the religious susceptibilities of many, but we are entitled to ask how it is possible for the sun to stand still in the sky in the presence of thousands of people collected in a particular area when it is seen nowhere else in the world and has been noted by no astronomical laboratory?)

(8) Mediums have been proved to be prepared to do the most extraordinary things in order to deceive a suggestible audience seated in semidarkness—e.g., the so-called " ectoplasm " (a supposedly psychic substance or materialisation) which exudes from the medium's body has been found before the séance, as have " apports " or objects apparently appearing from nowhere, half-way down the medium's throat or in the stomach ready to be regurgitated, and even in other bodily apertures.

It is not maintained that psychic phenomena do not happen, but that we must be extremely cautious in accepting the evidence of our own, or even more, other people's, senses, and much less free in our interpretation of what has been observed really means. See Poltergeist, Telepathy, Spiritualism.

Pyrrhonism, a sceptical philosophy which doubts everything.

# Q

Quakers. See Friends, The Society of.

Quartodecimani, an early Christian community who celebrated the Easter festival on the 14th day of the month, when the Jews celebrated their Passover. In consequence of the confusion caused, the practice was condemned by the Council of Nicaea in 325.

Quietism, a doctrine of extreme asceticism and contemplative devotion, embodied in the works of Michael Molinos, a 17th cent. Spanish priest, and condemned by Rome. It taught that the chief duty of man is to be occupied in the continual contemplation of God, so as to become totally independent of outward circumstances and the influence of the senses. Quietists taught that when this stage of perfection is reached the soul has no further need for prayer and other external devotional practices. Similar doctrines have been taught in the Moslem and Hindu religions. See Yoga.

# R

Racism, the doctrine that one race is inherently superior or inferior to others, one of the bases

of racial prejudice. It has no connection whatever with the study of race as a concept, or the investigation of racial differences, which is a science practised by the physical anthropologist (who studies physical differences), or the social anthropologist (who studies cultural differences). Racism is simply a vulgar superstition believed in by the ignorant or mentally unbalanced, and it may be categorically stated as a scientific fact that racial superiority is a myth believed in by no scientist of repute. There are, therefore, only two questions which it is necessary to answer: (1) If no race is superior to any other, why are there obvious differences between the backward and the technically advanced peoples? (2) If there are no inherent differences between races, then why does racial prejudice exist? Both of these are, strictly speaking, questions to which the scientists must give an answer; the former is answered in Section F, Part V, and Section Q, Part II; the latter under Anti-semitism, J3.

Ranters, a derisive term for the Primitive Methodists (see Methodism).

Rationalism is defined as " the treating of reason as the ultimate authority in religion and the rejection of doctrines not consonant with reason." In practice, rationalism has a double significance: (1) the doctrine as defined above, and (2) a 19th cent. movement which was given to what was then known as " free-thought," " secularism," or agnosticism—i.e., it was in the positive sense anti-religious and was represented by various bodies such as the Secular Society, the National Secular Society, and the Rationalist Press Association (founded in 1899).

In the first sense, which implies a particular philosophical attitude to the universe and life, rationalism is not easy to pin down although, at first sight, it would appear that nothing could be simpler. Does it mean the use of pure reason and logic or does it mean, on the other hand, the use of what is generally called the " scientific method " based on observation (i.e., the evidence of our senses) and experiment? If we are thinking in terms of the use of pure reason and logic then the Roman Catholic Church throughout most of its history has maintained, not that the whole truth about religion can be discovered by reason, but as St. Thomas Aquinas held, the basis of religion—e.g., the existence of God—can be rationally demonstrated. Nobody could have made more use of logic than the schoolmen of the Middle Ages, yet not many people today would accept their conclusions, nor would many non-Catholics accept St. Thomas's proofs of the existence of God even when they themselves are religious. The arguments of a first Cause or Prime Mover or the argument from Design on the whole leave us unmoved, partly because they do not lead us to the idea of a *personal God*, partly because we rightly distrust logic and pure reason divorced from facts and know that, if we begin from the wrong assumptions or premises, we can arrive at some very strange answers. If the existence of a Deity can be proved by reason, then one can also by the use of reason come to the conclusions, or rather paradoxes, such as the following: God is by definition all good, all knowing, all powerful—yet evil exists (because if it does not exist then it cannot be wrong to say " there is no God "). But if evil exists, then it must do so either because of God (in which case He is not all good) or in spite of God (in which case He is not all powerful).

Arguments of this sort do not appeal to the modern mind for two historical reasons: (1) many of us have been brought up in the Protestant tradition which—at least in one of its aspects—insists that we must believe in God by faith rather than by logic and in its extreme form insists on God as revealed by the " inner light "; (2) our increasing trust in the scientific method by direct observation and experiment. Thus, no matter what Aristotle or St. Thomas may say about a Prime Mover or a First Cause, we remain unconvinced since at least one scientific theory suggests that the universe did not have a beginning and if scientific investigation proved this to be so, then we should be entirely indifferent to what formal logic had to say.

The secularist and rationalist movements of

the 19th cent. were anti-religious—and quite rightly so—because at that time there were serious disabilities imposed even in Britain by the Established Church on atheism or agnosticism and freedom of thought. They are of little significance now because very little is left, largely thanks to their efforts, of these disabilities.

Finally, although most people are likely to accept the scientific method as the main means of discovering truth, there are other factors which equally make us doubt the value of " pure " logic and reason unaided by observation. The first of these is the influence of Freud which shows that much of our reasoning is mere rationalising—e.g., we are more likely to become atheists because we hated our father than because we can prove that there is no God. The second is the influence of a movement in philosophy which, in the form of logical positivism or logical analysis, makes us doubt whether metaphysical systems have any meaning at all. To-day, instead of asking ourselves whether Plato was right or wrong, we are much more likely to ask whether he did anything but make for the most part meaningless noises. Religion is in a sense much safer today than it ever was in the 19th cent. when it made foolish statements over matters of science that could be proved wrong; now we tend to see it as an emotional attitude to the universe or God (a " feeling of being at home in the universe," as William James put it) which can no more be proved or disproved than being in love.

**Realism** is a word which has so many meanings, and such contradictory ones, in various spheres, that it is difficult to define. We shall limit ourselves to its significance in philosophy. In philosophy, " realism " has two different meanings, diametrically opposed. (1) The most usual meaning is the one we should least expect from the everyday sense of the word—i.e., it refers to all those philosophies from Plato onwards which maintained that the world of appearance is illusory and that ideas, forms, or universals are the only true realities, belonging to the world beyond matter and appearance—the world of God or mind. In early mediaeval times St. Thomas Aquinas was the chief exponent of this doctrine which was held by the scholastics as opposed to the Nominalists (q.v.). (2) In its modern everyday meaning " realism " is the belief that the universe is real and not a creation of mind, that although all we really experience is the evidence of our senses there is a reality that causes the appearance, the " thing-in-itself " as Kant described it. Material things may not really be what they appear to be (e.g., a noise is not the " bang " we experience but a series of shock-waves passing through the atmosphere), yet, for all that, we can be sure that matter exists and it is very possible (some might add) that mind does not.

**Reformation,** the great religious movement of the 16th cent., which resulted in the establishment of Protestantism. John Wyclif (d. 1384), John Hus (d. 1415) and others had sounded the warning note, and when later on Luther took up the cause in Germany, and Zwingli in Switzerland, adherents soon became numerous. The wholesale vending of indulgences by the papal agents had incensed the people, and when Luther denounced these things he spoke to willing ears. After much controversy, the reformers boldly propounded the principles of the new doctrine, and the struggle for religious supremacy grew bitter. They claimed justification (salvation) by faith, and the use as well as the authority of the Scriptures, rejecting the doctrine of transubstantiation, the adoration of the Virgin and Saints, and the headship of the Pope. Luther was excommunicated. But the Reformation principles spread and ultimately a great part of Germany, as well as Switzerland, the Low Countries, Scandinavia, England, and Scotland were won over to the new faith. In England Henry VIII readily espoused the cause of the Reformation, his own personal quarrel with the Pope acting as an incentive. Under Mary there was a brief and sanguinary reaction, but Elizabeth gave completeness to the work which her father had initiated. See Lutheranism, Calvinism, Presbyterianism, Baptists, Methodism.

**Reincarnation,** the transmigration of souls. See Immortality, Hinduism, Buddhism.

**Renaissance** is defined in the Oxford English Dictionary as: " The revival of art and letters, under the influence of classical models, which began in Italy in the 14th century." It is a term which must be used with care for the following reasons: (1) Although it was first used in the form rinascita (re-birth) by Vasari in 1550 and people living at that time certainly were aware that something new was happening, the word had no wide currency until used by the Swiss historian Jacob Burckhardt in his classic The Civilization of the Renaissance in Italy (1860). (2) The term as used today refers not only to art in its widest sense but to a total change in man's outlook on life which extended into philosophical, scientific, economic, and technical fields. (3) Spreading from Italy there were renaissance movements in France, Spain, Germany, and northern Europe, all widely different with varying delays in time. As the historian Edith Sichel says: " Out of the Italian Renaissance there issued a new-born art; out of the Northern Renaissance there came forth a new-born religion. There came forth also a great school of poetry, and a drama the greatest that the world had seen since the days of Greece. The religion was the offspring of Germany and the poetry that of England."

The real cause of the Renaissance was not the fall of Constantinople, the invention of printing, the discovery of America, though these were phases in the process; it was, quite simply money. The rise of a new merchant class gave rise to individualist attitudes in economic affairs which prepared the way for individualism and humanism. The new wealthy class in time became patrons of the arts whereas previously the Church had been the sole patron and controller. Thus the artist became more free to express himself, more respected, and being more well-to-do could afford to ignore the Church and even, in time, the views of his patrons.

It is true that art continued to serve to a considerable extent the purposes of faith, but it was judged from the standpoint of art. Mediaeval art was meant to elevate and teach man: Renaissance art to delight his senses and enrich his life. From this free and questing spirit acquired from economic individualism came the rise of modern science and technology; here Italy learned much from the Arab scholars who had translated and commented upon the philosophical, medical, and mathematical texts of antiquity, while denying themselves any interest in Greek art and literature. Arabic-Latin versions of Aristotle were in use well into the 16th cent. The Byzantine culture, though it had preserved the Greek tradition and gave supremacy to Plato, had made no move forward. But the Greek scholars who fled to Italy after the fall of Constantinople brought with them an immense cargo of classical manuscripts. The recovery of these Greek masterpieces, their translation into the vernaculars, and the invention of printing, made possible a completer understanding of the Greek spirit. It was the bringing together of the two heritages, Greek science, and Greek literature, that gave birth to a new vision. But it was not only Aristotle and Plato who were being studied but Ovid, Catullus, Horace, Pliny and Lucretius. What interested Renaissance man was the humanism of the Latin writers, their attitude to science, their scepticism.

The period c. 1400–1500 is known as the Early Renaissance. During this time such painters as Masaccio, Uccello, Piero della Francesca, Botticelli, and Giovanni Bellini were laying the foundations of drawing and painting for all subsequent periods including our own. They concerned themselves with such problems as anatomy, composition, perspective, and representation of space, creating in effect a grammar or textbook of visual expression. The term High Renaissance is reserved for a very brief period when a pure, balanced, classical harmony was achieved and artists were in complete control of the techniques learned earlier. The High Renaissance lasted only from c. 1500 to 1527 (the date of the sack of Rome), yet that interval included the earlier works of Michel-angelo, most of Leonardo's, and all the Roman works of Raphael.

**Ritualism**, a tendency which, during the 19th cent., developed in the High Church section of the Church of England to make use of those vestments, candles, incense, etc. which are usually regarded as features of the Church of Rome. Since some opposition was aroused, a Ritual Commission was appointed in 1904 to take evidence and try to find some common basis on which High and Low Church could agree with respect to ceremonial. The report of 1906 in effect recommended the giving of greater powers to bishops to suppress objectionable practices. Although they are often associated together, it is worth while pointing out that there was no special connection between the Oxford Movement or Tractarians (*q.v.*) and Ritualism because Pusey disliked ritual and even Newman, who eventually went over to Rome, held extremely simple services at his church of St. Mary's.

**Roman Catholic Church**, the Christian organisation which acknowledges the Pope as the lawful successor of St. Peter, the apostle appointed by Christ to be the head of His Church. The reforming impulse at the Second Vatican Council (1962–5) has set in train great movements towards religious unity and the reform and modernisation of the Roman Catholic Church.

**Romantic Movement** or **Romanticism** is the name given not so much to an individual way of thinking but to the gradual but radical transformation of basic human values that occurred in the Western world round about the latter part of the 18th cent. It was a great breakthrough in European consciousness and arose through the writings of certain men living during the half-century or more following, say, 1760. It arose then because both time and place were propitious for the birth of these new ideas. There was a revolution in basic values—in art, morals, politics, religion, etc. The new view was of a world transcending the old one, infinitely larger and more varied.

To understand the Romantic movement it is necessary first to take note of the climate of thought preceding the great change; then to account for its beginning in Germany where it did (*see* Pietism) during the latter part of the 18th cent., and finally to appraise the writings of those men whose ideas fermented the new awakening. Briefly, the shift was away from French classicism and from belief in the all-pervasive power of human reason (the Enlightenment) towards the unfettered freedom that the new consciousness was able to engender. What mattered was to live a passionate and vigorous life, to dedicate oneself to an ideal, no matter what the cost (*e.g.*, Byron).

The ideas of the Enlightenment (*e.g.*, Fontenelle, Voltaire, Montesquieu) had been attacked by the Germans Hamann and Herder and by the ideas of the English philosopher Hume, but Kant, Schiller, and Fichte, Goethe's novel *Wilhelm Meister*, and the French Revolution all had profound effects on the aesthetic, moral, social, and political thought of the time. Friedrich Schlegel (1772–1829) said: "There is in man a terrible unsatisfied desire to soar into infinity; a feverish longing to break through the narrow bonds of individuality." Romanticism undermined the notion that in matters of value there are objective criteria which operate between men. Henceforth there was to be a resurgence of the human spirit, deep and profound, that is still going on.

**Rotarianism.** The Rotary Club is primarily an American association but has many members in Britain and presumably elsewhere since all Rotary Clubs are united in an international organisation. It consists of groups of business and professional men formed with the purpose of serving their community and humanity in general. The name is derived from the clubs entertaining in rotation.

# S

**Sabellian heresy.** During the 4th cent. great controversies raged within the Christian Church over the divinity of Jesus Christ. Arius (*see* Arianism) denied Christ's divinity and maintained that the Father alone was truly divine.

This doctrine was condemned at the Council of Nicaea (325), Arius being opposed by Athanasius who held the now orthodox view of the Trinity which was reaffirmed at the Council of Constantinople (381). The Sabellians, named after their founder Sabellius (*fl.* 215), a Libyan priest and theologian, held the view that God is indivisible but with three roles, appearing successively as the Father (the creator), as the Son (the redeemer), and as the Holy Spirit (the divine spirit within men). This view, which makes the person of Jesus Christ ultimately an illusion, was condemned.

**Salvation Army.** The religious movement which in 1878 became known by this name arose from the Christian Mission meetings which the Rev. William Booth and his devoted wife had held in the East End of London for the previous thirteen years. Its primary aim was, and still is, to preach the gospel of Jesus Christ to men and women untouched by ordinary religious efforts. The founder devoted his life to the salvation of the submerged classes whose conditions at that time were unspeakably dreadful. Originally his aim had been to convert people and then send them on to the churches, but he soon found that few religious bodies would accept these "low-class" men and women. So it was that social work became part of their effort. Practical help, like the provision of soup-kitchens, accompanied spiritual ministration. Soon, in the interests of more effective "warfare" against social evils, a military form of organisation, with uniforms, brass bands, and religious songs, was introduced. Its magazine *The War Cry* gave as its aim "to carry the Blood of Christ and the Fire of the Holy Ghost into every part of the world." There were persecutions: mobs, sometimes encouraged by the police, assaulted the Salvationists who, although not the aggressors, were often punished by the magistrates. General Booth saw with blinding clarity that conversion must be accompanied by an improvement of external conditions. Various books had earlier described the terrible conditions of the slums, but in 1890 he produced a monumental survey entitled *In Darkest England and the Way Out.* From that time forward the Army was accepted and its facilities made use of by the authorities. To-day the Army's spiritual and social activities have spread to countries all over the world; every one no matter what class, colour, or creed he belongs to is a "brother for whom Christ died."

**Sandemanians** or **Glassites**, an obscure religious sect whose sole claim to fame is that one of its members was the great Michael Faraday, founder of the science of electromagnetism, who never failed to attend its Sunday services.

**Sceptics.** From Thales of Miletus (*c.* 624–565 B.C.) to the Stoics in the 4th cent. B.C. philosophers had been trying to explain the nature of the universe: each one produced a different theory and each could, apparently, prove that he was right. This diversity of views convinced the Sceptic school founded by Pyrrho (*c.* 360–270 B.C.) that man is unable to know the real nature of the world or how it came into being. In place of a futile search for what must be for ever unknowable, the Sceptics recommended that men should be practical, follow custom, and accept the evidence of their senses.

**Schoolmen.** From the time of Augustine to the middle of the 9th cent. philosophy, like science, was dead or merely a repetition of what had gone before. But about that time there arose a new interest in the subject, although (since by then Western Europe was entirely under the authority of the Catholic Church) the main form it took was an attempt to justify Church teaching in the light of Greek philosophy. Those who made this attempt to reconcile Christian beliefs with the best in Plato and Aristotle were known as "schoolmen" and the philosophies which they developed were known as "scholasticism." Among the most famous schoolmen must be counted John Scotus Erigena (*c.* 800–*c.* 877), born in Ireland and probably the earliest; St. Anselm, archbishop of Canterbury (1033–1109); the great Peter Abelard whose school was in Paris (1079–1142); Bernard of Chartres, his contemporary; and the best-known of all, St. Thomas Aquinas of Naples (1225–74), who was given the name of the "Angelic Doctor."

The philosophies of these men are discussed under various headings (God and Man, Determinism and Free-will), but being severely limited by the Church their doctrines differed from each other much less than those of later philosophical schools. However, one of the great arguments was between the orthodox Realists (q.v.) and the Nominalists (q.v.) and a second was between the Thomists (or followers of St. Thomas Aquinas) and the Scotists (followers of John Duns Scotus—not to be confused with John Scotus Erigena). The two latter schools were known as the Ancients, whilst the followers of William of Occam, the Nominalist, were known as the Terminalists. All became reconciled in 1482 in face of the threat from humanism of which the great exponent was Erasmus of Rotterdam (1466–1536) who hated scholasticism.

Shakers, members of a revivalist group, styled by themselves "The United Society of Believers in Christ's Second Appearing," who seceded from Quakerism in 1747 though adhering to many of the Quaker tenets. The community was joined in 1758 by Ann Lee, a young convert from Manchester, who had "revelations" that she was the female Christ; "Mother Ann" was accepted as their leader. Under the influence of her prophetic visions she set out with nine followers for "Immanuel's land" in America and the community settled near Albany, capital of New York state. They were known as the "Shakers" in ridicule because they were given to involuntary movements in moments of religious ecstasy.

Central to their faith was the belief in the dual role of God through the male and female Christ: the male principle came to earth in Jesus; the female principle, in "Mother Ann." The sexes were equal and women preached as often as men at their meetings which sometimes included sacred dances—nevertheless the two sexes, even in dancing, kept apart. Their communistic way of living brought them economic prosperity, the Shakers becoming known as good agriculturists and craftsmen, noted for their furniture and textiles. After 1860, however, the movement began to decline and few, if any, are active today.

Shamans, the medicine men found in all primitive societies who used their magical arts to work cures, and protect the group from evil influences. The shaman was a man apart and wore special garments to show his authority. Shamanism with its magical practices, incantations, trances, exhausting dances, and self-torture is practised even today by tribes that have survived in a primitive state of culture.

Shiites or Shia, a heretical Moslem sect in Persia, opposed by the orthodox Sunnites. The dispute, which came almost immediately after the death of the Prophet and led to bitter feuding, had little to do with matters of doctrine as such, but with the succession. After Mohammed's death, there were three possible claimants: Ali, the husband of his daughter Fatima, and two others, one of whom gave up his claim in favour of the other, Omar. The orthodox selected Omar, who was shortly assassinated, and the same happened to his successor as Ali was passed over again. The Shiites are those who maintain that Ali was the true vicar of the Prophet, and that the three orthodox predecessors were usurpers.

Shintoism, the native religion of Japan, primarily a system of nature and ancestor worship. After the defeat of Japan in the second world war Hirohito disavowed his divinity as ancestor of the Sun-goddess.

Sikhism. The Sikh community of the Punjab, which has played a significant part in the history of modern India, came into being during a period of religious revival in India in the 15th and 16th cent. It was originally founded as a religious sect by Guru (teacher) Nanak (1469–1538) who emphasised the fundamental truth of all religions, and whose mission was to put an end to religious conflict. He condemned the formalism both of Hinduism and Islam, preaching the gospel of universal toleration, and the unity of the Godhead, whether He be called

Allah, Vishnu, or God. His ideas were welcomed by the great Mogul Emperor Akbar (1542–1605). Thus a succession of Gurus were able to live in peace after Nanak's death; they established the great Sikh centre at Amritsar, compiled the sacred writings known as the Adi Granth, and improved their organisation as a sect. But the peace did not last long, for an emperor arose who was a fanatical Moslem, in face of whom the last Guru, Govind Singh (1666–1708), whose father was put to death for refusal to embrace Islam, had to make himself a warrior and instil into the Sikhs a more aggressive spirit. A number of ceremonies were instituted by Govind Singh; admission to the fraternity was by special rite; caste distinctions were abolished; hair was worn long; the word singh, meaning lion, was added to the original name. They were able to organise themselves into 12 misls or confederacies but divisions appeared with the disappearance of a common enemy and it was not until the rise of Ranjit Singh (1780–1839) that a single powerful Sikh kingdom was established, its influence only being checked by the English, with whom a treaty of friendship was made. After the death of Ranjit Singh two Anglo-Sikh wars followed, in 1845–46, and 1848–49, which resulted in British annexation of the Punjab and the end of Sikh independence. In the two world wars the Sikhs proved among the most loyal of Britain's Indian subjects. The partitioning of the continent of India in 1947 into two states, one predominantly Hindu and the other predominantly Moslem, presented a considerable problem in the Punjab, which was divided in such a way as to leave 2 million Sikhs in Pakistan, and a considerable number of Moslems in the Indian Punjab. Although numbering less than 2 per cent. of the population (c. 8 million) the Sikhs are a continuing factor in Indian political life. In 1966 the Punjab was divided on a linguistic basis—Punjabi-speaking Punjab and Hindi-speaking Hariana.

Socialism, a form of society in which men and women are not divided into opposing economic classes but live together under conditions of approximate social and economic equality, using in common the means that lie to their hands of promoting social welfare. The brotherhood of man inspires the aims of socialism in foreign, colonial, social, and economic policies alike. The word "socialism" first came into general use in England about 1834 in connection with Robert Owen's "village of co-operation" at New Lanark. About the middle of the 19th cent. Charles Kingsley and others established a form of Christian socialism, and William Morris, John Burns, and others founded a Socialist League in 1886. With the development of trade unions the socialist movement took a more practical trend. Fabianism (q.v.) associated in its early days with the names of Beatrice and Sidney Webb and George Bernard Shaw, aims at the gradual reorganisation of society by creating intelligent public opinion by education and legislation. The British Labour Party believes in peaceful and constitutional approach to socialism by democratic methods based upon popular consent. A democratic programme of planned economy and public ownership of certain vital industries and services were features of socialist government from 1945–51 together with a comprehensive system of social security. Further radical reforms in the interest of social justice and industrial efficiency are in progress under the socialist government which has been in power since 1964. See also Section C, Part I.

Southcottians, followers of Joanna Southcott who died in 1814 shortly after announcing to them that (although aged over 50) she was about to give birth to a divine man named Siloh. It spite of the fact that she went through all the actions of a woman about to give birth it is not surprising that no Siloh appeared nor was she pregnant. She also announced that, 100 years after her death, great revelations would be made —but in 1914 people had other things to think about and no revelations were vouchsafed. Yet this unfortunate woman still has her followers who believe that Siloh will appear and that the "true" revelations will be made at some unspecified future date under the right conditions.

It is difficult to decide which is the stranger phenomenon, Joanna or her followers.

**Spiritualism** is a religion which requires to be distinguished from **psychical research** (*q.v.*) which is a scientific attempt carried on both by believers and non-believers to investigate psychic phenomena including those not necessarily connected with "spirits"—*e.g.*, telepathy or clairvoyance and precognition. As a religion (although for that matter the whole of history is filled with attempts to get in touch with the "spirit world") spiritualism begins with the American Andrew Jackson Davis who in 1847 published *Nature's Divine Revelations*, a book which is still widely read although it bears traces of the period in which it was written. Thus reference is made to the theories of "Mesmerism" and "magnetic influence" which really belong to the period when hypnosis was described as Mesmerism after the name of its first modern exponent, Anton Mesmer (d. 1815). The division of man into body, soul, and spirit is accepted and it is supposed that the "soul" is simply a sublimation of the body, needing food which after digestion by the body is refined into a more ethereal form. It even takes the actual form of the body which in reality is merely the covering by which soul communicates with the outer world before passing the messages on to the spirit which is a process of the Divine in which it will ultimately be absorbed. As we grow older there is a gradual separation between spirit or soul and the body—a process which Davis claimed to have observed in the clairvoyant state. According to his observations, the soul, still retaining the form of the body from which it was separating, moved above it but was still joined by a tenuous stream of "vital electricity" which Davis compared with the umbilical cord and took some time to vanish. Death in this view is literally a birth-process from a lower to a higher plane.

The earth is surrounded by a series of spheres from lower to higher, and although these are spiritual it is claimed that their actual distance from the centre of the earth can be measured in ordinary miles or metres. Davis supposed that the passage from lower to higher spheres is accompanied by an increase in moral perfection until the spirit is ultimately absorbed in God. In the lower spheres, however, it still retains something of the material which enables mediums to enter into contact with it. Therefore nearly all spiritualist meetings include a séance, and for the rest, there are prayers, sermons, and hymns. There are ministers, lay officers, and mediums; the latter usually are "freelance" and move about from one church to another. It is, as most people are well aware, perfectly possible for capable and knowledgeable men and women to be either "spiritualists" or (more commonly) interested in spiritualism, but for the most part those who attend services are people who come seeking for proof that their loved ones are not dead but have "passed on" and such are unlikely to retain a critical attitude on the subject however hard-headed they may be in other respects. In spite, or perhaps because of this, the Spiritualist Church is one with an ever-increasing membership especially in Britain and America. It is not permitted for Roman Catholics to hold or practise spiritualist beliefs.

**State and Man.** Most of the early civilisations such as those of Egypt and Babylonia were theocratic, that is to say, they were arranged in a hierarchy with, at the peak, a king who was also an incarnation of the god. Needless to say, in such circumstances there was no room for philosophising about the nature of the state and the relationship which ought to exist between state and citizens. As usual, we have to turn to ancient Greece for the beginnings of thought about this problem. We do so as briefly as possible since in general it is only the later philosophers whose work has much contemporary interest and, in any case, most people today realise that the political philosophy of a particular time is bound to reflect the actual conditions prevailing then and as such is of mainly theoretical interest today.

*The Greek Approach.* The early pre-Socratic

philosophers Democritus and the Pythagorean school, for example, held that the individual should subordinate himself to the whole; they had no doubt that the citizen's first duty was to the state. The Greeks until the time of Plato were not really thinking in terms of individual rights, nor had they given much thought to what form the state should take—they simply accepted it. The first great attempt to describe the ideal state is to be found in Plato's *The Republic* which is referred to elsewhere (*see* **Education**). His pupil Aristotle did not try to form a utopia but made many comments on the nature of government. Thus, while agreeing that the state was more important than any individual person, he distinguished between good and bad states, and pointed out that to the extent that the state does not enable its citizens to lead virtuous and useful lives it is evil. A good constitution must recognise the inequalities between human beings and confer on them rights according to their abilities: among these inequalities are those of personal ability, property, birth, and status, as freeman or slave. The best forms of rule were monarchy, aristocracy, and democracy; the worst forms—tyranny, oligarchy (or rule of a powerful few), and ochlocracy (or mob-rule). The later Greek thinkers of Hellenistic times held two opposed points of view. The Epicureans (*q.v.*) taught that all social life is based upon self-interest and we become members of a group for our own convenience; therefore there are no absolute rights and laws—what is good is what members decide at that time to be good, and when they change their minds the law must change too. Injustice is not an evil in any god-given sense; we behave justly simply because if injustice became the general rule, we ourselves should suffer. The Stoics (*q.v.*), on the other hand, held that the state must dominate the individual completely and everyone must carry out, first and foremost, his social duties and be willing to sacrifice everything for it; but the state of the Stoics was no narrowly national one, but one that strove to become a universal brotherhood.

*The Christian Approach.* The orthodox Christian view is expressed in St. Augustine's book *The City of God*. Here it is held that the church, as the worldly incarnation of the City of God, is to be supreme over the state, and the head of the church is to be supreme over secular rulers. In addition it must be recognised that, whilst the secular ruler can make mistakes, the church does not, since it is the representative of God's kingdom on earth.

*The Secular State.* During the Renaissance (*q.v.*) people began to think for themselves and the results of their cogitations were not always pleasant; for it was during this time that many rulers, petty and otherwise, were seeking absolute authority. Two notable thinkers at this stage were Niccolo Machiavelli (1469–1527) in Italy and Thomas Hobbes (1588–1679) in England, where, of course, the Renaissance arrived later in history. Both supported absolute monarchy against the former domination of the church. The name of Machiavelli has become a by-word for any behaviour that is cunning and unscrupulous, but he was not really as bad as he is usually painted. It is, indeed, true that in his book *The Prince* he showed in the greatest detail the methods by which a ruler could gain absolute control and destroy civic freedom, but this despotism was intended as merely a necessary intermediate stage towards his real idea which was a free, united Italian nation wholly independent of the church. Hobbes was a materialist whose thesis was that man is naturally a ferocious animal whose basic impulse is war and pillage and the destruction of whatever stands in his way to gain his desires. But if he allowed himself to behave in this way his life would be "nasty, brutish, and short" so he creates a society in which he voluntarily gives up many of his rights and hands them over to a powerful ruler in his own interest. But having done this he must obey; even when the ruler is unjust, as he has no right to complain because anything is better than a return to his natural state. The religion of the king must be the religion of the people and the only things no ruler has the right to do is to cause a man to commit suicide or murder or to make him confess to a crime.

*Views of Locke: Live and Let Live.* John Locke (1632–1704) disagreed with these views. Man is naturally peaceful and co-operative and therefore social life comes readily to him. He sets up an authority in order to preserve the group and that is why laws are made; but the function of the state is strictly limited to maintaining the public good and beyond this men are to be left free. Therefore absolute power and the doctrine of the Divine Right of Kings were wrong because power ultimately rests with the people who have the right to make and break governments. It is also wrong that those who make the laws should be able to execute them. This is the important British doctrine of the separation of powers between the legislature and the executive which, in Britain and America, is regarded as one of the bases of democracy.

*Rousseau's Social Doctrine.* The only other views we need consider here are those of Jean-Jacques Rousseau (1712–78) and Herbert Spencer (1820–1903), since the views of the two important intervening figures, Hegel and Karl Marx, are dealt with elsewhere (*see* **Dialectical Materialism**) and after Spencer we come to a stage where political philosophy begins to merge with sociology and the social sciences. Rousseau is a puzzling figure. On the one hand he has been hailed as the prophet of freedom and on the other as the father of modern totalitarianism. His book *Social Contract* (1762) begins with the words: " Man is born free, and everywhere he is in chains." He says that he is in favour, not merely of democracy, but of direct democracy in which everyone has to give his assent to all measures as in the Greek city-states and in Geneva, of which city he was a citizen. (This method is still in force in respect of some measures in the Swiss cantons.) Natural society is based on a " social contract " or mutual agreement and Rousseau speaks of a " return to nature " which would ensure the sovereignty of the people at all times. Thus far, he seems to agree with Locke but soon we find that he is more akin to Hobbes, since (as we are learning in our own day) nothing is more tyrannical than the absolute rule of all the people. (Public opinion is more Hitlerian than Hitler.) As it turns out, then, the "social contract " consists in " the total alienation of each associate, together with all his rights, to the whole community " and " each of us puts his person and all his power in common under the supreme direction of the general will." Rousseau admired direct democracy in the small city-state, but if his doctrine is applied to large states, then the " general will " becomes absolute. It is in this sense that he is regarded as the forerunner of totalitarianism. Herbert Spencer is quoted only as an example of the inappropriate application of a biological theory to social issues. Influenced by Darwin's thesis of natural selection, he saw in society a struggle in which the fittest survived and the less fit perished. Each individual had the right to preserve himself, but in the case of human beings this depended upon group life in which, to some extent, each individual is limited by the rights of others. But this should not go too far, and he condemned the socialism of J. S. Mill which (*a*) would give over-much protection to the unfit, and (*b*) would give the state powers which it has no right to since the best government is the least government. In accordance with Darwinism free competition was essential. Stoics, the followers of Zeno, a Greek philosopher in the 4th cent. B.C., who received their name from the fact that they were taught in the Stoa Poikile or Painted Porch of Athens. They believed that since the world is the creation of divine wisdom and is governed by divine law, it is man's duty to accept his fate. Zeno conceived virtue to be the highest good and condemned the passions. (*See* **God and Man, State and Man, Determinism** and **Free-will** for a more detailed account of their beliefs).

Sunnites, the orthodox sect of Islam as contrasted with the Shiites or Shia (*q.v.*).

Swedenborgianism. The Church of the New Jerusalem, based on the writings of Emanuel Swedenborg (1688–1772), was founded by his followers eleven years after his death. The New Church is regarded by its members not as a sect but as a new dispensation bearing the same relationship to Christianity as Christianity does to Judaism.

Syndicalism, a form of socialist doctrine which aims at the ownership and control of all industries by the workers, contrasted with the more conventional type of socialism which advocates ownership and control by the state. Since syndicalists have preferred to improve the conditions of the workers by direct action, *e.g.* strikes and working to rule, rather than through the usual parliamentary procedures, they have been closely related to anarchists (*q.v.*) and are sometimes described as anarcho-syndicalists. Under syndicalism there would be no state; for the state would be replaced by a federation of units based on functional economic organisation rather than on geographical representation. The movement had bodies in the United Kingdom, where guild socialism (*q.v.*) was strongly influenced by its doctrines, in France, Germany, Italy, Spain, Argentina, and Mexico, but these gradually declined after the first world war losing many members to the communists. Fascism (*q.v.*) was also strongly influenced by the revolutionary syndicalism of Georges Sorel in making use of his concept of the " myth of the general strike " as an emotional image or ideal goal to spur on the workers; with Mussolini the " myth " became that of the state. Mussolini was also influenced by Sorel's doctrine of violence and the justification of force. Syndicalism had a certain influence in the Labour Party in its early days, but was crushed by men like Ernest Bevin who began to fear that by involving the workers in direct responsibility for their industries, it would put them at a disadvantage when bargaining for wages.

# T

Taoism, a religion which, although in a degenerate state, is still one of the great Eastern creeds. Its alleged founder, Lao-tze, is said to have been born in Honan about 604 B.C.; he is also said to be the author of the bible of Taoism, the *Tao-te-ching*, or in English *The Way of Life*, and to have disapproved of Confucius. This, if true, would hardly be surprising; for Taoism is eminently a mystical religion recommending doing nothing and resisting nothing, whereas Confucianism (*q.v.*) is eminently a practical code of living and its founder insisted on intervening in everything to do with social life. But the truth as revealed by modern scholarship is rather different. We are told that the poems of the *Tao-te-ching* are anonymous and probably originated among recluses in lonely valleys long before the time of Confucius; they were collected and given form at some time late in the 3rd cent. B.C. and their authorship attributed to Lao-tze. It is entirely possible that no such person ever existed (unlike Confucius, who certainly did), but if there were such a man he appears to have used a pseudonym since " Lao " is not a surname but an adjective meaning " old " and it was customary to attribute important works to old men on account of their supposed wisdom. Lao-tze simply means " the old philosopher," and although the *Tao-te-ching* is one of the most remarkable and instructive books ever written it is as anonymous as the Border Ballads.

It is apparent that the religion learned both from the ancient Chinese mystics and from Brahmanism: *Tao*, the Way, is impalpable, invisible, and incapable of being expressed in words. But it can be attained by virtue, by compassion, humility, and non-violence. Out of weakness comes true strength whereas violence is not only wrong but defeats its own ends. There is no personal God and such gods as men imagine are mere emanations of *Tao* which gives life to all things. *Tao* is Being. Works ⸱re worthless and internal renunciation is far better than anything that follows from the use of force because passive resistance convinces the other from within that he is in error, whereas violence only compels the external ap-

**J43**

pearance of conviction whilst inwardly the individual is as before. "It is wealth to be content; it is wilful to force one's way on others."

Later Lao-tze became a divinity and indeed one of a Trinity each worshipped in the form of idols (which the founder had hated). Soon there was worship of the forces of nature: the stars, the tides, the sun and moon, and a thousand other deities among whom Confucius was one. The purest mysticism and wisdom had been utterly corrupted by contact with the world.

**Telepathy and Clairvoyance.** Telepathy is the alleged communication between one mind and another other than through the ordinary sense channels. Clairvoyance is the supposed faculty of "seeing" objects or events which, by reason of space and time or other causes, are not discernible through the ordinary sense of vision. Such claims have been made from time immemorial but it was not until this century that the phenomena were investigated scientifically. The first scientific studies were made by the Institute for Psychical Research. A new era in experimentation began with the work of J. B. Rhine at Duke University, North Carolina, and S. G. Soal of London University. The most common technique is card guessing using a special pack of cards with the Zener symbols (circle, square, cross, wavy lines, star), thus giving the subject one chance in five of guessing correctly. Although the results obtained have led to the conclusion that telepathic communication is a fact, scepticism still exists, partly because of criticism of the methods employed, the validity of the data obtained, and the assumptions drawn, and partly because telepathic theory appears to clash with existing scientific thought. Dr. Rhine uses the term extra-sensory perception (abbreviated to ESP) to include telepathy, clairvoyance, and precognition. His studies also include what is described as the PK effect or psychokinesis, the supposed influence of the human mind on the movements of physical bodies. The Psi force is the term used for the faculty behind ESP and PK. Reference should be made to the entry on Psychical Research in order to obtain the background relating to the various fallacies involved in accepting human evidence uncritically.

**Theism.** See God and Man.

**Theosophy** (Sanskrit *Brahma Vidya* = divine wisdom), a system of thought that draws on the mystical teachings of those who assert the spiritual nature of the universe, and the divine nature of man. It insists that man is capable of intuitive insight into the nature of God. The way to wisdom, or self-knowledge, is through the practice of **Yoga** (*q.v.*). Theosophy has close connections with Indian thought through Vedic, Buddhist, and Brahmanist literature. The modern Theosophical Society was founded by Mme H. P. Blavatsky and others in 1875, and popularised by Mrs. Annie Besant.

**Tractarianism,** a Catholic revival movement, also known as the **Oxford Movement** (not to be confused with the so-called Oxford Group), which had its beginnings at Oxford in 1833. The leaders included the Oxford high churchmen E. B. Pusey, J. Keble and J. H. Newman. Through the *Tracts for the Times* (1833–41), a series of pamphlets which were sent to every parsonage in England, they sought to expose the dangers which they considered to be threatening the church from secular authority. The immediate cause of the movement was the Reform Act (1832) which meant that the state was no longer in the safe keeping of Tories and Churchmen but that power was falling into the hands of Liberals and Dissenters. They advocated a higher degree of ceremonial in worship nearer the Roman communion. In *Tract 90* (the last) Newman showed how the Thirty-nine Articles themselves, which were regarded as the bulwark of Protestantism, could be made to square with Roman doctrine. It was obvious which direction the movement was taking and the romanizing tendency was widely resented. In 1845 Newman went over to Rome. Pusey and Keble persisted in their efforts to secure recognition of Catholic liturgy and doctrine in the Anglican Church. Catholicism of the Anglican type (*i.e.*, Catholic in ritual, ceremony, and everything save submission to the Pope) is termed Anglo-Catholicism (*q.v.*).

**Transmigration of Souls.** *See* Immortality, Buddhism, Hinduism.

**Transubstantiation,** the conversion in the Eucharist of the bread and wine into the body and blood of Christ—a doctrine of the Roman Catholic Church.

**Trotskyism,** a form of communism supporting the views of Leon Trotsky, the assumed name of Lev Bronstein (1879–1940) who, in 1924, was ousted from power by Stalin and later exiled and assassinated in Mexico. Trotsky held that excessive Russian nationalism was incompatible with genuine international communism and that Stalin was concentrating on the economic development of the Soviet Union to an extent which could only lead to a bureaucratic state with a purely nationalist outlook.

# U

**Unitarianism** has no special doctrines, although clearly, as the name indicates, belief is in the single personality of God, *i.e.*, anti-trinitarian. This general statement, however, can be interpreted with varying degrees of subtlety. Thus unitarian belief may range from a sort of Arianism which accepts that, although Christ was not of divine nature, divine powers had been delegated to him by the Father, to the simple belief that Christ was a man like anyone else, and his goodness was of the same nature as that of many other great and good men. Indeed, today, many Unitarians deny belief in a personal God and interpret their religion in purely moral terms, putting their faith in the value of love and the brotherhood of man. The Toleration Act (1689) excluded Unitarians but from 1813 they were legally tolerated in England. Nevertheless attempts were made to turn them out of their chapels on the ground that the preachers did not hold the views of the original founders of the endowments. But this ended with the Dissenting Chapels Act of 1845. In America no such difficulties existed, and in the Boston of the 19th cent. many of the great literary figures were openly unitarian both in belief and name: *e.g.*, Emerson, Longfellow, Lowell, and Oliver Wendell Holmes.

**Utilitarianism,** a school of moral philosophy of which the main proponents were J. S. Mill (1806–73) and Jeremy Bentham (1748–1832). Bentham based his ethical theory upon the utilitarian principle that the greatest happiness of the greatest number is the criterion of morality. What is good is pleasure or happiness; what is bad is pain. If we act on this basis of self-interest (pursuing what we believe to be our own happiness), then what we do will automatically be for the general good. The serious failing of this thesis is (1) that it makes no distinction between the quality of one pleasure and another, and (2) that Bentham failed to see that the law might not be framed and administered by men as benevolent as himself. J. S. Mill accepted Bentham's position in general but seeing its failings emphasised (1) that self-interest was an inadequate basis for utilitarianism and suggested that we should take as the real criterion of good the social consequences of the act; (2) that some pleasures rank higher than others and held that those of the intellect are superior to those of the senses. Not only is the social factor emphasised, but emphasis is also placed on the nature of the act.

**Utopias.** The name "utopia" is taken from a Greek word meaning "nowhere" and was first used in 1516 by Sir Thomas More (1478–1535) as the title of his book referring to a mythical island in the south Pacific where he sited his ideal society. Since then it has been used of any ideal or fanciful society, and here a few will be mentioned. (The reader may recall that Samuel Butler's 19th cent. novel, describing an imaginary society in New Zealand where criminals were treated and the sick punished, was entitled *Erewhon* which is the word "nowhere" in reverse.) It should be noted that not all utopias were entirely fanciful—*e.g.*, Robert Owen's and François Fourier's beliefs, although found to be impractical, were, in fact, tried out.

*Sir Thomas More.* More wrote at a time

when the rise of the wool-growing trade had resulted in farming land being turned over to pasture and there was a great wave of unemployment and a rise in crime among the dispossessed. More began to think in terms of the mediaeval ideal of small co-operative communities in which class interests and personal gain played a decreasing part, a society which would have the welfare of the people at heart both from the physical and intellectual points of view. His utopia was one in which there was no private property, because the desire for acquisition and private possessions lay at the root of human misery. There was, therefore, only common ownership of land and resources. Each class of worker was equipped to carry out its proper function in the economic scheme and each was fairly rewarded for its share in production so that there was neither wealth nor poverty to inspire conflict. Nobody was allowed to be idle, until the time came for him to retire when he became free to enjoy whatever cultural pleasures he wished, but, since the system was devoid of the waste associated with competition, the working day would be only six hours. There was to be compulsory schooling and free medical care for everybody, full religious toleration, complete equality of the sexes, and a modern system of dealing with crime which was free from vindictiveness and cruelty. Government was to be simple and direct by democratically-elected officials whose powers would be strictly limited and the public expenditure kept under close scrutiny. It will be seen that More was far in advance of his age, and to most democratically-minded people in advance of an earlier utopia, Plato's *Republic*,which is described under the heading of Education.

*James Harrington.* James Harrington published his book *The Commonwealth of Oceana* in 1656 and offered it to Oliver Cromwell for his consideration but without tangible results. Better than any other man of his time Harrington understood the nature of the economic revolution which was then taking place, and, like More, saw the private ownership of land as the main cause of conflict. He put forward the theory that the control of property, particularly in the shape of land, determines the character of the political structure of the state; if property were universally distributed among the people the sentiment for its protection would naturally result in a republican form of government. The Commonwealth of Oceana was a society " of laws and not of men "—*i.e.*, it was to be legally based and structured so as to be independent of the good or ill-will of any individuals controlling it. Thus there must be a written constitution, a two-house legislature, frequent elections with a secret ballot, and separation of powers between legislature and executive—all today familiar features of parliamentary democracy, but unique in his time.

*Saint-Simon.* The utopias of the late 18th and 19th cent. come, of course, into the period of the industrial revolution and of laissez-faire capitalism. Individual enterprise and complete freedom of competition formed the outlook of the ruling class. Naturally the utopias of this period tended to have a strongly socialist tinge since such theories are obviously produced by those who are not satisfied with existing conditions. Saint-Simon's *New Christianity* (1825) is one such, and by many, Claude Henri, Comte de Saint-Simon (1760–1825) is regarded as the founder of French socialism. His book urged a dedication of society to the principle of human brotherhood and a community which would be led by men of science motivated by wholly spiritual aims. Production property was to be nationalised (or " socialised " as he describes the process) and employed to serve the public good rather than private gain; the worker was to produce according to his capacity and to be rewarded on the basis of individual merit; the principle of inheritance was to be abolished since it denied the principle of reward for accomplishment on which the society was to be founded. Saint-Simon's proposals were not directed towards the poorer classes alone, but to the conscience and intellect of all. He was deeply impressed with the productive power of the new machines and his

scheme was, first and foremost, intended as a method of directing that power to the betterment of humanity as a whole.

*Fourier.* François Marie Charles Fourier (1772–1837), although by conviction a philosophical anarchist who held that human beings are naturally good if allowed to follow their natural desires, was the originator of what, on the face of it, one would suppose to be the most regimented of the utopias. It consisted of a system of " phalanxes " or co-operative communities each composed of a group of workers and technicians assured of a minimum income and sharing the surplus on an equitable basis. Agriculture was to be the chief occupation of each phalanx and industrial employment planned and so carefully assigned that work would become pleasant and creative rather than burdensome. One of his ideas was that necessary work should receive the highest pay, useful work the next, and pleasant work the least pay. The land was to be scientifically cultivated and natural resources carefully conserved. Most of the members' property was to be privately owned, but the ownership of each phalanx was to be widely diffused among members by the sale of shares. Such " parasitic and unproductive " occupations as stockbroker, soldier, economist, middle-man and philosopher would be eliminated and the education of children carried out along vocational lines to train them for their future employment.

The strange thing was that Fourier's suggestions appealed to many both in Europe and the U.S.A. and such men (admittedly no economic or technical experts) as Emerson, Thoreau, James Russell Lowell, and Nathaniel Hawthorne strongly supported them. An American Fourier colony known as Brook Farm was established and carried on for eight years when it was dissolved after a serious fire had destroyed most of its property.

*Robert Owen.* Robert Owen (1771–1858), a wealthy textile manufacturer and philanthropist, established communities founded on a kind of utopian socialism in Lanarkshire, Hampshire, and in America. Of his New Lanark community an American observer wrote: " There is not, I apprehend, to be found in any part of the world, a manufacturing community in which so much order, good government, tranquillity, and rational happiness prevail." The workers in Lanark were given better housing and education for their children, and it was administered as a co-operative self-supporting community in Scotland. Later in life Owen returned to sponsoring legislation that would remove some of the worst evils of industrial life in those days: reduction of the working day to twelve hours, prohibition of labour for children under the age of ten, public schools for elementary education, and so on. But he lived to see few of his reforms adopted. He also promoted the creation of co-operative societies, the formation of trades unions, labour banks and exchanges, the workers' educational movement, and even an Anglo-American federation. There can be no doubt that, if he saw little result himself, he left the imprint of his convictions to benefit future communities who may not even know his name.

# V

Vitalism, the philosophical doctrine that the behaviour of the living organism is, at least in part, due to a vital principle which cannot possibly be explained wholly in terms of physics and chemistry. This belief was at one time held strongly by the late Professor C. E. M. Joad and is implicit in Henri Bergson's (1858–1941) theory of creative evolution. It was maintained by Bergson that evolution, like the work of an artist, is creative and therefore unpredictable; that a vague need exists beforehand within the animal or plant before the means of satisfying the need develops. Thus we might assume that sightless animals developed the need to become aware of objects before they were in physical contact with them and that this ultimately led to the origin of organs of sight. Earlier this century a form of vitalism described as " emergent evolution " was put forward. This theory maintains that when two or more simple entities come together there may arise a new property which none of them previously possessed. Today biologists would say that it is the *arrangement* of atoms that counts, different arrangements exhibiting different properties, and that biological organisation is an essentially dynamic affair, involving the lapse of time.

## W

**Wahabis,** members of an Arabian sect of Islam which originated in the teaching of Muhammad Ibn 'Abd-al-Wahab, born at the end of the 17th cent. He was deeply resentful of the Turkish rule which, in addition to its tyranny, had brought about innovations in the religion which Muhammad regarded as a perversion of its original form. He proceeded to reform Islam to its primitive conditions and impressed his beliefs on Mohammed Ibn Saud, a sheikh who spread them with the aid of his sword. Under the successors of Ibn Saud the power of the Wahabis spread over much of Arabia where it is dominant today in Saudi Arabia. Its particular characteristic is that it refuses to accept symbolic or mystical interpretations of the words of the Prophet and accepts quite literally the teaching of Islam. It is, in fact, a sort of Moslem fundamentalism. Although crushed by the Turks in 1811–15, the movement remains an important element in Mohammedanism.

**Waldenses,** a movement also known as "The Poor Men of Lyons," founded by Peter Waldo of that city about the same time, and in the same part of southern France, as the Albigenses (*q.v.*) with whom, however, they had nothing in common. Their main belief was a return to Apostolic simplicity, based on reading the Bible in their own language; their doctrines were somewhat similar to those of the Mennonites and the Quakers. However, they did not wish to separate themselves from the Church and were originally protected by several popes until the Lateran Council of 1215 excluded them mainly for the crime of preaching without ecclesiastical permission. From this time they were subjected to persecution, yet maintained some contact with the Church until the Reformation when they chose to take the side of the Protestants. Situated mainly on the sides of the Alps, half in Piedmont and half in France, they were persecuted or not according to the contemporary political convenience of the Dukes of Savoy, and the major attempt to destroy them called forth Oliver Cromwell's intervention and the famous sonnet of Milton. In spite of torture, murder, deportation, and even the kidnapping of their children, to have them brought up in the Roman Catholic faith, the sect survived, and still exists, having been granted full equality of rights with his Roman Catholic subjects by Charles Edward of Piedmont in 1848.

**Witchcraft.** There are various interpretations and definitions of witchcraft from that of Pennethorne Hughes who states that "witchcraft, as it emerges into European history and literature, represents the old paleolithic fertility cult, plus the magical idea, plus various parodies of contemporary religions" to that of the fanatical Father Montague Summers who says that spiritualism and witchcraft are the same thing. A leading authority on witchcraft, however, the late Dr. Margaret Murray, distinguishes between Operative Witchcraft (which is really Magic (*q.v.*)) and Ritual Witchcraft which, she says, "embraces the religious beliefs and ritual of the people known in late mediaeval times as 'witches.'" That there were such people we know from history and we know, too, that many of them—the great majority of them women—were tortured or executed or both. Many innocent people perished, especially after the promulgation of the bull *Summis desiderantes* by Pope Innocent VIII in 1484. Himself "a man of scandalous life", according to a Catholic historian, he wrote to "his dear sons," the German professors of theology, Johann Sprenger and Heinrich Kraemer, "witches are hindering men from performing the sexual act and women from conceiving . . ." and delegated them as Inquisitors " of these heretical pravities." In 1494 they codified in the *Malleus Maleficarum*

(Hammer of Witches) the ecclesiastical rules for detecting acts of witchcraft. Dr. Murray points out that there have ordinarily been two theories about witchcraft: (1) that there were such beings as witches, that they possessed supernatural powers and that the evidence given at their trials was substantially correct; (2) that the witches were simply poor silly creatures who either deluded themselves into believing that they had certain powers or, more frequently, were tortured into admitting things that they did not do. She herself accepts a third theory: that there were such beings as witches, that they really did what they admitted to doing, but that they did not possess supernatural powers. They were in fact believers in the old religion of pre-Christian times and the Church took centuries to root them out. That there existed " covens " of witches who carried out peculiar rites Dr. Murray has no doubt whatever. The first to show that witchcraft was a superstition and that the majority of so-called witches were people suffering from mental illness was the physician Johann Weyer of Cleves (1515–88). His views were denounced by the Catholic Church.

**World Council of Churches,** a union of Christian Churches from all over the world (including the Churches of the Protestant, Anglican, and Orthodox traditions, but excluding the Roman Catholic Church), engaged in extending Christian mission and unity throughout the world. All Churches which " accept our Lord Jesus Christ as God and Saviour " are eligible. This modern ecumenical movement stems from the great World Missionary Conference held at Edinburgh in 1910. The World Council was founded in 1948 and meets for consultation from time to time; the fourth assembly met at Uppsala in 1968 to discuss the theme "All Things New."

## Y

**Yoga,** a Hindu discipline which teaches a technique for freeing the mind from attachment to the senses, so that once freed the soul may become fused with the universal spirit (*Atman* or *Brahman*), which is its natural goal. This is the sole function of the psychological and physical exercises which the Yogi undertakes, although few ever reach the final stage of *Samadhi* or union with *Brahman* which is said to take place in eight levels of attainment. These are: (1) *Yama,* which involves the extinction of desire and egotism and their replacement by charity and unselfishness; (2) *Niyama,* during which certain rules of conduct must be adopted, such as cleanliness, the pursuit of devotional studies, and the carrying out of rituals of purification; (3) *Asana,* or the attainment of correct posture and the reduction to a minimum of all bodily movement (the usual posture of the concentrating Yogi is the " lotus position " familiar from pictures); (4)–(5) *Pranayama,* the right control of the life-force or breath in which there are two stages at which the practitioner hopes to arrive, the first being complete absorption in the act of breathing which empties the mind of any other thought, the second being the ability almost to cease to breathe which allegedly enables him to achieve marvellous feats of endurance; (6) *Pratyahara* or abstraction which means the mind's complete withdrawal from the world of sense; (7) *Dharana* in which an attempt is made to think of one thing only which finally becomes a repetition of the sacred syllable OM, and perhaps by a kind of self-hypnosis, leads (8) to *Samadhi* the trance state which is a sign of the complete unity of soul with reality.

Yoga is very old, and when the sage Patanjali (c. 300 B.C.) composed the book containing these instructions, the *Yoga Sutras,* he was probably collecting from many ancient traditions. Some of the claims made by Yogis seem, to the Western mind, frankly incredible; but in the West and especially in recent years Yoga methods have been used at the lower levels in order to gain improved self-control, better posture, and improved health. Whether it achieves these ends is another matter, but the genuine Yogi regards this as a perversion of the nature and purpose of the discipline.

# Z

**Zen Buddhism,** a Buddhist sect which is believed to have arisen in 6th cent. China but has flourished chiefly in Japan; for some reason it has of recent years begun to attract attention in the West thanks to the voluminous writings of Dr. D. T. Suzuki and the less numerous but doubtless much-read books of Mr. Christmas Humphreys. But the fact that these writings exist does not explain their being read, nor why of all possible Eastern sects this particular one should be chosen in our times. What is Zen's attraction and why should anyone take the trouble to read about something (the word " something " is used for reasons that will become evident) that is not a religion, has no doctrine, knows no God and no after-life, no good and no evil, and possesses no scriptures but has to be taught by parables which seem to be purposely meaningless? One of the heroes of Zen is the fierce-looking Indian monk Boddhidharma (fl. *c.* 516–534) who brought Buddhism to China, of whom it is recounted that when the Emperor asked him how much merit he had acquired by supporting the new creed, the monk shouted at him: " None whatever! " The Emperor then wished to know what was the sacred doctrine of the creed, and again the monk shouted: " It is empty—there is nothing sacred! " Dr. Suzuki, having affirmed that there is no God in Zen, goes on to state that this does not mean that Zen denies the existence of God because " neither denial nor affirmation concerns Zen." The most concrete statement he is prepared to make is that the basic idea of Zen is to come in touch with the inner workings of our being, and to do this in the most direct way possible without resorting to anything external or superadded. Therefore anything that has the semblance of an external authority is rejected by Zen. Absolute faith is placed in a man's own inner being. Apparently the intention is that, so far from indulging in inward meditations or such practices as the Yogi uses, the student must learn to act spontaneously, without thinking, and without self-consciousness or hesitation. This is the main purpose of the *koan,* the logically insoluble riddle which the pupil must try to solve. One such is the question put by master to pupil: " A girl is walking down the street, is she the younger or the older sister? " The correct answer, it seems, is to say nothing but put on a mincing gait, to *become* the girl, thus showing that what matters is the experience of being and not its verbal description. Another *koan:* " What is the Buddha? " " Three pounds of flax " is attributed to T'ungshan in the 9th cent. and a later authority's comment is that " none can excel it as regards its irrationality which cuts off all passages to speculation." Zen, in effect, teaches the uselessness of trying to use words to discuss the Absolute.

Zen came to Japan in the 13th cent., more than five centuries after Confucianism or the orthodox forms of Buddhism, and immediately gained acceptance whilst becoming typically Japanese in the process. One of the reasons why it appealed must have been that its spontaneity and insistence on action without thought, its emphasis on the uselessness of mere words, and such categories as logical opposites, had an inevitable attraction for a people given to seriousness, formality, and logic to a degree which was almost stifling. Zen must have been to the Japanese what nonsense rhymes and nonsense books, like those of Edward Lear and Lewis Carroll, were to the English intellectuals. Lear's limericks, like some of the *koans,* end up with a line which, just at the time when one expects a point to be made, has no particular point at all, and *Alice in Wonderland* is the perfect example of a world, not without logic, but with a crazy logic of its own which has no relationship to that of everyday life. Therefore Zen began to impregnate every aspect of life in Japan, and one of the results of its emphasis on spontaneous action rather than reason was its acceptance by the Samurai, the ferocious warrior class, in such activities as swordsmanship, archery, Japanese wrestling, and later Judo and the Kamikaze dive-bombers. But much of Japanese art, especially landscape gardening and flower-arrangement, was influenced similarly, and Zen is even used in Japanese psychiatry. The very strict life of the Zen monks is based largely on doing things, learning through experience; the periods of meditation in the Zendo hall are punctuated by sharp slaps on the face administered by the abbot to those who are unsatisfactory pupils. Dr. Suzuki denies that Zen is nihilistic, but it is probably its appearance of nihilism and its appeal to the irrational and spontaneous which attracts the Western world at a time when to many the world seems without meaning and life over-regimented. However, it has influenced such various aspects of Western life as philosophy (Heidegger), psychiatry (Erich Fromm and Hubert Benoit), writing (Aldous Huxley), and painting (Die Zen Gruppe in Germany).

**Zionism,** a belief in the need to establish an autonomous Jewish home in Palestine which, in its modern form, began with Theodor Herzl (1860–1904), a Hungarian journalist working in Vienna. Although Herzl was a more or less assimilated Jew, he was forced by the Dreyfus case and the pogroms in Eastern Europe to conclude that there was no real safety for the Jewish people until they had a state of their own. The Jews, of course, had always in a religious sense thought of Palestine as a spiritual homeland and prayed " next year in Jerusalem," but the religious had thought of this in a philosophical way as affirming old loyalties, not as recommending the formation of an actual state. Therefore Herzl was opposed both by many of the religious Jews and, at the other extreme, by those who felt themselves to be assimilated and in many cases without religious faith. Even after the Balfour Declaration of 1917, there was not a considerable flow of Jews to Palestine, which at that time was a predominantly Arab state. But the persecutions of Hitler changed all this and, after bitter struggles, the Jewish state was proclaimed in 1948. Today Zionism is supported by the vast majority of the Jewish communities everywhere (although strongly disapproved of in the Soviet Union as " Western imperialism ") and Zionism is now an active international force concerned with protecting the welfare and extending the influence of Israel.

**Zoroastrianism,** at one time one of the great world religions, competing in the 2nd cent. A.D. on almost equal terms from its Persian home with Hellenism and the Roman Imperial Government. Under the Achaemenidae (c. 550–330 B.C.) Zoroastrianism was the state religion of Persia. Alexander's conquest in 331 B.C. brought disruption but the religion flourished again under the Sassanian dynasty (A.D. c. 226–640). With the advance of the Mohammedan Arabs in the 7th cent. Zoroastrianism finally gave way to Islam. A number of devotees fled to India there to become the Parsees. In Persia itself a few scattered societies remain.

The name Zoroaster is the Greek rendering of Zarathustra, the prophet who came to purify the ancient religion of Persia. It is thought that he lived at the beginning of the 6th cent. B.C. He never claimed for himself divine powers but was given them by his followers. The basis of Zoroastrianism is the age-long war between good and evil, Ahura Mazda heading the good spirits and Ahriman the evil ones. Morality is very important since by doing right the worshipper is supporting Ahura Mazda against Ahriman, and the evil-doers will be punished in the last days when Ahura Mazda wins his inevitable victory.

The sacred book of this religion is the *Avesta.* If Zoroastrianism has little authority today, it had a very considerable influence in the past. Its doctrines penetrated into Judaism (*q.v.*) and, through Gnosticism, Christianity. The worship of Mithra by the Romans was an impure version of Zoroastrianism. Manichaeism (*q.v.*) was a Zoroastrian heresy and the Albigensians of mediaeval times was the last relic of a belief which had impressed itself deeply in the minds of men.

# GAZETTEER OF THE WORLD

A complete index to the maps with up-to-date descriptive matter, together with a list of Commonwealth countries with their land areas and recent estimates of population.

# GAZETTEER OF THE WORLD

*This edition of the gazetteer has been revised from standard and authoritative sources. For the population figures the latest censuses have been used, where available, and where not available, the latest official estimates.*

*An endeavour has been made to include all the more important places throughout the world. The small scale of the maps included in the Cyclopædia does not enable all places included in the gazetteer to be named on the maps.*

*In regard to the spelling of place names, the general principle followed has been to adopt national spellings. For those countries where the Latin Alphabet is not used, the principles for transliteration laid down by the "Permanent Committee on Geographical Names" of the Royal Geographical Society have been followed. Chinese entries are in the conventional English form. New official Chinese form, based on Chinese romanised alphabet adopted 1958, is in brackets. There may be a few instances where the spelling shown on the map does not conform to that used in the gazetteer.*

## ABBREVIATIONS USED IN THE GAZETTEER

### GEOGRAPHICAL NAMES

| | | |
|---|---|---|
| *Ala.* = Alabama. | *La.* = Louisiana. | *Pac. Oc.* = Pacific Ocean. |
| *Ark.* = Arkansas. | *Mass.* = Massachusetts. | *Pa.* = Pasadena. |
| *A.S.S.R.* = Autonomous Soviet Socialist Republic. | *Md.* = Maryland. | *Penns.* = Pennsylvania. |
| | *Me.* = Maine. | *R.I.* = Rhode Island. |
| *Atl. Oc.* = Atlantic Ocean. | *Mich.* = Michigan. | *R.o.I.* = Republic of Ireland. |
| *B.C.* = British Columbia. | *Minn.* = Minnesota. | *R.S.F.S.R.* = Russian Soviet Federal Socialist Republic. |
| *Brit.* = British. | *Miss.* = Mississippi. | |
| *Cal.* = California. | *Mo.* = Missouri. | *S.C.* = South Carolina. |
| *Col.* = Colorado. | *Mont.* = Montana. | *Scot.* = Scotland. |
| *CSSR* = Czechoslovak Socialist Republic. | *N.B.* = New Brunswick. | *S.D.* = South Dakota. |
| | *N.C.* = North Carolina. | *S.S.R.* = Soviet Socialist Republic. |
| *Del.* = Delaware. | *N.D.* = North Dakota. | |
| *Eng.* = England. | *Neth.* = Netherlands. | *Tenn.* = Tennessee. |
| *E.R.* = East Riding. | *N.H.* = New Hampshire. | *U.A.R.* = United Arab Republic. |
| *Fla.* = Florida. | *N.J.* = New Jersey. | *U.S.S.R.* = Union of Soviet Socialist Republics. |
| *Fr.* = French. | *N.M.* = New Mexico. | |
| *Ga.* = Georgia. | *N.R.* = North Riding. | *Va.* = Virginia. |
| *Ill.* = Illinois. | *N.Y.* = New York. | *Vt.* = Vermont. |
| *Ind.* = Indiana. | *N.Z.* = New Zealand. | *Wash.* = Washington. |
| *Kan.* = Kansas. | *O.F.S.* = Orange Free State. | *W.I.* = West Indies. |
| *Ky.* = Kentucky. | *Okla.* = Oklahoma. | *Wis.* = Wisconsin. |
| | *Ore.* = Oregon. | *Wyo.* = Wyoming. |

*Abbreviations of names of Counties in Gt. Britain and Rep. of Ireland are those recognised by the General Post Office.*

### OTHER ABBREVIATIONS

| | | |
|---|---|---|
| *a.* = area. | *F.* = firth. | *p.* = population. |
| *agr.* = agriculture. | *fed.* = federal. | *par.* = parish. |
| *alt.* = altitude. | *fish. pt.* = fishing port. | *parlt.* = parliament. |
| *approx.* = approximate. | *fortfd.* = fortified. | *parly.* = parliamentary. |
| *arch.* = archaeological. | *ft.* = feet. | *prod.* = products. |
| *aut. rep.* = autonomous republic. | *G.* = gulf. | *prot.* = protectorate. |
| *ass.* = associated. | *gd.* = good. | *prov.* = province. |
| *bdy.* = boundary. | *gen.* = general. | *pt.* = port. |
| *bldg.* = building. | *gr.* = great, group. | *R.* = river. |
| *bor.* = borough. | *I.* = island. | *rep.* = republic. |
| *C.* = cape. | *impt.* = important. | *residtl.* = residential. |
| *c.* = city. | *inc.* = including. | *rly.* = railway. |
| *can.* = canton. | *indep.* = independent. | *rural dist.* = rural district. |
| *cap.* = capital. | *inds.* = industries. | *S.* = south or southerly. |
| *cas.* = castle. | *industl.* = industrial. | *shipbldg.* = shipbuilding. |
| *cath.* = cathedral. | *Is.* = islands. | *sm.* = small. |
| *ch.* = chief. | *L.* = lake. | *spt.* = seaport. |
| *co.* = county. | *lge.* = large. | *sq. m.* = square miles. |
| *co. bor.* = county borough. | *lgst.* = largest. | *St.* = Saint. |
| *col.* = colony. | *m.* = miles. | *st.* = state. |
| *colly.* = colliery. | *machin.* = machinery. | *sta.* = station. |
| *comm.* = commercial. | *mftg.* = manufacturing. | *sub.* = suburb. |
| *cst.* = coast. | *mkg.* = making. | *t.* = town. |
| *ctr.* = centre. | *mkt.* = market. | *terr.* = territory. |
| *cty.* = country. | *mnfs.* = manufactures. | *tr.* = trade. |
| *dep.* = department. | *mng.* = mining. | *trib.* = tributary. |
| *dist.* = district. | *mt.* = mount. | *univ.* = university. |
| *div.* = division. | *mtn.* = mountain. | *urb. dist.* = urban district. |
| *E.* = east or easterly. | *mun.* = municipality. | *vil.* = village. |
| *elec.* = electrical. | *mun. bor.* = municipal borough. | *W.* = west or westerly. |
| *engin.* = engineering. | *N.* = north or northerly. | *wat. pl.* = watering place. |
| *estd.* = estimated. | *nat.* = national. | *wks.* = works. |
| *exp.* = exports. | *nr.* = near. | *wkshps.* = workshops. |

*Land* = administrative division of W. Germany approx. corresponding to "province".

# A

**Aabenraa**, *spt.*, S.E. Jutland, Denmark; at head of Aabenraa fjord; cars, trailers, clothing; p. (1960) *14,219*.

**Aachen**, *t.*, N. Rhine–Westphalia, Germany; formerly Aix-la-Chapelle; one of the oldest cities in Germany, cath., famous baths; suffered badly from bombing in Second World War and was first large German town to be taken by the Allied Forces in 1944; non-ferrous metal inds. textiles, needles, footwear, elec. goods; p. (1963) *174,300*.

**Aaiun**, *cap.*, Saguia el Hamra region of Spanish Sahara.

**Aalborg**, *c.*, *spt.* Jutland, Denmark; shipbldg., cement, textiles, machin.; airport; p. (1965) *99,815*.

**Aalen**, *t.*, Baden-Württemberg, Germany; on R. Kocher; iron, textiles, lens mkg.; p. (1963) *33,700*.

**Aalst**, *see* Alost.

**Aar**, *R.*, Switzerland, flows through Brienz and Thun lakes, and thence into the Rhine, 181 m.; famous Aar gorges above Meiringen.

**Aarau**, *t.*, cap. Aargau can., Switzerland; precision tools and instruments, shoes, textiles; hydro-elec. plant; p. (1957) *14,280*.

**Aargau**, *can.*, N. Switzerland; a. 542 sq. m.; extensive vineyards, cereals, orchards, metal prod., textiles, salt mining; p. (1961) *360,940*.

**Aarhus**, *c.*, principal spt. on E. coast of Jutland, Denmark; famous Gothic cath., univ.; iron, metals, shipbldg, marine engin., textiles, paper, chemicals; p. (1965) *187,342*.

**Abaco**, Gt., Bahama Is., W. Indies; p. (1959) *3,407*.

**Abadan**, *c.*, Iran; oil refineries; intern. airpt.; tech. coll.; p. (1967) *339,121*.

**Abakan**, *t.*, R.S.F.S.R., on R. Jenisei; sawmilling, food inds.; p. (1959) *56,000*.

**Abbazia**, *see* Opatija.

**Abbeville**, *mftg. c.*, on the R. Somme (N. France); connected with Paris and Belgium by canals; sugar-milling, carpets, biscuits, beer; p. (1962) *26,899*.

**Abbeyleix**, *t.*, *rural dist.*, Laoighis, Ireland; quarries; p. (rural dist. 1961) *11,813*.

**Abbotsbury**, *par.*, Dorset, Eng.; world-famous swannery.

**Abbots-Langley**, *par.*, Herts, Eng., birthplace of Nicholas Breakspeare (Pope Adrian IV); p. (1961) *18,157*.

**Abeokuta**, *t.*, Nigeria; N. of Lagos; palm oil, hardwoods; p. (1953) *84,000*.

**Aberavon**, *t.*, Glamorgan, Wales; on R. Avon, 8 m. E. of Swansea; harbour Port Talbot; lge. coal and iron inds., metals, tinplate, cables; p. (1961) *31,226*.

**Aberayron**, *urb. dist.*, Cardigan, S. Wales; p. (1961) *1,220*.

**Abercarn**, *urb. dist.*, Monmouth, Eng.; coal and iron, tin-plate, knitting pins; p. (1961) *19,221*.

**Aberchirder**, *burgh*, Banff, Scot.; p. (1961) *755*.

**Abercorn**. *par.*, W. Lothian, Scot.; on the Forth; Roman wall built by Antoninus began here, and extended to Kirkpatrick on the Clyde; p. (1951) *806*.

**Abercorn**, *t.* Zambia; trading sta.; airfield; European p. (1959) *250*.

**Aberdare**, *urb. dist.*, Glamorgan, Wales, on the R. Cynon; wire cables; p. (1961) *39,044*.

**Aberdeen**, *co.*, Scot.; mtnous; agr., oats, barley, turnips, cattle; fisheries; granite, brewing, distilling, paper; a. 1,970 sq. m.; p. (1961) *298,503*.

**Aberdeen**, *c.*, Aberdeenshire and Kincardine, Scot.; at mouth of R. Dee, 100 m. N.E. of Edinburgh; univ.; sm. shipbldg., fishing, oats, whisky, paper mkg., granite, tourism; p. (1961) *185,379* of whom *23,254* S. of R. Dee are in Kincardine co.

**Aberdeen**, *t.*, S.D., U.S.A.; chemicals, foundry; p. (1960) *23,073*.

**Aberdeen**, *spt.*, Wash., U.S.A.; lumbering, salmon canning; p. (1960) *18,741*.

**Aberdovey**, *wat. pl.* Merioneth, Wales, on estuary of R. Dovey.

**Aberfeldy**, *burgh*, Perth, Scot., in Strath Tay, 4 m. below Loch Tay; mkt.; salmon and trout fishin resort; p. (1961) *1,469*. [[(1951) *1,133*.

**Aberfoyle**, *par.*, Perth, Scot.; tourist resort; p.

**Abergavenny**, *mun. bor.*, *t.*, Monmouth., on R. Usk; light engin., concrete prods.; p. (1961) *9,625*.

**Abergele**, *urb. dist.*, Denbigh, Wales; small wat. pl.; p. (1961) *7,982*.

**Aberlour**, Charlestown of, *burgh*, Banff, Scot.; on R. Spey, 12 m. S. of Elgin; p. (1961) *958*.

**Abernethy**, *burgh*, Perth, Scot.; on R. Tay, once the cap. of the Pictish Kings; p. (1961) *601*.

**Abersychan**, *par.*, Monmouth, Eng.; coal, iron, and steel; p. *25,743*.

**Abertillery**, *urb. dist.*, Monmouth.; coal, engin., leather goods; p. (1961) *25,160*.

**Aberystwyth**, *mun. bor.*, *wat. pl.*, on Cardigan Bay at the mouth of the R. Ystwyth, Cardigan, Wales; univ. college; Nat. Library of Wales; p. (1961) *10,418*.

**Abidjan**, *cap.*, Ivory Coast, W. Africa; palm oil, cocoa, copra, hardwood, rubber; oil refining at Vridi nearby; p. (1963) *212,000*.

**Abilene**, *t.*, Kansas, U.S.A.; univ.; food prod., oilseeds, oil-refining, cotton; p. (1960) *90,368*.

**Abingdon**, *mun. bor.*, Berks, Eng., on R. Thames; cars, leather goods; p. (estd. 1967) *16,770*.

**Abingdon**, *t.*, Va., U.S.A.; lumbering, flour milling; mnfs. condensed milk, chemicals, tobacco; tourist resort; p. (1960) *4,758*.

**Abington**, *t.*, Mass., U.S.A.; shoes, textile machin.; p. (1960) *10,449*.

**Abitibi**, *R.* and *L.*, R. flows into James Bay, Ontario, Canada; gold dist.

**Abo**, *see* Turku, Finland.

**Abomey**, *old cap.*, Dahomey, W. Africa; former slave mkt.; cotton; p. (estd. 1960) *18,900*.

**Abovyan**, *t.*, Armenian S.S.R.; 10 m. from Yerevan; new model t. founded 1963; planned p. *50,000*.

**Aboyne and Glentanner**, *par.*, Aberdeen. Scot.; hol. res. on R. Dee nr. Ballater; p. (1951) *1,651*.

**Abraham**, Plains of, nr. Quebec; Wolfe's victory over French under Montcalm, 1759.

**Abram**, *urb. dist.*, Lancs, Eng.; coal, engin., cotton mnfs.; p. (1961) *6,017*.

**Abrantes**, *t.*, Portugal, on the Tagus R.; French won battle here in Napoleonic Wars, 1807.

**Abruzzi**, *region* of Italy on the Adriatic, inc. provs. of Aquila, Chieti, Teramo; methane fields; p. (1961) *1,584,777*.

**Abu**, *mtn.*, Rajasthan, India, 5,653 ft.; Jain temples.

**Abukir** or **Aboukir**, *vil.* on Abukir Bay, U.A.R.; site of ancient Canopus; Battle of the Nile fought in the Bay, 1798; p. *7,086*.

**Abu Simbel**, Nile Valley, U.A.R.; famous anc. temples carved out of solid sandstone, one to Rameses II and the other to his Queen; rescue operation from rising waters behind Aswan High Dam undertaken.

**Abydos**, *ruined c.*, Upper U.A.R.; celebrated for its temple of Osiris.

**Abydos**. *ruined castled t.*, Anatolia on the Dardanelles, which resisted Philip of Macedon; famous for the story of Leander and Hero.

**Abyssinia**, *see* Ethiopia.

**Acadia** or **Acadie**, French name applied to previous possessions S. of St. Lawrence R., inc. Nova Scotia and New Brunswick and part of Maine.

**Acajutla**, *spt.*, Salvador, Central America; exp. coffee; cement, oil refining, fertilisers; p. (1960) *15,475*.

**Acambaro**, *t.*, Mexico; rly. junction; p. *17,643*.

**Acapulco**, *spt.*, Pacific coast, Mexico; tourism; exp. hides, cedar, fruit; p. (1960) *28,582*.

**Accra**, *spt.*, *cap.* Ghana, W. Africa; univ.; airport; pharmaceutics; p. (1960) *491,060* (inc. cap. dist. and rural a.).

**Accrington**, *mun. bor.*, *mftg. t.*, Lancs, Eng.; 20 m. N. of Manchester; cotton ctr., coal, textile machin., engin., bricks; p. (estd. 1967) *37,470*.

**Acerra**, *t.*, S. Italy; destroyed by Hannibal 216 B.C.; restored 210 B.C.; olive oil, wine, hemp; p. *16,460*.

**Achaia**, *prov.*, Greece; a. 1,206 sq. m.; chief currant-producing dist.; spt., Patras; p. (1961) *236,770*.

**Achalpur**, *t.*, W. Madhya Pradesh, India; cotton.

**Achill**, *I.*, off the W. coast of Mayo, Ireland; agr., fishing.

**Achill Head**, *cape*, Mayo.

**Achinsk**, *t.*, *industl.* *t.*, R.S.F.S.R., on R. Chulym; impt. rly. junction; manganese, cement; p. (1956) *42,400*. [*43,752*.

**Acireale**, *spt.*, Sicily; sulphur baths; p. (1961)

**Acklin**, *island*, Bahamas, W. Indies; timber, sponges; p. (1953) *1,273*.

Aconcagua, *mtn.*, Andes, Argentine, S. America, highest peak of New World, alt. 22,835 ft.

Aconcagua, *prov.*, Chile; a. 3,939 sq. m.; cap. San Felipe; alfalfa and Mediterranean fruits; p. (1957) *154,075.*

Aconquija, Sierra de, *mtn. range* N. Argentina, S. America; rises steeply from Chaco lowland to 18,000 ft.

Acqui, *ancient walled t.*, N. Italy, prov. Alessandria; famous cath., sulphur springs; p. *18,975.*

Acre (Akka), *c., spt.*, Israel, famous for its sieges during Crusades and in 1799 withstanding Napoleon for 61 days; *p. c. 18,000.*

Acre, *st.*, Brazil; a. 59,139 sq. m., cap. Rio Branco; rubber; p. (1960) *160,208.*

Acton, *former mun. bor.*, Middlesex, Eng.; now inc. in Ealing outer bor., Greater London. (*q.v.*), univ.

Ada, *t.*, Oklahoma, U.S.A.; p. (1960) *14,347.*

Adamawa, *prov.*, W. Africa, divided between Nigeria and Cameroun; a. 70,000 sq. m.; ivory, groundnuts.

Adams, *mfg. t.*, Mass., U.S.A.; paper, cottons, woollens, calcium quarrying; p. (1960) *11,949.*

Adam's Bridge, chain of sandbanks, 22 m. long, in Palk Strait, between India and Ceylon. Construction of rail causeway mooted.

Adam's Peak, *sacred mtn.*, S. Ceylon, alt. 7,352 ft.

Adana, *t.*, Turkey; on R. Seihan; wool, cotton, grain, tobacco; p. (1965) *290,515.*

Adapazari, *t.*, Turkey; rly. junction; agr. and tr. ctr., silk, linen; high grade concentrate from low grade iron ore deposits in Camdagi a.; p. (1965) *85,579.*

Adda, R., N. Italy, flows through L. Como to R. Po.

Addis Ababa, *cap.* Ethiopia; terminus of Jibuti rly.; p. (1960) *450,000.*

Adelaide, *c., spt., cap.*, S. Australia; on R. Torrens, which flows into G. of St. Vincent; transcontinental rly. connections; univ.; cars, steel tubes, electrical appliances, chemicals, sugar and oil refining; p. (with subs) (1966) *726,930.*

Adelboden, *t.* Bern can., Switzerland; 19 m. S.W. of Interlaken; health resort, mineral springs.

Adélie Land, Antarctica; French terr. and dependency of Réunion.

Adelsburg, *t.*, Jugoslavia; 20 m. N.E. of Trieste; extensive grotto and stalactite cavern.

Aden, *spt.*, Southern Yemen (1967), S. Arabia, former Brit. col.; bay behind headlands of Aden t. and Little Aden, excellent anchorage. *See also* Yemen, Southern.

Aden, Gulf of, Arabian Sea; 48 m. l., 180 m. wide.

Aderno, *t.*, Sicily, Italy; at base of Mt. Etna, ancient ruins; p. *24,307.*

Adige, R. in N. Italy; enters Adriatic N. of Po, length 240 m.

Adirondacks, *mtns.*, N.Y., U.S.A.; highest peak, Mt. Marcy, 5,345 ft.

Adiyaman, *t.*, Turkey; p. (1960) *17,021.*

Adlington, *urb. dist.*, Lancs, Eng.; nr. Chorley; cotton, coal-mining; p. (1961) *4,281.*

Admiralty G., N.W. of Western Australia.

Admiralty I., off Alaska mainland; belongs to U.S.A.; fishing, timber.

Admiralty Is., S.W. Pac. Oc. N. of New Guinea, comprise 40 sm. is.; Australian mandate; coconuts, copra; a. 663 sq. m.; p. *13,134.*

Adonara, *I.*, one of Nusa Tenggara Is., Indonesia; p. (estd.) *25,000.*

Adoni, *t.*, Andhra Pradesh, India; cotton market; p. (1961) *69,951.*

Adour, R., S.W. France; rises in Pyrenees, enters Bay of Biscay below Bayonne; length 207 m.

Adowa, *t.*, *cap.*, Tigre prov., N. Ethiopia; alt. over 6000 ft., tr. and mkt. centre; *p. c. 10,000.*

Adra, *spt., t.*, Almeria, S. Spain; nr. Guardia Viejas salt beds and Berja lead-mines; sugar-cane, fish, fruit and veg. canning; p. (1957) *13,687.*

Adrano, *t.*, Sicily, Italy; at S.W. foot of Etna; agr. mkt.; *p. c. 29,000.*

Adrar *oasis*, Sahara Desert, Algeria; salt, dates, grain; p. (1960) *44,116.*

Adria, *mkt. t.*, Rovigo, Italy; formerly on cst., now 14 m. inland, old Etruscan c.

Adrian, *c.*, Michigan, U.S.A.; 73 m. W. of Detroit; p. (1960) *20,347.*

Adrianople, *see* Edirne.

Adriatic Sea, branch of the Mediterranean, between Italy and Balkan Peninsula; forms G. of Venice on the N.; chief trading pts., Venice, Trieste, and Ancona on the N., Brindisi and

Dürres on the S.; a. 52,000 sq. m., length 450 m.

Adullam or Aidelma, *former dist.*, Palestine; S.E. Jerusalem. Site of Canaanite city; cave, David's hiding-place from King Saul.

Adwick le Street, *urb. dist.*, W.R. Yorks, Eng.; coal; p. (1961) *18,212.*

Adzhar, *rep.*, Georgian S.S.R.; tea, citrus fruits, oil-refining, engin.; ch. t. Batumi; a. 1,100 sq. m.; p. (1959) *242,000.*

Aegades, group of rocky Is. off W. coast of Sicily; ch. t. Favignana on I. of that name.

Aegean Is., between Greece and Turkey; called the Grecian Archipelago, inc. Crete, Cyclades, Sporades, and Dodecanese; a. 1,506 sq. m.; p. (1961) *477,476.*

Aegean Sea, branch of the Mediterranean; studded with Is., between Greece and Turkey; connected through the Dardanelles with Sea of Marmara and thence through the Bosphorus Strait with the Black Sea. [fisheries.

Aegina, *I.*, Greece; in G. of same name, sponge

Aerö, *I.* in the Baltic off Denmark; p. (1960) *10,109.*

Aetolia and Acarnania, *prov.*, N. Greece; cap. Missolonghi; p. (1961) *237,738.*

Afam, S. Nigeria; oilfield; pipe-line E. to Pt. Harcourt.

Afars and Issas, French Territory of the, N.E. Africa, formerly French Somaliland (renamed 1967); extends inland from straits of Bab-el-Mandeb; plain, mainly below 600 ft.; hot, dry climate; shark and mother of pearl fisheries; salt, coffee, hides, oilseed; cap. Djibouti; a. 8,900 sq. m.; p. (estd. 1965) *81,000.*

Affric, Glen, Inverness, Scot.; 30 m. S.W. of Inverness; hydro-elec. scheme, opened 1952.

Afghanistan, *mtn. cty.*, Asia; monarchy; cap. Kabul; comm. ctrs. Kabul, Kandahar; ch. rs., Kabul and Helm; climate, intense summer heat, severe winter cold, scanty rainfall; races, Afghans, aboriginal hill-tribes; languages, official Persian, spoken Pushtu; religion, Islam; cereals, fruit, sheep, horses, camels; inds. carpets, woollens, silks; coal-mining at Dara-i-Suf; natural gas at Shibarghan; rich copper, lead, iron resources undeveloped; a. 250,000 sq. m.; p. (est. 1964) *15,277,000.*

Afragola, *t.*, Napoli prov., S. Italy; 5 m. N.E. of Naples; cereals, fruit, hemp; p. (1961) *45,581.*

Africa, second largest *continent*; bounded on N. by Mediterranean, by Red Sea and Indian Ocean on E., by Atlantic Ocean on W.; adjoins Asia at Isthmus of Suez. Deserts in N., forests in centre, and lofty plateaux and veldts in S. Highest mtn., Kilimanjaro, 19,324 ft.; chief rivers, Nile, Congo, Niger, Zambesi; largest L. Victoria. Great Rift Valley (K69) in E. Africa. Rainfall heavy near equator, almost rainless in Sahara and Kalahari, elsewhere moderate. Agriculture: wine, olives, wheat, esparto grass in N.; cocoa, oil palm, groundnuts, coffee, cotton in centre; wheat maize, wool in S. Minerals: gold, diamonds, copper. Compared with only 4 at end of last war, 41 countries had achieved independence by 1969. Those still to become fully indep. are: the Spanish cols. of Sp. Sahara, Ifni; the Portuguese cols. of Angola, Port Guinea, Mozambique; Afars and Issas (French Terr.); Rhodesia, and S.W. Africa; a. (approx.) 11,500,000 sq. m.; p. (estd.) *225,000,000.*

Afyon Karahisar *t.*, Turkey; opium; p. (1960) *38,392.*

Agadir, *spt.*, S. cst. Morocco; wrecked by earthquake, 1960; new t. built S. of former c. in a. of greater geological stability; p. (estd. 1965) *30,000.*

Agawam, *t.*, Mass., U.S.A.; engin.; p. (1960) *15,711.*

Agder, E. and W., *two dists.*, Norway; (E.) a. 3,607 sq. m.; p. (1963) *77,639* (W.) a. 2,794 sq. m.; p. (1963) *112,012*

Agen, *t.* *cap.* Lot-et-Garonne, France; 85 m. from Bordeaux; cath.; p. (1962) *35,120.*

Agincourt, *vil.*, Pas-de-Calais, France; famed for battle in 1415 between English, led by Henry V, and French under d'Albert.

Agira, *t.*, Sicily, Italy; marble, cement, sulphur; p. *15,172.*

Agra, *c.*, Uttar Pradesh, India; on Jumna R., 115 m. S.S.E. of Delhi; formerly cap. of Mogul Empire; famous Taj Mahal mausoleum; univ.; p. (1961) *508,680.*

Agri, *t.*, Turkey, p. (1960) *19,786.*

Agrigento, *t.*, S. cst. Sicily, Italy; grain, sulphur salt; p. (1961) *47,094*. Agrigento (lately Girgenti, and formerly Agrigentum, Akragas), is also famous for its Greek temples.

Agrinion, *t.*, Greece; tobacco; p. (1951) *21,752*.

Aguadilla, *spt.*, Puerto Rico, Central America; exp. coffee and sugar; p. *c. 16,000*.

Aguascalientes, *st.*, Mexico; cap. Aguascalientes; a. 2,499 sq. m.; p. (1960) *243,363*.

Aguascalientes, *t.*, *cap.*, Aguascalientes, Mexico; alt. over 6000 ft.; 360 m. N.W. of Mexico City; wide range of local inds.; hot springs; p. (1960) *126,617*.

Aguilar de la Frontera, *t.*, S. Spain; wine, olives; Moorish castle, p. (1957) *15,224*.

Aguilas, *t. spt.*, Murcia, on E. cst. of Spain; exp. esparto, lead ores; p. *c. 15,000*.

Agulhas, *C.*, 100 m. E. of C. of Good Hope, most southerly point of Africa.

Ahaggar, *mtns.*, S. Algeria range 9,000–10,000 ft.

Ahlen, *t.*, N. Rhine–Westphalia, Germany; on R. Werse; coal mining, metal and engin. wks.; p. (1963) *42,200*.

Ahmedabad, *temporary cap.* Gujarat, India; Jain temple, splendid mosques, pottery, silk, gold, cotton; oilfield at Nawagam nearby; p. (1961) *1,149,918*.

Ahmadnagar, *c.*, Maharashtra, India; lge. trade in cotton and silk goods; p. (1961) *119,020*.

Ahmedi, *pt.*, Yemen; nr. Hodeida; oil storage.

Ahuachapán, *dep.*, Salvador; cap. Ahuachapán; trade in coffee, sugar, tobacco, cereals; p. (1960) *130,710*. [p. (1966) *21,401*.

Ahvenanmaa (Åland), *dep.*, Finland, a. 572 sq. m.;

Ahwaz, *c.*, cap. Khuzestan prov.; airpt.; oil, aluminium, steel pipes; p. (1967) *322,063*.

Aigion, *t.*, Greece; currants exported; p. *11,011*.

Aigues-Mortes, *t.*, Gard, France; on R. Rhône delta; canal centre, once spt. now 3 m. from Mediterranean; salt-works; p. (1962) *4,203*.

Ailsa Craig, *rocky I.*, off Ayrshire cst., Scot., alt. 1,114 ft.; gannetry.

Ain, *dep.*, France; mainly agr., vines, grains, sheep, tobacco, silk; a. 2,248 sq. m.; p. (1962) *327,146*.

Ain Sefra, *terr.*, S. Algeria.

Aintab, *t.*, Syria, military centre in the Middle Ages; hides, morocco leather; p. (1950) *72,743*.

Aintree, *vil.*, Lancs., Eng.; nr. Liverpool; nylon plant projected 1964. [indigo, senna.

Air or Asben, *oasis* in Sudan, cap. Agades; dates,

Air, *mtns.*, Niger, W. Africa; ch. t. Agadès.

Airdrie, *lge. burgh. mftg. t.*, N.E. Lanark, Scot.; 12 m. E. of Glasgow; coal-mng., iron inds., brick and concrete wks., steel tubes, pharmaceutics; p. (1961) *33,620*.

Aire, *R.*, W.R. Yorks, Eng.; trib. Ouse; l. 70 m.

Aireborough, *urb. dist.*, W.R. Yorks., Eng.; p. (estd. 1967) *29,370*.

Airlie, *par.*, Angus, Scot.; seat of the Earls of Airlie; p. (1951) *630* [tunnel.

Airolo, *vil.*, Switzerland; at S. end of St. Gotthard

Aisne, *dep.*, France; agr., timber, sugar, brewing, textiles; cap. Laon; a. 2,866 sq. m.; p. (1962) *512,920*.

Aisne, *R.*, N.E. France; trib. R. Oise; l. 150 m.

Aix, *t.*, Bouches-du-Rhône, France; 18 m. N. of Marseilles; old cap. of Provence; thermal springs; p. (1962) *72,696*.

Aix-la-Chapelle, *see* Aachen. [(1962) *18,270*.

Aix-les-Bains, *health resort*, Savoy, France; p.

Aizu-Wakamatsu, *t.*, N. Japan; lacquer ware, candles; p. (1965) *102,239*.

Ajaccio, *spt.*, *cap.* Corsica; timber, flour, olive oil, tobacco; p. (1962) *42,232*. [p. (1961) *231,240*.

Ajka, *t.*, Hungary; industl.; aluminium, glass.

Ajmer, *t.*, Rajasthan, India; cotton, salt, opium;

Aksu (Aqsu), *t.*, Sinkiang, China; walled town, impt. trading ctr. on caravan route; textiles, carpets, jade carving, tanning, metal wkg.; p. *50,000*.

Akaroa, *t.*, S. I. New Zealand; on Akaroa Harbour; scenic and historic interest.

Akershus, *co.*, Norway; a. 2,064 sq. m.; p. (1963) *249,760*; Akerhus fortress (14th cent.) at Oslo.

Akhisar, *t.*, Turkey; ancient Thyatira; manganese, tobacco, olives, cotton, grain; p. (1965) *47,422*.

Akhmim, *t.*, Upper U.A.R.; linen and cotton goods; limestone quarries.

Akhtyika, *t.*, Ukrainian S.S.R.; metal wks.

Akimiski I., *I.*, James Bay, Canada.

Akita, *t.*, Japan; silk, metals, rice, oil-refining; p. (1964) *219,000*.

Akmolinsk, *see* Tselinograd.

Akola, *t.*, Maharashtra, India; cotton; p. (1961) *115,760*.

Akosombo, *pt.*, Ghana; pt. and new t. around L. Volta; textile factory being built; planned p. *50,000*.

Akpatok I., *I.* in Ungava Bay, Labrador.

Akron, *mftg. c.*, Ohio, U.S.A.; lge. rubber mftg. ctr.; maize mills, woollens, machin., chemicals, plastics, tools; p. (1960) *290,351*.

Akrotiri, Cyprus; British sovereign a. within Rep.

Aksaray, *t.*, Turkey; p. (1960) *20,046*.

Aksehir, *t.*, Turkey; p. (1965) *25,265*.

Aktyubinsk, *t.*, N.W. Kazakhstan S.S.R.; at S. end of Ural Mtns.; ferro-alloys, engin., lignite, elec. power, chemicals, copper; p. (1967) *131,000*.

Akureyri, *t.*, N. Iceland; herring fishery; p. (1962) *9,152*. [exp. rice; p. *c. 42,000*.

Akyab, *spt.*, Burma; at mouth of Kaladan R.;

Alabama, *st.*, U.S.A.; cap. Montgomery, ch. pt. Mobile; minerals, cotton, cereals, sugar, fertilisers, chemicals, mng.; a. 51,609 sq. m.; p. (1960) *3,266,740*.

Alagôas, *maritime st.*, Brazil; cap. Maceio; sugar, cotton, tobacco, rubber, rice, textiles; a. 11,016 sq. m.; p. (1960) *1,271,062*.

Alajuela, *prov.*, Costa Rica, Central America; cap. Alajuela; coffee, sugar; p. (1963) *237,568*.

Alameda, *spt.*, Cal., U.S.A.; airport; lt. mnfs., shipbldg., fish-canning, resort; p. (1960) *61,316*.

Alamosa, *t.*, Col., U.S.A.; flour-milling, meatpacking, stockyards; p. (1960) *6,205*.

Aland Is. (Ahvenanmaa), group belonging to Finland at entrance of G. of Bothnia; a. 572 sq. m.; p. (estd. 1958) *21,967*.

Alasehir, *t.*, Turkey; ancient Philadelphia; mineral springs, wheat, tobacco, raisins; p. (1960) *13,923*.

Alaska, *st.*, U.S.A.; in Arctic N. America; mtnous.; furs, timber, salmon fishing, mng., natural gas, oil; severe earthquake, 28th March 1964; a. 586,400 sq. m.; p. (estd. 1965) *246,000*.

Alaska Highway, from Dawson Creek, B.C. to Fairbanks, Alaska, 1,527 m. long; built for Second World War programme; main supply base and H.Q., Edmonton, Alberta.

Alatau, *mtns.*, bdy. of W. Turkestan and Sinkiang, China; group of 5 ranges, outliers of Tien-Shan; alt. up to 15,000 ft.; highest peak Khan Tengri, 22,800 ft.

Alava, Basque *prov.*, N. Spain; ch. t. Vitoria; viticulture; a. 1,175 sq. m.; p. (1959) *130,887*.

Alba, *t.*, N. Italy; in Tanaro valley; mkt. for silk, cattle, grain, wine; p. (1936) *11,072*.

Albacete, *prov.*, S.E. Spain; cereals, fruit, sheep; a. 5,739 sq. m.; p. (1959) *384,849*.

Albacete, *t.*, *cap.*, Albacete, Spain; agr. mkt., fruit, saffron; p. (1959) *74,807*.

Alba-Iulia, *t.*, Romania; on R. Mures, formerly Carlsburgh; union of Transylvania with Romania proclaimed here 1918; p. (1956) *14,776*.

Alban Hills, *volcanic group*, 10 m. S.E. of Rome, Italy; circumference 35 m.; greatest alt. Monte Faete, 3,137 ft.; viticulture.

Albania, *rep.*, S. Europe; lying along Adriatic, adjacent Jugoslavia and Greece; rugged mtnous. cty., fertile Adriatic littoral and Koritsa Basin; maize, wheat, olive oil, cheese, tobacco, wool, hides, horses, bitumen; cap. Tiranë; a. 10,629 sq. m.; p. (estd. 1965) *1,814,000*.

Albany, *st. cap.*, New York, U.S.A.; on R. Hudson; river pt., iron, brass, chemicals, textiles, paper, machin. tools, car equipment; p. (1960) *129,726*.

Albany, *spt.*, *t.*, W. Australia; on King George Sound; agr. and pastoral; oil storage, wool, super-phosphates; p. (1966) *11,417*.

Albay, *t.*, Luzon I., Philippines, hemp, sugar, copra.

Albemarle I., lgst. of Galapagos in Pac. Oc.; alt. summit, 5,020 ft. above sea-level. [60 m.

Albemarle Sound, *inlet*, N. Carolina cst. U.S.A.

Albert, *t.*, Somme, France; on R. Ancre; almost destroyed First World War and damaged again Second World War; aircraft, machin., hardware; p. (1962) *10,423*.

Albert L., Africa; great reservoir of White Nile, extreme length 100 m., general breadth 20 m., alt. 2,100 ft.; greater part in Uganda.

Alberta, *prov.*, W. Canada; Rockies, in W.; preeminently agr.; wheat, alfalfa, dairying, livestock; coal, gas, oil, chemicals; cap. Edmonton; a. 255,285 sq. m.; p. (1961) *1,331,944*.

**Albertville**, *t.*, Congo; on W. of L. Tanganyika; comm. ctr., rail-steamer transfer point; p. *c.* 30,000.

**Albi**, *cap.*, Tarn, France; cath.; industl. and comm. ctr. in coal mining dist.; p. (1962) 41,268.

**Albigeois**, *sub-region*, Basin of Aquitaine, France; centred on Albi; rich farming, cereals and vines; sm. coalfield and associated industries.

**Albion**, *t.*, Mich., U.S.A.; mnfs. iron goods; p. (1960) 12,749.

**Albuquerque**, *c.*, N. Mex., U.S.A.; on Rio Grande; wool, hides, timber, metals, cement; univ.; (1960) 201,189.

**Albury**, *t.*, N.S.W., Australia; on Murray R.; sheep farming, wool ctr.; p. (1966) 32,019 with Wondonga, Vic.

**Alcalá de Henares**, *t.*, Spain; 20 m. E. of Madrid; univ.; birthplace of Cervantes; p. (1957) 19,415.

**Alcalá la Real**, *t.*, Andalusia, Spain; p. (1957) 29,165.

**Alcamo**, *t.*, Sicily, Italy; 24 m. S.W. of Palermo; olives, oranges, lemons, wines; ruins of anc. Segesta nearby; p. *c.* 44,000.

**Alcázar de San Juan**, *t.*, nr. Ciudad Real, Spain; soap, gunpowder, wine; p. (1957) 25,139.

**Alcázar Quivir (Al Kazral Kebir)**, *c.*, Morocco, N. Africa; 80 m. N.W. of Fez; p. (1960) 34,035.

**Alcester**, *t.*, *rural dist.*, Warwick, Eng.; needles and fish-hooks, agr. and mkt. gardening; p. (rural dist. 1961) 15,556.

**Alcoy**, *t.*, Spain; textiles, farm implements, mach., elec. engin., fine paper mkg.; p. (1959) 53,031.

**Alcudia**, *Roman walled t.*, Majorca I., Spain; 31 m. from Palma; site of Roman t. of Pollentia; p. (1957) 3,556.

**Aldan**, *navigable R.*, Siberia, U.S.S.R.; length 300 m.

**Aldeburgh**, *mun. bor. spt.*, E. Suffolk, Eng.; 30 m. from Ipswich; fisheries; H.Q. of gr. of Eng. writers and musicians; p. (estd. 1967) 3,100.

**Alderley Edge**, *urb. dist.*, Cheshire, Eng.; p. (1961) 3,618.

**Aldermaston**, Berkshire, Eng.; Atomic Weapons Research Establishment.

**Alderney**, most N. of Channel Is.; agr. and hort. prods., dairying; sand, grit, gravel; tourism; t. St. Anne; airpt.; a. 1,962 acres; p. (1961) 1,472.

**Aldershot**, *mun. bor.*, Hants, Eng.; bricks; lge. military camp; p. (estd. 1967) 36,080.

**Aldridge**, *urb. dist.*, Staffs, Eng.; plastics, pack ing-cases; p. (1961) 50,981.

**Aleksandrovsk**, *see* Zaporozhe.     [(1962) 27,024.

**Alençon**, *t.*, *cap.*, Orne, France; textiles, lace; p.

**Aleppo**, *c.*, ch. tr. centre N. Syria; grain, textiles, carpets, dairying, cement, sugar, brewing; p. (1961) 496,231.

**Alès**, *t.*, Gard, France; trades in raw silk pro duced in region; coal mining, chemicals, iron ore, pyrite, zinc; p. (1962) 43,370.

**Alessandria**, *c.*, N. Italy; 46 m. E. of Turin; linen, hats, macaroni; p. (1961) 92,291.

**Alesund (Aalesund)**, *spt.*, W. coast Norway; fish ing; p. (estd. 1960) 19,000.

**Aletsch**, *glacier*, Bernese Alps, Valais can., Switzer land; lgst. in Europe; length exceeds 15 m.

**Aletschhorn**, *mtn.*, Bernese Alps, Valais canton, Switzerland; alt. 13,763 ft.

**Aleutian Is.** (U.S.A.), N. Pac. Oc., chain of Is. stretching out 1,200 m. from the most S.W. point of Alaska towards Kamchatka.

**Alexander City**, *t.*, Ala., U.S.A.; formerly Young ville; textiles; p. (1960) 13,140.

**Alexandretta**, *spt.*, *see* Iskenderun.

**Alexandria**, *ch. pt.*, U.A.R., N.E. Africa; founded by Alexander the Great, 332 B.C.; floating dock; exp. cotton, wheat, rice, gum; p. (1960) 1,513,000.

**Alexandria**, *t.*, Dunbartonshire, Scot.; on W. side of vale of Leven; cotton printing, bleaching, dyeing, torpedo wks.

**Alexandria**, *t.*, Louisiana, U.S.A.; rice, foundries; p. (1960) 40,279.

**Alexandria**, *c.*, *spt.*, N.E. Virginia, U.S.A.; on Chesapeake Bay; mnfs. foodstuffs, thread, cotton, leather goods; p. (1960) 91,023.

**Alexandrina L.**, inlet, S. Australia; nr. Encounter Bay.

**Alexandroupolis**, *spt.*, Thrace, Greece; oak timber tr., many antiquities; p. (1961) 18,712.

**Alford**, *urb. dist.*, Lindsey, Lincoln, Eng.; agr. mkt., brewing, food-preserving; p. (1961) 2,134.

**Alfortville**, *t.*, Val-de-Marne, France; S.E. suburb of Paris, rubber, paper, glass, hosiery, metal wks.; p. (1954) 30,195.

**Alfreton**, *urb. dist.*, Derby, Eng.; coal, iron, stone, chemicals, textile, engin., hosiery, knitwear; p. (ested. 1967) 22,650.

**Algeciras**, *spt.*, Spain; on bay opposite Gibraltar; fishing, cork, oranges; winter health resort; oil refinery being built; p. (1959) 64,842.

**Algeria**, *indep. sov. st.* (3 July 1962), N. Africa; formerly under French rule; comprises 13 departments; fertile valleys, rugged mtns., barren plateaux; warm, moist winters, hot, dry summers; Berbers, Kabyles, Arabs, Tauregs; cap. Algiers; products: wine, fruit, olive oil, timber, tobacco, minerals; oil, natural gas and iron ore in Saharan regions; a. 919,600 sq. m.; p. (estd. 1963) 10,453,000.

**Alghero**, *spt.* on western coast of Sardinia; cath.; coral fisheries, fruit, wine.

**Algiers**, *cap. c.*, *pt.*, Algeria; strongly fortified; univ.; exp. wine, citrus fruit, iron ore; oil refining at Maison Carrée; airpt. at Maison Blanche, 10 m. E. of c.; p. (1963) 820,000.

**Algoa Bay**, about 425 m. E. of C. of Good Hope S. Africa.

**Algonquin Park**, Ontario, Canada; *park*, game reserve, tourist centre.

**Alhama**, *c.*, Granada, Spain; hot springs; p. (1957) 10,564.

**Alhambra**, *c.*, S. Cal., U.S.A.; oil refining equip ment, felt, clay, aircraft, p. (1960) 54,807.

**Alhaurin el Grande**, *t.*, S. Spain; rly.; olive oil, marble quarries; p. (1957) 11,537.

**Alicante**, *prov.*, S.E. Spain; ch. t. Alicante; a. 2,267 sq. m.; p. (1959) 696,165.

**Alicante**, *spt.*, *t.*, E. Spain; tourism; wine, fruits, minerals; p. (1959) 117,204.

**Alice**, *t.*, Cape Prov., S. Africa; health resort; timber inds.; p. (1960) 3,536 inc. 746 whites.

**Alice Springs**, *t.*, N. Territory, Australia; ctr. vast pastoral holdings; tourism; Stuart highway (arterial road) to Darwin; p. (1966) 6,001.

**Aligarh**, *t.*, Uttar Pradesh, India; univ.; wheat, cotton, gold and silver work; p. (1961) 185,020.

**Alingsås**, *t.*, Sweden, E. of Gothenburg; clothing ind.; p. (1961) 17,546.

**Aliwal North**, *t.*, Cape Prov., S. Africa; sulphur springs, health resort; p. (1960) 10,706 inc. 2,629 Europeans.

**Alkmaar**, *c.*, Netherlands; world cheese mkt.; p. (1967) 49,561.

**Allahabad**, *t.*, Uttar Pradesh, India; univ.; Hindu pilgrimage ctr.; p. (1961) 411,955.

**Allegan**, *t.*, Mich., U.S.A.; mkt. for dairy and fruit products of the district; mnfs. drugs; p. (1960) 4,822.

**Allegheny Mtns.**, U.S.A.; bold escarpment in the W. Section of the Appalachian system stretch ing from Pennsylvania to W. Virginia.

**Allegheny**, *R.*, U.S.A.; joins the Ohio R., Pitts burgh, Penns.; length 350 m.

**Allen, Bog of**, *peat morass*, Ireland; a. 372 sq. m.

**Allen, Lough**, *L.*, Ireland, length 5 m., breadth 3 m.; one source of R. Shannon.

**Allenstein**, *see* Olsztyn.

**Allentown**, *t.*, Penns., U.S.A.; on Lehigh R., furniture, silk, tobacco; lorries; p. (1960) 108,551.

**Aller**, *t.*, N.W. Spain; agr. mkt.; coal-, iron-, lead-mines; p. 23,600.

**Alliance**, *t.*, Ohio, U.S.A.; coal; p. (1960) 28,362.

**Allier**, *dep.*, France; coal- and iron-mining, mineral springs, wine, wheat; a. 2,848 sq. m.; p. (1962) 380,221.

**Allier**, *R.*, Central Massif, France; rises in Cevennes; trib. of R. Loire.

**Alloa**, *spt.*, *burgh*, Clackmannan, Scot.; on N. bank of R. Forth 5 m. E. of Stirling; engin., brass, bricks, tiles, woollens, glass, distilling; p. (1961) 13,395.

**Alma**, *R.*, Crimea, U.S.S.R.; great victory over Russia by Allies, 1854.

**Alma-Ata**, *cap.*, Kazakh S.S.R.; engin., textiles, leather, printing inds.; p. (1967) 636,000.

**Almada**, *t.*, Portugal; on R. Tagus opposite Lisbon; Salazar Bridge (opened 1966), links with Alcantara, sub. of L.; founded by English Crusaders; p. (1963) 30,688.

**Almaden**, *t.*, Sierra Morena, Spain; ancient Sisapon; quicksilver-mines; p. (1957) 12,375.

**Almansa**, *t.*, Spain; textiles, leather, shoes, soap, brandy; p. (1957) 15,990.

Almelo, *t.*, Overijssel, Netherlands; 25 m. S.E. of Zwolle; cotton textile mnfs.; p. (1967) 57,722.

Almendralejo, *t.*, Badajoz, Spain; wine, brandy; p. (1957) 21,394.

Almeria, *prov.*, S. Spain; ch. t. Almeria; a. 3,338 sq. m.; p. (1959) 367,833.

Almeria, *spt.*, *t.*, S.E. Spain; cath.; exp. grapes, oranges, esparto grass, lead; p. (1959) 83,653.

Almondbury, *t.*, W.R. Yorks, Eng.; joined to Huddersfield.

Aln, *R.*, Northumberland, Eng.

Alnwick, *urb. dist.*, Northumberland, Eng.; cas.; brewing, agr. machin.; p. (1961) 7,482.

Alor, *I.*, one of Nusa Tenggara Is., Indonesia.

Alor Star, *t.*, *cap.*, Kedah st., Malaya; on main road and rly., N. airport; p. 32,424.

Alost (Aalst), *t.*, Belgium; 14 m. N.W. of Brussels; rly.-junc.; weaving (linen, silk), brewing, rubber goods; p. (1962) 45,196.

Alpena, *c.*, Thunder Bay, Mich., U.S.A.; cement, paper, tanneries, sawmills; p. (1960) 14,682.

Alpes-Maritimes, *dep.*, S.E. France; ceded by Italy in 1860; ch. t. Nice; olives, wines, fruit; a. 1,443 sq. m.; p. (1962) 618,265.

Alphen on Rhine, *t.*, S. Holland, Netherlands; on Old Rhine, 10 m. S.E. of Leiden; mkt. for dairy produce; p. (1967) 30,980.

Alps, highest mtns. in Europe; 600 m. long from G. of Genoa to near Vienna; 130 m. broad in Tyrol; principal peaks: Mont Blanc (15,784 ft.), Mont Rosa (15,217 ft.), Matterhorn (14,782 ft.).

Alps, Apuan, limestone range near Viareggio, Italy; source of Carrara marble.

Alps, Australian, mtn. range between E. Victoria and N.S.W.; highest peak, Mt. Kosciusko, 7,328 ft.

Alps, Southern, mtn. ridge between Westland and Canterbury, New Zealand, highest peak Mt. Cook 12,349 ft.

Als, *I.*, Denmark, in the Little Belt, a. 130 sq. m.

Alsace-Lorraine, *prov.*, France; industl., agr., wooded, minerals; total a. 5,601 sq. m. Taken from France, in 1871, retroceded 1919; now divided into deps. of Bas-Rhin (1,848 sq. m. and p. (1962) 770,150); Haut-Rhin (1,354 sq. m. and p. (1962) 547,920; Moselle (2,403 sq. m. and p. (1962) 919,412.

Alsager, *urb. dist.*, *mkt. t.*, Cheshire, Eng.; motor vehicles; p. (1961) 7,800

Alsdorf, *t.*, N. Rhine-Westphalia, Germany; 10 m. N.E. of Aachen; tar-distillation plant; p. (1963) 31,900.

Alston, *t.*, Cumberland, Eng., on S. Tyne R. in N. Pennines; limestone quarrying, hosiery; p. (1961) 2,198.

Altai, *mtns.*, S. boundary of Siberia; extend from sources of Obi to Gobi Desert more than 2,500 m. Bieluka Peak, alt. 13,644 ft.

Altamaha, *R.*, Georgia, U.S.A.; flowing into Atlantic; length 150 m.

Altamira, *caves*, N. Spain; prehistoric shelters, paintings of animals (Magdalenian).

Altamura, *t.*, Apulia, Italy; at foot of the Apennines; wines, wool; p. (1961) 43,735.

Altdorf, *t.*, *cap.* Uri can., Switzerland; on R. Reuss; rubber goods, wood workings; p. (1961) 6,600.

Altena, *t.*, N. Rhine-Westphalia, Germany; site of ancient cas. of Counts von der Marck; metals, wine; p. (1963) 24,100.

Altenburg, *t.*, Leipzig, E. Germany; lignite mining, engin., metallurgy, mnfs. playing cards, textiles; p. (1963) 46,866. engin.; p. (1961) 9,158.

Alton, *urb. dist.*, Hants, Eng.; breweries, light

Alton, *t.*, Illinois, U.S.A.; machinery, glass, chemicals, flour; p. (1960) 43,047.

Altona, *t.*, part of Hamburg, Germany; iron, textiles, breweries, glasswks., soap, leather, tobacco, fish canning; p. (estd. 1954) 250,000.

Altona, *t.*, S. Victoria, Australia, 8 m. S.W Melbourne; oil refinery, chemicals.

Altoona, *c.*, Blair, Penns., U.S.A.; coal, rly. wks.; p. (1960) 69,083.

Altrincham, *mun. bor.*, Cheshire, Eng.; heavy engin.; p. (estd. 1967) 41,017.

Altus, *t.*, Okla., U.S.A.; cotton, livestock, grain mkt.; p. (1960) 21,225.

Altyn Tagh, part of Kunlun mtns., Tibet, 14,000 ft.

Alva, *burgh*, Clackmannan, Scot.; at S. foot of Ochil Hills, 3 m. N. of Alloa; woollens, printing, fruit and fish canning; p. (1961) 3,957.

Alvin, *t.*, Texas, U.S.A.; grain mkt., oil wells; p. (1960) 5,643.

Alvsborg, *co.*, Sweden; a. 4,919 sq. m.; p. (1961) 375,006.

Alyth, *mftg. burgh*, Perth., Scot.; in Strathmore, 17 m. N.E. of Perth; p. (1961) 1,862.

Amadeus, *large salt L.*, N. Terr., Australia; 92 m. long.

Amadjuak Lake, Baffin I., Canada.

Amagasaki, *t.*, Japan; sub. of Osaka; chemicals, polyethylene; iron and steel; oil refining; p. (1964) 485,000. [E. of Nagasaki.

Amakusa Bay, *inlet*, Kyushu, Japan; on W. cst.

Amakusa, *I.*, Japan; kaolin.

Amalfi, *spt.*, Italy; on G. of Salerno; tourist resort; fisheries. [p. 12,365.

Amalias, *t.*, W. Greece; grapes, wine, currants;

Amapá, *Fed. terr.*, Brazil; a. 53,059 sq. m.; cap. Macapá; manganese ore; p. (1960) 68,889.

Amara, *t.*, R. *pt.*, Iraq; on left bank of R. Tigris 250 m. below Baghdad; Arab t. and agr. mkt. at R. crossing; p. 18,000.

Amarillo, *t.*, Texas, U.S.A.; oil refining, creameries; p. (1960) 137,969.

Amasya, *t.*, Turkey; on Yeshil-Irmak; fruit, salt, silk, wine; p. (1965) 33,539.

Amazon, *R.*, S. America; lgst basin and extent of water of any river in the world; rises among the Andes as Alto Marañon, and flows 3,900 m. to the Atlantic. Ocean steamers penetrate to Iquitos, 1,935 m. from mouth. One of its affluents, the Madeira, has an extreme length of *c.* 2,000 m. Drains nearly 3 million sq. m.

Amazonas, *t.*, Brazil; rubber, timber; a. 616,148 sq. m.; cap. Manaus (*q.v.*); p. (1960) 721,215.

Amazonas, *dep.*, Peru; a. 13,943 sq. m.; cap. Chachapoyas; p. (1961) 117,525.

Amazonas, *fed. terr.*, Venezuela; cap. Puerto Ayacucho on Orinoco R.; a. 70,000 sq. m.; p. (1961) 15,000. [(1961) 105,507.

Ambala, *t.*, E. Punjab, India; cotton, flour; p.

Ambarchik, *spt.*, Yakut rep., U.S.S.R.; air base, gold-mining; p. 10,000.

Ambato, *c.*, Ecuador, S. America; S. of Quito, on slope of Mt. Chimborazo; alt. 8,859 ft.; textiles, canned fruits, leather gds.; p. (1950) 33,908.

Amberg, *t.*, Bavaria, Germany; on R. Vils; iron, mining, engin., textiles; p. (1963) 42,300.

Ambès, Gironde, France; nr. Bordeaux; oil refining.

Ambert, *t.*, Puy-de-Dôme, France; paper, cheese; p. (1962) 7,600.

Amble, *urb. dist.*, Northumberland, Eng.; exp. coal; p. (1961) 4,889.

Amblecote, *urb. dist.*, Staffs., Eng.; glass, fireclay, iron wks.; p. (1961) 3,008.

Ambleside, *sm. mkt. t.*, Westmorland, Eng.; nr. L. Windermere; tourist centre, slates.

Amboina, *I.*, Moluccas, Indonesia; a. 314 sq. m.; spices; p. 66,821.

Amboina, *t.*, *cap.*, *residency*, Molucca Is., Indonesia; pt. on S. cst. of Amboina I.; shipyards; p. (estd.) 17,334.

Amboise, *t.*, Indre-et-Loire, France; 15 m. E. of Tours; famous cas. and prison; p. (1962) 8,192.

Ambriz, *spt.*, Angola; sugar-cane, coffee, copper.

Ameland, *I.*, W. Frisian Is., Netherlands.

America, the lands of the Western hemisphere, comprising the continents of North and South America, separated by narrow Isthmus of Panama. Most N. point over 9,000 m. from C. Horn, the extreme S. point; (estd. 1965) 450,000,000. *See also* North, South, and Central America.

Amersfoort, *c.*, Utrecht, Netherlands; on R. Eem; textiles, leather, tobacco, steam turbines; rly. junc.; p. (1967) 75,312.

Amersham, *t.*, Bucks, Eng.; 17th-century mkt. hall; light inds.; Radio chemical centre of U.K. Atomic Energy Authority; p. (of rural dist.) (1961) 56,565.

Ames, *t.*, Iowa, U.S.A.; State College of Agriculture; p. (1960) 27,003.

Amesbury, *t.*, Mass., U.S.A.; 40 m. N. Boston; cotton; p. (1960) 9,625.

Amesbury, *t.*, *rural dist.*, Wilts, Eng.; nr. ancient British monuments of Stonehenge; p. (rural dist. 1961) 22,594.

Amherst, *t.*, Mass., U.S.A.; machin.; Univ. of Mass.; p. (1960) 10,306. [p. (1961) 10,788.

Amherst, *spt.*, Nova Scotia, Canada; shipbldg.;

Amiens, *c.*, Somme, N. France; on R. Somme; fine cath.; velvet, linen, woollens, silks; p. (1962) 109,869. [of Seychelles.

Amirante Is., British group, Indian Ocean; S.W.

**Amityville**, *t.*, N.Y., U.S.A.; Long I. sub. of New York; seaside resort; p. (1960) *8,318.*

**Amlwch**, *urb. dist., vat. pl.*, Wales; N. cst. of Anglesey; p. (1961) *2,910.*

**Amman**, *cap.*, Jordan; site of very ancient c.; aerodrome; p. (1962) *296,358.*

**Ammanford**, *urb. dist.*, Carmarthen, Wales; anthracite, brick mkg.; p. (1961) *6,264.*

**Ammendorf**, *t.*, Saxony-Anhalt, Germany; lignite mining, chemicals; p. (estd. 1954) *20,000.*

**Ammer**, *R.*, Germany; joins Neckar nr. Tübingen.

**Amorgos**, *I.*, Grecian Archipelago; p. *3,069.*

**Amoy (Xiamen)** *c.*, former treaty-pt., Fukien, China; rail link to Yingtang, Kiansi; tea, fruit, bricks; p. (estd. 1953) *224,000.*

**Amravati**, *t.*, Maharashtra, India; textiles; timber; p. (1961) *137,875.*

**Amritsar**, *c.*, Punjab, India; holy Sikh city; univ.; shawls and carpets; p. (1961) *376,295.*

**Amroha**, *t.*, Uttar Pradesh, India; pilgrimage ctr.; p. (1961) *68,965.* [W. cst. of Schleswig.

**Amrum**, *I.*, one of N. Frisian Is., Germany; off

**Amsterdam**, *spt., cap*, Netherlands; at junction of R. Amstel and the IJ; built on 96 Is. joined by 300 bridges, harbour can hold 1,000 ships; two univs., Royal Palace, Bourse; extensive tr.; exp. dairy prod., sugar, tobacco; shipbldg., diamond polishing, aeronautical, marine, elec. machin., oil refining; p. (1967) *866,421.*

**Amsterdam**, *t.*, N.Y., U.S.A.; woollens; p. (1960) *28,772.* [refining.

**Amuay**, *t.*, N. Venezuela, Paraguaná pen.; oil

**Amu Darya (Oxus)**, *R.*, U.S.S.R.; flows from the Pamir Mtns. to Aral Sea, length 1,350 m.

**Amur**, *R.*, flows from Mongolia between Manchuria and E. Siberia into the Pacific, opposite Sakhalin I.; length 3,000 m.

**Anaconda**, *t.*, Montana, U.S.A.; copper, zinc, manganese; p. (1960) *12,054.*

**Anadyr**, *R.*, U.S.S.R.; flows into Bering Sea.

**Anaheim**, *t.*, Cal., U.S.A.; p. (1960) *104,184.*

**Anahuac**, *depression*, central plateau, Mexico; average alt. 7,000 ft.; surr. by higher country inc. volcano Popocatapetl (17,887 ft.); contains Mexico City, a. approx. 1,500 sq. m.

**Anaiza**, *t.*, Nejd, Saudi Arabia; p. *25,000.*

**Ancash**, *dep.*, Peru; a. 14,700 sq. m.; ch. t. Huaraz; p. (1961) *586,889.* [joins the Humber.

**Ancholme**, *R.* Eng.; rises in Lincolnshire and

**Anchorage**, *t.*, Alaska, U.S.A.; timber, salmon fishing and canning; almost devastated by earthquake 28 Mar. 1964; p. (1960) *44,237.*

**Ancona**, *spt.*, Central Italy; on the Adriatic Sea; founded by Dorians, 1500 B.C.; sugar refineries, shipbldg.; p. (1961) *99,678.* [lead, copper.

**Andalusia**, *old div.*, S. Spain; citrus fruits, sherry,

**Andalusian Mtns. (Baetic Mtns.)**, S. Spain; young Alpine fold mtns. stretching from Atl. Oc. (Cadiz) to Mediterranean (Alicante); inc. Sierra Nevada (highest peak, Mulhacén, 11,420 ft.); some minerals, esp. lead and silver.

**Andaman and Nicobar Is.**, Bay of Bengal; constituted a Union Territory, India, 1 Nov. 1956; timber; a. 3,215 sq. m.; p. (1961) *63,548.*

**Andenne**, *t.*, Namur, Belgium; on the Meuse, mining, chalk quarrying, chemicals; p. (1962) *7,919.*

**Anderlecht**, *sub.* of Brussels, Belgium; spinning, weaving, dyeing; p. (1962) *96,454.*

**Andermatt**, *vil.*, Uri, Switzerland; at foot of Mt. St. Gotthard; tourist ctr., winter health resort.

**Andernach**, *t.*, Rhineland-Palatinate, Germany; on the Rhine, 70 m. N.W. of Coblenz; R. port; metallurgy; p. (1963) *21,200.* [(1960) *41,316.*

**Anderson**, *t.*, S.C., U.S.A.; cotton, lumber; p.

**Anderson**, *c.*, Indiana, U.S.A.; p. (1960) *49,061.*

**Anderson**, *R.*, N.W. Terr., Canada; flows into Arctic Ocean.

**Andes**, *great mtn. system*, S. America; 4,500 m. long; from Panama to C. Horn, 40 m. broad; volcanic; several of the peaks are over 20,000 ft. high. Rich in minerals.

**Andhra Pradesh**, *state*, E. India; cap. Hyderabad; a. 106,286 sq. m., p. (1961) *35,983,447.*

**Andizhan**, *t.*, Uzbekistan S.S.R.; formerly residence of Khans of Khokan; cotton, metals, petroleum, engin.; p. (1967) *164,000.*

**Andoeukhep**, *t.*, Cambodia; cotton ginning.

**Andorra**, *sm. st.*, E. Pyrenees, under joint suzerainty of Pres. of France and Bishop of Urgel (Spain), virtually indep.; livestock, wines, tobacco; a. 191 sq. m.; p. (estd. 1965) *11,000.*

**Andover**, *mun. bor., mkt. t.*, Hants, Eng.; prehistoric earthwks.; p. (1961) *16,972.*

**Andover**, *t.*, Mass, U.S.A., on R. Merrimac; woollens, rubber; p. (estd. 1967) *21,580.*

**Andria**, *t.*, S. Italy; wine, olive oil, cotton textiles; p. (1961) *70,831.* [p. (1953) *70,136*

**Andros**, *largest I.*, Bahamas; sponges, sisal hemp;

**Andros**, *sm. spt.*, Andros I., Cyclades, Greek Archipelago; on E. cst.; p. (estd. 1960) *2,600.*

**Andujar**, *t.*, Spain; on Guadalquivir R.; mineral springs, pottery, soap, textiles, tanning, uranium plant; p. (1957) *23,499.*

**Angara**, *R.*, Siberia, U.S.S.R.; trib. of Yenisei; navigable almost its entire length, rises nr. and flows through L. Baikal; length 1,300 m.

**Angarsk**, *t.*, E. Siberia; on R. Angara 20 m. N.W. Irkutsk; engin., saw milling; p. (1967) *179,000.*

**Angel Falls**, *waterfall*, Venezuela, nr. Ciudad Bolivar; 3,212-ft. drop. [Bothnia.

**Angermanälven**, *R.*, Sweden; falls into G. of

**Angermanland**, *old div.*, Sweden; now mainly in prov. of Vasternootland.

**Angermünde**, *t.*, Frankfurt, E. Germany; 40 m. N.E. Berlin; rly. ctr.; p. (1963) *12,784.*

**Angers**, *t., cap.*, Maine-et-Loire, France; on R. Maine; mkt. t. for local produce, fruit, vegetables, Anjou wines, Cointreau; textiles; cath.; p. (1962) *122,269.*

**Anglesey**, *I., co.*, N. Wales, separated from Caernarvon by Menai Straits; cattle rearing, farming; a. 276 sq. m.; p. (1966) *56,000.*

**Anglet**, *t.*, Basses-Pyrénées, France; airport, woodworking, cellulose mftg.; p. (1962) *16,676.*

**Angola** (Port. W. Africa), Portuguese possession, W. Africa; cap. Luanda; ch. prod. palm oil, rubber, coffee, maize, sugar, wax, diamonds; newly discovered oilfields; a. 481,350 sq. m.; p. (estd. 1966) *5,154,000.*

**Angoulême**, *mftg. t.*, Charente, France; on R. Charente; cognac, paper; fine cath.; suffered during Huguenot wars; p. (1962) *51,223.*

**Angra do Heroismo**, *cap.*, Azores Is.; exp. wine, pineapples, flax; p. (1960) *102,365.*

**Angren**, *t.*, Uzbekistan S.S.R.; lgst. ctr. of lignite mng. in C. Asia; p. (1959) *55,000.*

**Anguilla**, *I.*, Leeward Is., W.I.; cap. The Valley; a. 35 sq. m.; p. (1957) *5,109.*

**Angus**, *co.*, Scot., formerly Forfar; agr. and mftg.; a. 875 sq. m.; p. (1961) *278,370.*

**Anhalt**, *dist.*, Saxony-Anhalt, Germany; former duchy; agr. and mining.

**An Hoa**, *t.*, S. Vietnam; industl. fertilisers.

**Anholt**, *I.*, Kattegat, Denmark; p. (1960) *239.*

**Anhwei (Anhui)**, *prov.*, China; soya-beans, rice, tea, coal and iron; a. 54,319 sq. m.; cap. Hofei; p. (1953) *30,343,637.*

**Anjou**, *old div.*, France; on both sides of R. Loire within the Paris Basin; ch. t. Angers.

**Ankara**, *cap.*, Turkey; on the Sakarya R.; grain and fruit ctr.; mohair cloth; p. (1965) *902,218.*

**Anking (Anqing)**, *c.*, Anhwei prov., China; rice, cotton, wheat, tanning; p. (1953) *105,000.*

**Anklam**, *t.*, Neubrandenburg, E. Germany; on Peene R.; engin., sugar, furniture; p. (1963) *19,785.*

**Ankleshwar**, *t.*, Gujarat, India; natural gas, oil; gas pipelines to Ultaran and Barodi; p. (1961) *20,287.*

**Annaba (Bône)**, *spt.*, Algeria; 280 m. E. of Algiers; fertile plain; phosphates, iron and steel wks.; p. (1963) *155,000.*

**Annaberg**, *t.*, Karl-Marx-Stadt, E. Germany; in Erz Mtns.; cobalt, tin, uranium mng.; p. (1963) *29,005.*

**Annam**, *region*, N. and S. Viet-Nam; formerly within French Union; divided by 17th parallel bdy. (1957); rice, cotton, cinnamon, silk, tea, lacquer, minerals; a. 56,973 sq. m. ch. t. Hué.

**Annan**, *burgh*, Dumfries, Scot.; on R. Annan, 2 m. from its mouth in Solway Firth; cotton, ropes, gloves, boiler mkg., fishing; Chapelcross reactor sta.; p. (1961) *5,572.*

**Annapolis**, *cap.*, Maryland, U.S.A.; naval academy; p. (1960) *23,385.* [growing a.

**Annapolis Valley**, Nova Scotia; famous fruit

**Ann Arbor**, *c.*, Michigan, U.S.A.; on the Huron; University of Michigan; motor lorries, farm implements; p. (1960) *67,340.* [*43,251.*

**An Nasiriya**, *t.*, .Iraq.; on Euphrates R.; p. (1950)

**Annecy**, *industl t.*, France, dep. of Haute-Savoie; p. (1962) *45,715.* [p. *17,522.*

**Annen**, *t.*, Germany; coal, steel, chemicals, glass;

**Annonay**, *t.*, Ardèche, France; mnfs. paper, woollens, silk, leather goods; p. (1962) *18,323.*

Ansbach, *t.*, Bavaria, Germany; machin., metallurgy, furniture inds.; rly. ctr.; p. (1963) *32,600*.

Anshan, *industl. c.*, Liaoning, N. China; at foot of Changpai Shan, 60 m. S.W. of Mukden; ctr. of ch. worked deposits of iron-ore in China; iron, steel, engin.; p. (1953) *549,000*.

Ansong, *t.*, Central Korea; 40 m. S.E. of Seoul; rice, silk cocoons; p. (estd. 1950) *20,000*.

Ansonia, c., Conn., U.S.A.; machin., brass goods, cotton-braid inds.; p. (1960) *19,819*.

Antakya (Antioch), *ancient c.*, S. Turkey; on R. Orontes; tobacco, olives, maize, soap, silk; p. (1965) *57,584*.

Antalya, *t.*, Turkey; p. (1965) *71,632*.

Antarctica, *plateau continent* within Antarctic circle; 7,000–10,000 ft. high; volcanoes and several Is.; owned chiefly by Britain, Australia, New Zealand, France, Norway; penguins. *See also* Brit. Antarctic Terr.

Antarctic Ocean, lies approx. S. of 60° S.; contains Antarctica; whaling.

Antequera, *t.*, Spain; sugar, textiles; metallurgy, trade in olive oil; grain; p. (1957) *43,334*.

Antibes, *spt.*, France; Alpes-Maritimes; health resort; oranges, flowers for perfume mnfs.; p. (1962) *35,976*.

Anticosti, *barren I.*, N. of R. St. Lawrence, Canada; 140 m. by 28 m.; game preserve.

Antigua, *aut. st.*, in association with Gt. Britain; Leeward group, W.I.; sugar, molasses, pineapples; yacht harbour; oil refinery under construction; a. (inc. Barbuda and Redonda) 170 sq. m.; cap. St. Johns; p. (estd. 1967) *62,000*.

Anti-Lebanon, *mtn. range*, Syria; E. of Lebanon; length 60 m.; alt. 6,000–8,000 ft.

Antilles, Greater and Lesser, W. Indies, comprising the Archipelago enclosing the Caribbean Sea and G. of Mexico.

Antioquia, *dep.* Colombia, S. America; cap. Medellin; a. 25,402 sq. m.; maize, coffee, sugar, gold, silver, panama hats; p. (estd. 1962) *1,971,710*. [inhabited.]

Antipodes, *Is.*, New Zealand; in S. Pacific, un-

Antisana, *volcano*, Central Ecuador, S. America.

Antofagasta, *prov.*, Chile; exp. nitrates, copper; a. 47,502 sq. m.; p. (1960) *240,537*.

Antofagasta, *spt.*, Chile; cap. of prov.; nitrates, copper, lt. inds.; p. (1960) *91,400*.

Antony, *t.*, Hauts-de-Seine, France; brick wks., toys; p. (1962) *46,823*.

Antrim, *co.*, extreme N.E. of N. Ireland; co. t. Belfast; famous Giant's Causeway is on the N. coast; a. 1,098 sq. m.; p. (1966) *313,684*.

Antrim, *t.*, N. Ireland; on Six-Mile Water; linen, nylon; p. (1966) *5,468*. [18,460.]

Antsirabé, *t.*, Malagasy; thermal springs; p. (1957).

Antung (Andong), *c.*, Liaoning, China; on R. Yalu, 15 m. from mouth; Chinese frontier sta. main rly. from China into N. Korea; mkt. for agr. produce; lumbering; p. (1953) *360,000*.

Antwerp, *spt.*, Belgium; on R. Schelde; famous Gothic cath.; lge. refinery; great petroleum port; shpbldg., textiles, tobacco, distilling, diamond cutting, chemicals; p. incl. subs. (1965) *655,000*.

Antwerp, *prov.*, Belgium; grain, flax; a. 1,104 sq. m.; p. (1962) *1,455,644*.

Anyang, c., Honan prov., China; coal, cotton ind.; p. (1953) *125,000*.

Anzhero-Sudzhensk, *t.*, W. Siberia, U.S.S.R.; nr. Tomsk; coal-mng., mng. equipment, pharmaceutics; p. (1967) *118,000*.

Anzin, *t.*, Nord, France; chief coal-mining centre of France; p. (1954) *15,658*.

Aomori, *spt.* Honshu, Japan; on bay of same name; salmon; chemicals; p. (1965) *224,433*.

Aosta, *t., cap.*, Val d'Aosta, N. Italy; in valley of Dora Baltea at node of trans-Alpine routes; iron inds.; Mont Blanc road tunnel links to Martigny, Switzerland, opened 19 Mar. 64; p. (1951) *24,181*.

Apalachee Bay, Fla., U.S.A.; receives Apalachee R.

Apapa, *spt.*, sub. of Lagos, Nigeria; on mainland opposite I. on which Lagos is situated; modern pt. equipment, terminus of W. Nigerian rly. system; rly. wkshps.; exp. palm oil and kernels, hides and skins, ground-nuts, cocoa, rubber; imports cotton piece goods, machin.

Apeldoorn, c., Gelderland, Netherlands; favourite holiday resort; precision instruments, metalware; p. (1967) *116,548*.

Apennines, mtn. "backbone" of Italy; length

800 m., width 70–80 m.; highest part is in Gran Sasso, *q.v.*

Apia, *spt.*, Upolu, W. Samoa; p. c. *10,000*.

Apiskigamish, *L.*, Labrador, Canada.

Apolda, *t.*, Erfurt, E. Germany; textiles, engin. chemicals; p. (1963) *29,313*.

Appalachian Mtns., parallel ranges between At. and Mississippi, stretching from Maine to Alabama. Highest peak, Mt. Mitchell, 6,684 ft.

Appenzell, *can.*, N.E. Switzerland; divided into the half-cantons, Appenzell Inner-Rhoden. a. 67 sq. m., cap. Appenzell; p. (1961) *12,943*; and Appenzell Ausser-Rhoden. a. 94 sq. m. cap. Herisau; p. (1961) *48,920*.

Appenzell, *t., cap.*, Appenzell. Switzerland; on R. Sitter; linen tr.; p. (1957) *5,001*.

Appleby, *mun. bor., mkt. t.*, Westmorland, Eng.; on R. Eden; cas.; p. (estd. 1967) *1,860*.

Appleton, *c.*, Wis., U.S.A.; paper; p. (1960) *48,411*.

Appomattox, R., Va. U.S.A.; joins James R.

Apsheron, *peninsula* on W. side of the Caspian; petroleum wells (nr. Baku) and mud volcanoes.

Apulia, *S.E. region*, Italy; pastoral plain; grain, fruits, livestock; wine, oil; a. 7,470 sq. m.; p. (1951) *3,214,854*.

Apurímac, *dep.*, Peru, S. America; ch. t. Abancay; a. 8,187 sq. m.; sugar; p. (1961) *275,910*.

Apurímac, R., Peru; joins the Ucayali; l. 500 m.

Aqaba (Akaba), *pt.*, Jordan; loading of phosphates and discharging of oil; p. (1961) *9,223*.

Aqaba, *G.*, between Sinai Peninsula and Saudi Arabia. N.E. arm of the Red Sea.

Aquila degli Abruzzi, *t., cap.*, Abruzzi prov., Italy; on R. terrace of R. Aterno; mkt. and sm. inds. associated with local farming; holiday resort; cath.; p. (1961) *56,314*.

Aquitaine, Basin of, *geographical region*, S.W. France; to W. and S.W. of Central Massif, to N of Pyrenees, bordered on W. by Atl. Oc.; warm, wet, oceanic climate; rich agric. lowland; inc. Landes, reclaimed sandy area; ch. ts. Bordeaux, Toulouse.

Arab Emirates, Federation of, comprises the 7 Trucial States, Bahrain and Qatar (30 March 1968).

Arabia, S.W. peninsula of Asia; mainly desert plateau; coffee, dates, gums, horses, camels; petroleum; divided between Saudi Arabia, Yemen, Southern Yemen, Muscat and Oman, Trucial States, Kuwait, Bahrain, and Qatar; a. c. 1,000,000 sq. m.; p. c. 8,000,000.

Arabian Desert, U.A.R., N.E. Africa; between R. Nile and Red Sea; alt. approx. 1,200–6,000 ft.; a. c. 80,000 sq. m.

Arabian Sea, N.W. part of Indian Ocean, between Horn of Africa and India.

Aracajú, *spt. cap.* Sergipe st., Brazil; sugar, soap, textiles, tanneries; p. (1960) *115,713*.

Arad, *t.*, Israel; in Negev desert, E. of Beersheba; new t. inaugurated 21 Nov. 1962; ind. to be based on gasfields at Zohar and Kanaim; chemicals, fertilisers.

Arad, *t.*, Romania; on R. Maros, wine, corn, tobacco, textiles; p. (1963) *124,642*. [E. of Timor.

Arafura Sea, N. of Australia, S.W. of Papua, and Araguaia, R., Brazil; trib. of Tocatins; length 1,000 m.

Araish (Laraish, Larache), *spt.*, Morocco, N. Africa; on Atlantic cst., 45 m. S.W. of Tangier; tr. in grain and fruit, cork; p. (1960) *30,763*.

Arak, *t.*, Iran; carpets; p. (1956) *58,929*.

Aral Sea, large salt *L.*, Kazakhstan Rep. (U.S.S.R.); a. 26,166 sq. m.; receiving the Amu and Syr Darya Rs.; no outlet.

Aran, *Is.* group in Galway Bay, Ireland; fishing.

Aranjuez, *t.*, Spain; on R. Tagus; mkt. gardens; strawberries, asparagus; p. (1957) *24,667*.

Ararat, *mtn.*, Turkey; supposed resting-place of Noah's Ark.

Ararat, *t.*, Victoria, Australia; on Hopteins R., 131 m. from Melbourne; p. (1961) *7,930*.

Aras R. (the ancient Araxes), rising in Armenia, flows through Transcaucasia to the Kur, 500 m.

Arauan, *trading t.*, Sahara desert, N. Timbuktu.

Arauco, *prov.*, S. Chile; a. 2,222 sq. m.; cereals, alfalfa, fruit; p. (1961) *94,079*.

Aravalli Mtns., Rajasthan, India; Mt. Abu, 5,650 ft.

Araxes R., rises in Armenia, flows through Transcaucasia to Caspian Sea; bdy. between Persia and U.S.S.R.

Arbroath, *royal burgh*, Angus cst., Scot.; engin., textiles (flax, jute, cotton, woollens), fishing; holiday resort; p. (1961) *19,533*.

Arcachon, *t.*, Gironde, S.W. France; on S. side of Bassin d'Arcachon (Bay of Biscay); fish. pt.; health resort; p. (1962) *15,820*.

Arcadia, *div.* of Peloponnesus, Greece; cap. Tripolis; p. (1951) *154,318*.

Archangel (Archangelsk), *t., dist. ctr.*, U.S.S.R.; on E. side of Dvina estuary, White Sea; lge. harbour kept open in winter by ice-breakers; fishery headquarters; exp. and inds. connected with N. Russia's softwood resources; engin.. hydro-elec.; p. (1967) *308,000*.

Arcos, *t.*, Cadiz, Spain; on R. Guadalete; famous Gothic church, ancient fortifications; cattle; cork trees; p. (1957) *21,120*.

Arcot, *t.*, India; 65 m. W. of Madras; taken by Clive 1751; p. (1961) *25,029*.

Arctic Ocean, seas in the N. polar area.

Arcueil, *sub.*, Paris, Val-de-Marne, France; on both sides of Brière valley S. of Paris; varied light inds. concerned with chemicals, clothing, foodstuffs; p. (1954) *18,067*.

Ardabil, *t.*, Azerbaijan, Iran; dried fruits, carpets; p. (1956) *65,720*.

Ardèche, *dep.*, S. France; Cévennes Mtns.; olives, wine silk, minerals; cap. Privas; a. 2,144 sq. m.; p. (1962) *248,516*.

Ardennes, *dep.*, N.E. France; farming, woollens, iron; cap. Mézières; a. 2,027 sq. m.; p. (1962) *300,247*.

Ardennes, *hilly wooded dist.*, Belgium, France, Luxembourg.

Ardmore, *t.*, Oklahoma, U.S.A.; coal, cotton, oil refineries; p. (1960) *20,184*.

Ardnacrusha, Clare, Ireland; power sta. on R. Shannon 3 miles N. of Limerick.

Ardnamurchan, most westerly point of mainland of Scotland, Argyll.

Ardres, *t.*, France; Pas de Calais; nr. site of "Field of the Cloth of Gold," where Henry VIII and Francis I met in 1520; p. (1962) *3,137*.

Ardrishaig, *t., spt.*, Argyll, Scot.; on Loch Fyne; holiday resort.

Ardrossan, *burgh*, Ayr, Scot.; on Firth of Clyde, 25 m. S.W. of Glasgow; shipbldg., oil storage, road bitumen, engin.; p. (1961) *9,574*.

Arecibo, *c., spt.*, N. coast of Puerto Rico; W. Indies; coffee, sugar; p. (1960) *23,460*.

Arendal, *spt.*, Norway; on Skagerrak; wood pulp, aluminium, shipping; p. (1960) *11,395*.

Arequipa, *dep.*, Peru; minerals, wool; cap. Arequipa; a. 21,947 sq m.; p. (1961) *392,352*.

Arequipa, *c.*, Peru; comm. ctr.; alpaca wool inds.; being developed as Peru's 1st prov. industl. a.; steel rolling mill, cement wks.; projected wks. for plastics, nylon, pharmaceutics, asbestos, car assembly; p. (1961) *221,900*.

Arezzo, *t., cap.*, Arezzo prov., Tuscany, Central Italy; hill site in a basin within the Apennines at junction of valley routes; mkt. for silk, wine, olives; p. (1961) *74,245*.

Argentan, *t.*, Orne, France; gloves, lace; p. (1962) *13,411*. [p. (1962) *82,458*.

Argenteuil, *t.*, Val-d'Oise, France; industl.;

Argentina, *rep.*, S. America, bounded by Atlantic, Andes, and Parana, Uruguay, Paraguay and Pilcomayo Rs.; inc. Pampas and Patagonia; cap. Buenos Aires; agr. and pastoral; exp. meat, wool, wheat, maize, linseed, cotton; natural gas at Canadon Seco and Comodoro Rivadavia fields in S.; pipeline to Buenos Aires; a. 1,079,965 sq. m.; p. (estd. 1965) *22,137,000*.

Argenton-sur-Creuse, *t.*, Indre, France; gloves, linen, lace; p. (1962) *6,906*. [p. (1951) *85,389*.

Argolis, *prov.*, N.E. Morea, Greece; cap. Nauplion;

Argonne, *hill ridge*, S.E. Paris Basin, France; composed of greensand; wooded; alt. 1,000 ft.; a. approx. 250 sq. m.

Argos, *t.*, Greece; leading Dorian city prior to the 7th century B.C.; ancient acropolis, theatre; p. (1951) *14,706*.

Argostolion, *cap.*, Cephalonia I., Greece; shipbldg.; destroyed by earthquake 1953; p. (1961) *8,205*.

Argun, *R.*, N.E. Asia; headstream of Amur; rises in Heilungkiang, China, and for 500 m. forms frontier between U.S.S.R. and China; length 1,000 m.

Argyll, *co.*, W. Scotland; mountainous, deer forests, pastoral, fishing, distilling; a. 3,165 sq. m.; p. (1961) *59,345*.

Ariano Irpino, *t.*, Italy; pottery; ancient Aequum Tuticum; p. *22,855*.

Arica, *t., free spt.*, N. Chile; exp. sulphur, copper, silver; oil pipe-line connects to Sica-Sica (Bolivia); p. (1960) *46,542*.

Arichat, *spt.*, Madame I., off Cape Breton I., Nova Scotia, p. *675*. [*137,192*.

Ariège, *dep.*, S. France; livestock, fruit, iron, copper; cap. Foix; a. 1,892 sq. m.; p. (1962)

Arima, *bor.*, Trinidad, W.I.; nr. Port of Spain; cacao industry; p. (1960) *10,900*.

Arish, El, *t., cap.*, Sinai, Egypt; on Mediterranean at mouth of Wadi el Arish; p. (1947) *10,791*.

Arizona, *st.*, U.S.A.; bordering on Mexico; agr., stock-rearing, copper, silver, gold, cotton, oil; cap. Phoenix; a. 113,909 sq. m.; p. (1960) *1,302,161*.

Arjona, *t.*, Colombia, S. America; sugar; p. *10.410*.

Arkadelphia, *t.*, S.W. Ark., U.S.A.; cotton, lumber, flour mills; p. (1960) *8,041*.

Arkansas, *st.*, U.S.A.; cap. Little Rock; agr., bauxite, coal, petroleum, natural gas, timber; a. 53,102 sq. m.; p. (1960) *1,786,272*.

Arkansas, *R.*, U.S.A.; navigable 650 m.; length 1,450 m.

Arkansas City, *t.*, Kan., U.S.A.; oil, flour mills, packing plant; p. (1960) *14,262*.

Arklow, *urb. dist., spt.*, Wicklow, Ireland; fisheries, copper, lead, bog iron, pottery; fertiliser plant under const.; p. (1966) *6,056*.

Arles, *ancient Roman c.*, Bouches-de-Rhône, France; on the Rhône; corn, wine, hats, silk; p. (1962) *42,353*.

Arlington, *t.*, Mass., U.S.A.; residtl. sub. of Boston; p. (1960) *49,953*. [p. (1962) *13,373*.

Arlon, *t.*, cap. Luxembourg prvo., S.E. Belgium;

Armadale, *burgh*, West Lothian, Scot.; 10 m. S.W. Linlithgow; coal, iron, limestone, brick and fireclay wks., engin., hosiery; p. (1961) *6,193*.

Armagh, *co.*, Ulster, N. Ireland; a. 512 sq. m.; p. (1966) *125,031*.

Armagh, *urb. dist.*, Armagh, N. Ireland; cath.; linen, whisky; p. (1966) *11,000*.

Armavir, *old ruined cap.* of Armenia, U.S.S.R.; on the slope of the extinct volcano Algaghoz; grain, engin.; p. (1967) *134,000*.

Armenia, *const. rep.* U.S.S.R.; former area divided between Turkey, Russia, Iran; rich mineral deposits; agr., cattle rearing, forestry; hydro-elec. stas. under constr.; cap. Yerevan; a. 11,900 sq. m.; p (1959) *1,768,000*.

Armenia, *t.*, Colombia, S. America; coffee; p. (estd. 1959) *110,000*.

Armentières, *mftg. t.*, Nord, France; base of British operations against Lille in First World War; cloth, linen; p. (1962) *27,254*.

Armidale, *c.*, N.S.W. Australia; univ.; cath.; ctr. of wool industry; p. (1966) *14,990*.

Arnhem, *t.*, prov. cap., Gelderland, Netherlands; on R. Rhine; lge. tin smelter; light inds. using rubber and rayon; p. (1967) *134,921*.

Arnhem Land, N. part of N. Territory, Australia; with C. Arnhem.

Arno, *R.*, Central Italy; flows past Florence and Pisa into Mediterranean; Val d'Arno is the fruitful valley of the R..; length 75 m.

Arnold, *urb. dist.*, Sherwood Forest, Notts., Eng.; hosiery, brick mkg.; p. (estd. 1967) *30,640*.

Arnsberg, *t.*, N. Rhine–Westphalia, Germany; on R. Ruhr; metal and wood mftg.; spa; p. (1963) *21,700*.

Arnstadt, *t.*, Erfurt, E. Germany; on R. Gera, 10 m. S. of Erfurt; artificial silk, leather goods, engin.; p. (1963) *26,929*.

Arosa, *t.*, Grisons, Switzerland; health and holiday resort.

Arpino, *t.*, Italy, textiles, paper, marble quarries, p. *10,564*.

Arrah, *t.*, Bihar, India; famous in the Mutiny; p. (1961) *76,766*.

Arran, *I.*, Bute, Scot.; in Firth of Clyde; contains many summer resorts; a. 165 sq. m.; p. (1961) *3,705*.

Arras, *t., cap.*, Pas-de-Calais, France; famous for tapestry; grain; dyeing, brewing; battle, First World War (1917); p. (1962) *45,643*.

Arroux, *R.*, France; trib. of the Loire; flows past Autun; length 75 m.

Arrow Lakes, expansions of Columbia R., Brit. Columbia. [*82,504*.

Arta, *prov.*, Epirus, Greece; on R. Arta; p. (1961)

Arta, *t., cap.*, Arta, S. Epirus, Greece; on left bank of R. Arta, 10 m. N. of G. of Arta; purely agr. interests; p. (1961) *16,399*.

Arta, *G.*, between Albania and Greece; near which the Battle of Acitum was fought, 29 B.C.

Artem, *t.*, R.S.F.S.R.; 29 m. N.E. Vladivostok; ctr. of coal-mng. a.; p. (1959) *55,000.*

Artemovsk, *t.*, Ukrainian S.S.R.; salt, coal, iron, mercury; p. (1959) *61,000.*

Arth, *t.*, Schwyz, Switzerland; starting point of rly. up the Rigi; p. (1957) *2,904.*

Arthur's Pass, pass running through the Southern Alps, S. Island, New Zealand, alt. 3,109 ft.

Arthur's Seat, famous hill, Edinburgh, Scot.; 822 ft.

Artois, *old div.*, France; now dept. Pas de Calais.

Aru, *Is.*, group, Indonesia, off coast New Guinea; pearl, tortoise-shell; a. 3,244 sq. m.; p. *18,139.*

Aruba, *I.*, Leeward Is., Neth. Antilles; oil refining, shipping; a. 73 sq. m.; p. (1957) *57,213.*

Arun, *R.*, Sussex, Eng.; flows into English Channel at Littlehampton; length 40 m.

Arundel, *mun. bor., mkt. t.*, W. Sussex, Eng.; on the Arun; Arundel Castle, seat of Duke of Norfolk; p. (estd. 1967) *2,710.*

Aruppukkottai, *t.*, Tamil Nadu, India, 35 m. S. of Madura; p. (1961) *50,200.*

Aruwimi, *R.*, Central Africa; trib. of Congo; route of Stanley's famous forest march in 1887; length 1,800 m.

Arve, *R.*, Haute-Savoie, France; falls into Rhône near Geneva; length 45 m.

Arvida, *t.*, S. Quebec, Canada; aluminium plant; nearby Shipshaw power development; p. (1961) *14,460.*

Arvika, *t.*, N. of L. Vänern, Sweden; agr. machin. and implements, pianos, organs; p. (1961) *15,778.*

As, *t.*, W. Bohemia, ČSSR.; 12 m. N.W. of Cheb; textile mnfs.; p. (1961) *9,640.*

Asahigawa, *c.*, Hokkaido, Japan; industl. and transport ctr.; p. (1965) *245,246.*

Asansol, *t.*, W. Bengal, India; rly. junction; coal-mng., iron, steel; p. (1961) *103,405.*

Asbury Park, *t.*, N.J., U.S.A.; resort; elec. prod., seafood, trucks; p. (1960) *17,366.*

Ascension I., part of Brit. col. St Helena. 760 m. N.W.; settlement Georgetown; nesting pl. of sooty tern; Brit. earth satellite stn. (1966); airstrip known as miracle mile. a. 34 sq. m.; p. (1962) *418.*

Aschaffenburg, *t.*, Bavaria, Germany; on R. Main; cas.; inds. paper, textiles, engin.; transhipment pt.; p. (1963) *55,000.*

Aschersleben, *t.*, Halle, E. Germany; potash and lignite mining, chemicals, textiles, engin., horticulture; p. (1963) *35,558.*

Ascoli Piceno, *cath. c.*, Central Italy; cap. of prov. of same name; p. (1961) *49,070.*

Ascot, *par.*, Berks, Eng.; famous racecourse at Ascot Heath.

Asenovgrad, *t.*, Bulgaria; S.E. of Plovdiv; p. (1956) *25,265.*

Ashanti, *historic region*, Central Ghana; formerly powerful native state; timber, cocoa, goldmines; cap. Kumasi; a. 24,379 sq. m.; p. (1960) *1,108,548.*

Ashbourne, *mkt. t.*, Derby, Eng.; near Dovedale; quarrying, milk processing, corsetry; p. (1961) *5,656.*

Ashburton, *urb. dist.*, Devon, Eng.; old mkt. t. S. gateway to Dartmoor; p. (1961) *2,715.*

Ashburton, *t.*, S. Island, New Zealand; ctr. of great wheat-growing dist.; p. (1961) *11,604.*

Ashburton, *R.*, West Australia; flows into Indian Ocean at Onslow; length 400 m.

Ashby-de-la-Zouch, *urb. dist.*, Leicester, Eng.; hosiery, open-cast mining, soap mftg.; ruined cas. in which Mary Queen of Scots was imprisoned; p. (1961) *7,425.*

Ashby Woulds, *urb. dist.*, Leicester, Eng.; coal and clay mining, pottery; p. (1961) *3,313.*

Ashdod, *pt.*, Israel; new modern deep-water pt. on Med. cst., 20 m. S. of Jaffa (closed 1965).

Asheboro, *t.*, N.C., U.S.A.; chemicals, lumber, furniture, hosiery; p. (1960) *9,449.*

Asheville, *c.*, *winter resort*, N. Carolina, U.S.A.; leather, textiles, furniture; p. (1960) *60,192.*

Ashford, *urb. dist., mkt. t.*, Kent, Eng.; agr. implements, ironfounding; p. (estd. 1967) *34,070.*

Ashikaga, *c.*, Honshu, Japan; cultural ctr.; old silk-weaving ctr.; anc. school with library of Chinese classics; p. (1964) *150,000.*

Ashington, *urb. dist.*, Northumberland, Eng.; coal; p. (estd. 1967) *26,320.*

Ashio, *t.*, Japan; 65 m. N. of Tokyo; copper; commerce; p. (1947) *20,997.*

Ashland, *c.*, Kentucky, U.S.A.; on R. Ohio; iron, steel, lumber, leather; p. (1960) *31,283.*

Ashland, *t.*, Penns., U.S.A.; coal-mining, knitwear, mine pumps; p. (1960) *5,237.*

Ashland, *t.*, Wisconsin, U.S.A.; iron, steel; p. (1960) *10,132.*

Ashtabula, *t.*, Ohio, U.S.A.; near L. Erie; farm implements, leather; p. (1960) *24,559.*

Ashton-in-Makerfield, *urb. dist.*, Lancs., Eng.; near Wigan; coal; p. (estd. 1967) *23,350.*

Ashton-under-Lyne, *mun. bor., mftg. t.*, Lancs., Eng.; nr. Manchester; iron and steel, coalmining, textiles, light engin.; p. (estd. 1967) *49,050.*

Ashuapmuchuan, *L.*, Quebec, Canada.

Asia, *largest continent*, extends over nearly one-third of the land surface of the earth. Chief mtn. ranges: Himalayas, Kunlun, Tien Shan, Altai; Tibetan plateau; chief Rs.: Ob, Yangtze, Yenisei, Lena, Amur, Hwang-ho, Mekong; deserts: Arabia, Thar, Takla Makan, Gobi; some very fertile valleys and plains. Climate very varied, extreme in N., monsoonal in S. and E. Gold, coal, oil, iron, manganese, antimony, tin. Principal countries, in Asia: Turkey in Asia, Israel, Jordan, Iran, Iraq, Afghanistan, India, Pakistan, Ceylon, Burma, China, Viet-Nam, Indonesia, Thailand, Malaysia, Korea, Japan and Soviet Asia. Industrialisation greatest in Japan, China, India, and Soviet Asia; a. c. 17,700,000 sq. m.; p. c. *1,600,000,000* (half world's total).

Asiago, *t.*, Vicenza, Italy; straw hats; site of Austro-Italian battle, 1916; p. *2,861.*

Asia Minor (Anatolia), W. portion of Asia, part of Asiatic Turkey; chief c. Izmir, important spt. of Levant.

Asinara, *I.*, Mediterranean Sea; off N.W. coast Sardinia; 11 m. long; the ancient I. of Hercules.

Asir, part of Saudi Arabia, S. Arabia; cst. region between Yemen and Hejaz. [Ireland.

Askeaton, *t.*, on estuary of R. Shannon, Limerick.

Asmara, *c.*, cap. Eritrea, N.E. Africa; alt. c. 7,300 ft.; on rly. which connects Massawa and Agordat; p. (estd. 1958) *120,000.*

Asnières, *t.*, Hauts-de-Seine, France; dyes, perfumery; regattas; p. (1962) *82,201.*

Asolo, *t.*, N.E. Italy; Roman remains.

Aspra Spitia, *t.*, Central Greece; new industl. t. close to Andikira Bay; aluminium wks.

Aspropotamos, *R.*, Greece; longest R. in the country; length 115 m.

Aspull, *urb. dist.*, Lancs, Eng.; near Wigan; coal, cotton; p. (1961) *6,753.*

Assab, on Red Sea, Ethiopia; oil refinery.

Assam, *st.*, India; Brahmaputra R. flows through it; extensive tea plantations; rice, cotton, coal; oil development at Rudrasagar; cap. Shilong; a. 47,091 sq. m.; p. (1961) *11,872,772.*

Assen, *t.*, prov. cap. Drenthe, Netherlands; p. (1967) *35,080.*

Assens, *t.*, I. of Fyne, Denmark, on the Little Belt, p. (1960) *4,937.*

Assiniboine, *R.*, Manitoba, Canada; joins Red R. at Winnipeg; length 1,500 m.

Assisi, *t.*, Umbria, Central Italy; 15 m. S.E. of Perugia; birthplace of St. Francis; fine cath. and old cas.; p. *5,353.*

Assynt, *dist.*, *L.*, Sutherland, Scot., 7 m.; agr. and creameries; p. (1961) *831.*

Assyria, *heart of former empire*. N. plain of Mesopotamia (Iraq); drained by R. Tigris; now mainly pastoral farming a.; ruins of many ancient cas.; cap. Nineveh.

Astara, *spt.* on the Caspian, at frontier with Iran; important trading ctr.

Asterabad, *t.*, N. Iran; on S.E. shore of Caspian Sea; p. *28,000.*

Asti, *t.*, Alessandria, Italy; fine cath.; wines; silk, motor cycles; p. (1961) *60,217.*

Astipalaia, *I.*, Grecian Archipelago.

Astorga, *t.*, Spain, nr. Leon; cath.; p. (1957) *9,916.* [p. (1960) *11,239.*

Astoria, *t.*, Oregon, U.S.A.; salmon-canning;

Astoria, N.Y., U.S.A.; industl. and residtl.; part of Queen's bor., New York City; settled in 17th cent. as Hallet's Cove; renamed for J. J. Astor.

Astrakhan, *t.*, R.S.F.S.R.; on delta of R. Volga; univ.; fish, caviare, astrakhan wool, fruits, wheat, elec. power, engin.; p. (1967) *361,000.*

Astrolabe Bay, on N.E. coast of New Guinea; arm of the Pacific Ocean.

Asturias, *old prov.*, N. Spain; now Oviedo, on Bay of Biscay.

Asunción, *cap.*, Paraguay; on junction of Rs. Paraguay and Pilcomayo; cath.; tobacco, sugar, leather; p. (estd. 1960) *305,000.*

Aswan, *administrative div.*, Upper U.A.R., N.E. Africa; a. 337 sq. m.; p. (1960) *385,000.*

Aswan, *t.*, Upper U.A.R.; on Nile at 1st cataract, ancient name Syene; near famous ruins, temples, catacombs; tourism; p. (1960) *43,000.*

Aswan Dam, Aswan, Upper U.A.R.; built 1902 to control Nile flood in U.A.R.; High Dam under constr. to provide cheap electric power and irrigation of 2 million acres in Lower U.A.R.

Asyut (Assiut), *prov.*, Upper U.A.R.; cap. Asyut; a. 787 sq. m.; p. (1960) *1,329,558.*

Asyut, *t.*, Upper U.A.R., N.E. Africa; pottery, ivory work; p. (1957) *121,000.*

Atacama, *prov.*, N. Chile; cap. Copiapo; rich in minerals, nitrates, borax, guano; a. 30,834 sq. m.; p. (1960) *104,266.*

Atacama Desert, Chile; arid coastal tract. rich in nitrates.

Atami, *t.*, Honshu, Japan; on Sagami Bay; sea-side hot-spring resort; p. (1965) *54,540.*

Atar, *t.*, Mauritania, W. Africa; rly. terminus, chief inland town; p. (1954) *4,200.*

Atbara, *t.*, Sudan; at confluence of Atbara R. with Nile; rly. wkshps. cement; p. (estd. 1951) *36,100.*

Atbara R., or Black Nile, Ethiopia and Sudan; trib. of Nile; length 790 m.

Ath, *t.*, Hainaut, Belgium; sugar refining, furniture, chemicals, silk; p. (1962) *10,978.*

Athabaska, *R.*, Alberta, Saskatchewan, Canada; navigable by steamers, save at Grand Rapids, near mouth of Clearwater R.; length 740 m.

Athabaska, *L.*, Alberta, Saskatchewan, Canada; a. 3,085 sq. m.

Athelney, hill formerly encircled by marsh near Taunton, Somerset, Eng.; between the Rs. Tone and Parret; King Alfred's hiding-place.

Athenry, *mkt. t.*, Galway, Ireland; old Dominican monastery; p. (1951) *1,181.*

Athens, *cap.* Greece; most renowned c. in antiquity; ancient ctr. of Greek art and learning; Acropolis and many splendid temples; spinning, distilling, tanning, carpets; oil refinery nearby; p. of greater Athens (inc. Piraeus) (1961) *1,850,000,* of c. (1961) *628,000.*

Athens, *t.*, Georgia, U.S.A.; univ.; cotton goods, lumber; p. (1960) *31,355.*

Athens, *t.*, Ohio U.S.A.; univ.; coal, light inds.; p. (1960) *16,470.*

Atherstone, *mkt. t., rural dist.*, Warwick., Eng.; N. of Coventry; hats, coalmng., footwear, granite quarrying; p. (rural dist. 1961) *24,394.*

Atherton, *urb. dist.*, Lancs., Eng.; 13 m. N.W. Manchester; coal, cotton, light engin.; p. (estd. 1967) *20,510.* [*14,120.*]

Athis-Mons, *t.*, Seine-et-Oise, France; p. (1954)

Athlone, *urb. dist., military sta.*, Westmeath, Ireland; on R. Shannon; p. (1966) *9,616.*

Atholl, *dist.*, N. Perth, Scot.; extensive deer forests and grouse moors; a. 450 sq. m.

Athos, *mtn.*, Greece; on promontory of Chalkidike, known as the "Holy Mountain" and the "Monks' Peninsula"; self-governing monastic community; cap. Karyai; p. (1951) *3,100.*

Athy, *urb. dist.*, Kildare, Ireland; p. (1966) *4,055.*

Atikokan, *sm. t.*, Ontario, Canada; on Canadian National Rly., 110 m. W. of Fort William; ctr. of Steep Rock iron-ore mines.

Atiquizaya, *t.*, Ahuachapán, Salvador, Central America; p. *5,901.*

Atlanta, *cap. largest c.*, Georgia, U.S.A.; univ.; cotton, paper, farm implements, printing, clothing; p. (1960) *487,455.*

Atlantic City, *summer resort*, N.J., U.S.A.; p. (1960) *59,544.*

Atlantic Ocean, 2nd lgst ocean; a. (estd.) 31,830,000 sq. m.; conn. to Pac. Oc. by Panama Canal. Central ridge of volcanic activity runs S. from Iceland to Antarctic, some peaks emerging as Is. (*e.g.*, Azores, Ascension, Tristan da Cunha). Chief deeps: Milwaukee Deep (30,246 ft.) near Bahamas and Nares Deep (27,972 ft.) near Puerto Rico.

Atlántico, *dep.*, Colombia, S. America; cap. Barranquilla; a. 1,340 sq. m.; p. (estd. 1961) *612,170.*

Atlas, *great mtn. range*, N.W. Africa; extending 1,500 m. through Morocco and Algeria to Tunis. Highest point, Tizi-n-Tamjurt, 14,500 ft.

Atlit (Athlit), *t.*, Israel; S. of Haifa; site of Crusaders' pt.

Atmore, *t.*, Ala., U.S.A.; 35 m. N.E. of Mobile Bay; p. (1960) *8,173.*

Atoka, *t.*, Okla., U.S.A.; flour, lumber mills; p. (1960) *2,877.*

Atrato, *R.*, Colombia, S. America; flowing to G. of Darien, length 275 m.

Atrauli, *t.*, Uttar Pradesh, India; 16 m. from Aligarh; p. (1961) *17,936.*

Atrek, *R.*, Iran; enters Caspian Sea; length 250 m.

Atshan, *t.*, Fezzan, Libya, N. Africa; oil.

Attica, *dep.*, Greece; olives, grapes, figs; a. 1452 sq. m.; p. (1961) *2,057,994.*

Attica, *t.*, New York, U.S.A.; p. (1960) *2,758.*

Attleboro, *c.*, Bristol, S.E. Mass., U.S.A.; p. (1960) *27,118.*

Attock, *t.*, Pakistan; between Peshawar and Islamabad; oil wells; oil refining.

Atzcapotzalco, *t.*, Fed. Dist. Mexico; oil ref.; petro-chemicals.

Aubagne, *t.*, Bouches-du-Rhône, France; bricks, tiles, corks, meat processing; p. (1962) *21,889.*

Aube, *dep.*, N.E. France; cereals, fruit, livestock; cap. Troyes; a. 2,326 sq. m.; p. (1962) *255,099.*

Aube, *R.* France; trib. Seine; length 1,255 m.

Aubervilliers, *t.*, Seine, France; industl.; p. (1962) *70,836.*

Aubrac, *mtns.*, Auvergne, France.

Auburn, *t.*, Ind., U.S.A.; comm. ctr. for agr. area; light engin.; p. (1960) *6,350.*

Auburn, *c.*, Maine, U.S.A.; footwear; p. (1960) *24,449.*

Auburn, *t.*, N.Y., U.S.A.; shoes, woollens, farm implements; p. (1960) *35,249.*

Auch, *t., cap.*, Gers, France; cottons, woollens, poultry, wines; p. (1962) *20,384.*

Auchel, *t.*, Pas de Calais, F ance; coal; p. (1954) *14,825.*

Auchinleck, *par.*, Ayr., Scot.; coal; p.(1951) *6,808.*

Auchterarder, *burgh*, Scot.; 15 m. S.W. of Perth; health resort S. slopes of the vale of Strathearn; woollen inds.; p. (1961) *2,426.*

Auchterderran, *par.*, Fife., Scot.; coal; p. (1951) *17,599.*

Auchtermuchty, *burgh*, Fife., Scot.; at S. foot of Ochil Hills, 25 m. N.E. of Alloa; distilling, cotton spinning; p. (1961) *1,354.*

Auckland, *prov.*, N.I., New Zealand; farming, gold, Kauri gum, coal; a. 25,400 sq. m.; p. (1961) *996,281.*

Auckland, *spt..*, *c.*, N.I., New Zealand; lgst. c. in N.Z.; seat of government 1845–64; extensive tr. and shipping; univ.; sawmills, sugar refinery, shipbldg.; glass; steelwks projected 25 m. S. of A., in Waikato iron sand a.; p. (1964) *499,700* of c. *147,900.*

Auckland Is., uninhabited group in Southern Ocean; 200 m. off New Zealand, discovered by British in 1806.

Aude, *maritime dep.*, S.E. France; grain, fruit, wine; slate, iron; cap. Carcassonne; a. 2,448 sq. m.; p. (1962) *269,782.*

Audenshaw, *urb. dist.*, Lancs., Eng.; metals, leather, pharmaceutics; p. (1961) *12,112.*

Audincourt, *t.*, Doubs, France; forges, automobile and textile plants; p. (1962) *12,527.*

Audubon, *t.*, W. Iowa, U.S.A.; canneries; p. (1960) *2,928.*

Aue, *t.*, Karl-Marx-Stadt, E. Germany; nr. Zwickau; uranium-mining, metallurgy, textiles; p. (1963) *31,740.*

Auerbach, *t.*, Karl-Marx-Stadt, E. Germany; textiles; p. (1963) *19,082.*

Augsburg, *c.*, Bavaria, Germany; at confluence of Rs. Lech and Wertsch; cath; theological institute; textiles, aircraft and diesel engines; route ctr.; p. (1963) *210,500.*

Augusta, *t.*, Sicily, Italy; on sm. I. connected to E. cst.; good harbour used as naval base; fishing; lubricants; p. *25,437.*

Augusta, *spt.*, S.W. coast, W. Australia.

Augusta, *t., cap.*, Me., U.S.A.; on Kennebec R.; footwear, cotton goods, paper; p. (1960) *21,680.*

Augusta, *c.*, Ga., U.S.A.; on Savannah R.; cotton, cotton-seed oil, chemicals, foundries; p. (1960) *70,626.*

Augustow, *t.*, Poland; on Suwalki canal.

Aulnay-sous-Bois, *t.*, Siene-St-Denis, France; p. (1962) *47,686.*

Aunjetitz, *t.*, ČSSR.; site of early Bronze Age culture.

Aurangabad, *t.*, Maharashtra, India; textiles; p. (1961) *87,579.*

Auray, or Alrac, *t.*, Morbihan, Brittany, France; oysters, dairy produce; p. (1962) *8,354.*

Aurès, *mtn. massif* Algeria, N. Africa; Berber stronghold.

Aurignac, *commune*, Haute-Garonne, France; caves, paleolithic remains; tanneries.

Aurillac, *t.*, *cap.*, Cantal, France; industl.; p. (1962) *27,056.*

Aurora, *t.*, Col., U.S.A.; residtl. sub. 5 m. E. of Denver; p. (1960) *48,548.*

Aurora, *t.*, E. Ind., U.S.A.; lumber, mnfs. coffins, furniture; p. (1960) *4,119.*

Aurora, *rly. c.* Ill., U.S.A.; textiles, foundries; p. (1960) *63,715.*     [*4,683.*

Aurora, *t.*, Mo., U.S.A.; mining region; p. (1960)

Au Sable, *R.*, New York, U.S.A.; flows from the Adirondack Mtns. to L. Champlain.

Au Sable, *R.*, Mich., U.S.A.; emptying into L. Huron.

Aussig, *see* Usti.

Austin, *t.*, Minn., U.S.A.; food prods.; p. (1960) *27,908.*

Austin, *c.*, *cap.*, Texas, U.S.A.; on R. Colorado; st. univ.; farming ctr.; bricks, furniture; p. (1960) *186,545.*

Austral and Rapa Is., French group in Pacific Ocean; largest I. Rurutu; a. 115 sq. m.; p. (1962) *4,371.*

Australasia, div. of Oceania including Australia, Tasmania, New Zealand, New Guinea and neighbouring archipelagos.

Australia, Commonwealth of, largest I. in world; Cook took possession for Britain 1770; Commonwealth proclaimed 1901, federation of N.S.W., Victoria, Queensland, S. Australia, W. Australia and Tasmania; includes also federal cap. terr., N. Territory; cap. Canberra (administered separately). Mtns. in E.; most salient feature great interior plains, mainly arid; chief rivers: Murray, Darling, Swan; saline lakes. Climate: interior extremely hot and dry, cst. more moderate, N. coast tropical. Agr.: wheat, hay, cane-sugar, fruit; sheep, cattle, dairying; timber; great mineral resources: iron, bauxite, tin, gold, lead, silver, copper, zinc, coal; a. 2,974,581 sq. m.; p. (1966) *11,544,691.*

Australia, South, *st.* of the Australian Commonwealth, the "Desert State"; mainly undulating, interior forms part of central plateau of continent, mtns. in S. and S.E., 3,000 ft.; wheat crops, stock-raising, dairying, fruit, olives; lead, iron, uranium; exp. corn, wool, mutton; cap. Adelaide; a. 380,070 sq. m.; p. (1966) *1,090,723* plus *5,505* Aborigines.

Australia, Western,/st. Australia; lgst st., nearly a third of western part of continent; cap. Perth, on the Swan R.; wool, fruit, wheat, frozen meat; gold, bauxite, coal, high grade iron-ore, asbestos and ilmenite deposits; Kununurra Dam irrigation scheme for semi-arid northern regions; a. 975,920 sq. m.; p. (1966) *835,570* plus *11,542* Aborigines.

Australian Alps, *see* Alps, Australian.

Australian Antarctic territory, part of Antarctica; between 45° E. and 160° E.; inc. Oates Land, King George V Land, Wilkes Land, Queen Mary Land, Kaiser Wilhelm II Land, Princess Elizabeth Land, MacRobertson Land, Kemp Land, Enderby Land, MacDonald Is., together with the research stas. of Mawson, Davis, and Wilkes; a. (estd.) 2,472,000 sq. m.

Australian Bight, Great, large indentation on Australian S. coast between C. Catastrophe and C. Arid (850 m.)

Australian Capital Territory, area surrounding Canberra, seat of Fed. Govt. of Australia; predominantly pastoral; a. 910 sq. m.; p. (1966) *95,913.*

Austria, *rep.*, Europe; in 1938 forcibly incorporated in German Reich, liberated in 1945, and recovered its sovereignty and indep. 1955; mountainous, forested, drained by R. Danube; agr.; tourism; lignite, anthracite, iron, textiles, pianos, brewing; cap. Vienna; a. 32,393 sq. m.; p. (1961) *7,073,807.*

Austria, Lower, *st.*, Austria; cap. Vienna; a.

(excluding Vienna) 7,098 sq. m.; p. (excluding Vienna) (1961) *1,374,012.*

Austria, Upper, *st.*, Austria; cap. Linz; a. 4,625 sq. m.; p. (1961) *1,131,623.*

Autlán de Navarro, *t.*, Mexico; S.W. Jalisco state: p. *10,915.*

Autun, *c.*, Sâone-et-Loire, France; anc. Augustodunum; Roman remains; oil-shale refinery, leather, furniture, dyes, fertilisers; p. (1962) *17,165.*

Auvergne, old French prov. forming the present deps. of Puy-de-Dôme, Cantal and a small part of Haute-Loire.

Auvergne Mtns., *mtns.*, Central France; in N.W. of Central Plateau; highest peak, Mt. Dore, 6,188 ft.

Aux Cayes, *spt.*, Rep. of Haiti, W. Indies; on S. cst.; p. *25,000.*

Auxerre, *industl. c.*, *cap.*, Yonne, France; cath.; vines, bricks, iron and steel; p. (1962) *32,961.*

Auxonne, *fortfd. t.*, Côte d'Or, France; on R. Saône; mkt. gardening; p. (1962) *6,649.*

Ava, *c.*, Burma; on the Irrawaddy R.; former cap.; many pagodas, now ruins.

Avallon, *t.*, Yonne, France; on Cousin R.; ancient church; tourist ctr.; p. (1962) *6,371.*

Avebury (Abury), *par.*, *vil.*, Wilts., near Marlborough, Eng.; famous for its Megalithic remains.

Aveiro, *spt.*, *t.*, Portugal; wine; sardines; fruit; p. (1963) *16,011.*

Avellaneda, *industl. sub.* of Buenos Aires, Argentina; hides, wool; p. (1960) *170,000.*

Avellino, *t.*, *cap.*, Avellino prov., Italy; monastery; hazelnuts, linen, paper; p. (1961) *41,509.*

Averno, Alpine valley of Switzerland.

Aversa, *garrison t.* Italy; W. of Caserta; wine, hemp, soap and chemicals; p. (1961) *40,336.*

Aves (Bird Is.), group in the Caribbean Sea, W. Indies, belonging to Venezuela.

Avesta, *t.*, Kopparberg, Sweden; on Dal R.; iron, aluminium and charcoal wks.; p. (1961) *10,880.*

Aveyron, *dep.*, France; on rim of Central Plateau, watered by Rs. Lot, Aveyron, Tarn; extensive forests; grain, dairying, sheep; coal; cap. Rodez; a. 3,385 sq. m.; p. (1962) *290,442.*

Aviemore, *t.*, Inverness, Scot.; on R. Spey, 12 m. S.W. of Grantown; rly. junction; tourist resort.

Avigliano, *t.*, Lucania, Italy; 8 m. N.W. of Potenza; marble; p. *14,333.*

Avignon, *ch. t.*, Vaucluse, S.E. France; residence of Popes 1309–78, and anti-Popes 1378–1417; wines, silk-worm eggs, chemicals, leather; p. (1962) *75,181.*

Avila, *t.*, *cap.*, Avila prov.. Spain; univ., cath.; wool, pottery; p. (1957) *25,000.*

Aviles, *spt.*, Oviedo, Spain; exp. coal. lead, zinc, chemicals, fishing; p. (1957) *50,000.*

Avion, *t.*, Pas-de-Calais, France; coal-mining; p. (1954) *19,471.*

Avoca, *R.*, Ireland; drains Wicklow Mtns.

Avola, *t.*, Syracuse, Italy; almonds; p. (1936) *23,344.*

Avon, *R.*, Somerset, Eng.; enters Bristol Channel at Avonmouth; length 80 m.

Avon, *R.*, Warwick., Eng.; flows past Stratford to Severn at Tewkesbury.

Avon, *R.*, Wilts and Hants, Eng.; flows past Salisbury into English Channel at Christchurch; length 65 m.

Avonmouth, *spt.*, Gloucester, Eng.; outport of Bristol; at mouth of R. Avon; docks; seed crushing, petrol refinery, non-ferrous metals, chemicals.

Avranches, *t.*, Manche, France; typical Normandy mkt. t. dealing in cider and dairy produce; p. (1962) *10,127.*

Awaji, *I.* at entry of Inland Sea, Japan; a. 219 sq. m.; highest peak, Yurimbayama, 1,998 ft.

Awe, Loch, Argyll, Scot.; 8 m. W. of Inveraray, bordered by Ben Cruachan (16 sq. m.); salmon and trout fishing; hydro-elec. sta. at Cruachan under construction.

Axar, *fiord*, N. Iceland.

Axbridge, *rural dist.*, Somerset, Eng.; p. (1961) *30,761.*

Axe, *R.*, Somerset, Eng.; rising in Mendip Hills and flowing to Severn.

Axholme, I. of N.W. Lincs, Eng.; formed by Rs. Trent, Don and Idle. and comprising seven parishes; rural dist. agr. and engin.; p. (estd. 1961) *14,110.*

Axminster, *rural dist.*, Devon, Eng.; brushes; flour and saw mills; carpet and press tool mftg.; p. (1961) *14,350*

Axmouth, *t.*, E. Devon; fishing, holiday resort.

Ay, *t.*, Marne, France; Ay wine; p. (1954) *6,806*.

Ayacucho, *t.*, Peru; founded by Pizarro in 1539; univ.; cap. Ayacucho dept.; p. (1961) *22,000*.

Ayacucho, *dep.*, Peru, S. America; a. 18,185 sq. m.; p. (1961) *427,812*.

Ayamonte, *spt.* Spain; on Spanish–Portuguese frontier; p. (1957) *12,124*. [*6,586*.

Ayaviri, *t.*, Puno, Peru; N.W. of L. Titicaca; p.

Aydin, *t.*, Turkey; ancient Tralles; rly.; cotton, grapes, olives, magnesite, lignite and arsenic; p. (1965) *43,289*.

Aylesbury, *mun. bor.*, *co. t.*, Bucks, Eng.; mkt. t., dairying; p. (estd. 1967) *35,190*.

Aylesford, *t.*, Kent, Eng.; scene of battle between Britons and Saxons 445, death of Horsa; mkt. t., cement, paper mills; p. (1951) *3,644*.

Aylesham, *t.*, Kent, Eng.; N. of Dover; on Kent coalfield.

Ayr, *lge. burgh*, *spt.*, Ayr., Scot.; on Firth of Clyde, 30 m. S.W. of Glasgow; Burns born near by, 1759; racecourse; carpets, engin., footwear; p. (1961) *45,297*

Ayrshire, *co.*, S.W. Scot.; dairy produce, early potatoes; coal, iron, woollens, cottons; civil nuclear power-sta. at Hunterston; a. 1,132 sq. m.; p. (1961) *342,855*.

Ayre, Point of, northernmost point. Isle of Man.

Aysen, *prov.*, Chile; a. 34,348 sq. m.; p. (1957) *31,518*.

Azamgarh, *t.*, Uttar Pradesh, India; p. (1961) *32,391*.

Azbest, *t.*, Sverdlovsk dist., U.S.S.R.; asbestos quarries; p. (1959) *60,000*.

Azerbaijan (East), *prov.*, N. Iran, bordering U.S.S.R.; agr.; cap. Tabriz; p. (1967) *2,598,022*.

Azerbaijan (West), *prov.*, N.W. Iran, bordering U.S.S.R. and Turkey; agr.; cap. Rezayeh; p. (1967) *1,087,702*.

Azerbaydzhan, Transcaucasia, constituent rep. of the U.S.S.R.; impt. oil industry; chemicals, farming, cattle, fishing; cap. Baku; a. 33,460 sq. m.; p. (1959) *3,700,000*.

Azogues, *t.*, cap. Canar prov., Ecuador; straw hats; p. (1950) *6,579*.

Azores, Portuguese group of islands in mid-Atlantic; abt. 900 m. W. of Lisbon; volcanic; fruit, wine; ch. seaports : Ponta Delgada on San Miguel I., Horta on Fayal I. and Angra do Heroismo on Terceira I.; a. 922 sq. m.; p. (1960) *337,000*.

Azov, *t. spt.*, R.S.F.S.R., on R. Don; fisheries; p. *27,500*.

Azov, *sea*, U.S.S.R.; joins Black Sea by Kerchenski Strait; fisheries, caviare.

Azpeitia, *t.*, N. Spain; nr. birthplace of St. Ignatius Loyola; mineral springs; p. (1957) *8,991*.

Azraq Desert Nat. Park, first Jordanian nat. park around oasis of Azraq. 60 m. E. of Amman; a. 1,500 sq. m.

Azuay, S. *prov.*, Ecuador, S. America; cap. Cuenca; Panama hats; a. 3,873 sq m.; p. (1950) *243,920*.

Azul, *t.*, Buenos Aires, Argentina; cattle and mkt. ctr.; p. (1960) *45,000*.

Azusa, *t. spt.*, Cal., U.S.A., exp. citrus fruit; p. (1960) *20,497*.

# B

Baalbek, *c.*, Lebanon, S.W. Asia; old Heliopolis; ruins. [p. (1967)*23,355*.

Baarn, *t.*, Utrecht, Netherlands; summer resort;

Bab-el-Mandeb, *strait* connecting Red Sea and Indian Ocean, 20 m. wide. [(1967) *266,618*.

Babol, *c.*, Iran, Mazandaran prov.; airpt.; p.

Babushkin, *t.*, U.S.S.R.; residtl. and industl. sub. of Moscow; p. (1959) *112,000*.

Babuyan Is., group in Pac. Oc.; N. of Luzon in Philippines.

Babylon, *ancient cap.* of Babylonian Empire in Euphrates Valley about 60 m. S. of Baghdad, Iraq.

Bacacay, *t.*, Luzon, Philippines; hemp, copper deposits.

Bacau, *t.*, E. Romania; on R. Moldava; oil, sawmilling, textiles; p. (1963) *76,214*.

Back R., in N.W. Terr., Canada; falls into Arctic Ocean; length 360 m.

Bacolod, *t.*, *cap.* Negros I., Philippines; tr. ctr., sugar; p. (1960) *127,000*.

Bacup, *mun. bor.*, *mftg. t.*, S.E. Lancs, Eng.; 20 m. Manchester; cotton, iron, brass, footwear; p. (estd. 1967) *16,420*.

Badagri, *t.*, W. of Lagos, Nigeria, W. Africa; on the Bight of Benin, formerly a great slave pt.

Badajoz, *prov.*, Spain; great reclamation scheme in progress; a. 8,349 sq. m.; p. (1959) *865,004*.

Badajoz, *fortfd. t.*, Badajoz prov., Spain; on Guardina R.; cath.; woollens, wax; p. (1959) *98,088*.

Badakshan, *prov.*, Afghanistan; drained by Oxus and trib.; salt, lapis lazuli; cap. Faizabad.

Badalona, *t.*, Barcelona prov., Spain; p. (1959) *87,665*.

Baden, *former Land*, W. Germany, now merged with Baden-Württemberg.

Baden, *t.*, Switzerland; health resort, mineral springs; p. (1960) *12,000*.

Baden-Baden, *t.*, Baden-Württemberg, Germany; fashionable spa; p. (1963) *40,200*.

Baden-bei-Wien, *wat. pl.*, Austria; 14 m. S.W. of Vienna; p. (1961) *22,484*.

Badenoch, *dist.*, Inverness, Scot.; mountainous, drained by Spey; deer forest.

Badenweiler, *wat. pl.*, Baden, W. Germany; W. part of Black Forest.

Baden-Württemberg, *Land*, S.W. Germany; mountainous and afforested (Black Forest) with much mineral wealth; salt; cap. Stuttgart; a. 13,808 sq. m.; p. (1967) *8,566,000*.

Bad Lands, S. Dakota, U.S.A.; stretches of infertile badly eroded soil.

Badrinath, *mtn.* and *t.*, Uttar Pradesh, India; pilgrim shrine of Vishnu.

Badulla, *t.*, Ceylon; tea; p. *13,387*.

Badwater, *salt pool*, California, U.S.A.; 280 ft. below sea-level, lowest point in N. America.

Baena, *t.*, Spain; olive oil; horse-breeding; p. (1957) *22,031*

Baeza, *t.*, S. Spain; ancient Moorish city; olives, wine; p. (1957) *16,895*

Baffin Bay, Canada; W. of Greenland, joined to the Atlantic by Davis Strait and to Arctic Oc. by Smith Sound; open 4 months a year.

Baffin I., Canada; a. 236,000 sq. m.; inhabited by scattered Eskimos; iron ore deposit.

Bagamoyo, *spt.*, *tr. ctr.*, Tanzania, E. Africa; p. *5,000*.

Bagé, *t.*, S. Brazil; tr. ctr.; p. (1960) *47,930*.

Bagenalstown, *t.*, Carlow, Ireland; milling, granite; p. (1956) *1,984*.

Baghdad, *prov.* or *liwa*, Iraq; between Persia and Syrian Desert; inc. some of the most fertile lands in the Tigris and Euphrates valleys; p. (1956) *912,409*.

Baghdad, *cap.*, Iraq; on R. Tigris; airport, caravan ctr. textiles, gum, bricks, tiles, metal inds.; p. (1960) *552,000*.

Bagheria, *t.*, Sicily, Italy; p. *19,000*.

Bagirmi, *dist.*, Central African Rep.; S. of L. Chad; cap. Messenya.

Bagnacavallo, *t.*, prov. Ravenna, Italy; p. *3,676*.

Bagnara, *t.*, prov. Reggio, Italy; wine, honey; p. (1936) *11,580*.

Bagnères de Bigorre, *t.*, Pyrenees, France; mineral springs; (1962) *11,254*.

Bagnes de Chable, *wat. pl.*, Valais, Switzerland.

Bagneux, *t.*, Hauts-de-Seine, France; p. (1954) *13,774*.

Bagni di Lucca, *t.*, Italy; 13 m. N. of Lucca; warm springs; p. *14,000*.

Bagni de San Guiliano, *t.*, Italy, nr. Pisa; warm, radioactive springs; p. (1936) *21,894*.

Bagnolet, *t.*, Seine, France; sub. of Paris; famous for "plaster of Paris" from local gypsum; textiles; p. (1954) *26,779*.

Bagolino, *t.*, prov. Brescia, Italy; sulphur spring; p. *3,613*.

Bagshot, *rural dist.*, Surrey, Eng., adjoining heath of same name; historically old postal town. 26 m. S.W. of London; p. (1961) *16,744*.

Baguio, *summer cap.* of Philippine Is.; Mtn. prov.; p. (1960) *50,436*.

Bahamas, *Is.*, self-gov. Br. col., W. Indies; first land in New World sighted by Columbus, extending 780 m. from Florida to Turks Is.; collective cap. Nassau, New Providence; salt, tomatoes crawfish, sponges, Bahama hemp; a. 4,404 sq. m.; p. (estd. 1965) *134,000*.

**Bahawalpur**, *div.*, West Pakistan; a. 15,918 sq. m.; p. (1961) *3,205,000.*

**Bahia**, *spt.*, Ecuador, S. America; p. *10,820.*

**Bahia Blanca**, *spt.*, Argentina; industl. ctr., principle shipping point of S.; exports oil, grain, wool, hides; p. (1960) *150,000*

**Bahia de Caraquez**, *spt.*, Ecuador, S. America; p. *10,499.*

**Bahrein Is.**, sheikhdom group in Persian G.; famous pearl fisheries; oil-wells; cap. Manamah; a. about 213 sq. m.; p. (1965) *182,293.*

**Bahr El Benat Is.**, group in Persian G., off coast of Trucial Oman.

**Bahr-el-Ghaza**, *R.*, Sudan; trib. of White Nile R.

**Bahr-el-Ghazal**, *prov.*, Sudan, N.E. Africa; cap. Wau (*q.v.*); a. 77,820 sq. m.; p. (estd. 1951) *771,000*

**Baia**, *see* Salvador.

**Baia**, *st.*, Brazil; cap. Salvador; cocoa, thorium; a. 217,670 sq. m.; p. (1960) *5,990,605.*

**Baia**, *historic vil.*, Campania, Italy; beautifully situated on Bay of Naples; celebrated Roman pleasure resort.

**Baia-Mare**, *t.*, Romania; on Somes R.; gold, silver, lead, zinc, chemicals, uranium; p. (1963) *88,941.*

**Baie-St. Paul**, *t.*, Quebec, Canada; summer resort; hunting, fishing; p. (1961) *4,674.*

**Baij**, *t.*, on oil pipe-line, Iraq.

**Baikal**, *L.*, Siberia, U.S.S.R.; fresh-water; 6th lgst. in the world; frozen Nov.–May; skirted by Trans-Siberian Rly.; sturgeon, salmon; 40 m. wide; a. 13,700 sq. m.

**Baildon**, *urb. dist.*, W.R. Yorks, Eng.; nr. Bradford; p. (1961) *12,147.*

**Baile Atha Cliath**, *see* Dublin.

**Bailen**, *t.*, Spain; lead, ore; p. (1957) *10,129.*

**Bailleul**, *t.*, Nord, France; lace, linen; p. (1962) *12,926.*

**Baillieston**, *t.*, Lanark, Scot.; coal mining.

**Baird**, *t.*, Texas, U.S.A.; rly. junction; cotton, oil; p. *1,810.*

**Bairnsdale**, *t.*, Vic., Australia; on Mitchell R.; agr., timber, tourism; p. (1966) *7,785.*

**Bakar**, *pt.*, Jugoslavia; S. of Rijeka; new pt. and oil harbour.

**Bakchisaray**, *t.*, Crimea, U.S.S.R.; *old cap.* of Tartar Khans; p. (1956) *10,000.*

**Baker I.**, Pacific Ocean.

**Baker**, *L.*, N.W. Terr., Canada.

**Baker**, *t.*, Ore.–U.S.A.; gold, silver, lead, mineral springs; p. (1960) *9,986.*

**Bakersfield**, *c.*, S. Cal., U.S.A.; ctr. of oil-wells, refining; p. (1960) *56,848.*

**Bakewell**, *urb. dist.*, Derby, Eng.; tourist centre, Peak District; agr., mining, woollens; p. (1961) *3,603.*

**Bakhchisarai**, *t.*, Crimea, U.S.S.R.; leather, copper; p. *10,800.*

**Bakony Wald**, *mtns.*, forested, Hungary.

**Baku**, *cap.* Azerbaydzhan, S.S.R.; *pt.* of Caspian Sea; univ.; oil-wells; oil pipeline connects with Batumi; p. (1967) *1,164,000.*

**Bala**, *urb. dist.*, N. Wales; nr. Denbigh, Merioneth; light engin.; p. (1961) *1,603.*

**Bala**, *L.*, Merioneth, N. Wales; drained by the Dee.

**Balaka**, *t.*, S. Malawi; new t. 1966.

**Balashov**, *t.*, Saratov area, R.S.F.S.R.; on Khoper R.; engin, aircraft plant; p. (1959) *64,000.*

**Balasinor**, former Gujarat st. now merged into Bombay st., India.

**Balasore**, *spt.*, Orissa, India; p. (1961) *33,931.*

**Balaton**, *L.*, lgst. in Hungary; 50 m. S.W. of Budapest; 50 m. long, 2–7 m. wide.

**Balayan**, *t.*, Luzon, Philippine Is.; at head of G. of Balayan; p. (1948) *18,305.*

**Balboa**, *dist.*, S.E. Canal Zone, Central America; p. (1960) *30,623;* t., Pacific end of Panama Canal; p. (1960) *3,139.*

**Balbriggan**, *spt.*, Dublin, Ireland; hosiery; p. (1966) *3,249.*

**Balclutha**, *t.*, S.I., N.Z.; nr. Dunedin; p. (1961) *3,923.*

**Bald Head Peak**, Victoria, alt. 4,625 ft.; highest point in Dividing Range, Australia.

**Bald Mtn.**, peak in Front Range, Col., U.S.A.; alt. 12,000 ft.

**Baldock**, *urb. dist.*, Herts., Eng.; on N. edge of Chiltern Hills and Gr. N. Road; hosiery, malting, light engin.; p. (1961) *6,764.*

**Baldwin**, *t.*, N.Y., U.S.A.; on S. Long I.; fisheries; p. (1960) *30,204.*

**Baldwin**, *t.*, Penns., U.S.A.; p. (1960) *24,489.*

**Baldwinsville**, *t.*, N.Y., U.S.A.; agr., livestock natural gas; p. (1960) *5,985.*

**Balearic Is.**, Spain; include Majorca, Minorca, Iviza, Formentera; *ch.t.* Palma; fruit, fish, pigs; tourist ctr.; a. 1,936 sq. m.; p. (1959) *441,842.*

**Baleswar**, *R.*, one of the chief distributaries of the Ganges to Bay of Bengal.

**Bali**, off Java, Indonesia; mainly engaged in agr.; famous native dancers; a. (inc. Lombok) 3,937 sq. m.; p. (1961) *1,782,529.*

**Balikesir**, Turkey; p. (1965) *69,256.*

**Balikpapan**, *t.*, Kalimantan, Indonesia; oil; p. (1961) *91,706.*

**Baliuag**, *t.*, Luzon, Philippine Is.; rice, bamboo hats, mkt.; p. (1948) *30,670.*

**Balkan Mtns.**, Bulgaria; highest peak, 7,780 ft.; Shipka Pass.

**Balkan Peninsula**, the easternmost of the three great southern peninsulas of Europe, between the Adriatic and Ionian seas on the W., and the Black Sea, Sea of Marmara and the Ægean Sea on the E., with an area of, roughly, 200,000 sq. m.; includes Jugoslavia, Bulgaria, Albania, Greece; chief mtns.: Rhodope, Pindus, Balkan; ch. rivers: Danube, Maritza, Vardar; ch. lakes: Scutari, Okhrida.

**Balkh**, *dist.*, Afghanistan; between the Kabul and the Oxus; corresponding to the ancient Bactria, rival of Nineveh and Babylon.

**Balkh**, *t.*, Afghanistan; associated with Zoroaster, called the " Mother of Cities "; destroyed by Jenghis Khan in 1221; silk; p. *12,466.*

**Balkhash**, *L.*, U.S.S.R.; fresh water, nr. frontier of W. Mongolia receives the Ili R., but has no outlet, length 450 m., width 30–50 m.

**Balkhash**, *t.*, Kazakhstan S.S.R.; on N. shore of L.; copper, molybdenum; vermiculite discovered nearby; p. (1959) *53,000.*

**Ballachulish**, *vil.*, Argyll, Scot.; on S. shore of L. Leven, N.E. of Oban; tourism [(1951) *1,359.*

**Ballaghadorreen**, *t.*, Roscommon, Ireland; p.

**Ballantrae**, *par.*, Ayr., Scot.; fishing; p. (1951) *886.*

**Ballapali**, forest reserve, Tamil Nadu, India.

**Ballarat**, *c.*, Victoria, Autralia; 73 m. N.W., Melbourne, former gold-field dist.; mkt. ctr.; engin., timber, brick and tiles; p. (1966) *56,304.*

**Ballater**, *burgh* Aberdeen, Scot.; on R. Dee, 37 m. S.W. of Aberdeen; tourist resort, mineral wells; nr. the royal Highland residence of Balmoral; p. (1961) *1,132.*

**Ballenas Bay**, W. Coast, Lower California, Mexico.

**Balleny Is.**, S. Ocean; volcanic isles.

**Ballina**, *urb. dist., spt.*, Mayo, Ireland; agr. machin., flour mills; p. (1966) *6,187.*

**Ballina**, *t.*, N.S.W., Australia; at mouth of Richmond R.; resort, fishing; p. (1966) *4,924.*

**Ballinasloe**, *urb. dist.*, Galway and Roscommon, Ireland; large cattle fair; p. (1966) *5,826.*

**Ballinger**, *t.*, Texas, U.S.A.; grain, cattle, cottonseed oil, flour; p. (1960) *5,043.*

**Ballinrobe**, *rural dist.*, Mayo, Ireland; E. of L. Mask; p. (1961) *13,492.*

**Ballon d'Alsace**, *mtns.* (4,101 ft.), Vosges, France; highest peak Ballon de Guebwiller, 4,690 ft.

**Ballston Spa**, *vat. pl.*, Saratoga, N.Y., U.S.A., p. (1960) *4,991.*

**Bally L.**, Roscommon, Ireland, nr. Castlereagh.

**Ballycastle**, *spt., mkt. t., urb. dist.*, Antrim, N. Ireland; abbey and cas. ruins; seaside resort; p. (1966) *2,949.*

**Ballyclare**, *urb. dist.*, Antrim, N. Ireland; paper, linen, dyeing, asbestos-cement prod.; p. (1966) *4,583.*

**Ballycottin Is.**, Ballycottin Bay, Cork, Ireland.

**Ballymena**, *mkt. t., mun. bor.*, Antrim, N. Ireland; on R. Braid; linen and dyeing; p. (1966) *15,992.*

**Ballymoney**, *mkt. t., urb. dist.*, Antrim, N. Ireland; 40 m. N.W. of Belfast; linen, dairying; p. (1966) *3,520.*

**Ballyness Bay**, Donegal, Ireland.

**Ballyshannon**, *spt.*, Donegal, Ireland; at mouth of R. Erne; salmon fishery; p. (1966) *2,233.*

**Balmain**, *t.*, N.S.W., Australia; industl. sub. of Sydney; foundries, chemicals, glass, shipbldg., lumber.

**Balmoral Cas.**, Aberdeen, Scot.; royal residence, on R. Dee, 8 m. W. of Ballater.

**Balotra**, *t.*, Rajasthan, India; p. (1961) *12,110.*

**Balranald**, *t.*, N.S.W., Australia; on R. Murrumbidgee, p. *1,249.*

**Balsas**, *R.*, Mexico; flows S. to Pacific Ocean through impt. sugar-cane growing valley of Morelos; length approx. 500 m.

Balta L., Shetland Is., Scot.

Baltic Is. (Fyn, Lolland, Nykobing, etc.); farming div. of Denmark; a. 5,123 sq. m.; p. *1,291,772.*

Baltic Sea, an arm of the Atlantic, opens into N. Sea by narrow channels between Denmark and Sweden; joined to White Sea and Arctic by White Sea Canal; surrounded by Sweden, Denmark, Germany, Finland and the Baltic Reps. of the U.S.S.R.; 900 m. long, greatest width 200 m., a. 160,000 sq. m.; partly frozen in winter.

Baltic–White Sea Canal, *see* Volga Baltic Waterway.

Baltimore, *c., spt.,* Maryland, U.S.A.; nr. head of Chesapeake Bay; fine harbour; sugar refining, steel, radios, aircraft, clothing, machin., shipbldg., food canning; world's 1st nuclearpowered lighthouse; p. (1960) *939,024.*

Baluchistan, *reg.,* West Pakistan; S. of Afghanistan; largely desert and rugged barren mtns.; cap. Quetta; a. 52,900 sq. m.; cereals, potatoes, fruits, dates; p. (estd. 1951) *622,000.*

Baluchistan States, consisted of 4 states, Kalat, Las Bela, Kharan and Mekran, all of which were incorporated in W. Pakistan, 1955.

Bamako, *c.,* Mali; p. (1963) *135,000.*

Bamangwato, *tr. dist.,* Botswana, S. Africa.

Bamberg, *c.* Bavaria, Germany; cath.; philosophical and theological institute; textiles, elec., leather and engin. inds.; p. (1963) *73,700.*

Bamberg, *t.,* S.C., U.S.A.; agr., lumbering, pine timber; p. (1960) *3,081.*     [and iron dist.

Bambuk or Bambouk, Mali; W. Africa; gold

Bamburgh, *t.,* Northumberland, Eng.; birthplace of Grace Darling, cas.

Bamian, *t.,* Afghanistan, N.W. of Kabul; rockcut caves, colossal Buddhist statues.

Banam, *t.,* Cambodia; on Mekong R.; boat bldg., rice distilling; p. *28,000.*

Banana, L., Brazil; length 220 m., width 50 m.

Banana Is., sm. group nr. Sierra Leone.

Banat, *dist.,* Romania; N. of R. Danube and E. of R. Tisza; p. (1963) *1,241,832.*

Banbridge, *t. urb. dist.,* Down, N. Ireland; on Bann R.; linen; p. (1966) *6,551.*

Banbury, *mun. bor., mkt. t.,* Oxford, Eng.; 80 m. from London; aluminium ind., furniture, printing, ladies wear; p. (estd. 1967) *26,540.*

Banchory, *burgh,* Kincardine, Scot.; on R. Dee, 17 m. S.W. of Aberdeen; p. (1961) *1,918.*

Banda, *t.,* Uttar Pradesh, India; cotton; p. (1961) *37,744.*

Banda Is., group in Moluccas, in Banda Sea, Indonesia; nutmegs and mace.

Bandar, *spt.,* Andhra Pradesh, India, on Coromandel cst.; cotton mftg., rice; p. (1961) *101,417.*

Bandar Abbas, *spt.,* S. Iran; airpt.; import and export ctr. p. (1967) *163,133.*

Bandar-e-Bushehr (Bushire), *spt.,* S.W. Iran, on Persian G., Iran's major pt.; p. *c. 30,000.*

Bandar-e-Pahlavi, *spt.,* N. Iran, on Caspian Sea. p. (1967) *59,737.*

Bandar-e-Shah, *spt.,* N. Iran, on Caspian Sea, on rly. from Tehran.

Bandar-e-Shahpur, *spt.,* Iran, on Persian G., term. of rly. from Tehran; petrochemical plant being built.

Bandawe, *mission sta.* on L. Malawi, Africa.

Bandjarmasin, *t.,* Kalimantan, Indonesia; rubber; p. (1961) *214,096.*

Bandoeng or Bandung, *t.,* W. Java; quinine, rubber, chemicals; radio sta.; p. (1961) *973,000.*

Banff, *burgh, cap.,* Banff, Scot.; on Moray Firth at mouth of R. Deveron; fisheries; tourism; p. (1961) *3,329.*

Banff, *co.,* Scot.; oats, barley, fisheries, distilling, woollen mnfs.; a. 630 sq. m.; p. (1961) *46,400.*

Bangalore, *c.,* Mysore st., India; former Brit. military sta. and administrative H.Q.; silks, cottons, carpets, aircraft, machine tools; p. (1961) *905,134.*

Bangka (Banka), *I.,* between Sumatra and Kalimantan, Indonesia; tin; a. 4,611 sq. m.; p. (1930) *205,363.*

Bangkok (Krung Thep), *spt., cap.,* Thailand; on Menam R.; 20 m. from the sea; royal palace, univ.; rice, tea, teak; p. (1963) *1,608,000.*

Bangor, *c., mun. bor.,* Caernarvon, Wales; on S. shore of Menai Strait; cath., univ. coll.; slate, light engin.; p. (1961) *13,977.*

Bangor, *wat. pl., mun. bor.,* Down, N. Ireland; on S. shore of Belfast Lough, 10 m. N.E. of Belfast; lt. inds; carpets, hosiery; seaside resort; p. (1966) *26,385.*

Bangor, *pt.,* Maine, U.S.A.; on Penobscot R., lumber, boots, shoes, clothing, paper; p. (1960) *38,912.*

Bangor, *bor.,* E. Penns., U.S.A.; slate, agr., clothes; p. (1960) *5,766.*

Bangui, *cap.* of Ubangi-Shari terr., Central African Rep; on R. Ubangi; p. (1966) *237,971.*

Bangweulu, *L.,* Zambia; 150 m. long, 80 m. wide, contains 3 islands. Dr. Livingstone died at Illala, on S. shore of this L., in 1873.

Banias, *spt.,* Syria; terminus of oil pipe-line from Kirkuk, opened 1952.

Banjaluka, *t.,* Bosnia and Hercegovina, Jugoslavia; hot springs; tobacco; p. (1960) *45,000.*

Banka, *see* Bangka.

Banks I., Canada, Arctic Ocean; separated by Banks Strait from Melville I.

Banks Is., group of sm. Is. in S. Pacific; N.E. of New Hebrides.

Banks Peninsula, on E. coast of S.I., New Zealand.

Banks Strait, separating Furneaux Is. from Tasmania.

Bankura, *t.,* W. Bengal, India; on Hooghly R.; shellac, silk; p. (1961) *62,833.*

Bann, Upper and Lower R., N. Ireland; rises in co. Down, and flows through Lough Neagh to Atlantic nr. Coleraine; length 90 m.

Bannockburn, *vil.,* Stirling, Scot.; 3 m. S. of Stirling; Bruce's victory over Edward II, June 24th, 1314; coal, confectionery.

Bannu, *t.,* W. Pakistan; on Kurram R.; military sta.; sugar refining; p. *38,504.*

Banska Bystrica, *region,* Slovakia, ČSSR.; copper and silver mng., metal wks.; a. 3,564 sq. m.; p. (1961) *129,290.*

Banska Stiavnica, *t.,* ČSSR.; tr. ctr., gold, silver prod., lead, copper, zinc; p. (1947) (inc. Banska Bela) *11,870.*        [*41,950.*

Banstead, *urb. dist.,* Surrey, Eng.; p. (estd. 1967).

Bantam, *dist.,* W. Java; suffered severely from fever and volcanic eruption.

Bantry, *rural dist.* and *spt.,* Cork, Ireland; at head of Bantry Bay; fishing, farming; crude oil terminal on Whiddy Is.; p. (1961) *7,814.*

Banwy, R., Montgomery, Wales.

Banzyville, *t.,* Congo; on R. Uele; p. *1,000.*

Ba'quba, *t.,* Iraq; on Diyala R., 32 m. N.E. of Baghdad; agr., rly.; p. *10,000.*

Bar, *spt.,* Dalmatian cst. Jugoslavia; p. *5,500.*

Bar Harbor, *t.,* S.E. Me., U.S.A.; holiday resort; p. (1960) *2,444.*        [*6,726.*

Baraboo, *t.,* Wis., U.S.A.; agr. tr. ctr.; p. (1960)

Baracaldo, *t.,* Biscay, Spain; ironwks.; p. *36,165.*

Baracoa, *spt.,* Cuba; bananas, coconuts; p. *10,395.*

Barada, *R.,* Syria; in plain of Damascus.

Barajas, *vil.,* Madrid, Spain; airport; p. *1,800*

Baranovichi, *t.,* Byelorussian S.S.R.; 80 m. S.W. of Minsk; p. (1959) *58,000.*

Barauni, *t.,* N. Central Bihar, India; oil refining; oil pipelines to Gauhati, to Kanpur and from Haldia; p. (1961) *40,321.*

Barbacena, *t.,* E. Brazil; creameries; ceramics, glass; p. (1960) *41,931.*

Barbados, *I., indep. sov. st.,* within Brit. Commonwealth (1966); W.I.; sugar, molasses, rum, cotton; cap. Bridgetown; a. 166 sq. m.; p. (1966) *245,000.*

Barbary, *region,* N. Africa; includes Morocco, Algeria, Tunis, Tripoli, Barka and Fezzan.

Barbary Coast, general name applied to Mediterranean cst. of N. Africa between Strait of Gibraltar and C. Bon.

Barbastro, *t.,* Huesca, Spain; on R. Cinca; p. (1957) *9,381.*

Barberton, *t.,* Transvaal, S. Africa; citrus fruits, gold, asbestos, magnesite, talc, cotton; p. (1960) *11,016* inc. *2,705* whites.

Barberton, *t.,* Ohio, U.S.A., S.S.W. of Akron; tyre mftg.; p. (1960) *33,805.*

Barbizon, *vil.,* nr. forest of Fontainebleau; haunt of painters.

Barbuda and Redonda, *Is.,* Leeward Is., W.I.; dependencies of Antigua; sea-island cotton; a. 63 sq. m.; p. *1,000.*        [*1,780*]

Barcaldine, *t.,* Queensland, Australia; p. (1966.

Barcellona, *t.,* Sicily, Italy; silks; p. *25,580.*

Barcelona, *prov.,* N.E. Spain; cap. Barcelona; a. 2,942 sq. m.; p. (1967) *3,495,021.*

Barcelona, *c., spt., cap.,* Barcelona prov., Spain; "Manchester of Spain"; cottons, paper, leather, glass, soap; exp. olives, wines, cork; p. (1965) *1,656,000.*

Barcelona, *t.*, N. Venezuela; *cap.* of Azoátegui st.; agr. tr.; brewing; p. (1961) 44,773.

Barcoo R., *see* Cooper's Creek. [9,175.

Bardejov, *t.*, CSSR.; hot springs; p. (1961)

Bardera, *t.*, Somalia; head of navigation on Juba R.; p. 1,500.

Bardsey, I., Irish Sea; off coast of Wales, nr. N. point of Cardigan Bay; lighthouse.

Bareilly, *c.*, Uttar Pradesh, India; bamboo, furniture; p. (1961) 272,828.

Barents Sea, part of Arctic Ocean E. of Spitzbergen to N. Cape; cod, haddock.

Bari, *spt.*, S. Italy; on Adriatic, 69 m. N.W. of Brindisi; cath.; olive oil, wines, fruit, soap; p. (1965) 335,000.

Barinas, *t.*, cap. Barinas st., Venezuela; cattle, oil; p. (1961) 25,707.

Barisal, *t.*, East Pakistan; nr. Tetulia at mouth of Ganges; river pt.; great damage and loss of lives due to cyclone 1965; p. (1961) 59,900.

Barka, *dist.*, Libya, N. Africa.

Barking, *outer bor.*, E. London, Eng.; on R. Roding; inc. Dagenham; metal refining and smelting, insulation, cellulose; lge. power sta. and largest gaswks. in Europe; p. (1966) 171,000.

Barkly Tableland, N. Terr., Australia.

Barkly West, *t.*, Cape Province, S. Africa; diamonds.

Barkul, *t.*, Shensi, W. China; p. (estd. 1947) 19,097.

Barlad, *t.*, Romania, Moldavia; soap, textiles; p. (1963) 43,191.

Bar-le-Duc, *t.*, *cap.*, Meuse, France; cotton, hosiery; p. (1962) 20,168.

Barlee, L., W. Australia.

Barletta, *t.*, *spt.*, Italy; wine; p. (1961) 68,035.

Barlin, *t.*, Pas de Calais, France; coal-mines, lime, cement; p. (1954) 9,186.

Barmouth, *t.*, *urb. dist.*, Merioneth, Wales; on est. of Cardigan Bay; chemicals; p. (1961) 2,348.

Barnack, *rural dist.*, Huntingdon and Peterborough, Eng.; p. (1961) 4,420.

Barnard Castle, *mkt. t.*, *urb. dist.*, Durham, Eng.; health resort; woollens, penicillin; p. (1961) 4,969.

Barnaul, *t.*, W. Siberia, R.S.F.S.R.; chemicals, engin., textiles, sawmilling; p. (1967) 395,000.

Barnes, *see* Richmond upon Thames.

Barnesville, *t.*, Ga., U.S.A.; cotton mills; p. (1960) 4,919.

Barnesville, *t.*, Ohio U.S.A.; coal, natural gas, glass, paper, evaporatde milk; p. (1960) 4,425.

Barnet, *former urb. dist.*, Herts, Eng.; now outer bor., Greater London; comprising former bors. of Finchley and Hendon, and urb. dists. of Barnet, East Barnet and Friern Barnet; p. (1966) 317,000. [27,800.

Barneveld, *t.*, Gelderland, Netherlands; p. (1967)

Barnoldswick, *urb. dist.*, W.R. Yorks, E g.; p. (1961) 10,267. [p. 1,663.

Barnsdall, *t.*, N. Okla., U.S.A.; oil, gas, agr.;

Barnsley, *mftg. t.*, *co. bor.*, W.R. Yorks, Eng.; coal, machin., plastics; p. (estd. 1967) 75,910.

Barnstable, *t.*, Mass., U.S.A.; summer resort; fisheries; p. (1950) 10,480.

Barnstaple, *mkt. t.*, *mun. bor.*, Devon, Eng.; on R. Taw; seaside resort; concrete, glove mkg.; p. (estd. 1967) 16,340.

Baroda, *former st.*, India; now part of Gujarat st.; cereals, cotton, sugar, tobacco, opium; a. 2,961 sq. m.; p. (1961) 1,527,326.

Baroda, *t.*, Gujarat, India; univ.; palaces, Hindu temples; natural gas pipeline from Ankleshwar; oil refining nearby at Jawaharnagar; p. (1961) 295,326.

Barotseland, *prov.*, Zambia; savannah grasslands; livestock, grain, teak; a. 63,000 sq. m.; p. (1964) 378,000.

Barquisimeto, *t.*, Venezuela; sugar, coffee, cacao, cereals, cattle, copper, textiles; p. (1961) 196,557.

Barra Is., southerly groups, Outer Hebrides, Scot.; a. 348 sq. m.; lighthouse on Barra Head; p. 2,250.

Barrage, *vil.*, U.A.R., N.E. Africa; on Nile, 35 m. N. of Cairo.

Barranca Bermeja, *t.*, Colombia, S. America; oilfield, oil-refining, paper mkg., petro-chemicals; p. (estd. 1959) 65,000.

Barranqueras, *t.*, Chaco terr., N. Argentina; on Parana R.; exp. hardwoods, cotton.

Barranquilla, *pt.*, Colombia, S. America, on left bank nr. mouth of R. Magdalena; textiles, per-

fumes, saw mills, cement, pharmaceutics, river craft; p. (estd. 1962) 452,140.

Barre, *c.*, Vt., U.S.A.; granite; p. (1960) 10,387.

Barren I., volcano in Bay of Bengal.

Barren R., Ky. U.S.A.; length 120 m.

Barrhead, *mftg. burgh*, Renfrew, Scot.; 7 m. S.W. of Gasgow; iron and cotton; p. (1961) 14,422.

Barrie, *c.*, Ontario, Canada; light inds., boat bldg.; p. (1956) 16,573.

Barrier Ranges, *mtns.*, on boundary of S. Australia and N.S.W., Australia; alt. 2,000 ft.

Barrier Reef, Great, *coral reef*, Pac. Oc.; extending for 1,200 m. 10–150 m. from coast of Australia.

Barrington, *t.* R.I., U.S.A.; shipbuilding, fish. residtl. resort; p. (1960) 13,826.

Barron, *t.*, Wis., U.S.A.; dairy products, lumber; p. (1960) 2,338.

Barrow, *C.*, Mackenzie, Canada.

Barrow Falls, nr. Keswick, Cumberland, Eng.

Barrowford, *urb. dist.*, Lancs., Eng.; p. (1961) 4,531.

Barrow, R., Leinster, Ireland; rises in Slieve Bloom Mtns., and flows to Waterford Harbour.

Barrow-in-Furness, *spt.*, *co. bor.*, N. Lancs, Eng.; iron and steel, paper, shipbldg., engin.; p. (estd. 1967) 64,650.

Barrow-on-Soar, *rural dist.* and *t.*, Leicester, Eng.; p. (rural dist. 1961) 57,131.

Barrow Point, most northerly headland in Alaska, N. America.

Barry, *mun. bor.*, Glamorgan, Wales; "outport" of Cardiff; coal, tin-plate. chemicals, plastics; p. (1961) 42,039.

Barsac, *t.*, Gironde. France; Sauterne wine; p. (1954) 2,320.

Barsi, *t.*, Maharashtra, India; cotton, oil-seeds; p. (1961) 50,339.

Barstow, *t.*, Cal., U.S.A.; early silver mining and frontier town; p. (1960) 11,644.

Bar-sur-Aube, *t.*, Aube, France; wine, brandy; furniture; p. (1954) 4,387.

Bar-sur-Seine, *t.*, Aube, France; p. (1962) 2,763.

Barth, *spt.*, Rostock, E. Germany; shipyd. engin., furniture, sugar; p. (1963) 12,406.

Bartholomew Bayou, R., Ark., U.S.A., l. 275 m.

Bartin, *t.*, N. Turkey; p. (1960) 11,655.

Bartlesville, *t.*, Okla., U.S.A.; oil refining, zinc smelting, metal prod., leather goods; p. (1960) 27,893.

Barton-upon-Humber, *urb. dist.*, Lindsey, Lincs. Eng.; cycles, rope-making, bricks, tiles, chemical manure; p. (1961) 6,584.

Bartow, *t.*, Fla., U.S.A.; phosphates, citrus canneries, cigar-mkg.; p. (1960) 12,549.

Barvas, *par.*, Lewis, Scot.; p. 5,876.

Basel, *can.*, Switzerland; divided into the halfcantons, Basel-Stadt, a. 14 sq. m., cap. Basel; p. (1961) 225,588, and Baselland. a. 165 sq. m., cap. Liestal; farming, vines, forests; p. (1961) 148,282.

Basel, *c.*, *cap.*, Basel, Switzerland; head of barge navigation on Rhine; chemicals, ribbons; p. (1961) 205,800.

Bashee R., Cape Province, S. Africa.

Bashi L., gr. in Pac. Oc.; N. of Luzon in the Philippines.

Bashkir, *Rep.* R.S.F.S.R., U.S.S.R.; farming, gold, copper, coal, oil, engin., chemicals, textiles; cap. Ufa; p. (1959) 3,335,000.

Basildon, *t.*, Essex, Eng.; in lower Thames valley, 8 m. S.E. of Brentwood; one of "New Towns" designated 1949 to relieve population congestion in London; incorporated S. part of Billericay urb. dist. and N. part of Thurrock urb. dist; gen. and elec. engin., cars, clothing, tobacco, photographic apparatus; p. (estd. 1965) 66,486.

Basilicata, *dep.*, Italy; wheat, maize, vines, olive, oil; a. 3,855 sq. m.; p. (1961) 602,661.

Basingstoke, *mftg. and mkt. t.*, *mun. bor.*, N. Hants Eng.; 50 m. W. London; vehicles, farm implements, pharmaceutics; p. (estd. 1967) 38,230.

Basle, *see* Basel.

Basque Prov., Spain; comprising three provs., Alava, Guipuzcoa, Vizcaya, where Basque language is spoken and also N. of Pyrenees in France.

Basra, *prov.* or *liwa* on Euphrates, Iraq; 60 m. from the sea; p. (1956) 404,308.

Basra, *t.*, *river pt.*, Iraq; dates; p. (1956) 159,355.

Bass Rock, in Firth of Forth, opposite Tantallon Castle, E. Lothian, Scot.; gannetry.

Bass Strait, between Victoria and Tasmania; length about 200 m., breadth about 140 m.

Bassano, *t.*, Italy; on R. Brenta; vines, olives, majolica; p. *20,527.*

Bassein, *t.*, Burma; on mouth of Irrawaddy R., univ.; exp rice; airfield.

Bassein, *R.*, Burma.

Bassenthwaite, *L.*, Cumberland, Eng.; length 4 m., breadth 1 m.; fishing.

Basses-Alpes, *frontier dep.*, S.E. France; olives, wines; cap. Digne; a. 2,697 sq. m.; p. (1954) *84,335.*

Basses-Pyrénées, *dep.*, France; cattle, sheep, forest; cap. Pau; a. 2,977 sq. m.; p. (1954) *85,067.*

Basse-Terre, *ch. t.*, Guadeloupe, Fr. W. Indies; p. (estd. 1965) *12,000.*

Basseterre, *cap.*, St. Kitts I. Leeward group; W.I.; p. (1957) *35,873.*

Båstad, *summer resort*, Sweden; international tennis; p. *2,300.*

Bastia, *t.*, *spt.*, Corsica, France; p. (1962) *50,880.* [(1962) *5,893.*

Bastogne, *t.*, Belgium, nr. Luxembourg; p.

Bastrop, *t.*, N. La., U.S.A.; on Colorado R. mills; p. (1960) *15,193.*

Bastrop, *t.*, Texas, U.S.A.; on Colorado R.; lignite; p. (1960, *3,001.*

Basutoland, *see* Lesotho.

Bata, *ch. t.*, Spanish Guinea, W. Africa; p. *5,000.*

Bataan, *t.*, Philippine Is; plywoods and veneer, pulp, paper; oil refining nearby.

Batabanó, *t.*, Cuba; sponges; p. (1953) *5,075.*

Batangas, *prov.*, Philippine Is., oil refining; p. (1960) *681,414.*

Batavia, *see* Djakarta.

Batavia, *c.*, N.Y., U.S.A.; farm implements; p. (1960) *18,210.*

Bataysk, *t.*, Rostov region, R.S.F.S.R.; rly. junction; grain and cattle, engin., p. (1959) *52,000.*

Batesar, *t.*, Agra dist., India; on the R. Jumna; comm. ctr.

Batesville, *t.*, Ark., U.S.A.; marble, manganese; p. (1960) *6,109.*

Batesville, *t.*, Ind., U.S.A.; furniture; p. (1960) *3,349.*

Bath, *t.*, Maine, U.S.A.; on R. Kennebec; p. (1960) *10,717.*

Bath, *c.*, *co. bor.*, Somerset, Eng.; Roman baths, hot springs, medicinal waters; fine Regency architecture; univ.; elect. engin., metals and limestone; p. (estd. 1967) *85,870.*

Bathgate, *burgh*, West Lothian, Scot.; 6 m. S. of Linlithgow; coal-mng., quarrying, metal, elec., hosiery, cars; p. (1961) *12,686.*

Bathurst I., off coast of N. Terr., Australia; 30 m. long; Aborigines reserve; cypress pine milling.

Bathurst, *t.*, N.S.W., Australia; ctr. of pastoral, agr., fruit district; brewing, boots and shoes, lt. engin., cement pipes; p. (1966) *17,220.*

Bathurst, *sp.*, *cap.*, Gambia, W. Africa; at mouth of Gambia R.; airport; groundnuts; p. (1963) *27,809.*

Batina, fertile coastal plain Muscat and Oman, Arabia; produces early-ripening dates famous for flavour.

Batley, *industl. t.*, *mun. bor.*, W.R. Yorks, Eng.; woollens, shoddy; p. (estd. 1967) *41,160.*

Batna, *commune*, Algeria; N. Africa; rly. to Biskra; p. *10,322.*

Baton Rouge, *cap.*, Louisiana, U.S.A.; on Mississippi R.; cotton seed, oil-refining; p. (1960) *152,491.*

Battambang, *prov.*, Cambodia; 180 m. N.E. of Pnom-Penh; cotton mill; p. (1962) *551,860.*

Battam I., Malay Arch.; 20 m. S. of Singapore.

Battersea, *see* Wandsworth.

Batticaloa, *t.*, *cap.*, E. Prov. Ceylon; p. *12,984.*

Battle, *t.*, *rural dist.*, Sussex, Eng.; battle of Hastings fought here 1066; p. (rural dist. 1961) *30,558.*

Battle Creek, *c.*, Michigan, U.S.A.; on Kalamazoo R.; engin., cereal prod.; p. (1960) *44,169.*

Battleford, *N.*, *t.*, Canada; at junction of Battle R. with Saskatchewan R.; mixed farming; p. (1951) *7,489.*

Battle Harbour, nr. Strait of Belle I., Labrador.

Battle Mountain, *t.*, Nev., U.S.A.; copper-mines.

Batu Gajah, *t.*, Malaya; in valley Kinta R.; tin-mines; residtl.; p. (1947) *7,480.*

Batu, I., E. Indies, Indonesia.

Batumi, *t.*, *spt.*, Georgian S.S.R.; oil, engin., citrus fruits, tea; oil pipeline connects with Baku; p. (1959) *82,000.*

Bauchi, *t.*, central Nigeria; ctr. of impt. tin-mining a.; p. *10,000.*

Baud, *t.*, Orissa, India; on R. Mahanadi.

Bauld, *O.*, northernmost part of Newfoundland, N. America.

Baures, *R.*, E. Bolivia; flowing from L. Guazamire to R. Guapore; length 300 m.

Bautzen, *t.*, Dresden, E. Germany; on R. Spree; textiles, engin., iron inds.; p. (1963) *42,431.*

Bauya, *t.*, Sierra Leone, W. Africa; rly. junction.

Bavaria, *Land*, Germany; hilly, forested; ch. rivers; Danube, Main, Isar, Inn; ch. inds.; agr., dairying, rye, oats, hops, sugar-beet, brewing, glass, sugar, toys, chemicals, jewellery; cap. Munich (*q.v.*); a. 27,112 sq. m.; p. (1961) *9,514,000.*

Bavarian Alps, *mtns.*, Germany.

Bawdwin, *t.*, Burma; wolfram, lead, zinc, silver, rubles.

Bawtry, *mkt. t.*, W.R. Yorks, Eng.; 8 m. S. of Doncaster; p. (1951) *1,460.*

Baxley, *t.*, S.E. Ga., U.S.A.; pecan nuts, tobacco; p. (1950) *3,234.*

Baxter Springs, *t.*, S.E. Kan., U.S.A.; lead- and zinc-mines; p. (1960) *4,498.*

Bayamon, *t.*, Puerto Rico, W. Indies; fruit, tobacco, sugar, coffee; p. (1960) *72,134.*

Baybay, *t.*, Leyte, Philippine Is.; impt. comm. pt.; p. (1948) *50,725.*

Bayburt, *t.*, Turkey, p. (1960) *11,968.*

Bay City, *mftg. t.*, Mich., U.S.A.; on Saginaw R., 108 m. N.W. of Detroit; fishing, chemicals, beet-sugar; p. (1960) *53,604.*

Bay City, *t.*, Texas, U.S.A.; salphur, oil; p. (1960) *11,656.*

Bayeux, *t.*, Calvados, France; cath., museum, Bayeux tapestry; p. (1962) *10,641.*

Bay Is., group G. of Honduras, Central America; lgst., Ruatan; coconuts, bananas; p. (1961) *8,863.*

Bay of Islands, inlet and harbour on N.I., New Zealand.

Bayombong, *t.*, Philippine Is.; p. (1948) *14,079.*

Bayonne, *fortfd. t.*, Basses-Pyrénées, S.W. France; cath.; noted for fine hams, invention of bayonet; aircraft; p. (1962) *41,149.*

Bayonne, *t.*, N.J., U.S.A.; 6 m from New York; chemicals, oil-refining; p. (1960) *74,215.*

Bayport, *t.*, Minn., U.S.A.; on St. Croix R.; state prison; p. (1960) *3,205.*

Bayreuth, *c.*, Bavaria, S. Germany; home of Wagner; famous for musical festivals in magnificent national theatre; textiles, porcelain, engin.; p. (1963) *61,700.*

Baytown, *t.*, S.E. Texas, U.S.A.; oil-wells, toluene factory; p. (1960) *28,159.*

Baza, *t.*, S. Spain; W. of Lorca; lead, iron, mercury, sugar; p. (1957) *23,450.*

Beachy Head, 575 ft. high, on Sussex cst., loftiest headland in S. Eng.

Beaconsfield, *t.*, Tasmania, Australia; on W. of estuary of Tamar R.; tin mining.

Beaconsfield, *urb. dist.*, Bucks., Eng.; residtl.; p. (1961) *10,019.*

Beaconsfield, *t.*, Cape Province, S. Africa; diamonds.

Bear I., Arctic Ocean; 130 m. S. of Spitzbergen.

Bear L., on border of Idaho and Utah, U.S.A.

Bear L., Great, N.W. Terr., Canada; outlet to Mackenzie R. through Great Bear R.; a. 14,000 sq. m.

Béarn, *old prov.* now Basses-Pyrénées, France.

Bearsden, *burgh*, Dunbarton, Scot.; p. (1961) *17,022.*

Beas (Bias), *R.*, Punjab, India; trib. of Sutlej R.; one of the " five rivers."

Beas de Segura, *t.*, Spain; wine, oil, fruits, flax; p. *14,953.*

Beatrice, Neb., U.S.A.; health resort on Big Blue R.; p. (1960) *12,132.*

Beattock, *pass*, S. Uplands, Scot.; gives access from valley of R. Clyde to R. Annan; used by main W. cst. rly. route from Carlisle to Glasgow and Edinburgh; alt. 1,014 ft.

Beaucaire, *t.*, Gard, France; noted fair; p. (1962) *11,211.*

Beauce, *natural division* (" *pays* "), Central France; low. level, plateau of limestone S.W. of Paris and R. Seine; arid, few surface streams; thin layer of loam (limon) permits agr.; impt. wheat-growing area; population mainly grouped in lge. vlls.

**Beaufort**, *t.*, S.C., U.S.A.; S.W. of Charleston; canning and shipping point for farming and fishing region; tourist ctr.; p. (1960) *6,298*.

**Beaufort West**, *t.*, Cape Province, S. Africa; sheep, karakul; p. (1960) *16,323* inc. *5,297* whites.

**Beaujolais**, France; wine-growing dist.

**Beaulieu**, *par.*, Hants, Eng.; on Beaulieu R.; yachting; p. *1,201*.

**Beauly**, *R.*, Inverness, Scot.; flows to Beauly Loch.

**Beauly**, *t.*, Inverness, Scot.; on Beauly R.; p. *890*.

**Beaumaris**, *mun. bor., vat. pl.*, cap. Anglesey, N. Wales; on Menai Strait; cas., ruins; light engin.; p. (1961) *1,960*.

**Beaumont**, *c.*, E. Texas, U.S.A.; lumbering, petroleum; p. (1960) *119,175*.

**Beaune**, *t.*, Côte d'Or, France; wines, casks, farm implements; p. (1962) *15,882*.

**Beausoleil**, *t.*, Alpes-Maritime, France; p. (1962) *12,833*.

**Beauvais**, *t., cap.*, Oise, France; cath.; Gobelin tapestry; p. (1962) *36,533*.

**Beaver**, *R.*, Penns., Ohio, U.S.A.; rises in Allegheny Plateau, flows N. towards L. Erie, turns S.E. into R. Ohio just below Pittsburgh; valley provides easiest route from Pittsburgh to L. Erie pts.; contains many steel-mkg. ts., Youngstown, Newcastle, Warren; length 130 m.

**Beaver Dam**, *c.*, Wisconsin, U.S.A.; summer resort on L.; p. (1960) *13,118*.

**Beaver Falls**, *t.*, Penns., U.S.A.; machin., pottery, coal, natural gas; p. (1960) *16,240*.

**Beaver Meadows**, *bor.*, E. Penns., U.S.A.; anthracite, textiles; p. (1960) *1,392*.

**Beawar**, *t.*, Rajasthan, India; cotton; p. (1961) *53,931*.

**Bebington**, *mun. bor.*, Cheshire, Eng.; soap, chemicals, engin.; p. (estd. 1967) *55,520*.

**Becancourt**, *t.*, Quebec, Canada; on S. bank of St. Lawrence; integrated steel mill projected.

**Beccles**, *mun. bor.*, Suffolk, Eng.; printing, engin., malting; p. (estd. 1967) *7,850*.

**Béchar (Colom-Béchar)**, *t.*, N.W. Algeria; terminus of rly. through Oran dep.; p. (1960) *45,533*.

**Bechuanaland**, *see* Botswana.

**Be kenham**, *former mun. bor.*, Kent, Eng., now inc. in Bromley outer London bor. (*q.v.*); p. (1961) *77,265*.

**Beckley**, *c.*, S.W. Va., U.S.A.; coal; p. (1960) *18,642*.

**Beckum**, *t.*, N. Rhine-Westphalia, Germany; cement, chalk, engin. wks.; p. (1963) *21,200*.

**Bedale**, *mkt. t., rural dist.*, N.R. Yorks, Eng.; at N. end of Vale of York; tent mkg.; p. (rural dist. 1961) *8,215*.

**Beddgelert**, *par.*, Caernarvon, Wales; resort; slate.

**Beddington and Wallington**, *mun. bor.*, Surrey, Eng. nr. Croydon; p. (1961) *32,588*.

**Bedford**, *mun. bor.*, Beds, Eng.; on R. Ouse, 50 m. N. of London; general engin. inc. marine and elect., bricks, ironfounding, aero research; p. (estd. 1967) *67,300*.

**Bedfordshire**, S. Midland *co.*, Eng.; co. t. Bedford (*q.v.*); agr., mkt. gardening, brickmkg., cement, vehicles, engin.; a. 473 sq. m.; p. (1966) *428,000*.

**Bedford**, *t.*, Indiana, U.S.A.; p. (1930) *13,024*.

**Bedford**, *t.*, Ohio, U.S.A.; p. (1960) *15,223*.

**Bedford Level**, once over 400,000 acres of peat marsh in S. Fenland; first successful draining initiated by Earl of Bedford in 1634.

**Bedlington**, *urb. dist.*, Northumberland, Eng.; iron, coal; p. (estd. 1967) *30,810*.

**Bedloe's I.**, or Liberty I., N.Y. harbour, U.S.A.; on which statue of Liberty stands.

**Bedminster**, *t.*, Somerset, Eng.; sub. of Bristol.

**Bedourie**, *t.*, Queensland, Australia.

**Bedrashem**, *t.*, U.A.R., N.E. Africa; on R. Nile.

**Bedwas and Machen**, *urb. dist.*, Mon., Eng.; gas, coal and coke by-prods.; p. (1961) *10,231*.

**Bedwellty**, *urb. dist.*, Mon., Eng.; coal, iron, elec. goods, car upholstery; p. (1961) *27,336*.

**Bedworth**, *urb. dist.*, Warwick., Eng.; coal-mng., limestone quarrying, engin., textiles; p. (estd. 1967) *39,100*.

**Bedzin**, *t.*, S. Poland; coal, zinc, metals, chemicals, bricks, sugar-beet; p. (1965) *42,000*.

**Beechworth**, *t.*, Victoria, Australia; gold, pastoral and agr.

**Beechy Point**, *C.*, N.E. cst. Alaska, U.S.A.

**Beemaning Mtn.**, highest peak Blue Mtns., N.S.W., Australia; alt. 4,100 ft.

**Beenleigh**, *t.*, Queensland, Australia; 24 m. S. Brisbane.

**Beerberg**, *highest mtn.*, Thüringer Wald, Germany; alt. 3,266 ft.

**Beernem**, *t.*, W. Flanders, Belgium; p. (1962) *5,829*.

**Beersheba**, *t.*, Israel; ctr. for development of the Negev; p. (1953) over *20,000*.

**Beeskow**, *t.*, Germany; on R. Spree.

**Beeston and Stapleford**, *urb. dist.*, Nottingham, Eng.; engin., drugs, telephones; p. (estd. 1967) *62,070*.

**Beeville**, *c.*, Texas, U.S.A.; mnfs, oilfield equipment; oil-wells; p. (1960) *13,811*.

**Beg**, *L.*, Antrim, N. Ireland.

**Bega**, *R.*, S. Hungary; canalised trib. to R. Tisza.

**Bègles**, *t.*, Gironde, France; mftg.; p. (1954) *23,176*.

**Beheira**, *prov.*, Lower U.A.R., N.E. Africa; in delta of Nile R.; cotton; a. 1,639 sq. m.; p. (1960) *1,685,679*.

**Behistun**, *t.*, Iraq; in ruins; monuments of Darius the Great.

**Beilan**, *t., mtn. pass*, Syria-S.W. Asia; E. of G. of Iskenderun; ancient Amanus of "Syrian Gates."

**Beilngries**, *t.*, Bavaria, Germany; on Ludwig's canal.

**Beilstein**, *t.*, Germany; on R. Moselle.

**Beira**, *spt., cap.*, prov. Manica and Sofala, Mozambique; airport; rly. runs inland to Salisbury (Rhodesia) and Blantyre (Malawi); exp. sugar, maize, cotton; oil pipeline to Umtali; p. (1960) *64,600* inc. *16,000* Europeans.

**Beirut**, *cap.* Lebanon, S.W. Asia; most impt. *spt.* Syria and Lebanon; ancient historic t., now busy shipping and mercantile ctr.; silk, wool, fruits; p. (estd 1960) *500,000*.

**Beisan**, *t.*, Israel, in Jordan valley, *c.* 300 ft. below sea level; archaeological finds date from *c.* 1500 B.C.; rebuilt since 1948 by Israelis.

**Beit el Faki**, *t.*, Yemen, Arabia; coffee.

**Beit Jala**, *t.*, Jordan.

**Beit Jibrin**, *t.*, Israel, in Judaean Hills.

**Beja**, *dist.*, Portugal; pig-breeding dist.; olive oil, pottery; cr ch.; airfield under construction for training of German pilots; p. (1960) *253,152*.

**Bejaia (Bougie)**, *spt.*, Algeria; impt. tr. ctr.; exp. wood, hides; oil pipe-line connection to Hassi-Messoud; p. (1954) *43,934*.

**Bejar**, *t.*, Spain; cloth; p. *c. 13,000*.

**Bekes**, *t.*, Hungary; wheat; p. (1962) *24,100*.

**Békéscsaba**, *t.*, Hungary; milling; rly. junction; poultry processing plant; p. (1962) *50,664*.

**Belaya Tserkov**, *t.*, N. Ukrainian S.S.R.; agr. and comm. ctr.; p. (1959) *71,000*.

**Belbeis**, *t.*, U.A.R., N.E. Africa; agr. ctr. on W. edge of cultivated Nile delta.

**Belcher Is.**, two sm. groups in Hudson Bay, N.W. Terr., Canada.

**Belding**, *c.*, Mich., U.S.A.; silk mills; p. (1960) *4,887*.

**Belem**, *sub.* of Lisbon, Portugal; fine church, monastery.

**Belém**, *cap.*, Pará st., Brazil; cath., bishop's palace; arsenal, museum; coaling sta., rubber, rice, sugar; p. (1960) *402,170*.

**Belen**, *t.*, Catamarca, Argentina.

**Bélep Arch.**, about 7 m. N.E. of New Caledonia.

**Belfast**, *spt., co. bor., cap.* N. Ireland; Antrim (and partly Down), at head of Belfast Lough; linen mnf., rope, tobacco, shipbldg., distilling, aircraft, fertilisers, computers; oil refinery on E. side of harbour; univ.; Houses of Parliament, Stormont Cas.; p. (1966) *399,270*.

**Belfast**, *t.*, Maine, U.S.A.; p. (1960) *6,140*.

**Belfodio**, *t.*, Ethiopia; nr. border with Sudan; p. *1,000*.

**Belford**, *rural dist.*, Northumberland, Eng.; agr., whinstone quarrying; p. (1961) *4,994*.

**Belfort**, *fortress t.*, Belfort, France; between Jura and the Vosges; heavy inds., rly. wks., sm. cotton ind.; p. (1962) *51,230*.

**Belfort**, *dep.*, France; ch. t., Belfort; a. 235 sq. m.; p. (1962) *109,371*.

**Belgaum**, *t.*, Mysore, India; cotton; p. (1961) *126,727*.

**Belgian Congo.** *See* Congo.

Belgium, *ctry.*, W. Europe; climate temperate; ch. rivers: Scheldt, Meuse; races: Flemish, Walloon; languages: Flemish, French; religion: Roman Catholic; ch. inds.: agr., cereals, sugar-beet, potatoes, cattle, pigs, horses; minerals: coal; mnfs.: iron and steel machin., engin., metals, shipbldg., textiles, brewing, distilling; exp. mnf. goods; communications: rail, road, canal; cap. Brussels; ch. port, Antwerp; univ. at Brussels, Ghent, Liége, Louvain; a. 11,755 sq. m.; p. (1962) *9,251,414.*

Belgorod, *t.*, Kursk, R.S.F.S.R.; chalk, slate, lumber, soap, leather, engin.; p. (1959) *71,000.*

Belgorod-Dnestrovski, *t.*, Ukraine, U.S.S.R.; mouth of Dniester R.; wine, wool, fruit; p. (1956) *21,600.*

Belgrade (Beograd), *c. cap.*, Serbia, Jugoslavia; at junc. of Save and Danube; univ.; mnfs. tobacco, woollens, aircraft; p. (1961) *594,000.*

Belhaven, *t.*, N.C., U.S.A.; on Pamlico Sound; fishing, lumbering; p. (1960) *2,386.*

Belitung or Billiton, *I.* Between Sumatra and Kalimantan, Indonesia; tin; a. 1,866 sq. m.; p. *102,375.*

Belize, *R.*, Brit. Honduras, Central America; 150 m. long; rises in N.E. Guatemala and flows E. into G. of Honduras at B.

Belize, *t., cap..* British Honduras, Central America; mahogany, dyewoods, bananas; almost devastated by hurricane 31 Oct. 1961; cap. to be moved to new site 50 m. further inland; p. (1960) *32,824.*

Bell, *I.*, Newfoundland, E. Canada; in Conception Bay, 20 m. N.W. of St. Johns; impt. Wabana iron-ore deposits outcrop on N.W. cst., smelted on Pictou coalfield, Nova Scotia; a. 12 sq. m.; p. of Wabana (1956) *7,873.*      Bay.

Bell, *R.*, Quebec, Canada; flows N. into James Bay.

Bell, *t.*, Cal., U.S.A.; residtl. c. 5 m. S. of Los Angeles; p. (1960) *19,371.*

Bell Bay, *pt.*, Tasmania, Australia; on right bank of Tamar R.; modern pt. and site of aluminium refinery.

Bell Rock, Scot.; famous rock and lighthouse 12 m. S.E. of Arbroath.

Bellagio, *t.*, Italy; on L. Como; resort.

Bellaire, *mftg. t.*, Ohio, U.S.A. on Ohio R.; coal, limestone, glass, enamelware; p. (1960) *11,502.*

Bellary, *fortfd. c.*, Mysore, India; cotton; p. (1961) *85,673.*

Belleek, *par.* and *vil.*, Fermanagh, N. Ireland; on Erne R.; china; p. *1,300.*

Bellefontaine, *t.*, Ohio, U.S.A.; agr. ctr., light mnfs.; holiday resort; p. (1960) *11,424.*

Bellefonte, *bor.*, Penns., U.S.A.; limestone quarries; p. (1960) *6,088.*

Belle Fourche, *t.*, S.D., U.S.A.; on Belle Fourche R.; beet sugar, flour, bricks, dairy produce; p. (1960) *4,087.*

Bellegarde, *fort* on frontier of France and Switzerland, near Geneva.

Belle Ile, *I.* off S. coast of Brittany, France.

Belle Isle Strait, N. America; between Newfoundland and Labrador, on N. shipping route to Canada from Europe.

Bellenden Ker Hills, *mtn. range*, N. Queensland, Australia.

Belleville, *c.*, Ontario, Canada; dairying, fruit; deposit of white marble nearby; p. (1961) *30,655.*

Belleville, *t.*, Ill., U.S.A.; brewing, iron founding, shoes, flour; p. (1960) *37,264.*

Belleville, *t.*, N.J., U.S.A.; p. (1960) *35,005.*

Bellevue, *t.*, Ohio, U.S.A.; limestone, farm implements, car parts; p. (1960) *8,282.*

Bellevue, *t.*, Penns., U.S.A.; p. (1960) *11,412.*

Bellevue, *t.*, Queensland, Australia; goldfields.

Belley, *t.*, Ain, France; p. (1962) *6,442.*

Bellflower, *t.*, Cal., U.S.A.; p. (1960) *44,846.*

Bellingham, *rural dist.*, Hexham, Northumberland, Eng.; coal; p. (1961) *5,285.*

Bellingham, *t., spt.*, Wash., U.S.A.; saw-mills, paper-mills, salmon canning; p. (1960) *34,688.*

Bellingshausen, *sea*, S. Antarctic; lying W. of Graham Land.

Bellinzona, *t.*, Switzerland; on R. Ticino; 14 m. N. of Lugano; three castles built on hills dominating t.; p. (1957) *12,060.*

Bellot Strait, channel on Arctic coast, N. America; separates Boothia and N. Somerset.

Bellows Falls, *t.*, Vt., U.S.A., on Connecticut, R.; paper, farm implements; p. (1960) *3,831.*

Belluno, *c.*, Venetia, N. Italy; fine cattle; silk; p. (1961) *31,224.*

Belluno, *prov.*, Venetia, N. Italy; a. 1,276 sq. m.; p. (1961) *205,700.*

Belmar, *t.*, N.J., U.S.A.; seaside resort, fishing; p. (1960) *5,190.*

Belmez, *t.*, Córdoba prov., S. Spain; on N. flank of Sierra Morena, 38 m. N.W. of Córdoba; ctr. of sm. coalfield; p. (1959) *9,672.*

Belmont, *t.*, Cape Province, S. Africa; 56 m. S. of Kimberley.

Belmont, *t.*, Mass., U.S.A.; p. (1960) *28,715.*

Belmont, *t.*, N.C., U.S.A.; p. (1960) *5,007.*

Belo Horizonte, *t., cap.*, Minas Gerais st., Brazil; gold, iron, manganese; diamond-cutting; ctr. of agr. inds.; cotton; p. (1960) *693,328.*

Beloit, *c.*, Wisconsin, U.S.A.; on Rock R., diesel engines, farm implements; p. (1960) *32,846.*

Beloit, *c.*, Kan., U.S.A.; on Solomon R.; tr. ctr. for agr. region; p. (1960) *3,837.*

Beloretsk, *t.*, Bashkir A.S.S.R.; iron, metal inds.; p. (1959) *59,000.*

Belovo, *t.*, W. Siberia, R.S.F.S.R.; coal mng., zinc, engin.; p. (1967) *115,000.*

Beloyarsk, R.S.F.S.R.; atomic power sta. in Urals.

Belper, *urb. dist.*, Derby, Eng.; hosiery, textiles, paint, oil wks., iron foundries; p. (1961) *15,563.*

Belt, Great, *strait*, Denmark; separates Fyn I. from Själland I.; deep-water channel too winding for easy navigation; crossed by train ferry at its narrowest point (16 m.) between Nyborg and Korsor; approx. length 37 m.

Belt, Little, *strait*, Denmark; separates Fyn I. from Jutland; too shallow for large ships; bridged by road-railway bridge nr. Fredericia; approx. length 30 m.

Belterra, *dist.*, Para st., N.E. Brazil; on R. Tapajoz, 30 m. S. of confluence with R. Amazon at Santarem; experimental Ford rubber plantations; a. 950 sq. m.; p. (with Fordlandia) *12,000.*

Beltsy, *t.*, Moldavian S.S.R.; on trib. of Dniester R.; p. (1959) *67,000.*

Belturbet, *t., urb. dist.*, Cavan, Ireland; on R. Erne; distilling; p. (1951) *1,152.*

Bembridge, *vil.*, I. of Wight, Eng.; resort, yachting; p. *1,975* (par.).

Bemfica, Angola, W. Africa; oilfields.

Bemidji, *t.*, Minn., U.S.A.; lumber, cement, bricks, woollen goods; resort; p. (1960) *9,958.*

Ben Alder, *mtn.*, Grampian Range, Scot.; nr. Loch Erich; alt. 3,757 ft.

Ben Arthur, *mtn.*, Argyll, Scot.; alt. 2,891 ft.

Ben Attow, *mtn.*, Ross and Inverness, Scot.; alt. 3,383 ft.

Ben Avon, *mtn.*, Aberdeen, Scot.; alt. 3,834 ft.

Ben Cruachan, *mtn.*, Argyll, Scot.; alt. 3,689 ft.

Ben Doran or Doireann, *mtn.*, Argyll, Scot.; alt. 3,523 ft.

Ben Hope, *mtn.*, Sutherland, Scot.; alt. 3,040 ft.

Ben Lawers, *mtn.*, Perth, Scot.; by Loch Tay; alt. 3,984 ft.

Ben Ledi, *mtn.*, Perth, Scot.; N.W. of Callander; alt. 2,875 ft.

Ben Lomond, *mtn.*, Stirling, Scot.; E. side of L. Lomond; alt. 3,192 ft.

Ben Lomond, *mtn.*, New England range, N.S.W., Australia; alt. 5,000 ft.

Ben Lomond, *mtn.*, Tasmania, Australia; alt. 5,010 ft.; tin and wolfram mined on S.E. slopes.

Ben Macdhui, *mtn.*, S.W. Aberdeen, Scot.; Cairngorm gr; second highest peak in Brit. Is.; alt. 4,296 ft.

Ben More, *mtn.*, S.W. Perth, Scot.; 10 m. W. of Loch Earn; alt. 3,843 ft.; also mtns. in Sutherland, the Hebrides and the I. of Mull.

Ben Nevis, *mtn.*, Inverness, Scot.; at Lochiel; highest peak in Brit. Isles. alt. 4,406 ft.

Ben Nevis, *mtn.*, Otago, New Zealand; alt. 9,125 ft.

Ben Nevis, *mtn.*, Cornwall, Tasmania, Australia; alt. 3,910 ft.

Ben Venue, *mtn.*, nr. Loch Katrine, Perth, Scot.; alt. 2,393 ft.

Ben Vorlich, *mtn.*, Perth, Scot.; alt. 3,224 ft.

Ben Wyvis, *mtn.*, Ross, Scot.; nr. Dingwall; alt. 3,429 ft.

Benalla, *t., dist.*, Victoria, Australia; pastoral and agr.; p. (1961) *3,483.*

Benares, *see* Varanasi.

Benbecula I., Outer Hebrides, Inverness, Scot.; a. 36 sq. m.

**Benbecula Sound**, passage between the I. and S. Uist.

**Bendery**, *t.*, Moldavian S.S.R.; textiles, p. (estd. 1961) *63,000*.

**Bendigo**, *c.*, Victoria, Australia; former gold-mining dist., engin., brickwks., wool, eucalyptus oil and hardboard mftg., food processing; p. (1966) *42,191*.

**Benevento**, *prov.*, Italy; a. 819 sq. m., containing many Roman remains; p. (1961) *297,153*.

**Benevento**, *c.*, Italy; cath.; leather; p. (1961) *54,744*.

**Benfleet**, *urb. dist.*, Essex, Eng.; saw mills, joinery wks., light inds.; p. (estd. 1967) *43,890*.

**Bengal, West**, *st.*, India; a. 33,928 sq. m.; p. (1961) *34,926,279*; rice, oilseeds, sugar cane, tobacco, jute, silk, tea, coal, mesta, potatoes; served by 3 st. rlys.; Ganges alluvial plains and delta; ch. c. Calcutta which adjoins jute manuf. ctr. Howrah. (Former prov. of Bengal split 1947—W. Bengal to India, E. Bengal to Pakistan).

**Bengal, Bay of**, part of Indian Ocean washing E. shores of India and W. shores of the Indo-Chinese Peninsula; receives waters of Rs. Krishna, Ganges, Brahmaputra, Irrawaddy.

**Benghazi**, *spt.*, Libya, N. Africa; on the G. of Sidra; joint cap. with Tripoli; former starting-point for caravans to Egypt and the interior; cereals; p. (estd. 1954) *71,000*.

**Bengore Head**, *C.*, Antrim, N. coast Ireland; E. of Giant's Causeway.

**Benguela**, *c.*, Angola, S.W. Africa; rly. runs inland to Congo and Zambia; beeswax, maize, cattle, sugar; p. (1960) *52,300* inc. *11,500* whites.

**Benha**, *t.*, U.A.R.; impt. mkt. t., rail and road ctr. in heart of cultivated a. of Nile delta.

**Benholm**, *par.*, Kincardine, Scot.; ancient cas.; p. (1951) *1,028*.

**Beni**, *dep.*, N.E. Bolivia, S. America; cap. Trinidad; a. 93,354 sq. m.; p. (1962) *161,800*.

**Benicarlo**, *spt.*, Valencia, Spain; on Mediterranean cst.; wines; p. (1957) *9,385*.

**Benin**, W. Africa; between Niger delta and Dahomey; traversed by Benin R.; former African kingdom and slaving ctr.; now dist. incorporated in Nigeria; palm prod. and foodstuffs; famous African bronze ctr.; ch. t. Benin.

**Benin**, *t.*, Nigeria; W. Africa; cap. Mid-West region; palm oil, mahogany; p. (1953) *54,000*. [Africa.

**Beni Suef**, *t.*, U.A.R.; on Nile, 60 m. S. of Cairo; carpets, cotton; p. (1960) *79,000*.

**Benkulen**, *spt.*, Sumatra, Indonesia; p. *13,418*.

**Benmore**, *C.*, Antrim, N.E. point of N. Ireland; alt. 636 ft.

**Bennettsville**, *t.*, S.C., U.S.A.; yarn, tyre linings, lumber; p. (1960) *6,963*.

**Bennington**, *t.*, Vt., U.S.A.; p. (1960) *8,023*.

**Benoni**, *t.*, Transvaal, S. Africa; engin.; p. (1960) *135,467* (inc. *41,305* whites).

**Benrath**, *t.*, Germany; on Rhine R.; R. pt. and industl. t.; chemicals, machin.; p. *25,929*.

**Bensberg**, *t.*, N. Rhine–Westphalia, Germany; 10 m. from Cologne; iron-mining, foundries; p. (1963) *33,400*.

**Bensheim**, *t.*, Hessen, Germany; ctr. of fruit and wine dist.; textiles, paper, metallurgy; p. (1963) *24,800*.

**Bentang (Bintang)**, *t.*, Kalimantan, Indonesia.

**Bentley with Arksey**, *urb. dist.*, W.R. Yorks, Eng.; p. (estd. 1967) *23,650*.

**Benton**, *t.*, Ark., U.S.A.; p. (1960) *10,399*.

**Benton**, *t.*, Ill., U.S.A.; p. (1960) *7,023*.

**Benton Harbor**, *t.*, Mich., U.S.A.; midway along E. cst. L. Michigan; p. (1960) *19,136*.

**Benue**, *R.*, W. Africa; chief trib. of Niger.

**Benwell**, *t.*, Northumberland, Eng.; sub. of Newcastle.

**Ben-y-Gloe**, *mtn.*, Glen Tilt, Perth, Scot.; alt. 3,671 ft.

**Beograd**, *see* Belgrade.

**Beppu**, *t.*, Kyushu, Japan; hot spring resort; p. (1965) *118,938*.

**Berat**, *c.*, Albania; p. (1945) *11,872*.

**Berbera**, *beach pt.*, Somalia, N.E. Africa; on G. of Aden; former cap. of Br. Somaliland Prot.; exp. gum, raisins, skins; p. in hot season about *15,000*, in cold season about *30,000*.

**Berbice**, *co.*, Guyana, S. America; bauxite; p. (1946) *96,623*.

**Berchem**, *commune*, Belgium; sub. of Antwerp; metals; p. (1962) *48,880*.

**Berdichev (Ossipevsk)**, *t.*, Ukrainian S.S.R.; ctr. of sugar a.; engin., lt. inds.; p. (1959) *53,000*.

**Berck-Plage**, *seat. pl.*, France, on Eng. Channel; p. (1962) *15,543*.

**Berdyansk (Osipenko)**, *spt.*, Ukrainian S.S.R.; on Sea of Azov; a ctr. of the salt ind.; exp. grain, hemp, wool, agr. machin.; engin., oil refining; p. (1959) *65,000*.

**Berea**, *t.*, N. Ohio, U.S.A.; sandstone quarries, building blocks; p. (1960) *16,592*.

**Bere Regis**, *mkt. t.*, Dorset, Eng.

**Berezina**, *R.*, U.S.S.R.; trib. Dnieper; French disaster on the retreat from Moscow; length 350 m.

**Bereźniki**, *t.*, R.S.F.S.R., salt, chemicals, paper; p. (1967) *134,000*.

**Berga**, *t.*, Spain; medieval cas.; p. (1957) *8,023*.

**Bergama**, *t.*, Turkey; ancient Pergamos, ruins; p. (1960) *21,797*.

**Bergamo**, *c.*, Lombardy, Italy; 34 m. N.E. Milan; fine cath. and academy; silk industry; p. (1961) *113,512*.

**Bergedorf**, *t.*, Germany; sub. of Hamburg; on R. Elbe; glass, leather; p. *19,962*.

**Bergen**, *spt.*, W. coast Norway; univ.; most impt. comm. pt. in kingdom; shipping, fishing; mftg. inds.; p. (1963) *116,555*.

**Bergenfield**, *t.*, N.J., U.S.A.; clothing, light mnfs., pianos; p. (1960) *27,203*.

**Bergen op Zoom**, *c.*, N. Brabant, Netherlands; sugar-beet; p. (1967) *38,155*.

**Bergerac**, *t.*, Dordogne, France; on R. Dordogne; grain, wine; ancient Huguenot stronghold; p. (1962) *25,971*.

**Bergisch-Gladbach**, *t.*, N. Rhine–Westphalia, Germany; E. of Cologne; paper, metallurgy, textiles; p. (1963) *44,500*.

**Bering I.**, most W. of the Aleutian Is., N. America.

**Bering Sea**, part of N. Pac. Oc. between Aleutian Is. and Bering Strait, upwards of 1,600 sq. m.; fishing.

**Bering Strait**, *narrow sea* which separates Asia from N. America; 36 m. wide at narrowest part.

**Bering Current (Okhotsk Current, or Oyashio)**, *ocean current*, N. Pac. Oc.; flows through Bering Strait from Arctic, along E. cst. of Kamchatka and Japanese Is. Hokkaido, Honshu; relatively cold; moderate summer temperatures along cst. causes fogs.

**Berja**, *t.*, Almeria, Spain; wine and fruit; p. (1957) *11,011*.

**Berkeley**, *parish*, Gloucester, Eng.; nr. R. Severn, 2 m. S. of Sharpness; civil nuclear power-sta.

**Berkeley**, *c.*, Cal., U.S.A.; univ.; p. (1960) *111,268*.

**Berkeley Canal**, Gloucester, Eng.; connects Sharpness on S. side Severn estuary with Gloucester; navigable only for small coasting vessels; opened 1827; length 15 m., depth 11 ft.

**Berkhampstead (Berkhamsted)**, *urb. dist.*, Herts, Eng.; chemicals, wooden ware; p. (1961) *13,051*.

**Berkley**, *t.*, Mich., U.S.A.; sub. of Detroit; p. (1960) *23,275*.

**Berkshire**, *co.*, Eng.; downland including Inkpen Beacon, White Horse Hills, drained by Thames and tribs., Kennet, Cole, Pang; wooded; agr.; oats, dairying; biscuits; co. t. Reading; a. 725 sq. m.; p. (1966) *586,000*.

**Berlin**, *c.*, former cap. of Germany; on R. Spree; fourth c. on continent of Europe for population; enclave within East Germany; divided 1945 into 4 occupation zones; Soviet (East Berlin, p. *1,082,349*), British, American and French (West Berlin, p. *2,221,000*); total a. 890 sq. km.; inds. include elec. goods, optical and chemical prod., furniture, paper, foodstuffs, textiles, machin., publishing and printing; gr. route ctr. (each occupying force has an airfield).

**Berlin**, *t.*, New Hampshire, U.S.A.; p. (1960) *17,821*.

**Bermejo**, *t.*, Tarija dep., Bolivia; oil.

**Bermejo R.**, *trib.* R. Parana, Argentina.

**Bermeo**, *spt.*, Spain; nr. Bilbao, Bay of Biscay; fishing; p. (1957) *12,517*.

**Bermondsey**, *see* Southwark.

**Bermuda**, Brit. group coral islands (360 in number of which 20 are inhabited) N. Atlantic; about 600 miles E. of S. Carolina, U.S.A.; total area 21 sq. m.; Hamilton, on Long Island is the ch. t.; British and U.S. air and naval stations; favourite winter resort for Americans;

potatoes, onions, lily bulbs; bananas; p. (of gr.) (estd. 1965) 48,000.

Bermudez, asphalt lake, Venezuela, S. America; a. 2 sq. m.

Bernard, Great St., one of the Alps in the S. of the Valais, Switzerland; highest point 11,116 ft.; height of mtn. pass between Italy and Switzerland, 8,120 ft.; famous hospice for travellers in monastery on mtn. Great St. Bernard road tunnel, see K146.

Bernard, Little St., one of Graian Alps, Savoy, S. of Mt. Blanc, France; pass traversed by Hannibal 218 B.C.

Bernay, t., Eure, France; horse fair; dairying, clothing mftg., soap; p. (1962) 10,112.

Bernburg, t., Halle, E. Germany; cas.; chemicals, machin.; p. (1963) 44,738.

Berne, c., cap. can. Berne and fed. cap. Switzerland; on Aar R.; cath., univ.; textiles; p. (1961) 166,100.

Berne, can., Switzerland; fertile valleys, dairying; watches; tourist district; a. 2,657 sq. m.; p. (1961) 889,523.

Bernese Oberland, Switzerland; Alpine region; ch. peaks; Finsteraarhorn, Jungfrau; resorts: Interlaken, Grindelwald; summer and winter ctrs.

Bernina, pass and mtn., Switzerland; alt. 13,300 ft.

Beroun, t., Bohemia, ČSSR.; textiles, sugar ref., cement, coal, iron, limestone; p. (1961) 15,597.

Berri, oilfield, Saudi Arabia; 45 m. N.W. of Ras Tannura, between Qatif and Khursaniyah; the field extends offshore.

Berry, t., N.S.W., Australia; dairying.

Bertinoro, t., Forli, Italy; famous wines.

Berwick, maritime co., S.E. of Scot.; co. t. Duns; hilly; agr.; sheep, cattle; woollens, fishing, paper; a. 457 sq. m.; p. (1961) 22,441.

Berwick-upon-Tweed, spt., mun. bor., Northumberland, Eng.; fishing, light engin., tweeds, knitwear; p. (including Tweedmouth and Spittall) (estd. 1967) 11,650.

Berwyn, t., Ill., U.S.A.; p. (1960) 54,224.

Berwyn Mtns., range mid-Wales; alt. of highest peak 2,716 ft.

Besançon, t., Doubs, France; observatory; univ.; farm implements, textiles; watch- and clock-making; p. (1962) 101,729.

Besiklas, now Besiktas, dist. and sub., Istanbul, Turkey; p. (1950) 63,611.

Beskids, W. and E., min. range, Poland, Czechoslovakia, E. Europe; northern range of Carpathian mtn. system, seldom exceeds alt. 4,000 ft., many passes; forested; length 200 m.

Bessarabia, terr., ceded to U.S.S.R. by Romania, 1940, and now part of Moldavian S.S.R.; agr. region.

Bessbrooke, t., Armagh, N. Ireland; on Newry Canal; p. (1966) 3,325.

Bessèges, t., Gard, France; coal-mining, steel, silk; p. (1954) 5,823.

Bessemer, t., Ala., U.S.A.; iron and steel; p. (1960) 33,054.

Bessemer, t., Mich., U.S.A.; iron; p. (1960) 3,304.

Besshi, see Niihama.

Besuki, mountainous prov. E. Java, Indonesia.

Betanzos, t., Spain; wine; p. (1957) 10,824.

Bethany, vil. on Mt. of Olives 2 m. Jerusalem, now Elzariya.

Bethany, missionary sta., S.W. Africa; p. 544.

Bethel, anc. c., the modern Beitin, Jordan; 10 m. N. Jerusalem.

Bethel, t., Cape Province, S. Africa; rich farming a.; p. (1960) 11,952 inc. 4,003 whites.

Bethesda, t., Maryland, U.S.A.; p. (1960) 56,527.

Bethesda, urb. dist., Caernarvon, Wales; slate, light engin.; p. (1961) 4,151.

Bethlehem, t., Jordan; 5½ m. S.W. Jerusalem; birthpl.ce of Christ; p. (1961) 15,777.

Bethlehem, t., Penns., U.S.A.; 50 m. N. of Philadelphia; iron-wks.; p. (1960) 75,408.

Bethnal Green, see Tower Hamlets.

Bethphage, former vil. on Mt. of Olives, above Bethany, Israel, S.W. Asia.

Bethsaida, ancient vil. on W. side of Sea of Galilee, Israel, S.W. Asia.

Bethshemesh, t., Israel, S.W. Asia; 24 m. W. of Jerusalem; archaeological site.

Béthune, t., Pas de Calais, France; oil, salt, coal; p. (1962) 22,386.

Bettendorf, t., Iowa, U.S.A.; steel, oil burners; p. (1960) 11,534

Betteshanger, mining vil., Kent, Eng.; on N. flank of N. Downs, 4 m. W. of Deal.

Betws-y-Coed, urb. dist., Caernarvon, Wales; tourist and artists' resort; p. (1961) 778.

Betul, t., Madhya Pradesh, India; p. (1961) 19,860.

Betwa, R., of Bhopal, India, trib. of Jumna R.; length 360 m.

Beuel, t., N. Rhine–Westphalia, Germany; on R. Rhine opposite Bonn; chemicals, furniture; p. (1963) 33,000.

Beuthen, see Bytom.

Beuzeval, t., Calvados, France; on Eng. Channel; seaside resort; p. (1962) 2,363.

Beveland, I., S. Netherlands; between the old Maas and Hollands Diep.

Beverley, mkt. t., mun. bor., E.R. Yorks, Eng.; fine minster; p. (estd. 1967) 17,220.

Beverly, c., Mass., U.S.A.; boots, shoes, machin.; p. (1960) 36,108.

Beverly Hills, t., California, U.S.A.; p. (1960) 30,817.

Beverwijk, t., nr. Haarlem, N. Holland, Netherlands; p. (1967) 41,956.

Bewdley, mun. bor., Worcester, Eng.; p. (estd. 1967) 5,610.

Bexhill, mun. bor., Sussex, Eng.; resort; p. (estd. 1967) 32,350.

Bexley, former bor. W. Kent; now outer bor., Greater London, Eng., inc. Chislehurst and Sidcup (N. of the A.20) Crayford and Erith; p. (1966) 215,000.

Bexley, t., Ohio, U.S.A.; p. (1960) 14,319.

Beykoz, t., Turkey; on Bosporus Strait; p. (estd. 1960) 40,000.

Beyoglu, div. of Istanbul, Turkey; residtl. quarter of Europeans; p. (1945) 234,750.

Beypazari, t., Turkey; 65 m. W. of Ankara; rice, fruit, cotton; p. (1960) 8,866.

Beysehir, L., Turkey; 25 m. long; alt. 7,068 ft.

Bezhitsa, t., R.S.F.S.R.; fused with Bryansk (q.v.) in 1956.

Béziers, t., Hérault, France; wines, brandy; chemicals; p. (1962) 75,541.

Bezons, sub. of Paris, France; on Seine R.; light mnfs; p. (1954) 16,993.

Bezwade, see Vijayawada.

Bhadravati, t., Mysore, India; steel; p. (1961) 65,776; of new town 41,281.

Bhagalpur, t., Patna, Bihar, India; rice, maize; p. (1961) 143,850.

Bhamo, t., Upper Burma; on R. Irrawaddy; market ctr.; ruby mines; teak; p. c. 10,000.

Bhandara, dist., Maharashtra, India, a. 3,582 sq. m.; rice, oilseeds, wheat, bamboo, tobacco; p. (1961) 1,268,286.

Bhandara, cap. of Bhandara dist., Maharashtra, India; 30 m. E. of Nagpur; cotton cloth, brass mftg.; p. (1961) 27,710.

Bharatpur, t., Rajasthan, India; cloth; p. (1961) 49,776.

Bhatpara, t., W. Bengal, India; on R. Hooghly; p. (1961) 147,630.

Bhavnagar, dist., Gujarat, India; a. 4,652 sq. m.; p. (1961) 1,119,435.

Bhavnagar, t., spt., Gujarat, India; cotton, silk and gold embroidery; p. (1961) 176,473.

Bhilai, Madhya Pradesh, India; steel plant; rails and rly. sleepers; p. (1961) of industl. t. 86,116; of Durg 47,114.

Bhim-Gora, sacred pool, place of Hindu pilgrimage, Uttar Pradesh, India.

Bhir, dist., Maharashtra, India; a. 4,268 sq. m.; wheat, cotton, linseed, sugar; cap. Bhir, 190 m. E. of Bombay; p. (1961) 1,001,466.

Bhiwani, t., India; cottons; p. (1961) 58,194.

Bhopal, c., st. cap., Madhya Pradesh, India; impt. trade ctr.; p. (1961) 185,374.

Bhuj, ch. t., Kutch, Gujarat, Bombay, India; p. (1961) 33,953.

Bhutan, indep. st., E. Himalayas; cap. Thimphu; ch. prod.: Indian corn, millet, lac, rice, cloth; valuable forests; a. (approx.) 18,000 sq. m.; first motor road link with India constr. 1960–2; p. scattered and nomadic, c. 700,000.

Bhuvaneshwar, cap., Orissa, India; 18 m. from Cuttack; p. (1961) 38,211.

Biafra, Bight of, W. Africa; bay lying E. of the G. of Guinea between the Niger and Cape Lopez.

Biala-Krakowska, commine, Krakow dep., Poland; agr.; tr. ctr., cattle, textiles.

Bialogard, c., N.W. Poland; formerly in Germany; industl. and transport ctr.

Bialystok, prov., E, Poland; cap. Bialystok; a. 9,021 sq. m.; p. (1965) 1,160,000.

Bialystok, *t.*, Poland; *cap.* of Bialystok prov., nr. Grodno; engin., textiles, chemicals, saw-milling; p. (1965) *138,000*.

Biancavilla, *t.*, Sicily, Italy; oranges.

Biarritz, *t.*, Basses-Pyrénées, France; on Bay of Biscay; seaside resort; p. (1962) *25,514*.

Biba-El-Kubra, *t.*, U.A.R., N.E. Africa; on Nile; p. *1,000*.

Biberach, *t.*, Baden-Württemberg, Germany; on R. Riss; spa; wood, metal and engin. inds.; p. (1963) *23,100*.

Bicester, *urb. dist.*, Oxford. Eng.; rly. junction; lace; p. (1961) *5,513*.

Bida, *t.*, N. Nigeria, W. Africa; p. *10,000*.

Bidassoa, *R.*, on Spanish-French frontier.

Biddeford, *c.*, Maine, U.S.A.; cotton mnf.; resort; p. (1960) *19,255*.

Biddulph, *urb. dist.*, Stafford, Eng.; nr. Leek; coal mng., machin., textiles, furniture; p. (1961) *14,060*.

Bideford, *mun. bor.*, N. Devon, Eng.; on R. Torridge; ropes, sails, boat bldg., glove mkg.; p. (estd. 1967) *10,850*.

Biebrich, *t.*, Germany; on Rhine; dyes; p. *19,504*.

Biel (Bienne), *t.*, Berne, Switzerland; watches; p. (1961) *61,200*.

Bielawa, *t.* Wroclaw prov., S.W. Poland; textiles; p. (1965) *31,000*.

Bielaya-Tserkov, *t.*, Ukraine, U.S.S.R.; on trib. of Dnieper R.; fairs, tr. in cattle, beer, grain; p. *54,000*.

Bielefeld, *t.*, Rhine-Westphalia, Germany; ch. ctr. of linen industry; machin., bicycles; p. (1963) *172,800*.

Biella, *t.*, Novara, Italy; textiles; p. (1961) *50,209*.

Bielsko-Biala, *t.*, Katowice prov., Poland; woollens, linen, metal, chem.; p. (1965) *82,000*.

Bien-hoa, *t.*, nr. Saigon, S. Viet-Nam; sugar refining; cotton mills.

Bienne, *L.*, N.E. Neuchâtel, Switzerland.

Bierley, *par.*, W. Riding, Yorks. Eng.; coal, iron; p. *16,000*.

Bies-Bosch, reclaimed fenland area between N. Brabant and S.W. Netherlands; sugar refining, dairying; a. 55 sq. m.

Big Black, *R.*, trib. of Mississippi, U.S.A.

Big Bone Lick, *locality*, N. Ky., U.S.A.; E. of Ohio R.; deposit of fossil mammoth.

Biggar, *burgh*, Lanark, Scot.; in S. Uplands, 10 m. S.E. of Lanark; p. (1961) *1,403*.

Biggarsberg, *mtns.*, Natal, S. Africa; branch of the Drakensberg, highest point, Indumeni, 7,200 ft.

Biggleswade, *urb. dist.*, Beds, Eng.; in valley of R. Ouse, 9 m. S.E. of Bedford; ctr. of fruit-growing and mkt. gardening dist.; hydraulic machin. tools, hosiery, caravans; p. (1961) *8,047*.

Big Horn Mtns, Wyo. and Mont., U.S.A.; Rockies; highest alt., 12,000 ft.

Big Horn, *R.*, Wyo., U.S.A.; trib. of Yellow-stone R.

Bihač, *t.*, Jugoslavia; on R. Una; p. (1959) *14,000*.

Bihar, *state*, Indian Union; a. 67,196 sq. m.; cap. Patna (*q.v.*); ch. R., Ganges; agr.: rice, wheat, maize, sugar-cane, tobacco, oil-seeds; minerals: coal, iron, mica; ind.: iron and steel, oil refining at Barauni; p. (1961) *46,455,610*.

Bihé, *dist.*, Angola (Port. W. Africa).

Bihor Mtns., Romania.

Bisk, *c.*, Siberia, U.S.S.R.; p. (1967) *176,000*.

Bijapur, *t.*, Mysore, India; cotton; ruins; p. (1961) *78,854*.

Bijeljina, *t.*, Jugoslavia; p. (1959) *18,000*.

Bijnore, *t.* Uttar Pradesh, India; p. (1961) *33,610*.

Bikaner, *t.*, Rajasthan, India; p. (1961) *150,634*.

Bikini, *atoll*, Pacific Ocean; scene of atomic-bomb tests.

Bilaspur, *t.*, Madhya Pradesh, India; silks, cottons; p. (1961) *86,706*.

Bilbao, *spt.*, N. Spain; cap. Basque prov. of Viscaya; formerly famous for rapier making; iron ore, smelting; pipeline from Ayoluengo oilfield under construction; p. (1965) *356,000*.

Bilecik, *t.*, Turkey; p. (1960) *7,535*.

Bilina, *c.*, Bohemia, ČSSR.; wat. pl., mineral springs; p. (1961) *10,394*.

Billabong, *R.*, N.S.W., Australia.

Billericay, *mun. bor.*, Essex, Eng.; lost land and individuality to Basildon.

Billinge and Winstanley, *urb. dist.*, Lancs. Eng.; coal bricks; p. (1961) *6,941*.

Billingham, *t.*, *urb. dist.*, Durham, Eng.; on N. of Tees estuary; chemicals, shipbldg. and repairing, iron and steel, plastics, fertilisers; p. (1961) *32,130*.

Billings, *t.*, Montana, U.S.A.; cattle-raising, wool; p. (1960) *52,851*.

Billingsgate, London, Eng.; old river-gate and wharf, now chief fish mkt. of England.

Billiton (Belitung) I., Indonesia; tin.

Bilma, *oasis*, Niger, W. Africa; p. *1,000*.

Biloxi, *t.*, Miss., U.S.A.; fishing, tourist ctr.. U.S. Air Force base; p. (1960) *44,053*.

Bilsen, *t.*, Belgium; mkt. ctr. for fruit growing area; p. (1962) *6,517*.

Bilston, *mun. bor.*, Stafford, Eng.; coal mng., iron, steel, non-ferrous castings; p. (1961) *33,077*.

Bima, *t.*, Sumbawa, Indonesia.

Binab, *t.*, Azerbaijan, Persia; nr. L. Urmia.

Binalbagan, *t.*, Negros I., Philippine Is.; sugar.

Binan, *t.*, Luzon, Philippine Is.

Binangonan, *t.*, Luzon, Philippine Is.

Binche, *t.*, Belgium; lace, clothing; p. (1962) *10,426*.

Bingara, *t.*, N.S.W., Australia; wool, wheat, cattle.

Bingen, *t.*, Rhineland Palatinate, Germany; on Rhine R.; at S. entrance to Rhine gorge; wine; beautiful scenery; p. (1963) *20,500*.

Bingerville, *spt.*, Ivory Coast, W. Africa.

Bingham, *rural dist.*, Notts., agr.; p. (1961) *25,145*.

Bingham Canyon, *t.*, N. Utah, U.S.A.; copper, silver, gold, lead; p. (1960) *1,516*.

Binghamton, N.Y., U.S.A.; on Susquehanna R.; boot factories; p. (1960) *75,941*.

Bingley, *urb. dist.*, *mkt. t.*, W.R. Yorks, Eng.; on R. Aire, 16 m. N.W. of Leeds; textiles, engin., agr.; p. (estd. 1967) *24,590*.

Bingol-dag, *mins.*, Turkey; S. of Erzurum; highest peak 12,310 ft.

Bintang I., largest island of the Riouw Archipelago, Indonesia; bauxite.

Bio-Bio, *R.*, Chile; rises in Andes, flows N.W. to Pac. Oc. at Talcahuano; length 300 m.

Bio-Bio, *prov.*, Chile; cap. Los Angeles; a. 4,342 sq. m.; p. (1960) *179,984*.

Biratnagar, *t.*, S.E. Nepal, in the Terai; jute, sugar, cotton milling, stainless steel; p. (1961) *33,293*.

Birbhum, *dist.*, W. Bengal, India; cap. Suri; healthy climate; rice, sugar; mnfs. silk, cotton; a. 1,757 sq. m.; p. (1961) *1,446,158*.

Birchington, *t.*, Kent, Eng.

Birdsboro, *bor.*, Penns., U.S.A.; on Schuylkill R.; coal, steel; p. (1960) *3,025*.

Birjand, *t.*, Iran; p. *25,000*.

Birkenhead, *co. bor.*, Cheshire, Eng.; on R. Mersey, opp. Liverpool; docks, shipbldg., engin., clothing, metal, wood, glass; p. (estd. 1967) *143,550*.

Birket El Qarun, "Lake of the Horns," Fayum, Egypt, N.E. Africa.

Birmingham, *c.*, *co. bor.*, Warwick, Eng.; industl. cap. Midlands, second lgst. c. Gt. Britain; famous for its metal mnfs.; motors and cycles, plastics; univ., cath., town hall; p. (estd. 1967) *1,101,990*.

Birmingham, *t.*, *cap.*, Ala., U.S.A.; coal, iron, limestone, steel, aircraft, chemicals, textiles; p. (1960), *340,889*.

Birmingham, *t.*, Mich., U.S.A.; p. (1960) *25,525*.

Birnam, *vil.*, Perth, Scot.; location of Birnam Wood—Macbeth; former royal forest.

Birni, *t.*, Dahomey, W. Africa; p. *1,000*.

Birobidzhan, *t.*, U.S.S.R.; admin. ctr.; lt. and wood inds.; p. (1959) *41,000*.

Birr, *mkt. t.*, *urb. dist.*, Offaly, Ireland; on Little Brosna R.; farming; observatory; p. (1966) *3,266*.

Bir Tlacsin, Libya, Africa; 120 m. S.W. Tripoli; oilfields.

Bisbee, *t.*, Arizona, U.S.A.; very rich copper deposits, gold, silver, lead; p. (1960) *9,850*.

Biscarosse, Landes, France; 45 m. S.W. Bordeaux; rocket and missile testing range projected; p. (1962) *3,336*.

Biscay, *see* Vizcaya.

Biscay, Bay of, stormy a. of the Atl. W. of France and N. of Spain, from Ushant to C. Ortegal; the Roman Sinus Aquitanicus; heavy seas.

Bisceglie, *t.*, *spt.*; Apulia, Italy; on E. cst. 22 m. N.W. of Bari; fishing; p. (1961) *41,451*.

Bischheim, *t.*, Bas-Rhin, France; N.W. sub. of Strasbourg, furniture, porcelain; p. (1954) 11,430.

Bischoff, Mt., *t.*, Tasmania, Australia; tin.

Bischofswerda, *t.*, Dresden, E. Germany; quarrying, glass and iron inds.; rly. ctr.; p. (1963) 11,285.

Bishop, *t.*, Cal., U.S.A.; cattle, tungsten; p. (1960) 2,875.

Bishop Auckland, *urb. dist.*, Durham, Eng.; contains palace of Bishop of Durham: coal, iron, light engin.; p. (estd. 1967) 34,650.

Bishop Rock, *isolated rock, lighthouse*, Scilly Is., 36 m. S.W. of Land's End, Cornwall; recognised internationally as E. end of trans-Atlantic ocean crossing.

Bishop's Stortford, *mkt. t., urb. dist.*, Herts., Eng.; on Stort R.; grain; p. (estd. 1967) 21,010.

Bishop's Waltham, *par.*, Hants, Eng.; bricks.

Bishop Wearmouth, *t.*, pt. of Sunderland, Co. Durham.

Biskra, *c.*, Algeria, N. Africa; admin. ctr., winter resort; oasis nearby produces dates; p. *c.* 53,000.

Bisley, *t.*, Gloucester, Eng.; nr. Stroud.

Bismarck, *cap. c.*, N. Dakota, U.S.A.; on Missouri R.; p. (1960) 27,670.

Bismarck Arch., 3 large and several small islands off New Guinea, formerly German, now Australian Trust Terr.; total native p. (estd. 1962) 174,115.

Bissagos Is., off W. Africa, Port Guinea; ch. *t.* Bolama.

Bissao, *t.*, *spt.*, Port Guinea; p. 5,000.

Bistrita, *t.*, Romania; p. (1963) 23,346.

Bitetto, *t.*, *sm. spt.*, Apulia, Italy; on E. cst. 5. m. N.W. of Bari; fishing; p. 5,991.

Bitlis, *I.*, Turkey; p. (1945) 74,449.

Bitlis, *t.*, Turkey; minerals, Armenian massacre; p. (1960) 16,562.

Bitolj (Monastir), *t.*, Macedonia, Jugoslavia; many mosques, military H.Q., great tr. in corn, grain, flour, hides and woollen stuffs; tanning, carpets; p. (1959) 43,000.

Bitonto, *t.*, Apulia, on E. cst. 7 m. N.W. of Bari; Italy; olive oil, wine; fine cath.; p. 29,731.

Bitterfeld, *t.*, Halle, E. Germany; lignite mining; engin., chemicals; p. (1963) 30,900.

Bitterfontein, *t.*, Cape Province, S. Africa.

Bitter Lakes, Isthmus of Suez, U.A.R., utilised by Suez Canal.

Bitterroot, *mtns.*, U.S.A.; range of the Rockies, highest point Ajax Mtn., 10,900 ft.; rly. tunnel 2 m. long.

Bitton, *t.*, Gloucester, Eng.; mining.

Biwa, *L.*, Japan; a. 180 sq. m.; 330 ft. above sea-level; 300 ft. deep; connected by canal with Osaka.

Biyala, *t.*, Gharbiya prov.; Lower U.A.R.; N.E. Africa; rice, millet, cotton; p. (1947) 17,731.

Biysk, *t.*, W. Siberia, R.S.F.S.R.; engin., textiles; p. (1959) 146,000.

Bizerta, *spt.*, Tunisia, N. Africa; international dockyard; the ancient Hippo Zaritus; fishing; oil refining; steelwks, tyres; p. (1956) 46,681

Bizot, *commune*, N.E. Algeria; p. 10,845.

Bjelovar, *t.*, Croatia, Jugoslavia; p. (1959) 12,000.

Björnborg, *see* Pori.

Blaauw B. Mtns., Transvaal, S. Africa.

Blaavands Huk, Denmark; nr. Esbjerg.

Black Belt, *area* on coastlands of Miss. and Ala., U.S.A.; black soil prairie land, good for cotton.

Black Bluff, *mtn.*, N. Tasmania, Australia.

Blackburn, *co. bor.*, Lancs, Eng.; textiles, engin., light inds.; p. (estd. 1967) 100,910.

Black Country, Eng., Midlands; formerly impt. iron-working and coal-mining district round the Birmingham area.

Blackdown Hills, Devon, Eng.

Black Forest (Schwarzwald), *mtns.*, Germany; resort, forests, a. 1,844 sq. m.; highest peak Feldberg, alt. 4,696 ft.

Black Gang Chine, picturesque ravine on S. Coast, Isle of Wight, Eng.

Black Hawk, *mining t.*, Rocky Mtns., Colorado, U.S.A.

Black Head, *O.*, Galway Bay, Clare, Ireland.

Blackhead, *O.*, on N. entrance to Belfast Lough, N. Ireland; lighthouse.

Blackheath, *open common*, S.E. London, Eng.; a. 267 acres.

Black Hills, *mtns.*, between S.D. and Wyo., U.S.A.; highest, Horney Peak, alt. 7,240 ft.

Black Isle, *peninsula*, between Cromarty and Beauly Firths, Ross and Cromarty, Scot.; agr., fisheries, quarrying; a. 240 sq. m.

Black Lake, *t.*, S. Quebec, Canada; asbestos mines; p. (1961) 4,180.

Blackley, *t.*, S.W. Lancs, Eng.; N. sub. of Manchester; dye wks.

Black Mountain, *t.*, N.C., U.S.A.; resort.

Black Mtns., range of Appalachians, U.S.A.; Mt. Mitchell, alt. 6,684 ft.

Black Mtns., *range*, Brecknock, S. Wales; highest peak, Brecknock Van, alt. 2,631 ft.

Blackpool, *co. bor.*, seaside resort, Lancs, Eng. on cst. of Fylde dist.; p. (estd. 1967) 151,510.

Black Prairie, *region*, Texas, U.S.A.; extends 350 m. S.W. from Ouachita Mtns. to Austin; contains very fertile Black Waxy and Grande Prairie sub-regions devoted almost entirely to cotton growing; ch. ts., Dallas, Fort Worth, Austin; a. 30,000 sq. m.

Black River Falls, *t.*, Wis., U.S.A.; lumber, flour, dairying, poultry; p. (1960) 3,195.

Blackrock, *t.*, Ireland; sub. 4 m. from Dublin.

Blackrod, *urb. dist.*, Lancs, Eng.; nr. Chorley; weaving; p. (1961) 3,609.

Black Sea, *inland sea* between Russia and Turkey; 740 m. long, 390 m, broad; receives waters of Danube, Dnieper, Dniester, Don, Bug and other rivers; communicates with Mediterranean by Strait of Bosporus, Sea of Marmara and Dardanelles.

Blacksod Bay, coast of Mayo, Ireland.

Blackstone, *t.*, Mass., U.S.A.; textiles; p. (1950) 4,968.

Blackstone, *t.*, Va., U.S.A.; tobacco mkt.; p. (1960) 3,659.

Black Volta, *R.*, Upper Volta and Ghana; rises in Futa Jallon Plateau, flows E., S. and E. into R. Volta; length, over 800 m.

Black Warrior, *R.*, Ala., U.S.A.; flows through coalfields; navigable; water power.

Blackwater, *R.*, Hants and Essex, Eng.

Blackwater, *R.*, Ireland; three of this name.

Blackwater, *R.*, U.S.A. (Mont., Fla., and Va.).

Black Waxy, *see* Black Prairie.

Blackwell, *c.*, Okla., U.S.A.; gas, oil, wells, refining, zinc smelting; meat packing; p. (1960) 9,588.

Blaenau Ffestiniog, *see* Ffestiniog.

Blaenavon, *t.*, *urb. dist.*, Monmouth, Eng.; mining; p. (1961) 8,424.

Blagoevgrad, *t.*, formerly Gorna Dzhumaya, ch. *t.* Bulgarian Macedonia; p. (1956) 21,833.

Blagoveshchensk, *t.*, E. Siberia, R.S.F.S.R. on R. Amur; wat. p.; engin., sawmilling; p. (1967) 118,000.

Blair Atholl, *par.*, Perth, Scot.; tourist resort; p. (1951) 1,868.

Blairgowrie and Rattray, *burgh*, Perth, Scot.; at foot of Scot. Highlands, 18 m. N.E. of Perth; fruit; linen; agr. machin., canning inds.; p. (1961) 5,168.

Blairmore, *t.*, Alberta, W. Canada; on Canadian Pacific Rly., 160 m. S.W. of Medicine Hat, at approach to Crow's Nest Pass; coal-mining ctr. on Alberta Coalfield; p. (1961) 1,930.

Blairsville, *t.*, Penns., U.S.A.; p. (1960) 4,530.

Blakely, *t.*, Ga., U.S.A.; peanuts, lumber, turpentine; p. (1960) 3,580.

Blanc-Mesnil (Le), *t.*, Seine-et-Oise, France; p. (1954) 25,363.

Blanc, Mt., France; highest peak of Alps; alt. 15,782 ft.

Blanca Pk., Col., U.S.A.; alt. 14,390 ft.

Blanche Bay, on N.E. coast of New Britain, Bismarck Arch.; inner part site of Rabaul.

Blanchester, *t.*, Ohio, U.S.A.; textiles, pumps; p. (1960) 2,944.

Blanco, *t.*, Cape Province, S. Africa.

Blandford, or Blandford Forum, *mkt. t., mun. bor.*, Dorset, Eng.; lime and stone, agr. implements; p. (estd. 1967) 3,640.

Blanes, *spt.*, Spain; N.E. of Barcelona; holiday resort; p. (1957) 7,039.

Blankenberge, *spt.*, N. Belgium; seaside resort; p. (1962) 10,252.

Blantyre, *c.*, Malawi; in Shire Highlands; linked by rail to Beira; comm. ctr.; tobacco; p. (1966) 109,795.

Blantyre, *par.*, Lanark, Scot.; birthplace of Dr. Livingstone; aero engines; p. (1951) 17,766.

Blarney, *vil.*, 4 m. N.W. Cork, Ireland; cas. and Blarney stone; woollen mftg.

Blaydon, *urb. dist.*, Durham, Eng.; coal-mining; p. (estd. 1967) *31,880.*

Blekinge, *co.*, Sweden; a. 1,173 sq. m.; p. (1961) *144,468.*

Blenheim, *t.*, S.I., New Zealand; fruit; p. (1961) *11,942.*

Bletchley, *urb. dist.*, Bucks, Eng.; rly. junction, bricks, brushes; p. (estd. 1967) *24,980.*

Blida, *t.*, Algeria, N. Africa; flour, citrus fruits; p. (1954) *67,000.*

Bloemfontein, *t.*, *cap.*, O.F.S., S. Africa; cattle ctr.; engin., glass, bricks, meat canning; p. (1960) *140,924* inc. *61,213* Whites.

Blois, *c.*, Loire-et-Cher, France; on Loire; 30 m. S.W. of Orleans; château; wines; p. (1962) *36,426.*

Blood R., Natal, S. Africa.

Bloody-Foreland, *C.*, Donegal, N.W. Ireland.

Bloomfield, *t.*, Ind., U.S.A.; p. (1960) *2,224.*

Bloomfield, *t.*, N.J., U.S.A.; p. (1960) *51,867.*

Bloomington, *t.*, Ill., U.S.A.; coal, motor cars; p. (1960) *36,271.*

Bloomington, *t.*, Ind., U.S.A.; wheat, corn, alfalfa; furniture, structural glass, radios; p. (1960) *31,357.*

Bloomsburg, *t.*, Penns., U.S.A.; iron; p. (1960) *10,655.*

Blorca, *t.*, Java, Indonesia; teak; p. *18,451.*

Bludenz, *t.*, Austria; cotton, watches; p. (1961) *11,127.*

Bluefield, *t.*, W. Va., U.S.A.; coal, iron, limestone, steel foundries, silica, lumber; p. (1960) *19,256.*

Bluefields, *R.* in Nicaragua, Central America.

Bluefields, *t.*, Nicaragua; on E. cst.; bananas, timber; p. (1960) *11,376.*

Blue Grass, *dist.*, Ky., U.S.A., area where blue grass abundant; horse breeding.

Blue Mountains, chain in N.S.W., Australia; highest peak, 4,100 ft.

Blue Mountains, *t.*, N.S.W., Australia; tourist centre; p. (1961) *28,070.*

Blue Mountains, Jamaica, W. Indies.

Blue Nile (Bahr-el-Azrek), *R.*, rising in tablelands of Ethiopia, joins the White Nile at Khartoum; its seasonal flooding provides the bulk of water for irrigation in Sudan and U.A.R.

Blue Nile, *prov.*, Sudan; a. 54,577 sq. m.; cap. Wad Medani (*q.v.*); p. (estd. 1951) *1,840,600.*

Blue Point, Long I., U.S.A.; oysters.

Blue Ridge Mtns., U.S.A.; most E. ridge of Appalachian Mtns. in Virginia and North Carolina.

Bluff Harbour, S.I., New Zealand; 18 m. from Invercargill; spt. for Southland prov.

Bluffton, *t.*, Ind., U.S.A.; farm implements, lumber; p. (1960) *6,238.*

Blumenau, *t.*, Brazil; butter, sugar; p. (1960) *46,591*

Blyth, *spt. mun. bor.*, Northumberland, Eng.; exp. coal; shipbldg.; p. (estd. 1967) *36,120.*

Blytheville, *t.*, Ark., U.S.A.; tr. ctr. for agr. region; p. (1960) *20,797.*

Blythswood, *t.*, Cape Province, S. Africa.

Bo, *t.*, Sierra Leone, W. Africa; second lgst. t. in cty.; gold; adm. hdqtrs.; p. (1963) of dist. *209,000.*

Bobadilla, *t.*, S. Spain; N. of Málaga.

Bobbili, *t.*, Andhra Pradesh, India; tr. ctr. in agr. a.; p. (1961) *25,592.*

Bobbio, *t.*, Emilia-Rogmagna, Italy, in northern Apennines; ctr. European cultural life, 9th–12th cent.; St. Columban founded monastery, 612.

Bobigny, *t.*, Seine, France; p. (1954) *18,521.*

Bobrawa, *R.*, Lower Silesia; W. Poland; trib. of R. Oder; length 158 m.

Bobrek Karb, *t.*, Silesia, Poland; German before 1945; coal, coke, steel, ammonia; p. (1939) *22,095.*

Bobrinets, *t.*, Ukrainian S.S.R.; tobacco factories; p. *10,000.*

Bobruisk, *fortress*, *t.*, Byelorussian S.S.R., on R. Berezina; engin., sawmilling; p. (1967) *117,000.*

Bocas del Toro, *prov.*, Panama; cap. B. del T.; p. (1960) *32,600.*

Bochetta, La, *pass*, Liguria, Italy; used by main routes across Ligurian Apennines from Genoa to Lombardy Plain.

Bocholt, *t.*, N. Rhine–Westphalia, Germany; machin., textiles, elect. goods; p. (1963) *46,100.*

Bochum, *t.*, N. Rhine–Westphalia, Germany; 11 m.

M (78th Ed.)

W. of Dortmund; ctr. of steel ind.; coal and iron, chemicals, foodstuffs; p. (1963) *361,100.*

Bockum-Hövel, *t.*, N. Rhine–Westphalia, Germany; N.W. of Hamm; coal-mining; p. (1963) *24,700.*

Bodaïbo, *t.*, R.S.F.S.R.; N.E. of L. Baikal; gold, engin.; p. (1956) *14,600.*

Bodega Bay, Cal., U.S.A.; 20 m. W. of Santa Rosa; nuclear power sta.

Bodele, *area*, Chad, W. Africa; cotton, tobacco, forage grasses.

Boden, *t.*, Sweden; on Lulea R.; mil. ctr.; comm. ctr.; p. (1961) *13,719.*

Bodensee, *see* Constance, L.

Bodmin, *mun. bor.*, *co. t.*, Cornwall, Eng.; on S.W. flank of Bodmin Moor; china clay, lt. engin.; p. (estd. 1967) *7,370.*

Bodmin Moor, *upland*, N.E. Cornwall, Eng.; granite quarries, kaolin; lower slopes cultivated, higher slopes used for sheep pastures; average alt. 1,000 ft., highest point, Brown Willy, alt. 1,375 ft.

Bodö, *spt.*, Norway; within Arctic Circle at entrance to Salten Fjord, fishing, woollen goods; p. (1961) *12,445.*

Boeleleng, *spt.*, Bali, Indonesia; rice; harbour unsafe during monsoon.     [*114,474.*

Boeotia, *prov.*, Greece; a. 1221 sq. m.; p. (1961)

Bogalusa, *t.*, La., U.S.A.; p. (1960) *21,423.*

Bognor Regis, *t.*, *urb. dist.*, Sussex, Eng.; seaside resort; p. (estd. 1967) *30,840.*

Bogor, *t.*, Java, Indonesia; p. (1961) *154,092.*

Bogotá, *cap.*, Columbia, S. America in E. Cordilleras, 9,000 ft. above sea level; cath., museum, univ.; textiles, cement and brick mkg., leather, glassware, tyres, oil refining; p. (estd. 1965) *1,488,000.*

Bogovodsk, *see* Noginsk.

Bohemia, former W. prov. of Czechoslovakia; abolished 1948; plateau girdled by mountains, drained by R. Elbe; agr.; wheat, rye, hops, flax, sugar-beet; minerals; lignite, graphite; mnfs. textiles, sugar, pottery, machin., boots; p. inc. Moravia (1962) *9,566,753.*

Böhmerwald (Bohemian Forest) Mtns., forested range between Czechoslovakia and Bavaria; 150 m. long; highest points; Aber, alt. 4,848 ft., Rachelberg, alt. 4,743 ft.

Bohol, *I.*, Philippines; 1,492 sq. m.; p. (1960) *529,200.*

Boiro, *commune*, La Coruña, Spain; cattle, fishing, sardine canning; p. *11,663.*

Bois-Colombes, *t.*, Seine, France; p. (1954) *27,899.*

Boise City, *t.*, *cap.*, Idaho, U.S.A.; silver, hot springs; p. (1960) *34,481.*

Boise, *R.*, Idaho, U.S.A.

Bojador, *C.*, Rio de Oro, Africa.

Bokaro, *t.*, Bihar, India; 150 m. N.W. of Calcutta; steel plant.

Bokn Fjord, Norway; N. of Stavanger, 35 m. long, 10–15 m. wide.

Boksburg, *t.*, Transvaal, S. Africa; gold, coal; p. (1960) *70,933* inc. *27,806* whites.

Bolama, *spt.*, Port. Guinea; p. *4,000.*

Bolan Pass, Baluchistan, Pakistan; pass from Pakistan to Afghanistan; summit 5,900 ft.

Bolbec, *t.*, Seine-Maritime, France; 12 m. E. of Le Havre; p. (1962) *12,492.*     [*22,760.*

Boldon, *urb. dist.*, Durham, Eng.; p. (estd. 1967)

Boleslawiec (Bunzlau), *t.*, Lower Silesia, Poland, German before 1945; on the Bobrawa R., pottery; p. (1965) *27,000.*

Bolgrad, *t.*, Ukrainian S.S.R.; corn; p. *10,000.*

Bolivar, *t.*, Argentina; p. (1947) *13,773.*

Bolivar, *dep.*, Colombia, S. America, cap. Cartagena; a. 22,981 sq. m.; p. (estd. 1959) *780,650.*

Bolivar, *prov.*, Ecuador, S. America; cap. Guarando; a. 1,150 sq. m.; p. (1950) *109,305.*

Bolivar, *st.*, Venezuela; on L., Ciudad Bolivar; a. 91,868 sq. m.; p. (1961) *213,543.*

Bolivia, *inland rep.*, S. America, bounded by Brazil, Paraguay, Argentina, Chile and Peru; cap. nominally Sucre, actual administrative H.Q. La Paz; plateau, mountains; Boliv. Andes; volcanoes; L. Titicaca, Poopo, drained by tribs. of Amazon; climate varies with elevation; monkeys, jaguars; forests; savannahs; agr. in backward condition; rubber, quinine, cattle, hides; ch. exp. tin; petroleum; lead and zinc at Matilde; language, Spanish; a. 514,155 sq. m.; p. (1965) *3,668,000.*

Bolkhov, *t.*, Ukrainian S.S.R. monastery; impt. inds.; p. *10,000.*

Bollington, *t.*, *urb. dist.*, Cheshire, Eng.; nr.

Macclesfield, cotton, calico printing and dye wks.; p. (1961) *5,642*.

Bolobo, *t.*, Congo, Africa, on R. Congo.

Bologna, *ancient c.*, Emilia, N. Italy; on N. flank of Apennines; impt. route ctr. commanding road (over Futa Pass) and rly. (through Apennine Tunnel) across Apennines to Florence; mnfs. sugar, macaroni; nuclear research ctr.; p. (1965) *481,000*.

Bologna, *prov.*, Italy; a. 1,465 sq. m.; p. (1961) *848,440*.

Bologoye, *t.*, R.S.F.S.R.; depot and impt. junction on the Leningrad and Moscow Rly.; p. *10,000*.

Bolonchen, *t.*, Campeche, Mexico.

Bololondron, *mun. t.*, Matanzas, W. Cuba; p. (estd.) (of mun.) *11,823* (of t.) *3,710*.

Bolsa Island, Cal., U.S.A.; nuclear power and desalination project in progress.

Bolsena, *L.*, Latium region, Italy; occupies lge. extinct volcanic crater in S. of Tuscan Hills; a. (approx.) 50 sq. m.

Bolshoya Volga, *t.*, R.S.F.S.R.; 80 m. N. of Moscow, at junct. of Volga and Moscow Volga Canal; Soviet Institute of Nuclear Studies.

Bolsover, *urb. dist.*, Derby, Eng.; limestone, coal, textiles; p. (1961) *11,770*.

Bolsward, *c.*, Friesland, Netherlands; dairying, linseed, bricks; p. (1947) *7,389*.

Bolt Hd., *headland*, Devon, Eng.; alt. 430 ft.

Bolton, *co. bor.*, Lancs, Eng.; cotton, iron, coal, chemicals; p. (estd. 1967) *156,400*.  [abbey

Bolton, Abbey, W.R. Yorks, Eng.; famous ruined

Bolu, *t.*, Turkey; in ancient state of Bithynia; at Hija, S. of the t., are warm medicinal springs; p. (1960) *13,743*.

Bolus Head, *O.*, Kerry, Ireland.

Bolzano, *t.*, Venetia Tridentina, Italy; on R. Isarco at S. approach to Brenner Pass; resort; p. (1961) *89,070*.

Boma, *t.*, Congo, Africa, on Congo estuary; exports timber, cocoa, palm prods., bananas; p. *c. 32,000*.  [Bothnia.

Bomarsund, *strait*, Ahvenanmaa Is., Gulf of

Bombay, *former st.*, India; divided into sts. of Maharashtra and Gujarat 1 May 1960.

Bombay, Greater, *spt., cap.* Maharashtra, India; harbour, docks, rly. ctr.; univ.; greatest cotton ctr. in India; pt. handles nearly half of cty's foreign tr.; p. (1961) *4,152,056*.

Bomnak, *t.*, Chita Region, U.S.S.R.; on S. slopes of Stanovoi Mtns., in valley of R. Zeya; centre of alluvial gold workings.

Bonaca I., Honduras, Central America; in Caribbean Sea.

Bonaire I., Netherlands W. Indies; off N. cst. of Venezuela; goat rearing; scantily populated.

Bonavista Bay, Newfoundland, Canada.

Bonduku, *t.*, E. Ivory Cst., nr. Ghana; impt. trading sta.

Bondy, *commune*, France; N.E. sub. of Paris; brewing, chemicals; p. (1954) *22,411*.

Bône, *see* Annaba.

Bo'ness, *spt., burgh*, W. Lothian, Scot.; on Firth of Forth, 4 m. E. of Grangemouth; mng., quarrying, distilling, marine engin., iron-founding, fertilisers, chemicals; p. (1961) *10,194*.

Bonham, *t.*, Texas, U.S.A.; cotton; p. (1960) *7,357*.

Bonhill, *par.*, Dunbarton, Scot.; dyeing; p. (1951) *16,338*.

Bonifacio, *spt., fort.*, Corsica, France; opposite Sardinia, on Strait of Bonifacio; cork, olive-oil, oyster tr.; p. (1954) *2,157*.

Bonin Is., Pac. Oc., Japan; 15 islands, volcanic; 600 m. S. of Tokyo.

Bonn, *t.*, federal cap. W. Germany; at confluence of Rs. Sieg and Rhine; univ.; seat of W. German parliament; birthplace of Beethoven; metal, paper and elect. goods; p. (1963) *143,700*.

Bonne Terre, *c.*, E. Mo., U.S.A.; lead mines; p. (1960) *3,219*.

Bonneville Dam, Ore., Wash., U.S.A.; across R. Columbia 40 m. above Portland (Ore.); provides irrigation to valleys in Columbia–Snake Plateau; lge. hydro-electric power-sta.; locks permit navigation from Portland up middle courses of Columbia and Snake Rs.

Bonneville Salt Flats, Utah, U.S.A.; remains of ancient lake; world automobile speed tests, 1937–47.

Bonny, *t.*, S. Nigeria, W. Africa; at mouth of R. Bonny, Bight of Biafra; oil terminal.

Bonnyrigg and Lasswade, *burgh*, Midlothian Scot.; 7 m. S.E. of Edinburgh; paper, carpets; p. (1961) *6,331*.

Bonthe, *t.*, Sierra Leone, W. Africa; rutile production; p. (1963) of dist. *80,000*.

Boom, *t.*, Antwerp, Belgium; bricks, tanning, brewing; p. (1962) *17,431*.

Boone, *t.*, Iowa, U.S.A.; coal; p. (1960) *12,468*.

Booneville, *c.*, W. Ark., U.S.A.; lumber and cotton mills; tuberculosis sanatorium; p. (1960) *2,690*.

Boonton, *t.*, N.J., U.S.A.; agr. and industl. ctr.; p. (1960) *7,981*.

Boothia, *peninsula* (a. 13,100 sq. m.) and G. on Arctic coast; Franklin dist. Canada.

Bootle, *co. bor.*, Lancs, Eng.; on E. side of entrance to Mersey estuary; shipping, engin., timber, flour; p. (estd. 1967) *81,290*.

Boppard, *t.*, Rhineland Palatinate, Germany; p. (1946) *7,189*.

Borås, *t.*, S. Sweden; on R. Wiske, nr. Göteborg; cotton spinning and weaving textiles, hosiery, tyres; p. (1961) *67,069*.

Bordeaux, *spt.*, Gironde, France; nr. mouth of R. Garonne; cath., univ.; exp. wines, liqueurs, sugar, potatoes, pit props; oil refining nearby; p. (1962) *254,122*.

Bordentown, *c.*, N.J., U.S.A.; on Delaware R.; formerly impt. pt.; p. (1960) *4,974*.

Bordeyri, *t.*, Iceland; on Rumaflot inlet.

Bordighera, *t.*, Italy; Riviera winter resort.

Boreham Wood, *t.*, Herts, Eng.; light engin., computors, film studios.

Borger, *c.*, N.W. Texas, U.S.A.; gas and petroleum; p. (1960) *20,911*.

Borgerhout, sub. of Antwerp, Belgium; candle and tobacco factories; p. (1962) *51,115*.

Borgo, San Donnino, *t.*, Italy; cath.; p. *17,154*.

Borgo, San Lorenzo, *t.*, Italy; olives and wine.

Borgosesia, *commune*, N.W. Italy; on Sesia R.; textiles; p. *13,716*.

Borgo Val di Taro, *commune*, N. Italy; lignite; p. *15,209*.

Borinage, *dist.* round Mons, Belgium; coal.

Borislav, *c.*, Ukrainian S.S.R., formerly Polish; oilfield, natural gas, engin.; p. (1956) *29,600*.

Borisoglebsk, *t.*, R.S.F.S.R.; p. (1959) *54,000*.

Borisokova, *t.*, Kursk, U.S.S.R.; metals.

Borisov, *t.*, Byelorussian S.S.R.; scene of defeat of Napoleon, 1812; chemicals, saw mills, hardware; p. (1959) *59,000*.

Borispool, *t.*, Ukrainian S.S.R.; p. *25,000*.

Borlänge, *t.*, Sweden; iron, paper, engin. and chemical wks.; p. (1961) *26,685*.

Bormio, *vil.*, Lombardy, Italy; alpine resort; mineral springs; p. *1,910*.

Borna, *t.*, Leipzig, E. Germany; lignite, machin.; p. (1963) *19,331*.

Bornem, *t.*, Antwerp, Belgium; chemicals, elec. goods; p. (1961) *9,896*.

Borneo, lgst. island Malay Arch.; a. 285,000 sq. m., length 830 m., breadth 600 m.; Kinibalu Range, alt. 13,700 ft.; forests, jungle, swamps; rice, sago, spices, coconuts, rubber, hardwood; politically divided into Indonesian Borneo (Kalimantan) and Sabah.

Borneo, N., part of Fed. of Malaysia, *see* Sabah.

Bornholm, Danish I., Baltic; a. 210 sq. m.; agr.; fishing; porcelain, clay; cap. Rönne; p. (1960) *48,373*.

Bornu, *cty.*, Nigeria, Africa; S.W. Lake Chad; formerly a Negro kingdom, 51,000 sq. m.; p. (estd.) *5,000,000*.

Boroboedoer, Java, Indonesia; gr. Buddhist temple, once ruined, now restored under government care.

Boronga Is., in Bay of Bengal.

Borongan, *t.*, Philippine Is.; on cst., 36 m. E. of Catbalogan; coconut plantations; p. (estd.) *21,340*.

Borovichi, *t.*, R.S.F.S.R.; on Msta R., 160 m. S.E. of Leningrad; p. (estd.) *23,500*.

Borrolooia, N. Terr., Australia; sheep.

Borromean Is., four sm. islets in L. Maggiore; inci. Isola Bella, site of Stresa Conf., 1935.

Borrowdale, *valley*, Cumberland, Eng.; tourist resort; blacklead mines.

Borthwick, *par.*, Midlothian, Scot.; with old cas.; p. (1951) *3,163*.

Borzhom, *wat. pl.*, Georgian S.S.R.; hot mineral springs; p. (1959) *15,600*.

Boscastle, *sm. spt.*, Cornwall, Eng.; resort; pilchard fishing.

Bosham, *vil.*, Sussex, Eng.; 4 m. W. of Chichester; court of King Canute and Roman Emperor Vespasian; Saxon church; resort, yachting, fishing.

Boskoop, *vil.*, S. Holland, Netherlands; flowering-shrub nurseries; p. (1967) *10,641.*

Bosnia and Hercegovino, *fed. unit,* Jugoslavia; formerly part of Austria; cap. Sarajevo; mountainous, forested, fertile valleys; agr.; tobacco, cereals, fruit; cattle, sheep pigs; a. 19,768 sq. m.; p. (1960) *3,377,000.*

Bosporus or Strait of Constantinople, between Black Sea and Sea of Marmara.

Bossier City, *t.,* La., U.S.A.; p. (1960) *32,776.*

Boston, *t., mun. bor., spt.,* Holland, Lincs, Eng.; on R. Witham, 4 m. from the Wash; shipping, agr. mkt., timber, fruit and vegetable canning; p. (estd. 1967) *24,990.*

Boston, *spt. c., cap.* Mass., U.S.A.; univ., museum; fine harbour; 2nd Atlantic pt.; comm. fisheries; metal, leather, rubber and elec. goods, textiles, shoes; rly. ctr.; p. (1960) *697,197.*

Bosworth or Market Bosworth, *t., rural dist.,* Leics., Eng.; battle between Richard III and Henry VII, 1485; p. (rural dist. 1961) *27,493.*

Botany Bay, N.S.W., Australia; on E. cst., 10 m. S. of Sydney; resort; first settled by British in 1787; old penal colony.

Bothnia, G. of, N. of Baltic; between Finland and Sweden, breadth about 100 m.

Bothwell, *par.,* Lanark, Scot.; coal, iron; p. (1951) *63,185.*

Botosani, *t.,* N. Moldavia, Romania; rich pastoral cty.; flour milling, tanning; p. (1963) *47,319.*

Botswana, Rep. of, *indep. sov. st.* within Brit. Commonwealth (Sept. 1966), S.W. Africa; stretches from Orange R. to Zambesi R., and merges W. into Kalahari desert; Bamangwato ch. tribe; cap. Gaberones; cattle-rearing; lge. potential copper and nickel ores; a. 222,000 sq. m.; p. (estd. 1965) *548,000.*

Bottrop, *t.,* N. Rhine–Westphalia, Germany; N.W. of Essen; coal, coke, chemicals; p. (1963) *112,000.*

Botucatu, *t.,* Brazil; p. (1960) *33,878.*

Bouches-du-Rhône, *dep.,* S. France; cap. Marseilles; cereals, olives, vines; pottery, silk; a. 2,035 sq. m.; p. (1962) *1,248,355.*

Bougainville I., Solomon Is., Pac. Oc.; a. 4,100 sq. m.; p (1959) *53,130.* [Australia.

Bougainville, *O.,* jutting into Timor Sea, W.

Bougie, *see* Bejaia.

Bouillon, *t.,* Ardennes, Belgium; p. (1962) *3,042.*

Boulder, *t.,* West Australia; incl. in Kalgoorlie mun.; p. (1966) *19,892* (joint p.).

Boulder, *t., Col.,* U.S.A.; gold- and silver-mining dist.; univ.; p. (1960) *37,718.*

Boulder City, *t.,* Nevada, U.S.A.; nr. Great Boulder Dam, gr. engin. project; p. (1960) *4,059.*

Boulogne-Billancourt, S.W. sub. of Paris, France; p. (1962) *107,074.*

Boulogne-sur-Mer, *spt.,* Pas de Calais, France; resort; fishing; cement; chocolates; channel ferry; p. (1962) *50,036.*

Boundary, *t.,* Yukon, Canada.

Bound Brook, *bor.,* N.J., U.S.A.; paints, chemicals, asbestos, clothing; p. (1960) *10,263.*

Bountiful, *t.,* Utah, U.S.A.; mkt. gardens, fruit, especially cherries; irrigation necessary; p. (1960) *17,039.*

Bounty I., New Zealand, S. Pac. Oc.

Bourbonnais, *old prov.,* France.

Bourbonne-es-Bains, *t.,* France; mineral springs.

Bourg-en-Bresse, *t., cap.,* Ain dep., France; copper goods, pottery; p. (1962) *35,640.*

Bourges, *t., cap.,* Cher dep., France; cath.; brewing, cutlery, machin., aircraft; p. (1962) *63,479.*

Bourget, L., Savoy, France.

Bourg-la-Reine, *t.,* Seine, France; p. (1962) *17,908.*

Bourg-Madame, *vil.,* France; on Franco-Spanish border; international bridge.

Bourgoin, *t.,* Isère, France; industl.

Bourke, *t.,* N.S.W., Australia; on R. Darling nr. head of intermittent navigation, terminus of rly. running inland from Sydney and Newcastle; collects wool from sheep farms and despatches by R. to Adelaide (S. Australia) and by rail to Sydney; p. (1947) *2,205.*

Bourne, *urb. dist.,* Kesteven, Lincs., Eng.; agr. machin., manures, malting, seed growing; B.R.M. car mftg.; p. (1961) *5,339.*

Bournemouth, *co. bor.,* Hants, Eng.; on S. cst.,

E. of Poole Harbour; seaside resort; p. (estd. 1967) *150,000.*

Bournville, *model industl. t.,* Warwick., Eng.; 4 m. S.W. of Birmingham; initiated by Mr. Geo. Cadbury; chocolate and cocoa wks.

Bourtange, *t.,* Netherlands; nr. German frontier.

Boussu, *commune,* Belgium; coal, industl.; p. (1962) *11,488.*

Bouvet I., uninhabited island in S. Atlantic belonging to Norway, a. about 22 sq. m.

Boves, *t.,* Sommes dep., France; S.E. Amiens.

Bovino, *t.,* Apulia Italy.

Bow, *par.,* E. London, Eng.; industl.; properly Stratford-at-Bow.

Bow, *R.,* Alberta, N.W. Canada; head of Saskatchewan R.

Bow Fell, *mtn.,* W. Cumberland, at head of Borrowdale, 4 m. N.W. of Wast Water, alt. 2,960 ft.

Bowden, *urb. dist.,* Cheshire, Eng.; p. (1961) *4,478.*

Bowen, *spt.,* N. Queensland; on Port Denison, 725 m. N.W. of Brisbane; meat wks.; coke plant; p. (1966) *5,134.*

Bowes, *t.,* W.R., Yorks, Eng.; on R. Greta S.W. of Barnard Castle; mkt. t. for Stainmore dist. of Pennines.

Bowesdorp, *t.,* Cape Prov., S. Africa.

Bowie, *t.,* N. Texas, U.S.A.; oil, gas, coal, clay mining; p. (1960) *4,566.*

Bowland Fells, W. offshoot of mid-Pennines, W.R. Yorks., between Rs. Lune and Ribble; mountain limestone and millstone grit.

Bowland, Forest of, *hills,* Lancs, Eng.; millstone grit moors; many reservoirs supply water to industl. S. Lancs.

Bowling, *vil.,* Dumbarton, Scot.; on N. bank of R. Clyde, 10 m. N.W. of Glasgow; large oil refinery

Bowling Green, *t.,* Ky., U.S.A.; tr. ctr. for agr. a.; limestone; p. (1960) *28,338.* [7,397.

Bowmanville, *pt.* L. Ontario, Canada; p. (1961)

Bowness, *t.,* Westmorland, Eng.; on L. Windermere; tourist ctr.

Bowness, *par.,* Cumberland, Eng.; p. *1,050.*

Box Hill, nr. Dorking, Surrey, Eng.; E. of R. Mole gap through N. Downs; chalk; wooded, fine views.

Boyacá, *dep.,* Colombia, S. America; cap. Tunja; a. 24,928 sq. m.; p. (1962) *849,390.*

Boyle, *mkt. t.,* Roscommon, Ireland; on R. Boyle; dairying; p. (1966) *1,789.*

Boyne, *R.,* Leinster, Ireland; length 80 m.

Bozrah, *ancient c.,* S. Damascus, Syria, S.W. Asia; modern Busra; many arch. remains.

Bra, *t.,* Piedmont, Italy; 28 m. S. of Turin.

Brabant, *cent. prov.,* Belgium; fertile and wooded; many breweries; mnfs. linen, cloth, paper, lace; cap. Brussels (*q.v.*); a. 1,267 sq. m.; p. (1962) *2,011,842.*

Brabant, North, *prov.,* Netherlands; S. of Gelderland; N. half of former Duchy; cattle rearing; gram. hops, beetroot, etc.; cap. 's-Hertogenbosch; a. 1920 sq. m.; p. (estd. 1960) *1,512,787.*

Brac, *I.,* Adriatic Sea, Jugoslavia.

Bracadale, *vil.* and *L.,* Skye. Scotland.

Brackley, *mun. bor.,* Northants, Eng.; p. (estd. 1967) *4,040.*

Bracknell, *t.,* Berkshire, Eng.; on Thames Valley terrace, 10 m. S. of Windsor; one of " New Towns " designated 1949 to relieve population congestion in London; extends N. and W. of old vil. of Bracknell; engin., sealing compounds, plastics; central weather forecast sta.; p. (estd. 1965) *25,448.*

Brackwede, *t.,* N. Rhine–Westphalia, Germany; S.W. of Bielefeld; iron and machin.; p. (1963) *26,300.*

Brad, *t.,* Romania, on R. Muresul; p. (1956) *9,963.*

Braddock, *t.,* Penns., U.S.A.; iron and steel; p. (1960) *12,337.*

Bradford, *t.,* Penns., U.S.A.; oil; p. (1966) *15,061.*

Bradford, *co. bor., c.,* W.R. Yorks. Eng.; 9 m. W. of Leeds; univ.; ctr. wool-textile inds.; engin., and chemical inds.; p. (estd. 1967) *296,860.*

Bradford-on-Avon, *t., urb. dist.,* Wilts. Eng.; on R. Avon on E. flank of Cotswolds; mnfs. rubber goods, elect. instruments; p. (1961) *5,757.*

Brading, *par.,* Isle of Wight, Eng.; commands gap through central chalk ridge.

Bradwell, *par.,* Essex, mouth of R. Blackwater; civil nuclear power-sta.; p. (1961) *1,116.*

Brady, *t.,* Texas, U.S.A.; p. (1960) *5,333.*

**Braemar,** *par.,* in the Grampians, Aberdeen, Scot.; containing Balmoral estate; p. (1951 with Crathie) *1,291.*

**Braeriach,** *mtn.,* Scot.; Inverness and Aberdeen; alt. 4,248 ft.

**Braga,** *prov.,* N. Portugal; fruit growing, cattle, textiles; p. (1963) *615,500.*

**Braga,** *c., cap.* B. prov., N. Portugal, nr. Oporto; cath; steel; p. (1960) *40,977.*

**Bragança,** *dist.,* Tras-os-Montes, Portugal; silk; p. (1960) *238,588.*

**Bragança,** *t.,* Portugal; mediæval cas.; p. (1960) *8,075.* [length 1,800 m.

**Brahmaputra,** *R.,* India, Tsangpo in Tibet;

**Braich-y-Pwll,** S.W. point of Caernarvon, Wales.

**Braila,** *t.,* Romania; on Danube, nr. Galati; grain ctr.; p. (1963) *123,132.*

**Braintree,** *t.,* Mass., U.S.A.; p. (1960) *31,069.*

**Braintree** and **Bocking,** *urb. dist.,* Essex, Eng.; on Blackwater; rayon mftg., metal windows, engin.; p. (estd. 1967) *22,310.*

**Brakpan,** *t.,* Transvaal, S. Africa; p. (1960) *73,788.*

**Brampton,** *par.,* Cumberland, Eng.; tweeds; p. (1951) *2,526.*

**Brampton,** *t.,* Ontario, Canada; flower growing ctr., tanning, timber; p. (1961) *18,467.*

**Brancaster,** *par.,* Norfolk, Eng.; p. *900.*

**Branco,** *C.,* Brazil, Pernambuco st.

**Brandenburg,** *see* Neubrandenburg.

**Brandenburg,** *t.,* Potsdam, E. Germany; on R. Havel; steel, tractors, bicycles, textiles, machin.; p. (1963) *89,243.*

**Brandon,** *t.,* Manitoba, Canada; p. (1961) *28,166.*

**Brandon** and **Byshottles,** *urb. dist.,* Durham, Eng.; coal-mining; p. (1961) *19,531.*

**Brandywine Creek,** *R.,* Penns, U.S.A.; Americans defeated by British, 1777.

**Branford,** *t.,* Conn., U.S.A.; light mnfs., fishing, oysters; resort; p. (1960) *16,567.*

**Brantford,** *c.,* Ontario, Canada; farm implements, cycles, bus and truck parts; p. (1961) *55,201.*

**Brasilia,** *new cap.,* Brazil, Goiás st.; inaugurated 21 April 1960; 600 m. N.W. Rio de Janeiro; designed for pop. 500,000; p. (1960) *141,742.*

**Brasov,** *t.,* Romania; at foot of Transylvanian Alps; cloth, leather; p. (1963) *228,299.*

**Brass,** *t.,* Nigeria, W. Africa; at mouth of Brass R.; trading settlement.

**Bratislava,** *t.,* ČSSR.; on R. Danube 30 m. below Vienna; univ.; 2 palaces; rly. ctr.; textiles, chemicals, engin., oil refining; linked to Mozyr', U.S.S.R. by "Friendship Oil Pipeline"; p. (1966) *266,000.*

**Bratsk,** *t.,* central Irkutsk Oblast, R.S.F.S.R. on Angara R., at mouth of Oka R., 115 m. N.N.E. of Tulun; ship repair yards, lumber, iron-ore, wood processing, chemicals; large hydro-electric sta.; p. (1959) *51,000.*

**Brattleboro,** *t.,* Vt., U.S.A.; p. (1960) *9,315.*

**Brava,** *spt.,* Somalia; p. *4,000.*

**Bray,** *urb. dist.,* Wicklow, Ireland; on Irish Sea cst., 11 m. S. of Dublin; popular wat. pl.; p. (1966) *12,657.* [Dublin.

**Bray Head,** point on E. cst. of Ireland, S. of

**Brazil,** *rep.* S. America; length 2,600 m.; greatest breadth 2,690 m.; in S. Plateau bounded on E. by mtns., in N. Amazon; mainly tropical climate, temperate on plateaus; vast forests; ch. R Amazon and tribs.; agr.; coffee, maize, sugar-cane, cotton, rubber, fruits, hardwoods; cattle-raising; minerals; manganese, iron, gold, diamonds; mnfs.; textiles, brewing; religion R.C.; administered through 21 sts., fed. dist. and 3 terrs.; cap. Brasilia; a. 3,288,063 sq. m.; p. (estd. 1966) *84,600,000.*

**Brazil,** *t.,* Ind., U.S.A.; coal, clay, bricks, china; p. (1960) *8,853.*

**Brazil Current,** *ocean current;* flows S. along E. cst. of Brazil; relatively warm.

**Brazos,** *R.,* Texas, U.S.A.; length 950 m.

**Brazzaville,** *cap.,* Congo (ex French), Equat. Africa; connected by rly. with the Atlantic at Pointe-Noire; R. pt. under construction; airport; p. (1962) *135,632.*

**Breadalbane,** *mountainous dist.,* W. Perth, Scot.

**Brechin,** *par.,* Angus, Scot.; with ancient cath. on S. Esk; sail-cloth, linen, distilling, agr. machin., lt. engin.; p. (1961) *7,114.*

**Breckenridge,** *t.,* N. Texas, U.S.A.; oil, gas wells; exp. cattle, grain; p. (1960) *6,273.*

**Breckland,** *geographical region,* S.W. Norfolk,

N.W. Suffolk, Eng.; chalk, overlain by sand, gives dry soils; much heathland; sm. fertile valleys cultivated, wheat, rye, sugar-beet; ch. ts. Brandon, Lakenheath; a. 200 sq. m.

**Brecknock,** *co.,* Wales; mountainous; rs. Wye, Usk; cereals, dairy produce; timber; coal, iron; a. 744 sq. m.; p. (1966) *55,000.*

**Brecon,** (Brecknock), *mun. bor.,* Wales; agr.; p. (1961) *5,797.*

**Brecon Beacons,** *mtns.,* S. Wales 5 m. S. of Brecon; highest peak, 2,910 ft.; National Park.

**Breda,** *c.,* N. Brabant, Netherlands; rayon, linen carpets, soap, brewing; p. (1967) *119,239*

**Bredbury** and **Romiley,** *urb. dist.,* Cheshire, Eng.; iron, steel, paper; p. (estd. 1967) *27,620.*

**Bregenz,** *cap.,* Vorarlberg, Austria; at E. end of L. Constance; the Roman Brigantium; resort; p. (1961) *21,423.*

**Breidha Fjord,** large inlet, W. coast, Iceland.

**Bremen,** *t., spt., cap.* of *Land* Bremen, Germany; on R. Weser 40 m. from N. Sea; ocean liner, tr. and trans-shipment pt.; imports cotton, cereals, tobacco; inds.; cars, machin., textiles, tobacco, shipbldg., oil refining, steel mill; p. (1963) *577,900.*

**Bremen,** *Land,* W. Germany; cattle rearing, mkt. gardening; a. 156 sq. m.; p. (1961) *706,000.*

**Bremerhaven,** *spt.,* Germany; "outport" of Bremen at mouth of Weser R.; docks; impt. fish. pt., shipbldg.; p. (1963) *143,200.*

**Bremersdorp,** *see* Manzini.

**Bremerton,** *t.,* Wash., U.S.A.; on Puget Sound; naval dockyard; elec. equipment, machin.; p. (1960) *28,922.*

**Brenham,** *t.,* Texas, U.S.A.; oil, cotton, dairy produce; p. (1960) *7,740.*

**Brenner Pass,** Italy; famous pass leading from Italy into Austria, over Alps.

**Brent,** *outer bor.,* Greater London, Eng.; comprising the former mun. bors. of Wembley and Willesden; p. (1966) *295,000.*

**Brentford** and **Chiswick,** *former mun. bor.,* Middx., Eng. now inc. in Hounslow *(q.v.)*; brewing, soap, coal gas, light engin.; p. (1961) *54,832.*

**Brentwood,** *urb. dist., mkt. t.* Essex, Eng.; films, agr. implements, steel-tubing; p. (estd. 1967) *57,000.*

**Brentwood,** *sub.* of St. Louis, Mo., U.S.A.; residtl.; p. (1960) *12,250.*

**Brescia,** *t.,* Italy; cath.; palace; silks, woollens, iron and steel; p. (1961) *174,116.*

**Breslau,** *see* Wroclaw.

**Bressanone,** *t.,* N.E. Italy; ceded to Italy 1919 by Austria; cath., health resort; p. *9,503.*

**Bressay I.,** Shetland Is., Scotland.

**Brest,** *t., spt.,* Finistère dep., N.W. France; naval sta., arsenal; metal inds.; fishing, ropes, soap; oil refining nearby; p. (1962) *142,901.*

**Brest** (Brest Litovsk), *t.,* Byelorussian S.S.R., on Polish frontier; Treaty of Brest Litovsk, March, 1918; route ctr. and agr. mkt.; textiles; p. (1959) *73,000.*

**Bretton Woods,** N.H., U.S.A.; resort; site of U.S. monetary and financial conference, 1944.

**Brevik,** *t., pt.,* Norway; p. (1961) *12,338.*

**Brewer,** *t.,* Me., U.S.A.; on Penobscot R.; wood pulp, paper, bricks; p. (1960) *9,009.*

**Briançon,** *t.,* France; p. (1962) *10,105.*

**Bridgend,** *urb. dist., mkt. t.,* Glamorgan, S. Wales; industl. trading estate; iron, coal, stone, paper; p. (1961) *15,156.*

**Bridge of Allan,** *burgh* Stirling, Scot.; 2 m. N. of Stirling; mineral springs; glass; p. (1961) *3,312.*

**Bridgeport,** *t.,* Conn., U.S.A.; sewing machines, typewriters, valves, hardware, machin., rubber and elec. goods, chemicals, plastics; p. (1960) *156,748.*

**Bridgeport,** *t.,* Ohio, U.S.A.; on Ohio R.; glass, tin, sheet metal, boat bldg.; p. (1960) *3,824.*

**Bridgeport,** *bor.,* Penns., U.S.A.; iron and steel, woollens, quarrying; p. (1960) *5,306.*

**Bridgeton,** *t.,* N.J., U.S.A.; founded by Quakers; glasswks., fruit; p. (1960) *20,966.*

**Bridgetown,** *t.,* Barbados, W.I.; deep water harbour; p. (1966) *95,000.*

**Bridgewater,** *mfg. t.,* Mass., U.S.A.; nr. Boston; p. (1960) *10,268.*

**Bridgewater Canal,** Manchester–Runcorn–Leigh; crosses ship canal by means of Barton swing bridge, length 38 m.

**Bridgnorth**, *rural bor.*, Salop. Eng.; cas.; carpets, radio equipment; p. of t. (1961) *7,552*.

**Bridgwater**, *mun. bor.*, *pt.*, Somerset, Eng.; on R. Parrett, 10 m. from Bristol Channel; bricks and tiles, engin.. wire rope, fibre fabrics, cellophane; p. (estd. 1967) *26,580*.

**Bridlington** *mun. bor.*, E. Riding, Yorks, Eng.; on Bridlington Bay, S. of Flamborough Head; impt. fishing; seaside resort; p. (estd. 1967) *26,370*.

**Bridport**, *mun. bor.*, *mkt. t.*, Dorset, Eng.; rope, line and twine, engin., concrete prods.; sm. seaside resort; p. (estd. 1967) *6,510*.

**Brie**, *natural division* ("*pays*"), Central France; low, level, plateau of limestones and clays, S.E. of Paris; loam (limon) cover and plentiful water supply encourage agr.; grains, sugarbeet, fruit, dairy cattle; densely populated.

**Brieg**, *see* Brzeg.

**Brielle**, *spt.*, R. Maas, S. Holland, Netherlands; on Voorn I.

**Brienz**, *t.*, Switzerland; resort; wood carving; on L. Brienz; p. *2,637*.

**Brierfield**, *urb. dist.*, Lancs, Eng.; cotton weaving; p. (1961) *6,958*.

**Brierley Hill**, *urb. dist.*, Staffs., Eng.; on R. Stour; cut glass, castable metal goods, firebricks, roofing and tilling; p. (1961) *56,377*.

**Brigg**, *mkt. t.*, *urb. dist.*, Lindsey, Lincs, Eng.; ctr. of agr. dist. between Lincoln Heights and Wolds; sugar-beet, jam, seed crushing, hosiery; p. (1961) *4,906*.

**Brigham**, *t.*, Utah, U.S.A.; sugar-beet, peaches, canning, woollens; p. (1960) *11,728*.

**Brighouse**, *industl. t.*, *mun. bor.*, W.R., Yorkshire, Eng.; on R. Calder, 3 m. S.E. of Halifax; textiles and engin.; p. (estd. 1967) *32,710*.

**Brightlingsea**, *urb. dist.*, Essex, Eng.; on R. Colne; oysters, boat bldg.; p. (1961) *4,801*.

**Brighton**, *co. bor.*, E. Sussex, Eng.; 50 m. S. of London; lge. seaside resort and residtl *t.*; univ.; light inds.; p. (estd. 1967) *162,160*.

**Brindisi**, *spt.*, Apulia, S. Italy; on Adriatic cst. sea and air connections to Middle East; cath.; cas.; wine, olive oil, silk, petrochemicals; oil refining; p. (1961) *70,084*.

**Brinkley**, *t.*, Ark., U.S.A.; cotton, lumber; p. (1960) *4,636*.

**Brioude**, *t.*, Haute-Loire, France; tr. ctr. for agr. a.; p. (1962) *6,928*.

**Brisbane**, *t.*, *pt.*, *cap.*, Queensland, Australia; univ.; docks; shipbldg.; meats, wool, hides and skins; oil refining, fertilisers; p. (1966) *719,140*.

**Bristol**, *t.*, Conn., U.S.A.; foundries, ball bearings, clocks, bells; p. (1960) *45,499*.

**Bristol**, *c.*, *co.*, *co. bor.*, *spt.*, Gloucester–Somerset border, Eng.; on R. Avon 9 m. from Bristol Channel; "outport" at Avonmouth; cath.; univ.; docks; aircraft engin., tobacco, paint, printing and light inds.; p. (estd. 1967) *429,020*.

**Bristol**, *t.*, Penns., U.S.A.; cottons, woollens; p. (1960) *12,364*.     (p. (1960) *17,144*.

**Bristol**, *c.*, Va., U.S.A.; dairy produce, tobacco;

**Bristol**, *t.*, R.I., U.S.A.; fish, textiles, rubber goods, shoes, wire, yacht wks., yachting; p. (1960) *14,570*.

**Bristol**, *t.*, Tenn., U.S.A.; rayon, paper, leather goods, furniture, mining equipment, transport ctr., especially for cattle; p. (1960) *17,582*.

**Bristol Channel**, arm of the Atlantic between S. cst. of Wales and Somerset and Devon; noted tidal bores.

**British Antarctic Territory**, *Brit. col.*, created 3 March 1962; consists of all land and Is. S. of lat. 60° S. and between 20° and 80° W. longitude; comprising Graham Land peninsula, S. Shetlands, S. Orkneys and smaller Is., excluding S. Georgia and S. Sandwich Is. *See* K190.

**British Columbia**, *prov.*, Canada; mountainous, largely forested; principal Rs.: Columbia, Fraser, Kootenay, Peace; climate: temperate, rainy on coast, drier interior; communications: rlys.; lumbering, farming, dairying and livestock; fruit growing, canning, salmon fisheries; minerals: coal, copper, gold, lead, silver, oil in N.E.; cap, Victoria; a. 355,855 sq. m.; p. (1961) *1,629,082*.

**British East Africa**, formerly comprised Kenya, Tanganyika, Uganda, together with the islands of Zanzibar and Pemba. *See* under their respective headings.

**British Guiana**, *see* Guyana.

**British Honduras**, *self-gov.* *Br. col.*, Central America; heavy rainfall; tropical forests; mahogany, logwood, bananas; poor communications; cap. Belize; subject to tropical hurricanes; a. 8,866 sq. m.; p. (estd. 1965) *103,000*.

**British Indian Ocean Terr.**, *Brit. col.*, created Nov. 1965; consists of the Chagos Archipelago (of which Diego Garcia is lgst. I.) 1200 m. N.E. of Mauritius, and Is. of Aldabra, Farquhar, and Desroches in the W. Indian Oc.; p. (1965) *1,400*.

**British Is.**, *archipelago*, N.W. Europe, comprising 2 large islands: Great Britain, Ireland; and 5,000 small islands; a. 121,633 sq. m.

**British Solomon Is.**, *prot.*, W. Pacific; coconuts, rubber, pineapples, bananas; a. 11,500 sq. m.; p. (estd.) *137,000*.

**British Virgin Islands**, *see* Virgin Islands.

**British West Africa**, formerly comprised Gambia, Sierra Leone, Gold Coast (Ghana), Nigeria, and parts of Togoland and Cameroons. *See* under their separate headings.

**Briton Ferry**, *t.*, *pt.*, Glam., S. Wales; at mouth of R. Neath; steel wks., engin., ship-breaking.

**Brittany**, *prov.*, France; farming; fishing; a. 13,643 sq. m.; p. *3,000,000*.

**Brittle**, *L.*, Skye, Scot.

**Brive**, *t.*, Corrèze dep., France; vegetables, wines; truffles, straw; p. (1962) *43,683*.

**Brixham**, S. Devon, Eng.; incorporated in Torbay co. bor.; fishing; resort; p. (1961) *10,679*.

**Brixton**, *dist.*, S.W. London, Eng.

**Brno**, *t.*, CSSR.; brewing, cloth. engin.; cath. univ.; p. (1965) *327,000*.

**Broad Haven**, *t.*, New Town planned on St. Brides Bay, Wales.

**Broad Law**, *mtn.*, Peebles, Scot.

**Broads, The**, Norfolk, Eng.; yachting, fishing and fowling centre.

**Broadstairs**, *urb. dist.*, Kent, Eng.; seaside resort; 3 m. N.E. of Ramsgate; p. (estd. 1967) *20,300*.

**Broadway**, *par.*, Worcester, Eng.; tourist ctr., Cotswolds; p. *1,860*.

**Brocken**, Harz Mtns., Germany; highest point (3,745 ft.).

**Brockport**, *t.*, N.Y., U.S.A.; dairying, mkt. gardens; N.Y. St. Teachers' College; p. (1960) *5,256*.     [(1960) *72,813*.

**Brockton**, *c.*, Mass., U.S.A.; shoes, machin.; p.

**Brockville**, *c.*, Ont., Canada; entry pt. on R. St. Lawrence; farm implements; marine engin.; p. (1961) *17,744*.

**Brody**, *t.*, Ukranian S.S.R.; oil, linked to Czechoslovakia by "Friendship Oil Pipeline".

**Broken Hill**, *c.*, N.S.W., Australia; silver, lead, zinc; p. (1966) *30,001*.

**Broken Hill**, Zambia; comm. and mng. ctr., lead, zinc, vanadium; p. (1964) *43,000*.

**Brokopondo**, Surinam, S. America; aluminium smelter under construction 1966.

**Bromberg**, *see* Bydgoszcz.

**Bromborough**, *see* Bebington and Bromborough.

**Bromley**, *former mun. bor.*, Kent, Eng.; now outer bor., Greater London, inc. Beckenham, Chislehurst, and Sidcup (S. of the A.20) Orpington, Penge; p. (1966) *302,000*.

**Bromsgrove**, *urb. dist.*, *old mkt. t.* Worcs., Eng.; 13 m. S.W. Birmingham; wrought ironwk., lt. engin.; p. (estd. 1967) *38,480*.

**Bromyard**, *urb. dist.*, *mkt. t.*, Hereford, Eng.; hops, glove mkg., engin., floor-tiles; p. (1961) *1,681*.

**Bron**, *t.*, Rhône, France; airport; p. estd. *15,000*.

**Bronx**, one of the five boroughs of N.Y. City, U.S.A.; and connected by bridges with bor. of Manhattan; p. (1960) *1,424,815*.     [town.

**Bron y Mor**, *t.*, Cardigan Bay, Wales; new seaside

**Brookline**, sub. of Boston, Mass., U.S.A.; resdtl.; p. (1960) *54,044*.

**Brooklyn**, *bor.*, N.Y. City, linked with Manhattan bor. by Brooklyn, Manhattan and Williamsburgh suspension bridges across East R.; and with Staten I. by Verrazano-Narrows bridge (longest in world); mainly residtl. with numerous mftg. and comm. interests; p. (1960) *2,627,319*.

**Broom**, *loch* on N.W. cst. of Ross and Cromarty, Scot.

**Brora**, *t.*, Sutherland, Scot.; on E. cst., 12 m. N.E. of Dornoch Firth; ctr. of sm. coalfield; Harris Tweed ind.

**Brotton**, *t.*, N.R. Yorks, Eng., nr. Guisborough; iron and steel mftg.

**Brough**, *mkt. t.*, Westmorland, Eng.; in upper Vale of Eden, 4 m. N. of Kirkby-Stephen.

Broughshane, *vil.*, Antrim, N. Ireland.

Brownhills, *urb. dist.*, Staffs, coal-mining; p. (1961) 26,392.

Brownsville, *t.*, Texas, U.S.A.; livestock, sugar-cane; p. (1960) 48,040.

Brown Willy, *mtn.*, Cornwall, Eng.; alt. 1,375 ft.

Brownwood, *t.*, Texas, U.S.A.; exp. cotton, grain, wool, poultry, dairy prod.; p. (1960) 16,974.

Broxbourne, *t.*, Hertford, Eng.; on gravel terrace to W. of R. Lea about 20 m. N.E. of London; ctr. of very intensively cultivated district, mkt.-garden and glasshouse crops; light inds.; "dormitory" t. linked with London; p. (1961) 3,839.

Bruay-en-Artois, *t.*, Pas de Calais, France; p. (1962) 30,902.

Bruchsal, *t.*, Baden-Württemberg, Germany; tobacco, paper, machin.; p. (1963) 23,600.

Bruck, *t.*, Austria; p. (1961) 16,087.

Brue, *R.*, Somerset, Eng.

Bruges (Brugge), *t.*, *inland pt.*, Belgium; mkt.-hall with 13th-century belfry; univ.; impt. mkt. for grain, cattle, horses, engin., elec. goods; glass, textiles, lace; p. incl. subs. (1965) 105,000.

Brühl, *t.*, N. Rhine-Westphalia, Germany; 8 m. S. of Cologne; cas.; lignite, iron, sugar refining; p. (1963) 37,200.

Brunei, *Br. prot. st.*, N. Borneo; oilfields; cutch, rubber, sago, pepper, timber; a. 2,226 sq. m.; p. (est. 1965) 97,000.

Brünn, *see* Brno.

Brunsbüttelkoog, *t.*, mouth of Elbe, canal opposite Cuxhaven, Germany; p. (estd. 1954) 10,100.

Brunswick (Braunschweig), *c.*, Lower Saxony, Germany; on R. Oker; medieval bldgs.; canning, tinplate mftg., optics, pianos, drugs, vehicles; p. (estd. 1954) 236,900.

Brunswick, *t.*, Me., U.S.A.; p. (1960) 9,444.

Brussels, *c.*, *cap.* Belgium; town hall, palace, parliament houses, univ., museum; mnfs., lace, carpets, silk, cottons, rayon; p. (1962) 1,453,581 inc. subs.; of c. 169,211.

Bryan, *t.*, Texas, U.S.A.; mkt. ctr.; cotton gins, compresses; oil mills; p. (1960) 27,542.

Bryansk, *t.*, R.S.F.S.R.; sawmilling, engin. textiles, chemicals, phosphates, steel; oil pipeline from Kuybyshev; p. (1967) 276,000.

Brynmawr, *urb. dist.*, Brecon, Wales; iron, coal, steel, rubber goods; p. (1961) 6,471.

Brzeg (Brieg), *t.*, Silesia, Poland; German before 1945; on R. Oder; chemicals; p. (1965) 28,000.

Bua, *t.*, Fiji Islands, Pacific.

Bucaramanga, *t.*, cap. Santander, Colombia; coffee; cigar and cigarette mkg.; p. (estd. 1962) 221,779.

Buchan Ness, *C.*, nr. Peterhead, E. Scot.

Bucharest, *c.*, *cap.*, Romania; cath.; palace, univ.; textiles, grain, chemicals, pharmaceutics, oil refinery engin.; glass; p. (1963) 1,366,794.

Buckfast, S. Devon, Eng.; famous Abbey.

Buckfastleigh, *urb. dist.*, S. Devon, Eng.; wool, quarrying; p. (1961) 2,550.

Buckhannon, *t.*, W. Va., U.S.A.; agr. and pastoral ctr.; coal, gas, lumber, leather; p. (1960) 6,386.

Buckhaven, and Methil, *burgh*, Fife, Scot.; on N. side of Firth of Forth, 8 m. N.E. of Kirkcaldy; coal, oilsilk, brickmkg. inds; p. (1961) 21,104.

Buckie, *burgh*, Banff, Scot.; boat- and yacht-bldg.; fisheries; p. (1961) 7,666.

Buckingham, *co.*, England; wooded, beeches; includes Vale of Aylesbury; farming, dairy produce, ducks, sheep; mnfs., chairs, lace, paper; a. 749 sq. m.; p. (1966) 542,000.

Buckingham, *mun. bor.*, Bucks, Eng.; on Ouse R.; agr. bricks; p. (estd. 1967) 4,810.

Buckley, *urb. dist.*, Flint, Wales; small castings; (1961) 7,658.

Bucyrus, *t.*, Ohio, U.S.A.; machine-mnfs.; p. (1960) 12,276.

Budafoc, *sub.* of Budapest, Hungary; wine cellars.

Budapest, *twin-cap.*, Hungary; Buda on right bank and Pest on left bank of Danube; parit., univ.; steel, textiles, chemicals, engin., motorbuses, oil refining; mineral springs; p. (1965) 1,935,000.

Budaun, *t.*, Uttar Pradesh, India; sugar-cane, rice; ruins; p. (1961) 58,770.

Bude, *see* Stratton and Bude, Cornwall.

Budejovice, *t.*, ČSSR.; pencils, beet, porcelain, anthracite, domestic woodware; p. (1961) 63,949.      [p. (1961) 39,824.

Budge-Budge, *t.*, W. Bengal, India; hemp, rice;

Budleigh Salterton, *urb. dist.*, E. Devon; resort; p. (1961) 3,871.

Buena Park, *t.*, Cal., U.S.A.; citrus fruits, truck farms, oilfields; p. (1960) 46,401.

Buenaventura, *spt.*, Colombia; lumber yards, tanning, fish canning; p. (estd. 1962) 60,220.

Buenos Aires, *c.*, *cap.* Argentina; on Rio de la Plata, fine buildings, lgst. c. in S. hemisphere; univ.; tr. ctr.; carpets, cloth, cigars, boots and shoes, iron-ore; p. (estd. 1966) 3,876,000.

Buenos Aires, *prov.*, Argentina; a. 118,467 sq. m.; treeless plain; sheep and cattle; cereals, fruit, tobacco; p. (1960) 6,735,000.

Buffalo, *c.*, *pt.*, N.Y., U.S.A.; on L. Erie; univ.; iron, steel, oil refining, aircraft, car parts, elec. goods, textiles, meat packing, brewing; p. (1960) 532,759.

Bug, *R.*, in Ukraine, flows into Black Sea; length 348 m.

Bug, *R.*, Poland; trib. of Vistula R.; since 1939 frontier between Poland and Ukraine S.S.R.

Buga, *c.*, Colombia, S. America; tr. ctr. for sugar, coffee, cacao, rice, cotton; p. (estd. 1959) 75,220.

Buganda, *prov.*, Uganda, E. Africa; located W. of L. Victoria largely at alt. between 4,500 and 6,000 ft.; intensive cultivation, cotton (ch. comm. crop), plantains, millets; cap. Kampala. p. (1959) 61,000.

Bugisu, *dist.*, Uganda; coffee.

Bugulma, *t.*, Tatar A.S.S.R., R.S.F.S.R.; oil ctr.; p. (1959) 61,000.

Builth Wells, *urb. dist.*, N. Brecknock, Wales; on upper course, R. Wye; medicinal springs; p. (1961) 1,602.

Buitenzorg, *see* Bogor.      [12,796.

Bujalance, *c.*, Spain; E. of Cordova; p. (1957)

Bujumbura, *cap.* Burundi; p. (estd. 1965) 70,000.

Bukhara (Bokhara), *t.*, Uzbek S.S.R., U.S.S.R.; in Amu Darya valley at W. foot of Tien Shan; mkt. for cotton, sunflower seed, wheat grown in irrigated Bukhara Oasis; impt. tr. ctr. at W. terminus of ancient caravan route from China; linked by Trans-Caspian rly. to Krasnovodsk, by Turk-Sib. rly to Novo Sibivsk; natural gas nearby; pipeline to Urals; textiles; p. (1959) 69,000.

Bukittinggi, *t.*, Sumatra, Indonesia; p. (1957) 53,700.

Bukoba, *t.*, *pt.*, Tanzania, E. Africa; located midway along W. shore of L. Victoria; exp. coffee, rice, plantains and other foodstuffs to L. pts. in Kenya and Uganda.

Bukovina, Northern, formerly Romania, ceded to U.S.S.R. in 1940; now part of Ukraine; a. about 6,000 sq. km.; ch. t. Chernovitsy; Carparthian Mtns., forested; farming, cereals; cattle.

Bulawayo, *t.*, Rhodesia; impt. rly. and indus. ctr.; airpt.; agr. mnfs.; p. (1965) 237,000.

Buldan, *t.*, Turkey; p. (1960) 10,431.

Bulgaria, *rep.*, Eastern Europe; mountainous; Balkan Mtns., R. Danube N. boundary; climate: hot summer, cold winter, milder in S.; heavy summer rainfall; 5 lge. dams; hydro-electric stas.; religion: Greek Orthodox; communications: main rail from Central Europe passes through to Istanbul; grain, wines, rose-oil, pigs, iron, manganese, copper, lead, zinc. pyrites, salt, chemicals, oil, tobacco; a. 42,796 sq. m.; p. (1967) 8,334,000.

Bultfontein, *t.*, Cape Province, S. Africa; diamonds; p. (1960) 3,491 inc. 1,380 whites.

Bunbury, *t.*, *spt.*, W. Australia; on cst. 112 m. S. of Fremantle; pt. and comm. ctr. of lge. pastoral, agr., fruit growing and timber dist., wool, phosphates, oil; p. (1966) 15,453.

Buncrana, *urb. dist.*, Donegal Ireland; salmon; p. (1966) 3,120.

Bundaberg, *t.*, Queensland, Australia; on Burnett R.; sugar factories, timber, butter, iron; p. (1966) 25,404.

Bungay, *urb. dist.*, Suffolk, Eng.; on R. Waveney; printing, malting; p. (1961) 3,581.

Bunker Hill, Charlestown, now part of Boston, Mass., U.S.A.; battle between Americans and British, 1775.

Buntingford, *par.*, Herts, Eng.; on E. Anglian Heights, 10 m. N.W. of Bishop's Stortford; p. (1961) 1,559.

Bunzlau, *see* Boleslawiec.

Buraida, *t.*, Nejd, Saudi Arabia; p. (estd.) 50,000

Burbank, *c.*, Cal., U.S.A.; airport, aeroplanes; p. (1960) 90,155.

Burdur, t., Turkey; p. (1965) 28,960.

Bure, R., Norfolk, Eng.

Burg, t., Magdeburg, E. Germany; on Ihle Canal; leather goods, iron, furniture, machin.; p. (1963) 30,026.

Burgas, spt., Bulgaria; on Black Sea; copper, engin., chemicals, textiles; oil refining; pt. for oil tankers under construction; p. (1956). 72,795

Burgenland, prov., Austria; a. 1,526 sq. m.; p. (1961) 271,001.    [tiles; p. (1961) 13,990.

Burgess Hill, urb. dist., Sussex, Eng.; bricks,

Burghausen, t., W. Germany; oil refining; pipeline to Munich.

Burgos, c., Spain; cath.; hosiery, leather cloth, tyres; p. (1959) 87,520.

Burgos, prov., Old Castile, Spain; ch. t., Burgos; oil; a. 5,425 sq. m.; p. (1959) 401,891.

Burgstädt, t., Karl-Marx-Stadt, E. Germany; textiles, machin.; p. (1963) 17,167.

Burgundy, old prov., N.E. France; composed largely of upper valley of R. Saône; famous vineyards; strategic position on route leading between plateau of Vosges and Jura Mtns. from Rhône valley to Rhine valley.

Burhanpur, t., Madhya Pradesh, India; ancient walled Mogul city; textiles, brocades; p. (1961) 82,090.

Burlington, t., S. Ont., Canada, on L. Ontario, N.E. of Hamilton; in fruit-growing a.; indus-tl. development; tourism; p. (estd.) 47,000.

Burlington, c., Iowa, U.S.A.; on bluffs of Missis-sippi R.; machin., furniture; p. (1960) 32,430.

Burlington, pt., Vt., U.S.A.; E. side of L. Cham-plain; state univ.; timber; p. (1960) 35,531.

Burma (Union of), rep. 1948; ch. mtns.: Arakan Yoma, Pegu Yoma; chief rivers: Irrawaddy, Salween; forested; agr.: rice, fruit, tobacco; timber, teak; minerals: petroleum, precious stones, rubies, sapphires; textile, sugar and jute mills projected; cap. Rangoon; a. 261,789 sq. m., p. (1965) 24,229,000.

Burnham-on-sea, t., urb. dist., Somerset, Eng.; on Bridgwater Bay, 10 m. S. of Weston-super-Mare; resort; p. (1961) 9,850.

Burnham-on-Crouch, urb. dist., Essex, Eng.; yacht sailing, oysters, boat bldg.; p. (1961) 4,167.

Burnie, spt., Tasmania, Australia; pastoral and agr., paper pulp mftg.; chemicals; oil ter-minal; p. (1966) 18,028.

Burnley, industl. t., co. bor., Lancs. Eng.; cotton, weaving, coal; p. (estd. 1967) 78,060.

Burntisland, royal burgh, East Fife, Scot.; on F. of Forth, nr. Kirkcaldy; shipbldg., aluminium inds.; p. (1961) 6,036.

Burra, E. and W., two Shetland Is., Scot.

Burray, one of the Orkney Is., Scot.

Burriana, t., spt., Spain; oranges, wine; p. (1957) 17,697.

Burrinjuck, t., N.S.W. Australia; on Murrum-bidgee R., N. of Canberra; site of impt. dam providing irrigation in Riverina dist.

Burry Port, urb. dist., Carmarthen, Wales; p. (1961) 5,671.

Bursa, c., Turkey; 60 m. S. Istanbul; fruits, carpets, tapestry; cap. of Bithynia prior to the Christian Era, and later of the Ottoman Em-pire; p. (1965) 212,518.

Burslem, t., part of Stoke-on-Trent, Staffs.

Burton Latimer, urb. dist., Northants., Eng.; p. (1961) 4,401.

Burton-upon-Trent, industl. t., co. bor., Staffs, Eng.; brewing, malting, rubber goods, engin., steel, footwear, chemicals; p. (estd. 1967) 50,220.

Buru, I., Indonesia; W. of Serang.

Burujird, t., Iran; cotton, carpets; p. (1956) 49,228.

Burundi, indep. kingdom (1 July 1962), formerly Urundi, part of U.N. trust terr. of Ruanda-Urundi under Belgian adm.; cap. Bujumbura; coffee; a. 10,747 sq. m.; p. (est. 1965) 2,780,000.

Bury, industl. t., co. bor., S.E. Lancs.; on R. Irwell to S. of Rossendale Fells; cotton, textiles, engin., paper makg.; p. (estd. 1967) 64,540.

Bury St. Edmunds, mun. bor., W. Suffolk; mon-astic remains; farm implements, brewing, sugar-beet processing; p. (estd. 1967) 24,260.

Buryat, rep., R.S.F.S.R., U.S.S.R.; lge. deposit of graphite; ch. t. Ulan Ude; a. 135,500 sq. m.; p. (1959) 671,000.

Bushey, t., urb. dist., Herts., Eng.; p. (estd. 1967) 24,310.

Bushire, see Bandar-e-Bushehr.

Buskerud, co., Norway; a. 5,738 sq. m.; p. (1963 170,441.

Busto Arsizio, t., Varese prov., N. Italy; 19 m. N.W. of Milan; cotton milling ctr., iron, steel, rayon, textile machin.; p. (1961) 64,367.

Bute, I., co., Firth of Clyde, Scotland; 16 m. long and 3-5 m. broad; ch. t., Rothesay; a. 218 sq. m.; p. (1961) 15,129.      [Argyll.

Bute, Kyles of, strait, 6 m. between isles of Bute and

Buton, I., off coast of Sulawesi I., Indonesia.

Butt of Lewis, promontory with lighthouse; Lewis, Hebrides, Scot.

Butte, c., Montana, U.S.A.; copper, lead, silver; p. (1960) 27,877.

Buttermere, vil., Cumberland, Eng.; tourist resort.

Buttermere, L., Cumberland, Eng.; 1¼ m. long, ¼ m. wide.

Buxton, mun. bor., Derby, Eng.; wat. p . nr. High Peak dist.; spa t.; lime quarrying nearby; p. (estd. 1967) 19,730.

Buzau, t., Romania; rly. ctr.; cath.; wheat, timber, petroleum; p. (1963) 79,553.

Buzuluk, t., R.S.F.S.R.; in Urals; engin.; ctr. of agr. a.; p. (1959) 55,000.

Bydgoszcz, t., N. Central Poland; on R. Brda; R. pt., rly. ctr.; elec. equip., machine tools, chemicals; p. (1965) 255,000.

Bydgoszcz, prov., Poland; cap. B.; drained by Rs. Vistula, Brda and Notec; a. 8,031 sq. m.; p. c. 1,704,000.

Byelorussia (White Russia), constituent rep., U.S.S.R.; cap. Minsk; oil at Rechitsk; salt at Mozyr; a. 81,090 sq. m.; p. (1959) 8,060,000.

Byron C., most easterly point of Australia, Pacific coast of N.S.W.

Bytom (Beuthen), t., Upper Silesia, Poland; German before 1945; coal, zinc, lead and iron mining; iron inds.; p. (1965) 192,000.

# C

Cabinda, Port. enclave, W. Africa, admin. from Angola; hardwoods, coffee, cocoa, palm oil prods.; recent oil find; a. 2,794 sq. m.; p. c. 50,000.

Cabot Strait, entrance of Gulf of St. Lawrence between C. Breton I. and Newfoundland.

Cabra, t., Spain; 30 m. S.E. of Córdova; college; p. (1957) 22,174.

Cáceres, prov., W. Spain; pastoral; a. 7,705 sq. m.; p. (1959) 566,202.

Cáceres, t., Spain; largest bull-ring in Spain; ancient Castra Caecilia; p. (1957) 52,000.

Cachan t., Seine, France; p. (1954) 16,965.

Cachar, dist., Assam, India; tea-growing ctr.; a. 2,688 sq. m.; p. (1961) 1,378,476.

Cachoeira, t., nr. Salvador, Brazil; p. (1960) 39,470.

Cadarache, t., S. France; nr. Aix-en-Provence; nuclear research centre.

Cader Idris, mtn., Merioneth, Wales; alt. 2,929 ft.

Cadillac, t., Mich., U.S.A.; rubber tyres, wood and metal prod.; p. (1960) 10,112.

Cadiz, maritime prov., S. Spain; cap. Cadiz; a. 2,827 sq. m.; p. (1959) 811,581.

Cadiz, fortress t., spt., Andalusia, S. Spain; sherry, cork, fruit, olive oil, tunny fish; naval base; univ.; one of most ancient ts. in Europe, built by Phoenicians, c. 1100 B.C.; p. (1959) 113,325.

Caen, c. cap., Calvados, France; church and abbey, tomb of William the Conqueror; univ.; iron ore, lace, gloves exported; severely dam-aged in Second World War; p. (1962) 95,238.

Caerleon, urb. dist., Monmouth, Eng.; on R. Usk, 3 m. N.E. of Newport; Roman remains; agr. machin. tools, bricks; p. (1961) 4,184.

Caernarvon, royal bor., cap. Caernarvonshire, N. Wales; on S. shore of Menai Strait; cas. where first Prince of Wales (Edward II) was chris-tened; slate, bricks, plastics; p. (1961) 8,998.

Caernarvonshire, minous. marit. co., N. Wales; slate and stone quarries, lead-mines; oats, barley, sheep, cattle; highest peak, Snowdon (3,560 ft.); a. 569 sq. m.; p. (1966) 120,000.

Caerphilly, urb. dist., Glamorgan, S. Wales; cas.; coal, iron, light inds.; p. (1961) 36,008.

Caesar Mazaca, anc. c., Asia Minor; residence of the Cappadocian Kings; the modern Kayeri, Turkey.

Caesarea Palestinae, anc. c., Israel, 20 m. S. Mt. Carmel; cap. of Herod the Great.

Caeté, t., Minas Geraes st., Brazil; at foot of Serra do Espinhaço, 50 m. E. of Belo Horizonte; lge. iron and steel wks.

Cagayan, *prov.*, Luzon, Philippine Is.; p. (1960) *555,819*.

Cagliari, Italian *prov.*, comprising S. half of Sardinia; a. 5,179 sq. m.; p. (1961) *733,459*.

Cagliari, *spt.*, *cap.* Sardinia, on S. cst.; cath. and univ.; exp. lead, zinc; p. (1964) *200,000*.

Cagnes-sur-Mer, *t.*, Alpes-Maritimes dep., France; Riviera resort; p. (1954) *11,066*.

Caha, *mtns.*, on boundary of Cork and Kerry, Ireland; cas.; highest point 2,249 ft.

Cahir, *t.*, Tipperary, Ireland; on R. Suir; ancient cas. and abbey; p. (1966) *1,740*.

Cahirciveen, *t.*, Kerry, Ireland; p. (1966) *1,649*.

Cahors, *t.*, *cap.*, Lot, France; cath.; distilleries, shoe factories; p. (1954) *15,384*.

Caibarien, *t.*, Cuba; sugar pt.; p. (1953) *22,657*.

Caicos Is., *see* Turks and Caicos Is.

Cairngorm, *mtn.*, Inverness and Banff Scot.; alt. 4,084 ft.; national nature reserve.

Cairns, *spt.*, Queensland, Australia; on Trinity Bay; bulk sugar pt.; tourist ctr.; p. (1966) *25,555*.　　　　　　　　　　[alt. 4,241 ft.

Cairntoul, *mtn.*, Inverness and Aberdeen, Scot.;

Cairo, *c.*, *cap.* U.A.R.; on R. bank of Nile at head of Nile delta; univ.; tourist ctr.; mnfs. cotton, paper, silk; p. (1960) *3,346,000*.

Cairo, Ill., U.S.A.; confluence of Mississippi and Ohio; extensive traffic; p. (1960) *9,348*.

Caister, *vil.*, N. of Yarmouth, Norfolk, Eng.; ruined cas.; holiday resort.

Caithness, *co.*, Scot.; most N. part of mainland; flat, with much moorland; herring fishery; poor agr.; quarrying; ch. ts. Wick, Thurso; a. 686 sq. m.; p. (1961) *27,345*.

Caivano, *indostl. t.*, Italy; N.E. of Naples.

Cajalco Reservoir, S. Cal., U.S.A.; hill-top location nr. Riverside, 55 m. S.E. of Los Angeles; stores water brought 242 m. by aqueduct from Parker Res. on R. Colorado, for distribution throughout Los Angeles plain.

Cajamarca, *dep.* N. Peru; mining and agr.; gold and silver deposits found 1965; a. 12,538 sq. m.; p. (1961) *543,090*.

Cajamarca, *t.*, *cap.* Cajamarca prov., Peru; mng. ctr., dairying, cloth, leather, straw hats; thermal springs; p. (1961) *37,000*.

Calabar, *spt.*, S.E. Nigeria, W. Africa; exp. palm oil, kernals, rubber, ivory, cement; p. c. *47,000*.

Calabozo, *t.*, N. Venezuela, S. America; cattle, agr., tr. ctr.; p. *7,123*.

Calabria, *region*, extreme S.W. Italy; mountainous and fertile; highest point Mt. Pollino 7,325 ft.; ch. R. Crati; cereals, wine, olives, fruit; copper, marble; tunny fish; a. 5,830 sq. m.; p. (1961) *2,045,215*.

Calafat, *t.*, Romania; on Bulgarian frontier, opp. Vidin; p. (1956) *8,069*.

Calahorra, *t.*, Logrono, Spain; cath.; pimentoes, wine; on R. Ebro; p. (1957) *13,524*.

Calais, *spt.*, Pas de Calais, N.E. France; cross-channel ferry pt. opposite to and 21 m. distant from Dover; lace, fishing; p. (1962) *70,707*.

Calama, *oasis*, Antofagasta prov., N. Chile; in Atacama desert at foot of Andean Cordillera, 130 m. N.E. of Antofagasta on main rly. to La Paz; water from R. Loa supplies Antofagasta and used for irrigation locally.

Calamar, *t.*, Bolivar dep., Colombia; on R. Magdalena 60 m. from mouth, connected by rail to Cartagena; handles traffic between Cartagena and Magdalena valley; p. (estd. 1959) *21,000*.

Calamianes Is., Philippine Is.; between Mindoro and Palawan Is.　　　　　　　　　[p. *11,285*.

Calanas, *commune*, S. Spain; pyrites, olives;

Calarasi, *t.*, S.E. Romania; on the Danube; comm. ctr.; p. (1963) *29,474*.

Calasiao, *t.*, Luzon, Philippines; hats; p. (1948) *23,269*.

Calatafimi, *commune*, Sicily; Garibaldi defeated Neapolitans, May 1860; p. *11,484*.

Calatayud, *t.*, Spain; 55 m. S.W. Saragossa; cas.; weapons; flour milling; p. (1957) *18,762*.

Calbayog, *t.*, Samar, Philippine Is.; hemp trade, fisheries; p. (1960) *77,832*.

Calbe, *t.*, Magdeburg, E. Germany; on R. Saale; iron smelting, lignite mng., machin., chemicals; p. (1963) *16,859*.

Calcutta, *c.*, *spt.*, W. Bengal, India; on R. Hooghli; vast tr. from Ganges plain; univ.; jute-mills; exp. jute, cotton, sugar-cane, rice, tea, silk, coal; p. (1961) corporation a. *2,927,289*; metropolitan a. *5,500,195*.

Caldas, *dep.*, Colombia, S. America; cap. Manizales; a. 5,160 sq. m.; p. (1962) *1,399,590*.

Calder, *t.*, S.W. Midlothian; shale mines, oilwks.; p. *3,200*.

Calder, R., Lancs, Eng.; joins the Ribble.

Calder, R., W.R. Yorks, Eng.; trib. of Aire R.

Calder Hall, Cumberland; first full-scale nuclear power sta. in world (1956) owned and operated by U.K. Atomic Energy Authority; electricity and plutonium prod.

Caldwell, *t.*, Idaho, U.S.A.; p. (1960) *12,230*.

Caldy I., off Pembroke coast, Wales; lighthouse; Trappist monastery.

Caledonian Canal, from Moray Firth to Loch Linnhe, Scot., connecting North Sea with Atlantic; 62½ m. long; opened in 1822.

Calf of Man, *sm. I.*, S.W. I. of Man, Eng.; a. 620 acres.

Calgary, *ch. t.*, Alberta, Canada; ctr. of ranching country; lumber-mills, tanneries, oil refining; p. (1961) *279,062*.

Cali, *t.*, *cap.*, Valle del Cauca, Colombia; on Cauca R.; comm. ctr.; in rich agr. a.; coal mined nearby; textiles, tyres, paper, plastics; p. (estd. 1962) *693,120*.　　　　[spices; p. (1961) *192,521*.

Calicut, *spt.*, *mftg. t.*, Kerala, India; exp. coffee,

California, most impt. of Pacific States, U.S.A.; mountainous and forested but fertile valleys; salubrious climate; rich in minerals, oil, natural gas, gold, silver, copper, steel; oil refining; films; fruit; cap. Sacramento; ch. pt. San Francisco, lgst. c. Los Angeles; has 279 incorporated cities; a. 158,693 sq. m.; p. (1964) *18,084,000*.

California Current, E. Pac. Oc.; flows N. to S. along cst. of Ore., and Cal., U.S.A.; relatively cold water; reduces summer temp. and causes fog in cst. a. especially nr. San Francisco.

California, G. of, Mexico; 700 m.l.; inlet of Pac. Oc.

California, Lower, *terr.*, Mexico; between Gulf of C. and Pacific; cap. La Paz; chiefly a sterile region; some mineral wealth; a. 55,654 sq. m.; p. (1950) *287,366*.　　　　　　　　[Coast, India.

Calimere Point, most S. point of Coromandel

Calistoga, *t.*, Cal., U.S.A.; tr. ctr., wine, grapes; hot springs; p. (1960) *1,514*.

Callan, *rural dist.*, *mkt. t.*, Kilkenny, Ireland; on the King's R.; p. (1961) *5,963*.

Callander, *mkt. t.*, *burgh*, Perth, Scot.; on R. Teith, 15 m. N.W. of Stirling; "the gate of the Highlands," tourist resort; p. (1961) *1,654*.

Callao, *dep.*, Peru; cap. C.; a. 14 sq. m.; p. (1961) *213,206*.

Callao, *t.*, *spt.*, cap. Callao dep., Peru; linked by rly. to Lima; exp. sugar, cotton; oil refining; p. (estd. 1963) *214,186*.

Calne, *mkt. t.*, *mun. bor.*, Wilts, Eng.; on Marden R.; lge bacon factory; p. (estd. 1967) *9,290*.

Calonne-Ricouart, *commune*, Pas-de-Calais dep., France; coal; p. (1954) *10,897*.

Calota, gold-field dist., Colombia, S. America.

Calstock, *t.*, E. Cornwall, Eng.; on Tamar estuary.

Caltagirone, *t.*, Catania, Sicily; cath.; local mkt.; p. (1961) *44,212*.

Caltanissetta, *t.*, *cap.*, Caltanissetta prov., Sicily, Italy; cath.; sulphur; p. (1961) *62,115*.

Caluire-et-Clare, *t.*, Rhône, France, on Saône R; coal; p. (1954) *19,886*.

Calumet, *t.*, Mich., U.S.A.; on peninsula in L. Superior; copper-mining; p. (1960) 1,139.

Calvados, *dep.*, N.W. France; cap. Caen; livestock, dairying, fisheries, textiles, liqueur brandy; a. 2,197 sq. m.; p. (1962) *480,686*.

Calvinia, *t.*, Cape Province, S. Africa; p. *3,627*.

Cam, R., Cambridge, Eng.; trib. of Ouse; length 40 m.　　　　　　　　　[m.; p. (1953) *618,258*.

Camagüey, *prov.*, Cuba, W. Indies; a. 10,169 sq.

Camagüey, *t.*, *cap.*, Camagüey, Central Cuba; p. (1953) *110,388*.

Camagüey, *t.*, Peru; sugar-cane; p. (1953) *110,388*.

Camaiore, *t.*, Central Italy; foot of Apuan Alps, in prov. of Lucca; old church.

Camargue, *delta dist.*, Bouches-du-Rhône, France; at mouth of R. Rhône; famous col. of flamingoes; a. 300 sq. m.

Camarihes Norte, *prov.*, Luzon, Philippine Is.; mtns. and fertile land; agr., minerals; cap. Daet; a. 829 sq. m.; p. (1960) *188,091*.

Camas, *t.*, Wash., U.S.A.; agr., pulp, paper, fruit canning; p. (1960) *5,666*.

Cambay, G., separates Kathiawar peninsula from Gujerat st., India.

Camberwell, *see* Southwark.

Cambodia, *kingdom*, S.E. Asia, between Thailand and S. Vietnam; former associate st. of Fr. Union; cap. Phnom-Penh on Mekong R.; mainly agr.: rice, rubber, maize, pepper, kapok, livestock; Great L., or Tonle Sap., impt. for fisheries; car assembly, cigarette mkg., textiles, plywood, paper, tyres, cement; oil refinery nr. Sihanoukville; a. 70,000 sq. m.; p. (estd. 1965) *6,200,000.*

Camborne, *t.*, Cornwall, Eng.; 11 m. S.W. Truro; old tin- and copper-mines; engin., radio-television assembly, textiles and chemicals; p. (Camborne–Redruth urb. dist.) (estd. 1967) *37,600.*

Cambrai, *t.*, Nord dep., France; on Schelde R.; linen, brewing, soap; p. (1954) *29,567.*

Cambridge and Isle of Ely, *co.*, Eng.; Rs. Ouse, Nen, Cam; wheat, oats, potatoes, fruit, dairying, light engin., light indus.; p. (1966) *294,000.*

Cambridge, *mun. bor., univ. c., co. t.*, Cambridge, Eng.; on Cam R.; famous univ. with residtl. colleges; radio, scientific instruments, asphalt, boat bldg.; p. (estd. 1967) *100,340.*

Cambridge, *t.*, Md.,U.S.A.; oysters; p. (1960) *12,239.*

Cambridge, *c.*, Mass., U.S.A., 3 m. from Boston; seat of Harvard Univ.; mnftg.; impt. research ctr.; p. (1960) *107,716.*

Cambridge, *t.*, Ohio, U.S.A.; coal, iron, clay, oil; glassware, pottery; p. (1960) *14,562.*

Cambuslang, *par.*, Lanark, Scot.; turkey red dye-works, hosiery, engin, plate mill; on Clyde R.; p. (1951) *26,861.*

Camden, *inner bor.*, N. London, Eng.; incorporating former bors. of Hampstead, Holborn and St. Pancras; p. (1966) *240,000.*

Camden, *mftg. and residtl. c.* N.J., U.S.A.; on Delaware R., suburban and opposite Philadelphia; iron foundries, chemicals, glass, wireless sets, shipbldg.; p. (1960) *117,159.*

Camden Town, *industl. and residtl. dist.*, London, Eng.; N.E. of Regent's Park.

Camel, *R.*, E. Cornwall, Eng.; length 30 m.

Camerino, *c.*, Macerata, Central Italy, in Apennines; the ancient Camerium annexed to Papal States in 16th century; univ. cath.

Cameron, *c.*, Texas, U.S.A.; p. (1960) *5,640.*

Cameron Bay, *t.*, N.W. Terr., Canada; by Gr. Bear Lake; radium.

Cameroons, British (North and South), former U.N. trust terrs. under British adm. (Northern part achieved independence as part of Nigeria (Sardauna prov.), and Southern part as part of Cameroun (Western prov.) (1961); a. 34,081 sq. m.; p. (estd 1960) *1,621,000.*

Cameroun, Fed. Rep. of, *ind. sovereign st.* (Jan. 1960); comprises Eastern Cameroun (former U.N. trust terr. under French adm.) and Western Cameroun (former U.N. trust terr. under British adm.). Fed. cap. Yaoundé; timber, cocoa, palm kernels, palm oil, groundnuts, bananes, coffee; a. 143,500 sq. m.; p. (estd. 1965) *5,150,000.*

Camiguin, *I.*, Philippines; in Mindanao Sea; mtns.; sugar, rice, tobacco; a. 96 sq. m.; p. (1960) *11,000.*

Campagna, Italy; malarial coastal plain round Rome; now being drained; new commune of Latina founded 1932.

Campanha, *t.*, Minas Geraes, Brazil; industl.

Campania, *region*, S. Italy; ch. t. Naples; a. 5,250 sq. m.; p. (1961) *4,756,094.*

Campaspe, *R.*, Victoria, Australia; rises in Grampian Mtns., flows N. into R. Murray at Echuca; supplies water for irrigated area between Rochester and Echuca; length, 140 m.

Campbellton, *t.*, *spt.*, New Brunswick, Canada; lumbering, fishing; (1961) *9,873.*

Campbelltown, *t.*, N.S.W., Australia; dairy and poultry ctr.; proposed as satellite t. for Sydney; p. (1966) *22,812.*

Campbeltown, *burgh*, *spt.*, Argyll, Scot.; on Firth of Clyde cst. of peninsula of Kintyre; distilling, fishing; p. (1961) *6,525.*

Campeche, *st.*, Yucatan, Mexico; hot, flat and unhealthy; rice, cotton, logwood, chicle, sisal; a. 19,670 sq. m.; p. (1960) *168,219.*

Campeche, *cap. t. of st., spt.*, Mexico; on G. of Mexico; exp. logwood, sisal, hemp; p. (1960) *31,272.* [lands; battle 1797.

Camperdown, *vil.* on dunes, N. Holland, Nether-

Campinas, *t.*, Brazil; 55 m. N. of São Paulo; coffee; machin.; rubber gds.; p. (1960) *179,797.*

Campine or Kempenland, *dist.*, provs. Limburg and Antwerp, Belgium; coalfield.

Campo Belo, *t.*, Minas Geraes st., Brazil; 200 m. by rail N.E. of Guanabara; impt. cattle ctr.

Campobasso, *prov.*, Italy; in Appenines; a. 1,692 sq. m.; p. (1961) *332,121.*

Campobasso, *fortfd. t.*, 50 m. N.E. Naples, Italy; famous for cutlery and arms; p. (1961) *34,314.*

Campobello di Licata, *t.*, Sicily; sulphur-mines.

Campobello di Massara, *t.*, Sicily; quarrying.

Campos, *c.*, Rio de Janeiro, Brazil; coffee, sugar, alcohol distilling; p. (1960) *90,601.*

Campsie Fells, *range of hills*, Stirling, Scot.; highest point, 1,894 ft.

Campulung, *t.*, Muscel, Romania; N.W. of Bucharest.; summer resort; p. (1963) *22,696.*

Canada, Dominion of, N. America; dominion founded 1867, and now inc. all Brit. N. American Federation of ten provinces: Nova Scotia, New Brunswick, Prince Edward I., Quebec, Ontario, Manitoba, Saskatchewan, Alberta, Brit. Columbia, Newfoundland with Labrador, and the terr. of Yukon and N.W. Territories (Franklin, Keewatin, Mackenzie); cap. Ottawa; Great Lakes; Rocky Mtns.; Great Plains; St. Lawrence, Saskatchewan, and Mackenzie Rs.; Trans-Canada Highway 4860 m. long runs from St. John's (Newfoundland) to Victoria (B.C.) opened 3 Sept. 1962; extreme climate, Pacific seaboard mild; conniferous forest belt except for Central grass-lands, tundra in N.; agr.: wheat, oats, dairying; pulp, paper; coal, gold, copper, nickel, zinc, lead, radium, uranium; oil, natural gas; fisheries; furs; hydro-electric power; impt. mnfs.; a. 3,851,809 sq. m.; p. (estd. 1966) *20,014,800.*

Canada Dam, Bihar, Indian Union; on R. Mayurakshi, 160 m. from Calcutta.

Canadian Coast Range, *mtns.*, B.C., W. Canada; extend N.W. to S.E. along cst.; penetrated by deep inlets (fjords) with very little cst. plain; drained by short, swift Rs., crossed only by R. Skeena in N., R. Fraser in S., which give access to interior; marked climatic barrier, to W. equable climate with heavy all-year rain, to E. more extreme semi-arid climate, especially on valley floors.

Canadian R., trib. (flowing from New Mexico) of Arkansas R., U.S.A.; length 900 m.

Canal du Centre, *canal*, Saône-et-Loire dep., France; links Rhône–Saône valley at Chalon-sur-Saône with R. Loire at Digoin; serves Le Creusot Coalfield; length 60 m.

Canal Zone, Panama; strip of land leased to U.S.A. for Panama Canal; a. 648 sq. m. (276 sq. m. water); p. (1960) *42,122.*

Cananea, *t.*, Mexico; cattle, copper, silver, lead, zinc; p. *11,006.*

Cañar, *prov.*, Ecuador; cap. Azoques; Inca remains; agr., Panama hats; a. 1,521 sq. m.; p. (estd. 1962) *112,618.*

Canaries Current, *ocean current*; flows S. along N.W. cst. of Africa from Casablanca to C. Verde; relatively cold and has very marked cooling effect on Saharan coastlands.

Canary Is., or Canaries, N. Atl. Oc.; group of 7 Is. belonging to Spain, 60 m. off cst. Africa and 700 m. S. of Gibraltar; compr. Tenerife I., the lgst. (cap. Santa Cruz), Gran Canaria (cap. Las Palmas), Palma, Gomera, Hierro, Fuerteventura, Lanzarote; tropical produce; ch. exp., bananas, oranges, tomatoes, vegetables and tobacco; wine, cochineal; a. 4,685 sq. m.; p. (1962) *967.177.*

Canastota, *t.*, N.Y., U.S.A.; engin., furniture, plastics; p. (1960) *4,896.*

Canberra, Australian Capital Territory, Australia; in Gr. Dividing Range (alt. *c.* 6,000 ft.) 200 m. S.W. of Sydney; *seat of govt.* of Commonwealth; univ.; 911 sq. m.; p. (of t. 1966) *92,199.*

Cancale, *t.*, Ille-et-Vilaine dep., N. France; St. Michael's Bay; oysters; p. (1954) *5,463.*

Candia (Herakleion), *c.*, Crete; midway along N. cst.; olive oil, raisins; p. (1961) *64,492.*

Canea, *see* Khania.

Canelones, *dep.*, Uruguay; wine; a. 1,834 sq. m.; p. (1953) *201,359.*

Cañete, *sm. spt.*, Lima dep., Peru, S. America; 75 m. S.E. of Callao; exp. cotton grown under irrigation in Canete valley.

Cangas de Onis, *commune*, Spain; agr., cattle; coal, copper, tanning; p. (1957) *10,713.*

Cangas de Tineo, *t.*, Oviedo, Spain; nr. N. cst., 35 m. E. of Oviedo; woollens, linens; p. (1957) *21,500.*

Canicatti, *t.*, Sicily; sulphur; in fruit-growing dist.; p. *27,860.*

Canna, *sm. I.*, Hebrides, Scot.; basaltic pillars.

Cannanore, *t.*, Kerala, India; exp. timber, coconuts; p. (1961) *48,960.*

Cannet (Le), *t.*, Alpes-Maritimes, France; p. (1954) *11,601.*

Cannes, *spt.*, dep. Alpes-Maritimes, France; 20 m. S.W. Nice; famous winter resort; perfumes; p. (1962) *59,173.*

Cannock and Hednesford, *urb. dist.*, Staffs, Eng., on S.W. flank of Cannock Chase, 7 m. N.E. of Wolverhampton; coal-mng., engin., bricks, tiles, tools, elec. goods, car parts; p. (estd. 1967) *52,030.*

Canonsburg, *bor.*, Penns., U.S.A.; coal, gas, oil; p. (1960) *11,877.*  [Serapis.

Canopus, *anc. c.*, Lower U.A.R.; gr. temple to

Canosa, *t.* Apulia, S. Italy; cath.; the Roman Canusium; ctr. of olive-growing dist.; p. *27,341.*

Cantabrians, *mtns.*, N. Spain, from Pyrenees to Cape Finisterre, hgst. pk. Peña Vieja (8,736 ft.).

Cantal, *mountainous dep.*, Central France; mineral springs, grain, dairying; coal, marble; cap. Aurillac; a. 2,229 sq. m.; p. (1962) *172,977.*

Canterbury, *c.*, *co. bor.*, Kent, Eng.; at foot of N. Downs on R. Stour; famous cath. founded A.D. 597 by St. Augustine; shrine of the murdered Thomas à Becket, a place of pilgrimage for centuries; univ.; fruit growing, tanning; p. (estd. 1967) *32,910.*

Canterbury, *prov.*, S.I., N.Z.; cap. Christchurch; a. 13,940 sq. m.; p. (1961) *339,883.*

Canterbury Plains, rich grazing and wheat-growing dist. S.I., N.Z.; along E. cst., famous for "Canterbury Lamb"; ch. t. Canterbury; ch. pt. Lyttelton.

Can Tho, *t.*, S. Vietnam; on Mekong R.; rice, fish; tr. ctr.; p. *27,000.*

Canton (Guangzhou) *ch. c.*, Kwantung, S. China; on bank of Chu-kiang (Pearl R.); former treaty pt; impt. tr. ctr.; thermal power stas; machin. bldg. plant; p. (1957) *1,840,000.*

Canton, *t.*, Ill., U.S.A.; mnfs.; p. (1960) *13,588.*

Canton, *industl. and agr. c.*, Ohio, U.S.A.; coal, farm machin., engin.; p. (1960) *113,631.*

Canton R., *see* Chukiang.

Canvey I., *urb. dist.*, Essex; fronting the Thames; resort; radio components, bookbinding, iron and wire wk., oil storage; oil refinery projected; liquid gas terminal; p. (estd. 1967) *22,170.*

Cap-de-la-Madeleine, *t.*, Que., Canada; p. (1961) *26,925.*

Cap Haitien, *spt.*, Rep. of Haiti; on N. cst.; bombarded by British 1865; p. (1961) *24,959.*

Capannori, *t.*, Lucca, Italy; silk ind.; p. *39,527.*

Cape Breton I., Nova Scotia, E. Canada; farming, timber, fishing; ch. t. Sydney; a. 3,120 sq. m.

Cape Chidley, *I.* off N. point of Labrador.

Cape Coast, *t.*, Ghana; on cst. 60 m. S.W. of Accra; palm oil; p. (1960) *41,143.*

Cape Giradeau, *t.*, Mo., U.S.A.; p. (1960) *47,924.*

Cape Kennedy, E. Fla., U.S.A., on Atl. Oc., seaward extremity of barrier is. sheltering Bahama R. Lagoon; mil. base for testing missiles.

C. of Good Hope, S. Africa; famous headland, S. of Cape Town, 1,000 ft. high.

Cape Province (formerly Cape of Good Hope Colony), *prov.*, Rep. of S. Africa; physical features: Drakensberg Mtns., Orange and Caledon R., Gr. Karroo, Lit. Karroo; scanty rain except S. and E. cst.; sheep raising; wheat, citrus fruits, grapes, tobacco; fisheries; diamond and copper mng. in Namaqualand; automobile assembly, textiles, food canning; includes Transkeian terrs. in east.; a. 278,465 sq. m.; p. (1960) *5,362,853* incl. *1,003,207* whites.

Cape Town, *c.*, *spt.*, cap. of Cape Province, and legislative cap. of Rep. of S. Africa; on Table Bay, 30 m. N. of C. of Good Hope; communication by rail direct with Rhodesia, Transvaal, Orange and Natal; docks; cath.; univ.; exp. wool, gold, diamonds; oil refinery under construction at Milnerton 6 m. N.E., p. (1960) *745,942* (inc. *286,418* Whites).

C. Verde Islands, Portuguese Is., in Atlantic, 350 m. W. of C. Verde, Africa; divided into two groups, Barlavento (Windward) and Sotavento (Leeward); 15 Is. and islets; a. 1,557 sq. m.; agr., sugar, and fruit-growing; cap. Praia; São Vicente coaling sta. for all navigation to S. America; p. (estd. 1965) *220,000.*

Capernaum, in time of Christ impt. place in Palestine, on the N. shore of the L. of Galilee; the modern Tell Hum (Israel).

Capo d'Istria, *see* Koper.

Cappoquin, *t.*, Waterford, R.o.I. on Blackwater R.

Capraja, Italian I. in the Mediterranean, 16 m. E. Corsica; anciently called Capraria.

Caprera, Italian I. off N.E. Sardinia, where Garibaldi lived.

Caprese, *commune*, Tuscany, Italy; birthplace of Michelangelo; p. *3,195.*

Capri, *I.* and *t.*, in Bay of Naples; tourist resort; residence of Augustus and Tiberius; the ancient Caprae; famous Blue Grotto; fine wines; p. (*t.*) *4,500*; (*I.*) *8,050.*

Capua, *ancient fort. c.*, Campania, Italy; 20 m. N. of Naples; founded by the Etruscans, came under Roman rule, sacked by the Saracens; modern t. 2 m. N. of site of ancient Casilinum; fireworks-mkg.; cath.; p. *14,375.*

Carácas, *cap.*, Venezuela; 8 m. inland from its pt., La Guaira; alt. about 3,000 ft.; cath.; univ.; coffee, cacao, textiles, soaps, detergents, steel, car assembly; underground rly. projected; p. (1961) *739,255.*

Caravaca, *t.*, Murcia, Spain; iron, tanning; p. (1957) *21,700.*  [(1957) *20,965.*

Carballo, *t.*, Corunna, Spain; industl.; fishing; p.

Carbon County, N. Utah, U.S.A.; contains immense reserves of good coking coal suitable for blast furnaces; not yet developed.

Carbondale, *t.*, Penns., U.S.A.; anthracite; p. (1960) *13,595.*

Carbonia, *t.*, Sardinia; built 1937–38 nr. lignite and barite area; p. *12,000.*

Carcagente, *t.*, W. of Cullera, Valencia, Spain; oranges; p. (1955) *18,002.*

Carcar, *t.*, Cebu, Philippine Is.; sugar ind.; p. (1948) *32,818.*

Carcassonne, *t.*, Aude, France; on Aude R.; historic citadel guarding impt. routeway from Aquitaine to Rhône valley; farm implements; wines, cloth; p. (1962) *43,709.*

Carchi, *prov.*, Ecuador; cap. Tulcan; a. 1,495 sq. m.; p. (1962) *93,824.*

Cardamon Hills, Travancore, S. India; forms extreme S.W. edge of Deccan plateau; drained W. by R. Periyan, E. by R. Vaigai; rainfall less seasonal than over most of India; "China" tea plantations on middle slopes; rise to over 8,000 ft. alt.

Cardenas, *t.*, Matanzas, Cuba; sugar, rice, rum; p. (1953) *47,750.*

Cardiff, *cap. c.*, *spt.*, *co. bor.*, Glamorgan, Wales; univ.; docks, coal, iron, steel, engin., elect. goods, brewing, paper; p. (1961) *256,270.*

Cardigan, *mun. bor.*, *co. t.*, Cardigan, S. Wales; on Teifi R.; p. (1961) *3,780.*  [N. and S.

Cardigan Bay, *lge. bay*, W. Wales, 70 m. extent

Cardiganshire, *maritime co.*, S. Wales; mountainous; mainly agr., mines and quarries; a. 692 sq. m.; p. (1966) *53,000.*  [oil refining.

Cardón, *t.*, N. Venezuela, Paraguaná peninsula;

Cardross, *industl. vil.*, Dunbarton, Scot.; on R. Clyde; Robert Bruce d. 1329 in Cardross Castle.

Cardwell, *t.*, Queensland, Australia; harbour; gold-mining dist.  [(1960) *3,722.*

Carey, *t.*, Ohio, U.S.A.; mkt. gardening; p.

Cargenbridge, *t.*, Kirkcudbright, Scot.; chemicals, plastics.

Caribbean Sea, between W. Indies and Central and S. America; a. 7,500 sq. m.

Caribou Range, *mtns.*, B.C., W. Canada; mass of ancient crystalline rocks inside the gr. bend of R. Frazer; widespread occurrence of lode and alluvial gold; mainly above 5,000 ft.

Caribou, *t.*, Maine, U.S.A.; p. (1960) *8,305.*

Caribrod, *t.*, Jugoslavia; on Nisava R.; p. *4,000.*

Carimata I., off S.W. Borneo, Indonesia.

Carinthia, *prov.*, Austria; cap. Klagenfurt; mtnous.; mineral springs; rye, oats; lead, iron; a. 3,681 sq. m.; p. (1961) *495,226.*

Carisbrooke, *t.*, I. of Wight, Eng.; cas. prison of Charles I (1647–8); p. (1951) *5,232.*

Carlingford, *t.*, *spt.*, Louth, Ireland; on Carlingford Bay; oysters.  [Louth. Ireland.

Carlingford, Lough, *inlet* of sea between Down and

Carlinville, *t.*, Ill., U.S.A.; bricks and tiles, agr. machin.; p. (1960) *5,440.*

Carlisle, *t.*, *co. bor.*, Cumberland, Eng.; on Eden R.; 8 m. from Solway Firth; impt. route ctr.; ancient cas. and cath.; textiles, biscuits, metal boxes; p. (estd. 1967) *70,950.*

Carlisle, *bor.*, Penns., U.S.A.; boots and shoes; p. (1960) *16,623.*

Carlow, *co.*, Leinster, Ireland; co. t., Carlow; a. 346 sq. m.; p. (1966) *33,479.*

Carlsbad, *see* Karlovy Vary.

Carlsbad, t., N.M., U.S.A.; p. (1960) *25,541.*

Carlsbad Cavern, N.M., U.S.A.; gr. cave in limestone through which flows R. Pecos; stalactites, stalagmites; tourist attraction; length 4,000 ft., width 600 ft., height of roof 300 ft.

Carlsruhe, *see* Karlsruhe.     [p. (1960) *6,042.*

Carlstadt, *bor.*, N.J., U.S.A.; brass, marble;

Carlton, *urb. dist.*, Notts. Eng.; 2 m. N.E. of Nottingham; lace, hosiery; p. (estd. 1967) *41,660.*

Carluke, t., *par.*, Lanark, Scot.; engin., mng., fruit growing and preserving; p. (1951) *11,415.*

Carmagnola, *mftg. t.*, N. Italy; on Melba R.; p. *12,241.*

Carmarthen, *mun. bor., co. t.,* Carmarthenshire, Wales; on Towy R.; anthracite, limestone quarrying; p. (1961) *13,249.*

Carmarthen Bay, Carmarthen, Wales; 18 m. across.

Carmarthenshire, *co.*, S. Wales; co. t., Carmarthen; mountainous; mining; mainly pastoral land; a. 920 sq. m.; p. (1966) *166,000.*

Carmaux, t., Tarn, France; glass mftg.; p. (1954) *11,485.*

Carmel, Mt., *mtn.*, N.W. Israel, extends 12 m. to Med.; hgst. peak, 1,818 ft.; in biblical times ass. with prophets Elijah and Elisha.

Carmen de Bolivar, *spt.*, Campeche Bay, Mexico.

Carmiel c., N. Israel; new t. built between Acre and Safad, in the Galilean hills; planned for p. *50,000.*     [(1957) *27,115.*

Carmona, t., Spain; olives, wine, fruit; p.

Carnac, *vil.*, Morbihan, N.W. France; S.E. of Lorient; prehistoric stone monuments and circles.

Carnarvon, t., W. Australia; on R. Gascoyne; NASA tracking sta.; p. *4,000.*

Carnatic, *region*, S.E. India, between E. Ghats and Coromandel cst. where earliest European settlements were established.     [(1960) *11,587.*

Carnegie, *bor.*, Penns., U.S.A.; steel, iron; p.

Carnew, *vil.*, Wicklow, Ireland; granite, slate.

Carnforth, t., *urb. dist.*, Lancs, Eng.; rly. ctr.; p. (1961) *4,113.*

Carnoustie, *burgh*, Angus, Scot., on N. Sea; 6 m. S.W. of Arbroath; resort; p. (1961) *5,511.*

Carnsore Point, S. Wexford, Ireland.

Carntogher Mtns., *range of mtns.*, Londonderry, N. Ireland.

Carnwath, *vil.*, Lanark, Scot.; coal, shale, iron.

Caro, t., Mich., U.S.A.; sugar-beet refining; p. (1960) *3,534.*

Carolina, *see* N. and S. Carolina.

Caroline Is., *archipelago* in W. Pac. Oc.; 549 in number, lying between the Philippines and the Marshall Gr., former Japanese mandate now part of U.S. Pac. Trust Terr.; ch. exp. copra.

Caroni R., Venezuela, S. America; hydro-elec. complex at confluence Orinoco R. under constr.

Carpathian Mtns., *range* separating Czechoslovakia and Hungary from Galicia, and Transylvania from Moldavia, 805 m. long; highest point, Tatra 8,740 ft.

Carpentaria, G. of, North Australia; between C. Arnhem and C. York.

Carpentras, c., Vaucluse, France; on R. Auzon; many antiquities; p. (1954) *15,076.*

Carpi, *industl. t.*, Modena, Central Italy; cath.; p. (1961) *45,208.*

Carrantuohill Mtn., Kerry, Ireland; loftiest in Magillicuddy's Reeks and all Ireland, alt. 3,414 ft.

Carrara, t., Massa-e-Carrara, Central Italy; famed for white marble; p. (1961) *64,901.*

Carrickfergus, *spt., mun. bor.*, Antrim, N. Ireland; on N. shore of Belfast Lough; textiles, nylon fibres, tobacco inds.; p. (1966) *10,926.*

Carrickmacross, *mkt. t., urb. dist.*, Monaghan, Ireland; hand made lace; p. (1966) *2,094.*

Carrick-on-Shannon, co. t., *rural dist.*, Leitrim, Ireland; p. (of t.) (1966) *1,636.*

Carrick-on-Suir, *mkt. t., urb. dist.*, Tipperary, Ireland; coal, timber; p. (1966) *4,830.*

Carrizal-Bajo, t., Atacama prov., Chile; port for Carrizal-Alto, 25 m. E.     [*10,973.*

Carrollton, t., Ga., U.S.A.; textiles; p. (1960)

Carron, *vil.*, Stirling, Scot.; nr. Falkirk; famous ironwks.

Carron, Loch, *inlet*, W. cst., Ross and Cromarty, Scot.; followed by rly. from Dingwall to Kyle and Lochalsh.

Carse of Gowrie, Perth, Scot.; fertile cstl. dist. between Perth and Dundee, S. of Sidlaw Hills; sm. fruits, especially raspberries.

Carshalton, *see* Sutton.

Carson City, *st. cap.*, Nevada, U.S.A.; silver- and gold-mining dist.; p. (1960) *5,163.*

Carstairs, *vil.*, Lanark, Scot.; N.E. of Lanark t.

Cartagena, *spt., cap.*, dep. Bolivar, Colombia, S. America; shares with Barranquilla tr. brought down Magdalena R.; platinum, coffee, chemicals, textiles, fertilisers; oil pipe terminal; p. (estd. 1962) *185,160.*

Cartagena, *spt.*, Murcia, E. Spain; fine wharves and harbour; naval arsenal; cath.; shipbldg., metal-wkg.; p. (1959) *123,301.*

Cartago, t., Cauca, Colombia, S. America; coffee, tobacco, cattle; p. (estd. 1959) *64,830.*

Cartago, *prov.*, Costa Rica, Central America; cap. C.; coffee, fruits; p. (1963) *154,500.*

Carteret, *bor.*, N.J., U.S.A.; metal and oil refining, chemicals, tobacco; p. (1960) *20,502.*

Carter Fell, *mtn.*, Northumberland, Eng., 1,815 ft.

Carterton, *bor.*, Wellington, N.I., New Zealand; p. (1961) *3,077.*

Carthage, c., N.E. Tunis, N. Africa; with ruins of ancient Carthage, destroyed by the Romans 146 B.C.

Carthage, t., Mo., U.S.A.; coal; p. (1960) *11,264.*

Cartmel, *par.*, Lancs, Eng.; near Ulverston.

Carupano, *spt.*, Venezuela, S. America; exp. coffee, cacao; airport; p. (1961) *30,000.*

Carvine, t., Pas-de-Calais, France; p. (1954) *15,780.*

Casablanca, autonomous c., Morocco, N. Africa; motor plant; p. (1960) *965,277.*

Casablanca, t., Valparaiso, Chile.

Casa Branca, t., S.E. of Lisbon, Portugal.

Casale, t., Piedmont, Italy; cath.; cement; p. (1961) *40,827.*

Casalmaggiore, t., Italy; on R. Po, near Parma; p. *15,012.*

Casas Grandes, t., N.W. Chihuahua st., Mexico; Aztec ruins; p. *2,000.*

Cascade Range, N. America; extends N. and S. through Brit. Columbia, Washington and Oregon between Rocky Mtns. and Pacific cst. Highest peak, Mt. Rainier, 14,408 ft.

Cascade Tunnel, longest rly. tunnel in N. America, Wash., U.S.A.; carries trunk rly. from Spokane to Seattle through Cascade Mtns.; length 7⅘ m.

Cascina, t., Pisa, Italy; on R. Arno; silk mnfs.

Caserta, t., Italy; on N. edge of Plain of Naples; royal palace; cath.; silks; p. (1961) *50,810.*

Cashel, c., *urb. dist.*, Tipperary, Ireland; cath. (ruined) on Rock of Cashel; p. (1966) *2,632.*

Casino, t., N.S.W., Australia; ctr. for mkt., forestry and meat processing; p. (1966) *8,498.*

Casiquiare, R., Venezuela, joins Orinoco to the Rio Negro, a trib. of the Amazon.

Caspe, t., Spain; on R. Guadalupe; p. *9,033.*

Casper, t., Wyo., U.S.A.; petroleum; p. (1960) *38,930.*

Caspian Sea, U.S.S.R.; 760 m. long, 270 m. wide, 170,000 sq. m., between Asia and Europe; lgst. inland sea in the world; surface 85 ft. below ocean; fisheries; pts.: Astrakhan, Baku, Derbent.

Casquets, *dangerous rocks*, 7 m. W. of Alderney, Channel Is; lighthouse.

Cassaba (Kassaba), *see* Turgutlu.

Cassel, t., *see* Kassel.

Cassilis, t., N.S.W., Australia; 115 m. N.W. of Newcastle in impt. gap in Gr. Dividing Range between Hunter and Liverpool Ranges, giving access from Newcastle to interior.

Cassino, t., Campania, Italy; formerly San Germano; the ancient Casinum nr. famous monastery.

Castelbuono, t., Sicily; mineral springs.

Castelfiorentino, t., Tuscany, nr. Florence, Italy.

Castelfranco, t., Bologna, Italy; p. *2,925.*

Castelfranco, t.; Treviso, Italy; fine church and paintings; silk; p. *4,240.*

Castellamare, *dockyard t.*, Italy; on Bay of Naples at foot of Vesuvius; mineral springs; wat. pl.; p. (1961) *64,618.*

Castellamare del Golfo, *spt.*, N.W. Sicily; wat. pl., tuna fishing; p. *18,032.*

Castellón de la Plana, *prov.*, Spain; on Mediterranean, part of ancient Valencia, mainly mtns., a. 2,579 sq. m.; cap. Castellón; p. (1959) *334,472.*

Castellón de la Plana, *t.*, Spain; porcelain, oranges, carob-wood, onions, wines; oil refining; p. (1959) *57,780*.

Castelnaudary, *t.*, Aude, France, on Languedoc canal, burned by Black Prince, 1355; p. (1954) *8,760*.

Castelo Branco, *c.*, Portugal; *cap.* of dist. same name; p. of dist. (1960) *325,800*.

Castelvetrano, *t.*, Sicily, Italy; industl.; wine; p. *24,746*.

Castiglione, *t.*, Sicily, Italy; near Catania; sulphur refining.

Castiglione Fiorentino, *t.*, Italy; nr. Arezzo; sericulture.

Castile, formerly a kingdom of Spain; now div. into Old and New Castile.

Castine, *t.*, Me., U.S.A.; on Penobscot Bay; resort; fishing.

Castlebar, *urb. dist.*, *cap.*, Mayo, Ireland; " Race of Castlebar " battle fought here in 1798 Rebellion; bacon curing, hat-mkg.; p. (1966) *5,630*.

Castleblayney, *urb. dist.*, Monaghan, Ireland; nr. Dundalk; p. (1961) *2,125*.

Castle Cary, *mkt. t.*, Somerset, Eng.; N.E. of Yeovil; dairying; p. (1951) *1,664*.

Castlecary, *vil.*, Stirlingshire, Scot.; sta. on Roman wall; silica, fire-clay deposits.

Castlecomer, *rural dist.*, N. Kilkenny, Ireland; p. (1961) *7,323*.

Castle Donington, *t.*, *rural dist.*, Leics. Eng.; p. (of dist. 1961) *9,809*.

Castle Douglas, *burgh*, Kirkcudbright, Scot.; 15 m. S.W. of Dumfries; cattle fairs; p. (1961) *3,253*.

Castleford, *mun. bor.*, W.R. Yorks, Eng.; 10 m. S.E. of Leeds at confluence of Rs. Aire and Calder; coal-mng., chemical, glass and clothing mnfs., flour-milling, brick-mkg.; p. (estd. 1967) *39,630*.

Castleisland, *t.*, Kerry, Ireland; agr. ctr.; p. (1966) *1,673*.

Castlemaine, *t.*, Victoria, Australia; at foot of Gr. Dividing Range, 25 m. S. of Bendigo; dairying, sheep; engin; wool; p. (1966) *7,082*.

Castlerea, *rural dist.*, Roscommon, Ireland; p. (of dist.) (1961) *18,337*.

Castletown, *t.*, Isle of Man; former cap.; p. (1956) *1,755*.

Castletown Berehaven, *spt.*, Cork, Ireland; on Bantry Bay.

Castres, *t.*, Tarn, France; on R. Agoût; former Huguenot stronghold; cath.; textiles, soap, earthenware; p. (1962) *40,005*.

Castries, *cap.*, *spt.*, St. Lucia, Windward Is., W.I., greatly damaged by fire June 1948; fine harbour; p. (1957) *25,000*.

Castro del Rio, *t.*, Andalusia, Spain; on R. Guadjo; industl.; p. (1957) *14,126*.

Castrogiovanni, *see* Enna.

Castrop-Rauxel or Kastrop Rauxel, *t.*, N. Rhine-Westphalia, Germany; industl.; coal, cement, tar prod., tiles, brandy; p. (1963) *88,500*.

Castro Urdiales, *spt.*, Santander, N. Spain; sardines, iron ore; p. (1957) *11,646*.

Castrovillari, *hill t.*, S. Italy; built on cliff above R. Coscile; mkt. ctr. for local cereals, wine, oil and silkworms; p. (estd.) *10,000*.

Cat I. (or Guanahani), Bahamas, W. Indies; a. 340 sq. m.; p. (1953) *3,201*.

Catacaos, *t.*, Piura dep., Peru; Panama hats.

Catalonia, *old prov.*, N.E. Spain; mountainous; wooded; cereals; mnfs.: cottons, woollens, silks; rich in minerals; cap. Barcelona; nuclear power sta. projected; a. 12,427 sq. m.; p. (1957) *3,240,000*.

Catamarca, *prov.*, N.W. Argentina; cap. C.; farming; gold, silver, copper mng.; a. 40,942 sq. m.; p. (1960) *172,000*.

Catamarca, *t.*, *cap.*, Catamarca prov., N.W. Argentina; located in Andean foot-hills 80 m. S. of Tucuman; ctr. of irrigated oasis producing vines, apricots, cherries, cotton; thermal springs; p. (1960) 29,000.

Catanduanes, *I.*, off Luzon, Philippines; hilly, fertile; rice, corn, cotton, hemp, coconuts; a. 552 sq. m.; p. (1960) *1,563,000*.

Catania, *prov.*, Sicily; ch. t., Catania; a. 1907 sq. m.; p. (1961) *884,447*.

Catania, *c.*, Sicily; on E. cst. at foot of Mt. Etna; city several times rebuilt in consequence of earthquakes; cath.; univ.; textiles, dyeing; p. (1965) *396,000*.

Catanzaro, *c.*, S. Italy; univ.; silks, velvets; p. (1961) *72,723*.

Catasauqua, *bor.*, Penns., U.S.A.; industl.; flour, cement, textiles; p. (1960) *5,062*.

Catastrophe, C., S. extremity of Eyre Peninsula, S. Australia.

Catawba, *R.*, N.C., U.S.A.; rising in Blue Ridge Range; length 300 m.

Caterham and Warlingham, *urb. dist.*, Surrey, Eng.; on N. Downs; residtl.; p. (estd. 1967) *36,910*.

Cathay, ancient name for China and E. Tartary.

Catoche, C., N.E. point of Yucatan, Mexico.

Catrine, *t.*, Ayr, Scot.; mftg.

Catskill Mtns., N.Y., U.S.A.; gr. in Appalachians, W. of Hudson R.; holiday resort.

Cauca, *I.*, Colombia; trib. of Magdalena; length 600 m.

Cauca, *dep.* Colombia Rep.; cap. Popayán; a. 11,657 sq. m.; p. (1962) *529,040*.

Caucasia, region between Black Sea and Caspian, divided by Caucasus Mtns. into N. or Cis-Caucasia and Trans-Caucasia.

Caucasus, *lofty mtn. range* between Caspian and Black Sea; highest summits Mt. Elbruz (18,463 ft.) and Kasbek (16,546 ft.); length of system about 900 m., greatest width 120 m.; many lofty passages and lge. glaciers.

Caudebec, *ancient t.*, Seine-Maritime, France; oil refinery nearby; p. (1962) *9,270*.

Cauderan, *commune*, Gironde, France; sub. of Bordeaux; p. (1954) *26,543*.

Caudete, *t.*, Albacete, Spain; p. (1957) *7,862*.

Caudry, *t.*, Nord, France; lace and tulle; p. (1962) *13,475*. [*12,987.*

Cauquenes, *t.*, Chile; cap. of Maule prov.; p.

Causses, Les, *limestone plateau*, Aveyron, Tarn deps., S. France; on S.W. flank of Central Plateau; caverns, gorges of Rs. Lot and Tarn; sheep provide milk for Roquefort cheese; alt. 3,000–6,000 ft.

Cauterets, *vil.*, dep. Hautes-Pyrénées; France; mineral springs.

Cautin, *prov.*, S. Chile; cap. Temuco; a. 6,705 sq. m.; p. (1960) *475,121*.

Cauvery, *R.*, S. India; rises in the W. Ghats, flows into Bay of Bengal through Mysore and Madras; length 400 m.

Cava or La Cava, *t.*, Salerno, Italy; summer resort; textiles; p. (1961) *42,235*.

Cavaillon, *commune*, Vaucluse, France; cath.; p. (1962) *17,218*.

Cavan, *inland co.*, Ulster, Ireland; a. 746 sq. m.; agr.; distilling; p. (1966) *53,815*.

Cavan, *urb. dist.*, *co. t.*, Cavan, Ireland; 72 m. S.W. Belfast; p. (1966) *4,165*.

Cavarzere, *t.*, Venice, N. Italy; on R. Adige; industl.; p. *22,321*.

Cavite, *spt.*, Luzon, Philippines; oil refining nearby; p. (1960) *54,891*.

Cavour Canal, *irrigation canal*, Piedmont and Lombardy regions, N. Italy; links R. Po nr. Chivasso with R. Ticino 10 m. N.E. of Novara; provides water for 250,000 acres of rice-fields and meadow-land; length 80 m.

Cawnpore (Kanpur), *cap.*, Cawnpore dist., Uttar Pradesh, India; on the Ganges; 130 m. N.W of Allahabad; grain, cotton, woollens, aircraft mftg.; p. (1961) *947,793*.

Caxias, *t.*, Maranhão, Brazil; on Itapecuru R.; cotton, rice; p. (1960) *60,607*.

Cayambe, *mtn.*, Andes, Ecuador; alt. 19,355 ft.

Cayenne, *spt.*, *cap.*, Fr. Guiana, S. America; famous for pepper; p. (estd. 1965) *19,000*.

Cayey, *t.*, S.E. Puerto Rico; tobacco, coffee, sugar; p. *5,622*.

Cayman Is., West Indies, a. 100 sq. m.; p. (estd. 1965) *8,853*; consists of Grand Cayman, cap. Georgetown; Little Cayman; and Cayman Brac.; turtle and shark fishing.

Cazalla de la Sierra, S.W. Spain; iron and lead; aniseed; p. (1957) *11,347*.

Ceará, *st.*, N. Brazil; sugar, cotton, coffee, rubber; cap. Fortaleza; a. 59,168 sq. m.; p. (1960) *3,337,856*.

Ceara, *see* Fortaleza.

Cebu, *I.*, Philippines; mtnous, forested; copper, cement; a. 1,702 sq. m.; p. (1960) *1,185,600*.

Cebu, *ch. t.*, Cebu I., trade ctr. of Visayan Is.; p. (1960) *251,000*.

Cedar or Red Cedar, *R.*, Iowa, U.S.A.; trib. of Mississippi R., length 400 m.

Cedar Falls, *t.*, Iowa, U.S.A.; p. (1960) *21,195*.

Cedar Mountain, *hill*, Va., U.S.A.; here Stonewall Jackson defeated Banks 1862.

Cedar Rapids, c., Iowa, U.S.A.; rly. ctr.; farm machin., lumber; p. (1960) 92,035.

Cedartown, t., Ga., U.S.A.; textiles, rubber tyres; cottonseed oil; p. (1960) 9,340.

Cedros, I., off W. coast, Lower Cal., Mexico.

Cefalù, spt., Palermo, N. Sicily; famous Norman cath. with mosaics; vines, oranges; fishing; p. c. 13,000.

Ceglie, c., Lecce, S. Italy; wine, olive oil, building stone; p. c. 21,000. [15,830.

Cehegin, t., Murcia, Spain; on R. Quipar; p. (1957)

Celaya, t., Guanajuato, Mexico; ctr. rich farming a.; many inds.; p. c. 35,000.

Celebes, see Sulawesi.

Celina, t., W. Ohio, U.S.A.; resort; furniture, canning; p. (1960) 7,659.

Celje, t., Slovenia, Jugoslavia; lignite, zinc smelting; p. (1960) 29,000.

Celle, t., Lower Saxony, Germany; on R. Aller; former residence of the Dukes of Brunswick-Lüneberg; cas.; metal, leather, paints, textiles, oil; p. (1963) 59,000.

Cenis, Mont, see Mont Cenis.

Cento, t., Ferrara, Italy; industl.; p. 4,942.

Central African Republic, ind. sov. st. within French Community, Equatorial Africa; cap. Bangui; a. 238,000 sq. m.; p. (1966) 2,088,000.

Central America, between Mexico and S. America, from the Isthmus of Tehuantepec to that of Panama; includes Guatemala, Honduras, Nicaragua, Salvador, Costa Rica, Panama, Brit. Honduras; tropical climate; forests, savannahs p. (estd. 1965) 30,000,000.

Central Asia, usually applied to regions between 30° and 40° N. lat. and 55° and 85° E. long.; Russian C.A. is the land between China and Afghanistan and the Caspian, now consisting of various Soviet Reps.

Central Falls, c., Rhode Is., U.S.A.; nr. Pawtucket; cotton goods; p. (1960) 19,858.

Central Greece and Euboea, geographical div., Greece; contains the cap. Athens; a. 9,704 sq. m.; p. (1961) 2,323,658.

Central Province, prov., Iran, cap. Tehran; p. (1967) 4,950,394.

Centralia, t., Ill., U.S.A.; p. (1960) 13,904.

Centuripe, commune, Enna, Sicily; sulphur, marble; p. 10,802.

Cephalonia, see Kephallenia.

Ceram (Serang), I., Moluccas, Indonesia; a. 6,621 sq. m.; tobacco, sago; p. 83,000.

Ceres, t., Cape Province, S. Africa; on R. Hex; health resort; p. (1960) 6,173.

Cerignola, t., Foggia, Italy; Spanish victory over French 1503; p. (1961) 49,287.

Cerigo, see Kythera.

Cernauti, see Chernovtsy.

Cernavoda, t., Dobrogea, Rumania; on R. Danube, 70 m. S. of Braila; p. (1956) 8,802.

Cerro de Pasco, t., dep. Junin, Peru; silver, coal, lead; copper smelting; large vanadium mines W. of t.; p. (1961) 19,354.

Cerro Rico, mtn., Bolivia; in Andes, W. of Potosi; alt. 15,680 ft.; v. rich silver, tin, tungsten ores.

Certaldo, commune, Firenze, Italy; anc. cas.; home of Boccaccio; p. 12,094.

Cesena, old industl. t., Forli, Italy; cath.; antiquities; sulphur-mines, wines; p. (1961) 79,704.

Ceská Lípa, t., ČSSR.; on R. Ploucnice N. o Prague; industl.; p. (1961) 14,038.

Ceská Trebová, old t., ČSSR.; W. of Pardubice; engin., textiles; p. (1961) 13,031.

Ceské Budejovice, t., ČSSR.; on R. Vltava 80 m. S. of Prague; pencils, porcelain, brewing, anthracite; p. (1961) 63,949.

Cesky Tesin, (Teschen), Silesia, ČSSR., (divided between Poland and Czechoslovakia); coal and ironwks.; p. (1961) 15,508.

Cessnock, t., N.S.W., Australia; coal-mining declining 1968; clothing wks.; p. (1966) 15,329 inc. Bellbird.

Cette, see Sète.

Ceuta, spt., Morocco; opposite to and 16 m. from Gibraltar; cath.; the ancient Abyla, one of the Pillars of Hercules; p. (1950) 59,936.

Cévennes, mtns., S. France; separating basins of Rhône, Loire and Tarn; highest point Mt. Mézenc, alt. 5,794 ft.

Ceylon, I., indep. sov. st. within Br. Commonwealth (1948); in Indian Ocean, S.E. of India; fertile plains, mountainous interior; principal prod.: rice, rubber, tea, coconuts, fruits and spices; rubber tyres and tubes, hardware, tiles;

cap. and ch. spt. Colombo; steel mill at Oruwala; a. 25,332 sq. m.; p. (1965) 10,965,000.

Chacabuco, t., E. Argentina; agr. ctr.; p. 15,000.

Chachapoyas, t., cap. of Amazonas dep., N. Peru; agr., forest prod.; p. (1946) 5,494.

Chaco, terr., N. of Argentina; part of Gran Chaco; farming and prairie land; cap. Resistencia; a. 38,468 sq. m.; p. (1960) 535,000.

Chad, L., lge sheet of water of N. Central Africa; a. 50,000 sq. m. when in flood, varies in extent with season, and is drying up, shallow, many Is., lies between the wooded region of the Sudan and the steppes leading to the Sahara desert.

Chad, ind. sov. st. within French Community, Equatorial Africa; cap. Fort Lamy; a. 495,000 sq. m.; p. (estd. 1965) 2,830,000.

Chadderton, urb. dist., Lancs. Eng.; cotton and chemical mftg.; p. (estd. 1967) 31,880.

Chagford, par., Devon, Eng.; stone circles.

Chagos, Is., Indian Ocean; administered from Mauritius; fine harbour in Diego Garcia.

Chagres, spt., Panama, S. America; on N. side of Isthmus of Panama; p. 1,300.

Chaguaramas, Trinidad, W.I., part of naval base leased to U.S.A. since 1941.

Chahar Mahal Bakhtiiyari, region, Iran; W. of Isfahan; mainly mtnous.; cap. Sharkord; a. 6,072 sq. m.; p. (1967) 209,057.

Chakray-Ting, t., Cambodia; cement plant.

Chalcidice, see Khalkidhiki.

Chalcis, t., Euboea, Greece; p. (1961) 24,745.

Chaleur Bay, Canada; between N. Brunswick and Gaspé Peninsula, Quebec.

Chalon-sur-Saône, ancient industl. c., Saône-et-Loire, E. France; glass, iron; p. (1962) 45,993.

Chalons-sur-Marne, c., Marne, N.E. France; 20 m. E. of Epernay; cath.; military ctr.; brewery ind.; p. (1962) 45,348. [11,473.

Chamalières, t., Puy-de-Dôme, France; p. (1954)

Chaman, t., Baluchistan, Pakistan; on Afghan frontier; terminus of rly. through Quetta.

Chamba, t., Himachal Pradesh, India; 100 m. N.E. of Amritsar; p. (1961) 8,609.

Chambal, R., trib. of R. Jumna rising in Vindhya hills; length 650 m.

Chambersburg, bor., Penns., U.S.A.; foundries, brewing; p. (1960) 17,670.

Chambéry, t., cap., Savoie, S.E. France; silk, leather; p. (1962) 47,447. [wines.

Chambolle-Musigny, commune, Côte d'Or, France;

Chambon-Feugerolles, t., Loire, France; coal, iron, steel mftg.; p. (1954) 17,695.

Chamonix, t., Haute-Savoie, France; at foot of Mont Blanc, in valley of R. Arve; winter sports ctr.; road tunnel links to Aosta; p. (1954) 5,699.

Champagne, old prov., N.E. France; famous for its wine; wheat, sheep, impt. tr. fairs in Middle Ages.

Champagne Humide, natural division (" pays "), Central France; clay vale, runs 100 m. N.E. from Auxerre to Bar-le-Duc; drained by Seine, Aube, Marne, Aisne and many tribs.; heavily wooded, marshy; where cleared and drained, grain cultivation.

Champagne Pouilleuse, natural division (" pays "), Central France; barren chalk plateau, extends 80 m. N.E. from Sens to Reims; drained by Aisne, Vesle, Seine, Aube, Marne; dusty downland pastures; sheep; vine growing on S.-facing valley sides and S.E.-facing escarpment of Falaise de l'Ile de France favours production of Champagne wines, ch. producing ctrs.: Châlons-sur-Marne, Reims, Epernay.

Champaign, t., Ill., U.S.A.; foundries; p. (1960) 49,583.

Champerico, spt., S.W. Guatemala; coffee.

Champigny-sur-Marne, t., Seine, France; embroidery; piano keys; p. (1962) 57,925.

Champlain, L., U.S.A.; N. frontier of N.Y., state; discharges by Richelieu R. into St. Lawrence; flanked by trunk route from New York to Montreal; a. 600 sq. m.

Champlain Canal, N.Y., U.S.A.; follows gap between Adirondack Mtns. and Green Mtns. occupied by Hudson R.; links Albany with L. Champlain and allows through barge traffic between New York and St. Lawrence valley.

Chanaral, spt., N. Atacama, Chile; lies in gold and copper mng. ctr.; p. (1960) 21,098.

Chancelade, commune, Dordogne, France; arch. type-site of Chancelade culture (late paleolithic).

Chanda, *t.*, Nagpur, Maharashtra, India; ancient temples; p. (1961) *51,484.*

Chanda, *dist.*, Maharashtra, India; teak forests, coal, iron; a. 9,200 sq. m.; p. (1961) *1,238,070.*

Chandausi, *t.*, Uttar Pradesh, India; cotton, hemp; rly. ctr.; p. (1961) *48,557.*

Chandernagore, *t.*, W. Bengal, India; on Hooghly R.; French 1816–1949; cotton; p. (1961) *67,105.*

Chandigarh, *Union terr.*, E. Punjab, India; situated on plateau at foot of Himalaya, S.W. of Simla; built 1951–3 by Le Corbusier; univ.; cap. of Punjab and Hariana sts., p. (1961) *89,321.*

Changchow (Changzhou), *c.*, Kiangsu, China; in Yangtze Kiang valley, on Grand Canal 70 m. S.E. of Nanking; mkt. for intensively cultivated dist.; silk; p. (1953) *297,000.*

Changchun, *c.*, Kirin, China; rly. ctr.; p. (1953) *855,000.*

Changnacheri, *t.*, Kerala, S. India; tea, cotton spinning, silk; p. (1961) *42,376.*

Changpai Shan, *mtns.*, form bdy. between China and N. Korea; drained by Rs. Yalu, Ertao, Tumen; highest point, Peiktusan, alt. 8,005 ft.

Changsha, *c.*, *cap.*, Hunan prov., China; tea, rice, antimony; p. (1953) *651,000.*

Changshu, *c.*, Kiangsu, China; in Yangtze Kiang valley 65 m. N.W. of Shanghai; mkt. for local agr. produce; p. (1953) *101,000.*

Channel Islands, gr. of self-governing Is. belonging to the British Crown off N.W. cst. France, of which the lgst. are Jersey, Guernsey, Alderney and Sark; part of the old Duchy of Normandy; vegetables, flowers, fruit, granite; two famous breeds of dairy cattle; tourist resort; German occupation, 1940–45; ch. t. St. Helier, Jersey; total a. 75 sq. m.; p. (1961) *110,503.*

Chantaburi, *t.*, *spt.*, Thailand, rubies and other precious stones.

Chantada, *commune*, N.W. Spain; cattle, leather, soap, bricks, linen; p. (1957) *14,467.*

Chantilly, *t.*, Oise, France; famous race-course; p. (1946) *5,105.*

Chanute, *mkt. t.*, Kan., U.S.A.; oil, gas; refineries, cement; p. (1960) *10,849.*

Chaochow (Chaozhou), *c.*, Kwangtung, S. China; on Han R. 20 m. N. of Swatow; ctr. of cultivated plain; rice, sugar, tea; linked to Swatow by rly.; p. (1953) *101,000.*

Chapala, *L.*, Mexico; chiefly in Jalisco st.; a. 1,300 sq. m.

Chapayev, *see* Gurev.

Chapayevsk, *t.* Kuibyshev Region, R.S.F.S.R.; chemicals, agr. machin.; p. (1959) *83,000.*

Chapelcross, nr. Annan, Dumfriesshire, Scot.; nuclear reactor sta.; power and plutonium prod.

Chapel-en-le-Frith, *mkt. t.*, *rural dist.*, Derby, Eng.; p. (1961 rural dist.) *18,366.*

Chapelizod, *sub.* of Dublin, Ireland; on R. Liffey.

Chapra, *t.*, Bihar; on Ganges R.; ctr. of saltpetre and indigo tr.; p. (1961) *75,580.*

Chard, *mun. bor.*, Somerset, Eng.; lace, iron, engin., shirt and cotton mftg.; p. (estd. 1967) *6,910.*

Chardzhou, *t.*, Turkmen S.S.R.; on the Central Asia Rly.; textiles, chemicals; p. (1959) *66,000.*

Charente, *dep.*, W. France; cap. Angoulême; ctr. of distilling tr., cognac; a. 2,305 sq. m.; p. (1962) *327,658.*

Charente, R., W. France; flows into Bay of Biscay below Rochefort.

Charente-Maritime, *dep.*, S.W. France; cap. La Rochelle; wine, wheat; oysters, pilchards; a. 2,791 sq. m.; p. (1962) *470,897.*

Charenton-le-Pont, *commune*, Seine dep., France; N.E. sub. of Paris; boats, pottery, rubber; p. (1954) *22,079.*

Charleroi, *t.*, Hainaut, Belgium; on R. Sambre; coal-mng.; glass; p. (1965) *233,000* (inc. subs.).

Charleroi, *t.*, Penns., U.S.A.; steel, glass; p. (1960) *8,148.*        [(1960) *9,964.*

Charles City, *c.*, Iowa, U.S.A.; on Cedar R.; p.

Charleston, *t.*, Ill., U.S.A.; dairy produce, flour, shoes; p. (1960) *10,505.*

Charleston, *c.*, *spt.*, S. Carolina, U.S.A.; lumber, metal, concrete, fertilisers, chemicals, plastics, cigars, fabrics; p. (1960) *60,182.*

Charleston, *t.*, *cap.*, W. Virginia, U.S.A.; on Kanawha R.; in bituminous coal dist.; chemicals, glass, tools, oil, natural gas, lumber, coal processing; p. (1960) *85,796.*

Charlestown, *ch. t.*, Nevis I., Leeward Group; p. (1957) *15,446.*

Charleville, *see* Rathluirc.

Charleville-Mézières, *t.*, Ardennes dep., N.E. France; on Meuse R.; iron, bricks, nails, hardware; p. (1962) *50,229.*

Charleville, *t.*, Queensland, Australia; on Warrego R., 400 m. W. of Brisbane; pastoral dist.; p. (1966) *4,799.*        [(1960) *2,751.*

Charlevoix, *pt.*, *t.*, L. Michigan, U.S.A.; p.

Charlotte, *c.*, N.C., U.S.A.; key rly. junction; machin., chemicals, textiles; p. (1960) *201,564.*

Charlotte, *t.*, S. Mich., U.S.A.; furniture, car parts; p. (1960) *7,657.*

Charlottenburg, *t.*, Germany; on R. Spree; sub. of Berlin; palace; china, beer, machin.

Charlottesville, *t.*, Va., U.S.A.; on Rivanna R.; univ.; Monticello—home of Thomas Jefferson; p. (1960) *29,427.*

Charlottetown, *spt.*, *cap.*, Prince Edward I., Canada; Parliament buildings; iron foundry, shipyards, fisheries; p. (1961) *18,318.*

Charlton Kings, *t.*, *dist.*, Gloucester, Eng.; at foot of Cotswolds nr. Cheltenham; p. (1961) *7,744.*

Charnwood Forest, *upland district*, Leicester, Eng.; to W. of Soar valley, 12 m. N.W. of Leicester; composed of ancient rocks; stone-crushing; largely forests; used for recreation by industl. ts. of E. Midlands; alt. 600–900 ft.

Charters Towers, *t.*, N. Queensland, Australia; 925 m. by rail from Brisbane; pastoral ctr.; p. (1966) *7,533.*

Chartres, *c.*, *cap.*, dep. Eure-et-Loir, France; fine Gothic cath.; milling, brewing, distilling; p. (1954) *28,750.*        [near Grenoble.

Chartreuse, La Grande, France, famous monastery

Chateaubriant, *t.*, Loire-Inférieure, France; rly. ctr.; p. (1946) *7,965.*        [p. (1946) *7,243.*

Château Thierry, *t.*, Aisne, France; on R. Marne;

Châteauroux, *t.*, Indre, France; 60 m. S.E. of Tours on R. Indre; woollens, machin.; p. (1962) *46,772.*

Châtelet, *t.*, Hainaut, Belgium; on R. Sambre; coal, pottery; p. (1962) *15,483.*        [*20,095.*

Châtelineau, *t.*, Hainaut, Belgium; p. (1962)

Châtellerault, *t.*, Vienne, France; 40 m. S. of Tours; cutlery, small arms; p. (1954) *23,583.*

Châtenay-Malabry, *t.*, Seine, France; p. (1954) *14,269.*

Chatham, *mun. bor.*, *dockyard*, (*former naval arsenal*), Kent, Eng.; on estuary of R. Medway; light inds.; p. (estd. 1967) *53,560.*

Chatham, *t.*, *spt.*, New Brunswick, Canada; lumbering, fish exporting; p. (1961) *7,109.*

Chatham, *c.*, Ontario, Canada; farming, fruit, machin., canned vegetables; p. (1961) *29,826.*

Chatham, Is., New Zealand dependency; a. 372 sq. m.; lgst. I., Wharekauri; (1961) *487.*

Châtillon-sur-Seine, *t.*, Côte d'Or, France; on R. Seine, 45 m. S.E. of Troyes; p. (1954) *12,526.*

Chatou, *t.*, Seine-et-Oise, France; p. (1954) *15,338.*

Chatsworth, *par.*, Derby, Eng.; on R. Derwent; seat of Duke of Devonshire.

Chattanooga, *c.*, Tenn., U.S.A.; on Tennessee R.; univ.; rly. ctr.; cottons; iron, steel, chemicals, paper, metals; p. (1960) *130,009.*

Chatteris, *urb. dist.*, Cambridge and Isle of Ely, Eng.; mkt. t.; p. (1961) *5,490.*

Chaudière Falls, on Ottawa R., above Ottawa, Canada; hydro-electric power-sta.

Chauk, *t.*, Burma; on Irrawaddy R.; chemical fertiliser plant being built, due for completion 1970.

Chaumont, *t.*, Haute-Marne, France; gloves, leather; p. (1954) *19,346.*

Chauny, *t.*, Aisne, France; on R. Oise; chemicals, glass; p. (1954) *10,544.*

Chautauqua, *L.*, N.Y. st., U.S.A.; summer resort.

Chaux-de-Fonds, La, *t.*, *can.*, Neuchâtel, Switzerland; ctr. of watchmkg. ind.; p. (1957) *33,300.*

Chaves, *t.*, N. Portugal; cath.; hot salt springs; linen silk; p. (1960) *13,156.*

Chaville, *t.*, Seine-et-Oise, France, p. (1954) *14,508.*

Cheadle, *rural dist.*, Staffs, Eng.; coal pits, metal mnfs.; p. (1961) *38,153.*

Cheadle and Gatley, *urb. dist.*, Cheshire, Eng.; textile finishing and bleaching; p. (estd. 1967) *54,920.*

Cheb, *t.*, ČSSR.; nr. Bavarian frontier; industl. ctr.; motor cycles, machin., textiles; p. (1961) *20,590.*

Cheboksary, *t.*, cap. R.S.F.S.R.; textiles, hydroelec., engin., wood-working; p. (1967) *170,000.*

Cheboygan, *t.*, Mich., U.S.A.; on L. Huron; sawmills: p. (1960) *5,859*.

Cheddar, *vil.*, Somerset, Eng.; famous limestone caves in Mendips; cheese, strawberries.

Cheduba I., Bay of Bengal, Burma; fertile, well-wooded; a. 240 sq. m.

Chefoo (Yantai), *c., former treaty pt.*, Shantung, China; on N. cst. of peninsula; p. (1953) *116,000*.

Chekiang (Zhijiang), *maritime prov.*, S.E. China; cap. Hangchow; exp. silk, cotton, etc.; a. 39,486 sq. m.; p. (1953) *22,865,747*.

Cheling Pass, on bdy. between Kwangtung, Hunan, S. China; historic route across Nanling mtns., now followed by Hankow to Canton trunk rly.; alt. 984 ft. [*19,539*.

Chelles, *t.*, Seine-et-Marne, France; p. (1954)

Chelm, *t.*, E. Poland; nr. Lublin; cath.; 1944 Manifesto of Poland's Liberation issued here; p. (1965) *35,000*.

Chelmer, *R.*, Essex, Eng.; joins R. Blackwater at Maldon.

Chelmno (Kulm), *t.*, Poland; on R. Vistula; ancient wells; large oil mills, engin., impt. tr.; p. (1946) *11,634*.

Chelmsford, *co. t., mun. bor.*, Essex, Eng.; 30 m. N.E. London; cath.; agr. mkt.; radio, elec. engin., brewing; p. (estd. 1967) *55,210*.

Chelsea, *see* Kensington and Chelsea.

Chelsea, *t.*, Mass., U.S.A.; rubber goods, shoes, paper; p. (1960) *33,749*.

Cheltenham, *t., mun. bor.*, Gloucester Eng.; spa; educational ctr.; aircraft mftg. and repair, precision instruments; p. (estd. 1967) *75,640*.

Chelyabinsk, *t.*, R.S.F.S.R.; on Mijas R. W. Siberian lowlands; metallurgy and machin.; pipeline to natural gas field Gazli opened Nov. 1963; p. (1967) *820,000*.

Chelyuskin C., most N. point of Asia.

Chemnitz, *see* Karl-Marx-Stadt.

Chemulpo, *see* Inchon.

Chenab, *R.*, W. Punjab, Pakistan; one of " five rivers " of Punjab; rises in Himalayas, flows S.W. into R. Sutlej; dams at Merala and Khanki provide water for Upper and Lower Chenab Irrigation Canal Systems; length approx. 900 m.

Chengchow (Zhengzhou), *c., cap.* Honan prov., China; 15 m. S. of Hwang-Ho, where it emerges on to N. China Plain; impt. route ctr. and rly. junction where Peking to Hankow rly. crosses Sian to Tunghai rly.; p. (1953) *595,000*.

Chengtu (Chengdu), *c., cap.* Szechwan prov., China; silk, rice; p. (1957) *1,107,000*.

Chepstow, *mkt. t., urb. dist.*, Monmouth, Eng.; on R. Wye 2 m. above confluence with R. Severn; Severn Bridge links to Aust (Glos.); fine ruined cas.; light engin., brush mkg., asphalt, limestone; p. (1961) *6,041*.

Chequers, *seat*, Bucks, Eng.; official residence of Prime Minister.

Cher, *central dep.*, France; cap. Bourges; grain, wines, iron, porcelain; a. 2,819 sq. m.; p. (1962) *293,514*. [Auvergne Mtns.

Cher, *R.*, France, trib. of R. Loire, flowing from

Cherbourg, *spt.*, Manche, France; N. cst. of Contentin Peninsula; opposite to and 80 m. dist. from Portsmouth; naval arsenal, ship-bldg.; metals, ropes, fishing; p. (1962) *40,018*.

Cheremkhovo, *t.*, R.S.F.S.R.; N.W. of Irkutsk; coal, engin., chemicals; p. (1967) *111,000*.

Cherepovets, *c.*, R.S.F.S.R.; steel, engin., saw-mills; p. (1967) *159,000*.

Cheribon, *spt.*, Java, Indonesia; N. cst., 120 m. E. of Jakarta; rice, tea, coffee; p. *54,079*.

Cherkassy, *t.*, Ukrainian S.S.R.; nr. Kiev, on Dnieper R.; sugar, engin.; p. (1959) *83,000*.

Chernigov, *t.*, Ukrainian S.S.R.; on Desna R.; caths.; univ.; flour, textiles, chemicals; p. (1967) *132,000*.

Chernogorsk, *t.*, R.S.F.S.R.; 10 m. N. of Abakan; ctr. of Minusinsk coal-mng. basin; p. (1959) *51,000*.

Chernovtsy, *t.*, Ukrainian S.S.R.; univ.; Greek cath.; wheat. dairy produce, textiles, engin., chemicals; p. (1967) *175,000*.

Chernyakovsk (Insterburg), *t.*, Lithuanian S.S.R.; chemicals, textiles; p. (1959) approx. *50,000*.

Cherokee, *t.*, Iowa, U.S.A.; p. (1960) *7,724*.

Cherrapunji, *t.*, Assam, India; in Khasi Hills; reputed wettest place in world, av. annual rainfall 500 in.

Chertsey, *urb. dist.*, Surrey, Eng.; on S. bank of R. Thames, 4 m. below Staines; residtl; air-

craft components, cement; p. (estd. 1967) *44,710*.

Cherwell, *R.*, trib. of Thames, nr. Oxford; l. 30 m.

Chesapeake Bay, *inlet* on Atlantic coast, U.S.A.; extending 200 m. from mouth of Susquehanna R. to C. Charles; shellfish ind.; bridge-tunnel (opened 1964) spans entrance to Bay.

Chesham, *residtl. t., urb. dist.*, Bucks, Eng.; in heart of Chiltern Hills; printing, textiles, light engin.; p. (1961) *16,236*.

Cheshire, *co.*, Eng.; cap. Chester; plain; Rs. Mersey and Dee; dairying, mkt. gardening; salt, coal; mnfs.; textiles, chemicals, ship-bldg.; a. 1,056 sq. m.; p. (1966) *1,472,000*.

Cheshire, *t.*, Conn., U.S.A.; agr., formerly copper, and barytes mined; p. (estd. 1967) *42,900*.

Cheshunt, *urb. dist.*, Herts, Eng.; in Lea valley, 7 m. S. of Hertford; bricks, mkt. gardening, horticulture; p. (1961) *35,371*.

Chesil Bank, Dorset, Eng.; shingle ridge from Portland to Bridport.

Chester, *c., co. bor.*, Cheshire, Eng.; at head of estuary of R. Dee; cath., ancient walls and old timbered houses; engin., metal goods; p. (estd. 1967) *60,360*.

Chester, *t.*, S.C., U.S.A.; cotton mnfs.; flour; granite; p. (1960) *6,906*. [p. (1960) *63,658*.

Chester, *t.*, Penns., U.S.A.; large inds., textiles

Chesterfield, *mkt. t., mun. bor.*, colly. dist., Derby, Eng.; on Rother R.; 8 m. S. of Sheffield; iron, steel, engin., coal-mng., glass, elec. lamps, galvanised goods, chemicals; p. (estd. 1967) *70,020*.

Chesterfield Inlet, arm of Hudson Bay, Canada; 250 m. by 25 m.

Chesterfield Is., *dep.*, New Caledonia, Pac. Oc.; French; about 342 m. W. of N.C.

Chester-le-Street, *urb. dist.*, Durham, Eng.; clothing, confectionery; p. (estd. 1967) *20,300*.

Chesterton, *sub.* of Cambridge, Eng.; p. *35,950*.

Cheviot, *t.*, S.W. Ohio, U.S.A.; clothes, leather goods; flour; p. (1960) *10,701*.

Cheviot Hills, between Scot. and Northumberland, Britain; highest point The Cheviot, 2,676 ft.

Cheyenne, *R.*, S.D., U.S.A.; trib. of Missouri; length 500 m.

Cheyenne, *cap.*, Wyo., U.S.A.; cattle-ranching dist.; rly. ctr.; p. (1960) *43,505*.

Chiana, Val de, *valley*, central Italy; longitudinal depression separating Tuscan Hills from Central Apennines; occupied by upper course of R. Arno, middle course of R. Tiber; followed by main route from Florence to Rome.

Chiangmai, *prov.*, N.W. Thailand; cap. Chiangmai; a. 8,839 sq. m.; p. (1960) *798,483*.

Chiangmai, *c.*, Chiangmai prov., N.W. Thailand; on Ping R.; tr. ctr., teak; p. (1960) *65,736*.

Chiapas, *Pacific st.*, Mexico; cap. Tuxtla-Gutierrez; mountainous, forested; coffee, tobacco, sugar and cocoa, cattle; a. 28,729 sq. m.; p. (1960) *1,210,370*. [(1956) *19,200*.

Chiatura, *t.*, Georgian S.S.R.; manganese; p.

Chiavari, *t.*, Liguria, Italy; on the Riviera; shrine of the Madonna; p. *17,586*.

Chiba, *cap.* of Chiba prefecture, Japan; on E. Tokyo Bay; impt. tr. ctr.; giant shipyard; oil refining; aluminium, chemicals; new airpt. projected 1972; p. (1964) *301,000*.

Chicago, *c.*, Ill., U.S.A.; on S. shore of L. Michigan; second lgst. U.S. c.; economic heart of Mid-West; comm. ctr. called " The Loop "; immense tr. by rail and Great Lakes, flourishing univ.; grain mkt., pork, beef canning, agr. implements, iron and steel, machin., clothing, furs, electronic equipment, metals, chemicals, petrol, coal; lgst. airpt. in world; p. (1960) *3,550,404*.

Chichester, *c., mun. bor.*, W. Sussex, Eng.; on S. cst. plain, 11 m. W. of Arundel; fine cath.; agr.; p. (estd. 1967) *20,640*.

Chickamauga Creek, U.S.A.; branch of the Tennessee R. above Chattanooga; Civil War battles; site of National Park.

Chickasha, *t.*, Okla., U.S.A.; maize, cotton; p. (1960) *14,866*. [*13,262*.

Chickerell, E. Dorset, Eng.; 3 m. N.W. of Weymouth; site for nuclear power sta.; on shores of East Fleet R.

Chiclana, *mftg. t.*, Spain; nr. Cadiz; p. (1957)

Chiclayo, *ch. t.*, Lambayeque dep., Peru; rice, sugar, wheat, coffee; p. (1961) *54,400*.

Chico, *t.*, N. Cal., U.S.A.; food processing, lumber, cement; p. (1960) *14,757*.

Chicopee, *t.*, Mass., U.S.A.; on Connecticut R.; hardware, carpets, cars; p. (1960) *61,553.*

Chicoutimi, *t.*, Quebec, Canada; on Chicoutimi R.; hydro-elec. power-sta.; lumber, pulp, paper; p. (1961) *31,657.*

Chidambaram, *t.*, Tamil Nadu, India; nr. Cuddalore; p. (1961) *40,694.*

Chidley C., most N. point of Labrador, Hudson Strait, Canada. [ft. above sea-level.

Chiem, *L.*, large lake nr. Munich, Germany, 1,500

Chieri, *t.*, Piedmont, Italy; nr. Turin; was mediæval republic; Gothic church; silks, cottons; p. *14,747.* [*347,824.*

Chieti, *prov.*, S. Italy; a. 1,142 sq. m.; p. (1961)

Chieti, *t.*, prov. Chieti, S. Italy; the ancient Teate Marrucinorum; Europe's lgst. glass plant, using methane from Abruzzi field; p. (1961) *48,011.*

Chigirik, *t.*, Uzbek S.S.R.; new town being built (1963), 21 m. S. of Tashkent.

Chignecto Bay, inlet of Bay of Fundy, Canada.

Chigwell, *urb. dist.*, Essex, Eng.; on borders of Epping Forest; Hainault Estate, now incorporated in Redbridge, Greater London; residtl.; p. (estd. 1967) *56,040.*

Chihli, see Hopei.

Chihli, G. of, see Pohai, Gulf of.

Chihuahua, *st.*, Mexico; adjoining the U.S.A.; mining, stock-raising and agr.; a. 94,822 sq. m.; p. (1960) *1,226,793.*

Chihuahua, *c., cap.*, Chihuahua st., Mexico; fine cath.; on Mexican Central Rly.; silver, cottons, woollens; p. (1960) *150,430.*

Chikchi, *pen.*, R.S.F.S.R.; world's first Arctic nuclear power sta. being built.

Chikuho, *t.*, N. Kyushu, Japan; largest coal-mines in the country. [Valley.

Chilcoot, *R., pass.*, Alaska, leading into Yukon

Chile, *rep.*, S. America, independent of Spain since 1818; Pacific coastal strip rising sharply to Andes; Atacama Desert in N., fertile valleys in ctr., heavy rains in S.; Spanish language; Roman Catholic; forested in S.; dairying, sheep, wool; gr. nitrate output, copper, iron ore, coal, iodine, paper, petroleum; cap. Santiago; ch. pt. Valparaiso; length 2,660 m., breadth 69–270 m., a. 285,133 sq. m.; p. (estd. 1965) *8,515,000.*

Chilka, *L.*, inlet, E. coast, Orissa, India.

Chillán, *c., cap.* Nuble prov., Chile; destroyed 1939 by one of world's worst recorded earthquakes; since rebuilt; agr. and comm. ctr.; p. (1961) *32,947.*

Chillicothe, *c.*, Ohio, U.S.A.; on Scioto R., mftg.; furniture, leather; p. (1960) *24,957.*

Chilliwack, *t.*, B.C., Canada; on Fraser R.; dairy produce, fruit, lumber; p. (1961) *5,259.*

Chiloé, *I.* and S. *prov.* Chile; cap. San Carlos, suffered earthquakes 1939 and 1960; ch. pt. Ancúd destroyed 1960; a. 9,058 sq. m.; p. (1960) *98,662.* [p. (1960) *12,673.*

Chilpancingo, *c., cap.*, Guerrero st., Mexico;

Chiltern Hills, *chalk hills*, Oxon., Bucks., Beds. and Herts., Eng.; highest point 904 ft. nr. Wendover.

Chimborazo, *mtn.*, Ecuador, Andes; extinct volcano, alt. 20,610 ft.

Chimborazo, *prov.*, Ecuador; cap. Riobamba; a. 2,089 sq. m.; p. (estd. 1962) *279,607.*

Chimbote, *spt.* Peru; steel, iron-ore, coal; tinned fish, fish-meal; p. (1961) *90,000.*

Chimkent, *t.*, Kazakh S.S.R.; chemicals, engin., textiles; lead smelting; p. (1967) *209,000.*

China, People's Republic of, Asia, consists of 27 provs. (inc. Taiwan, the aut. regions of Kwangsi Chuang, Ningsia, Inner Mongolia, Sinkiang Uighur, and Tibet). Total a. 3,643,000 sq. m.; mountainous in N. and W., fertile valleys and plains in E.; Rs.: Hwang-ho, Yangtze, Si-kiang; climate, extreme in N.; monsoon in S.; wheat, barley, maize, millet in N.; rice (staple food), sugar in S.; cotton, tea, hemp, jute, flax; livestock; cotton, woollen and silk mnfs.; flour- and rice-milling; great mineral wealth; coal, iron, tin, antimony, wolfram, bismuth, molybdenum; oil; rural electrification; p. (1966) *710,000,000.*

China Sea, part of W. Pacific between Korea and Philippines; divided by the narrow Formosa Strait into two areas; N. China Sea, including Yellow Sea, and S. China Sea.

Chinandega, *t.*, Nicaragua, Central America; cotton, sugar, bananas; iron wks.; p. (1960) *19,025.*

Chincha Is., gr. off cst. of Peru; p. (of ch. t.) *14,763.*

Chinchow (Jinzhou), *c.*, Liaoning prov., China; cement, glass, bricks, tiles, paper and wood pulp, oil; p. (1953) *352,000.*

Chincoteague, *t.*, and *I.*, E. Va., U.S.A.; fisheries, poultry; p. (1960) *2,131.*

Chindwin, *R.*, Burma; ch. trib. of Irrawaddy; rising in Patkoi Hills, navigable in rainy season.

Chindwin, Upper and Lower, *provs.*, Burma; fertile plains and extensive teak forests, rice.

Chingford, see Waltham Forest.

Chingleput, *t.*, India; S. of Madras; cotton weaving, salt mnfs.; p. (1961) *25,977.*

Chingola, *t.*, Zambia, copper-mng.

Chinju or Shinshu, *t.*, S. Korea; cotton; p. *30,269.*

Chinkiang (Zhenjiang), *c.*, Kiangsu, China; former treaty pt. Yangtse-kiang, 48 m. below Nanking; tr. ctr.; p. (1953) *201,000.*

Chinkolobwe, *mines*, Congo; uranium.

Chinon, *t.*, Indre-et-Loire, Central France; on R. Vienne, industl.; ruined cas., once a royal residency; nuclear power sta.; p. (1954) *6,743.*

Chinquinquira, *t.*, Boyaca, Colombia; pilgrimage ctr.; comm. ctr.; coffee, cattle; p. (estd. 1959) *24,150.*

Chinwangtao (Qinhuangdao), *c., spt., former treaty pt.*, Hopeh, N. China; on Yellow Sea cst., 150 m. N.E. of Tientsin; only good natural harbour on N. China cst.; exp. coal from Kailan mines; p. (1953) *187,000.*

Chioggia, *spt., cath. c.*, N. Italy; on I. in G. of Venice; fishing; p. (1961) *47,151.*

Chios, see Khios.

Chippenham, *t.*, *mun. bor.*, Wilts, Eng.; mkt. t. on R. Avon; rly. signal and brake equipment, bacon curing, tanning; p. (estd. 1967) *18,640.*

Chippewa Falls, *c.*, Wis., U.S.A.; flour, lumber; p. (1960) *11,708.*

Chipping Campden, *vil.*, Gloucester, Eng.; in Cotswold Hills; formerly impt. for woollens.

Chipping Norton, *mun. bor., mkt. t.*, Oxford, Eng., nr. Banbury; p. (estd. 1967) *4,420.*

Chipping Sodbury, *mkt. t.* Gloucester, Eng.; 8 m. N.E. of Bristol.

Chirchik, *t.*, Uzbekistan S.S.R.; 20 m. N.E. of Tashkent; engin., chemicals; hydro-elec. stas.; p. (1959) *65,000.* [*188,350.*

Chiriqui, *prov.*, Panama; cap. David; p. (1960)

Chirk, *t.*, Denbigh, Wales; on R. Cleriog, S. of Wrexham; slate, coal.

Chisinau, see Kishinev.

Chislehurst and Sidcup, see Bexley and Bromley.

Chistyakovo, see Thorez.

Chita, *t., rly. junct.* Siberia, R.S.F.S.R.; on upper Amur R., 400 m. E. of L. Baikal; coal, engin., chemicals, sawmilling; p. (1967) *201,000.*

Chitral, *st.*, Pakistan; N.W. Frontier Provs.

Chittagong, *dist.*, East Pakistan; ch. t., Chittagong; p. (estd. 1951) *11,783,000.*

Chittagong, *c., spt.*, East Pakistan; on E. cst. of Bay of Bengal; exp. jute, tea; oil-refining; steel mill; suffered severe damage by cyclone May 1963; p. (1961) *364,205.*

Chittaranjan, *t.*, W. Bengal, India; new t. on Barakhar R., in steel ctr., of Asasol and Tatanagan; rly. locomotive wks.; p. (1961) *25,957.*

Chobrum, see Godwin-Austen Mt.

Choctawhatchee, *R.*, Ala. and Fla., U.S.A.; length 180 m.

Choisy-le-Roi, *t.*, Seine, France; cloth factories; p. (1962) *41,269.*

Cholet, *t.*, Maine-et-Loire, France; cotton, linen, flannel mnfs.; p. (1962) *37,557.*

Cholon, *t.*, S. Viet-Nam; 10 m. S.W. of Saigon; rice; p. inc. with Saigon (1964) *1,371,000.*

Cholula, *ancient c.* of Puebla, prov., Mexico; Aztec temple, pyramid of Cholula, and other remains.

Chomutov, *mftg. t.*, ČSSR.; p. (1961) *33,152.*

Chonos Archipelago, Chile; about 120 islands on W. coast of Patagonia.

Chooz, *t.*, Ardennes, France; pressurized water reactor; nuclear power sta. linked with Belgian grid.

Chorley, *industl. t.*, *mun. bor.*, N. Lancs, Eng.; on W. flank of Rossendale Fells, 7 m. S.E. of Preston; cotton, engin.; proposals for expansion as "New Town" with Leyland (50,000 acres); p. (estd. 1967) *31,170.*

Chorley Wood, *urb. dist.*, Herts, Eng.; p. (1961) *6,964.*

Chorrilos Pass, Argentina; in E. cordillera of Andes at alt. 14,655 ft.; used by rly. from Tucuman to Antofagasta.

Chorzow (Królewska Huta), *t.*, Upper Silesia, Poland; coal, iron and steel, chemicals, engin.; p. (1965) *154,000*.

Choukoutien, *vil.*, Hopeh prov., N.E. China; site of discovery of bones of extinct Pekin man.

Chowtsun, *t., former treaty pt.*, Shantung, N.E. China; silk; rly.; p. *46,200*.

Christchurch, *t., mun. bor.*, Hants, Eng.; on S. cst. 5 m. E. of Bournemouth; holiday resort, aircraft, light inds.; p. (estd. 1967) *30,270*.

Christchurch, *cap.*, Canterbury, S.I., N.Z.; univ.; cath., mus.; comm. ctr. of lamb, wool and grain prov.; airpt.; p. (1964) *237,000* of c. *156,900*.

Christiansand, *see* Kristiansand.

Christianshaab, Danish settlement on Disco Bay, W. Greenland; meteorological sta.

Christianstad, *see* Kristianstad.

Christiansund, *see* Kristiansund.

Christmas I., in Indian Oc., Australian terr. since Oct. 1, 1958; a. 62 sq. m., healthy climate, phosphate deposits; p. (1960) *3,099*.

Christmas I., lge. coral atoll in Pacific, one of Line Is.; discovered by Cook 1777; 100 m. in circum; U.K. nuclear test site, 1957–64. [*15,514*.

Chrudim, *t.*, ČSSR.; horse mkt., mnfs.; p. (1961)

Chrzanow, *commune*, S. Poland; 27 m. from Krakow; coal, locomotives, leather, bricks; p. (1965) *23,000*.

Chu, *R.*, Kazakh S.S.R., U.S.S.R.; rises in Tien Shan, flows N.W. for 500 m. into inland drainage basin; Chumysh Dam provides hydro-electricity and water for intensive cultivation under irrigation of cotton, sugar-beet, citrus fruits.

Chuanchow (Quanzhou), *c.*, Fukien prov.; China; rice, wheat, sugar cane; p. (1953) *108,000*.

Chuchow (Zhuzhou), *c.*, Hunan prov., China; p. (1953) *127,000*.

Chu Kiang (Canton R. or Pearl R.), Kwangtung, S. China; one of most impt. waterways of China; fertile delta known as "land of fish, rice and fruit"; around Canton network of elec. drain-age and irrigation stas., built since 1959.

Chubut, *prov.*, Argentine; cap. Rawson; a. 87,152 sq. m.; agr.; p. (1960) *142,000*.

Chudleigh, *mkt.*, Devon, Eng.; on R. Teign; stone quarrying; p. (1951) *1,944*.

Chudskoye, *L.*, between R.S.F.S.R. and Estonia S.S.R.; 70 m. long. [gold deposit.

Chukotkaa, *pen.*, U.S.S.R.; extreme N.E.; rich

Chula Vista, *t.*, Cal., U.S.A.; agr., aircraft; p. (1960) *42,034*.

Chungking (Zhongqing), *t., former treaty pt.*, Szechwan, China; on Yangtze-Kiang; comm. ctr., S.W. China; exp. silk, soya-beans, sugar; p. (1957) *2,121,000*.

Chuquibamba Mtns. (alt. 21,000 ft.), Peru.

Chuquicamata, *part of* Calama *commune*, N. Chile; lgst. copper-mines in the world; p. (1960) *30,476*.

Chuquisaca, *dep.*, Bolivia; cap. Sucre; a. 36,132 sq. m.; p. (1962) *307,600*.

Chur (Coire), *t., cap.* Grisons can., Switzerland; Upper Rhine Valley; cath. and hist. bldgs.; fruit and wine; p. (1960) *20,000*.

Church, *urb. dist., sub.* Accrington, Lancs, Eng.; cotton weaving and engin.; p. (1961) *5,380*.

Church Stretton, *urb. dist.*, Salop, Eng.; p. (1961) *2,712*.

Churchill, *R.*, Canada; enters Hudson Bay at Churchill; 925 m.; fine harbour.

Churchill, *R.*, formerly Hamilton R. flows into H. inlet, cst. of Labrador, Canada; magnificent waterfall, Churchill Falls.

Churchill, *t.*, Manitoba, Canada; terminus of Hudson Bay rly.; summer wheat route from prairie provs. [tea, rice.

Chusan I., off E. cst. of China; cap. Tinghai;

Chusovoy, *t.*, R.S.F.S.R.; in Urals; iron and steel; p. (1959) *60,000*.

Chuvash, *rep.*, A.S.S.R., U.S.S.R.; a. 7,107 sq. m.; p. (1959) *1,098,000*.

Cibao, *lowland area*, Dominican Republic, Central America; extends along N. side of Cordillera de Cibao for approx. 100 m.; cacao, tobacco, maize; densely populated, ch. t. Santiago.

Cicero, *t.*, Ill., U.S.A.; p. (1960) *69,130*.

Ciechanów, *t.*, Poland; 49 m. N.W. of Warsaw; agr. inds.; p. (1965) *21,000*.

Cienaga, *spt.*, N. Colombia; exp. cotton, bananas, cacao; p. (estd. 1962) *69,900*.

Cienfuegos, *t., spt.*, Cuba; sugar, tobacco; p. (1953) *57,991*.

Cieszyn, *t.*, Katowice, Poland; p. (1965) *24,000*.

Cieza, *t.*, Murcia, Spain; in fertile raisin and orange-growing dist.; p. (1957) *23,328*.

Cilicia, *ancient prov.*, S.E. Anatolia, Turkey.

Cincinnati, *c.*, Ohio, U.S.A.; on Ohio R.; "the Queen City"; univ.; pork-packing, machin., tools, soap, electrotypes, seed processing, chemi-cals; p. (1960) *502,550*.

Cinderford, *lge. vil.*, Gloucester, Eng.; in Forest of Dean, 12 m. S.W. of Gloucester; ch. mining ctr. on sm. F. of D. coalfield.

Cinque Ports, five ancient English pts. on cst. of Kent and Sussex; Sandwich, Dover, Hythe, Romney and Hastings.

Cinto, *mtn.* Corsica.

Cintra, *see* Sintra.

Circleville, *t.*, Ohio, U.S.A.; agr. ctr., maize; wheat; p. (1960) *11,059*.

Cirencester, *t., urb. dist.*, Gloucester, Eng.; the Roman Corineum; p. (1961) *11,836*.

Citlaltépetl, (Aztec name for Orizaba), *mtn.*, vol-canic peak, Veracruz st., Mexico, highest point in Mexico; 18,701 ft.

Cittadella, *t.*, Venetia, Italy; nr. Padua; mediæval walls and towers; p. *12,679*.

Cittanova, *t.*, Reggio, Italy; built on ruins of Casalnuovo; olive-oil ind.

Citta Vecchia, *c.*, Central Malta; former cap.

Ciudad Bolivar, *spt.*, Bolívar st., Venezuela; on R. Orinoco; (formerly called Angostura); great comm. ctr.; coffee; cattle; p. (1961) *56,032*.

Ciudad Juarez, *t.*, Mexico; p. (1960) *261,683*.

Ciudad Madero, *t.*, Mexico; styrene and detergent plants.

Ciudad Real, *prov.*, S. Central Spain; grazing grounds, forest and quicksilver mines; cap. Ciudad Real; a. 7,622 sq. m.; p. (1959) *583,930*.

Ciudad Rodrigo, *c.*, Salamanca, Spain; captured by French 1707 and 1710, by the English 1706, stormed by Wellington in 1812; fine cath.; p. (1957) *12,600*.

Ciudad Trujillo, *see* Santo Domingo.

Civitavecchia, *spt.*, Latium, Italy; on W. cst., 30 m. N. of mouth of R. Tiber; sulphur springs; p. *34,400*.

Clackmannan, *smallest co.*, Scot.; flat in Carse, and hilly elsewhere; co. t. Alloa; coal, textiles (esp. woollens), metal work, brewing, distilling, agr.; a. 54½ sq. m.; p. (1961) *41,391*.

Clacton-on-Sea, *t., urb. dist.*, Essex, Eng.; on E. cst., 12 m. S.E. of Colchester; seaside resort; light inds.; residtl.; p. (estd. 1967) *34,250*.

Clairton, *t.*, S.W. Penns., U.S.A.; coal, iron, steel, chemicals; p. (1960) *18,389*.

Clairvaux, *vil.*, Aube, France; famous Cistercian Abbey.

Clamart, *t.*, Seine, France; p. (1962) *43,290*.

Clanwilliam, *t.*, Cape Province, Rep. of S. Africa, on Oliphant R.; p. *1,463*.

Clare, *co.*, Munster, Ireland; co. t. Ennis; oats, potatoes; sheep, cattle; oysters, salmon; a. 1,294 sq. m.; p. (1966) *73,539*.

Clare, *t.*, S. Australia; on W. flank of Flinders Mtns., 70 m. N.E. of Adelaide; ctr. of wine-producing dist.; p. (1966) *1,584*.

Clare I., Clew Bay, Mayo, Ireland.

Clarence Strait, between Melville I. and P. Darwin, N. Terr., Australia.

Clarence, *R.*, N.S.W., Australia; length 240 m.

Clarksburg, *t.*, W. Virginia, U.S.A., machin., glass, pottery; p. (1960) *28,112*.

Clarksdale, *t.*, Miss., U.S.A.; p. (1960) *21,105*.

Clarksville, *t.*, Tenn., U.S.A.; on Cumberland R.; tobacco mkt.; p. (1960) *22,021*.

Claustal-Zellerfeld, *t.*, Lower Saxony, Hanover, Germany; iron, lead, copper, silver, zinc; tourist ctr.; p. (estd. 1954) *17,200*.

Clawson, *t.*, Mich., U.S.A.; p. (1960) *14,795*.

Clay Cross, *urb. dist.*, Derby, Eng.; coal and iron; p. (1961) *9,173*.

Clayton-le-Moors, *urb. dist.*, Lancs, Eng.; nr. Blackburn; textile machin., cotton and blanket weaving, bristles, soap; p. (1961) *6,421*.

Clear, Alaska; site of American ballistic missile early warning station. [off S.W. cst.

Clear, C. (southernmost point of Ireland), Clear I.,

Clearwater, *t.*, Fla., U.S.A.; citrus fruit, flowers, fish; resort; p. (1960) *34,653*.

Cleator Moor, *colly. t.*, Cumberland, Eng.; p. *8,291*.

Cleburne, *t.*, Texas, U.S.A.; rly wks., flour; p. (1960) *15,381*.

Cleckheaton, *mftg. t.*, Yorks, Eng.; nr. Bradford; woollens, blankets.

Clee Hills, Salop, Eng.; between Rs. Severn and Teme; alt. 1,800 ft.

Cleethorpes, *t.*, *mun. bor.*, Lindsey, Lincs, Eng.; on E. cst. 3 m. S. of Grimsby; resort; p. (estd. 1967) *33,970.*

Clent, *hills*, N.E. Worcester, Eng.; about 10 m. S.W. of Birmingham, on S. edge of S. Staffordshire coalfield, overlooking valley of R. Stour; well wooded; used for recreation by industl. ts. around Birmingham; maximum alt. 1,036 ft.

Clerkenwell, *industl. dist.*, London, Eng.; immediately N. of the City.

Clermont-Ferrand, *t.*, Puy-de-Dome, France; fine Gothic cath.; former cap. of Auvergne; rubber; chemicals; food ind.; p. (1962) *134,263.*

Clevedon, *urb. dist.*, Somerset, Eng.; at mouth of R. Severn; seaside resort; quarrying, bricks, footwear; p. (1961) *10,642.*

Cleveland, *hilly agr. dist.*, N.R. Yorks, Eng.; between R. Tees and Whitby.

Cleveland, *c., port*, Ohio, U.S.A.; on L. Erie; rly. ctr.; steamboat mnfs.; machin., iron foundries, lumber, coal, oil-refining, meat canning, steel, metals, aircraft, refrigerators, chemicals; p. (1960) *876,050.*

Clew Bay, Mayo, Ireland; 10 m. by 7 m.

Clichy, *t.*, Seine, France; p. (1962) *56,495.*

Clifton, *sub.*, Bristol, Eng.; on R. Avon; mineral springs; famous suspension bridge.

Clifton, *t.*, New Jersey, U.S.A.; nr. Passaic; p. (1960) *82,084.*

Clinton, *c.*, Iowa, U.S.A.; on Mississippi R.; iron and steel; p. (1960) *33,589.*

Clinton, *t.*, Mass., U.S.A.; on Nashua R.; machin., carpets; p. (1960) *12,848.*

Clinton Golden Lake, *L.*, Mackenzie, N.W. Terr., Canada.

Clipperton I., Pacific Oc., S.W. of Mexico; belongs to France (since 1931).

Clitheroe, *t.*, *mun. bor.*, Lancs, Eng.; on R. Ribble; cotton weaving, limestone quarrying; p. (estd. 1967) *12,640.*

Clonakilty, *urb. dist.*, Cork, Ireland; nr. Bandon; corn, farming; p. (1966) *2,341.*

Cloncurry, *t.*, Queensland, Australia; in pastoral and copper-producing dist. S. of the G. of Carpentaria; p. (1966) *2,174.*

Clones, *mkt. t.*, *urb. dist.*, nr. Dundalk, Monaghan, Ireland; rly. ctr.; p. (1951) *2,107.*

Clonfert, *c.*, Galway, Ireland; famous monastery.

Clonmel, *t.*, *urb. dist.*, Tipperary, Ireland; on R. Suir; agr. ctr.; fairs; cider, footwear; p. (1966) *11,026.*

Clovelly, *par.*, Devon, Eng.; seaside resort, picturesque fishing vil.

Clovis, *t.*, N.M., U.S.A.; rly. junction, tr. ctr., wheat, cattle; p. (1960) *23,713.*

Cloyne, *mkt. t.*, nr. Middleton, Cork, Ireland.

Cluj, *c.*, Romania; textiles, uranium, engin.; p. (1963) *204,400.*     [Ballarat.

Clunes, *gold-mining t.*, Victoria, Australia, nr.

Clutha R., S.I., New Zealand.

Clwyd, *R.*, Denbigh, N. Wales; flows into Irish Sea at Rhyl; length 30 m.

Clydach, *t.*, Glamorgan, Wales; on R. Tawe, 5 m. N.E. of Swansea; steel wks., nickel refineries.

Clyde, *R.*, Lanark, S.W. Scot.; navigable to Glasgow; greatest shipbldg. ctr. in world; length 96 m.; twin-road tunnel under R. in Glasgow (Whiteinch–Linthouse) completed 1963.

Clyde, Firth of, Scot.

Clydebank, *burgh*, Dunbarton, Scot.; on the Clyde adjoining Glasgow; shipbldg., sewing machin., tyres, biscuits; p. (1961) *49,654.*

Clydesdale, *valley* of R. Clyde, S.W. Scot., agr.; fine horses.

Coachella Valley, Cal., U.S.A.; part of old bottom of G. of Cal. which lies N.W. of Stalon Sea; arid; dates and citrus fruits under irrigation from Imperial Valley irrigation system.

Coahuila, *st.*, Mexico; cap. Saltillo; maize, cotton; silver, copper, coal, gold; a. 55,062 sq. m.; p. (1960) *907,734.*

Coalbrookdale, *vil.*, Salop, Eng.; old coal- and iron-mines.

Coalville, *t.*, *urb. dist.*, Leics. Eng.; nr. Ashby-de-la-Zouch; coal-mining, engin., elastic webbing; p. (estd. 1967) *28,150.*

Coanza, R., Angola; length 660 m.

Coast Range, *mtns.*, U.S.A.; along Pacific cst.

Coatbridge, *burgh*, Lanark, Scot.; 10 m. E. of Glasgow; coal, iron and steel, prefabricated houses, tubes, engin.; p. (1961) *53,946.*

Coatesville, *t.*, Penns., U.S.A.; iron, steel, brass, textiles; p. (1960) *12,971.*

Coats I., S. of Southampton I., Hudson Bay, Canada.

Coatzacoalcos (Puerto México), *spt.*, Mexico; on G. of Campeche; oil refinery; chemicals, fertilisers; p. (1961) *43,740.*

Cobalt, *t.*, Ontario, Canada; silver, cobalt, arsenic, nickel; p. (1961) *2,209.*

Coban, *t.*, Guatemala, Central America; coffee and Peruvian bark tr.; p. (estd. 1960) *42,300.*

Cobar, *t.*, N.S.W., Australia; copper; sawmills; p. (1966) *2,348.*

Cobh (Queenstown), *spt.*, *urb. dist.*, Cork, Ireland; fine harbour and docks; p. (1966) *5,608.*

Cobija, *cap.* of Pando dep., N.W. Bolivia; rubber; p. (1962) *2,537.*

Cobourg, *t.*, Ontario, Canada; on L. Ontario; dairying, fruit, woollens; p. (1961) *10,646.*

Coburg, *t.*, Bavaria, Germany; old cas.; wickerwork, furniture, metal, machines, toy inds.; p. (1963) *43,100.*

Cochabamba, *dep.*, Bolivia; a. 25,288 sq. m.; p. (1962) *550,300.*

Cochabamba, *t.*, *cap.*, dep. Cochabamba, Bolivia; cath.; oil refining, shoes, rubber tyres, fruit, canning; modern milk plant; hydro-elec. plant projected; p. (1962) *92,003.*

Cochin, *spt.*, Kerala, India; Malabar cst.; exp. coconut oil, tea; oil refining; p. (1961) *35,076.*

Cochin China, name formerly applied to the whole E. part of Indo-China, now limited to S.E. of the peninsula; since 1946 within S. Viet-Nam; rice, silk, coffee, rubber, maize, cotton; cap. Saigon; a. 26,476 sq. m.; p. *5,600,000.*

Cockburn Land, N. of Baffin I., Arctic Canada.

Cockenzie and Port Seton, *burgh*, East Lothian, Scot.; on Firth of Forth, 9 m. E. of Edinburgh; p. (1961) *3,462.*

Cockermouth, *t.*, *urb. dist.*, Cumberland, Eng.; coal, agr., shoe mfg.; p. (1961) *5,323.*

Cocle, *prov.*, Panama, Central America; cap., Penonomé; p. (1960) *93,156.*

Cocos or Keeling Is., *2 coral atolls*, Indian Ocean; since 1955 terr. of Australia; ch. prod. coconuts; strategic psn. S.E. of Ceylon, 530 m. W. of Christmas I., N.E. of Mauritius; radio and cable sta.; civil aviation marine base; German raider beached and destroyed on N. Keeling I. in 1914; a. 5 sq. m.; p. (estd. 1965) *620.*

Cod, C., S.E. point of Mass. Bay, U.S.A.; summer resort; fishing, boat bldg.; p. (estd. 1960) *55,000.*

Coesfeld, *t.*, N. Rhine-Westphalia, Germany; textiles, machin.; p. (1963) *20,700.*

Coeur d'Alene, *t.*, Idaho, U.S.A.; lead, silver, lumber; p. (1960) *14,291.*

Coffeyville, *t.*, Kan., U.S.A.; p. (1950) *17,133.*

Coggeshall, *par.*, Essex, Eng.; on Blackwater R. silk; isinglass; p. (1961) *3,027.*

Cognac, *t.*, Charente, France; cognac, bottles; p. (1954) *19,026.*

Cohoes, *c.*, N.Y., U.S.A.; on Hudson R.; hosiery, paper, foundries; p. (1960) *20,129.*

Coimbatore, *t.*, Tamil Nadu, India; coffee, sugar, cotton spinning; p. (1961) *286,305.*

Coimbra, *c.*, Portugal; cath., univ., wine-growing, earthenware mnfs.; p. (1960) *46,313.*

Coin, *commune* Malaga, Spain; soap, paper, textiles, oil, wine, marble; p. (1957) *20,000.*

Cojutepeque, *t.*, El Salvador, Central America; cigars; rice, sugar, coffee in a.; p. (1960) *18,536.*

Colac, *t.*, Victoria, Australia; nr. Melbourne; farming and dairying dist; flax, engin., and brickmaking; p. (1966) *9,497.*

Colchagua, *prov.*, Chile; cap. San Fernando; stock raising; a. 3,422 sq. m.; p. (1961) *181,593.*

Colchester, *mun. bor.*, Essex, Eng.; on R. Colne; univ.; light inds.; engin.; oyster fisheries; p. (estd. 1967) *72,600.*

Cold Harbour, *vil.*, Va., U.S.A.; battles between Grant and Lee, 1864.

Coldstream, *burgh*, Berwick, Scot.; on R. Tweed; agr. engin., and knitwear; p. (1961) *1,227.*

Coldwater, *t.*, Mich., U.S.A.; engin.; flour, cement, leather goods; p. (1960) *8,880.*

Coleford, *t.*, Gloucester, Eng.; in Forest of Dean; ctr. of sm. coal-mining dist.; p. *2,800.*

Colenso, *t.*, Natal, S. Africa; on R. Tugela; battle 1899; p. *2,145.*

Coleraine, *urb. dist. spt.*, Londonderry, N. Ireland; on R. Bann, 4 m. from sea; univ.; linen, acrilan mftg., distilling; p. (1966) *13,578.*

Coleshill, *t.*, Warwick, Eng.; lurgi gasification plant projected; new colliery 1965; p. *3,177.*

Colima, *volcano* (30 m. N.E. of c.), Mexico, alt. 12,685 ft.

Colima, *st.*, Mexico; on Pacific cst.; cap. Colima; a. 2,009 sq. m.; p. (1960) *164,450.*

Colima, *c.*, Mexico; on Colima R. in fertile valley; p. (estd.) *25,000.* [ster fishing ind.

Coll, *i.*, off coast of Mull, Argyll, Scot.; agr., lobster fishing ind.

Colle di Val d'Elsa, *commune*, Siena, Italy; cath.; metal mftg.; p. *11,052.* [p. (1966) *7,616.*

Collie, *t.*, Western Australia; sub-bituminous coal;

Collingswood, *t.*, N.J., U.S.A.; p. (1960) *17,370.*

Collingwood, *t.*, Ontario, Canada; on L. Huron; shipbldg., steel; p. (1961) *8,385.*

Collinsville, *t.*, Ill., U.S.A.; coal, zinc smelting, canning; women's clothes; p. (1960) *14,217.*

Colmar, *t.*, cap. Haut-Rhin dep., France; vines, textiles, rayon, brewing; p. (1962) *54,264.*

Colne, *t.*, *mun. bor.*, E. Lancs, Eng.; cotton mnfs.; p. (estd. 1967) *18,850.*

Colne, *R.*, Essex, Eng.; oysters.

Colne Valley, *urb. dist.*, W.R. Yorks; woollens; p. (estd. 1967) *20,760.*

Cologne, (Köln), *c.*, *Land* N. Rhine–Westphalia, Germany; on R. Rhine at N. end of Rhine gorge; cath.; univ.; eau-de-Cologne, electrotechnical ind., machin., metallurgy, paper, wood, chemicals, cars, oil refining, textiles; impt. R. pt. and route ctr.; p. (1963) *832,400.*

Colomb-Béchar, *see* Béchar. [p. (1962) *77,090.*

Colombes, *t.*, Seine, France; mftg. sub. of Paris;

Colombia, *rep.*, S. America, mountainous in W. (Cordilleras), swampy, llanos in E.; climate mainly tropical. Rs.: Magdalena, Cauca and tribs. of Amazon; Spanish language; Roman Catholic; coffee, tobacco, cocoa, cattle; gold, platinum, oil, emeralds; oilfield in Amazon a.; cap. Bogotá; a. 439,997 sq. m.; p. (estd. 1963) *16,525,000.*

Colombo, *cap.*, *pt.* Ceylon; exp. tea, rubber, coconuts; p. (1963) *510,947.*

Colón, *c.*, Panama, Central America; at Atlantic end of Panama Canal; comm. ctr., oil refining nearby; p. (1960) *59,598.*

Colonia, *dep.* Uruguay; cap. Colonia; a. 2,193 sq. m.; p. (1953) *135,033.*

Colonsay, *I.*, Inner Hebrides, Scot.; 8 m. long; ecclesiastical antiquities; p. (inc. Oronsay) *233.*

Colorado, *st.*, U.S.A.; in Rocky Mtns.; agr. with irrigation; pastoral; gold, copper, silver, coal, petroleum, uranium; cap. Denver (*q.v.*); a. 104,247 sq. m; p. (1960) *1,753,947.*

Colorado, *R.*, W. of N. America, formed by union of Grand and Green Rs. (2,000 m. long, navigable for 600 m.), with cañon (6,000 ft. deep).

Colorado, *R.*, Texas, U.S.A.; length 900 m.

Colorado, *R.*, flows into Blanca Bay, Argentina.

Colorado Springs, *wat. pl., health resort*, Col., U.S.A.; 64 m. S. Denver; smelting; p. (1960) *70,194.*

Colton, *t.*, S.E. Cal., U.S.A.; fruit and vegetable canning; mkt. gardening; p. (1960) *18,666.*

Columbia, *c.*, Mo., U.S.A.; st. univ.; flour, lumber; p. (1960) *36,650.* [*12,075.*

Columbia, *t.*, Penns., U.S.A.; mnfs.; p. (1960)

Columbia, *cap.*, S.C., U.S.A.; burned 1865; univ.; cotton mills; ironwks.; p. (1960) *97,433.*

Columbia, *t.*, Tenn., U.S.A.; mftg.; livestock mkt.; p. (1960) *17,624.*

Columbia, *R.*, on Pacific slope of N. America; rises in Brit. Columbia, flows through Wash., U.S.A.; salmon fishing; length 1,400 m.

Columbia, Dist. of, U.S.A.; on left bank of Potomac R.; contains Washington, the federal cap. of U.S.A.; a. 69 sq. m.; p. (1960) *763,956.*

Columbia, Mt., Alberta, Canada (alt. 12,294 ft.).

Columbus, *st. cap.*, Ohio, U.S.A.; rly. ctr.; st. univ.; machin., paper, aircraft machin., chemicals; p. (1960) *471,316.*

Columbus, *t.*, Ga., U.S.A.; cotton goods, machin.; p. (1960) *116,779.*

Columbus, *t.*, Ind., U.S.A.; engin.; leather goods; p. (1960) *20,778.* [p. (1960) *24,771.*

Columbus, *t.*, Miss., U.S.A.; cotton, dairying;

Colwyn Bay, *t.*, *mun. bor.*, on cst., 6 m. E. of Llandudno; Denbigh, N. Wales; seaside resort; diamond tools; p. (1961) *23,090.*

Comacchio, *c.*, Italy; nr. the Adriatic, 20 m. N. Ravenna; p. *12,609.*

Comayagua, *c.*, Honduras Rep., Central America; cath.; univ.; p. (1961) *5,192.*

Combe Capelle, *rock shelter*, nr. Dordogne, France; discovery of race type of Aurignacian period, 1909.

Combe Martin, *vil.*, Devon, Eng.; 5 m. E. of Ilfracombe; popular seaside resort; p. (1951) *1,920.*

Comber, *t.*, Down, N. Ireland; linen; p. (1966) *3,925.*

Comiso, *t.*, Sicily, Italy; medicinal spring, porcelain mnfs.; p. *29,555.*

Commentary, *t.*, Allier, France; nr. Moulins; mining; p. (1954) *9,259.*

Como, *c.*, N. Italy; at foot of Alps, on L. Como; silk ind.; oranges, olives; p. (1961) *82,070.*

Como, *L.*, N. Italy (35 m. long), tourist resort.

Comodoro Rivadavia, *spt.*, Chubut prov. Argentina; on San Jorge Gulf, 550 m. S.W. of Bahia Blanca; military zone; ch. source of oil in Argentine; p. (1960) *40,000.*

Comorin, C., most S. point of India.

Comoro Is., unit of French Community with full intern. aut., Mozambique channel, midway between Africa and Malagasy; cap. Dzaoudzi on Mayotte I.; total a. about 838 sq. m.; turtle fishing; vanilla, copra, sisal, timber, perfume plants; p. (estd. 1965) *197,000.*

Compiègne, *t.*, Oise, France; sugar-mills, rope; Armistice signed between Allies and Germany 1918; French surrendered to Hitler in 1940; p. (1954) *22,325.*

Compton, *t.*, Cal., U.S.A.; heavy engin., glass, oil refining; p. (1960) *71,812.*

Conakry, *cap.*, Guinea; experimental fruit gardens; textiles; airfields; p. (estd. 1965) *113,000.*

Concarneau, *t.*, Finistère, France; on I. nr. Quimper; salted fish and preserve tr.; p. (1954) *10,341.*

Concepción, *prov.*, Chile; cap. Concepción; Lota-Coronel coalfield, lgst in Chile; a. 2,201 sq. m.; p. (1961) *535,633.*

Concepción, *c.* prov. cap., Chile; shipping ctr. through its pt. Talcahuano; univ.; comm. and cultural t.; severe earthquakes 1939 and 1960; p. (1961) *186,700.*

Concepción, *t.*, Paraguay; trade ctr.; p. (estd. 1960) *34,000.*

Concepción C., on cst. of California, U.S.A.

Conception Bay, Newfoundland, Canada; N.W. of St. Johns.

Conchos, *R.*, Chihuahua prov., Mexico, Central America; flows N.E. from Sierra Tarahumare to Rio Grande; cotton under irrigation in upper valley.

Concón, *t.*, Chile; on N.E. point of Valparaiso Bay; oil refining.

Concord, *t.*, Mass., U.S.A.; literary ctr.; textiles; p. (1960) *12,275.*

Concord, *t.*, N.C., U.S.A.; cotton, textiles; p. (1960) *17,799.*

Concord, *t.*, *cap.*, N.H., U.S.A.; on Merrimore R.; granite, machin., textiles; p. (1960) *28,991.*

Concordia, *t.*, Argentina; on Uruguay R.; p. (1960) *56,000.* [R. Darling.

Condamine, *R.*, Queensland, Australia; trib. of

Conegliano, *commune*, N. Italy; silks, wines, light mftg.; p. *15,434.*

Coney I., *t.*, N.Y., U.S.A.; on Long I., 5 m. long, comprises Manhattan Beach, Brighton Beach, W. Brighton and W. End; seaside resort.

Congleton, *t.*, *mun. bor.*, E. Cheshire, Eng.; on S.W. margin of Pennines; agr., salt, clothing, textiles; p. (estd. 1967) *18,650.*

Congo, Rep. of the, *ind. sov. st. within French Community*, Equatorial Africa; cap. Brazzaville; a. 132,000 sq. m.; p. (1962) *864,684.*

Congo, Rep. of the, *ind. sov. st.* (ex-Belgian); Central Africa; div. into 8 provs.: Bandundu, Central Congo, East Kasai, Eastern Province, Equator, Katanga, Kivu, West Kasai; climate: uniformly hot, heavy rains; tropical forests; agr., palm oil, cotton, rice, copal, coffee, ivory, rubber; minerals: copper, gold, diamonds, tin, uranium; communications mainly river, some rail; cap. Kinshasha; ch. ts. Buma, Kinsangani, Lubumbashi; a. 905,400 sq. m.; p. (estd. 1965) *15,449,000.*

Congo, *R.*, greatest R. in Africa, numerous tribs.; estd. length 3,000 m.; drains 1,500,000 sq. m., navigable from sea to Matadi for ocean steamers.

from Matadi to Stanley Pool interrupted by rapids and falls, again navigable to Stanley Falls; estuary, 7–10 m. wide.

Conisborough, *t.*, *urb. dist.*, W.R., Eng.; limestone, bricks, tiles; p. (1961) *17,596*.

Coniston, *t.*, Ontario, Canada; on rly. 8 m. E. of Sudbury; nickel smelting; town built by and for nickel-mining company.

Coniston Old Man, *mtn.*, nr. L. Coniston, Lancs. Eng. (alt. 2,575 ft.).

Coniston Water, *L.*, N. Lancs. Eng.; length 5½ m.; tourist resort.

Conjeeveram (Kancheepuram), *t.*, Tamil Nadu. S. India; pilgrimage ctr.; silk, cotton, weaving; p. (1961) *92,714*.

Connacht, *prov.*, Ireland; (includes cos. Galway, Mayo, Sligo, Leitrim, Roscommon); mntnous. in W.; farming, fishing; a. 6,863 sq. m.; p. (1966) *401,518*.

Connah's Quay, *urb. dist.*, Flint, Wales; p. (1961) *8,355*.

Connaught, *see* Connacht.

Connaught Tunnel (Can. Pac. Rly.), B.C., Canada; longest in N. America (5 m.), 5,000 ft. under Mt. Sir Donald (Selkirk Mtns.).

Connecticut, *st.*, New England, U.S.A.; cereals, tobacco, dairying; fishing; watches and clocks, firearms, aircraft, engin., copper, brass, machin.; cap. Hartford; lgst. c. New Haven; a. 5,009 sq. m.; p. (1960) *2,535,234*.

Connecticut, *R.*, flows S. to Long I. Sound, U.S.A.; length 450 m.

Connellsville, *t.*, Penns., U.S.A.; coke, machin., motor cars; p. (1960) *12,814*.

Connemara, *mtns.*, *dist.*, W. of Ireland, Galway; many lakes and bogs; tourist resort.

Conowingo Dam, Penns., U.S.A.; situated on lower Susquehanna R.; hydro-electric powersta. supplies power to inds. in Philadelphia.

Conroe, *t.*, Texas, U.S.A.; oil, timber; p. (1960) *9,192*.

Consett, *urb. dist.*, Durham, Eng.; on edge of Pennines, 10 m. S.W. of Newcastle; iron, steel, coke, coal; p. (estd. 1967) *37,500*.

Conshohocken, *bor.*, Penns., U.S.A.; iron, steel, surgical instruments, textiles; p. (1960) *10,259*.

Constance (Konstanz), *c.*, Baden-Württemberg, Germany; on L. Constance; cath.; textiles, machin., chemicals, elect. inds.; route ctr.; p. (1963) *55,100*.

Constance, L., or Bodensee, between Switzerland and Germany; 45 m. long, 9 m. broad; a. 207 sq. m.; R. Rhine flows through.

Constanta, *spt.*, Romania; on the Black Sea; exp. petroleum, wheat; p. (1963) *153,371*.

Constantina, *t.*, Andalusia, Spain; p. (1957) *14,619*.

Constantine, *dep.*, N. Algeria; cap. Constantine; p. (1960) *1,411,000*.

Constantine, *t.*, N. Algeria; wheat, woollens, leather; stands 2,130 ft. high upon a rock; p. (1960) *223,000*.

Constantinople, *see* Istanbul.

Conversano, *c.*, Bari, S. Italy; cath.; olives, citrus fruits; mnfs.

Conway, *t.*, S.C., U.S.A.; river pt.; cotton, tobacco, lumber; p. (1960) *8,563*.

Conway, *mun. bor.*, *spt.*, Caernarvon, N. Wales; at mouth of R. Conway; sm. seaside resort; cas.; quarrying, light engin.; p. (1961) *11,392*.

Cooch Behar, *dist.*, W. Bengal, India; a. 1,289 sq. m.; rice, jute, tobacco; p. (1961) *1,019,806*.

Cooch Behar, *t.*, Cooch Behar, India; on Torsha R.; p. (1961) *41,922*.

Cook, *mtn.*, alt. 12,349 ft.; highest point in S. Alps, New Zealand.

Cook Inlet, S. cst., Alaska; U.S.A. (200 m. long); oil; pipeline connects oilfields of Granite Point with marine terminal at Drift R.

Cook Is., British group (Rarotonga, lgst.) in S. Pacific, annexed to New Zealand, 1901; internal self govt. 1965; bananas, oranges, copra; p. (estd. 1965) *20,000*.

Cook Strait, *channel* between N. and S. Is. of N.Z.; 15–18 m. wide; undersea cable completed 1965.

Cookham, *t.*, *rural dist.*, Berks., Eng.; on R. Thames nr. Maidenhead; p. (rural dist. 1961) *17,169*.

Cookstown, *mkt. t.*, *urb. dist.*, Tyrone. Ireland; cement wks.; p. (1966) *5,542*.

Coolin Mtns., *see* Cuillin Hills.

Cooma, *t.*, N.S.W., Australia; mkt. t. and pastoral ctr.; tourism; H.Q. of Snowy Mts. Authority; p. (1966) *9,101*.

Coonoor, *t.*, Tamil Nadu, India; sanatorium 6,000 ft. above sea-level; p. (1961) *30,690*.

Coopers Creek (Barcoo), *R.*, Central Australia; rises in Warrego Range, Gr. Dividing Range, flows S.W. into marshes of L. Eyre; flow is intermittent and seasonal, but provides water for livestock in this semi-arid region; length approx. 900 m.

Coorg, *former st.*, now inc. in Mysore, India; mountainous, forests; coffee, rice, rubber, tea; cap. Mercara; a. 1,587 sq. m.; p. (1961) *322,829*.

Coorong, The, S. Australia; lagoon and long tongue of land on cst.

Coosa, *R.*, Ala., U.S.A.; length 350 m.

Cootamundra, *t.*, N.S.W., Australia; agr. and mftg.; p. (1966) *6,207*.

Cootehill, *mkt. t.*, *urb. dist.*, Cavan, Ireland; Bellamont forest; p. (1951) *1,489*.

Copeland Is., gr. off N.W. coast of Down, N. Ireland, at entrance to Belfast Lough.

Copenhagen, *ch. spt.*, *cap.*, Denmark; on E. cst. of Själland I.; royal palace, univ.; library; naval sta.; steel, metal, textiles, clothing, breweries; airport; p. (1965) *1,377,605*.

Copiapo, *cap.*, Atacama prov., Chile; impt. copper and iron mng. ctr.; p. (1960) *37,224*.

Copparo, *commune*, Ferrara, N. Italy; drained agr. land, in R. Po delta; p. *23,777*.

Coppercliff, *t.*, E. Ontario, Canada; mining, nickel-copper smelting; p. (1961) *3,600*.

Coppermine, *R.*, N.W. Terr., Canada; flows N. into Arctic Ocean; length 300 m.

Coquet I., off cst. Northumberland, Eng.

Coquilhatville *see* Mbandaka.

Coquimbo, *prov.*, Chile, on Argentine border; copper-mining dist.; cap. La Serena; a. 15,397 sq. m.; p. (1960) *393,664*.

Coquimbo, *spt.*, Chile; prin. exps: iron, copper, and manganese ores; p. (1962) *52,250*.

Coracora, *t.*, S. Peru; mining; pt. Chala; p. *8,000*.

Coral Sea, Pacific Ocean, extending from the New Hebrides to Australia.

Coraopolis, *bor.*, S.W. Penns., U.S.A.; iron, steel, glass; p. (1960) *9,643*.

Corato, *t.*, Apulia, Italy; farming ctr., olive oil, wine; p. *44,139*.

Corbeil-Essonnes, *t.*, Essonne, France; on R. Seine, 12 m. S.E. of Paris; flour mills, printing, paper; p. (1962) *27,038*.

Corbridge, *t.*, Northumberland, Eng.; on R. Tyne, nr. Hexham; p. *2,415*.

Corby, *t.*, Northants, Eng.; 7 m. N. of Kettering; steel wks.; one of "New Towns," designated 1950; steel wks., shoes, clothing, lamps; p. (estd. 1967) *46,580*.

Cordeli, *t.*, S.W. Ga., U.S.A.; tr. ctr.; peanuts, cotton mills, sawmills; p. (1960) *10,609*.

Córdoba, *agr. prov.*, Argentina; cap. Córdoba; a. 65,195 sq. m.; p. (1960) *1,760,000*.

Córdoba, *c.*, Argentina; univ.; wheat, flour, wool, shoes; car and aircraft prod.; p. (1960) *600,000*.

Córdoba, *dep.*, Colombia, S. America; cap. Monteria; p. (estd. 1959) *377,690*.

Córdoba, *t.*, Veracruz, Mexico; cottons, woollens, coffee; p. (1960) *32,883*.

Córdova, *prov.*, Andalusia, Spain; cap. Córdova; agr., olives, vines, livestock; a. 5,299 sq. m.; p. (1959) *805,150*.

Córdova, *t.*, Andalusia, Spain; cap. of C. prov.; on Guadalquivir R.; cath.—formerly a sacred mosque of Mohammedans; textiles, leather, distilling; p. (1965) *215,000*.

Corentyne, *R.*, forms bdy. between Brit. and Netherland Guiana; length 400 m.

Corfe Castle, *par.*, Dorset, Eng.; cas. ruins; mkt., potter's clay.

Corfu, *see* Kerkyra.

Corigliano, *t.*, S. Italy; 4 m. from E. cst. of Calabria; agr.; p. *15,926*.

Coringa, *t.*, Madras, India; at mouth of Godavari R.

Corinth, Isthmus of, divides the Saronic G. from G. of Corinth, Greece; cut across by Ship Canal.

Corinth Canal, *ship canal*, S. Greece; traverses Isthmus of Corinth, links G. of Corinth and Ionian Sea with Saronic G. and Ægean Sea; opened 1893; length 3½ m., depth 26 ft.

Corinthia, *prov.*, Greece; p. (1961) *112,491*.

Corinto (Corinth), *c.*, Greece; at W. end of Isth. of Corinth; occupies a site 3 m. distant from the ancient classic c. destroyed by earth quake. 1858; currants, olive oil, silk; p. (1961) 15,892.

Corinto, *ch. spt.*, N.W. Nicaragua; exp. hides, sugar, coffee; p. (1960) 7,096.

Cork, *co.*, S. Ireland; lgst. and most S.; mtns.; dairying, brewing, agr., fisheries; cap. Cork; a. 2,890 sq. m.; p. (1966) 339,525.

Cork, *spt., co. bor.*, Cork, Ireland; at mouth of R. Lee; univ.; woollens, butter, cattle, brewing, cars, rubber; p. (1966) 122,066.

Cork Harbour, pt. of call (Cobh) for Atlantic steamers.

Corleone, *t.*, Palermo, Sicily, Italy; mineral springs; p. 13,704.

Corlu, *t.*, Turkey in Europe; grain mkt.: p. (1965) 27,156.

Cormeilles-en-Parisis, Seine-et-Oise, France; p. (1954) 10,638.

Corner Brook, *c.*, W. Newfoundland; gd. harbour; pulp, paper; p. of E. and W. (1961) 25,185.

Corning, *t.*, N.Y., U.S.A.; dairying, tobacco; p. (1960) 17,085.

Cornwall, *co.*, S.W. Eng.; mkt. gardening, oats, cattle, fishing, minerals, kaolin, granite, tin, lt. engin.; extreme point Land's End; co. to. Bodmin; a. 1,357 sq. m.; fp. (1966) 353,000.

Cornwall, *c.*, Ontario, Canada; on St. Lawrence R.; H.Q. of Seaway Authority; textiles, pulp, paper, flour; p. (1961) 43,639.

Cornwallis Is., Arctic Ocean, Brit. N. America.

Coro, *t.*, Venezuela; agr.; p. (1950) 28,307.

Corocoro, *sm. t.*, La Paz dep., Bolivia; at alt. 13,000 ft. in Central Andes, 50 m. S. of La Paz; impt. copper-mining ctr.; p. (1946) 4,500.

Coromandel Cst., cst. of S.E. Tamil Nadu, India.

Coronado, Cal., U.S.A.; fashionable seaside resort; p. (1960) 18,039.

Coronation Gulf, arm of Arctic Ocean; extreme point N. Canada; discovered by Franklin.

Coronel, *spt.*, Chile; p. 28,027.

Coronel Oviedo, *t.*, Paraguay; p. (1945) 33,098.

Corpus Christi, *c.*, Texas, U.S.A.; cotton; p. (1960) 167,690.

Corrèze, *mtnous. dep.*, S. Central France; cap. Tulle; cereals, wines, cattle, timber, coal, granite, iron; a. 2,272 sq. m.; p. (1962) 237,926.

Corrib, Lough, *L.*, Galway and Mayo, R.o.I.; a. 68 sq. m.; R. Corrib flows from it into Atl.

Corrientes, *prov.*, Argentina; cap. Corrientes; a. 34,325 sq. m.; p. (1960) 543,000.

Corrientes, *t.*, Argentina; on Parana R.; univ.; cattle, sugar, rice, cotton; p. (1960) 104,000.

Corrientes, C., Mozambique, Port. E. Africa.

Corry, *t.*, Penns., U.S.A.; oil, engin., metal wks., furniture; p. (1960) 7,744.

Corsham, *mkt. t.*, Wilts, Eng.

Corsica (Corse), French I. and dep. in Mediterranean; forested, mtns.; agr., olives, lemons, chestnuts, vine growing; cap. Ajaccio; a. 3,367 sq. m.; p. (1962) 275,465, excluding Bastia.

Corsicana, *t.*, Texas, U.S.A.; p. (1960) 20,344.

Corso, C., N. point of Corsica.

Cortland, *t.*, N.Y., U.S.A.; stoves, wine; p. (1960) 19,181.

Cortona, *t.*, Tuscany, Italy; nr. Perugia; silk factories; p. 30,222.

Coruh, *prov.*, N.E. Turkey, a. 3,408 sq. m.; p. (1960) 193,684, *spt.*, the *cap.* p. 13,861.

Corum, *prov.*, N. Central Turkey in Asia, a. 4,339 sq. m.; p. (1955) 485,847. t. its *cap.* p. (1965) 41,200.

Corumba, *port*, Mata Grosso, Brazil; on R. Paraguay; p. (1960) 36,744.

Corunna, *see* La Coruña.

Corvallis, Ore., U.S.A.; rich farming section, canning, lumber; p. (1960) 20,669.

Coryton, *t.*, Essex, Eng.; on Thames, oil refining; oil pipeline to Stanlow refinery under constr.

Coseley, *t.*, Staffs., Eng.; W. edge of Black Country; heavy iron steel wks.; p. (1961) 39,557.

Cosenza, *c.*, S. Italy; ctr. for figs, oranges, olive oil, wine, silk; cath., cas.; p. (1961) 77,590.

Cosenza, *prov.*, Calabria, Italy; a. 2,566 sq. m.; p. (1951) 685,572.

Coshocton, *t.*, Ohio, U.S.A.; coal, gas, oil; pottery, enamelware; p. (1960) 13,106.

Cosne, *t.*, Nièvre, France; on R. Loire; pottery.

Costa Brava, *reg.*, Catalonia, Spain; tourism.

Costa del Sol, *reg.*, Malaga cst., Spain; tourism.

Costa Rica, *rep.*, Central America; cap. Sap José; volcanic mtns.; agr., coffee, bananas, rubber, gold; a. 19,656 sq. m.; p. (estd. 1965) 1,430,000.

Costa Smerelda, N.E. Sardinia, Italy; deserted cst. being developed

Côte d'Or Mtns., N.E. part of Central Massif; max. alt. 1,968 ft.

Côte d'Or, *dep.*, E. France; traversed by R. Saône; cap. Dijon; wines, live-stock, iron and steel; a. 3,391 sq. m.; p. (1962) 387,869.

Cotentin, *peninsula*, N. France; 50 m. long; Cherbourg, at its extremity, 80 m. from Portsmouth.

Côtes-du-Nord, *agr. dep.*, Brittany, W. France; cap. St. Brieuc; wheat, flax, iron, slate, fishing, linen-mkg.; a. 2,787 sq. m.; p. (1962) 501,923.

Cotopaxi, *vol.*, (alt. 19,613 ft.) in the Andes of Ecuador, nr. Quito; loftiest active volcano in the world; recent eruptions have caused great damage to Ecuador.

Cotopaxi, *prov.*, Ecuador, S. America; cap. Latacunga; a. 2,595 sq. m.; p. (estd. 1962) 193,929.

Cotrone, *spt.*, Catanzaro, S. Italy; good tr. in wine, olive oil, etc.; p. 21,496.

Cotswold Hills, W. Eng., between Lower Severn and Upper Thames; highest point, Cleeve Cloud, 1,031 ft.; fine sheep pastures.

Cottbus, *t.*, Cottbus, Germany; on R. Spree; textiles, metallurgy; rly. ctr.; p. (1963) 71,390.

Coudekerque-Branche, S. E. sub. of Dunkerque, Nord dep., France; tar and lubricant refinery, textiles; p. (1954) 15,334.                    [11,092.

Coueron, *t.*, Loire Atlantique, France; p. (1954)

Coulsdon and Purley, *former urb. dist.*, Surrey, Eng., now inc. in Croydon outer bor. Greater London; in dry valley of N. Downs, 4 m. S. of Croydon; residtl.; chalk quarries; p. (1961) 74,738.

Council Bluffs, *c.*, Iowa, U.S.A.; on Missouri R.; rly. ctr., farm implements, paper, machin.; p. (1960) 54,361.

Coupar Angus, *mkt. burgh*, Perth, Scot.; 16 m. S.W. of Forfar; p. (1961) 2,049.

Courbevoie, *t.*, industl. sub. of Paris, France; on R. Seine; p. (1962) 59,941.

Courcelles, *t.*, Hainaut, Belgium; coal, linen, factories; p. (1962) 17,331.

Courneuve (La), *t.*, Seine, France; p. (1954) 18,349.

Courtrai, *see* Kortrijk.

Cove and Kilcreggan, *burgh*, Dunbarton, Scot.; at junction of Loch Long and R. Clyde; p. (1961) 577.

Coventry, *mftg. c., co. bor.*, N. Warwick, Eng.; 18 m. E.S.E. of Birmingham; ctr. of cycle, motor-cycle, motor-car ind.; aircraft, tools; chemicals; projectiles, textiles; cath.; univ.; p. (estd. 1967) 333,830.                      [23,091.

Covilha, *t.*, Portugal; cloth factories; (1960)

Covington, *industl. c.*, Ky., U.S.A.; on R. Ohio, opp. Cincinnati; machin., leather, furniture; p. (1960) 60,376.

Covington, *t.*, Va., U.S.A.; X-ray equipment, paper, rayon, textiles; p. (1960) 11,062.

Cowbridge, *mun. bor.*, Glamorgan, S. Wales; nr. Cardiff; p. (1961) 1,065.

Cowdenbeath, *burgh*, Fife, Scot.; 5 m. N.E. of Dunfermline; coal; p. (1961) 11,918.

Cowes, *t., urb. dist.*, I. of Wight. Eng.; on both sides of estuary of R. Medina; home of the Royal Yacht Squadron; regattas and yacht bldg.; aircraft, p. (1961) 16,974.

Cowley, *sub.*, Oxford, Oxfordshire, Eng.; 3 m. S.E. of Oxford; mnfs. motor vehicles.

Cowra, *t.*, N.S.W., Australia; famous wheat dist. and site of state experimental farm; sm. mftg ctr.; p. (1966) 7,082.

Cozenza, *t., cap.*, prov. Cozenza, Italy; iron and steel; p. 40,032.

Cozumel I., E. of Yucatan Peninsula; Mexico.

Cracow, *see* Kraków.

Cradle, Mt., *mtn.*, Tasmania, alt. 5,069 ft.

Cradock, *t.*, Cape Province; wool tr.; p. (1960) 19,476 inc. 5,200 whites.

Craigavon *t.*, N. Ireland; new "city in a garden" under constr.

Crail, *burgh*, Fife, Scot.; p. (1961) 1,066.

Craiova, *cap.*, Oltenia, Romania; p. (1963) 140,526.

Cramlington, *t.*, Northumberland, Eng; 8 m. N. of Newcastle; "New Town" designated 1964 (local authorities and private enterprise); proposed p. 48,000; major industl. estate to be established.

Cranbrook, *rural dist., mkt. t.*, Kent, Eng.; hops and grain; p. (rural dist. 1961) 14,153.

Cranford, *t.*, N.J., U.S.A.; iron. chemicals; p. (1960) 26,424. [66,766.

Cranston, *c.*, Rhode I., U.S.A.; mnfs.; p. (1960)

Crater L., Ore., U.S.A.; in National Park, is a gr. body of water 2,000 ft. deep and 6 m. across, set in a crater of an extinct gigantic volcano, 8,000 ft. high.

Crathie and Braemar, *pars.*, Aberdeenshire, Scot.; adjoining Balmoral Cas. and Abergeldie Cas. estates; p. (1951) 1,291.

Crato, *t.*, Ceara st., Brazil; at foot of Chapados de Araripe, approx. 300 m. by rail S. of Fortaleza; ctr. of irrigated area producing cotton, sugar, rice; p. (1960) 27,649.

Crau, La, *region*, Bouches-du-Rhône dep., S.E. France; dry, pebbly area E. of Rhône delta; winter pasture for sheep.

Craven, *dist.*, Central Pennines, Eng.; relatively low limestone plateau, alt. mainly below 800 ft. except where capped by grits in N. Craven; typical limestone features, caves, stalactites and stalagmites, steep-sided valleys (dales); drained by R. Ribble to S.W., R. Aire to S.E.; largely moorland, sheep rearing in valleys, rearing of cattle for fattening elsewhere, cultivation of root and fodder crops; R. valleys give the only easy routes across Central Pennines, Leeds to Preston, Leeds to Carlisle; ch. mkt. ts. and route ctrs., Skipton, Settle.

Crawfordsville, *t.*, Ind., U.S.A.; p. (1960) 14,231.

Crawley, *t.*, Sussex, Eng.; on N.W. flank of the Weald 9 m. S. of Reigate; one of "New Towns" designated 1947 to relieve population congestion in London; extends from vil. of Crawley N. towards Horley; engin., pharmaceutics, metals, leather, wooden goods; p. (estd. (1967) 62,200.

Crayford, *former urb. dist.*, Kent, Eng.; now inc. in Bexley, Greater London; engin., fabric printing, oil and resin ref. [4,422.

Crediton, *mkt. t., urb. dist.*, Devon, Eng.; p. (1961)

Creil, *t.*, Oise, France; on R. Oise, 30 m. N. of Paris; machin. mnf.; p. (1954) 13,500.

Crema, *commune*, Cremona, N. Italy; cath.; wine, silk, linen, lace, hats; p. 25,163.

Cremona, *c.*, N. Italy; on R. Po; silk, cotton, stringed instruments; birthplace of Stradivari; p. (1961) 74,242.

Crete, *I.*, E. Mediterranean; 60 m. from Greek mainland; cap. Khania (Canea), Heraklion (Candia) lgst. c.; incorporated into Greece after Balkan Wars (1913); exp. fruit, oil, etc.; a. 3,235 sq. m.; p. (1961) 483,258.

Créteil, *t.*, Seine, France; p. (1954) 13,793.

Creus, C., juts out into Mediterranean Sea, Spain, nr. French border.

Creuse, *dep.*, Central France; agr., etc.; cap. Gueret; a. 2,164 sq. m.; p. (1962) 163,515.

Creusot, Le, *t.*, Saône-et-Loire, France; lge. ordnance works; p. (1954) 23,663.

Creutzwald-la-Croix, *t.*, Moselle dep., N.E. France; coal, iron foundries; p. (1954) 10,183.

Crevillente, *t.*, Spain; wine, wheat and fruit; p. (1957) 12,636.

Crewe, *t., mun. bor.*, Cheshire, Eng.; 20 m. S.E. of Chester; lge. rly. wks.; impt. rly. junction; aircraft and refrigerator wks., clothing, engin., motor vehicles; p. (estd. 1967) 52,400.

Crewkerne, *mkt. t., urb. dist.*, Somerset, Eng.; 8 m. S.W. of Yeovil; sailcloth, twine, webbing, gloves, concrete prod.; p. (1961) 4,215.

Criccieth, *t., urb. dist.*, Caernarvon, N. Wales; on N. shore of Cardigan Bay; sm. seaside resort; p. (1961) 1,671.

Crickhowell, *rural dist., mkt. t.*, Brecon, S. Wales; on R. Usk; paper; p. (rural dist. 1961) 7,483.

Cricklade, *t., rural dist.*, N. Wilts., Eng.; on R. Thames, 8 m. N.W. of Swindon; p. (rural dist. 1961) 17,869.

Crieff, *burgh, summer resort*, Perth, Scot.; on R. Earn, 15 m. W. of Perth; egg hatchery, preserve wks.; p. (1961) 5,773.

Crimea Peninsula, jutting into Black Sea, U.S.S.R.; wheat, tobacco, fruit; campaign 1854-55 between Russia and the Allied Force of Turkey, Britain, France and Sardinia was chiefly fought out here (Alma, Balaclava and Sevastopol).

Crimmitschau, *t.*, Karl-Marx-Stadt, E. Germany, nr. Zwickau; woollen-cloth, machin.; p. (1963) 30,891.

Crinan Canal, across peninsula of Kintyre, S.W. Scot.; connecting Loch Gilp with the Atlantic; length 6 m.

Cristóbal, *dist.*, Panama Canal Zone, Central America; adjoins Colón at N. entrance to Canal; p. (1960) 11,499; of t. (1960) 817.

Croaghpatrick, *mtns.*, Mayo, Ireland, 2,510 ft.

Croatia, *fed. unit*, Jugoslavia; formerly part of Austria; mtns.; cereals, potatoes, tobacco, timber, pigs, sheep, cattle; cap. Zagreb; a. 16,418 sq. m.; p. (estd. 1960) 4,207,000.

Crockett, *t.*, E. Texas, U.S.A.; lumber, cottonseed oil, pecan nuts; p. (1960) 5,356.

Crocodile R., *see* Limpopo.

Croix, *t.*, Nord, France; p. (1954) 18,702.

Cromarty, *burgh*, Ross and Cromarty, Scot.; off N.E. cst. of Black Isle; p. (1961) 605.

Cromer, *t., urb. dist.*, Norfolk, Eng.; on N. cst. of E. Anglia; seaside resort; p. (1961) 4,895.

Crompton, *mftg. t., urb. dist.*, Lancs, Eng.; 2 m. S. of Rochdale; cotton, engin., elec. lamps; p. (1961) 12,707.

Crooked I., Bahama Is., W. Indies; p. (1953) 836.

Crosby or Great Crosby, *mun. bor.*, S. Lancs., Eng.; on Liverpool Bay, 3 m. N. of Bootle; residtl.; seaside resort; p. (estd. 1967) 59,650

Cross, *R.*, S.E. Nigeria; rises in Cameroon Highlands, flows W. and S. into G. of Guinea at Calabar; useful inland waterway; length approx. 400 m.

Cross Fell, *mtn.*, Cumberland, Eng.; on E. border of co.; alt. 2,930 ft.

Crow Head, *C.*, Kerry, Ireland.

Crowley, *t.*, S. La., U.S.A.; rice mills, rice experiment sta.; p. (1960) 15,617.

Crows Nest Pass, B.C., Alberta, Canada; southernmost pass across Canadian Rocky Mtns.; used by rly. from Medicine Hat to Spokane (U.S.A.); alt. summit 4,459 ft.

Croydon, *residtl. t., former co. bor.*, Surrey, Eng., now outer bor. Greater London; inc. Coulsdon and Purley; lt. inds.; formerly airpt. (closed 1959); p. (1966) 327,000.

Crozet Is., mountainous uninhabited group in S. Indian Ocean; French.

Cruzeiro, *t.*, S. Brazil, on trib. of Uruguay R.; coffee, tobacco; p. (1960) 27,005.

Csepel, *sub.*, Budapest, Hungary; iron and steel, oil refining, leather, paper; p. (1965) 60,000.

Csongrad, *mkt. t., agr. dist.*, Hungary; at junction of Rs. Theiss and Koros; p. (1962) 20,399.

Cuba, *I.*, W. Indies; taken from Spain by the U.S.A., but later constituted an independent rep.; climate, insular tropical, plentiful rainfall; tropical forest; agr., sugar-cane, tobacco, maize, fruits, mahogany and cedar, hardwoods, iron, copper, rayon, cement; cap. Havana; a. 44,206 sq. m.; p. (estd. 1965) 7,468,000.

Cubango, *R.*, S. Africa, enters L. Ngami.

Cuckfield, *mkt. t., urb. dist.*, Sussex, Eng.; p. (estd. 1967) 23,800.

Cuckmere, *R.*, Sussex, Eng.; rises in High Weald and flows S. into English Channel 4 m. W. of Beachy Head; passes through S. Downs in very beautiful gap; length 23 m.

Cucuta, *t.*, cap. Santander del Norte, Colombia, S. America; coffee, tobacco, cattle; p. (estd. 1959) 131,410.

Cudahy, *t.*, Wis., U.S.A.; p. (1960) 17,975.

Cuddalore, *spt.*, Tamil Nadu, India; nr. Pondicherry; exp. oil-seeds, cottons; p. (1961) 79,163.

Cuddapah, *t.*, Andhra Pradesh, India; cotton, cloth factories, millet, rice; p. (1961) 49,027.

Cudillero, *commune*, Oviedo, N.W. Spain; manganese; p. 10,630. [9,042.

Cudworth, *urb. dist.*, W.R Yorks, Eng.; p. (1961)

Cue, *t.*, W. Australia; goldfields.

Cuenca, *c.*, Cuenca, Spain; on R. Jucar; p. (1949) 25,215.

Cuenca, *agr. and mining prov.*, Central Spain; furniture, leather, paper; a. 6,588 sq. m.; p. (1959) 326,753.

Cuenca, *cap.*, Azuay, Ecuador; univ.; cath.; sugar, tyres, flour mills; p. (1962) 63,000.

Cuernavaca, *cap.*, Morelos St., Mexico; ancient Indian t. captured by Cortés; p. 30,567.

Cuesmes, *coal mng. t.*, adjoining Mons, Belgium; p. (1962) 10,799.

Cuiabá, *c., cap.*, Mato Grosso, Brazil; ctr. pastoral a.; gold and diamonds produced; galena deposit nearby; p. (1960) 57,860.

Cuidadela, *t.*, Balearic Is., Spain; W. cst. of Minorca; cath.; ancient ruins; cheese mnfs.; p. 10,716. [Sgurr Alasdair; alt. 3,251 ft.

Cuillin Hills, I. of Skye, Scot.; highest peak

Culebra, *valley and mtns.*, N. New Mexico.

Culebra, *spt. and I.*, Puerto Rico; W. Indies.

Culgoa, *R.*, trib. of Darling R., Queensland and N.S.W., Australia.

Culiacau, *cap.*, Sinaloa, Mexico; p. (1950) *144,550.*

Cullen, *burgh*, Banff, Scot.; between Buckie and Portsoy; p. (1961) *1,327.*

Cullera, *spt.*, Valencia, Spain; on R. Jucar; p. (1957) *14,831.* [mining ind.

Cullinan, *t.*, Transvaal, S. Africa; ctr. of diamond-

Culloden Moor, 6 m. E. of Inverness, Scot.; defeat of Bonnie Prince Charlie, 1746.

Cullompton (Cullumpton), *mkt. t.*, Devon, Eng.; paper, mftg., leather; p. 2,737. [514.

Culross, *burgh*, F. of Forth, Fife, Scot.; p. (1961)

Culver City, Cal., U.S.A.; large motion-picture plant; p. (1960) *32,163.*

Cumaná, *spt.*, c., Sucre. Venezuela; coffee, cacao; sardine canning; airport; p. (1961) *73,400.*

Cumaná, *G.*, N. cst., Venezuela.

Cumberland, *co.*, Eng.; S.E. part of Lake Dist., ch. mtns.; Scafell, Helvellyn, Skiddaw; ch. Ls.; Ullswater, Derwentwater, Thirlmere; oats, sheep rearing, dairying, fishing, coal, iron ore, iron and steel, shipbldg.; a. 1,516 sq. m.; p. (1966) *296,000.*

Cumberland, *industl. t.*, Md., U.S.A.; on Potomac R.; iron and steel; p. (1960) *33,450.*

Cumberland, *t.*, R.I., U.S.A.; iron, cotton, silk, granite; p. (1960) *18,763.* [700 m.

Cumberland, *R.*, Ky., U.S.A.; trib. of Ohio;

Cumberland Gap, Ky., U.S.A.; ch. break in high E. wall of Cumberland Plateau; gives access from upper Tennessee valley to Cumberland and Ohio valleys; very impt. routeway in colonisation of Ky.

Cumberland Is., off coast of Queensland, Australia.

Cumberland Plateau, *mtn. region*, Ky., Tenn., Ala., U.S.A.; forms S.W. zone of Appalachian mtn. system terminating abruptly towards Tennessee valley to E., Cumberland valley to W.; drained W. by tribs. of Cumberland and Ohio Rs.; composed of horizontal sandstones overlying coal; thinly populated by backward farming communities except where mining ts. occur in valleys cut down to coal; mainly between 1,200 and 3,000 ft.

Cumbernauld, Dunbarton, Scot.; designated "New Town" 1955; to accommodate 50,000 "over-spill" from Glasgow; adding machines; p. (estd. 1965) *16,448.*

Cumbrae, *Is.*, in F. of Clyde, off cst. of Ayr, Scot.

Cumbrian Mtns., Lake District, Cumberland, Westmorland and Lancashire, Eng.

Cumnock and Holmhead, *sm. burgh, mng. dist.*, Ayr, Scot.; p. (1961) *5,403.*

Cundinamarca, *dep.*, Colombia, S. America; contains the fed. cap. Bogotá; a. 9,106 sq. m.; p. (1962) *2,121,680.*

Cunene, see Kunene, R.

Cuneo, *prov.*, Italy; a. 2,870 sq. m.; p. (1961) [529,968.

Cuneo, *cap.*, Cuneo prov., Italy; cath.; cotton, paper; p. (1961) *45,709.*

Cupar, *burgh*, Fife, Scot.; on R. Eden, W. of St. Andrews; linen; sugar beet; p. (1961) *5,495.*

Curaçao I. (Netherlands Antilles), in the Carib-bean, off N. cst. of Venezuela; oil refining, phosphates, salt, aloes, resin, hides, skins; a. 210 sq. m.; p. (1963) *127,164.*

Curanilahua, *commune*, Arauco, Chile; coal-mining; p. *13,026.*

Curepipe, *t.*, Central Mauritius; health resort; p. (estd. 1968) *50,000.* [116,391.

Curico, *prov.*, Chile; a. 2,214 sq. m.; p. (1961)

Curico, *t.*, Chile; agr. and comn. ctr.; flour milling, brewing, wines; p. (1961) *82,600.*

Curitiba, *cap.*, Paraná st., Brazil; univ.; coffee, matches, porcelain, yerba maté; p. (1960) *361,309.*

Curtea de Arges, *t.*, Romania; on S. slopes of the Transylvanian Alps; p. (1956) *10,764.*

Curwensville, *bor.*, Penns., U.S.A.; firebrick, leather, clay, clothing; p. (1950) *3,332.*

Curzola or Korcula, *I., t.*, Dalmatia, Jugoslavia; in the Adriatic; fishing, seafaring, agr.

Cushing, *t.*, Okla., U.S.A.; oil, gas, refineries, industl. ctr.; p. (1960) *8,619.*

Cuttack, *t.*, Orissa st., India; on Mahanadi R.; long famous for gold and silver filigree work; p. (1961) *146,308.*

Cuxhaven, *spt.*, Lower Saxony, Germany; out-port of Hamburg at the mouth of R. Elbe; fine harbour, docks, fishing; p. (1963) *44,900.*

Cuyahoga, *R.*, in N. Ohio, U.S.A., flowing into L. Erie at Cleveland; length 85 m.

Cuyahoga Falls, *t.*, Ohio, U.S.A.; p. (1960) *47,922.*

Cuyapo, *mun.*, Luzon, Philippines; rice, sugar, tobacco, hemp; p. *24,570.*

Cuyuri, *R.*, Venezuela, enters sea Brit. Guiana.

Cuzco, *ancient t.*, Peru; in the Andes at alt. 11,400 ft. in valley of Urubamba R.; once cap. of the Incas; temple and fortress; be-sieged and sacked by Manco Inca in 1536; cath.; cottons, woollens; p. (1961) *68,000.*

Cuzco, *dep.*, Peru; a. 55,716 sq. m.; p. (1961) *590,958.*

Cwmamman, *urb. dist.*, Carmarthen, Wales; on R. Loughor, 12 m. N.E. of Llanelly; p. (1961) *4,272.*

Cwmbran, *t.*, Monmouth, Eng.; in valley of Avon-Lwyd, 5 m. N. of Newport; one of "New Towns" designated 1949 comprises bulk of Cwmbran urb. dist. and extends N. towards Pontypool; iron, motor accessories, wire, elec. goods, bricks, tiles, pipes; p. (estd. 1965) *35,860.*

Cyclades, group of about 220 Is. Grecian arch.; ch. t. Hermopolis (Syros); a. 1,023 sq. m.; p. (1961) *99,931.*

Cyprus, Republic of, *I.*, indep. Commonwealth nation, E. Mediterranean; 40 m. from Anatolia, 60 m. from Syria; cap. Nicosia; salt, iron, copper, agr., sponge fishing; a. 3,572 sq. m.; p. (1965) *591,000.*

Cyrenaica, see Libya.

Czechoslovak Socialist Republic (ČSSR.), Central Europe; country divided into 11 regions; mtns.; former provs. of Bohemia, Moravia, Slovakia of geographical significance only; fer-tile valleys; agr.; potatoes, sugar-beet, cereals, hops, lumbering; coal, iron, sugar, textiles, glass, stoneware, machin., chemicals, footwear, cars, cycles; cap. Praha (Prague); a. 49,381 sq. m.; p. (1961) *13,741,770.*

Czeladz, *t.*, S.W. Poland; coal; p. (1965) *31,000.*

Czernowitz, see Chernovtsy.

Czestochowa, *c.*, Katowice prov., S. Poland; on Warta R.; old pilgrimage monastery; rly. and industrl. ctr.; iron and steel, textiles; p. (1965) *175,000.*

Czirknitzer (Zirknitzer), *L.*, with I. in Carniola, Jugoslavia, S. of Ljubljana, 6 m. long; extra-ordinary variations in depth.

# D

Daanbantayan, *mun.*, N. Cebu, Philippine Is.; rice, sugar; p. *24,198.*

Dabhoi, *t.*, Gujarat, India; architectural remains; p. (1961) *30,841.*

Dabrowa Gornicza *t.*, Poland; 38 m. N.W. of Kraków; coal, zinc, iron ore; p. (1965) *60,000.*

Dacca, ch. *c.*, E. Pakistan; univ.; on Buriganga R., old channel of Ganges; jute, muslin; medi-cal radioisotope ctr.; p. (1961) *556,712.*

Dachau, *t.*, Bavaria, Germany; paper, elec. goods, brewing; p. (1963) *30,000.*

Dachstein, *mtn.*, Salzkammergut, Austria; alt. 9,830 ft.

Dade City, *t.*, Fla., U.S.A.; ctr. of mkt. gardening and citrus region; kaolin; p. (1960) *4,759.*

Dadra and Nagar Haveli, Union Terr., India; admin. ctr. Silvassa; a. 189 sq. m.; p. (1962) *57,963.*

Dagenham. *former mun. bor.*, Essex, Eng.; on N. bank of R. Thames, 10 m. E. of London; now inc. in Barking outer London bor. (except N. Chadwell Heath Ward inc. in Redbridge); motor cars, drugs, chemicals; p. (1961) *108,363.*

Dagestan, Caucasian prov. of R.S.F.S.R., U.S.S.R.; one of the most mountainous dists. in the world; cap. Makhachkala; cotton, orchards and vineyards; machin., engin, oil; a. 19,400 sq. m.; p. (1959) *1,063,000.* [Finland.

Dago (Hiiumaa), *I.*, Estonia, at entrance G. of

Dagupan, *t.*, Pangasinan, Luzon, Philippines; on Lingayen Bay; comm. ctr.; p. (1960) *83,191.*

Daharki Mari *t.*, Pakistan; 350 m. N.E. of Karachi; fertiliser plant projected.

Dahlak Archipelago, gr. of Is. in Red Sea, nr. Massawa; pearl fishing.

Dahomey, *ind. sov. st. within French Community*, W. Africa; forests, palm-oil; cap. Porto Novo; a. 44,000 sq. m.; p. (1965) *2,300,000.*

Daimiel, *mkt. t.*, Ciudad Real, Spain; cheeses, oil, wine; p. (1957) *20,204.*

Dairen, see Talien.

Dakar, *spt.*, *air and naval base*, Senegal, W. Africa, S.E. of Cape Verde behind Gorée I., impt. adm. ctr.; airpt. for S. America; groundnuts; p. (1960) *383,000*.

Dakhla, *oasis*, Libyan Desert, U.A.R.; 170 m. S.W. of Asyut; dates, olives; stage on caravan route from Cyrenaica to Upper U.A.R.

Dakota, *R.*, trib. of Missouri R., U.S.A.

Dakovica, *t.*, Jugoslavia; 80 m. E. of Cetinje; p. (1959) *20,000*.

Dalälven, *R.*, S. Central Sweden; length 325 m.

Dalaguete, *t.*, Cebu, Philippines; sugar, maize; p. *30,000*. [nuclear reactor (1963).

Dalat, *t.*, S. Viet-Nam; 140 m. N.E. Saigon;

Dalbeattie, *burgh*, Kircudbright, Scot.; granite, dairy prod. gloves; p. (1961) *3,104*.

Dalby, *t.*, Queensland, Australia; likely to increase with devel. of Moonie oilfield; dairying, timber; p. (1966) *8,370*. [posed p. *10,000*.

Dalgety, *t.*, on Fife cst., Scotland; New t. pro-

Dalhousie, *health resort*, Chamba, Himachal Pradesh, India; 7,687 ft. above sea-level.

Dalhousie, *spt.*, N.B., Canada; lumber, lobsters, salmon; resort; p. (1961) *5,856*.

Dalkeith, *burgh*, Midlothian, Scot.; 6 m. S.E. of Edinburgh; coal; ironwks.; p. (1961) *8,864*.

Dalkey, *t.*, Dublin, Ireland; on E. cst.; 4 m. N. of Wicklow border; seaside resort; residtl.; p. (1956) *5,526*.

Dallas, *c.*, Texas, U.S.A.; in cotton and grain-growing region; machin., aeroplanes; p. (1960) *679,684*.

Dalmatia, *dist.*, N.E. Adriatic cst., Jugoslavia; limestone (Karst) plateau; olive oil, wine; a. 4,916 sq. m.; p. *622,000*. [p. (1960) *17,363*.

Dalton, *t.*, N. Ga., U.S.A.; cotton and sawmills;

Daltonganj, *t.*, Bihar, India; on R. Koël; shellac, cement; p. (1961) *25,270*.

Dalton-in-Furness, *t.*, *urb. dist.*, N. Lancs, Eng.; limestone quarrying, woollens, felt mftg.; abbey ruins; p. (1961) *10,317*. [Bay.

Daly, *R.*, N. Terr., Australia; flowing into Anson

Daman (Damao), *spt.*, India; 100 m. N. Bombay; fishing, ship-bldg., cotton; p. (1960) *22,388*.

Damanhur, *t.*, U.A.R.; on E. margin of Nile delta, 25 m. S.E. of Alexandria; mkt. for local agr. produce; p. (1960) *126,000*.

Damaraland, formerly part of German S.W. Africa now administered by Union of S. Africa; only pt., Walvis Bay; cattle rearing.

Damascus (Arabic Esh-Sham), *cap.*, Syria; 57 m. S.E. of its pt. Beirut; claims to be oldest continuously inhabited c. in world; metal-wk., glass, cement; p. (1961) *507,503*.

Dambovitza, *R.*, Romania; rises in Mt. Omul (Transylvanian Alps), flows S. through Bucharest to R. Danube; flows through impt. oilfields; length 150 m.

Damghan, *t.*, Iran; nr. Caspian Sea; p. *16,500*.

Damietta, *t.*, Nile Delta, U.A.R.; cotton; p. (1960) *72,000*. [ctr. and mkt.; p. (1961) *44,673*.

Damoh, *t.*, N. Madhya Pradesh, India; agr.

Dampier, *spt.*, W. Australia; mouth of Fitzroy R.; new pt. (1965) for shipping of iron ore; solar salt evaporation plants projected.

Dampier Archipelago, *gr.* of *sm. Is.*, off N.W. Australia.

Dampier Strait, *channel* between N.W. of New Guinea and Waigeu I.

Dampier Strait, Bismarck archipelago, between Umboi and New Britain. [p. (1962) *10,012*.

Dampremy, *commune*, Hainaut, Belgium; coal;

Danakil or Dankali Country, Eritrea; cst. land between Red Sea and Ethiopia; potash being exploited; sm. pt. and road projected.

Danao, *t.*, Cebu, Philippines; rice and sugar dist.; p. (1960) *32,326*.

Danbury, *t.*, Conn., U.S.A.; hat-mkg. ind. since 1780; p. (1960) *22,928*.

Dandenong, *c.*, Victoria, Australia; 19 m. E. of Melbourne; growing industl. ctr.; p. (estd. 1968) *23,700*.

Dannemora, *t.*, Sweden; 25 m. N.E. of Uppsala; iron ore worked since 1579; p. *1,062*.

Dannevirke, *t.*, N.I., N.Z.; p. (1961) *5,517*.

Dansalan, *chartered c.*, cap. of Lanao prov., Philippine Is.; resort; p. (1948) *19,557*.

Danube, *R.* second longest R. in Europe; rises in Black Forest, Germany, and flows E. into Black Sea; navigation for steamers from Ulm to the sea; Vienna, Budapest, Belgrade and other large cs. on its banks; length 1,750 m.

Danvers, *t.*, Mass., U.S.A.; p. (1960) *21,926*.

Danville, *c.*, Ill., U.S.A.; coal; p. (1960) *41,856*.

Danville, *t.*, Ky., U.S.A.; mkt. for tobacco, hemp; horses; p. (1960) *9,010*.

Danville, *c.*, Va.; cotton, tobacco; p. (1960) *46,577*.

Danzig, see Gdansk.

Darbhanga, *t.*, Bihar, India; rice, oil-seeds, grain, sugar; p. (1961) *103,016*.

Dardanelles, *strait* between Europe and Turkey, connecting Ægean Sea with Sea of Marmara; (the ancient Hellespont), 40 m. long.

Dar-es-Salaam, *spt.*, *cap.*, Tanzania, E. Africa; univ. coll.; textile mill projected; oil refining; 1,000 m. oil products pipeline to Ndola, Zambia; p. (1957) *128,732*, incl. *4,478* Europeans, *93,363* Africans. [*6,881*.

Darveld, *urb. dist.*, W.R. Yorks, Eng.; p. (1961)

Darfur, *prov.*, Sudan, N.E. Africa; between Kordofan and Wadai; inhabited by Arabs and Negroes; cap. El Fasher; a. 133,150 sq. m.; p. (1947) *832,300*.

Darien, *region*, Panama; tortoiseshell, pearls, gold; p. (1960) *19,715*.

Darjeeling, *hill t.*, West Bengal, India; tea, quinine; has suffered from earthquake and landslips; p. (1961) *40,651*.

Darkhan, *new t.*, Mongolia; on R. Hara; industl.

Darlaston, *urb. dist.*, Staffs, Eng.; nuts, bolts, fabricated steel mnfs., drop forgings, car components, pot and tile mkg.; p. (1961) *21,732*.

Darling, *R.*, N.S.W., Australia; rises in Gr. Dividing Range, flows S.W. into Murray R. at Wentworth; length 1,702 m.

Darling Downs, *plateau*, S.E. Queensland, Australia; grazing cty.; ch. t. Toowomba.

Darling Range, *mtns.*; granite range; gt. grazing cty. of W. Australia; parallel with cst., highest peak, 3,500 ft.

Darlington, *t.*, *co. bor.*, Durham, Eng.; locomotive, wagon and bridge bldg., woollen yarn mnf.; engin.; p. (estd. 1967) *84,720*.

Darmstadt, *t.*, Hessen, Germany; on Darm R.; cas.; metallurgy, paper, machin., radio, chemicals, plastics; p. (1963) *139,600*.

Dart, *R.*, Devon, Eng.; rises in Dartmoor, flows S. into English Channel at Dartmouth; l. 46 m.

Dartford, *mkt. t.*, *mun. bor.*, Kent, Eng.; nr. S. cst. of Thames Est. 15 m. E. of London; Dartford–Purfleet road tunnel (1963); engin., chemicals, quarrying, paper; p. (estd. 1967) *46,520*.

Dartmoor, *high stony plateau*, S.W. Devon, Eng.; granite; kaolin; sheep and ponies; a. 220 sq. m.; highest point, High Willhays, 2,039 ft.

Dartmouth, *spt.*, *mun. bor.*, S. Devon, Eng.; on W. of estuary of R. Dart; Royal Naval College; pottery; p. (estd. 1967) *7,190*.

Dartmouth, *t.*, Nova Scotia; p. (1961) *46,966*.

Dartmouth, *t.*, Mass., U.S.A.; p. (1960) *14,464*.

Dartmouth, *pt.*, Richmond Bay, Prince Edward I., Canada. [coal; p. (1961) *14,111*.

Darton, *urb. dist.*, W.R. York., Eng.; nr. Barnsley

Darvel, *burgh*, Ayr, Scot.; on R. Irvine, 8 m. E. Kilmarnock; curtains, carpet; p. (1961) *3,255*.

Darwen, *t.*, *mun. bor.*, N.E. Lancs, Eng.; on flank of Rossendale Fells, 3 m. S. of Blackburn; cottons, tile and glaze brick, paint and paper, mftg.; p. (estd. 1967) *28,810*.

Darwin, *c.*, *spt.*, N. Terr., Australia; landing place of world airlines—England to Australia; p. (1966) *20,261*.

Dashava, settlement in Lvov Oblast, W. Ukraine, U.S.S.R.; ctr. of rich natural gas field and starting point of gas pipe-line to Kiev and Moscow, built after 2nd. World War.

Datia, *t.*, Madhya-Pradesh, India; stone-walled, palaces; p. (1961) *29,430*.

Datteln, *t.*, N. Rhine–Westphalia, Germany; coal, leather, iron; p. (1963) *31,200*.

Daugavpils, *t.*, Latvian S.S.R., on Dvina R.; textiles, engin., rly. repair wks.; p. (1959) *65,000*.

Daura, *t.*, nr. Baghdad, Iraq; oil refining.

Davão, *t.*, Mindanao, Philippines; p. (1960) *225,712*.

Davenport, *c.*, Iowa, U.S.A.; at foot of Rock I.; rapids; on Mississippi R.; flour mills; p. (1960) *88,981*.

Daventry, *t.*, *mun. bor.*, Northampton, England.; 9 m. S.E. of Rugby; boot-mkg., light engin.; wireless-transmission sta.; p. (estd. 1967) *6,860*.

David, *t.*, cap. Chiriqui prov., Panama; timber, coffee, cacao, sugar; p. (1960) *22,924*.

Davis Strait, *channel* between Greenland and

**Baffin Land**, N.W. Terr., Canada; connects Atlantic with Baffin Bay.

**Davos-Platz**, *Alpine winter resort*, Grisons, Switzerland; alt. 4,845 ft.; p. *9,259*.

**Dawley**, *t.*, *urb. dist.*, Shropshire, Eng.; on S.E. flank of The Wrekin; ironwks., pipe, cement, roadstone, asphalt and brick wks., engin.; "New Town" designated 1963; p. (estd. 1966) *21,240*.

**Dawlish**, *t.*, *urb. dist.*, S. Devon, Eng.; on S. cst. between estuaries of Rs. Exe and Teign; seaside resort; p. (1961) *7,807*.

**Dawson**, *t.*, Yukon Terr., Canada; on Yukon R., nr. the Klondyke goldfields; asbestos mng. projected 1968; p. (1961) *846*.

**Dax**, *t.*, Landes, S.W. France; on Adour R.; hot sulphur spring; horse mart; p. (1962) *18,422*.

**Dayton**, *c.*, Ohio, U.S.A.; on Great Miami R.; univ.; aeroplanes, elec. machin., rubber goods; p. (1960) *262,332*.

**Daytona Beach**, *t.*, Fla., U.S.A.; resort, tr. and shipping, ctr.; p. (1960) *37,395*.

**De Aar**, *t.*, *rly. junction*, Cape Province, S. Africa; 500 m. from Cape Town; rlys. from N.W. (Luderitz, Walvis Bay) and S.E. (Pt. Elizabeth, E. London) join Cape Town to Johannesburg trunk rly.; p. *9,137*.

**Dead Sea**, *salt-water L.*, between Israel and Jordan; surface 1,286 ft. below level of the Mediterranean; a. 340 sq. m., length 47½ m., greatest width 9¼ m., greatest depth 1,309 ft.; receives waters of Jordan; high mineral content.

**Deal**, *mun. bor., ancient spt.*, E. Kent, Eng.; on S.E. cst. 7 m. N.E. of Dover; opposite Goodwin Sands; seaside resort; Julius Cæsar is said to have first landed nr.; p. (estd. 1967) *26,780*.

**Dean, Forest of**, Gloucester, Eng.; between Wye and Severn Rs.; coal-mining.

**Dearborn**, *t.*, Mich., U.S.A.; p. (1960) *112,007*.

**Dearne**, *urb. dist.*, W.R. Yorks, Eng.; p. (estd. 1967), *26,720*.

**Death Valley**, *depression*, Cal., U.S.A.; in Mohave Desert, 150 m. N.E. of Los Angeles; completely arid; floor covered with saline deposits; tourist attraction; depth of valley floor 276 ft. below sea-level.

**Debar**, *t.*, Jugoslavia; nr. Drin R.; tr. ctr., cattle breeding, sulphur springs; p. *6,913*.

**Debra Markos**, *cap.*, Gojjam prov., Ethiopia; p. approx. *5,000*.

**Debrecen**, *t.*, Hungary; 114 m. E. of Budapest; univ.; ctr. of pastoral dist.; fairs; pharmaceutics, medical instruments; p. (1965) *146,000*.

**Decatur**, *t.*, Ala., U.S.A.; steel, textiles; p. (1960) *29,217*.

**Decatur**, *t.*, Ga., U.S.A.; p. (1960) *22,026*.

**Decatur**, *c.*, Ill., U.S.A.; mnfs., coal; p. (1960) *78,004*.

**Decazeville**, *t.*, Aveyron, S. France; coalmine (due for closure); p. (1962) *12,032*.

**Deccan, The**, gr. upland of S. India, bounded by the Narbada and Kistna Rs.

**Dedham**, *t.*, Mass., U.S.A.; p. (1960) *23,869*.

**Dedza**, *t.*, S. Malawi, new t., p. (1966) *2,261*.

**Dee**, *R.*, N. Wales and Cheshire; length 90 m.

**Dee**, *R.*, Aberdeen and Kincardine, Scot.; length 87 m.

**Dee**, *R.*, Kirkcudbright, Scot.; length 38 m.

**Dee**, *R.*, Louth, Ireland; flowing to Dundalk Bay; length 20 m.

**Defiance**, *t.*, N.W. Ohio, U.S.A.; light mftg., trade and agr. ctr.; p. (1960) *14,553*.

**De Funiak Springs**, *t.*, Fla., U.S.A.; in agr. region; turpentine; p. (1960) *5,282*.

**Dehdasht**, *c.*, Iran; cap. Kuhgilvieh and Boer Ahmadi dist.; p. (1967) *112,544*.     [*111,013*.

**Dehiwala** (Mt. Lavinia), *t.*, Ceylon; p. (1963)

**Dehra Dun**, *t.*, Uttar Pradesh, India; p. (1961) *156,341*.

**Deir-ez-Zor**, *t.*, Syria; on Euphrates R.; on motor route between Damascus and Baghdad; p. (1961) *59,757*.

**Dej**, *t.*, on Szamos R., Romania; lge. distillery; p. (1963) *22,327*.

**Delabole**, *vil.*, Cornwall, Eng.; on N.W. flank of Bodmin Moor; lge. slate quarries.

**Delagoa Bay**, *natural harbour*, Mozambique; Port E. Africa; ch. pt. Lourenço Marques.

**Delaware**, *Atlantic st.*, U.S.A.; agr., lumber, fertilisers, minerals, leather, chemicals, machin.; cap. Dover; ch. pt. Wilmington; a. 2,057 sq. m.; p. (1960) *446,292*.

**Delaware**, *R.*, flows from New York State along the Pennsylvania border, through New Jersey to Delaware Bay; length 350 m.

**Delaware Bay**, *inlet*, Atlantic cst., U.S.A.; drowned estuary of R. Delaware, extends 80 m. inland from C. May into heart of highly industl. a. of Philadelphia.

**Delaware**, *c.*, Ohio, U.S.A.; p. (1960) *13,282*.

**Delemont**, *t.*, Berne, Switzerland; watchmkg.; p. (1960) *8,000*.

**Delft**, *c., pt.*, S. Holland, Netherlands; on Schie R., nr. Rotterdam; famous techn. univ.; ceramics (delftware), tool mftg., precision instruments; 13th cent. Old church and 15th cent. New church; p. (1967) *79,805*.

**Delhi**, *union terr.*, India; hot and arid region between Indus valley and alluvial plain of Ganges; irrigation to support agr.; New Delhi (*q.v.*) and Old Delhi chief ctrs.; a. 578 sq. m.; p. (1961) *2,359,408*.

**Delitzsch**, *t.*, Leipzig, E. Germany; 16 m. E. of Halle; sugar, chemicals; p. (1963) *23,614*.

**Delmenhorst**, *t.*, Lower Saxony, Germany; nr. Bremen; jute, woollens, linoleum, foodstuffs; p. (1963) *59,300*.

**Delphi**, in ancient Phocis, Central Greece, north of Gulf of Corinth; famous for Delphic oracle on Mt. Parnassus.

**Del Rio**, *spt.*, Texas, U.S.A.; mkt. for agr a., grapes; exp. wool, sheep; p. (1960) *18,612*.

**Demavend**, *mtn.*, 17,604 ft.; highest peak, Elburz Mtns., N. Persia, extinct volcano.

**Demerara**, *co.*, Guyana; between Essequibo and Demerara Rs.; exp. sugar, molasses, rum; p. (1946) *220,639*.

**Demirkapu**, "The Iron Gate," rocky defile, through which the Danube rushes, in the Transylvanian Alps.

**Demirtas**, *t.*, Turkey; nr. Bursa; car wks.

**Demmin**, *t.*, Neubrandenburg, E. Germany; sugar ind.; p. (1963) *16,735*.     [p. (1962) *29,467*.

**Denain**, *t.*, Nord, N. France; nr. Douai; coal;

**Denbigh**, *co.*, Wales; sheep, dairying, coal, slate, quarrying; a. 669 sq. m.; p. (1966) *176,000*.

**Denbigh**, *mun. bor., co. t.*, Denbigh, N. Wales; dairying, slate; in Vale of Clwyd, 10 m. S. of Rhyl; p. (1961) *8,044*.

**Denby Dale**, *urb. dist.*, W.R. Yorks, Eng.; 8 m. W. of Barnsley; coal-mining, woollen textiles; p. (1961) *9,304*.

**Dendermonde** or **Termonde**, *t.*, E. Flanders, Belgium; nr. Ghent; p. (1962) *9,740*.

**Den Haag**, *See* Hague, The

**Denham**, *vil.*, Bucks., Eng.; 1 m. E. of Gerrards Cross; impt. ctr. of film industry; residtl.

**Den Helder**, *see* Helder.

**Denholme**, *t.*, *urb. dist.*, W.R. Yorks, Eng.; nr. Bradford; dairying, textiles; p. (1961) *2,596*.

**Denia**, *spt.*, Spain; 45 m. N.E. of Alicante; oranges, raisins, grapes, onions; toy mkg.; p. (1957) *11,859*.

**Denison**, *t.*, Iowa, U.S.A.; ctr. of agr. region; p. (1960) *4,930*.

**Denison**, *c.*, Texas, U.S.A.; on Red R.; cotton, lumber; p. (1960) *22,748*.

**Denizli**, *t.*, Anatolia, Turkey; 47 m. S.W. of Izmir; gardens—"the Damascus of Anatolia"; nr. site of Laodicea; p. (1965) *61,520*.

**Denmark**, *kingdom*, N.W. Europe; consisting of peninsula of Jutland and islands in Baltic; agr. and associated inds.; coastal fisheries; shipbldg., diesel engines; cap. Copenhagen; a. 16,576 sq. m.; p. (1965) *4,767,597*.

**Denny and Dunipace**, *burgh*, Stirling, Scot.; 6 m. W. of Falkirk; steel castings, precast concrete; p. (1961) *7,761*.

**Dent Blanche**, *mtn.*, in Pennine Alps, S. Switzerland; height 14,318 ft.

**Dent du Midi**, *mtn.*, Valais Alps, Switzerland; alt. 10,778 ft.

**Denton**, *urb. dist.*, Lancs, Eng.; nr. Manchester; felt-hat mkg.; p. (estd. 1967) *37,900*.

**D'Entrecasteaux Is.**, gr. off S.E. New Guinea, administered by Australia.

**D'Entrecasteaux Point**, *C.*, S.W. extremity of Australia.

**Denver**, *c., cap.*, Col., U.S.A.; on the E. slope of Rocky Mtns., on South Platte R.; univ.; oil, electronic equipment, mng. machin., livestock, canning; tourism; p. (1960) *493,887*.

**Deoband**, *t.*, Uttar Pradesh, India; nr. Meerut; p. (1961) *29,980*.

**Deogarh**, *t.*, Santal Pargans dist., Bihar, India;

numerous temples, place of pilgrimage; p. (1961) *30,813*. [p. (1961) *9,383*.

**Deori,** *t.,* Madhya Pradesh, India; nr. Sagar;

**De Pere,** *t.,* Wis., U.S.A.; agr. ctr.; mftg.: boots, paper, chemicals, bricks; p. (1960) *10,045*.

**Deptford,** *see* Lewisham.

**De Quincy,** *t.,* La., U.S.A.; oil, gas, lumber, rice, sugar; p. (1960) *3,928*.

**Dera Ghazi Khan,** *cap.,* West Punjab, Pakistan; W. side of R. Indus; silk, brass, ivory goods, handsome mosques; p. *25,000*.

**Dera Ismail Kahn,** *div.,* W. Pakistan; p. (1961) *2,085,000*.

**Dera Ismail Khan,** *t.,* W. Pakistan; on Indus R.; adm. ctr., caravan ctr.; p. (1961) *46,100*.

**Derbent,** *t., spt.,* R.S.F.S.R.; on W. side of Caspian Sea; textiles, petrol; p. (1956) *41,800*.

**Derby,** *co. bor., co. t.,* Derbyshire, Eng.; on R. Derwent; rly. wks., pottery, aircraft engine mnf. and repair, vehicles, textiles; natural gas beneath Calow vil; p. (estd. 1967) *127,910*.

**Derby,** *t.* Conn., U.S.A.; rubber, metal, hardware mftg.; p. (1960) *12,132*.

**Derby,** *sm. spt.,* W. Australia; on natural harbour of King Sound on N.W. cst. of Australia; hinterland little developed but potential gold and cattle-ranching within a. of artesian basin.

**Derbyshire,** *co.,* Eng.; hilly and rich in minerals; lge. part of N. and W. scheduled as Nat. Park; E. part highly industl.; *co. t.,* Derby; a. 1,041 sq. m.; p. (1960) *912,000*.

**Dereham,** East, *t., urb. dist.,* Norfolk, Eng.; 14 m. W. Norwich; agr. implements; p. (1961) *7,197*.

**Derg,** Lough, in basin of R. Shannon, Ireland, separating Galway and Clare from Tipperary.

**Derg,** *L.,* Donegal, with cave on I. much visited by R.C. pilgrims and known as " St. Patrick's Purgatory."

**Derna,** *spt.,* Libya, N. Africa; p. (estd. 1951) *15,600*.

**Derry,** *t.,* N.H., U.S.A.; boots, shoes; p. (1960) *6,987*.

**Derwent,** *R.,* Cumberland, Eng.; length 33 m.

**Derwent,** *R.,* Derby, Eng.; length 60 m.

**Derwent,** *R.,* Yorks, Eng.; length 57 m.

**Derwent,** *R.,* trib. of the Tyne R., Eng.; length 30 m. [Bay; length 30 m.

**Derwent,** *lgst. R.,* Tasmania; flowing to Storm

**Derwentwater,** *L.,* Cumberland, Eng.; nr. Keswick; 3 m. long. [L. Titicaca.

**Desaguadero,** *R.,* Bolivia, S. America; outlet of

**Desaguadero,** *plateau,* S. Peru and W. Bolivia between the Andes ranges, the second highest in the world.

**Desborough,** *t., urb. dist.,* Northants, Eng.; boot and shoe mnfs., iron; p. (1961) *4,555*.

**Désirade,** *I.,* Fr. W. Indies; nr. Guadeloupe; a. 10 sq. m.; p. *1,581*.

**Des Moines,** *R.,* Iowa, U.S.A.; trib. of Mississippi rising in Minnesota; length 550 m.

**Des Moines,** *c., cap.* Iowa State, U.S.A.; rly. and mftg. ctr.; p. (1960) *208,982*.

**Des Plaines,** *t.,* Ill., U.S.A.; p. (1960) *34,886*.

**Desna,** *R.,* trib. of Dnieper R., U.S.S.R.; length 550 m.

**Despoto Dagh,** *mtn. range,* Balkans; alt. 7,800 ft.

**Dessau,** *t.,* Halle, E. Germany; at confluence of Mulde and Elbe Rs.; cas.; machin., rly. carriages, paper, sugar, chemicals; route ctr.; p. (1963) *95,730*.

**Detmold,** *t.,* N. Rhine–Westphalia, Germany; cas.; paints, wood inds.; p. (1963) *30,600*.

**Detroit,** *ch. c., pt.,* Mich., U.S.A.; busy comm. and industl. ctr.; univ.; gt. grain mart; and ctr. of the " Ford " motor-car wks., aeroplanes, military tanks, synthetic diamonds, pharmaceutics, tools, chemicals, steel; lgst. exporting t. on Great Lakes; p. (1960) *1,670,144*.

**Detroit,** *R.,* channel between L. St. Clair and L. Erie (25 m.), separates st. of Michigan from Ontario, Canada; carries more shipping than any other inland waterway in the world; navigable for eight months in the year.

**Deurne,** *t.,* Belgium; nr. Antwerp; p. (1962) *69,498*.

**Deventer,** *t.,* Overijssel, Netherlands; on IJssel R.; industl. ctr., machin., textile and carpet inds.; Hanse t. in Middle Ages; p. (1967) *61,623*.

**Deveron,** *R.,* Aberdeen and Banff, Scot.; flows into Moray Firth; length 61 m.

**Devizes,** *mkt. t., mun. bor.,* N. Wilts, Eng.; on Kennet Avon Canal at N. foot of Marlborough Downs; tobacco and snuff, bricks, tiles, bacon curing; p. (estd. 1967) *9,000*.

**Devon,** *R.,* trib. of Forth, Scot.; length 34 m.

**Devonport,** *fortfd. spt.,* S. Devon, Eng.; adjoins Plymouth on Tamar estuary; royal dockyards and naval sta.; road bridge to Saltash across Tamar; p. included with Plymouth.

**Devonport,** *spt.,* Tasmania Australia; 82 m. from Launceston; agr. dist.; canning, foundry inds.; p. (1966) *14,848*.

**Devonport,** *suburban bor.,* Auckland, N.Z.; naval base and dockyard; p. (1961) *10,949*.

**Devonshire,** *maritime co.,* S.W. Eng.; between English and Bristol Channels; famous for cream and cider; ch. ts. Exeter and Plymouth; a. 2,611 sq. m.; p. (1966) *865,000*.

**Dewsbury,** *t., co. bor.,* W.R. Yorks, Eng.; on R. Calder, 8 m. from Leeds; heavy woollens, coal-mining, dyewks.; p. (estd. 1967) *52,730*.

**Dexter,** *t.,* Mo., U.S.A.; cotton, flour, poultry; p. (1960) *5,519*.

**Deyeth,** *t.,* Cambodia; plywooods.

**Dez Dam,** Iran, over Dez R., Khurzistan prov., opened 16 Mar. 1963.

**Dhahran,** *spt.,* Saudi-Arabia; oil.

**Dhanbad,** *t.,* Bihar, India; lead, zinc, tools, radio assembly; p. (1961) *46,756*.

**Dhanushkodi,** *t.,* Tamil Nadu, India; on I. Palk Strait; ferry pt. for passenger traffic from India to Ceylon.

**Dhar,** *t.,* Madhya Pradesh, India; cultural and tr. ctr.; p. (1961) *28,325*.

**Dharmsala,** *hill sta.,* E. Punjab, India; 100 m. N.E. of Amritsar; sanatorium; alt. 6,000 ft.; imposing mtn. scenery; p. (1961) *10,255*.

**Dharwar,** *t.,* Mysore, India; 70 m. E. of Goa, Carnatic; univ.; cotton mnf.; p. (1961) *77,163*.

**Dhaulagiri,** *mtn.,* Himalayas, Nepal; alt. 26,810 ft.

**Dhekelia,** Cyprus; Brit. sovereign a. within Rep.; p. (1960) *3,602*.

**Dholpur,** *t.,* Rajasthan, India; p. (1961) *27,412*.

**Dhrangadhra,** Saurashtra, India; 75 m. W. of Ahmedabad; chemicals, salt, cotton, bldg. stone, brass vessels, pottery; p. (1961) *32,197*.

**Dhufar,** *fertile prov.,* Muscat and Oman, Arabia; sugar-cane, cattle; ch.t.Salalah; ch.pt.Mirbat.

**Dhulia,** *t.,* Khandesh dist., Maharashtra, India; cotton ind., p. (1961) *98,893*.

**Diamante,** *t.,* E. Argentina; on Paraná R.; grain, cattle; p. *11,518*.

**Diamante,** *R.,* Mendoza prov., Argentina; rises in Andes, flows E. to R. Salado; irrigates oasis of San Rafael; length 200 m.

**Diamantina,** *t.,* Minas Gerais, Brazil; ctr. of diamond dist.; p. (1960) *52,170*.

**Diber,** *prefecture,* Albania; p. (estd.) *83,491*.

**Dibrugarh,** *t.,* Assam, India; terminus of rail and river communications along Brahmaputra from Calcutta; coal, tea; p. (1961) *58,480*.

**Dickson I.,** Kara Sea, Arctic Ocean, U.S.S.R.

**Didymoteikhon,** *t.,* Thrace, Greece; on R. Maritza; p. *10,150*.

**Diego Garcia,** *I.,* Brit. Indian Oc. Terr.; coaling sta.; 12½ m. long, 6½ m. wide; ch. exp. coconut oil, tortoise-shell; p. (1962) *660*.

**Diego Suarez,** *t., Bay,* extreme N. of Malagasy; meat preserving; p. (1957) *38,212*.

**Dieppe,** *cross-Channel pt.,* Seine-Maritime, France; 35 m. N. of Rouen; fisheries, shipbldg., machin.; p. (1962) *30,327*.

**Differdange,** *t.,* S.W. Luxembourg; iron ore, cattle; p. (1960) *17,637*. [p. (1961) *35,028*.

**Digbol,** N.E. Assam, India; oil fields and refinery;

**Digne,** *t.,* Basses-Alpes, France; nr. Aix; cath.; p. (1962) *13,660*.

**Dijon,** *t.,* Côte-d'Or, E. France; the Roman *Divonense castrum*; cath.; bathing; casino; gt. wine tr., tobacco, brewery, textiles; p. (1962) *141,104*. [p. (1962) *3,867*.

**Diksmuide,** *t.,* W. Flanders, Belgium; on Yser R.;

**Dillingen,** *t.,* Bavaria, Germany; on R. Danube; 20 m. downstream from Ulm; p. *6,500*.

**Dilolo,** *L.,* Angola; nr. source of Zambesi R.

**Dimitrovgrad,** *t.,* Bulgaria; founded 1947; fertilisers, chemicals, super phosphate plant, iron, thermo-electric sta.; p. (1956) *34,162*.

**Dimitrovo,** *t.,* Bulgaria, formerly Pernik; steel blast furnaces; p. (1956) *59,721*.

**Dinan,** *t.,* Côtes-du-Nord, France; nr. St. Brieux; medieval houses and ramparts; mineral water; p. (1962) *16,438*.

**Dinant,** *fortfd. t.,* Namur, Belgium; on R. Meuse; brass, copperware, summer resort; p. (1962) *6,808*.

Dinapore, *military t.*, Bihar, India; on Ganges R., nr. Patna; p. (1961) *70,766*.

Dinard, *hol. res.*, Ille-et-Vilaine, France; op. St. Malo; ch. wat. pl. of Brittany; p. (1962) *9,432*.

Dinaric Alps, *mtn. range*, Jugoslavia; highest peak, Dinara, alt. 6,007 ft.

Dindigul, *t.*, Tamil Nadu, India; 25 m. S. of Trichinopoly; cigars, tobacco; p. (1961) *92,947*.

Dingras, *mun.*, Luzon, Philippine Is.; rice, hemp, tobacco; p. *22,434*.

Dingwall, *burgh*, Ross and Cromarty, Scot.; at head of Cromarty Firth; rly. junction; livestock mkt. ctr.; distilling, hand-loom weaving; p. (1961) *3,752*.

Dinslaken, *t.*, N. Rhine–Westphalia, Germany, N. of Duisburg; coal, steel, iron, footwear, timber; oil pipeline from Wesseling under construction; p. (1963) *46,400*.

Diomede Is., two barren granitic islets in Behring Strait between Alaska and Siberia; accepted bdy. between Soviet and U.S. territory.

Diourbel, *t.*, Senegal, W. Africa; hides, groundnuts; p. *18,006*.

Diredawa, *t.*, Ethiopia; 25 m. N. of Harar, rly. wks.; p. (estd. 1960) *40,000*.

Dirk Hartog I., off Shark Bay, W. Australia.

Disko I., off W. cst. of Greenland in Baffin Bay; contains harbour of Godhavn, cap. N. Greenland; rendezvous for whalers; a. 3,200 sq. m.

Dismal Swamp, *morass*, S. Virginia and N. Carolina, U.S.A.; contains L. Drummond and extends 30–40 m. S. from nr Norfolk.

Diss, *mkt. t.*, *urb. dist.*, Norfolk, Eng.; on R. Waveney 28 m. S.W. of Norwich; agr. implements; p. (1961) *3,682*.

Ditchling Beacon, nr. Brighton, Sussex, Eng.; alt. 813 ft. [p. *14,916*.

Dittersbach, *commune*, S.W. Poland; coal, drugs;

Diu, *spt.*, *I.*, off S. coast of Bombay, India; oil nearby at Kayakoy; a. 20 sq. m.; p. (1960) *14,271*. [p. (1954) *11,187*.

Divion, *commune*, Pas de Calais France; coal;

Divnogorsk, *t.*, R.S.F.S.R.; 25 m. W. of Krasnoyarsk on R. Yenisei; dam builders' t.; p. (1963) *25,000*.

Dixon Entrance, *channel* between Queen Charlotte I. and Alaska, Brit. Columbia, Canada.

Diyarbakir, *t.*, Anatolia, Turkey; on Tigris R.; head of navigation; ancient Amida, old walls, gates, citadel; morocco leather, filigree work; p. (1965) *102,624*. [p. (1956) *52,153*.

Dizful, *t.*, Persia; 32 m. N.W. of Shushtar; indigo;

Djakarta (Batavia), *t.*, cap., Java, Indonesia; comm. ctr.; textiles; p. (1961) *2,973,052*.

Djambi, *dist.* and *t.*, Sumatra, Indonesia; on E. cst. plain 100 m. N.W. of Palembang; productive oil-field; a. (dist.) 17,345 sq. m.; p. (1961) of dist. *744,381* of t. *113,080*.

Djapara-Rembang, *prov.*, N.E. Java; petroleum, sugar, rice; a. 2,339 sq. m.; p. *1,885,548*.

Dneprodzerzhinsk, *t.*, Ukrainian S.S.R.; W. of Dnepropetrovsk on Dnieper R.; iron and steel, engin., chemicals; hydro-elec. sta. nearby; p. (1967) *219,000*.

Dnepropetrovsk, *t.*, Ukrainian S.S.R.; on Dnieper R.; univ.; coal, iron, steel, manganese, engin., chemicals, sawmilling, tyres; p. (1967) *790,000*.

Dneprorudnyy, *t.*, Ukrainian S.S.R.; new t. on S. shore of Kakhovta reservoir, tentatively called Dneprograd, now renamed; p. (1964) *6,000*.

Dneprostroy, *see* Zaporozhe.

Dnieper, R., S.E. Europe; rises in U.S.S.R., flows into the Black Sea; connected by canals with Baltic, etc.; the Dneprostroy dam, a barrage erected across the R. at Kichkas by the Soviet Government, feeds the lgst. power-sta. in the world; length 1,400 m.

Dniester, R., S.E. Europe; rises in Carpathians and flows into the Black Sea; length 700 m.

Doab, *dist.*, between "two rivers" Jumna and Ganges, Uttar Pradesh, India.

Döbeln, *t.*, Leipzig, E. Germany; machin., metallurgy, wood, cigar and sugar inds.; p. (1963) *29,327*.

Dobrich, *t.*, *see* Tolbukhin.

Dobruja, *dist.*, E. Romania; a. 6,102 sq. m., ch. pt. Constanta, traversed by ancient wall of Trajan; p. (1963) *517,016*.

Dobsina, *t.*, ČSSR.; cave containing ice-field of 2 acres; asbestos, iron ore; p. *5,300*.

Doce, R., Brazil; flows to Atlantic; length 400 m.

Dodecanese, gr. of 12 Greek Is. in Ægean Sea, to S. of Greek Archipelago; Italian 1912–46; a. 1,055 sq. m.; p. (1961) *122,346*.

Dodge City, *t.*, Kan., U.S.A.; p. (1960) *13,520*.

Dodoma, *mkt. t.*, Tanzania, E. Africa; 250 m. W. of Dar-es-Salaam on central Tanganyika rly. from Dar-es-Salaam to Kigoma; also on main N. to S. motor road.

Dodworth, *urb. dist.*, W.R. Yorks, Eng.; nr. Barnsley; coal; p. (1961) *4 139*.

Dogger Bank, *sandbank* in N. Sea, between England and Denmark; depth varies from 6 to 20 fathoms; valuable fishing ground; action between British fleet under Beatty and German fleet under Hipper; *Blücher* sunk Jan. 1915.

Dogs, I. of, *riverside dist.*, formed by bend in the R. Thames off Greenwich, London, Eng.; Millwall docks and shipbldg. yards.

Dokai Bay, *inlet*, N. Kyushu, Japan; landlocked bay on S. side of Shimonoseki Straits; flanked by highly industl. zone inc. Yawata, Wakamatsu, Tobata cs.; requires constant dredging; length 4 m., width ½–1½ m.

Dokkum, *t.*, Friesland, Netherlands; p. *5,073*.

Dôle, *t.*, Jura, E. France; on R. Doubs, nr. Dijon; ancient cap. of Franche-Comté, ceded to France in 1678; birthplace of Pasteur; p. (1954) *22,022*.

Dolgarrog, *sm. t.*, N.E. Caernarvon, Wales; aluminium, milling; p. (1951) *572*.

Dolgelly, *urb. dist.*, *ch. t.*, Merioneth, N. Wales; agr., quarrying, timber; p. (1961) *2,267*.

Dollar, *burgh*, Clackmannan, Scot.; at foot of Ochil Hills, 6 m. N.E. of Alloa; p. (1961) *1,955*

Dollar Law, *min.*, nr. Peebles, Scot.; alt. 2,680 ft.

Dolomites, *gr. of limestone mtns.*, S. Tyrolese Alps, N.E. Italy; tourist district; peaks assume fantastic forms; principal peak, Marmolata 11,000 ft.

Dolon-Nor, *t.*, Mongolia, China; Buddhist temples; brass idols; p. *30,000*.

Dom, *mtn.*, Valais, Switzerland; alt. 14,942 ft.

Dominica, *aut. st.* in association with Gt. Britain; Windward Is., W.I.; limejuice, sugar, cacao, fruits, spices; extremely beautiful; cap. Roseau; a. 290 sq. m.; p.(estd. 1967) *65,000*.

Dominican Rep, indep. Spanish-speaking E. part of I. of Hispaniola, Antilles; cap. Santo Domingo; sugar, coffee, cacao, bananas, tobacco, bauxite, iron ore, cement; a. 19,332 sq. m.; p. (estd. 1965) *3,573,000*.

Domodossola, *frontier t.*, Piedmont, N. Italy, nr. Simplon; tourist ctr.; p. *10,350*.

Don, R., Aberdeen, Scot.; flows into N. Sea; salmon; length 82 m.

Don, R., W.R. Yorks, Eng.; trib. of R. Ouse, length 70 m.

Don, R., Maine-et-Loire, France; length 40 m.

Don, *lge. R.*, W. Russia; falls into Sea of Azov below Rostov; navigable to Voronezh; access to the Volga by the Don–Volga Canal.

Donaghadee, *spt.*, *urb. dist.*, Down, N. Ireland; nearest point to Scot.; carpets; seaside resort; p. (1966) *3,649*.

Donaueschingen, *t.*, Baden–Württemberg, Germany; at confluence of Rs. Brigach and Breg forming R. Danube; cas.; textiles; p. (estd. 1954) *8,900*.

Donawitz, *commune*, Styria prov., Austria; lignite, iron and steel; p. *17,623*.

Donbas, *industl. region*, Ukraine, U.S.S.R.; in valleys of Rs. Donetz and lower Dnieper; about 9,000 sq. m.; produces 60% Russia's coal; adjoins Krivoi Rog ironfields; many lge. industl. ts. [wine, fruit; p. *21,095*.

Don Benito, *t.*, Badajoz, Spain; tr. in wheat,

Doncaster, *t.*, *co. bor.*, W.R. Yorks, Eng., on Don R. 17 m. N.E. of Sheffield; rly. wks. mnfs. nylon; racecourse; p. (estd. 1967) *85,910*.

Donchery, *ancient t.*, Ardennes, France, on R. Meuse, nr. Sedan; scene of gr. battle 1870.

Donegal (Tirconnail), *co.*, N.W. Ireland; ch. t. Donegal, a. 1,865 sq. m.; p. (1966) *108,486*.

Donegal, *spt.*, *cap.*, Co. Donegal, Ireland; on W. cst. of Donegal Bay; homespun tweeds, carpets; p. (1966) *1,507*.

Donets, R., Ukraine S.S.R., U.S.S.R.; rises in uplands of central Russia, flows S.E. 400 m. into R. Don; crosses impt. Donets coalfield. *See* Donbas.

Donetsk (Stalino), *t.*, Ukraine S.S.R.; coal, iron, steel, engin., chemicals; p. (1967) *823,000*.

Donges, Loire Atlantique, France; nr. St. Nazaire; oil refinery.

Dongola, New, *t.*, Sudan; left bank of R. Nile above 3rd Cataract; replaced Old D., now in ruins; p. *5,000*.

Donna, *t.*, S. Texas, U.S.A.; sugar refining, fruit and vegetables; p. (1960) 7,522.

Donzère-Mondragon, Provence, France; site of gr. barrage on Rhône supplying hydro-elec. power, completed 1952.

Doon, *R.*, Ayr. Scot.; flows from Loch Doon to Firth of Clyde; length 26 m.

Dora Baltea, *R.*, N. Italy; rises in Mt. Blanc, flows E. and S. through Val d'Aosta to R. Po at Chivasso; impt. routeway from N. Italy to Switzerland (through Gr. St. Bernard Pass) and France (through Little St. Bernard Pass); length 95 m.

Dora Riparia, *R.*, Italy; trib. of R. Po. flowing from Cottian Alps past Turin; length 60 m.

Dorchester, *mun. bor. co. t.* Dorset, Eng.; on R. Frome: Roman remains: lime, agr., engin., tent mkg.; p. (estd. 1967) 13,570.

Dorchester, *pt. of entry*, N.B., Canada; on Penticodiac R.; p. 1,000.

Dordogne, *dep.*, S.W. France; a. 3,550 sq. m.; cap. Périgueux; p. (1962) 375,455.

Dordogne, *R.*, France; joins Garonne to form the Gironde; length 290 m.

Dordrecht, *c.*, nr. Rotterdam, Netherlands, on R. Merwede; timber, shipbldg., seaplanes; p. (1967) 88,475.

Dorking, *mkt. t.*, *urb. dist.*, Surrey, Eng.; on R. Mole to S. of gap through N. Downs; residtl.; light inds.; p. (estd. 1967) 23,010.

Dornoch, *burgh*, Sutherland, Scot.; on N. side of Dornoch Firth; health resort; p. (1961) 933.

Dorohoi, *t.*, Moldavia, Romania; 33 m. S.E. of Chernovtsy; gr. annual fair; p. (1956) 14,771.

Dorp, *t.*, Germany; on R. Wupper, nr. Cologne; mnfs.; p. 14,000.

Dorset, *co.*, S. Eng.; mainly agr.; sheep: Purbeck marble, Portland stone; co. t. Dorchester; a. 988 sq. m.; p. (1966) 333,000.

Dorset Heights, *hills*, extend E. to W. across Central Dorset, Eng.; chalk, smooth slopes, few streams; short, dry, grass; pastoral farming, sheep; some cultivation where soil is deep enough; rise to 800–900 ft.

Dorsten, *t.*, N. Rhine-Westphalia, Germany; on R. Lippe; coal, iron, elec., chemical inds.; p. (1963) 37,600.

Dortmund, *t.*, N. Rhine-Westphalia, Germany; impt. Ruhr comm. ctr.; coal, iron. steel, machin., brewing; p. (1963) 650,900.

Dortmund-Ems Canal, N. Rhine-Westphalia, Germany; links Dortmund on Ruhr Coalfield with R. Ems 5 m. above Lingen; impt. coal, iron-ore traffic; length 90 m.

Dorval, *t.*, Quebec, Canada; p. (1961) 18,592.

Dothan, *t.*, Ala., U.S.A.; p. (1960) 31,440.

Douai, *t.*, Nord, France; nr. Lille on Scarpe R.; coal, iron and engin. wks.; bell founding, arsenal; p. (1962) 50,104.

Douarnenez, *spt.*, Finistère, N.W. France; on D. Bay; sardine fisheries; p. (1962) 20,304.

Doubs, *dep.*, E. France; traversed by the Jura range and the R. Doubs; chiefly agr.; watch-mkg. ind.; cap. Besançon; a. 2,052 sq. m.; p. (1962) 384,881.

Douglas, *cap.*, I. of Man; 75 m. W. of Liverpool, Eng.; seaside resort; p. (1956) 20,361.

Douglas Point, on shore of L. Huron. Ont., Canada; nuclear power sta.      [reactor.

Dounreay, Caithness, Scot.; fast-breeder nuclear

Douro, *R.*, Portugal and Spain; enters Atlantic below Oporto; known as Duero R. in Spain; length 485 m.

Douro Littoral, *prov.*, Portugal; textiles, wine, fruit, cattle; cap. Oporto; a. 1,314 sq. m.; p. (1950) 1,237,170.

Dove, *R.*, Derby and Staffs, Eng.; trib. of Trent; flows through beautiful dales; length 45 m.

Dover, *spt.*, *mun. bor.*, Kent, Eng.; one of old Cinque pts.; nearest spt. to France, the Strait of D. being only 21 m. wide; chief pt. for passenger and mail traffic with Continent; p. (estd. 1967) 36,060.

Dover, *cap.*, Del., U.S.A.; p. (1960) 7,250.

Dover, *t.*, N.H., U.S.A.; p. (1960) 19,131.

Dover, *t.*, N.J., U.S.A.; iron, munitions, explosives; knitwear, silk; p. (1960) 13,034.

Dovercourt, *sub.*, Harwich, Essex, Eng.; seaside resort.

Dowlais, *mining dist.*, Merthyr Tydfil, S. Wales; fertilisers, nylon.

Down, *maritime co.*, N. Ireland; agr. and fisheries; industl. round Belfast; cap. Downpatrick; a. 957 sq. m.; p. (1966) 286,930.

Downers Grove, *t.*, N.E. Ill., U.S.A.; dairy produce; tools, furniture; p. (1960) 21,194.

Downey, *t.*, Cal., U.S.A.; agr.; aircraft, cement, asbestos prod., machin., soap.; p. (1960) 82,505.

Downham Market, *t.*, *urb. dist.*, Norfolk, Eng.; on R. Ouse; flour-milling, malting, sheet-metal wks.; p. (1961). 2,650

Downpatrick, *urb. dist.*, *co. t.*, Down, N. Ireland; on R. Quoile; linen; p. (1966) 4,291.

Downs, *roadstead*, natural harbour of refuge for shipping between Kent coast and Goodwin Sands in the English Channel.

Downs, North and South, two chiefly pastoral broad chalk ridges in S.E. Eng.; N. Downs ending at Dover, and S. Downs at Beachy Head and enclosing the Weald; fine grazing ground for sheep.

Downton, *t.*, S. Wilts, Eng.; nr. Salisbury; on R. Avon; agr. college.

Drachenfels, *mtn. peak* on the Rhine, the steepest of the Siebengebirge range, nr. Königswinter; alt. 1,065 ft.; ascended by light rly.; famous cave of legendary dragon.

Draguignan, *cap.*, Var. dep., S.E. France; nr. Toulon; p. (1962) 16,085.

Drakensberg, *mtn. chain* between Natal and Orange Free State, S. Africa; extending 500 m. from Gt. Fish R. to Olifants R.; highest peak Mont-aux-Sources 10,763 ft.; rly. crosses range by Van Reenen Pass.

Drama, *pref.* Macedonia, Greece; cap. Drama; p. (1961) 120,936.

Drammen, *spt.*, Norway; nr. Oslo, on the Drammen R.; shipyard; exp. timber, wood-pulp, paper; p. (estd. 1960) 31,000.

Drancy, *t.*, Seine, France; p. (1962) 65,940.

Drava, *R.*, Jugoslavia; trib. of Danube, flows from the Tyrol across Carinthia and Styria, joining D. nr. t. of Osijek; length 450 m.

Drenthe, *E. prov.*, Netherlands; on German frontier; cap. Assen; a. 1,028 sq. m.; p. (1967) 348,001.

Dresden, *t.*, Dresden, E. Germany; on R. Elbe 50 m. E. of Leipzig; fine art collections; cigarette, engin., chem., brewing, gen. inds., optical and photographic apparatus, porcelain, glass, impt. route ctr.; oil pipeline from Schwedt under construction; p. (1963) 499,014.

Dreux, *t.*, Eure-et-Loir, France; nr. Chartres; hardware, heavy iron mnfs.; p. (1954) 16,813.

Driffield, *urb. dist.*, E.R. Yorks, Eng.; on Yorks. Wolds 13 m. N. of Beverley; oil-cake wks.; p. (1961) 6,890.

Drina, *R.*, trib. Sava, Jugoslavia, separating Serbia from Bosnia; length 300 m.

Dröbak, *spt.*, S.E. Norway; winter pt. for Oslo; summer resort; p. (1961) 2,735.

Drogheda, *spt.*, Louth, Ireland; considerable tr. in agr. produce, salmon, etc.; stormed by Cromwell in 1649; p. (1966) 17,823.

Drogobych, *t.*, Ukrainian S.S.R.; petroleum, engin.; p. (1959) 42,000.

Drohobycz, *t.*, Ukraine, U.S.S.R.; 40 m. S.W. of Lwow; ctr. of lge. oilfields, refineries; p. 32,622.

Droitwich, *t.*, *mun. bor.*, Worcester, Eng.; brine baths, salt wks., wireless-transmission sta.; light inds.; p. (estd. 1967) 8,970.

Drôme, *dep.*, S.E. France; traversed by Alps and watered by Rs. Rhône, Drôme and Isère; cap. Valence; agr., forestry, sericulture, textile ind.; a. 2,533 sq. m.; p. (1962) 304,227.

Dromore, *mkt. t.*, *urb. dist.*, Down, N. Ireland; on Lagan R.; linen; p. (1966) 2,081.

Dronfield, *t.*, *urb. dist.*, Derby, Eng.; between Chesterfield and Sheffield; iron, coal, edged tools, engin. and agr. implements; p. (1961) 11,294.

Droylsden, *urb. dist.*, Lancs., Eng.; sub. of Manchester; cotton spinning; chemicals; p. (estd. 1967) 25,340.

Drummondville, *t.*, Quebec, Canada; 45 m. N.E. of Montreal; woollens; p. (1961) 27,909.

Drummoyne, *c.*, N.S.W., Australia; sub. of Sydney, on Parramatta R.

Drumochter Pass, Grampian Mtns., Scot.; carries main Perth to Inverness rly. from Glen Garry into valley of R. Spey; highest alt. reached by any main rly. in Gr. Britain, 1,484 ft.

**Duala**, *spt.*, Cameroun Rep., W. Africa; rly. to Yaoundé; p. *18,000*. [(estd.) *60,000*.

**Dubai**, *ch. t. and pt.*, Trucial States, Arabia; p.

**Dubbo**, *t.*, N.S.W., Australia; on Macquarie R., 180 m. N.W. of Sydney; in extensive pastoral and agr. dist.; timber, wool, flour, meat; p. (1966) *15,568*.

**Dublin**, *co.*, Ireland; co. t. Dublin; a. (inc. c. of Dublin) 356 sq. m.; p. (1966) *793,790*.

**Dublin** (Baile Atha Cliath), *co. bor., cap.* Rep. of Ireland; at mouth of R. Liffey; cath., univ., cas.; spirit and chemical produce, stout, glass, etc.; p. (1966) *568,271*.

**Dubois**, *c.*, Penns., U.S.A.; 75 m. N.E. of Pittsburgh; coal; p. (1960) *10,667*.

**Dubrovnik** (Ragusa), *c.*, W. coast of Jugoslavia; oil, silk, leather inds.; p. (1960) *21,000*.

**Dubuque**, *c.*, Iowa, U.S.A., on Mississippi R.; clothing, carriage wks.; p. (1960) *56,606*.

**Duchov**, *t.*, N.W. Bohemia, ČSSR.; 5 m. S.W. of Teplice; glass, pottery; p. *15,000*. [nickel.

**Dudinka**, Arctic *spt.* on R. Yenisei, R.S.F.S.R.;

**Dudley**, *t.*, *co. bor.*, Worcester, Eng.; 8 m. N.W. Birmingham; engin., clothing, leather goods, firebricks, chains, cables; p. (estd. 1967) *177,760* inc. p. of a. in Staffs. added to bor. 1966.

**Dudweiler**, *t.*, nr. Saarbrücken, Saarland; coalmines and ironwks.; p. (1963) *29,700*.

**Dueñas**, *mun.*, Panay, Philippine Is.; rice, hemp; p. *16,310*.

**Duffel**, *commune*, Antwerp, Belgium; foundries, distilleries, paper, coarse woollen cloth; p. (1962) *13,365*.

**Duisburg**, *t.*, R. *pt.*, N. Rhine–Westphalia, Germany; on E. bank of R. Rhine at confluence with R. Ruhr, 10 m. N. of Düsseldorf; extensive iron and steel inds., machin., textiles, chemicals, impt. route and R. tr. ctr.; p. (1963) *501,100*.

**Dukeries**, *dist.*, Sherwood Forest, Notts. Eng.; so called from ducal mansions in dist.

**Dukinfield**, *t.*, *mun. bor.*, Cheshire, Eng.; 6 m. S.E. of Manchester; textiles, engin., rope and twine; p. (estd. 1967) *17,120*.

**Dukla**, *pass*, Carpathian Mtns., Central Europe; easy route N. from Hungarian Plain to Poland; alt. 1,650 ft. ▪ [rice, cotton, sugar; p. *28,59*

**Dulag**, *mun.*, Leyte I., Philippine Is.; hemp,

**Dulcigno** (Ulcinj), *ancient c.*, Montenegro, Jugoslavia; tobacco, olive oil; p. *5,000*.

**Dülken**, *t.*, N. Rhine–Westphalia, Germany; nr. Krefeld. machin., textiles, leather goods; p. (1963) *21,300*.

**Duluth**, *pt.*, Minn., U.S.A.; at W. end of L. Superior; gr. tr. in grain, timber and iron ore; natural gas pipeline into the Mesabi Iron Range; p. (1960) *106,884*.

**Dumbarton**, *burgh.*, *co. t.*, Dunbarton, Scot.; on N. bank of R. Clyde, 12 m. below Glasgow; shipbldg, valve and tube-mkg., iron and brassware; p. (1961) *26,335*.

**Dum-Dum**, South, t., W. Bengal, India; ammunition; p. (1961) *111,284*.

**Dumfries**, *maritime co.*, S. Scot.; on Solway Firth; N. parts mtns., much of the remainder pastoral; lead ore, coal, sandstone; a. 1,068 sq. m.; p. (1961) *88,423*.

**Dumfries**, *co. burgh*, Dumfries, Scot.; on R. Nith, 10 m. from Solway Firth; p. (1961) *27,275*.

**Dunaujváros**, *t.*, Hungary; New Town built from vil. of Dunapentele; iron and steel wks.; paper inds., engin.; p. (1962) *34,998*.

**Dunbar**, *spt.*, *burgh*, E. Lothian, Scot.; 25 m. E. of Edinburgh; potatoes; p. (1961) *4,003*.

**Dunbarton**, *co.*, W. Scot.; agr., stock-raising, shipbldg., chemicals, dyeing, paper-mkg., mining, quarrying. lt. engin.; a. 246 sq. m.; p. (1961) *184,546*.

**Dunblane**, *mkt. burgh*, Perth, Scot.; on Allan Water, 5 m. from Stirling; ancient cath.; woollen ind., light engin.; p. (1961) *2,922*.

**Duncan**, *c.*, Okla., U.S.A.; oil; oilwell machin.; asphalt, cottonseed oil; p. (1960) *20,009*.

**Duncan Bay**, *t.*, Vancouver I., B.C.; newsprint.

**Duncansby Head**, *promontory*, Caithness, N.E. Scot.

**Dundalk**, *spt.*, *urb. dist., cap.*, Louth, Ireland; impt. rly. ctr.; engin., footwear, tobacco, brewing; p. (1966) *19,834*.

**Dundas**, *t.*, N.S.W., Australia; p. *6,017*.

**Dundas**, *t.*, Ontario, Canada; at W. end of L. Ontario; leather, paper; p. (1961) *12,912*

**Dundee**, *c.*, *spt.*, Angus, Scot.; on Firth of Tay, 50 m. N. Edinburgh; preserves, shipbldg.,

**textile** machin., cash registers, adding machin., linoleum, oil refining; univ.; p. (1961) *182,959*.

**Dundee**, *t.*, N. Natal, S. Africa; coal; p. *7,073*.

**Dundonald**, *vil.*, coast of Ayr, 5 m. S.W. of Kilmarnock; coal; p. (par.) *18,400*.

**Dunedin**, *cap.*, Otago, S.I., N.Z.; named after the old name of Edinburgh; univ.; wool and dairy produce; p. (1961) *105,053* of c. *73,226*.

**Dunfermline**, *burgh*, Fife, Scot.; at foot of Leven Hills, 14 m. E. of Alloa; damask linen tr., rubber; p. (inc. Rosyth) (1961) *47,159*.

**Dungannon**, *t.*, Tyrone, N. Ireland; p. (1966) *7,335*.

**Dungarvan**, *spt.*, *urb. dist.*, Waterford, Ireland; brewing, woollens; p. (1966) *5,376*

**Dungeness**, *headland of shingle*, Kent, Eng.; 10 m. S.E. of Rye; civil nuclear power-sta. (1964); a second to be built; linked by power cable to France 1961.

**Dunkeld**, *t.*, *par.*, Perth, Scot.; on R. Tay at entrance to Strathmore; cath.; tourist resort; p. (1951) *833*.

**Dunkirk** or **Dunkerque**, *spt.*, Nord, France; strong fort; gd. harbour and tr.; fisheries, shipbldg., oil refining; steel mill; scene of evacuation of B.E.F. 1940; p. (1962) *28,383*.

**Dunkirk**, *pt.*, N.Y., U.S.A.; on L. Erie; p. (1960) *18,205*.

**Dun Laoghaire** (Kingstown), *spt.*, *co. bor.*, Dublin, Ireland; mail packet sta., fishing; p. (1966) *55,585*. [Kerry, Ireland.

**Dunloe, Gap of**, *mtn. pass*, nr. L. of Killarney.

**Dunmanway**, *t.*, Cork, Ireland; on R. Brandon; tweeds, blankets; p. (1951) *1,439*.

**Dunmore**, *t.*, Penns., U.S.A.; nr. Scranton; anthracite; p. (1960) *18,917*.

**Dunmow**, Gr., *mkt. t.*, Essex Eng.; on R. Chelmer; 10 m. N.W. of Chelmsford; p. (par.) (1961) *3,827*.

**Dunmow**, Little, *vil.*, 2 m. E. of Gr. Dunmow; "Dunmow Flitch" trial here annually; p. (1961) *359*.

**Dunnet Head**, *promontory*, Caithness, N.E. Scot.

**Dunnottar**, *par.*, Kincardine, Scot.; nr. Stonehaven; ruined cas.; p. (1951) *1,514*.

**Dunoon**, *burgh*, *vat. pl.*, Argyll, Scot.; on N. side of Firth of Clyde, nearly opp. Greenock, ancient cas.; holiday resort; p. (1961) *9,211*.

**Duns**, *burgh*, Berwick, Scot.; agr. and allied inds.; p. (1961) *1,838*.

**Dunsinane**, *hill*, Sidlaws, Scot.; nr. Perth; alt. 1,012 ft.; referred to by Shakespeare in "Macbeth."

**Dunsmuir**, *t.*, N. Cal., U.S.A.; summer resort; hunting, fishing; p. (1960) *2,873*.

**Dunstable**, *t.*, *mun. bor.*, Beds, Eng.; on N. edge of Chiltern Hills, 4 m. W. of Luton; motor vehicles, sparking-plugs, car components, engin., cement, rubber and plastic goods; p. (estd. 1967) *28,940*.

**Duque de Caxias**, *t.*, Rio de Janeiro st., Brazil; oil refining; p. (1960) *173,077*.

**Duquesne**, *c.*, Penns., U.S.A.; 9 m. S.E. of Pittsburgh; steelwks.; p. (1960) *15,019*.

**Du Quoin**, *c.*, Ill., U.S.A.; meat packing, flour, leather goods, shoes; p. (1960) *6,558*.

**Durance**, *R.*, S.E. France; trib. of Rhône; rapid current; length 217 m.

**Durango**, *inland st.*, N.W. Mexico; mining, agr., stock-raising; a. 42,272 sq. m.; p. (1960) *760,836*.

**Durango**, *cap.*, D. state, Mexico; cath.; silver, gold, copper, iron-ore; p. (1960) *70,000*.

**Durant**, *c.*, S. Okla., U.S.A.; cotton gins and compresses, cottonseed oil; p. (1960) *10,467*.

**Durban**, *spt.*, Natal, Rep. of S. Africa; ch. comm. t. in S.E. Africa; maize, wool, hides, oil and sugar refining, chemicals, textiles, engin.; oil pipeline to Johannesburg; p. (1960) *655,370* (inc. *194,276* Whites).

**Düren**, *t.*, N. Rhine–Westphalia, Germany; on R. Ruhr, 23 m. S.W. of Cologne; textiles, leather, machin., rly ctr.; p. (1963) *52,600*.

**Durgapur**, *t.*, W. Bengal; steel plant, coke oven plant; p. (1961) *41,696*.

**Durham**, *cath. c.*, *mun. bor.*, *co. t.*, Durham, N.E. Eng.; univ.; carpet, organ, confectionery mftg.; p. (estd. 1967) *24,410*.

**Durham Co.**, N.E. Eng.; fertile valleys, moorland; coal, limestone; cattle; shipbldg., iron, steel, chemicals; a. 1,015 sq. m.; p. (1966) *1,542,000*.

**Durham**, *c.*, N.C., U.S.A.; tobacco factories; p. (1960) *78,302*.

**Duriach**, *t.*, Baden–Württemberg, Germany;

2¼ m. E. Karlsruhe; cas.; cycles, machin.; p. (estd. 1954) *25,000.*

**Dürres (Durazzo),** *spt.* Albania, on Adriatic; pt. for Tirana; tobacco ind.; p. (1960) *32,000.*

**Dursley,** *t.,* Glos., Eng.; 13 m. S. by W. of Gloucester; engin. inds., agr. mach.; p. *5,355.*

**Duryea,** *bor.,* Penns., U.S.A.; anthracite; silk; p. (1960) *5,626.*

**Dushanbe** (former Stalinabad), *t.* cap. Tadzhik S.S.R.; univ.; engin., textiles; p. (1967) *323,000.*

**Düsseldori,** *cap.,* N. Rhine–Westphalia, Germany; on R. Rhine, 20 m. N. of Cologne; admin. and cultural ctr., art and medical academies; iron, steel, machin., soap, cars, paper, chemical inds.; impt. trans-shipment pt.; p. (1963) *704,000.*

**Dust Bowl,** *region,* U.S.A.; name applied to Great Plains on E. flank of Rocky Mtns.; subject to severe soil erosion by wind, particularly in drought years (1933, 1936) due to destruction of natural vegetation by excessive ploughing.

**Dutch Guiana,** *see* Surinam.

**Dutch Harbour,** *t.,* Unalaska I., Aleutian gr., N. Pac. Oc.; strategic American naval base.

**Dvina,** *R.,* (N.) flows to White Sea at Arkhangelsk, and is formed by the junction of the Rs. Sukhona and Vychegda, U.S.S.R.; connected by canal with Neva and Volga; length 1,000 m.

**Dvina,** *R.,* Latvia, U.S.S.R.; rises near sources of Volga and Dnieper, flows to G. of Riga; l. 65 m.

**Dysart,** *spt., mun. bor.,* Fife, on F. of Forth, Scot.; linen, coal; p. *9,068.*

**Dzaudzhikau,** *see* Ordzhonikidze.

**Dzerzhinsk,** *industl. t.,* R.S.F.S.R.; W. of Gorki; chemicals (fertilisers, explosives); p. (1967) *196,000.*

**Dzhalil,** *t.,* R.S.F.S.R.; new t. 30 m. N.E. of Almetyevsk to serve new A. oilfield.

**Dzhambul,** *t.,* Kazakhstan S.S.R.; on R. Talis and Turksib rly.; chemicals; p. (1967) *152,000.*

**Dzhezkazgan,** *t.,* Kazakh S.S.R.; 350 m. W. of L. Balkhash; copper-mines; manganese ore near-by; p. (1956) *29,100.*

**Dzierzoniow,** *t.,* S.W. Poland, formerly Germany; ceded to Poland at Potsdam conference; tex-tiles, machin.; cattle, grain mkt.; p. (1965) *31,000.*

**Dzungaria,** *broad trench* leading to the Mongolian plateau from the lowlands round L. Balkhash; formerly independent state.

## E

**Eagle Grove,** *c.,* N. Iowa, U.S.A.; gypsum, agr.; p. (1960) *4,381.*

**Ealing,** *outer bor.,* Greater London; comprising former bors. of Acton, Ealing and Southall; p. (1966) *304,000.*

**Earby,** *urb. dist.,* W.R. Yorks, Eng.; cotton, plastic, cloths, agr. machin.; p. (1961) *4,983.*

**Earlestown,** *mftg. t.,* S. Lancs., Eng.; included in Newton le Willows urb. dist.; engin., glass.

**Earn,** *R.,* Perth, Scot.; issues from Loch Earn (6¼ m. long) and flows into the Tay R.; length 46 m.

**Earnslaw,** *mtns.,* S. I., N.Z.; highest peak, 9,165 ft.

**Easdale,** *I.,* off W. Argyll, Scot.; nr. Oban; slate quarries. [gas terminal.

**Easington,** *t.,* E.R. Yorks.; nr. Hull; natural

**East C.,** extreme N.E. point of Asia.

**East C.,** extreme E. point of New Zealand, named by Capt. Cook on his first voyage in 1769.

**East African Community,** comprises Kenya, Uganda, Tanzania (formed 1 Dec. 1967).

**East Anglia,** *dist.,* comprising Norfolk and Suffolk, Eng.; former Anglo-Saxon kingdom.

**East Anglian Heights,** *hills,* extend S.W. to N.E. across N.E. Hertfordshire, N. Essex and S.W. Suffolk, Eng.; chalk overlain by glacial clays and sands; smooth, rolling surface; region of lge. farms and lge. fields, mixed farms mainly grain; rarely exceed 600 ft. alt.

**East Barnet,** *former urb. dist.,* Herts, Eng., now inc. in Barnet outer bor., Greater London (*q.v.*); residtl.; p. (1961) *40,641.*

**East Bengal,** E. *div* of Pakistan; includes part of former Bengal Presidency; rice, jute, cotton; a. 5,091 sq. m.; p. (estd. 1951) *42,119,000.*

**East Chicago,** *c.,* Ind., U.S.A.; L. Michigan; iron and steel wks., oil refining; p. (1960) *57,669.*

**East Cleveland,** *t.,* Ohio, U.S.A.; residtl.; p. (1960) *37,991.*

**East Greenwich,** *t.,* Rhode I., U.S.A.; light mftg.; shellfish; summer resort; p. (1960) *6,100.*

**East Grinstead,** *t., urb. dist.,* E. Sussex, Eng.; in ctr. of the Weald, 9 m. W. of Tunbridge Wells; agr. mkt.; famous hospital for plastic surgery; p. (1961) *15,421.*

**East Ham,** *former co. bor.,* Essex, Eng.; mftg. sub. E. of London, docks; chemicals; now inc. in Newham bor., Greater London.

**East Indies (Malay Archipelago),** gr. of Is. be-tween Asia and Australia, inc. Borneo, Sulawesi, New Guinea, Sumatra, Java, Bali, Timor (see under Kalimantan and Indonesia); sugar, coffee, spices, fruits, rubber, tobacco, sago, tapioca, canes.

**East Kilbride,** *t.,* N. Lanark, Scot., 7 m. S.S.E. of Glasgow; designated " New Town " 1947; lge. agr. machin., aero engines, engin., elec. goods; seawater distillation plant; knitwear, clothing; p. (estd. 1965) *45,933.*

**East Liverpool,** *c.,* Ohio, U.S.A.; pottery mnfs.; p. (1960) *22,306.*

**East London,** *spt.,* C. Prov., S. Africa; at mouth of Buffalo R.; holiday resort; trading ctr.; inds. inc. car assembly, textiles, engin.; p. (1960) *114,584* (inc. *48,725* Whites).

**East Lothian (Haddington),** *co.,* S.E. Scot.; cereals, potatoes, sheep, coal; *co. t.,* Hadding-ton, a. 267 sq. m.; p. (1961) *52,653.*

**East Main R.,** Labrador, Newfoundland, Canada; flowing into James Bay.

**East Moline,** *t.,* Ill., U.S.A.; p. (1960) *16,732.*

**East Orange,** *t.,* N.J., U.S.A.; residtl. sub., New York; p. (1960) *77,259.*

**East Pakistan,** *prov.,* Pakistan; comprises E. terrs. of prov. of Bengal and former Assam dist. of Sylhet; divided into 3 divs. and 17 dists.; cap. Dacca; a. 54,501 sq. m.; p. (1961) *50,844,000.*

**East Palestine,** *t.,* Ohio, U.S.A.; clay, coal, oil, pottery; p. (1960) *5,232.* [*41,955.*

**East Providence,** *t.,* Rhode I., U.S.A.; p. (1960)

**East Retford,** *mun. bor.,* Notts, Eng.; on R. Idle, 6 m. E. of Worksop; rubber, wire ropes, engin.; p. (estd. 1967) *18,770.*

**East Riding, Yorkshire,** *see* Yorkshire, East Riding.

**East River,** *tidal strait* about 16 m. long and from 600 to 4,000 ft. wide; the R. separates the bors. of Manhattan and Bronx from the bors. of Queens and Brooklyn.

**East St. Louis,** *c., R. pt.,* Ill., U.S.A.; on Missis-sippi R.; large stockyards; meat packing; p. (1960) *81,712.*

**East Stonehouse,** *t.,* Devon, Eng.; adjoining Plymouth and Devonport.

**Eastbourne,** *t., co. bor.,* E. Sussex, Eng.; on S. cst. to E. of Beachy Head; seaside resort; p. (estd. 1967) *66,800.* [images, ruins; p. *250.*

**Easter I.,** E. Pac. Oc., W. of Chile; stone

**Eastern Province,** Zambia; groundnuts, maize, tobacco; prov. ctr. Fort Jameson; a. 22,350 sq. m.; p. (1964) *507,000.*

**Eastham,** *vil.,* Cheshire, Eng.; on S. of Mersey estuary, nr. entrance to Manchester Ship Canal.

**Easthampton,** *t.,* Mass., U.S.A.; p. (1950) *10,694.*

**Eastleigh,** *t., mun. bor.,* Hants, Eng.; locomotives; p. (estd. 1967) *43,070.*

**Easton,** *t.,* Mass., U.S.A.; p. (1960) *9,069.*

**Easton,** *c.,* Penns., U.S.A.; on Delaware R.; rly. ctr., coal, steel, machin., furniture; p. (1960) *31,955.*

**Eastview,** *t.,* Ontario, Canada; p. (1961) *24,555.*

**Eastwood,** *t., urb. dist.,* Notts, Eng.; coal; p. (1961) *10,585.*

**Eau Claire,** *c.,* Wis., U.S.A.; on Chippewa R.; timber, paper, furniture; p. (1960) *37,987.*

**Eaux Bonnes, Les,** *wat. pl.,* Pyrenees, S. France.

**Eaux Chaudes,** *wat. pl.,* Pyrenees, S. France.

**Ebal, Mt.,** Israel; opposite Gerizim; alt. 2,986 ft.

**Ebbw Vale,** *t., urb. dist.,* Monmouth, Eng.; 17 m. N.W. of Newport; coal, iron, steel, tinplate, bricks, pipes, precast concrete; p. (1961) *28,631.*

**Eberswalde,** *t.,* Frankfurt, E. Germany; N.E. of Berlin; iron, wood and cardboard wks.; p. (1963) *32,906.*

**Ebingen,** *c.,* Württemberg, Germany; knitwear, velvet, precision tools; p. (1963) *21,400.*

**Eboli,** *t.,* Campagna, Italy; E. of Salerno.

**Ebro, R.,** N.E. Spain; flows to Mediterranean from Cantabrian Mtns.; length 440 m.

**Ebury, R,** Monmouth, Eng.; trib. of Usk R.

**Eccles,** *mun. bor.,* Lancs, Eng.; 4 m. W. of Man-chester; iron and steel, cotton, textiles, leather, chemicals, coal-mining; p. (estd. 1967) *41,400.*

**Ecclesfield,** *t.,* W.R. Yorks, Eng.; N. of Sheffield; cutlery.

Eccleshall, *mkt. t.*, Staffs, Eng.; 6 m. N.W. of Stafford; p. *3,630*.

Echague, *t.*, Philippine Is.; tobacco ctr.

Echternach, *t.*, Luxembourg; famous abbey; Whitsun dancing-procession; p. (1960) *9,320*.

Echuca, *t.*, Victoria, Australia; on R. Murray; 50 m. N.E. of Bendigo; rly. ctr.; irrigation wks.; diary prods., timber; p. (1966) *8,014*.

Ecija, *t.*, Seville, Spain; olive oil, wine, pottery; the Roman Astigi; p. *34,944*.

Eck, Loch, *L.*, Argyll, Scot.; 6 m. long.

Eckernförde, *spt.*, Schleswig-Holstein, Germany; on Baltic N.W. of Kiel; fishing; resort; p. (1963) *20,400*.

Eckington, *t.* Derby, Eng.; S.E of Sheffield; coal, agr. implements; p. *14,614*.

Ecorse, *t.*, Mich., U.S.A.; p. (1960) *17,328*.

Ecuador, *rep.*, S. America; on Equatorial Pacific cst.; Andes mtns.; Chimborazo, 20,600 ft.; climate: lowlands tropical, uplands cool and dry; race chiefly Indian speaking the Quechua language; poor communications; cocoa, sugar, coffee, cereals, fruits, gold, copper, silver, Panama hats; cap. Quito; a. 106,508 sq. m.; p. (estd. 1965) *4,877,000*.

Edam, *t.*, S. Holland, Netherlands; on cst. IJsselmeer; cheese, tool mftg.; p. (1967) *16,558*.

Eday, *I.*, Orkney Is., Scot.; the Ocelli of Ptolemy.

Ed Damar, *cap.*, Northern Prov., Sudan; p. (estd. 1949) *8,000*.

Eddystone, *rock with lighthouse*, Eng. Channel; 15 m. S.W. of Plymouth.

Ede, *t.*, Gelderland, Netherlands; livestock; pianos; p. (1967) *67,558*.

Ede, *t.*, W. Prov., Nigeria; p. *57,500*.

Eden, *R.*, Westmorland, Eng.; rises in Pennines, flows N.W. to Solway Firth below Carlisle; length 65 m.

Edenton, *t.*, N.C., U.S.A.; groundnuts, cotton, herring fisheries; p. (1960) *4,458*.

Edessa (Edhessa), *t.*, *cap.*, Pella prefecture, Macedonia, Greece; p. (1961) *15,534*.

Edfu, *see* Idfu.

Edgbaston, *residtl. dist.*, Birmingham, Eng.

Edgehill, *ridge*, 15 m. S. Warwick, Eng.; first battle in Civil War, 1642.

Edgewater, *t.*, N.J., U.S.A.; sub., connected by ferry with New York; p. (1960) *4,113*.

Edgware, *t.*, Middlesex, Eng.; N. sub. of London; residtl.; p. (1961) *20,127*.

Edina, *t.*, Minn., U.S.A.; p. (1960) *28,501*.

Edinburgh, *c.*, Midlothian; cap. Scot.; royal burgh on F. of Forth; univ., cas.; palace (Holyrood); printing, publishing, brewing; Edinburgh Festival in August; Leith, with docks is joined to E.; p. (1961) *468,378*.

Edirne, *c.*, Turkey; on left bank of the Marica R.; greatly developed by Hadrian 125; residence of the Sultans 1366–1453; wine, tobacco, silk, perfume; p. (1965) *46,264*.

Edjelé, *t.*, nr. Tripoli, Algeria, Africa; oilfields.

Edmonton, *c.*, cap. Alberta, Canada; fast-growing c. (46 sq. m.) on both sides of N. Saskatchewan R.; high-level bridge links Strathcona; immense war-time activity (" invasion "), now major Canadian military ctr.; univ.; international air ctr.; oilfields and farming; oil and chemical inds.; p. (1961) *337,568*.

Edmonton, *former mun. bor.*, Middix., Eng.; now inc. in Enfield outer bor., Greater London (*q.v.*); residtl.; light inds.; p. (1961) *91,956*.

Edremit, *t.*, Balikesir, N.W. Turkey; cereals, opium; silverwk.; p. (1960) *22,246*.

Edward, *L.*, on frontier of Uganda and the Congo (ex-Belgian), one of the sources of R. Nile; alt. 3,000 ft., length 44 m., breadth 32 m

Edwardsville, *t.*, Ill., U.S.A.; p. (1960) *9,996*.

Eekloo, *t.*, E. Flanders, Belgium; textiles; p. (1962) *18,571*.

Eger, *c.*, Hungary; wine, soap; cath.; p. (1962) *35,532*.

Egersund, *spt.*, S. cst., Norway; pottery, china, engin.; fishing; p. (1960) *3,868*.

Eggan, *R. pt.*, Ilorin, Nigeria; p. *10,000*.

Egham, *urb. dist.*, Surrey, Eng.; on R. Thames, nr. Staines; contains field of Runnymede, where King John signed Magna Carta; residtl.; p. (estd. 1967) *31,670*.

Egmont, *mtn.*, N.I., N.Z.; volcanic; alt. 8,200 ft.

Egremont, *mkt. t.*, Cumberland, Eng.; 10 m. S. of Whitehaven; limestone, iron ore; p. *16,727*.

Egypt, *see* United Arab Republic.

Ehen, *R.*, Cumberland, Eng.; issues from Ennerdale Water to Irish Sea; length 12 m.

Ehrenbreitstein, *t.*, *fort.*, Germany; on R. Rhine opposite Koblenz.

Eibar, *c.*, Guipuzcoa, N. Spain; iron, steel mftg., ordnance wks.; p. (1957) *16,318*.

Eibenstock, *t.*, Saxony, Germany; p. *7,760*.

Eider, *R.*, Germany; connected with Kiel canal; length 90 m.

Eifel, *plateau of ancient rocks*, W. Germany; lies N. of R. Moselle, terminates in steep slope forming W. edge of Rhine gorge between Koblenz and Bonn; drained by Kyll, Ahr, Rur; formerly cultivated, now largely woodland and moorland; farming in valleys; rises to just over 2,000 ft.

Eiger, *mtn.*, one of the highest peaks of the Bernese Oberland, Switzerland; alt. 13,042 ft.

Eigg, *I.*, Inner Hebrides, Scot.; 15 m. S.W. of Mallaig; basaltic rocks on cst.; rises to 1,289 ft.

Eilat, *new spt.*, Negev, Israel; on Gulf of Akaba; oil; copper at Timna; p. (estd. 1953) *400*.

Eildon Hills, Roxburgh, Scot.; S. of Melrose; highest point 1,385 ft.

Eilenburg, *t.*, Leipzig, E. Germany; rly. junction; machin., chemicals; p. (1963) *21,050*.

Eindhoven, *c.*, N. Brabant, Netherlands; electronic equipment, motor vehicles, tobacco and textile inds.; techn. univ.; p. (1967) *183,637*.

Einsiedeln, *t.*, Schwyz, Switzerland; monastery, pilgrim ctr.

Eire, *see* Ireland, Republic of.

Eisenach, *t.*, Erfurt, E. Germany; on R. Hörsel, at foot of Thuringian forest; ctr. of Werra potash field; cars, machin., textiles; birthplace of J. S. Bach; p. (1963) *47,854*.

Eisenberg, *t.*, Gera, E. Germany; pianos, porcelain, cement, machin.; p. (1963) *13,666*.

Eisenerz Alps, *mtn. range*, Austria; most northerly range of Alps, overlooking Danube valley between Linz and Vienna; impt. iron-ore deposits; alt. from 6,000 to 9,000 ft.

Eisenhüttenstadt, *t.*, Frankfurt, E. Germany; iron smelting; p. (1963) *35,671*.

Eisleben, *t.*, Halle, E. Germany; birthplace of Luther; machin., copper- and silver-mining ctr.; p. (1963) *33,589*.

Ekibastuz, *t.*, Kazakhstan S.S.R.; 75 m. S.W. of Pavlodar; ctr. of rapidly developing mng. a. coal, gold, metals; coal-fed generating plant projected, to supply power to European Russia; p. (1956) *15,000*.

El Alamein, *vil.*, U.A.R.; in Libyan Desert 60 m. S.W. of Alexandria, scene of gr. Allied victory, Second World War; oilfield nearby; terminal nr. Sidi Abd el-Rahman.

El Callao, *t.*, Bolivar st., Venezuela; in ctr. of Guiana Highlands, 125 m. S.E. of Ciudad Bolivar; ctr. of impt. gold-mining region.

El Centro, Cal., U.S.A.; rich agr. a. reclaimed from the desert; p. (1960) *16,811*.

El Dorado, *t.*, Ark., U.S.A.; oil; p. (1960) *25,292*.

El Dorado, *t.*, Kan., U.S.A.; p. (1960) *12,523*.

El Faiyûm or El Fayum, *oasis t.*, *cap.* of Faiyûm prov., U.A.R.; nr. L. Moeris; predynastic arch. finds; lgst. cultivated a. of U.A.R. outside Nile flood plain; uranium; p. (1960) *102,000*.

El Fasher, *cap.*, Darfur Prov., Sudan; p. (estd. 1961) *28,462*.

El Hasa, *dist.*, Saudi Arabia; on Persian Gulf, ch. t. Hofuf.

El Jadida (Mazagan), *spt.*, Morocco; grain and wool tr.; p. (1960) *40,302*.

El Khârga, *oasis*, Libyan desert, U.A.R.; 85 m. S.W. of Asyut; p. *5,000*.

El Misti, *volcano*, Peru, S. America; N.E. of Arequipa; alt. 19,170 ft.

El Obeid, *cap.*, Kordofan, Sudan; 200 m. S.W. of Khartoum; ivory, gums, ostrich feathers; p. (estd. 1961) *56,970*.

El Oro, *prov.*, Ecuador; cap. Machala; a. 2,238 sq. m.; p. (estd. 1962) *162,591*.

El Paso, *c.*, Texas, U.S.A.; on Rio Grande; natural gas distribution, ore refining; p. (1960) *276,687*.

El Quantara (El Kantara), *t.*, U.A.R.; on E. bank of Suez Canal, 21 m. S. of Pt. Said; terminus of Palestine Rly. system; linked by ferry across canal (and temporary swing bridge) to El Quantara (W.) on Egyptian Rly. systems.

El Teniente, *t.*, central Chile; copper-mines; p. *11,761*.

Elan, *R.*, Radnor, Wales; rises on S.E. sides of Plynlimon, flows S.E. then N.E. into R. Wye at Rhayader; lower valley contains series of 4 lge. reservoirs, length 4 m., capacity 10,000 million gall.; ch. source of water for Birmingham.

Elâzig, *t.*, E. Turkey; dam and hydro-elec. project planned at Keban, 30 m. to N.W. at confluence of E. and W. branches of Euphrates; p. (1965) 73,899.

Elba, *I.*, off Tuscan cst., Italy; iron ore, wine, marble, salt; Napoleon's first exile here; ch. t. Porto Ferrajo; a. 140 sq. m.; p. (1960) 26,000.

Elbasan, *prefecture*, Albania; cap. Elbasan; p. (1958) 430,000.

Elbe, *R.*, Czechoslovakia, Germany; the Roman "Albis"; rises in Bohemia and flows into N. Sea at Cuxhaven, 65 m. below Hamburg; navigable for 500 m. of total length 725 m.

Elbert, *mtn.*, Col., U.S.A.; alt. 14,420 ft.

Elbeuf, *t.*, Seine-Maritime, France; woollens; p. (1954) 17,293.

Elblag (Elbing), *spt.*, N. Poland (since 1945), formerly in E. Prussia; shipbldg., machin., vehicles; p. (1965) 85,000.

Elbruz Mt., Caucasus, highest in Europe (18,480 ft.), over-topping Mont Blanc by 2,698 ft.

Elburz, *mtn. range*, N. Iran; bordering on Caspian Sea; highest peak, Demavend, 18,500 ft.

Elche, *t.*, Alicante, Spain; 15 m. S.W. of Alicante; palm groves; oil, soap; p. (1959) 72,706.

Eldorado, *radium mine*, N.W. Terr., N. Canada; situated on E. shore of Gr. Bear Lake nr. Arctic Circle; produces 40% of world's radium, sent to Pt. Hope, Ontario, for refining.

Electra, *t.*, N. Texas, U.S.A.; oil; drilling tools and equipment; p. (1960) 4,759.

Electrona, Tasmania, Australia; carbide wks. based on local limestone and hydroelec. power; unique in S. hemisphere.

Elektrenai, *t.*, Lithuanian S.S.R.; new township nr. Vievis, at site of thermal power sta.

Elektrostal, *t.*, R.S.F.S.R.; 35 m. E. of Moscow; steel, engin.; p. (1967) 116,000.

Elephant Butte Dam, N.M., U.S.A.; on Rio Grande, 125 m. above El Paso; built to control flood water; lake, a. 60 sq. m., supplies irrigation water to 780 sq. m. in N.M. and Texas, water also supplied to Mexico.

Elephanta, *I.*, Bombay Harbour, India; cave sculptures.

Elephantine, *I.*, in Nile, Upper U.A.R.; site of nilometer.　　　　　　　　　　　[engin. wks.

Eleusis, *t.*, Greece; nr. Athens; ship repair yard;

Eleuthera, *I.*, Bahamas, T.W.I.; p. (1953) 6,070.

Elgin, *t.*, Ill., U.S.A.; watches, elec. goods, machin. chemicals, wood prod.; p. (1960) 49,447.

Elgin, *co. t.*, *burgh*, Moray, Scot.; ancient ruined cath.; woollens; p. (1961) 11,971.

Elgon Mt., *extinct volcano*, on bdy. of Kenya and Uganda; 40 m. in diam.; alt. 14,100 ft.; cave dwellings on slopes.

Elie and Earlsferry, *burgh*, Fife, Scot.; summer resort; p. (1961) 1,128.

Elisabethville, *see* Lubumbashi.

Elizabeth, *mftg. t.*, N.J., U.S.A.; univ.; sewing machines, iron, oil-ref.; p. (1960) 107,698.

Elizabeth, satellite t. 17 m. N. of Adelaide, S. Australia; p. (1966) 47,000, proposed p. 60,000.

Elizabeth, *t.*, N.C., U.S.A.; timber ind.; p. (1960) 14,062.

Elizabethton, *t.*, Tenn., U.S.A.; manganese; rayon; p. (1960) 10,896.

Elkhart, *t.*, Ind., U.S.A.; E. of Chicago; paper, machin.; p. (1960) 40,274.

Elk Mtns., *lofty range*, W. Col., U.S.A.; highest point Castle Peak, alt. 14,115 ft.

Elland, *t.*, *urb. dist.*, W.R. Yorks, Eng.; on R. Calder, 3 m. S.E. of Halifax; woollens; p. (1961) 18,353.

Ellesmere, *t.*, Shropshire, Eng.; 8 m. N.W. of Wem; mkt. agr.; p. (1961) 2,254.

Ellesmere, *agr. dist.*, S.I., N.Z.; on Canterbury Plain nr. Christchurch.

Ellesmere I., lge. I. extreme north of Arctic Canada; barren, uninhabited; a. 41,000 sq. m.

Ellesmere Port, *t.*, *mun. bor.*, N.W. Cheshire, Eng.; on Manchester Ship Canal and 9 m. S.S.E. of Liverpool; impt. petrol docks and refinery; metal mftg., paper, engin.; p. (estd. 1967) 52,950.

Elliot Lake, *t.*, N. Ontario; ctr. of uranium mines; p. 25,000.

Ellis I., New York harbour, U.S.A.; served as ch. immigration ctr., 1892–1943.

Ellon, *burgh*, Aberdeen, Scot.; on R. Ythan; p. (1961) 1,456.

Ellwood, *t.*, Penns., U.S.A.; p. (1960) 12,413.

Elmhurst, *t.*, Ill., U.S.A.; p. (1960) 36,991.

Elmina, *t.*, Ghana, W. Africa; fortress; tr. in palm oil, ivory, gold; p. 15,200.

Elmira, *mftg. t.*, N.Y., U.S.A.; rly. goods, farm implements; burial place of Mark Twain; p. (1960) 46,517.

Elmshorn, *t.*, Germany; N.W. of Hamburg; p. (1963) 35,400.　　　　　　[p. (1960) 26,658.

Elsinore (Helsingor), *t.*, *spt.*, Denmark; shipbldg.;

Elstree, *t.*, Herts., Eng.; 4 m. W. of Barnet; residential; films, light engin., silk hosiery; p. (1961) 24,782.　　　　　　　　　　　[London.

Eltham, *residtl. dist.*, Kent, Eng.; S. sub. of

Eluru, *t.*, Andra Pradesh, India; cotton; carpets, hosiery, oil; p. (1961) 108,321.

Elvas, *c.* (*fortfd.*), Portugal; on Guadiana R.; plums, olives; p. (1960) 11,742.

Elwood, *industl. t.*, Ind., U.S.A.; on Duck Creek; grain, tinplate; p. (1960) 11,793.

Ely, *c.*, Cambridge and I. of Ely, Eng.; on S. fringe of the Fens; mkt., cath.; agr. ctr. (fruit, roots); p. (1961) 9,815.

Ely, I. of, *see* Cambridge and Isle of Ely.

Elyria, *t.*, Ohio, U.S.A.; mftg.; p. (1960) 43,782.

Emba, *R.*, Kazakh S.S.R.; rises in S. end of Ural Mtns., flows S.W. to Caspian Sea; crosses productive Ural–Emba oilfield.

Emden, *spt.*, Lower Saxony, Germany; nr. mouth of R. Ems; freighting, shipbldg., cars; fishing prod., imports iron ore, corn; exp. coal and iron from Ruhr; p. (1963) 46,100.

Emilia-Romagna, *region*, N. Italy; S. of Po R.; agr. (grain, wine, fruits); a. 8,542 sq. m.; p. (1961) 3,646,507.

Emmaus, *bor.*, Penns., U.S.A.; textiles, rubber prod.; p. (1960) 10,262.

Emmen, *t.*, Drenthe, Netherlands; 30 m. S.E. of Groningen; elec. machin., ball bearings, tinplate, iron wks.; p. (1967) 75,660.

Empedrado, *t.*, Argentina; oranges, rice in a.; p. (1960) 21,000.

Empoli, *t.*, Florence, Italy; textile mnfs., straw plaiting, leather goods, pottery; p. 21,000.

Emporia, *t.*, Kan., U.S.A.; stock-raising; p. (1960) 18,190.　　　　　　　　　　　[p. 7,070.

Ems, *t.*, Germany; on Lahn R.; spa, silver, lead;

Ems, *R.*, N. Germany; rises in Teutoburger Wald, flows N. to N. Sea at Emden; length 205 m.

Emscher, *R.*, W. Germany; rises in Sauerland, flows W. through heart of Ruhr coalfield to enter R. Rhine at Hamborn; canalised for most of its course; length 55 m.

Emsdetten, *t.*, Germany; on R. Ems; textiles; p. (1963) 26,000.

Encarnación, *pt.*, *cap.*, Ipatua dep., S.E. Paraguay; on Paraná R.; exp. timber, maté, tobacco, cotton, hides; p. (estd. 1960) 35,000.

Encounter Bay, S. Australia, receives Murray R.

Enderby Land, *terr.*, Antarctica; S. of C. of Good Hope.　　　　　　　　　　　[18,775.

Endicott, *t.*, N.Y., U.S.A.; shoe mftg.; p. (1960)

Endrick, *R.*, Stirling, Scot.; flows to Loch Lomond; length 29 m.　　　　　[(1960) 1,485.

Enez, *t.*, S. Turkey-in-Europe; nr. Gallipoli; p.

Enfield, *former mun. bor.*; Middlesex Eng.; now outer bor. Greater London; comprising former bors. of Edmonton, Enfield and Southgate; p. (1966) 268,000.

Engadine, Switzerland; upper valley of Inn R.; health resort; chief t. St. Moritz.

Engaño, *c.*, S. extremity of Luzon, Philippine Is.

Engelberg, *t.*, Unterwalden, Switzerland; tourists; old monastery; p. 2,403.

Engels, *t.*, R.S.F.S.R.; on Volgar R. opposite Saratov; textiles, chemicals, petroleum refining; p. (1967) 120,000.

Enghien-les-Bains, *t.*, Seine-et-Oise, France; p. (1962) 12,504.

England (with Wales), forms S. and lgst. div. Gr. Britain; length 420 m., greatest breadth 360 m.; ch. mtns.: Cheviot Hills, Pennine Chain, Cumbrian Gr., Cambrian Mtns., Dartmoor, Exmoor; ch. Rs.: Thames, Severn, Trent, Mersey, Gr. Ouse, Yorkshire Ouse; climate: temperate maritime; vegetation: woods, moor, heath, grassland; ch. inds.: agr.; arable, pastoral, dairying; ch. crops: wheat, barley, oats, sugar-beet, potatoes, hops, fruit.

livestock; cod, haddock; coal, iron; iron and steel mnfs., machinery, machine tools, engin. prods., road vehicles and aircraft, ships, textiles, pottery; good road and rail comm.; cap. London; a. 50,875 sq. m.; p. (1961) *46,071,604*.

Englewood, *t.*, N.J., U.S.A.; p. (1960) *26,057*.

English Channel (La Manche), *narrow sea* separating England from France; extends from Strait of Dover to Land's End in Cornwall; length 300 m., greatest width 155 m.

Enham-Alamein, Hants.; rehabilitation ctr. for disabled ex-service men; 2½ m. N. of Andover; light inds.          [ments; p. (1960) *38,359*.

Enid, *t.*, Okla., U.S.A.; ironwks., farm imp

Enkhuizen, *c.*, *spt.*, N. Holland, Netherlands; on W. cst. IJsselmeer; picturesque c., p. (1967) *11,231*.

Enna (Castrogiovanni), *t.*, Sicily; rocksalt, sulphurmines; famous for its connection with the Proserpine legend; p. (1961) *28,145*.

En Nahud, *t.*, central Sudan; tr. in cattle, ivory, cotton, ostrich feathers; p. *19,300*.

Ennepetal, *t.*, N. Rhine-Westphalia, Germany; on R. Ennepe; t. created 1949 with merging of Milspe and Voerde; iron, machin.; p. (1963) *32,000*.

Ennerdale Water, *L.*, Cumberland, Eng.

Ennis, *mkt. t.*, *urb. dist.*, Clare, Ireland; farming, flour; p. (1966) *5,831*.

Enniscorthy, *mkt. t.*, *urb. dist.*, Wexford, Ireland; brewing, tanning; p. (1966) *5,762*.

Enniskillen, *co. t.*, *mun. bor.*, Fermanagh, N. Ireland; brewing, nylon mftg., meat processing; p. (1966) *7,154*.

Enns, *R.*, Austria; S. trib. of Danube; 112 m.

Enschede, *c.*, Overijssel, Netherlands; cottonspinning, weaving, textile mach., engin.; techn. univ.; p. (1960) *123,799*.

Entebbe, *t.* Uganda, E. Africa; on L. Victoria; univ.; cotton ginning; p. (estd.) *11,000*.

Enterprise, *c.*, Ala., U.S.A.; peanuts; p. (1960) *11,410*.

Entre Rios, *prov.*, Argentina; between Paraná and Uruguay Rs.; wheat, linseed, livestock; cap. Paraná; a. 29,427 sq. m.; p. (1960) *804,000*.

Entrocamiento, *t.*, Central Portugal, on Tagus R.

Enugu, *cap.* E. prov., Nigeria; coal; p. (1953) *63,000*.          [(1962) *22,799*.

Epernay, *t.*, Marne, France; champagne; p.

Ephesus, *ruined c.*, Turkey, S. of Izmir.

Ephrata, *t.*, S.E. Penns., U.S.A.; cattle rearing, printing; p. (1960) *7,688*.

Epinal, *cap.*, Vosges dep., France; on Moselle R.; textiles, printing; p. (1962) *37,808*.

Epirus, *dist.*, N.W. Greece; a. 3,688 sq. m.; p. (1961) *352,604*.

Epping, *t.*, *urb. dist.*, Essex, Eng.; mkt. gardening, dairying; p. (1961) *10,001*.

Epping, *forest*, Essex, Eng.

Epsom and Ewell, *mun. bor.*, Surrey, Eng.; 18 m. S.W. of London; residtl., racecourse; drain pipes, brick tiles; p. (estd. 1967) *72,320*.

Equatoria, *prov.*, Sudan; a. 76,995 sq. m.; cap. Juba; p. (estd. 1951) *632,900*.

Equatorial Guinea, *Rep.*, W. Africa; (formerly Span. overseas prov.) consists of mainland terr. of Rio Muni and Is. of Fernando Po, Annobon, Corisco, Elobey Grande and Elobey Chico; total a. 10,832 sq. m.; total p. (1968) *245,000*; cap. Santa Isabel. (*See* Feranado Po and Rio Muni.)

Erandio, *t.*, N. sub. of Bilbao, Spain; iron ore, paper, tobacco, wine; p. *11,268*.    [Antarctica.

Erebus, *mtn.*, active volcano, Victoria Land,

Eregli, *spt.*, Black Sea, Turkey; rly. to Zonguldak coal-mines; steel wks.; p. (1960) *8,815*.

Erfurt, *c.*, *cap.*, Erfurt, E. Germany; cath., ctr. of mkt. gardening and seed-growing dist., textiles, machin., foodstuffs, footwear, radios, heavy engin.; p. (1963) *189,817*.

Ericht, *loch*, Perth, Inverness, Scot.; in central Grampians; 15¼ m. long; hydro-elec. scheme.

Erie, *lake*, N. America; separating Canada from U.S.A.; a. 9,940 sq. m.; 241 m. long, 57 m. broad.

Erie, *industl. c.*, *lake pt.*, Penns., U.S.A.; iron and steel ind., engin.; p. (1960) *133,440*.

Erie Canal, *see* New York State Barge Canal.

Eriskay, I., Outer Hebrides, Scot.

Erith, *former mun. bor.*, Kent, Eng.; on S. bank of Thames estuary 5 m. below London; engin., oil refining, cables, plastics, paints and varnishes, timber, concrete prods.; p. (1961) *45,043*; now inc. in Bexley bor., Greater London.

Eritrea, *prov.*, Ethiopia; fed. within Ethiopia 1952; former Italian col., N.E. Africa; tobacco, cereals, pearl fishing; cap. Asmara, a. *45,754* sq. m.; p. (estd. 1960) *1,000,000*.

Erivan, *cap.* Armenian S.S.R., U.S.S.R.; situated in deep valley in Caucasus Mtns.; woollen mnfs., fruit canning, machine tools; p. (1939) *200,000*.

Erlangen, *t.*, Bavaria, Germany; univ.; textiles, elec. and precision engin., gloves; p. (1963) *73,200*.          [hides; p. (1961) *117,253*

Earnakulam, *t.*, Kerala, India; cotton, coffee,

Erne, *R.*, (72 m.) and *L.*, N. Ireland, flows to Donegal Bay.

Erode, *t.*, S. Tamil Nadu, India; cotton; p. (1961) *73,762*.

Erskine, *t.*, Renfrewshire, Scot.; new satellite t.

Erzgebirge (Ore Mns.), *mtn. range*, Germany; highest peak, 4,122 ft.

Erzurum, *t.*, Turkey; agr. ctr. on fertile plateau 6,200 ft. a.s.l.; formerly of gr. strategic impt.; p. (1965) *106,301*.

Esbjerg, *spt.*, Denmark; W. cst. of Jutland; export harbour on N. Sea cst.; exp. agr. prod.; fishing; airport; p. (1965) *55,882*.

Escanaba, *t.*, Mich., U.S.A.; iron, shipping, lumber, chemicals; p. (1960) *15,391*.

Escatrón, *t.*, Spain; on Elbro R.

Esch-sur-Alzette, *t.*, Luxembourg; mining ctr.; p. (1960) *27,954*.

Eschwege, *t.*, Hessen, Germany; cas.; machin., textiles, leather, cigars, chemicals; p. (1963) *24,000*.

Eschweiler, *t.*, N. Rhine-Westphalia, Germany; N.W. of Aachen; lignite mng., steel, iron, metallurgy, leather, textiles; p. (1963) *40,000*.

Escondido, *t.*, Cal., U.S.A.; p. (1960) *16,377*.

Esdraelon, *plain*, Israel; S.W. Asia; between Carmel and Gilboa Mtns.

Esfahan. *See* Isfahan.

Esher, *urb. dist.*, Surrey, Eng.; on R. Mole, residtl.; Sandown Park racecourse; p. (estd. 1967) *62,980*.

Eshowe, *health resort*, Natal, S. Africa; 40 m. from Tugela R.; p. (1960) *4,919* inc. *1,945* whites.

Esk, *R.*, Dumfries, Scot., rises in S. Uplands, flows S. into Solway Firth; length 50 m.

Esk, *R.*, N.R. Yorks., Eng.; flows E. into N. Sea at Whitby; length 28 m.

Eskilstuna, *t.*, Sweden; on R. of same name; iron, steel, machin.; p. (1961) *59,072*.

Eskisehir, *t.*, Turkey; W. of Ankara, anc. Dorylaeum; rly. ctr.; meerschaum; p. (1965) *174,451*.

Esmeralda, *t.*, Venezuela, S. America; on Orinoco R.

Esmeraldas, *prov.*, Ecuador, S. America; cap. E. on R. of same name; cacao, tobacco; a. 5,464 sq. m.; p. (estd. 1962) *124,742*.

Esmeraldas, *pt.*, Ecuador; bananas, timber, tobacco, cacao, rubber; gold mines nearby; p. (1962) *13,169*.

Espirito Santo, *maritime st.*, Brazil; sugar, cotton, coffee, fruits, forests, thorium; cap. Vitória; a. 15,785 sq. m.; p. (1960) *1,188,665*.

Essaouira (Mogador) *spt.*, Morocco, N. Africa; cereals, almonds, gum-arabic, crude oil; p. (1960) *26,392*

Essen, *t.*, N. Rhine-Westphalia, Germany; ch. t., in W. Ruhr; coal-mng., steel (Krupp), elec. and light engin.; p. (1963) *729,400*.

Essendon, *sub.*, Melbourne, Victoria, Australia; racecouse, air-port.

Essentuki, *t.*, Stavropol, U.S.S.R.; light mnfs., medicinal springs; p. *23,000*.

Essequibo, *R.*, Guyana; length 620 m.

Essex, *co.*, Eng.; bounded on S. by Thames, on E. by North Sea; co. t. Chelmsford; lies mainly on London Clay and chalk; agr.; wheat, barley, sugar-beet; market gd.; S.W. part of Greater London with manf. subs.; motor wks. at Dagenham; oil refs. at Shell Haven; civil nuclear power-stn. at Bradwell; univ. at Colchester; a. 1,528 sq. m.; p. (1966) *1,244,000*.

Esslingen, *t.*, Baden-Württemberg, Germany; on R. Neckar; mach. and rly. shops; textiles, chemicals, leather goods; Liebfrauen church (1440); p. (1963) *83,900*.

Este, *t.*, N.E. Italy; ancient fortress; iron, pottery, chemicals; p. *14,433*.          [*53,872*.

Esteli, *dep.*, W. Nicaragua; a. 772 sq. m.; p.

Estepona, *spt.*, Malaga, Spain; wine, olives, citrus fruit, sardines; p. (1957) *12,913*.

Eston, *t.*, *urb. dist.*, N.R. Yorks, Eng.; 3 m. E. of Middlesbrough; iron and steel, shipbldg. and repairing; p. (1961) *37,160*.

Estonia, *constituent rep.*, U.S.S.R.; formerly independent st.; climate: severe winter, mild summer, moderate rainfall; farming and dairying, textiles, matches, leather; a. 17,610 sq. m.; cap. Tallin; p. (1959) *1,196,000.*

Estoril, watering-place and thermal spa, Portugal; N. side of Tagus estuary.

Estrela, Serra da, *mtn. range*, Portugal; highest peak 7,524 ft.

Estremadura, *prov.*, Portugal; cap. Lisbon; a. 2,064 sq. m.; p. (1950) *1,595,067.*

Esztergom, *t.*, Hungary; weaving; mineral springs; cath.; p. (1962) *23,716.*

Etampes, *t.*, Seine-et-Oise; France; 30 m. S. of Paris; commerce; p. (1962) *13,658.*

Etang de Berre, *lagoon*, Bouches-du-Rhône, S.E. France; lies E. of Rhône delta, separated from Gulf of Lions by low Chaîne de l'Estaque; traversed by Rhône–Marseille Canal; salt pans; oil refineries in a.; approx. a. 100 sq. m.

Etaples, *t.*, Pas de Calais, France; seaside resort; p. (1962) *8,647.*

Etawney, *L.*, Manitoba, Canada.

Ethiopia (Abyssinia), *indep. sovereign st.*, Africa; under Italian domination 1936–41; federated with Eritrea 1952; tableland with average height 3,000 ft. intersected deep valleys; Samen Mtns. 15,000 ft.; summer rains; pastoral, farming, coffee; cap. Addis Ababa. a. 400,000 sq. m.; p. (estd. 1965) *22,200,000.*

Etna, *volcano*, N.E. Sicily, Italy; recent eruptions have raised height from 10,768 ft. to 11,121 ft.

Etna, *t.*, Penns., U.S.A.; p. (1960) *5,519.*

Eton, *t.*, *urb. dist.*, Bucks, Eng.; on N. bank of R. Thames opposite Windsor; famous public school, founded by Henry VI, p. (1961) *3,901.*

Etowah, *R.*, Ga., U.S.A.; trib. of Coosa R.

Etruria, *t.*, Staffs, Eng.; potteries, ironwks.

Ettelbrück, *t.*, Luxembourg; p. *4,373.*

Etterbeek, *commune*, sub. Brussels, Belgium; carpets, brewing; p. (1962) *53,091.*

Ettrick, *R.*, Selkirk, Scot.; length 32 m.

Eucla, *t.*, W. Australia; close to bdy. of S. Australia on Transcontinental rly.; artesian wells.

Euclid, *t.*, Ohio, U.S.A.; p. (1960) *62,998.*

Eucumbene Dam and L., N.S.W., Australia, major storage of Snowy Mtns. hydroelec. scheme; will hold eight times as much water as Sydney Harbour when completed.

Eugene, *t.*, Ore., U.S.A.; univ.; ironwks.; p. (1960) *50,977.*      [*11,326.*

Eunice, *t.*, La., U.S.A.; cotton, rice; p. (1960)

Euphrates, *lgst. R.* in S.W. Asia; rises in Armenian uplands and joined by the Tigris, enters Persian G. at Shatt-et-Arab; length 1,780 m.

Eure, *dep.*, Normandy, France; agr., fruit, livestock, textiles; cap. Evreux; a. 2,331 sq. m.; p. (1962) *361,904.*

Eure-et-Loir, *dep.*, N. France; flour, textiles, iron, paper; cap. Chartres; a. 2,291 sq. m.; p. (1962) *277,546.*

Eureka, *c.*, Cal., U.S.A.; timber; p. (1960) *28,137.*

Europe, *continent*; a. 3,900,000 sq. m.; greatest length N. to S. 2,400 m. breadth E. to W. 3,000 m.; ch. mtns.: Alps, Pyrenees, Carpathians, Balkans, Apennines, Sierra Nevada, Urals, Caucasus; ch. Rs.: Volga, Danube, Rhine, Dnieper, Ural, Don; ch. lakes: Ladoga, Onega, Peipus, Vänern, Vättern; climate: Arctic border, long cold winter, short cool summer, snow; W. seaboard, cool summer, mild winter, abundant rainfall; Continental, warm summer, cold winter; Mediterranean, hot dry summers, warm wet winters; vegetation: N. tundra; Scandinavia and N. Russia, coniferous forests; European plain, woodlands; Mediterranean, drought-resisting evergreens; S. Russia, steppe; Caspian shores, desert; ch. inds.: agr., cereals, fruits, sugar-beet, potatoes, flax, hemp; pastoral, cattle-rearing, dairying, fishing; forestry; wood pulp, paper; mining, iron, coal, petroleum; hydro-elec. power; mountainous regions. Politically divided into reps., kingdoms, principalities and a grand duchy; p. (est.) *533,000,000.*

Europort, name of the latest expansion of the Rotterdam docks; capable of handling 100,000-ton oil-tankers; oil refining.

Euros, *prefecture*, Thrace, Greece; cap. Alexandroupolis; p. (1961) *157,901.*

Euskirchen, *t.*, N. Rhine–Westphalia, Germany; W. of Bonn; cloth, glass, wood, paper wks.; p. (1963) *21,000.*

Evanston, *t.*, Ill., U.S.A.; on L. Michigan; sub. of Chicago, seat of N.W. Univ.; p. (1960) *79,283.*

Evanston, *t.*, Wyo., U.S.A.; coal, oil, iron; dairying, agr.; p. (1960) *4,901.*

Evans Strait, divides Southampton Land from Coats I., Hudson Bay, Canada.

Evansville, *mftg. c.*, Ind., U.S.A.; on Ohio R.; hardwood tr., coal, farm implements; p. (1960) *141,543.*

Everest, Mt. (Chomolungma = Goddess Mother of the Earth), Himalaya, on frontier of Nepal and Tibet; alt. 29,028 ft.; highest mtn. in the world; Hillary and Tenzing first to reach summit in 1953.

Everett, *mftg. t.*, Mass., U.S.A., nr. Boston; iron and steel; p. (1960) *43,544.*

Everett, *t.*, Wash., U.S.A.; timber, salmon, fruit; p. (1960) *40,304.*

Everglades, Fla., U.S.A.; extensive marshes.

Evesham, *mkt. t.*, *mun. bor.*, Worcester, Eng.; on R. Avon, in Vale of Evesham, 15 m. S.E. of Worcester; fruit ctr.; p. (estd. 1967) *13,140.*

Evora, *cap.*, Evora prov., Portugal; iron, cork; famous for its mules; p. (1960) *24,144.*

Evreux, *t.*, *cap.*, Eure, France; iron, glass, textiles; p. (1962) *40,153.*

Evvoia (Euboea), *Greek I.*, Ægean Sea; 115 m. long; wheat, olive oil, wine; cap. Khalkis; p. (1951) *163,720.*

Ewing, *t.*, N.J., U.S.A.; p. (1960) *26,628.*

Exe, *R.*, Somerset and Devon, rises on Exmoor, flows S. to English Channel at Exmouth; length 44 m.

Exeter, *c.*, co. bor., co. *t.*, mkt. *t.*, Devon, Eng.; E. of Dartmoor on R. Exe 8 m. from the sea; univ.; cath.; aircraft components, leather goods; p. (estd. 1967) *92,550.*      [(1950) *5,130.*

Exeter, *bor.*, Penns., U.S.A.; coal, timber; p.

Exmoor, *moorland tract*, Somerset, Devon, Eng.; highest point, Dunkery Beacon, 1,707 ft.

Exmouth, *t.*, *urb. dist.*, Devon, Eng.; on E. side of estuary of R. Exe; holiday resort; p. (estd. 1967) *22,420.*      [p. *3,000.*

Exmouth, *t.*, W. Australia; new t. opened 1967;

Exploits, *R.*, Newfoundland, Canada; length 150 m.

Extremadura, *old prov.*, S.W. Spain; largely plateau, alt. 1,500–3,000 ft.; heathy moorland; sheep; less arid conditions than in remainder of central Spain allow olives, vines, cereals; irrigation in valleys of Tagus, Guadiana; gov. project to develop a. in progress.

Exuma, *gr. sm. Is.*, Bahamas, W.I.; p. (1953) *2,919.*

Eye, *mkt. t.*, *mun. bor.*, Suffolk, Eng.; 18 m. N. of Ipswich; anc. church; p. (estd. 1967) *1,640.*

Eyemouth, *burgh*, Berwick, Scot.; on E. cst., 9 m. N. of Berwick; fishing; p. (1961) *2,160.*

Eyre, *L.* (salt), N. part of S. Australia; a. 4,000 sq. m., 38 ft. below sea-level; practically dried up.

Eyre Peninsula, S. Australia; between G. of St. Vincent and Spencer G.

Eyzies, Les, *commune*, Dordogne dep., France; caves, arch. interests, Paleolithic paintings, Cromagnon type site.

# F

Faaborg, *spt.*, Fyn I., Denmark; p. (1960) *5,135.*

Fabriano, *mftg. t.*, Marches, Italy; 30 m. S.W. of Ancona; fine cath.; paper; p. *26,625.*

Fabrizia, *t.*, nr. Monteleone, Italy; p. *4,150.*

Facone, *sacred L.*, Honshu, Japan; 57 m. from Tokyo.

Faenza, *t.*, Ravenna, Italy; at foot of Apennines, 15 m. S.W. of Ravenna; pottery (faience), silk; p. (1961) *51,085.*

Fagersta, *t.*, Vastmanland, Sweden; iron, steel smelting; p. (1961) *15,527.*

Failsworth, *t.*, *urb. dist.*, Lancs, Eng.; N.E. of Manchester; textiles, elec. goods; p. (estd. 1967) *22,520.*

Fair I., midway between Shetland and Orkney, Scot.; bird sanctuary; famous for brightly patterned, hand-knitted articles.

Fairbanks, *t.*, Alaska, U.S.A.; p. (1960) *13,311.*

Fairfield, *t.*, Ala., U.S.A.; p. (1960) *15,816.*

Fairhaven, *t.*, Mass., U.S.A.; p. (1960) *14,233.*

Fairhead, *O.*, N.W. Antrim, N. Ireland.

Fair Lawn, *t.*, N.J., U.S.A.; p. (1960) *26,628.*

Fairmont, *t.*, W. Va., U.S.A.; p. (1960) *27,477.*

Fairweather, *mtn.*, Alaska, N. America; alt. 14,872 ft.

Faiyum, *see* El Faiyum.

Faizabad, *ch. t.*, Badakhshan, N.E. Afghanistan.

Fakenham, *t.*, Norfolk, Eng.; on R. Wensum.

Fal, *R.*, Cornwall, Eng.; flows to the English Channel; length 23 m.

Falaise, *t.*, Calvados, France; birthplace of William the Conqueror; scene of rout of a German Army, 1944; p. (1962) *6,711*.

Falaise de l'Ile de France, *low S. E.-facing escarpment*, 50 m. S.E. and E. of Paris, France; overlooks " pays " of Champagne Pouilleuse; ch. vine-growing dist. for champagne-wine ind. of Rheims, Epernay.

Falcón, *st.*, Venezuela; bordering Caribbean Sea; cap. Coro; p. (1961) *340,450*.

Falkirk, *burgh*, Stirling, Scot.; 10 m. S.E. of Stirling; foundries, bricks, chemical, aluminium wks., concrete, timber yards; battles 1298 and 1746; p. (1961) *1,032*.

Falkland, *burgh*, Fife, Scot.; 3 m. S. of Auchtermuchty; mkt.; p. (1961) *1,032*.

Falkland Is., *Brit. Crown col.*, S. Atlantic, comprises E. and W. Falkland and adjacent Is.; sheep rearing (for wool); cap. Port Stanley on E. Falkland I.; a. 4,700 sq. m.; p. (1962) *2,172*.

Falkland Is. Dependencies, comprise S. Georgia (ctr. of whaling ind.) and S. Sandwich Is. (S. Shetland, S. Orkney Is., and Graham's Land were constituted a separate col. in 1962 and now form British Antarctic Territory (*q.v.*)).

Fall River *industl. c.*, Mass., U.S.A.; cottons, dyeing, brewing, iron; p. (1960) *99,942*.

Falmouth, *spt., mun. bor.*, Cornwall, Eng.; on W. side of estuary of R. Fal, 10 m. S. of Truro; fine sheltered harbourage; seaside resort; fisheries, ship repairing, mng., quarrying, lt. engin.; p. (estd. 1967) *17,350*.

False Bay, *inlet* on E. side of C. of Good Hope peninsula.

Falster, *I.* in the Baltic, Denmark; cap. Nyköbing; p. (1960) *46,662*. [*13,305*.

Falticeni, *t.*, N.E. Romania; timber; p. (1956)

Falun, *t.*, Kopparberg, Sweden; iron, paper, pyrites, zinc and lead ore; p. (1961) *18,813*.

Famagusta, *t., spt.*, Cyprus; on E. cst., 2½ m. S. of ruins of ancient Salamis; p. (1960) *34,774*.

Famatina, *t.*, La Rioja prov., Argentina; in foothills of Andes, 360 m. N.W. of Cordoba; coppermines.

Fannich, *loch*, Ross, Scot.; (6½ m. long), drains to Cromarty F.

Fanning, *Brit. I.*, Gilbert and Ellice Is. col.; N. Pac. Oc.; a. 15 sq. m.; guano, mother-of-pearl; p. *196*.

Fano, *t.*, Italy; on Adriatic cst., N. of Ancona; resort; p. (1961) *41,033*.

Fanö, *I.*, Denmark; off W. cst. of Jutland, opposite Esbjerg; a. 20 sq. m.; p. (1960) *2,675*.

Farafra, *oasis*, Libyan Desert, U.A.R.; 200 m. W. of Asyut; dates; stage on caravan route from Cyrenaica to Upper U.A.R.

Farciennes, *commune*, S.W. Belgium; coal, mftg.; p. (1962) *11,359*.

Fareham, *t., urb. dist.*, Hants., Eng.; at N.W. corner of Portsmouth Harbour; sm. boats, ceramics; p. (estd. 1967) *75,330*.

Farewell, *C.*, southernmost tip of Greenland.

Farewell, *C.*, most northerly point S.I., N.Z.

Fargo, *c.*, N.D., U.S.A.; on Red R.; grain, farmmachin.; p. (1960) *46,662*.

Faribalut, *t.*, Minn., U.S.A.; flour, factories; p. (1960) *16,928*.

Faridpur, *t.*, E. Bengal. Pakistan; cloth, carpets; p. (1961) *28,300*.

Faringdon, *mkt. t.*, Berks, Eng.; on N. edge of Vale of White Horse; p. *11,450*.

Farmington, *t.*, N.M., U.S.A.; p. (1960) *23,786*.

Farmington, *t.*, N. Conn., U.S.A.; residtl. and industl.; p. (1960) *10,798*.

Farnborough, *t., urb. dist.*, Hants, Eng.; 3 m. N. of Aldershot military camp; Royal Aircraft Establishment; p. (estd. 1967) *40,020*.

Farne Is., off Northumberland cst., Eng.; a. 80 acres; since 1923 bird sanctuaries.

Farnham, *mkt. t., urb. dist.*, Surrey, Eng.; at N. Foot of N. Downs, 10 m. W. of Guildford; pottery, engin., coach mkg.; p. (estd. 1967) *29,840*.

Farnworth, *mftg. t., mun. bor.*, Lancs, Eng., nr. Bolton, cotton mnfs.; p. (estd. 1967) *26,700*.

Faro, *prov.*, Portugal; cap. Faro; fruit, fishing, wines, salt; a. 2,028 sq. m.; p. (1963) *314,900*.

Faro, *spt. cap.*, Faro prov., Portugal; wine, fruit, cork; p. (1963) *18,909*.

Faro, *C.*, N. point of Sicily, nearest to Italy.

Faroe Is., 200 m. N.W. of the Shetlands, Scot.; cap. Thörshavn (Strömö I.); Danish possession; fishing, agr.; a. 540 sq. m.; p. (1960) *34,596*.

Farrell, *t.*, Penns., U.S.A.; p. (1960) *13,793*.

Farrukhabad, *t.*, Uttar Pradesh, India; on Ganges R.; gold, lace, brass wk.; p. (1961) *94,591*.

Fars, *prov.*, S. Iran; agr.; cap. Shiraz; p. (1967) *1,499,472*.

Fasa, *t.*, Fars Prov., Iran; silk, wool; p. *10,000*.

Fasano, *t.*, Bari, Italy; industl.; p. over *20,000*.

Fastnet, *lighthouse* in Atlantic, 4½ m. S.W. C. Clear, Irish cst.

Fatehpur, *t.*, Uttar Pradesh, India; hides, grain; p. (1961) *28,323*.

Fatima, *hamlet*, W. Portugal, near Leiria; R.C. pilgrimage ctr.

Fatshan (Foshan), *c.*, Kwangtung, China; S.W. of Canton; iron and steel, textiles; p. (1953) *123,000*.

Faucilles, Les Monts, *range of hills*, connecting Vosges and Langres plateau, E. France; highest point about 1,600 ft.

Favara, *t.*, Sicily, Italy; sulphur, marble.

Faversham, *old mkt. t., mun. bor.*, Kent, Eng.; 10 m. W. Canterbury; fruit, hops, bricks, brushes, engin.; p. (estd. 1967) *14,260*.

Fawley, *t.*, Hants, Eng.; on W. shore of Southampton Water, 2 m. N.W. of Calshot; oil refining; p. (1951) *6,515*.

Fayal I., Azores; orange growing; cap. Horta.

Fayetteville, *t.*, Ark., U.S.A.; univ.; rly. and tr. ctr., agr. implements, resort; p. (1960) *20,274*.

Fayetteville, *t.*, N.C., U.S.A.; p. (1960) *47,106*.

Fear, *C.*, point of the N. Carolina cst. U.S.A.

Feather, *R.*, Cal., U.S.A.; trib. of Sacramento R.

Featherstone, *t., urb. dist.*, W.R. Yorks, Eng.; coal; p. (1961) *14,633*.

Fécamp, *sm. spt., wat. pl.*, Seine-Maritime, France; 12th cent. abbey; fishing; p. (1962) *19,851*.

Fedchenko, *glacier*, lgst in U.S.S.R.; in Pamir-Altai mtns of central Asia; 50 m.l.

Federal Dist., *st.*, Mexico; a. 431 sq. m.; p. (1960) *4,871,000*.

Fehmarn, *I.*, in W. Baltic Sea; pastureland; belongs to Schleswig-Holstein, Germany; a. 72 sq. m.; p. *12,000*.

Feilding, *t.*, Wellington, N.Z.; p. (1951) *5,810*.

Foldberg, *mtn. peak*, Black Forest, Germany; alt. 4,900 ft.

Foldkirch, *t.*, Vorarlberg, Austria; on Swiss frontier; p. (1961) *17,343*.

Felixstowe, *t., urb. dist.*, E. Suffolk, Eng.; 12 m. S.E. Ipswich; seaside resort, fertilisers; dock development; p. (1961) *17,254*.

Feltham, *see* Hounslow. [*19,000*.

Feltre, *t.*, Venetia, Italy; cath.; silk, wine; p.

Fenny Stratford, *mkt. t.*, Bucks, Eng.; 2 m. E. of Bletchley; straw-plaiting; p. *4,300*.

Fens, The, *low-lying dist.* round Wash; protected by high embankments against flooding by spring tides; includes parts of 6 English cos.

Fenton, *t.*, Staffs, Eng.; nr. Stoke-on-Trent; earthenware wks.

Feodosiya, *spt.*, Crimea, U.S.S.R.; harbour; tobacco, hosiery; p. (1956) *42,600*.

Ferbane, *vil.*, Co. Offaly, Ireland; milled peat elec. generating sta.

Ferentino, *t.*, prov. Rome, Italy; wine, olive oil; cath.; p. *14,625*.

Ferghana, *region*, Uzbek S.S.R., U.S.S.R.; deep basin at W. end of Tien Shan Mtns.; drained W. by R. Syr Darya; semi-arid but extensive irrigation system allows intensive cultivation of cotton, citrus fruits, silk, rice; ch. ts., Kokand, Namangan.

Ferghana, *t.*, Uzbekistan S.S.R.; hydro-elec., petroleum refining, textiles; deposits of ozocerite located nearby; p. (1959) *80,000*.

Fergus Falls, *t.*, Minn., U.S.A.; flour, dairy produce; p. (1960) *13,733*.

Fermanagh, *inland co.*, N. Ireland; bisected by R. Erne and lakes; cap. Enniskillen; stockraising, dairying, stone; a. 714 sq. m.; p. (1966) *49,876*.

Fermo, *c.*, Ascoli, Italy; p. *25,000*.

Fermoy, *t.*, Cork, Ireland; on R. Blackwater; p. (1966) *3,207*.

Fernando de Noronha, *st.*, consisting of Is. off E. cst. Brazil; penal sta.; p. (1960) *1,389*.

Fernando Po, *I.*, Equatorial Guinea, W. Africa; in Bight of Biafra; mtnous; coffee, cocoa, bananas, timber; p. (1968) *61,000* inc. *4,900* Europeans.

**Ferndale**, *t.*, Mich., U.S.A.; p. (1960) *31,347.*

**Fernie**, *t.*, Brit. Columbia, Canada; in Rockies, nr. Crows Nest Pass; coal.      [*97,932.*

**Ferozepore**, *t.*, Punjab, India; wheat; p. (1961)

**Ferrara**, *prov.*, N. Italy; cap. Ferrara; a. 1,019 sq. m.; p. (1961) *393,663.*

**Ferrara**, *fortfd. c.*, N. Italy; nr. head of delta of R. Po; cath., univ.; mnfs. silk, hemp, wine; mkt. for fertile plain; oil refinery nearby; petrochemicals; p. (1961) *151,145.*

**Ferro**, *most S.W. I.*, Canary Is.; a. 106 sq. m.; was chosen by Fr. scientists (1630) as first meridian; cap. Valverde.

**Ferrol**, *spt.*, *naval arsenal*, Spain; on N.W. cst. nr. Corunna; p. (1950) *77,030.*

**Ferryhill**, *vil.*, Durham, Eng.; 5 m. S. of Durham, in gap through limestone ridge which separates Wear valley from Tees valley; commands main N. to S. route along lowland E. of Pennines.

**Fertile Crescent**, an arc of fertile land from the Mediterranean Sea, N. of the Arabian Desert, to Persian Gulf; home of some very early civilisations and migrations.

**Festiniog**, *see* Ffestiniog.

**Fethiye**, *spt.*, Turkey; opp. Rhodes; p. (1960) *7,652.*

**Fetlar I.**, Shetland Is., Scot.; 6¼ m. long by 2¾ m. wide.

**Feuerbach**, *industl. c.*, Baden–Württemberg, Germany; N.W. sub. of Stuttgart; sandstone; p. (1963) *27,000.*

**Fez**, *c.*, Morocco, N. Africa; lies inland 100 m. E. of Rabat; one of the sacred cities of Islam; univ. attached to mosque (one of lgst. in Africa); impt. comm. ctr.; p. (1960) *216,133.*

**Fezzan**, *prov.*, Libya, N. Africa; numerous wells and inhabited oases.

**Ffestiniog (Festiniog)**, *urb. dist.*, Merioneth, N. Wales; at head of Vale of Ffestiniog 9 m. E. of Portmadoc; contains vils. of Ffestiniog and Blaenau Ffestiniog; impt. slate quarries; world's lgst pumped-storage hydroelec. sta. (1963); cement; p. (1961) *6,677.*

**Fianarantsoa**, *t.*, Malagasy; p. (1957) *34,845.*

**Fichtelgebirge (Fir Mtns.)**, *mtn. range*, N.E. Bavaria, Germany; highest peak, Schneeberg; alt. 3,454 *ft.*

**Fife**, *peninsula, co.*, E. Scot.; between the F. of Tay and Forth; *co. t.* Cupar; a. 492 sq. m.; p. (1961) *320,541.*

**Fife Ness**, extreme E. point, Fife, Scot.

**Figuéira da Foz**, *t.*, Portugal; resort at mouth of R. Mondego; corn, wine; p. (1960) *10,855.*

**Figuéras**, *fortfd. t.*, Gerona, Spain; nr. French frontier; glass, cork, leather; p. (1957) *16,589.*

**Fiji**, *archipelago of* 322 coral Is. (106 inhabited) in S. Pac.; Brit. Crown Col.; forests, bananas, coconuts, sugar-cane; cap. Suva on Viti Levu I.; a. 7,083 sq. m.; p. (estd. 1965) *449,000.*

**Filey**, *t.*, *urb. dist.*, E.R. Yorks, Eng.; on E. cst. 5 m. S.E. of Scarborough; seaside resort; p. (1961) *4,705.*

**Filton**, Bristol, Glos., Eng.; aircraft wks.

**Finchley**, *former mun. bor.*, Middx., Eng., now inc. in Barnet outer bor., Greater London, (*q.v.*); residtl.; p. (1961) *69,370.*

**Findhorn**, *fishing vil.*, Moray, Scot.; resort.

**Findlay**, *mftg. t.*, Ohio, U.S.A.; on Blanchard R.; p. (1960) *30,344.*

**Findochty**, *sm. burgh.*, Banff, Scot.; p. (1961) *1,331.*

**Findon or Finnan**, *fishing vil.*, Kincardine, Scot.

**Fingal's Cave**, Staffa I., Inner Hebrides, W. Scot.; basaltic columns.

**Finistère**, *dep.*, N.W. France; cap. Quimper; cereals fruit, livestock; coal, granite; fishing; a. 2,730 sq. m., p. (1962) *749,558.*

**Finisterre**, *C.*, extreme N.W. point of Spain.

**Finland**, *rep.*, Europe, low-lying tableland, glaciated, innumerable lakes; forested; oats, rye, barley, potatoes; timber, wood-pulp, textiles; iron mining; official languages, Finnish and Swedish (Swedish names mainly as alternatives on W. cst.); mainly agr.; cap. Helsinki; a. 117,975 sq. m.; p. (1966) *4,626,956.*

**Finland**, G. of, E. arm of Baltic Sea, 250 m.

**Finnart**, Dunbartonshire, Scot.; oil terminal situated in Loch Long, N.W. Glasgow; pipeline to Grangemouth.

**Finnmark**, *most northerly co.*, Norway; inhabited by Lapps; whale fisheries; lge. copper deposits discovered nr. Reppan fjord; a. 18,581 sq. m.; p. (1963) *73,229.*

**Finsbury**, *see* Islington.

**Finsteraarhorn**, *mtn.*, Switzerland, (14,023 ft.) highest peak in Bernese Oberland.

**Finsterwalde**, *t.*, Cottbus, E. Germany; textiles, furniture, metallurgy, glass; p. (1963) *21,117.*

**Finucane I.**, *pt.*, W. Australia; deepwater pt. to ship iron ore and new t. projected.

**Fir Mountains**, *see* Fichtelgebirge.

**Firenze**, *see* Florence.

**Firminy**, *mftg. t.*, Loire, France; S.E. of St. Etienne; p. (1954) *21,161.*

**Fishguard and Goodwick**, *spt.*, *urb. dist.*, N. Pembroke, Wales; on S. of Cardigan Bay; steamer connection to Cork and Rosslare (Ireland); p. (1961) *4,898.*      [machin.; p. (1960) *43,021.*

**Fitchburg**, *c.*, Mass., U.S.A.; woollens, paper,

**Fitzroy**, *R.*, W. Australia; flows into King Sound.

**Fiume**, *see* Rijeka.      [p. *17,550.*

**Fivizzano**, *t.*, Tuscany, Italy; mineral springs;

**Flagstaff**, *t.*, Arizona, U.S.A.; seat of Lowell Univ.; p. (1960) *18,214.*

**Flamborough Head**, *C.*, Yorks cst. Eng.; chalk cliffs, alt. 500 ft.; lighthouse.

**Fläming**, *heathland*, Potsdam, E. Germany; occupies low sandy ridge, alt. below 800 ft., 50 m. S.W. of Berlin; heathland, coniferous woodland; former military training a.

**Flanders**, *dist.*, Belgium. divided into two provs. of W. (1,248 sq. m., p. (1962) *1,075,949*) and E. (1,147 sq. m., p. (1962) *1,276,803*; caps. Bruges and Ghent.      [*4,515.*

**Flat River**, *c.*, Mo., U.S.A.; lead mines; p. (1960)

**Flattery Cape**, on Pacific cst., Wash., U.S.A.

**Flèche, La**, *t.*, Sarthe, France; nr. Le Mans; p. (1962) *14,392.*

**Fleet**, *t.*, *urb. dist.*, Hants, Eng.; 4 m. N.W. of Aldershot; p. (estd. 1967) *20,650.*

**Fleetwood**, *spt.*, *mun. bor.*, Lancs., Eng.; at mouth of Wyre; fishing; lge. chemical plant projected nearby; p. (estd. 1967) *28,630.*

**Flémalle**, 2 *communes*, Liége prov., Belgium; glass; p. (1962) *13,857.*

**Flensburg**, *spt.*, Schleswig-Holstein, Germany; on Baltic cst.; coal; shipbldg., machin., iron, chemicals, fishing; p. (1963) *97,000*

**Flevosted**, *t.*, Netherlands; administrative ctr. of new S.E. Polder.      [G. of Carpentaria.

**Flinders**, *R.*, Queensland, Australia; flowing to

**Flinders Range**, *mtns.*, S. Australia; extend 250 m. N.E. from head of Spencer G.; alt. 3,900 ft.

**Flin Flon**, *t.*, Manitoba, Canada; 90 m. by rly. N. of The Pas; ctr. of gold-mining a.; p. (1961) *11,104.*

**Flint**, *co.*, Wales; stock-raising; coal, iron, steel, textiles, chemicals; a. 257 sq. m.; p. (1966) *161,000.*

**Flint**, *c.*, Mich., U.S.A.; motor cars, lumber, woollens, aeroplane engines; p. (1960) *196,940.*

**Flint**, *mun. bor.*, *co. t.*, Flint, Wales; viscose textile yarn, pulp; p. (1961) *13,690.*

**Flint I.**, (Brit.), Pac. Oc.; uninhabited.

**Flodden**, *vil.*, Northumberland, Eng.; on R. Till; famous battle 1513, James IV of Scotland defeated by the Earl of Surrey.

**Flora**, *c.*, Sogn og Fjordane, Norway; new c. 85 m. N. of Bergen; p. (1965) *7,700.*

**Florange**, *t.*, Moselle, France; p. (1962) *14,270.*

**Florence (Firenze)**, *c.*, Tuscany, Italy; on R. Arno; leather-work; famous for art treasures, cath. and churches; ruled by Medici 1421–1737; birthplace of Dante and Michelangelo; severely affected by heavy floods Nov. 1966; p. (1965) *454,000.*

**Florence**, *c.*, N.W. Ala., U.S.A.; iron, textiles, lumber, food; airport; p. (1960) *31,649.*

**Florence**, *t.*, S.C., U.S.A.; p. (1960) *24,722.*

**Flores**, *I.*, most north-westerly of the Azores gr.; Portuguese; cap. Santa Cruz; French to set up ballistic missiles tracking sta.

**Flores**, *I.*, Indonesia; divided between Indonesia and Portugal; mountainous, volcanic, densely forested; a. 8,870 sq. m.; p. *500,000.*

**Flores**, *dep.*, Uruguay; cap. Trinidad; a. 1,744 sq. m.; p. (1953) *35,565.*      [nesia.

**Flores Sea**, between Sulawesi and Flores, Indo-

**Florianopolis**, *spt.*, cap. Santa Catarina st., Brazil; cst tr.; p. (1960) *98,520.*

**Florida**, *st.*, U.S.A.; between Atlantic and G. of Mexico; resort a.; tourism; lumber, paper, minerals; fruit, vegetables, sugar, cotton; cattle raising; cap. Tallahassee; a. 58,560 sq. m.; p. (1960) *4,951,560.*

**Florida**, *dep.*, Uruguay; cap. Florida; a. 4,673 sq. m.; p. (1953) *106,284.*

Floridabanca, *t.*, Luzon, Philippine Is.; sugar, rice; p. *17,521.*

Florida Strait, between Florida and Bahama Is.; course of " Gulf Stream " from Gulf of Mexico.

Florina, *see* Phlorina.

Fiume, The, picturesque gorge, Franconia Mtns., N.H., U.S.A.

Flushing, *see* Vlissingen.

Flushing Meadow, *t.*, Flushing Bay, Long Island, N.Y., U.S.A.; U.N.O. meeting place.

Fly, *R.*, New Guinea; flows S.E. to G. of Papua.

Fochabers, *vil.*, Moray, Scot.; nr. mouth of Spey; tourist resort; food canning ind.

Focsani, *t.*, Putna dist., Romania; on R. Milkov; soap, petroleum (1963) *36,854.*

Foggia, *prov.*, Apulia, S. Italy; a. 2,683 sq. m.; p. (1961) *632,332.*

Foggia, *t.*, S. Italy, Apulia; cath.; industl.; p. (1961) *117,485.*

Fogo, *I.*, Atl. Oc.; in Cape Verde gr.; volcanic.

Folda Fjord, W. coast, Norway.

Foligno, *t.*, Perugia, Italy; remarkable grotto; numerous factories; p. (1961) *48,069.*

Folkestone, *spt.*, *mun. bor.*, Kent, Eng.; seaside resort, pt. for Folkestone–Boulogne route to France 29 m.; p. (estd. 1967) *43,880.*

Fond du Lac, *mfg. t.*, Winnebago Lake, Wis., U.S.A.; cath.; p. (1960) *32,719.*

Fonsagrada, *industl. t.*, Lugo, Spain; p. (1957) *13,925.*

Fonseca Bay, *inlet* on Pacific cst. of C. America, bordering on Nicaragua; U.S.A. naval base; (U.S.A. have acquired the option for a canal route through Nicaragua).

Fontainebleau, *t.*, Seine-et-Marne, France; on R. Seine, 35 m. S.E. of Paris; magnificent forest (a. 42,500 acres) and palace; porcelain; Ecole d'Artillerie; p. (1962) *22,704.*

Fontenay-le-Comte, *industl. t.*, Vendée, France; p. (1962) *12,104.* [Paris: p. (1954) *36,739.*

Fontenay-sous-Bois, *t.*, Seine, France; sub. of Fontenoy, *vil.*, Belgium; nr. Tournai; battle, 1745; Marshall Saxe defeated the Allies under Duke of Cumberland; p. (1962) *639.*

Fontevrault, *t.*, dep. Maine-et-Loire, France.

Foochow (Fuzhou), *c.*, Fukien, China; former treaty pt.; gr. tea-exporting ctr.; p. (1953) *553,000.*

Foots Cray, *sm. t.*, Kent, Eng.; paper-mills.

Forbach, *t.*, Moselle, France; p. (1962) *22,106.*

Forbes, *t.*, N.S.W., Australia; mkt. ctr.; sm. mnfg.; p. (1966) *7,370.*

Fordingbridge, *mkt. t.*, Hants, Eng.; on R. Avon, sail-cloth; p. *3,394.*

Fordlandia, *t.*, Para, N.E. Brazil; on Tapajoz R.; one of the Ford rubber plantations.

Foreland, N. and S., two headlands, on E. cst. of Kent, Eng.; lighthouse.

Forest Hill, *t.*, Ontario, Canada; p. (1961) *20,489.*

Forest Hills, *residtl. a.*, part of Queen's bor., N.Y., U.S.A.; on Long I.; p. *21,400.*

Forest Park, *t.*, Georgia, U.S.A.; p. (1961) *14,201.*

Forfar, *burgh.*, Angus, Scot.; in Strathmore, 17 m. S.W. of Montrose; linen, jute; p. (1961) *10,252.*

Forlì, *ancient c.*, Emilia Italy; silk factories, ironwks.; felt; p. (1961) *91,146.*

Formby, *t.*, *urb. dist.*, Lancs, Eng.; on W. cst., 6 m. S.W. of Southport; p. (1961) *11,730.*

Formentera, *I.*, Balearic Is., S. of Ibiza; 13 m. long; cereals, wine, tunny fishing; p. (1957) *2,657.*

Formia, *t.*, Caserta, Italy; the ancient Formiæ.

Formigine, *t.*, Modena prov., N. Italy; silk, leather; p. *10,985.*

Formosa, *see* Taiwan.

Formosa, *prov.*, N. Argentina; bordering on Paraguay; timber; cap. Formosa; a. 27,825 sq. m.; p. (1960) *178,000.*

Fornaes, *c.*, extreme E. point of Jutland.

Forres, *burgh.*, Moray, Scot.; nr. mouth of R. Findhorn, 25 m. E. of Inverness; distilling, oat and woollen mills; p. (1961) *4,780.*

Forst, *t.*, Cottbus, E. Germany; on R. Neisse; E. section of t. Polish since 1945; textiles; p. (1963) *28,931.*

Fort Augustus, *vil.*, Inverness, Scot.; at S.W. end of Loch Ness; on Caledonian Canal; Fort now Abbey.

Fort Collins, *c.*, Col., U.S.A.; ctr. of rich farming a.; grain, sugarbeet, livestock; site of Colorado State Univ.; p. (1960) *25,027.*

Fort de France (formerly Fort Royal), *cap.*, Martinique, W. Indies; has a land-locked harbour of some 16 sq. m.; exp. rum, sugar; p. (estd. 1960) *60,648.*

Fort Dodge, *t.*, Iowa, U.S.A.; on Des Moines R., in rich agr. cty.; grain, pottery, coal; p. (1960) *28,399.*

Fort Frances, *t.*, Ontario, Canada; pulp, lumbering; p. (1961) *9,481.*

Fort George, *R.*, Labrador, Canada; flowing into James Bay.

Fort Johnson, *t.*, S. Malawi, on L. Malombe; new t., 1966; tobacco; airpt.

Fort Lamy, *t.*, *cap.*, Chad, Africa; p. (1965) *92,000.*

Fort Lamy, *t.*, *cap.*, Chad, Africa; p. *18,465.*

Fort Landerdale, *t.*, Fla., U.S.A.; prefab. bldg. mftg., concrete prod., fertilisers; p. (1960) *83,648.*

Fort Madison, *c.*, Iowa, U.S.A.; meat packing; p. (1960) *15,247.*

Fort Myers, *t.*, Fla., U.S.A.; p. (1960) *22,523.*

Fort Pierce, *t.*, Fla., U.S.A.; p. (1960) *25,256.*

Fort St. John, *t.*, B.C., Canada; on Peace R.; oilfield; p. (1961) *3,619*

Fort Scott, *t.*, Kan., U.S.A.; maize, wheat, cattle; p. (1960) *9,410.*

Fort Smith, *c.*, Ark., U.S.A.; on Arkansas R.; rly. ctr., cotton, maize, wagons, furniture; p. (1960) *52,991.*

Fort Victoria, *t.*, Rhodesia; agr. and mining ctr., cattle; historic ruins in Zimbabwe Nat. Park; p. (1958) *10,700* (incl. *1,700* Europeans).

Fort Wayne, *c.*, Ind., U.S.A.; rly.-carriage bldg. and machine shops; p. (1960) *161,776.*

Fort William, *c.*, Ontario, Canada; on L. Superior; grain pt.; p. (1961) *45,214.*

Fort William, *burgh*, Inverness, Scot.; nr. head of Loch Linnhe, at base of Ben Nevis; aluminium factory; pulp- and paper-mill at Corpach; p. (1961) *2,715.*

Fort Worth, *c.*, Texas, U.S.A.; rly. and comm. ctr. on Trinity R.; livestock and grain mkt.; petroleum, meat packing, aeroplanes, oilfield equipment; site of Texas Christian Univ.; p. (1960) *356,268.*

Fort Yukon, Alaska, U.S.A.; trading sta. on Yukon R.; p. *274.*

Fortaleza, *cap.*, Ceará st., Brazil; exp. sugar, rubber, cotton, carnauba wax; p. (1960) *514,818.*

Fortescue, *R.*, W. Australia.

Forth, *R.*, Scot.; rises on Ben Lomond, and flows E. into F. of Forth nr. Alloa; length 65 m.

Forth Bridge, *rly. bridge*, Scot.; spans F. of Forth between N. and S. Queensferry; length 1½ m. Forth road bridge (suspension) just upstream opened 1964; length 5,980 ft.

Forth, Firth of, *lge. inlet*, E. cst. of Scot.; submerged estuary of R. Forth; navigable by lge. vessels for 40 m. inland to Grangemouth; [other pts., Leith, Rosyth (naval), Bo'ness; length (to Alloa) 50 m., width varies from 1 to 13 m.

Forth and Clyde Canal, Scot.; links F. of Forth at Grangemouth, and F. of Clyde at Glasgow; length 38 m.

Fortrose, *t.*, *burgh*, Ross and Cromarty, Scot.; on S. cst. of Black Isle, on Moray Firth; p. (1961) *902.* [Canada.

Fortune Bay, *inlet*, S. cst. of Newfoundland, Fossano, *t.*, Italy; nr. Turin; cath.; paper, silk; p. *21,850.*

Fos-sur-mer, *t.*, Bouches-du-Rhône, S. France; nr. Marseilles; deepwater pt.; oil refinery.

Fostoria, *t.*, Ohio, U.S.A.; glass, quarries, stockyards; p. (1960) *15,732.*

Fotheringhay, *vil.*, on R. Nene, Northampton, Eng.; Mary Queen of Scots beheaded in F. Castle, 1587.

Fougères, *t.*, Ille-et-Vilaine, France; cas.; p. (1962) *25,171.*

Fougerolles, *t.*, Haute-Saône, France; p. (1962) *4,234.*

Foula, *I.*, Shetland Is., Scot.; westward of main gr.

Foulness Island, Essex, Eng.

Foulweather, *C.*, Ore., U.S.A.

Fountains Abbey, fine ruin, Cistercian, founded 1132, W.R. Yorks, Eng.; nr. Ripon.

Fourmies, *t.*, Nord, France; nr. Valenciennes; p. (1954) *13,414.*

Foveaux Strait, N.Z.; separates S.I. from Stewart I.

Fowey, *spt.*, *mun. bor.*, Cornwall, Eng.; on W. of Fowey estuary, 22 m. W. of Plymouth; seaside resort, fishing; exp. kaolin; p. (1961) *2,237.*

**Fox Is.**, one of the Aleutian Is. gr.

**Foxe Basin and Channel**, to N. of Hudson Bay, between Baffin I. and Southampton I.

**Foxe Peninsula**, Baffin I., Franklin, Canada.

**Foyers**, *falls*, Inverness, Scot. ; E. of Loch Ness, nr. Fort Augustus ; aluminium wks., hydro-elec. scheme.

**Foyle, Lough**, estuary of Foyle R., between Donegal and Londonderry, N. Ireland.

**Foynes Is.**, R.O.I. ; oil terminal on N. side, E. of Battery Point.

**Framingham**, *industl. t.*, Mass., U.S.A. ; 10 m. W. of Boston ; p. (1960) 44,526.

**Framlingham**, *mkt. t.*, E. Suffolk, Eng. ; 15 m. N.E. of Ipswich.

**Franca**, *c.*, São Paulo st., Brazil ; 160 m. N. of Campinas ; p. (1960) 47,244.          [p. 21,375.

**Francavilla**, *t.*, Lecce, Italy ; wine, oil, leather ;

**France**, *rep.* (*former monarchy and empire*), W. Europe, bounded N. by Belgium and English Channel, W. by the Bay of Biscay, S. by the Pyrenees and the Mediterranean, E. by Italy, Switzerland and Germany. Greatest length about 600 m., greatest breadth 540 m. ; a. 212,600 sq. m., or 3½ times size of England and Wales ; F. is divided into 90 metropolitan deps. ; ch. ts. are Paris (the cap., the fifth lgst. c. in Europe), Bordeaux, Marseilles, Lyons, Lille, Nice and Toulouse : 19 univs. ; ch. mtns. : Cevennes, Jura, Vosges, Pyrenees ; ch. Rs.: Seine, Loire, Rhône, Garonne ; climate, temperate ; agr. : wheat, oats, potatoes, sugar-beet, vine, fruits, silk, cattle, sheep, dairying ; minerals : coal, iron, bauxite, potash ; mnfs.: iron and steel, machin., textiles ; communications excellent ; p. of the Rep. (1965) 48,492,700. The French Community was set up in 1959 as successor to the French Union.

**Franceville**, *t.*, Gabon, Equatorial Africa ; on R. Ogowe ; manganese mines opened 1962.

**Francisco Morazán**, *dep.* central Honduras ; a. 3,870 sq. m. ; p. (1961) 284,540.

**Francis Lake**, *L.*, Yukon Canada.    [p. 10,000.

**Francistown**, *gold-mining t.*, Botswana, Africa ;

**Frankental**, *t.*, Rhineland Palatinate, Germany ; N.W. of Mannheim ; engin., farm implements, metallurgy, cork ; p. (1963) 35,800.

**Frankfort**, *t.*, Ky., U.S.A. ; mining, horse-breeding ; p. (1960) 18,365.

**Frankfort**, *t.*, Ind., U.S.A. ; p. (1960) 15,302.

**Frankfurt-on-Main**, *c.*, Hessen, W. Germany ; restored cath. ; univ. ; birthplace of Goethe ; machin., cars, chemicals, publishing, elec. engin., transhipment pt., airfield ; p. (1963) 694,200.

**Frankfurt-on-Oder**, *t.*, E. Germany ; 50 m. from Berlin ; gr. route ctr. ; machin., iron ; E. section of t. (Slubice) Polish since 1945 ; p. (1963) 58,339.

**Frankischer (Franconian) Jura**, *plateau with steep N.-facing edge*, S.W. Germany ; runs 80 m. S.W. from Fichtel Gebirge (Fir Mtns.), highest elevation just exceeds 3,000 ft. ; drained by Regnitz Altmühl ; slate quarrying ; vine, maize in sheltered valleys.

**Franklin**, *t.*, N.H., U.S.A. ; p. (1960) 6,742.

**Franklin**, *bor.*, N.J., U.S.A. ; ctr. of U.S. zinc ind. ; p. (1960) 3,624.

**Franklin**, *c.*, Penns., U.S.A. ; petroleum, oil-well tools, rolling stock ; p. (1960) 9,556.

**Franklin**, *t.*, Tasmania, Australia ; 20 m. from Hobart ; principal fruit-growing dist. in the island.

**Franklin**, *dist.*, N.W. Terr., Canada ; comprising the Is. of Arctic Canada from Banks I. to Baffin I., including Boothia Peninsula and Melville Peninsula ; sparsely populated ; furs ; a. 554,032 sq. m.

**Frantiskové Lázne** (Franzensbad), *t.*, W. Bohemia ; famous spa ; ČSSR

**Franz Josef Land**, U.S.S.R., *archipelago* in Arctic Ocean ; N. of Novaya Zemlya ; a. 7,050 sq. m. ; mainly ice-covered.

**Frascati**, *t.*, Italy ; 12 m. S.E. of Rome ; summer resort ; famous villas and arch. remains ; nuclear research ctr. ; p. 11,425.

**Fraser**, *R.*, B.C., Canada ; rises at 6,000 ft. on W. slopes Rocky Mtns. ; famous salmon fisheries ; lenth 850 m.

**Fraserburg**, *agr. t.*, Cape Province, S. Africa ; supply sta. for stock-raisers between Calvinia and Carnarvon.

**Fraserburgh**, *cst. burgh*, N.E. Aberdeen, Scot. ; extreme N.E. of Buchan peninsula ; impt. herring

fishery ; tool factory ; p. (1961) 10,462.

**Fraserville**, *t.*, Quebec, Canada ; on St. Lawrence R.

**Fratta Maggiore**, *t.*, Italy ; 6 m. from Naples ; p. 13,100.

**Frauenfeld**, *cap.*, Thurgau, Switzerland ; cas. ; cotton ; p. (1957) 10,048.

**Fray Bentos**, *t.*, *cap.*, Rio Negro, Uruguay ; on R. Uruguay 50 m. from its mouth ; meat canning and salting, meat extracts ; p. (1963) 14,000.

**Frechen**, *t.*, N. Rhine–Westphalia, Germany ; W. of Cologne ; lignite, pottery ; p. (1963) 28,000.

**Fredericia**, *spt.*, *t.*, Vejle, Jutland, Denmark ; traffic ctr., barracks ; new bridge over Little Belt ; textiles, silver and plates wks., art. fertilisers ; oil refinery projected ; p. (1960) 29,870.

**Frederick**, *c.*, Md., U.S.A. ; canning, tanning ; p. (1960) 21,744.

**Fredericksburg**, *t.*, Va., U.S.A. ; scene of severe Federal rebuff, Civil War ; p. (1960) 13,639.

**Fredericton**, *t.*, *cap.*, N.B., Canada ; on St. John R. ; univ., cath. ; lumbering ; p. (1961) 19,683.

**Frederiksberg**, *sub..* Copenhagen, Denmark ; p. (1965) 110,847.

**Frederikshaab**, *sm. spt.* on W. cst. of Greenland.

**Frederikshavn**, *spt.*, *fishing t.*, N. cst. of Jutland ; iron wks., canneries ; p. (1960) 22,522.

**Frederikstad**, *t.*, Norway ; at mouth of Glommen R. ; tr. ctr. ; pulp, paper, electrotechnical inds., shipbldg., whale oil refining ; p. (1960) 13,746.

**Fredonia**, *t.*, N.Y., U.S.A. ; p. (1960) 8,477.

**Freehold**, *t.*, N.J., U.S.A. ; p. (1960) 9,140.

**Free Port**, *mftg. t.*, Ill., U.S.A., on the Pecatonica R. ; p. (1960) 26,628.            [(1960) 34,419.

**Free Port**, *t.*, Long Island, N.Y. ; U.S.A. ; p.

**Freeport**, *spt.*, Texas ; sulphur, chemicals, magnesium from sea ; p. (1960) 11,619.

**Freetown**, *cap.*, Sierra Leone, W. Africa ; univ. ; coaling sta. ; exp. palm oil ; diesel power plant ; oil refinery being built ; p. (1963) 125,000.

**Fregenal de la Sierra**, *t.*, Spain ; nr. Badajoz ; p. (1957) 11,716.

**Freiberg**, *c.*, Karl-Marx-Stadt, Germany ; cath. ; cas. ; metallurgy, textiles, glass, porcelain ; p. (1963) 48,062.

**Freiburg (Fribourg)**, *can.*, Switzerland ; much forest and unproductive land ; a. 645 sq. m. ; p. (1961) 159,194.

**Freiburg**, *cap.*, Freiburg, Switzerland ; between Berne and Lausanne ; fine viaduct and bridges ; univ. ; machin., chocolate ; p. (1957) 29,005.

**Freiburg**, *t.*, Baden-Württemberg, Germany ; in Black Forest ; cath., univ. ; textiles, paper, metallurgy ; p. (1963) 150,400.

**Freising**, *c.*, Bavaria, Germany ; cath. ; agr. machin., textiles, brewing ; p. (1963) 28,800.

**Freital**, *t.*, Dresden, E. Germany ; coal-mining, iron, leather, glass, uranium ore processing ; p. (1963) 35,805.

**Fréjus**, *cst. t.*, Var. France ; p. (1962) 20,313.

**Fréjus**, Col de, the Alpine pass under which the Mont Cenis tunnel runs.

**Fremantle**, *c.*, *spt.*, W. Australia ; at mouth of Swan R., 12 m. S.W. from Perth, principal pt. of commerce in W. Australia and first Australian pt. of call for mail steamers ; oil refining ; whe.t, wool ; p. (1966) 32,134.

**Fremont**, *t.*, Cal., U.S.A. ; p. (1960) 43,790.

**Fremont**, *t.*, Nebraska, U.S.A. ; on Platte R. ; 33 m. from Omaha ; flourmills, canneries ; p. (1960) 19,698.

**Fremont**, *c.*, Ohio, U.S.A. ; on Sandusky R. ; petroleum field ; p. (1960) 17,573.

**Fremont's Peak**, highest peak of Wind River Range, Wyoming St., U.S.A. ; alt. 13,570 ft.

**French Equatorial Africa**, formerly comprised the French African cols. Gabon (cap. Libreville), Middle Congo (cap. Brazzaville), Ubangi-Shari (cap. Bangui), and Chad (cap. Fort Lamy) ; timber, ivory ; a. 953,740 sq. m. ; p. (1957) 4,879,000. These sts. are now indep. within Fr. Community. *See* under separate headings: Gabon, Congo, Central African Rep., Chad.

**French Guiana**, *col.*, S. America ; forests ; cocoa, gold, phosphates ; lge. deposits of bauxite at Kaw Mt. to be exploited ; poor communications ; cap. Cayenne ; a. 34,740 sq. m. ; p. (estd. 1965) 36,000.

**French**, *R.*, Ontario, Canada ; the outlet of L. Nipissing into L. Huron.

**French Somaliland**, *see* Afars and Issas.

**French Soudan**.  *See* Mali.

**French West Africa**, comprised former French cols. of Dahomey, Ivory Coast, Mauritania, Niger,

French Guinea, Upper Volta, Senegal, French Soudan.

Freshwater, *sm. t., bathing resort,* I. of Wight, Eng.; at W. end of I., 8 m. W. of Newport.

Fresnillo, *t.,* Zacatecas St., Mexico; p. *25,000.*

Fresno, *c.,* Cal., U.S.A.; ctr. of impt. irrigated fruit-growing dist.; dairying, copper, petroleum; p. (1960) *133,929.*

Friedrichshafen, *t., L. pt.,* Germany; on L. Constance; machin., boat bldg., motors; p. (1963) *39,300.*

Friedrichstal, *t.,* Saar; coal-mining, steel wks.; p. (estd. 1954) *16,400.*

Friendly Is. (Tonga), Pac. Oc.; 400 miles S.E. Fiji; independent Polynesian kingdom under Brit. protection; mild and healthy climate; ch. I., Tongatapu; cap. Nukualofa in Tongatapu; copra, bananas; a. 270 sq. m.; p. (estd.) *71,000*

Friern Barnet, *former urb. dist.,* Middx., Eng.; now inc. in Barnet outer bor., Greater London (*q.v.*); residtl.; p. (1961) *28,813.*

Friesland, *prov.,* Netherlands; cap. Leeuwarden; dairying, horses, cattle; natural gas on Ameland I.; a. 1,325 sq. m.; p. (1967) *506,311.*

Frimley and Camberley, *urb. dist.,* Surrey, Eng.; 3 m. N. of Farnborough (Hants); light engin., plastics; p. (estd. 1967) *40,660.*

Frinton and Walton, *urb. dist.,* Essex, Eng.; on E. cst., 5 m. N.E. of Clacton; deaside resort; p. (1961) *9,576.* [linen; p. *10,667.*

Friol, *commune,* Lugo, N.W. Spain; leather.

Frisches Haff, *shallow freshwater lagoon,* Baltic cst. of Poland; 53 m. long, 4–11 m. broad.

Frische Nehrung, *sandspit,* G. of Gdansk, Baltic Sea; astride bdy. between Poland, U.S.S.R.; almost separates Frisches Haff (Zalew Wislany) from G. of Gdansk; length 36 m.

Frisian Islands, *chain of Is.* stretching from Zuyder Zee and N. to Jutland, along the csts. of the Netherlands and N. Germany; ch. Is. are Texel, Vlieland and Ameland.

Friuli-Venezia Giulia, *aut. reg.* (created 1963), N.E. Italy; comprising 3 provs. Udine (p. *800,000*), Gorizia (p. *140,000*), and Trieste (p. *300,000*); cap. Trieste.

Frobisher Bay, *inlet* in S. Baffin I., N. Canada, extending 200 m. between Cumberland Sound and Hudson Strait.

Frodingham, *t.,* Lincoln, Eng.; on W. flank of limestone ridge, Lincoln Edge; impt. iron-ore open-cast mines; mnfs. iron and steel; p. (1961) *67,257* (with Scunthorpe).

Frodsham, *mkt. t.,* Cheshire, Eng.; 10 m. N.E. Chester; chemicals.

Frome, *mkt. t., urb. dist.,* Somerset, Eng.; on R. Frome, 11 m. S. of Bath; woollens, printing, brewing, iron, metal and plastic wks.; p. (1961) *11,440.*

Frontignan, *t.,* Herault, S. France; oil refining; oil pipeline under sea from Sete; p. (1962) *8,309.*

Frosinone, *industl. t.,* Lazio, Italy; on R. Cosa; p. (1961) *30,796.*

Froward, *C.,* Magallanes prov., Southern Chile.

Frunze, *cap.,* Kirgiz S.S.R.; univ.; meat packing, engin., textiles; p. (1967) *370,000.*

Fthiotis and Focis, *pref.,* Greece; cap. Lamia; p. (1951) *199,794.*

Fucino, *L. (now drained),* Aquila, Central Italy; old volcanic crater. [(1957) *10,027.*

Fuente de Cantos, *industl. t.,* Badajoz, Spain; p.

Fuente-Ovejuna, *t.,* Cordoba, Spain; ctr. of lead-mining dist., honey prod.; p. (1957) *17,000.*

Fuerteventura, *I.,* Canary gr.; a. 663 sq. m.; p. (1962) *18,333.*

Fujisawa, *t.,* Honshu, Japan; bearings machin.; p. (1965) *175,183.*

Fujiyama, extinct volcano, Japan, 60 m. S.W. of Tokyo; pilgrim resort; alt. 12,395 ft.

Fukien (Fujian) *prov.,* China; cap. Foochow (Fuzhou); tea, rice, cotton, sugar, tobacco; paper, coal, gold, silver; a. 45,845 sq. m.; p. (1953) *13,142,721.* [169,636.

Fukui, *t.,* Honshu, Japan; silk, paper; p. (1965)

Fukuoka, *t.,* Kyushu, Japan; comm. ctr.; silk, fabrics, dolls; p. (1965) *749,808.*

Fukushima, *c.,* N. Japan; chemicals, coal, iron prod.; pears, cherries; p. (1965) *173,678.*

Fukuyama, *t.,* S. Hokkaido, Japan; p. (1964) *161,000.*

Fulda, *c.,* Hessen, Germany; nr. Cassel; on R. Fulda; palace, abbey; textiles, metallurgy, rubber; route ctr.; p. (1963) *44,900.*

Fulda, *R.,* Central Germany; with the Werra forms the R. Weser.

Fulham, *see* Hammersmith.

Fullerton, *t.,* Cal., U.S.A.; p. (1950) *56,180.*

Fulton, *t.,* Mo., U.S.A.; firebrick and shoe factories; p. (1960) *11,131.*

Fulton, *c.,* N.Y., U.S.A.; woollens, cutlery, paper; p. (1960) *14,261.*

Fulwood, *urb. dist.,* Lancs, Eng.; 2 m. N.E. of Preston; p. (1961) *15,966.*

Funchal, *t., spt., cap.,* Madeira; winter resort; wine; p. (1960) *43,301.*

Fundy, Bay of, *inlet* between Nova Scotia and New Brunswick, Canada. [Tasmania.

Furneaux, *Is.,* gr. in Bass Strait, belonging to

Furness, *dist.,* N.W. Lancs, Eng.; between Morecambe Bay and the Irish Sea; haematite iron ore.

Fürstenwalde, *industl. t.,* Frankfurt, E. Germany; on R. Spree; metallurgy, leather; p. (1963) *31,881.*

Fürth, *t.,* Bavaria, Germany; nr. Nürnberg; furniture mftg., toys, metallurgy, glass, paper, radio, footwear; p. (1963) *98,300.*

Fusan, *see* Pusan.

Fushiki, *t., spt.,* Honshu, Japan; on Toyama Bay to E. of Noto Peninsula; lge. coastwise tr. in rice from Koga and Toyama plains; exp. chemicals, lumber, metals; imports metals, coal, bean-cake, flax.

Fushun, *c.,* Liaoning, N. China; at foot of Changpai Shan, 22 m. S.E. of Mukden; most impt. coal-mines in Far East; possesses world's thickest bituminous coal seam (417 ft.) worked by deep and open-cast mines; p. (1953) *679,000.*

Fushimi, *c.,* Honshu, Japan; sub. of Kyoto; p. (1965) *128,281.*

Fusin (Fuxin), *c.,* Liaoning prov., China; coal mng.; agr.; p. (1953) *105, 000.*

Futa, La, *pass,* Tusco-Emilian Apennines, N. Italy; used by main road from Bologna to Florence; alt. 2,962 ft.

Futa Jalon, *upland dist.,* mostly in Guinea, W. Africa, with outliers in Liberia and Sierra Leone.

Futuna and Alofi, *Is.,* S. of Wallis Is., dependency of Fr. col. of New Caledonia; p. about *2,000.*

Fylde, *rural dist., geographical sub-region,* W. Lancs., Eng.; extends along W. cst. between estuaries of Ribble and Wyre; low, flat plain behind coastal sand dunes, covered by fertile glacial deposits; cultivated where drained, grain, vegetables; impt. pig and poultry rearing dist.; ch. t., Blackpool, famous holiday resort; p. (rural dist., 1961) *16,928.*

Fylingdales, ballistic missile early warning station on Yorkshire moors.

Fyn, *I.,* Denmark; in the Baltic Sea; a. 1,320 sq. m.; cap. Odense; p. (1960) *376,872.*

Fyne, *loch* on Argyll cst. W. Scot.; an arm of F. of Clyde; length 40 m. [(1961) *88,296.*

Fyzabad, *t.,* Uttar Pradesh, India; sugar; p.

# G

Gabes, *spt.,* Tunisia, on G. of Gabes, 200 m. S. of Tunis; dates, henna, wool; p. (1961) *24,400.*

Gaberones, *cap.,* Botswana, S.W. Africa; cattle, sorghum, maize; manganese mng.; p. (estd. 1965) *12,000.*

Gabon, *ind. sovereign st.,* within Fr. Community, Equatorial Africa; cap. Libreville; ivory, ebony, palm-oil; a. 103,000 sq. m.; p. (estd. 1965) *458,000.*

Gadag-Betgeri, *t.,* Mysore, India; cotton and silk weaving; p. (1961) *76,614.*

Gadsen, *industl., c.,* Ala., U.S.A.; cotton, cars, coal, iron, steel; p. (1960) *58,088.*

Gaeta, *spt., fort,* Caserta, Italy; 40 m. N.W. of Naples; the ancient Caietae Portus; cath.; p. *22,882.*

Gaffney, *t.,* S.C., U.S.A.; limestone, textiles; p. (1960) *10,435.*

Gafsa, *t.,* Tunisia; phosphates; p. (1961) *24,300.*

Gaillac, *t.,* Tarn, France; wines; p. (1962) *9,058.*

Gaillard Cut, *excavated channel,* Panama Canal Zone; carries Panama Canal through Culebra Mtn. from L. Gatun to Pac. Oc.; length 7 m.

Gainesville, *t.,* Fla., U.S.A.; p. (1960) *29,701.*

Gainesville, *t.,* Ga., U.S.A.; p. (1960) *16,523.*

Gainesville, *t.,* Texas, U.S.A.; p. (1960) *13,093.*

Gainsborough, *mkt. t., urb. dist.,* Lincs., Eng.; on R. Trent, 15 m. N.W. of Lincoln; shipping, agr. implements, engin., milling, malting, timber; p. (1961) *17,276.*                [broad.

Gairdner, *L.,* S. Australia; 130 m. long, 23 m.

Galápagos, *volcanic Is.,* Pac. Oc.; 600 m. W. Ecuador; consists of 12 lge. and several 100 sm. Is.; only 5 inhabited; administered by Ecuador; peculiar fauna and flora; guano; a. 2,868 sq. m.; p. (1962) *2,412.*

Galashiels, *burgh,* Selkirk, Scot.; on Gala Water, 2 m. above confluence with R. Tweed; tweeds, woollens; p. (1961) *12,374.*

Galați, *Black Sea pt.,* Romania, on Danube R.; naval base; engin., steel; p. (1963) *111,906.*

Galatina, *t.,* Apulia, Italy; p. *20,300.*

Galena, *t.,* Ill., U.S.A.; lead, zinc, marble, granite; p. (1960) *4,410.*

Galesburg, *t.,* Ill., U.S.A.; engin.; p. (1960) *37,243.*

Galicia, *former Austrian prov.,* Polish 1918–39, since 1939 E. part transferred to Ukrainian S.S.R. and W. remaining Polish (provs. Kraków and Rzeszów).

Galicia, *old prov.,* N.W. Spain; now forming provs. of La Coruña, Lugo, Orense and Pontevedra; mountainous; dairying; mining, lead, copper, iron; p. (1957) *2,600,000.*

Galilee, *N. div.* of Palestine in Roman period, containing Capernaum, Nazareth.

Galilee, Sea of (Lake Tiberias), also known as L. Gennesaret; 13 m. l., 6 m. wide, 150 ft. deep, 680 ft. below level of Med.; Israel plans to draw water from L. to irrigate Negev.

Galion, *t.,* Ohio, U.S.A.; mftg.; rly. ctr.; p. (1960) *12,650.*

Galla and Sidamo, *prov.,* Ethiopia.

Galle, *spt.,* Ceylon; on S.W. cst.; extensive tr. in tea, coconut oil, cement; p. (1963) *64,942*

Galleana, *mkt. t.,* Leon Prov., Mexico; at foot of Sierra Madre Oriental, 120 m. S. of Monterrey; focus of tr. between tropical lowlands and high plateau.

Gallego, *R.,* N.E. Spain; rises in Pyrenees, flows S. to R. Ebro at Zaragoza; R. provides water for irrigation around Zaragoza; valley used by main rly. across Pyrenees from Pau (France) to Zaragoza; length 110 m.

Gallegos, *t., cap.,* Santa Cruz terr., Argentina; p. *7,003.*                    [p. *12,200.*

Gallipoli, *spt.,* Italy; on E. shore G. of Taranto;

Gallipoli, *see* Gelibolu.

Gallipolis, *t.,* Ohio U.S.A.; p. (1950) *7 871.*

Gällivare, *dist.,* N. Sweden; inside Arctic Circle, 120 m. N.W. of Lulea; iron ore; p. *26,200.*

Galloway, *dist.,* S.W. Scot.; inc. the cos. of Wigtown and Kirkcudbright.

Galloway, Mull of, extreme S.W. point of Scot.

Gallup, *t.,* N.M., U.S.A.; coal, wool, sheep, cattle rearing; p. (1960) *14,089.*

Galston, *burgh,* Ayr, Scot.; on R. Irvine, nr. Kilmarnock; hosiery, lace; p. (1961) *4,023.*

Galt, *t.,* Ontario, Canada; mnfs.; p. (1961) *27,830.*

Galty Mtns., Tipperary, Ireland; alt. 3,000 ft.

Galveston, *c., spt.,* Texas, U.S.A.; on I. in G. of Mexico; gr. cotton pt.; mills, foundries; p. (1960) *67,175.*

Galway, *co.,* Galway Bay, Connacht, Ireland; fishery, cattle, marble quarrying; a. 2,452 sq. m.; p. (1966) *148,190.*

Galway, *t. cap.,* Galway, Ireland; univ.; p. (1966) *24,495.*

Gambela, *tr. sta.,* leased to Sudan by Ethiopia.

Gambia, *indep. sov. st.* within Brit. Commonwealth (1965), W. Africa; narrow terr., average 20 m. wide, extends 200 m. inland astride R. Gambia; hot all year, summer rain; savannah grassland; ground-nuts, palm-kernals, beeswax, hides; cap. Bathurst; a. 4,003 sq. m.; p. (estd. 1964) *315,999.*

Gambia, *R.,* Fr. W. Africa and Gambia, rises in Futa Jallon Plateau, flows N. and W. into Atl. Oc. at Bathurst; forms main means of communication through Gambia.                [(1961) *5,725.*

Gander, *airport.* Newfoundland, Canada; p.

Gandhinagar, *new cap.,* Gujarat, India; on Sabarmati R. 13 m. N. of Ahmedabad; under construction; planned initial p. *75,000* rising to *200,000.*

Gandia, *t. spt.,* Valencia, Spain; fruit exp.; silk spinning p. (1957) *20,160.*

Ganges (Ganga), *gr. sacred R.,* India; rises in Himalayas and flows to Bay of Bengal, by several delta mouths, on one of which stands Calcutta. Delta very fertile and densely populated. Navigable for lge. ships from Allahabad; length 1,500 m.

Gangtok, *t., cap.* Sikkim, E. Himalayas; trade ctr., carpets; p. (1965) *12,000.*      [(1961) *1,872.530.*

Ganjam, *dist.,* Orissa, India; a. 4,324 sq. m.; p.

Gap, *c.,* Hautes Alpes, S.E. France; silk and other textiles; p. (1962) *21,935.*

Gard, *Mediterranean dep.,* France; cap., Nîmes; vines, olives, sericulture; a. 2,270 sq. m.; p. (1962) *435,482.*

Garda, *L.,* between Lombardy and Venezia, Italy; a. 143 sq. m.; greatest depth, 1,135 ft.

Garden City, *t.,* Mich., U.S.A.; p. (1960) *38,017.*

Garden City, *t.,* N.Y., U.S.A.; p. (1960) *23,948.*

Garden Grove, *t.,* Cal., U.S.A.; p. (1960) *84,238.*

Gardena, *t.,* S.W. Cal., U.S.A.; mkt.-gardening; p. (1960) *35,943.*

Gardiner, *t.,* Me., U.S.A.; p. (1960) *6,897.*

Gardner, *t.,* Mass., U.S.A.; chair mftg.; p. (1960) *19,038.*

Garfield, *t.,* N.J., U.S.A., p. (1960) *29,253.*

Garfield Heights, *t.,* Ohio, U.S.A.; iron, steel, oil refineries, abrasives; p. (1960) *38,455.*

Garforth, *urb. dist.,* W.R. Yorks, Eng.; p. (1961) *14,641*

Garigliano, Italy; nuclear power plant projected.

Garland, *t.,* Texas, U.S.A.; p. *38,501.*

Garmisch-Partenkirchen, *t.,* Bavaria, Germany; winter sports; p. (1963) *26,600.*

Garo Hills, *mountainous dist.,* Assam, India; a. 3,119 sq. m.; dense forests; p. (1961) *307,228.*

Garonne, *R.,* S.W. France; rises at foot of Mt. Maladetta (Pyrenees), and enters the Gironde estuary 20 m. below Bordeaux; length 350 m.

Garonne, Haute, *dep.,* S. France · a. 2,458 sq. m.; p. (1962) *594,633.*

Garrigue, *region,* Languedoc, S. France; low limestone hills, run N.E. to S.W., W. of Rhône delta; semi-arid; scanty vegetation; winter pasture for sheep, olives; Montpellier, Nîmes located on S. flank.

Garston, *spt.,* southern end Bootle and Liverpool docks; Lancs, Eng.; docks; p. *28,000.*

Garut, *t.,* W. Java, Indonesia; mtn. resort; p. *24,219.*

Gary, *c.,* Ind., U.S.A.; at S. end of L. Michigan; steel, tin-plate, cement, soap, chemicals, oil refining; p. (1960) *178,321.*

Gascony, *ancient prov., duchy,* S.W. France.

Gaspé, *peninsula,* Quebec, Canada; on S. side of St. Lawrence.

Gastein, *t.,* Salzburg, Austria; mineral springs.

Gastonia, *c.,* N.C., U.S.A.; p. (1960) *37,276.*

Gateshead, *t., co. bor.,* Durham, Eng.; on R. Tyne, opp. Newcastle; engin.; p. (estd. 1967) *100,780.*

Gatineau, *R.,* Canada; trib. of Ottawa R., which it joins nr. Ottawa; length 300 m.

Gatooma, *t.,* Rhodesia; farming, mining and cotton mnfs., gold, mineral deposits; p. (1958) *10,000* (incl. *2,000* Europeans).

Gatun, *artificial L.,* Panama Canal Zone, Central America; passed through by Panama Canal; alt. 40 ft. above Caribbean Sea; a. 250 sq. m.

Gatwick, Surrey–Sussex border; 25 m. S. London; 1st airport in world where trunk road, main rly. line and air facilities combined in one unit.

Gauhati, *t.,* Assam, India; univ.; silk, cotton, lace, oil refinery; oil pipeline from Barauni; p. (1961) *100,702.*

Gauri-Sankar, *mtn.* in Himalayas; 35 m. W. of Mt. Everest; alt. 23,440 ft.

Gävle, *spt.,* Sweden; timber, textiles, steel, porcelain; p. (1961) *54,768.*

Gävleborg, *co.,* Sweden; ch. t., Gävle; a. 7,610 sq. m.; p. (1961) *293,070.*

Gaya, *t.,* Bihar, India; famous Buddhist pilgrim ctr.; cottons, silks; p. (1961) *151,105.*

Gayyarah, Mosul, Iraq; bitumen refinery.

Gaza, *spt.,* U.A.R.; exp. cereals, wool; p. *c. 100,000.*

Gaza Strip, *cstl. a.* under Egyptian admin. since 1949; occupied by Israeli troops, Nov. 1956–March 1957, and since June 1967.

Gaziantep, *t.,* Turkey; S.W. of Malatya; p. (1965) *158,367.*

Gazli, Uzbekistan S.S.R.; 60 m. N.W. of Bukhara; natural gas field discovered mid-1950's; pipeline to Chelyabinsk opened Nov. 1963.

Gdansk *prov. (woivodship),* Poland; ch. t. Gdansk (Danzig); a. 4,290 sq. m.; p. (1965) *1,853,000.*

Gdansk (Danzig), *spt.,* Poland; on R. Vistula; impt. Baltic pt.; Prussian, 1814–1919; free city under Treaty of Versailles; annexed to Germany, 1939; restored to Poland, 1945; industr. and comm. ctr.; shipbldg., machin., chemicals, metals; p. (1965) *319,000*.

**Gdynia**, *spt.*, Poland; built by Poland as pt. after 1924 when Danzig was a free city; impt. comm. pt.; rly. ctr.; metal, machin., food inds.; p. (1965) *165,000*.

**Géant, Aiguille du,** *mtn.* in Savoy Alps, France; alt. 13,170 ft.; nearby Col du Géant, pass from Chamonix to Italy, alt. 11,145 ft.

**Geel,** *t.*, Belgium; 30 m. E. of Antwerp; nuclear power plant projected.

**Geelong,** *spt.*, Port Phillip, Victoria, Australia; fine harbour; tr. in flour, wool; oil refining; aluminium, agr. machin.; superphosphates; cars, carpets; p. (1966) *104,974*.

**Geislingen,** *t.*, Wurttemberg, Germany; p. (1963)

**Gela,** *t.*, S. Sicily, Italy; in cotton growing a.; petro chemicals; p. (1961) *54,774*.

**Gelderland,** *prov.*, Netherlands; E. and S. of Utrecht prov.; a. 1,939 sq. m.; cap. Arnhem; cereals, tobacco; cattle rearing; p. (1967) *1,434,439*.

**Gelibolu, (Gallipoli),** *t.* and *peninsula* on the Dardanelles, Turkey; vines, sericulture; scene of unsuccessful landing by British and Anzac troops 1915; p. (1960) *12,956*.

**Gelligaer,** *t.*, *urb. dist.*, Glamorgan, Wales; 4 m. N.E. of Pontypridd; mining; p. rural dist. (1961) *34,572*.

**Gelsenkirchen,** *t.*, N. Rhine–Westphalia, Germany; nr. Dortmund; collys., ironwks., glass, chemicals, oil refining; p. (1963) *380,600*.

**Gemmi,** *mtn.* pass across Swiss Alps, Valais to Berne; alt. 7,600 ft. [cattle; p. *14,500*.

**General Pico,** *t.*, S. central Argentina; grain,

**Geneva,** *c.*. *cap. can.* Geneva, Switzerland; at W. end of L. Geneva, R. Rhone flows through c.; cath., univ.; former H.Q. of League of Nations, H.Q. of I.L.O., W.H.O., I.T.U., International Red Cross; watch-mkg., jewellery, elec. goods, chocolate; tourist resort; p. (1961) *179,400*.

**Geneva,** *can.*, Switzerland; a. 109 sq. m.; p. (1961) *259,234*.

**Geneva,** *L.*, S.W. corner of Switzerland; length 40 m., greatest breadth 8¼ m.; a. 108 sq. m.

**Geneva,** *t.*, N.Y., U.S.A.; engin.; p. (1960) *17,286*.

**Génissiat,** France; site of gr. barrage and hydro-elec. power sta. on Rhône below Geneva; completed 1950. [p. (1962) *49,483*.

**Genk,** *t.*, Limburg, Belgium; stainless steel wks.

**Gennevilliers,** *t.*, Seine, France; p. (1962) *42,611*.

**Genoa,** *maritime prov.*, Liguria, N. Italy; a. 1,582 sq. m.; p. (1961) *1,044,633*.

**Genoa (Genova),** *spt.*, *comm. c.*, on G. of Genoa; fine palaces, cath., univ.; shipbldg., engin., tanning, sugar, textiles; p. (1965) *848,000*.

**Gentilly,** *t.*, Seine, France; p. (1954) *17,497*.

**Gentilly,** Quebec, Canada; nuclear power sta. being built.

**George,** *t.*, Cape Province, S. Africa; footwear, sawmilling, hops; p. (1960) *14,505* inc. *8,635* whites.

**Georgetown,** *cap.*, Guyana, S. America; on Demerara R.; exp. sugar, cocoa, coffee, timber, gold, diamonds, bauxite; p. (1962) *98,350*.

**Georgetown,** *t.*, S.C., U.S.A.; fish, lumber, cotton; p. (1960) *12,261*.

**Georgetown,** *t.*, Washington D.C., U.S.A.; on R. Potomac; univ., cath.

**Georgetown,** *c.*, *spt.*, Penang, Malaya; p. *189,068*.

**Georgia,** *st.*, U.S.A.; on Atlantic cst.; forested; agr.; cotton, tobacco, corn, peanuts, fruit; textiles, lumber, chemicals, steel,; chief ts.; Atlanta (cap.) and Savannah; a. 58,876 sq. m.; p. (1960) *3,943,116*.

**Georgia,** *constituent rep.*, U.S.S.R.; maize, tobacco, wheat; engin., metallurgy, manganese mng., oil, gold deposit discovered nr. R. Inguri in a. of new h.e.p. project 1965; cap. Tbilisi; a. 37,570 sq. m.; p. (1959) *4,049,000*.

**Georgian Bay,** *lge. inlet*, Ontario, Canada; E. shore of L. Huron; many impt. lake ports. (Owen Sound, Parry Sound) where Prairie wheat is transhipped for rly. for despatch to Montreal; a. approx. 4,500 sq. m.

**Gera,** *t.*, Gera, E. Germany; lignite, woollens, printing; p. (1963) *104,198*.

**Geraldton,** *spt.*, W. Australia; 306 m. from Perth; in agr. and pastoral dist.; exp. gold, copper, wool; natural gas nearby; p. (1961) *10,878*.

**Germany,** after defeat in Second World War

divided into E. and W. Germany. W. Germany is Federal st. (declared sovereign May 5, 1955) of 9 Länder, Schleswig-Holstein, Hamburg, Lower Saxony, Bremen, North Rhine–Westphalia, Hesse, Rhineland, Palatinate, Baden-Württemberg, and Bavaria. Previously divided into British, American, and French zones; a. 94,716 sq. m.; admin. ctr. Bonn; Saar incorporated, 1956; a. 991 sq. m.; p. (1968) *59,948,000* inc. Saar, and W. Berlin; E. Germany comprises 14 dists., Rostock, Schwerin, Neubrandenburg, Magdeburg, Potsdam, Frankfurt, Erfurt, Halle, Leipzig, Cottbus, Suhl, Gera, Karl-Marx-Stadt, Dresden. Previously the Soviet zone, became sovereign st., March 25, 1954; a. 41,571 sq. m.; p. (1968) *17,067,000*. Berlin under four-Power control; ch. German inds.: agr.: rye, oats, wheat, potatoes, sugarbeet, wines; pastoral; cattle, pigs, sheep; forests, timber; minerals; coal, lignite, iron, potash, copper, zinc, salt; mnfs., machine., shpbldg., textiles, chemicals, dyes, printing, etc.; commerce; communications very good.

**Germiston,** *t.*, Transvaal, S. Africa; nr. Johannesburg; gold mng.; rly. wkshps., engin., machin., chemicals; gas pipeline from Sasolburg, O.F.S.; p. (1960) *204,605* (inc. *84,419* Whites).

**Gerona,** *maritime prov.*, N.E. Spain; cap. G.; textiles, coal, paper; a. 2,264 sq. m.; p. (1959) *345,320*.

**Gerrards Cross,** *t.*, S.E. Bucks, Eng.; 9 m. E. of High Wycombe; residtl.; p. (1951) *2,942*.

**Gers,** *dep.*, S.W. France; cap. Auch; grain, vines, brandy; a. 2,429 sq. m.; p. (1962) *182,264*.

**Gers,** *R.*, rising in the Pyrenees, flows to the Garonne; length 75 m.

**Gettysburg,** *t.*, Penns., U.S.A.; Federal victory 1863; granite; p. (1960) *7,960*.

**Gevelsberg,** *c.*, Westphalia, Germany; iron stoves; p. (1963) *32,100*.

**Gezira,** *dist.*, Sudan, N.E. Africa; situated between Blue and White Niles above confluence at Khartoum; approx 4,700 sq. m. capable of irrigation by water drawn from Blue Nile at Sennar Dam; large-scale growing of high-quality cotton; total a. approx. 7,800 sq. m.

**Ghadames,** *oasis*, Sahara Desert, Libya; N Africa; at point where terr. of Tunis, Algeria, Libya converge 300 m. S.W. of Tripoli; impt. focus of caravan routes.

**Ghaghara (Gogra),** *sacred R.*, India; rising in Tibet, flows through Uttar Pradesh; trib. of Ganges; length 300 m.

**Ghana, Rep. of,** W. Africa; sovereign and ind. st. within British Commonwealth since 6 March 1957; agr.; cocoa, palm-oil, groundnuts; mahogany, manganese, gold, diamonds; cap. Accra; harbours at Takoradi and Tema; total a. 91,843 sq. m.; p. (1965) *7,600,000*.

**Ghardaia,** *t.*, S. Algeria; p. (1960) *58,327*.

**Ghats, E. and W.,** *two mtn. ranges* bordering the triangular upland of S. India, the Deccan; alt. of ch. summits, 4,700–7,000 ft.

**Ghazipur,** *t.*, N. India; on Ganges R., E. of Varanasi; agr. school; p. (1961) *37,147*.

**Ghazni,** *fortfd. town*, t., Afghanistan; 78 m. S.W. of Kabul; gr. tr. ctr.; cap. of the Empire of Mahmud, c. A.D. 1000; p. *10,500*.

**Ghazvin,** *c.* and *dist.*, Central Prov., Iran; agr.; irrigation plant.

**Ghent,** *c.*, Belgium; cap. of E. Flanders, on R. Scheldt; cath. univ.; extensive cotton, woollen, sugar inds.; plastics, photographic materials; oil refinery under construction; p. (1965) *229,000*. inc. subs.

**Giant's Causeway,** *famous basaltic columns*, on promontory of N. cst. of Antrim, Ireland.

**Giarre,** *t.*, Sicily, Italy; nr. Mt. Etna; industl.; p. *20,050*.

**Gibara,** *t.*, Oriente prov., Cuba, W. Indies; exp. bananas; p. *8,045*.

**Gibraltar,** *Brit. fortress and naval base* of gr. strategic importance, W. end of Mediterranean; on rocky peninsula (1,396 ft.), extreme S. of Spain; captured by British in 1704; a. 2¼ sq. m.; civilian p. (estd. 1965) *24,386*.

**Gibraltar, Strait of,** connects Atlantic and Mediterranean; its narrowest breadth is 9 m.

**Gibson Desert,** centre of W. Australia.

**Gibson Island,** *t.*, Queensland, Australia; nr. N. bank of Brisbane R.; fertiliser wks.

**Giessen,** *t.*, Hesse, Germany; on R. Lahn; univ.; tobacco, engin., textiles; p. (1963) *69,800*.

Gifu, *t.*, Central Honshu, Japan; silk; paper; cormorant fishing; p. (1965) *358,190.*

Gigha, *I.*, Argyll, Scot.; off W. cst.; 6 m. long, 2 m. wide; p. (with Cara) *243.*

Gijón, *spt.*, Oviedo, Spain; on Bay of Biscay; gd. harbour; tobacco, petroleum, coal, earthenware; steel wks. nearby; p. (1959) *121,692.*

Gila, *R.*, New Mexico and Arizona, U.S.A.; trib. of Rio Colorado; water used for irrigation in Imperial Valley; length 650 m.

Gilan, *prov.*, N.W. Iran, on Caspian Sea, bounded by U.S.S.R.; sub-tropical climate; agr., inc. cotton and rice; cap. Rasht; p. (1967) *1,754,650.*

Gilbert and Ellice Islands Colony, *gr.* of coral *Is.* (Brit.), Micronesia, Pac. Oc.; ch. crops: pandanas fruit and coconuts; exp. phosphates and copra; a. 369 sq. m.; p. (estd.) *50,000.*

Gilgit, *cap.*, G. extreme N.W. dist. of Kashmir.

Gilgit, *R.*, of the Punjab rising in Chitral, trib. of the Indus, flowing along the Gilgit valley into Kashmir.

Gill, Lough, *L.*, on borders of cos. Sligo and Leitrim, Ireland.

Gillespie, *t.*, Ill., U.S.A.; coal; p. (1960) *3,569.*

Gillingham, *t.*, *mun. bor.*, Kent, Eng.; 2 m. E. of Chatham; cherry orchards, cement, light inds.; p. (estd. 1967) *83,930.*

Gilly, *t.*, Hainaut, Belgium, nr. Charleroi; coal; p. (1962) *23,878.*

Gilolo I., *see* Halmahera I.

Gilp Loch, Argyll, Scot.; inlet of Loch Fyne, at head of Crinan Canal.

Gioja del Colle, *c.*, Bari, S. Italy; olive oil, wine, wool; p. *24,000.*

Giovinazzo, *spt.*, S. Italy; on the Adriatic, N. of Bari; p. *12,150.*

Gippsland, *dist.*, S.E. Victoria, Australia; a. 13,900 sq. m.; mntous.; farming, grazing; coal.

Girardot, *t.*, Colombia, S. America; impt. R. pt. and airport on upper course of R. Magdalena, 685 m. upstream from Caribbean Sea; linked by rly. (70 m.) to Bogotá; coffee, hides, ceramics; p. (estd. 1959) *50,000.*

Giresun, *spt.*, Black Sea, Turkey, W. of Trabzon; p. (1960) *19,946.*

Girga, *t.*, Upper U.A.R.; on R. Nile; p. *1,000.*

Girga, *admin. div.*, Upper U.A.R., N.E. Africa; a. 595 sq. m.; p. (1960) *1,574,000.*

Girgenti, (same as Agrigento, *q.v.*) *t.*, S. Sicily, Italy; famous for its Greek temples.

Girishk, *t.*, Afghanistan; on Helmand R.; ctr. of agr. dist.

Gironde, *dep.*, France; vineyards, grain, fruit, wines; cap. Bordeaux; a. 4,140 sq. m.; p. (1962) *935,443.*

Gironde, *R.*, *estuary*, S.W. France; formed by junction of Rs. Garonne and Dordogne; navigable to Pauillac.

Girton, *par.*, nr. Cambridge, Eng.; women's college.

Girvan, *burgh*, Ayr, Scot.; on F. of Clyde, 18 m. S.W. of Ayr; summer resort; p. (1961) *6,159.*

Gisborne, *spt.*, N.I., N.Z.; on Poverty Bay, 60 m. N.E. of Napier; freezing-wks.; p. (1961) *25,064.*

Gisburn, *t.*, W.R. Yorks.; on R. Ribble, nr. Clitheroe.

Giugliano, *t.*, Italy; N.W. of Naples; mnfs.; p. *20,500.*

Giulianova, *t.*, Teramo, Italy; fruit, grain; p. *20,000.*

Giurgiu, *pt.*, Romania; on R. Danube; opposite Ruse; good tr.; timber; p. (1963) *51,520.*

Givet, *t.*, Ardennes, N.E. France; on R. Meuse; tanneries; p. (1962) *7,925.*

Givors, *t.*, Rhône dep., France; on Rhône R.. 10 m. S. of Lyons; mnfs.; oil refining nearby at Feyzin; p. (1962) *17,232.*

Giza, *admin div.*, U.A.R.; cap. Giza; a. 392 sq. m.; p. (1960) *1,337,000.*

Giza, *t.*, Lower U.A.R.; on the Nile, 3 m. S.W. of Cairo; nr. pyramids of Khafra (Chephren), Khufu (Cheops) and Men-ka-va; also the Sphinx; contains Museum of Egyptian antiquities; film ind.; p. (1960) *250,000.*

Gjinokastër (Argyrocastro), *prefecture*, Albania; cap. G.; p. (estd.) *159,695.*

Gjövik, *t.*, S. Norway; on L. Mjosa; furniture, footwear, light inds.; p. (1961) *7,738.*

Gjuhëzës, C. (Glossa C.), Albania, Strait of Otranto.

Glace Bay, *t.*, Nova Scotia, Canada; coal; p. (1961) *24,186.*

Gladbeck, *t.*, N. Rhine–Westphalia, Germany; N. of Essen; coal-mining, chemicals, rly. junc-

tion; p. (1963) *83,700.*

Gladewater, *t.* N.E. Texas, U.S.A.; oil, lumber; p. (1960) *5,742.*

Gladstone, *t.*, Queensland, Australia; alumina refining, oil, chemicals; p. (1966) *12,372.*

Gladstone, *t.*, S. Mich., U.S.A.; harbour; mnfs. sports equipment; p. (1960) *5,267.*

Glamorgan, *co.*, S. Wales; immense coal and iron deposits; copper and tin smelting; machin.; chemicals; co. t. Cardiff; a. 813 sq. m.; p. (1966) *1,252,000.*

Glamorgan, Vale of, *see* Gwent, Plain of.

Glarus, *can.*, Switzerland; E. of Schwyz; a. 264 sq. m.; sheep, cheese, cottons; p. (1961) *40,148.*

Glarus, *c.*, *cap.*, can. G., Switzerland; on R. Linth, nr. Weesen; p. (1957) *5,724.*

Glasgow, *c. burgh*, Lanark, Scot.; on R. Clyde; third lgst. c. in Gr. Britain; many thriving mnfs.; shipbldg., heavy and light engin., printing; ctr. of great industrial belt; univ. and famous cath.; p. (1961) *1,054,913.*

Glasport, *bor.*, Penns., U.S.A.; tools, steel, hoops, glass; p. (1960) *8,418.*

Glastonbury, *t.*, *mun. bor.*, Somerset. Eng.; at foot of Mendip Hills, 5 m. S.W of Wells; noted 8th-century abbey with legend of thorn planted by Joseph of Arimathea, also adjacent to Avalon, burial I. of King Arthur; gloves, sheepskin rug and slipper mnfs.; p. (estd. 1967) *6,220.*

Glatz, *see* Klodzko.

Glauchau, *t.*, Karl-Marx-Stadt, E. Germany; on R. Mulde; woollens, calicoes, dyes, machin.; p. (1963) *33,370.*

Glazov, *t.*, R.S.F.S.R., in Urals; saw-milling, metal inds.; p. (1959) *59,000.*

Gleiwitz, *see* Gliwice.

Glen, The, beautiful valley and resort in White Mountain dist. of New Hampshire, U.S.A.

Glen Affric, Inverness, Scot.; drained E. to Moray Firth; hydro-elec. scheme.

Glen Garry, Inverness, Scot.; used by Perth to Inverness rly. on S. approach to Drumochter Pass.

Glen Innes, *hill t.*, N.S.W., Australia; alt. 3,518 ft.; pastoral and agr. dist.; p. (1966) *5,754.*

Glen More. Scottish valley traversed by Caledonian canal, from Fort William to Inverness; cattle-ranching being attempted.

Glen Roy, Inverness, Scot.; 15 m. N.E. of Fort William; remarkable terraces, remains of series of glacial lakes. [Fort William rly.

Glen Spean, Inverness, Scot.; used by Glasgow to Glencoe, Argyll, Scot.; S.E. of Ballachulish; scene of massacre of MacDonalds, 1692.

Glendale, *t.*, Cal., U.S.A.; p. (1960) *119,442.*

Glendalough, *valley*, Wicklow, Ireland; scenic beauty; ecclesiastical ruins; tourists.

Glendora, *t.*, Cal., U.S.A.; p. (1960) *20,752.*

Glenelg, *R.*, S.W. Victoria, Australia; length 200 m.

Glenelg, *t.*, S. Australia; on Holdfast Bay; now incl. in met. a. of Adelaide; 1st settlement on mainland.

Glenolden, *bor.*, Penns., U.S.A.; surgical instruments; p. (1960) *7,249.*

Glenrothes, *t.*, Fifeshire, Scot.; one of the "New Towns" designated 1948; coal, transistor factory, mng. machin.; photo precision ind.; p. (estd. 1965) *17,443.*

Glens Falls, *t.*, N.Y., U.S.A.; on Hudson R.; lime kilns and many mnfs.; lumber, paper; p. (1960) *18,580.*

Glenside, *t.*, S.E. Penns., U.S.A.; mnfs. rubber and wood prod.; paints, toys; p. (1950) *9,654.*

Glittertind, *mtn.*, Opland co., S. Norway; highest peak in Scandinavia; alt. 8,140 ft.

Gliwice, (Gleiwitz), *t.*, Upper Silesia, Poland; German before 1945; nr. Katowice; chemicals, iron and steel; p. (1965) *164,000.*

Globe, *t.*, Ariz., U.S.A.; copper, manganese, gold, silver, vanadium, tungsten mining; p. (1960) *6,141.*

Glogów (Glogau), *c.*, Poland, German before 1945; on R. Odra; cath.; sugar, wood, iron inds.; rly. junction; p. (1946) *1,681.*

Glommen R., Norway; lgst. Norwegian R., flows S. in Skaggerak. [Albania.

Glossa, C. (*see* Gjiuhëzës, C), *strait*, Otranto,

Glossop, *mkt. t.*, *mun. bor.*, Derby, Eng.; at W. foot of Pennines, 12 m. S.E. of Manchester; cotton, paper, food canning; p. (estd. 1967) *19,480.*

Gloucester, *co.*, W. of Eng.; fertile valleys, Cotswold Hills; dairying, cheese, sheep, coal machin., textiles, glass, broadcloth; a. 1,257 sq. m.; p. (1966) *1,054,000.*

Gloucester, *cath. c., co. bor.*, on R. Severn; aircraft mftg. and repair, wagon wks., engin., matches, nylon; p. (estd. 1967) *88,050.*

Gloucester, *t.*, Mass., U.S.A.; fishing; granite; p. (1960) *25,789.*                                [*21,741.*

Gloversville, *c.*, N.Y., U.S.A.; gloves; p. (1960)

Glyder Fach, *mtn.*, Caernarvonsh., N. Wales; alt. 3,262 ft.                                      [3,279 ft.

Glyder Fawr, *mtn.*, Caernarvonsh., N. Wales; alt. N. of Maesteg; coal, iron; p. (1961) *9,902.*

Glyncorrwg, *urb. dist.*, Glamorgan, Wales; 4 m.

Gmünd, *t.*, Austria, on Czechoslovakian border.

Gmünd, *t.*, Baden-Württemberg, Germany; on R. Rems, nr. Stuttgart; clocks, metallurgy, glass, costume jewellery; p. (estd. 1954) *34,100.*

Gniezno (Gnesen), *mftg. t.*, Poland: E. of Poznan; cath.; linen; p. (1965) *47,000.*

Gôa, Daman and Diu, Union Terr. of, India, former Port. India; iron pyrites, manganese, cocunuts, fish, spices, cashew nuts, salt, copra; p. (1960) *626,978.*

Goajira, *peninsula* on G. of Maracaibo, N. cst. of S. America; crossed by bdy. of Venezuela and Colombia.

Goalunda, *pt.*, Pakistan; at junction of Rs. Ganges and Brahmaputra.                    [2,866 ft.

Goat Fell, *mtn.*, I. of Arran, Bute, Scot.; alt.

Gobi, steppes and stony or sandy desert in Central Asia; divided into two principal divs.: Shamo in Central Mongolia, and the basins of the Tarim, E. Turkestan; length about 1,500 m. (E. to W.), breadth 500–700 m.; average elevation 4,000 ft.; crossed by Kalgan–Ulan Bator highway.

Godalming, *t.*, *mun. bor.*, Surrey, Eng.; 4 m. S.W. of Guildford; 1st public supply of elec. 1881; tanning, timber yards, corn mills, knitwear; Charterhouse School; p. (estd. 1967) *17,810.*

Godavari, *R.*, India; flows E. across Deccan to Bay of Bengal; forms large delta; length 900 m.

Goderich, *pt.*, Ont., Canada; on S.E. cst. L. Huron; transh. wheat from prairies; p. (1961) *6,411.*

Godesberg, Bad, N. Rhine–Westphalia, Germany; nr. Bonn; famous Spa; chalybeate springs; p. (estd. 1954) *46,700.*

Godhavn, Danish settlement, Disco I., W. of Greenland; whaling; scientific sta.

Godhra, *t.*, Gujarat, India; timber tr.; tanneries; p. (1961) *52,167.*

Godstone, *vil.*, *rural dist.*, Surrey, Eng.; nr. Reigate; p. (1961) rural dist. *40,068.*

Godthaab, *t.*, Greenland; first Danish col. 1721; p. (1960) *4,306.*

Godwin Austen (K²), Mt., Himalaya, second highest in the world; alt. 28,250 ft. Summit reached by Prof. Desio in July 1954. Mt. named Chobrum.                    [(1961) *5,472.*

Gogo, *spt.*, Gujarat, India; on G. of Cambay; p.

Gogra, *see* Ghaghara R.

Goiánia, *cap.*, Goiás State, Brazil; p. (1960) *153,505*

Goiás, *st.*, Central Brazil; mountainous, forested; stock raising; tobacco; gold, diamonds; cap. Goiánia, on Vermelho R.; a. 240,334 sq. m.; p. (1960) *1,954,862.*

Golborne, *t.*, *urb. dist.*, Lancs. Eng.; man-made fibres; p. (1961) *26,100.*

Golconda, *fort and ruined c.*, nr. Hyderabad, S. India; famous for diamonds in former days and mausoleums of ancient kings.

Gold Coast, *see* Ghana.

Gold River, *t.*, B.C., Canada; on W. cst. of Vancouver I. at junct. of Heber and Gold Rs. new t. 1967.                    [*7,118.*

Golden, *c.*, Col., U.S.A.; nr. Denver; p. (1960)

Golden Gate, entrance of Bay of San Francisco, California, U.S.A.; famed Golden Gate Bridge, opened 1937.

Golden Horn, *peninsula* on the Bosporus, forming the harbour of Istanbul.

Golden Vale, *dist.*, Limerick, Tipperary, Ireland; lies between Slieve Bloom Mtns. and Galtee Mtns., drained W. to Shannon and E. to Suir; rich farming, beef and dairy cattle, pigs.

Golden Valley, *t.*, Minn., U.S.A.; p. (1960) *14,559.*

Goldsboro, *t.*, N.C., U.S.A.; on Neuse R.; cotton, tobacco; p. (1960) *28,873.*

Golspie, *co.t.*, Sutherland, Scot.; fishing pt.

Gomal Pass, from Afghanistan to W. Punjab, Pakistan over Sulaiman mtns.

Gomel, *t.*, Byelorussia S.S.R.; on R. Sozh; engin., chemicals, clothing inds.; p. (1959) *166,000.*

Gomera, *I.*, Canaries; 13 m. S.W. Tenerife; cap. San Sebastian; p. (1962) *30,747.*

Gometray I., Hebrides, included in co. Argyll, Scot.; fishing, sta., and harbour.            [*21,000.*

Gonaives, *spt.*, Haiti, W. Indies; on W. cst.; p.

Gonda, *t.*, Uttar Pradesh, India; p. (1961) *43,496.*

Gondar, *t.*, Amhara prov., Ethiopia; p. *22,000.*

Good Hope, *t.*, N.W. Terr., Canada; on Mackenzie R.

Good Hope, C. of, *see* C. of Good Hope.

Goodenough Bay, *inlet*, N. coast of Papua, New Guinea.

Goodwin Sands, *dangerous sand-banks* off E. cst. of Kent, Eng.; shielding the Down roadstead.

Goole, *t.* *mun. bor.*, W.R. Yorks, Eng.; second pt. to Hull on Humber est.; iron, shipbldg., flour milling, fertilisers, alum and dextrine mftg.; p. (estd. 1967) *18,570.*

Goonhilly, Cornwall, Eng.; space communications sta. of G.P.O., likely to be one of most advanced satellite communication stas. in world.

Goose Bay, *t.*, Labrador, Canada; on Hamilton R.

Göppingen, *t.*, Baden-Württemberg, Germany; between Ulm and Stuttgart; machin., iron, wood, chemicals; p. (1963) *48,600.*

Gorakhpur, *t.*, Uttar Pradesh, India; on the Rapti R., 100 m. N. of Varanasi; grain, timber; fertilisers; Govt. agr. school; p. (1961) *180,255.*

Gore, *t.*, Southland, S.I., N.Z.; p. (1961) *7,270.*

Gorgan, *c.*, Iran, Mazandaran prov.; p. (1967) *309,878.*

Gorgonzola, *t.*, N. Italy; 12 m. N.E. of Milan, famous for its cheese.

Gori, *t.*, Georgia, U.S.S.R.; grain, timber; p. (1961) *33,100.*                    [*24,736*

Gorinchem, *t.*, S. Holland, Netherlands; p. (1967)

Gorki (formerly Nizhni-Novgorod), *t.*, R.S.F.S.R.; at confluence of Rs. Oka and Volga; gr. comm. ctr.; engin., chemicals, petroleum refining, steel, textiles, cars, glass; p. (1967) *1,100,000.*

Gorleston, Norfolk, Eng.; at mouth of R. Yare; seaside resort; inc. in co. bor. of Gt. Yarmouth.

Görlitz, *t.*, Dresden, E. Germany; on W. Neisse R.; iron, wood, metallurgy, machin.; p. (1963) *89,578.*

Gorlovka, *t.*, Ukrainian S.S.R.; in Donets Basin; coal, chemicals, engin.; oil pipeline connects with Groznyy oilfields; p. (1967) *348,000.*

Gorno-Altaysk, *t.*, R.S.F.S.R.; 60 m. S.E. of Biysk, nr. Chuya highway to Mongolia; p. (1959) *27,000.*

Gornyy Snezhnogorsk, *t.*, R.S.F.R.S.; new town in Siberian Arctic on R. Hantaiki, 35 m. W.N.W. Komsomolsk; tin mng.

Gorseinon, *vil.*, Glamorgan, S. Wales; nr. Loughour estuary, 4 m. N.W. of Swansea; steel-wks., zinc refineries.

Gort, *rural dist.*, Galway, Ireland; p. (1961) *8,187.*

Gorizia (Görz), *c.*, cap. Gorizia prov., N.E. Italy; cas.; agr. mkt., fruit, wine; cotton mills, textile mach.; p. (1961) *41,854.*

Göschenen, *vil.*, Switzerland; at W. end of St. Gotthard tunnel.

Gosford, *t.*, N.S.W., Australia; 50 m. N. of Sydney; resort and commuter t.; food processing, bldg. materials; p. (1966) *11,312.*

Gosforth, *t.*, *urb. dist.*, sub. to Newcastle-on-Tyne, Eng.; coal; p. (estd. 1967) *27,540.*

Goshen, *c.*, Ind., U.S.A.; p. (1960) *13,718.*

Goslar, *t.*, Lower Saxony, Germany; at foot of Harz Mtns.; clothing mnfs., wood inds.; rly. junction; p. (1963) *41,000*

Gosport, *mun. bor.*, *spt.*, Naval depot, Hants, Eng.; W. side of Portsmouth harbour; shipbldg., engin.; p. (estd. 1967) *75,320.*

Gossau, *vil.*, St. Gallen, Switzerland; embroidery, lace; agr. ctr.; butter and cheese wks.; p. *7,914.*

Göta, *R.*, Sweden; flows from L. Vänern to the Kattegat; also canal connecting L. Vänern with the Baltic; the G. Canal provides a popular tourist trip from Stockholm to Göteborg.

Götaland, southernmost of 3 old provs. of Sweden; a. 39,000 sq. m.; name used only in weather forecasts.

Göteborg and Bohus, *prov.*, Sweden; on cst. of Kattegat; a. 1,989 sq. m.; p. (1961) *624,762.*

Göteborg, *c.*, *cap.*, Göteborg and Bohus, Sweden; at mouth of R. Göta; second c. in Sweden for commerce and ind.; shipbldg., oil refining; deepwater tanker terminal; p. (1960) *404,758.*

Gotha, *t.*, Erfurt, E. Germany; iron, machin.,

porcelain, printing, cartography; p. (1963) *56,611.*

Gotland I., *fertile Swedish I.* in the Baltic; cap. Visby; a. 1,225 sq. m.; p. (1961) *54,322.*

Gottesberg, *t.*, S.W. Poland; coal, mftg.; assigned to Poland at Potsdam conference; p. *8,000.*

Göttingen, *t.*, Lower Saxony, Germany; univ.; scientific instruments, pharmaceutics, film studios; p. (1963) *82,600.*

Gottwaldov (Zlín), *industl. t.*, ČSSR.; 40 m. E. of Brno; footwear, leather and domestic woodware inds.; p. (1961) *54,189.*

Gouda, *c.*, S. Holland, Netherlands; on R. Hollandse IJssel 11 m. from Rotterdam; cheese, candle mnfg.; ceramics, pipes; p. (1967) *46,823.*

Gough I., Atl. Oc. dependency of St. Helena; breeding ground of the great shearwater.

Goulburn, *c.*, N.S.W., Australia; commands route across Gr. Dividing Range; in agr. dist. W. of Sydney; cath.; wool, shoes; p. (1966) *20,849.*

Goulburn R., Victoria, Australia.

Gourock, *burgh*, Renfrew, Scot.; on Firth of Clyde, 2 m. W. of Greenock; p. (1961) *9,609.*

Gouverneur, *t.*, N. N.Y., U.S.A.; mines talc, lead, zinc; mnfs. wood pulp, silk; p. (1960) *4,946.*

Govan, *par.*, Lanark, Scot.; on the Clyde, part of Glasgow; shipbldg.; p. (1951) *312,911.*

Governor's I., *fort*, Boston Harbour; also fortfd. islet in harbour of N.Y., U.S.A.

Govindpura, *t.*, Madhya Pradesh, India; nr. Bhopal; heavy elec. goods; p (1961) *20,747.*

Gower, *peninsula*, W. Glamorgan, Wales.

Gowerton, *vil.*, Glamorgan, S. Wales; S. cst. of Loughour estuary, 4 m. W. of Swansea; new steel-wks.

Gowrie, Carse of, fertile tract N. side Firth of Tay, Scot.; includes Dundee, Kinnoul, Perth.

Goya, *t.*, Argentina; on R. Paraná; cattle; p. (1960) *40,000.*

Goyanna, *comm. t.*, Brazil; 40 m. N. of Recife.

Gozo, *Br. I.* in Mediterranean, nr. Malta; the ancient Gaulos; surrounded by perpendicular cliffs; a. 26 sq. m.; p. *27,612.*

Graaff-Reinet, *t.*, Cape Province, S. Africa; fruit growing, wool; p. (1960) *16,703* inc. *5,565* whites.

Graciosa, *I.*, Azores gr., N.W. of Terceira.

Grado, *commune*, Oviedo, N.W. Spain; iron foundries; p .(1957) *17,385.*

Grado-Aquileia, N. Adriatic, prov. Gorizia, Italy; pleasure resort and former Roman spt.; rich in early Christian mosaics and other antiquities; p. (est.) *3,000.*

Graengesberg, *dist.*, Kopparberg co., Sweden; on S. fringe of Scandinavian mtns.; iron ore deposits.

Grafton, *t.* N.S.W., Australia; on Clarence R.; dairy prod., timber; p. (1966) *15,944.*

Graham, *t.*, N. Texas, U.S.A.; oil refining, flour milling; p. (1960) *8,505.*

Graham I., the lgst. of the Queen Charlotte gr. in the Pacific; off cst. of Brit. Columbia.

Graham Land, Falkland Is. Dependencies, Antarctica; mtnous, icebound; discovered 1832.

Grahamstown, *c.*, Cape Province, S. Africa; univ.; cath.; p. (1960) *32,611* inc. *10,668* Europeans.

Graian Alps, *mtns.* between Savoy and Piedmont; highest point Gran Paradiso; alt. 13,320 ft.

Grain Coast, general name formerly applied to cst. of Liberia, W. Africa; "grain" refers to pepper, spices, etc.

Grammichele, *t.*, E. Sicily, Italy; 23 m. S.W. of Catania; marble; p. *14,014.*

Grammont, *t.*, E. Flanders, Belgium; nr. Ghent, on Dender R.; mftg; p. (1962) *9,585.*

Grampians, *highest mtns.* of Scot.; highest point Ben Nevis; alt. 4,406 ft.; includes Cairngorms, high granitic mtns.

Granada, *prov.*, S. Spain; traversed by Sierra Nevada; wheat, olives, textiles, liqueurs, paper; a. 4,838 sq. m.; p. (1959) *779,434.*

Granada, *ancient c.*, Granada, S. Spain; at foot of Sierra Nevada; formerly cap. of the Moorish Kingdom of G., now cap. of fertile maritime prov.; famous 14th-century Alhambra; p. (1959) *145,169.*

Granada, *c.*, Nicaragua, Central America; distilling, soap, furniture; p. *38,918.*

Granby, *c.*, Quebec, Canada; on Yamaska R.; sawmills, leather; p. (1961) *31,463.*

Gran Chaco, *extensive dist.*, N. Argentina and Paraguay; flat with lge. areas of forest; quebracho.

Grand Bank, *submarine plateau*, extending S.E. from Newfoundland, Canada; a. 500,000 sq. m.; impt. cod fisheries.

Grand Bassam, *t.*, *spt.*, Ivory Cst., W. Africa; exp. bananas, palm-kernels; p. *5,743.*

Grand Bahama, one of the Bahama Is., W. Indies; p. (1953) *4,095.*

Grand Canal, *canal*, N. China; about 1,000 m. long from Tientsin to Hangchow; built between A.D. 605–18 and 1282–92; now silted up and cst. or rail transport more impt.

Grand Canal, main water thoroughfare through Venice, Italy. [(1962) *404,581.*

Grand Canary, *I.*, Canaries; cap. Las Palmas; p.

Grand Canyon, Arizona, U.S.A.; narrow gorge, 3,000 to over 5,000 ft. deep of Colorado R.

Grand Cayman I., T.W.I.; a. 85 sq. m.; coconuts; cap. Georgetown; p. (estd. 1957) *6,636.*

Grand Combin, *min.* in the Alps, N. of Aosta, Italy; alt. 14,141 ft. [*14,458.*

Grand-Comme (La.), *t.*, Gard, France; p. (1962)

Grand Coulée Dam, Wash., U.S.A.; across R. Columbia 110 m. below Spokane; world's lgst. dam; reservoir formed 151 m. long, a. 130 sq. m. supplies irrigation water to 1,900 sq. m. between Rs. Columbia and Snake; hydro-elec. power sta. when complete will generate 2,700,000 h.p.

Grande Chartreuse, La, *monastery*, Isère, France; 15 m. N. of Grenoble; famous for its liqueur.

Grande Prairie, *t.*, Alberta, Canada; wheat; p. *8,000.*

Grand Forks, *t.*, N.D., U.S.A.; on Red R.; in wheat region; p. (1960) *34,451.*

Grand Island, *c.*, Nebraska, U.S.A.; cattle and grain t.; p. (1960) *25,742.*

Grand Junction, *t.*, Col., U.S.A.; p. (1960) *18,694.*

Grand Lake, *lgst. L.*, Newfoundland; a. about 200 sq. m.

Grand Lahon, *t.*, Ivory Cst., W. Africa; p. *1,000.*

Grand' Mère, *t.*, Quebec, Canada; pulp and paper mills; p. (1961) *15,806.*

Grand Prairie, *see* Black Prairie.

Grand Rapids, *c.*, Mich., U.S.A.; on Grand R.; furniture mkg., car and aircraft parts, chemicals, paper; p. (1960) *177,313.*

Grand R., Mich., U.S.A.; enters L. Mich. at Grand Haven, navigable to Grand Rapids; length 250 m.

Grand R., W. Colorado and E. Utah, U.S.A.; trib. of the Colorado R.; length 350 m.

Grand Turk I., *seat of government*, Turks and Caicos Is.; p. *1,693.*

Grange, *t.*, *urb. dist.*, N. Lancs, Eng., on N. cst. of Morecambe Bay; sm. summer resort; p. (1961) *3,117.*

Grangemouth, *burgh*, Stirling, Scot.; on F. of Forth, 20 m. W. of Leith; shipbldg. and repair, marine engin., oil refining, petroleum prods., chemicals, pharmaceutics; electronics and elec. ind; oil pipeline to Finnart; p. (1961) *18,860.*

Granite City, Ill., U.S.A.; p. (1960) *40,073.*

Gran Sasso d'Italia, *rugged limestone highlands*, Abruzzi, Central Italy; highest part of Apennines, Monte Corno alt. 9,584 ft.; winter sports ctr., Aquila.

Grantham, *t.*, *mun. bor.*, Lincoln, Eng.; on Witham R.; tanning, agr. machin., engin., brewing, malting, basket mkg.; p. (estd. 1967) *26,350.*

Grant Land, *region*, N. of Ellesmere I., Arctic Canada.

Grantown-on-Spey, *burgh*, Moray, Scot.; on R. Spey; health resort; p. (1961) *1,581.*

Grants Pass, *t.*, S.W. Ore., U.S.A.; fruit growing; lumber, mining, fishing; p. (1960) *10,118.*

Granville, *spt.*, *wat. pl.*, Manche, France; at mouth of the Bosq; fisheries; p. (1962) *11,482.*

Granville, *sub.*, Sydney, N.S.W., Australia.

Grasmere, *vil.*, Westmorland, Eng.; at head of Grasmere L.; home of Wordsworth.

Grasse, *t.*, *health resort*, Alpes-Maritimes, S.E. France; perfumes; p. (1962) *27,226.*

Graubünden (Grisons), *can.*, Switzerland; cap. Chur; a. 2,746 sq. m.; p. (1961) *147,458.*

Graudenz, *see* Grudziadz.

's-Gravenhage, *see* Hague.

Graves, Pointe de, N. point of Médoc Peninsula, France; in famous wine dist.

Gravesend, *spt.*, *mun. bor.*, Kent, Eng.; S. bank R. Thames facing Tilbury; shipping, paper, cement, tyres, engin.; p. (estd. 1967) *54,930.*

Gravina, *industl. c.*, Apulia, Italy; p. *20,775.*

Gray's Peak, Rocky Mtns., Col., U.S.A.; alt. 14,341 ft.

Grays Thurrock, *urb. dist.*, Essex, Eng.; on the

Thames, nr. Tilbury Fort; oil refining, metal refining, cement, paper board, margarine, soap mftg.; p. (estd. 1967) *121,670*.

Graz, *t.*, Austria; on R. Mur; machin., iron and steel, rly. wks.; p. (1964) *249,000*.

Great Altai, *range of mtns.*, lying mainly in outer Mongolia but also in Western Siberia.

Great Atlas, *mtns.*, N.W. Africa; alt. 7,000 ft.

Great Australian Basin, *artesian basin*, Australia; underlies plains of S.W. Queensland, N.W. New South Wales, N.E. of S. Australia; water supply used on sheep-farms, cattle-ranches, in a. from Normanton in N. to Renmark in S., Ooodnadatta in W. to Roma in E.; a. 570,000 sq. m.

Great Australian Bight, *wide inlet*, S. of Australia, between C. Arid and Port Whidbey; 850 m.

Great Barrier Reef, *coral reef barrier*, off N.E. cst. of Australia; 1,000 m. long, 75-100 m. from cst.

Great Basin, *high plateau region* between the Wasatch and Sierra Nevada Mtns., U.S.A., inc. most of Nev., parts of Utah, Cal., Idaho, Ore., Wyo.; inland drainage ctr. Great Salt Lake; a. 210,000 sq. m.; much desert; sparse p.

Great Bear Lake, on the Arctic Circle, in N.W. Terr., Canada, over 150 m. long; a. 14,000 sq. m.; outlet through Great Bear R. to Mackenzie R.

Great Belt, *strait*, separating I. of Fyn from Sjaelland, Denmark.

Great Britain, *see* England, Scotland, Wales, British Isles.

Great Dividing Range, *mtn. system*, E. Australia; extends, under different local names, from Queensland to Victoria and separates E. cst. plains from interior; reaches max. alt. in Mt. Koskiusko (7,328 ft.), in Australian Alps, on bdy. between Victoria and New South Wales.

Great Falls, *t.*, Mont., U.S.A.; on Missouri R.; wool; gold, silver; lead and copper smelting; p. (1960) *55,357*.

Great Fish R., Cape Province, S. Africa.

Great Fisher Bank, *submarine sandbank* in N. Sea; 200 m. E. of Aberdeen, 100 m. S.W. of Stavanger; valuable fishing-ground; depth of water, from 25 to 40 fathoms.

Great Gable, *mtn.*, Cumberland, Eng.; alt. 2,949 ft.

Great Harwood, *t.*, *urb. dist.*, Lancs. Eng.; 5 m. N.E. of Blackburn; cotton weaving, textiles, engin.; p. (1961) *10,718*.

Great Karroo, Cape Province, S. Africa; high plateau; ostrich farming.

Great Lakes, N. America; comprising 5 fresh-water Ls.: Superior, Michigan, Huron, Erie, Ontario; frozen 4 to 5 months in winter; enormous L. traffic in cereals, iron, coal, etc.; a. 96,000 sq. m. *See* St. Lawrence Seaway.

Great Makarikari, Botswana, South Africa; salt pan.

Great Namaqualand, S. region of S.W. Africa.

Great Ormes Head, *promontory*, N. Wales; nr. Llandudno.

Great Plains, *lowland area* of central N. America, extending E. from Rocky Mtns. and S. from Mackenzie to S. Texas.

Great Rift Valley, geological fault extending from S.W. Asia to E. Africa, 3,000 m. in length; includes L. Tiberias, Jordan Valley, Dead Sea, Gulf of Aqaba, Red Sea, and chain of Ls. from Rudolf to Nyasa; a branch runs through Ls. Tanganyika, Edward and Albert.

Great St. Bernard, *pass*, Switzerland. *See* K146.

Great Salt Lake, Utah, U.S.A.; in the Great Basin plateau of N. America; 90 m. long; a. over 2,000 sq. m.; alt. 4,218 ft.; receives Bear, Jordan and Beaver Rs.; no outlet.

Great Sandy Desert, N. part, W. Australia.

Great Slave Lake, N.W. Terr., Canada; length 300 m.; greatest breadth 50 m., outlet Mackenzie R.

Great Slave R., Canada, flowing between L. Athabaska and the Great Slave L.

Great Smoky Mtns., Tenn., U.S.A.; with Blue Ridge Mtns. form E. Zone of Appalachian Mtn. system; rise to alt. over 6,000 ft.; largely preserved as National Park.

Great Victoria Desert, W. and S. Australia, lies north of Nullarbor Plain.

Greater Antilles Is., W. Indies.

Greece, *kingdom, S.*, part of Balkan Peninsula, bounded on N. by Albania, Jugoslavia and Bulgaria, on W. and S. by the Mediterranean, and on the E. by the Ægean Sea, and inc. Is. in the Mediterranean, Ægean and Ionian Seas;

cap. Athens; agr.: cereals, tobacco, currants vines, fruit; sheep, goats, cattle; minerals iron, lead, magnesite, lignite; mnfs.: olive oil, wine, textiles, chemicals, shipyds., oil refining; a. 51,182 sq. m.; p. (estd. 1965) *8,550,000*.

Greeley, *t.*, Col., U.S.A.; nr. Denver, site of st. college of education; lumber, flour; p. (1960) *26,314*.

Green Bay, *c.*, Wis., U.S.A.; tr. in timber, flour, etc., paper, coal; p. (1960) *62,888*.

Greenfield, *t.*, Mass., U.S.A.; p. (1960) *14,389*.

Greenhithe, Thames-side, nr. Dartford, Kent, Eng.

Greenland, *I.*, between Arctic Ocean and Baffin Bay; lofty ice-capped plateau; peopled by coastal settlements of Eskimos; whale oil, seal skins; some coal, lead, zinc; U.S. base at Thule; part of Danish kingdom; cap. Godthaab; a. 840,000 sq. m., of which 708,000 sq. m. are under a permanent ice-cap; p. (estd. 1965) *37,000*.

Greenlaw, *t.*, Berwick, Scot.

Green Mtns., Vermont section of Appalachian mtns.; highest peak, alt. 4,430 ft.

Greenock, *burgh*, Renfrew, Scot.; on S. shore of Firth of Clyde, 20 m. W. of Glasgow; shipbldg., sugar-refining, woollens, chemicals, aluminium casting, tin plate inds.; p. (1961) *74,578*.

Greenore, *cape*, Louth, Ireland; separating Dundalk Bay from Carlingford, Lough.

Green R., trib. of Grand R., Utah, U.S.A.; length 750 m. [p. (1960) *119,574*.

Greensboro', *c.*, N.C., U.S.A.; cotton, tobacco;

Greensburg, *t.*, Penns., U.S.A.; iron and glass factories; p. (1960) *17,383*.

Greenville, *t.*, Miss., U.S.A.; on Miss. R.; cotton tr.; p. (1960) *41,502*.

Greenville, *c.*, S.C., U.S.A.; in the cotton belt; p. (1960) *66,188*.

Greenville, Texas, U.S.A.; cotton, rayon, shipping; p. (1960) *19,087*.

Greenwich, *inner bor.*, London, Eng.; inc. most of former bor. of Woolwich on S. bank of R. Thames; famous for its Hospital, Observatory (now moved to Herstmonceux) and R.N. College; longitudes conventionally calculated Greenwich meridian either E. or W.; p. (1966) *232,000*.

Greenwood, *t.*, Miss., U.S.A.; p. (1960) *20,436*.

Greenwood, *t.*, S.C., U.S.A.; p. (1960) *16,644*.

Greifswald, *spt.*, Rostock, E. Germany; on Baltic inlet; shipbldg., textiles, wood inds.; p. (1963) *47,563*.

Greiz, *t.*, Gera, E. Germany; paper, textiles, chemicals; p. (1963) *38,470*.

Grenaa, *t.*, Randers, Jutland, Denmark; textiles, furniture, engin.; p. (1960) *9,088*.

Grenada, *I.*, *aut. st.* in association with Gt. Britain; W.I.; cap. St. George's; fruit, cocoa, spices a. (inc. the Grenadines) 133 sq. m.; p. (estd. 1967) *89,000*.

Grenadines, Brit. *gr. of sm. Is.*, between Grenada and St. Vincent, Windward Is.; sea-island cotton; p. (1960) *6,433*.

Grenoble, *fortfd. c.*, Isère, S.E. France; on R. Isère; 60 m. from Lyons; gloves, buttons, machin., liqueurs, cement; joint Franco-German nuclear research reactor; p. (1962) *162,764*. [(1960) *21,967*.

Gretna, *t.*, La., U.S.A.; on the Mississippi R.; p.

Gretna Green, *vil.*, Dumfriesshire, Scot., on Eng. border; famous as place of runaway marriages, 1754-1856.

Grey Range, *mtns.*, S.W. Queensland, Australia; extends S.W. from Gr. Dividing Range towards Flinders Range and Spencer G.; forms divide between streams draining E. to R. Darling and those draining W. to L. Eyre.

Greymouth, *spt.*, S.I., N.Z.; on W. cst. at mouth of Grey R.; ch. t. prov. of Westland; coal; p. (1961) *8,877*.

Greytown, *see* San Juan del Norte.

Griffin, *c.*, Ga., U.S.A.; cotton factories and tr.; p. (1960) *21,735*.

Grim, *C.*, N.W. Tasmania.

Grimaldi, *caves*, N.W. Italy; remains of prehistoric man, late Paleolithic, found there.

Grimsby, *spt.*, *co. bor.*, Lincoln, Eng.; on S. bank of R. Humber; fishing, shipbldg., fertilisers, chemicals, engin., paper mkg., tanning, cod liver oil, acrylic fibre; p. (estd. 1967) *95,110*.

Grimsel Pass, Bernese Alps, Switzerland; alt. 7,100 ft.

Grindelwald, *vil.*, Bernese Oberland, Switzerland; tourist ctr.

Griqualand East, *dist.*, Cape Province, S. Africa;

pastures, wool; ch. t. Kokstad; a. 6,602 sq. m.; p. 265,000.

Griqualand W., dist., Cape Province, S. Africa; diamonds; ch. t., Kimberley; a. 15,197 sq. m.; p. 160,793. [French cst. to Dover.

Gris-Nez, C., N.E. France; nearest point on

Grisons (Graubünden), can., Switzerland; one-half only productive, many glaciers, contains the mtn. health resorts of Davos-Platz (alt. 5,115 ft.), St. Moritz (alt. 6,089 ft.), Arosa (alt. 6,108 ft.); a. 2??46 sq. m.; p. (1960) 145,600.

Grivegnee, t., Belgium; nr. Liége; ironwks.; p. (1962) 23,340.

Grodno, t., W. Byelorussia (Polish until 1939); agr.; engin., textiles, chemicals; p. (1959) 72,000.

Grodzisk Mazowiecki, commune, Poland; 12 m. S.W. of Warsaw; p. 18,737.

Gronau, t., N. Rhine–Westphalia, Germany; nr. Dutch frontier; textiles, rly. junction; p. (1963) 26,000.

Grong, spt., Norway, on Falda Fjord; p. (1961) 2,052.

Groningen, c., cap. Groningen, Netherlands; comm. ctr.; univ.; woollens, glucose, shipbldg.; p. (1967) 156,208.

Groningen, prov., N.E. Netherlands; agr. and dairying; natural gas deposits at Slochteren; a. 883 sq m.; p. (1967) 508,173.

Groote Eylandt. I., G. of Carpentaria; off cst. of N. Terr., Australia; manganese ore mng.

Grootfontein, t., S.W. Africa; copper- and lead-mining; world's lgst. known meteorite on nearby farm; p. (1960) 3,722 inc. 1,195 whites.

Grosseto, prov., central Italy; ch. t. Grosseto, a. 1,735 sq. m.; p. (1963) 216,704.

Grosseto, t., cap. Grosseto prov., Central Italy; severely affected by heavy floods Nov. 1966; p. (1961) 51,004.

Groton, industl. t., Conn., U.S.A.; opp. New London at mouth of Thames R.; p. (1960) 10,111.

Grottaglie, t., Lecce, Apulia, Italy; nr. Brindisi; white glaze pottery; p. 14,850.

Grove City, bor., Penns., U.S.A.; engines, carriages; p. (1960) 8,368.

Groznyy, t., N. Caucasia, R.S.F.S.R.; on R. Terek; naphtha wells, refinery, engin.; starting point of oil pipelines to Makhachkala Tuapse and Gorlovka; p. (1967) 319,000.

Grudziadz (Graudenz), t., on R. Vistula, Polish Pomerania; sawmilling; p. (1965) 71,000.

Grünberg, see Zielona Gora.

Gruyère, dist., can. Fribourg, Switzerland; cheese.

Gstaad, fashionable summer and winter res., Bernese Oberland, Switzerland.

Guadalajara, c., Mexico; cap. of Jalisco st.; cotton and wool mnfs.; cath.; gas pipe-line from Salamanca; p. (1960) 736,800.

Guadalajara, prov., Spain; agr. and salt mines; a. 4,709 sq. m.; p. (1959) 195,637.

Guadalajara, mftg. t., G. prov., Spain; woollens, leather; p. (1957) 15,700.

Guadalaviar, R., E. Spain; flows into Mediterranean, nr. Valencia; length 130 m.

Guadalcanal, I., Brit. Solomon Is., Pac. Oc.

Guadalquivir, R., Spain; flows through Andalusia to Atlantic; length 375 m.

Guadalupe Hidalgo, t., Mexico; treaty signed 1848 ending Mexican–U.S. war; p. (estd.) 29,000.

Guadeloupe and Dependencies, Leeward gr.; a. 722 sq. m.; sugar produce; ch. pt. Pointe à Pitre; p. (1931) 282,000. French Overseas Dept.; Leeward gr. consists of Guadaloupe (p. 113,412, ch. t. Basse-Terre), Grande Terre p. (113,545, ch. t. Pointe à Pitre); united a. of Is., 583 sq. m.; and 5 smaller Is., Marie Galante, Désirade, St. Barthelemy and St. Martin (total p. 304,000) still inhabited by white descendants of French emigrants of 300 years ago; mountainous; rum, sugar, coffee, bananas.

Guadiana, R., forms part of Spanish and Portuguese frontier; flows into Bay of Cadiz; length 510 m.; Extremadura valley reclamation scheme in progress.

Guadiana del Caudillo, new t., nr. Badajoz, Spain; linen, hemp goods, cattle foods.

Guadix, c., Granada, S. Spain; cath.; hats, hemp, brandy, pottery, mats, carpets; p. (1957) 30,088.

Guaira, La, spt., Venezuela; motor road to Carácas; exp. hides, cocoa, coffee; p. (1961) 20,275.

Gualdo Tadino, commune, central Italy; cath.; pottery; p. 12,791.

Gualeguaychu, t., Entre Rios, Argentina; cattle and agr. ctr.; p. (1960) 43,000.

Guam, I., most S. and lgst. of Marianas Archipelago, N. Pacific; naval sta. of the U.S.A.; Polaris submarine base at Apra harbour; ch. t. Agaña and spt. is Piti; maize, sweet potatoes, bananas; a. 209 sq. m.; p. (1960) 67,044.

Guanabacoa, industl. t., nr. Havana, Cuba; p. 21,999.

Guanabara, st., Brazil; formerly fed. dist. of Rio de Janeiro; q.v. [p. (1963) 141,523.

Guanacasta, prov., Costa Rica, Central America;

Guanajuato, st., Central Mexico; very fertile, productive and prosperous; a. 11,804 sq. m.; p. (1960) 1,735,490.

Guanajuato, ch. t., G. st., Mexico; 250 m. from Mexico c.; cotton, silver, lead; p. (1960) 23,379.

Guanta, spt., Anzoategui st., Venezuela, S. America; on Caribbean Sea, linked by road to Barcelona (10 m.); exp. oil.

Guantanamo, t., Cuba; sugar, coffee, bananas, cacao; p. (1953) 64,671.

Guapore, R., Brazil, S. America; joins the Mamore; length 900 m. [9,094.

Guarda, t., Portugal; alt. over 3,000 ft.; p. (1960)

Guarda, wine-growing dist., Portugal; between Rs. Tagus and Douro; p. (1963) 279,100.

Guardafui, C., most E. point of Africa.

Guatemala, republican st., Central America; adjoins Mexico, Br. Honduras and El Salvador, coffee, bananas, chicle; lead, zinc, and cadmium mined in sm. quantities; a. 45,452 sq. m.; p. (estd. 1965) 4,304,000.

Guatemala City, cap. c., Guatemala; cath.; univ.; minerals: gold, silver, copper, lead; p. (estd. (1965) 573,000.

Guayaquil, ch. pt., Ecuador, S. America; on Guayas R., 30 m. above its entrance into the Bay of Guayaquil; devastated by fire in 1896 and 1899; univ.; cath.; sawmills, foundries, machin., brewing; p. (1963) 506,000.

Guayas, prov., Ecuador; cap. Guayaquil; a. 8,331 sq. m.; p. (1960) 825,600.

Guaynabo, t., Puerto Rico W.I.; p. (1960) 40,257.

Gubat, mun., Luzon, Philippine Is.; hemp, coconuts, sugar-cane region; p. 22,380.

Gubbio, t., Perugia Italy; lustre ware; p. 30,350.

Gubin (Guben), t., R. pt., on R. Neisse between E. Germany and Poland; formerly in Prussian prov. of Brandenburg; comm. ctr.; textiles, machin., leather, synthetic fibre; p. (estd. 1939) 45,800.

Gudbrandsdal, gr. valley, S. Norway; leads S.E. from Dovre Fjeld towards Oslo; drained by R. Logan; used by main road Oslo to Trondheim; provides relatively lge. a. of cultivable land; hay, oats, barley, dairy cattle.

Gudiyatam, t., Tamil Nadu, India; p. (1961) 50,384.

Guebwiller, t., Haut-Rhin, France; cottons; p. (1962) 10,864.

Guelph, c., Ontario, Canada; cloth, yarn, pottery, agr. and veterinary colleges; p. (1961) 39,838.

Guernsey, Channel Is., between cst. of France and England; tomatoes, grapes (under glass), flowers, cattle; tourist res.; t. and ch. spt. St. Peter Port; a. 15,654 acres; p. (1961) (inc. Herm and Jethou) 45,126.

Guerrero, Pacific st., Mexico; cereals, cotton, coffee, tobacco; cap. Chilpancingo; ch. pt. Acapulco; a. 24,885 sq. m.; p. (1960) 1,186,716.

Guiana, region, S. America; a. 179,000 sq. m.; comprises Guyana and Fr. Guiana and Surinam.

Guiana Highland, plateau, S. America; extends approx. 900 m. from E. to W. across S. parts of Venezuela, Guyana, Surinam, Fr. Guiana; steep sides, rounded tops approx. 3,000 ft. alt. but rises to 8,635 ft. in Mt. Roraima; chiefly composed crystalline rocks rich in minerals.

Guienne, old French prov., separated by R. Garonne from Gascony.

Guildford, c., co. t., mun. bor., Surrey, Eng.; 30 m S.W. London; on gap cut by R. Wey through N. Downs; cath.; univ.; vehicles, agr. implements, light inds.; residl., p. (estd 1967) 55,470.

Guinea, ind. rep. (Oct. 1958), formerly Fr. Guinea; member of Union of African States; iron-ore, bauxite, diamonds, groundnuts, palm oil; cap. Conakry; a. 94,900 sq. m.; p. (1965) 3,420,000.

Guinea, general name for W. African coastlands round the greatest bend of G. of G. from the Gambia to the Congo.

Guinea, Portuguese. See Portuguese Guinea.

Guinea, Spanish. See Spanish Guinea.

Guinea Current, *ocean current*, flows W. to E. along Guinea Cst., diverted away from cst. in Bight of Benin by C. Three Points. [*22,669.*

Güines, *t.*, Havana, Cuba, W. Indies; sugar; p.

Guinobatan, *mun.*, Luzon, Philippine Is.; hemp; lime deposits; p. *26,419.*

Guipuzcoa, *Basque prov.*, Spain; mftg., minerals, agr.; cap. San Sebastian; tourism; a. 728 sq. m.; p. *(1959) 455,388.*

Guisborough, *t.*, *urb. dist.*, N.R. Yorks, Eng.; in Cleveland iron-mng.; a. S.E. of Middlesbrough; steel, sawmilling, clothing; p. *(1961) 12,079.*

Gujarat, *st.*, India; formerly part of Bombay st.; cap. temporarily Ahmedabad; new cap. Gandhinagar, 13 m. N. of A. under construction; oil development in Cambay area; fertiliser plant projected; a. 72,245 sq. m.; p. *(1961) 20,633,350.*

Gujranwala, *c.*, W. Pakistan; N. of Lahore; power plant projected; p. *(1951) 120,860.*

Gujrat, *t.*, W. Pakistan; on Chenab R.; pottery and furniture; p. *(1941) 22,000.* [*53,000.*

Gukhovo, *t.*, N. Caucasus, R.S.F.S.R.; p. *(1959)*

Gulbarga, *t.*, Gulbarga dist., Mysore, India; oil, cotton, flour, paint; p. *(1961) 97,069.*

Gulf Basin, W. Australia; artesian well basin.

Gulfport, *t.*, Miss., U.S.A.; p. *(1960) 30,204.*

Gulf Stream, current of the Atlantic, issuing from Gulf of Mexico by Florida Strait.

Gulf Stream Drift, *see* North Atlantic Drift.

Gummersbach, *t.*, N. Rhine–Westphalia, Germany; textiles, leather, metallurgy, paper, machin.; p. *(1963) 32,400.*

Gumti, *R.*, trib. of Ganges, India; flows past Lucknow. [p. *(1961) 187,122.*

Guntur, *t.*, Andhra Pradesh, India; cotton mftg.;

Gurgan (Asterabad), *t.*, N. Persia; nr. S.E. end of Caspian Sea; carpets, cotton, rice.

Guryev, *t.*, Kazakh S.S.R.; on mouth of R. Ural, entrance to Caspian Sea; petrol refining, engin.; oil pipeline to Orsk; p. *(1959) 78,000.*

Gus-Khrustalnyy, *t.*, R.S.F.S.R., 40 m. S. of Vladimir; impt. ctr. of glass ind.; p. *(1959) 53,000.*

Güstrow, *t.*, Schwerin, E. Germany; S. of Rostock; cas.; steel and wood inds.; rly. junction; p. *(1963) 38,897.*

Gütersloh, *t.*, N. Rhine–Westphalia, Germany; nr. Bielefeld; silk and cotton inds.; famous for its Pumpernickel (Westphalian rye bread); machin., furniture, publishing, metallurgy; p. *(1963) 53,300.*

Guyana, *indep. sov. st.* within Brit. Commonwealth *(1966)*, S. America; flat, swampy cst., interior highlands; climate, very hot, heavy rainfall along cst.; tropical forests; agr.: sugar, rice, coffee; cattle; hardwoods; minerals: bauxite, diamonds, gold, manganese; copper in Cuyuni and Groete Creek areas; iron ore nr. Essequibo estuary; molybdenum at Eagle Mt.; poor communications; cap. Georgetown; a. 83,000 sq. m.; p. *(estd. 1965) 650,000;* option of becoming rep. after beginning of 1969.

Gwadar, *t.*, W. Pakistan; p. *15,000.*

Gwalior, *dist.*, Madhya Pradesh, India; a. 2,002 sq. m.; p. *(1961) 657,876.*

Gwalior, *t.*, Madhya Pradesh, India, formerly Lashkar, 76 m. S. of Agra; cotton spinning, muslin, carpets, cereals, sugar-cane; bauxite; p. *(1961) 300,587* inc. Morar. [Pakistan.

Gwatar, *spt.* on G. of Oman, Persia; by border of

Gwelo, *t.*, Rhodesia; impt. indust. ctr.; p. *(1961) 37,590* inc. 8,590 Europeans.

Gwent, Plain of (Vale of Glamorgan), *lowland dist.*, Glamorgan, S. Wales; lies S. of moorland of S. Wales Coalfield, extends E. into Monmouth; fertile soils; mixed farming except in industl. areas of Cardiff, Barry.

Gympie, *t.*, Queensland, Australia; on Mary R., 106 m. from Brisbane; former goldfield; now dairying and pastoral dist., tropical fruits, especially pineapples; p. *(1966) 11,277*

Györ, *c.*, Hungary; at junction of R. Raab with arm of R. Danube; cath.; horses, textiles, chemicals, engin., rolling stock, bridge parts, p. *(1962) 72,319.*

# H

Haarlem, *t.*, cap. N. Holland prov., Netherlands; textiles, printing, brewing, bulb growing; cath.; p. *(1967) 172,263.*

Habab, *dist.*, W. coast Red Sea, Ethiopia.

Hachioji, *c.*, Honshu, Japan; weaving, silk–cotton mixtures; p. *(1964) 178,000.*

Hackensack, *t.*, N.J., U.S.A.; iron foundries, silk, jewellery, paper; p. *(1960) 30,521.*

Hackney, *inner bor.*, N.E. London, Eng.; incorporates former bors. of Shoreditch and Stoke Newington; furniture, clothing, footwear; p. *(1966) 251,000.*

Haddington, *burgh*, *cap.*, E. Lothian, Scot.; on R. Tyne 16 m. E. of Edinburgh; woollen mnf.; grain mkt., corn mills, lt. engin., hosiery; p. *(1961) 5,506.*

Haderslev, *t.*, Denmark; tobacco, clothing, knitted goods p. *(1960) 19,735.*

Hadhramaut, *dist.*, Southern Yemen; ch. pt. and c. Mukalla; fertile coastal valley; frankincense, aloes, tobacco, shawls, carpets; p. *150,000* (estd.).

Hadsund, *t.*, Jutland, Denmark; p. *(1960) 3,424.*

Hafnarfjördur, *t.*, S. of Reykjavik, Iceland; p. *(1962) 7,490.*

Hagen, *t.*, N. Rhine–Westphalia, Germany, N.E. of Wuppertal; iron, steel, chemicals, textiles, paper; p. *(1963) 198.800.*

Hagenau, *t.*, Bas-Rhin, France; textiles, porcelain, soap, beer; p. *(1962) 21,841.*

Hagerstown, *c.*, Md., U.S.A.; machin., furniture, chemicals; p. *(1960) 36,660.*

Hagonoy, *mun.*, Luzon, Philippine Is.; maize, rice, sugar.

Hague, C. de La, Cotentin Peninsula, France; French fleet defeated by British 1692.

Hague, The, or 's-Gravenhage or Den Haag, *t.*, S. Holland, Netherlands; seat of government; permanent court of international justice; adm. ctr.; urban inds., mach. and metal wares; engin., printing; p. *(1967) 586,187.*

Haifa, *ch. spt.*, Israel; on Bay of Acre at foot of Mt. Carmel; terminus of Iraq oil pipeline; inds. include oil refining, car assembly, steel, chemical wks, petro-chemicals; Technion univ.; p. (estd. 1951) *190,000.*

Hail, *t.*, Neid, Saudi Arabia; p. over *10,000.*

Hailsham, *mkt. t.*, *rural dist.*, Sussex, Eng.; 5 m. N. of Eastbourne; mats, rope and twine; p. (rural dist. 1961) *42,372.*

Hainan, *I.*, S. coast of China; ch. t. Kiungchow; densely wooded, camphor, mahogany, rosewood; a. 13,974 sq. m.

Hainaut, *prov.*, Belgium, adjoining N.E. border of France; industl. and agr.; coal- and iron-mines; a. 1,436 sq. m.; p. *(1962) 1,249,536.*

Hainburg, *t.*, Austria; on R. Danube; tobacco; Roman remains; p. *(1961) 6,437.*

Haine, *R.*, Belgium, and Nord, France; trib. of R. Scheldt; length 40 m.

Haiphong, *t.*, *ch. port*, N. Viet-Nam; thriving tr.; cotton, thread, soap, glass, enamel ware, fish canning; p. *(1960) 369,000.*

Haiti, *rep.* (the "Black Republic"), W. Indies; consists of W. portion of I. of Hispaniola; cap. Port au Prince; language French; coffee, sisal, sugar, textiles, soap, cement, rum; a. 10,204 sq. m.; p. (estd. 1964) *4,000,000.*

Hakodate, *spt.*, Hokkaido, Japan; fishing ctr., sulpher, dried fish, timber; p. *(1965) 243,418.*

Hal, *t.*, central Belgium; flax; p. *(1962) 19,508.*

Halberstadt, *c.*, Magdeburg, E. Germany; cath.; metallurgy, rubber inds., engin.; rly. junction; p. *(1963) 46,355.*

Halden, *t.*, S.E. Norway; wood-pulp, paper, footwear, cotton spinning; nuclear research reactor; p. *(1960) 10,006.*

Haldensleben, *t.*, Magdeburg, E. Germany; leather, stoneware; p. *(1963) 21,254.*

Haldia, *pt.*, W. Bengal, India; nr. mouth of R. Hooghli; satellite pt. for Calcutta to handle coal, ore, grain; oil pipeline to Barauni; refinery.

Halesowen, *industl. t.*, *mun. bor.*, S.W. of Birmingham, Worc., Eng.; coal, weldless tubes, elec. gds., stainless steel forgings, engin.; p. (estd. 1967) *50,390.*

Halesworth, *t.*, *urb. dist.*, E. Suffolk, Eng.; on R. Blyth, 7 m. S. of Beccles; farming, corn mills, malting, engin.; p. *(1961) 2,252.*

Halifax, *spt.*, *cap.*, Nova Scotia, Canada; gr. tr.; univ.; naval sta. and dockyard, open in winter; machin., iron foundries, boots and shoes, oil refining; p. *(1961) 183,946.*

Halifax, *t.*, *co. bor.*, W.R. Yorks, Eng.; E. flanks Pennines, 8 m. S.W. of Bradford; carpets, textiles and machine tools; p. (estd. 1967) *94,770.*

Hall Peninsula, S.E. Baffin Land, Canada; between Cumberland Sound and Frobisher Bay.

Hallamshire, S., *dist.*, W.R. Yorks. Eng.; inc. Sheffield and Ecclesfield. [*170,060.*

Halland, *co.*, Sweden: a. 1,901 sq. m.; p. (1961)

Halle, *t.*, Halle, E. Germany; on R. Saale: univ.; lignite, potash, engin., chemicals; p. (1963) *273,729.*

Hallein, *t.*, Salzburg, Austria; on Austro-German frontier, 13 m. S. of Salzburg; impt. salt-mines; p. (1961) *13,329.* [culture type site.

Hallstatt, *vil.*, Upper Austria; early Iron Age

Halluin, *frontier industl. t.*, Nord, France; on R. Lys; p. (1962) *14,138.*

Halmahera, *I.*, Indonesia; mountainous, active volcanoes, tropical forests; spices, pearl fisheries; grows sago and rice; a. 6,648 sq. m.

Halmstad, *spt.*, Kattegat, Sweden; iron and steel wks., machin. engin., cycles, textiles, leather, jute, wood-pulp; p. (1961) *39,032.*

Hals, *t.*, Jutland, Denmark; on Lim Fjord.

Halstead, *t.*, *urb. dist.*, Essex, Eng.; on R. Colne, 12 m. N.W. of Colchester; rayon weaving, farming; p. (1961) *6,465.* [p. (estd. 1967) *50,660.*

Haltemprice, *t.*, *urb. dist.*, E. Riding, Yorks, Eng.;

Haltom City, *t.*, Texas, U.S.A.; p. (1960) *23,133.*

Haltwhistle, *mkt. t.*, *rural dist.*, Northumberland, Eng.; on R. Tyne; coal, paint wks., agr.; p. (rural dist. 1961) *6,884.*

Ham, *t.*, Somme dep., N. France; on R. Somme, nr. Amiens; old cas.; p. (1962) *4,449.*

Hama, *c.*, Upper Syria; on R. Orontes; the ancient Hamath, cap. of a kingdom in time of Kings David and Solomon; cement wks.; p. (1961) *116,362.*

Hamadan, *dist.*, W. Iran; cold in winter; cap. Hamadan; p. (1967) *888,663.*

Hamadan, (*anc.* Ecbatana), *c.* Iran, cap. prov.; carpets, pottery; airpt.; tomb of Avicenna; p. (1967) *553,598.*

Hamamatsu, *t.*, S. Honshu, Japan; on cst. plain 60 m. S.E. of Nagoya; ctr. of impt. cotton-mftg. region; textiles, dyeing, musical instruments, motor cycles; p. (1964) *370,000.*

Hamar, *t.*, Norway; on L. Mjösa; ctr. of rich agr. dist.; tr. and mftg. inds.; p. (estd. 1960) *13,000.*

Hamburg, *Land*, W. Germany; cap. Hamburg; a. 299 sq. m.

Hamburg, *gr. spt.*, *industl. and comm. t.*, *Land* Hamburg, N. Germany; astride R. Elbe, 85 m. upstream from N. Sea; second lgst. German t., and ch. pt.; univ. and hydrographic institute; handles vast tr., inc. liner traffic and barge traffic down Elbe from Saxony and Bohemia (Czechoslovakia), also much trans-shipment of goods; imports fuel, raw materials for inds., foodstuffs; exports textiles, leather goods, chemicals, light-engin. prod.; ch. inds., shipbldg., fishing, food processing, leather, brewing, tobacco, textiles, rubber, oil, wood; impt. airport; p. (1963) *1,851,000.*

Hamburg, *t.*, N.Y., U.S.A.; optical goods; mkt. gardening; p. (1960) *9,145.*

Hamburg, *bor.*, S.E. Penns., U.S.A.; coal, mnfs.; p. (1950) *3,805.* [m.; p. (1966) *608,091.*

Hame (Tavastehus), *dep.*, Finland; a. 7,118 sq.

Hamelin (Hameln), *t.*, Lower Saxony, Germany; on R. Weser; iron, textiles; legend of "The Pied Piper"; p. (1963) *49,500.*

Hamilton, *cap.* Bermudas (on largest I.); p. (estd. 1957) *3,000.*

Hamilton, *t.*, W. Victoria, Australia; mkt. ctr. for dairying and grazing a.; p. (1966) *10,052.*

Hamilton, *c.* and *L. pt.*, S.E. Ontario, Canada; at W. end of L. Ontario; varied metallurgical mnfs. and has been called the "Birmingham" and "Manchester" of Canada; fruit ctr.; univ.; p. (1961) *395,189.* [p. (1961) *50,433.*

Hamilton, *c.*, N.I., N.Z., on Waikato R.; univ.;

Hamilton, *burgh*, Lanark, Scot.; in Clyde valley, 10 m. S.E. of Glasgow; elec. goods, iron and steel foundries, carpet mftg., cotton, woollen and knit-wear goods; p. (1961) *41,928.*

Hamilton, *c.*, Ohio, U.S.A.; on the Gr. Maine R., thriving ind. and tr.; p. (1960) *72,354.*

Hamilton, *R.*, *see* Churchill R.

Hamlet, *t.*, N.C., U.S.A.; rly. ctr. in peach- and tobacco-growing region; p. (1950) *5,061.*

Hamm, *t.*, N. Rhine–Westphalia, Germany; on R. Lippe, nr. Dortmund; rly. marshalling yards, iron inds.; p. (1963) *71,300.*

Hamme, *t.*, E. Flanders, Belgium; rope, linen and lace factories; p. (1962) *18,880.*

Hammerfest, *spt.*, Norway; world's most northerly t.; fishing; p. (1961) *5,604.*

Hammersmith, *Thames-side inner bor.*, London, Eng.; inc. former bor. of Fulham; industl., residtl.; elec. and car accessories, synthetic rubber; p. (1966) *214,000.*

Hammond, *c.*, Ind., U.S.A.; ironwks., pork packing; p. (1960) *111,698.* [p. (1960) *10,563.*

Hammond, *t.*, La., U.S.A.; strawberry culture;

Hamoaze, estuary of R. Tamar, Plymouth, Eng.

Hampshire, *co.*, Eng.; ch. town Southampton; farming; shipbldg., brewing, tanning; a. 1,503 sq. m.; p. (1966) *1,483,000.*

Hampstead, *see* Camden.

Hampton, *Thames-side t.*, inc. in Richmond upon Thames, outer London bor., Eng.; Hampton Court Palace in the par.; Hampton Wick is a mile E. of H. Court.

Hampton, *t.*, S.E. Va., U.S.A.; oldest English community in the U.S.; fishing, oyster and crab packing; p. (1960) *89,258.*

Hamtramck, *t.*, Mich., U.S.A.; p. (1960) *34,137.*

Han Kiang, *R.*, Hupeh, China; rises in E. edge of Tibet plateau, flows S.E. between Tsinling Shan and Tapa Shan into Yangtze-Kiang at Hankow; upper course crosses fertile Nancheng valley, length 60 m., width 12 m.; lower course interrupted by many deep gorges, especially below Ankang; ch. trib. of Yangtze-Kiang, length over 1,000 m.

Hanau, *t.*, Hessen, Germany, on R. Main; rubber and non-ferrous metals inds., jewellery; p. (1963) *48,500.*

Hancock, *t.*, Mich., U.S.A.; copper-mines; iron and brass mnfs.; p. (1960) *5,022.*

Hangchow (Hangzhou), *c.*, *cap.*, Chekiang, China; head of H. Bay; former treaty pt.; extensive tr.; ctr. of silk-weaving ind.; p. (1953) *697,000.*

Hanko, *t.*, on S. point, Finland; p. (1966) *9,414.*

Hankow, *c.*, *former treaty pt.*, Hupeh, China; 700 m. from mouth of Yangtze-Kiang; great tea mart, also lge. tr. in opium, raw silk, cotton, etc., iron and steel wks., textiles, flour. *See also* Wuhan.

Hanley, *industl. t.* (now inc. in co. bor. of Stoke-on-Trent), Staffs, Eng.; pottery, china.

Hannibal, *c.*, Mo., U.S.A.; on R. Mississippi; timber and wagon bldg.; p. (1960) *20,028.*

Hanoi, *c.*, *cap.*, N. Viet-Nam; ancient "Ke-Sho" or "great market" on the Red R.; old Annamese fort, now modern comm. ctr.; univ.; cotton, silks, tobacco, pottery; superphosphate and magnesium phosphate nearby; bricks, concrete, rubber; p. (1960) *644,000.*

Hanover, *t.*, *cap.*, Lower Saxony, Germany; W. of Brunswick; iron, textiles, machin., paper, biscuits, cigarettes, cars, rubber processing, chemicals; gr. route ctr.; p. (1963) *571,300.*

Hanover, *bor.*, Penns., U.S.A.; mnfs. shoes, jute, wire cloth; p. (1960) *15,538.* [*24,991.*

Hanwell, *t.*, Middlx., Eng.; on R. Brent; p. (1961)

Hanyang, *industl. c.*, China; opp. Hankow, on Yangtze-kiang; lge. iron wks. *See also* Wuhan.

Haparanda, *spt.*, N. Sweden; salmon fishing; exp., timber and prod. of the Lapps; p. (1961) *3,394.*

Hapur, *t.*, W. Uttar Pradesh, India; tr. in sugar, timber, cotton, brassware; p. (1961) *55,243.*

Harar, *cap.* Harar prov., Ethiopia; hides and skins, ivory, cattle; p. approx. *25,000.*

Harbin, *c.*, Heilungkiang, China; former treaty pt.; rly. junction; soya-beans, flour, tanning, distilling; machin.; p. (1953) *1,163,000.*

Harbour Grace, *t.*, *pt.*, Conception Bay, New-foundland, Canada; p. (1961) *2,650.*

Harburg, *spt.*, Hanover, Germany; on R. Elbe, nr. Hamburg; linseed-crushing, india-rubber ind., etc.

Hardanger Fjord, W. cst. Norway; 75 m. long.

Hardt Mtns., W. Germany; northward continuation of Vosges on W. of Rhine rift valley; formerly forested, now lgely cleared for pasture; highest points reach just over 2,000 ft.

Hardwar, *t.*, Uttar Pradesh, India; on R. Ganges; gr. annual fair and pilgrimage; p. (1961) *58,513.*

Harelbeke, *t.*, N.W. Belgium; tobacco; p. (1962) *16,998.*

Hariana, *st.*, India, formed 1966 when Punjab st. was partitioned on linguistic basis; Hindu speaking; joint cap. with Punjab st. Chandigarh; p. (estd. 1966) *7,000,000.*

Haringey, *outer bor.*, Greater London, Eng.; comprising former bors. of Hornsey, Tottenham and Wood Green; p. (1966) *255,000.*

Hari-Rud, *R.*, N. Afghanistan and Iran; the ancient "Arius"; length 650 m.; (*Rud* = river).

# ATLAS OF THE WORLD

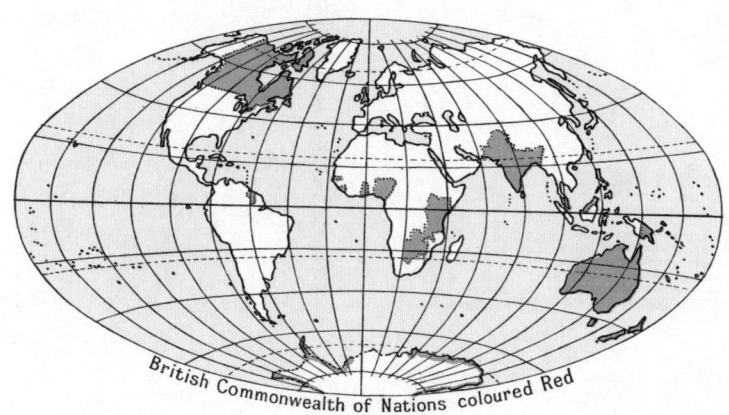

British Commonwealth of Nations coloured Red

## CONTENTS

©

PRINTED BY JOHN BARTHOLOMEW AND SON, LTD.,
AT THE GEOGRAPHICAL INSTITUTE, EDINBURGH

3645

2

POLITICAL DIVISIONS OF
THE WORLD
On Mercator's Projection
Railways thus

EUROPE

English Miles

0  100  200  300  400  500

Railways thus

ENGLAND AND WALES

English Miles

0   20   40   60   80   100

Railways thus

N O R T H   S E A

SCOTLAND

EDINBURGH

Leith

Glasgow

Greenock

Ayr

Firth of Clyde

Kintyre

Arran

North Channel

Stranraer

Portpatrick

Donaghadee

Belfast

Lurne

Dundrum B.

IRELAND

DUBLIN

Dúnlaoghaire

IRISH SEA

ISLE OF MAN

Peel

Ramsey

Douglas

Castletown

Pt of Ayre

Calf of Man

Dumfries

Berwick

Coldstream

Hawick

R. Tweed

Flodden

Cheviot Hills

Wooler

Holy I.

Farne Is.

Alnwick

Coquet I.

Morpeth

NORTHUMBERLAND

Tynemouth

Whitley Bay

Blyth

R. Tyne

Newcastle

N. Shields

S. Shields

Sunderland

Gateshead

Hexham

DURHAM

Durham

Hartlepool

Stockton

R. Tees

Darlington

Middlesbrough

Saltburn

Whitby

Scarborough

Filey

Flamborough Hd.

Bridlington & Bay

Hornsea

Withernsea

YORK

NORTH RIDING

EAST RIDING

WEST RIDING

Richmond

Northallerton

Thirsk

Malton

Pickering

Beverley

Hull

R. Humber

Goole

Doncaster

Sheffield

Rotherham

Barnsley

Wakefield

Leeds

Bradford

Halifax

Huddersfield

Ripon

Harrogate

Pontefract

LINCOLN

LINDSEY

Gainsborough

Louth

Mablethorpe

Sutton-on-Sea

Spurn Head

Grimsby

CUMBERLAND

Carlisle

Penrith

Keswick

Whitehaven

WESTMORLAND

Kendal

Appleby

PENNINE

LANCASHIRE

Lancaster

Morecambe

Fleetwood

Blackpool

Lytham

Southport

Preston

Blackburn

Burnley

Bolton

Wigan

Salford

MANCHESTER

Oldham

Stockport

Macclesfield

Liverpool

Birkenhead

Chester

Anglesey

Amlwch

Holyhead

CAERNARVON

# LONDON

## SHOWING RAILWAYS AND PLACES OF INTEREST

UNDERGROUND
OTHER RAILWAYS - - - - -

# LONDON DISTRICT

| | | |
|---|---|---|
| 5 | 10 | 15 Miles |

Main Roads ——
Secondary Roads ====
Other Roads ——
Railways ====

**LONDON**

Aylesbury · Leighton Buzzard · Ivinghoe · Kensworth · Markyate Street

BUCKINGHAM · Thame · Stone · Stanbridge · Wendover · Princes Risborough · Chesham · Berkhamstead · Hemel Hempstead · King's Langley · Chipperfield · Chenies · Watford

Chinnor · Lane End · Stokenchurch · Missenden · Amersham · Chorleywood · Rickmansworth · Radlett · Mimms · Barnet

Henley on Thames · Marlow · Hurley · Hargrave · Bourne End · High Wycombe · Beaconsfield · Chalfont · Gerrard's Cross · Denham · Uxbridge · Harrow · Stanmore

READING · Wargrave · Twyford · Cookham · Maidenhead · Taplow · Burnham · Slough · Eton · WINDSOR · Staines

HERTFORD · Ware · Hatfield · Welwyn · Hatfield Heath · Hertford · Hoddesdon · Wormley · Cheshunt · Hatfield · St. Albans · Waltham Abbey · Enfield

Leaden Roding · Hatfield Broad Oak · Harlow · Potter Street · Epping · Ongar · Chipping Ongar · Ingatestone

CHELMSFORD · Writtle · Roxwell · Fyfield · Chignall

Baddow · Stock · Billericay · Brentwood · Brook Street · Noak Hill · Romford · Barking

Danbury · Cold Norton · Rettendon · Rochford · SOUTHEND ON SEA · Shoeburyness · Shoebury Ness

Maldon · Steeple · Burnham · Wakering · Gt. Wakering · Foulness

Pitsea · Benfleet · Canvey I. · Thames · Sheerness · STEPPEY · Sheppey

Grays · Tilbury · Gravesend · Cliffe · Allhallows · Grain · SHEERNESS

Dartford · Swanscombe · Northfleet · Strood · ROCHESTER · Chatham · GILLINGHAM · Rainham · Sittingbourne

Bexley · Crayford · Erith · Wilmington · Eynsford · Farningham · Meopham · Cobham · Snodland · Boxley

Bromley · Orpington · Sevenoaks · Seal · Kemsing · Wrotham · West Malling · MAIDSTONE · Loose

Croydon · Caterham · Godstone · Westerham · Brasted · Ide Hill · Leigh · Tonbridge · Hadlow · Yalding · Marden

SURREY · Richmond · Kingston · Esher · Epsom · Sutton · Carshalton · Wallington · Beckenham · Penge

Sunbury · Walton · Weybridge · Cobham · Leatherhead · Dorking · Reigate · Redhill · Merstham · Oxted · Edenbridge · Hever · Penshurst · KENT

Chertsey · Woking · Byfleet · Ripley · Send · Ockham · Wotton · Limpsfield · Lingfield · Crockham Hill · New Chapel

Aldershot · Farnham · Farnborough · Frimley · Bagshot · Bisley · Chobham · Worplesdon · GUILDFORD · Godalming · Milford · Bramley · Horsley

Ascot · Sunningdale · Windlesham · Bracknell · Wokingham · Crowthorne · Sandhurst · Yateley · Hook

8

SCOTLAND

English Miles
0    10    20    30    40

Railways thus

*Same Scale*

Unst
Yell
*Fetlar*
SHETLAND
*Whalsey* *Sula Sgear*
*Nth Rona*
Lerwick
Bressay
*Sandness*
Fitful Hd.
*Sumburgh Hd.*

ORKNEY
*Pt. Nth Ronaldsay*
Westray
*Rousay* Sanday
*Eday* Stronsay
*Shapinsay*
*Skara Brae*
Stromness Kirkwall
Hoy *South*
Pentland Firth *St. Ronaldsay*

C. Wrath
*L. Eriboll*
*Kyle of Tongue*
Scrabster *Scaby Pt.*
Dunnet Hd.
*Dounreay* Duncansby Hd.
Thurso *Jn O'Groats Ho.*
Noss Hd.
Wick

CAITHNESS
Morven

NORTH

SEA

*L. Laxford*
Eddrachillis
*Pt. of Stoer*
*L. Assynt*
*L. Enard*
*Ben More Assynt*
SUTHERLAND
*L. Naver*
*L. Shin*
Lairg Brora
Golspie
Helmsdale

OUTER HEBRIDES

Stornoway
Lewis
North Minch
Harris
Tarbert
*St. Kilda's*

58

Uig
N. Uist
*Lochmaddy*
Benbecula
South Uist
*L. Broom*
*L. En...*
Ullapool
*L. Grunard*
*L. Maree*
Ben Dearg
Dingwall
Cromarty
ROSS & CROMARTY
Dornoch Firth
Dornoch
Tain *Tarbat Ness*
*Moray Firth*

Little Minch
*L. Torridon*
*Ben Wyvis*
*Fannich*
Beauly
Fortrose
Nairn
NAIRN
Forres
*Elgin*
*Fochabers*
MORAY
Keith
BANFF
Banff
*Macduff*
*Portsoy*
*Cullen*

Skye
*Cuillin Hills*
*L. Bracadale*
*Raasay*
*Scalpa*
Kyle of Lochalsh
*Glenelg*
Inverness
*L. Ness*
*R. Spey*
Grantown on Spey
Huntly
Inverurie
ABERDEEN
Aberdeen
Peterhead
*Fraserburgh*
*Buchan Ness*
*R. Ugie*

Canna
*Eriskay*
Barra
*Barra Hd.*

Rum
Eigg
Muck
Coll
Tiree
Staffa
Iona
*Skerryvore L.H.*

*Ardnamurchan Pt.*
*Sleat*
*L. Hourn*
*L. Arkaig*
*L. Lochy*
Fort Augustus
*L. Oich*
INVERNESS
Kingussie
Aviemore
Cairn Gorm
Ben Macdhui
*Balmoral Castle*
Ballater
Aboyne
Banchory
*R. Dee*

*L. Eil*
Fort William
Ben Nevis
4406
Kinlochleven
*L. Leven*
Lydoch
*L. Laggan*
Grampian Mountains
Ben Glee
*L. Ericht*
Blair Athol
*Killiecrankie Pass*
Pitlochry
*V. Esk*
KINCARDINE
Inverbervie
Stonehaven

ATLANTIC

OCEAN

56

*Scarba*
Colonsay
*Corryvreckan*
Oronsay
Jura
Islay
*Bowmore*
*Port Ellen*
*Mull of Oa*
Gigha
*Mull of Kintyre*

Mull
Ben More
Tobermory
*Sound of Mull*
*Lismore*
*L. Sunart*
*L. Linnhe*
Oban
ARGYLL
*L. Awe*
*L. Etive*
Inveraray
*Firth of Lorn*
*L. Fyne*
*L. Long*

Ben Cruachan
Ben More
Ben Lawers
*L. Earn*
PERTH
Crieff Perth
Scone
Ben Lomond
*L. Tay*
Aberfeldy
Dunkeld
*L. Rannoch*
Schiehallion
Coupar Angus
Brechin
ANGUS
Forfar
Montrose
Arbroath
*Bell Rock*
Dundee
*R. Tay*
Cupar
St. Andrews
FIFE
*Fife Ness*
*Leven*
Methil
*I. of May*

Ben Ledi
*L. Katrine*
Callander
*Dunblane*
Dumbarton
STIRLING
Stirling
CLACKMANNAN
Kinross
KINROSS
Dunfermline
*Firth of Forth*
*Nth Berwick*
Dunbar

*Kintyre*
Campbeltown
*Machrihanish*

Bute
Rothesay
Greenock
Port Glasgow
Paisley
GLASGOW
RENFREW
*Barrhead*
Airdrie
Coatbridge
*Wishaw*
Hamilton
LANARK
Lanark
MIDLOTHIAN
Edinburgh
Leith
*Dalkeith*
*Pentland Hills*
PEEBLES
Peebles
E. LOTHIAN
Haddington
*St. Abbs*
BERWICK
Greenlaw
Coldstream
Duns
*Lammermuir Hills*

NORTH CHANNEL

Arran
Brodick
*L. Fyne*
Kilmarnock
Irvine
Troon
Prestwick
Ayr
AYR
Kilwinning
Ardrossan
Saltcoats
*Tinto*
Galashiels
*Broad Law*
SELKIRK
Selkirk
*Teviot*
ROXBURGH
Hawick
*Cheviot Hills*
Jedburgh
Kelso

*Turnberry*
*Ailsa Craig*
Girvan
Maybole
*L. Doon*
*R. Doon*
Sanquhar
Cumnock
Leadhills
*Lowther Hills*
Moffat
*Tweedsmuir Hills*
Langholm

Merrick
*L. Ken*
*R. Ken*
DUMFRIES
Lockerbie
Dumfries
Annan

*Corsewall Pt.*
Newton Stewart
Stranraer
Portpatrick
WIGTOWN
Wigtown
KIRKCUDBRIGHT
Castle Douglas
Kirkcudbright
*Southerness Pt.*
Solway Firth
Carlisle

Londonderry
Larne

IRELAND
Belfast

*Luce Bay*
*Burrow Hd.*
*Mull of Galloway*
*Wigtown Bay*

ENGLAND

IRELAND

*English Miles*

0   10   20   30   40   50

*Railways thus*

FRANCE AND
ADJOINING COUNTRIES

English Miles

0     100     200

Railways thus

Lisbon to Bordeaux 730

Liverpool to Bordeaux 780

# GERMANY, POLAND AND CENTRAL EUROPE

English Miles

Railways thus ———

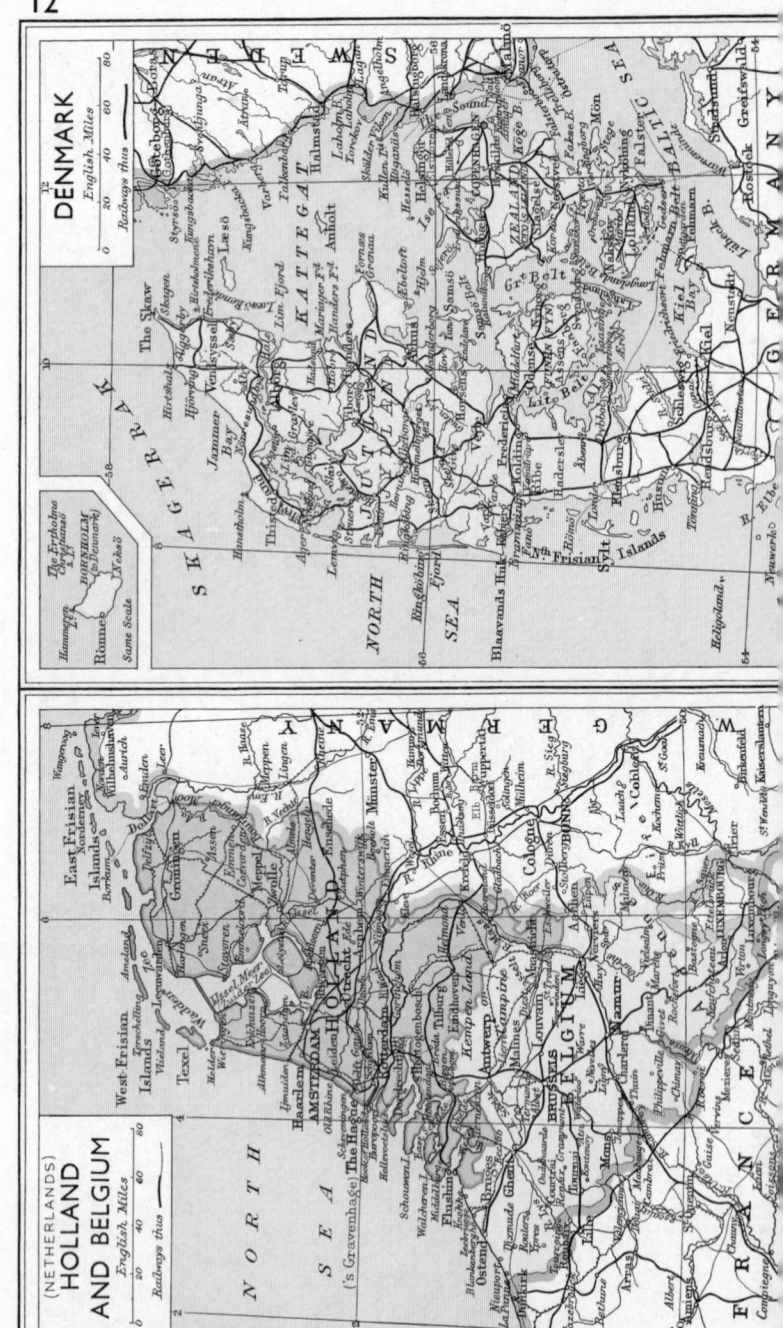

DENMARK

English Miles

0    20    40    60    80

Railways thus

S W E D E N

BORNHOLM
(to Denmark)

The Ertholms
(to Denmark)

Hammeren
Rönne
Nexö

Same Scale

S K A G E R R A K

KATTEGAT

The Skaw

J U T L A N D

NORTH

SEA

Nth. Frisian Islands

Heligoland

R. Elbe

G E R M A N Y

BALTIC

SEA

ZEALAND

COPENHAGEN

FALSTER

LOLLAND

(NETHERLANDS)

HOLLAND
AND BELGIUM

English Miles

0    20    40    60    80

Railways thus

NORTH

SEA

East Frisian Islands

West Frisian Islands

Texel

HOLLAND

AMSTERDAM

Haarlem

The Hague
('s Gravenhage)

BELGIUM

BRUSSELS

Antwerp

Bruges

Ostend

G E R M A N Y

Cologne

BONN

Aachen

LUXEMBOURG

F R A N C E

SWITZERLAND

13

On the same scale

**ICELAND**

Horn (North C.)
Isafjördur
Siglufjördur
Akureyri
Langanes
Breidha
Bordeyri
Seydisfjordur
Faxaflói
Vatna Jökull
REYKJAVIK
Öræfa J. 6930
Djupivogur
Hafnarfjördur
Hekla
Vestmannaeyjar
Surtsey

# SCANDINAVIA AND BALTIC LANDS

*English Miles*

0   50   100   200   300

Railways thus ————

North Cape
Nordkyn
Hammerfest
Vardö
Vadsö
Varanger Fd.
Tana
Tromsö
Kirkenes
Pechenga
Kola B.
Murmansk
Senja
Finnes
Lake Inari
Polyarnyi
Kola
Lofoten
Islands
Gjastad
Narvik
Kiruna
Kandalaksha
Vest Fd.
Torne
Kolari
Bodö
Saltdal
Harsprånget
Gällivare
Kemijärvi
Arctic Circle
Horn avan
Boden
Kemi
Taivalkoski
Mosjöen
Piteå
Oulu
Vikna I.
Stensele
Skellefteå
Raahe
Folda Fd.
Vilhelmina
Namsos
Grong
Vannas
Umeå
Kokkola
Iisalmi
Nurmes
Levanger
Trondheim fd.
Östersund
Örnsköldsvik
Vaasa
Seinäjoki
Kuopio
Kristiansund
Trondheim
Stor L.
Bräcke
Sollyftea
Kristinankaupunki
Mikkeli
Ålesund
Molde
Dovre
Röros
Hede
Härnösand
Sundsvall
Pori
Tampere
Saimaa
Dombas
Galdhöpiggen
Siegemon
Hudiksvall
Rauma
Lahti
Söderhamn
Sogn Fd.
Jostedals
bree
Glittertind
Gävle
Åland Is.
Kuhmäki
Turku
HELSINKI
Kotka
Bergen
Mjösa L.
Hamar
Falun
Avesta
Viipuri
Vik
Hönefoss
Uppsala
Gulf of Finland
Hanko
Hangö
Kronstadt
Stord
Odda
Kongsvinger
Hankö
Tallinn
Narva
Haugesund
Drammen
Arvika
Fredrik
Karlstad
Västerås
STOCKHOLM
Hiiumaa
Paldiski
Lake Peipas
Böknf.
Stavanger
Larvik
Dano
L. Vänern
Vkbro
Majen
ESTONIA
Tartu
Pskov
Egersund
Arendal
Uddevalla
Mariestad
Norrköping
Saaremaa
Pärnu
Ostrov
Flekkefjord
Kristiansand
Skagerrak
Grenen
Vänersborg
Linköping
Gulf of Riga
Valga
Cesis
Madona
Rezekne
The Naze
NORTH
Fredrikshavn
Borås
Jönköping
Västervik
Visby
Ventspils
Gotland
RIGA
Thisted
Varberg
Oskarshamn
Fishy
Jelgava
W. Dvina
Daugavpils
SEA
Viborg
Kattegat
Halmstad
Kalmar
Öland
Liepāja
(Libau)
LATVIA
Ringköbing
Randers
Hälsingborg
Karlskrona
Klaipeda
Telsiai
Siauliai
Polotsk
DENMARK
Helsingör
Lund
Kristianstad
Mamel
LITHUANIA
Lepel
Esbjerg
Frederica
COPENHAGEN
Sovetsk
Kaunas
Sylt
Nordre
Funen Zealand
Trelleborg
VILNIUS
(VILNA)
Schleswig
Lolland
Falster
Bornholm
(Den.)
Kaliningrad
(Königsberg)
Lida
MINSK
Heligoland
Altona
Sassnitz
Rügen
Kolobrzeg
Gdynia
Gdansk
(Danzig)
Elbląg
Elblag
Shwalki
Grodno
WHITE
Horn Reef
Emden
Hamburg
Lübeck
Rostock
Świnoujście
(Swinemünde)
Szczecin
(Stettin)
Bydgoszcz
Toruń
Łomża
Białystok
RUSSIA
HOLL.
Zwolle
WEST
Bremen
EAST
Berlin
Frankfurt
POZNAŃ
WARSAW
Brest
(Brest Litovsk)
Pinsk
Pripet
Marshes
GERMANY
Brunswick
Münster
POLAND

15

ATLANTIC OCEAN

SPAIN AND
PORTUGAL

English Miles

0    100    200

Railways thus

Marseilles to Tunis 470, Malta 655
Marseilles to Philippeville 395
Marseilles to Bougie 395
Marseilles to Algiers 400

MEDITERRANEAN SEA

SPAIN

PORTUGAL

Gulf of Lions

Barcelona

Minorca

Majorca

Balearic Is.

Madrid

Valencia

Andalusia

LISBON

Seville

Cadiz

Strait of Gibraltar

Gibraltar

Ceuta

MOROCCO

ALGERIA

Plymouth to Gibraltar 1050

C. Finisterre

C. St. Vincent

16

# ITALY, CENTRAL EUROPE
## AND THE BALKANS

English Miles

0    100    200

Railways thus

U.S.S.R.

English Miles

200  400  600  800

Railways thus

19

S.W. ASIA

English Miles

0   100   200   300   400

Railways thus

**21**

INDIA, PAKISTAN
CEYLON & BURMA

English Miles
0    100  200  300  400  500  600
Railways thus

CHINA AND JAPAN

## S.E. ASIA

English Miles

Railways thus

PACIFIC OCEAN

MARIANAS OR LADRONES IS.

CAROLINE ISLANDS

(U.S.A. Trust Terr.)

PHILIPPINES

LUZON

MANILA

MINDANAO

SOUTH CHINA SEA

INDO-CHINA

NAM

THAILAND

LAOS

KAMPOT

Siam

Gulf of

MALAY PENINSULA

SINGAPORE

MALACCA STRAIT

SUMATRA

SULU SEA

CELEBES SEA

BORNEO

SABAH

SARAWAK

KALIMANTAN

EAST

WEST

CENTRAL

CELEBES

MOLUCCAS

Halmahera

BANDA SEA

WEST IRIAN

NEW GUINEA (AUST.)

Equator

CORAL SEA

ARAFURA SEA

TORRES STRAIT

AUSTRALIA

TIMOR SEA

JAVA SEA

JAVA

JAKARTA

INDIAN OCEAN

AFRICA

English Miles

0 100 200 300 400 500        1000

Railways thus

T.F.A.I.—Territoire Français des Afars et des Issas.

27

## UNITED STATES

English Miles

0  100  200  300  400  500

Railways thus

MEXICO,
CENTRAL AMERICA
AND WEST INDIES

English Miles

Railways thus

SOUTH AMERICA

English Miles

0        500        1000

Railways thus

PACIFIC OCEAN

On Mercator's Projection

Railways thus ————

Harlech, *t.*, Merioneth, Wales; on Cardigan Bay, 10 m. N. of Barmouth; famous cas.; farming.

Harlem, *R.*, N.Y., U.S.A.; and Spuyten Duyvil Creek together form a waterway c. 8 m. long, extending from the East R. to Hudson R., and separates the bors. Manhattan and Bronx.

Harlingen, *spt.*, Friesland, Netherlands; margarine, mixed farming, fish; natural gas; p. *10,400*.

Harlow, *t.*, Essex, Eng.; in valley of R. Stort, 22 m. N.E. of London; one of "New Towns" designated 1947; spreads S.W. from nucleus of old mkt. t. of Harlow; engin., glass, furniture mkg., metallurgy; p. (estd. 1967) *71,370*.

Harnosand, *t.*, Sweden; on G. of Bothnia; engin., saw-mills, pulp, graphite prod.; p. (1961) *17,163*.

Harpenden, *t.*, *urb. dist.*, Herts, Eng.; in Chiltern Hills, 5 m. N. of St. Albans; Rothamsted agr. experimental sta.; rubber, hosiery, basket mftg., engin.; p. (estd. 1967) *22,020*.

Harringay, *see* Haringey.

Harris, *par.*, Lewis I., Outer Hebrides, Scot.; inc. several sm. islets; tweeds, fishing; p. *4,467*.

Harrisburg, *c.*, *cap.*, Penns., U.S.A.; iron, steel factories, machin., cigarettes, cotton goods; p. (1960) *79,697*.

Harrisburg, *t.*, Ill., U.S.A.; p. (1960) *9,171*.

Harrison or East Newark, *industl. t.*, N.J., U.S.A.; p. (1960) *11,743*.

Harrogate, *t.*, *mun. bor.*, spa, W.R. Yorks, Eng.; in valley of R. Nidd, 14 m. N. of Leeds; numerous chalybeate springs; p. (estd. 1967) *60,720*.

Harrow, *outer bor.*, Greater London, Eng.; famous public school; camera mftg.; p. (1966) *209,000*.

Harstad, *ch. t.*, Lofoten Is., N.W. Norway; herring ind., woollen goods; p. (1960) *4,028*.

Hart Fells, *mtn.*, between Peebles and Dumfries, Scot.; alt. 2,651 ft.

Hartebeestpoort Dam, Transvaal, Rep. of S. Africa; on R. Crocodile (Limpopo), 25 m. W. of Pretoria; supplies water for cultivation, under irrigation, of cotton, maize, tobacco.

Hartford, *cap.*, Conn., U.S.A.; lge. comm. ctr., seat of Trinity College; small arms, typewriters, elec. machin., aircraft engin., ceramics, plastics; p. (1960) *162,178*.

Hartford City, Ind., U.S.A.; p. (1960) *8,053*.

Hartland Point, Barnstaple Bay, N. Devon, Eng.

Hartlepool, *spt.*, *co. bor.*, Durham, Eng.; on E. cst., 3 m. N. of estuary of R. Tees; iron inds., shipbldg., light inds., timber; good sands for holiday-makers to the S.; p. (estd. 1967) *98,040*.

Hartsville, *t.*, S.C., U.S.A.; cotton, rayon, silk, textiles; nuclear power plant being built; p. (1960) *6,392*.

Harvey, *t.*, N.E. Ill., U.S.A.; rolling stock, diesel engines, heavy machin.; p. (1960) *29,071*.

Harwell, *vil.*, Berkshire, Eng.; 12 m. S. of Oxford; Atomic Energy Research Estab.; nuclear power research and prod. of radioisotopes.

Harwich, *spt.*, *mun. bor.*, Essex, Eng.; on S. cst. of estuary of R. Stour; packet sta. for Belgium, Netherlands, Denmark; docks, naval base, fisheries, light inds.; p. (estd. 1967) *14,400*.

Harz Mtns., *range* in Hanover and Brunswick, Germany; highest peak the Brocken; 1,142 m. forested slopes rich in minerals; length 57 m.

Haslemere, *mkt. t.*, *urb. dist.*, Surrey, Eng.; 13 m. S.W. of Guildford, on hills of Hindhead and Blackdown; residtl.; lt. inds.; p. (1961) *12,528*.

Haslingden, *t.*, *mun. bor.*, Lancs, Eng.; on Rossendale Fells, 3 m. S. of Accrington; cotton, stone quarrying, engin.; p. (estd. 1967) *14,150*.

Hasselt, *t.*, prov. Limbourg, Belgium; gin distilleries; p. (1962) *37,198*.

Hassi Messoud, *t.*, Algeria, Africa; lge. oilfield; 24 inch pipe-line to Bejaia.

Hassi R'Mel, *t.*, Algeria, Africa; natural gas.

Hastings, *t.*, *co. bor.*, E. Sussex, Eng.; on S. cst., midway between Beachy Head and Dungeness; seaside resort; one of the Cinque Ports; p. (estd. 1967) *66,850*.

Hastings, *t.*, N.I., N.Z.; on Hawke's Bay, nr. Napier; p. (1961) *32,479*.

Hastings, *t.*, Nebraska, U.S.A.; p. (1960) *21,412*.

Hastings-on-Hudson, *t.*, N.Y., U.S.A.; residtl.; mnfs. copper chemicals; p. (1960) *8,979*.

Hatay (formerly Sanjak of Alexandretta), ceded to Turkey by France 1939; p. (1960) *441,209*.

Hatfield, *t.*, Herts, Eng.; on Great North Road, 19 m. N. of London; one of "New Towns"

N　(78th Ed.)

designated 1948 growing around old t. of Bishops Hatfield; light engin., aircraft; p. (estd. 1965) *23,635*.

Hathras, *t.*, Aligarh dist., W. Uttar Pradesh, India; sugar, cotton, carved work; p. (1961) *64,045*.

Hatteras, C., N.C., U.S.A.; stormy region.

Hattiesburg, *t.*, Miss., U.S.A.; p. (1960) *34,989*.

Hattingen, *t.*, N. Rhine–Westphalia, Germany; S.E. of Essen; machin., textiles; p. (1963) *30,700*.

Hatvan, *mkt. t.*, Hungary; E. of Budapest; sugar refining; canning; p. (1962) *20,080*.

Haugesund, *spt.*, S. Norway; on S.W. coast, 35 m. N. of Stavanger; ch. ctr. of herring fishery; canning inds.; p. (estd. 1960) *20,000*.

Hauraki, *G.*, E. cst. N.I., N.Z.

Hautmont, *t.*, Nord, France; p. (1954) *15,978*.

Haut-Rhin, *see* Rhin-Haut.

Haute-Garonne, *see* Garonne-Haute.

Haute-Loire, *see* Loire-Haute.

Haute-Marne, *see* Marne-Haute.

Haute-Saône, *see* Saône-Haute.

Haute-Savoie, *see* Savoie-Haute.

Haute-Vienne, *see* Vienne-Haute.

Hautes-Pyrénées, *see* Pyrénées, Hautes.

Havana, *prov.*, Cuba; cap. H.; lge. exp. tr.; a. 3,173 sq. m.; p. (1953) *1,538.803*.

Havana, *spt.*, *cap.*, Cuba; ch. c. of the W. Indies; cigars, tobacco, sugar, rum, coffee, woollens, straw hats, iron-ore; oil refining on outskirts of t.; p. (estd. 1960) *788,000*.

Havant and Waterloo, *urb. dist.*, Hants, Eng.; at foot of Portsdown Hill, 6 m. N.E. of Portsmouth; malting, brewing, tanning; p. (estd. 1967) *99,830*.

Havel, *R.*, Germany; flowing to R. Elbe (221 m.).

Haverfordwest, *co. t.*, *mun. bor.*, Pembrokeshire, Wales; 6 m. N.E. of Milford Haven; agr. mkt.; Norman cas.; p. (1961) *8,372*.

Haverhill, *t.*, *urb. dist.*, Suffolk, E. Eng.; p. (1961) *5,446*. 　　　　　　　　　[(1960) *46,346*.

Haverhill, *t.*, Mass. U.S.A.; boot factories; p.

Havering, *outer bor.*, E. London, Eng.; inc. Hornchurch and Romford (q.v.); p. (1966) *250,000*.

Haverstraw, *t.*, N.Y., U.S.A.; brick-mkg.; p. (1960) *5,771*.

Havre, Le, *spt.*, Seine-Maritime, France; on English Channel at mouth of R. Seine; fine boulevards; ship-bldg., engin., chemicals, ropes, cottons, oil refining; pipeline to Grandpuits; p. (1962) *184,133*.

Havre de Grace, *t.*, Md., U.S.A.; resort; duck shooting; p. (1950) 7 *809*.

Hawaii, *I.*, lgst. of Hawaiian gr.; three great volcanic mtns., Mauna Kea (13,796 ft., highest island mtn. in world, dormant), Mauna Loa (13,680 ft., world's most active volcano), Hualali (last erupted, 1801); ch. pt. Hilo (devastated by tidal wave, 1946); lava deserts, bamboo forests; sugar-cane, cattle, coffee; tourism; deep-sea fishing; p. (1960) *61,332*.

Hawaiian Is. (Sandwich Is.), *st.*, Pac. Oc., admitted 1959 as 50th st. of U.S.A.; chain of coral and volcanic Is.; a. 6,424 sq. m.; cap. Honolulu on S.E. cst. of Oahu I.; p. (1960) *632,772*.

Hawarden, *t.*, *rural dist.*, Flint, N. Wales; steel plant; p. (rural dist. 1961) *36,290*.

Hawash, *R.*, Ethiopia, flows E. of Shoa frontier; length 500 m.

Hawera, *t.*, N.I., N.Z.; p. (1961) *7,537*.

Hawes Water, *L.*, Westmorland, Eng. (2½ m.).

Hawick, *burgh*, Roxburgh, Scot.; on R. Teviot, 18 m. S.W of Kelso; hosiery, tweed and woollens; p. (1961) *16,204*.

Hawke's Bay, *prov. dist.*, N.I., N.Z.; on E. cst.; cap. Napier; a. 4,260 sq. m.; p. (1961) *114,516*.

Hawkesbury, R., N.S.W., Australia; length 330 m.

Hawkesbury, *t.*, Ontario, Canada; p. (1956) *7,874*.

Haworth, *t.*, W.R. Yorks, Eng.; nr. Keighley; home of the Brontës.

Hawthorne, *t.*, S.W. Cal., U.S.A.; residtl.; in gas- and oil-producing area; p. (1960) *33,035*.

Hawthorne, *bor.*, N.J., U.S.A.; paint, glass textiles, dyewks.; p. (1960) *17,735*.

Hay, *R.*, Alberta, Canada; flows into G. Slave Lake. 　　　　　　　　　　　　[p. (1961) *1,321*.

Hay, *urb. dist.*, Brecknock, Wales; on R. Wye;

Hay, *t.*, N.S.W., Australia; situated on R. Murrumbidgee on N. edge of Riverina dist.; collecting ctr. for fruit and wheat grown under irrigation, for despatch by rail E. to Narandera and Sydney, or by river W. to Adelaide.

Hayange, *t.*, Moselle, France; ironwks.; p. (1954) *11,060.*

Hayden, *Mt.*, or Grand Teton peak, Rockies, Wyo., U.S.A.; alt. 13,600 ft.

Haydock, *t.*, *urb. dist.*, Lancs, Eng.; coal-mining; p. (1961) *12,070.*

Hayes and Harlington, *former urb. dist.*, Middx., Eng.; now inc. in Hillingdon outer bor., Greater London (*q.v.*); residtl.; elec. goods, gramophones, aeroplane mftg.; p. (1961) *67,912.*

Hayle, *t.*, Cornwall, Eng.; nr. St. Ives; engin.; p. *5,800.*

Hayling Island, *resort*, Hants, Eng.; E. of Portsmouth.

Haystack, *summit* of the Adirondacks, Vt., U.S.A.; alt. 4,919 ft.

Hayward, *t.*, Cal., U.S.A.; p. (1960) *72,700.*

Hayward's Heath, *mkt. t.*, Sussex, Eng.; nr. Cuckfield; cattle mkt.; p. *5,400.*

Hazard, *t.*, Ky., U.S.A.; gas, coal, sawmills, steel mills; p. (1960) *5,958.*                     [*40,958.*

Hazaribagh, *t.*, Bihar, India; coal, mica; p. (1961)

Hazebrouck, *t.*, France, Nord; rly. ctr., textiles, grain, livestock; p. (1954) *15,525.*

Hazel Grove and Bramhall, *urb. dist.*, Cheshire, Eng.; p. (estd. 1967) *34,800.*

Hazleton, *c.*, Penns., U.S.A.; anthracite region; coal, iron, textiles, iron and steel mnfs.; p. (1960) *32,056.*                     [residtl.

Headingley, *sub.*, Leeds, Yorks, Eng.; mainly

Healdtown, *mission sta.*, nr. Fort Beaufort, Cape Province, S. Africa.

Heanor, *t.*, *urb. dist.*, Derby, Eng.; 7 m. N.E. of Derby; coal, hosiery, rly. wagons, pottery, prefabricated timber bldgs. mftg.; p. (estd. 1967) *24,270.*

Heard, *I.*, S. Indian Ocean; 280 m. S.E. of Kerguelen I.; Australian possession.

Heathrow, *vil.*, Middx, Eng.; on W. margin of built-up area of London; site of London Airport; arterial road link with London.

Hebburn, *t.*, *urb. dist.*, Durham, Eng.; on R. Tyne, 4 m. below Gateshead; shipbldg., engin., and colliery inds.; p. (estd. 1967) *24,940.*

Hebden Royd, *urb. dist.*, W.R. Yorks, Eng.; cotton factories, dyewks., heavy engin.; p. (1961) *9,409.*

Hebrides or Western Is., Scot., grouped as Outer and Inner Hebrides; ch. t. Stornoway, Lewis; a. 2,850 sq. m.

Hebron, *t.*, Jordan; 16 m. S.W. of Jerusalem; p. (1961) *37,911.*

Heckmondwike, *t.*, *urb. dist.*, W.R. Yorks, Eng.; p. (1961) *8,420.*

Hedmark, *co.*, Norway; on Swedish border; a. 10,621 sq. m.; p. (1963) *177,730.*

Heerenveen, *commune*, Friesland prov., N. Netherlands; livestock; p. (1967) *29,758.*

Heerlen, *t.*, Limburg, Neth.; 14 m. E. of Maastricht; traces of Roman occupation; coal mng.; p. (1967) *76,940.*

Heide, *t.*, Schleswig-Holstein, Germany; ctr. of petroleum dist.; machin., food preserving; p. (1963) *20,100.*

Heidelberg, *famous univ. t.*, Baden-Württemberg, Germany; on R. Neckar, nr. Mannheim; cas.; tobacco, wood, leather, rly. carriages; rly. junction; nylon plant projected; p. (1963) *126,500.*

Heidenheim, *t.*, Baden-Württemberg, Germany; N.E. of Ulm; textiles, machin., metallurgy, furniture; p. (1963) *50,000.*

Heilbronn, *t.*, *r. pt.*, Baden-Württemberg, Germany; engin., vehicles, foodstuffs; p. (1963) *92,400.*

Heilungkiang (Heilungjiang), *prov.*, N. China; a. c. 180,000 sq. m.; tractor farming, lumbering; coal, gold; cap. Harbin; p. (1953) *11,897,309.*

Hejaz, *region*, Saudi Arabia; mainly desert; very poor communications; ch. t. Mecca; a. 150,000 sq. m.; p. *1,000,000* (estimated).

Hekla, *volcano*, Iceland; alt. 5,095 ft.

Helder (Den Helder), *t.*, N. Holland, Netherlands; on strait between peninsula and I. of Texel; naval base; on cst. 50 m. N. of Amsterdam; p. (1967) *55,727.*

Helena, *t.*, Ark., U.S.A.; on Mississippi R.; shipping ctr. for cotton; p. (1960) *11,500.*

Helena, *cap.*, Mont., U.S.A.; gold, silver, iron, smelting; p. (1960) *20,227.*

Helensburgh, *residtl. burgh*, Dunbarton, Scot.; on N. side of Firth of Clyde at entrance to Gare Loch; metal goods; p. (1961) *9,605.*

Heletz, Negev, Israel; oilwells.

Heligoland, *German I.*, N. Sea, off mouth of Elbe; formerly British.

Helikon, *mtn.*, Greece; between G. of Corinth and L. Kopais; alt. 5,736 ft.

Hell Gate R., Mont., U.S.A.; trib. of Bitter Root R.

Hellendoorn, *commune* Overijssel, Netherlands; textiles; p. (1967) *23,252.*

Hellespont, *see* Dardanelles.

Hellin, *t.*, Albacete, Spain; sulphur-mines; p. (1957) *30,026.*

Helmond, *t.*, N. Brabant, Netherlands; on the Zuid-Willemsvaart (canal); textiles; p. (1967) *46,834.*

Helmsley, *mkt. t.*, ctr. of rural dist., N.R. Yorks. *See also* Pickering, Vale of.

Helmstedt, *t.*, Lower Saxony, Germany; E. of Brunswick; coal and potassium mining, textiles, machin.; p. (1963) *29,100.*

Helmund, *R.*, Afghanistan; falls into L. Hamun; length 650 m.

Helsingborg or Hälsingborg, *spt.*, Sweden; on the Sound, opposite Helsingör, Denmark; shipyd., engin., textiles, rubber goods, chemicals; p. (1961) *76,574.*

Helsingör, *t.*, Själland, Denmark; shipyds, textiles, rubber boots; p. (1960) *26,658.*

Helsinki (Helsingfors), *spt.*, *cap.* Finland; on G. of Finland, harbour ice-bound Jan. to April except for channel opened by ice-breaker; univ.; timber prod., textiles, carpets, etc.; p. (1966) *508,353.*

Helston, *mkt. t.*, *mun. bor.*, Cornwall, Eng.; on R. Cober, 8 m. W. of Falmouth; tourist ctr. famous for its festival of the Furry or Floral Dance (8 May); p. (estd. 1967) *9,240.*

Helvellyn, *mtn.*, Cumberland, Eng.; 9 m. S.E. Keswick; alt. 3,118 ft.

Helwan, *t.*, U.A.R.; 15 m. S. of Cairo; iron and steel complex projected.

Hemel Hempstead, *t.*, Herts, Eng.; on S. slopes of Chilterns, 9 m. N. of Watford; one of "New Towns" designated 1947; consists of bulk of mun. bor. of Hemel Hempstead with new growth to E. and S.E.; mun. bor. exists as separate entity; scientific glass, elec. engin., cars; p. (estd. 1967) *64,100.*

Hempstead, *t.*, Long I., N.Y., U.S.A.; p. (1960) *34,641.*

Hemsworth, *urb. dist.*, W.R. Yorks, Eng.; 6 m. S.E. of Wakefield; p. (1961) *14,401.*

Henderson, *c.*, Ky., U.S.A.; tobacco, cotton, coal; p. (1960) *16,892.*

Henderson, *t.*, N.C., U.S.A.; cotton, tobacco, mkt. and mnfs.; p. (1950) *10,996.*

Hendon, *former mun. bor.*, Middx., Eng.; now inc. in Barnet outer bor. Greater London, (*q.v.*); many light inds.; p. (1961) *115,843.*

Hengelo, *t.*, Overijssel, Neth.; industl. ctr., metals; cattle mkt.; lace mkg., textiles; p. (1967) *68,007.*

Hengyang, *c.*, Hunan, China; on Siang Kiang in foot-hills to S. of Yangtze plain; nr. impt. lead- and zinc-mng. dist.; p. (1953) *235,000.*

Hénin-Liétard, *t.*, Pas-de-Calais, France; p. (1962) *25,660.*

Henley-on-Thames, *mun. bor.*, Oxford, Eng.; 5 m. N.E. of Reading; mkt. gardening, brewing; p. (estd. 1967) *10,550.*          [p. (1962) *11,899.*

Hennebont, *t.*, Morbihan, France; on R. Blavet;

Henrietta Maria, *C.*, Ontario, Canada; on Hudson Bay.

Henry, *C.*, Va., U.S.A.; at S.entrance to Chesapeake Bay.

Hensbarrow, *upland a.*, Cornwall, Eng.; granite; impt. kaolin-mining dist., kaolin exported by sea from Par, Fowey; rises to over 1,000 ft.; a. 30 sq. m.

Henzada, *t.*, Burma, on R. Irrawaddy; p. *28,542.*

Herat, *cap. c.* of prov. same name, Afghanistan; on Hari Rud; strongly fortified; has been called "the key of India"; crude petroleum and chrome ore in a.; p. (1948) (of prov.) *1,142,343;* (of t.) (1964) *62,000.*

Hérault, *dep.*, S. France; wines, fruit, olives, cheese, sheep-rearing; cap. Montpellier; a. 2,402 sq. m.; p. (1962) *516,658.*

Herculaneum, *buried c.*, Italy; 7 m. E.S.E. Naples; re-discovered in 1709.

Heredia, *prov.*, Costa Rica, Central America; cap. Heredia; p. (1963) *83,878.*

Hereford, *co.*, Eng.; on Welsh border; fertile;

fruit, cereals, hops, cattle, sheep, cider, salmon, limestone; a. 842 sq. m.; p. (1966) *140,000.*

**Hereford,** *c.,* *mun. bor., co. t.,* Hereford, Eng.; on R. Wye; cath.; steel for turbines and aircraft rockets, tiles, engin., timber, cider and preserves, p. (estd. 1967) *46,120.*

**Herenthals,** *commune,* N. Belgium; mftg.; p. (1962) *17,697.*

**Herford,** *t.,* N. Rhine–Westphalia, Germany; on R. Werra; cotton, flax, furniture, cigars, confectionery, metallurgy; p. (1963) *55,700.*

**Herisau,** *t., cap. can.* Appenzell Ausser–Rhoden, Switzerland; muslin mftg., embroidery, dyeing; p. (1957) *13,407.*

**Herm,** *sm. I.* of Channel Is., English Channel; 4 m. N.W. Sark and N.E. of Guernsey; remarkable shell-beach; a. 320 acres; p. *90.*

**Hermon,** *mtn.,* Syria; in Anti-Lebanon mtns.; alt. 9,385 ft.

**Hermosillo,** *t., cap.,* Sonora, Mexico; on Sonora R; univ.; impt. tr.; distilling, silver; p. (1960) *50,000.* [(1961) *14,402.*

**Hermoupolis,** *spt., cap.,* Cyclades, Greece; p.

**Herne,** *t.,* N. Rhine–Westphalia, Germany; nr. Dortmund; coal, iron, machin., chemicals; p. (1963) *111,200.*

**Herne Bay,** *t., urb. dist.,* Kent, Eng.; on cst., 62 m. from London; p. (estd. 1967) *24,100.*

**Herning,** *t.,* Jutland, Denmark; knitting ind.; p. (1960) *24,790.*

**Heröya,** S. Norway; nuclear power plant projected. [*61,672.*

**Herrera,** *prov.,* Panama, cap. Chitré; p. (1960)

**Hersfeld,** *c.,* Hessen, Germany; textiles; machin., wood, iron, leather, mineral baths; p. (estd. 1954) *22,800.*

**Herstal,** *t.,* Belgium; nr. Liége; repeating rifle wks., aero-engines; p. (1962) *29,698.*

**Herstmonceux,** *vil.,* nr. Hastings, Sussex, Eng.; cas.; site of Royal Greenwich Observatory.

**Herten,** *t.,* N. Rhine–Westphalia, Germany; coal, machin.; p. (1963) *52,300.*

**Hertford,** *co.,* Eng.; undulating parks, woods, wheat, fruit; light inds., elec. engin., pharmaceutics; a. 632 sq. m.; p. (1966) *872,000.*

**Hertford,** *co. t., mun. bor.,* Hertford, Eng.; on R. Lea, 20 m. N. of London; pharmaceutics, flour milling, rolling stock, diesels, brewing; p. (estd. 1967) *18,660.*

**'s-Hertogenbosch,** *t.,* Netherlands; on Rs. Dommel and Aa; cap. of N. Brabant prov.; famous cath.; cattle mkt.; industl. development; p. (1967) *79,151.*

**Hessen,** *Land,* Germany; a. 7,931 sq. m.; cap. Wiesbaden; p. (1961) *4,814,000.*

**Hessen Nassau,** *former Prussian prov.,* Germany; a. 6,472 sq. m.; cap. Cassel; forested, cereals, tobacco, flax, potatoes, mineral springs, iron, coal, copper.

**Heston and Isleworth,** *see* Hounslow.

**Hetch Hetchy Dam,** Cal., U.S.A.; on R. Tuolumne 100 m. upstream from St. Joaquin R.; ch. source of irrigation for middle St. Joaquin valley; supplies water and hydro-elec. to San Francisco; height 430 ft., capacity 1,466,000 million gallons.

**Hetton,** *t., urb. dist.,* Durham, Eng.; 5 m. N.E. of Durham; coal; p. (1961) *17,463.*

**Héverlé,** *commune,* central Belgium; mkt. gardens; p. (1962) *16,495.*

**Hex,** *R.,* Cape Province, Rep. of S. Africa; rises in Lange Berge, flows S.W. to Gr. Berg R. at Worcester; valley gives access to Gr. Karroo and Central African tableland, is used by trunk rly. from Cape Town to Johannesburg.

**Hexham,** *mkt. t., urb. dist.,* Northumberland, Eng.; on R. Tyne, 20 m. W. of Newcastle; p. (1961) *9,897.*

**Heysham,** *see* Morecambe and Heysham.

**Heywood,** *t., mun. bor.* Lancs, Eng.; 3 m. E. Bury; coal, cotton, chemicals; p. (estd. 1967) *30,400.*

**Hiawassee,** *R.,* Tenn., U.S.A.; trib. Tenn. R.

**Hibbing,** *t.,* Minn., U.S.A.; iron ore; p. (1960) *17,731.*

**Hickory,** *t.,* N.C., U.S.A.; p. (1960) *19,328.*

**Hidalgo,** *st.,* Mexico; cap. Pachuca; mng., coffee, sugar, tobacco; a. 8,057 sq. m.; p. (1960) *994,598.* [*62,063.*

**High Point,** *c.,* N.C., U.S.A.; textiles; p. (1960)

**High Wycombe,** *t., mun. bor.,* Bucks, Eng.; 15 m. N.W. of Windsor; furniture, paper mkg.; freeze dry egg processing; p. (estd. 1967) *55,980.*

**Higham Ferrers,** *mkt. t., mun. bor.,* Northants, Eng.; 3 m. E. of Wellingborough; footwear and leather dressing; p. (estd. 1967) *4,380.*

**Highgate,** *residtl. dist.,* London, Eng.; on hill N. of Camden bor.; p. (1961) *15,580.*

**Highland, Park,** *t.,* Mich.. U.S.A.; motor cars; p. (1960) *38,064.*

**Highland Park,** *t.,* N.I., U.S.A.; non-metallic sta. of U.S. Bureau of Mines; p. (1960) *11,049.*

**Hilden,** *t.,* N. Rhine–Westphalia, Germany; S.E. of Düsseldorf; textiles, iron, chemicals; p. (1963) *39,900.*

**Hildesheim,** *c.,* Lower Saxony, Germany; at foot of Harz Mtns.; cath.; machin., farm implements, textiles, ceramics; p. (1963) *98,800.*

**Hilla,** *liwa,* Iraq; on R. Euphrates; nr. ancient Babylon; p. (1956) *274,567.*

**Hilleröd,** *t.,* N.E. Själland, Denmark; agr. implements; p. (1960) *11,605.*

**Hillingdon,** *outer bor.,* Greater London, Eng.; comprising former urb. dists. of Hayes and Harlington, Ruislip and Northwood, Yiewsley and W. Drayton and mun. bor. of Uxbridge; p. (1966) *233,000.*

**Hillside,** *t.,* N.J., U.S.A.; engines; speed boats; drugs; lumber; p. (1960) *22,304.*

**Hilo,** *c.,* Hawaii; nr. lgst. active volcano in the world, Mauna Loa; alt. 13,600 ft.

**Hilversum,** *t.,* Netherlands; nr. Utrecht; outstanding modern architecture; floorcloth factories, wireless equipment; broadcasting sta.; p. (1967) *102,756.*

**Himachal Pradesh,** *Union terr.,* India; cap. Simla; p. (estd. 1966) *2,855,000.*

**Himalayas,** *vast chain of mtns.* along N. border of India; 1,600 m. long; highest peak, Mt. Everest, 29,028 ft.

**Himeji,** *industl. t.,* S. Honshu, Japan; on shore of Inland Sea, 30 m. W. of Kobe; iron and steel ind., heavy engin.; oil refining; p. (1964) *359,000.*

**Hinckley,** *mkt. t., urb. dist.,* on border of Leicester and Warwick, Eng.; hosiery, boots, cardboard boxes, dye wks., engin.; p. (estd. 1967) *43,910.*

**Hinckley Point,** Somerset, Eng.; civil nuclear power-sta.; 2nd sta. now being built.

**Hindenburg,** *see* Zabrze. [nr. Haslemere, Eng.

**Hindhead,** *hilly common and health resort,* Surrey.

**Hindiya Barrage,** *dam,* Iraq; across R. Euphrates, 30 m. above Hilla; provides flood control and irrigation in a. between Shatt el Hilla and R. Euphrates.

**Hindley,** *t., urb. dist.,* Lancs, Eng.; 2 m. S.E. of Wigan; cotton, paint knitwear, asbestos; p. (estd. 1967) *21,900.*

**Hindu Kush,** *mtn. range,* mainly in N.E. Afghanistan; highest peak Tirich Mir (25,426 ft.) in Chitral dist., W. Pakistan; Salang tunnel (opened 1964) with 2-lane motor highway cuts H.K. at height of 11,000 ft., runs 800 ft. below mtn. top, 1½ m.

**Hindustan,** former name of part of N. India between Himalayas and Vindhya ranges.

**Hinojosa del Duque,** *commune,* S. Spain; copper; agr.; textiles; p. (1957) *15,629.*

**Hirado,** *I.,* off W. cst. Japan; nr. Sasebo; famous for blue and white porcelain.

**Hirfanli Dam,** project on R. Kizilirmak 90 m. S.E. Ankara, Turkey, 1961.

**Hirosaki,** *t.,* Honshu, Japan; castle; lacquer ware; p. (1965) *151,624.*

**Hiroshima,** *spt., c.,* central Honshu, Japan; close to the "Island of Light" with its famous Shinto temple; first city to be destroyed by atomic bomb (6 Aug. 1945); now rebuilt; p. (1965) *504,245.*

**Hirschberg,** *see* Jelenia Gora.

**Hispaniola,** Greater Antilles, W. Indies; *lge. I.,* divided between the Haiti and Dominican Reps; a. 29,536 sq. m.

**Hispar,** *glacier,* Karakoram mtns., length 38 m.

**Hitchin,** *mkt. t., urb. dist.,* Herts, Eng.; in gap through Chiltern Hills, 35 m. N. of London; light engin., tanning, chemicals, distilling; p. (estd. 1967) *26,240.* [185 sq. m

**Hjälmaren Lake,** Sweden; S.W. of L. Malar; a.

**Hjorring,** *t.,* Jutland, N. Denmark; biscuit and clothing wks.; p. (1960) *15,035.* [Martaban.

**Hlaing (Rangoon),** *R.,* Burma; flows to G. of

**Hobart,** *spt., cap.,* Tasmania, Australia; on R. Derwent; univ.; gr. fruit exp.; zinc, cadmium, superphosphates, textiles; p. (1966) *119,415.*

**Hobbs,** *t.,* N.M., U.S.A.; oil-well area; supply ctr.; p. (1960) *26,275.*

Hoboken, *t.*, Antwerp, Belgium; shipbldg.; refractory metals; p. (estd. 1957) *30,552.*

Hoboken, *c.*, N.J., U.S.A.; lge. ocean commerce; p. (1960) *48,441.*

Hobro, *spt.*, Jutland, Denmark; at W. end of Mariager Fjord; cattle feed factory; p. (1960) *8,203.* [*15,791.*

Höchst, *t.*, Hessen; Germany; on R. Main; p.

Hochstetter, *mtn.*, S.I., N.Z.; in Southern Alps; alt. 11,200 ft.

Hoddesdon, *t.*, *urb. dist.*, Herts, Eng.; in Lea valley, 4 m. S. of Ware; nursery trade, tomatoes, etc.; p. (estd. 1967) *20,640.*

Hodeida, *spt.*, Yemen, Arabia; on Red Sea; naval base; p. *50,000.*

Hodmezovarsarhely, *t.*, S.E. Hungary; wheat, fruit, tobacco, cattle; natural gas pipeline from Szeged; p. (1962) *53,228*

Hof, *t.*, Bavaria, Germany; on R. Saale; textiles, iron, machin., porcelain, glass, brewing; p. (1963) *56,200.*

Hofei (Hefei), *c.*, *cap.* Anhwei prov., China; rice growing a.; cotton and silk; p. (1953) *184,000.*

Hoffman, *mtn. peak* of the Sierra Nevada, California; alt. 8,108 ft. [*100,000.*

Hofuf, *t.*, Hasa, Saudi Arabia; p. (estd. 1956)

Hog's Back, Surrey, Eng.; chalk ridge; alt. 505 ft.

Hohe Tauern, *Alpine range*, Tyrol, Austria; rugged crystalline rocks; highest point, Grau Glockner, alt. 12,461 ft.

Hohenlimburg, *t.*, N. Rhine–Westphalia, Germany; nr. Dortmund; cas.; textiles, iron, steel; p. (1963) *26,800.*

Hohenstein-Ernstal *t.*, Karl-Marx-Stadt, E. Germany; textiles, metal goods; p. (1963) *17,136.*

Hohenzollern, *former prov.*, Germany; Upper Danube; a. 441 sq. m.

Hoihow (Haikou), *c.*, Kwangtung prov., China; comm. ctr.; p. (1953) *135,000.*

Hokitika, *t.*, S.I., N.Z.; on W. cst., 20 m. S. of Greymouth; p. (1961) *3,005.*

Hokkaido, *lge. I.*, Japan, N. of Honshu; a. 34,276 sq. m.; p. (1962) *5,000,000.*

Holbaek, *t.*, Sjaelland, Denmark; W. of Copenhagen; engin. and motor wks.; p. (1960) *15,475.*

Holbeach, *mkt. t.*, S. Lincoln, Eng.; in Fens, 7 m. E. of Spalding; agr., brewing; p. (1948) *5,382.*

Holborn, *see* Camden.

Holderness, *div.*, E.R. Yorks, Eng.; between R. Humber and N. Sea; agr. and pastoral.

Holguin, *t.*, E. Cuba, W. Indies; exp. cattle, maize, tobacco, hardwoods; p. *171,997.*

Holland, *see* Netherlands.

Holland, Parts of, *admin. div.* of Lincoln, Eng.; adjoining the Wash; ch. ts. Boston, Spalding; a. 419 sq. m.; p. (1961) *103,327.*

Holland, *t.*, Mich., U.S.A.; p. (1960) *24,777.*

Holland, N., *prov.*, Netherlands; a. 1,051 sq. m.; p. (1967) *2,200,602.* [p. (1967) *2,902,572.*

Holland, S., *prov.*, Netherlands; a. 1,130 sq. m.;

Hollandia, *see* Kota Baru.

Holidaysburg, *bor.*, Penns, U.S.A.; coal, iron ore, limestone; foundries, machine shops; p. (1960) *6,475.*

Holloway, N. dist., Islington bor., London, Eng.

Hollywood, sub. Los Angeles, Cal., U.S.A.; ctr. of film industry.

Holmesdale, Vale of, *geographical sub-region*, Kent, E. Surrey, Eng.; extends along foot of N. Downs escarpment E. from Dorking; drained by Rs. Mole, Darent, Medway, Len, Stour; heavy clay soils; woodland or rich meadowland; dairy farming; some cultivation along N. and S. fringe; ch. ts., Dorking, Reigate, Sevenoaks, Maidstone, Ashford have grown up on gaps through hills to N. and S. of the Vale; length 60 m., average width 1 m.

Holmfirth, *t.*, *urb. dist.*, W.R. Yorks, Eng.; 5 m. S. of Huddersfield; textiles, engin.; p. (1961) *18,391.*

Holroyd, *t.*, N.S.W., Australia; sub. of Sydney.

Holstein, former Danish Duchy, now inc. in Schleswig-Holstein *Land* of Germany.

Holston, *R.*, U.S.A.; head of Tenn. R.; flows through Va. and Tenn.; length 300 m.

Holsworthy, *rural dist.*, *mkt. t.*, N. Devon, Eng.; p. (1961) rural dist. *5,795*; t. *1,619.*

Holt, *t.*, Denbigh, Wales; on R. Dee, 7 m. S. of Chester. [Sheringham.

Holt, *mkt. t.*, N. Norfolk, Eng.; 5. m. S.W. of

Holyhead, *spt.*, *urb. dist.*, Anglesey, Wales; on Holyhead I.; mail packet sta. for Ireland;

light engin,. woodwkg.. clocks; site for aluminium smelter; I. is 7½ m. long, width ½ m. to 4 m.; p. (1961) *10,408.*

Holy I., off cst. of Anglesey, Wales.

Holy I., Scot., in F. of Clyde, nr. I. of Arran.

Holy I. (Lindisfarne), off cst. of Northumberland. Eng.

Holyoke, *c.*, Mass., U.S.A.; impt. mftg. ctr., paper, machin.; on Connecticut R.; seat of Mount Holyoke College for women; p. (1960) *52,689.*

Holytown *t.*, Lanark, Scot.; nr. Glasgow; coal, steel; p. *20,669.*

Holywell, *mkt. t.*, *urb. dist.*, Flint, N. Wales; woollen, rayon and paper inds.; p. (1961) *8,459.*

Holywood, *spt.*, *urb. dist.*, Down, N. Ireland; on S. shore of Belfast Lough; seaside resort; p. (1966) *7,795.*

Holzminden, *t.*, Lower Saxony, Germany; on R. Weser; chemicals, machin., lumber; p. (1963) *22,900.*

Homberg, *t.*, N. Rhine–Westphalia, Germany; on R. Rhine opposite Duisburg; coal-mining. machin., chemicals; p. (estd. 1954) *32,200.*

Homburg, *t.*, Hessen, Germany; spa, cas.; iron, machin., dyes, leatherwk.; p. (1963) *35,500.*

Homburg, *t.*, Saar; univ.; iron, wood, glass, brewing; p. (1963) *31,000.*

Home Counties, term applied to the geographical counties adjoining London, *i.e.*, Middlesex, Surrey, Essex, and Kent; sometimes Hertfordshire, Buckinghamshire, and Berkshire are included, and occasionally Sussex.

Homestead, *bor.*, Penns., U.S.A.; ironwks.; p. (1960) *7,562.*

Homs, *t.*, W. Syria; on R. Orontes; ancient Emesa; silk, textiles, cement; oil refinery; pipeline from Karachok fields; p. (1961) *164,362.*

Honan (Henan), *fertile prov.*, N.E. China; traversed by Yellow R.; cap. Kaifeng; cereals, coal; a. 64,545 sq. m.; p. (estd. 1957) *48,670,000.*

Honda, *t.*, Tolima dep., Colombia; coffee; p. (estd. 1959) *21,000.*

Honduras, *rep.*, Central America; mtnous.; bananas, coconuts, coffee, hardwoods; panama hat mkg.; silver and lead mng.; cap. Tegucigalpa; a. 43,227 sq. m.; p. (1965) *2,163,000.*

Honduras, British, *see* British Honduras.

Honesdale, *bor.*, Penns., U.S.A.; coal, textiles, shoes, glass; p. (1960) *5,569.*

Honfleur, *spt.*, Calvados, France; fine harbour; p. (1962) *9,132.*

Hong Kong, *Brit. I.* and *Crown Col.*, China; at mouth of R. Canton; inc. peninsula of Kowloon and Is.; cap. c. Victoria; total a. 398 sq. m.; univ.; military and sm. naval base; engin., textiles (50 per cent of total exports), plastics, transistor radios, shipbldg.; p. (estd. 1967) *4,000,000* (mainly Chinese).

Honiton, *mkt t.*, *mun. bor.*, E. Devon, Eng.; on R. Otter, 16 m. E. of Exeter; trout fishing; p. (estd. 1967) *5,260.*

Honolulu, *c.*, *cap.*, Hawaiian Is.; on the I. of Oahu; gd. harbour, fruit, canning, sugar; p. (1960) *294,179.*

Honshu, *lgst. I.* of Japan; oil; a. 88,019 sq. m.

Hood Mt., highest peak Cascade range, Ore., U.S.A.; alt. 11,225 ft.

Hoogeven, *t.*, Drenthe, Netherlands; canned fruits and vegetables; p. (1967) *33,730.*

Hooghli or Hughli, *R.*, W. branch of R. Ganges, India; flows into Bay of Bengal; Calcutta on its banks.

Hook of Holland, *spt.*, Netherlands; packet sta. with steamer connections to Harwich, Eng.

Hooker Mt., Rockies, Brit. Columbia, Canada.

Hoole, *t.*, *urb. dist.*, Cheshire, Eng.; 2 m. N.E. of Chester; mnfs.; p. (1951) *9,054.* [Vet R.

Hoopstad, *t.*, Orange Free State, S. Africa; on

Hoorn, *old fishing t.*, N. Holland, Netherlands; on IJsselmeer, 20 m. N. of Amsterdam; cheese and cattle mkts.; birthplace Tasman, discoverer of Tasmania and New Zealand, founder of Batavia; p. (1967) *17,072.* [U.S.A.

Hoosack, *mtns.*, part of Green Mtn. range, Mass.,

Hoosick Falls, *t.*, N.Y., U.S.A.; paper, elec. goods; agr. implements; p. (1960) *4,023.*

Hopedale, *t.*, Labrador cst., Newfoundland, Canada.

Hopeh (Hebei), *prov.*, N.E. China; cap. Tientsin; cereals, cotton, iron ore; a. c. 75,000 sq. m.; p. (estd. 1957) *44,720,000.*

Hopetown, *t.*, Cape Province, S. Africa; on Orange R.; p. (1960) *2,631.*

Hopewell, *t.*, Va., U.S.A.; synthetic textiles, chemicals, pottery; p. (1960) *17,895.*

Hopkinsville, *c.*, Ky., U.S.A.; p. (1960) *19,465.*

Hoquiam, *spt.*, Wash., U.S.A.; lumber, salmon, tuna fishing, oysters, canning; p. (1960) *10,762.*

Hor, unlocated biblical mtn. between Dead Sea and G. of Aqaba, the place of Aaron's death.

Horbury, *urb. dist.*, W.R. Yorks, Eng.; nr. Wakefield; p (1961) *8,642.*

Hordaland, *dist.*, Norway; a. 6,043 sq. m.; ch. t. Bergen; p. (1963) *230,937.* [steel; p. *35,000.*

Horde, *t.*, Germany; nr. Dortmund; coal, iron,

Horeb, *mtn.*, another name for Mt. Sinai.

Horley, *sm. t.*, Surrey, Eng.; on R. Mole, 7 m. S.E. of Dorking. [in Hormuz Strait.

Hormuz, *I.*, off S. cst. of Iran and nr. Qishm I.;

Horn, C., most S. point of S. America; noted for severe gales encountered there.

Horn (North C.), N. point of Iceland.

Horncastle, *mkt. t.*, *urb. dist.*, Lindsey, Lincoln, Eng.; at confluence of Rs. Bain and Waring at foot of Lincoln Wolds; impt. cattle fairs, malting, corn, horse fairs; p. (1961) *3,768.*

Hornchurch, *former urb. dist.*, Essex, Eng.; nr. Romford; residtl.; general engin.; now inc. in Havering bor., Greater London; p. (1961) *131,014.* [*13,907.*

Hornell, *c.*, N.Y., U.S.A.; rly. car wks.; p. (1960).

Hornsea, *t.*, *urb. dist.*, E.R. Yorks, Eng.; on E. cst.. 13 m. N.E. of Hull; seaside resort; p. (1961) *5,949.*

Hornsey, *see* Haringey.

Horsens, *spt.*, Jutland, Denmark; brewing, diesel engines, weaving, etc. goods; p. (1965) *37,106.*

Horsforth, *t.*, *urb. dist.*, W.R. Yorks, Eng.; in Aire valley 4 m. N.W. of Leeds; cloth, tanning, light engin.; p. (1961) *15,351.*

Horsham, *t.*, *urb. dist.*, W. Sussex, Eng.; on R. Arun at W. end of forested dist. of the High Weald; agr., timber, engin., and chemicals; p. (1967) *24,690.*

Horsham, *t.*, Victoria, Australia; on R. Wimmera; pastoral, dairying and agr. dist.; agr. machin.; p. (1966) *10,557.*

Horta, *ch. spt.*, Fayal I., Azores, Atl. Oc.; cap. of dist.; fruit, wine, winter resort; p. of dist. (1960) *49,735*, of t. *7,109.*

Horten, *spt.*, Norway; nr. Oslo; naval base; shipbldg., mftg. inds.; p. (1960) *13,289.*

Horton, *R.*, N.W. Terr., Canada; flows into Arctic Ocean.

Horwich, *t.*, *urb. dist.*, S. Lancs, Eng.; on W. edge of Rossendale Fells, 4 m. N.W. of Bolton; bleaching and cotton spinning, calico printing, paper, coal, stone; p. (1961) *16,067.*

Hoshangabad, *t.*, Madhya Pradesh, India; on Narbada R.; p. (1961) *19,284.*

Hoshiarpur, *t.*, Punjab, India; lacquer wks., inlaid goods; p. (1961) *50,739.*

Hospitalet, *t.*, Spain; p. (1965) *176,000.*

Hot Springs, *c.*, Ark., U.S.A.; health resort; p. (1960) *28,337.*

Houdeng-Goegnies, *commune*, S.W. Belgium; coal, smelting, glassworks; p. (1962) *8,769.*

Houghton-le-Spring, *t.*, *urb. dist.*, Durham, Eng.; 5 m. S.W. of Sunderland; coal; p. (estd. 1967) *31,610.*

Houilles, *t.*, Seine-et-Oise, France; p. (1954) *22,974.*

Hounslow, *outer bor.*, Greater London, Eng.; inc. former bors. of Brentford and Chiswick, Heston and Isleworth, Feltham and Hounslow; p. (1966) *207,000.*

Housatonic, *R.*, Conn. and Mass., U.S.A.; empties into Long Island Sound; length 150 m.

Houston, *t.*, Renfrewshire, Scot.; new satellite t.

Houston, *c.*, *spt.*, Texas, U.S.A.; on Buffalo Bay; rly. ctr., canal to est., oil refineries, machin.; meat pkg., steel, chemicals, cotton; p. (1960) *938,219.*

Houston Ship Canal, Texas, U.S.A.; links Houston to head of shallow Galveston Bay and continues through bay to deep water; provides site for heavy inds., cement, paper, fertilisers, oil-refining, etc.; opened 1915; total length 45 m.

Hove, *t.*, *mun. bor.*, E. Sussex, Eng.; on S. cst., continuous with Brighton; residtl; holiday resort; p. (estd. 1967) *72,140.*

Howe, *C.*, Victoria; S.E. extremity of Australia.

Howell, *t.*, S.E. Mich., U.S.A.; dairy prod.; p. (1960) *4,861.*

Howrah, *c.*, W. Bengal, India; faces Calcutta across Hooghli R.; jute, cotton, shipbldg.; p. (1961) t. *512,598*, dist. *2,038,477.*

Howth, *hill*, nr. Dublin; alt. 563 ft.

Hoy, *I.*, Orkneys, Scot.

Hoylake, *t.*, *urb. dist.*, Cheshire, Eng.; on N. cst. of Wirral peninsula; residtl; p. (estd. 1967) *32,400.*

Hoyland Nether, *urb. dist.*, W.R. Yorks, Eng.; p. (1961) *15,707.*

Hradec Králové, *t.*, ČSSR.; p. (1961) *55,147.*

Hron, *R.*, ČSSR.; trib. of R. Danube.

Huacho, *spt.*, Peru, S. America; pt. for cotton and sugar, cottonseed oil; p. (1963) *27,219.*

Huancavelica, *dep.*, Central Peru; a. 8,297 sq. m.; cap. H.; p. (1961) *298,892.*

Huancayo, *cap.*, Junin, Peru; woollen mills, artificial silk; p. (1961) *20,000.*

Huanuco, *dep.*, Central Peru; a. 15,426 sq. m.; ch. t. Huanco; p. (1961) *339,388.*

Huaras, *ch. t.*, Ancash, Peru; mineral springs, copper, silver, coal; p. (1961) *11,628.*

Hubli, *t.*, Mysore, India; E. of Goa; cotton, silk-weaving; p. (1961) *171,326.*

Hucknall, *industl. t.*, *urb. dist.*, Nottingham, Eng.; 5 m. N. of Nottingham; hosiery, coal; p. (estd. 1967) *25,720.*

Huddersfield, *mfg. t.*, *co. bor.*, W.R. Yorks, Eng.; on edge of Pennines, 10 m. S. of Bradford; wool. textiles, chemicals, engin.; p. (estd. 1967) *132,120.*

Hudiksvall, *spt.*, Sweden; on inlet of G. of Bothnia; salting and engin. wks., sawmills; p. (1961) *11,979.*

Hudson, *t.*, N.Y., U.S.A.; cement, textiles, machin.; p. (1960) *11,075.*

Hudson, *R.*, N.Y., U.S.A.; flows from the Adirondacks to New York Harbour; with valley of Mohawk R. makes gr. highway of tr. between Gr. Lakes and New York; length 350 m.

Hudson Bay, *inland sea*, Canada; communicating by Hudson's Strait (400 m. long) with Davis Strait; salmon, cod; a. 540,000 sq. m.

Hué, *c.*, S. Viet-Nam; nr. mth. of Hué R.; royal palace; glass factories; impt. tr.; p. (1960) *103,870.*

Huelva, *maritime prov.*, S.W. Spain; copper-mining, vine and olive growing, stock-raising, fisheries, brandy distillery, etc.; a. 3,906 sq. m.; p. (1959) *403,090.*

Huelva, *spt.*, cap. Huelva, Spain; on G. of Cadiz; oil refining; chemicals; p. (1959) *76,845.*

Huercal Overa, *t.*, Almeria, S.E. Spain; silver-, lead- and copper-mining; p. (1957) *13,963.*

Huesca, frontier prov., N.E. Spain; mtnous.; forested; a. 5,849 sq. m.; p. (1959) *242,332.*

Huesca, *t.*, *cap.*, Huesca prov., Spain; on R. Isuela; cath.; gr. wine and timber tr. with France, pottery, leather, cereals; p. (1957) *25,500.*

Hugh Town, *cap.*, St. Mary's I. Scilly Isles.

Huhehot, *c.*, Inner Mongolia, China; p. (1953) *148,000.*

Huila, *dep.*, Colombia, S. America; a. 7,990 sq. m.; cap. Neiva; p. (estd. 1959) *353,090.*

Huizen, *commune*, Netherlands, prov. N. Holland; radio sta.; fishing; plastics; p. (1967) *19,502.*

Hulan, *t.*, N. China; 20 m. N. of Harbin; tr. ctr.; on Harbin-Aigun rly.

Hull or Kingston-upon-Hull, *c.*, *spt.*, *co. bor.*, E.R. Yorks, Eng.; third pt. of U.K.; at influx of R. Hull, in estuary of the Humber; univ.; impt. mnfs. and gr. shipping tr.; docks, fishing, ship repairing, rope, machin., chemicals, tanning, veg. oils, flour milling, seed crushing, paint, cement; p. (estd. 1967) *295,900.*

Hull, *c.*, Quebec, Canada; faces Ottawa across R. Ottawa; sawmills, paper; p. (1961) *56,929.*

Humber, *estuary* of Rs. Ouse and Trent, separating Yorks and Lincoln, Eng.; fine waterway; 1-7 m. wide, length 38 m.

Humboldt Bay, *inlet*, Cal., U.S.A.; nuclear experimental breeder reactor.

Humboldt, *mtn. range*, E. Nevada, U.S.A.

Humboldt Current, *see* Peru Current.

Hume Lake, *artificial lake*, N.S.W., Australia; formed by dam where R. Murray leaves Gr. Dividing Range, just below confluence with R. Mitta Mitta; supplies water for irrigation in upper Riverina dist.; approx. capacity 4,000 million cu. ft.

Hunan, *inland prov.*, China; coal, zinc, tea, wheat, rice. tung oil; cap. Changsha; a. 79,378 sq. m.; p. (1953) *33,226,954.*

Hungary, *rep.*, Central Europe; ch. physical features; central plain of treeless steppes; R. Danube, R. Tisza, Carpathian mtns., L.

Balaton; hot, dry summer, rainfall moderate; race, Magyar; agr., wheat, maize, potatoes, sugar-beet; livestock, poultry; mach., textiles, metal prods., chemicals; coal, lignite, bauxite, oil; communications good; cap. Budapest; a. 35,912 sq. m.; p. (1963) *10,138,000.*

Hungerford, *mkt. t., rural dist.,* Berks, Eng.; on R. Kennet, p. (rural dist. 1951) *9,411.*

Hunmanby, *t.,* E.R. Yorks, Eng.; S. of Scarborough; bricks and tiles.

Hunsrück, *mtn. a.,* Rhineland-Palatinate, Germany; highest point, 2,677 ft.

Hunstanton, *urb. dist.,* Norfolk, Eng.; S.E. shore of Wash; seaside resort; p. (1961) *4,843.*

Hunter, *R.,* N.S.W., Australia; rises in Liverpool Range, Gr. Dividing Range, flows S. and E. into Tasman Sea at Newcastle; valley of Hunter and ch. trib. Goulburn lead from Newcastle up to Cassilis Gate through Gr. Dividing Range to interior; length, approx. 250 m.

Hunterston, Ayrshire, Scot.; civil nuclear power station.

Huntingdon and Peterborough, *inland co.,* Eng; mkt. gardening, fruit-growing, agr.; p. (1966) *184,000.*

Huntingdon, *co. t.,* Hunts, Eng.; on R. Ouse, 6 m. above St. Ives; birthplace of Oliver Cromwell; canning, engin., processed rubber, confectionery; Huntingdon and Godmanchester, *mun. bor.,* p. (estd. 1967) *14,760.*

Huntington, *t.,* Ind., U.S.A.; on Little R.; rly. and wool wks.; p. (1960) *16,185.*

Huntington, *c.,* W. Va., U.S.A.; on Ohio R.; machine wks., lumbering; p. (1960) *83,627.*

Huntly, *mkt. burgh,* Aberdeen, Scot.; at confluence of Rs. Bogie and Deveron; farming, woollens; p. (1961) *3,952.*

Huntly, *t.,* N.I., N.Z.; on Waikato R.; 65 m. S. of Auckland; coal; p. (1961) *4,617.*

Huntsville, *t.,* Ala., U.S.A.; cotton-mills; p. (1960) *72,365.*

Huon, *I.,* 170 m. N. of and *dep.* of New Caledonia, Pacific; very barren group.

Hupeh (Hubel), *prov.,* China; N. of the Yangtze-Kiang; cap Wuhan; tea, cotton, wheat, coal, paper; a. 71,955 sq. m.; p. (1953) *27,789,693.*

Hurlford and Crookedholme, *ts.,* Ayr, Scot.; nr. Kilmarnock; iron, fireclay, worsteds, coal-mng.

Huron, *L.,* between Canada and U.S.A.; one of the Gr. Lakes of the St. Lawrence basin; a. 23,610 sq. m.; 280 m. long. [*14,180.*

Huron, *t.,* S.D., U.S.A.; meat prod.; p. (1960)

Hurstville, *sub.,* S. of Sydney, N.S.W., Australia; p. *22,667.*

Hürth, *t.,* N. Rhine–Westphalia, Germany; S.W. of Cologne; lignite-mining, machin., chemicals; impt. elec. power sta.; p. (1963) *47,500.*

Husi, *mftg. t.,* Romania; tobacco, wine; p. (1956) *18,155.*

Huskvarna, *t.,* Sweden; S. extremity of L. Vättern; lt. inds.; p. (1961) *13,763.*

Husum, *spt.,* Schleswig-Holstein, Germany; rly. junction; p. (1963) *24,600.*

Hutchinson, *c.,* Kan., U.S.A.; p. (1960) *37,574.*

Hutt, *urb. a.,* N.I., N.Z.; p. (1964) *108,700.*

Huy, *t.,* Belgium; on R. Meuse; nr. Liége; vinegrowing dist.; p. (1962) *13,493.*

Huyton with Roby, *urb. dist.,* Lancs, Eng.; sub. of Liverpool; p. (estd. 1967) *69,180.*

Hwai Ho (Huai Ho), *R.,* N. China; rises in Tungpeh Shan, flows E. between N. China plain and lower Yangtze; subject to disastrous floods and changes of course; since 1950 flood control and irrigation canal to sea.

Hwainan (Huainan), *c.,* Anhwei prov., China; impt. coalfield; p. (1953) *287,000.*

Hwang Hai (Yellow Sea), arm of the Pac. Oc. between Korea and China; branches into the Gs. of Pohai and Liaotung; greatest width 400 m., length 600 m.

Hwang Ho (Yellow R.), China; rises nr. source of Yangtze-Kiang, Tibet, flows through N.W. China into G. of Pohai; l. 2,600 m.

Hwangshih (Huangshi), *c.,* Hupeh prov., China; cement and lime wks.; p. (1953) *111,000.*

Hyde, *industl. mkt. t., mun. bor.,* Cheshire, Eng.; on R. Tame, 5 m. S.E. of Manchester; textiles, clothing, engin., leathercloth, rubber, paper prod.; p. (estd. 1967) *33,760.*

Hyderabad, *dist.,* Andhra Pradesh, India; rice, cotton, wheat; a. 1,957 sq. m.; p. (1961) *2,062,995.*

Hyderabad, *ch. t.,* of Andhra Pradesh, India; on R. Musi; walled t. and impt. comm. ctr.; univ.; p. (1961) *1,251,119.*

Hyderabad, *t.,* W. Pakistan; on R. Indus; arsenal; univ.; silks, gold and silver wk., pottery, cement; heavy elec. plant; p. (1961) *434,537.*

Hyderabad, *dist.,* W. Pakistan; p. (1961) *2,342,000.*

Hydra, *I.,* Greece; off Morea; a. 26 sq. m.; p. *3,693.*

Hyères, *winter health resort,* Var, France; vines, oranges, flowers, fruit; p. (1962) *33,693.*

Hyères, Iles d', *sm. archipelago of Is.,* off French Riviera cst. [rubber plant.

Hythe, nr. Southampton, Hants., Eng.; synthetic

Hythe, *t., mun. bor.,* Kent, Eng.; on S. cst., 3 m. W. of Folkestone; one of the Cinque Ports; Royal school of musketry; p. (estd. 1967) *11,180.*

# I

Iasi, *see* Jassy.

Iba, *spt., mun.,* cap. of Zambales prov., Luzon, Philippine Is.; uranium, lumbering; p. *3,299.*

Ibadan, *t.,* cap. Western prov., Nigeria; 60 m. N. of Lagos; silk, tobacco, cotton; univ.; p. *600,000.*

Ibagué, *cap.,* Tolima, Colombia, S. America; cotton, tobacco, sugar, leather gds.; p. (estd. 1959) *133,380.*

Ibarra, *t.,* Ecuador, S. America; at foot of Volcano of Imbabura; p. (1962) *14,031.*

Iberian Peninsula, S.W. peninsula of Europe; containing sts. of Spain and Portugal; derived from the Iberian people who lived along the R. Ebro (Iberus); a. 229,054 sq. m.; p. *35,470,953.* [*7,588.*

Iberville, *t.,* Quebec, Canada; lt. engin.; p. (1961)

Ibicui, *t.,* S. Paraguay; iron ore; p. *14,350.*

Ica, *cst. dep.,* Peru; cap. Ica; a. 9,796 sq. m.; p. (1961) *243,617.*

Iceland, *I.,* N. Atl. Oc.; 130 m. E. Greenland; independent rep.; barren and mtnous., with ice-covered plateaus and volcanoes; glacier fields cover 5,000 sq. m.; highest peak, Oraéfa Jökull, alt. 6,950 ft.; main ind. fishing; cap. Reykjavík; a. 39,709 sq. m.; p. (1962) *183,478.*

Ichang, *pt.,* Hupeh, China; on Yangtze-Kiang; cotton, rice, oil; large tr.; p. *107,940.*

Ichinomiya, *t.,* S.E. Honshu, Japan; ancient Shinto shrine; textiles, pottery; p. (1964) *192,000.*

Ichow, *c.,* Shantung, China; at foot of Shantung highlands, 80 m. N.E. of Tungshan (Suchow); silk ind.; p. (estd.) *100,000.*

Icknield Way, *ancient highway* in S. Eng.; from nr. Bury St. Edmunds, through Wantage to Cirencester and Gloucester.

Icod, *commune,* N.W. Tenerife, Canary Is.; agr.; silk; p. *13,263.*

Ida, *mtn.,* Central Crete, Greece; famous in Greek mythology; 8,058 ft.

Idaho, *mtn. st.,* U.S.A.; part of Rocky Mtns. in st.; rich mineral region; cap. Boise City; a. 83,557 sq. m.; p. (1960) *622,356.*

Idaho Falls, *t.,* Idaho, U.S.A.; food processing, lumbering; silver, lead, and gold mines near by; nuclear experimental breeder reactor; p. (1960) *33,161.*

Idar-Obestein, *t.,* Rhineland-Palatinate, Germany; gem cutting, jewellery; p. (1963) *30,400.*

Idle, *mftg. t.,* W.R. Yorks, Eng.; in Aire valley, 3 m. N. of Bradford; woollens, motor cars.

Idle, *R.,* Notts, Eng.; trib. to R. Trent.

Idrija, *t.,* N.W. Jugoslavia; ancient cas.; mercury mines; cinnabar; p. *10,317.*

Ifni, *Span. overseas prov.,* enclave S. Morocco; cap. Sidi Ifni; a. 700 sq. m.; p. (1963) *54,000.*

Igarka, *sm. t.,* Siberia, R.S.F.S.R.; on R. Yenesei, 400 m. from its mouth; graphite plant, nickel-mines, lumber-mills; p. (1956) *15,200.*

Iglesias, *t.,* Sardinia, Italy; N.W. of Cagliara; cath.; p. *23,575.*

Igualada, *t.,* Barcelona, Spain; leather, textiles; ctr. of wine-producing dist.; p. (1957) *16,945.*

Iguassu, *R.,* S. Brazil; famous falls. [*6,983*

Iisalmi, *t.,* Finland; E. of Kokkola; p. (1966)

IJ, *inlet,* IJsselmeer, now separated by locks, forming part of canal system of Amsterdam.

IJmuiden, *t.,* N. Holland, Netherlands; on cst. at mouth of N. Sea Canal; fishing; gasification plant, steel-mill; p. (1967) *135,089.*

IJsselmeer (Lake IJssel), Netherlands; shallow expanse of water, formerly Zuider Zee; separated from N. Sea by Wieringen–Friesland Barrage (length 19 m.) constructed 1932; active land reclamation in progress, lgst. a. being Northeast Polder (185 sq. m.); chief c. on inlet (IJ) is Amsterdam; when reclamation complete, water a. will be reduced to 408 sq. m.

**Ilagan,** *t.,* Mindanao, Philippines; integrated steel mill; p. (1960) *58,433.*

**Ilam,** *dist.,* W. Iran; p. (1967) *170,567;* cap. Ilam, p. (1967) *91,545.*

**Ilchester,** *t.,* Somerset, Eng.; on R. Yeo; N.W. of Yeovil; birthplace of Roger Bacon.

**Ile-Ife,** *t.,* Nigeria, W. Africa; 54 m. from Ibadan.

**Iletsk,** *t.,* Kazakh. S.S.R., on R. Ilek, trib. of R. Ural; S. of Chkalov; rock salt; p. *13,010.*

**Ilford,** *former mun. bor.,* Essex, Eng.; E. sub. of London on R. Roding; bordering on Hainault Forest, now inc. in Redbridge Outer London bor. (*q.v.*); paper-mills, elec. and radio equipment, films and photoplate wks.; p. (1961) *178,024.*

**Ilfracombe,** *t., urb. dist.,* N. Devon, Eng.; on cst. of Bristol Channel; seaside resort; p. (1961) *8,701.*

**Ilhéus,** *spt.,* Baia, Brazil; exp. cacao, timber; p. (1960) *46,000.*

**Ili,** *R.,* Central Asia; rises in Tien Shan and flows into L. Balkhash; length 850 m.

**Ilia** (Elis), *prefecture,* S. Greece; cap. Pyrgos; p. (1951) *188,274.*

**Ilion,** *t.,* N.Y., U.S.A.; firearms; office equipment; p. (1960) *10,199.*

**Ilkeston,** *t., mun. bor.,* Derby, Eng.; 7½ m. W. of Nottingham; coal, iron, engin., locknit fabrics, needles, plastics; p. (estd. 1967) *35,340.*

**Ilkley,** *t., urb. dist., spa,* W.R. Yorks, Eng.; on R. Wharfe 15 m. N.W. of Leeds; local mkt.; p. (1961) *18,519.*

**Ill,** *R.,* E. France; rises in Jura Mtns., flows N. through Mulhouse, Colmar, Strasbourg, enters Rhine 12 m. below Strasbourg; length 135 m.

**Illawara,** *dist.,* N.S.W., Australia; forming belt of land between S. tableland and cst.; very fertile; dairy farming; coal seams; ch. ts., Kiama, Wollongong, Bulli, Geringong.

**Ille-et-Vilaine,** *dep.,* N.W. France; on English Channel; a. 2,699 sq. m.; agr.; cap, Rennes; p. (1962) *614,263.*

**Illimani, Mt.,** nr. La Paz, Bolivia; 21,184 ft.

**Illinois,** *st.,* U.S.A.; named after its principal R.; a large trib. (360 m.) of Mississippi R.; cap. Springfield; lgst. t. Chicago; iron and steel, coal and oil; agr.; a. 56,400 sq. m.; p. (1960) *10,081,158.*

**Illogan,** *vil.,* Cornwall, Eng.; N.W. of Redruth; tin, copper; p. (par.) *8,300.*

**Illyria,** *region,* mainly Jugoslavia, stretching along Adriatic Sea from Trieste in N. to Albania in the S. and inland as far as Rs. Danube and Morava.

**Ilmen,** *L.,* S. of Novgorod, Russia; a. 360 sq. m.; fisheries.

**Ilmenau,** *t.,* Suhl, E. Germany; at N. base of Thüringer Wald, S.S.E. of Gotha; porcelain, toys, glass; p. (1963) *19,115.*

**Ilminster,** *t., urb. dist.,* Somerset, Eng.; 10 m. S.E. of Taunton; cutstone, concrete, collars, radio valves; p. (1961) *2,784.*

**Ilobasco,** *c.,* Salvador, Central America; cattle, coffee, sugar, indigo; p. *21,225.*

**Iloilo,** *cap.,* prov of Iloilo, Panay Philippines; coconut oil, fishing ind.; p. (1960) *151,266.*

**Ilorin,** *t.,* N. Nigeria, W. Africa; on Lagos–Kano rly.; agr. and caravan ctr.; govt. sugar growing scheme at Bacita; p. *54,686.*

**Imabari,** *t., spt.,* N.W. Shikoku, Japan; on shore of Inland Sea; mnfs. cotton textiles, paper, canned fruits; p. (1965) *104,470.*

**Imbabura,** *prov.,* Ecuador; a. 2,414 sq. m.; cap. Ibarra; p. (1960) *182,700.*

**Imbros, Turkish I.,** Ægean Sea; fertile fruit-growing dist.

**Immingham,** *pt.,* Lindsey, Lincoln, Eng.; on S. cst. of Humber, 8 m. N.W. of Grimsby; lge. docks; new dry dock; chemicals, engin., refinery nearby at Killingholme.

**Imola,** *t.,* Italy; S.E. of Bologna; cath.; glass, pottery; p. (1961) *51,239.*

**Imperial Valley,** S. Cal., U.S.A.; extends 30 m. S.E. from Salton Sea to Mexican bdy.; mainly below sea-level; hot, arid climate; cotton, dates, wheat under irrigation; water brought from Colorado R. by Imperial Canal (Laguna Dam) and All-American Canal (Imperial Dam) nr. Yuma; total irrigated a. (1938) 700 sq. m.

**Imphal,** *ch. t.,* Manipur, India; p. (1961) *67,717.*

**Inari L.,** *extensive L.,* Lappi, Finland; outlet into Barents Sea; a. 685 sq. m.

**Inca,** *t.,* I. of Majorca, Spain; p. (1957) *12,522.*

**Ince-in-Makerfield,** *urb. dist.,* Lancs., Eng.; nr. Wigan; coal, cotton, engin., wagon-bldg.; p. (1961) *18,027.*

**Inchgarvie,** *islet,* F. of Forth, Scot.; forms central support of the Forth rail bridge.

**Inchkeith,** *fortfd. I.,* F. of Forth, Fife, Scot.

**Inchon,** *spt.,* S. Korea; on W. cst.; soya beans, rice; glass; diesel engines; p. (1962) *430,000.*

**Indan,** *mun.,* Luzon, Philippine Is.; rice; p. *11,240.*

**Independence,** *t.,* Mo., U.S.A.; on prairie, S. of Missouri R.; p. (1960) *62,328.*

**Independence,** *t.,* Iowa, U.S.A.; p. (1960) *7,069.*

**Independence,** *t.,* Kan., U.S.A.; p. (1960) *11,222.*

**India,** *peninsula subcontinent,* Asia; comprises India, Pakistan, and Ceylon; ch. mtns.: Himalayas (Everest 29,028 ft.), E. and W. Ghats, Sulaimain range, Hindu Kush, Karakoram; Ganges Plain, Thar desert; ch. Rs.: Indus, Ganges, Brahmaputra; climate: monsoonal; vegetation: dense forests in region of high rainfall; sal, teak; elsewhere savannah or jungle, bamboo; coconuts on cst.; variety of races; inds.: agr., rice, wheat, millet, sugar-cane, cotton, jute, tea, rubber, linseed, cattle, sheep, goats; forests, timber; minerals: coal petroleum, manganese, lead, gold, silver; mnfs.: cottons, jute, milling, engin., machin., brass, carpets; communications: good rail and sea; total a. 1,606,742 sq. m.; total p. (1961) approx. *542,851,695.*

**India, Republic of (Indian Union),** *indep. sov. st.* within Br. Commonwealth (1947), consists of 17 states and 10 centrally adm. terrs.; cap. New Delhi; mainly agr.; ch. crops, rice wheat, sugar-cane, millet, maize, barley; prin. expts. tea, cottons, fabrics, raw cotton, leather, fruits, nuts, iron and other metal ores; industl. expansion; intern. airpts., New Delhi, Calcutta, Bombay; a. 1,178,995 sq. m.; p. (1966) *498,000,000.*

**Indian Harbour,** Labrador cst., nr. Hamilton Inlet, Canada.

**Indian Ocean** extends from S. of Asia and E. of Africa to the C. of Good Hope and C. Leeuwin in Australia, separated from the Pacific by the Malay Archipelago and Australia; a. 29,340,000 sq. m.

**Indian Territory,** since 1907 part of the st. of Okla., U.S.A.

**Indiana,** *st.,* between Kentucky and Michigan, Illinois and Ohio, U.S.A.; agr., coal, limestone, clay, petroleum, cement, glass; cap. Indianapolis; a. 36,291 sq. m.; p. (1960) *4,662,498.*

**Indianapolis,** *cap.,* Ind., U.S.A.; on White R.; impt. rly. ctr.; meat packing, jet engines, aircraft parts, chemicals, pharmaceutics; p. (1960) *476,258.*

**Indigirka R.,** Yakut, U.S.S.R.; flows into Laptev Sea; length 1,100 m.

**Indo-China,** S.E. Asia; federation in French Union until end of hostilities July 1954. Consisted of the three sts. of Viet-Nam, Cambodia and Laos.

**Indonesia, Republic of,** S.E. Asia (comprising Java, Sumatra, Kalimantan, Sulawesi, West Irian, 15 minor Is., thousands of smaller ones); climate: tropical, abundant rainfall; equatorial forest; race: Malay; agr.: rice, maize, sweet potatoes, sugar-cane, coffee, tea, tobacco, oil palms, cinchona, spices, rubber; petroleum, tin, coal, bauxite; mineral wealth; cap. Djakarta (Batavia); p. (1967) *112,300,000.*

**Indore,** *t.,* Madhya Pradesh, Indian Union; in valley of R. Narbada; cotton-mills; p. (1961) *394,941.*

**Indre,** *dep.,* Central France; agr. and industl.; cap. Châteauroux; a. 2,666 sq. m.; p. (1962) *251,432.*

**Indre-et-Loire,** *dep.,* Central France; to the N.W. of Indre; agr., vines, silk factories; cap. Tours; a. 2,377 sq. m.; p. (1962) *395,210.*

**Indus, R.,** W. Pakistan; rises in Tibet, and flows through Kashmir, Punjab, Sind, to the Arabian Sea; length 1,800 m.; 5 tribs.: Jhelum, Chenab, Ravi, Beas, Sutlej, one of world's major R. systems; Indus Waters irrigation scheme under development.

**Inebolu,** *spt.,* Anatolia, Turkey; on cst. of Black Sea; tr. in mohair and wool; p. (1960) 5,586.

**Ingersoll,** *t.,* Ontario, Canada; N.E. of Hamilton; p. (1961) 6,874.

**Ingleborough,** *mtn.,* near Settle, Yorks. Eng.; limestone; underground caves, stalactites, stalagmites; alt. 2,373 ft.

**Inglewood,** *c.,* S.W. Cal., U.S.A.; chinchilla farms; furniture; light engin.; p. (1960) 63,390.

**Ingolstadt,** *t.,* Bavaria, Germany; on Danube, nr. Munich; cas.; machin., cars, tobacco, oil refining; oil pipeline from Genoa; transalpine pipeline under construction from Trieste, through N.E. Italy and Austria to Ingolstadt.; p. (1963) 64,600.

**Inhambane,** *spt.,* Mozambique; sugar, copra, oil-seeds, bricks, soap, tiles; p. (1960) 67,265.

**Inishmore,** *lgst. of Aran Is.,* Galway, Ireland; 30 m. S.W. of Galway; fishing; p. 1,800.

**Inkerman,** *t.,* Crimea, U.S.S.R.; nr. E. extremity of Sevastopol harbour; battle 1854.

**Inkpen Beacon,** *hill,* Berks., Eng.; W. end of N. Downs, 7 m. S.W. of Newbury; highest point reached by chalk hills in Eng.; alt. 975 ft.

**Inkster,** *t.,* S.E. Mich., U.S.A.; residtl.; p. (1960) 39,097.

**Inland Sea,** Japan; length 250 m., breadth 10–40 m.; ch. spts.: Hiroshima, Okayama, Kobe.

**Inn,** *R.,* traversing Switzerland, the Austrian Tyrol and Bavaria; enters R. Danube at Passau; the ancient Œnus; length 320 m.

**Innerleithen,** *burgh and health resort,* Peebles, Scot.; on R. Tweed, 5 m. S.E. of Peebles; woollen cloth and knitwear; p. (1961) 2,299.

**Inner Mongolia,** *aut. region,* N. China; stretches along S. border of Mongolian People's Rep.; cap. Huhehot; p. (1957) 9,200,000.

**Innisfail,** *t.,* Queensland, Australia; ch. sugar-producing ctr. of Australia; p. (1966) 7,419.

**Innsbruck,** *cap.,* the Tyrol, Austria; on R. Inn; commands N. approach to Brenner Pass; univ.; military stronghold; p. (1963) 108,000.

**Inowrocław,** *t.,* N. Poland; nr. Bydgoszcz; rock-salt, iron pyrites; agr. prod.; p. (1960) 47,000.

**Insterburg,** *see* Chernyakovsk.

**Interlaken,** *t.,* Bernese Oberland, Berne, Switzerland; on R. Aar, between Ls. Thun and Brienz; tourist resort; p. (1957) 4,368.

**Inuvik,** *t.,* Canadian Arctic; built above the permanent frost.

**Inveraray,** *burgh,* Argyll, Scot.; nr. head of Loch Fyne; herring fishing; p. (1961) 501.

**Inverbervie,** *burgh,* Kincardine, Scot.; on E. cst., 8 m. S. of Stonehaven; linen, rayon inds.; p. (1961) 921.

**Invercargill,** *c.,* S.I., N.Z.; on S.E. cst.; sawmills, freezing wks.; aluminium smelter; served by Bluff Harb.; p. (1961) 41,087.

**Inverell,** *t.,* N.S.W., Australia; 383 m. N. of Sydney; wheat and lamb cty.; tin; p. (1966) 8,411.

**Invergordon,** *burgh, spt.,* Ross and Cromarty, Scot.; on N. side of Cromarty Firth, 12 m. N.E. of Dingwall; naval pt.; lge. chemical ind. and aluminium smelter projected; p. (1961) 1,640.

**Inverkeithing,** *burgh,* Fife, Scot.; on F. of Forth, nr. Dunfermline; shipbreaking, paper mkg., quarrying; p. (1961) 4,069.

**Inverkip,** *par., vil.,* Renfrew, Scot.; 6 m. S.W. of Greenock; par. contains Gourock; wat. pl.; p. (1951) 17,288.

**Inverness,** *co.,* Scot.; mountainous and well wooded; rising to Ben Nevis 4,406 ft.; Caledonian Canal crosses co.; little cultivation; deer forests and grouse moors, fishing, sheep breeding, distilleries; hydroelec. schemes at Foyers, Glen Cannich, and Lochaber; a. 4,351 sq. m.; p. (1961) 83,425.

**Inverness,** *burgh, co. t.,* Inverness, Scot.; on Moray Firth nr. N.E. end of Caledonian Canal; distilleries, light engin., tweeds; fisheries and agr.; p. (1961) 29,773.

**Inverurie,** *burgh,* Aberdeen, Scot.; on R. Don, 14 m. N.W. of Aberdeen; rly. ctr., wool fair; tourism; p. (1961) 5,152.    [tralia.

**Investigator I.,** off cst. of Eyre Peninsula, S. Aus-

**Inyokern,** *t.,* E. Cal., U.S.A.; naval ordnance research sta.; p. (1960) 11,684.

**Ioannina** (Janina), *prefecture,* Epirus, Greece; ch. t. Ioannina; p. (1961) 154,201.

**Ioannina** (Janina), *t.,* Epirus, Greece; nr. Albanian frontier; embroidery; p. (1961) 34,997.

**Iona,** *I.,* off cst. of Mull, Argyll, Scot.; early Scottish Christian ctr.; restored abbey; St. Columba's burial place; ancient burial place of Scottish kings.

**Ionian Is.,** gr. in Mediterranean, belonging to Greece, formerly under British protection; comprising Kerkyra, (Corfu), Kephallenia, Zákynthos, Levkás, Ithake, Paxos and Kytherá; suffered from severe earthquakes in Aug. 1953; total a. 752 sq. m.; p. (1961) 212,573.

**Ionian Sea,** Mediterranean; between Greece on E; Italy and Sicily on W.

**Iowa,** *st.,* U.S.A.; prairie cty.; over 1,000 ft. above sea-level; watered by Mississippi and Missouri; farming, dairying, maize, wheat, oats, potatoes; coal; cars, chemicals; cap. Des Moines; a 56,290 sq. m.; p. (1960) 2,757,537.

**Iowa City,** Iowa, U.S.A.; farming, stockbreeding; p. (1960) 33,443.

**Ipin** (Yibin), *c.,* Szechwan prov., China; cereals, match mfg.; p. (1953) 176,000.    [80,874.

**Ipoh,** *t.,* Perak, Malaya; tin; textiles; p.

**Ipswich,** *co. t., co. bor.,* Suffolk, Eng.; at head of estuary of R. Orwell; agr. implements, brewing, clothing, printing; p. (estd. 1967) 121,570.

**Ipswich,** *c.,* S.E. Queensland, Australia; coal, woollens; rly. wks.; bricks, earthenware, hardboard; p. (1966) 53,396

**Iquique,** *c.,* N. Chile, a pt. on Pacific; exports nitrates and iodine from Atacama desert; fish canning; p. (1960) 53,800.

**Iquitos,** *ch. t.,* Loreto, Peru; shipyards, docks; rubber, cotton, saw-mills, oil refining; p. (1961) 54,300.

**Iraklion** (Heraklion), *prefecture,* Crete; cap. Iraklion; p. (1961) 207,437.

**Iraklion** (Candia), *cap.,* Crete; central position on N. cst. at foot of terraced hill slopes; wine, olive oil, fishing; p. (1961) 63,458.

**Iran** (Persia), *kingdom,* S.W. Asia; central tableland 3,000–5,000 ft.; ch. range Elburz mtns., (Demavend 18,500 ft.); Rs. few; centre mainly arid, N. cst. and parts of W. very fertile; climate varies widely; agr.; rice, cotton, tobacco, fruits, nuts; impt. oil ind., carpet mnfg.; heavy ind. and mng. developing; exp. of natural gas to U.S.S.R. projected; cap. Tehran; a. 628,000 sq. m.; p. (1967) 25,781,000.

**Irapuata,** *c.,* central Mexico; agr. ctr.; p. 60,000.

**Iraq,** *rep.* (since July 1958), S.W. Asia; approx. co-extensive with ancient Mesopotamia; ch. Rs.: Tigris, Euphrates; climate: hot, rainless, in summer, cool in winter, scanty rainfall; agr. depends on irrigation; ch. crops, dates, cotton, wheat, maize, barley; impt. oilfields; lgst. pt. Basra; cap. Baghdad; dam and power sta. on Euphrates projected; a. 116,600 sq. m.; p. (1965) 7,085,000.

**Irbit,** *t.,* Sverdlovsk region, U.S.S.R.; engin., motor cycles, wood-wkgs., pharmaceutics; mkt., famous fair; p. (1956) 41,200.

**Ireland,** 2nd. largst. I., Brit. Is.; ch. physical features; L. Neagh in N.E., Rs. Shannon, Boyne, Blackwater, Barrow, Nore, Suir, Liffey; ch. mtn. groups—all near cst.—Mourne Mtns., Wicklow Mtns., Mtns. of Kerry; climate, mild and damp; called " the emerald isle " because of its grasslands; a. 32,000 sq. m.; p. (1961) 4,321,411.

**Ireland, Republic of** (Eire), *sov. ind. st.* covering 26 of the 32 cos. of Ireland inc. the 3 provs. of Leinster, Munster and Connaught (Cannacht) together with 3 of the cos. (Cavan, Monaghan and Donegal), of the former prov. of Ulster. Ceased to be member of Brit. Commonwealth in 1949; mainly agr.; root crops, oats, barley; livestock; fisheries; main industl. development around cap. Dublin; a. 26,600 sq. m.; p. (1966) 2,880,752.

**Irish Sea,** Brit. Is.; between Gt. Britain and Ireland, connecting N. and S. with Atl. Oc.; 200 m. long; 50–140 m. wide; greatest depth 140 fathoms; a. 7,000 sq. m.

**Irkutsk,** *t.,* R.S.F.S.R.; on R. Angara; on Trans-Siberian Rly.; univ.; engin., sawmilling, petroleum refining, chemicals; hydro-elec. power stn.; p. (1967) 409,000.

**Irlam,** *t., urb. dist.,* Lancs, Eng.; steel, engin., tar, soap, glycerine, margarine; p. (1961) 15,365.

**Iron Country,** Utah, U.S.A.; vast reserves of iron ore; undeveloped due to inaccessibility.

Iron Gate, Romania; famous rapids in R. Danube; Romanian-Yugoslavian hydro-elect. and navigation project, 1964-71.

Iron Mountain, t., Mich., U.S.A.; former iron mining ctr.; p. (1960) 9,299.

Ironton, c., Ohio, U.S.A.; machin.; coal, iron, fireclay; p. (1960) 15,745.

Ironwood, t., Mich., U.S.A.; iron-mining, lumbering; p. (1950) 11,466.

Irrawaddy, R., Burma; flows S. to Bay of Bengal; navigable for lge. steamers 900 m.; irrigation wks.; length 1,300 m.

Irthlingborough, t., urb. dist., Northants., Eng.; p. (1961) 5,125.

Irtysh, R., Siberia, U.S.S.R.; trib. of R. Ob; two-thirds navigable; crossed by Trans-Siberian Rly. at Omsk; length 2,500 m.

Irun, t., N.E. frontier, Spain; nr. San Sebastian; tanning and brandy distillery; paper mills, iron; Roman remains; p. (1957) 19,956.

Irvine, royal burgh. spt., Ayr, Scot.; nr. mouth of R. Irvine, 7 m. W. of Kilmarnock; "New t" designated 1966; hosiery, lt. engin., bottle, chemical wks.; p. (1961) 16,910, estd. final p. 80,000.

Irvington, t., N.J., U.S.A.; p. (1960) 59,379.

Irvington, t., N.Y., U.S.A.; residtl.; light engin.; p. (1960) 5,494.

Irwell, R., S. Lancs, Eng.; flows past Manchester to the Mersey; length 30 m.

Isa Town, new t., Bahrain; 4 m. from Manamah; proposed p. 35,000.

Isarco, R., N. Italy; rises nr. Brenner Pass, flows S. into R. Adige at Bolzano; used by main rail and road routes from N. Italy to Austria; length 50 m.

Ischia, I., in G. of Naples, Italy; saline baths; cap. I.; a. 26 sq. m.; p. 30,000.

Ischl, t., Austria; wat. pl., saline baths; p. (1961) 12,703. [S. of Haifa.]

Isdud (Ashdod), ancient Philistine c., Israel; 20 m.

Ise Bay, inlet, S. Honshu, Japan; flanked by ch. textile mftg. a. of Japan with 5 million people ctred. on Nagoya; length 40 m. width 15-20 m.

Iselle, t., N.W. Italy; S. terminal of Simplon Pass and tunnel.

Isère, dep., S.E. France; drained by Rs. Isère and Rhône; cap. Grenoble; mtnous.; cereals; wine, butter cheese; iron, coal, lead, silver, copper; gloves, silks; a. 3,178 sq. m.; p. (1962) 729,739.

Isère, R., S.E. France; rises in W. Alps (Grande Sassière), flows W. into R. Rhône nr. Valence; used to generate hydro-elec.; used, with trib. R. Arc, by main rly. from France to N. Italy through Mt. Cenis (Fréjus) Tunnel.

Iserlohn, t., N. Rhine-Westphalia, Germany; iron, steel, metalwks.; needles; p. (1963) 56,300.

Iseyin, t., Lagos st., Nigeria, W. Africa.

Isfahan (anc. Aspadana), c., central Iran; prov. cap.; historical and picturesque c., noted for its carpets and metalware; steel mill under constr.; tourism; airpt.; p. (1967) 862,454.

Ishikari, t., Hokkaido, Japan; on cst. of Otaru Bay, 10 m. N. of Sapporo; ctr. of second lgst. coalfield in Japan; sm. petroleum production.

Ishimbay, t., Bashkir A.S.S.R., R.S.F.S.R.; on R. Belaya; ctr. of Ishimbay oilfields; p. (1956) 44,400.

Ishpeming, c., Mich., U.S.A.; machin., gold, silver, iron, marble; p. (1960) 8,857.

Isiro (Paulis), t., N.E. Congo; admin. offices; cotton ginneries; rly. repair shops.

Isis, R., head stream of R. Thames, Eng.; so named until its confluence with Thames at Dorchester, Oxfordshire.

Iskenderun, spt. Hatay, Turkey; pt. and rly. terminus; oil; fertilisers; p. (1965) 69,259.

Islamabad, cap., Pakistan; outside Rawalpindi below Himalayas; nuclear power sta.

Islay, I., Inner Hebrides; Argyll, Scot.; 13 m. W. Kintyre; a. 235 sq. m.; farming, dairying, distilleries.

Isle of Grain, rural a., Kent; flat promontory once separated from mainland by a tidal estuary; lge. oil refinery.

Isle Royale, I., in L. Superior, Mich., U.S.A.; length 40 m.

Isleworth, see Hounslow.

Islington, inner bor., London, Eng.; N. of City; incorporates former bor. of Finsbury; univ.; industl. and residtl.; p. (1966) 255,000.

Ismailia, t., U.A.R., at mid-point of Suez Canal on L. Timsah, 45 m. N.N.W. of Suez; has rail connections with Cairo, Suez and Port Said; p. (1960) 25,194.

Isna (Esneh), t., Upper U.A.R.; caravan ctr.; barrage; p. (1947) 13,458.

Isonzo, R., Illyria, Italy; flows into Adriatic Sea.

Isparta, t., Turkey; N. of Antalya; p. (1965) 42,963. [research ctr.]

Ispra, t., Varese, Italy, nr. L. Maggiore; nuclear

Israel, indep. Jewish rep., since 1948; part of former Palestine mandate; cap. Jerusalem; impt. ts. Tel Aviv, Haifa; mainly agr.; grains, vegs., olives, citrus-fruit prod.; processed foods, textiles, wearing apparel, pharmaceuticals; little mineral wealth except for potash and other chemicals from Sea of Galilee and Dead Sea; a. 8,050 sq. m.; p. (1964) 2,525,600.

Issoudun, t., Indre, France; leather, parchment, woollens, farm implements; p. (1962) 14,483

Issy, t., France; on R. Seine; sub. of Paris; p. (1962) 53,298.

Issyk-kul, L., Kirgizia, U.S.S.R.; alt. 4,476 ft.; a. 250 sq. m.; drained by R. Chu.

Istanbul (Constantinople), ch. spt., former cap., Turkey; on Golden Horn pen. on European cst. at entry of Bosporus into Sea of Marmara; div. into old "Stamboul" on S. side and dists. of Galata and Beyoglu (Pera) on N.; the ancient Byzantium; magnificent mosque of Sta Sophia; light inds.; car wks. nearby; p. (1965) 1,750,642.

Istria, peninsula, N. Adriatic Sea; formerly Italian, now divided between Jugoslavia and Italy; agr., olives, vines, oranges, maize; rural p. mainly Slavs, ts. mainly Italian.

Ita, c., S. Paraguay; cattle, agr.; leather; p. 16,892.

Itabira, t., Minas Geraes st., Brazil; on Brazilian Plateau, 60 m. N.E. of Belo Horizonte; lgst. deposits of iron ore in Brazil. [54,268.]

Itabuna, c., E. Brazil; coffee, tobacco; p. (1960)

Itajaí, t., at mouth of Itajaí R., S. Brazil; exp. lumber, tobacco, starch, sassafras oil; p. (1960) 55,000.

Italy, rep., S. Europe; peninsula 750 m. long and 100-120 m. broad; many Is. (ch. Sardinia, Sicily); mtns. in N. (Alps) and in ctr. and S. (Apennines); ch. R. Po; climate, Mediterranean; wheat and other cereals; vines, olives, fruit; cattle, sheep; sulphur, iron and iron pyrites, mercury, lead, zinc; Carrara marble; hydro-elec. power, natural gas; mnfs.; cottons, silks, sugar, glass, furniture, olive oil; gen. engin., cars; fisheries; cap. Rome; a. 116,235 sq. m.; p. (1963) 52,520,000.

Itasca, L., a source of Mississippi R., Minn., U.S.A.; alt. 1,575 ft.

Itatiaia, mtn., highest mtn. in Brazil; 9,255 ft.

Itaugua, t., S.W. Paraguay; lace mkg.; p. 11,300.

Itchen, R., Hants, Eng.; flows to Southampton Water; length 25 m.

Ithaca, t., N.Y., U.S.A.; on Cayuga L.; seat of Cornell Univ.; elec. clocks; p. (1960) 28,799.

Ithake, one of the Ionian Is., Greece; a. 37 sq. m.; ch. t. Ithake; severe earthquake, 1953.

Ito, t., Honshu, Japan; on E. cst. of Izu pen.; hot-spring resort; p. (1965) 59,404.

Itzehoe, t., Schleswig-Holstein, Germany; on Stor R.; wood, cement, machin.; p. (1963) 36,900. [(1959) 66,000.]

Ivano-Frankovsk, t., Ukrainian S.S.R.; oil; p.

Ivanovo, t., R.S.F.S.R.; N.E. of Moscow; textiles, iron and chemical wks.; peat-fed power stas.; p. (1967) 398,000. [cryolite.]

Ivigtut, Danish sttlement, S.W. Greenland;

Iviza, I., Balearic gr. in the W. Mediterranean; Spanish; cath., fortress.

Ivory Coast, ind. sov. st., within French Community, W. Africa; climate, tropical; maize, coffee, rubber, mahogany; dense forests; cap. Abidjan; a. 124,000 sq. m.; p. (1963) 3,750,000.

Ivrea, t., Italy; on the Dora Baltea, nr. Turin; silks, cotton mnfs.; p. 14,473.

Ivry-sur-Seine, t., France; on R. Seine, sub. of Paris; organs, chemicals, iron and steel; p. (1962) 53,646.

Iwamizawa, t., W. Hokkaido, Japan; rly. junction; coalfield; p. (1965) 65,508.

Iwanai, spt., S.W. Hokkaido, Japan; copper, coal, sulphur; fisheries; p. (1947) 20,394.

Iwo, t., Nigeria, W. Africa; nr. Ibadan; p. (1953) 100,000.

Izegem, commune, N.W. Belgium; linen, tobacco; p. (1962) 17,157. [360,000.]

Izhevsk, t., R.S.F.S.R.; steel, engin.; p. (1967)

Izieux, *t.*, Loire, France; nr. St. Etienne.

Izmail, *former prov.* of Bessarabia, Romania; ceded to U.S.S.R. in 1940, and now part of Ukrainian S.S.R.

Izmail, *t.*, Ukrainian S.S.R.; on R. Danube; food inds.; p. (1956) *43,400.*

Izmir (Smyrna), *c.*, Turkey; at head of G. of Smyrna, Anatolia; exp. figs, raisins, tobacco, carpets, rugs; anc. and historic c.; ch. comm. ctr. of the Levant; p. (1965) *417,413.*

Izmit, *t.*, Turkey; E. end of Sea of Marmara; cereals, tobacco, oil refinery and polythene plant under construction; p. (1965) *90,061.*

Izúcar, *t.*, Puebla, Mexico; nr. Popocatepetl; p. *7,065.*

# J

Jabbok, *R.*, Syria, trib. of R. Jordan; length 45 m.

Jablonec, *t.*, ČSSR.; on R. Neisse; artificial jewellery; p. (1961) *27,266.*

Jaboatoa, *c.*, E. Brazil; sub. of Recife; p. (1960) *33,963.*

Jaca, *fortfd. t.*, N. Spain; at foot of Pyrenees; p. (1957) *9,035.*

Jachymov, *t.*, ČSSR.; spa; uranium-mines, pitch-blende, lead, silver, nickel, cobalt; p. *6,806.*

Jackson, *c.*, Mich., U.S.A.; on Grand R.; loco-motives, motor-car accessories; p. (1960) *50,720.*

Jackson, *t.*, cap. Miss., U.S.A.; cotton tr.; p. (1960) *144,422.*

Jackson, *t.*, Tenn., U.S.A.; univ.; cotton, cotton-seed oil, engines, sewing-machines; p. (1960) *33,849.*

Jackson, *t.*, Ohio, U.S.A.; foundries, gas wells; p. (1960) *6,980.*

Jacksonville, *t.*, Ark., U.S.A.; p. (1960) *14,488.*

Jacksonville, *c.*, *pt.* Fla., U.S.A.; univ.; on St. John's R.; chemicals, shipbldg. and repair, printing, lumber, cigar mftg.; p. (1960) *201,030.*

Jacksonville, *t.*, Texas, U.S.A.; rly., ctr.; fruit, vegetables, cotton; p. (1960) *9,540.*

Jacksonville, *c.*, Ill., U.S.A.; woollens, rly. wks.; p. (1960) *21,690.*

Jacobabad, *frontier sta.*, Sind, Pakistan; one of hottest places in the Indian sub-continent; p. (1961) *35,200.*

Jacobina, *t.*, Baia, Brazil; on R. Itapicura; p. *4,389.*

Jacobsdal, *t.*, Orange Free State, S. Africa; on Riet R.

Jacobstadt, *see* Yekabpils.

Jacques-Cartier, *R.*, Quebec, Canada; trib. of St. Lawrence.

Jacques-Cartier, *t.*, Quebec, Canada; p. (1961) *40,807.*

Jacuhy, *R.*, S. Brazil; rises in S. edge of Brazilian Plateau, enters Atl. Oc., through lagoon, Lagoa dos Patos; length 350 m.

Jade, or Jahde, *estuary*, N. Sea, Germany; fine harbour and entrance to pt. of Wilhelmshaven.

Jaduguda, Bihar, India; uranium plant.

Jaen, *prov.*, S. Spain; mines, wine, garden produce, leather, weaving; a. 5,209 sq. m.; p. (1959) *773,563.*

Jaen, *t.*, *cap.*, Jaen, S. Spain; N. of Granada; p. (1959) *60,395.*

Jaffa–Tel Aviv, *t.*, Israel; orange-growing dist.; spt. closed 1965; p. (estd. 1956) *364,000.*

Jaffna, *t.*, *spt.*, N. Ceylon; p. (1963) *94,248.*

Jagdalpur, *t.*, Madhya Pradesh, India; p. (1961) *20,412.*

Jagersfontein, *t.*, O.F.S., S. Africa; most impt. diamond mine; p. (1960) *3,885* inc. *785* whites.

Jahrom, *t.*, Fars, Iran; tobacco, dates; p. *15,000.*

Jakarta, *see* Djakarta.

Jaipur, *cap. c.*, Rajasthan, India; comm. ctr.; univ.; p. (1961) *403,444.*

Jalalabad, *t.*, S. of Kabul R., Afghanistan; cane sugar; p. (estd. 1964) *44,000.*

Jalapa, *dep.*, S.E. Guatemala; maize, beans; cap. Jalapa; a. 797 sq. m.; p. (1964) *97,996.*

Jalapa, *cap.*, Veracruz st., Mexico; p. (1960) *60,000.*

Jalgaon, *t.*, *dist.*, Maharashtra, India; cotton, linseed; p. (1961) of t. *80,351;* of dist. *1,765,047.*

Jalisco, *Pacific st.*, Mexico; well timbered, agr.; mining; cap. Guadalajara; a. 31,149 sq. m.; p. (1960) *2,443,261.*

Jallieu, *commune*, Isère, S.E. France; light mnfs.; p. (1954) *5,241.*

Jalna, *t.*, Maharashtra, India; E. of Aurangabad; p. (1961) *67,153.*

Jalon, *R.*, Spain; rises in Iberian Mtns., flows N.E. into R. Ebro nr. Zaragoza; valley forms main rly., road route from Madrid to Ebro Valley.

Jaluit, *I.*, Marshall Is., Pa., Oc.

Jamaica, *I.*, *indep. sov. st.* within Br. Common-wealth (1962); W.I., divided into three cos., Middlesex, Surrey and Cornwall; mountainous, highest peak (in Blue Mtns.) 7,420 ft.; cap. Kingston; univ.; bauxite, alumina, cement, sugar, rum, molasses, coffee, bananas, cocoa; tourism; a. 4,411 sq. m.; p. (estd. 1965) *1,745,000.* [*57,039.*

Jamalpur, *t.*, N.E. Bihar, Indian Union; p. (1961)

Jambes, *commune*, S. Belgium; sub. of Namur; glass, engin.; p. (1962) *13,426.*

James (or Powhattan), *R.*, Va., U.S.A.; flows from Blue Ridge to Chesapeake Bay; length 450 m.

James Bay, S. part of Hudson Bay, Canada; length about 1,250 m.

Jamestown, *c.*, N.D., U.S.A.; cattle; food processing; p. (1960) *15,163.*

Jamestown, *spt.*, *cap.*, St. Helena I.; flax; p. (1961) *1,700.*

Jamestown, *c.*, N.Y., U.S.A.; summer resort and mftg.; p. (1960) *41,818.*

Jamestown, *t.*, *dist.*, Va., U.S.A.; nr. mouth of James R., where first English permanent settle-ment was founded 1607.

Jammer Bay, *bay*, W. cst. of Vendsyssel, Jutland, Denmark.

Jammu and Kashmir, *st.*, N.W. India and N.E. Pakistan; divided along cease-fire line; traver-sed by ranges of the Himalayas; in Jhelum valley is the celebrated vale of Kashmir, pro-ducing abundant crops of wheat and rice; cap. Srinagar; winter cap. Jammu; a. 92,780 sq. m.; p. (1961) *3,560,976.*

Jamshedpur, *t.*, Bihar, India; W. of Calcutta; Tata iron and steel wks.; p. (1961) *328,044.*

Jämtland, *co.*, Sweden; a. 19,967 sq. m.; p. (estd. 1963) *134,200.*

Janesville, *t.*, Wis., U.S.A.; in agr. region; textiles, machin.; p. (1960) *35,164.*

Janina, *see* Ioannina.

Janiuay, *t.*, Panay, Philippines; fine woven fabrics.

Jan Mayen I., between Spitzbergen and Iceland, Arctic Ocean; belongs to Norway; seal and whale fisheries; government weather-forecast sta.; a. about 144 sq. m.

Japan, *cty.*, E. Asia; chs. Is. Shikoku, Hokkaido, Honshu, Kyushu; mtnous.; 18 active vol-canoes; subject to earthquakes; industl., comm., and financ. nation; 25 per cent agr.; climate varies according to latitude, in N. temperate, in S. sub-tropical, warm summers, abundant rainfall; vegetation, broad-leaved forest and meadows, coniferous forest; fine harbours, good communications; ch. inds.; agr., rice, cereals, mulberry and silk, tobacco, cotton, tea; coal, iron, copper; lumber; fisheries; textiles, silks, cottons, woollens; shipbldg., engin., machin., chemicals, electronics, metal mnfs., paper; oil from Honshu; cap. Tokio; a. 182,700 sq. m.; p. (1966) *99,180,000.*

Japan, Sea of, portion of Pac. Oc. between Korea, U.S.S.R. and Japan.

Japan Current, *see* Kuroshio.

Jappan I., Geelvink Bay, New Guinea, Indonesia.

Japura, *R.*, Colombia, Brazil, S. America; rising in the Andes of Colombia, and flowing through Brazil to R. Amazon; length 1,300 m.

Jarocin, *t.*, Poland; S. of Poznan; p. *11,818.*

Jaroslaw, *mftg. t.*, Rzeszow, Poland; on R. San; garrison; p. (1965) *27,000.*

Jarrahi, *R.*, S.W. Iran; flows into Persian G.

Jarrow, *t.*, *mun. bor.*, Durham, Eng.; on S. bank of R. Tyne, 7 m. below Gateshead; ship repairing and engin.; steel and tube wks., oil storage; birthplace of Venerable Bede; diecastings and knitting wool mkg. at Bede Trading Estate; p. (estd. 1967) *29,120.*

Jasper, *t.*, E. Texas, U.S.A.; cattle, agr., lumber; p. (1960) *4,580.*

Jasper Place, *t.*, Alberta, Canada; p. (1961) *30,530;*

Jassy (Lasi), *t.*, Romania; former cap. Moldavia, in vineyard dist.; textiles, chemicals; p. (1963) *159,541.*

Jászbereny, *t.*, Hungary; on R. Zagyva; engin.; p. (1962) *30,454.*

Jativa, *t.*, Valencia, Spain; wine, oil, fruit; p. (1957) *18,092*.

Jau, *c.*, São Paulo st., S.E. Brazil; coffee; p. *18,655*.

Jauf, *t.*, Nejd, Saudi Arabia; p. exceeds 10,000.

Jauja, *t.*, Junín, Central Peru; E. of Lima; p. *8,276*.

Jaunpur, *t.*, Uttar Pradesh, India; on R. Gumti; perfumes; p. (1961) *61,851*.

Java, *ch. I.*, Indonesia; mtns. (many volcanic); loftiest peak, 12,057 ft.; agr., rubber, tobacco, sugar, coffee, tea; oil palms, cinchona, spices; coal, tin, gold, silver; teak forests; petroleum; steel plant in W. densely populated; cap. Djakarta; a. 51,000 sq. m.; p. (inc. Madura) (1967) *72,600,000*.

Javari (Yavari), *R.*, forms bdy. between Peru and Brazil; trib. of R. Amazon.

Java Sea, part of the Pac. Oc. between N. cst. Java, Borneo and Sumatra.

Jaworzno, *industl. t.*, Poland; nr. Cracow; coal; p. (1965) *59,000*.

Jaxartes R., *see* Syr Darya.

Jayuya, *mun.*, central Puerto Rico, W. Indies; sugar, tobacco, cotton; p. *14,589*.

Jeanerette, *t.*, S. La., U.S.A.; sugar, pecan nuts, rice; p. (1960) *5,568*.

Jeanette, *bor.*, Penns., U.S.A.; natural-gas region; p. (1960) *16,565*.

Jebba, *t.*, Nigeria, W. Africa; on R. Niger.

Jebel Aulia, *vil.*, Sudan; S. of Khartoum; proposed site for dam across White Nile R.

Jebel ed Druz, *terr.*, S.E of Hauran, Syria; ch. t. Es Suweida.

Jebel-Hauran, high tableland of Syria; alt. 6,000 ft.

Jebel Serbal, *min.*, Sinai peninsula, U.A.R., alt. 6,760 ft.

Jebl-us-Siraj, *t.*, Afghanistan; cement wks.

Jedburgh, *burgh*, Roxburgh, Scot.; on R. Jed, 12 m. S.W. of Kelso; abbey ruins, tweeds, woollens, rayon; p. (1961) *3,647*.

Jefferson, *t.*, Texas, U.S.A.; near oilfield; cattle, grain; p. (1960) *3,082*.

Jefferson City, *cap.*, Mo., U.S.A.; on R. Missouri, 100 m. W. of St. Louis; shoes, tiles, farm implements; p. (1960) *28,228*.

Jeffersonville, *mftg.*, Ind., U.S.A.; on Ohio R.; p. (1960) *19,522*.

Jehol, former *prov.*, China; divided 1955 among Hopei and Liaoning provinces and Inner Mongolian Region; p. (1953) *5,160,822*.

Jelenia Góra (Hirschberg), *t.*, Lower Silesia, Poland, German before 1945; spa, rly. junction; p. (1965) *54,000*.

Jelep-la, *high pass*, leading from Sikkim, N. India, to Tibet; alt. 14,390 ft.

Jelgava (Mitau), *t.*, Latvia U.S.S.R.; on R. Aa; textiles, sugar; p. (1956) *31,600*.

Jemappes, *industl. t.*, Hainaut, Belgium; on the Haine R.; coal, iron; French victory over Austria 1792; p. (1962) *12,950*.

Jena, *t.*, Gera, E. Germany; on R. Saale; univ.; observatory; glass, books, pianos, optical mftg. (Zeiss); p. (1963) *83,451*.

Jennings, *t.*, La., U.S.A.; agr.; oil wells; p. (1960) *11,587*.

Jenolan Caves, N.S.W., Australia; in Blue Mtns., 20 m. S.W. of Katoomba; lge. natural caves in limestone, stalactites, stalagmites.

Jeremie, *spt.*, S.W. Haiti; p. *6,000*.

Jerez de la Frontera, *t.*, Andalusia, Spain; 14 m. N.E. of Cadiz; sherry; p. (1959) *127,194*.

Jerez de los Caballeros, *commune*, S.W. Spain; marble, cork, tr. ctr. for agr. region; p. *16,154*.

Jericho, *vil.*, Jordan Valley, Jordan; estd. through recent excavations as oldest t. in the world (6000 B.C.); p. (1961) *10,284*.

Jersey, *I.*, lgst. of Channel Is., 13 m. W. of Fr. cst; potatoes, tomatoes, cauliflowers, flowers, fruit, cattle; tourist resort; t. St. Helier; a. 45 sq. m.; p. (1961) *63,345*.

Jersey City, *spt.*, N.J., U.S.A.; opp. New York on Hudson R.; canning, iron, steel, tobacco, chemicals; rly. ctr.; p. (1960) *276,101*.

Jerusalem, *c.*, Holy Land; 2,660 ft. above sealevel, between Dead Sea and Mediterranean; the "Holy City" of the Jews and sacred c. of Christians and Mohammedans; divided between Israel and Jordan; Israel sector cap. of Israel; Old City annexed by Israel June 1967;

p. (estd. 1960 Israel) *164,000*; (1961 Jordan) *60,337*.

Jervis Bay, *Commonwealth terr.*, acquired as site for port for Canberra by Federal Government of Australia 1909; a. 28 sq. m.; p. *360*.

Jesi. *t.*, Ancona, Italy; cath.; p. *23,600*.

Jesselton, *see* Kota Kinabalu.

Jhansi, *t.*, Uttar Pradesh, India; p. (1961) *169,712*.

Jharia, *t.*, Bihar, India; firebricks; p. (1961) *33,683*.

Jhelum, *R.*, W. Punjab, Pakistan; most W. of the five Rs. of the Punjab; Mangla Dam, under Indus Waters Treaty, completed 1967.

Jibuti (Djibouti), *pt.* on G. of Aden, cap. French Somaliland; rly. link with Addis Ababa; impt. transit trade; p. (estd. 1965) *41,000*.

Jičin, *t.*, N.E. Bohemia, ČSSR.; mkt.; p. (1961) *12,970*.

Jidda, *spt.*, *t.*, Hejaz, nr. Mecca, Saudi Arabia; steel mill projected; p. (estd.) *150,000*.

Jihlava, *t.*, Moravia, ČSSR.; timber, grain, textiles; p. (1961) *34,744*.

Jimena de la Frontera, *t.*, Spain; nr. Cadiz; p. *10,123*.

Jimma, ., *prov.*, Ethiopia; ch. prod. Jimma coffee; connected by road with Addis Ababa.

Jinja, *t.*, Uganda, E. Africa; on N. shore of L. Victoria where R. Nile drains from L. over Ripon Falls; hydro-elec. power scheme; cotton mnfs., copper smelting, flour and maize milling; brewing; rly. to Kampala; p. (1960) *29,741*.

Jinotega, *t.*, Nicaragua; coffee; p. (1961) *50,325*.

João Pessôa, *cap.*, Paraíba st., Brazil; sugar, cotton, mandioca, sisal; p. (1960) *155,117*.

Joban, *dist.*, N.E. Honshu, Japan; third lgst. coalfield in Japan; ch. t. Fukushima.

Joda, Orissa, India; ferromanganese plant.

Jodhpur, *t.*, Rajasthan, Indian Union; p. (1961) *224,760*.

Joênsuu, *t.*, on chain of Ls., S.E. Finland; p. (1966) *32,677*. [*11,034*.

Joeuf, *t.*, Meurthe-et-Moselle, France; p. (1954)

Jogjakarta, *c.*, Java; 40 m. S. of Semarang; connected with Jakarta by rail; citadel, with palace; p. (1961) *313,000*.

Johanna, *I.*, of the Comoro gr. in Mozambique Channel; p. *12,370*.

Johannesburg, *c.*, Transvaal, S. Africa; univ.; gold-mining ctr. of Witwatersrand; diamond cutting, engin., textiles, chemicals; oil pipeline from Durban; p. (1960) *1,110,905* (inc. *398,517* whites).

John o' Groat's House, *place* nr. Duncansby Head, Caithness, Scot.

Johnsonburg, *bor.*, Penns., U.S.A.; chemicals, paper, iron and steel; p. (1950) *4,567*.

Johnson City, *t.*, N.Y., U.S.A.; leather, chemicals, paper; p. (1960) *19,113*.

Johnson City, N.E. Tenn., U.S.A.; mkt., iron, textiles; p. (1960) *29,892*.

Johnston, *t.*, Providence, Rhode I., U.S.A.; p. (1960) *16,898*.

Johnstone, *mftg. burgh*, Renfrew, Scot.; on R. Black Cart, nr. Paisley; iron, brass, machine tools, textile ind.; p. (1961) *18,369*.

Johnstown, *t.*, N.Y., U.S.A.; glove mftg.; p. (1960) *10,390*.

Johnstown, *c.*, Penns., U.S.A.; on Connemaugh R.; immense steel wks.; p. (1960) *53,949*.

Johore, *st.*, Malaysia, at S. end of Malaya; forested; rubber, rice, copra, tin, iron, bauxite; a. 7,330 sq. m.; p. (1961) *1,084,351*.

Johore Bharu, *t.*, cap. Johore, Malaya; across the Strait from Singapore; p. (1957) *126,099*.

Joina Falls, Mali; dam projected for hydro-elec. and irrigation purposes, under auspices of Organisation of Riparian States of R. Senegal (Guinea, Mali, Mauritania, Senegal).

Joinville, *t.*, Santa Catarina, Brazil; exp. timber, matté tea; textiles, machin., car parts, plastics; p. (1960) *45,500*.

Jökulsa, *R.*, flowing into Axar Fjord, Iceland.

Joliet, *t.*, Ill., U.S.A.; rly. and mftg. ctr.; p. (1960) *66,780*.

Joliette, *t.*, Quebec, Canada; woollens, paper, tobacco; p. (1961) *18,088*.

Jonesborough, *t.*, Ark., U.S.A.; p. (1960) *21,418*.

Jönköping, *co.*, Sweden; cap. Jönköping; a. 4,447 sq. m.; p. (1961) *285,271*.

Jönköping, *t.*, cap. Jönköping, Sweden; paper matches, textiles, footwear; p. (1961) *50,652*.

Jonquière, *t.*, S. Quebec, Canada; lumber, rly. shops; p. (1961) *28,588.*

Joplin, *t.*, Mo., U.S.A.; lead-mng; p. (1960) *38,958.*

Jordan, *kingdom*, bounded by Israel, Syria, Saudi Arabia and Iraq; agr. but lge. areas of desert; phosphate deposits and potash; cap. Amman; a. 34,750 sq. m.; p. (1962) *1,824,614.*

Jordan, *R.*, famous in Bible history; flowing S. from Anti-Lebanon along a sinuous course, mostly below sea-level to the Dead Sea, its rapidity and variant depth render it unnavigable, and no t. of any importance has ever been built on its banks; length 120 m.

Jorullo, *volcano*, Michoacan st., Mexico, 4,265 ft.

Jos, *t.*, central Nigeria; on Bauchi Plateau, 60 m. S.W. of Bauchi; impt. tin-mines; on branch line linking with E. Nigerian rly. system to Pt. Harcourt.

Jotunheimen, *mtn. region*, central Norway; Gold-hopiggen, 8,097 ft., Glittertind, 8,048 ft.

Joyce's Country, *minous. dist.*, Galway, Ireland.

Juan de Fuca Strait, between Vancouver I. and Washington st., U.S.A.

Juan Fernandez, *rocky I.*, S. Pac. Oc.; belonging to Chile; a. 38 sq. m.; famous for Alex. Selkirk (Robinson Crusoe), 1704–9. [Equator.

Juba, *R.*, E. Africa; flows to Indian Ocean, nr. the

Juba, *cap.*, Equatorial Prov., Sudan; p. *10,000.*

Jubbulpore, *t.*, Madhya Pradesh, India; carpets, cottons; oil mills, ordnance wks.; p. (1961) *367,215.*

Juby, *O.*, Rio de Oro., N.W. Africa.

Jucar, *R.*, E. Spain; rises in Serrania de Cuenca, flows S.E. to G. of Valencia, Mediterranean Sea; length 250 m.

Juchitan, *t.*, S.E. Mexico; mkt. for rich agr. region; p. (1950) *14,550.*

Judaea, *div.* of Palestine in the Roman period.

Judenburg, *t.*, Styria, Austria; on R. Mur; p. (1961) *9,869.*

Juggernaut, *see* Puri.

Jugoslavia, *Federal People's Rep.*, comprising former terrs. of Serbia, Montenegro, Croatia, Dalmatia, Bosnia, Herzegovina and Slavonia; farming, wheat, maize, barley, rye, oats, fruits, plums; sheep, cattle, pigs, goats; timber, coal, iron, copper, lead, cement, chromium, salt, bauxite; cap. Belgrade; a. 98,386 sq. m.; p. (1960) *18,643,000.*

Juiz de Fora, *mftg. t.*, E. Brazil; textiles, lumber, brewing, sugar refining; p. (1960) *124,979.*

Jujuy, *prov.*, Argentina; cap. San Salvador de Jujuy; a. 16,859 sq. m.; p. (1960) *240,000.*

Julfa, *c.*, N. Iran; on frontier with U.S.S.R., impt. customs and transit ctr. on overland route from Europe.

Julian Alps, *mtn. range*, Venetia, Carinthia, Carniola and Croatia; highest peak, Triglav, 9,394 ft. [well.

Julianehaab, *sta.*, Greenland; N.W. of C. Fare-

Jülich, *t.*, Germany; nr. Aachen; "pebble bed" nuclear reactor projected.

Jullundur, *t.*, Punjab, India; cotton and silk mnfs.; p. (1961) *222,569.*

Jumet, *t.*, Belgium; nr. Charleroi; mftg. and mining; p. (1962) *28,653.*

Jumilla, *t.*, Murcia, Spain; exp. fabrics; p. (1957) *20,851.*

Jumna, *R.*, N. India; ch. trib. of R. Ganges; rises in the Himalayas and flows past Delhi and Agra to Allahabad; length 860 m.

Junction City, Kan., U.S.A.; p. (1960) *18,700.*

Jundiaí, *t.*, S.E. Brazil; rly. junction; textiles, steel; p. (1960) *79,536.*

Juneau, *c.*, cap., Alaska, U.S.A.; at foot of Chilkoot mtns.; lumbering; fisheries; gold settlement (1881); p. (1960) *6,797.*

Jungfrau, *peak*, Bernese Oberland, Switzerland; height 13,642 ft.; electric rly. from Kleine Scheidegg to Jungfraujoch.

Juniata, *R.*, Penns., U.S.A.; flows to the Susquehanna at Petersburg.

Junin, *inland dep.*, Peru; traversed by the Andes; copper, silver, lead; ch. t. Huancayo; a. 22,814 sq. m.; p. (1961) *507,908.*

Jura, *mtns.*, Switzerland and France; highest peak Crête de la Neige; alt. 5,654 ft.; length 180 m., width up to 30 m.

Jura, *dep.*, E. France; named from the mtns.; many vineyards; forests, cereals, watches, toys; a. 1,951 sq. m.; p. (1962) *225,682.*

Jura, *I.*, Argyll, Scot.; off W. cst.; a. 146 sq. m.

Jurua R., trib. of R. Amazon.

Jutland, *peninsula*, Denmark; intensive agr. and poultry farming; a. 11,411 sq. m.; p. (1960) *2,018,168.*

Jyväskylä, *t.*, central Finland; mkt.; pulp and paper; p. (1966) *53,004.*

# K

K², *see* Godwin-Austen, Mt.

Kabankalan, *mun.*, Negros Occidental, Philippine Is.; agr.; p. *29,315.*

Kabansk, *t.*, E. Siberia, U.S.S.R.; nr. L. Baikal; agr. and industl.

Kabarda-Balkar, A.S.S.R., Transcaucasia, U.S.S.R.; non-ferrous metals, gold, platinum, iron ore, coal, arsenic; a. 4,800 sq. m.; p. (1959) *420,000.*

Kabinda, *t.*, Angola, W. Africa; on W. cst., 30 m. N. of Congo estuary; p. *1,000.*

Kabul, *c.*, cap., Afghanistan; on R. Kabul, S. of the Hindu Kush; 6,900 ft. above sea level; univ.; excellent climate; wool, leather wks.; p. (estd. 1964) *400,000.*

Kabul, *R.*, flowing through Afghanistan to the R. Indus at Peshawar, Pakistan; length 270 m.

Kachin State, *div.*, Burma; comprising former Myitkyina and Bhamo dists; 29,500 sq. m.

Kadiyevka, *t.*, Ukrainian S.S.R.; coal, iron and steel, synthetic rubber; p. (1967) *138,000.*

Kaduna, *t.*, N. Nigeria; cap. of Northern Provs.; impt. rly. junction with main rlys. to Lagos, Pt. Harcourt; aluminium wks.; p. *10,000.*

Kaffraria, *extensive dist.*, Cape Province, S. Africa; comprising Griqualand E., Tembuland, Transkei, and Pondoland.

Kafue, *R.*, Zambia; famous gorge.

Kafue, *t.*, Zambia; 28 m. S. of Lusaka; iron and steel mill being built.

Kagoshima, *spt.*, at S. end of Kyushu I., Japan; rocket launching site nearby at Uchinoura; p. (1965) *328,446.* [inhabited.

Kahoolawe, *I.*, Hawaiian Is.; a. 45 sq. m.; un-

Kai Islands, *Is.*, Indonesia; between New Guinea and Timor; timber; a. 680 sq. m.; p. *51,000.*

Kaiapoi, *t.*, S.I., N.Z.; on the Waimakariri R., 14 m. by rail from Christchurch; woollens; p. (1961) *3,109.*

Kaieteur Falls, Guyana, S. America; located where R. Potaro leaves Guiana Highlands; among world's highest falls (741 ft.).

Kaifeng, *c.*, *cap.*, Honan, China; on Hwang-Ho R.; one of the most ancient cities in China; cottons; p. (1953) *299,000.*

Kaikoura, *t.*, S.I., N.Z.; on E. cst., 80 m. N.E. of Lyttelton; in this region are the Kaikoura ranges, in which the highest peaks are Tapuaenuku (9,465 ft.) and Alarm (9,400 ft.).

Kainji Dam, Nigeria; power sta. transmission system and river transportation on R. Niger, projected.

Kaiping, *t.*, Hopeh, N. China; 80 m. N.E. of Tientsin; second lgst. coal-mining a. (Kailan mines) in China; coal exported through Chinwangtao.

Kairouan, *holy c.* of the Moslems, Tunisia N. Africa; 80 m. S.S.E. of Tunis; founded *c.* A.D. 670; mosque; p. (1961) *34,000.*

Kaiserslautern, *t.*, Rhineland Palatinate, Germany; nr. Mannheim; iron, textiles, machin., tobacco, wood; p. (1963) *86,900.*

Kaiser Wilhelm's Land, *Australian dependency*, Antarctica.

Kaishu, *cap.* of Kokai prov., W. Korea; p. *29,688.*

Kajaani, *t.*, on Oulu L., Finland; p. (1966) *17,780.*

Kakamega, *t.*, Kenya, E. Africa; 30 m. N. of Kisumu; ctr. of gold-mining dist.

Kakhovka, *t.*, Ukrainian S.S.R.; on R. Dnieper; hydro-elec. sta.; p. (1956) *19,200.*

Kakinada, *t.*, *spt.*, Andhra Pradesh, India; cotton, oil seeds; p. (1961) *122,865.*

Kalahari Desert, *gr. infertile tract* of S. Central Africa, between the R. Orange and the Zambesi; mainly in Botswana; alt. 3,700 ft.; a. 20,000 sq. m.; inhabited chiefly by Bushmen.

Kalamata, *t.*, Peloponnese, Greece; nr. Sparta; silk ind., figs, currants, olive oil exp.; p. (1961) *38,211.*

Kalamazoo, *c.*, Mich., U.S.A.; rly. ctr., engin.; college; p. (1960) *82,089.*

Kalat, *div.*, W. Pakistan; a. 53,995 sq. m.; p. (1961) *539,000.*

**Kalgan** (Zhangjiakou), *c.*, Hopeh prov., China; nr. Gt. Wall 110 m. N.W. of Peking; tea, wool, hides; p. (1953) *229,000.*

**Kalgoorlie**, *t.*, W. Australia; on transcontinental rly. route 350 m. E. of Perth; semi-desert conditions; gold-mng. a.; p. (1966) *19,892* incl. Boulder.

**Kalimantan** (Indonesian Borneo); oil, rubber, rice, hardwood; a. 208,286 sq. m.; quartzites discovered in S.E.; p. (1961) *4,101,475.*

**Kalinin**, *t.*, R.S.F.S.R.; on trib. of R. Volga; cath.; engin., textiles, chemicals; p. (1967) *311,000.*

**Kaliningrad**, *prov.*, R.S.F.S.R., U.S.S.R.; cap. K., oil discovered in a.

**Kaliningrad** (formerly Königsberg), *t.*, formerly E. Prussia, now U.S.S.R.; on R. Pregel; cath.; fine bldgs; shipbldg., machin., wood-pulp, chemicals, sugar-beet; tea ctr.; p. (1967) *261,000.*

**Kalisz**, *t.*, Poland; on R. Prosna; industl. ctr., textiles; oldest Polish t., mentioned in 2nd century A.D. by Ptolemy; p. (1965) *75,000.*

**Kalmar**, *co.*, S. Sweden; cap. Kalmar; a. 4,485 sq. m.; p. (1961) *235,770.*

**Kalmar**, *spt.*, Sweden; on E. cst.; matches, shipbldg., food inds.; p. (1961) *30,839.*

**Kalna**, *vil.*, on Mt. Trara Planina, Yugoslavia; uranium mine and plant; nuclear power sta.

**Kalocsa**, *t.*, Hungary; on R. Danube; cath., palace; wine; p. (1962) *13,786.*

**Kalpakkam**, nr. Madras, India; nuclear power sta. being built.

**Kaluga**, *t.*, R.S.F.S.R.; on R. Oka; chemicals, engin., hydro-elec.; p. (1967) *176,000.* [*73,482.*

**Kalyan**, *spt.*, Thana, Maharashtra, India; p. (1961)

**Kama**, *R.*, U.S.S.R.; trib. of R. Volga, which it joins S. of Kazan; length 1,400 m.

**Kamaishi**, *t.*, *spt.*, N.E. Honshu, Japan; serves Kamaishi–Sennin iron-ore field, lgst. worked deposits and reserves in Japan; impt. iron and steel ind.; p. (1947) *26,200.*

**Kamakura**, *t.*, Honshu, Japan; on shore of Sagami Bay; tourism; p. (1965) *118,329.*

**Kamaran I.**, Red Sea; Southern Yemen, formerly under Brit. occupation, 1915–67; a. 22 sq. m.; p. c. *2,200.*

**Kamchatka**, *peninsula*, E. Siberia, U.S.S.R.; mtns. with volcanoes (Klyuchevsk, alt. 16,512 ft.); mineral wealth, fisheries on cst., climate cold, wet and foggy; cap. Petropavlovsk.

**Kamenets Podolski**, *t.*, Ukrainian S.S.R.; brewing, tobacco; p. (1956) *33,000.*

**Kamensk-Shakhtinskiy**, *t.*, R.S.F.S.R.; on R. Severskiy Donets; coal-mng., engin., artificial fibres; p. (1959) *58,500.*

**Kamensk Uralsk**, *t.*, R.S.F.S.R.; aluminium, iron, steel, engin.; p. (1967) *159,000.*

**Kamet**, *mtn.*, N. Garhwal dist., Himalayas; alt. 25,477 ft.; until 1953 (Everest) highest mtn. climbed (Smythe, 1931).

**Kamloops**, *c.*, B.C., Canada; on Thompson R.; formerly Fort Thompson; in "Wild West" area; on transcontinental rlys.; supply ctr. for mining and grazing dist.; p. (1961) *10,076.*

**Kampala**, *cap.*, Uganda, E. Africa; univ. coll.; ch. comm. ctr.; lt. inds.; coffee processing; p. (1959) *46,780.*

**Kampar**, *t.*, Perak, Malaysia; p. *17,449.*

**Kampen**, *t.*, Overijssel, Netherlands; on R. IJssel; cigar mkg.; p. (1967) *28,942.*

**Kamp-Lintfort**, *t.*, N. Rhine–Westphalia, Germany; abbey; coal-mng.; p. (1963) *35,900.*

**Kampot**, *prov.*, Cambodia; pepper; cement plant at Chakrey Ting; p. (1962) *337,879.*

**Kamyshin**, *mftg. t.*, R.S.F.S.R.; on R. Volga; textiles; mkt. gardening, grain; p. (1959) *55,000.*

**Kan**, *R.*, S. China; rises in Nan Shan, flows N. into L. Poyang; valley provides route for main road from Kiangsi prov. to Kwangtung prov. over Meiling Pass.

**Kanawha**, *R.*, W. Va., U.S.A.; rises in Allegheny Mtns., flows S.W. to Hinton, then turns N.W. across Allegheny Plateau into R. Ohio; lower course runs through ch. mining a. of W. Va. coalfield nr. Charleston; length 350 m. approx.

**Kanazawa**, *t.*, Kaga, Honshu, Japan; silks, ceramics, lacquer ware; p. (1965) *335,823.*

**Kanchenjunga**, *mtn.*, on Nepal–Sikkim bdy., N.E. India; 3rd highest mtn. in world; alt. 28,146 ft.

**Kandahar**, *prov.*, S. Afghanistan; mountainous; cap. K.; p. (1948) *1,063,496.*

**Kandahar**, *c.*, former cap., Afghanistan; alt. 3,400 ft.; 370 m. from Herat; linked by road to Kushka (Turkmenia) via Herat; fruit pre-

serving and canning; textiles; p. (estd. 1964) *115,000.*

**Kandy**, *t.*, Ceylon; in ctr. of I., 75 m. from Colombo at alt. 3,000 ft.; resort in hot season; tea and cocoa; p. (1963) *67,768.*

**Kangaroo I.**, S. Australia; eucalyptus; p. (1966) *3,380.*        [machin.; p. (1960) *27,666.*

**Kankakee**, *t.*, Ill., U.S.A.; farm implements;

**Kano**, *c.*, N. Nigeria, W. Africa; gr. emporium for the whole Sudan region; impt. airport and rly. terminus; brewing; p. (1953) *130,000.*

**Kanpur**, *t.*, Uttar Pradesh, India; fertilisers.

**Kansas**, *st.*, U.S.A.; called the "Sunflower State"; prairie; farming, maize, wheat; cattle, dairying, pigs; coal, petroleum, natural gas, lead, meat-packing, flour-milling, aircraft, chemicals, machin.; cap. Topeka; a. 82,276 sq. m.; p. (1960) *2,178,611.*

**Kansas City**, Mo., U.S.A.; on right bank of R. Missouri; univ.; gr. livestock mart., car and aircraft assembly, steel, metal; meat pkg., food processing; p. (1960) *475,539*, adjoins Kansas City, Kansas; p. (1960) *121,901.*

**Kansk**, *t.*, R.S.F.S.R., on Trans-Siberian Rly.; ctr. of industl. a.; textiles, wood-working; p. (1959) *74,000.*

**Kansu** (Gansu), *prov.*, N. China; bordering Inner Mongolia; cap. Lanchow; wheat, cotton, tobacco; livestock; mineral resources; a. 151,161 sq. m.; p. (1953) *12,928,102.*

**Kant**, *t.*, Kirgiz S.S.R.; 12 m. E. of Frunze; to be expanded to industl. c.; proposed p. *100,000.*

**Kaohsiung**, *spt.*, Taiwan; on S.W. cst.; exp. rice, sugar; oil refining, aviation spirit, diesel oil; p. (1962) *276,000.*

**Kapfenberg**, *commune*, Austria; iron, chemicals, paper; resort; p. (1961) *23,859.*

**Kaposvar**, *t.*, Hungary; textiles; p. (1962) *45,054.*

**Kara-Bogaz**, *lge. G.* on E. cst. of Caspian Sea, Turkmen S.S.R.; very high salinity, impt. deposits of Glauber's salt used in local chemical ind.; a. 7,000 sq. m.      [p. (1965) *47,660.*

**Karabuk**, *t.*, Turkey; N. of Ankara; steel wks.;

**Karachi**, Fed. Terr. of, *div.*, W. Pakistan, on the Indus delta; univ.; spt., air ctr.; oil refining; industl. gases; steel mill; natural gas from Sui; nuclear power sta. under construction; a. 8,400 sq. m.; p. (1961) *2,153,000.*

**Karaganda**, *t.*, Kazakh S.S.R.; on impt. coalfield; engin.; iron and steel wks.; p. (1967) *489,000.*

**Karakorum Mtns.**, Kashmir, India; on border with China; hgst peak Godwin-Austen.

**Kara-Kum**, *sand desert*, Turkmen S.S.R.; canal 510 m. long across desert completed 1962.

**Kara Sea**, Arctic Ocean; E. of Novaya Zemlya; navigation open July–Sept.

**Karbala**, *t.*, Iraq; N.W. of Hilla; ctr. of pilgrimage; sacred c. of Shiites; p. (1961) *219,015.*

**Karcag**, *t.*, E. Hungary; tortoiseshell goods; p. (1962) *25,787.*

**Karelia** A.S.S.R., U.S.S.R., incorporated into R.S.F.S.R. July '56; cap. Petrozavodsk; rich in timber, minerals, precious metals; a. 69,720 sq. m.; p. (1959) *649,000.*

**Kariba Dam**, in Kariba gorge of Zambezi R., on Rhodesia–Zambia border; operated jointly by the two govts.; one of lgst dams in world with vast artificial lake supplying hydroelec. power to Rhodesia, Malawi, and the Copperbelt of Zambia; completed 1960.

**Karikal**, *former Fr. prov.*, united with India 1954: on E. cst.; p. (1961) *22,252.*

**Karkonosze** (Riesengebirge), *mtn. range*, between Polish Silesia and Bohemia; highest peak Sniezka (Schneekoppe), 5,275 ft.

**Karl-Marx-Stadt**, *t.*, Karl-Marx-Stadt, E. Germany; cottons, woollens, machin., cars, furniture, chemicals, engin.; p. (1963) *288,597.*

**Karlovac**, *t.*, Croatia, Jugoslavia; S.W. of Zagreb; chemicals; p. (1959) *30,000.*

**Karlovy Vary**, *t.*, *vat. pl.*, ČSSR.; on R. Ohre; health resort; porcelain; p. (1961) *42,819.*

**Karlshamn**, *t.*, Sweden; oil refining, demagnetising sta.; p. (1961) *11,657.*

**Karlskoga**, *mkt. t.*, Sweden; E. of L. Vänern; armaments, iron and steel; p. (1961) *35,606.*

**Karlskrona**, *ch. naval sta.*, Sweden; on the S. cst.; lighting fixtures, china; p. (1961) *32,977.*

**Karlsruhe**, *t.*, Baden-Württemberg, Germany; chemicals, engin., elec., tobacco ind, oil refining; rly. junction; outport on Rhine; nuclear reactor projected (1957); oil pipeline to Lavera, nr. Marseilles, opened 1963; p. (1963) *249,500.*

Karlstad, *t.*, Sweden; on N. shore L. Vänern; ironwks. hy. engin., machin.; p. (1961) *43,064.*

Karnak, *vil.* Upper U.A.R.; on Nile, the site of ancient Thebes; ruined temples.

Karpathos, *I.*, Dodecanese, Greece; Mediterranean Sea; between Rhodes and Crete, p. *8,747.*

Karoos, Gr. and Little, extensive treeless plateau between mtn. ranges covered by scrub, W. Cape Prov., S. Africa.

Kars, *c.*, Turkey; woollens, carpets; p. (1965) *41,236.*      [(1961) *46,842.*

Karvina, *t.*, ČSSR.; coal, iron, chemicals; p.

Kasai, *R.*, Angola and Congo, Central Africa; rises in Bihé Plateau (Angola) and flows over 1,200 m. into R. Congo 120 m. above Kinshasa.

Kasanlik, *t.*, Central Bulgaria; captured from Turks at surrender of Sipka Pass 1878; famous for attar of roses; p. (1956) *30,934.*

Kashan, *c.*, Iran; Isfahan prov.; carpets, velvet; p. (1967) *153,986.*      [R. Yarkand.

Kashgar, *R.*, E. Turkestan; flowing 500 m. to the

Kashing, *t.*, N. Chekiang, E. China; on Grand Canal; mkt. and tr. ctr.; p. *c. 86,000.*

Kashmir, *see* Jammu and Kashmir.

Kassala, *prov.*, Sudan; a. 134,450 sq. m.; p. (estd. 1951) *788,200.*

Kassel, *t.*, Hessen, Germany; on R. Fulda; cas.; iron, machin., cars, wood; route ctr.; p. (1963) *211,800.*

Kastamonu, *t.*, Karasu, Turkey; cap. of Turkish I. same name; great comm. ctr.; fruit, cotton, mohair; p. (1960) *19,450.*      [*10,162.*

Kastoria, *t.*, N. Greece; E. of Vérroia; p. (1961)

Katanga, *prov.*, Congo; cap. Lubumbashi; copper, radium, uranium; cattle; a. 180,000 sq. m.; p. *1,178,029.*

Katmandu, *cap.*, Nepal; on Vishnumati R., 75 m. from Indian frontier; highway to Kodari; hydro-elec. sta.; brick and tile wks.; p. (1961) *195,260.*

Kathiawar, *peninsula*, Gujarat, India.

Katoomba, *t.*, N.S.W., Australia; holiday resort; alt. 3,300 ft.; p. (1966) *10,513.*

Katowice, *prov.*, S. Poland; cap. K.; mng. and industl. a., drained by upper Vistula and upper Warta Rs.; a. 3,674 sq. m.; p. (1965) *3,253,000.*

Katowice, *c.*, S. Poland; ch. mng. and industl. ctr.; heavy machin., chemicals; p. (1965) *286,000.*

Katrine, Loch, S.W. Perth, Scot.; on R. Teith, 8 m. long; principal source of Glasgow water supply; beautiful scenery.

Kattegat, arm of North Sea linked with Baltic; separates Denmark (Jutland) from Sweden; 40–70 m. wide.

Katwijk, *t.*, Neth., S. Holland; on N. Sea, 15 m. from the Hague; resort; synthetic resins; p. (1967) *33,666.*      [*23,176.*

Kauai, *I.*, Hawaiian Is.; a. 555 sq. m.; p. (1960)

Kaunas (Kovno), *t.*, Lithuanian S.S.R.; on R. Niemen; old-time cap.; univ.; metal goods, chemicals, textiles; hydro-elec. sta. under construction; p. (1967) *276,000.*

Kavalla, *prefecture*, Macedonia, Greece; ch. t. Kavalla; p. (1961) *140,445.*

Kavalla, *t.*, Kavalla, Greece; on Bay of Kavalla; gr. tobacco ctr.; p. (1961) *44,517.*

Kavaratti, *I.*, Laccadive, Minicoy and Amindivi Is., India; admin. ctr. of Union terr.; p. (1961) *2,828.*

Kawasaki, *c.*, Honshu, Japan; S. sub. of Tokyo; pilgrims; engin.; steel plate, petro-chemicals, synthetic resins, rubber; p. (1964) *789,000.*

Kawerau, *t.*, N.I., N.Z.; pulp and paper mill; p. (1961) *4,413.*

Kawthoolei, *div.*, Burma; former Karen st. extended to include areas in Tenasserim and Irrawaddy, inhabited by Karens.      [*126,913.*

Kayseri, *t.*, Turkey; S.E. of Ankara; p. (1965)

Kazakhstan, *constituent rep.*, U.S.S.R.; cap. Alma-Ata; steppe with stock-raising; lge. desert areas, being made fertile by irrigation; grain in N.; coal at Karaganda; asbestos at Dzhetygara; metaborite (richest boron mineral); minerals, oil; atomic power sta. being built in W., on Caspian Sea; a. 1,072,797 sq. m.; p. (1959) *9,301,000.*

Kazan, *t.*, R.S.F.S.R.; impt. tr. ctr. for E. U.S.S.R., Turkestan Bokhara and Iran; cath., univ.; engin., chemicals, synthetic rubber, textiles, oil refining, paper; natural gas pipeline to Minnibayevo (Tatar A.S.S.R.); p. (1967) *804,000.*

Kazan Retto (Volcano Is.), *gr. of Is.*, Pac. Oc.; S. of Ogasawara Is. and of Japan.

Kazerun, *t.*, S.W. Iran; oranges, cotton, opium; p. (1956) *30,659.*      [*17,477.*

Kazincbarcika, *t.*, Hungary; chemicals; p. (1962)

Kazvin, *t.*, Navistain, Iran; good transit tr.; p. (estd. 1950) *80,000.*

Kearny, *t.*, N.J., U.S.A.; mnfs.; p. (1960) *37,472.*

Kearsley, *urb. dist.*, Lancs. Eng.; chemicals and paper, cotton; p. (1961) *10,302.*

Keban Dam, S.E. Turkey; at confluence of the E. and W. branches of Euphrates; projected.

Kecskemet, *t.*, Hungary; nr. Budapest; fruit canning, wine distilling; p. (1962) *68,327.*

Kedah, *st.*, Malaysia, N.W. Malaya; rice, rubber, coconuts; a. 3,660 sq. m.; cap. Alor Star; p. (1961) *794,086.*

Kedzierzyn, *t.*, Opole, Poland; p. (1965) *26,000.*

Keeling Is., *see* Cocos Is.

Keelung, *c.*, N. Taiwan; naval base and prin. pt.; chemicals; gold, sulphur and copper mng.; p. (estd.) *226,400.*

Keene, *c.*, N.H., U.S.A.; mnfs.; p. (1960) *17,562.*

Keeper, *mtn.*, Tipperary, Ireland; alt. 2,265 ft.

Keewatin, *dist.*, N.W. Terr., Canada; chiefly " barren lands "; a. 228,160 sq. m.

Kei (Kai) Is., *gr.* off cst. of W. Irian, Indonesia, in Banda Sea; densely forested; p. *50,648.*

Keighley, *t.*, *mun. bor.*, W.R. Yorks., Eng.; in Aire valley, 15 m. N.W. of Leeds; engin., textiles; p. (estd. 1967) *55,710.*

Keith, *burgh*, Banff, Scot.; on Isla R.; mftg. inds.; in agr. dist.; p. (1961) *4,208.*

Kelaniya, *t.*, Ceylon; tyre factory.

Kelantan, *st.*, Malaysia; N.E. Malaya; rice, coconuts, rubber; a. 5,720 sq. m.; cap. Kota Bharu; p. (1961) *579,246.*      [(1960) *5,061.*

Kellogg, *c.*, N.E. Idaho. U.S.A.; lead-mines; p.

Kelso, *burgh*, Roxburgh, Scot.; at confluence of Rs. Teviot and Tweed; p. (1961) *3,964.*

Kelvin, *R.*, Scotland, flows S.W. to Clyde at Partick; length 21 m.

Kemerovo, *t.*, R.S.F.S.R.; S.E. of Tomsk; iron, chemicals, coal, textiles; p. (1967) *358,000.*

Kemi (Kymmene), *dep.*, Finland; a. 3,537 sq. m.; cap. K.; p. (1966) *347,696.*

Kempsey, *t.*, N.S.W., Australia; dairy prod. timber; p. (1966) *8,173.*

Kempston, *urb. dist.*, Bedford, Eng.; on R. Ouse, 3 m. S.W. of Bedford; p. (1961) *9,173.*

Kempten, *t.*, Bavaria, Germany; nr. L. Constance; Benedictine Abbey; textiles, furniture, paper; rly. junction; p. (1963) *44,500.*

Ken, *R.*, N. India, flows to the Jumna; length 230 m.

Kena, *see* Qena.

Kendal, *mkt. t.*, *mun. bor.*, Westmorland, Eng.; engin., footwear, woollens; p. (estd. 1967) *19,140.*

Kenilworth, *mkt. t.*, *urb. dist.*, Warwick, Eng.; 4 m. S.W. of Coventry; ruined cas.; lt. engin., agr. repair wk.; p. (estd. 1967) *20,450.*

Kenitra. *See* Mina Hassan Tani.      [*6,982.*

Kenmare, *rurl dist.*, *t.*, Kerry, Ireland; p. (1961)

Kenmore, *t.*, N.Y., U.S.A.; p. (1960) *21,261.*

Kennebec, *R.*, Maine, U.S.A.; flows to Atlantic; length 200 m.

Kennet, *R.*, Wilts and Berks, Eng.; trib. of R. Thames; followed by main rly. London to W. of England; length 44 m.

Kenosha, *c.*, Wis., U.S.A.; on W. shore of L. Michigan; mnfs.; p. (1960) *67,899.*      [London.

Kensal Green, *dist.*, Middx, Eng.; sub. N.W.

Kensington and Chelsea, Royal Borough of, *inner bor.*, W. London, Eng.; mainly residtl.; contains K. Palace and Gardens; p. (1966) *215,000.*

Kent, *maritme co.*, S.E. Eng.; agr., stock-raising, hops and cherries; co. t. Maidstone; a. 1,525 sq. m.; p. (1966) *1,325,000.*

Kentucky, *E. central st.*, Mississippi basin, U.S.A.; agr., coal, fluorspar, petroleum, natural gas; tobacco, chemicals, machin., metal, steel, hemp, asphalt; tobacco, hay, corn; cattle and horse raising; cap. Frankfort; lgst. c. Louisville, at falls of Ohio R.; a. 40,395 sq. m.; p. (1960) *3,038,156.*

Kentucky, *R.*, U.S.A.; flows from Cumberland Mtns. to the Ohio R.; length 350 m.

Kenya, Rep. of, *indep. sov. st.* within Brit. Commonwealth (1963), E. Africa; cst. strip flat, interior elevated; climate varies according to elevation; vegetation tropical; forests on cstal. belt, semi-desert and grasslands on uplands, hydroelec. stns. at Wanjii, Tana, and Kindaruma (under constr.); mainly agr.; maize;

sugar, coconuts, sisal, cotton, coffee, pyrethrum; cattle, sheep; bamboo, pencil cedar, hardwoods; gold; oil refining at Changamwe; cap. Nairobi; a. 224,960 sq. m.; p. (estd. 1964) *8,676,000*.

**Kenya, Mt.,** *volcanic pk.,* Kenya; 17,040 ft.

**Keokuk,** *industl., c.,* S.E. Iowa, U.S.A.; on Mississippi at foot of Des Moines rapids; p. (1960) *16,316.* [(1961) *62,090.*

**Keos (Chios),** Ægean Is., Greece; cap. Keos; p.

**Kephallenia (Cephalonia),** one of the Ionian Is., Greece; currants, olive oil; cap. Argostolion; devastated by earthquake 1953; a. 315 sq. m.; p. (1961) *46,302.*

**Kerala,** *st.,* India; cap. Trivandrum; plantations producing rubber, tea, pepper; zircon; a. 15,002 sq. m.; p. (1961) *16,903,715.*

**Kerch,** *spt.,* Ukrainian S.S.R.; iron and steel, manganese, vanadium and phosphorus; ship-bldg.; fisheries; p. (1967) *115,000.*

**Kergulen,** *French archipelago,* dependency of Madagascar, S. of Indian Ocean; whaling and fishing sta.; a. 1,400 sq. m.

**Kerkrade,** *t.,* Limburg, Neth.; anc. Abbey; music ctr.; p. (1967) *50,566.*

**Kérkyra (Corfu),** most N. of Ionian Is., Greece; a. 274 sq. m.; mtnous.; p. (1961) *101,555.*

**Kérkyra,** *spt., cap.,* Kérkyra I., Greece; wine, fruits, olives; p. (1961) *26,991.*

**Kermadec Is.,** S. Pac. Oc., gr. belonging to New Zealand, 600 m. N.N.E. of New Zealand; a. 13 sq. m.; meteorological sta. on Sunday I. (lgst. of gr.); p. (1961) *10.*

**Kerman,** *prov.,* S. Iran; mtnous, much desert land; agr.; carpets; coal and iron ore mng. being developed; recent copper find; major irrigation scheme projected; p. (1967) *243,770.*

**Kerman,** *c.,* S. Central Iran; prov. cap.; airpt.; p. (1967) *163,689.* [airpt.; p. (1967) *424,978.*

**Kermanshah,** *c.,* Iran; cap. Kermanshahan prov.;

**Kermanshahan,** *prov.,* Iran; frontier Iraq; oil-fields; p. (1967) *779,336.*

**Kern, R.,** E. Cal., U.S.A.; one of most impt. power-generating Rs. in st.

**Kerry,** *maritime co.,* Munster, Ireland; a. 1,816 sq. m.; cap. Tralee; p. (1966) *112,642.*

**Keski Soumen,** *dep.,* Finland; p. (1966) *248,282.*

**Kesteven,** *administrative div.,* Lincoln, Eng.; ch. ts. Grantham, Stamford and Sleaford; a. 724 sq. m.; p. (1961) *49,946.*

**Keswick,** *mkt. t., urb. dist.,* Cumberland, Eng.; on Greta R.; at N. end of L. Derwentwater; tourist ctr.; pencils; p. (1961) *4,752.*

**Ketchikan,** *t.,* Alaska, U.S.A.; halibut, salmon; pulp, lead, zinc; p. (1960) *6,483.*

**Kettering,** *mkt. t., mun. bor.,* Northants, Eng.; nr. Wellingborough; iron, steel, boots, shoes; p. (estd. 1967) *39,270.*

**Kettering,** *t.,* Ohio, U.S.A.; p. (1960) *54,462.*

**Kew,** *sub.* London, Surrey, Eng.; on R. Thames opp. Brentford; contains Kew Gardens. (Kew Observatory is in Old Deer Park, Richmond.)

**Kewaneo,** *t.,* N.W. Ill., U.S.A.; agr.; coal, engin.; p. (1960) *16,324.* [15,144.

**Keynsham,** *t., urb. dist.,* Somerset, Eng.; p. (1961)

**Key West,** *c.,* Fla., U.S.A.; on sm. I. same name about 100 m. from the mainland; naval sta., and cigar factories; nearest U.S.A. pt. to the Panama Canal; p. (1960) *33,956.*

**Khabarovsk,** *t.,* R.S.F.S.R.; on Amur R.; cath.; oil refining, aircraft engin., sawmilling; oil pipeline connects with oilfields in N. Sakhalin; cellulose, cardboard; p. (1967) *420,000.*

**Khairpur,** *div.,* W. Pakistan; a. 6,050 sq. m.; p. (1961) *2,586,000.*

**Khalkidhiki (Chalcidice),** *prefecture,* Macedonia, Greece; cap. Poliyicos; p. (1961) *79,838.*

**Khamgaon,** *t.,* Maharashtra, India; cotton; p. (1961) *44,432.* [refinery; p. *5,000.*

**Khanaqin,** *t.,* Iraq; nr. E. frontier; oil-fields,

**Khandwa,** *t.,* Madhya Pradesh, India; S. of Indore; cotton, oil-pressing; p. (1961) *63,505.*

**Khania (Canea),** *prefecture* I. of Crete; cap. Khania; p. (1961) *130,898.*

**Khania (Canea),** *cap.* Crete; in sheltered bay on N.W. cst.; p. (1961) *33,467.*

**Khanka Lake, L.,** on Manchurian border, U.S.S.R.

**Kharan,** *dist.,* W. Pakistan; a. 18,508 sq. m.; p. (estd. 1951) *54,000.*

**Kharkov,** *c.,* Ukrainian S.S.R.; on R. Donets; univ., cath.; rly. ctr.. farm implements, engin., paper, chemicals; p. (1967) *1,092,000.*

**Khartoum,** *prov.,* Sudan; a. 5,700 sq. m.; p. with Omdurman (1956) *275,000.*

**Khartoum,** *cap.* Sudan; at confluence of White and Blue Niles; univ.; ivory, gum, ostrich feathers, brewing; p. (estd. 1956) *87,000.*

**Khartoum North,** *t.,* Sudan; lge. textile mill; p. (1961) *39,081.*

**Khashm el Girba,** *t.,* Sudan; new t. on Atbara R., between Khartoum and Ethiopian border; for p. of Wadi Halfa which will be inundated by Aswan Lake; sugar refinery.

**Khasi Hills,** Assam, N.E. India; form abrupt S. edge to middle Brahmaputra valley; very heavy monsoon rains on S.-facing slopes; lower slopes forested; middle slopes constitute impt. tea-growing region; rise to over 6,000 ft.

**Khaskovo,** *t.,* Bulgaria; woollens, carpets. silk, tobacco; p. *27,294.*

**Kherson,** *t.,* Ukrainian S.S.R.; 10 m. up R. Dnieper from Black Sea; grain, oil refining, engin., textiles, shipbldg.; p. (1967) *222,000.*

**Khingan,** Gr. and Little, *mtn. ranges,* Inner Mongolia and Heilungkiang prov., N.E. China; rich timber resources.

**Khios,** *I.,* Ægean Is., Greece; wines, figs, fruits, marble; cap. Khios; p. (1961) *62,090.*

**Khiva,** *originally vassal st.* of Russia; now part of Uzbekistan, U.S.S.R.

**Khiva,** *t.,* Uzbekistan, U.S.S.R.; silks, cottons, carpets; p. (estd.) *25,000.*

**Khmelnitskiy (Proskurov),** *t.,* Ukrainian S.S.R.; on R. Bug; machin. tools. textiles, food inds.; p. (1959) *62,000.*

**Khor Abdulla,** Iraq; in Persian G. nr. Basra; deep water oil loading island terminal in-augurated 1963.

**Khorramshahr,** *spt.,* S.W. Iran; leading pt. on Persian G.; import and export ctr.; p. (1967) *156,323.*

**Khotin,** *c.,* Ukrainian S.S.R., in Bessarabia, on Dniester R.; food processing plants.

**Khovu-Aksy,** *t.,* Tuva A.S.S.R.; on R. Elegest, 50 m. S.W. of Kyzyl; new town 1956; cobalt deposit being developed.

**Khurasan,** *prov.,* Iran; W. of Afghanistan; ch. prod. wool; cap. Meshed; p. (estd. 1956) *1,300,000.* [p. (1961) *41,491.*

**Khurja,** *t.,* Uttar Pradesh, India; cotton, pottery;

**Khorasan,** *prov.,* N.E. Iran; bounded by U.S.S.R. and Afghanistan; agr.; wool; turquoise; cap. Mashhad; p. (1967) *2,494,283.*

**Khuzestan,** *prov.,* W. Iran; frontier Iraq; leading petroleum ctr.; large dams; cap. Ahwaz; p. (1967) *1,614,576.*

**Khyber,** *difficult mtn. pass,* between W. Punjab, Pakistan and Afghanistan; followed by route from Peshawar to Kabul, traversed by Alexander the Great and by two British expeditions.

**Kiamusze (Jiamusi)** *c.,* Heilungkiang prov. China; p. (1953) *146,000.*

**Kiang-si (Jiangxi),** *inland prov.,* China; S. of the Yangtze-Kiang; cap. Nanchang; rice, wheat, tea, silk, cotton; a. 66,600 sq. m.; p. (1953) *16,772,865.*

**Kiangsu (Jiangsu),** *maritime prov.,* China; exp. much silk; a. 42,085 sq. m.; cap. Chinkiang; p. (1953) *41,252,192.* [Peninsula, China.

**Kiaochow Bay,** *inlet* on S. side of Shantung

**Kicking Horse Pass,** *mtn. pass,* over Rocky Mtns., B.C., Canada; used by Canadian Pac. Rly.

**Kidderminster,** *t., mun. bor.,* Worcester, Eng.; on R. Stour 4 m. above its confluence with R. Severn; carpets, engin., sugar-beet refining, textile machin., elec. vehicles, drop forgings; p. (estd. 1967) *45,510.*

**Kidsgrove,** *mftg. t., urb. dist.,* " Potteries," Staffs., Eng.; 3 m. N.W. of Stoke-on-Trent; chemicals, metal wks., rayon, silk and nylon spinning, precast concrete, ceramics; p. (estd. 1967) *21,790.*

**Kiel,** *spt.,* cap. Schleswig-Holstein, Germany; univ.; Baltic naval pt.; shipbldg. and allied inds., elec. goods, textiles, fishing; p. (1963) *270,800.*

**Kiel Canal (Kaiser-Wilhelm-Kanal),** Germany; 61 m. long, connects N. Sea with the Baltic; opened in 1895, reconstructed 1914.

**Kielce,** *co.,* Central Poland; minerals, agr.; cap. K.; a. 17,000 sq. m.; p. (1965) *1,899,000.*

**Kielce,** *t.,* Central Poland; tr. ctr., metal inds., sawmills, glass and food processing factories; dates from 12th cent.; p. (1965) *102,000.*

**Kiev,** *c., cap.,* Ukraine, U.S.S.R.; on R. Dnieper; once cap. of Muscovite Empire; cath.; univ.; machin., grain, in a. of rich mineral deposits, engin.; natural gas pipeline runs from Dashava; p. (1967) *1,371,000*.

Kigoma, *impt. tr. t.*, Tanzania, Africa; W. terminus of the Central Rly. on L. Tanganyika; p. (1957) *3,970*. [*31,000*

Kikinda, *t.*, Vojvodina, Jugoslavia; p. (1959)

Kilauea, *crater*, 3,646 ft. high, on S.E. slope of Mauna Loa, Hawaii, one of lgst. active craters in world; over 2 miles in diameter.

Kildare, *inland co.*, Leinster, Ireland; a. 654 sq. m.; p. (1966) *66,486*.

Kildare, *mkt. t., cap.*, Kildare, Ireland; cath.; close by is the famous racecourse, the Curragh of Kildare; p. (1966) *2,731*.

Kilimanjaro, *volcanic mtn.*, Tanzania, E. Africa; highest peak in the continent; alt. 19,321 ft.

Kilindini, *spt.*, Kenya; adjoins Mombasa; the finest harbour on E. cst. of Africa.

Kilkenny, *inland co.*, Leinster, Ireland; cap. Kilkenny; pastoral farming, coal, black marble; a. 796 sq. m.; p. (1966) *60,472*.

Kilkenny, *t.*, cap. Kilkenny, Ireland; on R. Nore; local mkt.; p. (1966) *10,057*. [Ireland.

Kilkieran Bay, *lge. intricate indentation*, Galway,

Kilkis, *prefecture*, Macedonia, Greece; cap. Kilkis; p. (1961) *102,847*.

Killarney, *t., urb. dist.*, Kerry, Ireland; local mkt. and tourist ctr.; p. (1966) *6,870*.

Killarney, Is. of, Lower, Middle and Upper, celebrated for their beauty; tourist resorts.

Killiecrankie, Pass of, Scot.; on R. Garry; at S. approach to Drumochter Pass; used by main rly. Perth to Inverness.

Kill van Kull, channel between N.J. and Staten I., N.Y., c., U.S.A.

Killybegs, *t.*, Donegal, Ireland; on Donegal Bay.

Killyleagh, *t.*, on Stangford L., Down, N. Ireland; p. (1966) *2,169*.

Kilmarnock, *rly. ctr., lge. burgh*, Ayr, Scot.; on R. Irvine, 11 m. N.E. of Ayr; carpet factories, textile and ironwks.; p. (1961) *47,509*.

Kilmore, *t.*, Victoria, Australia; 30 m. N. of Melbourne in impt. gap between Grampian Mtns. and Australian Alps.

Kilo-Moto, *goldfield*, Congo, Central Africa; in N.E. of st., 50 m. W. of L. Albert; linked by motor road to R. Congo (Stanleyville) and L. Albert (Kasenyi).

Kilpatrick, New, *par.*, Dunbarton, Scot.; north of R. Clyde; p. (1951) *54,931*.

Kilpatrick, Old, *par.*, Dunbarton, Scot.; on bank of R. Clyde, 9 m. N.W. of Glasgow; lowest ferry across Clyde; p. (1951) *49,248*.

Kilrenny and Anstruther, *burgh*, Fife, Scot.; at entrance to Firth of Forth; fishing, hosiery, oilskin mnfs.; p. (1961) *2,888*.

Kilrush, *spt., urb. dist.*, S.W. Clare, Ireland; on R. Shannon; p. (1966) *2,734*.

Kilsyth, *burgh*, Stirling, Scot.; at S. foot of Campsie Fells, 10 m. W. of Falkirk; whinstone quarries, coal-mining; p. (1961) *9,831*.

Kilwinning, *burgh*, N. Ayr, Scot.; 5 m. E. of Ardrossan; p. (1961) *7,287*; to be incorporated in new t. Irvine.

Kimberley, *c.*, Cape Province, S. Africa; 20 m. from R. Vaal; diamond-mng. dist.; asbestos, manganese, iron, cement, engin.; p. (1960) *91,816* inc. *27,460* Europeans.

Kimberley, *goldfield dist.*, W. Australia; big deposits of bauxite discovered 1965.

Kimberly, *t.*, B.C., Canada; on R. Kootenay in valley between Selkirk Range and Rocky Mtns.; site of Sullivan Mine; lg. lead–zinc mine; ores smelted at Trail; p. (1956) *5,730*.

Kincardine, *maritime co.*, E. Scot., between Angus and Aberdeen; agr. and fishing; co. t. Stonehaven; a. 383 sq. m.; p. (1961) *48,810*.

Kinder Scout, *mtn.*, N. Derby, Eng.; highest point of the Peak dist.; alt. 2,088 ft.

Kindu, *t.*, Congo, Central Africa; on R. Congo; p. *10,628*.

Kineshma, *t.*, U.S.S.R.; N.W. of Gorki; pt. for Ivanovo industl. a.; textiles; p. (1959) *84,000*.

Kineton, *mkt. t.*, Warwick, Eng.; nr. Stratford-on-Avon.

King George's Sound, W. Australia; nr. Albany; fine harbour and bay.

Kinghorn, *burgh*, Fife, Scot.; on Firth of Forth, 3 m. S. of Kirkcaldy; p. (1961) *2,112*.

Kingsbridge, *mkt. t., urb. dist.*, S. Devon, Eng.; at head of Kingsbridge estuary, 10 m. S.W. of Dartmouth; p. (1961) *3,283*.

Kingsclere and Whitchurch, *mkt. t., rural dist.*, N.

Hants, Eng.; on R. Test, 10 m. S.W. of Basingstoke; p. (rural dist. 1961) *23,264*.

Kings Langley, *t.*, Herts, Eng.; 5 m. N. of Watford; paper, light engin.; p. (1961) *4,255*.

King's Lynn, *spt., mun. bor.*, Norfolk, Eng.; on R. Ouse, 3 m. above its mouth; docks; fishing, agr. machin., canning, chemical fertilisers, shoes; p. (estd. 1967) *28,370*.

King's River, Cal., U.S.A.; flows from Sierra Nevada to L. Tulare. [p. (1960) *26,314*

Kingsport, *t.*, N.E. Tenn., U.S.A.; varied mnfs.;

Kingston, *c.*, Ont., Canada; E. end of L. Ontario; cap. of United Canada, 1841–4; univ., military college; lge inds; p. (1961) *53,926*.

Kingston, *cap.*, Jamaica, W. Indies; oil refining; p. (estd. 1962) *180,000*. [(1960) *29,260*.

Kingston, *t.*, N.Y., U.S.A.; tobacco mftg.; p.

Kingston, *t.*, Penns., U.S.A.; p. (1960) *20,261*.

Kingston-upon-Hull, *see* Hull.

Kingston-upon-Thames, *former co. t., mun. bor.*, Surrey, Eng.; now The Royal Borough of Kingston-upon-Thames, *outer bor.*, Greater London; inc. bors. of Malden and Coombe and Surbiton; residtl.; with Royal Park; aircraft parts; p. (1964) *145,977*.

Kingstown, *see* Dun Laoghaire.

Kingstown, *spt., cap.*, St. Vincent, W.I.; cath., botanic gardens; p. (1956) *6,500*.

Kingsville, *t.*, Texas, U.S.A.; in ranching area; agr., light inds.; p. (1960) *25,297*.

Kingswood, *urb. dist.*, Gloucester, Eng.; nr. Bristol; elec. vehicles, motor cycles, boots, brushes, tools; p. (estd. 1967) *28,710*.

Kington, *mkt. t., urb. dist.*, N.W. Hereford, Eng.; 12 m. W. of Leominster; p. (1961) *1,861*.

Kingussie, *burgh*, Inverness, Scot.; between Cairngorm Mtns. and Monadhliath Mtns., on R. Spey; summer resort; p. (1961) *1,079*.

King William I., off Boothia peninsula in Arctic Ocean, Canada.

King William's Town, *t.*, Cape Prov., S. Africa; on Buffalo R.; industl. ctr.; p. (1960) *14,328* inc. *6,873* whites.

Kinhwa, *c.*, Chekiang, China; in fertile, intensively cultivated basin, 85 m. S.W. of Hangchow p. (estd. 1947) *211,140*.

Kinibalu, *mtn.*, Sabah; alt. 13,455 ft.

Kinlochleven, *vil.*, Argyll, Scot.; at head of Loch Leven; hydro-elec. power sta., aluminium smelting. [N.E. Aberdeen cst., Scot.

Kinnaird Head, *promontory*, nr. Fraserburgh, on N.E. Aberdeen cst., Scot.

Kinross, *sm. inland co.*, Scot.; between Fife and Perth; hilly; oats, potatoes, sheep, cattle; a. 78 sq. m.; p. (1961) *6,704*.

Kinross, *co. burgh*, Kinross, Scot.; on Loch Leven, 16 m. N.E. of Alloa; coal, linen mnfs.; p. (1961) *2,365*.

Kinsale, *spt., urb. dist.*, on K. Harbour, Cork, Ireland; p. (urb. dist. 1961) *7,993*.

Kinshasa (Leopoldville), *cap.*, Congo; above the cataracts on R. Congo; founded by Stanley; p. (1964) *403,000*. [deposits of alluvial tin.

Kinta Valley, S.E. Perak, Malaya; very impt.

Kintyre, *peninsula*, Argyll, Scot.; length 40 m., greatest breadth 11 m.; S. point the Mull of Kintyre.

Kioga, *L.*, Uganda, E. Africa; on R. Nile midway between L. Victoria and L. Albert; very shallow, fringed with marsh; land reclamation.

Kiölen or Kjölen, *mtn. range*, Scandinavia; highest point Mt. Sulitelma; alt. 6,150 ft.

Kirgiz Steppes, *gr. plains and uplands*, Kirghizia S.S.R., U.S.S.R.; N. of the Caspian and Aral Seas, inhabited by the wandering Mongolian Tatar race numbering nearly *3,000,000*.

Kirghizia, *constituent rep.*, U.S.S.R.; S.W. of Siberia; livestock breeding, mineral resources; a. 75,900 sq. m.; cap. Frunze; p. (1959) *2,063,000*. [iron ore mng.

Kiriburu, *t.* on border of Bihar and Orissa, India;

Kirin (Jilin), *prov.*, China; S. of the Sungari R. and N. of Korea and the Liaotung Peninsula; fertile; soyabeans; timber; good rly. services; cap. Kirin, a. 34,616 sq. m.; p. (1953) *11,290,073*.

Kirin (Jilin), *c., cap.*, Kirin, N.E. China; on Sungari R. at outlet of Sungari reservoir; impt. position on rly. from Changchun to coastal ports, p. (1953) *435,000*.

Kirkburton, *urb. dist.*, W.R. Yorks, Eng.; S.E. of Huddersfield; woollens; p. (1961) *18,066*.

Kirkby, *urb. dist.*, Lancs., Eng.; p. (estd. 1967) *63,800*.

**Kirkby in Ashfield**, *t.*, *urb. dist.*, Notts, Eng.; 10 m. N.W. of Nottingham; coal; p. (estd. 1967) *22,450*.

**Kirkby Moorside**, *mkt. t.*, *rural dist.*, N.R. Yorks., Eng.; sailplanes, gliders; p. (1961) *4,402*.

**Kirkcaldy**, *spt. t.*, *burgh*, Fife, Scot.; on N. side of F. of Forth; shipping; linoleum, potteries, linen bleaching, engin.; p. (1961) *52,371*.

**Kirkcudbright**, *maritime co.*, S.W. Scot.; abutting on Irish Sea and Solway Firth; chiefly agr.; a. 909 sq. m.; p. (1961) *28,877*.

**Kirkcudbright**, *co. burgh*, Kirkcudbright, Scot.; on Kirkcudbright Bay, Solway Firth, 25 m. S.W. of Dumfries; agr., hosiery; p. (1961) *2,425*.

**Kirkenes**, *t.*, Finnmark, N. Norway; on S. arm of Varanger Fjord, nr. Norway–U.S.S.R. bdy.; iron-ore mines. [weaving; p. (1961) *4,760*.

**Kirkham**, *t.*, *urb. dist.*, Lancs., Eng.; cotton

**Kirkintilloch**, *burgh*, Dunbarton, Scot.; on Forth and Clyde Canal; iron, coal-mng; p. (1961) *18,257*.

**Kirkland Lake**, *t.*, Ontario, Canada; on rly. nr. Quebec–Ontario bdy., 45 m. N. of Cobalt; ctr. of impt. gold-mng. dist.; p. (estd. 1956) *19,000*.

**Kirkstone Pass**, *min. pass*, Westmorland, Eng.; used by main road between Ullswater and Windermere Lakes.

**Kirksville**, *industl. t.*, Mo., U.S.A.; p. (1960) *13,123*.

**Kirkuk**, *t.*, Iraq; mart for Arab horses; lge. oilfield with pipelines to Tripoli, Haifa and Banias; p. (1956) *89,917*.

**Kirkwall**, *burgh*, Pomona I., Orkneys, Scot.; off the N.E. Scottish cst.; p. (1961) *4,315*.

**Kirkwood**, *sub.*, St. Louis, Mo., U.S.A.; p. (1960) *29,421*.

**Kirov**, *t.*, R.S.F.S.R.; on trans-Siberian Rly.; engin., sawmilling, chemicals, leather inds.; p. (1967) *302,000*.

**Kirovabad**, *t.*, W. Azerbaydzhan S.S.R.; copper-manganese mines; textiles, petroleum, aluminium plant under construction; p. (1967) *170,000*.

**Kirovgrad**, *t.*, Urals; copper; p. (1954) *50,000*.

**Kirovograd**, *t.*, Ukrainian S.S.R.; engin.; p. (1967) *161,000*.

**Kirovsk**, *t.*, R.S.F.S.R.; on Kola peninsula; apatite, nephelite, chemicals; p. (1954) *50,000*.

**Kirriemuir**, *burgh*, Angus, Scot.; on N. margin of Strathmore, 5 m. W. of Forfar; jute weaving, oat milling; p. (1961) *3,485*.

**Kiruna**, *t.*, N. Sweden; inside Arctic Circle, N.W. of Lulea; linked by rly. to Narvik (Norway); impt. deposits of iron ore; p. (1961) *26,804*.

**Kisangani** (Stanleyville), *t.*, Congo, Africa; on R. Congo nr. Stanley Falls.

**Kiselevsk**, *t.*, W. Siberia, R.S.F.S.R.; coalmng., engin.; p. (1967) *139,000*.

**Kishinev**, *cap.* Moldavian S.S.R., U.S.S.R.; univ.; agr., engin.; vineyards; p. (1963) *254,000*.

**Kislovodsk**, *t.*, R.S.F.S.R.; spa; p. (1959) *79,000*.

**Kissimee R.**, Fla., U.S.A., flows to L. Okeechobee; length 90 m.

**Kistna**, *see* Krishna.

**Kisumu**, *spt.*, *cap.*, Nyanza prov., Kenya, E. Africa; at head of Kavirondo G. on L. Victoria; original W. terminus of rly. from Mombasa; still handles bulk of cotton from Buganda and coffee from N. Tanzania for transhipment E. by rail; p. (1962) *23,200*.

**Kitakyushu City**, *c.*, N. Kyushu, Japan; one of Japan's largest municipalities on merging (1963) of ts. Moji, Kokura, Tobata, Yawata and Wakamatsu; sixth lge. t. to enjoy special aut. rights; p. (1965) *1,042,389*.

**Kitchener**, *c.*, Ontario, Canada; agr. machin., tyres, hardware, p. (1961) *74,485*.

**Kittatinny Mtns. or Blue Mtns.**, *range* in Penns. and N.J., U.S.A.; a continuation of the Appalachian system.

**Kitwe**, *t.*, Zambia; contiguous to mine township of Nkana, ctr. of copperbelt; p. (1964) *110,000*.

**Kiukiang**, *c.*, *former treaty pt.*, Kiangsi, China; Yangtze-Kiang; p. (1948) *180,897*.

**Kiungchow**, *c.*, *cap.*, Hainan Is., China; on N. cst.; former treaty pt.

**Kivu**, *L.*, Central Africa; N. of L. Tanganyika by which it is joined by Russisi R.; length 55 m.; a. 1 100 sq. m.

**Kizel**, *t.*, R.S.F.S.R., in Urals; ctr. of coal mng. a.; mng. equipment; p. (1959) *60,000*.

**Kizilirmak (or Red River)**, the lgst. R. of Turkey in Asia; rises in Kisil Dagh, flows to Black Sea via Sivas; l. 600 m.

**Kladno**, *mng. t.*, ČSSR.; 10 m. N.W. of Prague; coal, iron, steel, engin.; p. (1961) *49,561*.

**Klagenfurt**, *t.*, *cap.*, Carinthia, Austria; winter sports ctr.; varied mnfs.; p. (1961) *69,218*.

**Klaipeda (Memel)**, *spt.*, Lithuanian S.S.R.; nr. N. extremity Kurisches Haff; exp. timber, textiles, chemicals, paper; p. (1967) *125,000*.

**Klamath**, *L.*, Cal. and Ore., U.S.A.; discharges by K. R. (275 m.) to Pacific.

**Klamath Falls**, *t.*, Ore., U.S.A.; p. (1960) *16,949*.

**Klamono**, *t.*, New Guinea, nr. Klasafet R.; oil pipe-line to Sorong harbour.

**Klang**, *t.*, Selangor, Malaya; designated future st. cap.; coffee, rubber; p. *33,506*.

**Klatovy**, *t.*, S.W. Bohemia, ČSSR.; mkt.; rose-growing a., textiles; p. (1961) *14,004*.

**Klerksdorp**, *t.*, S. Transvaal, S. Africa; gold, diamonds; p. (1962) *48,500* inc. *22,000* whites.

**Kleve**, *t.*, N. Rhine–Westphalia, Germany; nr. Netherlands frontier; foodstuffs, leather, machin., tobacco; p. (1963) *22,100*.

**Klin**, *t.*, R.S.F.S.R., 45 m. from Moscow; glass, textiles; p. (1959) *53,000*.

**Klondyke**, *R.*, Yukon, Canada; small trib. of Yukon in gold-mine region.

**Klodzko (Glatz)**, *t.*, Lower Silesia, Poland, German before 1945; on R. Nisa (Neisse); rly. junction; p. (1965) *25,000*.

**Knaresborough**, *mkt. t.*, *urb. dist.*, W.R. Yorks., Eng.; 3 m. N.E. of Harrogate; p. (1961) *9,311*.

**Knighton**, *mkt. t.*, *urb. dist.*, Radnor, Wales; on R. Teme; p. (1961) *1,817*.

**Knockmealdown Mtns.**, cos. Waterford and Tipperary, Ireland; highest point 2,609 ft.

**Knossos**, *ruined c.*, *cap.* of ancient Crete; S.E. of Candia; ctr. of Cretan Bronze Age culture, c. 1800 B.C.

**Knottingley**, *t.*, *urb. dist.*, W.R. Yorks, Eng.; on R. Aire, 12 m. S.E. of Leeds; engin., glass, tar distilling, chemicals, shipbldg.; p. (1961) *11,153*.

**Knoxville**, *c.*, Tenn., U.S.A.; univ.; textiles; marble, plastics, chemicals, aluminium; agr. tobacco; p. (1960) *111,827*.

**Knutsford**, *mkt. t.*, *urb. dist.*, Cheshire, Eng.; 6 m. N.E. of Northwich; p. (1961) *9,389*.

**Kobe**, *t.*, *spt.*, Honshu, Japan; at E. end of Inland Sea; shipbldg., silk-weaving; steel wks.; gr. tr.; p. (1965) *1,216,666*.

**Koblenz (Coblenz)**, *t.*, Rhineland Palatinate, Germany; at confluence of Rs. Rhine and Moselle; fine buildings, wine, paper, machin., leather, ceramics; p. (1963) *101,200*.

**Kocaeli**, *prov.*, Turkey; on G. of Sea of Marmara.

**Kochi**, *c.*, Shikoku, Japan; industl.; fishing; p. (1965) *217,839*.

**Kodiak I.**, N. Pac. Oc.; the lgst. I. of W. Alaska; (90 m. long); fur-trading, extensive salmon fishing, canning; ch. settlement St. Paul, on Chiniak R.; suffered earthquake damage 28 Mar. 1964; p. (1960) *2,628*.

**Kofu**, *c.*, Honshu, Japan; silk, vegetables, grapes; p. (1964) *172,000*.

**Kohat**, *t.*, N.W. Pakistan; on trib. of Indus; military t.; cement wks.; p. (1961) *49,800*.

**Koh-I-Baba Mtns.**, Afghanistan, spur of the Hindu Kush; highest point 17,640 ft.

**Kohima**, *dist.*, Nagaland, India; a. 2,374 sq. m.; p. (1961) *108,924*. [engin.; p. (1967) *123,000*.

**Kokand**, *t.*, Uzbek S.S.R.; textiles, chemicals,

**Kokiu (Gejiu)**, *c.*, Yunnan prov., China, tin-mng.; p. (1953) *160,000*.

**Kokkola (Gamla Karleby)**, *t.*, Finland; on cst. G. of Bothnia; p. (1961) *16,153*.

**Kokomo**, *c.*, Ind., U.S.A.; on Wild Cat R.; steel, glass, agr. region; p. (1960) *47,197*.

**Koko-Nor**, *salt L.*, Tsinghai prov., China; a. 2,040 sq. m.; no outlet.

**Kokura**, *c.*, N. Kyushu, Japan; 40 m. N.E. of Fukuoka; steel, chemicals, porcelain ware, textiles, p. (1960) *286,000*.

**Kola**, *peninsula*, R.S.F.S.R.; extension of Lapland.

**Kola**, *t.*, R.S.F.S.R.; nr. Murmansk, on Kola Peninsular. [*146,811*.

**Kolar Gold Fields**, Mysore, India; p. (1961)

**Kolding**, *mkt. t.*, Vejle, Denmark; good harbour; engin., lt. inds.; p. (1960) *35,101*.

**Kolguev**, *I.*, Arctic Oc.; at entrance of Cheshsk G., N.E. of Arkhangelsk. [(1961) *187,442*.

**Kolhapur**, *t.*, Maharashtra, India; bauxite; p.

**Kolo**, *t.*, Poland; on I. of the Warta; pottery.

**Kolobrzeg (Kolberg)**, *c.*, *spt.* W. Pomerania, Poland, German before 1945; cath.; resort; fishing; p. (1965) *22,000*.

**Kolomna**, *t.*, R.S.F.S.R., 72 m. S.E. of Moscow; engin., locomotives, machin.; p. (1967) *131,000*.

Kolyma R., flows into E. Siberian Sea, R.S.F.S.R.

Komárno, *industl. t.*, ČSSR.; on R. Danube; textiles; p. (1961) *24,009.* [p. (1962) *25,832.*

Komlo, *t.*, Hungary; new mng. t.; coking coal;

Komotene, *cap.*, Rhodope, Thrace, Greece; p. (1961) *23,335.* [mill; textiles.

Kompong Cham, *t.*, Cambodia, cotton ginning

Komsomolsk, *c.*, R.S.F.S.R.; built by volunteer youth labour, after 1932; heavy industl. development; oil refining; pipeline connects with oilfield in N. Sakhalin; p. (1967) *207,000.*

Komsomoloskiy, *c.*, Mordvinian A.S.S.R.; on site of present workers' settlement; planned p. *50,000.*

Konigshütte, *see* Chorzow.

Konotop, *t.*, Ukrainian S.S.R.; rly. junct. on Moscow–Kiev line; engin., metals; p. (1959) *53,000.*

Konstantinovka, *industl. t.*, Ukraine, S.S.R. U.S.S.R.; in heart of Donbas industl. region, 38 m. N. of Donetsk; heavy engin., iron and steel, zinc smelting; p. (1959) *89,000.*

Konya, *l.*, Turkey; well wooded; opium; ch. t. K. (the ancient Iconium); impt. tr.; p. (1965) *157,301.*

Koolyanobbing, *t.*, W. Australia; mng. t., high-grade haematite and limonite ores; linked to rly. between Kwinana and Kalgoorlie 1968.

Kootenay R. (Flat Bow R.), trib. of the Columbia R. flowing in Mont., U.S.A., and B.C.; length 450 m.

Koper (Capo d'Istria), *spt.*, Jugoslavia; cath., old fort; Austro-Italian disputes over ownership since very early days; p. (1960) *10,100.*

Kopeysk, *t.*, R.S.F.S.R.; in Urals; lignite mng., agr. and mng. machin.; p. (1967) *167,000.*

Köping, *t.*, Sweden; W. of L. Malaren; iron ore and minerals; p. (1961) *17,692.* [(1961) *285,862.*

Kopparberg, *co.*, Sweden; a. 11,649 sq. m.; p.

Korangi, *t.*, W. Pakistan; oil refinery.

Korba, *t.*, Madyha Pradesh, India; mng. a.; fertilizers; p. (1961) *12,424.*

Korce (Koritza), *t.*, S.E. Albania; sugar refining, brewing; p. (1960) *34,000.*

Kordofan, *prov.*, Sudan, Africa; a. 146,930 sq. m.; cap. El-Obeid; p. (estd. 1951) *1,671,600.*

Korea, *rep.*, *peninsula*, E. Asia; extending between Yellow Sea and Sea of Japan; annexed by Japan in 1910; after Second World War separated into 2 zones along 38th parallel, N. under Russian influence, the S. under American. Korea, N.: a. 46,814 sq. m.; mainly agr.; iron ore, steel ingots, oilwells; ch. t. Pyongyang; p. (1963) *11,100,000.* Korea, S.; a. 38,452 sq. m.; mainly agr.; tungsten, salt; oil refining at Ulsan; cap. Seoul; p. (1963) *28,155,000.*

Korkino, *t.*, R.S.F.S.R.; in Urals; coal mng.; p. (1959) *85,000.*

Korsör, *spt.*, Sjaelland I., Denmark; fine harbour; glass wks.; p. (1960) *14,276.*

Kortrijk (Courtrai), *t.*, W. Flanders, Belgium; linen, lace; p. (1962) *43,894.*

Kos (Cos), *I.*, Dodecanese Is., Greece; ch. t., Kos; p. (1940) *20,982.*

Kosciusko, *peak*, Australian Alps, N.S.W., Australia; highest peak in Gr. Dividing Range; alt. 7,328 ft.

Kosi, *barrage*, Bhimnagar, nr. Nepalese–Indian frontier below foothills of Himalayas, inaugurated 1965; hydroelec. plant. projected.

Košice, *c.*, ČSSR.; Gothic cath.; univ.; magnesite, chemicals, textiles, sheet steel; p. (1962) *79,581.*

Kosova-Metohija, *aut. reg.*, Yugoslavia; p. (1959) *950,000.*

Kostroma, *c.*, R.S.F.S.R.; at confluence of Rs. Volga and Kastromo; textiles, engin.; p. (1967) *205,000.*

Koszalin (Köslin), *t.*, Poland; N.E. of Szczecin; paper mftg., engin., textiles; p. (1965) *52,000.*

Koszalin, *prov.*, N.W. Poland; cap. K.; mainly agr.; a. 6,930 sq. m.; p. *680,400.*

Kota Baru *see* Sukarnapura

Kota Kinabalu, *spt.*, *cap.*, Sabah, Malaysia; on W. cst.; rubber; p. (1960) *21,719.*

Kotah, *t.*, Rajasthan, India; on R. Chambal; muslins; p. (1961) *120,345.*

Köthen, *t.*, Halle, E. Germany; N. of Halle; cas.; metallurgy, sugar, machin., chemicals; rly. junction; p. (1963) *38,773.* [(1966) *52,859.*

Kotka, *spt.*, on Gulf of Finland; wood pulp; p.

Kotri, *t.*, W. Pakistan; on R. Indus, opposite Hyderabad; barrage 4¼ m. N. of the t., started to help irrigate Sind; p. *7,617.*

Kottayam, *t.*, Kerala, India; p. (1961) *52,685.*

Koulikoro, *t.*, Mali, W. Africa; on upper course of R. Niger; mkt. for ground-nuts, gum-

arabic, sisal; linked by R. to Timbuktu and Gao; rly. terminus, 760 m. from Dakar.

Kovrov, *t.*, R.S.F.S.R.; on Gorki rly. line and R. Klyazma; impt. agr. exp. ctr.; engin., textiles; p. (1967) *114,000.*

Kowloon, *spt.*, S.E. China; on mainland opp. Hong Kong I.; tr. ctr.; p. (1961) *726,976.*

Koyali, *nr.* Baroda, Gujarat, India; oil refining.

Kozani, *prefecture*, Macedonia, Greece; cap. Kozani; p. (1961) *190,607.*

Kragerö, *spt.*, Telemark, Norway; exp. ice, timber, wood-pulp, etc.; p. (1961) *4,329.*

Kragujevac, *t.*, central Serbia, Jugoslavia; cath., college, arsenal, garrison; p. (1960) *46,000.*

Kra, Isthmus of, between G. of Siam and Indian Oc.; connects Malaya with Asian mainland.

Krakatao, *volcanic I.*, Strait of Sunda, Indonesia; greater part destroyed by eruption, 1883.

Kraków, *prov.*, Poland; cap. Kraków; a. 6,367 sq. m.; p. (1965) *2,127,000.*

Kraków, *t.*, Poland; machin., chemicals, farm implements; univ.; p. (1965) *520,000.*

Kramatorsk, *c.*, E. Ukraine, U.S.S.R.; heavy engin., metallurgy; p. (1967) *136,000.*

Kramfors, Sweden; on G. of Bothnia; paper mill and sulphite pulp wks. projected.

Krasnodar, *t.*, R.S.F.S.R.; on R. Kuban; oil refining, engin., textiles; p. (1967) *395,000.*

Krasnoturinsk, *t.*, R.S.F.S.R.; in Urals, 6 m. N.W. of Serov; aluminium, coal; p. (1959) *62,000.*

Krasnovodsk, *t.*, Turkmen S.S.R.; oil refining, engin.; p. (1958) *38,000.*

Krasnoyarsk, *t.*, R.S.F.S.R.; on Trans-Siberian Rly. at crossing of R. Yenesei; oil refining, engin., synthetic rubber; copper deposits nearby; polyester fibre plant projected; chemical plants; iron ore deposits to be developed; p. (1967) *557,000.*

Krasnyy Luch, *t.*, Ukrainian S.S.R.; coal mng.; Shterovka power sta. nearby; p. (1959) *94,000.*

Krefeld, *t.*, N. Rhine–Westphalia, Germany; ctr. of German silk ind.; steel, machin., chemicals, soap; rly. junction; p. (1963) *216,900.*

Kremenchug, *t.*, Ukrainian S.S.R.; on R. Dnieper; timber, engin., textiles; hydro-elec. sta.; oil refining; p. (1967) *129,000.*

Krems, *industl. t.*, Austria; on R. Danube; vinegar, white lead; p. (1961) *21,046.*

Kreuznach, *t.*, N. Rhine–Westphalia, Germany; on R. Nahe; metallurgy, leather, optical and chemical inds.; viticulture; mineral baths; p. (estd. 1954) *31,800.*

Krishna, R., S. India; rises in W. Ghats, flows E. across Deccan plateau into Bay of Bengal; lower valley and delta under intensive rice cultivation; densely populated; length 850 m.

Kristiansand, *spt.*, Norway; 160 m. S.W. of Oslo; cath.; tr., inds., shipping; p. (1960) *27,748.*

Kristianstad, *co.*, Sweden; a. 2,485 sq. m.; p. (1961) *256,475.*

Kristianstad, *t.*, Sweden; 10 m. from the Baltic; clothing, machin.; p. (1961) *25,813.*

Kristiansund, *spt.*, W. cst. Norway; exp. dried fish; p. (1960) *17,105.*

Kristinehamn, *L.*, *pt.*, Sweden; on L. Vänern; egin., machin.; p. (1961) *21,547.*

Krivoi Rog, *t.*, Ukrainian S.S.R.; on R. Ingulats; rich coal and iron dist.; p. (1967) *498,000.*

Krkonose (Riesengebirge), range between Polish Silesia and Bohemia; highest peak Snežka (Schneekoppe) 5,275 ft.

Kroměříz, *t.*, Moravia, ČSSR.; mnfs., engin.; p. (1961) *20,583.* [(1961) *158,977.*

Kronoberg, *co.*, Sweden; a. 3,828 sq. m.; p.

Kronstadt, *spt.* (*strongly fortfd.*), on I. in G. of Finland; Baltic pt. and naval sta., R.S.F.S.R.; scene of naval mutiny which precipitated the Russian Revolution; p. (1954) *50,000.*

Kroonstad, *t.*, O.F.S., S. Africa; on R. Valseh; agr. and rly. ctr.; engin., milling; p. (1960) *42,433* inc. *13,068* whites.

Kropotkin, *t.*, E. Krasnodar terr. R.S.F.S.R.; grain; engin.; p. (1959), *54,000.*

Krugersdorp, *t.*, Transvaal, S. Africa; named after President Kruger; gold-mining, uranium, manganese; p. (1960) *89,493* inc. *30,241* whites.

Krumlov, *t.*, Bohemia, ČSSR.; on N. slopes of Böhmer Wald; graphite-mines; p. (1961) *8,931.*

Krusevac, *t.*, Jugoslavia; mkt.; munitions; p. (1959) *25,000.*

Kuala Lumpur, *c.*, West Malaysia; cap. of Fed. of Malaysia and of Selangor st.; univ.; p. (1959) *477,238.*

Kubango (Okovango), *R.*, flows from Angola into L. Ngami, Botswana.

Kuching, *cap.*, Sarawak, Malaysia; gold discovered nearby at Bau; p. (1960) *50,579*.

Kuchinoerabu, *I.*, Japan; S. of Kyushu; mtns.

Kuçovë, nr. Berat, Albania; oil prod. and refining; pipe-line connects to Vlonë.

Kufra, *oasis*, Libya.

Kuhgilvieh and Boer Ahmad, *dist.*, W. Iran; cap. Dehdasht; p. (1967) *165,112*.

Kuibyshev, *t.*, R.S.F.S.R.; on R. Volga; at head of central Asian and Siberian rlys.; comm. ctr.; engin., sulphur, paper, oil refining; p. (1967) *969,000*. [mines; p. (1953) *108,000*.

Kuldja (Yining), *c.*, Sinkiang, China; iron, coal

Kulmbach, *t.*, Bavaria, Germany; textiles, cars, brewing; p. (1963) *23,100*. [*407,052*.

Kumamoto, *spt.*, W. Kyushu, Japan; p. (1965)

Kumasi, *ch. t.*, Ashanti, Ghana; univ.; aerodrome; p. (1960) *190,323*.

Kumbakonam, *t.*, *sacred c.*, Tamil Nadu, India; Cauvery delta; silks, cottons; p. (1961) *92,581*.

Kumta, *t.*, Mysore, India; on sea cst.: sandalwood; carving; p. (1961) *16,223*.

Kunene (Cunene), *R.*, Angola; lower course forms bdy. between Angola and South-West Africa; *c.* 750 m.

Kungur, *t.*, R.S.F.S.R., S.E. Perm.; agr.; leather; kaolin; oil ind. equip.; p. (1959) *65,000*.

Kun Lun (Kwen Lun), *mtns.*, Tibet; extend 1,800 m. E. from Pamirs along N. edge of high plateau of Tibet; drained N. into inland drainage basin of Lop Nor; alt. frequently exceeds 18,000 ft. [industl.; p. (1953) *699,000*.

Kunming, *c.*, Yunnan, China; univ.; comm. ctr.;

Kununurra Dam, Ord R., W. Australia; opened 1963; to irrigate 200,000 acres of semi-arid land for cotton, rice, and cattle.

Kuopio, *dep.*, Finland; p. (1966) *267,853*.

Kuopio, *t.*, Finland; on L. Kalki; p. (1966) *52,097*.

Kur, *R.*, Transcaucasia, U.S.S.R.; flows to Caspian S.; length 520 m.

Kurdistan (Country of the Kurds), includes parts of E. Turkey, Soviet Armenia, N.E. Iraq, and N.W. Iran.

Kure, *c.*, S.W. Honshu, Japan; spt. and naval base; engin.; mnfs.; p. (1965) *225,013*.

Kurgan, *t.*, R.S.F.S.R.; on the Trans-Siberian Rly. nr. Tobolsk; tr. in cattle and foodstuffs, agr. engin.; p. (1967) *205,000*.

Kuria Muria Is., Muscat and Oman, off cst. of Oman, consisting of 5 barren islands.

Kuril Is., *chain of sm. Is.*, N. Pacific, U.S.S.R.; extending from Kamchatka to Hokkaido; mainly mtns.

Kurisches Haff (Kurštu Martos), *shallow lagoon*, Baltic cst. of Lithuanian S.S.R., U.S.S.R.; receives water of R. Niemen; narrow entrance to Baltic Sea at N. end of lagoon commanded by pt. of Klaipeda (Memel); length, 60 m., maximum width, 20 m.

Kurische Nehrung, *sandspit*, Baltic Sea; almost cuts off Kurisches Haff from Baltic Sea; length, 55 m.

Kurnell, *t.*, Australia; oil refining.

Kuroshio (Japan Current), *ocean current*, flows N.E. along Pacific cst. of Kyushu, Shikoku and S. Honshu, relatively warm water, exerts slight warming influence on this cst. in winter.

Kushiro, *spt.*, S.E. Hokkaido, Japan; exp. lumber; p. (1965) *174,105*.

Kursk, *region*, adj. N. Ukraine, R.S.F.S.R.

Kursk, *t.*, R.S.F.S.R.; in fruit-growing dist.;[?] gr. annual fair; engin., textiles, synthetic rubber; p. (1967) *249,000*. [inds.; p. (1967) *114,000*.

Kustanay, *t.*, Kazakh S.S.R.; on R. Tobol; light

Kustendil, *t.*, Bulgaria; on trib. of R. Struma; fruit-growing dist; p. (1956) *25,025*.

Kütahya, *t.*, W. Central Turkey; agr. market ctr., ceramics; p. (1965) *49,227*.

Kutaisi, *c.*, Georgian S.S.R.; on R. Rion; chemicals, textiles, barium, engin.; big coal deposits being mined; p. (1967) *156,000*.

Kutaradja, *t.*, N. Sumatra, Indonesia; p. (1958)

Kutch, *peninsula*, N.W. cst., India, Gujarat st.; largely barren except for fertile strip along Arabian Sea; p. (1961) *696,440*.

Kutch, Rann of, *desert region* covered with salt, but flooded during monsoons; nine-tenths belongs to India; one-tenth to Pakistan.

Kutchan, *t.*, S.W. Hokkaido, Japan; 45 m. N.W. of Muroran; ctr. of second lgst. iron-ore field in Japan; ore smelted at Muroran.

Kutno, *t.*, Lodz, Poland; p. (1965) *27,000*.

Kuwait, *indep. sov. st.*, Arabia; on N.W. cst. of Persian G.; sand, bricks; impt. oil wells, petrochem. ind. projected; p. (1961) *321,000*.

Kuzbas (Kuznetsk Basin), *industl. reg*, Siberia, U.S.S.R.; lies S. of Trans-Siberian Rly. in upper valleys of Rs. Ob and Tom; second lgst. coal output in U.S.S.R., iron and steel mftg., heavy metallurgical ind.; ch. ts., Novosibirsk, Novokuznetsk, Kemerovo, Leninsk-Kuznetsky.

Kwangchow, *spt.*, Kwantung, China; on S. cst. opposite Hainan I.

Kwangsi Chuang (Guang Zhuang), *aut. reg.*, China; cap. Nanning; sugar, tobacco, rice, indigo, silk; a. 85,452 sq. m.; p. (1953) *19,560,822*.

Kwangtung (Guangdong), *prov.*, China; cap. Canton; rice, tea, sugar, silk; a. 85,447 sq. m.; p. (1953) *34,770,059*.

Kwanto Plain, S.E. Honshu, Japan; lgst. a. of continuous lowland in Japan, extends 80 m. inland from Tokyo; composed of: (1) low, badly-drained alluvial plain devoted to intensive rice cultivation; (2) higher, drier terraces under mulberry, vegetables, tea, tobacco; very dense rural p., especially on lower ground; lge. number of urban ctrs. inc. Tokyo, Yokohama; a. 5,000 sq. m. [of Kowloon Bay.

Kwan Tong, *t.*, Hong Kong; new industl. t. on E.

Kwanza (Cuanza), *R.*, Angola, W. Africa; rises in Bihé and flows to Atlantic; length 700 m.

Kweichow (Guizhou), *prov.*, S.W. China; cap. Kweiyang; cereals, silk, timber, gold, silver, mercury; a. 68,139 sq. m.; p. (1953) *15,037,310*.

Kweilin (Guilin), *c.*, Kwangsi Chuang, China; univ.; textiles, sugar refining, timber; p. (1953) *145,000*.

Kweiyang (Guiynag), *c.*, Kweichow prov., China; univ.; comm. and industl.; p. (1953) *271,000*.

Kwidzyn (Marienwerder), *c.*, Poland, German before 1945; cath.; cas.; p. (1965) *22,000*.

Kwinana, *t.*, W. Australia; 12 m. from Fremantle on shores of Cockburn Sound; oil refinery and steel plant, alumina reduction, blast furnace; integrated steelwks. by 1978.

Kyle of Lochalsh, *vil.*, *sm. spt.*, Ross and Cromarty, Scot.; at entrance to Loch Alsh, facing S. end of I. of Skye; terminus of rly. across Highlands from Dingwall; ch. pt. for steamers to N.W. cst., I. of Skye, Outer Hebrides; p. (1951) *1,525*. [Bute, Scot.

Kyles of Bute, *sound*, between Argyll cst. and N.

Kymore, *t.*, Madhya Pradesh, India; nr. Katni; cement wks.; p. (1961) *12,319*.

Kyoto, *c.*, *cap.* Kyoto *prefecture*, Honshu, Japan; univ.. temples; former cap. of Japan; p. (1965) *1,713,764*.

Kyrenia, *t.*, Cyprus; on N. cst.; p. (1960) *3,498*.

Kythera (Cerigo), *I.*, S. of Peloponnesos, Greece; a. 107 sq. m.

Kyushu, one of the lge. Is. of Japan; W. of Shikoku; mtns.; rice, wheat, tea, hemp, coal, copper; ch. t. Nagasaki; a. 16,247 sq. m.

Kyustendil, *t.*, Bulgaria; in foothills of Osogovo Mts.; lge lead and zinc deposits; combined plant for mng. and ore dressing projected.

Kzyl Orda, *R.*, Kazakh S.S.R.; large dam being constructed to irrigate rice plantations.

# L

La Ceiba, *spt.*, Honduras; on Atlantic cst.; exp. bananas; p. (1961) *24,868*.

La Coruña, *prov.*, N.W. Spain; cap. La Coruña; oil refinery; a. 3,051 sq. m.; p. (1959) *1,010,695*.

La Coruña, *spt.*, cap. La Coruña prov., N.W. Spain; fishing; import. tr.; p. (1965) *182,000*.

La Crosse, *t.*, W. Wis., U.S.A.; mkt., agr.; light mnfs.; rubber; p. (1960) *47,575*.

La Estrada, *c.*, N.W. Spain; mineral springs; agr., cattle; p. *27,240*.

La Grange, *t.*, Ga., U.S.A.; p. (1960) *23,632*.

La Grange, *t.*, Ill., U.S.A.; p. (1960) *15,285*.

La Guaira, *see* Guaira, La.

La Libertad, *dep.*, Peru; a. 10,206 sq. m.; ch. t. Trujillo; p. (1961) *586,631*. [p. (1959) *61,119*.

La Línia, *t.*, Spain, nr. Gibraltar; vegetables, fruit;

La Madeleine, *t.*, Nord, France; p. (1954) *22,831*.

La Mancha, *see* Mancha, La.

La Paz, *dep.*, Bolivia; traversed by the Andes; cap. La Paz; cocoa, coffee, rubber, minerals; tin mng. at Catari; a. 40,686 sq. m.; p. (1962) *1,140,300*.

La Paz, t., Bolivia, seat of govt., Sucre is legal cap.; impt. comm. ctr.; copper, alpaca wool, cinchona, textiles; p. (1960) 347,394.

La Plata, c., spt., Argentina; cap. Buenos Aires prov.; univ.; refrigerated meat prods.; oil refining; p. (1960) 340,000.

La Plata, Rio de (R. Plate), lge. estuary, between Argentina, Uruguay, S. America; receives water of Rs. Parana, Uruguay; cst. provides sites for lge. spts. Buenos Aires, La Plata, Montevideo; length 200 m., max. width 50 m.

La Porte, t., Ind., U.S.A.; flour, iron and steel, woollens; p. (1960) 21,157.

La Puebla, t., Majorca, Balearic Is.; p. 10,147.

La Rioja, prov., Argentina; a. 33,394 sq. m.; cap. La R.; p. (1960) 128,000.

La Rochelle, t., spt., cap., Charante-Maritime, France; locomotives, glass, sugar, fish; cath.; p. (1962) 68,445.

La Salle, c., Ill., U.S.A.; coal; p. (1960) 11,897.

La Salle, t., Quebec, Canada; p. (1961) 30,904.

La Serena, cap. Coquimbo prov., Chile; cath.; p. (1962) 61,500.

La Skhirra, pt., on G. of Gabes, Tunisia; oil; pipe-line to Edjelé under construction.

La Tuque, t., S. Quebec, Canada; R. pt.; lumbering; resort; p. (1961) 13,023.

La Unión, t., Spain; nr. Cartagena; iron, manganese, sulphur; p. (1957) 10,131.

Laaland, I., Danish, Baltic Sea; a. 462 sq. m.; forests; cap. Maribo.

Labrador, peninsula, Newfoundland, Canada; sterile, climate severe, fisheries; cap. Battle Harbour; a. 110,000 sq. m.

Labrador City, t., Newfoundland, Canada; new t. built 1965, nr. Wabush L. to house workers of iron ore mines.

Labuan, I., Sabah, Malaysia; rubber, rice, coconuts; cap. Victoria; a. 35 sq. m.; p. (1960) 14,904.

Laccadive, Is., Arabian Sea; about 200 m. off Malabar cst. joined with Minicoy and Amindivi Is. to form Union Territory, India; coir, coconuts; cap., Kavaratti; p. of Territory (1961) 24,108.

Lachine, t., Quebec, Canada; at head of L. rapids; summer resort, timber, bridge-bldg., wire, rope; p. (1961) 38,630.

Lachine Canals, Quebec, E. Canada; skirt Lachine Rapids on St. Lawrence R. immediately above Montreal; give access to Montreal from Gr. Lakes for steamers of 14 ft. draught; length 9 m.

Lachlan, R., N.S.W., Australia; trib. R. Murrumbidgee; length 700 m.

Lackawanna, t., N.Y., U.S.A.; on L. Erie; iron and steel; p. (1960) 29,564.

Laconia, div. of Peloponnesus, Greece; cap. Sparta; p. (1961) 118,449.

Laconia, G., S. Peloponnesus, Greece.

Laconia, c., N.H., U.S.A.; hosiery, rly. wks.; p. (1960) 15,288.

Lacq, t., S.W. Aquitaine, France; 15 m. N.W. Paris; oil, natural gas, sulphur.          [monastery.

Lacroma, I., Jugoslavia; holiday resort, château.

Lacrosse, c., Wis., U.S.A.; rly. ctr., flour, timber; p. (1960) 47,575.

Ladakh, dist., of the Upper Indus, bordering Tibet; ch. t. Leh; p. (1961) 88,651.

Ladoga, L., nr. Leningrad, U.S.S.R. (lgst. in Europe); a. 7,100 sq. m.; drained to G. of Finland by R. Neva.

Ladrones, see Marianas Is.

Ladybank, burgh, Fife, Scot.; 5 m. S.W. of Cupar; rly. wks., malt, linen; p. (1961) 1,207.

Ladysmith, t., Natal, S. Africa; rly. wks., coal, cotton mills; besieged by Boers 1899-1900; p. (1960) 22,997 inc. 7,260 Europeans.

Lafayette, c., Ind., U.S.A.; univ.; timber, farm implements; p. (1960) 42,330.

Lafayette, t., La., U.S.A.; timber, cottonseed oil; p. (1960) 40,400.              [alt. 5,259 ft.

Lafayette, peak, White mtns. range, N.H., U.S.A.;

Lagan, R., N. Ireland; flows into Belfast Lough; length 35 m.

Lagoa dos Patos, L., Brazil; drained by Rio Grande do Sul; length 140 m.

Lagoa Mirim, L., on bdy. between Brazil and Uruguay; drains N.; length 110 m.

Lagos, spt., cap., Nigeria; good natural harbour; univ.; exp. palm oil and kernels, cocoa, groundnuts, hides; imports machin., cotton piece goods; rly. wks.; p. (1963) 675,352.

Laguna, dist., Durango st. Mexico; former L. bed irrigated by R. Nazas and Aguanaval; ch. cotton-growing region in Mexico; ch. t., Torréon; a. 100,000 sq. m.

Laguna Dam, see Imperial Valley.

Laguna de Terminos. inlet, Campeche, Mexico; 70 m. by 40 m.

Laguna Madre, lagoon, Texas, U.S.A.; 110 m. by 14 m.

Lahn, R., Germany; enters R. Rhine at Koblenz; length 135 m.

Lahore, div., W. Pakistan; ch. t. Lahore; p. (estd. 1951) 5,340,000.

Lahore, ch. c., W. Pakistan; univ., cath., temples, mosques; textiles, pottery, carpets, industl. gases; atomic research ctr.; p. (1961) 1,296,477.

Lahr, t., Baden-Württemberg, Germany; at W. edge of Black Forest; tobacco, cardboard, leather, precision mechanics; p. (1963) 22,800.

Lahti, t., S. Finland; p. (1966) 81,652.

Laibach, see Ljubliana.

Lake Charles, t., La., U.S.A.; oil, rice, timber; holiday resort; p. (1960) 63,392.

Lake District, mountainous dist., Cumberland and Westmorland, Eng.; tourist resort, beautiful scenery, inc. Ls. Windermere, Ullswater, Derwentwater, etc.

Lake Forest, t., Ill., U.S.A.; on L. Michigan; p. (1960) 10,687.

Lake of the Woods, L., E. of Winnipeg, Ontario, on bdy. between Canada and U.S.A.

Lake Success, vil., N.Y., U.S.A.; temporary H.Q. of U.N.O. since 1946; p. (1960) 2,954.

Lakeland, t., Fla., U.S.A.; agr., fruit ctr., phosphates; holiday resort; p. (1960) 41,350.

Lakeview, t., Ont., Canada; thermal elec. power plant projected; to be lgst. in world.

Lakeview, Ore., U.S.A., uranium mill; p. 3,262.

Lakewood, t., N.J., U.S.A.; winter resort; p. (1960) 13,004.

Lakewood, t., Ohio, U.S.A.; sub. of Cleveland; grapes; p. (1960) 66,145.

Lalin, t., N.W. Spain; agr. ctr., paper, tanning; p. 18,620.

Lambay, I., off cst. Dublin co., Ireland.

Lambayeque, dep., N. Peru; sugar, cotton, tobacco; cap. Chiclayo; a. 4,613 sq. m.; p. (1961) 363,297.

Lambersart, commune, Nord, France; sub. Lille; spinning; p. (1954) 19,092.

Lambeth, inner bor., London, Eng.; inc. part of former bor. of Wandsworth (Clapham and Streatham); L. Palace, residence of Archbishop of Canterbury; p. (1966) 339,000.

Lambezellec, t., Finistère, France; tr. ctr.; p. (1946) 19,227.

Lambourn, par., Berks, Eng.; agr.; training stables; p. 2,316.

Lamesa, t., N.W. Texas, U.S.A.; cotton, maize, cattle; p. (1960) 12,438.

Lamia, cap., Phthiotis prefecture, Greece; p. (1961) 21,509.

Lammermuir Hills, E. Lothian, Scot.; highest peak Lammer Law, alt. 1,733 ft.

Lampedusa, I., Mediterranean; S. of Malta.

Lampeter, mkt. t., mun. bor., Cardigan, S. Wales; on R. Teifi; St. David's College; p. (1961) 1,853.

Lamu, I., off cst. of Kenya; p. 3,576 (non-African).

Lanai, one of the Hawaiian Is.; fruit, sugar, cotton, livestock; a. 141 sq. m.; p. 3,360.

Lanark, co., Scot.; coal, iron, steel, textiles; co. t. Lanark; a. 897 sq. m.; p. (1961) 1,626,317.

Lanark, burgh, co. t., Lanark, Scot.; in Clyde valley 22 m. S.E. of Glasgow; hosiery, chenille fabrics, tanning; p. (1961) 8,436.

Lancashire, mftg. dist., industl. co., N.W. Eng.; Liverpool most impt. spt.; Manchester gr. comm. ctr.; Preston adm. hdqrs.; mnfs. inc. textiles, engin. prod., chemicals, foodstuffs; coal-mining; co. t. Lancaster; a. 1,875 sq. m.; p. (1966) 5,189,000.

Lancaster, c., mun., bor., co. t., Lancs, Eng.; 6 m. up R. Lune; cas.; univ.; linoleum, cotton, artificial silk inds.; p. (estd. 1967) 47,060.

Lancaster, t., Ohio, U.S.A.; in natural-gas region; agr.; flour, machin., glass; p. (1960) 29,916.

Lancaster, bor., Penns., U.S.A.; agr. ctr.; mnfs. light and heavy iron and steel prod.; p. (1960) 61,055.                                [wde.

Lancaster, sound, N.W. Terrs., Canada; 50 m.

Lanchow (Lanzhou), c., cap., Kansu, China; on R. Hwang-Ho; silk, tobacco, grain tea-tr. ctr., oil refining; p. (1953) 397,000.

Lanciano, *t.*, Abruzzi e Molise, Italy; wine, fruit, oil, silk, linen; p. *22,450.*

Lancing, *vil.*, Sussex, Eng.; on S. cst., 2 m. E. of Worthing; seaside resort; college; light inds.; p. *13,000.*

Landau, *t.*, Rhineland-Palatinate, Germany; on R. Queich; cigar mftg., wine, iron ind.; here the carriages called Landaus were first made; p. (1963) *30,000*

Landes, *dep.*, S.W. France; on Atlantic cst.; agr., vineyards, resin; cap. Mont-de-Marson; a. 3,604 sq. m.; p. (1962) *260,495.*

Landes, Les, *coastal sub-region*, Aquitaine, S.W. France; fringes Bay of Biscay from Pointe de Grave to Biarritz; coastal sand dunes and lagoons backed by low, flat plain of alternate sandy tracts and marsh; reclaimed by drainage and afforestation, now over half a. covered by pine forests; turpentine, timber; oilfield; length 150 m., maximum width of dune belt 7 m., of plain 40 m.

Landrecies, *t.*, Nord, France; on R. Sambre.

Land's End, extreme S.W. point of Eng. on Cornish cst.

Landshut, *t.*, Bavaria, Germany; on R. Isar; cas.; elec. inds., glass, metallurgy, textiles, coal; rly. junction; p. (1963) *50,600.*

Landskrona, *spt.*, Sweden; shipping and tr. ctr.; hy. machin., lt. inds.; p. (1961) *28,526.*

Lanett, *t.*, E. Ala., U.S.A.; textiles; p. (1960) *7,674.*

Langanes, *C.*, N.E. cst., Iceland.

Langebergen, *mtns.*, Cape Province, Rep. of S. Africa; extend 150 m. E. to W. parallel to S. cst. of Africa; form barrier to access from cst. plain to Little Karroo, broken across by valley of R. Gouritz; max. alt. exceeds 4,500 ft.

Langefjell, *mtn. gr.*, Romsdal, Norway; highest peak 8,101 ft.

Langeland, *I.*, Gr. Belt, Denmark; a. 111 sq. m.; p. (1960) *18,692.*

Langholm, *mkt. burgh*, Dumfries, Scot.; on R. Esk; 18 m. N. of Carlisle; woollen mills, tanning; p. (1961) *2,369.*          [Eng.

Langley, *industl. dist.*, nr. Birmingham, Worcs.,

Langnau, *t.*, Switzerland; ch. t. of the Emmental; cheese, cloth mills, pottery; p. *8,300.*

Langreo, *t.*, Asturias, Spain; hilly, agr. and fruit-growing dist., colly. and iron-wks.; p. (1959) *64,347.*

Langres, *fortfd. t.*, Haute-Marne, France; the ancient Andematunnum; cath.; grain, livestock, cutlery, wine; p. (1962) *10,493.*

Languedoc, *prov.*, S. France; wine.

Languedoc, *canal*, S. France; unites Mediterranean with R. Garonne at Toulouse, France.

Lannemazan, *sub-region*, Aquitaine, S.W. France; belt 50 m. wide stretches over 100 m. along foot of Pyrenees W. of Toulouse; consists of immense deltas of glacial gravel deeply cut by tribs. of Rs. Garonne and Adour; valleys liable to severe floods in summer, intervening plateau dry, bare; scantily populated.

Lansdowne, *t.*, *sub.*, Philadelphia, S.E. Penns., U.S.A.; p. (1960) *12,612.*

Lansford, *bor.*, Penns., U.S.A.; p. (1950) *1,487.*

Lansing, *cap.*, Mich., U.S.A.; tr., mnfs. iron goods; cars; chemicals; p. (1960) *107,807.*

Lanzarote, *I.*, Canary Is.; volcanic, mountainous; grapes, cochineal; cap. Arrecife; p. (1962) *36,519.*

Laoag, *t.*, N. Luzon I., Philippines; cereals, tobacco, cotton, sugar; p. *40,800.*

Laoighis or Leix Co., Leinster, Ireland; mtns. and bog; inland pasture and tillage; cap. Port Laoighise (Maryborough); a. 664 sq. m.; p. (1966) *44,662.*

Laon, *cap.*, Aisne, France; fort, cath.; metal, linen mftg.; p. (1962) *27,261.*

Laos, *kingdom*, former associate st. of Fr. Union; mtnous. and densely forested; a. 89,320 sq. m.; cereals, sugar, cotton, cattle, some minerals but only tin mined in sm. quantities; cement; modern saw and rice mills; admin. cap. Vientiane; p. (estd. 1962) *2,200,000.*

Lapeer, *t.*, E. Mich., U.S.A.; wooden prod.; p. (1960) *6,160.*

Lapland, *terr.*, N. Europe, in Norway, Sweden, Finland and U.S.S.R., extending from the Norwegian cst. to the White Sea; mainly mtn. and moorland, with many lakes; a. 130,000 sq. m.; p. *100,000.*

Lappi (Lappland), *dep.*, N. Finland; a. 36,308 sq. m.; p. (1966) *220,003.*

Laptev Sea (Nordenskiöld Sea), *inlet* of Arctic Ocean; between Severnaya Zemlya and N. Siberian Is., R.S.F.S.R.

Larache, *spt.*, Morocco; on Atl. cst. 40 m. S. of Tangier; cork; p. (1960) *30,763.*

Laramie, *c.*, Wyo., U.S.A.; univ., cattle; p. (1960) *17,520.*

Larbert, *par.*, Stirling, Scot.; brass and copper wares, chemicals, confectionery; p. *13,763.*

Laredo, *c.*, Texas, U.S.A.; frontier *c.* on Rio Grande; iron, steel, oil, bricks, hides, wool; p. (1960) *60,678.*

Largo, *par.*, Fife. Scot.; fishing, holiday resort; p. (1951) *2,499.*

Largs, *burgh*, Ayr, Scot.; on F. of Clyde opposite Is. of Bute and Cumbrae; seaside resort, fishing; battle 1263; p. (1961) *9,100.*

Larissa, *prefecture*, Thessaly. Greece; cap. Larissa; p. (1961) *237,653.*

Larissa, *t.*, Thessaly, Greece; silk, cotton goods; p. (1961) *55,391.*

Laristan, *prov.*, S. Iran; on Persian G.; mainly mtns., camels, silk; cap. Lar.

Lark, *R.*, Cambridge, Eng.; trib. of R. Ouse; length 26 m.

Larkhall, *t.*, Lanark, Scot.; Industl. Estate; foundry, hosiery, silk dye wks.; p. *14,055.*

Larnaca, *spt.*, Cyprus; the ancient Citium; grain, cotton, fruit; oil refinery projected; p. (1960) *19,824.*

Larne, *spt.*, *mun. bor.*, Antrim, N. Ireland; at entrance to Larne Lough, 18 m. N. of Belfast; cross channel service to Stranraer; p. (1966) *17,278.*

Larvik, *spt.*, Norway; S.W. of Oslo; seaside resort; engin., pulp, stone; p. (1961) *10,479.*

Las Bela, *dist.*, Baluchistan, W. Pakistan; a. 7,132 sq. m.; p. (estd. 1951) *76,000.*

Las Cruces, *t.*, N.M., U.S.A.; agr. with irrigation; lead, fluorspar mining; p. (1960) *29,367.*

Las Palmas, *Spanish prov.*, Canary Is.; comprising Gran Canaria, Lanzarote, Fuerteventura and smaller Is.; bananas, potatoes, tomatoes, fishing; a. 1,565 sq. m.; p. (1962) *459,433.*

Las Palmas, *t.*, Gran Canaria, Canary Is.; cap. of Las Palmas prov.; p. (1965) *239,000.*

Las Tres Marias, *Is.*, off W. cst. Mexico.

Las Vegas, *t.*, Nevada, U.S.A.; resort; p. (1960) *64,405.*

Las Vegas, *t.*, N. Mexico, U.S.A.; E. of Santa Fé; p. (1960) *6,028.*

Las Villas, *prov.*, Cuba; a. 8,264 sq. m.; p. (1953) *1,030,162.*

Lashio, *t.*, Burma; on R. Salween; end of the Burma Road to China; p. *4,638.*

Lashkar, *see* Gwalior.          [(1961) *73,843.*

Lasithi, *prefecture*, Crete; cap. Ayios Nikolaos; p.

Lasswade, *see* Bonnyrigg and Lasswade.

Latacunga, *cap.*, Cotopaxi prov., Ecuador; tr. ctr., paper, malt; p. (1960) *29,423.*

Latakia, *spt.*, Syria; tobacco, olive oil, sponges; p. (1961) *68,498.*

Latin America, the Spanish-, Portuguese- and French-speaking countries of N. America, S. America, Central America and the West Indies, incl. the reps. of Argentina, Bolivia, Brazil, Chile, Colombia, Costa Rica, Cuba, Dominican Republic, Ecuador, El Salvador, Guatemala, Haiti, Honduras, Mexico, Nicaragua, Panama, Paraguay, Peru, Uruguay and Venezuela; sometimes Puerto Rico, French West Indies, and other Is. of the West Indies are included, and occasionally Brit. Honduras, Guyana, French Guiana, and Surinam.

Latina, *see* Littoria.

Latium, *see* Lazio.

Latrobe, *t.*, S.E. Penns., U.S.A.; p. (1960) *11,932.*

Latronico, *t.*, Potenza, Italy; p. *5,175.*

Latvia, *constituent S.S. rep.*, U.S.S.R., on the Baltic Sea; former independent st.; mainly agr.; cap. Riga; principal spts. Ventspils, Liepaya; a. 24,800 sq. km.; p. (1959) *2,094,000.*

Lauenburg, *see* Leborrk.

Launceston, *t.*, *mun. bor.*, Cornwall, Eng.; agr. mkt.; mng., quarrying, lt. engin.; p. (estd. 1967) *4,600.*

Launceston, *c.*, Tasmania, Australia; wool, textiles, fruit; cars; p. (1966) *60,453.*

Laurel, *t.*, Miss., U.S.A.; p. (1960) *27,889.*

Laurens, *t.*, S.C., U.S.A.; cotton, glass; p. (1960) *9,598.*

Laurentide, *escarpment* of Laurentian plateau, E. Canada.

Laurium, *hills, dist.*, Greece; silver and lead.

Laurium (formerly Calumet), *vil.*, Mich., U.S.A.; copper; p. (1950) *3,211.*

Lausanne, *cap.*, Vaud, Switzerland; nr. L. Geneva; cath., univ.; rly. junction, iron, chocolate, paper; p. (1961) *130,500.*

Lauterbrunnen, *vil.*, Bern can., Switzerland; highest and most famous of its waterfalls (Staubbach 980 ft.); tourist ctr.; p. *2,958.*

Lautoka, *spt.*, Viti Levu, Fiji Is.; sugar ctr.

Lauven, R., Norway; length 200 m.

Lavagna, t., Genoa, Italy; shipbldg., marble; p. *8,100.*

Laval, t., *cap.*, Mayenne, France; cotton, paper, machin., marble; cas.; p. (1962) *43,196.*

Lavera, *pt.*, nr. Marseilles, commencement of 470 m. oil pipeline to Karlsruhe, W. Germany, operated April 1963; oil refining.

Laverton, t., W. Australia; 200 m. N. Kalgoorlie.

Lawndale, t., Cal., U.S.A.; p. (1960) *21,740.*

Lawrence, c., Kan., U.S.A.; st. univ., paper, machin.; p. (1960) *32,858.*

Lawrence, c., Mass., U.S.A.; on Merrimac R., N.W. of Boston; textiles paper, footwear, engin.; p. (1960) *70,933.*

Lawrenceburg, t., Tenn., U.S.A.; textiles, cheese, phosphates; p. (1950) *5,442.*

Lawton, t., Okla., U.S.A.; p. (1959) *61,697.*

Laxey, *vil.*, I. of Man; lead-mining.

Lazio, *region*, Italy; a. 6,634 sq. m.; p. inc. Vatican City and Rome; p. (1961) *3,922,783.*

Le Bouscat, t., Gironde, France; p. (1954) *19,558.*

Le Havre, *see* Havre, Le.

Le Maire, *strait*, between Staten I. and Tierra del Fuego, S. America.

Le Mans, *cap.*, Sarthe, France; cath.; linen, ironmongery, chemicals, motor cars, aeroplanes; motor-racing; p. (1962) *136,083.*

Le Puy, t., Haute-Loire, France; p. (1962) *28,648.*

Lea, R., Eng.; rises in Chiltern Hills nr. Luton, flows E. and S. into R. Thames; length 46 m.

Lead, t., S.D., U.S.A.; gold, mnfs. jewellery, mng. equipment; resort; p. (1960) *6,211.*

Leader Water, R., Scot.; trib. of R. Tweed, which it joins nr. Melrose; length 21 m.

Leadgate, t., Durham, Eng.; 2 m. N.E. of Consett; coal, mftg.

Leadhills, *mng. vil.*, S.W. Lanark, Scot.; lead.

Leadville, c., Col., U.S.A.; in Arkansas valley; mining ctr.; p. (1960) *4,008.*

Leaf, R., flowing into Ungava Bay, Labrador, Canada.

Leam, R., Warwick, Eng.; trib. of R. Avon; length, 25 m.

Leamington, t., Ont., Canada; tobacco, canned vegetables; p. (1961) *9,030.*

Leamington (Royal Leamington Spa), t., *mun. bor.*, Warwick, Eng.; on R. Leam, 24 m. S.E. of Birmingham; fashionable spa; gen. (engin.) inds.; p. (estd. 1967) *44,860.*

Leaside, t., Ontario, Canada; p. (1961) *18,579.*

Leatherhead, t., *urb. dist.*, Surrey, Eng.; on R. Mole to N. of gap through N. Downs; boiler mftg., engin.; p. (estd. 1967) *33,090.*

Leavenworth, c., Kan., U.S.A.; on Missouri; rly. ctr. and military post, furniture, machin., bricks, coal; p. (1960) *22,052.*

Lebanon, *rep.*, S.W. Asia; mountainous; mainly agr.; textiles, garments, wooden, metal goods; cap. Beirut; a. 3,400 sq. m.; p. (estd. 1965) *2,250,000.*

Lebanon, *mtn. range*, Lebanon st. and N. Israel; highest peaks Dahr-el-Khadeb (10,052 ft.) and Timarum (10,539 ft.).

Lebanon, t., Penns., U.S.A.; coal, iron, steel, mnfs.; rubber, food, tobacco; p. (1960) *30,045.*

Lebork (former German Lauenburg), t., Poland; p. (1965) *23,000.* [(1961) *12,560.*

Lebu, *spt.*, *cap.*, Arauco prov., Chile; coal; p.

Lecce, t., Apulia, Italy; cas.; p. (1961) *74,123.*

Lecco, t., Italy; on L. Como; silk, cotton, copper, iron; p. (1961) *48,230.*

Lech, R., Germany; trib. of Danube; 177 m.

Leczyca, t., Poland; p. *20,996.*

Ledbury, t., *urb. dist.*, Hereford, Eng.; at W. foot of Malvern Hills; mkt., fruit preserving, tanning; p. (1961) *3,632.*

Ledeberg, t., Belgium; nr. Ghent; industl.; p. (1962) *11,127.*

Lee, R., Cork, Ireland; flows past Cork c. to Cork harbour; length 50 m.

Lee-on-Solent, t., Hants, Eng.; on Southampton Water; p. *4,000.*

Leeds, c., co. bor., W.R. Yorks, Eng.; on R. Aire; at E. margin of Pennines; univ.; lge. clothing ind., varied engin. mnfs., furniture, tanning; p. (estd. 1967) *507,780.*

Leek, *mkt. t., urb. dist.*, Staffs, Eng.; 11 m. N.E. of Stoke-on-Trent; silk mnfs.; p. (1961) *19,173.*

Leer, *pt.*, Lower Saxony, Germany; nr. confluence of Leda and Ems; iron, machin., textiles; harbour and route ctr.; p. (1963) *20,200.*

Lees, *urb. dist.*, Lancs. Eng.; cotton; p. (1961) *3,729.*

Leeston, t., S.I., N.Z.; on Canterbury Plain, nr. Christchurch; agr. ctr.; p. (1951) *738.*

Leete's I., Conn., U.S.A.; on Long I. sound.

Leeton, t., N.S.W., Australia; New t., ctr. of fruit and rice farming as part of Murrumbidgee Irrigation A.; p. (1966) *5,814.*

Leeuwarden, *prov. cap.*, Friesland, Netherlands; agr.; iron, metal goods, bicycles; p. (1967) *86,805.*

Leeuwin, C., S.W. point of Australia.

Leeward Is., W.I.; inc. Antigua, Barbuda, Redonda, Montserrat, Virgin Is., St. Kitts, Nevis, Anguilla, Sombrero; ch. prod., sugar, fruit; Is. cap. St. John's, Antigua; total a. 423 sq. m.; p. (1952) *119,700.*

Leeward Is. (Dutch), part of Neth. Antilles, consisting of St. Maarten (a. 34 sq. m.; p. *1,697*), St. Eustatius (a. 31 sq. m.; p. *945*), Saba (a. 9 sq. m.; p. *1,150*).

Leeward Is. (French), E. Pacific, inc. Huahiné Raiatéa, Tahaa, Bora-Bora-Maupiti; p. (1962) *16,177.*

Leghorn or Livorno, *prov.*, Italy; a. 133 sq. m.; p. (1961) *313,599.*

Leghorn or Livorno, *spt.*, *prov. cap.*, Italy; on W. cst., 10 m. S. of mouth of R. Arno; shipbldg., glass, wire, olive oil, hats, marble; p (1961) *159,973.* [p. (1965) *20,000.*

Legionowa, t., Warsaw, Poland; new town (1951):

Legnago, t., Lombardy, Italy; on R. Adige; fort, sugar, cereals; p. *20,175.*

Legnano, t., Lombardy, Italy; N.W. of Milan; cotton, silk, machin.; p. (1961) *42,460.*

Loh, ch. t., Ladakh, Kashmir, India; on R. Indus; caravan ctr.; p. (1961) *3,720.*

Lehigh, R., Penns., U.S.A.; trib. of Delaware R.; length 120 m. [p. (1960) *6,318.*

Lehighton, bor., Penns., U.S.A.; anthracite.

Leicester, c., co. t., co. bor., Leics., Eng.; on R. Soar; univ.; footwear, hosiery, knitwear, engin., and elec. goods, chemicals; p. (estd. 1967) *282,800.*

Leicestershire, co., Eng.; mainly agr.; co. t. Leicester; a. 832 sq. m.; p. (1966) *716,000.*

Leichhardt, W., sub. of Sydney, N.S.W., Australia; p. *31.500.*

Leiden (Leyden), t., S. Holland, Neth.; printing, textiles, medical apparatus; univ.; p. (1967) *102,425.*

Leigh, t., *mun. bor.*, S.W. Lancs, Eng.; 5 m. S.E. of Wigan; mkt.; coal-mining; silks, cottons, brass, iron; p. (estd. 1967) *46,600.*

Leigh-on-Sea, t., Essex, Eng.; on N. cst. of Thames estuary, 2 m. W. of Southend; holiday resort, fishing; p. (1961) *10,059.*

Leigh's L., Wyo., U.S.A.; links with Snake R.

Leighton Buzzard, t., Bedford, Eng.; at N.E. end of Vale of Aylesbury; tiles, engin., sand quarrying; p. (1961) *11,649.*

Leine, R., N.W. Germany; trib. of R. Aller; length 130 m.

Leinster, S.E. prov., Ireland; a. 7,620 sq. m.; agr.; p. (1966) *1,412,465.*

Leipzig, c., Leipzig, E. Germany; at junction of Rs. Pleisse, Elster and Parthe; univ., cath.; comm., publishing, metal, textile, chemical, steel, paper, machin. and elec. inds., vehicles; birthplace of Wagner; p. (1963) *588,135.*

Leiston-cum-Sizewell, t., *urb. dist.*, E. Suffolk, Eng.; on cst., 4 m. E. of Saxmundham; agr. implements; p. (1961) *4,119.*

Leith, *spt.*, Midlothian, Scot.; Edinburgh sub.; shipbldg., timber, whisky; p. *81,618.*

Leith Hill, Surrey, Eng.; nr. Dorking; alt. 993 ft.

Leitmeritz, *see* Litoměřice.

Leitrim, co., Connacht, Ireland; agr.; cap. Carrick-on-Shannon; a. 613 sq. m.; p. (1966) *30,532.*

Leix, co., *see* Laoighis.

Leixões, *spt.*, Portugal; at mouth of R. Douro.

**Lek,** *R.,* Netherlands; one of the branches of the Neder Rijn; from Wijk-bij-Duurstede to Krimpen nr. Rotterdam; length 40 m.

**Leland,** *t.,* Miss., U.S.A.; cotton, vegetables, nuts; p. (1960) *6,295.*

**Lema,** *Is.,* Sea of Hong Kong in China Sea.

**Lemgo,** *t.,* N. Rhine–Westphalia, Germany; E. of Bielefeld; furniture, textiles; p. (1963) *21,700.*

**Lemnos,** *I.* (Greek), Ægean Sea; 20 m. long; fertile valleys; tobacco, fruit, sheep, goats; cap. Kastron; p. *4,000.*

**Lemvig,** *spt.,* Jutland, Denmark; fishing, agr. machin.; p. (1960) *5,783.*

**Lena,** *gr. R.,* Siberia, R.S.F.S.R.; rising in mtns. W. of Lake Baikal and flowing N. to the Arctic Ocean; length 2,800 m.

**Lenin Dam (Dnieper Dam),** *see* Zaporozhe.

**Leninabad,** *t.,* Tadzhik S.S.R.; on R. Syr Darya, S. of Tashkent; cottons, silks, fruit-preserving; hydro-elec. sta.; p. (1959) *77,000.*

**Leninakan,** *t.,* Armenian S.S.R.; silk, textiles, engin.; p. (1967) *130,000.*

**Leningrad,** *c.,* R.S.F.S.R.; at mouth of R. Neva; cath., palaces, univs.; engin., oil ref., chemicals, textiles, synthetic rubber, steel, paper; founded by Peter the Gr. as St. Petersburg; p. (1967) *3,665,000.*

**Leninogorsk,** *t.,* Kazakh S.S.R.; lead, zinc, silver, copper, gold; p. (1959) *67,000.*

**Leninsk-Kuznetski (Charjui),** *t.,* R.S.F.S.R.; heavy engin., power-sta., coal, gold; p. (1967) *140,000.*

**Lenkoran,** *spt.,* Azerbaydzhan S.S.R.; on Caspian Sea; ctr. of rice, citrous fruits, tea a.; p. (1956) *30,800.*

**Lennox,** *ancient Scottish div.,* comprising Dunbarton, parts of Stirling, Perth and Renfrew.

**Lennox Hills,** *mtn. range,* between Dunbarton and Stirling, Scot.

**Lennoxtown,** *t.,* Stirling, Scot.; coal-mining, bleaching, print and alum wks.; p. *2,550.*

**Lennoxville,** *t.,* Quebec, Canada; on St. Francis R.; univ.; p. *1,927.*

**Lens,** *t.,* Pas de Calais, France; on canal of same name; ironwks., soap, sugar; p. (1962) *42,733.*

**Lentini or Leontini,** *t.,* Sicily, Italy; on plain of Catania; cereal, oil, wine; p. *23,150.*

**Leoben,** *old mining t.,* Styria, Austria; walls and tower; p. (1961) *36,257.*

**Leominster,** *t., mun. bor.,* Hereford, Eng.; 13 m. N. of Hereford; rly. junction, mkt., cider, cattle, agr. tools, glove mkg.; p. (estd. 1967) *6,930.*

**Leominster,** *c.,* Mass., U.S.A.; wood prod., light mnfs.; p. (1960) *27,929.*

**León,** *t.,* Nicaragua; cath., univ.; footwear, textiles; p. (1960) *46,000.*

**León,** *t.,* Mexico; textiles, leather, gold, silver; p. (1960) *209,469.*

**León,** *prov.,* Spain; agr., livestock, coal, iron; cap. León; a. 5,937 sq. m.; p. (1959) *591,231.*

**Leonforte,** *t.,* Sicily, Italy; sulphur-mines, cattle, oil, wine; p. *19,400.*

**Leonidion,** *t.,* Greece; on G. of Nauplia; p. *3,452.*

**Leonora,** *sm. t.,* W. Australia; 140 m. N. of Kalgoorlie; gold-mines.

**Léopoldville.** *See* Kinshasa.

**Lercara,** *t.,* Sicily, Italy; macaroni mftg., sulphur-mines; p. *11,000.*

**Lerici,** *coastal t.,* Italy; nr. Spezia; macaroni mftg.; old cas.

**Lérida,** *prov.,* Spain; wine, olive oil, livestock, wool, timber; a. 4,656 sq. m.; p. (1959) *334,807.*

**Lérida,** *t., cap.* of L. prov., Spain; on R. Segre; 2 caths.; textiles, leather, glass; p. (1959) *59,040.*

**Lerins,** *Is.* (French), in Mediterranean; nr. Cannes.

**Leros,** *Is.,* Dodecanese, Greece.

**Lerwick,** *cap.,* Shetland Is., Scot.; on Mainland; fishing; p. (1961) *5,906.*

**Les Baux,** *commune,* Bouches-du-Rhône, France; bauxite first discovered here; not impt. now.

**Les Causses,** *see* Causses, Les.

**Les Landes,** *see* Landes, Les.

**Les Lilas,** *commune,* Seine, France; glass, chemicals, metallurgy; p. (1954) *18,590.*

**Les Sables d'Olonne,** *commune,* Vendée, France; shipbldg.; fish, canning; p. (1962) *19,256.*

**Lesbos,** *see* Mytilene I.

**Leskovac,** *t.,* Serbia, Jugoslavia; on R. Morava; hemp, flax, tobacco; p. (1959) *29,000.*

**Leslie,** *burgh,* Fife, Scot.; 7 m. N. of Kirkcaldy; paper, flax, bleaching; p. (1961) *3,421.*

**Lesotho (Basutoland),** *indep. sov. st.,* S. Africa; at head of Orange R., and enclosed on S. by

**Drakensberg Mtns;.** mtnous plateau; univ. at Roma; mainly agr., maize, wool, mohair; cap. Maseru; a. 11,716 sq. m.; p. (estd. 1965) *733,000.*

**Lesser Antilles,** *see* Antilles.

**Lesser Slave,** *L.,* Central Alberta, Canada.

**Lesvos (Lesbos),** *Greek prefecture* and *I.* in Ægean Sea; cap. Mitilini (Mytilene); p. (1961) *140,144.*

**Leszno,** *t.,* Poznan, W. Poland; engin., distilling, tobacco; p. (1965) *31,000.*

**Letchworth (Garden City),** *t., urb. dist.,* Herts, Eng.; at foot of Chiltern Hills, 2 m. N.E. of Hitchin; model residtl. and industl. t.; all types of engin., office equipment; p. (estd. 1967) *28,110.*

**Lethbridge,** *t.,* Alberta, Canada; coal, oil; p. (1961) *35,454.*

**Letterkenny,** *t.,* Donegal, Ireland; on Lough Swilly; tourist ctr.; p. (1966) *4,513.*

**Leucadia,** *see* Levkas.

**Leuna,** *t.,* Halle, E. Germany; 3 m. S. of Merseburg; chemicals; oil pipeline from Schwedt; p. (1963) *12,702.*

**Levanger,** *spt.,* Norway; at N. end of Trondheim Fjord; p. (1961) *1,711.*

**Levant,** French and Italian name for E. cst. of Mediterranean.

**Leven,** *burgh,* Fife, Scot.; on N. side of F. of Forth, 10 m. N.E. of Kirkcaldy; linen, coal; p. (1961) *8,872.*

**Leven,** *L.,* Kinross, Scot.; associated with escape of Mary Queen of Scots from Castle I., 1568.

**Leven,** *salt-water L.,* Argyll, Inverness, Scot.

**Levenshulme,** *industl. t.,* Lancs, Eng.; sub. of Manchester.

**Leverkusen,** *t.,* N., Rhine–Westphalia, Germany; on R. Rhine, N. of Cologne; iron, machin., textiles, chemicals; p. (1963) *99,300.*

**Levin,** *t.,* N.I., N.Z.; p. (1961) *7,940.*

**Levis,** *t.,* Quebec, Canada; on St. Lawrence R., opposite Quebec; rly. terminus, landing place for Transatlantic passengers; p. (1961) *15,112.*

**Levkas (Santa Maura),** Ionian Is., Greece; ch. t. and spt.. L.; mtns.; grapes, currants; a. 110 sq. m.; p. (1961) *23,969* of t. *6,552.*

**Levoča,** *t.,* ČSSR.; N.W. of Kosice; industl.; p. (1961) *13,768.*

**Lewes,** *co. t., mun. bor.,* E. Sussex, Eng.; on R. Ouse at N. entrance to gap through S. Downs; mkt., agr. ctr.; old buildings; iron wks.; p. (estd. 1967) *14,080.*

**Lewis,** *I..* Outer Hebrides, Scot.; fishing, tweeds; ch. t. Stornoway; a. 770 sq. m.; p. *31,687.*

**Lewisham,** *inner bor.,* London, Eng.; inc. former bor. of Deptford; residtl.; industl.; p. (1966) *289,000.*

**Lewiston,** *t.,* Idaho, U.S.A.; gold, silver, lead; agr., lumber; p. (1960) *12,691.*

**Lewiston,** *c.,* Maine, U.S.A.; textiles, machin., timber; p. (1960), *40,804.*

**Lexington,** *c.* Ky., U.S.A.; univ.; tobacco, horse-rearing; p. (1960) *62,810.*

**Lexington,** *t.,* Mass., U.S.A.; nr. Boston; mftg.; first battle in American War of Independence, 1775; p. (1960) *27,961.*

**Leyburn,** *t.,* N.R. Yorks, Eng.; in lower Wensleydale; mkt.; lead, lime; p. *1,440.*

**Leyden,** *see* Leiden.

**Leyland,** *t., urb. dist.,* Lancs, Eng.; 5 m. S. of Preston; motors, cotton, paint and varnish, rubber goods; p. (1961) *19,241.*

**Leyre,** *R.,* S.W. France; length 40 m.

**Leyte,** *I.,* Philippines; a. 2,785 sq. m.; p. (1960) *1,072,600.*

**Leytha (Leitha),** *R.,* Austria; flowing to the Danube below Vienna.

**Leyton,** *see* Waltham Forest.

**Leytonstone,** part of Waltham Forest, Eng.; p. (1961) *12,254.*

**Lhasa (Lasa),** *c., cap.,* Tibet, China; " forbidden " c.; Buddhist ctr., temple, monasteries, shrines; caravan tr. in carpets, silk, lace, gold, tea; p. (1953) *50,000.*

**Liao-ho,** *R.,* Liaoning, N.E. China, flows into G. of Liaotung, Yellow Sea; navigable for last 400 m. of course; length approx. 1,000 m.

**Liaoning,** *prov.,* N.E. China; incl. lower course and delta of Liao-ho; extremely fertile; gr. mineral resources; cap. Mukden; p. (1953) *18,545,147.*

**Liaotung,** *peninsula,* N.E. China; nr. G. of same name.

**Liaoyang,** *c.,* Liaoning, N.E. China; in fertile valley of Liao-ho; p. (1953) *102,000.*

Liaoyuan, c., Kirin, China; p. (1953) 120,000.

Liberal, t., S.W. Kan., U.S.A.; natural gas, flour, machin.; p. (1960) 13,813.

Liberec, t., ČSSR.; on R. Neisse; univ.; textiles, chemicals, tr. ctr.; p. (1962) 65,267.

Liberia, rep., W. Africa; rubber, palm kernels, palm oil, cocoa, timber; rich iron ore deposits, diamond mng.; cap. Monrovia; a. 43,000 sq. m.; p. (1961) 1,250,000.

Libmanan, mun., Luzon, Philippine Is.; hemp, rice; p. 23,000.

Libourne, t., Gironde, France; on R. Dordogne; vineyards, brandy, sugar, woollens; p. (1954) 19,474.

Libreville, c., cap. Gabon; pt. on G. of Guinea; exp. tropical hardwoods, rubber, cacao; p. c. 31,000.

Libya, indep. sov. st. (1951), formerly Italian col., adm. after Second World War by Britain and France, N. Africa; cap. Beida; some agr., fruits, fishing, oil; a. 679,400 sq. m.; p. (1961) 1,195,000.

Libyan Desert, part of the Sahara, Africa.

Lichfield, c., mun. bor., Staffs, Eng.; 7 m. N.W. of Tamworth; cath.; agr. and light inds.; p. (estd. 1967) 22,100.

Lichtenstein, t., Karl-Marx-Stadt, E. Germany; textiles; p. (1963) 13,978.

Lick Observatory, on Mt. Hamilton, Cal., U.S.A.

Lickey Hills, Worcester, Eng.; 4 m. S.W. of Birmingham; sm. l. of ancient rocks; largely wooded; rise to 956 ft.

Licking, R., Ky., U.S.A.; trib. of Ohio R.; length 220 m.

Licosa, C., Italy; S. side of G. of Salerno.

Liddel, R., Roxburgh, Dumfries, Scot.; trib. of R. Esk.; valley used by "Waverley Route" rly. from Carlisle to Edinburgh.

Lidköping, t., Sweden; on L. Vänern; iron, porcelain inds.; p. (1961) 16,853.

Liechtenstein, sm. principality, Europe; between Austria and Switzerland; agr., cattle, cotton weaving and spinning, leather goods; cap. Vaduz; a. 62 sq. m.; p. (1960) 16,628.

Liége, prov., Belgium; minerals; cap. Liége; a. 1,525 sq. m.; p. (1962) 1,007,516.

Liége (Luik), c., prov. cap., Belgium; at junction of Rs. Meuse and Ourthe; cath., univ.; textiles, machin., coal, iron, glassware, fire-arms; p. (1965) 452,000 incl. subs.

Lier, t., Belgium; textiles, mnfs.; p. (1962) 28,887.

Liepaja, spt., Latvian S.S.R.; fishing inds.; engin, steel, chemicals; p. (1959) 71,000.

Liestal, cap. of the half-can. Baselland, Switzerland; p. 7,211.

Liévin, mflo. t., Pas-de-Calais, France; adjoining Lens; coal-mining; p. (1954) 31,808.

Liévres, R., Quebec, Canada; trib. of St. Lawrence R.

Liffey, R., Ireland; flows from Wicklow to Dublin Bay; length 50 m.

Lifu, I. (French); Loyalty Is., Pacific.

Ligao, t., Luzon, Philippine Is.; sugar, rice.

Lightning Ridge, N.S.W., Australia; black opal field.

Lignice (Liegnitz), t., Silesia, Poland; German before 1945; cas.; foodstuffs, textiles, rly junction; p. (1965) 72,000.

Liguria, region, N.W. Italy; inc. provs. of Genoa and Porto Maurizio; a. 2,089 sq. m.; p. (1961) 1,717,630.

Ligurian Sea, Mediterranean; N. of Corsica.

Lika, R., Jugoslavia; partly underground; length 30 m.

Lille, cap., Nord, France; on R. Deule; univ.; linens, cottons, rayons, iron, sugar, chemicals; p. (1962) 199,033.

Lillehammer, t., Norway; in R. Lagen valley; tourist ctr.; car., lumbering; p. (1961) 6,153.

Lilongwe, t., cap., Central Prov. Malawi; p. (1966) 19,176.

Lim Fjord, shallow strait, Jutland, Denmark; connects N. Sea with Kattegat; length 100 m.

Lima, dep., Peru; a. 15,048 sq. m.; p. (1961) 2,321,198.

Lima, cap., Peru; univ.; comm. ctr., textiles, leather, furniture, iron-ore; spt. Callao; p. (1963) 1,960,000.

Lima, c., Ohio, U.S.A.; on Ottawa R.; rly. wks., oil, car bodies, refrigerators; p. (1960) 51,037.

Limassol, spt., Cyprus; wine, grapes, raisins; p. (estd. 1959) 37,000.

Limavady, t., urb. dist., Londonderry, N. Ireland; mkt.; linen; p. (1966) 4,811.

Limbach, t., Karl-Marx-Stadt, E. Germany; hosiery, textiles, machines; p. (1963) 26,287.

Limbe, t., Malawi, Africa; merged with Blantyre (q.v.); elec. and power plants; p. 7,140.

Limburg, prov., Belgium; agr., livestock, gin, sugar-beet, mftg.; cap. Hasselt; a. 930 sq. m.; p. (1962) 586,279.

Limburg, prov., Neth.; drained by R. Maas (Meuse); cap. Maastricht; agr., cattle, coal, iron; a. 846 sq. m.; p. (1967) 980,276.

Limburg, c., Hessen, Germany; on R. Lahn; cath.; iron, machin., glass, paper; rly. junction; p. (estd. 1954) 15,800.

Limehouse, par., Tower Hamlets, E. London, Eng.; on R. Thames; p. (1961) 7,552.

Limeira, t., Sao Paulo, Brazil; ctr. of orange cultivation; hats, matches; p. (1960) 54,000.

Limerick, co., Munster, Ireland; agr., livestock, fishing; a. 1,307 sq. m.; p. (1966) 137,276.

Limerick, co. bor., spt., cap., Limerick, Ireland; at head of Shannon estuary; bacon, tanning, shipbldg.; p. (1966) 55,885.

Limmat, R., Switzerland; trib. of R. Aar; flows through c. of Zurich; length 80 m.

Limoges, ch. t., Haute-Vienne France; porcelain, kaolin paste; p (1962) 120,596.

Limón, prov., Costa Rica, Central America; p. (1963) 68,263.

Limón, prov. cap., spt., Costa Rica, Central America; comm. ctr.; oil refining nearby; p. (1963) 22,505.

Limousin, old prov., and natural division (" pays "), Central France; located W. of Auvergne plateau, average alt. 1,000 ft., composed of old crystalline rocks; exposed, damp climate; rich pasture favours raising of dairy cattle, horses; kaolin deposits; ch. t., Limoges.

Limpopo, or Crocodile R., S. Africa.

Linares, prov., Chile; a. 3,790 sq. m.; cap. L.; p. (1961) 190,350.

Linares, t., Chile; wine, fruit, cereals, vegetables; p. (1961) 51,481.       [(1959) 58,327.

Linares, t. Spain; lead-mining and mftg.; p.

Lincoln, agr. co., Eng.; a. 2,665 sq. m.; divided into 3 administrative dists.; Holland, p. (1966) 105,000; Kesteven, p. (1966) 226,000; Lindsey, engin., agr. machin.; p. (1966) 453,000.

Lincoln, c., co. bor., co. t., Lincoln, Eng.; on R. Witham in gap through Lincoln Edge; cath.; heavy engin., iron foundries, bricks, lime, seed milling, malting; p. (estd. 1967) 77,320.

Lincoln, c., Ill., U.S.A.; coal, agr.; pottery; p. (1960) 16,890.

Lincoln, cap., Nebraska, U.S.A.; rly. ctr., flour; agr. machin., watches, cars, chemicals, rubber goods; p. (1960) 128,521.

Lincoln, t., R.I., U.S.A.; limestone, textiles; p. (1960) 13,545.

Lincoln Edge, hill ridge, Lincoln, Eng.; runs N. from Ancaster through Lincoln to Humber; narrow ridge with steep scarp slope to W., broken across by R. Witham at Lincoln; composed of limestone, little surface drainage; iron-ore deposits worked in N. nr. Scunthorpe; sheep, barley; rarely exceeds 300 ft. alt.

Lincoln Park, sub. of Detroit, Mich., U.S.A.; residtl.; p. (1960) 53,933.

Lincoln Wolds, low plateau, Lindsey, Lincoln, Eng.; runs N. 45 m. from Wash to Humber; chalk covered with glacial deposits; mixed farming, grains, roots, sheep; lge. farm units; scantily populated; rise to approx. 450 ft.

Lindau, t., Bavaria, Germany; situated on I. in L. Constance; foodstuffs, machin., elec. goods; route ctr.; p. (1963) 25,500.

Linden, t., N.J., U.S.A.; p. (1960) 39,931.

Lindsey, N. div., Lincoln, Eng.; ch. ts. Lincoln, Grimsby; a. 1,520 sq. m.; p. (1961) 504,678.

Lingen, t., Lower Saxony, Germany; on Dortmund-Ems Canal; oil refining, textiles, cheese, cellulose; route ctr.; p. (1963) 25,400.

Linköping, t., S E. Sweden; hy. engin., aeroengin., pianos, furniture; p. (1961) 65,237.

Linlithgow, burgh, co. t., W. Lothian, Scot.; 15 m. W. of Edinburgh; paper, glue, chemicals, distilling, brewing; p. (1961) 4,327.

Linnhe, L., Argyll, Scot.; 21 m. long; entrance to Caledonian canal.

Linosa, I. (Italian), Mediterranean, W. of Malta.

Linslade, t., urb. dist., Bucks, Eng.; 1 m. N.W. of Leighton Buzzard; p. (1961) 4,127.

Linwood, *t.*, N.E. Renfrew, Scotland; 3 m. W. of Paisley; cars.

Linz, *c.*, *cap.*, Upper Austria; on Danube; boats, brewing, printing, iron, steel, textiles; cath.; p. (1964) *202,000*.

Lions, G. of, Mediterranean, S. France.

Lipa, *t.*, Luzon, Philippine Is.; sugar, tobacco, cocoa, maize; p. (1960) *69,036*.

Lipari Is., Italy; volcanic, Stromboli 3,155 ft.; a. 45 sq. m.; olives, grapes, wine, sulphur; lgst. I. and cap. L.; p. *19,500*.

Lipetsk, *industl t.*, R.S.F.S.R.; on the R. Voronezh; iron, engin., ferro-alloys; p. (1967) *237,000*.

Lippe, *R.* Germany; trib. of Rhine; length 110 m.

Lippstadt, *t.*, N. Rhine–Westphalia, Germany; on R. Lippe; metallurgy, textiles, rly. ctr.; p. (1963) *38,500*.

Liri, *R.*, Central Italy; rises in Alban Hills, flows S.E. to Cassino and then S.W. to G. of Gaeta; valley followed by main road from Rome to Naples; length 105 m.

Lisbon, *spt.*, *cap.*, Portugal; on R. Tagus; cas., cath.; univ.; cotton, silk, gold, silver, chemicals; p. (1960) *818,000*.

Lisburn, *t.*, *urb. dist.*, Antrim, N. Ireland; on R. Lagan, 6 m. S.W. of Belfast; tyre valves; p. (1966) *21,538*.

Lisieux, *t.*, Calvados, France; cath.; flannel, dairying, footwear, machin.; p. (1962) *22,472*.

Liskeard, *mkt. t.*, *mun. bor.*, Cornwall, Eng.; on R. Looe at S. edge of Bodmin Moor; mining, tanning, chemicals; p. (estd. 1967) *4,700*.

Lisle, *t.*, Tasmania; gold.

Lismore, *mkt. t.*, *rural dist.*, on R. Blackwater, Waterford, Ireland; p. (1961) *8,027*.

Lismore, Scot., *I.*, 12 m. long in Loch Linnhe near Oban; p. *200*.

Lismore, *t.*, N.S.W., Australia; dairying, sugar-refining, maize, potatoes, textiles, engin.; p. (1966) *19,740*.

Lissa, *I.*, Jugoslavia; wine.

Listowel, *urb. dist.*, Kerry, Ireland; on R. Feale; cas. ruins; p. (1961) *2,858*. [(1960) *7,330*.

Litchfield, *c.*, Ill., U.S.A.; natural gas, oil; p.

Litherland, *urb. dist.*, Lancs, Eng.; N. sub. of Liverpool; tanning, rubber processing, tar distilling, tin smelting; p. (estd. 1967) *24,320*.

Lithgow, *t.*, N.S.W., Australia; coal-mining, ironwks., potteries; p. (1961) *14,222*.

Lithuania, *constituent rep.*, U.S.S.R.; former independent st.; agr., livestock, timber; cap. Vilnius; a. 31,600 sq. m.; p. (1959) *2,713,000*.

Litomerice, *t.*, ČSSR.; on R. Elbe; brewing, agr. ctr.; p. (1961) *16,584*.

Little Bahama, one of the Bahama Is., W.I.

Little Belt, *strait*, separating Jutland from I. of Fyn, Denmark.

Little Cayman, *I.*, *see* Cayman Is.

Little Colorado, *R.*, Arizona, U.S.A.; trib. of Colorado R. [timber; p. (1960) *7,551*.

Little Falls, *c.*, Minn., U.S.A.; on R. Mississippi;

Little Falls, *t.*, N.Y., U.S.A.; on Mohawk R.; paper, leather, bicycles, knitted goods; p. (1960) *8,935*.

Little Lever, *urb. dist.*, Lancs, Eng.; residtl and industl.; p. (1961) *5,088*.

Little Rock, *c.*, Ark., U.S.A.; on Arkansas R.; oil, cotton-seed cakes, cotton, machin., and many diversified inds.; livestock; p. (1960) *107,813*. [length 300 m.

Little Sioux, *R.*, Iowa, U.S.A.; trib. of Missouri;

Littleborough, *t.*, *urb. dist.*, Lancs, Eng.; 3 m. N.E. of Rochdale; cotton, woollens, dyeing; p. (1961) *10,514*.

Littlehampton, *t.*, *urb. dist.*, W. Sussex, Eng.; on S. cst. at mouth of R. Arun; holiday resort, sm. spt.; p. (1961) *15,647*.

Littleport, *mkt. t.*, Cambs, Eng.; N. of Ely; agr.; p. (par.) *4,709*.

Littleton, *t.*, N.H., U.S.A.; mftg.; p. (1960) *3,355*.

Littoria (Latina), *t.*, Lazio, Italy; in ctr. of reclaimed area of Pontine Marshes, 38 m. S.E. of Rome; mkt. ctr., on which planned road system converges; built since 1932; nuclear power sta. nearby; p. (1961) *43,395*.

Liverpool, *c.*, *spt.*, *co. bor.*, Lancs, Eng.; 2nd lgst. pt. in Gr. Britain, on N. bank at entrance to Mersey estuary; shipping and shipbldg.; elec. mnfs. and engin., flour milling, sugar refining, seed and rubber processing, cars; cath., univ.; p. (estd. 1967) *705,310*.

Liverpool, *t.*, N.S.W., Australia; within met. a. of Sydney; mkt. and processing ctr. for dairy prod.; elec. goods, woollens; p. (1966) *60,552*.

Liversedge, *t.*, W.R. Yorks, Eng.; woollens, chemicals, machin.; p. *15,000*. [*8,229*.

Livingston, *t.*, Mont., U.S.A.; industl.; p. (1960)

Livingston, "new town" (designated 1962), on bdy. of W. Lothian and Midlothian, Scot.; p. (estd. 1968) *6,500*.

Livingstone Falls, cataracts on R. Congo, Africa.

Livingstone, *t.*, Zambia; on Zambesi R. where the rly. bridges the r., stands at 3,000 ft.; former cap.; impt. saw-mills ctr.; p. (1962) *31,560* inc. 4,000 Europeans. [9,600 ft.

Livingstone, *mtns.*, Tanzania, highest point,

Livorno, *see* Leghorn.

Livry-Gargain, *t.*, Seine-St-Denis, France; p. (1962) *29,688*.

Lizard, The, *C.*, Cornwall, Eng.; S. point of Eng.

Ljubljana, *cap.*, Slovenia, Jugoslavia; on Laibach R.; textiles, chemicals, bell mftg. engin.; p. (1960) *155,000*.

Llanberis, *t.*, Caernarvon, Wales; tourist ctr. at base of Snowdon; p. *2,370*.

Llanberis, *pass*, Caernarvon, N. Wales; between mtns. Snowdon and Clyder Fawr; road carries heavy tourist traffic; summit alt. 1,168 ft.

Llandaff, *c.*, Glamorgan, S. Wales; part of Cardiff; cath.; p. *13,227*.

Llandarcy, *vil.*, Glamorgan, S. Wales; on cst. Swansea Bay, Bristol Channel; lge. oil-refinery; pipe-line to Angle Bay, Pembroke.

Llandilo, *t.*, *urb. dist.*, E. Carmarthen, Wales; on R. Towy, 10 m. E. of Carmarthen; agr. mkt.; p. (1961) *1,906*.

Llandovery, *t.*, *mun. bor.*, N.E. Carmarthen, Wales; on R. Towy, 11 m. N.E. of Llandilo; agr., forestry; fertilisers, cattlefood, bricks, tourist ctr.; p. (1961) *1,896*.

Llandrindod Wells, *t.*, *urb. dist.*, mid-Radnor, Wales; medicinal waters; p. (1961) *3,243*.

Llandudno, *t.*, *urb. dist.*, Caernarvon, Wales; between Gr. and Little Orme's Head; resort; elec. domestic goods; p. (1961) *17,852*.

Llandysul, *t.*, S. Cardigan, Wales, on R. Teifi; woollen milling; p. (1961) *2,590*.

Llanelli, *spt.*, *mun. bor.*, Carmarthen, Wales; on N. cst. of Loughor estuary; coal-mng., steel and tin-plate wks., mng. machin.; p. (1961) *29,994*.

Llanera, *commune*, N.W. Spain; horticulture; p. *11,424*.

Llanfairfechan, *t.*, N. Caernarvon, Wales; under Penmaenmawr Mt.; seaside resort; granite quarrying; p. (1961) *2,861*.

Llanfair Caereinion, *t.*, Montgomery, Wales; mkt., flannel; p. *1,665*.

Llanfyllin, *t.*, *mun. bor.*, Montgomery, Wales; 11 m. S.W. of Oswestry; brewing, malting; Roman remains; p. (1961) *1,251*.

Llangefni, *t.*, *urb. dist.*, Anglesey, Wales; in ctr. of the I.; mkt. and agr. t.; p. (1961) *3,209*.

Llangollen, *t.*, *urb. dist.*, Denbigh, Wales; on R. Dee; mkt., tourist ctr., flannel mftg., light engin., slate quarrying; p. (1961) *3,050*.

Llanidloes, *t.*, *mun. bor.*, Montgomery, Wales; on R. Severn; leather, ironfoundry, engin. wks.; p. (1961) *2,375*.

Llanos, *lowland region*, Venezuela and Colombia, S. America; drained by R. Orinoco and tribs.; high temperatures throughout year, but rain chiefly in summer; ch. vegetation, coarse grass which withers during dry season (Dec. to May); little developed, some cattle-rearing.

Llanos de Urgel, *upland region*, Lérida, N.E. Spain; semi-arid; formerly steppe-land, now irrigated by R. Segre; vine, olive, maize, tobacco. [(1960) *152,181*.

Llanquihue, *prov.*, Chile; a. 7,005 sq. m.; p.

Llanrwst, *t.*, *urb. dist.*, Denbigh, Wales; on R. Conway; 10 m. S. of Conway; mkt., tourist ctr.; p. (1961) *2,571*.

Llanstephan, *vil.*, Carmarthen, Wales; cas.

Llantrisant, *rural dist.*, Glamorgan, Wales; iron, coal, quarrying; Royal Mint; p. (rural dist. 1961) *27,125*.

Llanwrtyd Wells, *t.*, *urb. dist.*, Brecknock, Wales; iron, farming; p. (1961) *536*.

Lleyn, *peninsula*, *rural dist.*, Caernarvon, N. Wales; extends W. from Snowdonia to Bardsey I., separates Cardigan Bay from Caernarvon Bay; crystalline rocks form hills in E., otherwise low, undulating; pastoral farming, sheep, cattle; settlements mainly on cst., fishing vils. and sm. seaside resorts; ch. t.,

**Pwllheli**; a. 180 sq. m.; p. rural dist. (1961) 16,521. [24,903.

**Llwchwr**, *urb. dist.*, Glam., S. Wales; p. (1961)

**Loa**, *R.*, N. Chile.

**Loango**, *spt.*, Congo (ex-French), Eq. Africa; N. of mouth of R. Congo; rubber, palm-oil exp.

**Loanhead**, *burgh*, Midlothian, Scot.; 5 m. S.E. of Edinburgh; coal, iron ore, engin.; p. (1961) 5,023. [16,805.

**Löbau**, *industl. t.* Dresden, E. Germany; p. (1963)

**Lobaye**, *R.*, Congo rep., Eq. Africa.

**Lobito**, *spt.*, Angola, Africa; N. of Benguela; exp. copper, maize; rly. terminus; p. (1960) 79,600 (inc. 15,000 whites). [Talara: oil-wells.

**Lobitos**, *t.*, Piura dep., Peru; on cst. 20 m. N. of

**Locarno**, *t.*, Switzerland; on L. Maggiore; tourist ctr.; L. treaty 1925; figs, olives, pomegranates; p. 7,700 (inc. subs. 12,000).

**Lochaber**, *mountainous dist.*, S. Inverness, Scot.; contains Ben Nevis.

**Lochalsh**, *see* Kyle of Lochalsh.

**Lochgelly**, *burgh*, Fife, Scot.; nr. Dunfermline; coal-mining; p. (1961) 9,114.

**Lochgilphead**, *co. t.*, Argyll, Scot.; at head of Loch Gilp, 2 m. N. of Ardrishaig; tourist ctr.; p. (1961) 1,208.

**Lochmaben**, *burgh*, Dumfries, Scot.; in Annandale, 7 m. N.E. of Dumfries; p. (1961) 1,279.

**Lochy, Loch**, Inverness, Scot.; used by Caledonian Canal; 10 m. long; R. Lochy flows 8 m. to Fort William from S. end of the loch.

**Lockerbie**, *burgh*, Dumfries, Scot.; in Annandale 10 m. E. of Dumfries; sheep mkt.; p. (1961) 2,826. [agr.; p. (1960) 6,084.

**Lockhart**, *t.*, Texas, U.S.A.; cotton, petroleum

**Lock Haven**, *c.*, Penns., U.S.A.; on Susquehanna R.; timber; p. (1960) 11,748. [7,560.

**Lockport**, *t.*, Ill., U.S.A.; rly. ctr.; p. (1960)

**Lockport**, *c.*, N.Y., U.S.A.; on Erie canal; machin., paper pulp, fruit; p. (1960) 26,443.

**Loddon**, *R.*, Victoria, Australia; rises in Grampian Mtns., flows N. into R. Murray at Swan Hill; water used for irrigation in N. Victoria; length approx. 200 m. [p. (1962) 7,234.

**Lodève**, *t.*, Hérault, France; cloth mftg.; cath.;

**Lodi**, *c.*, Italy; on R. Adda; cheese, majolica ware; cath.; p. 29,000.

**Lodi**, *t.*, Cal., U.S.A.; in San Joaquin valley; agr., especially grapes; packing plants; p. (1960) 22,229.

**Lodi**, *t.*, N.J., U.S.A.; p. (1960) 23,502.

**Lodore**, *waterfall*, nr. Keswick, Cumberland, Eng.

**Lodz**, *prov.*, Central Poland; a. 7,904 sq. m.; p. (1965) 1,665,000.

**Lodz**, *t.*, Central Poland; the "Manchester of Poland"; textiles, paper, engin.; p. (1965) 744,000.

**Lofoten Is.**, *storm-swept gr.*, off N.W. cst. Norway; stretching 175 m.; mainly mtns.; cod and herring fishing.

**Loftus**, *t.*, *urb. dist.*, N.R. Yorks, Eng.; on N.E. flank of Cleveland Hills; stone, iron and steel; p. (1961) 8,111.

**Logan**, *c.*, Utah, U.S.A.; p. (1960) 18,731.

**Logan**, *t.*, Ohio, U.S.A.; coal, natural gas, oil; leather, wool mnfs.; p. (1960) 6,417.

**Logansport**, *c.*, Ind., U.S.A.; on Wabash and Erie canal; timber, fruit, grain, machin., woollens; p. (1960) 21,106.

**Logroño**, *prov.*, N. Spain, cap. Logroño; a. 1,946 sq. m.; p. (1959) 232,386.

**Logroño**, *c.*, N. Spain, ctr. of wine growing a.; comm. and agr. mkt. t.; p. (1957) 55,465.

**Loir**, *R.*, France; trib. of R. Sarthe; length 150 m.

**Loire**, *R.*, France; lgst. in cty., flows from Cévennes Mtns. to Atlantic; length 625 m.

**Loire**, *dep.*, France; agr. (potatoes vineyards), mining, mftg.; cap. St. Etienne; a. 1,853 sq. m.; p. (1962) 696,348.

**Loire, Atlantique**, *dep.*, W. France; cap. Nantes; a. 2,695 sq. m.; p. (1962) 803,372.

**Loire, Haute**, *dep.*, France; cap. Le Puy; a. 1,930 sq. m.; p. (1962) 211,036.

**Loiret**, *dep.*, France; agr., vineyards, distilling, mftg.; cap. Orléans; a. 2,630 sq. m.; p. (1962) 389,854.

**Loir-et-Cher**, *dep.*, Central France; cap. Blois; a. 2,479 sq. m.; p. (1962) 250,741.

**Loja**, *prov.*, Ecuador; cap. Loja; a. 3,705 sq. m.; p. (estd. 1962) 285,351.

**Lokeren**, *t.*, Belgium; textiles, chemicals, tobacco; p. (1962) 25,975.

**Lokoja**, *t.*, Nigeria; at confluence of Rs. Niger and Benue; military sta.; importance decreased since rlys. opened; p. 2,122.

**Lolland**, *I.*, Danish Baltic Sea; a. 462 sq. m.; forests; cap. Maribo; p. (1960) 83,170.

**Lombardy**, *region*, N. Italy; in R. Po Valley; a. 9,190 sq. m.; p. (1961) 7,390,492.

**Lombardy, Plain of**, N. Italy; extensive lowland flanked by Alps, Apennines, Adriatic Sea; built up by alluvium from R. Po, its tribs. and R. Adige; zone bounding main Rs. liable to floods, elsewhere irrigation necessary on account of hot summers; intensively cultivated, rice, maize, flax, clover, lucerne, wheat, apples, dairy cattle, mulberry; densely populated; many industl. ts., Milan, Novara, Pavia, etc.; length 250 m., width from 50 to 120 m.

**Lombok**, one of the lesser Sunda Is., Indonesia, Malay Archipelago; mtns., peak of Lombok 11,810 ft., volcanic; Wallace's Line passes between Lombok and Bali; ch. t. Mataram; p. 701,298.

**Lomé**, *spt.*, *cap.*, Togo, W. Africa; on G. of Guinea; deep water pt. exp. cacao, cotton, palm prods.; phosphates; p. (estd. 1964) 80,000.

**Lomme**, *commune*, Nord, France; spinning, hats; p. (1954) 23,483.

**Lomond, L.**, between Dunbarton and Stirling cos., Scot.; contains 30 Is.; lgst. loch in Scot.; length 20 m.; a. 27 sq. m.

**Lomond Hills**, Kinross and Fife, Scot.; alt. 1,713 ft. and 1,471 ft.

**Lomza**, *t.*, Poland; on Narew R.; grain, timber; p. (1965) 22,000.

**London**, *cap. c.*, *spt.*, Eng.; on R. Thames; inc. 12 inner and 20 outer bors.; tourist ctr., lge. tr., gr. fin., industl. and cult. ctr.; univ.; many historic bldgs.; p. (1966) 7,914,000 (Greater London); (1966) 4,600 (c.).

**London**, *t.*, Ontario, Canada; on R. Thames, 65 m. W. of Hamilton; industl. ctr.; univ.; p. (1961) 181,283.

**Londonderry**, *co.*, N. Ireland; a. 816 sq. m.; p. (1966) 118,664.

**Londonderry** (or Derry), *co. bor.*, N. Ireland; on left bank of R. Foyle, 4 m. upstream from Lough Foyle; shirt mftg.; textiles; acetylene from naphtha; training ctr. for ind.; p. (1966) 55,681.

**Londonderry**, *O.*, jutting into Timor Sea, W. Australia.

**Long Beach**, *c.*, Cal., U.S.A.; tourism; petrol, shipbldg., fishing, canning, aircraft, chemicals; p. (1960) 344,168.

**Long Beach**, *t.*, Long I., N.Y., U.S.A.; holiday resort; p. (1960) 26,473.

**Longbenton**, *t.*, *urb. dist.*, Northumberland, Eng.; 3 m. N.E. of Newcastle; coal-mng.; p. (estd. 1967) 48,480.

**Long Branch**, *c.*, N.J., U.S.A.; seaside resort; p. (1960) 26,228.

**Long Eaton**, *t.*, *urb. dist.*, Derby, Eng.; on R. Trent. 5 m. S.W. of Nottingham; rly. wks., lace mftg., elec. cables, flexible tubing, hosiery; p. (estd. 1967) 32,430.

**Longford**, *co.*, Leinster, Ireland; peat bogs; dairy farming; a. 421 sq. m.; p. (1966) 28,943.

**Longford**, *co. t.*, Longford, Ireland; agr. ctr.; p. (1966) 3,421.

**Long Forties Bank**, *submarine sandbank*, N. Sea; 80 m. E. of Aberdeen; valuable fishing-grounds; depth of water, from 25 to 40 fathoms.

**Long I.**, part of N.Y., U.S.A.; separated from mainland by East R.; contains Queens and Brooklyn, bors. of New York City; mkt. gardening, fisheries, oysters, holiday resorts; a. 1,682 sq. m.

**Long I.**, Bahamas Is., W.I.; p. (1953) 3,755.

**Long I. City**, part of Queen's bor., N.Y., U.S.A.; industl. ctr.; food, engin., leather.

**Long, Loch**, *arm of sea*, between Dunbarton and Argyll, Scot.; length 17 m.

**Longmeadow**, *t.*, S.W. Mass., U.S.A.; residtl.; p. (1960) 10,547.

**Longreach**, *t.*, Queensland, Australia; in ctr. of Gr. Australian (artesian) basin, 400 m. W. of Rockhampton; where rly. from cst. crosses R. Thompson; collecting and forwarding ctr. for cattle and wool; p. (1966) 3,864.

**Longridge**, *t.*, *urb. dist.*, Lancs, Eng.; 6 m. N.E. of Preston; cotton, nails; p. (1961) 4,677.

**Long's Peak**, *mtn.*, Col., U.S.A.; alt. 14,271 ft.

Longueuil, *t.*, Quebec, Canada; p. (1961) *24,131*.

Longview, *t.*, Texas, U.S.A.; p. (1960) *40,050*.

Longview, *t.*, Wash., U.S.A.; p. (1960) *23,349*.

Longwy, *t.*, Meurthe-et-Moselle, France; fortfd.; iron, porcelain; p. (1962) *22,214*.

Long Xuyen, *mkt. t.*, S. Vietnam; p. *148,000*.

Lons-le-Saunier, *cap.*, Jura, France; salt springs; wine, agr.; livestock; p. (1962) *19,041*.

Looe, *urb. dist.*, Cornwall, Eng.; on Looe estuary; holiday resort; p. (1961) *3,878*.

Lookland, *t.*, S.W. Ohio, U.S.A.; chemicals, paper, light mnfs.; p. (1960) *5,292*. [p. (1954) *14,882*.

Loos, *t.*, Pas-de-Calais, France; coal-mining;

Lop Nor, *marsh*, Sinkiang, W. China; in Tarim Basin at foot of Altyn Tagh; ctr. of inland drainage, receives water from R. Tarim.

Lorain, *c.*, Ohio, U.S.A.; on L. Erie; shipbldg., steelwks., fisheries; p. (1960) *68,932*.

Lorca, *t.*, Murcia, Spain; agr. prod., woollens, chemicals; bishop's palace; p. (1959) *61,557*.

Lord Howe I., Australian I., S. Pac. Oc., length 7 m., width 1½ m.; *c.* 436 m. N.E. of Sydney; palm seed ind.; p. (1958) *223*.

Lorena, *c.*, S.E. Brazil; cotton, coffee; p. *10,262*.

Lorestan, *see* Luristan.

Loreto, *t.*, Ancona, Italy; pilgrim ctr.; p. *6,700*.

Loreto, *dep.*, Peru; rubber; cap. Iquitos; a. 119,270 sq. m.; p. (1961) *330,335*.

Lorient, *spt.*, Morbihan, France; on Bay of Biscay; govt. dockyds. and arsenal; metals, fishing; p. (1962) *63,924*.

Lörrach, *t.*, Baden–Württemberg, Germany; N.E. of Basle; textiles, tobacco, chocolate mnfs., machin.; p. (1963) *31,200*.

Lorraine, *prov.*, France; agr. wine, iron.

Los Angeles, *c.*, S. Cal., U.S.A., booming modern c. (" the city of angels "), busiest pt. in Cal.; fine harbour; one of world's lgst. urban areas; 400 m. of freeway (1,500 m. planned by 1980); many prosperous inds., inc. aircraft, missiles, chemicals, machin., electronic equipment, food processing; film ctr.; fine climate; p. (1960) *2,479,015*; of Greater Los Angeles *c.* 7,000,000.

Los Angeles, *cap. c.*, Bio Bio, Chile; wine, fruit, timber; p. (1960) *79,000*.

Losinj, *I.*, Jugoslavia; summer resort, tr.

Los Rios, *prov.*, Ecuador, S. America; a. 2,295 sq. m.; cap. Babahoyo; p. (estd. 1962) *244,651*.

Los Santos, *prov.*, Panama, Central America; cap. Las Tablas; p. (1960) *70,554*.

Lossiemouth, *burgh*, Moray, Scot.; on Moray F., 5 m. N. of Elgin; fishing; p. (1961) *5.855*.

Lot, *R.*, S. France; trib. of Garonne R.; length 272 m.

Lot, *dep.*, S.W. France; livestock, wine, cereals, coal, iron; a. 2,018 sq. m.; cap. Cahors; p. (1962) *149,929*. [(1961) *51,679*.

Lota, *pt.*, Chile; coal-mng. ctr.; ceramics; p.

Lot-et-Garonne, *dep.*, S.W. France; agr. (cereals, vines, fruit); cap. Agen; a. 2,079 sq. m.; p. (1962) *275,028*.

Lothians, *Scottish dist.*, S. of F. of Forth, cos. Mid Lothian, W. Lothian and E. Lothian.

Lötschental, *picturesque valley*, can. Valais, Switzerland; ch. vil., Kippel.

Loughborough, *t.*, *mun. bor.*, Leicester, Eng.; on R. Soar 10 m. N. of Leicester; engin., elec. gds., chemicals, textiles; univ.; p. (estd. 1967) *39,580*.

Loughor, *R.*, Glamorgan, S. Wales; rises in Black Mtns., flows S.W. into Bristol Channel; lower valley submerged to form estuary, length 8 m., width 4 m., around which cluster steel-wks. and zinc refineries of Llanelly, Bynea, Gorseinon, Gowerton, etc.

Loughton, *t.*, Essex, Eng.; on border of Epping Forest; residtl.; p. (1961) *33,864*.

Louisiana, *st.*, U.S.A.; agr., tobacco, cotton, sugar, timber, minerals and mfg., oil, gas; cap. Baton Rouge; ch. spt. New Orleans; a. 48,523 sq. m.; p. (1960) *3,257,022*.

Louisville, *c.*, Ky., U.S.A.; on Ohio R.; univ.; lgst. tobacco mkt. in world; chemicals, paints, cars, machin., elec. goods, synthetic rubber; p. (1960) *390,639*.

Loulé, *t.*, Portugal; esparto-grass ctr.; porcelain, leather; p. *23,000*.

Lourdes, *t.*, France; on R. Pau; great pilgrim ctr.; slate, marble; p. (1962) *16,376*.

Lourenço Marques, *cap.*, *spt.*, Mozambique, Port. E. Africa; rly. terminus, coaling-sta., oil refining; lge deposits of bentonite being worked in a. p. (1961) *183,798* inc. 62,000 Europeans.

Louth, *t.*, *mun. bor.*, Lindsey, Lincoln, Eng.; on E. edge of Lincoln Wolds; abbey ruins; cattle mkt., farm implements, rope mkg., lime, malting, canning; p. (estd. 1967) *11,470*.

Louth, *maritime co.*, Leinster, Ireland; mtns., bog and barren land; salmon fishing; cap. Dundalk; a. 316 sq. m.; p. (1966) *69,162*.

Louvain, *t.*, Belgium; univ.; lace, brewing, tobacco mftg.; p. (1962) *32,474*.

Louviers, *t.*, Eure, France; on R. Eure; cloth mftg.; p. (1962) *13,668*.

Loveland, *t.*, N. Col. U.S.A.; beet-sugar refined, vegetables, fruit canning; p. (1960) *9,734*.

Low Archipelago, *see* Tuamotu Is.

Low Countries. Name applied to Belgium and The Netherlands. *See under separate headings.*

Lowell, *c.*, Mass., U.S.A.; at junction of Merrimac and Concord Rs.; 30 m. N. of Boston; textiles, machin., chemicals, carpets; James Whistler, the artist, born here; p. (1960) *92,107*.

Lower Austria, *prov.*, Austria; industl., agr.; ch. t. Vienna; a. 7,098 sq. m.; p. (1961) *1,374,012*.

Lower Hutt, *c.*, N.I., New Zealand; p. (1964) *55,900*.

Lower Saxony, *Land*, Germany; a. 18,226 sq. m. p. (1961) *6,641,000*.

Lowestoft, *spt.*, *mun. bor.*, Suffolk, Eng.; on E. Anglian cst. 9 m. S. of Gr. Yarmouth; holiday resort, fishing ctr., boat bldg., engin., vehicle mftg.; p. (estd. 1967) *49,160*.

Lowther Hills, *mtns.*, between Dumfries and Lanark, Scot.; highest point 2,403 ft.

Loyalty Is., S. Pac. Oc.; included in French administration of New Caledonia; copra; lgst. Is., Maré, Lifou, Uvéa; a. about 800 sq. m.

Loyang, *c.*, Honan prov., China; industl.; ball bearing and mng. machin.; p. (1958) *500,000*.

Lozère, *dep.*, S.E. France; traversed by Cévennes Mtns.; agr., silkworm-rearing, stock-raising; cap. Mende; a. 1,996 sq. m.; p. (1962) *81,868*.

Lualaba, *R.*, Congo, Central Africa; rises nr. Elisabethville in Katanga prov., flows N. approx. 500 m. to Kikondja, where joined by R. Lufira to form R. Congo; name also applied to main stream of R. Congo as far downstream as Ponthierville.

Luanda, *cap.*, *pt.*, Angola; oil refining; hydroelec. wks; p. (1962) *220,000* inc. 55,000 whites.

Luang Prabang, *c.*, Laos, on Mekong R.; silk, ivory, rubber; pagoda; (1962) *8,000*.

Lubbock, *c.*, N. Texas, U.S.A.; p. (1960) *128,691*.

Lübeck, *c.*, *spt.*, cap. Schleswig-Holstein, Germany; on R. Trave; cath.; shipbldg., machin., chemicals, textiles, iron, foodstuffs; pt. and rly. junction; p. (1963) *236,000*.

Lublin, *prov.* E. Poland; agr.; a. 10,834 sq. in. p. (1965) *1,901,000*.

Lublin, *t.*, *prov. cap.*, Poland; textiles, engin. agr. tr.; cath., 2 univs.; p. (1965) *203,000*.

Lubnaig, *Loch*, Perth, Scot.; drains to R. Teith by the R. Leny.   [engin., chemicals; p. *23,332*.

Lubny, *t.*, Ukrainian S.S.R.; on rly. E. of Kiev;

Lubumbashi (Elizabethville), *t.*, Katanga, Congo; copper mng. ctr.; p. (1959) *183,808* inc. 13,808 whites.

Lucca, *c.*, *cap.* Lucca, Tuscany, Italy; nr. Pisa; cath., churches; jute mftg., tobacco, silk, cotton, and oil-refining inds.; p. (1961) *85,940*.

Lucena, *t.*, Córdoba, Spain; olive oil, ceramics, gilt metals; p. (1957) *35,830*.

Lucenec, *t.*, ČSSR.; on Hungarian border; magnesite, textiles, sawmilling; p. (1961) *16,102*.

Lucera, *t.*, Apulia, Italy; 8 m. W. of Foggia; cas., cath.; silk mftg.; p. *17,000*.

Lucerne (Luzern), *can.*, Switzerland; agr., pastoral, vineyards; oil refinery projected at Schötz/Ettiswil; cap. Lucerne; a. 576 sq. m.; p. (1961) *253,446*.

Lucerne (Luzern), *t.*, *cap.*, Lucerne can., Switzerland; at W. end of L. Lucerne; light inds.; impt. tourist ctr.; p. (1961) *70,600*.

Lucerne, *L.*, Switzerland; also known as Lake of the Four Cantons; length 23 m.

Luchow (Luzhou), *c.*, Szechwan, China; coal, iron, kaolin; synthetic ammonia plant; p. (1953) *289,000*.

Luckenwalde, *t.*, Potsdam, E. Germany; on R. Nuthe; textiles, footwear, machin., wood and metals, chemicals; p. (1963) *28,741*.

Lucknow, *c.*, cap. Uttar Pradesh India; on R. Gumti; rly. ctr., muslin embroidery, brocade mftg.; famous defence of L. in Indian Mutiny 1857; univ.; p. (1961) *655,673*.

Lüdenscheid, t., N. Rhine–Westphalia, Germany; S.E. of Barmen; hardware; p. (1963) 58,500.

Lüderitz, t., S.W. Africa; on cst. of Kalahari desert; linked by rly. to S. African rly. system at De Aar; diamonds; p. (1960) 3,604.

Ludhiana, t., Punjab, India; nr. R. Sutlej, W. of Simla; p. (1961) 244,032.

Ludington, t., Mich., U.S.A.; on Lake M.; wood-wkg.; p. (1960) 9,421.

Ludlow, rural bor., Salop., Eng.; at foot of Clee Hills on R. Teme; agr. mkt., agr. implements, meters, gauges; p. of t. (1961) 6,774.

Ludvika, t., Sweden; elec. goods; p. (1961) 12,253.

Ludwigsburg, t., Baden-Württemberg, Germany; N. of Stuttgart; cas.; textiles, foodstuffs, machin., toys; p. (1963) 75,500.

Ludwig's Canal, Germany; unites Rs. Danube and Main; length 110 m.

Ludwigshafen, t., Rhine-Palatinate, Germany; on R. Rhine, opposite Mannheim; chemicals, marine diesel engines, metallurgy, glass; R. pt. and rly. junction; oil pipeline from Rotterdam under construction; p. (1963) 171,500.

Lufkin, c., Texas, U.S.A.; lumber, engin.; food prod.; p. (1960) 17,641.

Lug, R., trib. of R. Wye, Hereford, Eng.

Lugano, t., Ticino, Switzerland; on L. Lugano; tourist ctr., silk, paper; p. (1957) 19,112.

Lugano, L., Italy-Switzerland; length 16 m.

Lugansk, industl. t., Ukraine S.S.R.; S. of R. Donets in Donbas region; impt. rly. eng. factories; textiles; p. (1967) 339,000.

Lugnaquilia, mtn., Wicklow, Ireland; highest point in Wicklow Mtns., alt. 3,039 ft.

Lugo, prov., N.W. Spain; fisheries, leather; cap. Lugo; a. 3,815 sq. m.; p. (1959) 500,643.

Lugo, t., prov. cap., Spain; on R. Minho; tanning, textiles; p. (1959) 50,137.

Luichow (Luizhou), c., Kwangsi Chuang, China; comm. ctr.; p. (1953) 159,000.

Lukuga, intermittent outlet of L. Tanganyika, Africa, linking with R. Congo.

Luleå, spt., N. Sweden; on Lule R. at head of G. of Bothnia; iron ore, timber, engin.; p. (1961) 65,237.

Lulworth Cove, sm. inlet, Dorset, Eng.; on S. cst., 9 m. E. of Weymouth; formed by sea breaching hard coastal rocks and eroding softer rocks behind; tourists.

Lumbira, t., on N. shore of L. Nyasa, Tanzania.

Lund, t., Sweden; nr. Malmö; univ.; packaging ind.; steam boilers; p. (1961) 40,380.

Lundy I., Bristol Channel; 12 m. N.W. of Hartland Point, N. Devon, Eng.; 2½ m. long by 1 m. wide.

Lune, R., Lancs. and Westmorland, Eng.; flows [45 m. to Irish Sea.

Lüneburg, t., Lower Saxony, Germany; S.E. of Hamburg, on Ilmenau R.; chemicals, wood, iron, paper; rly. junct.; p. (1963) 60,900.

Lünen, t., N. Rhine–Westphalia, Germany; N.E. of Dortmund; coal, metallurgy, glass, wood; R. pt. and rly. ctr.; p. (1963) 72,200.

Lunéville, t., Meurthe-et-Moselle, France; S.E. of Nancy, on R. Meurthe; cottons, woollens, hosiery, porcelain; p. (1962) 24,463.

Lungchow, t., Kwangsi, China; nr. Vietnam frontier; military sta.; p. 13,600.

Lungi, t., Sierra Leone, W. Africa; nr. Freetown; only civil airport in st.

Lupata Gorge, Mozambique, Port. E. Africa; narrow pass occupied by R. Zambesi.

Lurgan, t., mun. bor., Armagh, N. Ireland; textiles, tobacco mftg.; p. (1966) 20,677.

Luristan (Lorestan), dist., W. Iran; mainly mtnous; cap. Khorramabad; p. (1967) 688,139.

Lushun, see Port Arthur.

Luta, special mun., S. Liaoning prov., China: comprising Port Arthur Naval Base District and the pts. of Port Arthur and Talien (Dairen).

Luton, t., co. bor., Beds., Eng.; in Chiltern Hills nr. source of R. Lea; motor vehicles, engin., hat mkg., aircraft, gear instruments, chemicals; p. (estd. 1967) 153,520.

Lutong, pt., N. Sarawak, Malaysia; oil refining.

Lutsk, t., Ukrainian S.S.R.; comm. ctr., mnfs.; p. (1959) 49,000.

Luxembourg, prov., S.E. Belgium; on French border; wooded and hilly; a. 1,705 sq. m.; cap. Arlon; p. (1962) 216,975.

Luxembourg, grand duchy, Europe; on borders of France, Germany, Belgium; upland, much over 1,000 ft.; very impt. deposits of iron ore;

cap. Luxembourg; a. 999 sq. m.; p. (1960) 314,889.

Luxembourg, t., cap., Luxembourg; in S. of Grand Duchy; iron and steel, heavy engin., leather, paper inds.; p. (1960) 71,653.

Luxor, vil., Upper U.A.R.; on E. bank of R. Nile; site of Thebes; ruined temples; p. 5,000.

Luzon, I., lgst. in Philippines; mtns.; cotton, coffee, sugar, cereals, coal, copper; cap. Manila; a. 40,420 sq. m.; p. (1960) 12,875,100.

Lvov, (Pol. Lwów, Ger. Lemberg), c., Ukraine, U.S.S.R.; ceded by Poland 1939; univ., 3 caths.; engin., textiles, chemicals oil-refining, sawmilling; p. (1967) 502,000.

Lyallpur, t., W. Punjab, Pakistan; univ.; cotton, chemicals, fertilisers; p. (1961) 425,200.

Lydd, mkt. t., mun. bor., Kent, Eng.; on Romney Marsh, 4 m. S.W. of New Romney; "lyddite" shells, concrete; airport; p. (estd. 1967) 4,170

Lydda, c., Israel; rly. junction, airport; mentioned in the Bible, and the reputed birthplace of St. George; p. (estd.) 20,000.

Lydenburg, t., Transvaal, S. Africa; gold, cotton, wheat, sheep; p. (1960) 7,393 inc. 3,306 whites.

Lydford, par. and vil., Devon, Eng.; old stannary ctr. for Devon; p. 2,200.

Lydney, par., Gloucester, Eng.; in Forest of Dean; iron, coal; p. 4,158. [alt. 2,000 ft.

Lyell, mtn., Stanley Range, N.S.W., Australia;

Lyell, mtn., Cal., U.S.A.; in Sierra Nevada; alt. 13,190 ft.

Lyme Regis, spt., mun. bor., Dorset, Eng.; on bdy. between Devon and Dorset; holiday resort, p. (estd. 1967) 3,300.

Lymington, t., mun. bor., Hants, Eng.; on The Solent at mouth of R. Lymington; small spt., yachting; p. (estd. 1967) 32,580.

Lymm, t., urb. dist., Cheshire, Eng.; 5 m. W. of Altrincham; salt mftg.; mainly residtl.; p. (1961) 7,330. [19,881

Lynbrook, t., Long I., N.Y., U.S.A.; p. (1960)

Lynchburg, c., Va., U.S.A.; footwear, agr. implements, tobacco; p. (1960) 54,790.

Lyndhurst, t., N.J., U.S.A.; synthetic perfumery; p. (1960) 21,867.

Lynemouth, nr. Blyth, Northumberland, Eng.; aluminium smelter projected.

Lynher, R., Cornwall, Eng.; length 26 m.

Lynn, spt., Mass., U.S.A.; footwear, elec. appliances; p. (1960) 944,78. [of Chatham strait.

Lynn Canal, fiord. Alaska, U.S.A.; continuation

Lynton, t., urb. dist., N. Devon, Eng.; 17 m. W. of Minehead on Bristol Channel; seaside tourist ctr. of Exmoor; p. (1961) 1,918. [31,614.

Lynwood, t., S.W. Cal., U.S.A.; engin.; p. (1960)

Lyon, c., Iowa, U.S.A., on Mississippi R.; p. (1960) 14,468. [38 m.

Lyon, R., Perth, Scot.; trib. of R. Tay; length

Lyonnais, mtns., France; W. of Lyons.

Lyons, c. cap., Rhône dep., France; at confluence of Rs. Saône and Rhône; comm. ctr., silk, rayon, chemicals, engin.; heavy lorries; univ.; oil refinery nearby; world ctr. for cancer research; p. (1962) 535,784.

Lys, R., Belgium and France, trib. of R. Scheldt; length 100 m. [length 25 m.

Lysterfiord, N.E. arm of the Sogne fiord, Norway;

Lytham St. Annes, t., mun. bor., N. Lancs, Eng.; on N. cst. of Ribble estuary, 4. m. S. of Blackpool; holiday ctr., shipbldg.; p. (estd. 1967) 36,620.

Lyttelton, spt., S.I., N.Z.; on N. cst. of Banks Peninsula; ch. pt. of Canterbury Plain; exp. mutton, wool, wheat; p. (1961) 3,403.

Lyubertsy, t., R.S.F.S.R., industl. sub. on Moscow-Kazan rly.; agr. engin.; p. (1967) 115,000.

# M

Ma'an, t., S. Jordan, term. of rly. through Amman to Beirut; restoration of Hijaz rail line to Medina (1964–7); p. (1961) 6,899.

Maas, R., Dutch name for the R. Meuse after it has entered the Netherlands.

Maasin, mun., S.W. Leyte, Philippine Is.; cst. tr.; hemp; p. 29,264.

Maastricht, t., cap., Limburg, Neth.; on R. Meuse; pottery, glass, textiles, brewing; p. (1967) 95,393.

Mablethorpe and Sutton, t., urb. dist., Lindsey, Lincs, Eng.; on E. cst., 15 m. N. of Skegness; holiday resort; p. (1961) 5,389.

Macao, *Port. terr.*, S. China; consists of peninsula and 2 sm. Is. (Taipa and Colôane) to S. of estuary of Canton R.; a. 6 sq. m.; oldest European col. in Asia (1557); p. (estd. 1965) *174,000.*

Macao, *c.*, Macao terr., S. China; occupies peninsula section of the terr.; impt. fisheries.

Macapá, *cap.*, Amapa st., Brazil; at mouth of R. Amazon; p. (1960) *46,905.*

Macassar, *ch. t., pt.*, Sulawesi, *see* Makasar.

Macassar, *strait*, Indonesia, *see* Makasar.

Macau, *spt.*, Rio Grande do Norte, Brazil; p. *6,556.*

Macclesfield, *t., mun. bor.*, Cheshire, Eng.; at foot of Pennines, 10 m. S. of Stockport; on R. Bollin; mkt., textiles, clothing, paper prods., engin.; p. (estd. 1967) *40,900.*

Macdonald Is., *terr.* of Australia, Antarctica.

Macdonnell Range, *mtns.*, Northern Terr., Australia; highest part of desert tableland, centrally situated within the continent; some gold and mica mines, but development hampered by aridity and isolation; highest alt. 4,482 ft.

Macduff, *spt. burgh*, Banff, Scot.; 2 m. E. of Banff; fishing; p. (1961) *3,479.*

Macedonia, *dist.*, Greece; cereals tobacco, fruit, opium, fishing; p. (1961) *1,890,654.*

Macedonia, *fed. unit*, Jugoslavia; cap. Skopje; a. 10,598 sq. m.; p. (1960) *1,387,000.*

Maceió, *spt., cap.*, Alagoas st., Brazil; cotton, sugar, tobacco, soap, sawmills, distilleries; p. (1960) *170,134.*

Macerata, *prov. cap.*, Italy; cath., univ.; terra-cotta, glass, chemicals; p. (1961) *37,464.*

Macgillicuddy's Reeks, *mtns.*, Kerry, Ireland; highest peak, Carrantuohill, alt. 3,414 ft.

Machala, *t.*, S.W. Ecuador; cocoa, coffee, leather, gold; p. (1962) *22,730.*

Machynlleth, *t., urb. dist.*, Montgomery, Wales, on R. Dovey; tourist ctr., clothing mftg.; p. (1961) *1,903.*

Macintyre, *R.*, N.S.W., Australia; forms border between Queensland and N.S.W.; trib. of R. Darling; length 350 m.

Mackay, *spt.*, Queensland, Australia; on R. Pioneer; sugar, dairying and banana ctr.; p. (1966) *24,566.*

Mackenzie, *township*, Guyana; bauxite; p. approx. *15,000* mostly Negro.

Mackenzie, *dist.*, N.W. Terrs., Canada; a. 527,490 sq. m.; forests and tundra; oil, radium, uranium; furs and timber.

Mackenzie, *R.*, N.W. Terrs., Canada; rises in Rocky Mtns. as Athabaska R. and flows into L. Athabaska, leaves as Slave R. and thence into Gr. Slave L., which it leaves as M. R. into Beaufort Sea; length 2,350 m.

Mackinac Sound, connects Ls. Michigan and Huron, N. America.

Mackinney, *c.*, N.E. Texas, U.S.A.; cotton ctr.; (1960) *13,763.*

Macmillan, *R.*, N.W. Terrs., Canada; trib. of Yukon R.

Macnean, *L.*, cos. Leitrim and Fermanagh, Ireland.

Macomb, *c.*, Ill., U.S.A.; industl.; p. (1960) *12,135.*

Mâcon, *t., cap.*, Saône-et-Loire, France; on R. Saône; ruined cath.; agr. implements, wines, copper; rope; p. (1962) *30,671.*

Macon, *c.*, Ga., U.S.A.; on Ocmulgee R.; univ.; rly. junction, ironwks., cotton mftg.; p. (1960) *69,764.*

Macon, *t.*, E. Miss., U.S.A.; cotton, dairying, lumbering; p. (1960) *2,432.*

Macquarie, I., *Australian I.*, S. Pacific; 900 m. S.E. of Tasmania, Australia; 21 m. long, 2 m. wide; uninhabited except for meteorological and research base.

Macquarie, *R.*, N.S.W., Australia; trib. of R. Darling; length 350 m.

Macroom, *t.*, Cork, Ireland; on R. Sullane; agr. tr., fishing; p. (1961) *2,169.*

Mactan, *I.*, off Cebu, Philippine Is.; mangroves, coconuts; a. 24 sq. m.; p. *40,103.*

Madagascan Republic, *see* Malagasy.

Madang, *t.*, Papua–New Guinea; copra ctr.; p. *500.*

Madawaska, *t.*, Me., U.S.A.; spt.; lumber, pulp, paper-mills; p. (1960) *4,035.*

Madawaska, *R.*, Ontario, Canada; trib. of Ottawa R.; length 230 m.

Maddalena, *I.*, off N.E. cst. of Sardinia, Italy.

Maddaloni, *t.*, Naples, Italy; p. *21,975.*

Madeira, *Portuguese I.*, Atl. Oc.; wine, sugar, fruits; holiday resort; cap. Funchal; a. 315 sq. m.; p. (1963) *268,700.*

Madeira, *R.*, Brazil; trib. of R. Amazon; together with Mamoré R.; l. 2,000 m.

Madeley, *t.*, Salop, Eng.; on R. Severn; mkt., coal- and iron-mining; p. *7,300.*

Madera, *t.*, central Cal., U.S.A.; agr., lumber, wines; p. (1960) *14,430.*

Madhya Bharat, formerly a st., absorbed by Madhya Pradesh, 1 Nov. 1956.

Madhya Pradesh, *st.*, Indian Union; absorbed the sts. of Bhopal, Uindhya Pradesh, and Madhya Bharat 1 Nov. 1956; rice, jute, pulses, oilseeds, cotton; forests; manganese, coal, marble, limestone; cotton textiles; cap. Bhopal; a. 171,217 sq. m.; p. (1961) *32,372,408.*

Madinat Al Shaab, *cap.*, South Yemen People's Rep.

Madison, *c.*, Ind., U.S.A.; on Ohio R.; mftg.; p. (1960) *10,097.*

Madison, *t.*, Ill., U.S.A.; heavy engin. wks.; p. (1960) *6,861.*

Madison, *cap.*, Wis., U.S.A.; univ.; agr. tools, machin., footwear; p. (1960) *126,706.*

Madison Heights, *t.*, Mich., U.S.A.; p. (1960) *33,343.*

Madisonville, *t.*, Ky., U.S.A.; p. (1960) *13,110.*

Madras, *see* Tamil Nadu.

Madras, *c.*, *spt., cap.*, Tamil Nadu, S. India; on S.E. (Coromandel) cst.; cath., univ.; comm. ctr., cottons, tanning, brewing, potteries, rly. coaches; oil refinery projected; p. (1961) *1,729,141.*

Madre de Dios, *dep.*, E. Peru; ch. t. Maldonado; forested; gold, silver; a. 58,827 sq. m.; p. (1961) *13,437.*

Madre de Dios, *R.*, Bolivia; trib. of R. Madeira; rises in Peru.

Madrid, *cap.*, Spain; on R. Manzanares; univ., cath., palace; Prado; gold and silver work; leather goods; chemicals, furniture mftg.; p. (estd. 1967) *3,000,000.*

Madrid, *prov.*, Spain; agr., freestone, granite, gypsum quarried; a. 3,089 sq. m.; cap. M.; p. (1967) *3,270,000.*

Madura, I., Indonesia; off N.E. of Java; cereals, coconuts, fishing, cattle rearing, salt; a. 1,770 sq. m.; p. (1930) *1,962,462.*

Madurai, *c.*, Tamil Nadu, India; univ.; coffee, muslin, brasswk., wood carving; p. (1961) *424,810.*

Maebashi, *c.*, Honshu, Japan; mulberry trees, silk production; p. (1964) *190,000.*

Maelstrom, *whirlpool*, N.W. cst., Norway.

Maentwrog, *vil.*, Merioneth, N. Wales; in Vale of Festiniog, 2 m. E. of Festiniog; ch. hydro-elec. power-sta. in N. Wales.

Maesteg, *t., urb. dist.*, Glamorgan, Wales; dorm. t. for steel wks. at Pt. Talbot; coal-mining, cos-metics; p. (1961) *21,652.*

Mafeking, *t.*, C. Prov., S. Africa; famous siege, 1899–1900; p. (1960) *3,279* inc. *4,159* whites.

Magadan, *spt.* R.S.F.S.R.; on N. side of Sea of Okhotsk; engin.; p. (1959) *62,000.*

Magallanes, *prov.*, Chile; sheep-rearing; cap. Punta Arenas; fox breeding; petroleum; a. 52,271 sq. m.; p. (1960) *73,037.*

Magdalen, Is., G. of St. Lawrence, Canada.

Magdalena, *dep.*, Colombia; coffee, cotton, rubber; cap. Santa Marta; a. 20,813 sq. m.; p. (estd. 1961) *500,640.*

Magdalena, *R.*, Colombia; length 1,000 m.

Magdeburg, *c.*, Magdeburg, E. Germany; on R. Elbe; cath.; beet-sugar, chemicals, iron, steel, mng. machin., heavy engin.; route ctr. and R. pt.; p. (1963) *267,733*

Magelang, *t.*, Java, Indonesia; tr. ctr.; p. (1961) *96,454.*

Magellan, *strait*, between Tierra del Fuego and Chile, S. America.

Magenta, *t.*, N. Italy; nr. Milan; silk, matches; p. *12,650.*

Magenwil, Aargau, Switzerland; oil refinery projected.

Maggiore, *L.*, N. Italy–Switzerland; a. 82 sq. m.; contains Borromean Is.; tourist re-sort.

Maghreb, collective name given to Arabic speaking countries bordering Mediterranean in N. Africa (Morocco to Libya).

Magnet Mtn., S. Urals, R.S.F.S.R.; very rich

deposit of magnetite iron ore; smelted at Magnitogorsk, and in Kuzbas region.

**Magnitogorsk**, *t.*, R.S.F.S.R.; at S. end of Ural Mtns.; iron, steel, engin., iron ore, chemicals; term. of oil pipeline from Shkapovo in Bashkiria; p. (1967) 352,000.          [p. (1961) 13,139.

**Magog**, *t.*, S. Quebec, Canada; textiles, mnfs.;

**Mahad Al-Dhahab**, *t.*, Hejaz, Saudi-Arabia; between Mecca and Medina; gold-mining.

**Mahalla El Kubra**, *t.*, Lower U.A.R.; p. (1960) 63,000.

**Mahanadi**, *R.*, India; flows from Orissa to Bay of Bengal; length 520 m.          [p. (1960) 8,536.

**Mahanoy City**, *t.*, Penns., U.S.A.; anthracite;

**Maharashtra**, *st.*, India; ch. ts.: Greater Bombay (cap.), Poona, Nagpur, Sholapur, Kolhapur, Amravati, Nasik, Malegaon, Nagar, Akola, Ulhasnagar, Thana; a. 118,717 sq. m.; p. (1961) 39,553,718.

**Mahé**, *former Fr. prov.*, S. India; united with India 1954; cap. Mahé.          [cheese; p. 18,220.

**Mahon**, *spt. cap.*, Minorca, Balearic Is., Spain;

**Maidenhead**, *t.*, *mun. bor.*, Berks, Eng.; on R. Thames, 9 m. above Windsor; light engin., printing, jam mkg.; p. (estd. 1967) 43,700.

**Maidens, The**, *gr. of dangerous rocks*, nr. Larne, off Antrim cst., N. Ireland.

**Maidstone**, *co. t.*, *mun. bor.*, Kent, Eng.; on R. Medway; hops, fruit ctr.; brewing, paper, agr. tools, confectionery; p. (estd. 1967) 65,790.

**Maikop**, *t.*, Adgeysk, U.S.S.R.; oil-refineries; woodwkg., food inds.; p. (1959) 82,000.

**Main**, *R.*, Germany; trib. of R. Rhine; l. 304 m.

**Main**, *Hudson Bay Co's.* fort, at mouth R. Main R., Labrador, Canada.

**Maine**, *st.*, New England, U.S.A.; mtns., with much forest; potatoes, paper pulp, metals, woollens, shoes, processed foods; cap. Augusta; ch. spt. Portland; a. 33,215 sq. m.; p. (1960) 969,265.

**Maine**, *R.*, France; formed by junction of Sarthe and Mayenne, flows 7 m. to R. Loire at Angers.

**Maine-et-Loire**, *dep.*, France; agr., vineyards; cap. Angers; a. 2,811 sq. m.; p. (1962) 556,272.

**Mainland**. (1) *I.*, lgst. of Shetlands, Scot. (2) *I.*, lgst. of Orkneys, *see* Pomona.

**Mainz**, *c.*, *cap.* Rhineland-Palatinate, Germany; at confluence of Rs. Rhine and Main; R. pt.; cath., univ. cas.; cement, engin., optical glass, food processing; p. (1963) 139,400.

**Maioli**, *t.*, Taiwan; fertilisers.

**Maison-Carrée**, *commune*, N. Algeria; 5 m. E. of Algiers; p. 24,341.

**Maisons-Alfort**, *t.*, Seine, France; p. (1962) 51,689.

**Maisons-Laffitte**, *t.*, Yvelines, France; p. (1962) 19,385.

**Maitland**, *t.*, N.S.W., Australia; on R. Hunter, nr. Newcastle; agr., pastoral ctr., coal-mining, textiles; p. (1966) 23,105.

**Maizuru**, *c.*, *spt.*, Honshu, Japan; naval base; sheet glass; p. (1960) 99,615.

**Majorca or Mallorca**, *see* Balearic Is.

**Majunga**, *spt.*, Malagasy; on N.W. cst., at mouth of R. Ikopa; p. (1957) 50,356.          [384,000.

**Makasar**, *ch. t.*, *pt.*, Sulawesi, Indonesia; p. (1961)

**Makasar**, *strait*, Indonesia; separates Kalimantan from Sulawesi; 240 m. wide.

**Makeyevka**, *t.*, Ukrainian S.S.R.; iron and steel, engin. coal; p. (1967) 410,000.

**Makhachkala**, *spt.*, R.S.F.S.R.; oil-refining, chemicals, textiles, engin.; p. (1967) 153,000.

**Makó**, *t.*, Hungary; agr.; flour milling; p. (1962) 29,541.          [m.; p. (estd.1951) 143,000.

**Makran**, *reg.*, W. Pakistan-Iran; a. 26,000 sq.

**Makurdi**, *t.*, Nigeria, W. Africa; on R. Benue, 150 m. upstream from confluence with R. Niger at Lokoja; mkt. for palm prod., ground-nuts; site of rly. bridge across R. Benue on E. main rly. from Pt. Harcourt to Kaduna.

**Makwar**, *vil.*, Sudan, N.E. Africa; on R. Blue Nile, 200 m. upstream from Khartoum; site of Sennar Dam.

**Malabar Coast**, India; name applied to W. cst. of India from Goa to southern tip of peninsula at Cape Comorin; sand dunes backed by lagoons; coastlands intensively cultivated, rice, spices, rubber, coconuts; ch. pt. Cochin.

**Malacca**, *st.*, S.W. Western Malaysia; originally part of Brit. Straits Settlements (*q.v.*); cap. M.; a. 640 sq. m.; p. (1961) 341,319.          [Peninsula.

**Malacca**, *strait*, separates Sumatra from Malay

**Maladetta**, with Pic d' Anéto, highest point in the Pyrenees; alt. 11,174 ft.

**Málaga**, *Mediterranean prov.*, S. Spain; agr.,

exp. wine, fruits, olive oil; a. 2,813 sq. m.; p. (1959) 772,517.

**Málaga**, *spt.*, *cap.*, Málaga, Spain; red oxide, olive oil, wine and fruit; oil pipeline from Puertollano refinery; p. (1965) 322,000.

**Malagasy Republic**, *I.*, *indep. sov. st.*, E. African cst.; within Fr. Community; cap. Tananarive; ch. spt. Tamatave; a. 227,800 sq. m.; p. (estd. 1965) 6,180,000.

**Malakal**, *cap.*, Upper Nile, Sudan; p. (1956) 9,680.

**Malakoff**, *t.*, S.W. Paris, France; residtl.; p. (1954) 28,576.

**Malang**, *t.*, Java, Indonesia; p. (1961) 342,000.

**Mälar**, *L.*, S.E. Sweden; connected with the Baltic by Södertelge canal, has 1,260 Is.; length 80 m.; a. 477 sq. m.          [(1965) 105,207.

**Malatya**, *t.*, central Turkey; fruit, opium; p.

**Malawi, Rep. of**, *indep. sov. st.* within Brit. Commonwealth (1964), Central Africa; along W. cst. L. Malawi; hot wet summers, cool dry winters; savannah vegetation, subtropical forest; tea, tobacco, groundnuts, cotton, coffee, ivory; cap. Lilongwe; a. 47.747 sq. m.; p. (1966) 4,042,412.

**Malawi, L.**, Central Africa, southward extension of the Great Rift Valley; 1,500 ft. above sealevel; length 350 m., breadth 40 m.; drains by R. Shire into R. Zambesi.

**Malay Archipelago**, *lge. gr. of tropical Is.* extending 4,800 m. from the Nicobar Is. in Bay of Bengal to the Solomon Is. in the Pacific; inc. Sumatra, Java, Borneo, Celebes, Philippines, New Guinea, Bismarck Archipelago.

**Malaysia, East**, name given in 1966 to Sarawak and Sabah (the two Borneo terrs. forming part of Fed. of Malaysia), separated from West Malaysia by South China Sea.

**Malaysia, Federation of**, *indep. fed.* within Brit. Commonwealth (1963), comprising West Malaysia and East Malaysia; plantation inds., mineral wealth; fed. cap. Kuala Lumpur; a. 127,198 sq. m.; p. (1963) 9,148,000.

**Malaysia, West**, name given in 1966 to mainland Malaya (9 Malay sts., Penang and Malacca); rubber, tin, iron ore, timber, palm oil prods., fruit; cap. Kuala Lumpur; a. 50,840 sq. m.; p. (1963) 7,810,000.

**Malbork (Marienburg)**, *t.*, Poland, German before 1945; on R. Nogat; cas.; rly. junction; p. (1965) 28,000.

**Malden**, *c.*, Mass., U.S.A.; mftg. sub. of Boston; rubber gds., hosiery furniture; p. (1960) 57,676.

**Malden I.**, Line Is., Central Pac. Oc.; a. 35 sq. m.; guano, uninhabited. British, discovered 1825.

**Malden and Coombe**, *former mun. bor.*, Surrey, Eng.; now inc. in *Royal Borough* of Kingston-upon-Thames; light inds.; p. (1961) 46,587.

**Maldive Is.**, *indep. sultanate* (1965), 2,000 lowlying coral Is., under Brit. prot. 1887–1965; 400 m. S. W. of Ceylon, about 215 of which are inhabited; cap. Malé; Britain retains facilities on Addu Atoll (incl. airfield on Gan I.) until 1986; coconuts, millet, fruit, fishing, coir and lacemkg.; p. (estd.) 93,000.

**Maldon**, *t.*, *mun. bor.*, Essex, Eng.; at head of Blackwater estuary; agr. machin., steel window-frames, flour milling; p. (estd. 1967) 12,010.

**Maldonado**, *dep.*, Uruguay; a. 1,587 sq. m.; p. (1953) 67,933.

**Malham Cove**, W. R. Yorks, Eng.; in Craven dist. of N. Pennines, 10 m. N.W. of Skipton; semicircular amphitheatre surrounded by limestone cliffs from base of which emerges R. Aire.

**Malin Head**, Donegal, Ireland; most N. point.

**Mali, Republic of**, *ind. sovereign st.*, W. Africa; millet, sorghum, rice, maize, groundnuts, cotton; cap. Bamako; a. 460,200 sq. m.; p. (1961) 4,100,000.          [p. 15,089.

**Malinao**, *mun.*, Luzon, Philippine Is.; hemp:

**Malines (Mechelen)**, *c.*, Belgium; on R. Dyle; cath.; rly. ctr., furniture, textiles, leather, car assembly, detergents, paint; p. (1962) 64,547.

**Malita**, *t.*, Mindanao, Philippines; p. 30,755.

**Mallaig**, *vil.*, S.W. Inverness, Scot.; on Sound of Sleat; rly. terminus; fish; p. 1,000.

**Malleco**, *prov.*, S. Chile; cap. Angol; a. 5,511 sq. m.; p. (1960) 207,477.

**Malling**, *t.*, *rural dist.*, Kent, Eng.; 3 m. W. of Maidstone; mkt., fruit ctr., chemicals; p. (rural dist. 1961) 40,680.

**Mallow**, *mkt. t.*, Cork, Ireland; on R. Blackwater; agr., fishing, flour mills, tanneries, condensed milk, dehydrated foods; p. (1966) 5,539.

Malmédy, t., Belgium; transferred to Belgium from Germany after the First World War; tanning, dyeing, paper-wks.; p. (1962) 6,357.

Malmesbury, t., mun. bor., Wilts, Eng.; on R. Avon, 8 m. N. of Chippenham; mkt.; abbey; elec. eng. ind.; p. (estd. 1967) 2,680.

Malmesbury, t., Victoria, Australia; on R. Campaspe, 20 m. S.E. of Bendigo; dam across R. provides water for domestic and mining purposes to Bendigo.

Malmesbury, t., S.W. Cape Prov., S. Africa; mineral springs; p. 5,731.

Malmö, spt., S. Sweden; on The Sound; docks; shipbldg., textiles, cement; p. (1961) 229,388.

Malmöhus, co., Sweden; a. 1,872 sq. m.; p. (1961) 625,667.

Malo-les-Bains, sub. of Dunkerque, Nord, France; seaside resort; p. (1954) 12,101. [8,737.

Malone, t., N.Y., U.S.A.; iron-mining; p. (1960)

Malta, I., indep. sov. st. within Brit. Commonwealth (1964); in Mediterranean, 60 m. S. of Sicily; cap. Valetta; received George Cross for heroism in Second World War; deep water quay; dry docks; no raw materials; a. (inc. Gozo and Comino) 122 sq. m.; p. (estd. 1962) 329,285. [(1961) 13,691.

Maltby, urb. dist., W. Riding, Yorks, Eng.; p.

Malton, mkt. t., urb. dist., N.R. Yorks, Eng.; on R. Derwent, in S.W. of Vale of Pickering; brewing, ironwks.; p. (1961) 4,430.

Maluti, mtn. range, Lesotho, S. Africa; highest peak Machacha, alt. 10,990.

Malvern or Great Malvern, t., urb. dist., Worcester, Eng.; at E. foot of Malvern Hills; spa; annual dramatic festival; stone quarrying, agr. machin., motor-cars, electronics wks., plastics; p. (estd. 1967) 28,630.

Malvern Hills, narrow ridge forming bdy. between Worcester and Hereford, Eng.; rises very abruptly from Severn Valley to over 1,000 ft. between Malvern and Bromsberrow; moorland, woodland on lower slopes; length 8 m., width, under 1 m., maximum alt., 1,395 ft.

Malverne, t., N.Y., U.S.A.; on Long I.; residtl. sub. of New York; p. (1960) 9,968.

Mamaroneck, t., N.Y., U.S.A.; textiles, mnfs. oils; p. (1960) 17,673.

Mammola, t., Reggio, S. Italy; p. 9,925.

Mammoth Caves, Ky., U.S.A.; Green R.; stalactite formations in avenues aggregating 150 m. long.

Mamore or Rio Grande, R., Bolivia; trib. of R. Beni; length 500 m. [3,862 ft.

Mam Soul, mtn., Ross and Inverness, Scot.; alt.

Man, I. of, in Irish Sea; 30 m. from England (Cumberland), and N. Ireland (Down), 20 m. from Scotland (Wigtown); tourist ctr.; agr., sheep, lead, zinc; ch. t. Douglas; old cap. Castletown; administered according to own laws; refinery on N.W. cst. between Rue Point and Point of Ayre under construction; a. 227 sq. m.; p. (1961) 48,151.

Mana, R., Fr. Guiana, S. America; 175 m.

Manabí, prov., Ecuador; on W. slope of the Andes; cap. Puertoviejo; cacao, sugar; a. 7,891 sq. m.; p. (estd. 1962) 614,803.

Manacor, t., Majorca, Spain; 30 m. from Palma; artificial pearls, wine; 7 m. from its spt. Porto Cristo; stalactite caves of Drach and Hams; p. (1957) 18,956.

Managua, cap., Nicaragua; nr. Lake M.; univ., palace; coffee, cotton; p. (1960) 207,000.

Manamah, cap., Bahrein Is., Persian Gulf; p. (1965) 62,000. [5,000.

Mananjary, t., E. Malagasy, sugar, coffee; p.

Manaqil Canal, fed by waters from Blue Nile released through Semnar dam; helps cultivate 600,000 acres of Gezira desert. [Ceylon.

Manar, G., with Palk Strait separates India from

Manasarowar, sacred L., Tibet.

Manatee, t., Fla., U.S.A.; lumber, fruit and vegetable canning; p. (1950) 3,582.

Manáus (Manaos), c., cap., Amazonas st., N.W. Brazil; on Rio Negro nr. confluence with Amazon; impt. R. pt., airpt.; oil ref.; former rubber ctr.

Mancha, La, plain, Cuidad-Real prov., S. Spain; in shallow depression on central plateau, average alt. between 1,500 and 3,000 ft., drained by headstreams of R. Guadiana; semi-arid climate with hot summers, cold winters; widespread salt deposits; Merino sheep, esparto grass; Spain's lgst. grape-growing region.

Manche, maritime dep., N.W. France; on English Channel; agr. and dairying; cap. Saint Lo; ch. port Cherbourg; a. 2,475 sq. m.; p. (1962) 446,873.

Manchester, c., spt., co. bor., S. Lancs, Eng.; on R. Irwell (which separates it from Salford); inland terminus of Manchester Ship Canal; ctr. of cotton tr. and ind.; also engin. heavy, light and elec., and aircraft, paper, foodstuffs; univ.; gr. comm., cultural and recreational cap. of N.W. England; p. (estd. 1967) 616,520.

Manchester, t., E. Iowa, U.S.A.; tr. ctr.; flour milling; woollen goods; p. (1960) 4,402.

Manchester, c., N.H., U.S.A.; at Amoskeag Falls, on the Merrimac R.; textiles, footwear, machin.; p. (1960) 88,282.

Manchester, t., Conn., U.S.A.; textiles (silk); p. (1960) 41,906.

Manchester Ship Canal, ship canal, S. Lancs, Ches., Eng.; joining Manchester to Mersey estuary at Eastham; can be used by ocean steamers; length 35½ m.

Manchuria, former Chinese outer terr., no longer exists as administrative unit, comprised nine provs.—Liaoning, Kirin, Heilungkiang, Liaopeh, Nunkiang, Hsingan, Sunkiang, Hokiang and Antung; mountainous, N.W. and E.; drained to N. by Sungari and S. by Liao Rs.; forested; soya-beans, wheat, coal, iron, gold, silver.

Mandal, t., Norway; steel, hempropes; p. (1961) 5,156.

Mandalay, c., Upper Burma; on the R. Irrawaddy, 400 m. N. of Rangoon; formerly cap. of kingdom; silk, old carved wooden palace and many pagodas; p. (1955) 182,367.

Manduria, t., Italy; tr. ctr.; p. 17,675.

Mandvi, spt., Kutch, India; p. (1961) 26,609.

Manfredonia, spt., Foggia, Italy; cath.; cereals, fruit; p. 18,600.

Mangalore, spt., Mysore, India; exp. coffee, coconuts, rice, spices, fertilisers; p. (1961) 142,669.

Mangere, N.I., N.Z., 13 m. S. of Auckland; international airport (opened 1965).

Mangerton, mtn., Kerry, Ireland.

Mangla Dam, W. Pakistan, world's lgst. earth-filled dam, on Jhelum R., part of Indus Basin irrigation scheme.

Mangotsfield, urb. dist., Gloucester, Eng.; p. (1961) 24,092.

Manhattan, I., N.Y., U.S.A.; at mouth of Hudson R.; a. 22 sq. m., forms major part of bor. of Manhattan (p. 1960) 1,698,281) of N.Y. City.

Manica and Sofala, prov., Mozambique; comprises dists. of Beira and Tete; cap. Beira; p. (1962) 779,462.

Manicouagan, R., Canada; flows S. from Quebec prov. to St. Lawrence, S.W. of Baie Comeau where there is dam and hydroelec. plant; length 300 m.

Manihiki, Cook Is., N.Z.; p. 454.

Manila, c., cap. Philippines, S.W. Luzon; ch. pt. of Is.; univ., cath.; general tr.; fishing ind.; p. (1960) 1,138,611.

Manipur, Union Terr., India; rice, cotton, fruits; cap. Imphal; a. 8,628 sq. m.; p. (1961) 780,037.

Manisa, t., Turkey; comm. ctr., cotton, silk; p. (1965) 69,394.

Manistee, c., Mich., U.S.A.; on L. Michigan; timber, salt, fruit; p. (1960) 8,324.

Manistique, t., Mich., U.S.A.; on M. R.; p. (1960) 4,875.

Manitoba, prov., Canada; wheat, minerals, furs, oil; cap. Winnipeg; a. 246,512 sq. m.; p. (1961) 921,686.

Manitowoc, c., Wis., U.S.A.; on L. Michigan, shipbldg., iron, aluminium goods, flour; p. (1960) 32,275.

Manizales, cap., Caldas, Colombia; coffee, textiles, leather gds., chemicals; p. (estd. 1962) 176,080.

Manjil Dam, Iran; on Sefid Rud (white river), Gilan prov.; 352 ft. high.

Mankato, c., Minn., U.S.A.; agr. tools, flour, brewing; p. (1960) 23,747.

Mannheim, t., Baden-Württemberg, Germany; gr. R. pt. at confluence of Rs. Neckar and Rhine; cas.; machin., vehicles, cellulose, steel, elec., foodstuffs, tobacco, wood, textiles, chemicals; p. (1963) 321,100.

Manningtree, par., Essex, Eng.; head of Stour estuary; fishing, yachting; p. (1961) 524.

Manorhamilton, t., Leitrim, Ireland; rly. wks.; p. 1,012. [ironwks.; p. (1957) 40,452.

Manresa, t., Spain; textiles, paper, chemicals,

Mans, Le, *see* Le Mans.                          [Coats I.
Mansel I., Hudson Bay, Canada; S.E. of Pennines, 12 m. N. of Nottingham; iron, coal, hosiery, footwear mftg., sand-quarrying, metal box wks., lace, cotton, lt. engin.; p. (estd. 1967) *55,540*.
Mansfield, I., Hudson Bay, Canada; S.E. of
Mansfield, t., mun. bor., Notts, Eng.; on E. flank of Pennines, 12 m. N. of Nottingham; iron, coal, hosiery, footwear mftg., sand-quarrying, metal box wks.. lace, cotton, lt. engin.; p. (estd. 1967) *55,540*.
Mansfield, t., Mass., U.S.A.; textiles, engin.; confectionery; p. (1960) *4,674*.
Mansfield, c., Ohio, U.S.A.; machin., farm tools, paper, rubber goods; p. (1960) *47,325*.
Mansfield Woodhouse, t., urb. dist., Notts, Eng.; 2 m. N. of Mansfield; stone quarries; Roman remains; p. (estd. 1967) *23,600*.
Mansura, t., Lower U.A.R.; cotton mftg.; p. (1960) *152,000*.
Manta, t., Ecuador; coffee, panama hats.; p. (1962) *19,228*.
Mantanzas, t., Venezuela; on S. bank of R. Orinoco; steel wks.
Mantes-la-Jolie, t., Yvelines, France; on R. Seine; cath., agr. prod., hosiery, musical instruments; p. (1962) *19,227*.
Mantiqueira, mtn. range, Brazil; N.W. of Rio de Janeiro; highest peak Itatiaia 9,255 ft.
Mantua, prov., Italy; a. 903 sq. m.; p. (1961) *382,515*.                          [p. (1961) *61,580*.
Mantua, t., N. Italy; on R. Mincio; ironwks.; Manukau Harbour, N.I., N.Z.; lge. shallow inlet on W. cst. of Auckland Peninsula which is here less than 6 m. wide; provides additional harbour facilities for spt. of Auckland but shallow water limits usefulness; mainly used for recreational sailing.
Manych, R., U.S.S.R.; trib. of R. Don; length 300 m.; canal is being built through R. to the Caspian to provide through connection with Black Sea.
Manzala (Menzala), lagoon, Mediterranean cst., Egypt, N.E. Africa; extends E. from Damietta mouth of Nile to Pt. Said; fringed by salt marsh; a. 800 sq. m.
Manzanares, R., Spain; trib. of R. Jarama.
Manzanares, t., Spain; 30 m. E. of Ciudad Real; soap, bricks, pottery mftg., agr. prod.; p. (1957) *18,204*.                          [*42,252*.
Manzanillo, spt., Cuba; sugar, rice; p. (1960)
Manzanillo, spt., Colima, Mexico; Mexico's chief inlet and outlet on Pac. Oc.; p. (1961) *13,030*.
Manzini, (Bremersdorp), t., Swaziland, S. Africa.
Mar, ancient dist., Aberdeen, Scot.; between Rs. Don and Dee.
Maracaibo, spt., cap., Zulia st., Venezuela; on W. of narrow entrance to L. Maracaibo; univ.; oil, coffee, cocoa, and hide exp.; shipbldg.; p. (1961) *432,902*.
Maracaibo, G., and L., Zulia st., Venezuela, S. America; brackish lake, 120 m. long, 60 m. wide; oil-wells on fringes and drilled into lake floor.
Maracay, t., W. Venezuela; mftg. and military ctr.; p. (1961) *134,120*.          [(1956) *36,556*.
Maragheh, t., Iran; on N. end of L. Urmia; p. Marajó, I., at mouth of the Rs. Amazon and Pará, Brazil; a. 173 sq. m.
Maralinga, S. Australia; 200 m. N.E. Eucla; joint U.K.–Australian atomic testing ground; first weapon exploded here 27 Sept. 1956.
Maranhão, st., N.E. Brazil; rice, cotton, sugar, tobacco, coffee, cattle, gold, copper; oil in the Barrierinhas a.; cap. São Luiz; a. 129,271 sq. m.; p. (1960) *2,492,139*.
Marañon, R., see Amazon, R.
Marans, t., Charente-Maritime, France; industl.; p. (1962) *3,836*.
Maras, t., S. central Turkey; tr. in Kurdish carpets; p. (1965) *63,315*.
Marathon, plain, Greece; battle between Greeks and Persians 490 B.C.
Marazion, mkt. t., Cornwall, Eng.; on Mount's Bay; pilchard fisheries; p. *1,100*.
Marbella, spt., Malaga, Spain; cas.; iron mines; oranges, sugar cane, cotton; p. (1957) *9,921*.
Marble, I., Keewatin, N.W. Terrs., Canada.
Marble Bar, t., W. Australia; located 85 m. inland by rail from Pt. Hedland; ctr. of Pilbara goldfields.
Marblehead, spt., Mass., U.S.A.; holiday resort, footwear; p. (1960) *18,521*.
Marburg, t., Hessen, Germany; univ., cas.; instruments, pharmaceuticals, wall-paper mftg.; p. (1963) *47,800*.          [*10,475*.
Marcaria, t., Italy; on R. Oglio; industl.; p.

March, mkt. t., urb. dist., I. of Ely, Eng.; in Fens. 12 m. N.W. of Ely; impt. rly. junction; mkt., farm tools; p. (1961) *13,119*.
Marchena, t., Spain; on R. Guadalquivir; mftg.; p. (1957) *20,326*.
Marches, The, region, central Italy; extending from eastern slopes of Apennines to Adriatic cst.; embracing provs. of Macerata, Ascoli-Piceno, Acona, and Pesaro e Urbino; maize, wine, tobacco, silk, paper; a. 3,744 sq. m.; p. (1961) *1,347,234*.
Marchienne-au-Pont, t., Belgium; on R. Sambre; tr. ctr.; p. (1962) *19,370*.
Marcq-en-Barœul, commune, sub. Lille, Nord, France; textiles, foundries; p. (1954) *24,564*.
Marcus Hook, t., Del., U.S.A.; on right bank of R. Del. 15 m. below Philadelphia.
Mar del Plata, t., Argentina; on C. Corrientes; seaside resort; p. (1960) *300,000*.
Mardin, t., Turkey; agr., textiles; p. (1965) *31,123*.
Maree, L., Ross and Cromarty, Scot.; length 12½ m., breadth 2½ m.; contains many Is.
Mareotis or Birket-et-Mariut, L., Lower Egypt; separated from Mediterranean by ridge of sand on which stands Alexandria; length 50 m., width 20 m.
Margam, t. in Pt. Talbot mun. bor., W. central Glamorgan, S. Wales; on cst. of Swansea Bay; lge. new steel-wks., lgst. steel-rolling mill in Europe; p. (estd. 1955) *18,300*.
Margarita, I., Venezuela; in the Caribbean S.; pearl fisheries, fishing, fibre wks.; cap. Asuncion, a. 450 sq. m.; p. (1961) *87,500*.
Margate, t., mun. bor., Kent, Eng.; W. of N. Foreland, in the Isle of Thanet; seaside resort; p. (estd. 1967) *49,060*.
Margelan, t., E. Uzbek S.S.R.; agr. ctr., tr. especially cotton and silk; p. (1959) *68,000*.
Mari, autonomous Soviet Socialist rep., U.S.S.R.; cap. Ioshkar Ola; p. (1959) *647,000*.
Mariana, t., Minas Gerais, Brazil; tr. ctr;. gold mng.; p. (1960) *34,500*.
Mariana Is., chain of Is., W. Pacific; U.S. Trust Terr.; most impt. are Guam, Saipan and Tinian; a. c. 370 sq. m.; p. c. *75,000*.
Marianské Lázne (Marienbad), t., ČSSR.; spa; antimony; p. (1961) *12,597*.
Maribor, t., Slovenia, Jugoslavia; fruit ctr., leather goods, wine, rly. wks.; p. (1960) *84,000*.
Marie Galante, I., Lesser Antilles gr.; Fr. possession; sugar-cane; p. (1960) *16,037*.
Marienburg, see Malbork.
Marienwerder, see Kwidzyn.
Marietta, t., Ohio, U.S.A.; at confluence of Muskingum R. with Ohio R.; timber, ironwks., coal, oil, natural gas; p. (1960) *16,847*.
Marigliano, t., Campagna, Italy; p. *14,155*.
Mariinsk Canal, see Volga Baltic Waterway.
Marin, spt., N.W. Spain; fishing; textiles; naval school; p. (1957) *17,592*.
Marinette, t., Wis., U.S.A.; on L. Michigan; paper, pulp, timber; p. (1960) *13,329*.
Marino, t., Sicily, Italy; p. *6,625*.
Marion, c., Ind., U.S.A.; natural gas, iron, paper, glass, wireless sets; p. (1960) *37,854*.
Marion, t., Ohio, U.S.A.; agr. implements, steam shovels, tractors; p. (1960) *37,079*.
Marion, c., S. Ill., U.S.A.; fruit; coal; engin.; p. (1960) *11,274*.
Maritime Alps, mtn. ranges, S. France–Italy.
Maritime Provinces, embraces Canadian provs. of Nova Scotia, New Brunswick, Pr. Edward I.
Maritsa, R., Bulgaria and Greece; length 260 m.
Maritzburg, see Pietermaritzburg.
Mariupol, see Zhdanov.
Marken, I., nr. Amsterdam, Netherlands; tourist ctr.
Market Deeping, t., Lincoln, Eng.; on R. Welland; brewing, rope; p. *876*.
Market Drayton, t., urb. dist., Salop, Eng.; on R. Tern, 5 m. S. of Newcastle-under-Lyme; agr. implements, nylon mftg.; p. of t. (1961) *5,853*; of urb. dist. (estd. 1966) *16,000*.
Market Harborough, t., urb. dist., Leicester, Eng.; on R. Welland, 8 m. N.W. of Kettering; elec. engin., foodstuffs, corsetry; p. (1961) *11,556*.
Market Rasen, t., urb. dist., Lindsey, Lincoln, Eng.; 14 m. N.E. of Lincoln; agr. ctr.; p. (1961) *2,257*.

Market Weighton, *t.*, E.R. Yorks, Eng.; malting, iron; p. *1,735.*

Markinch, *burgh*, Fife, Scot.; 8 m. N. of Kirkcaldy; paper mftg., whisky blending and bottling; p. (1961) *2,446.*

Marl, *t.*, N. Rhine–Westphalia, Germany; in the Ruhr; coal-mining and chemicals; p. (1963) *73,300.* [(1960) *18,819.*

Marlboro, *c.*, Mass., U.S.A.; boot mftg.; p.

Marlborough, *t.*, *mun. bor.*, Wilts, Eng.; on R. Kennet in heart of Marlborough Downs; agr., tanning, brewing; public school; p. (estd. 1967) *5,910.*

Marlborough, *prov. dist.*, S.I., N.Z.; pastoral; a. 4,220 sq. m.; cap. Blenheim; p. (1961) *27,740.*

Marlborough Downs, *hills*, Wilts, Eng.; chalk; highest point, Milk Hill, 976 ft.

Marlin, *t.*, Texas, U.S.A.; hot artesian water; oil; cotton; dairying; p. (1950) *7,099.*

Marlow, *t.*, *urb. dist.*, Bucks, Eng.; on R. Thames; mkt., tourist ctr.; brewing and chair mkg.; p. (1961) *8,704.*

Marmande, *t.*, Lot-et-Garonne, France; on R. Garonne; brandy, liqueur, woollens, iron; p. (1962) *14,004.*

Marmara, *sea*, separates Europe from Anatolia.

Marmolata, highest point of Dolomite Alps, S. Tyrol, Italy; alt. 11,045 ft.

Marne, *R.*, Central France; rises in Plateau de Langres, flows N.W. and W. across Champagne Humide, Champagne Pouilleuse and Beauce, joins R. Seine just above Paris; with Marne–Rhine and Marne–Saône Canals it forms impt. inland waterway linking Seine with Rhine and Rhône valleys; length (approx.) 325 m.

Marne, *dep.*, N.E. France; agr., wines, textiles, minerals; cap. Chalons-sur-Marne; a. 3,168 sq. m.; p. (1962) *442,195.*

Marne, Haute, *dep.*, France; a. 2,420 sq. m.; cap. Chaumont; p. (1962) *208,446.*

Maros, *R.*, Hungary; trib. of R. Theiss; length 400 m.

Marple, *t.*, *urb. dist.*, Cheshire, Eng.; 3 m. E. of Stockport; textiles; p. (estd. 1967) *23,300.*

Marquesas, *I. gr.* (Fr.), Pac. Oc.; a. 480 sq. m.; lgst. Is. Nukuhiva and Hivaoa; bananas, sugar-cane, copra; p. (1962) *4,837.*

Marquette, *c.*, Mich., U.S.A.; on L. Superior; iron-ore deposits, timber, rly. wks.; p. (1960) *19,824.*

Marradi, *t.*, Italy; p. *8,275.*

Marrakesh, *c.*, Morocco; tourist ctr., leather goods; p. (1960) *243,134.*

Marree, *sm. t.*, S. Australia; on rly. from Pt. Augusta to Alice Springs; terminus of overland stock route from Queensland.

Marsa el-Brega, *new pt.*, Gulf of Sirte, Libya; oil pipeline from Zelten; one projected from Raguba oilfield; refinery projected.

Marsala, *spt.*, Sicily, Italy; wine ctr.; p. (1961) *81,327.* [(1960) *4,347.*

Marseilles, *t.*, N. Ill., U.S.A.; paper, bricks; p.

Marseilles, *c.*, *spt.*, cap. Bouches-du-Rhône, S. France; cath., univ., palace; comm. pt., coal, iron, bauxite, marine engin., aircraft, glass, agr. prod., wines, oil refining; oil pipeline to Karlsruhe (1963); p. (1962) *783,738.*

Marshall, *c.*, Mo., U.S.A.; p. (1960) *9,572.*

Marshall, *c.*, Texas, U.S.A.; rly. wks., canning, foundries; p. (1960) *23,846.*

Marshall, *spt.*, W. Liberia, W. Africa; exp. rubber; p. *1,000.*

Marshall, *I. gr.*, N. Pac. Oc.; U.S. Pac. Trust Terr., formerly Japanese mandate; total a. 150 sq. m.; sugar-cane, copra; ch. I. Jaluit; p. (1958) *13,928.*

Marshalltown, *t.*, Iowa, U.S.A.; on I. R.; iron, steel, machin., food canning; p. (1960) *22,521.*

Marshfield, *spt.*, Ore., U.S.A.; fishing, lumber, mining; p. (1950) *5,218.*

Marshfield, *t.*, Wis., U.S.A.; mftg. ctr. in timber region; p. (1960) *14,153.*

Martaban, *t.*, Burma; on R. Salween.

Martha's Vineyard, *I.*, Mass., U.S.A.; holiday resort, ch. ts. Vineyard Haven, Oak Bluffs, Edgartown; 21 m. long.

Marti, *t.*, Cuba; sugar, sisal; p. *5,060.*

Martigny, *t.*, Valais, Switzerland; peaches, tourist resort; linked by road tunnel to Aosta, Italy; p. (1957) *6,572.*

Martigues, *t.*, Bouches-du-Rhône, France; nr. Marseilles; p. (1962) *21,526.*

Martinao, *t.*, Italy; industl., tr. ctr.; p. *38,325.*

Martinez, *c.*, W. Cal., U.S.A.; industl., oil refineries, copper smelting; p. (1960) *9,604.*

Martinique, *I.*, (Fr.) W. Indies; cap. Fort-de-France; sugar, rum; a. 385 sq. m.; p. (estd. 1965) *310,000.*

Martinsburg, *c.*, W. Va., U.S.A.; in Shenandoah valley; rly. wks., cider, textiles; p. (1960) *15,179.*

Martin's Ferry, *t.*, Ohio, U.S.A.; on O. R., iron and steel mftg., coal-mining; p. (1960) *11,919.*

Marton, *t.*, N.I., N.Z., p. *2,810.*

Martos, *t.*, Andalusia, Spain; agr. ctr., wines, sulphur springs; p. (1957) *30,404.*

Mary, *t.*, Turkmen. S.S.R.; cereals, fruit, textiles; p. (1959) *48,000.*

Maryborough, *t.*, *pt.*, Queensland, Australia; fruit ctr., mng. and sugar mill machin., cars, ships, sawmills; p. (1966) *20,381.*

Maryborough, *t.*, Victoria, Australia; rly. ctr.; agr., pastoral, wool, engin.; p. (1966) *7,694.*

Maryborough, *see* Port Laoighise, Ireland.

Mary Kathleen, *t.*, Queensland, Australia; new t., nr. uranium field in Cloncurry a.

Maryland, *st.*, U.S.A.; steel, copper, smelting and refining, coal, asbestos, potash, salts, aircraft, chemicals; agr., livestock; cap. Annapolis; lgst. c. Baltimore; a. 10,577 sq. m.; p. (1960) *3,038,156.*

Maryport, *mkt. t.*, *urb. dist.*, Cumberland, Eng.; on the Irish Sea; coal, iron, plastics, footwear; p. (1961) *12,334.*

Marysville, *t.*, Cal., U.S.A.; fruit; p. (1960) *9,553.*

Marysville, *t.*, Kan., U.S.A.; rly. ctr. in rich agr. region; p. (1960) *4,143.*

Marysville, *t.*, Ohio, U.S.A.; mkt., grass seed, livestock; p. (1960) *4,952.*

Maryville, *c.*, E. Tenn., U.S.A.; lumber; clothes; quarries; p. (1960) *10,348.*

Masai Land, *dist.*, S. Kenya, Africa.

Masaya, *cap. c.* of M. dep. S.W. Nicaragua; agr., tobacco; p. (1959) *99,573.*

Masbate, *I.*, Philippines; a. 1,262 sq. m.; p. (1960) *280,300.*

Mascara, *t.*, Algeria; wine, oil, cereals; p. (1948) *35,078.*

Mascarene Is., collective name of Mauritius, Rodriguez and Réunion, in Indian Ocean.

Masham, *t.*, N.R. Yorks, Eng.; on R. Ure; 9 m. N.W. of Ripon; mkt., sheep fair; p. *1,702.*

Mashhad (Meshed), *c.*, N.E. Iran; prov. cap. Khorassan; pilgrimage ctr.; shrine (*meshed*) of Imam Riza; agr.; carpets; turquoise; p. (1967) *707,884.* [cultivation.

Mashonaland, *prov.*, Rhodesia; tobacco and maize

Masira, *I.*, off est. of Oman, Arabia.

Mask, *L.*, Mayo and Galway, Ireland; length 12 m., width 2–4 m.

Mason City, *t.*, Iowa, U.S.A.; on the Sheel Rock R.; cement, bricks, sugar-beet; p. (1960) *30,642.*

Massa or Massa Carrara, *t.*, Italy; olive oil, paper, tobacco, marble; p. (1961) *55,831.*

Massachusetts, *st.*, New England, U.S.A.; fisheries, agr., textiles, footwear, iron and steel goods, elec. machin., rubber goods, leather, paper, wood pulp; cap. Boston; a. 8,257 sq. m.; p. (1960) *5,148,578.*

Massafra, *t.*, Italy; industl.; p. *12,275.*

Massarosa, *commune*, Tuscany, Italy; agr.; p. *12,546.*

Massawa, *spt.*, Eritrea; pt. for Ethiopia, on Red Sea; fine harbour; pearl fishing; p. c. *25,000.*

Massena, *t.*, N.Y., U.S.A.; p. (1960) *15,478.*

Messenya, *t.*, Central African Rep., nr. L. Chad; cap. of Bagirmi.

Massillon, *c.*, Ohio, U.S.A.; coal, machin., glass, aluminium ware; p. (1960) *31,236.*

Masterton, *t.*, N.I., N.Z.; p. (1961) *15,121.*

Matabeleland, *dist.*, Rhodesia; cereals, sugar, cotton, gold. [23,000.

Matadi, *pt.*, Congo; nr. mouth of R. Congo; p.

Matagalpa, *t.*, Nicaragua; coffee, cattle; gold mng. in a.; p. (1961) *14,000.* [(1941) *14,090.*

Matale, *t.*, Ceylon; Buddhist monastery; p.

Matamoros, *t.*, Mexico, on Rio Grande; livestock tr. ctr.; p. (1960) *93,334.*

Matanzas, *prov.*, Cuba; sugar, tobacco, rice; a. 3,259 sq. m.; p. (1953) *395,780.*

Matanzas, *spt.*, *prov. cap.*, Cuba; exp. sugar, cigars; rayon plant; p. (1953) *63,916.*

Matapan, *C.*, W. side of G. of Laconia, Greece.

Matara, *spt.*, S. Ceylon; p. *22,908.*

Matarani, S. Peru; oil refinery being built.

Mataro, *spt.*, Spain; nr. Barcelona; fisheries, textiles, chemicals, paper; p. (1957) *31,642.*

Matera, *t.*, Italy; N.W. of Taranto; tr. ctr., leather, oil; p. (1961) *38,233.*

Matlock, *t., urb. dist.*, Derby, Eng.; on R. Derwent; 15 m. N. of Derby; health resort, tourist ctr., quarrying, light inds.; p. (1961) *13,486.*

Mato Grosso, *st.*, Brazil; cap. Cuiaba; a. 487,482 sq. m.; p. (1960) *910,262.*

Mato Grosso, *plateau*, Mato Grosso st., Brazil; average alt. 3,000 ft., acts as divide between Amazon and Parona–Paraguay R. systems; reserves of gold, diamonds, manganese but largely undeveloped.

Matrah, *t.*, Muscat and Oman, Arabia; tr. route ctr.; p. *8,500.*

Matsue, *t.*, Honshu, Japan; p. 1965) *110,534.*

Matsumoto, *t.*, Japan; silkworm tr.; p. *c.* (1964) *150,000.*

Matsuyama, *c.*, Japan; p. (1965) *282,651.*

Matterhorn, German name for (Fr.) Mt. Cervin, (It.) Monte Cervino; Pennine Alps, Switzerland; alt. 14,678 ft, (*see* Zermatt).

Mattoon, *c.*, Ill.. U.S.A.; ironwks., flour, bricks, agr. tr.; p. (1960) *19,088.*

Maturin, *t.*, Venezuela; comm. ctr.; airport; p. (1961) *53,445.*

Matyásföld, *sub.* Budapest, Hungary; lge bus wks., refrigerator vans. [Gänserndorf; oil.

Matzen, *vil.*, E. Lower Austria; 4m. N. of Mauban, *spt.*, Luzon, Philippine Is.; p. *14,332.*

Maubeuge, *t.*, Nord, France; metal, glasswks.; p. (1962) *27,287.*

Mauch Chunk, *bor.*, E. Penns., U.S.A.; coal, carnotite, clothing; p. (1950) *2,959.*

Mauchline, *par.*, Ayr, Scot.; associated with Robert Burns; p. *4,000.* [*42,576.*

Maui, *I.*, Hawaiian Is.; a. 728 sq. m.; p. (1960)

Maule, *prov.*, Chile; a. 2,172 sq. m.; p. (1961) *93,942.*

Maumee, *R.*, Ind., U.S.A.; flows to L. Erie; length 180 m.

Mauna Kea, *volcano*, Hawaii; alt. 13,823 ft.

Mauna Loa, *volcano*, Hawaii; alt. 13,675 ft.

Mauritania, Islamic Republic of, *ind. sov. st.* within French Community, W. Africa; livestock, gum, salt; cap. Nouakchott; a. 430,000 sq. m.; p. (1961) *727,000.*

Mauritius, *I., indep. sov. st.* within Brit. Commonwealth (1968); Indian Ocean; 500 m. E. of Malagasy; sugar, rum; cap. Port Louis; a. 720 sq. m.; p. (estd. 1968) *773,000.*

Mawddach, *R., estuary*, Merioneth, Wales; 19 m.

Mawson, Australian national research base, Antarctica. [textiles, timber.

Maxwelltown, *t.*, Dumfries, Scot.; on R. Nith;

May, *I.*, Firth of Forth, Fife, Scot.

Mayaguana I., Bahamas, W. Indies; p. (1953) *615.*

Mayagüez, *c.*, *spt.*, Puerto Rico; sugar, coffee, tobacco; p. (1960) *50,808.*

Maybole, *burgh*, Ayr, Scot.; 8 m. S. of Ayr; footwear, agr. implements; p. (1961) *4,677.*

Mayen, *c.*, Rhine prov., Germany; mftg., brewing; leather; quarries; p. *14,327.*

Mayenne, *dep.*, N.W. France; pastoral and agr.; cap. Laval; a. 1,987 sq. m.; p. (1962) *250,030.*

Mayenne, *R.*, France; trib. of R. Sarthe; 125 m.

Mayfield, *t.*, S.W. Ky., U.S.A.; tobacco; dairy prod.; clothing; p. (1960) *10,762.*

Mayo, *maritime co.*, Connacht, Ireland; broken cst., much barren mtn. land, many large lakes; agr., fishery; co. t. Castlebar, a. 2,126 sq. m.; p. (1966) *115,588.*

Mayotte, *ch. I.*, Fr. col., Comoro Archipelago, Mozambique Channel; sugar-cane, vanilla, cacao, a. 140 sq. m.; p. *18,000.*

Maywood, *t.*, Ill., U.S.A.; adjoining Chicago; residtl., some mnfs.; p. (1960) *27,330.*

Mazagan, *see* El Jadida. [p. (1962) *17,891.*

Mazamet, *t.*, Tarn, France; tanning, leather wks.;

Mazandaran, *prov.*, N.E. Iran; Caspian Sea, frontier U.S.S.R.; subtropical climate; agr.; cap. Sari; p. (1967) *1,843,388.*

Mazar, *t.*, Afghanistan; 200 m. N. of Kabul; chemical fertilisers from natural gas and thermal elec. plant projected; p. (estd. 1964) *40,000.*

Mazarron, *t.*, Murcia, Spain; metal wks., flour, soap; p. (1957) *15,225.*

Mazatenango, *t.*, S.W. Guatemala; coffee, cacao, sugar, fruit; p. (1960) *26,120.*

Mazatepec, *t.*, Puebla, Mexico; hydro-elec. plant.

Mazatlán, *spt.*, W. cst. Mexico; hides, minerals, fruit; oil refinery being built; p. (1960) *50,000.*

Mazingarbe, *t.*, Pas-de-Calais, France; p. (1954) *10,311.*

Mazzara, *t.*, Sicily, Italy; cath., ruined cas.; agr. prod.; p. *24,250.*

Mazzarino, *t.*, Sicily, Italy; mftg.; p. *21,580.*

M'babane, *t.*, Swaziland; alt. 3,800 ft.; administrative ctr.; European p. (1960) *1,092.*

Mbandaka (Coquilhatville), *t.*, Congo; at confluence of Rs. Congo and Ruki. [refinery.

M'Bao, Senegal, W. Africa; 11 m. from Dakar; oil

McAlester, *t.*, Okla., U.S.A.; coal-mining ctr., rly. wks.; p. (1950) *17,875.*

McClintock Channel, *strait*, between Prince of Wales's land and Victoria I., Arctic Canada.

McComb, *t.*, Miss., U.S.A.; p. (1960) *12,020.*

McKeesport, *c.*, Penns., U.S.A., on Monongahela R.; coal, iron and steel; p. (1960) *45,489.*

McKees Rocks, *t.*, Penns., U.S.A.; on Ohio R.; iron, glass; p. (1960) *13,185.* [I., Canada.

M'Clure, *strait*, between Banks I. and Melville

McPherson, *t.*, Yukon, Canada; on Peel R.

McPherson, *t.*, Kan., U.S.A.; in oil-field region; refining plants; p. (1950) *8,689.*

Mead, *L.*, Cal., U.S.A.; on R. Colorado behind Boulder (Hoover) Dam; world's lgst. reservoir; stores water for irrigation in Imperial Valley and Yuma dist.; length 115 m.

Meadowfield, Durham, nr. Brandon; major industl. estate proposed.

Meadville, *c.*, Penns., U.S.A.; on French Creek; univ.; rly. wks., rayon yarn; p. (1960) *16,571.*

Mealfuarvonie, *mtn.*, on side of L. Ness, Scot.; alt. 2,284 ft.

Meath, *maritime co.*, Leinster, Ireland; pastoral; co. t., Trim; a. 906 sq. m.; p. (1966) *67,279.*

Meathus Truim, *see* Edgeworthstown.

Meaux, *t.*, Seine-et-Marne, France; on R. Marne; cath.; dairying; p. (1962) *23,305.*

Mecca, *holy c.*, Saudi Arabia; Mohammedan pilgrim ctr.; p. (estd.) *200,000.*

Mechanicsburg, *bor.*, S. Penns., U.S.A.; steel; clothes; p. (1950) *6,786.*

Mechelen, *see* Malines.

Mecklenburg, former *Land*, Soviet Zone, Germany; bordering on Baltic Sea; abolished as admin. unit, 1952; Schwerin was the cap.; a. 8,856 sq. m.

Medan, *cap.*, E. Sumatra, Indonesia; rubber, tobacco; p. (1961) *479,000.*

Medellin, *c.*, Colombia, S. America; univ.; textiles, tobacco, coffee, cement, glass, steel; hydroelec. plant; p. (estd. 1962) *690,710.*

Medford, *t.*, Mass., U.S.A.; sub. of Boston; residtl.; chemicals, machin., textiles; p. (1960) *64,971.* [leather; p. *14,903.*

Medicina, *commune*, N. Italy; textiles, agr.;

Medicine Bow, *mtns.*, Col. and Wyo., U.S.A.

Medicine Hat, *t.*, Alberta, Canada; on S. Saskatchewan R.; rly. junction; coal, natural gas, flour; p. (1961) *24,484.*

Medina, *t.*, W. Australia; oil refinery.

Medina, *t.*, N. Ohio, U.S.A.; bees, honey, beeswax; p. (1960) *8,235.*

Medina, *c.*, Saudi Arabia; tomb of Mohammed; rail line to Ma'an restored (1964–7); harbour at Yenbo (Yanbu); fruit, dates; p. (estd.) *50,000.* [*14,889.*

Medinia-Sidonia, *t.*, Spain; agr. prod.; p. (1957)

Mediterranean, *gr. inland sea*, almost tideless, dividing Europe from Africa; and communicating with the Atlantic by the Strait of Gibraltar and Black Sea by the Dardanelles, Sea of Marmara and Bosporus, E. part touches Asia in the Levant; total length W. to E. 2,200 m.; greatest width of sea proper about 700 m.; water a. 900,000 sq. m.; greatest depth 14,695 ft.; ch. Is.: Corsica, Sardinia, Sicily, Crete, Cyprus, and the Balearic, Lipari, Maltese, Ionian grs., also Grecian Archipelago.

Médoc, *old dist.*, Gironde, France, extending for about 48 m. along Garonne R.; noted for wines.

Medveditsa, *R.*, U.S.S.R.; trib. of R. Don; length 330 m.

Medway, *R.*, Kent, Eng.; length 70 m.; Medway Bridge (part of London–Dover motorway) completed 1962.

Meekatharra, *t.*, Murchison goldfields, W. Australia.

Meerane, *t.*, Karl-Marx-Stadt, E. Germany; textiles, machin., chemicals; p. (1963) *24,170.*

Meerut, *c.*, Uttar Pradesh, India; scene of outbreak of Indian Mutiny, 1857; p. (1961) *283,997.*

Megara, *t.*, Greece; p. (1951) *14,118.*

Mehsana, *t.*, Gujarat, India; rice, cotton, toabcco; p. (1961) *32,571.*

Meiktila, *dist.*, Upper Burma; teak forests; cap. M.; paper mill; p. (of t.) *8,830.*

Meiling Pass, on bdy. between Kwangtung, Kiangsi, S. China; provides historic routeway across Nanling mtns., followed by old imperial highway from Nanking to Canton; alt. approx. 1,000 ft.

Meiningen, t., Suhl, E. Germany; on R. Werra; cas.; machin., chemicals; p. (1963) 24,379.

Meiringen, t., Switzerland; nr. to Aar Gorge; resort, wood carving, hand weaving; p. 3.285.

Meissen, c., Dresden, E. Germany; on R. Elbe; cath.; famous porcelain wks., textiles, iron, furniture, elec. machine.; p. (1963) 47,676.

Meknès, c., Morocco, N. Africa; one of the caps. of M.; agr. ctr., olives; p. (1960) 175,943.

Mekong, R., S.E. Asia; rises in Tibet and separates Laos and Thailand; length 2,800 m.

Melanesia, chain of I. grs., S. Pacific: New Britain, Solomon, Santa Cruz, New Hebrides, New Caledonia, Loyalty and other archipelagos

Melbourne, spt. cap., Victoria, Australia; at mouth of Yarra R.; comm. ctr.; textile and knitting mills, machin. mftg., cars; botanical gardens; univ., caths.; p. (1966) 2,108,499.

Meld, t., Potenza, Italy; cath.; p. 14,300.

Melilla, spt., Morocco, N. Africa; exp. iron ore; convict settlement; p. (1950) 85,010.

Melipilla, t., central Chile; agr., dairy prod.; p. (1940) 9,316.

Melitopol, t., Ukrainian S.S.R.; engin.; ctr. of rich fruit growing a.; p. (1967) 115,000.

Melksham, t., urb. dist., Wilts, Eng.; on R. Avon, 5 m. N.E. of Bradford-on-Avon; rubber wks., heavy engin., flour mills, creameries, rope and matting; p. (1961) 8,279.

Mělník, t., ČSSR.; p. (1961) 13,100.

Melrose, burgh, Roxburgh, Scot.; on R. Tweed; 4 m. E. of Galashiels; ruined abbey, dist. ass. with Sir Walter Scott; p. (1961) 2,123.

Meltham, t., urb. dist., W.R. Yorks, Eng.; 4 m. S.W. of Huddersfield; woollen textiles; p. (1961) 5,413.

Melton Mowbray, t., urb. dist., Leicester, Eng.; on Lincoln Heights, 15 m. N.E. of Leicester; mkt., hunting dist.; famous pork pies; footwear, wool spinning mills; p. (1961) 15,913.

Melun, t., cap. Seine-et-Marne, France; on R. Seine; agr. tools and prod.; p. (1962) 23,796.

Melville I., off N. cst., Arnhem Land, Australia.

Melville I., N.W. Terrs., Arctic Canada. [Vjosa.

Memaliaj, t., Albania; new mng. t. on banks of R.

Memmingen, t., Bavaria, Germany; rly. junction; machin., textiles; p. (1963) 31,300.

Memphis, ancient c., Egypt; on R. Nile; 10 m. S. of Cairo; near by are Sakkara ruins.

Memphis, c., Tenn., U.S.A.; on R. Mississippi; rly. ctr., timber, cotton seed, ironwks., oil; textiles, chemicals; p. (1960) 497,524.

Mena, t., W. Ark., U.S.A.; lumber, bricks, cotton, flour; tourist resort; p. (1960) 4,388.

Menado, t., Sulawesi, Indonesia; p. (1961) 129,912.

Menai Bridge, urb. dist., Anglesey, Wales; p. (1961) 2,337.

Menai Strait, separates Isle of Anglesey from Caernarvon, Wales; crossed by Britannia rly. and Menai suspension bridges; 14 m. long, ¼ m. to 2 m. wide.

Menam, R., W. Thailand, length 750 m.

Menasha, t., Wis., U.S.A.; on L. Winnebago; mnfs.; p. (1960) 14,647.

Mende, t., cap. Lozère, France; on R. Lot; serge mftg.; p. (1962) 10,061.

Menden, t., N. Rhine–Westphalia, Germany; metallurgy, elec. prod.; p. (1963) 28,400.

Menderes, R., Anatolia, Turkey; length 200 m.

Mendip Hills, Somerset, Eng.; limestone range containing many karst features inc. Cheddar Gorge and Wookey Hole; length 20 m.; highest point 1,067 ft. [(1960) 6,154.

Mendota, c., Ill., U.S.A.; nr. Chicago, mftg.; p.

Mendoza, prov., W. Argentina; alfalfa, vines, olives, fruit, peppermint; cap. Mendoza; a. 57,445 sq. m.; p. (1960) 826,000.

Mendoza, t., cap. Mendoza prov., Argentina; on Transandine Rly.; wine-producing dist.; petroleum; p. (1960) of c. 110,000 greater M. 250,000.

Menen, t., W. Flanders, Belgium; tobacco tr., textiles, rubber gds., soap; p. (1962) 22,520.

Menfi, t., Sicily, Italy; industl.; p. 10,225.

Mengtsz, c., Yunnan, China; ruined in Tai-ping rebellion; tin, cotton ginning ctr.; p. 193,004.

Menominee, Mich., U.S.A.; on M. R.; industl. ctr. for lumber, sugar beets, dairy prod.; p. (1960) 11,289.

Menomonie, c., Wis., U.S.A.; on Red Cedar R.; farm ctr. and dairy prod.; p. (1960) 18,276.

Menteith, L., of, S.W. Perth, Scot.; between Rs. Forth and Teith; a. 2¼ sq. m.

Menton, t., Alpes-Maritimes, S. France; on Mediterranean cst.; health resort, olive oil, wines, perfumes; p. (1962) 20,069.

Meppel, t., Drenthe, Netherlands, 13 m. N. of Zwolle; shipbldg.; p. (1967) 19,192.

Merano, t., Tyrol, N. Italy; health resort; p.30,350.

Merced, t., Cal., U.S.A.; p. (1960) 20,068.

Mercedes, cap., Soriano dep., Uruguay; livestock ctr.; resort; p. (1963) 34,000.

Mercedes, t. S. Texas, U.S.A.; cotton, oil, fruit; veg. canning; p. (1960) 10,943.

Merchantville, bor., N.J., U.S.A.; paper, lead mnfs.; p. (1960) 4,075. [fishing.

Mergui, archipelago, Burma; teak, rice, pearl

Mergui, t., Tenasserim, Lower Burma; on Bay of Bengal; pearl fishing; p. 20,405.

Mérida, t., Badajoz, Spain; on R. Guadiana; agr. dist., textiles; p. 28,886.

Mérida, cap., Yucatán, Mexico; univ.; sisalhemp, ropes, cigars, brandy; p. (1960) 170,834.

Mérida, t., cap. Mérida st., Venezuelan Andes; univ., cath; tourist ctr.; world's highest cable rly. to Espejo peak (15,380 ft.); p. (1961) 40,404. [p. (1960) 51,850.

Meriden, c., Conn., U.S.A.; hardware mftg.;

Meridian, t., Miss., U.S.A.; in cotton-growing region; p. (1960) 49,374.

Mérignac, commune, Gironde dep., S.W. France; cattle mkt.; p. (1954) 23,050.

Merioneth, maritime co., N. Wales; pastoral and mining; nuclear power-sta. at Trawsfynydd; co. t., Dolgellau; a. 600 sq. m.; p. (1966) 38,000.

Meriti, c., S.E. Brazil; 10 m. N. Rio de Janeiro; p. (1947) 38,645. [Galilee, Israel.

Merom, Waters of, L., modern Hule L., Upper

Merrick, mtn., Kirkcudbright, Scot.; highest peak in S. Uplands of Scot.; alt. 2,764 ft.

Merill, t., N. Wis., U.S.A.; wooden goods, paper, knitwear; p. (1960) 9,451.

Merrimac, R., N.H. and Mass., U.S.A.

Merse, geographical sub-region, S.E. Scot.; comprises lower valleys of Rs. Tweed and Teviot below Melrose and Hawick; glacial deposits form low hillocks en échelon, which largely influence the pattern of streams, roads, settlements, etc.; most favoured part of Scot. for crop growing, wheat, barley, root crops (for feeding to cattle, sheep); ch. ts. Hawick, Kelso, Berwick-on-Tweed (Eng.); a. approx. 220 sq. m.

Mersea, I., at mouth of R. Colne, Essex, Eng.; oysters; holiday resort; length 5 m., width 2 m.

Merseburg, c., Halle, E. Germany; on R. Saale; cath., cas.; paper, machin., tobacco, chemicals; p. (1963) 52,545.

Mersey, R., between Lancs and Cheshire, Eng.; enters Irish Sea by fine estuary at Liverpool; length 68 m.

Merseyside, lge. conurbation, S.W. Lancs and N. Cheshire, Eng.; comprises: (1) spt. and industl. a. either side of lower Mersey estuary; (2) residtl. a. of W. Wirral Peninsula; a. 150 sq. m.; p. (1961) 1,385,702. See also under Bebington, Birkenhead, Bootle, Crosby, Ellesmere Pt., Hoylake, Huyton, Litherland, Liverpool, Neston, Wallasey, Wirral.

Mersey Tunnel, biggest underwater tunnel in world, linking Liverpool and Birkenhead; opened 1934; main tunnel 2 m. l., with branch bores, 3 m.; second tunnel (two-way) planned.

Mersin, spt., Turkey; oil refining; textiles, fruit, cereals, timber; p. (1965) 87,267.

Mertert-Grevenmacher, R. pt., on Moselle, Luxembourg.

Merthyr Tydfil, t., co. bor., Glamorgan, S. Wales; in narrow valley of R. Taff, 22 m. N.W. of Cardiff; hosiery, aircraft, bricks, elec. domestic goods; p. (1961) 59,008.

Merton, outer bor., Greater London, Eng.; inc. former bors. of Mitcham, Wimbledon, and Merton and Morden; p. (1966) 184,000.

Meru, mtn., Tanzania, E. Africa; extinct volcano overlooking E. arm of Gr. Rift valley; coffee plantations at alt. 5,000–6,000 ft., some rubber below 4,000 ft.; alt. summit 14,953 ft.

Merv, see Mary.

Mesa, t., Arizona, U.S.A.; agr. and cotton ginning ctr.; helicopter mftg.; p. (1960) 33,772.

Mesabi Range, hills, N.E. Minn., U.S.A.; about

100 m. long, alt. 200–500 ft.; vast iron-ore deposits.

Mesagna, *t.*, S. Italy; mnfs.; p. *17,300*.

Meshed, *see* Mashhad.

Mesopotamia, *see* Iraq.

Messina, *c.*, *spt.*, Sicily, Italy; opposite Reggio; univ.; exp. fruit, wine, silk, oil; silk mnf.; p. (1965) *265,000*.

Messina, *strait*, between Sicily and Italian mainland; length 22 m. minimum width 3 m.

Messinia, *prefecture*, Peloponnese, Greece; cap. Kalamaí; p. *210,728*.

Mesta, *R.*, Bulgaria, Greece; rises in Rhodope Mtns., flows S.E. into Ægean Sea 15 m. E. of Kaválla; valley famous for tobacco; known in Greece as Nestos; approx. length 175 m.

Mestre, *t.*, Italy; on lagoon at landward end of causeway linking Venice to mainland; p. *11,750*.

Mesurado, *R.*, Liberia, Africa; 300 m. long.

Meta, *R.*, Colombia and Venezuela; navigable for 400 m.; trib. of R. Orinoco; length 750 m.

Metemma, *t.*, Sudan; opposite Shendi, on R. Nile.

Methil, *t.*, Fife, Scot.; on F. of Forth; united with Buckhaven.

Methuen, *t.*, Mass., U.S.A.; textiles, footwear; p. (1960) *28,114*.                [(1960) *7,339*.

Metropolis, *c.*, Ill., U.S.A.; on R. Ohio; p.

Mettmann, *t.*, N. Rhine–Westphalia, Germany; nr. Düsseldorf; iron, machin.; p. (1963) *25,800*.

Metuchen, *bor.*, N.J., U.S.A.; residtl., chemicals, needles, rubber; p. (1960) *14,041*.

Metz, *c.*, cap. Moselle, France; on R. Moselle 25 m. N. of Nancy; cath.; metals, wines, leather goods, preserved fruits; p. (1962) *109,678*.

Meudon, *t.*, Hauts-de-Seine, France; nr. Versailles; observatory; glass, linen, ammunition; p. (1962) *35,824*.

Meurthe, *R.*, France; length 70 m.

Meurthe-et-Moselle, *dep.*, E. France; agr., vineyards, mining; cap. Nancy; a. 2,037 sq. m.; p. (1962) *678,073*.

Meuse, *dep.*, N.E. France; livestock, mining, wine; cap. Bar-le-Duc; a. 2,408 sq. m.; p. (1962) *215,985*.

Meuse (Maas), *R.*, France; rises in Haute-Marne, flows past Verdun into Belgium past Namur and Liége into the Netherlands and joins the Waal, left arm of the Rhine; length 570 m.

Mevagissey, *vil.*, Cornwall, Eng.; fishing and fish canning; tourist resort; p. *1,739*.

Mexborough, *t.*, *urb. dist.*, W.R. Yorks, Eng.; on R. Don, 10 m. above Doncaster; potteries, iron; p. (1961) *17,095*.              [500 m.

Mexcala, *R.*, S. Mexico; flows into Pacific; length

Mexia, *t.*, Texas, U.S.A.; rly. ctr.; cotton, oil, engin.; p. (1960) *6,121*.

Mexicali, *cap.*, N. Terr., Lower California, Mexico; p. (1960) *174,540*.

Mexico, *fed. rep.*, S. of N. America; contains much forest, fertile land and mtn. dists.; rich in minerals, silver, copper, arsenic, oil, zinc, lead; stock-raising and agr. are the ch. occupations in the N States; cap. Mexico City; a. 761,600 sq. m.; p. (estd. 1965) *40,913,000*.

Mexico City, *cap. c.*, Mexico; in plain, alt. 7,460 ft. above sea-level; many noteworthy bldgs.; extensive tr. and inds.; p. (1960) *2,832,133*.

Mexico, *st.*, Mexico; a. 8,267 sq. m.; cap. Toluca; p. (1960) *1,897,851*.

Mexico, *c.*, Mo., U.S.A.; firebrick and shoe factories; p. (1960) *12,889*.

Mexico, G. of, *lge. inlet* of the Atlantic (1,000 m. E. to W. by 800 m. N. to S.) lying S. of U.S.A. and E. of Mexico. Communicates by Florida Strait with the Atlantic and by Channel of Yucatán with the Caribbean Sea.

Meycauayan, *mun.*, Luzon, Philippines; rice, sugar, maize; p. *16,082*.

Mezhdurechensk, *t.*, R.S.F.S.R.; W. Siberia, on R. Tom'; new coalmng. ctr.; p. (1959) *55,000*.

Mézières, *see* Charleville-Mézières.

Mezőkövesd, *t.*, Hungary; agr. and industl.; p. (1962) *18,640*.              [(1962) *23,329*.

Mezőtúr, *t.*, Hungary; mkt., flour, pottery; p.

Mhow, *t.*, Madhya Pradesh, India; cotton; p. (1961) *48,032*.

Miagao, *t.*, Panay, Philippines; tr. ctr., mnfs.

Miami, *c.*, Fla., U.S.A.; on Biscayne Bay, at mouth of Miami R.; famous resort and recreational ctr.; varied inds.; intern. airpt.; p. (1960) *291,688*.

Miami, *t.*, Okla., U.S.A.; tr. ctr., agr., cattle; packing, mining; p. (1960) *12,869*.

Miamisburg, *t.*, Ohio, U.S.A.; p. (1960) *9,893*.

Miani, *t.* N.W. Punjab, Pakistan; salt; p. about 6,000.                        [(1951) *550,000*.

Mianwali, *dist.*, W. Punjab, Pakistan; p. (estd.

Miass, *t.*, R.S.F.S.R. in Urals, 56 m. S.W. Chelyabinsk; gold mng. ctr.; cars; p. (1967) *119,000*.

Michigan, *st.*, U.S.A.; in valley of Gr. Lakes; industl.; cars, iron and steel goods, petroleum, minerals; some agr.; cap. Lansing; a. 58,216 sq. m.; p. (1960) *7,823,194*.

Michigan, *L.*, N. America; in basin of St. Lawrence R., enclosed by two peninsulas of the st. of M. and by Wis., Ill. and Ind.; a. 23,900 sq. m.; discharges by Straits of Mackinac to L. Huron.

Michigan City, *t.*, Ind., U.S.A.; on L. M.; rly. wks., furniture, hosiery; (1960) *36,653*.

Michipicoten, *R.*, Ontario, Canada; flows 125 m. to L. Superior.

Michoacan, *st.*, Mexico; on the Pacific; mtnous. and rich in minerals; cap. Morelia; a. 23,200 sq. m.; p. (1960) *1,851,876*.

Michurinsk, *t.*, R.S.F.S.R.; N.W. of Tambov; engin., textiles, food inds.; agr. exp. ctr.; p. (1959) *80,000*.

Micronesia, *grs. of sm. Is.*, S. Pacific; includes Carolines, Marianas (Ladrones), Marshall, Pelews, etc.

Middleburg, *t.*, cap. Zeeland, Neth.; on Walcheren I. nr. Flushing; margarine, timber, optical instruments; p. (1967) *27,996*.

Middelburg, *t.*, Transvaal, S. Africa; coal, iron, copper, cobalt; p. (1960) *12,907* inc. *4,886* Europeans.

Middelfart, *t.*, Fyn, Denmark; off Fredericia; p. (1960) *8,801*.

Middleboro, *t.*, Mass., U.S.A.; agr. ctr.; p. (1960) *6,003*.

Middle Congo, fmr. Fr. col. *See* Congo, Rep. of.

Middlesboro, *t.*, Ky., U.S.A.; p. (1960) *12,607*.

Middlesbrough, *spt.*, Cleveland dist., N.R. Yorks., Eng.; enlarged M. now forms co. bor. of Teeside; on S. side of Tees estuary; impt. iron and steel ind., heavy engin., shipbldg. and coal exp.; oil refinery projected; p. (1961) *157,308*.

Middlesex, *former co.*, S.E. Eng.; N. of R. Thames; completely absorbed in Greater London 1964; a. 232 sq. m.; p. (1961) *2,230,093*.

Middleton, *mkt. t.*, Durham, Eng.; civil airport projected; on R. Tees.

Middleton, *t.*, *mun. bor.*, S.E. Lancs, Eng.; mkt.; textiles, engin., chemicals; p. (estd. 1967) *53,140*.

Middletown, *c.*, Conn., U.S.A.; on C. R.; univ.; p. (1960) *33,250*.

Middletown, *c.*, N.Y., U.S.A.; on Walkill R.; ironwks.; p. (1960) *23,475*.

Middletown, *c.*, Ohio, U.S.A.; in Miami and Erie canal; p. (1960) *42,115*.

Middletown, *bor.*, Penns., U.S.A.; on Susquehanna R.; p. (1960) *11,182*.

Middlewich, *t.*, *urb. dist.*, Cheshire, Eng.; on Rs. Dane, Wheelock, and Croco, 5 m. N. of Crewe; salt, chemicals, silk, clothing; p. (1961) *6,533*.

Midhurst, *t.*, Sussex, Eng.; on R. Rother; mkt., agr. ctr.; brick, timber, lime wks.; p. *1,812*.

Midland, *t.*, Mich., U.S.A.; chemicals, salt, oil; p. (1960) *27,779*.

Midland, *t.*, Texas, U.S.A.; oilfield ctr., cotton ginning, natural gas; p. (1960) *62,625*.

Midleton, *urb. dist.*, Cork, Ireland; mkt.; p. (1966) *4,173*.

Midlothian, *co.*, Scot.; dairying, coal-mining, paper, brewing, fishing; a. 362 sq. m.; p. (1961) *580,332*.            [(1961) *59,532*.

Midnapore, *t.*, W. Bengal, India; silkworm tr.; p.

Midway, *Is.*, Pac. Oc.; calling-place on air-routes between San Francisco and Asia, mid-way between Asia and U.S.A. (to which it belongs).

Miechowice, *t.*, S.W. Poland; coal, iron foundries; p. *14,608*.              [leather; p. *16,837*.

Miedzyrzecz (Meseritz), *t.*, E. Poland; agr.,

Mieres, *t.*, Spain; on R. Leno, nr. Oviedo; minerals, agr. prod.; p. (1959) *69,623*.

Mihama, Fukui, Japan; nuclear reactor under construction 1968.

Mihoro, Gifu, Japan; power plant under construction.

Mikkeli (St. Michel), *dep.*, Finland; a. 6,750 sq. m.; p. (1966) *230,144*.

Milan, *c.*, N. Italy; on R. Olona; cath., univ.; textiles, machin., motors, chemicals, procelain;

cultural. comm. and industl. ctr.; p. (1965) *1,673,000.*

Milas, *t.,* S.W. Turkey in Asia; agr., fruit; carpets; p. (1960) *11,676.*

Mildenhall, *t.,* W. Suffolk, Eng.; on R. Lark, 10 m. N.W. of Bury St. Edmunds; mkt., flour; p. *3,235.*

Mildura, *c.,* Victoria, Australia; on R. Murray; irrigation ctr., fruit, canning, food processing; p. (1966) *12,931.*

Miles City, *c.,* Mont., U.S.A.; on Yellowstone R.; cattle; p. (1960) *3,665.*

Milford, *t.,* Conn., U.S.A.; residtl., resort; fish; light engin.; p. (1960) *41,662.* [13,722.

Milford, *t.,* Mass., U.S.A.; boot mnfs.; p. (1960)

Milford Haven, *spt., urb. dist.,* Milford Haven, Pembroke, Wales; major oil pt., providing access and anchorage for 100,000-ton oil tankers; refinery, fishing, trawlers built and repaired, net mkg., beryllium; p. (1961) *12,802.*

Milford Sound, *inlet,* at S. extremity of S.I. N.Z., tourist restort; noted for grandeur of scenery, and rare birds.

Milianah, *t.,* Algeria; tr. ctr.; p. *5,000.*

Militello, *t.,* Sicily, Italy; agr., interests; p. *10,770.*

Milk, *R.,* Mont., U.S.A.; trib. of Missouri R.; length 500 m.

Millau, *t.,* Aveyron, France; on R. Tarn; glove mnfs.; p. (1962) *22,174.*

Millbrook, *t.,* Hants, Eng.; at mouth of R. Test, nr. Southampton.

Millersburg, *bor.,* Penns., U.S.A.; machin., shoes; p. (1950) *2,861.* [7,318.

Millinocket, *t.,* Me., U.S.A.; paper; p. (1960)

Millom, *t.,* Cumberland, Eng.; on N.W. cst. of Duddon estuary; ironwks. (closed 1968 after 100 years); p. *8,708.*

Millport, *burgh,* Bute, Scot.; on Gr. Cumbrae I., in F. of Clyde; resort; cath.; quarries; p. (1961) *1,592.*

Millville, *c.,* N.J., U.S.A.; on Maurice R.; glass, iron, cotton; p. (1960) *19,096.*

Milnerton, *t.,* S. Africa; nitrogenous fertiliser plant.

Milngavie, *burgh,* Dunbarton, Scot.; 5 m. N.W. of Glasgow; textiles; p. (1961) *8,594.*

Milnrow, *t., urb. dist.,* S.E. Lancs, Eng.; sub. of Rochdale; cotton and waste spinning, engin., brick mkg., paper and tube mftg.; p. (1961) *7,819.*

Milos, *I.,* Cyclades, Greece; volcanic; length 13 m.; fruits, gypsum, sulphur; famous statue of Venus found here in 1820. [p. *11,291.*

Milspe, *commune,* Westphalia, Germany; ironwks.;

Milstin, *peak,* Atlas Mtns., Morocco, N. Africa; alt. 11,400 ft.

Milton, *t.,* Mass., U.S.A.; sub. of Boston; p. (1960) *26,375.*

Milton, *t.,* Penns., U.S.A.; on Susquehanna R.; ironwks.; p. (1960) *7,972.*

Milton Keynes, *vil.* Bucks; a. 3 sq. m.; site and name of new c. for London overspill to comprise Bletchley, Wolverton and Stoney Stratford; a. 34 sq. m. [mkt.

Milverton, *t.,* Somerset, Eng.; 6 m. W. of Taunton.

Milwaukee, *c.,* Wis., U.S.A.; on L. Michigan, 70 m. N. of Chicago; univ.; rly. ctr., cars, meat canning, agr. tools, machin., iron and steel castings, generators; dairying; p. (1960) *741,324.*

Mimico, *t.,* Ontario, Canada; p. (1961) *18,212.*

Minab, *t.,* Iran; orchards; p. about *10,000.*

Mina Hassan Tani (Kenitra), *t.,* Morocco; 18 m. N. of Rabat; developed since 1912; exp. grain; p. (1960) *86,775.* [Canada.

Minas Basin, *E. arm,* Bay of Fundy, Nova Scotia,

Minas Gerais, *st.,* Brazil; extensive mining, diamonds, gold, iron, manganese, aluminium, cotton, coffee, agr.; cap. Belo Horizonte; a. 224,701 sq. m.; p. (1960) *9,798,880.*

Minas Novas, *t.,* Minas Gerais, Brazil.

Minatitlán, *t.,* E. Mexico; petroleum refineries; petrochemicals; p. (1940) *13,539.*

Minch, The, *channel* between the Outer and Inner Hebrides; 24 m. to 40 m. wide.

Minchinhampton, *t.,* Gloucester, Eng.; in Cotswold Hills, 4 m. S.E. of Stroud; mkt., woollens, brewing; p. *3,500.*

Mincio, *R.,* Italy; trib. of R. Po; drains L. Garda; length 38 m.

Mindanao, 2nd lgst. I. of Philippines; pineapples, hemp, coconuts, coffee; iron, gold, coal, copper,

plywoods and veneer; paper, pulp; ch. ts. Zamboanga, Davao; off N.E. cst. is Mindanao Deep (c. 35,000 ft), one of greatest known ocean depths; a. 36,536 sq. m.; p. (1960) *5,358,900.*

Minden, *c.,* N. Rhine–Westphalia, Germany; on R. Weser at crossing of Mittelland Canal; cath.; glass, tobacco, metal, wood, leather, meat prod.; p. (1963) *48,900.*

Minden, *t.,* La., U.S.A.; exp. cotton; petroleum, natural gas; p. (1960) *12,785.*

Mindoro, *I.,* Philippines, S. of Luzon; a. 3,759 sq. m.; p. (1960) *291,100.*

Minehead, *t., urb. dist.,* Somerset, Eng.; at N. foot of Exmoor, on Bristol Channel cst.; mkt., holiday resort; p. (1961) *7,674.*

Mineo, *t.,* Sicily, Italy; mftg.; p. *11,400.*

Mineola, *t.,* N.Y., U.S.A.; sub. N.Y. c.; glass, packing; p. (1960) *20,519.*

Minersville, *bor.,* Penns., U.S.A.; on Schuylkill R.; p. (1960) *6,606.*

Minervino, *t.,* S. Italy; industl.; p. *18,375.*

Minho, *R.,* separates Portugal from Spain in N.W.; length 170 m.

Minia, *t.,* U.A.R.; on R. Nile; cotton, tr. ctr; p. (1960) *94,000.*

Minicoy Is., Arabian Sea, joined with Laccadive and Amindivi Is. to form *Union terr.* (India).

Minneapolis, *c.,* Minn., U.S.A.; on Mississippi R., at Falls of St. Anthony; univ.; flour, timber, agr. machin., linseed oil; chemicals, textiles, paper; p. (1960) *482,327.*

Minnesota, *st.,* U.S.A.; iron-ore, agr., flour, timber, meat; cap. St. Paul; a. 84,068 sq. m.; p. (1960) *3,413,864.*

Minnick, Water of, *R.,* Ayr and Kirkcudbright, Scot.; trib. of R. Cree; length 15 m.

Minorca (Menorca), Spanish I., Balearic Is., Mediterranean Sea; fruits, olives, cereals, cattle, minerals; cap. Mahón; a. 283 sq. m.; p. (1957) *42,473.*

Minot, *t.,* N.D., U.S.A.; p. (1960) *30,604.*

Minsk, *cap.,* Byelorussian S.S.R.; univ.; engin., textiles, elec. power; p. (1967) *717,000.*

Minya Konka, *mtn.,* Szechwan, China; at E. end of Plateau of Tibet; highest mtn. in China; alt. approx. 23,000 ft.

Miosnavo, *L.,* Norway; length 24 m.

Miquelon, *I.,* French, off S. cst. Newfoundland, Canada; fisheries.

Mira, *t.,* Italy; on Brenta Morta; p. *19,600.*

Miranda, *st.,* N. Venezuela; pastoral and agr.; cap. Los Teques; p. (1961) *492,349.*

Miranda, *t.,* N.E. Spain; on R. Ebro; p. (1957) *18,094.*

Mirandola, *t.,* Modena, Italy; p. *20,875.*

Mirano, *t.,* N. Italy; p. *14,600.*

Mirfield, *t., urb. dist.,* W.R. Yorks, Eng.; on R. Calder, 3 m. S.W. of Dewsbury; woollens; p. (1961) *12,289.*

Miri, *t.,* Sarawak; oil ctr.; p. (1960) *13,350.*

Mirim, *L.,* Brazil and Uruguay; 115 m. long, 20 m. wide.

Mirzapur, *t.,* Uttar Pradesh, India; on R. Ganges; carpets, brassware; p. (1961) *100,097.*

Misburg, *vil.,* Lower Saxony, Germany; on Weser-Elbe Canal, 5 m. E. of Hanover; oil refining; p. (estd.) *8,830.*

Mishawaka, *c.,* Ind., U.S.A.; on St. Joseph R.; agr. implements; p. (1960) *33,361.*

Misilmeri, *t.,* Sicily, Italy; p. *11,420.*

Misiones, *terr.,* Argentina; farming and stockraising; cap. Posadas; a. 11,749 sq. m.; p. (1960) *391,000.*

Miskolcz, *t.,* Hungary; univ.; porcelain, textiles, iron and steel, cement, bricks, refrigeration plants; p. (1965) *167,000.*

Misoöl, *I.,* N. of Ceram, Indonesia.

Mission, *t.,* S. Texas, U.S.A.; fruit, cotton, vegetables; engin.; p. (1960) *14,081.*

Mississinewa, *R.,* Ind., U.S.A.; trib. of Wabash R.; length 140 m.

Mississippi, *st.,* U.S.A.; cotton, sweet potatoes, pecan nuts, rice, sugar cane, sorghum cane; cable; petroleum, natural gas, chemicals, shipbldg.; cap. Jackson; a. 47,716 sq. m.; p. (1960) *2,178,101.*

Mississippi, *R.,* Canada; trib. of Ottawa R.; length 100 m.

Mississippi, *R.,* U.S.A.; length c. 2,350 m. (Mississippi-Missouri-Red Rock, c. 3,860 m.).

Missolonghi, *c., spt., cap.,* Aetolia and Acarnania, Greece; currants; p. (1961) *11,266.*

Missoula, c., Mont., U.S.A.; on Klark R.; univ.; rly. wks., agr., fruit, oil ref.; p. (1960) 27,090.

Missouri, st., U.S.A.; livestock, maize, coal, iron, tobacco; cap. Jefferson City; ch. t. St. Louis; a. 69,674 sq. m.; p. (1960) 4,319,813.

Missouri, R., U.S.A.; trib. of Mississippi R.; length (including the Madison) 3,047 m., navigable 2,400 m.

Missouri Coteau, hill ridge, N. America; runs N.W. to S.E. across prairies of Saskatchewan (Canada), N. and S. Dakota (U.S.A.); rises abruptly from 1,600 to 2,000 ft.

Missouri, Little, R., U.S.A.; trib. of M. R.; length 450 m.

Mistassini, L., Quebec, Canada; 100 m. long.

Mistretta, t., Sicily, Italy; mnfs.; p. 10,800.

Misurata, t., Tripolitania, Libya, N. Africa; on cst. of Mediterranean, 110 m. E. of Tripoli; mkt. for local agr. produce; fishing; p. (1954) 66,735.

Mitau, see Jelgava.

Mitcham, former mun. bor., Surrey, Eng.; now inc. in Merton outer London bor.(q.v.); paint, calico printing, elec. engin.; p. (1961) 63,653.

Mitchell, R., Queensland, Australia; flows into G. of Carpentaria.

Mitchell, t., S. Dakota, U.S.A.; univ.; farming; p. (1960) 12,555.

Mitchell, mtn. pk., Black Mtns., N. Carolina, U.S.A.; alt. 6,684 ft.; also called the " Black Dome."

Mitchelstown, t., Cork, Ireland; nr. Fermoy; p. (1966) 2,617.

Mitidja, plain, Algeria, N. Africa; borders Mediterranean 25 m. E. and W. of Algiers; intensive cultivation of vine; [ch. ts. Algiers, Blida.

Mito, c., N. Japan; lime tree growing; p. (1965) 154,983.

Mitrovica, t., Jugoslavia; on R. Sava; livestock, mkt.; p. (1959) 22,000.

Mittelland Canal, inland waterway system, N. Germany; system of canals and canalised Rs.; links Dortmund-Ems Canal nr. Rheine through Minden, Hanover, Magdeburg, Berlin to R. Oder at Frankfurt-on-Oder; makes use of natural E.–W. troughs across the N. German Plain.

Mittweida, t., Karl-Marx-Stadt, E. Germany; metallurgy, textiles; p. (1963) 20,592.

Miyazaki, c., Kyushu, Japan; famous shrine; chemicals, lumbering; p. (1965) 132,870.

Mizen Head, C., S. Ireland; W. of C. Clear.

Mjösa, lost. L., Norway; 55 m. long.

Mlada Boleslav (Jungbunzlau), t., Bohemia, ČSSR.; religious ctr., chemicals; p. (1961) 25,694.

Mljet, I., Adriatic Sea; part of Jugoslavia.

Moanda, Leopoldville, Congo; oil refinery.

Moate, t., W. Meath Ireland; p. (1951) 1,274.

Moberly, c., Mo., U.S.A.; rly. wks., grain, iron, hosiery, footwear; p. (1960) 13,170.

Mobile, c., spt., Ala., U.S.A.; on R. M.; shipbldg., cotton exp.; p. (1960) 202,779.

Moçâmedes, pt., Angola, W. Africa; ore pier; linked by rail to Cassinga mines.

Mocha, fortfd. spt., Yemen, Arabia; on Red Sea; coffee; p. 5,000.

Modane, t., S.E. Savoie, France; commands routes via Mont Cenis Pass and tunnel; p. (1962) 5,137.

Modder, R., C. Prov., S. Africa; trib. of Orange R.

Modena, t., prov. cap., Italy; cath., univ.; textiles, fruit, grain, leather; p. (1961) 139,496.

Modesto, t., Cal., U.S.A.; fruit, vegetables; p. (1960) 36,585.

Modica, t., Sicily, Italy; cheese, macaroni, grain, wines; p. (1961) 44,050.

Modjokerto, t., E. Java, Indonesia; sugar; fossil man discovered 1934; p. 23,600.

Mödling, t., Austria; on R. Brühl, metalwks., sulphur-baths; p. (1961) 17,274.

Moers, t., N. Rhine-Westphalia, Germany; N.E. of Krefeld; cas.; coal-mining, metal ind.; p. (estd. 1954) 36,300.

Moffat, burgh, Dumfries, Scot.; in Annandale, 15 m. N.W. of Lockerbie; health resort; p. (1961) 1,917.

Moffat Tunnel, Col., U.S.A.; carries trunk rly. from Chicago to San Francisco under Rocky Mtns. between Denver and Salt Lake City; length 6¼ m.

Mogadishu, cap., Somalia, N.E. Africa; fish canning, hides; p. (1958) 86,643.

Mogador, see Essaouira.

Mogilev, c., Byelorussian S.S.R.; on R. Dnieper; engin., textiles, chemicals; p. (1967) 164,000.

Mogilev Podolski, t., Ukrainian S.S.R.; on Dniester R.; tr., flour, sugar refining; p. (1939) 22,271.

Mohác, t., Hungary; on R. Danube; R. pt.; flour, brewing; p. (1962) 18,100.

Mohammedia, t., Morocco, N. Africa; oil refining; p. (1960) 35,010.

Mohawk, R., N.Y., U.S.A.; trib. of Hudson R.; followed by impt. road, rly. and canal routes across Appalachian Mtns.; length 175 m.

Moidart, L., cst. dist., S.W. Inverness, Scot.

Moisie, R., Labrador, Canada, flows S. into G. of St. Lawrence.

Moissac, t., France; on R. Tarn; abbey; p. 7,435.

Mojave, desert, Cal., U.S.A.

Moji, spt., Kyushu, Japan; now part of Kitakyushu City newly formed 1963 (q.v.); exp. coal, cement, timber, sugar, cotton, thread; p. (1960) 152,081.

Mokan, R., S.I., N.Z.

Mokpo, spt., W. cst. S. Korea; ctr. of food-processing and cotton-ginning; p. (1955) 113,492.                           [ctr.; p. (1962) 25,404.

Mol, t., N.E. Belgium; nuclear energy research

Mola di Bari, spt., Apulia, Italy; grain, livestock, olives, wine; p. 18,775.

Mola di Gaeta, t., Italy; p. 15,950.

Mold, co. t., urb. dist., Flint, N. Wales; on R. Alyn; chemicals, roadstone; p. (1961) 6,857.

Moldau, see Vltava.

Moldavian S.S.R., const. rep., U.S.S.R.; viniculture, fruit-growing, mkt. gard.; cap. Kishinev; a. 13,200 sq. m.; p. (1959) 2,880,000.

Moldavia, prov. Romania; a. 14,660 sq. m.; wine; ch. t. Jassy; p. 2,350,063.

Mole, R., Surrey, Eng.; rises in central Weald, flows N. into R. Thames nr. Molesey; cuts impt. gap through N. Downs between Dorking and Leatherhead; length approx. 50 m.

Molenbeek-Saint-Jean, t., Belgium; nr. Brussels; large mftg. ctr.; p. (1962) 63,433.

Molesey, E. and W. t., Surrey, Eng.; at junction of Rs. Mole and Thames; residtl.; p. 8,500.

Molfetta, spt., Apulia, Italy; olive oil, macaroni, wine; p. (1961) 61,684.

Molina de Segura, commune, S.E. Spain; tinned food and jams; salt wks; p. (1957) 14,683.

Moline, c., Ill., U.S.A.; on Mississippi R.; agr. implements, ironwks., flour; p. (1960) 42,705.

Molise, region, S. Central Italy, on Adriatic; cap. Campobasso.                           [18,000.

Mollendo, spt., Peru; bricks, fishing; p. (1961)

Mölndal, c., S.W. Sweden; paper, textiles; margarine; p. (1961) 26,502.

Molokai, I., Hawaiian Is.; a. 260 sq. m.; p. 5,258.

Molotov, see Perm.

Molsheim, t., Bas-Rhin, France; W. of Strasbourg; sword and bayonet mkg; p. (1962) 5,197.

Molucca or Spice Is., Indonesia; between Sulawesi and West Irian; spices, sago, timber, pearls, rice, copra; ch. t. Ternate; a. 191,681 sq. m.; p. (1961) 789,534.

Mombasa, spt., Kenya; ch. harbour, Killindini; rly. terminus; oil refinery; exp. tropical produce (ivory, hides, rubber, etc.); p. (1962) 178,400.

Mön, I., off cst. of Själland, Denmark; a. 90 sq. m.; cap. Stege; p. (1960) 13,107.

Mona Passage, strait, Caribbean Sea; separates Hispaniola from Puerto Rico.

Monaca, bor., Penns., U.S.A.; glass, light engin.; p. (1960) 8,394.

Monaco, principality, S. France; divided into 3 sections, Monaco Ville, La Condamine and Monte Carlo (famous Casino); tourism; olive oil, perfumes; a. 8 sq. m.; p. (1961) 20,441.

Monadhliath Mtns., Inverness, Scot.; on W. side Strathspey; highest peak Carn Mairg, 3,087 ft.

Monaghan, inland co., Ireland; mainly pastoral and agr.; a. 500 sq. m.; p. (1966) 45,726.

Monaghan, co. t., Monaghan, Ireland; on the Ulster Canal; cath.; p. (1966) 4,019.

Monaro, mtn. plateau, N.S.W., Australia; a. 8,335 sq. m.

Monastir, see Bitolj.

Moncalieri, commune, Piedmont, N.W. Italy; on R. Po; industl.; p. 21,181.

Mönch or "The Monk", mtn., Bernese Alps, Switzerland; alt. 13,468 ft.

Mönchen-Gladbach, t., Land, North Rhine-Westphalia, Germany; 16 m. W. of Düsseldorf; rly. ctr., cotton and wool; p. (1963) 153,400.

Monchique, *t.*, Algarve, Portugal; spa; wine, oil, chestnuts; p. *10,000.*

Monclova, *t.*, N.E. Mexico; coffee; copper, silver, zinc, lead-mines; p. (1941) *7,181.*

Moncton, *t.*, N.B., Canada; rly. ctr., textiles; oil near by; p. (1961) *43,840.*

Mondego, *R.*, Portugal; length 130 m.

Mondovi, *t.*, Cuneo, Italy; porcelain, paper, silk; p. *20,900.* [wire; p. (1960) *18,428.*

Monessen, *t.*, Penns., U.S.A.; steel, tinplate,

Monfalcone, *commune*, N.E. Italy; chemicals, shipbldg., cotton mills; p. (1948) *19,634*

Monferrato, *low hills*, Piedmont, N. Italy; S. and S.E. of Turin between valleys of R. Po and R. Tanaro; celebrated vineyards, produce Asti Spumante wines; alt. never exceeds 1,500 ft.

Monforte, *t.*, Galicia, Spain; soap, linen; p. (1957) *21,682.*

Monghyr, *dist.*, Bihar, India; a. 3,975 sq. m.; agr., mica; p. (1961) *3,387,082.*

Mongla, *pt.*, E. Pakistan; on Pussur R.; shipping pt. under construction.

Mongol-Buryat, A.S.S.R., U.S.S.R.; E. of L. Baikal; cattle breeding.

Mongolia, *vast elevated plateau*, in heart of Asia between China and U.S.S.R. See Mongolian People's Republic and Inner Mongolia.

Mongolia, Inner, *see* Inner Mongolia.

Mongolian People's Republic (Outer Mongolia), *indep. st.*, Asia; bordered by China on W., S. and E. and by U.S.S.R. on N.; mainly plateau 5,000–10,000 ft. with Altai mtns. in N.W. and Gobi Desert in S.; watered by numerous Rs.; many Ls.; cap. Ulan Bator; livestock, wool, hides, skins; gold, coal; close links with U.S.S.R.; a. 604,000 sq. m.; p. (estd. 1965) *1,050,000.* [546 sq. m.; p. (1966) *462,000.*

Monmouth, *co.*, Eng.; coal, iron, steel, agr.; a.

Monmouth, *co. t., mun. bor.*, Monmouth, Eng.; at confluence of Rs. Wye and Monnow; mkt. ctr.; tinplate, timber, crushed limestone, wrought ironwk.; p. (estd. 1967) *6,010.*

Monmouth, *t.*, Ill., U.S.A.; mnfs., coal; p. (1960) *10,372.*

Monnow, *R.*, Monmouth and Hereford, Eng.; trib. of R. Wye; length 28 m.

Monongahela, *R.*, W. Va., U.S.A.; joins Allegheny R. at Pittsburgh to form Ohio R.

Monongahela City, Penns., U.S.A.; mining, natural gas; p. (1960) *8,388.*

Monopoli, *spt.*, Apulia, Italy; oil, wine, fruit, flour tr.; p. *26,725.* [p. *18,525.*

Monreale, *t.*, Sicily, Italy; cath.; fruit, almonds;

Monroe, *c.*, La., U.S.A.; cotton ctr., natural gas, paper, printing ink; p. (1960) *52,219.*

Monroe, *t.*, Mich., U.S.A.; paper, machin.; p. (1960) *22,968.* [p. (1960) *10,882.*

Monroe, *t.*, N.C., U.S.A.; marble quarries; mftg.;

Monrovia, *cap., spt.*, Liberia, Africa; at mouth of R. St. Paul; exp. rubber, palm oil; p. estd. (1965) *81,000.*

Mons, *t.*, Belgium; on R. Trouville; cath.; rly. junction; coal, cotton, rayon, iron, engin., glass, brewing, radios, aluminium ware; H.Q. of NATO(SHAPE) nearby at Casteau; p. (1962) *27,062.*

Monserrat or Montserrat, *mtn.*, Spain; alt. 4,000 ft.

Monsummano, *t.*, Italy; N.W. of Florence; health resort; some mnfs.; p. *9,125.*

Montagnana, *t.*, Italy; p. *12,100.*

Mont Blanc, *mtn.*, Alps; on confines of Italy and France; alt. 15,782 ft.; longest road tunnel in world (opened to traffic 1965) linking Courmayeur (Italy) and Chamonix (France), length 7½ m.

Mont Cenis Pass, W. Alps; on bdy. between France and Italy; approached from W. by Isère–Arc valleys, from E. by Dora Riparia; alt. 6,876 ft.

Mont Cenis Tunnel, W. Alps; on bdy. between France and Italy; carries main rly. from Lyons to Turin under Col de Fréjus; approached from W. by Isère–Arc valleys, from E. by Dora Riparia; opened 1871; length 7½ m.

Mont-d'Or, *mtns.*, France; highest peak, 6,188 ft.

Mont Genèvre, *mtn.*, Cottian Alps, France; alt. 6,100 ft. [power project.

Mont St. Michel, *I.*, N. France; tourist ctr; tidal

Montalcino, *t.*, Italy; industl.; p. *9,925.*

Montana, *st.*, U.S.A.; cap. Helena; Rocky Mtns.; copper, silver, gold, lead; pastoral, agr.; a. 147,138 sq. m.; p. (1960) *674,767.*

Montargis, *t.*, Loiret, France; hosiery, chemicals, rubber; p. (1962) *17,645.*

Montauban, *t.*, Tarn-et-Garonne, France; on R. Tarn; cath.; silk, agr. produce, wines; p. (1962) *43,401.*

Montbéliard, *t.*, Doubs, France; S. of Belfort; watch, textiles, mngs., agr. tr.; p. (1962) *23,374.*

Montceau-les-Mines, *t.*, Saône-et-Loire, France; coal, textiles, metal-working; p. (1962) *29,364.*

Montclair, *t.*, N.J., U.S.A.; residtl. suburb of New York; paper goods mnfs.; p. (1960) *43,129.*

Mont-de-Marsan, *t.*, Landes, France; p. (1962) *23,254.*

Monte Bello Is., *gr.*, off N.W. cst., Australia, about 85 m. N. of pt. of Onslow; first British atomic weapon exploded here 3 Oct. 1952.

Monte Carlo, *t.*, Monaco; tourist resort, casino; p. (1961) *9,516.*

Monte Corno, *mtn.*, Italy; in Central Apennines; alt. 9,583 ft.

Monte Gargano, *peninsula*, S. Italy; projects into Adriatic Sea nr. plain of Foggia; formed by limestone plateau, alt. over 3,000 ft.; pasture on upper slopes, woodland on lower slopes; a. approx. 400 sq. m. [p. *5,575.*

Monte Maggiore, *t.*, Sicily, Italy; agr. interests;

Monte Perdu, *mtn.*, Pyrenees, Spain; alt. 10,997 ft.

Monte Rosa, *gr.*, Pennine Alps, on border of Italy and Switzerland; highest peak 15,203 ft.

Monte Rotondo, *highest mtn.*, Corsica; alt. 9,071 ft.

Monte Sant-Angelo, *t.*, Italy; pilgrim ctr.; p. *24,550.*

Monte Viso, *mtn.*, Cottian Alps, Italy; alt. 12,605 ft.

Montecristi, *t.*, W. Ecuador; Panama hats; copra mkt.; p. (estd. 1962) *4,000.*

Montefrio, *t.*, Spain; W. of Granada; cas.; alcohol, soap, cotton mnfs.; p. *12,000.*

Montégnée, *commune*, Liége prov., E. Belgium; mftg. sub. Liége; p. (1962) *11,503.*

Montego Bay, *spt.*, Jamaica; famous for its beauty; p. (1947) *11,547.*

Monteleone di Calabria, *t.*, Italy; cas.; p. *15,675.*

Montélimar, *t.*, Drôme, France; nr. R. Rhône; bricks, tiles, "nougat," coal-mining; p. (1954) *16,632.*

Montenegro, *dist.*, Jugoslavia; agr., pastoral; cap. Cetinje; a. 13,837 sq. m.; p. (1960) *489,000.*

Montereau-faut-Yonne, *t.*, Seine-et-Marne, France; on R. Seine; agr. tools, footwear, brick mftg.; p. (1962) *14,121.*

Monterey, *c.*, Cal., S. of San Francisco; resort of artists and writers; impt. sardine indus., fruit, and veg. canneries; p. (1960) *22,618.*

Monteria, *t.*, cap. Cordoba, Colombia, S. America; tobacco, cacao, cotton, sugar; p. (1959) *96,150.*

Monterrey, *t., cap.*, Nuevo León, Mexico; cath.; textiles, brewing, ironwks., minerals; thermoelec. plant; sheet metal; p. (1960) *596,993.*

Montespertoli, *mkt. t.*, Italy; S.W. Florence; p. *11,850.* [p. *15,300.*

Montevarchi, *t.*, Italy; on R. Arno; industl.;

Montevideo, *spt., cap.*, Uruguay; on N. cst. of La Plata estuary; univ.; livestock prod. mnfs. and exp.; p. (estd. 1956) *922,385.*

Montezuma, *t.*, Ga., U.S.A.; mkt. for winter mkt. garden produce, cottonseed oil; p. (1950) *2,921.*

Montgomery, *co.*, N.E. Wales; cap. Montgomery; a. 797 sq. m.; p. (1966) *44,000.*

Montgomery, *co. t., mun. bor.*, Montgomery, N.E. Wales; in upper Severn valley, 8 m. N.E. of Newtown; agr. mkt.; p. (1961) *970.*

Montgomery, *c., cap.*, Ala., U.S.A.; cotton, timber, fertilisers; comm. ctr.; rly. wks.; p. (1960) *134,393.*

Montgomery, *t.*, W. Punjab, Pakistan; livestock; leather, cotton; p. (1961) *25,100.*

Montichiari, *commune*, Lombardy, N. Italy; mftg.; p. *11,650.*

Montignies-sur-Sambre, *t.*, Belgium; coal, ironwks.; p. (1962) *24,092.*

Montigny-lès-Metz, *commune*, Moselle, France; residtl. sub. Metz; botanic gardens; p. (1954) *19,271.*

Montilla, *commune*, S. Spain; agr., wines; textiles, pottery, soap; p. (1957) *24,002.*

Montluçon, *t.*, Allier, France; on R. Cher; agr. ctr.; machin., cutlery, chemicals, mirrors; p. (1962) *58,855.* [16,682.

Montmorency, *t.*, Val d'Oise, France; p. (1962)

Montoro, *c.*, S.W. Spain; on R. Guadalquivir; agr. prod., olive oil; p. (1957) *15,396.*

Montpelier, *c.*, cap. Vt., U.S.A.; on Winooski R.; varied inds.; p. *8,000.*

Montpellier, *t.*, cap. Hérault, France; univ., wines, fruit, silk, chemicals, agr.; p. (1962) *123,367.*

Montreal, c., spt., Quebec, Canada; at confluence of Ottawa and St. Lawrence Rs.; caths., univ.; rly. ctr.; brewing, tobacco, footwear, oil refining; comm. ctr.; lgst. c. and spt. in Canada; p. (1961) 2,109,509.

Montreuil-sous-Bois, t., Seine, France; mnfs., fruit; p. (1962) 92,316.

Montreux, t., Switzerland; on L. Geneva; health resort; p. 19,000.

Montrose, spt., burgh, Angus, Scot.; on E. cst. at mouth of S. Esk R.; chemicals, and rope wks., linen, fisheries; p. (1961), 10,702.

Montrouge, t., Seine, France; paper, perfumes precision tools; p. (1962) 45,324.

Montserrat, I., Leeward Is., W.I.; limes, fruits, carrots and onions; ch. t. Plymouth; a. 32 sq. m.; p. (estd. 1965) 13,000.     [p. (1960) 1,060.

Montville, t., S.E. Conn., U.S.A.; paper, textiles.

Monza, t., Lombardy, Italy; cath.; comm., textiles, leather, hats; p. (1961) 84,445.

Moonie, t., Queensland, Australia; 200 m. W. of Brisbane; oilfields; pipeline to Lytton, at mouth of Brisbane R.

Moorea, one of the ch. Is., the Society gr., Pac. Oc.; a. 50 sq. m.; p. (1962) 4,147.

Moorfoot Hills, range, Peebles and Midlothian, Scot.; alt. 2,136 ft.

Moorhead, t., W. Minn., U.S.A.; potatoes, dairying, poultry; p. (1960) 22,934.          [Bay.

Moose R., Ontario, Canada; flows to James

Moosehead, L., Me., U.S.A.; source of Kennebec R.; 35 m. long, 10 m. wide.

Moose Jaw, c., Saskatchewan, Canada; rly. junction; agr. ctr.; agr. implements, oil refining; p. (1961) 33,206.

Moquegua, dep., S. Peru; cotton, maize, fruit; cap. M.; a. 5,549 sq. m.; p. (1961) 51,315.

Moquegua, t., Peru; wines; p. (1961) 3,885.

Mora, t., Spain; industl.; p. (1957) 10,844.

Moratalla, t., Spain; N.W. of Murcia; cloth, alcohol, wines; p. 14,536.

Moratuwa, t., Ceylon; p. (1946) 50,700.

Morava, R., Czechoslovakia and Austria; trib. of R. Danube; length 212 m.

Morava, R., Jugoslavia; rises in Crna Gora (S. of Dinaric Alps), flows N. into R. Danube 50 m. below Belgrade; valley used by trunk rly. from Belgrade to Thessaloniki (Salonika) and Athens, Sofia and Istanbul (Constantinople); length approx. 350 m.

Moravia, old prov., Czechoslovakia; agr., forestry, coal, textiles; p. inc.,Bohemia (1962) 9,566,753.

Moray, co., N.E. Scot.; cereals, fisheries, distilling, woollens; co. burgh, Elgin; a. 482 sq. m.; p. (1961) 49,156.

Moray Firth, arm of N. Sea; on Scottish E. cst., between Ross and Cromarty, and Nairn, Moray cos.

Morbihan, dep., France; on Bay of Biscay; agr. (apples), mining, fishing; cap. Vannes; a. 2,739 sq. m.; p. (1962) 530,333.

Morceux, t., Landes, France; p. (1962) 4,166.

Mordov A.S.S.R., U.S.S.R.; between Rs. Oka and Volga; agr.; a. 9,843 sq. m.; p. (1959) 1,000,000.

Morea, see Peloponnisos.

Morecambe and Heysham, t., mun. bor., N. Lancs, Eng.; on S. shore of Morecambe Bay; Morecambe, holiday resort; Heysham, port for N. Ireland and oil refinery; nuclear power sta. to be built on cst. S. of Morecambe; p. (estd. 1967) 40,810.

Moree, t., N.S.W., Australia; in agr. and grazing region; mkt.; p. (1966) 7,774.

Morelia, c., cap., Michoatán, Mexico; cath.; textiles, sugar; p. (1960) 100,828.

Morelos, inland st., Mexico; mtns., forested; cap. Cuernavaca; a. 1,916 sq. m.; p. (1960) 386,264.     [(1963) 214,879.

Möre Og Romsdal, dist., Norway; a. 5,812 sq. m.;

Moret-sur-Loing (Moret les Sablons), t., 40 m. S. of Paris on picturesque R. Loing.

Morez, t., S.E. Jura, France; precision instruments, optical equipment, winter sports.

Morgan, t., R. pt., S. Australia; on R. Murray, where it suddenly turns S. approx. 150 m. from its mouth; handles transhipment of Murray and Darling R. traffic to rail for despatch to Adelaide.

Morgantown, t., W. Va., U.S.A.; coal, oil, gas fields; chemicals, heavy ind.; p. (1960) 22,487.

Morioka, c., N. Honshu, Japan; textiles, ironwks.; p. (1964) 171,000.

Morlaix, spt., Finistère, France; tobacco, paper, brewing, agr.; p. (1962) 20,248.

Morley, t., mun. bor., W.R. Yorks, Eng.; 3 m. S.W. of Leeds; woollens, coal-mining, stone quarrying, tanning; p. (estd. 1967) 43,790.

Morocco, ind. sovereign st., since March 1956 (formerly French and Spanish prots.) N.W. Africa; cap. Rabat; chief ts. Casablanca, Marrakesh, Tangier, Fez, Meknès, Tetuan, Oujda, Safi, Mina Hassan Tani; !agr., forest, and animal prod.; fruits; phosphates, manganese, iron ore, lead, zinc; coal, petroleum, sugar refining; a. 171,000 sq. m.; p. (1961) 11,626,000.

Morogoro, t., Tanzania, E. Africa; on E. edge of Central African plateau, alt. approx. 3,000 ft., 110 m. by rail W. of Dar-es-Salaam; ctr. of sisal- and cotton-growing a.

Moron, t., Venezuela; on Caribbean cst. nr. Puerto Cabello; industl.; natural gas.

Morón de la Frontera, commune, S.W. Spain; olives; iron ore; marble; p. (1957) 30,137.

Morotai I., N. of Molucca, Indonesia.

Morpeth, mun. bor., Northumberland, Eng.; nr. Newcastle; coal-mining, iron; p. (estd. 1967) 14,340.

Morrinsville, t., N.I. N.Z.; agr. ctr.; p. (1961) 4,111.

Morriston, vil., Glamorgan, S. Wales; on R. Tawe, 2 m. N.E. of Swansea; zinc smelting and refining steel.

Morristown, t., N.J., U.S.A.; holiday ctr., fruit; p. (1960) 17,712.

Morrisville, bor., Penns., U.S.A.; on Delaware R.; rubber prod.; p. (1960) 7,790.

Morro Velho, mng-dist., Minas Geraes, Brazil; in Serra do Espinhaco, 10 m. S. of Belo Horizonte; deep rich gold-mines; ch. t. Nova Lima.

Mors, I., N. Jutland, Denmark; a. 138 sq. m.; p. (1960) 26,766.

Morven, mtn., Aberdeen, Scot.; nr. Ballater; alt. 2,862 ft.        [alt. 2,313 ft.

Morven, mtn., Caithness, Scot.; nr. Berriedale;

Morwell, t., Victoria, Australia; industl.; coal mng.; p. (1966) 16,578.

Moscow, c., R.S.F.S.R.; cap., U.S.S.R.; on R. Moskva; caths., univ., Kremlin, palaces; leading cultural, political and comm. ctr.; textiles, steel, engin., oil refining, chemicals; p. (1967) 6,464,000.

Moscow Sea (Ucha Reservoir), artificial L., R.S.F.S.R.; created behind dam on R. Volga at Ivankovo; supplies water to Moscow, maintains level on Moscow–Volga Canal, and supplies water to 8 hydro-elec. power-stas.; a. 127 sq. m.

Moscow–Volga Canal, R.S.F.S.R.; links R. Volga at Ivankovo with Khimki suburb of Moscow; forms part of Leningrad–Moscow inland waterway; opened 1937; length 80 m.

Moselle, dep., N.E. France; cap. Metz; a. 2,403 sq. m.; p. (1962) 919,412.

Moselle, R., France and Germany; trib. of R. Rhine; length 328 m.; canalised between Thionville and Coblenz (168 m.).

Moshi, t., Tanzania, E. Africa; on S.E. flank of Mt. Kilimanjaro; ctr. of coffee-growing dist. at alt. approx. 5,500 ft.; despatches coffee by rail to Tanga or Mombasa.        [249 m.

Moskva, R., U.S.S.R.; trib. of R. Oka; length

Mosonmagyaróvár, t., Hungary; aluminium wks.; agr. machin.

Moss, spt., Norway; pulp, paper, machin., textile inds.; p. (1960) 20,461.

Mossamedes, spt., Angola, Africa; exp. rubber; fishing, fertilisers; p. 8,977.

Mossel Bay, spt., C. Prov., S. Africa; oysters, whaling; wool, cereals; p. (1960) 12,178 inc. 4,333 whites.        [steel; p. 6,000.

Mossend, t., Lanark, Scot.; nr. Glasgow; iron and

Mossgiel, t., S.I., N.Z.; woollens; p. (1961) 6,463.

Mossley, mun. bor., Lancs, Eng.; 3 m. E. of Oldham; mkt. t., textiles, iron and steel; p. (estd. 1967) 9,630.

Most, t., ČSSR.; lignite, chemicals; Druzhba crude oil pipeline extended to chemical wks.; p (1961) 44,490.

Mostar, t., Herzegovina, Jugoslavia; on R. Naretva; bauxite, lignite, aluminium plant; p. (1960) 43,000.

Mosul, t., Iraq; on R. Tigris; comm. ctr., impt. during crusades; agr. prod., livestock, textiles; p. (1960) 341,000.

Motala, t., on L. Vättern, Sweden; radio sta.; engin., woollen goods; p. (1961) 27,143.

Motherwell and Wishaw, *burgh*, Lanark, Scot.; in Clyde valley, 15 m. S.E. of Glasgow; coal, iron, steel, machin., engin., silk, nylon; p. (1961) 72,799.                                     [p. (1957) 23,420.

Motril, *spt.*, Spain; minerals, cotton, sugar, fruits;

Mottarone, Monte, *mtn.*, Italy, between L. Maggiore and L. Orta; alt. 4,892 ft.          [3,310.

Motueka, *t.*, S.I., N.Z.; fruit, tobacco; p. (1961)

Moulins, *t.*, cap. Allier, France; on R. Allier; cath., ruined château; timber wks., brewing; p. (1954) 24,437.  [timber; p. (1955) 101,720.

Moulmein, *spt.*, Burma on R. Salween; rice,

Moundsville, *c.*, W. Va., U.S.A.; on Ohio R.; coal, glass, zinc; p. (1960) 15,163.

Mount Adams, *peak*, White Mtns., N.H., U.S.A.; alt. 5,679 ft.                             [fruit.

Mount Barker, *t.*, extreme S.W. of W. Australia;

Mount Carmel, *bor.*, Penns., U.S.A.; on Wabash R.; coal-mng., clothing mftg.; p. (1960) 10,760.

Mount Clemens, *t.*, Mich., U.S.A.; on Clinton R.; mineral springs; p. (1960) 21,016.

Mount Desert, *I.*, Me., U.S.A.; a. 100 sq. m.; mtns.; summer resort.

Mount Goldsworthy *t.*, W. Australia; new t. being developed in iron ore mng. a.

Mount Gambier, *t.*, S. Australia; pastoral. agr. ctr.; timber, dairy prod. processing; p. (1966) 17,146.

Mount Holly, *t.*, N.J., U.S.A.; textiles, clothes, leather; p. (1960) 13,271.

Mount Isa, *t.*, W. Queensland, Australia; in Selwyn Range 80 m. W. of Cloncurry, linked by rly. through Cloncurry to E. cst. at Townsville; copper mng.; p. (1966) 16,713.

Mount Kennedy, *mtn.*, Yukon, 3 m. E. of Mt. Hubbard on Alaskan border; alt. 14,000 ft.

Mount Lofty Range, *mtn. range*, S. Australia; lies immediately E. of Adelaide approx. 5 m. from St. Vincent G.; forms barrier to routes leaving Adelaide N.E. and E.; lower slopes support vineyards and outer suburbs of Adelaide; rises to over 3,000 ft.

Mount Pleasant, *t.*, Mich., U.S.A.; oil, lumber, sugar-beet, dairy prod.; p. (1960) 14,875.

Mount Prospect, *t.*, Ill., U.S.A.; p. (1960) 18,906.

Mount Tom Price *t.*, W. Australia; new t., being developed in iron ore mng. a.

Mount Vernon, *c.*, Ill., U.S.A.; timber, flour, woollens, coal; p. (1960) 15,566.

Mount Vernon, *c.*, N.Y., U.S.A.; on Bronx R.; sub. of N.Y.; residtl.; p. (1960) 76,010. Takes its name from George Washington's house on the Potomac, in Virginia, 15 m. S. of Washington, D.C.; varied inds. incl electronic equipment.

Mount Vernon, *c.*, Ohio, U.S.A.; on Kokosing R.; timber goods, mnfs.; p. (1960) 13,284.

Mountain Ash, *urb. dist.*, Glamorgan, Wales; in narrow valley 3 m. S.E. of Aberdare; coal; p. (1961) 29,590.

Mountain Province, *prov.*, N. Luzon, Philippines; rice, metal working; copper; h.e.p. at Ivogon; a. 5,458 sq. m.; p. 296,874.

Mountain View, *t.*, Cal., U.S.A.; p. (1960) 30,889.

Mountmellick, *t.*, *rural dist.*, Laoighis, Ireland; mkt., tanning, malting; p. (rural dist. 1961) 22,596.                        [wide; fishery grounds.

Mount's Bay, *inlet*, S. cst. Cornwall, Eng.; 20 m.

Mourenx, *t.*, S.W. Aquitaine, France; nr. Lacq; new town in oil dist.; p. (1966) 8,660.  [2,796 ft.

Mourne Mtns., Down, N. Ireland; highest peak,

Mouscron, *t.*, Belgium; cotton- and wool-weaving; p. (1962) 36,595.

Mouse or Souris, *R.* Canada and U.S.A.; trib. of Assiniboine R.; length 500 m.

Moy, *R.*, Mayo and Sligo, Ireland; length 35 m.

Mozambique, *Portuguese col.*, E. Africa; sugar, oil-nuts, cotton, maize; oil refining, cement; rich deposits of coal, iron ore, and semi-precious stones near Namapa; cap. Lourenco Marques; a. 302,327 sq. m.; p. (1962) 6,592,983.

Mozambique Channel, *strait*, Indian Ocean; separates Malagasy from mainland of Africa; length 1,000 m., width from 250 to 600 m.

Mozambique Current, *ocean current*, flows N. to S. along E. cst. of Mozambique and Natal, E. Africa; relatively warm water.

Mozdok, *t.*, R.S.F.S.R.; on Rostov–Baku rly.; oil pipe-lines; p. 14,003.

Much Hoole, Lancs.; S.W. Preston, Eng.; site for nuclear power sta.

Much Wenlock, *see* Wenlock.

Muck, *I.*, Inner Hebrides, Scot.; S. of Eigg.

Mühlhausen, *t.*, Erfurt, E. Germany; on R.

Unstrut; textiles, machin., tobacco; p. (1963) 45,362.

Mukachevo (Munkács), *t.*, Ukrainian S.S.R.; furniture, textiles, tobacco; p. (1956) 44,000.

Mukden (Shenyang), *c.*, *cap.*, Liaoning, N.E. China; on Hun-Ho in narrowest part of lowland with hilly country on both sides; impt. rly. junction with main routes N. to Harbin and Trans-Siberian Rly., S. to Peking, Luta and into Korea; gr. comm. and educational ctr.; machin, bldg. plant; p. (1956) 2,290,000.

Mula, *t.*, Spain; tr. ctr.; p. (1957) 15,127.

Mulde, *R.*, Germany; trib. of R. Elbe; length 130 m.

Mulhacén, *mtn.*, Sierra Nevada range, Spain; alt. 11,420 ft. (highest peak Europe, outside Alps).

Mülheim-an-der-Ruhr, *t.*, N. Rhine–Westphalia, Germany; on R. Ruhr; cas.; coal-mining, iron, steel, tobacco, engin., elec., oil refining; airport; p. (1963) 189,900.

Mulhouse, *t.*, Haut-Rhin. France; textiles, machin.; p. (1962) 110,735.

Mull, *I.*, Argyll, Scot., included in Hebrides; a. 357 sq. m.; granite, pastoral farming; ch. t. Tobermory.

Mull of Galloway, S. point of Wigtown, Scot.

Mullet, The, *peninsula*, W. cst. Mayo, Ireland.

Mullingar, *co. t.*, Westmeath, Ireland; on Brosna R.; mkt., agr. ctr., tanning; p. (1966) 6,453.

Multan, *div.*, W. Punjab, Pakistan; ch. t., Multan; p. (1961) 6,953,000.

Multan, *t.*, W. Punjab, Pakistan; on R. Chenab; carpets, silks, pottery; steel, thermal sta.; gas pipeline to Lyallpur; p. (1961) 358,000.

Muncie, *t.*, Ind., U.S.A.; on White R.; iron, steel, glass and paper; p. (1960) 68,603.

Münden, *t.*, Germany; on R. Weser; picturesque medieval t., cas.; leather and rubber goods tobacco fact.; p. 22,000.

Munhall, *t.*, Penns., U.S.A.; p. (1960) 17,312.

Munich (München), *c.*, cap. Bavaria, Germany; on R. Isar; univ., cath., palace, museum, " English Garden "; comm. ctr.; scientific instruments; machin., brewing, textiles, tobacco, chemicals, elec. engin.; film studios; route ctr.; p. (1965) 1,210,000.

Münster, *c.*, N. Rhine–Westphalia, Germany; cath., univ., cas.; leather, metal machin., rly. junction; p. (1963) 189,700.

Munster, *prov.*, S.W. Ireland; includes cos. Waterford, Kerry, Cork, Limerick, Clare Tipperary; a. 9,475 sq. m.; p. (1966) 969,902.

Muonio, *R.*, part of boundary between Finland and Sweden; flows into G. of Bothnia.

Mur, *R.*, Austria; trib. of R. Drava; length 250 m.                                      [Canada.

Murchison, *O.*, Hall Peninsula, Baffin I.,

Murchison, *R.*, W. Australia; length 800 m.

Murchison, *peak*, Rocky Mtns., B.C., Canada; alt. 13,500 ft.

Murchison Falls, on Victoria Nile, Uganda.

Murcia, *prov.*, S.E. Spain; former kingdom; minerals, cereals, fruit; cap. Murcia; a. 4,369 sq. m.; p. (1959) 803,610.

Murcia, *c.*, *cap.*, Murcia, Spain; on R. Segura; cath., univ.; silk, glass, hats, gloves; p. (1965) 259,000.

Murfreesboro, *t.*, Tenn., U.S.A.; p. (1960) 18,991.

Murg, *R.*, Germany; trib. of R. Rhine; length 40 m.                           [m. to desert swamps.

Murgab or Murghab, R., Afghanistan; flows 250

Murmansk, *spt.*, R.S.F.S.R., U.S.S.R.; on Kola-peninsula; ice-free throughout year; engin., elec. power; fishing, shipbldg.; marine power sta. utilising tidal energy projected; p. (1967) 279,000.

Muron, *t.*, R.S.F.S.R.; mkt. gardening; textiles, engin.; p. (1959) 73,000.

Muroran, *spt.*, Hokkaido, Japan; on W. cst.; industl.; iron ore; p. (1965) 161,252.

Murray, *R.*, separates N.S.W. and Victoria, Australia; lgst. R. in continent, length 1,600 m.

Murray, R., dist., N.E. Victoria, Australia.

Murray, *t.*, N. Utah, U.S.A.; sub. Salt Lake City; lead smelting; p. (1960) 16,806.

Murrumbidgee, *R.*, N.S.W., Australia; trib. of R. Murray; length 1,350 m.

Murshidabad, *t.*, W. Bengal, India; silk, weaving, ivory carving, gold and silver embroidery; p. (1961) 16,990.

Murupara, *t.*, N.I., N.Z.; in Kaingaroa Forest a.; timber inds.; p. (1961) 1,560.

Murwillumbah, *t.*, N.S.W., Australia; sugar, butter processing ctr.; p. (1966) *7,304.*

Murzuk, *t.*, Libya, N. Africa; in Fezzan Oasis; tr. ctr.; p. *1,000.*

Mus, *t.*, Turkey; W. of L. Van; p. (1960) *12,015.*

Musa Jebel, *mtn.*, Egypt; alt. 7,375 ft.; identified with the Biblical Sinai.

Muscat and Oman, *sultanate*, Arabia; agr., fruit (dates), oil; cap. Muscat; a. 82,000 sq. m.; p. *565,000.*

Muscat, *t.*, *cap.*, Muscat and Oman, Arabia; on S. cst. of G. of Oman: sm. tr.; pearl fisheries; p. (estd. 1962) *6,200.*

Muscatine, *c.*, Iowa, U.S.A.; on Mississippi R.; meat packing, timber ind.; p. (1960) *20,997.*

Muscle Shoals, *rapids*, in Tennessee R., U.S.A.; site of Wilson dam.

Musgrave Range, *mtns.*, on bdy. between S. Australia and N. Terr., Australia; isolated highland in ctr. of continent; arid; rise to over 3,000 ft.

Muskegon, *c.*, Mich., U.S.A.; engin., motor cars, accessories, aeroplane engines; p. (1960) *46,485.*

Muskingum, *R.*, Ohio, U.S.A.; trib. of Ohio R.; length 240 m.

Muskogee, *t.*, Okla., U.S.A.; rly. wks., oil refining, cotton, flour; p. (1960) *38,059.*

Musselburgh, *anc. burgh*, Midlothian, Scot.; on S. Firth of Forth at mouth of R. Esk; wire, cables, nets, twine; paper mkg.; golf course; p. (1961) *17,273.*

Mussel Shell, *R.*, Mont., U.S.A., trib. of Missouri R.

Mussomeli, *t.*, Sicily; agr. interests; p. *12,500.*

Mutankiang (Mudanjiang), *c.*, Heilungkiang prov., China; pulp, paper, machin., flour milling; p. (1953) *151,000.*

Muttra or Mathura, *t.*, Uttar Pradesh, India; on R. Jumna; Hindu ctr.; p. (1961) *125,258.*

Muz Tagh, *mtn. pass*, Karakoram Mtns., E. Turkestan; alt. 18,980 ft.

Muzaffarpur, *t.*, Bihar, India; univ.; p. (1961) *109,48.* [p. (1959) *5,000.*

Muzo, *mun.*, central Colombia; emerald-mining.

Muzuntan, *t.*, U.S.S.R.; goldfields in operation nearby.

Mwanza, *t.*, N. Tanzania, E. Africa; pt. on L. Victoria; rly. terminus; shirt-mkg.; p. *6,000.*

Mweelrea, *mtn.*, Mayo, Ireland; alt. 2,688 ft.

Mweru, *L.*, between Congo and N. Rhodesia; a. 2,700 sq. m. [awa; p. *7,773.*

Myaungmya, *dist.*, Lower Burma; ch. t. Patan-

Mycenae, *ancient c.*, Greece; ruined.

Mykonos, *I.*, N. Cyclades, Greece; p. *4,188.*

Mymensingh, *t.*, Bengal, Pakistan; rice, jute; p. (1961) *53,200.*

Mynyddislwyn, *t.*, *urb. dist.*, Monmouth, Eng.; in narrow valley of W. Ebbw R., 7 m. N.W. of Newport; coal-mng., elec. goods, kerb- and flagstones; p. (1961) *15,433.*

Mynydd-Mawr, *mtn.*, N. Wales; alt. 2,293 ft.

Myslowice, *t.*, Poland; nr. Katowice; rly. junc.; coal, flax mills, bricks; p. (1965) *44,000.*

Mysore, *st.*, S. India; hydro. elec. power; gold, iron and steel, manganese; coffee, tea, cotton; cap. Bangalore; a. 74,210 sq. m.; p. (1961) *23,586,772.* [ctr.; p. (1961) *253,524.*

Mysore, *c.*, Mysore, India; univ.; carpets, comm.

Mytishchi, *t.*, R.S.F.S.R., 12 m. N.E. Moscow; lorries, coaches; p. (1967) *110,000.*

Mytilene (Lesbos), *I.*, Greece, in Aegean Sea; highest point 3,080 ft.; olives, figs, lemons, oranges, grapes; antimony and marbles; ch. t. Mytilene; a. 618 sq. m.; p. (1951) *154,683.*

Mytilene, *cap.*, *spt.*, M.I., Greece; ip. (1951) *27,125.*

Mzombe, *R.*, Kenya; trib. of Ruaha R.; length 110 m.

Mzymta, *R.*, U.S.S.R.; flows to Black Sea; length 80 m.

# N

Naab, *R.*, Bavaria, Germany; joins R. Danube nr. Ratisbon; length 90 m.

Naarden, *c.*, N. Holland, Neth.; nr. Hilversum; arboriculture; ceramics; p. (1967) *17,003.*

Naas, *mkt. t.*, *cap.*, Kildare, Ireland; former cap. Leinster; p. (1966) *4,523.* [*15,000.*

Nabeul, *t.*, Tunisia, N. Africa; winter resort; p.

Nabi Saleh, *I.*, forming part of st. of Bahrein, Arabia; about 2 m. in circumference.

Nablus, *c.*, Jordan; N. of Jerusalem; nr. Old Testament c. of Shechem (Sichem, Sychem), the first Palestinian site mentioned in Genesis;

Jacob's Well and Mt. Gerizim adjacent; p. (1961) *45,653.*

Nachod, *t.*, CSSR.; on R. Mettaj at entrance to Lewin Nachod Pass; Prussian victory over Austrians 1866; cotton spinning, dyeing; p. (1961) *17,848.* [mftg.; p. (1960) *12,674.*

Nacogdoches, *t.*, Texas, U.S.A.; lignite; mkt.;

Naestved, *mkt. t.*, Själland, Denmark; paper, iron, footwear; p. (1960) *19,617.*

Nagaland, *st.*, India (1963): incorporates Naga Hills and Tuengsang; tribal a., formerly parts of Assam; adm. ctr. Kohima; a. 6,366 sq. m.; p. (1961) *369,000.*

Nagano, *c.*, central Honshu, Japan; on R. Sinanogawa, 100 m. S.W. of Niigata; cultural ctr.; silk mftg., reed organs, computers; p. (1965) *172,836.*

Nagaoka, *t.*, N.W. Honshu, Japan; lge. oil production ctr.; p. (1960) *148,254.*

Nagapattinam, *t.*, Tamil Nadu, India; at mouth of R. Vettar; rly. terminus; cotton, tobacco, groundnuts; p. (1961) *59,063.*

Nagasaki, *c.*, *spt.*, Kyushu, Japan; engin., shipbldg., enamelled and lacquer ware; 2nd c. to be destroyed by atomic bomb in Second World War; since rebuilt; p. (1965) *405,479.*

Nagh Hamadi (Nag' Hammâdi), *t.*, Upper U.A.R., N. Africa; on R. Nile 160 m. above Asyût; site of barrage (opened 1930) to regulate Nile flood and ensure irrigation of Girga prov.; barrage carries Cairo-Shellal rly. across Nile; junction for light rly. to Kharga Oasis.

Nagina, *t.*, Uttar Pradesh, India; sugar; p. (1961) *30,427.*

Nagoya, *c.*, Owari, Honshu, Japan; thriving cap., gr. tr., ch. ceramic ind. ctr., cotton and silk wks.; oil refining; p. (1965) *1,935,430.*

Nagpur, *t.*, Maharashtra, India; univ.; Hindu temples; salt, grain, cotton; p. (1961) *643,659.*

Nagy Banya, *mining t.*, Romania; gold, silver, lead.

Nagy Becskerek, *industl. t.*, Jugoslavia; on R. Bega.

Nagyenyed, *t.*, Transylvania, Romania; on R. Maros; wood carving, educational ctr., famous for wine in Middle Ages.

Nagykanizsa, *t.*, Hungary; distilling, milling; glasswks., machin.; p. (1962) *34,491.*

Nagykikinda, *t.*, Torontál, Jugoslavia; flour and fruit ctr. [*25,250.*

Nagykoros, *mkt. t.*, Hungary; wine; p. (1962)

Naha, *spt.*, Ryuku Is., Japan; U.S.A. control; mkt., textiles; U.S.A. air base; p. (1950) *44,779.*

Nahe, *R.*, Germany, flows 69 m. to R. Rhine, nr. Bingen. [fertilisers; p. (1961) *8,877.*

Nahorkatiya, N.E. Assam, India; oil-fields;

Nailsworth, *t.*, *urb. dist.*, Gloucester, Eng.; in Cotswold Hills, 4 m. S. of Stroud; woollens; p. (1961) *3,613.* [(1967) *40,289.*

Nain, *c.*, Iran; noted for very fine carpets; p.

Nairn, *mar. co.*, Scot., on Moray F. between Moray and Inverness; much moorland; farming, quarries, fishing; a. 200 sq. m.; p. (1961) *8,421.*

Nairobi, *c.*, *cap.*, Kenya, E. Africa; 327 m. from Mombasa; univ.; Uganda Rly. ctr.; lt. inds.; big-game shooting; p. (1962) *266,700.*

Naivasha, *L.*, Kenya; located on floor of Gr. African Rift Valley; alt. 6,000 ft.

Najibabad, *t.*, Uttar Pradesh, India; tr. in timber, sugar, metal mnfs.; p. (1961) *34,310.*

Nakhichevan, *t.*, Azerbaydzhan S.S.R.; salt mines in a.; food and wine inds.; p. (1959) *25,000.*

Nakhodka, *t.*, R.S.F.S.R.; pt. on Sea of Japan, 45 m. E. of Vladivostok; pt. of call for foreign ships; new town 1950; p. (1959) *63,000.*

Nakhon Ratchasima, *t.*, Thailand; copper mkt.; p. (1960) *42,218.*

Nakhornsri-Ayuthaya, *t.*, Thailand; 42 m. N. of Bankok; temples; p. (1960) *32,368.*

Nakuru, *t.*, Kenya rift valley (6,024 ft.), E. Africa; protected bird sanctuary (flamingoes) on L. Nakuru; wool processing, fertilisers; p. (1962) *37,900.*

Nakshov, *spt.*, Laaland I., Denmark; sugar refining; p. (1960) *16,639.* [*114,000*

Nalchik, *t.*, R.S.F.S.R.; N. Caucasus; p. (1967)

Namaqualand, *region*, south west cst. of Africa; divided by Orange R. into Great N. in S.W. Africa, and Little N. in Cape Province, Rep of S. Africa; semi-arid; a. 100,000 sq. m.; copper. diamonds.

Namangan, *industl. t.*, Uzbekistan, S.S.R.; on the Syr Daria; textiles, leather; p. (1967) *154,000.*

Nam Dinh, *impt. tr. t.*, N. Vietnam, nr. mouth of Red R.; p. *25,000.*

Nam Ngum, in Mekong R. a.; hydro-electric power plant projected.

Namrup, *t.*, Assam, India; fertilisers.

Namoi, *R.*, in N.S.W., Australia; trib. of Darling R.; 270 m. [p. *5,000.*

Nampula, *ch. t.*, Mozambique, Port. E. Africa;

Namsos, *spt.*, central Norway; on Folda Fjord lumber, fish canning; textiles; copper; p. (1961) *5,269.*

Namur, *prov.*, Belgium; bordering on France; collieries, iron ore, woodland; a. 1,413 sq. m.; p. (1962) *370,870.*

Namur, *fortfd. c.*, Belgium; at confluence of Meuse and Sambre Rs.; p. (1962) *32,396.*

Nanaimo, *c.*, *pt.*, B.C., Canada; on Vancouver I.; timber and allied inds.; fisheries; harbour; boating and yachting; p. (1961) *14,135*; Greater N., *37,000.*

Nanchang, *c.*, Kiangsi, China; on Kan-Kiang; tea, rice, cotton; tractors; p. (1963) *398,000.*

Nanchung (Nanchong), *c.*, Szechwan, China; agr. tr. ctr.; p. (1953) *165,000.*

Nancy, *ch. t.*, Meurthe-et-Moselle, France; old cap. Lorraine; gr. industl. activity, metals, cottons, woollens, chemicals, embroidery; p. (1962) *133,532.*

Nanda Devi, *mtn.*, Uttar Pradesh, India; alt. 25,645 ft.; first climbed by British team, 1936.

Nanded, *t.*, Maharashtra, India; on R. Godovari; muslins and tr. ctr.; p. (1961) *81,087.*

Nanga Parbat, *mtn.*, N.W. Kashmir, India, in W. Himalayas; alt. 26,660 ft.

Nanking (Nanjing), *gr. c.*, Kiangsu, China; on Yangtze-kiang; cap. during Kuomintang régime, 1928–49; famous seat of learning; cotton cloth, silk, ink; contains tombs of founders of the Ming dynasty; road-rail bdge. over lowest reaches of Yangtse R. opened 1.10.1969; p. (estd. 1952) *1,020,000.*

Nanling (Nanshan), *mtns.*, S. China; form divide between Rs. flowing N. to Yangtze-kiang and S. to Si-kiang; crossed by historic Cheling and Meiling Passes; alt. mainly below 6,000 ft.

Nanning, *cap., former treaty pt.*, Kwangsi, China; on the Yu-kiang; ch. mkt. on S. frontier; p. (1953) *195,000.*

Nan Shan, *mtns.*, Central China; between Yangtze-kiang basin and that of the Si-kiang.

Nanterre, *t.*, Seine, France; nr. Paris; noted for cakes; aluminium mftg.; p. (1962) *83,523.*

Nantes, *t.*, cap. Loire-Atlantique, France; on R. Loire; univ.; locomotives, biscuit mftg., wood pulp, bell foundries, machine wks., chemicals, sugar, oil, textiles, stained glass, nursery gardens; p. (1962) *246,227.*

Nanticoke, *t.*, Penns., U.S.A.; on Susquehanna R.; anthracite, canning; p. (1960) *15,601.*

Nantucket, *I.*, Mass., U.S.A.; official W. end of trans-Atlantic sea-crossing; summer resort; fishing; p. (1960) *2,804.*

Nantung (Nantong), *c.*, Kiangsu, China; on N. bank of Yangtze-kiang estuary 20 m. N.W. of Hai-men; p. (1953) *260,000.*

Nantwich, *mkt. t.*, *urb. dist.*, Cheshire, Eng.; on R. Weaver, 3 m. S.W. of Crewe; brine baths, fox-hunting ctr.; clothing, food prodn.; p. (1961) *10,454.*

Nantyglo and Blaina, *urb. dist.*, Monmouth, Eng.; in narrow valley 2 m. N. of Abertillery; coal, iron, footwear, rubber prods.; p. (1961) *10,950.*

Nao, *C.*, E. cst. Spain; opposite Balearic Is.

Napier, *c.*, *cap.*, Hawke's Bay, N.I. N.Z.; fine esplanade, suffered great damage by earthquake 1931, rebuilt by 1933; exp. frozen meat; p. (1961) *32,767.*

Naples (Napoli), *c.*, *spt.*, Campania, S. Italy; on Bay of N., at foot of Vesuvius, opposite site of ancient Pompeii; sanctuary of Madonna di Pompeii; grotto of Pozzuoli, Castel del Ovo, grand cath.; votive church of San Francesco di Paola; monastery of San Martino; subject to earthquakes and volcanic eruptions; impt. shipping; mnfs.; macaroni, vermicelli, wine, olive-oil, shipbldg.; p. (1965) *1,236,000.*

Napo, *R.*, Ecuador; trib. of Amazon; length 800 m. [(1960) *6,739.*

Napoleon, *t.*, N.W. Ohio, U.S.A.; light mnfs.; p.

Nara, *t.*, Honshu, Japan; S. of Kyoto; shrines and temples, colossal image of Buddha; old cap. of Japan; lacquer ware; p. (1965) *134,577.*

Narbada, *see* Narmada.

Narbeth, *mkt. t.*, *urb. dist.*, Pembroke, Wales; nr. head of Milford Haven; p. (1961) *960.*

Narbonne, *t.*, Aude, France; wines, sulphur, tiles; p. (1962) *35,899.*

Nardo, *t.*, Lecce, Italy; textiles; p. *20,558.*

Narenta, *R.*, Jugoslavia; flowing 140 m. to Adriatic. [length 200 m.

Narew, *R.*, Poland; flows to R. Bug, nr. Warsaw;

Narino, *dep.*, Colombia, S. America; a. 11,545 sq. m.; cap. Pasto; p. (estd. 1959) *628,840.*

Narmada, *R.*, Central India; flowing W. through Madhya Pradesh and Gujarat to G. of Cambay; length 800 m.

Narni, *t.*, Perugia, Italy; linoleum.

Narrabri, *t.*, N.S.W., Australia; 300 m. N. of Sydney; observatory with stellar interferometer (1964); p. (1966) *5,953.* [Rhode I., U.S.A.

Narragansett Bay, *inlet* of the Atlantic off cst. of

Narrandera, *t.*, N.S.W., Australia; on R. Murrumbidgee on N. margin of Riverina dist.; collecting ctr. for wool, mutton, wheat, fruits produced in irrigated a. fringing Murrumbidgee from Narrandera to Hay; p. (1966) *4,897.*

Narrogin, *t.*, W. Australia; p. (1966) *4,864.*

Narva, *t.*, Estonian S.S.R.; founded in 1223 by the Danes; cath.; textile factories, engin.; hydro-elec.; p. (1956) *21,000.*

Narvik, *t.*, N.W. Norway; opposite Lofoten Is.; ice-free throughout year, linked by rly. to impt. iron-ore fields in N. Sweden; exp. iron ore; p. (1960) *13,311.*

Nashua, *c.*, N.H., U.S.A.; cotton, paper, carpets, ironwks.; p. (1960) *39,096.*

Nashville, *c.*, *cap.*, Tenn., U.S.A.; on Cumberland R.; river pt., rly. ctr; fine capitol and other public bldgs.; impt. comm. and educat. ctr.; univs. and colleges; cellophane, rayon, food and tobacco prods., shoes, printing and publishing; p. (1960) *170,874.*

Nasik, *t.*, Maharashtra, India; on R. Godavari; Hindu pilgrim ctr.; metal work, cotton weaving; p. (1961) *131,103.*

Nasirabad, *t.*, Ajmer dist., Rajasthan, India; p. (1961) *24,143.*

Naso, *t.*, nr. Messina, Sicily; industl.; p. *8,000.*

Nassau, *I.*, Cook Is., S. Pac. Oc.; New Zealand terr.; uninhabited.

Nassau, *t.*, cap. Bahamas, W. Indies; all impt. Is. of the Bahamas connected with N. by radio telegraphy; resort; pearls, sponges, fruit; p. (estd. 1965) *55,000.*

Nasser City, rural development at Kom Ombo, N. of Aswan, for resettlement of 50,000 Nubians before formation of Lake Nassar behind the High Dam. [p. *18,400.*

Nässjö, *t.*, S. Sweden; rly ctr.; furniture, textiles;

Natal, *cap.*, Rio Grande do Norte, Brazil; sugar, cotton, salt, carnauba wax, hides; p. (1960) *162,537.*

Natal, *prov.*, Rep. of S. Africa; sub-tropical coastal climate; sugar-cane, tea, cereals; minerals (especially coal); oil discovered at Dannhauser; cap. Pietermaritzburg; a. 33,578 sq. m.; p. (1961) *2,979,920.*

Natanz, *prov.*, Iran; in hill cty. between Kashan and Isfahan; pears and other fruits.

Natchez, *c.*, Miss., U.S.A.; in rich cotton-growing dist.; p. (1960) *23,791.*

Natchitoches, *t.*, La., U.S.A.; on Red R.; p. (1960) *13,924.* [*25,831.*

Natick, *t.*, Mass., U.S.A.; boots, shoes; p. (1960)

Natick, *t.*, R.I., U.S.A.; cotton, light mnfs.; p. *3,660.*

Naturaliste, C., N.E. Tasmania.

Naturaliste, C., S. of Geographe Bay, W. Australia.

Naucratis, *ancient c.*, between Cairo and Alexandria; excavated by Flinders Petrie and Gardiner.

Naugatuck, *industl. t.*, Conn., U.S.A.; mnfs. rubber, iron castings; p. (1960) *19,511.*

Naumburg, *c.*, Halle, E. Germany; at confluence of Rs. Unstrut and Saale; annual Hussite feast; cath.; textiles, leather, toys, chemicals; p. (1963) *37,905.*

Naupila, *see* Navplion.

Nauru, *I.*, *indep. sov. st.* (1968); phosphate ind.; world's smallest indep. st.; a. 8 sq. m.; p. (1968) *3,000.*

Nauta, *t.*, Peru; on confluence of Rs. Maranon and Ucayali.

Navan (An Uamh), *urb. dist.*, Meath, Ireland; p. (1961) *3,996.*

Navanagar, *see* Bhavnagar.

Navarino or Neocastro, *spt.*, Greece; on W. cst.

Morea; Turkish–Egyptian fleet destroyed in the harbour by allied English, French and Russians in 1827.

Navarra, *prov.*, *old kingdom*, N. Spain; bounded by the Pyrenees; cap. Pamplona; grain, fruits, olives, wines, cattle-rearing, copper, silver, lead; a. 4,055 sq. m.; p. (1959) *399,033*.

Navasota, *t.*, E. Texas, U.S.A.; mkt., cotton processing mills; p. (1960) *4,937*.

Navsari, *t.*, Gujarat, India; cotton, leather, metalwork; p. (1961) *51,400*.

Naxos, *I.*, Greece; lgst. of the Cyclades; a. 164 sq. m.; famous for wine and fruit.

Nayarit, *st.*, Mexico; a. 10,444 sq. m.; cap. Tepia; p. (1960) *389,929*.

Nazareth, *t.*, Israel; 21 m. S.E. Acre; associations with early life of Christ; p. (1963) *26,400*.

Naze, The, *c.*, S. point of Norway.

Nazilli, *t.*, S.W. Turkey; on R. Menderes; agr., esp. olives; p. (1965) *41,121*.

Ndola, *t.*, Zambia, Central Africa; nr. bdy. with Katanga prov., Congo, 110 m. by rail N. of Broken Hill; ctr. of rich copper-mng. a., less impt. lead- and zinc-mng; minerals despatched by rail E. to Beira and W. to Lobito Bay; p. (1964) *84,000*.

Neagh, Lough, *L.*, N. Ireland; lgst freshwater L. in Brit. Is.; a. 153 sq. m.; drained by R. Bann.

Neath, *t.*, *mun. bor.*, Glamorgan, Wales; 6 m. up R. Neath from Swansea Bay; coal, aluminium inds., oil ref.; p. (1961) *30,884*.

Nebit-Dag, *t.*, Turkmen S.S.R.; 95 m. S.E. of Krasnovodsk; ctr. of oil and ozokerite a.; p. (1956) *30,400*.

Nebraska, *st.*, U.S.A.; mainly prairie; cap. Lincoln; farming, meat-packing, oats, wheat, maize, hay, potatoes, sugar-beet, apples, wool, livestock, petroleum, cement, mng., minerals; a. 77,227 sq. m.; p. (1960) *1,411,330*.

Nebraska, *R.*, trib. of Missouri R., U.S.A.

Neckar, *R.*, Germany; rising between the Swabian Jura, nr. Schwenningen, and the Black Forest; through Württemberg–Baden to the Rhine at Mannheim; length 240 m.

Neder Rijn, *R.*, Netherlands; more northerly of two branches of main Rijn; length 40 m.

Needham, *t.*, Mass., U.S.A.; nr. Boston; mnfs.; p. (1960) *25,793*.

Needham Market, *t.*, Suffolk, Eng.; on R. Gipping.

Needles, *gr. of rocks*, jutting out at W. extrem. I. of Wight, Eng.

Neemuch, *t.*, Madhya Pradesh, India; p. (1961) *36,287*.

Neenah, *c.*, Wis., U.S.A.; timber yards, flour and paper mills; summer resort; p. (1960) *18,057*.

Neftyne Kamni, *t.*, built on piles over Caspian Sea for Russian oil workers.

Negapatam, *see* Nagapattinam.

Negev, *reg.*, S. Israel, pioneering a.; natural gas.

Negoiul, *mtn.*, Transylvanian Romania; 8,346 ft.

Negombo, *spt.*, *urb. dist.* N.W. prov., Ceylon; native work in metal, leather; p. (1963) *47,028*.

Negotin, *t.*, E. Jugoslavia; on Romanian border; p. *6,633*.

Negril Beach, Jamaica; 25 m. W. of Montego Bay; new resort to further Jamaica's tourist tr.

Negri Sembilan, *st.*, Malaysia; S.W. Malaya; a. 2,580 sq. m.; cap. Seremban; p. (1961) *430,227*.

Negritos, *t.*, Piura dep., Peru; on cst., 15 m. S. of Talara; impt. oil-field.

Negro, Rio, *prov.*, Argentina; a. 77,610 sq. m.; cap. Viedma; p. (estd. 1960) *204,200*.

Negro Rio, *R.*, Argentina; flows into G. of St. Mathias.

Negro, Rio, Brazil, Colombia, S. America; one of the ch. tribs. of R. Amazon; rises in Colombia, joins the Amazon in N. Brazil.

Negros, *I.*, Philippines; S. of Mindanao; copper, a. 4,905 sq. m.; p. (1960) *1,362,500*.

Nehbandan Range, *mtns.*, E. Persia.

Neheim-Hüsten, *t.*, N. Rhine–Westphalia, Germany; at confluence of Rs. Möhne and Ruhr; lamps, metals, chemicals; p. (1963) *34,700*.

Neikiang (Neijiang), *c.*, Szechwan prov., China; agr. ctr.; p. (1953) *190,000*.

Neilston, *par.*, nr. Glasgow, Renfrew, Scot.; bleachfields, cotton, coal.

Neisse or Nisa, *R.*, tribs. of R. Oder, (1) Western Neisse, now frontier between Poland and Germany to Czechoslovak frontier, (2) Eastern Neisse in E. Silesia.

Neiva, *t.*, Colombia, S. America; on R. Magdalena;

cattle, coffee, panama hats; p. (estd. 1959) *71,170*.

Nejd, *dist.*, Central Arabia; with Hejaz, forms kingdom of Saudi Arabia; mainly desert; impt. oil wells, horses, camels, dates, various fruits; cap. Riyadh; p. *4,000,000* (estimated).

Nellore, *t.*, Andhra Pradesh, India; dyeing; rice; p. (1961) *106,797*.

Nelson, *mftg. t.*, *mun. bor.*, Lancs, Eng.; on N. flank of Rossendale 3 m. N.E. of Burnley; cotton, rayon, iron and brick wks., light engin.; p. (estd. 1967) *30,630*.

Nelson, *prov.*, S.I. N.Z.; cap. Nelson; a. 10,870 sq. m.; p. (1961) *74,281*.

Nelson, *t.*, S.I. N.Z.; nr. head of Tasman Bay; fruit packing, timber, cath.; p. (1961) *25,310*.

Nelson, *R.*, Canada; drains L. Winnipeg to Hudson Bay; length (with its gr. trib. the Saskatchewan) 1,450 m.

Nemunas, *R.*, U.S.S.R.; flowing to the Kurisches Haff, S.E. Kaliningrad; length 50 m.

Nenagh, *mkt. t.*, *urb. dist.*, Tipperary, N. Riding, Ireland; p. (1966) *4,542*.

Nene, *R.*, Northants, Eng., rises nr. Naseby and flows 90 m. to the Wash. [length 450 m.

Neosho, *R.*, Kan., U.S.A.; trib. of Arkansas R.;

Neosho, *t.*, S.W. Mo., U.S.A.; mkt., lumber, agr., lead-mining; p. (1960) *7,452*.

Nepal, *ind. kingdom*, Himalayas; bounded on N. by Tibet, on E. by Sikkim, on S. and W. by India; exp. cattle, hides and skins, opium and other drugs, timber; cigarette and sugar factories at Janakpur and Brijung; cap. Katmandu; a. 54,362 sq. m.; p. (1961) *9,407,127*.

Nepalgant, *t.*, S.W. Nepal; in the Terai; tr. ctr.; cereals, oilseeds, hides; p. (1961) *15,817*.

Nephin, *mtn.*, Mayo, Ireland; alt, 2,646 ft.

Nepanagar, *t.*, E. Nimar, Madhya Pradesh, India; India's only newsprint plant; p. (1961) *8,780*.

Nerbudda, *see* Narbada.

Nerchinsk, *t.*, R.S.F.S.R.; on Nertcha R., S.E. Siberia; gold, non-ferrous metals; p. (1956) *11,600*.

Ness, Loch, *L.*, Inverness, Scot.; occupies N.E. end of Glenmore; forms link in Caledonian Canal; very deep; 22½ m. long.

Neston, *t.*, *urb. dist.*, Cheshire, Eng.; on N. side of Dee estuary; residtl.; p. (1961) *11,836*.

Nestos, *R.*, *see* Mesta.

Nesvizh, *t.*, W. Byelorussia, U.S.S.R.; p. *10,000*.

Netherlands, *kingdom*, W. Europe; divided into 11 provinces; bounded by the N. Sea, Germany, and Belgium; ch. cs.: Amsterdam (cap.), Rotterdam (ch. pt.), The Hague (seat of Government), Utrecht, Eindhoven, Haarlem, Groningen; country low-lying, cst. protected by dykes; fertile and productive; agr., butter- and cheese-mkg., mkt. gardening, distilling and various mnfs., shipbldg., machin., tobacco, sugar, diamond-cutting, electronic equipment, electric lamps, motor cars, lorries; Delta plan, lgst. of its kind in world, for sealing off Rhine and Scheldt estuaries of Zeeland and S. Holland by series of great dykes and sea walls, due for completion late 1970s; a. 12,868 sq. m.; p. (estd. 1967) *12,535,307*.

Netherlands Antilles (Curaçao), grs. of Is., Caribbean Sea; off N. cst. Venezuela; consist of Neth. Windward and Leeward Is.; a. 403 sq. m.; cap. Willemstad; p. (1963) *196,100*.

Netze, *see* Notec.

Neubrandenburg, *dist.* E. Germany; mng. and agr.; p. (1963) *650,877*.

Neubrandenburg, *t.*, Neubrandenburg, E. Germany; fibreglass, machin., chemicals; p. (1963) *38,762*.

Neuchâtel, *can.*, Switzerland; mountainous dist., Jura Mtns.; cattle, cheese, chocolate, watches, cutlery, cottons, hosiery; a. 309 sq. m.; p. (1961) *147,633*.

Neuchâtel, *t.*, *cap.*, Neuchâtel, Switzerland; on N.W. shore of Lake N.; watchmkg., jewellery, condensed milk; oil refinery projected nearby; p. (1964) *35,600*.

Neuchâtel, *L.*, Switzerland; at S.E. foot of Jura Mtns. at the W. end of the central Swiss plateau; drains N.E. to R. Aar; length 36 m., width 3–5 m.

Neugersdorf, *t.*, Dresden, E. Germany; ironwks., textiles; p. (1963) *12,083*.

Neuhausen, *commune*, N. Switzerland; aluminium wks.; p. (1941) *6,355*.

Neuilly-sur-Seine, *sub.*, W. of Paris, France; fine bridge and cas.; p. (1962) *73,315*.

**Neumünster**, *t.*, Schleswig-Holstein, Germany; N. of Hamburg; tanning, cloth, machin., chemicals; p. (1963) *75,000.*

**Neunkirchen**, *t.*, Saar, Germany; iron, coal; p. (1963) *46,100.*

**Neuquén**, *prov.*, Argentina; agr. and stock-raising; a. 37,245 sq. m.; cap. Neuquén; p. (1960) *111,000.*

**Neuquen**, *t.*, cap. Neuquen Prov., Argentina; fruit farming; p. (1960) *17,500.*

**Neu-Ruppin**, *t.*, Potsdam, Germany; on L. Ruppin; fire extinguishers, chemicals; p. (1963) *22,102.*

**Neusalz**, *see* Nowa Sól.

**Neusandetz**, *see* Nowy Sacz.

**Neusatz (Novi Sad)**, *t.*, Jugoslavia; on R. Danube; formerly a royal free c.; almost destroyed by the Austrians in 1849; literary and comm. ctr.; coal; p. (estd. 1959) *97,000.*

**Neuse**, *R.*, N.C., U.S.A.; flows to Pamlico Sound; length 300 m.

**Neuss**, *c.*, N. Rhine–Westphalia, Germany; mnfs. iron goods, textiles, paper; rly. junction; p. (1963) *101,400.*

**Neustadt**, *see* Wiener-Neustadt.

**Neustadt**, *t.*, Rhineland-Palatinate, Germany; on R. Haardt; metal, paper, textiles; p. (1963) *30,800.*

**Neustrelitz**, *t.*, Neubrandenburg, E. Germany; machin.; p. (1963) *28,334.*

**Neutitscheim**, *see* Novy Jičin.

**Neutra**, *see* Nitra.

**Neuwied**, *t.*, Rhineland-Palatinate, Germany; on R. Rhine; cas.; ironwk., wood, pumice stone; p. (1963) *26,600.*

**Neva**, *R.*, R.S.F.S.R.; drains L. Ladoga S.W. via Leningrad to G. of Finland; 40 m. long.

**Nevada**, *mtn. st.*, U.S.A.; between Utah, Oregon and Idaho, and bounded S. and W. by California; mining: gold, silver, copper, tungsten, gypsum, iron, lead; livestock, agr.; timber; tourism; cap. Carson City; a. 110,540 sq. m.; p. (1960) *285,278.*

**Nevada**, *c.*, Mo., U.S.A.; zinc-mining and smelting; p. (1960) *8,416.*

**Nevers**, *c.*, cap. Nièvre, France; on R. Loire; cath.; the Roman Noviodunum; porcelain and faience industry; iron goods; farm implements; aircraft; p. (1962) *41,051.*

**Neves**, *t.*, S.E. Brazil; sugar, coffee; p. (1960) *85,741.*

**Nevis**, *I.*, Leeward Is., W.I.; ch. prod. cotton; ch. t. Charlestown; a. 50 sq. m.; p. *11,383.*

**Nevis, Loch**, *arm of sea*, off cst. of Inverness, Scot.; 14 m. long.

**New Albany**, *c.*, Ind., U.S.A.; on R. Ohio; glass, furniture, leather, iron and steel, car bodies; p. (1960) *37,812.*

**New Amsterdam**, *t.*, Guyana; on Berbice R.; p. (1962) *15,000.*

**New Amsterdam**, *t.*, Manhattan I., U.S.A., taken by English from Dutch, 1664, and renamed New York.

**New Antwerp**, *t.*, on Congo R., Congo.

**New Bedford**, *c.*, *spt.*, Mass., U.S.A.; on estuary of R. Acushnet; whale-fishery ctr.; mnfs. cottons, cordage, glass, shoes; p. (1960) *102,477.*

**New Bern**, N.C., U.S.A.; tr. in timber, tobacco, cotton; p. (1960) *15,717.*

**New Braunfels**, *c.*, Texas, U.S.A.; cotton goods, leather; lime; beauty spot; p. (1960) *15,631.*

**New Brighton**, *t.*, Cheshire, Eng.; at entrance to Mersey estuary; residtl.; resort.

**New Brighton**, *bor.*, Penns., U.S.A.; coal-mining; p. (1960) *8,397.*

**New Brighton**, *t.*, S.I., *seaside resort*, nr. Christchurch, New Zealand; p. (1961) *10,219.*

**New Britain**, *lgst. I.*, Bismarck Archipelago, Papua–New Guinea; a. (with adjacent Is.) 14,600 sq. m.; p. (1957) *100,375* (inc. approx. *3,856* non-indigenous).

**New Britain**, *c.*, Conn., U.S.A.; iron and brass mnfs.; p. (1960) *82,201.*

**New Brunswick**, *prov.*, Canada; forest-clad, mtns., many Ls.; lumber, pulp, paper, agr., fishing, canning; lead, zinc, barytes, natural gas; mnfs.; cap. Federiction; combined road and rail tunnel, bridge and causeway link with Prince Edward I. projected (1966–70); a. 27,985 sq. m.; p. (1961) *597,936.*

**New Brunswick**, *c.*, N.J., U.S.A.; on Raritan R.; chemicals, motor lorries, motor parts, leather, hosiery and hardware; p. (1960) *40,139.*

**New Caledonia**, *I.*, *Fr. Col.*, S. Pacific; coffee copra, chrome ore, nickel, iron, manganese; cap. Nouméa; a. 8,548 sq. m.; p. (estd. 1965) *89,000*

**New Castle**, *t.*, Ind., U.S.A.; steel mnfs., motor parts; p. (1960) *20,349.*

**New Castle**, *t.*, Penns., U.S.A.; tinplate, glass, steel wire, iron, coal; p. (1960) *44,700.*

**New Cumberland**, *bor.*, Penns., U.S.A.; tobacco, clothes; p. (1960) *9,257.*

**New Delhi**, *c.*, cap. India; on Jumna R.; adm. and trade ctr.; textile mills, printing, light inds.; univ.; government house; adjoining is Old Delhi, anc. cap. of Mogul empire; p. *260,272* (incl. Old Delhi, *292,429*).

**New Dongola** or **Maraka**, *t.*, Nubia, Sudan; on R. Nile; p. *10,000.*

**New England**, the six N.E. Atlantic sts. of U.S.A.: Me., N.H., Vt., Mass., R.I., Conn.

**New Forest**, *woodland region*, Hants, Eng.; a. 93,000 acres; ch. t. Lyndhurst. [*57,451.*

**New Forest**, *rural dist.*, Hants. Eng.; p. (1961)

**New Galloway**, *burgh*, Kirkcudbright, Scot.; on R. Dee; p. (1961) *327.* [*9,782.*

**New Glasgow**, *spt.*, Nova Scotia, Canada; p. (1961)

**New Granada**, former name of the United States of Colombia, S. America.

**New Guinea (Australian)**, *see* Papua–New Guinea.

**New Guinea, West**, *see* West Irian.

**New Hampshire**, *st.*, New England, U.S.A.; touching the Canadian border; forested and mountainous; agr. and fruit-growing extensively pursued; paper and forest products, textiles, shoes; granite; cap. Concord; ch. spt. Portsmouth; principal mftg. ctr. Manchester; a. 9,304 sq. m.; p. (1960) *606,921.*

**New Haven**, *c.*, *pt.*, Conn., U.S.A.; on New Haven Harbour, inlet of Long I. Sound; Yale Univ.; firearms, clocks, hardware, radiators, rubber goods; meat-packing; p. (1960) *152,048.*

**New Hebrides Condominium**, *I.*, Pac. Oc.; roughly 500 m. W. of Fiji and 250 m. N.E. of New Caledonia; administered jointly by France and Britain; 3 active volcanoes, on Tanna, Ambrym and Lopevi: earth tremors frequent; forested; meat canning, soap; a. 5,700 sq. m.; p. (1964) *66,000.*

**New Holland**, *vil.*, rly. term., ferry pt. for crossing to Hull; on R. Humber, Lincoln, Eng.

**New Iberia**, *sm. pt.*, La., U.S.A.; fishing, sugar, cotton, rice; timber tr.; p. (1960) *29,062.*

**New Ireland**, *I.*, Bismarck Archipelago, Papua–New Guinea; a. (with adjacent Is.) 3,800 sq. m.; p. (1957) *36,512* (native), (1954) *713* (non-indigenous).

**New Jersey**, *Atlantic st.*, U.S.A.; adjoining New York; mixed farming, petroleum-refining, smelting, chemicals, sanitary ware, motor vehicles; glass sand, zinc, iron ore, clay; cap. Trenton; ch. cs.; Newark and Jersey City; a. 7,836 sq. m.; p. (1960) *6,066,782.*

**New Kensington**, *t.*, Penns., U.S.A.; aluminium ind.; p. (1960) *23,485.*

**New Lexington**, *t.*, Ohio, U.S.A.; coal, oil and natural gas; p. (1960) *4,514.*

**New London**, *c.*, *pt.*, Conn., U.S.A.; at mouth of R. Thames; harbour; fishing, engin., machin., silk and woollen wks.; p. (1960) *34,182.*

**New Mexico**, *st.*, U.S.A.; N. of the Mexican Rep., and S. of Colorado st.; traversed by the Rocky Mtns.; uranium, potash salts, pumice, beryllium, copper, petroleum; agr.: cereals, fruit, vegetables, cotton, livestock; cap. Santa Fé; a. 121,666 sq. m.; p. (1960) *951,023.*

**New Milford**, *t.*, Milford Haven, Pembroke, Wales.

**New Milford**, *t.*, N.W. Conn., U.S.A.; dairy prods., tobacco, foundries, textiles, chemicals; p. (1960) *3,023.*

**New Mills**, *industl. t.*, *urb. dist.*, Derby, Eng.; at W. foot of Pennines 6 m. S.E. of Stockport; textile printing, bleaching and dyeing, rayon, paper, emery and glass-cloth mftg., iron and brass mnfs.; p. (1961) *8,510.*

**New Mirpir**, *t.*, W. Pakistan; new t. 2 m. from old Mirpur submerged by Mangla Lake on 29 Aug. 1967; planned p. *40,000.*

**New Norfolk**, *t.*, Tasmania, Australia; hops, apples; p. (1966) *5,775.*

**New Orleans**, *c.*, *spt.*, La., U.S.A.; on delta of Mississippi R.; the gr. cotton mart of America, and a busy comm. and mftg. ctr.; univ., cult. tr.; p. (1960) *627,525.*

**New Philadelphia**, *c.*, Ohio, U.S.A.; impt. rly. and canal ctr.; p. (1960) *14,241.*

New Plymouth, *spt.*, *cap.*, Taranaki, N.I., N.Z.; on W. cst. at N. foot of Mt. Egmont; sm. oil deposits; ctr. of dairy-farming dist.; p. (1961) *32,374.*

New Providence, *I.*, Bahama Is., W. Indies; contains cap., Nassau; p. (1953) *46,125.*

New Quay, *t.*, *urb. dist.*, Cardigan, Wales; on cst. of Cardigan Bay, 18 m. S.W. of Aberystwyth; p. (1961) *951.*

New Radnor, *rural dist.*, *co. t.*, Radnor, Wales; on slope of Radnor Forest, 6 m. S.W. of Presteign; p. (of dist. 1961) *2,050.*

New River, *artificial aqueduct*, Herts to Islington, London, Eng.; length 36 m.

New Rochelle, *c.*, N.Y., U.S.A.; on Long I. Sound; residtl.; p. (1960) *76,812.*

New Romney, *t.*, *mun. bor.*, Kent, Eng.; nr. S. cst. to E. of Dungeness; one of the Cinque Ports, in the rich agr. dist. Romney Marsh; old harbour silted up by shingle, and now a mile from sea; p. (estd. 1967) *3,620.*

New Ross, *mkt. t.*, *urb. dist.*, Wexford, Ireland; brewing and malting; p. (1966) *4,568.*

New South Wales, *st.*, S.E. Australia; much mineral wealth in tablelands and mtns.; silver, lead, coal, zinc, iron and steel; agr., corn, potatoes, fruit-growing, sheep, wool, cattle, meat; Snowy Mtns. hydroelec. scheme; cap. Sydney; a. 309,433 sq. m. (exclusive of Capital Terr. of Canberra); p. (1966) *4,235,030.*

New Waterway (Nieuwe Waterweg), *ship canal*, S. Holland, Neth.; connects R. Lek 7 m. below Rotterdam with N. Sea cst. at Hook of Holland.

New Westminster, *t.*, B.C., Canada; at mouth of R. Fraser; former cap. col.; exp. timber, canned salmon; p. (1961) *33,654.*

New York, *st.*, U.S.A.; one of the original sts.; touching Canada on the N., and reaching the Atlantic on the S.; known as the " Empire State "; inc. Long I. and Staten I.; mixed agr., Portland cement, iron ore, stone, sand and gravel, zinc, petroleum, gypsum, titanium concentrate, steel; Albany is the state cap. a. 49,576 sq. m.; p. (1964) *17,915,000.*

New York, *c.*, *spt.*, N.Y., U.S.A.; ch. comm. ctr. of U.S.A. and W. hemisphere; originally founded by Dutch settlers as New Amsterdam on Manhattan I.; gr. portion situated on Long I.; fine parks and bridges, skyscrapers, gd. harbour; world's longest bridge (Verrazano) spans mouth of N.Y. harbour opened 1964; univ.; ch. inds.; cloth textiles, printing and publishing, iron and steel wks., machin., sugar-refining, meat packing, chemicals, leather; p. (1960) *7,781,984*; of Greater N.Y. (1965) *11,348,000.*

New York State Barge Canal (Erie Canal), N.Y. st., U.S.A.; links Tonawanda on Niagara R. with Hudson R. via the Mohawk gap through Appalachian Mtns.; provides through water route from N.Y. to Gr. Lakes; opened as Erie Canal 1825, improved 1918; length 339 m. (with branches 525 m.), depth 12 ft.

New Zealand, *Brit. Dominion*, S. Pac. Oc.; E. of S.E. Australia and Tasmania, just over 1,200 m. from Sydney, N.S.W.; it consists of two main Is., N.I. and S.I. (a. 102,375 sq. m.), Stewart I. (670 sq. m.), Chatham Is. (372 sq. m.), Cook I. and several smaller Is.; the Is. are mountainous and contain numerous Ls., thermal springs and geysers; the scenery being varied and beautiful, and the climate everywhere healthy; there are active and dormant volcanoes in N.I.; cap. Wellington; principal exp.; wool, butter, frozen meat, cheese, hides, skins and pelts; p. (1966) *2,670,000* (Maori *198,188*) excluding Cook, Niue and Tokelau Is.

Newark, *t.*, Del., U.S.A.; univ.; p. (1960) *11,404.*

Newark, *mkt. t.*, *mun. bor.*, Notts, Eng.; on R. Trent 17 m. N.E. of Nottingham; ball bearings, brewing and malting; p. (estd. 1967) *25,030.*

Newark, *c.*, N.J., U.S.A.; meat packing, printing, elec. goods, paints, chemicals, cars, aircraft, leather; p. (1960) *405,220.*

Newark, *c.*, Ohio, U.S.A.; on R. Licking; rly. carriage wks., mnfs.; p. (1960) *41,790.*

Newark, *t.*, N.Y., U.S.A.; horticulture, glass, light mnfs.; p. (1960) *12,868.*

Newbiggin-by-the-Sea, *t.*, *urb. dist.*, on E. cst., 4 m. N. of Blyth; sm. seaside resort; coal-mining; Northumberland; Eng.; p. (1961) *10,066.*

Newburgh, *burgh*, Fife, Scot.; on S. side of Firth of Tay, 8 m. E. of Perth; p. (1961) *2,079.*

Newburgh, *c.*, N.Y., U.S.A.; on Hudson R.;

clothing and machin. mftg.; p. (1960) *30,979.*

Newburn, *t.*, *urb. dist.*, Northumberland, on R. Tyne, 3 m. W. of Newcastle; Eng.; pure graphite for nuclear reactors; p. (1961) *27,379.*

Newbury, *mkt. t.*, *mun. bor.*, Berks, Eng.; on R. Kennet, 17 m. S.W. of Reading; engin., furniture, paper, cardboard boxmaking; p. (estd. 1967) *21,050.*

Newburyport, *c.*, *spt.*, Mass., U.S.A.; on Merrimac R.; boot and shoe factories, comm. and fisheries; p. (1960) *14,004.*

Newcastle, *spt.*, *urb. dist.*, on Dundrum Bay; Down, N. Ireland; resort; p. (1966) *4,336.*

Newcastle, *t.*, W. Natal, S. Africa; coal, iron, steel, wood, grain, hemp; p. (1960) *17,539* inc. *3,212* whites.

Newcastle, Greater, *c.*, N.S.W., Australia; at mouth of R. Hunter; 2nd c. of st.; gr. coal depot of S. hemisphere and leading provincial industl. ctr.; iron and steel, engin., shipbldg., chemicals; p. (1966) *233,967.*

Newcastle Emlyn, *urb. dist.*, Carmarthen, Wales; on R. Teifi; p. (1961) *643.*

Newcastle-under-Lyme, *t.*, *mun. bor.*, Staffs., Eng.; 2 m. W. of Stoke-on-Trent, on Lyme Brook; iron and steel, mng., quarrying, textiles, non-ferrous metals, bricks, tiles; p. (estd. 1967) *77,950.*

Newcastle upon Tyne, *c.*, *spt.*, *co. bor.*, Northumberland, Eng.; on N. bank of R. Tyne, 10 m. from the N. Sea; connected by bridges with Gateshead, Durham; great shipbldg. and colly. pt.; univ., cath., many fine public bldgs.; coal-mining, heavy engin., iron and steel, heavy chemicals; p. (estd. 1967) *251,650.*

Newcomerstown, *t.*, E. Ohio, U.S.A.; coal, steel, tinplate, bricks; p. (1960) *4,273.*

Newent, *mkt. t.*, *rural dist.*, Gloucester, Eng.; 8 m. S. of Ledbury; p. (rural dist. 1961) *3,724.*

Newfoundland, *I.*, *prov.* Canada; E. of the G. of St. Lawrence; in E. low, in W. rugged mtns., many Ls.; coniferous forest; fishing, cod, salmon, halibut, lobster, seal; lumber, wood-pulp, paper; iron ore, lead, zinc, copper, asbestos; hydro-elec. power; climate is severe; cap. St. John's; supposedly Viking village discovered at L'Anse-aux-Meadows at N. tip of I. a. *156,185* sq. m.; p. (1961) *457,853.*

Newham, *outer bor.* Greater London, Eng.; comprising the former co. bors. of East and West Ham, part of Barking, (W. of Barking Creek), Woolwich (N. of Thames); p. (1966) *259,000.*

Newhaven, *spt.*, *urb. dist.*, E. Sussex, Eng.; on S. cst. at mouth of R. Ouse, 9 m. E. of Brighton; the passenger pt. for Dieppe; boat bldg. and light inds.; p. (1961) *8,325.*

Newlyn, *picturesque vil.*, Cornwall, Eng.; on Mount's Bay, 1 m. W. of Penzance; fishing and fish canning; p. *3,902.*

Newmarket, *t.*, *urb. dist.*, Suffolk, Eng.; at foot of E. Anglian Heights, 11 m. N.E. of Cambridge; horse-racing ctr.; famous Heath (partly in Cambridgeshire); mkt. gardening, agr. and agr. engin.; p. (1961) *11,207.* [p. (1961) *8,932.*

Newmarket, *t.*, S.E. Ont. Canada; leather mnfs.;

Newmilns and Greenholm, *burgh*, Ayr, Scot.; on R. Irvine, 12 m. E. of Kilmarnock; muslin and lace curtain mnf.; p. (1961) *3,541.*

Newport, *t.*, *mun. bor.*, *cap. of I.*, I. of Wight, Eng.; on R. Medina, in gap through central Chalk ridge; mkt.; brewing, joinery and coach wks., bait mnfs.; p. (estd. 1967) *19,690.*

Newport, *t.*, *co. bor.*, Monmouth, Eng.; on R. Usk, 5 m. from its mouth; timber terminal and deep-water berth; shipbldg., engin., iron and steel, aluminium, coal, paper-board, confectionery, chemicals, plastics; p. (1961) *108,107.*

Newport, *mkt. t.*, *urb. dist.*, Salop, Eng.; 8 m. N.E. of Wellington; p. (1961) *4,370.*

Newport, *burgh*, Fife, Scot.; on S. side of Firth of Tay, opp. Dundee; p. (1961) *3,326.*

Newport, *c.*, Ky., U.S.A.; on Ohio R.; a. residtl. sub. of Cincinnati, with impt. local inds.; p. (1960) *30,070.*

Newport, *c.*, R.I., U.S.A.; on Narragansett Bay; seaside resort; permanent p. (1960) *47,049.*

Newport, *spt.*, S. Vietnam; on N. outskirts of Saigon; lge pt. inaugurated 1967.

Newport News, *c.*, *spt.*, Va., U.S.A.; on north shore of estuary of James R. on Hampton Roads; lge. harbour; shipbldg.; outlet for Virginian tobacco and Appalachian coal; p. (1960) *113,662.*

**Newport Pagnell**, *mkt. t., urb. dist.*, Bucks, Eng.; on R. Ouse, 11 m. S.W. of Bedford; p. (1961) *4,722*.

**Newquay**, *t., urb. dist.*, Cornwall, Eng.; on N. Cornish cst.; seaside resort; p. (1961) *11,877*.

**Newry**, *t., urb. dist.*, Down, N. Ireland; at head of Carlingford Lough; machin., rope, brewing, granite; p. (1966) *12,214*.

**Newton**, *c.*, Kan., U.S.A.; silks, worsted; p. (1960) *14,877*.

**Newton**, *c.*, Mass., U.S.A.; on R. Charles; mnfs.; p. (1960) *92,384*.      [(1966) *47,194*.

**Newtonabbey**, *urb. dist.*, Antrim, N. Ireland; p.

**Newton Abbot**, *mkt. t., urb. dist.*, Devon, Eng.; at head of Teign estuary; rly. junction; pottery, lt. engin.; p. (1961) *18,066*.

**Newton Aycliffe**, *t.*, Durham, Eng.; 6 m. N.W. of Darlington; one of "New Towns" designated 1947; engin. prod., textiles, plastics, paints; p. (estd. 1965) *16,040*.

**Newton-le-Willows**, *t., urb. dist.*, Lancs., Eng.; famous Vulcan locomotive wks. founded by George Stephenson (now being closed down); paper, textiles; p. (estd. 1967) *22,300*.

**Newton-Stewart**, *burgh*, Wigtown, Scot.; on R. Cree, 5 m. N. of Wigtown; wool, creameries and agr. inds.; p. (1961) *1,980*.

**Newtown**, *c.*, N.S.W., Australia; S. sub. Sydney; ironwks., paint; p. (1947) *25,293*.

**Newtown and Llanllwchaiarn**, *mkt. t., urb. dist.*, Montgomery, Wales; on R. Severn, 8 m. S.W. of Montgomery; precision instruments, machin. tools; p. (1961) *5,512*; plan for expansion, p. *11,000*.

**Newtownards**, *spt., mkt. industl. t., mun. bor.*, Down, N. Ireland; 7 m. E. of Belfast; hosiery; p. (1966) *12,928*.

**Neyland**, *t., urb. dist.*, Pembroke, Wales; on Milford Haven; rly. terminus; p. (1961) *2,149*.

**Nezhin**, *t.*, Ukrainian S.S.R.; rly. junction on Kiev–Moscow line; p. (1954) *50,000*.

**Ngami**, *L.*, Botswana, S. W. Africa; swamp, the remnant of a much larger L.     [alt. 7,515 ft.

**Ngauruhoe**, *mtn.*, N.I., N.Z.; an active volcano;

**Niagara**, *R.*, forming part of boundary between Canada and U.S.A.; flows from L. Erie to L. Ontario; has rapids and the famous falls (167 ft.); gr. hydro-elec. power-sta.; length 35 m.

**Niagara Falls**, *t.*, Ontario, Canada; opp. the falls; carborundum, canning, silverware, castings; p. (1961) *22,351*.

**Niagara Falls**, *c.*, N.Y., U.S.A.; extending along the summit of cliff for 3 miles; paper, flour, aluminium; p. (1960) *102,394*.

**Niamey**, *t.*, Niger rep., W. Africa; one of the termini (the other is Zinder) of the trans-Sahara motor routes; p. (estd. 1963) *42,000*.

**Nias**, *I.*, W. of Sumatra, Indonesia; 95 m. long.

**Niassa**, *prov.*, Mozambique, Port. E. Africa; ch. t. Nampula; p. (1962) *276,795*.

**Nicaragua**, *rep.*, Central America; tropical forest; heavy rain in summer; uniformly hot; coffee, cocoa, sugar, bananas; gold and silver; cap. Managua; a. 57 145 sq. m.; p. (estd. 1965) *1,597,000*.

**Nicastro**, *mftg. t.*, Calabria, Italy; W. of the Apennines; olives, wine; p. *24,869*.

**Nice**, *c., spt., cap.*, Alpes Maritimes, France; on Mediterranean cst., at the foot of the Alps; beautiful climate and surroundings; joins ancient t. of Cimiez; ceded to France in 1860 by Sardinia; winter health resort; fruit and flower exp., perfume mftg.; p. (1962) *294,976*.

**Nicobar Is.**, *see* Andaman and Nicobar Is.

**Nicosia**, *c., cap.*, Cyprus; the ancient Ledra; fortified, mosques; hand weaving; cap. of admin. dist. same name; p. (1965) *103,000*.

**Nicoya, G. of**, *inlet*, Costa Rica.

**Nictheroy**, *see* Niteroi.

**Nidd**, *R.*, trib. of R. Ouse, W.R. Yorks, Eng.

**Nidwalden**, *can.*, Switzerland; a. 106 sq. m.; p. (1961) *22,188*.

**Niederhernsdorf**, *t.*, S.W. Poland; formerly Germany; coal, explosives; p. *11,706*.

**Niederwald**, *hill*, opposite Bingen-on-the-Rhine, Germany; national monument commemorating German triumph over France 1870–71, and formation of the G. Empire.

**Niemen or Memel**, *R.*, Poland and U.S.S.R.; flowing to the Kurisches Haff; length 500 m.

**Nienburg**, *t.*, Lower Saxony, Germany; on R. Weser; glass, metal, wood, chemicals; p. (1963) *23,300*.

**Nieuwveld Range**, *mtns.*, C. of Gd. Hope, Union of S. Africa; part of S. terminal escarpment of African tableland; overlooks Gr. Karroo to its S.; forms impenetrable barrier to routes; mainly over 5,000 ft., max. alt. 6,276 ft.

**Nièvre**, *central dep.*, France; traversed by Morvan Mtns.; forests, livestock, coal, iron, steel; cap. Nevers; a. 2,659 sq. m.; p. (1962) *245,921*.

**Nigde**, *t.*, Turkey; p. (1960) *18,010*.

**Nigel**, *t.*, Transvaal, S. Africa; gold mng.; industl.; p. (1960) *33,896* inc. *7,580* whites.

**Niger**, *gr. R.*, W. Africa; rises nr. sea in outer mtn. zone of W. Africa, as R. Tembi, and sweeps round by Timbuktu to a delta in the G. of Guinea, on a circuitous course of 2,600 m., receiving its gr. trib. the R. Benue, about 250 m. from the mouth; navigable for 1,000 m.

**Niger**, *indep. sovereign st.*, W. Africa; millet, groundnuts, rice; sheep, goats; cap. Niamey; a. 494,000 sq. m.; p. (1961) *2,870,000*.   [1964.

**Niger Dam**, Nigeria; at Kainji L.; dam projected

**Nigeria, Republic of**, *indep. sovereign st.*, within Br. Commonwealth (Oct. 1, 1960), West Africa; occupying lower basin of R. Niger, with region adj. up to Lake Chad; exp. world's lgst. supply of palm kernels and palm oil; groundnuts, cocoa, rubber, cotton, bananas; tin, asbestos, coalmng.; natural gas pipeline from fields at Owaza to Aba, E. Nigeria; oil in the Niger delta a.; cap. Lagos, lgst. c. Ibadan; fed. divided into 12 sts. in lieu of regions May 1967; total a. 356,669 sq. m.; p. (1963) *55,600,000*.

**Nightingale**, *I.*, most S. of Tristan da Cunha gr., S. Atlantic.

**Niigata**, *c., port*, Honshu, Japan; coal, petroleum; gas pipeline to Tokio under constr.; p. (1964) *345,000*.

**Niihama**, *c.*, N. Shikoku, Japan; on cst. of Inland Sea 20 m. S.E. of Imabari; refines copper obtained from Besshi Mines 12 m. to the S.; petrochemicals; p. (1966) *125,155*.

**Niitakayama**, *mtn.*, Taiwan I., China; highest mtn. of Niitaka Chain; alt. 12,939 ft.

**Nijar**, *t.*, Almeria, Spain; fruit, nuts, grain; textiles, porcelain; lead, manganese, iron ore; p. *10,107*.

**Nijmegen**, *c.*, E. Neth.; on R. Waal, nr. Arnhem; univ.; mnfs. ale, Prussian blue, cigars, pottery, metal-work; p. (1967) *144,004*.

**Nijni-Novgorod**, *see* Gorki.

**Nikaria**, *I.*, Dodecanese Archipelago, Greece.

**Nikko**, *t.*, Honshu, Japan; famous temples and shrines; beautiful tourist resort; p. (1966) *32,031*.

**Nikolayev**, *fortfd. t.*, Ukrainian S.S.R.; nr. Kherson, at head of estuary R. Bug; 2nd lgst. shipbldg. ctr. in U.S.S.R.; engin., petroleum refining; p. (1967) *289,000*.

**Nikolayevsk**, *t., pt.*, R.S.F.S.R.; on R. Amur; iron ore, engin., oil refining; p. (1954) *50,000*.

**Nikopol**, *t.*, Ukrainian S.S.R.; on R. Dnieper; manganese prod.; engin., steel; p. (1959) *81,000*.

**Nikšic**, *t.*, Montenegro, Jugoslavia; N. of Cetinje; p. (1960) *16,000*.

**Nile**, *the longest R.* in the world (*see* White Nile (Bahr-el-Abiad) and Blue Nile (Bahr-el-Azrek)); flows through a longer stretch of basin (over 2,450 m. in a direct line) than any other R. in the world, and along all its windings measures 4,145 m.; on Upper Nile navigation is hindered by sudd (floating vegetation); R. rises April, overflows Sept.; formerly cultivation entirely dependent on annual floods, but now assisted by dams, at Asyût, Aswan, Sennar, for regulating flow and navigation; first stage of Aswan High Dam completed 1964 when Nile waters were diverted.

**Niles**, *t.*, Ohio, U.S.A.; p. (1960) *19,545*.

**Nilgiri Hills**, Tamil Nadu, S. India.

**Nimes**, *t.*, Gard, France; Roman antiquities, educational institutions; silk, cottons, carpets, machin., wine tr.; p. (1962) *105,172*.

**Nineveh**, *celebrated ancient c.*, Iraq, stood on E. bank of upper R. Tigris, opp. modern Mosul.

**Ningpo (Ningbo)**, *c., spt.*, Chekiang, China; 100 m. from Shanghai; leading fishing pt., comm. and mnf. ctr. p. (1953) *238,000*.

**Ningsia**, *aut. reg.*, N.W. China; bounded on N. by Inner Mongolia; cap. Yinchwan; p. (estd. 1957) *1,810,000*.

**Ninh Binh**, *t.*, N. Viet-Nam; p. *25,000*.

**Ninove**, *t.*, Belgium; on R. Dender; industl.; p. (1961) *11,898*.

**Niobrara**, *R.*, U.S.A.; trib. of Missouri R.; flows from Wyoming to Nebraska; length 450 m.

**Niort**, *t.*, Deux-Sèvres, France; noted for its mkt. gardens, and leather mnf. (gloves); p. (1962) *44,630*.

**Nipigon**, *L.*, in Thunder Bay dist., Ontario, Canada; 70 m. long, 50 m. wide, 1,000 Is.; discharges by N. R. to Lake Superior; 30 m. wide.

**Nipissing**, *L.*, Ontario, Canada; 50 m. long, 35 m. wide.

**Niriz**, *t.*, Fars prov., S.W. Iran; on old caravan route from Kerman to Shiraz; p. *9,000*.

**Niš**, *t.*, Jugoslavia; on R. Nishava; p. (1960) *75,000*.

**Nišava**, *R.*, Jugoslavia; rises in Stara Planina, flows N.W. into R. Morava nr. Niš; valley used by trunk rly. from Belgrade to Sofia and Istanbul (Constantinople); length over 100 m.

**Niscemi**, *commune*, Caltanissetta prov., Sicily; sulphur. agr.; p. *20,281*.

**Nishapur**, *mkt. t.*, N.E. Iran; Khurasan.; in fertile a.; cotton, fruits; famous turquoise mines nearby; birthplace of Omar Khayyám; impt. archaeological finds dating 9th and 10th cent.; p. *c. 30,000*.

**Nishinomiya**, *c.*, S. Honshu, Japan; brewing, vegetable oils; p. (1964) *317,000*.

**Niterói**, *t.*, *cap.*, Rio de Janeiro st., Brazil; soap, textiles; p. (1960) *245,467*.

**Nith**, *R.*, S.W. Scot.; flows to Solway Firth, S. of Dumfries; followed by main rly. from Carlisle to Kilmarnock and Glasgow; length 71 m.

**Nitra (Neutra)**, *R.*, ČSSR.; trib. of R. Waag; length 100 m.

**Nitra**, *t.*, ČSSR.; on R. Nitra; p. (1961) *34,242*.

**Niue or Savage I.**, Pac. Oc.; one of Cook Is., but under separate admin.; belongs to New Zealand; ch. pt. Alofi; copra, plaited basketware, sweet potatoes; a. 100 sq. m.; p. (1959) *4,781*.

**Nivelles**, *t.*, Brabant, Belgium; rly. wkshps., paper; p. (1962) *14,483*.

**Nivernais**, *old prov.*, France, now forming Nièvre prov. and part of Cher.

**Nizampatam**, *t.*, *spt.*, Tamil Nadu, India; formerly called Pettipollee after the neighbouring village of Pedapalle; first trg. estab. made by the Brit. in the Madras presidency in 1611.

**Nizheudinsk**, *t.*, W. Irkutsk, R.S.F.S.R.; new mftg. t.; p. *10,342*.

**Nizhniy Tagil**, *t.*, R.S.F.S.R.; in Ural mtns.; iron ore, iron and steel, railway cars, engin., chemicals; p. (1967) *375,000*.    [Ogowe.

**Njole**, *t.*, Congo Rep., Equatorial Africa; on R.

**No**, *L.*, Bahr-el-Ghazal prov., Sudan, N.E. Africa; vast swamp a. 350 m. S.W. of Khartoum receiving Rs. Bahr-el-Jebel and Bahr-el-Ghazal (to form White Nile); flow of water blocked by papyrus reed and floating weed (sudd); gr. loss of water by evaporation.

**Noakhali**, *dist.*, and *t.*, Chittagong div., Pakistan; p. (of t.) *13,063*.

**Nobi Plain**, S. Honshu, Japan; located at head of Ise Bay; composed of: (1) low, badly drained alluvial plain on W. under intensive rice cultivation, (2) higher, drier, terraces on E. under mulberry, vegetables, pine-woods; very dense urban and rural p.; ch. textiles and pottery mftg. a. in Japan; inc. cities Nagoya, Gifu, Yokkaichi; a. 720 sq. m.

**Noblesville**, *t.*, Ind., U.S.A.; agr., horse breeding; p. (1960) *7,664*.

**Nocera Inferiore**, *t.*, Italy; nr. Naples; the ancient Nuceria Alfaterna; p. (1961) *43,050*.

**Nogent-sur-Marne**, *t.*, Seine, France; S.E. sub. Paris; chemicals, knives; p. (1954) *23,581*.

**Noginsk**, *t.*, R.S.F.S.R.; nr. Moscow; textiles, metals; natural gas pipeline from Central Asia projected; p. (1959) *93,000*.

**Noisy-le-Sec**, *t.*, Seine, France; p. (1954) *22,337*.

**Nola**, *t.*, Italy; at foot of Vesuvius, 12 m. N.E. of Naples; was an ancient c. of Campania, noted for its vases; p. *20,253*.

**Nome**, *cst. t.*, Alaska, U.S.A.; gold; (1960) *2,316*

**Noordoostpolder**, Overijssel, Neth.; land reclaimed from Zuider Zee, 1942; a. 185 sq. m.; p. (1967) *31,016*.

**Noordwijk**, *resort*, W. cst., Neth.; p. (1967) *20,563*.

**Noranda**, *t.*, Quebec, Canada; 12 m N.E. of Rouyn; goldmines; p. (1961) *11,477*.

**Norcia**, *t.*, Italy; old walls, cath.; famous for pork and terra-cotta.

**Nord**, *N. dep.*, France; on Belgian frontier and N. Sea; flourishing agr., mining, iron and coal, textile and chemical mnfs.; cap. Lille; a. 2,229 sq. m.; p. (1962) *2,293,112*.

**Nordenham**, *pt.*, Lower Saxony, Germany; on Lower Weser; cables, textiles, metals, shipbldg., fishing pt.; p. (1963) *27,100*.

**Norderney**, *I.*, Frisian Is., Germany; resort.

**Nordhausen**, *c.*, Erfurt, E. Germany; in Harz Mtns.; cath.; engin., agr. machin., clothing inds.; rly. junction; p. (1963) *41,401*.

**Nordhorn**, *t.*, Lower Saxony, Germany; nr. Neth. frontier; textiles; p. (1963) *40,200*.

**Nordkapp or N. Cape**, *most N. point*, Europe; on Magerö I., Norway.

**Nordkyn**, *most N. point*, with N. Cape, of the European mainland, Norway, opposite N. Cape.

**Nordland**, *co.*, Norway; a. 14,728 sq. m.; p. (1963) *240,314*.

**Nördlingen**, *t.*, Bavaria, Germany; carpet factories; p. *8,800*.

**Nore, The**, *sandbank*, *lightship*, Thames estuary, Eng.

**Nore**, *R.*, Ireland; trib. of R. Barrow; length 70 m.

**Norfolk**, *co.*, E. Eng.; noted for shallow lake expanses known as the Broads, popular yachting region; farming, corn, potatoes, cattle, fisheries (Yarmouth), brewing, boots, mustard, farm machin.; cap. Norwich; a. 2,055 sq. m.; p. (1966) *586,000*.

**Norfolk**, *c.*, Nebraska, U.S.A.; on Elkhorn R.; in farming country; p. (1960) *13,111*.

**Norfolk**, *c.*, Va., U.S.A.; impt. naval sta.; spt.; shipbldg. and repair, car assembly, food processing, lumber, fertilisers; p. (1960) *305,872*.

**Norfolk I.**, *fertile Australian I.*, Pac. Oc.; 800 m. E. of N.S.W. partial autonomy 1957; formerly a penal settlement; discovered by Captain Cook, 10 Oct. 1774; bean seed, whaling; a. 13 sq. m.; p. (1966) *1,152*.

**Noric Alps**, *mountainous region*, Styria, S. Austria.

**Norilsk**, *t.*, E. Siberia, R.S.F.S.R.; most N. t. in Russia; coal mng., uranium, nickel, copper; natural gas pipeline from W. Siberia; p. (1967) *127,000*.

**Normal**, *t.*, Ill., U.S.A.; mkt. gardening, fruit, plants; univ.; p. (1960) *13,357*.

**Norman**, *t.*, Okla., U.S.A.; oil-field; cotton processing; agr.; univ. of Okla.; p. (1960) *33,412*.

**Norman Wells**, *t.*, N.W. Terr., Canada; at confluence of R. Mackenzie and G. Bear R., 70 m. W. of G. Bear L.; ctr. of rich oil-field.

**Normandy**, *old French prov.*, on Eng. Channel; mainly agr.; now divided into deps. Manche, Calvados, Eure, Seine-Maritime and part of Orne; Rouen was cap.; the Roman Lugdunensis; later a powerful Dukedom; conquered England, 1066.

**Normanton**, *t.*, *urb. dist.*, W.R. Yorks, Eng.; on R. Calder 2 m. E. of Wakefield; coal-mining, rly. wks.; p. (1961) *18,307*.

**Norrbotten**, *co.*, N. Sweden; a. 40,754 sq. m.; cap. Piteå; p. (1961) *261,672*.

**Norris Dam**, Tenn., U.S.A.; across R. Clinch at confluence with R. Tenn., N.W. of Knoxville; lgst. dam Tenn. Valley Authority (TVA); built for flood control and hydro-elec.

**Norristown**, *bor.*, Penns., U.S.A.; textiles, hosiery, carpets; p. (1960) *38,925*.

**Norrköping**, *pt.*, *t.*, Sweden; N.E. of Linköping; textiles, margarine, paper; agr. machin.; ocean-going shipping through Lindö Canal; p. (1960) *91,661*.

**Norte de Santander**, *dep.*, Colombia, S. America; a. 8,295 sq. m.; cap. Cucuta; p. (estd. 1959) *412,440*.

**North Adams**, *c.*, Mass., U.S.A.; on R. Hoosac; textiles, boots, and shoes; p. (1960) *19,905*.

**North America**, *northern continent*, of Western hemisphere, comprising Mexico, U.S.A., Canada, Greenland and excl. Central America and the W. Indies; cst. much indented; on W. high chain of mtns., lower range in E., and central plain. Climate varies considerably owing to wide range of latitude and altitude; great extremes of temperature; abundant rainfall on E. cst. and N. of W. cst.; S. of W. cst. Mediterranean; Mexico, sub-tropical and tropical. Vegetation diverse, varying with alt., latitude and climate; coniferous forests in N.; originally deciduous forests from E. cst. to approx. 100° W., then grassland to mtn. vegetation of W. range; semi-desert in S.W. Prairies once home of bison. Agr.: temperate and tropical prod., cereals, cotton, tobacco, sugar-beet, potatoes, etc.; lumbering; rich in minerals, coal, petroleum, iron, manganese, etc. Gen. inds., comm., shipbldg. Formerly inhabited by Red Indians; now mainly occupied by White races, with many negroes in S.; p. (estd. 1965) 255,106,000.

North Atlantic Drift, drift of surface waters of Atl. Oc. N.E. from Gulf Stream towards Europe; relatively warm; supplies prevailing S.W. winds with warmth and moisture to modify climate of Brit. Is. and countries on N.W. margin of European Continent. *See* Gulf Stream, Section L.

North Attleboro, *t.*, Mass., U.S.A.; jewellery mnfs.; p. (1960) 14,704.

North Bay, *c.*, Ontario, Canada; p. (1961) 23,781.

North Berwick, *burgh*, E. Lothian, Scot.; on S. of F. of Forth, 20 m. E .of Edinburgh; seaside resort; golf course; p. (1961) 4,161.

North Brabant, *prov.*, Neth.; cap. 's-Hertogenbosch; a. 1,920 sq. m.; p. (estd. 1967) 1,700,866.

North Braddock, *t.*, Penns., U.S.A.; p. (1960) 13,204.

North Cape, *see* Nordkapp.

North Cape, *most northerly point*, N.I., N.Z.

North Carolina, *S. Atlantic st.*, U.S.A., E. of Tennessee and S. of Virginia; agr., maize, cotton-growing and mftg., tobacco culture and mftg., timber, scrap mica, textiles; cap. Raleigh; ch. pt., Wilmington; a. 52,712 sq. m.; p. (1960) 4,556,155.

North Channel, Brit. Is.; gives access from Atl. Oc. to Irish Sea between S.W. Scotland (Galloway) and N.E. Ireland (Antrim); length 60 m.; narrowest width 15 m.

North Chicago, *t.* Ill., U.S.A.; chemicals, metallurgy, elec. goods; p. (1960) 20,517.

North Crimean Canal, *canal*, U.S.S.R.; linking R. Dnieper with Black Sea and Sea of Azov, crossing steppes of S. Ukraine and the Crimea, terminating at Kerch; 1st section (77 m. long) opened Oct. 1963; when completed will be 220 m. long, 125 m. of which will be navigable.

North Dakota, *N.W. st.*, U.S.A.; mainly rolling prairie; agr., wheat, maize, oats, barley, flax, cattle, horses, sheep; coal, petroleum; cap. Bismarck; a. 70,665 sq. m.; p. (1960) 632,446.

North Downs, range of low chalk hills across S. Eng., forming cliffs at Dover; alt. about 800 ft.

North Eastern New Guinea, part of New Guinea under Australian administration as Trusteeship terr. under United Nations; a. 69,700 sq. m.

North East Passage, along N. cst. Europe and Asia between Atlantic and Pacific. *See* Gen. Inf.

North Holland, *prov.*, Neth.; a. 1,051 sq. m.; cap. Haarlem; natural gas in Schermer Polder nr. Alkmaar; p. (1967) 2,200,602.

North Island, *lge I.*, New Zealand; dairy prod.; lge. clay deposits at Matauri Bay; processing at Kaeo; a. 44,281 sq. m.; p. (1964) 1,320,118.

North Little Rock, *t.*, Ark., U.S.A.; p. (1960) 58,032.

North Osetian, A.S.S.R., U.S.S.R.; a. 3,100 sq. m.; cereals, livestock, petroleum; p. (1959) 449,000.

North Platte, *c.*, Nebraska, U.S.A., on N. Platte R.; in irrigated reg. of the Great Plains; grain, livestock, processed meat; p. (1960) 17,184.

North Platte, *R.*, rises N. Colorado, flows 680 m. through Wyoming, across W. Nebraska to join S. Platte at c. of North Platte; extensive power and irrigation developments.

North Providence, *see* Nassau.

North Rhine-Westphalia, *Land*, Germany; a. 13,153 sq. m.; p. (1961) 15,902,000.

North River, Kwangtung, S. China; rises in Nan Ling mtns., flows S. into Canton delta; length 300 m.

North Sea, arm of the Atlantic, E. of Gr. Brit., W. of Norway, Sweden and N. Germany, and N. of Holland, Belgium and France; length 600 m., width 400 m.; good fisheries.

North Sea Canal, *ship canal*, N. Holland, Neth.; connects Amsterdam to N. Sea at IJmuiden; depth 46 ft., length 16 m.

North Shields, *mkt. t.*, Northumberland, Eng.; Tyne pt. and part of the borough Tynemouth; marine engines, chain cables, anchors, rope.

North Sydney, *spt.*, C. Breton I., Nova Scotia, Canada; docks, coal; p. (1961) 8,657.

North Tonawanda, *c.*, N.Y., U.S.A.; on Niagara R.; mnfs.; p. (1960) 34,757.

O (78th Ed.)

North Walsham, *mkt. t.*, *urb. dist.*, Norfolk, Eng.; 13 m. N.E. of Norwich; p. (1961) 5,010.

North-West Frontier Province, *former prov.* (dissolved 1955), now incl. in Peshawar div., W. Pakistan; mtnous, fertile valleys; bounded by Hindu Kush and Afghanistan on N., and on S. by Baluchistan and Punjab; ch. c., Peshawar; wheat, barley, sugar cane, tobacco, cotton; iron, copper, marble quarrying; irrigation wks.; a. 14,263 sq. m.; p. (estd. 1951) 3,239,000.

North-West Passage, between Atl. and Pac. along Arctic cst. of Canada. *See* Section L.

North-West Staging Route, a daisy chain of airfields built during last war linking Edmonton, Alberta, with Whitehorse, Yukon.

North-West Territories, Canada; N.W. region of Canada between Yukon on W., Hudson Bay on E., and B.C., Alberta, Saskatchewan and Manitoba on S.; divided into 3 dists., Franklin, Mackenzie and Keewatin; cap. Yellowknife; gold- and silver-mng., petroleum, furs, fisheries; a. 1,304,903 sq. m.; p. (1961) 22,998.

North York. Moors, *limestone plateau*, N.R., Yorkshire; lies 8 of estuary of R. Tees; drained N. to R. Tees, S. to R. Derwent and to N. Sea by R. Esk; heather moorland; some pastoral farming on lower slopes; impt. iron-ore quarrying along N. edge in Cleveland dist.; alt. varies from 1,000 to 1,500 ft.

Northallerton, *t.*, *urb. dist.*, N.R. Yorks, Eng.; in broad gap between Cleveland Hills and Pennines; dairy farming and agr. dist.; car and agr. engin., leather; p. (1961) 6,720.

Northam, *t.*, W. Australia; on R. Avon. 66 m. from Perth, Australia; timber, metal wks.; p. (1966) 7,392.

Northampton, *S. Midland co.*, Eng.; chiefly agr.; iron, mining and mftg.; footwear, lace, leather, flax, light engin.; co. t., Northampton; a. 998 sq. m.; p. (1966) 428,000.

Northampton, *t.*, *co. bor.*, Northampton, Eng.; on R. Nene; footwear mftg., leather goods, light engin.; p. (estd. 1967) 121,890.

Northampton, *c.*, Mass., U.S.A.; textiles, paper; univ.; p. (1960) 30,058.

Northampton, *t.*, Penns., U.S.A.; cement; beer; clothes; quarrying; p. (1960) 8,866. [10,476.

Northbridge, *industl. t.*, Mass., U.S.A.; p. (1950)

Northcote, *t.*, Victoria, Australia; N. sub. Melbourne; mnfs.

Northern Ireland, consists of the administrative cos. of Antrim, Armagh, Down, Fermanagh, Londonderry and Tyrone, and administrative bors. of Belfast and Londonderry. Has its own parliament and executive Government under a Governor appointed by the Crown. Returns 12 members to British House of Commons; agr., oats, potatoes; textiles, chemicals, tobacco ind., electronic equip.; shipbldg; tourism; univs.; cap. Belfast; a. 5,238 sq m.; p. (1966) 1,484,770.

Northern Rhodesia, *see* Zambia.

Northern Territories, Ghana, West Africa; lies N. of latitude 8° N.; ch. t. Tamale; incl. Togoland a. 41,063 sq. m.; p. (1948) 1,076,696.

Northern Territory, a large tract of land N. of S. Australia; stock-raising, copper, gold, uranium, manganese, salt, bauxite; silver, mica, tin, tungsten; lead-zinc; rice at Humpty Doo, 30 m. S. of Darwin; a. 523,620 sq. m.; ch. t. Darwin; p. (1966) 37,166. [(1960) 8,707.

Northfield, *c.*, S. Minn., U.S.A.; agr., dairying; p.

Northfleet, *t.*, *urb. dist.*, Kent, Eng.; on S. bank of R. Thames, adjoining Gravesend; cement, paper, rubber, tyres, cables; p. (estd. 1967) 24,660.

Northumberland, *N. maritime co.*, Eng.; on border of Scot.; pastoral, mining, coal and lead, mftg.; chemicals, glass, engin., and shipbldg. on Tyneside; cap. Newcastle-upon-Tyne; a. 2,019 sq. m.; p. (1961) 818,988.

Northumberland Straits, separates Prince Edward I. from Nova Scotia and New Brunswick; 9 m. combined road and rail tunnel, bridge and causeway to link provs. projected.

Northwich, *mkt. t.*, *urb. dist.*, Cheshire, Eng.; on R. Weaver, 10 m. S.E. of Runcorn; chemicals, salt, engin.; p. (1961) 19,374. [(1950) 4,315.

Norton, *t.*, S.W. Va., U.S.A.; coal, mftg.; p.

Norton, *t.*, *urb. dist.*, E.R. Yorks, Eng.; on R. Derwent opposite Malton; p. (1961) 4,773.

Norton Sound, *inlet*, W. cst. Alaska, Behring Sea; 200 m. long.

**Norwalk**, *t.*, Conn., U.S.A.; on Long I. Sound; good harbour, oysters, iron foundries, clothing; p. (1960) *67,775*. [*88,739*.

**Norwalk**, *t.*, Cal., U.S.A.; oil refining; p. (1960)

**Norwalk**, *bor.*, Ohio, U.S.A.; mftg. ctr. of farming dist.; p. (1960) *12,900*.

**Norway**, *kingdom*, N. Europe; fjord cst., mtnous; climate influenced by prevailing winds, heavy rain and snowfall cstal regions; barley, forest prod., aluminium, pyrites; fisheries; hydro-elec. power; cap. Oslo; a. 124,556 sq. m.; p. (1963) *3,654,030*.

**Norwich**, *c.*, *co. bor.*, *co. t.*, Norfolk, Eng.; on R. Wensum just above confluence with R. Yare; univ.; cath., old cas., cult. ctr., agr. ctr.; boots, shoes, textiles, gen. inds., chemicals; p. (estd. 1967) *118,610*.

**Norwich**, *c.*, Conn., U.S.A.; firearms, cutlery and machin., textiles; p. (1960) *38,506*.

**Norwood**, S., *sub. div.*, Lambeth, Surrey, Eng.; mainly residtl. [(1960) *34,580*.

**Norwood**, Ohio, U.S.A.; *sub.*, Cincinnati; p.

**Norwood**, *t.*, Mass., U.S.A.; p. (1960) *24,898*.

**Nossi Bé**, *Is.*, Indian Ocean; off W. cst of Malagasy; a. 130 sq. m.; rice, coffee, tobacco.

**Noteć (Netze)**, *R.*, Poland; trib. R. Warta; 140 m.

**Noto**, *c.*, Sicily; W. of Syracuse; cath.; wine, olive oil, mnfs.; p. *32,575*.

**Notodden**, *t.*, S. Norway; hydro-elec. power; iron smelting; nitrates; p. (1961) *7,383*.

**Notre Dame Bay**, N. cst., Newfoundland, Canada.

**Nottingham**, *midland co.*, Eng.; wheat, oats, barley, cattle, coal, oil; co. t. Nottingham; a. 844 sq. m.; p. (1961) *902,966*.

**Nottingham**, *c.*, *co. bor.*, *co. t.*, Nottingham, Eng.; on R. Trent, at S.E. end of Pennines; ctr. of English lace ind.; univ., R.C. cath., fine buildings, cas., museum, gr. mkt. square; hosiery, engin., pharmaceutical ind., chemicals, cycles; p. (estd. 1967) *309,740*.

**Nouakchott**, *cap.*, Mauritania, W. Africa; p. (estd. 1962) *6,000*. [p. (1962) *35,000*.

**Nouméa or Port de France**, *cap.*, New Caledonia;

**Nova Lima**, *t.*, Minas Gerais st., Brazil; in Serra do Espinhaço, 10 m. S. of Belo Horizonte; adjacent to impt. gold-mines of Morro Velho; p. (1960) *21,135*.

**Nova Lisboa (Huambo)**, *t.*, Angola, Africa; E. of Benguela; rly. repair shops; p. (1960) *60,800* (inc. *14,000* whites). [p. *458,905*

**Novara**, *Alpine prov.*, N. Italy; a. 2,548 sq. m.;

**Novara**, *mftg. t.*, nr. Milan; p (1961) *86,190*.

**Nova Scotia**, *maritime prov.*, Canada; mainly fertile uplands and rich valleys, but with mtns. along the cst. nr. Bay of Fundy; agr., fruit, livestock, dairying, much mineral wealth, coal and gypsum, and very valuable fisheries; cap. Halifax; a. 21,068 sq. m.; p. (1961) *737,007*.

**Nova Zembla (Novaya Zemlya)**, *Is.*, Arctic Ocean, U.S.S.R.; furs, walrus, whale, seal fisheries, lead, zinc and copper; nuclear testing a. [mftg.; p. (1961) *22,041*.

**Nové Zamky**, *t.*, Slovakia, ČSSR.; mkt. and

**Novgorod**, *t.*, R.S.F.S.R.; sawmills, engin., p. (1959) *61,000*.

**Novi Ligure**, *t.*, Alessandria, Italy; nr. Genoa; noted for silk mftg.; p. *21,575*.

**Novi Pazar**, *t.*, Serbia, Jugoslavia; on R. Rashka; p. (1959) *17,000*.

**Novi Sad (Neusatz)**, *t.*, Jugoslavia; on R. Danube; opposite Petrovaradin; formerly royal free c., almost destroyed by Austrians 1849; tr. in fruit, wine, vegetables, corn; p. (1959) *97,000*.

**Novocherkask**, *t.*, R.S.F.S.R.; 20 m. N.E. of Rostov; engin., chemicals; p. (1967) *116,000*.

**Novokuybyshevsk**, *t.*, R.S.F.S.R.; Volga region; lge. oil processing plant; p. (1959) *63,000*.

**Novokuznetsk (Stalinsk)**, *t.*, R.S.F.S.R.; Kuznets; coal, iron, steel, engin., chemicals, aluminium; p. (1967) *484,000*.

**Novomoskovsk (Stalinogorsk)**, *t.*, R.S.F.S.R.; on R. Don; lignite, fertilisers, chemicals; p. (1967) *124,000*.

**Novorossiisk**, *spt.*, R.S.F.S.R.; on N.E. cst. of Black Sea; engin., textiles; lgst. cement producer in U.S.S.R.; p. (1967) *120,000*.

**Novoshakhtinsk**, *t.*, R.S.F.S.R.; on Rostov–Kharkov highway; coalmng., chemicals; p. (1967) *108,000*.

**Novosibirsk**, *t.*, R.S.F.S.R.; on R. Ob; hydro-elec., steel, tin smelting, engin., textiles, chemicals, sawmilling; p. (1967) *1,049,000*.

**Novo Troitsk**, *t.*, R.S.F.S.R.; in Urals, 11 m. S.W.

of Orsk; cement, iron and steel; p. (1959) *57,000*. [power sta.

**Novovoronezh**, U.S.S.R., on R. Don; nuclear

**Nový Jičín (Neutitschein)**, *t.*, Moravia, ČSSR.; farm machin. and engin.; p. (1961) *16,560*.

**Nowa Huta**, *t.*, Poland; S.E. Kraków, on R. Vistula; newly developed metallurgical ctr.; p. (1954) *50,000*.

**Nowa Sól (Neusalz)**, *t.*, Lower Silesia, Poland; on R. Oder; chemicals; p. (1965) *29,000*.

**Nowata**, *t.*, N.E. Okla., U.S.A.; agr., natural gas, oil-field gear; p. (1950) *3,965*.

**Nowawes**, *c.*, Brandenburg, Germany; textiles, engin., chemicals; p. *26,975*.

**Nowra-Bomaderry**, *t.*, N.S.W., Australia; on E. cst. at mouth of Shoalhaven R.; collecting ctr. for agr. and pastoral prod. of coastal plain; at S. terminus of rly. along E. cst. of Australia; paper mill; p. (1966) *9,642*.

**Nowy Sacz**, *industl. t.*, Krakow, S. Poland; on R. Dunajec; lignite; p. (1965) *37,000*.

**Nsanje (Port Herald)**, *t.*, Malawi, Africa; pt. on Shire R.

**Nubia**, *region*, Africa, extending on both sides of Nile from Aswan, U.A.R., southwards to Khartoum, Sudan.

**Nubian Desert**, Sudan, N.E. Africa; between R. Nile and Red Sea; alt. 1,200–9,000 ft.; a. approx. 90,000 sq. m.

**Nuble**, *prov.*, Chile; bordering on Argentina; a. 5,484 sq. m.; cap. Chillan; p. (1961) *327,105*.

**Nueces**, *R.*, Texas, U.S.A.; flows to G. of Mexico; length 400 m. [p. (1961) *89,492*.

**Nueva Esparta**, *st.*, Venezuela; cap. La Asuncion;

**Nuevo Laredo**, *c.*, E. Mexico; agr., cotton, maize, cattle rearing; p. (1960) *107,473*.

**Nuevo León**, *st.*, Mexico; agr. and stock raising, sugar; cap. Monterrey; a. 25,134 sq. m.; p. (1960) *1,078,848*.

**Nukualofa**, *cap.* of Polynesian kingdom of Tonga.

**Nukus**, *t.*, Uzbek S.S.R.; in Khorezm oasis; p. (1959) *39,000*.

**Nullarbor Plain**, S. Australia; low, level, limestone plateau fringing Gr. Australian Bight; arid; treeless, salt-bush scrub; crossed by Transcontinental Rly. between Naretha (W. Australia) and Ooldea; rly. is dead straight dead level for 298 m.

**Nun**, *ch. mouth* of R. Niger, Africa.

**Nun**, *R.*, Inner Mongolia, Heilungkiang, N. China; trib. of Sungari; length 500 m.

**Nun**, *R.*, on S. frontier of Morocco, N. Africa; with t. thereon; length 130 m.

**Nuneaton**, *mkt. t.*, *mun. bor.*, Warwick, Eng.; on R. Anker, 18 m. E. of Birmingham; coal-mining, quarrying, textiles, engin., lt. inds.; p. (estd. 1967) *63,420*.

**Nuremberg (Nürnberg)**, *t.*, Bavaria, Germany; cas., museum, cultural academy and many historic bldgs.; elec. mnfs., machin., heavy vehicles, toys, pencils and crayons; rly. junction; p. (1968) *466,100*.

**Nusa Tenggara**, *Is.*, Indonesia; p. (1961) *3,775,127* inc. Bali *5,557,656*.

**Nutley**, *t.*, N.J., U.S.A.; p. (1960) *29,513*.

**Nyasa**, *L.*, see Malawi, L.

**Nyasaland**, see Malawi.

**Nyborg**, *t.*, Denmark; on Fyn I.; p. (1960) *11,667*.

**Nyeri**, *t.*, Kenya; p. (1962) *7,400*.

**Nyiregyháza**, *mftg. t.*, Hungary; wine, farming; implements; p. (estd. 1957) *55,000*.

**Nykobing**, *spt.*, Falster I.,Denmark; light engin., food-packing, margarine, sugar-refining, tobacco ind.; p. (1960) *17,850*.

**Nyköping**, *spt.*, Sweden; at head of inlet on cst., comm. and industr.; cars; p. (1961) *24,250*.

**Nystad (Uusikapunki)**, *spt.*, Abo-Björneborg, Finland; on G. of Bothnia; p. (1966) *5,074*.

# O

**Oadby**, *urb. dist.*, Leics, Eng.; 3 m. S.E. of Leic.; boots and shoes; p. (1961) *12,266*.

**Oahu**, *I.*, Hawaiian Is., Pac. Oc.; sugar, pineapples; tourist tr.; cap. Honolulu; a. 604 sq. m.; p. (1960) *500,409*.

**Oak Park Village**, *t.*, Ill., U.S.A.; now included in Chicago; p. (1960) *61,093*.

**Oakengates**, *t.*, urb. dist., Salop, Eng.; 15 m. N.W. of Wolverhampton; iron and steel, precast concrete, engin.; expansion of t. projected; p. (1961) *12,158*.

Oakham, *co. t., urb. dist.*, Rutland, Eng.; 9 m. S.E. of Melton Mowbray; mkt.; hosiery; p. (1961) *4,571.*

Oakland, *c.*, Cal., U.S.A.; on San Francisco Bay; residtl. sub.; cars, shipbldg., fruit canning, elec. machin., clothing, tanneries, chemicals; p. (1960) *367,548.* [p. (1961) *12,401.*

Oamaru, *bor., spt.*, S.I., N.Z.; wool, frozen meat;

Oaxaca, *st.*, Pacific cst., Mexico; cereals, rubber, coffee, mining; cap. Oaxaca; a. 36,371 sq. m.; p. (1960) *1,727,266.*

Oaxaca, *c., cap.*, Oaxaca st., Mexico; alt. 4,800 ft.; ctr. of cochineal tr.; table linen weaving, wool zarapes; coffee; silver, gold; cattle; p. (1960) *60,000.*

Ob, *G.*, U.S.S.R.; inlet of Arctic Oc.; length 600 m.

Ob, *R.*, W. Siberia, U.S.S.R.; flows from the Altai Mtns. to the G. of Ob; length (with trib. R. Irtish) 2,600 m.

Oban, *spt., burgh*, Argyll, Scot.; on F. of Lorne; summer resort of Highland tourists; terminus of rly. from Stirling; ctr. for local shipping; woollens, tartans; p. (1961) *6,859.*

Obed, Alberta, Canada; 150 m. W. of Edmonton; major natural gas a.

Oberlahnstein, *t.*, Germany; at junction of Rs. Rhine and Lahn; cas., ancient walls; mng.

Oberammergau, *vil.*, Upper Bavaria, Germany; scene of decennial Passion Play; p. *1,500.*

Oberhausen, *t.*, N. Rhine–Westphalia, Germany; nr. Duisburg; cas.; coal, iron, steel, zinc, chemicals, rly. junction; p. (1963) *259,800.*

Obi I., *sm. I.*, between Halmahera and Serang, Indonesia.

Obidos, *t., R. pt.*, Brazil; 500 m. up R. Amazon; cacao, cotton; p. (1960) *3,500.*

Obihiro, *t.*, Hokkaido, Japan; p. (1947) *36,555.*

Obninsk, *t.*, R.S.F.S.R.; 60 m. S.W. of Moscow; atomic power sta.

Obok, *spt.*, Fr. Somaliland, N.E. Africa; in the Red Sea; coaling sta.; p. *1,000.*

Obuasi, *t.*, Ghana, W. Africa; p. (1960) *23,000.*

Obwalden, *can.*, Switzerland; a. 190 sq. m.; p. (1961) *23,135.*

Ocaña, *ancient t.*, Toledo, Spain; on Ocaña plateau; cas.; pottery, wine; p. (1957) *6,840.*

Ocaña, *t.*, Magdalena st., Colombia; coffee, hides; p. (estd. 1959) *21,200.*

Ocean I., Brit. col., Gilbert and Ellice Is., Pac. Oc.; high-grade phosphate; p. (1956) *2,446.*

Oceania, name given to the Is. of the Pacific; comprising Australasia, Polynesia, Melanesia, Micronesia; copra, sugar, fruit, timber; pearl fishing; gold, minerals, phosphates; a. 3,201,000 sq. m.; p. approx. *11,000,000.*

Ochil Hills, Scottish range reaching from the F. of Tay to nr. Stirling; highest peak, Ben Cleugh, 2,363 ft.

Ockmulgee, *R.*, Ga., U.S.A.; trib. of Altamaha R.; length 280 m. [length 250 m.

Oconee, *R.* Ga., U.S.A.; joins the Ockmulgee;

Odawara, *t.*, Japan; nr. Tokyo; gr. tr.; p. (1965) *143,377.*

Odda, *t.*, S. Norway; on Haugesund; electro-chem. and metallurgic inds.; p. (1961) *7,383.*

Odemiş, *t.*, Asiatic Turkey; N.E. of Aydin; tobacco, cereals, silk, cotton, flax, olives, raisins, figs; minerals; p. (1965) *30,621.*

Odendaalsrust, *t.*, O.F.S., S. Africa; gold ctr.; p. (1960) *15,047* inc. *6,070* whites.

Odense, *co.*, Denmark; now includes all N.W. Fyn; a. 699 sq. m.; p. (1965) *218,667.*

Odense, *spt.*, cap. of Fyn, Denmark; ancient c. said to have been founded by Odin; birthplace of Hans Andersen; elec. motors, shipyd., engin., textiles, footwear; p. (1965) *132,978.*

Odenwald, *mtns.*, Hessen, Germany; wooded; highest point Katzenbuckel, 2,057 ft.

Oder or Odra, *R.*, Central Europe; flowing from Moravia to Baltic through Polish Silesia, forming (since 1945) frontier between Poland and Germany, flows past Wroclaw (Breslau), Frankfurt and Szczecin (Stettin); length 560 m.

Odessa, *t.*, Texas, U.S.A.; impt. oil ctr., chemicals, foundry prod.; p. (1960) *80,338.*

Odessa, *spt.*, Ukrainain S.S.R.; on Black Sea; cath., univ.; gr. grain exp.; engin., oil-refining, chemicals; ice-bound for a few weeks in winter; bombarded by English and French 1845; p. (1967) *753,000.*

Offaly, *co.* (late King's co.), prov Leinster, Ireland; much marshy land (inc. Bog of Allen),

barren uplands (Slieve Bloom and other mtns.); fertilising factory for ammonium nitrate from peat in Blackwater Bog; ch. t. Tullamore; a. 772 sq. m.; p. (1966) *51,707.*

Offenbach, *t.*, Hessen, Germany; on R. Main; cas., leather museum; machin., chemicals, leather goods, metals; p. (1963) *118,000.*

Offenburg, *t.*, Baden–Württemberg, Germany; on R. Kinzig; textiles, glass, rly. junction; p. (1963) *28,600.*

Ogbomosho, *t.*, Nigeria; p. (1953) *140,000.*

Ogden, *c.*, Utah, U.S.A.; nr. the Great Salt L.; rly. ctr.; beet sugar, meat packing, flour milling; p. (1960) *70,197.*

Ogdensburg, *c., pt.*, N.Y., U.S.A.; on St. Lawrence R., opp. Prescott; gd. tr.; p. (1960) *16,122*

Ogeechee, *R.*, Ga., U.S.A.; flows to Atlantic, S. of Savannah; length 200 m.

Oglio, *R.*, Italy; traverses L. Iseo; flows to the Po; length 135 m.

Ogmore and Garw, *t., urb. dist.*, Glamorgan, Wales; in narrow valley, 6 m. N. of Bridgend; industl.; p. (1961) *20,955.*

Ogowe, *R.*, Gaboon, Africa; length 750 m.

Ohau, *L.*, Mt. Cook dist., S.I., N.Z.; fed by glaciers; 12 m. by 22 m.; hydroelec. plant projected.

O'Higgins, *prov.*, Chile; a. 2,745 sq. m.; p. (1961) *292,296.*

Ohio, *R.*, U.S.A.; trib. of Mississippi R.; formed in Penns., by the junction of the Monongahela and Allegheny Rs. at Pittsburgh, thence navigable for 975 m. to Cairo in Kentucky, 1,200 m. from the mouth of the Mississippi R.

Ohio, *st.*, U.S.A.; drained by Ohio R. and tribs.; gr. agr. and industl. region; maize, wheat, oats, cattle; lime, sand and gravel, salt, coal, petroleum, gas, iron and steel wks., machin., timber; cap. Columbus; lgst. cs. Cleveland and Cincinnati; a. 41,122 sq. m.; p. (1960) *9,706,397.*

Ohre (Eger), *R.*, Bohemia, Czechoslovakia; rises in Fichtelgebirge, flows N.E. into Labe (Elbe) at Litoměřice; flows through several sm. lignite fields, spas of Karlovy Vary (Karlsbad); length 140 m. [(1959) *15,000.*

Ohrid, *t.*, S. Jugoslavia; nr. Albanian border; p.

Oich, Loch, *L.*, Great Glen, Inverness, Scot.; 6 m. long, 1 m. wide.

Oil City, Penns., U.S.A.; on Allegheny R.; oil, machin.; p. (1960) *17,692.*

Oise, *dep.*, N. France; traversed by R. Oise; forests, cereals, fruits, iron, textiles; cap. Beauvais; a. 2,272 sq. m.; p. (1962) *481,289.*

Oise, *R.*, trib. of R. Seine, France; canalised, navigable to Chauny; length 186 m.

Oita, *spt.*, Japan; exp. coal; cattle; p. (1964) *229,000.*

Ojos del Salado, *mtn.*, N.W. Argentina; alt. 22,572 ft.

Oka, *R.*, U.S.S.R.; trib. of R. Volga at Gorki; length 929 m. [length 500 m.

Oka, *R.*, Siberia, U.S.S.R.; trib. of R. Angora;

Okanagan, R. and *L.*, B.C., Canada; fruit-growing dist.

Okasaki, *t.*, Honshu, Japan; nr. G. of Ovari; industl.; p. (1965) *194,409.*

Okayama, *t.*, Honshu, Japan; exp. paper, minerals, firebricks; shipbldg.; rly. ctr.; cattle rearing; p. (1965) *291,825.*

Okehampton, *mkt. t., mun. bor.*, Devon, Eng.; on N. flank of Dartmoor; stone; p. (estd. 1967) *3,810.*

Okha, *spt.*, E. cst. Sakhalin I., R.S.F.S.R.; exp. petroleum; lge. refinery projected; p. (1954) *50,000.*

Okhotsk, Sea of, N.E. Asia; 1,000 m. by 500 m.; enclosed by the Siberian mainland, Kamchatka, the Kurils and Sakhalin I.

Oki Is., off cst. of Honshu, Japan; a. 135 sq. m.

Okinawa, *I.*, Ryuku Is., Japan, under U.S. control; lgst. and most impt. of Ryuku Is., cap. Naha; 2 lgst. U.S. air bases Kadena and Naha; a. 579 sq. m.; p. (1956) *665,315.*

Oklahoma, *st.*, U.S.A.; prairie, plains and mtns.; cereals, cotton, stock-raising, petroleum, gas, zinc, coal, gypsum, lead; ch. ind. petroleum refining; cap. Oklahoma City; a. 69,919 sq. m.; p. (1960) *2,328,284.*

Oklahoma, *c.*, Okla., U.S.A.; univ.; oil and by-prod., oil processing, field machin., iron, steel, flour mills, meat pkg.; p. (1960) *324,253.*

Okmulgee, *t.*, Okla., U.S.A.; p. (1960) *15,951.*

Oktyabrsky, *t.*, Bashkir., A.S.S.R.; on R. Ik; in new oil-mng. dist., the "New Baku"; p. (1959) *65,000.*

Öland, I., Baltic Sea; off E. cst. Sweden; separated from mainland by Kalmar Sound; a. 533 sq. m.; ch. t. Borgholm, a seaside resort.

Old Castile, historical div., Spain; now divided into Santander, Soria, Segovia, Logrono, Avila, Valladolid, Palencia and Burgos provs.

Old Fletton, urb. dist., Hunts, Eng.; on R. Nene opposite Peterborough; bricks, gen. and elec. engin., beet sugar, fruit and vegetable canning, tar distilling; p. (1961) 11,673.

Old Forge, bor., Penns., U.S.A.; anthracite coal; p. (1960) 8,923.

Old Kilpatrick, see Kilpatrick, Old.

Oldbury, mun. bor., Worcs., Eng.; nr. Birmingham; iron, steel, chemical, brick, glass inds.; p. (1961) 53,935.

Oldbury-on-Severn, Glos., Eng.; nuclear power sta.

Oldenburg, t., Lower Saxony, Germany; on R. Hunte; grand-ducal palace; impt. horse fair; food processing, lt. inds.; rly. junction; natural gas nr. to cst.; p. (1963) 126,200.

Oldham, mftg. t., co. bor., Lancs, Eng.; on R. Medlock, 4 m. N.E. of Manchester; cotton, textile, and machin. mftg.; p. (estd. 1967) 109,840.

Oldmeldrum, burgh, Aberdeen, Scot.; 4 m. N.E. of Inverurie; p. (1961) 1,083.

Olean, t., N.Y., U.S.A.; on Allegheny R.; oil region; p. (1960) 21,868.

Olenek, R., Ukrainian S.S.R.; flows W. of the Lena, into Laptev Sea, Arctic Ocean; length 800 m.

Oléron, Ile d', I., Bay of Biscay; lies off estuary of R. Charente, Aquitaine, France; vine, oysters, salt; length 18 m., maximum width 7 m.

Olga, spt., R.S.F.S.R.; on cst. of Japan Sea; iron ore; p. 1,000. [16,017.

Olhão, t., Faro, Portugal; fisheries; p. (1960)

Olifant, R., Transvaal, S. Africa; trib. of Limpopo.

Olinda, c., Pernambuco st., Brazil; seaside resort; phosphates; p. (1960) 100,545.

Oliobiri, S. Nigeria; oilfields; pipe-line to Pt. Harcourt, 80 m. W.

Oliva, t., Valencia, Spain; nr. Alicante; wine dist., ducal palace; p. (1957) 13,343.

Olivenza, t., Spain; nr. Portuguese frontier; p. (1957) 13,334. [p. (estd. 1960) 160,000.

Olivos, sub., Buenos Aires, Argentina, S. America;

Olkhon, I., L. Baykal, R.S.F.S.R.; manganese.

Olmutz, see Olomouc.

Olney, t., N. Bucks, Eng.; 11 m. S.E. Northampton; boots, shoes, lace; dairying; p. 2,651.

Olomouc (Olmütz), c., ČSSR.; formerly one of the ch. fortresses of Austria; cath., univ.; iron and steel engin., textiles; p. (1962) 70,116.

Oloron, t., Basses-Pyrénées, France; on Gave d'Oloron; cath.; p. (1962) 13,593.

Olsnitz, t., Saxony, Germany; on Weisse Elster; carpet mnfs.

Olsztyn (Allenstein), t., N.W. Poland, cap. Olsztyn prov.; on R. Alle, 100 m. N. of Warsaw; cas.; machin., wood inds.; p. (1965) 75,000.

Olt, R., Romania; joins R. Danube at Nikopol.

Olten, t., Switzerland; on R. Aare; rly. junction; motor, cement, machin. wks.; p. (1957) 16,435.

Oltenita, t., Romania; on R. Danube, nr. Bulgarian border; p. (1956) 14,111.

Olvarria, t., E. Argentina; 200 m. S.W. Buenos Aires; rly. ctr.; p. 24,326.

Olvera, t., Spain; nr. Cadiz; on R. Guadalete; p. (1957) 10,232.

Olympia, plain, Peloponnesus, Greece, on R. Ellis where the Olympic Games were held.

Olympia, cap., Washington st., U.S.A.; timber, machin., farm prod.; p. (1960) 18,273.

Olympus, mtn., Thessaly, Greece; W. of G. of Thessalonika; alt. 9,753 ft.; home of ancient Greek Gods.

Olympus, mtn., Turkey; nr. Troy.

Olympus, Mt., Wash., U.S.A.; alt. 8,150 ft.

Om, R., Siberia, R.S.F.S.R.; trib. of R. Irtish; length 330 m.

Omagh, t., urb. dist., Tyrone, N. Ireland; on R. Strule 28 m. S. of Londonderry; corn, tanning; shirt factories; tourist ctr.; p. (1966) 9,857

Omaha, c., Nebraska, U.S.A.; on Missouri R.; gr. tr., cnr. of one of the lgst. livestock and meat-packing ctrs. in the U.S., gold and silver smelting and refining, steel fabrication, industl. alcohol prod.; p. (1960) 301,598.

Oman, see Muscat and Oman.

Oman, G. of, Arabian Sea; connected through

strait of Hormuz to Persian G.; length 300 m., width 130 m.

Omaruru, t., S.W. Africa; creamery, aerodrome; p. (1960) 2,689 inc. 743 whites.

Ombai Is., Indonesia; N. of Timor.

Omdurman, c., Sudan on R. Nile, opp. Khartoum; built by the Mahdi; old Dervish cap.; here Kitchener defeated the Dervishes, 1898; tr. in ivory, gum arabic, cattle, camels; p. (estd. 1956) 130,000.

Ometepe, I., L. Nicaragua, Central America, with volcano; alt. 5,747 ft.

Omine, t., Japan; anthracite coal-mines.

Omsk, t., W. Siberia, R.S.F.S.R.; on the R. Irtish; on Trans-Siberian Rly., caravan ctr.; cath.; engin., chemicals, textiles, oil refining; p. (1967) 746,000.

Omuta, t., Kyushu, Japan; coal; p. (1964) 221,000.

Onahama, pt., N.E. Japan; copper refinery under construction.

Onate, t., Guipuzcoa, Spain; nr. Bilbao; industl; p. (1957) 7,225.

Onega, L., R.S.F.S.R.; 85 m. from L. Ladoga; a. 3,765 sq. m.; connection with R. Volga by canal.

Onega, R., R.S.F.S.R.; flows to G. of Onega; length 400 m.

Oneglia, spt., Italy; on G. of Genoa, nr. Nice, Italy; olive-oil tr.

Onehunga, spt., bor., N.I., N.Z.; nr. Auckland; p. (1961) 16,375.

Oneida, L., N.Y., U.S.A.; nr. Syracuse; 20 m. by 6 m.; discharges via Oneida R. to Seneca R.

Oneonta, t., N.Y., U.S.A.; on Susquehanna R.; rly. wagon wks.; p. (1960) 13,412.

Onomichi, t., Honshu, Japan; p. (1947) 48.726.

Onstwedde, t., Groningen, Neth.; mnfs.; p. (1967) 27,666.

Ontario, L., N. America; smallest of the Gr. Lakes of the St. Lawrence basin, separating the Canadian prov. of O. from N.Y., U.S.A.; a. 7,500 sq. m.; depth 740 ft.

Ontario, prov., Canada; formerly called Upper Canada; St. Lawrence and Ottawa Rs., Gr. Lakes; extreme climate, milder in peninsula in S.; coniferous forest; good communications; hydro-elec. power; nuclear power sta. at Chalk R.; wheat, oats, fruit, dairying, cattle, lumbering, gold, silver, copper, lead, uranium, nickel, oil, farm implements, rly. rolling stock, motor vehicles, machin., textiles, furs, wood pulp, newsprint, cap. Toronto; contains Ottawa; a. 412,582 sq. m.; p. (1961) 6,236,092.

Onteniente, t., Valencia, Spain; on R. Clariano; woollen gds., paper mills; p. (1957) 14,689.

Oodnadatta, t., S. Australia; on uncompleted N. to S. trans-continental rly.; p. 100.

O'okiep, t., Cape Province, S. Africa; copper-mining dist.; p. (with neighbouring villages—whites and non-whites) 5,000.

Oosterhout, t., N. Brabant, Netherlands; nr. Breda; mnfs.; p. (1967) 23,677.

Ootacamund, t., Tamil Nadu, India; ch. t. in Nilgiri Hills; summer headquarters of Tamil Nadu Govt.; sanatorium; p. (1961) 50,140.

Opala, t., Congo; on Lomami R.; palm-nuts, gum copal.

Opalton, t., Queensland, Australia; opals.

Opatija, (former It. Abbazia), t., Jugoslavia, tourist resort known as the "Nice" of the Adriatic.

Opava, (former Troppau), t., ČSSR.; textiles, paper, sugar; p. (1961) 42,523. [gold.

Ophir, dist., N.S.W., Australia; nr. Bathurst;

Ophir, mtn., S. Malaya, alt. 4,186 ft.

Ophir, mining t., S.I., N.Z.; nr. Dunedin.

Opladen, t., N. Rhine–Westphalia, Germany; on R. Wupper; metals, textiles, chemicals; p. (1963) 36,300.

Opobo, spt., Nigeria; exp. palm-oil and kernels.

Opole (Oppeln), t., S. Poland, cap. Opole prov.; on R. Oder; R. pt., rly. junc.; trade ctr.; cement, metals, furniture; former cap. Prussian prov. of Upper Silesia (1919–45); p. (1965) 75,000.

Oporto, spt., Portugal; on R. Douro; second c. in Portugal; comm.; royal palace of Torre de Marca; cath.; univ.; ctr. of port-wine tr., sardine fisheries, cottons, woollens, silks, distilling, sugar refineries; fruit; oil refinery projected; p. (1960) 310,000.

Opotiki, t., N.I., N.Z.; ctr. of maize dist.; p. (1961) 2,559.

Oppeln, see Opole.

**Oppland**, *co.*, Norway; a. 9,608 sq. m.; p. (1963) *166,823.*

**Oradea**, (former Nagyvarad), *t.*, Romania; nr. Hungarian border; rly. junction, farming pottery, engin.; p. (1963) *122,535.*

**Öraefa Jokull**, *highest mtn.*, Iceland; alt. 6,409 ft.

**Oran** *dep.*, N. Algeria; p. (1948) *1,990,729.*

**Oran**, *c.*, *spt.*, N. Algeria; tr. in wines, wool, cereals, meat, skins; founded by Moors; occupied by French 1831–1962; fine roadstead Mers-el-Kebir; former French naval and military sta.; p. (1960) *393,000.*

**Orange**, *t.*, N.S.W., Australia; fruit packing, meat, wool, bricks, elec. machin.; p. (1966) *22,200.*

**Orange**, *ancient t.*, Vaucluse, France; silks, sugar, fruit; p. (1954) *17,473.*

**Orange**, *t.*, Mass., U.S.A.; p. (1960) *3,689.*

**Orange**, *c.*, N.J., U.S.A.; adj. Newark; calculating machines, radio, textiles, drugs; p. (1960) *35,789.*

**Orange**, *C.*, N. Brazil, S. America.

**Orange**, *R.*, Cape Province, S. Africa; flows from Basutoland to the Atlantic; part forms S. bdy. between Cape Province and Orange Free State; length 1,300 m.

**Orange Free State**, *prov.*, Rep. of S. Africa; plateau land, Drakensberg to N.E., Rs. Orange, Vaal and Caledon; sheep, cattle, horses, wheat, maize, fruit, tobacco, coal, diamonds; cap. Bloemfontein; a. 49,647 sq. m.; p. (1960) *1,386,547* (inc. *276,745* whites).

**Oranienburg**, *t.*, Potsdam, E. Germany, on R. Havel; industl.; chemicals, metals, machin.; p. (1963) *21,075.*

**Oras**, *t.*, Samar, Philippines; p. *20,962.*

**Orastie**, *t.*, Romania; on R. Muresul; p. (1956) *10,488.*

**Orbetello**, *t.*, Tuscany, Italy; cath.; p. *10,631.*

**Ord** of Caithness, *hill*, *headland*, nr. Helmsdale, Scot.; alt. 1,200 ft.

**Ordos**, *desert region*, Inner Mongolia; lies S. and E. of Yellow R.; pastoral nomads; mean alt. 3,300 ft.

**Ordu**, *spt.*, Turkey; on Black Sea; gd. tr.; exp. manganese; p. (1965) *27,307.*

**Ordzhonikidze**, *t.*, Caucasia, R.S.F.S.R.; on R. Terek; hydro-elec., lead, silver and zinc smelting; natural gas pipeline to Tbilisi; p. (1967) *212,000.*

**Örebro**, *co.*, Sweden; timber, machin., matches; cap. Örebro; a. 3,650 sq. m.; p. (1961) *262,239.*

**Örebro**, *t.*, *cap.*, Örebro, Sweden; footwear, textiles, paper; p. (1961) *75,434.*

**Oregon**, *Pacific st.*, U.S.A.; Cascade, Cst. and Blue Mtns.; Colombia R. and tribs.; L., valleys; rainy cst., drier interior (agr with irrigation); cereals, sugar-beet, fruit, cattle, gold, silver, copper, coal, uranium; fisheries, canning, meat-packing, timber, milling; cap. Salem; a. 96,891 sq. m.; p. (1960) *1,768,687.*

**Oregon City**, Ore., U.S.A.; on Willamette R. at the falls; p. (1950) *7,682.*

**Orekhovo-Zuyevo**, R.S.F.S.R.; E. of Moscow, on R. Klyazma; cottons, woollens, silk, linen and knitted goods; p. (1967) *117,000.*

**Orel**, *t.*, R.S.F.S.R.; on R. Oka; univ.; engin.; p. (1967) *202,000.*

**Orenburg**, *c.*, R.S.F.S.R.; on Ural R.; engin., leather, silk; p. (1967) *316,000.*

**Orense**, *inland prov.*, N.W. Spain; timber and fruit-growing, agr.; cap. Orense; a. 2,694 sq. m.; p. (1959) *468,242.*

**Orense**, *t.*, cap. Orense, Spain; on R. Minho; flour, leather, iron; p. (1959) *64,747.*

**Ore Sound**, *str.*, between Sjaelland and S. Sweden; freezes occasionally.

**Orford Ness**, *cst. prom.*, Suffolk, Eng.; 2¼ m. long.

**Oriente**, *prov.*, Cuba; a. 14,128 sq. m.; p. (1953) *1,797,606.*

**Oriente**, *terr.*, S. America; in dispute between Peru and Ecuador; situated E. of Andes, between R. Putumayo and R. Marañon; mainly dense forest, reputedly rich in minerals.

**Orihuela**, *t.*, Alicante, Spain; on R. Segura; leather, silks, textiles, wine, cereals, fruit; p. (1957) *44,979.*       [p. (1961) *15,345.*

**Orillia**, *t.*, Ont., Canada; wood-working, metal;

**Orinoco**, *R.*, Venezuela; rises Parima mtns., flows circuitously to Atlantic opposite Trinidad; its trib., the Cassiquiare, connects it with the Rio Negro and the Amazon; length 1,480 m.

**Orissa**, *st.*, India; agr. with few ts.; Hirakud dam across Mahanadi R.; Paradeep being devel. as

pt.; rice; cap. Bhuvaneshwar; a. 60,164 sq. m.; p. (1961) *17,548,846.*

**Orizaba**, *t.*, Veracruz, Mexico; textiles, paper mills, breweries; p. (1960) *70,000.*

**Orizaba**, *mtn.*, Veracruz, Mexico; volcanic; called Citlaltépetl in Aztec times; alt. 18,701 ft.

**Orkney**, *co.*, Scot.; a gr. of 68 Is. in the N. Sea, 29 being inhabited; principal Is. Pomona, Sanday, Westray; antiquarian remains, stone circles; farming, fishing; cap. Kirkwall; total a. about 360 sq. m.; p. (1961) *18,743.*

**Orlando**, *c.*, Fla., U.S.A.; winter resort; citrus fruit; industl.; p. (1960) *88,135.*

**Orléanais**, *old prov.*, France, corresponding mainly to deps. Loire-et-Cher, Eure-et-Loire Loiret.

**Orléans**, *c.*, Loiret, France; on R. Loire; cap. of Orléanais; cath.; univ.; gr. tr. in wine, brandy, textiles, chemicals; farm implements; statue of Joan of Arc; p. (1962) *88,105.*

**Orleans, I. of**, Quebec, Canada; in St. Lawrence R., nr. Quebec; a. 70 sq. m.

**Ormes Head, Great and Little**, promontories on cst. Caernarvon, N. Wales.

**Ormoc**, *t.*, Leyte, Philippines; p. (1960) *62,764.*

**Ormskirk**, *t.*, *urb. dist.*, Lancs., Eng.; 14 m. N.E. of Liverpool; light engin., clothing, timber, agr.; p. (estd. 1967) *25,440.*

**Orne**, *dep.*, Normandy, France; agr., dairying, stock-keeping, fruit-growing, cider, mineral springs, iron; cap. Alençon; a. 2,372 sq. m.; p. (1962) *280,549.*    [dustl. ctr.; p. *8,400.*

**Örnsdköldsvik**, *t.*, Sweden; on G. of Bothnia; in-

**Oronsay**, *sm. I.*, S. Colonsay, Argyll, Scot.

**Orontes**, *R.*, Lebanon, Syria, Turkey; rises in Lebanon Mtns., flows N. in deep trench between Lebanon and Anti-Lebanon Mtns. to Plain of Antioch (Antakya), then turns W. and breaks through mtns. to Mediterranean Sea; upper valley above Hama forms cultivated belt, width 10 m., used by Aleppo–Beirut rly.; middle valley is marshy; lower valley and Plain of Antioch intensively cultivated, mulberry, citrus and hard fruits, grain; length over 400 m.

**Oroquieta**, *t.*, Mindanao, Philippines; p. *26,640.*

**Oroshaza**, *mkt. t.*, S.E. Hungary; in agr. and pig-keeping dist.; p. (1962) *31,867.*

**Oroszlany**, *t.*, Hungary; coalmng.; p. (1967) *16,700.*

**Orotava**, *t.*, Tenerife, Canary Is.

**Oroya**, *t.*, Peru, S. America; copper smelting; lead refining; p. (1961) *15,000.*

**Orpington**, *see* Bromley.    [p. (1961) *10,663.*

**Orrell**, *t.*, *urb. dist.*, Lancs., Eng.; W. of Wigan;

**Orsha**, *t.*, Byelorussian S.S.R.; on R. Dnieper; textiles, metal workings; p. (1959) *64,000.*

**Orsk**, *t.*, R.S.F.S.R.; on R. Ural; growing industl. t. of the Ural industl. reg.; iron and steel, locomotives, iron–chrome–nickel ores; term. of oil pipeline; p. (1959) *176,000.*

**Orsova**, *mkt. t.*, Romania; on R. Danube, nr. the Iron Gates Pass; oil-refining; p. (1965) *6,527.*

**Orta**, *L.*, Italy; W. of Lago Maggiore; a. 7 sq. m.

**Orta**, *t.*, Foggia prov., Italy; on shore of L. Orta.

**Ortegal**, *C.*, N. cst. Spain.

**Orthez**, *t.*, Basses-Pyrénées, France; scene of Wellington's victory over Soult (1814); leather, hams, chocolate; p. (1962) *8,829.*

**Ortona**, *t.*, Abruzzi Molise, Italy; cap. of ancient Frentani; on Adriatic; cath.; wines; p. *19,104.*

**Oruro**, *dep.*, Bolivia; a. 20,657 sq. m.; cap. Oruro; p. (1962) *265,400* (large proportion Indians).

**Oruro**, *t.*, Bolivia; alt. 12,160 ft.; gold, silver, copper, tin; p. (1962) *86,985.*

**Oruwala**, *t.*, Ceylon; steel rolling mill.

**Orvieto**, *t.*, Umbria, Italy; on R. Paglia; cath.; Etruscan antiquities; wines, olive oil, cereals; pottery, lace; p. *20,352.*

**Orwell**, *R.*, Suffolk, Eng.; estuary of R. Gipping; runs from Ipswich to Harwich.

**Osaka**, *lge. spt.*, *c.*, *comm. ctr.*, Honshu I., Japan; gr. tr.; silk, cotton, rayon cloth, tea, iron, glass, shipbldg., sugar-refining, arsenal; Shinto and Buddhist temples; p. (1965) *3,156,222.*

**Oschersleben**, *t.*, Magdeburg, E. Germany; sugar, chemicals, engin.; p. (1963) *19,123.*

**Ösel I. (Saaremaa)**, Baltic, Estonian S.S.R.; ch. t. Kuressare.    [*65,000.*

**Osh**, *t.*, Kirghiz, S.S.R.; silk, food inds.; p. (1959)

**Oshawa**, *c.*, Ontario, Canada; motors; p. (estd. 1965) *69,000.*

**Oshima**, *I.*, Tokyo Bay, Japan; lgst and most

northerly of Izu-shichito gr.; site of volcanic Mt. Mihara (2,477 ft.).

Oshkosh, c., Wis., U.S.A.; on Fox R.; meat pkg., farming, flour, motors; p. (1960) 45,110.

Oshogbo, t., Nigeria; p. (1953) 123,000.

Osijek (Esseg), t., Croatia, Jugoslavia; nr. Hungarian front.; cottons, silks, beet-sugar, glass, oil refining; p. (1959) 75,000.

Osinniki, t., R.S.F.S.R.; W. Siberia; new ctr. of coal mng.; thermal power sta.; p. (1959) 68,000.

Osipenko, see Berdyansk.

Oskaloosa, t., Iowa, U.S.A.; in agr. and colly. region; p. (1960) 11,053.

Oskarshamn, spt., Sweden; on Kalmar Sound; seldom icebound; shipbldg.; p. 12,900.

Oslo (formerly Christiania), c., cap., ch. spt., Norway; on fjord of same name; cath., univ.; woollens, cottons, condensed milk, paper; exp. timber, fish, matches; p. (1963) 482,495.

Osnabrück, c., Lower Saxony, W. Germany; on R. Hase, linked by canal with Ems–Weser Canal; inland pt. and industl. ctr.; iron and steel mills; mach., textile and paper mnfs.; p. (1963) 141,000.

Osorno, t., Chile; agr. ctr.; in beautiful, forested cty.; Germanic atmosphere; p. (estd.) 93,686.

Osorno, mtn., Chile; volcanic peak, 8,790 ft.

Osorno, prov., S. Chile; p. (1960) 160,156.

Ossa (Kissavos), mtn., Thessaly; N. of Vale of Tempe and Olympus; alt. 6,194 ft.

Ossett, mun. bor., W.R. Yorks, Eng.; 3 m. W. of Wakefield; woollens, coal-mining, engin.; p. (estd. 1967) 16,460.

Ossining, t. N.Y., U.S.A.; on Hudson R.; famous "Sing-Sing" prison; p. (1960) 18,662.

Ostend, spt., Belgium; passenger route between Britain and continent of Europe; popular resort; casino, fisheries, shipbldg.; textiles, tobacco; p. (1962) 56,811.

Östergötland, co., Sweden; on Baltic cst.; a. 4,266 sq. m.; cap. Linköping; p. (1961) 357,693.

Östersund, t., Jämtland, Sweden; on Stor L.; mil. ctr.; rly. wkshps., bricks; p. (1961) 24,866.      [206,073.

Östfold, dist., Norway; a. 1,613 sq. m.; p. (1963)

Ostia, ancient pt., Italy; at mouth of R. Tiber; marshy situation; arch. remains, cath.

Östra Kvarken, channel, Gulf of Bothnia, between Sweden and Finland.

Ostrava, t., ČSSR.; univ.; coal, iron, steel, chemicals, oil-refining; p. (1965) 259,000.

Ostrog, t., on Horýn R., W. part of Ukrainian S.S.R. (Volhynia), U.S.S.R.

Ostrogochsk, t., R.S.F.S.R.; nr. R. Don; tallow and cattle tr., tanneries; p. 10,000.

Ostrow Wielkopolski, t., Poznan, Poland; agr. machin.; perfume; p. (1965) 46,000.

Ostrowiec Swietokrzyski (Ostrovets), t., Kielce, Poland; on trib. Oder; lignite, iron ore, iron; cattle mkt.; p.(1965) 43,000.

Ostuni, t., Leece, Italy; mnfs. and tr.; p. 27,502

Osuna, t., Seville, Spain; p. (1957) 23,250.

Oswaldtwistle, t., urb. dist., Lancs, Eng.; at N. foot of Rossendale Fells, 3 m. E. of Blackburn; cotton weaving, spinning and dyeing; chemicals; p. (1961) 11,915.

Oswego, c., N.Y., U.S.A.; on L. Ontario; taken by Montcalm 1756, and the British 1814; waterpower; hosiery, matches, textiles, engines; p. (1960) 22,155.

Oswestry, rural bor., Salop, Eng.; at foot of Welsh mtns., 18 m. N.W. of Shrewsbury; cas.; rly. engine wks.; p. (of t. 1961) 11,193.

Oswiecim, t., Krakow, Poland; p. (1965) 36,000.

Otago, dist., S.I., N.Z.; mtnous., afforested, rich in gold; farming, sheep, fruit; lge. deposit of jade found at head of L. Wakatipu; cap. Dunedin (q.v.); a. 25,220 sq. m.; p. (1961) inc. Southland 270,067.

Otago Harbour, Otago dist., S.I., N.Z.; Dunedin and Port Chalmers are ports on this harbour.

Otanmäki, Finland; rich deposit of magnetite-ilmenite ore found 1953.

Otaru, spt. Hokkaido, Japan; herring fisheries; coal-mining, lumbering; p. (1965) 196,771.

Otira Tunnel, S.I., N.Z.; carries rly. from Christchurch to Greymouth through S. Alps nr. Arthur's Pass; length 5½ m.

Otley, t., urb. dist., W.R. Yorks, Eng.; on R. Wharfe, 10 m. N.W. of Leeds; printing, machin., wool, paper mkg., leather, furnishings; p. (1961) 11,930.

Otranto, fishing t., S. Italy; on Strait O.; cas.;

submarine cable sta.; once a flourishing c.; cath., fine mosaic pavement; bauxite exp.

Ottawa, c., Ontario, Canada; cap. of Dominion of Canada; on R. Ottawa, 100 m. W. of Montreal; univ., caths., parliament bldgs.; hydro-elec. power, lumbering, sawmills, paper, flour, leather, matches, machin., ironware; p. (1961) 429,750.

Ottawa, R., Canada; trib. of St. Lawrence, forming boundary between Ontario and Quebec; length 625 m.

Ottawa, t., Ill., U.S.A.; at mouth of Fox R.; grain, glass; p. (1960) 19,408.

Ottawa, t., Kan., U.S.A.; on Osago R.; rly. wks.; p. (1960) 10,673.

Ottery St. Mary, mkt. t., urb. dist., Devon, Eng.; 10 m. E. of Exeter; silk, rope, brushes; birthplace of S. T. Coleridge; p. (1961) 4,121.

Ottoshoop, t., Transvaal, S. Africa; gold, fluorspar.

Ottumwa, c., Iowa, U.S.A.; on Des Moines R.; in midst of great coalfield and agr. dist.; iron and steel, meat packing; p. (1960) 33,871.

Otway, hills, S.W. Victoria, Australia; sheep.

Otwock, t., Warsaw, Poland; (1965) 38,000.

Ouachita or Washita, R., Arkansas, U.S.A.; trib. of Red R.; length 550 m.

Oudenaarde (Audenarde), t., Belgium; Allies defeated French 1708; textiles; p. (1962) 6,906.

Oudtshoorn, t., Cape Province, S. Africa; on Olifants R.; ostrich farms, tobacco, fruit: tourism; caves; p. (1960) 22,186 inc. 8,921 whites.

Oued Gueterini, t., Algeria, 70 m. S.E. Algiers, oil.

Ouagadougou, t., cap ; Voltaic Rep., W. Africa; p. 18,000.

Oughter, L., lough, Cavan, Ireland.

Oughterard, t., Galway, Ireland; marble quarries, farming, fishing; p. (1951) 498.

Oujda, t., Morocco; phosphate dist.; p. (1960) 128,645.

Oullins, t., dep. Rhône, France; nr. Lyons; locomotive repair shops; textiles, glass, leather; p. (1954) 19,224.

Oulton Broad, t., Suffolk, Eng.; nr. Lowestoft.

Oulu (Uleåborg), co., N. Finland; partly forest and partly agr.; cap. Oulu; a. 21,887 sq. m.; p. (1966) 419,889.

Oulu (Uleåborg), t., cap., Oulu, Finland; on G. of Bothnia (Baltic Sea) at mouth of R. Oulu; lumbering; p. (1966) 78,950.

Oulu, L., Finland; 40 m. long.

Oundle, mkt. t., urb. dist., Northants, Eng.; on R. Nene, 7 m. S.W. of Peterborough; public school; p. (1961) 2,546.

Ouro Preto, t., Brazil; former cap. of Minas Gerais st.; iron, manganese, gold; textiles; p. (1960) 31,400.

Ourthe, R., Belgium; trib. of R. Meuse; l. 90 m.

Ouse or Great Ouse, R., Norfolk, Eng.; flows N.E. to the Wash; length 156 m.

Ouse, R., Yorks, Eng.; formed by Rs. Swale and Ure, flows to Humber estuary; length 130 m.

Ouse, R., Sussex, Eng.; flows to English Channel at Newhaven; length 30 m.

Outremont, t., Quebec, Canada; p. (1961) 30,753.

Ovalle, t., Coquimbo prov., Chile; fruit, wool; manganese, mng.; p. (1960) 46,553.

Ovar, t., Beira Litoral, Portugal; on Avera lagoon; onions and other vegetables, sardines, wine, wheat; p. 12,729.

Overijssel, prov., Neth.; dairying, fishing, cottons; a. 1,299 sq. m.; p. (1967) 887,261.

Overton, t., rural dist., Flint, N. Wales; 5 m. S.E. of Wrexham; p. (rural dist. 1951) 6,760.

Oviedo, maritime prov., N. Spain; agr., fruit, sardine, and other fisheries; cap. O.; a. 4,204 sq. m.; p. (1959) 995,233.

Oviedo, t., cap., Oviedo, Spain; on S.W. cst. of Georgian Bay, L. Huron; E. terminus Gothic cath., univ.; coal; textiles, leather, matches; gr. mkt.; p. (1959) 128,766.

Owatonna, t., Minn., U.S.A.; p. (1960) 13,409.

Owendis, pt., Liberia; deep water pt. being built to serve iron-ore mines at Belinga.

Owen Falls Dam, Uganda; inaugurated 1 Apr. 1954; converts L. Victoria into reservoir for irrigation of U.A.R. and Sudan; also to supply Uganda industries with hydro-elec. power.

Owen Sound, t., L. pt., Ontario, Canada; on S.W. cst. of Georgian Bay, L. Huron; E. terminus of lgst. wheat-carrying L. steamers; linked by rly. to Toronto (125 m.) and Montreal; p. (1961) 17,421.

Owen Stanley, *range*, Papua, New Guinea; highest peak Mt. Victoria; alt. 13,121 ft.

Owens, L., S. Cal., U.S.A.; on E. flank of Sierra Nevada 20 m. S.E. of Mt. Whitney; water taken by 225-m.-long aqueduct to Los Angeles; a. 120 sq. m.

Owensboro', *t.*, Ky., U.S.A.; petroleum, farming, stock-raising, tobacco; p. (1960) 42,471.

Owosso, *c.*, Mich., U.S.A.; on Shiawassee R.; timber tr.; p. (1960) 17,006.           [length 350 m.

Owyhee, *R.*, Ore.. U.S.A.; trib. of Snake R.;

Oxelösund, Sweden; on Baltic cst., S. of Stockholm; steelwks., tarcoke, glass; p. (1961) 10,007.

Oxford, *co.*, S. Midlands, Eng.; mainly agr.; cereals, paper, gloves, blankets, agr. implements, motor cars; cap. O.; a. 749 sq. m.; p. (1966) 349,000.

Oxford, *co. bor., univ. c., co. t.*, Oxford, Eng.; between Thames and its trib. Cherwell, 63 m. from London by rail; famous univ. with residtl. colleges, printing, steel wks., motor wks. at Cowley; p. (estd. 1967) 109,350.

Oxnard, *t.*, Cal., U.S.A.; citrus fruits, sugar beet, oil refining; p. (1960) 40,265.

Oxus R., *see* Amu Darya.

Oyashio, *see* Bering Current.

Oyo, *t.*, Nigeria; p. (1953) 72,000.

Oyster Bay, *t.. cst. resort*, N.Y., U.S.A.; on Long I.; home of Theodore Roosevelt; p. (1950) 5,215.                                  [ch. *t.* Joplin.

Ozark Mtns., Okla. and Ark., U.S.A.; lead, zinc;

Ozd, *t.*, Hungary; iron and steel; p. (1962) 35,959.

# P

Paarl, *t.*, Cape Province, S. Africa; summer resort; wines, fruit, tobacco; flour, saw and textile mills; p. (1960) 41,540.(inc. 14,128 whites).

Pabianice, *t.*, Poland; nr. Lodz; textiles, farming implements, paper; p. (1965) 59,000.

Pabna, *t.*, Bengal, E. Pakistan; oil, carpets; p. (1961) 40,700.

Pacasmayo, *spt.*, Peru, S. America; exp. rice, sugar, cotton, cacao, hides, copper, lead, zinc, silver; p. (1961) 6,000.

Pachitea, *R.*, Peru, S. America; rises in Andes, flows N. to R. Ucayali; sm. German immigrant colonies in upper valley; length 320 m.

Pachmarhi, Madhya Pradesh, India; summer cap., tourist ctr.; p. (1961) 6,142.

Pachuca, *cap.*, Hidalgo st., Mexico; silver; p. (1960) 70,000.

Pacific Ocean; a. 68,000,000 sq. m.; lgst. ocean in the world; extends from W. cst. of America to E. cst. of Asia and Australia and the S. Ocean in the S.; enters Arctic Ocean via Bering Strait; greatest length N. to S. 8,000 m.; breadth, 10,000 m.; mean depth 12,560 ft., greatest depth 37,800 ft. in the Marianas Trench (1960 dive).

Padang, *spt.*, Sumatra, Indonesia; coffee, spices, rubber, tobacco, copra; p. (1961) 143,699.

Paddington, *see* Westminster, City of.

Paderborn, *c.*, N. Rhine–Westphalia, Germany; cath., other historic bldgs.; foodstuffs, textiles, metals; p. (1963) 56,600.

Padiham, *urb. dist.*, Lancs, Eng.; at N. foot of Rossendale Fells, 4 m. S.W. of Nelson; textiles; p. (1961) 9,893.

Padstow, *t., spt., urb. dist.*, Cornwall, Eng.; on W. side of Camel estuary 4 m. N.W. of Wadebridge; light inds.; sm. seaside resort; p. (1961) 2,676.

Padua, *t.*, Italy; cath., arcades, ancient bridges; machin., chemicals, silks, cloth, distilling; p. (1964) 212,000.

Paducah, *c.*, Ky., U.S.A.; on Ohio R.; saw-mills, tobacco, railway wks.; p. (1960) 34,479.

Paeroa, *bor.*, N.I., N.Z.; p. (1961) 2,896.

Pag, *I.* and *spt.*, Jugoslavia; timber, salt; cath.; p. (of I.) 4,349.

Pagan, *t.*, Burma; ruins; lacquer work.

Pago-Pago, *spt.*, Samoan Is., Pac. Oc.; U.S. naval sta.; p. (1950) 1,586.

Pahang, *st.*, Malaysia; central Malaya; cap. Kuala Lipis; forested; a. 13,280 sq. m.; p. (1961) 359,739.

Pahiatua, *bor.*, N.I., N.Z.; dairying; p. (1961) 2,577.

Pahlevi, *t.*, Iran; nr. Resht, on Caspian Sea; rice, hides, skins, fruit; p. (estd. 1949) 48,000.

Pai, *R.*, Hopeh, China; unites with Yungting R. Huto R., and flows to G. of Chihli; length 300 m.

Paignton, *t.*, S. Devon, Eng.; incorporated in Torbay co. bor.; resort; farming, cider; p. (1961) 30,289.

Paimpont, *fishing pt.*, Cotes du Nord, N.W. France; on N. cst. of Brittany, 20 m. N.W. of St. Brieuc; lobster fishing; p. (1962) 1,791.

Painted Desert, area of bare, multi-coloured rocks, Arizona, U.S.A.

Paisley, *burgh*, Renfrew, Scot.; 5 m. W. of Glasgow; ancient abbey; thread and rope spinning, shipbldg., chemicals, engin., preserves, car bodies; p. (1961) 95,753.

Paita, *pt.*, Peru, S. America; exp. cotton, wool, flax, panama hats; lge. whaling sta. to S.; p. (1961) 6,958.

Pakhoi, *former treaty pt.*, Kwangtung prov., China; indigo, groundnuts, hides, leather, sugar, fish; p. (1931) 36,000.

Pakistan, Islamic Republic of, *indep. sov. st.* within Br. Commonwealth (1947), forming part of sub-continent of India; consists of 3 provs.: West Pakistan (cap. Lahore), East Pakistan (cap. Dacca) and Fed. Terr. of Karachi; prin. expts. raw jute, cotton, hides and skins, oilseeds, tea; cap. Islamabad; a. 365,529 sq. m.; p. (1961) 93,831,982.

Paknampoh, *t.*, Thailand; on R. Meinam, at upper limit of steam navigation.

Pakokku, *t.*, Burma; comm. ctr.; sugar, rice, tobacco, oil-fields, teak; p. 23,115.

Palagruz, *I.*, Adriatic Sea; formerly Italian; ceded to Jugoslavia by peace treaty 1947.

Palanpur, *t.*, Gujarat, India; p. (1961) 29,139.

Palatinate, *see* Rhineland Palatinate, Germany.

Palau Is., *group of Is.*, in Pac. Oc.; p. (1958) 8,845.

Palawan, *I.*, Philippines; coffee, resin, timber; a. 4,550 sq. m.; p. (1960) 104,500.

Palayamcottai, *t.*, Tamil Nadu, India; rice, coffee, cotton, tobacco; p. (1961) 51,002.

Palembang, *t.*, Sumatra, Indonesia; cap. P. residtl.; cotton, rubber, coffee; fertilisers; tyres; p. (1961) 475,000.

Palencia, *inland prov.*, Old Castile, Spain; partly fertile plain, partly wooded and mntainous; cap., Palencia; a. 3,093 sq. m.; p. (1959) 239,041.

Palencia, *t., cap.*, Palencia, Spain; N. of Valladolid; ctr. of rich wheat-growing dist.; iron-founding and weaving; p. (1957) 50,000.

Palermo, *spt.*, Sicily, Italy; cath., univ.; machin., chemicals, wines, fruit, tobacco; p. (1965) 633,000.

Palestine or The Holy Land, historic region, bounded by Syria and Lebanon on the N., Jordan on the E., the Egyptian prov. of Sinai on the S., and the Mediterranean on the W.; a. when under British mandate 10,429 sq. m.; p. (estd. 1948) 782,000. *See* Israel.

Palestine, *t.*, Texas, U.S.A.; agr. and forest region; p. (1960) 13,974.

Palghat, *t.*, Kerala, India; p. (1961) 77,620.

Palitana, *t.*, Gujarat, India; a. c. of Jain temples inhabited by priests and their servants; p. (1961) 24,581.

Palk Strait, India; separating India from Ceylon.

Palm Beach, *t.*, Fla., U.S.A.; Atl. coastal resort.

Palm Beach, *t.*, N.S.W., Australia; N. of Sydney; tourist resort.

Palma, *spt.*, Majorca I., Spain; cath., palaces; wine, fruit, silk; cap. Balearic Is.; p. (1965) 171,000.

Palmarola I., Pontine Is., Italy; vineyards.

Palmerston North, *c.*, N.I., N.Z.; dairying, sheep; univ; rly. junction; p. (1961) 43,164.

Palmira, *t.*, Colombia; tobacco, coffee, rice, cocoa, sugar, grain; p. (estd. 1959) 124,000.

Palmyra (ancient Tadmor), *c.*, in Syrian desert, 120 m. N.E. of Damascus; extensive ruins; p. 10,000.                                  [coconuts; p. 32.

Palmyra Is., Pac. Oc., U.S.A.; coral islets;

Palni Hills, *range*, between E. and W. Ghats, S. Deccan, India; highest peak 7,050 ft.

Palos, *spt.*, Huelva, S. Spain; on Río Tinto; starting point for Columbus in 1492.

Palos, C. de, Mediterranean, S.E. cst. of Spain.

Palua, *pt.*, Venezuela; pt. of shipment for iron mines at El Pao; nearby Caroni hydro-elec. plant built to serve steel wks. and aluminium plant.

Pamiers, *t.*, Ariège, France; elec. steel furnaces; wine; leather; p. (1962) 13,953.

Pamir Mtns., *high mtn. plateau* ("roof of the world"), Tadzik S.S.R., Central Asia; Mt.

Communism (24,590 ft.) climbed by Russo-British team 1962.

Pamlico Sound, lge. lagoon, on E. cst. of N.C., U.S.A.; length 75 m., width 25 m.

Pampa, La, terr., Central Argentina; stock-rearing; cap. Santa Rosa; a. 55,669 sq. m.; p. (1947) 166,929.

Pampas, Argentina; vast plains stretching from the Rio Negro on the S. to the Gran Chaco in the N., and E. from the Andes to the Atlantic; woodless, level country; rich pastures in E., supporting countless numbers of sheep and cattle, W. mostly barren.

Pampilla, t., Peru; on cst. N. of Callao; oil refinery under construction.

Pamplona, t., Colombia; coal, gold, coffee, cocoa, wheat, brewing, textiles; p. (estd. 1959) 22,800.

Pamplona, t., Spain; cath., fortress, univ.; textiles, leather, paper, flour, soap, earthenware; p. (1959) 88,410.

Panama, rep., Central America; mountainous; climate hot throughout year, abundant rains; languages Spanish; religion R.C.; communications poor; cattle-raising, farming; pearls, bananas, cocoa, coconuts, rubber, sugar, coffee, timber, shrimps; cap. Panama City; a. 28,575 sq. m.; p. (estd. 1965) 1,244,000.

Panama, canal zone, Panama; strip of land 47 m. long by 10 m. wide, extending 5 m. on either side Panama Canal, under U.S. jurisdiction; p. (1960) 41,683 (inc. Forces personnel).

Panama Canal, Canal Zone, Panama; length 51 m. ranging in width from 300 to 1,000 ft., minimum depth 41 ft.; time of transit through canal 7-8 hours; canal starts at Cristobal (Atlantic), to Gatun locks, through Gatun Lake, Culebra cut, Pedro Miguel locks, Miraflores locks to Balboa (Pacific). See also Section L.

Panama City, c., spt., cap. Panama; harbour at S. entrance to Canal; cath.; oil refining, steel rolling mill, cement plant, lt. inds.; p. (1960) 369,280.

Panarukan, spt., Java, Indonesia; exp. tobacco, sugar; p. 7,455.

Panay, I., Philippines; between Negros I. and Mindoro I.; a. 4,446 sq. m.; cotton, rice, sugar, coffee; p. (1960) 1,746,500.

Pancevo, t., Voivodina, Jugoslavia; wheat, maize, timber, glass, textiles, ironwks., oil refining; (1959) 40,000. [on R. Damodar.

Panchet Hill Dam and power sta.; Bihar, India;

Pandharpur, t., Maharashtra, India; on R. Bhima; temple, pilgrimages; p. (1961) 45,421.

Pando, dep., Bolivia; p. 18,600; cap. Cobija; p. (1962) 24,400.

Panevezys, t., Lithuanian S.S.R.; textiles; p. (1954) 60,000.

Pangalanes Canal (Canal Des Pangalanes), Malagasy; follows E. cst. from Farafangana to Tamatave, through series of lagoons; 300 m.

Pangani, spt., Tanzania, E. Africa; copra, sisal hemp, maize; p. 3,000.

Pangkalanbrandan, spt., Sumatra, Indonesia; oil-refining and exp.

Panipat, t., E. Punjab, India; silver and brass, cotton goods, blankets, carpets, pottery; p. (1961) 67,026.

Panjsher Valley, Afghanistan; silver-mines, unexploited; mica-mine.

Pantar I., Lesser Sunda Is., Indonesia; mtns.; p. 8,000.

Pantelleria, volcanic I., Mediterranean, Italy; midway between W. Sicily and Tunisia; a. 58 sq. m.; ch. t. P. on N.W. cst.; figs, raisins, vines, capers, cereals; fishing; p. 10,000.

Pantin, sub., Paris, France; glasswork, sugar ref., tobacco factories, chemicals, leather, tallow; p. (1962) 46,401.

Paoki (Baoji), c., Shensi prov., China; cotton weaving; millet, wheat; p. (1953) 130,000.

Paoting (Baoding), c., Hopeh prov., China; on the Yungting R.; gr. tr.; p. (1953) 197,000.

Paotow (Baotou), c., Inner Mongolia; on left bank of Yellow R., on road and rly. routes to E. China; airfield; terminus of caravan routes through Gobi desert and Tarim basin to Turkestan; gr. tr. and industl. ctr.; steelwks.; p. (1958) 650,000.

Papeete, t., pt., Tahiti I. Pac. Oc.; cap. Tahiti and of French Settlements in Oceania; exp. copra, vanilla, phosphates and mother-of-pearl; p. (1962) 19,903.

Paphos, administrative dist., Cyprus; ancient c.,

ruins; serious eathquake 1953; rich deposits of copper and iron pyrites, sulphur in Vretsia a.; p. (1960) of dist. 58,159 of t. 9,083.

Papua-New Guinea, terr., Eastern New Guinea; administered by Australia; adm. H.Q. Port Moresby (cap. of Papua); gold, copra, rubber, timber; oil 30 m. offshore; Sirinumu Dam (q.v.) opened 1963; total a. 183,540 sq. m.; p. (1966) 1,562,153 indigenous and2 0,286 non-indig. mainly Australian.

Pará, st., Brazil; densely forested; rubber, fruits, cacao, Brazil nuts; cap. Bélem; a. 464,780 sq. m.; p. (1960) 1,550,935.

Pará, spt., Brazil, see Bélem.

Paraguay, rep., S. America; undulating cty., swamps, forests; Rs., Paraguay, Pilcomayo, Paraná; climate, hot summers, warm winters, moderate rainfall; religion, R.C.; communications poor; fertile; cattle, yerba maté, oranges, sugar, maize, cotton, tobacco, lumber, quebracho extract; iron, manganese, copper; meat packing; oil refining at Villa Elisa; cap. Asinción; a. 157,006 sq. m.; p. (estd. 1965) 1,996,000.

Paraguay, R., S. America; rises in plateau of Mato Grosso, flows S. and joins R. Paraná nr. Corrientes; forms bdy. between Brazil and Bolivia, Brazil and Paraguay; approx. length 1,200 m.

Paráiba, st., Brazil; cotton, cocoa, sugar, rubber, tobacco; cap. João Pessôa; a. 21,730 sq. m.; p. (1960) 2,018,023.

Paráiba, R., Brazil; flows to Atlantic in st. of P.; length 200 m.

Paráiba, R., S. Brazil; rising in São Paulo st., and flowing between Rio de Janeiro and Minas Gerais to the Atlantic N.E. of Rio de J.; length 658 m.

Paramaribo, spt., cap., Neth. Guiana; (Surinam); on R. Surinam; ch. exp., bauxite, timber, rubber, rice, fruit; p. (1959) 113,473.

Paraná, cap., Entre Rios prov., Argentina; pt. for grain, cattle, sheep; road tunnel to Santa Fé under construction; p. (1960) 109,600.

Paraná, st., Brazil; extensively forested; cap. Curitiba; a. 77,717 sq. m.; p. (1960) 4,277,763.

Paraná, R., Brazil; formed by junction of Rs. Rio Grande and Parnaiba; flows W. between Paraguay and Argentina; flows into Rio de la Plata; navigable to Brazil frontier nr. Iguassú Falls; length 2,000 m.

Paranaguá, spt., Paraná st., Brazil; ch. pt. for Paraná; in lagoon harbour; exp. maté, timber, bananas, iron ore; p. (1960) 27,723.

Pardubice, t., CSSR.; univ.; saw-milling; brewing, distilling; p. (1961) 52,655.

Parentis, t., Landes, France; nr. L. Biscarosse, 40 m. S.S.W. Bordeaux; oil: lignite mined nearby; p. (1962) 2,493.

Parenzo, spt., Italy; cath.; fishing; Roman remains.

Pariñas, C., Peru, S. America.

Paris, c., cap., France, on R. Seine, 110 m. from mth.; cultural ctr.; 12 boulevards radiate from Arc de' Triomphe; Notre Dame, Louvre, Tuileries, Palais Royal; oldest bridge Pont Neuf (1578-1604); royal forests and palaces nearby, e.g., Fontainebleau, Rambouillet, Chantilly; univ. (founded 12th cent.); German siege 1870-71; German occupation 1940-44; luxury inds., publishing, furniture, food, clothing; heavy inds. in northern subs.; admin. a. called "Ville de Paris"; oil refineries at Grandpuits, 25 m. S.E., and Porcheville in W.; p. (1964) 2,790,100; of Greater Paris (1962) 8,468,63.

Paris, t., Texas, U.S.A.; cotton, fruit, canned goods; p. (1960) 20,977.

Parkersburg, c., W. Va., U.S.A.; on Ohio R.; iron- and steel-wks., oil and natural gas, coal, glassware, rayon, porcelain; p. (1960) 44,797.

Parkes, t., N.S.W., Australia; mkt.; rly. junction; p. (1966) 8,431.

Parma, prov., Emilia, Italy; a. 1,258 sq. m.; p. (1961) 381,624.

Parma, t., N. Italy; between Apennines and R. Po; univ., cath.; tr. ctr.; food processing, wine, cheese; precision instruments; agr. machin., footwear, felt hats; p. (1961) 140,844.

Parnaiba, R., rises in Brazil, flows into N. Atlantic Ocean, forms bdy. between Maranhão and Piaui; length 750 m.

**Parnaiba,** *spt.,* Piaui, Brazil; cotton, cattle; p. (1960) *39,951.*

**Parnassos,** *mtn. ridge,* Greece; 83 m. N.W. of Athens, nr. the ancient Delphi, the modern Liakhura; highest summit, Licoreia, alt. 8,068 ft.

**Parnu,** *t.,* Estonian S.S.R.; on G. of Riga; resort; flax, timber, wood pulp, woollens; p. (1956) *33,600.*

**Páros,** *I.,* Grecian Archipelago; W. of Naxos; a. 63 sq. m.; cap. P.

**Parramatta,** *c.,* N.S.W., Australia; pt. near head of Parramatta R. (spanned by lgst concrete bridge in world) in met. a. of Sydney; expts. woollen and leather goods; p. (1966) *107,006.*

**Parrett,** *R.,* Somerset, Eng.; flows to Bristol Channel, nr. Bridgwater; length 35 m.

**Parry (Mauke),** *I.,* Pac. Oc.; part Cook Is., N.Z.; p. 773.

**Parry Sound,** *t.,* Ont., Canada; lumbering; p. (1961) *6,004.*

**Parsons,** *t.,* Kan., U.S.A.; coal, natural gas, machin.; p. (1960) *13,929.*

**Partinico,** *t.,* Sicily, Italy; silk; p. *22,080.*

**Pasadena,** *c.,* Cal., U.S.A.; N. of Los Angeles; in fruit-growing region, base of San Gabriel Mtns.; 200-in. telescope on Mt. Palomar; famous for its carnival; p. (1960) *116,401.*

**Pasco,** *t.,* Wash., U.S.A.; on Snake R.; p. (1960) *14,522.*

**Pasco,** *see* Cerro de Pasco.

**Pas-de-Calais,** *dep.,* N. France; coal, iron; farming, sugar distilling, paper, pottery; cap. Arras; a. 2,606 sq. m.; p. (1962) *1,366,282.*

**Pasig,** *t.,* Luzon, Philippines; comm. ctr. of the L. region; p. *29,170.*

**Pasir Mas,** *t.,* Kelantan, Malaysia; rly. junction.

**Passage West,** *urb. dist., spt.,* Cork, Ireland; shipping, fishing; p. (1951) *2,658.*

**Passaic,** *c.,* N.J., U.S.A.; silk, chemicals, dyes, rubber goods, mill machin., springs, steel cabinets, tin cans; p. (1960) *53,963.*

**Passaic,** *R.,* N.J., U.S.A.; flows 100 m. to Newark Bay.

**Passau,** *t.,* Germany, at confluence of Rs. Danube, Inn and Ilz; near Austrian frontier; transshipment base, inds. inc. leather, porcelain, tobacco and brewing; p. (1963) *31,200.*

**Passchendaele,** *t.,* Belgium; impt. strategic point in First World War; p. (1962) *3,115.*

**Passero I.,** Mediterranean Sea; off S.E. cst. of Sicily, Italy.

**Pasto,** *t., cap.,* Nariño dep., Colombia; on flank of Pasto volcano; univ.; gold near by; p. (estd. 1959) *110,790.*

**Pasuruan,** *spt.,* Java, Indonesia; exp. sugar, tapioca; p. *36,973.*

**Patagonia,** Argentina; extensive region, E. of Andes; elevated plateau, arid, sterile; principal Rs., Colorado, Rio Negro and Chubut; oil and minerals, unworked; lge. tracts of grazing for sheep, horses and cattle.

**Patan,** Gujarat, India; swords, silk and cotton goods; p. (1961) *50,264.*

**Patan,** *valley t.,* Nepal; p. (1961) *135,230.*

**Patani,** *spt.,* Thailand; tin exp., fishing; p. *109,252.*

**Paterno,** *t.,* Sicily, Italy; N.W. of Catania; mineral springs, wines; p. (1961) *42,935.*

**Pater Noster Is.,** Indonesia; coconuts.

**Paterson,** *c.,* N.J., U.S.A.; principal ctr. silk mftg.; aeroplane engines; textiles; machin.; p. (1960) *143,663.*

**Pathankot,** *t.,* E. Punjab, India; fruit preserving; p. (1961) *46,330.*

**Patia R.,** Colombia; gold, platinum found.

**Patiala,** *t.,* Punjab, India; iron and steel mftg.; flour; p. (1961) *125,234.*

**Patino Mines,** *see* Uncia.

**Patkai,** *hills,* India; Chaukan; alt. 9,020 ft.

**Patmos,** *I.,* one of the Dodecanese, Aegean Sea; a. 13 sq. m.; p. (estd.) *3,000.* (According to Rev. 1. 9. the exiled St. John wrote the Revelation here.)

**Patna,** *cap.,* Bihar, India; univ.; rice, indigo, cotton, salt.; p. (1961) *364,594.*

**Patras,** *spt.* "Peloponnese", Greece; citadel and cas.; currants, raisins, figs, olives, wine, skins, etc.; p. (1961) *95,364.*

**Pau,** *t.,* Basses Pyrénées, France; on Gave du Pau; cas.; health resort; linen, chocolate, hams, wine; natural gas nearby; p. (1962) *61,468.*

**Pauillac,** *t.,* Gironde, France; oil refining; natural gas; p. (1962) *5,725.*

**Paulis,** *see* Isiro.

**Paulo Affonso,** *falls,* São Francisco R., Brazil; 260 ft.; Tres Marias dam and power sta. inaugurated 1960.

**Pavia,** *t.,* Italy; cath. univ.; walled city; battle site 1525; olives, silk, wine; Parmesan cheese; oil refining at Spineto; p. (1961) *73,503.*

**Pavlodar,** *pt.,* Kazakh, S.S.R.; on R. Irtysh; chemicals, sulphates, agr. machin., locomotives, aluminium, oil processing; p. (1967) *145,000.*

**Pavlovo,** *t.,* R.S.F.S.R.; on R. Oka; iron and steel, engin.; p. (1956) *42,600.*

**Pawtucket,** *c.,* R.I., U.S.A.; on P. R. used for water-power, woollen, cotton and silk goods; machin.; chemicals; first cotton-spinning factory established in the U.S.A. 1790; p. (1960) *81,001.*

**Paysandu,** *dep.,* Uruguay; p. (1953) *92,417.*

**Paysandu,** *t.,* Uruguay; meat, cattle, sheep, wool; footwear, soap; p. (estd. 1956) *60,000.*

**Pazardzhik,** *t.,* Bulgaria; on main rly. line to Istanbul; p. (1956) *39,499.*

**Paz de Rio,** *t.,* Boyaca, Colombia; steel; iron ore, coal, limestone nearby; hydro-elec. sta. projected.

**Peace,** *R.,* Canada; rises in Rocky Mtns., and flows to L. Athabaska; length 1,000 m.

**Peak, The,** *Pennine hill dist.,* mid-Eng.; extending from Chesterfield to Buxton, and Ashbourne to Glossop; mainly composed of limestone with typical Karst features; tourists; highest point Kinder Scout, alt. 2,080 ft.

**Pearl,** *R., see* Chu Kiang.

**Pearl Harbour,** *landlocked harbour,* Oahu I., Hawaiian Is., one of finest natural harbours in E. Pacific; U.S. Naval base. Attacked by Japanese without warning on 7 Dec. 1941.

**Peary Land,** Greenland.

**Peč,** *t.,* Jugoslavia; nr. Albanian border; tobacco, fruit; p. (1959) *25,000.*

**Pechelbronn,** Alsace, France; oilfields.

**Pechenga (Petsamo),** *spt.,* R.S.F.S.R., U.S.S.R.; on left bank of R. Petsamon 10 m. upstream from Barents Sea; formerly Finnish, ceded to U.S.S.R. Sept. 1944; ice-free throughout year, thanks to influence of N. Atlantic Drift; exp. nickel, timber, cobalt.

**Pechora,** *R.,* flowing into Arctic Ocean, R.S.F.S.R. 1,000 m. long, 700 m. navigable.

**Pecos,** *R.,* N.M. and Texas, U.S.A.; trib. of Rio Grande; length 764 m.

**Pécs,** *t.,* Hungary; cath., univ., airport; coal, chemicals, majolica; p. (1965) *134,000.*

**Peebles,** *bor., co. t.,* Peebles, Scot.; on upper course of R. Tweed; hydro. woollen cloth knitwear; p. (1961) *5,545.*

**Peebles,** *co.,* Scot.; hilly, Broad Law, 2,754 ft.; sheep, woollen cloth, knitwear; a. 346 sq. m.; p. (1961) *14,117.*

**Peekshill,** *t.,* N.Y., U.S.A.; on Hudson R.; ironwks.; p. (1960) *18,737.*

**Peel,** *t.,* I. of Man, Eng.; midway along W. cst.; cas., cath., ruins; resort; fisheries; p. *2,612.*

**Peel Fell,** *mtn.,* Northumberland, Eng.; 1,964 ft.

**Pegasus,** *Bay,* S.I., N.Z.

**Pegu,** *dist.,* Lower Burma; annexed by Brit. 1852; teak forests; industl. a.; p. *2,961,249.*

**Pegu,** *c.,* Pegu prov., S. Burma; R. pt., rly. junc.; founded *c.* 825 A.D.; many temples, inc. Shwe May Daw Pagoda; bronze statuettes mnfd.; p. *c. 48,000.*

**Pegu Yoma,** *mtns.,* Burma; separate valleys of Rs. Irrawadi and Sittang.

**Pei Kiang,** *see* North River

**Peine,** *t.,* Lower Saxony, Germany; N.W. of Brunswick; iron, furniture, textiles; p. (1963) *30,300.*

**Peipus,** *see* Chudskoye.

**Peiraieus,** *spt.,* Greece; pt. of Athens; principal pt. of Greece; arsenal; wines, brandy, currants, vinegar; marble; machin.; p. (1961) *1,853,000* inc. Athens.

**Pekalongan,** *t.,* N. cst. Java, Indonesia; exp. sugar, rubber; p. (1961) *102,380.*

**Pekan,** *t.,* Pahang, Malaya; p. *5,000.*

**Pekin,** *t.,* Ill., U.S.A.; cereal prods., distilling, leather, metal goods; p (1960) *23,146.*

**Peking (Peiping),** *c., cap.,* China; cultural ctr. and c. of gr. arch. beauty; for hundreds of years seat of the Chinese emperors (Mongol, Ming and Manchu régimes); surrounded by 22 m. of towering walls broken by 16 gates; p. (estd. 1958) *5,420,000.*

**K130**

Pelée, *mtn.*, Martinique; active volcano, devastated town of St. Pierre 1902, loss of over 30,000 lives, later eruption caused further 2,000 deaths; alt. 4,400 ft.

Pelew Is., Caroline Is., Pac. Oc.; coral, primitive agr.; bauxite; p. *12,798.*

Pella, *prefecture*, Macedonia, Greece; cap. Edessa; p. (1961) *133,128.*

Pelly, *R.*, trib. of R. Yukon, N.W. Terr., Canada.

Peloponnesos, *peninsula*, S. part of Greece, separated from mainland proper by G. of Corinth; a. 8,356 sq. m.; p. (1961) *1,096,390.*

Pelotas, *t.*, Rio Grande do Sul, S. Brazil; at S. end of Lagôa dos Patos; tr. in sheep, cattle from interiors; mnfs. woollens, leather, wine; p. (1960) *121,280.*

Pelvoux, *mtn.*, France; between Isère and Hautes Alpes; alt. 12,920 ft.

Pemba, *I.*, part of indep. st. of Zanzibar; E. Africa; a. 380 sq. m.; cloves and copra, coconuts, exp. mangrove bark for tannin; p. (1958) *133,858.*

Pembroke, *t.*, Ont., Canada; lumbering; p. (1961) *16,791.*

Pembroke, *co.*, Wales; fertile; stock-raising, steel, fishing, shipbldg.; a. 617 sq. m.; p. (1966) *97,000.*

Pembroke, *mkt. t.*, *mun. bor.*, Pembroke, Wales; on S. side of Milford Haven; cas., ruins of Monkton Priory; naval dockyard, light engin.; metal ind., woollens; p. (1961) *12,737.*

Pembroke Dock, Pembroke, Wales.

Penang, *I.*, *st.* West Malaysia; cap. Georgetown, pt. for N. Malaya handling rubber and tin; paper mill; the first Brit. Straits Settlement (*q.v.*); a. 400 sq. m.; p. (1961) *651,399.*

Penarth, *urb. dist.*, Glamorgan, Wales; on Severn estuary 2 m. S. of Cardiff; ship repairing, wood, cement, bricks; p. (1961) *20,897.*

Pendleton, *t.*, Ore., U.S.A.; p. (1960) *14,434.*

Penge, see Bromley.

Pengpu (Bengbu), *c.*, Anhwei, China; on Hwai Ho 105 m. N.W. of Nanking; on Tientsin-Nanking rly.; p. (1953) *253,000.*

Penicuik, *burgh*, Midlothian, Scot.; on N. R. Esk, 7 m. S. of Edinburgh; paper, iron; p. (1961) *5,824.*

Penistone, *mkt. t.*, *urb. dist.*, W.R. Yorks., Eng.; on R. Don; steel; p. (1961) *7,071.*

Penki (Benqi), *c.*, Liaoning prov., China; metallurgical ctr.; p. (1953) *449,000.*

Penmaenmawr, *t.*, *urb. dist.*, Caernarvon, Wales; 4 m. W. of Conway; resort; p. (1961) *3,754.*

Pennine Alps, Switzerland; division of Alpine system; ch. peaks; Matterhorn (14,782 ft.), Weisshorn (14,804 ft.). Mischabelhörner (14,942 ft.); includes Zermatt; winter sports.

Pennine Range, *mtn. range*, running N. to S. from Cheviot Hills to Derby, Eng.; length 140 m.

Pennsylvania, *st.*, U.S.A.; originally proprietary colony of Penn family, and later one of the 13 original sts. in the Union; traversed N.E. to S.W. by Appalachians; ch. Rs.: Delaware, Susquehanna, Allegheny and Monongahela; iron and steel, coal (bituminous and anthracite); natural gas, petroleum; maize, wheat, oats, rye; textiles, machin., motor cars, tobacco; cap. Harrisburg; ch. ts.: Pittsburgh, Philadelphia; a. 45,333 sq. m.; p. (1960) *11,319,366.*

Penrhyn, *dist.*, Caernarvon, Wales; nr. Bethesda; slate quarries.

Penrith, *mkt. t.*, *urb. dist.*, Cumberland, Eng.; at N. foot of Shap Fell, 18 m. S.E. of Carlisle; ruined cas.; agr. mkt.; agr. implements, egg-packing sta.; tourist ctr.; p. (1961) *10,931.*

Penrith, *t.*, N.S.W., Australia; in Sydney met. a.; ctr. for mkt. gardening; p. (1966) *35,970.*

Penryn, *t.*, *mun. bor.*, Cornwall, Eng.; on estuary of R. Fal, 2 m. N.W. of Falmouth; fishing; granite quarries; p. (estd. 1967) *4,990.*

Pensacola, *spt.*, Fla., U.S.A.; safest land-locked harbour in G. of Mexico; naval sta.; fish, naval requisites, wool, hides, cotton and lumber mills; p. (1960) *56,752.*

Penticton, *t.*, B.C., Canada; fruit farming, canning; p. (1961) *13,859.*

Pentire Point, headland, Cornwall, Eng.

Pentland Firth, strait between Orkney and the Caithness cst., N. Scot.

Pentland Hills, *range*, Scot.; running from Lanark-Edinburgh-Peebles; highest point Scald Law, 1,896 ft.

Pentland Skerries, *small Is.*, Pentland Firth, Scot.

Penybont, *rural dist.*, Glamorgan, Wales; coalmining; p. (1961) *41,992.*

Pen-y-Ghent, peak in Pennine Range, W.R. Yorks., Eng.; 2,231 ft.

Penza, *t.*, R.S.F.S.R.; between Penza and Kuibyshev; grain, sawmills, paper, soap and candles, engin.; "Druzhba" oil pipeline from Mozyr; p. (1967) *324,000.*

Penzance, *t.*, *mun. bor.*, Cornwall, Eng.; on Mounts Bay; seaside resort, good harbour; pilchard fishing, copper, tin, and china clay, textiles, lt. engin.; p. (estd. 1967) *18,900.*

Peoria, *c.*, Ill., U.S.A.; river pt.; farming implements, grain; distilling, brewing, mng.; p. (1960) *103,162.*

Perak, *st.*, Malaysia; N.W. Malaya; cap. Ipoh; tin; a. 8,030 sq. m.; p. (1961) *1,404,952.*

Pereira, *t.*, Caldas, Colombia; cath.; coffee, brewing, thread mkg.; p. (estd. 1959) *183,730.*

Perekop, Isthmus of, connects Crimea with Ukraine, and rail focus in ctr. of maize-growing a.

Pergamino, *t.*, Buenos Aires prov., Argentina; on Pampas 60 m. S. of Rosario; impt. road and rail focus in ctr. of maize-growing a.

Périgueux, *t.*, *cap.*, Dordogne, France; on R. L'Isle; cath.; china, iron, woollens, figs, truffles; pâté de foie gras; marshalling yards; rly. repair shops; p. (1962) *41,134.*

Perim, *I.*, Straits of Bab-el-Mandeb at southern entrance to Red Sea; Southern Yemen; formerly part of Brit. col. of Aden; a. 5 sq. m.; p. (1946) *360.*

Perlis, *st.*, Malaysia; N. Malaya; cap. Kangar; rice, tin, coconuts; a. 310 sq. m.; p. (1961) *102,726.*

Perm, *formerly* Molotov, *t.*, R.S.F.S.R.; on R. Kama, N.W. of Sverdlovsk; hydro-elec., oil, textiles, engin., chemicals, copper; p. (1967) *785,000.*

Pernambuco, *st.*, Brazil; sugar, fruits; mntnous interior, cst. fertile; cotton, coffee; cap. Recife; a. 37,458 sq. m.; p. (1960) *4,136,900.*

Pernis, *t.*, opp. Rotterdam, Netherlands; lge oil refinery; oil pipeline to Wesserling (nr. Cologne); pipeline to carry ethylene to Terneuzen.

Perovo, *t.*, R.S.F.S.R.; nr. Moscow; engin., chemicals, agr. research institutes; p. (1959) *143,000.*

Perpignan, *fortfd. t.*, Pyrénées-Orientales, France; cath.; wine, brandy, silk, wool; p. (1962) *86,156.*

Perreux-sur-Marne, *t.*, Seine, France; p. (1962) *27,900.*

Persepolis, *ruins*, ancient cap. of Persia.

Pershore, *mkt. t.*, *rural dist.*, Worcs, Eng.; on R. Avon, 8 m. S.E. of Worcester; abbey church; preserves, machin.; p. (1961) *17,599.*

Persia. See Iran.

Persian G., arm of Indian Oc., through G. of Oman and Strait of Ormuz, between Iran and Arabia; ch. pts. Bandar-e-Bushehr (Bushire), Abadan, Kuwait; Bahrein, lgst. I.

Perth, *co.*, Scot.; Trossachs and P. of Killiecrankie; noted for beautiful scenery; crossed by Grampians in N. and W.; ch. peaks, Ben More, Ben Lowers, Schiehallion; ch. Rs.: Tay, with tribs. Isla, Garry, Tummel, Sarn; pastoral; fruit; distilling; textiles; a. 2,493 sq. m.; p. (1961) *127,018.*

Perth, *burgh*, Perth, Scot.; on R. Tay, in gap between Sidlaw and Ochil Hills; cap. of Scot. till assassination of James I in 1437; near by is Scone Palace; cath.; linen, winceyettes, brewing, rope, dyeing; p. (1961) *41,199.*

Perth, *c.*, cap. W. Australia; 12 m. above pt. of Fremantle; univ., observatory, race-courses; lge. bauxite deposit nearby; p. (1966) inc. subs. *449,494.*

Perth Amboy, *spt.*, N.J., U.S.A.; terracotta wks.; shipyards and dry docks; p. (1960) *38,007.*

Peru, *rep.*, S. America; traversed N. to S. by the Andes, attaining 22,000 ft.; ch. Rs., Marañon, Ucayali; in S.E., L. Titicaca (12,450 ft.) lgst. L. in S. America; climate, eastern, very hot, drenching rains, central or mountain zone, sun intensely hot, but shade temperatures low; W. and Pacific cst., heat not excessive, scanty rainfall; religion R.C.; poor communications; sugar, cotton, coffee, wool, hides, timber, cocoa, wheat, tobacco, petroleum, silver, copper, iron ore, fertilisers; cap. Lima; a. 482,258 sq. m.; p. (estd. 1965) *11,854,000* (Indians 46 per cent., mestizos and whites 53 per cent).

Peru (Humboldt), Current, *ocean current*, S. Pac. Oc.; flows N. along cst. of N. Chile and Peru;

relatively cold water causes lower air temperatures and produces cloud and fog.

**Perugia,** *spt.,* Umbria, Italy; on R. Tiber; univ., observatory; woollens, silks, lace; foodstuffs, furniture, pottery, chemicals, agr. machin.; p. (1961) 109,596.

**Pervouralsk,** *t.,* R.S.F.S.R.; in Urals, 25 m. W. of Sverdlovsk; pipe rolling mill; p. (1967) 109,000.

**Pesaro,** *Adriatic spt.,* Italy; N.W. of Ancona; resort; figs, wines, oil, silks; majolica ware; sulphur; sugar-refining; p. (1961) 65,601.

**Pescadores Is.,** *group of Is.,* 30 m. W. of Formosa; total a. about 51 sq. m.; since 1945 Chinese, formerly Japanese.

**Pescara,** *t.,* Italy; at estuary of R. Aterno. E. cst.; olive oil, soap, pasta, pottery; fishing; p. (1961) 87,076.

**Peshawar,** *t.,* W. Pakistan; on rly. to Khyber Pass commanding route Afghanistan–India; military sta.; univ.; coal, fruit, sugar; cottons, ambroidery, wood carving, copper ware, boat bldg., marble; p. (1961) 218,691.

**Peshawar,** *div.,* W. Pakistan; p. (1961) 5,088,000.

**Pesquilerto,** *R.,* trib. of Rio Grande del Norte, Mexico.

**Pest,** *c.,* Hungary; on left bank of R. Danube, opposite Buda, and connected therewith by suspension bridge, the two cs. forming the Hungarian cap. of Buda-Pest (see Budapest).

**Petah Tiqva,** *t.,* Israel; agr. ctr.; oranges; textiles, chemicals, metal goods, tanning; p. (1960) 62,700.

**Petaling Jaya,** *t.,* West Malaysia; industl. estate nr. Kuala Lumpur; tyres, aluminium rolling mill.

**Peter I.,** *uninhabited I.,* Antarctic Ocean; belonging to Norway; a. about 94 sq. m.

**Peterborough,** *t.,* Ont., Canada; flour milling, elec. machin., trailers, agr. equipment, plastics, textiles, paper; p. (1961) 47,185.

**Peterborough, Soke of,** *see* Huntingdon and Peterborough.

**Peterborough,** *c., mun. bor.,* Huntingdon and Peterborough, Eng.; on R. Nene at the margin of The Fens; cath.; rly. ctr.; engin., bricks, paper, milling; p. (estd. 1967) 66,100.

**Peterhead,** *spt., burgh,* E. Aberdeen, Scot.; on E. cst., 27 m. N.E. of Aberdeen; herring fisheries, tweed; granite quarries; p. (1961) 12,497.

**Peterlee,** *t.,* Durham, Eng.; on plateau of E. Durham, 11 m. E. of Durham; one of " New Towns " designated 1948; ctr. of coal-mng. dist.; mohair and worsted spinning; clothing and wood-wool mftg.; p. (estd. 1965) 17,963.

**Petermann Peak,** Greenland; alt. 9,175 ft.

**Petersburg,** *c.,* Va., U.S.A.; tobacco, meat-canning, cotton; optical goods; p. (1960) 36,750.

**Petersfield,** *t., urb. dist.,* Hants, Eng.; on R. Rother, 12 m. N.W. of Chichester; college; malting, brewing; p. (1961) 7,379.

**Petit Morin,** *R.,* France; trib. of R. Marne.

**Petra,** *ancient t.,* Jordan; temples, rock tombs and Roman ruins.

**Petra,** *t.,* Majorca, Spain; birthplace of founder of San Francisco.

**Petropavlovsk,** *spt.,* Kamchatka Pen., U.S.S.R.; fishing; p. (1967) 119,900.

**Potropavlovsk,** *t.,* Kazakh. S.S.R.; on R. Ishim; flour, leather, meat canneries; furs, engin.; p. (1967) 162,000.

**Petropolis,** *t.,* Rio de Janeiro, Brazil; health resort, 2,300 ft. above sea-level; p. (1960) 93,849.

**Petrosani,** *t.,* Romania; S. of Deva; coal; p. (1963) 134,245.

**Petrovgrad,** *t.,* N.W. Jugoslavia; p. 32,833.

**Petrovsk,** *t.,* S.E. Siberia, R.S.F.S.R.; iron and steel, non-ferrous metallurgy; p. (1954) 50,000.

**Petrozavodsk,** *t.,* R.S.F.S.R.; L. Onega; univ.; mica, paper, engin.; p. (1967) 164,000.

**Petsamo,** *see* Pechenga.

**Petten,** *t.,* Netherlands; 30m. N.W. of Amsterdam, on cst.; atomic research ctr.

**Petworth,** *mkt. t., rural dist.,* W. Sussex, Eng.; in Rother valley, 12 m. N.E. of Chichester; building stone; p. (rural dist. 1961) 9,463.

**Pevensey Levels,** *marshy area,* E. Sussex, Eng.; lie behind coastal sand-bars between Eastbourne and Bexhill, extend 5 m. inland to Hailsham; now largely drained, cattle pastures; a. 24 sq. m.

**Pewsey,** *vil., rur. dist..* Wilts, Eng.; in Vale of Pewsey, 7 m. E. of Devizes; farming, iron, bricks, tiles; p. (rural dist. 1961) 16,971.

**Pforzheim,** *t.,* Baden–Württemberg, Germany; S.E. of Karlsruhe; gold, silver, metal wks. jewellery; p. (1963) 86,100.

**Phan Rang,** ctr. of irrigation scheme, S. Viet-Nam.          [fish; p. 5,000.

**Phan Thiet,** *spt.,* S. Viet-Nam; exp. dried and salt

**Pharsala,** *c.,* Thessaly, Greece; S. of Larissa; Cæsar's triumphs over Pompey.

**Philadelphia,** *c., pt.,* Penns., U.S.A.; univ., R.C. cath. masonic temple; mint, academy of fine arts; shipbldg., locomotives, machin., surgical instruments, carpets, woollens, cottons, worsteds; sugar, and petroleum refining; ctr. of War of Independence, from 1790 to 1809; fed. cap. founded by Wm. Penn 1682; p. (1960) 2,002,512.

**Philae,** *I.,* Upper U.A.R.; in Nile above Aswan Dam; temples dating from late Egyptian and classical times incl. famous temple to Isis; submerged by dam waters.

**Philippeville,** *t., spt.,* Algeria; wine, sheep, cattle, cereals, cork, cigarettes, mineral water, macaroni, fish canning; p. (1954) 70,000.    [1,554.

**Philippeville,** *t.,* Namur, S. Belgium; p. (1962)

**Philippine Is.,** *rep.,* Asia; comprising over 7,000 Is., lgst. being Luzon, Mindanao, Mindoro and Palawan; mountainous, many volcanoes, highest Apo, 10,312 ft.; coal, iron, copper, gold; dye-woods, rice, maize, tobacco, coffee, cotton, Manila hemp; coconuts, cigars, pearl fisheries; cap. Quezon City; p. (1967) 34,656,000.

**Philippopolis,** *see* Plovdiv.

**Philipstown,** *see* Daingean.

**Phillipsburg,** *c.,* N.J., U.S.A.; on Delaware R.; water-power, machin., rly. wks.; silk and pulp; p. (1960) 18,502.     [ing; p. (1960) 30,364.

**Phitsnulok,** *t.,* central Thailand; temples; weaving-

**Phlorina (Florina),** *pref.,* Greece; occupied by Bulgaria, April 1941, restored to Greece by peace treaty of 1947; cap. Phlorina; p. (1961) 67,238.

**Phlorina (Florina),** *t.,* Phlorina, Greece; in basin at alt. 3,000 ft., 10 m. from Jugoslav border, 15 m. from Albanian border, purely agr. interests; p. (1961) 11,933.

**Phnom-Penh,** *t.,* R. *pt.,* cap. Cambodia, on Mekong R.; univ., airpt.; rice, cotton; hydro-elec. and storage dam project being built to W.; p. (1965) 404,000.

**Phnom Sar,** *t.,* Cambodia; brewing, fertilisers, bricks; abattoir.

**Phoenix,** *c.,* Arizona, U.S.A.; winter resort; iron, steel, aircraft, electronics, clothing; p. (1960) 439,170.

**Phoenix Group,** *Is.,* Pac. Oc.; part of Gilbert and Ellice I. colony; a. 16 sq. m.; U.S. now have some rights over Canton and Enderbury; Canton used as international airport; p. (1956) 1,257.

**Phthiotis,** *pref.,* Greece; cap. Lamia; p. (1961) 159,373.

**Phuket,** *t.,* S. Thailand; tin smelting plant projected; p. (1960) 28,033.

**Piacenza,** *prov.,* Emilia, Italy; a. 965 sq. m.; p. (1961) 282,813

**Piacenza,** *t.,* Italy; cath., palaces, arsenal; motor cars, chemicals, cement; p. (1961) 87,930.

**Pianosa I.,** Italy; penal settlement; cereals, vineyards, olives; p. 1,000.

**Pias,** *t.,* Alentejo Baixo. S. Portugal; E. of Beja.

**Piatra-Neamt,** *t.,* Moldavia, Romania; timber, pharmaceuticals, soap; p. (1963) 48,572.

**Piaui,** *st.,* Brazil; cattle, cotton, sugar, tobacco, rubber; silver, iron and lead; a. 96,262 sq. m.; cap. Teresina; p. (1960) 123,368.    [125 m.

**Piave,** *R.,* N.E. Italy; flows to Adriatic; length

**Piazza Armerina,** Sicily, Italy; oil, wines and nuts; remarkable Roman mosaics (recently discovered); p. 28,420.

**Picardy,** *old prov.,* France; which included all the Somme dep. and parts of Pas de Calais, Aisne and Oise; old battle sites, Agincourt and Crécy.

**Pichincha,** *prov.,* Ecuador; cap. Quito—the cap. of Ecuador; a. 6,218 sq. m.; p. (1950) 386,520.

**Pickering,** *mkt. t., urb. dist.,* N.R. Yorks, Eng.; on N. margin of Vale of Pickering, 6 m. N. of Malton; church with murals; iron, bricks; p. (1961) 4,193.

**Pickering, Vale of,** E.R. Yorks, Eng.; wide, flat-floored vale, once occupied by glacial lake; bounded to N. by N. York Moors, to S. by York Wolds; drained W. by R. Derwent, which leaves Vale through Kirkham gap; alluvial soils, marshy in ctr.; crop-farming along margins, grain, fodder crops; cattle grazing on damper meadows in ctr.; ch. ts. Pickering, Malton, Helmsley.

Pico da Bandeira, *mtn.*, Brazil; alt. 9,462 ft.

Picton, *t.*, S.I., N.Z.; freezing wks.; tourist and fishing ctr.; p. (1961) *2,320.*

Pidurutalagala, *mtn.*, Ceylon; alt. 8,295 ft.; highest peak in Ceylon.

Piedmont, *region*, N. Italy; rice, wheat, vines, fruits; silk, cottons, woollens; a. 9,813 sq. m.; p. (1961) *3,889,962.*

Piedras Negras, *frontier t.*, Mexico; cattle mkt., coal, silver, zinc and copper; p. *15,663.*

Pierre, *t., cap.*, S.D., U.S.A.; on Missouri R.; p. (1960) *10,088.*

Pietermaritzburg, *t., cap.*, Natal, S. Africa; 30 m. N.W. of Durban; named after Piet Retief and Gerhardus Maritz, two Boer leaders; lt. inds.; tanning; iron-ore mng. in a.; p. (1960) *95,124* inc. *39,472* Europeans.

Pietersburg, *t.*, Transvaal, S. Africa; gold, asbestos, tin; cereals, tobacco, cotton, oranges, lemons; p. (1962) *28,000* inc. *11,000* whites.

Piet Retief, *t.*, Transvaal, S. Africa; tobacco, fruit, mealies, wattle gr. in dist.; p. (1960) *8,604* inc. *2,745* whites.

Pikes Peak, *mtn.*, Col., U.S.A.; alt. 14,109 ft.

Pila (Schneidemühl), *t.*, N.W. Poland (since 1945); formerly in Prussian prov. of Pomerania; trade ctr., lignite mines nearby; p.(1965) *38,000.*

Pilar, *t.*, Paraguay; cotton, timber, hides, oranges; p. (estd. 1960) *10,000.*

Pilatus, *mtn.*, Switzerland; alt. 6,988 ft.

Pilawa (Pilau), *t., spt.*, R.S.F.S.R.; shipbldg., fishing.

Pilbara, *dist.*, W. Australia; metal ores inc. gold, copper, tin; iron ore; ch. mining ctr., Marble Bar.

Pilbara, *new t.*, W. Australia; iron ore mng.

Pilcomayo, *R.*, rising in S. Bolivia, and flowing through the Gran Chaco, separates W. Paraguay from Argentina; trib. of the Paraguay; length 1,400 m.

Pilibhit, *t.*, Uttar Pradesh, India; rice, pepper, sugar; p. (1961) *57,527.*

Pilion, *celebrated mtn.*, S. of Mt. Ossa, Thessaly, Greece; alt. 5,310 ft.

Pillon Pass, Switzerland; alt. 5,092 ft.

Pimlico, *dist.*, Westminster, London, Eng.

Pinar del Rio, *prov.*, W. Cuba, W. Indies; tobacco, asphalt; a. 5,211 sq. m.; p. (1953) *448,422.*

Pinar del Rio, *t.*, Cuba, W. Indies; tobacco; p. (1953) *38,885.*

Pinawa, *t.*, Manitoba, Canada; 55 N.E. of Winnipeg; nuclear research; p. (1965) *8,000.*

Pind Dadan Khan, *t.*, W. Pakistan; coal; p. *11,445.*

Pindus, *mtn. chain*, between Thessaly and Albania, Greece; highest peak 8,050 ft.

Pine Bluff, *c.*, Ark., U.S.A.; cotton, motor-cars; p. (1960) *44,037.*

Pine Creek, *t.*, Arnhem Land, N. Terr., Australia; gold; p. *115.*

Pinerolo, *t.*, Italy; S.W. of Turin; cath.; silk, cotton, woollens; p. *22,890.*

Pines, Is. of, *dependency* of Fr. col. New Caledonia; a. 58 sq. m.; convict settlement.

Pinetown, *t.*, Natal; residtl., industl.; p. (1960) *12,799* inc. *6,965* Europeans.

Pinios R., Greece; flows into G. of Thessaloniki.

Pinjarra, *t.*, W. Australia; rly. junction; timber and stock-raising dist.

Pinneberg, *t.*, Schleswig-Holstein, Germany; N.W of Hamburg; rose cultivation, metals, leather; p. (1963) *29,900* [a. 1,180 sq. m.

Pinos I. (I. of Pines), Caribbean Sea; S. of Cuba;

Pinsk, *t.*, Byelorussia, U.S.S.R.; paper, woodworking inds.; p. (1956) *36,500.*

Piombino, *t.*, Italy; port for Elba I.; steel wks.; p. *26,238.*

Piotrkow Trybunalski, *industrl. t.*, Poland; S. of Lodz; p. (1965) *57,000.*

Pique, *t.*, Ohio, U.S.A.; N. of Dayton; ironwks.. woollens; nuclear reactor; p. (1960) *19,219.*

Piraeus, *see* Peiraieus. [olives; p. *14,875.*

Piran, *spt.*, Istria, Jugoslavia; salt, wines.

Piracicaba, *t.*, São Paulo, Brazil; sugar, cattle, coffee, oranges; p. (1960) *80,670.*

Pirmasens, *t.*, Rhineland-Palatinate, Germany; S.W. of Mannheim; footwear, leather goods; p. (1963) *53,100.*

Pirna, *t.*, Dresden, E. Germany; on R. Elbe; textiles, paper, glass; p. (1969) *41,076.*

Pirot, *t.*, Jugoslavia; nr. Bulgarian border; Jugoslavia; p. *13,033.* [*365,882.*

Pisa, *prov.*, Italy; a. 1,180 sq. m.; p. (1961)

Pisa, *c.*, Italy; at head of Arno delta, 12 m. N.E. of Leghorn; famous leaning tower, cath., univ.; mineral baths, cotton, silk; p. (1961) *91,108.*

Pisco, *spt.*, Peru, S. America; cotton; lead, zinc; whaling; p. (1961) *17,000.*

Pisco, *dep.*, Peru, S. America; p. (1961) *123,917.*

Pisek, *t.*, ČSSR.; brewing, iron foundries, textiles; p. (1961) *19,542.*

Pistoia, *t.*, Tuscany, Italy; on Arno plain, N.W. of Florence; iron and steel goods, silk, macaroni; p. (1961) *82,401.*

Pitcairn I., E. Pacific; British col.; incs. Henderson, Ducie, and Oeno Is.; sweet potatoes, bananas, oranges, coconuts; a. 2 sq. m.; p. (1965) *186*, mostly descendants of the mutineers of the *Bounty*.

Pitch Lake, Trinidad I., W.I.; located in the S. of the I., 10 m. S.W. of San Fernando; natural deposit of asphalt; tourism; a. 212 acres.

Pitea, *spt.*, N. Sweden; on G. of Bothnia; saw mills; p. (1961) *7,426.*

Pitesti, *t.*, Romania; on Arges R.; petroleum, fruit, grain; lge. automobile plant; oil refinery under construction; p. (1963) *67,236.*

Pitlochry, *burgh*, Perth, Scot.; on R. Tummel, 4 m. S. of Pass of Killiecrankie; summer resort; distilleries, hydros; p. (1961) *2,051.*

Pittenweem, *burgh*, Fife, Scot.; at entrance to Firth of Forth; fisheries; p. (1961) *1,576.*

Pittsburgh, *c.*, Penns., U.S.A.; univ.; R.C. cath., coll., Carnegie Library and Institute; port on Ohio R.; ctr. of richest American coalfield; natural gas, petroleum, iron and steel, machin., metal goods, meat packing, glass, aluminium, chemicals; p. (1960) *604,332.*

Pittsfield, *c.*, Mass., U.S.A.; textiles, paper, plastics, elec. machin., hol. resort; p. (1960), *57,879.*

Pittston, *t.*, Penns., U.S.A.; anthracite, coal, machin.; p. (1960) *12,407.* [*716,837.*

Piura, *N. dep.*, Peru; a. 15,190 sq. m.; p. (1961)

Piura, *t.*, Peru; p. (1961) *32,100.*

Pladju, *t.*, S. Sumatra, Indonesia; oil refining; linked by pipe-line with Tempino and Bejubang.

Plainfield, *c.*, N.J., U.S.A.; sub. New York City; printing, motor lorries, machin., chemicals, hosiery; p. (1960) *45,330.*

Plaistow, *dist.*, E. London, Eng.; p. (1961) *10,424.*

Planitz, *t.*, Saxony, Germany; S.W. of Zwickau; textiles, tobacco; p. (estd. 1954) *25,100.*

Plate R., or Rio de la Plata, estuary of the Rs. Paraná and Uruguay flowing to the Atlantic between Argentina and Uruguay, length 170 m.; width at head 25 m., at mouth 138 m.

Plattsburg, N.Y., U.S.A.; pt. of L. Champlain, tourist ctr.; military post; p. (1960) *20,172.*

Plauen, *t.*, Karl-Marx-Stadt, E. Germany; textiles, machin., cable, leather, paper, radios; rly. junction; p. (1963) *79,111.*

Plenty, Bay of, N.I., N.Z.; on E. cst.; 130 m. wide.

Plettenberg, *t.*, N. Rhine–Westphalia, Germany; on R. Lenne; iron wks.; p. (1963) *29,000.*

Pleven, *fortfd. t.*, Bulgaria; many mosques; famous siege 1877; woollens, silks, wines; p. (1956) *57,758.*

Plock, *t.*, Poland; on R. Vistula, nr. Warsaw agr.; oil refinery and petrochemical plant; p. (1965) *54,000.*

Ploesti, *t.* Prahova dist., Romania; petroleum, engin.; p. (1963) *170,894.*

Plovdiv (Philippopolis), *c.*, Bulgaria; on R. Marica; univ., Greek cath.; wheat, fruit, silks, woollens, tobacco, leather, attar of roses, cars; p. (1956) *162,518.*

Plumstead, *dist.*, S.E. London, Eng.

Plymouth, *c., spt., co. bor.*, S. Devon, Eng.; on Plymouth Sound; comprises the "three towns" of Plymouth, Devonport and Stonehouse; R.C. cath., guildhall, museum; shipbldg.; seaside resort; fishing and fish canning, light inds.; p. (estd. 1967) *247,400.*

Plymouth, *spt.*, Mass., U.S.A.; Pilgrim Hall, Pilgrim Fathers landed in 1620 from *Mayflower*, established first English colony; textiles, cordage, machin., cottons, woollens; p. (1950) *10,540.*

Plymouth, *ch. t.*, Montserrat I., T.W.I.; p. (1957) *2,500.*

**Plymouth**, *t.*, Penns., U.S.A.; coal; p. (1960) *10,401*.

**Plynlimmon**, *mtn.*, Montgomery and Cardigan, Wales; alt. 2,469 ft.

**Plzen (Pilsen)**, *t.*, ČSSR.; coal, iron ore, steel, engin., chemicals; p. (1965) *142,000*.

**Po**, *R.*, Italy; flows from Monte Viso, through Piedmont and Lombardy to the Adriatic; length, 340 m.; natural gas deposits Po valley.

**Pocatello**, *t.*, Idaho, U.S.A.; rly. wks.; livestock; cheese; p. (1960) *28,534*.

**Pocklington**, *mkt. t.*, *rural dist.*, E.R. Yorks, Eng.; at foot of York Wolds, 12 m. E. of York; milling, malting, bricks, tiles, agr.; p. (rural dist. 1961) *13,933*.

**Podolsk**, *t.*, R.S.F.S.R.; S. of Moscow; engin., tin smelting, cement; p. (1967) *160,000*.

**Podrinye**, *dist.*, W. Serbia, Jugoslavia; antimony.

**Pohai (Chihli)**, G. of, N. China; together with G. of Liaotung forms shallow expanse of water almost cut off from Yellow Sea by Liaotung and Shantung peninsulas; receives water and silt of Hwang Ho; a. approx. 15,000 sq. m.

**Pohjois Karjalan**, *dep.*, Finland; p. (1966) *198,063*.

**Point Clairette**, Equatorial Africa; oilfield.

**Point-à-Pierre**, Trinidad; oil refinery; natural gas pipeline from Forest Reserve field.

**Pointe-à-Pitre**, *ch. t.*, Grande Terre I., Guadeloupe, Lesser Antilles; p. (1960) *26,160*.

**Point-Claire**, *t.*, Quebec, Canada; p. (1961) *22,709*.

**Pointe-des-Galets**, *ch. pt.*, Ile de la Réunion, Indian Ocean (Fr.).

**Pointe-Noire**, *impt. spt.*, Congo Rep. (ex-French), Equatorial Africa; aerodrome; copper ore, potash, timber, groundnuts; p. (1962) *54,643*.

**Point Fortin**, Trinidad; oil field and refinery.

**Poitiers**, *t.*, Vienne, France; univ.; Black Prince defeated French (1356); brewing, hosiery, cloth; p. (1962) *62,222*.

**Pola**, *see* Pula.

**Poland**, *rep.*, Europe; bounded by Germany, the Baltic Sea, Russia, and Czechoslovakia; largely lowland, rising from Baltic to Carpathians on S. border; ch. Rs.; Vistula and tribs.; climate: hot summers, very cold winters, moderate rainfall; good communications; agr.: cereals, potatoes, sugar-beet, forests, cattle, sheep, horses, pigs; minerals: coal, iron, steel, petroleum, natural gas, potash; cap. Warsaw; a. 121,131 sq. m.; p. (1965) *31,551,000*.

**Pollokshields**, *S.W. sub.*, Glasgow, Scot.; industl. and residtl.

**Polotsk**, *t.*, Byelorussian S.S.R.; cath.; gasoline prod., oil refining; oil pipeline to Latvian pt. of Ventspils; p. (1965) *38,100*.

**Polotskiy**, *t.*, Byelorussian S.S.R.; 8 m. W. of Polotsk; new oil workers' t. 1963.

**Poltava**, *industl. t.*, Ukrainian S.S.R.; horses, cattle, grain, engin., textiles; synthetic diamond plant; p. (1967) *177,000*.

**Polynesia**, *sub-div.*, Oceania; I. groups in Pacific within 30° N. and S. of the equator; between 135° E. and W. longitude.

**Pomerania**, *former prov.*, N. Germany; in postwar redivision part E. of R. Oder to Poland; part W. of R. Oder incorporated in *Land* Mecklenburg, E. Germany; farming, shipbldg. fishing.

**Pomona or Mainland**, lgst. of the Orkney Is., Scot. Kirkwall (cap.) and Stromness on I.

**Pomona**, *c.*, Cal., U.S.A.; fruit-culture; p. (1960) *67,157*.     [8,012 sq. m.

**Pomorze**, *prov.*, Poland; cap. Bydgoszcz; a.

**Pompeii**, *ruined c.*, Italy; stood 13 m. S.E. of Naples, at foot of Vesuvius; destroyed A.D. 79 by volcanic eruption, site re-discovered in 1748; many most interesting excavations; also modern c. near by; fine church with famous collection of silver and gold plate.

**Ponape I.**, Caroline Is., Pac. Oc.; copra, ivory, nuts, starch, bauxite; a. 134 sq. m.; p. (1958) *14,335*.

**Ponca City**, *t.*, Okla., U.S.A.; p. (1960) *24,411*.

**Ponce**, *c.*, Puerto Rico, W. Indies; coffee, sugar, rum; p. (1960) *114,965*.

**Pondicherry**, *cap.*, former Fr. Settlements in India; united with India 1954; cotton, rice; a. of dist. 185 sq. m.; p. (1961) *369,079*; of c. *40,421*.

**Pont-à-Mousson**, *t.*, Meurthe-et-Moselle, France; R. Moselle; ironwks., paper, velvet, cement wks.; p. (1962) *13,037*.

**Ponta Delgada**, *ch. t.*, *spt.*, San Miguel I., Azores; p. (1960) *22,316*.

**Ponta Grossa**, *t.*, Paraná, Brazil; rly. junction;

maté, rice, timber, tobacco, bananas, cattle, jerked beef; p. (1960) *77,803*.

**Pontardawe**, *vil.*, Glamorgan, S. Wales; on R. Tawe, 9 m. N.E. of Swansea; zinc smelting and refining, steel wks.

**Pontchartrain**, Lake, *shallow lake*, lower Mississippi flood plain, U.S.A., connected by canal to New Orleans which lies 6 m. to the south, and by deltaic channels to the gulf of Mexico.

**Pontefract**, *t.*, *mun. bor.*, W.R. Yorks, Eng.; 7 m. E. of Wakefield; cas. ruins; coal, furniture, confectionery; p. (estd. 1967) *29,630*.

**Pontevedra**, *prov.*, Spain, on Atl. cst., bordering Portugal; agr., livestock, fisheries; cap. Pontevedra; a. 1,695 sq. m.; p. (1959) *736,069*.

**Pontevedra**, *spt.*, cap. Pontevedra prov.; Spain; fishing; p. (1949) *46,168*.

**Ponthierville**, *t.*, Congo, Africa; nr. Stanley Falls, Congo R.; p. *1,000*.

**Pontiac**, *c.*, Mich., U.S.A.; on Clinton R.; fishing and shooting, motor cars, rubber goods, machin., varnish; p. (1960) *82,233*.

**Pontianak**, *t.*, *cap.*, Kalimantan, Indonesia; exp. rubber, copra; p. (1961) *150,220*.

**Pontine Is.**, off W. cst. of Italy; in Tyrrhenian Sea; a. 4½ sq. m.; p. *6,000*.

**Pontine Marshes**, *region*, Latium, S. Italy; coastal zone S.E. of Rome extending from Velletri to Terracina; formerly highly malarial fens, largely drained and colonised 1930–35; 3,200 new farms, 4 new ts.; ch. t. Littoria; a. c. 250 sq. m.     [Moritz; tourist resort.

**Pontresina**, *t.*, Grisons, Switzerland; E. of St.

**Pont-y-mister**, *vil.*, Monmouth, Eng.; in valley of R. Ebbw, 6 m. N.W. of Newport; lge. steel-wks., zinc refineries.

**Pontypool**, *t.*, *urb. dist.*, Monmouth, Eng.; coal, iron, steel, glass, bricks, tin galvanising, nylon at Manhilad; p. (1961) *39,879*.

**Pontypridd**, *t.*, *urb. dist.*, Glamorgan, Wales; on R. Taff, 12 m. N.W. of Cardiff; coal, iron; p. (1961) *35,536*.

**Ponza I.**, Pontine Is., Italy; wine, wheat, flax; fishing; bentonite-mining; a. 3 sq. m.

**Poole**, *mkt. t.*, *spt.*, *mun. bor.*, E. Dorset, Eng.; on Poole Harbour, 4 m. W. of Bournemouth; seaplane base; yachting; marine engin., tent mkg., bricks, chemicals; p. (estd. 1967) *97,520*.

**Poona**, *t.*, Maharashtra, India; univ.; cotton, sugar, rice; p. (1961) *737,426*.

**Poopo**, *L.*, Oruro dep., Bolivia; S. America; situated in Andes at alt. 12,120 ft.; very shallow; fed from L. Titicaca by R. Desaguadero, which flows over saline beds; no outlet, therefore salt-water; max. length 50 m., width 30 m.

**Popayan**, *cap.*, Cauca Dep., Columbia; cath.; univ.; gold, silver, platinum, copper near by; p. (estd. 1959) *57,770*.

**Poperinghe**, *t.*, W. Flanders, Belgium; woollens linens, hops; p. (1962) *12,409*.

**Poplar**, *see* Tower Hamlets.     [17,887 ft.

**Popocatepetl**, *volcano*, nr. Pueble, Mexico; alt.

**Porbandor**, *spt.*, Gujarat, India; cement, silk, cotton; imports coal, dates, timber, machin., petroleum; birthplace of Mahatma Gandhi; p. (1961) *75,081*.

**Porcupine Hills**, *t.*, Ont., Canada; on rly. 40 m. S. of Cochrane; ctr. of impt. gold-mng dist.

**Pordenone**, *dist.*, *t.*, within Friuli-Venezia Giulia reg.; Italy; cath; cottons, silks, pottery.

**Pori (Björneborg)**, *spt.*, S. Finland; at mouth of R. Kokemäen; copper refinery, rolling mills, match, paper and pulp wks.; p. (1966) *60,205*.

**Porjus**, *t.*, Norrbotten, N. Sweden; on R. Lulea, where it leaves Stora Lulevatten; impt. hydro-elec. power-sta. supplies power to iron-ore mining dists. of Gällivare and Kiruna, also to Narvik rly.     [6,121.

**Porrentruy**, *t.*, Berne, Switzerland; watches; p.

**Porsgrunn**, *spt.*, Norway; timber, shipping, engin., porcelain, explosives; p. (1961) *10,604*.

**Port Alfred**, *pt.*, Canada; Upper St. Lawrence R.; imports bauxite for smelting at Arvida (lgst. smelter in world, 1959).

**Port Alfred**, *t.*, Cape Province, S. Africa; resort; p. (1960) *6,171* (inc. *1,112* whites).

**Port Amelia**, *spt.*, Mozambique; sisal, coconuts, cotton, maize, groundnuts; p. (1960) *55,902*.

**Port Antonio**, *t.*, Jamaica, W. Indies; p. *5,482*.

**Port Arthur**, *c.*, S.W. Liaoning prov., China; naval base at entrance to Pohai R.; p. (estd.) *200,000*. *See* Luta.

Port Arthur, *L. pt.*, Ontario, Canada; on N.W. cst. of L. Superior; lumbering, mining, grain-milling, exp. ctr.; p. (1961) *45,276.*

Port Arthur, *t.*, Texas, U.S.A.; p. (1960) *66,676.*

Port Arzew, *pt.*, Algeria; world's 1st comm. plant to liquefy natural gas for exp. opened 1964; oil pipeline from Haoud el Hamra projected; oil refinery being built.

Port Assab, *t.*, Ethiopia; oil refining.

Port au Prince, *spt.*, Haiti, W. Indies; coffee, cacao; p. (estd. 1964) *200,000.*

Port Augusta, *t., spt.*, S. Australia; at head of Spencer G.; fine harbour; salt field; exp. wheat, fruit; p. (1966) *10,123.*

Port Blair, *spt. cap.*, Andaman and Nicobar Is. p. (estd.) *16,000.*

Port Chalmers, *t., bor.*, S.I., N.Z.; docks, ship-yards; p. (1961) *3,120.*

Port Chester, *t.*, N.Y., U.S.A.; on Long I. Sound; summer resort, cottons and woollens; p. (1960) *24,960.*

Port Colborne, *t.*, Ont., Canada; port on L. Erie; iron smelting; nickel, copper refining; p. (1961) *14,886.*

Port Elizabeth, *spt.*, Cape Province, S. Africa; on Algoa Bay; bilingual univ.; exp. skins, wool, ostrich feathers, mohair; foundries, soap, chemicals, car assembly, food preservation, sawmills; p. (1960) *270,815* (inc. *94,085* whites).

Port Erin, *vil.*, I. of Man, Eng.; on S.E. cst.; seaside resort, fisheries.

Port Essington, *N. point.* of Coburg Peninsula, N. Terr., Australia; pearl culture experiments.

Port Francqui, *t.*, Congo; present terminus of Congo rly. on Kasai R.; p. *5,000.* [p. *1,000.*

Port Fuad, *t.*, U.A.R.; N. entrance to Suez Canal;

Port Gentil, *spt.*, Gabon, Eq. Africa; exp. palm oil, mahogany, ebony; sawmills, fishing; oil refining; p. *5,000.*

Port Glasgow, *burgh, spt.*, Renfrew, Scot.; on S. bank of R. Clyde, 17 m. below Glasgow; ship-bldg. and repairing, textiles, rope, canvas mftg.; p. (1961) *22,551.*

Port Harcourt, *spt.*, Nigeria; 30 m. from sea on E. branch of Niger delta; terminus of E. Nigerian rly. system; tin, palm oil, groundnuts; bitumen plant, tyres; oil refining; p. (1953) *72,000.*

Port Hedland, *sm. spt.*, W. Australia; on N.W. cst. 285 m. S.W. of Broome; exp. gold and other metals from Pilbarra gold-field; imports food and machin.; linked to Marble Bar by narrow-gauge rly.; new t. being bult 5 m. inland to absorb impact of Mt. Newman iron ore project; twin ts. to be linked by industl. belt.

Port Hope, *t.*, Ont., Canada; midway along N. shore of L. Ontario; fruit, dairying, radium refining; p. (1961) *8,091.* [castle.

Port Hunter, N.S.W., Australia; port for New-

Port Huron, *t.*, Mich., U.S.A.; on L. Huron; summer resort, mineral springs, dry docks, grain elevators; motor-car parts; p. (1960) *36,084.* [for Sydney.

Port Jackson, N.S.W., Australia; *natural harbour*

Port Kembla, *spt.*, N.S.W., Australia; S. of Wollongong; iron and steel wks., gold refining, textiles. [mills; p. (1966) *3,435.*

Port Laoighise, *mkt. t.*, Laoighis, Ireland; corn-

Port Lincoln, *spt.*, S. Australia; exp. wheat, frozen meat, tallow, wool; fertilisers; p. (1966) *3,867.*

Port Louis, *c. cap., pt.*, Mauritius, Indian Ocean; ch. comm. ctr.; p. (estd. 1968) *135,000.*

Port Lyautey (Kenitra), *see* Mina Hassan Tani.

Port Macquarie, *t.*, N.S.W., Australia; on Hastings R.; resort; p. (1966) *7,090.*

Port Mahon, *see* Mahon.

Port Moody, *terminus*, Canadian Pacific Rly., Vancouver, Brit. Columbia; p. *1,512.*

Port Moresby, *spt., ch. t.*, Papua, New Guinea; promising copper deposits; exp. copra, sandalwood, coffee, rubber, shell; univ.; p. (estd. 1963) *14,000.*

Port Natal, *see* Durban.

Port Nelson, *spt.*, Manitoba, Canada; on cst. of Hudson Bay at mouth of R. Nelson; linked by rly. to trans-continental systems via The Pas; exp. wheat, minerals; closed by ice for 7 months each year.

Port Nolloth, *spt.*, Cape Province, Rep. of S. Africa; pt. serving copper- and diamond-mining dists.

Port of Spain, *cap.*, Trinidad, W.I.; cocoa, sugar, asphalt; natural gas pipeline from Penal; p. (estd. 1963) *94,000.*

Port Phillip, *lge. inlet*, Victoria, Australia; land locked bay, Melbourne on N., Geelong on W.

Port Pirie, *c., spt.*, S. Australia; smelting ores, gold refining; exp. wheat, minerals; p. (1966) *15,549.*

Port Radium, *t.*, N.W. Terr., Canada; on Gr. Bear L.; pitchblende deposits; p. *300.*

Port Said, *spt.* U.A.R.; N. end Suez Canal; Free Trade a.; coaling sta.; p. (1960) *246,000.*

Port St. Mary, *vil.*, I. of Man, Eng.; on S.E. cst.; resort; fisheries, boat-bldg.

Port Shepstone, *t.*, Natal, S. Africa; sugar, bark, fibre, maize, fruit, dairying, poultry; cement; p. (1960) *4,233* inc. *1,775* whites.

Port Stanvac, S. Australia; 15 m. S. of Adelaide; oil refining.

Port Sudan, *spt.*, Sudan; 30 m. N. of Suakin; linked by rail to Atbara and Khartoum; oil refining; p. (1960) *51,790.*

Port Sunlight, Cheshire, Eng.; modern garden village founded 1888 by Lord Leverhulme for the employees of Lever Brothers' Port Sunlight factories; p. *6,000.*

Port Swettenham, *spt.*, Selangor, Malaysia; exp. tin, rubber, copra, pineapples; p. *11,300.*

Port Talbot, *t., mun. bor.*, Glamorgan, S. Wales; on E. side of Swansea Bay; impt. iron and steel ind., copper, coal; harbour projected; p. (1961) *50,223.* [p. *1,000.*

Port Taufiq, *spt.*, U.A.R.; S. end of the Suez canal;

Port Vendres, *spt.*, Pyrénées-Orientales, France; nr. Perpignan; p. (1962) *5,085.*

Portadown, *t., mun. bor.*, Armagh, N. Ireland; on R. Bann, 25 m. S.W. of Belfast; linen, lace, farming; p. (1966) *20,710.*

Portaferry, *spt.*, Down, N. Ireland; shipping, fisheries; p. (1966) *1,426.*

Portage, *t.*, Wis., U.S.A.; iron; p. (1960) *7,822.*

Portage la Prairie, *spt.*, Manitoba, Canada; grain exp.; p. (1961) *12,388.*

Portalegre, *t.*, Portugal; cath.; mkt.; p. (1960) *11,017.*

Portarlington, *t.*, Offaly, Ireland; farming; first place to have elec. power-sta. using local peat fuel; p. (1966) *2,804.*

Portbou, *t.*, on Fr. side of Franco–Spanish border, opposite Rosas on Mediterranean cst.

Porthcawl, *t., urb. dist.*, Glam., Wales; on cst. 10 m. S.E. of Pt. Talbot; resort; p. (1961) *11,082.*

Portici, *spt.*, Campania, S. Italy; on Bay of Naples 5 m. S.E. of Naples; dockland sub. of Naples; p. (1961) *50,373.*

Portishead, *t., urb. dist.*, Somerset, Eng.; on Severn estuary 3 m. S.W. of Avonmouth; shipping; p. (1961) *6,440.*

Portknockie, *burgh*, Banff, Scot.; on N. Buchan cst., 5 m. E. of Buckie; sm. fishing pt.; p. (1961) *1,245.*

Portland, *urb. dist.*, Dorset, Eng.; 4 m. S. of Weymouth on sheltered N.E. side of I. of Portland; lge. artificial harbour; p. (1961) *11,542.*

Portland, *t., spt.*, Me., U.S.A.; comm. cap. of Me.; lge. fisheries; paper, pulp, lumber, processed food, clothing; p. (1960) *72,566.*

Portland, *c.*, Ore., U.S.A.; gr. wheat and wool tr.; flour milling, shipbldg., fishing and canning, aluminium, lumber; p. (1960) *372,676.*

Portland Canal, *fjord*, N.W. cst. of America, forming boundary between Alaska and B.C.

Portland, I. of, *peninsula*, Dorset, Eng.; limestone mass, linked to mainland by shingle spit, Chesil Bank, terminates S. in Portland Bill; naval base, prison, Borstal inst.; limestone quarrying; masonry wks.

Portmadoc, *spt., urb. dist.*, Caernarvon, Wales; on Tremadoc Bay; linked by light rly. to Ffestiniog; copper and slate exp.; p. (1961) *3,419.*

Porto, *see* Oporto.

Porto Alegre, *c., cap.*, Rio Grande do Sul st., Brazil; exp. lard, preserved meats, rice, timber, tobacco; textiles, chemicals, furniture, brewing, metallurgy; oil refinery under construction; pipeline connects with Rio Grande do Sol; p. (1960) *641,173.*

Porto Empedocle, *spt.*, Sicily, Italy; sulphur refining, flour, furniture, lime, gypsum; p. *14,764.*

Porto Marghera, *spt.*, Venezia, N. Italy; extends along cst. S. from landward end of the causeway linking Venice to the mainland; the modern pt. of Venice, reached by ship canal dredged through shallow lagoon; oil-refineries.

Porto Novo, *t.*, *cap.*, Dahomey, W. Africa; nr. Bight of Benin; p. (1965) *65,000.*

Porto Vecchio, *t.*, Corsica; on E. cst.; p. *5,304.*

Porto Velho, *cap.*, Rondonia St., Brazil; p. (1960) *51,049.*

Portobello, *resort*, Midlothian, Scot.; on Firth of Forth, 3 m. E. of Edinburgh; bricks, pottery, paper.

Porto Torres, *spt.*, Sardinia, Italy; exp. iron ore; p. *7,251.*

Portree, *t.*, *par.*, I. of Skye, Scot.; on sound of Raasay; fishing, tweed mill; p. *2,120.*

Portrush, *spt.*, *urb. dist.*, Antrim, N. Ireland; 5 m. N. of Coleraine; tourism; p. (1966) *4,357.*

Ports and Isles of Persian Gulf, *dist.*, Iran; along E. cst. Persian G.; extensive oil ind.; very hot; cap. Bandar-e-Bushehr; p. (1967) *346,784.*

Ports and Isles of Oman Sea, *dist.*, S. Iran; arid, very hot; cap. Bandar Abbas; p. (1967) *336,784.*

Portsdown Hill, *chalk ridge*, Hants, Eng.; extends E. to W. behind Portsmouth from Havant to Fareham; water-storage reservoirs supply Portsmouth; lined with early 19th-century fortifications for defence of Portsmouth; length 6 m., alt. 400 ft.

Portsea Is., *fortfd. I.*, between Portsmouth and Langston Harbours.

Portslade-by-Sea, *urb. dist.*, E. Sussex, Eng.; 1 m. W. of Hove; p. (1961) *15,750.*

Portsmouth, *c.*, *co. bor.*, *naval pt.*, Hants, Eng.; opposite I. of Wight; has lgst. naval establishment in the world; Portsmouth is the garrison t.; Portsea has the naval dockyards, Landport is residtl., and Southsea is a popular wat. pl. within the bor. a.; across the harbour is Gosport; aircraft, light engin.; p. (estd. 1967) *219,110.*

Portsmouth, *t.*, N.H., U.S.A.; summer resort, naval dockyard, cotton; the 1905 Peace Treaty between Japan and Russia was negotiated here; p. (1960) *25,833.*

Portsmouth, *c.*, Ohio, U.S.A.; iron and steel goods, aircraft, boots, shoes, bricks; p. (1960) *33,637.*

Portsmouth, *spt.*, Va., U.S.A.; naval dockyard; farm produce, cotton, rly. wks.; p. (1960) *114,775.*

Portsoy, *spt.*, *burgh*, Banff, Scot.; 5 m. W. of Banff; fisheries, meal milling; p. (1961) *1,690.*

Portugal, *rep.*, Iberian peninsula, S.W. Europe; interior mountainous, with wide, fertile valleys; mild winter, hot summers; agr.; cereals, fruit, etc.; livestock; cork, pine and other timbers; copper; fisheries; textiles, pottery, tanning, wine, olive oil; cap. Lisbon; a. 35,404 sq. m.; p. (1963) *8,889,000* (inc. Azores and Madeira).

Portugalete, *spt.*, Biscay prov., Spain; nr. Bilbao; p. (1957) *12,211.*

Portuguesa, *st.*, Venezuela; cap. Guanare; p. (1961) *203,707.* [length 200 m.

Portuguesa, *R.*, Venezuela, trib. of R. Apure;

Portuguese Guinea, Portuguese col., W. Africa; on Atlantic cst.; cap. Bissau; palm nuts, groundnuts, rubber, wax; a. 13,900 sq. m.; p. (estd. 1960) *510,000.*

Portuguese Timor, *col.*, E. Indies; mtns.; copra, coffee, cocoa beans, maize, rice, hides, wax, timber; cap. Deli; a. 7,330 sq. m.; p. (1950) *442,378*

Porvenir, *spt.*, Chile; chief t. Tierra del Fuego; wool; p. mainly Jugoslav. [(1966) *13,687.*

Porvoo, *spt.*, Finland; engin. forest inds.; p.

Porz, *t.*, N. Rhine–Westphalia, Germany; on R. Rhine, S.E. of Cologne; glass, metals, paper; p. (1963) *51,000.*

Posadas, *t.*, Spain; on R. Guadalquivir, nr. Cordova; p. (1957) *7,491.*

Posados, *cap.*, Misiones Terr., Argentina; on Alto Paraná R., on border of Paraguay; yerba-maté, tobacco; p. (1960) *44,000.*

Posen, *see* Poznan.

Pössneck, *t.*, Gera, E. Germany; S.E. of Weimar; porcelain, textiles, leather; p. (1963) *19,455.*

Postillon Is., Lesser Sunda Is., Indonesia; coconuts.

Potchefstroom, *t.*, Transvaal, S. Africa; on the Mooi R.; univ.; agr.; malt, timber, engin.; p. (1962) *44,000* inc. *21,000* whites.

Potenza, *t.*, Italy, cap. of prov. Potenza; situated on hill above R. Basento 2,700 ft. above sea-level; agr. and ind. ctr.; p. (1961) *42,659.*

Potgietersrust, *t.*, Transvaal, S. Africa; agr. ctr.; cattle; citrus fruits; p. (1961) *11,000* (inc. *5,400* whites).

Poti, *spt.*, Georgian S.S.R.; manganese, saw-mills, engin.; p. (1956) *42,500.*

Potomac, *R.*, U.S.A.; dividing Virginia from Maryland; flowing past Washington to Chesa-peake Bay; length 400 m.

Potosi, *dep.*, Bolivia, adjoining Chile and Argentina; famous for silver- and tin-mines; cap. Potosi; a. 45,031 sq. m.; p. (1962) *619,600.*

Potosi, *c.*, Bolivia; on slope of Cerro Gordo de Potosi, 13,350 ft. above sea-level; tin, silver, copper, lead; p. (1962) *55,233.*

Potsdam, *cap.*, Potsdam E. Germany; lies on R. Havel 18 m. S.E. of Berlin; beautiful parks and gardens, and many palaces, inc. former Imperial residence; scene of conference between Allies on boundary questions, 1945; motor and locomotive wks., engin.; p. (1963) *115,093.*

Potteries, The, *dist.*, N. Staffs, Eng.; ctr. of earthenware ind., comprising ts. Burslem, Hanley, Fenton, Tunstall, Stoke, and Longton.

Potters Bar, *t.*, *urb. dist.*, Herts., Eng.; residtl.; p. (estd. 1967) *24,730.*

Pottsdown, *t.*, Penns., U.S.A.; iron and steel, farm implements, silk; p. (1960) *26,144.*

Pottsville, *c.*, Penns., U.S.A.; iron and steel, rly. wks.; p. (1960) *21,659.*

Poughkeepsie, *c.*, N.Y., U.S.A.; on Hudson R.; clothing and iron factories; agr. implements; oil clarifiers; p. (1960) *38,330.*

Poulton-le-Fylde, *urb. dist.*, Lancs, Eng.; 4 m. N.E. of Blackpool; farming; p. (1961) *12,767.*

Povenets, *t.*, R.S.F.S.R.; on L. Onega; cellulose, paper; p. *2,000.*

Powis, Vale of, Montgomery, Wales; runs 12 m. N.E. from Montgomery between Welsh Mtns. and Long Mtn.; drained by R. Severn; cattle-rearing; ch. t. Welshpool; av. width 2 m.

Poyang Hu, *lge. L.*, Kiangsi, China; on S. margin of Yangtze-Kiang plain; receives water of Kan Kiang and tribs., drains N. into Yangtze-Kiang; surrounded by flat, intensively cultivated land, rice, sugar, mulberry; size varies greatly with season, max. a. (in late summer) 1,800 sq. m.

Poznan, *prov.*, W. Poland; stock-raising, mining, mnfs. inc. locomotives; a. 15,152 sq. m.; p. (1965) *2,126,000.*

Poznan, *t.*, *cap. of prov.*, oldest *cap. of* Poland; on R. Warta; cath., univ.; engin., iron founding, chemicals; p. (1965) *438,000.*

Pozoblanco, *t.*, Spain; cattle fairs, lead-mines; p. (1957) *14,703.*

Pozzuoli, *t.*, Italy; 2 m. W. of Naples; ancient Puteoli; mineral baths, ordnance wks.; notable Roman ruins; p. (1961) *51,308.* [p. (1960) *1,528.*

Praest, *t.*, Sjalland, Denmark; on Fakse fjord;

Prague (Praha), *c.*, *cap.*, ČSSR.; picturesque, anc. c. on R. Vltava; comm. and cultural ctr.; univ. (founded 1348); extensive mnfs.; machin., sugar, leather, milling, chemicals; p. (1965) *1,020,000.*

Prahova, *R.*, Walachia, Romania; rises in Tran-sylvanian Alps, flows S. through impt. Ploesti oilfield into R. Ialomita; length approx. 110 m.

Prato, *t.*, Italy; 8 m. N.W. of Florence; cath., medieval cas. and fortifications; straw plaiting, cottons, woollens, machin.; p. (1961) *111,285.*

Prebalkhash (Balkhash), *t.*, Kazakh. S.S.R.; copper; p. (1954) *50,000.*

Predeal Pass, Romania; carries main road and rly. across Transylvanian Alps from Bucharest to Brasov; alt. over 4,000 ft.

Preesall, *urb. dist.*, Lancs, Eng.; N. of Blackpool; p. (1961) *2,356.*

Pregel, *R.*, Poland; flows to Frisches Haff, nr. Kaliningrad; length 125 m.

Prek Ihnot, Cambodia; power and irrigation development project on Lower Megong R.

Prenzlau, *t.*, Neubrandenburg, E. Germany; p. (1963) *19,955.*

Prerov, *t.*, ČSSR.; S.E. of Olomouc; hardware, textiles; p. (1961) *30,511.*

Prescelli Myndd, *mtns.*, N.E. Pembroke, Wales.

Prescot, *mfg. t.*, *urb. dist.* S.W. Lancs, Eng.; 4 m. S.W. of St. Helens; mkt., elec. cable ind.; p. (1961) *13,077.*

Prescott, *pt.*, Ontario, Canada; on R. St. Lawrence; p. (1961) *5,366.*

Presidio St. Vicente, *t.*, N.M., U.S.A.; on Rio Grande del Norte.

Prešov, *t.*, ČSSR.; linen mnfs.; p. (1961) *35,121*

Prestatyn, *t.*, *urb. dist.*, Flint, Wales; on N. cst., 3 m. E. of Rhyl; seaside resort; p. (1961) *10,771.*

Prestea, *t.*, Ghana; gold-mining region.

Presteign, *mkt. t.*, *urb. dist.*, Radnor, Wales; on R. Lugg, 10 m. N.W. of Leominster; p. (1961) *1,190.* [11,577.

Preston, *t.*, Ont., Canada; furniture; p. (1961)

Preston, *t.*, *pt.*, *co. bor.*, Lancs, Eng.; on R. Ribble; textiles, engin., aircraft wks.; p. (estd. 1967) *106,010.*

Prestonpans, *burgh*, E. Lothian, Scot.; on S. side of Firth of Forth, 9 m. E. of Edinburgh; "Bonnie Prince Charlie" defeated British here in 1745; bricks, soap, brewing; p. (1961) *3,104.*

Prestwich, *industl. t.*, *mun. bor.*, Lancs, Eng.; in valley of R. Irwell, 3 m. N.W. of Manchester; cotton bleaching and dyeing, soap, furnishings; p. (estd. 1967) *33,480.*

Prestwick, *burgh*, Ayr, Scot.; on Firth of Clyde, 3 m. N. of Ayr; impt. golfing ctr. and trans-Atlantic airport; resort; p. (1961) *12,564.*

Pretoria, *admin. cap.*, Transvaal, Rep. of S. Africa; fine admin. bldgs., univ.; impt. tr. ctr.; inds. inc. engin., chemicals, iron and steel; p. (1960) *422,590* inc. *207,202* whites.

Préveza, *prefecture*, Greece; cap. Préveza; p. (1961) *62,387.*

Préveza, *fortfd. t.*, Préveza, Greece; on G. of Arta; gd. shipping tr.; p. (1961) *11,172.*

Pribalkhash, *see* Balkhash.

Pribram, *t.*, Bohemia, ČSSR.; lead-, silver-mng. zinc, barium, antimony; p. (1961) *25,729.*

Prichard, *t.*, Ala., U.S.A.; meat packing, canning, fertilisers, wood and paper prod.; p. (1960) *47,371.*

Prieska, *t.*, Cape Prov., S. Africa; on Orange R.; sheep, cattle, horses; blue asbestos; p. (1960) *6,464* (inc. *1,738* whites).

Prijedor, *t.*, Croatia, Jugoslavia; on E. flank of Dinaric Alps, 65 m. S.E. of Zagreb; iron-ore mines.

Prilep, *t.*, Macedonia, Jugoslavia; p. (1959) *36,000.*

Prince Albert, *t.*, Saskatchewan, Canada; lumbering, furs; p. (1961) *24,168.*

Prince Albert Peninsula, *dist.*, Victoria I., Arctic Canada.

Prince Albert Sound, *inlet*, Victoria I., Arctic Canada.

Prince Edward I., *prov.*, Canada; dairying, fishing, agr.; bridge-tunnel link with New Brunswick projected; cap. Charlottetown; a. 2,184 sq. m.; p. (1961) *104,629.*

Prince George, *t.*, B.C., Canada; oil refining; p. (1961) *13,877.*

Prince of Wales I., off cst. of C. York Peninsula, Queensland, Australia.

Prince of Wales, *C.*, Bering Strait, Alaska.

Prince Rupert, *t.*, B.C., Canada; Pacific pt. of Canadian National Rly.; p. (1961) *11,987.*

Princes Risborough, *mkt. t.*, Bucks, Eng.; at N. foot of Chiltern Hills, in gap used by main rly.; chairs, brewing; p. *2,435.*

Princeton, *bor.*, N.J., U.S.A.; seat of Princeton Univ.; p. (1960) *11,890.* [son.

Princetown, *vil.*, Devon, Eng.; nr. Dartmoor pri-

Principe and S. Tomé, *Portuguese Is.*, G. of Guinea, Africa; products, cacao, coffee, coconuts, etc.; a. 372 sq. m.; p. (1960) *63,435.*

Pripet (Pripyat), *R.*, Byelorussian S.S.R.; trib. of R. Dnieper; length 350 m.

Pripet Marshes, Byelorussian S.S.R.; a. 30,000 sq. m.; greater part reclaimed.

Priština, *t.*, *cap.*, Kosmet, Jugoslavia; on R. Sitnic; many mosques; sugar and coffee; p. (1959) *32,000.*

Progreso, *spt.*, Yucatan, Mexico; sisal; warehousing; p. (1960) *14,000.*

Prokopevsk, *t.*, S.W. Siberia, R.S.F.S.R.; nr. Novokuznetsk; metallurgy, coal; p. (1967) *291,000.*

Prome, *t.*, Burma; on R. Irrawaddy; silk, rice, cotton, tobacco; p. *23,295.*

Proskurov, *see* Khmelnitsky. [m.

Prosna, *R.*, Poland; trib. of R. Warta; length 120

Prostějov, *t.*, CSSR.; match-mkg., brewing, malt and sugar; geese-breeding; p. (1961) *35,519.*

Provence, *old maritime prov.*, S.E. France; now deps. Var, Basses-Alpes, Bouches-du-Rhône, and part of Vaucluse.

Providence, *c.*, R.I., U.S.A.; at head of Narragansett Bay; univ.; jewellery, textiles, silverware, rubber goods, machin., oil, coal; p. (1960) *207,498.*

Provo, *c.*, Utah, U.S.A.; at base of Wasatch mtns., nr. shore of Utah Lake; flour, bricks, blast furnaces; p. (1960) *36,047.*

Prudhoe, *urb. dist.*, Northumberland, Eng.; coal; p. (1961) *9,959.*

Prussia, *old st.*, former kingdom, Germany; cap. Berlin; E. Prussia partitioned between Russia and Poland.

Pruszkow, *t.*, Poland; nr. Warsaw; elec. plant; engin; p. (1965) *39,000.*

Prut, *R.*, flows between Romania and Bessarabia from the Carpathian Mtns. to the Black Sea; length 360 m.

Przemysl, *frontier t.*, Poland; on bdy. between Poland and Ukrainian S.S.R.; timber, leather, corn, chemicals; p. (1965) *50,000.*

Psel, *R.*, U.S.S.R.; flows to the R. Dnieper at Kremenchug; length 300 m.

Pskov, *t.*, R.S.F.S.R., U.S.S.R.; on R. Velykaya; flax tr., leather, sawmills, flour mills, cordage; p. (1959) *81,000.*

Pucallpa, *R. pt.*, Peru; on R. Ucayali; sawmills, rosewood oil; p. (1961) *20,000.*

Pudsey, *t.*, *mun. bor.*, W.R. Yorks, Eng.; between Leeds and Bradford; mnfs., woollens; p. (estd. 1967) *37,380.* [50,483.

Pudukkottai, *t.*, Tamil Nadu, S. India; p. (1961)

Puebla, *st.*, Mexico; agr.; coffee and sugar growing; a. 13,124 sq. m.; p. (1960) *1,973,837.*

Puebla, *c.*, Mexico; one of the oldest and most impt. cs.; alt. 7,137 ft.; cath.; cottons, onyx, glazed tiles; p. (1960) *289,049.*

Pueblo, *c.*, Col., U.S.A.; on R. Arkansas; coal; iron- and steel-wks.; copper, gold and silver smelted; p. (1960) *91,181.*

Puenteareas, *t.*, Spain; nr. Vigo; vine growing, porcelain; p. (1957) *14,987.*

Puente Genil, *t.*, Córdoba, Spain; olive oil, quince pulp; p. (1957) *30,465.*

Puerto Barrios, *pt.*, Guatamala; rly. term.; oil refining; p. (estd. 1960) *30,980.*

Puerto Berrio, *R. pt.*, Colombia; on R. Magdalena; serves Medellin; p. (estd. 1959) *12,500.*

Puerto Cabello, *spt.*, Venezuela; on the Caribbean S., nr. Valencia; lge. exp.; asbestos, vegetable oils, soap, candles; p. (1961) *48,000.*

Puerto Colombia, *t.*, Colombia; resort; former ocean pt. for Barranquilla; p. (1947) *4,896.*

Puerto Cortes, *spt.*, Honduras rep., Central America; p. (1961) *17,412.*

Puerto de Santa Maria, *spt.*, Cadiz, Spain; wine, glass; p. (1957) *28,300.*

Puerto la Cruz, *t.*, Venezuela; 10 m. from Barcelona; oil refining; p. (1961) *45,000.*

Puerto Limon, Costa Rica; oil refinery under construction.

Puerto México, *see* Coatzacoalcos.

Puerto Montt, *spt.*, Chile; in sheep-farming dist.; S. term. of rlys.; devastated by earthquake, May 1960; lumber, cattle, potatoes; p. (1961) *45,400.* [p. (1961) *11,705.*

Puerto Natales, *spt.*, Chile; wool, frozen meat;

Puerto Ordaz. *See* Santo Tomé de la Guayana.

Puerto Plata, *t.*, Dominican rep. Central America; p. (1960) *26,139.*

Puerto Real, *spt.*, Andalusia, Spain; summer resort; wine and oil tr.; p. (1957) *13,061.*

Puerto Rico, *W. Indian I.*, Greater Antilles; ceded by Spain to U.S.A. in 1898 (since 1952 free cmwlth. ass. with U.S.A.); nuclear reactor at Punta Higuera; sugar, tobacco, rum, textiles, iron ore, salt, marble, white clay; cap. San Juan; a. 3,423 sq. m.; p. (estd. 1965) *2,650,000* mainly natives of mixed Spanish and aboriginal descent.

Puerto Salinas, *spt.*, Venezuela; oil-transhipment.

Puerto Saurez, *R. pt.*, Bolivia; on R. Paraguay; collecting ctr. for rubber, coffee, Brazil nuts.

Puerto Varas, *t.*, Chile; tourist ctr. in Chilean "Switzerland"; p. (1961) *26,615.*

Pugoda, *t.*, Ceylon; cloth mill.

Puget Sound, Washington, U.S.A.

Puket, *t.*, ch. Thailand pt. on Malay Peninsula; tin-mines; p. *30,000.*

Pula, *spt.*, Croatia, Jugoslavia; arsenal, naval base; cement; ship-breaking; footwear, tar, flour, tobacco, fishing; p. (1959) *35,000.*

Pulacayo, *t.*, Bolivia; alt. 13,600 ft.; silvermines; p. *8,000.*

Pulo Tantalum, strip of land connecting Burma with Malay Peninsula, Thailand.

Pulo Wai I., Sumatra, Indonesia; hilly, forests; ch. pt. Sabang.

Pumpherston, *vil.*, nr. Edinburgh, Scot.; oil refining.

Puna, bleak, uninhabited plateau of Peru and Bolivia; alt. 12,000–18,000 ft.

Punjab, *geographical region*, comprising N.W. of Indus plains, Indian sub-continent; extensive irrigation from the "five rivers"—Jhelum, Chenab, Ravi, Bias, Sutlej; cotton, sugar, cereals; now divided politically between India and Pakistan.

Punjab (East), *st.*, India; partitioned on linguistic basis in 1966: Punjabi-speaking Punjab st., and Hindi-speaking Hariana st.; certain hill areas transferred to Himachal Pradesh; joint cap. Chandigarh; p. of Punjab st. *12,000,000* (inc. 55% Sikh.)

Puno, *dep.*, Peru, S. America; p. (1961) *687,077.*

Puno, *t.*, Peru; p. (1961) *15,880.*

Punta Arenas, *t.*, *free pt.*, Magallanes prov., Chile; most S. c. in the world; mutton, wool; whaling; coal nearby; natural gas pipeline from Kimiri-Aike; p. (1961) *46,872.*

Puntarenas, *prov.*, Costa Rica; p. (1963) *155,599.*

Puntarenas, *spt.*, Costa Rica, Central America; one of the ch. comm. pts. of the country, stands on Gulf of Nicoya; p. (1963) *33,378.*

Purbeck, I. of, *dist.*, Dorset, Eng.; Corfe cas. in ctr.; limestone (Purbeck "marble") quarries.

Puri, *dist.*, Orissa, India; cap. P. famous for its temple and festival of the god Vishnu and his monster car, Juggernaut; p. (1961) *1,365,439.*

Purley, *former urb. dist.*, Surrey, Eng.; now inc. in Croydon outer bor. Greater London.

Purnea, *t.*, Bihar, Indian Union; tobacco; p. (1961) *40,602.*

Pursat, *mkt. t.*, Cambodia, Indo-China; between Pnompenh and Thailand frontier; p. *96,000.*

Purús, *R.*, Peru; trib R. Amazon; 1,400 m.

Pusan (Fusan), *pt.*, S. Korea; on S.E. cst.; silk, hides, rice; elec. apparatus, cars; iron and steel mill at Pohang nearby; p. (1962) *1,271,000.*

Puteaux, *sub.*, Paris, France; woollens, dyes; p. (1962) *39,687.*  [London.

Putney, *S.W. residtl. and industl. Thames-side sub.*,

Putrid Sea, *see* Sivash.

Putumayo, *R.*, Ecuador; trib. of R. Amazon; length 700 m.  [alt. 4,806 ft.

Puy-de-Dôme, *peak*, Auvergne Mtns., France;

Puy-de-Dôme, *dep.*, France; drained by R. Allier; generally mountainous; agr., vineyards; coal, silver, lead; cap. Clermont-Ferrand; a. 3,090 sq. m.; p. (1962) *508,928.*

Puy, Le, *cap.*, Haute-Loire, France; lace-mkg.; p. (1962) *23,648.*

Puymorens Tunnel, Pyrenees, on bdy. between France and Spain; carries main rly. between Toulouse and Barcelona.

Pwllheli, *spt.*, *mun. bor.*, Caernarvon, N. Wales; on S. cst. of Lleyn peninsula; seaside resort; inshore fishing, boat bldg.; p. (1961) *3,642.*

Pyatigorsk, *t.*, Caucasus, R.S.F.S.R.; spa, sulphur springs; engin., radio equip.; p. (1959) *69,000.*

Pyinmana, *t.*, Burma; rly. junction; sugar mills projected; p. *17,556.*

Pylos, *t.*, S.W. Peleponnese, Greece; shipblbg. and repair yard and heavy metalworking factory projected.

Pyongyang, *cap. c.*, N. Korea; located 40 m. up Taedong R.; coal and iron ore deposits; silk, textiles; p. (1960) *940,000.*

Pyrenees, *range of mtns.*, S.W. Europe; dividing France from Iberian Peninsula; 270 m. long; hgst. peak Pic d'Anéto (Maladetta) 11,174 ft.

Pyrénées, Basses, *dep.*, S.W. France; mainly agr. and livestock rearing; cap. Pau; a. 2,978 sq. m.; p. (1962) *466,038.*

Pyrénées, Hautes, *dep.*, S. France; agr., vines, nuts, livestock, marble quarries; cap. Tarbes; a. 1,750 sq. m.; p. (1962) *211,433.*

Pyrénées-Orientales, *dep.*, S. France; on Mediterranean; wheat, wine, silk-worm culture, stock-rearing; cap. Perpignan; a. 1, 599 sq. m.; p. (1962) *251,231.*

Pyrgos, *t.*, Elis, Greece; prov. Elis, nr. Patras; has suffered from earthquakes; p. (1961) *20,558.*

## Q

Qaiyara, Al, *t.*, Iraq; route ctr.; oil resources undeveloped.

Qalyub, *t.*, U.A.R.; rly. junction; p. *5,000.*

Qalyûbîya, *administrative div.*, Egypt; a. 364 sq. m.; p. (1947) *690,156.*

Qara Dagh, *t.*, Iraq; gum.

Qarun (Karun), *see* Birket el Qarun.

Qasr el Azraq, *t.*, Jordan; oasis; rice.

Qasvin, *c.*, Iran; p. (1956) *66,386.*

Qatar, *sheikdom*, Arabia; includes Q. Peninsula, Persian G.; oil-mining; a. 4,000 sq. m.; p. (1962) *55,000.*

Qatif, *fortfd. t.*, El Hasa, Saudi Arabia.

Qatlava Depression, N. Egypt; a. 7,000 sq. m.

Qena, *t.*, Egypt; on R. Nile; water jars and bottles; p. (1960) *58,000.*

Qishm, *I.*, part of Prot. of South Arabia (Aden); off S. cst. of Iran, at entrance of Persian G.; hilly; cereals, vegs., fruit, salt; p. *15,000.*

Qisil-Qum, *desert region*, central Asia; covering dried-up a. of extended Pleistocene Aral Sea.

Qizan, *spt.*, Saudi Arabia; cereals, pearl-fishing, salt.

Quantock Hills, Somerset, Eng.; S. of Bridgwater Bay; highest pt., 1,262 ft., officially designated (1957) as a place of "outstanding natural beauty."

Quaregnon, *t.*, Hainaut prov., Belgium; Mons colly. dist.; ironwks. and tobacco factories; p. (1962) *18,063.*  [and Istria.

Quarnero, *G.*, Adriatic Sea; between Croatian cst.

Quarto, G. oi, *arm*, G. of Cagliari, Sardinia.

Quathlamba Mtns., *see* Drakensberg.

Quatre Bras, *nr.* Waterloo, S. Brabant, Belgium.

Queanbeyan, *t.*, N.S.W., Australia; pastoral, dairying and mixed farming dist.; mkt. and service ctr.; bldg. materials; p. (1966) *12,489.*

Quebec, *prov.*, Canada; pulp, paper, textiles; metal smelting, chemicals; agr., forestry, mng., elec. power; cap. Quebec, lgst. c. Montreal; a. 594,860 sq. m.; p. (1961) *5,259,211.*

Quebec, *c. cap.*, Quebec, Canada; on St. Lawrence R.; univ.; fine harbour, handsome gov. bldgs.; furs, textiles, leather, paper; oil refinery at St. Romauld under construction; p. (1961) *357,568.*

Quebec-Labrador Trough, Canada; geological formation extending through central Quebec prov. to Ungava Bay, Hudson Strait; immense reserves of iron-ore (locally "red gold ").

Quedlinburg, *c.*, Halle, E. Germany; at foot of Hartz Mtns.; cas. cath.; cheese; aniline dyes, metals, engin.; p. (1963) *31,251.*

Queen Alexandria Ra., Antarctica; highest pk., Mt. Kirkpatrick, 14,600 ft.

Queenborough, *t.*, *mun. bor.*, Kent, Eng.; on R. Swale, I. of Sheppey; chemicals, glass, pottery, glue, iron; p. (1961) *3,044.*

Queen Carola Harbour, W. cst. Buka Is., Solomon Is., Pac. Oc.

Queen Charlotte's Is., *group*, N. of Vancouver I., off cst. of Brit. Columbia; ch. Is.: Graham I., Moresby I.; valuable halibut fishing ind.

Queen Charlotte Sound, *strait* separating Vancouver I. from Brit. Columbia mainland, a continuation of Johnstone Strait.

Queen Maud Land, Antarctica; claimed by Norway; ice crystal mtns., 10,000 ft. high for 100 m. along cst.

Queens, *bor.*, N.Y. City, U.S.A.; p. (1960) *1,809,578.*

Queensferry, *burgh*, W. Lothian, Scot.; on S. side of Firth of Forth, 8 m. N.W. of Edinburgh; S. end of Forth Bridge and ferry across Firth; whisky; tourism; p. (1961) *2,929.*

Queensferry N., *vil.*, Fife, Scotland.

Queensland, *st.*, N.E. Australia; great grassy plains and cst. highlands; agr.; maize, wheat, sugar-cane, cotton, pineapples, bananas; dairying; cattle, sheep, wool; timber; coal, copper, gold, uranium; oil at Moonie and Alton; cap. Brisbane; a. 670,500 sq. m.; p. (1966) *1,661,240.*

Queenstown, *see* Cobh.

Queenstown, *t.*, Cape Province, S. Africa; in the Great Kei R. valley; prosperous agr. region; p. (1960) *33,126* (inc. *9,743* whites).

Queenstown, *t.*, Tasmania, Australia; mng.; p. (1966) *4,292.*

Quelimane, *pt.*, Port. E. Africa; rly. term.; rubber, almonds, copra, coffee, cotton, sisal, tea, tobacco, sugar, wax, ivory; p. (1960) *156,587.*

Quelpart (Cheju Do), *I.*, Yellow Sea; 60 m. S. of Korea (40 m. by 17 m.) belonging to S. Korea; agr. and pearl-fishing.

Quemoy, *gr. of Is.*, off Chinese mainland near Amoy, held by Nationalist forces; p. (estd.) *50,000* (plus garrison of *40,000*).

Que Que, *t.*, Rhodesia; alt. 3,979 ft.; gold-mining, farming, ranching dist. ctr.; iron and steel; tobacco, vegs., citrus fruit; p. (1958) *11,200* (incl. *2,200* Europeans).

Quequen, *t.*, E. Argentina; seaside resort.

Querétaro, *st.*, central Mexico; agr.; minerals, famous for opals; a. 4,432 sq. m.; p. (1960) *355,045*.

Querétaro, cap. Q., Mexico; at alt. 6,346 ft., cotton mills; an Aztec c., Emperor Maximilian executed here (1867); p. (1960) *60,000*.

Querimba Is., off Mozambique.

Quesnel, *t.*, B.C., Canada; on R. Frazer, 360 m. N. of Vancouver; impt. alluvial gold workings.

Quetta, *t.*, W. Pakistan; at end of Bolan Pass, on road to Kandahar; tr. and military ctr.; thermal sta. under construction; lge. coal reserves nearby; iron ore deposits; p. (1961) *106,633*.

Quetta, *div.*, W. Pakistan; coloured marble in the Chagai a.; p. (1961) *585,000*.

Quezaltenango, *c.*, Guatemala, Central America; on slopes of Cerro Quemado volcano; ctr. of tr. for W. part of the rep.; textiles; p. *50,750*.

Quezon City, *cap.*, Philippines; N. E. of Manila; nuclear reactor; p. (1960) *398,000*.

Quibdó, *t.*, Colombia, S. America; on R. Atrato; p. (estd. 1959) *41,350*.

Quiberon, *t.*, Morbihan, France; on Quiberon Bay, nr. Lorient; p. (1962) *4,540*.

Quibor, *t.*, Venezuela; 40 m. S.S.W. Barquisimeto; blankets from local wool.

Quicamao, *t.*, st. Rio de Janeiro, Brazil; nr. Camos; industl.

Quillota, *comm. t.*, Valparaiso, Chile; nr. Santiago; p. *17,232*.

Quilmes, *industl. sub.*, Buenos Aires, Argentina; brewing, textiles, ironware, glass; Eng. public school; p. (estd. 1960) *120,000*.

Quilon, *t.*, Kerala, India; on Malabar cst., gd. tr.; coconuts, pepper, timber; p. (1961) *91,018*.

Quilpie, *t.*, Queensland, Australia; rly. connects interior with Brisbane.

Quimper, *fortfd. t.*, Finistère, France; nr. Brest; pilchards, pottery, paper, leather, brewing; p. (1962) *50,670*.

Quimperlé, *t.*, Finistère, France; 34 m. E.N.E. Quimper; industl.; p. (1962) *11,163*.

Quincy, *t.*, Ill., U.S.A.; milling, tobacco, ironware, machin.; p. (1960) *43,793*.

Quincy, *c.*, Mass., U.S.A.; granite, foundries, shipbldg.; p. (1960) *87,409*.

Quindío, *pass*, Columbia; provides impt. routeway through Cordillera Central; 11,099 ft.

Qui Nhon, *t.*, S. Viet-Nam; rice, coconut oil, copra, dried fish, groundnuts; p. *10,000*.

Quintana Roo, *terr.*, Mexico; cap. Chetumal; a. 19,438 sq. m.; p. (1960) *50,169*.

Quintero, *t.*, Chile; naval air sta.; copper refining.

Quintin, *t.*, dep Côtes-du-Nord, France; nr. St. Brieuc.

Quinto, *R.*, Argentina; flows S.E. from the Sierra de San Luis and becomes lost in a morass; length 250 m.

Quiringua, *ruined ancient t.*, nr. Isabel, Guatemala, Central America; on R. Mohtagua.

Quistello, *t.*, Mantua, Italy; on R. Secchia; p. *9,450*.

Quito, *c.*, *cap.*, Ecuador; in the Andes, 15 m. S. of the Equator; alt. 9,350 ft.; textiles, shoes, soap, pharmaceutics; p. (1963) *368,000*.

Qum (Qom), *c.*, Iran, pilgrimage ctr.; shrine of Fatima (daughter of Mohammed and sister of Imam Riza); rly. junc.; p. (1967) *179,434*.

Quorndon, or Quorn, *sm. t.*, Leicester, Eng.; on R. Soar, 3 m. S. of Loughborough; ctr. of fox-hunting dist.

Quorra, *R.*, Africa; one of the names given to the R. Niger; below Timbuktu.

Quseir, *t.*, U.A.R.; on Red Sea cst.; caravan tr. ctr.; uranium; p. *1,000*.

Quyquyo, *t.*, S. Paraguay; copper, manganese; p. *6,590*.

# R

Raab, *see* Györ.

Raalte, *vil.*, Overijssel, Neth.; nr Zwolle; industl.; p. (1967) *13,306*.

Raasay, *I.*, E. of Skye, Inverness, Scot.; 13 m. long, 3½ m. wide.

Rab I., at head of Adriatic, Jugoslavia; marble, silk mnfs.; resort; a. 74 sq. m.; p. *6,354*.

Rabat or New Salle, *c.*, *spt.*, Morocco; at mouth of Bu Regreg; cath., univ.; leather and carpet mnfs.; p. (1960) *227,445*.

Rabaul, *spt.*, New Britain, Papua-New Guinea; copra ctr.; p. *4,500*.

Rabot, *t.*, Malta; on Gozo I.

Racalmuto, *t.*, Girgenti, Sicily; agr.; p. *13,825*.

Race, *C.*, S.E. Newfoundland, Canada.

Racibórz (Ratibor), *t.*, Upper Silesia, Poland; German before 1945; on R. Oder; textiles, metals, wood, engin.; p. (1965) *36,000*.

Racine, *c.*, Wis., U.S.A.; on L. Michigan, 10 m., S. of Milwaukee; motor cars, farm implements; p. (1960) *89,144*.

Radauti, *t.*, Bukovina, Romania; paper, glass, engin.; p. (1956) *15,949*.

Radcliffe, *mun. bor.*, Lancs, Eng.; nr. Manchester; paper-mkg., cotton weaving, engin.; p. (estd. 1967) *27,610*.

Radebeul, *t.*, Dresden, E. Germany; on R. Elbe; machin.; p. (1963) *40,177*.

Radford, *t.*, Va., U.S.A.; iron smelting, lumbering; p. (1960) *9,371*.

Radnorshire, *inland co.*, S. Wales; oats, wheat; sheep rearing, breeding Welsh ponies, mineral springs; cap. Presteign; a. 471 sq. m.; p. (1966) *18,000*.

Radom, *industl. t.*, Kielce, Poland; nr. Warsaw; engin.; p. (1965) *143,000*. [*29,000*.

Radomsko, *t.*, Poland; S. of Lodz; p. (1965)

Radomsyl, *t.*, Ukrainian S.S.R.; textiles.

Radstock (Norton Radstock), *t.*, *urb. dist.*, Somerset. Eng.; 10 m. S.E. of Bristol; collieries; p. (1961) *12,732*.

Radzionkow, *t.*, Katowice, Poland; New Town (1951) p. (1965) *27,000*.

Rafah, *t.*, U.A.R., on Israel bdy.

Raffadali, *t.*, Girgenti, Sicily, Italy; agr.; p. *10,825*.

Ragaz, Bad, *t.*, *resort*, St. Gall, Switzerland; on R. Tamina; hot springs; ancient Abbey of Pfäfers, 2,697 ft. above sea-level.

Ragusa, *c.*, Syracuse, Italy; cheese factories; oil; p. (1961) *55,274*.

Ragusa, *see* Dubrovnik.

Rahad, *R.*, Sudan; trib. of Blue Nile.

Rahmánfya, El, *t.*, Lower U.A.R.; nr. Rosetta; on R. Nile.

Rahway, *c.*, N.J., U.S.A.; on R. Rahway; residtl. for New York business men; p. (1960) *27,699*.

Raiatéa, *I.*, Society Is., Pac. Oc.; lgst. of Fr. Leeward gr. 130 m. N.W. Tahiti; p. (1962) *6,210*.

Raichur, *t.*, Mysore, India; pottery; p. (1961) *63,329*.

Raigarh, *t.*, cap. Raigarh *dist.*, Madhya Pradesh, India; silk mnfs.; rice; p. (1961) *36,933*.

Rainford, *urb. dist.*, Lancs, Eng.; nr. St. Helens; coal; p. (1961) *5,385*.

Rainier, *mtn.*, Washington, U.S.A.; 14,530 ft.

Rainton, E. and W., *colly. dists.*, nr. Durham, Eng.

Rainy, *L.*, on border of Canada and Minn., U.S.A., drained by Rainy R. to Lake of the Woods.

Raipur, *t.*, Madhya Pradesh, India; p. (1961) *139,792*.

Raismes, *t.*, Nord, France; nr. Valenciennes; lace ind.; p. (1954) *14,577*.

Rajahmundry, *t.*, Andhra Pradesh, India; on the delta of the Godivari R.; p. (1961) *130,030*.

Rajasthan, *st.*, India; farming, millet, cotton, pulses, textiles, ivory; ch. towns, Jaipur, (cap.), Udaipur, Alwar, Jodhpur; section of canal scheme inaugurated 1961 at Hanumangarh, 200 m. N.W. of New Delhi; nuclear power sta. projected; copper mines and ore processing at Khetri; a. 132,077 sq. m.; p. (1961) *20,155,602*.

Rajkot, *t.*, Gujarat, India; p. (1961) *194,510*.

Rajshahi, *t.*, Rajshahi *dist.*, E. Pakistan; on R. Ganges; univ.; silk inds.

Raki-Ura I., *see* Stewart I.

Rakka, *t.*, Nigeria, W. Africa; on Lower Niger R.

Rakos Palota, *sub.* Budapest, Hungary.

Rakovnik, *t.*, Bohemia, ČSSR.; mkt., mining; p. (1961) *11,979*.

Raleigh, *c.*, N.C. U.S.A.; educational ctr.; rly. wks., cotton-mills; p. (1960) *93,931*.

Ralick, *chain of Is.*, Marshall gr., Pac. Oc.; parallel with Ratack chain.

Ramacca, *commune*, E. Sicily; marble; linen; agr.; p. *12,521*.

Rambervilliers, *t.*, Vosges, France; nr. Nancy; p. (1962) *7,060*.

Rambouillet, t., Yvelines, France; nr. Versailles; ancient château; p. (1962) 12,593.

Rameswaram, t., S. India; on Rameswaram I., Palk Strait; contains a great Dravidian temple, one of the Hindu holy places of pilgrimage; p. (1961) 6,801.

Ramgunga, R., India; trib. of R. Ganges, which it joins nr. Cawnpore; length 300 m.

Ramle, t., Israel; S. of Lydda; p. (1946) 16,380.

Ramleh, t., U.A.R.; E. of Alexandria; p. 52,000.

Ramme, t., Ringkjobing, Jutland, Denmark.

Ramnad, t., Tamil Nadu, India; on peninsula projecting towards Rameswaram I.

Râmnicu-Sârat, t., Romania; scene of several battles; petroleum; p. 19,267.

Râmnicu-Vâlcea, c., Romania; on R. Olt; cath.; monasteries; salt-mining; hot springs; p. 15,162.

Rampur, t., Uttar Pradesh, India; N.W. of Bareilly; damask, sugar, pottery; p. (1961) 135,407.

Ramree I., Bay of Bengal, Indian Ocean; off cst. Arakan, Lower Burma; 50 m. long.

Ramsbottom, t., urb. dist., Lancs, Eng.; on R. Irwell, 4 m. N. of Bury; cottons, bleaching, dyeing, engin., paper mftg., p. (1961) 13,813.

Ramsey, mkt. t., urb. dist., Hunts, Eng.; on edge of The Fens, 7 m. N. of St. Ives; engin., agr.; p. (1961) 5,697.

Ramsey, t., spt., I. of Man; on N.E. cst.; holiday resort; p. (1956) 4,621.

Ramsey, residtl. bor., N.J., U.S.A.; ctr. of dairying region; p. (1960) 9,527.

Ramsey L., off cst. of Pembroke, Wales.

Ramsgate, t., mun. bor., Kent, Eng.; on S. cst. of I. of Thanet; seaside resort; p. (estd. 1967) 38,810.

Rana Pratap Sagar, Rajasthan, India; nuclear power sta.

Rancagua, c., Colchagua prov., Chile; agr. tractors; p. (1961) 61,832.

Rance, R., Brittany, France; world's first major tidal hydro-elec. sta. (opened 1966).

Ranchi, hot-weather seat of govt., Bihar, India; technical institute; rice, tea, shellac; p. (1961) 140,253.

Rand, gold-mining dist., Transvaal, S. Africa (see Witwatersrand).

Randazzo, t., Catania, Sicily; on S. slopes of Mt. Etna; 2,474 ft. above sea-level; p. 16,325.

Randers, t., Denmark; medieval monastery; machin., foundries; exp. dairy produce; p. (1965) 42,923.        [10,000.

Ranenburg, t., U.S.S.R.; on R. Voronezh; p.

Rangiora, t., S.I., N.Z.; 20 m. N.W. of Christchurch; ctr. of lge. agr. dist.; p. (1961) 3,540.

Rangitaiki R., N.I., N.Z.; flows N. into Bay of Plenty.

Rangoon, c., cap., Burma; on E. arm of Irrawaddy delta; 2 caths., many mosques, temples and pagodas; gr. tr., and many impt. mnfs.; rice, oil, lumber; ivory and wood carving; textiles; p. (estd. 1965) 1,530,000.

Rangpur, t., E. Pakistan; on R. Ghaghat; jute; p. (1961) 40,600.        [p. (1961) 30,113.

Raniganj, t., W. Bengal, India; iron, coal-mines;

Rani-Nur, famous rock-cave, Khandgiri Hill, Puri dist., Orissa, India.

Rannoch, Loch, Perth, Scot.; 9 m. long, 1 m. wide; drained to R. Tay.

Rapallo, t., wat. pl., Liguria, N.W. Italy; on G. of Genoa, 22 m. E. of Genoa; most celebrated resort on Italian Riviera di Levante; p. (1946) 14,675.

Rapanui or Easter I., I., Pac. Oc.; W. of Chile.

Raphoe, par., co. Donegal, Ireland; cath.; mkt.; woollens, esp. tweeds; p. 2,600.

Rapid City, t., S.D., U.S.A.; p. (1960) 42,399.

Rappollsweiler, t., Bas Rhin, France; nr. Selestat; walled; known as "the pipers' town."

Raqqa, t., Syria; on R. Euphrates; p. 2,000.

Raritan, t., N.J., U.S.A.; p. (1960) 15,334.

Rarotonga, volcanic I., Pac. Oc.; cap. of Cook Is.; fruit canning; ch. t. and pt. Avarua; p. 7,368.

Ras-al-Had, O., E. extremity Arabia.

Ras-al-Khaima, t., on Persian G., st. of Bahrain, Arabia.

Rasgrad, t., Bulgaria; nr. Ruschuk, on R. Ak-Lom.

Ras Lanuf, oil terminal, on G. of Sidra, Libya; pipeline from Hofra oilfield.

Ras Mohammed, S. point, Sinai Peninsula.

Ras Tannura, spt., Nejd, Saudi Arabia; lge. oil-refinery.

Rashin, t., N. Korea; nr. U.S.S.R. frontier.

Rasskazovo, t., Tambov reg., U.S.S.R.; ironwks.; wheat; p. 25,168.

Rastrick, industl. t., W.R. Yorks, Eng.; on R. Calder, nr. Halifax.

Rat Is., group of Is., Aleutian Archipelago.

Ratack, chain of Is., Marshall Gr., Pac. Oc., parallel with Ralick chain.

Rathenow, t., Potsdam, E. Germany; on R. Havel; optical glass; p. (1963) 29,491.

Rathkeale, mkt. t., rural dist., Ireland; nr. Limerick; p. (rural dist. 1961) 11,726.

Rathlin, I., off Fair Head, N. Antrim, N. Ireland; 5 m. by 1 m.

Rathven, par., Banff, Scot.; farming, sandstone, limestone, slate; p. 15,404.

Ratibor, see Raciborz.

Ratingen, t., N. Rhine–Westphalia, Germany; N.E. of Düsseldorf; textiles, machin., glass; p. (1963) 37,200.

Ratisbon, see Regensburg.

Ratnagiri, pt., Maharashtra, India; all weather pt.; p. (1961) 31,091.

Ratnapura, t., Ceylon; graphite; p. 12,441.

Rattray Head, Aberdeen, Scot.    [(1966) 23,952.

Rauma, spt., Finland; on G. of Bothnia; p.

Raunds, t., urb. dist., Northants, Eng.; 5 m. N.E. of Wellingborough; p. (1961) 4,593.

Raurkela, t., Orissa, India; steel, tinplate, iron, fertilisers; p. (1961) 90,287.

Rava Ruskaya, t., Ukrainian S.S.R.; oil processing; quarrying; lignite; p. 12,000.

Ravenglass, t., Cumberland, Eng.; nr. mouth of R. Esk.

Ravenna, region, Emilia, Italy; a. 715 sq. m.; p. (1961) 328,969.

Ravenna, c., Emilia, N. Italy; on marshy plain, nr. the Adriatic, 45 m. E. of Bologna; cath., archiepiscopal palace, famous mosaics; agr. mkt. and ctr. for sugar-beet and beet sugar; sericulture; oil refining, petrol chemicals; p. (1961) 115,205.        [p. (1960) 10,913.

Ravenna, t., N.E. Ohio, U.S.A.; engin., rubber;

Ravensburg, t., Baden–Württemberg, Germany; nr. Konstanz; p. (1963) 31,800.

Ravenscraig, t., nr. Motherwell, Lanark., Scot.; hot strip steelmill; cold reduction mill at Gartcosh 8 m. away.        [Dewsbury.

Ravensthorpe, industl. t., W.R. Yorks, Eng.; nr.

Ravi, R., Punjab, India; trib. of the Chenab; used for irrigation; length 450 m.

Rawalpindi, div., W. Pakistan; between Lahore and Peshawar; p. (1961) 3,879,000.

Rawalpindi, t., Pakistan; on R. Leh, W. Pakistan; fortfd.; admin., comm. and rly. ctr.; rly. wks., brewing, foundries, oil refining, industl. gases; p. (1961) 340,175.

Rawlins, t., S. Wyo., U.S.A.; mkt., coal, oilfields, ranching; p. (1950) 7,415.

Rawmarsh, t., urb. dist., W.R. Yorks, Eng.; 2 m. N.E. of Rotherham; engin.; p. (1961) 19,603.

Rawson, spt., cap., Chubut terr., Argentina; S. of Valdes Peninsula; fish, fruit, livestock; p. 2,500.

Rawson, industl. t., nr. Leeds, Yorks, Eng.

Rawtenstall, t., mun. bor., Lancs, Eng.; on R. Irwell in ctr. of Rossendale Fells; cotton weaving; p. (estd. 1967) 22,630.

Ray, C., S.W. Newfoundland, Canada; beginning of Long Range, of which the highest peak is 2,673 ft.

Rayleigh, t., urb. dist., Essex, Eng.; 5 m. N.W. of Southend; light inds.; p. (estd. 1967) 24,850.

Raynham, t., S.E. Mass., U.S.A.; mkt. ctr. for agr. products, poultry, eggs; p. 2,141.

Razeim, L., Dobrodea, Romania; 25 m. long.

Ré or Rhe, I., W. cst. Charente-Inférieure, France; opp. a. Rochelle; salt mftg.; ch. t. St. Martin.

Reading, t., co. bor., Berks, Eng.; at confluence of Rs. Thames and Kennet; univ.; biscuits, engin., electronics, seed-growing and mkt. gardening, tin-box mftg., printing; p. (estd. 1967) 126,380.

Reading, t., Mass., U.S.A.; nr. Boston; p. (1960)

Reading, c., Penns., U.S.A.; on Schuylkill R.; ironwks.; p. (1960) 98,177.

Recanati, t., Macerata, Italy; industl.; p. 16,325.

Recife, spt., cap., Pernambuco, Brazil; univ.; exports sugar, cotton, coffee; called the Brazilian Venice; fine natural harbour; p. (1960) 788,580.

Recklinghausen, t., N. Rhine–Westphalia, W. Germany; nr. Dortmund; collieries, iron, machin., textiles, chemicals; p. (1963) 130,100.

Recôncavo, *dist.*, Bahia st., N.E. Brazil; surrounds bay at mouth of R. Paraguassu; intensive cultivation of sugar-cane, cotton, tobacco, rice, by Negro farmers; ch. ts. São Salvador, Cachoeira.

Red Basin, *see* Szechwan.

Red Bay, Antrim, N. Ireland.

Red Deer R., trib. of Saskatchewan R., Alberta, Canada. [gold.

Red Lake, *t.*, Ontario, Canada; nr. L. Winnipeg;

Red R. (China), *see* Song-koi.

Red R., U.S.A.; trib. Mississippi, flows from New Mexico through the Staked Plain; length, 1,600 m.

Red R. of the North, U.S.A.; rises in Minnesota and flows N., separating N. Dakota and Minnesota, U.S.A., and thence into Manitoba, Canada, to join Assiniboine R.; length 650 m.

Red Sea, *arm of the sea* separating Arabia from Africa; connects with the Indian Ocean by the Straits of Bab-el-Mandeb; length 1,400 m., greatest width 230 m.

Red Wing, *c.*, Minn., U.S.A.; on the Mississippi R., at head of L. Pepin; flour mills, grain tr.; p. (1960) 10,528.

Redbank, *t.*, N.J., U.S.A.; summer resort, fishing, mkt. gardens, light mnfs.; p. (1960) 12,482.

Redbridge, *outer bor.*, E. London, Eng.; incorporating former bors. of Ilford, Wanstead and Woodford, Chigwell (Hainault Estate), Dagenham (N. Chadwell Heath ward); mainly residtl.; p. (1966) 247,000.

Redcar, *t.*, *mun. bor.*, N.R. Yorks, Eng.; on E. cst.. nr. mouth of R. Tees; seaside resort; steel wks., engin., slag bricks, toys; p. (1961) 31,460. [p. (1966) 26,999.

Redcliffe, *t.*, Queensland, Australia; holiday t.;

Redding, *c.*, N. Cal., U.S.A.; lumber, mining, agr.; tourists; p. (1960) 12,773.

Redditch, *t.*, *urb. dist.*, Worcester, Eng.; 12 m. S. of Birmingham; needles, fish tackle, cycles, springs, aluminium alloys, chromium and cadmium plating; designated "New Town" 1964; p. (estd. 1967) 36,900.

Rede, *R.*, Northumberland, Eng.; trib. of R. Tyne.

Redhill, *t.*, Surrey, Eng.; at foot of N. Downs, adjoining Reigate; residtl.; refractory sands.

Redlands, *t.*, Cal., U.S.A.; p. (1960) 26,829.

Redonda, *I.*, Leeward group, Caribbean Sea; between Montserrat and Nevis.

Redondela, *t.*, Pontevedra, Spain; on Vigo estuary; old feudal castle; p. (1957) 17,024.

Redruth, *t.*, part of Camborne–Redruth urb. dist., Cornwall, Eng.; tin-mine dist., chemicals, engin., textiles; p. (1961) (with Camborne) 36,090.

·Redwood City, *c.*, W. Cal., U.S.A.; shipbldg., saltwks.; exp. sequoia; p. (1960) 46,290.

Ree, Lough, L., Ireland; between Roscommon, Longford and Westmeath, an extension of R. Shannon; 17 m. long. [14,250.

Regello, *t.*, Val d'Arno, Italy; nr. Florence; p.

Regensburg (Ratisbon), *c.*, Bavaria, Germany; N.E. of Munich on R. Danube; cath.; brewing, machin., wood, chemicals; p. (1963) 125,300.

Reggio di Calabria, *c.*, Calabria, Italy; on Strait of Messina; cath.; perfumes, silks, terracotta; train ferry to Messina (Sicily); has suffered from earthquakes; p. (1961) 150,334.

Reggio nell' Emilia, *c.*, *cap.*, Emilia-Romagna, Italy; at N. foot of Apennines, 40 m. N.W. of Bologna; locomotives, aircraft; fine church of the Madonna della Ghiara; sericulture, cheese-mkg.; p. (1961) 116,515.

Regina, *t.*, *cap.*, Saskatchewan, Canada; foundries, oil-wks., sawmills; helium gas exp.; p. (1961) 112,141.

Region Oriental, Ecuador; a. 219,095 sq. m.; p. 295,200; consists of provs.—Napo Pastaza and Santiago Zamora; about 110,000 sq. m. of region inhabited.

Regla, *t.*, Cuba, W. Indies; nr. Havana; p. 23,037.

Rehoboth, *t.*, S.W Africa; salt. mining, cattle; p. 9,727. [p. *c.* 10,500.

Rehovoth, Israel; agr. (citrus) and scientific ctr.;

Reichenbach, *t.*, Karl-Marx-Stadt, E. Germany; paper, metals; p. (1963) 29,189.

Reichenberg, *see* Liberec.

Reidsville, *t.*, N.C., U.S.A.; tobacco mkt., mnfs., textiles, turpentine; p. (1960) 14,267.

Reigate, *mkt. t.*, *mun. bor.*, Surrey, Eng.; at foot of N. Downs, 5 m. E. of Dorking; residtl.; fuller's earth, freestone; p. (estd. 1967) 56,340.

Reims, *t.*, Marne, France; on R. Vesle; famous Gothic cath.; univ.; champagne ctr., cloth factories, woollen inds. and tr., dye wks.; p. (1962) 138,576.

Reindeer L., Saskatchewan, Canada.

Rembang, *t.*, Java; oil, teak, rubber; p. 13,791.

Remscheid, *t.*, N. Rhine–Westphalia, Germany; nr. Düsseldorf; cutlery. machin., textiles; p. (1963) 128,600.

Renaix (Ronse), *t.*, Belgium; nr. Ghent; linen, woollens; dyeing, bleaching; p. (1962) 25,122.

Rendsburg, *t.*, Schleswig-Holstein, Germany; on N. Sea–Baltic Canal; metals, elec. goods, shipbldg.; p. (1963) 35,100.

Renfrew, *maritime co.*, W. Scot.; S. of R. Clyde; agr., mftg. and comm., coal, iron, shipbldg., machin., printing; ch. industl. ctrs. Paisley and Greenock; a. 245 sq. m.; p. (1961) 338,815.

Renfrew, *co. t.*, *burgh*, Renfrew, Scot.; nr. R. Clyde, 5 m. W. of Glasgow; p. (1961) 17,946.

Renfrew, *t.*, Ontario, Canada; p. (1961) 8,935.

Renmark, *t.*, S. Australia; on Murray R.; ctr. of fruit-growing dist., wine mkg.; p. (1966) 3,047.

Rennes, *c.*, *cap.*, Ille-et-Vilaine, France; 40 m. S. of St Malo; univ.; dairying and agr. dist.; farm implements, sail-cloth, oil refining nearby; p. (1962) 157,692.

Reno, *t.*, Nevada, U.S.A.; seat of Univ. of Nevada; st. agr. college; famous for easy divorce procedure; p. (1960) 51,470.

Rensselaer, *t.*, N.Y., U.S.A.; on R. Hudson facing Albany; p. (1960) 10,506.

Repton, *rural dist.*, Derbyshire, Eng.; agr., clay, coal-mining, sanitary ware; p. 29,780.

Republican Fork or Pawnee, *R.*, trib. of Kansas R., Col., U.S.A.; length 550 m.

Repulse Bay, on S. side of Melville Peninsula, N. Canada.

Requeña, *t.*, Valencia, Spain; sulphur springs of Fuentepodida; p. (1957) 20,253.

Resht (Rasht), *c.*, Iran; prov. cap. Gilan, in a. producing rice, cotton, silk; carpets; nearby Pahlevi serves as pt.; p. (1967) 353,172.

Resina, *t.*, S. Italy; on Bay of Naples at W. foot of Vesuvius; p. (1961) 45,148.

Resistencia, *t.*, *cap.*, Chaco, Argentina; cotton, quebracho, cattle; p. (1960) 94,000.

Resolution, *t.*, N.W. Terr., Canada; on S. shore of Gr. Slave L.

Resolution I., off S.W. cst. of S.I., New Zealand.

Resolution Is. (Brit.), N. of Labrador, at entrance Hudson Strait, Franklin, Canada.

Resolven, *t.*, N. Glamorgan, Wales, on R. Neath 6 m. N.E. of Neath; aluminium; p. (1951) 4,353.

Retalhulen, *t.*, *cap.*, R. dep., Guatemala, Central America; coffee, sugar; p. (1960) 29,361.

Rethymnon, *prefecture*, I. of Crete; cap. Rethymnon; p. (1961) 69,843. [14,999.

Rethymnon, *cap.*, Rethymnon, Crete; p. (1961)

Réunion. Ile de la (formerly Bourbon), Fr. I.. Indian Ocean; between Mauritius and Malagasy; sugar growing; cap. St. Denis; a. 970 sq. m.; p. (estd. 1965) 387,000.

Reus, *t.*, Tarragona, Spain; textiles, leather, soap; p. (1957) 35,950.

Reuss, R., Switzerland; flows N. from the St. Gotthard Pass through L. Lucerne, joining Aar R. near Brugg; length 98 m.

Reutlingen, *t.*, Baden-Württemberg, Germany; S. of Stuttgart; textiles, metals, machin., leather; p. (1963) 70,600.

Reval, *see* Tallin.

Revda, *t.*, R.S.F.S.R.; in Urals, 29 m. W. of Sverdlovsk; iron, copper, chemicals; p. (1959) 55,000.

Revere, *t.*, Mass., U.S.A.; sub. of Boston; resort; p. (1960) 40,080.

Revilla Gigedo Is., *gr. of Is.*, belonging to Mexico, Pac. Oc.; ch. Is., Socorro, San Benito.

Rewa, *t.*, Madhya Pradesh, India; rice, coal; p. (1961) 43,065.

Rewari, *t.*, Punjab, India; S.W. of Delhi; turban and brass-ware mnfs.; p. (1961) 36,994.

Reykjavik, *c.*, *cap.*, Iceland; on S.W. cst.; univ., cath.; exp. fish, skins, wool; aluminium smelting at Straumsvik nearby; p. (1964) 87,000.

Reynella-Port Noarlunga, *t.*, S. Australia; abattoirs, wine mkg.; p. (1966) 11,775.

Rezayeh, *c.*, Iran; prov. cap. W. Azarbayejan; p. (1967) 291,369.

Rezé, *t.*, Loire Atlantique,France; p.(1954) 19,000.

Rheine, *t.*, N. Rhine–Westphalia, Germany; on R. Ems; textiles, machin.; p. (1963) 46,400.

Rheinhausen, *t.*, N. Rhine–Westphalia, Germany; on R. Rhine; S. of Duisburg; coal-mining, iron, textiles; p. (1963) 70,500.

Rheinkamp (Repelen-Baerl before 1950), *t.*, N. Rhine–Westphalia, Germany; on R. Rhine, N.W. of Duisberg; coal-mng.; p. (1963) 38,900.

Rheydt, *t.*, N. Rhine–Westphalia, Germany; W. of Düsseldorf; textiles, machin., rly. junction; p. (1963) 96,000.

Rhin (Bas), *dep.*, N.E. France; cap. Strasbourg; a. 1,848 sq. m.; p. (1962) 770,150.

Rhin (Haut), *dep.*, N.E. France; cap. Colmar; a. 1,354 sq. m.; p. (1962) 547,920.

Rhine, *R.*, rises in Switzerland, can. Grisons, passes through L. Constance, skirts Baden, traverses Hesse, Rhineland, and the Neth., flowing to N. Sea by two arms, Oude Rijn and the Waal (the latter discharging finally by the Maas); famous for its beauty, especially between Bonn and Bingen; ch. falls at Schaffhausen; once a natural barrier between E. and W. Europe, the Rhine is now spanned by 30 rly. bridges, and its navigation declared free in 1868; length 800 m.

Rhineland Palatinate (Rheinland-Pfalz), *Land*, Germany; a. 7,665 sq. m.; cap. Mainz; p. (1961) 3,417,000.

Rhinns (Rins), *peninsula*, on W. cst. Islay I., Inner Hebrides, Scot.; lighthouse.

Rhio-Lingga Archipelago, *gr. of Is.*, Indonesia; mainly in Malacca Strait; a. 12,235 sq. m.

Rhode Island, *st.*, New England, U.S.A.; washed by the Atlantic, and surrounded by Massachusetts and Connecticut; divided by Narragansett Bay, with many islands, lgst. being that from which the st. takes its name; jewellery, silverware, textiles, rubber, granite; agr., fisheries; cap. Providence; a. 1,214 sq. m.; p. (1960) 859,488.

Rhodes (Rhodos), *I.*, Dodecanese Is.; off S.W. cst., Anatolia, belonging to Greece; cap. R.; figs, oranges, grapes; p. (1940) 61,791.

Rhodes, *t., cap.*, I. of Rhodes, Greece; on N.E. cst.; p. (1951) 24,186.

Rhodesia, *self-gov. Brit. col.* central Africa; tobacco, maize, fruit, cattle; gold, coal, asbestos, chrome ore, magnesite; crystalline graphite ore deposits being developed; cap. Salisbury; a. 150,333 sq. m.; p. (estd. 1965) 4,210,000.

Rhodope Mtns., *range*, S. Bulgaria; rise to 10,200 ft. [tīni; p. (1961) 109,194.

Rhodopi, *prefecture*, Thrace, Greece; cap. Komo-

Rhöngebirge, *mtn. gr.*, Thuringia, Germany; highest peak 3,100 ft.

Rhondda, *t., urb. dist.*, Glamorgan, Wales; in narrow Rhondda valley, 7 m. N.W. of Pontypridd; coal-mining; p. (1961) 100,314.

Rhône, *R.*, Switzerland and France; rising in the Rhône glacier of the St. Gotthard mtn. gr., and flowing through the L. of Geneva and E. France to the G. of Lyons in the Mediterranean; length 507 m.; power stas. at Sion and Geneva; canals, dams, locks and power stas. form part of French Rhône Valley project (1937–72).

Rhône, *dep.*, S.E. France; drained by R. Rhône, and its trib. R. Saône, which unite at Lyons; agr., grain, potatoes, wine; vine-growing, many mnfs., silks, textiles; cap. Lyons; a. 1,104 sq. m.; p. (1962) 1,116,664.

Rhyl, *t., urb. dist.*, Flint, N. Wales; between Bangor and Chester, at entrance Vale of Clwyd; resort; furniture mkg.; p. (1961) 21,825.

Rhymney, *t., urb. dist.*, Monmouth, Eng.; on R. Rhymney, 4 m. E. of Merthyr Tydfil; mining; p. (1961) 8,859. [of comm.

Rialto, *I.* and *dist.*, on Grand Canal, Venice; ctr.

Ribadesella, *spt.*, Spain; W. of Santander; iron mines; p. (1957) 7,692.

Ribatejo, *prov.*, Portugal; a. 2,794 sq. m.; p. (1950) 459,853.

Ribe, *mkt. t.*, Jutland, S. Denmark; on W. cst.; iron wks.; p. (1960) 7,809.

Ribble, *R.*, Yorks and Lancs, Eng.; followed by main rly. route Leeds to Carlisle; length 75 m.

Ribeira, *t.*, Galicia, Spain; on peninsula of Arosa estuary; agr., cattle-rearing, fishing.

Ribeirão Preto, *c.*, S.E. Brazil; mkt. in rich agr. a. esp. coffee, cotton, sugar; p. (1960) 116,153.

Riberalta, *R. on.*, Colonia Terr., Bolivia, S. America; on R. Beni above rapids which limit navigation to upper course; collecting ctr. for wild rubber.

Richborough, *pt.*, Kent, Eng.; at mouth of R.

Stour; pt. was derelict but now being developed as a private pt.; chemicals, antibiotics.

Richelieu or Chambly, *R.*, Quebec, Canada; flows from L. Champlain to the St. Lawrence R. at L. St. Peter; length 80 m.

Richmond-upon-Thames, *outer bor.*, Greater London, Eng.; inc. former bors. of Barnes, Richmond and Twickenham; industl. and residtl.; beautiful park and riverside scenery; p (1966) 180,000.

Richmond, *t., mun. bor.*, N.R. Yorks, Eng.; at E. foot of Pennines on R. Swale; p. (estd. 1967) 7,300. [71,854.

Richmond, *t.*, Cal., U.S.A.; oil refining; p. (1960)

Richmond, *c.*, Ind., U.S.A.; on R. Whitewater; mnfs.; p. (1960) 44,149.

Richmond, *c.*, Ky., U.S.A.; in tobacco-growing and horse-rearing region; p. (1960) 12,168.

Richmond, one of the five bors. of New York City, U.S.A.; p. (1957) 210,146.

Richmond, *c., cap.*, Va., U.S.A.; on falls on R. James; gr. tobacco mftg. ctr. and mart; chemicals, iron and steel, lumber; p. (1960) 219,958.

Rickmansworth, *mkt. t., urb. dist.*, Herts, Eng.; at confluence of Rs. Colne and Chess, 3 m. S.W. of Watford; paper, brewing; residtl.; p. (estd. 1967) 30,290.

Rideau Canal, Canada; from Ottawa R., to Kingston on L. Ontario; length 132 m.

Ridgefield, *t.*, N.J., U.S.A.; p. (1960) 10,788.

Ridgewood, *t.*, N.J., U.S.A.; p. (1960) 25,391.

Riesa, *t.*, Dresden, E. Germany; on R. Elbe, nr. Meissen; steel wks., sawmills; p. (1963) 38,929.

Riesengebirge, *mtns.*, Germany; (Czech Krkonose, Polish Karkonosze).

Riesi, *t.*, Sicily, Italy; industl.; p. 20,200.

Rieti, *t.*, Perugia, Italy; an ancient Sabine t. in famous fertile dist.; mnfs.; p. (1961) 34,580.

Riff (Er Rif), *mtns.*, Morocco, N.W. Africa; extend E. along N. African cst. for 200 m. from Straits of Gibraltar; inaccessible and economically unattractive, terr. of semi-nomadic tribes; rises to over 7,000 ft. in many places.

Riga, *cap.*, Latvian S.S.R.; at head of G. of Riga; gr. industl. activity; machin., glass, paper, cottons; rly. and shipbldg., exp. wheat, flax, hemp, dairy produce; p. (1967) 666,000.

Rigi, *mtn.*, nr. L. Lucerne, Switzerland; alt. 5,905 ft.

Rijeka-Susak, *t.*, Jugoslavia; formerly Fiume; belonged to Austria-Hungary before First World War, then to Italy; ceded to Jugoslavia by Italy after Second World War; rival pt. to Trieste; petrol refining, tobacco, chemicals, hydro-elec., shipbldg.; p. (1959) 87,000.

Rimac, *R.*, Lima dep., Peru; S. America; rises in W. cordillera of Andes and flows W. to Pac. Oc.; provides water for irrigation and for c. of Lima; length 75 m.

Rimini, *t.*, Emilia, Italy; on the Adriatic cst.; mineral springs, sea-bathing, thriving inds.; p. (1961) 92,912.

Rimnic, *t.*, Romania; on R. Rimnic. nr. Bucharest; industl; p. (1963) 22,242.

Rimouski, *t.*, Quebec, Canada; on S. bank St. Lawrence R.; lumber; tourists; p. (1961) 17,739.

Ringerike, *c.*, Buskerud, Norway; new c. 25 m. N.W. of Oslo and inc. former t. of Hönefoss; p. (1965) 27,900.

Ringköbing Fjord, *inlet*, W. cst. Jutland, Denmark.

Ringwood and Fordingbridge, *mkt. t., rural dist.*, Hants, Eng.; on R. Avon, nr. Christchurch; p. (rural dist. 1951) 23,908.

Rio Branco, *R.*, Brazil; prov. Baia, trib. of Rio Grande; length 120 m.

Rio Branco, *R.*, N. Brazil; flowing to Rio Negro; length 370 m. [47,882.

Rio Branco, *terr.*, Brazil; cap. Boa Vista; a. 82,749 sq. m.; p. (1960) 29,489.

Rio Cuarto, *t.*, Cordoba prov., Argentina; agr. ctr.; p. (1960) 70,000. [length 500 m.

Rio das Mortes, *R.*, Brazil; trib. of the Araguay.

Rio de Janeiro, *maritime st.*, Brazil; a. 16,443 sq. m.; coffee plantations, sugar, cotton, tobacco; thorium; cap. Niterói; p. (1960) 3,402,728.

Rio de Janeiro, *c., spt.*, former fed. cap. Brazil; on Bay of Rio de Janeiro; many fine bdgs., flourishing tr. and inds.; rly. wks.; shipyards; mnfs. iron, steel, cement, textiles, sugar, tyres, pharmaceutics, china, sheet glass; p. (1960) 3,307,163.

Rio de la Plata, *see* Plate R.

Rio de Oro, *prov.*, Spanish Sahara; a. 70,000 sq. m.

Rio de San Juan, *R.*, Utah, New Mexico and Colorado, U.S.A.; length 350 m. [400 m.

Rio Dulce, *R.*, Santiago st., Argentina; length

Rio Grande, *headstream* of the R. Paraná, Brazil.

Rio Grande City, *t.*, S. Texas, U.S.A.; on Rio Grande R.; mkt., agr., oil, natural gas; p. (1960) *5,835*. [Pacific.

Rio Grande de Santiago, *R.*, Mexico; flows into the

Rio Grande del Norte, *R.*, flows from st. of Colorado through New Mexico to the G. of Mexico; forms bdy. between Texas, U.S.A. and Mexico; length 1,800 m.

Rio Grande do Norte, *st.*, Brazil; sugar, cotton, cattle-rearing; cap. Natal; a. 20,482 sq. m.; p. (1960) *1,157,258*.

Rio Grande do Sul, *st.*, S. Brazil; cap. Porto Alegre; a. 109,067 sq. m.; p. (1960) *5,448,323*.

Rio Grande do Sul, *spt.*, Brazil; textiles, oil refining; cattle, agr.; p. *45,000*.

Rio Muni, Equatorial Guinea, W. Africa, on cst. between Cameroun and Congo; with Fernando Po and other Is. forms Equatorial Guinea; ch. t. Bata; cacao, coffee, bananas, timber; a. 10,040 sq. m.; p. (1968) *183,000* inc. *3,000* Europeans.

Rio Negro, *R.*, Argentina; rises in the Andes, and flows through the terr. of Rio Negro to the Atlantic; length 650 m.

Rio Negro, *prov.*, Argentina; S. of Pampa; cap. Viedma; cattle-rearing region; a. 77,610 sq. m.; p. (1960) *193,000*.

Rio Negro, *R.*, S. America; rises in Colombia, and flows through N. Brazil to the Amazon; length 1,350 m.

Rio Negro, *dep.*, Uruguay; cap. Fray Bentos; a. 3,269 sq. m.; p. (1953) *51,954*.

Rio Piedras, *t.*, Puerto Rico, W. Indies; univ.; merged with San Juan 1951.

Rio Salada, *R.*, Argentina; rises in the Andes, and flows S.E. to R. Paraná, at Buenos Aires; length 1,000 m.

Rio Tinto, *t.*, Spain; at W. end of Sierra Morena, 40 m. N.E. of Huelva; lead- and copper-mines; p. (1957) *10,000*.

Riobamba, *c.*, Chimborazo, Ecuador; on R. St. Juan; woollens, cotton gds., cement, ceramics; Inca palace ruins; p. (estd. 1960) *35,099*.

Rioja, *region*, N. Spain, Upper Ebro; famous for wines, orange groves; ch. ctr. Logroño.

Rioja, La, *prov.*, Argentina; gold- and copper-mines; cap. La Rioja; a. 33,394 sq. m.; p. (1960) *128,000*.

Riom, *t.*, Puy-de-Dôme, France; nr. Clermont Ferrand; p. (1962) *15,416*.

Rion, *R.*, Georgian S.S.R.; flows from Caucasus to Black Sea; lower half navig.; hydro-elec. sta. at Kutais. (In Greek mythology the R. Phasis of the Argonauts.)

Rionero, *t.*, Potenza prov., S. Italy; nr. Melfi; industl.; p. *12,025*.

Ripley, *mkt. t.*, *urb. dist.*, Derby, Eng.; 7 m. N.E. of Derby; coal, iron, heavy engin., bricks, agr. implements; p. (1961) *17,601*.

Ripley, *t.*, W. Tenn., U.S.A.; lumbering; veneer; cottonseed processing; p. (1960) *3,782*.

Ripon, *c.*, *mun. bor.*, W.R. Yorks, Eng.; on R. Ure; cath.; paint, varnish, prefabricated concrete structures; p. (estd. 1967) *11,520*.

Ripon, *t.*, Wis., U.S.A., on Green L., p. (1950) *5,619*.

Ripon Falls, *see* Jinja.

Riposto, *t.*, Sicily, Italy; on E. cst. nr. Taormina; wine export; p. *10,725*.

Ripponden, *urb. dist.*, W.R. Yorks, Eng.; nr. Halifax; p. (1961) *5,765*.

Risca, *t.*, *urb. dist.*, Monmouth, Eng.; on R. Ebbw, 5 m. N.W. of Newport; coal, iron and steel, bricks, tiles, plastics; p. (1961) *14,008*.

Rishton, *t.*, *urb. dist.*, Lancs, Eng.; at N. foot of Rossendale Fells, 4 m. N.E. of Blackburn; p. (1961) *5,431*.

Risley, nr. Warrington, Lancs., Eng.; headquarters of Engineering Group of U.K. Atomic Energy Authority; site of Manchester's New t.; proposed p. *50,000*.

Riva, *t.*, Trentino, Italy; battle zone in First World War, Nov.–Dec. 1915; p. *12,950*.

Rivas, *spt.*, Nicaragua, Central America; p. (1960) *19,159*.

Rive-de-Gier, *t.*, Loire, France; on R. Gier, nr. Lyons; mining ctr.; p. (1962) *16,677*.

Rivera, *dep.*, Uruguay; cap. Rivera; a. 3,793 sq. m.; p. (1953) *91,740*.

Riverina, *pastoral cty.*, N.S.W., Australia; between Lachlan-Murrumbidgee and Murray Rs.; sheep, agr. with irrigation; gold, coal; ch. ts., Wagga Wagga, Albury; a. 26,600 sq. m.

River Rouge, *t.*, Mich., U.S.A.; p. (1960) *18,147*.

Riverside, *t.*, Cal., U.S.A.; p. (1960) *84,332*.

Riverside, *t.*, N.J., U.S.A.; p. (1960) *8,474*.

Riverside, *t.*, Ontario, Canada; p. (1961) *13,089*.

Riviera, the belt of cst. between the mtns. of the shore of the G. of Genoa, N. Italy, from Spezia to Nice; picturesque scenery, sheltered, mild climate; fashionable health resort.

Riyadh, *t.*, *cap.*, Saudi Arabia; 230 m. inland from Persian G.; palace; univ.; p. (estd.) *300,000*.

Rizal, *prov.*, *t.*, central Luzon, Philippine Is.; chiefly agr.; food processing, steel mill, cement; a. 791 sq. m.; p. of t. (1960) *132,673*.

Rize, *t.*, Turkey; nr. Trabzon, on Black Sea; p. (1965) *27,069*.

Rjukan, *t.*, Telemark, S. Norway; 35 m. N.W. of Notodden, impt. nitrate factories; p. (1961) *5,637*.

Road Town, *spt. cap.*, Tortola and Virgin Is.; p. (1960) *900*.

Roanne, *t.*, Loire, France; nr. St. Etienne; textile, cottons, woollens, silk; p. (1962) *53,203*.

Roanoke, *I.*, off cst. N.C., U.S.A.; 13 m. long.

Roanoke, *R.*, Va., and N.C., U.S.A.; flows into Albemarle Sound; length 230 m.

Roanoke, *t.*, Ala. U.S.A.; cotton mnfs., clothes; p. (1960) *5,283*. [wks.; p. (1960) *97,110*.

Roanoke, *c.*, S.W. Va., U.S.A.; on R. R.; iron-

Roaring Creek, Brit. Honduras, C. America; site of new cap. 50 m. inland, at junction of W. Highway with Hummingbird Highway.

Roatan Is., Honduras, in G. of H.

Robin Hood's Bay, *picturesque inlet with fishing vil. on cst.*, N.R. Yorks, Eng.; nr. Whitby.

Robson, Mt., Alberta, Canada, 12,972 ft.

Roca, C. da, most W. point of estuary of R. Tagus, Portugal.

Roch, *R.*, Lancs, Eng.; rises in E. of Rossendale Fells, central Pennines, flows S.W. into R. Irwell nr. Bury; with R. Calder provides relatively easy route across Pennines from Leeds to Manchester; used by rail, road, canal; length approx. 20 m.

Rocha, *dep.*, Uruguay; a. 4,280 sq. m.; cap. Rocha; p. (1953) *86,334*.

Rochdale, *t.*, *co. bor.*, Lancs, Eng.; at S. foot of Rossendale Fells, on R. Roch; textiles, textile engin., rayon spinning, elec. engin.; co-operative movement started here, 1844; p. (estd. 1967) *86,960*.

Rochefort, *t.*, S. Belgium; p. (1962) *3,996*.

Rochefort, *fortfd. pt.*, Charente-Maritime, France; with arsenal and sm. cst. tr.; famous cheese; p. (1962) *33,584*.

Rochelle, La, *fortfd. spt.*, *cap.*, Charente-Maritime, France; on Bay of Biscay; shipbldg., chemical wks., fisheries; p. (1962) *68,445*.

Roches Point, E. side of Cork harbour, Co. Cork, Ireland.

Rochester, *c.*, *mun. bor.*, Kent, Eng.; on R. Medway, adjoining Chatham; cath., cas.; aeronautical, elec. and mechanical engin., paint, varnish; p. (estd. 1967) *55,100*.

Rochester, *c.*, Minn., U.S.A.; in grain-growing dist.; p. (1960) *40,663*.

Rochester, *t.*, N.H., U.S.A.; on Salmon Falls and Cocheco Rs.; boot factories; p. (1960) *15,927*.

Rochester, *c.*, N.Y., U.S.A.; on Genesee R.; univ.; hydro-elec. power; cameras, films, optical instruments, thermometers, electronic equipment; p. (1960) *318,611*.

Roche-sur-Yon, La, *t.*, Vendée, France; on R. Yon; cas.; called formerly Bourbon Napoleonville; p. (1962) *25,456*.

Rochford, *t.*, *rural dist.*, Essex, Eng.; 3 m. N. of Southend; timber wharves, boat bldg., brick mkg.; p. (rural dist. 1961) *30,306*.

Rockall, *sm. I.*, N. Atl. Oc.; lies 200 m. W. of Outer Hebrides; forms highest part of submarine bank which forms good fishing-ground; uninhabited. Annexed by Britain, 1955.

Rockall Deep, *submarine trench*, N. Atl. Oc., between N.W. Ireland and Rockall I.; depth exceeds 1,600 fathoms.

Rockaway, *bor.*, N.J., U.S.A.; iron founding and products; textiles, leather; p. (1960) *5,413*.

Rockaway Beach, *summer resort*, on sandbar of

Long I.; now incorporated with Queens, one of the 5 bors. of New York City, U.S.A.

Rockford, *c.*, Ill., U.S.A.; machin. and furniture mftg.; p. (1960) *126,706.*

Rockhampton, *c., pt.,* Queensland, Australia; on R. Fitzroy; comm. cap. of Central Queensland; meat-preserving; fruit canning; cotton ginning; rly. wks.; p. (1966) *45,349.*

Rock Hill, *c.* S.C., U.S.A.; industl.; p. (1960) *29,404.*

Rockingham, *t.,* N.C., U.S.A.; cotton mnfs., paper, lumbering, peaches; p. (1950) *3,356.*

Rock Island, *c.,* Ill., U.S.A.; on R. Mississippi; lumbering, flour mills, glass, farm implements; elec. equipment; p. (1960) *51,863.*

Rockland, *c., spt.,* Ma., U.S.A.; on Penobscot Bay; shipbldg., granite quarrying; p. (1950) *9,234.*

Rockland, *t.,* Mass., U.S.A.; shoemkg., engin.; p. (1960) *13,080.*

Rock River, Wis., U.S.A.; trib. of the Mississippi; length 375 m.

Rockville, *c.,* Conn., U.S.A.; on Hockanum R.; silks, woollens; p. (1960) *9,478.*

Rocky Mount, *t.,* N.C., U.S.A.; p. (1960) *32,147.*

Rocky Mountains, *extensive chain,* N. America; extending along the W. portions of Canada and the U.S.A. from Alaska to Mexico; the highest accurately measured point in the U.S.A. system is Mt. Massive (14,418 ft.); other high peaks are Mt. Elbert (14,431 ft.), Blanca Peak (14,390 ft.), Mt. Harvard (14,399 ft.), La Plata Peak (14,340 ft.), and Mt. Uncompahgre (14,306 ft.). Mt. St. Elias, in Alaska, is computed to be 18,008 ft. high, and was long held to be the highest peak in N. America, but is now known to be surpassed by the adjacent Mt. Logan (19,850 ft.) and by Mt. Orizaba (18,701 ft.) in Mexico.

Rodas, *mun.,* Cuba; sugar; p. *21,288.*

Rödby, *t.,* Denmark; on S. cst. of Lolland; p. (1960) *3,551.*

Rodewisch, *t.,* Karl-Marx-Stadt, E. Germany; engin., textiles; p. (1963) *12,458.*

Rodez, *t., cap.,* Aveyron, France; on R. Aveyron; cath.; woollens; p. (1962) *24,352.*

Rodosto, *see* Tekirdag.

Rodriguez, *I.,* British dependency of Mauritius, Indian Ocean; 350 m. N.E. of Mauritius; principal exp., cattle, beans, salt, fish and goats; 42 sq. m.; p. (estd. 1968) *20,000.*

Roebling, *t.,* N.J., U.S.A.; established by steel-cable mkg. company; p. (1960) *3,272.*

Roermond, *t.,* Limburg, Neth.; on R. Maas; minster; paper, beer, cloth; p. (1967) *36,842.*

Roeselare, *t.,* W. Flanders, Belgium; on R. Lys, nr. Courtrai, cotton, linen, lace; p. (1962) *35,662.*

Roes Welcome, channel between Southampton I. and N.W. Terr. Canada.

Rogaland, *co.,* Norway; a. 3,546 sq. m.; p. (1963) *244,103.*

Rogers, *t.,* Ark., U.S.A.; fruit, vegs.; tourists; p. (1960) *5,700.*

Rogerstone, *t.,* S. Monmouth, Eng., on R. Ebbw 3 m. W. of Newport; aluminium; p. (1951) *4,453.*

Rohtak, *t.,* Punjab, India; mkt., cotton textiles; fortifications; p. (1961) *88,193.*

Rokko, *O.,* Honshu, Japan; jutting into Sea of Japan.

Rolphton, Ontario, Canada; nuclear power plant.

Roma, *t.,* Queensland, Australia; in agr. dist. nr. Mt. Horrible; natural gas; oil; p. (1966) *6,000.*

Roman, *t.,* Romania; on R. Moldava; cath.; p. (1963) *45,930.*

Romania, *rep.,* E. Europe; bounded by U.S.S.R., Hungary, Jugoslavia and Bulgaria, consisting of provs. of Oltena, Muntenia (Wallachia), Dobrogea (Dobruja), Moldova (Moldavia), S. Bucovina, Transylvania, Banat, Crisana and Maramures; plain drained by Danube and tribs. Prut, Siret, Dambovita, Olt Jiu; except Transylvania, mountainous, Carpathians, Transylvanian Alps; very warm summers, severe winters, rainfall moderate, chiefly in summer; agr., maize, wheat, barley, oats; sheep, cattle, pigs, horses; forests, timber; minerals, petroleum, natural gas, lignite, copper, salt; flour-milling, brewing, distilling, oil-refining, chemicals; cap. Bucharest; a. 91,671 sq. m.; p. (1963) *18,813,131.*

Romans, *t.,* Drôme, France; on R. Isère; formerly seat of ancient abbey; p. (1962) *27,662.*

Romblon Is., *prov.,* of Philippine Is.; low, fertile;

ch. crops, abaca and copra; gold, marble; a. 512 sq. m.; p. (1960) *16,700.*

Rome, *c., cap.,* Italy; on R. Tiber, 15 m. from the sea; one of the most famous cities in the world; ctr. of the Roman Catholic Church and former cap. of the greatest st. in the ancient world; situated on the original " seven hills " of the old Roman metropolis, and in the valleys between, along the R.; contains the celebrated cath. ch. of St. Peter, in the Vatican City, many historical monuments, a univ. and several institutions devoted to art and learning; created cap. of mod. United Italy in 1871; mnfs. and tr.; p. (1965) *2,514,000.*

Rome, *c.,* Ga., U.S.A.; on Coosa R.; in cotton region; p. (1960) *32,226.*

Rome, *c.,* N.Y., U.S.A.; on the Mohawk R.; dairying ctr.; p. (1960) *51,646.*

Romford, *former mkt. t., mun. bor.,* Essex, Eng.; 12 m. E. of London; now inc. in Havering bor. Greater London; brewing, light inds.; p. (1961) *114,584.*

Romilly-sur-Seine, *t.,* Aube, France; nr. Troyes; textile factories; p. (1962) *15,966.*

Romney, *see* New Romney.

Romney Marsh, *coastal marsh,* Kent, Eng.; formed by blocking of R. Rother by shingle spit of Dungeness which extends from Rye to Hythe; now largely drained; pastures for special Romney Marsh breed of sheep; a. 50 sq. m.

Romsdal, Möre Og, *dist.* Norway; cap. Molde; a. 5,812 sq. m.; p. (1961) *212,020.*

Romsey, *mun. bor.,* Hants, Eng.; on R. Test, 8½ m. N.W. of Southampton; mkt. ctr.; p. (estd. 1967) *7,660;* rural dist. with Stockbridge (1961) *21,615.*

Ronaldshay, N. and S., Is. of the Orkneys.

Roncesvalles, *mtn. pass.,* in the Pyrenees, Spain; 20 m. N.E. of Pamplona, Navarra; Charlemagne's army under Roland, who was slain, defeated here, 778.

Ronda, *t.,* Malaga, Spain; ancient Moorish t. 42 m. N. of Gibraltar; mnfs. chocolate, leather, fruit, wines; p. (1957) *30,962.*

Rondonia *st.,* Brazil; on Bolivian border; cap. Porto Velho; p. (1960) *70,783.*

Rongotai, Wellington, N.Z.; international airport.

Rönne, *t.,* Denmark; on W. cst. of Bornholm; granite; p. (estd.) *13,000.*

Ronse, *see* Renaix.

Roodepoort-Maraisburg, *t.,* Transvaal, S. Africa; mng. and industl.; p. (1960) *94,740* (inc. *40,711* whites).

Rooppur, nr. Ishurdi, East Pakistan; nuclear power plant projected 1964.

Roorkee, *t.,* Uttar Pradesh, India; univ.; p. (1961) *45,801.*

Roosendaal, *industl. t.,* S.W. of N. Brabant, Neth.; nr. Breda; p. (1967) *44,102.*

Roosevelt, *R.,* trib. of Madeirj R., Brazil.

Roosevelt Dam, Arizona, U.S.A.; on R. Salt 130 m. above Phoenix on edge of Colorado Plateau; supplies irrigation for cultivation of 360 sq. m. in lower valley of R. Salt and upper valley of R. Gila; hydro-elec. power-sta.

Roper R., N.E. Northern Terr., Australia; navigable for about 90 m. inland.

Roquefort-sur-Soulzon, *t.,* S.E. Aveyron, France; caves in limestone cliffs used for ripening cheese.

Roraima, *mtn.,* Guyana, Venezuela bdy.; alt. 9,000 ft.

Rorschach, *t.,* Switzerland; lace; p. (1957) *11,325.*

Rosa Monte, highest pk., Pennine Alps, Italy; alt. 15,217 ft.

Rosario, *t.,* Santa Fé, Argentina; on R. Paraná; rly. terminus; univ.; chemicals, metals, leather, bricks, milling; p. (1960) *760,000.*

Rosas, *t.,* Spain; on Franco-Spanish border, opp. Portbou on the Mediterranean cst; fishing pt.; p. (1957) *2,720.*

Roscommon, *inland co.,* Connaught, Ireland; a. 949 sq. m.; p. (1966) *56,130.*

Roscrea, *mkt. t.,* Tipperary and Offaly, Ireland; on Little Brosna R.; p. (1966) *3,510.*

Roseau, *t.,* Dominica, Windward Is.; p. (1957) *13,500.*

Roseburg, *t.,* S.W. Ore., U.S.A.; roses, fruit, poultry; canning, sawmills; p. (1950) *8,390.*

Roselle, *t.,* N.J., U.S.A.; p. (1960) *21,032.*

Rosenheim, *t.,* Bavaria, Germany; on R. Inn, 35 m. S.E. of Munich; sulphur springs; impt. brine wks., machin., wood, iron, textiles, brewing; rly. junction; p. (1963) *32,000.*

Rosetta (Rashid), *t.*, Lower U.A.R.; on W. distributary of R. Nile, 43 m. N.E. Alexandria; p. (1947) *28,698.*

Roseville, *t.*, E. Cal., U.S.A.; exp. fruit. wines; p. (1960) *13,421.*

Roskilde, *mkt. t.*, Denmark; 20 m. W. of Copenhagen; fine cath. containing tombs of Kings and Queens of D.; royal palace; dairy prod.; leather; p. (1960) *31,923.*

Ross, *mkt. t., urb. dist.*, Hereford, Eng.; on R. Wye, cider; p. (1961) *5,643.*

Ross and Cromarty, *cst. and Highland co.*, Scot.; total a. 3,202 sq. m.; ch. t. Dingwall; p. (1961) *57,607.*

Ross Dependency, Antarctica, N.Z.; p. (1961) *198.*

Ross I., Victoria Land, Antarctica.

Ross Sea, *sea* extending to 85° S. in the Antarctic.

Rossan Pt., *headland*, N. side of Donegal Bay, Ireland.

Rossano, *c.*, Cosenza, S. Italy; nr. G. of Taranto; old t. under the Byzantine Empire; alabaster and marble quarries; silk, olive oil; p. *17,425.*

Rossendale Fells (Rossendale Forest), *upland region*, S.E. Lancs, Eng.; forms W. extension of Pennines between Mersey and Ribble valleys; composed of hard, impervious millstone grit; covered by boggy moorland; many reservoirs store soft water for cotton-spinning ts. along S. edge (Bolton, Bury, Rochdale), cotton-weaving ts. along N. edge (Blackburn, Accrington, Burnley) and sm. industl. ts. in Irwell valley within Rossendale; alt. mainly above 1,200 ft.

Rosslare, *spt.*, Wexford, Ireland; on extreme S.E. of Ireland; steamer connections to Fishguard (Wales).

Rostock, *spt.*, Rostock, E. Germany; nr. mouth of R. Warnow; univ.; shipbldg.; ship repair ind.; fisheries; deep-water harbour; oil pt.; p. (1964) *170,000.*

Rostov, *t.*, *pt.*, R.S.F.S.R.; on R. Don, 10 m. up from Sea of Azov (Black Sea); a gr. grain mart and comm. and industl. ctr.; engin., elec. power, paper; p. (1967) *737,000.*

Roswell, *t.*, N.M., U.S.A.; p. (1960) *39,593.*

Rosyth, *t.*, Fife, Scot.; naval dockyard.

Rothamsted, *hamlet*, Herts, Eng.; in Chiltern Hills, 1 m. S. of Harpenden; lge. agr. experimental sta.

Rother, *R.*, Sussex and Kent, Eng.; rises in the Weald, flows S.E. into English Channel at Rye; length 31 m.

Rother, *R.*, Hants and Sussex, Eng.; trib. of R. Arun; length 24 m.

Rother, *R.*, Derby and Yorks, Eng.; flows to R. Don at Rotherham; length 21 m.

Rotherham, *t., co. bor.*, W.R. Yorks; on R. Don, 4 m. N.E. of Sheffield; iron, steel, coal, glass; p. (estd. 1967) *86,670.*

Rotherhithe, *S.E. Thames-side-dist.*, London, Eng.

Rothes, *burgh*, Moray, Scot.; on R. Spey, 12 m. S.E. of Elgin; p. (1961) *1,105.*

Rothesay, *burgh*, Bute, Scot.; on E. cst. of I. of Bute in Firth of Clyde; tourism; p. (1961) *7,656.*

Rothwell, *t., urb. dist.*, Northants, Eng.; 3 m. N.W. of Kettering; boots, shoes; p. (1961) *4,766.*

Rothwell, *t., urb. dist.*, W.R. Yorks, Eng.; on R. Aire, 3 m. S.E. of Leeds; mining; chemicals, bricks, tiles, copper tubes, stone and sand quarrying; p. (estd. 1967) *27,130.*

Rotondo, *mtn.*, Corsica, France.

Rotorua, *t.*, N.I., N.Z.; health resort; hot springs; p. (1961) *25,074.*

Rotterdam, *spt., wealthy comm. c.*, Neth.; on R. Nieuwe Maas; linked to N. Sea at Hook of Holland by "New Waterway" ship canal; Europe's lgst. pt., second in world; breweries, sugar-ref., oil-ref., shipbldg., chemicals, clocks; p. (1967) *723,955.*

Rotti, *I.* (50 m. by 20 m.) off cst. of Timor, Malay Archipelago, Indonesia; p. *59,221.*

Roubaix, *t.*, Nord, France; nr. Lille; on the Roubaix canal 1 m. from the Belgian frontier; woollen mnfs., grape and tomato forcing; gr. tr., many educational institutions and fine bldgs.; p. (1962) *113,163.*

Rouen, *c.*, Seine-Maritime, France; over 50 m. up R. Seine; textiles, chemicals, oil refining; magnificent cath. and church; badly damaged Second World War; p. (1962) *123,474.*

Roulers, *see* Roeselare.

Roumania, *see* Romania.

Roukela, *see* Raukela.

Rousay, Orkney Is., Scotland.

Roussillon, *old prov.*, S. France; lies in depression at E. end of Pyrenees, in dep. of Pyrénées Orientales; largely irrigated by many sm. streams; olive, vine, wheat.

Rouyn, *mining t.*, Quebec, Canada; at end of L. Abitibi; gold, copper, zinc; p. (1961) *18,716.*

Rovereto, *c.*, S. Tyrol, Italy; on R. Adige; silk, leather, paper, cottons; p. *20,575.*

Rovigo, *prov.*, Venetia, Italy; cap. Rovigo; a. 684 sq. m.; p. (1961) *270,983.*

Rovigo, *t.*, *cap.*, Rovigo prov., Italy; on R. Adige, 20 m. S. of Padua; agr. mkt.; p. (1961) *45,271.*

Rovno, *t.*, Ukrainian S.S.R.; 110 m. N.E. of Lvov; comm. ctr.; p. (1959) *57,000.*

Rowley Regis, *industl. t., mun. bor.*, Staffs, Eng.; adjoins Dudley; p. (1961) *43,166.*

Roxboro', *t.*, N.C., U.S.A.; cotton, tobacco, mnfs.; p. (1950) *4,321.*

Roxburgh, *inland co.*, S. Scot.; stretching halfway along the Eng. border; hilly; sheep-rearing; woollens, tweed; cap. Jedburgh; a. 670 sq. m.; p. (1961) *43,171.*

Royal Leamington Spa, *see* Leamington.

Royal Oak, *t.*, Mich., U.S.A.; p. (1960) *80,612.*

Royan, *t.*, Charente-Maritime, France; S. of Rochelle; fishery, tr., industl.; p. (1962) *17,232.*

Royersford, *bor.*, S.E. Penns., U.S.A.; light iron and steel mnfs.; glass; p. (1950) *3,562.*

Royston, *mkt. t., urb. dist.*, Herts, Eng.; at N. foot of E. Anglian Heights, 7 m. N.E. of Baldock; p. (1961) *6,166.*

Royston, *urb. dist.*, W.R. Yorks, Eng.; coalmining; p. (1961) *8,490.*

Royton, *t., urb. dist.*, Lancs, Eng.; 4 m. N.E. of Manchester; cotton spinning; p. (1961) *14,476.*

Roznava, *t.*, ČSSR.; W. of Košice; antimony; p. (1961) *10,227.*

Ruabon, *par.*, Denbigh, N. Wales; on Salop border; coal, iron, tile wks., chemicals; p. *3,333.*

Ruanda-Urundi, *see* Rwanda and Burundi.

Ruapehu, *highest mtn.*, N.I., N.Z.; volcanic peak at S. extremity of central volcanic dist.; alt. 9,175ft.

Rubicon, *R.* of Central Italy, flowing to the Adriatic, crossed by Julius Caesar and his armies in 49 B.C. Has been identified with the Fiumicino or the Uso. There is a R. Rubicon (It. Rubico) a few m. N. of Rimini and S. of Cervia.

Rubtsovsk, *t.*, W. Siberia, R.S.F.S.R.; agr. engin.; p. (1967) *140,000.*

Ruby Mines, *dist.*, Mandalay, Upper Burma; hilly region of the Shan plateau, rich in precious stones; H.Q. t. Mogôk, in ctr. of the mining dist.

Ruda Slaska, *t.*, Katowice, Poland; industl; p. (1965) inc. Nowy Bytom *141,000.*

Rudnyy, *t.*, Kazakh S.S.R.; new town 30 m. S.W. of Kustanay; iron ore mining and dressing plant supplying Magnitogorsk; p. (1958) *c. 40,000*

Rudolf, L., N.W. Kenya, in Great Rift Valley; a. 3,500 sq. m.

Rudolph I., N. of Franz Josef Land, Arctic Ocean; Russian naval base; met. sta.

Rudolstadt, *t.*, Gera, E. Germany; on R. Saale; cas.; porcelain, metals; p. (1963) *23,474.*

Rueil Malmaison, *t.*, Seine-et-Oise, France; nr. Paris; p. (1962) *56,024.*

Rufiji, *R.*, Tanzania; E. Africa; flows to the Indian Ocean; length 450 m.

Rugby, *mkt. t., mun. bor.*, Warwick, Eng.; on R. Avon, 11 m. E. of Coventry; famous Public school; elec. and gen. engin., motor and aircraft patterns; p. (estd. 1967) *56,450.*

Rugeley, *mkt. t., urb. dist.*, Staffs, Eng.; on R. Trent, 9 m. S.E. of Stafford; coal, iron, tanning; p. (1961) *13,012.*

Ruhr, *industl. dist.*, W. Germany; lies to E. of R. Rhine, on either side of R. Ruhr; rich coalfield; impt. iron and steel, heavy engin. inds. based on local coal and iron ore from Luxembourg, Spain, Sweden; water communications to N. Sea along R. Rhine and Dortmund-Ems Canal; ch. ts. Essen,Duisburg,Düsseldorf,Dortmund,Bochum.

Ruislip-Northwood, *former urb. dist.*, Middlesex, Eng.; now inc. in Hillingdon bor. Greater London (*q.v.*); residtl.; p. (1961) *72,791.*

Rukwa, *L.*, E. Africa; between L. Tanganyika and L. Malawi in the rift valley; 30 m. by 12 m., a. increasing.

Rum, *I.*, Inner Hebrides, Argyll, Scot.; 8½ m. by 8 m.

Rumaila, Iraq; oilfield; pipe-line links to the Zubair-Fao system.

Rumania, *see* Romania.

Rum Jungle, N. Terr., Australia; 70 m. S.E. of Darwin; uranium mng.; silver, lead and copper deposits.

Runcorn, *industl. t., urb. dist.*, Cheshire, Eng.; on S. side of Mersey estuary; new Runcorn-Widnes bridge over Mersey and Manchester Ship canal opened 1961 (lgst. span arch in Europe); designated " New Town " 1964; chemicals; p. (estd. 1967) *30,650.*

Rupert, *R.*, Canada; flows from L. Mistassini to James Bay; length 300 m.

Ruse, *t.*, Bulgaria; on R. Danube, opp. Giurgiu in Romania; univ., arsenal, barracks; beer. sugar, tobacco; p. (1956) *53,523.*

Rushden, *t., urb. dist.*, Northants, Eng.; 3 m. E. of Wellingborough; shoes; p. (1961) *17,370.*

Rusholme, *t.*, E. of Manchester, S.E. Lancs. Eng.; industl. and residtl.

Russell *t.*, Kan., U.S.A.; mkt. in agr. and cattle region, oil and gas fields; p. (1960) *6,113.*

Rüsselsheim, *t.*, Hessen, Germany; on R. Main, E. of Mainz; car mftg. (Opel); p. (1963) *44,100.*

Russian Soviet Federal Socialist Republic (R.S.F.S.R.) *ch. constituent rep.*, U.S.S.R.; ch. inds.: wheat, rye, oats, barley, potatoes, sugar-beet, fruits, sunflower, cotton, hemp, tobacco; sheep, cattle, dairying, pigs, horses; lumbering, timber, wood-pulp; coal, petroleum, iron, manganese, etc.; machin., textiles, oil-refining, cement, bricks; a. 6,310,594 sq. m.; cap. Moscow; p. (1959) *117,494,000.*

Rustavi, *t.*, Georgian S.S.R., new t. 20 m. S.E. Tbilisi; metallurgical plant; p. (1959) *62,000.*

Rustenburg, *t.*, Transvaal, Rep. of S. Africa; on N.W. edge of High Veld, 60 m. W. of Pretoria; local mkt. for agr. produce, sorghum, maize, cotton; p. (1960) *20,866* (inc. *10,648* whites).

Rutbah, *t.*, Iraq; on oil pipe-line from Iraq to Haifa.

Rute, *t.*, Cordova, Spain; nr. Lucerna; industl.; p. *18,903.*

Ruthenia, *dist.*, U.S.S.R.; formerly part of Romania, ceded to U.S.S.R. in 1945, now part of Ukrainian S.S.R.

Rutherford, *t.*, N.J., U.S.A.; p. (1960) *20,473.*

Rutherfordton, *t.*, N.C., U.S.A.; gold, lumber, textiles; agr.; p. (1950) *3,146.*

Rutherglen, *burgh*, Lanark, Scot.; on R. Clyde, S.E. of Glasgow; industl., chemicals, tubes, paper, wire ropes, bolts, chenilles, webbing; p. (1961) *25,067.*

Ruthin, *t., mun. bor.*, Denbigh, Wales; Vale of Clwyd, 8 m. S.E. of Denbigh; p. (1961) *3,502.*

Rutigliano, *t.*, Bari, Italy; agr.; p. *10,650.*

Rutland, *midland co.*, Eng.; smallest in cty.; agr. farming, livestock; cheese, stone, iron; a. 152 sq. m.; cap. Oakham; p. (1966) *23,000.*

Rutland, *c.*, Vt., U.S.A.; marble quarries, machin. and furniture; p. (1960) *18,353.*   [p. *25,225.*

Ruvo, *t.*, Bari, Italy; cath.; olive-oil presses;

Ruwenzori, *mtn. range*, on Uganda-Congo border, overlooking W. arm of Gr. Rift Valley, midway between L. Albert and L. Edward; hgst peaks, Mt. Margherita (16,798 ft.), Mt. Alexandra (16,750 ft.); lower slopes covered in equatorial rain forest, coffee plantations on middle slopes above 5,000 ft.

Rwanda, *indep. rep.*, (1 July 1962), formerly kingdom of Ruanda, part of U.N. trust terr. of Ruanda-Urundi under Belgian adm.; coffee; cap. Kigali; a. 10,169 sq. m.; p. (estd. 1962) *2,634,000.*

Ryan Loch, *arm of sea*, on cst. Wigtown, Scot.; 8 m. by 2 m.

Ryazan, *t.*, R.S.F.S.R.; S.E. of Moscow; distilling, leather, engin.; p. (1967) *297,000.*

Rybinsk, *t., R. pt.*, R.S.F.S.R.; on R. Volga; engin., textiles, hydro-elec.; p. (1967) *209,000.*

Rybinsk Sea (Rybinsk Reservoir), R.S.F.S.R.; artificial L.; created behind dams on R. Volga and R. Sheksna at Rybinsk; part of scheme to regulate flow of R. Volga and to incorporate it in a vast inland waterway system; opened 1945; approx. a. 1,500 sq. m.

Rybnik, *t.*, S.W. Poland; engin., brewing, furniture-mkg.; p. (1965) *33,000.*

Rydal Water, *L.*, nr. Ambleside, Westmorland, Eng.; vil. adjacent contains Rydal Mount, where Wordsworth lived.

Ryde, *t., mun. bor.*, I. of Wight, Eng.; on N.E. cst.; yachting ctr. and seaside resort; boat and yacht bldg.; steamer connection across Spithead to Portsmouth; p. (estd. 1967) *21,200.*

Rye, *t., mun. bor.*, Cinque Pt., E. Sussex, Eng.;

at mouth of R. Rother to W. of Dungeness; shipbldg. and fishing; p. (estd. 1967) *4,400.*

Ryton, *t., urb. dist.*, Durham, Eng.; on R. Tyne W. of Newcastle; ironwks.; p. (1961) *13,485.*

Ryuku Archipelago, *chain of Is.*, 650 m. long, between Taiwan and Kyushi I., Japan; total a. 1,808 sq. m.; incl. Amami-gunto, Okinawa and Sakishima; ch. t. Naha on Okinawa.; mtnous., volcanic; sugar, pineapple, tobacco; steel bars, chemical adhesives; under U.S. control since end of war; self-gov. since 1962; p. (1956) *807,400.*

Rzeszow, *prov.*, S.E. Poland; a. 7,110 sq. m.; agr.; p. (1965) *1,693,000.*

Rzeszow, *t.*, S.E. Poland; industl. development since 1950; p. (1965) *69,000.*

Rzhev, *t.*, R.S.F.S.R.; on R. Volga; industl. and comm. engin.; p. (1956) *42,000.*

# S

Saale, *R.*, Halle and Gera, Germany; trib. of R. Elbe; length 225 m.

Saalfeld, *t.*, Gera, E. Germany; on R. Saale; famous cas. and grottos; machin., chocolate mftg.; p. (1963) *29,635.*

Saane, *R.*, Switzerland; flows to R. Aar, nr. Berne; length 65 m.

Saar, *R.*, Lorraine, Saarland, Palatinate; rises in the Vosges and flows N.W. to R. Moselle, nr. Trier; length 153 m.

Saar, *st.*, W. Europe; in valley of Saar; administered by League of Nations 1919–35 and returned to Germany after plebiscite; economic attachment of Saar to France agreed upon by Allied powers after Second World War; reunited politically with German Federal Republic 1 Jan. 1957 as a *Land.* Impt. coalfields, iron; ch. t. Saarbrucken; p. (1961) *1,072,000.*

Saarbrücken, *cap.*, Saarland, on R. Saar, opp. Sanct, Johann; cas.; rich coalfield; iron and steel wks., textiles, leather, paper, oil refining at Klarenthal nearby; p. (1963) *133,100.*

Saarebourg, *t.*, Moselle, France; on R. Saar, 30 m. N.W. of Strasbourg; mnfs. gloves, watch springs; p. (1962) *13,280.*

Saare Maa (Ösel), *I.*, Baltic Sea; at entrance to G. of Riga, Estonian S.S.R., U.S.S.R.; consists of low plateau, bleak and barren; ch. t., Kuresaare; a. approx. 900 sq. m.

Saarlouis, *t.*, Saarland, Germany; on R. Saar; coal-mng., wood, metals; p. (1963) *36,800.*

Sabac, *t.*, Jugoslavia; on R. Sava; old cas.; fruit, cattle, pigs, coal, zinc; p. (1959) *22,000.*

Sabadell, *t.*, Spain; N.W. of Barcelona; linen and cloth mills, flour, paper, distilling, iron founding; p. (1959) *86,417.*

Sabah, East Malaysia, *formerly* N. Borneo; tropical climate but equable, heavy rainfall; largely forested; hardwoods, rubber, tobacco, copra, cutch, hemp; cap. Kota Kinabalu; a. 29,387 sq. m.; p. (estd. 1963) *518,000.*

Sabahiyah, *t.*, Kuwait; new t. being built between Ahmadi and Fahahil.

Sabang, *spt.*, Sumatra, Indonesia; bunkering sta.; p. *6,855.*

Sabara, *t.*, Minas Gerais, Brazil; iron and steel; p. (1960) *16,800.*

Sabine, *R.*, Texas and La., U.S.A.; flows through S. Lake (an expansion of the R. 18 m. long) to Gulf of Mexico; length 500 m.

Sable Cape, *S. point*, Fla., U.S.A.

Sable I., off S.E. cst., Nova Scotia; 45 m. long.

Saclay, France; ENEA Neutron Data Compilation Centre.

Saco, *c.*, Me., U.S.A.; cotton mnfs.; p. (1960) *10,515.*

Saco, *R.*, U.S.A.; flows from White Mtns. in New Hampshire to Saco B., Mne.; 160 m. long.

Sacramento, *c., cap.*, Cal., U.S.A.; on the R. Sacramento; Capitol and R.C. cath.; rail wkshps., smelting, meat and fruit packing, flour, lumber, metal prods., rocket and missiles ind.; p. (1960) *191,667.*

Saddleback (Blencathara), *mtn.*, Cumberland, Eng.; nr. Keswick; alt. 2,847 ft.

Saddleworth, *t., urb. dist.*, W.R. Yorks, Eng.; in Pennines, 5 m. N.E. of Oldham; woollen, paper mkg., engin.; p. (1961) *17,010.*

Sado, *I.*, off cst. of Honshu, Japan; gold and silver mines; rice, fishing; a. 331 sq. m.

Sadon, *t.*, R.S.F.S.R.; zinc. lead, lead smelting.

Safad, *t.*, N. of Sea of Galilee, Israel; p. *11,300.*

**Saffron Walden**, *mkt. t., mun. bor.*, Essex, Eng.; on E. Anglian Heights 12 m. N. of Bishops Stortford; agr., hort. and engin.; p. (estd. 1967) 9,410.

**Safi**, *spt.*, W. cst. Morocco; resort; poor harbour, gr. grain and wool tr.; lge. phosphate plant; fishing; p. (1960) 81,072.    [p. (1955) 126,432.

**Saga**, *t.*, Kyushu, Japan; coal-mining, fishing;

**Sagaing**, *div.*, Upper Burma; mtn. ridges, fertile plains; rice, wheat, peas, cotton; a. 50,086 sq. m.; p. 2,322,675.

**Sagaing**, *t.*, Upper Burma; on R. Irrawaddy; pagodas; groundnuts, cotton, millets, tobacco, cattle; textile mill projected; p. c. 15,000.

**Saganoseki**, *sm. t.*, N.E. Kyushu, Japan; on Bungo Strait, 15 m. E. of Oita; impt. gold-, copper-, silver-mines.       [104,676.

**Sagar**, *t.*, Madhya Pradesh, India; univ.; p. (1961)

**Sagastyr**, *I.*, at mouth of R. Lena, R.S.F.S.R.

**Saginaw**, *c.*, Mich., U.S.A.; on R. Saginaw; in agr. and timber region; machin., railwks., beet-sugar; p. (1960) 98,265.

**Sagua la Grande**, *t.*, Cuba; on R. of same name; machin., chemicals, bricks, tiles, salt; p. (1953) 26,187.

**Saguenay**, *R.*, Quebec, Canada; length from L. St. John to St. Lawrence R. about 100 m.; of gr. depth, beautiful scenery; hydro-elec. power developed.

**Sagunto**, *t.*, Spain; nr. Valencia; p. (1957) 26,932.

**Sahara**, the gr. N. African desert between the Sudan and the Barbary sts., extending from the Atlantic to the Nile, inc. Tripoli and Fezzan; a. 3,500,000 sq. m.; the E. portion is known as the Libyan desert, that part E. of the R. Nile, being often called the Nubian Desert; numerous oases with ts. and tr. ctrs.; oil pipe lines to Algerian and Tunisian csts.; p. (estd. 2,500,000), nomadic Arab and Berber tribes.

**Saharan Atlas**, S. range of Atlas mtns. in Algeria; ch. pks., J. Aures, 7,644 ft., J. Aissa, 7,350 ft., J. Ksel, 6,594 ft.

**Saharan Oases**, *terr.*, S. Algeria; p. 39,575.

**Saharanpur**, *c.*, Uttar Pradesh, India; rly. wks., wood carving; furniture, paper, tobacco, mnfs.; p. (1961) 185,213.        [(1961) 31,409.

**Sahibganj**, *t.*, Bihar, India; on R. Ganges; p.

**Saida**, *see* Sidon.

**Saidabad** or **Sirdjan**, *t.*, Laristan, Iran; S.W. of Kerman, nr. Kuh-i-Lalehzar mtn.; p. 10,000.

**Saigon**, *c.*, *spt.*, S. Viet-Nam; on R. Saigon, to E. of Mekong delta, 60 m. from sea; lge. comm. ctr.; cath., citadel, arsenal and naval yd.; spices, rice; paper mill; p. (1964) 1,371,000 (with Cholon).

**Saih-El-Maleh**, *pt.*, Muscat and Oman; oil terminal.

**Saimaa**, *L.*, Finland; a. of water which forms basin of R. Vuoksi; total expanse of water 390 sq. m.; canal connects with G. of Finland and runs partly through Soviet terr.

**St. Abb's Head**, *rocky promontory*, Berwick, Scot.

**St. Agnes Head**, Cornwall, Eng.

**St. Albans**, *c.*, *mun. bor.*, Herts, Eng.; on N. margin of Vale of St. Albans, 20 m. N.W. of London; faces remains of Roman Verulamium across R. Ver; light inds., electronics, instrument mkg.; cath.; residtl.; p. (estd. 1967) 52,470.

**St. Albans**, *t.*, Vt., U.S.A.; dairy farming; p. (1960) 8,806.      [industl.; p. (1954) 10,765.

**St. Amand**, *t.*, Cher., France; on R. Cher;

**St. Andrews**, *burgh*, Fife, Scot.; on N.E. cst. of Fife; seaside resort; univ.; famous golf course; p. (1961) 9,888.

**St. Anne**, *t.*, Alderney, Channel Is.; church designed by Sir George Gilbert Scott.

**St. Anthony**, *waterfalls*, on R. Mississippi; U.S.A. predominant factor in site of Minneapolis (Minn.).

**St. Asaph**, *c.*, *rural dist.*, Flint, N. Wales; on R. Clwyd, 4 m. N. of Denbigh; cath.; optical glass mkg.; p. (rural dist. 1961) 9,478.

**St. Augustine**, *t.*, Fla., U.S.A.; resort; p. (1960) 14,734.

**St. Austell**, *mkt. t.*, *urb. dist.*, Cornwall, Eng.; on S. flank of Hensbarrow, 14 m. N.E. of Truro; holiday resort; china clay, stone quarrying. engin., wood and cork; p. (estd. 1967) 28,990.

**St. Barthélemy**, *French I.*, W. Indies; dependency of Guadeloupe; p. (1960) 2,079.

**St. Bees Head**, *promontory*, 2½ m. N.W. of St. Bees, Cumberland, Eng.; freestone quarries, tin.

**St. Benoît**, *t.*, Ile de la Réunion, Indian Ocean; connected by rail with ch. port, Pointe-des-Galets.

**St. Bernard Pass, Great**, on Italian–Swiss bdy., W. Alps; carries main road from W. Switzerland to Plain of Lombardy; approached from N. by trib. of upper Rhône, from S. by Val d'Aosta; 8,120 ft. above sea level. The Great St. Bernard road tunnel (3½ m.) constr. 1958–62 links Cantine de Proz (Valais can., Switzerland) and St. Rhémy (Italy); under tunnel will run projected 260 m. pipeline from Genoa to Aigle.

**St. Bernard Pass, Little**, on French–Italian bdy., W. Alps; links Isère valley with Val d'Aosta; alt. approx. 5,000 ft.

**St. Boniface**, *t.*, Manitoba, Canada; sub. of Winnipeg; p. (1961) 37,600.

**St. Bride's Bay**, Pembroke, Wales.

**St. Brieuc**, *t.*, Côtes-du-Nord, France; college, cath.; ironwks., textiles, timber and cst. tr.; p. (1962) 47,307.

**St. Catharines**, *c.*, Ont., Canada; on Welland Canal; mkt. for Niagara fruit-growing reg.; agr. implement wks., timber mills, flour mills, tanneries and varied inds.; (1961) 48,472.

**St. Chamond**, *t.*, Loire, France; nr. St. Etienne; silk, ribbons, rayon; rly. wks.; coal-mining; p. (1962) 36,589.

**St. Charles**, *c.*, Mo., U.S.A.; nr. St. Louis; tobacco and flour; p. (1960) 21,189.

**St. Clair**, *L.*, Canada–U.S.A.; part of link between L. Huron and L. Erie.

**St. Clair**, *R.*, N. America; flows from L. Huron through L. of St. Clair into L. Erie; forms bdy. between Michigan (U.S.A.) and Ontario (Canada); impt. link in Gr. Lakes waterway; length 85 m., depth dredged to 20 ft.

**St. Clair Shores**, *t.*, Mich., U.S.A.; residtl. sub. of Detroit; p. (1960) 76,657.

**St. Claude**, *t.*, Jura, France; at confluence of Rs. Tacon and Bienne; cath.; fancy shell, horn and ivory mnfs.; p. (1962) 12,649.

**St. Cloud**, *t.*, Hauts-de-Seine, France; 6 m. from ctr. of Paris; fine park, château; residtl.; porcelain; p. (1962) 26,746.

**St. Cloud**, *t.*, Minn., U.S.A.; on R. Mississippi; timber yds., dairying, farming; p. (1960) 33,815.

**St. Croix**, *I.*, Virgin Is., gr., U.S.A.; ch. inds. sugar cultivation, stock raising, vegetable growing, rum mnf.; a. 82 sq. m.; p. (1950) 12,096.

**St. Croix**, *R.*, Wis., U.S.A.; trib. of the Mississippi; length 200 m.

**St. Davids**, *c.*, Pembroke, Wales; 15 m. S.W. of Fishguard; cath., ruins of Bishop's Palace; p. 1,595.

**St. Davids Head**, *prom.*, on cst. of Pembroke, Wales.

**St. Denis**, *t.*, N. *sub.*, Paris, France; industl. and residtl.; abbey, burial pl. of Kings of France; chemicals, machin., spirits, soap; p. (1962) 95,072.

**St. Denis**, *spt.*, *cap.*, Ile de la Réunion (French), Indian Ocean; p. (estd. 1965) 65,000.

**St. Dié**, *t.*, Vosges, France; on R. Meurthe; cath.; iron, copper, machin., hosiery; p. (1962) 24,373.

**St. Dizier**, *t.*, Haute-Marne, France; on R. Marne; iron, steel, copper, boats; p. (1962) 36,361.

**St. Elias**, *mtn.*, Alaska, U.S.A.; alt. 18,024 ft.

**St. Etienne**, *t.*, *cap.*, Loire, France; nr. Lyons; ribbon-weaving, boot-lace, silk, velvet, engin., armaments, motor-cycles, cycles, chemicals, and iron mftg. ctr., in coal-field dist.; p. (1962) 203,633.

**St. Eustatius**, one of the Neth. Antilles, W. Indies; a. 31 sq. m.; p. (1963) 1,103.

**St. Francis R.**, Quebec, Canada; hydro-elec. power.

**St. Francis**, *R.*, Mo., U.S.A.; trib. of R. Mississippi; forms bdy. of Ark.; length 450 m.

**St. Gall (St. Gallen)**, *can.*, Switzerland; mountainous; forest; vineyards; cattle raising; cotton spinning, lace; cap. St. G.; a. 777 sq. m.; p. (1961) 339,489.

**St. Gail**, *t.*, Switzerland; on R. Steinach; cath.; cottons and embroidery; p. (1961) 76,700.

**St. George**, *bay*, W. cst. Newfoundland, Canada.

**St. George**, *I.*, Grenada Is., Brit. W. Indies; wireless sta.        [quarried; p. 1,169.

**St. George**, *spt.*, N.B., Canada; various granites

**St. George's Channel**, Brit. Isles; part of Irish Sea separating Wales from Ireland.

**St. George's I.**, Fla., U.S.A.

**St. Germain-en-Laye**, *t.*, Yvelines, France; on R.

Seine; former royal château; cottons, woollens; p. (1962) *37,391*.

St. Germans, *mkt. t., rural dist.*, Cornwall, Eng.; 4 m. W. of Saltash; p. (rural dist. 1961) *14,775*.

Saint Gotthard, *mtn. gr.*, Alps, S. central Switzerland, crossed by St. Gotthard Pass (6,935 ft.). St. Gotthard Rly. passes through St. Gotthard tunnel (9½ m., max. alt. 3,786 ft.). Road tunnel (6½ m.) under pass Göschenen to Airolo projected; motorways linking pass with Zurich, Basle and Lugano being built.

St. Gowan's Head, *promontory*, Pembroke, Wales.

St. Helena, *I., Brit. col.*, Atl. Oc.; 1,200 m. from W. cst. Africa; spt. and only t. Jamestown; Napoleon imprisoned 1815–21, and Boer captives 1900; famous for its wirebird, species of plover peculiar to I.; a. 47 sq. m.; p. (estd. 1965) *4,526*.

St. Helens, *t., co. bor.*, Lancs, Eng.; 12 m. E. of Liverpool; connected by canal with R. Mersey; coal, iron, alkali; copper smelting, glass, fibreglass, plastics; p. (estd. 1967) *103,320*.

St. Helier, *spt.*, Jersey, Channel Is.; p. *26,484*.

St. Hyacinthe, *c., spt.*, Quebec, Canada; on Yamaska R.; cath.; farm machin., woollens, leather; p. (1961) *22,354*.

St. Ives, *t., mun. bor.*, Cornwall, Eng.; at entrance to St. Ives Bay; fishing, holiday resort; p. (estd. 1967) *8,780*.

St. Ives, *mkt. t.*, Huntingdon, Eng.; on R. Ouse, 4 m. E. of Huntingdon; timber, gravel, concrete prod., engin., canning, agr. machin.; p. (1961) *4,076*.

St. James, *t.*, Man., Canada; p. (1961) *33,977*.

St. Jean, *t.*, Quebec, Canada; rly. junction; porcelain, pottery, tiles; p. (1961) *26,988*.

St. Jérôme, *t.*, Quebec, Canada; pulp, paper, knitted goods, woollens, rubber goods, cement, bricks; p. (1961) *24,546*.

St. John, *c., spt.*, N.B., Canada; cottons, woollens, machin., paper, lumbering, sugar refinery; fisheries; corn tr.; p. (1961) *95,563*.

St. John, *I.*, U.S. Virgin Is. gr.; a. 19 sq. m.; ch. inds. charcoal, stock-raising, tourists; was noted for bay leaf oil, but ind. now dormant.

St. John, *L.*, Quebec, Canada; on Saguenay R.

St. John, *R.*, N.B., Canada; flows to Bay of Fundy; length 450 m.      [*12,000*.

St. John, *t., cap.*, Antigua, W. Indies; p. (1957)

St. John's Point, *C.*, Down, Northern Ireland; forming N. side of Dundrum Bay.

St. Johns R., Fla., U.S.A.; flows to Atlantic; length 350 m.

St. John's, *spt., c., cap.*, Newfoundland, Canada; on E. cst.; first Eng. settlement in America; univ.; gr. tr. in fish, cod, oil, etc.; p. (1961) *90,838*.

St. John's Wood, *residtl. dist.*, N.W. London, Eng.; contains Lord's Cricket Ground.

St. Joseph, *t.*, Mich., U.S.A.; on L. Mich.; resort; industl.; p. (1960) *11,755*.

St. Joseph, *c.*, Mo., U.S.A., on M. R.; rly. ctr.; meat packing, clothing, farm implements; p. (1960) *79,673*.      [paper; p. *6,449*.

St. Joseph d'Alma, *t.*, Quebec, Canada; pulp,

St. Joseph Lake, Ontario, Canada.

St. Junien, *t.*, Haute Vienne, France; on R. Vienne; fine churches, shrine; gloves, leather; porcelain wks.; p. (1962) *11,424*.

St. Just, *t., urb. dist.*, Cornwall, Eng.; nr. Lands End, 6 m. W. of Penzance; dairying; tinmining; p. (1961) *3,636*.

St. Kilda, *rocky I.*, most W. of the Hebrides, Scot.; 3 m. long; bird sanctuary, famous for its wren, a sub-species.

St. Kilda, *wat. pl.*, Victoria. Australia; nr. Melbourne; p. *26,000*.

St. Kitts-Nevis-Anguilla, Leeward gr. of Is., W.I.; *aut. st.* in assocn. with Britain (Anguilla unilaterally seceded from union 1967); sugar, sea island cotton, molasses; a. 136 sq. m.; cap. Basse-Terre; p. (estd. 1967) *58,000*.

St. Laurent, *t.*, Quebec, Canada; p. (1961) *49,805*.

St. Laurent des Eaux, *t.*, Loir-et-Cher, France; 15 m. S.W. Orleans; nuclear power sta.; p. (1962) *992*.

St. Laurent du Maroni, *t.*, Fr. Guiana; penal admin. ctr.; p. *2,000*.

St. Lawrence, G. of, Canada; arm of Atlantic, partly enclosed by Newfoundland and Nova Scotia; impt. fisheries.      [100 m. long.

St. Lawrence I., Alaska, U.S.A.; in Bering Sea.

St. Lawrence, *gr. R.*, of N. America; length from the source of its headstream, the St. Louis, 2,100 m.; forms the outlet of the great lakes

(Superior, Michigan, Huron, Erie and Ontario) and the bdy. between the st. of N.Y., U.S.A. and Ontario, Canada; ch. tribs.; Ottawa, Richelieu, St. Maurice, Saguenay.

St. Lawrence Seaway, N. America; joint Canada-U.S.A. project links head of the Gr. Lakes with Atl. Oc., providing channel 27 ft. min. depth enabling lge. ocean-going vessels to reach American continent; provides major source of hydroelectric power to industl. areas; opened 1959.

St. Lawrence Ship Canal, Canada. Channel deepened to provide safe navigation for ocean-going vessels from deep water to Montreal; depth 35 ft. at low water; links St. Lawrence Seaway at Montreal.      [seaside resort.

St. Leonards, *t.*, Sussex, Eng.; W. of Hastings.

St. Lô, *t.*, Manche, France; on R. Vire; cath.; cloth mnfs.; p. (1962) *17,035*.

St. Louis, *t.*, Senegal, W. Africa; at mouth of R. Senegal; cath., pal.; rly. and road ctr.; airport; exp. oilseeds and skins; p. (1948) *51,000*.

St. Louis, *t.*, Ile de la Réunion, Indian Ocean; p. (1960) *25,220*.

St. Louis, *c.*, Mo., U.S.A.; on R. Mississippi 10 m. below confluence of Rs. Miss. and Mo.; two univs., impt. rly. and river junction; mkt. for furs, livestock, grain, farm prod.; banking and fin. ctr.; varied mnfs.; mach., cars, aircraft, leather goods, beer, chemicals; p. (1960) *750,026*.

St. Louis Park, *t.*, Minn., U.S.A.; tools, dental supplies; p. (1960) *43,310*.

St. Lucia Bay, *inlet* of the Indian Oc. at mouth of R. Umvolozi, S. of St. Lucia L., Natal, S. Africa.

St. Lucia I., *aut. st.* in association with Gt. Britain; Windward Is., W.I.; exp. sugar, cocoa, lime juice, etc.; coaling sta.; a. 238 sq. m.; cap. Castries; p. (estd. 1967) *99,000*.

St. Malo, *fortfd. spt.*, Ile-et-Vilaine, France; cas. and church (formerly a cath.); agr. prod., shipping, fishing, and tourist inds.; p. (1962) *17,800*.

St. Maria di Leuca, *C.*, S. Italy.

St. Marie, *C.*, S. point of Malagasy.

St. Martin, *French I.*, W. Indies; dependency of Guadeloupe; p. (1946) *6,786*.

St. Martin, *I.*, Neth. Antilles, W. Indies; a. 13 sq. m.; p. (1948) *1,697*.

St. Marylebone, *see* Westminster, City of.

St. Mary's I., Scilly Is., Brit. Isles.

St. Matthew I., Alaska; U.S.A.; in Bering Sea.

St. Maur-des-Fosses, *sub.*, Paris, Seine, France; garden city; p. (1962) *70,681*.

St. Maurice, *vil.*, Valais, Switzerland; nr. Martigny; 6th-century abbey; once a leading Burgundian t.; p. *2,699*.

St. Maurice, *R.*, Quebec, Canada; trib. of St Lawrence R.; hydro-elec. power developed; length 400 m.

St. Mawes, *vil.*, Cornwall, Eng.; on E. cst. of estuary of R. Fal; holiday resort, fishing.

St. Michael's Mt., *castled rock*, Cornwall, Eng.; the ancient Ictis; alt. 230 ft.

St. Michel, *t.*, Que., Canada; p. (1956) *24,540*.

St. Mihiel, *t.*, Meuse, France; on R. Meuse, nr. Bar-le-Duc; industl.; Benedictine abbey; lace; p. (1962) *5,366*.

St. Monance, *burgh*, Fife, Scot.; p. (1961) *1,406*.

St. Moritz, *picturesque t., health resort*, Switzerland; in the Upper Engadine; winter sports; alt. 6,090 ft.; spa; p. *4,000*.

St. Nazaire, *t.*, Loire-Atlantique, France; at mouth of R. Loire, nr. Nantes; docks and shipping; steelwks., aircraft; exp. wine, sardines, silk, oil refining nearby; p. (1962) *59,181*.

St. Neots, *mkt. t., urb. dist.*, Hunts, Eng.; on R. Ouse, 10 m. N.E. of Bedford; shoes, brewing, milling, paper mkg., sports equipment, plastics; (1961) *5,570*.

St. Niklaas, *mftg. t.*, E. Flanders, Belgium; nr. Antwerp; cottons, woollens, lace, rayon, carpets; p. (1962) *48,019*.      [p. *14,662*.

St. Ninians, *par.*, Stirling, Scot.; woollens, nails;

St. Omer, *t.*, Pas-de-Calais, France; cath., abbey ruins; brewing, distilleries, soap, linen; p. (1962) *20,911*.

St. Ouen, *t., sub.*, Paris, France; on R. Seine; light inds., copper, aluminium goods, furniture, gloves; power sta.; p. (1962) *52,103*.

St. Pancras, *see* Camden.

St. Paul, *c., cap.*, Minn., U.S.A.; faces Minneapolis across the R. Mississippi; cath.; univ.; meatpacking, foundries, cars, electronics, industl. abrasives; p. (1960) *313,411*.

St. Paul, *spt.*, Ile de la Réunion (French), Indian Ocean; p. (1960) *28,681.*

St. Paul, *R.*, Liberia; flows to the Atlantic nr. Monrovia; length 300 m.

St. Paul de Loanda, *t.*, Angola; exp. rubber, ivory, palm oil, coffee, coconuts, rum.

St. Peter, *L.*, Canada; expansion of St. Lawrence R. above Three Rivers; 20 m. by 9 m.

St. Peter Port, *seaport, cap.*, Guernsey, Channel Is.; wat. pl.; fruit, flowers, vegetables; p. *15,706.*

St. Petersburg, *c.*, Fla., U.S.A.; resort; p. (1960) *181,298.*

St. Pierre, *t.*, Martinique I., Fr. W. Indies; ch. t. in Fr. W. Indies; completely destroyed by eruption of Mt. Pelée, 1902.

St. Pierre and Miquelon, *French terr.*, consisting of 8 sm. Is. off S. cst. of Newfoundland; a. of St. Pierre gr., 10 sq. m.; a. of Miquelon gr., 83 sq. m.; ch. t. St. Pierre, fisheries; p. of St. P. and M. (1958) *4,904.*

St. Pierre-des-Corps, *t.*, Indre-et-Loire, France; p. (1954) *10,656.*     [*27,573.*

St. Pierre, *t.*, Réunion, Indian Ocean; p. (1960)

St. Pölten, *t.*, Lower Austria; nr. Vienna; cotton spinning and hardware mftg.; p. (1961) *40,112.*

St. Quentin, *t.*, Aisne, France; on R. Somme; lace, tulle, woollens, chemicals, ironwks.; p. (1962) *62,579.*     [antiquities.

St. Rémy, *t.*, Bouches-du-Rhône, France; Roman

St. Servan, *spt.*, Ille-et-Vilaine, France; opp. St. Malo; p. (1954) *13,763.*

St. Thomas I., *see* São Tomé.

St. Thomas, *I.*, Virgin Is. gr., Atl. Oc.; belongs to U.S.A.; rum and bay rum, sugar, truck-farming, cattle, deep-sea fishing; bunkering of ships, handicrafts, tourism; a. 32 sq. m.; p. (1950) *14,559* (with St. John).

St. Thomas, *t.*, Ontario, Canada; rly. wkshps., flour, flax; p. (1961) *22,469.*

St. Trond, *t.*, Limbourg, Belgium; brewing, distilling; p. (1962) *20,976.*

St. Valéry-sur-Somme, *spt.*, Somme, France; resort of pilgrims; here William the Conqueror embarked for Eng. 1066; fishing; p. *3,071.*

St. Vincent, *C.*, S.W. Portugal; Spanish fleet defeated by British 1797.

St. Vincent, Gulf of, *lge. inlet*, S. Australia; penetrates 100 m. inland, max. width 35 m.; Pt. Adelaide located on E. side.

St. Vincent, *I.*, *aut. st.* in association with Gt. Britain; one of Windward gr.; W.I.; sugar, arrowroot, cotton, peanuts; cap. Kingstown; a. 150 sq. m.; p. (estd 1967) *85,000.*

Sainte Agathe des Monts, *t.*, Quebec, Canada; tourist resort; p. (1961) *5,725*

Sainte Croix, Virgin Is., W. Indies; former possession of Denmark, now U.S.A.

Saintes, *t.*, Charente-Maritime, France; cath.; Roman antiquities; suffered in Huguenot wars; agr. implements; earthenware; p. (1954) *23,768.*

Saipan I., Marianas, Pac. Oc., U.S.A. trusteeship; sugar, coffee , fruit; a. 71 sq. m.; p. (1958) *7,250.*

Sakai, *spt.*, Japan; local import ctr.; iron machin., vinyl pipe plant; oil refining; p. (1964) *439,000.*

Sakania, *t.*, Congo; frontier sta. on rly. between Elizabethville and N. Rhodesia; p. *25,095.*

Sakata, *t.*, Honshu, Japan; p. (1965) *95,982.*

Sakhalin, *I.*, off E. cst. Asia; S. half ceded by Japan to U.S.S.R., 1945; a. about 13,930 sq. m.; herring fisheries, coal, naphtha, alluvial gold, oil, timber, natural gas; oil pipeline connects to Komsomolsk and Khabarovsk refineries; p. (1959) *651,000* inc. Kurile Is.

Sakishima, *Is.*, E. of Formosa.

Sakmara, *R.*, R.S.F.S.R.; rises in Ural Mtns., trib. of R. Ural; length 350 m.

Sala, *t.*, Västmanland, Sweden; silver-mine worked for over 400 years, now to limited extent; lime, bricks; p. (1961) *11,015.*

Saladillo, *R.*, N. Argentina; upper course of R. Dulce.

Salado Rio, *R.*, Argentina; trib. of the R. Paranà; length 1,000 m.     [Norte.

Salado, Rio, *R.*, Mexico; trib. of Rio Grande del

Salamanca, *t.*, Guanajuato st., Mexico; oil refining; ammonia plant; natural gas pipeline to Guadalajara.

Salamanca, *prov.*, Leon, W. Spain; cap. Salamanca; a. 4,756 sq. m.; p. (1959) *422,114.*

Salamanca, *t.*, *cap.*, Salamanca prov., Spain; on R. Tormes; oldest Spanish univ.; 2 caths., many convents; p. (1959) *88,316.*   [Terr.; gold.

Salamaua, *t.*, *pt.*, New Guinea, Australian Trust.

Salamis, *I.*, Greece; opposite harbour of Athens; famous naval battle, 480 B.C.

Salamis, *spt.*, Greece; naval base; p. *17,312.*

Salar de Uyuni, windswept, dry, salt flat, S.W. Bolivia.

Salavat, *t.*, R.S.F.S.R.; in Bashkiria, 90 m. S. of Ufa; ctr. of oilfield; glass factory; became t. in 1954; p. (1959) *60,000.*   [lgst., 180 sq. m.

Salayer Is., *gr.*, S. of Celebes, Indonesia; a. of

Sala-y-Gomez I., Pac. Oc.; Chilean; uninhabited.

Salazar, Mexico, nr. Mexico City; at alt. 9,500 ft.; nuclear reactor for radioisotopes for medical, industl. and agr. purposes.

Salcombe, *t.*, *urb. dist.*, S. Devon, Eng.; 4 m. S. of Kingsbridge; resort; fishing; p. (1961) *2,558.*

Saldanha B., *inlet* on W. cst. C. of Good Hope, S. Africa; whaling, fishing; granite, quarrying; length 17 m.

Sale, *t.*, *mun. bor.*, Cheshire, Eng.; on R. Mersey, 2 m. S. of Stretford; p. (estd. 1967) *55,140.*

Sale, *t.*, Victoria, Australia; 128 m. from Melbourne; ctr. of lge. agr. and pastoral dist.; plastics, engin.; p. (1966) *8,648.*

Salé or Salch, *spt* , Fez, Morocco; formerly pirate headquarters; p. (1960) *75,799.*

Salekhard, *t.*, *R. pt.*, N.W. Siberia, R.S.F.S.R.; on R. Ob; fisheries, collecting ctr. for furs; exp. timber; p. (1956) *16,000.*

Salem, *t.*, Tamil Nadu, India; carpets, weaving, farming ctr.; p. (1961) *249,145.*

Salem, *c.*, Mass., U.S.A.; 15 m. from Boston; cottons, lumber products, leather goods, machin. wireless valves; p. (1960) *39,211.*

Salem, *t.*, N.J., U.S.A.; in fruit-growing dist.; p. (1960) *8,941.*

Salem, *c.*, Ohio, U.S.A.; steel; p. (1960) *13,854.*

Salem, *c.*, *cap.*, Ore., U.S.A.; on Williamette R.; univ.; fruit-packing, flour milling and canning; p. (1960) *49,142.*     [p. *19,100.*

Salemi, *t.*, Sicily, Italy; the ancient Halicyae; p. (1960)

Salerno, *spt.*, Campania, Italy; on G. of Salerno, 30 m. S.E. of Naples; cottons, silks, printing, leather; vine-growing dist.; p. (1961) *113,171.*

Salford, *c.*, *co. bor.*, Lancs, Eng.; on R. Irwell, adjoining Manchester; engin., clothing mftg.; p. (estd. 1967) *143,430.*

Salgótarján, *t.*, N Hungary; coalmng., agr. machin., tools, glass; p (1962) *30,000.*

Salima, *t.*, Malawi, S. Africa; alt. 1,672 ft.; term. of rly. from Beira on L. Malawi; p. (1966) *2,301.*

Salina, *c.*, Kan., U.S.A.; on Smoky Hill R.; univ.; flour milling, cattle mkt., farm implements; p. (1960) *43,202.*

Salina, *I.*, Lipari Is., Italy; in the Mediterranean, 6 m. long; 2 volcanic cones.

Salina Cruz, *t.*, *spt.*, Oaxaca, Mexico; terminal pt. of Tehuantepec rly.; shallow harbour; dyewoods, coffee, hemp, hides and skins; p. *3,243.*

Salinas, *t.*, Ecuador; cable sta.; holiday resort; 118 m. from Guayaquil.

Salinas, *R.*, Cal., U.S.A.; rises in U.S. Coast Range, flows N.W. into Bay of Monterey, Pac. Oc.; fertile valley floor irrigated to produce hard and stone fruits, mkt.-garden produce (especially lettuce), alfalfa; length, 140 m.

Salinas-Grandes, *gr. marsh a.*, Argentina; N. of Córdoba.

Salisbury, *cath. c.*, *mun. bor.*, Wilts, Eng.; at S. foot of Salisbury Plain at confluence of Rs. Avon and Wily; cath., pure Early English with tallest spire in Eng. (404 ft.); mkt. t.; eng. inds.; p. (estd. 1967) *35,990.*

Salisbury, *c.*, *cap.* Rhodesia; airways ctr.; univ.; ctr. gold mng. a.; inds. inc. fertilisers, tobacco, machin.; p. (1965) *327,000.*

Salisbury, *t.*, Md., U.S.A.; iron and steel goods, woodwork, canning; p. (1960) *16,302.*

Salisbury, *t.*, N.C., U.S.A.; cotton, grain, timber, textiles, refrigerators; p. (1960) *21,297.*

Salisbury Plain, Wilts Eng.; undulating upland N. of Salisbury; Stonehenge; army training-ground.     [*14,541.*

Sallaumines, *t.*, Pas-de-Calais, France; p. (1954)

Salmon, *R.*, Idaho, U.S.A.; trib. of Snake R.; length 450 m.

Salon, *t.*, Bouches-du-Rhône, France; on Canal de Craponne; soap and oil wks.; p. (1962) *22,629.*

Salpau Selka, Finland; most southerly gravel ridge; forested; winter sports.

Salsette I., N. of Bombay, India; a. 241 sq. m.; connected by bridge and causeway with Bombay; cave antiquities and temples.

Salt, *R.*, Arizona, U.S.A.; rises in Colorado Plateau, flows W. into Gila R. 20 m. below Phoenix; length 240 m. *See also* Roosevelt Dam.

Salt Fork, *R.*, Okla., U.S.A.; trib. of Arkansas R.

Salt Lake City, *c.*, *cap.*, Utah, U.S.A.; nr. Gr. Salt Lake, H.Q. of Mormonism; temple and univ.; mng.; agr.; steel, oil, textiles, meat pkg.; livestock; p. (1960) *189,454.*

Salta, *N. prov.*, Argentina; sugar, vines, oranges, oil; cap. Salta; a. 62,511 sq. m.; p. (1960) *413,000.*

Salta, *c.*, Argentina; on R. Salta; sugar, vines, oranges, tobacco, oil, minerals; cath., college; p. (1960) *120,000.*

Saltash, *mkt. t.*, *mun. bor.*, Cornwall, Eng.; on W. side of Tamar estuary; lowest bridge (rly.) and road bridge to Devonport across Tamar; farming, fishing, malting; p. (estd. 1967) *8,410.*

Saltburn, *t.*, *urb. dist.* (with Marske), N.R. Yorks, Eng.; on E. cst. 3 m. S.E. of Redcar; seaside resort; p. (1961) *12,482.*

Saltcoats, *sm. burgh*, Ayr, Scot.; on Firth of Clyde, 2 m. S. of Ardrossan; chemicals, shipyards and rly. sheds; p. (1961) *14,187.*

Saltillo, *cap.*, Coahuila st., Mexico; cottons, flour, woollens, cereals, gold, silver, lead, copper, iron, zinc, coal; p. (1960) *99,101.*

Saltney, *t.*, Flint, Wales; on R. Dee, 2 m. S.W. of Chester; oil and fat refining; p. (1951) *2,642.* [p. (1953) *108,030.*

Salto, *dept.*, Uruguay; cap. Salto; a. 4,865 sq. m.;

Salto, *cap.*, S. dep., Uruguay; leather, salted meats, sugar cane and beet; p. (estd. 1956) *60,000.*

Salton Sea, *L.*, S. Cal., U.S.A.; 263 ft. below sea-level in depression which extends N.W. from head of G. of Cal.; ctr. of inland drainage; a. 270 sq. m. *See also* Imperial Valley.

Salton Sink, Cal., U.S.A.; inland depression 287 ft. below sea-level.

Saluggia, *t.*, Piedmont; N. Italy; nuclear reactor.

Saluzzo, *t.*, Italy; nr. Cunei; cath., cas.; leather, silks, hats; p. *17,000.*

Salvador, El, *rep.*, Central America; on Pacific cst.; very hot, abundant summer rain but dry winter; coffee, sugar, rubber, tobacco, gold, silver, iron, mercury, ginned cotton; h.e.p. sta. at Guayabo Rapids; smallest and most densely populated of Central American States; cap. San Salvador; a. 13,173 sq. m.; p. (estd. 1965) *2,824,000.*

Salvador, *spt.*, Baia, Brazil; coffee, cocoa, tobacco, hides, castor seed, sisal; oil field and refinery at Matanipe; p. (1960) *655,735.*

Salween, *R.*, Burma; rises in Tibet, flows S. to G. of Martaban; many rapids; length 1,800 m.

Salzach, *R.*, Austria; trib. of R. Inn; length 130 m.

Salzburg, *prov.*, Austria, adjoining Bavaria and the Tyrol; on N. slope of E. Alps; many L., thermal springs; much mineral wealth; cap. Salzburg; a. 2,762 sq. m.; p. (1961) *347,292.*

Salzburg, *c.*, Austria; on R. Salzach; cath., cas.; birthplace of Mozart; tourist resort; salt, dairying, musical instruments; annual musical festival; p. (1964) *115,000.*

Salzgitter, *t.*, Lower Saxony, Germany; S.W. of Brunswick; steel, engin., wagon bldg., fertilisers; p. (1963) *113,200.* [mines.

Salzkammergut, *lake dist.*, Upper Austria; salt-

Salzwedel, *t.*, Magdeburg, E. Germany; on R. Jeetze; chemicals, sugar, metals; p. (1963) *20,567.* [tion.

Samakh, *t.*, Israel; on Sea of Galilee; rly. junc-

Samar, *I.*, Philippines; S. of Luzon; 147 m. long, 50 m. wide; a. 5,050 sq. m.; copper; p. (1960) *735,700.*

Samara, *see* Kuibyshev.

Samaria, *ancient c.*, Jordan, now Sabastye.

Samarinda, *t.*, Borneo, Indonesia; on E. cst.; p. *11,046.*

Samarkand, *c.*, Uzbek S.S.R.; E. of Bukhara; mosques and ancient ruins; univ.; textiles, engin.; p. (1967) *240,000.*

Samarra, *t.*, Iraq; on R. Tigris; Moslem holy c.; p. *8,000.*

Samawa, *t.*, Iraq; on R. Euphrates; cereals, carpets; p. *10,000.*

Sambalpur, *t.*, Orissa, India; on R. Mahanadi; ruined fort, old temples; cottons, silks; p. (1961) *38,915.*

Sambar, *C.*, S.W. Kalimantan, Indonesia.

Sambhal, *t.*, Uttar Pradesh, India; p. (1961) *68,940.*

Sambhar, *t.*, Rajasthan, India; p. (1961) *14,139.*

Sambre, *R.*, Belgium and N.E. France; trib. R. Meuse at Namur; length 110 m.

Samburu, *t.*, Kenya; rly. sta.

Samnan, *t.*, Iran; iron, sulphur ores, petroleum.

Samoa, Western, *ind. sov. st.* since Jan. 1962; not a member of Brit. Commonwealth but treated under N.Z. law as such; *gr.* of 9 Pacific Is. in Pac. Oc.; lgst., Savaii (a. 700 sq. m.); exp. copra, cacao beans, bananas; p. (estd.) *109,000.*

Samoa Is., Samoan gr. Pac. Oc.; E. of 171° long., W. of Greenwich; belong to U.S.A.; a. 76 sq. m.; lgst. I. Tutuila; ch. pt. Pago Pago; admin. ctr. Fagatogo; American naval sta.; p. (1960) *20,051.*

Samokov, *t.*, Bulgaria; S. of Sofia; industl.; p. (1956) *16,743.*

Samos, *I.*, Ægean Sea; Greek terr.; off W. cst. Anatolia; fine wine, silk, tobacco, cotton; cap. Vathéos; a. 180 sq. m.; p. (1961) *52,034.*

Samothrake, *ruggea I.*, Ægean Sea; alt. 5,248 ft.; the "Thracian Samos"; sulphur springs, sponges; a. 71 sq. m.; p. mainly Greeks.

Samshui, *t.*, *former treaty pt.*, Kwangtung, China; good tr. with Hong Kong; p. (1931) *9,160.*

Samsö, *I.*, Kattegat, Denmark; a. 42 sq. m.; p. (1960) *6,429.*

Samsun, *spt.*, Trabzon, Turkey; on Black Sea cst.; exp. tobacco, grain, timber, wax, wool, skins, copper goods, antimony; p. (1965) *106,921.*

San, *R.*, S.E. Poland; trib. of R. Vistula, bdy. between Poland and Ukraine.

San Ambrosia, *I.*, off cst. Chile.

San Angelo, *t.*, Texas, U.S.A.; on R. Concho; cattle, wool, mohair mkt.; dairy produce, petroleum, machine-shop prod.; p. (1960) *58,815.*

San Antonio, *sm. coastal t.*, Angola, Africa; at mouth of R. Congo; serves as occasional pt. of embarkation for travellers from lower regions of Congo (ex-Belgian).

San Antonio, *spt.*, Chile; nearest pt. for Santiago; holiday resort; exp. copper; p. (1961) *64,722.*

San Antonio, *c.*, *winter resort*, Texas, U.S.A.; at mouth of San Pedro R.; cath., fort., arsenal, univ.; producing, refining and mnftg. oil prod. and equipment, textiles, machin; meat pkg., food processing; p. (1960) *587,718.*

San Antonio, *C.*, most westerly point of Cuba.

San Benito, *spt.*, G. of Tehuantepec, Mexico.

San Bernardino, *t.*, Paraguay; holiday resort.

San Bernardino, *c.*, Cal., U.S.A.; railroad ctr.; citrus-fruit packing and shipping ctr.; p. (1960) *91,922.* [*124,756.*

San Carlos, *t.*, Luzon, Philippines; p. (1960)

San Carlos de Bariloche, *t.*, Argentina; on S. shore of L. Nahuel Huapi; tourist ctr.; p. (1960) *18,000.* [p. *14,325.*

San Casciano, *t.*, Italy; nr. Florence; industl.

San Cataldo, *t.*, Sicily; Italy; good tr.; p. *22,700.*

San Cristóbal, (formerly Cuidad Real), *t.*, Chiapas, Mexico; cath.; textiles; p. (1940) *11,763.*

San Cristóbal, *c.*, *cap.*, Táchira st., Venezuela; cath.; cement; wireless sta.; p. (1961) *96,102.*

San Diego, *t.*, Cal., U.S.A.; on Pacific cst., 10 m. N. of Mexican border; naval installation; fine harbour, winter health resort; fish-canning, aircraft, marble, onyx, missiles, electronics; p. (1960) *573,224.*

San Felipe, *cap.*, Yaracuy St., Venezuela; sugar, cacao, cotton, maize, fruits, rice, hides; p. (1961) *29,274.*

San Felipe de Aconcagua, *t.*, Chile; nr. Valparaiso; agr. ctr., copper and gold mng.; p. (1961) *27,149.* [*37,834.*

San Fernando, *t.*, Chile; agr. ctr.; p. (1961)

San Fernando, *t.*, B. of Cadiz, S. Spain; pt. has naval arsenal; salt mftg.; much of surrounding marshland now reclaimed; p. (1957) *41,196.*

San Fernando, *t.*, Venezuela; at confluence of Apuré and Portuguesa Rs.; ctr. cattle ranching region of upper Llanos; oil concessions not yet developed; p. (1961) *21,544.*

San Fernando, *spt.*, Trinidad I., W.I.; on W. cst. of Trinidad, 25 m. S. of Port of Spain; exp. sugar, asphalt, petrol; p. (estd. 1957) *38,850.*

San Francisco, *t.*, Argentina; on rly. between Córdoba and Santa Fé.

San Francisco, *c.*, *spt.*, Cal., U.S.A.; on the San

F. bay; entrance spanned by Golden Gate Bridge, second longest single-span bridge in the world; univ.: engin., canning, lumber mills, printing, publishing, chemicals, machin., petrol; p. (1960) *742,855.*

San Francisco Pass, Argentina–Chile; across Andes at alt. 15,505 ft.

San Francisco de Macoris, *t.,* Dominican rep., W. Indies; p. *18,108.*

San Geronimo, *t.,* Oaxaca st., Mexico; rly. junction.

San Giovanni a Teduccio, *t.,* S. Italy; at foot of Vesuvius; iron mines, rly. wkshps.; p. *27,475.*

San Giovanni in Persiceto, *t.,* N. Italy; nr. Bologna; p. *20,450.*

San Isidro, *t.,* E. Argentina; N. sub. Buenos Aires; resort; p. (1960) *80,000.*

San Jerónimo, *t.,* Rio Grande do Sul, Brazil; low-grade coal.

San José, *prov.,* Costa Rica, Central America; cap. San J.; bauxite mng. nr. San Isidro del General projected and road connecting S.I. del G. with Punta Uvita where sm. pt. will be built.

San José, *t., cap.,* Costa Rica; cath., univ., observ.; coffee tr.; p. (1963) *267,454.*

San José, *c.,* Cal., U.S.A.; in Santa Clara valley; nr. is Lick Observatory; resort; fruit and vegetable canning; lumber prod., woollens, leather; p. (1960) *204,196.*

San José, *dep.,* Uruguay; a. 2,688 sq. m.; cap. San J.; p. (1953) *96,842.*

San José, *t., cap.,* San José, Uruguay; grain, flour milling; p. (1963) *20,000.*

San Juan, *prov.,* Argentina; at foot of the Andes; a. 34,432 sq. m.; cap. San Juan; gold, copper; p. (1960) *352,000.*

San Juan, *t., ca.,* San Juan, Argentina; wine, fruit, cattle; p. *112,286.*

San Juan, *c., cap.,* Puerto Rico, Central America; cath.; univ.; naval sta., airport; distilleries, sugar; p. (1960) *431,705.*

San Juan R., Central America; divides Nicaragua and Costa Rica; plans made for its canalisation, which would give both countries a clear water-way from Caribbean to Pacific; length 90 m.

San Juan, R., Mexico; trib. of Rio Grande; length 160 m.

San Juan del Norte (Greytown), *spt.,* S.E. pt. of Nicaragua on Caribbean Sea.

San Juan del Rio, *t.,* Durango, Mexico; p. *6,694.*

San Juan del Sur, *spt.,* Nicaragua, Central America; coffee, timber, sugar; p. (1960) *4,223.*

San Juanito, *spt.,* Lower Cal., Mexico; on W. cst.

San Lorenzo, *min.,* S. Argentina; alt. 12,000 ft.

San Lorenzo, *t.,* Argentina, 14 m. N. Rosario; lge. chemical wks.

San Lucas, *O.,* point of Lower Cal., Mexico.

San Luis, *prov.,* Argentina; oranges, grapes; a. 29,700 sq. m.; cap. S.L.; p. (1960) *174,000.*

San Luis, *t., cap.,* St. Luis, Argentina; cattle, grain, wines; onyx quarrying; p. (1960) *38,000.*

San Luis Obispo, *t.,* Cal., U.S.A.; p. (1960) *20,437.*

San Luis Potosi, *st.,* Mexico; agr. and mining; cap. San Luis Potosí; a. 24,415 sq. m.; p. (1960) *1,048,297.*

San Luis Potosi, *t., cap.,* San Luis Potosí st., Mexico; arsenic plant, clothing, cottons, rly. wks., lead-, silver- and gold-refining; sulphur fields; wool hides, cattle; p. (1960) *159,980.*

San Marco in Lanis, *t.,* Foggia, Italy; p. *19,275.*

San Marino, *small republic;* on spurs of Apennines, Italy; ch. exp.: wine, woollen goods, hides, building stone; farming, cattle-raising; wine; a. 23·8 sq. m.; cap. San Marino; p. (estd. 1962) *17,000.*

San Marino, *t., cap.,* San Marino; on hill-top, alt. over 1,200 ft., 12 m. S.W. of Rimini; tourists; wine, curios for sale to tourists; p. *2,200.*

San Martin, *dep.,* Peru; ch. t. Moyobamba; a. 17,448 sq. m.; p. (1961) *162,592.*

San Mateo, *t.,* Cal., U.S.A.; residtl. sub. San Francisco; p. (1960) *69,870.*

San Miguel, *c.,* El Salvador, Central America; on Rio Grande; nr. malarial swamps; cotton, sisal, coffee, cattle; p. (1960) *80,759.*

San Miguel, *principal I.,* Azores, Portugal; hot sulphur springs, oranges, etc.; 41 m. by 9 m.; cap. Ponta Delgada.

San Nicolas, R. *pt.,* Argentina; on Paraná R.; cattle, flour, agr. produce, distillery; steel plant; p. (1960) *55,000.*

San Pedro, *spt.,* Cal., U.S.A.; sub. Los Angeles; naval base; p. (1950) *36,527*

San Pedro de Macoris, *t.,* Dominican Rep., W. Indies; p. (1948) *24,200.*

San Pedro Sula, *t.,* Honduras, Central America; ctr. for banana and sugar inds.; rice mill; p. (1961) *58,931.*

San Quintin Bay, *spt.,* Lower Cal., Mexico.

San Rafael, *t.,* W. Argentina; agr., cattle, fruit; p. *32,663.*

San Remo, *sm. pt.,* Italy; famous winter seaside resort on Italian riviera; flower mkt., olive oil, lemons, wine; 12th cent. church; p. *31,525.*

San Roque, *O.,* E. Brazil.

San Roque, *t.,* Andalusia, Spain; nr. Gibraltar; p. (1957) *15,333.*

San Salvador or Watling's I., Bahama Is., W. Indies; discovered by Christopher Columbus, 1492; p. (1953) *694.*

San Salvador, *cap.,* El Salvador; univ., observatory; silks, cottons, cigars; p. (estd. 1965) *253,000.*

San Salvador de Jujuy, *t.,* Argentina; wheat, maize, sugar; minerals, timber; p. (1960) *52,000.*

San Sebastian, *c., spt., cap.,* Guipuzcoa, Spain; captured by Wellington 1813; gd. tr. and fisheries; sailcloth, cottons, paper, glass; p. (1959) *129,395.*

San Severo, *mkt. t.,* S. Italy; hill-top site, 15 m. N.W. of Foggia, Apulia; cath.; wine ctr., cream of tartar, bricks; p. (1961) *43,443.*

San'a, *cap.,* Yemen, Arabia; walled c. 7,270 ft. above sea-level; tr. in silk, cottons and china; jewellery, arms, fruit; p. (estd. 1965) *100,000.*

Sanandaj, *c.,* Iran; prov. cap. Kordestan; p. (1967) *204,676.*

Sanchez, *spt.,* Dominican Rep., W. Indies; situated on the Bahia de Sumana, at E. end of Cibao lowland dist.; linked to Santiago by rail; exp. cacao, tobacco.

Sancti Spiritus, *c.,* Santa Clara, Cuba; in grazing dist.; sugar, tobacco; p. (1953) *37,740.*

Sandakan, *impt. tr. c.,* Sabah, E. Indies; N.E. cst.; fine natural harbour; exp. timber, rubber, copra, hemp, salt fish; p. (1960) *28,806.*

Sandalwood (Sumba), *I.,* in Malay Archipelago, S. of Flores, Indonesia; very fertile; horse-breeding; rice, maize, tobacco, timber, cinnamon; *cap.* Waingapu; a. 4,305 sq. m.; p. *251,126.*

Sanday, *I.,* Barra Is., Orkney, Scot.

Sandbach, *t., urb. dist.,* Cheshire, Eng.; 5 m. S.E. of Middlewich; salt, chemicals, motor vehicles; p. (1961) *9,856.*

Sandoa, *t.,* Congo; on upper Lulua R.; admin. ctr.; p. *5,000.*

Sandown-Shanklin, *t., urb. dist.,* I. of Wight, Eng.; on Sandown Bay; holiday resort; p. (1961) *14,257.*

Sandringham, *par.,* Norfolk, Eng.; Royal residence; farming. [p. *5,529.*

Sandur, *t.,* Mysore st., India; manganese, iron;

Sandusky, *c.,* Ohio, U.S.A.; on S. cst., L. Erie; tr. in coal, fruit, and foodstuffs; paper, farm implements, chemicals; p. (1960) *31,989.*

Sandwich, *t., mun. bor., Cinque pt.,* Kent, Eng.; at mouth of Stour R.; mkt., light inds., chemicals nearby; p. (estd. 1967) *4,590.*

Sandwich Is., *dependency* of Falkland Is., Brit. Crown Col. S. Atlantic.

Sandy, *t., urb. dist.,* Beds, Eng.; 3 m. N.W. of Biggleswade; mkt. gardening; p. (1961) *3,392.*

Sandy Hook, *peninsula,* N.J., U.S.A.; projecting into lower bay of N.Y.; yachting ctr.

Sanford, *t.,* Fla., U.S.A.; p. (1960) *19,175.*

Sanga, R., trib. of Congo R.; Equatorial Africa.

Sangir (Sangihe), *Is.,* Indonesia; between Philippines and Celebes; eruption of volcano on ch. I. killed 12,000 inhabitants, 1856.

Sankt Ingbert, *t.,* Saarland, N.E. of Saarbrücken; coal-mining, iron, glass, machin., textiles, leather; p. (1963) *28,700.*

Sankuru, R., trib. of Kasai R., Congo, Central Africa.

Sanlucar, *t.,* Cadiz, Spain; nr. mouth R. Guadalquivir; wines and agr. produce; ruined cas.; p. (1957) *35,363.*

Sanniya Hor, L., Iraq; linked to R. Tigris; shallow, acts as flood control reservoir.

Sannois, *t.,* Seine-et-Oise, France; p. (1954) *13,644.* [p. *11,176.*

Sanok, *t.,* Poland; nr. Rzeszów; metallurgy;

Sanquhar, *burgh,* Dumfries, Scot.; in upper Nithsdale; carpets, coal, bricks; p. (1961) *2,182.*

Sansanding, *t.*, Mali, W. Africa; lge. barrage across R. Niger.

Santa Ana, *c.*, El Salvador, Central America; municipal palace, barracks; coffee, sugar; p. (1959) *130,976.*

Santa Ana, *t.*, Cal., U.S.A.; fruit farming, oilfields, mnfs. farm implements, preserved fruits; p. (1960) *100,350.*

Santa Bárbara, *dist.*, Honduras; Panama hats; p. (1962) *145,100.*

Santa Barbara, *t.*, *winter resort*, Cal., U.S.A.; at foot of Santa Inez mtns.; fruit, oil; p. (1960) *58,259.*

Santa Catarina, *st.*, Brazil; inc. Santa Catarina I.; a. 36,435 sq. m.; mineral wealth; cap. Florianopolis; p. (1960) *2,146,909.*

Santa Clara, *t.*, Cuba; at alt. over 1,200 ft.; sugar, tobacco, cattle; p. (1964) *121,000.*

Santa Clara Valley, Cal., U.S.A.; extends S. from San Francisco Bay; intensive fruit-growing under irrigation, prunes; ch. t. San José.

Santa Cruz, *spt.*, Patagonia, Argentina; sheep; p. *3,000.*

Santa Cruz, *prov.*, S. Argentina; sheep, horses; cap. Gallegos; a. 93,952 sq. m.; p. (1960) *53,000.*

Santa Cruz, *t.*, Bolivia; alt. 1,500 ft.; univ.; sugar, coffee, rice, cattle; oil refining; Japanese settlement nearby; p. (1962) *72,703.*

Santa Cruz, *dep.*, Bolivia; cap. S. C.; p. (1962) *326,900.*

Santa Cruz, *c.*, Cal., U.S.A.; on Monterey Bay; popular seaside resort, fruit, and vegetable canning; fishing; p. (1970) *25,596.*

Santa Cruz, *t.*, cap. Tenerife I., Canary Is.; p. (1962) *133,100.*

Santa Cruz Is., Pac. Oc.; Brit. Solomon Is.

Santa Cruz de la Sierra, *t.*, Bolivia; on R. Piray; sugar, flour; distilling; p. *33,000.*

Santa Cruz de Tenerife, *prov.* (Spanish), Canary Is., Atl. Oc.; inc. Is. of Tenerife, Palma, Gomera, Hierro; a. 1,329 sq. m.; p. (1962) *507,744.*

Santa Fé, *prov.*, Argentina; agr. and stock farming; cap. Santa Fé; a. 52,056 sq. m.; p. (1960) *1,866,000.*

Santa Fé, *t.*, Argentina; on I. in R. Salado; cath., univ.; dairy prod.; zinc and copper smelting; road tunnel to Panama under construction; p. (1960) *203,300.*

Santa Fé, *t.*, N.M., U.S.A.; at base of Sangre de Cristo range; oldest capital in U.S. founded by Spaniards 1610; p. (1960) *34,676.*

Santa Isabel, *cap.*, Equatorial Guinea, W. Africa; harbour; p. (estd. 1965) *37,000.*

Santa Maria, *t.*, Rio Grande do Sul, Brazil; rly. ctr.; tanning, hats, brewing, maté, wine timber, rice; p. (1960) *78,632.*

Santa Maria, *t.*, Campania, Italy; on site of ancient Capua; cath.; glass, leather; p. *36,637.*

Santa Maria de Garona, Spain; nr. Burgos; nuclear power plant being built.

Santa Marta, *spt.*, *cap.*, Magdalena dep., Colombia, S. America; cath.; bananas; p. (1960) *64,400.*

Santa Maura, see Levkás.

Santa Monica, *c.*, Cal., U.S.A.; sub. Los Angeles; residtl.; p. (1960) *83,249.*

Santa Rosa, *t.*, *cap.*, La Pampa terr., Argentina; p. (1960) *17,000.*

Santa Rosa, *t.*, Cal., U.S.A.; fruit, grain, dairying; p. (1960) *31,027.*

Santa Rosalia, *t.*, peninsula of Lower Cal., Mexico; located E. cst. on G. of Cal.; impt. copper-mines.

Santander, *dep.*, Columbia, S. America; E. of the Magdalena R.; cap. Bucaramanga; a. 12,379 sq. m.; p. (estd. 1959) *838,430.*

Santander, *prov.*, Spain; agr., grape growing, fisheries; cap. Santander; a. 2,108 sq. m.; p. (1959) *427,235.*

Santander, *spt.*, *cap.*, Santander prov., Spain; former summer resort of the Court; cath.; exp. iron and zinc ore; p. (1959) *113,116.*

Santarém, *t.*, Para, Brazil; rubber, cacao, Brazil nuts, sugar; p. (1960) *24,924.*

Santarem, *dist.*, *t.*, Portugal; in fertile valley of R. Tagus; cap. S.; p. (1960) of dist. *480,038*, of t. *16,449.*

Santiago, *prov.*, Chile; cap. Santiago; a. 5,557 sq. m.; p. (1961) *2,283,977.*

Santiago de Chile, *c.*, *cap.*, Chile; on R. Mapocho; most populous t. on Pacific side of S. America; cath., univ.; national library; leather, textiles, chemicals, cars; p. (1961) *2,114,000.*

Santiago de Compostella, *c.*, Corunna, Spain;

on R. Sar; cath. (with tomb of St. James); univ.; beer, spirits, paper, linen; p. (1950) *55,553.*

Santiago de Cuba, *c.*, *spt.*, Cuba, W. Indies; on S. cst.; former cap. of I.; cath.; iron foundries, tanneries, ctr. of mineral dist.; exp. sugar, coffee, tobacco; Spanish fleet destroyed by U.S.A. warships here 1898; p. (1964) *231,000.*

Santiago de los Caballeros, *t.*, Dominican Rep., W. Indies; p. (1964) *329,808.*

Santiago del Estero, *t.*, Argentina; on R. Dulce; p. (1960) *92,000.*

Santiago del Estero, *prov.*, Argentina; cap. S. del E.; a. 52,511 sq. m.; p. (1960) *477,000.*

Santiago-Zamora, *prov.*, Ecuador; p. (1950) *21,046.*

Säntis, *mtn.*, on bdr. Swiss cans. St. Gallen and Appenzell, alt. 8,216 ft.; Europe's highest television transmitter on summit.

Santo Domingo, *spt.*, *cap.*, Dominican Rep.; cath. univ.; p. (estd. 1965) *529,000.*

Santoña, *spt.*, Spain; on No. cst., E. of Santander.

Santorene, *see* Thera.

Santos, *c.*, *spt.*, São Paulo, Brazil; world's ch. coffee pt.; also exp. oranges, bananas, cotton, and industl. prod.; tog. with São Vicente and nearby Guarujá resort ctr.; p. (1960) *265,753.*

Santo Tomé de la Guayana, *c.*, S.E. Venezuela; new industl. c. nr. confluence of Orinoco and Caroni Rs.; iron mines, steel, hydroelec. power and aluminium plants in a.; vast industl. complex projected.

São Carlos, *t.*, São Pau'o st., Brazil; 120 m. N.W. of São Paulo; ctr. of coffee-growing a.; textiles, refrigerators, furniture; p. (1960) *50,010.*

São Francisco, *R.*, Brazil; flows from Minas Gerais prov., to Atlantic; navigable for 150 m. below cataract of Paulo Afonso; length 1,600 m.

São Leopoldo, *t.*, Rio Grande do Sul st., S. Brazil; 20 m.½N. of Porto Alegre, mkt. t; (1960) *41,023.*

São Luiz, *cap.*, Maranhao st., Brazil; cultural ctr.; p. (1960) *159,628.*

São Paulo, *st.*, Brazil, on Atlantic cst.; major industl. a. of S. America; coffee, cotton, sugar, rice, maize; vehicles, elec. gds., chemicals, textiles, telecomm. equipment, metal-wkg. plants; cap. São Paulo, Santos lgst pt. in Brazil; a. 95,454 sq. m.; p. (1967) *15,909,012.*

São Paulo, *c.*, *cap.* São Paulo st., Brazil; fast-growing c., comm. and industl. ctr. of Brazil and leading c. of S. America; vehicles, machin., elec. gds., textiles, pharmaceutics; aluminium a. refinery projected; nearby pt. Santos ships rich agr. prod. from hinterland; p. (1967) *5,383,194* (mun. a.); of Greater São Paulo *5,885,561.*

São Roque, *c.*, Rio Grande do Norte st., N.E. Brazil; most N.E. point of S. America.

São Tomé with Principe Is. in the G. of Guinea; p. (1965) *64,000.*

Saône, *R.*, France; rises in Vosges, and flows to R. Rhône at Lyons; length 282 m.

Saône-et-Loire, *dep.*, France; mtnous; noted vineyards; cap. Mâcon; a. 3,331 sq. m. p. (1962) *535,772.*

Saône-Haute, *dep.*, France; mainly agr.; cap. Vesoul; a. 2,074 sq. m.; p. (1962) *208,440.*

Sapporo, *c.*, Hokkaido, Japan; industl., admin., educational ctr.; oil, iron, non-ferrous metals; p. (1965) *794,908.*

Saqqâra, *t.*, U.A.R.; tombs and pyramids; nr. site of Memphis.

Saragossa, *see* Zaragoza.

Sarajevo, *t.*, *cap.*, Bosnia and Herzegovina, Jugoslavia; the assassination here, on 28 June 1914, of the Archduke Francis Ferdinand precipitated the First World War; weaving carpets, pottery, flour, silks, sugar; p. (1959) *176,000.*

Saransk, *t.*, R.S.F.S.R.; Mordov A.S.S.R. 145 m. S.E. of Gorkiy; univ.; elec. equipment; engin.; p. (1967) *146,000.*

Sarapul, *R. pt.*, R.S.F.S.R., on R. Kama; boots, shoes, gloves, engin.; p. (1959) *68,000.*

Saratoga Springs, N.Y., U.S.A.; summer resort at foot of Adirondack mtns., mineral springs; p. (1960) *16,630.*

Saratov, *t.*, *pt.*, R.S.F.S.R.; on R. Volga; univ.; engin., ball-bearings, textiles, oil-refining, saw-milling; p. (1967) *699,000.*

Sarawak, *st.* East Malaysia; exp. sago, rubber, oil, pepper; cap. Kuching; a. 47,071 sq. m.; p. (estd. 1963) *820,000.*

Sardinia, *I.*, *aut. region*, Italy; Mediterranean; mtnous.; sheep, cattle, fishing, wheat, barley, fruit, wine; oil refining at Sarroch on S. cst.; cap. Cagliari; part of former kingdom of Sardina belonging to house of Savoy; a. 9,302 sq. m.; p. (1961) *1,413,289.*

Sargasso Sea, *zone,* situated in S.W. of North Atlantic; relatively still sea within swirl of warm ocean currents. Noted for abundance of gulf-weed on its surface, rich in marine life. Named by Columbus.       [*206,463.*

Sari, *c.,* Iran, prov. cap. Mazandaran; p. (1967)

Sark, *I.,* Channel Is.; 6 m. E. of Guernsey; picturesque scenery; farming; tourist ctr.; a. 1,274 acres; p. inc. Brechou *560.*

Sark, *R.,* forms extreme W. bdy. between Scot. and Eng.

Sarnia, *t.,* Ontario, Canada; on St. Clair R.; car parts, machin., oil refineries, petro-chemical inds.; p. (1961) *50,976.*

Sarpsborg, *t.,* Norway; on R. Glommen; mftg. inds.; lgst. pulp and paper concern in kingdom; p. (estd. 1960) *13,500.*

Sarreguemines, *t.,* Moselle, France; 7 m. S.E. of Saarbrücken; porcelain, plush leather, matches; p. (1962) *23,243.*

Sarria, *t.,* Lugo, Spain; p. (1957) *16,142.*

Sarthe, *dep.,* N.W. France; undulating surface; farming, apples, livestock; coal, linen, potteries; cap. Le Mans; a. 2,412 sq. m.; p. (1962) *443,019.*

Sarthe, *R.,* France; trib. of R. Loire; l. 165 m.

Sàrzana, *t.,* Liguria, Italy; nr. Spezia; cath.; silks; p. *13,550.*

Sasebo, *spt.,* Kyushu, Japan; p. (1965) *247,069.*

Saseno I., Adriatic Sea; off cst. of Albania.

Saskatchewan, *prov.,* Canada; coniferous forests and plains; Rs. Saskatchewan and Churchill; many lge. Ls.; extreme climate; good rail communications; hydro-elec. power; gr. wheat prov.; livestock, dairying; oil, coal, copper, potash, helium, furs, fisheries; cap. Regina; a. 251,700 sq. m.; p. (1961) *925,181.*

Saskatchewan, *R.,* Canada; flows from Rocky mtns. through L. Winnipeg and thence by R. Nelson to Hudson Bay; length 1,450 m.

Saskatoon, *c.,* Saskatchewan Canada; univ.; flour, cement, oil refining; p. (1961) *95,526.*

Sasolburg, *t.,* O.F.S., S. Africa; oil from coal production; gas pipeline to Germiston a. p. (1960) *12,557* (inc. *6,723* whites).

Sasovo, *t.,* R.S.F.S.R.; wood inds.; p. *10,000.*

Sassari, *t.,* Sardinia, Italy; nr. G. of Asinara; cath., univ., palaces; tobacco and macaroni wks.; oil, grain; p. (1961) *89,482.*

Satara, *t.,* Maharashtra, India; p. (1961) *48,709.*

Sattahip, *pt.,* Thailand; new pt. inaugurated 1967.

Satu-Mare, *t.,* N.W. Romania; pottery, textiles; p. (1963) *63,656.*

Saudi Arabia, *lgst. kingdom,* pen. of Arabia; cap. Riyadh; formerly kingdom of Hejaz (cap. Mecca) and Nejd (cap. Riyadh); mainly desert; nomadic pop; Moslem; dates, wheat, barley; impt. oil concessions; oil refining at Jeddah; a. 1,500,000 sq. m.; p. (estd) *6,000,000.*

Sauerland, *dist., Land,* N. Rhine–Westphalia, W. Germany; plateau, alt. from 500 to 1,500 ft., E. of Rhine and between valleys of Sieg and Ruhr; agriculturally poor, largely forested; crossed by R. Wupper, with which are associated industl. ts. Wuppertal (textiles), Solingen and Remscheld (cutlery and special steel).

Sault Ste. Marie, *c.,* Mich., U.S.A.; on L. Superior at rapids; flour, woollens, locomotives; p. (1960) *18,722.*

Sault Ste. Marie, *c.,* Ontario, Canada; on L. Superior at rapids; pulp, paper, iron, steel; p. (1961) *43,088.*

Saulte Ste. Marie Canals ("Soo"), Canada and U.S.A.; twin canals on Canadian and American side of shallow channel linking L. Superior and L. Huron; traversed by all wheat and iron-ore traffic from L. Superior pts.; length (Canadian) 1 m.; depth 18 ft.

Saumur, *t.,* Maine-et-Loire, France; on R. Loire, 30 m. S.W. of Tours; wines, enamels, tinware; p. (1962) *22,876.*       [Gujarat st.

Saurashtra, *former st.,* India; now absorbed into

Sava or Save, *R.,* N. Jugoslavia; trib. of Danube; length 550 m.

Savage or Niue, Cook Is., Pac. Oc.; under N.Z.; ch. exp. native plaited ware, bananas, copra, and sweet potatoes; ch. pt. Alofi; a. 100 sq. m.

Savaii I., *lgst. of Samoan gr.,* Pac. Oc.; a. 703 sq. m.

Savannah, *c., spt.,* Ga., U.S.A.; Kraft paper,

sugar refining, ship bldg. and repair, fertilisers, paint; p. (1960) *149,245.*

Savannah, *R.,* U.S.A.; flows between Ga. and S.C. to Atl. Oc.; length 450 m.

Save, *B.,* France; trib. of R. Garonne; 65 m. l.

Saverne, Col de, *low pass,* N.E. France; carries trunk rly. from Paris to Strasbourg and the Orient between Vosges and Hardt Mtns.; gradual approach from W., steep descent to E. into Rhine valley.

Savigliano, *t.,* Piedmont, Italy; silk; p. *18,725.*

Savoie or Savoy, *dep.,* S.E. France; on Italian border; mountainous; mineral springs, pastoral, dairying; cap. Chambéry; Vanoise Park (1st French nat. park); a. 2,389 sq. m.; p. (1962) *266,673.*

Savoie (Haute), *dep.,* France; mountainous; farming, wine, cheese; cap. Annecy; a. 1,774 sq. m.; p. (1962) *329,230.*

Savona, *spt.,* Genoa, Italy; cath.; iron, shipbldg., glass and tinplate wks.; exp. preserved fruits and tomatoes; p. (1961) *71,007.*

Sawbridgeworth, *t., urb. dist.,* Herts, Eng.; on R. Stort, 4 m. S. of Bishops Stortford; malting, fruit preserving; p. (1961) *4,633.*

Saxmundham, *mkt. t., urb. dist.,* Suffolk, Eng.; 18 m. N.E. of Ipswich; p. (1961) *1,538.*

Saxony, *former Land,* E. Germany; farming, printing, toy-founding, toys, textiles, lace, spirits, beer, coal, iron, mineral springs; ch. ts. Dresden. Leipzig, Karl-Marx-Stadt.

Saxony-Anhalt, *former Land,* E. Germany

Sayan Mtns., *range of mtns.,* between Rs. Yenisei and Angra, R.S.F.S.R.

Scafell Pike, *mtn.,* Cumberland, Eng.; in N. Pennines; highest in Eng.; alt. 3,210 ft.

Scalby, *t., urb. dist.,* N.R. Yorks, Eng.; 3 m. N.W. of Scarborough; p. (1961) *7,251.*

Scalpay, *I.,* off E. cst. of Skye, Scot.

Scalpay, Harris, Outer Hebrides, Scot.

Scalloway, Shetlands, on W. cst. of Mainland; the anc. cap.; ruined castle.

Scandinavia, Sweden, Norway and Denmark.

Scapa Flow, *strait,* N. Scot.; between Pomona and Hoy, Orkney Is., surrendered German fleet scuttled, 1919.

Scarba, *I.,* Argyll, Scot.; off N. end of Jura.

Scarborough, *t., mun. bor.,* N.R. Yorks, Eng.; on E. cst. 18 m. N.W. of Flamborough Head; seaside resort; p. (estd. 1967) *42 200.*

Scarpanto, *I.,* Dodecanese, Greece; E. Mediterranean; between Rhodes and Crete,; p. *3,747.*

Schaan-Vaduz, *t.,* Liechtenstein; point where Arlberg Express (Paris–Vienna) passes through the principality.

Schaffhausen, *most N. can.,* Switzerland; on R. Rhine; pastoral and afforested; cap. Schaffhausen; p. (1961) *65,981.*

Schaffhausen, *t.,* cap. Schaffhausen can., Switzerland; on the Rhine; cath., cas.; famous falls, iron, steel, aluminium, cottons, brewing, distilling; p. (1957) *25,971.*

Schaumburg-Lippe, *former st.,* between provs. of Hanover and Westphalia, Germany, now part of Lower Saxony; farming; coal-mining.

Schefferville, *t.,* Canada; 360 m. N. of St. Lawrence estuary and connected to it (at Seven Islands) by rly.; ctr. of iron-ore mines of Quebec-Labrador trough; p. (estd.) *3,500.*

Scheldt (Scheldt), *R.,* France, Neth. and Belgium; rises in Aisne, France, flows to N. Sea; 248 m.

Schenectady, *c.,* N.Y. U.S.A.; foundries, wireless-transmitting apparatus, locomotive; synthetic diamonds; p. (1960) *81,682.*

Scheveningen, *seaside resort,* Neth.; 2 m. N.W. of The Hague; fishing.

Schiedam, *t.,* Neth.; W. of Rotterdam; distilleries, gin; shipyds., mnfs., chemicals, machin.; p. (1967) *82,222.*

Schiehallion, *mtn.,* Perth, Scot.; alt. 3,547 ft.

Schiltigheim, *t.,* Bas-Rhin, France; machin., factory equipment; p. (1954) *22,793.*

Schlei, *narrow inlet* of Baltic, Schleswig-Holstein, Germany; 25 m. long.

Schleswig, *c., pt.,* Schleswig-Holstein, Germany; cath., cas.; rope wks., tanning, freighting; p. (1963) *33,600.*

Schleswig-Holstein, *Land,* N. Germany; retroceded from Denmark 1920; cap. Kiel; moors and plain farming, livestock; textiles, tobacco; oil; a. 6,048 sq. m.; p. (1961) *2,316,000.*

Schlettstadt, *see* Sélestat.

Schneidemühl, *see* Pila.

**Schoonebeek**, *vil.*, Drente, Neth.; S. of Emmen; lge. oilfield; p. (1967) 7,473.

**Schönebeck**, *t.*, Magdeburg, E. Germany; on R. Elbe; metals, chemicals, brewing; p. (1963) 45,035. [Bay; p. 25,487.

**Schouten I.**, West Irian, Indonesia; in Geelvink

**Schouwen I.**, Zeeland, Neth.; in N. Sea.

**Schuylkill R.**, Penns., U.S.A.; flows into Delaware R.; length 130 m.

**Schwabach**, *t.*, Bavaria, Germany; S. of Nürnberg; metal inds.; p. (1963) 23,900.

**Schwäbisch-Gmünd**, *c.*, Baden-Württemberg, Germany; E. of Stuttgart; cath.; clocks, glass, optical, precious metal and jewellery inds.; p. (1963) 40,500.

**Schwarzwald (Black Forest)**, *forest belt*, Land Baden-Württemberg, W. Germany; a. 1,844 sq. m.; highest peak Feldberg, alt. 4,900 ft.

**Schwechat**, *t.*, Austria; nr. Vienna; oil refining; oil pipeline to Trieste; p. (1961) 13,403.

**Schwedt**, *t.*, Frankfurt, E. Germany; on R. Oder; lge. oil refinery; oil pipeline from Mozyr; p. (1963) 14,775.

**Schweinfurt**, *t.*, Bavaria, Germany; on R. Main, N.E. of Würzburg; metals, machin., ball bearings, dyes, brewing; p. (1963) 57,800.

**Schwelm**, *t.*, N. Rhine-Westphalia, Germany; E. of Wuppertal; metals machin., textiles, paper; p. (1963) 34,200.

**Schwenningen**, *t.*, Baden-Württemberg, Germany; clocks, metals, footwear; p. (1963) 32,600.

**Schwerin**, *cap.*, Schwerin, E. Germany; indust. and educational; cath. palace; p. (1963) 94,786.

**Schwyz**, *forest can.*, Switzerland; cap. Schwyz; a. 350 sq. m.; p. (1961) 78,048. [(1957) 12,464.

**Schwyz**, *t.*, Switzerland; nr. L. of Lucerne; p.

**Sciacca**, *spt.*, Sicily, Italy; nr. Agrigento; cath.; H.Q. of Mediterranean coral fishery; sardines, olives; mineral springs; p. approx. 25,000.

**Scilla**, *promontory*, Strait of Messina, Calabria, Italy.

**Scilly Is.**, *gr.*, 30 m. S.W. of Land's End, Cornwall, Eng.; total a. 10 sq. m.; lgst. I., St. Marys; cap. Hugh Town; flowers, vegetables; p. (1961) 2,273. [mouth; length 250 m.

**Scioto, R.**, Ohio, U.S.A.; joins Ohio at Portsmouth.

**Scone**, *par.*, Perth, Scot.; place of residence and coronation of early Scottish kings; from here Edward I. removed the Stone of Destiny to Westminster Abbey in 1297; tourist ctr.; civil aerodrome.

**Scotland**, Brit. Is.; N. part of Gr. Britain; contains 33 cos.; home affairs administered by Dep. of Secretary of State for Scot.; physically divided into Highlands (many islands on W.), Middle Lowlands and S. Uplands; highest peaks, Ben Nevis 4,406 ft. and Ben Macdhui 4,296 ft.; ch. Ls., L. Lomond, L. Ness; ch. Rs., Clyde, Tweed, Tay, Spey, Dee, Forth; climate, maritime; agr. in E., grazing in W.; oats, barley, wheat, potatoes, fruit; coal, iron, oil-shale, granite; fisheries; mnfs., textiles, ship-bldg.; machin., distilling, sugar-refining, printing; hydroelectric development in Highlands; cap. Edinburgh; Glasgow, ch. comm. and industl. t.; a. 29,796 sq. m.; p. (1961) 5,178,490.

**Scranton**, *c.*, Penns., U.S.A.; on R. Susquehanna; anthracite, iron foundries, steel wks., locomotives, and silk mnfs.; p. (1960) 111,443.

**Scunthorpe**, *t.*, *mun. bor.*, Lindsey, Lincs, Eng., on Lincoln Edge, 6 m. S. of the Humber; iron-mng. and smelting, steel girders, engin., chemicals, tar distillation, hosiery, lt. inds.; p. (estd. 1967) 71,010.

**Scutari** (Albania), see Shkodra.

**Scutari** (Turkey), see Usküdar.

**Seaford**, *t.*, *urb. dist.*, E. Sussex, Eng.; 3 m. E. of Newhaven; seaside resort; p. (1961) 10,994.

**Seaforth Loch**, Lewis, Outer Hebrides, Scot.; 14 m. long.

**Seaham**, *spt.*, *urb. dist.*, Durham, Eng.; Seaham Harbour, on E. cst. 4 m. S. of Sunderland; modern colly. workings, extending under sea; p. (estd. 1967) 25,200.

**Seathwaite**, *vil.*, Cumberland, Eng.; 7 m. from Keswick, close to Styhead (1,430 ft.); exceptionally heavy annual rainfall (above 150 in.).

**Seaton**, *t.*, *urb. dist.*, S. Devon, Eng.; on Lyme Bay at mouth of R. Axe; seaside resort; freestone quarries; p. (1961) 3,410.

**Seaton Carew**, Durham, Eng.; within Hartlepool co. bor.; proposed site for nuclear power sta. nr. mouth of R. Tees.

**Seaton Valley**, *t.*, *urb. dist.*, Northumberland, Eng.; nr. Blythe; coal-mining; p. (estd. 1967) 28,410.

**Seattle**, *spt.*, Wash., U.S.A.; univ.. cath.; shipbldg., aeroplanes, glass, fish-canning, fishing, packing, lumbering, chemicals, trucks, buses; p. (1960) 557,087.

**Sebnitz**, *t.*, Dresden, E. Germany; p. (1963) 14,520. [sta.; p. (1961) 78,412.

**Secunderabad**, Andhra Pradesh, India; military

**Sedalia**, *c.*, Mo., U.S.A.; farming, meat-packing; machin., textiles, coal; rly. ctr. and wks.; p. (1960) 23,874.

**Sedan**, *t.*, Ardennes, France; on R. Meuse; weaving; machin., metal ware, woollens, flour; battle 1870; p. (1962) 22,284.

**Sedgley**, *industl. t.*, *urb. dist.*, Staffs, Eng.; nr. Wolverhampton; coal-mng., metal wks., bricks, engin., fireclay goods; p. (1961) 27,927.

**Segezha**, *t.*, R.S.F.S.R.; on L. Vyg; cellulose, paper, sawmilling.

**Sego**, *L.*, R.S.F.S.R.; 20 by 20 m.; N.W. of L. Onega; outlet into White Sea.

**Ségou**, *t.*, *R. pt.*, Mali, W. Africa; on R. Niger; ctr. of irrigation scheme; cotton, hides, cattle, wax, salt; p. (1957) 21,000.

**Ségou Canal**, W. Africa; leaves R. Niger 4 m. below Bamako, extends 130 m. N.E. to Ségou; irrigates 3,000 sq. m. on right bank of Niger and assists navigation.

**Segovia**, *prov.*, Old Castile, Spain; agr., stock-keeping, and mftg.; cap. Segovia; a. 2,682 sq. m.; p. (1959) 204,484.

**Segovia**, *c.*, Spain; nr. R. Eresma; cath.; iron-ware, cloth, earthenware, paper, flour; p. (1957) 34,700.

**Segre, R.**, Lérida, N.E. Spain; rises in E. Pyrenees, flows S.W. into R. Ebro; water irrigates the a. around Lerida, the lgst. block of irrigated land in Spain; length approx. 170 m.

**Segura, R.**, Spain, flows to Mediterranean at Guardamar; 180 m.

**Seibersdorf**, Austria; ENEA experimental food irradiation project.

**Seikan Tunnel**, project to link main Japanese I. of Honshu with northern I. of Hokkaido under Tsugaru Straits; length 23 m. (14 m. under seabed); expected completion 1970.

**Seim, R.**, Ukrainian S.S.R.; trib. of R. Desna; length 300 m.

**Seine, R.**, France; rising in Côte d'Or dep., and flowing past Paris and Rouen to English Channel at Havre; length 473 m.

**Seine-et-Marne**, *dep.*, N. France; agr., stock-raising, dairying; "Brie" cheese; porcelain, gypsum, flagstone; cap. Melun; a. 2,275 sq. m.; p. (1962) 537,543.

**Seine-Maritime**, *dep.*, N. France; undulating and fertile; grain, dairying, textiles, iron, shipbldg., flax, chemicals; fisheries; cap. Rouen; a. 2,448 sq. m.; p. (1962) 1,035,844.

**Seine-Saint-Denis**, *dep.*, N.E. Paris, France; mkt. gardens; p. (1964) 1,083,700.

**Seistan and Baluchistan**, *twin prov.*, Iran; co. ts. Zabol, Zahedan (rly. term. Pakistan rly. from Quetta through Mirjaveh, the customs post on Iranian frontier).

**Sekondi**, *spt.*, Ghana, W. Africa; connected with and largely superseded as a pt. by Takoradi harbour; p. (1965) 104,000 (inc. Takoradi).

**Selangor**, *st.*, W. Malaysia; central Malaya; cap. Kuala Lumpur (to relieve congestion, Klang designated future cap.); chemicals; a. 3,150 sq. m.; p. (1961) 1,150,413.

**Selby**, *mkt. and industl. t.*, *urb. dist.*, W.R. Yorks, Eng.; on R. Ouse, 13 m. S. of York; ancient abbey church; flour-milling, flax, oil-cake; p. (1961) 9,869.

**Sele, R.**, S. Italy; rises in S. Apennines, flows W. into G. of Salerno; headwaters now carried 13 through gr. Apennine tunnel (7 m.) to irrigate plateau of Apulia in S.E. Italy.

**Selenga, R.**, Mongolia and Siberia; flows into L. Baikal; length 750 m.

**Selkirk**, *co.*, Scot.; mountainous (Broad Law 2,723 ft.); sheep, oats, woollens; cap. Selkirk; a. 267 sq. m.; p. (1961) 21,055.

**Selkirk**, *bor.*, *co. t.*, Selkirk, Scot.; on Ettrick Water; 4 m. S. of Galashiels; tartans, tweeds; p. (1961) 5,634.

**Selkirk Mtns.**, B.C., Canada; run N.W. to S.E. parallel with Rocky Mtns. and occupy inside of the great bend of R. Columbia; ancient rocks, highly mineralised; pierced by Connaught

Tunnel on Canadian Pacific Rly. route through Kicking Horse Pass to Vancouver; rise to over 9,000 ft.

Selma, c., Ala., U.S.A.; on Alabama R.; in cotton-growing dist.; also dairying, lumbering, ironwks., fertilisers; p. (1960) 28,385.

Selsey, t., Sussex, Eng.; on Selsey Bill, 7 m. S. of Chichester; coastal resort; fishing.

Selsey Bill, peninsula, between Bognor Regis and Portsmouth, Sussex, Eng.

Selukwe, t., Rhodesia; alt. 4,734 ft.; goldmng., chrome ore, molybdenum; ranching, agr.

Selwyn Range, mtns., Queensland, Australia; extends 350 m. W. from Gr. Dividing Range; forms divide between Rs. flowing N. to G. of Carpentaria and Rs. flowing S. to Darling; gold, copper; alt. mainly below 1,500 ft.

Semarang, spt., Java, Indonesia; exp. sugar, tobacco, tapioca, kapok; shipbldg., tc. repairs, cement, sawmills; p. (1961) 503,000.

Seminole, t., Okla., U.S.A.; p. (1960) 11,464.

Semipalatinsk, t., Kazakh. S.S.R.; on R. Irtysh; lge meat-packing plant; textiles, sawmilling, engin.; rich gold deposit found in a. 1965; p. (1967) 197,000.

Semlin, see Zemun.

Semmering Pass, low pass, Austria; provides route across E. Alps for rly. from Vienna to Venice· alt. below 3,000 ft.

Semnan, dist., N. Iran; much desert land; cap. Semnan; p. (1967) 59,152.

Sena, t., Mozambique; on R. Zambesi.

Sendai, t., Honshu, Japan; salt, fish; p. (1964) 480,000.

Senegal, R., W. Africa; flowing from Kong mtns. W. and N.W. to Atlantic at St. Louis, above Cape Verde; length 1,000 m.

Senegal, indep. sovereign st., within Fr. Community; N. of R. Gambia; groundnuts; chromium 375 m. E. of D.; cap. Dakar; a. 78,000 sq. m.; p. (estd. 1965) 3,400,000.

Senekal, t., O.F.S., S. Africa; tr. ctr.; wool, wheat; p. (1960) 7,409 (inc. 1,984 whites).

Senigallia, t., Italy, N.W. of Ancona; p. 26,345.

Sennar, t., Sudan; on Blue Nile, on rly. route to Khartoum, Suakin, Pt. Sudan; dam for irrigation and control of Nile floods; hydro elec. power sta.; p. 1,000.

Sennin, see Kamaishi.

Sens, t., Yonne, France; on R. Yonne; cath., the ancient Agedincum; farm implements, boots, chemicals, cutlery; p. (1962) 21,742.

Sensuntepeque, t., E. Salvador, Central America; pottery, distilling; p. (1960) 27,070.

Senta, t., Jugoslavia; on R. Tisa; flour, leather, sugar, wine, agr., machin., chemicals, paper; p. (1959) 20,000.

Seoul, cap., S. Korea; brassware, pottery, silk; processing clinker into cement; p. (1963) 3,376,000.     [alt. 7,611 ft.

Septimer, mtn. pass, Swiss Alps, can. Grisons;

Seraing, t., Liége, Belgium; extensive ironwks.; engin.; p. (1962) 40,706.

Serampore, t., W. Bengal, India; former Danish settlement; cotton and silk weaving, pottery, jute- and paper-mills; p. (1961) 91,521.

Serang, I., Indonesia, N. of Amboina; a. 6,612 sq. m.; tobacco; p. (estd.) 105,000.

Serbia, fed. unit, Jugoslavia; former independent kingdom; a. 33,930 sq. m.; cap. Belgrade; p. (1960) 7,593,000.     [25,000.

Seremban, t., cap., Negri Sembilan, Malaya; p.

Seres, see Sérrai.     [290 m.

Sereth, R., Romania; trib. of R. Danube; length

Sergipe, cst. st., Brazil; forested; tobacco, maize, sugar, cotton; oil deposits; cap. Aracaju; a. 8,129 sq. m.; p. (1960) 760,273.

Sergo, see Kadiyevka.

Seria, t., Brunei; oil ctr.; linked by pipe-line with Lutong.     [Ægean Sea.

Sériphos, I., Cyclades gr., Grecian Archipelago,

Serov, t., R.S.F.S.R., in Urals; iron and steel; natural gas pipeline from Ingrim; p. (1967) 105,000.

Serowe, c., Botswana, S.W. Africa; p. (1964) 34,000.

Serpukhov, t., R. pt., R.S.F.S.R.; on R. Oka, S. of Moscow; engin., textiles; p. (1967) 120,000.

Serra da Mantiqueira, mtn. range, highest in Brazil;

Serra do Espinhaço, mtns., Brazil; highest peak, Itambe, 6,705 ft.; iron-ore deposits.

Serra do Mar, mtns., Brazil; form steep E. edge of Brazilian Plateau S. from Rio de Janeiro.

Sérrai (Seres), prefecture Macedonia, Greece; cap. Sérrai; p. (1961) 248,045.

Sérrai (Seres), t., Macedonia, Greece; on Struma R.; woollens, cottons, carpets; p. (1961) 40,063.

Sesto San Giovanni, sub., Milan, Italy; machin., glass, chemicals, plastic; p. (1961) 71,384.

Sète (formerly Cette), spt., Hérault, France; on Mediterranean cst.; chemicals, fisheries; exp. oysters, brandy, wine; oil pipeline under the sea to Frontignan; p. (1962) 37,816.

Setif, mkt. t., E. Algeria; alt. 3,596 ft.; cereals, horses; p. (1948) 51,674.

Setouchi, coastal region, S.W. Honshu, N. Shikoku, Japan; flanks shores of Inland Sea; sm. plains backed by terraced hillsides; intensive agr., rice, mulberry, tea, citrus fruits; many sm. ts. engaged in fishing, local tr. and varied inds. inc. textiles, salt-extraction from brine.

Setté Cama, spt., Gaboon, Equat. Africa; open roadstead, landing difficult owing to swell; exp. timber; oil nearby.

Settle, mkt. t., rural dist., W.R. Yorks, Eng.; on R. Ribble in heart of Craven dist.; caves with remains of extinct fauna; thread, cotton; p. (rural dist 1961) 13,782.

Settsu Plain, S. Honshu, Japan; located at head of Osaka Bay at E. end of Inland Sea; intensively cultivated alluvial lowlands, ch. crops, rice, vegetables, oranges; gr. industl. belt extends along cst. through Kobe, Osaka, Kishiwada; engin., chemicals, textiles; a. 500 sq. m.

Setubal, c., spt., Lisbon, Portugal; on R. Sado; boatbldg., fishing, sardine-curing, lace, salt, fertilizers, etc.; p. (1960) 44,435.

Seul Lac, L., S. of St. Joseph L., Ont., Canada.

Sevan (Gokcha), lge. L., Armenian S.S.R.; alt. 6,340 ft.; never freezes; surrounded by high, barren mtns.

Sevan, t., Armenian S.S.R.; underground hydro-elec. power sta.

Sevastopol, spt., Ukrainian S.S.R.; built on ruins left after famous siege 1855; Black Sea resort; naval arsenals; leather, tiles, machin.; exp. grain; p. (1967) 200,000.

Seven Islands, pt., on St. Lawrence, Quebec, Canada; iron brought by rail from Schefferville; airline service but no highway.

Sevenoaks, mkt. t., rural dist., Kent, Eng.; in Vale of Holmesdale, 5 m. N.W. of Tonbridge; residtl; agr., light inds.; Knole Park; p. (1961) 17,604.

Severn, R., W. of Eng. and N. Wales; rises in Montgomery and flows to Bristol Channel; length 215 m.; suspension bridge at estuary opened 1966.

Severn, R., Ontario, Canada; flows to Hudson Bay; length 350 m.

Severn Tunnel, Eng.; under estuary of R. Severn between Pilning (Glos.) and Severn Tunnel Junction (Mon.); carries main rly. from London to S. Wales; longest main-line rly tunnel in Brit. Is.; length nearly 4½ m.

Severodvinsk, t., R.S.F.S.R.; on Dvina Bay, White Sea; metals, bldg. materials; p. (1959) 79,000.

Seville, prov., Spain; agr., mining; cap. Seville; a. 5,430 sq. m.; p. (1959) 1,226,730.

Seville, pt., cap., Seville, Spain; on R. Guadalquivir; Gothic cath.; palace, univ.; ironware, machin., cigars, silks, porcelain, brewery, cotton and wool mills, aircraft; exp. lead, iron, mercury, cork, oranges, lemons, wine; birthplace of Velasquez and Murillo; p. (1965) 549,000.

Sèvres, t., Hauts-de-Seine, France; on R. Seine; celebrated porcelain mnfs.; p. (1962) 20,290.

Sevres (Deux), dep., N. France; p. (1962) 321,118.

Seychelles Is., Brit. col., Indian Ocean; consisting of 92 Is., lgst. I. Mahé; cap. Victoria; exports prods. of coconut palm, phosphate, essential oils and spices; famous for species of nut; total a. 156 sq. m.; p. (estd. 1965) 46,000.

Seyne or La Seyne-sur-Mer, t., Var, France; nr. Toulon; shipbldg.; p. (1962) 34,270.

Sfax, spt., Tunisia; admin. ctr.; exp. phosphate, olive oil, salt, esparto grass, cereals, dates, hides; imports food, coal, textiles, soap; sponges; fishing; natural gas found in a. p. (1966) 250,000.

Sgurr Mor, mtn., Ross and Cromarty, Scot.; alt. 3,483 ft.

Shabani, t., Rhodesia; asbestos; p. (1958) 7,930 (incl. 1,700 Europeans).

Shadrinsk, t., R.S.F.S.R.; W. Siberia, 160 m. S.E. of Sverdlovsk; car parts, printing presses; p. (1959) 52,000.

Shaftesbury, *mkt. t.*, *mun. bor.*, Dorset, Eng.: 10 m. N. of Blandford; agr. implements, chemicals, glove mftg.; p. (estd. 1967) *3,434.*

Shahjahanpur, *c.*, Uttar Pradesh, India; on Deoha R.; sugar; p. (1961) *117,702.*

Shahpur, *t.*, W. Punjab, Pakistan; cotton; p. *8,545.*      [*36,460.*

Shaker Heights, *t.*, Ohio, U.S.A.; p. (1960)

Shakhty (Alexandrovsk Grushevski), *t.*, R.S.F.S.R.; coal, engin., elec. power; p. (1967) *208,000.*

Shamaldy-Say, *t.*, Kirghiz S.S.R.; new town on site of Uch-Kurgan hydroelec. sta.

Shamokin, *bor.*, Penns., U.S.A.; iron mftg., anthracite; p. (1960) *13,674.*

Shan State, *div.*, Burma; a. 57,500 sq. m.; p. *2,500,000*; elevated plateau through which flows R. Salween; iron, lead, silver, zinc; former Federated Shan States and Wa States, E. Burma.

Shandaken Tunnel, N.Y. st., U.S.A.; carries water under Catskill Mtns. to augment water supply of c. of N.Y.; length 18 m.

Shanghai, *c.*, *pt.*, Kiangsu, China; on Whangpoo trib. of Yangtze-Kiang; most impt. of the former Chinese treaty pts., considerable exp. silk and tea; mnfs. paper, cigarettes, cotton; shipbldg., engin., machin., chemicals, plastics, nylon, synthetic fibres; p. (estd. 1957) *7,100,000.*

Shangkiu (Shangqiu), *c.*, Honan prov., China; agr. ctr.; silk weaving; p. (1953) *134,000.*

Shanklin, *see* Sandown-Shanklin.

Shannon Airport, Clare, Ireland; N.W. of Limerick; on main transatlantic air route; ctr. of industl. estate.

Shannon, *R.*, Ireland; separating Connaught from provs. of Leinster and Munster, and flowing to Atlantic at Loop Head; length 224 m.

Shansi (Shanxi), *inland and hilly prov.*, N. China, bounded W. and S. by the Hwang-Ho; coal, iron ore, petroleum, salt; cap. Taiyuan; a. 60,394 sq. m.; p. (1953) *14,314,485.*

Shantung (Shandong), *maritime prov.*, China, on the G. of Chihli and the Yellow Sea; fertile plain; grain, silk, fruit; coal, iron, lead, copper; cap. Tsinan; a. 56,447 sq. m.; p. (1953) *48,876,548.*

Shaohing (Shaoxing), *c.*, Chekiang prov., China; rice, wheat, cotton; p. (1953) *131,000*

Shaoyang, *c.*, Hunan prov., China; coal and iron mng.; timber; p. (1953) *127,000.*

Shap, *par.*, Westmorland, Eng.; near by is Shap Summit 914 ft., an impt. pass traversed by rly. and by a main road; granite.

Shapinsay, Orkney Is., Scot.

Shari, *R.*, Mali, W. Africa; flows from the S. to L. Chad; navigable for greater part of course; length 70 m.

Sharkord, *t.*, prov. cap. Chahar Mahal Bakhtiiari; p. (1967) *178,607.*

Sharon, *plain*, Israel; citrus fruits, vines, poultry.

Sharon, *c.*, Penns., U.S.A.; ironwks., bricks, elec. goods; p. (1960) *25,267.*      [estuary.

Sharpness, *vil.*, Glos., Eng.; on S. shore, Severn

Shasta, *mtn.*, Cal., U.S.A.; 14,380 ft.

Shatt-al-Arab, *R.*, Iraq; formed by union of Tigris and Euphrates, flows thence to head of Persian G.; length 120 m.

Shatura, *t.*, R.S.F.S.R.; E. of Moscow; elec. power-plant; p. (1954) *50,000.*

Shawinigan Falls, *c.*, Quebec, Canada; pulp and paper; p. (1961) *32,169.*

Shawnee, *c.*, Okla., U.S.A.; cottons, meat-preserving; p. (1960) *24,326.*

Sheaf, *R.*, W.R., Yorks, Eng.; rises in S.E. Pennines, flows N.E. to join R. Don at Sheffield; for last 2 m. narrow valley crowded with smaller factories of Sheffield; valley provides main route to S. (Chesterfield) and S.W. (Manchester via Totley); length 11 m.

Shebelinka, natural gas fields nr. Kharkov, Ukraine; pipelines to Kharkov-Bryansk and Dnepropetrovsk-Odessa.

Sheboygan, *c.*, Wis., U.S.A.; on L. Michigan; furniture mftg., pianos, gloves, enamelled ware; p. (1960) *45,747.*

Shechem, *see* Nablus.

Sheerness, *spt.*, *urb. dist.*, Kent, Eng.; on I. of Sheppey at entrance to estuary of R. Medway; former royal dockyard and garrison; deepwater comm. pt.; electronics, furniture, coach bldg.; p. (1961) *14,123.*

Sheffield, *c.*, *co. bor.*, W.R. Yorks, Eng.; on cramped site at confluence of Rs. Sheaf and

---

Don; univ.; gr. cutlery, steel, iron, brass mftg. ctr., machin., instruments, electro-plate; p. (estd. 1967) *534,100.*

Shelbyville, *t.*, Ind., U.S.A.; on Big. Blue R.; mftg. ctr. in colly. and agr. region; p. (1960) *14,317.*

Shellal (Esh Shellal), *t.*, *R. pt.*, Upper U.A.R., N.E. Africa; on right bank of R. Nile. 2 m. above Aswan Dam; S. terminus of Egyptian rly. system; river-steamer service connects with Wadi Halfa, 160 m. upstream, N. terminus of Sudan rly. system.

Shellhaven, *oil refineries*, Essex, Eng.; on N. side of Thames estuary, nr. Stanford-le-Hope.

Shelton, *t.*, Conn., U.S.A.; old vil. of Huntingdon, has 18th-century houses; p. (1960) *18,190.*

Shenandoah, *t.*, Penns., U.S.A.; anthracite; p. (1960) *11,075.*

Shenandoah, *R.*, Va., U.S.A.; trib. of Potomac R.

Shenao, Taiwan; E. of Keelung; oil refinery being built.

Shendi, *t.*, Sudan; on R. Nile; p. *14,300.*

Shensi (Shenxi), *prov.*, China; W. of Hwang-Ho; wheat, cotton; coal, petroleum; cap. Sian; a. 72,919 sq. m.; p. (1953) *15,881,281.*

Shenyang, *see* Mukden.

Shepparton, *t.*, Victoria, Australia; 118 m. N.N.E. of Melbourne; ctr. of veg. and orchard a.; fruit canning, metal, brick wks.; p. (1966) *17,523.*

Sheppey, I. of, Kent, Eng.; in Thames estuary E. of mouth of R. Medway; 9 m. long, 5 m. wide; cereals, sheep-raising.

Shepshed, *t.*, *urb. dist.*, Leicester, Eng.; 3 m. W. of Loughborough; gloves, boots, shoes, needles; p. (1961) *7,179.*

Shepton Mallet, *mkt. t.*, *urb. dist.*, Somerset, Eng.; at foot of Mendip Hills, 5 m. S.E. of Wells; shoes, cider; p. (1961) *5,518.*

Sherborne, *mkt. t.*, *urb. dist.*, Dorset, Eng.; 4 m. E. of Yeovil; famous abbey and school; p. (1961) *6,062.*

Sherbrooke, *c.*, Quebec, Canada; at confluence of Rs. St. Francis and Magog; woollens, cottons, carpets, machin., sawmills; p. (1961) *66,554.*

Sherchell, *sm. spt.*, Algeria; mkt.; p. *12,650.*

Sheridan, *t.*, Wyo., U.S.A.; p. (1960) *11,651.*

Sheringham, *t.*, *urb. dist.*, Norfolk, Eng.; on E. cst. 4 m. W. of Cromer; seaside resort; fishing; p. (1961) *4,836.*

Sherman, *t.*, Texas, U.S.A.; tr. in cotton and corn; p. (1960) *24,988.*      [Eng.

Sherwood Forest, *ancient royal woodland*, Notts.

Shetland Is., Scot.; in Zetland co., 50 m. N.E. of the Orkneys; about 100 in gr., ch. I., Mainland; textile, fishing; cattle, sheep, ponies; potatoes; ch. t. Lerwick; a. 551 sq. m.; p. (1961) *17,809.*

Sheyenne, *R.*, Dakota, U.S.A.; trib. of Red R.; length 325 m.

Shifnal, *mkt. t.*, *rural dist.*, Shropshire, Eng.; 5 m. S.E. of Wellington; malting, coal, iron; p. (rural dist., 1961) *14,234.*

Shigatze, *t.*, Tibet; on R. Tsangpo; tr. ctr. on main caravan routes; p. *9,000.*

Shihkiachwang (Shijiazhuang), *c.*, Hopeh prov., China; cotton milling, glass mftg.; p. (1953) *373,000.*      [and silk; p. over *62,000.*

Shikarpur, *t.*, N. Sind, Pakistan; tr. ctr., gems

Shikoku, *one of the lge. Is.* Japan; S. of Honshu; rice, salt, paper, fish, lumber; a. 7,248 sq. m.

Shildon, *t.*, *urb. dist.*, Durham, Eng.; 3 m. S. of Bishop Auckland; rly. wks.; p. (1961) *14,372.*

Shilka, *R.*, E. Siberia; R.S.F.S.R.; trib. of R. Amur; length 760 m.

Shillong, *cap.*, Assam, India; at alt. 4,500 ft. in Khasi Hills; ctr. of impt. tea-growing dist.; p. (1961) *102,398.*      [44,175.

Shimabara, *t.*, Japan; holiday resort; p. (1966)

Shimizu, *spt.*, Japan; tea ctr.; oranges, paper, tinned fruit and fish; p. (1965) *219,000.*

Shimoda, *spt.*, Honshu, Japan; between Nagoya and Yokohama; p. (1965) *63,493.*

Shimonoseki, *spt.*, Honshu I., Japan; at extreme S.W. of I.; tunnel links island of Kyushu; impt. rail and steamer ctr.; p. (1965) *254,376.*

Shin, Loch, Sutherland, Scot.; 16½ m. long; drained by R. Shin to the R. Oykell.

Shipka Pass, Bulgaria; over the Balkan Mtns., 47 m. N.E. of Plovdiv.

Shipley, *t.*, *urb. dist.*, W.R. Yorks, Eng.; on R. Aire, 8 m. N.W. of Leeds; worsted mnfs.; p. (estd. 1967) *29,480.*

Shiraz, *c.*, *cap.*, Fars, Iran; beautifully sited in

vine-growing dist.; textiles, rugs, metalwk., light elec. ind.; tourist ctr.; tombs of Saadi and Hafez (brothers of Imam Riza); known as "city of roses and nightingales"; pleasant winter climate; airpt.; p. (1963) *230,000*.

Shire, *R.*, flows from L. Malawi to R. Zambesi; on it are the famous Murchison Falls, up to which the R. is navigable; length 380 m.

Shirwa or Chilwah, *shallow L.*, nr. Malawi, Africa; 40 m. long, 14 m. wide; has 4 Is.

Shizuoka, *spt.*, Honshu, Japan; tea refining, blending, packing; oranges, fruit tinning; woodwork; textiles; p. (1965) *367,705*.

Shkodra (Scutari), *L.*, 29 m. long; on borders of Montenegro and Albania; outlet via R. Bojana into Adriatic.

Shkodra (Scutari), *t.*, Albania; stands at foot of S. L. (ancient cap. Illyria); cas. cath.; tobacco ind., cement; p. (1960) *41,000*.

Shoa, *st.*, Ethiopia; S.E. Amhara.

Shoalhaven, *t.* and *R.*, N.S.W., Australia; tourism.

Shoeburyness, *t.*, Essex, Eng.; on N. side of Thames estuary, 3 m. E. of Southend; barracks, gunnery school, bricks; p. (1961) *10,855*.

Sholapur, *c.*, Maharashtra, India; between Hyderabad and Poona; lge. bazaar, temples, etc., silk, cotton cloth; p. (1961) *337,583*.

Shoreditch, *see* Hackney.

Shoreham-by-Sea, *t.*, *urb. dist.*, W. Sussex, Eng.; at mouth of R. Adur, 4 m. E. of Worthing; old spt. and mkt. t.; oil jetty; boat bldg., chemicals, soap, preserves; p. (1961) *17,391*.

Shoshone Falls, on Snake R., Idaho, U.S.A.; height 200 ft.

Shott esh Shergui, lgst. saline L., Algeria.

Shotts, *plateau*, N. Africa; upland region with salt Ls., within Atlas mtns.

Shreveport, *c.*, La., U.S.A.; industl. ctr. in cotton-growing dist.; petroleum; p. (1960) *164,372*.

Shrewsbury, *co. t.*, *mun. bor.*, Salop, Eng.; on R. Severn 12 m. above Ironbridge gorge between The Wrekin and Wenlock Edge; agr. and dairy equipment, machin., elec. goods; impt. cattle and sheep mkt.; famous public school; fine churches, Shire Hall, Guildhall; p. (estd. 1967) *53,870*.

Shropshire (Salop), *N.W. midland co.*, Eng.; bordering on Wales; fine pastoral country with hills and woodland, agr. and dairying; iron; mnfs.; cap. Shrewsbury; a. 1,347 sq. m.; p. (1966) *322,000*.

Shumen (Kolarovgrad) *t.* Bulgaria; S.E. of Ruse; cloth; occupied by Russians, 1878; p. (1956) *41,670*.

Shurma, *t.*, Hejaz, Saudi Arabia; S. of Medina.

Shusha, *t.*, Azerbaydzhan S.S.R.; spa; p. massacred by Moslems 1926; p. (1956) *5,700*.

Shustar, *t.*, Iran; carpets, woollens, pottery, etc.; shallow-draught boats can reach Shallili, nr. S. by R. Karun; p. *20,000*.

Shuya, *t.*, R.S.F.S.R.; engin., textiles; p. (1959) *64,000*.

Shwebo, *t.*, Central Burma; on R. Irrawaddy.

Si Kiang, *ch. R.*, S. China; headstreams rise in Yunnan plateau, form main R. nr. Sunchow; R. then flows E., enters S. China Sea through lge. delta nr. Hong Kong; lower valley intensively cultivated, rice, sugar-cane, tea; tropical climate permits continuous cultivation of most crops throughout year; valley very densely populated.

Sialkot, *t.*, W. Pakistan; N.E. of Lahore; sports goods, musical and surgical instruments, paper; p. (1961) *164,346*.

Siam. *See* Thailand.

Siam, G. of, *lge. inlet*, S. China Sea; 385 m. from Sian (Xian), *c.*, *cap.*, Shensi, China; mkt.; oil- and saw-mills; p. (estd. 1957) *1,500,000*.

Siangtan (Xiangtan), *c.*, Hunan prov., China; tea ctr.; rice, cotton, hemp; coal-mng. in a.; p. (1953) *184,000*.

Siauliai, *t.*, Lithuanian S.S.R.; 115 m. N.W. of Vilnius; impt. rly junction; food inds.; p. (1959) *60,000*.

Šibenik, *t.*, Jugoslavia; naval base; fishing, weaving, woollens, chemicals; bauxite; p. (1959) *23,000*.

Siberia, *terr.*, U.S.S.R.; from the Ural Mtns. to Sea of Okhotsk and Bering Strait, bounded by the Arctic on the N., and on the S. by Mongolia and Turkestan; climate mostly severe; ch. ts. Novosibirsk (cap. W.S.) and Irkutsk (cap. E.S.); rich in coal, iron, minerals; oil and gas in W. Siberian lowland; resources not yet fully

known; a. 4,210,420 sq. m.; p. (1959) *18,225,000*.

Siberut, *I.*, S. of Sumatra, Indonesia.

Sibi, *t.*, W. Pakistan; gypsum mng.

Sibiu, *t.*, Central Romania; linen, leather, brewing; p. (1963) *100,659*.

Sibu, *t.*, Sarawak, E. Malaysia; 80 m. up R. Rejang; p. (1960) *29,630*.

Sicily, *the lgst. I.*, Mediterranean Sea; former kingdom and now an aut. region of Italy; produces corn, oranges, olives, silk, almonds, sardines, sulphur and salt; oil in dist. of Ragusa, Gela Fontasarossa; pleasant climate; mountainous, highest point the volcano Mt. Etna; ch. ts. Palermo, Catania, Messina; severe earth tremors, 1968; a. 9,926 sq. m.; p. (1961) *4,711,783*.

Sicuani, *t.*, S. Peru, S. America; alt. 11,650 ft.; agr. and pastoral dist. ctr.; p. *15,000*.

Sidamo, *see* Galla and Sidamo.

Sidi-bel-Abbès, *t.*, W. Algeria; wheat, barley, tobacco, olives, vines; cattle, wool; footwear, bricks, furniture, cheese, macaroni; p. (1960) *105,000*.

Sidi-Kacem (Petit Jean) *t.*, Morocco, N.W Africa; oilfield and refinery; p. (1960) *19,473*.

Sidlaw Hills, *low mtn. range*, Angus, Perth, Scot.

Sidmouth, *mkt. t.*, *urb. dist.*, Devon, Eng.; on S. cst., 15 m. S.E. of Exeter; seaside resort; Honiton lace, gloves; p. (1961) *11,139*.

Sidon, *cst. t.*, Lebanon; on Mediterranean, S. of Beirut; terminal of oil pipe-line from Saudi Arabia; refinery; p. *17,695*.      [*36,000*.

Siedlce, *t.*, Poland; E. of Warsaw; p. (1965)

Siegburg, *t.*, N. Rhine-Westphalia, Germany; on R. Sieg; Benedictine abbey; dyes, iron, ceramics.; p. (1963) *34,100*.

Siegen, *t.*, N. Rhine-Westphalia, Germany; on R. Sieg; 2 cas.; iron-mining and smelting, machin., leather; p. (1963) *49,600*.

Siemianowice Slaskie, *t.*, Poland; nr. Katowice; (1965) *66,000*.

Siena, *hill-town*, Tuscany, Italy; 32 m. S. of Florence; spreads over three hilltops with Piazza del Campo in between where celebrated Palio festival (horse-races) are held; 13th- and 14th-cent. arch., cath.; agr. mkt., tanning, glass, textiles, bricks; *panforte* confectionery; tourist ctr.; p. (1961) *62,215*.

Siero, *t.*, Oviedo, Spain; on R. Nora; agr., livestock-raising, coal-mining; p. *30,931*.

Sierra da Estrella, *see* Estrella, Sierra da.

Sierra de Baudo, *mtn. range*, Columbia, S. America.

Sierra de Gata, *mtn. range*, Portugal–Spain.

Sierra de Gredos, *mtn. range*, Central Spain.

Sierra de Guadarrama, *mtn. range*, Central Spain.

Sierra Leone, *ind. sov. st.* within British Commonwealth (1961), W. Africa, situated between Guinea and Liberia; covered with ranges of hills; ch. prod., palm kernels, ginger, piassava, kolas; iron ore, diamonds, chromite, gold; cap. Freetown; a. 27,925 sq. m.; p. (1963) *2,183,000*.

Sierra Madre, *mtn. range*, W. cst., Mexico and Guatemala.

Sierra Mojada, *mtn. range*, Central Mexico.

Sierra Morena, *mtn. range*, Spain; between Guadalquivir and Guadiana basins, highest point 5,500 ft.

Sierra Nevada, *mtn. range*, Granada, Spain; highest summit, Mulhacen.

Sierra Nevada, *mtn. chain*, Cal., U.S.A.; highest peak Mt. Whitney, alt. 14,898 ft.

Sierra Nevada de Mérida, *mtn. range*, W. Venezuela; S. America; extends N.E. from San Cristóbal to Barquisimeto; extension of E. range of Andes, alt. over 16,000 ft.; impt. coffee plantations from 3,000 to 6,000 ft. on slopes.

Sierra Nevada de Santa Marta, *mtns.*, Colombia, S. America; summits over 19,000 ft.

Sighet, *t.*, N. Romania on U.S.S.R. frontier; p. (1963) *27,523*.      [*2,625*.

Siglufjörd, *spt.* N. Iceland; herrings; p. (1962)

Siguiri, *t.*, Guinea, W. Africa; on R. Niger; gold; p. *11,000*.      [refining.

Sihanoukville, *t.*, Cambodia; tractors; oil

Siirt, *t.*, Turkey; S. of Bitlis; p. (1965) *25,397*.

Sikasso, *t.*, Mali, W. Africa; mkt., route ctr.

Sikkim, *st.* E. Himalayas, adjoining Tibet, Nepal and Bhutan; dense forests, with rich flora and orchidaceæ, but rice and corn grown in clearings; India–Tibet tr. routes run through st.; cap. Gangtok; lge. copper deposits nr. Ranikhola, Gangtok; a. 2,745 sq. m.; p. (1961) *161,080*.

Sila La, *min. massif*, Calabria, S. Italy; granite mass occupying full width of peninsula; alt. over 3,500 ft., max. 6,327 ft.

Silchester, *par.*, Hants, Eng.; between Basingstoke and Reading; impt. ctr. of the Roman road system; many Roman remains.

Silesia (Polish Śląsk, Czech Slezsko), *geographical region*, Europe; extends on both sides of Oder R.; rich in coal, zinc, iron, arsenic; farming, sugar-beet, cereals, fruit, general ind.; has frequently changed hands, in 1919 was divided between Germany (70%), Poland (25%), and Czechoslovakia (5%); in 1945 the former German part became Polish, now forms 2 provs., caps. Katowice and Wrocław; p. 4,764,500; the Czechoslovakian part is united with Moravia; p. 200,000.

Silistra, *t.*, Bulgaria; on N.E. Romanian border, on Danube R.; cloth, distilleries, sawmills, grapes; p. (1956) 20,350.

Silkeborg, *t.*, Jutland, Denmark; W. of Aarhus; paper, textiles; (1960) 24,465.　　[coal, grain.

Silksworth, *t.*, Durham, Eng.; adjoining Sunderland bor.; new t. projected.

Silloth, *resort*, on Solway Firth, Cumberland, Eng.

Silver City, *t.*, N.M., U.S.A.; gold, iron, silver; cattle; health resort; p. (1960) 6,972.

Silvermines, *vil.*, Co. Tipperary, R.o.I.; 5 m. S.W. of Nenagh; lead and zinc.

Silver Spring, *t.*, Md., U.S.A.; sub. to Wash.; p. 43,294.

Simalur, *I.*, S. of Sumatra, Indonesia.

Simcoe, *L.*, N. of L. Ontario, Canada; 30 m. by 18 m.

Simeto, *R.*, Sicily, Italy; rises in central Sicily, flows E. across plain of Catania into Mediterranean; lower course bordered by malarial marshes; length 54 m.

Simferopol, *t.*, Ukrainian S.S.R.; on R. Salghir nr. Sevastopol; soap, candles, fruits, engin.; p. (1967) 217,000.

Simla, *t.*, Punjab, India; alt. 7,075 ft. above sea, with sanatorium; p. (1961) 42,597.

Simonstown, W. Cape Prov., S. Africa; naval sta., docks; p. (estd. 1963) 10,220 inc. 5,120 Europeans.

Simplon, *mtn.*, Switzerland; alt. 11,695 ft.; the pass over the Simplon (alt. 6,594 ft.) from Domodossola, Italy, to Brig in the Rhône valley, Switzerland, was originally made by Napoleon I. The Simplon rly. tunnel leads from Brig on the Swiss side to Iselle in the Val di Vedro on the Italian and is the longest in the world, 12¼ m.

Simpson Desert, S.E. of Alice Springs, Northern Terr.. extending into S. Australia.

Sinai, *peninsula*, easternmost part of Egypt, between Gs. of Aqaba and Suez, at head of Red Sea; a. 11,055 sq. m., mainly desert in N., granitic ridges in S. rising to 8,500 ft. at Jebel Katrun; Jebel Musa or Mt. Sinai (7,359 ft.) is one of numerous peaks; mineral resources; coalmine at Maghâra; occupied by Israeli troops, Nov. 1956–March 1957, and since June 1967.

Sinaloa, *st.*, Mexico; on G. of Cal.; agr. and mining, rich in gold, silver, copper, iron and lead; cap. Culiacán; a. 22,580 sq. m.; p. (1960) 838,404.

Sind, *prov.*, W. Pakistan; lower Indus valley; agr. depends on irrigation; Gudda barrage (1933) to irrigate large a.; adm. ctr. Karachi; cereals, hemp, cotton, indigo; a. 50,443 sq. m.; p. (1951) 4,619,000.

Sindara, *t.*, Gabon, Africa; admin. ctr.

Sindri, *t.*, Bihar, India; fertiliser plant; p. (1961) 41,315.

Singapore, *I.* and *c.*, S. E. Asia; at tip of Malay pen.; Republic within Brit. Commonwealth on secession from Malaysian Fed. 1965; Brit. Govt. retained right to maintain military base; univ.; vast *entrepôt* tr.; chemicals; a. 291 sq. m.; p. (1959) 1,550,000.

Singen, *t.*, Baden-Württemberg, Germany; N.W. of L. Constance; foodstuffs, metals; p. (1963) 35,500.

Singhbhum, *dist.*, Bihar, India; iron- and steelwks; a. 5,191 sq. m.; p. (1961) 2,049,911.

Sinhailien (Xinhailien), *c.*, Kiangsu, China; formed by merger of Sinpu, Tunghai and Lienyienkang; p. (1953) 208,000.

Sining (Xining), *c.*, Tsinghai prov., China; wool, salt, timber; p. (1953) 94,000.

Sinkiang-Uighur (Xinjiang), *aut. region*, China, bordering on Soviet Union and Kashmir; cereals, cotton, wool, silk; cap. Urumchi; a. 705,962 sq. m.; p. (1953) 4,873,608.

Sinneh, *t.*, Iran; carpets; p. 32,000.

Sinop, *Turkish t.*, on Black Sea; timber, silk; p. (1960) 9,899.

Sinsiang (Xinxiang), *c.*, Honan prov., China; cotton weaving, flour milling; p. (1953) 171,000.

Sintra (Cintra), *t.*, Portugal; summer resort, 18 m. from Lisbon; convention of S., 1808.

Sion, *cap.*, Valais, Switzerland; on R. Rhône; built on two castled hills; cath.; hydroelec. plant nearby; p. (1957) 10,904.

Sioux City, Iowa, U.S.A.; on R. Missouri; meatpacking, foundries, elec. goods, cement; p. (1960) 89,159.

Sioux Falls, *t.*, S.D., U.S.A.; on Big. Sioux R.; in rich wheat region; machin., cars, farming implements; nuclear reactor; p. (1960) 65,466.

Sir Edward Pellew, *gr. of Is.*, N. Australia; in G. of Carpentaria.

Sistan and Baluchestan, *twin prov.*, Iran; bounded by Afghanistan and Pakistan; cap. Zahedan; much desert land; arid, very hot; p. (1967) 456,435.　　　　　　　　　　[53,884.

Sitapur, *t.*, Uttar Pradesh, India; p. (1961)

Sitka (formerly Novo Archangelsk), *t.*, S.E. Alaska, U.S.A.; on Baranof I., in Sitka Sound; was ch. pt. of former Russian America; gold-mines; lumbering, canning; naval and coaling sta.; p. (1960) 3,237.

Sitra, *I.*, Persia G.; forming part of st. of Bahrain, Arabia, 3 m. long and 1 m. wide; oil pipeline and causeway carrying road extends out to sea for 3 m. to deep-water anchorage.

Sittang, *R.*, Burma; rises in Pegu Yoma, flows S., enters G. of Martaban, Andaman Sea through delta; valley intensively cultivated; rice; delta forested; length 610 m.

Sittang Bridge, *t.*, Burma; lge. paper mills.

Sittingbourne and Milton, *mkt. t., urb. dist.*, Kent, Eng.; on Milton Creek, 9 m. E. of Chatham; paper-mills, brick-wks.; cement; insecticides; ctr. of fruit-growing dist.; p. (estd. 1967) 28,470.

Sivas, *prov.*, Turkey; rich in minerals, has mineral springs with fertile grain-growing soil, fine orchards and vineyards, besides timber forests; cap. Sivas; p. (1965) 705,077.

Sivas, *t.*, Turkey; in the Kizil Irmak valley; mnfs. woollens; p. (1965) 109,165.　　[U.S.S.R.

Sivash or Putrid Sea, lagoon on E. side of Crimea,

Siwa, *oasis*, Egypt; in Libyan Desert, 300 m. S.W. of Alexandria; dates, olives, remains of temple of Ammon and the fountain of the Sun; 20 m. long, 1 m. wide; p. 1,000.

Sizewell, Suffolk, Eng.; nuclear power sta.

Sjælland, *I.*, Denmark; lgst. I.; agr., fishing, mnfs.; ch. t. Copenhagen; a. 2,840 sq. m.; p. (1960) 1,771,557.

Skagen, *t.*, N. Denmark; on cst. of the Skagerrak; fishing, tourism; p. (1960) 10,390.

Skagerrak, arm of N. Sea, giving access to the Kattegat, between Norway and Denmark, 70–90 m. wide.

Skagway, *sm. spt.*, Alaska, U.S.A.; at head of Lynn Canal inlet, 400 m. N.W. of Prince Rupert; linked by rly. to Whitehorse on Upper R. Yukon; boomed in gold rush (in 1898, p. 15,000), subsequently declined; p. (1960) 659.

Skåne (Scania), *peninsula*, extreme S. of Sweden; corresponds approx. to cos. Malmöhus, Kristianstad; most favoured part of Sweden in relief, soil, climate; intensive farming, wheat, barley, sugar-beet, fodder crops, dairy cattle; ch. ts. Malmo, Lund, Hälsingborg; a. approx. 4,000 sq. m.　　　　　　　　　　　　　　　[250,180.

Skaraborg, *co.*, Sweden; a. 3,269 sq. m.; p. (1961)

Skarzysko-Kamienna, *t.*, Kielce, Poland; p. (1965) 37,000.　　　　　　　　　　　　　　　[mark.

Skaw, The (Grenen), *C.*, at extreme N. of Denmark.

Skeena, *R.*, B.C., Canada; rises in N. Rocky Mtns., flows S.W. to Pac. Oc. at Prince Rupert; lower valley used by Canadian National Rly. from Edmonton (Alberta) to Prince Rupert via Yellowhead Pass; length approx. 400 m.

Skegness, *t., urb. dist.*, Lindsey, Lincoln, Eng.; on E. cst.; farming, vegetables; resort; light engin.; p. (1961) 12,843.

Skelleftea, *t.*, N. Sweden; on Bothnia G., mng., chiefly copper, gold.; p. (1961) 22,730.

Skelmersdale, *t., urb. dist.*, Lancs. Eng.; coal, bricks, drainpipes; designated "New Town" 1961; spun yarn; p. (estd. 1965) 8,695.

Skelton and Brotton, *t., urb. dist.*, N.R. Yorks, Eng.; at N. foot of Cleveland Hills, 10 m. E. of Middlesbrough; steel flooring; p. (1961) 13,186.

**Skiddaw**, *mtn.*, Cumberland, Eng.; E. of Bassenthwaite L.; alt. 3,054 ft.

**Skien**, *spt.*, Bratsberg, Norway; on R. Skien; saw-mills, ice, and timber tr.; p. (1960) *15,502.*

**Skierniewice**, *t.*, Lodz, Poland; S.W. of Warsaw; p. (1965) *24,000.*

**Skipton**, *t.*, *urb. dist.*, W.R. Yorks, Eng.; on R. Aire, 6 m. N.W. of Keighley; cotton and rayon; cas.; p. (1961) *12,988.*

**Skive**, *t.*, N. Jutland, Denmark; fishing; rly. ctr.; p. (1960) *15,558.* [engin.; p. *16,740.*

**Skopin**, *t.*, R.S.F.S.R.; S.E. of Moscow; lignite,

**Skopje**, *t.*, *cap.*, Macedonia, Jugoslavia; the ancient Scupi, one of oldest ts. in Balkans; almost completely destroyed by earthquake 26 July 1963 (over 1 000 deaths); chrome mines in neighbourhood; iron and steelplate wks.; p. (1959) *167,000.*

**Skövde**, *t.*, Sweden; between Ls. Vänern and Vättern; garrison t., cars, cement; p. (1961) *23,946.*

**Skowhegan**, *t.*, Me., U.S.A.; p. (1950) *6,183.*

**Skye**, *I.*, lgst. of the Inner Hebrides, Inverness, Scot.; mountainous; sheep-farming and fisheries; only town, Portree; a. 547 sq. m.

**Skyros**, *I.*, Grecian Archipelago, E. of Evvoia (Euboea).

**Slagelse**, old *t.*, Sjaelland, Denmark; food inds.; iron and silver wks.; p. (1960) *20,562.*

**Slanic**, *t.*, Wallachia, Romania; on S. flank of Carpathian Mtns., 22 m. N. of Ploesti; impt. salt deposits; p. (1956) *6,842.*

**Slask**, *see* Silesia.

**Slatina**, *t.*, Romania; on R. Olt, 87 m. W. of Bucharest; ancient churches; p. (1956) *13,381.*

**Slave**, *R.*, N.W. Terr., Canada; flows into Gr. Slave L.

**Slave Coast**, portions of Guinea cst., W. Africa, embracing Dahomey and Nigeria.

**Slavonia**, former Crown land (with Croatia) of Hungary; now Jugoslavia.

**Slavyansk**, *t.*, Ukrainian S.S.R.; coal, chemicals, salt, engin.; p. (1959) *83,000.*

**Sleaford**, *mkt. t.*, *urb. dist.*, Kesteven, Lincoln, Eng.; 12 m. N.E. of Grantham; agr. and agr. implements, malting, seeds; p. (1961) *7,834.*

**Sleepers, The**, *gr. of Is.*, Hudson Bay, Canada.

**Slezsko**, *see* Silesia.

**Slieve Bloom**, *hill range*, Offaly and Laoghis cos., Ireland; highest point 1,733 ft.

**Slieve Donard**, *mtn.*, N. Ireland; highest of the Mourne Mtns., co. Down; alt. 2,796 ft.

**Sligo**, *cst. co.*, Connacht, Ireland; pasture, tillage, barren mtn., and turf; livestock, fishing; a. 737 sq. m.; p. (1966) *51,078.*

**Sligo**, *t.*, Sligo, Ireland; on Sligo Bay; distilling, flour, fisheries; p. (1966) *13,297.*

**Slioch**, *mtn.*, Ross and Cromarty, Scot.; 3,217 ft.

**Sliven**, *t.*, E. Roumelia, Bulgaria; famous for black wine; p. (1956) *46,383.*

**Slough**, *t.*, *mun. bor.*, Bucks, Eng.; on river terrace N. of R. Thames, 23 m. W. of London; many light inds.; p. (estd. 1967) *86,860.*

**Slovakia**, *old prov.*, ČSSR.; consists largely of Carpathian Mtns.; ch. t. Kosice; a. 18,902 sq. m.; p. (1961) *4,175,017.*

**Slovenia**, *fed. unit*, Jugoslavia; cap. Ljubljana (Laibach); a. 6,266 sq. m.; p. (1959) *1,589,000.*

**Slupsk (Stolp)**, *t.*, Pomerania, Poland; German before 1945; cas.; machin., agr. implements; p. (1965) *59,000.*

**Småland**, *dist.*, S. Sweden; barren upland area S. of L. Vättern; moorland, deciduous forest; contrasts greatly with remainder of S. Sweden.

**Smederevo**, *t.*, Serbia, Jugoslavia; nr. Belgrade; p. (1959) *22,000.*

**Smethwick**, *co. bor.*, Staffs, Eng.; N.W. sub. of Birmingham; machin., engin., iron, glass; p. (1961) *68,372.*

**Smichov**, *t.*, ČSSR.; on R. Vltava; connected by bridge with Prague; mnfs.; p. *54,370.*

**Smith Sound**, Arctic Canada; connects Kane Bay with Baffin Bay.

**Smoky Hill**, *R.*, Col., Kan., U.S.A.; trib. of Kansas R.; length 400 m.

**Smolensk**, *c.*, R.S.F.S.R.; on both banks of the R. Dnieper; tallow, linen, iron and copper smelting, engin.; p. (1967) *189,000.*

**Smyrna**, *see* Izmir.

**Snaefell**, *highest mtn.*, I. of Man; alt. 2,034 ft.

**Snake R. or Lewis Fork**, trib. of Columbia R., flows from Wyo. to Wash., U.S.A.; length 1,050 m.

**Sneek**, *c.*, Friesland, Neth.; nr. Leeuwarden; yachting ctr.; mnfs.; p. (1967) *24,464.*

**Sneeuwbergen**, *mtn. range*, Cape Prov., S. Africa.

**Snizort, Loch**, *arm of sea* (14 m. long), N. of I. of Skye, Scot. [Norway; alt. 7,565 ft.

**Snohetten**, *mtn.*, highest in Dovrefjeld range,

**Snowdon**, *mtn.*, nr. Caernarvon, Wales; (highest in Eng. and Wales); alt. 3,571 ft.

**Snowy**, *R.*, N.S.W. and Victoria, Australia; rises in Mt. Kosciusko, flows S. into Bass Strait 80 m. W. of C. Howe; length 270 m. Snowy Mtns. project (1950–75) to provide hydroelec. power and irrigation.

**Soar**, *R.*, Leicester, Nottingham, Eng.; rises in uplands of S. Leics, flows N.W. through Leicester, Loughborough, into R. Trent nr. Long Eaton; hosiery and knitwear inds. in lower valley; 43 m. long.

**Sobat**, *R.*, Sudan, N.E. Africa; rises in S.W. of Abyssinian Highlands, flows N.W. into R. Nile 80 m. below L. No; one of ch. sources of Nile flood-water; Abyssinia receives monsoon rains April to Oct., max. discharge into White Nile, Nov. and Dec.; length over 500 m.

**Soche**, *see* Yarkand.

**Sochi**, *t.*, R.S.F.S.R.; on Black Sea at foot of main Caucasian range; health resort with sub-tropical climate and sulphur springs; developed since 1933; p. (1967) *182,000.*

**Society Is.**, *archipelago*, S. Pac. Oc.; between the Tuamotu Archipelago and Friendly Is., under Fr. protection; ch. I. Tahiti; ch. prod. phosphate and copper; cap. Papeete·; p. *37,303.*

**Socotra**, *Brit. I.*, G. of Aden, Indian Ocean; S. of Arabia and E. of C. Guardafui; livestock; exports "Dragon's Blood", myrrh, frankincense, aloes; a. 1,382 sq. m.; p. c. *9,000.*

**Sodbury**, *rural dist.*, Glos, Eng.; aircraft, bricks, quarrying, coal-mining; p. (1961) *44,826.*

**Söderhamn**, *spt.*, Sweden; on G. of Bothnia, N. of Gavle; timber, wood-pulp, iron, engin.; p. (1961) *13,010.*

**Södermanland**, *co.*, Sweden; S.W. of Stockholm; a. 2,634 sq. m.; p. (1961) *227,615.*

**Södertälje**, *t.*, Sweden; on L. Malar; engin., tools, machin., cars, aluminium; p. (1961) *33,152.*

**Soerabaya or Surabaya**, *spt.*, Java, Indonesia; dockyards and arsenal; oil; coffee, rice, cotton, sugar, tapioca; glass; p. (1961) *1,007,000.*

**Soerakarta, or Solo**, *t.*, Java, Indonesia; p. (1961) *363,000.* [iron ind.; p. (1963) *34,200.*

**Soest**, *c.*, N. Rhine–Westphalia, Germany; cath.;

**Soest**, *t.*, Utrecht, Neth.; artistic earthenware toys; p. (1967) *32,958.*

**Sofala and Manica**, *prov.*, Mozambique; N. of Inhambane; by some identified with the "Land of Ophir" of the Bible; cap. Beira.

**Sofia**, *t.*, *cap.*, Bulgaria; the ancient Sardica, and the Triaditza of the Byzantine Greeks; on Golem Isker R.; univ.; sugar, beer, flour, leather, silk, tobacco, maize, linen, engin., chemicals; p. (1967) *853,876.*

**Sogn og Fjordane**, *co.*, Norway; a. 7,135 sq. m.; p. (1963) *100,467.*

**Sogne Fjord**, longest in Norway.

**Sohåg**, *t.*, U.A.R.; on R. Nile; p. (1960) *62,000.*

**Soignies**, *t.*, Belgium; on R. Senne; granite, flax; p. (1962) *10,946.*

**Soissons**, *t.*, Aisne, France; iron, copper, farm implements, glass, sugar; p. (1954) *20,484.*

**Söke**, *t.*, Turkey; liquorice, fruits, cereals, livestock; emery, lead; p. (1965) *27,140.*

**Sokoto**, *t.*, Nigeria, W. Africa; groundnuts, rice, cotton, cattle, hides and skins. Founded 1809 as cap. of native st. of S., pop. mainly Hausa and Fulani. p. *48,000.*

**Sol Iletsk**, *t.*, R.S.F.S.R.; near Kazakhstan border; potash; p. *10,000.*

**Solefttea**, *t.*, Västernorrland, Sweden; on G. of Bothnia; p. (1961) *9,888.*

**Solent, The**, *strait* separating the I. of Wight from the mainland; extends from Hurst Castle to Calshot.

**Soleure (Solothurn)**, *can.*, N. Switzerland; arable, pastoral, and afforested; a. 306 sq. m.; p. (1961) *200,816.*

**Solihull**, *co. bor.*, Warwick, Eng.; 5 m. S.W. of Birmingham; motor wks., drawing office equipment, stellite alloys mftg.; p. (estd. 1967) *105,890.*

**Solikamsk**, *t.*, R.S.F.S.R.; on R. Kama; potash and magnesium salts; chemicals, fertilisers, paper; p. (1956) *41,200.*

Solingen, *t.*, N. Rhine–Westphalia, Germany; 15 m. E. of Düsseldorf; cutlery ctr.; p. (1963) *172,200.*

Sóller, *t.*, Majorca, Spain; p. (1957) *9,377.*

Solna, *t.*, nr. Stockholm, Sweden; p. (1961) *51,094.*

Solnechnyy, *see* Gornyy Snezhnogorsk.

Solomon Is., *Brit. prot.*, S. Pac.; inc. all Is. in 900-m. archipelago, S. and S.E. of large I. of Bougainville; copra, trochus shell, timber; bauxite, nickel; volcanic soil; a. 11,500 sq. m.; (1959) *124,076.*

Solor I., Lesser Sunda Is., Indonesia; a. 114 sq. m.

Solothurn, *can.*, N.W. Switzerland; crossed by Jura mtns. and R. Aar; agr., pastoral, industl.; a. 306 sq. m.; p. (1961) *200,816.*

Solothurn (Soleure), *t.*, *cap.*, can. Solothurn, Switzerland; on R. Aar; watches, jewellery, cottons, motor production; p. (1957) *16,744.*

Sölvesborg, *spt.*, Sweden; tanneries; p. *4,246.*

Solway Firth, *arm* of Irish Sea, between Dumfries, Kirkcudbright, Scot., and Cumberland; length 40 m.

Somaliland, *region*, N.E. Africa; "the Eastern Horn of Africa," from the Strait of Bab-el-Mandeb S. to the Equator.

Somaliland, French. *See* Afars and Issas.

Somali Republic, *ind. sovereign st.* since 1 July 1960, comprising former U.N. trust terr. under Italian adm. (cap. Mogadishu) and former British Somaliland Prot. (cap. Hargeisa) which achieved ind. June 26, 1960; consists of torrid coastal strip from bdy. of Kenya N. along Indian Oc. up to 300 m. inland and strip along G. of Aden, up to 150 m. inland; hot, dry climate (tempered inland by alt.); cattle, maize, food-crops, hides; total a. 246,200 sq. m.; p. (1961) *1,990,000.*

Sombor, *t.*, Serbia, Jugoslavia; cattle, grain; p. (1962) *37,800.*

Sombrero I., Brit. Leeward Is., W.I.; phosphate of lime; Board of Trade lighthouse.

Somerset, *S.W. co.*, Eng.; bounded inland by Glos, Devon, Wilts and Dorset; pasture, arable, orchard and woodland, with mines, quarries and mnfs.; impt. fisheries; co. t. Taunton; a. 1,620 sq. m.; p. (1966) *638,000.*

Somerset West, *t.*, Cape Province, S. Africa; wine, fruit, veg.; explosives, fertilisers, chemicals; p. (1960) *8,234* inc. *4,225* whites.

Somersworth, *t.*, N.H., U.S.A.; on Salmon Falls R.; mnfs.; p. (1960) *8,529.*

Somerville, *c.*, Mass., U.S.A.; sub. of Boston; varied mnfs.; p. (1960) *94,697.*

Somme, *dep.*, N. France; mainly agr. with thriving textile inds.; cap. Amiens; a. 2,443 sq. m.; p. (1962) *488,225.*

Somme, *R.*, France; flows in deps. Aisne and Somme to English Channel; length 116 m.

Sommen, *L.*, Sweden (25 m. by 8 m.) 15 m. E. of L. Vättern.

Somport Tunnel, on bdy. France–Spain; carries main rly. from Pau to Zaragoza under Central Pyrenees; length 5 m.

Sönderborg, *spt.*, S. Jutland, Denmark; resort; cas. (military barracks); p. (1960) *20,653.*

Sondrio, *prov.*, Lombardy, Italy; silk; a. 1,233 sq. m.; cap. Sondrio; p. (1961) *18,717.*

Songea, *t.*, Tanzania, E. Africa; admin. ctr.; wheat, coffee, tobacco.

Song-koi (Red R.), *R.*, rises in Yunnan plateau, S.W. China, flows S.E. through N. Vietnam, enters G. of Tongking; Hanoi is nr. head of delta; Haiphong nr. one of R. mouths; lower valley densely populated and intensively cultivated; length approx. 800 m.

Sonneberg, *t.*, Suhl, E. Germany; toys; p. (1963) *29,231.*

Sonora, *st.*, Mexico; on G. of Cal.; silver-mines, stock-raising, grain, cotton, sugar, fruit, tobacco growing; cap. Hermosillo; a. 70,477 sq. m.; p. (1960) *783,378.*

"Soo" Canals, *see* Saulte Ste. Marie Canals.

Soochow (Suzhou), *c.*, Kiangsu, China; nr. Shanghai; former treaty pt.; silk, weaving and exp.; cotton, rice; p. (1953) *474,000.*

Sopot, *spa, seaside resort*, Poland; on W. shore of Gdańsk B.; p. (1965) *45,000.*

Sopron, *t.*, N.W. Hungary; on R. Hunte; holiday resort; viticulture; p. (1962) *42,333.*

Sorata, *t.*, Bolivia; 57 m. W. La Paz; nr. Andes peak of Ancohuma (Illampu).

Sorau, *see* Zary.

Sorel, *t.*, Quebec, Canada; sawmills, foundries, engin.; p. (1961) *17,147.*

Soria, *prov.*, Old Castile, Spain; agr. and cattle-rearing, with cheese, timber, wool and salt exp.; cap. Soria; a. 2,977 sq. m.; p. (1959) *154,987.*                                      [(1957) *21,500.*

Soria, *t.*, *cap.*, Soria, Spain; on R. Douro; p.

Soriano, *dep.*, Uruguay; a. 3,561 sq. m.; cap. Mercedes; p. (1953) *99,927.*

Sormova, *industl. sub.*; 6 m. W. of Gorkiy on R. Volga; Byelorussian S.S.R.; machin., diesel motors, boilers, ships, tanks.

Soro, *t.*, Själland, Denmark; p. *3,191.*

Sorocaba, *t.*, Brazil; rly. wks.; textiles, cement, footwear, wines, fertilisers; p. (1960) *109,258.*

Sorrento, *cst. t.*, S. Italy; nr. S. extremity G. of Naples; popular resort, anciently celebrated for its fine wines; p. *26,325.*

Sör-Tröndelag, *see* Tröndelag.

Sosnowiec, *t.*, S.W. Poland; rly. junction; coal, iron, textiles; p. (1965) *140,000.*

Sotteville-lès-Rouen, *t.*, Seine-Maritime, France; rly. wks.; p. (1954) *25,626.*

Soufrière, *mtn.*, Basse-Terre I., Lesser Antilles Gr. W. Indies; volcanic; highest peak in Lesser Antilles; alt. 4,869 ft.

Sound, The, *channel* between the Kattegat and the Baltic, 3 m. across at narrowest part.

Sousse (Susa), *spt.*, Tunisia; p. (1956) *48,172.*

South Africa, Republic of, *ind. rep.* (withdrew from Br. Commonwealth May 31, 1961), compr. provs. Cape Province, Natal, Transvaal and O.F.S.; climate, Mediterranean to tropical; vegetation, evergreens in C. region, grassland (veld) in E.; cereals, cotton, sugar, vines, citrus fruit, sheep and cattle, ostriches, gold, diamonds, coal, copper, tin, various mnfs.; admin. cap. Pretoria, legislative cap. Cape Town; a. (inc. Walvis Bay) 472,685 sq. m.; p. (1966) *18,298,000* (inc. *3,481,000* whites).

South America, southern continent of Western hemisphere incl. Argentina, Bolivia, Brazil, Chile, Colombia, Ecuador, Paraguay, Peru, Uruguay, Venezuela and Guyana; physical features, cst. regular except in S.W., Andes Mtns. along whole of W. cst., Brazilian Highlands on E. cst., rolling plains in ctr.; climate, diverse, varying with latitude and alt.; equatorial, hot and wet; Atacama, a rainless desert on middle W. cst. In S. temperate; vegetation, varying with latitude, alt.; climate, from coniferous, deciduous and tropical forest to tropical and temperate grasslands and deserts; ch. inds.; temperate and tropical agr.; cocoa, coffee, sugar-cane, rubber, cereals; cattle, sheep; minerals; gold, silver, copper, tin, diamonds, nitrates; factory inds. developing gradually; races: Europeans, mainly o. Spanish and Portuguese descent, Indians, Negroes, mulattoes and mestizos (mixed races); a. 7,300,000 sq. m.; p. (estd. 1965) *164,000,000.*

South Arabia, Federation of. *See* Yemen, Southern.

South Bend, *c.*, Ind., U.S.A.; carriage and wagon wks., iron foundries, paper- and flour-mills, farming implements, aeroplanes; seat of Notre Dame University; p. (1960) *132,445.*

South Carolina, *st.*, U.S.A.; level in E., and mtns. in W.; cereals, cotton, tobacco; textiles, chemicals, lumber; cap. Columbia; ch. pt., Charleston; a. 31,055 sq. m.; p. (1960) *2,382,594.*

South Coast, *t.*, Queensland, Australia; p. (1957) *22,800.*

South Dakota, *st.*, U.S.A.; mixed farming, wheat; gold, silver, gypsum, lumbering, flourmilling, butter, cheese, meat-packing; cap. Pierre; a. 77,047 sq. m.; p. (1960) *680,514.*

South Downs, *range chalk hills*, Sussex and Hants, Eng.

Southern Arabia, Protectorate of, the name adopted by Aden on accession to Federation (Jan. 1963).

South Gate, *industl. t.*, Cal., U.S.A.; paint, chemicals, tiles, furniture, tires, machin.; p. (1960) *53,831.*

South Georgia, *Brit. I.*, S. Atl. Oc.; a. 1,450 sq. m.; mtns., whaling ctr.

South Holland, *prov.*, Neth.; flat, intersected by Rs. and dykes; cap. The Hague; a. 1,130 sq. m.; p. (1960) *2,706,810.*

South I., *lge. I.*, N.Z.; contains S. Alps (highest Mt. Cook, 12,349 ft.), Canterbury Plains; wool, mutton, dairy prod., fruit; Benmore hydroelec. sta., on Waitiki R.; a. 58,093 sq. m.; p. (1964) 770,669.

**South Kensington**, dist., in W. London; contains Victoria and Albert Museum, Geological and Science Museums, British Museum of Natural History, Commonwealth Institute, Albert Hall.

**South Molton**, mkt. t., mun. bor., Devon, Eng.; at S. foot of Exmoor, 10 m. S.E. of Barnstaple; textiles, cosmetics; p. (1961) 2,994.

**South Orange**, t., N.J., U.S.A.; p. (1960) 16,175.

**South Orkney Is.**, Antarctica; whaling; met. sta.

**South Portland**, c., Me., U.S.A.; on Portland harbour; p. (1960) 22,788.

**South Sandwich Is.**, Antarctica; whaling.

**South Shetland**, Brit. archipelago, S. Atlantic; 400 m. S. C. Horn.

**South Shields**, t., co. bor., Durham, Eng.; on S. bank at mouth of R. Tyne; coming holiday resort; coal, engin., lingerie; p. (estd. 1967) 107,760.

**Southall**, t., former mun. bor., Middlesex, Eng., now inc. in Ealing outer bor. Greater London (q.v.); residtl.; many varied light inds.; p. (1961) 52,983.

**Southam**, mkt. t., rural dist., Warwick, Eng.; 5 m. S.E. of Leamington; lime, cement, mineral spring; p. (1961) 15,457.

**Southampton**, c., spt., co. bor., Hants, Eng.; at head of Southampton Water on peninsula between estuaries of Rs. Test and Itchen; univ.; extensive docks for passenger-liners and other shipping; ship repairing, oil refining, cable mkg., electronics, synthetic rubber; p. (estd. 1967) 209,790.

**Southampton, O.**, S. pt. of Coates I., Hudson Bay, Canada.

**Southampton Water**, inlet, Hants, Eng.; comprises drowned estuaries of Rs. Itchen and Test; gives access from Solent and Spithead to spt. of Southampton; length 9 m., width 1–1½ m.

**Southborough**, t., urb. dist., Kent, Eng.; in ctr. of The Weald, 2 m. N. of Tunbridge Wells; residtl.; chalybeate spring; p. (1961) 9,770.

**Southbridge**, t., Mass., U.S.A.; optical instruments and cutlery; p. (1960) 15,889.

**Southend-on-Sea** t., co. bor., Essex, Eng.; on N. side of Thames estuary; wireless factory, varied light inds.; air ferry terminal; p. (estd. 1967) 165,760.

**Southern Alps**, range of mtns., S.I., N.Z.

**Southern Cross**, t., rly. junction, W. Australia; on main Transcontinental Rly. 220 m. E. of Perth; gold-mines, now declining.

**Southern Ocean**, surrounds Antarctica; pack ice.

**Southern Rhodesia**, see Rhodesia.

**Southgate**, former mun. bor., Middlesex, Eng.; now inc. in Enfield outer bor. Greater London (q.v.); residtl.; p. (1961) 72,359.

**Southland**, prov.; S.I., N.Z.; cap. Invercargill; big agr. a.; wheat, meat, wool; a. 11,170 sq. m.; p. (1961) 93,697.

**Southport**, t., co. bor., Lancs, Eng.; on S. side of Ribble estuary; 18 m. N. of Liverpool; seaside resort; residtl.; p. (estd. 1967) 79,710.

**Southport**, vat. pl., Queensland, Australia; 50 m. S. of Brisbane; pastoral, dairying, fruit-growing and timber dist.; p. (1947) 8,432.

**Southsea**, dist., Portsmouth, Hants, Eng.; seaside resort.

**Southwark**, inner bor., London, Eng.; incorporating former bors. of Bermondsey and Camberwell; p. (1966) 304,000.

**Southwell**, mkt. t., rural dist., Notts, Eng.; cath.; coal-mining, agr.; p. (rural dist. 1961) 45,818.

**South-West Africa**, terr., under U.N. responsibility; mostly desert, scanty rainfall; cattle, ostriches; diamonds, tin, copper; cap. Windhoek; a. 318,261 sq. m.; p. (1961) 525,064.

**Southwick**, urb. dist., W. Sussex, Eng.; on S. cst. 4 m. W. of Brighton; p. (1961) 11,874.

**Southwold**, spt., mun. bor., E. Suffolk, Eng.; on E. cst. 8 m. S. of Lowestoft; fishing; resort; p. (estd. 1967) 2,140.

**Soviet Harbour**, spt., G. of Tartary, R.S.F.S.R.; sawmilling; p. (1954) 75,000.

**Sowerby Bridge**, t., urb. dist., W.R. Yorks, Eng.; on R. Calder, 3 m. W. of Halifax; woollens; p. (1961) 16,224.

**Sowjetsk (Tilsit)**, t., R.S.F.S.R.; German before 1945; on R. Memel; cas.; foodstuffs. machin., wood; p. (1956) 34,100.

**Sozh, R.**, Ukrainian S.S.R.; trib. of R. Dnieper; length 240 m.

**Spa**, t., Liége, Belgium; mineral springs, resort; [p. (1962 9,040.

**Spain**, kingdom (without a sovereign), S.W. Europe; interior plateau; climate varied, very hot summers, warm rainy winters, N.W. mild, and wet, central plateau extremes of heat and cold; evergreen trees and shrubs; cereals, vines, citrus fruits, olives, nuts; sheep, goats, pigs; coal, copper, iron, lead, zinc, mercury, colophony, turpentine, cork; mnfs. wine, sugar, silk, brewing; oil refining; leading ind. tourism; cap. Madrid; a. 189,890 sq. m.; p. (1967) 32,275,434.

**Spalding**, mkt. t., urb. dist., Holland, Lincoln, Eng.; in The Fens, 10 m. up the R. Welland from The Wash; agr., bulb mkt., agr. machin., sugarbeet, fruit canning; p. (1961) 14,521.

**Spandau**, t., Potsdam, E. Germany; firearms, gunpowder; previously agr. military ctr.

**Spanish Guinea**, see Equatorial Guinea.

**Spanish Sahara**, Spanish col., N.W. African cst.; comprising Rio de Oro and Saguia el Hamra; lge. reserves of phosphate at El Aiun being exploited; a. 105,000 sq. m.; p. (estd. 1963) 26,000 (nomadic).

**Spanish Wells**, l., Bahamas, W. Indies; p. (1953) 665.

**Sparrows Poin`**, t., Md., U.S.A.; situated on Chesapeake Bay at entrance to Bear Creek; impt. iron and steel ind.

**Sparta**, famous ancient c., the Morea, Greece; on the R. Eurotas; passed under Roman rule, 146 B.C.; p. (1961) 10,412.

**Spartanburg**, t., S.C., U.S.A.; cotton; p. (1960) 44,352.

**Spartel, O.**, International Zone, N.E. Africa.

**Spartivento, O.**, Italy; most S. point of Italian mainland.

**Spenborough**, mun. bor., W.R. Yorks, Eng.; textiles, plastics, wire; p. (estd. 1967) 33,440.

**Spencer Gulf**, lge. inlet, S. Australia; penetrates 240 m. inland, max. width 75 m.

**Spennymoor**, t., urb. dist., Durham, Eng.; 5 m. S. of Durham; mnfs.; p. (1961) 19,104.

**Sperrin Mtns.**, Tyrone and Londonderry, N.Ireland.

**Spey, R.**, Inverness, Moray, and Banff, the most rapid in Scot., flows N.E. to Moray Firth; length 107 m.

**Speyer**, c., Rhineland-Palatinate, Germany; cas.; its famous Diet of 1529 condemning the Reformation gave rise to the term "Protestant"; textiles, tobacco, machin., footwear, beer, sugar, paper; oil refining; p. (1963) 39,800.

**Spezia, La**, spt., Liguria, Italy; on Bay of Spezia; arsenal, docks, maritime inds., elec. machin., and olive oil; p. (1961) 121,191.

**Spice Is.**, see Moluccas.

**Spitalfields**, par., E. London, Eng.; former silkweaving dist., introduced by Huguenots, 17th. cent.

**Spithead**, roadstead, between Portsmouth and the I. of Wight, Eng.; used by ships of Royal Navy.

**Spitsbergen (Svalbard)**, I., gr., belonging to Norway; well within Arctic Circle; mountainous; sealing and whaling; coal-mining; asbestos, copper, gypsum, iron, marble, mica, zinc and phosphate deposits; a. 24,294 sq. m.; p. (1956) Norwegian 1,530, Russian 2,746.

**Split (Spalato)**, c., Jugoslavia; wine, olive oil, bauxite, shipping; p. (1959) 84,000.

**Spltigen Pass**, Rhaetian Alps; between Lombardy and Grisons, Switzerland; alt. 6,939 ft.

**Spokane, R.**, Idaho, U.S.A.; flows to the R. Columbia at Washington; length 120 m.

**Spokane**, t., Wash., U.S.A.; on R. Spokane, at the fall which is used for hydro-elec. power; gr. timber tr., flour and sawmills, mng.; cement, elec. goods; p. (1960) 181,608.

**Spoleto**, t., Perugia, Italy; truffles; p. 32,600.

**Spondon**, t., Derby, Eng.; on R. Derwent, 3 m. E. of Derby; textiles; nylon plant projected 1964.

**Sporades, I.**, Grecian Archipelago in the Ægean and neighbouring seas; belonging to Greece; includes Samos, Kos, etc.

**Spree, R.**, E. Germany; flowing W. past Berlin to the Havel at Spandau; length 227 m.

**Spremberg**, t., Cottbus, Germany; on R. Spree; lignite, mining, glass, elec., metals, cloth, bicycles, machin.; p. (1963) 22,931.

**Springbok**, t., cap., Namaqualand, Cape Prov., S. Africa; copper-mining; p. (1960) 3,111

Springfield, *c., cap.*, Ill., U.S.A.; gr. rly. ctr.; iron, watches, etc.; p. (1960) *83,271.*

Springfield, *c.*, Mass., U.S.A.; mnfs. cars, elec. apparatus and paper; p. (1960) *174,463.*

Springfield, *c.*, Mo., U.S.A.; flour milling; Congregational college; p. (1960) *95,865.*

Springfield, *c.*, Ohio, U.S.A.; agr. implements, motor lorries; p. (1960) *82,723.*

Springfontein, *t.*, O.F.S., S. Africa; rly. ctr.; p. (1960) *2,850 inc. 758 whites.*

Springs, *t.*, Transvaal, Rep. of S. Africa; E. of Johannesburg; gold mng., engin., machin., cars, elec. goods; uranium plant; p. (1960) *135,231 inc. 36,445 whites.*

Spurn Head, *C.*, E. Yorks, Eng.; at mouth of Humber estuary.

Sretensk, *t.*, R.S.F.S.R.; coal, machin., leather, woodworking.

Srinagar, *t., cap.*, Kashmir, India; on R. Jhelum in W. Himalayas; 5,263 ft. above sea-level; silver and copper wares, carpet weaving, paper; univ.; p. (1961) *285,257.*

Sriracha, *t.*, Thailand; sawmills; oil refinery (p. 1960) *10,472.*

Stade, *t.*, Lower-Saxony, Germany; nr. Hamburg; leather, wood, textiles; p. (1963) *31,400.*

Staffa, *I.*, the Inner Hebrides, W. Scot.; 6 m. N. Iona, off W. cst. Mull; Fingal's Cave, 227 ft. long, with other basaltic caves.

Stafford, *co. t., mun. bor.*, Staffs, Eng.; on R. Sow, 15 m. N. of Wolverhampton; elec. engin., concrete; engin., footwear, salt; p. (estd. 1967) *52,560.*

Staffordshire, *W. midland co.*, Eng.; rich in iron and coal, the "Black Country" being famous; also lge. Potteries dist., famous breweries, and many thriving mnfs.; co. t. Stafford; a. 1,153 sq. m.; p. (1966) *1,802,000.*

Staines, *mkt. t., urb. dist.*, Middx., Eng.; on R. Thames, 4 m. S.E. of Windsor; linoleum, machin., petrol engines; p. (estd. 1967) *55,190.*

Stainmore, *pass*, N.R. Yorks, Eng.; crosses N. Pennines from Greta valley into upper Eden valley; used by main road but only minor rly.; alt. 1,370 ft

Staithes, N.R. Yorks., Eng.; 9 m. N.W. of Whitby; potash mng.

Stalin, *see* Brasov.

Stalin Canal, *see* Volga Baltic Waterway.

Stalinabad *see* Dushanbe.

Stalingrad, *see* Volgograd.

Stalino *see* Varna.

Stalino, *see* Donetsk.

Stalinogorsk, *see* Novomoskovsk.

Stalinsk, *see* Novokuznetsk.

Stalybridge, *t., mun. bor.*, Cheshire, Eng.; on R. Tame, 5 m. E. of Manchester; cotton and wool, engin., plastics, rubber goods, elec. cables; p. (estd. 1967) *21,770.*

Stamboul, *see* Istanbul.

Stamford, *c.*, Conn., U.S.A.; on shore of Long I. Sound; p. (1960) *92,713.*

Stamford, *mkt. t., mun. bor.*, Kesteven, Lincoln, Eng.; 10 m. N.W. of Peterborough; agr. inds., elec. goods, plastics; p. (estd. 1967) *13,120.*

Standerton, *t.*, Transvaal, S. Africa; on R. Vaal; livestock, oats; p. (1960) *16,868 inc. 6,698* Europeans.

Standish-with-Langtree, *urb. dist.*, Lancs, Eng.; 4 m. N.W. of Wigan; coal-mining, silk mftg.; p. (1961) *9,689.*

Stanger, *t.*, Natal, S. Africa; tea, sugar, maize, wattle; p. (1960) *9,557 inc. 1,740 whites.*

Stanimaka *see* Asenovgrad.

Stanislaus, *R.*, Cal., U.S.A.; trib. of the San Joaquin R.; length 200 m.

Stanislav, *see* Ivano-Frankovsk.

Stanley, *t., urb. dist.*, Durham, Eng.; 10 m. N.W. of Durham; mnfs.; p. (estd. 1967) *44,690.*

Stanley, *spt., cap.*, Falkland Is.; whaling; p. (estd. 1958) *1,135.*

Stanley, *urb. dist.*, W.R. Yorks, Eng.; p. (1961) *16,749.*

Stanley Falls, on the Upper Congo R., Congo, Africa; nr. the Equator, named after the explorer, Sir H. M. Stanley.

Stanley Pool, an expansion of the Lower Congo, Africa; 25 m. long. 16 m. wide.

Stanleyville, *see* Kisangani.

Stanlow, inc. in Ellesmere Port, urb. dist., Cheshire; petrol ref., oil-storage dks. and terminal; chemicals.

Stanovoi Mtns., *range of mtns.*, U.S.S.R.; extends

from N. of R. Amur to nr. Sea of Okhotsk.

Stans, *cap.*, half-can. Nidwalden, Switzerland; mkt. t., orchards; p. *4,200.*

Star of the Congo, *t.*, Katanga, Congo, Africa; copper-mining.

Stara Planina (Balkan Mtns.), Bulgaria; highest peak, 7,780 ft.

Stara Zagora, *t.*, Central Bulgaria; copper smelting, mineral springs; nitrogen fertiliser plant; p. (1956) *55,322.*

Stargard Szczecinski, *t.*, Poland; prev. in Prussia; woollens, machin., cottons, spirits; p. (1965) *38,000.*

Start Point, *C.*, nr. Dartmouth, Devon, Eng.

Stassfurt, *t.*, Magdeburg, E. Germany; potash salts, chemicals, machin., metals; p. (1963) *26,166.*

Staten I., the most S. point N.Y. st., U.S.A.; shipyards; linked with Brooklyn by Verrazano-Narrows bridge (opened 1964); also island off Tierra del Fuego, S. America, 45 m. long.

States of the Church or Papal States, former indep. terr. under the temporal rule of the popes, prior to 1870; comprised Latium, Umbria, the Marches, E. Emiglia-Romagna.

Stavanger, *spt.*, Rogaland, Norway; margarine and preserved-food, woollen mills, fish curing and canning, shipbldg.; oil refinery at Sola under construction; p. (1960) *52,799.*

Staveley, *t., urb. dist.*, Derby, Eng.; 3 m. N.E. of Chesterfield; coal, iron, chemicals; p. (1961) *18,071.*

Stávnice, *t.*, ČSSR.; impt. mining ctr., producing silver, copper, lead.

Stavropol, *see* Togliatti.

Stawell, *t.*, Victoria, Australia; 150 m. N.W. of Melbourne; agr. pastoral, viticulture ctr.; p. (1966) *5,904.*

Steelton, *bor.*, Penns., U.S.A.; steel foundries; p. (1960) *11,266.*

Steep Holm I., Bristol Channel, Eng.

Steep Rock, *see* Atikokan.

Stellenbosch, *t.*, C. Prov., Rep. of S. Africa; 25 m. E. of Cape Town; univ.; wines, sawmilling, brick and tile mkg.; p. (1960) *22,233* inc. *10,673* Europeans.

Stendal, *c.*, Magdeburg, E. Germany; cath.; iron, sugar wks.; p. (1963) *37,204.*

Stepney, *see* Tower Hamlets.

Sterlitamak, *t.*, Bashkir, R.S.F.S.R.; on S.W. flank of Ural Mtns., 120 m. N.E. of Chkalov (Orenburg); impt. oil-refineries on "Second Baku" oilfield; linked by pipeline to Stavropol; p. (1967) *156,000.*

Sternberk, *t.*, Moravia, ČSSR.; N. of Olomouc; textile mftg.; p. (1961) *11,215.*

Stettin, *see* Szczecin.

Steubenville, *c.*, Ohio, U.S.A.; iron, steel, paper, glass, coal, natural gas; p. (1960) *32,495.*

Stevenage, *t.*, Herts, Eng.; 4 m. S.E. of Hitchin; one of "New Towns" designated 1946; agr., light engin., school furniture, elec. goods, chemicals, aircraft parts; p. (estd. 1967) *58,690.*

Stevenston, *sm. burgh*, Ayr, Scot.; p. (1961) *10,174.*    [Canada.

Stewart, *R.*, trib. of R. Yukon, N.W. Terr., Stewart I., S. or S.I., N.Z.; a. 670 sq. m.; oysters.

Stewarton, *burgh*, Ayr, Scot.; 5 m. N. of Kilmarnock; woollens, carpets; p. (1961) *3,387.*

Steyning, *vil.*, E. Sussex, Eng.; on R. Adur, 4 m. N. of Shoreham at entrance to gap through S. Downs; residtl.; p. *1,875.*

Steyr, *t.*, Austria; on R. Enns. nr. Linz; bicycles, lorries, small-arms factories; p. (1961) *38,306.*

Stilton, *vil.*, Huntingdon, Eng.; 6 m. S.W. Peterborough; famous for cheese.

Stinchar, *R.*, Ayr, Scot.; flows W. to sea at Ballantrae; length 30 m.

Stirling, *ancient burgh*, Stirling, Scot.; on R. Forth in gap between Campsie Fells and Ochil Hills; cas.; univ.; coal-mng., engin., concrete, rock, wool, rubber gds; p. (1961) *27,553.*

Stirling, *midland co.*, Scot., borders Firth of Forth; coal-mining, agr., textiles; a. 466 sq. m.; p. (1961) *194,858.*

Stockerau, *t.*, Austria; machin., chemicals; p. (1961) *11,853.*

Stockholm, *c., cap.*, Sweden; on Is. at outlet of L. Malar; called the "Queen of the Baltic" for the beauty of its surroundings; comm. ctr.; machin., textiles, leather, sugar, chemicals; many academic institutions; p. (1961) *808,484.*

Stockport, *t., co. bor.,* Cheshire, Eng.; on R. Mersey, 5 m. S.E. of Manchester; cotton, hats, engin.; p. (estd. 1967) *141,030.*

Stocksbridge, *urb. dist.,* W. R. Yorks; p. (1961) *11,137.*

Stockton, *t.,* Cal., U.S.A.; farm implements, flour, lumber; p. (1960) *86,321.*

Stockton-on-Tees, *mkt. t., mun. bor.,* Durham, Eng.; 4 m. W. of Middlesbrough; impt. iron and steel inds., plywood; first rly. for passenger traffic opened in 1825 between Stockton and Darlington; 18th cent. town hall; racecourse; p. (1961) *81,198.*

Stoke-on-Trent, *c., co. bor.,* Staffs, Eng.; at S.W. foot of the Pennines; formed in 1910 by union of the "five towns" of Arnold Bennett's novels, Hanley, Burslem, Tunstall, Longton, and Fenton (with Stoke-upon-Trent); ceramics, coal, iron and steel, engin., brick and tile wks., precast concrete; p. (estd. 1967) *275,730.*

Stoke Newington, *see* Hackney.

Stokesley, *mkt. t., rural dist.,* N.R. Yorks, Eng.; 7 m. S. of Middlesbrough; agr.; p. (rural dist. 1961) *25,571.*

Stolberg, *t.,* N. Rhine–Westphalia, Germany; E. of Aachen; metals, glass, wood, chemicals; p. (1963) *33,200.*

Stolp, *see* Slupsk.

Stone, *mkt. t., urb. dist.,* Staffs, Eng.; on R. Trent, 7 m. S. of Stoke-on-Trent; footwear, tiles, porcelain, scientific glassware; p. (1961) *8,791.*

Stoneham, *t.,* Mass., U.S.A.; boots and shoes; p. (1960) *17,821.*

Stonehaven, *fishing t., burgh,* Kincardine, Scot.; on E. cst., 14 m. S. of Aberdeen; distilling, net mftg.; p. (1961) *4,500.*

Stonehenge, *prehistoric gr. of monumental stones,* on Salisbury Plain, Wilts, Eng.; date of erection estd. between 1860–1560 B.C.

Stonehouse, *par.,* Lanark, Scot.; coal, linen; p. *4,204.*

Stony Stratford, *mkt. t.,* Bucks, Eng.; on R. Ouse, nr. Buckingham; engin., lace.

Stornoway, *spt., burgh,* Ross and Cromarty, Scot.; on E. cst. of I. of Lewis, Outer Hebrides; ctr. Harris Tweed ind.; fishing ctr.; p. (1961) *5,221.*

Stour, *R.,* Kent, Eng.; flows past Canterbury to Pegwell Bay; length 40 m.

Stour, *R.,* Somerset, Dorset, and Hants, Eng.; trib. of R. Avon; length 55 m.

Stour, *R.,* Suffolk and Essex, Eng.; flows E. to sea at Harwich; length 42 m.

Stour, *R.,* Worcs, and Staffs, Eng.; trib. of R. Severn; length 20 m.

Stourbridge, *t., mun. bor.,* Worcs, Eng.; on R. Stour, 9 m. W. of Birmingham; coal, iron and steel, brick and glass wks.; p. (estd. 1967) *51,300.*

Stourport-on-Severn, *urb. dist., mkt. t.,* Worcs, Eng.; at confluence of Rs. Stour and Severn; carpets, iron and steel goods, porcelain, ceramics; p. (1961) *11,751.*

Stowmarket, *t., urb. dist.,* Suffolk, Eng.; on R. Gipping, 11 m. N.W. of Ipswich; I.C.I. paint factory ctr.; p. (1961) *7,790.*

Strabane, *t., urb. dist.,* Tyrone, N. Ireland; salmon fishing, agr. ctr.; p. (1966) *8,813.*

Straits Settlements, *former Brit. crown col.,* Malay Peninsula; comprised Penang, Malacca, and Singapore, estbl. 1867, dissolved 1946; Christmas I., the Cocos Is. and Labuan were at various times part of the col. *See* West Malaysia.

Stralsund, *spt.,* Rostock, E. Germany; opposite Rügen I.; grain tr., machin., metals, fish smoking, shipbldg.; p. (1963) *68,791.*

Strand, *t.,* Cape Province, S. Africa; resort; p. (1960) *13,313* inc. *7,067* whites.

Strangford Lough, *arm of sea,* Down, N. Ireland; 18 m. long, 6 m. wide at entrance.

Stranraer, *burgh,* Wigtown, Scot.; at head of Loch Ryan; steamer service to Larne, Antrim, N. Ireland; creameries, brewing, knitwear; p. (1961) *9,249.*

Strasbourg, *fortfd. c., cap.,* Bas-Rhin, France; on R. Ill just above confluence with R. Rhine; captured 1870, regained 1918; fine cath., univ., imperial palace, many handsome new public bldgs.; extensive tr.; oil refining; machin., textiles, chemicals; p. (1962) *233,549.*

Stratford, *dist.,* E. London, Eng.; in bor. Newham; mftg.

Stratford, *c.,* Ontario, Canada; woollens, farm machin., flour, sawmills, engine wks.; p. (1961) *20,467.*

Stratford, *t.,* on R. Housatonic, Conn., U.S.A.; aircraft; p. (1960) *44,712.*

Stratford-on-Avon, *c., mun. bor.,* Warwick, Eng.; on R. Avon, 11 m. S.W. of Leamington; birth-place of Shakespeare; memorial theatre, library, tourist ctr.; light inds.; p. (estd. 1967) *18,600.*

Strathaven, *t.,* Lanark, Scot.; cas.; knitwear, agr. engin., fibre glass; p. *4,207.*

Strathmore, *lowland belt.,* central Scot.; extends from Crieff N.E. to Montrose; flanked to N. by Scot. Highlands, to S. by Sidlaw, and Ochil Hills; drained by Rs. Earn, Tay, Isla, S. Esk; famous for cereals and small fruits; length 60 m., width 7–10 m.

Strathpeffer, *wat. pl.,* Ross and Cromarty, Scot.; 5 m. W. of Dingwall; spa.

Strathspey, *valley of the Spey,* Scot.; 70 m. long.

Stratton and Bude, *resort,* N. Cornwall, Eng.; 12 m. S. of Hartland Point; p. (1961) *5,095.*

Straubing, *t.,* Bavaria, Germany; on R. Danube; cas.; brewing, tiles, chemicals, machin.; p. (1963) *36,700.*

Strawberry, *R.,* Utah, U.S.A.; on E. slopes of Wasatch Mtns. 80 m. S.E. of Salt Lake City; dammed to supply irrigation water, led through 3¾ m. tunnel under Wasatch Mtns. to 100 sq. m. cultivable land round L. Utah.

Streator, *c.,* Ill., U.S.A.; bricks, glass, hardware, farm implements; p. (1960) *16,864.*

Street, *t., urb. dist.,* Somerset, Eng.; at foot of Polden Hills, 7 m. S.W. of Wells; footwear, leather, vehicle wks.; p. (1961) *6,660.*

Stresa, *vil.,* Piedmont, Italy; favourite health resort on L. Maggiore; p. (estd.) *4,500.*

Stretford, *mun. bor.,* S.E. Lancs, Eng.; sub. of Manchester; engin., chemicals; p. (estd. 1967) *60,010.*

Stromboli, *I.,* Lipari Is., N. of Sicily, Tyrrhenian Sea; active volcano, alt. 3,038 ft.; p. *853.*

Stromness, *mkt. burgh, pt.,* Mainland, Orkney Is., Scot.; 13 mm. W. Kirkwall; p. (1961) *1,477.*

Stromstad, *spt.,* Sweden; on Skagerrak; seaside resort; shipbldg.; fishing; p. (1961) *4,039.*

Stronsay, Orkney Is., Scot.

Stroud, *mkt. t., urb. dist.,* Eng.; in Cotswold Hills, on R. Frome; cloth, carpets, plastics, engin.; p. (1961) *17,461.*

Strumble Head, *promontory,* N. Pembroke, Wales.

Stryj, *R.,* Poland; trib. of R. Dniester.

Stryj, *t.,* Poland; sawmills, matches; p. *25,000.*

Stungmeanchy, *t.,* Cambodia; glass plant.

Sturminster Newton, *mkt. t., rural dist.,* Dorset, Eng.; on R. Stour, 6 m. N.W. of Blandford; creameries; p. (rural dist. 1961) *9,566.*

Sturt Desert, area N.E. of S. Australia.

Stuttgart, *c. cap.,* Baden-Württemberg, Germany; on R. Neckar; cas., cath.; cars, machin., elec. engin., hosiery, knitwear; route ctr.; oil refinery nearby; p. (1963) *640,500.*

Styr, *R.,* Poland; trib. of R. Prypel (Pripet); length 250 m.

Styria, *prov.,* Austria; grain, wine and fruit; stock-rearing, tourist tr.; a. 6,326 sq. m.; p. (1961) *1,137,865.*

Styrian Alps, that portion of the Alpine mtn. system E. of the Hohe Tauern.

Suakin, *former pt.,* Sudan, N.E. Africa; on Red Sea; now used only for pilgrim traffic to Jeddah.

Suanhwa (Xuanhua), *c.,* Hopeh prov., China; iron mng.; p. (1953) *114,000.*

Subotica, *t.,* Serbia, Jugoslavia; boots, rly. material, farming, stock-raising; tri-phosphate wks.; p. (1959) *80,000.*

Suceava, *t.,* S. Bukovina, Romania; former residence of Moldavian princes; fancy leather; p. (1963) *62,557.*

Suchan, *t.,* R.S.F.S.R.; coal; p. (1956) *43,900.*

Süchow (Suzhou), *c.,* Kiangsu, China; on Tai-Hu, 40 m. W. of Shanghai; gr. comm. and industl. ctr., silks, cottons, rice; p. (1953) *c. 373,000.*

Sucre, *cap.,* Chuquisaca dep. and legal cap. of Bolivia; univ. and cath.; cement plant.; p. (1962) *54,270.*

Sucre, *st.,* Venezuela; cap. Cumana; p. (1961) *401,992.*

Sudan, The, *ind. sovereign st.* since Jan. 1956, N.E. Africa; formerly Anglo-Egyptian condominium; bounded by Egypt, Libya, Chad, Central African Rep., Congo, Uganda, Ethiopia, and Red Sea; cotton, gum arabic, hides, ground nuts, sugar; iron ore mng.; cap. Khartoum; a. 967,500 sq. m.; p. (1961) 12,109,000.

Sudanese Republic. See Mali.

Sudbury, t., mun. bor., W. Suffolk, Eng.; on R. Stour, 12 m. N.W. of Colchester; p. (estd. 1967) 7,060.	[(1956) 46,025.

Sudbury, t., Ontario, Canada; nickel, copper; p.

Sudeten Mtns., range, Poland, Czechoslovakia; separating Bohemia and Moravia from Silesia.

Suez, spt., U.A.R., N.E. Africa; at head of G. of Suez (arm of Red Sea) and S. entrance of Suez Canal, which crosses the Isthmus of Suez to the Mediterranean at Port Said and is of very gr. value to shipping; the ancient Arsinoë; Port Tewfiq adjoining has quay and docks; p. (1960) 203,000.

Suez, G., Red Sea; N.W. arm of Red Sea between Arabian Desert and Sinai Peninsula, Egypt; southern approach to Suez Canal; length 190 m., width varies from 12 to 25 m.

Suez Canal, ship canal, U.A.R., N.E. Africa; connects Mediterranean Sea (Pt. Said) with Red Sea (Suez) through Ls. Manzala, Timsah and Bitter; saves over 4,000 m. on journey N.W. Europe to India, 1,000 m. to Australia; opened 1869; length, 101 statute m.

Suffolk, most E. maritime co., Eng.; bounded by Essex, Norfolk, Cambridge and the N. Sea; mixed agr., dairying; fisheries; mnf. of agr. implements; civil nuclear power-sta. at Sizewell (1966); co. t. Ipswich; a. 1,482 sq. m. divided for admin. purposes into Suffolk E. p. (1966) 371,000 and Suffolk W. p. (1966) 148,000.

Suhl, t., Suhl, E. Germany; toys, armaments; p. (1963) 26,907.

Sui, Baluchistan, W. Pakistan; natural gas; pipeline to Karachi.

Suir, R., Ireland; flows E. to Waterford Harbour.

Sukarnapura, formerly Kota Baru, cap., West Irian, Indonesia.

Sukhumi, spt., Georgian S.S.R.; resort; sawmilling; p. (1959) 64,000.

Sukkur, t., Pakistan; on R. Indus, 230 m. N.E. of Karachi; gr. dam for irrigation; thermal sta. under construction; p. (1961) 103,000.

Sulaiman, mtns., Asia; range bounding the Punjab and Baluchistan.	[272,442.

Sulaimaniya, liwa, Iraq; a. 4,554 sq. m.; p. (1956).

Sulawesi (Celebes), I., Indonesia; mtnous., forested; copra, coffee, bauxite; ch. pt. Menado, Makasar; a. 73,160 sq. m.; p. (1961) 7,079,349.

Sulina, t., Romania; at mouth of Sulina branch of Danube R.; considerable grain tr.; p. 3,622.

Sullana, t., N. Peru; rly. ctr.; maize, cotton, cinchona bark, fishing, whaling; p. (1961) 23,000.

Sultanabad, t., Persia; carpet mftg.; p. 55,000.

Sulu Is., Philippines; archipelago between Borneo and the Philippines; a. 950 sq. m.; acquired by the U.S.A. 1898.

Sumatra, I., Malay Archipelago, Indonesia; coffee, sugar, rice, pepper; gold, tin, petroleum coal; a. 161,612 sq. m.; p. (1967) 18,300,000.

Sumba, I., Indonesia; part of Timor Archipelago.

Sumbawa, one of the Nusa Tenggara Is., Indonesia; in E. Indian Archipelago, E. of Lombok; a. (inc. nearby Is.) 5,240 sq. m.; p. 314,843.

Sumgait, t., Azerbaydzhan S.S.R.; on Caspian Sea; 25 m. N.W. of Baku; metallurgical ind.; chemicals; p. (1959) 52,000.

Sumy, t., Ukrainian S.S.R.; engin., chemicals, textiles; p. (1967) 135,000.	[m. long.

Sunart, Loch, sea arm, Argyll cst., W. Scot.; 19½

Sunbury-on-Thames, urb. dist., Middx., Eng.; W. of London; residtl., water wks., gravel pits; petrol research establishment; p. (1961) 33,437.

Sunda Strait, between Java and Sumatra, Indonesia; 13 m. wide, contains the volcanic I. of Krakatao.

Sundarbans, The, tract of forest and swamps, fringing the delta of the Ganges, E. Pakistan; 165 m. long, 81 m. wide; rice grown in N.; tigers and crocodiles found in S.

Sunday I., lgst. of Kermadec Is., N.Z.; 20 m. in circuit and with a p. of 10 is the only one of the Kermadec Is. that is inhabited; met. and radio sta. established on I. [Algoa Bay; 200 m. long.

Sunday, R., Cape Prov., S. Africa; flows into

Sunderland, spt., co. bor., Durham, Eng.; at mouth of R. Wear; gr. shipbldg. and coal-exp. ctr. (inc. Monkwearmouth and parts of Bishopwearmouth), best gas coal, also engin., glass, paper and rope; fine harbour, piers and docks; p. (estd. 1967) 219,270.

Sundsvall, spt., Västernorrland, Sweden; on a wide bay of the Baltic nr. Hernösand; timber and wood-pulp inds.; p. (1961) 29,493.

Sungari, R., N. China; trib. of R. Amur; inc. the Nonni; length over 1,000 m.

Sungpan, t., Szechwan, China; silver, gold, lead; linseed oil, paper; smelting, engin.

Superior, c., Wis., U.S.A.; at head of L. Superior; gr. tr. in grain, timber, coal, shipbldg. and flour mills; oil refining; p. (1960) 33,563.

Superior, L., N. America; lgst. sheet of fresh water in the world; lies between Canada and the U.S.A.; one of the chain of gr. Ls. in the St. Lawrence system; outlet to L. Huron by the St. Mary's R., receives the waters of the St. Louis, Pigeon and Nipigon; a. 32,000 sq. m.

Surat, c., Gujarat, India; on R. Tapti; cotton, silk, embroidery; p. (1961) 288,026.

Surbiton, former mun. bor., Surrey, Eng., on R. Thames, nr. Kingston; now inc. in Royal Borough of Kingston-upon-Thames (q.v.); residtl.; light engin., bricks, tiles, elec. components; p. (1961) 62,940.

Suresnes, t., Seine, France; p. (1962) 40,151.

Surinam, R., Neth. Guiana, S. America; flows N. to Atl. Oc. nr. Paramaribo; length 300 m.

Surinam (Neth. Guiana), Dutch col., S. America; ch. exp. bauxite, timber, rubber, rice, fruit; cap. Paramaribo; a. 55,000 sq. m.; p. (1956) 350,000.

Surinumu Dam, 30 m. from Port Moreby, Papua; part of hydro-elec. scheme; opened 1963.

Surrey, S. co., Eng.; S. of R. Thames; cereals, livestock, vegetables; residtl.; a. 722 sq. m.; p. (1966) 977,000.

Surry, Va., U.S.A.; nuclear power sta. being built on James R.

Sus, R., S. prov. Morocco, N. Africa; flowing to the Atlantic nr. Agadir; length 130 m.

Susa, see Sousse.

Susquehanna, R., N.Y., Penns., and Md., U.S.A.; flows to Chesapeake Bay through highly industl. a.; routeway, W. from Philadelphia and Baltimore across Appalachian Mtns.; length 422 m.

Sussex, maritime co., S.E. Eng.; adjoining Surrey, Kent and Hants, and washed by Eng. Channel; traversed E. to W. by the S. Downs; co. t. Lewes; a. 1,457 sq. m.; divided administratively into Sussex E. p. (1966) 710,000 and Sussex W. p. (1966) 450,000.

Susten Pass, modern alpine road, alt. 7,296 ft., between Haslital and Reuss valley, links Bernese Oberland with Gotthard road.

Sutherland, N. co., Scot.; N.W. Moray Firth, washed by Atlantic and N. Sea; grazing and forest land, most sparsely pop. in Scot.; mountainous, with many lochs; co. t. Dornoch; a. 2,102 sq. m.; p. (1961) 13,442.

Sutlej, R., West Pakistan; rises in the Himalayas and flows to the R. Indus; used for lge.-scale irrigation; length 1,000 m.

Sutton, outer bor., Greater London, Eng.; inc. former bors. of Beddington and Wallington, Sutton and Cheam, and Carshalton; p. (1966) 166,000.

Sutton Coldfield, t., mun. bor., Warwick, Eng.; 6 m. N.E. of Birmingham; hardware, plastics; television transmitter; p. (estd. 1967) 81,630.

Sutton-in-Ashfield, t., urb. dist., Notts, Eng.; 3 m. S.W. of Mansfield; coal, light engin.; hosiery; p. (estd. 1967) 40,630.

Suva, c., cap., Fiji Is.; on Viti Levu I., fine harbour; p. (estd. 1965) 38,000.

Suwalki, t., N.E. Poland; nr. Lithuanian S.S.R. bdy.; timber, grain, woollens; p. (1965) 22,000.

Suwannee, R., Fla., and Ga., U.S.A.; flows to G. of Mexico; known as "Swanee River," length 250 m.

Svalbard, see Spitsbergen.

Svendborg, spt., Fyn, Denmark; mnfs., earthenware, tobacco, exp. butter; p. (1960) 23,892.

Sverdlovsk, t., R.S.F.S.R.; on R. Iset, at E. base of the Ural Mtns.; steel, engin., chemicals, textiles; p. (1967) 940,000.	[of White Sea.

Sviatoi Nos, C., Arctic cst., U.S.S.R.; nr. entrance

Svir, R., U.S.S.R.; flowing between L. Onega and L. Ladoga; length 125 m.

Svistov, t., Bulgaria; on R. Danube, Romanian border; p. (1956) 18,448.

Svobodnyy, t., R.S.F.S.R.; on R. Zeya, 105 m. N. of Blagoveshchensk; agr. equipment, sawmilling; p. (1959) 57,000.

Svolær, spt., Norway; ch. t. Lofoten Is.; fishing; p. (1961) 3,821.	[cap. Augsburg.

Swabia, dist., Bavaria, Germany; a. 3,807 sq. m.;

Swabian Alps, *mtns.*, Württemberg, Germany; inc. the Swabian Jura range between valleys of Neckar and Danube.

Swadlincote, *t., urb. dist.*, Derby, Eng.; 3 m. E. of Burton-on-Trent; collys., potteries, engin., clothing; p. (1961) *19,222.*

Swaffham, *mkt. t., urb. dist.*, Norfolk, Eng.; forestry; p. (1961) *3,210.*  [R. Ouse; length 60 m.

Swale, *R.*, N.R. Yorks, Eng.; joins R. Ure to form

Swale, *channel*, between I. of Sheppey and Kentish mainland, Eng.; 16 m. long.       [nr. Perth.

Swan, *R.*, W. Australia; flows to Indian Ocean,

Swan Hill, *t.*, Victoria, Australia; fruit growing and dairying under irrigation; canning; p. (1966) *7,376.*

Swanage, *mkt. t., urb. dist.*, Dorset, Eng.; on bay, E. cst. I. of Purbeck; seaside resort; stone quarries; p. (1961) *8,112.*

Swanland, *region*, W. Australia; consists of extreme S.W. corner of W. Australia; hot, dry summers and mild winter with adequate rain; forests of Karri and Jarrah; agr. vines, citrus and deciduous fruits, wheat; highest pop. density in W. Australia; ch. ts. Perth, Fremantle, Bunbury.

Swansea, *spt., co. bor.*, Glamorgan, Wales; on Swansea Bay, Bristol Channel; univ. coll.; coal and iron, copper, steel, zinc, chemicals; lge. exp. anthracite, aluminium wire and cable, refrigerators; p. (1961) *166,740.*

Swat, *dist.*, Malakand, N.W. Frontier Agencies and Tribal Areas, Pakistan.

Swatow (Shantou), *c., spt.*, Kwangtung, S. China; on S.E. cst. nr. mouth of Han Kiang, 200 m. N.E. of Hong Kong; gd. harbour; fishing; sm. coastal tr. mainly with Hong Kong; exp. tangerines; p. (1953) *280,000.*

Swaziland, *indep. kingdom* within Brit. Commonwealth (Sept. 1968), S. Africa; S.E. of the Transvaal; agr., sugar, citrus, cotton, rice; iron ore and coal-mng., hydroelectr. power; timber and pulp ind.; asbestos, gold, tin, barytes; cap. Mbabane; a. 6,704 sq. m.; p. (1966) *389,000.*

Sweden, *kingdom*, N. Europe; forming E. (and larger) part Scandinavian Peninsula; mountainous W., but otherwise flat and dissected by Rs. and many Ls., while one-fourth of the land is forest; gr. timber exp. and mining of iron ore, lead, silver, arsenic; cereals, root crops, hay, livestock; mnfs., textiles, matches, machin., glass, chemicals, etc.; cap. Stockholm; a. 173,426 sq. m.; p. (1961) *7,495,129.*

Swidnica (Schweidnitz), *t.*, Lower Silesia, Poland; German before 1945; textiles, machin.; p. (1965) *44,000.*             [(1961) *12,186.*

Swift Current, *t.*, Saskatchewan, Canada; p.

Swilly, Lough, *arm of the Atlantic*, cst. of Donegal, Ireland; 25 m. long.

Swindon, *t., mun. bor.*, Wilts, Eng.; in upper Thames Valley (Vale of White Horse), 27 m. S.W. of Oxford; gr. rly. wks.; impt. rly. junction; mkt. for local dist.; heavy engin., textiles, tobacco, cars; p. (estd. 1967) *97,920.*

Swinemünde, *see* Swinoujscie.

Swinoujscie (Swinemünde), *spt.*, Pomerania, Poland, German before 1945; on I. of Usedom (Uznam), Baltic Sea; spt. for Szczecin; spa and summer resort; p. (1965) *22,000.*

Swinton, *t., urb. dist.*, W.R. Yorks, Eng.; in Don valley, 3 m. N.E. of Rotherham; coal, iron, potteries, bricks and tiles; p. (1961) *13,420.*

Swinton and Pendlebury, *mun. bor.*, Lancs, Eng.; 5 m. W. of Manchester; cotton spinning, coal, engin., accumulator mftg.; p. (estd. 1967) *40,760.*

Switzerland, *fed. rep.*, Cen. Europe; upland region, with Jura Mtns. on N. and Alps to S.; dairying, butter, cheese, chocolate, etc., wine; watches and clocks, elec. machin.; very dependent on lge. tourist tr.; 4 national languages; cap. Bern; a. 15,944 sq. m.; p. (1961) *5,429,061.*

Sydenham, *S.E., sub.*, London, Eng.; residtl.; site of the Crystal Palace, burnt down 1936.

Sydney, *c., cap.*, N.S.W., Australia; principal spt. on shore of Pt. Jackson Bay; many beautiful bdlgs. and parks, stretching S. to Botany Bay; univ.; lge. comm. and active inds.; magnificent bridge, harbour and docks; six-lane highway bridge under constr. oil refinery under construction; p. (1966) *2,444,735.*

Sidney or S. Sydney, *spt.*, C. Breton I., Nova Scotia; iron and steelwks., coal, chemicals; p. (1956) *32,162.*

Sydney Mines, *t.*, Nova Scotia, Canada; coal; p. [(1961) *9,122.*

Syktyvkar, *t.*, R.S.F.S.R.; on Vychegda R.; sawmilling, engin.; p. (1959) *64,000.*

Syra, *I.* of the Cyclades, Ægean Sea; part of Greece; p. (1951) *33,775.*

Syracusa, *t.*, Sicily, Italy; on I. of Ortygia, off E. cst.; cath.; exp. olive oil, oranges, lemons, locust beans, almonds, wine, chemicals, pottery, etc; chemicals at Priolo; p. (1961) *90,333.*

Syracuse, *c.*, N.Y., U.S.A.; air conditioners, electronic equipment, jet engines; chemicals, salt, machin., cars, seat of Syracuse Univ.; p. (1960) *216,038.*           [into Aral sea.

Syr Darya, *R.*, Kazakhstan, U.S.S.R.; flowing

Syrian Arab Republic, *rep.*, S.W. Asia; seceded from United Arab Rep. 28 Sept. 1961; stretches along E. shore of Mediterranean and E. to the R. Euphrates; chiefly agr.; cereals, olives, fruit, goats, sheep; silk, wool, cement, soap; oil; pipeline from Karachok fields to Homs and Tartus; phosphate deposits; cap. Damascus; a. 66,046 sq. m.; p. (estd. 1962) *4,839,000.*

Syzran, *t.*, R.S.F.S.R.; on R. Volga; petroleum refining, engin.; p. (1967) *167,000.*

Szarvas, *t.*, Hungary, S. of Mezőtur; industl.; p. (1962 *18,950.*          [sq. m.; p. (1965) *848,000.*

Szczecin, *prov.*, Poland; cap. Szczecin; a. 12,100

Szazhalombatta, *t.*, Hungary, on R. Danube, 15 m. S. of Budapest; lgst. oil refinery in Hungary; oil supplied through Druzhba pipeline.

Szczecin (Stettin), *spt.*, Pomerania, Poland, German before 1945; at mouth of R. Odra (Oder); cas.; engin., iron, textiles, paper; p. (1965) *310,000.*

Szczecinek (formerly German Neustettin), *t.*, W Polish Pomerania; p. (1965) *26,000.*

Szechwan (Sichuan), *prov.*, China; cereals, sugar, tea, cotton, silk, coal, iron, salt, petrol; cap. Chengtu; a. 144,996 sq. m.; p. (1953) *62,303,999.*

Szeged, *t.*, Hungary; on Theiss R., 100 m. S.E. of Budapest; univ.; cath.; gr. comm. and industl. ctr.; leather, breweries, textiles; oil nearby at Tape; natural gas pipeline from deposit under oilfield; p. (1965) *113,000.*

Székesfehérvár, *t.*, Hungary; nr. Budapest; aluminium and metal processing; radios, cycles; p. (1962) *57,757.*

Szentes, *t.*, Hungary; p. (1962) *30,979.*

Szeping (Siping), *c.*, Kirin prov., China; agr. distributing ctr.; cement; p. (1953) *126,000.*

Szolonok, *t.*, Hungary; on R. Tisza, E. of Budapest; machin., paper ind., cellulose, chemicals; p. (1962) *47,919.*

Szombathely, *t.*, Hungary; cath.; rly. ctr.; textiles, tanning, shoe mkg.; p. (1962) *55,849.*

Szóny, *t.*, Hungary; oil refining, linked to U.S.S.R. by "Friendship Oil Pipeline;" p. (1962) *4,600.*

# T

Taasinge, *I.*, Denmark; S. of Fyn; 9 m. long; p. (1960) *4,366.*   [charcoal; fishing; p. *1,500.*

Tabarka, *spt.*, Tunisia; mkt. exp. cork, tanning,

Tabasco, *maritime st.*, Mexico; on Bay of Campeche, adjoining Guatemala; cacao, sugarcane, tobacco, rubber, pepper, maize, rice and hard-woods; cap. Villa Hermosa; a. 9,782 sq. m.; p. (1960) *496,340.*      [and Amazon.

Tabatinga, *t.*, Brazil; on junction of Rs. Javari

Table Bay, *inlet of Atlantic*, cst. of C. of Gd. Hope, S. Africa; site of Cape Town.

Table Mountain, Cape Prov., S. Africa, nr. Cape Town; alt. 3,549 ft.

Tabor, *t.*, ČSSR.; S. of Prague, on R. Luznice; cigars, beer; p. (1961) *19,561.*

Tábor, Mt., N. Palestine; S.E. of Nazareth.

Tabora, *t.*, Central Tanzania; E. Africa; at junction of rlys. from Dar es Salaam and L. Victoria; agr.; p. (1960) *15,350.*

Tabriz, *c.*, Iran, cap. E. Azarbayejan; metal inds., machine tool complex projected; famous blue mosque; airpt.; p. (1967) *806,631.*

Tachira, *st.*, Venezuela, S. America; cap. San Cristobal; p. (1961) *399,163.*

Tacna, *dep.*, Peru; terr. transferred by treaty from Chile, 1929; mainly desert; nitrate of soda, silver, copper; subject to earthquakes; a. 4,930 sq. m.; ch. t. T.; p. (1961) *69,176.*

Tacna, *t.*, Peru, airport, p. (1961) *18,000.*

Tacoma, *spt.*, Wash., U.S.A.; on Puget Sound;

shipping, fishing, iron, steel, copper, electro-chemicals, aluminium; p. (1960) *147,979.*

**Tacuarembo,** *dep.* Uruguay, S. America; a. 8,112 sq. m.; cap. Tacuarembo; p. (1963) *19,658.*

**Tadcaster,** *rural dist., mkt. t.,* on R. Wharfe, W.R. Yorks, Eng.; brewing, stone, paper board; p. (rural dist. 1961) *26,725.*

**Tadmor,** *see* Palmyra.

**Tadoussac,** *t.,* Quebec, Canada; on R. Saguenay, where it enters St. Lawrence R.; tourist ctr.; oldest settlement in Canada (1599).

**Tadzhik,** *constituent rep.,* U.S.S.R., cereals, cotton, fruit, horticulture, cattle breeding; minerals, gold, petroleum, coal; magnetic iron ore prospecting in the Kara Mazar mtns.; cap' Dushanbe; a. 55,700 sq. m.; p. (1959) *1,982,000*

**Taegu,** *c.,* S. Korea; silk-spinning and cotton-ginning mills; nylon yarn; p. (1962) *717,000.*

**Taejon,** *t.,* S. Korea; S. of Seoul; fish, petroleum, cereals; p. (1962) *269,000.*

**Taff,** *R.,* Glamorgan, Brecknock, Wales; rises in Brecon Beacons, flows S.E. across coalfield to Bristol Channel at Cardiff; length 40 m.

**Tafilalet,** Morocco, N. Africa; oasis of the Sahara, E. of Atlas; ch. t. Abuam; dates.

**Taganrog,** *spt ,* R.S.F.S.R.; on Sea of Azov; steel, engin.; p. (1959) *201,000.*

**Tagliamento,** *R.,* N.E. Italy; rises in Carnic Alps, flows S. into Adriatic Sea (G. of Venice); valley used by rly. from Venice to Vienna via Semmering Pass; length 100 m.

**Tagus,** *R.,* Spain and Portugal; flows W. across Meseta to Atlantic at Lisbon; length 540 m.

**Tahiti,** *principal I.,* of Society gr, French Polynesia; Pac. Oc.; fertile cst. land, picturesque; a. 402 sq. m.; cap. Papeete; p. (1962) *45,430.*

**Tahoe,** *L.,* Cal., Nevada, U.S.A.; in Yosemite National Park, Sierra Nevada, at alt. 6,225 ft., surrounded by summer resorts; a. 200 sq. m.

**Taichow (Taizhou),** *c.,* Kiangsu prov., China; rice ctr.; p. (1953) *160,000.*

**Taif,** *t.,* Hejaz, Saudi Arabia; 50 m. W. of Mecca; 5,900 ft. above sea-level; summer resort; honey, fruit, mat mkg., boat bldg.; p. *25,000.*

**Taihape,** *t., N.I., N.Z.;* 161 m. N.E. of Wellington; in the King Country, on Hautapu R.; sheep and dairy farming, saw-milling; p. (1961) *2,684.*

**Tai Hu,** *L.,* Kiangsu, China; focus of intensive system of sm. canals and waterways 60 m. N. of Shanghai; a. approx. 100 sq. m.

**Taima,** *t.,* Saudi Arabia; cereals, dates, fruit, tobacco, rock salt.

**Taimyr Peninsula,** N. cst., Siberia, U.S.S.R.; terminates with C. Chelyuskin.    [*229,500.*

**Tainan,** *t.,* Taiwan, China; sugar, rice; p. (1957)

**Taipei,** *cap.,* Taiwan; fertiliser plant; p. (1964) *1,085,000.*

**Taiping,** *t.,* Malaya; p. *41,361.*

**Taiwan (Formosa),** *I.,* China, 100 m. E. of mainland; U.S.A. protection; fishing, rice, tea, sugar, coal, gold, oil, natural gas, textiles; cap. Taipei; a. 13,890 sq. m.; p. (1959), *10,431,341* (excluding armed forces *600,000*).

**Taiyuan,** *c.,* Shansi, China; on Fuen-Ho; p. (1953) *721,000.*    [p. (1965) *243,444.*

**Takamatsu,** *t.,* Japan; N. cst. Shikoku; gr. tr.;

**Takaoka,** *t.,* Honshu, Japan; ctr. of rice tr.; lacquer wk.; cars; p. (1965) *140,000.*

**Takasaki,** *t.,* Honshu, Japan; coal mines, raw silk; radiation chemistry research ctr.; p. (1965) *174,000.*

**Takhnan,** *t.,* Cambodia; tyres.

**Takoradi,** *spt.* Ghana, West Africa; as spt. has superseded Sekondi; rly. to Kumasi thence to Accra; exp. cocoa, palm-oil, rubber, bauxite, gold, manganese, industl. gases; p. (1960) *41,000.*

**Talara,** *t.,* N. Peru, S. America; on C. Pariñas; oil refining; p. (1961) *40,000.*

**Talavera,** *c.,* Spain; on Tagus R.; cloth, leather, wine; p. (1957) *22,152.*

**Talca,** *prov.,* Chile; cap. Talca; a. 3,721 sq. m.; p. (1961) *226,052.*

**Talca,** *t.,* cap. Talca prov., Chile; S. of Santiago; lge. mftg. ctr.; matches, footwear, paper and flour mills, foundries; p. (1961) *80,277.*

**Talcahuano,** *spt.,* Chile, nr. Concepción; naval sta.; grain and repair ctr.; steel plant at Huachipato; p. (1961) *99,231.*

**Talence,** *t.,* Gironde, France; p. (1962) *26,911.*

**Talien (Dairen),** *c., spt.,* S. Liaoning prov., China; on Liaotung pen., Bay of Korea; together with Port Arthur adm. as part of special mun. of Luta (*q.v.*); p. (estd. 1957) *1,508,000.*

**Tallahassee,** *c.,* Fla., U.S.A.; cigars; p. (1960) *48,174.*

**Tallahatchee,** *R.,* trib. of Miss., U.S.A.; flows S.W. and becomes R. Yazoo; length 240 m.

**Tallin,** *spt., cap.,* Estonian S.S.R., U.S.S.R.; timber, shipbldg., textiles; p. (1967) *335,000.*

**Taltal,** *spt.,* Chile; S. of Antofagasta; exp. nitrates and silver; p. (1961) *5,897.*

**Tamale,** *ch. t.,* Northern Terr., Ghana, W. Africa; aerodrome; p. (1960) *49,223.*

**Tamar,** *R.,* Devon and Cornwall, Eng.; flows S. to Plymouth Sound; length 45 m.

**Tamar,** *R.,* Tasmania, Australia; formed at confluence of North Esk and South Esk at Launceston, flows into Bass Strait nr. Georgetown.

**Tamatave,** *one of the ch. pts.,* Malagasy; lge. meat-preserving factories; exp. graphite, hides, raffia; oil refinery; p. (1959) *48,627.*

**Tamil Nadu** (*formerly* Madras), *st.,* India; rice, millet, oilseeds, cotton, indigo, spices, tobacco, tea; fertilisers; ch. ts. Madras, Madurai, Tiruchirapalli; a. 50,331 sq. m.; p. (1961) *33,686,953.*

**Tamaulipas,** *st.,* Mexico; on G. of Mexico, S. of Texas; nitrates, cereals, sugar, coffee, cattle, petroleum; cap. Ciudad Victoria; a. 30,731 sq. m.; p. (1960) *1,024,182.*

**Tambov,** *t.,* R.S.F.S.R.; on R. Oka; synthetic rubber, engin., chemicals; p. (1959) *170,000.*

**Tampa,** bay on W. cst. Fla., U.S.A.; 40 m. long.

**Tampa,** *c.,* Fla., U.S.A.; popular winter resort, cigar factories, phosphates, electronics; fruit growing and canning; p. (1960) *274,970.*

**Tampere (Tammerfors),** *t.,* S. Finland; on rly. between Helsinki and Vaasa; textiles, leather, paper; p. (1966) *144,175.*

**Tampico,** *spt.,* Mexico; on the R. Panuco, 9 m. from the G. of Mexico; fruits, sugar, maize; p. (1960) *122,197.*

**Tampico,** *R.,* Mexico, flows to G. of Mexico; length 200 m.

**Tamworth,** *t.,* N.S.W., Australia; on R. Peel; milling; ch. comm. ctr. of Northern Tableland; bldg. inds., agr. engin.; p. (1966) *21,682.*

**Tamworth,** *t., mun. bor.,* Staffs, Eng.; on R. Tame, 5 m. S.E. of Lichfield; ancient cas.; coal, light engin.; p. (estd. 1967) *34,600.*

**Tana,** *lge. L.,* N. Ethiopia, nr. Gondar, source of Blue Nile, 45 m. long, 40 m. wide; surrounded by marsh, papyrus swamp.

**Tana,** *R.,* forming part of bdy. between Finland and Norway, flows into Arctic Ocean.

**Tana R.,** *ch. R.,* Kenya, E. Africa.

**Tananarive,** *c., cap.,* Malagasy; air-line to Paris; ctr. of commerce and communications; lge. meat-preserving factories; p. (1965) *254,000.*

**Tanaro,** *R.,* N. Italy; trib. of R. Po; 125 m. long.

**Tandil,** *t.,* Argentina; resort; granite quarried nearby; p. (1960) *70,000.*

**Tandjoengbalei,** *spt.,* Sumatra, Indonesia; exp. tobacco, copra, shipyards.

**Tanga,** *spt.,* Tanzania, E. Africa; rly. terminus; on plateau overlooking Tanga Bay; hydroelec. sta.; p. *38,000.*

**Tanganyika,** *gr. L.,* E. Central Africa; 400 m. long, greatest width 45 m.; a. about 12,700 sq. m.; 2,800 ft. above sea; discovered by Burton and Speke in 1868, and since explored by Livingstone, Stanley and others.

**Tanganyika, Rep. of,** *see* Tanzania.

**Tanimbal Is.,** S. Moluccas, Indonesia; gr. of 66 islands; forests, swamps; maize, rice, coconuts, sago; p. *31,847.*

**Tangier,** *free pt.,* Morocco, N. Africa; on Strait of Gibraltar; no longer internationalised zone but integral part of kingdom of Morocco; summer cap.; shipyd.; cigarettes, fishing; p. of t. (1960) *141,714.*

**Tangshan,** *c.,* Hopeh prov., China; mun. limits incl. whole Kailan coal mng. a.; p. (1953) *693,000.*

**Tanta,** *t.,* Lower U.A.R.; 55 m. N. of Cairo; impt. rly. junction; religious fairs; p. (1960) *184,000.*

**Tanzania, United Rep. of,** *indep. sov. st.,* E. Africa; within Brit. Commonwealth; comprising former sts. of Tanganyika and Zanzibar; climate tropical, varies with elevation; ch. prod., sisal, coffee, cotton, groundnuts, pyrethrum, copra, cloves, ebony, hardwoods; sugar mill and refinery projected in Kilombero Valley; diamond deposits discovered nr. Kahama, 80 m. N. of Tabora; cap. Dar es Salaam; a. 363,708 sq. m.; p. (estd. 1964) *9,710,000.*

**Tapachula**, *ch. t.*, S. Mexico; coffee, cattle, tobacco, sugar refineries, sawmills; p. (1940) *43,032*.

**Tapajóz**, *R.*, trib. of R. Amazon.

**Tapti**, *R.*, W. India; flows W. to G. of Cambay at Surat from Betul dist., Madhya Pradesh; length 450 m.

**Tapungato**, *mtn.*, W. Argentina; alt. 22,300 ft.

**Taquari**, *R.*, Brazil; trib. of R. Paraguay; length 400 m.      [length 200 m.

**Tara**, *R.*, Siberia, R.S.F.S.R.; trib. of R. Irtysh.

**Tarakan**, *spt.*, Borneo, Indonesia; on Tarakan I.; oil; p. (of I.) *12,000*.

**Taranaki**, *prov.*, N.I., N.Z.; a. 3,750 sq. m.; [p. (1961) *99,721*.

**Taranto**, *t.*, Lecce, Italy; on G. of Taranto, inlet of Ionian Sea; maritime arsenal with gr. comm. and industl. interests; strong cas.; cottons, velvets, soap, oil; steel wks.; cement; oil refinery; famous for its oyster and mussel fisheries; p. (1964) *205,000*.

**Tarapaca**, *prov.*, N. Chile; nitrates, silver; cap. Iquique; a. 21,340 sq. m.; p. (1960) *133,775*.

**Tarapore**, *t.*, Maharashtra, India, nr. border of Gujarat; 62 m. N. of Bombay, atomic power sta.

**Tarascon**, *t.*, Bouches-du-Rhône, France; connected by bridges with Beaucaire on opposite bank of R. Rhône; old cas. famous festival; silk and fruit; p. (1962) *8,910*.

**Tarawera Mtn.**, *volcanic peak*, N.I., N.Z.; *c.* 1,000 ft.; in Hot Springs dist.; eruption in 1886 destroyed L. Rotomahana.

**Tarbat Ness**, *promontory*, N. Side of Moray Firth, Ross and Cromarty, Scot.

**Tarbela Dam**, W. Pakistan; on R. Indus 30 m. upstream from Attack and 40 m. N.W. of Rawalpindi; projected.

**Tarbes**, *t.*, *cap.*, Hautes-Pyrénées, France; on R. Adour; cath., paper, flax, woollens, machin., metals, aircraft, leather; p. (1962) *50,715*.

**Taree**, *t.*, N.S.W., Australia; dairying, agr., fishing, timber and fibre-boards; p. (1966) *10,559*.

**Târgu-Jiu**, *t.*, Romania; coal, petroleum, timber; p. *17,698*.

**Târgul-Mures**, *t.*, Romania; on R. Maros; famous old fort, with Gothic Calvinist cath., where in 1571 religious liberty was promulgated for the first time in Europe; gd. tr.; p. (1945) *41,118*.

**Tarifa**, *c.*, Spain; on Gibraltar Strait; most S. point of mainland of Europe; fish tr., cereals, oranges, wines; p. (1957) *18,098*.

**Tarija**, *prov.*, Bolivia; cap. Tarija; a. 24,786 sq. m.; p. (1962) *142,600*.

**Tarija**, *t.*, *cap.*, Tarija prov., Bolivia; S.E. of Potosí; maize, wheat, vines; p. (1962) *20,851*.

**Tarma**, *t.*, Peru, S. America; alt. 9,980 ft.; maize, cotton, oranges, bananas; p. (1961) *7,860*.

**Tarn**, *R.*, France; trib. of R. Garonne; has famous rocky gorge 31 m. long in its upper course; length 235 m.

**Tarn**, *dep.*, S. France, watered by Tarn and its tribs.; wheat and wine; cap. Albi; a. 2,232 sq. m.; p. (1962) *319,560*.

**Tarn-et-Garonne**, *dep.*, W. France; corn, wine, woollens, paper, silk; cap. Montauban; a. 1,440 sq. m.; p. (1962) *175,847*.

**Tarnow**, *t.*, Poland; E. of Kraków; agr.; farm implements, glass; industl. development since 1950; p. (1965) *77,000*

**Tarragona**, *prov.*, Spain; on the Mediterranean; vineyards and agr.; cap. Tarragona; a. 2,426 sq. m.; p. (1959) *364,075*.

**Tarragona**, *fortfd. spt.*, cap. Tarragona, Spain; at mouth of R. Franconi; mnfs. alcohol, liqueurs, chocolate, paper, silk, fish-salting; p. (1957) *42,000*.

**Tarrasa**, *t.*, Barcelona, Spain; in fruit and vine-growing dist.; royal college; thriving inds.; p. (1959) *86,469*.

**Tarsus**, *ancient c.*, Turkey; nr. Adana, opposite Cilician Gates; orange and citron groves; ruined Roman temple; birthplace of Apostle Paul; exp. cotton, wool, hides; p. (1965) *57,035*.

**Tartary** or **Tatary**, *region*, Central Asia; now divided into Chinese or E. Turkestan, and W. Turkestan, U.S.S.R.

**Tartary, Gulf of**, *arm of the Sea of Japan*, separating Sakhalin from the Siberian mainland.

**Tartu** (formerly Dorpat), *t.*, Estonian S.S.R.; univ.; saw milling, engin.; p. (1959) *74,000*.

**Tarudant**, *t.*, Morocco, N. Africa; mkt., orange water, leather, pottery, copper, brass; p. *12,877*.

**Tashkent**, *cap.*, Uzbek. S.S.R. on Syr Darya R.;

univ.; extensive silk mnfs.; engin; pipeline from Gazil natural gas field; p. (1967) *1,127,000*.

**Tasman Bay**, *lge. inlet*, S.I., N.Z.; penetrates N. cst., between Separation Point and D'Urville I.; enclosed by mtns., sheltered, fertile, coastal fringe; ch. ts. Nelson, Motueka.     [the world.

**Tasman Glacier**, S.I., N.Z.; one of the lgst. in

**Tasmania** (formerly Van Diemen's Land), *I., st.*, Australia; plateau with fertile valleys; temperate climate; forest and grasslands, grain, fruit, cattle-raising; aluminium, copper, zinc, lead, tin, silver; electro-metallurgical inds.; cap. Hobart; a. 26,215 sq. m.; p. (1966) *369,401*.

**Tatar**, A.S.S.R., U.S.S.R.; oil, natural gas; ch. t. Kazan on R. Volga; p. (1956) *2,847,000*.

**Tatra Mtns.** (High Tatra), highest Carpathian gr., Czechoslovakia, alt. 8,743 ft.

**Tatung** (Datong), *c.*, Shansi prov., China; impt. coalfield; p. (1953) *229,000*.

**Taubaté**, *t.*, Brazil; p. (1960) *64,863*.

**Tauber**, *R.*, Germany; trib. of R. Main; l. 74 m.

**Taunton**, *co. t.*, *mun. bor.*, Somerset, Eng.; on R. Tone at W. end of Vale of Taunton; old cas.; apples, cider, clothing tr., engin., plastics; p. (estd. 1967) *37,180*.     [ries; p. (1960) *41,132*.

**Taunton**, *c.*, Mass., U.S.A.; cotton, iron found-

**Taunus**, *mtn. range*, Hessen, Germany; between the R. Lahn and the Rs. Rhine and Main.

**Taupo**, *L.*, N.I., N.Z.; lgst. L. in N.Z.; geysers, hot springs in vicinity; 25 m. by 17 m.

**Taurida** or **Krim**, *dist.*, Crimean Peninsula, U.S.S.R., separated from Ukraine by Perekop Peninsula, divided by R. Salgir; a. 24,540 sq. m.; wheat, tobacco, fruit.

**Taurus Mtns.**, *range*, S. Turkey.

**Tavastehus** (Häme), *dep.*, Finland; cap. Tavastehus; a. 7,118 sq. m.; p. (1958) *573,444*.

**Tavistock**, *mkt. t.*, *urb. dist.*, Devon. Eng.; on R. Tavy, 12 m. N. of Plymouth; impt. mkt.; p. (1961) *6,086*.

**Tavoy**, *t.*, Burma; between Thailand and the Bay of Bengal, W. of Bankgok; rice, tin-mining.

**Tavy**, *R.*, Devon, Eng.; trib. of R. Tamar; length 20 m.

**Taw**, *R.*, Devon, Eng.; flows from Dartmoor to Barnstaple Bay; length 50 m.

**Taxco**, *t.*, Mexico; alt. 5,600 ft.; gold- and silver-mining; tourist ctr.; p. (1960) *10,076*. [jected.

**Taxila**, *t.*, W. Pakistan; heavy machin. wks. pro-

**Tay**, *R.*, Scot.; flows S.E. from Loch Tay in Perth to the Firth of Tay; longest R. in Scotland.

**Tay Bridge**, *rly. bridge*, E. Scot.; spans Firth of Tay from Wormit (Fife) to Dundee (Angus); carries main E. cst. rly. from Edinburgh to Aberdeen; length 2 m.; road bridge (longest in Britain) spanning R. at Dundee, opened 1966.

**Tay**, Firth of, *lge. inlet*, E. cst. Scot.; extends inland almost to Perth; length 27 m., max. width 3 m.

**Tayabas**, *t.*, Luzon, Philippines; on slope of extinct volcano Banajao; in rice- and coconut-growing dist.

**Tayeh**, *industl. t.*, Hupeh, China; lies to S. of Yangtze-Kiang, 42 m. S.E. of Wuhan; ctr. of very impt. iron-ore deposits; iron and steel inds., heavy engin.

**Tayport**, *burgh*, Fife, Scot.; at entrance to Firth of Tay; opposite Broughty Ferry; linen, jute; p. (1961) *3,151*.

**Taz**, *R.*, Siberia, R.S.F.S.R.; flows to Bay of Tazovsk in Gulf of Obi; length 300 m.

**Tbilisi** (Tiflis), *cap.*, Georgian S.S.R.; petroleum refining, engin., textiles; natural gas pipeline to Ordzhonikidze; p. (1965) *823,000*.

**Tczew** (Dirschau), *t.*, Pomerania, Poland; on R. Vistula; rly. wks., sugar, agr. implements; p. (1965) *37,000*.

**Team Valley**, Durham, Eng.; impt. trading estate has been developed here.

**Te Aroha**, *t.*, N.I., N.Z.; between Hamilton and Thames; one of the ch. resorts in the thermal springs dist.; p. (1961) *3,053*.

**Te Awamutu**, *t.*, N.I., N.Z.; S. of Hamilton agr. and dairying dist.; p. (1961) *5,423*.

**Tebessa**, *t.*, Algeria; alt. 2,789 ft.; mkt.; embroidery, carpets; phosphate deposits near by.

**Tecuci**, *t.*, Romania; N.W. of Galati; battle, 1476 (between Stephen the Great and the Turks); p. (1963) *27,226*.

**Teddington**, *S.W. sub.* of London, inc. in Greater London outer bor. of Richmond-upon-Thames; National Physical Laboratory; p. (1961) *13,455*.

**Tedzhen,** *R.,* Turkmen and N. Persia; flowing into Hari-Rud.

**Tees,** *R., N.* Eng.; flows E. from Pennines to N. Sea between Yorks and Durham; length 70 m.

**Teeside,** *co. bor.,* N.R., Yorks. Eng.; formed by enlarged Middlesborough; p. (estd. 1968) *392,500.*

**Teesport,** *oil refinery,* between Redcar and Middlesbrough.

**Tefte,** *R.,* Brazil; trib. of R. Amazon; length 500 m. [*89,016.*]

**Tegal,** *spt.,* Java, Indonesia; sugar; p. (1961)

**Tegucigalpa,** *c., cap.,* Honduras, central America; lies on R. Choluteca; alt. 3,200 ft. above sealevel; univ.; inter-ocean highway, connecting the t. with both Caribbean and Pacific constructed; bananas, p. (1965) *154,000.*

**Tehran,** *cap. c.,* Iran, 70 m. due S. of Caspian Sea; mftg. and comm. ctr., incl. car assembly; modern bldgs. and hotels; gas pipeline to U.S.S.R. projected; nuclear ctr. for CENTO; intern. airpt.; p. of t. and dist. (1965) *2,317,000.*

**Tehri-Garhwal** formerly Himalayan princely st., India, now merged tog. with Kampur and Benares, into st. of Uttar Pradesh.

**Tehuantepec,** *t.,* Mexico; on the Tehuantepec R., nr. the Pacific cst. of the Isthmus; once an Indian cap.; cath.; p. *10,087.*

**Tehuantepec, Isthmus of,** separates G. of Mexico from the Pacific at narrowest point of Mexico; width 130 m.

**Teifi,** *R.,* S.W. Wales; rises in Cambrian Mtns. nr. Strata Florida, flows S.W. and W. into Cardigan Bay 14 m. N.E. of Fishguard; forms bdy. between Cardigan and Carmarthen, Cardigan and Pembroke; sm. flannel ind. in ts. and vils. in lower valley; length 94 m.

**Teign,** *R.,* Devon, Eng.; flows to sea at Teignmouth from Dartmoor; length 30 m.

**Teignmouth,** *t., urb. dist.,* Devon, Eng.; at mouth of R. Teign, 13 m. S. of Exeter; resort; yacht-bldg.; p. (1961) *11,576.*

**Tei-pei,** *c., cap.,* Taiwan, China; on cst. plain at N. end of I. of Taiwan; p. (1957) *759,200.*

**Tekirdag,** *t.,* Turkey in Europe; on Sea of Marmara, W. of Istanbul; grain; p. (1965) *26,964.*

**Tela,** *spt.,* Honduras Central America; on Atlantic cst.; p. (1961) *13,408.*

**Tel Aviv,** *c.,* Israel, founded by Zionists, 1909; first all-Jewish c.; many mnfs.; p. with Jaffa (1960) *387,000.* [*152,073.*]

**Telemark,** *co.,* Norway; a. 5,837 sq. m.; p. (1963)

**Tellicherry,** *t., spt.,* Kerala, India; exp. coffee, cardamoms, sandalwood, and coconuts p.; (1961) *44,763.*

**Telok Betong,** *spt.,* Sumatra, Indonesia; exp. pepper, agr. products; p. *25,170.*

**Tema,** *new pt., t.* nr. Accra, Ghana, opened 1962; big industr. devel., incl. aluminium smelter, deep-water harbour, oil refinery.

**Teme,** *R.,* on border of Wales and Worcester, Eng.; trib. of R. Severn; length 70 m.

**Temes,** *R.,* S.W. Romania; flows to R. Danube, nr. Belgrade; length 180 m.

**Temir-Tau,** *t.,* Kazakh S.S.R.; iron, steel, synthetic rubber, soda; lge thermal power sta.; p. (1967) *147,000.*

**Temperley,** *t.,* nr Buenos Aires, Argentina; impt. rly. junction; p. (1960) *105,000.*

**Temple,** *rly. t.,* Texas, U.S.A.; in cotton-growing dist.; p. (1960) *30,419.*

**Templemore,** *mkt. t., urb. dist.,* Tipperary, Ireland; on R. Suir; p. (1966) *2,031.*

**Temuco,** *c.,* cap. Cautin prov., Chile; cath.; cereals, apples, timber; p. (1961) *117,115.*

**Tenasserim,** *div.,* lower Burma; on Siamese border; tin, rice; p. *2,110,420.*

**Tenasserim,** *t.,* lower Burma; on cst. at mouth of R. Tenasserim; length 250 m.; p. *10,000.*

**Tenby,** *mkt. t., mun. bor.,* Pembroke, Wales; on W. side of Carmarthen Bay, Bristol Channel; seaside resort; p. (1961) *4,752.*

**Tenedos,** *I.,* Ægean Sea; off W. cst. Turkey; 7 m. long; Turkish possession.

**Tenerife,** *I.,* Canary Is.; tourist resort; wheat, fruits, wines, oil refining; contains extinct volcanic peak of Tenerife; alt. 12,182 ft.; cap. Santa Cruz; a. 782 sq. m.; p. (1962) *394,456.*

**Tengri-Nor,** *L.,* Tibet; N.W. Lhasa; 80 m. long, 40 m. wide.

**Tennant Creek,** *t.,* N. Terr., Australia; in arid cty; gold, copper, silver; p. (1966) *991.*

**Tennessee,** *R.,* Tenn., Ky., U.S.A.; lgst. and most impt. branch of the Ohio; its valley once liable

to flooding, now controlled by dams, and land improved by the Tennessee Valley Authority; length 782 m.

**Tennessee,** *S. central st.,* U.S.A.; between Mississippi R. and the Appalachian Mtns.; agr.: cotton, pecans, sorghum, maize; oil, natural gas, lignite, cement, salt; inds.: chemicals, synthetic rubber, primary magnesium (from sea-water), steel wks.; cap. Nashville; ch. pt. Memphis; a. 42,244 sq. m.; p. (1960) *3,567,089.*

**Tenos,** *I.,* Greek Archipelago, Ægean Sea; one of the Cyclades.

**Tenterden,** *mkt. t., mun. bor.,* Kent, Eng.; 8 m. N. of Rye; church with famous steeple; p. (estd. 1967) *5,620.*

**Tepic,** *cap.,* Nayarit st., Mexico, p. *54,000.*

**Teplice,** *wat. pl.,* ČSSR., N.W. of Prague; textile and hardware inds.; p. (1961) *42,893.*

**Teramo,** *prov.,* Abruzzi, Italy; a. 1,067 sq. m.; cap. Teramo; p. (1961) *238,303.*

**Teramo,** *t.,* Italy; pottery and silks; ancient Interamnium; p. (1961) *41,629.*

**Terek,** *R.,* N. Caucasia, R.S.F.S.R.; flows to Caspian Sea; length 350 m.

**Teresina,** *t., cap.,* Piaul st., Brazil; cotton, sugar, rice, cereals; p. (1961) *144,799.*

**Termini,** *spt.,* Sicily, Italy; S.E. of Palermo; tunny fishing, macaroni, olive oil; wine, sulphur; p. *19,050.* [p. (estd.) *9,000.*]

**Ternate,** Moluccas Is., Indonesia; sago, spices;

**Terneuzen,** *t.,* Neth.; on W. Schelde R.; pipeline to be constructed to carry ethylene from Pernis; p. (1967) *20,029.*

**Terni,** *t.,* Perugia, Italy; amongst the Apennines; iron and steelwks., arms factory, jute; p. (1961) *94,015.*

**Ternopil (Tarnopol),** *t.,* Ukrainian S.S.R.; E. of Lvov; engin.; p. (1959) *52,000.*

**Terranova,** *t.,* Sardinia, Italy; on N.E. cst.; textiles, fishing; p. *10,157.*

**Terre Adélie,** name given to Fr. terr. and I. in Antarctic; estd. a. 160,000 sq. m.

**Terre Haute,** *c.,* Ind., U.S.A.; coal, natural gas, flour, paper, glass, foundries; p. (1960) *72,500.*

**Terschelling,** *I.,* Frisian Is., Neth.; at entrance to Zuyder Zee.

**Teruel,** *prov.,* S. Aragon, Spain; timber forests, coal, weaving, etc.; cap. Teruel; a. 5,721 sq. m.; p. (1959) *225,434.* [p. (1949) *19,047.*]

**Teruel,** *t., cap.,* Teruel prov., on R. Turia; cath.

**Teslin Lake,** S. of Yukon, N.W. Terr., Canada; source of R. Lewes. [Southampton Water.

**Test or Anton,** *R.,* Hants, Eng.; flows to head of

**Tettenhall,** *urb. dist.,* Staffs, Eng.; industl.; p. (1961) *14,800.* [*101,352.*]

**Tetuan,** *ch. spt.,* Morocco, N. Africa; p. (1960)

**Tetyukhe,** *t.,* R.S.F.S.R.; on cst N.E. of Vladivostock; cadmium refinery; p. *5,000.*

**Teutoburger Wald,** *mtn. range,* Germany.

**Teviot,** *R.,* Roxburgh, Scot.; trib. of R. Tweed; length 37 m.

**Tewkesbury,** *mkt. t., mun. bor.,* Glos, Eng.; on R. Avon. 1 m. above confluence with R. Severn; milling, light engin.; p. (estd. 1967) *8,250.*

**Texarkana,** *c.,* Texas and Ark., U.S.A.; bdy. passes down middle of main street; timber and cotton region; rly. wkshps.; total p. (1960) *50,006.*

**Texas,** *st.,* S.W. U.S.A.; a. 263,644 sq. m.; prairie, mtns. in W.; chemicals, oil, gas, wood and leather products; meat pkg., fishing, mng.; agr. cotton; cap. Austin; ch. pt. Galveston; a. 267,339 sq. m.; p. (1960) *9,579,677.*

**Texel,** *I.,* W. Frisian Is., Neth.; a. 83 sq. m.; scene of several naval battles; p. (1967) *11,003.*

**Tezcuco or Texocco,** *L.,* Mexico; a. 77 sq. m.; less than 2 ft. deep; contains no fish.

**Thailand (Siam),** *kingdom,* S.E. Asia much jungle; hot, abundant summer rainfall; mainly agr.; rice, rubber, teak-wood, jute, maize; cotton, tobacco, iron ore, copper, tin, chem. fertilisers; cap. Bangkok; a. 200,418 sq. m.; p. (1960) *25,519,965.*

**Thai Nyuyen,** *t.,* N. Vietnam, S.E. Asia; iron and steel plant.

**Thame,** *mkt. t., urb. dist.,* Oxford, Eng.; on R. Thame, 7 m. S.W. of Aylesbury, p. (1961) *4,197.*

**Thame,** *R.,* trib. of R. Thames, Eng.; length 35 m.

**Thames,** *R.,* Eng.; rises in the Cotswold Hills, Glos, and flows past Oxford, Reading, Windsor and London to the Nore; length 210 m.

**Thames,** *R.,* Ontario, Canada; flows into L. St. Clair; length 160 m. [length 86 m.

**Thames,** *R.,* N.Z., flows N. to G. of Hauraki;

**Thameshaven**, *lge. oil refinery*, Essex, Eng.; on N. cst. of Thames estuary 8 m. below Tilbury.

**Thanet, I. of**, *lge. promontory*, N.E. extremity, Kent, Eng.; formed by bifurcation of R. Stour; contains Margate, Ramsgate and Broadstairs, with other seaside resorts.

**Thanjavur**, *t.*, Tamil Nadu, India; silks, carpets, jewellery, inlaid metals; impt. Brahman ctr.; p. (1961) *111,099.*

**Thar Desert**, on bdy. between India and W. Pakistan; covers slopes between N.W. Deccan and irrigated valley of R. Indus; completely barren, lack of Rs. or level land prevents irrigation; crossed only by caravan routes.

**Tharawaddy**, *dist.*, Pegu, Lower Burma; mainly forest, with rice fields in the clearings; a. 2,815 sq. m.; p. of dist. *508,319;* of t. *7,131.*

**Thaton**, *dist.*, Tennasserim div., Burma; rice and tobacco.

**Thaya**, *R.*, Austria; trib. of the R. March; length 130 m.

**Thebes**, *ruined ancient cap.*, Upper U.A.R.; on both banks of R. Nile; site now partly occupied by vils. Karnak and Luxor; impt. arch. discoveries in Valley of the Kings in 1923.

**Theiss**, *see* Tisa.

**The Pas**, *t.*, Manitoba, Canada; on R. Saskatchewan 80 m. upstream from L. Winnipegosis; rly. junction on line from Prairie Provs. to Churchill on Hudson Bay; branch line to Flin Flon.

**The Sound**, *see* Sound, The.

**Thera**, *volcanic I.*, Greek archipelago, Ægean Sea; 10 m. long; cap. Thera.

**Thermopylæ** or **Pylæ**, celebrated pass between Mt. Æta and the sea, N.E. Greece; battle between Persians and Spartans, 480 B.C.

**Thesprotia**, *prefecture*, Epirus, Greece; cap. Hegoumenitsa; p. (1961) *52,075.*

**Thessaloniki** (Salonika), *prefecture*, Greece; p. (1961) *542,880.*

**Thessaloniki**, *t.*, Greece; at head of G. of Thessaloniki; woollens, soap, cottons, brewing, import and exp. tr.; oil refining; contains fiscal free zone; p. (1961) *250,920.*

**Thessaly**, *dist.*, Central Greece; containing two main prefectures, Larisa and Trikkala; horse-breeding; a. 5,208 sq. m.; p. (1961) *695,385.*

**Thetford**, *t.*, *mun. bor.*, Norfolk, Eng.; on Little R. Ouse; industl. estate for London overspill projected; fruit and vegetable canning, pulp mftg., engin.; p. (estd. 1967) *10,400.*

**Thetford Mines**, *t.*, Quebec, Canada; asbestos mining ctr.; p. (1956) *19,316.*

**Thibodaux**, *t.*, S.E. La., U.S.A.; comm. and mkt. ctr. for agr. dist.; petroleum; p. (1960) *13,043.*

**Thielt**, *t.*, Belgium; 17 m. W. of Ghent; lace, wool, cotton, linen; p. (1962) *3,732.*

**Thiers**, *t.*, Puy-de-Dôme, France; cutlery; p. (1962) *17,442.*

**Thiès**, *t.*, Senegal, W. Africa; rly. ctr. and wkshps.; groundnuts; p. (1957) *39,100.*

**Thika**, *t.*, Kenya, E. Africa; nylon processing.

**Thimphu**, *cap.*, Bhutan; hydro-elec. plant; 110 m. road-link to Phuntsholing (Sikkim), 1968.

**Thionville**, *t.*, Moselle, N. France; nr. Luxembourg border; fruit, vegetables, tanning, brewing; p. (1962) *33,669.*

**Thirlmere**, *L.*, Cumberland, Eng.; 3 m. long; furnishes part of the water supply of Manchester by a conduit of 96 m.

**Thirsk**, *mkt. t.*, *rural dist.*, N.R. Yorks, Eng.; in wide gap between Pennines and Cleveland Hills, 7 m. S.E. of Northallerton; flour; p. (rural dist. 1961) *13,060.*

**Thisted**, *t.*, Thyland, Denmark; on Lim Fjord; p. dairy prod., brewing; p. (1960) *8,768.*

**Tholen**, *I.*, S.W. Netherlands; a. 46 sq. m.; p. *15,000.*

**Thok-Jalung**, *t.*, Tibet; in Aling Kangri Mtns.; gold-mining ctr.

**Thomar**, *t.*, Portugal; paper, cheese; route ctr.; *11,333.*

**Thomasville**, *t.*, Ga., U.S.A.; cotton region; p. (1960) *18,246.*

**Thompson**, *R.*, B.C., Canada; rises in Monashee Mtns. flows S.W. into R. Frazer 140 m. upstream from Vancouver; valley forms impt. routeway used by trunk rlys. from Vancouver E. towards Yellowhead Pass (Canadian National Rly.) and Kicking Horse Pass (Canadian Pacific Rly.); length approx. 280 m.

**Thompson**, *t.*, Manitoba, Canada; nickel producing a.

**Thonburi**, *c.*, Thailand; industl. ctr.; rice and saw mills, fertilisers, tyres; p. (1964) *460,000.*

**Thonon-les-Bains**, *t.*, Haute Savoie, France; resort on L. Geneva; p. (1962) *18,501.*

**Thorez**, *t.*, Ukrainian S.S.R.; formerly Chistyakovo; coalmng.; p. (1959) *92,000.*

**Thornaby-on-Tees**, *t.*, *mun. bor.*, N.R. Yorks; opposite Stockton-on-Tees; iron and steel mnf., heavy engin., wire ropery, flour and sugar milling; p. (1961) *22,786.*

**Thornbury**, *mkt. t.*, *rural dist.*, Glos, Eng.; 10 m. N. of Bristol; aircraft mftg.; p. (rural dist. 1961) *30,685.*

**Thornton Cleveleys**, *t.*, *urb. dist.*, Lancs, Eng.; 4 m. N.E. of Blackpool; p. (estd. 1967) *24,430.*

**Thórshavn**, *cap.*, *pt.*, Faroe Is.; p. (1960) *7,447.*

**Thousand Isles**, *L.*, at outfall of L. Ontario; the islets really number 1,500–1,800, and are partly situated in N.Y. State and partly in Canada.

**Thrace**, ancient name of terr. in S.E. Europe, part of which has been added to Greece; successively under Macedonian, Roman, Byzantine and Turkish rule, before passing to Greece; tobacco; a. 3,315 sq. m.; p. (1961) *356,555.*

**Three Kings**, *gr. of Is.*, N. of N.Z.; plants and shrubs of extreme rarity. [of Benin.

**Three Points**, *c.*, Ghana; W. extremity of Bight

**Three Rivers** (Trois Rivières), *c.*, *pt.*, Quebec, Canada; at confluence of St. Maurice and St. Lawrence Rs.; wood-pulp mnf.; exp. grain, cattle; p. (1956) *50,483.*

**Thule**, N.W. Greenland; 1,000 m. from N. Pole; American air base and site of ballistic missile early warning sta.; spt. open 2–3 mths. p.a.

**Thumba**, Kerala, India; space science and technological ctr.

**Thun**, *L.*, Berne can., Switzerland; occupies valleys of R. Aar where it leaves Alpine region; separated from L. Brienz by deltaic neck of land on which is Interlaken; a. 38 sq. m.

**Thun**, *t.*, Berne, Switzerland; on N.W. end of L. Thun, 16 m. S.E. of Berne; mil. training ctr.; cas. on hill above t.; p. (1957) *24,157.*

**Thur**, *R.*, Switzerland; flows to R. Rhine, nr. Schaffhausen; length 70 m.

**Thurgau**, *can.*, N.E. Switzerland, on L. Constance, dairying, fruit, textiles; cap. Frauenfeld; a. 388 sq. m.; p. (1961) *166,420.*

**Thuringia**, *former Land*, E. Germany, bordered on Bavaria to S., Saxony-Anhalt, Lower Saxony and Hesse to N. and E.; drained by Rs. Saale and Werra; crossed by Thuringer Wald and extending to Harz mtns.; cap. Weimar; now dists. of Erfurt, Suhl and Gera.

**Thuringian Forest** or **Thüringer Wald**, *wild, wooded hill range*, Central Germany; 95 m. long; famous for romantic scenery and legends.

**Thurles**, *mkt. t.*, Tipperary (N. Riding), Ireland; on R. Suir; horse fair; p. (1966) *6,743.*

**Thursday, I.**, Torres Strait, Queensland; pearl and trochus fishery ctr.; p. (1966) *2,549.*

**Thurso**, *burgh*, Caithness, Scot.; on Thurso Bay; most N. t. on Scottish mainland; ancient stronghold of the Northmen; p. (1961) *8,038.*

**Tiaret**, *t.*, W. Algeria, N. Africa; in strategic pass; walled; agr. mkt.; cereals, wool, cattle; p. *22,344.*

**Tiber**, *R.*, Italy; flows from Apennines to Mediterranean, passing through Rome; l. 220 m.

**Tiberias**, *t.*, Israel; on Sea of Galilee (Lake Tiberias); gypsum quarried near by; inland pt.; p. (1946) *17,810.*

**Tibesti**, *mtns.*, on bdy. between Libya and Chad, Equatorial Africa; barren in spite of slight rainfall; mainly above 6,000 ft., maximum alt. 11,155 ft.

**Tibet**, *aut. reg.*, China; lofty plateau, called " the roof of the world ", its lowest plains being 12,000 ft. above sea-level; semi-desert; Chinese suzerainty restored, 1951; network of roads being built, inc. one across Himalayas to Katmandu; exp. wool, musk, gold, skins, and drugs; cap. Lhasa; a. 70,003 sq. m.; p. c. *6,900,000.*

**Ticino** or **Tessin**, *can.*, Switzerland; forests, vineyards, olives, agr.; contains parts of Ls. Maggiore and Lugano; cap. Bellinzona; lgst. t. Lugano; a. 1,086 sq. m.; p. (1961) *195,566.*

**Ticino**, *R.*, Switzerland and Italy; trib. of Po; forms S. approach to St. Gotthard Pass; length 150 m.

Tickhill, *urb. dist.*, W.R. Yorks., Eng.; cas.; p. (1961) *2,584*.    [fruit; a. 30 sq. m.; p. *19,126*.

Tidore I., Moluccas, Indonesia; coffee, tobacco,

Tien Shan or Celestial Mtns., *lofty chain*, N. frontier China, Sinkiang-Kirghizia; hgst. peak 24,000 ft.

Tientsin (Tianjing), *c., former treaty pt., mun. prov.*, Hopei, China; 70 m. S.E. Peking; cottons silks; exp. wool, skins, soya-beans; tractor plant; p. (1953) *2,693,831*.

Tierra del Fuego, *archipelago*, S. America, separated from Patagonia by Strait of Magellan, divided politically between Chile and Argentina; a. (Argentine part) 8,344 sq. m.; p. *7,500*; oil field at Rio Grande.

Tiffin, *c.*, Ohio, U.S.A.; milling, brewing, foundries; p. (1960) *21,478*.    [dom; cap. Adua.

Tigre, *st.*, Ethiopia, formerly an independent kingdom.

Tigre, *R.*, S. America; rises in Ecuador and flows mainly through Peru to the R. Marañón (Amazon); length 400 m.

Tigris, *R.*, Turkey; rising in mtns. of Armenia and Turkestan, flowing S.E. to join the Euphrates 40 m. N.W. of Basra; length 1,100 m.; dam projected 35 m. N. of Mosul.

Tikhvin, *t.*, R.S.F.S.R.; on R. Syas; aluminium ores; p. (1954) *50,000*.

Tilburg, *c.*, N. Brabant, Neth.; nr. Breda; woollens, textiles, tobacco, leather; p. (1967) *148,497*.

Tilbury, *t.*, Essex, Eng.; on N. bank of R. Thames, 20 m. E. of London; docks; shoe mftg; p. (1961) *18,387*.    [Tweed; length 32 m.

Till, *R.*, N. Northumberland, Eng.; trib. of R.

Tillicoultry, *burgh*, Clackmannan, Scot.; on Devon R.; woollen, worsted, paper mkg.; p. (1961) *3,963*.

Tilmanstone, *mining vil.*, Kent, Eng.; on N. flank of N. Downs, 4 m. S.W. of Deal; on Kent coalfield, coal despatched by overhead cable to Dover.    [p. (1961) *26,419*.

Timaru, *t.*, S.I., N.Z.; wool, milling, skins;

Timbuktu, Mali, Africa; 8 m. N. of the N. bend of R. Niger, on border of the Sahara desert; agr. tr. ctr.; p. (1957) *7,000*; flourished as comm. mart. and Moslem ctr., 14–16th cent.

Timisoara, *t.*, W. Romania; impt. comm. and industl. ctr., tobacco, petroleum, paper; fortress, cas., cath.; p. (1963) *167,907*.

Timmins, *t.*, Ontario, Canada; gold running out; vast deposits of copper, zinc, silver, discovered 1964; p. (1961) *29,270*.

Timor, *Portuguese possession*, E. Indies; consists of E. part of T.I. in Malay Archipelago, together with Ambeno, Pulo Cambing and Pulo Jako; ch. products coffee, sandalwood, copra, wax; cap. and ch. spt. Dili; total a. 7,330 sq. m.; p. (1965) *551,000*.

Timor Archipelago, *gr. of Is.*, Indonesia; of which the lgst. is Timor (E. part Portuguese; remainder Indonesian); total a. 24,450 sq. m.; fishing, exp. copra; p. *1,657,376*.

Timor Sea, that part of the Indian Ocean N.W. of W. Australia, and S. of Timor I.

Timsah, *L.*, U.A.R., N.E. Africa; sm. L. midway along Suez Canal; formerly used for recreational purposes by Brit. garrison in Canal zone.

Tinogasta, *t.*, Catamarca prov., Argentina; in E. foot-hills of Andes 120 m. N.W. of Catamarca; impt. copper-mines.

Tintagel, *vil.*, Cornwall, Eng.; ruined cas.; reputed birthplace of King Arthur; tourists.

Tinto, *R.*, Huelva, Spain; flows W. to the Atlantic; length 65 m.

Tinto Hills, Lanark, Scot.; highest peak 2,300 ft.

Tipperary, *inland co.*, Munster, Ireland; a. 1,659 sq. m.; divided into Tipperary co. (N.R.), p. (1966) *53,532*; and Tipperary co. (S.R.), p. (1966) *58,946*.

Tipperary, *t.*, Tipperary. Ireland; 29 m. S.E. Limerick; mftg., butter lace; p. (1966) *4,507*.

Tipton, *t., mun. bor.*, Staffs Eng'; 2 m. W. of W. Bromwich; metals, engin.; p. (1961) *33,091*.

Tiranë, *t., cap.*, Albania; univ.; textiles, metal-lurgy; p. (1966) *153,000*.

Tiraspol, *t.*, Moldavian S.S.R.; on R. Dniester; heat and power-sta. recently constructed; milling, tobacco; p. (1959) *62,000*.

Tire, *t.*, Aydin, Turkey; raisins, tobacco, cotton; p. (1965) *27,248*.

Tiree, *I.*, Inner Hebrides, Scot.; off cst. of Mull; sm. fresh-water lochs and Scandinavian forts.

Tirlemont (Flemish Thienen), *t.*, ctr. of Belgian sugar-refining; Brabant, Belgium; machin.,

P  (78th Ed.)

woollens, leather; captured by Marlborough, 1705; p. (1962) *22,766*.

Tiruchirapalli, *formerly* Trichinopoly, *t.*, Tamil Nadu, India; on R. Cauvery; cigars, goldsmith's wk.; boiler plant; p. (1961) *249,862*.

Tisa (Tisza), *R.*, U.S.S.R., Hungary, Jugoslavia; rises in E. Carpathians, flows N.W. to Cop, thence S. across flat, agr. plain of Gr. Arföld into R. Danube 45 m. below Novi Sad; approx. length 600 m.; navigable in part.    [ctr.

Tiszapalkonya, *t.*, Hungary; new town; chemical

Titicaca, *L.*, Bolivia, Peru, S. America; between 2 ranges of the Andes, on borders of Bolivia and Peru; 12,645 ft. above the sea; a. 3,200 sq. m.; average width 27 m. length 101 m.; almost cut in two by peninsula of Copacabana; nearly 700 ft. deep on E. side, shallow W. and S.; contains numerous Is., lgst. Titicaca; it is drained on the S. side by the R. Desaguadero.

Titograd (Podgorica), *t.*, Montenegro, Jugoslavia; nr. Albanian frontier; p. (1959) *22,000*.

Titov Veles, *t.*, Jugoslavia; on R. Vardar, and main rly. to Belgrade; maize, silk; p. (1960) *25,100*.

Tiverton, *mkt. t., mun. bor.*, Devon, Eng.; 14 m. N. Exeter; lace and silk mftg.; p. (estd. 1967) *14,879*.

Tivoli, *t.*, Rome, Italy; sulphur baths.

Tjirebon, *t.*, Java, Indonesia; oil refining; p. (1961) *158,299*.

Tlaxcala, *st.*, Mexico; adjoining Puebla; a. 1,555 sq. m.; cap. Tlaxcala; p. (1960) *346,699*.

Tlemcen, *t.*, Algeria, N. Africa; exp. textiles, carpets, ostrich feathers, olive oil, grain and onyx; p. (1954) *73,000*.

Tobago, *I.*, with Trinidad *indep. st.* within Brit. Commonwealth (1962); exp. sugar, rum, rubber, cotton, tobacco, coffee, etc.; cap. Scarborough on S. side; a. 116 sq. m.; p. (1960) *33,200*, nearly all Negroes.

Tobata, *c., spt.*, N. Kyushu, Japan; now part of Kitakyushu City newly formed 1963 (*q.v.*) on S. shore of Shimonoseki Strait at ent. to Tokai Bay; iron and steel ind., engin., sugar-refining, glass, bricks; lge. mod. coal docks.

Tobermory, *burgh*, Argyll, Scot.; on I. of Mull at N. entrance to Sound of Mull; p. (1961) *668*.

Tobol, *R.*, W. Siberia, R.S.F.S.R.; trib. of R. Irtysh; length 500 m.

Tobolsk, *t.*, W. Siberia, R.S.F.S.R.; on R Irtysh; shipbldg., sawmilling, fishing; p. (1956) *35,300*

Tobruk, *spt.*, Libya, N. Africa; on cst. 220 m. E. of Benghazi; p. (estd. 1951) *2,500*.

Tocantins, *R.*, provs. Pará and Goiaz, Brazil; flows N. through the Pará estuary to the Atlantic; navigation interrupted by rapids 200 m. above Pará; length, 1,700 m.

Toce, *R.*, N. Italy; rises in Lepontine Alps, flows S. and S.E. into L. Maggiore; valley used by trunk rly. from Milan to Berne as S. approach to Simplon Tunnel; length, 54 m.

Tocopilla, *spt.*, Chile; exp. nitrate, copper ore, sulphates, iodine; p. (1960) *22,244*.

Todmorden, *mkt. t., mun. bor.*, W.R. Yorks, Eng.; nr. source of R. Calder, 6 m. N.E. of Rochdale; cottons, machin.; p. (estd. 1967) *16,100*.

Togliatti, *t.*, R.S.F.S.R., U.S.S.R.; formerly Stavropol; on R. Volga, 35 m. W.N.W. of Kuybyshev; engin., motor wks., natural gas; (1967) *171,000*.

Togo Republic of, *indep. sov. st.* (April 1960), W. Africa, formerly U.N. trust terr. under French adm.; cap. Lomé; mainly agr.; yams, sweet potatoes, green peppers, beans, millet, sorghum, coffee, cocoa; phosphate plant; a. 21,220 sq. m.; p. (1961) *1,440,000*. (Br. Togoland integrated in Ghana on achieving independence 1957.)

Tokaimura, *vil.*, Ibaraki, Japan; nuclear reactor and lge. nuclear power sta.

Tokat, *t.*, Turkey; on Tokat I., N. of Sivas; copper and yellow leather mftg.; Armenian massacre 1895; p. (1965) *33,006*.

Tokelau or Union Isles, gr. of 3 Is., Brit. col., Pac. Oc.; 300 m. N. of W. Samoa administered by N.Z.; a. 4 sq. m.; p. (1959) *7,861*.

Tokio, *c., spt., cap.*, Japan; on Tokio Bay, S.E. cst. of Honshu; univ. imperial palace; gr. comm. ctr; silks, machin., lacquer, pottery, "chlorela" artificial food production, metal tableware, chemicals; p. (1965) *8,893,094*; of Greater Tokio *10,869,000*.

Tokoroa, *t.*, N.I., N.Z., township to serve Kinleith; kraft paper, pulp, and sawn timber; p. (1961) *7,054*.

Tokushima, *t.*, E. cst. Shikoku, Japan; cottons, reed organs; p. (1965) *193,233*. [*42,815*.

Tolbukhin, *t.*, Bulgaria, former Dobrich; p. (1956)

Toledo, *prov.*, Spain; mtnous.; agr., vineyards, stock-raising; a. 5,925 sq. m.; p. (1959) *531,324*.

Toledo, *ancient c.*, *cap.*, Toledo, Spain; on R. Tagus; with cath., and many specimens of Gothic, Moorish and Castillian architecture in its picturesque narrow streets; famous Alcázar palace citadel; sword-mkg. still flourishes; p. (1957) *46,465*.

Toledo, *c.*, Ohio, U.S.A.; on Maumee R.; gr. rly. ctr. covering 28½ sq. m.; glass, car parts, oil refining; p. (1960) *435,000*. [alt. 18,143 ft.

Tolima, *volcano*, Andes, Columbia, S. America;

Tolima, *dep.*, Colombia, S. America; a. 8,874 sq. m.; cap. Ibague; p. (estd. 1961) *875,650*.

Tolna, *t.*, Hungary; on R. Danube; nuclear power sta. projected.

Toluca, *t.*, Mexico; brewing, flour, cottons; p. (1960) *60,000*. [length 400 m.

Tom, *R.*, Siberia, R.S.F.S.R.; trib. of R. Obi:

Tomaszow Mazowiecki, *c.*, Lodz prov., Poland; woollens, synthetic fibres, agr. tools; p. (1965) *52,000*. [the Mobile; length 500 m.

Tombigbee, *R.*, Miss., U.S.A.; flows S. to form

Tomsk, *region*, Siberia, R.S.F.S.R.; adjoining Chinese frontier; agr., dairying, stock-raising, fisheries, mining, mftg.

Tomsk, *c.*, Siberia, U.S.S.R.; on R. Tom, and branch of Trans-Siberian rly.; univ., cath.; engin., chemicals; p. (1967) *311,000*.

Tonawanda, *t.*, N.Y., U.S.A.; on Niagara R.; mnfs.; p. (1960) *21,561*.

Tonbridge, *t.*, *urb. dist.*, Kent, Eng.; on R. Medway, 13 m. S.W. of Maidstone; malting, brewing rly. wks.. elec. apparatus, light inds.; p. (estd. 1967) *28,550*.

Tönder, *t.*, Denmark; old houses; cattle-breeding; lace; p. (1960) *7,192*.

Tonga Is., *see* Friendly Is.

Tongariro, *volcanic peak*, N.I., N.Z.; in ctr. of volcanic dist.; alt. 6,458 ft.; hydroelec. plant projected. [mineral springs; p. (1962) *16,240*.

Tongeren (Tongres), *episcopal c.*, Belgium;

Tongking, *region*, N. Viet-Nam; formerly within French Union; rice, sugar-cane, tobacco, coffee, cotton, silk, coal, tin, limestone; a. 40,530 sq. m.; ch. t. Hanoi; ch. pt. Haiphong.

Tonk, *t.*, Rajasthan, India; mica; p. (1961) *43,413*.

Tonlé Sap, *L.*, Cambodia, Indo-China; one of world's lgst. fishing ctrs.

Tönsberg, *t.*, Norway; on Bay nr. entrance to Oslo fjord; tr. ctr.; shipping; H.Q. of sealing-and whaling-fleet, oil mills; p. (estd. 1960) *12,500*.

Toowoomba, *c.*, Queensland, Australia; wheat, pastoral and dairying dist., flour-milling. tanning, brewing, wine, engin., agr. machin.; p. (1966) *52,120*.

Topeka, *t.*, *cap.*, Kan., U.S.A.; on Kansas R.; flour-milling, engin., machin., lge. tr.; p. (1960) *119,484*.

Torbay, *co. bor.*, S. Devon, Eng.; formed by amalgamation of Torquay, Paignton and Brixham; p. (estd. 1968) *98,657*.

Torcello, *I.*, with ancient Byzantine cath.. on lagoon nr. Venice, Italy. [(1962) *13,599*.

Torhout, *t.*, W. Flanders, Belgium; textiles; p.

Tormes, *R.*, Spain; trib. of Douro; length 150 m.

Toronto, *c.*, *pt.*, *metrop. a.*, *cap.* Ontario, Canada; on Bay of Toronto, L. Ontario; spacious harbour; univ.; extensive tr. and mnfs.; oil refining; fine parliament bldgs., parks; a. 240 sq. m.; p. (1961) of met.a. *1,824,481*; of c. *672,000*.

Torontoy, *gorge*, Cuzco dep., Peru; located on R. Urubamba 50 m. N.W. of Cuzco.

Torpoint, *urb. dist.*, Cornwall, Eng.; on Plymouth Sound; p. (1961) *4,260*.

Torquay, *t.*, S. Devon, Eng.; incorporated in Torbay co. bor.; on N. Side of Tor Bay; seaside resort with all-year season.

Torre Annunziata, *t.*, *spt.*, Italy; on Bay of Naples; arms factory, macaroni mftg., seri-culture; p. (1961) *58,400*.

Torre del Greco, *spt.*, Italy; on Bay of Naples; at foot of Mt. Vesuvius; seaside resort; lava quarries, shipbldg; p. (1961) *77,576*.

Torredonjimeno, *t.*, Jaen, Spain; wine, wheat, fruit; p. *16,069*.

Torremolinos, cst. resort Spain; S. of Malaga.

Torrens, *L.*, S. Australia; 130 m. long, 20 m. wide; varies from brackish lake to salt marsh.

Terreón, *t.*, Coahuila, Mexico; ctr. of comm. agr.; oil pipe-line connects to Chihuahua; thermo-elec. plant; p. (1960) *179,955*.

Torres Strait, between C. York, Queensland, Australia, and New Guinea; 90 m. wide, dangerous navigation.

Torridge, *R.*, Devon, Eng.; flows from Hartland Dist. to Bideford Bay; length 53 m.

Torrington, *t.*, Conn., U.S.A.; metal-plate wk., woollens; p. (1960) *30,045*.

Torrington, *t.*, *mun. bor.*, Devon, Eng.; on R. Torridge, 4 m. S.E. of Bideford; ball clay; glass wks.; p. (estd. 1967) *2,920*.

Tortona, *t.*, N. Italy; the Roman Dertona; cath.; p. *21,813*.

Tortosa. *fortfd. t.*, Spain; on R. Ebro; wine, oil, fruit, paper, leather; p. (1957) *45,672*.

Tortuga, *I.*, Caribbean Sea; off N.W. cst. of Hispaniola; provides shelter from N.E. trade winds for Port de Paix; 25 m. by 10 m.

Torun (Thorn), *t.*, S. Pomerania, Poland; on R. Vistula; univ.; grain, timber; p. (1965) *114,000*.

Tosya, *t.*, Turkey; grapes, rice, cotton, wool, mohair, weaving; p. (1960) *13,690*.

Totnes, *t.*, *mun. bor.*, Devon, Eng.; on R. Dart, 6 m. N.W. of Dartmouth; cider; p. (estd. 1967) *5,630*.

Totonicapan, *t.*, Guatemala, Central America; hot springs, gardens; pottery. furniture, textiles; p. (estd. 1960) *40,100*.

Tottenham, *former mun. bor.*, Middx., Eng.; now. inc. in Haringey outer bor., Greater London (*q.v.*); industl. and resdtl.; p. (1961) *113,249*.

Tottington, *urb. dist.*, Lancs. Eng.; cotton and artificial silk goods; p. (1961) *6,133*.

Touggourt or Tuggurt. *t.*, S. Algeria; edge of Sahara; rly. terminus; dates; p. (1960) *107,561*.

Toul, *t.*, Meurthe-et-Moselle, France; on R. Moselle; wines, brandy, earthenware, lace; p. (1962) *15,031*.

Toulon, *t.*, *spt.*, *naval sta.*, Var, France; on Mediterranean cst.; arsenal, fine bldgs., shipbldg, lace-mkg., vines, olive oil, fisheries; Port-Cros nat. park nearby; p. (1962) *172,586*.

Toulouse, *t.*, Haute-Garonne, S. France; on R. Garonne; cath.; paper, leather, stained glass, aircraft engin.; projected aeronautical and space research ctr.; p. (1962) *330,570*.

Touraine, *former prov.*, France; now divided into Indre-et-Loire and part of Vienne deps.

Tourane, *t.*, S. Vietnam; weaving wks., elec. plant, cotton mills.

Tourcoing, *t.*, Nord France; 10 m. N.E. of Lille; textiles, carpets, cement; p. (1962) *90,105*.

Tournai, *t.*, Hainaut, Belgium; on R. Scheldt; nr. Mons; famous cath.; textiles, carpet mftg.; p. (1962) *33,346*.

Tours, *t.*, Indre-et-Loire, France; cath.; iron. steel, wines, leather, textiles; p. (1962) *96,472*.

Towcester, *mkt. t.*, *rural dist.*, Northants, Eng.; 9 m. S.W. of Northampton; boot-mkg.; p. (rural dist. 1961) *15,198*.

Tower Hamlets, *inner bor.*, E. London, Eng., inc. former bors. of Bethnal Green, Stepney and Poplar; industl.; p. (1966) *203,000*.

Tow Law, *urb. dist.*, Durham, Eng.; in Wear Dale, 10 m. N.W. of Bishop Auckland; p. (1961) *2,920*.

Townsville, *spt.*, Queensland, Australia; on E. cst., 2nd pt. of st.; exp. prods. of rich dairying, pastoral, and mining terr.; copper refining; gen. inds.; p. (1966) *56,687*. [Bay; length 65 m.

Towy, *R.*, S. Wales; flows S.W. to Carmarthen

Towyn, *mkt. t.*, *urb. dist.*, Merioneth, Wales; on cst. of Cardigan Bay, 3 m. N.W. of Aberdovey; p. (1961) *4,466*.

Toyama, *c.*, Honshu, Japan; located centrally on Etchu plain to E. of Noto Peninsula; administrative and comm. ctr. of region; aluminium smelting; p. (1964) *218,000*.

Trabzon, *spt.*, Turkey; on Black Sea cst.; caravan ctr.; exp. tobacco. carpets, hides; reputed to be the ancient Trapezus; p. (1965) *65,598*.

Trafalgar, *C.*, S.W. cst., Cadiz, Spain; Nelson's famous victory, 1805.

Trail, *t.*, B.C., Canada; lgst. metallurgical smelter in Brit. Commonwealth; p. (1961) *11,580*.

Tralee, *cst.*, *t.*, Kerry, Ireland; on R. Lee; exp. grain, butter; p. (1966) *11,211*.

Tranent, *burgh*, E. Lothian. Scot.; 10 m. E. of Edinburgh; coal; p. (1961) *6,317*.

Trani, *spt.*, Apulia, Italy; on the Adriatic; 12th-century cath.; p. *30,551*.

Transbaikal, *dist.*, Siberia, R.S.F.S.R.; E. of L. Baikal; mineral wealth; ch. t., Chita.

Transcaucasia, name given to region of U.S.S.R. which comprises the constituent reps. of Georgia, Armenia, and Azerbaydzhan; ch. t., Tbilisi.

Transkei, *Bantu reserve*, E. Cape, S. Africa; cereals, fruits, cattle, sheep; limited Bantu self-gov., pop. mainly employed in mines in Transvaal and Orange Free State; cap. Umtata; a. 16,544 sq. m.; p. (1963) 1,300,000.

Transvaal, *prov.*, Rep. of S. Africa; hot summers, temperate winters; grassland, agr., maize, tobacco, sheep, wool, cattle, gold, diamonds; coal, copper, tea, engin., brewing, pottery; a. 110,450 sq. m.; cap. Pretoria; nuclear reactor in the N.; p. (1960) 6,273,477 (inc. 1,468,305 whites).

Transylvania, *former prov.*, Hungary, now in Romania; cereals, tobacco, sheep, cattle, horses; surrounded and traversed by the Carpathians.

Transylvanian Alps, *range of high mtns.*, Romania.

Trapani, *fortfd. spt.*, W. Sicily, Italy; salt, wine, olive oil, fish, alabaster, coral, mother-of-pearl; exp.; p. (1961) 75,537.

Traralgon, *t.*, Vic., Australia; paper, cement, clothing; p. (1966) 14,080.

Trasimeno, *L.*, Umbria, central Italy; occupies lge. extinct volcanic crater; drained S. to R. Tiber; a. approx. 60 sq. m.

Trás-os-Montes e Alto-Douro, *prov.*, N. Portugal; ch. t. Tua; a. 47,340 sq. m.; p. (1950) 636,322.

Traun, *R.*, Austria; trib. of R. Danube; enters L. known as Traun See; length 100 m.

Travancore-Cochin, *former st.*, S. India; included in Kerala st. 1 Nov., 1956; rice, coconuts, pepper, tapioca, hardwoods; univ.

Traverse City, *t.*, Mich., U.S.A.; timber inds., tr.; p. (1960) 18,432.                        [p. (1961) 1,951

Trawden, *urb. dist.*, Lancs, Eng.; cotton, engin.;

Trawsfynydd, Merioneth, Wales; within N. Wales Nat. Pk.; atomic power sta.

Trebizond, *see* Trabzon.

Tredegar, *mining t.*, *urb. dist.*, Monmouth, Eng.; in narrow valley 3 m. W. of Ebbw Vale; p. (1961) 19,792.

Treforest, *t.*, Glam., Wales; on R. Taff; lge. trading estate established in 1930s to alleviate unemployment in primary inds. of S. Wales; aircraft accessories, electronics, chemical, pharmaceutical, rayon, metal wks.

Treinta y Tres, *dep.*, Uruguay; a. 3,682 sq. m.; cap. Treinta y Tres; p. (1953) 72,063.

Trelew, *t.*, Patagonia, Argentina; ch. comm. t.; sheep; p. (1960) 11,500.

Trelleborg, *spt.*, S. Sweden; most impt. rubber fact. in cty.; p. (1961) 19,209.

Tremadoc Bay, N. Wales; N. part of Cardigan Bay between Lleyn pen. and Merioneth cst.

Trengganu, *st.*, Malaysia; N. E. Malaya; rice, rubber, coconuts; tin, iron; cap. Kuala Trengganu; a. 5,050 sq. m.; p. (1961) 320,431.

Trent, *R.*, Eng.; rises in N. Staffs, and flows to join the Ouse in forming the estuary of the Humber; length 170 m.

Trentino-Alto Adige, *aut. region*, N. Italy; a. 5,252 sq. m.; p. (1961) 785,491.

Trento, *t.*, *cap.*, Venezia Tridentina, N. Italy; on R. Adige; p. (1961) 74,766.

Trenton, *c.*, *cap.*, N.J., U.S.A.; on Delaware R.; ironwks., pottery, rubber, and other mnfs.; p. (1960) 114,167.          [ctr.; p. (1960) 40,000.

Tres Arroyos, *t.*, E. Argentina; agr. and livestock

Treviglio, *t.*, Lombardy, Italy; E. of Milan; silk mftg.; p. 19,615.

Treviso, *t.*, Lombardy, Italy; cath.; majolica ware, silks, woollens; p. (1961) 75,217.

Trichinopoly, (*see* Tiruchirapalli).

Trier, *c.*, Rhineland-Palatinate, Germany; on R. Moselle; cath.; Roman antiquities (Porta Nigra); wine cellars, tobacco, leather, textiles, machin., brewing; p. (1963) 87,400.

Trieste Free Territory, *former free st.*, on the Adriatic; constituted by Peace Treaty with Italy, 1947, as compromise between conflicting Jugoslav and Italian claims; a. 287 sq. m.; military government terminated Oct. 1954; Zone A handed over to Italy, Zone B to Yugoslavia.

Trieste, *spt.*, *cap.*, Friuli-Venezia Giulia, N. E. Italy; shipbldg., fishing; cath., cas., Roman antiquities; oil pipeline to Schwechat, nr. Vienna; p. (1964) 280,000.

Trikkala, *prefecture*, Thessaly, Greece; cap Trikkala; p. (1961) 142,450.

Trikkala (the ancient Trikal), *t.*, Thessaly, Greece; nr. Larissa; mosques; grain p. (1961) 27,876.

Trincomalee, *t.*, *naval sta.*, N.E. cst., Ceylon; gd. harbour; tobacco, rice, palms; p. 32,507.

Tring, *mkt. t.*, *urb. dist.*, Herts. Eng.; in gap through Chiltern Hills, 9 m. N.W. of Hemel Hempstead; dairy farming; p. (1961) 6,051.

Trinidad, *I.*, with Tobago, *indep. st.*, within Brit. Commonwealth (1962); W.I.; oil, natural gas, asphalt, sugar, rum, coconut oil, molasses, cocoa, citrus fruits; tourism; cap. Pt. of Spain; a. 1,864 sq. m.; p. (estd. 1964) 850,000 inc. Tobago.

Trinidad, *cap.* Beni, Bolivia; p. (1962) 14,505.

Trinidad, *t.*, Cuba, W.I.; exp. honey; p. 16,756.

Trinity, *R.* Texas, U.S.A.; flows S.E. to Galveston Bay; length 500 m.

Trino, Piedmont, N. Italy; 11 m. S.S.W. of Vercelli; nuclear power sta.

Tripoli, *spt.*, Lebanon; S.W. Asia; terminus of oil pipe-line from Iraq; p. (estd. 1956) 80,000.

Tripoli, *prov.*, Libya, N. Africa; extends W. to Tunisia, E. to Cyrenaica, S. into Sahara Desert; largely composed of desert, scattered oases; cap. Tripoli; p. (1964) 976,177.

Tripoli, *t.*, *cap.*, Tripoli prov. Libya, N. Africa; expanded under Italian colonial administration; exp. wool. hides; p. (1964) 245,000.

Tripolis, *cap.*, Arcadia, Peloponnese, Greece; tapestries, leather; p. (1961) 13,500.

Tripura, Union Terr., India; hilly; rice, jute, cotton, sugar cane; cap. Agartala; a. 4,036 sq. m.; p. (1961) 1,142,005.

Tristan da Cunha, *sm. gr. of Brit. Is.*, S. Atl. Oc.; ch. I. Tristan; evacuated 1961 (volcanic eruption) but resettled 1963; p. (1964) 270.

Trivandrum, *t.*, Kerala, S. India; univ.; woodcarving; p. (1961) 239,815.

Trnava, *t.*, ČSSR.; on R. Vah; cloth, sugar; p. (1961) 31,732.                              ]16,182.

Trnovo (Tirnovo), *t.*, Bulgaria; copper wk.; p. (1959) 76,000.

Troitsk, *t.*, S. Urals. R.S.F.S.R.; leather, knitwear; lge. thermal power sta.; p. (1959) 76,000.

Trollhättan, *t.*, Sweden; famous waterfalls, with generating-sta.; cars; p. (1961) 32,051.

Trombay, *I.*, off Bombay, India; oil refining; atomic reactor; zirconium metal produced; fertilisers.                                [129,219.

Troms, *dist.*, Norway; a. 10,006 sq. m.; p. (1963)

Tromsö, *spt.*, Troms, Norway; on sm. I. of Tromsö, in Tromsö Sound; seal and walrus fishing; canning; p. (1960) 12,316.

Tronador, *volcano*, Andes, S. America; on Argentine-Chilean bdy.; alt. 11.352 ft.

Tröndelag, N., *co.*, Norway; a. 8,659 sq. m.; p. (1963) 116,469                    [p. (1963) 215,274.

Tröndelag, S., *co.*, Norway; a. 7.241 sq. m.;

Trondheim, *spt.*, Norway; on W. cst. on S. side of Trondheim Fjord; shipbldg., engin.; exp. timber and wood-pulp, butter, fish, copper; contains ancient cath., burial place of early Norwegian kings and place of coronation of recent sovereigns; p. (1960) 59,271.

Troon, *burgh*, Ayr, Scot.; on Firth of Clyde, 6 m. N. of Ayr; gd. harbour and graving docks; shipbldg., hosiery; seawater distillation research ctr. projected; p. (1961) 9,932.

Troppau, *see* Opava.

Troste, nr. Llanelly, Wales; steel strip mill, tin plate; newly developed 1952.

Trossachs, *mtn. defile*, Perth, Scot.; tourist resort.

Trowbridge, *mkt. t.*, *urb. dist.*, Wilts. Eng.; 3 m. S.E. of Bradford-on-Avon; cloth wks., bacon curing, dairying, engin.; p. (1961) 15,833.

Troy, *c.*, N.Y., U.S.A.; at confluence of Rs. Hudson and Mohawk; great shirt-mftg. ctr.; p. (1960) 67,492.

Troyes, *c.*, Aube, France; on R. Seine; former cap. Champagne; magnificent cath., hosiery, iron, looms, mnfs.; p. (1962) 68,898.

Trucial States, *seven sts.*, E. Arabia, along Persian G.; ch. t. Dubai; Brit. prot. to be withdrawn by end 1971; a. 32,000 sq. m.; p. 111,000.

Trujillo, *spt.*, Honduras. Central America; on Atlantic cst.; p. (1958) 3,016.

Trujillo, *ch. t.*, La Libertad, Peru; univ.; cath.; cocaine mftg., sugar, brewing, tanneries, rice mills; p. (1961) 122,000.

Trujillo, *old t.*, Spain; N.E. Badajoz; wheat, wine, fruit; birthplace of Pizarro; p. (1957) 14,587.          [coffee; cap. T.; p. (1961) 326,634.

Trujillo, *st.*, Venezuela, S. America; cocoa

Truk Is., Caroline Is., Pac. Oc., U.S.A. Trusteeship; coral, copra, dried fish; a. 50 sq. m.; p. (1958) 19,807.

Truro, c., mun. bor., Cornwall, Eng.; at confluence of Rs. Kenwyn and Allen; cath.; tin smelting, jam wks., light engin., textiles; p. (estd. 1967) 14,430.

Truro, t., Nova Scotia, Canada; on Salmon R.; hosiery; p. (1961) 12,421.

Trutnov, t., ČSSR.; at foot of Riesengebirge; coal, linen; p. (1961) 22,961.

Tsamkong (Zhanjiang), c., Kwangtung prov., China; cotton milling, leather mnfs.; p. (1953) 166,000.

Tsangpo, R., Tibet; one of the headstreams of the R. Brahmaputra; length 850 m.

Tschenstokov, see Czestochowa.

Tselinograd, t., Kazakhstan, S.S.R.; nr. Karaganda coalfield; engin.; p. (1967) 171,000.

Tsinan (Jinan), c., Shantung, China; on the south bank of the Hwang Ho, 100 m. from the G. of Chihli; mnfs. glass, textiles, precious stones; p. (1953) 680,000.

Tsinghai (Qinghai), prov., China; between Nan Shan and Kunlun mtns.; cap. Sining; a. 269,187 sq. m.; p. (1953) 11,676,534.

Tsingtao (Qingdao), c., Shantung, China; salt, silk; former treaty pt.; p. (1953) 917,000.

Tsitsihar (Qiqihar), c., Heilungkiang, N. China; on the Vladivostock portion of the Trans-Siberian rly.; p. (1953) 345,000.

Tsugaru Strait, Japan; separates Is. Hokkaido and Honshu; links Sea of Japan with Pac. Oc.; length 45 m., width 15–20 m.

Tsumeb, t., S.W. Africa; rly. terminus; copper, lead, zinc; p. (1960) 7,769 inc. 2,987 whites.

Tsuruga, spt., Japan; on W. cst. Honshu; rayon textiles, cotton, atomic power plant projected; p. (1965) 32,343.

Tuam, mkt. t., rural dist., Galway, Ireland; Roman Catholic and Protestant caths.; p. (1961) (of dist.) 25,676 (of t. 1966) 3,621.

Tuamotu, coral archipelago, S. Pac. Oc.; belonging to France; a. of gr 330 sq. m.; pearl fisheries; p. of gr. (1962) 7,097.

Tuapse, spt., R.S.F.S.R., U.S.S.R.; at foot of Caucasus Mtns. on N. cst. of Black Sea; at W. end of oil pipe-line from Baku and Makhach Kala; impt. oil refineries; p. (1954) 50,000.

Tubarao, t., Santa Catarina st., S. Brazil; on E. cst., 175 m. N. W. of Porto Alegre; coal-mines; p. (1960) 29,615.

Tübingen, t., Baden-Württemberg, Germany; on R. Neckar; univ. cas.; machin., paper, textiles; p. (1963) 53,300.

Tucson, c., Arizona, U.S.A.; on Santa Cruz R.; founded in 1560 by a Jesuit mission, and from 1867 to 1877 was the cap. of Arizona; seat of Univ. of Arizona; winter resort; aircraft, electronics, clothing; p. (1960) 212,892.

Tucumán, prov., Argentina; agr. and stock-raising; cap. Tucumán; a. 8,817 sq. m.; p. (1960) 780,000.

Tucumán, San Miguel de, c., cap. Tucumán prov., Argentina; on R. Sali; univ.; breweries, sawmills, flourmills, sugar; p. (1960) 290,000.

Tugela, R., Natal, S. Africa; rises in Drakensberg Mtns. and flows to Indian O.; length 300 m.

Tuggurt, see Touggourt.

Tula, region, R.S.F.S.R., U.S.S.R.; S. of Moscow; pasturage, stock-keeping, iron and coal.

Tula, t., R.S.F.S.R., U.S.S.R.; on both banks R. Upa; engin., iron ore nearby; p. (1967) 371,000.

Tulare, L., S. Cal., U.S.A.; ctr. of inland drainage 40 m. S. of Fresno; streams feeding it used for irrigation; in drought years L. dries up completely; a. 90 sq. m.

Tulbagh, t., Cape Prov., Rep. of S. Africa; on Gr. Berg R., 65 m. N.E. of Cape Town.

Tulcea, t., Dobroja, Romania; on Danube; chemicals, copper; p. (1963) 29,932.

Tulenovo, Balchik dist., on Black Sea, Bulgaria; oil production.                [p. (1961) 19,343.

Tulkarm, t., Jordan; agr. ctr.; rly. junction;

Tullamore, mkt. t., urb. dist., Offaly, Ireland; on Grand Canal; farming, distilling, brewing; p. (1966) 6,650.                [20,790.

Tulle, t., cap., Correze, France; cath.; p. (1962)

Tulsa, c., Okla., U.S.A.; 2nd lgst. c. in st.; oil-well machin., aeroplanes; p. (1960) 261,685.

Tumbes, dep., Peru, S. America; cap. Tumbes; a. 1,590 sq. m.; p. (1961) 52,403.

Tummel, R., Perth, Scot.; trib. of R. Tay; used by Perth to Inverness rly. as S. approach to Drumocheter Pass.

Tunbridge Wells, mkt. t., Royal mun. bor., Kent, Eng.; on border of Sussex, 5 m. S. of Tonbridge; chalybeate waters; p. (estd. 1967) 43,490.

Tung Hai or Eastern China Sea, name of part of the Pac. Oc. bordering S. China.

Tunghwa (Tonghua), c., Kirin prov., China; p. (1953) 129,000.

Tungting Hu, lge. L., Hunan, China; on S. margin of Yangtze-Kiang plain; receives waters of Yuan Kiang and Siang Kiang, drains N. to Yangtze-Kiang; surrounded by flat, intensively cultivated land, rice, sugar, mulberry; size varies greatly with season; maximum a. (in late summer) 2,500 sq. m.

Tunguska, Upper, Stony and Lower, Rs., Siberia, U.S.S.R.; all rise in Sayan Mtns. nr. L. Baikal and flow N.W. through forested country into R. Yenesel.

Tunis, ch. t., Tunisia, N. Africa; spt. on bay off G. of Tunis; univ., notable mosques; tourist ctr.; many inds., much tr.; the ruins of ancient Carthage are to the N.E.; p. (1956) 680,000.

Tunisia, ind. sovereign st. since March 1956, formerly French prot., N. Africa; agr., stock-rearing, mineral and phosphate wkg., silk and carpet weaving, pottery mftg., fishing (inc. sponges), also fruit- and flower-growing and perfume distillation; lge. steelwks. at Menzel-Bourguiba projected; oil deposits in El Borma a.; cap. Tunis; a. 48,330 sq. m.; p. (1961) 4,168,000.                [63,500

Tunja, t., cap. Boyaca, Colombia; p. (estd. 1959)

Turda, t., Transylvania, Romania; salt-mines; p. (1963) 63 421.

Turfan (Tulufan), c., Sinkiang, China; below sea-level on the S. side of the Tian-Shan Mtns.

Turgal, dist., U.S.S.R.; N. of Sea of Aral, forms part of Kazakh. rep.; a. 175,219 sq. m.; agr. and cattle-breeding; antimony p. 500,000 (largely nomadic Kirghiz).

Turgutlu (Kassaba), t., Manisa prov., Turkey; 30 m. E.N.E. of Izmir; lignite, cotton, melons; p. (1965) 35,079.

Turin (Torino), c., N. Italy; on Rs. Po and Dora; former cap. Piedmont and Sardinian sts.; cath., univ., royal palace and cas., and Palazzo Carignano; leather, textiles, engin.; extensive tr.; p. (1965) 1,107,000.

Turkestan E., terr. included in Sinkiang, China; separated from W. or former Russian Turkestan by Pamir plateau; mainly desert.

Turkey, rep., Europe and Asia; has lost much of 19th-century terrs.; evergreen trees, shrubs, livestock, cereals, tobacco, figs, fruits, copper, silver, coal, carpets, silk, wine, olive oil; oil nr. Iskenderun and along shores of Marmara Sea; cap. Ankara; lgst. t. Istanbul; a. 296,107 sq. m.; p. (1965) 31,391,207.

Turkmenistan, const. rep., U.S.S.R.; agr. based on irrigation, fruit, cotton, wool; sulphates, petroleum, mnfs., carpets; cap. Ashkhabad; a. 189,603 sq. m.; p. (1959) 1,520,000.

Turks and Caicos, Is., Caribbean Sea; West Indies; about 30 sm. Is., geographically the S.E. continuation of the Bahamas; Caicos Is. separated by narrow channel from Turks Is.; ch. prod., salt, conches, sisal, sponges. Total a. 166 sq. m.; p. (estd. 1965) 6,272.

Turku (Abo), spt., S. Finland; Swedish and Finnish univs., archiepiscopal see; p. (1966) 140,139

Turku-Pori (Abo-B[orneborg), dep., Finland; a. 8,500 sq. m.; p. (1966) 674,073.

Turner Valley, dist., Alberta, Canada; oilfield; natural gas.

Turnhout, t., Belgium; nr. Antwerp; textiles, lace, playing-card mnf.; p. (1962) 36,701.

Turnu Severin, t., Romania; below the Iron Gate cataracts of R. Danube; grain, salt, petroleum; p. (1963) 36,831.

Turriff, burgh, Aberdeen, Scot.; nr. R. Deveron; p. (1961) 2,686.

Turton, t., urb. dist., Lancs, Eng.; 4 m. N. of Bolton; mnfs.; p. (1961) 13,673.

Tuscaloosa, t. Ala., U.S.A.; st. univ.; p. (1960) 63,370.

Tuscany, region, former grand duchy, Italy; includes provs. Arezzo, Florence, Leghorn, Siena, Grosseto, Lucca, Pisa, and Massa and Carrara;

cereals, olive oil, wine, copper, lead, mercury, marble, textiles, porcelain; a. 8,876 sq. m.; p. (1961) *3,267,374.*

**Tuticorin,** *spt.,* Madras, India; cotton-spinning, salt, pearls; p. (1961) *124,273.*

**Tuttlingen,** *t.,* Baden-Würtemberg, Germany; on R. Danube; musical instruments, tanning, footwear, steel, textiles; p. (1963) *25,200.*

**Tuva,** *aut. rep.,* U.S.S.R.; formerly Tannu Tuva rep., bounded on E., W., and N. by Siberia, and on S. by Mongolia; cap. Kyzyl; pastoral; asbestos ctr. at Ak-Tovurak, a. about 64,000 sq. m.; p. (1959) *172,000.*

**Tuy Hoa,** *t.,* S. Vietnam; fertilisers, tyres, sugar mill.

**Tuxla Gutierrez,** *t.,* Chiapas, Mexico; alt. 1,500 ft.; ctr. for sisal, tobacco, coffee, cattle; p. (1960) *23,262.*

**Tuzla,** *t.,* Jugoslavia; salt-springs, coal, timber, livestock, grain, fruit; p. (1959) *49,000.*

**Tweed,** *R.,* S.E. Scot.; rises in Peebles, and reaches sea at Berwick; dividing Berwick from the Eng. co. Northumberland; famous for its salmon fisheries; length 97 m.

**Twelve Pins,** star-shaped *mtn. range.* Galway, Ireland; Benbaum, alt. 2,395 ft.

**Twickenham,** *former mun. bor.,* Middx., Eng., now inc. in Richmond upon Thames (*q.v.*); Rugby Football Union ground; p. (1961) *100,322.*

**Tychy,** *t.,* Katowice, Poland; p. (1965) *63,000.*

**Tyldesley,** *t., urb. dist.,* Lancs, Eng.; 4 m. S. of Bolton; mnfs.; p. (1961) *16,513.*

**Tyler,** *c.,* Texas, U.S.A.; fruit, livestock, cotton; p. (1960) *51,230.* [zinc, copper

**Tynagh,** *mine* on Longhrea, Galway, R.O.I.; lead,

**Tyne,** *R.,* Durham and Northumberland, Eng.; formed by junction of N. and S. Tyne at Hexham; flows E. to sea at Tynemouth and S. Shields; valley gives easy route across mtns. from Newcastle to Carlisle; forms a continuous harbour (with shipbldg. and other wks.) from Newcastle to Tynemouth; length 80 m.; road tunnel between Wallsend and Jarrow under constr.

**Tynemouth,** *t., spt. co. bor.,* Northumberland, Eng.; at mouth of R. Tyne, on its N. bank; inc. in its a. the townships of Tynemouth, N. Shields, Cullercoats, Chirton, Preston, Percy Main, E. Howden and New York; favourite wat. pl. with old priory and cas.; gd. harbour; fishing, ship repairing, coal bunkering, laminated plastics; oil storate; p. (estd. 1967) *72,440.*

**Tyneside,** *lge. conurbation,* S.E. Northumberland, N.E. Durham, Eng.; comprises highly industl. built-up a. astride R. Tyne for 14 m. from its mouth to Scotswood Bridge; huge exp. of coal, abroad and round Brit. csts.; shipbldg., heavy engin.; a. 90 sq. m.; p. (1961) *852,341. See also under* Gateshead, Newcastle upon Tyne, S. Shields, Tynemouth, Jarrow, Wallsend, Felling, Hebburn, Gosforth, Longbenton, Newburn, Wickham, Whitley Bay.

**Tyrol,** *mountainous region,* Alps, Europe; falls within Austria and Italy; between Munich and Verona, which are linked by the Brenner Pass; the Tyrol embraces all the highest peaks of the Austrian Alps, culminating in the Ortler Spitz; two-fifths forest; cap. Innsbruck; mtn. pasture, vineyards, silk inds.; a. 4,884 sq. m.; p. of Austrian T. (1961) *462,899.*

**Tyrone,** *inland co.,* N. Ireland; agr. and dairying; cap. Omagh; a. 1,260 sq. m.; p. (1966) *135,634.*

**Tyrrhenian Sea,** part of Mediterranean between Italy and Corsica, Sardinia and Sicily.

**Tyumen,** *t.,* R.S.F.S.R.; on R. Tura, engin., textiles; natural gas nearby in Berezovo vil.; oil pipeline connects with Shaim; p. (1967) *218,000.*

**Tzekung** (Zigong), *c.,* Szechwan, China; petroleum, natural gas, salt wks.; p. (1953) *291,000.*

**Tzepo** (Zibo), *c.,* Shantung, China; formed by merging 1950 coal mng. ts. of Tzechwan and Poshan and 1954 addition of Changchow; p. (estd.) *234,000.*

# U

**Uanapú** or **Anapú,** *R.,* Brazil; trib. of R. Pará; length 400 m.

**Ubangi,** *R.,* central Africa; trib. of R. Congo; with R. Congo forms W. bdy. between Central African Rep. and Congo; length 1,400 m.

**Ubangi-Shari,** *see* Central African Republic.

**Ube,** *spt.,* S. Honshu, Japan; chemical cement machin., coal; p. (1965) *159,000.*

**Ubeda,** *t.,* Jaen, Spain; on R. Guadalquivir; in vineyard and fruit-growing dist.; old walls; p. (1957) *30,249.*

**Uberaba,** *t.,* Minas Gerais, Brazil; cattle, maize, manioc, rice, sugar; p. (1960) *72,053.*

**Ucayali,** *R.,* Peru, S. America; head-stream of R. Amazon; over 1,400 m. long navigable for 1,000 m. [(1962) *73,169.*

**Uccle,** *t.,* Belgium; nr. Brussels; industl.; p.

**Uckfield,** *mkt. t., rural dist.,* E. Sussex, Eng.; 8 m. N.E. of Lewes; p. (rural dist. 1951) *43,132.*

**Udaipur,** *t.,* Rajasthan, India; 2,469 ft. above sea-level; marble palace of the Maharajah; temple of Siva; embroidery, cotton cloth; p. (1961) *111,139.*

**Uddevalla,** *spt.,* S. Sweden; N. Göteborg; prefab. houses, timber, granite quarrying, textiles; p. (1961) *34,290.*

**Udi,** *t.,* S. Nigeria, W. Africa; 100 m. N. of Pt. Harcourt; impt. mining ctr. on Enugu coal-field; linked by rail to Kaduna and Pt. Harcourt.

**Udine,** *t.,* N.E. Italy; between Alps and G. of Venice; old cas. (now barracks); silk, velvet, and cotton inds.; p. (1961) *85,205.*

**Udmurt,** *autonomous Soviet Socialist Rep.,* part of R.S.F.S.R., U.S.S.R., cap. Izhevsk.

**Uelzen,** *t.,* Lower Saxony, Germany; on Lüneberger Heath; machin. chemicals, sugar; p. (1963) *24,500.*

**Ufa,** *t.,* R.S.F.S.R.; in W. Urals at confluence of Rs. Ural and Belaia; iron and copper foundries and machin. wks., saw-mills, textiles, oil; p. (1967) *683,000.*

**Uganda,** *indep. sov. st.* within Br. Commonwealth (1962); E. Central Africa; ch. R. Nile; Ruwenzori Range, Mt. Elgon on Kenya border; Ls. inc. parts of Victoria, Edward, Albert, and whole of Kioga; moderate rainfall; cotton, coffee, tea, oilseeds, tobacco, groundnuts, maize; copper, beryl, tin; timber; Owen Falls hydro-elec. power plant; cap. Kampala; a. 93,981 sq. m. inc. 13,680 sq. m. swamp and water; p. (estd. 1964) *6,845,000.*

**Ughelli,** *t.,* Nigeria; glass wks.

**Uinta,** *min. range.* Utah, U.S.A.; its highest points are Emmons (13,694 ft.), Gilbert Peak (13,687 ft.), and Wilson (13,300 ft.).

**Uist, N.,** *I.,* Outer Hebrides, Inverness, Scot.; separated from I. of Skye by Little Minch; length 17 m., width 3-13 m.

**Uist, S.,** *I.,* Outer Hebrides, Inverness, Scot.; most S. lge. I. of Outer Hebrides gr.; length 22 m., width 8 m.

**Uitenhage,** *t.,* Cape Prov., S. Africa; summer resort, fruit, wool, rly. wks., tyres, car assembly, textiles; p. (1960) *48,755* inc. *17,531* whites.

**Ujiji,** *t.,* in sm. terr. same name (a. 920 sq. m.) on E. shore L. Tanganyika, E. Africa; where Stanley found Livingstone, 1871; p. (1957) *12,149.* [p. (1947) *63,093.*

**Ujiyamada,** *t.,* Japan; sacred c. of Shintoism;

**Ujjain,** *t.,* Madhya Pradesh, India; sacred c. and formerly cap. of Malwa; univ.; p. (1961) *144,161.*

**Ujpest,** *t.,* Hungary; nr. Budapest; elec. engin.; leather, shoes, textiles, furniture, pharmaceutrics; p. *76,000.*

**Ukerewe,** *I.,* on L. Victoria, Central Africa.

**Ukpilla,** *t.,* Nigeria; cement wks.

**Ukraine,** *constituent rep.,* U.S.S.R.; fertile "black earth" region; agr., wheat, maize, barley; tobacco, sheep, pigs; coal, iron-ore, manganese; mnfs., flour, sugar, brewing, chemicals, smelting, hydro-elec., oil; cap. Kiev; a. 225,000 sq. m.; p. (1959) *41,893,000.*

**Ulan Bator,** *t., cap.,* Mongolian People's Republic; in stock-raising region; comm. ctr.; iron, metals, machin.; woollen inds., furniture; p. (1962) *218,000.*

**Ulan-Ude** (Verkhneudinsk), *t.,* Siberia, R.S.F.S.R.; on L. Baikal; engin., textiles, glass, leather; p. (1967) *220,000.*

**Ulcinj,** *ancient c.,* Montenegro, Jugoslavia; tobacco, olive oil; p. *5,000.*

**Uleåborg** (Oulu), *spt.,* Finland; on G. of Bothnia; shipbldg exp. pitch, timber, hides, butter; p. (1961) *59,163.*

**Ulhasnagar,** *c.,* Maharashtra, India; new c. built for refugees from Pakistan; p. (1961) *107,760.*

**Ullswater,** *L.,* on border Cumberland and Westmorland, Eng.; 8 m. long; outlet by R. Eamont to the Eden

**Ulm,** *c.,* Baden-Württemberg, W. Germany; on R. Danube; cath.; machin., textiles, cars, radios; rly junction; p. (1963) *94,400.*

**Ulsan,** *t.,* S. Korea; oil refining, fertilisers.

**Ulster,** *anc. Irish prov.;* comprised nine counties; six of these (Down, Antrim, Armagh, Fermanagh, Londonderry and Tyrone) now form Northern Ireland, a. 5,238 sq. m.; p. (1961) *1,423,127;* three counties (Cavan, Monaghan, Donegal) are in the Rep. of Ireland; largely agr. tourism; gr. industl. expansion; a. 3,123 sq. m.; p. (1966) *208,027.*

**Ulva,** *I.,* Argyll, Scot.; off W. cst. of Mull; 5 m. long.

**Ulverston,** *t., urb. dist.,* N.W. Lancs, Eng.; nr. Morecambe Bay; paper-mills, hardware mftg.; iron, corn, brewing; p. (1961) *10,515.*

**Ulyanovsk,** *t.,* R.S.F.S.R.; on R. Volga; engin., textiles; p. (1967) *275,000.*

**Uman,** *t.,* Ukrainian S.S.R.; iron; p. (1954) *50,000.*

**Umbria,** *region,* Italy; between Tuscany and the Marches, and Rome and the Abruzzi; comprising the prov. of Perugia; mtnous., fertile valleys; a. 3,271 sq. m.; p. (1961) *788,546.*

**Ume älv,** *R.,* Sweden; flows S.E. to the G. of Bothnia; length 250 m.

**Umeå,** *t.,* Sweden; at mouth of Ume älv; woodpulp; cultural ctr.; p. (1961) *22,623.*

**Umtali,** *t.,* Rhodesia; impt. distr. ctr.; timber, fruit, veg., car assembly, engin., textiles; oil refinery at Feruka; pipeline to Beira p. (1961) *41,900* inc. *8,410* whites.

**Umtata,** *c.,* S. Africa; cath.; veg., dehydration, fruit canning; rly. terminus; p. (1960) *12,287* inc. *3,439* whites.

**Una,** *R.,* N. Jugoslavia; trib. of R. Sava.

**Unalaska,** *lge. I.,* Alaska, U.S.A.; in Aleutian gr.; mtnous., treeless; ch. pt. of Bering Strait.

**Uncia,** *t.,* Oruro dep., Bolivia; alt. 13,000 ft. in E. Cordillera of Andes, 60 m. S.E. of Oruro; site of impt. Patino tin-mines.

**Ungava Bay,** *arm of Hudson Strait,* projecting into Labrador, N.E. Canada; lge. forests in the S., minerals abundant, recent exploitation of impt. medium and low-grade iron deposits.

**Union of African States,** union formed by Ghana, Guinea, Mali (1 July 1961).

**Union of Central African States,** union formed by the Congo (Kinshasa) Chad, and the Central African Rep. (2 April 1968).

**Union of South Africa**—*see* South Africa, Rep. of.

**Union of Soviet Socialist Republics,** *cty.,* Europe, Asia; stretches across two continents from the Baltic Sea to the N. Pac. Oc. and from the Arctic to the Black Sea, bounded on the W. by Finland, Poland, Hungary and Romania, on the S. by Turkey, Persia, Afghanistan, and China; The Union consists of 15 Union Republics; R.S.F.S.R., Ukrainian, Byelorussian, Azerbaydzhan, Georgian, Armenian, Turkmen, Uzbek, Tadzik, Kazakh, Kirghiz, Moldavian, Estonian, Lithuanian and Latvian S.S.R.'s. These reps. are divided into 126 terrs. and regions which include 18 autonomous reps., 10 autononomous regions and 10 national areas. European portion, separated in the E. from Asia by Ural Mtns., is a vast low plain with Caucasus Mtns. in the S. In Asia the ctr. and N. is occupied by the vast plain of Siberia, rising in the S. to lofty mtn. ranges, Pamirs, Tien Shan, Sayan, Yablonovy, Stanovoi, etc. Rs. are impt. Dnieper, Volga, Ural and Don in Europe flowing southwards; Ob, Yenisei and Lena in Asia flowing northwards into Arctic Ocean; and Amur into Pac. Oc. N. and central regions—long, cold winters; short, cool summers, S. regions—temperate and sub-tropical; desert and semidesert E. of Caspian Sea. In N. tundra and immense forests with lumbering and associated inds.; agr., wheat, oats, barley, rye, flax, potatoes, sugar-beet, tobacco, cotton, silk, rubber, vines, tea, rice; rich fisheries; impt. minerals; coal, oil, lignite, iron ore, manganese, chrome ore, platinum, copper, lead, zinc, nickel, uranium, asbestos, mica, apatite, nepheline bauxite; many hydro-elect. plants inc. lgst. in Europe; nuclear power stas.; good rly. and canal systems; highly developed inds. inc. metallurgical prods., textiles, chemicals, cellulose-paper and lumbering, leather goods, foodstuffs preparation. Ch. spts. Leningrad, Murmansk, Arkhangelsk, Vladivostok (kept open by icebreakers), Odessa, Sevastopol,

Novorossik, Batumi; cap. Moscow; a. 8,708,070 sq. m.; p. (1966) *233,000,000.*

**Union City,** *t.,* N.J., U.S.A.; p. (1960) *52,180.*

**United Arab Republic** (Egypt), *ind. sovereign st.,* since Feb. 1958; desert, except fertile Nile valley; agr. depends on annual rise of the Nile waters and irrigation (Aswan High Dam); climate: hot, dry summers, warm winters with little rain; agr.: wheat, barley, rice, onions, cotton; phosphates; communications; Nile rly., several surfaced roads across desert; oil offshore 11 m. W. of El Tor, and at Ras Amir. Moslem; cap. Cairo; chief spt. Alexandria; a. 386,100 sq. m.; p. (1961) *26,059,000.*

**United Arab States,** Federation of United Arab Republic and Yemen.

**United Kingdom,** *cty.,* N.W. Europe; separated from continent of Europe by Eng. Channel; consists of Gr. Britain (Eng., Wales, Scot.) and N. Ireland. *See under separate headings.*

**United Provinces, India.** *See* Uttar Pradesh.

**United States,** *federal rep.,* N. America: ch. physical features: Great Ls., lgst. freshwater a. in the world; ch. Rs.: Mississippi-Missouri, Rio Grande del Norte, Colorado, Hudson, Susquehanna, Savannah, Columbia; ch. mtns.: Rocky Mtns., Coast Range, Sierra Nevada, Appalachian Mtns.: Great Basin, great plains, Piedmont plateau, coastal plains; climate in N.E.—cool, temperate, rainfall all year round, warm summers, cold winters; in central plains and Gr. Basin—continental climate of extremes; in N.W.—cool temperate with abundant rainfall warm summers, cold winters; in S.W. on Pacific cst.—Mediterranean climate of very warm summers and drought, mild winters with rainfall, dense fogs off Pacific cst.; in S. and S.E. sub-tropical, hot summers, mild winters with abundant rainfall in the S.E. decreasing towards the W.; ch. inds.: agr., maize, wheat, oats, etc., fruit, potatoes, hay, alfalfa, cane- and beet-sugar, cotton, tobacco; pastoral farming, ranching, dairying, sheep, wool, cattle, pigs, horses; lumbering, timber, wood-pulp; fishing off Grand Bank, Newfoundland, for cod, etc., and in W. for salmon; minerals: coal, petroleum, natural gas, phosphate, iron ore, copper, lead, gold, silver, zinc, aluminium, mercury; mftg. of all kinds; commerce: comprises 50 sts. and Dist. of Columbia; cap. Washington; lgst. ts. New York, Chicago, Los Angeles, Philadelphia; total a. (inc. possessions) *3,608,787* sq. m.; p. (1966) *196,600,000.*

**University City,** *t.,* Mo., U.S.A.; p. (1960) *51,249.*

**Unna,** *t.,* N. Rhine-Westphalia, Germany; coalmng., machin., iron; p. (1963) *31,000.*

**Unst,** *I.,* Shetlands; most N. of gr.; length 12½ m.

**Unstrut,** *R.,* Saxony, Germany; trib. of R. Saale, length 110 m.

**Untersee,** W. portion of L. of Constance.

**Unterwalden,** *old can.,* Switzerland; now subdivided into Obwalden and Nidwalden; dairying, fruit and livestock; ch. ts. are Sarnen and Stans.

**Upholland,** *t., urb. dist.,* Lancs, Eng.; 4 m. W. of Wigan; bricks; p. (1961) *7,451.*

**Upper Austria,** *prov.,* Austria; cap. Linz; a. 4,625 sq. m.; p. (1961) *1,131,623.*

**Upper Nile,** *prov.,* Sudan, N.E. Africa; cap. Malakal; a. 92,270 sq. m.; p. (1964) *1,037,736.*

**Upper Seal Lake,** Labrador, Newfoundland, Canada.

**Upper Volta,** see Voltaic Republic.

**Uppsala,** *co.,* E. Sweden; N. of L. Mälar; cap. Uppsala; a. 2,056 sq. m.; p. (1961) *167,735.*

**Uppsala,** *t.,* cap. Uppsala, Sweden; on R. Sala; 45 m. from Stockholm; univ., cath.; lt. inds.; p. (1961) *77,518.*

**Ur,** *ancient* Chaldean c. Iraq; 130 m. W.N.W. of Basra; ruins; flourished about 3,000 B.C.

**Ural Mtns.,** R.S.F.S.R.; mtns. separating Asia from Europe; 2,050 m. long; highest summit, Tolposis Mtn., 5,430 ft.

**Ural,** *R.,* R.S.F.S.R.; flows S.W. and S. to the Caspian Sea; length 1,500 m.

**Uralsk,** *t.,* Kazakh S.S.R.; on R. Ural; graintrading and cattle-mart. ctr.; flour, leather, woollens, iron-ware; p. (1967) *119,000.*

**Uranium City,** N. Saskatchewan, Canada; nr. N. shore of L. Athabasca, ctr. of Beaverlodge uranium-mining a.; founded 1951; p. (1953) approx. *500.*    [of st. univ.; p. (1960) *27,294.*

**Urbana,** *c.,* Ill., U.S.A.; on Embarrass R.; seat

**Urbino,** *t.,* N. Marche, Italy; cath., univ.; silk, cheese, olive oil; p. *20,375.*

Ure, *R.*, N.R. Yorks., Eng.; flows E. and S.E. to the Swale to form the Ouse; length 50 m.

Urfa, *t.*, Turkey; nr. Syrian border; gd. local tr.; p. (1965) *72,873*.

Uri, *can.*, Switzerland; S. of L. of Lucerne; forest and mtn.; traversed by St. Gotthard Rly. and R. Reuss; cap. Altdorf; a. 415 sq. m.; p. (1961) *32,021*.

Urmia (Rizaieh), *t.*, Azerbaijan, Iran; birthplace of Zoroaster; p. *64,000*.

Urmia, L. of, nr. Tabriz, N.W. Iran; 85 m. by 30 m.; salt and shallow.                  [*43,300*.

Urmston, *urb. dist.*, Lancs., Eng.; p. (estd. 1967)

Urubamba, *R.*, Peru, S. America; rises in E. Cordillera of Andes; forms one of head streams of R. Amazon; length 350 m.

Urubupunga, *t.*, Brazil; new t. for 10,000 at site of hydro-elec. sta.

Uruguaiana, *t.* Brazil; on R. Uruguay; cattle ctr.; jerked beef, soap, candles; p. (1960) *43,358*.

Uruguay, *rep.*, S. America; climate, temperate; moderate rainfall; vegetation temperate and sub-tropical grasslands; language, Spanish; religion, R. C.; cattle- and sheep-rearing, wheat, olives, grapes, gold, textiles; cap. Montevideo; a. 72,153 sq. m.; p. (1965) *2,682,000*.

Uruguay, *R* , S. America; rises n S. Brazil, and flows between Argentina and Brazil and Uruguay to Río de la Plata; length 850 m.

Urumchi (Wulumuchi), *c.*, Sinkiang, China; p. (1953) *141,000*.                             [wide.

Urup, *I.*, Kurile gr., Pac. Oc.; 50 m. long; 12 m.

Usa, *R.*, U.S.S.R.; flows E. from the Urals to the Pechora; length 220 m.

Usak, *t.*, Turkey; connected by rail with Izmir; noted for pile carpet-weaving; p. (1965) *33,315*.

Usedom (Uznam), *I.*, Baltic Sea; off mouth of R. Oder; since 1945 the E. part belongs to Poland, the W. (the larger part) to Germany; I. is 30 m. long and 14 m. wide.

Ushant, *I.*, off cst. of Finisterre, France; at entrance to Eng. Channel; it was off Ushant that Lord Howe gained his great naval victory on the " glorious first of June," 1794.

Ushuaia, *t.*, Argentina; most southerly t. in world; sheep farming, timber, furs; freezing plant; p. *6,000*.

Usk, *R.*, S. Wales and Monmouth, Eng.; flows S. to Bristol Channel; length 57 m.

Üsküdar (Scutari), *t.*, Turkey; on the Bosporus, opposite Istanbul; silks, cottons, muslin; p. (estd. 1960) *85,000*.

Uspallata Pass, Andes, Argentina; used by the Mendoza–Valparaíso Transandine rly.

Ussuri, *R.*, N. China; rises in Maritime prov. of R.S.F.S.R., flowing c. 500 m. to R. Amur; final 300 m. forms Sino-Soviet boundary.

Ussuriysk (Voroshilov), *t.*, R.S.F.S.R.; 70 m. N. of Vladivostok; rly. junction; soya oil, sugar; p. (1967) *123,000*.

Ust Kamenogorsk, *t.*, Kazakhstan, U.S.S.R.; lead refining; hydro-elec. power sta. nearby on R. Irtish; p. (1967) *207,000*.

Ustica, *I.*, Italy; hilly; fruit, olives, grain, osiers; fishing; a. 3 sq. m.

Ustí Nad Labem, *t.*, ČSSR.; on the Elbe; chemicals, coal; p. (1962) *63,819*.

Usumacinta, *R.*, Mexico and Guatemala, Central America; trib. of R. Tabasco; length 400 m.

Usumbura, *t.*, Burundi, Africa; cotton ginnery, soapwks.; exp. cotton, coffee, hides; p. (estd. 1949) *17,188*.

Utah, *W. st.*, U.S.A.; farming, wheat, maize, barley, rye, livestock, sugar-beet, fruits; copper, silver, lead, gold, coal, uranium, vanadium; petroleum; fruit-canning; cap. Salt Lake City; a. 84,916 sq. m.; p. (1960) *890,627*.

Utah, *L.*, U.S.A., drains by R. Jordan to Gr. Salt L., 23 m. by 8 m.

Utica, *c.*, N.Y., U.S.A.; on Mohawk R.; clothing and other mnfs.; p. (1960) *100,410*.

Utiel, *t.*, Spain; W. of Valencia; brandies, wines; p. (1957) *13,365*.

Utrecht, *prov.*, Neth.; between Gelderland and N. and S. Holland; fertile agr., cattle rearing, horticulture; a. 526 sq. m.; p. (1967) *758,007*.

Utrecht, *c.*, Neth.; on Old R. Rhine; univ., cath.; chemical and cigar factories; printing, machin., woollens, silks, velvets; p. (1967) *274,485*.

Utrera, *t.*, Spain; S.E. of Seville; industl.; p. (1957) *34,893*.

Uttar Pradesh, *st.*, India; Himalayas on N. bdy., drained by Ganges and Jumna; splendid irriga-

tion; wheat, rice, millet, barley, maize, cotton, sugar, oil-seeds; ch. ts. Allahabad, Lucknow (cap.), Varanasi, Cawnpore, Agra, Meerut; a. 113,410 sq. m.; p. (1961) *73,746,401*.

Uttoxeter, *t.*, *urb. dist.*, Staffs, Eng.; on R. Dove, 10 m. N.W. of Burton-on-Trent; machin., biscuit mftg.; p. (1961) *3,163*.

Uusimaa, *dep.*, Finland; a. 4,435 sq. m.; cap. Helsinki; p. (1966) *942,947*.

Uvira, *pt.*, Congo, Central Africa; on N.W. cst. of L. Tanganyika; exp. coffee, cotton, hides; bricks, cotton ginning.

Uxbridge, *mkt. t.*, *former mun. bor.*; Middx. Eng.; on R. Colne; now inc. in Hillingdon outer bor., Greater London; residtl.; light inds., film studio; p. (1961) *63,941*.

Uzbekistan, *constituent rep.*, U.S.S.R.; intensive farming based on irrigation; rice, cotton, fruits, silk, cattle, sheep; cap. Tashkent; alluvial gold deposits and bauxite in Kyzyl-Kum desert; a. 159,170 sq. m.; p. (1959) *8,113,000*.

Uzen, (Gr. and Little), *Rs.*, U.S.S.R., flowing 250 m. to the Caspian Sea.

Uzgen, *region*, Kirghiz, S.S.R., U.S.S.R.; coal cotton. engin.

Uzhgorod, *t.*, Ukrainian S.S.R.; univ.; woodworkings, food inds.; engin.; p. (1959) *47,000*.

Uzhoi Cape, *promontory*, on Ob. Bay, N. Siberia, U.S.S.R.

Uzlovaya, *t.*, R.S.F.S.R.; 30 m. S.E. of Tula; coal mng.; impt. rly. junction; p. (1959) *54,000*.

## V

Vaal, *R.*, S. Africa; rises in Drakensberg Mtns., and flows between the Transvaal and Orange Free State to join the Orange R. nr. Kimberley; length 560 m.

Vaasa (Vasa), *dep.*, Finland; cap. Vaasa; p. (1966) *448,509*.

Vaasa, *t.*, *pt.*, *cap.*, Vaasa, Finland; on G. of Bothnia; oats, butter, cattle exp.; p. (1966) *47,528*.

Vác, *t.*, Hungary; on R. Danube; chemicals, textiles, cement, boat-mkg.; p. (1962) *26,679*.

Vaduz, *t.*, *cap.*, Liechtenstein; p. (1960) *3,393*.

Váh, *R.*, Czechoslovakia; trib. of R. Danube; length 200 m.

Val de Chiana, *see* Chiana, Val de.

Valais, *can.*, Switzerland; comprising upper valley of R Rhône; surrounded by high mtns.; cap. Sion; a. 2,021 sq. m.; p. (1961) *177,783*.

Valdai Hills, U.S.S.R.; N.W. of Moscow; highest summit, 1,100 ft.                      [power sta.

Valdecañas, Spain, 120 m. S.W. Madrid; dam and Valdepeñas, *t.*, Central Spain; mineral springs, wine; p. *26,000*

Valdivia, *prov.*, S. Chile; cap. Valdivia; a. 7,721 sq. m.; p. (1960) *302,779*.

Valdivia, *t.*, cap. Valdivia, S. Chile; on R. Callecalle nr. the sea (pt. Corral); damaged by earthquake and tidal wave, May 1960; univ.; metal, wood and leather goods; paper, flour, brewing; p. (1961) *85,000*.

Valdosta, *t.*, Ga., U.S.A.; rly. ctr., cotton mills, light engin.; p. (1960) *30,652*.

Valence, *t.*, cap. Drôme, France; on left bank of R. Rhône; metal-founding, silks, hosiery, vineyards; p. (1962) *55,023*.

Valencia, *prov.*, Spain; on Mediterranean; agr., vineyards, olive-, fig-, and orange-growing, stock-rearing, silk, tapestry carpet mftg.; cap. Valencia; a. 4,239 sq. m.; p. (1959) *1,451,037*.

Valencia, *t.*, cap. Valencia, Spain; on R. Turia, 3 m. from the Mediterranean; univ., museum, cath.; active industl. and comm. ctr.; mnfs., linen, leather, cigars, silks, exp. wine, fruits, corn, etc.; p. (1965) *585,000*.

Valencia, *l.*, S.W Kerry, Ireland; 6 m. by 2 m.

Valencia, *t* , Venezuela, S. America; univ.; ctr. of agr. a.; most industrialised town in rep.; p. (1961) *161,410*.

Valencia, *L.*, Venezuela; a. 216 sq. m.; surrounded by swampy flats used for cattle-grazing.

Valenciennes, *fortfd. t.*, Nord. France; on R. Escaut; lace; metallurgical inds., starch, chemicals coal, iron; p. (1962) *46,643*.

Valera, *t.*, Trujillo, Venezuela; airport; p. (1961) *44,820*.

Valladolid, *prov.*, Central Spain; agr., vineyards, livestock, mnfs.; cap. Valladolid; a. 3,155 sq. m.; p. (1959) *368,049*.

Valladolid, *t.*, cap. Valladolid, Spain; on R.

Pisuerga; seat of army corps, univ., cath.; thriving inds. and tr.; p. (1965) *172,000*.

Vallecas, *sub.* Madrid, Spain.

Valle d'Aosta, *aut. region*, N.W. Italy; a. 1,260 sq. m.; p. (1961) *99,754*.

Valle del Cauca, *dep.*, Colombia, S. America; cap. Cali.; a. 8,083 sq. m.; p. (estd. 1959) *1,596,650*.

Vallejo, *c.*, Cal., U.S.A.; exp. fruit and corn, milling; p. (1960) *60,977*.

Vallenar, *t.*, Atacama prov., Chile; agr. ctr.; dried fruit, wines; iron ore nearby; p. (1960) *30,793*.

Valletta, *ch. t.*, *spt.*, Malta; on N.E. cst. of I.; strongly fortifd., fine harbour; univ.; cath.; p. (1960) *18,000*.      [paper; p. (1961) *27,297*.

Valleyfield, *t.*, Quebec, Canada; textiles, glazed

Valona, *see* Vlonë.

Valparaiso, *prov.*, Chile; cap. Valparaiso; a. 1,860 sq. m.; p. (1961) *648,449*.

Valparaiso, *c.*, *spt.*, cap. Valparaiso, Chile; the most impt. pt. on the Pacific cst. of S. America, and the ch. mftg. comm. and industl. ctr. of the Rep. of Chile; locomotives rolling-stock, sugar-refining, textiles, chemicals, tanneries; p. (1961) *259,241*.

Van, *fortfd.*, *c.*, Turkey; on E. side of L. Van, S. of Erzurum; p. (1965) *31,010*.

Van, *prov.*, Turkey; mtnous., pastoral; sulphur springs, petroleum wells; p. (1965) *267,111*.

Vancouver, *spt.*, B.C., Canada; international airport and terminus of trans-continental rly.; univ.; lumbering, shipbldg., fishing; oil- and sugar-refining; p. (1961) *790,165*.

Vancouver, *t.*, Wash., U.S.A.; dairying, milling, fruit, lumbering, canning; p. (1960) *32,464*.

Vancouver, *I.*, B.C., Canada; off W. cst.; forestry, fishing, dairying, coal, tourism; cap. Victoria; a. 12,408 sq. m.; p. (1956) *361,952*.

Vandellos, Tarragona, Spain; nuclear power sta.

Vanderbijlpark, *t.*, Transvaal, S. Africa; on Vaal R.; ctr. for steel wks.; p. (1960) *41,318* (inc. *21,857* whites.)

Van Diemen Gulf, between Darwin and Coburg Peninsula, N. Terr., Australia.

Vänern, *lge. L.*, Sweden; W.N.W. of L. Vättern, with which it is connected by canal (and thence with the Baltic); a. 2,149 sq. m.

Vänersborg, *L. pt.*, Sweden; on a tongue of land between the R. Göta and the Vasobotten (the southernmost bay of L. Vänern); footwear, wood and sulphite pulp; p. (1961) *18,491*.

Vannes, *ch. t.*, Morbihan, France; on S. cst. Brittany; shipbldg., ironwks., breweries, ropes, leather, oysters; p. (1962) *34,107*.

Var, *R.*, Alpes-Maritimes, France; flows S. to the Mediterranean Sea; length 60 m.

Var, *dep.*, S. France; on the Mediterranean; pasture, vineyards, sericulture, wines, olives, paper; cap. Draguignan, Toulon lgst. c.; a. 2,333 sq. m.; p. (1962) *469,557*.

Varanasi (formerly Benares) *t.*, India; on Ganges, Hindu holy city; annual pilgrimage; temples, mosques, palaces, univ.; brocade, gold, silver, lacquer, locomotives; p. (1961) *489,864*.

Varanger Fjord, an inlet of the Arctic Ocean into Finnmark, Norway's most N. prov

Varazdin, *t.*, Croatia, Jugoslavia; on R. Drava; woollens, coal; p. (1959) *23,000*.

Varberg, *spt.*, Halland, Sweden; resort; granite quarries; p. *11,874*.

Vardar, *R.*, Jugoslavia, Greece; flows S. into G. of Thessalonika; length 280 m.

Varde, *t.*, W. Jutland, Denmark; recently developed as agr. and route ctr.; food processing; steelwks.; p. (1960) *9,577*.

Varese, *t.*, N. Italy; silk-spinning, wine, paper, leather, aircraft; p. (1961) *64,977*.

Värmland, *co.*, Sweden; a. 7,427 sq. m.; p. (1961) *291,085*.

Varna, *fortfd. spt.*, Bulgaria; on Black Sea; univ.; shipbldg., textiles, grain; trading ctr.; p. (1956) *119,769*.

Varpalota, *t.*, Hungary; lignite mines; aluminium, fertilisers, oil; p. (1962) *22,853*.

Vásárhely *or* Hódmező Vásárhely, *t.*, Hungary; wine, tobacco

Västerås, *t.*, *cap.*, Västmanland, Sweden; on N. bay of L. Malar; Gothic cath. (with episcopal library), 16th-century cas.; impt. elec. inds.; power sta.; p. (1961) *77,946*.

Västerbotten, *co.*, Sweden; a. 22,839 sq. m.; p. (1961) *239,625*.

Västernorrland, *co.*, Sweden; a. 9,925 sq. m.; p. (1959) *288,231*.

Västervik, *t.*, Sweden; on Baltic cst.; engin., iron, wire, nails, chemicals, paper; p. (1961) *18,193*.

Västmanland, *co.*, Sweden; N. of L. Malar; cap. Västeras; a. 2,611 sq. m.; p. (1961) *232,589*.

Vathéos, *spt.*, Samos I., Greece; exp. wine, olive oil, leather, tobacco, raisins.

Vatican City, the Papal st. of Italy; a. 108.7 acres; p. (estd.) *1,000*.

Vatna Jökull, *mtn.*, Iceland; elevated snowfield.

Vättern, *L.*, Sweden; 25 m. S.E. L. Vänern; a. 733 sq. m.

Vaucluse, *dep.*, S.E. France; ag., wines, sericulture, linen, silks, pottery; cap. Avignon; a. 1,381 sq. m.; p. (1962) *303,536*.

Vaud, *or* Pays de Vaud, *can.*, W. Switzerland; N. of L. of Geneva; timber, forests and vineyards; cap. Lausanne; a. 1,239 sq. m.; p. (1961) *429,512*.

Växjö, *t.*, S. Sweden; engin., timber wks., hosiery; p. (1961) *24,041*.

Vecht, *R.*, Neth.; branch of Rhine, flows into IJsselmeer.

Vecses, *t.*, Hungary; p. (1962) *15,540*.

Véjer de la Frontera, *t.*, Spain; nr. C. Trafalgar; agr. and stock-rearing; p. (1957) *12,569*.

Vejle, *spt.*, Jutland, Denmark; gd. harbour and tr.; textiles, iron ind., leather, soap; p. (1960) *31,362*.

Velbert, *t.*, N. Rhine–Westphalia, Germany; N.W. of Wuppertal; metal ind. locks and keys; p. (1963) *53,000*.

Veleki Bečkerek, *see* Zrenjanin.

Veles, *see* Titov Veles.

Velez Málaga, *c.*, Malaga, Spain; famous for wine, raisins, sugar, olive oil; p. (1957) *31,610*.

Veliki Ustyug, *t.*, R.S.F.S.R.; on R. Sukhona; shipbldg., silver craft; p. (1956) *35,800*.

Velletri, *t.*, Italy; foot of the Alban Hills overlooking Pontine Marshes; gd. wine; at this spot Garibaldi gained a victory over the King of Naples, 1849; p. (1961) *40,053*.

Vellore, *t.*, Tamil Nadu, India; perfumes, etc.; p. (1961) *113,742*.

Veluwe, *dist.*, Gelderland, Neth.; between Arnhem and IJsselmeer (Zuiderzee); low hills of glacial sands and sand-dunes; heathland and pine-woods; relatively low p. density.

Vendée *or* La Vendée, *dep.*, W. France; on Bay of Biscay; agr. pasturage, vineyards, fishery, sea-salt, coal and some mnfs.; cap. La Roche-sur-Yon; a. 2,692 sq. m.; p. (1962) *408,923*.

Vendôme, *t.*, Loir-et-Cher, France; on R. Loire; leather goods, cottons; p. (1962) *14,176*.

Venetia (Veneto *or* Venezia Euganea), *div.* N.E. Italy; between the Alps and the Adriatic; embraces provs. Vicenza, Verona, Venice, Udine, Treviso, Padua, Belluno and Rovigo; cap. Venice; a. 7,098 sq. m.; p. (1961) *3,833,537*.

Venetia Tridentina, *div.*, N. Italy; mountainous, lying between Austrian and Swiss frontiers and L. Garda; embraces provs. Trento and Bolzano; cap. Trento; a. 5,250 sq. m.; p. (1961) *747,221*.

Venezia Giulia, *see* Friuli-Venezia Giulia.

Venezuela, *rep.*, S. America; on Caribbean cst.; climate tropical, with temperate uplands, wet summers, dry winters, tropical forests, and grasslands (llanos); petroleum (one of the lgst. oil producing ctys. of the world), gold, copper, iron ore, coal, asphalt; new inds. in petrol a. inc. aluminium, cars, textiles, glass, agr. implements; pearl fishing, coffee, cocoa, sugar, maize, cotton, indigo, balata, tobacco; cap. Carácas; a. 352,143 sq. m.; p. (estd. 1965) *8,722,000*.

Venice, *maritime c.*, Italy; built on group of islets within a lagoon in G. of Venice, at head of the Adriatic; splendid architecture; rich in art treasures and historic associations; glassware, gold, silver, embroidery, lace, damask, shipbldg.; p. (1965) *364,000*.

Venlo, *t.*, Neth.; on the Maas; brewing, leather, ceramics, needles, tobacco; p. (1967) *60,773*.

Vennachar, *Loch*, Perth. Scot.; expansion of R. Teith.

Ventimiglia, *t.*, *cst. resort*, Italy; on Mediterranean cst. nr. Fr. border; cath.; p. *17,081*.

Ventnor, *t.*, *urb. dist.*, I. of Wight, Eng.; on S. cst., 11 m. S. of Ryde; mild climate, tourist and health resort; p. (1961) *6,410*.

Ventolene I., Pontine Is., Italy; vineyards, fruit.

Veracruz, *c.*, *pt.*, Veracruz, Mexico; on G. of

Mexico; exp. ores, precious metals, textiles, raw cotton and petrol; p. (1960) *144,232.*

Veracruz, *prov.*, Mexico; contains volcano Orizaba; cap. Jalapa: a. 27.736 sq. m.; p. (1960) *2,727,399.* [Santiago; p. (1968) *157,400.*

Veraguas, *prov.*, Panama, central America; cap.

Vercelli, *c.*, Piedmont, Italy; cath.; cottons, woollens, machin., aircraft parts; exp. rice; p. (1961) *50,197.*

Verde, C., *most W. point*, Africa, Senegal.

Verden, *c.*, Lower Saxony, Germany; S.E. of Bremen; cath.; machin., glass, tobacco; p. (estd. 1954) *19,900.*

Verdun, *t.*, Quebec, Canada; p. (1961) *78,317.*

Verdun, *fortfd. t.*, Meuse, France; on R. Meuse; 12th-century cath.; confectionery, liqueur, hardware factories; scene of famous battle in First World War; p. (1962) *25,238.*

Vereeniging, *t.*, Transvaal, S. Africa; coal, iron and steel, bricks; Treaty of Vereeniging (31 May 1902) ended Boer War; p. (1962) *88,008* inc. *26,234* whites.

Verkhneudinsk, *see* Ulan-Ude.

Verkhneuralsk, *t.*, R.S.F.S.R.; on Upper Ural R.; tanneries, distilleries; p. (1956) *11,000.*

Verkhoyansk, *t.*, Yakutsk A.S.S.R., R.S.F.S.R.; in N.E. Siberia; coldest place in world; mean January temp. of -59° F.; ctr. of fur trapping a.; p. (1956) *1,800.*

Vermont, *st.*, New England, U.S.A.; adjoining Quebec prov., Canada; traversed by the Green Mtns.; farming, dairying, stock-raising, lumbering, quarrying, machin. tool and textile mnftg.; cap. Montpelier; a. 9,609 sq. m.; p. (1960) *389,881.*

Vern, Ille-et-Vilaine, France; nr. Rennes; oil refining. [p. (1961) *10,250.*

Vernon, *t.*, B.C., Canada; fruit, farming, canning;

Verona, *fortfd. c.*, Venetia, Italy; on R. Adige; beautiful cath.; Roman antiquities; active tr. and inds.; iron goods, machin., paper, silk; p. (1964) *240,000.*

Verona, *prov.* of Venetia region, Italy; a. 1,188 sq. m.; p. (1961) *665,053.*

Verroia, *t.*, N. Greece; S.E. of Thessaloniki; ancient Berea; p. (1961) *25,765.*

Versailles, *pref.*, Yvelines, France; 12 m. W.S.W. of Paris; famous royal palace; mkt. gardening, distilleries, etc.; Treaty of Versailles 1919; p. (1962) *95,149.*

Verulamium, *site of ancient Roman t.*, Herts, Eng.; on R. Ver, opposite St. Albans; impt. during Roman occupation.

Verviers, *t.*, Belgium; nr. Liége; cloth mnfs., glass, polystyrene mftg.; p. (1962) *35,125.*

Veszprem, *t.*, Hungary; in Bakony; univ. for chemical ind.

Vest Fjord, *strait*, separates Lofoten Is., from mainland, Norway.                                    [*177,438.*

Vestfold, *co.*, Norway; a. 96,359 sq. m.; p. (1963)

Vesuvius, *famous active volcano*, S. Italy; on side of Bay of Naples; alt. 3,984 ft.; its eruption in A.D. 79 destroyed Pompeii and Herculaneum, and frequent eruptions have since occasioned havoc; funicular rly. from the base of the mtn. to the edge of the crater since 1880.

Veurne (Furnes), *t.*, W. Flanders, Belgium; sugar-refining; warehouses; p. (1962) *7,315.*

Vevey, *t.*, Vaud, Switzerland; on N.E. shore of L. of Geneva; chocolate, watches, machin.; p. (1957) *14,264.*

Veyangoda, *t.*, Ceylon; textiles.

Viacha, *t.*, Bolivia, S. America; rly. junction nr. La Paz; cement; p. *2,000.*

Viana do Castello, *dist.*, Portugal; cap. Viana do Castello; a. 814 sq. m.; p. (1960) *280,100.*

Viana do Castello, *t.*, Portugal; at mouth of R. Lima, nr. Oporto; p. (1960) *14,371.*

Viareggio, *spt.*, *resort*, Italy; on Mediterranean, nr. Pisa; monument to the poet Shelley; p. (1961) *47,323.*                                 [dustrial.

Viazma, *t.*, R.S.F.S.R.; N.E. of Smolensk, in-

Viborg, *t.*, Jutland, Denmark; comm. and admin. ctr., knitted goods; cath.; p. (1960) *23,265.*

Viborg (Viipuri), *spt.*, R.S.F.S.R., U.S.S.R.; on G. of Finland; impt. industl. and transport ctr.; agr. machin., timber; p. (1959) *51,000.*

Vicenza, *c.*, Italy; woollens, cottons, silks, pottery, furniture mkg.; p. (1961) *97,617.*

Vich (Vique), *c.*, Spain; nr. Barcelona; cath.; mnfs.; p. (1957) *16,975.*

Vichuga, *t.*, R.S.F.S.R., N.E. of Ivanovo; ctr. of cotton ind.; p. (1959) *51,000.*

Vichy, *t.*, *wat. pl.*, Allier, France; 35 m. S. of Moulins; mineral springs, lge. exp. of waters; seat of Gov. during German occupation. p. (1962) *32,178.*

Vicksburg, *c.*, Miss., U.S.A.; on cliffs above a "cut-off" L. on R. Mississippi; furniture, machin.; mftg. ctr. in cotton and timber region; prominent in American Civil War, Confederate surrender 1863; p. (1960) *29,130.*

Victoria, *st*, Australian Commonwealth; mixed farming, grapes, mnfs., machin., hardware, textiles, wine, gold, coal, tin; oil refining at Crib Point, 45 m. from Melbourne; natural gas off E. cst.; cap. Melbourne; a. 87,884 sq. m.; p. (1968) *3,217,832.*

Victoria, *c.*, *cap.*, B.C., Canada; on Vancouver I., sawmills, cement, chemicals, fish-canning; p. (1961) *154,152.*                              (p. *42,873.*

Victoria, *spt.*, *cap.*, Espirito Santo st., Brazil;

Victoria, *t.*, *cap.*, Seychelles, Ind., Oc.; gd. harb.

Victoria, *t.*, *cap.*, Labuan I., Sabah; fine harbour; p. (estd. 1957) *2,526.*

Victoria, *t.*, *cap.*, Hong Kong; built on reclaimed land; p. (estd. 1965) *675,000.*

Victoria Falls, on the R. Zambesi, Zambia, discovered by Livingstone in 1855; falls are 1,860 yd. wide and broken by islands and rocks.

Victoria, *L.*, Kenya, Uganda, Tanzania, E. Africa; lgst. L. of Africa; lies on the Equator; a. 25,000–26,000 sq. m.; discharges to the N. by R. Nile; 3,705 ft. above sea; discovered by Captain Speke in 1858.

Victoria, *L.*, on Gr. Pamir, Central Asia; 13,870 ft. above sea-level; supposed to be ch. source of the R. Oxus.

Victoria, *R.*, flows into Queens Channel, N.W. cst. of Northern Terr. Australia.

Victoria Land, *terr.*, N. Canada; S.E. of Prince Albert Land.                                  [Ross in 1841.

Victoria Land, *region*, Antarctica; discovered by

Victoria Nile, *R.*, Uganda, E. Africa; name of R. Nile from its source at L. Victoria until it enters L. Albert.

Victoria Strait, separates Victoria I. from King William I., Arctic Canada.

Victoria West, *t.*, Cape Province, S. Africa; p. *2,535.*

Victoriaville, *t.*, Quebec, Canada; woodworking; p. (1961) *18,720.*

Vidin, *fortfd. t.*, Bulgaria; on R. Danube; ruined mosque and palace; p. (1956) *23,932.*    [*7,000.*

Vledma, *t.*, *cap.*, Rio Negro Argentina; p. (1960)

Vienna (Wien), *cap.*, Austria; on branch of R. Danube; ranks also as prov.; univ., gothic cath. (St. Stephen's Church), Rathaus, Parliament bldgs., magnificent Prater park; thriving comm. and mnfs., silks, iron, steel, breweries, etc.; p. (1964) *1,639,000.*

Vienne, *R.*, France; trib. of the Loire; l. 220 m.

Vienne, *dep.*, W. France; grain, wine, cutlery, arms; cap. Poitiers; a. 2,711 sq. m.; p. (1962) *331,619.*

Vienne, *t.*, Isère, France; nr. Grenoble, on R. Rhône; textiles, gloves; p. (1962) *28,163.*

Vienne, Haute (Haute-Vienne), *dep.*, France; fruits, cereals, livestock, porcelain; cap. Limoges; a. 2,119 sq. m.; p. (1962) *332,514.*

Vientiane, *cap.*, Laos; p. (estd. 1962) *100,000.*

Viersen, *t.*, N. Rhine-Westphalia, Germany; S.W. of Krefeld; textiles, machin., furniture, paper ind.; p. (1963) *42,200.*

Vierzon, *t.*, Cher, France; nr. Bourges; mnfs.; p. (1962) *31,951.*

Viet-Nam, S.E. Asia; formerly within the French Union, covering 3 countries of Tongking, Annam and Cochin-China. Since 1954 div. into 2 zones. S. zone (Rep. of Vietnam) a. 66,300 sq. m., p. (estd. 1960) *14,100,000*; cap. Saigon; rice, rubber. N. zone (Dem. Rep. of Vietnam) a. 63,000 sq. m., p. (1960) *15,903,000*; cap. Hanoi; rice, coal, cement, apatite (phosphate).

Viet-Tri, *t.*, N. Vietnam; 80 m. N.W. of Hanoi; chemicals, paper mill, sugar refining.

Vigevano, *t.*, Lombardy, Italy; on R. Ticino; cath.; silks; p. (1961) *57,069.*

Vigo, *fortfd. t.*, Galicia, Spain; on Rio de Vigo; impt. fishery and shipping inds.; flour, sugar, petroleum, leather; p. (1965) *166,000.*

Vijayavada, *t.*, Andhra Prad., India; irrigation dam, Kistna R., rice; p. (1961) *230,397.*

Vila de João Belo (Chai Chai), *t.*, Mozambique, Port. E. Africa; on R. Limpopo; exp. sugar, rice, timber, maize.

Vila Nova de Gala, *t.*, Portugal; sub. of Oporto;

on R. Douro; pottery, wine-casks, tobacco and glass factories; p. (1960) *45,739*.

Vila Real, *dist.*, Portugal; a. 1,636 sq. m.; p. (1960) *333,156* of t. *10,263*.

Villa Hermosa, *cap.*, Tabasco, Mexico; p. (1960) *33,587*.

Villa Maria, *t.*, Argentina; rly. junction; grain, timber, dairying; p. (1960) *50,000*.

Villach, *t.*, Austria; iron, timber, leather, beer; tourist ctr.; p. (1961) *32,971*.

Villanueva de la Serena, *t.*, prov., Badajoz, Spain; wine, wheat, hemp and fruit; p. (1957) *18,391*.

Villanueva y Geltrú, *spt.*, Spain; nr. Barcelona; cotton ind., tyres; p. (1957) *19,483*.

Villarrica, *t.*, Paraguay; cath.; tobacco, cotton, sugar, yerba-maté, hides, wines; p. (estd. 1960) *30,700*.

Villavicencio, *t.*, cap. Meta, Colombia, S. America; cattle raising; p. (estd. 1962) *48,355*.

Villaviciosa, *spt.*, Spain; on N. cst. 10 m. E. of Gijon; p. (1957) *20,348*.

Villefranche, *t.*, Rhône, France; on R. Rhône, nr. Lyons; cottons, wines; p. (1962) *24,957*.

Villejuif, *t.*, Seine, France; p. (1962) *46,130*.

Villena, *t.*, Alicante, Spain; silk, salt, brandy; p. (1957) *19,994*.

Villeneuve St. Georges, *t.*, Val-de-Marne, France; marshalling yards; p. (1962) *25,231*.

Villeurbanne, *t.*, Rhône, France; sub. Lyons; silk, rayon, metallurgy, chemicals, leather, glass; p. (1962) *107,630*.

Villingen, *t.*, Baden-Württemberg, Germany; in the Black Forest; clocks, elec., metals; p. (1963) *34,000*.

Vilnius (Wilno, Vilna), *cap.*, Lithuanian S.S.R.; Polish from 1919 to 1939; univ., cath.; timber, chemicals, engin.; p. (1967) *305,000*.

Vilvorde, *t.*, Brabant, Belgium; on R. Senne; oil and chemical factories; p. (1962) *32,133*.

Viña del Mar, *t.*, Chile; social resort; textiles, sugar; p. (1960) *126,441*.

Vincennes, *t.*, Ind., U.S.A.; milling, glass, steelwks.; p. (1960) *18,046*.

Vincennes, *sub.*, Paris, France; p. (1962) *50,499*.

Vindhya, *mtn. range*, Madhya Prad., India; separating the Deccan from the Ganges basin

Vindhya Pradesh, *former st.* Indian Union; now absorbed into Madhya Pradesh 1 Nov. 1956; cereals, oil seeds; coal, iron, copper, bauxite.

Vinnitsa, *t.*, Ukrainian S.S.R.; on R. Bug, 120 m. S.W. of Kiev; agr. mkt. t.; engin., chemicals, textiles; p. (1967) *154,000*.

Virginia, *st.*, U.S.A.; S. of Md.; tobacco culture; famous for natural bridge in Rockbridge County and mineral springs; "Virginia Leaf" tobacco is the finest the U.S. produces; rayon, shipbldg., iron, coal, chemicals; cap. Richmond; a. 40,815 sq. m.; p. (1960) *3,966,949. See also* W. Virginia. [Eng.

Virginia Water, *artificial L.*, nr. Windsor, Berks.

Virgin Is. (Brit.), part of Leeward Is. gr., W. Indies, a. 59 sq. m.; lgst. I. Tortola; fruit, vegetables, charcoal, rum, sugar, tobacco; p. (estd. 1965) *8,500*.

Virgin Isles (U.S.A.), gr. in the W. Indies; E. of Puerto Rico; purchased by U.S.A. from Denmark 1917, comprising the Is. of St. Croix, St. Thomas and St. John, and about 50 sm. Is.; total a. 133 sq. m.; oil refinery projected at St. Croix, p. (1950) *26,665*.

Visby, *old spt.*, Sweden; on Gotland I. in Baltic Sea; rich in historic interest; Gothic churches; resort; p. (1961) *15,604*.

Viscaya, *Basque prov.*, Spain; on Bay of Biscay; mineral inds., shipping, etc.; cap. Bilbao; a. 836 sq. m.; p. (1959) *722,030*.

Vistula, *R.*, Poland; rising in Silesia, and flowing past Krakow and through Poland to the Baltic nr. Gdańsk; navigable from Krakow to the sea; length 693 m.

Vitebsk, *t.*, Byelorussian S.S.R.; on R. Dvina, 354 m. W. of Moscow; textile, machin. tools, food inds.; rly. junction; p. (1967) *194,000*.

Viterbo, *c.*, Italy; N. of Rome; alum mines, matches; p. (1961) *49,543*.

Vitim, *R.*, E., Siberia, R.S.F.S.R.; flows to R. Lena; length 900 m.

Vitória, *spt.*, Brazil; exp. coffee, cocoa, fruit, iron ore; sugar refining, boots, shoes, textiles, cement; p. (1960) *85,242*.

Vitoria, *cap.*, Alava, Spain; wine, hardware, mules, horses; p. (1959) *60,148*.

Vittoria, *t.*, Sicily, Italy; silk mftg.; p. *38,628*.

Vittorio Veneto, *t.*, Italy; N. of Venice; resort; mineral springs; silk; p. *24,234*.

Vizagapatam, *impt. spt.*, E. cst. India; Andhra Prad.; exp. manganese and other mineral ores, tobacco, oil-seed, myrabalams and coir; sm. shipyard; oil-refining; fertilisers; p. (1961) *182,004*.

Vizcaino Bay, Lower Cal., Mexico.

Vizcaya, *prov.*, N. Spain; cap. Bilbao; a. 836 sq. m.; p. (1950) *569,188*.

Vizeu, *dist.*, Portugal; cap. Vizeu; a. 1,955 sq. m.; p. (1960) *498,292*. [*76,808*.

Vizianagram, *t.*, Andhra Prad., India; p. (1961)

Vlaardingen, *fishing t.*, S. Holland, Neth.; on R. Nieuwe Maas; p. (1967) *74,582*.

Vladimir, *c.*, R.S.F.S.R.; between Gorki and Moscow; cath.; farm produce, fruit, tobacco, engin., chemicals; p. (1967) *203,000*.

Vladivostok, *t.*, *ch. spt.*, Siberia, U.S.S.R.; univ., H.Q. Army of the Far East; terminus of the Trans-Siberian rly. and airline from Moscow; oil-refining; p. (1967) *379,000*. [Neth.

Vlieland, *Friesian I.*, at entrance to IJsselmeer.

Vlissingen, *spt.*, *wat. pl.*; Walcheren I., Zeeland, Neth.; summer resort, fishing and shipbldg. ctr.; p. (1967) *38,564*.

Vlonë, *spt.*, Albania; on Strait of Otranto, Adriatic Sea; salt; oil pipe-line connects from Kuçovë; p. (1960) *33,000*.

Vltava, *R.*, Bohemia, Czechoslovakia; flows to R. Elbe, below Prague; length 262 m.

Voghera, *t.*, Italy; silks; p. *30,422*.

Voi, *t.*, *impt. rly. junction*, Kenya, E. Africa; 90 m. N.W. of Mombasa on rly. to Nairobi; branch connection with Tanzania rly. system allows agr. produce from Arusha and Moshi dists. to pass through Mombasa as alternative to Tanga.

Voiron, *t.*, Isère, France; on R. Isère nr. Grenoble; p. (1962) *15,585*.

Volga, *R.*, U.S.S.R.; rises on Vladai plateau, flows in a serpentine course to the Caspian at Astrakhan; frozen in winter; 2,325 m. long.

Volga Baltic Waterway (Mariinsk Waterway), R.S.F.S.R.; inland deep water navigation network linking Black Sea and Caspian Sea in S. with Baltic Sea and White Sea in N.

Volgograd (former Stalingrad), *c.*, R.S.F.S.R.; on R. Volga, S. of Saratov; steel, engin., chemicals, oil-refining, hydro-elec. sta.; fierce siege and successful defence Sept. to Nov. 1942 turning point of the last war; p. (1967) *720,000*.

Volhynia, *dist.*, part of Ukraine S.S.R., U.S.S.R.; on Polish frontier (Polish 1919–39); a. 13,750 sq. m.; now prov. of Lutsk and Rovno.

Volkhov, *R.*, R.S.F.S.R.; flows from L. Ilmen to L. Ladoga; length 130 m.

Völklingen, *t.*, Saarland; on R. Saar; coal-mining, metallurgy; p. (1963) *42,900*.

Volksrust, *t.*, Transvaal, S. Africa; dairying; rly. wkshps.; p. (1960) *8,096* inc. *3,776* Europeans.

Vologda, *t.*, R.S.F.S.R., U.S.S.R.; engin., textiles, sawmilling; p. (1967) *166,000*. [(1951) *51,134*.

Vólos, *spt.*, Greece; at head of G. of Vólos; p.

Volpiano, nr. Turin, Italy; oil refinery under construction; pipeline to Geneva projected.

Volsk, *t.*, R.S.F.S.R.; on R. Volga; gd. tr.; iron-wks., tanneries, milling; p. (1959) *62,000*.

Volta Redonda, Rio de Janeiro, Brazil; steel plants; p. (1960) *83,973*.

Volta (White Volta), *R.*, drains extensive terr. in Niger Bend, flows S. through Ghana |to delta on Guinea cst. 70 m. E. of Accra; forms main means of communication; rapids make through navigation impossible; length 950 m. Volta R. project for industrialisation of Ghana: dam and power plant at Akosombo, aluminium smelter at Tema. *See also* Black Volta.

Voltaic Republic (former Upper Volta), *ind. sov. st.*, W. Africa; cap. Ouagadougou; a. 122,000 sq. m.; p. (1961) *3,635,000*.

Volterra, *hill t.*, Tuscany, Italy; Etruscan and mediaeval walls; alabaster; p. *19,054*. [*10,000*.

Voltri, *t.*, Italy; shrine, shipbldg., ironwks.; p.

Volzhskiy, *t.*, R.S.F.S.R.; new town 10 m. E. of Volgagrad; p. (1959) *67,000*.

Vorarlberg, *prov.*, Austria; cap. Bregenz (*q.v.*); a. 1,004 sq. m.; p. (1961) *226,323*. [*11,780*.

Vordingborg, S., *t.*, Zealand, Denmark; p. (1960)

Vorkuta, *dist.*, Siberia, R.S.F.S.R.; about 120 m. W. of mouth of R. Ob; new coal-mining ctr. which supplies entire European north U.S.S.R.; p. of Vorkuta t. (1959) *55,000*.

Voronezh, *region*, R.S.F.S.R., U.S.S.R.; agr.

stock-rearing, woodwork and domestic mnfs.; cap. Voronezh.

Voronezh, t., R.S.F.S.R., U.S.S.R.; on R. Voronezh nr. its junction with R. Don; univ.; impt. comm. ctr.; synthetic rubber, engin.; p. (1967) 592,000.

Voroshilovgrad see Lugansk.

Voroshilovsk, t., Ukrainian S.S.R.; 25 m. S.W. of Lugansk; ctr. of iron, steel and coking inds.; p. (1956) 98,000.

Vosges, mtn. chain, E. France; 190 m. long; highest summit, the Ballon de Guebwiller (4,672 ft.).

Vosges, E. frontier dep., France; agr., dairying, vineyards, textiles, coal, stone; cap. Epinal; a. 2,305 sq. m.; p. (1962) 380,676.

Voskresensk, t., R.S.F.S.R.; S.E. Moscow; lignite, chemicals, fertilisers; p. (1954) 50,000.

Votkinsk, t., R.S.F.S.R.; 38 m. N.E. of Izhevsk; lge. engin. plant; p. (1959) 59,000.

Voyusa, R., rises in Greece, flows N.W. through Albania into Strait of Otranto.

Vranja, t., Jugoslavia; flax and hemp culture and mnf.; nr. is health resort of Vranyskas Banya; p. (1959) 15,000.

Vratca, t., Bulgaria; on R. Vratcanska; jewellery, wine, silk, tanning; p. (1956) 26,582.

Vrede, t., O.F.S., S. Africa; agr. ctr.; horse-breeding; p. (1960) 6,770 (inc. 2,106 whites).

Vrsac, t., Jugoslavia; milling, wine, brandy; p. (1959) 30,000.

Vryburg, t., Cape Province, S. Africa; gold field in a.; stock-raising; p. (1960) 14,597 (inc. 4 809 whites).

Vryheid, t., Natal, S. Africa; coal, iron, copper, gold, silver, lead mines; p. (1960) 10,783 (inc. 4,920 whites).　　[Romania and Transylvania.

Vulcan Pass, in the Carpathian Mtns., between

Vulcano, I., Lipari gr., Tyrrhenian Sea; located 12 m. off N.E. cst., Sicily; active volcano; gave its name as generic title for this type of mtn.

Vychegda, R., Komi A.S.S.R., R.S.F.S.R.; flows W. to N. Dvina R.; length 700 m.

Vyrnwy, L., artificial reservoir, Montgomery, Wales; with a dam 1,180 ft. long furnishing water for Liverpool; 5 m. long; a. 1,121 acres

Vyshni-Volochek, t., R.S.F.S.R., U.S.S.R.; 74 m. N.W. of Kalinin; flour-milling, textiles, glass inds.; p. (1959) 66,000.

# W

Waag, see Vah.

Waal, R., Neth.; S. arm of R. Rhine.

Wabana, see Bell I.　　　　　　　　　[12,621.

Wabash, c., Ind., U.S.A.; rly. ctr.; p. (1960)

Wabash, R., Ohio and Ind., U.S.A.; trib. of R. Ohio; length 550 m.

Wabash and Erie, canal, Ind., U.S.A.; longest canal in U.S.A.; 476 m. long.

Wabush, t., Labrador, Canada; iron ore mines; p. (1965) 2,700.

Waco, c., Texas, U.S.A.; on Brazos R.; univ.; cotton ctr., woollens, grain, iron, leather; p. (1960) 97,807.

Wadai, dist., Equatorial Africa; nr. L. Chad; desert and oases; pastoral; ivory, ostrich feathers; a. 17,000 sq. m.; p. (1947) 1,000,000.

Wadden Zee, G., between W. Frisian Is. and N. Neth.

Waddington, mtn., B.C., Canada; alt. 13,260 ft.

Wadebridge, spt., rural dist., Cornwall; at head of Camel estuary 6 m. N.W. of Bodmin; china clay; p. (rural dist. 1961) 14,907.

Wädenswil, t., Zürich, Switzerland; on L. Zürich; silk, wool, textiles; wine, fruit; p. 10,000.

Wadi Halfa, t., Sudan, N.E. Africa; on R. Nile; at 2nd cataract; rly. terminus of Sudan rlys.; to be inundated by Aswan L.; new t. Khashm el Girba for inhabitants.

Wad Medani, t., cap., Blue Nile Prov., Sudan, Africa; grain, oil, soap; p. (1956) 57,000.

Wadsworth, t., Ohio, U.S.A.; matches, valves, engin.; p. (1960) 10,635.

Wagadugu, see Ouagadougou.　　　　　[Canada.

Wager Bay, inlet, of Hudson Bay, N.W. Terr.,

Wagga Wagga, c., N.S.W., Australia; on R. Murrumbidgee; wheat, agr. pastoral ctr., dairying; large stock mkt., timber, rubber; p. (1966) 25,939.

Wahiawa, t., Oahu I., Hawaii; pineapples; p. (1960) 15,512.　　　　　　　　　[Indonesia.

Waigeo, I., off N. cst., Dutch New Guinea,

Waihi, t., N.I., N.Z.; gold-mining; p. (1961) 3,164.

Waikaremoana, L., N.I., N.Z.; hydro-elec. power plant.　　　　　　　[length 220 m.

Waikato, R., N.I., N.Z.; the longest in N.Z.;

Waimate, t., S.I., N.Z.; agr. ctr., soft fruits; p. (1961) 3,308.

Wairakei, t., N.I., N.Z.; on L. Taupo; health resort; geothermal power sta. opened Nov. 1958.

Wairoa, t., N.I., N.Z.; on R. Wairoa; p. (1961) 4,301.

Waitaki, t., Otago, S.I., N.Z.; Benmore hydro-elec. power plant projected; p. (1961) 11,018.

Waitzen, t., Hungary; on R. Danube.

Wakamatsu, t., Kyushu, Japan; now part of Kitakyushu City newly formed (1963) (q.v.); lacquer ware, mnfs.; p. (1960) 106,975.

Wakatipu, L., Otago, S.I., N.Z.; 52 m. long, 3 m. wide; 1,200 ft. deep; 1,070 ft. above sea-level.

Wakayama, spt., Honshu, Japan; cotton; p. (1964) 313,000.

Wake I., Pac. Oc.; between Marianas and Hawaii; calling-place on trans-Pacific air-routes; belongs to U.S.A.

Wakefield, c., co. bor., W.R. Yorks, Eng.; on R. Calder; 8 m. S. of Leeds; cath.; woollens, brewing, coal, iron, boiler mkg.. chemicals, glass, engin.; p. (estd. 1967) 60,200.

Wakefield, t., Va., U.S.A.; George Washington's birthplace; p. 687.

Walachia, dist., S. Romania; cereals, fruits; ch. t. Bucharest; a. 29,561 sq. m.; p. 5,029,212.

Walbrzych (Waldenburg), t., Silesia, Poland; German before 1945; textiles, coal, porcelain, iron ware; p. (1965) 125,000.

Walcheren, I., Zeeland, Neth.; 12 m. long, low-lying, agr.; was flooded to stop German advance in Second World War.

Waldeck, see Hessen-Nassau.

Waldenburg, see Walbrzych.

Wales, principality, S.W. of Gr. Britain; flanked by Irish Sea, St. George's Channel and Bristol Channel; mtns.; coal, slate, oats, barley, good pasturage. smelting tin, copper, iron; cap. Cardiff; a. 7,388 sq. m.; p. (1961) 2,196,943 (excluding Monmouthshire).

Walker, t., Northumberland, Eng.; on R. Tyne; industl. sub. of Newcastle.

Wallaceburg, t., Ontario, Canada; glass, brass, iron; sugar, flour; p. (1961) 7,881.

Wallaroo, spt., S. Australia; clothing, fertilisers; p. (1966) 2,093.

Wallasey, co. bor., on Mersey estuary, adjoining Birkenhead, Cheshire, Eng.; residtl., seaside resort (New Brighton); p. (estd. 1967) 102,470.

Walla Walla, t., Wash., U.S.A.; on Mill Creek; cereal and fruit ctr., agr. tools, flour. leather; p. (1960) 24,536.

Wallensee, L., Switzerland; 11 m. long.

Wallhamn, pt., Sweden; on Tjörn I., 20 m. N.W. of Göteborg.

Wallingford, t., mun. bor., Berks, Eng.; on R. Thames, to N. of its gap between Chiltern Hills and Lambourn Downs; p. (estd. 1967) 5,870.

Wallingford, t., Conn., U.S.A.; steel, brass, silver and nickel ware; tools, wire; p. (1960) 29,920.

Wallington, t., N.J., U.S.A.; curtains, paints; p. (1960) 9,261.

Wallis Archipelago, I. gr., S. Pacific; a. 40 sq. m.; status as overseas terr. Fr. Community (1962); p. (1959) 6,000.

Wallsend, t., mun. bor., Northumberland, Eng.; on N. bank of R. Tyne; 4 m. below Newcastle; coal-mining, shipbldg., engin., iron, plywood, plastics and quartz glass; p. (estd. 1967) 45,290.

Walmer, t., Kent, Eng.; 2 m. S. of Deal; holiday resort; cas.. residence of Warden of Cinque Ports; p. 5,335.

Walney, I., off cst. of Lancs., Eng.; opposite Barrow.

Walpole, t., Mass., U.S.A.; nr. Boston; p. (1960) 14,053.

Walpole, I., dep. of New Caledonia; Pac. Oc.; Fr. possession, lies S.E. of Maré (Loyalty Is.).

Walsall, t., co. bor., Staffs, Eng.; 5 m. E. of Wolverhampton; leather and iron goods, engin., steel tubes; p. (estd. 1967) 183,680.

Walsham, N., see North Walsham.

Walsingham, C., on Cumberland Peninsula, Baffin I., Canada.

Walsum, t., N. Rhine-Westphalia, Germany; at confluence of Emscher and Rhine; coal-mining, paper, cellulose; p. (1963) 46,400.

Waltham, c., Mass., U.S.A.; nr. Boston; watchmkg., textiles, motors, furniture, shoes, paper; p. (1960) *55,413.*

Waltham Abbey (Waltham Holy Cross), *t.*, Essex, Eng.; 13 m. N.E. London, on edge of Epping Forest; glasshouses (tomatoes); Norman nave of abbey part of parish church; gunpowder factories S. of t.; p. (1961) *11,655.*

Waltham Forest, *outer bor.*, E. London, Eng.; incorporating former bors. of Chingford, Leyton, Walthamstow; industl. and residtl.; p. (1966) *240,000.*

Walthamstow, *see* Waltham Forest.

Walton and Weybridge, *urb. dist.*, Surrey, Eng.; on R. Thames, 17 m. S.W. of London; engin., aircraft; p. (estd. 1967) *51,190.*

Walton-le-Dale, *t.*, *urb. dist.*, N.E. Lancs, Eng.; on R. Ribble, 2 m. E. of Preston; mkt. gardening, cottons, timber; p. (estd. 1967) *24,350.*

Walvis Bay, *dist.* and *spt.*, administered by S.W. Africa; a. 374 sq. m.; fishing, whaling; p. (1961) *16,490* (inc. *5,067* Europeans).

Wandsbeck, *t.*, Germany; sub. of Hamburg; beer, brandy, tobacco; p. *40,000.*

Wandsworth, *inner bor.*, S.W. London, Eng.; inc. Battersea; on R. Wandle at influx into Thames; oil-mills, metal-wks., paper, brewing; p. (1966) *332,000.*

Wanganui, *c.*, N.I., N.Z.; on R. Wanganui; wool, grain, meat, dairy prod.; p. (1961) *35,718.*

Wanganui, *R.*, N.I., N.Z.; l. 160 m., famous for its beauty.

Wangaratta, *c.*, Victoria, Australia; 145 m. from Melbourne; agr. dist.; nylon and woollen wks.; p. (1966) *15,167.*

Wankie, *t.*, Rhodesia: site of coalmng. ind.; 215 m. N.W. Bulawayo; p. (1958) *19,610* (incl. 2,460 Europeans). [Hills: lead-mines.

Wanlockhead, *vil.*, Dumfries, Scot.; in Lowther

Wanne-Eickel, *t.*, N. Rhine-Westphalia, Germany; N.W. of Bochum; coal-mining, chemicals; p. (1963) *107,800.*

Wansbeck, *R.*, Northumberland, Eng.; flows E. from Pennines into N. Sea 3 m. N. of Blyth; length 23 m.

Wanstead and Woodford, *see* Redbridge.

Wantage, *mkt. t.*, *urb. dist.*, Berks, Eng.; in Vale of the White Horse; hempen cloth, brass; p. (1961), *5,940.*

Wapping, *Thames-side dist.*, London, Eng.; contains the London Docks; industl.; p. *3,200.*

Warangal, *t.*, Andhra Prad., India; p. (1961) *155,106.*

Waratah, *t.*, N. Tasmania, Australia; tin-mining ctr.; magnetite ore on R. Savage, 25 m. W.S.W.

Warburg, *t.*, Germany; on R. Diemel; industl.

Wardha, *R.*, Madhya Pradesh, India; trib. of R. Wainganga; length 254 m.

Ware, *mkt. t.*, *urb. dist.*, Herts, Eng.; on R. Lea; 2 m. N.E. of Hertford; malting, bricks; p. (1961) *9,987.*

Wareham, *mkt. t.*, *mun. bor.*, Dorset, Eng.; on R. Frome, on N. of I. of Purbeck, 8 m. S.W. of Poole; agr. engin., pipes; p. (estd. 1967) *3,490.*

Waremme (Borgworm), *t.*, Belgium; p. (1962) *6,818.* [dairying, iron; p. (1963) *19,693.*

Waren, *t.*, Neubrandenburg, E. Germany; timber,

Warley, *t.*, *co. bor.*, Worc., Eng.; p. (estd. 1967) *169,440.*

Warminster, *t.*, *urb. dist.*, Wilts, Eng.; on Wylye watershed at edge of Salisbury Plain; agr. mkt., gloves, silk; p. (1961) *9,855.*

Warnemünde, *spt.*, Germany; ferry pt. for rail traffic between Berlin and Copenhagen; shipbldg., resort; p. *6,374.*

Warragamba Dam, 40 m. W Sydney, New S. Wales, Australia; 450 ft. high, opened Oct. 14, 1960; when in full operation a 36-mile lake will be formed behind dam, impounding 460,000 millions gallons of water.

Warrego, *R.*, Queensland, N.S.W., Australia; trib. of R. Darling; length 400 m.

Warren, *c.*, Ohio, U.S.A.; on Mahoning R.; coal and iron-mining, iron and steel mftg.; p. (1960) *59,648.*

Warren, *bor.*, Penns., U.S.A.; on Allegheny R.; natural gas, petroleum, oil-refining; furniture, tools; p. (1960) *14,505.*

Warrenpoint, *spt.*, *urb. dist.*, Down, N. Ireland; at head of Carlingford Lough; holiday resort; p. (1966) *3,579.*

Warrenton, *t.*, Cape Province, S. Africa; cheesemkg.; p. (1960) *5,980* (inc. *1,559* whites).

Warrington, *t.*, *co. bor.*, Lancs., Eng.; on R. Mersey, 18 m. E. of Liverpool; aluminium rolling and drawing, soap, chemicals, brewing, iron and steel; to be expanded as New Town with p. *205,000* by 1991; p. (estd. 1967) *73,880.*

Warrnambool, *c.*, *spt.*, Victoria, Australia; mkt., agr. dairying, wood, timber, plastics, engin.; p. (1966) *17,497.*

Warsak Dam, W. Pakistan; on Kabul R., 15 m. N. of Peshawar, nr. Khyber Pass; hydroelec. power and irrigation project.

Warsaw or Warszawa, *prov.*, Poland; on Vistula and Bug Rs.; a 10,900 sq. m.; p. (1965) *2,453,000.*

Warsaw or Warszawa, *cap.*, Poland; on R. Vistula; cath., univ.; rly. ctr.; iron and steel, engin., textiles, chemicals; p. (1965) *1,253,000.*

Warsop, *t.*, *urb. dist.*, Notts, Eng.; 4 m. N.E. of Mansfield; limestone, gravel; p. (1961) *11,596.*

Warta, *R.*, Poland; trib. of R. Oder; length 450 m.

Warwick, *t.*, Queensland, Australia; coal, agr., sawmilling; p. (1962) *9,813.*

Warwick, *co.*, Eng.; coal, iron, limestone, fruit, livestock, motors, metal goods; co. t. Warwick; a. 976 sq. m.; p. (1966) *2,095,000.*

Warwick, *co. t.*, *mun. bor.*, Warwick, Eng.; on R. Avon, 8 m. S.W. of Coventry; cas.; agr. implements, brewing, malting rope, iron; p. (estd. 1967) *17,700.*

Warwick, *c.*, R.I., U.S.A.; on Narragansett Bay; cotton mnfs.; p. (1960) *68,504.*

Wasatch Mtns., *range*, Utah and Idaho, U.S.A.

Wash, The, *bay*, N. Sea between Lincs and Norfolk, Eng.; 22 m. long, 15 m. wide; partly reclaimed.

Washa, *L.*, La., U.S.A.; 14 m. long.

Washburne, *mtn range*, Yellowstone National Park, U.S.A.; highest summit 10,345 ft.

Washington, *t.*, *urb. dist.*, Durham, Eng.; 5 m. S.E. of Gateshead; coal, iron and steel, stone quarrying, chemicals; designated "New Town" 1964; p. (estd. 1965) *20,000.*

Washington, *st.*, U.S.A.; coal, iron, minerals, forests, agr.; cap. Olympia; ch. ts. Seattle and Tacoma; a. 68,192 sq. m.; p. (1960) *2,853,214.*

Washington, *c.*, *cap.*, U.S.A.; in Dist. of Columbia, on Potomac R.; White House, Capitol, 4 univs., etc.; printing and engraving; world's first weather ctr. 1965; p. (1960) *746,958.*

Washington, *t.*, Penns., U.S.A.; coal, petroleum, steel, glass, chemicals; p. (1960) *23,540.*

Washington I., Pac. Oc. (Gilbert and Ellice Is. col.); a. 6 sq. m., coral atolls; copra; p. *86.*

Washita, *R.*, Ark. and La., U.S.A.; trib. of Red R.; length 400 m. [(1962) *13,923.*

Wasmes, *t.*, Belgium; nr. Mons; coal-mining; p.

Wasquehal, *t.*, Nord, France; textiles, chemicals, oil-refineries; p. (1954) *12,363.*

Wast Water, *L.*, Cumberland, Eng.; 3 m. long.

Watchet, *t.*, *urb. dist.*, Somerset, Eng.; on cst. of Bristol Channel; 5 m. E. of Minehead; paper mkg., fishing; p. (1961) *2,596.*

Waterbury, *c.*, Conn., U.S.A.; on Naugatuck R.; watches, pins, brass goods, elec. and photographic goods, chemicals; p. (1960) *107,130.*

Waterford, *co.*, Munster, Ireland; agr., livestock, fisheries; co. t., Waterford; a. 721 sq. m.; p. (1966) *72,986.*

Waterford, *co. t.*, *spt.*, Waterford, Ireland; on R. Suir; cath.; brewing, fishing; p. (1966) *29,642.*

Waterloo, *vil.*, Belgium; battle, 1815; p. (1962) *12,261.*

Waterloo, *c.*, Iowa, U.S.A.; on Cedar R.; agr. produce and tools; p. (1960) *71,755.*

Waterloo, *t.*, Ontario, Canada; p. (1961) *21,366.*

Waterloo-(with-Seaforth), *urb. dist.*, Lancs, Eng.; at mouth of R. Mersey; N. sub. of Liverpool; residtl.; p. *15,447.* [cattle; agr. ctr.

Waterpoort, *t.*, Transvaal, S. Africa; on R. Sand;

Watertown, *t.*, Conn., U.S.A.; plastics, textiles, hardware, wire prods.; p. (1960) *14,812.*

Watertown, *t.*, Mass., U.S.A.; on Charles R.; arsenal; p. (1960) *39,092.*

Watertown, *c.*, N.Y., U.S.A.; on Black R.; carriage wks., steam-engines, silk, agr. tools; p. (1960) *33,306.* [packing; p. (1960) *14,077.*

Watertown, *t.*, S.D., U.S.A.; machin., meat-

Watertown, *c.*, Wis., U.S.A.; on Rock R.; univ.; mnfs.; p. (1960) *13,943.*

Waterville, *c.*, Me., U.S.A.; on Kennebec R.; univ : cotton mnfs., rly wks.; p. (1960) *18,695.*

Watervliet, *c.*, N.Y., U.S.A.; on Hudson R.;

arsenal; iron goods, woollens, asbestos goods; p. (1960) *13,917.*

**Watford**, *t., mun. bor.*, Herts, Eng.; on R. Colne, 16 m. N.W. of London; mkt.; many varied inds., inc. light and elec. engin., paper, printing; p. (estd. 1967) *76,310.*

**Wath**, *t., urb. dist.*, W.R. Yorks, Eng.; 4 m. N. of Rotherham; coal, quarrying; p. (1961) *15,191.*

**Watling**, *Brit. I.*, Bahamas, W. Indies; reputed landing place of Columbus.

**Watlington**, *t.*, Oxford, Eng.; at N. foot of Chiltern Hills, 5 m. S.W. of Princes Risborough; lace; p. *1,386.*      [holiday resort

**Watson's Bay**, N.S.W., Australia; nr. Sydney;

**Wattenscheid**, *t.*, N. Rhine–Westphalia, Germany; E. of Essen; coal, metals, footwear; p. (1963) *79,700.*

**Wattrelos**, *t.*, Nord, France; nr. Lille; textiles, mnfs.; p. (1962) *41,319.*

**Watu Bella Is.**, Moluccas, Indonesia; coconuts, sago.

**Wau**, *cap.*, Bahr-el-Ghazal, Sudan, N.E. Africa; p. *6,000.*

**Waukegan**, *c.*, Ill., U.S.A.; on L. Michigan; summer resort; steel, brass, motors, sugar refining; livestock, agr. ctr.; p. (1960) *55,719.*

**Waukesha**, *t.*, Wis., U.S.A.; health resort; p. (1960) *30,004.*

**Wausau**, *c.*, Wis., U.S.A.; on Wisconsin R.; timber, paper, machin., leather, silver-fox farms; p. (1960) *31,943.*

**Wauwatosa**, *c.*, Wis., U.S.A.; sub. of Milwaukee; p. (1960) *56,923.*      [50 m.

**Waveney**, *R.*, Norfolk and Suffolk, Eng.; length

**Waverly**, *t.*, N.Y., U.S.A.; dairying, tr. ctr.; p. (1960) *5,950.*      [(1960) *12,749.*

**Waxahachie**, *t.*, Texas, U.S.A.; rly. ctr.; p.

**Wayatinah**, Tasmania, Australia; hydro-elec. commission vil. (1956), dam, lagoon and power sta.; at confluence of Nive and Derwent Rs.

**Waycross**, *t.*, Ga., U.S.A.; rly. wks., timber, naval stores, machin., agr. prods.; p. (1960) *20,944.*

**Waynesboro**, *t.*, Penns., U.S.A.; industl.; p. (1960) *10,427.*      [(1960) *26,203.*

**Wazan** or **Ouezzan**, *sacred c.*, Morocco; p.

**Waziristan**, *dist.*, N.W. frontier, Pakistan; mtns.; a. 5,000 sq. m.; p. (1951) *264,000.*

**Weald, The**, wooded and pastoral tracts S.E. Eng., extending from Folkestone, Kent, through Surrey, Hants and Sussex to the sea about Beachy Head.

**Wear**, *R.*, Durham, Eng.; rises in the Pennines, flows through Durham to N. Sea at Sunderland; length 60 m.      [length 45 m.

**Weaver**, *R.*, Cheshire, Eng.; trib. of R. Mersey;

**Weaver Hills**, Staffs, Eng.; alt. 1,300 ft.

**Webb City**, *c.*, Mo., U.S.A.; lead, zinc mining; p. (1960) *6,740.*

**Webster**, *t.*, Mass., U.S.A.; on French R.; textiles, footwear; p. (1960) *12,072.*

**Webster Grove**, *t.*, Mo., U.S.A.; p. (1960) *28,990.*

**Weddell Sea**, arm of S. Atl. Oc., Antarctica; whaling and sealing.

**Wednesbury**, *t., mun. bor.*, Staffs, Eng.; 8 m. N.W. of Birmingham; iron, aluminium, metal inds.; rly. carriages, elec. goods; p. (1961) *34,511.*

**Wednesfield**, *urb. dist.*, Staffs, Eng.; nr. Wolverhampton; locks and keys, metal refining, engin.; p. (1961) *32,936.*

**Wed Zem**, *t.*, Morocco; impt. production of phosphate; p. *12,223.*

**Weehawken**, *t.*, N.J., U.S.A.; coal depot, rly. ctr.; mnfs.; p. (1960) *13,504.*      [*34,308.*

**Weert**, *t.*, Limburg, Neth.; industl.; p. (1967)

**Wei** *R.*, Shensi, China; rises in highlands of Kansu, flows E. between highlands of Shansi and Tsinling Shan to join Yellow River nr. Tungkwan; valley contains very fertile loess soils; formed cradle of Chinese civilisation; length approx. 500 m.

**Weiden**, *t.*, Bavaria, Germany; porcelain, glass, textiles; p. (1963) *42,200.*

**Weifang**, *c.*, Shantung, China; coal-mng. ctr.; tobacco processing; p. (1953) *149,000.*

**Weihai** *spt.*, Shantung, China; cotton, silk, oil-seed; summer resort; p. *222,000.*

**Weimar**, *t.*, Erfurt, E. Germany; on R. Ilm; 2 cas., Goethe and Schiller houses; cultural institutes; elec., metal, footwear, textiles, machin.; p. (1963) *64,406.*

**Weinheim**, *t.*, Baden-Württemberg, Germany; cas.; leather, machin., rubber; p. (1963) *28,800.*

**Weipa**, Queensland, Australia; new t., pt., and alumina plant; bauxite.

**Weissenfels**, *t.*, Halle, E. Germany; on R. Saale; cas.; footwear, paper, metals; p. (1963) *46,600.*

**Weisshorn**, *mtn. peak*, Switzerland; alt. 14,770 ft.

**Weisskirchen**, *see* Bela Crkva.

**Wejh**, *spt.*, Hejaz, Saudi Arabia.

**Welkom**, *t.*, O.F.S., S. Africa; ctr. of O.F.S. goldfields; p. (1964) *128,000.*

**Welland**, *t.*, Ont., Canada; on Welland Canal; farm machin., steel tubing, castings, rope; p. (1956) *15,935.*

**Welland**, *R.*, Northants and Lincs, Eng.; rises in Northampton Heights, flows N.E., enters The Wash 10 m. below Spalding; length 70 m.

**Welland Ship Canal**, Ontario, Canada; connects Ls. Erie and Ontario; length 27 m.; 2-lane waterway projected. 1963.      [*26,071.*

**Wellesley**, *t.*, Mass., U.S.A.; residtl.; p. (1960)

**Wellesley Is.**, *gr.*, in the Gulf of Carpentaria, belonging to Queensland, Australia.

**Wellingborough**, *t., urb. dist.*, Northants, Eng.; on R. Nene, 9 m. N.E. of Northampton; mkt., footwear, iron smelting, brewing; p. (estd. 1967) *33,520.*

**Wellington**, *mkt. t., urb. dist.*, Shropshire, Eng.; 12 m. E. of Shrewsbury; steel wks., brewing, toys, storage tanks, timber yds., agr.; its ancient name was Watling Town, because it stood on the line of Watling Street; p. (1961) *13,630.*

**Wellington**, *mkt. t.*, Somerset, Eng.; 6 m. S.W. Taunton, anc. woollen ind. still survives; dairy prod.; p. (1961) *7,523.*

**Wellington**, *c., spt.*, N.I., cap. N.Z.; univ.; foundries, cold storage, soap, candles, footwear; p. (1964) *158,700* of c. *125,900.*

**Wellington**, *prov.*, N.I., N.Z.; a. 10,870 sq. m.; p. (1961) *473,621.*

**Wellington**, *t.*, Cape Prov., S. Africa; tanning, dried fruits, wine, jam, textiles; p. (1960) *10,330* (inc. *3,736* whites).

**Wellington**, *L.*, Gippsland, Victoria, Australia; shallow; fishing.

**Wells**, *c., mun. bor.*, Somerset, Eng.; at W. foot of Mendip Hills; cath., bishop's palace; paper, brushes, textiles, scientific inst.; p. (estd. 1967) *7,620.*

**Wells-next-the-Sea**, *t., urb. dist.*, Norfolk, Eng.; ancient pt. on N. cst. of E. Anglia, 14 m. W. of Sheringham; whelks, cockles and mussels; p. (1961) *2,490.*

**Wellston**, *c.*, Ohio, U.S.A.; rly. ctr.; furniture; p. (1960) *5,728.*

**Wellsville**, *c.*, Ohio, U.S.A.; on Ohio R.; coal-mining, agr.; p. (1960) *7,117.*

**Wels**, *t.*, Austria; machin., leather, paper; natural gas; p. (1961) *41,060.*

**Welshpool**, *mkt. t., mun. bor.*, Montgomery, Wales; on R. Severn, 7 m. N. of Montgomery; nr. is Powis Castle; lt. inds. based on agr., hosiery; p. (1961) *6,332.*

**Welwyn Garden City**, *urb. dist.*, Herts, Eng.; 21 m. N. of London. Founded by Sir Ebenezer Howard in 1920 as the first of the satellite ts. of London; one of the " New Towns " designated 1948, inc. Hatfield, Hertford, and Welwyn rural dist.; pharmaceutics, plastics, radio, and electronics, light inds.; p. (estd. 1967) *41,460.*

**Wem**, *t.*, Salop, Eng.; nr. Shrewsbury; mkt., flour, tanning, malting; p. (1961) *2,603.*

**Wembley**, *former mun. bor.*, Middx., Eng.; now inc. in Brent outer bor. Greater London, (*q.v.*); light ind., sports ctr.; p. (1961) *124,892.*

**Wemyss**, *par.*, Fife, Scot.; fishing pt., coal-mining; p. *26,619.*

**Wemyss Bay**, *t.*, Renfrew, Scot.; holiday resort, residtl.; impt. ctr. for Clyde steamers.

**Wenatchee**, *t.*, Wash., U.S.A.; fruit (apple) ctr. and inds.; p. (1960) *16,726.*

**Wenchow (Wenzhou)**, *c., spt.*, Chekiang, China; nr. mouth of Wu Kiang 230 m. S.W. of Shanghai; textile, silk inds.; exp. wood, tea, agr. prod.; fishing; coastal tr.; p. (1953) *202,000.*

**Wendover**, *t.*, Bucks, Eng.; at N. foot of Chiltern Hills, 4 m. S.E. of Aylesbury, at entrance to wind gap; agr. mkt.; p. (1961) *6,151.*

**Wengen**, *vil.*, Bernese Oberland, Switzerland; alt. 4,200 ft.; resort; p. *1,230.*

**Wenlock** or **Much Wenlock**, *t., mun. bor.*, Salop, Eng.; on N.E. end of Wenlock Edge, 11 m. S.E. of Shrewsbury; iron and coal; p. (1961) *14,929.*

Wenlock Edge, *narrow ridge*, Shropshire, Eng.; extends 18 m. S.W from Much Wenlock to Craven Arms; limestone; moorland, woodland on margins, particularly steep N.W. flank; width 1–1½ m., mainly above 950 ft. alt.

Wensleydale, N.R. Yorks, Eng.; valley in N. Pennines drained E. by R. Ure; cattle reared for fattening on lowland farms; some dairying (cheese); length 35 m.

Wentworth, *t., R. pt.*, N.S.W., Australia; at confluence of Rs. Murray and Darling; ships wool downstream to Morgan and round to Adelaide.

Werdau, *t.*, Karl-Marx-Stadt, E. Germany; on R. Pleisse; textiles, machin., tools; p. (1963) 24,634.

Werdohl, *t.*, N. Rhine–Westphalia, Germany; metal goods, glass; p. (1963) 22,800.

Wermelskirchen, *t.*, N. Rhine–Westphalia, Germany; S.E. of Remscheid; footwear, iron, textiles; p. (1963) 25,200.

Wernigerode, *t.*, Magdeburg, E. Germany; cas.; elec., glass, wood, metals, sugar; p. (1963) 33,161.

Wervicq, *t.*, Belgium; nr. Ypres; tobacco factories; p. (1962) 12,384.

Wesel, *c.*, N. Rhine–Westphalia, Germany; at confluence of Rs. Lippe and Rhine; cath.; machin., potteries; p. (1963) 32,100.

Weser, *R.*, Germany; flows N. to N. Sea at Bremerhaven; navigable for 270 m.; total length 440 m.

Wesermünde, *t.*, Bremen, Germany; nr. mouth of R. Weser; adjoins Bremerhaven; brewing, bricks; p. (1946) 77,491.

Wesseling, *t.*, N. Rhine–Westphalia, Germany; on R. Rhine, S. of Cologne; oil refining, petrochemicals; p. (1963) 21,200.

Wessex, *ancient kingdom*, S. Eng.; inc. Berks, Hants, Wilts, Dorset, Somerset and Devon.

West Allis, *t.*, Wis., U.S.A.; iron and steel goods; p. (1960) 68,157.

West Bengal, *st.*, India; delta of Ganges; rice, jute, oilseeds; cap. Calcutta; a. 33,945 sq. m.; p. (1961) 34,967,634.

West Bridgford, *t., urb. dist.*, Notts, Eng.; at junction of Grantham canal with R. Trent; p. (estd. 1967) 23,030.

West Bromwich, *t., co. bor.*, Staffs, Eng.; on R. Thame, 5 m. N.W. of Birmingham; heavy engin. and allied inds., chemicals, springs, oil red.; p. (estd. 1967) 172,550.

West Chester, *bor.*, Penns., U.S.A.; residtl. sub. Philadelphia; mkt gardening, dairying, agr. tools; p. (1960) 15,705.

West Dean, *rural dist.*, Gloucester, Eng.; coalmining, forestry; p. (1961) 17,472.

West Ham *former co. bor.*, Essex, Eng.; sub. to E. of London; bordered by Rs. Thames and Lea; now inc. in Newham bor., Greater London; residtl.; extensive docks, rubber, soap, jutewks., engin., smelting, chemicals; p. (1961) 157,367.

West Hartford, *t.*, Conn., U.S.A.; residtl. sub. of Hartford; metal goods, ctr. for dairying, tobacco-growing dist.; p. (1960) 62,210.

West Hartlepool, *see* Hartlepool, W.

West Haven, *bor.*, Conn., U.S.A.; sub. of New Haven; p. (1960) 42,526.

West Indies or Antilles, *I. grs.*, Atl. Oc.; extend between the csts of Florida and Venezuela, separating the Caribbean Sea and the G. of Mexico from the Atlantic; sugar, tobacco, fruits, cotton, coffee, cocoa; inc. Cuba, Haiti, Dominican Rep., Bahamas, Barbados, Jamaica, Leeward Is., Trinidad and Tobago, Windward Is., Guadeloupe, Martinique, Curacao, Puerto Rico, Virgin Is.

West Irian, Indonesia; formerly West New Guinea and Dutch col.; came under Indonesian adm. 1 May 1963; cap. Sukarnapura (formerly Kota Baru); a. (inc. Ternate) 115,861 sq. m.; p. (1961) 753,396.

West Lothian, *co.* Scot.; agr., coal, iron, bricks, engin., hosiery; co. t. Linlithgow; a. 120 sq. m.; p. (1961) 92,764.

West New York, *t.*, N.J., U.S.A.; on Hudson R.; grain elevators, silks rubber goods, cotton-seed oil; p. (1960) 35,547. [39,895.

West Orange, *t.*, N.J., U.S.A.; industl.; p. (1960)

West Pakistan, *prov.*, Pakistan; divided into 10 divs.: Karachi, Hyderabad, Khairpur, Bahawalpur, Quetta, Dera Ismail Khan, Peshawar, Lahore, Rawalpindi, and Kalat; ch. c. Lahore;

5 gt. Rs.: Indus with tribs. Jhelum, Chenab, Ravi, and Sutlej; wheat, cotton, rice, oilseeds, rocksalt; a. 300,839 sq. m.; p. (1961) 40,815,000 (excl. Fed. terr. of Karachi).

West Point, *military sta.*, N.Y., U.S.A.; on Hudson R.; Military Academy.

West Springfield, *t.*, Mass., U.S.A.; industl.; p. (1960) 25,385.

West Virginia, *st.*, U.S.A.; coal, salt, petroleum, agr. (cereals, tobacco), pastoral; cap. Charleston; a. 24,181 sq. m.; p. (1960) 1,860,421.

West Warwick, *t.*, R.I., U.S.A.; p. (1960) 21,414.

Westbrook, *c.*, Me., U.S.A.; paper, cottons, silks; p. (1960) 13,820.

Westbury, *t., urb. dist.*, Wilts, Eng.; at N. foot of Salisbury Plain; rly. junction; woollens, bricks, glove mnfs.; p. (1961) 5,409.

Westerwald, *plateau of old volcanic rocks*, W. Germany, ending in steep slope E. of R. Rhine between Koblenz and Bonn; drained to Rhine by R. Lahn and R. Sieg; fertile soil; pastureland or deciduous woodland; sm. quantities of iron ore in Siegerland.

Westfield, *t.*, Fife, Scot.; Lurgi gas plant.

Westfield, *c.*, Mass., U.S.A.; cigars, paper, machin., bicycles, radiators; p. (1960) 26,302.

Westfield, *t.*, N.J., U.S.A.; p. (1960) 31,447.

Westgate-on-Sea, *t.*, Kent, Eng.; nr. Margate; agr., seaside resort; p. 4,554.

Westhoughton, *urb. dist.*, S.E. Lancs, Eng.; coal-mining, cottons; p. (1961) 16,254.

Westland, *prov.*, S.I., N.Z.; coal, timber, gold; cap. Hokitika; a. 4,880 sq. m.; p. (1961) 17,954.

Westmeath, *co.*, Leinster, Ireland; pasture, agr., dairying; with much bog; co. t. Mullingar; a. 708 sq. m.; p. (1966) 52,349.

Westminster, City of, *inner bor.*, London, Eng.; on N. bank of R. Thames; W. of City of London; incorporates former bors. of Paddington and St. Marylebone; contains Houses of Parliament, Westminster Abbey, Government offices, Royal Palaces (Buckingham Palace and St. James's); p. (1966) 263,000.

Westmorland, *co.*, N.W. Eng.; covering part of the Lake Dist. (Windermere, Ullswater, Grasmere, etc.); sheep, oats, bldg.-stone, tourist ind.; cap. Appleby; most populous t., Kendal; a. 789 sq. m.; p. (1966) 67,000.

Westmount, *t.*, Que. Canada; p. (1961) 25,012.

Weston-super-Mare, *t., mun. bor.*, Somerset, Eng.; on Bristol Channel, 20 m. S.W of Bristol; holiday resort; p. (estd. 1967) 44,170.

Westphalia, *see* N. Rhine–Westphalia.

Westport, *spt., urb. dist.*, Mayo, Ireland; on Westport Bay; mkt., cereals; p. (1961) 2,583.

Westport, *spt.*, S.I., N.Z.; on R. Buller; cst. shipping; coal; p. (1961) 5,464.

Westport, *t.*, Conn., U.S.A.; residtl.; woollens, twine, soap, disinfectants; p. (1950) 11,667.

Westray, *I.*, Orkney Is., Scot.; 10 m. long; p. 1,270. [Bay; seaside resort.

Westward Ho!, *vil.*, N. Devon, Eng.; on Bideford

Westwood, *t.*, Queensland, Australia; coal-mining.

Wetherby, *t.*, W.R. Yorks, Eng.; on R. Wharfe; mkt., malting, brewing; p. 2,126.

Wethersfield, *t.*, Conn., U.S.A.; oldest regular settlement in C.; lge. st. prison; agr. implements, seeds; p. (1960) 20,526.

Wetteren, *t.*, Belgium; on R. Schelde; textiles; p. (1962) 20,250.

Wetterhorn, *mtn.*, Switzerland; alt. 12,165 ft.

Wetzlar, *c.*, Hessen, Germany; on R. Lahn; cath.; optical instruments, metals, radios, textiles, footwear; p. (1963) 37,800.

Wewoka, *t.*, Okla., U.S.A.; oil wells; agr., bricks, petrol; p. (1960) 5,954.

Wexford, *maritime co.*, Leinster, S.E. Ireland; pasture agr., dairying, fishing; cap. Wexford; a. 901 sq. m.; p. (1966) 83,355.

Wexford, *t., cap.*, Wexford; Leinster, S.E. Ireland; on R. Slaney; p. (1966) 11,533.

Wey, *R.*, Hants, Surrey, Eng.; rises in W. Weald, flows N. into R. Thames nr. Weybridge; cuts impt. gap through N. Downs at Guildford; length 35 m.

Weybridge, *see* Walton and Weybridge.

Weymouth and Melcombe Regis, *t., mun. bor.*, Dorset, Eng.; on Weymouth Bay, 8 m. S. of Dorchester; torpedo and boatbldg., bricks, tiles, engin.; holiday resort; p. (estd. 1967) 42,160.

Weymouth, *t.*, Mass., U.S.A.; footwear mnf.; p. (1960) 48,177.

**Whakatane**, *t.*, N.I., N.Z.; on Bay of Plenty; board mills; p. (1961) *7,169*.

**Whales, Bay of**, *inlet* in Ross Dep. Antarctica; exploration base.

**Whangarei**, *t.*, N.Z.; agr., fruit; oil refining; natural gas pipeline from Kapuni; p. (1961) *17,865*.

**Whangpoo**, *R.*, Kiangsu, China; tidal creek upon which Shanghai is situated; runs 14 m. inland from Yangtze-Kiang estuary nr. Woosung.

**Wharfe**, *R.*, W.R. Yorks, Eng.; trib. of R. Ouse; length 60 m.

**Wheeling**, *c.*, W. Va., U.S.A.; on Ohio R.; rly. and comm. ctr., iron and steel, pottery; p. (1960) *53,400*.

**Whernside**, *mtn.*, W.R. Yorks, Eng.; alt. 2,414 ft.

**Whickham**, *t.*, *urb. dist.*, Durham, Eng.; nr. Gateshead; coal-mining, iron and steel, chemicals, rope mnf.; p. (estd. 1967) *27,890*.

**Whitburn**, *burgh*, W. Lothian Scot.; 20 m. S.W. of Edinburgh; coal, limestone; p. (1961) *5,902*.

**Whitby**, *spt.*, *urb. dist.*, N.R. Yorks, Eng.; at mouth of R. Esk. 17 m. N.W. of Scarborough; abbey; holiday resort; fisheries; potash to be mined nearby; p. (1961) *11,662*.

**Whitby** (formerly Windsor), *t.* Canada; on L. Ontario; p. (1961) *14,685*.

**Whitchurch**, *t.*, Salop, Eng.; 13 m. S.W. of Crewe; mkt., malting, cheese; p. (1961) *7,159*. [length 350 m.

**White**, *R.*, Ark., U.S.A.; trib. of Mississippi R.;

**White**, *R.*, Ind., U.S.A.; trib. of Wabash R.; length 330 m.

**White**, *R.*, Ark., Mo., U.S.A.; trib. of Mississippi R.; 300 m. navigable; length 800 m.

**White Mtns.**, part of Appalachian system, N.H., U.S.A.; highest summit, Mt. Washington, 6,288 ft.

**White Nile (Bahr-el-Abiad)**, *R.*, Sudan, N.E. Africa; strictly, name applied to stretch of R. Nile between L. No and Khartoum; distance over 500 m.

**White Plains**, *t.*, N.Y., U.S.A.; on Bronx R.; residtl.; battle 1776; p. (1960) *50,485*.

**White Russia**, *see* Byelorussia.

**White Sea or G. of Arkangelsk**, *inlet* of the Arctic Ocean, R.S.F.S.R.; a. 47,346 sq. m.

**Whiteadder**, *R.*, Berwick, Scot.; trib. of R. Tweed; length 34 m.     [p. (1961) *14,370*.

**Whitefield**, *urb. dist.*, Lancs, Eng.; cotton mnf.;

**Whitehall**, *t.*, N.Y., U.S.A.; at head of L. Champlain; timber tr.; p. (1960) *4,016*.

**Whitehaven**, *spt.*, *mun. bor.*, Cumberland, Eng.; on Solway Firth, 3 m. N. of St. Bees Head; coal, methane gas, tanning chemicals, flour and silk mills; p. (estd. 1967) *27,050*.

**Whitehead**, *t.*, *urb. dist.*, Antrim, N. Ireland; at entrance to Belfast Lough; seaside resort; p. (1966) *2,740*.

**Whithorn**, *royal burgh*, Wigtown, Scot.; 9 m. S. of Wigtown; cath.; p. (1961) *986*.

**Whitehorse**, *c.*, cap. Yukon Terr., Canada; ctr. coal and copper mng., hunting and fur trapping; once a gold " boom town "; H.Q. Royal Canadian Mounted Police; end of Alaska highway linking Edmonton, Alberta; p. (1961) *5,031*.

**Whitley Bay**, *mun. bor.*, Northumberland, Eng.; 3 m. N. of Tynemouth; seaside resort; plastics; p. (estd. 1967) *38,380*.     [alt. 14,898 ft.

**Whitney**, *mtn.*, Sierra Nevada, Cal. U.S.A.;

**Whitstable**, *spt.*, *urb. dist.*, Kent Eng.; on Thames estuary, 6 m. N. of Canterbury; holiday resort, oysters; p. (estd. 1967 *22,510*.

**Whittington or Whittington Moor**, *par.*, Derby, Eng.; nr. Chesterfield; coal-mining iron, steel; p. *8,317*.

**Whittlesey**, *t.*, *urb. dist.*, I. of Ely, Eng.; in The Fens, 8 m. W. of March; bricks, mkt. gardening; p. (1961) *9,324*.

**Whitworth**, *urb. dist.*, S E. Lancs, Eng.; cottons, coal, slate; p. (1961) *7,031*.

**Whyalla**, *c.*, *spt.*, S. Australia; impt. steel and shipbldg. inds.; ironstone, pig-iron, steel; p. (1966) *22,126*.

**Wichita**, *c.*, Kan., U.S.A.; in Arkansas valley; rly. wks.; oil refineries and equipment; meatpacking ctr. in agr. and stock-raising region; p. (1960) *254,698*.

**Wichita**, *R.*, Texas, U.S.A.; trib. of Red R.; length 225 m.

**Wichita Falls**, *c.*, Texas, U.S.A.; oil-refining; p. (1960) *101,724*.

**Wick**, *spt.*, *burgh*, Caithness, Scot.; on E. cst.

14 m. S. of John O'Groats; herring-fisheries ctr.; p. (1961) *7,397*.

**Wicklow**. *maritime co.*, Leinster, Ireland; pastoral and agr.; cap. Wicklow: a. 781 sq. m ; p. (1966) *60,281*.

**Wicklow**, *t.*, *cap.*, Wicklow, Leinster, Ireland; on S.E. cst., 35 m S. of Dublin; mkt.; sm. seaside resort; p. (1966) *3,340*.

**Wicklow**, *mtns.*, Wicklow, Ireland; highest summit, Lugnaquillia, 3,039 ft.

**Widnes**, *t.*, *mun. bor.*, Lancs, Eng.; on R. Mersey, 12 m. E of Liverpool; anhydrite acid, asbestos, cement, wire cables chemicals, explosives fertilisers, copper and zinc; p. (estd. 1967) *54,600*.

**Wiener Neustadt**, *t.*, Lower Austria; 20 m. S. of Vienna; machin., pottery; p. (1961) *33,845*.

**Wieringermeer Polder**, *reclaimed a.*, N. Holland, Neth.; located in N.W. of IJsselmeer; reclaimed in 1930, maliciously flooded by Germans but drained again 1945; largely meadowland; a. 78 sq. m.

**Wiesbaden**, *cap.*, Hessen Germany; at S. edge of the Taunus; spa; cas.; chemicals, cement, engin ; p. (1963) *258,000*.

**Wigan**, *t.*, *co. bor.*, S.W. Lancs. Eng.; 16 m. N.E. of Liverpool; coal, cotton. engin., chemicals, cement; p. (estd. 1967) *79,720*.

**Wight, I. of**, *co.*, Eng.; Eng. Channel, separated from Hants by Spithead and The Solent; wheat, sheep, cement; holiday resort; ch. ts.: Newport, Cowes, Ryde; a. 147 sq. m.; p. (1966) *97,000*.

**Wigston**, *t.*, *urb. dist.*, Leic., Eng.; 4 m. S. of Leicester; rly. wks., engin., hosiery; p. (estd. 1967) *26,630*.

**Wigtown**, *maritime co.*, S.W. Scot.; agr., mainly dairying, creameries; agr. implements; cap. W.; a. 485 sq. m.; p. (1961) *29,107*.

**Wigtown**, *burgh*, Wigtown. Scot.; on Wigtown Bay, Solway Firth; fishery; creamery, distillery; p. (1961) *1,201*.

**Wilcannia**, *t.*, *R. pt.*, N.S.W., Australia; on R. Darling, 350 m. upstream from Wentworth sends wool and minerals downstream to Morgan, Murray Bridge, Echuca for transhipment by rail to Adelaide or Melbourne.

**Wilhelmshaven**, *spt.*, Lower Saxony, Germany; 40 m. N.W. of Bremen; shipbldg., machin., textiles, furniture, elect., wood, leather; harbour; oil pipeline; p. (1963) *100,400*.

**Wilkes-Barre**, *c.* Penns., U.S.A.; on Susquehanna R.; anthracite-mining, machin., locomotives, iron and steel, textiles; p. (1960) *63,551*.

**Wilkes Land**, Antarctica; featureless plateau, alt. 9,500 ft.; immense glaciers; U.S. base taken over by Australia in 1959.

**Wilkinsburg**, *bor.*, Penns., U.S.A.; Pittsburgh sub.; residtl.; timber wks.; p. (1960) *30,066*.

**Willamette**, *R.*, Ore., U.S.A.; rises in Cascade Mtns., flows N. into Columbia R. below Portland; valley gives rich agr. land, wheat, rootcrops, dairy produce, hard and soft fruits; ch. ts. Portland, Salem; length approx. 300 m.

**Willemstad**, *pt.*, *cap.*, Neth. Antilles; on Curaçao I.; oil refining; p. (estd. 1963) *60,000*.

**Willenhall**. *urb. dist.*, Staffs, Eng.; 4 m. E. of Wolverhampton; lock and key drop forgings, castings, car accessories; p. (1961) *32,317*.

**Willesden**, *former mun. bor.*, Middx,. Eng.; now inc. in Brent outer bor., Greater London, (*q.v.*); impt. rly. junction; residtl. and industl.; p. (1961) *171,001*.

**Williamsburg**, *c.*, Va., U.S.A.; oldest incorporated c. in America; p. (1960) *6,832*.

**Williamsport**, *c.*, Penns. U.S.A.; on Susquehanna R.; rly. ctr., timber, machin., silks; summer resort; p. (1960) *41,967*.

**Williamstown**, *spt.*, *sub.*, Melbourne, Victoria, Australia; at mouth of Yarra R.; naval dockyds., shipbldg., railway wks., rifle range; p. (1958) *30,388*.

**Willimantic**, *c.*, Conn., U.S.A.; on Willimantic R.; textiles, thread; p. (1960) *13,881*.

**Wilmette**, *t.*, Ill., U.S.A.; residtl. sub. Chicago; p. (1960) *28,268*.

**Wilmington**, *c.*, *spt.*, Del., U.S.A.; on Delaware R.; shipbldg., gunpowder, machin., iron- and steel-wks.; chemicals; leather, cork, rubber goods; p. (1960) *95,827*.

**Wilmington**, *spt.*, N.C., U.S.A.; exp. cotton, tobacco, timber, fertilizers; shipbldg., textiles, chemicals; p. (1950) *45,043*.

Wilmslow, *t.*, *urb dist.*, Cheshire, Eng.; on R. Bollen, 6 m. S.W. of Stockport; residtl., cotton mnfs.; p. (estd. 1967) *28,160*.

Wilsden, W.R. Yorks, Eng.; nr. Bradford; worsted mnfs.; p. *2,500*.

Wilson, *t.* N.C., U.S.A.; tobacco, cotton, timber; p. (1950) *23,019*.                [Victoria, Australia.

Wilson's Promontory, juts into Bass Strait,

Wilton, *t.*, *mun. bor.*, Wilts, Eng.; on R. Wylye, 3 m. W. of Salisbury; agr. mkt., carpets, felt; p. (estd. 1967) *4,240*.

Wilton, *industl. estate*, Cleveland, Yorks.; S. side of Tees estuary; heavy organic- and petro-chemicals; nylon polymer plant projected 1964.

Wiltshire, *S.W. inland co.*, Eng.; agr. and pastoral; cap. Salisbury; a. 1,345 sq. m.; p. (1966) *471,000*.

Wimbledon, *former mun. bor.*, Surrey, Eng.; now inc. in Merton outer London bor.; residtl.; famous common and internationally famous tennis tournament; p. (1961) *56,994*.

Wimborne Minster, *t.*, Dorset, Eng.; on R. Stour; agr. machin., car body bldg.; p. (1961) *4,156*.

Wimmera, *N.W. dist.*, Victoria, Australia; a. 24,000 sq. m.; pastoral areas of fruit-growing under irrigation.

Winburg, *t.*, O.F.S., S. Africa; was the first cap. of O.F.S.; tr. ctr.; p. (1960) *1,454* whites.

Wincanton, *t.*, Somerset, Eng.; at N.W. foot of Salisbury Plain; mkt., agr., cheese; p. *2,047*.

Winchcomb, *t.*, Gloucester, Eng.; nr. Cheltenham; silk, flour, tanning; cas.; p. *2,546*.

Winchelsea, *ancient t.*, Sussex, Eng.; 2 m. S.W. of Rye; formerly an impt. walled spt., now 2 m. inland; p. *693*.

Winchester, *c.*, *mun. bor.*, Hants, Eng.; on R. Itchen, 12 m. N. of Southampton; ancient cap. of the Saxons; cath., famous Public School, barracks; brewing, malting, agr. produce; p. (estd. 1967) *30,740*.

Winchester, *t.*, Ky., U.S.A.; agr., livestock; p. (1960) *10,187*.

Winchester, *t.*, Mass., U.S.A.; sub. of Boston; p. 1960) *19,376*.

Winchester, *c.*, Va., U.S.A.; in Shenandoah valley; p. (1960) *15,110*.

Windermere, *lgst. Eng. L.*, in Westmorland and Lancs; outlet to Morecambe Bay; 10 m. long, 1 m. wide.

Windermere, *urb. dist.*, Westmorland, Eng.; on E. shore of L.; tourist ctr.; p. (1961) *6,556*.

Windhoek, *cap.*, S.W. Africa; fruit, silver, copper, lead; p. (1962) *43,000* inc. *25,200* Europeans.

Windorah, *t.*, Queensland, Australia; pastoral, sheep and cattle.

Wind River Mtns., Wyo., U.S.A.; range of Rockies; Fremont's Peak, 13,576 ft.

Windrush, *R.*, Oxford, Gloucester, Eng.; trib. of R. Thames.

Windscale, Cumberland, Eng.; nuclear reactors for defence purposes.

Windsor, *t.*, N.S.W., Australia; farming ctr.; p. (1961) *12,015*.

Windsor, *c.*, *pt.*, Ontario, Canada; linked to Detroit, U.S.A., by tunnel bridge and ferry; cars, tyres, paint, drugs, salt; p. (1961) *193,365*.

Windsor, *t.*, Conn., U.S.A.; on Connecticut R.; (1960) *19,346*.

Windsor, New, *t.*, *mun. bor.*, Berks, Eng.; on R. Thames, 20 m. W. of London; famous royal cas. (founded by William the Conqueror) and park, St. George's Chapel and the Royal Mausoleum; p. (estd. 1967) *29,920*.

Windward, Is., W.I., consisting of Grenada, St. Vincent, St. Lucia and Dominica; a. 826 sq. m.; p. *336,000*.

Windward Is., (Neth.) part of Neth. Antilles, W. Indies; consisting of 3 Is.; Curaçao, Aruba, and Bonaire.

Windward Passage, *channel*, 60 m. wide, between Cuba and Haiti.

Winfield, *c.*, Kan., U.S.A.; on Walnut R.; educational and comm. ctr., agr.; p. (1960) *11,117*.

Winfrith Heath, Dorset, Eng.; UKAEA Atomic Energy Establishment (ENEA *Dragon* pro ect inaugurated 1964).

Winneba, *t.*, Ghana, W. Africa; p. (1960) *25,000*.

Winnebago, *L.*, Wis. U.S.A.; 27 m. long.

Winnipeg, *c.*, *cap.*, Manitoba, Canada; at junction of Red and Assiniboine Rs ; caths., univ.; rly. ctr.; ch. world wheat mkt.; meat packing and food processing plants; lgst. garment mnf. ctr. in Canada; p. (1961) *475,989*.

Winnipeg, *L.*, Manitoba, Canada; 40 m. N. of Winnipeg; 260 m. long, 25–60 m. wide; contains several lge. Is. (Reindeer, 70 sq. m.; Big I., 50 sq. m.).

Winnipegosis, *L.*, Manitoba and Saskatchewan, Canada; a. (exclusive of Is.) 2,000 sq. m.; 50 m. W. of L. Winnipeg, into which it drains.

Winnipesaukee, *L.*, N.H., U.S.A.; 24 m. long.

Winona, *c.*, Minn., U.S.A.; on R. Mississippi; rly. ctr., timber, grain tr., medicines, shoes, furs.; p. (1960) *24,895*.

Winooski or Onion, *R.*, Vt., U.S.A.; length 90 m.

Winsford, *urb. dist.*, Cheshire, Eng.; on R. Weaver; 4 m. S. of Northwich; only rock salt mine still working in Brit. Is.; p. (1961) *12,733*.

Winslow, *t.*, Bucks, Eng.; mkt., agr. ctr.; p. *1,539*.

Winston-Salem, *c.*, N.C., U.S.A.; tobacco and cotton mnfs.; p. (1960) *111,135*.

Winterswijk, *t.*, Gelderland, Neth.; industl.; p. (1967) *26,243*.

Winterthur, *t.*, Zurich, Switzerland; on Eulach R.; rly. ctr., locomotives, machines, cottons, wine; p. (1961) *84,300*.

Winthrop, *cst. t.*, Mass., U.S.A.; residtl. sub. of Boston, summer resort; p. (1960) *20,303*.

Wipper, *R.*, Germany, trib. of R. Rhine; length 50 m.

Wirl, *t.*, New Zealand, 15 m. S. of Auckland; aluminium fabricating mill.

Wirksworth, *t.*, *urb. dist.*, Derby, Eng.; in Pennines, 5 m. S. of Matlock; lead-mng., limestone, fluorspar wks.; p. (1961) *4,930*.

Wirral, *urb. dist.*, W. Cheshire, Eng.; between estuaries of Dee and Mersey; residtl.; p. (estd. 1967) *25,650*.

Wisbech, *t.*, *mun. bor.*, of Ely, Cambs., Eng.; on R. Nene, 11 m. from its mouth in the Wash; mkt. gardening, fruit growing and canning, agr. implements; p. (estd. 1967) *17,410*.

Wisconsin, *st.*, U.S.A.; leading dairy st. of Union; timber, iron ore, lead, zinc, stone, sand, and gravel; agr. machin., cars, engin.; cap. Madison; ch. t. Milwaukee; a. 56,154 sq. m.; p. (1960) *3,951,777*.

Wisconsin, *R.*, Wis. U.S.A.; trib. of R. Mississippi; length 600 m.

Wishaw, *burgh*, Lanark, Scot., joined with Motherwell; rly. wks., engin., coal, iron, steel.

Wiske, *R.*, N.R. Yorks, Eng.; trib. of R. Swale; length 24 m.

Wismar, *spt.*, Rostock, E. Germany; on Baltic Sea, N. of Schwerin; metals, sugar, canning, shipbldg.; p. (1963) *57,277*.

Witbank, *t.*, Transvaal. S. Africa; power sta.; coal-mng.; carbide, cyanide, steel; p. (1960) *24,510* (inc. *8,482* whites).

Witham, *R.*, Rutland and Lincs, Eng.; flows into The Wash; length 80 m.

Witham, *t.*, *urb. dist.*, Essex, Eng.; 9 m. N.E. of Chelmsford; agr., mkt. gardening; malting, metal windows; p. (1961) *9,459*.

Withernsea, *t.*, *urb. dist.*, E.R. Yorks, Eng.; on E. cst. 15 m. E. of Hull; holiday resort; agr., fishing; p. (1961) *4,963*.

Withnell, *t.*, *urb. dist.*, Lancs, Eng.; at N. foot of Rossendale Fells, 3 m. S.W. of Blackburn; textiles, stone, paper; p. (1961) *2,840*.

Witney, *t.*, Oxford, Eng.; on R. Windrush, 10 m. W. of Oxford; woollens, blankets, gloves; p. (1961) *9,217*.

Witten, *t.*, N. Rhine–Westphalia, Germany; on R. Ruhr; glass, machin., metals, chemicals, optical inds.; p. (1963) *97,400*.

Wittenberg, *t.*, Halle, E. Germany; on R. Elbe; cas.; ctr. of Reformation and burial place of Luther; he burnt Papal bull against him here in 1520; iron, machin., textiles; p. (1963) *46,544*.

Wittenberge, *t.*, Schwerin, E. Germany; on R. Elbe; woollens, machin., rly. junction; p. (1963) *32,828*.                [mining.

Witwatersrand, *dist*. Transvaal, S. Africa; gold-

Wivenhoe, *t.*, *urb. dist.*, Essex, Eng.; on R. Colne; boatbldg., oysters, lt. inds.; p. (1961) *2,729*.

Wloclawek, *t.*, *pt.*, N. Poland; on R. Vistula; brewing, iron-wks., pottery, nitrate fertilising; p. (1965) *68,000*.

Woburn, *t.*, Bedford, Eng.; 5 m. N.E. of Leighton Buzzard; Woburn Abbey (seat of Dukes of Bedford).                [p. (1960) *31,214*.

Woburn, *c.*, Mass., U.S.A.; chemicals, footwear;

Woking, *t.*, *urb dist.*, Surrey, Eng.; 4 m. N. of

Guildford; wireless parts, aeroplane equipment; mkt., residtl.; p. (estd. 1967) *78,840.*

Wokingham, *t., mun. bor.,* Berks, Eng.; 5 m. S.E. of Reading; mkt., agr. and agr. machin., bricks; p. (estd. 1967) *17,980.*

Wolds, The, *chalk hill range,* Lincoln. E.R. Yorks, Eng.; pastoral; 45 m. long.

Wolf Rock, *isolated rock, lighthouse;* at approach to Eng. Channel from Bay of Biscay; 9 m. S.W. of Lands End, Cornwall.

Wolfe, *I.,* in L. of 1,000 Is., St. Lawrence R., Canada.

Wolfenbüttel, *t.,* Lower-Saxony Germany; S. of Brunswick; cas., Lessing museum; textiles, machin., canning; p. (1963) *39,700.*

Wolfsburg, *t.,* Lower Saxony, Germany; on R. Aller N.E. of Brunswick; Volkswagen wks.; p. (1963) *74,100.*

Wollaston, *L.,* N.W. Terr., Canada; 50 m. long.

Wollongong, Greater, *c.,* N.S.W., Australia; coal-mining, iron- and steel-wks., fertilisers, chemicals, bricks; dairying; p. (1966) *162,535.*

Wolmaransstad, *t.,* Transvaal, S. Africa; diamonds; p. (1960) *6,041* inc. *2,474* whites.

Wolsingham, *t.,* Durham, Eng.; on R. Wear; woollens, coal, agr. tools, marble; p. *3,535.*

Wolverhampton, *t., co. bor.,* Staffs, Eng.; 15 m. N.W. of Birmingham; ironwks., coal, metal goods, elec. engin., elec. apparatus, car and cycle components, rayon, nylon, rubber goods; p. (estd. 1967) *266,890.*

Wolverton, *t., urb. dist.,* Bucks, Eng.; on R. Ouse, 15 m. S.W. of Bedford; rly.-carriage wks.; p. (1961) *13,116.*

Wolyn (*former* Wollin), *I.,* Baltic Sea; off mouth of R. Oder; Polish; a. 133 sq. m.; p. *21,000.*

Wombwell, *urb. dist.,* W.R. Yorks, Eng.; at E. foot of Pennines, 7 m. N. of Sheffield; coal-mining, bricks; p. (1961) *18,701.*

Wonokromo, *sub.* of Soerabaya, Indonesia; oil refining.

Wonsan, *spt.,* N. Korea; exp. rice, cattle, hides, fish; p. (estd. 1942) *122,185.*

Wonthaggi, *t.,* Victoria, Australia; clothing, engin.; p. (1966) *4,672.*

Woodbridge, *t., urb. dist.,* E. Suffolk, Eng.; on R. Deben; engin., brush mkg.; p. (1961) *5,927.*

Woodbridge, *t.,* N.J., U.S.A.; tiles, bricks, terra-cotta; p. (1960) *78,846.*

Woodbury, *t.,* N.J., U.S.A.; nr. Philadelphia; (1960) *12,453.*

Wood Green, *former mun. bor.,* Middx., Eng.; now inc. in Haringey outer bor., Greater London, (q.v.); p. (1961) *47,945.*

Woodhall Spa, *t., urb. dist.,* Lindsey, Lincs, Eng.; 4 m. S.W. of Horncastle; health resort; p. (1961) *1,990.*

Woodside, *burgh* Aberdeen, Scot.; on R. Don; paper; p. *7,698.*

Woodstock, *t.* Ontario, Canada; on R. Thames; dairying, woollens, agr. tools; p. (1961) *20,486.*

Woodstock, *t., mun. bor.,* Oxford, Eng.; on Glynne R. 7 m. N.W. of Oxford; glove mnfs.; Blenheim Palace; p. (estd. 1967) *2,260.*

Wookey Hole, *cave,* Mendip Hills, Somerset, Eng.; at foot of limestone hills, 2 m. N.W. of Wells; R. Axe emerges from the cave.

Woolgar, *l.,* Queensland, Australia; gold.

Woolwich, *former met. bor.,* London, Eng.; a. S. of R. Thames incorporated in Greenwich; a. N. of Thames incorporated in Newham; Royal Ordnance Factory (Woolwich Arsenal) to be closed by 1966; of total Defence Department estate of 1,193 acres, 500 acres to be developed by GLC for housing purposes; free ferry across Thames; p. (1961) *146,603.*

Woomera, S. Australia; about 270 m. N.W. of Adelaide; base for joint U.K.–Australian guided-weapon testing range extending N.W. across the continent; established 1947.

Woonsocket, *c.,* R.I., U.S.A.; on Blackstone R.; textiles, rubber goods; p. (1960) *47,080.*

Wooster, *c.,* Ohio, U.S.A.; univ.; agr. ctr.; p. (1960) *17,046.* [Bassett.

Wootton Bassett, *see* Cricklade and Wootton

Worcestershire, *midland co.,* Eng.; W. of Warwick; agr.; pasturage, hops, orchards, minerals, mnfs.; co. t. Worcester; a. 699 sq. m; p. (1966) *663,000.*

Worcester, *c., co. bor.* Worcester, Eng.; on R. Severn, 24 m. N. of Gloucester; cath.; porcelain, glove mkg., machin.; p. (estd. 1967) *70,230.*

Worcester, *t.,* C. Prov., S. Africa; viticultural and industrl. ctr., Goudini spa nearby; p. (1960) *32,301* inc. *10,858* Europeans.

Worcester, *c.,* Mass. U.S.A.; univ.; iron, foot-wear, tools; p. (1960) *186,587.*

Workington, *spt., mun. bor.,* Cumberland, Eng.; on Solway Firth, at mouth of Derwent R.; coal, iron, steel, shipbldg., cycles, motors; p. (estd. 1967) *29,900.*

Worksop, *t., mun. bor.,* Notts, Eng.; 15 m. S.E. of Sheffield; coal-mining, timber, glasswks., knitwear, refractory bricks; quarrying; p. (estd. 1967) *35,580.*

Worms, *c.,* Rhineland-Palatinate, Germany; on R. Rhine, cath.; "Nibelungen city"; wine ctr.; chemicals, leather textiles, machin., metals; p. (1963) *63,100.*

Worms Head, *promontory,* on Glamorgan cst., Gower Peninsula, Wales.

Worsborough, *urb. dist.,* W.R. Yorks, Eng.; coal-mng., timber, gunpowder; p. (1961) *14,577.*

Worsley, *urb. dist.,* S.E. Lancs. Eng.; cottons, iron, coal; p. (estd. 1967) *48,750.*

Worthing, *t., mun. bor.,* W. Sussex, Eng.; on S. cst., 10 m. W. of Brighton; holiday resort, mkt. gardening, horticulture; p. (estd. 1967) *81,200.*

Wotton-under-Edge, *t.,* Gloucester, Eng., nr. Stroud; mkt., agr. ctr., woollens; p. *3,121.*

Wowoni I., Celebes, Indonesia.

Wrangel I., Arctic Ocean; off N. cst., R.S.F.S.R.

Wrangel, *t.,* Alaska, U.S.A.; p. (1960) *1,315.*

Wrangell, *min.,* Alaska, U.S.A.; alt. 17,500 ft.

Wrath, *C.,* N.W. Sutherland, Scot.

Wrekin, *hill,* Salop, Eng.; alt. 1,320 ft.

Wrexham, *t., mun bor.,* Denbigh, Wales; 11 m. S.W. of Chester; steel, engin., textiles, brick wks., chemicals, tanning; tyres; p. (1961) *35,427.*

Wroclaw (Breslau), *prov.,* Poland–Lower Silesia; industrl., coal, ironwks., agr.; cap. Wroclaw; a. 9,552 sq. m.; p. (1965) *1,967,000.*

Wroclaw (Breslau), *c.,* Silesia, Poland; German before 1945; on R. Oder; univ., cath.; metals, textiles, machin., foodstuffs; p. (1965) *474,000.*

Wrotham, *t.,* Kent, Eng.; nr. Sevenoaks; hops, fruit; p. *4,510*

Wuchang, *c.,* Hupeh, China; on Yangtze-Kiang, opp. Hankow; cottons, tea; comm. ctr. See Wuhan.

Wuchow (Wuzhou), *R.pt.,* Kwangsi, China; on Si-Kiang; tr. ctr.; exp. tung oil, hides, aniseed; p. (1953) *111,000.*

Wuhan, *industl. c.,* Hupeh, China; at head of navigation by ocean-going steamers of Yangtze-Kiang; formed by amalgamation of Hankow, Hanyang, Wuchang; combined p. (1953) *1,427,000. See also under separate headings.*

Wuhu, *c.,* Anhwei, China; on Yangtze-Kiang; tea, silk, coal; p. (1953) *242,000.*

Wupper, *R.,* Germany; trib. of R. Rhine; length 40 m.

Wuppertal, *t.,* N. Rhine–Westphalia, Germany; formed by amalgamation of Barmen and Elberfeld; textiles, rubber goods, paper, metals, pharmaceuticals; p. (1963) *422,900.*

Württemberg-Hohenzollern, *Land,* Germany; now merged with Baden-Württemberg.

Würzburg, *c.,* Bavaria, Germany; on R. Main; univ.; machin., metals, chemicals, printing, engin.; route ctr.; p. (1963) *119,700.*

Wurzen, *c.,* Leipzig, E. Germany; on R. Mulde; cath., cas.; machin., furniture, leather, foodstuffs; p. (1963) *23,524.*

Wusih (Wuxi), *c.,* Kiangsu, China; on N. shore of Tai Hu, 75 m. W. of Shanghai; silk, cotton-weaving; p. (1953) *582,000.*

Wutungkiao (Wutongqiao), *c.,* Szechwan prov., China; 15 m. S.E. of Loshan; p. (1953) *199,000.*

Wyalong, N.S.W., *see* West Wyalong.

Wyandotte, *c.,* Mich., U.S.A.; on Detroit R.; chemicals; p. (1960) *43,519.*

Wye, *R.,* Bucks, Eng.; rises in Chiltern Hills above High Wycombe, flows S.E. to R. Thames at Cookham. [length 20 m.

Wye, *R.,* Derby, Eng.; trib. of R. Derwent; flows S.E. into R. Severn at Chepstow; length 130 m. [sta. projected.

Wye, *R.,* Eng. and Wales; rises in Plynlimmon, [sta. projected.

Wylfa Head, Anglesey, N. Wales; nuclear power

Wymondham, *t.,* Norfolk, Eng.; 9 m. S.W. of Norwich; mkt.; brush-making; Benedictine abbey, founded 1107; p. (1961) *5,896.*

**Wyoming,** *st.,* U.S.A.; livestock, agr., coal-mining, minerals, petroleum; cap. Cheyenne; a. 97,914 sq. m.; p. (1960) *330,066.*

**Wyoming,** *valley,* N.E. Penns., U.S.A., on Susquehanna R.; coal; length 30 m.

**Wyre.** *R.,* Lancs, Eng.; rises in Pennines, flows W. into Lancaster Bay at Fleetwood; length 28 m.

**Wyvis, Ben,** *mtn.,* Scot., *see* Ben Wyvis.

# X

**Xanthi,** *t.,* Thrace, Greece; on R. Mesta; tobacco; p. (1961) *26,377.*

**Xanthus,** *ruined c.,* Turkey; on R. Xanthus.

**Xauen,** *t.,* Morocco, N. Africa; p. *14,473.*

**Xenia,** *c.,* Ohio, U.S.A.; in Miami valley; twine, footwear, agr. ctr.; p. (1960) *20,445.*

**Xeres,** *see* Jerez de la Frontera.

**Xingu,** *R.,* Brazil; trib. of the Amazon; navigable in its lower course; length 1,200 m.

**Xochicalco,** *ruins,* Mexico.

**Xochimilco, L.,** Mexico; formerly contiguous with L. Tezcuco.

**Xochimilco,** *sub.,* Mexico City; famous for flower-lined canals; on L. Xochimilco; p. *14,370.*

**Xois,** *ancient c.,* Lower U.A.R.; cap. Ancient Egypt in 17th century B.C.

# Y

**Yablonovy,** *mtn. range,* Siberia, Asiatic R.S.F.S.R.; E. of L. Baikal; highest peak, Sokhondo, *c.* 8,230 ft.; crossed by Trans-Siberian rly.

**Yaila Mtns.,** Ukrainian S.S.R., U.S.S.R.; form S.E. margin of Crimea Peninsula, extend from Sevastopol to Kerch; forested on middle slopes, pasture on upper slopes; forms marked climate barrier between mild winters of Mediterranean cst. to the S. and cold winters to the N.

**Yakima,** *t.,* Wash., U.S.A.; agr., livestock; p. (1960) *43,284.*

**Yakima, R.,** Wash., U.S.A.; trib. of Columbia R.; length 208 m.

**Yakova,** *t.,* Albania; nr. Shkodra.

**Yakushima,** *I.,* Osumi Gr., Japan; S. of Kyushu; mtns., forest.

**Yakut, A.S.S.R.,** U.S.S.R.; gold-mining; a. 1,530,253 sq. m.; p. (1959) *247,000.*

**Yakutsk,** *t.,* R.S.F.S.R.; on R. Lena; p. (1959) *74,000.*

**Yala,** *t.,* S. Thailand; tin-mining.

**Yalta,** *spt.,* Ukrainian S.S.R.; on Black Sea; p. (1956) *34,100.*

**Yalu, R.,** forms bdy. between Manchuria and N. Korea; flows into Yellow Sea.

**Yamagata,** *t.,* Honshu, Japan; mnfs.; p. (1966) *193,737.*

**Yamaguchi,** *t.,* Honshu, Japan; p. (1966) *98,977.*

**Yamal,** *peninsula,* R.S.F.S.R.; jutting into Arctic Ocean; lge oil and gas deposits nearby.

**Yambol,** *t.,* Bulgaria; on R. Tunja; ruined mosque; corn tr.; p. (1956) *42,038.*

**Yamethin,** *dist.,* Upper Burma; teak forests, rice; ch. t. Yamethin; p. *9,291.*

**Yamina,** *t.,* Gambia, W. Africa; p. *6,700.*

**Yamina or Nyamina,** *t.* Nigeria, W. Africa; on R. Niger; tr. ctr.

**Yana, R.,** Siberia, U.S.S.R.; length 1,000 m.

**Yanago,** *t.,* Japan; business ctr.; cotton textiles; p. (1947) *50,027.*

**Yanaon or Yanam,** *prov., t.* formerly Fr. Orissa, united with India 1954; p. (1961) *7,032.*

**Yanbu,** *spt.,* Arabia; on E. cst. of Red Sea; pt. for Medina.

**Yangchow (Yangzhou),** *c.,* Kiangsu, China; on Grand Canal; comm. ctr.; p. (1953) *180,000.*

**Yangchuan (Yangqan),** *c.,* Shansi prov., China; ironworking ctr.; p. (1953) *177,000.*

**Yangi-yer,** *t.,* Uzbek S.S.R., founded 1957 as ctr. for new irrigated cotton lands of the Hunger steppe.

**Yangtze River,** China; rises in plateau of Tibet, flows E. to E. China Sea, Pac. Oc. nr. Shanghai; traverses " Red Basin " of Szechwan, a deep gorge above Ichang, and finally a broad, level plain; many lge. cs. on its banks, Chungking, Ichang, Wuhan (Hankow, Hayang, Wuchang), Nanking, Chinkiang; navigable by ocean-going vessels 1,800 m. to Ichang; total length 3,500 m.

**Yannina,** *see* Ioánnina.

**Yaoundé,** *cap.,* Cameroun Rep., W. Africa; p. (estd. 1965) *93,000.*

**Yap, I.,** Carolines, Pac. Oc., U.S.A. trusteeship; a. 79 sq. m.; cable sta.; p. (1958) *5,459.*

**Yapura, R.,** Brazil and Colombia, S. America; trib. of R. Amazon; navigable for 600 m.; length 1,500 m.

**Yaracuy,** *st.,* Venezuela; cap. San Felipe; p. (1961) *175,291.*

**Yare, R.,** Norfolk, Eng.; flows E. to N. Sea at Gorleston; length 50 m.

**Yaritagua,** *t.,* Venezuela; tobacco, coffee, cocoa, sugar; p. *5,399.*

**Yarkand (Soche),** *c.,* Sinkiang, China; tr. ctr.; wheat, rice, beans, fruit, carpets, textiles; p. (estd.) *60,000.*

**Yarkand, R.,** Sinkiang, China; trib. of Tarim R.; length 500 m.

**Yarmouth,** *spt.,* Nova Scotia, Canada; shipbldg., fisheries; p. (1961) *8,636.*

**Yarmouth** *par.,* I. of Wight, Eng.; on N.W. cst., 8 m. W. of Newport; holiday resort; p. *893.*

**Yarmouth, Great,** *spt. co. bor.,* Norfolk Eng.; at mouth of R. Yare; holiday resort; fisheries, herrings, timber, shipyds.; p. (estd. 1967) *51,910.*

**Yaroslavl,** *t.,* R.S.F.S.R.; on R. Volga; cath.; synthetic rubber, engin., textiles, chemicals, sawmilling; p. (1967) *486,000.*

**Yarra, R.,** Victoria, Australia; length 100 m.

**Yasan, N.** Bulgaria; nr. Pleven and oil reservoir Dolni Dubnik; lge. refinery under construction.

**Yatsushiro,** *t.,* Kyushu, Japan; p. (1965) *103,000.*

**Yavary, R.,** S. America; on Brazilian–Peruvian frontier; trib. of R. Marañon; length 450 m.

**Yawata,** *t.,* Kyushu, Japan; now part of Kitak-yushu City newly formed 1963 (*q.v.*); chemicals, iron and steel; p. (1960) *332,000.*

**Yazd,** *c.,* Iran, Isfahan prov.; carpets, textiles; p. (1967) *280,442.*

**Yazoo,** *c.,* Miss., U.S.A.; on Yazoo R.; agr. tr.; p. (1960) *11,236.* [length 280 m.

**Yazoo, R.,** Miss., U.S.A.; trib. of R. Mississippi;

**Yazoo,** *dist.,* Miss., U.S.A.; very flat, low-lying flood plain of R. Mississippi and R. Yazoo, extends 220 m. along R. from Memphis to Vicksburg; very fertile alluvial soil, but subject to disastrous floods; one of ch. cotton-growing dists. in U.S.A.

**Yecla,** *t.,* Spain; mkt.; p. (1957) *24,046.*

**Yeddo,** old name of Tokio, Japan.

**Yegoryevsk,** *t.,* R.S.F.S.R.; 72 m. S.E. of Moscow; lge. textile ind.; p. (1959) *59,000.* [Dvina.

**Yekabpils,** *t.,* Kurland, Latvian S.S.R.; on R.

**Yeletz,** *t.,* R.S.F.S.R.; on R. Sosna; grain and cattle tr.; p. (1959) *78,000.*

**Yell, I.,** Shetlands, Scot.; 17 m. long; p. *1,883.*

**Yellow R.,** *see* Hwang Ho.

**Yellow Sea (Hwang-hai),** *arm* of Pacific Ocean, between China and Korea; length 600 m., greatest width 400 m.; max. depth 500 ft.

**Yellowhead Pass,** B.C., Alberta, Canada; most N. and lowest of main passes across Rocky Mtns.; carries Canadian National Rly. on route from Edmonton to Vancouver and Prince Rupert; summit alt. 3,700 ft.

**Yellowknife,** *t.* N.W. Terr., Canada; on N. shore of Gr. Slave L.; ctr. of impt. gold-mining dist.; linked by air to Edmonton, Alberta.

**Yellowstone, L.,** Wyo., U.S.A.; 20 m. long, 15 m. wide; alt. 7,740 ft.; in Y. National Park.

**Yemen,** *republic,* S.W. Arabia; bounded by Saudi Arabia on N., Southern Yemen on S.; prin. c. Sana; barley, wheat, millet, coffee, hides; a. 75,000 sq. m.; p. c. *5,000,000.*

**Yemen, Southern, People's Republic of,** *indep. sov. st.* (1967), S.W. Arabia, on G. of Aden; comprises former Brit. Aden col., Prot. of South Arabia, and the Is. of Perim and Kamaran; cap. Madinat al Shaab; a. 111,075 sq. m.; p. (estd.) *1,220,000.*

**Yenakievo,** *t.,* Ukrainian S.S.R.; coal, iron and steel; p. (1959) *92,000.*

**Yenangyaung,** *t., R. pt.,* Burma; on left bank of R. Irrawaddy, 280 m. N. of Rangoon; ctr. of Burma oilfields.

**Yenesei, R.,** Siberia, R.S.F.S.R.; rises in Sayan Mtns., flows N. into Arctic Ocean; ch. tribs. Upper, Stony and Lower Tunguska Rs.; length 3,300 m.

**Yentai,** *see* Chefoo.

**Yeo or Ivel, R.,** Dorset, Somerset, Eng.; trib. of R. Parrett; length 24 m.

Yeovil, *t.*, *mun. bor.*, Somerset, Eng.; on R. Yeo; 22 m. S.E. of Taunton; glove mnf., aeroplane wks. engin.; dairying; p. (estd. 1967) *25,450.*

Yerevan, *cap.*, Armenian S.S.R.; engin., chemicals, synthetic rubber, textiles, aluminium; p. (1967) *643,000.*

Yeshil-Irmak, *R.*, Turkey; flows N. to Black Sea; length 200 m.

Yeshil Kul, *L.*, Chinese Turkestan (Sinkiang).

Yes Tor, *2nd highest summit*, Dartmoor, Devon, Eng.; alt. 2,028 ft.

Yevpatoriya (Eupatoria), *spt.* Ukrainian S.S.R.; chemicals, leather, locks, dried fish; new port being built 1963; p. (1959), *57,000.*

Yeysk, *t.*, R.S.F.S.R.; N. Caucasus, pt. on Taganrog Bay; resort; engin.; p. (1959) *55,000.*

Yezd, *t.*, *prov. cap.*, Iran; caravan ctr.; p. (estd. 1949) *56,000.*

Yezo, see Hokkaido.

Yiewsley and West Drayton, *former urb. dist.*, Middx., Eng.; now inc. in Hillingdon outer bor. Greater London; varied light inds.; p. (1961) *23,723.*

Yingkow (Yingkou), *c.*, Liaoning prov., China; 20 m. up R. from mouth of Liao-ho; soyabean prods.; p. (1953) *131,000.*

Ykspihlaja, *sub.* of Kokkola, W. Finland; foundries, chemicals.

Yokkaichi, *industl. c.*, *spt.*, S. Honshu, Japan; on W. cst. of Ise Bay, 23 m. S W. of Nagoya; silk, cotton and woollen goods, petro chemicals, synthetic rubber; p. (1964) *221,000.*

Yokohama, *ch. spt.*, Honshu, Japan; W. side of Tokio Bay; silks, tea, cars; p. (1965) *1,788,915.*

Yokosuka, *spt.*, Honshu, Japan; S. of Tokio; holiday resort; thermal power sta.; p. (1965) *317,411.*

Yola, *t.*, N. Nigeria Africa; nr. R. Benue; agr. tr.; p. *5,310.*

Yonkers, *c.*, N.Y., U.S.A.; on Hudson R.; light inds.; p. (1960) *190,634.*

Yonne, *dep.*, France; agr., wines, minerals; cap. Auxerre; a. 2,894 sq. m.; p. (1962) *269,826.*

York, *c.*, *co. bor.*, *co. t.*, Yorks, Eng.; on R. Ouse; in central position in Vale of York; cath. cas. univ.; mkt., confectionery; p. (estd. 1967) *105,550.*

York, *I. or.*, Torres Strait (between New Guinea and Australia).

York, *R.*, tidal estuary of Chesapeake Bay, U.S.A.

York, *c.*, Nebraska, U.S.A.; rly. ctr.; p. (1960) *6,173.*

York, *c.*, Penns., U.S.A.; agr. tools, confectionery, tobacco; p. (1960) *54,504.*

York, *C.*, Hayes Peninsula, Greenland

York, *C.*, Queensland, Australia; most N. point on mainland of Australia.

York Factory, *t.*, on Nelson R., Hudson Bay, Manitoba, Canada.

York, Vale of, *broad lowland*, Yorks, Eng.; extends N. to S. between Pennines to W. and N. Yorks Moors and Yorks Wolds to E.; drained to Humber by R. Ouse and tribs. from N. by Rs. Don and Trent from S.; flar apart from low transverse ridge Stamford Bridge to Harrogate; glacial and alluvial soils have required draining; crop farming, wheat, barley, root-crops, associated with fattening of beef cattle; settlement mainly marginal; ch. t. York; length 60 m.; width varies from 10 m. in N. to 30 m. in S.

Yorke, *peninsula*, S Australia; separates Spencer G. and G. of St. Vincent; 100 m. long, 30 m. wide.

Yorkshire, *lgst. co.*, Eng.; divided into 3 Ridings, N., E. and W.; cap. York; a. 6,081 sq. m.; p. (1961) *4,722,561.*

Yorkshire, East Riding, *admin. co.*, Yorks, Eng.; farming, pastoral on Wolds, arable elsewhere; ch. t. Hull; a. 1,172 sq. m.; p. (1966) *543,000.*

Yorkshire, North Riding, *admin. co.*, Yorks, Eng; farming, pastoral on Moors, mixed elsewhere; iron-ore mng. in Cleveland Hills; heavy inds. around Middlesbrough; ch. t. Middlesbrough; a. 2,128 sq. m.; p. (1966) *584,000.*

Yorkshire, West Riding, *admin. co.*, Yorks, Eng.; pastoral farming on Pennines, but highly industl. on coalfield at foot of Pennines; woollens, steel, engin.; ch. ts. Leeds (in N.), Sheffield (in S.); a. 2,780 sq. m.; p. (1966) *3,736,000.*

Yorkshire Moors, *hills*, N.R. Yorks, Eng.; inc.

North Yorks Moors, Cleveland Hills and Hambleton Hills; bounded to N. by Tees Valley, S. by Vale of Pickering, W. by Swale Valley, E. by sea; composed of oolitic limestone; good sheep pastures; impt. iron-ore deposits worked in Cleveland Hills; maximum alt. 1,489 ft.

Yorkshire Wolds, *hills*, E.R., Yorks, Eng.; extend N.E. from Humber and terminate in Flamborough Head; composed of chalk; smooth slopes and short grass give gd. sheep pasture; average alt. 600 ft.

Yorkton, *t.*, Saskatchewan, Canada; agr. ctr.; p. (1961) *9,995.*

Yoruba, *dist.*, Nigeria; ch. ts., Oyo, Ibadan, Abeokuta and Illorin.

Yosemite Falls, 3 cataracts, of Yosemite Creek, Cal., U.S.A.

Yoshkar-Ola, *t.*, Mariy A.S.S.R.; R.S.F.S.R.; 80 m. N.W. of Kazan; wood processing, food inds.; p. (1967) *133,000.*

Youghal, *spt.*, *urb. dist.*, Cork, Ireland; on estuary of the Blackwater, Cork, Ireland; fisheries; p. (1966) *5,093.*

Youngstown, *industl. c.*, Ohio, U.S.A.; on Beaver R., 60 m. N.W. of Pittsburgh; iron- and steel-mkg., heavy engin.; p. (1960) *166,689.*

Yoyang, *c.*, Hunan, China; at outlet of Tung Ting L. on the bank of the R. Yangtze; p. *4,800.*

Yozgat, *t.*, Turkey; p. (1960) *18,263.*

Ypres (Ieper), *t.*, Belgium; automatic textile loom mkg.; 2 battles, First World War; p. (1962) *18,213.*

Ypsilanti, *c.*, Mich., U.S.A.; on Huron R.; agr. mkt., mnfs.; p. (1960) *20,957.*

Ysselmeer. See IJsselmeer.

Yssingeaux, *t.*, Haute-Loire, France; nr. Le Puy; mnfs.; p. (1962) *5,889.*

Ystad, *spt.*, S. Sweden; on Baltic Sea; agr. machin., soap; p. (1961) *13,711.*

Yuba, R., Cal., U.S.A.; trib. of Feather-Sacramento R.

Yucatan, *st.*, Mexico; cereals, cotton; cap. Merida; a. 23,926 sq. m.; p. (1960) *614,049.*

Yucatan, *strait*, connects G. of Mexico with Caribbean Sea.

Yuan Kiang, *R.*, Hunan, China; length 400 m.

Yugoslavia, see Jugoslavia.

Yukon, *R.*, Canada–Alaska; flows N.W. and W. into Bering Strait; navigable for 1,200 m.; length 2,000 m.

Yukon, *terr.*, Canada; mountainous; coal. minerals; chief ts. Dawson, and Whitehorse (cap.); a. 207,076 sq. m.; p. (1961) *14,628.*

Yuma, *t.*, Arizona, U.S.A.; at confluence of Rs. Gila and Colorado nr. Mexican–U.S.A. bdy.; ctr. of irrigated agr., obtaining water from Laguna and Imperial Dams; cotton, citrus fruits, alfalfa; p. (1960) *23,974.*

Yunnan, *S.W. prov.*, China; adjoining Burma; mountainous; agr., minerals; cap. Kunming; a. 162,342 sq. m.; p. (1953) *17,472,737.*

Yuzhno-Sakhalinsk, *t.*, R.S.F.S.R.; at S. end of Sakhalin I; paper, light inds.; p. (1959) *86,000.*

Yverdon, *t.*, Switzerland; cas.; tourist ctr.; p. *10,865.*

# Z

Zaandam, *t.*, N. Holland, Neth.; paper, oil, timber, cement; p. (1967) *57,099.*

Zabrze (Hindenburg), *t.*, Upper Silesia, Poland; German before 1945; steel, coal, engin., chemicals; p. (1965) *200,000.*

Zacapa, *t.*, Guatemala, Central America; sulphur springs; tobacco; p. (estd. 1960) *35,300.*

Zacatecas, *st.*, Mexico; silver-mines; cereals, fruit, sugar; a. 28,122 sq. m.; p. (1960) *817,831.*

Zacatecas, *t.*, *cap.*, Zacatecas, Mexico; silver, pottery, comm. ctr.; p. (1960) *24,454.*

Zacatecoluca, *t.*, El Salvador, Central America; cigar mkg., hand looms; coffee, cotton, sugar, vanilla in a.; p. (1960) *30,810.*

Zadar (Zara), *spt.*, Jugoslavia; formerly Italian; cath.; maraschino, flour, glass; p. (1959) *22,000.*

Zagan (Sagan), *t.*, Silesia, Poland; German before 1945; on R. Bober; cas.; textiles, paper, lignite; p. (1965) *21,000.*

Zagazig, *t.*, Egypt; on Nile Delta; cotton, grain tr.; p. (1960) *124,000.*

Zagorsk, *t.*, R.S.F.S.R.; 44 m. N.E. of Moscow; woodcarving, toy mkg.; p. (1959) *73,000.*

**K188**

Zagreb, t., Jugoslavia; on R. Sava; cath., univ.; engin., textiles, chemicals, paper, asbestos; p. (1961) 457,000. [14,921 ft.

Zagros, mtns., Persia; highest, Zardeh Kuh.

Zahedan, c., Iran, prov. cap. Sistan and Baluchestan; airpt.; term. of rly. from Pakistan; p. (1967) 79,257.

Zahle, t., Lebanon, S.W. Asia; on slopes of L. mtn.; p. (estd 1950) 78,031.

Zakopane, t., Poland; in High Tatra mtns.; tourist resort; p. (1965) 26,000.

Zakynthos, Ionian I. Greece; cap. Zante; currants; devastated by severe earthquake, 1953; a. 277 sq. m.; p. (1961) 35,451.

Zalaegerszeg, t., Hungary; in Göcsej dist.; oilfields.

Zambesi, R., S.E. Africa; flows E. to Mozambique Channel, Indian Ocean; navigable for 1,700 m.; length 2,200 m. [p. (1961) 1,369,961.

Zambesia, prov., Mozambique; ch. t., Quelimane;

Zambia, indep. sov. st. within Brit. Commonwealth (1964), Central Africa; landlocked, bordering Congo, Angola, South-West Africa, Rhodesia, and Botswana (50-yd. frontier across Zambesi); tropical climate, moderate rains; savannah vegetation; maize, tobacco, wheat, coffee; zinc, copper, vanadium, gold, ivory; fishing ind.; irrigation system under development on Kafue Flats; mica in the Lundazi a.; cap. Lusaka; a. 288,130 sq. m.; p. (estd. 1964) 3,500,000.

Zamboanga, t., Mindanao, Philippines; rice, sugar, tobacco, timber, copper; p. (1960) 131,489. [sq. m.; p. (1959) 320,335.

Zamora, prov., Spain; cap. Zamora; a. 40,835

Zamora, t., cap., Zamora, Spain; on R. Duero; olive oil, wines; p. (1957) 45,000.

Zamosc, old t., Poland; bentwood furniture mnf.; p. (1965) 30,000. [machin., p. (1960) 39,077.

Zanesville, t., Ohio, U.S.A.; textiles, pottery, machin.; p. (1960) 39,077.

Zanjan, c., Iran, prov. cap. Gilan; p. (1967) 461,588.

Zante, t., Zakynthos, Greece; p. (1961) 9,506.

Zanzibar, I., E. Africa; joined with former st. of Tanganyika to form Tanzania; cloves, coconuts, copra; cap. Zanzibar; a. 1,020 sq. m.; p. (estd. 1965) 325,000.

Zapala, t., W. Argentina; in Andes; rly. term.; oilfield.

Zaporozhe (Dneprostroy), industl. t., Ukrainian S.S.R.; on R. Dnieper, 45 m. S.E. of Dnieperpetrovsk; nr. Lenin (Dnieper) Dam and hydroelec. power-sta. (558,000 kW.); iron- and steelwks., ferro-alloys, engin., aluminium, chemicals, cars, elec. equipment; p. (1967) 571,000.

Zaragoza, prov., Spain; cap Zaragoza; a. 6,611 sq. m.; p. (1959) 643,825.

Zaragoza, t., Spain; on R. Ebro; 2 caths., univ., citadel; captured by Moors 8th century, once cap. of Aragon; beer, spirits, woollens, iron ware; p. (1965) 393,000.

Zarate, t., Entre Rios, Argentina; paper wks.; p. (1960) 52,000.

Zaria, t., N. Nigeria, Africa; univ.; cotton ctr.; p. (1953) 54,000.

Zary (Sorau), t., Brandenburg, Poland; German before 1945; textiles, pottery; p. (1965) 28,000.

Zastron, t., O.F.S., S. Africa; alt. 5,507 ft.; agr. ctr.; p. (1960) 4,440 inc. 1,625 whites.

Zawiercie, t., Poland; industr. ctr.; coal, iron, textiles, glass; p. (1965) 37,000.

Zdunska Wola, t., Poland; nr. Lodz; p. (1965) 27,000.

Zealand (Sjaelland), I., Denmark; between Kattegat and Baltic; a. (with Is. attached) 2,709 sq. m.; ch. t. Copenhagen; p. 1,771,557.

Zeebrugge, spt., Belgium; connected with Bruges by ship canal; glass ind.; petrol storage and conditioning depot; oil refinery; rolling mill equip.; p. (1947) 8,450.

Zeeland, prov., S.E. Neth.; fishing; cap. Middelburg; a. 690 sq. m.; p. (estd. 1967) 295,374.

Zeilah, t., Somali Rep., E. Africa; on G. of Aden; p. 1,000.

Zeist, t., Utrecht Neth.; metalware, Meccano toys, silverware; p. (1967) 55,501.

Zelenodolsk, t., R.S.F.S.R., on R. Volga 25 m. W. of Kazan; rly. junction; sawmills; p. (1959) 60,000.

Zelten, Libya, N. Africa; 200 m. S. of Benghazi; oil field; pipeline Mersa al-Brega.

Zenica, t., Jugoslavia; lge. iron and steel wks; p. (1959) 47,000.

Zerbst, t., Magdeburg, E. Germany; on R. Nuthe, S.E. of Magdeburg; cas.; machin.; p. (1963) 18,862.

Zermatt, vil., Valais, Switzerland; at foot of Matterhorn; tourist ctr. [39,000.

Zgierz, t., Poland; nr. Lodz; linens; p. (1965)

Zhdanov (Mariupol), spt., Ukrainian S.S.R.; on Azov Sea; iron and steel, zirconium, chemicals; p. (1967) 373,000.

Zhitomir, t., Ukrainian S.S.R.; engin.; p. (1967) 133,000.

Zielona Gora (Grünberg), t., Silesia, Poland; German before 1945; lignite mining, viticulture; p. (1965) 62,000. [(1965) 26,152.

Zile, t., Turkey; cereals, fruit, wool, rugs; p.

Zillertal, valley, Tyrol, Austria; drained by R. Ziller, trib. of R. Inn; length 50 m.

Zillertal Alps, mtns., Austria; in Tyrol.

Zinder, t., Niger, W. Africa; terminus of trans-Saharan motor route; tr. ctr.

Zipaquira, t., Colombia; 30 m. N. of Bogota; cattle farming; salt mines; p. (estd. 1959) 29,580.

Zistersdorf, t., N.E. Austria; recently developed oilfields.

Zittau, t., Dresden, E. Germany; on R. Mandau; woollens, linens, machin., cars, chemicals; p. (1963) 42,863.

Žižkov, t., ČSSR.; sub. of Prague; p. 91,082.

Zlatoust, t., R.S.F.S.R.; in the Ural Mtns.; steel, chemicals, sawmilling; p. (1959) 161,000.

Zlin, see Gottwaldov.

Znojmo or Znaim, t., ČSSR.; pottery, textiles, mkt. gardening; p. (1961) 23,956.

Zomba, t., Malawi, 2,900 ft. above sea level on slopes of Zomba mtn., 42 m. N.E. Blantyre; univ.; p. (1966) 19,616.

Zonguldak, t., Turkey; p. (1965) 60,565.

Zorita De Los Canos, Guadalajara, Spain; on R. Tagus; nuclear power plant.

Zorritos, t., Tumbes dep., Peru, S. America; on cst., 10 m. from Ecuador bdy.; oilfield.

Zoutpansberg, dist., N.E. Transvaal, S. Africa; goldfields, mtns.

Zrenjanin (Veliki Bečkerek), t., Vojvodina, Jugoslavia; on R. Begej; flour, leather, timber, sugar, wine, paper, agr., machin.; p. (1960) 52,100.

Zug, can., Switzerland; cap. Zug; a. 93 sq. m.; p. (1961) 52,489.

Zugspitze, mtn., Bavarian Alps, highest peak in Germany, 9,722 ft.

Zuider Zee, see Ijselmeer.

Zulia, st., Venezuela, S. America; cap. Maracaibo; p. (1963) 1,044,000.

Zululand, prov., Natal; livestock, cereals, fruit, sugar, coffee, tea, gold, coal; a. 10,427 sq. m.

Zungeru, t., Nigeria, Africa; on Lagos-Kano rly.

Zurich, can., Switzerland; cottons, silks; a. 668 sq. m.; p. (1961) 952,304.

Zurich (Zürich), c., Switzerland; on L. Zurich and R. Limmat, lgst. t.; cap. of Z. prov.; cath., univ.; paper, silks, cottons, machin.; p. (1961) 439,600.

Zutphen, c., Gelderland, Neth.; on R. IJssel; paper, tanning,engin.; p. (1967) 27,017.

Zveitina, Libya; new oil terminal 1968; pipeline from Idris field.

Zwartebergen, mtns., Cape Province, Rep. of S. Africa; extending 200 m. E. to W. flanked by Gr. Karroo to N. Little Karroo to S.; form impenetrable barrier except where broken across by headstreams of R. Gouritz; rise to over 7,000 ft.

Zwartsluis, t., Neth.; nr. Zwolle; p. 3,348.

Zweibrücken, t., Rhineland-Palatinate, Germany; nr. Saarbrücken; cas.; machin., footwear, textiles; p. (1963) 33,300.

Zwickau, t., Karl-Marx-Stadt, E. Germany; on R. Zwickhauser Mulde; cas.; coal, motors, machin., textiles; p. (1963) 129,389.

Zwolle, c., Overijssel, Neth.; canal ctr.; cattle mkt., cottons, ironwks.; p. (1967) 59,877.

Zyrardow, t., Poland; nr. Warsaw; mnfs.; p. (1965) 91,000.

Zyryanovsk, t., Kazakhstan S.S.R.; lead, zinc; p. (1959) 54,000.

# THE COMMONWEALTH

The Commonwealth is a free association of independent member nations together with their dependencies at various stages of political advance. Member nations include Britain, Canada, Australia, New Zealand whose membership of the Commonwealth dates from the Statute of Westminster, 1931, India (1947), Pakistan (1947), Ceylon (1948), Ghana (1957), the Federation of Malaya (1957), which in 1963 became Malaysia, the Federation (now the Federal Republic) of Nigeria (1960), Cyprus (1961), Sierra Leone (1961), Tanganyika (1961), which in 1964 united with Zanzibar (1963) to become Tanzania, Jamaica (1962), Trinidad and Tobago (1962), Uganda (1962), Kenya (1963), Malawi (1964), Malta (1964), Zambia (1964), the Gambia (1965), Singapore, which seceded from the Malaysian Federation (1965), Botswana (1966), Guyana (1966), Lesotho (1966), Barbados (1966), Mauritius (1968), and Swaziland (1968). Nauru, which became independent in 1968, has the status of "special membership" of the Commonwealth. *See also* Section C, Part II.

## I.—MEMBERS OF THE COMMONWEALTH
(including territories for which members other than the U.K. are responsible).

| Country | Land Area (sq. miles) | Recent Population Estimates |
|---|---|---|
| United Kingdom | 94,209 | 55,068,000 |
| Canada (incl. Newfoundland and Labrador) | 3,851,809 | 20,334,000 |
| Australia (Commonwealth of) | 2,974,581 | 11,929,000 |
| Cocos Islands | 5 | 607 |
| Christmas Island | 55 | 3,099 |
| Norfolk Island—*Colony* | 13½ | 1,048 |
| Papua—*Colony* | 90,540 | 523,000 |
| New Guinea—*Trusteeship* | 93,000 | 1,449,000 |
| Antarctic territory | 2,333,624 | — |
| New Zealand | 103,736 | 2,781,000 |
| Island Territories (Cook Is. self-gov. st.) | 194 | 24,478 |
| Ross Dependency | 160,000 (estimated) | 262 |
| India (Republic of) | 1,178,995 | 511,298,000 |
| Pakistan (Republic of) | 365,529 | 102,876,000 |
| Ceylon | 25,332 | 10,582,000 |
| Ghana (Republic of) | 91,843 | 7,945,000 |
| Nigeria (Federal Republic of) | 356,669 | 55,000,000 |
| *Cyprus (Republic of) | 3,572 | 614,000 |
| Sierra Leone | 27,925 | 2,183,000 |
| Tanzania (United Republic of) | 363,708 | 12,231,000 |
| Uganda | 93,981 | 7,740,000 |
| Jamaica | 4,411 | 1,893,000 |
| Trinidad and Tobago | 1,980 | 828,000 |
| Kenya (Republic of) | 224,960 | 9,104,000 |
| Malaysia (Federation of) | 127,298 | 9,880,000 |
| Malawi (Republic of) | 45,747 | 4,042,000 |
| Malta and Gozo | 122 | 318,000 |
| Zambia (Republic of) | 288,130 | 3,894,000 |
| Gambia | 4,003 | 330,000 |
| Singapore (Republic of) | 291 | 1,956,000 |
| Botswana (Republic of) | 222,000 | 576,000 |
| Guyana | 83,000 | 692,000 |
| Lesotho | 11,716 | 1,000,000 |
| Barbados | 166 | 251,000 |
| Mauritius | 720 | 803,000 |
| Swaziland | 6,704 | 389,000 |

* The United Kingdom retains sovereignty over areas totalling about 99 sq. m.

The West Indian Associated States (Antigua, St. Kitts-Nevis-Anguilla, Dominica, St. Lucia, St. Vincent and Grenada) enjoy a special relationship with Britain. They are fully self-governing but Britain retains general responsibility for their defence and external relations. This relationship can be terminated either by the island territory concerned or by the British Government. Anguilla unilaterally seceded from the St. Kitts union in 1967.

## II.—TERRITORIES FOR WHICH THE U.K. IS RESPONSIBLE AND WHICH ARE ADMINISTERED THROUGH THE FOREIGN AND COMMONWEALTH OFFICE.

(Some of the very small, or practically uninhabited, islands have been omitted.)

| Region and Territory | Status | Land Area (sq. miles) | Recent Population Estimates |
|---|---|---|---|
| **Central Africa:** | | | |
| Rhodesia | Colony (self-gov.) | 150,333 | 4,330,000 |
| **Far East:** | | | |
| Brunei | Protected state (self-gov.) | 2,226 | 84,000 |
| Hong Kong | Colony | 398 | 3,527,000 |
| **Mediterranean:** | | | |
| Gibraltar | Colony | 2¼ | 25,000 |
| **Caribbean:** | | | |
| Montserrat | Colony | 32 | 14,500 |
| Cayman Is. | Colony | 100 | 7,600 |
| British Honduras | Colony (intern. self-gov.) | 8,866 | 114,000 |
| Virgin Islands | Colony | 59 | 8,600 |
| **Western Pacific:** | | | |
| Fiji | Colony | 7,095 | 477,000 |
| Pitcairn | Colony | 2 | 186 |
| Tonga | Protected State | 270 | 77,000 |
| Western Pacific High Commission Territories: | | | |
| British Solomon Islands Protectorate | Protectorate | 11,500 | 146,000 |
| Gilbert and Ellice Islands Colony | Colony | 369 | 52,000 |
| New Hebrides | Anglo-French Condominium | 5,700 | 66,000 |
| **Atlantic Ocean:** | | | |
| Falkland Islands | Colony | 4,700 | 2,122 |
| Dependencies: | | | |
| S. Georgia | Dependency of Falkland Islands | 1,450 | 531 |
| S. Sandwich Is. | Dependency of Falkland Islands | | Uninhabited |
| British Antarctic Territory: | | | |
| S. Shetlands, S. Orkneys, Graham's Land | Colony | 500,000 | No permanent inhabitants |
| Bahamas | Colony (intern. self-gov.) | 4,404 | 146,000 |
| Turks and Caicos Is. | Colony | 166 | 6,272 |
| Bermuda | Colony | 21 | 50,000 |
| St. Helena | Colony | 47 | 5,000 |
| Ascension | Dependency of St. Helena | 34 | 1,217 |
| Tristan da Cunha | Dependency of St. Helena | 38 | 270 |
| **Indian Ocean:** | | | |
| Seychelles | Colony | 156 | 49,000 |
| †British Indian Ocean Territory | | | 1,400 |

*Note.*—An illegal declaration of independence was declared in Rhodesia on 11 November 1965. *See* Section C, Part II.

† This territory consists of the Chagos Archipelago (formerly part of Mauritius) and Aldabra, Farquhar and Desroches Islands (formerly part of Seychelles).

# GENERAL
# INFORMATION

Some three thousand entries, including a number of scientific terms
and explanations.   Cross references
direct the reader to fuller information elsewhere in the book.   A
list of Nobel Prize Winners will be
found at the end of the section.

# GENERAL INFORMATION

## A

**Aard-vark** (Dutch *aarde* = earth + *vark* = pig), name given by the Boers to a genus of ant-eating mammals peculiar to Africa. They are nocturnal and burrowing, with an arched back, and usually grow to a length of 5 ft.

**Abacus,** a device for making arithmetical calculations, consisting of parallel bars on which are strung movable coloured beads. The earliest form of this instrument was used in Mesopotamia about 3000 B.C., and its use spread westwards throughout the Græco–Roman world and eastwards to China. An efficient form of the abacus is still used today in parts of Asia.

**Abdication.** The term usually refers to the renunciation of the royal office by a reigning monarch. Both Edward II (1327) and Richard II (1399) were forced to abdicate, James II left the throne vacant without waiting for a formal deposition, and the abdication of Edward VIII was effected by the Declaration of Abdication Act, 1936. Since 1688 when Parliament declared James II to have abdicated by reason of desertion and subversion of the constitution, no British monarch can abdicate without the consent of Parliament.

**Aberration,** in astronomy, is the apparent displacement of a star due to the speed of the observer with the earth (see Parallax). In optics (i) spherical aberration is when there is blurring of the image and fringes of colour at its edges, due to failure of lens to bring light to a single focus; (ii) chromatic aberration is due to the refractive index of glass being different for light of different colours. For instance, violet light is bent more than red.

**Abiogenesis,** or spontaneous generation; the origination of living from non-living matter. The term is applied to such discredited ideas as that frogs could be generated spontaneously by the action of sunlight on mud, or maggots arise spontaneously in dead meat without any eggs from which the maggots hatch being present. Spallanzani (1729–99) upset the hypothesis of spontaneous generation; Pasteur dealt it a death-blow.

**Abominable Snowman.** *See* Yeti.

**Aborigines,** a term first applied to an ancient mythical people of central Italy, derives from the Latin *ab origine* = from the beginning. It now signifies the original inhabitants of any country, in particular the aboriginal tribes of Australia. In contrast to their highly complex social and religious customs, the material culture of Australian aborigines is very low and ill adapted to stand up to contact with European civilisation. Originally estimated at 300,000, their number has dropped in the last 200 years to some 40,000. A referendum held in 1967 showed that the majority of Australians wished to give the Aborigines citizen rights and thus end the discrimination against them.

**Absolute Temperature, Absolute Zero.** This is a refined notion requiring some study of thermodynamics for its full understanding. For setting up an absolute temperature scale one must first assign a numerical value to one fixed temperature. For this, the triple point of water has been chosen, *i.e.*, the temperature at which solid, liquid, and gaseous water are all in equilibrium. The triple point is defined to be 273·16° K where °K is read " degrees Kelvin " (after Lord Kelvin). This temperature is 0·01° C on the Celsius scale (*q.v.*) and is thus very close to the melting point of ice. Suppose the pressure and volume of a mass of gas are measured (i) at the triple point of water, giving $(pV)_{tr}$ as the product of the pressure and volume; and (ii) at any unknown temperature $T°$ K, giving $(pV)$ as the product. Then the absolute temperature, $T°$ K, is defined by

$$T° \text{ K} = 273·16 \frac{(pV)}{(pV)_{tr}}$$

It is to be understood that the gas pressure is very low. The nature of the gas is immaterial. More subtly, it can be shown that the temperature so defined is identical with that derived in a rather abstract way in the science of thermodynamics. The absolute scale is therefore also called the thermodynamic scale. Absolute temperatures can be obtained from Celsius temperatures by adding 273·15; thus the absolute temperature of melting ice is 273·15° K. Conversely, absolute zero is a temperature 273·15° K below the temperature of melting ice, *i.e.*, −273·15° C. Theory shows that absolute zero is unattainable, but it has been approached to within about 1 millionth of a degree. Within ten or so degrees of absolute zero, matter develops some remarkable properties. *See* Cryogenics, Superconductor, Helium.

**Absolution,** an ecclesiastical term denoting the liberation of a person guilty of sin from its consequences by the act or intercession of religious authority.

**Abstract Art,** a term applied to 20th cent. plastic arts in which form and colour possess aesthetic value apart from the subject. Usually represented as a modern movement beginning with Cézanne. The idea is ancient, abstract design being found in the Neolithic period, in folk-art, and particularly in Moslem art (which forbids naturalistic representations especially of the human figure). Among those in the tradition are Kandinsky, Braque, Mondrian, Calder.

**Acetic Acid,** an organic acid produced when ordinary (ethyl) alcohol is fermented by the organism called *Acetobacter aceti*. The same oxidation process yields vinegar; this is a weak and crude solution of acetic acid obtained by trickling dilute alcoholic liquor over beechwood shavings at 35° C. The souring of wine is due to the same process. Acetic acid is used as a food preservative and flavouring material, and in the manufacture of cellulose acetate and white lead.

**Acetylene,** a compound of carbon and hydrogen prepared from calcium carbide and water. A very reactive gas, it is used industrially on a large scale to prepare acetaldehyde, chlorohydrocarbon solvents, and many intermediates for plastics manufacture. Burns in air with a highly luminous flame, formerly used for lighting purposes, but is now widely used, with oxygen, in welding. For safe storage and transportation it is dissolved in acetone.

**Acids,** substances having a tendency to lose a positive ion (a proton). This general definition overcomes difficulties of earlier views which merely described their properties and asserted that they are chemically opposite to bases. As a whole acids contain ionisable hydrogen, replaceable by a metal, to form a salt. Inorganic acids are compounds of non-metals or metalloids, *e.g.*, sulphuric, phosphoric acid. Carboxylic acids contain the group –COOH. **F22.**

**Acolyte,** one who assists the priest at Mass by saying the responses and by waiting on him.

**Act of God,** a natural catastrophe that could not be foreseen or averted.

**Advent,** a period devoted to religious preparation for the coming celebration of the Nativity (Christmas). It comprises four Sundays, and commences on the one nearest to St. Andrew's Day (Nov. 30). Advent was not observed before the 4th cent.

**Advocatus Diaboli** (" the devil's advocate "), a Roman Catholic functionary who presents opposing evidence in regard to the life of any deceased person it may be proposed to canonise.

**Aeolian Harp,** a musical instrument once very popular. It consists of catgut stretched over a wooden sound-box which, when placed out of doors in the wind, can be made to emit many pleasing harmonies.

**Aerenchyma.** Plant tissue which is spongy because there are large air spaces between the cells in which gases can circulate. This aerating tissue is characteristic of marsh and water-plants.

**Aerodynamics,** the science of gases (especially air) in motion, particularly in relation to aircraft (aeronautics). The idea of imitating the birds by the use of wings is of ancient origin. Leonardo da Vinci first carried out experiments in a scientific manner. The invention of the balloon in 1783 and the researches of scientists and engineers in the 19th cent. ultimately led to the development of the aeroplane.

**Aerolites,** the name given to the class of meteorites composed chiefly of heavy silicates. The other two main classes are *siderolites* (nickel–iron and silicates) and *siderites* (nickel–iron).

**Aerosol,** a suspension of a liquid in a gas; for example, a fog is very small drops of water suspended in air. Formed by spraying the liquid in air, aerosols are used to disperse liquids over a wide area in crop spraying, air freshening, and pest control.

**Afrikander,** type of cattle bred in South Africa.

**Afrikaner,** an Afrikaans-speaking South African, usually of Dutch descent.

**After-damp** is a mixture of carbon dioxide and nitrogen that occurs in a mine after an explosion and causes suffocation to human beings. It is also called " choke damp " and "black damp."

**Agape,** a " love-feast " held by the early Christians in commemoration of the Lord's Supper. *See* J28 (1).

**Agar-agar,** a vegetable jelly obtained from sea-weeds, widely used in jellies, canned meat and poultry, and as a constituent in medicinal and cosmetic preparations. Used by bacteriologists to solidify broth and blood upon which bacteria are cultivated. Chief sources of supply: Far East and California.

**Agaric,** large fungi of the family *Agaricaceae,* which includes the mushroom and what are popularly called " toadstools," though the idea that these two lay terms sharply differentiate between edible and poisonous fungi is an incorrect one. Characteristic of the agarics is the presence of a cap or *pileus* (bearing underneath the spore-shedding gills) and a stalk or *stipe.*

**Agate,** a variety of chalcedony. Parallel bands of colour are often characteristic. Germany, Brazil, and India furnish the main supplies, and Scotland has a species of agate called Scotch pebble.

**Agave,** the American aloe or Century Plant which sometimes does not attain to flowering maturity under sixty or seventy years, and then dies. The flower spray may reach a height of 20 feet and in its development the rush of sap is so great that the Mexicans collect for brewing the strong spirit called mescal. 1,000 litres of sap can be obtained from a single plant. Some species of agave yield sisal used for making cord and rope.

**Agnus Dei** (Lamb of God), a short anthem said or sung at a certain point of the Roman Catholic Mass or Anglican communion service. (John i. 29.)

**Air** is a mixture of gases forming the atmosphere we breathe. Nitrogen, oxygen, and argon are always present in air; a typical sample of dry air might contain these gases in the following proportions (by volume): nitrogen, $78 \cdot 06\%$; oxygen, $21\%$; argon, $0 \cdot 94\%$. A small quantity of carbon dioxide is present, about 3 parts in 10,000 parts of air. This carbon dioxide is the source of carbon compounds built up by green plants in photosynthesis (F28); in the process carbon dioxide is absorbed from the air and oxygen returned, the reverse of the respiratory process of animals. Air also contains a quantity of water vapour, and traces of ammonia, nitrogen oxides, hydrogen, sulphur dioxide, hydrogen sulphide, ozone and of the rare gases helium, krypton, neon, and xenon. In a city smoke and dust particles may be as abundant as 100,000 particles per cc. A litre of air at $0°$ C. and 700 mm. pressure weighs $1 \cdot 2932$ grams. *See also* Atmosphere, Pollution.

**Alabaster,** a soft crystalline form of sulphate of lime, or granulated gypsum, easily worked for statuary and other ornamental articles, and capable of being highly polished. Volterra, in Tuscany, yields the finest; that in highest ancient repute came from Alabastron in Egypt, near to the modern Antinoë.

**Alb,** white vestment reaching to the feet, worn by priests in religious ceremonies.

**Albatross,** a large sea-bird of almost pure white black and white, or brown plumage. It nests in colonies on remote islands, but at other times rarely approaches land. Of the thirteen species, nine are found in the southern oceans, one in the tropics, and the three others in the North Pacific.

**Albert Memorial,** a large Gothic monument designed by Sir George Gilbert Scott, and embellished with sculptures by eminent artists. Erected in memory of Prince Albert in Kensington Gardens at a cost of £120,000.

**Alcázar,** the palace at Seville, famed for the beauty of its halls and gardens, in ancient days the residence of the Moorish kings.

**Alcohols.** A class of organic compounds of general formula R–OH, where R is an aliphatic radical. " Alcohol " is the name used for ethyl alcohol (ethanol); this is produced by distilling fermented liquors, and synthetically from ethylene, a product of petroleum cracking. Industrially ethyl alcohol is used in the manufacture of chloroform, ether, perfumes, etc. Diluted with wood alcohol or other denaturants ethyl alcohol is called " methylated spirits "; the denaturants are varied according to the industrial purposes for which it is required, the methylated spirits then being largely exempt from duty. Wood alcohol (methyl alcohol or methanol) can be obtained by distilling wood, or synthetically from water gas. *See* F24(1).

**Alcoholic Strength.** In Great Britain the standard is the proof gallon which is an imperial gallon of spirits containing $49 \cdot 28$ per cent. of alcohol by weight or $57 \cdot 1$ per cent. by volume at $60°$ F. In Europe the strength of spirits is usually measured by the Guy-Lussac hydrometer. In the U.S.A., because of the smaller gallon, $1 \cdot 37$ U.S. proof gallons $= 1$ British proof gallon. In Britain the alcoholic content of spirits and liqueurs appears on the bottle in degrees proof. Whisky, for example, at $70°$ proof (or $30°$ under proof) contains $70/100 \times 57 \cdot 1$ alcohol, or about 40 per cent. The alcoholic content of wines is not shown on the label.

**Aldehyde,** the generic term for a class of chemical compounds of general formula R·CHO, where R is an organic radical. Except for formaldehyde, which is a gas, aldehydes are volatile liquids. They are produced by oxidation of primary alcohols. Most important aldehyde is formaldehyde used in making the plastics described as formaldehyde resins. Formalin (formaldehyde solution in water) is much used for preserving zoological specimens.

**Alder,** a river-side tree of the genus *Alnus,* including some 30 species and found in north temperate regions and the Andes. The only species native to Britain is *A. glutinosa,* which has been described as " guardian of river-banks " because of the way its roots bind together the sand and stones, and so slow down erosion. The wood is used for furniture and charcoal.

**Aldine Editions** are the beautiful books printed in Venice by the Renaissance printer Aldo Pio Manuzio and his family between 1490 and 1597. Italics were first introduced in these books.

**Algae,** flowerless plants living mostly in water. Seaweeds and the green pond scums are the best known algae. The green powder found on trees is composed of a microscopic alga (*Protococcus*).

**Algebra,** a branch of mathematics in which symbols are used in place of numbers. Sir Isaac Newton styled it the " universal arithmetic." The Chinese were able to solve the quadratic equation before the Christian era but it was Al-Khowarizmi, an Arab mathematician of the early 9th cent., who introduced algebra to Europe.

**Alhambra,** the ancient palace of the Moorish kings at Granada in Spain, built in the 13th and 14th cent. Though part of the castle was turned into a modern palace under Charles V., the most beautiful parts of the interior are still preserved—the graceful halls and dwelling-rooms grouped round the Court of Alberca and the Court of Lions, with their fountains, arcades, and lovely gardens.

**Aliphatic** describes derivatives of hydrocarbons having chains of carbon atoms, as distinct from rings of carbon atoms as in benzene (*see* Aromatic). The gas butane is aliphatic.

**Alkali,** the general name given to a number of chemicals which are bases (*q.v.*). The term should be limited to the hydroxides of metals in the first and second group of the periodic table and of ammonia, e.g., NaOH, KOH. They are used commercially in the manufacture of paper, glass, soap, and artificial silk. The word comes from the Arabic al-kali meaning calcined wood ashes. Alkalis are extremely soluble in water and neutralise acids to form salts and water.

**Alkaloids,** a large group of natural products which contain nitrogen; they are usually basic. Isolated from plants and animals, they include some hormones, vitamins, and drugs. Examples are nicotine, adrenalin, and cocaine. Many alkaloids are made synthetically for medicinal use, e.g., morphine, quinine. Their function in plants is not well understood. See Belladonna.

**Alligator,** the crocodile of America, common in the lower Mississippi and adjacent lakes and marshes, varying in length from 2 to 20 feet.

**Alloys** are combinations of metals. They are made because of their valuable special properties, e.g., durability, strength, lightness, magnetism, rust-resistance, etc. Some well-known ones are brass (zinc + copper), coinage bronze (copper + zinc + tin), steels (iron + carbon + various other materials), soft solder (tin + lead), dental fillings (mercury + various ingredients).

**All Saints' Day** (Nov. 1) is common to both the English and Roman Catholic Churches, and is in commemoration of the saints generally, or such as have no special day set apart for them. Instituted by Pope Boniface IV., early in the 7th cent., this ecclesiastical festival was formerly called " All Hallows."

**All Souls' Day** (Nov. 2) is a festival of the Roman Church, intended for the mitigation by prayer of the sufferings of souls in purgatory. The commemoration was enjoined by Abbot Odilo of Cluny during the 11th cent. upon the monastic order over which he presided, and was afterwards adopted generally throughout the Roman Communion.

**Allspice,** a flavouring obtained from a West Indian tree of the myrtle family, Pimenta officinalis. The essential oil of its unripe fruit is a powerful irritant, and the bruised berries are carminative.

**Alluvium,** accumulations of sand, mud, gravel, etc., washed down by rivers and forming distinct deposits.

**Almond,** the fruit of the Amygdalus communis, originally indigenous to Persia, Asia Minor, and N. Africa; now cultivated in Italy, Spain, France, the U.S.A., and Australia. It yields both bitter and sweet oil. Bitter almond oil is obtained by macerating and distilling the ripe seeds; it is used for flavouring and scenting purposes, its fragrant odour being due to the presence of benzaldehyde and hydrogen cyanide. When the seeds are pressed sweet almond oil results: this is used in perfumery, and also as a lubricant for very delicate machinery.

**Almuce,** a fur stole worn by certain canons.

**Aloe,** large plants of the lily family, with about 180 species found mainly in the S. African veldt and Karroo. The bitter purgative drug (aloes) is prepared by evaporating the plant's sap. See Agave.

**Alpaca,** a South American ruminant related to the llama whose long, fine wool is woven into a soft dress fabric known by the same name. Sir Titus Salt first manufactured alpaca cloth (1836). Saltaire, near Bradford, remains to evidence the success which for many years attended the enterprise.

**Alpha Particle,** or alpha-ray, fast-moving helium nucleus ejected by some radioactive atoms, e.g., polonium. It is a combination of 2 neutrons and 2 protons. See F11(1).

**Alphabet** (so called from the first two letters of the Greek alphabet—alpha, beta) is the term applied to the collection of letters from which the words of a language are made up. It grew out of the knowledge that all words can be expressed by a limited number of sounds arranged in various combinations. The Phoenicians were the first to make use of an alphabetic script derived from an earlier Semitic alphabet (earliest known inscriptions c. 1500–950 B.C.) from which all other alphabets have sprung. The stages in the development of the alphabet were mnemonic (memory aids), pictorial (actual pictures),

ideographic (symbols), and lastly phonetic. All the ideographic systems died out, with the exception of that of the Chinese.

**Altimeter,** an instrument used in aircraft to estimate altitude; its usual essential feature is an aneroid barometer which registers the decrease of pressure with height. Roughly 1 millibar corresponds to 30 ft. To read an aircraft altimeter correct for its destination, the zero setting must be adjusted for difference of ground height and difference of surface pressure, especially when pressure is falling or when flying towards low pressure.

**Altitude,** an astronomical term used to signify the angular elevation of a heavenly body; this is measured with a quadrant or sextant. In aeronautics it is the height (in feet or metres) above sea-level.

**Alto-Relievo,** a term applied to sculptured designs which are depicted in prominent relief on a flat surface, technically signifying that the projection exceeds one-half the true proportions of the objects represented. Basso-relievo is carving kept lower than one-half such projection.

**Alum** is a compound salt used in various industrial processes, especially dyeing, its constituents being the sulphate of one univalent metal or radical (e.g., potassium, sodium, ammonium, rubidium, caesium, silver, thallium) and the sulphate of a tervalent metal (e.g., aluminium, iron, chromium, manganese), and water of crystallisation.

**Alumina** is the oxide of aluminium. Very valuable as a refractory material. The ruby is almost 100 per cent. alumina; so also are the emerald, oriental amethyst, etc. An hydrated aluminium oxide is bauxite, chief ore of aluminium from which the metal is extracted electrolytically.

**Aluminium** is a light metal which conducts electricity well. Its specific gravity at 20° C. is 2·705. Melting point of aluminium is 660·2° C. It is made commercially by electrolysing bauxite dissolved in cryolite (double fluoride of aluminium and sodium). Aluminium alloys because of their strength and lightness are being increasingly used for the construction of railway coaches, automobiles, aeroplanes, etc.

**Amadavat,** a popular cage bird of the weaver family, mainly crimson with white spots, so named because the first specimens came from Ahmadabad in India about 1700.

**Amalgam** is the term applied to any alloy of which mercury forms a part.

**Amber,** a brittle resinous substance; in origin, fossilised resin. Obtained mostly from the Baltic coasts, and used for ornaments, pipe mouth-pieces, etc.

**Ambergris** is a waxy substance produced in the intestines of the sperm whale, and generally found floating on the sea. It is a valuable perfumery material.

**Amblyopsis,** a species of fish, practically sightless, and with inoperative organs of hearing and feeling, that inhabit the Mammoth Cave of Kentucky. A remarkable illustration of the failure of senses not brought into use.

**America's Cup,** a prize trophy first offered in 1851 by the Royal Yacht Squadron and open to yachts of all nations. It was won in the first year by the " America," a New York yacht, and has remained on that side of the ocean ever since, despite attempts to recapture it by Lord Dunraven, Sir Thomas Lipton, Mr. T. O. M. Sopwith, and others. The last attempt by Great Britain was in 1964, when Sovereign was beaten by the American Constellation. Australia challenged for the first time in 1962 with Gretel, and in 1967 with Dame Pattie, but unsuccessfully. See also U32(2).

**Amethyst,** the violet variety of quartz, used as a precious stone, containing traces of manganese, titanium, and iron. The finest coloured specimens come from Brazil and the Urals.

**Amice,** a linen vestment worn about the neck by Roman and many Anglican priests over the alb when officiating at Mass or Holy Eucharist. Formerly worn on the head by priests and pilgrims.

**Amines,** organic chemicals composed of carbon, hydrogen, and nitrogen. They are derived from ammonia, which they resemble in smell and chemical characteristics. The smell of bad fish is due to the presence of amines. Important industrially as intermediates in a wide variety of products, for example, the synthesis of dye-stuffs and man-made fibres such as nylon.

**Amino acids,** organic compounds containing an amine group and an acid group. They are the " building bricks " of proteins (q.v.). See F27(1), 29.

**Ammeter,** an instrument for measuring the current flowing in an electric circuit. A contraction of ampere-meter. See Ampere.

**Ammonia,** a colourless gaseous compound comprising three atoms of hydrogen to one of nitrogen. Formerly it was made by heating the horns and hoofs of deer, acquiring the name of spirits of hartshorn. The ammonia of commerce is now procured by coal decomposition in the course of gas-making and by direct synthesis. In the very important Haber process of ammonia production by fixation of atmospheric nitrogen, the nitrogen is made to combine with hydrogen and the ammonia so prepared is converted into nitric acid, ammonium nitrate or ammonium sulphate. The Haber process made Germany self-sufficient in nitrates in the first world war, and was afterwards exploited all over the world.

**Ammonites,** extinct animals related to the Nautilus. The chambered shell is coiled, usually in a plane spiral, and they are confined to Mesozoic rocks.

**Ammonium,** the basic radical of ammonium salts. Composed of one atom of nitrogen and four of hydrogen, it behaves chemically like an ion of a monovalent alkali metal. Ammonium chloride is known as " sal ammoniac." " Sal volatile " is ammonium carbonate.

**Amnesty,** an act of grace by which a ruler or governing power pardons political offenders.

**Amorphous,** a term used to indicate the absence of crystalline form in any body or substance.

**Ampere,** unit of electric current in the SI system of units; named after André Marie Ampère, who in the 1820s helped to lay the foundations of modern electromagnetism. Defined as that constant current which, if maintained in two parallel rectilinear conductors of infinite length, of negligible circular cross section, and placed at a distance of one metre apart in a vacuum, would produce between these conductors a force equal to $2 \times 10^{-7}$ newton per metre length. See N13.

**Amphibia.** See F33(2).

**Amphioxus** or **Lancelet,** a primitive chordate occurring in sand-banks around British shores and elsewhere.

**Ana,** a collection of criticisms, observations, or opinions about a particular person, place or subject. Used as a suffix especially applies to a person's memorable sayings, anecdotes about or publications bearing on, as in Johnsoniana, Alexandriana, Victoriana.

**Anabolism.** See Catabolism.

**Anarchism.** See J3.

**Anchor,** an instrument used for keeping ships stationary. Great improvements have been introduced in recent years, stockless anchors being now chiefly used, consisting of a shank and a loose fluke. Lloyds' rules prescribe the number and weight of anchors which must be carried by merchant ships.

**Anchorite** is a religious person who retires into solitude to employ himself with holy thoughts. Among the early Christians, anchorites were numerous, but in the Western Church they have been few. Their reputation for wisdom and prescience was high, and kings and rulers in olden days would visit their cells for counsel. An anchorite or " ankret " was in mediæval times a source of fame and profit to the monastic house within which he was voluntarily immured.

**Anchovy,** a fish of the herring family, distinguished by its large mouth and projecting snout, plentiful in the Mediterranean and much esteemed when cured.

**Ancient Lights** are rights of light enjoyed by a property owner over adjoining land. Such a right is obtained either by uninterrupted enjoyment for twenty years, or by written authority, and once legally established cannot be upset, no building being permissible that would seriously interfere with the privilege.

**Anemometer,** an instrument for measuring the strength of the wind. In the most widely used pattern the rotation, about a vertical axis, of a group of hemispherical or conical cups gives a measure of the total flow of air past the cups, various registering devices being employed. The Dines anemograph provides a continuous record of the variation in both velocity and direction; changes of pressure produced in a horizontal tube, kept pointing into the wind by a vane, cause a float, to which a pen is attached, to rise and fall in sympathy with the gusts and lulls. The recently devised hot-wire anemometer, depending upon the change of electrical resistance experienced by a heated wire when cooled, enables very gentle air currents to be investigated.

**Aneroid** is the kind of barometer which does not depend upon atmospheric support of a mercury (or other liquid) column. It consists of a metallic box, partially exhausted of air, with a corrugated lid which moves with atmospheric changes. A lever system magnifies the lid movements about 200 times and atmospheric pressure is read from a dial. The construction of the vacuum chamber provides automatic compensation for temperature changes. An aneroid barometer is the basic component of an altimeter.

**Angelica,** an aromatic plant of the Umbelliferae order, Angelica officinalis, valuable as a flavouring and possessing medicinal properties. In olden times supposed to protect against poison.

**Angelus,** a church bell rung in Roman Catholic countries, at morn, noon, and sunset, to remind the faithful to say their Angelic Salutation.

**Angevin Dynasty** includes the Plantagenet kings from Henry II. to Richard II. The name was derived from Henry II.'s father, Geoffrey, Count of Anjou.

**Angles,** a northern tribe originally settled in Schleswig, who with the Saxons and Jutes invaded Britain in the 5th cent.

**Angstrom,** a unit of wavelength, named after the Swedish physicist A. J. Angstrom (1814–74), equal to one hundred-millionth of a centimetre ($10^{-8}$ cm). It is used to measure wavelengths of light, X-rays, etc.

**Aniline,** a simple aromatic compound related to benzene and ammonia. It is obtained from coal-tar. The name recalls the fact that it was first prepared by distilling indigo (anil is Portuguese for indigo). In 1856 W. H. Perkin (1838–1907) discovered the first aniline or coal-tar dye, mauve, and thus founded the modern dyestuff industry.

**Animal Kingdom.** See F32.

**Anise,** an umbelliferous plant (Pimpinella anisum) found in Egypt and the Levant, and valued for its fruit, aniseed, possessing certain medicinal properties and yielding an aromatic, volatile oil. Also used in cooking. The anise of the Bible is Anethum graveolens, i.e., dill.

**Annates** were acknowledgments formerly paid to the popes by way of fee or tax in respect of ecclesiastical preferment, and consisted usually of a proportion of the income (" first-fruits ") of the office. Introduced into England in the 13th cent.; annexed to the Crown under Henry VIII; transferred to a perpetual fund for the benefit of the poorer clergy in 1704. See Queen Anne's Bounty.

**" Annual Register,"** a yearly record of political and literary events, founded by Edmund Burke (as editor) in 1759 and Robert Dorsley, the bookseller.

**Annunciation, Feast of the** (March 25), is a church festival commemorating the message of the incarnation of Christ brought by the angel Gabriel to the Virgin Mary, hence the title Lady Day.

**Anointing** is the pouring of consecrated oil upon the body as a mark of supreme honour. In England it is restricted chiefly to the ceremony of the monarch's coronation, and the spoon with which the oil is applied forms part of the English regalia. In the Roman Catholic Church anointing represents the sacrament of extreme unction.

**Ant.** There are about 6,000 species of ants, which belong to the same order (Hymenoptera) as the bees, wasps, and ichneumon flies. They are social in habit, living in communities of varying size and development. There are three basic castes in ants—the females or queens, the males, and the workers (the last-named being neuter), although specialised forms of workers are sometimes found, e.g., the soldiers of the harvesting ants. In the communities of those species of ants which evolved most recently there is a highly complex social life and well-developed division of labour. Some species of these ants make slaves of other species, stealing the cocoons before the adult forms emerge. Many ants " milk " greenflies, which they protect for their honey-like secretion, and most ants' nests contain many " guests," such as beetles and silver fish. Some ants harvest grains of corn, and others, from S. America, live on fungi which they cultivate in underground " mushroom beds."

**Antarctic Exploration.** In earlier centuries it was thought that a great continent must exist in the southern hemisphere, around the South Pole, to balance the known land masses in the north. Its supposed extent was greatly reduced in the 18th cent., particularly when Capt. Cook sailed for the first time south of the Antarctic Circle and reached the edge of the ice pack. A portion of the ice-covered continent—the coast of Graham Land—was first sighted by Lieut. Edward Bransfield in 1820. Explorers of several other nations sighted portions of the coast-line in other quarters, but the first extensive exploration was made by Capt. James Clarke Ross, who with the *Erebus* and *Terror* penetrated into the Ross Sea in 1841, and discovered the great Ross Ice Barrier in 78° South lat. Interest in the Antarctic did not revive until after 1890, when an international scheme of research was drawn up. A Norwegian, C. E. Borchgrevink, in 1898–1900, was the first to winter in the Antarctic and to travel on the ice barrier. The British share in this work was carried out by Capt. R. F. Scott's expedition in the *Discovery*, 1901–4. Scott's party sledged across the barrier to 82° 17′ South, then a record " farthest south." A little later, Ernest Shackleton beat this by travelling to within 100 miles of the South Pole. In 1910 Scott organised his second expedition of the *Terra Nova*, and became engaged against his will in a " race for the Pole," when, after his departure, the Norwegian Arctic explorer, Roald Amundsen, suddenly announced that he was sailing for the Antarctic. Amundsen set up his base at the eastern end of the Barrier, and relying on dog teams for hauling his sledges, reached the Pole on December 14, 1911. Meanwhile Scott and his party, their start delayed by adverse weather, were marching southwards, man-hauling their sledges, for Scott was against the use of dogs. After an arduous journey they reached the Pole one month after Amundsen. The return was a struggle against the weather and increasing weakness, probably due to scurvy, until at last they perished within a few miles of their base. After the First World War the development of the whaling industry greatly stimulated further exploration. Outstanding expeditions included that of Admiral R. E. Byrd, 1929, when he flew over the South Pole; The British Graham Land expedition, 1934, which carried out the first extensive mapping of any part of the Antarctic continent; and the U.S. Navy's Antarctic Expedition of 1940, when the whole continent was circumnavigated and great areas photographed from the air. In recent years valuable work has been done by the first International expedition, the Norwegian–British–Swedish Expedition to Queen Maud Land, and by the French in Adélie Land. The Falkland Island Dependencies Survey, set up during the war, has continued the scientific exploration of Graham Land. The Antarctic was the scene of high adventure during the International Geophysical Year (1957–58), when scientists from many countries participated in the explorations. The Commonwealth Trans-Antarctic Expedition set out from opposite sides of the continent and met at the South Pole, the U.K. party, led by Sir Vivian Fuchs, from the Falklands, and Sir Edmund Hillary and his party from New Zealand. The U.K. party accomplished the first crossing of the White Continent in 99 days. Their scientific work included the making of seismic and complementary gravimetric studies at frequent intervals along the 2,200-mile traverse. Since the Antarctic is becoming important for many reasons, in weather forecasting, in the

whaling industry, and as a possible centre for world air routes, the tempo of exploration and research will become even faster in the future.

**Anteater.** There are two unrelated families of anteaters, the Myrmecophagidae and the Manidae. Among the former the Great Anteater (*Myrmecophaga jubita*) is the largest species, over 6 ft. in length, occurring in Central and S. America. Only half its size is the lesser Anteater (*Tamandua tetradactyla*); this is found in forests of tropical America and Trinidad. The Two-toed Anteater (*Cyclopes didactylus*) belongs to South America and Trinidad. These three animals live mostly on termites; they are adapted to this diet, having large claws for digging out ants, and a tubular mouth with a long sticky tongue. The Manidae are the Scaly Anteaters or Pangolins, widely distributed over Africa and the Orient. The difference between the two families is that the first has hair covering the body, the latter has horny scales instead.

**Antennae,** paired feelers of insects and crustacea.

**Anthem,** a choral composition, with or without instrumental accompaniment, usually sung after the third collect in the Church of England service. The words are from the Scriptures, and the composition may be for solo voices only, for full choir, or for both. Among the chief British composers of anthems are Tallis, Purcell, Croft, Boyce, Goss, and Stainer.

**Anthracite** is a black coal with a brilliant lustre. It contains 92% and over of carbon and burns slowly, without smoke or flame. *See* Coal.

**Anthropoid,** meaning " resembling man," a suborder of the primate mammals including man and also the gibbon, chimpanzee, orang-utan, and gorilla.

**Antibiotics.** *See* Index to Section P.

**Anticyclone,** a region where barometric pressure is greater than that of its surroundings. Such a system is distinguished on weather charts by a pattern of isobars, usually circular or oval-shaped, enclosing the centre of high pressure where the air is calm. In the remaining areas light or moderately strong winds blow spirally outwards, in a clockwise direction in the Northern Hemisphere (and in the reverse direction in the Southern Hemisphere), in accordance with Buys Ballot's law (an observer with back to wind in Northern Hemisphere has lower pressure to left; in Southern to right). Over the British Isles anticyclonic weather is generally quiet and settled, being fair, warm, and sunny in summer and either very cold and often foggy or overcast and gloomy in winter. These systems move slowly and sometimes remain practically stationary for days at a time, that over Siberia being particularly well defined. Extensive belts of almost permanent anticyclones occur in latitudes 30° N. and 30° S. Persistent anticyclonic weather with easterly winds during the months December to March, 1962–3, brought the coldest and hardest winter to Britain since 1740 (taking the Midlands as representative).

**Antimony.** Metal element, symbol Sb. In group V of the periodic table. Exists in various forms, the stable form being a grey brittle metal with a layer structure. The other forms are non-conductors. On being burned, it gives off dense fumes of oxide of antimony. By itself it is not of special utility; but as an alloy for hardening other metals, it is much used. As an alloy with lead for type-metal, and with tin and copper or zinc for Britannia-metal, it is of great value. Most important antimony ore is stibnite (antimony sulphide).

**Anti-Pope,** one elected in opposition to one held to be canonically chosen; commonly applied to the popes Urban VI. and Clement VII., who resided at Avignon during the Great Schism (1378–1417).

**Anti-proton,** the " negative proton," an atomic particle created in high energy collisions of nuclear particles. Its existence was confirmed in Oct. 1955. *See* F14.

**Antisemitism.** *See* J3.

**Antlers** are the branched horns of deer, the branches being called tines. Antlers originate as outgrowths of the frontal bone, and are usually shed once a year. Except in the reindeer and caribou they are restricted to the male.

**Apartheid.** *See* J4.

**Ape**, a term applied to the gorilla, chimpanzee, orang-utan, and gibbon—the anthropoid apes.

**Aphelion**, the point in the orbit of a planet farthest from the sun; the opposite of perihelion.

**Aphids.** See T29 (2).

**Apis**, the sacred bull worshipped by the ancient Egyptians; also the scientific name for the bee.

**Apocalyptic writings** are those which deal with revelation and prophecy, more especially the Revelation of St. John.

**Apocrypha** (hidden writings), the books which were included in the Septuagint (Greek) and Vulgate (Latin) versions of the Old Testament but excluded from the sacred canon at the Reformation by the Protestants on the grounds that they were not originally written in Hebrew nor regarded as genuine by the Jews. The books include: 1 and 2 Esdras, Tobit, Judith, additions to Esther, Wisdom of Solomon, Ecclesiasticus, Baruch, Song of the Three Holy Children, History of Susannah, Bel and the Dragon, Prayer of Manasses, 1 and 2 Maccabees. The term is usually applied to the additions to the old Testament, but there are also numerous Christian writings of the same character.

**Apogee**, that point in the orbit of a heavenly body which is farthest from the earth; used in relation to the sun, moon, and artificial satellites. The sun's apogee corresponds to the earth's aphelion; the moon's apogee is the point in its orbit most remote from the earth. See Perigee.

**Apostasy** is a revolt, by an individual or party, from one form of opinions or doctrine to another. Julian, the Roman Emperor (331–63), brought up as a Christian, became converted to paganism and on coming to the throne (361), proclaimed religious toleration. Hence his name, Julian the Apostate.

**Apostles.** The twelve apostles who were disciples of Jesus were: Simon Peter and Andrew (his brother), James and John (sons of Zebedee), Philip, Bartholomew, Thomas, Matthew, James, Thaddaeus, Simon, and Judas Iscariot. After the Ascension Matthias was chosen to take the place of Judas. St. Paul is always referred to as the chief apostle, though he is not one of the twelve. St. Barnabas has also been called an apostle.

**Apostles' Creed**, applied to the most ancient of the Church's statements of its belief: " I believe in God the Father Almighty; and in Jesus Christ his only Son our Lord, who was born of the Holy Ghost and the Virgin Mary. . . ." A later version is used in the Church of England at morning and evening prayer.

**Apostolic Fathers** were the immediate disciples or followers of the Apostles, especially such as left writings behind. They included Barnabas, Clement of Rome, Ignatius of Antioch, Hermas, Papias of Hieropolis, and Polycarp.

**Appeasement Policy.** The name of the policy during 1937 and 1938 of yielding to the demands of Hitler and Mussolini in the hope that a point would be reached when the dictators would co-operate in the maintenance of peace. The policy culminated in the Munich Agreement (which was the subject of much criticism) after a series of concessions including the recognition of the Italian conquest of Abyssinia and the German annexation of Austria. The policy was finally demonstrated as futile when Hitler seized Czechoslovakia in March 1939.

**Appian Way**, the oldest and finest of the Roman roads originally laid by Appius Claudius (312 B.C.) from Rome to Capua and thence to Brundisium (Brindisi).

**Approved Schools** are residential schools, subject to Home Office inspection, for the training of young persons under 17 who, because of disturbed behaviour as a result of unfavourable influences such as bad environment or parental neglect, are guilty of offences or in need of care and protection and have been sent to them by magistrates from juvenile or other courts. Corporal punishment is being phased out and many people think that there should be more psychiatric help available. See also Detention Centre, Borstal.

**April**, the fourth month of the year, from the Roman *Aprilis* derived from *aperire* " to open " —the period when the buds begin to open.

**Apse** is a semicircular recess, arched or dome-

roofed, at the end of the choir, aisles, or nave of a church.

**Aquatint** is a method of etching on copper, by which imitations of drawings in water-colours, Indian ink, bistre, and sepia are produced.

**Aqueducts** are conduits in which water flows or is conveyed from its source to the place where it is to be used. Most famous builders were the Romans and the oldest Roman aqueduct was the Aqua Appia, which dates from about 310 B.C. Among modern aqueducts may be mentioned that of Glasgow, which brings water to that city from Loch Katrine; that of Manchester, which taps Thirlmere; that of Liverpool, with Lake Vyrnwy in North Wales as its source, and the Fron Aqueduct, Radnorshire, which carries water from the Elan Valley to Birmingham.

**Arabesque**, the term applied to the elaborate decoration based on flowing lines used in Moorish art.

**Arabian Nights**, a collection of fascinating tales of the Orient, of mixed Indian, Persian, Arabic, and Egyptian origination, and first made known in Europe by Antoine Galland, a French Oriental scholar whose original translation was called *The Thousand and One Nights.*

**Arabic Numerals.** The modern system of numbering 0, 1, 2, 3, 4, 5, 6, 7, 8, 9, in which the digits depend on their position for their value, is called the Arabic numerical notation. The method is, in fact, of Indian origin. By the 9th cent. Hindu science was available in Arabic, and the Persian mathematician Al-Kwarizimi (c. 830) in his *Arithmetic* used the so-called "Arabic" system of numbering. Gradually the method spread to Europe, taking the place of the Roman system which was useless for calculation. The West is indebted to the Arabs for the zero symbol, the lack of which had been a serious drawback to Greek mathematics. It made the invention of decimal fractions possible.

**Aragonite**, the unstable form of calcium carbonate found as a mineral in some young deposits. It crystallises in the orthorhombic system but tends to revert to calcite (q.v.).

**Aramaic Languages**, the Semitic dialects current in Mesopotamia and the regions extending southwest from the Euphrates to Palestine from about the 12th cent. B.C. until after the rise of Islam, when Aramaic was superseded by Arabic. Both Aramaic and Greek were spoken in Palestine during the time of Christ. See M37(2).

**Archaeopteryx**, a fossil bird providing a connecting link between reptiles and birds. It had feathers, jaws with teeth, no bill, reptilian bones and skull, a long tail, and it probably used its fore-limbs for gliding flight. The first specimen, found in 1861, in the Solenhofen limestone of Bavaria, is in London's Natural History Museum.

**Archbishop**, the chief of the bishops of an ecclesiastical province in the Greek, Roman, and Anglican churches. In the Church of England there are two archbishops, the Archbishop of Canterbury, called the Primate of *all* England, and the Archbishop of York, styled the Primate of England.

**Archimedes' Principle.** When a body is weighed in air and then in any fluid, the apparent loss in weight is equal to the weight of fluid displaced. This scientific fact was noted by the Syracusan philosopher Archimedes (287–212 B.C.) and is frequently used as a basis for density measurements.

**Architecture**, the art and science of building. The provision of shelter for mankind by the orderly arrangement of materials in a manner which expresses man's attitude to living. The forms which buildings take are the outcome of the function for which they are to be used, of the architect's aesthetic sensibility and of the structural method adopted. Until the last hundred years structural methods were limited to timber frames, and columns, lintels, load-bearing walls, arches, vaults, and domes in brick or stone. From these few basic elements have evolved the great variety of historic styles of building to be found throughout the world. To give but one example, the Greeks created those systems of decorated columns and beams, known as the Orders, which were adapted by the Romans, revived decoratively rather than structurally during the Renaissance and are still used in debased form on the more presumptuous type of modern building. In recent years, however, architecture has taken on a new meaning. Once confined to the rich, in the form of Church, State, or Commerce, it is now, with the coming of democracy, recognised as an essential social service for all. This, and the development of new structural techniques and materials (steel, aluminium, sheet glass, reinforced concrete, plastics, and plywoods, to name a few), have made the interest in historic styles, the mainstay of the older architect, of secondary importance. Modern architecture is the creation of buildings with the highest possible standards of functional performance in terms of efficient planning and structure, good artificial and natural lighting, adequate heating or cooling, and proper acoustic conditions consistent with the price the client can afford to pay. At the same time the architect's task is to design a structure, and the spaces the structure delimits, internally and externally, which are æsthetically stimulating and satisfying, and well related to the land and buildings around.

Arctic Exploration. Modern exploration of the Arctic begins in the 16th cent., when men sought to reach the East Indies by sailing through the Arctic to the Pacific Ocean. The North-east Passage, via the shores of northern Asia, was the first attempted. In 1553 and 1554 the English navigators Sir Richard Chancellor and Stephen Burrough sailed into the White Sea, but were prevented by storms and ice from advancing farther eastwards. The project was later revived by the Dutch; Barendts in 1594 discovered Spitsbergen, but also failed to get beyond Novaya Zemlya. It was not, in fact, until 1879 that the Swede, A. E. Nordenskiöld, in the *Vega*, succeeded in reaching the Pacific. The attempts to find a North-west Passage were more numerous and determined. In 1585 John Davis penetrated Davis Strait and coasted along Baffin Island. Hopes ran high when Henry Hudson discovered Hudson Bay in 1610, but a practicable passage continued to elude explorers. The problem was to find a navigable route through the maze of channels in the short summer season, and to avoid being frozen in with supplies exhausted. After the Napoleonic Wars the Admiralty sent out many naval expeditions which culminated in Sir John Franklin's expedition with the *Erebus* and *Terror* in 1845. The ships were beset by ice in Victoria Channel and, after Franklin's death, were abandoned by their crews, who perished from scurvy and starvation on their march southwards. To ascertain their fate, several further expeditions were despatched, and the crew of the *Investigator*, commanded by R. J. M'Clure, sailing eastwards from Bering Strait, were the first to make the Passage, though in doing so they were obliged to abandon their ship. It was thirty years before the Norwegian, Roald Amundsen, succeeded in sailing the *Gjoa* from east to west. In the meantime, the North Pole had become the goal of explorers. Nansen, in 1893, put the *Fram* into the ice-pack to drift across the Polar basin, and himself made an unsuccessful attempt on the Pole across the pack. This was eventually achieved by the American explorer Robert E. Peary, who after several expeditions in the North Greenland region, sledged to the Pole with Eskimo companions in 1909. The next phase was the employment of airships and aeroplanes in Arctic exploration. In 1926 Admiral Byrd made the first flight over the Pole, and in the same year Amundsen and Lincoln Ellsworth flew the airship *Norge* from Spitsbergen to Point Barrow, Alaska. Two years later, the *Italia*, commanded by the Italian, Nobile, was wrecked on a return flight from the Pole, and Amundsen lost his life in an attempt to rescue the survivors. With modern developments in aircraft and navigation, flights over the Polar basin are almost a routine matter, and passenger flights between Europe and America via northern Greenland are being pioneered. The first voyage under the North Pole was made in August 1958 by the American nuclear-powered submarine *Nautilus*.

Arenaceous Rocks, the rocks composed of grains of sand, chiefly sandstones; quartz is the most abundant mineral in these rocks.

Argillaceous Rocks are a sedimentary group, including the shales and clays.

Argon, chemical element, symbol A. This was the first of the inert gases (*q.v.*) to be isolated from air by Rayleigh and Ramsay in 1894. Argon is used for filling gas-filled metal filament electric lamps. In gas discharge tube it gives a blue glow.

Arithmetic, the branch of mathematics that deals with numerical calculations as in counting, measuring, weighing. The early civilisations used simple arithmetic for commercial purposes, employing symbols and later letters of the alphabet as numerals. When Hindu-Arabic numerals replaced Roman numerals in the Middle Ages it meant a great step forward and led to rapid developments—the invention of logarithms, slide-rule, calculating machines.

Ark of the Covenant was the sacred chest of the Hebrews and symbolised God's presence. It was overlaid with gold inside and outside. It accompanied the Israelites into battle and was once captured by the Philistines. Eventually it found a resting-place in Solomon's Temple.

Armada, Spanish, the naval expedition fitted out by Philip II. of Spain in 1588 against England, commanded by the Duke of Medina Sidonia. It comprised 129 ships, was manned by 8,000 sailors and carried 19,000 soldiers and more than 2,000 cannon. Against this formidable force Elizabeth had only 80 ships, manned by 9,000 sailors, under Lord Howard of Effingham, under whom served Drake, Hawkins, and Frobisher. The British Fleet awaited the Armada off Plymouth, and at Tilbury there was a considerable defensive land force under the command of the Earl of Leicester. On July 19 the ships of the Armada were sighted off the Lizard, disposed in a crescent seven miles long from horn to horn. The excellent manoeuvring of the English, their fire-ships, and a gale from the N.W. combined so effectively to cripple the Spanish ships that the Armada was scattered in confusion, a very small remnant contriving to reach home via the North of Scotland. It was impossible to embark the army of Parma waiting in the Netherlands. Elizabeth had a medal struck bearing in Latin the inscription, "God blew, and they were scattered."

Armadillo, a genus of animals related to the sloths and anteaters, belonging to South America, and carrying a hard bony covering over the back, under which one species (*Tolypeutes*) can completely conceal itself when attacked, rolling itself up like a hedgehog.

Armageddon, according to the Revelation of St. John, the great battle in which the last conflict between good and evil is to be fought.

Armillary Sphere, an early form of astronomical apparatus with a number of circles representing equator, meridian, ecliptic, etc. Used by Hipparchus and Ptolemy and up to the time of Tycho Brahe for determining the position of the stars.

Aromatic. A term used by chemists, originally to describe compounds like benzene, having a characteristic smell. It is a term which implies a collection of chemical characteristics, the salient features being a flat ring structure and a general similarity to benzene.

Arsenic, a metalloid element, symbol As, in group V of the periodic table, usually met with as a constituent of other minerals, sometimes by itself. Its compounds are very poisonous. Lead arsenate is a powerful insecticide used for spraying fruit trees. The more stable allotropic form (grey) has a layer structure, and conducts electricity.

Artesian Wells take their name from Artois in France, where the first wells of this kind were constructed in 1126. They are to be found only when a water-bearing bed is sandwiched between two impervious beds. When a boring is made to the lower part of the bed, the pressure of water is sufficient to cause the water to overflow at the surface. Artesian wells were known to ancient Egypt and China, and have existed in the Sahara since the earliest times. The fountains in Trafalgar Square are fed by artesian wells sunk through the London clay into the chalk about 400 ft.

Arthur's Seat, a hill of volcanic origin, 823 ft. high,

dominating Holyrood Park, to the south-east of Edinburgh.

**Articles.** The *Six Articles* are those contained in an Act of Henry VIII, and were of Roman Catholic origin. The *Thirty-nine Articles* were drawn up for the English church at the Reformation. They are printed at the back of the Prayer Book. Candidates for holy orders in the Church of England are required to subscribe to them, though the form of assent has recently been modified.

**Art Nouveau,** a term applied to the "new art" which spread across Europe and the U.S.A. during the 1890s. It was mainly a style of architecture and interior decoration which attempted to break with the old traditions of darkness and "heaviness" by the use of the new materials of cement, steel, and glass from which it created patterns characterised by: (*a*) over-elaboration; (*b*) relatively naturalistic but tortuous representations of plants, etc.; (*c*) a ubiquity which left no surface undecorated. Typical of the extravagances of Art Nouveau are the cast-iron lilies with copper tendrils, the cupboard doors and chair-backs with heart-shaped holes, and the furniture shaped like animals, examples of which are still with us. In Britain the movement was basically a continuation of the Arts and Crafts movement of William Morris; Aubrey Beardsley represented this essentially fin-de-siècle school in his drawings.

**Arts and Crafts Movement,** the English revival of decorative art which began about 1875 as a revolt against the existing vulgarity of internal decoration and furnishings and the pettiness of academic art. Inspired by William Morris and Burne-Jones together with Rossetti, it was strongly influenced by the former's mediaevalism, his hatred of industrialism, and his own version of socialism which included the regeneration of man by handicrafts. His firm of Morris & Co. produced wallpapers, tapestries, furniture, stained-glass windows, carpets, and fabrics in a style totally different from that of contemporary Victorian decoration. Morris's Kelmscott Press did much to raise the standards of book design and printing. *See* Art Nouveau.

**Arum,** a genus of plants of the Araceae family, of which there is but one British species, the wake-robin or cuckoo-pint, sometimes also styled "Lords and Ladies." Its pointed leaves and spikes of scarlet poisonous berries are familiar in the hedgerows.

**Arundel Marbles,** a collection of ancient Greek sculptures formed by Thomas Howard, Earl of Arundel, in the 17th cent. and presented to Oxford University by his grandson, Henry Howard, who became Duke of Norfolk.

**Aryans,** nomadic peoples who made their way in successive waves from the Eurasian steppes to the Indus and the Nile during the first half of the 2nd millennium B.C. They crossed the Hindu Kush into N.W. India and settled in the valleys of the Indus and Ganges, where an earlier Indus civilisation had flourished, *c.* 3250–2750 B.C. Their religious ideas are reflected in the Veda (oldest Hindu scriptures, written down many centuries later in Vedic, parent language of Sanskrit). Those who made their way to Syria and Egypt founded the Hyksos empire (*c.* 1680–1580 B.C.). The Aryans introduced the horse-drawn chariot and spoke a language from which the great Indo-European family of languages is derived, with one group in India and Iran, and another in Europe. *See* M37.

**Asafoetida,** an acrid, strong-smelling gum resin exuded from the stem of an umbelliferous plant, *Ferula foetida*, found in Persia and Afghanistan. Formerly used medicinally to treat hysteria; still used in cooking in India, Iran, and France.

**Ascension Day,** or Holy Thursday, is the 40th day after Easter.

**Ascot Races** are an annual fashionable function dating from 1711 and taking place on Ascot Heath, only six miles from Windsor, in June. These races have always had royal patronage. The course is nearly two miles long.

**Ash,** a familiar deciduous tree of the genus *Fraxinus*, of over 60 species, native to North-temperate regions. The ash held an important place in Norse mythology, as it was supposed to support the heavens with its roots in Hell. The species native to Britain, and to Europe,

is *F. excelsior*, a tall tree with compound leaves, greenish flowers, winged seeds, and black buds in winter. It is a valuable timber tree, tough and elastic, and largely used for wheels and handles. The rowan, or mountain ash, *Sorbus aucuparia*, with similar leaves and orange berries, belongs to a different family. *F. pendula* or weeping ash is a weeping strain which makes an ideal natural summer house.

**Ashes, The,** the symbol which distinguishes the winning cricket team in the Australian Test Matches. In 1882 the Australians won at the Oval by 7 runs. After the match the following epitaph appeared in the *Sporting Times*: "In affectionate remembrance of English Cricket which died at the Oval on Aug. 29, 1882, deeply lamented by a large circle of sorrowing friends and acquaintances. R.I.P. NB. The body will be cremated and the ashes taken to Australia." When the English Eleven went to Australia the same winter it was said that they had come to recover the "ashes." England won two out of three matches, and after the third match the ashes of what is now generally believed to have been a stump were presented in an urn to Ivo Bligh, later Lord Darnley. He bequeathed the urn to the M.C.C., and it now stands in the Memorial Gallery at Lord's.

**Ash Wednesday,** first day of Lent, the seventh Wednesday before Easter.

**Asp,** a small poisonous snake, often mentioned in ancient literature and traditionally supposed to have been used by Cleopatra in killing herself. Probably the Egyptian Horned Viper (*Cerastes*).

**Assassination,** treacherous murder for political ends, usually of a ruler or distinguished person. Among the most famous assassinations of history were: Julius Caesar, 44 B.C.; Thomas à Becket, 1170; David Rizzio, 1566; William the Silent, 1584; Henry IV. of France, 1610; Jean Paul Marat, 1793; Abraham Lincoln, 1865; Alexander II. of Russia, 1881; Archduke Francis Ferdinand of Austria, 1914; Dr. Dollfuss, 1934; King Alexander of Yugoslavia, 1934; Mahatma Gandhi, 1948; King Abdullah of Jordan, 1951; Liaquat Ali Khan, 1951; King Feisal of Iraq, 1958; Mr. Bandaranaike, 1959; President Kennedy, 1963; Malcolm X, 1965; Dr. Verwoerd, 1966; Dr. Martin Luther King, 1968; Senator Robert Kennedy, 1968.

**Asteroids** are minor planets most of whose orbits lie between those of Mars and Jupiter; they were unknown until the discovery of Ceres by Piazzi in 1801. More than a thousand have been named and many thousands are believed to exist. After 1891 they were identified by their paths on exposed photographic plates. Most of them have a diameter of well under 50 miles. Ceres, with a diameter of *c.* 480 m., is the largest, then there are Pallas (*c.* 304 m.), Juno (120 m.), Vesta (240 m.), Astraea, Adonis, Hermes, Hidalgo, Eros, Amor, Apollo, and the Trojan group which all take their names from Homer's *Iliad*—Achilles, Patroclus, Hector, Nestor, Priam, Agamemnon, Ulysses, Aeneas, Anchises, Troilus, Ajax, and Diomede. The asteroid Icarus (diameter *c.* ¼ mile) makes the closest approach to the Sun, and was within a few miles of the Earth on June 14, 1968. A full list of asteroids has been issued by the Spanish astronomical historian, Prof. A. Paluzie-Borrell.

**Astrolabe,** a mediæval scientific instrument for taking altitudes, observing the sun by day and the stars by night, and used for telling the time and finding the latitude. Used by the ancient Greeks, later by the Arabs and Persians, and introduced into Europe by way of Spain in the 14th cent. Chaucer is said to have sent his son Lois, a ten-year-old student at Oxford, an astrolabe with a treatise on its use in 1391.

**Astronomical unit,** the mean distance from the centre of the earth to the centre of the sun, or half the major axis of the earth's elliptical orbit. It has been known for some 300 years that the earth–sun distance is roughly 93 million miles, but over the past 60-odd years astronomers have attempted to determine it with ever-greater accuracy, using various methods of computation. Spencer Jones (1931) deduced a value of 93,004,000 miles; the American astronomer E. K. Rabe (1950) obtained a value of 92,914,800 miles; and data from the *Pioneer V* space probe gave a value of 92,925,100 miles. The earth–sun distance is a fundamental value in astronomy.

**Astrology.** *See* J5.

**Astronomy,** the oldest and one of the most fascinating of sciences, was in early times associated with astrology, but by a long series of observations and mathematical calculations a gradual knowledge of the movements of the heavenly bodies grew up. Pythagoras (520 B.C.) understood the revolution of the earth upon its axis, but it was not until two thousand years later that his theory gained general acceptance, when the keen and spacious minds, first of Copernicus, and then of Tycho Brahe and Galileo, demonstrated the truth of the Pythagorean theory. With the setting forth of the Copernican system, astronomy was placed on a sure foundation, and the movements of the planets began to be more clearly comprehended. The studies of Kepler and Galileo, making their observations with the telescope, resulted in an immense increase of astronomical knowledge. Newton, to whom we owe the discovery of the law of gravitation, the improvement of the telescope and many other discoveries, placed physical astronomy on well-defined lines. Two great landmarks in more recent times were the discovery of Uranus by Herschel in 1781 which extended the solar system as then recognised, and the estimation by Hubble in 1924 of the distance of Andromeda of nearly a million light years (more recent determinations give 1,500,000 light years), which showed that our Galaxy was just one of many. Today radio-telescopes and space probes are advancing astronomical knowledge and making it possible to explore regions beyond the scope of optical telescopes. The following have held the position of Astronomer Royal (period of office in brackets): John Flamsteed (1675–1719), Edmund Halley (1719–42), James Bradley (1742–62), Nathaniel Bliss (1762–65), Nevil Maskelyne (1765–1811), John Pond (1811–35), Sir George Airy (1835–81), Sir William Christie (1881–1910), Sir Frank Dyson (1910–33), Sir Harold Spencer Jones (1933–55), Sir Richard Woolley (1956–   ). *See* F5–7.

**Astrophysics,** a branch of astronomy concerned with the physical nature and constitution of celestial bodies. The application of spectroscopy and photometry since the second half of the 19th cent. and of space research in recent years has been responsible for the great advance in this branch of science.

**Athanasian Creed,** one of the three ancient creeds of the Christian Church, often referred to as the *Quicunque Vult,* is a statement of the doctrine of the Trinity and the Incarnation, and though named after St. Athanasius, the view is now widely held that it is the work of St. Ambrose (339–97). *See also* Apostles' Creed and Nicene Creed.

**Athodyd,** also called "Ramjet" or "Propulsive Duct." This can be considered as an extremely simple gas-turbine engine, without any rotating parts. A power plant with great possibilities for high-speed aerial flight, it consists of a diffuser, combustion chamber, and exhaust chamber; its thrust results from the fact that the gases leaving the athodyd have a higher velocity than the gases entering it.

**Atmosphere** is the gaseous envelope of the earth, and consists of a mixture of gases (*see* Air) and water vapour, the variability of the latter being of great importance meterologically. The ozone layer, which absorbs ultra-violet radiation which would be lethal to plant life if it reached the ground, is concentrated at about 20 miles above the earth but extends to about twice that height. The lower level of the atmosphere up to a height of about 7 miles (6 miles at the Poles and 10 miles at the Equator) is known as the *troposphere,* and it is in this region that nearly all weather phenomena occur. This is the region of most interest to the forecaster studying temperature, humidity, windspeeds, and the movement of air masses. Temperature falls with height by about 1° C. per 500 ft. in this layer. The *tropopause* is the boundary between the troposphere and the *stratosphere.* Temperature varies little in the lower levels of this region: it is mainly cloudless, and has no vertical currents. Strangely enough, the lowest temperatures of the atmosphere are to be found not at the Poles, but at about 11 miles above the Equator, where a temperature as low as −80° C. has been recorded! Temperatures begin to rise about 20 miles from the earth's surface at about the same rate as they fall in the troposphere, owing to the absorption of solar radiation by the concentration of ozone. The stratospheric air is extremely dry. Near the 60-mile level a number of important atmospheric phenomena occur. Above this level the oxygen becomes predominantly monatomic in contrast to the normal diatomic form at lower altitudes. This is the *ionosphere,* extending to heights over 500 miles from the earth's surface. This layer acts as an electrical radio mirror which makes long-distance radio transmission possible. The auroras are most frequently observed at altitudes near 60 miles but do extend at times far higher. *See also* Ionosphere.

**Atmospherics** are electrical impulses which are believed to originate in atmospheric electrical discharges such as lightning. They give rise to crashing background noises in the loudspeakers of radio sets, interfering with reception at distances of up to 4,000 miles from the centre of the disturbance. The location of atmospherics with the aid of radio direction-finding methods gives warning of the approach of thunderstorms.

**Atom.** *See* F9–14, F20.

**Atomic Pile,** an apparatus containing a fissionable element and a moderator, such as heavy water or graphite, in which a self-sustaining fission process proceeds at a controllable rate. The first atomic pile, constructed on a squash court at Chicago, was operated for the first time on December 2, 1942, under the direction of Dr. Enrico Fermi. The pile contained 12,400 lb. of uranium. *See also* Nuclear Reactors.

**August,** named after the Emperor Augustus, because it was his "lucky" month.

**Auks,** duck-like sea-birds, black and white, with short, narrow wings, compact bodies, and legs set well back. Breed in colonies on rocky coasts of N. Europe (incl. British Isles) and spend most time in coastal waters. Migrate south in winter. The Auk family includes the Razorbill, Little Auk, Guillemot, and Puffin. The Great Auk became extinct in the 19th cent. after ruthless hunting for the sake of its feathers. Except for the Black Guillemot, they lay only one egg a year.

**Aulic Council,** a supreme court of the Holy Roman Empire, established by Maximilian I., in 1501.

**Aurora polaris.** This wonderful phenomenon of the night sky is a common sight in some high latitudes, north and south. It is visible less often in temperate latitudes, and only very seldom in the tropics. As seen in the northern hemisphere it is called the aurora borealis or northern lights, and in the south, the aurora australis or southern lights. The zone of maximum frequency surrounds the north magnetic pole and includes Greenland, northern Canada, and the north coast of Alaska. Auroral displays may take several forms, *e.g.,* a faint glow, a diffuse ribbon of light crossing the heavens, great folded waving curtains like draperies; the whole sky may be a grand panoply of light. Both the aurora and the magnetic storm associated with it are ascribed to the envelopment of the earth in a great cloud or stream of solar gas shot out from stormy areas on the sun (sunspots) that has travelled to the earth at a speed of over a thousand miles a second. The gas is mainly atomic hydrogen, but the atoms are broken up into their two parts, protons and electrons. These are both electrically charged. This renders them subject to the influence of the earth's magnetic field, which deflects many of them to the high latitudes where the aurora is most commonly seen. The aurora is a kind of light essentially different from that of the rainbow which is a partly subjective phenomenon. Each beholder sees his own rainbow, whose light is sunlight refracted and reflected by many raindrops. The raindrops that produce his rainbow depend on his position as well as on the direction of the sun. The aurora, on the contrary, is a light as objective as that of a candle, though produced differently. It is a self-luminescence of the air in particular regions of the atmosphere that lie far above the clouds. By simultaneous observation from stations twenty or more miles apart it is possible to locate the position of the luminous air, *i.e.*, to determine the height of the aurora, its location in plan, and its form and volume.

**Austerlitz, Battle of,** was fought near Brünn, in Moravia, on December 2, 1805, when Napoleon defeated the Russians and Austrians under Kutuzon.

**Auto-da-Fé,** or Act of Faith, was the ceremony connected with the sentencing of heretics under the Inquisition of Spain and Portugal, the persons found guilty being imprisoned or burned alive. The ceremony took place in some public square, sometimes in the presence of the king and court.

**Automation** is a recently coined word, used to designate the adoption of methods of automatic control either of manufacturing processes or of any business process involving a large mass of routine work. The word is used in broader and narrower senses. In its broadest sense it covers any form of mechanisation which largely replaces human labour by the work of automatic or semi-automatic machines, such as has been in progress continuously since the Industrial Revolution; but it is better kept to a narrower meaning, in which it is confined to the recent development of electronic or similar devices, involving feedback (automatic detection and correction of malfunction). Human labour is eliminated save for that needed for watching and maintaining the elaborate machines used. In this sense, automation began mainly in the United States, but has been spreading rapidly to other advanced countries. *See* G12(1).

**Autumn,** the third season of the year, begins with the autumnal equinox, and ends with the winter solstice, but the term is generally understood as covering the period from mid-August to mid-November.

**Auxins,** " plant hormones," organic substances produced by plants to regulate growth. Synthetic auxins are now widely used, *e.g.*, for promotion of root formation in cuttings, differential weed control, prevention of premature dropping of fruit, in storage of potatoes and hard fruit, and to overcome frost damage to fruit buds.

**Average** is a single number designed to give a typical example of a set of numbers, *e.g.*, a cricketer's batting average for a season gives an idea of his typical score. There are several kinds of average and their uses are studied in the science of statistics (*q.v.*). A statement that " so and so is the average value " can be misleading if one does not know which average is meant. Three common averages are: the arithmetic average (or mean), the mode, and the median. The arithmetic average of *n* numbers is found by adding them together and dividing by *n*; this is a very common method of averaging. The mode of *n* numbers is the most frequently occurring number. The median is the middle number, *i.e.*, the number which is smaller than just as many of the other numbers as it exceeds. Of the numbers 1, 2, 2, 2, 2, 3, 4, 5, 6, 8, 9, the arithmetic mean is 4, the mode is 2, the median is 3.

**Avocet,** a graceful wading bird related to the stilts, of black-and-white plumage, bluish legs, and slender upturned bill. There are four species. Avocets nest in colonies and there is one in the sanctuary on Havergate Island, Suffolk.

**Avogadro's Hypothesis.** This is a fundamental concept of chemistry. Equal volumes of all gases under the same conditions of temperature and pressure contain the same number of molecules. This law was instrumental in assigning the formulæ of molecules. The hypothesis was put forward in 1811, but was not generally accepted until 1860. *See* F21(2).

**Aztecs,** the name of a native and powerful race found in Mexico when the Spaniards first discovered that country, and with difficulty subdued.

## B

**Babiroussa,** a ferocious, long-legged wild pig, native of the Celebes, sometimes called the horned-hog, because of the long upper tusks in the male, which are developments of the canine teeth which grow upwards, piercing the upper lip, and curving backwards, often broken in fighting.

**Baboon,** monkeys belonging to the African genus *Papio.* They are considered the lowest of the Old World (Catarrhine) monkeys, and walk on all fours. In the main terrestrial, but take to trees after food. The mandrill is closely related.

**Babylonian Captivity,** the period spent by the Jews in Babylon after Jerusalem was captured by Nebuchadnezzar, the Babylonian emperor, in 586 B.C. Traditionally the captivity lasted 70 years, but when Babylon was in turn taken by Cyrus in 538 B.C., the exiles were permitted to return to Jerusalem. The term is also applied in church history to the period 1309–78 when the papacy moved to Avignon, into the control of the French monarchy.

**Badger,** a carnivorous mammal related to the weasel, of nocturnal and burrowing habits, inoffensive, subsisting chiefly on roots and insects, though sometimes mice, young rabbits, and eggs form part of its diet. Badger-baiting was a favourite sport in Britain until it was prohibited in the middle of the 19th cent. The badger does little harm and quite a lot of good; badger digging is to be condemned as a cruel sport.

**Bagpipe.** Once popular all over Europe, this instrument is still played in Scotland, Ireland, Brittany, and elsewhere. The bag acts as a reservoir of air and, when squeezed by the player's arm, forces air through the pipes. One of these, the Chanter pipe, provides the tune and is played by the fingers as in a flageolet. The remainder, the Drone pipes, give a continuous, unvarying note.

**Bailey Bridge,** invented by Sir Donald Bailey and first used in N. African campaign 1942–3. Built up of pre-fabricated girders, it can be easily transported and erected.

**Bailie,** is a Scottish term for the magistrate of a municipal corporation or royal burgh.

**Bailiwick,** a feudal term denoting the limits of a bailiff's jurisdiction. The term has survived in the Channel Islands, where Jersey and Guernsey are Bailiwicks.

**Bakelite.** A plastic material made from phenol, formaldehyde, and urea. It is used in the manufacture of electrical fittings because of its insulating properties.

**Balance of Power** was the doctrine in British policy whereby European groups should be so balanced as to prevent the emergence of a dominating Power. Thus the balance was maintained between the Triple Alliance (Germany, Austria and Italy) and the Triple Entente (Great Britain, France and Russia) and preserved peace from 1871 to 1914. After the first world war there was tentative support of Germany's recovery to counterweight a possible French hegemony; but when Germany's power grew under Hitler culminating in the second world war, Britain, France and Russia again became allies. By the end of the war the old system of a balance of power centred upon Europe collapsed to give way to a thermonuclear balance of power between the super-Powers, the Soviet Union (Warsaw Pact) and the United States (Nato alliance).

**Baldachin** (It. *Baldachino*), a canopy usually supported by four pillars over throne, altar, or other sacred object. The name is also applied to the silken canopy used in processions and borne by the priest who carries the Host.

**Balearic Crane,** the crowned crane of the Balearic Islands and the North African mainland, distinguished by its yellowish, black-tipped occipital tuft and by its trumpet note.

**Baleen** *or* " whalebone " the name given to a series of horny plates growing from the roof of the mouth in those whales classified as Whalebone or Baleen Whales (Mystacoceti) There are 300–400 or so plates on each side, and their inner edges are frayed, the whole system constituting a filter for collecting minute organisms used for food. The Baleen Whales include the Right-Whales, the Pacific Grey-Whale, and the Rorquals. *See* Whales.

**Ballet** is a combination of four arts; dancing, music, painting, and drama, each of which is ideally of equal importance. The movement of the individual dancers and the "orchestration" of the whole group is in the hands of the choreographer. The dancer's training follows certain basic rules but save in classical ballet there is considerable freedom of movement. Ballet as we know it today developed professionally at the Court of King Louis XIV. of France, though it owes its origins to Italy and in the earliest times to Greece and Rome. Its movements were made up from the dances of courtiers, country folk and tumblers. Technique grew more complex as costume became modified, the body gaining complete freedom with the invention of tights. A succession of great dancers—French, Italian and latterly Russian left their imprint on the art. Contemporary ballet reflects the aesthetic of the Russian, Sergei Diaghilev. In England Dame Ninette de Valois has laid the foundation of a national ballet, at Sadler's Wells and Covent Garden, with a personality that reflects the national character. A Royal Charter was granted in 1957 setting up the Royal Ballet to co-ordinate the activities of the Sadler's Wells group.

**Ballistics,** the science dealing with the motion of projectiles, especially shells, bombs, and rockets. Great advances have been made in this science in recent years.

**Balloon,** the modern balloon consists of a bag of plastic material inflated with a gas lighter than air. The first ascent by man in a hot-air balloon was made on Nov. 21, 1783, and in a hydrogen balloon on Dec. 1, 1783. The most famous of the early scientific flights by manned balloons were those of the Englishmen Coxwell and Glaisher, in 1862, when a height of 7 miles was reached. The first aerial crossing of the English Channel by Blanchard and Jeffries was made on 7 Jan. 1785. Piccard's ascent to 10 miles, in 1931, marked the conquest of the stratosphere. Four years later the huge American balloon Explorer II, inflated with nearly 4 million cubic feet of helium, carried a team of scientists with their floating laboratory to an altitude of 14 miles. In 1957 a pressurised balloon carrying an American doctor rose 19 miles above the Earth. Captive kite-balloons were widely used in the war as defensive measures against air attack. Meteorologists send their instruments up in balloons to collect data about the upper atmosphere, and of recent years physicists have learned much about cosmic radiation from the study of photographic plates sent to the upper regions in balloons. The American balloon satellites *Echo I* and *II* move round the Earth in orbits several hundred miles high, and, as the brightest of the earth satellites, can be seen with the naked eye as brilliant points moving across the sky. Ballooning as a hobby is carried on by a number of enthusiasts.

**Balsam,** a big genus (140 species) of flowering plants. Many species are cultivated for their showy flowers, *e.g. Impatiens noli-me-tangere,* the yellow balsam or "touch-me-not," so called because the fruit explodes when touched, slinging out the seeds. Balsam fir is a conifer (*Abies balsamea*) from which Canada balsam gum is obtained.

**Baltimore Bird,** a lively black-and-orange bird of the oriole sub-family extending from Brazil to Canada; builds a well-constructed hanging nest, and has a fine voice.

**Bamboo,** a genus of strong grasses, some species growing to over 120 ft. in height; much used by oriental peoples for all kinds of purposes. The young shoots of some species are tender and esculent. *See* T5(2).

**Banana** (family *Musaceae*), a large herbaceous plant cultivated in moist regions of the tropics, and one of the most productive plants known. The main areas of commercial cultivation are in tropical America, the Canary Islands, and West Africa. World production is estimated at 20 million tons, of which only 3 million are for trade.

**Bandicoots,** Australasian marsupial mammals, of the size of a large rat or rabbit. They are burrowing animals living largely on insects. The rabbit-eared bandicoot, restricted to Australia, has shrew-like snout, long ears like a rabbit, long crested tail, and a silky coat. The long-nosed bandicoot has a spiny coat and comes from E. Australia. The pig-footed bandicoot has two functional toes on the foot, like a pig.

**Bantu** (native word = people), term loosely used for large family of Negro races of Southern Africa. *See* Negroes, African languages, M35.

**Baobab,** a tropical African tree. The species *Adansonia digitata* is one of the largest trees known, though not the tallest; the trunk can reach 30 ft. in thickness. The fruit is woody, but its juice provides a cooling beverage. The bark yields a fibre used for making rope and cloth.

**Barbary Ape,** a large monkey belonging to the genus *Macaca*. It is the only monkey living in relative freedom in Europe, a small colony being found on the Rock of Gibraltar. It has no tail.

**Barberry,** a genus of berry-producing shrubs containing a hundred species. Several species are cultivated for their flowers and bright berries. Has an interesting pollination mechanism; the base of each stamen is sensitive to touch, and insects probing for nectar cause top of stamen to spring inwards, so dusting visitor's head with pollen which can then be carried to the next flower visited. The common barberry (*Berberis communis*) harbours one stage of the fungus that causes rust of wheat.

**Barbican,** a fortified entrance to a castle or city, with projecting towers. In the London street called Barbican there was formerly a barbican in front of the city gates.

**Barbiturates.** A group of drugs derived from a parent compound called barbituric acid; phenobarbitone is the best-known example. They induce sleep and are used in the manufacture of sleeping pills and sometimes as anaesthetics, but they have the disadvantage of being habit forming. *See also* P23(2).

**Barbizon School,** a school of mid-19th-cent. landscape painters whose main tenet was a return to nature with an exact rendering of peasant life and country scenery painted on the spot. It was named after the village of that name in the Forest of Fontainebleau, where its chief members—Millet, Theodore Rousseau, Daubigny, and Diaz—made their home. Their practice of painting direct from nature, which was far from universal at that time, made them the precursors of Impressionism (*q.v.*).

**Barcarolle,** a Venetian gondolier's song applied to instrumental as well as vocal compositions.

**Bard,** among the ancient Celts a poet or minstrel whose mission was to sing of heroic deeds. He was supposed to have the gift of prophecy, and was exempt from taxes and military service.

**Barilla,** soda carbonate or soda ash obtained by burning certain salt-marsh plants (*e.g.* the saltwort, *Salsola kali*). It used to be in great demand, until the product of the Leblanc and then the Solvay ammonia-soda process was made available by the chemical industry.

**Barium,** metal element, symbol Ba. In group II of the periodic table. The metal is soft and easily cut. It occurs as the sulphate and carbonate in nature. It was first prepared by Sir Humphry Davy in 1808, as an amalgam, by electrolysis of barium chloride. The pure metal was not isolated until 1901.

**Barium meal.** Barium sulphate is opaque to X-rays and before taking X-ray pictures of the alimentary canal radiologists give a "barium meal" to the patients so that the alimentary canal shows up more clearly.

**Barnacles** constitute a sub-class (*Cirripedia*) of the Crustacea. The barnacle fouling the bottom of ships is the Goose Barnacle, which has a long muscular stalk and a shell composed of five plates. The Acorn Barnacles, which cover rocks, breakwaters, etc., just below high-water mark are similarly constructed, but have no stalk. The manner of feeding of barnacles was vividly described by T. H. Huxley, who said the barnacle is "a crustacean fixed by its head kicking the food into its mouth with its legs." It was a naval surgeon, J. Vaughan Thompson, who discovered in 1830 that barnacles have a free-swimming larva (or nauplius). In the Middle Ages a curious myth grew up to the effect that the Barnacle changed into a sea-bird called, for that reason, the Barnacle Goose.

**Barometer** is an instrument for measuring atmospheric pressure, invented at Florence by Torricelli, pupil of Galileo, in 1644. The standard method consists of balancing the air column against a column of mercury, used on account of its high density. The mercury is contained in a long glass tube, closed at one end, and inverted in a cistern also containing mercury. The height of the mercury column, supporting the air column, is taken as the pressure at the time, and can be read off very accurately by means of a vernier scale. Present-day tendency is to express the readings in units of pressure instead of length, the millibar being adopted (1 mb = 1000 dynes per sq. cm.; 1000 mb ≡ 29·53 inches of mercury approx.). The standard instrument is correct for pressures at 0° C in Lat. 45°, so that corrections have to be applied for temperatures and latitudes other than these. Also a correction has to be made for reducing the pressure to mean sea level. *See* Aneroid.

**Baron,** title given in feudal England to a man who held his land directly from the king by military or other honourable service. The first baron created by letters patent was John Beauchamp de Holt, Baron of Kidderminster, in 1387. A baron is a member of the fifth and last grade of the peerage of the United Kingdom and is addressed as "Lord." Life peers and life peeresses rank with hereditary barons and baronesses according to the date of their creation. In Scotland the term baron is used of the possessor of a fuedal fief, or the representa-tive by descent of such a fief. The equivalent of the English baron, as a rank of the Scottish peerage, is Lord of Parliament.

**Baronet,** the lowest hereditary title, instituted by James I. to provide funds for the colonisation of Ulster. The first baronet was Sir Nicholas Bacon. Since 1964 no recommendations for hereditary honours have been made.

**Baroque,** a term used for the art style of the period *c.* 1600–1720 which was the artistic accompani-ment of the Jesuit counter-Reformation. Its most obvious characteristics are: (*a*) its emo-tional appeal and dramatic intensity both related to its deliberate intention as propa-ganda ("a good picture makes better religious propaganda than a sermon" said one of its exponents); (*b*) in architecture, a style which is heavily and sometimes almost grotesquely or-nate, plentifully covered with voluptuous sculp-ture on which draperies float rather than hang, with twisted and spiral instead of plain or fluted columns, and unnecessary windows or recesses added for ornament rather than use; (*c*) its emphasis on the whole at the expense of the parts such that a building's sculpture merges into its architecture and both into its painting (Baroque paintings are as closely knit as a jig-saw puzzle so that one cannot isolate individual figures as would be possible in a Renaissance one). Baroque architecture owing to its origin is found mainly in the Catholic countries; Italy, France, Austria, Bavaria, *e.g.*, the Barberini Palace, Rome, designed by its greatest exponent Bernini and others; the Church of the Invalides, Paris. Baroque artists include Caravaggio, Guido Reni, Murillo, and Rubens, the greatest Northern Baroque painter. The Baroque style merges gradually into Rococo (*q.v.*).

**Barque,** a small sailing vessel with three or four masts. A three-masted barque has fore- and mainmasts square-rigged, the mizzenmast fore- and aft-rigged.

**Barrow** is an ancient artificial mound of earth or stone raised over the site of a burial. In Britain barrows were built from 2500 B.C. until the late Saxon period, but the Egyptian are the earliest barrows known, the great pyramids being a spectacular development of the custom of ceremonial burial. Silbury Hill, south of Avebury, is the biggest artificial mound in Europe, 1680 ft. in circuit at the base, 315 ft. at top, and 135 ft. high.

**Bartholomew, Massacre of St.,** occurred in Paris on the night of Aug. 24, 1572, when over two thousand Huguenots were massacred by order of the Catholic French Court.

**Basalt Rocks** are fine-grained, dark coloured, of igneous origin and occur either as lava flows as in Mull and Staffa, or as intrusive sheets, like the Edinburgh Castle Rock and Salisbury Craig. One of the most noted examples of columnar basalt is that of the Giant's Cause-way in Ireland.

**Basanite.** A smooth black siliceous mineral, or flinty jasper; a crypto-crystalline quartz,

used as a touchstone for testing the purity of gold, etc., by means of the mark left after rubbing the metal with it. Sometimes styled the Lydian stone.

**Base,** a substance having a tendency to accept a proton (H$^+$). This is a wide definition and covers unconventional types of compounds. In aqueous solution bases dissolve with forma-tion of hydroxyl ions, and will neutralise an acid to form a salt. In non-aqueous solvents, like liquid ammonia or hydrogen fluoride, compounds classically regarded as salts can be bases, *e.g.*, sodium fluoride is a base in hydrogen fluoride solution. *See* F22.

**Basilisk,** is a lizard of aquatic habits, with an elevated crest (which it can erect or depress at will) down the centre of its back.

**Basques,** people of N. Spain and S.W. France, oldest surviving racial group in Europe, who have preserved their ancient language which is unrelated to any other tongue.

**Bas-Relief** ("low relief"), a term used in sculpture to denote a class of sculptures the figures of which are only slightly raised from the surface of the stone or clay upon which the design is wrought.

**Bastille,** a castle or fortress in Paris, built in the 14th cent., and used as a state prison, especially for political offenders. Its bad repute as an instrument of despotism excited the hatred of the populace, who stormed and demolished it on July 14, 1789, at the beginning of the Revo-lution.

**Bastinado,** an oriental punishment, by beating with a pliable rod or cane on the soles of the feet.

**Bats.** These mammals fly by means of a mem-brane stretched between each of the long fingers of the hand and between the fifth finger and the body. Another membrane stretches between the legs and the tail. There are twelve British species; namely, the Noctule, Leisler's B., Serotine, Pipistrelle, Long-eared B., Dauben-ton's B., Natterer's B., Whiskered B., Bech-stein's B., Barbastelle, Greater Horseshoe, and Lesser Horseshoe Bats. Bats avoid obstacles and locate their prey by emitting pulses of very high frequency sound, inaudible to the human ear (unless a bat detector is used). Blindness does not affect this ability but deafness leaves them comparatively helpless. Bats are mostly insectivorous, catching the insects in their open mouths while flying; some eat fruit. During the winter they survive on their stored fat. The Vampire Bats, feeding exclusively on blood, are confined to tropical America.

**Bath, Order of the,** believed to have been estab-lished by Henry IV. at his coronation in 1399; remodelled in 1725 as a military order; formally instituted in three classes in 1815; civil division added in 1847. In the Order are three classes: G.C.B., or Knight Grand Cross of the Bath; K.C.B., or Knight Commander of the Bath; C.B., or Companion of the Bath. Companion-ship of the Bath does not carry knighthood nor entitle the holder to the prefix "Sir." The motto of the order is *Tria juncta in uno* (Three joined in one). The insignia for civil and mili-tary and the three classes vary. *See* Knight-hood.

**Battery, Electric,** the common term for an electric cell but really meaning a combination of two or more cells. A cell is a device for converting stored chemical energy into electricity which can then be used for heat, light, traction, or any desired purpose. A *primary* cell will do this until the chemical action is completed and the cell is then useless. In a *secondary* cell, the chemical actions are reversible and the cell can be returned to its initial condition and used again. This is done by passing an electric current through—a process called recharging. A common primary cell is the Leclanché dry cell used in torches. This works by the action of sal-ammoniac on electrodes made of zinc and carbon. About a century after it came into com-mon use it is still the chief source of power for portable equipment in armed forces. A com-mon secondary cell is the lead and sulphuric acid accumulator used in cars. Many other types of cell are known and some are under development because the demands of space travel, medicine, warfare, etc., call for batteries of lighter weight, greater reliability, or special properties. *See* Fuel Cell, Energy Conversion.

**Bauhaus,** a German institution for the training of architects, artists, and industrial designers, founded in 1919 at Weimar by Walter Gropius. It was closed by Hitler in 1933 and re-opened at Chicago. The Bauhaus doctrine held that there should be no separation between architecture and the fine and applied arts; that art, science, and technology should co-operate to create "the compositely inseparable work of art, the great building." Thus it was an organisation with a social purpose. The original institution, at the instigation of Gropius, included on its teaching staff not only architects and technicians but also such noted artists as Paul Klee and Wassily Kandinsky.

**Bauxite,** the chief ore of aluminium. Chemically it is aluminium oxide. Aluminium metal is made industrially by electrolysing purified bauxite dissolved in fused cryolite. Chief producing areas: Surinam, Guyana, U.S.A., France, Hungary, Indonesia, U.S.S.R., Yugoslavia, Italy.

**Bayeux Tapestry,** a famous tapestry representing the conquest of England by William the Conqueror. It is embroidered on a band of linen 231 ft. long and 20 in. wide in blue, green, red, and yellow, divided into 72 scenes ranging over the whole story of the conquest. The accepted view is that the tapestry was commissioned for Bayeux Cathedral, but a new interpretation is that it is an Anglo-Norman secular work of art, much influenced by the contemporary *chansons de geste* (songs of deeds), executed by English embroiderers for a Norman patron. A representation can be seen in the Victoria and Albert Museum in London.

**Beagle,** a small hound that tracks by scent, and formerly used for hare hunting.

**Bears** belong to the Ursidae family of the Carnivora. They are plantigrade mammals, walking (like man) on the soles of their feet. Found in most parts of the world except Australia. The common Brown Bear was once spread over the whole of Europe; it became extinct in England about the 11th cent.; 7–8 ft. in length, and stands 3 ft. or more at the shoulder. The Grizzly Bear of N. America is larger, and the coat is shorter and greyer. The Polar Bear is remarkable in having a white coat all the year round; it spends much time in water, and unlike the other bears it is entirely carnivorous. Bear-baiting was made illegal in England in 1835.

**Beaufort Scale** of wind force is used to specify numerically the strength of the wind. Since the introduction of anemometers to measure the actual velocity, equivalent values of the ranges in miles per hour at a standard height in the open have been assigned to the Beaufort numbers. *See* N33.

**Beaver,** a genus of mammals of the Rodentia order, with short, scaly ears, webbed hind feet, and a long broad scaly tail. They grow up to 4 ft. long, and live in communities, constructing dams and lodges where they breed. Found in N. America, Russia, and Poland. Hunted mercilessly by trappers for its valuable pelt before protective laws were passed.

**Bedford Level** comprises parts of Norfolk, Suffolk, Huntingdon, Northampton, Lincoln, and Cambridge, generally called the Fens, 70 miles long and 20 to 40 miles broad. It was reclaimed and drained in the 17th cent. by the Earl of Bedford and the Dutch engineer Cornelius Vermuyden.

**Bedlam** (a corruption of Bethlehem) was a priory in Bishopsgate, afterwards converted into a hospital for lunatics. The asylum was transferred to St. George's Fields, Lambeth, in 1815. The term "bedlamite" came to be applied to any person behaving like a madman.

**Beech,** a deciduous tree belonging to the genus *Fagus* of some eight or nine species found in north temperate regions. The common beech, *F. sylvatica,* is believed to be native to Britain and is one of our finest trees, with massive trunk, long, pointed winter buds, and smooth, grey bark. There is little undergrowth under its dense shade. It is shorter lived than the oak, taking about 200 years to reach full size and then declining. The timber of beech has a variety of uses, *e.g.,* spoons, handles, tools, and chairs.

**Bee-eater,** name of a family of brilliantly coloured birds closely related to the rollers and kingfishers inhabiting the tropical and sub-tropical parts of Africa, Asia and Europe. The European species successfully nested in Britain for the first time in 1955 and a pair nested in Alderney in 1956. With their long curved beaks they catch insects on the wing, especially bees and butterflies, and lay their eggs in dark nest tunnels.

**Beefeater.** *See* Yeomen of the Guard.

**Beeswax,** the secretion of the bee, used for the formation of the cells or honey-comb of the hive; when melted it is what is commercially known as yellow wax, white wax being made by bleaching. Being impervious to water, it acts as a good resistant and is an article of much utility.

**Beetles** (Coleoptera) constitute one of the biggest orders of insects, numbering over 200,000 species. There are two pairs of wings; the hind pair are used for flight, while the front pair are hardened to form a pair of protective covers (elytra). Some beetles have lost the power of flight and then the elytra are joined together.

**Bel and the Dragon** is the title of certain supplementary chapters to the "Book of Daniel" of an apocryphal character. First appeared in the Septuagint, but the Jewish Church did not accept it as inspired. In 1546 the Council of Trent declared it to be canonical.

**Bell,** a hollow body of metal used for making sounds. Bells are usually made from bell-metal, an alloy of copper and tin. Small bells used for interior functions are often made of silver, gold, or brass. Ordinary hand-bells are of brass. From the 7th cent. large bells have been used in England in cathedrals, churches, and monasteries. The greatest bell in the world is the "King of Bells" in the Kremlin at Moscow, which weighs about 198 tons, is 20 ft. 7 in. high and 22 ft. 8 in. in diameter. It was cast in 1733, but cracked in the furnace (the broken part weighed 11 tons) and is now preserved as a national treasure. Other large bells in Russia, include the 171-ton one at Krasnogvardersk, near Leningrad, and the one of 110 tons at Moscow. The Great Bell (Great Paul) at St. Paul's, cast in 1881, weighs 16¾ tons, and is the largest in the United Kingdom. Other gigantic bells are the Great Bell at Peking (53 tons); Nanking (22 tons); Cologne Cathedral (25 tons); Big Ben, Westminster (13½ tons); Great Peter, York Minster (10 tons). The Curfew bell is rung in some parts of England to this day, notably at Ripon. The number of changes that can be rung on a peal of bells is the *factorial* of the number of bells. Thus four bells allow 24 and eight bells 40,320.

**Belladonna** *or* **Deadly Nightshade** (*Atropa belladonna*), a well-known poisonous wild plant found in Southern Europe and Western Asia. The alkaloid atropine it contains is valuable in medicine, although a large dose is poisonous.

**Bell, Book, and Candle.** To curse by "bell, book, and candle" was a form of excommunication in the Roman Church ending with the words: "Do to the book, quench the candle, ring the bell."

**Benedicite,** the canticle in the Book of Common Prayer, known also as "The Song of the Three Holy Children."

**Benedictines** are monks and nuns of the Benedictine Order who live under the rule of St. Benedict—the monastic code whose influence on the religious and cultural life of the West has been so powerful. The rule is marked by an absence of extravagant asceticism. The greatest of the early Benedictines was Pope Gregory I (590–604) who sent St. Augustine of Canterbury to Anglo-Saxon England. Gregorian plainsong is named after him. *See also* J30(1).

**Benedictus,** a canticle used in the morning service of the English Church, and deriving its name from the first word of the Latin verse, *Benedictus,* blessed.

**Benzene.** An aromatic hydrocarbon obtained from coal tar and some petroleum fractions. It is a volatile inflammable liquid with a characteristic smell. The molecule consists of a flat ring of six carbon atoms, each bound to one hydrogen atom. Benzene is the parent member of many aromatic organic compounds and is widely used in industry to synthesise intermediates for fibres, dyestuffs, explosives, and pharmaceutical chemicals.

**Bergamot**, an essential oil obtained from the rind of a species of citrus grown chiefly in Calabria, and largely used in perfumery. Also a hardy herbaceous perennial.

**Beryl**, a mineral, of which the emerald is a grassgreen variety. Composed of beryllium and aluminium silicates. The pure mineral is colourless; the colour of most beryl comes from traces of impurities, notably iron and chromium. Otherwise it is yellowish, greenishyellow, or blue, and is found in veins which traverse granite or gneiss, or embedded in granite, and sometimes in alluvial soil formed from such rocks.

**Beryllium.** Metallic element, symbol Be. Very similar to aluminium, it is stronger than steel and only one-quarter its weight. It is not very abundant, its main source is the mineral, beryl. Copper containing 2% beryllium is used for making springs. Because of its special properties the metal is used as a component in spacecraft, missiles and nuclear reactors. This accounts for its recent development on a technical scale. The metal powder is toxic.

**Bessemer Process**, for making steel depends on the forcing of atmospheric air into molten pig iron to burn out the impurities. *See* Steel.

**Betel**, the leaf of an Indian climbing plant, of pungent, narcotic properties. It is destructive to the teeth, and reddens the gums and lips.

**Bhang**, the Indian name for the hemp plant *Cannabis sativa*, the leaves and seed-capsules of which are chewed or smoked. The potent drug which comes from flowers of the female plant is called hashish in Arabia and marihuana in the United States and Mexico. *See* P23(2).

**Bible**—The Old Testament and the New Testament. The Old Testament—the prehistoric portion—consists of 39 books, and is divided into three parts: (1) the Law, (2) the Prophets, (3) Miscellaneous Writings. The Old Testament was written in Hebrew except for parts of Ezra and Daniel, which were in Aramaic. It was not until the 9th cent. A.D. that a complete Hebrew text was made, the so-called Massoretic text. Before that the main versions were the Alexandrian Greek translation (Septuagint) made in the 2nd cent. B.C. and St. Jerome's Latin Vulgate of the 4th cent. A.D. Portions were translated into the Anglo-Saxon in the 8th cent. and the Venerable Bede put the greater part of St. John's gospel into English, but it was not until 1535 that a complete printed English version appeared—the Coverdale Translation. The Authorised Version dates from 1611 in the reign of James I., and because of its beautiful phraseology it has had a lasting appeal. The Revised Version dates from 1885. A new translation of the Bible in the English language of today is in progress (*The New English Bible*); the New Testament was published in 1961 and the Old Testament and the Apocrypha will be ready later. The finding of the Dead Sea Scrolls (since 1947) has added to our knowledge of Scripture.

**Billion**, in English usage, a million million, or $10^{12}$; in American and French usage, a thousand million, or $10^9$.

**Bill of Rights**, or Declaration of Rights, was the document setting forth the conditions upon which the British throne was offered to William and Mary in 1688. This was accepted and ultimately became an Act of Parliament.

**Binary Notation**, for numbers, is a way of representing numbers using only two digits, 0 and 1. Electronic digital computers handle numbers in this form and many people these days are having to learn it. Many school children find it both easy and fascinating—as did the great philosopher and mathematician Leibniz. The ordinary, or decimal numbers, 0, 1, 2, 3, 4, 5, 6, 7, 8, 9, 10 are written in binary notation as follows: 0, 1, 10, 11, 100, 101, 110, 111, 1000, 1001, 1010. The reader might divine the rules from this. The point is that you "carry 1." *i.e.*, move the digit 1 a place to the left, when you reach 2. In decimal notation you move 1 a place left when you reach 10. In other words, instead of columns for units, tens, hundreds, thousands, etc., the columns are for units, twos,

fours, eights, etc. In binary notation: "1+1 = 0 with 1 to carry." Since every digit in binary notation is either 0 or 1 it requires one bit of information to specify a binary digit. *See* Bit.

**Biological Warfare**, is the use for warlike purposes of bacteria, viruses, fungi, or other biological agents. These can be used to spread distress, incapacity, disease, or death among the enemy's people or livestock. One of the strange uses to which mankind puts its science is to make naturally infective organisms even more virulent for military use. This sort of research can be done in many countries; it is much cheaper and easier to hide than nuclear weapons development. Secret attack by biological agents is supposed to be easy and it may affect the populations without damaging buildings or bridges. However, the true effectiveness of biological warfare is largely unknown—meteorological conditions alone might render an attack completely unreliable.

**Birch**, a genus of deciduous trees including about 40 species and found only in northern regions. Birches native to Britain, and to Europe generally, are of two species—the silver birch, *Betula pendula*, with its graceful, drooping branches and triangular leaves, and the white birch, *Betula pubescens*, which has erect branches and soft oval leaves. Birch timber is an important plywood timber, the bark is used for tanning leather, and wintergreen oil comes from the bark of black birch, *Betula lenta*, a North American species. The birch is not a long-lived tree, few standing for more than a hundred years. The tallest recorded is at Woburn in Bedfordshire, 102 ft. high.

**Birds**, or Aves, are, next to mammals, the highest class of animal life. There are two kinds of modern birds—*Carinatae*, possessing keeled breast-bones and having power of flight; *Ratitae*, having raft-like breast-bones, and incapable of flight; and a sub-class of fossil birds, Archaeornithes, including *Archaeopteryx*. It is estimated that there are about 120 million land birds breeding in Great Britain, including 10 million each of the chaffinch and blackbird, 7 million each of the starling and robin and about 2 million sparrows.

The wheatear is usually the first of the migratory birds to return, often reaching Britain at the end of February and always before the middle of March; the sand martin is the first of the " early swallows " to return, followed by the house martin. The first cuckoo arrives about the middle of April, and the whinchat, garden warbler, and sedge warbler during the last week in April. The nightjar, spotted flycatcher, and red-backed shrike are not seen until the first week in May. The swift is among the last to return from Africa and the earliest to depart. Bird-nesting is illegal in Britain. *See also* F33, Z21.

**Birds of Paradise**, over 40 species of tropical birds inhabiting the dense forests of New Guinea and neighbouring islands. The male birds are remarkable for their brilliant plumage, long tail feathers, and ruffs on wings and neck, which are displayed to advantage during courtship. Related to the Bower Birds of Australia, and crows.

**Biretta**, a four-cornered head-covering worn by ecclesiastics of the Roman Church and varying in colour according to the rank of the wearer. A cardinal's biretta is red, a bishop's purple, a priest's black.

**Bise**, a keen dry north wind prevalent in Switzerland and South France.

**Bishop** is a Christian ecclesiastic, a person consecrated for the spiritual government of an area, a diocese or province, to the spiritual oversight of which he has been appointed (diocesan bishops), or to aid a bishop so appointed (suffragan bishops). In the Church of England there are forty-three diocesan bishops, all nominated by the Crown. Two, Canterbury and York, are archbishops having primacy in the respective provinces. The archbishops of Canterbury and York and the bishops of London, Durham, and Winchester and twenty-one other diocesan bishops in the order of seniority are spiritual peers, and sit in the House of Lords. The (Disestablished) Church of Ireland has two archbishops and twelve bishops; the (Disestablished) Church of Wales an archbishop and five bishops and the Episcopal Church in Scotland seven bishops. *See also* **Cardinal.**

**Bismuth,** metallic element symbol Bi, in group V of the periodic table. Like antimony, its stable form is a grey, brittle, layer structure; electrical conductor. It is readily fusible, melting at 264° C and boiling at about 1420° C. Wood's metal, an alloy with one of the lowest melting points (under 150° F, so that a spoon made of it will melt when placed in a cup of hot tea), contains four parts bismuth, two parts lead, one part tin, one part cadmium.

**Bison,** a genus of wild cattle, distinguished from the ox by its shorter, wider skull, beard under the chin, high forequarters, and, in winter, a great mane of woolly hair covering head and forequarters. There are two species, the European and the American bison, both now protected in game preserves.

**Bit,** formerly the word often referred to the metal piece in the mouth of a bridled horse, now more likely to be a technical expression in the mouth of a computer expert. A bit is a unit of information; it is the information that can be conveyed by indicating which of two possibilities obtains. Any object that can be either of two states can therefore store one bit of information. In a technical device, the two states could be the presence or the absence of a magnetic field, or of an electric voltage. Since all numbers can be represented in the binary system (*see* Binary Notation) by a row of digits which are *either* 0 or 1, it takes one bit of information to specify a binary digit. Bit is short for binary digit.

**Bittern,** a bird of the heron genus, with long, loose plumage on the front and sides of the neck. It is a solitary bird inhabiting marshes, but rare in Britain.

**Bivalves,** shell-fish whose shell consists of two hinged valves, lying one on each side of the body, such as mussels, oysters, and cockles.

**Blackbird, or Merle,** a member of the Thrush family, a familiar song bird in Britain. Male is all-black with orange bill; female is mottled brown with brown bill; the young are spotted brown.

**Blackcock and Greyhen** (as the female is called) are closely related to the Capercaillies but smaller. They nest on the ground and prefer wooded country to open moors. Found in northern half of northern hemisphere. Polygamous, they perform excited courtship dances; the male is a handsome blue-black bird with white undertail, the female dark brown mottled.

**Black Death,** the plague which swept across Europe in the years 1348-50, beginning in the ports of Italy, brought in by merchant ships from Black Sea ports. It was the worst scourge man has ever known; at least a quarter of the European population was wiped out in the first epidemic of 1348. It reached England in the winter of that year. The disease was transmitted to man by fleas from black rats, though this was not known at the time, the specific organism being *Bacillus pestis.* The disease continued to ravage Europe in recurrent outbreaks up to the late 17th cent. The epidemic which raged in England in 1665 wiped out whole villages and one-tenth of London's population of 460,000. Samuel Pepys wrote a grim account of it in his *Diary. See also* Labourers, English Statute of.

**Black Hole of Calcutta,** the name given to the place where a captured British garrison was confined in 1756, during the struggle for India between the French and British. Into a noisome space, about 20 ft. square, 146 persons were driven and only 23 were found alive the next morning. The authenticity of the story has been called into question, but after sifting the evidence Professor H. H. Dodwell, in the *Cambridge History of the British Empire,* believes it to be substantially true.

**Black-letter,** the Old English or Gothic type first used in printing blocks.

**Black Woodpecker** (*Dryocopus martius*), a large, black bird about the size of a rook, with slightly crested scarlet crown, found in many parts of Europe.

**Blenny,** a group of marine fishes with spiny rays part of the fin running along the back. Several species are found around the British coast.

**Blood Groups.** *See* Index to Section P, also F47.

**Bloody Assizes,** the assizes, conducted in 1685 by George Jeffreys, Lord Chief Justice, at which participants in the Duke of Monmouth's rebellion against King James II. were tried. They were marked by relentless cruelty.

**Bluebird,** a migratory bird of North America, deriving its name from its deep blue plumage. It is one of the few song birds of America, and familiar in the woods from early spring to November. In India and Malaya there is the Fairy Blue-bird; the male is black with shiny blue upper parts. The bluebird was used as the symbol of happiness by Maeterlinck in his play *The Blue Bird.*

**Blue Peter,** a blue flag with a white square in the centre, is hoisted 24 hours before a ship leaves harbour (the letter P in the alphabet of the International Code of Signals).

**Blue Ribbon,** a term in general use to denote the highest honour or prize attainable in any field or competition. Thus the Derby is the blue ribbon of the turf. The expression is derived from the highest Order of Knighthood in the gift of the British Crown, the insignia of which is a garter of blue velvet.

**Blue Stocking,** a term used to describe a learned or literary woman, particularly if pedantic and undomesticated. It is said that the term derives from the Bas-Bleu club of Paris, which was attended by the literary savantes of the 17th cent. In England a similar literary club was formed about 1780, whose members were distinguished by their blue stockings.

**" Blue "** Sun, Moon, etc., a phenomenon caused by the scattering of sunlight by transparent particles suspended in the atmosphere, the effect being that blue light is transmitted and red light extinguished to direct vision. The dust from the Krakatoa eruption in 1883 and the drifting layer of smoke from the forest fires in Alberta, Canada, in September 1950 gave rise to " blue " moons and suns, phenomena sufficiently rare to be described as occurring " once in a blue moon." In the cold climatic conditions of the Pamirs and the far north, vegetation is said to look " blue " on account of the rays of high calorific value (red, yellow, green) being absorbed, while only the blue and violet are transmitted. It was Tyndall who first explained the blue colour of the sky.

**Boa,** a term applied to a family of snakes of large size, some attaining a length of 30 ft. They are not poisonous, but kill their prey by crushing —constriction—hence the name "boa constrictor." They occur both in the Old World and the New, but are more abundant in the latter. Most Boas retain the eggs within the body until young are fully developed, whereas the Pythons almost all lay leather-shelled eggs.

**Boar, or Wild Hog,** an animal largely distributed over the forest regions of Europe, Asia, Africa, and South America. It has a longer snout and shorter ears than its descendant the domestic hog, and is provided with tusks. Having to forage for itself, it is a more active and intelligent animal than the pig of the sty, and offers good sport to the hunter.

**Boat,** an open vessel, propelled by oars or sails, or both. The boats of a ship of war are the launch, barge, pinnace, yawl, cutters, jolly boat, and gig; of a merchant vessel, the launch, skiff, jolly boat or yawl, stern boat, quarter-boat, and captain's gig. Every ship is compelled to carry adequate, fully provisioned and equipped lifeboats.

**Bode's Law,** a numerical relationship formulated by Bode in 1772, which states that the relative mean distances of the planets from the sun are found by adding 4 to each of the terms 0, 3, 6, 12, 24, 48, 96. The actual mean distances (in millions of miles) are: Mercury, 36; Venus, 67·2; Earth, 92·9; Mars, 141·6; Jupiter, 483·3; Saturn, 886·0; Uranus, 1782·8. The gap between Mars and Jupiter caused Bode to predict the existence of a planet there, which was later confirmed by the discovery of Ceres and other minor planets. The law breaks down, however, for Neptune and Pluto.

**Boer War,** lasted from Oct. 11, 1899, when the Boers invaded Natal, to May 31, 1902, when the Treaty of Vereeniging ended hostilities. At first the operations of the British troops in

Cape Colony were unsuccessful and disastrous reverses were sustained. Lord Roberts was then sent out as Commander-in-Chief, with Lord Kitchener as Chief-of-Staff, and from February, 1900 when Kimberley was relieved and Cronje was compelled to surrender and Ladysmith and Mafeking were relieved, the struggle was practically over.

**Boiling-point** is the temperature at which a liquid boils. At that point the pressure of the vapour is equal to the pressure of the atmosphere. Under increased pressure the b. p. rises and under less pressure, as on the top of a mountain, it is lower. As represented on the Centigrade scale the b. p. of water is 100°; alcohol 78·4°; and ether, 35·6°. On the Fahrenheit scale, the b. p. of distilled water is 212°. Boiling points are given for a standard pressure (760 millimetres of mercury).

**Books, Sizes of.** *See* N14.

**Books, Classification of.** All libraries are classified to facilitate reference, but the favourite system is the Dewey Decimal System, which divides the whole field of knowledge into ten Main Classes: General Works; Philosophy; Religion; Sociology; Philology; Natural Science; Useful Arts and Applied Science; Fine Arts; Literature; History (including geography and travel and biography). Each of these Main Classes is again subdivided into ten main divisions. As an example: the main class of Sociology receives the number 300. This range 300 to 400 (the next main class) is graduated into tens, and Economics is 330. The range 330 to 340 is again graduated, and the subject of Labour and Capital is 331. This process is carried on by decimals so that 331·2 deals with Remuneration for Work, 331·22 with Wage Scales, and 331·225 with Extra Pay.

**Borax (Sodium Pyroborate)** is a white, soluble, crystalline salt. It is widely and diversely used, *e.g.*, as a mild antiseptic, in glazing pottery, in soldering, in the making of pyrex glass, as a cleansing agent and sometimes as a food preservative. Borax occurs naturally in the salt lakes of Tibet, where it is called tincal, in California (Borax Lake, Death Valley), and elsewhere

**Bore.** In physical geography, an almost vertical wall of water which passes upstream along certain estuaries. Its formation requires special conditions of river flow, incoming high tide, and shape of river channel. It can be spectacular and dangerous on some rivers. In Britain the best known is the Severn bore which can be a few feet high and move at 10 or 12 m.p.h. In some parts of Britain the bore is called an eagre.

**Boron.** A metalloid element, symbol B. There are two forms, one crystalline, the other amorphous. It is not very abundant in nature but occurs in concentrated deposits. It is best known in boric acid, which is used as a mild antiseptic (called boracic acid) and borax (*q.v.*). Boron compounds are essential to some plants, *e.g.*, beans. Used in the preparation of various special-purpose alloys, such as impact resistant steel. Compounds of boron and hydrogen are used as rocket fuels.

**Borstal**, an institution where young offenders between 15 and 21 on conviction may be sent for detention and reform by a court of quarter sessions or assize. The first was opened in 1902 at the village of Borstal, near Rochester in Kent. Administered by the Home Office.

**Boston Tea Party,** an incident which occurred on Dec. 16, 1773, on board some tea-ships in Boston Harbour. High taxation imposed by the British Parliament under George III. had caused bitter feelings, and instigated by popular meetings, a party of citizens, disguised as Indians, boarded the tea-ships and threw the tea overboard. This incident was a prelude to the American War of Independence (1775–83).

**Bounds Beating,** an old Anglo-Saxon custom. The parish clergyman and officials go round the parish boundaries accompanied by boys who beat the boundary stones with long sticks of willow. The ceremony takes place on the Rogation days preceding Ascension Day.

**Bourgeoisie,** a term used by Marxists to indicate those who do not, like the proletariat, live by the sale of their labour. They include, on the one hand, industrialists and financiers or members of the liberal professions and, on the other, small artisans and shop-keepers who, although their standard of living may not be appreciably higher (and today is often lower) than that of the proletariat, are described as the "petty bourgeoisie." According to the Marxist view of history, the bourgeoisie arose with modern industrialism after it had overthrown the old feudal aristocracy and replaced it as ruling class.

**Bow,** an instrument for propelling arrows, and, in the days when it was a weapon of war, was usually made of yew or ash, and was about 6 ft. long, with an arrow 3 ft. long. It was the weapon with which Crécy, Poitiers, and Agincourt were won. The cross-bow was Italian and was adopted in France, but did not become popular in Britain.

**Bow Bells** is the peal of the London church of St. Mary-le-Bow, Cheapside, within sound of which one must be born to be entitled to be called a "cockney." Bow Bells had not been heard since 1939, but they once again rang out over the City of London on Dec. 20, 1961.

**Bowdlerize,** to expurgate a book. Derived from Thomas Bowdler (1754–1825), the editor of the Family Shakespeare, in which "those words and expressions are omitted which cannot with propriety be read aloud in a family." He treated Gibbon's *History of the Decline and Fall of the Roman Empire* in the same way, omitting "all passages of an irreligious and immoral tendency." Such prudery met with ridicule and hence the words "bowdlerism," "bowdlerist," etc.

**Bower Bird,** native to Australia and New Guinea and related to the Bird of Paradise, though often less striking in appearance. In the mating season the male builds a "bower" of sticks and grasses for courtship displays and as a playground. The Gardener Bower Bird of Papua makes a lawn in front of his bower and adorns it with bright coloured pebbles and flowers which are replaced as they wither. The female builds her nest away from the bower.

**Boycott,** a term used in connection with a person that the general body of people, or a party or society, refuse to have dealings with. Originally used when Captain Boycott (1832–97) was made the victim of a conspiracy by the Irish Land League which prevented him making any purchases or holding any social intercourse in his district. He had incurred the League's hostility by a number of evictions.

**Brass,** an exceedingly useful alloy of copper and zinc. Much brass is about two-thirds copper, but different proportions give different properties. It is harder than copper and easily worked. Brass in the Bible (Matt. x, 9) probably refers to bronze.

**Breadfruit Tree** (*Artocarpus altilis*), a native of the South Sea Islands; the fruits are a brownish green, about the size of a melon, and contain a white pulpy substance which is roasted before being eaten. The tree grows 40 ft. or more. Captain Bligh's ship *Bounty* was on a voyage to Jamaica carrying a cargo of 1,000 breadfruit trees when the mutiny occurred.

**Breeder Reactor,** a kind of nuclear reactor (*q.v.*) which besides producing energy by the fission process also produces ("breeds") more nuclear fuel at the same time. A typical reaction is: a neutron induces fission of a U-235 nucleus which breaks up into two medium-sized nuclei and some neutrons; one of the latter then enters a U-238 nucleus turning it into U-239 which then decays radioactively *via* neptunium into plutonium which is useful fuel. There are technical problems in breeder reactors which have delayed their practical use but the "breeding" principle is so valuable that experiments have gone on for many years in, *e.g.*, Scotland and Idaho, and breeder reactors will no doubt increase in importance the more the supply of natural nuclear fuel appears to become depleted.

**Breviary** (Lat. *breviarium*=abridgment), the short prayer-book of the Roman Catholic Church which gives the Divine Office, *i.e.*, the canonical hours or services. The directions for Mass are in the Missal. The modern Roman breviary is a reformed version of the 11th-cent. breviary and was produced by Pope Pius V. in 1568 in response to a decree of the Council of Trent. All Roman Catholic priests are required to recite the whole of the breviary services allotted for each day. *See also* Matins.

Bridges are structures for continuing a road, railway, or canal across a river, valley, ravine, or a road or railway at a lower level. From early times bridges were made of timber, stone, or brick, and it was not until the 19th cent. that wrought- and cast-iron were used. Today the materials mostly used are steel and reinforced concrete. Among the most famous of ancient bridges is that of S. Angelo at Rome, built by Hadrian as the Pons Aelius, A.D. 134. The Rialto bridge at Venice dates from 1588. The Ponte Santa Trinita at Florence, one of the finest Renaissance bridges and deemed the most beautiful in the world, was destroyed by German mines in 1944 but has now been reconstructed just as it was before. The first stone bridge across the Thames was begun in 1176. It had 19 arches and was lined with houses and stood until 1831 when it was replaced by the granite bridge designed by Sir John Rennie. By 1970 this will have been replaced by a new three-span concrete bridge with a six-lane carriageway and two footways. The first cast-iron bridge was at Ironbridge, Madeley, Shropshire, built in 1779 and now in need of repair. Telford's Menai suspension bridge (1825) has since been enlarged but the original design has been maintained. Another example of Britain's supremacy in constructional iron-work was Robert Stephenson's tubular bridge across the Menai Straits (1850), the prototype of all modern plate girder railway bridges. Other famous bridges are the Niagara (suspension), Forth railway bridge (cantilever), London Tower bridge (suspension), Tay bridge in Scotland, Victoria Jubilee bridge across the St. Lawrence at Montreal (an open steel structure), Sydney Harbour bridge, Lower Zambesi bridge, Storstrom bridge in Denmark, Howrah bridge at Calcutta, with the third largest cantilever span in the world, the Volta bridge of Ghana and the Auckland Harbour bridge, both built in recent years, the Verrazano-Narrows bridge spanning New York's harbour from Brooklyn to Staten I., the world's longest bridge, exceeding by 60 ft. the centre span of San Francisco's Golden Gate bridge, until 1964 the world's longest. Britain is engaged in the largest bridge building programme for over a century. The new road suspension bridge across the Firth of Forth, completed in 1964, has the largest single span in Europe (3,300 ft.). The Medway bridge, completed in 1963, is one of the largest pre-stressed concrete structures in the world. The Severn and the Tay road bridges were completed in 1966, the Tinsley viaduct, near Sheffield, was opened in 1968.

Britannia Metal, an alloy of tin, antimony, and copper, harder than pure tin, corrosion-resistant, used for teapots, and jugs (often electroplated).

British Association for the Advancement of Science, The, was founded in 1831 by a group of British scientists under the leadership of Charles Babbage (1792–1871) to stimulate scientific inquiry and promote research in the interest of the nation. Its meetings are held annually in different cities of the United Kingdom. It is divided into sections which include the chief physical and biological sciences, economics, anthropology and archaeology, psychology and education, engineering, forestry, agriculture, and there is also a division for studying the social and international relations of science. Sir Peter Medawar, F.R.S., was elected President for 1969, when the meeting was to be held in Exeter.

British Museum, was created by an Act of Parliament in 1753, when the Sir Hans Sloane collection, which the British Government had acquired for £20,000, was added to the Cottonian Library and the Harleian Manuscripts. It was opened to the public in 1759 at Montagu House, Bloomsbury. The acquisition of the library of George III. (now known as the King's Library) in 1823 made larger premises necessary, and the present building in Great Russell Street was completed in 1847 from designs by Sir Robert Smirke. The great domed Reading Room was opened in 1857, and the Natural History Department was transferred to South Kensington in the eighties. As a museum it is perhaps the most famous in the world, since, apart from its colossal library of books and manuscripts, it has many priceless collections of sculptures, antiquities, prints and drawings, coins and medals. *See also* Libraries.

British Railways. The name under which the railways of Britain were unified on January 1, 1948. Instead of the former four main railway systems six regions were formed: London Midland region (former L.M.S.R.) Western (former G.W.R.), Southern (formerly S.R.), Eastern (southern area of former L.N.E.R.), N.E. region (N.E. of former L.N.E.R.), Scottish region (Scottish system of the former L.M.S.R. and L.N.E.R.). The most far-reaching change in the modernisation and re-equipment programme since 1955 has been the replacement of steam traction by electric and diesel locomotives. Under the chairmanship of Lord (then Dr.) Richard Beeching the British Railways Board planned a viable railway system by closing uneconomic branch lines, by developing new services on the liner train principle, and by utilising a more limited trunk route system. Under the Labour Government an integrated system of transport is being worked out, embracing rail, road, canals, shipping, etc., itself integrated in the pattern of the country's social and economic needs. A 11,000-mile basic network has been fixed (8,000 route miles previously proposed) and a further 2,500 miles are under review. Unremunerative services necessary on social grounds are to receive a Government subsidy. The name was changed to British Rail in 1964.

British Standard Time, which is one hour ahead of Greenwich Mean Time, was introduced throughout the year in Britain on 18 February 1968. This brought Britain into line with countries in Western Europe where Central European Time is observed. Previously in Britain, British Summer Time (one hour fast on Greenwich) was observed in the summer and Greenwich Mean Time in the winter months.

Brocken-spectre or Glory. The series of co oured rings which an observer sees around the shadow of his own head (or an aeroplane in which he is travelling) as cast upon a bank of mist or thin cloud. This effect is produced by reflection and refraction of sunlight in minute water-droplets in the air just as in a rainbow.

Bromine. A non-metal element, symbol Br, member of the halogen family (*q.v.*). It is a red, evil-smelling liquid (Greek *bromos*, a stink). It is an abundant element In the U.S.A. bromide is extracted from sea-water on a large scale. It unites readily with many other elements, the products being termed bromides. Its derivatives with organic compounds are used in synthetic chemistry. Bromoform is a liquid resembling chloroform. Bromides are used in medicine to calm excitement.

Bronze is primarily an alloy of copper and tin, and was one of the earliest alloys known, the Bronze Age in the evolution of tool-using man coming between the Stone Age and the Iron Age. Some modern bronzes contain zinc or lead also, and a trace of phosphorus is present in " phosphor-bronze."

Bubble Chamber. An instrument used by physicists to reveal the tracks of fast fundamental particles (*e.g.*, those produced in large accelerating machines) in a form suitable for photography; closely related to the Wilson cloud chamber (*q.v.*), but the particles leave trails of small bubbles in a superheated liquid (often liquid hydrogen) instead of droplets of liquid in a supersaturated gas; invented in 1952 by the American physicist, Dr. D. Glaser, Nobel Prizeman, 1960, and developed by Prof. L. W. Alvarez, Univ. of California, Nobel Prizeman, 1968.

Buckingham Palace, London residence of British sovereigns since 1837. Originally built for the Duke of Buckingham (1703); bought by George III. in 1762 and remodelled by Nash 1825–36.

Buddhism. *See* J6.

Bulk Purchase. Arrangements for bulk purchase involve undertakings by a country, or by some agency within it, to buy from another country specified quantities of its products, either at prices fixed in advance or with provision for adjusting the prices at specified intervals to take account of general price movements. Such long-term arrangements may be, but need not be, combined with undertakings by the seller to buy specified quantities, or specified values, of the products of the purchasing country in exchange. The purpose of bulk-purchase arrangements is, on the one hand, to provide the seller of the goods in question with assured markets and, on the other, to assure the buyers of needed supplies of their goods.

**Buntings,** name of a group of finches, seed-eating birds, usually found in open country. The Yellowhammer, Reed Bunting, Corn Bunting, and Cirl Bunting are resident in Britain; the Snow Bunting (which breeds in small numbers in Scotland) and Lapland Bunting are regular winter visitors, and the Ortolan is among the rare visitors.

**Butane,** a colourless inflammable gas made of carbon and hydrogen; formula $C_4H_{10}$. Found in natural gas and made as a by-product of oil refining. Butane, like propane (*q.v.*), can easily be liquefied and moved safely in cans and tanks. It is thus useful as a " portable gas supply "; also used in internal combustion fuels.

**Byzantine Art** developed in the eastern part of the Roman empire after Constantine founded the city of Constantinople (A.D. 330). It has many sources—Greek, Syrian, Egyptian, and Islamic —and reached its zenith in the reign of Justinian (527–65). The major art form was ecclesiastical architecture, the basic plan of which was Roman—either basilican (symmetrical about an axis) or centralised (symmetrical about a point). Arched construction was developed, and the dome became the most typical feature, although, unlike the Roman dome which was placed on a round apartment, the Byzantine dome was placed on a square one on independent pendentives. Frequently small domes were clustered round a large one as in the case of the great church of Santa Sophia (537), the climax of Byzantine architecture. Usually the churches were small and include those of SS. Sergius and Bacchus, Sta. Irene (in Constantinople), S. Vitale in Ravenna, and the much later and larger St. Mark's in Venice. Byzantine art also took the form of miniatures, enamels, jewels, and textiles, but mosaics, frescos, and icons (*q.v.*) are its greatest treasures.

## C

**Cacao,** *Theobroma cacao,* is an evergreen tree, from 15 to 20 ft. high, growing abundantly in tropical America, West Africa, the West Indies, Ceylon, etc., yielding seeds, called cocoa beans, from which cocoa and chocolate are manufactured. The fruit is 7–10 in. long, hard and ridged; inside are the beans, covered with a reddish-brown skin, which are first fermented, then dried. The trees mature at five to eight years and produce two crops a year.

**Cactus,** a family of flowering plants numbering about a thousand species adapted to living in very dry situations. The stem is usually fleshy, being composed of succulent tissue, remarkably retentive of water; commonly equipped with sharp thorns which deter animals from eating them. The roots are generally very long, tapping soil water over large area; a " prickly pear " cactus may have roots covering a circular area 25 ft. or more in diameter. The leaves are commonly insignificant or absent, and the stem takes over the photosynthetic leaf function and becomes accordingly flattened to expose greater area to sunlight and air. In some kinds of cactus (*e.g. Echinocactus*) the stem is shaped almost like a sea-urchin.

**Cadmium.** A metallic element, symbol Cd, chemically similar to zinc and mercury. Used in alloys to lower the melting point, as in Wood's metal with bismuth and tin. Alloyed with copper to make electric cables. Like zinc, it is a protective metal and is used in electro-plating. The cadmium-vapour lamp gives a characteristic frequency used in measuring wavelength.

**Caesium,** also spelt Cesium, is an alkali metal element, symbol Cs, in first group of the periodic table. It resembles rubidium and potassium and was discovered by Bunsen and Kirchhoff in 1860. It was the first element whose existence was discovered spectro-

scopically. The caesium atom consists of a heavy nucleus surrounded by 55 electrons, 54 of which are arranged in stable orbits, and one of which, known as the valency electron, is in a less stable orbit surrounding them. Used in the construction of photo-electric cells and as an accurate time standard (atomic clock).

**Calcite,** the stable, naturally-occurring form of calcium carbonate; very abundant; crystallises in the hexagonal system.

**Calcium,** a silvery-white metallic element, symbol Ca. It melts at 810° C. and is very reactive. It was discovered by Sir Humphry Davy in 1808, but not until 1898 was it obtained pure, by Moissan. Does not occur as metal in nature, but calcium compounds make up a large part of the earth's crust. Most important calcium sources are marble, limestone, chalk (all three are, chemically, calcium carbonate); dolomite, which is the double carbonate of calcium and magnesium; gypsum, a hydrated calcium sulphate; calcium phosphate and calcium fluoride. Igneous rocks contain much calcium silicate. Calcium compounds are essential to plants and are used in fertilisers. Animals require calcium and phosphorus for bone and teeth formation; deficiency is treated by administration of calcium phosphate. Strontium is chemically similar to calcium, and the radioactive strontium 90 from atomic " fall-out " is therefore easily assimilated by the body.

**Calendar,** a collection of tables showing the days and months of the year, its astronomical recurrences, chronological references, etc. The Julian Calendar, with its leap year, introduced by Julius Cæsar, fixed the average length of the year at 365¼ days, which was about 11 minutes too long (the earth completes its orbit in 365 days 5 hours 48 minutes 46 seconds of mean solar time). The cumulative error was rectified by the Gregorian Calendar, introduced in Italy in 1582, whereby century years do not count as leap years unless divisible by 400. This is the rule we now follow. England did not adopt the reformed calendar until 1752, when she found herself 11 days behind the Continent.

**Calends,** the first day of the month in the Roman calendar, when interest fell due, and proclamations as to the order of days were made.

**Calorie.** Unit of quantity of heat. The " small " or fundamental calorie is the amount of heat required to raise the temperature of 1 gram of water from 14·5° to 15·5° C. This is the gram-calorie used in physics and chemistry. The large Calorie (written with a capital C), commonly used in nutritional connotations, is equal to 1000 small calories and is called the kilogram-calorie.

**Calvinism.** *See* J7.

**Calypso,** West Indian song in the form of a doggerel lampoon composed spontaneously and sung to a guitar.

**Cambridge University** had a sufficiently good teaching reputation to attract Oxford students in 1209, when lectures at their own university were suspended. In 1226 it had a Chancellor who was recognised by King and Pope. The first college to be founded was Peterhouse in 1284. The university was reorganised and granted a Charter of Incorporation by an act of Elizabeth in 1571. The colleges with their dates of foundation are Christ's (1505), Churchill (1960), Clare (1326), Clare Hall (1966), Corpus Christi (1352), Darwin (1964), Downing (1800), Emmanuel (1584), Fitzwilliam (1966), Gonville and Caius (1348), Jesus (1496), King's (1441), Magdalene (1542), Pembroke (1347), Peterhouse (1284), Queens' (1448), St. Catherine's (1473), St. Edmund's House (1896), St. John's (1511), Selwyn (1882), Sidney Sussex (1596), Trinity (1546), Trinity Hall (1350), University (1966). The women's colleges are: Girton (1869), Newnham (1875), New Hall (1954), Hughes Hall (formerly Cambridge T.C.) (1885), and Lucy Cavendish Collegiate Society (1966) (for women research students and other graduates). Women were admitted to degrees (though not allowed to sit for examination) in 1920, and to full membership of the University in 1948.

**Camel,** a large ruminant quadruped, inhabiting Asia and Africa, where it is largely used as a beast of burden. There are two species—the Arabian camel or dromedary, with only one hump; and the Bactrian, or double-humped camel. There are no wild dromedaries, and the only wild bactrians occur in the Gobi Desert. The camel is able to go for long periods without water, not, as was formerly believed, because it stored water in its hump, but because of the unique mechanism of its physiology which enables it to conserve water at the expense of not sweating until 104° F. is reached.

Campanile, or bell-tower, is separate from but usually adjoining its parent church. The most famous are in Italy. Giotto's tower at Florence, adjoining the cathedral of Santa Maria del Fiore, is architecturally the finest in the world. Others are at Cremona, the loftiest in Italy (364 ft.) and Pisa (the leaning tower). The magnificent pointed campanile of St. Mark's, Venice, which collapsed in 1902 and has since been rebuilt in its original form, was begun in 902.

Canal, an artificial watercourse used for navigation which changes its level by means of locks. The completion of the Bridgewater Canal in 1761 to take coal from Worsley to Manchester marked the beginning of canal building in industrial Britain. There are some 2,500 miles of navigable inland waterways in Great Britain today, 1,850 miles of which are under the control of the British Waterways Board set up by the Transport Act, 1962. The English network is based on the four great estuaries Mersey, Humber, Severn, and Thames.

Canary, a light, sweet wine from the Canaries and chief export until the grape blight of 1853. Much consumed in Britain from Tudor to Georgian times. Also, a popular cage bird bred from a small finch, *Serinus canarius*. See Z22.

Candela, unit of luminous intensity, so defined that the brightness of a total radiator, or black body, at the temperature of solidification of molten platinum is 60 candelas per sq. cm.

Candlemas, an English and Roman Church festival in celebration of the Purification of the Virgin Mary. The date is February 2.

Canon, a term applied to signify a recognised rule for the guide of conduct in matters legal, ecclesiastical, and artistic, or an authoritative ordinance: thus we have Canonical Scriptures, Canon Law, etc. A Canon is also a dignitary of the Church, usually a member of a cathedral chapter in the Anglican communion, or in the Roman Church a member of an order standing between regular monks and secular clergy.

Canonical Hours were seven in number in the Western Church; Matins and Lauds, before dawn; Prime, early morning service; Terce, 9 a.m.; Sext, noon; Nones 3 p.m.; Vespers, 4 p.m.; Compline, bed-time.

Canonisation, the entering of one of the faithful departed on the list of saints of the Roman Catholic Church. The rules governing canonisation were simplified by papal decree in 1969. The proof-gathering is now left to the bishop, who must consult regularly with the Holy See and show in advance " that the cause itself is based upon a legitimate and solid foundation." Beatification, by which a person is called blessed, is usually followed by canonisation, but not necessarily.

Canticles, the name given to the scriptural passages from the Bible sung by the congregation in the various Christian liturgies. They are the *Benedicite, Benedictus, Magnificat, Nunc Dimittis*.

Capercaillie, the largest of the grouse family, found in the Scottish highlands and the pine forests and mountainous regions of Northern and Central Europe and Asia.

Capet, the family name of the royal house of France, founded by Hugh Capet in 987, with its collateral branches. The main line of the dynasty came to an end in 1328 with the death of Charles IV when the throne passed to the related house of Valois. The direct Valois line ended in 1498 with the death of Charles VIII. The first of the Bourbon line was Henry IV whose descendants ruled France (except during the French Revolution and the Napoleonic era) until 1848.

Capitalism. See J7.

Capuchins are members of a mendicant order of Franciscans, founded in the 16th cent. with the aim of restoring the primitive and stricter observance of the rule of St. Francis, so called from the capuce or pointed cowl worn by them.

Carat, a term used in assessing the value of gold

and precious stones. In connection with gold, it represents the proportion of pure gold contained in any gold alloy, and for this purpose the metal is divided into 24 parts. Thus 24-carat indicates pure gold, and any lesser number of carats shows the proportion of gold contained in the alloy. The carat as a measure of weight is now obsolete, having been replaced by the *metric carat* of 0·2 grams.

Caravan, a band of travellers or traders journeying together for safety across the Eastern deserts, sometimes numbering many hundreds. There are several allusions to caravans in the Old Testament. The great caravan routes of this period from Egypt to Babylon and from Palestine to Yemen linked up with the Syrian ports and so with western sea commerce. Many wars have been fought in the past over their control.

Carbohydrates, group of organic compounds composed of carbon, hydrogen and oxygen, *e.g.*, sugars, starches, cellulose. Play an essential rôle in all living processes. See P40, F23.

Carbon, a non-metallic chemical element which occurs in crystalline form as diamonds and graphite; amorphous forms of carbon include charcoal and soot, while coke consists mainly of elementary carbon. The biochemistry of plants and animals largely hinges upon carbon compounds. The study of carbon compounds is called Organic Chemistry. Carbon 14, a radioactive isotope of carbon, with a half-life c. 6,000 years, used in following the path of compounds and their assimilation in the body. Also used in determination of the age of carbon-containing materials such as trees, fossils, and very old documents. See F24.

Carbonari, members of a secret political society originated in Naples, and at one time very numerous. Their chief aim was to free Italy from foreign rule, and they exerted considerable influence in the various revolutionary movements in the first half of the 19th cent. Their name was adopted from the charcoal-burners (*carbonari*), and their passwords, signs, etc., were all in the phraseology of the fraternity.

Carbon dioxide. Commonest of the oxides of carbon. It is formed when carbon and its compounds are burnt with abundant supply of air, and when carbon compounds are oxidised in the respiration process of animals. The atmosphere contains carbon dioxide to the extent of about three parts in 10,000; this figure remains more or less constant because, while carbon dioxide is always being added by animal respiration and the burning of fuels, such as coal and oil by man, plants are constantly removing it in the process known as photosynthesis (F28) or carbon assimilation.

Carbon monoxide is a colourless gas with no taste or smell. It is formed when coal and coke are burnt with a restricted supply of air; the blue flame to be seen in a coke brazier, for instance, is the flame of carbon monoxide. This gas is very poisonous, forming with the haemoglobin of the blood a compound which is useless for respiration and cherry red in colour, which gives a visible symptom of poisoning by carbon monoxide. With nickel it forms a volatile compound, called nickel carbonyl, and this reaction is the basis of the Mond process for extracting nickel.

Cardinal, one of the chief dignitaries of the Roman Catholic Church who constitute the Pope's council, or Sacred College, and when the papal chair is vacant elect a Pope from among themselves. There are three orders: cardinal bishops, members of the Roman Curia (the central administration of the Church) and bishops of sees near Rome; cardinal deacons, also members of the Curia, holding titular bishoprics; and cardinal priests who exercise pastoral duties over sees removed from Rome, though some are members of the Curia. Their numbers were fixed by Pope Sixtus V in 1586 at 6, 14, and 50 respectively. Both Pope John XXIII and Pope Paul VI increased the number and since 1969 there have been 136, the highest number in the history of the Church. Their insignia was trimmed of embellishment by papal decree in 1969 with the abolition of the famous red hat (the galero) and the shoes with buckles.

Cardinal Virtues, according to Plato these were justice, prudence, temperance, fortitude—

*natural* virtues as distinct from the *theological* virtues of the Roman Catholic Church, faith, hope, charity. The phrase "seven cardinal virtues," combining the two, figures in mediæval literature. *See* Sins, Seven Deadly.

**Carmelites,** a body of mendicant friars taking their name from Mount Carmel, where the order was first established in the 12th cent. The original rule of the order required absolute poverty, abstinence from meat and a hermit life. The rigidity of the rule of the order was mitigated by Innocent IV. They wear a brown habit with white mantle, hence their name of White Friars. The order of Carmelite nuns was instituted in the 15th cent.

**Carolingians,** dynasty of Frankish rulers founded in the 7th cent. The family was at its height when represented by Charlemagne. It ruled, with interruptions, until 987 when the Capetian dynasty succeeded.

**Carp,** a well-known fresh-water fish, found in plenty in most European and Asiatic still waters; reaches a length of about 2 ft., and under favourable conditions lives for about 40 years. Familiar British members of the family are the roach, rudd, dace, chub, gudgeon, tench, minnow, barbel, bream and bleak. The goldfish, popular in ornamental ponds, is the domesticated variety of a Far Eastern member of the carp family.

**Carthusians,** an order of monks founded in 1084 by St. Bruno at the Grande Chartreuse, near Grenoble, and introduced into England about a century later. They built the Charterhouse (corruption of Chartreuse) in London in 1371. The chief characteristics of the order are a separate dwelling-house in the precincts of the charterhouse for each monk, and the general assembly in the Church twice in the day and once at night. They wear a white habit, with white scapular and hood. The liqueur *Chartreuse* was invented by the order and is still their secret. For many years they have derived large revenues from its sale. The order of Carthusian nuns was founded in the 12th cent.

**Casein,** the chief protein in milk and cheese. It is coagulated by the action of rennet or acid. An important class of plastics (" casein plastics ") are produced from it, and these plastics are converted into buttons, knitting-needles, etc. 8000 gallons of milk yield about a ton of casein.

**Cassowary,** a genus of ostrich-like birds which, together with the emu, form a separate order found only in Australasia. All species are black, with brightly coloured necks, and with a horny crest on the head. Noted for fleetness.

**Castor-oil Plant** (*Ricinus communis*), an African shrub now cultivated in most tropical countries. It has broad palmate leaves and bears a spiny fruit containing seeds which when pressed yield the well-known oil.

**Cat,** the general name for all members of the class *Felidae* of the carnivorous order, from the lion down to the domestic cat. The latter is believed to be descended from the European and African wild cats. Egypt is credited with having been the first country in which the cat was domesticated. *See* Z9–12.

**Catabolism, Anabolism,** are the terms used to describe the two types of metabolic pathway. Catabolic pathways are routes by which large organic molecules are broken up by enzymes into their simpler constituents *e.g.,* starch into glucose. The anabolic pathways are the routes by which complex molecules are synthesised from simple sub-units, *e.g.,* proteins from amino acids.

**Catalyst.** A substance which speeds up a chemical reaction without being changed itself. Various aluminium and titanium compounds are catalysts in the formation of polythene from ethylene. Palladium catalyses the reaction of hydrogen with oxygen (hence its use in gas lighters). Enzymes in the body hasten the breakdown of carbohydrates and proteins by catalytic action. *See* F24(2).

**Cataracts** are gigantic waterfalls. The most famous are those of Niagara in North America, the Orinoco in South America, the Victoria Falls on the Zambesi in Africa, the Falls of the Rhine at Schaffhausen, and the Cascade of Gavarni in the Pyrenees.

**Catechism,** an elementary book of principles in any

science or art, but more particularly in religion, in the form of questions and answers. There is a great variety of these, including the Lutheran, prepared by Luther in 1529, Calvin's Geneva (in 1536), and the Anglican, in the Book of Common Prayer.

**Catenary,** the name of the curve taken up by a flexible uniform chain or clothes line supported at its two ends.

**Caterpillar,** the larva of a butterfly or moth, worm-like in its segmented body, with 3 pairs of jointed true legs, often curiously marked and coloured, and frequently more or less hairy.

**Cathedral,** the chief church of a diocese, so called from its containing a Bishop's seat, or episcopal chair. The town in which it is situated is a cathedral city. Some celebrated cathedrals are St. John Lateran of Rome, Notre Dame of Paris, the cathedrals of Cologne and Milan, St. Paul's in London, Canterbury Cathedral, York Minster, and the cathedrals of Durham, Bristol, Gloucester, Peterborough, Exeter, Liverpool, and Coventry (destroyed by bombs, now rebuilt).

**Catholicism.** *See* J7.

**Cat's-eye,** a kind of quartz, much valued as a gem, opalescent, and of various shades.

**Cavalier,** a name adopted during the troubles of the Civil War to designate the Royalist party; it is also used generally in reference to a knightly, gallant, or imperious personage.

**Caves,** natural hollow places in the earth, frequently found in Carboniferous limestone areas. The underground caves are formed by the action of rainwater carrying carbon dioxide, a dilute acid which slowly attacks the limestone rocks. The main caves in the British Isles are in the Mendips, Derbyshire, Yorkshire, S. Wales, and in County Clare. The floods of Sept. 1968 moved masses of debris in some of the British caves, redistributing it in a major way; new routes were blocked and old passages reopened. The scientific study of caves is known as speleaology.

**Cedar,** a dark-leaved, cone-bearing, horizontal-branched evergreen tree that grows to a considerable height and girth, the best known species in Britain being the Lebanon Cedar, which was introduced in the 17th cent.

**Celluloid,** one of the first synthetic thermoplastic materials, discovered by Alexander Parkes in 1865 when he was attempting to produce synthetic horn. It is made by treating cellulose nitrate with camphor and alcohol. Photographic film is made of a similar, but less-inflammable material, formed by the use of cellulose acetate instead of the nitrate.

**Cellulose,** a carbohydrate, and a constituent of nearly all plants. Cellulose occurs in an almost pure state in the fibres of linen (flax), absorbent cotton, jute, and filter-paper (used in laboratories).

**Celsius** was an 18th cent. Swedish scientist (B17) after whom the modern Celsius temperature scale is named. Since 1954, $^{\circ}C$ stands for " degree Celsius " instead of " degree Centigrade " but this is only a change in name. Both symbols refer to the temperature scale which calls the melting point of ice $0^{\circ}C$ and the boiling point of water at one atmosphere pressure $100^{\circ}C$. *See* Absolute Temperature.

**Celts,** an ancient race of W. Europe, originally from southern Germany (2nd millennium B.C.), united by a common language and culture, who spread westward into Spain, northward into Britain, eastward to the Black Sea, reaching Galicia in Asia Minor. The " La Tène " iron age Celts invaded Britain 250 B.C. After Britain was conquered by the Romans and invaded by the Angles and Saxons there remained as areas of Celtic speech only Wales (Brythonic speakers), Ireland, Scotland, Isle of Man (Gaelic speakers). The late Celtic period in Britain produced a distinctive Christian art (*e.g.,* the Lindisfarne Gospel *c.* 700, and the Irish Book of Kells, dating from about the same time).

**Centrifuge,** a machine which produces large accelerations by utilising the radial force caused by rotating a body about a fixed centre. Centrifuges have found extensive application in modern science. They can be used for the separation of one size of particle from another (for this use in biochemistry see F20) or in the training of astronauts where the accelerations occuring during rocket lift-off can be simulated in a centrifuge on the ground.

**Ceramics,** are substances in which a combination of one or more metals with oxygen confers special and valuable properties. These include hardness, and resistance to heat and chemicals. Ceramic comes from the Greek word for pottery, and pottery materials of mud and clay were probably the first man-made ceramics. Nowadays the range is enormous and growing; apart from all the pottery materials, there are fire-bricks, gems, glasses, concretes, nuclear reactor fuel elements, special materials for electronic devices, coloured pigments, electrical insulators, abrasives, and many other things. The scientific study of ceramics is part of materials science (*see* Materials Science). The need to design ceramic objects has inspired great art, and the production of ceramics is a major industry.

**Cerium,** a scarce metallic element discovered by Berzelius in 1803. A mixture of cerium and thorium nitrates is used in the manufacture of gas mantles, which owe their incandescent property to the deposit of cerium and thorium oxide with which they are coated.

**Chain reaction.** *See* F12(1).

**Chalcedony,** a mixture of crystalline silica and amorphous hydrated silica, *i.e.,* of quartz and opal. It has a waxy lustre, and is much used by jewellers for necklaces, bracelets, etc. Commonly it is white or creamy. Its bright orange-red variety is called carnelian; its brown variety, sard. Chrysoprase, plasma, bloodstone are varieties which are respectively pale apple-green, dark leek-green, green with red spots.

**Chalk,** a white limestone, calcium carbonate, found in the Upper Cretaceous deposits (formed from the shells of minute marine organisms). In southern England the chalk is a soft rock, but in Yorkshire, Scotland, and Ireland it is solid limestone. French chalk is hydrated magnesium silicate, a variety of talc.

**Chamberlain, Lord,** the senior officer of The Royal Household who is responsible for all ceremonial within the palace (levées, courts, garden parties, entertainment of foreign royalties and heads of state) but not the coronation or state opening of parliament. He is also in charge of appointments to The Royal Household. His office as censor of plays was abolished in 1968.

**Chamberlain, Lord Great,** one of the great officers of state whose duties are now mainly ceremonial. He attends the monarch at the state opening of parliament and at the coronation and is custodian of the Palace of Westminster (Houses of Parliament). The office is hereditary, dating from Norman times, and is held for one reign in turn by the descendants of the De Veres, Earls of Oxford.

**Chameleon,** a family of lizards with numerous species. Their ability to change colour is well known, but exaggerated, and is due to the movement of pigment cells beneath the skin. They are slow in movement, arboreal, and mainly insectivorous. Found in Africa, India, Ceylon, Madagascar, and Arabia.

**Chamois,** a species of antelope, native of Western Europe and Asia. About the size of a goat, it lives in mountainous regions, and possesses wonderful leaping power, so that it is very difficult to capture. Its flesh is much esteemed, and from its skin chamois leather is made, although to-day sheep and goat skins are usually substituted. The mating season is Oct.–Nov. and the fawns are born in May or June. Live to be 20–25 years old.

**Channel Tunnel,** a scheme to bore a tunnel through 20–30 miles of chalk under the sea between Dover and Calais has been a subject for discussion ever since Albert Mathieu first conceived the idea as a practical possibility in 1802. In the 1830s proposals for a bridge were made. Investigations have been undertaken from time to time, the most recent being that of the Channel Tunnel Group, composed of British, French, and American interests, which was set up in 1957. In 1964 it was announced that the British and French Governments had decided in principle to go ahead with a rail tunnel, thus accepting the recommendations of the Anglo-French study group published in 1963. In 1968 the Minister of Transport said that if studies

confirmed the case for the tunnel, it should be possible to complete it by 1976. It is to be financed by private capital but operated by a Franco-British public authority. Estimated cost (1968) £300 million.

**Chapel Royal,** the church dedicated to the use of the Sovereign and Court. There are, among others, chapels royal at St. James's Palace, Buckingham Palace, Windsor, Hampton Court, the Tower, and Holyrood.

**Characterology.** *See* J7.

**Charcoal,** a term applied to wood that has been subjected to a process of slow smothered combustion. More generally it refers to the carbonaceous remains of vegetable, animal, or combustible mineral substances submitted to a similar process. Charcoal from special woods (in particular buckthorn) is used in making gunpowder. Bone charcoal finds use in sugar refining, as it removes dark colouring matter present in the crude syrup.

**Chasuble,** a sleeveless vestment worn by ecclesiastics over the alb during the celebration of Mass. It is supposed to symbolise the seamless coat of Christ. Its use in English churches was prohibited in 1552, but again permitted after 1559. It gradually fell into disregard, however, but about 100 years ago its use was revived in the Church of England.

**Cheese,** an article of food made from the curd of milk, which is separated from the whey and pressed in moulds and gradually dried. There are about 500 varieties differing with method of preparation and quality of milk. They used to be made in the regions after which they are named but nowadays many of them are mass-produced, *e.g.,* Cheddar is made not only in all parts of Britain but in Canada, New Zealand, Australia, Holland, and the U.S.A. Cheeses may be divided into 3 main classes: (1) soft, *e.g.,* Camembert, Cambridge, Port l'Evêque; (2) blue-veined, *e.g.,* Stilton, Gorgonzola, Roquefort (made from ewe's milk), (3) hard-pressed, *e.g.,* Cheddar, Cheshire, Gruyère, Parmesan, Gouda.

**Cheetah** or "hunting leopard," the large spotted cat of Africa and Southern Asia whose ability to run at 45 m.p.h. for 500 yards makes it the swiftest four-footed animal alive.

**Chemistry** is the science of the elements and their compounds. It is concerned with the laws of their combination and behaviour under various conditions. It had its rise in alchemy (J2) and has gradually developed into a science of vast magnitude and importance. Organic chemistry deals with the chemistry of the compounds of carbon; inorganic chemistry is concerned with the chemistry of the elements; physical chemistry is concerned with the study of chemical reactions and with the theories and laws of chemistry. *See* F20–6.

**Chestnut,** the fruit of the chestnut tree; those of the Spanish chestnut, *Castanea vesca,* furnish a favourite esculent. The wood is used in carpentry; while the horse-chestnut (*Æsculus hippocastanum*) is much employed in brushmounting and in cabinet work.

**Chiaroscuro,** a term used in painting to denote the arrangement of light and shade in a picture.

**Chiltern Hundreds,** three hundreds—Stoke, Burnham, and Desborough—the stewardship of which is now a nominal office under the Chancellor of the Exchequer. Since about 1751 the nomination to it has been used as a method of enabling a member of Parliament to resign his seat on the plea that he holds an office of honour and profit under the crown. (This has been a disqualification for Parliament since 1707.)

**Chimpanzee,** a large anthropoid ape, a native of tropical West Africa, of a dark brown colour, with arms reaching to the knee, and capable of walking upright. Its brain is about a third of the weight of the human brain, but is anatomically similar. The animal has considerable intelligence and powers of learning. A suitable subject for space flight experiments.

**China Lobby,** the name applied to the body of opinion and pressure in American politics which strenuously opposes recognition of Communist China, and advocates support of Chiang Kai-shek.

**Chinchilla,** a South American burrowing rodent.

Grey in colour, and white underneath. It is greatly esteemed for its beautiful fur.

**Chippendale Furniture** was introduced in the reign of George I. by Thomas Chippendale, a cabinet-maker from Yorkshire who migrated to London and set up for himself in St. Martin's Lane, Charing Cross. He was fonder of inventing designs for furniture than of making it, and in 1752 published a book of patterns; the London furniture-makers of the day soon began to model their work upon it.

**Chirognomy.** *See* J8.

**Chivalry,** an international brotherhood of knights formed primarily during the 13th cent. to fight against the infidels in the Crusades. For the French the major battle was against the Mos-lems in the Holy Land and North Africa, the Spaniards fought the same enemy in their own country, and the Germans were concerned with the heathen of Baltic lands, but Chaucer's " very perfect gentle knight " had fought in all these areas. One did not easily become a knight who had to be of noble birth and then pass through a period of probation, beginning as a boy page in the castle of some great lord, serving his elders and betters humbly while he was taught good manners, singing, playing musical instru-ments, and the composition of verse. Probably he learned Latin, but he certainly learned French, which was the international language of knights as Latin was of scholars. At fourteen he became a squire and learned to fight with sword, battle-axe, and lance, and to endure conditions of hard living while carrying out his duties of waiting on his lord, looking after his horses, and in time accompanying him in battle. Only if he showed himself suitable was he finally knighted by a stroke of the hand or sword on the shoulder from the king or lord. Knighthood was an international order and had its special code of behaviour: to honour one's sworn word, to protect the weak, to respect women, and defend the Faith. To some extent it had a civilising effect on the conduct of war (*e.g.*, knights of opposing sides might slaughter each other in battle but feast together after), but, since war was regarded as the supreme form of sport, it cannot be said to have contributed to peace.

**Chlorine,** a gaseous element of the halogen family, first isolated in 1774 by Scheele by the action of manganese dioxide on hydrochloric acid. It unites easily with many other elements, the compounds resulting being termed chlorides. The gaseous element is greenish-yellow, with a pungent odour. It is a suffocating gas, injuring the lungs at a concentration as low as 1 part in 50,000, and was used during the first world war as a poison gas. Has a powerful bleaching action, usually being used in form of bleaching powder, made by combining lime and chlorine. Also a valuable disinfectant; used, for instance, in rendering water of swimming baths sterile.

**Chloroform,** a volatile colourless liquid, com-pounded of carbon, hydrogen, and chlorine. It is a powerful solvent, not naturally occurring but synthesised on a large scale. When the vapour is inhaled it produces unconsciousness and insensibility to pain. It owes its discovery to Liebig, and its first application for medical purposes to Sir James Young Simpson (P5(2).

**Chlorophyll,** the green pigment contained in the leaves of plants, first discovered by P. J. Pelletier (1788–1829) and J. B Caventou (1795–1877) in 1818. Enables the plant to absorb sunlight and so to build up sugar. The total synthesis of chlorophyll was reported in 1960 by Prof. R. B. Woodward. This is an out-standing achievement in the field of organic chemistry. *See* Photosynthesis, F28.

**Chouans,** the name given to the band of peasants, mainly smugglers and dealers in contraband salt, who rose in revolt in the west of France in 1793 and joined the royalists of La Vendée. Balzac gives a picture of the people and the country in which they operated in his novel *Les Chouans.* They used the hoot of an owl as a signal—hence the name.

**Chough,** a member of the crow family, of glossy blue-green-black plumage, whose long curved bill and legs are coral red. It used to be abun-dant on the cliffs of Cornwall, but its haunts are now restricted to the rocky outcrops of the western coasts and in the mountains near by. It nests in cleft rocks and caves. The Alpine chough with yellow bill inhabits the mountain-ous districts of Europe and Asia and is not found in Britain. It was found at 27,000 ft. on Everest.

**Christmas** means " mass of Christ " from the old English *Cristes maesse,* which is celebrated by the Western church on December 25. The ac-tual day on which Christ was born is not known and there is some uncertainty about the year. December 25 as the day of Nativity was not generally observed until the 5th cent. A.D., though, as the winter solstice, it had long been observed as a pagan festival of *sol invictus* (un-conquered sun). The first Christmas card dates from about 1843 and the Christmas tree, of pagan origin, was introduced into England from Germany by Queen Adelaide, wife of William IV. Santa Clause is a corruption of Saint Nicolas, patron saint of children, whose feast day properly falls on December 6.

**Chromatic Scale,** a scale proceeding in intervals of one semitone. *E.g.,* chromatic scale in C: C–D♭–D–E♭–E–F–G♭–G–A♭–A–B♭–B–C.

**Chromium,** a very hard, bluish-white metal ele-ment, symbol Cr, melting at a very high temperature (above 1900° C.). Its chief ore is chromite or chrome iron-ore (ferrous chromite). " Ferro-chrome " is produced by heating chromite and anthracite in an electric furnace, and chrome steels are prepared by adding the pre-calculated amount of ferro-chrome to melted steel. Best known chrome steel is stain-less steel first made by Brearley in 1912 and since then developed greatly at Sheffield. A typical formula is 18 per cent. chromium, 8 per cent. nickel, 74 per cent. iron. Equally important are Stellite alloys, containing chromium, cobalt, tungsten (or molybdenum), which have made possible modern high-speed cutting tools. Dies used in manufacture of plastics are commonly of chrome steel. The elementary metal finds little use alone except in chromium-plating for motor cars, etc.

**Chromosomes,** the structures contained within the nucleus of every animal and plant cell by which genetic information is transmitted. The chromosome number in somatic (body) cells is constant for each species of plant and animal, *e.g.,* man (46), cat (38), mouse (40), honey bee (16), fruit fly *Drosophila* (8), potato (48). Chromosomes are long molecules composed of deoxyribonucleoproteins (*i.e.,* proteins and DNA). Human chromosomes have been the subject of much recent research since it has been found that certain disorders are associated with chromosomal aberration, *e.g.,* in Mongolism an extra chromosome is present. *See also* Genes, Cell Division, F30(2).

**Church Commissioners.** The Church Commis-sioners were established in 1948 by the amalga-mation of Queen Anne's Bounty (established 1704) and the Ecclesiastical Commissioners (es-tablished 1836) to administer Church revenues and to manage Church property generally. The Commissioners own in investments and real estate a total of over £300 million.

**Church of England.** *See* J9.

**Cid, The,** a famous Spanish hero of the 11th cent. Don Rodrigo Diaz de Vivar, who, before he was twenty, led a Spanish force against the Moors, and drove them out of Spain. He is celebrated in poem, play, and romance.

**Cilia,** minute hair-like projections on the surface of some cells, which beat together in wavelike movements like the wind over a corn-field. These movements can be used as a means of locomotion as in the aquatic organism parame-cium. Cilia are also found on the outer layers of the human trachea where they waft particles upwards to the throat, thus protecting the lungs. *See* F34, P31, *also* Flagella.

**Cinchona,** the tree native to the Andes which is famous for its bark, source of the drug quinine. It was introduced into Ceylon, India, and Java, the latter becoming the main supplier of quinine.

**Cinque Ports,** a number of seaport towns on the coast of Kent and Sussex, originally five: Hastings, Romney, Hythe, Dover, and Sand-wich. Winchelsea and Rye were added later. These ports were required to furnish a certain number of ships, ready for service, and in return they were granted many privileges. The official residence of the Lord Warden (Sir Robert Menzies) is Walmer Castle, near Dover.

Cistercians, an order of monks and nuns taking their names from Cîteaux, near Dijon, where their first monastery was established in 1098. The order was noted for the severity of its rule. They were famous agriculturists. The habit is white, with a black cowl or hood. The order declined, and in the 17th cent. there was a reform movement instituted by the Trappists, who were later organised into a separate order.

Citron, a species of citrus (*Citrus medica*) related to the lemon, whose fruit has thick rind used for candied peel.

Civil List is the annual sum payable to the Sovereign to maintain the Royal Household and to uphold the dignity of the Crown. The amount is granted by Parliament upon the recommendation of a Select Committee and has to be settled afresh in the first six months of a new reign. The Civil List of Queen Victoria was £385,000; Edward VII. and George V., £470,000; Edward VIII. and George VI., £410,000; Elizabeth II., £475,000. The annuities payable to members of the Royal Family do not form part of the Civil List but are a charge on the Consolidated Fund; Queen Mother, £70,000; Duke of Edinburgh, £40,000; Duke of Gloucester, £35,000; Princess Margaret, £15,000; Princess Anne (at 21) £6,000 (£15,000 on marriage); Prince Andrew (at 21) £10,000 (£25,000 on marriage). Prince Charles has his own income from the Duchy of Cornwall.

Cleopatra's Needle on the Thames Embankment is of the time of Tuthmosis III. (1500–1450 B.C.). The monolith had nothing to do with Cleopatra, as it only came to Alexandria after her death. It was first erected at the Biblical On (Greek Heliopolis), sacred City of the Sun. It was presented to the British Government by Mehemet Ali in 1819, but not brought to this country until 1878. Weight, 180 tons; height, 68¼ ft.

Climate is a generalised representation of the day-to-day weather conditions throughout the year, the combination of all weathers thus determining the climate of a place. Averages and extremes of temperature, variation of humidity, duration of sunshine and cloud cover, amount of rainfall and frequency of snow, frost, gales, etc., are amongst the data normally investigated. The interiors of great land masses are characterised by large ranges of temperature and low rainfall (continental climate), while proximity to oceans has an ameliorating effect with increase in rainfall (oceanic climate). Presence of mountain ranges and lakes and configuration generally produce local modifications of climate, also apparent between the centre and the outlying suburbs of a city. There is evidence that vast changes of climate have occurred during geological time. Since the mid-19th cent. most of the world has shown a tendency to be warmer; the rise in annual mean temperature is now over 1° C. But this trend now seems to be easing off. Latitude introduces zones of climate, e.g., tropical rain, subtropical steppe and desert, temperate rain and polar.

Clock, a device for measuring the passage of time. The earliest timekeeper was the shadow-clock, a primitive form of sundial, used in Ancient Egypt about 1500 B.C. To find the time at night the water-clock or clepsydra was used. The sand-glass dates from the 15th cent. No one knows when the first mechanical clocks were invented, but it is known that a complicated mechanical clock driven by water and controlled by a weighbridge escapement was built in Peking in 1090. The Dover Clock in the Science Museum is not the earliest surviving clock in England, as was once believed, but early 17th cent. The Salisbury Cathedral clock dates from 1386 and that of Wells Cathedral from 1392. The pendulum clock was invented by the Dutch scientist Christiaan Huygens (1625–95). The first watches were made in Nuremberg shortly after 1500. The marine chronometer is a high-precision timepiece used at sea for giving Greenwich mean time. The quartz-crystal clocks are accurate to one thousandth of a second a day, and the improved atomic clock,

recently developed at the British National Physical Laboratory, which makes use of the natural vibrations of the caesium atom, is said to be an almost absolute measure of time (accurate to 1 sec. in 300 years, *i.e.*, one part in $10^{10}$).

Cloisonné, a kind of fine pottery with enamelled surface, decorated with elaborate designs, the outlines of which are formed by small bands or fillets of metal. The Byzantines excelled in this work, but in the 20th cent. Japan and China led in Cloisonné-ware.

Cloud chamber, an apparatus invented by C. T. R. Wilson in which the tracks of atomic particles can be made visible. Just as the vapour trails tell of the track of an invisible aircraft high up in the air, so the vapour trails of an unseeable particle can tell of its behaviour. The rays under investigation pass through a chamber containing a gas, *e.g.*, air thoroughly cleansed of dust, supersaturated with water- or alcohol-vapour. As the particle passes through it forms a track of tiny water droplets which can be photographed. After a long and honourable history this wonderful instrument is now virtually obsolete. A later ingenious device for tracking fast fundamental particles is the Bubble chamber (*q.v.*).

Clouds are formed by the ascent of moist air, the type depending on the way the air ascends and the height at which condensation occurs. There are three main classes: (1) high cloud (above 20,000 ft.)—cirrus (delicate and fibrous), cirrostratus (thin white veil), and cirrocumulus (delicately rippled) consisting of ice crystals; (2) medium cloud (above 7,000 ft.)—altostratus (dense, greyish veil) and altocumulus (broken flattened cloudlets)—chiefly water particles, often supercooled; (3) low cloud (from near ground to 7,000 ft.)—cumulus (fair weather, broken, dome-topped), cumulonimbus (heavy, towering to great heights), stratocumulus (layer of globular masses or rolls), stratus (like fog but off the ground), nimbostratus (low, rainy cloud). The highest clouds of all, and the rarest, are the noctilucent, seen only on summer nights in high latitudes. They form at about 50 miles above the earth and consist of ice-coated dust from meteors.

Clover, plants of the *Trifolium* genus, family *Leguminosae*, with about 250 species. These are "nitrogen fixing" plants and include red clover, white clover, alsike clover, and crimson clover. They are of great importance in agriculture because in a good pasture they supply directly or indirectly most of the protein available to the animals. Seed of "wild white" clover has been accepted since about 1939 as the indispensable plant of good United Kingdom grassland, largely through the efforts of pioneers like D. A. Gilchrist (1859–1927).

Cloves are the dried flower-buds of a species of myrtle (*Eugenia caryophyllata*) grown principally in Zanzibar and Madagascar.

Coal. Until recently the most important single fuel has been coal. It is a mineral of organic origin, formed from the remains of vegetation which over millions of years has changed to coal by the effects of heat and pressure from overlying rock or water. All coal contains moisture, inflammable volatiles, mineral impurities (some of which remain as coal ash after the coal is burnt), and fixed carbon (the coke that is left after the volatiles have been driven off). The relative proportions vary—from Anthracite, a hard coal containing the highest proportion of fixed carbon, to Lignite or brown coal which is little more than a hard peat. World reserves of bituminous coal have been estimated at $7\cdot5 \times 10^{12}$ tons. If one adds the reserves of brown coal and lignite, this figure is increased by about 15 per cent. The proportion of the reserves that could be economically recovered varies from country to country and estimates vary from 50 to 100 per cent of the reserves. The reserves are highly localised—over half being located in the Soviet Union. In the United Kingdom coal has formed the basis of past industrial prosperity. Peak output occurred in 1913 when 287 million tons were mined, one third of which was exported. At the end of the Second World War (1946) production had fallen to 183 million tons and was far below demand. During the next ten years great efforts were made to increase coal output but, quite suddenly in 1956, demand for coal fell as oil became a popular fuel and since then the problem has been to cut back the coal industry without causing undue social problems. A future market of about 170 to 180 million tons is envisaged beyond 1970. In 1947 the British coal industry was brought under public ownership and all its assets were vested in the National Coal Board.

**Coal Tar.** A by-product in coal-gas and coke manufacture, it is a valuable source of organic intermediates, indeed over 20 different compounds have been isolated, many of which find use in such fields as the manufacture of soaps, fuel, cosmetics, detergents, and drugs as well as dyes. *See* Benzene, Aniline.

**Coat of Arms,** in heraldry, is a device containing a family's armorial bearings. In mediæval times it was an actual coat upon which such device was embroidered, and knights wore it over their armour.

**Cobalt,** a white metal melting at 1490° C. Two main ores are *cobalt glance* (in which the element is combined with arsenic and sulphur) and *smaltite* (cobalt arsenide). The principal sources are Ontario and the Congo. Various cobalt alloys are important, *e.g.*, stellite, ferrocobalt and carboloy. Its monoxide is an important colouring medium, and is used for colouring glass and porcelain-blue.

**Cobra,** hooded and very venomous snakes. The best known species are the Indian Cobra, the Egyptian Cobra, and the Black-necked Cobra. Their food consists chiefly of small rodents. The King Cobra is almost exclusively a snake-eater. " Spitting " Cobras (or Ringhals) of S. Africa are a related genus, capable of spitting their venom several yards.

**Coca,** a S. American shrub, *Erythroxylon coca*, also cultivated in Java. The leaves yield cocaine, classified as a dangerous drug; used medicinally as a local anaesthetic, especially on the eyes and in dentistry. When the natives chew the leaves they are enabled to withstand astonishing amounts of hunger and fatigue, as cocaine acts both as a mental stimulant and as an anaesthetic on the mucous lining of the stomach.

**Cochineal** *or* **Carmine,** a dyestuff consisting of the dried bodies of the female scale insect (*Dactylopius coccus*) which feeds on cacti. Of ancient origin, the dye was well known to the Aztecs, and was used widely in the Middle Ages. The famous scarlet tunics worn by the English during the Napoleonic wars owed their colour to carmine. To-day it is almost entirely replaced by aniline dyes.

**Cockatoo,** a member of the parrot family, bearing a crest of feathers on the head, native to Australia and adjacent regions. Predominant colour is white tinged with yellow or scarlet while some species have dark plumage. The great black cockatoo of New Guinea is slaty black with pale red cheeks and can crack Kanary nuts which usually require a hammer to break them open.

**Cockchafer** (*Melolontha*), one of the most destructive of beetles, the larvae feeding on roots. It is about 1 inch in length, of a brownish colour, and emits a loud whirring sound when flying.

**Cockle,** the popular name of the bi-valve shell-fish of the genus *Cardium*, found plentifully in sandy bays near low-water line; there are numerous British species.

**Cockroach,** inaccurately called the " black beetle "; a pest of bakeries and kitchens. In Britain two species are commonly found: the Common Cockroach (*Blatta orientalis*), resident since the time of Elizabeth I, dark brown, about an inch long, with the wing covers long in the male and short in the female; and the German Cockroach (*Blatta germanica*), now the most common, half the size, dark yellow, with both sexes fully winged. All species have long antennae and flattened, leathery, shiny bodies. They are nocturnal and omnivorous.

**Cocoa.** *See* Cacao.

**Coconut Palm** (*Cocos nucifera*), a tropical tree, growing to a height of 100 ft., with a slender, leaning trunk surmounted by giant feather-like leaves. One of the most important sources of food and raw material for people living in the tropics. The juice of the fruit, or coconut, is drunk; the kernel is eaten fresh or dried to form copra, which yields animal feeding stuffs and oil, used in the manufacture of soap, margarine, cosmetics, synthetic rubber, etc.; leaves are used for thatching; leaf stalks for canes, fence posts, needles, etc., and the trunk for houses and bridges. Main producing areas: Indonesia, Philippines, Malaysia, Ceylon, and S. India.

**Codes,** a term used to designate a system of laws properly classified. The Code of Hammurabi, king of Babylon, *c.* 1700 B.C., had extensive influence over a long period. The Romans formulated several codes of historic importance including the Theodosian Code which summarised the Roman laws from the time of Constantine to 438 A.D. The final codification was made under order of the Emperor Justinian by his chief minister Tribonian and published in 529 with a new edition in 534. The most important of modern codes is the *Code Napoléon*, compiled between 1803 and 1810, and still in force. It has been used as an example for the codification of the laws of a number of countries from America to Japan. Under Frederick the Great the law of Prussia was codified. English law has never been codified, although the law on certain subjects has been gathered up into a single statute. The Law Commission Act, 1965, was passed to consolidate and codify the law wherever possible. *See* D5(2).

**Codex,** a manuscript volume of the Scriptures comprising the Sinaitic codex of the 4th cent., the Vatican codex of the same period, the Alexandrine codex of the 5th cent., and others. The British Museum, in 1933, purchased the *Codex Sinaiticus* from the Soviet Government for £100,000.

**Coffee,** a shrub found originally in Arabia and Abyssinia, but now extensively grown in the West Indies, Brazil, India, and Central America. It yields a seed or berry which, after undergoing the necessary preparation, is ground and largely used in most countries as a popular breakfast beverage. The best coffee is the Mocha, an Arabian variety. The stimulating effect of coffee is due to the caffeine, which is also present in tea. The beverage was introduced into Europe in the 16th cent., and the first London coffee shop was opened in 1632.

**Coke** is the solid residue remaining when coal is carbonised and nearly all the volatile constituents have been driven off. Used as fuel, and as an agent for reducing metallic oxides to metals, *e.g.*, iron ore to iron, in the manufacture of steel.

**Colorado Beetle,** a serious pest of potato crops. Both adults and larvae feed on the foliage where the orange eggs are laid. The grub is reddish, with two rows of small black spots on each side. The adults are about ½ in. long with yellow and black striped wing cases. The beetle is avoided by birds because of its nasty taste, and is controlled by arsenical sprays.

**Colosseum,** the name of the Flavian amphitheatre at Rome, begun by Vespasian and finished by Titus A.D. 80. In general outline it still remains one of the most magnificent ruins in the world. In the arena of this great building the famous gladiatorial displays and mimic naval battles used to be given, and about 50,000 spectators could be accommodated.

**Colossus** is the name which the ancients gave to any statue of gigantic size. The Colossus at Rhodes, which was a bronze statue of the sun god, Helios, was the most famous, and reckoned among the seven wonders of the world. It stood over 100 ft. high at the mouth of the harbour. There is no truth in the legend that ships could pass between its legs. It fell in an earthquake in 224 B.C.

**Coluga,** also known as " flying lemur ", caguan or kubuk, a remarkable mammal which may be regarded as an aberrant insectivore or an aberrant form of the earliest ancestor of the bats. It has nothing to do with lemurs. There are two genera, one inhabiting the Philippines and one inhabiting Malaya. They have a parachute-like membrane which covers them from the neck to the tip of the tail, by means of which they can glide from treetop to ground a distance of up to 70 yards.

**Column,** in architecture, is an upright solid body serving as a support or decoration to a building. Columns consist of a pedestal, a shaft, and a capital, over which the supported entablature rises. They are named according to the styles of architecture of which they form part, being Doric, Tuscan, Ionic, Corinthian, or Composite as the case may be.

Comets are celestial bodies which move about the solar system in elliptical or hyperbolic orbits. Usually these star-like bodies are accompanied by a long shining tail. The hyperbolic comets are seen once only, and do not reappear; the elliptical comets are periodic, and their recurrence can be calculated with accuracy. The head of a comet is believed to consist of small lumps of solid matter accompanied by dust particles and gases such as carbon dioxide and methane. It used to be thought that the tail was produced by the pressure of sunlight on the cometary material but a modern explanation is that it is produced by the combined action of the solar wind (a continuous stream of ionised hydrogen originating in the sun) and the interplanetary magnetic field. When they run parallel the effect is to produce a long streaming tail pointing away from the sun. Chief among the periodic comets is Edmund Halley's, the first to return as predicted in 1757. It reappears about every 76 years and is next due in 1985. The most spectacular comet of the 19th cent. was that found by Donati in 1858.

Common Law, See D4.

Commons are the remnants of the mediaeval open fields round villages in which the villagers had rights in common, e.g., (i) estover—the right of taking wood for house building or firewood; (ii) pasture—the right of grazing beasts; (iii) turbary—the right of digging turf; (iv) piscary—the right to fish. Many of these common lands were enclosed during the agrarian revolution which went on steadily in England from the 15th cent. onwards, and with their enclosure common rights vanished. A Royal Commission on Common Land described the commons in 1965 as the "last reservoir of uncommitted land" which provide, as far as the public is concerned, by far the largest part of the accessible open spaces of the country. Under the Commons Registration Act, 1965, it is the duty of County Councils and County Borough Councils to make a register of all common land and all town and village greens in their areas.

Commons, House of, the Lower House of the British Parliament. See Section C, Part II.

Commune of Paris has twice played a dramatic part in the history of France. In 1792 it was able, through its control of the administrative organisation of Paris, to override the National Assembly. In 1871, after the withdrawal of the Prussian troops, it tried to assert its authority. Public buildings were destroyed by members of the Commune and civil war raged during April and half May, but Government troops suppressed the rising.

Communism. See J9.

Compass or Mariner's Compass is an instrument by which the magnetic meridian is indicated, and comprises a horizontal bowl containing alcohol and water, a card upon which the thirty-two points of the compass are marked, and the steel needle which always points to the meridian. Although the discovery of the directive property of a magnet is credited to the Chinese, the first practical use of this property in a compass was made in western Europe in the 12th cent. Aircraft and ships now largely employ gyrostatic compasses which are not affected by electrical and magnetic disturbances. Sperry, Brown, and Anschutz are three important types of gyroscopic compass.

Computer, a technical device for accepting an input of information, processing this information according to some prescribed programme of operations and supplying an output of processed information. Many types of operation can be performed on many types of information and computers are now indispensable in science, business, warfare, government, and other activities. Early thinkers in this field were Pascal (17th cent.), Babbage (19th cent.) and Turing (1930s), but electronic computers as we know them appeared during the Second World War and the first commercial machine was on sale in 1950. Computers are millions of times faster than human beings at computing; and the introduction of computers into an organisation does more than just speed up the calculations, it tends to transform the whole nature of the organisation. The possibilities for future developments seem enormous. Analogue computers and digital computers are two different kinds stemming from the difference between measuring and counting. Analogue types handle data that is represented by physical quantities of continuously variable size such as voltages or lengths. These quantities can be made to vary like the quantities in a problem which the computer is set to solve; the problem is thus solved by analogy. A slide rule is a rudimentary analogue computer in which numbers are represented by lengths of rule. Digital computers handle actual numbers expressed in digits and the quantities in the problem are represented by discrete numbers. These can all be expressed in binary form and thus stored or handled in bits. See Bit, Binary Notation.

Conclave, an assembly of Roman Catholic cardinals met together to elect a pope. The last Conclave was held in the Vatican in June 1963 when Cardinal Montini, archbishop of Milan, was elected Pope Paul VI.

Concordat, an agreement or convention between the pope and a secular government regarding ecclesiastical matters. The Concordat of Worms in 1122 between Calixtus II. and the Emperor Henry V. was famous as deciding a long struggle in regard to investiture. In 1801, Napoleon concluded a concordat with Pius VII. defining the restored relations between the head of the Church and the French Roman Catholics.

Condor, a large eagle of brilliant black plumage with a circlet of white feathers round its neck. It is a native of the Andes.

Confederation is a free association of sovereign states united for some common purpose. It is to be distinguished from a Federation, which is a union of states with one central government, each state relinquishing its sovereignty, though retaining some independence in internal affairs.

Confucianism. See J10.

Coniferae are cone-bearing trees, including firs, pines, cedars, cypresses, junipers, yews, etc., and are widely distributed in temperate regions.

Conservatism. See J10.

Consistory, a council or meeting of councillors; also the higher ecclesiastical courts and senates of the Anglican and Roman Churches.

Constitution, the fundamental organic law or principles of government of a nation, state, society, or other organised body, embodied in written documents, or implied in the institutions and customs of the country or society. The government of the U.S.A., unlike Great Britain, works upon a written Constitution. It was framed when the U.S.A. came into existence as a sovereign body, when the Constitution built a republic out of a federation of thirteen states, based on representative government. The constitution was adopted in 1789, and its strength has been tested by the fact that, substantially unchanged, it is now the groundwork for a federation which now comprises fifty states.

Continent, a word used in physical geography to denote the larger continuous land masses in contrast to the great oceans of the earth. They are: Eurasia (conventionally regarded as 2 continents, Europe and Asia), Africa, North America, South America, Australia and Antarctica.

Continental Drift. The hypothesis of drifting continents is due to F. B. Taylor, an American geologist who published his theory in 1908, and to the Austrian meteorologist Alfred Wegener in 1910. The latter was impressed by the matching coasts of South America and Africa, which seemed to him to fit together like the pieces of a jigsaw puzzle. Since then many other people have taken up and developed the idea. According to Wegener, at one time there were two primary super-continents, Laurasia and Gondwanaland. The one in the northern hemisphere consisted of North America, Europe, and the northern part of Asia. Its southern counterpart included Antarctica, Australia, India, Africa and South America. These super-continents broke up, and their various bits moved apart. In particular, the southern hemisphere continents drifted radially northwards away from the south pole, and the two Americas shifted westwards from Europe and Africa. What would have been the leading edges of the land masses on this hypothesis, are now heavily buckled up into mountain belts, such as the Cordillera and the Alpine-Himalayan chain. The resistance afforded to drifting by the strong ocean floors may well have been the cause of such structures. Despite the wealth of geological facts which have a bearing on the problem of continental drift, none of these has been able to decide the issue in a conclusive manner. Further studies of rock magnetism (q.v.) and of fossil climates should ultimately establish the concept of continental drift on a firm basis.

Conurbation, a term which has been defined as "an area occupied by a continuous series of dwellings, factories, and other buildings, harbours, and docks, urban parks and playing fields, etc., which are not separated from each other by rural land; though in many cases in this country such an urban area includes enclaves of rural land which is still in agricultural occupation." The term has been widely adopted for the contiguous densely populated areas which form continuous urban areas. The seven officially recognised in Britain are: Greater London, West Midlands, S.E. Lancashire, West Yorkshire, Merseyside, Tyneside, Clydeside.

Convention is an assembly of delegates, representatives, members of a party met to accomplish some specific civil, social, political, ecclesiastical or other important object.

Convocation, an assembly called together to deliberate ecclesiastical affairs. In the Church of England the provinces of Canterbury and York each have their convocation. The term is also applied to assemblies of the graduates of certain universities.

Coot. A very widely distributed bird of the rail family and a common resident of the British Isles. The adult is black with a conspicuous white bald shield on the forehead and a white bill. The juvenile is brownish grey with whitish breast and throat. The coot flies heavily, but swims well. It dives frequently and can remain submerged for a considerable time. It is pugnacious and in winter gregarious. The food is chiefly vegetable. The large nest is usually built among aquatic vegetation and the young are fed by both parents. Another species, the Crested Coot, occurs in S. Europe.

Copper, one of the most familiar of metals, symbol Cu, used in ancient times as an alloy with tin in producing bronze, and preceding iron as an industrial material. Copper ores are most abundant in the U.S.A., Chile, Canada, Zambia, and the Congo. All copper compounds are poisonous. Copper sulphate is largely used in calico-printing and in the production of blue and green pigments.

Copyright. Under the Copyright Act, 1956, copyright subsists in every original literary, dramatic, musical, and artistic work if the author is a British subject or a citizen of the Republic of Ireland or resident in the United Kingdom, or if the work is first published in the United Kingdom. The Act provides that, except in certain special cases, the author of the work shall be the first owner of the copyright, and there are no formalities, such as registration or payment of fees, to be accomplished. Copyright includes the right to reproduce the work in any material form, to perform the work in public, or, if the work is unpublished, to publish the work. The Act also protects sound recordings, films, and television and sound broadcasts. Literary, dramatic, musical, and artistic works which enjoy the protection of the Act are automatically protected in those countries which are parties to the Berne Copyright Convention or the Universal Copyright Convention. In general, copyright in literary, dramatic, musical, and artistic works is vested in the author for the period of his lifetime and 50 years following, after which it passes into the public domain and becomes freely available to any who wish to make use of it. The Copyright Libraries, entitled to receive copies of books published in the United Kingdom are given under Libraries. A new copyright convention was signed in Stockholm in 1967 which

gives "under-developed" countries the right to reproduce, without payment if they choose, any books to be used for teaching, study, or research. The Government Department responsible for matters in connection with copyright is the Industrial Property Department, Board of Trade, 25, Southampton Buildings, London, W.C.2.

Coral, an order of small marine animals closely related to the sea-anemone, but differing from it in their ability to develop a limy skeleton. They multiply sexually and by budding. The structure of the coral secretions assumes a variety of forms, fan-like, tree-like, mushroom shape, and so forth. Red coral (the skeleton of Corallium rubrum) is mainly obtained from the Mediterranean. The coral reefs of the Pacific and Indian Oceans are often many miles in extent. Living corals occur only in warm seas at about 23° C.

Cordite, a smokeless explosive adopted for small arms and heavy artillery by the British Government in the naval and military services in 1889, and composed of 58 parts of nitro-glycerine, 37 of gun-cotton, and 5 of vaseline. It is a jelly or plastic dough, and used in the form of sticks.

Cork, the bark of a species of oak, Quercus suber, grown largely in the South of Europe and North America. The cork tree is said to yield bark every six to ten years for 150 years, and grows to a height of from 20 to 40 ft. Its lightness, impermeability, and elasticity enable it to be used for a variety of commercial purposes, especially for stoppers of bottles.

Cormorant, a large, long-billed water-bird which captures fish by diving. It has bronze-black plumage with white cheeks and sides and is found around the sea coasts of most parts of the world, including the British Isles. It nests in colonies on sea cliffs and rocky ledges. The Shag or Green Cormorant is a smaller bird with green-black plumage and a crest.

Corncrake. See Landrail.

Corn Laws were statutes intended for the benefit of British agriculture, and restricted import and export of grain. From the 14th to the mid-19th cent. such laws were in force, and were often of a stringent nature. They became so oppressive and caused corn to reach so high a price that the poorer classes were plunged into distress. A powerful anti-corn law agitation was organised, of which Cobden, Bright, and Villiers were the leaders, and Sir Robert Peel, in 1846, at the time of the Irish potato famine, carried through free trade. The repeal of the Corn Laws marked an important phase in the transformation of an agricultural to an industrial Britain.

Coronae, series of luminous rings surrounding sun or moon produced by the diffraction of light by water droplets in the atmosphere. Usually seen when sun shines through altostratus clouds. The outside of the ring is red and the inside bluish. See Halo.

Corpus Christi Festival is one of the great celebrations of the Roman Catholic Church, and takes place on the Thursday after Trinity. It was instituted by Pope Urban IV. in 1264.

Cortes, the name of the Parliamentary assemblies of Spain and Portugal.

Cosmic Rays, a form of radiation coming from outer space, of deep penetrating power and of great scientific interest. The rays are believed to consist chiefly of fast protons, with a few α-particles and other positive nuclei. By interacting with the gas of the atmosphere, these rays initiate a complex series of events, in the course of which other particles ("secondary radiations") are generated. The secondary rays contain virtually all the particles listed on F14; indeed, several particles were first discovered as secondary cosmic rays. Cosmic rays are investigated at and below sea-level, on mountains, in mines, in balloons, rockets, and satellites. Origin still uncertain. See F3(2).

Cosmology is the science which studies the whole universe, its origin, its nature, its size, and evolution. At present it is a very active science partly because new techniques such as radioastronomy are revealing more facts about distant parts of the universe and partly because of fruitful clashes between theoretical ideas. See F3–7.

Cotton, the name of a plant of several species,

bearing large yellow flowers with purple centres. These centres expand into pods, which at maturity burst and yield the white fibrous substance known as cotton. The raw cotton contains a large proportion of seeds which are removed by "ginning." Long before the Christian era, cotton had been grown and used with great skill in India to make fabrics. The industry was not introduced into England until the middle of the 17th cent. when Protestant refugees from Flanders came to settle in the wool textile districts of East Anglia and Lancashire. With improvements in machinery and expansion of overseas trade in the 18th and 19th cent., Lancashire became the centre of the world's cotton industry. Since the first world war there has been a marked decline in Britain's cotton industry. Cotton reacts with nitric acid to form gun cotton, which is combined with more sensitive explosives to give a more safely handled substance.

Coulomb, a unit of electric charge, named after the French naval engineer, Charles Augustin de Coulomb (1736–1806), equal to the quantity of electricity transferred in one second by a current of one ampere.

County. The word county was introduced after the Norman conquest as an equivalent of the old English "shire." England has 41 geographical counties, Wales 13, Scotland 33, and Ireland 32. The number of administrative counties differs from the number of geographical counties because the division for Local Government purposes is made on grounds of convenience. Under the London Government Act, 1963, the county of Middlesex was completely absorbed in Greater London.

Coup d'Etat, a violent change in the government of a state carried out by force or illegally. Examples are the overthrow of the French Republic in 1851 by Louis Napoleon, who then became Emperor, and more recently the military coups in the Middle East which brought about the abdication of Farouk of Egypt in 1952 and the assassination of Feisal of Iraq in 1958.

Court Leet, a court of record held annually before the steward of any particular manor or lordship; originally there was only one court for a manor, but in the time of Edward I. it branched into two, the court baron and the court leet.

Coypu or Nutria rat, a large beaver-like rodent found in S. America; now wild in E. Anglia, where it is causing damage to dykes, reeds, and crops, having escaped from farms where it is bred for its fur.

Crane, a large, graceful wading-bird with elegant long legs and neck, greyish plumage, superficially resembling the heron and related to the bustard. They migrate in V or W formation and have trumpet-like voices. There are several species, found in all continents except S. America, including the Crowned Crane with golden coronet and the Demoiselle with tuft-like crest of white feathers. The Common Crane nested in East Anglia in mediaeval times but now comes only as a rare visitor from the Continent.

Credit is an advance of money or of goods or services in consideration of a promise of payment later. Trade credit is such an advance from trader to customer; bank credit is an advance of money by a bank to a client, whether a business firm or a private person, in consideration of an interest payment by the borrower.

Creed, a brief enumeration of a particular belief or religion. The three important Christian creeds are the Apostles' Creed, the Nicene Creed, and the Athanasian Creed.

Cremation, the ancient custom, revived in modern times, of burning the dead. Cremation was first legalised in Great Britain in 1885 and the first crematorium opened at Woking in that year. Application for cremation must be accompanied by two medical certificates.

Cricket, a genus of insects of the grasshopper order which move by leaps. The male produces a chirping noise by rubbing its wing-covers together.

Crimean War (1853–56). This war between Russia and the allied powers of Turkey, England, France, and Sardinia, was connected with the Eastern Question (q.v.) and the desire of Russia for a port on the Mediterranean. Chief engagements were the Alma, Balaclava, and Inkerman. Fighting virtually ceased with fall of Sevastopol in Sept. 1855. Treaty of Paris signed March 30, 1856.

Crocodile, the name of the largest existing reptile, and classed with the alligator and the gavial. The crocodile inhabits the Nile region, the alligator the lower Mississippi, and the gavial is found in many Indian rivers.

Crow, a family of birds including many well-known species such as the rook, raven, jackdaw, carrion crow, hooded crow, magpie, nutcracker, jay, and chough.

Crusades were military expeditions undertaken by some of the Christian nations of Europe with the object of ensuring the safety of pilgrims visiting the Holy Sepulchre and to retain in Christian hands the Holy Places. For two centuries nine crusades were undertaken: First, 1095–99, under Godfrey of Bouillon, which succeeded in capturing Jerusalem; Second, 1147–49, led by Louis VII. of France, a dismal failure, which ended with the fall of Jerusalem; Third, 1189–92, in which Richard I. of England took part, making a truce with Saladin; Fourth, 1202–4, led by French and Flemish nobles, a shameful expedition, resulting in the founding of a Latin empire in Constantinople; Fifth, 1217–21, led by John of Brienne; Sixth, 1228–29, under the Emperor Frederick II.; Seventh, 1248–54, under St. Louis of France; Eighth, 1270, under the same leadership, but cut short by his death on an ill-judged expedition to Tunis; Ninth, 1271–72, led by Prince Edward of England, which accomplished nothing. Millions of lives and an enormous amount of treasure were sacrificed in these enterprises and Jerusalem remained in the possession of the "infidels." The chief material beneficiaries were the Italian maritime cities; the chief spiritual beneficiary was the pope; but in literature and the arts both Europe and the Levant benefited enormously from the bringing together of the different cultures.

Cryogenics (Greek roots: productive of cold) is the science dealing with the production of very low temperatures and the study of their physical and technological consequences. "Very low " is often taken to mean below about −150°C. The growth of cryogenics (essentially a 20th-cent. science) is connected with the discovery of how to liquefy all gases including even helium which resisted liquefaction until 1908. Scientifically, cryogenics is important partly because special phenomena (e.g., superconductivity (q.v.)) appear at low temperatures and partly because more can be learned about ordinary properties by studying them in the absence of heat. Technologically, cryogenics is becoming more and more significant, for example, liquefied gases are rocket propellants, superconductors make valuable magnets, tissue-freezing techniques (using very cold liquids) have been introduced into surgery. See Absolute Temperature.

Crystal, in everyday usage, a solid chemical substance bounded by plane surfaces which show a regular geometrical arrangement as, e.g., quartz crystals, rock salt, snow flakes. In physics the term means any solid whose atoms are arranged in a regular three-dimensional array. This includes most solids, even those not particularly crystalline in appearance, e.g., a lump of lead. Common non-crystalline substances are liquids, jellies, glass.

Cubism, the name of a revolutionary movement in art created in the years 1907–9 by the two painters Picasso and Braque. Rejecting purely visual effects, they approached nature from an intellectual point of view, reducing it to mathematical orderliness. Its respectable grandparent was Cézanne who had once written: " you must see in nature the cylinder, the sphere, and the cone "—a concept which, together with the contemporary interest in Negro sculpture, moved the two founders of the movement to experiment with the reduction of natural forms to their basic geometrical shapes. In practice, this meant combining several views of the object all more or less superimposed in order to express the idea of the object rather than any one view of it. The name Cubism was derisive and the movement aroused the same opposition as Impressionism, Fauvism, and the later Futurism. Picasso's *Young Ladies of Avignon* was the first Cubist painting and his "Head" (1909) the first Cubist sculpture. Three phases are recognised: (1) Cubism under the influence of Cézanne; (2) high or analytical Cubism (c. 1909–12) concentrating on the breaking-down of form to the exclusion of interest in colour; (3) synthetic Cubism (c. 1913) making use of *collage* in which pieces of pasted-on paper (illustrations, wallpaper, newspaper) and other materials were used in addition to paint. Amongst other early cubist painters were Metzinger, Gris, Duchamp, and Léger.

**Cuckoo**, a well-known migratory bird which is found in Great Britain from April to July, hawk-like in shape, with a very characteristic note, uttered during the mating season only by the male. The hen has a soft bubbling call. It lays its eggs in the nests of other birds, e.g., the meadow pipit and hedge sparrow, but only one egg in each nest. Feeds mainly on insects, particularly hairy caterpillars.

**Cuneiform**, the term applied to the written arrow-headed characters found in Assyria, Persia, and Mesopotamia. Good examples may be seen in the British Museum, some of them several thousand years old.

**Curfew** (Old Fr. *covre-feu* = cover fire), a regulation common throughout Europe in mediæval times by which, at a fixed hour in the evening, the church bell was rung as a signal that fires were to be put out and the people were to go to bed. The custom originated in the fear of fire when buildings were built of timber. Nowadays a curfew is imposed by the military in areas where riots or disturbances are expected, compelling the civilian population to remain indoors after nightfall.

**Curia**, the central government of the Roman Catholic Church. By the reform which came into force on Jan 1, 1968, its twelve Sacred Congregations or "ministries" were reorganised and reduced to nine. Top Curial appointments are for 5 years instead of for a lifetime, renewable only at the Pope's discretion. The new "finance ministry" is called the Prefecture of Economic Affairs, the "foreign ministry" the Sacred Council for the Church's Public Affairs. The aim of the reform was to streamline the Curial offices so that the Church's machinery can cope with modern problems, so favouring the desires expressed by the Ecumenical Council convened by Pope John.

**Curie**, a measure of the rate at which radioactive material emits radiation. One curie is a disintegration rate of $3.7 \times 10^{10}$ disintegrations per second.

**Curlew**, a wading-bird of which there are several species. It frequents marshy places, feeds on worms, insects, molluscs, and berries and possesses a very long, down-curved bill.

**Currency** is the name given to the types of cash money—metal or paper—in use in an area (e.g. pound, sterling, dollar, franc). It also designates the actual coins or notes issued. Its amount is usually subject to regulation by the Government, or by a Central Bank acting on the Government's behalf. Britain proposes to change over to a £-based decimal currency in Feb. 1971. *See also* N10, 27.

**Cybernetics**, the science concerned with the automatic control and communication processes in both animals and machines. Thus it is concerned with brain function, information theory, electronic computers, and automation.

**Cyclone**, a term usually applied to a tropical revolving storm. Cyclones often occur towards the end of the hot seasons and are mainly confined to tracks in the western areas of the oceans, being known as hurricanes (Caribbean and Pacific), cyclones (Indian Ocean), and typhoons (China Seas). The circulation of air in a cyclone is similar to that in the *depression* of temperate latitudes, but the region of low pressure is much more localised and the pressure gradients steeper. Winds of hurricane strength and torrential rain occur generally, although at the centre of the storm there is a small area, known as the "eye," where fair, calm weather prevails.

**Cyclotron**, a machine for accelerating charged particles such as protons to very high energies. Devised by E. O. Lawrence in California in 1930, it uses a magnetic field to make the particles traverse nearly circular paths and an electric field to give them an additional pulse of energy each time round. The accelerated particles impinge on targets, and the resulting events are a basic source of information for nuclear physicists. The cyclotron is obsolescent and has led to the development of other machines, e.g., betatrons, synchrotrons. Britain has two major national high-energy machines: *Nimrod* (7-GeV proton accelerator) and *Nina* (4-GeV electron accelerator).

# D

**Dactylopterus**, a fish of the gurnard family, with wing-like pectoral fins; sometimes known as the flying fish, though that appellation is more generally given to *Exocaetus exiliens*.

**Dadaism** (French *Dada* = hobby-horse) was a hysterical and nihilistic precursor of Surrealism (q.v.) resulting from the shock produced by the first world war. Beginning in Zurich about 1915, it spread to other continental cities, such as Berlin and Paris, dying out in 1922. The movement was deliberately anti-art, destructive, and without meaning; it intended to scandalise by such tricks as "compositions" made out of anything that came to hand—buttons, bus tickets, pieces of wire, bits of tin, etc. Other excesses included incoherent poetry, Dada night-clubs, plays, and short-lived newspapers. Many Dadaist painters became Surrealists at a later stage, but where Surrealism is a deliberate attempt to present subconscious and dream-like images, Dadaism was sheer anarchism. Among its chief exponents were Hans Arp, Marcel Duchamp, André Breton, Guillaume Apollinaire, and Max Ernst, all of whom subsequently became noted in more reputable ways.

**Daddy Longlegs**, or Crane-fly, a slender long-legged fly of the family Tipulidae. The larvae which do damage to lawns and plants are called leather-jackets. The Americans call Harvestmen (q.v.) daddy longlegs.

**Dafila**, a genus of river duck, with long, supple tail, found in Europe, Asia, and America, related to the pintail duck.

**Daguerreotype**, a first practical photographic process, invented in Paris by M. Daguerre during the years 1824–39. The light-sensitive plate was prepared by bringing iodine in contact with a plate of silver. After exposure a positive image came by development of the plate in mercury vapour. Even for open-air scenes the first daguerreotypes involved exposure of 5–10 minutes. The wet collodion process (1851) rendered the technique obsolete.

**Dail Eireann**, the name of the national parliament of the Irish Republic.

**Dalmatic**, a wide-sleeved ecclesiastical vestment, reaching below the knee. Worn by bishops and deacons over the alb or stole.

**Damaskeening**, the art of inlaying one metal upon another, largely practised in the East in mediaeval times, especially in the decoration of sword blades.

**Dandies**, the name given to a class of exquisites prominent in early Victorian days, and who attracted attention by excessive regard for dress. Their feminine counterparts were the dandizettes.

**Danegeld**, a tax imposed in England in Anglo-Saxon times to raise funds for resisting the Danes or to buy them off. Edward the Confessor abolished the tax, but it was revived by the Conqueror and subsequently retained, under another name, after the danger from the Danes was past. It is the basis of all taxation in this country. Domesday Book (q.v.) was originally drawn up for the purpose of teaching the State how to levy the tax.

**Danelaw**, the law enforced by the Danes in the kingdoms of Northumbria, East Anglia, and in the districts of the five (Danish) boroughs—lands grouped round Leicester, Nottingham, Derby, Stamford, and Lincoln—which they occupied during the Viking invasions of the 9th and 10th cent. The country occupied was also called the Danelaw or Danelagh.

**Darter, 1.** Snakebirds, a genus of the pelican family, with long, pointed bill and serpent-like neck and resembling cormorants in appearance. There are 5 species. 2. Numerous species of small freshwater fish belonging to the Perch family, found in N. America.

**Date Palm**, *Phoenix dactylifera*, one of the oldest known food plants widely cultivated in N. Africa and W. Asia. It grows to 100 ft. and continues to bear for 2 or 3 centuries, its fruit being of great value as a food. From the leaves the Africans make roofs for their huts; ropes are made from the fibrous parts of the stalks; and the sap furnishes a stimulating beverage.

**Dauphin**, the title borne by the eldest sons of the Kings of France from 1349 to the Revolution of 1830.

**Day** is the most natural unit of time and may be defined as the period of rotation of the earth relative to any selected heavenly body. Relative to the sun it is called the *solar day*. Relative to a fixed star it is called the *sidereal day*. Owing to irregularities in the earth's movements, the time taken for the earth to rotate through 360° relative to the sun is variable, and so the *mean solar day* of 24 hours has been introduced, which is the average throughout the year. The *mean solar day* is our standard, used for purposes of the calendar, and astronomers use *sidereal* clocks to check mean solar time. In practice, for convenience, the sidereal day is determined by the earth's rotation relative to the vernal equinox or first point of Aries, and is equal to 23 hours 56 minutes and 4·091 seconds of mean solar time (*i.e.*, about 4 minutes shorter than a solar day). *See* Time.

**D.D.T.** (dichloro-diphenyl-trichloroethane). A very powerful insecticide which has had wide success in the control of diseases, such as malaria and typhus, which is carried by insects. Mosquito swamps are sprayed with D.D.T. to kill the carriers.

**Deacon**, an ecclesiastical official, who assists in some of the smaller ministerial duties in church or chapel; in the Anglican Church he ranks below a priest.

**Dead Languages** are such as the ancient Greek and Roman tongues, which are no longer spoken but are preserved in literature.

**Dead Sea Scrolls**, a group of ancient Jewish documents, consisting of scrolls and fragments which have been recovered since 1947 in the vicinity of Qumran near the Dead Sea and which represent one of the most important finds ever made in the field of biblical archæology and Christian origins. The scrolls, written in Hebrew or Aramaic, were found in caves, the first by chance by an Arab shepherd in 1947. These consisted of biblical texts older by a thousand years than the earliest Hebrew manuscript of the Old Testament (A.D. 895). Many fragments have since been discovered, comprising the whole of the Old Testament with the exception of Esther. In addition there are commentaries and other non-biblical writings, including one called "The War of the Sons of Light with the Sons of Darkness." The writing on the scrolls indicates that they were written over a period of two centuries, the greater portion before the birth of Christ. A nearby ruin is believed to have been the home of a religious sect called the Essenes (**J15**), to whom the scrolls belonged. By the aid of the latest scientific techniques, including radiocarbon tests, the age of the scrolls is being accurately determined.

**Dean**, a Church of England dignitary, ranking below a bishop, and the head of the chapter of a cathedral. A rural Dean supervises a *deanery* or group of parishes. There are also Deans of Faculties in some universities, and at Oxford and Cambridge the *Dean* is in charge of chapel services and disciplinary arrangements.

**Death Watch Beetle** (*Xestobium rufovillosum*), a wood-boring beetle, larger than the common furniture beetle, found chiefly in the old oak beams of churches and other historic buildings. The grub bores from 4–12 years. The name "death watch" comes from the superstition that the ticking sound, made by the beetle striking its head against the wood, is a sign of approaching death. The death watch beetle in the roof of Westminster Hall is being smoked out by means of an insecticide called gamma benzine hexachloride. *See also* Furniture Beetle, Woodworm.

**Decalogue**, name given to the Ten Commandments of the Old Testament. There are two versions of them, differing in detail: Exodus xx. 2–17 and Deuteronomy v. 6–21. They are of Hebrew origin and are recognised by Jews and Christians as the divine law given by God to Moses on Mt. Sinai. Most of them are prohibitions in contrast to the beatitudes (pronounced by Christ in the Sermon on the Mount) which are positive, *e.g.*, Blessed are the merciful.

**December**, the last month of the year in our calendar, and the tenth in the old Roman.

**Deciduous Trees** are such as shed their leaves at certain seasons as distinguished from evergreens or permanent foliaged trees or shrubs.

**Decimal System** is based on the unit of 10. Duodecimal System is based on the unit of 12. Fractional numbers are expressed as divisions of 10 and 12 respectively. Thus:

| Fraction | Decimal | Duodecimal |
|---|---|---|
| ½ | 0·5 | 0:6 |
| ⅓ | 0·3333 | 0:4 |
| ¼ | 0·25 | 0:3 |
| ⅕ | 0·2 | 0:2497 |
| ⅙ | 0·1666 | 0:2 |
| ⅛ | 0·125 | 0:16 |
| 1⁄12 | 0·0833 | 0:1 |
| 1⁄24 | 0·04166 | 0:06 |

Decimal currency was imposed on France in 1795. A changeover to decimal coinage in 1971, keeping the £ as the basic unit, has been accepted by the British government. The six new coins are:

| Denomination | Value | Metal |
|---|---|---|
| ½ new penny | 1·2d. | bronze |
| 1 new penny | 2·4d. | bronze |
| 2 new pence | 4·8d. | bronze |
| 5 new pence | 1s. | cupro-nickel |
| 10 new pence | 2s. | cupro-nickel |
| 50 new pence | 10s. | cupro-nickel |

*See also* Metric System; **N11, G38**.

**Declaration of Independence** was an Act by which the American Congress, on July 4, 1776, declared the American colonies to be independent of Great Britain. "Independence Day" is a holiday in the United States.

**Defender of the Faith** (*Defensor Fidei*), a title conferred upon Henry VIII. by Pope Leo X. in 1521 for entering the lists against Luther with his book on *The Assertion of the Seven Sacraments*. In 1554 the title was confirmed by Parliament and has been used even since by English sovereigns.

**Deflation** is a policy designed to bring down costs by reducing the supply of means of payment. It is usually advocated as a remedy for inflation, and in this connection is often referred to as Disinflation. It usually results in a fall in employment. The "credit squeezes" in Great Britain were designed to have a disinflationary effect.

**Dehydrate**, to eliminate the water from a substance. The process of dehydration is now used in the food industry, as a result of wartime research, in making such things as dried egg and packet soups. Most vegetables contain over 90% of water, and much of this can be removed under vacuum at low temperatures without appreciably impairing the flavour. The lightness of the dehydrated products is an advantage when supplies have to be transported.

**Deliquescence**, the process of dissolving by the absorption of moisture from the atmosphere. For instance, chromic acid crystals on exposure to the air quickly deliquesce.

**Delta**, a triangular tract of land between diverging branches of a river at its mouth, and so called from its general resemblance to the Greek letter Δ *delta*. The best-known examples are the deltas of the Nile, the Ganges, the Niger, and the Mississippi.

**Deluge**, a flood, commonly applied to the story of the Deluge in the Bible, in which Noah and the Ark figure. A similar tradition lingers in the mythologies of all ancient peoples.

**Democratic Party**, one of the two great American political parties, originated about 1787, advocating restrictions on the federal governments and in opposition to the federalists. It was in 1825 that a group who were in favour of high tariffs seceded, later to become the Republican Party.

The Democratic Party was split again over slavery before the Civil War (1861–65), and in the main the southern states have been supporters of the Democrats. The economic depression helped the Democrats to power in 1932 (*see* New Deal) and they held office until 1953 when Eisenhower became President. In 1960 Kennedy narrowly won the Presidency and in 1964 Lyndon Johnson swept in with a landslide victory over the Republican candidate In 1964 Humphrey was beaten by Nixon, the Republican candidate. The symbol of the party is a donkey, invented, like the Republican's elephant, by the cartoonist Nash.

**Demoiselle**, the Numidian crane, a wading-bird. Also, a sub-order of dragon flies which close their wings over their backs when at rest.

**Dendrite**, any stone or mineral on or in which appears natural tracery resembling trees, leaves, or flowers, the result of the action of the hydrous oxide of manganese.

**Density**, a measure of the mass per unit volume of a material, usually expressed in grams per cubic centimetre. *Specific gravity* is the ratio of the density of a material at the temperature under consideration to that of water at the temperature of its maximum density (4° C.). In grams per cubic centimetre the density of gold is 19·3, silver 10·5, lead 11·3, water 0·99997, air 0·00129.

**Depreciation of a currency** is a fall in its relative value in terms of gold or of other currencies. The term is most often used to indicate a fall in the value of one country's money in relation to others.

**Depression**, a region where barometric pressure is lower than that of its surroundings. These areas of low pressure enclosed by the isobars are usually less extensive than anticyclones and may vary from 100 to 1,000 miles in diameter. The winds, often of gale force when the depression is deep, blow round the system in an anticlockwise direction in the Northern Hemisphere (in the reverse direction in the Southern Hemisphere) and inwards across the isobars. The majority of depressions which cross the British Isles travel from the Atlantic, sometimes in series or families, at rates of between a few miles and 700 miles in a day, bringing their generally unsettled weather with them.

**De Profundis** (out of the depths), the first two words of the Latin version of the 130th Psalm, and commonly used to designate this psalm.

**Deserts**, vast, barren, stone or sandy wastes where there is almost no rainfall and little or no vegetation. These regions are found in the interior of the continents Africa, Asia, and America between 20° and 30° north and south of the equator. Europe is the only continent without deserts. The most famous are the Sahara, the largest in the world, the Gobi desert of central Asia, the Kalahari desert of south-west Africa, and the great Australian desert.

**Detention Centres** in Britain are for young people (boys and girls) aged at least 14 but under 21 who have been found guilty of an offence for which an adult could be sent to prison. Controlled by the Home Office.

**Deuterium** or "heavy hydrogen." The second isotope of hydrogen; the third is called tritium. Deuterium atoms have in their nuclei a neutron as well as a proton; tritium nuclei have two neutrons and one proton. In ordinary hydrogen gas about one out of every 5,000 atoms is a deuterium atom. Deuterium was discovered in 1932 by Professor Harold Urey. The oxide of deuterium corresponding to water is called "heavy water." The nucleus of the deuterium atom is called a deuteron. An anti-deuteron consisting of an anti-proton and an anti-neutron was produced at Brookhaven in 1965, the first compound anti-nucleus ever to be produced.

**Devaluation** is a definite, official downward valuation of a country's currency in terms of its exchange value with other currencies. The £ was devalued in 1949, when an official exchange rate of £1 = $2.8 was established, and again in 1967, to a rate of £1 = $2.4.

**Devonian System** in geology refers to the strata between the Silurian and the Carboniferous Formations. It includes the Old Red Sandstone Formation. The fauna of the Devonian include the group of fishes known as the Rhipidistra (on the evolutionary route towards the

amphibians), Actinistia (coelacanth), and the Dipnoi or lung fishes. *See* F41.

**Dew**, moisture deposited by condensation of water vapour on exposed objects especially during calm, cloudless nights. The loss of heat from the ground after sunset, by radiation, causes the layer of atmosphere close to the surface to be chilled below the temperature, known as the dew-point, at which the air is saturated with vapour. Part of the vapour condensed may be transpired from blades of grass and foliage of plants.

**Dew Pond** is a shallow artificial pond which is on high ground and rarely dries up, even during prolonged droughts, despite being used by cattle and sheep as a drinking source. The name arose from the belief that dew deposits at night provided the moisture for replenishment. Drainage of rain-water and mist condensed on neighbouring trees and shrubs are probably more important factors.

**Dialectical Materialism.** *See* J12.

**Diamond**, a mineral, one of the two crystalline forms of the element carbon (the other is graphite), the hardest known substance, used as a gem and in industry. India was the first country to mine diamonds (the Koh-i-noor, known since 1304, came from Golconda near Hyderabad). The celebrated diamond mines of South Africa were discovered in the 1870s. Other important diamond producing countries are Angola, Sierra Leone, Congo, Tanzania, Guyana, and the Soviet Union. Diamonds can be made artificially by subjecting carbon to very high temperatures and pressures; many industrial diamonds are made this way. Antwerp is the main diamond centre of the world, London the main diamond marketing centre, Amsterdam the main diamond cutting centre.

**Diatoms.** One-celled algae, common in fresh and salt water. Distinctive feature is the siliceous wall which is in two halves, one fitting over the other like the lid of a box. These walls are often very finely and beautifully sculptured. The diatoms constitute a class of the plant kingdom known as the Bacillariophyta. *Diatom ooze* is a deep-sea deposit made up of diatom shells. *Diatomite* or *diatomaceous earth* is the mineral form that such diatom oozes assume (sometimes known as kieselguhr which mixed with nitroglycerine yields dynamite).

**Diatonic Scale.** The ordinary major and minor scales on which most European music is built, *e.g.,*

C major     C – D – E – F – G – A – B – C
Tone intervals   1 – 1 – ½ – 1 – 1 – 1 – ½
C minor     C – D – E♭ – F – G – A♭ – B♭ – C
Tone intervals   1 – ½ – 1 – 1 – ½ – 1 – ½

**Dies Irae** (the Day of Wrath), a famous 13th-cent. Latin hymn of the Roman Catholic Church, part of the Requiem Mass.

**Diesel Engine.** A compression-ignition engine. The air in the cylinder is compressed to over 500 lb. per sq. in. and its temperature is about 800° F.; oil injected into the hot compressed air ignites immediately. The modern oil engine has been evolved mainly from the principles enunciated by Herbert Akroyd-Stuart in his patent of 1890 and, like the steam and other inventions, represents the improvements achieved by many men, including those by Rudolf Diesel of Germany, in respect of high compression pressures and greater fuel economy.

**Diet**, in German history, an assembly of dignitaries or delegates called together to debate upon and decide important political or ecclesiastical questions. The most famous imperial Diets were those held at Worms (1521), Speyer (1529), and Augsburg (1530), all of which dealt with matters of religious conflict arising from the Reformation.

**Diffusion** is the process of mixing which occurs when two liquids or gases are in contact. It is most rapid between gases and, as laid down by Graham's law, "the rates of diffusion of different gases are in the inverse proportion to the square roots of their relative densities." Diffusion arises through the continual movement of molecules. Even in solids diffusion can occur. If a block of gold and a block of silver are welded together, after some time particles of gold are found in the silver, and *vice versa*.

**Dimensions** in common speech are the magnitudes

of length, breadth, and thickness giving, the size of an object, thus a line has only one dimension: length; a plane surface two: length and breadth; and a solid three: length, breadth, and thickness. In mathematics, hypothetical objects with any number of dimensions are considered. In physics and mechanics, dimensions are numbers which relate the units in which any quantity is measured to the so-called fundamental units. The latter are usually but not necessarily those of length, mass, and time. " Dimensional analysis " is an important technique of scientific reasoning. See N14.

Dimorphism, the quality of assuming two distinct forms. For instance, carbon, which is graphite in one form, is the diamond in another.

Dinosaur, the name given to a group of extinct reptiles of the Mesozoic period, some of which were of immense size—much larger than crocodiles. See Diplodocus.

Diocese, a territory under the pastoral authority of a bishop. The term originated in the time of the Roman Empire to signify an administrative rather than an ecclesiastical territory.

Diopside, a variety of pyroxene occurring in prismatic crystals, chemically calcium magnesium silicate. Two light-green varieties, malacolite and alalite are gemstones.

Diorite, an igneous rock of crystalline structure composed of felspar and hornblende. It used to be classed as greenstone.

Dip Needle. Instrument for measuring the *dip* or inclination of the earth's magnetic field.

Diplodocus, one of the best known of the extinct mammoth dinosaurs. Fossil remains have been discovered in the Jurassic rocks of the United States. Some reached a length of over 80 ft.

Dipnoi *or* Lung Fishes. These have the air bladder adapted to function as a lung, and they can remain alive when the stream or marsh in which they live dries up. Species of lung fish occur in Australia, Africa, and S. America.

Diptera, an order of insects. Their main characteristic is that they are two-winged, and the common house-fly is the best-known example. There are at least 50,000 species of these insects, including gnats, blow-flies, mosquitoes, tsetses.

Diptych was a folding two-leaved tablet of wood, ivory, or metal, with polished inner surfaces, utilised for writing with the style by the ancient Greeks and Romans. The same term was applied to the tablets on which the names of the persons to be commemorated were inscribed in the early Church. In art any pair of pictures hinged together is styled a diptych.

Discus, a circular piece of metal or stone about 12 in. in diameter, used in athletic contests by the ancient Greeks and Romans. Throwing the discus was a very favourite game, which was deemed worthy of celebration in Myron's famous *Discobolus* (c. 460 B.C.–450 B.C.), the best copy of which is in Rome.

Disk, an astronomical term denoting the seemingly flat surface of celestial bodies as seen by the eye.

Distillation, a process used to separate liquids of different boiling points. This is effected by placing the mixture in a distillation apparatus and heating. The liquid with the lower boiling point distils over first, the vapour being condensed and collected, forming the first *fraction*. With continued heating the second liquid reaches its boiling point, distils over and the mixture is said to be *fractionated*. Mixtures of liquids with close very high boiling points require more elaborate apparatus. Fractional distillation is a common process in the chemical industry, particularly in the refining of petroleum.

DNA (Deoxyribonucleic acid), a polymer molecule in the form of a double-strand helix containing many thousands of sub-units. Contains the genetic information coded in sequences of sub-units called bases. The Nobel Prize for medicine was awarded in 1962 for the discovery of the structure of DNA; that for 1968 for interpreting the genetic code and its function in protein synthesis. See Nucleic Acids, *also* L128.

Docks are enclosed water spaces where ships rest while being loaded or unloaded, or waiting for cargo. There are three main types: the wet dock (*e.g.*, King George V. dock, London) is for

loading and unloading; the dry dock, or graving dock (*e.g.*, King George V. dock, Southampton) is for overhauling and repairing vessels, and is so constructed that, after a ship has been docked the water can be drawn off; the floating dock is a type of dry dock.

Dodo, an extinct bird, giant and flightless, which lived on the island of Mauritius up until 250 years ago. Another species, the white dodo, lived on Réunion. Some reached exceptional sizes. By the end of the 17th cent. Mauritius, Rodriguez, and Réunion had all been colonised, and the dodo along with many other birds vanished forever because of their inability to stand up to man and the animals imported into the islands.

Dog-days, a period of 40 days (3 July–11 Aug.) when Sirius rises and sets with the sun. The ancient superstition, which can be traced back in Greek literature to Hesiod (8th cent. B.C.), was that this star exercised direct influence over the canine race.

Doge, the chief magistrate in the former republics of Venice (697–1797) and Genoa (1339–1797, 1802–5).

Dogfish, a large family of small sharks, seldom more than 3 ft. in length. The flesh is sold as " rock salmon." The eggs are contained in horny cases called " mermaid's purses." The commonest of the British dogfishes are the spurdogs.

Dog Licences are necessary for household dogs of six months of age or over. The cost per dog is 7s. 6d., and the licence can be obtained at any Post Office. Dogs for tending sheep or cattle, or for leading blind persons, are exempt.

Doldrums, a nautical term applied to those areas of the Atlantic and Pacific towards which the trade winds blow and where the weather is calm, hot, and sultry but liable to change suddenly in squall, rendering navigation difficult.

Dolomite, a name applied to a limestone containing appreciable magnesium; also the mineral dolomite, a double carbonate of magnesium and calcium.

Dolphin, an ocean mammal of the whale order, from 6 to 8 ft. long, with a long, sharp snout, and of an active disposition. They abound in most temperate seas and swim in shoals. A few species live in large rivers (Ganges and Amazon). They can cruise for long periods at around 15 knots and produce bursts of speed in the region of 20 knots, the water apparently flowing smoothly past their bodies. Dolphins are some of the most intelligent of mammals and are currently the subject of scientific experiments in communication.

Dome, a large cupola, hemispherical in form, rising over the main building of a cathedral or other prominent structure. The finest existing dome, that of the Pantheon at Rome, is also the oldest, dating from the time of the Emperor Hadrian. It is 142 ft. in diameter and about the same in height. The dome of St. Peter's, in the same city, has a double shell, is 330 ft. high and 140 ft. in diameter. The dome of the cathedral at Florence is 139 ft. in diameter and 310 ft. high, and that of St. Paul's, London, has 3 shells and is 112 ft. in diameter and 215 ft. high. The circular reading-room of the British Museum has a dome 140 ft. in diameter and is 106 ft. high. Malta's Mosta dome is also famous.

Domesday Book is the famous register of the lands of England framed by order of William the Conqueror. According to Stowe, the name was derived from *Domus dei*, the name of the place where the book was deposited in Winchester Cathedral; though by others it is connected with doom in the sense of judgment. Its compilation was determined upon in 1084, in order that William might compute what he considered to be due to him in the way of tax from his subjects. William sent into each county commissioners to make survey. They were to inquire the name of each place, the possessor, how many hides of land were in the manor, how many ploughs were in demesne, how many homagers, villeins, cottars, serving men, free tenants, and tenants in soccage; how much wood, meadow, and pasture; the number of mills and fish ponds; what had been added to or taken away from the place; what was the gross value at the time of Edward the Confessor. So minute was the survey that the Saxon chronicler of the time reports " there was not a single hide, nor one vintage of land, nor even, it is shame to tell, though it seemed no shame to do, an ox, nor a cow, nor a swine was left that was not set down." The record, which did not take in Northumberland, Cumberland, Durham, and parts of Lancashire and Westmorland, was completed on Nov. 15, 1085, and was comprised in two volumes—one a large folio, sometimes called the Little Domesday, which deals with Essex, Norfolk, and Suffolk, the other a quarto, sometimes called the Great Domesday. The first is written on 384 double pages of vellum in one and the same hand, and in a small but plain character, each page having a double column. The quarto is written on 450 pages of vellum, but in a single column and in a large, fair character. The original is preserved in the Public Record Office. *See also* Danegeld.

**Dominicans,** an order of mendicant preaching friars founded by St. Dominic in Languedoc in 1215 and confirmed by the Pope in 1216. The rule of the order was rigorous. The dress was a white habit and scapular with a long black mantle. This gave them the name of Black Friars. Their official name is Friars Preachers.

**Donjon,** the keep, or inner tower of a castle, and the strongest and most secure portion of the structure. This was the last refuge of the garrison, and there was usually a prison on the lower floor, hence the name *dungeon.*

**Don Juan,** the legendary hero of many famous works, supposedly based on the life and character of the unscrupulous gallant Don Juan Tenorio of 14th-cent. Seville. The first dramatisation of the legend and the most famous is Tirso de Molina's *El Burlador de Sevilla.* Don Juan was also the subject of Molière's *Le Festin de Pierre,* Mozart's *Don Giovanni,* Byron's *Don Juan,* and José Zorilla's *Don Juan Tenorio.* The latter is played on All Saints' Day throughout Spanish-speaking countries.

**Don Quixote,** the " knight of the doleful countenance," the hero and title of Cervantes' classic novel of 16th-cent. Spain. Don Quijote de la Mancha, a gentle country gentleman of lofty but unpractical ideals, having read many chivalric romances, believes he is called upon to redress the wrongs of the world. Mounted on his nag Rosinante and accompanied by his companion Sancho Panza, a hard-headed and practical peasant, he sets out on his journeys of knight-errantry

**Dormouse,** a family of small, squirrel-like rodents widely distributed throughout Europe and Asia, and living mainly on fruit and nuts. It is of nocturnal habits and sleeps through the winter.

**Dot,** a French term indicating the property which a wife brings to her husband on marriage, and is usually settled on the woman, being her separate property, though the income from it may go towards the general household expenses.

**Dotterel,** a handsome bird of the plover family found in northern Europe and Siberia. Nests in the Cairngorms, the Crampians, and E. Ross. Very tame.

**Doukhobors.** *See* J12.

**Drachm (or Drachma),** an ancient Greek silver coin and weight. One drachma was equivalent to six obols. The word has survived as the name of a weight: Avoirdupois, one-sixteenth part of an ounce: Apothecaries' Weight, one-eighth part of an ounce.

**Drag.** Term used in mechanics for resistance offered by a fluid to the passage of a body moving through it. When speed of sound is reached drag increases abruptly. The lift/drag ratio gives the aeroplane designer his measure of aerodynamic efficiency.

**Dragon,** a fabulous monster common to folk-lore in most countries; generally represented as a winged reptile, with fiery eyes and breath of flame. A dragon guarded the garden of the Hesperides; in the New Testament there is mention of the "dragon, that old serpent, which is the devil"; St. George, England's patron saint, is supposed to have overcome the dragon; mediaeval legend abounds in dragons; in heraldry the dragon has also a conspicuous place; and in China it was the imperial emblem.

**Dragonade,** the term given to the series of persecutions of Huguenots in France in the reign of Louis XIV., just before and after the revocation of the edict of Nantes, dragoons being chiefly employed in the work. Since then the term has been used in reference to any onslaught on the people by soldiers.

**Dragonet,** the name of the fish of the *Callionymus* genus, beautifully coloured, and about a foot in length. They are common on the British coast and in the Mediterranean.

**Dragon Fly,** the common name of a well-known order of insects having two pairs of membraneous wings, and often of very brilliant colours. They are swift of flight and may be seen hovering over sheets of water in the sunshine all through the summer. Their chief food is mosquitoes.

**Dragon's Blood,** a dark-red resinous substance obtained from the fruit of a Malay palm, and possessing medicinal virtues. In a special technique used for making line blocks in printing, dragon's blood is used.

**Drama.** *See* M32; Contemporary Theatre, I1–34.

**Drawbridge,** a bridge that can be lifted up so that no passage can be made across it. It was a usual feature of a fortified castle in the Middle Ages, and was raised or lowered by chains and levers. It spanned the fosse, and on the approach of an attacking party was raised and formed a special barricade to the gate. Modern drawbridges are such as are raised to allow of the passage of boats up and down a river or estuary. The Tower Bridge is a famous London bridge of this type.

**Drongo.** The King Crow or Indian Black Drongo is frequently seen in India perched on branches or telegraph wires, darting suddenly to catch insects and to attack crows and hawks. Other members of the family are found in Asia, Africa, and Australia. Its plumage is black with steel-blue gloss.

**Drosophila** *or* **Fruit Fly.** More has been learnt by geneticists from breeding experiments with this insect than with any other.

**Dross,** the name generally applied to the refuse of molten metal, composed of slag, scales, and cinders.

**Drought,** a period of dry weather, is a normal and recurring condition in many warm climates, and is frequently provided against by irrigation. In the British Isles really long rainless spells are somewhat rare, and an " absolute drought " is defined officially as a period of at least fifteen days on each of which the rainfall is less than $\frac{1}{100}$ inch. The summer of 1959 was wholly without precedent in all parts of Britain for lack of rainfall, abundant sunshine, and warm weather. In South Yorkshire an absolute drought lasted 59 days, the longest period in British records.

**Drupe** is the scientific term for stone fruit. The stone forms the inner part (endocarp) of the fruit, and encloses a seed or kernel which is liberated after the fleshy part (pericarp) has rotted.

**Dry-rot,** the term was first used about 1775 to describe the fungal decay of timber in buildings. Creosote distilled from coal tar is the standard material for preservation of timber, and pentachlorophenol and copper naphthenate are two compounds now extensively used. Dry wood always escapes dry-rot. Chief fungi causing dry-rot are *Merulius* and *Poria.*

**Duck,** water bird smaller than the related goose and swan, which together form the family Antidae. Duck refers to the female, drake to the male. The duck family falls into two separate groups: the river or freshwater (surface feeding) ducks, such as the mallard, pintail, wigeon, shoveler, mandarin, teal, garganey; and the sea (diving) ducks, such as the goldeneye, pochard, scoter, eider, and the fish-eating mergansers or " sawbills." The ancestor of all domestic breeds, with the exception of the muscovy, is the mallard.

**Duck-bill,** *Ornithorhynchus anatinus,* also duckbilled platypus, a fur-covered, egg-laying, nestbuilding mammal inhabiting Australia and Tasmania. It has webbed feet and a muzzle like a duck's bill and is about 20 in. long.

**Ductility** is a property possessed by most metals which renders them capable of being stretched without breaking. Gold is the most, and lead the least ductile of metals, the order being gold, silver, platinum, iron, copper, palladium, aluminium, zinc, tin, lead. In animated nature the spider and the silkworm produce secretions of notable ductility.

**Dugong.** A marine mammal belonging to the order Sirenia (sea-cows). Inhabits Red Sea and Indian Ocean; also found as far East as the Philippines and Australia. Lives on sea-weed. Related to the Manatee.

**Duke,** the highest rank in the British peerage next to that of a royal prince. Edward, the Black Prince, eldest son of Edward III., who died before his father, was the first English duke, being created Duke of Cornwall in 1337. Since then all Princes of Wales have held that title.

**Dukeries,** a range of English woodland and park country, mainly in Nottinghamshire, comprising the adjacent demesnes of several English dukes and nobles. The Dukeries include Sherwood Forest and the estates of Welbeck Abbey, Clumber Park, Worksop Manor, and Thoresby Hall.

**Dunes.** Sand dunes are elliptical or crescent-shaped mounds of loose sand produced by wind action. The dune has a gentle slope on windward side; a steep slope on the leeward side.

**Dunlin,** very common small wading-bird of the Sandpiper family nesting in Britain. Its range extends to other areas where it also breeds.

**Dunmow Flitch,** a custom which originated in the parish of Little Dunmow, Essex, in the reign of Henry III., which was that the husband who was prepared to swear before the prior, convent, and townsfolk of Dunmow that he had not repented of marriage or quarrelled with his wife for a year and a day, should be rewarded with the gift of a flitch of bacon. The custom has frequently been revived.

**Dunnock** (*Prunella modularis*), a small bird of rich brown and dark grey plumage common in gardens and hedgerows. Sings a cheerful song all the year round. Called hedge-sparrow in southern England. Another member of the same family, the larger Alpine Accentor (*Prunella collaris*), is found on rocky mountain slopes of Europe and Asia.

**Duodecimo,** a sheet of paper folded into twelve leaves, written " 12mo."

**Durbar,** a term used in India from the Persian word *darbár* meaning " court " or " audience." It may be either a council for administering affairs of state, or a purely ceremonial gathering. The word was applied to great ceremonial gatherings like Lord Lytton's durbar for the proclamation of the Queen-Empress in 1877 and the Delhi durbar of 1911.

**Dust,** solid particles of matter floating in the atmosphere, produced chiefly by volcanic eruptions, sand-storms in desert regions, and industrial and domestic smoke. When the island of Krakatoa erupted in 1883, more than 1 cubic mile of dust was thrown into the air and carried three times round the earth by the explosion wave. The particles in dust-storms are much finer than those in sand-storms and are swept up to far greater heights. The local whirlwinds which form over loose dry soils are termed dust-devils.

**Dyke.** A wall-like intrusion of igneous rock which cuts across the bedding or other layered structure of the country rock; the word also signifies in alternative usage, a sea-wall and an open drain.

**Dynamite,** a powerful explosive whose chief element is nitro-glycerine. It was discovered by Nobel in 1867, who absorbed nitro-glycerine in kieselguhr; has a disruptive force of about eight times that of gunpowder.

**Dynamo.** Machine for transforming mechanical energy into electrical energy. Depends on principle of electromagnetic induction whereby a current is produced in a conductor (*e.g.*, copper wire) traversing a magnetic field. The two essential parts of a dynamo are the conductors or *armature* and the *field magnets*.

**Dynasty,** a succession of monarchs of the same family, as the Carlovingian dynasty, the Bourbon dynasty, the Plantagenet dynasty, etc.

# E

**Eagle,** large bird of prey with huge hooked bill, related to the buzzard, kite, hawk, harrier, falcon, and vulture, together forming the family Falconidae. There are many species to be found throughout the world, the Golden, Imperial, Tawny, Spotted, and Lesser Spotted being found in Europe. The Golden Eagle, a magnificent-looking bird, nests in the Scottish Highlands, and the White-tailed Sea Eagle, which used to breed in Britain, is now only an occasional visitor. The eagle has been the symbol of royal power since the earliest times, and the American or Bald Eagle is the emblem of the United States.

**Earl,** a British title of nobility of the third rank, duke and marquis coming first and second. The title dates from Saxon times, and until 1337 ranked highest in our peerage.

**Earl-Marshal,** in England ranks as the eighth of the great officers of state, is head of the College of Arms, attends the sovereign in opening and closing the session of Parliament, arranges state processions (especially coronations) and assists in introducing newly created peers in the House of Lords. The office is hereditary in the family of the Dukes of Norfolk.

**Earth,** our habitable globe, is the third of the planets of the solar system in order from the sun, and on an average throughout the year takes 24 hours to turn completely round relative to the sun, the whole earth revolving round the sun in a slightly elliptical orbit once in a year of 365·2564 days. The mean distance of the earth from the sun is 93,004,000 miles. The shape of the earth is that of an oblate spheroid, its equatorial and polar axes measuring 7,926 miles and 7,900 miles respectively. Earth satellite studies have shown that it is also slightly pear-shaped, with the stalk towards the north pole. The scale of this effect is such that the south pole is 50 ft. nearer the centre of the earth than the north pole. The crust consists of an outer layer of surface soil of varying thickness, beneath which there is a mass of hard rock several miles deep, the percentage (by weight) of the principal elements present being oxygen 47, silicon 28, aluminium 8, sodium and potassium 5, iron 4·5, calcium 3·5, magnesium 2·2, titanium 0·5, hydrogen 0·2, carbon 0·2, phosphorus and sulphur 0·2. Mass of the earth is estimated to be 6,000 million million million tons. Two-thirds of the earth's surface is covered with water. It has only one satellite, the moon. The earth receives more light from the sun in 13 seconds than it does from the moon in one year. Weather changes are independent of the moon. A recent estimate of the age of the earth's crust is 5,000 million years. Recent discoveries suggest that the earth is embedded in the atmosphere of the sun and that some of the heat that reaches us from the sun gets here by direct conduction through interplanetary space. *See* F8-9.

**Earthquake,** a sudden violent disturbance of the earth's crust; the region of the surface immediately above the " focus," or source where the earthquake originates, is termed the " epicentre." On account of their destructive power earthquakes have attracted attention from the earliest times, but accurate study dates only from the last century and the development of a world-wide network of recording stations from the present one. The majority of severe earthquakes result from fractures, usually along existing faults, in underlying rock strata subjected to great strains, the shearing movement sometimes extending to the surface. These dislocations set up vibrations which are propagated as waves throughout the bulk of the earth or round the crust. Frequently the main shock is followed by a series of smaller after-shocks. Minor local earthquakes may be attributed to the effects of volcanic activity, but most of the larger ones originate in non-volcanic regions along well-marked lines of weakness in the earth's crust. Generally the ground is felt to tremble, undergoing oscillations which may gradually or suddenly increase to a maximum and accompanied by sounds. Where there is movement of the sea-bed a tidal wave may result. One of the greatest of historic times was that which destroyed and flooded Lisbon in 1755. Among the notable shocks of the present century rank those of San Francisco (1906), Messina, Italy (1908), China (1920), Japan (1923). Napier, New Zealand (1931), N.E. Assam (1950), Ionian Is. (1953), Agadir, Morocco (1960), Chile (1960), Iran (1962), Yugoslavia (1963), E. Turkey (1966), W. Sicily (1968).

**Earthworm**, of which there are several species, has a cylindrical body, tapering at both ends, and segmented into rings. It moves by contraction of its rings, aided by retractive bristles; is eyeless, but has a mouth, gullet, and stomach. Earthworms exist in immense numbers, and perform an important part in the scheme of nature by loosening the soil and rendering it more amenable to tillage. They also form a valuable food for birds and many mammals, and are unequalled as bait for certain kinds of fish.

**Earwig**, a genus of insects possessing two pairs of wings and anal forceps. It is nocturnal living on vegetable matter, and hides by day under stones or in flowers, e.g., dahlias. The old belief that it deliberately creeps into people's ears is altogether unfounded. See T30(2).

**Easter**, the annual Christian festival in commemoration of the resurrection of Christ, the English name being derived from Eostre, goddess of Spring. The date cannot fall earlier than March 22 nor later than April 25. Many disputes arose among the early Christians as to the proper time to celebrate this day which governs all other movable feasts. It was eventually ruled at the Council of Nicaea in 325 that Easter Day should be the first Sunday after the full moon following the vernal equinox. If this happens to be a Sunday, then Easter Day is the Sunday after. It should be remembered, however, that this moon is a hypothetical moon of the ecclesiastical calendar, quite imaginary, and generally one or two days later than the real moon we see in the heavens. In fact the reverend fathers at Nicaea did us a bad turn in having anything to do with the moon but then they had no Astronomer Royal to advise them of the complications. See also N25.

**Eastern Question**, a term formerly applied to the problems arising from the instability of the Mohammedan power of Turkey and its relations with the other nations of Europe. Later connected with other problems of the Near East, such as the possession of Constantinople and the position of the Balkan states.

**East India Company** was incorporated by Elizabeth in 1600. In 1613 the Company set up a factory at Surat, India, and in 1662 Bombay came under the Company's influence and developed into an important trading port. Dupleix wanted to establish French power in India and a struggle for supremacy took place. Clive gained the victory for England and thenceforward British dominion in India remained undisputed except by native princes. In 1772 Warren Hastings was appointed the first Governor-General and in 1784 Pitt's India Act established a Board of Control for the India Company. A great increase of trade resulted, and this rule continued down to 1858, when, as a result of the mutiny, the Crown assumed the sovereignty. With the passing of the Indian Independence Act of 1947, British dominion ended and India was handed back to the Indians.

**Eau-de-Cologne**, a popular distilled perfume first manufactured at Cologne in the 18th cent. by Johann Maria Farina, an Italian, and since made in large quantities in Cologne and elsewhere.

**Ebony**, a name applied to various hard black woods, the best of which are grown in Mauritius and Ceylon. There are also Indian and American varieties. Only the inner portions, the heartwood, of the trees are of the necessary hardness and blackness. Ebony is largely used in ornamental cabinet work, for piano keys, canes, etc.

**Ecce Homo** (" Behold the Man! "), used in reference to the pictures and sculptures representing Christ crowned with thorns.

**Ecclesiastical Courts**, courts for administering ecclesiastical law and maintaining the discipline of the Church of England. Introduced by the Normans. Originally they had jurisdiction over both clergy and laity. See also D24(1).

**Eclipse**, an obscuration of the light of the sun, moon, or other heavenly body by the passing of another body either between it and the eye or between it and the source of its light. The sun is eclipsed by the moon intervening between it and the earth; the moon by the earth passing between it and the sun. Total eclipses of the sun have occurred over parts of the British Isles in the years 1424, 1433, 1598, 1652, 1715, 1724, 1927, 1954 (visible from the Shetland Is.), and the next will be seen only from near Land's End on Aug. 11, 1999.

**Ecliptic** is the sun's apparent path in the sky: the great circle described by the sun from west to east in the course of a year. The sun is exactly on the equator on approx. March 21 and Sept. 23, and the points where the celestial equator and ecliptic intersect on these days are called the equinoctial points. On approx. June 21 and Dec. 22 the sun reaches its greatest and least midday elevation and its greatest distance north and south of the equator, and the points on the ecliptic on these days are called the solstices (see Seasons, N25). These four points are equidistant from each other by 90°. The equinoctial points are not fixed. The angle of inclination of the ecliptic to the equator is called the obliquity of the ecliptic, which is also variable, being influenced by the gravitational action of the other planets on the earth. At present the angle is 23½°.

**Ecumenical Council**, a general council of the Christian Church summoned when important questions of Church doctrine and policy are to be decided. The early councils were predominantly Greek and convoked by the emperor. Those summoned by the pope when they meet at the Lateran Palace in Rome are called Lateran Councils; others have met at Constance, Florence, Trent, and the Vatican. Their decisions are not binding on the rest of Christendom. Only 21 Ecumenical Councils have been held in the history of Christendom. The first was held at Nicaea in 325 when the mystery of the Trinity was defined. The 21st (known as the 2nd Vatican Council), convened by Pope John, opened in Oct. 1962 in St. Peter's Rome, and ended in Dec. 1965. Two of the principal themes were the reunion of all Christians with the Church of Rome and the Church's place in the modern world. At the last session of the Council the Pope announced his decision to establish for the first time an international synod of bishops in Rome for consultation and collaboration in the government of the Roman Church. This Senate of Bishops will provide the balancing factor alongside the Curia, which represents the Papacy and not the episcopacy.

**Edda**, the name given to two important collections of early Icelandic literature—the Elder or Poetic Edda, poems handed down from the 9th and 10th cent., probably Norwegian in origin, and the Younger or Prose Edda of Snorri Sturluson compiled about 1230. They treat of mythical and religious legends of an early Scandinavian civilisation.

**Eddystone Lighthouse**, 13 miles south of Plymouth, is one of the most isolated in the world. The tower is 168 ft. high, and its light can be seen for 17½ miles. The present structure is the fourth that has occupied this dangerous position. The first was of wood, completed by Winstanley in 1698, but it was destroyed by storm in 1703. In 1708 a second and stronger lighthouse was built by Rudyerd. This lasted until 1755, when it was destroyed by fire. Smeaton built the third lighthouse of granite and this withstood storm and tempest for over a hundred years, 1759–1881. The present lighthouse, also of granite, was built 1879–81 on a nearby rock by Sir James Douglass.

**Edelweiss**, a white perennial flower of the daisy order, common in Alpine regions.

**Education, History of**. See J13.

**Eels**, edible fishes of the order Apodes, with snakelike body covered with minute scales embedded in the skin. The common or freshwater eel Anguilla anguilla is found in the Atlantic coastal areas of N. America and Europe and in the Mediterranean, and breeds S.E. of Bermuda. The electric eel of S. America is a variety of great interest, being able to cause electric shocks.

**Egg-plant** or **Aubergine**, a plant cultivated for its ovate fruit, varying in colour from dark purple to white.

**Egret**, a slender, graceful bird of the heron family, of pure white plumage, famed for its beautiful silky plumes (aigrettes), which appear in the

**L36**

breeding season, and for which it was ruthlessly hunted and would have been exterminated had not international action been taken to protect it. The Little Egret with black bill, black legs, and yellow feet breeds in Mediterranean lands.

**Egyptian Vulture** is smaller than other vultures. Found in S. Europe, frequents native villages and scavanges for offal.

**Eider,** a large diving duck, found along the rocky coasts of northern latitudes, well known for the beautifully warm soft down, called " eider down," which the female bird plucks from her breast to line her nest. In Norway and Iceland the haunts of the eider are preserved and the birds protected by law on account of the much prized " eider down," which is collected from the nests just before the breeding season. " Eider down " is so elastic that a pound or two of it will fill an ordinary bed covering.

**Eiffel Tower,** built by the French engineer Alexandre Gustave Eiffel (1832–1923) for the Paris Exhibition of 1889. The tower which is made of iron is 985 ft. high and weighs about 7,000 tons.

**Eisteddfod** (a sitting) was originally a congress of Welsh bards and minstrels, and dates from before the 12th cent. These assemblies, discontinued for a long period, were resumed in 1819, and have been held yearly since, each lasting three or four days. Their object is to foster the Welsh patriotic spirit; they are devoted to orations and competitions in poetry, singing, and harp-playing, prizes being awarded to the successful contestants.

**Eland,** largest species of antelope, native of Africa; large pointed horns, stands 5 feet high at the withers, and weighs several hundred pounds.

**Elder,** small trees of the *Sambucus* genus, with pinnate leaves, and clusters of white flowers and, later, small purplish-black berries. The black elder, the best known, is common in most parts of Europe, and thrives in Britain. A wine is made from its berries.

**El Dorado,** a " golden land," was an idea much favoured in the days of the early Spanish explorers. It was believed that somewhere on the South American continent there was a country abounding in gold and precious stones. Many expeditions were fitted out to discover it. Sir Walter Raleigh also went forth on this illusive quest. The term is still used in regard to any place of rich promise.

**Electret,** a piece of solid matter which retains a permanent electric polarisation analogous to the magnetic polarisation of a permanent magnet. There are various recipes for making them; carnauba wax is a common constituent.

**Electricity.** *See* F13, *also* Energy Conversion.

**Electric Light** is produced in several ways, commonly by causing a tungsten wire to heat up to incandescence by passing a current through it. Current may also be forced through ionised gases, causing them to glow. Such discharges include neon lights, sodium and mercuryvapour street-lamps, and various intense electric arcs used for technical purposes. In fluorescent lights an electric discharge causes ultra-violet (invisible) light, which then excites luminosity in certain chemical substances called luminescent materials. Other forms of electric lighting are being investigated.

**Electric Telegraph** may be said to date from 1836, when Sir Charles Wheatstone and his co-inventor Cooke introduced their Single-Needle instrument, which was soon followed by the Double-Needle apparatus. Morse, in 1837, invented his famous recording instrument. The first electric cable was between Dover and France, and was laid in 1850. The first Atlantic cable was laid in 1858, and the second in 1866. It was in 1899 that the first Marconi wireless telegraph messages were sent between England and France.

**Electrolysis** is the condition established when an electric current passes through a conducting substance, between electrodes, resulting in decomposition and separation into constituents. Water thus becomes decomposed into hydrogen and oxygen.

**Electromagnetic waves.** *See* F13.

**Electrometer,** an instrument for measuring differences of electrical potential. The moving part, perhaps a needle, is affected by electrostatic forces and no current flows through the instrument. High sensitivity can be obtained.

**Electron.** *See* F10, 14.

**Electron Microscope.** A microscope in which beams of electrons are focused by magnetic lenses in a manner analogous to the focusing of light beams in the ordinary optical microscope. Modern electron microscopes have very high resolving power and can magnify up to 1,500,000 times, making it possible to explore the cell and the virus. A development of the electron microscope is the scanning electron microscope (stereoscan), recently developed at Cambridge, which can examine an essentially thick object, giving a very large depth of focus. *See* F27(2).

**Electronvolt,** unit of energy used in nuclear physics. It is the amount of energy required to move one electronic charge through a potential difference of one volt. It is very small— $1·6 \times 10^{-12}$ ergs—and therefore suited to atomic physics. 1 MeV = a million electronvolts and this larger unit is used in nuclear energy physics.

**Electronics.** The science which deals with the behaviour and control of free electrons. It started with the discovery of the electron by Sir J. J. Thomson in 1897. The practical applications, constituting electronic engineering, have given us radio, radar, photo-electric cells, cathode-ray oscillographs, electron microscopes, television. Nowadays electronics uses devices like transistors such that the electrons move inside solid matter instead of *in vacuo.* This is sometimes referred to as " solid state electronics."

**Electrophorus,** a simple device for producing static electricity, consisting of a smooth disc of resin or ebonite mounted on a metal base and with a metal cover carrying an insulated handle. The disc is first electrified (negatively) by rubbing it with a dry catskin or flannel and the cover replaced, the upper surface receiving a positive charge and the lower a negative. On lifting off the cover, after having touched it with the finger, the negative charge leaks away to earth and the positive charge is isolated on the cover. The action may be repeated a number of times before it is necessary to replenish the original charge on the disc. Of historical interest only.

**Elements.** In chemistry, an element is a substance in the simplest form to which it has been reduced. Ninety elements are found naturally on the earth, one is observed spectroscopically in the stars, and a further twelve have been made artificially. Between them these elements can appear in some 1,200 different isotopes, of which 317 occur in Nature. (There are 274 stable isotopes among 81 stable elements.) *See* F20, N34.

**Elephant,** a proboscidian mammal of which only two species survive—the Asiatic, in India, and the African elephant. No other animals possess a trunk. Both males and females have large ivory tusks, of considerable commercial value. The Indian elephant is usually about 9 ft. high and weighs about 3 tons; African elephants are larger, weigh about 6 tons, and are usually much fiercer. Several fossil elephants of still larger bulk have been discovered, including the mammoth and the mastodon. The Indian elephant is domesticated and used as a beast of burden, and may live 70 years.

**Eleusinian Mysteries,** festivals common throughout ancient Greece, agricultural in their symbolism.

**Elgin Marbles,** a collection of ancient Greek sculptures and architectural fragments got together by the 7th Earl of Elgin and brought to England between 1802 and 1812. These celebrated treasures had originally formed part of the Parthenon at Athens, and were probably carved by pupils of the sculptor Phidias. Lord Elgin expended over £70,000 upon them, and they were purchased for £35,000 for the British Museum, where they can now be seen displayed.

**Elk,** the largest animal of the deer family, possessing enormous antlers, and standing, when mature, about seven feet high. The American moose is of the same family.

**Elm,** a stately, wide-spreading tree having some 20 species spread over north-temperate regions, several of which are native and peculiar to Britain. The grandest of the field elms is the English elm, *Ulmus procera,* which may reach a height of 140 ft. and a girth of 25 ft. The wych elm, *U. glabra*, or Scots elm, is a valuable hardwood and used in boat-building.

Elzevir, the name of a celebrated family of Dutch printers, who produced editions of Latin, French, and German classics, which were highly valued for their beauty of type and accuracy of printing. They flourished in the 17th cent.

Embalming, the process by which dead bodies are preserved from decay by means of spices and drugs. The art reached perfection in ancient Egypt, as the mummies which still exist so powerfully testify. In modern times many experiments in embalming have been tried, with various degrees of success.

Ember-days are set apart for fasting and prayer in the Western Church, at the periods appointed for ordination, viz., the Wednesday, Friday, and Saturday after the first Sunday in Lent, Whit-Sunday, Sept. 14 (Holy Cross Day), and Dec. 13 (St. Lucia's Day). They are of very ancient origin.

Embossing, the art of stamping in relief letters or designs upon pliant substances.

Embryology, that branch of biology which deals with embryos, tracing their development from fertilisation of the germ or seed to birth.

Emerald. The rich green variety of beryl (beryllium aluminium silicate). The colour is due to the presence of chromium oxide.

Emery, a granular substance of the corundum order, generally mixed with other metallic substances, and used in a powdered state for polishing and grinding purposes. Emery is mined in Asia Minor and the Grecian archipelago.

Enamel, a vitrified substance applied as a coating to pottery and porcelain. The art was practised by the Assyrians and Egyptians, and was introduced into Europe by way of Greece. Enamels are all either of the transparent or opaque kind, and are susceptible to an immense variety of colouring, according to the metallic oxides introduced.

Encaenia, a festival commemorating a dedication; at Oxford University the annual commemoration of benefactors, accompanied by the conferring of honorary degrees, is held in June.

Encyclical Letters, a term used in reference to letters addressed by the Pope to his bishops upon matters of doctrine or discipline.

Encyclopaedists, a term first applied to the eminent writers who collaborated in the French *Encyclopédie* (1751–65). They included Diderot, D'Alembert, Voltaire, Helvetius; their writings generally were sceptical as to religion, destructive as to politics, and had great influence in popularising the social ideas which afterwards resulted in the French Revolution.

Energy. One of the most fundamental concepts of science. A body in motion possesses *kinetic energy* as a result of the *work* done by the forces creating the motion. But a force which does work to stretch a spring does not create motion. Instead, the work is stored up in the spring and is one example of *potential energy*. A raised body also possesses potential energy which turns into kinetic when the body falls. The *heat energy* contained in a body is the sum of the kinetic and potential energy of the constituent atoms which are vibrating all the time. Heat and motion are obtainable from electrical, magnetic, chemical, atomic, and other sources, and physicists therefore define corresponding forms of energy. The vital point is that all forms of energy are transferable into one another *without loss or gain*. This is the Law of Conservation of Energy. It is one of the most fundamental laws of science, and its general validity is the reason why energy is an important idea. Since Einstein, it has been recognised that mass also is interchangeable with energy. See F15, *also* Nuclear Energy.

Energy Conversion. For practical purposes it is frequently necessary to change energy from one into another of its many forms; indeed almost every activity does this in one way or another. The primary sources of energy are the sun, uranium and other elements from which nuclear energy can be drawn, and the tides. The sun is not much used *directly* because its heat is intermittent and not very intense, but solar cookers and refrigerators have been invented and solar batteries (*q.v.*) are used in spacecraft. The sun can be used *indirectly* because it has produced, *via* living processes, fossil fuels like coal and oil and still continues to generate winds, rain, and rivers and hence hydroelectric and wind power. Commonly both fossil fuels and the energy of river or tidal waters are converted into electricity. Wind-mill type electricity generators are also quite common. The bulk of electricity production is a two-stage process: first fossil or nuclear fuel is used to create heat (*see* Nuclear Reactors); then the heat is used to raise steam and drive generators. Efforts are being made to convert heat into electricity more directly, *e.g.*, by using thermoelectric or thermionic effects (*q.v.*), but these have not been used for large-scale production. Once electrical energy is available, factories can make chemical batteries in great numbers and these can then be used as portable energy sources, as can petrol and other refined forms of fossil fuel. See Battery, Fuel Cell.

English Language. *See* M36.

Engraving is the art of cutting or otherwise forming designs of pictures on wood, stone, or metal surfaces for reproduction by some method of printing. Wood-engraving was the earliest in the field, dating from the 15th cent. Later, engraving on steel and copper plates was introduced, and mezzotint, lithography, stipple, aquatint, etc. With the development of photography, and an increased knowledge of the use of acids, many readier methods of engraving were adopted, and now wood-engraving, which was formerly resorted to for all general engraving purposes, is comparatively little used. What is styled "process" engraving is the most utilised.

Ensilage, a method of storing and preserving fodder, vegetables, etc., in pits dug in the ground and excluded from air or light. The system was practised in ancient Rome and revived in England in the 19th cent.

Entablature, that portion of a building which surmounts the columns and extends to the roof of the tympana of the pediments; it comprises the architrave, the frieze, and the cornice.

Entomology is the study of insects. *See* Insects.

Entrepreneur. An entrepreneur, or undertaker, is a firm which brings together the factors of production needed for producing goods or services, undertaking the risks and uncertainties involved—though it may transfer some of them by insurance or by other methods. The entrepreneur may be either an individual or a company or corporation, private or public.

Enzymes. Organic catalysts which accelerate chemical processes occurring in living organisms. There are a large number present in the cell, and most have a high degree of specificity. Enzyme mechanisms are the key to basic biological processes. See F25(1), 30(1).

Epaulette, a shoulder badge fringed with cord, worn by English army officers until 1855; now confined to naval officers, and varying in form and richness according to the rank of the wearers.

Ephemeroptera *or* May-flies, an order of insects. In the larval condition they exist from two to three years aquatically, but no sooner do they arrive at maturity than their lives are hurried to a close. They rise up in pyramids on warm summer nights, take no food, propagate, and perish. The Latin name expresses the fact that the adults have an ephemeral existence.

Ephod, a vestment worn by a Jewish high priest, and sometimes by priests of lower rank. In olden times it was of rich texture and set with gems.

Epiphany, a church festival celebrated on January 6, Twelfth Day.

Equator, the imaginary great circle of the earth, every point of which is 90 degrees from the earth's poles, and dividing the northern from the southern hemisphere. It is from this circle that the latitude of places north and south is reckoned. The celestial equator is the circle in which the plane of the earth's equator meets the celestial sphere (the imaginary sphere, in which the observer is at the centre, used for representing the apparent positions of the heavenly bodies).

Equinox, the time when the sun crosses the plane of the earth's equator, making day and night of equal length. *See* N25.

Eras are distinctive periods of time associated

with some remarkable historical event or personage. *The Christian era* is computed according to a 6th-cent. reckoning to begin with Jesus's birth, A.D. 1. The date is placed some years too late. Scholars now believe that Jesus was born *c.* 6 B.C. The *Jewish era* dates from 3761 B.C.; the *Julian era* from the alteration of the calendar by Julius Caesar, 45 B.C.; the *Mohammedan era* from the date of the *Hejira*, or the flight of Mohammed from Mecca to Medina, which is A.D. 622, July 16, in the Gregorian Calendar.

**Erbium,** belongs to the group of rare-earth metals discovered by Mosander in 1842.

**Erg,** the unit of work and energy in the centimetre-gram-second system; the energy involved when a force of 1 dyne moves its point of application through a distance of 1 cm.

**Erl-King,** a forest fiend of German mythology, who lured children from their homes and carried them off. In Goethe's ballad the "Erlkönig" it is a traveller's child who is lured to destruction.

**Ermine.** *See* Stoat.

**Ernie,** the name given to the "electronic random number indicator equipment", the electronic machine which selected the prizewinning numbers in the first Premium Bond draw held June 1–2, 1957.

**Eros.** This asteroid is 15–20 miles in diameter. It comes closer to the earth than any other member of the solar system with the exception of the moon and several very small asteroids. Determination of solar parallax based on observations of Eros in 1930–31 yielded the most accurate estimate of the distance of the sun from the earth (93,004,000 miles).

**Erse,** a term used by Lowland Scottish, and English writers for the Gaelic language spoken in the Highlands of Scotland. Sometimes erroneously applied to Irish, the Gaelic language as spoken in Ireland and revived as an official language in recent times. Dr. Johnson, Sir Walter Scott, and other writers used "Erse" to signify Scottish Gaelic. The language of the Scottish Lowlands (that used by Robert Burns) is related to the English language and not to Gaelic and is variously termed Scots, Braid Scots, the Doric, the Scottish vernacular, and, fashionably of late, Lallans.

**Escutcheon,** a shield-shaped surface called a field, upon which a man's armorial bearings are represented. A woman's is lozenge-shaped.

**Esparto Grass** grows in great abundance in Spain and North Africa, and the pulp is largely used for paper-making as well as for other purposes.

**Esperanto,** an artificial international language created by L. Zamenhof of Warsaw and first published in 1887. It does not seek to replace national languages but to serve as a second language for international communication. It is based on the internationality of many words in the principal modern languages, and is entirely phonetic in spelling and pronunciation.

**Esquire,** formerly a title applied to a young man of noble birth who attended on a knight and carried his shield. The title ranked next below that of knight and was applied to the eldest sons of knights and the younger sons of peers. Later it became a courtesy title and given to any man as a mark of respect.

**Essential Oils** are oils derived from plants by distillation or expression, and much used in perfumery as well as to some extent in medicine.

**Estate Duty** is the duty payable upon the value of all property passing on the death of any person. In his 1969 Budget the Chancellor proposed to raise the exemption limit to £10,000 and to recast the estate duty scales, introducing a "slice" system under which duty is charged at increasing rates on successive slices of the estate. The changes affect deaths occurring after 15 April 1969. As from 19 March 1968 gifts made by deceased during his life are liable to duty if made within seven years before death, subject to graduation of the charge in the case of gifts made more than four years before death. Gifted insurance policies and other gifts in which the deceased never had an interest are subject to aggregation with other property chargeable. Gifts made for charitable purposes are liable to duty if made within one year before death. There are also exemptions in respect of gifts made in consideration of marriage (parties to the marriage and their issue) and of buildings and land of special interest bequeathed to non-profit-making bodies for preservation. Gifts not exceeding £100 in value (or in certain circumstances £500) also exempt.

**Estates of the Realm** in Great Britain are the Lords Spiritual, the Lords Temporal, and the Commons. They are the great classes invested with distinct political powers, and whose concurrence is necessary to legislation.

**Esters.** Organic chemicals formed by combining an alcohol with an acid. They have a pleasant smell, and occur naturally in plants as the scent of flowers. Manufactured for use in the perfumery industry, and as flavourings in food. Some esters are used as solvents, notably amyl-acetate ("pear drops") in quick-drying paints. The polymeric fibre "Terylene" consists of chains of molecules containing many ester groups, formed by reacting an alcohol having two alcoholic (OH) groups with an acid having two acid (COOH) groups.

**Etching,** a process of engraving, on copper usually, the design being drawn with a steel needle, and the lines produced by the action of an acid or mordant.

**Ether,** in chemistry, is a volatile inflammable liquid composed of carbon, hydrogen, and oxygen. It is a valuable anaesthetic obtained by heating alcohol with sulphuric acid. In physics, in the 19th cent., all space was supposed to be filled with a substance called ether, the chief property of which was to carry light waves, *i.e.*, light was supposed to be waves in this all-pervading medium known as the ether. Speculation and experiment concerned with the ether were very fruitful in advancing physics. Ultimately the attempts by Michelson and Morley to detect the motion of the earth through the ether were unsuccessful in this respect but profoundly successful in stimulating the theory of relativity. The ether concept has now been abandoned. *See also* **F15(1)**

**Ethylene.** A gas compounded of carbon and hydrogen, it is related to acetylene and ethane. Industrially it is obtained as a by-product in petroleum refining. It has wide uses as a starting material in the industrial manufacture of intermediates, especially alcohol. Its most important application is in the production of polythene (poly-ethylene). *See* Catalyst.

**Etruscans,** people believed to have come from Asia Minor who colonised Italy about 900 B.C., settled in what is now Tuscany and part of Umbria, reached the height of their civilisation about 500 B.C., and were ultimately absorbed by the Romans. They were skilled technicians in bronze, silver, and goldwork, and excelled in the art of granular decoration.

**Etymology** treats of the science and structure of words, including classification and derivation.

**Eucalyptus.** This genus includes 300 species of evergreen, leathery-leaved trees native to Australia. The oils yielded by different species vary a great deal in their scent and other properties and are chiefly used in pharmacy and perfumery; about 30 species produce oils suitable for medicinal purposes. Various species produce timber.

**Europium,** element discovered by Demarcay in 1906. A member of the rare-earth metal group.

**Evaporation** is the process by which a solid or liquid is resolved into vapour by heat. The opposite process is condensation. Wherever a liquid or solid surface is exposed, evaporation takes place into the space above. If the vapour is continually removed the solid or liquid vanishes into vapour; the higher the temperature the quicker the process. If the vapour is confined, then it collects, getting more concentrated until as many atoms of vapour are condensing as are evaporating. The vapour is then said to be saturated. Evaporation of water from sea, soil, plants, skin, etc., is continuously in progress, so it is a process of fundamental importance to meteorology, botany, physiology, industry, not to speak of human comfort and homely activities such as laundry.

**Everest Expeditions.** For many years after Mt. Everest had been shown to be the highest mountain in the world, political conditions in Nepal, lying south of the summit, and in Tibet, to the north, prevented mountaineers from attempting an ascent. At last in 1921 the Tibetan authorities gave permission, and the first expedition, organised, as were all subsequent British expeditions, by a joint committee of the Royal Geographical Society and the Alpine Club, and led by Col. C. K. Howard-Bury, was sent out. This was primarily a reconnaissance; besides mapping the northern flanks, it found a practicable route up the mountain. By 1939, six further expeditions had climbed on the northern face. Some were baulked by bad weather, others by problems previously little known, such as the effect of high altitudes on the human body and spirit. Nevertheless, notable climbs were accomplished. In 1924, for example, Col. E. F. Norton reached 28,163 ft., and it was on this expedition that G. L. Mallory and Andrew Irvine were seen going well at about the same height. They never returned, however, and what disaster befell them is not known. After the war, political conditions again closed the Tibet route; permission was eventually obtained from the Nepalese Government to make the attempt from the south. In 1951 a reconnaissance expedition under Eric Shipton reached the ice-fall at the exit of the Western Cwm (a high valley lying south-west of the massif), and reported favourably on the prospects for an ascent. The first attempt from this side was made the following year by a Swiss expedition led by Dr. E. Wyss-Dunant, two members of which made an attempt on the summit, but were stopped at approx. 28,200 ft. by the intense cold and the very strong winds. When the British 1953 Expedition, led by Col. (now Brig. Sir) John Hunt, was being organised, stress was laid on three main points: proper acclimatisation of the climbers; use of oxygen for the final stages; and the establishment of very high altitude camps, so that the final assault parties would set out fresh and unencumbered. Great attention was also paid to recent developments in diet, clothing, and equipment. In all these matters the 1953 expedition was able to draw on the accumulated experience of their predecessors. By the end of April, a base camp had been established below the ice-fall, and with the aid of thirty-four Sherpa porters supplies had been carried up into the Western Cwm. The next critical stage was the ascent of the steep head of the cwm, the Lhotse face, with the threat of avalanches always present. By most strenuous efforts, a camp was established on the South Col (25,800 ft.) on May 21. From this camp on May 26, T. D. Bourdillon and R. C. Evans climbed the South Peak of Everest (28,720 ft.), then the highest altitude ever attained. On May 28, Edmund Hillary and the Sherpa leader, Tenzing Norkey, spent the night at the highest camp (27,900 ft.) and on the following day, May 29, climbed to the South Summit, negotiated the difficult final ridge, and reached the summit of Everest—the climax of a long, arduous, and stirring endeavour.

**Evolution,** in the words of Sir Julian Huxley, " a natural process of irreversible change which generates novelty, variety, and increase of organisation." The theory, as laid down by Darwin, is that all existing species, genera, and classes of animals and plants have developed from a few simple forms by processes of change and selection. Up to the time of Darwin a large part of the civilised world believed that life had been created suddenly at the beginning of the world which God had created, according to Archbishop Usher, on 22 Oct. 4004 B.C. The evidence of the rocks, however, has given a more convincing theory of creation, and by studying the fossils preserved in the various layers of the earth's crust the past history of the earth's life has been pieced together. Darwin has been called the Newton of biology. *See* **F43.**

**Excommunication,** exclusion from the rights and privileges of the Church. It is of two kinds—the major, which means a total cutting off, and the minor, which shuts out only from participation in the Eucharist. In mediæval times, major excommunications were often launched against rulers and leaders.

**Exchequer,** which derives its name from the checkered tablecloth on which accounts were calculated in early Norman times, is a term connected with the revenues of the Crown. In former times it had jurisdiction in all revenue matters. The term Exchequer is now applied to the Governmental department which deals with the public revenues, the working head of which is the Chancellor of the Exchequer.

**Existentialism.** *See* **J15.**

**Exploration.** Modern exploration began in the second half of the 15th cent. with the voyages of the great Portuguese and Spanish discoverers. They were followed by sailors of other European nations, who profited from their developments in navigation and from their charts, and in less than one hundred years the coast-lines of much of the Americas, Africa, and south-west Asia had been revealed and the globe circumnavigated. The motives of these early explorers were mixed: they were seeking adventure, trade, plunder, national power, and the conversion of the heathen. Few if any were directly interested in advancing scientific knowledge. But from the reports of their voyages and travels, scholars at home compiled descriptions of the strange new world which stimulated their successors to undertake more systematic enquiries. One of the earliest English expeditions to be despatched for scientific research was that of William Dampier on the *Roebuck,* which was sent out by the Admiralty in 1699 to examine the coasts of North-west Australia. In the 18th cent. British explorers were at work mainly in the Pacific Ocean, with the object of breaking the Spanish monopoly of trade. Capt. James Cook sailed thither in 1769 to observe the first the transit of Venus at Tahiti, and then to search for the alleged great southern continent. On this voyage he discovered and charted much of the coasts of New Zealand and the east coast of Australia. On his second voyage he was the first to sail across the Antarctic Circle, and he showed that the southern continent was much smaller than had been supposed. By 1800 the general outlines of the continents, except for Antarctica were known, and explorers in the 19th cent. were largely engaged in opening up the interiors. In Africa British explorers solved two problems which had puzzled men for centuries: Mungo Park and Richard Lander established the true course of the River Niger, and Sir Richard Burton, J. H. Speke, Sir Samuel Baker, and others revealed the true sources of the Nile. The greatest African explorer of that age was undoubtedly David Livingstone, the missionary, who in three great journeys explored the Zambesi and the region of the Great Lakes, spreading the Gospel, fighting the slave trade, and opening up the interior to settlement and trade. In North America Alexander Mackenzie was the first to cross the main breadth of the continent from sea to sea. In Asia motives were also mixed; men like Charles Doughty, who explored in Arabia, and Sir Francis Younghusband, who journeyed from China to India across the Gobi and the Himalaya, were impelled by a love of adventure and the quest for knowledge, but political considerations were often involved. In recent years, with the main features of the world's surface known, exploration has become more intensive. Teams of scientists go out to study restricted areas in detail. An Antarctic expedition can contribute to our knowledge of world weather, or by biological research into the life history of whales, can help to improve our food supplies. Similarly, expeditions in Africa can help to check the loss of valuable agricultural land through soil erosion, or to develop areas of settlement by schemes for irrigation and power. And there are still great areas to be adequately mapped. All these problems are inter-related, and in solving them the modern explorer can call on many improved techniques and instruments—the aeroplane, the aerial camera, tracked motor vehicles, radio, in fact all the resources of modern science. But the human element is still vital, and for those with the old explorers' spirit there will always be problems left to solve.

**Explosives,** substances which burn violently to produce gases in such volume that an explosion is induced. Gunpowder was the first explosive to be used; Roger Bacon's powder, consisting of charcoal, sulphur, and nitre, was the only practical explosive for centuries. 1845 brought gun-cotton, made by treating cotton with a mixture of sulphuric and nitric acids; but it was not until 1865 that Sir Frederick Abel perfected the process of manufacture that made it safe enough to store and use. In 1867 Alfred Nobel discovered how to make dynamite by absorbing nitro-glycerine in kiesulguhr; in 1886 he produced cordite, evaporating a solution of gun-cotton and nitro-glycerine in acetone, the resultant jelly being squeezed through jets to form cords. Cordite came into general use as a propellant. High explosives, providing bursting charge for shells and bombs, include: T.N.T. (trinitrotoluol), picric acid (known as lyddite, melinite, etc.), cyclonite (R.D.X.). Chemical explosives have been eclipsed by nuclear explosives which have developed from the first atom bomb (dropped on Hiroshima 6 August 1945) to the 100-megaton hydrogen bomb.

**Expressionism,** a modern art movement confined primarily to the non-Latin countries of Europe which sought to give expression to intimate and personal emotions by means of distortions of line and colour and simplified style which carried a greater impact in terms of feeling. Broadly speaking, this has been characteristic of northern art in general. (*See* Gothic) The term is usually used of the modern movement which influenced the Post-impressionists and subsequent movements in France. Tired of the naturalism of the Impressionists, such artists as van Gogh, Gauguin, Matisse, and Rouault together with the Fauvists (*q.v.*) made use of simple outlines and strong colours. Apart from Toulouse-Lautrec, the principal Expressionists were Norwegian, like Munch, or German, like the painters of *Die Brücke* and *Der Blaue Reiter* groups. Individual artists were Ensor, Kokoschka, Nolde, Rouault, and Soutine.

**Extreme Unction,** the final sacrament of the Roman Catholic and Greek Churches, administered to a dying person, and consisting of the anointing with holy oil, after confession and absolution.

# F

**Fabian Society.** *See* J16.

**Fables** are fictitious narratives intended to enforce some moral precept, and may be either in prose or verse, and deal with personified animals and objects or with human beings. Aesop in ancient times and Hans Christian Andersen and the Brothers Grimm (in many of their stories) in later days, have given fables. Mention must also be made of La Fontaine's and Krylov's fables.

**Faience,** a kind of decorated glazed earthenware invented in Faenza, Italy, about the end of the 13th cent. Wedgwood-ware is a notable example of modern faience.

**Fairs** were established in mediæval times as a means of bringing traders and customers together at stated periods, and formed the chief means of distribution. The great English fairs of early times were those of Winchester and Stourbridge near Cambridge. Traders from the Netherlands and the Baltic gathered there with the great merchants of London, and goods of every kind, wholesale and retail, were sold. The British Industries Fair is the modern counterpart of the mediaeval trade fair. One of the biggest trade fairs was at Nijni-Novgorod, founded in the 17th cent.; other big continental fairs are those of Leipzig (founded in the 12th cent.), Lyons, and Prague.

**Fairy Rings** are the circles caused in grassland by certain fungi. The circles expand outwards as the fungus spreads, the fruiting bodies being at the periphery. Farther inward where the fungi are decaying the grass grows more strongly, fertilised by the nitrogen released from the rotting fungi. In olden times these rings were held to be the scene of fairy dances.

**Falcon,** name given to diurnal birds of prey which belong to the same family, *Falconidae*, as the hawk, eagle, buzzard, kite, and harrier. They are swift of wing and feed on birds and small mammals. These birds have long, pointed wings, strong, hooked and notched bill, long, curved claws, and an eye of great power. They are found all over the world. Those that breed in Britain are the Kestrel (the most common), Hobby (one of the swiftest of European birds), Merlin, and Peregrine, a swift and magnificent bird with slate-grey back, blackish crown, black "moustache" and whitish breast. Other members of the family are the Gyr Falcon from northern latitudes, Iceland and Greenland, which is a winter visitor to Britain, the Lanner, Saker, Eleonora's falcon, Red-footed falcon, and the Lesser Kestrel. The Gyr Falcon and the Peregrine were used in the sport of falconry in olden times. Because of its fearlessness and larger size, the female bird was used. When the quarry was sighted, the bird was unhooded, set free, and after mounting high into the air would dart swiftly down to strike the prey. The heron was the usual victim.

**Fall-out.** Radioactive material produced by nuclear explosions which may cause bodily and genetic damage. (1) *Local fall-out,* due to the return to earth of larger particles, occurs locally, and within a few hours after the explosion; (2) *Tropospheric fall-out,* due to particles which remain in the troposphere and come down within a month or so, possibly all over the world, but within the altitude in which the explosion occurred; (3) *Stratospheric fall-out,* which comes from fragments taken up into the stratosphere and then deposited, in the course of many years uniformly all over the globe. The two radioactive materials which have given rise to the greatest concern for the health of the individual are strontium-90 and iodine-131. Both these materials are liable to become concentrated in certain parts of the human body, strontium-90 in bone and iodine-131 in the thyroid gland. Iodine-131 gives off radiation, but after a few weeks this becomes negligible; the risk is likely to be limited to children under one year old. Strontium-90 continues to give off radiation for many years, and particular attention is therefore paid to levels of strontium-90 in milk and in the bones of young children who are growing rapidly. Radiation exposure may produce genetic effects, that is effects which may show up in succeeding generations. So far as these genetic effects are concerned, the most important components of fall-out are caesium-137 and carbon-14.

**Fandango,** a lively Spanish dance executed by two persons, who usually mark time with castanets.

**Fantail,** a variety of the domestic pigeon; also a genus of Australian birds of the *Muscicapidae* family. A small New Zealand bird is called a fantail.

**Fan Tracery,** a complicated style of roof-vaulting, elaborately moulded, in which the lines of the curves in the masonry or other material employed diverge equally in every direction. It is characteristic of the late Perpendicular period of Gothic architecture, and may be seen in St. George's Chapel at Windsor and the Chapel of Henry VIII. at Westminster Abbey.

**Farmer-General,** the name given to the financiers who in the days of the old French monarchy farmed certain taxes, contracting to pay the Government a fixed sum yearly, on condition that the specified taxes were collected and appropriated by themselves. The revolution of 1789 swept Farmers-General away.

**Fascism.** *See* J16.

**Fata Morgana,** the name given to a curious mirage often observed over the Straits of Messina, attributed to the magic of the fairy Morgana, half-sister of King Arthur, who was fabled to live in Calabria.

**Fathers of the Church** were early writers who laid the foundations of Christian ritual and doctrine. The earliest were the Apostolic Fathers, (*q.v.*). The Four Fathers of the Latin Church were St. Ambrose, St. Jerome, St. Augustine, and St. Gregory the Great. The Four Fathers of the Greek Church were St. Basil, St. Gregory Nazianzen, St. John Chrysostom, and St. Athanasius.

**Fathom,** a nautical measure, the six-foot stretch of a man's arms. It is to be replaced by the metre on British Admiralty charts, but will continue on yachtsmen's coastal charts.

**Fats** are important foodstuffs. In physiology they constitute a valuable form of reserve food. They contain carbon, hydrogen and oxygen: chemically they are described as esters of glycerol (glycerine). Commonest fats are stearin, palmitin, and olein, esters formed by the combination of glycerol with stearic, palmitic, and oleic acid respectively. Fats are converted into soap by alkali; this process (saponification) also releases glycerol.

**Fault**, a term designating a breakage coupled with displacement of geological strata.

**Fauvism** (Fr. *fauve* = wild beast), a term contemptuously applied to the work of a group of French painters led by Matisse who exhibited at the Salon d'Automne in Paris in 1905. Their belief was that a painting must be not only a consistent and harmonious decoration but the expression of an idea or feeling. Forms and colours are emotive in their own right. The objects painted by the Fauves, though simplified, distorted, and often violently coloured, are easily recognisable. Inspiration for their highly decorative canvasses came from many sources: Byzantine and Persian art in the case of Matisse; German Expressionism in the case of Derain and Vlaminck. The Fauves paved the way for the Cubists (Braque joined Picasso in 1909) who approached nature in more arrogant mood, from a more intellectual point of view.

**February**, the second month of the year, contains in ordinary years 28 days, but in leap years 29 days. When first introduced into the Roman calendar by Numa *c.* 700 B.C. it was made the last month of the year, preceding January, but in 452 B.C. the position of the two months was changed, February following January.

**Federation.** *See under* Confederation.

**Félibrige**, a movement founded in 1854 to revive the ancient glories of Provence, initiated by the French poet Frédéric Mistral.

**Felspar**, the name given to a group of minerals, silicates of aluminium with some calcium and sodium, or potassium, which make up probably more than half of the earth's crust. It is formed in granite and other rocks, both igneous and metamorphic.

**Fenestella**, the niche set apart on the south side of the altar for the piscina in Roman Catholic churches.

**Fermentation**, the action of chemical ferments or *enzymes* in bringing about chemical changes in the materials of living animals and plants, *e.g.*, the breaking-down of sugar by yeast into alcohol.

**Ferret**, a carnivorous animal of the Pole-cat family, with a pointed head and long sinuous body, well adapted for following rabbits and game into their burrows and hiding-places, it being kept in this country for that purpose. It is a native of Spain and Africa, and does not exist in England in a condition of natural freedom. *See* Z12.

**Ferrites** are compounds containing iron, oxygen, and one or two of a certain range of other possible metallic elements. Ferrites have recently become very important technically, because, unlike ordinary magnetic materials, they combine strong magnetism with electrical insulating properties. Ferrite-rod aerials are now common in portable radios, and ferrite devices are used in radar. *See* F20(1).

**Feudalism.** *See* J17.

**Fieldfare**, the largest member of the thrush family, a regular winter visitor to Britain from Scandinavia. It is brown in colour with a lighter spotted breast and a grey head.

**Field-Marshal**, the highest ranking title in the British army, and only bestowed on royal personages and generals who have attained great distinction. The first British Field-Marshal was created in 1736, when John, Duke of Argyll, had the title conferred upon him by George II.

**Fifth Column.** When Franco, the Spanish dictator, revolted against the Spanish Republic in 1936 and attacked Madrid with four armies, he declared that a group of fascists within the city was assisting the besiegers. The term is used to describe a body of spies behind a fighting front.

**Fighting-Fish**, small pugnacious Siamese fish with long caudal and ventral fins. They are kept in glass globes in Siam, and when brought into contact will fight to the death, these encounters being the occasion of much gambling.

**Filibuster**, a name first given to pirates and buccaneers in the 17th cent. who took possession of small islands or lonely coast lands, and there maintained themselves apart from any governing authority. In later times the term was used to specify men taking part in expeditions whose object was to appropriate tracts of country, and settle upon them in disregard of international law. The most notable expeditions of this kind in modern times were those of Narcisco Lopez against Cuba in 1850–51, and of William Walker against Nicaragua, between 1855 and 1860. Both leaders were captured and executed. The term is also used to express the right of a minority in the United States Senate for unlimited debate, which is used on occasions to delay legislation for an unlimited period.

**Finches**, a large family of small birds belonging to the Passerine or perching order of birds. There are about 200 species, including greenfinch, hawfinch, chaffinch, goldfinch, siskin, bullfinch, crossbill, linnet, twite, and buntings.

**Fir**, a cone-bearing tree with small evergreen leaves and of considerable use as timber. There are two types: the Silver Firs and the Douglas Firs numbering about 25 species. All these firs attain to a considerable height, and all yield turpentine or other resinous material.

**Fire-Fly**, a small winged insect of the *Elateridae* family, is able to throw out a strong phosphorescent light in the dark. There are some remarkable specimens in tropical countries.

**Fire of London**, of 1666, extended from East to West, from the Tower to the Temple church, and northward to Holborn Bridge. It broke out in a baker's shop in Pudding Lane, and lasted four days, and destroyed 87 churches, including St. Paul's Cathedral, and many public buildings, among them the Royal Exchange, the Custom House, and the Guildhall. In the ruins were involved 13,200 houses and 400 streets. About 100,000 people were made homeless yet in about 10 years all the houses had been rebuilt. The plague had not disappeared from London when the fire occurred.

**Firkin**, a former measure of capacity, the fourth part of a barrel, now only used in reference to a small cask or tub for butter, lard, tallow, etc.

**Fischer-Tropsch Process.** A process for making synthetic petrol from carbon monoxide and hydrogen. The synthesis is accelerated by cobalt-thoria and nickel-thoria catalysts.

**Fish Louse.** Parasitic crustacea found on marine and fresh-water fishes and whales.

**Fission, Nuclear.** A nuclear reaction in which the nucleus of an atom (*e.g.*, uranium 235, plutonium) captures a neutron, and the unstable nucleus so produced breaks into two nearly equal fragments and throws out several neutrons as well. In biology the term fission is applied to reproduction by fragmentation of a single-cell organism, as in amœba. *See* F12(1).

**Flagella**, single hair-like projections found on many micro-organisms. Their sole function is, by complicated motion, to move the organism about. They are longer and less versatile than cilia (*q.v.*).

**Flag Officer**, a British naval officer who enjoys the right of carrying a flag at the mast-head of his ship, and is of the rank of Admiral, Vice-Admiral, or Rear-Admiral.

**Flagship**, the ship that flies the Admiral's flag, and from which all orders proceed.

**Flamingo**, a strangely beautiful, extremely slender wading bird of white and rose-pink plumage with long, slender legs and neck and a long, down-curved bill with which it rakes the mud and obtains its food of worms and molluscs. The wings are bright crimson, bordered with black, and a flock in flight is a picture of singular beauty. There is a large and famous colony in the Camargue.

**Flash-Point.** This is found by heating an oil in a special cup and taking the temperature at which sufficient vapour is produced to ignite when a small flame is applied. It is an index of the inflammability of oils.

**Flea.** Fleas are small parasitic insects belonging to the order *Aphaniptera* (so called because these creatures have no wings). They obtain their food by sucking blood from their host. They are laterally compressed, which immediately distinguishes them from lice. The human flea

(*Pulex irritans*) is able to jump vertically a distance of over 7 in.

**Fleet Prison**, a noted debtors' prison that stood in Farringdon Street, London, where the Congregational Memorial Hall now stands, taking its name from the Fleet Ditch. Notorious for the cruelties inflicted on prisoners. It was pulled down in 1846.

**Fleet Street**, a famous thoroughfare in London, now the centre of journalism and newspaperdom, though it was long celebrated for its taverns where the literary coteries of the day were wont to meet. It takes its name from the Fleet stream which used to run from Hampstead through Holborn to the Thames at Blackfriars.

**Flemings**, the people of Flanders, whose ancestors of mediaeval times excelled in the textile arts; England owes its early eminence as a manufacturing nation to the migration of numbers of Flemings to this country in the 16th and 17th cent. *See also* Walloons.

**Fleur de Lis**, the former national emblem of France, the flower of the lily. It was superseded by the Tricolour in 1789, but is still adhered to by the supporters of the old French royalties.

**Flint**, consists of granular chalcedony with some opaline silica, and occurs as nodules and bands in the Chalk. It is hard and has a conchoidal fracture, so enabling it to be used in making cutting implements in prehistoric times. Before the invention of lucifer matches, it was used along with steel for striking lights.

**Flint implements** are objects found in the younger geological strata, and constituting evidence of the condition and life of the period. They include knives, clubs, arrow-heads, scrapers, etc., used as weapons, tools and possibly as surgical instruments and in religious ceremonies. At the end of the Neolithic Period and the beginning of the Bronze Age a people using a new type of stone axe became evident in Europe, advancing towards the south and central regions, and supposed by many to be the ancestors of the present European stock, or Aryans. Similar to prehistoric specimens are the flint and obsidian implements of some of the primitive peoples of today. Ritual weapons and sacrificial knives continued to be made of stone long after the introduction of metals for practical purposes.

**Flounder**, one of the most familiar of the smaller flat fishes common round the British coasts, and seldom attaining a weight of over three pounds.

**Fluorine**, a chemical element, member of the halogen family, symbol F, it is found in combination with calcium in fluorspar, and occurs in minute quantities in certain other minerals. Discovered by Scheele in 1771, it was first obtained by Moissan in 1886. A pale yellow gas, it is very reactive and combines with most elements except oxygen. Its acid, hydrogen fluoride, etches glass, the fluorine combining with the silicon to form volatile silicon fluoride. Organic fluorine compounds have found use as very stable polymers which resist a wide variety of chemical actions.

**Fluorescent Lamp.** *See* Electric Light and Ultra-Violet Rays.

**Fluorspar**, a mineral; chemically, calcium fluoride. Can be colourless, green, or yellow, but is most commonly purple. Blue fluorspar under the name of Derbyshire "blue John" has been used for ornamental purposes.

**Fly**, the popular name for a large number of insects with one pair of wings and a proboscis terminating in a sucker through which fluid substances can be drawn up. The best-known species are the common house-fly, the bluebottle, and the blow-fly. In the larval form flies are maggots, and feed upon decaying substances, animal flesh, etc. Flies are able to walk upon ceilings or upright surfaces by having suckers at the soles of their feet. *See* Diptera.

**Flycatcher**, name of a large family of small birds, the Muscicapidae. They are insect feeders, catch their food in the air, and are distributed over most countries of the world. The spotted and the pied nest in Britain, which they visit from April to September.

**Flying Fish** are frequently to be seen in southern waters, and are capable of gliding considerable distances without touching the water. To build up speed for its "take-off" the fish swims rapidly, to break the surface at 15–20 miles an hour. Maximum air speed is about 40 m.p.h.

**Flying Fox**, a member of the bat family, but of much larger size, and confined to the tropical and sub-tropical Old World. Like the bats, it is nocturnal, but it feeds entirely on fruits.

**Flying Lemur.** *See* Colugo

**Flying Lizard**, or *Draco*, an Asiatic lizard, possessing wing-like projections from each side, which enable it to make flying leaps through the air, though not sufficient for continuous flight.

**Flying Saucers**, the name given to certain saucer-like shapes which have on occasion been seen travelling through the atmosphere. For some time speculation was rife, especially in America, but it is now believed that when not hallucinations, meteorological or cosmic-ray balloons, they are nothing more than atmospheric phenomena like mirages or mock suns caused by unusual atmospheric conditions. Described by Dr. Menzel, astrophysics professor at Harvard, "as real as rainbows are real, and no more dangerous". It has been suggested that the study of some of the people who report the sighting of unidentified flying objects (UFOs) would be more rewarding than the investigation of what they saw!

**Flying Squirrel**, rodents of which there are several species in Europe, Asia and America. It possesses a parachute-like fold of skin by means of which it projects itself through the air. In appearance they are much like ordinary squirrels, to which they are related. The African flying squirrels belong to a different family.

**Fog** is caused by the presence of particles of condensed water vapour or smoke in the surface layers of the atmosphere, the term being applied meteorologically when the resulting obscurity is such as to render objects invisible at distances of up to 1 km. Fogs are frequently formed when the air near the ground is cooled below its dew-point temperature by radiation on a still, cloudless night; by flowing over a relatively cold land or water mass; or by mixing with a colder air stream. An accumulation of smoke over a large city may cause a high fog cutting off the daylight and producing gloom. *See* Pollution and also Aerosol.

**Foliation**, a geological term applied to rocks whose component minerals are arranged in parallel layers as the result of strong metamorphic action.

**Folio**, a printing term for a sheet of paper folded once, a half sheet constituting a leaf.

**Folklore** concerns itself with the mental and spiritual life of the people—both civilised and primitive—as expressed in the traditional beliefs, customs, institutions, and sayings that have been handed down from generation to generation by word of mouth, and with the observation recording, and interpretation of such traditions. (The word *folklore* itself was first suggested and used—as two words *Folk Lore*—by W. J. Thoms in the *Athenæum* of August 22nd, 1846, and was at once absorbed into the English language.) Traditional lore of the kind included in the term folklore takes many forms and ranges from omens of good and bad luck (spilling the salt breaking a mirror, dropping an umbrella, etc.) and the wearing of amulets or the possession of talismans (such as the horseshoe) as protection against misfortune, to elaborate ceremonial dances such as the Abbots Bromley Horn Dance, the Hobby horses of Padstow and Minehead, the Northern sword-dances, and the Christmas mummers' plays. Especially important are the beliefs and customs associated with birth, babyhood, marriage, and death such being occasions when the individuals concerned require special protection or when unusual happenings can be used for foretelling their future. The child born on a Sunday will be the luckiest; rocking an empty cradle will ensure the speedy arrival of a new baby; throwing an old shoe after a newly-married couple brings them luck; the bride should be carried over the threshold of the new home; on the sea-coast, death is believed to take place at the ebb-tide; the bees must be told of the death of the master of the house, or they will leave the hive. Another very large section of the subject deals with the traditional sayings and practices associated with particular days and seasons of the year—calendar customs, as they are called. The eating of pancakes on Shrove Tuesday; Mother Sunday customs and the simnel cake; Good Friday as the right day for planting potatoes, but emphatically the wrong day for washing clothes or cutting one's finger-nails; the necessity of wearing something new on Easter Sunday; the children's maypole dances and May garlands; midsummer fires; All Hallowe'en as the most favourable occasion for divining the future—especially in respect of marriage—and for games and sports such as apple-bobbing; the numerous practices accompanying the harvest. All these are examples of calendar customs; their full story would occupy several volumes. Folklorists are interested in all such oral tradition because they think that to a large extent it represents what folk have mentally stored up from the past and transmitted to their descendants throughout the centuries, and because therefore it is able to assist other historic methods—ethnographical linguistic, archaeological, etc.—in the elucidation of the early story of man. In those countries with a great diversity of peoples in all stages of culture, a knowledge of folklore and what it can teach of the mind of man is of great importance to administrators. The Folk-Lore Society was founded in 1878, and that part of the subject represented by song and dance has now its own organisation in the English Folk Dance and Song Society.

**Force**, as a term in physics, signifies an influence or exertion which, when made to act upon a body, tends to move it if at rest, or to affect or stop its progress if it be already in motion. In the c.g.s. system, the unit of force is the dyne; in the foot-pound-second system, the poundal; in the SI system, the newton. *See* N14.

**Formaldehyde.** Chemically it lies between methyl alcohol and formic acid; oxidation of methyl alcohol yields formaldehyde, and oxidation of formaldehyde produces formic acid. It is used as a disinfectant, in silvering mirrors, and in the manufacture of phenol-formaldehyde plastics (of which bakelite is the best-known example). Solutions of formaldehyde in water, formalin, are used to preserve biological specimens.

**Forme**, a body of letterpress type, composed and secured for printing from; or a stereotype or electrotype. The former is used more for newspaper formes and the latter in good book work.

**Formic Acid** can be obtained from a colourless fluid secreted by ants and other insects and plants. It is a strong irritant. Commercially it is obtained from sodium formate, which is synthesised by the absorption of carbon monoxide in caustic soda. It is used in the electroplating, tanning, and textile industries.

**Formula**, in mathematics and physics a statement of certain facts in symbolical form. In chemistry a representation of the composition of a compound.

**Fossils.** Remains of animals and plants, or direct evidence of their presence, preserved in rocks. They include petrified skeletons and shells, leaf imprints, footprints, etc.

**Four Freedoms**, a phrase coined by President Roosevelt in January, 1941, embodying what should be the goal of the Allies. They were (1) Freedom of speech and expression; (2) Freedom of every person to worship God in his own way; (3) Freedom from want; (4) Freedom from fear.

**Fox**, carnivorous animal of the canine family, found in considerable numbers in most parts of the world. The common fox *Vulpes vulpes* of Europe is a burrowing animal of nocturnal habits, living upon birds, rabbits, and domestic poultry, in the capture of which it displays much cunning. The fox in Britain is preserved from extinction chiefly for hunting purposes. Among other notable species are the Arctic fox and the red fox of North America, of which the valuable silver fox, coveted for its fur, is a variety.

**Fox-Shark**, *or* Thresher Shark, a large species of shark common in the Atlantic and in the Mediterranean. It is very destructive to small fish, but although it attains a length of 15 ft. it is not dangerous to man.

**Franciscans.** *See* Friars.

**Franco-German War** (1870–71) was opened by a declaration of war by Napoleon III., but the Germans who were better prepared than the French, won victory after victory. In September Napoleon and the whole French army were made prisoners at Sedan, a republic was then proclaimed, and Paris sustained a four months' siege. In the end France ceded Alsace and part of Lorraine to Germany, who claimed a war indemnity of over £20 million.

**Francolin**, a genus of birds closely related to the common partridge, belonging to Africa. It includes the spur-legged partridge, and the black partridge which ranges from Cyprus to Assam.

**Frankincense** is of two kinds, one being used as incense in certain religious services and obtained from olibanum, an Eastern shrub, the other is a resinous exudation derived from firs and pines, and largely used in pharmacy.

**Franklin**, the name given in feudal times to a country landowner who was independent of the territorial lord, and performed many of the minor functions of local government, such as serving as magistrate.

**Fresco**, a painting executed upon plaster walls or ceilings, a technique which has remained unchanged since it was practised by the great Renaissance artists.

**Freshwater Shrimp**, a small crustacean abounding in British streams, and feeding on dead fish or other decomposing matter. Although of shrimp-like form it is not closely related to saltwater shrimps. Its generic name is *Gammarus*.

**Friars**, members of certain mendicant orders of the Roman Catholic Church. The four chief orders are the Franciscans or Grey Friars, the Dominicans or Black Friars, the Carmelites or White Friars, and the Augustinians (Austin Friars).

**Friday**, the 6th day of the week, named after Frigga, the wife of Odin. It is the Mohammedan Sabbath, a general abstinence day of the Roman Catholic Church, and according to popular superstition, an unlucky day.

**Friends, The Society of.** *See* J17.

**Frigate-Bird**, a web-footed bird widely distributed over tropical latitudes, and deriving its name from its great expanse of wing and forked tail, resembling the shape of a swift vessel. It feeds on flying fish mostly, being unable to dive and also steals from other birds. A frigate-bird was found dying on the Hebridean island of Tiree in July 1953: only twice previously had one been recorded in Europe—the first on the German coast in 1792, and the second on the coast of France in 1902.

**Frog**, a familiar amphibian, breathing through gills in the earlier (tadpole) part of its existence, and through lungs later. It remains three months in the tadpole stage. The frog hibernates underwater in the mud during the winter.

**Frost** occurs when the temperature falls to, or below, 0° C., which is freezing point. Hoar frost is applied to the needles or feather-like crystals of ice deposited on the ground, in the same manner as dew. Glazed frost is the clear icy coating which may be formed as a result of rain falling on objects whose temperatures are below the freezing point. These layers of ice, often rendering roads impassable for traffic, damaging overhead power and communication systems and endangering aircraft, can also be caused by condensation from warm, damp winds coming into contact with very cold air and freezing surfaces.

**Froth-Hopper** *or* **Frog-Hopper.** A family of bugs (belonging to the insect order *Hemiptera*) which in the larval stage surround themselves with a protective mass of froth (" cuckoo spit "). These insects, which suck the sap of plants, bear a faint resemblance to frogs, and the adults possess great leaping powers.

**Fuel Cells.** A recent development is a type of battery into which the active chemicals are fed from external fuel tanks. This is the *fuel cell*, which is being developed in a number of versions in several countries. One was demonstrated in action when in 1959 Bacon of Cambridge University used his fuel cell to drive a fork-lift truck and a welding machine. The Bacon fuel cell consists of two electrodes of porous nickel dipping into a solution of caustic potash in water. One electrode is supplied with hydrogen gas from an outside cylinder and the other with oxygen. These gases, forming layers on the nickel, are the active chemicals. The oxygen combines with water to make two negatively charged ions, each consisting of an oxygen and a hydrogen atom joined together (a hydroxyl ion). The hydroxyl ions travel through the solution to the hydrogen electrode, where they combine with hydrogen to form neutral water. Their negative charge (one electron per ion involved) has now arrived at the hydrogen electrode and is ready to flow back to the other electrode through any outside circuit that is provided. This flow constitutes the useful electric current, and it has been provided at the expense of creating water out of the original hydrogen and oxygen. The water can be removed in the form of steam. What is the advantage of all this? In the first place the fuel gases are easy to make and to store in cylinders. Supplying a new gas cylinder is easier and quicker than recharging an ordinary accumulator. Furthermore, a fuel cell is lighter for a given power than an accumulator; satellite designers have found them useful. The fuel cell is not damaged by heavy overloading, and this is valuable for application to vehicle driving. Fuel-cell-driven buses could combine the advantages of diesel buses and trolleybuses. Fuel cells are still in the development stage. It is not certain how they will compete with combustion engines or, in the oil-less future, with improved ordinary batteries.

**Fulani,** a non-Negro people of Hamitic stock widely distributed in N.W. Africa, chiefly in Nigeria. There are two main branches: the dark-skinned Fulani, settled farmers and city dwellers, Moslem in religion, and the light-coloured Bororo'en who are semi-nomadic herdsmen. The Fulani are different from any tribe in W. Africa though they resemble in some ways the Masai of E. Africa. The Fulani conquered the Hausa states at the beginning of the 19th cent. which passed under British suzerainty after 1903. Sokoto, built in 1810, was capital of the Fulani empire.

**Fuller's Earth,** a special kind of clay or marl possessing highly absorbent qualities, originally used in the " fulling "—that is, cleansing and felting—of cloth. Now used in clarifying oils. Deposits in America and in south of England.

**Function.** In mathematics, one quantity $y$ is said to be a function of another quantity $x$, written $y = f(x)$, if a change in $x$ results in some corresponding change in $y$. Thus $\sin x$ or $\log x$ are functions of $x$. If $y$ depends not only on $x$ but on several other quantities as well, $y$ is called a function of many variables.

**Functionalism,** in architecture, a movement originated by Le Corbusier, Swiss-born French architect and town-planner, who applied the austere principles of the Purist movement in painting to his own art. From about 1924 he designed in concrete, steel, and glass, buildings in which every part had a significance in terms of function on the theory that objects created to carry out their particular function to perfection cannot help being beautiful. " A house is a machine for living in." The style was in vogue between the two wars, and although its severity became somewhat modified, it is still the basis of most modern architecture.

**Fungi,** a class of simple plants, which reproduce from spores and lack the green colouring matter *chlorophyll.* It includes moulds, rusts, mildews, smuts, mushrooms, etc. Potato blight is a fungus disease which caused the failure of the potato crop in Ireland in 1846. 50,000 different fungi are known. *See also* F39(2), P8(1).

**Furniture Beetle** (*Anobium punctatum*). The common furniture beetle is responsible for 80 per cent of all woodworm damage and is the great pest of the comparatively modern house, causing damage in the main to softwood roofing and flooring timbers. Adults one-eighth of an inch long. The grub tunnels for about 33 months. *See also* Woodworm, Death Watch Beetle.

**Futurism,** the only important modern art movement to arise outside France, initiated by Marinetti, an Italian writer and mountebank friend of Mussolini at a later period. Its origin took the form of a manifesto published in Paris in 1909 in which Marinetti glorified violence,

war, and the machine age. In its aggression it favoured the growth of fascism. One of the distinctive features of Futurist art was the use of the principle of " simultaneity " in which the same figure (*e.g.,* a woman descending a flight of stairs) is represented in successive positions like film " stills " superimposed on each other. In spite of two further manifestos it was not until 1911 that the first examples of Futurist painting and sculpture appeared by the artists Severini, Balla, and Boccioni. Apart from the principle of simultaneity, Futurism derived from Cubist and Post-impressionist techniques. The movement faded out early in first world war.

# G

**Gabardine,** a long, loose, coarse, over-garment, worn by men of the common class in the Middle Ages, and prescribed by law as the distinctive garment of the Jews. The name is now given to a closely woven cloth of wool and cotton used to make raincoats.

**Gabbro,** a kind of igneous rock, often very coarse-grained, containing a good deal of plagioclase felspar, and monoclinic pyroxene; it may occasionally also include biotite, magnetite, ilmenite, and hornblende. A gabbro containing nickel at Sudbury in Canada is one of the richest sources known of that metal.

**Gadfly,** a widely distributed family of flies with only one pair of wings, including the horse fly. The females are very voracious, being able to bite through the skin and suck the blood of animals. The males are harmless.

**Gadolinium.** An element belonging to the rare-earths metals discovered in 1886 by Marignac. It is strongly magnetic.

**Gaelic,** relating to the Gaels and their language, a term now applied only to the Celtic people inhabiting the Highlands of Scotland, but formerly also to the Celts of Ireland and the Isle of Man.

**Galago,** " Bush Babies," related to the lemur, native to Africa, large-eyed, in keeping with its nocturnal characteristics.

**Galaxy** *or* **Milky Way Galaxy** is the huge disk-shaped cloud of gas and stars (some 100,000 million, one of which is the sun) that is turning in space like a great wheel, with a diameter of about 100,000 light years. The Milky Way (that part of the heavens in Milton's words " powdered with stars ") is really only a small part of this disk, and every star in the galaxy is moving round the centre under the gravitational control of the whole. The sun and planets lie near the edge of the disk, and it takes them about 250 million years to travel once round. The number of stars that can be seen with the unaided eye is about 3,000, and they all belong to the Milky Way Galaxy, as do most of the stars that can be seen with anything but the greatest telescopes. With the large modern optical and radar telescopes many other systems, similar in size and weight to our galaxy, have been discovered, scattered more or less uniformly through space, and the universe is said to include at least 10,000 million such galaxies. *See also* F3–6.

**Gale,** a high wind now technically defined as one of at least Beaufort force 8. Between thirty and forty gales a year occur on the north and west coasts of the British Isles and only about half of this number in the south-east. At St. Ann's Head, Pembroke, the anemometer registered a gust of 113 m.p.h. on Jan. 18, 1945, which is a record for these islands. Gusts exceeding 70 m.p.h. are rarely experienced in London. Gale warnings are issued for specified areas by the Meteorological Office, the warnings taking the form of radio broadcasts and the hoisting of storm signals at certain points on the coast. *See* Beaufort Wind Scale, N33.

**Gall,** abnormal vegetable growths caused by insects, mites, bacteria, or fungi, found on all parts of the plant. Oak-apples, Robin's pin-cushion (on wild rose), " witches brooms " (on trees) are examples. Some are useful commercially, *e.g.,* oak apples yield tannic acid and the black oak gall is used in America as animal food.

**Galleon,** the name given to the old three-decked Spanish treasure vessels employed in conveying the precious minerals from the American colonies to Spain. The term is often applied to any large, especially stately, sailing vessel.

**Galley,** an oar-propelled sea-boat used by the ancient Greeks and Romans for transport purposes, manned by slaves. Boats of a similar class were used by the French down to the middle of the 18th cent., and manned by convicts.

**Gallic Acid,** obtained from gall nuts, sumach, tea, coffee, and the seeds of the mango, is used in the manufacture of inks and as an astringent in medicine. It was discovered by C. W. Scheele (1742–86), a Swedish chemist.

**Gallium,** a white metal, symbol Ga, related to aluminium, but which can be cut with a knife. It was discovered spectroscopically by L. de Boisbaudran in 1875. Long before Mendeleyev had predicted that an element with its properties would be found to fill the then existing gap in the Periodic Table; this gap came immediately below aluminium, so he suggested the name " eka aluminium " for it.

**Gallup Poll,** a system, introduced by Dr. Gallup of the United States, for testing public opinion on topical subjects by taking a test poll on questions framed to elicit opinions.

**Galvanised Iron** is iron coated with zinc. The name comes from the fact that such a coat protective against rust could be deposited electrolytically. Electrodeposition is sometimes used, but the cheaper and more common process depends on dipping the iron in a bath of molten zinc.

**Gamboge,** a resinous gum obtained from the sap of *Garcinia morella*, a tree native to Thailand, Cambodia, and Ceylon, and used as a yellow pigment in paints and also as a purgative.

**Game** is the term applied to wild animals which are protected from indiscriminate slaughter by Game Laws. In the United Kingdom game comprehends deer, hares, pheasants, partridges, grouse, black game, moor game, woodcocks, bustards, and certain other birds and animals of the chase. Game can only be killed (with few exceptions) by persons holding game licences. Occupiers of land and one other person authorised by them in each case are allowed to kill hares and rabbits on their land without licence. Game cannot be sold except by a person holding a proper licence. There is a " close time " prescribed for the different classes of game; for instance, the selling or exposing for sale of any hare or leveret during March, April, May, June, or July is prohibited by law. Grouse cannot be shot between Dec. 11 and Aug. 11; patridges between Feb. 2 and Aug. 31; pheasants between Feb. 2 and Sept. 30; and black game between Dec. 11 and Aug. 10. In regard to foxes, stags, and otters, custom and not Parliament prescribes a certain law which sportsmen rigidly adhere to. Game reserves are legally protected areas where natural vegetation and wild life are allowed to remain unmolested by sportsmen or those who might destroy for economic ends. See British Game Seasons, N25.

**Gaming,** *or* **Gambling**—*i.e.,* staking money on the chances of a game—differs from betting in that it depends upon the result of a trial of skill or a turn of chance. The Betting and Gaming Act of 1959, passed by the Macmillan administration, replaced all the old laws on gaming, which went back to an Act of 1541 entitled " An Acte for Mayntenance of Artyllarie and debarringe of unlauful games," under which some games were unlawful if played for money in any circumstances. Roulette and any game of dice were among such games. Under the 1959 Act any game was lawful, subject to certain conditions. Since then the Betting, Gaming and Lotteries Act, 1963, and the Gaming Act, 1968, have been passed, to deal with unlawful gaming and to prevent the exploitation of gaming by commercial interests.

**Gammexane,** a powerful insecticide, used particularly to kill the tsetse fly and mosquito.

**Gangue.** Useless minerals associated with metallic ores.

**Gannet,** a fish-eating bird which dives on its prey from a great height, swallowing it under water; is found in large numbers off the coast of Scotland, and has breeding stations in the Hebrides, St. Kilda, Ailsa Craig, the Bass Rock, Grassholme Island, and on Ortac and Les Etacs (rocks

off Alderney). It is a bird of white plumage, black tips to long narrow wings and wedge-shaped tail, and weighs about 7 lb. The gannet breeds in colonies on ledges of steep, rocky, island cliffs. Related to the cormorants, pelicans, and frigate-birds.

**Garden Cities** in England were founded by Ebenezer Howard (1850–1928), and his ideas were put forward in his book *Tomorrow—A Peaceful Path to Real Reform* (later re-issued as *Garden Cities of Tomorrow*). New towns should be so placed and planned as to get the best of town and country life, an adaptation of the model villages of certain industrial philanthropists such as Salt, Richardson, Cadbury, Leverhulme, and others. The Garden City Association (later the Town and Country Planning Association) was formed in 1899, and the first garden city was begun at Letchworth in 1903 and successfully established. Welwyn Garden City was also Howard's foundation, established in 1919.

**Gardener-Bird,** a bird possessing many of the characteristics of the bower-bird, and found only in Papua–New Guinea. *See also* Bower Bird.

**Gargantua,** the giant hero of Rabelais' satire, of immense eating and drinking capacity, symbolical of an antagonistic ideal of the greed of the Church.

**Gargoyle,** a projecting spout for carrying off water from the roof gutter of a building. Gargoyles are only found in old structures, modern waterpipe systems having rendered them unnecessary. In Gothic architecture they were turned to architectural account and made to take all kinds of grotesque forms—grinning goblins, hideous monsters, dragons, and so forth.

**Garlic,** a bulbous plant of the same genus as the onion and the leek, and a favourite condiment among the people of Southern Europe. It possesses a very strong odour and pungent taste and its culinary use is agelong.

**Garnet,** a group of minerals; chemically they are orthosilicates of the metals calcium, magnesium, titanium, iron, aluminium. Garnets can be coloured yellow, brown, black, green, or red; the blood-red garnet is an important gemstone.

**Garrotte,** a method of strangulation used as capital punishment in Spain, and consisting of a collar which is compressed by a screw that causes death by piercing the spinal marrow. Garroting was also applied to a system of highway robbery common in England in 1862–63, the assailants seizing their victims from behind, and by a sudden compression of the windpipe disabling them until the robbery was completed.

**Garter.** The Most Noble Order of the Garter was founded (c. 1348) by King Edward III., and is the premier order of knighthood in Great Britain. The traditional story associating the garter and the motto with the Countess of Salisbury, who it was said dropped her garter while dancing with the King, who remarked " honi soit qui mal y pense " cannot be accepted. The order was originally limited to the Sovereign and 25 knights, but the number has been extended, and it may now be bestowed on royal personages and leading representatives of the British peerage. The insignia of the order are the garter of dark-blue velvet with the motto in letters of gold, the mantle of dark-blue velvet lined with white silk, the surcoat and hood, and the gold-and-enamel collar. The garter is worn on the left leg below the knee and by women as a sash over the left shoulder. *See* Knighthood.

**Gas** is an elastic fluid substance, the molecules of which are in constant rapid motion, and exerting pressure. The technique whereby gases are liquefied depends on increasing pressure and diminishing temperature. Each gas has a critical point; unless the temperature is brought down to this point no amount of pressure will bring about liquefaction. Last gas to be liquefied was helium (1908) which boils at −209° C. *See* F17(1).

**Gas** from coal was first used as an illuminating agent by William Murdoch towards the end of the 18th cent. in Birmingham, and about 1807 was introduced in London, one side of Pall Mall being lighted with it. It became widely used as an illuminant, and for space heating and cooking. In the United Kingdom there has been increasing attention paid to the possibility of using a primary fuel—natural gas—instead of producing gas from coal or oil. *See* Gas, Natural.

Gas, Natural, natural mixture of gases often present with deposits of petroleum, found issuing from the ground in many parts of the world—in the oilfields of Venezuela and the Caucasus, in China, Saudi-Arabia, but chiefly in North America. Its chief component is methane. Large industrial centres have made use of this gas since the latter part of the 19th cent., but much of this valuable fuel still goes to waste. Pipelines have been constructed to deliver the gas to where it is wanted. Britain began to ship liquid methane from the Saharan oilfield in 1964. Natural gas reserves have recently been discovered in the North Sea and are being actively exploited. Domestic gas appliances have to be modified if the natural product is substituted for ordinary town gas because the burning characteristics are different. *See* North Sea Gas, Section F, Part VI.

Gas Turbine. In this kind of engine mechanical movement is produced by a jet of gas impinging on a turbine wheel; used in aeroplanes, locomotives, and ships. These engines are mechanically simple compared with internal combustion engines, and require less maintenance. It has been stated that the jet-propelled Comet cruises at 450 m.p.h. burning less than ⅓ lb. of kerosene per passenger mile.

Gauge, a standard dimension or measurement, applied in various branches of construction. Thus, the standard railway gauge is 4 ft. 8½ in. in the United Kingdom, United States, Canada, France, Germany, Austria, Holland, Egypt, Belgium, Denmark, Italy, Hungary, Sweden, Switzerland, and Turkey. In India, Ceylon, and Spain the gauge is 5 ft. 6 in. In Soviet Russia and Finland, 5 ft., Ireland, 5 ft. 3 in. Narrow railway gauges of different standards are in use on very steep inclines in various countries. Other standard gauges are fixed in building and gun-boring.

Gauls were inhabitants of ancient Gaul, the country which comprised what is now France, Belgium, and parts of the Netherlands, Switzerland, and Germany.

Gault, a stratum of blue clay between the Lower Greensand and the Chalk. A typical section of the Gault can be seen at Folkestone.

Gauss, a unit of magnetic induction in the c.g.s. system, named after the great German mathematician and astronomer, K. F. Gauss.

Gavelkind, an old English custom of land tenure in Kent and other places in England, whereby on the death, intestate, of a property owner, his property is divided equally among his children and not according to the law of primogeniture. Abolished by the Law of Property Act, 1922, and the Administration of Estates Act, 1925.

Gazelle, an animal of the antelope family, of small and delicate shape, with large eyes and short cylindrical horns. It is of a fawn colour, a native of North Africa, and easily domesticated.

Gecko, the name of a family of drab lizards common in or near the tropics. They are nocturnal, insectivorous, and harmless.

Geiger Counter, an electrical device, invented by Geiger, which can detect individual atomic particles, *e.g.*, electrons, protons, etc. It often consists of a tube of gas at a few cm. Hg pressure, fitted with two electrodes—a cylinder and an axial wire. A high voltage is kept across the electrodes, and the passage of a charged particle through the gas releases ions which permit a momentary discharge between the electrodes. Electronic circuits register this discharge as a " count." Geiger counters are widely used to detect and measure radioactivity and cosmic rays, both for technical and research purposes.

Gelatine, a transparent, tasteless, organic substance obtained from animal membranes, bones, tendons, etc., by boiling in water. It is of various kinds, according to the substance used in making it. Isinglass, the purest form of it, is made from air-bladders and other membranes of fish, while the coarser kind—glue—is made from hoofs, skin, hides, etc. Its constituents are carbon, hydrogen, oxygen, and nitrogen. Gelatine is applied to an immense variety of purposes, from the making of food jellies to photographic materials.

Gemsbok, a large South African antelope, with long straight horns and tufted tail. Light fawn in colour, it has a black streak across its face, and is very fleet of foot.

General, a military title next in rank to that of Field-Marshal, the highest officer in the army. Ranking below full General are Lieutenant-General, Major-General, and Brigadier.

Generation, a time-measure reckoned at about 30 years when children are ready to replace parents; also the body of persons existing at the same time or period.

Generation, Spontaneous. *See* Abiogenesis.

Genes, the elementary units of heredity. They exist as highly differentiated regions arranged along the length of the chromosomes which the nuclei of cells carry. A chromosome may carry hundreds or even thousands of genes, each with its own particular structure and specific properties. The position of a particular gene on a chromosome is called its locus. The material of the gene is DNA (*q.v.*). *See* Cell Division, F30(2).

Genesis, the first book of the Pentateuch, compiled in the 5th cent. B.C. from earlier documents, which carries the scriptural narrative from the creation to the death of Joseph. Sometimes there is disagreement, as in the story of the creation, Gen. i and ii. Gen. i reflects the views of the ancient Greek scientist Thales (c. 640–546 B.C.) and may be said to be the first scientific account of the creation of the world. The conditions described around the figures of Abraham, Isaac, Jacob, and Joseph have a genuine historical basis.

Genet, one of the smaller carnivorous animals, about the size of a cat, but with longer tail and spotted body. It is a native of Southern Europe, North Africa, and Western Asia.

Genetic Code The elucidation of the structure of DNA (*q.v.*) for which Crick, Wilkins, and Watson were jointly awarded the 1962 Nobel Prize for medicine, revealed the code or chemical dictionary out of which messages serving as blueprints for living structures can be made. *See* Protein synthesis, F29(2).

Geneva Convention, an agreement made by the European Powers at Geneva in 1864, establishing humane regulations regarding the treatment of the sick and wounded in war and the status of those who minister to them. All persons, hospitals, hospital ships are required to display the Geneva cross—a red cross on a white ground. A second conference held at Geneva in 1868 drew up a supplementary agreement. An important result of this Convention was the establishment of the Red Cross Society in 1870.

Genouillieres, ancient metal caps for covering the knees of an armed man; an example may be seen on the Black Prince's monument in Canterbury Cathedral.

Gentian, the name for plants of the *Gentiana* genus, many of which have intensely blue flowers. The gentian-root of *G. lutea* is used in pharmacy.

Genus, a term applied in biology to designate a group of similar species. A group of similar genera is called a family.

Geodesy, the science of calculating the configuration and extent of the earth's surface, and determining exact geographical positions and directions, with variations of gravity, etc. Land-surveying is a branch of geodesy.

Geography, the science which describes the earth's surface, its physical peculiarities, and the distribution of the various animals and plants upon it. It is usual to divide the subject into two main branches—physical geography, which deals with the composition of the earth's surface and the distribution of its living occupants, animate and inanimate; and human geography, which includes economic, political, and social geography.

Geology, the science which deals with the condition and structure of the earth, and the evidence afforded of ancient forms of life. The geological strata are classified in the following categories: *Primary* or *Palaeozoic* (the oldest fossil-bearing rocks including the Cambrian, Ordovician, Silurian, Devonian, Carboniferous, Permian); *Secondary* or *Mesozoic* (Triassic, Jurassic, Cretaceous); *Tertiary* or *Cainozoic*

(Eocene, Oligocene, Miocene, Pliocene, Pleistocene); *Post tertiary* (most recent rocks). *See* **F41.**

**Geometrical Progression** is a term used to indicate a succession of numbers which increase or decrease at an equal ratio—as 3, 9, 27; or 64, 16, 4.

**Geometry** is the branch of mathematics which demonstrates the properties of figures, and the distances of points of space from each other by means of deductions. It is a science of reason from fundamental axioms, and was perfected by Euclid about 300 B.C. The books of Euclid contain a full elucidation of the science, though supplemented in modern times by Descartes, Newton and Carnot. Of recent years non-Euclidean geometry has been developed.

**Geophysics**, the branches of physics which are concerned with the earth and its atmosphere. Meteorology, geomagnetism, aurora and air-glow, ionosphere, solar activity, cosmic rays, glaciology, oceanography, seismology, nuclear radiation in the atmosphere, rockets, and satellites—all these are geophysical subjects. The object of the International Geophysical Year, 1957–58, was to investigate the physical phenomena occurring on and around the earth by means of carefully co-ordinated observations made simultaneously all over the globe.

**George-Noble**, a gold coin, so called from St. George and the dragon depicted on its obverse. First issued in the reign of Henry VIII.

**German Silver**, an alloy of copper, zinc, and nickel, and used in the manufacture of table-ware, such as spoons, forks, etc.

**Germanium.** A grey, hard, brittle chemical element, symbol Ge, chemically related to silicon and tin. Discovered by Winkler in 1886. Its richest ore is germanite containing 6% of the metal. Coal is also a relatively rich source. Since 1948 it has assumed great importance as a semi-conducting material for making transistors (*q.v.*). Because of this it has been so intensively studied that more is known about its physical properties than about those of any other element.

**Gesta Romanorum** (Latin = deeds of the Romans), a mediaeval collection of Latin stories of unknown authorship which circulated widely in Europe during the Middle Ages. First printed in the 15th cent. The stories were used by Chaucer, Shakespeare and other writers who found many romantic incidents and legends which they were able to turn to good account.

**Gestation**, the carrying of young in animals during pregnancy, varies considerably in its length. In the case of an elephant, the period is 21 months; a camel, 12 months; a cow, 9 months; a cat, 8 weeks; a horse, 48 weeks; a dog, 9 weeks; and a pig, 16 weeks. Hens " sit " for 21 days; geese, 30; swans, 42; turkeys, 28; pigeons, 18.

**Geysers**, hot springs of volcanic origination and action, are remarkable for the fact that they throw out huge streams of boiling water instead of lava as in the case of a volcano. The most famous geysers are those of Iceland, which number over a hundred, the principal one having an opening 70 ft. in diameter and discharging a column of water to a height of 200 ft. There are also geysers in the Yellowstone region of America, and some in New Zealand. Also a device now in common domestic use for heating running water quickly by gas or electricity.

**Ghost-Moth** or **Ghost Swift**, an interesting nocturnal insect (*Hepialus humuli*), common in England, possessing in the male a white collar and known for its habit of hovering with a pendulum-like action in the twilight over a particular spot where the female is concealed.

**Giambeaux**, metal armour for the legs and shins, worn by the warriors of Richard II.'s reign.

**Gibbon**, the name of a long-armed ape mainly inhabiting S.E. Asia. It is without tail, and possesses the power of very rapid movement among the trees of the forests.

**Gin**, a well-known spirit distilled from malt or barley and flavoured with the juniper berry. The principal varieties are the English and American, known as " Gin " or " Dry Gin ", and the Dutch, referred to as " jenever " or " Hollandse jenever ". In Germany and Austria it is called " Schnapps ". The word " Gin " is an ab-

breviation of " Geneva ", both being primarily derived from the French genièvre (juniper).

**Ginger** is obtained from a reed-like perennial plant grown in tropical countries. There are two varieties, black ginger and grey ginger. The former is obtained by peeling and drying the root, the latter by scalding and drying. Ginger is largely used as a condiment.

**Giraffe**, the tallest of existing animals, reaching a height of from 18 to 20 ft. when full grown. Its sloping back and elongated neck seem to be the natural evolution of an animal that has to feed on the branches of trees. It is a native of Africa, is of a light fawn colour marked with darker spots, and has a prehensile tongue.

**Giralda**, a beautiful and remarkable example of Arabian art, erected in 1195 at Seville, still in existence. Minarets similar to the Giralda are to be found at Morocco, Tunis, and Tetuan.

**Glaciers** form in the higher Alpine ranges, and are immense consolidated masses of snow, which are gradually impelled by their force down the mountain-sides until they reach a point where the temperature causes them to melt, and they run off in streams. From such glaciers the five great rivers, the Rhine, the Po, the Rhône, the Inn, and the Adige, have their source. The longest of the Swiss glaciers is the Gross Aletsch, which sometimes extends over 10 miles. Some of the glaciers of the Himalayas are four times as long. The Muir in Alaska is of enormous magnitude, and that of Justeldals Brae in Norway is the largest in Europe.

**Gladiators** were professional athletes and combatants in ancient Rome, contesting with each other or with wild beasts. At first they were drawn from the slave and prisoner classes exclusively, but so much were the successful gladiators held in esteem that men came to make a profession of athletics, and gladiatorial training schools were established. When a gladiator was vanquished without being killed in combat, it was left with the spectators to decide his fate, death being voted by holding the hands out with the thumb turned inward, and life by putting forth the hands with the thumb extended. Gladiatorial shows were the chief public displays in Rome from the 3rd to the 4th cent. A.D.

**Glass**, a substance obtained from the fusion of silica (sand) with various bases, and is more or less transparent. There are numerous kinds of glass, but they group themselves under one or other of the following classifications:—Flint glass, or crystal, whose components are potash, silica, and oxide of lead; window glass, made from soda, lime, and silica; Bohemian glass, containing potash, lime, and silica; and bottle glass, composed of soda, lime, alumina, silica, and oxide of iron. Heat-proof glasses used for making cooking utensils contain boron. Glass was made by the Phoenicians, and was familiar in ancient Egypt. The Egyptians introduced it into Rome. In the Middle Ages Venice was famed for its glass manufactures, but after the 17th cent. Bohemia acquired pre-eminence. English glass reached its highest level of artistic design in the 17th and 18th cent. Window glass was not used in this country for dwellings until the end of the Middle Ages.

**Glass-Snake**, genus, *Ophisaurus*, of legless lizards with long fragile tails capable of re-generation when broken. Six species are known; in S.E. Europe, S.W. Asia, Indo-China, and N. America. Attains a length of about 2 ft.; main colouring, green, with black and yellow markings.

**Glauconite.** A green mineral, chemically a hydrated silicate of potassium and iron. Commonly found in marine sands (hence these rocks are known as " greensands ") and sandstones.

**Glaucus** is a curious genus of sea slugs often called the Sea Lizard belonging to the molluscs. It is without shell and has a soft body, with horny mouth and four tentacles. It is a native of the Atlantic, and is not more than 12 in. in length.

**Glee**, an unaccompanied piece for three or more voices. Glee-singing was popular in England during the 18th and early 19th cent. and glee-clubs are still in existence.

**Globigerina**, an oceanic unicellular animalcule with a perforated shell, and occurring in certain parts of the Atlantic in such vast numbers as to form a bed of chalk ooze with their empty shells.

**L48**

**Glockenspiel**, an instrument composed of metal bars each of which is tuned to a note. The bars are struck by hand-hammers and give forth chiming sounds.

**Gloria in Excelsis** (" Glory to God in the highest ") is the opening of the Latin hymn adapted from Luke ii. 4, and the most prominent hymn of the ecclesiastical rites in the Christian liturgies.

**Gloria Patri**, the lesser Doxology, with which chants are generally concluded in the English Church service—" Glory be to the Father, and to the Son."

**Glow-worm**, a beetle, possessing the power (much stronger in the female than the male) of emitting phosphorescent light from the hind end of the body. The female is wingless.

**Glucinium.** *See* **Beryllium.**

**Glucose, Dextrose** *or* **Grape Sugar** is a carbohydrate (*q.v.*). It is produced by hydrolysis from cane sugar, dextrine, starch, cellulose, etc., by the action of reagents. It also occurs in many plants, fruits, and honey. For brewing purposes glucose is prepared by the conversion of starch by sulphuric acid. Malt also converts starch into glucose.

**Glutton** *or* **Wolverine**, the biggest animal of the weasel family, inhabits the northernmost parts of Europe and America. In build it resembles the bear, and is rather larger than a badger. Its fur is of a brown-black hue, but coarse.

**Glycerine** *or* **Glycerol**, occurs in natural fats combined with fatty acids, and is obtained by decomposing those substances with alkalies or by superheated steam. It is colourless and oily and sweet, and is put to a variety of commercial uses, being widely utilised for medicaments, for lubricating purposes, and in the manufacture of nitro-glycerine.

**Glycols.** Organic compounds containing two alcohol groups. Ethylene glycol is the most widely known example: it is used as an anti-freeze in motor-car radiators on account of its property of greatly reducing the freezing point of water. Also used in the manufacture of " Terylene." *See* **Esters.**

**Glyptoden**, an extinct species of gigantic armadillo, fossil remains of which have been discovered in S. America. It was some 9 ft. long, carried a huge tortoise-like shell, and had fluted teeth.

**Gneiss**, a metamorphic rock usually containing quartz, felspar, and mica. It is banded, the light-coloured minerals being concentrated apart from the dark minerals.

**Gnosticism.** *See* **J18.**

**Gnu**, an animal of the antelope family, combining the characteristics of the buffalo in its head and horns, the ass in its neck and mane, and the horse in its long and bushy tail. There are two species, the common and the brindled, and they are about the size of an ass. They abound in Africa and congregate in herds.

**Goat-Moth** (*Cossus cossus*), a large moth of the *Cossidae* family, common in Britain, evil-smelling, and very destructive in the larval stage to trees of the poplar and willow genus, into the wood of which the caterpillar bores during its three years' period of development.

**Goats** are horned ruminant quadrupeds, indigenous to the Eastern Hemisphere, but now domesticated in all parts of the world. Though related to the sheep, they are a much hardier and more active animal. The male has a tuft of hair under the chin. Many species, including those of Cashmere and Angora, are valuable for their hair, which is used for fine textile fabrics. The milk of the goat is nutritive, and goat-skins are in good demand for leather for gloves, shoes, etc.

**Gobelin Tapestry** was originated by a family of dyers named Gobelin in the 15th cent. in Paris. The Gobelin establishment, which produced this beautiful tapestry, made of silk and wool, or silk and cotton, was taken over by the Government of Louis XIV., in 1662, and since then has been the French national factory for that class of fabric.

**God and Man.** *See* **J18.**

**Gog and Magog**, two legendary City of London giants, supposed to be the offspring of certain wicked daughters of the Emperor Diocletian and a band of demons. They were brought captive to London and made to serve as prisoners at the Palace of Brute, which stood on the site of Guildhall. Effigies of the giants have stood in Guildhall since the time of Henry V. They were destroyed in the Great Fire of 1666, replaced in 1672, and used to be carried through the streets of London in the Lord Mayor's Show. The present figures, newly carved in lime wood by Mr. David Evans, replaced those carved in 1708 by Richard Saunders, which were destroyed in an air raid during the last war.

**Gold.** Metallic element, symbol Au (Latin *Aurum*) related to silver and copper, the coinage metals. The greatest amount of gold is obtained by treating gold-bearing quartz by the cyanide process. The gold is dissolved out by cyanide solution, which is then run into long boxes filled with zinc shavings when the gold is precipitated as a black slime. This is melted with an oxidising agent which removes the zinc.

**Gold-Beaters' Skin** is the outside membrane of the large intestine of the ox, specially prepared and used by gold-beaters for placing between the leaves of gold while they beat them. This membrane is of great tenacity, and gets beaten to such extreme thinness that it is used to put on cuts and bruises.

**Gold Standard.** Under the gold-standard system, which was widely prevalent up to 1914, each gold-standard country fixed the value of its currency in terms of a weight of gold of a certain fineness and was, broadly speaking, ready to exchange its currency freely for gold, which could then be exported without restriction. This involved keeping a gold reserve big enough to meet all likely demands and also to serve as a backing for the issue of notes. The gold standard had to be given up during the First World War; and though it was in substance restored in Great Britain in 1925 (when Churchill was Chancellor), the restoration was never complete, as the gold reserve remained too small for complete freedom to export to be practicable. Sterling had to be devalued in the financial crisis of 1931 (which brought about the fall of the Labour Government) and Great Britain was forced off the gold standard. Most of the currencies important in world trade and payments are now convertible. The monetary crisis of March 1968 led to the present two-tier gold price system. *See* **Section G, Part IV.**

**Goldeneye**, a species of wild duck, widely distributed over Arctic regions. It is a passage-migrant and winter-visitor to the British Isles. Has nested in Cheshire. Distinguished by a large white spot in front of each eye on a dark ground.

**Golden Number**, the number of any year in the metonic cycle of 19 years, deriving its name from the fact that in the old calendars it was always printed in gold. It is found by adding 1 to the number of the year A.D. and dividing by 19, the remainder being the Golden Number; or, if no remainder, the Golden Number is 19. The only use to which the Golden Number is put now is in making ecclesiastical calculations for determining movable feasts.

**Goldsmiths Company**, one of the richest London City Companies; the official assayers of gold and silver, invested with the power of " hall-marking " the quality of objects made from these metals. First charter granted in 1327.

**Gondola**, the old regulation black boats so common on the canals of Venice, propelled by a gondolier with one oar who stands at the stern, his passengers being accommodated in a covered space in the centre.

**Gonfalon**, the pennon affixed to a lance, spear, or standard, consisting usually of two or three streamers, and made to turn like a weather-cock.

**Gophers.** Rodent mammals. The pocket gophers are stout-bodied burrowers common in the U.S.A. The slender burrowing gophers, also called " ground squirrels," occur in central and western U.S.A. The sisel or suslik is a related European species. They are a great pest among grain crops.

**Gordon Riots** of 1780 were an anti-popery agitation fomented by Lord George Gordon. Called also " No-Popery Riots."

**Gorilla**, the largest of the anthropoid apes, found in the forests of Equatorial Africa, and at maturity standing from 4 to 5 ft. high.

**Goshawk** (*Accipter gentilis*), a diurnal bird of prey

**L49**

fearless and extremely agile; loves wooded country and is very destructive of poultry and game-birds. It resembles the peregrine falcon in appearance, but has shorter, rounded wings. This bird was a great favourite of falconers in mediaeval times.

**Gospels** are those portions of the New Testament which deal with the life, death, resurrection, and teachings of Christ. They are the gospels of Matthew, Mark, Luke, and John, and the first three are called the *synoptic gospels* because of their general unity of narrative. That of John is of somewhat wider scope, and gives in addition to the story of the Passion an account of the ministry in Judaea.

**Gothic.** A term applied to a style of architecture which followed the Romanesque, appeared in France during the 12th cent., and is typical of northern Europe. It was not generally appreciated south of the Alps. The high and sharply pointed arches, the walls supported outside by flying buttresses, the traceried windows, often filled with stained glass, and the lofty spires are in sharp distinction to the semicircular arches and the massive walls characteristic of the more sturdy Romanesque style. Yet the transition was gradual. The cathedrals of Chartres, Laon, and the Benedictine church of St. Denis just outside Paris are typical of early Gothic. The style found its full expression in the French cathedrals of the 13th and 14th cent.: Reims, Notre Dame, Beauvais, Bourges, and Amiens. From France the style spread to other lands in each of which it developed its own characteristics; thus the English churches tended to have massive towers and delicate spires and, as at Salisbury, were often set in open grounds surrounded by lawns; Flemish and Dutch churches were sometimes built of brick as were those in north Germany and Scandinavia; in Spain the Flamboyant style was followed. The main Gothic cathedral in Italy, that of Milan, although begun in 1386 was not completed until the early 19th cent. The lofty character of Gothic has been attributed by the romantic to pious aspiration, as if the spires were striving towards heaven and this concept may well have played a part. The more concrete reasons however were somewhat different: Romanesque churches were thick-walled, sturdy, small-windowed, and set often in open country or on heights (a) because architects had not yet discovered how to support a heavy roof without massive walls; and (b) because, being built in dangerous times, they had a defensive function. Gothic churches began to be raised in less troublesome times and were tall for the same reason that New York skyscrapers are tall (i.e., the increasing price of land). Also they were built in growing cities where not much space was available and they were lavish in style because wealth was increasing and rich merchants were willing to contribute. Late English Gothic is seen, for example, at King's College Chapel, Cambridge, Henry's Chapel at Westminster, and St. George's Chapel at Windsor (all c. 1500). Gothic is also found in secular buildings, e.g., Little Wenham Hall in Suffolk, the castle at Ghent, the town halls of Louvain and Middelburg, and the streets of Gothic houses in Bruges still in use today. Virtually Gothic as a style (excluding the " Gothic revival " of 19th cent. England) ended at the close of the 15th cent. Gothic art is best seen in the illuminated manuscripts of the 13th and 14th cent. and in the church sculpture. Its characteristic is a complete departure from the cool, perfectionist realism of classical times with distortion to produce emotional effects. The human figures are not ideal forms but recognisable as people we might meet in the street; yet there was also the element of wild imagination, intricate design, and a wealth of feeling which might be grotesque, humorous, macabre, or even obscene. This element of distortion and sometimes wildly " unrealistic " colouring which produced an effect more dramatic than the literal representation of the classic schools remained an important element in German art (see Expressionism) right up to modern times and is used by other modern schools.

**Goths.** A Teutonic people who originally came from southern Sweden (Gotland) and by the 3rd cent. were settled in the region north of the Black Sea. They began to encroach on the Roman Empire and early in the 4th cent. split into two divisions: the " wise " Goths or Visigoths between the Danube and the Dniester (referred to as the West Goths), the " bright " Goths or Ostrogoths in southern Russia on the Dnieper (referred to as the East Goths). The Ostrogoths were conquered by the Huns c. 370, while the Visigoths under Alaric devastated Greece and sacked Rome in 410. Eventually the Visigoths spread to France and Spain and their last king Roderick fell in battle against the Moors in 711. The Ostrogoths regained their independence on the death of Attila in 453 and under their king Theodoric the Great conquered Italy in 493. They lost their identity after Justinian regained Italy, 525–552.

**Gourd Family** *or* **Cucurbitaceæ.** This family of about 650 species of flowering plants includes the gourds, pumpkins, cantaloupes, cucumber, gherkin, water-melon and squashes. Most abundant in the tropics, the cucurbits are mainly climbing annuals with very rapid growth. The bath-room loofah is the skeleton of one curcurbit fruit, *Luffa cylindrica*. The squirting cucumber is another member of the family.

**Governor.** A device attached to an engine, turbine, compressor, etc., which automatically controls the engine's speed in accordance with power demand. Most governors depend upon the centrifugal action of two or more balls which are thrown outwards as their speed of rotation increases and actuate a throttle valve or cut-off. The centrifugal governor was invented by Thomas Mead, patented by him in 1787, and used on windmills. Watt adapted it to the steam engine.

**Grail, Legend of the Holy,** a tale of Celtic origin which became part of Arthurian legend and the subject of many mediaeval quest-romances. According to the Christian version the grail was the cup which Christ used at the Last Supper, brought to England by St. Joseph of Arimathea.

**Grand Prix,** the " French Derby," was established by Napoleon III., in 1863. It is the chief French race and is an international competition of three-year-olds.

**Granite** is a coarsely crystalline igneous rock consisting of quartz and alkali felspars plus mica or hornblende. It is a much used ornamental and building stone; it forms the high ground of Dartmoor and Bodmin Moor.

**Graphite** *or* **Plumbago,** commonly called blacklead, is a form of carbon occurring in foliated masses in marble, schist, etc. It is soft, will make black marks on paper or other plain surfaces, and is mainly used for lead pencils. It is also a valuable lubricant. Pure graphite has found a new use with the construction of atomic piles. Important deposits occur in Siberia, Ceylon, Madagascar, Canada, and the U.S.A.

**Graptolites,** fossil animals confined to Cambrian, Ordovician and Silurian strata. Once classified as hydrazoa but now considered more likely to be hemichordates.

**Grasshopper.** There are many species of these leaping insects which are related to the locusts and crickets. Most are vegetarians; some eat flies and caterpillars also. The chirping sound they make is made by scraping the hind legs against the wings; in some species a noise is produced by rubbing the wings together.

**Gravitation.** One of the four types of force known to physics. The others are electromagnetic forces and two types of nuclear force (F15(2)). Gravitational forces are an attraction that one piece of matter has for another; they dominate astronomical phenomena, but inside the atom they are negligible compared with the other three types of force. Einstein's General Theory of Relativity is the only theory at present extant which attempts to interpret gravitational forces in terms of more fundamental concepts. See F15(2).

**Graylag,** the ordinary wild grey goose of Europe, the species from which domestic geese are derived; frequents fens and marshes; breeds in Iceland, Scandinavia, and Scotland; distinguished by pinkish legs and feet and lack of black markings on bill.

**Grayling,** a fresh-water fish of the salmon family

having a large dorsal fin, and averaging about 1 lb. in weight.

**Grebe,** a diving bird of beautiful plumage found over a great part of the world on lakes and oceans. The two species familiar in Great Britain are the Dabchick or Little Grebe and the large and handsome Great Crested Grebe, which has a feathery tuft, lost in the autumn, on each side of the head. Grebes have remarkable courtship displays. The breast feathers are of a downy softness and silver lustre, for which they were formerly much hunted.

**Greek Art.** *See* Hellenic Art.

**Greek Fire,** a combustible, supposed to have been composed of sulphur, nitre, naphtha, and asphalt, used with destructive effect by the Greeks of the Eastern Empire in their wars.

**Greek Kalends,** equivalent to never, as only the Romans, not the Greeks, had kalends.

**Greenwich Mean Time.** The first Nautical Almanac, for the use of navigators and astronomers, was published by the Astronomer Royal in 1767. It was based on the meridian at Greenwich, with longitude measured east and west of 0°. A master clock, which still exists, was built at Greenwich Observatory in 1852 to control the railway station clocks and Greenwich Mean Time, or Railway Time as it was sometimes called, prevailed. In 1884 Greenwich was chosen as the prime meridian of the world and GMT became known as Universal Time. Continuously from Feb. 18, 1968, clocks in Britain are one hour fast on GMT but GMT remains as the standard time by which the time zones of the world are calculated. *See* British Standard Time.

**Gregorian Calendar.** *See* Calendar.

**Gregorian Chant,** ritual music with a system of harmony suitable for church use. First established by Pope Gregory I.

**Gresham's Law** states that if good money, *i.e.*, money with the higher intrinsic value, and bad money are in circulation together, the bad money will tend to drive out the good money from circulation. For instance, the good money is more likely to be melted down or demanded in payment by foreign creditors.

**Gretna Green,** a celebrated village in Dumfries, just over the border from England, where runaway marriages were performed from 1754 to 1856, though only completely stopped during present century.

**Griffin,** in ancient mythology, a winged creature with an eagle's head and body of a lion, found in ancient sculptures of Persia and Assyria. Its origin is traced to the Hittites. It had the same religious significance as the winged sphinx of Egypt. The griffin vulture is a bird named after the mythological creature, found in Europe, Africa and India.

**Grilse,** a young salmon that has only been once to the sea.

**Grimm's Law,** formulated by Jacob Grimm, an eminent German philologist, lays down a principle of consonantal change in the Germanic languages. For instance, Lat. *pater*, Eng. *father*, Ger. *Vater*; Lat. *frater*, Eng. *brother*, Ger. *Bruder*; Lat. *decem*, Eng. *ten*, Ger. *zehn*.

**Grog,** the beverage served out to sailors, and compounded of spirit and water in prescribed proportions. The name, it is said, was derived from the fact that Admiral Vernon, who introduced it into the English navy in 1745, wore Grogram breeches.

**Grogram** (French = *gros grain*), a kind of rough fabric made of wool and some other fibre, such as silk, mohair, or cotton, formerly much used for commoner kinds of wearing apparel.

**Grotto,** a natural or artificial cave. Among the most famous are the blue grotto of Capri and the stalactite grotto of Antiparos (Cyclades, Aegean). The latter has been known since 1673 and is of singular picturesqueness.

**Ground Wave,** is that part of the energy emitted by a radio transmitter which travels along the ground; as opposed to the sky wave which is reflected back to earth by the ionosphere. With the lower radio-frequencies, the ground wave can be picked up over several thousand miles; in the broadcasting band, over a hundred or so miles; it is virtually useless at high frequencies.

**Grouse,** game bird of the northern latitudes where some 20 species occur. They are stout, compact, ground-dwelling birds, protectively plumaged (the willow grouse turns white in winter), the male usually being larger and more brightly coloured than the female. The red grouse of the British moorlands has been introduced into Belgium and W. Germany. Of the same family are the blackcock, ptarmigan, capercaillie, American prairie-hen, and the common partridge. Grouse shooting begins in Britain on Aug. 12.

**Guanaco,** a large species of llama, common to South America, and utilised as a beast of burden.

**Guano,** the excrement of sea-birds, found in large quantities on the rocky islands of the western coasts of South America and Nauru Is. It forms a useful fertilising agent, being rich in phosphate and ammonia, and first came into use in 1841, since which time Peruvian guano has been a recognised article of commerce. Beds of guano from 50 to 60 ft. in thickness are not uncommon. Fish guano and bat guano from caves in South America and the Bahamas are also used as fertilisers.

**Gudgeon,** a small fresh-water fish of the carp family with 2 small barbels on the upper lip.

**Guelph and Ghibelline,** italianised forms of the German words "Welf" and "Waiblingen," the names of two rival princely families whose conflicts made much of the history of Germany and Italy during the Middle Ages. The feuds between these two factions continued in Italy during the campaigns of Emperor Frederick I., and later developed into the fierce struggles of the 13th cent. between emperor and pope. In Italy the Ghibellines supported the side of the German emperors and the Guelphs the cause of the pope. The present Royal Family of England is descended from the Guelphs, through the ducal House of Brunswick (the name of Windsor was assumed during the first world war).

**Guildhall,** the place of assembly of the members of a guild, and at one time, when guilds were in full strength, was practically the Town Hall. The London Guildhall is to-day the hall of meeting for the City of London Corporation.

**Guilds** for the fostering and protection of various trades have existed in England since Anglo-Saxon times, and from the 12th to the 16th cent. exercised great influence and enjoyed many privileges. There were trades' guilds and craftsmen's guilds, and in all large cities and towns there was a guild hall. Their successes in the Middle Ages led to many monopolistic abuses, and in the end it became necessary to free the country from their restrictive power. The City Guilds (Livery Companies of the City of London) derive their name from the distinctive dress assumed by their members in the 14th cent. There are 83 Guilds in existence.

**Guild Socialism.** *See* J21.

**Guillemot,** a genus of sea-birds of the auk family, common in Northern Europe, two species—the Common Guillemot and the Black Guillemot—being natives of our own sea coasts, nesting on the cliffs. Brünnich's Guillemot, an Arctic species, is a rare straggler in the British Isles.

**Guinea,** an English gold coin of the value of twenty-one shillings, current from 1663 to 1817, and deriving its name from the first guinea coinage having been struck from gold obtained on the coast of Guinea.

**Guinea-Pig,** a rodent of the cavy family about 10 in. in length and with a tail so short that it does not project outside the body. It makes an excellent pet, though easily frightened. Its ancestors were species of the wild cavy of S. America said to have been domesticated by the Incas of Peru. *See* Z15(2).

**Gules,** a heraldic term, denoting a rose of red tincture, indicated by vertical lines drawn or engraved without colour.

**Gulf Stream** is confined entirely to the western side of the N. Atlantic and is the warm-water current flowing through the Straits of Florida from the Gulf of Mexico parallel to the American coast up as far as Cape Hatteras. From there it continues north-eastwards as a slower, broader, cooler (yet even so, relatively warm) drift of water, merging with the North Atlantic Drift and losing its identity about 40° N. Lat., 60° W. Long. It is a common error to attribute the warmth of the British Isles and Western Europe generally to the Gulf Stream but this has no influence whatever except in so far as it feeds the North Atlantic Drift. Both the Gulf Stream and the North Atlantic Drift owe their movement to the direction of the prevailing winds, and it is the south-westerly airstream coming from warmer regions and passing over the surface waters of the Atlantic Drift that brings the warmth inland to influence the climate of Western Europe.

**Gull.** An extremely well-known, long-winged sea-bird with rather short legs and webbed feet. In almost all adults the body and tail are white whilst the back and most of the wings are grey or black. In the majority of cases the plumage of juveniles is partly or entirely dusky. Gulls are omnivorous, and are very useful as scavengers. They follow ships and quickly seize upon any refuse which may be thrown overboard. There are 44 species, which vary in size from moderately small to large. With certain exceptions, such as the Kittiwake in the North Atlantic, they are not found very far from land. They are sociable and mostly breed in colonies on cliff-ledges, on islands, beaches and sandhills, and among vegetation in swamps, sometimes a long way from the sea. The nest is usually substantial, and the eggs generally number from two to three. Of the 29 species breeding in the northern hemisphere, 14 occur in the British Isles. The pure white Ivory Gull is the most northerly of birds. Sabine's and the Swallow-tailed Gull have forked tails. Ross's Gull has a black ring round the neck and one species, Franklin's Gull, migrates from the North, where it breeds, to pass the winter in the Southern hemisphere.

**Gums** are glutinous compounds obtained from vegetable sources, soluble in cold or hot water, but not in alcohol. There are innumerable varieties. Gum Arabic is exuded from a species of acacia grown in Senegal, the Sudan, Arabia, India and other countries, and is a valuable commercial product, used in dyeing, ink-making, as a mucilage, and in medicine. India-rubber is an elastic gum. Gums are also made from starch, potatoes, wheat, etc., from seeds, bark, roots, and weeds. Many so-called gums are resins.

**Gun-Cotton,** a powerful explosive manufactured by subjecting a prepared cotton to the prolonged action of a mixture of three parts sulphuric acid and one part of nitric acid. It burns without explosion on ignition, but by percussion explodes with a force five times greater than that of gunpowder.

**Gunpowder,** also called "black powder," the oldest of explosive mixtures, consists of salt-petre, sulphur, and charcoal, intimately mixed, the proportions being varied for different intended uses.

**Gunpowder Plot** was a conspiracy by a desperate band of Roman Catholics in the reign of James I, to avenge the harsh treatment to which Catholics were subjected. Barrels of gunpowder were secreted in the vaults underneath the Houses of Parliament, and it was proposed to fire these when the King and his Ministers assembled on Nov. 5, 1605. The plot was betrayed and Guy Fawkes and his co-conspirators were arrested and executed. The date serves to perpetuate the ancient custom of burning the effigy of Fawkes, a custom in which young people are the most enthusiastic participants, with bonfires, fireworks, etc.

**Gurnard,** a sea-fish, with large, bony head and diminutive body, of which there are some forty species. They are plentiful in British waters.

**Gymnasium,** originally the name given in ancient Greece to the public places where Greek youth used to exercise and receive instruction. Plato, Aristotle, and other great teachers lectured there. The Greek institution was never very popular with the Romans, and it was not until the 18th and 19th cent, that the cult of combining physical with intellectual activity again found a place in educational systems. In Germany the name was applied to the classical grammar school; in this country and America to the halls where gymnastics were practised.

**Gypsies,** a nomadic race, believed to be of Indian origin; their language, Romany, is related to the languages of N.W. India. They are spread over many parts of the world, but are most common in Europe where they appeared towards the end of the Middle Ages. The English name *gypsy* comes from the Spanish *gitano* = Egyptian; other European names are *Zigeuner* (Ger.), *zingaro* (It.), *tzigany* (Magyar), all resembling the Persian *zingar* = a saddler. Their history has been one of persecution. Hitler treated them like the Jews. In Britain since the war they have been kept increasingly on the move, but in 1968 Parliament passed a Bill to make the provisions of sites a duty of local authorities. The Netherlands passed a similar Bill in 1918! It is now more usual to speak of gypsies as "travellers." Economic pressure has largely removed their traditional crafts of tinkering, basket-making, peg-making. The majority now deal in scrap-iron, paper, and rags.

**Gypsum,** a whitish mineral consisting of hydrated sulphate of calcium. The finest gypsum is alabaster. When heated gypsum is converted into the powder called Plaster of Paris; the water it loses can be taken up when the plaster is wetted, and the reconversion of Plaster of Paris into gypsum accounts for the way in which the former sets hard. The name "Plaster of Paris" came from the location of important gypsum quarries in the Montmartre district of Paris. It was found after the flood disasters of Jan. 1953 that gypsum could undo the effect of sea-water. By spreading it for the rain to wash into the soil, thousands of acres of farmland in Holland and Britain were made productive again.

**Gyroscope** is a symmetrical rapidly rotating object, typically wheel-like, which because of its mass and rotation possesses a lot of the dynamical property known as angular momentum. Basic dynamical laws tell us that angular momentum is conserved and a consequence of this is that the axis of rotation tends to stay pointing in the same direction. Disturbing influences make a gyroscope's motion complicated but the general effect of the presence of a gyroscope attached to any body is to help to stabilise the body's motion. This is made use of in reducing the rocking of ships and in compasses and control systems in aircraft, torpedoes, and missiles.

# H

**Habeas Corpus,** the name given to a writ ordering the body of a person under restraint or imprisonment to be brought into court for full inquiry into the legality of the restraint to be made. The first Habeas Corpus Act was passed in 1679, though nominally such a right had existed from Magna Carta, but some of the more despotic kings had disregarded it. In times of public peril the privilege of *habeas corpus* is sometimes temporarily suspended, many instances occurring in the history of Ireland and during the First and Second World Wars.

**Haber Process,** the important industrial process for synthesising ammonia from atmospheric nitrogen. Nitrogen and hydrogen are made to combine at high pressure (200 atmospheres or upwards) in an electric arc.

**Haddock,** one of the best-known fishes abounding in northern seas and averaging about 4 lb. in weight. Related to the cod. Largely used for curing, and sold as "finnan haddies."

**Hade** of veins, a mining term indicating the particular inclination that any vein, seam, or strata may have from the perpendicular; thus, in Weardale the veins mainly "hade" to the north.

**Hadrian's Wall.** *See* Roman Walls.

**Haematite,** ferric oxide, one of the principal iron ores, containing about 70% of the metal. It is usually found in kidney-shaped masses, and is specular, red or brown, in thin fragments, but greyish in bulk.

**Haemocyanin,** the respiratory pigment of crustaceans and molluscs. It functions like haemoglobin, from which it differs in containing copper instead of iron and being blue when oxidised instead of red. *See* F36(2).

**Haemoglobin,** the pigment containing iron which gives red blood corpuscles their colour. It is a respiratory pigment, having the property of picking up oxygen when the blood passes through the lungs to produce the compound known as oxyhaemoglobin. In other parts of the body the oxyhaemoglobin breaks down, liberating oxygen, which is used in the oxidation process (respiration) that the body tissues carry on. *See* F36(2).

**Hafiz**, besides being the pseudonym of a famous Persian poet, is a title conferred upon any Mohammedan who has committed the whole of the Koran to memory.

**Hafnium**, a metallic element discovered by Coster and Hevesy in 1922 and important in the atomic-energy field. It occurs in most zirconium minerals to the extent of about 5 per cent.

**Hag-fish**, a blind, eel-like parasitic sea-fish with soft backbone; found within the bodies of other fish, and called sometimes the "borer," or "the glutinous hag-fish." Related to the Lamprey.

**Hagiarchy**, the rule or order of Saints.

**Hagiology**, a branch of literature that is wholly given up to the history of the saints, and the setting forth of the stories and legends associated with their names.

**Hail**, hard, roughly spherical balls of ice, consisting of white cores covered by layers of both transparent and opaque ice, frequently falling during thunderstorms. They usually do not exceed 1 in. in size, but hailstones larger than apples and weighing more than 2 lb. have been observed. The general theory of a hailstone is that near the top of a cumulonimbus cloud a raindrop becomes frozen, grows in size by condensation and through collisions with snow particles, and eventually becomes so weighty as to overcome the ascending air currents in the cloud. Falling, it first encounters supercooled water drops, immediately freezing on it, increasing the white core, and then at lower levels ordinary water drops, freezing more slowly, producing a layer of clear ice. Before the hailstone arrives at the ground gusts and lulls may transport it several times up and down both regions, adding alternate coatings of soft white and hard clear ice.

**Hake**, a fish of the cod family, found in large numbers in the seas of Europe, but not in high favour for the table with fastidious feeders.

**Halcyon**, a term associated in olden times with the kingfisher and days of soothing calm. "halcyon days" being a frequently used expression. The legend was that the kingfisher laid its eggs on the surface of the sea at the time of the winter solstice when the sea was unruffled. Halcyon is the Greek for kingfisher.

**Halibut**, one of the largest of the flat fishes, averaging when full grown from 4 to 6 ft. in length, and highly esteemed for the table. Specimens of still larger size occasionally occur. It is plentifully distributed. Its two eyes are on the right side of the head.

**Hall-mark.** A mark or group of marks, impressed by an assay office on gold or silver articles guaranteeing the standard of fineness of the precious metal used in them. These marks, which have been applied to silver made in London since the beginning of the 14th cent. and perhaps earlier, make it possible to establish the year and place of assay as also the name of the maker. English pieces of silver usually have not less than four marks, viz., (1) town mark; (2) maker's mark; (3) date letter; (4) sterling mark.

The town mark is rarely changed; in London a crowned leopard's head was used from the earliest days until 1820 with only minor modifications, except for the period 1697–1720 when a lion's head erased was substituted; since 1820 the crown has been omitted.

Until the late 17th cent. a symbol was often used as a maker's mark, from 1696 to 1720 the first two letters of the maker's surname, and subsequently the maker's initials. Owing to the destruction of the earlier mark plates at Goldsmiths' Hall no maker's name prior to the late 17th cent. can be identified with certainty.

The London date letter is changed at the end of May each year, so each letter covers seven months of one year and five months of the following. The London date cycle has usually consisted of twenty letters; the alphabet of each cycle is of different style, and the letters are enclosed in shields of different shape.

The sterling mark, the lion passant, was introduced in 1544 and continued in use until 1697, when the higher Britannia standard was introduced in order to discourage the practice current amongst goldsmiths of melting down coin of the realm to make plate. The leopard's head crowned and the lion passant were then replaced by a figure of Britannia and a lion's head erased. Though the regulation imposing the higher standard was withdrawn in 1720, a small amount of Britannia standard silver continued to be made and still is made.

From 1784 until 1890 a plate tax was levied on all silver assayed in Great Britain and an additional duty mark, the sovereign's head, was used during this period. A Jubilee mark bearing the head of George V and of Queen Mary was used in between the years 1933 and 1935, and in 1953 a coronation mark with the head of Queen Elizabeth was introduced.

The tables of hall-marks in Gen. Comp. (N16-18) give the London date letter cycles from 1598 to 1955. The form of town mark and sterling mark used during each cycle is given at the head of each column. Where a major alteration took place in either of these marks during a date-letter cycle, the alternative forms are also shown. The date of the change can be established by reference to the notes above. At the bottom of each page the marks used by the major provincial, Scottish and Irish assay offices are shown. Owing to lack of space, the complete date-letter cycles are not shown, but two examples only from the 17th, 18th or 19th cent. Where a provincial assay office was established in the 17th cent. or earlier, the marks of one year in the 17th and 18th cent. respectively are shown, where the office was not established until the 18th cent., the marks of one year in the 18th and 19th cent. are given.

**Halloween** (Oct. 31), the eve of All Saints' Day, a time associated, especially in Scotland, with certain pleasing superstitions attractively set forth in Burns's famous poem "Hallowe'en." It is the night when young men and maidens are supposed, by observing certain rites, to have their future wives and husbands disclosed to them.

**Hallucinogen**, a drug which acts upon the brain to create sensory illusions or hallucinations with a variety of emotional effects. One of the most widely studied is LSD (*q.v.*) which will produce symptoms very similar to those found in some mental disorders. *See* P67(2).

**Halo**, a luminous circle usually of 22° radius, surrounding sun or moon, produced by the refraction and reflection of light by ice crystals of high cirrus cloud. It is a very common occurrence, in the British Isles almost one day in three. The inner side is red and the outer a whitish-yellow colour. "Mock suns," *i.e.*, patches of light at the same elevation as the sun are much rarer occurrences, sometimes being of great beauty and brilliance. Halo is the Greek for threshing-floor. *See* Coronae.

**Halogens**, the group name for the four non-metallic elements fluorine, chlorine, bromine, and iodine. The term "halogen" means "salt-producer."

**Halteres**, the modified hind-wings of the two-winged flies or *Diptera* (*e.g.*, the house-fly). The equilibrium in flight of these insects depends on the halteres, which are commonly called "balancers."

**Hampton Court Conference**, presided over at Hampton Court Palace by James I. in 1604 and which brought about his authorised translation of the Bible, had an important bearing on the religious differences of the time. James refused to grant tolerations to the Puritans. This sowed the seeds of civil war. Following the conference three hundred English Puritan clergy were ejected from their livings.

**Hanaper Office**, a former Chancery office, deriving its name from the fact that its writs and papers were kept in a hanaper (hamper). The Chancellor's officer thus came to be known as the Hanaper. The Comptrollers of the Hanaper were abolished in England in 1842.

**Hand**, a measure of four inches, the average size of the palm; used in reckoning height of horses.

**Handfasting**, an informal marriage custom once prevalent in Scotland, whereby a man and woman bound themselves to cohabit for a year and a day, and at the end of that period either confirmed their contract by a regular marriage or separated.

**Hansard,** the title given to the official reports of Parliamentary debates, so named after Luke Hansard who in 1774 became partner in a firm of printers to the House of Commons. His son T. C. Hansard was first the printer and then the publisher of an unofficial series of parliamentary debates inaugurated by William Cobbett in 1803. In 1909 production was taken over by H.M. Stationery Office and today's volumes contain full, substantially verbatim, reports of what is said in both Houses of Parliament.

**Hanseatic League** was a confederation of North German towns established about 1241 for purposes of mutual protection in carrying on international commerce. The League became so powerful that it was able to dominate the foreign trade of Norway, Sweden, Denmark, and even to some extent of London. A branch was established in London and had its guild hall in Cannon Street for hundreds of years. The League existed down to the middle of the 17th cent. Hamburg, Lübeck, and Bremen are the only cities which, as free ports, still by commercial courtesy retain the name of Hanse towns. *Hansa* is Old High German for Association or Merchants' Guild.

**Hapsburg** (*Ger.* Habsburg), the ruling house of Austria, 1282–1918; held title of Holy Roman Emperor, 1438–1806, except for 1740–5. The aggrandisement of the Hapsburg family was mainly brought about by a series of fortunate marriages. In 1521 when the Hapsburg power was at its zenith, Charles V divided his dominions into two branches—Austrian Hapsburg and Spanish Hapsburg. The Hapsburg Danubian Monarchy dates from 1526 when the Hungarian and Bohemian crowns were united with the Austrian patrimony of the Hapsburg. The triple union lasted 400 years. The murder of the heir to the Hapsburg thrones, Francis Ferdinand, at Sarajevo in 1914, provoked the outbreak of the First World War. Francis Joseph's great-nephew, Charles, abdicated in 1918. (Prof. C. A. Macartney's authoritative work, *The Habsburg Empire, 1790–1918,* was published in 1969.)

**Hare,** species of the *Lepus genus,* distributed widely through the N. hemisphere. Noted for having four upper front teeth, one pair behind the other, short tufted tail, a cleft upper lip and longer ears and limbs than the rabbit. It does not burrow. The young are born with hair and able to see. A swift animal hunted with greyhounds in the sport called "coursing." *See* Game.

**Harleian MSS.** comprise some thousands of volumes of MSS. and documents, collected by the first Earl of Oxford (1661–1724) and his son Edward. After the death of the latter, his widow handed the MSS. over to the nation for £10,000, and they are deposited in the British Museum.

**Harlequin,** the buffoon of ancient Italian comedy. As adapted to the British stage, however, harlequin is a pantomime character only, in love with Columbine, appearing in parti-coloured garments and carrying a wand, by which he exercises a magic influence in thwarting the fantastic tricks of the clown and pantaloon.

**Harmattan,** a dry wind which may blow between January and May across the Sahara to the Gulf of Guinea. Although affording relief from the tropical heat, vegetation withers because of its extreme dryness and much irritation is caused by the clouds of fine dust which it carries.

**Harmonic Motion,** regular periodic motion of the kind exemplified by a ball bobbing up and down at the end of a spring, and by the piston in a steam engine. It may be simple (simple harmonic motion) or composed of two or more simple harmonic motions. In simple harmonic motion the acceleration is proportional to the distance of the moving body from its original rest position.

**Harp-seal,** the ordinary Greenland seal, with a dark harp-shaped marking on its back, hence its name. It abounds in Newfoundland waters and further northward towards the Arctic.

**Harpy Eagle,** a large bird of prey named from the winged monsters of Greek mythology, inhabiting the forest regions of Central and South America. There are eight species, one with handsome grey plumage and large crest which attacks and kills animals much larger than itself, and was called by the Aztecs "winged wolf."

**Harrier,** a bird of prey of the falcon family; of the various species distributed over the world, three breed in Britain: the moorland Hen harrier, the Marsh harrier, and Montagu's harrier. They are large birds with long tails, long legs, long wings, and gliding flight. They nest on the ground and eat small mammals, frogs, lizards, and small birds.

**Hartebeest,** common African antelope of a greybrown colour, with ringed and knotted horns bending backward and tapering to sharp points; gregarious, of large size, and capable of domestication. There are several species.

**Harvest Bug,** a very small insect, of a dark red colour, which appears in large numbers in the fields in autumn, and is peculiarly irritating to animals and man by the tenacity with which it attaches itself to the skin and burrows underneath. Probably the larvae of spinning mites (Trombidoids). In the U.S.A. they are called "chiggers."

**Harvest Moon,** the full moon that occurs nearest to the autumn equinox, in September. It rises for several nights running about the same time, and yields an unusually brilliant series of moonlight nights.

**Harvestmen** are, like spiders, members of the arachnid class but belong to the distinctly different order of Phalangida. They are common in the countryside in autumn and have small oval bodies and eight long slender legs which besides being mere organs of locomotion also act as sense organs. Known as "daddy longlegs" in America.

**Hashish,** an Arabic word for the narcotic substance prepared from the hemp plant (*Cannabis sativa*). It is known by a variety of names, *e.g.,* bhang in India and marijuana in America.

**Hatchment,** in heraldry, is a square board, in vertical diagonal position, placed outside a house or on the tomb at the death of a member of a family and so arranged that it indicates the sex and condition of the deceased.

**Hawfinch,** a well-known European bird of the finch family, having a variegated plumage, a sturdy bill, and black-and-white tail. In England it is found in the Midland and Eastern Counties, and locally in Scotland.

**Hawk.** This name is applied to almost any diurnal bird of prey other than eagle, falcon, or vulture, but in its strict sense applies only to the *Accipiter* genus—the small Sparrow Hawk and the larger Goshawk, round-winged, long-tailed birds with barred under-parts. They prey upon small birds captured in flight and small mammals.

**Hawk-moths,** large species of moths, thick of body and strong of wing, which fly with rapid swooping motion, hence its name. There are numerous handsome species in Britain.

**Hearth-Money** was a tax laid on hearths (in all houses paying the church and poor rates). Charles II. introduced it in 1662, and it was repealed in the reign of William and Mary.

**Heat,** after prolonged controversy over whether or not heat is a "substance" (formerly called "caloric"), it was established in the 19th cent. that heat is a form of energy; it is in fact the combined kinetic and potential energy of the atoms of which a body is composed. Heat can be turned into other forms of energy, *e.g.,* a red hot body loses heat by radiating it in the form of electromagnetic waves ("radiant heat"—chiefly infra-red rays). Heat may also be transferred from one place to another by conduction and, in fluids, by convection. All three processes occur when a glowing fire heats a room. A unit quantity of heat is the calorie, which is the amount of heat sufficient to raise the temperature of 1 gm. of water by 1° C. In general, adding heat to a body raises its temperature. The number of calories required per gram of material to raise the temperature 1° C is called the *specific heat* of the material. However, adding heat may not raise the temperature but may instead cause a change of state, *e.g.,* from solid to liquid (melting) or liquid to gas (evaporation). The amount of heat required to melt 1 gram of a solid is called the latent heat of melting. Similarly, there is a latent heat of evaporation. Strictly speaking, the specific and latent heats of a substance depend on how much its pressure and volume are allowed to vary during the measurements. Water has a high specific heat, and this makes the oceans a vast heat reservoir, a factor of great meteorological significance. The science of heat is called thermodynamics, and is of great importance in physics and chemistry. *See* F17.

**Heath,** flowering plants of the *Ericaceae* family. Heaths are widely distributed over uncultivated spaces of Europe and Africa. In Britain they are represented by heather (of which there are several species) and ling (*Calluna vulgaris*), which cover thousands of acres of moorland. Some of the African or Cape heaths are very beautiful and much prized by florists. One species of heath (*Erica arborea*) which grows in S. Europe and N. Africa has close-grained woody root-stock used for making briar pipes. *See* T7(2).

**Heat Wave** is a spell of very hot weather, due chiefly in the British Isles to a warm southerly current of air caused by the presence of an anticyclone over western or central Europe at the same time as a depression is stationary over the Atlantic. High humidity increases the discomfort.

**Hegira,** an Arab term signifying departure or flight, and used in reference to Mohammed's departure from Mecca for Medina, A.D. 622, from which date the Mohammedan era is reckoned.

**Helicopter,** heavier-than-air aircraft which obtains its lift from blades rotating above the fuselage in windmill-fashion. The first successful heli-copters were the Focke-Wulf 61, a German machine (1936), and the VS-300, designed by Igor Sikorsky, flown in 1937. Helicopters can hover, and rise and descend vertically, in addition to being capable of horizontal flight.

**Heliotrope,** a favourite sweet-scented flowering plant, common in tropical and sub-tropical countries; the Peruvian heliotrope is the "cherry pie" of our summer garden borders. *See* T9(1).

**Helium,** a gaseous element first discovered by means of the spectroscope in the sun's atmo-sphere. This discovery, made in 1868 by the astronomer Sir Norman Lockyer, was followed in 1895 by Sir William Ramsay's proof that the element existed on earth. He found it in the uranium ore, clevite. Later it was established that helium is formed by the radioactive decay of many elements which emit $\alpha$-particles (nuclei of helium atoms) and is contained in all radioactive minerals. The largest source of helium is natural gas, the richest in helium being the gas from certain wells in Utah, U.S.A. Next to hydrogen, helium is the lightest gas known, has a lifting power equal to 92% of hydrogen and the advantage that it is inert and non-inflammable. It is used for inflating air-ships. Ordinary air contains 1 part in 200,000 of helium. It was the last gaseous element to be liquefied, this being achieved by Onnes in 1908 in Leyden. Liquid helium has many re-markable properties only imperfectly under-stood. As well as being scientifically fascinat-ing it is indispensable in cryogenics (*q.v.*) as a medium for cooling other substances to tem-peratures near absolute zero. Hydrogen fusion in the " H bomb " produces helium.

**Hellebore,** a plant of the *Ranunculaceae* (buttercup) family. The best-known British examples are the green and stinking varieties. There is also a garden kind which flowers in December called the Christmas Rose. Hellebore yields a bitter substance which forms a drastic purgative, but is now little used. *See* T9(1).

**Hellenic Art.** The art of ancient Greece may be roughly divided into three periods: the pre-historic period (*c.* 1500–1000 B.C.) of the bronze age Mycenaeans; the archaic period (*c.* 600–500 B.C.); and the classical period (*c.* 500–300 B.C.). Of the first period centred on Mycenae in Peloponnesus but extending to the coasts of Asia and the city of Troy we can mention only the massive stone gateways and the shaft graves of Mycenae, where the archaeologist Schliemann discovered painted vases, gold cups, bronze swords, and ornaments of what had once been a great, if primitive, civilisation. During the

archaic period sculpture was the principal form of art expression. The magnificent male and female figures are reminiscent of Egyptian art, but are distinctive in liveliness of facial expres-sion. The vase-paintings of this period became more elaborate, depicting scenes from mytho-logy or ceremonial events. Typical of classical Greek art is the representation of the beautiful and healthy human body deliberately posed and often carrying out heroic or athletic acts. The vast majority of these statues are known to us only through Roman copies. The *Hermes* of Praxiteles (born *c.* 385 B.C.) is possibly the only existing statue which can be assigned with any degree of certainty to an individual artist. Almost the whole of the Greek genius in archi-tecture was expended on temples which are all basically similar in design—a rectangle with a low-pitched gabled roof resting on side walls. The three orders Doric, Corinthian, and Ionic mainly referred to the type of column used, but naturally the whole building was influenced thereby. Some of the main buildings are on the Acropolis, a hill outside Athens, on which stand the Parthenon (from the outer frieze of which the Elgin marbles, now mostly in the British Museum, were taken), the Erechtheum, famous for its Porch of Maidens, and the gateway known as the Propylaea with its broad flight of marble steps. Apart from that on vases, no Greek painting has come down to us, although Greek painters existed and were noted in their time. All we have are copies in mosaic and fresco made by the Romans, at Naples and Pompeii. Of Greek literature in prose, verse, and the drama little can be said here. To the early period (*i.e.*, the archaic age) belong Homer's *Iliad* and *Odyssey*, Hesiod's long poem *Work and Days*, and Sappho's love poems, and Pindar's Odes. The period of Pericles in the 5th cent. B.C. produced more great literature than any comparable period in history: the philosophical writings of Plato and Aristotle, the tragedies of Aeschylus, Euripides, and Sophocles, the comedies of Aristophanes—all these are still part of the European tradition, and together with Greek architecture played a major part in the Renaissance (*see* J38).

**Hellenistic Art,** the art of the period of Greek civilisation which began with the conquests of Alexander the Great (356–323 B.C.) and lasted until his former empire (which encompassed most of the Middle East and part of North Africa) was conquered by the Romans in 146 B.C. Culturally it was an important period because it spread Greek culture far beyond its original boundaries—even as far as the north of India, and its centres spread from Athens to the cities of Alexandria in Egypt, Antioch in Syria, and Pergamum in Asia Minor. But equally Eastern culture spread to the West: democracy was replaced by absolute monarchy, cosmopoli-tanism took the place of the Greek tendency to believe that all who were not Greeks were bar-barians, and mystical philosophies took the place of Greek rationalism. This was a sensuous, secular, pleasure-loving, rootless society, and these tendencies were reflected in its art. Hellenistic sculpture was sensual, effeminate, and violently emotional, yet it depicted indivi-duals and not always noble or beautiful ones. (Classical Greek sculpture was idealistic, showed types rather than individuals, and appealed to the intellect rather than the emotions.) Some of the best examples came from the school at Pergamum and later from the island of Rhodes, and the titles themselves speak of their nature: *The Dying Gaul, Gaul Slaying his Wife and Himself*, and the famous *Laocoön* (representing Laocoön and his two sons being crushed by two enormous serpents). All these date from about 240 to 50 B.C.—for the culture did not imme-diately end with the Roman conquest. The enormous frieze of the altar of the temple in Pergamum depicts a battle between gods and giants with tremendous realism and brutal violence far removed from the serene art of classical times. Portrait sculpture is typical of Hellenistic art, where it may almost be said to have been invented, since such ventures in the past had been idealistic rather than realistic. The great Hellenistic cities were geometrically planned and fine public buildings made their appearance in which the slender and graceful Ionic or the ornate Corinthian columns took the place of the more austere and heavy classical ones. Alexandria was famed for its library of 700,000 books and was the centre of philosophical schools such as the Stoics and Epicureans. Here too worked the mathematicians Euclid and Archimedes, the physicians Erasistratus and Herophilus, and the geographer Pytheas. But Hellenistic literature was a pale reflection of the glories of the past and we mention only the comedies of Menander and the pastoral verse of Theocritus of Syracuse.

**Hemiptera,** the order of insects to which belong the true bugs. Their wing structure is in most species incomplete, hence the term hemiptera. This order includes the familiar water insects, the water boatman and water skater, also the aphids, cicadas, leaf hoppers, scale insects. *See* T29(2).

**Hemlock,** a plant of the *Umbelliferae* family, growing in all parts of Britain, and containing a strong alkaloid poison. Used medicinally, this alkaline substance is of considerable service, being a powerful sedative. According to Pliny, hemlock was the poison used by the Athenians in putting criminals to death.

**Hemp** (*Cannabis sativa*), name of a plant native to Asia, now cultivated widely for the valuable fibre contained in the stalk or in some species in the leaves. Hemp fibre has been replaced by cotton for textiles and by jute for sacks and is now chiefly used for cordage and twine. It contains a resinous substance from which the narcotic hashish is made. The seed yields a valuable oil. The term hemp is also used for other fibre plants, including manila hemp from the Philippines, sunn hemp from India, sisal from W. and E. Africa and phorium from New Zealand.

**Henbane,** a plant found in Britain and other parts of Europe and Northern Asia. It belongs to the potato family *Solanaceae*, grows mostly on waste ground, and bears yellow-brown flowers veined with purple. The leaves yield a poisonous alkaloid substance which, medicinally prepared and administered, is of great use. Tincture of henbane is often preferred to laudanum.

**Heptarchy,** a word derived from the Greek *hepta*, seven, and denoting the seven kingdoms (*archai*) into which Anglo-Saxon England was divided before 900. The seven were Kent, Essex, Sussex, Wessex, Mercia, East Anglia, and Northumbria.

**Heracleum,** a plant of the *Umbelliferae* family, common in southern and central Europe, though only one species, the cow parsnip, grows in England. It has a bitter root, and from the juice of the stem an intoxicating liquor is occasionally prepared.

**Herald,** an officer of state empowered to make formal proclamations and deliver messages from the sovereign or other high personage whom he serves. In the developments which took place in armorial bearings, the herald was the functionary charged with the duty of their proper depiction.

**Heraldry,** the knowledge of armorial bearings, was mainly the outcome of the love of outward distinction which prevailed in mediaeval times. " Heraldry," says Stubbs, " became a handmaid of chivalry, and the marshalling of badges, crests, coat-armour, pennons, helmets, and other devices of distinction grew into an important branch of knowledge." The *shield*, or *escutcheon*, is the ground upon which armorial signs are traced, the colour of the shield being called the *tincture*, the signs recorded the *charges*. There are seven *tinctures—or* (gold), *argent* (silver), *gules* (red), *azure* (blue), *vert* (green), *purpure* (purple), and *sable* (black). The *charges* are classed as " Honourable " and " Subordinate " ordinaries, comprising lines and geometrical forms; and " Common " ordinaries, which latter includes all representations of natural objects. There is also a system of external signs, such as crowns, coronets, mitres, helmets, mantlings, wreaths, and crests, each having its distinctive significance. For other distinguishing marks see Hatchments, Quartering, Rampant, Pean.

**Heralds' College or College of Arms,** was incorporated by Richard III. in 1483. Its head is the Earl Marshal (an office hereditary in the

family of the Dukes of Norfolk), and there are three Kings of Arms, six Heralds, and four Pursuivants. The business transacted is wholly connected with the tracing of genealogies and the granting of armorial bearings. In Scotland the Heraldic functions are performed by the Lord Lyon King of Arms.

**Herbarium,** a systematically classified collection of preserved plants. One of the largest in the world is at the Royal Botanic Gardens at Kew.

**Heredity** is the study of the transmission of physical and mental characteristics from one generation to another. Gregor Mendel (1822–84), a great experimenter in the field of inheritance, established the principle embodied in Mendel's law in his work published in 1866. The ideas which he then put forward were forgotten until the early years of this century, but today they form the basis of the modern study of genetics. Genes are the units of heredity; they are contained in the chromosomes of the cell nucleus. In human cells there are 46 chromosomes—22 pairs of characteristic shape, and a 23rd (the sex chromosomes) similar in women and dissimilar in men, which unite in the process of fertilisation. An individual can only develop, even under the most favourable surroundings, as far as his inherited characteristics, *i.e.*, his genes will allow him to do so. It is in the development of personality that the interplay between heredity and environment becomes most apparent. *See* The Evolution of Organisms, F42, *and* Section Q, Part I.

**Hermaphrodite,** animals or plants possessing both male and female reproductive organs, *e.g.*, snail, earthworms, most flowering plants.

**Hermit Crab,** a decapod, with a soft asymmetrical body which it protects by thrusting it into an empty gastropod shell, *e.g.*, whelk, which it carries about, only abandoning it when necessary for a larger one. Found in all seas, many live in commensal relationship with sea anemones, etc.

**Heron,** a large wading bird with long curved neck and pointed bill, is a member of the *Ardeidae* family, of which there are many species. Egrets and bitterns are included as herons. Herons are to be met with in marsh lands and near rivers and lakes, where they feed on fish and frogs. They nest in trees in large numbers, these colonies being called heronries. The common heron is native to England, and other species from the Continent are frequent visitors.

**Herring,** a common sea-fish, related to the sardine and pilchard, abounding in northern seas and found in large numbers round the British coasts. The herring fishing is the most important fish industry in this country, a large fleet being engaged in it. The fishing season proper lasts from May to October, the enormous shoals being followed as they move from place to place. The spawning season is about the end of August. One female herring may produce 20 to 50 thousand eggs, which sink to the sea-bed, where they develop.

**Hibernation,** the dormant condition in which numerous mammals, reptiles, amphibians, insects, plants, etc., pass the winter. The rate of metabolism slows down, and the body temperature drops to that of the surroundings. Work on these low temperatures and their physiological effect has led to improved surgical techniques. Animals of the torrid regions pass through an analogous period (aestivation) during the hot season, when the sources of food are dried up.

**Hickory,** several species of American tree of the walnut family, remarkable for its very hard, solid, heavy white wood, and bearing an edible, four-lobed nut.

**Hieratic Art,** a type of art (typified by the major part of the art of ancient Egypt) which is (a) exclusively religious, and (b) conventionally based on earlier forms and traditions.

**Hieroglyphics** are the earliest form of pictured symbolic expressions, and are supposed to have been introduced by the ancient Egyptians. They consist of rude depictions of animals, plants, signs, and objects, and in their later examples express, in abridged form, ideas and records from which significant historical information has been gleaned. The deciphering of

Egyptian hieroglyphics long formed an ardent study, but gradually the key to the riddle was discovered, and most of the ancient records can now be understood. Besides the Egyptian there are also Hittite, Minoan and Mayan hieroglyphic scripts. *See* Rosetta Stone.

**Hi-Fi** means high fidelity and refers to gramophones, tape recorders, and similar apparatus which will *faithfully* reproduce sounds. It is not too difficult these days to amplify electrical signals without distorting them much; it is more difficult to turn electrical impulses into exactly equivalent sound waves (with a loudspeaker, for example) or *vice versa* (with a microphone or gramophone pick-up). Pick-up and loudspeaker are therefore often the weak links in domestic hi-fi and faults in their design, deficiencies in the electronic amplifiers, imperfect gramophone motors can all contribute to audible results ranging from the tolerable to the execrable. Almost perfect sound reproduction is however available to enthusiasts possessing a suitable combination of discrimination, know-how, and financial resources. There are periodical magazines which provide guidance.

**Hindi,** the official language of India. *See* M36.

**Hinduism.** *See* J21.

**Hindustani,** the spoken form of Hindi (written in Devanagari script) and Urdu (written in Arabic characters).

**Hippogriff,** a fabulous animal, like a horse in body, but with the head, wings, and front legs and claws of an eagle. The monster frequently appears in the romances of the Middle Ages.

**Hippopotamus** or "river-horse," the largest living representative of the hog family, widely distributed over Africa, where it lives in herds. It is of immense bulk, attaining a length of 12 ft. and a weight of 4 tons and stands about 5 ft. high. Its skin is hairless and about 2 in. thick, and it has a pair of tusks often weighing as much as 6 lb. It spends most of its time in the water, and lives entirely on vegetation, both aquatic and terrestrial. The pigmy hippopotamus, which occurs in forests and swamps in W. Africa, is only half the size.

**Histology** is the study of the structure of plant and animal tissues. These mainly consist of groups of cells with similar functions, *e.g.*, muscle, brain tissue.

**Hittites,** an ancient race (often mentioned in the Old Testament) who inhabited Cappadocia (region of Eastern Asia Minor) from the third to the first millennium B.C. Excavations have revealed that they attained a high level of civilisation round about 1350 B.C. The Hittites were rivals of Egypt, disputing with the Pharaohs the mastery of the Middle East. They were the first to smelt iron successfully.

**Hobby,** a bird of the falcon family, 12–14 in. long. Local breeding visitor to England and Wales, April–Sept.; irregular visitor to Scotland and Ireland. They winter in Africa.

**Hog,** the common name of animals of the Suina family, including the wild boar, pig, and sow. The wild boar, *Sus scrofa*, is the common ancestor. The skin of the hog is covered with bristles, the snout truncated, and each foot has four hoofed toes. Hogs are omnivorous feeders and eat almost anything that is given them.

**Hogmanay,** the Scottish New Year's Eve festival and a national holiday of the country. The custom of demanding Hogmanay bread is still upheld in many parts of Scotland.

**Hogshead,** a cask of varying capacity, also a specific measure. In the old English measure a hogshead was 63 old gallons of wine (= 52½ imperial gallons). Of beer 54 old gallons make a hogshead.

**Hollands, Schiedam,** or **Schnapps,** a kind of gin made mostly in Holland from rye and malt, with a flavouring of juniper berries.

**Holly,** a hardy evergreen shrub, largely grown in England. Its bright dark green prickly curved leaves and clusters of red berries are familiar in all parts of the country, and used as house decoration between Christmas Eve and Twelfth Night, probably a relic from Roman and Teutonic customs. Its wood is white and hard, valued for carved work, while its bark yields a gummy substance which is coveted into birdlime.

**Hologram,** a photographic record, taken under special optical conditions, of light reflected from a scene or object. The hologram is typically a piece of film. However it is nothing like a photographic negative of the ordinary kind; for one thing it will show an unintelligible pattern of light and dark patches. Nevertheless if it is illuminated (again under special optical conditions) the light coming through it will form a *three dimensional* image of the original object. Another radical difference between a hologram and an ordinary film is that if the hologram is cut up, each fragment can be used to construct the entire image. Holography, as a method of recording and reproducing photographic information, was conceived by Gabor in 1947 but was only fully realised in practice after the invention of the laser (*q.v.*). The use of laser light is one of the "special conditions" referred to above. Technical applications are being explored in many laboratories.

**Holy Alliance,** an alliance ostensibly for conserving religion, justice and peace in Europe, but used for repressing popular tendencies towards constitutional government. Formed by Alexander I. of Russia, Francis I. of Austria and Frederick William III. of Prussia, at Paris on Sept. 26, 1815. Subsequently joined by all the sovereigns of Europe, except the Pope and the King of England. It ended after the 1830 revolution in France.

**Holy Coat of Trèves,** a garment preserved in the Cathedral of Trèves and said to have been worn by Christ. It was brought from Jerusalem by the Empress Helena in the fourth century.

**Holy Rood,** an annual Roman Catholic festival held on Sept. 14 to celebrate the Elevation of the Cross in commemoration of its re-erection in Jerusalem by the Emperor Heraclius in 628 after retaking it from the Persians. Also included in the Church of England calendar.

**Holyrood,** the ancient royal palace at Edinburgh, dating from the 15th cent., and inhabited by many Scottish sovereigns, notably Mary Stuart, the rooms occupied by her (including the one in which Rizzio was murdered) being still shown. It is now known as Holyrood House and is still used as a royal residence.

**Holy Roman Empire,** the title which the German Empire received in 962 when Pope John XII. crowned Otto I. at Rome. It endured until 1806 when Francis II. became Emperor of Austria.

**Holy Water,** water blessed by a priest and kept in small fonts at the entrance to Roman Catholic churches, and used by worshippers going in, and out, or by priests in sprinkling.

**Holy Week** is the week preceding Easter Sunday, and includes the days of the Sufferings of Christ, ending on Good Friday.

**Honey,** the sweet syrup formed by bees from the nectar of flowers, the sucrose in the nectar being converted into a mixture of the simple sugars, glucose and fructose. Hybla, an ancient town of Sicily, on the southern slope of Mt. Etna, was famous for its honey.

> " For your words, they rob the Hybla bees
> And leave them honeyless." (*Julius Caesar*).

**Honey-eater,** an Australian bird (of which there are many species) provided with a long curved bill and tufted tongue. It lives by sucking the " nectar " from the flowers which abound in rural parts of Australia and New Zealand.

**Hookah,** an Oriental pipe for tobacco smoking, the smoke being drawn through the water of a goblet (commonly a coconut shell) by means of a long flexible tube.

**Hoopoe,** a remarkably handsome bird with vivid black and white-barred wings and tail and black-tipped crest which opens like a fan. Ranges over Europe, Asia, and Africa. It has bred in England and Wales and occurs in the British Isles in small numbers at all seasons. Other species are confined to Africa, Madagascar, and India.

**Hops,** the female " cones " of the hop plant used in brewing; their essential oils give beer an aromatic flavour, and their tannin and resin act as a preservative as well as accounting for the bitter taste desired. The hop is a perennial climber belonging to the mulberry family. The male and female organs are on separate plants;

as only the female flower-heads are commercially useful, female plants predominate in a hop garden, only a very few male plants being grown so that the female flowers can be fertilised.

**Horizon,** the limit of vision, the apparent line where sea and sky, or land and sky meet. This is termed the *sensible* or visible horizon. An ordinary person at the height of 5 feet can see for 3 miles, at 20 feet 6 miles, at 50 feet 9½ miles, and at 1,000 feet 42 miles. The figures are approximate.

**Horn** *or* **French Horn,** a brass instrument of the trumpet family (*i.e.,* played by three valves) whose tube is very thin and long (Horn in F = 12 ft.). In consequence the tube is curled in a complicated manner. Owing to the sweet tone it is capable of producing, the Horn sometimes plays as part of the wood-wind.

**Hornbill,** large bird found in Africa and oriental regions, remarkable for its having an immense horned upward-curved helmet, growing over its downward curved beak. It inhabits tropical regions, and feeds on fruits. When the female nas laid her eggs in the hollow of a tree, the male bird stops up the entrance, and keeps her imprisoned until the hatching is completed and the young ones are able to fly. There are about 45 species.

**Horneblende,** the commonest member of the amphibole group of minerals, a silicate of calcium, magnesium, iron and aluminium, of a dark green colour. It is a constituent of numerous rocks, including diorite, syenite, and hornblende schist.

**Horned Viper,** a curious African genus of *Viperidae,* with a small pointed bone over each eyebrow; a venomous species, found in Egypt, is thought by some to be identical with the " adder " mentioned in Genesis xlix. 17.

**Hornet,** a general name for many of the bigger wasps. It usually nests in hollow trees, and despite its rather fiercesome appearance does not sting unless unduly provoked.

**Horology,** the science of time-measurement, including the construction and management of clocks, watches, etc. Instruments of this kind are not known to have existed before the 12th cent. and until the introduction of the pendulum in the 17th cent., clocks were ill-regulated and inaccurate. The time-recording mechanisms of the present day include (*a*) the *clock,* which shows the hours and minutes by hands, and strikes the hours, and sometimes quarters; (*b*) the *timepiece,* which is not generally a fixture and shows the time, but does not strike; (*c*) the *watch,* which is a pocket time-keeper; (*d*) the *chronometer,* which indicates the minutest portions of time; (*e*) electric timepieces, mains electric clocks; (*f*) the highly accurate quartz-crystal and atomic clocks used for astronomical purposes. *See* Clocks.

**Horse Chestnut,** one of the large forest trees, with ample branches, and full foliage, and much esteemed for parks and ornamental grounds. The bark and fruit seeds yield substances of commercial value, but the timber is not worth much. The tree came originally from Asia about the 16th cent.

**Horse Guards,** the building in Whitehall which until 1872 was the headquarters of the Commander-in-Chief of the British Army. The archway is still sentinelled by mounted guards.

**Horse Latitudes,** the latitudes of the sub-tropical high pressure systems, between the trade winds and the prevailing westerlies, characterised by light variable winds and low humidity.

**Hospitallers, Knights,** were of the order of St. John of Jerusalem, at first devoted to the aid of the sick, but afterwards military monks, who became prominent figures in the Crusades of the 12th cent. They adopted the Benedictine black habit with the eight-pointed cross worn by the modern St. John's Ambulance Brigade. In 1309 they took Rhodes, but were expelled by the Ottomans in 1522. In 1530 the emperor Charles V gave them the island of Malta, which, as Knights of Malta, they held until 1798, when they were dislodged by Napoleon. The Knights still survive as a sovereign order, with headquarters in Rome. *See* Templars and Teutonic Order.

**Hottentots,** name given to certain African natives by Dutch settlers in the 17th cent. They used to occupy the greater part of Cape Colony, and though driven out a number still survive in S.W. Africa. Appear to be related to the Bushmen, though their culture is more advanced. In addition to herding, they practise some farming and know how to smelt iron.

**Hounds** are dogs that were originally bred and trained for hunting, such as the greyhound, foxhound, bloodhound, wolfhound, deerhound, beagle, harrier, etc., but now often kept also as domestic dogs. The greyhound, deerhound, and wolfhound hunt by sight, the others, with the bloodhound first in order, track by scent.

**Hour-glass,** a glass instrument tapering to the middle to a narrow orifice, through which a sufficient quantity of fine sand gravitates to mark an hour of time. When the sand has run through from one end, it can be reversed and made to count the hour in the opposite direction. The same kind of glass with smaller supplies of sand will indicate shorter periods, as an egg-glass, which runs its course in three minutes—time to boil an egg by, or to gauge the length of a telephone trunk call.

**House Flies** are world-wide and prolific. Their eggs are hatched within 24 hours of being laid, and full maturity is attained in a month. They feed mainly on decayed animal and vegetable matter.

**Hovercraft,** or air cushion vehicle, is a craft which is lifted on a pad of air underneath it. This pad or cushion must be at a pressure higher than that of the atmosphere and it is made by sucking in air above the craft and ejecting it in a downward stream all round the lower edge. The stream is guided by a flexible skirt and the high pressure air pad is contained partly by the skirt and partly by the air stream itself which forms a continuous air curtain all round the vehicle. Hovercraft are being intensively developed and there are variations in the basic scheme just described and also in the means of propulsion which can be by air or water jets or propellers. Hovercraft were devised by Cockerell in the 1950s and a full-scale example appeared before the British public in June 1959. Craft of over 100 tons are made commercially and much bigger ones conceived. The air pad support means that hovercraft can move over land, water, or marsh. Cross-Channel hovercraft were introduced in 1966.

**Howler Monkey,** a genus of South American monkey noted for a laryngeal conformation which enables it to emit a loud reverberant noise something between a yell and a howl, as the name suggests.

**Huanuco-bark,** a medicinal bark, brought from the Peruvian town of that name, and derived from the *Cinchona micrantha* tree. *See* Cinchona.

**Huguenots,** a name applied to the French Protestant communities of the 16th and 17th cent. Henry of Navarre, by the Edict of Nantes in 1598, granted them religious freedom, but more than a quarter of a century before—Aug. 24, 1572—thousands had been put to death in the massacre of St. Bartholomew. The revocation of the Edict of Nantes by Louis XIV. in 1685 drove thousands into exile in England, Holland, Germany, and America.

**Humanism.** *See* J21.

**Humble-bee** or **Bumble-bee,** the common name of the insects of the genus *Bombus,* of the Hymenoptera order. They live in small communities comprising males, females, and drones, their habitations being underground. They do not have one queen bee only like the hive bee, but several females occupy the same nest, and these alone live through the winter, breeding and forming new colonies in the spring. Although this large bee buzzes loudly, it does not sting.

**Humidity,** the state of the atmosphere with respect to the water-vapour it contains. "Absolute humidity " is defined as the density of the vapour present, while "relative humidity," more frequently employed indicates the degree of saturation, *i.e.,* the ratio of the actual vapour pressure to the saturation vapour pressure at the particular temperature, expressed as a percentage.

**Humming Birds** are so called because of the humming noise made by the vibration of their wings in flying. They are of radiant plumage, and are among the smallest birds. The smallest bird in the world is the Fairy or Princess Helen's humming bird of Cuba. The body is 2 in. long and the eggs are $\frac{3}{10}$ in. long. There are from four to five hundred species, and they are confined wholly to North and South America, being most numerous in the tropical latitudes. They have long, slender bills and tubular tongues which reach down into flowers to suck up the nectar on which they feed.

**Hummum**, the original name for what is now called the Turkish Bath in this country. One of the first of these baths to be established in London was the Hummums in Covent Garden.

**Hundred**, the ancient divisional name given to a portion of a county for administration or military purposes. It is supposed to imply the territory occupied by a hundred families; or the space of a hundred hides of land, or the capacity of providing 100 soldiers. Each hundred had its hundred court, with powers similar to those of a manor court, but this was abolished in 1867 by County Court Act.

**Hundred Days**, the interval of time between Napoleon Bonaparte's entry into Paris after his escape from Elba and his departure after his abdication, extending from March 20, 1815 to June 28. During this period occurred the battle of Waterloo, June 18.

**Hundred Years' War**, a term applied to the almost incessant contest between England and France, lasting from 1338 to 1453, including such famous battles as Crécy, Poitiers, and Agincourt, and engaging successively Edward III., Henry V., and Henry VI., among English kings.

**Huns**, a fierce Asiatic race which swept over eastern Europe in the 4th cent. Under Attila about the middle of the 5th cent. they obtained control of a large portion of central and eastern Europe, forcing even Rome to pay tribute. Their defeat at Châlons-sur-Marne in 451 by a mixed army of Romans, Goths, and Teutonic tribes, and the death of Attila in 453, terminated their empire.

**Hurdy-Gurdy**, an Italian rustic so-called musical stringed instrument of the lute order, the sounds of which are produced by the action of a rosined wheel turned by the left hand, the notes being made by the fingering of the right hand.

**Hurricane.** *See* Cyclone *and* Wind.

**Hydra**, an aquatic animal of simple structure, whose body is in the form of a cylindrical tube, with a disc-shaped base by which it attaches itself to any shifting substance. Its mouth is surrounded by tentacles by which it catches its food. The Hydra has the power of reproducing lost parts.

**Hydrates** are compounds containing water of crystallisation.

**Hydraulic Ram**, a form of automatic pump, used to raise water to a height by the action of its own falling velocity.

**Hydraulics**, the science of applied hydrodynamics, or water-machine engineering, ranging from pumps to marine engines.

**Hydrocarbons** are compounds of carbon and hydrogen. They include the *paraffins*, which are saturated compounds (*e.g.*, methane); the ethylene, acetylene and other series which are unsaturated; compounds with ring structures, *e.g.*, benzene, naphthalene, and anthracene. Petroleum is composed almost entirely of hydrocarbons. *See* F23.

**Hydrochloric Acid**, a solution of hydrogen chloride gas in water, and resulting in considerable quantities as a by-product of the soda-ash or salt-cake manufacture. Its solution forms the common hydrochloric or muriatic acid of commerce. It is present to the extent of nearly half a per cent. in the digestive juice secreted by the stomach.

**Hydrocyanic Acid**, cyanide of hydrogen or prussic acid; very poisonous, and of the odour of bitter almonds. It is formed by the action of acids on sodium or potassium cyanide. Used to kill wasps (and in the gas chamber in the U.S.A.). It is a very important chemical on account of the reactions of its derivatives in many synthetic fields. Discovered by Scheele in 1782.

**Hydroelectric Schemes.**—The sun's energy has been indirectly exploited in the past by harnessing the energy of the winds and rain. Our climate is due, essentially, to differential heating of the earth. The resulting convection currents in the air (the motion of which is complicated by the rotation of the earth) give rise to winds.

Moisture is collected from the sea and deposited high up on mountains as rain. Some of the gravitational energy may be collected as hydropower. Simple windmills or waterwheels are so undependable that they have not been used to any extent since the beginning of the Industrial Revolution. However, the modern form of the waterwheel—the hydroelectric generation plant —is extensively used in mountainous countries and about a third of the world's electricity is produced by this means. The essential requirements for a modern hydroelectric scheme are a river with a sufficient flow of water to provide the required power, a large " head " of water so that a cheap, compact turbine can be used and a dam so that water can be stored until it is required. In some cases a hydroelectric scheme is made economic by being associated with an irrigation or drainage scheme. Such multi-purpose schemes are especially important in certain Commonwealth countries, notably India and Pakistan, where most hydro projects are of this type. Other well-known examples include the Snowy Mountains Scheme in Australia and the Aswan High Dam in Egypt. Although over 90 per cent. of the electricity in certain individual countries, notably Norway, Sweden, Portugal, Switzerland, and Uganda is produced from hydroelectric schemes, only a relatively small fraction of the total potential has been exploited. This fraction varies from about a third in Western Europe to a quarter in the United States to a very small fraction in Alaska, Canada, Africa, and the hinterland of Asia.

**Hydrofluoric Acid** is obtained by distillation of fluorspar with sulphuric acid, and is a compound of fluorine and hydrogen. Its action is highly corrosive; a valuable agent in etching on glass, and a rapid decomposer of animal matter.

**Hydrogen**, Symbol H, the simplest element, atomic number (*q.v.*) of 1, colourless, and the lightest of all substances. Cavendish in 1766 was the first to recognise that it was an element. It is 14·4 times as light as air, and is found in a free state in volcanic regions. It can be obtained by the action of metals on acids, and forms an explosive mixture with air, burning with oxygen to form water. Commercially it is used to produce the very hot flame of the oxy-hydrogen blowpipe for cutting metals; to fill balloons and airships; to harden certain oils and render them suitable for margerine- and soap-production. The gas can be liquefied, and the presence of the isotope deuterium was detected by Urey in 1931 in the residue of the evaporated liquid. The third isotope, tritium, is very rare. *See also* Deuterium, Tritium, *and* F22, F23.

**Hydrography**, the science of water measurement, as applied to seas, rivers, lakes, currents, rocks, reefs, etc., and embracing the whole art of navigation.

**Hydrometer**, an instrument for measuring the specific gravity of liquids, especially for ascertaining the strength of spiritous liquors and solutions. It is usually in the form of a glass bulb, to the lower end of which a smaller bulb, containing mercury, is attached, which forces the instrument to sink into the liquid which it is to test. The larger bulb has a scale fixed to it, and the indication on this scale of the sinking point shows the specific gravity. There are many varieties: Twaddell's—a pear-shaped bulb containing mercury: Beaumé's of similar construction, but applicable to liquids both heavier and lighter than water: Sykes's, largely employed for determining the strength of alcohol: and Nicholson's, used for taking the specific gravities of solids.

**Hydropathy**, the method of treating disease with water, either by bathing or drinking. Natural springs of special chemical and therapeutic properties, such as sulphur springs, and other mineral sources, have been used since prehistoric times for this purpose. It is probably one of the most ancient methods of cure. Recently the beneficial effects of pure water treatment have been advocated. Hydropathic establishments have been set up in many health resorts.

**Hydroponics**, the culture of plants without soil. The plants are grown with their roots dipping into a solution of nutritive mineral salts; or they may be rooted in sand which is watered with such a solution.

**Hydrostatics,** the science of the pressure and equilibrium of liquids that are non-elastic.

**Hydrozoa** are a class of water animals of the *Coelenterata phylum* to which Hydra (*q.v.*) belongs. In one order of the Hydrozoa, free-swimming colonies showing marked division of labour between the individual units occur; this order includes the Portuguese man-of-war.

**Hyena,** a nocturnal carnivore with powerful jaws. The striped hyenas inhabit N. Africa, India, and S.W. India. The brown hyenas with long shaggy hair are natives of S. Africa. The spotted, or laughing hyena, noted for the peculiar cry from which its name is derived, is also confined to Africa.

**Hygrometer,** an instrument for measuring the amount of water vapour in the atmosphere. A simple form of hygrometer, known as the wet-and-dry bulb, consists of two vertical thermometers affixed to a frame. One bulb is exposed to the air, and the other is covered with muslin which dips into a water-bath to keep it moist. If the air is saturated, it takes up no moisture from the wet bulb and the two thermometers read the same. If the air is not saturated, evaporation takes place from the wet bulb, latent heat is absorbed from the air, and the temperature of the wet bulb is lower than that of the dry bulb. Relative humidity and dew-point of the air can then be derived from suitable tables. Hygrometers depending upon the expansion of human hair and gold-beater's skin and the deposition of dew on a polished surface, when cooled sufficiently, are also in general use. *See* Humidity.

**Hymenoptera,** the order of insects to which bees, wasps, hornets, ants and sawflies belong. They have a well-defined waist, two pairs of membranous wings coupled together, mouth parts modified for biting or sucking; the females possess an ovipositor used for depositing eggs and is sometimes modified for stinging. There are about 70,000 species in this order and many live in highly organised communities. *See also* Ichneumon Fly.

**Hyperbola.** A curve described by certain comets that go round the sun and never return.

**Hypsometer,** an instrument formerly used by mountaineers to find the height above sea-level by indirectly measuring the atmospheric pressure by determining the boiling point of water at the particular height. Based on the fact that as pressure decreases with height so the boiling point is lowered. Superseded by the aneroid barometer.

# I

**Ibex,** wild goats of several species found in the mountain regions of Europe, Asia, and Africa. The male has exceedingly large curved ridged horns. The species that lives in the Alps is called the Steinbock or bouquetin.

**Ibis,** belongs to a family of birds related to the stork. The sacred ibis of ancient Egypt is now extinct in Egypt but is found in the lakes and swamps of the Sudan near the Upper Nile. It has white and black plumage and a long curved beak. Other species are found elsewhere, the Glossy Ibis (black plumage glossed with purple and green) occasionally visiting England.

**Ibo,** a large tribe of S.E. Nigeria, numbering between 5 and 6 million. Since the end of British rule they have been active in their struggle for national independence and under their leader, Ojukwu, embarked upon the secessionist state of Biafra and the civil war against Federal forces. The Hausa and the Yoruba are the other main Nigerian groups.

**Ice** is frozen water. It is a colourless, crystalline and brittle solid. Being only 92% as dense as water, it floats on the latter; the expansion which occurs as water changes into ice causes the fracture of water-pipes, though the fracture only becomes obvious when the ice melts and leaks out through the crack. The temperature at which ice forms is $0°$ C., $32°$ F. Ice can be melted by pressure, and the ease and smoothness with which one is able to skate on ice depend on this phenomenon.

**Ice Ages.** Periods during which the continents were partly or largely covered by ice-sheets and glaciers. The present-day ice-sheets of Greenland and Antarctica are relics of the latest Ice Age, which began in the Pleistocene. Much of the southern hemisphere experienced an ice age at the end of the Carboniferous Period; ice ages are recorded from isolated localities during the Pre-Cambrian, but there is no evidence that these were simultaneous. *See* F9(1), 45(2), A2.

**Icebergs** are detached masses of glacier which subside into the sea and float as wind or current may take them. About one ninth of an iceberg is above sea-level. The North Atlantic is the chief home of icebergs, which reach the ocean from the ice-clad plateaux of Greenland. Some of these floating masses of ice are of enormous proportions, and constitute in the spring and early summer seasons a great menace to the safety of ships, as was disastrously shown in the *Titanic* catastrophe of 1912. For some years past these menaces to N. Atlantic shipping have been kept under close observation by vessels specially detailed for this work.

**Ice-breaker,** a special heavy bow-plated ship for forcing a way through ice and used especially at ports of the Baltic Sea and the Great Lakes region of Canada which freeze during the winter months. The Soviet atomic ice-breaker *Lenin*, the first of its kind in the world, launched in Dec. 1957, is designed to cut a channel through ice of any thickness. Her icebreaking performance will allow the sea-route to the north of Siberia to be kept open throughout the year.

**Icelandic Literature,** the Old Norse literature, centred about Iceland, which includes numerous works of poetry, mythology, and history of interest and importance. Much of this literature is in the saga form. *See also* Edda.

**Iceland Moss,** a kind of lichen (*Cetrario islandica*) which grows in great quantities in the mountain regions of Iceland and other Northern countries. It possesses certain nutritive qualities and is of some value in medicine.

**Iceland Spar,** a colourless form of calcite (calcium carbonate), frequently found in association with metallic ores; it has the power to produce strong double refraction of light so that two images are seen of an object viewed through a piece of Iceland spar. It was formerly used in optical apparatus for producing polarised light.

**Iceni,** an ancient British race who in early times lived in Norfolk and other parts of Eastern England. Their most famous ruler was Queen Boadicea, who led her people against the Romans in A.D. 61.

**Ice Plant,** also called " dew plant " and " diamond plant." A South African mesembry-anthemum commonly grown in British gardens. Introduced in 1690.

**Ice Saints,** St. Mamertus, St. Pancras and St. Servatius, so called because of the legendary cold on these Saints' Days, namely, May 11–13.

**Ichneumon,** the Egyptian mongoose, popularly known as "Pharaoh's Rat." It is of great use in checking the multiplication of reptiles. It is frequently domesticated.

**Ichneumon Fly,** a numerous group of parasitic hymenopterous insects abounding in many lands, and all having the peculiarity of depositing their eggs in the bodies of other insects. It destroys swarms of caterpillars, which become the unwilling hosts of their progeny.

**Ichthyology,** the natural history of fishes.

**Ichthyosaurus** was a gigantic marine reptile of the Mesozoic age. The fossils are mostly found in the lias formation. Some were over 30 ft. in length.

**Icons.** Icons are religious paintings designed for devotional use either by the individual or in church rituals. In size they range from the very small to large ones in two or three panels on church screens dividing the nave from the chancel (these are known as diptych and triptych respectively). The icon style of painting derives from the tomb paintings of Hellenistic and Roman Egypt, where it had become the custom to leave a portrait of the dead over the mummy's face. Icons of the earlier periods are rare, those of the 6th cent. probably having been destroyed and those of the 9th–12th cent. mostly removed to Russia. They were essentially simple with the Virgin and Child, or the Virgin, Christ, and John the Baptist as subject. From the 13th cent. icons were more complex, dealing with New Testament scenes or scenes from the lives of the saints, and by this time schools of painting, each with their own style, were arising in other countries, including Russia, which accepted the Eastern Church. The 16th-cent. icons begin to show Italian influence just as Italian painting was influenced by Byzantine. Most icons were painted on wood, but mosaic was sometimes used, and some icons were of metal.

**Ides,** in the ancient Roman Calendar, the 15th of March, May, July, October, and the 13th of all other months; always the eighth day after the Nones.

**Idiom,** an expression characteristic of a country, district, dialect or language, which usually gives strength and force to a phrase or sentence. The idioms of a language are its distinctive marks, and the best writers are the most idiomatic.

**Idris,** a famous giant belonging to the myths of Wales, commemorated by a chair of rock on the top of the Cader Idris mountain in Merionethshire.

**Igneous Rocks** are such as have been molten under conditions of great heat at some stage in their history: e.g., granite, basalt. See F8(2).

**Ignis Fatuus** or "Will-o'-the-wisp," a phosphorescent light which may often be seen on summer and autumn evenings hovering over marshy ground or graveyards. Its nature is hardly understood, though it is generally believed to be the result of the spontaneous combustion of the gases from decaying organic matter. In olden times when marshy grounds were more common than now, this "dancing light" was very frequently visible and was regarded with superstition.

**Iguana,** large South American lizards, with a long tail, a scaly back and head, a thick fleshy tongue and a prominent dew-lap in the throat. Specimens of the different species average 4–5 ft. in length, and they live mostly in trees, though they are equally at home on land or in the water. The flesh of some species is good eating, as are also the eggs.

**Iguanodon,** a genus of extinct dinosaurs, whose fossils are found in the Jurassic and Cretaceous rocks. Iguanodons were 15–25 ft. long, and walked on their hind legs, the front legs being small and adapted for grasping the branches of trees on the leaves of which they fed.

**Ilex,** mentioned by classical authors, is the holm- or holly-oak, which flourishes round the Mediterranean. To botanists Ilex is the genus to which the holly and maté plant belong. See T9(2).

**Iliad,** the great epic poem of ancient Greece attributed to Homer (c. 700 B.C.). It consists of ancient folk tale and saga, welded into an artistic unity, having as plot the carrying off of Helen by Paris to Troy and the subsequent siege of Troy. See H19.

**Illuminated MSS.** of great value and beauty of decoration exist in most public museums and in many private collections, some of them being of great antiquity, especially those of ancient Egypt executed on papyri. Greek and Latin specimens are also numerous, and the British Museum contains fine examples of all these kinds and also an extensive collection of mediæval English MSS.

**Ilmenite,** a mineral widespread in igneous rocks: chemically it is an oxide of iron and titanium. Rich deposits have recently been found in the Allard Lake area of Quebec; the Travancore sands are also a source of ilmenite.

**Immortality.** See J22.

**Immortelles** are wreaths, crosses, or other designs made from what are called everlasting flowers, which are obtained from certain plants of the Composite order, and retain their colours and compactness for a long time. Immortelles are largely used as mementoes for decorating graves, especially in France.

**Impeachment,** a special arraignment, usually before Parliament or other high tribunal, of a person charged with some offence against the State. The custom in England was for the impeachment to be made in the House of Commons, and the trial to be before the House of Lords. The first instance occurred in 1376 when Lord Latimer was impeached. With present parliamentary procedure, impeachment is no longer necessary, since the Cabinet is responsible for the individual actions of its ministers, who, acting as a team, must carry the Commons with them, or resign, when it falls to the Leader of the Opposition to form a new Cabinet. Other famous impeachments were those of the Lord High Chancellor Francis Bacon (1621), Earl of Strafford and Archbishop Laud (1640), Warren Hastings (1788), the last being that of Lord Melville (1805). Under the constitution of the United States public officials may be impeached by the House of Representatives and tried by the Senate. The most famous case was that of President Andrew Johnson.

**Imperialism.** See J22.

**Impluvium,** a basin or tank in the hall or atrium of an ancient Roman house, serving the purpose of receiving the rain that dropped through the open space in the roof.

**Impressionism,** the name given contemptuously to the first modern movement in painting, being derived from the title of Claude Monet's picture Impression: soleil levant, which showed the play of light on water with the observer looking straight into the rising sun. Although intended to be the ultimate form of naturalism the inspiration of the school had been the scientific study of light with an attempt to render the play of light on the surface of objects. Feeling that putting a line around a form was bound to cause it to look unnatural, they used bright colours corresponding to the spectrum and unmixed on the palette, and noted that an object of any given colour casts a shadow tinged with the complementary one (e.g., red-green, yellow-blue). Hence bright sunlight was represented in clear yellows and orange with violet shadows. The first Impressionist exhibition held in Paris in 1874 aroused derision with its paintings by Monet, Renoir, Sisley, Pissaro, Cézanne, and Degas among others. Impressionism subsequently led to the entirely artistic and anti-naturalist movement of Post-impressionism. Cézanne, who felt that he wanted to produce "something solid and durable, like the art of the museums," was only dubiously impressionist, as were also Degas and Renoir. Of course, in the wider sense of the word (i.e., the recording of an ephemeral impression of a scene), Whistler, Turner, and even Rembrandt used the technique.

**Impressment,** the forced seizure of persons for military service resorted to by many countries before the establishment of conscription. Press gangs forcibly recruited men for British warships especially during the Napoleonic wars, but such measures were abandoned after about 1850.

**Imprimatur,** originally an official licence to print, and an important formula in the early days of printing. The term is now used in the wider significance of authority, or endorsement.

**Inbreeding,** mating of closely related animals and plants. Close inbreeding has long been held to be harmful, but this is not necessarily so, for if practised with selection, stock can be purged of the undesirable qualities and the race improved.

**Incas,** an Indian people who inhabited ancient Peru, founded a great empire, and reached a high level of civilisation: overthrown by the Spaniards in 1533.

**Incense,** an aromatic resinous substance which, under combustion, exhales a pungent odour, and is used, mixed with certain fragrant perfumes, in the celebration of Mass in Roman Catholic churches. Olibanum or frankincense is ordinarily the leading ingredient.

**Incisors,** the sharp-edged cutting teeth at the front of mammalian jaws. Rodents have long, sharp incisor teeth. Elephant tusks are modified incisors.

**Income Tax,** a tax on annual income charged under the following schedules:
  Schedule A.—On the beneficial occupation of land (including buildings). Finally abolished as from 1964–65. Rents now assessed under Schedule D.
  Schedule B.—Abolished as from 1963–64 on amenity lands (parks, gardens). Restricted to woodlands managed on a commercial basis.
  Schedule C.—On dividends, interest, annuities from public revenue. Income Tax deducted at source.
  Schedule D.—On profits from trade, profes-

sion, or vocation; remittances from abroad; interest on government stocks not taxed at source, Post Office Savings, etc.; sundry profits; short-term gains; rents.

*Schedule E.*—On salaries, wages, pensions, emoluments, directors' fees, etc. Taxed under P.A.Y.E.

The income-tax year is from April 6 to the following April 5. Rates of tax on taxable income for the year 1969–70 are as follows:— on the first £260, 6s. (or 30 per cent.); on the balance 8s.3d. (or 41·25 per cent.). *Taxable* income is found by deducting from *Total* income certain allowances.

(1) *Earned Income* allowance of two-ninths to £4,005 and one-ninth to £9,945.
(2) *Personal* allowance of £255 to single persons and married women in employment; to married man living with his wife, or if wife though not living with, is wholly maintained by means of a voluntary allowance, £375. If the wife is maintained under a Court Order or under a binding legal agreement the allowance is reduced to £255. Personal allowances for a parent reduced by £42 for each child for whom family allowance is due.
(3) *Child* allowance of £115 for each child under 11; £140 over 11; and £165 over 16 if still being educated; provided child does not have income in own right of more than £115. With effect from 1969–70, investment income of minor children (under 18) aggregated with that of their parents.
(4) *Dependent Relative* allowance, £75; for single woman, widow, divorced or separated woman solely supporting dependent relative, £110. (Dependent's income limit: £245).
(5) *Daughter's Services*, necessary owing to old age or infirmity, allowance of £40.
(6) *Additional Personal* allowance of £100 to widows and widowers and certain other persons who have single-handed responsibility for a young child resident with them.
(7) *Housekeeper* allowance of £75 (certain restrictions).
(8) *Age relief* of two-ninths of unearned income where taxpayer (or his wife) is over 65 and total income does not exceed £1,000. Marginal allowances.
(9) *Life Insurance.* Life assurance policies taken out after 19 March 1968 which do not satisfy certain new conditions do not qualify for income tax relief on premiums and are subject to a charge to surtax in respect of the proceeds (less premiums).

*Age* Exemption: no tax payable by single persons aged 65 or over if income does not exceed £425; £680 for married couples where either is 65 or over. Appropriate marginal allowances.

*Pensions* qualify for the earned income relief of two-ninths.

*Small Income Relief.* All incomes up to £450 are treated as Earned Income.

*Surtax* is on a sliding scale, increasing from 2s. in the £ with the size of the income. Surtax on earned income, in effect, begins at £5,000, or more if personal reliefs are due. *See also* Surtax.

**Independence Day,** commemorates the adoption of the Declaration of Independence on July 4, 1776. July 4 is celebrated as a holiday in the United States.

**Index.** The name given to a list of books, prepared by papal authority, which are declared to be dangerous to faith and morals, and therefore forbidden to Roman Catholics, called the *Index librorum prohibitorum.* One of the reforms of the Vatican Council was the closing in 1966 of the Curia office which judged writings for the Church's Index of forbidden books, though the Index itself still remains. The Pope ordered that nothing should be placed on the Index until the author had been given a chance of explaining his views. The first Index was issued by Pope Pius IV, in 1559.

**India Office Library** (since 1947 called the Library of the Commonwealth Relations Office (Division B)). This is an orientalist library, which specialises in Indian studies. It was founded in 1801 by the East India Company, and contains 20,000 manuscripts in European languages and in Sanskrit, Persian, modern Indian, and other oriental languages, and a

quarter-of-a-million printed books, of which three-quarters are in oriental languages. There are also collections of drawings, photographs, and other objects of oriental interest. It was announced in 1965 that a judicial tribunal was to decide on legal ownership of library.

**Indian Ink,** a pigment made from lampblack and gum or glue, originally prepared in China and Japan. It is dried and marketed in small sticks and used mainly by artists for shading and lettering.

**Indian Mutiny.** This turning-point in the history of modern India occurred in 1857–58. The ostensible cause was the serving out to the native troops of cartridges greased with animal fat, for contact with this was forbidden both by the Hindu and Mohammedan faiths. A rebellious feeling, however, had long been developing, and when the Sepoys at Meerut in May 1857 refused to obey the English officers, overpowered and put them to death, the mutiny spread like wildfire. The rebels took Delhi and Lucknow, and for many months terrible massacres and atrocities were committed; men, women and children were slain in thousands. Order was re-established in the autumn of 1858 when the governing power was transferred from the East India Company to the Crown.

**Indian Summer** is applied to a warm spell of weather occurring in the late autumn.

**Indicators,** substances which by a marked change in colour are used to indicate the course of a chemical reaction. Litmus paper, for instance, is red with acids and blue with alkalis. In biological work some radioactive substances are used as tracer elements.

**Indigo,** the substance obtained from the plant *Indigofera tinctoria,* a native of S. Asia, India being the chief producing country. The colouring matter is the result of the decomposition and fermentation of a glucoside contained in the plant. This is afterwards dried and becomes the caked indigo of commerce. Natural indigo has been eclipsed by artificial indigo, a coal-tar dye which came into commercial production at the end of the last century, which is cheaper and more uniform in quality.

**Indium,** a scarce lead-coloured metal, symbol In, found in zinc blende in Saxony and certain other ores. This element was discovered in 1863 by Reich and Richter. It is an important material in the manufacture of transistors.

**Indo-European Languages.** *See* M37.

**Indulgence.** In the Roman Catholic Church the remission granted by ecclesiastical authority to a repentant sinner of the temporal punishment still due after the guilt of sin has been forgiven by God. The indiscriminate sale of Indulgences by Tetzel and other Papal agents in the 16th cent. was one of the grievances which led to the Reformation (*see* J38).

**Indulgence, Declaration of,** was the proclamation by which James II. suspended the penal laws against Roman Catholics and Dissenters. It was issued in 1688, but the clergy as a body refused to obey, and the trial of the Seven Bishops and their acquittal by a jury followed. An invitation was thereupon sent to William of Orange to become King.

**Industrialisation** is simply a name for industrial development. It is customarily used in particular to designate the course of events in a hitherto underdeveloped country which is seeking to increase its wealth and productivity by the introduction of more advanced techniques and by the establishment of industries previously not carried on within it. The word usually covers not only the development of modern industrial production but also the provision of electric power-stations, irrigation works, and transport and other developments designed to improve production in any field by methods involving large capital investments. The outstanding example in our time of rapid industrialisation has been the Soviet Union, which, unable to get the capital from abroad, has had to carry it through by ruthless restriction of the people's consuming power so as to achieve an unprecedentedly high ratio of investment to total production. Industrialisation has in practice meant a high concentration on the expansion of the basic heavy industries and of power supply, coupled with much slower development of the industries supplying consumers' goods and of agricultural production; but there is no reason why this should always be the case. It may well be that in most underdeveloped countries development can but be devoted largely to the industries making consumers' goods and to measures designed to increase agricultural production and productivity.

**Industrial Revolution.** The name, first given by Engels in 1844, to describe the radical changes that took place in Britain during 1760–1840 to transform a mainly agricultural country into one predominantly industrial. It began with the mechanisation of the textile industry (Hargreave's spinning jenny, 1764, Arkwright's water-frame, 1769, Comptons' mule, 1770, and Watt's steam-engine, 1785), with subsequent major developments in mining, transport, and industrial organisation. It was based on Britain's rich mineral resources, particularly coal and iron ore. With the use of the steam-engine as power, industry became concentrated round the coalfields and the great new industrial towns developed—Birmingham, Manchester, Newcastle and Glasgow. Britain became supreme in constructional ironwork (Telford, George and Robert Stephenson). Canals, bridges, railways, and ships were built, and great advances were made in the practical application of scientific principles. Aided by colonial exploitation Britain became the most prosperous country in the world. The new industrial capitalists began to replace the country squires as ruling class. But the great accumulation of wealth at one pole of society was matched at the other by poverty and misery, for child labour, long working hours, low wages, and slums were features of the industrial revolution in its infancy. As with all great technological developments, the industrial revolution produced related changes in all fields of social life—in politics, art, religion, literature, and morals, and with the rise of democracy, social reforms. *See also* Section Q, Part II.

**Inertia,** a term used in mechanics for the property of matter by which it offers resistance to a change in its state of rest or in its state or direction of motion.

**Inertial Navigation,** an automatic method of dead-reckoning which at present finds its chief application in guided missiles, submarines, and aircraft. Navigation by this means is carried out with reference to inertial space (*i.e.*, space which is stationary with respect to the fixed stars) and not to the surface of the earth as in normal navigation (latitude and longitude). This is done by means of high-accuracy gyroscopes combined with highly sensitive accelerometers in an apparatus known as the Ship's Inertial Navigation System. The American nuclear-powered submarine *Nautilus* pioneered the new north-west passage under the polar ice pack by this method of dead-reckoning in Aug. 1958.

**Inflorescence,** a flowering shoot. Many arrangements of the flowers are possible and there are many kinds of inflorescence; *e.g.*, the spike, catkin, umbel, capitulum (in composites).

**Inflation.** *See* G4(2).

**Infra-red Rays** *or* **Radiation.** This is the range of rays which come between the visible red rays and the ultra-short Hertzian radiation. The wave-lengths involved range from about 0·00076 millimetre (7,600 Angstrom units) to 0·4 millimetre. Infra-red rays penetrate haze; hence landscapes obscured by haze or cloud can be photographed using plates sensitive to infra-red. Many substances strongly absorb these rays and thereby become hot; this happens in toasting bread. Many industries use infra-red lamps for drying paints and lacquers. Very important to chemists, as a tool in the investigation of the structure of compounds, since various groups of elements absorb infra-red radiation at a characteristic frequency.

**Infula,** a sacred fillet, of woollen material, worn on the forehead by priests, magistrates and rulers in Roman times, also by persons fleeing for protection to sanctuary. Later, each of the two lappets of a bishop's mitre.

**Ingoldsby Legends,** a series of whimsical metrical tales full of droll humour written by the Rev. R. H. Barham, and first published in *Bentley's Miscellany* in 1837. The best known is the *Jackdaw of Rheims.*

**Ink,** a liquid pigment ordinarily made from an infusion of nut-galls, copperas, and gum arabic. Shumac is substituted for nut-galls for inferior inks. An acid is sometimes added to prevent oxidation, and for the blue-black inks a small quantity of solution of indigo serves for colouring. Copying ink contains glycerine or sugar, which keeps the ink moist. Lampblack used to be the leading ingredient in printer's ink but now new methods of manufacturing have been developed. Marking ink is composed of a solution of nitrate of silver, gum, ammonia, and carbonate of soda. For red, blue, and other coloured inks, colouring solutions are used, for example, Prussian blue. The earliest examples of ink writing (on wooden tablets) ever found in Britain were recovered from the well of a Roman villa (3rd cent A.D.) during excavations in 1954 at Chew Stoke, Somerset.

**Ink Sac,** a glandular organ found in squids and other cephalopods which contains an inky solution. When roused the animal discharges the contents of the ink sac into the water, to make a cloud through which its enemies cannot see. The pigment, sepia, comes from the ink sac of the cuttlefish.

**Inlaying** is the introduction of one class of substance into another in some artistic or other design, such as silver let into zinc, copper, or lead, and called *bidri*; the insertion of gold and silver into iron or steel, which is *damascening*; the mingling of brass with tortoiseshell, *buhl work*; the inlaying of woods, *marquetry*; of stone, *pietra dura*; and of the arrangement of small pieces of stone, for floors, walls, etc., *mosaic.*

**Innocents' Day,** a festival day in Roman, Greek, and Anglican Churches in commemoration of the killing of the children of Bethlehem by Herod, Dec. 28.

**Inns of Court,** the four bodies in London which enjoy the privilege of calling candidates to the bar after they have studied for a certain number of terms and passed certain examinations. The Inns are: the Inner Temple, the Middle Temple, Lincoln's Inn, and Gray's Inn.

**Inquisition,** a Roman Catholic ecclesiastical court which became a formidable weapon of the Church in the 13th cent. under Pope Innocent III. in dealing with charges of heresy. It was effectively set up in the various Catholic countries of the Continent, obtaining its fullest and most sweeping organisation in Spain in the days of Ferdinand and Isabella, when Torquemada was made Grand Inquisitor, and used its powers with terrible severity. *See* Auto-da-fé. In the 18th cent. its influence began to wane, and the jurisdiction of the Congregation of the Holy Office at Rome was limited to the suppression of heretical literature (*see* Index).

**Insectivorous Plants,** plants which trap insects with special mechanisms. Plant enzymes or bacteria digest the prey, providing the plants with nitrogen usually scarce in the soil in which they grow. The most common British species are the Sun-dew and the Bladderwort.

**Insects.** This huge class of invertebrate animals (*see* Arthropods, (F33)) includes about 100,000 species. Insects are ubiquitous except in the sea, only a very few species being adapted to marine existence. Characteristic features are: the body is divided into three parts, head, thorax, and abdomen: the head carries a pair of antennae, the thorax three pairs of legs, and usually two pairs of wings. The most primitive insects constituting the sub-class *Apterygota* are wingless. The other sub-class, *Pterygota*, is divided into the *Exopterygota* (*Hemimetabola*), which have a simple metamorphosis, *e.g.*, cockroach, and the *Endopterygota* (*Holometabola*), with a complex metamorphosis, *e.g.*, butterfly, bee. Although many are parasitic on man, animals and plants, innumerable animals and some plants use them as food, and many flowering plants are dependent on a variety of insects for pollination leading to the development of seeds and fruits. *See* F33(1), 38(2), T28(1).

**Insignia,** marks or badges of office or honour, such as stars, ribbons, crosses, medallions or other designating objects, worn by members of special Orders or holders of prominent offices.

**Instinct.**—*See* F38(1).

**Institut de France** was formed in 1795, and after various modifications was in 1832 organised on its present basis. Its five academies are—the Académie Française, Académie des Inscriptions et Belles-Lettres, Académie des Sciences, Académie des Beaux-Arts, Académie des Sciences morales et politiques. It is restricted to 40 members.

**Instruments, Musical.** Musical instruments may be classified in a number of ways, but in general they fall into one of the three main classes, String, Wind, and Percussion, according to how the sound is produced. Stringed Instruments are those which produce the sound by the vibration of a string: (*a*) by plucking, as in Harp, Lyre, Psaltery, Zither, Lute, Guitar, Balalaika, Ukelele, Harpsichord; (*b*) by friction (bowed), as in Crwth, Rebec, Viol, Violin, Marine Trumpet, Hurdy-Gurdy; (*c*) by striking (hammered), as in Dulcimer, Pianoforte, Clavichord; (*d*) by wind (blown), as in the Aeolian Harp. Wind Instruments are those in which the air in the instruments is set in vibration: (*a*) by blowing into a tube (flue-voiced), as in Recorder, Pandean Pipe, Flute, Organ; (*b*) by means of reeds (reed-voiced), as in Oboe, Clarinet, Saxophone, Bagpipe, Cor Anglais, Bassoon, Organ reed-stops; (*c*) those in which the sound is produced by the vibration of the player's lips against the mouthpiece (lip-voiced), as in Bugle, Horn, Trumpet, Tuba, Trombone, Saxhorn, Flügelhorn, Cornet. In a modern orchestra these are known as the *Brass*: instruments of the flute, oboe, and clarinet families as the *Woodwinds*. Then there are the Percussion Instruments, which include the Drums, Cymbals, Tambourines, Castenets.

**Insulator,** a substance that will not conduct electric current. Many solids, liquids, and gases are important insulators—rubber, cotton, silk, plastics, porcelain, glass, air, oil. If the applied voltage is too high, all insulators will " break down ", *i.e.*, conduct electricity perhaps with resulting breakage, puncture, or charring. Thermal insulators will not conduct heat; they are usually the same kinds of substance as electrical insulators.

**Insulin** is a hormone which controls the supply of sugar from the blood to muscles. The breakdown of sugar provides energy. In diabetes there is a lack of insulin, causing a build-up of blood sugar which can be released by the injection of insulin. It is secreted by the islet tissue of the pancreas, from which it was isolated in 1922 by Banting and Best. Dr. F. Sanger of Cambridge University was awarded the 1958 Nobel Prize for his work in determining the chemical structure of insulin.

**Intaglio,** engraving or carving on a sunken ground, a method frequently adopted in the ornamentation of stones and rings.

**Intelligence.** Intelligence has been variously defined as the innate potential of a person to learn and understand; to make appropriate judgments; to see the relationships between things; to profit from experience; or to meet adequately new problems and conditions in life. There are many lines of evidence to show that intellectual capacity is closely related to heredity and influenced by environmental factors. The idea of intelligence testing was first devised by the French psychologist Binet at the beginning of this century. He was asked by the French government to invent a test which would weed out backward children in state schools, and thus save public money and avoid holding back the work of the class by teaching children who were incapable of learning at a given standard. Briefly, a series of problems are given to a large number of children and it is thus found out which series can be solved by the average child of a given age-group; if a child of 7 can only pass the tests suitable to the average child of 6, then his mental age is 6. The intelligence quotient or I.Q. is discovered by dividing his mental age by his chronological age and multiplying by 100. A gifted child can usually be spotted at an early age. Although I.Q. tests are the standard method of estimating intelligence, they are not universally accepted as a criterion; a teacher's

general judgment may be the best assessment. High intelligence may be inherited, but fail to develop to the full because facilities for education are not available. Recent research suggests that the growth of the brain may be permanently affected by undernutrition at the time of its fastest growth (the last weeks before birth, and, to a lesser extent, the first weeks after birth). At this vulnerable period even quite minor deprivation can effect the rate and ultimate extent of growth of the brain. This has significance not only for the severely undernourished babies in the poor parts of the world, but for babies of low birth weight in our own communities. *See also* Section Q, Part I.

**Interest** is the payment made for the use of borrowed money over time. The rate of interest is the rate per cent per annum charged for such loans. There are many such rates, varying with the plenty or scarcity on borrowable money, with the length of time for which the loans are made, and with the degree of risk, if any, that the loans will not be duly repaid. Short-term loans are usually cheaper than long-term: the lowest rates are usually for " call money " repayable immediately on demand. These are used principally in short-term financial transactions, such as bill discounting. Bank loans, though usually made for fairly short terms, command higher rates. Long-term loans are made chiefly to public authorities, or as bonds or debentures to business concerns. The rates obtained vary with the demand and the supply of such accommodation.

**Interferon,** the name given to a substance discovered in 1957 by Drs. Isaacs and Lindenmann at the National Institute for Medical Research. It is produced by the interaction of viruses with living cells and has the important property of inhibiting virus reproduction. Its development may lead to a new approach to the therapy of viral diseases.

**International Date Line,** a line along the 180° meridian, marking the difference in time between E. and W. For the westward-bound traveller crossing the line the date would be put forward one day, for the eastward-bound, back one day. To avoid difference of date in adjacent land areas, the line deviates from the 180° meridian where this crosses land.

**Interval,** in music indicates the differences in pitch between two notes. This is often expressed numerically. Thus the interval between C and the E above it is a major third, that between C and E flat is a minor third, that between C and G is a fifth, that between C and A is a sixth.

**Introit,** the psalm sung by the choir as the priest approaches the alter to celebrate the Eucharist.

**Invention of the Cross,** a Roman Catholic festival held on May 3, to celebrate the finding of the alleged True Cross at Calvary by the Empress St. Helena in 326. Also included in the Church of England calendar. *See* Holy Rood.

**Iodine,** a non-metal element, symbol I, member of the halogen family (*q.v.*), a substance formerly exclusively obtained from the ribbon-wrack seaweeds. These were burnt and the ashes (kelp) extracted with water. After concentrating the iodides, these were distilled with manganese dioxide and sulphuric acid to yield iodine vapour which was condensed in stoneware bottles. Nearly all iodine now in use is derived from the iodine salt present in Chili saltpetre (sodium nitrate). Iodine is used in photography, as an antiseptic solution in alcohol or potassium iodide (tincture of iodine), and in medicine. Discovered by Courtois in 1812.

**Ions,** electrically charged atoms, or groups of atoms. Atoms of the metals lose electrons to become positively charged ions, *e.g.*, the sodium ion ($Na^+$) has one electron less than the atom. The non-metal ions are negatively charged, *e.g.*, the chloride ion ($Cl^-$) has one electron more than the atom. Similarly, a group like the sulphate ion ($SO_4^{2-}$) has more electrons than the constituent atoms. Thus, the hydrogen atom without its electron is a hydrogen ion or *proton* and the helium atom without its two electrons is a helium ion or *alpha-particle*. When an electric force is applied to certain solutions, the ions into which molecules of the dissolved substance are broken up are attracted to the oppositely charged electrodes, their movements constituting an electric current through the solution. In the same way gases, including air, conduct electricity by virtue of free ions (*see* F12(2)). Combustion, radio-activity, and ultra-violet and cosmic radiations produce ionisation.

**Ionic Order** of architecture is one of the five classic orders, its leading characteristics being the volute of its capital, which has on each side distinctive curved or scrolled ends.

**Ionosphere,** a succession of ionized layers of the earth's atmosphere lying above the stratosphere. In this region free electrically charged particles —electrons and positive ions—occur in sufficient concentration to affect substantially the propagation of radio waves through the region. It extends upwards from a height of 60 miles to several hundred miles, being most concentrated at an altitude of 200 miles. The behaviour of the upper atmosphere is strongly influenced by the sun. A great deal of new information about the ionosphere above an altitude of 150 miles (the topside ionosphere) has been obtained by the use of instruments carried in satellites. *See also* Atmosphere.

**Ipecacuanha,** a flowering plant of the Brazilian forests. Various alkaloids are isolated from ipecacuanha, one is emetine, which is used in medicine to cause vomiting and so remove poisons from the stomach. Another is used as an expectorant in cough mixtures.

**Iridium,** a white and very hard metal, symbol Ir, discovered by Tennant in 1804. It occurs naturally as an alloy with platinum or osmium; tips for fountain-pen nibs have been made from the former native alloy. The former standard metre was composed of platinum–iridium alloy (*see* Metre) as are parts of scientific apparatus and surgical tools that must be non-corrodible.

**Iris,** the typical genus of the botanical order *Iridacae,* with tuberous rhizomes and sword-shaped leaves, many of the family having beautiful flowers. About 100 species of Iris are recorded from the northern temperate zone, the most common species wild in Britain being the yellow flag. Orris root, used in perfumery, comes from another iris species.

**Iron** is a metallic element, symbol Fe (Latin *ferrum*), occurring widely in nature in such ores as haematite, loadstone (magnetic iron oxide), spathic ore, and iron pyrites. It is extracted by a process known as smelting, with coke and limestone in a furnace. Its many uses are familiar, the most important being in the manufacture of cast- and wrought-iron products and of steels, which are alloys mainly of iron with added carbon and various metals. Iron rust is formed by the action of oxygen and water, and is a coating of iron oxide. *See* Smelting.

**Ironclads,** ships of war cased in iron or steel plates of sufficient thickness to resist projectiles. They were first introduced (1858) in the French Navy, and in 1860 the first British ironclad, the *Warrior,* was launched.

**Iron Curtain.** In a speech at Fulton, U.S.A., on March 5, 1946, Sir Winston Churchill used this phrase to describe the dividing line behind which, he said, lie all the capitals of the ancient States of Central and Eastern Europe—Warsaw, Berlin, Prague, Vienna, Budapest, Belgrade, Bucarest, and Sofia. These famous cities and the populations around them, said Sir Winston, lie in the Soviet sphere and are subject " to a very high and increasing measure of control from Moscow."

**Ironsides** were Cromwell's special troopers, so called because of their solidity and firmness in battle.

**Irredentists,** a political party organised in Italy about 1878 with the object of incorporating within Italy neighbouring regions. Also a person, group, or party advocating policies for the restoration to their country of territory formerly belonging to it but later lost.

**Irrigation,** an artificial method of providing water for the growth of plants on lands where the natural supply of water is deficient. The science has made immense progress during the last fifty years, and has been the means of bringing into profitable cultivation vast tracts of territory in India and Western America which

had previously been arid wastes. The systems are various and are utilised according to the special conditions of the land to be irrigated, but the success which has attended these experiments has been very gratifying. In fact, irrigated lands are often more productive than lands which receive a fair amount of moisture from the elements; the irrigation supply can be distributed and regulated exactly according to requirements. Irrigation also serves the purpose of supplying *warmth* in winter; *e.g.,* in the English water-meadows, and in the more highly developed Italian *marcite* and winter-meadows, where the water is mostly applied in winter when there is plenty of rain. There are several other functions of irrigation; *e.g.,* washing out of excess salts.

**Isinglass,** a gelatinous substance manufactured from the swim bladders of certain fish; used to preserve eggs, to keep beer free from sediment, and to make a glue.

**Islam.** *See* J23.

**Isobars** are the lines drawn on charts linking together points of equal barometric pressure.

**Isochasms,** lines connecting places at which there is an equal probability of seeing an aurora, taking the average over a number of years, based on the auroral catalogue of Fritz.

**Isomers** are chemical compounds having the same composition but different structural arrangements, and consequently different physical and chemical properties. For example, ethyl alcohol and methyl ether are isomers, since the molecules of both are built up of two atoms of carbon, six of hydrogen, and one of oxygen, *viz.,* $C_2H_6O$; ethyl alcohol, $C_2H_5OH$; and methyl ether, $CH_3OCH_3$.

**Isotherms** are lines drawn on charts through points of equal temperature.

**Isotopes.** When one talks of an element, say, uranium or lead, the name of the element is a generic name for a collection of uranium species and lead species. The different species are called isotopes. For any particular element, the number and arrangement of electrons around the nucleus are the same in all the isotopes, so all the isotopes have the same chemical properties. Soddy has described isotopes as " elements, the atoms of which have similar outsides but different insides." For example, in the nucleus of the uranium isotopes, U 235, U 238, and U 239, there are respectively 143, 146, and 147 neutrons, but all have 92 protons. The isotopes have different atomic weights, in this instance respectively 235, 238, and 239. But all have the same chemical properties. *See* F10(2)

**Ivory,** the dentine substance of which the tusks of the elephant, hippopotamus, walrus, etc., are composed. The tusks of the African elephant sometimes weigh as much as 100 lb., and reach a length of 8 or 9 ft.

**Ivory Gull,** a small, beautifully shaped sea-bird with striking all-white plumage and black legs which breeds on the rocky shores of the Arctic, being found farther north than any other bird; it occasionally wanders south in the winter.

**Ivy,** the well-known climbing shrub, chiefly ever-green; furnishing a sudorific, the berries having also emetic properties.

# J

**Jabiru,** the Brazilian name for the giant stork of South America.

**Jacamar,** from *Jacameri,* the Brazilian name for a smallish bird with long, sharply pointed bill and brilliant plumage which inhabits the tropical regions of South America east of the Andes. These birds are seen sitting motionless on trees, darting off at intervals, like flycatchers, to catch insects on the wing.

**Jacana,** a tropical bird (the water-hen of Brazil and the warmer parts of America) of wide range, beautiful of plumage, with slim body and narrow wings, and long, pointed beak. It feeds on seeds and insects, inhabits marshy lands, and is related to the plovers.

**Jack,** a small schooner-rigged vessel, used in the Newfoundland fisheries; a pike; an oscillating lever; a device used in roasting meat.

**Jackal,** *Canis aureus,* a small wild dog related to the wolf and resembling a fox. The Common

**Jackal** is found in S.E. Europe, India, and Ceylon; other species inhabit Africa and Egypt. The jackal is a well-known scavenger. It hunts singly or in pairs, unlike the wolf, which usually hunts in packs.

**Jackdaw**, one of the smaller members of the Crow family. This European bird is typically black with grey collar. It is easily tamed, makes an amusing pet, and delights in making off with and taking to its nest bright objects, such as silverware.

**Jacobins**, a French revolutionary club or party, formed in 1789, and accustomed to meet at a Jacobin convent, hence the name. It became a controlling force in the Revolution, especially in the movement which led to the Terror. Robespierre was its chief spokesman.

**Jacobites**, adherents of the Stuart cause after the abdication of James II. First James himself, then his son (the Old Pretender), and later his grandson (the Young Pretender) tried to fan the flame of rebellion in Scotland and Ireland, but after the defeat at Culloden in 1746 the cause was lost. Also the name of the monophysite heretics of Syria (see Section J), so named after their leader Jacobus Baradaeus in the 6th cent. A.D.

**Jade**, a green mineral found in China, America, and New Zealand, and used for making vases, bracelets, and other ornamental articles. There are many varieties, and there is evidence that the stone was in common use in prehistoric times for weapons and utensils.

**Jaguar**, a South American carnivorous animal resembling the leopard, but much larger and more powerful, the largest of the Felidae.

**Janeite**, a devotee of Jane Austen and her writings.

**Janissaries**, an élite band of Ottoman foot soldiers who acted as the Sultan's bodyguard. They were conscripts, raised by the "tribute of children" from conquered Christian countries, mainly Serbia and Albania. First recruited under Murad I (14th cent.). They were not allowed to marry. They gained great power under the Ottoman Empire. In 1826 the Sultan Mahmud II had them massacred.

**January**, the first month of the year, named after Janus, the two-faced god of the Romans. It was the *Wolf monath* and *Aefter Yule* of the Saxons.

**Jasmine**, a graceful climber belonging to the olive family with odoriferous blossom, originally a Persian plant, but now acclimatised in many varieties in almost all parts of the world. Two species of jasmine (the common jasmine and the Spanish jasmine) yield oils used in perfumery.

**Jasper**, a precious stone of the chalcedony variety, opaque, and coloured red, brown, yellow and sometimes green. It was greatly esteemed by the ancients, the Bible having numerous allusions to it.

**Jay**, a gaily-coloured bird of the Crow family, of many species—the Blue jay of N. America, the Canada jay, sometimes called "whisky jack," the Siberian jay, and the British jay, fawn-coloured with black and whitish crest and bright blue feathers in the wings. It lives in woods and like the magpie, takes the eggs and young of small nesting birds.

**Jazz**, a rhythmical syncopated music character-ised by a strong element of improvisation in the performance, probably originating among the Negro population of the Southern States of the U.S.A. It became popular during the first world war and, in a commercialised form, has held the popular field ever since. Modern dance music and popular songs are based on the jazz idiom, which has also had a profound effect upon contemporary music of a more serious kind.

**Jean**, a stout kind of twilled cotton cloth much worn in olden times, and resembling fustian. Blue *jeans*, adopted by American city young-sters from farmworkers, are now the fashion elsewhere and worn not only as overalls by workmen but by both sexes in leisure time.

**Jelly-fish.** The jelly-fishes, which have gelatinous, translucent bodies fringed at the margin with delicate tentacles, constitute the coelenterate order *Scyphozoa*. The mouth, with a squarish opening, is seen on the underside, and there are four horseshoe-shaped sex organs.

**Jerboa**, small jumping mammals of the Rodent order. These mice-like animals have long tufted tails and very long hind legs, the front legs not being used for locomotion.

**Jeremiad**, any utterance or writing in which sorrow or complaint is the chief characteristic, so named as recalling the style of the "Lamen-tations of Jeremiah," in the Old Testament.

**Jerusalem Chamber**, a room in Westminster Abbey, deriving its name from the circumstance of its having originally been decorated with a view of Jerusalem. Henry IV. died in this chamber, and the Committee for the Revision of the Bible met there in 1870 and later.

**Jesuits**, members of the Roman Catholic teaching order founded by Ignatius Loyola in 1534. A long and vigorous course of study is pre-scribed before they are admitted into the privileges of full membership. They are required to take the vows of voluntary poverty, perfect chastity, perfect obedience, and com-plete submission to the Pope. The Society played an important part in politics.

**Jet**, a deep black fossil substance admitting of a high polish and much used for jewellery, orna-ments, and trimming. It is a form of lignite, the most important British deposit being found near Whitby, where jet manufacture has been an established industry for a long period.

**Jet Engine**, an aeroplane engine which derives its thrust from the high velocity of the gases it ejects. The essential units in a jet engine are a rotary compressor and a gas turbine, the latter driving the compressor. The first reliable, high-performance jet propulsion engine for aircraft was invented by Air Commodore Sir Frank Whittle.

**Jet Stream**, a meteorological term coined in 1946 to describe the relatively narrow belt of strong winds (100–200 m.p.h.) at levels in the atmo-sphere from 3 to 7 miles. These winds are im-portant in forecasting weather, and can be a valuable aid to aircraft. From the ground, where there may be little wind, the jet stream can sometimes be seen as high cirrus cloud moving across the sky at high speed.

**Jew's Harp.** The name is believed to be a corruption of "jaws harp." This instrument consists of a metal frame with a central tongue of spring steel. The frame is pressed against the teeth, and the tongue of the harp is twanged with the finger, the mouth acting as a resonat-ing chamber. By altering the shape of the mouth the resonant frequency and therefore the note can be varied.

**Jockey Club**, the governing body that, although possessing no legal status, frames rules and laws by which horse-racing and turf matters generally are regulated. The club-house is at New-market.

**John Bull**, the typical figure of an Englishman, bluff, big, and burly. Arbuthnot's *History of John Bull* is supposed to have originated the character.

**John Dory**, a fish found in most temperate seas and common in British waters. It is of a golden-yellow colour (*jaune doré*), has a high dorsal fin with long filaments projecting from the spines, very protractile jaws, and is much valued as a table fish. According to legend the dark spot on each side of its body is the thumbprint of St. Peter who took a coin from the fish's mouth Matt. XVII. 24–7).

**John o' Groat's House**, W. of Duncansby Head, Caithness, popularly named as the northern-most point of Scotland. According to legend the house, which has now disappeared, was built in octagonal form by a Dutchman Jan de Groot who came to live there in the 16th cent. The site is marked and an inn was erected near it in 1876.

**Jongleurs** were minstrels and jesters who wan-dered from town to town singing songs, playing musical instruments, dancing, and giving entertainments in mediæval France and Norman England. Jongleurs were low-born in contrast to the Troubadours, who were often of the nobility.

**Joule**, a unit of energy in the SI system of units, defined as the work done when the point of application of a force of one newton is displaced through a distance of one metre in the direction of the force. Named after J. P. Joule (1818–89). The relationship between mechanical energy and heat energy is called the mechanical equivalent of heat and was found by Joule to be 778 ft lbf in lb °F units, or $4.18 \times 10^7$ ergs in gram °C units. *See* F17, N13.

**Jousts** were military tiltings in the nature of tournaments, where the contestants strove against each other on horseback with blunted lances. It was the sport of nobles in feudal times.

**Judaism.** *See* J24.

**Julian Calendar,** named after Julius Cæsar, who in 46 B.C., finding the Roman year 90 days in advance of the real time, was the first to adopt the calculation of time by the solar year, the average length being fixed at 365¼ days. There was still an overplus of a few minutes every year, and this was rectified by the Gregorian Calendar, introduced in Italy in 1582 and adopted in England in 1752, from which date what is called the " New Style " begins.

**Julus,** a genus of millipedes with cylindrical bodies and two pairs of legs to each segment, the latter being 40 to 50 in number. In South America specimens 5 or 6 in. long are frequent, but those found in England are small.

**July,** the seventh month of the year, named after Julius Cæsar. It was the *Maed monath* (Meadmonth) of the Saxons.

**June,** the sixth month of the year, containing 30 days and deriving its name from Juno. It was the *Sear* (Dry) *monath* of the Saxons.

**Jungle-Fowl,** birds related to the peacocks and peacock-pheasants. At least four species are known from the jungles of India, Ceylon, and Java. The domestic chicken has been derived from the Red Jungle-Fowl (*Gallus gallus*).

**Junkers,** name of the ruling class of Prussia, military in spirit, who were the party of reaction and defenders of the landed interests. Supported Bismarck prior to the Franco-Prussian war and helped bring Hitler to power.

**Jupiter,** the largest planet. It is believed to have a rocky core surrounded by ice layers thousands of miles thick. There is an outer atmosphere containing ammonia and methane, both presumably in the liquid or solid state owing to the very low temperatures of the outer layers (−120° C). In 1610 Galileo made history by discovering the four major satellites of Jupiter, which he named Medicean planets after his patron Cosimo Medici; these are visible with good field-glasses. There are eight others. For distance of Jupiter, etc., *see* F7. Also the supreme mythical deity of the Romans, identified with the Greek Zeus (H38).

**Jurassic Formation,** a series of rocks (the evidences of which are most marked in the Jura Mountains) coming between the Cretaceous and Triassic groups and including the Oolite and the Lias. It is a formation rich in fauna, abounding in echinoids, lamellibranchs, ammonites, and belemnites; large reptiles, marine and land, are common, as are the plants called cyads. In Britain the Jurassic outcrop extends from the Dorset coast to the Yorkshire moors. *See* F34.

**Jury,** a body of private citizens chosen and sworn to hear and pass verdict upon evidence brought forward at a trial, inquest, or inquiry. The origin of the English jury is obscure, but it is thought to have been introduced by the Normans. The jurors are the sole judges of the true facts upon the evidence laid before them. Under the Criminal Justice Act of 1967 their verdicts in criminal courts in England and Wales no longer have to be unanimous but by a majority of 10 to 2. In Scotland 45 jurors are summoned in criminal cases, of whom 15 are chosen by ballot, and majority verdicts are accepted: not guilty, not proven, and guilty.

**Jute,** the name given to the fibre of a plant grown largely in Pakistan in the Ganges delta and used for the manufacture of coarse cloths, cordage, and packs. Calcutta is the biggest jute-manufacturing centre of the world, as Dundee was in the 19th cent.

**Jutes,** a Low German race who in the 5th cent. invaded the south-eastern part of England, establishing themselves in Kent and making Canterbury their capital.

**Juvenile Courts.**—This is a special kind of Magistrates' Court to deal with accused persons under the age of seventeen. The Magistrates chosen are specially qualified for the work, and where possible a woman is appointed as one of the Magistrates who constitute the Court (*see* D44 ).

The Court is held in private away from the ordinary court room. The object of the Juvenile Court is to introduce into the trial a plan to reform the offender by providing for the care and protection which he may need, by removal from undesirable surroundings, and by subsequent education or training. In these objectives the Court has the co-operation of social workers, including Probation Officers (*q.v.*). Radical changes in methods of preventing and treating juvenile delinquency were proposed in a Government White Paper in 1968 called *Children in Trouble*. These proposals emphasised the necessity of helping and supporting the child as far as possible in his own family and community, with resort to formal procedures only where allegations were denied or control was necessary in the interest of society or of the child. The prosecution of children from 10 to 14 would cease; they would be dealt with in the same way as children under 10—by social casework or by care and protection proceedings. Over 14 to 17 there could be (would be in the case of homicide) prosecution, but it would involve an imposed system of co-operation between police, children's officer, probation officer, education authority, and the courts. Detention centres for the under-14s would be abolished.

# K

**Kagu,** native name for a curious bird related to the sun-bittern and the only member of the Rhinochetinae family, found inhabiting New Caledonia when that island was colonised by the French.

**Kakapo,** the Maori name for the New Zealand owl-parrot, a peculiar and interesting species, possessing wings but not able to use them for flight (though it can glide); of sap-green plumage, nocturnal in its habits, and nesting in burrows. Still to be found in the larger forest areas of the South I.

**Kangaroo,** pouched (marsupial) mammals of Australia and adjacent islands. There are over 20 species, the smaller ones being known as " wallabies." Kangaroos leap in a succession of springy bounds 10–20 ft. long, the forefeet not touching the ground. They can reach a height of over 6 ft. and a weight of 200 lb. First seen by white men when Capt. Cook's expedition visited Australia in 1770. Related genera include the tree kangaroos, rat kangaroos, and the Tasmanian Jerboa kangaroo.

**Kaolin** *or* **Kaolinite,** a fine clay much used in the manufacture of high-class pottery. It results from the decomposition of felspar, and is found in China, Japan, Devon, Cornwall, at Limoges in France, and in parts of the United States.

**Karst,** geological formations typical of limestone regions in which the drainage is by underground channels. Rain water carries part of the limestone away in solution, leaving the surface dry and barren and pitted with innumerable hollows. The name comes from the Karst (Slav *Kras*) region of N.W. Yugoslavia where the rocks are massive pure limestone; the barren plateau is characterised by fissures, caves and subterranean rivers.

**Katydid,** large long-horned insects of the grasshopper family, common throughout the United States east of the Rockies. Their name comes from the sound these insects make.

**Kauri Pine,** a large coniferous tree yielding a fine copal resin which ranges from Malay to New Zealand. The New Zealand Kauri. *Agathis australis,* is found only in the N. Island. Some of the best Kauri gum comes from fossilised pines and is dug out of the soil far from any living trees.

**Kava,** a refreshing drink made from the pounded root of the pepper plant (*Piper methysticum*) and the national drink of Tonga.

**Keep,** the central tower or chief stronghold of an ancient castle, sometimes called the donjon.

**Kelvin.** Lord Kelvin, an important 19th-cent. physicist, gave his name to the degree Kelvin, written °K. This is a measure of temperature on the absolute scale. *See* Absolute Temperature.

**Kentish Rag,** a fossiliferous clayey limestone of Cretaceous age found in Kent. Used in building.

**Keratin**, a hard protein material of which horns, nails, claws, hoofs, and reptiles' scales are made.

**Kestrel**, the most common British falcon, well known for its habit of hovering for minutes at a time with vibrating wings and then swooping down to attack mice and insects. The male has spotted chestnut-brown back, greyish head and tail, which has a broad black band near tip.

**Ketones.** A class of organic compounds, related to aldehydes, of general formula $R_2CO$ (where R is an organic radical). The simpler ketones, especially acetone, are widely used as solvents for lacquers, synthetic rubber, and polymers, such as cellulose acetate and perspex. More complex ketones occur in nature, and some are used in the perfumery industry, muscone (from the musk deer (q.v.)) is an example.

**Kew Gardens**, officially known as the Royal Botanic Gardens, are among the most celebrated gardens in the world. They were started in 1759 by Princess Augusta of Saxe-Gotha, widow of Frederick, Prince of Wales, and mother of George III. They remained private property until 1841, when control passed to the Commissioners of Woods and Forests. They now cover 300 acres and are administered by the Min. of Agriculture, Fisheries, and Food. Since 1841 the gardens have been open to the public, and form one of the most attractive resorts near London.

**Keys, House of**, is the Manx representative assembly. See Tynwald.

**Keystone**, the stone which occupies the centre and highest point of an arch and is usually the last to be inserted.

**Khaki**, a clay-coloured cloth adopted for uniforms in the British Army in the time of the war with the Boers, and used in the first and second world wars. First used by Indian regiments.

**Kilderkin**, once a common liquid measure in England, representing 18 gallons.

**Kilogram**, unit of mass, defined as the mass of the international prototype kilogram of platinum-iridium kept at the International Bureau of Weights and Measures at Sèvres. A new determination of the imperial standard pound in terms of the international kilogram was made recently by the National Physical Laboratory (1 international pound = 0·45359237 kilogram). See also N12, 13.

**Kilowatt.** Unit of power, equal to one thousand watts. See Watt.

**Kinetic Energy**, the energy (q.v.) possessed by a particle or body in virtue of its motion. If the motion is destroyed, e.g., by the impact of the body with an obstacle, the kinetic energy vanishes, being turned into some other form of energy such as heat and sound. If the body has mass $m$ and speed $v$ its kinetic energy (leaving out corrections due to relativity) is $\frac{1}{2}mv^2$.

**Kinetic Sculpture**, a development of equipoised sculpture (i.e., sculpture independent of gravity in the sense of resting on a base either horizontally, vertically, or obliquely) intended to appear as "a weightless poising of volumes, relationships, and interpenetrations." Since in the literal sense this is impossible, the Constructivists (Pevsner, Gabo, and Moholy-Nagy) used glass and invisible wire as supports, giving the impression that their creations were in fact independent of gravity. However, the American, Alexander Calder, has made constructions of balls and wire which he calls "mobiles," and in this form they are now known to everyone as they delicately dangle and rotate suspended from the ceiling.

**King Crab**, remarkable arthropods now classified separately from both Arachnids and Crustacea which they resemble, inhabiting the sea coasts of America, Japan, India, and Malay Peninsula, carrying a shield-shaped shell, and having a long pointed spine projecting from the posterior. The body comprises three separate sections articulated together. These crabs—in America known commonly as the horseshoe crab because of their shape—are from 18 in. to 2 ft. in length. Fossil king-crabs are found as far back as the Silurian. There are about six living species.

**Kingfisher**, a well-known family of brilliant-plumaged birds, found in all continents, comprising some 250 species and sub-species. The British kingfisher, *Acedlo atthis*, haunts the rivers and streams, and is one of the most beautiful of native birds, having iridescent blue-green, white, and rich chestnut in its plumage and bright-red feet. All kingfishers have long, dagger-shaped bills. In the Malayan region, New Guinea, the Moluccas, and Australia the varieties are very numerous. The quaint *Laughing Jackass* of Australia is among the largest of the kingfisher family. The European kingfisher is the bird of the Greek legend of the Halcyon.

**King-of-Arms**, the name of the chief officials of the Heralds' College. There are several in England —the principal being those of the Garter, Norroy and Ulster, Clarenceux. See Heralds' College.

**Kiosk**, a word of Russian or Turkish origin meaning a small open pavilion of light construction much used in Eastern countries as a place of shade and rest. Similar structures are common in the streets of Paris as news and advertisement stands, and in London as telephone offices.

**Kirimon** (*Kiri no go Mon*) and **Kikumon** (*Kiki no go Mon*), the two Japanese imperial crests, the first a design of leaves, stems, and flowers of the Paulownia plant, and the other representing the sixteen-petalled chrysanthemum.

**Kite**, name of several birds of prey, widely distributed, related to the hawks and eagles, graceful in flight, and distinguished by their long wings and deeply forked tails. The red kite, light chestnut brown, once the most familiar bird of prey in Britain, seen scavenging the streets of London, is now the rarest, and found only in Wales. The Egyptian kite and the pariah kite of India, notorious for their daring thefts, are closely related to the black kite, a smaller European species, with less forked tail and blackish-brown plumage.

**Kittiwake**, a beautiful white and pearl-grey gull with black legs, dark eyes, and greenish-yellow bill. Its range is wide, and includes the British Isles, where it is a local resident. The flight of this only truly oceanic gull, which excepting in the breeding-season, is generally found off-shore, is graceful, swift, and buoyant. A triangular black patch, noticeable on the ends of the wings when open, is characteristic of the species, as is the call kitti-wake, from which the bird derives its name. It nests in colonies on the ledges of caves and steep cliffs.

**Kiwi**, flightless, stoutly-built birds of New Zealand, now very rare and carefully protected by the Government. They are little larger than a domestic hen, and lay astonishingly large eggs for their size. Incubation and care of chicks fall to the male bird. They have rudimentary wings concealed by the plumage, and the feathers are hair-like. They are nocturnal in habit.

**Knighthood** is a degree of honour or title common in Europe since the Middle Ages, and was at first exclusively a military order. In Great Britain the four main orders of knighthood are those of the Garter, the Bath, the Thistle, and St. Patrick; in addition to which there are several other orders, such as the Order of St. Michael and St. George, the Star of India, etc. There are also Knights Bachelors, such as are not associated with any special order. The title is not hereditary, and therefore ranks below that of a baronet, though both are entitled to the prefix "Sir."

**Knot**, a nautical measure of speed (1 sea mile per hour), and formerly measured by a log-line, divided by knots at equal distances $\frac{1}{120}$ of a geographical mile. The number of knots travelled by the ship in half a minute corresponded to the number of sea miles it travelled per hour. A sea mile is equal to about 1⅛ of a statute mile. Also, a grey and white wading bird, usually a winter visitor to Britain found in flocks on the coast.

**Knout**, formerly a Russian instrument of punishment, consisting of a whip of many thongs, used upon Russian criminals since the 15th cent. A hundred and twenty strokes were considered equivalent to a sentence of death, half that number sufficing to kill in many instances. Tsar Nicholas I., however, changed the form of the knout, and made it a much milder instrument.

**Koala**, the Australian arboreal marsupial mammal that looks like a toy teddy-bear, with ashy-grey fur, bushy ears, and rudimentary tail. It feeds on the leaves and shoots of certain eucalyptus trees, and is not more than 2 ft. in length.

**Kohl,** a powder prepared from antimony or burnt almond shells, and in common use by the women of the East for darkening the eyelids.

**Koto,** a musical instrument in general use in Japan consisting of a series of 13 silken strings stretched across a curved wooden surface, and played with the fingers. Each string is 5 ft. long, and has a separate bridge so fixed as to give the vibration necessary for the note it has to produce. It is a sort of horizontal harp, and in the hands of an expert player is capable of giving forth excellent music.

**Kremlin,** the citadel or walled city within a Russian city which during the Middle Ages served as an administrative and religious centre and offered protection. That of Moscow, now the headquarters of the Russian government, contains the cathedral where the Tsars were crowned, an imperial palace, and the bell-tower of Ivan the Great. Its walls which are topped with towers were built in the 15th cent.

**Krypton,** one of the rare gases, symbol Kr, occurring in the air to the extent of 1 part in 20 million. It was discovered in 1898 by Ramsay and Travers. It is used in gas-filled electric lamps.

**Kusti,** the sacred cord or girdle of the Parsees, consisting of 72 threads—the number of the chapters of the Izashue—and two branches, each branch containing six knots, together standing for the 12 months of the year.

**Kyrie Eleison** (" Lord, have mercy "), the name of a common form of prayer in the Anglican, Roman Catholic, and Greek Churches; also applied to the English Church responses after the recital of the commandments.

**Kyrie Society,** named after Pope's " Man of Ross," John Kyrle, founded by Miss Miranda and Miss Octavia Hill in 1875, and having for its object, the decoration of workmen's clubs, hospitals, etc. and the promotion among the poor of a taste for literature, music, and outdoor recreation.

# L

**Labarum,** the standard of Constantine the Great, adopted after his conversion to Christianity, marked with his seal, and represented upon the coinage.

**Labourers, English Statute of,** was passed 1350–51, with the object of compelling labourers to accept a certain rate of wages and not leave their employers' service, the Plague having rendered labourers so scarce that they were in great demand and had been insisting on higher pay. These enactments were bitterly opposed and led to the " Peasants' Revolt," headed by Wat Tyler.

**Labradorite,** a felspar rich in calcium and of a pearly lustre on cleavage, found in masses in igneous rocks, the best samples of which come from Labrador.

**Labyrinth,** or **Maze,** a combination of roads and passages so constructed as to render it difficult for anyone ignorant of the clue to trace the way to the central part. The Egyptian labyrinth near Lake Moeris had 3,000 rooms, half of them subterranean and the remainder above ground. The labyrinth in Crete, according to Greek myth, was built by Dædalus to house the Minotaur. There was one at Lemnos, renowned for its stalactite columns; and another at Clusium constructed by Porsenna, King of Etruria, about 520 B.C. The labyrinth in which Fair Rosamond was concealed was at Woodstock. Hampton Court maze dates from the 16th cent.

**Labyrinthodonts,** gigantic fossil amphibians which get their name from the curious labyrinthine structure of their teeth, probably an evolutionary link between fishes and reptiles. They occur in the Carboniferous, Permian, and Triassic formations, and remains have been found in Britain and other parts of Europe. Their heads were several feet long, and their footprints, by which they were discovered, closely resemble the prints of the human hand.

**Lac,** a resinous matter deposited on the branches of a number of tropical trees by the females of the lac insect, the exudation including eggs and a viscous covering. At the gathering time the twigs are broken off and dried in the sun, when the insects die, and the lac that remains is termed *stick-lac*. From this, by the removal

of extraneous accretions and dissolving, *seed-lac* is produced. *Shell-lac* is seed-lac after it has been melted and otherwise prepared, and this is the best known of the lacs, being used in printing and the manufacture of varnishes and sealing-wax, and for other commercial purposes.

**Lace,** a delicate fabric of linen, silk, or cotton threads, made by hand or machinery, and worked in various ornamental designs. The kinds of lace are many, deriving their distinctive names either from the method employed in production or from the place where any special variety was originally made. The best-known makes are pillow or bobbin-lace, woven and plaited by hand; needle-point lace, worked by the needle over a traced design; and machine lace, which practically dates from Heathcote's invention of the early part of the 19th cent. Some of the most famed laces are the following: *Alencon*, a needle-point lace; *Brussels*, a very fine kind, with needle-point sprigs and flowers; *Chantilly*, a silk variety with flowers and openwork; *Cluny*, a netlace with darned stitch; *Honiton*, a delicate kind with dainty sprigs and figures; *Mechlin*, generally made in one piece and very varied in design; and *Valenciennes*, or bobbin lace, of great durability, the pattern and ground of which are made at the same time, being one of the best and most costly of laces, now manufactured mainly in Belgium. Nottingham is famous for its lace.

**Lace-Wings,** insects with frail, transparent, and much-veined wings whose grubs eat large numbers of insect pests such as aphids. The eggs are borne at the ends of threads attached to plants.

**Lachesis,** a genus of venomous snakes of the rattlesnake family confined to tropical countries, and including the " deadly bushmaster," of Surinam, and several Crotalidae pit-vipers of Guiana and Brazil.

**Lacquer,** a varnish made from shellac and certain colouring matters, and utilised for imparting lustre to various surfaces of metal or wood. In China and Japan the production of lacquer ware of a decorative character has long been an important industry, bringing into use gold, coral, vermilion, sprinkled, and other lacquers, with pleasing effect.

**Ladybird,** the common name of a large family of beetles—the *Coccinellidae*. The insect is usually of a red or yellow colour with small black or coloured spots. Ladybirds are of good service to the gardener because their larvae feed on aphids. There are about 2,000 species.

**Lady-Day,** the day of the festival of the Annunciation of the Virgin Mary, Mar. 25. One of the four English quarter days.

**Lagoon,** a stretch of shallow water opening out upon the sea. Venice is built on lagoons.

**Lake Dwelling,** the name given to certain prehistoric habitations which were thought to have stood on platforms over lakes, like villages in certain Pacific islands. Recent excavations at the Lake of Burgäschi in Switzerland show that the prehistoric Swiss pile dwellings probably stood on the shores of lakes, not on platforms over the water.

**Lakes** are bodies of water collected in depressions of the earth's surface. The most notable lakes are the Great Lake series of North America, including Superior, Michigan, Huron, Erie, and Ontario, all discharging into the St. Lawrence River. Africa has an enormous area of lakes, including the Albert Nyanza and the Victoria Nyanza, forming the sources of the White Nile, Lakes Tanganyika, Nyassa, Tchad, etc. Smaller lakes are numerous in other countries—Switzerland, Germany, Italy, England, Ireland, Scotland, all having their lake regions, where the scenery is invariably beautiful and romantic.

**Lake School,** the name given, at first in ridicule, to a distinguished trio of poets—Wordsworth, Coleridge, and Southey—who made their homes in the English Lake District.

**Lamellibranchs (Pelecypods),** the class of aquatic, bi-valve molluscs to which the oysters, cockles, mussels, clams, and scallops belong. In these animals the body, which is compressed laterally, is enclosed in two hinged shells held together by muscular action. The gills are thin plates hence the name " lamellibranch." *See* **F33(1),** **33(2).**

**Lamination,** stratification on a very fine scale, as in shales.

**Lammas Day** is one of the oldest of the Church festivals, probably derived from the loaf-mass (hláfmæsse) of the Anglo-Saxons. It occurs on August 1. In the olden times it was the day when loaves were given in place of first-fruit offerings.

**Lammergeyer,** the bearded vulture of alpine regions, resembling an eagle in appearance. It has a white head with black tufts at base of the bill, and its general plumage is dark brown, nearly black. It is found in the remote mountain ranges from Southern Spain to China, and is becoming scarce.

**Lampblack,** a carboniferous pigment obtained from flame-smoke, and now produced in specially constructed furnaces in which bodies rich in carbon, such as tar, resin, petroleum, etc., are burned. The smoke or soot resulting is collected from the sides of the furnace, and forms lampblack. It finds use in making printer's ink, black paint, etc. Being a very pure form of carbon, it is also utilised in the manufacture of dynamo brushes and arc-lamp carbons.

**Lamprey.** Eel-like fish having no scales, bones, paired fins, or jaws. They attach themselves by their mouths to fish whose blood they suck. Together with the hagfishes, the lampreys are placed in a special class—the Cyclostomes. There are three British lampreys.

**Lancelet.** *See* Amphioxus.

**"Lancet,"** the name of a noted English medical journal, established in 1823 by Dr. Wakley.

**Land Crab,** a family of crabs (*Gecarcinidae*) which live mainly on land, though migrating to the sea to deposit their eggs.

**Land League,** an association formed in 1879, with Parnell as president, for compelling a reduction in the rents of land, and a reconstruction of the land laws in Ireland, and in case of non-compliance refusing to pay rent. For a time this League exercised great political influence and was an important aid to the Home Rule agitation.

**Landrail,** popularly known as the Corncrake, was a regular summer visitor to Britain two generations ago, but no longer. Its harsh and piercing note was a familiar sound in English cornfields. Still found in Ireland.

**Landslip,** a sudden downward sliding under gravity of large masses of rock, soil, etc.; often set off by earthquake shock or saturation of a particular stratum with water. Many serious landslides have occurred from time to time. In 1618, an earthfall happened at Plurs, on Lake Como, involving the destruction of many buildings and the loss of numerous lives. In 1806 a portion of Rossberg mountain in Switzerland slipped from its position, and falling into the valley below buried many villages and hamlets and over 800 people. A chalk cliff from 100 to 150 ft. high and three-quarters of a mile long fell at Lyme Regis, in Dorsetshire, in 1839, doing great damage. Over 200 people were killed by a landslip in Naini Tal, in India, in 1880; and at Quebec, in 1889, a rocky eminence called Cape Diamond gave way, many buildings being destroyed and lives lost. Notable landslips in recent times have occurred at Amalfi (Italy) in 1924, and at Murchison (New Zealand) in 1929.

**Langue d'oc and Langue d'oïl,** the two principal mediæval French dialects, *oc* and *oïl* being their respective words for the affirmative particle (modern French *oui*). *Langue d'oc,* spoken south of the Loire, was the language of the troubadours. Provençal, one of its dialects had a literary revival in the 19th cent. under the influence of the poet Frédéric Mistral. *Langue d'oïl* was spoken in northern France, and it was the dialect of the Paris region which developed into modern French.

**Lantern Fly,** bugs belonging to the family *Fulgoridae* in which the head is drawn out to form a lantern-like structure. In no instance is the "lantern" luminous, though naturalists used to think it was.

**"Lantern of England."** Bath Abbey possesses so many windows that it is called sometimes the "Lantern of England." Among numerous interesting monuments Bath Abbey contains that of Malthus, author of *Essay on Population.*

**Lanthanum,** a metal belonging to the rare earth group of metals, discovered by Mosander in 1839.

**Lapis Lazuli,** an azure-blue mineral, being a silicate of aluminium and sodium. The pigment ultramarine is made by grinding it, though artificial ultramarine has largely superseded it. The mineral (also called *lazurite*) has been used as a gemstone since ancient times.

**Lapwing** *or* Green Plover, familiar British bird on moors and marshlands with iridescent greenish-black plumage, white underparts, and black crest. Often called "peewit" from its cry. Protected under Protection of Birds Act, 1967.

**Larboard** is the old nautical term indicating the left-hand side of a ship, and changed by Admiralty order to "port" in 1844. Starboard is the right-hand side.

**Larch,** a familiar coniferous tree in the mountain regions of northern Europe, and though not native to Britain, the Common Larch is successfully cultivated in various parts of the kingdom. It is one of the best of all turpentine-yielding trees, and the bark is valued for tanning. The larch is an unusual conifer in being deciduous.

**Larid,** a bird of the *Laridae* or gull family.

**Lark,** a family of song birds (*Alaudidae*) of many species, some of which—notably the skylark—are famed for their habit of soaring into the air, singing all the while. They build their nests on the ground in the open country and, except for the black lark of Russia, have streaked brown plumage. The skylark and woodlark are the best known British species, while the crested lark and shore lark are among the occasional visitors. Africa has the greatest number of larks: America has only one species, the horned lark.

**Larkspur,** the common name of the genus *Delphinium,* a favourite flower introduced into British gardens from Switzerland in 1573. The common larkspur is *D. consolida.*

**Larva,** the undeveloped form of any animal which, before maturity, undergoes metamorphosis, usually different from the adult in structure and habits.

**Laser.** A remarkable kind of light source that was discovered in 1960. With the laser it is possible to probe the behaviour of matter under the influence of enormous energy densities, range and survey vast distances to microscopic accuracy, and send millions of telephone and television messages between any two points that can see each other with telescopes. Laser light, in contrast to natural light, is coherent and can be expressed as a regular progression of waves carrying energy along a particular path. Thus the essential difference is that laser light is an orderly sort of wave motion in contrast to ordinary light which is inherently unsteady and therefore an inefficient carrier of information in time. The name *maser,* which is the microwave parent of the laser, derives from the expression "*microwave amplification by the stimulated emission of radiation.*" Upon application to light wavelengths the microwave part of the name lost its meaning and the term maser became generally descriptive of any device in which stimulated emission dominates.

**Latent Heat** is the quantity of heat required to convert 1 gram of a substance from one form into another. For example, when a solid changes into a liquid or a liquid into a gas, the addition of heat to bring about the change produces no rise in temperature, the energy being absorbed in the form of latent heat. An equal amount is released when the process is reversed. The latent heat of fusion of ice is about 79·6 calories per gram, that of the vaporisation of water about 539 calories per gram.

**Lateran Councils** were the religious conventions held in the Lateran basilica at Rome for deciding important questions of Church doctrine. The most brilliant was that of 1215, which pronounced in favour of a Crusade. *See* Ecumenical Councils.

**Laterite,** a residual deposit formed in the tropics by weathering and decomposition of igneous rocks. It consists mainly of hydrated ferric and aluminium oxides and is difficult to cultivate.

**Latin America.** The Spanish-speaking, Portuguese-speaking, and French-speaking countries of N. America, S. America, Central America, and the W. Indies. *See* K93.

**Latitude** of a point on the earth's surface is its

angular distance from the equator, measured on the surface of the earth in degrees, minutes, and seconds. Thus the equator is 0° Lat. and the poles 90° Lat. (N. or S.). First determined by Hipparchus of Nicaea about 160 B.C.

**Laughing Gas.** *See* Nitrous oxide.

**Launce** *or* **Sand Eel,** a family of eel-like sea fishes found in large numbers on the coasts of North America and Europe. There are two species common to British waters. These fishes are of a bright silvery hue, and live much in the sand underneath the water. They are prized as human food and as bait.

**Laurentian Shield** refers to the Pre-Cambrian rocks in the region of the Upper Lakes of Canada, nearly 2 million sq. m. in extent. Of enormous importance to Canada on account of the mineral wealth, forests yielding valuable timber and wood-pulp, and water-power.

**Lava,** the molten rock which is erupted from a volcanic vent or fissure. Also the same material which has cooled and solidified.

**Lawn,** very fine sun-bleached linen, in olden time called " cloth of Rheims."

**Lead,** a soft malleable metal, symbol Pb (Latin *plumbum*), occurring in numerous ores, which are easily smelted. Its most important source is the mineral galena which consists chiefly of lead sulphide; rarely is it found free. Lead is largely used in plumbing on account of its pliability, and in nuclear reactors as a shield against radiation because of its very high density. As an alloy element it combines in the formation of type metal, stereo metal, shot metal, pewter, and many other compounds. Oxides of lead are used in some types of glass and in the manufacture of paints (red lead). All lead compounds are poisonous. Leading producers of lead are the United States (Missouri), Australia (Broken Hill) and the Soviet Union.

**Leaf Insect,** a group of insects related to the locusts, grasshoppers and stick insects which in colour and form closely resemble leaves.

**Leaf Miners,** insect larvae which tunnel between the upper and lower skins of leaves. Most leaf miners are caterpillars of tiny moths; some sawfly larvae have the same habit.

**Leagues,** or combinations of kings, countries, communities, have been frequent since the kings of Canaan united against the Israelites. Among the most famous leagues may be mentioned the Holy or Catholic League, which prevented the accession of Henry IV. of France until he became a Roman Catholic; and the League of Augsburg against Louis XIV. of France in 1686.

**League of Nations,** was founded on Jan. 10, 1920, with the object of promoting international peace and security. The original members were the signatories to the Peace Treaties at Versailles, and membership grew to fifty-three and new nations and ex-enemy States were admitted. Two notable absentees were the United States and Soviet Russia, the latter not being represented until 1934. Germany was a member from 1926 to 1933. The League had an Assembly which met at Geneva every year and a Council which met five or six times a year. The Permanent Court of International Justice sits at The Hague. The final Assembly of the League was held at Geneva between April 8 and 18, 1946. Its place has been taken by the United Nations. The International Labour Organisation, set up by the League of Nations met on April 20, 1944, at Philadelphia and resumed its old quarters at Geneva under the new organisation in 1946.

**Leap Year** *or* **Bissextile,** was fixed by Julius Caesar, 45 B.C., the addition of one day in every four years bringing the measure of the calendar year even with the astronomical year with three minutes per year over. The Gregorian Calendar corrected this by dropping leap year at the centuries not divisible by 400. For instance, 1700, 1800, and 1900 were not leap years.

**Learning.**—*See* F38(1).

**Leather** was made in ancient Egypt, Greece, and Rome, and has through succeeding centuries played an important part in the service of man. It consists of the dressed hides or skins of animals after the process of tanning has been gone through. Untanned skins are known as pelts.

Leather is classed either according to the skins from which it is made or the system of preparation employed. The best-known kinds are morocco, kin, Russian, chamois, Cordovan, grained, patent, russet, tan, calf, Hungarian.

**Leech,** an aquatic blood-sucking worm, mostly found in fresh-water ponds. Each end of the body is provided with a sucker, but that at the head end has jaws and teeth. The medicinal leech has three jaws. The leech attaches itself with avidity to animal bodies and sucks until glutted. Its saliva contains an anti-coagulant.

**Leeward,** a nautical term, meaning the sheltered side of a vessel—that is, the opposite side to that from which the wind is blowing.

**Legion,** a body of Roman troops, varying in numbers at different periods. A legion was divided into 10 cohorts, and every cohort into three maniples. Three legions composed the Roman army of occupation in Britain.

**Legion of Honour,** the French order for distinguished services, military or civil, was instituted by Napoleon I. in 1802, and confirmed and modified under later rules. There are five grades—Grands Croix, Grands Officiers, Commandeurs, Officiers, and Chevaliers.

**Legume,** the fruit typical of the pea, bean family, or *Leguminosae.*

**Lemming,** small light-brown rodents with dark spots, abounding in Scandinavian countries and in Siberia, about 5 in. long, with a short stump of a tail. The migrations of the lemming are famous, probably caused by overbreeding when food is plentiful. So insistent is the urge to keep moving that these animals will march on into the sea in their thousands and be drowned.

**Lemur,** the most primitive member of the Primate order of mammals (to which man, apes, and monkeys also belong). They are noted for having strong pliant toes enabling them to use their feet as hands, and also well-developed thumbs on the hands. They have long squirrel-like tails, fox-shaped heads, and large staring eyes, and are distributed over the tropical parts of the Old World, being most abundant in Madagascar.

**Lend-Lease.** During the earlier phases of the Second World War the bulk of British investments in the U.S.A. had to be either sold or pledged to Americans in payment for dollar supplies. After the United States entered the war this drain was stopped by the Lease-Lend arrangement, under which Great Britain met the costs of American consumption in Great Britain, while the United States paid for British supplies from America. This arrangement was abruptly terminated on the ending of hostilities; and Great Britain and other belligerent countries found themselves without means of paying in dollars for indispensable American supplies, including the foodstuffs, materials and capital goods needed for economic reconstruction. In these circumstances Great Britain negotiated with the United States and also with Canada a large loan, which was used for buying dollar supplies and played an important part in helping the West European economies to maintain themselves and feed their peoples while they were carrying through the earlier stages of postwar reconstruction. These loans involved large charges for interest and amortisation in future years, but proved far too small to meet the dollar deficit for more than a short period. In face of this situation the United States launched the Marshall Plan (*q.v.*).

**Lenses,** pieces of transparent material designed to focus an image of an illuminated object. Usually of glass, but plastic lenses are common, and quartz, etc. are used for special purposes. The surfaces of the simplest lenses are parts of spheres. Lenses which are thickest, or thinnest, at the centre are called convex and concave respectively. Lenses of complex shape are often used in microscopes, etc. Electron lenses are arrangements of electric or magnetic fields which focus beams of electrons, *e.g.*, on to television screens.

**Lent,** the forty days' period of fasting that precedes Easter.

**Lepidoptera,** the order of insects with scaly wings and bodies, to which the 90,000 butterflies and moths belong.

**Leptons.** A group of particles which includes

electrons, neutrinos and muons. All are much lighter than protons or any of the baryons. *See* **F14.**

**Lepus,** the constellation of the Hare, situated under the Orion group, and one of the constellations with which the ancients were familiar.

**Lettres de Cachet,** sealed letters which the kings of France issued to their agents to secure the imprisonment of distrusted or disliked persons without trial. Abolished in 1789.

**Levée,** a State reception held by the Sovereign or his representative and attended by men only.

**Lever,** a rigid bar of metal or wood used for raising heavy bodies, and worked by means of a support called the fulcrum placed underneath the lever.

**Lewis,** a contrivance for stone-lifting, the principle of which was known to the ancient Romans; it consists of two dovetail tenons of iron or other metal, expanded by an intervening key in a dovetail-shaped mortice in the stone, and shackled by a ringed bolt to the hoisting chain.

**Leyden Jar,** the earliest form of electrical condenser. Its invention is usually credited to Muschenbroeck of Leyden (1745). It consisted of a jar coated inside and out with tinfoil for about two-thirds of its height and having its inner coating connected with the top by a brass knob and chain. The jar was charged by connecting it to an electrostatic machine.

**Lias,** a geological term referring to the lower section of the Jurassic group, and mainly comprising shales and limestones.

**Liberalism.** *See* **J25.**

**Libraries,** before the invention of printing, were few, and collected together at enormous cost. At Nineveh remains of libraries, consisting of tablets of baked clay, have been discovered. There were two libraries at Alexandria containing a vast collection of rolls or volumes, founded by Ptolemy I Soter (367–283 B.C.) and established by Ptolemy II Philadelphus (309–246 B.C.). Among the great libraries of later times may be mentioned the Vatican Library at Rome, moved to its present premises in 1588; the Royal Library in Paris which later became the Bibliothèque Nationale; The Astor Library, New York; and in England, the Bodleian Library, Oxford, and the British Museum Library at Bloomsbury. Since 1850 public libraries have been established in all the chief cities and towns of the kingdom. The first lending library was opened in Edinburgh in 1726. In most villages there is a " county library centre " to which collections of books are sent by the County Library. In Great Britain there are 24,000 centres of this kind in village clubs, halls, shops, schools, and even homes. In some counties there is a library van or the bibliobus, as it has been called by a French writer. This travelling library tours on a pre-arranged time-table so that everyone knows exactly when it will arrive. The British Museum Library in London, the National Library of Scotland, in Edinburgh, that of Wales in Aberystwyth, the Bodleian Library of Oxford and the Cambridge University Library comprise the " copyright " libraries, entitled to receive a copy of each new book published in Britain. Other national libraries are the National Lending Library for Science and Technology, under the Department of Education and Science, at Boston Spa, Yorkshire, and the National Central Library, which is responsible for inter-lending at national and international level. Four of the best special libraries in the world are open to the public in London. They are:

1. The Library of the Natural History Museum (for zoology, geology, and related subjects).

2. The Library of the Science Museum (all branches of science and technology, except medicine).

3. The Patent Office Library.

4. The Library of the Victoria and Albert Museum, which is the national art library containing volumes and photographs on all aspects of fine, applied, and decorative art.

Full details of the large number of specialist libraries in London (including that of the British Library of Political and Economic Science, one of the best collections in the world on this subject,

at the London School of Economics) will be found in *The Student's Guide to the Libraries of London,* by R. A. Rye, published by the University of London Press and *The Libraries of Greater London,* by L. M. Harrod, published by G. Bell. *See also* **British Museum, India Office Library.**

**Libration,** an astronomical term referring to an apparent irregularity in the moon's course, which may be libration in longitude or latitude, or diurnal, and due to a variety of causes.

**Lichens.** In every lichen, two plants are associated, one being an alga and the other a fungus. The fungus derives its food from the alga; probably the alga gains too from the association, being protected against desiccation by the fungus (an example of symbiosis). Lichens are the first plants to colonise bare rocks.

**Life-Boat** was invented by three men, Lionel Lukin who converted a coble into a boat for saving life in 1785; William Wouldhave, who discovered how to make a boat right herself if she capsized, and Henry Greathead, who built a life-boat, partly from Wouldhave's model, in 1789. This boat was stationed at South Shields, which was the first permanent life-boat station to be established. It was not until 1851 that the first life-boat able to self-right was built, and a motor was first installed in a life-boat in 1904. Modern motor life-boats have engines of from twin-18 h.p. to twin-80 h.p., with a speed of nearly 10 knots. All coastal life-boats in this country are maintained by the Royal National Lifeboat Institution founded by Sir William Hillary in 1824.

**Light,** a particular kind of electromagnetic disturbance capable of travelling through space, and some kinds of matter, and of affecting our eyes to cause vision. Its finite speed was first demonstrated by O. Römer, using observations of the eclipses of Jupiter's satellites in 1675. In 1860 Maxwell showed that light waves are electromagnetic. Since Einstein's theory of relativity (1905) it has been generally realised that the speed of light is a fundamental natural constant. Visible light with wavelengths between about 4 and 6 $\times$ 10$^{-5}$ cm. is only a small part of the electromagnetic spectrum. Subtle modern methods give the speed as 2·997930 $\times$ 10$^{10}$ cm. per sec. (about 186,000 miles per sec.).

**Light Year.** A measure of astronomical distance, equal to the distance light travels in the course of a year. A light year is thus 5·88 million million miles. *See also* **F3(2).**

**Lighthouses,** to warn ships of dangerous places and indicate coasts, points, harbours, etc., have existed since the building of the Pharos, a tower of white marble 600 ft. high, built by Ptolemy II Philadelphus at Alexandria about 280 B.C. In early lighthouses the lights were simple fires. The most famous and one of the earliest British lighthouses is the Eddystone (*q.v.*). Dungeness lighthouse, opened in 1960, is very modern in design, capable of automatic operation and the first of its kind to incorporate the xenon electric arc lamp as a source of illumination. The electric fog signal consists of sixty loud-speaker units built into the tower just below the lantern, giving a honeycomb effect. The lighthouses of England and Wales, the Channel Islands, and Gibraltar are under the control of Trinity House; Commissioners of Northern Lighthouses control those of Scotland; and the Commissioners of Irish Lights control the coasts of Ireland. Particulars of lights in all parts of the world are published for the guidance of navigation in the *Admiralty Lists of Lights,* compiled annually by the British Admiralty.

**Lightning,** the flash of a discharge of electricity between two clouds, or between a cloud and the earth, when the strength of the electric fields becomes so great as to break down the resistance of the intervening air. With " forked " lightning the actual path, often branched, is visible, while with " sheet " lightning the flash is hidden by the clouds which themselves are illuminated. " Ball " lightning or fireballs is the name given to the luminous balls which have been seen floating in the air during a thunderstorm. The Boys camera has provided much information regarding the sequence of events in a lightning discharge. It is found that a flash consists of a number of separate strokes, usually four or five, and that the discharge of electricity to earth begins with a faintly luminous "leader" moving downwards and branching at intervals. As the ground is approached a much brighter luminosity travels back along the conducting channels, lighting up the several branches. The multiple strokes which follow in fractions of a second have the same "return" nature and are rarely branched. Lightning flashes to earth damage structures, cause loss of life and endanger overhead power systems, often interrupting electricity supply. Such storms generally affect radio transmissions and present hazards to aircraft. Thunder-clouds may develop energy far exceeding the capacity of our largest power generating stations.

Lightning Conductor, a metal rod, the upper part of which is of copper with a conical point, the lower portion being iron, which extends into the earth. Its effect is to gather to itself the surrounding electricity and discharge it into the earth, thus preventing its falling upon the protected building. In ships, lightning conductors are fixed to the masts and carried down through the ship's keel-sheathing. Benjamin Franklin was the first to realise the possibilities of lightning protection and, in 1752, carried out his famous experiment of drawing electricity from thunder-clouds, with the aid of a sharp-pointed conductor fixed to a kite.

Lillibulero, an old marching song composed by Purcell. With words by Wharton, it is said to have "sung James II. out of three kingdoms." During the second world war it was used by the B.B.C. as a station identification signal preceding news bulletins.

Lily Family (Liliaceae), one of the largest families of flowering plants, with 200 genera and 2,500 species. It includes the true lilies (Lilium), tulips and hyacinths. Useful vegetables belonging to the family are the onion and asparagus.

Limes, trees of the genus Tilia, including some 30 species spread over north temperate regions. The word is a corruption of "linden." Limes native to Britain are the small-leaved T. cordata and the broad-leaved T. platyphyllos. The hybrid T. vulgaris was introduced into Britain from the Continent during the 17th cent. and is frequently seen in streets and parks. Lime-wood was used by Grinling Gibbons for his fruit, flower, and bird decorations.

Limestone is carbonate of calcium. It is found in every geological formation, and is often highly fossiliferous. Marble is limestone that will polish after cutting.

Linen, a textile fabric manufactured from flax fibre, known to the ancient Egyptians, and first manufactured in England under Henry III. by Flemish weavers. The chief seat of the manufacture is Ulster, with Belfast as the centre, Dunfermline (famous for its damasks) and Manchester are also large linen-producing towns.

Ling, a sea-fish common on the coasts of Britain, and abounding in more northern waters. It averages from 3 to 4 ft. in length, and is a voracious feeder, living chiefly on small fish. Ling is also the name applied to Calluna vulgaris, the plant which most people called "heather."

Linguistics. See M35(1).

Linseed, the seed of the flax plant, containing, apart from its fibrous substance, certain oily and nitrogenous matter of considerable commercial value. This yields linseed oil, and some of the residue is used to make cattle food.

Lion, the most impressive of the Cat family (Felis leo or genus Panthera). It is chiefly found in open bush country in Africa, being comparatively rare in Asia. Its large square head, its flowing mane (in the males only), and its tufted tail distinguish it. From tip to tip it can reach a length of 10 ft.; a weight of 500 lb. Only weak, old lions are liable to attack man, usually they avoid him.

Lion and Unicorn, the supporting figures of the royal arms of Great Britain, date from the union of Scotland with England at the accession of James I. (James VI. of Scotland), the lion representing England and the unicorn Scotland.

Liqueurs are essences combined with alcoholic liquid, and are of many kinds, named according to their flavourings or place of production, and include Maraschino, Chartreuse, Curacoa, Benedictine, Noyau, Kümmel, etc.

Liquid, the name given to matter in such state that it takes its shape from the containing vessel. The volume it occupies is independent of the container, however. See F17, 18.

Litanies were first used in church processions in the 5th cent. The first English litany was commanded to be recited in the Reformed churches by Henry VIII, in 1544.

Lithium, a soft metallic element, symbol Li, similar to sodium. It is very reactive and is stored under paraffin oil. It is the lightest metal element.

Lithography, the art of drawing on stone and printing therefrom, was discovered by Alois Senefelder about 1796, and was introduced into England a few years later. Many improvements in the art have been made in recent years, especially in chromo-lithography and photolithography.

Litre, a metric measure, was abolished in 1964 as a scientific unit of volume, but remains as an everyday unit, e.g., of wine in countries that use the metric system for everyday purposes.

Liturgy, the name given to the Church ritual, though strictly applying only to the portion used in the celebration of the Eucharist or Lord's Supper. The Anglican liturgy is laid down in the Book of Common Prayer (1662). Parliament gave its consent in 1965 for changes in the form of worship.

Liverworts (Hepatics), a class of simple green plants related to the mosses. There is no differentiation into stem and leaves. Liverworts are most common in damp situations, such as the banks of ditches.

Lizard, the name given to a diversified order of reptiles, of which there are about 1,600 species. Included among the lizards are the geckos, chameleons, glass snakes, skinks, and blind worms.

Llama, mammals related to the camels, from which they differ in small size, absence of humps, and more woolly coat. The domestic llama of S. America is used as a beast of burden, also providing wool, meat, and milk. See also Alpaca, Guanaco.

Loadstone or Lodestone, an oxide of iron, found chiefly in Sweden and Norway. Its scientific name is magnetite. It has the power of attracting pieces of iron and served as the first magnets used in compasses. One of the class of non-metallic magnetic materials nowadays known as "ferrites."

Lobby Correspondents are political correspondents of newspapers who do not report the actual proceedings of Parliament—this is done by Parliamentary Correspondents—but interpret political news and events.

Lobsters are marine crustacean animals existing in large numbers in the northern seas of Europe and America, and in fair proportion on some parts of the British coasts, especially in the neighbourhood of the Channel Islands.

Locarno, Treaty of, 1925, whereby Germany, France, and Belgium undertook to maintain their present frontiers and to abstain from the use of force against each other. Hitler broke the pact by re-occupying the Rhineland, the demilitarisation of which had been recognised by Germany.

Locust, insects of the grasshopper family, but much more powerful. They are inhabitants of hot countries, and often make their appearance in untold millions, like clouds, devastating all the vegetation that comes within their course. The locust-tree (Ceratonia siliqua) is supposed to have furnished food to St. John the Baptist in the wilderness, and its "beans" have accordingly been styled "St. John's Bread."

Loess, a deposit of silt or marl laid down by wind action. The biggest loess deposits are in Asia, the source of the dust of which they are composed probably being the deserts of Central Asia.

Log, a line used for reckoning the speed at which a ship is travelling. It was first used in the 16th cent. The line is divided into spaces of 50 ft. marked off by knots and measured by a half-minute sand glass, bearing the same proportion to an hour as 50 ft. bear to a mile.

Logarithms, a system of calculation invented by John Napier in 1614, and developed by Henry Briggs a few years later. Thus if a number is expressed as the power of another number, *i.e.*, if $a = b^n$, then $n$ is said to be the logarithm of $a$ to base $b$, written $\log_b a$. Common logs are to base 10 and Napierian to base $2.7182818\ldots$, expressed as $e$. Their use represents a great saving of time.

**Logical Positivism.** *See* J25.

**Lollards.** *See* J25.

**Lombards,** a German people, originating on the Elbe, who settled in Italy in the 6th cent., occupying northern and central regions, and establishing a kingdom with Pavia as capital. They were conquered by Charlemagne in 774, but left their name to the region of Lombardy. Lombard Street, London, takes its name from the Lombard merchants and bankers who came to settle there in the 12th cent.

**London Clay,** geological stratum which occupies much of the London Basin and part of the Hampshire Basin. It represents the lower stratum of the Eocene. Outside the metropolis, brickfields utilise the clay for brickmaking. Water held above this impervious stratum is tapped by a number of artesian wells in London. The tunnels of the Capital's underground railways run through the London Clay.

**London University** comprises nearly one-third of the academic activity of the United Kingdom, and is recognised as one of the great universities of the world. Originated in the foundation of a non-sectarian college in Gower Street in 1828. Among the chief colleges are: University, Kings, Imperial College of Science and Technology, London School of Economics, School of Oriental and African Studies, Queen Mary, Birkbeck, Royal Holloway, Bedford, Westfield, and Queen Elizabeth College. London University was the first to throw open all degrees to women (1878).

**Long Distance Routes.** The National Parks and Access to the Countryside Act 1949 provided for the establishment in England and Wales of Long Distance Footpaths and Bridleways. The following have been approved but only the Pennine Way has been completed: Pennine Way (a magnificent hill walk of 250 miles from Edale in Derbyshire along the Pennines over the Cheviots to the Scottish border); Pembrokeshire Coast Path; Offa's Dyke Path (168 miles along the marches of Wales); South Downs Way (Beachy Head to Salisbury); South-West Peninsula Coast Path (North Cornwall, South Cornwall, South Devon, Somerset and North Devon, Dorset); Yorkshire Coast and North York Moors. *See also* National Parks.

**Longitude** of a point on the earth's surface is the angle which the meridian through the poles and that point makes with some standard meridian. The meridian through Greenwich is usually accepted as the standard meridian and the longitude is measured east or west of that line. As the earth revolves through 360° in 24 hrs., 15° longitude represent 1 hour's difference in apparent time.

**Long Parliament** (1640–60), marked the end of Charles I's 11-year attempt to govern without parliament. It carried through what has come to be called "the English Revolution" and was the parliament of the civil war (1642–49).

**Lord Chamberlain.** *See* Chamberlain, Lord.

**Lord Lieutenant** is the Queen's representative in the county, and his office is now largely ceremonial. On his recommendation the magistrates or Justices of the Peace are appointed by the Lord Chancellor. The office was created in 1549 to take over the military duties of the sheriff.

**Lords, House of,** the Upper House of the British Parliament composed of Lords Spiritual and Lords Temporal. The former consist of the two Archbishops and twenty-four English Bishops and the latter of Peers and Peeresses. The full membership (1969) is 1062. The right of the Lords to veto Bills passed by the Commons is restricted by the Parliament Acts of 1911 and 1949. The Lord High Chancellor presides over the House of Lords. *See* Section C, Part II.

**Louse,** parasitic insect found on the skin of birds and mammals. The bird or biting lice belong to the order *Mallophaga*; the true or sucking lice to the order *Anoplura*. Two species of lice parasitise man, and one of these, the body louse, is a carrier of typhus.

**Louvre,** one of the old royal palaces of Paris, was built in its present form partly by Francis, I. and added to by later monarchs, Louis XIV. completing the edifice. Napoleon I. turned it into a museum and enriched it with the plunder of many foreign art galleries. The great extension to the Louvre building begun by Napoleon I. was completed under Napoleon III. in 1857. Much injury was done to the building during the Commune of 1871. Amongst other famous treasures it houses the Venus de Milo and Leonardo da Vinci's masterpiece, *La Gioconda*.

**Lovebird,** a vivid little bird native to Africa, resembling a parrakeet but with a short, wide tail and short body.

**LSD** (d-lysergic acid diethylamide). This hallucinogenic drug has achieved wide notoriety because of its use by certain people to give themselves abnormal mental experiences. Doctors have frequently warned against the dangers of its use. It is active in extremely small quantities and a dose as small as a fifty-millionth part of a gram can cause marked disturbances of the mental function in man. LSD has been used in the study of mental disease because it produces symptoms very similar to mental disorders such as schizophrenia. *See* Section P, Part III.

**Luddites,** a combination of workmen formed in 1811, in a period of great distress, with the object of destroying the new textile machinery then being largely adopted, which they regarded as the cause of their troubles. Their first outbreak was at Nottingham, and was stated to have been started by a young apprentice named Ned Ludd. Afterwards, serious Luddite riots occurred in various parts of the country, especially in the West Riding of Yorkshire, where many people were killed, mills were destroyed, and numbers of rioters were tried and executed. Charlotte Brontë used the period in her novel, *Shirley*.

**Lunar Month.** *See* Month.

**Lung Fishes** *or* Dipnoi. *See* Dipnoi.

**Lutecium,** element of the rare-earth metal group discovered in 1907 by Urbain.

**Lutheranism.** *See* J25.

**Lynx,** cats of sturdy build, with tufted ears and spotted fur, inhabiting many parts of the world, including Northern and Central Europe. They commit serious ravages among sheep and goats and are very fierce.

**Lyon King of Arms,** the President of the Scottish Lyon Court, and head of the heraldic organisation for Scotland.

**Lyre-Bird,** a remarkable family of Australian birds, the males of which possess a beautiful lyre-shaped tail. The bird is not more than 15 in. long, but its tail, displayed during its remarkable courtship dance, is 23 in. in length. There are two species: the Superb and Albert's Lyrebird.

# M

**Macaque.** A family of monkeys which include the Barbary ape (specimens of which live on Gibraltar), the Rhesus macaque (the organ grinder's monkey and the one used for experimental work in the investigation of disease), the Bonnet monkey of southern India and Ceylon, the Crab-eating, and the Pig-tailed monkeys of south-eastern Asia.

**Macaw,** a genus of large parrots with brilliant scarlet and sky-blue plumage, with interminglings of green. Native to South and Central America.

**Mace,** originally a weapon of offence, now an ensign of authority borne before officers of state and other dignitaries. In the House of Commons the mace is handed to an official of the Crown by the Sergeant-at-Arms at the close of a parliamentary session.

**Mach Number.** Unit of flight speed. The ratio of speed of flight to speed of sound under same conditions of pressure and density. Speed of sound at sea-level is 762 m.p.h., so flight speed of 381 m.p.h. is equivalent to a Mach Number of ½. At supersonic speeds the Mach Number is greater than 1; subsonic speeds, less than 1.

**Mackerel,** a familiar sea-fish existing in large numbers in the northern waters of both hemispheres. In May and June immense shoals are to be found round the British coasts.

**Macromolecules** are very large molecules about 10,000 times or more as heavy as ordinary small molecules like hydrogen. Most are built up from a large number of simple sub-units, *i.e.*, are polymers (*q.v.*). The term macromolecule is often used in biology, *e.g.*, starch and cellulose are biological macromolecules, both built from glucose sub-units. Other important ones are proteins and nucleic acids. The properties of macromolecules depend on the sub-units of which they are composed.

**Madder**, one of the most important of dye-stuffs, largely used in producing Turkey-red dye, but now superseded by synthetic alizarin. Natural madder is the root of the *Rubia tinctorum*.

**Madrier**, a term in military engineering for a beam used to support the earth in a mine or fortification, or to receive the mouth of a petard.

**Maelstrom**, a great whirlpool. The most famous is that off the coast of Norway, between the islands of Moskenes and Mosken, of the Lofoten group, the power of which has been much exaggerated.

**Mafia**, a secret Sicilian society formed for purposes of vengeance, private and public, prominent about 1860, and again after the second world war. Signor Dolci (*see* B26) is working to end Mafia exploitation, intimidation, and violence in Sicily. It was not until 1962 that the Italian Parliament finally admitted that the Mafia existed and decided to set up a commission to study it and the means of eradicating it. The American branch of the Mafia, the Cosa Nostra, has infiltrated many city governments by bribing officials.

**Magellan, Clouds of,** the name given to a pair of small galaxies, satellite systems of our own galaxy, visible only from the southern hemisphere. On account of their relative nearness to the earth (186,000 light-years), they are receiving much attention from astronomers.

**Magenta**, a blue-red aniline dye discovered in 1859 by Sir W. H. Perkin, and named after the great battle of that year between the French and Austrians.

**Magic.** *See* J26.

**Magistrates** *or* **Justices of the Peace** preside over courts of petty sessions, and are appointed by the Lord Chancellor on the recommendation of the Lord Lieutenant of the County. Most J.P.s are laymen and are unpaid. In certain big towns a legally-qualified, paid, full-time magistrate is appointed, known as a stipendiary magistrate. In London stipendiaries are known as Metropolitan Stipendiary Magistrates. J.P.s are no longer appointed over the age of 60 and they must retire when they reach 70. There are now arrangements for the training of magistrates. By the Justices of the Peace Act, 1968, *ex officio* J.P.s are abolished, except for the Lord Mayor and aldermen of the City of London. *See* D37, 43, 44.

**Magma**, molten rock material rich in volatile constituents prior to its eruption at the surface. On eruption and loss of volatiles it becomes lava.

**Magna Carta** was sealed by King John at Runnymede on June 15, 1215, in obedience to the insistent demands of the barons, and has been confirmed many times by later monarchs. It was not a revolutionary document. It laid down what the barons took to be the recognised and fundamental principles for the government of the realm and bound king and barons alike to maintain them. Its main provisions were that no man should be punished without fair trial, that ancient liberties generally should be preserved, and that no demands should be made by an overlord to his vassal (other than those recognised) without the sanction of the great council of the realm.

**Magnesium**, a metallic element, symbol Mg, first isolated in 1808 by Sir Humphry Davy, who prepared it by electrolysing the chloride. Its chief ores are magnesite and dolomite. Industrially it is obtained by electrolysis. Many important light alloys contain magnesium. The metal burns with a very bright light, and for this reason it is used in photographers' flash bulbs and also in firework manufacture.

**Magnetic Pole.** Either one of two regions of a magnet where the attraction appears concentrated.

**Magnetic Storms**, large irregular disturbances superimposed upon the normal magnetic field of the earth. They may occur at any time, but are most frequent during equinoctial months and in years of sunspot maxima. World-wide in extent, magnetic storms are most pronounced in the polar regions, being due apparently to intense electric currents located in the upper atmosphere near to the zones of greatest auroral frequency. One theory attributes the high ionisation of these belts to solar radiation. Magnetic storms cause radio fade-outs and interfere with telegraphic communication.

**Magnetism**, originally the name given to the quality of attraction for iron possessed by lodestone (*q.v.*). Now known to be a phenomenon inseparably connected with electricity (F18). Strong magnetic attraction is possessed by a comparatively small class of substances; iron, nickel, and cobalt are the most common elements, but there are several less well known, *e.g.*, gadolinium. Many alloys have valuable magnetic properties which make possible numberless technical devices. New magnetic substances are always being developed (*see* Ferrite). The earth acts like a huge magnet with its axis inclined at about 11° to the axis of rotation, the magnetic poles being on the Boothia Peninsula (North Canada) and South Victoria Land (Antarctica). The magnetic field at the surface consists of the regular field of a magnetised sphere with an irregular field superimposed upon it. Variation in the magnetic forces occurs from place to place and from time to time, and maps showing the distribution over the globe of points of the same declination (*i.e.*, the angle which the magnetic meridian makes with the geographical one) are of the utmost importance in navigation. In the south-east of the British Isles, at present, a magnetic needle points 9° and in the north-west 14° west of true north. Little is known regarding the origin of the main (regular) field of the earth, but it is believed that the irregularities are due to the presence of intense electric currents in the upper atmospheres and local magnetisation of rock strata. In 1967 the discovery was claimed of isolated magnetic poles, *i.e.*, north and south magnetic poles existing separately, just as positive and negative electrical charges exist separately. If this is confirmed it will probably rank as one of the most important experimental results of the 20th cent., because of its significance for the theory of electromagnetism and fundamental particles.

**Magnetohydro-dynamics.** A current-carrying wire always experiences a force if it is in a magnetic field. This is the well-known electrodynamic force, and electric motors work because of it. If the current is carried in a fluid, *e.g.*, a liquid metal or a plasma, these forces cause bodily movements of the fluid, which are in general very difficult to calculate. The forces are then called *magnetohydro-dynamic forces*. Now magnetic fields are themselves produced by electric currents; so a current flowing in a fluid produces a magnetic field, which then reacts on the fluid itself by means of the magnetohydro-dynamic forces. In the Harwell machine Zeta, used in studying the technical problems of thermonuclear reactions, this effect acts so as to constrict the electric discharge on to the axis of the tube and thus keeps it away from the walls. This action is assisted by an extra magnetic field produced by a separate current flowing in metallic conductors outside the tube. Thus the hot plasma is contained by magnetohydro-dynamic forces and not at all by the material tube wall. In practical devices of the future magnetic forces may have to sustain plasma pressures of 60 atmospheres—a pressure for which a thick steel wall would normally be used! *See also* Plasma Physics.

**Magnificat**, the hymn of the Virgin Mary, given in Luke 1, 46 beginning in the Vulgate with the words "Magnificat anima mea Dominum" ("My soul doth magnify the Lord"), and used in the services of all Christian Churches.

**Magnitude** in astronomy is a measure of the apparent brightness of a star, which is inversely proportional to the square of its distance. A low number indicates a bright star, and a high one a faint star. The *absolute magnitude* is a measure of *real* brightness, *i.e.*, the brightness a star would have at a standard distance away of 32·6 light years. The distance can be calculated if the apparent and absolute magnitudes are known.

**Magnolia,** species of the family *Magnoliaceae* comprising many beautiful trees, and shrubs with large and fragrant flowers, and chiefly native to North America and Asia. Introduced in 1688.

**Magpie,** a well-known bird of the crow family, of glossy black and white plumage, famed for its mischievous propensities.

**Magyars,** the Hungarian race who came to eastern Europe from S.W. Asia and settled in Hungary in the 10th cent. Their language belongs to the Finno-Ugrian group.

**Mahdi,** an Arab leader of great influence, invested with powers akin to those of a Messiah in the Mohammedan mind. The title was taken by Mohammed Ahmed, who overran the Egyptian Sudan, and in 1885 captured Khartoum.

**Mahogany,** a fine hard wood susceptible of a very high polish, and distinguished for the beauty of its colour and markings. Obtained chiefly from the trees of the genera *Swietenia* (Spanish or Cuban mahogany) and *Khaya* (African mahogany) of the family Meliacaea. According to tradition Raleigh had a mahogany table made for Queen Elizabeth.

**Maidenhair Tree** *or* **Ginkgo.** This tree takes its name from the shape of its leaves, which resemble those of the maidenhair fern. Widely cultivated in China and Japan. It is the only survivor of an order of gymnosperms which flourished in Mesozoic times. Botanically interesting because the male gametes are motile.

**Malmaison,** château at Rueil-Malmaison, a western suburb of Paris. It derives it name from having been inhabited in the 11th cent. by the Norman brigand Odon, and afterwards, according to the tradition, by evil spirits, exorcised by the monks of St. Denis. It was the residence of Napoleon and of the Empress Josephine after her divorce. She died there in 1814 as the result of a chill caught while showing the Russian Emperor round the grounds. In 1900 it was given to the nation.

**Malmsey,** a strong, sweet wine originally made in Greece, but now also in Spain, Madeira, and the Azores; known also as Malvoisie.

**Maltose,** a sugar formed in cereal grains during germination. It is produced by hydrolysis of starch, and further hydrolysis converts the maltose into glucose.

**Mamluks,** commonly known as Mamelukes, were originally—in the 13th cent.—a bodyguard of Turkish and Circassian slaves in the service of the Sultan of Egypt, and attained such influence that in 1250 they were strong enough to appoint one of their own body to the throne of Egypt. After that a succession of Mamluk Sultans reigned down to 1517. Then the Turks annexed Egypt, and the Mamluks were taken into the service of the Beys. They again came to the front after Napoleon's conquest of Egypt, and for a time resumed governmental sway; but in 1811 they were decoyed into the citadel of Cairo and massacred by order of Mehemet Ali.

**Mammoth,** extinct elephants of gigantic size. In 1799 the first perfectly preserved specimen was found in Siberia in a block of ice. It was in prehistoric times an inhabitant of Britain and other parts of Europe, as well as of Asia and America.

**Mammoth Cave** of Kentucky, about 10 miles long, is one of a series of spacious caverns formed in the limestone rock formation, and is from 40 to 300 ft. wide and at one point 300 ft. high. Stalactites and stalagmites abound.

**Manatee,** an aquatic mammal of the sea cow (Sirenia) order of mammals, averaging when full grown from 10 to 12 ft. in length, with shovel-shaped tail, and four limbs and nails which almost give the appearance of arms and hands. In spite of their ungainly aspect, these creatures are believed to have given rise to the legend of mermaids.

**Manchus,** the original nomadic race inhabiting northern Manchuria who invaded China early in the 17th cent. A Manchu dynasty occupied

the imperial throne of China from 1644 to 1911.

**Mandarin,** the name given to a powerful Chinese official, civil or military, under the old régime, whose rank was shown by the wearing of a button on the cap. Mandarin is the major language of N. China (*see* M36).

**Mandible,** the lower jaw in human anatomy. The two parts of a bird's beak are known as the upper and lower mandible. The term is also used for biting jaws in arthropods.

**Manganese,** a metallic element, symbol Mn, discovered by Scheele in 1774. It is silver-white, not very hard (it forms a hard alloy with carbon), brittle, and tarnishes when exposed to air. Its chief ore is pyrolusite (manganese dioxide). Steels containing manganese are very tough, and used for making machine parts.

**Maniple,** eucharistic vestment worn over left arm.

**Manna,** a tree of the ash genus, *Fraxinus ornus,* growing in the South of Europe and in the East and exuding a sweet substance which is gathered, boiled, and eaten.

**Manometer,** instrument used to measure gas pressure. Usually a U-tube containing water or mercury, one end open to the atmosphere, the other to the gas whose pressure is to be measured. More sensitive for small pressures than the Bourdon gauge.

**Manors** were estates originally granted in Anglo-Saxon times as rewards for knightly service, and included the privilege of a special court with jurisdiction, criminal and civil, within the manorial territory. *See* Court-Leet.

**Mansion House,** the official residence of the Lord Mayor of London, stands opposite to the Bank of England, and was erected in 1739–53 from the designs of George Dance.

**Mantis.** Large insects belonging to the same order as the locusts and grasshoppers. The manner in which the forelegs are held, as though in suppliance, has gained for these insects the common name of "praying mantis." They are distributed throughout the warmer countries of the world.

**Manx,** the Celtic dialect (Manx Gaelic) of the Isle of Man, now on the point of extinction.

**Maoris,** the race found in New Zealand at the time of its discovery by Europeans. The Maoris are believed to have migrated from Polynesia about 1350. They number 165,000 (1961), and being very intelligent people have adapted themselves with considerable success to the conditions of civilised life. Until 1870 they were frequently in arms against the Government, but since then have settled down with the Whites as equal citizens.

**Maple,** trees native to the northern hemisphere. There are over 100 species. The sycamore is the best-known species growing in Britain. The sugar maple abounds in Canada and the eastern parts of the United States. The sugar is tapped by boring holes in the tree in Feb. and Mar., and the juice that escapes is collected and evaporated. The maple-leaf is the Canadian national emblem.

**Maquis,** name of the dense scrub in Mediterranean France and Corsica, providing good cover for bandits and outlaws. The French resistance movement adopted the name Maquis during the German Occupation, 1940–45.

**Marble** is limestone in its hardest and most crystalline form. There are many varieties—33 were used in the building of the Paris Opera House—but white is the purest and rarest. White marble was used by the ancient Greeks for their temples and statues. Among the famous marbles of Italy are the Carrara and Siena marbles, which were used by Renaissance sculptors. Devonshire and Derbyshire yield some beautiful marbles and Connemara furnishes a serpentine-marble.

**March,** the third month of the year, and the first of the old Roman Calendar. It was named after the god Mars, and was the *Hlyd* (storm) *monath* of the Anglo-Saxons.

**Mardi Gras,** the last day of the Carnival in France, Shrove Tuesday.

**Marionettes** are puppets moved by strings. They originated in the *Fantoccini* of the 15th cent. which had such a vogue in Italy and elsewhere on the Continent. The English *Punch and*

*Judy* is a version of Punchinello. Puppet shows were known in the earliest civilisations.

**Marl,** a rock composed partly of clay and partly of carbonate of lime.

**Marlinspike,** a pointed iron tool used by sailors to splice wire. The instrument used when rope splicing is called a fid.

**Marmoset,** small monkeys confined to the New World. Very squirrel-like in appearance, with long bushy tails, and thick woolly fur, they are pretty little animals and the smallest of all monkeys. There are claws, not nails, on their digits, the big toe excepted.

**Marprelate Tracts,** seditious pamphlets written with great maliciousness by a group of Elizabethan puritans about 1586, and intended to discredit the episcopacy, caused a great sensation in their time, and led to the execution of their supposed author, John Penry.

**Marquess** *or* **Marquis,** the title next in precedence to that of duke. The first English marquess was Rovery de Vere, Earl of Oxford, who had the honour conferred upon him by Richard II. in 1385.

**Marquetry,** a kind of inlaying in which thin layers of coloured woods are wrought into a design, and mainly used in ornamental floors.

**Mars,** the fourth nearest planet to the sun, being 141,500,000 miles distant. Its diameter is 4,215 miles as against the earth's 7,920. There has been much speculation about certain dark lines which some observers have seen on the surface of Mars; photographs give no support to the theory of an artificially constructed network of canals, but it is possible they represent areas covered by some simple form of vegetation of the lichenous type. The temperature of the planet's surface would allow living organisms as we know them to exist, but the quantity of oxygen in the atmosphere would be almost certainly too little to support animal life. American (*Mariner IV*) and Russian (*Zond II*) spacecraft launched in 1964 reached the planet in the summer of 1965. *Mariner IV* took close-up pictures of part of the Martian surface. Like the moon it is pitted with craters. Mars has two small moons—Phobos and Deimos.

**Marseillaise,** the French national hymn, written and composed by Rouget de L'Isle, a French engineer officer, who was inspired to write it in 1792 to encourage the Strasburg conscripts. It immediately became popular, and received its name from the fact that it was sung by the Marseillaise troops while marching into Paris.

**Marshalsea Prison,** a once well-known house of detention in Southwark. It stood near St. George's Church, and was originally a prison for royal servants convicted of offences, but from 1842 to 1849 was a debtors' prison. It was abolished in 1849. Dickens described it in *Little Dorrit*.

**Marsh Gas.** *See* Methane.

**Marsh Tortoise,** an amphibious animal of the order *Chelonia*, spread over many countries and inhabiting ponds and small rivers. There are 42 species, and they are all carnivorous.

**Marston Moor,** near York, was the scene of the famous battle between Prince Rupert and Cromwell on July 2, 1644. Cromwell's victory was the turning-point in the Civil War.

**Marsupials,** members of the order of pouched animals. Except for the opossums of America, all marsupials occur in Australasia. Well-known marsupials are the kangaroos, wallabies, and wombats.

**Martello Towers,** circular forts erected on the coasts of England and Jersey early in the 19th cent. as defences against the threatened Napoleonic invasion. So called from the circular fort at Mortella (Corsica), which resisted an English fleet in 1794.

**Marten,** carnivorous animals of the weasel family, one species of which was once common in Britain, but now seldom met with. Many valuable furs come from martens, *e.g.*, the sable of N. Asia and the marten of N. America.

**Martial Law** is a term loosely employed to indicate the suspension of the administration of normal civil law and its replacement by military authority when this is rendered desirable by such circumstances as war or rebellion.

**Martin,** a well-known bird-visitor to Britain. It belongs to the swallow family, and the two species that spend their summers here are the house-martin, which makes its nest of mud under the eaves of houses, and the sand martin, which builds in sandy banks.

**Martingale,** a long strap or thong of leather, one end of which is fastened to the girth of a horse, between the fore legs, and the other to the bit, or to a thin mouthpiece of its own.

**Martinmas** *or* **St. Martin's Day,** falls on Nov. 11, and is one of the Scottish quarter days. St. Martin was a popular Saint with our ancestors, and Martinmas was a busy time for the mediæval housewife. It was the date when "Martlemas Beef" was dried in the chimney, and enough bacon and mutton cured to last until the spring, because, owing the the scarcity of winter fodder, fresh meat could seldom be obtained. This diet of dried meat without vegetables caused scurvy, King's evil, leprosy, and other maladies. Originally the goose belonged to Martinmas, not to Michaelmas, the legend being that when Martin was elected Bishop of Tours he hid himself, but was betrayed by the cackling of geese. He died in the 4th cent. The spell of fine weather sometimes occurring at Martinmas is called St. Martin's Summer.

**Martyrs.** People who suffer death in testimony to their faith. Stephen was the first Christian martyr in 39. The first English martyr was St. Alban, 286, and in Tudor times many eminent churchmen went to the stake at West Smithfield, in London, and at Oxford, where now exists the "Martyrs' Memorial." There is a Martyrs' Memorial Church in St. John St., Clerkenwell, near the scene of the Smithfield fires.

**Marxism.** *See* J27.

**Mason and Dixon's Line** is the boundary line separating the old slave states of America from the free state of Pennsylvania. It was drawn by two English surveyors, Charles Mason and Jeremiah Dixon, between 1763 and 1767.

**Masques** were light dramatic compositions set to music and performed on special occasions. One of the best-known examples is Milton's "Comus," which was given at Ludlow Castle in 1634.

**Mass,** the service in the Roman Catholic Church in which are enacted and enshrined Christ's words and actions at the Last Supper. It is high or low, *i.e.*, performed with full choial service, or merely by the rehearsal of prayers without singing. Mass was first celebrated in Latin in the 4th cent., and was introduced into England in the 7th cent. The use of a vernacular language was sanctioned by the Second Vatican Council (1965).

**Mass Spectrograph,** an instrument for separating isotopes. It works by sorting electrified particles according to their masses; the particles stream through a magnetic and possibly an electric field, and the lightest particles undergo the greatest deflection.

**Massorah,** a collection of criticisms on the Hebrew text of the Scriptures, and rules for its correct interpretation.

**Mast,** a long round piece of timber or tubular steel or iron, standing upright in a vessel, and supporting the yards, sails, and rigging in general. The earliest ships had only one mast, carrying a simple sail. The number increased until there were 4 or 5, or even more. Above the lower mast of a sailing-ship comes the topmast, and above that, the topgallantmast and royalmast. The position of each mast is indicated by a prefix, as foremast, foretopmast, foretopgallantmast, foreroyalmast, mainmast, maintopmast, etc. The foremast is in the fore of the ship, the mainmast in the centre, and the mizzen nearest the stern. In large vessels nowadays the mast does not extend to the keel, as it formerly did, but is usually stopped at the second deck.

**Master of the Revels** was an important Court official upon whom devolved the arrangement of Court festivities. The office is at least as old as the time of Edward III. By 1737 it seems to have died.

**Master of the Rolls,** one of the English judges, formerly a judge of Chancery, but since 1881 a judge of the Court of Appeal only. In addition he has charge of the rolls or records of Chancery and ranks next to the Lord Chancellor and Lord Chief Justice.

**Mastodon,** an extinct order of quadruped closely

resembling the elephant in structure, but much larger.

**Materials Science** is a blend of science and technology; it is the use of scientific research methods to study and improve materials for practical use. The deeper understanding so obtained enables scientists to design new substances with hitherto unknown combinations of properties that are useful in engineering, aircraft, nuclear power, surgery, etc. Materials science institutes or university departments will usually contain an assortment of chemists, physicists, metallurgists, ceramicists, engineers, and others because materials science brings to bear on materials a great many specialised techniques. The scientific study of materials is bringing continual improvement in metals, ceramics, plastics, fibres, and many valuable combinations of these.

**Mathematics** is the language of physics, and uses symbols for expressing measurements, theories, and laws. Mathematical formulae summarise and condense in exquisite simplicity the results of vast numbers of observations and experiments.

**Matins**, the first of the canonical hours or services of the day in the Roman Catholic Church and Morning Prayer in the Anglican Church. The daily service in the Roman breviary (*q.v.*) consists of eight offices or " hours," fixed by canon, for prayer and devotion. Formerly, Matins was recited or sung at midnight, Lauds at sunrise, Prime at 6 a.m., Terce at 9 a.m., Sext at midday, Nones at 3 p.m., Vespers at sunset, and Compline before retiring for the night. Lauds are now commonly joined to Matins.

**Mau-Mau**, a secret, anti-European, terrorist movement which agitated the Kikuyu tribe of Kenya during the years 1953–57. Mau-mau was a symptom of native insecurity and discontent; emergency powers were lifted in Nov. 1959, an large-scale reforms were instituted. Kenya attained independence in Dec. 1963 with Mr. Jomo Kenyatta as Prime Minister.

**Maundy Thursday**, the day before Good Friday, commemorates the Last Supper. " Maundy " derives from Christ's command (mandatum) to his disciples on that day to love one another. It was the custom in the monasteries for the monks to wash the feet of the poor on this day, and for many centuries the sovereigns of England, through their almoners, have distributed money, food, and clothing to " as many old men and as many old women as the Sovereign is years of age." The Royal Maundy ceremony is still observed, special silver money granted by the Royal Almonry is coined for the occasion and the distribution takes place in Westminster Abbey. *See* **U.K. Coinage, Section N.**

**Mausoleum**, a special place of sepulture, generally for the reception of the remains of members of a royal or other family of distinction. The name is derived from the tomb of King Mausolus at Halicarnassus, erected about 350 B.C., and forming one of the seven wonders of the world.

**Mauve**, a colouring matter produced from lichens by Dr. Stenhouse in 1848, but in 1856 obtained from aniline by William Perkin (1838–1907), who gave it the name Mauveen. This was the first synthetic organic dyestuff ever to be produced, which led to the building up of the great synthetic dyestuffs industry (which Germany dominated before the First World War).

**May**, the fifth month of the year, but the third of the ancient Roman calendar. Supposed to be named after Maia, the mother of Mercury, to whom sacrifices were offered on the first day of this month. In England in former days May Day was made the occasion of many festivities, including the crowning of the May Queen, dancing round the Maypole, etc.

**" Mayflower,"** the name of the ship which in 1620 conveyed the Pilgrim Fathers, 101 in number, from England to America. *See* **Pilgrim Fathers.**

**May Fly.** *See* **Ephemeroptera.**

**Mazarin Bible**, an edition of the Latin Vulgate, acknowledged as the masterpiece of the Gutenberg press (1456). It was the first book completely printed from movable types. It is called the Mazarin Bible because the first copy to capture the attention of scholars was found in the library of Cardinal Mazarin, in Paris. Sometimes called the Gutenberg or the 42-line Bible.

**Mazurka**, a Polish dance in 3-beat time. Chopin wrote many Mazurkas as concert-pieces for the pianoforte.

**Meal-Worm** is the larva of a beetle—*Tenebrio molitor*—and is found in corn mills, granaries, and bakeries, where it does considerable damage. It is largely used for feeding birds.

**Mean.** In statistics and mathematics generally understood to be the arithmetic mean. The geometric mean between two quantities is the square root of their product. *See* **Average.**

**Mechanical Equivalent of Heat.** *See* **Joule.**

**Medals**, as decorations for military service, were first issued in this country by Charles I., who ordered medals for gallantry to be distributed to certain soldiers in 1643. Medals were also issued to officers and men who were victorious against the Dutch fleet in 1653. After Lord Howe's victory in 1794 a naval medal was instituted. Medals were also struck for the victory of Waterloo, and since that time special medals have been issued in connection with all our wars. The Victoria Cross, a special reward for personal gallantry in the Navy, Army, and Air Force, was instituted in 1856. The George Cross for gallantry instituted in 1940 ranks next to the Victoria Cross. The Military Cross was instituted in 1914.

**Median.** *See* **Average.**

**Medlar**, a tree of which the fruit is about 1 in. in diameter and hard fleshed when gathered, but after being stored for a few weeks it softens. It has a peculiar flavour. Its large white flowers give it a decorative appearance.

**Meerschaum**, a white or yellow-white earthy mineral, found in beds in Asia Minor, Greece, and other places, is a silicate of magnesium allied with water. Its chief use is in making pipe-bowls.

**Megalith**, a prehistoric monument, consisting of a large single stone or a group of such stones, in a circle as at Stonehenge or in burial chambers as at New Grange, Ireland. Megalithic monuments have been constructed by different peoples in different parts of the world since the third millennium B.C.

**Meiosis**, a special type of cell division by which the gametes or sex cells are generated, resulting in the sperm or ovum receiving only half the number of chromosomes found in a somatic cell. *See* **Mitosis.**

**Mendelian Law.** The first statistical rules of inheritance, determining the ratio of variation of characteristics in the offspring of differing individuals, and the classification of characters discontinuously inherited, were first formulated by the Austrian monk Gregor Mendel. The results of his most important experiments in the crossing of peas were published in 1866, and showed that when two races are crossed, the resultant hybrids will exhibit the dominant features of one parent, but the offspring of the second generation will show those of both grandparents. *See* **F44.**

**Mendicant Friars**, certain religious orders which spread over Europe in the 13th cent., and comprised the Franciscans, Dominicans, Augustines, and Carmelites. Originally they depended entirely on alms.

**Mercator's Projection**, a method of indicating meridians and parallels of latitudes on maps, introduced by Mercator in the 16th cent., and still universally used in navigator's charts.

**Mercury**, one of the smaller planets and the nearest to the sun, being 36 million miles distant. It has no satellite. *See* **F7.**

**Mercury** *or* **Quicksilver**, symbol Hg (Latin *hydrargyrum*) is one of the oldest-known metals, whose chief ore is the sulphide, cinnabar, found in certain parts of Spain, China, Japan, Mexico, and South America. It is liquid at ordinary temperature and is used in the construction of barometers and thermometers. Alloys of mercury are called amalgams. It is also of great value in medicine. The metal is used in the mercury-vapour (or " sunlight ") lamp, since the vapour gives a bright yellow-white glow in an electric discharge.

**Mercy Killing.** *See* **D6(2).**

**Meridian**, an imaginary circle extending through the North and South Poles and any given place. When the sun is at its midday height at any place it is " on the meridian "; hence the terms ante-meridian (a.m.) and post-meridian (p.m.). *See also* **Greenwich Mean Time.**

**Merino Sheep** were imported into England from Spain in 1788, and had great influence in improving native breeds, especially in regard to the quality of the wool.

**Merit, Order of,** founded by King Edward VII. in 1902 as a special distinction for eminent men and women without conferring a knighthood upon them. The Order has twenty-four British companions in addition to foreign honorary members limited in number, as the choice of members is, by the Sovereign's pleasure. Lord Kelvin was the founder companion. General Eisenhower (1945), and Dr. Sarvepalli Radhakrishnan (1963) are honorary members. Florence Nightingale (1907) and Professor Dorothy Hodgkin (1965) are the only women to have received this coveted decoration.

**Merovingians,** the name given to the family that ruled over France from about 500 to 750. Clovis was first of the line and Childeric the last.

**Mesons** (from Greek *meso* = middle), a family of unstable particles of mass between that of an electron and that of a proton. Some are positive, some negative, some neutral. No stable meson is known, the longest-lived particle having a lifetime of only two-millionths of a second. The first of these particles was discovered in cosmic radiation in 1937 and called the mu-meson or *muon*. In 1947 a heavier type was discovered called the pi-meson or *pion*, which behaved like the meson predicted on theoretical grounds by Yukawa in 1935. The pion is connected with the theory of nuclear forces. *See also* F13, 14.

**Mesozoic.** The geological era which includes the Triassic, Jurassic, and Cretaceous rocks. *See* F41.

**Metabolism,** the general term for the physical and chemical processes occurring within a living organism. *See* F26.

**Metalloid,** an element which has properties intermediate between those of a metal and a non-metal. Arsenic is a metalloid.

**Metamorphic Rocks** are such geological deposits as have undergone alterations of structure and mineral reorganisation. The most active agents in producing these metamorphic changes are heat, water, and pressure. *See* F8(2).

**Metamorphosis,** period of development from egg to adult, during which the animals have different forms, as found, *e.g.*, in the life histories of frog and butterfly.

**Meteorites.** The word meteor originally signified any natural phenomenon, but in modern usage meteors are small bodies coming from interplanetary space which become luminous by friction on entering the earth's atmosphere. Popularly called "shooting stars." Larger meteors are known as fireballs. Some of these reach the ground. The object which has been a meteor in flight then becomes a meteorite. In some meteorites iron is the predominating element, others are like rock. The iron meteorites are more common amongst those which have been preserved, but falls of rocklike meteorites occur more frequently. At l'Aigle in France in 1803 from 2000 to 3000 meteorite stones fell; this fall is famous because it convinced scientists that meteorites really came from outside our atmosphere. (The largest meteorite stone actually known to have fallen to earth is one which descended in Emmott County, Iowa, in 1870, weighing 437 pounds.) A meteorite weighing no less than 36½ tons found in Greenland is now in New York. On June 30, 1908, an enormous object fell in Siberia in a sparsely-inhabited region. A hot blast destroyed all trees within a radius of about 5–10 miles, the explosion waves being recorded by barographs as far distant as London, Washington, and Batavia. For the next few nights there was in Europe in the northern sky brilliant illumination due to sunlight falling on clouds of dust at a great height in the atmosphere. Whether this dust had accompanied the object in its journey through space like the tail of a comet or whether the dust had come from Siberia is unknown. (Many Russian astronomers now believe this Siberian meteorite, as it is commonly called, was the nucleus of a small comet.) When the place where the object fell was visited in 1927 some 200 craters were found, but no considerable

meteorite had been recovered. Meteorites are possibly débris from the disintegration of a body in the solar system.

**Meteorology,** the science of the atmosphere considered as a heat engine. Deals with weather, climate, optical phenomena, atmospheric electricity, physical processes such as radiation and precipitation, the dynamics and structure of cyclones, anticyclones, etc. Wide application to problems of aviation, agriculture, commerce and shipping. Meteorological observing stations are in operation all over the world, and on the simultaneous or synoptic reports of their instrument readings and estimates of pressure, temperature, humidity, speed and direction of wind, rain, character and amount of cloud, visibility, etc., forecasts, gale, snow and frost warnings are based. Instruments carried by earth satellites outside the atmosphere can make systematic observations on a world-wide basis of the atmospheric circulation, through observation of cloud cover and of the thermal radiation into space from the atmosphere. Such observations are of great importance for meteorology. For example, in 1961, the development of a hurricane in mid-Atlantic was first detected by an American weather satellite, one of the *Tiros* series which have since been used for Weather Bureau routine forecasts.

**Methane.** The simplest hydrocarbon, compounded of one carbon atom and four hydrogen atoms. This gas occurs over marshes and swamps, where it is liberated in the decay of vegetable matter. It is the main constituent of natural gas, and also occurs in coal-mines, where it is called "fire-damp" because of the explosive character of its mixture with air. Formerly this natural gas was removed from the coal seams and ran to waste; now in many countries (including Britain) it is being used for commercial purposes.

**Methodism.** *See* J27.

**Methylated Spirit,** a mixture of 90 parts by volume ethyl alcohol, 9½ parts wood naphtha (methyl alcohol), ⅛ part crude pyridine, together with small amounts of petroleum oil and methyl violet dye. Industrial methylated spirit consists of a mixture of 95 parts by volume ethyl alcohol and 5 parts wood naphtha. It is used as a solvent and a fuel.

**Metre.** *See* English Verse, M22.

**Metre,** unit of length in the metric system; since 1960 the wavelength of the orange-red light of krypton 86 has been adopted as the basis of the international unit of length. Before that (since 1889) the platinum–iridium bar kept at Sèvres was the international prototype metre.

**Metric System,** the system of weights and measures based on the gram and the metre, smaller and larger units being decimals and multiples of the primary units respectively. A decimal currency was adopted in France in 1795 and the metric system of weights and measures in 1799. (In that year the quadrant of the earth was surveyed and the standard metre adopted.) Nevertheless the change was accepted slowly, and as late as 1837 the French Government had to pass a law forbidding the use of the old measures. Since then the metric system has been adopted in most of the continental countries and is used universally in scientific work. Although there have been many attempts to get the system adopted in Britain, it was not until 1965 that the Government announced that it was encouraging the adoption of the metric system of weights and measures. By 1975 the greater part of British industry should have effected the change. The change-over to decimal coinage is to be made on 15 Feb. 1971, and the first of the new coins were issued in 1968. *See* N11.

**Mezzotint,** an engraving from copper or steel produced by instruments which burnish and scrape away portions of the surface, and yield an impression effectually graded in light and shade.

**Mica.** The mica of commerce is a nearly transparent mineral, which has great heat-resisting power, and can be split into thin plates. The most important micas are muscovite (potassium mica), the commoner variety, phlogopite (magnesium mica), and biotite, the magnesium and iron mica.

**Michael, St., and George, St.,** an order of knighthood originally founded for the Ionian Isles and Malta in 1818, and reorganised in 1869, so as to admit Crown servants connected with the Colonies. The Earl of Derby, Earl Russell, and Earl Grey were the first of the new knights.

**Michaelmas Day,** the festival day of St. Michael and All Angels, Sept. 29th, one of the English quarter days.

**Microbe,** a term proposed by Sédillot in 1878 to denote any microscopic organism, vegetable or animal, or found on the borderland between the two great natural kingdoms. The term is commonly used, but not by scientists.

**Microelectronics** is a rapidly developing technology of the 1960s which reduces entire electronic circuits to minute size and embeds them in tiny chips of solid material. These are then called integrated circuits. A circuit consisting of, say, a dozen transistors and fifty resistors can be built into a small piece of semiconductor (*q.v.*) measuring not more than a couple of millimetres in any direction. Hundreds of these circuits can be made simultaneously in pennysize wafers of silicon about one-hundredth of an inch thick. There are great advantages in cheapness, reliability, robustness, and speed of electronic performance. The small size is in itself an advantage in space vehicles and medical instruments. Applications to missile control systems, computers, and communications equipment are no doubt only the first fruits of this new achievement of the current technological revolution.

**Micrometer,** an instrument for measuring minute distances; usually attached to the eye-pieces of a microscope or telescope, and consisting of two very fine hairs or wires stretched across the field of view, one fixed, the other movable. It was invented by William Gascoigne in the 17th cent. and improved by later inventors. Sir Joseph Whitworth made one in 1858 to measure the millionth part of an inch.

**Micro-organisms,** the collective term applied to several types of organism, the most important of which are fungi, viruses, bacteria, and protozoa. It is a classification of convenience in biological studies. These organisms are generally simple in their environmental requirements (*e.g.*, have simple nutritional needs) and in cellular organisation. This makes them very suitable for modern biological research. Much of the information on the nature of the genetic code (F31) was obtained from experiments on these organisms.

**Microphone,** device for converting the acoustic energy of sound waves into waves of electrical energy, used in sound amplifying systems. Developed independently by Edison (1877) and Hughes (1878).

**Microscope,** invented about 1590 by Janssen, and improved by Galileo, Fontana, and others, is an instrument which by a lens system magnifies minute objects. Microscopes are simple, compound, and binocular. The more powerful instruments have a magnifying capacity of as much as 10,000 diameters. *See also* Electron Microscope.

**Middle Ages** (*c.* A.D. 400–1500), usually considered to be the period between the decline and fall of the Western Roman Empire and the fall of Constantinople to the Turks (*see* A4–7). The period covers (*a*) an earlier part ending with the 12th cent. (sometimes called the Dark Ages) when science was dead, when theology was the main preoccupation, and when the language of the learned West was Latin; and (*b*) a later age of Arabian influence when alchemy and astrology (at that time indistinguishable from astronomy) were central interests, technology was advancing, and Greek learning was transmitted by Arab scholars. Characteristic features of the mediaeval scene were monasticism (J29), the Crusades (*q.v.*), Gothic art (*q.v.*), feudalism (J17), and the supremacy of Islam in the field of learning. The period came to an end with the ushering in of the Renaissance (J38).

**Midrash,** name given to the homiletical interpretation of some of the Hebrew Scriptures in which allegory and legendary illustration were freely used. Compiled by Jewish rabbis from *c.* A.D. 200.

**Millenary Petition** was presented to James I. in 1603, on behalf of nearly 1,000 Puritan Ministers against certain of the rites and ceremonies of the Church of England. The Hampton Court Conference was the outcome of this petition.

**Millennium,** a period of a thousand years. The term is specifically used of the period of a thousand years during which, according to Rev. xx. 1–5, Christ will reign in person on earth. The Millenarians are a sect that interprets the "Millennium" as beginning with the commencement of the 6001st year from the Creation, which, according to Archbishop Ussher (1581–1650), was in 4004 B.C.

**Millipede.** Arthropods allied to the centipedes, from which they differ in having two pairs of legs to each body segment (except the first three) instead of one pair. Worm-like in shape but with a pair of antennæ on the head, they are vegetarians and can do much harm to garden plants. *See* T29(1).

**Millstone-Grit,** a series of grits and sandstones of deltaic origin underlying the coal measures of the Carboniferous system and attaining in England a thickness in parts of 5,000 ft. It is from this rock that millstones have been made from time immemorial.

**Mimicry,** protective similarity of an animal to another animal or to inanimate objects. Examples of the former are the hover flies, which mimic wasps and bees; of the latter, leaf insects, stick insects, and caterpillars that look like dead twigs.

**Mink.** Semi-aquatic mammals closely related to polecats. There is one American species and one European. The fur, which varies light to dark brown, is soft and thick, and is among the most valuable of commercial furs.

**Minnesingers** were minstrel poets of Germany who, during the 12th and 13th cent., composed and sang verses of heroism and love. They were of knightly rank, the counterpart of the French troubadours. *See* E3(2).

**Minnow,** a small fresh-water fish of the carp family, abounding in all the waters of Europe; it has a mottled back and silvery belly, and forms a popular bait for trout.

**Minstrels** were originally specially appointed instrumentalists and singers—pipers, harpers, and gleemen—engaged by barons and manorial lords to amuse their tenants. Later, minstrels assumed nomadic habits, made their way into the houses of the great, and were generally welcome. By Elizabeth's time, however, they were too numerous, and were classed as "rogues and vagabonds," along with actors.

**Miracle Plays,** popular in England in the 15th cent., were usually religious in character, representing some of the dramatic incidents of the Bible. Staging of plays was one of the many activities of the Guilds of those days. *See* M33.

**Mirage,** an optical illusion often observed in desert regions when the objects on the surface of the earth often seem some distance away appear as if reflected in a surface of water. Mirage is due to the unequal heating of the different parts of the atmosphere, which bends the light rays, and so produces distorted images.

**Mishna,** the first part of the Talmud, setting forth the "Oral Law" of the Jews.

**Missal,** the name of the mass-book of the Roman Church compiled 492–96 by Pope Gelasius I., and revised by Gregory I., 590–604. The present Roman Missal was sanctioned by the Council of Trent 1545–63. In the Anglican Communion the Book of Common Prayer superseded the Missal in 1549.

**Mistle Thrush** receives its name from its partiality to the mistletoe-berry. Larger than the song-thrush, with spotted breast rather than speckled.

**Mistletoe,** a parasitic evergreen with white berries used as a decoration at Christmas-time. The familiar mistletoe of Europe is the *Viscum album*, which grows on the boughs of lime, willow, apple, poplar, maple, ash, hawthorn, but seldom on oak-trees. It was sacred to the Druids, and in Norse mythology it was a mistletoe dart that killed the god Baldur.

**Mistral,** a cold, dry, northerly wind peculiar to the French coast of the Mediterranean.

**Mitosis,** cell division whereby each daughter cell receives the same number of chromosomes as the parent cell. When the gametes (sex cells) are formed a special type of division occurs (meiosis) in which the number of chromosomes is halved. *See* F23(2).

**Mitre,** the twofold pointed head-dress of bishops and certain abbots of the Western Church, and occasionally of other ecclesiastics.

**Moa,** the name for several species of ostrich-like extinct birds related to the New Zealand kiwi. The largest species, *Diornis maximus*, stood 8 ft. 7 in. high. Became extinct about 500 years ago.

**Moabite Stone,** a stone of the 9th cent. B.C. containing the earliest known inscription in Phoenician characters, and discovered in the highlands of Moab in 1868. It is now in the Louvre, Paris. It records the campaign between Moab and Israel, a differing account of which is given in the Old Testament.

**Mode.** *See* Average.

**Moderator,** a material used to slow down neutrons in an atomic pile. Examples of moderators are pure graphite and heavy water. *See* Nuclear Reactors.

**Mohole Project,** a scheme to bore through the earth's crust to take samples of the mantle rocks beneath. Drilling trials, led by an American team of geophysicists, began in 1961 near the island of Guadalupe off the Mexican coast in the Pacific. The project, however, was cancelled in 1966 on account of the escalating cost. Russian geophysicists have already started on a similar experiment, but are boring through land rocks where the digging will have to be much deeper and higher temperatures are likely to be met with. The name " Anti-Cosmos " has been given to the project. The boundary between the earth's crystal and mantle rocks is known as the Mohorovičić Discontinuity, or, more simply, as the Moho. *See* F8(1).

**Molasses,** sugar-cane juice in its uncrystalised form after boiling. The crystallised part is the raw sugar. Used to make rum.

**Mole,** a small burrowing animal with long, sensitive nose, about the size of a small rat, with short legs and forefeet armed with strong claws for digging in the earth. Their subterranean dwellings are of curiously ingenious construction, and they do not often leave them except to make raids on mice, frogs, snails, etc. The earth-worm, however, is the mole's chief item of food. Not to be confused with the vole which has a blunt nose.

**Mole,** or gram molecular weight. *See* F21(2).

**Molecular Biology,** a rapidly expanding branch of science mainly concerned with cell structure and function at a molecular level, in particular with genes and enzymes and the interaction between the two. Recent work in Britain has led to the unravelling of the structure of DNA, the hereditary substance of the genes, and has played a major part in uncovering the molecular mechanism of the transfer of hereditary information and the nature of the genetic code. Crystallisation of the first enzyme (urease) took place in 1929; the gene as a definite chemical entity was discovered in 1943. *See* F26–32.

**Molecule.** A group of atoms held together by chemical forces. *See* F12(2), 20, *also* Macromolecule.

**Molybdenum,** symbol Mo, a fairly hard white metal with properties resembling those of chromium. Its commonest ore is the sulphide, molybdenite. The chief use of the metal is in the manufacture of alloy steels.

**Monasticism.** *See* J29.

**Monazite,** a cerium mineral containing some thorium. Occurs as grains, often as sand (" monazite sands "), derived from granites. Deposits occur in India (Travancore), Russia, Norway, Madagascar, S. Africa, Brazil, U.S.A.

**Monday,** the second day of the week, called by the Anglo-Saxons *Monandaeg* (moon-day).

**Mongoose,** species of mammals related to the civets, feeding on vermin and reptiles. These animals, which have long tails and short legs, occur in Africa and Asia (especially India). The biggest mongoose is the Egyptian ichneumon, and this has been introduced into the W. Indies because of its ability to kill large poisonous snakes.

**Monitor,** a family of lizards most resembling dragons. There are about 30 species widely distributed over the tropical parts of Asia, Australia, and Africa.

**Monroe Doctrine,** a principle of American policy declining any European intervention in political affairs of the American continent, outlined by President Monroe in 1823. At the same time interference was disclaimed with existing European colonies in the Western Hemisphere. The American Civil War hampered the application of the doctrine for some time, but afterwards the United States firmly insisted on it. The Doctrine is not international law, but a national policy of the U.S.A.

**Monsoons,** regular persistent winds which blow at certain seasons in middle latitudes, mainly in South and East Asia. Their occurrence is related to the great changes of pressure which take place between summer and winter over the land mass. In India the south-west monsoon (June–Oct.) is moisture-laden from its long passage over the sea and in the higher regions, especially, there is heavy rainfall. Sudden reversal of the wind results in the cold north-east monsoon (Oct.–March) which is dry on account of the shelter afforded by the mountain ranges to the north. Frequently the term " monsoon " is applied to denote the associated rainfall without reference to the actual winds.

**Monstrance,** an ornamental transparent receptacle in which the Sacred Host is carried in procession or exposed for adoration.

**Month,** the 12th part of the calendar year. A lunar month is the interval of new moon to new moon or full moon to full moon; mean length, 29 days, 12 hours, 44 minutes, 2·87 seconds. A sidereal month represents the time of the moon's revolution from a given star back to the same again, 27 days, 7 hours, 43 minutes, 11·5 seconds. In English law, since 1926, a month, unless otherwise expressed, means a calendar month.

**Monument of London,** a 202 ft. column, overlooking Billingsgate, designed by Wren and erected (1671–77) to mark the starting-point of the Great Fire of London (1666). The original inscription upon it ascribed the fire to " the treachery and malice of the popish faction," which stood down to 1831, when the words were erased as objectionable. The black marble staircase has 345 steps (311 to the balcony).

**Moon,** the earth's satellite, 2,160 miles in diameter and 238,857 miles distant from the earth. It rotates in the same time as it revolves round the earth (27 days 7 hours 43 minutes), so that the same face is always presented to the earth. In 1959 Russia launched her first three moon probes. The second succeeded in hitting the moon and recorded no magnetic field. The third photographed that part of the moon's surface which is never visible from the earth. The U.S. hard-landing *Rangers* in 1964–5 sent back a series of photographs of the surface. From these pictures and from those taken by the Russian *Luna 9* and *13* and the U.S. *Surveyor 1*, which made soft landings in 1966, it is clear that there are craters on the moon's surface. From their shape and distribution it is a reasonable conclusion that the surface is not covered by any great thickness of soft dust. The success of the U.S. *Apollo* missions in Dec. 1968 and March 1969 increased the feasibility of a manned spacecraft landing on the moon in 1969. The exploration of the moon at close range by means of space-craft was made possible only by parallel developments in several branches of technology —rocket propulsion, long-range radio and television transmission, electronic computer control.

**Moorhen,** a widely distributed bird of the rail family, a common resident in the British Isles. The adult is blackish with white under tail-coverts, a white line on the flanks, and a yellow-tipped bill. The frontal shield and the base of the bill are vermilion. It bobs its head, flirts its tail, and dives well. The nest is usually placed close to the water's edge or on an overhanging branch. In feeding the young the parents are sometimes helped by their offspring of a previous brood of the season. In N. America the bird is known as the Florida Gallinule.

**Moors,** the name given to the Moslems who live in N.W. Africa and to those who once lived in Spain. In 711 Moorish Arabs invaded Spain and spread beyond the Pyrenees into France, where they were driven back by the end of the century. Spain, however, remained virtually under Moorish domination until the 11th cent., and during that period was the most civilised and prosperous part of Western Europe. In the arts and sciences the impact of Moorish culture was profound and lasting. Examples of the brilliant splendour of Moorish architecture are still to be seen in Toledo, Córdoba, Seville, and Granada. During the long struggle for the Christian reconquest thousands were killed and expelled, and in 1492 Granada, their last remaining kingdom, was forced to surrender. They were virtually exterminated by the Inquisition, and the last were expelled in 1609.

**Moose**, the largest members of the deer family. The N. American Moose stands 5½–6¾ ft. high, and has huge palmate antlers. There is another New World species, occurring in Alaska. The European species is known as the elk.

**Morse Alphabet**, a system of dots and dashes, intended to be used in combination with the indicator in telegraphy; but usually read by sound, the receiving operator writing down the words in the same as transmitted. This system of signals was invented by the American inventor and artist Samuel Finley Breese Morse (1791–1872) of Charlestown, Massachusetts.

**Mosaic**, art of arranging small pieces of coloured glass, marble, or other materials in such a fashion as to produce a decorative pattern. Some of the best examples of Byzantine mosaics are to be seen at Ravenna, Rome, Venice, and Sicily.

**Mosque**, a Mohammedan church, the greatest being that of Santa Sophia at Istanbul, now converted into a museum of Byzantine art.

**Mosquito**, small two-winged flies with long legs and slender body. Their larvae are aquatic. The females of some species are blood-suckers, and thus come to transmit the blood parasites which cause malaria and yellow fever, for example. See **D.D.T.** and **Gammexane**.

**Mosses.** Most mosses live in moist habitats, but there are some species that can withstand desiccation and are adapted to live on rocks and tree trunks.

**Moths**, of the insect order, *Lepidoptera*, differing from butterflies which have clubbed antennae, in having feathery, sometimes thin, pointed antennae, rarely clubbed. Most are nocturnal, and the pupae are usually brown and enclosed in a cocoon unlike those of the butterfly, which are usually naked. See also **Lepidoptera**.

**Motion, Laws of.** According to Newton: (1) A body continues in its state of rest or uniform motion in a straight line except in so far as it is compelled by external forces to change that state. (2) Rate of change of momentum is proportional to the applied force, and takes place in the direction in which the force acts. (3) To every action there is an equal and opposite reaction. These laws are the basis of almost all engineering and everyday mechanics. Corrections to them have been made by relativity and the quantum theory. See **F15, 16**.

**Mule**, a hybrid between horse and ass. Also the name of the spinning machine invented by Crompton in 1779 which combined the principle of Hargreaves' spinning jenny with the machine invented by Arkwright.

**Mullions**, the vertical bars dividing the lights in a window, forming a highly decorative feature in the Tudor period of English Gothic architecture. The cross-beam or horizontal bar of wood or stone in a mullioned window is styled a transom. See **Windows**.

**Munich Agreement.** In Sept. 1938 Mr. Neville Chamberlain and M. Daladier, British and French Premiers, reached agreement with Hitler at Munich for the dismemberment of Czechoslovakia, primarily for the benefit of Germany. Czechoslovakia itself was not consulted, nor Russia who with Britain and France had jointly pledged themselves to uphold the independence of Czechoslovakia. Hitler had been threatening that country for some time, but every concession had been met by further demands. After three visits to Germany, during which Hitler raised his demands, the British and French statesmen gave way. Mr. Chamberlain declared on return that he had secured " Peace in our Time." The Agreement

was the subject of much controversy. Hitler seized Czechoslovakia in March 1939.

**Muscles.** See **F34(1)**.

**Musk Deer**, a small deer of the Himalayas, standing about 20 in. high. It is grey in colour, slightly brindled, and carries a small pouch in the abdominal region, containing what is commercially known as musk, an article which is of great value in the manufacture of various perfumes. The active constituent of musk, muscone, is now made synthetically. The species was becoming rare on account of its slaughter for its musk.

**Mutton Bird**, an Australasian name of controversial origin for a shearwater or petrel, *e.g.*, the Short-tailed and Sooty Shearwaters and the Great-winged, Kermadec, and White-headed Petrels. The young are taken by hand from their burrows for human food.

**Myrrh**, a resinous substance obtained from a tree of the natural order *Amyridaceae*, growing plentifully in Abyssinia and Arabia. Its use for embalming, medical, and aromatic purposes may be traced back to the most remote times.

**Mysteries, Greek**, secret mystic ceremonies of the ancient Greeks, religious drama accompanied by dancing, the most well known being the Eleusinian and Orphic ceremonies.

**Mystery Plays** were the mediaeval religious dramas performed by the priests at great ecclesiastic festivals, particularly in France and Bavaria, staging the Nativity, Passion, and Resurrection. See **M33**.

# N

**Nadir**, one of the two poles of the horizon, the other being the zenith. The nadir is the pole vertically below the observer's feet.

**Nahum**, one of the books of the Minor Prophets of the Old Testament. It is a prophecy of doom on the approaching sack of Nineveh which fell in 612 B.C. to the Medes and Babylonians.

**Naiad**, a water-nymph of classic mythology, beautiful and mystic; celebrated by Virgil, Ovid, Homer, and other ancient writers.

**Nantes, Edict of**, was a decree promulgated by Henry IV. of France in 1598, giving full freedom of worship to the Protestants of the country. It was the revocation of this edict in 1685 by Louis XIV. that drove hundreds of thousands of French Huguenots to this country.

**Naphtha**, a liquid combustible believed to have been one of the ingredients of " Greek fire." Naphtha is a light, highly inflammable oil obtained by distilling petroleum, shale oil, or coal tar. The petroleum naphtha consists of a mixture of paraffins; that from shale contains olefines as well as paraffins. Coal-tar naphtha contains xylol.

**Naphthalene** is an aromatic hydrocarbon; it is obtained from coal tar, and its derivatives are much used in the manufacture of colours for dyers and printers. " Moth balls " are made of naphthalene.

**Narcotic**, a medical dictionary definition is that a narcotic is a drug that produces stupor, complete insensibility, or sleep. In terms of drug addiction, a narcotic has been defined as altering and distorting the user's perception of himself and of the external world, being taken primarily for that purpose. See **P22–24**.

**Nardus**, a genus of coarse grasses, growing on bleak upland heaths and hill slopes. *Nardus stricta*, known as " mat-weed," is a British species.

**Narghile**, an oriental tobacco pipe so constructed that the smoke passes through water and up a long flexible tube before reaching the lips of the smoker.

**Narrative Art**, a type of art popular during the late 19th cent. based on the principle: " every picture tells a story "—*e.g.*, such paintings as the little Royalist boy surrounded by his anxious family and confronted across a table by the Roundheads bearing the title: " When did you last see your father? " The term, although often applied derisively, suitably describes many works of considerable artistic merit: *e.g.*, Hogarth's *Marriage à la Mode*, his series of eight engravings entitled *A Rake's Progress*, the Bayeux Tapestry, and many Babylonian and Egyptian friezes.

**Naseby, Battle of**, was fought on June 14, 1645,

between the Royalists under the command of Prince Rupert and the King, and the Parliamentarians under Fairfax and Cromwell. It resulted in a complete defeat for Charles.

**National Anthem,** a musical composition with words, officially adopted for ceremonial use as an expression of patriotism and loyalty to a national cause. The national anthem of the United Kingdom is "God Save the Queen" which has been in use since about the middle of the 18th cent. There is some doubt about its origin. It has been variously attributed to Dr. John Bull, Henry Carey, and James Oswald.

**National Assembly,** the name taken by the body responsible for the opening stages of the French Revolution and subsequently by other sovereign bodies in France and elsewhere.

**National Covenant,** an oath and declaration subscribed to by the Scottish Presbyterians in 1638 to maintain their religion against Charles I.'s episcopalianising designs.

**National Gallery,** established in 1824 at Pall Mall, London, with the Angerstein Collection of 38 pictures, purchased for £60,000 as a nucleus. The existing building which was opened in 1838 has been enlarged several times. The National Gallery at Millbank, the Tate Gallery, was given to the nation by Sir Henry Tate in 1897.

**Nationalisation** is the taking over by the State of the ownership and operation of an industry or service—*e.g.*, coal-mining, railway transport, gas, and electricity. Where this is done without revolution, compensation is usually paid to the previous owners at what is regarded as a fair market price; the compensation is sometimes paid in cash, but more often in fixed-interest-bearing bonds issued either by the State or by the administration of the nationalised service, which is usually a publicly appointed Board or Corporation acting, with greater or lesser autonomy, under the direction of a Minister responsible to Parliament. In some cases the State becomes a partner with private investors in the ownership of a particular enterprise, *e.g.*, oil companies, such as the former Anglo-Iranian and some recent French examples. Nationalisation is usually brought about by a separate Act of Parliament relating to each industry or service taken over. These Acts, in Great Britain, include provision for joint consultation at all levels between the administering boards or commissions and the workers employed and their Trade Unions. When, as in the Soviet Union, nationalisation occurs as an outcome of social revolution no compensation is paid to the dispossessed owners.

**National Parks.** Under the National Parks Act 1949 a National Parks Commission was set up to create National Parks in England and Wales. Ten have been established: Peak District, Lake District, Snowdonia, Yorkshire Dales, Exmoor, Brecon Beacons, Dartmoor, Pembrokeshire Coast, North Yorks Moors, and Northumberland. They cover an area of some 5,260 square miles, or 9 per cent of the total area of England and Wales. It is not intended to change the character of these territories but to control their development so as to harmonise with the two dominant principles: (*a*) that the characteristic beauty of the landscape within the Park area shall be preserved and (*b*) that the visiting public shall have ample access and facilities for recreation and enjoyment. The National Parks Commission also has power to designate areas in England and Wales outside the national parks as "areas of outstanding natural beauty." Twenty-four areas had been designated by 1968: Gower, Quantock Hills, Lleyn, Surrey Hills, Dorset, Northumberland Coast, Cannock Chase, Shropshire Hills, Malvern Hills, Cornwall, N. Devon, S. Devon, E. Devon, E. Hampshire, Isle of Wight, Forest of Bowland, Chichester Harbour, and Solway Coast, Chilterns, Sussex Downs, Cotswolds, Anglesey, South Hampshire Coast, and Norfolk Coast. Under the Countryside Act, 1968, the National Parks Commission has been reconstituted as the Countryside Commission. *See also* Long Distance Routes.

**National Physical Laboratory,** situated at Teddington, is one of the world's largest and best-equipped laboratories. It was first established in 1900 under the control of the Royal Society.

In 1918 DSIR took over financial liability and in 1964 it became part of the Ministry of Technology. It conducts research in its three main groups: Measurement, Materials, and Engineering Sciences, and maintains British primary standards and physical units.

**National Portrait Gallery,** established in 1856 and now located in a building in St. Martin's Lane adjoining the National Gallery. Contains portraits of eminent people in history, literature, art, etc., and a valuable collection of medals and autographs.

**National Trust,** founded in 1895. "A non-profit-making organisation incorporated by Act of Parliament for the purposes of promoting the permanent preservation of lands and buildings of historic interest or natural beauty for the benefit and access of the people." As a consequence of gifts of public-spirited individuals the Trust now owns many acres of magnificent scenery and property, including mediaeval castles, bird sanctuaries, ancient monuments, birthplaces and homes of famous men, and classic examples of domestic architecture, preserved for the enjoyment of present and future generations. Since 1946 lands and houses of interest to the nation may be given to the National Trust in lieu of death duties.

**Nativity.** There are three nativity festivals of the Christian Church: Christmas, 25 December, the festival of the birth of Christ; the birthday of the Virgin Mary (8 Sept.); and of St. John the Baptist (24 June).

**Natterjack,** a curious warty, prominent-eyed, brown toad (*Bufo calamita*), having a bright yellow line down the middle of its back. It utters a muttering sort of croak, hence its name.

**Natural Law.** *See* J32.

**Naturalisation,** the grant of British nationality to an alien. Before an application can be made to the Secretary of State for the grant of a certificate an alien must have qualified by 5 years' residence in the U.K. or service under the Crown, during the 8 years immediately passed.

**"Nautical Almanac,"** published under the authority of the Admiralty, is always issued four years in advance, and contains information specially prepared for the use of navigators and astronomers. It first appeared in 1767.

**Nautilus,** a term now applied only to the pearly-shelled nautilus, the sole surviving example of the four-gilled section of the *Cephalopoda*. Its fossil relatives are called Ammonites. The spiral shell is divided into a number of compartments, the animal living in the last and largest chamber. There are three or four species, all living in tropical seas. The Paper Nautilus is not related to the Pearly Nautilus, belonging to the same order as the octopus.

**Nave** is the body or main open portion of a cathedral or church, and extends from the chief entrance to the choir, or chancel, and is usually flanked by aisles. A nave, in mechanics, indicates the "hub" or central part of a wheel.

**Neandertal,** the name of the valley lying between Düsseldorf and Wuppertal, where in a limestone cave a now famous skull of a very early species of prehistoric man was discovered in 1856. Fossils of Neandertal man have been found over a wide area, and from archaeological evidence he began to disappear from Europe during the last Ice Age, about 40,000 B.C. *See* F45(2).

**Necromancy,** "the black art," was in olden times much believed in, and supposed to be an occult power by which its practitioners could converse with the spirits of the dead and learn the future.

**Negroes** are the dark-skinned, woolly-headed races, natives of tropical Africa, or descendants of such natives. There are many different racial types, including the Ashanti of Ghana, the Kikuyu of Kenya, the Yoruba of Nigeria, the Pygmies (nomadic hunters living in the equatorial forests), the Bushmen of the Kalahari Desert, the Hottentots of South Africa (who have largely lost their identity), the so-called Bantu peoples of Central and Southern Africa, and many others. Their culture is rich in folklore, and they have great artistic gifts in music, dancing and sculpture. About 25 million people of Negro descent are in N. and S. America, the European slave trade having taken them there from W. Africa. *See also* African Languages, M35.

**Negus,** the name given to any mixture of wine and water, and said to have been named after Colonel Francis Negus about 1714. The sovereign of Abyssinia is styled the Negus.

**Nekton,** term used to differentiate actively swimming aquatic organisms (*e.g.*, fishes) from the "drifters" or plankton.

**Nelson Column,** in Trafalgar Square, London, designed by Mr. William Railton, was chosen from among a number of designs—temples, obelisks and various sculptural groups—sent in as a result of a competition held in 1839. The erection of the column was begun in 1840. Twenty-six years later the lions designed by Landseer were set up at the foot of the completed column. The statue of Nelson himself was made by E. H. Bailey and the bronze reliefs at the base executed by Carew, Woodington, Ternouth, and Watson, representing the Battles of the Nile, St. Vincent, Copenhagen, and Trafalgar. Height 170 ft., executed in Portland stone instead of granite, as originally planned, at a cost of £46,000.

**Néné or Hawaiian Goose.** At the Severn Wildfowl Trust at Slimbridge Mr. Peter Scott has saved this bird from extinction.

**Neo-Classical School of Art,** a French school of painting and sculpture belonging to the late 18th and early 19th cent. and founded by Jacques David, the Academician, republican, and later admirer of Bonaparte. His classicism probably arose from his republican sympathies, which caused him to paint such works as the *Oath of the Horatii* (Louvre) drawing analogies between revolutionary France and Rome. Because of these views he revolted against the romantic and sensual art of Watteau and Greuze and equally against the realism of Chardin. Among his many famous pupils was Ingres, who later assumed leadership of the school.

**Neodymium,** an element belonging to the rare earth metal group. Discovered by Welsbach in 1885.

**Neo-Impressionism,** a development of Impressionism (*q.v.*) by Seurat and Signac during the 1880s who devised the method of painting known as *pointillism* (the application of pure colours in minute touches to form a composite whole, based on a knowledge of the laws of colour and optics). One of the best-known examples of this technique is Seurat's *Sunday Afternoon on the Grand Jatte*.

**Neon,** inert gas present in air to the extent of about 1 part in 65,000. The crimson glow produced when an electric discharge passes through the gas is familiar in advertising signs.

**Neoprene,** generic name for a class of synthetic rubbers made from acetylene.

**Nepotism,** the bestowal of patronage by reason of relationship rather than of merit. It had its origin in the custom of certain Popes to enrich their families out of the offices of the Church.

**Neptune.** Apart from Pluto this is the most distant of the planets, estimated to be about 2,793 million miles from the sun, and taking about 165 years to revolve around it. Discovered by the German astronomer Galle on Sept. 23, 1846, after its existence had been predicted by Leverrier and Adams.

**Neptunium,** element 93, one of the four new elements discovered during the progress of the atomic bomb project in the second world war. Neptunium is formed when a neutron enters a nucleus of Uranium 238, and it decays radioactively to yield plutonium.

**Neutrino,** a neutral particle which carries energy and spin and although possessing little or no mass plays an important part in the interaction of other fundamental particles. The discovery that there are in fact two distinct neutrinos, each with its counterpart, was discovered in 1962 as a result of an experiment made with the 30,000 million-electronvolt proton accelerator at Brookhaven. *See* **F14.**

**Neutron,** a neutral particle present in all atomic nuclei except the hydrogen nucleus which is a single proton. In the development of nuclear science and technology the neutron has played a most important role and neutrons produce the radioisotopes now widely used in medicine, agriculture, and industry. Neutrons and protons are termed nucleons. *See* **F10, 14.**

**New Deal.** The measures taken by President Roosevelt in U.S.A. in 1933 to overcome the great economic crisis which broke out at the end of 1929 and to restore the social security threatened by it. The measures were drawn up by a group of experts called a Brains Trust and they provided for recovery by a programme of public works, including large-scale construction of houses and large-scale assistance to farmers. Loans were granted and authorities formed to stimulate activities which reduced the workless from 17 millions to between 7 and 10 millions. Unemployment relief was regulated and enlarged; and social insurance (which for decades had been a subject of dispute, being held to be contrary to American principles of self-help) was introduced. Many of the changes have become a permanent part of American legislation though some laws were repealed by the U.S. Supreme Court as being unconstitutional.

**Newgate Prison,** now pulled down and replaced by the Central Criminal Court, opened in 1907, was situated near the point where once stood one of the old London city gates. There is a record of a prison upon this spot in the 13th cent. Later a new one was built by the executors of Richard Whittington, but this was destroyed by the Great Fire in 1666. Still another new prison on this site was erected between 1778 and 1780. In the Gordon Riots of the latter year it was destroyed by fire and re-erected. It was not used as a prison after 1880.

**News Letters** were an early form of newspaper, popular in the time of Charles II. They consisted of items of news and gossip collected at the various coffee-houses and other places of public resort. They often included blank pages on which readers wrote their private letters.

**Newspapers.** The first news-books to be published at regular intervals in Britain appeared in 1662 with news of what was going on abroad translated from German and Italian news-sheets. Licence to print was obtained from the Star Chamber, which until its abolition in 1641 allowed only the printing of foreign news. With the lifting of the ban on domestic news the Press became free. In the reign of Queen Anne English newspapers employed writers of great intellectual power and versatility. Despite the newspaper tax introduced in 1712, the number of newspapers published in London in 1776 had increased to 53, though the standard of writing was below that of earlier times. The development of the Press was greatly assisted in the 19th cent. by the abolition of the "taxes on knowledge," by the introduction of the cheap postal system, and by improvements in printing, distribution, collection of news, and advertising. The *London Gazette*, founded in 1665 (and still appearing twice weekly as the official organ of the Government), is the oldest newspaper living. *The Times*, known throughout the world, began as the *Daily Universal Register* in 1785, and adopted its present title in 1788. The *Manchester Guardian* (renamed *Guardian* in 1959), once a provincial but now a national newspaper with a world-wide reputation, began as a weekly in 1821, and became a daily in 1855. The *Scotsman*, founded as a weekly in 1817 and established as a daily in 1855, and the *Glasgow Herald*, which began as the *Glasgow Advertiser* in 1783, are the leading Scottish newspapers. The London Press, which is national, publishes 11 daily, 2 evening, and 7 Sunday Newspapers.

**Newt,** amphibians of lizard shape and mottled markings. There are three British species, the largest being the Great-Crested Newt (*Trilurus cristatus*), which attains a length of 6 in.

**Newton,** the unit of force in the metre–kilogram–second (MKS) system. Under its influence a body with a mass of 1 kilogram will accelerate at a rate of 1 metre per second each second.

**Newton's Rings.** Concentric circular rings, due to the phenomenon of interference, which are seen around the point of contact of a slightly convex lens with a flat plate of glass.

**New Towns.** The new towns in Britain established under New Town Acts, 1946, 1959, and 1965, with dates of designation are: Basildon (1949), Bracknell (1949), Corby (1950), Crawley (1947), Cwmbran (1949), East Kilbride (1947), Glenrothes (1948), Harlow (1947), Hatfield (1948), Hemel Hempstead (1947), Newton

Aycliffe (1947), Peterlee (1948), Stevenage (1946), Welwyn Garden City (1948); Cumbernauld (1956), Dawley (1963), Irvine (1966), Livingston (1962), Milton Keynes (1967), Newtown (mid-Wales) (1967), Peterborough (1967), Redditch (1964), Runcorn (1964), Skelmersdale (1961), Washington (1964); designated under Town Development Act 1952 Killingworth (1959) and Cramlington (1963); designated under New Towns Act of N. Ireland 1965 Craigavon (1965), and Antrim/Ballymena (1967). In addition a new regional city is to be built in the Preston–Leyland–Chorley area of Lancashire and the new town of Dawley with neighbouring Wellington and Oakengates will form the new town of Telford. It is also proposed to expand Ipswich, Northampton, and Warrington and to build cities along the Tay, Solway, and Humber estuaries.

**New Year's Day,** Jan 1. The first New Year's festival of which we have record is that constituted by Numa 713 B.C., and dedicated to Janus.

**Nibelungenlied,** the German epic of the early 13th cent. comprising numerous mythical poems or sagas of which several English translations exist. Wagner's *The Ring of the Nibelungs* was based largely on Norse legends and on the Nibelungenlied.

**Nicene Creed,** a summary of the principles of Christian faith, first issued in 325 by the Council of Nicaea (summoned by the emperor Constantine the Great) for the purpose of thwarting the Arian heresy and asserting the godhead of Christ. Date of Easter fixed at Council of Nicaea.

**Nickel,** silver-coloured metal, symbol Ni, fairly soft though harder than iron. Chief source of the metal is the nickel sulphide in iron–copper pyrites deposits in Ontario. Chief uses are: in electroplating, in coins, as an element in alloy steels. A novel method of making pure nickel (by treating the metal with carbon monoxide and heating the resulting liquid, nickel carbonyl) was developed in 1890 by Mond. This discovery led to many technical advances in industrial chemistry, one of which is the production of catalysts for a variety of processes.

**Niello Work** was in considerable vogue in the Middle Ages, and is said to have suggested the idea of engraving upon copper. It was produced by rubbing a mixture of silver, lead, copper, sulphur, and borax into engravings on silver, and some highly decorative results were obtained.

**Night Heron,** a stocky, short-legged heron of black and white plumage, red eyes, and yellowish legs, crepuscular except in breeding season, and an occasional visitor to Britain.

**Nightingale,** a familiar singing bird which visits the southern counties of England every summer, and is sometimes found as far north as Yorkshire. It is a shy, brown bird, not often seen, but the song of the male, usually heard in the late evening or at early morn, is of remarkable sweetness and variety. After its wooing period is over its song ceases.

**Nightjar,** nocturnal, insectivorous bird, owl-like in appearance, with mottled brown plumage of "dead leaf" pattern, and a churring song. It is a common breeding visitor to the British Isles, Apr. to Sept., and lays its eggs on bare ground.

**Niobium** is a metal element, symbol Nb, related to vanadium. Technical development has been slow because of its rare occurrence, although niobium is now used in ferrous alloys to increase resistance to corrosion and produce steel which can be used at high temperatures.

**Nitre** *or* **Saltpetre,** is now mostly manufactured by the double decomposition of sodium nitrate and potassium chloride. Its chief use is the manufacture of gunpowder and fireworks. It has been manufactured in England since 1625.

**Nitrogen,** a non-combustible gaseous element, symbol N, devoid of taste or smell, and constituting nearly four-fifths of the atmospheric air. Nitrogen compounds are essential to plants and animals, and are used in fertilisers.

**Nitro-Glycerine,** an explosive yellow fluid produced by mixing small quantities of glycerine with a combination of one part of nitric acid and two parts of sulphuric acid. By itself it is a dangerously explosive substance to handle. In 1867, Nobel produced dynamite, a safe

explosive made by absorbing nitro-glycerine in kieselguhr.

**Nitrous Oxide,** a compound of nitrogen and oxygen possessing mild anaesthetic power. Termed "laughing gas" on account of its exhilarating effect. It is still used in dentistry, and for minor operations and has proved useful in a new technique for finding leaks in water mains.

**Nobel Prizes.** The Nobel Foundation was established at the beginning of the century to give effect to the wishes expressed by Alfred Nobel in his Will. By the terms of the Will the judges are the Swedish Academy of Science, the Caroline Medico-Surgical Institute, the Swedish Academy, and five members of the Norwegian Storting. The award of a Nobel Prize is accepted as the highest form of international recognition in the field in which it is given; physics, chemistry, medicine, literature, peace, and, since 1969, economics. *See* L126–8.

**Nones** were dates of the Roman calendar which fell on the 5th of each month, excepting Mar., May, July, and Oct., when they fell on the 7th.

**Non Nobis Domine!** ("Not unto us, O Lord!"), a musical canon, sung as a grace at public feasts (traditionally attributed to Byrd).

**Norman Architecture** is English Romanesque (*q.v.*), which flourished from the time of the Norman Conquest and was gradually superseded through a transition period (c. 1175–1200) by the introduction of the pointed arch characteristic of the Early English (first Gothic style). Typical of Norman churches are the round arches, thick walls, massive cylindrical columns, with throughout the basic pattern of the square and the circle. Some churches (*e.g.*, the Temple church in London or the chapel at Ludlow Castle) are wholly circular. Roofs in the early days were flat and towers, usually placed at the "crossing," were square but occasionally round; the spires of all these towers have perished, but it seems likely that they were squat and pyramidal.

**North-East Passage,** from the North Atlantic to Bering Strait has been rapidly developed by the U.S.S.R. in recent years as a northern sea route to render accessible vast areas of northern Siberia. Attempts to find a north-east passage were made by Englishmen and Dutchmen in the 16th cent. but they were always defeated by the ice, for the sea is completely frozen for some 3,000 miles for 9 months of the year. A Swede succeeded in sailing from Europe to Japan via the Arctic in the late 19th cent. *See also* Arctic Exploration.

**North-West Passage,** from the Atlantic to the Pacific through the Arctic Seas, has been the dream of navigators for centuries. Attempts to find it were made in the 16th and early 17th cent. by John and Sebastian Cabot, Frobisher, Gilbert, Davis, Hudson, and Baffin. Two centuries later Ross, Parry, Franklin, and others made the attempt; but it was not until 1903–5 that Amundsen, discoverer of the South Pole, made the complete voyage. The American nuclear-powered submarine, *Nautilus*, opened up a new short sea route between the Atlantic and the Pacific when she made her epic voyage under the North Pole in Aug. 1958.

**Notre Dame,** the famous Paris cathedral, was founded in 1163, and is one of the finest specimens of Gothic architecture in Europe. The best descriptions of the buildings are to be found in Victor Hugo's "Hunchback of Notre Dame."

**November,** the 9th month of the year originally, but from c. 700 B.C., when Numa added Jan., and Feb., it became the 11th month.

**Nuclear Energy.** Atomic nuclei consist of protons and neutrons joined in various proportions (F10). The heaviest naturally occurring nucleus contains 238 particles (92 protons, 146 neutrons) and is uranium 238 ($U^{238}$); the lightest is hydrogen, which consists of 1 proton. Neutrons and protons attract one another by very strong forces which are not at all well understood; they are called *nuclear forces*. Consequently it requires energy to be supplied if a nucleus is to be pulled apart into its constituent particles. The energy is required to overcome the attractions of the nuclear forces. Conversely, when the particles rush together to form a nucleus, energy is released in the form of heat or radiation. The energy released when protons and neutrons coalesce to form a nucleus is called *Binding Energy*. The binding energy of a nucleus divided by the number of particles involved is called the binding energy per particle, which we will call B. It is very difficult to overestimate the importance of B to the human race. B varies from nucleus to nucleus, and the exact form of its variation is only roughly understood at the present time. But the most significant thing is that B is greatest for elements of medium atomic weight and lowest at the heavy (uranium) and light (hydrogen) ends of the periodic table. This means that if middleweight nuclei can be formed either from heavy ones or from light ones, B increases and *energy is released in either case.*

**Nuclear Fission.** *See* F12(1).

**Nuclear Fusion.** If light nuclei are hurled at high speeds into intimate contact they sometimes coalesce and release binding energy (*see* Nuclear Energy). This has been studied in laboratories where powerful and energy-consuming machines accelerate small numbers of particles for purely experimental purposes. If useful amounts of energy are to be gained these fusion reactions will have to occur on a bigger scale in an apparatus from which the resulting heat can be extracted in a controlled way. The one " useful " fusion device so far made is the thermonuclear bomb (" H-bomb "). Thermonuclear is the important word. If a suitable gas can be raised to a very high temperature the nuclei are stripped of their electrons and all particles move with very high speeds. The gas is then called a plasma. High enough temperatures will make speeds great enough for fusion reactions to occur and nuclear energy to be released. This is a thermonuclear reaction. For example, in deuterium gas, at temperatures over a million degrees Centrigrade, the deuterium nuclei (*i.e.*, heavy hydrogen nuclei consisting of 1 proton joined to 1 neutron) interact to produce helium nuclei. To obtain a net gain in energy from this process, the temperature must be raised to about 300 million degrees C and maintained long enough; otherwise the energy released is less than that required to heat the fuel and to make up for heat losses. Many attempts to study the staggering technical problems are being made, and fusion research is very active in Britain, the U.S.A. and Russia.

**Nuclear Power Stations.** Britain generates about 11 per cent of her electricity in nuclear power stations and the proportion is expected to rise to about 13 per cent in 1970. Britain has so far produced as much electricity by nuclear power as the rest of the world put together. The Atomic Energy Authority has five main stations at Calder Hall, Cumberland, Chapelcross, Dumfriesshire, the AGR station at Windscale, Cumberland, the experimental fast breeder station at Dounreay, Caithness, and the Steam Generating Heavy Water Moderated Reactor (SGHWR) at Winfrith, Dorset. The nine nuclear power stations operated by the electricity authorities are at Berkeley (1962), Bradwell (1962), Hinkley Point (1964), Hunterston (1964), Trawsfynydd (1964), Dungeness " A " (1965), Sizewell (1965), Oldbury (1967), and Wylfa, in Anglesey (1968–69). They have all been developed from the classic Calder Hall type, burning natural uranium inserted in a graphite moderator and cooled by carbon dioxide gas. They are called Magnox stations because the fuel elements of natural uranium rods are encased in magnesium alloy cans. The second nuclear power programme for 1970–75, is based on the advanced gas-cooled reactor system. The third programme planned for the end of the 1970s is to be based on the fast breeder reactor.

**Nuclear Reactors** are pieces of apparatus designed to permit nuclear chain reactions to occur under controlled conditions. (Uncontrolled chain reactions are dangerous, *e.g.*, atomic bombs.) The success of a reactor depends on the neutrons reaching the $U^{235}$ nuclei to produce more fissions and not being wasted in irrelevant processes or simply escaping through the wall of the apparatus (neutrons are quite difficult to contain). The neutrons leaving the scene of fission are rapidly moving, and they stand more chance of causing another fission if they are slowed down.

Consequently a material other than the uranium has to be present to facilitate this, and it is called a moderator. A useful moderator is pure graphite. Thus a reactor may consist of alternate blocks of uranium and graphite. If the reactor is too small so many neutrons escape that there are not enough to keep the chain reaction going. The reactor must therefore be greater than a certain *critical size*. In order to intensify or damp down the chain reaction, it is arranged for pieces of neutron-absorbing material, such as cadmium, to be inserted or withdrawn as required. While the chain reaction is proceeding countless numbers of fissions are occurring, each one liberating energy which turns into heat. The temperature therefore increases, and to prevent a catastrophic rise, cooling has to be provided. The reactor therefore has cooling pipes through which a fluid coolant is pumped. The coolant carries the heat away and, in a reactor designed to produce electrical power, the heat is taken to steam-raising boilers and the high-pressure steam is led to turbines which drive the electric generators. What has been briefly described is the type of reactor first used for serious power production at Calder Hall. This is a graphite-moderated, gas-cooled reactor using as fuel natural uranium (*i.e.*, fissile $U^{235}$ greatly diluted with $U^{238}$). It is also possible to make reactors work without slowing the neutrons with a moderator; these are called *fast reactors*. The design of the prototype fast reactor (PFR) now being built at Dounreay in N. Scotland is based on experience gained with the Dounreay experimental fast breeder reactor which was the first in the world to produce electricity on a commercial scale (1962) and has achieved the highest power output of any of its type in the world. These fast reactors can produce new nuclear fuel in the course of their operation and therefore offer great economies. The British-designed advanced gas-cooled reactor (AGR) successfully developed at Windscale and chosen for the new Dungeness " B " and Hinkley " B " nuclear power stations, promises to produce electricity more cheaply than conventional sources. The alternative method to nuclear fission is nuclear fusion (*q.v.*). The problem of achieving a controlled thermonuclear reactor is one of the outstanding challenging problems of applied physics and although considerable understanding of the phenomena involved has been gained, the solution is still as distant as ever. *See also* Breeder Reactor.

**Nucleic Acids.** Living matter is built up of cells, each of which has a nucleus surrounded by cytoplasm. Cell nuclei are composed chiefly of substances called nucleoproteins, which consist of a protein attached to a nucleic acid (this original name is still used, although nucleic acids are found in the cytoplasm as well as the nucleus). Nucleic acids are complex organic structures made up of chains of compounds called nucleotides (F22(1)). Nucleotide molecules have a sugar group attached to a nitrogenous base and a phosphate group. Only two sugar groups are found in the nucleotides, ribose, giving rise to ribonucleic acids (R.N.A.s, found mainly in the cytoplasm) and deoxyribose, which forms deoxyribonucleic acids (D.N.A.s, found mainly in cell nuclei). Seven different nitrogenous bases have been isolated, so that a number of different nucleotides are possible. A repeating, regular pattern of nucleotides is linked by the phosphate groups, forming nucleic acids. The functions of nucleic acids are of fundamental importance. They are concerned in the process of transmission of inherited qualities in reproduction and in building up body proteins. Lord Todd of Cambridge University was awarded the 1957 Nobel Prize in Chemistry for his work on the structures of nucleic acids; the 1962 Nobel Prize in Medicine (*see* L128) was awarded for the discovery of the molecular structure of D.N.A. *See* F28(2), 29.

**Nuremberg Trial.** On Nov. 21, 1945, an International Military Tribunal, consisting of one American, one British, one Russian, and one French member, began the trial of twenty-four Nazi leaders. There were four counts: the conspiracy of Nazism; wars of aggression;

war crimes; and crimes against humanity. Twelve were condemned to hanging of whom ten were hanged on Oct. 16, 1946. Goering committed suicide; Bormann has never been found; Papen, Schacht, and Fritsche were acquitted. The rest received varying terms of imprisonment.

**Nuthatch,** name of a number of tree-creeping birds, plump, with short tail, bluish-grey plumage, and black stripe under eye. Nest in holes and wedge nuts in bark of trees, hammering them to get a kernel. There are three European species, one, *Sitta europaea*, resident in England.

**Nylon,** a generic term for any long-chain synthetic polymeric amide which has recurring amide groups as an integral part of the main polymer chain, and which is capable of being formed into a filament in which the structural elements are orientated in the direction of the axis. The first nylon of commerical interest was made in 1935, and the world's first nylon factory—in the United States—began production in 1940.

# O

**Oak,** a tree of the genus *Quercus*, including some 300 species distributed over the northern hemisphere and into the tropics. Two species are native to Britain, where the oak is the commonest tree (1 in 3)—*Q. petraea*, more common in the west and north on shallower, lighter soils, and *Q. robur*, more common in the south on deeper, heavier soils. Oak timber is much prized for its strength and durability, and from the time of the Spanish Armada to Nelson's day was in great demand for naval construction. It has always been used for building, flooring, furniture, and cabinet work. The oak is attacked by many insects, the round nut-like oak galls, or oak-apples, being produced by the sting of certain minute gall wasps.

**"Oaks,"** a famous race for three-year-old fillies run at Epsom two days after the " Derby."

**Obelisk,** a tapering monolithic column, square at the base and pyramidal at the top, regarded by the ancient Egyptians as a sacred stone and usually found at the entrance to the sun temples. Many were transported from Egypt and set up at various times: there is one in the Place de la Concorde in Paris, and one on the Thames Embankment in London—Cleopatra's Needle—originally erected at Heliopolis, centre of the sun-cult, by Tuthmosis III c. 1500 B.C.

**Observatories** existed in ancient Babylon and Egypt. They were erected on tombs and temples. The most famous observatory of Egypt was that of Alexandria, erected by Ptolemy Soter, 300 B.C. It was not until the 16th cent., however, that an observatory adequately equipped for astronomical investigations was built. This was at Cassel. Tycho Brahe's observatory at Uranienburg was erected in 1576. The Royal Observatory at Greenwich was completed in 1675. Mount Wilson Observatory in California has had a 100-in. reflector telescope working since 1917 but Mount Palomar Observatory, also in California, has a 200-in. reflector—the largest in the world, completed in 1949—which can reveal remote galaxies out to a limiting distance of 2,000 million light years. It is known as the *Hale* telescope in memory of Dr. George Ellery Hale, the founder of the Mount Wilson Observatory. The 98-in. telescope, the *Isaac Newton*, for the Royal Greenwich Observatory at Herstmonceux Castle was completed in 1967. A number of observatories are devoted to meteorological and geophysical work, the most important in the British Isles being those at Eskdalemuir (Dumfries), Kew, Lerwick, and Valencia (Eire). *See also* Astronomy *and* Telescopes.

**Obsidian,** a form of volcanic rock of vitreous structure, and usually a silicate of aluminium, lime, magnesium, etc. Produced when acid lavas are rapidly congealed, it is usually black and fractures like pitch.

**Occam's Razor.** *See* J32.

**Occultation,** in astronomy, refers to the concealment of a celestial body by the passing before it of some other heavenly body. The most frequent occultation is the eclipse of a star or planet by the moon.

**Ocean** comprises the great body of water which covers five-eighths of the surface of the earth, and has an average depth of 2 miles. The principal oceans are the Pacific, Atlantic, Indian, and Arctic. *See* F3.

**Ocean Currents** are well-defined streams running over certain portions of the ocean and caused mainly by wind-friction, slope of the sea surface and differences in density of the water, all movements being influenced by the deflective forces due to the earth's rotation. The climatic importance of the great ocean currents is that they constitute one of the means whereby heat is transferred from lower to higher latitudes.

**Ocelot,** the most common wild cat of S. America. It is about 4 ft. in length, including tail, and of a grey or tawny colour and spotted. Closely related to the Leopard cats.

**Octane Number,** the index of the knock-rating of petrol. It is based on the arbitrary scale in which iso-octane (which does not cause " knocking ") has a value of 100, and normal heptane (which is prone to " knocking ") has a value of 0. A good fuel for modern cars must have an octane number greater than 80.

**Octarch,** the kings of the English heptarchy, Hengist (455) being the first, and Egbert (800) the last.

**October,** the 10th month, but the 8th in the old Roman calendar. It was held sacred to Mars.

**Octopus,** a genus of marine molluscs with eight tentacles that bear suckers.

**Odyssey,** Homer's epic setting forth the incidents of the wanderings of Odysseus on his way back to Ithaca after the Siege of Troy. *See* H23.

**Oeil-de-boeuf,** meaning bull's eye, is the name of a small octagonal vestibule lighted by a small round window in the palace of Versailles. The term is used in architecture for a small round or oval window in friezes, roofs, or domes of buildings.

**Oersted,** a unit of magnetic-field intensity in the c.g.s. system.

**Ohm's Law,** propounded by G. S. Ohm in 1827, is expressed in the equation: electromotive force (in volts) = current (in amperes) × resistance (in ohms). The ohm is the unit of electrical resistance in the metre-kilogram-second system.

**Oil.** The great expansion in energy demand over recent years has been met to a large extent by petroleum oil. This contains a wide range of hydrocarbon molecules of varying complexity. The various components are separated from each other by making use of their different boiling points. Crude oil is heated in the base of a fractionating tower; the various components condense at different temperatures in trays at different levels of the tower. The fraction of a given composition can be increased by " cracking " or breaking down the heavier hydrocarbons into lighter ones. The total world reserves of petroleum oil are still uncertain since large parts of the world are still not fully prospected. However, such information as exists suggests that total reserves from all sources may be between $5 \times 10^{11}$ and $10^{12}$ tons of oil.

**Okapi,** nocturnal ruminant mammal, smaller than the giraffe, chestnut brown in colour with zebra-striped legs, native to the African Congo.

**Olbers' Comet** was discovered in 1815 by Olbers the German astronomer. Olbers also discovered the asteroids Pallas and Vesta (1802–07).

**Old Red Sandstone,** the continental rocks formed during the Devonian. *See* F41.

**Olefines,** a series of hydrocarbons, in which the hydrogen atoms are double the number of carbon. The first member of the series is ethylene.

**Oleic Acid,** an important fatty acid present in lard and olive- and cotton-seed oils. Used in soap-making. Olein is the ester formed by the reaction of oleic acid and glycerine.

**Oléron Laws or Judgments,** were a code of maritime laws, introduced into England in the reign of Richard I. in the 12th cent. Oléron is an island off the west coast of France, opposite the mouth of the Charente.

**Olive.** This small tree, whose fruit yields olive oil, is a native of the eastern Mediterranean countries, but has been introduced into cultivation elsewhere. Its oil is used for cooking, in packing sardines, and in soap making; the green unripe fruit is pickled for table olives.

**Olympiads** were periods of four years which elapsed between each celebration of the Olympic games, held at Olympia in honour of Zeus. These festivals included competitions in literature, art, drama, rhetoric, music, and gymnastics, and they were continued, with intervals, from 776 B.C. to A.D. 394. Athletic revivals have taken place at Athens 1896, Paris 1900, St. Louis 1904, London 1908, Stockholm 1912, Antwerp 1920, Paris 1924, Amsterdam 1928, Los Angeles 1932, Berlin 1936, London 1948, Helsinki 1952, Melbourne 1956, Rome 1960, Tokyo 1964, Mexico City 1968, and it is planned to hold the 1972 Olympic Games at Munich. *See* U33, 36.

**Onomasticians** are scientists who study the fascinating subject of names—names of places and names of people—to find out their origins. They tell us, for example, that Cambridge is an Anglo-Norman corruption of *Grantabrycg* = bridge over the Granta; that Harrow-on-the-Hill was an early Anglo-Saxon settlement— " heathen temple on the hill "; that we owe the ridings of Yorkshire to the Vikings (Old Norse *thrithungr* = third part); that in Scotland *-ton* and *-toun* indicate not a town but a hamlet or village. Onomasticians are also concerned with the international standardisation of place names.

**Onyx** or **Sardonyx,** a variety of chalcedony built up of different-coloured layers, which are parallel and straight (not curved as in agate).

**Oolite,** a geological term for the Jurassic oolitic limestones existing through a long stretch of country extending from Yorkshire to Dorsetshire. It abounds in fossils of molluscs and reptiles. The term " oolite " derives from the fact that these rocks are made of egg-shaped particles of calcium carbonate.

**Opal,** a mineral consisting of hydrous silica, occurring in numerous varieties and colours. Precious opal displays a beautiful internal opalescence, the result of the interference of light waves on the surfaces of layers differing in their water-content. Opal miners are called gougers. Chief source, the Andamooka and Coober Pedy fields of South Australia.

**Opera.** *See* Section E.

**Opium** was known to the ancients, and used by them as a medicine. It is obtained from the poppy (*papaver somniferum*), the unripe " head " or seed capsule of that flower yielding a juice which when dried becomes the opium of commerce. The poppy is cultivated in India, Persia, Turkey, Macedonia, and China for the sake of this juice, which yields various alkaloids, such as morphine, narcotine, codeine, etc. These days the drug is rarely used medicinally. *See also* P22(2).

**Opossum,** marsupial mammals found in the more southerly parts of the United States, South America, and Australasia. They are arboreal except for the water-opossum, which eats fish.

**Optics,** the branch of physics which investigates the nature and properties of light and the phenomena of colour. Burning lenses were known to the ancient Greeks and Ptolemy wrote a treatise on optics A.D. 150. Lenses as visual aids were known in ancient China but eyeglasses were not in use until the 13th cent. Spectacles were in more general use after the invention of printing in the 15th cent. The camera obscura was invented in the 16th cent. and the telescope and microscope at the beginning of the 17th cent.

**Oracles** were in ancient times supposed to be words spoken by the gods, and it was the custom on important occasions to consult them about the future. The Greeks had the Oracles of Zeus at Dodona, and Apollo at Delphi, while the Romans consulted the Oracles of Mars, Fortune, and others.

**Orange,** a fruit growing in most sub-tropical climates and in universal demand. It is grown on an evergreen tree that attains a height of about 20 ft. at maturity.

**Orang-utan,** one of the largest of the anthropoid apes, found only in the swampy forests of Borneo and Sumatra. When full-grown it stands over 4 ft. in height and weighs about 150 lb.

**Orchestra,** a group of instruments and instrumentalists whose playing is under the direction of a conductor. The composition of a typical symphony orchestra is as follows: STRINGS: 1st Violin (16), 2nd Violin (16), Viola (12),

Violoncello (12), Double Bass (8). WOOD-WIND: Flute (3–4), Piccolo (1), Oboe (3), Cor Anglais (1), Bass Oboe (1), Clarinet (3), Bass Clarinet (1), Bassoon (3), Contra-bassoon (1). BRASS: Horn (6), Trumpet (5), Trombone (3–4), Tuba (2). PERCUSSION: Timpani (3–6), Side Drum (1), Bass Drum (1), Cymbals (1), Harp (2).

**Orders in Council** are issued by the sovereign on the advice of a few selected members of the Privy Council. They must not seriously alter the law of the land. Another class of Orders in Council are issued by authority of an Act of Parliament for the carrying out of its provisions.

**Ordination,** the ceremony of installing ministers or clergymen in clerical offices, has existed from the earliest times. In the Anglican and Roman Catholic Churches the rites of Ordination are performed by bishops; among Nonconformists the power of ordination rests with the governing bodies of the different Churches.

**Organ** is a musical wind instrument of ancient origin whose tones are produced by the vibrations of air in pipes of varying length. Basically, an organ consists of a number of pipes grouped in rows or ranks according to their special tone-character. The air is fed by bellows or, in modern organs, by a rotary fan, electrically driven. Each rank is controlled by a slider, and the knob that controls the slider is called a stop. The organist pulls out the stops to give the tones he wants, the other pipes being kept out of action by the slider. When a particular note on the keyboard is depressed the player may hear, by pulling out the appropriate stop, not only the normal pitch but the note in several octaves. A stop of which the notes are of normal pitch is called an 8-foot stop, a 16-foot stop would give an octave lower, a 4-foot stop an octave higher, and a 2-foot stop two octaves higher. The hand keyboard is called a manual, and the foot keyboard the pedal board. The basic tone of an organ is its diapason tone, and is normally of 8-foot length and pitch. Most large organs have four manual keyboards and one pedal board. The most important manual is the great organ which comprises the majority of basic stops. The next in importance is the swell organ, so called because the pipes are enclosed in a box fitted with movable shutters operated by a swell-pedal. The effect provides a controlled crescendo or diminuendo. The tone of a typical English swell has a reedy character. The third manual controls the choir organ— a collection of stops suitable for vocal accompaniment. The fourth manual controls the solo organ—a group of stops which, singly or in combination, may provide a solo melody which the remainder of the organ accompanies. The pedal keyboard controls most of the bass stops. In some very large organs there is a fifth manual controlling the echo organ. This is a small group of stops usually set high in the roof of the building to give the effect of distant music. Most church organs have two or three manuals. Modern cinema organs may have some normal stops but rely chiefly on a number of effects unknown to the straight organ.

**Organic Chemistry.** The chemistry of compounds containing carbon and usually associated with living organisms. *See* F24–5.

**Oriel Window** is a window projected from the front of a building, rectangular, triangular, or pentagonal. The ordinary bay window and bow window are varieties of Oriel. When an Oriel window does not reach to the ground it usually rests upon moulded sills supported by corbels.

**Oriflamme,** the name of the original banner of the abbey of St. Denis, and adopted by Louis VI. as his standard. It remained the national emblem of France for three centuries. The flag was of red silk, the outer edge being cut in the form of flames.

**Original Sin,** according to Christian doctrine the corruption that is born with us, as a result of Adam's fall.

**Orioles,** brilliantly coloured birds, members of the passerine family *Oriolidae,* found in the tropical regions of Asia, Africa, and Australia. The golden oriole, perhaps the most beautiful of them all, with brilliant yellow plumage, black wings and tail, winters in Africa, visits England, and is known to have nested here.

**Orion**, a famous constellation of the heavens, comprising nearly a hundred stars, all visible to the naked eye. It contains three stars of the second magnitude in a line, and these are called " Orion's Belt."

**Ormer**, a shellfish (*Haliotis tuberculata*) which occurs in the Channel Islands and on parts of the French coast. It is considered a great delicacy.

**Ornithology**, the scientific study of birds.

**Ornithorhynchus.** *See* Duck-bill.

**Orogeny**, large-scale earth movements, including faulting and folding and sometimes igneous activity, which produce a linear belt of mountains, *e.g.*, the Alpine orogeny in Europe which produced the Alps.

**Orphism.** *See* J33, H117–128.

**Orphrey**, the name of an ornamental border of gold and silver embroidered on ecclesiastical vestments.

**Orrery**, an instrument used in the 18th and early 19th cent. which showed the motions of the planets round the sun and the satellites round their primaries. The first orrery made was named after Charles Boyle, Earl of Orrery.

**Orthodox Eastern Church.** *See* J33.

**Osborne House**, near Cowes, in the Isle of Wight. Queen Victoria's favourite winter-residence, and where she died. It was given to the nation by Edward VII., and is now a convalescent home.

**Osier**, a species of willow growing in damp soils and yielding branches utilised in basket-making.

**Osmium**, a very hard, bluish-white metal, symbol Os, of the platinum group and one of the heaviest of known metals. It is obtained from certain sands of South America, California, Australia, and Russia. The alloy of osmium and iridium (osmiridium) provides long-wearing tips for gold fountain-pen nibs.

**Osmosis**, The process by which absorption of liquids through semi-permeable membranes takes place. A solution exerts osmotic pressure (O.P.) or suction in proportion to concentration but also depending on kind of dissolved substance. The roots of the higher plants are covered with fine root-hairs, within the cell-walls of which the sap is normally of a higher concentration than the dissolved matter in the surrounding soil. The root-hairs, therefore, draw into themselves these weaker salt-solutions. (The explanation of water and salt exchanges is complicated by the selective ability of some cells (*e.g.*, roots) to accept or reject particular dissolved substances along with the water. The absorption of salts by a plant is selective, each plant selecting through the semi-permeable membranes of its root-hairs those substances which are most suited to itself.)

**Osprey** (*Pandion haliaëtus*), a large and magnificent bird of prey, dark brown above and nearly white below. The head is whitish with a dark band from eye to nape. To the British Isles it is a rare passage migrant. In 1959, thanks to the energy and vigilance of the Royal Society for the Protection of Birds, a pair nested in a Scots pine in Inverness-shire and reared three young. Since then more young ospreys have been safely fledged in this sanctuary. The food consists almost entirely of fish, which the bird seizes with its talons. The so-called osprey plumes do not come from this bird but from the egret.

**Ostrich**, the largest living bird, related to the rhea, emu, and extinct moa, now found only on the sandy plains of Africa and parts of S.W. Asia. The male has beautiful white plumes on wings and tail. The wings are useless in flight, but the birds have a fleetness of foot exceeding that of the swiftest horse. An ostrich's egg weighs 3 lb.

**Otary**, any seal which has external ears (as opposed to the *true seals* which lack them). The eared seals make up the family *Otariidae*, which includes the Sea-Lion and the Fur-seal of the N. Pacific.

**Otter**, an aquatic carnivorous mammal widely distributed over Europe, and at one time very common in England and Wales. The otter averages about 2 ft. in length, exclusive of tail, has web-feet, and is a very expert swimmer. Otters are harmless and their hunting is a cruel and senseless blood sport.

**Ounce**, a carnivorous member of the cat family, spotted like a leopard and having a long bushy

tail. It is only found at high altitudes on the Himalayas, and is often called the " snow leopard."

**Outcrop.** Where a bed of rock appears at the surface of the ground, there is an outcrop of the particular rock. Outcrop coal is surface coal; the mining of such coal is called open-cast mining.

**Oviparous**, a zoological term referring to animals which lay eggs to be hatched outside the body of the parent.

**Ovipositor**, the organ by means of which female insects lay their eggs.

**Owls**, nocturnal birds of prey, distributed over the greater part of the world. Their forward-looking eyes, embedded in rings of feathers, give them a characteristic " owl-like " appearance, and their plumage, usually a mottled blend of browns and greys, is so soft that their flight is almost noiseless. Owls live on small mammals, reptiles, birds, insects, and fish, and are very valuable birds to the farmer. British owls include the barn owl (screech owl), short-eared owl, long-eared owl, tawny owl, little owl. Snowy owls have recently nested in the Shetland Is.

**Ox**, the popular name of the mammals included in the genus *Bos*. They are hollow-horned ruminants and hoofed quadrupeds, and include the various classes of domestic cattle as well as the different wild species. The adult male is called a bull, the female a cow, and the young a calf. The best-known breeds of domesticated cattle are the Durham or Shorthorn, the Angus, the Jersey, Ayrshire, Suffolk, and Hereford.

**Oxalic Acid**, an organic acid obtained from numerous plants, such as sorrel and rhubarb, and produced artificially for commercial purposes from sawdust, treated with caustic potash or caustic soda. It combines with metals to form oxalates; used in the manufacture of ink.

**Oxford Clay**, a geological formation consisting of a bed of blue clay hundreds of feet thick, and forming the lower portion of the Upper Jurassic. It makes good bricks.

**Oxford University.** The early history of the university is obscure. There was a school at Oxford as early as 1115 and it is known that Robert Pullen, a theologian from Paris, lectured there in 1133. Allusions to Oxford as the most celebrated centre of learning in England occurred in a work of Gerald of Wales in 1184–5. The earliest colleges to be founded were University College (1249), Balliol (about 1263), Merton (1264). In 1571 the university was reorganised and granted a Charter of Incorporation by an Act of Elizabeth. Other colleges and halls with their dates of foundation are: All Souls (1438), Brasenose (1509), Christ Church (1546), Corpus Christi (1517), Exeter (1314), Hertford (1874), Jesus (1571), Keble (1868), Linacre (1962), Lincoln (1427), Magdalen (1458), New College (1379), Nuffield (1937), Oriel (1326), Pembroke (1624), Queens' (1340), St. Antony's (1950), St. Catharine's (1962), St. Cross (1965), St. Edmund Hall (1270), St. John's (1555), St. Peter's (1929), Trinity (1554), Wadham (1612), Wolfson (1965), Worcester (1714), Campion Hall (1962), St. Benet's Hall (1964), Mansfield (1886), Regent's Park (1958), Greyfriars Hall (1953). The women's colleges are:—Lady Margaret Hall (1878), Somerville (1879), St. Hugh's (1886), St. Hilda's (1893), St. Anne's (1952). Women were not admitted to degrees (though allowed to sit for examination) till 1920.

**Oxygen** is the most abundant of all terrestrial elements, symbol O. In combination, this gaseous element forms about 46% of the earth's crust; one-fifth of the atmosphere; eight-ninths by weight of all water. Discovered independently by Scheele (c. 1773) and Priestley (1774). It is colourless, tasteless, and odourless, and forms the chief life-supporting element of animal and vegetable life.

**Oyster**, a bivalve mollusc, of the genus Ostrea, having very numerous species and abounding in nearly all seas. The shell is rough and irregular. Oysters are exceedingly prolific, spawning in May and June. In England and Scotland deep-sea oysters are not allowed to be sold between June 15 and Aug. 4, and other kinds between May 14 and Aug. 4. In Ireland, no oysters may be taken between May 1 and Sept. 1, except in certain waters. The Whitstable oyster beds have existed since pre-Roman times; "clocks" are dead oysters.

Oystercatcher, a wading bird with black-and-white plumage and long, orange bill, inhabiting estuaries and sea-shores. Feeds on mussels, shell fish, etc., but not oysters.

Ozone, a modified form of oxygen, containing three atoms of oxygen per molecule instead of two. It is prepared by passing oxygen through a silent electric discharge. When present in air to the extent of 1 part in 4 million parts of air it kills bacteria, and has been used for this purpose in ventilating systems, e.g., that of underground railways. It is present in extremely small quantities in the lower atmosphere but is comparatively plentiful at heights of about 20 miles. The belief widely held that seaside air is particularly rich in ozone is untrue. As ozone absorbs ultra-violet light of certain wavelengths spectroscopic methods, involving the analysis of sunlight, are chiefly used in ozone determinations. *See also* Atmosphere.

# P

Paca, a genus of large rodents found in Central and South America, and resembling the guinea-pig. It is of nocturnal habits, has a streaked and spotted fur, and lives on fruits and plants.

Pacific Ocean. The first European to recognise the Pacific as distinct from the Atlantic was the Spanish explorer, Vasco Nuñez de Balboa, who discovered its eastern shore from a peak in Panama in 1513. The first European to sail upon it was Magellan, who entered it by the strait that bears his name in 1520. Sir Francis Drake was the first Englishman to sail upon it in 1577. The world's greatest ocean depth (6,297 fathoms or just over 7 miles) was established by a British survey ship in 1962 in the Mindanao trench in the Philippine Sea.

Pagan, a person who does not worship God; a heathen. The word is derived from the Latin *paganus* (a countryman or uncultivated person). In the Middle Ages the term was used largely to describe Mohammedans (Moors, Saracens, etc.).

Pagoda, the name given in China, India, and other Asiatic countries to a high pyramidal tower, usually, but not necessarily, connected with a temple.

Palaeontology, the science which is devoted to the investigation of fossils: animal (palaeozoology) and plants (palaeobotany). By studying the markings and fossils of living things in the stratified rocks, palaeontologists have been able to establish with astonishing accuracy a record of the evolution of life through geological time. The geologist at the same time with the evidence of the fossils has been able to work out the order and the age of the rocks. *See also* F41.

Palatinate, a term formerly applied to two German electorates or provinces, the Upper and Lower Palatinates. They are now provinces of Bavaria.

Pale, the name given to the part of Ireland colonised by the English and comprising portions of the counties of Louth, Dublin, Meath, and Kildare. The Anglo-Saxon rulers were styled "Lords of the Pale."

Palimpsests are ancient MSS. or parchments which have been partly effaced and used for fresh writings. Many valuable MSS. were thus lost, but sometimes the second writing has been washed out, enabling the original writings to be deciphered. Among such restorations are a dialogue of Cicero's, a portion of a book of Livy, etc.

Palladium, a scarce metallic element, symbol Pd, similar to platinum, with which it is usually found. It is an expensive metal, with desirable properties as a catalyst in reactions involving hydrogen, since it has a remarkable capacity for absorbing this gas; for example, coal gas and air will inflame in the presence of palladium at room temperature. It forms a silver-white alloy with gold, and this is used in some kinds of jewellery. It is used in expensive watches to make non-magnetic springs.

Pallium, a vestmental ornamentation of white wool presented by the Pope to archbishops on their appointment, and the sign of Papal confirmation.

Palm, a large straight-trunked plant or tree common to tropical countries, and usually fruit-yielding, such as dates, coconuts, etc. Many commodities useful to man are obtained from plants of the Palm family (*Palmaceae*).

Palm Sunday, the Sunday before Easter, upon which occasion it is customary to carry palms to the churches in some countries, in commemoration of Christ's entry into Jerusalem for the Feast of the Passover, when the people went forth to greet Him with palm branches.

Panama Canal. In 1903 the United States signed a treaty with Panama (which had previously seceded from Colombia) which gave the United States rights in perpetuity over a ten-mile-wide strip of land extending across the isthmus for the purposes of building and running the canal. The canal connects the Atlantic and Pacific Oceans, is just over fifty miles long (with sea approaches), and the depth varies from 41 to 85 ft. It is constructed above sea-level, with locks, and has been available for commercial shipping since Aug. 3, 1914. Studies are in progress for the building of a new sea-level canal to replace the present one.

Panda, *or* Cat-Bear, is related to the Raccoon, Dogs and the Bear. There are two kinds, the Red or True Panda, resembling a large domestic cat, which lives in the eastern Himalayas and S.W. China, and the Giant Panda, which is more like a bear in appearance and inhabits the mountains of western China. Both frequent the dense bamboo forests of these regions.

Pangolin, the scientific name of the "scaly ant-eater," a toothless mammal, found in W. Africa and S.E. Asia. It has a long extensible tongue which it uses in catching ants and termites, its chief food. When attacked the pangolin rolls itself into a ball, and its scales assume the form of sharp spikes. Pangolins have an Order of their own—the Pholidota, the scale-bearers.

Pantagruel, the leading character in one of the satires of Rabelais.

Pantheon, the famous temple in Rome, originally consecrated to the gods, built by Agrippa in 27 B.C. and rebuilt in the 2nd cent. by Hadrian. Its splendid dome and portico make it one of the most interesting architectural monuments of ancient days. Since the 7th cent. it has been used as a Christian church.

Panther, another name for the leopard, *Panthera pardus*, related to the lion, carnivorous, active climber, found in India, and other parts of Asia, also in Africa.

Papal Infallibility. *See* J33.

Paper has been known in one form or another from very early times. The papyrus reeds of the Nile swamps served the ancient Egyptians for sheets upon which to inscribe their records. The Chinese and Japanese, centuries later, were using something more akin to modern paper in substance, an Asiatic paper-mulberry, yielding a smooth fibrous material, being utilised. With the spread of learning in Western Europe the necessity of a readier medium made itself felt and paper began to be manufactured from pulped rags and other substances. The first known English paper-mill was Sele mill near Stevenage, built about 1490, which produced the paper for an edition of Chaucer in 1498. Other mills were set up under Elizabeth, using linen and cotton as raw material. Other papermaking staples were later introduced, such as surat, esparto grass, and wood-pulp. The chief raw material in the world paper industry is wood-pulp, the main exporters being the timber-growing countries of Canada, Sweden, and Finland. Canada is the world's chief producer of newsprint and supplies a large proportion of U.S. requirements.

Papier mâché means pulped-paper and is a composition of paper pulp and other substances, to which, when moulded into form, coatings of japan, with gilt and coloured inlayings, are added. Elegant and decorative objects are made of papier-mâché. A ceramic papier-mâché is very durable.

Papyrus, the earliest known paper made in Egypt at a very remote period from a large species of reed, *Cyperus papyrus*. This plant is to be found all over tropical Africa, especially in the "sudd" region of the White Nile.

Parachute, the umbrella-shaped safety device used in emergency by the crew and passengers of aircraft. The first parachute descent from a great height was made in 1797 by André Garnerin who dropped 3,000 ft. from a balloon. *See also* Parachute Jumping, U21.

Paraclete (the Holy Ghost, or Comforter), the name used in the English translations of St. John's Gospel, and adopted by Abelard to designate the convent in Champagne founded by him, and of which Héloïse became the abbess.

Paradise, a Persian word used by the translators of the Old Testament to designate the Garden of Eden, and since meaning any place of happiness.

Paraffin, a mixture of hydrocarbons of higher boiling point than petrol. Paraffin was first obtained by distillation of coal, the process being discovered about 1830. About 1848, Mr. James Young procured it from mineral oil, and Irish peat also yielded it. The main source of paraffin supply to-day is crude petroleum. It is largely used in the manufacture of candles, for waterproofing, and numerous other purposes.

Parakeets, various small parrots of vivid plumage native to Australia, Polynesia, Asia, and Africa. One of the loveliest of the parakeets is the budgerigar of Australia. *See* Z21, 23.

Parallax, the change in direction of a body caused by a change in position of the observer. If the parallax is measured (in degrees of angle) and the distance between the two observation points is known the distance of the observed body can be calculated. The distance of heavenly bodies has been found this way. The first stellar distances were so obtained in 1838 by Henderson, Struve, and Bessel. Stellar distances are so great that even when the two observations are made at opposite points of the earth's orbit round the sun the parallax is always less than $1 \cdot 0''$ of arc. *See* Aberration.

Parchment, made chiefly from the skins of animals, usually of goats and sheep, was employed in olden times before printing was invented and superseded papyrus as writing material. Vegetable parchment, invented by W. E. Gaine in 1853, though not equal in strength and durability to skin parchment, is about five times stronger than ordinary paper. Vellum is parchment made from the skins of young calves or lambs.

Paris University, of which the Sorbonne forms a part was founded in the 12th cent. and is one of the greatest educational institutions of Europe.

Parliament, is the name given to the supreme legislature of the United Kingdom. It consists of the Queen, the Lords spiritual and temporal, and the Commons. It meets in two houses: the House of Lords (the Upper or Second Chamber) and the House of Commons. It derives from the Anglo-Saxon *Witans* (*see* Witan). The Statute of Westminster (1275) first uses " parlement " of the Great Council in England, which comes from the French word meaning discourse. *See* Central Government, Section C, *also* D5.

Parliamentary Correspondents sit in the Press Gallery of the House of Commons and describe its proceedings for newspapers either by impressions or a summary of the debate.

Parquetry, the name of a style of flooring consisting of small rectangular wooden blocks laid down according to geometrical pattern.

Parrot, the popular name of a widely distributed family of tropical birds, including the African grey parrot, the green parrot of South America —both familiar cage pets in this country—and the various parakeets, cockatoos, macaws, lories, etc. Many of these birds possess a remarkable gift of imitating sound, especially that of the human voice.

Parsec, unit of distance used by astronomers for expressing distances between stars; equivalent to about three and a quarter light-years.

Parthenogenesis. The development of animals from unfertilised eggs. The drones of the honey bee are parthenogenetic, and the phenomenon is also common among aphids.

Parthenon, the famous Temple of Athena on the Acropolis at Athens, was built under the rule of Pericles between 447 B.C. and 432 B.C. It was made wholly of marble without mortar. The famous sculptured friezes, known as the Elgin Marbles, are now in the British Museum.

Partridge, a well-known British game bird. Close time: Feb. 2 to Aug. 31. Two species are common in Britain.

Passeriformes, the order of perching birds which includes about half the known species.

Passport is an official document issued to a person by his own government, certifying to his citizenship and permitting him to travel abroad. Passports to British subjects are granted by the Foreign Office, authorise bearer to leave the country and guarantee him the state's protection. Passports now cost £2.—and are issued for a period of 10 years. Passports for children under 16 are issued for 5 years in the first instance, renewable then for a further 5 years without fee on production of new photographs, etc. A simplified form of travel document (British visitor's passport) is issued for British subjects wishing to pay short visits to certain foreign countries for a fee of 7s. 6d., valid for 12 months.

Patricians, the aristocracy of ancient Rome.

Paul's Cathedral, St., is the third cathedral church to be built on the site. It was preceded by a Norman building which was practically destroyed by the Great Fire in 1666. This followed a Saxon church which was burnt in 1086. The present building was designed by Sir Christopher Wren. The foundation stone was laid in 1675 and the structure was completed in 1710. It cost a little under £748,000. Its central feature is the dome, crowned by its cupola and lantern with the golden ball and cross. It escaped serious damage during the air raids of the second world war, but many of the surrounding buildings were laid waste.

*p*C Value, introduced by Dr. C. L. Whittles in 1935 as a measure of salinity of aqueous solutions (soil extract, irrigation water, etc.); defined as the negative logarithm of specific electrical conductivity in reciprocal ohms. Alone or joined with *p*H (below) is useful as an index of osmotic pressure (*see* Osmosis) and related hindrance to plant growth resulting from excess of fertiliser or soil salts. If manuring is balanced, growth is best about *p*C 3.3.

Peacock, a bird of large size and beautiful plumage, its characteristic feature being a tail of brilliant " eyed " feathers, which it can erect and spread out, the males possessing resplendent feathering to a much greater extent than the females. It is related to the pheasant; one species is found wild in the forests of India, and another inhabits Burma and the Malayan regions, in Africa there is the Congo Peacock.

Pean, a term in heraldry indicating one of the furs borne in coat armour, the ground of which is black, with ermine spots of gold.

Peanut, Ground Nut *or* Monkey Nut. A member of the pea family native to S. America, but now cultivated in many parts of the world. After pollination, the flower stalk bends down and buries the pod containing the peas (" nuts ") in the ground. The oil from these " nuts " can be used for margarine manufacture.

Pearl is produced by certain shelled molluscs, chiefly the oyster. The inner surface of the shells of the pearl oyster yield " mother-of-pearl," and distinct pearls are believed to be morbid secretions, caused by some external irritation. Many fine pearls are found in the actual body of the oyster. The Persian Gulf, Ceylon, the north-west coast of Western Australia, many Pacific islands, and the Gulf of Mexico are among the most productive pearl-fishing grounds. In ancient times Britain was renowned for its pearl fisheries, the pearls being obtained from a species of fresh-water mussel. Western Australia has produced a 40-grain pearl, the finest the world has seen. The largest pearl ever found was the " Beresford-Hope Pearl," which weighed 1,800 grains, over six times as much as the oyster that produced it.

Peat, decayed vegetable matter found mostly in marshy positions, and common in Ireland and Scotland. Peat is coal in its first stage of development; burnt for fuel in many cottage homes.

Peccary, a pig-like animal native to the Americas. There are two species: the collared peccary and the white-lipped peccary, the latter being a vicious and dangerous animal.

Pelican, a genus of bird with long depressed bill pouched underneath so that it can hold a number of fish in reserve for future consumption. It has immense wings and webbed feet.

**Pemmican,** venison or other meat, sliced, dried, pounded and made into cakes, used by explorers and others when out of reach of fresh meat.

**Penguin,** a genus of flightless, fish-eating sea-birds of the southern hemisphere. They are stout-bodied, short-necked, and of small, moderate, or large size. The Emperor and King Penguins make no nest but protect and incubate the single egg by carrying it in the down feathers between the feet and the body. Other species brood in the usual way and may lay as many as three eggs. Penguins use their flippers for swimming under water. All 16 species are bluish-grey or blackish above and white below. They are very sociable and breed in colonies.

**Penicillin.** An antibiotic drug produced by the mould *Penicillium notatum*, and discovered by Sir Alexander Fleming in 1928. It is one of the most effective chemotherapeutic agents known. The mould produces a number of penicillins, all of which are effective antibiotics. *See* P4(2), 9(1).

**Peninsular War** lasted from 1808 to 1814. Fought in Spain and Portugal (the Iberian peninsula) by the British, Spanish, and Portuguese forces, chiefly under Wellington, against the French. The latter were defeated.

**Pentagon,** government office in Washington (the largest in the world), housing many thousands of military and civilian workers in the War Department of the United States (Army, Navy, and Air Force).

**Pentateuch,** the first five books of the Old Testament—Genesis, Exodus, Leviticus, Numbers, and Deuteronomy.

**Pepys Diary,** by Samuel Pepys, was first published in 1825. It gives a picture of the social life of the period 1 Jan. 1660 to 31 May 1669. He bequeathed the manuscript, together with his library, to Magdalene College, Cambridge.

**Perch,** a well-known family of fresh-water fish, with dark striped sides. The common perch of the British rivers and lakes falls an easy prey to the angler because of its voracity.

**Perfumes** are essences or odours obtained from floral and other substances. The chief flower perfumes are those obtained from rose, jasmine, orange flower, violet, and acacia. Heliotrope perfume is largely obtained from vanilla and almonds. Among the aromatic herbs which yield attractive perfumes are the rosemary, thyme, geranium, lavender, etc., while orange peel, citron peel, musk, sandalwood, patchouli, and other vegetable products are largely drawn upon. In recent times chemistry has been called into play in aid of the perfumer, and many of the popular perfumes of to-day are chemically prepared in simulation of the scents of the flowers or other natural substances the names of which they bear. *See* **Musk Deer.**

**Periclase,** a mineral form of magnesium oxide.

**Perigee.** The moon or the sun is said to be in perigee when it is at its least distance from the earth. The opposite of apogee (*q.v.*).

**Perihelion.** That point in a planet's orbit when it is nearest to the sun. The opposite of aphelion.

**Peripatus,** an animal which stands as a link between the annelid worms and the arthropods. Wormlike with short unjointed legs it breathes by a system of air tubes like those in insects. Certain other points of internal structure point to a relationship with annelid worms. There are some fifty species, the best known being the S. African *Peripalus capensis.*

**Perjury,** the offence of giving false evidence. The ancient Romans threw the perjurer from the Tarpeian Rock, and after the Empire was Christianised, those who swore falsely upon the Gospel had their tongues cut out. The usual punishment in England from the 16th to the 19th cent. was the pillory, fine, and imprisonment.

**Permian Formation,** a group of rocks lying between the Trias and the Carboniferous strata. It has three subdivisions. Upper, Middle and Lower Permian. *See* F41.

**Per Procurationem** signature means that the subject of the correspondence has been put into the writer's care by his principal for him to use his personal judgment in the matter, and that he is authorised to sign on behalf of his principal. Normally contracted to *per pro* or *p.p.*

**Peruke,** the name given to the wigs worn by men

in the latter half of the 18th cent. The custom of wearing wigs was gradually superseded by powdering the natural hair. Wigs are still worn by the Speaker of the House of Commons, judges, and barristers.

**Petrel,** the name given to a member of a large, widely-distributed family of sea-birds of great diversity of size and colouring and distinguished by tube-like external nostrils. They usually skim low over the waves, and some, for this reason, are known as shearwaters. The storm petrel or Mother Carey's chicken occasionally patters along the surface, and is often called Little Peter—a reference to St. Peter walking on the water. Except when breeding, petrels are always at sea. They mostly nest in holes and crevices on islands and lay one egg, which is invariably white. The storm petrel, Leach's petrel, Manx shearwater, and the fulmar petrel are resident in the British Isles. *See also* Mutton Bird.

**Petroleum.** *See* Oil.

**Pewter,** alloy of tin and lead formerly much used for making household utensils and ornaments.

**pH Value.** Introduced in 1909 by the Danish chemist Sørensen to indicate hydrogen-ion concentration on the basis of electrical conductivity and a view of ionisation since discarded; is now taken as a logarithmic scale of acidity or alkalinity of aqueous solutions: acidity 0–7, neutrality at 7·0, alkalinity 7–14. The $pH$ of blood is about 7·6 (faintly alkaline). *See* F22.

**Phalanger,** pouched marsupial mammals. They are arboreal and superficially resemble squirrels. There are two genera of flying phalangers or flying squirrels, which have a remarkable membrane along each side of the body enabling the animals to glide through the air. The members of the phalanger family are confined to the Australasian and oriental regions.

**Phalangid,** a member, of the arachnid family Phalangida: popularly known as " harvesters."

**Phalanx,** a name applied by the ancient Greeks to a body of troops drawn up in close array, with overlapping shields, and eight, ten, or more rows deep. The Macedonians stood sixteen deep. A Greek phalanx consisted of 8,000 men.

**Pharmacopoeia,** an official publication containing information on the recognised drugs used in medicine. Each country has its own pharmacopoeia. The British Pharmacopoeia (B.P.) is published under the direction of the General Medical Council. The Pharmaceutical Society issues the British Pharmaceutical Codex (B.P.C.); there is also an International Pharmacopoeia (2 vols.) which is issued by the World Health Organisation.

**Pharos,** the name of the first lighthouse, built by Ptolemy II. about 280 B.C., on the Isle of Pharos, at the entrance to the harbour of Alexandria. It was 600 ft. high, and one of the " seven wonders."

**Pheasant,** game birds related to the partridges, quails, peacocks, chickens, and turkeys, distinguished by their brilliant plumage and long tapering tail. First found by the Greeks in Georgia where the River Phasis flows through to the Black Sea. Close time: Feb. 2 to Sept. 30.

**Philippics,** the orations delivered by Demosthenes, 352–341 B.C., against Philip of Macedon—remarkable for their acrimonious invective. The word was also used for Cicero's speeches against Antony. In modern use, any impassioned invective.

**Philosopher's Stone.** *See* Alchemy, J2.

**Phoenix,** a fabled bird of Egyptian mythology.

**Phosphorus** is a non-metal element, symbol P. Most familiar as a waxy, yellow solid which is spontaneously inflammable in air. It has chemical similarities to arsenic, like which it is very poisonous. It was discovered by Brandt in urine in 1669. It is found in most animal and vegetable tissues. It is an essential element of all plants and of the bones of animals. In combination with various metals it forms different phosphates, which are largely utilised as manures. The chief commercial use of phosphorus is in the preparation of matches.

**Photoelectric Cell,** a device which gives a useful electrical response to light falling on it. There are several kinds depending on the different effects which light may have on a suitably chosen solid (usually a semiconductor), viz., the emission of electrons from the surface ("photo-emissive cell"); change in electrical resistance ("photoconducting cell"); generation of electric current from a specially designed sensitive structure ("barrier layer" or "photo-voltaic cell", "solar battery"). Different cells respond differently to lights of various wavelength and must be chosen for each application. *See also* Solar Battery.

Photogrammetry, the science of measurement from photographs taken from an aircraft. Aerial photography has many uses and is of great value to military intelligence and for map-making.

Photon. When light behaves like a stream of discrete particles and not like waves, the particles are called photons. *See* F13(1), 14.

Photosynthesis. *See* F28.

Phrenology. *See* J34.

Phylloxera, a genus of plant-lice related to the aphids, which attacks the grape vine. Many vineyards of France, in common with the rest of Europe, were replanted with native vines grafted on immune stocks from California in 1879 after being ravaged by the insect (which came from America). Curiously enough, the remedy also came from America, the vine stocks there being immune to *phylloxera*.

Picts, inhabitants of Scotland in pre-Roman times, are held by some historians to be a branch of the old Celtic race, by others to have been of Scyth-ian origin. They occupied the north eastern portion of Scotland, and were subdued by the Scots in Argyll in the 9th cent., Kenneth Mac-Alpin becoming king of a united kingdom of the Picts and Scots—the kingdom of Alban.

Pike, a familiar fresh-water fish abundant in the temperate regions of both hemispheres. It forms good sport for the angler in rivers and lakes, and sometimes attains a weight of from 20 to 30 lb. It is extremely voracious, is covered with small scales, and has a ferocious-looking head

Pilchard, a fish of the herring family, but with smaller scales and more rounded body. It appears off the Cornish coasts in vast shoals every summer.

Pilgrimage, the undertaking of a journey to a distant place or shrine to satisfy a religious vow or secure spiritual benefit, was resorted to in early Christian times. The first recorded pilgrimage is that of the Empress Helena to Jerusalem in 326. In the Middle Ages pilgrim-ages became common, and were undertaken by monarchs and people of rank in all Christian countries. Moslems have been making pil-grimages to Mecca since the death of the Prophet, such duty being enjoined by the Koran. Among the great centres of Christian pilgrimages are Jerusalem, Rome, the tomb of Becket at Canterbury, and the holy places of Lourdes and La Salette in France.

Pilgrim Fathers, the 101 English Puritans, who, after living some years in exile in Holland, to escape persecution in their own country, set sail for America in the *Mayflower*, Sept. 6, 1620, land-ing at Plymouth, Mass., Dec. 4. They founded the settlement of Plymouth, and are regarded as the pioneers of American colonisation although 13 years earlier a small Virginian colony had been established.

"Pilgrim's Progress," Bunyan's famous allegory, written in Bedford gaol. The first part was issued in 1678. It is the greatest work of its kind. *See* M32(1).

Pillory, a wooden instrument of punishment in use in England until 1837. It consisted of a pair of movable boards with holes through which the culprit's head and hands were put, and was usually erected on a scaffold. While a person was undergoing this punishment the mob generally pelted him with stones and rubbish, sometimes to his serious injury. People con-victed of forgery, perjury, or libel were often condemned to the pillory, but from 1816 to 1837 the only offence for which it could be inflicted was perjury.

Pine, a conifer of the genus *Pinus*, which flourishes all over the northern hemisphere and includes 80–90 species, which afford valuable timber and yield turpentine and tar. The Scots Pine, *Pinus silvestris*, with its blue-green, short

needles, set in pairs, and its rosy-orange branches, is native to Britain, as it is to the whole of Europe. It provides the red and yellow deal in everyday use.

Pipa, a species of toad inhabiting Guiana, and not found elsewhere. It is of considerable size, and is remarkable for the fact that the female carries its eggs on its back until they are hatched, her-self depositing them in that position. Generally known as the "Surinam toad."

Pitcairn Islanders were originally the mutineers of the *Bounty*. They took possession of the island in 1790, and it was not until 1814 that their whereabouts was ascertained, accidentally, by a passing ship. The mutineers, under their leader, Adams, had settled down to a communal existence, married Tahitian women, and in-creased so in numbers that in the course of years they were too many for the island to sup-port, and in 1856 they were removed by the British Government to Norfolk Island. A small number returned to Pitcairn.

Pitchblende *or* Uraninite, a relatively scarce mineral. It is nearly all uranium oxide, but lead, thorium, etc., are also present. Pitch-blende from Joachimstal in Czechoslovakia was the material in which radium was discovered by the Curies. Pitchblende also occurs in Saxony, Rumania, Norway, Cornwall, the Congo, and at Great Bear Lake in Canada.

Plainsong, a style of musical composition sung in unison (all voices singing the same tune with-out harmony), familiar in the Western Church from very early times and still performed, principally in the Roman Catholic Church. Though restrained and contemplative in spirit, it is capable of expressing deep emotion. *See* E3(2).

Planetarium, a complex optical system which pro-jects into the interior of a dome a replica of all the phenomena of the sky that can be seen by the naked eye, *e.g.*, sun, moon, planets, stars, comets, meteors, aurora, eclipses, and clouds. There is a planetarium in the Marylebone Road, London, and another (opened in 1966) at Armagh Observatory, N. Ireland.

Planets, the name give to such celestial bodies as revolve round the sun in elliptical orbits. The name was first used by the Greeks to indicate their difference from the fixed stars. There are nine planets, Mercury, Venus, Earth, Mars, Jupiter, Saturn, Uranus, Neptune, Pluto. Many important questions can be answered by means of probes sent to the neighbourhood of the planets. These include the measurement of the magnetic field, if any, of the planets, the study of their atmospheres, much of which can be done without actually penetrating to the surface. With instruments landed gently on the surface it is possible to investigate surface conditions and composition by many methods. Even without a soft landing information on these questions can be obtained by photography and subsequent transmission of the picture back to earth by some form of television scanning. For example, the American Mars probe, *Mariner IV*, transmitted pictures of the Martian surface in 1965 when it was at its closest approach to the planet, and the Russian *Venus IV* in 1967 made a soft landing on Venus. *See* F7, *also* Venus, Section F, Part VI.

Plankton, a word which first came into biological use in 1886 to describe the usually microscopic plants and animals floating, swimming, and drifting in the surface waters of the sea. To be distinguished from *nekton* (swimming animals like fishes and squids) and *benthos* (plants and animals living on the sea bottom, like fixed algae, sponges, oysters, crabs, etc.). Of great economic importance, providing food for fish and whales.

Plantagenets, the kings who reigned in England between 1154 and 1485 and included the Houses of Lancaster and York. More correctly they are styled Angevins, from Anjou, of which Geoffrey, father of Henry II., was Count, and whose badge was a sprig of broom (*planta genista*).

Plasma Physics is the physics of wholly ionised gases, *i.e.*, gases in which the atoms initially present have lost practically the whole of the electrons that usually surround their nuclei, so that the gas consists of a mixture of two com-ponents, positively charged ions and negatively charged electrons. The physical properties of a *plasma* are very different from those of an un-ionised gas. In particular, a plasma has a high electrical conductivity and can carry large currents. *See also* Nuclear Fusion.

**Plastics,** a broad term covering those substances which become plastic when subjected to increased temperatures or pressures. The Plastics Industry is based on synthetic organic examples of this group. There are two classes of plastics: the *thermoplastic*, which become plastic every time they are heated (*e.g.* cellulosic plastics) and *thermosetting*, which undergo chemical change when heated, so that once set they cannot be rendered plastic again (*e.g.* Bakelite). Plastics are composed of long-chained molecules, *e.g.*, polyethylene.

**Platinum,** a metal element, symbol Pt. It is a scarce white metal generally allied with iridium, osmium, ruthenium, and palladium. It can only be melted in an oxyhydrogen or electric furnace, but can be rolled out into a film-like sheet, or drawn out to the finest wire; being resistant to acids it is termed a noble metal.

**Platonic Solids,** five regular solid figures known to the ancient world. They are: the tetrahedron (4 triangular faces), cube (6 square faces), octahedron (8 triangular faces), dodecahedron (12 five-sided faces), icosahedron (20 triangular faces). All the faces and angles of each solid are identical.

**Plebeians** were the ordinary citizens of Rome as distinct from the patricians. There was a long struggle between the two orders for political equality.

**Pleiades,** famous cluster of stars in the constellation of Taurus. Of the seven principal stars in the group, one is rather faint, and many myths have sprung up about this "lost pleiad".

**Pleistocene** the geological period that succeeded the Pliocene. During the Pleistocene, also known as the *Great Ice Age*, there were four cold periods, when the ice sheets covered northern Europe and N. America, separated by warm periods when the glaciers drew back into the mountains. From recent studies based on rock magnetic measurements the transition to Pleistocene took place about 1,850,000 years ago.

**Pliocene,** the geological period preceding the Pleistocene, and the last major division of the Tertiary strata. It began about fifteen million years ago. *See* F41.

**Plough Monday,** the first Monday after the Epiphany, when in olden times the rustic population returned to work after the Christmas festivities.

**Plover,** wading birds, widely distributed over marshy places of Europe. Several species occur in Britain, including the Golden-plover, which breeds on the moors of Devon, Somerset, Wales, N.E. Yorkshire, and Scotland, and the Ringed plover, Kentish plover, and Dotterel.

**Pluto,** the last planet to be discovered; existence established by C. W. Tombaugh at the Flagstaff Observatory in Arizona in Jan. 1930 from reckonings made by P. Lowell in 1914. It is the most distant of all the known planets; diameter about 3,650 miles. Mean distance from the sun estimated at 3,671 million miles.

**Plutonium,** a chemical element, symbol Pu, capable of nuclear fission in the same way as Uranium 235. Not until after it had been synthesised in atomic piles during the second world war was it shown to occur in infinitesimally small traces in nature. Its synthesis in the atomic pile depends on the capture by Uranium 238 nuclei of neutrons; immediate product of this reaction is the element neptunium, but this undergoes rapid radioactive disintegration to plutonium. Because of its explosive power and poisonous character, an American scientist once remarked: "If ever there was an element which deserved a name associated with hell, it is plutonium."

**Poet Laureate** is the poet attached to the royal household, an office officially established in 1668, though its origins go back to the early Middle Ages, when minstrels were employed at the courts of English kings. Chaucer, Skelton, and Spenser, though not court poets, were all unofficial poets laureate. Ben Jonson has been called the first "official laureate" (1616), but the office was not officially recognised until 1668, when Dryden was formally granted the

office. It is customary for the poet laureate to write verse in celebration of events of national importance. Cecil Day-Lewis succeeded John Masefield as poet laureate in 1967.

**Pogrom.** Russian word meaning "destruction." First used to describe the Tsarist attacks on the Jews in 1881 in Russia. In 1938 Hitler ordered a general pogrom in Germany: all synagogues were destroyed and nearly all Jewish shops and homes, Jewish hospitals and children's homes suffered. During the subsequent war Jews of central Europe were systematically exterminated in cold blood by the Nazis.

**Poitiers, Battle of,** was fought on Sept. 19, 1356, during the Hundred Years' War, when Edward the Black Prince gained a complete victory over John, King of France, who was taken prisoner and brought to London.

**Polecat,** an animal of a dark-brown colour, about 18 in. in length, exclusive of tail; the ears and face-markings are white or light brown. It is carnivorous and belongs to the weasel family. Like the skunk, it emits an offensive odour.

**Pole-Star** is of the second magnitude, and the last in the tail of the Little Bear constellation. Being near the North pole of the heavens—never more than about one degree from due north—it always remains visible in the Northern hemisphere; hence its use as a guide to seamen.

**Police,** a regular force established for the preservation of law and order and the prevention and detection of crime. The powers they have vary from country to country and with the type of government; the more civilised and democratic the state, the less police intervention. England, compared with countries abroad, was slow to develop a police force, and it was not until 1829 that Sir Robert Peel's Metropolitan Police Act established a regular force for the metropolis, later legislation establishing county and borough forces maintained by local police authorities throughout England and Wales. Up to that time police duties were discharged by individual constables and watchmen appointed by local areas in England and Wales. Under the Police Act, 1964, the former 121 regular police forces in England and Wales are being reduced, by amalgamation, to 49. The forces are defined according to area of responsibility:

   1. County forces, under a Police Committee.

   2. Borough forces, under Watch Committees, elected by the borough councils.

   3. Combined forces covering more than one county or borough, under a body representing the constituent areas.

   4. The Metropolitan Police Force, covering a 15-miles radius from Charing Cross, under the control of the Home Secretary.

   5. The City of London force, under a committee of the Common Council.

As a result of the amalgamations county forces have grown at the expense of borough forces. The Metropolitan Police, with an establishment of over 25,000 are unaffected by the current changes. Central authority rests with the Home Secretary in England and Wales and the Secretary of State for Scotland in Scotland. In Northern Ireland the police force is controlled by an Inspector General, who is responsible to the Minister of Home Affairs.

**Pollution** of the atmosphere is due chiefly to the incomplete combustion of fuels, especially coal, large particles of soot being deposited fairly quickly close to their place of origin and smaller particles (including smoke) remaining suspended in the air for a long time. Corrosion of exposed objects and damage to buildings result from the production of sulphuric acid. The introduction of more efficient furnaces, the washing of flue gases and the introduction of smokeless zones have assisted in the abatement of smoke and other forms of pollution. Estimation of polluting substance is carried out systematically in Great Britain by the Department of Scientific and Industrial Research, the dust and matter brought down with the rain being collected in large deposit gauges; automatic filters provide continuous records of the variation of the floating solid impurities; and apparatus is employed to measure the concentration of sulphur dioxide. Nuclear tests add to the load of pollution in the atmosphere (*see* Fall-out). " Smog " (smoke-laden fog) which reduces visibility to zero and affects the respiratory organs, is liable to occur when the air near the earth is cooled below the dew-point temperature by radiation on a still, cloudless night when an accumulation of smoke over a large city cuts off daylight and produces gloom, and absence of wind or vertical currents prevents the lower layers of the air from getting away. Such conditions are associated with the smoke-laden atmosphere of large industrial towns during a winter anticyclone. During the great London smog of 1952 there were 2,000 deaths over and above those expected for the time of year. Since the Clean Air Act of 1956 pollution by smoke and sulphur dioxide has continued to diminish in London. The Act allows local authorities to control emissions of dark smoke, grit, and dust and to establish smoke control areas in which the emission of any type of smoke is prohibited. Householders in smoke control areas may apply for a grant towards the cost of installing appliances to burn smokeless fuel.

**Polonium,** a radioactive element, symbol Po, discovered by Madame Curie in 1898, and named after her native land of Poland.

**Poltergeist.** *See* J35.

**Polymerisation** is the linking together of small molecules to make a large long-chain molecule. The general name for polymers of ethylene is Polythene, a wax-like plastic solid which because of its special qualities is used in a variety of ways today.

**Polytheism.** *See* God and Man, J18.

**Pomander,** name of a small ball or box containing perfumes and spices, formerly carried suspended from the neck or girdle as a protection against infection so it was believed.

**Pomology,** the science of fruit-growing.

**Pontifex,** the title assigned in ancient Rome to members of the college of pontifices. " Pontifex maximus " was the official head of Roman religion. It was as " pontifex maximus " that Julius Caesar revised the calendar in 46 B.C., and when after the rise of Christianity the popes took over the title the revision fell to them.

**Pope, The,** the head of the Roman Catholic Church, recognised by that Church as the lawful successor of St. Peter. He is elected by the body of Cardinals. Since 1870, when the King of Italy deposed the holder from temporal power, no pope had left the Vatican between appointment and death until 1929, when peace was made between the Church and State in Italy and compensation was paid to the Holy See for the loss of temporal power. Cardinal Montini, Archbishop of Milan, was elected Pope Paul VI in 1963 on the death of Pope John XXIII.

**Porcelain.** The word is thought to be derived from the Italian *porcellana,* indicating the texture of a piglet. The majority of porcelain made on the continent was of " hard-paste ", or true porcelain, similar to that discovered by the Chinese as early as the T'ang Dynasty (A.D. 618–907). It was composed of *kaolin* (china-clay) and *petuntse* (china-stone) which when fired in a kiln at a temperature of *c.* 1300° C. became an extremely hard and translucent material. The recipe of " hard-paste " porcelain remained a secret of the Chinese until 1709, when it was re-discovered in Europe by Johann Böttger of the Meissen factory (popularly known as Dresden). Aided by disloyal Meissen workmen, factories were later established at Vienna, Venice and in many parts of Germany. Plymouth and Bristol were the only English factories to produce this type of porcelain, from 1768 to 1781. Elsewhere, both in England and France, the material manufactured was known as " soft-paste " or artificial porcelain which was made by blending varying white-firing clays with the ingredients of glass. The French factory of Sèvres began to make some hard-paste porcelain by 1768 and by the 19th cent. such porcelain was the only type being made throughout the whole of the continent. In England Josiah Spode is credited with the introduction of " bone-china " about 1794. This hybrid-paste was quickly adopted by many other factories and today remains the

most popular type of English porcelain. *See* Pottery and Porcelain Marks, Section N.

**Porcupine,** a rodent whose back is covered with long, sharp, black and white spikes, which form a powerful means of defence. There are two families of porcupines; one is confined to the Old World and the other contains the American porcupines.

**Porphyry,** a form of crystalline rock of many varieties that in ancient Egypt was quarried and used for the decorative portions of buildings and vessels. The term is applied generally to the eruptive rocks in which large well-formed crystals of one mineral are set in a matrix of other minerals.

**Porpoise,** a highly intelligent marine mammal of the dolphin and whale family, and a common inhabitant of northern seas. Porpoises travel in shoals, their progression being marked by constant leapings and plungings. Their average length is from 4 to 5 ft. There are several species, nearly all being confined to northern oceans.

**Port,** a special kind of red Portuguese wine, taking its name from Oporto. It was little known in England until the Methuen Treaty of 1703, when it was permitted to be imported at a low duty.

**Portcullis,** a strong, movable timber or iron grating let into the wall of the gateway to a feudal castle, and capable of being lowered or raised at will. It formed an effective protection against attack in the days before firearms.

**Portland Vase,** one of the most renowned specimens of ancient art, long in the possession of the Portland family. In 1810 it was loaned to the British Museum. Here it was shattered in 1845 by a stone from a maniac's hand, but has been skilfully restored. It is said to have been found in the 17th cent. in an ancient tomb near Rome. It was purchased from the Barberini family in 1770 by Sir Wm. Hamilton, subsequently sold to the Duchess of Portland. The vase, which is actually a two-handled urn, stands about 10 ins. high, is of transparent dark blue glass, ornamented with figures cut in relief in overlaid white opaque glass. It was purchased by the British Museum in 1945.

**Portreeve** in olden times was an official appointed to superintend a port or harbour, and before the name of mayor was used the chief magistrate of London was styled the Portreeve.

**Positivism.** *See* J35.

**Positron,** the " positive electron," an atomic particle having the same mass but an electric charge equal but opposite to that of an electron. It was discovered in 1932. *See also* F14.

**Post-Impressionism,** a term introduced by Roger Fry to describe the exhibition of paintings sponsored by himself in London (1910–11) officially entitled " Manet and the Post-Impressionists." The exhibition included paintings by Manet, Cézanne, Gauguin, Van Gogh, Seurat, Signac, works by Matisse, Rouault, and the *Fauves* (*q.v.*), and sculpture by Maillol. In a second exhibition, held in 1912, Picasso and the Cubists were also represented. The term therefore refers to the movement in modern art which reacted against the transient naturalism of the Impressionists by concerning itself primarily with colour, form, and solidity. Most artists today would include Cézanne, Van Gogh, and Gauguin as the main Post-Impressionists and maintain that it prepared the way for Fauvism, Cubism, and Expressionism.

**Potassium,** a metal, symbol K (German *Kalium*). It is similar to sodium, like which it reacts violently with water. It was discovered by Sir Humphry Davy in 1807, and now generally obtained by the electrolysis of fused potassium hydroxide or chloride/fluoride mixture. Its principal minerals are carnallite and kainite, and it is relatively common in rocks, accounting for about 2¼% of the earth's crust. An essential element for healthy plant growth; the ashes of plants are relatively rich in potassium.

**Potsdam Agreement** was signed by Truman, Stalin, and Attlee in Aug., 1945. By this Agreement a Council of Foreign Ministers was established, representing the five principal Powers: China, France, Soviet Russia, the United Kingdom, and United States of America, with the task of drawing up the peace treaties for submission to the United Nations. It laid down, *inter alia* that German militarism and Hitlerism should be destroyed; that industrial power should be so reduced that Germany would never again be in a position to wage aggressive war; that surplus equipment should be destroyed or transferred to replace wrecked plant in allied territories; that Germany should be treated as an economic whole; and that local self-government should be restored on democratic lines as rapidly as was consistent with military security. The Potsdam Agreement became a dead letter with the creation of a communist régime in the Russian zone of Germany, and marked the beginning of the " cold war."

**Prado Gallery,** the great public picture collection of Madrid, containing a superb collection of paintings by Velasquez, Murillo, Raphael, Titian, Dürer, Van Dyck, Rubens, Holbein, etc.

**Pragmatism.** *See* J35.

**Prefect,** chief magistrates in ancient Rome. The title is now applied to the chiefs of administration of the departments of France.

**Pre-Raphaelite Brotherhood** was the name given to their school of thought by three British artists, Dante Gabriel Rossetti, J. E. Millais, and W. Holman Hunt, who in 1848 revolted against the academic art of their time and advocated a return to the style of the Italian painters prior to Raphael—the simple naturalism of the Primitives, such as Botticelli, Fra Angelico and Filippo Lippi. Thus they avoided the use of heavy shadows and painted on a white ground in bright colours—a technique which aroused the ire of those used to the dark and murky canvases of the contemporary romantic artists. Although they held these principles in common the three members of the " P.R.B.", as it was popularly called, were really quite different in other respects. Thus Rossetti (who for some reason is always thought of as the typical Pre-Raphaelite) produced works of a highly romanticised mediaevalism which, apart from certain aspects of technique, bear not the slightest resemblance to the sentimental naturalism of Millais or the much more dramatic realism of Holman Hunt (*e.g.*, in *The Scapegoat*). The Brotherhood was later joined by a number of lesser artists, but its works are not commonly accepted with enthusiasm to-day when the general feeling is that they are sentimental and religiose rather than the product of deeply-felt emotions. Ruskin in his writings defended their work but the movement came to an end in 1853.

**Presbyterianism.** *See* J35.

**Press-Gang,** a body of sailors employed to impress men into naval service, frequently resorted to in England, especially during the war with France in the early 19th cent. Press gangs were not used after about 1850.

**Primitive Art.** The word " primitive " has a number of different meanings: (1) the art of prehistoric communities (*e.g.*, the famous animal cave-drawings of the Aurignacians, c. 25,000 B.C., at Altamira in Spain); (2) the art of modern primitive communities (*e.g.*, Bushman rockpaintings); (3) child art; (4) peasant art which springs from a spontaneous desire to impart beauty to objects of daily use and shows a tendency towards abstraction. Peasant art has many features in common the world over, the woodcarving of the Norsemen being almost indistinguishable from that of the Maoris; (5) the modern school of primitive painting in which naïveté of presentation is either the aim of a highly sophisticated mind (*e.g.*, the self-taught French painter Le Douanier Rousseau (d. 1910)), or arises naturally from a simple one (the American " grandma " Moses (d. 1961) who began to paint in her seventies).

**Printing** by movable types was first used in Europe in 1454 by Johann Gutenberg, a citizen of Mainz. The invention is also claimed for Laurens Koster of Haarlem. It was introduced into England by Caxton, who set up a printing press in Westminster in 1476. Gothic characters were first used, being superseded by Roman letters in 1518. In 1798 Earl Stanhope replaced the wood printing press by one of iron. In 1814 Friedrich Koenig applied the principle of steam power to the press. Mr. John Walter, of *The Times* newspaper, was the first to use the steam press. Improvements were introduced by Applegarth and Cowper in 1828 and great strides were made in 1858 when the Hoe machine was put on the market. Then came the Walter press in 1866 which printed on continuous rolls of paper from curved stereotyped plates. The Monotype machine casts single letters and the Linotype whole lines. The term letterpress is used for all printing methods using plates where the characters stand in *relief*. The other main printing methods are *intaglio* and *planographic*.

**The Privy Council** is the Queen's own Council, consisting of over 300 distinguished men drawn from all walks of life. Its function is to give private advice to the Queen. From it have sprung many organs of the constitution. For example, the Judiciary or courts of justice have grown from the Queen's Council sitting as a Court of Justice, and today the Judicial Committee of the Privy Council is a body of distinguished lawyers acting as a Court of Appeal from courts of the Commonwealth. Many of our Government Departments have grown from Committees of the Privy Council.

**Probation Officers** are attached to particular Courts, sometimes a Magistrates' or a higher court. Sometimes an offender is not sentenced to punishment, but is released " on probation," that is on the condition that he behaves well and follows directions given by the Court or by a probation officer. Such an officer is a trained man (or woman) who advises, assists, and befriends people who have been committed to his care by a court of law. The probation officer, by his assessment of the social background of the offender, can advise the court upon the wisdom of putting the offender on probation. The probation officer by his understanding can so befriend an offender as to provide a basis for his rehabilitation. He undertakes the " after care " of those released from prison or Borstal or approved schools, to which juveniles are sent. *See also* Juvenile Courts.

**Productivity.** Physical productivity is the output of products during a time unit, *e.g.*, so many products per man hour, or day, or year. Total productivity is the sum of all the units of product created during the given time. Labour productivity is the part of the total that is attributed to labour as a factor of production. Productivity of capital is the element attributed to capital as a factor. Productivity of land is the element attributed to the natural powers of the soil, as distinct from what is contributed by the application to it of capital or labour. The term productivity is also used to refer not to the quantity of output, but to its money value. There have been many attempts to compare the productivities of different economies—*e.g.*, Great Britain and the United States or advanced and underdeveloped countries.

**Propane,** a colourless inflammable gas made of carbon and hydrogen; formula $C_3H_8$. It is easily liquefied and transported liquid in cylinders and tanks. In this form it is familiar as a " portable gas supply " for domestic and industrial uses. It is sometimes mixed with butane (*q.v.*) for this purpose. Propane occurs in natural gas and is a by-product of oil refining.

**Proteins** are the main chemical substances of living matter: they are a part of every living cell and are found in all animals and plants. Proteins have many functions, and occur in structural matter such as bones, tendons, skin, hair, and hoof, and in some vitamins and hormones. Lean meat, fish, and eggs are almost entirely proteins. Their composition varies with the source, but all proteins are basically constructed of carbon, hydrogen, oxygen, and nitrogen, and some contain sulphur, phosphorus (nucleoproteins), and iron (haemoglobin). Proteins are built up of very long chains of amino-acids connected by amide linkages (the synthetic polymers such as " nylon " and casein plastics (from milk) are built up of the same linkages). Enzymes, which bring about chemical reactions in living cells, are proteins having specific properties. *See* F27(1).

**Proton,** a basic constituent of the atomic nucleus, positively charged, having a mass about 1836 times that of the electron. It is a positive hydrogen ion. *See* F10(2), 14.

**Protoplasm.** See F19(2).

**Prout's hypothesis.** The English chemist William Prout (1785–1850) advanced the idea that all atoms are made of hydrogen, and their weights are exact multiples of the weight of a hydrogen atom. With the modification that neutrons as well as protons occur in the nucleus, Prout's belief, though rejected for many years, has been substantially vindicated.

**Provost,** a Scottish official similar in rank to an English mayor. The Provosts of Edinburgh, Glasgow, Aberdeen, Perth, and Dundee are styled Lords Provost. The title of provost is also given to the heads of certain colleges.

**Prud'hommes** (Prudent Men), Councils of, were French trade tribunals, of masters and workmen, formed to decide on disputes. Originally a mediaeval institution, they were revived by Napoleon in 1806, and were carried on by the Third Republic.

**Psalms,** Book of, for many years attributed to David, but present-day scholars are of opinion that the psalms were written by a series of authors at different times and for different purposes, and that few, if any, were written by David. The Holy Scriptures contain 150.

**Psychic Research.** See J36.

**Ptarmigan,** birds of the grouse family, one species of which inhabits the Scottish Highlands. In the winter the bird assumes a white plumage.

**Ptomaines,** amino acids produced during the putrefaction of proteins of animal origin. Not a cause of food poisoning, as was once generally supposed, which is almost invariably due to certain specific bacteria.

**Publicans,** under the Roman Empire, were people who farmed the public taxes. It is this class of officials that is alluded to in the " publicans and sinners " phrase in the New Testament.

**Public Corporations,** statutory bodies which operate major industries and services in the public interest, e.g., UK Atomic Energy Authority, Bank of England, B.B.C., Electricity Authorities, Gas Council, National Coal Board, British Steel Corporation, British Railways Board. They are accountable to Parliament but their staffs are not civil servants. The Post Office is to become a public corporation in 1969.

**Public Schools.** The Public Schools Act of 1864 named nine " public " schools: Eton, Harrow, Rugby, Winchester, Westminster, Shrewsbury, Charterhouse, St. Paul's, and Merchant Taylors. Today the term embraces many more, and can be applied to all those schools which are financed by bodies other than the State and whose headmasters belong to the Headmasters' Conference as distinct from the Headmasters' Association. There are about 200 such schools in Britain, including among others: Bedford Grammar School (founded 1552); King Edward's School, Birmingham (1552); Brighton College (1845); Charterhouse School, Godalming (1611); Cheltenham College (1841); Christ's Hospital, West Horsham (1552); City of London School (1442); Clifton College, Bristol (1862); Dulwich College (1619); Eton College (1440); Felsted School (1564); Haileybury College (1862); Harrow School (1571); Malvern College (1865); Manchester Grammar School (1515); Marlborough College (1843); Merchant Taylors' School (1561); Mill Hill School (1807); Oundle (1556); Radley (1847); Repton School, Derbyshire (1557); Rugby School (1567); St. Paul's School (1509); Sherborne School (1550); Shrewsbury School (1552); Stonyhurst College (1594); Tonbridge School (1553); Uppingham School (1584); Wellington College (1859); Westminster School (1339); Winchester College (1387); and Warwick (914). Public schools for girls include: Christ's Hospital, Hertford (1552), Cheltenham Ladies College (founded by Miss Beale in 1853), North London Collegiate School (founded by Miss Buss in 1850), Roedean (1885), Wycombe Abbey (1896).

**Pulsars,** cosmic objects discovered in 1967 by the radio astronomy group at Cambridge; of great scientific interest because they are probably made of highly compressed matter. See F5.

**Puma,** a carnivorous mammal of the cat family found in the New World from Canada to Patagonia.

**Pyramids of Egypt,** on the west bank of the Nile, are vast stone or brick-built structures with inner chambers and subterranean entrances, built by the Pharaohs as royal tombs and dating from about 3000 B.C. The most celebrated are at Giza built during the 4th dynasty. The largest, originally 481 ft. high, is called the Great Pyramid, one of the seven wonders of the world, built by the Pharaoh Khufu, better known as Cheops, and there he was buried, 100,000 men, according to Herodotus, being employed for 20 years upon it. Chephren, successor of Cheops, erected the second pyramid, and the third was built by Mycerinus, a son of Cheops. The pyramid at Meidum built by King Snefru, founder of the 4th dynasty, is the most imposing of all. American and Egyptian scientists are cooperating in a project to X-ray (by means of cosmic rays) the interior of the Pyramid of Chephren.

**Pyrite,** the brassy-yellow crystalline form of iron disulphide. It can often be seen in coal; known as " fool's gold ".

**Pythons,** large snakes, non-poisonous, and destroying their prey by crushing it. Some species average 30 ft. in length, and prey upon deer and other small mammals. Found in Asia, Africa, and Australia. They lay eggs.

# Q

**Quadrant,** an astronomical instrument for measuring altitudes, superseded for navigational purposes in modern times by the sextant. It consists of a graduated arc of 90° with a movable radius for measuring angles on it.

**Quai d'Orsay.** An embankment in Paris where the French Foreign Office is situated.

**Quail,** an edible bird of the partridge family, of which only one species, the Common Quail, is found in England. It is not more than 8 in. long. It is found in most of the warmer regions of the world. In England and Wales the Quail is covered by the Wild Bird Protection Acts.

**Quair,** an old name for a pamphlet or little book.

**Quantum Theory.** The rapid development of quantum theory has been almost entirely due to the experimental and theoretical study of the interactions between electromagnetic radiation and matter. One of the first steps was taken when it was discovered that the electrons emitted from metals due to the action of ultraviolet radiation have an energy which is not related to the intensity of the incident radiation, but is dependent on its wavelength. Einstein showed in 1905 that this could only be explained on the basis that energy is transferred between radiation and matter in finite amounts, or *quanta*, which are inversely proportional to wavelength. See F13(1).

**Quarks** are hypothetical subnuclear particles recently postulated by theoretical physicists concerned with the so-called elementary particles. There are supposed to be three kinds, all carrying electrical charges which are fractions of those carried by familiar particles like electrons and protons. This and other special properties of quarks make them suitable for explaining the existence of the large number of other particles referred to on F13, 14. The physical existence of quarks may be demonstrated by experiment at any time and if this happens it will be an exciting truimph for speculative theoretical physics.

**Quartering,** in heraldry, is the disposition of various escutcheons or coats of arms in their proper " quarters " of the family shield, in such order as indicates the alliances with other families.

**Quartermaster,** a military officer charged with the provisioning and superintendence of soldiers in camp or barracks, and holding the equivalent rank to a lieutenant. The Quartermaster-General is an officer who presides over the provisioning department of the whole army. A Quartermaster in the Navy is a petty officer responsible to the Officer of the Watch; at sea for the correct steering of the ship and in harbour for the running of the ship's routine.

**Quarto,** a sheet of paper folded twice to make four leaves, or eight pages; usually abbreviated to " 4to."

**Quartz** is a common and usually colourless mineral, occurring both crystallised and massive. In the first form it is in hexagonal prisms, terminating in pyramids. When pure its specific gravity is 2·66. It is one of the constituents of granite, gneiss, etc. Among the quartz varieties are *rock crystal* (colourless), *smoky quartz* (yellow or brown), *amethyst* (purple), *rose quartz* (pink), and *milky quartz* (white). Quartz veins in metamorphic rocks may yield rich deposits of gold. Mining for gold in the rock is termed quartz-mining.

**Quasars**, or in preferred terminology, quasi-stellar radio-sources, form a new class of astronomical object, first identified in the period 1960 to 1962. They have small size, *i.e.*, they are like stars not galaxies; they have enormous energy output, and are at vast distances. Many are strong sources of radio waves and fluctuate in intensity. Their nature and cosmological significance have presented the major astronomical problem of the 1960s. *See* F5.

**Queen Anne's Bounty**, established by Queen Anne in 1704 for the augmentation of the maintenance of the poor clergy. Since April 1, 1948, Queen Anne's Bounty and the Ecclesiastical Commissioners ceased to exist and became embodied in the Church Commissioners for England.

**Queen's (or King's) Speech** is the speech prepared by the Government in consultation with the Queen and delivered by Her Majesty in person or by her deputy, at the opening or closing of a Parliamentary session.

**Quicksilver.** *See* Mercury.

**Quince**, a well-known hardy orchard tree, bearing fragrant, yellow, pear-shaped fruit. The correct botanical name for the Japanese quince or japonica is *Chaenomeles speciosa*. *See* T6.

**Quinine**, a vegetable alkaloid obtained from the bark of several trees of the *Cinchona* genus. It is colourless and extremely bitter. The drug, sulphate of quinine, is one of the most valuable medicines, forming a powerful tonic. It is antiperiodic, antipyretic, and antineuralgic. In cases of malaria it is the most efficacious remedy of natural origin known.

**Quintal metrique**, a French weight of 100 kilogrammes, or 220 lb, avoirdupois.

**Quirinal**, one of the seven hills of Rome.

**Quisling**, term which came into use during the second world war to denote traitor, collaborator, or fifth-columnist. After Vidkun Quisling, who became head of the puppet government after the German invasion of Norway in 1940.

**Quorum**, the number of members of any body or company necessary to be present at any meeting or commission before business can be transacted. The House of Commons needs a quorum of 40, the Lords a quorum of 3.

## R

**Rabbi**, a Jewish term applied to specially ordained officials who pronounce upon questions of legal form and ritual, and also generally accorded to any Jewish scholar of eminence.

**Rabbit.** *See* Z17.

**Raccoon**, plantigrade carnivorous mammals common to the American continent. There are several species. The common Raccoon (*Procyon lotor*) is about 2 ft. long, with a bushy ringed tail and sharp snout. Its skin is valuable.

**Race.** In the old text-books anthropologists were much concerned with the differences between the various races of Man: they described the Black Man (Negro), the Yellow Man (Mongol), the Red Man (American Indian), the Brown Man (Indian), and the White Man (European). Those who study Man from this point of view further subdivide each group into others. Thus White Man may be divided into Nordic, Alpine, and Mediterranean; Black Man into Hamitic, Bushman, and so on. Each of these groups tends to have physical traits which its members hold in common, although, of course, there are no *pure* racial types. All existing races have been fairly thoroughly mixed. What, in view of recent experience, is really important, is that races or even nations do not have psychological traits—at least not *innate* traits. Anthropology dismisses all theories of a superior race as unscientific: there is not the slightest evidence that one race differs in any way from another in its psychological

potentialities. Jews, Irish, Scots, Italians do differ (so do the inhabitants of Edinburgh and London): but their differences are due to their situation and not to anything inborn. *See* F46.

**Raceme**, an inflorescence in which the main stem bears stalked flowers, *e.g.*, lupin, foxglove. The youngest flowers are at the tip of this axis.

**Radar.** The basic principle of radar is very similar to that of sight. We switch on a light in the dark, and we *see* an object because the light waves are reflected from it and return to our eye, which is able to detect them. Similarly, the radar station *sees* an object because the invisible radio waves sent out from the transmitter are reflected from it and return to the receiver, which is able to detect them. Thus radar is the use of radio signals that man broadcasts.

The utilisation of radio waves for the detection of reflecting surfaces began with the classical experiment of the late Sir Edward Appleton in 1925, which he conducted in order to demonstrate the existence of the Heaviside layer in the upper atmosphere. During the course of the last war developments took place which tremendously improved the methods and instruments used. As in the case of so many of the inventions primarily developed for the purpose of waging war, many useful applications have been found for radar in times of peace, and, in particular, it has proved of great service as an aid to aerial and marine navigation, and in meteorology and astronomy. Radar astronomy investigates the solar system with the echoes of signals sent out from the Earth.

**Radiation**, energy emitted in the form of a beam of rays or waves, *e.g.*, acoustic (sound) radiation from a loudspeaker, radiant heat from a fire, $\beta$-radiation from a radioactive substance. The radiation of electromagnetic waves from a body depends on its temperature, the amount of energy radiated per second being proportional to the fourth power of the absolute temperature. The hotter the body, the shorter the wavelengths of the radiation; thus the colour of a glowing body depends on its temperature. Of paramount importance to us is radiation from the sun. Amongst other radiations, the sun sends ultra-violet, visible, and infra-red (heat) waves. The principal gases of the atmosphere are transparent to practically all of the solar and sky radiation and also that which the earth re-transmits to space. Carbon dioxide and water vapour, however, strongly absorb certain types, the latter, as clouds, playing an important rôle in regulating the temperature of the globe. The cooling of the ground on a clear night is a result of the outgoing long-wave radiation exceeding that coming down from the sky; at sunrise cooling ceases as the incoming radiation becomes sufficient to compensate for the loss of heat.

**Radiation, Cosmic.** *See* F3(2).

**Radio.** The theory of electromagnetic waves—of which the radio wave is one—was originated by the British physicist James Clerk Maxwell (F12). He showed that both electrical and optical phenomena in space are essentially similar in character, and that the waves if short in wavelength are those of light, and if of longer wavelength those of radio waves. Heinrich Hertz made many useful discoveries about the waves themselves, and about their behaviour under differing conditions, and also about the apparatus for producing them. Marconi developed the use of radio waves as a practical means of communication.

Radio methods are vital for the transmission of observed data from space vehicles back to earth, a process known as "telemetering." This is done by converting the observations into electrical pulses which actuate a suitable radio transmitter so that it radiates a signal, in coded form, which can be received at a ground station and decoded. The transmission of such a signal can also be remotely controlled by means of signals from the earth. Photographic and television techniques may also be employed for obtaining the desired information and sending it back to earth, as in the case of the Russian picture of the reverse side of the moon and the American pictures of the lunar surface. The information may be stored within the spacecraft for a time, and then, upon receipt of a particular radio signal from the earth transmitted by the spacecraft at a time convenient for its reception. Soviet scientists, by a special technique, were able in the case of their *Venus IV* probe (Oct. 1967) to parachute an instrumented canister from the spacecraft so that it could descend slowly to the surface of the planet—a feat described by Sir Bernard Lovell, who was recording the enterprise at Jodrell Bank, as "an experiment of classic elegance." *See also* Radio Astronomy, Telemetry.

**Radioactivity** is the spontaneous transformation of atomic nuclei, accompanied by the emission of ionising radiations. It was discovered in 1896 by Becquerel, who noticed that salts containing uranium sent off radiations which, like X-rays, can blacken a photographic plate. Two years later Marie and Pierre Curie discovered several new chemical elements which possessed the same property, but many times more intense than uranium, the most important of these was radium. Shortly afterwards it was established, mainly by Rutherford, that three types of radiations called α-, β-, and γ-rays, are emitted from radioactive substances. It was also Rutherford who, jointly with Soddy, deduced that the emission of the radiations is associated with the spontaneous disintegration of atoms which result in the transformation of one radioactive substance into another. A series of such transformations ends when a stable element is produced. All of the heavy radioactive elements can be arranged in three radioactive series, called, the uranium, thorium, and actinium series. Initially, radioactivity was thought to be a property confined only to a few elements occurring in nature. In 1934, however, Irene and Frederick Joliot-Curie discovered that ordinary elements can be transformed into radioactive forms by subjecting them to bombardment with α-particles. Following this, it was found that beams of other fast particles produced in accelerators can also render ordinary substances radioactive. Nowadays it is known that radioactivity is a general property of matter; any chemical element can be produced in one or more radioactive forms, or isotopes. *See* **F11.**

**Radio Astronomy.**—The science of radio astronomy makes use of radio apparatus and techniques for the observation of events occurring in far distant parts of the universe, and, in so doing, is able to enlarge upon the observational field of optical astronomy in a remarkable way. By means of radio telescopes it is possible to observe parts of the universe so far distant that the radio waves received have taken thousands of millions of years to travel from their source to the earth, and thus to observe happenings which may have occurred near the beginning of the history of the universe. Thus radio astronomy works with signals that are broadcast by objects in space.

There are two main types of radio telescope. The first, known as the interferometer, uses aerials spaced at large distances so as to cover a wide tract of ground. This has a high "resolution" but suffers from the disadvantage that it can "observe" only a very limited area of the sky overhead, as the earth turns upon its axis. The second, and "steerable," type, is that of the radio telescope at Jodrell Bank, Cheshire, which consists of an enormous concave metal bowl, with the radio aerials at its centre. This, though it has a lower "resolution," can be directed or "steered" on to any part of the sky which is above the horizon, and so can undertake a much more comprehensive observational programme. It can be used either to receive radio waves coming from desired sources or to transmit them and then pick up the echo from, for example, the moon or a planet, as in radar.

One source of radio waves which can be detected by radio telescopes is our own sun, whose behaviour under "quiet" and "abnormal" conditions can be observed in this way. Some of the planets also appear to emit radio waves from parts of their surface. But much more remarkable are the waves which are received from quasars (*q.v.*).

**Radiosonde,** a weather station in miniature carried aloft by a free balloon to heights normally in the neighbourhood of 10 miles. Signals representative of values of atmospheric pressure, temperature and humidity are transmitted simultaneously by radio to ground receiving apparatus. The position of the balloon at any instant can be determined by radar, enabling the speed and direction of the upper winds to be deduced.

**Radium,** a radioactive metal, symbol Ra, discovered by Marie and Pierre Curie in 1898. Atomic weight 226. The Radium Institute, founded and equipped by Lord Iveagh and Sir Ernest Cassel, was opened in 1911 for the treatment of patients and research into the effect of radium on the human system. Radiotherapy (use of X-rays from radium) is used in the treatment of cancer.

**Radon,** a radioactive gaseous element, symbol Rn, formed by radioactive decay of radium. Its discovery completed the series of elements known as the inert (or rare) gases.

**Rail,** a well-known genus of the *Rallidae* family, including the Water Rail, the Moorhen, Corncrake, and Coot, resident in the British Isles.

**Rain.** When moist air rises into lower temperatures and becomes saturated, condensation takes place on the numerous hygroscopic particles present in the atmosphere. If the temperature is above freezing a cloud of small droplets is formed, and as the air continues to rise they grow in size until the weight is great enough to make them fall to the earth as rain. The formation of large raindrops has been attributed to coagulation of smaller drops of different sizes, while another mechanism depends upon the presence in the cloud of ice crystals as well as water drops. In temperate latitudes snowflakes falling from the freezing level melt in the warmer air below, producing large raindrops which grow in their flight through the lower part of the cloud.

**Rainbow,** a beautiful colour effect visible to an observer with back to the sun and facing a rain shower, caused by the refraction and reflection of sunlight in minute water-droplets in the air. From high in the air it would be possible to see a rainbow as a complete circle, but from the ground the most that can be seen is a semicircle when the sun is just on the horizon; the higher the sun is, the smaller the arc of the rainbow. When conditions are suitable two bows are seen, the secondary with the colours of the spectrum reversed. The colours of the rainbow are seven: red, orange, yellow, green, blue, indigo, and violet—the colours of the spectrum. *See also* Aurora.

**Raingauge,** an instrument consisting of a deep metal funnel whose stem dips into a graduated glass jar from which the depth of the rain water collected can be read. Continuous records of rainfall are provided by self-registering instruments.

**Rain Making** is a facility long desired by mankind, especially in the drought-ridden regions, and attempted throughout history by numerous non-scientific means. Since the Second World War it has been proved that clouds can sometimes be made to rain or snow by dropping into them from an aeroplane very cold particles of solid carbon dioxide or certain chemicals. This makes the moisture of the cloud form tiny ice crystals which grow big and finally fall out of the cloud. The process is quite complicated and not fully understood and the practical exploitation is somewhat chancy at present, but experiments have been made in many countries and the United States has a considerable programme of study. As well as scientific there are commercial and legal problems; premature commercial exploitation has resulted in disillusionment in some cases.

**Rambouillet,** a royal French château (14th cent., rebuilt 18th cent.), near Paris, and the official summer residence of the President of the French Republic. Also the name of the famous literary salon of the Marquise de Rambouillet (1588–1665).

**Rampant,** in heraldry, is a term applied to the figure of an animal with forelegs elevated, the dexter uppermost. When the animal is shown side-faced it is *rampant displayed,* when full-face, *rampant guardant*; when looking back, *rampant requardant*; and when in sitting position *rampant sejant*.

**Rape,** a cruciferous plant yielding coleseed or rape-seed, extensively grown in all parts of Europe and India. Rape oil or colza is made from the seeds, and the leaves and refuse are used for sheep-food. Rape oil is a yellow, thick oil, of considerable commercial importance as a lubricant and for other purposes. It was at one time much used as an illuminant.

**Rare Gases** (also called **Inert Gases**). These are a group of elements which are chemically inert, comprising helium, neon, argon, krypton, xenon, and radon. Cavendish in 1785 noticed that there was in air some gas which was not oxygen, nitrogen, or carbon dioxide, but it was not until 1894 that the first of the rare gases was found by Rayleigh and Ramsay. This they called argon (inert). After the discovery of helium in 1895 Kayser, Rayleigh and Travers soon isolated the other gases except radon, which was later detected as a radioactive decay product of radium. Some of these inert gases are used to fill electric-light bulbs, and helium is used in balloons, since it is very light.

**Rat,** a well-known order of rodent embracing many species. The *brown rat* appeared in Europe early in the 18th cent., coming from the East and entering by way of Russia; now it is widespread and met with in Britain and all parts of the Continent. The *black rat*, which was the common rat before the arrival of the brown species, is a smaller animal and now comparatively scarce. There are numerous other kinds, all of them gross feeders, and existing in such numbers in many places as to constitute a pest. *See* Z13.

**Rationalism.** *See* J37.

**Rattlesnake,** venomous snakes which obtain their name from the possession of a rattle in the end of their tail, consisting of horny pieces so arranged that when vibrated they make a rattling sound. They are only found in N. and S. America.

**Raven,** a black-plumaged bird of the crow family, with raucous voice and massive bill. Occurs in many parts of Europe, Asia, and America. Ravens are easily domesticated and form interesting pets. Dickens had one which he described in *Barnaby Rudge*.

**Ray,** fish with a very flat body and broad and fleshy pectoral fins, related to the sharks. There are about 140 species. In Britain they are generally called *skate*.

**Razorbill,** a sea-bird of the auk family, having a high, furrowed bill and black-and-white plumage. It inhabits rocky cliffs during the breeding season, and at other times is mostly out on the open sea.

**Realism** is a vague term. For its use in philosophy *see* J38(1). As a movement in art it can be said to have started with Gustave Courbet in the mid-19th cent. in his revolt against the classicism of Ingres and the romanticism of Delacroix. He was a man of strong radical views, and like Zola, Balzac, and Flaubert in literature, turned to the actuality of everyday life, recording it with frankness and vigour. Some young English painters, notably Bratby, of the "kitchen sink" school, practise what some describe as social realism. In another sense, realism is an attitude concerned with interpreting the essential nature of the subject, revealing truths hidden by the accidentals of ordinary visual appearance. Thus form becomes more significant than content. Beginning with Cézanne and Van Gogh this trend passes on to Cubist and Abstract painting.

**Record Office,** in Chancery Lane, London, the place where the Public Records of England are preserved, including Domesday Book, the various Rolls of Charters, and important historical documents.

**Rectifier,** an electrical device which will allow electric current to flow in one direction only and can therefore be used for turning alternating current into direct current. Since electricity is usually supplied in alternating form and frequently needed in direct form, rectifiers are of very common use both in industry and the home, for example in radio and television and for battery chargers. Rectifying properties are possessed by a number of different devices, one of which is a thermionic diode (*see* Valve).

Very large valves filled with mercury vapour are often used for rectifying heavy currents for industrial purposes. Many other rectifiers use semiconductors in close contact with metals or with other semiconductors because such junctions have the property of passing electric current easily only in one direction.

**Recusants,** people who refused to attend the Anglican Church or to acknowledge the ecclesiastical supremacy of the Crown in the 16th and 17th cent.

**Red Crag,** the name given to a strata of gravel or sand, containing certain fossil mollusc deposits, found on the Suffolk and Norfolk coasts.

**Red Cross.** *See* Geneva Convention.

**Red-Letter Day,** a Church festival day indicated in the Prayer Book by red letters, now a popular term for any day of special significance.

**Redstart,** a small bird of the Thrush family of handsome plumage and striking song. Two species visit Great Britain; the Common Redstart, with bright chestnut rump and tail, white forehead, and black cheeks, favours wooded country, and the Black Redstart, with black breast and throat, chestnut tail and white wing bars, prefers rocky ground or bombed buildings, and has recently begun to breed in S. England.

**Redwing,** a bird of the Thrush family which finds its way to this country for the winter. Resembles the song thrush, but distinguished by smaller size, buffish-white eye-stripe, chestnut flanks and underwings. It has bred in Scotland and on Fair Isle.

**Redwood** *or* **Sequoia.** This genus of coniferous tree comprises two species of Redwoods occurring in N.W. America. Specimens of one species, the Giant Redwood, reach a height of over 300 ft. and a thickness of 36 ft. The age of the largest, the General Sherman tree, is put at 3,500 years.

**Referendum and Initiative,** two methods by which the wishes of electors may be expressed with regard to proposed legislation. It is developed to the highest extent in Switzerland. In a referendum some specific matter is referred to the electors. The Initiative is the means by which electors can compel their representatives to consider a specific issue. After consideration by the legislature it must then be submitted to the electorate for approval (*i.e.*, a referendum). Gen. de Gaulle has made use of the referendum in seeking the consent of the French nation for his policies. In a democracy a referendum should be preceded by a programme of education and public debate.

**Reformation.** *See* J38, 25.

**Reform Bills.** The principal Bills have been passed for the reform of the Parliamentary franchise. The first was the great Reform Bill of 1832, introduced by Lord John Russell and enacted under the Whig administration of Lord Grey. In addition to a sweeping redistribution of seats, this Act greatly extended the franchise but still left many people without the right to vote. The second Bill, passed by Disraeli in 1867, by giving the vote to workers in towns, established household suffrage. A third Bill, passed in 1884 under a Gladstone ministry, removed the distinction between borough and county franchises, enfranchised agricultural workers, and thus gave the vote to all men over 21. Women had to wait until 1918 to get the vote at the age of 30. The Representation of the People (Equal Franchise) Act, 1928, gave them the right to be registered as Parliamentary electors at the age of 21, thus making England into a true democracy. The Representation of the People Act, 1948, abolished the representation of the universities and the separate representation of the City of London and the business-premises vote.

**Refraction.** The change of direction which light rays and other rays undergo when passing from one medium to another. The phenomenon is due to the fact that in different media light (and other forms of radiation) has different speeds.

**Refractory,** a substance capable of standing high temperatures and therefore useful for making furnaces and allied apparatus. Some insulating refractories are fire-clay, alumina, porcelain, carborundum, graphite, and silica. Some refractory metals are platinum, molybdenum, tungsten, tantalum, and the alloys nichrome, chromel, alumel.

**Reindeer,** a genus of deer horned in both sexes, occurring only in northerly regions. It has an average height of 4 ft. 6 in., is very fleet of foot, and the Laplanders utilise it for draught purposes and for food.

**Relativity.** The laws of relativity have been substantially proved and have revolutionised our ideas as to the nature of space, time, matter, and energy and forced us to think along new lines. In 1949 a new theory by Einstein was announced which sets forth in a series of equations the laws governing both gravitation and electromagnetism, which is said to bridge the gap that separates the universe of the stars and galaxies and the universe of the atom. At present the one is explained by relativity, and the other rests on the quantum theory. *See* F15.

**Relief** in sculpture is of three kinds—high relief (*alto-relievo*), in which the figures stand out to the extent of one-half of their natural proportions, low-relief (*basso-relievo*) when the figures project but slightly; and middle-relief (*mezzo-relievo*), when the projection is intermediate.

**Renaissance.** *See* J38.

**Republican Party** of the United States was born by the fusion in 1854 of the group who called themselves National Republicans, having split from the Democrats over tariffs in 1825, and the northern Democrats, both of them being opposed to slavery. It came to power when Abraham Lincoln was elected President in 1860 and won 14 of the 18 presidential elections held between 1860 and 1932. It was defeated in 1932 largely as a result of the economic depression and reached its lowest ebb in the years of Roosevelt's New Deal (*q.v.*). The Party went on being defeated every four years until Eisenhower's victory in 1952. Nixon narrowly failed to defeat Kennedy in 1960 and Goldwater was decisively beaten by Lyndon Johnson in 1964. In 1968 Nixon was successful in winning the Presidency. The Party has its interventionist and its isolationist wings, its hawks (conservatives) and its doves (liberals). The symbol of the party is an elephant, the invention of Nash, a cartoonist, in 1874. *See also* C22(1).

**Requiem.** Properly a mass for the dead, the term is extended to cover musical settings by Palestrina, Mozart, Verdi, and others.

**Reredos,** the ornamental screen at the back of the altar or communion table. It is often of a highly decorative character and is an architectural feature in many churches in Spain. Other examples are to be found in the following cathedrals in England: Southwark, St. Albans, Winchester, Durham, and Liverpool.

**Resins,** natural resins are vegetable compounds largely employed in the industrial arts. They comprise india-rubber, amber, mastic, copal, etc. "Synthetic resins" is a term sometimes used as a synonym for "plastics."

**Reuter,** an international news agency, organised since 1941 as a trust and owned by the newspapers of Britain, Australia, and New Zealand, founded by Baron J. de Reuter in 1849.

**Rhea,** a large flightless bird, the "ostrich" of S. America, distinguished from the ostrich proper by smaller size, longer beak, larger wings, no tail and 3 toes instead of 2. There are 2 species.

**Rheology,** the science of flow. *See* F17(2).

**Rhesus Factor.** *See* Index to Section P.

**Rhinoceros,** a large hoofed quadruped, of which there are nine existing species native to the river and marsh regions of Africa, India, Borneo, and Java. It is remarkable for its thick hide and upturned snout, from which springs a long horn. The white rhinoceros, which is scarce, is the biggest species, attaining a length of 10–12 ft. and a height of from 5 to 6 ft.

**Rhodium,** a metallic element, symbol Rh, discovered by Wollaston in 1804. It is found in platinum ores in small amounts, generally less than 2 per cent. With platinum it gives a very hard and durable alloy. It is also used, instead of silver, in putting the reflecting layer on a mirror.

**Ribbon Fish** *or* **Oarfish,** a deep-sea fish, deriving its name from its ribbon-like shape. Though many feet in length, it is only an inch or two thick. The ribbon fish is rarely met with because of its habitat, and most of what is known about it has been learnt from specimens occasionally cast ashore during storms.

**Rice,** a grain-yielding grass, of which thousands of strains are known today, extensively cultivated in China, India, and certain parts of America, and forming the main food of the peoples of China, Japan, India, and the Malayan regions. Some 95 per cent. of the world's rice is produced and consumed in the Orient. The grain with the husk is known as " paddy." Arrack, an alcoholic liquor, is made from fermented rice seeds.

**Rime,** a crystalline deposit of ice formed on objects exposed to wet fog at the same time as frost.

**Rinderpest** *or* Cattle Plague, is a highly contagious disease affecting cattle, sheep, and other ruminants. In Europe the disease has been eradicated, but it was formerly very widespread and caused great loss of life amongst cattle. The disease is caused by a filtrable virus, and is attended by fever and congestion of the mucous membranes.

**Ring Dove** *or* Wood Pigeon, a blue-grey bird, distinguished from other pigeons by larger size (16 in.), white wing-bar, glossy green-and-purple neck, and white half-collar. It is very common in Britain.

**Rituale,** the book of rites used in the Roman Catholic Church for the administration of certain sacraments and other church ceremonies. Like the Roman breviary, it dates in its present form from the Council of Trent.

**RNA.** (Ribonucleic Acid). *See* Nucleic Acids.

**Roaring Forties,** name applied to the prevailing westerly winds over the oceans in the temperate latitudes of the Southern Hemisphere.

**Robin** (or **Redbreast**). A small bird with olive-brown upper parts and orange-red forehead, throat, and breast; both sexes look alike. The young are speckled, lacking the red breast. Its wide European distribution includes the British Isles, where it is the national bird. It also occurs in N. Africa and W. Asia. The nest is placed in a great variety of situations including holes in banks, trees, and walls; in sheds, amongst ivy, and sometimes in old tins. Nesting-boxes are readily adopted, but care should be taken to ensure that the entrance-hole is small enough to exclude starlings. Robins are pugnacious and defend their territories with vigour. Their attractive appearance, trustful disposition, engaging ways, and sweet song make them extremely popular. The name robin is also applied to a number of very different birds, one of which, the American Robin, occasionally wanders to Europe.

**Rock Dove,** the grey pigeon *Columba livia* of Europe and Asia, ancestor of the domestic pigeons as Darwin was the first to show.

**Rockets** for use in war were first studied by Sir William Congreve early in the 19th cent., and proved very destructive in siege operations. They were invented by the Chinese as long ago as the 11th cent. The Germans devised the huge V2 rocket, carrying a ton of explosive, which was used near the end of the war to bombard London. Rockets are propelled by the burning of fuel (*e.g.*, oxygen or nitric acid), the exhaust, being ejected at high velocity, thrusts the rocket forward. For the study of the properties of the atmosphere vertical sounding rockets are used. Rocket flight in outer space was first presented as practicable by the Russian rocket expert, K. E. Tsiolkovsky, in 1903. The provision of sufficient launching velocity involves the use of rocket motors with adequate thrust. To launch a satellite into an orbit circulating within a few hundred miles of the surface a velocity of 18,000 m.p.h. must be imparted. This may be done by using a multi-stage launching system. When the first-stage motor has burned out it drops off, so that, when the second-stage motor ignites, it does not have to support the weight of the first-stage, and so on. If the launching velocity is increased to 25,000 m.p.h. the vehicle will not return to the neighbourhood of the earth but pass out of the range of the earth's gravitational pull completely. Unless the launching velocity reaches 100,000 m.p.h. it will not escape from the sun and will become an artificial planet. *See also* Space Research.

**Rock Magnetism.** The study of naturally occurring magnetism in rocks is a subject which has gained considerable importance in recent years.

There are two principal reasons for this. One is that this so-called "fossilised magnetism" may be able to tell us more about the past history of the earth's magnetic field. The other is that after many years of heated dispute between geologists rock magnetism promises to settle once and for all the controversy as to whether or not the continents have changed their relative positions in past times (continental drift theory (*q.v.*)). This branch of geophysical research, in addition to its academic interest, may well have important economic consequences. It might, for instance, become possible to locate mineral deposits once accumulated under special conditions at certain latitudes but now drifted to other places. Salt and similar deposits formed by the continuous evaporation of solutions in hot countries are one example; oil may well be another. There has been a *steady* change in rock magnetisation direction with geological time. It is now known with some accuracy that the most recent reversal took place 700,000 years ago. It has been found that the older the rock, the farther removed is its fossil magnetisation from the present field.

**Rococo**, an architectural style which was, in effect, the final stage of Baroque (*q.v.*). The name first came into use about 1830 to describe the period 1720–70 and means "shell-shaped" (French *Rocaille*), since the shell was a favourite motif in Rococo ornamentation. About the beginning of the early 18th cent. the heavy older type of Baroque began to show even less restraint than had characterised it in the past; it became still less utilitarian, and showed a kind of playful lighthearted vitality which manifested itself in a wealth of ornamental invention. Baroque was flamboyant and robust, Rococo frivolous. In architecture Rococo is naturally found in those areas where the Baroque had flourished, *i.e.*, Munich, Prague, Vienna, and Dresden. In painting, the best expressions of Rococo are to be seen in the works of the French painters Watteau (d. 1721), Boucher (d. 1770), a favourite of Mme de Pompadour, and famous as a decorator of boudoirs, and Fragonard (d. 1806). (As in the case of Baroque, it was typical of Rococo that the sculpture, painting, and the decorative arts of a building all expressed the same spirit.)

**Roe**, popular name given to organs in fish which produce eggs and sperms. "Hard roe" is that of the female and consists of eggs; that of the male is the soft roe or milt.

**Roebuck**, a deer that was formerly common in the forests and parks of Britain, but is now only found at large in the northern parts of Scotland.

**Roller**, a tropical Old World bird of the *Coraciidae* family, related to the hoopoe, kingfisher and bee-eater, of strikingly brilliant blue, chestnut, greenish-blue plumage. There are fifteen species, one of which breeds in the far north and visits the British Isles on its migrations to and from its winter quarters in Africa.

**Romanesque Architecture**, prevailed throughout Europe from the mid-10th to the 13th cent., and implies an art which developed from that of the Romans. Notable in Romanesque style were the rounded arch and masonry vaulting. Romanesque led to the graceful and more complex Gothic (*q.v.*). The Italians never regarded Gothic highly and Romanesque churches, generally based on the basilican plan (oblong with double colonnades and a semi-circular apse at the end), continued to be built there until the beginning of the 15th cent. Some of the best examples can be seen at Pisa (11th cent.), Florence (San Miniato, 1013), Lucca (12th cent.), and Milan (the 12th cent. San Ambrogio, most famous of all). In Germany Romanesque architecture flourished longer than in France or England; the most famous churches are in the valley of the Rhine, at Cologne (completely destroyed during the second world war), Mainz and Speyer. In France Romanesque churches are found in Burgundy, Provence and Normandy. For English Romanesque *see* Norman Architecture.

**Roman Roads**, highways constructed by the Romans. They were of great durability. The best known British roads were Ermine Street (London, Lincoln, York), Fosse Way (Lincoln through Leicester, Cirencester, Bath, Exeter), Watling Street (London to Shropshire).

**Romanticism**, a term for a movement in the arts—whether in music, painting, sculpture or literature—which seeks to give expression to the artist's feelings about his subject rather than to be concerned with form or reality. The romantic view is that art is nature seen through a temperament; the realist view is that art is a slice of life. In painting Delacroix (1798–1863) is the romantic artist par excellence with his uncontrolled expression of the passions and love of the exotic. In literature the Romantic movement reached its finest form in the works of Goethe, Schiller, and Heine; in the poetry of Byron, Keats, Wordsworth, Shelley and Blake; and in the writings of Victor Hugo. Since Romanticism is partly a matter of temperament in the artist just as Classicism is, it may be found at all times and places, although whether or not it becomes predominent depends on contemporary taste. Cubism, for example, with its attention to form is classical, whereas Surrealism with its attention to content is romantic. *See also* Romantic Movement. J39.

**Roman Walls** were built as frontier barriers under the Emperors Hadrian (76–138) and Antoninus Pius (86–161). Hadrian's works, linking Wall-send-on-Tyne with Bowness-on-Solway, comprised a twenty-foot stone wall, ditches, turrets, "milecastles," fortresses, and a double earthen mound, or "Vallum." Impressive ruins are still visible at Chesters and Housesteads. Antoninus Pius, Hadrian's successor, made a further advance, but the turf wall which he built between Forth and Clyde was soon abandoned. Septimius Severus (146–211) restored Hadrian's wall after the assassination of Commodus and the subsequent civil wars. It was finally abandoned between 380 and 390.

**Rood Screen**, an ornamental partition, separating the choir from the nave in a church, and supporting a crucifix or rood.

**Rook**, a member of the crow family, abounding in most parts of the British Isles and found in Europe, Asia, and N. Africa. It has been introduced into New Zealand. Rooks usually nest in colonies in tall trees. They are highly intelligent birds, and their ways have long been the subject of much careful study.

**Rosary**, a circular chain of beads, used by Catholics when reciting a particular form of sustained prayer. Each bead represents an entire prayer, and the combined prayers constitute the Rosary.

**Roses, Wars of the** (1455–85), between the rival houses of York and Lancaster, for the possession of the English crown, began in the reign of Henry VI, and ended with the death of Richard III. on Bosworth Field. The emblem or badge of the Lancastrians was the red rose and of the Yorkists the white rose. All rivalry between the Roses ended by the marriage of Henry VII., the Lancastrian, with the Princess Elizabeth, daughter of Edward IV., the Yorkist.

**Rosetta Stone**, discovered in 1799 by the French at Rosetta in Egypt, and deposited in the British Museum. It is a piece of black basalt about 3 ft. long, and contains a decree of the Egyptian priests of Ptolemy V. Epiphanes (205–181 B.C.) in (1) hieroglyphics, (2) demotic, and (3) Greek characters. It was by means of the three different inscriptions on the same stone that hieroglyphic writing was first able to be deciphered.

**Rotten Row**, a corruption of *route de roi* (king's drive), the famous riding resort in Hyde Park.

**Rouge et Noir**, a well-known gambling card game played on a table divided into two sections and marked with two black and two red lozenges. Any number of players can take part, and the money is staked on the red or black spaces. The cards are dealt out, first to Noir, until the pips aggregate more than 30; then in like manner to the Rouge, and the packet coming nearest to 31 wins the stakes.

**Roulette**, a gambling game played on a table carrying a revolving wheel divided into 37 compartments. Each compartment bears a number, 0 (zero) and 1 to 36. The numbers are mixed and do not follow any particular order. Of these 37 numbers 18 are black and 18 are red, whereas zero is green. The players stake their money on any compartment, colour, or combination of numbers they please.

The wheel is whirled round and a ball is set rolling in the opposite direction, dropping finally into one of the compartments, thus deciding the winning number and colour.

**Roundhead.** In the reign of Charles I. and later, a Puritan or member of the Parliamentary party who wore his hair cut short. It was originally a term of derision applied by the Royalists, who usually wore ringlets.

**Round Towers,** high circular towers with conical roof and massive masonry walls, built during the early Middle Ages (c. 10th cent.) It is believed that they served as refuges and lookouts. These buildings are numerous in Ireland, and three remain in Scotland, including that at Brechin which is attached to the church.

**Royal Academy of Arts** was founded in London in 1768, under the patronage of George III. The early exhibitions of the Academy were held first in Pall Mall, and after in Somerset House, where the exhibitions continued to be held until 1836, when the National Gallery being built, the Academy moved its quarters to that building. In 1869 the present Royal Academy at Burlington House was opened. The Academy numbers 58 R.A.s and about 30 A.R.A.s. List of presidents: Sir Joshua Reynolds (1768), Benjamin West (1792), James Wyatt (1805), B. West (1806), Sir Thomas Lawrence (1820), Sir M. A. Shee (1830), Sir C. Eastlake (1850), Sir F. Grant (1866), Lord Leighton (1878), Sir J. E. Millais (1896), Sir E. J. Poynter (1896), Sir Aston Webb (1919), Sir F. Dicksee (1924), Sir William Llewellyn (1928), Sir E. Lutyens (1938), Sir A. J. Munnings (1944), Sir Gerald F. Kelly (1949), Sir A. E. Richardson (1954), Sir Charles Wheeler (1956) and Walter T. Monnington (1966). The Academy holds an exhibition of pictures, statuary, and architectural designs every summer.

**Royal Hospital,** Chelsea, built by Wren, was opened in 1694 as an institution for invalid soldiers.

**Royal Institution,** established 1799, and incorporated by Royal Charter in 1800 for "the promotion, extension, and diffusion of Science and of Useful Knowledge." It was in the building of the Institution that Faraday conducted his experiments. It supports four professors: natural philosophy, astronomy, chemistry, and physiology. Famous also for its Christmas lectures designed for a juvenile audience.

**Royal Society** was founded in 1660 and incorporated by Royal Charter in 1662, Viscount Brouncker being named the first president. Its *Philosophical Transactions* date from 1665. Among those who served as president of the Royal Society are Sir Christopher Wren, Pepys, Sir Isaac Newton, Sir Joseph Banks, Sir Humphry Davy, Prof. T. H. Huxley, Lord Rayleigh, Sir Archibald Geikie, Sir J. J. Thomson, O.M., Prof. Sir C. S. Sherrington, O.M., G.B.E., Lord Rutherford, O.M., Sir William Henry Bragg, O.M., Sir Henry Dale, O.M., Sir Robert Robinson, O.M., Lord Adrian, O.M., Sir Cyril Hinshelwood, O.M., Lord Florey, O.M., and Lord Blackett O.M. (1966).

**Rubber,** produced from the juice of certain trees and shrubs of tropical countries, is in such extensive demand now for tyres and other purposes that rubber plantations have been established in almost every part of the world where rubber can be grown, particularly in Malaysia and Indonesia. The best kinds come from the Amazon valley. In recent years great advances have been made in the production of synthetic rubber.

**Rubicon,** a small river falling into the Adriatic, and forming one of the Italian boundaries, the crossing of which anciently involved decisive action and constituted a declaration of war. Thus the phrase "crossing the Rubicon", denoting an act from which there is no withdrawal.

**Rubidium,** a metallic element, symbol Rb, most closely resembling potassium. It is silver-white and very soft, and was discovered in 1861 by Bunsen and Kirchoff, using the spectroscope. It is rare, occurring in small amounts in the mica called lepidolite and in potash salts of the Strassfurt deposits in Germany.

**Rubrics** are instructions in regard to the ceremonies of the Church, appearing in red in the Prayer Book.

**Ruby** is a deep red variety of Corundum (aluminium oxide); one of the most valued of precious stones. Burma yields some of the finest, and rubies of inferior colour are found in Siam, Ceylon, South Africa, and Brazil.

**Rudd,** a fresh-water fish of wide distribution, plentiful in the rivers of Britain, and found in most other parts of Europe, also in Asia Minor. It is of a reddish-gold colour, with a greenish-blue beard.

**Ruff,** a bird related to the common sandpiper, at one time common in the Fen districts. The males have a ruff of feathers round the neck in the breeding season. The female is the Reeve.

**Ruffe** or **Pope,** a small fresh-water fish common in most parts of central Europe, and similar in appearance to the ordinary perch. It is found in British rivers.

**"Rule, Britannia !"** the national sea-song of England, was written by James Thomson (1700–48), the author of the "Seasons," and set to music by Dr. Arne about 1740. The poet's words were "Britannia, rule the waves!" but it is usually rendered "Britannia rules the waves."

**Rum,** an ardent spirit distilled from molasses, and containing from 40 to 50 per cent. of alcohol. It is chiefly manufactured in the West Indies, and derives its special flavour from a volatile oil.

**Ruminants,** animals that chew the cud, being provided with a compartmented stomach, enabling them to swallow food, and later to bring it back to the mouth for mastication; e.g., sheep, goats, oxen, etc. While in the rumen, or storage compartment, some digestion of food, especially cellulose, takes place by bacterial action.

**Runcible spoon,** a kind of fork used for pickles having three broad prongs. The word was used by Edward Lear about 1870 as a nonsense word and may be derived from *Rouncival* meaning large or huge from the bones said to have been dug up at *Roncesvalles* where Roland fell. Rouncival peas are the large peas called "marrowfats."

**Runes,** certain characters of an alphabet found in inscriptions in the Germanic languages, discovered cut upon stone monuments and implements found in many parts of Europe, including England. The runic alphabet originally had 24 letters. Scholars agree that some of the runes derive from Greek and others from Latin.

**Ruskin College,** the first residential college for working people, founded at Oxford in 1899 by Mr. Walter Vrooman, an American.

**Rusts,** parasitic fungi, some common species of which have reddish spores which in a mass have a rusty appearance. A well-known species is the Wheat Rust (*Puccinia graminis*), which has an alternative host in the barberry.

**Ruthenium,** a greyish-white metallic element, symbol Ru, discovered by Claus in 1845. It is harder and more brittle than platinum, in whose ores it occurs.

**Rutile,** mineral titanium dioxide. It is found in many igneous rocks, and in gneisses and schists. Its commonest colour is reddish-brown.

## S

**Sabaoth,** a Hebrew word, meaning an army or host, and applied sometimes to the Supreme Being, e.g., "the Lord of Hosts" (Rom. ix. 29).

**Sabbath and Sunday.** Sunday, or the Lord's Day, is the first day of the week in the Christian year. It was substituted for the Jewish Sabbath in the 1st cent. A.D. as the Christian day of worship in commemoration of the Resurrection. The Sabbath, in the Jewish system, was the last day of the week (Saturday in the Christian calendar), designated as the day of religious rest in the fourth commandment of the Decalogue. It was the Puritans at the time of the Reformation who applied the term Sabbath to the Christian Sunday and the two terms have been used indiscriminately ever since.

**Sabbatical Year** was instituted by the Jews in ancient times for the purpose of giving the soil a rest from cultivation. This was every seventh year. In universities a sabbatical year is a year of absence from duty for the purpose of study and travel, granted to professors at certain intervals.

**Sable,** a furred mammal of the weasel family

mainly inhabiting Siberia. It is bright brown in colour, and has a long, bushy tail. American sable is a marten.

**Saccharin,** a white crystalline solid manufactured from toluene, 550 times as sweet as cane sugar. It is used as a sweetening agent; as a substitute for sugar when sugar is forbidden, as in certain diseases, or when there is a shortage. It has no value as a food.

**Sack,** the white dry wines of Spain and Madeira, canary being the most popular.

**Safety Lamp,** as used in coal mines, was invented by Sir Humphry Davy in 1816. The flame is enclosed in a cage of fine-meshed wire which allows air to enter and promote burning, but conducts away the heat generated in combustion so that no product of combustion escapes at a temperature high enough to ignite explosive gases in the mine.

**Sainfoin,** a widely cultivated forage plant, especially adapted for sheep. It is of strong, leafy growth and bears bright red flowers. It belongs to the same family of flowering plants as peas and beans.

**St. Elmo's Fire,** a glowing brush-like discharge of electricity which takes place from sharp-pointed objects on mountains or the masts of ships exposed to the intense electric fields of thunder-clouds.

**Salamanders** are amphibia superficially resembling lizards, from which they differ in having a moist skin and no scales.

**Salic Law** was probably instituted in France in the 5th cent. for the purpose of excluding females from inheriting the Crown. The Bourbons introduced the same law into Spain, but this was abolished by decree in 1830 to enable Isabella II. to succeed.

**Salicylic Acid** can be obtained from the flowers of the meadow-sweet, and from oil of wintergreen, but is now usually prepared by the action of carbon dioxide on sodium phenate under pressure. The acid is then prepared from the sodium salicylate. It is used as an antiseptic and has been used as a food preservative. Aspirin is a derivative of salicylic acid.

**Salmon,** a familiar fish notable for its habit of ascending rivers from the sea in the autumn and there depositing its spawn, not returning to the sea until the early spring. The salmon fishing season varies from place to place.

**Saltpetre.** See Nitre.

**Salvarsan,** the organic arsenical compound arsphenamine, which Ehrlich discovered was able to kill inside the human body the spirochæte germ that causes syphilis. Also known as "606." It has been superseded by neosalvarsan.

**Salvation Army.** See J39.

**Sanctuaries** were places where offenders against the law were free from arrest, and previous to 1697, when sanctuaries were suppressed, several parts of London were treated as sanctuaries. The chief of these refuge localities was in Whitefriars. There were others in the Minories, Mitre Court, the Savoy, Westminster, and the Mint. Other sanctuaries were at Beverley and at St. Burian's in Cornwall.

**Sanderling,** small wading bird of sandpiper family; breeds in tundra regions of far north, and is seen on sandy beaches of Britain as a winter visitor. Conspicuous white wing stripe and, like Curlew, Sandpiper, Knot, Dunlin, and other members of sandpiper family, has marked change of plumage between winter and summer.

**Sandpiper,** small- to medium-sized wading birds of several species whose migratory powers are so great that they are found in most parts of the world. They include the Common Sandpiper, a bird about 7 in. long, greenish-brown head and back, white under-parts; beak long and slender. Other species met with in Britain are the Green, Purple, Wood, and Curlew-Sandpipers.

**Sans-culottes** (French = without knee breeches), a term applied by the French aristocrats to the revolutionary leaders during the French Revolution who wore long trousers instead of knee breeches.

**Sanskrit** is the language of ancient India, spoken by the Brahmins, and existing in early Oriental literature. It was the language of literature and government and is now confined to temples and places of learning. Its relationship to the modern Indian languages is rather like that of Latin and Greek to modern European languages. See also M37(1).

**Saponin.** The term is a generic one applied to a range of organic compounds which produce frothy, soapy solutions. Saponins are extracted from the soapwort root, horse chestnut seeds, etc. Saponin is the basis of the "foam" used for fire fighting; it can be used like soap to make insecticides and fungicides adhere to the leaves of plants. Also used as detergents.

**Sapphic Verse,** a form of verse said to have been invented by Sappho, the lyric poetess of Lesbos, who flourished about 600 B.C.

**Sapphire,** a valuable deep blue variety of Corundum (aluminium oxide) found mostly in India, Ceylon, and Northern Italy. Synthetic sapphire is often used for gramophone styli.

**Saprophytes.** A term applied to plants which feed on dead organic matter. Many fungi are saprophytes.

**Saracen,** the name given in classic times to the Arab tribes of Syria and adjacent territories. In the Middle Ages the current designation among the Christians for their Muslim enemies.

**Sarcophagus,** the name given to a stone coffin, such as was used by the ancient Egyptians, Greeks, and Romans, for receiving the remains of their famous dead. These sarcophagi were often decorated with rich carvings and sculptures.

**Sardonyx.** See Onyx.

**Sarrusophone,** bears the same relation to the Oboe as the Saxophone does to the Clarinet (i.e., it has a metal tube and a double-reed mouthpiece). The Contrabass Sarrusophone is sometimes used instead of the Double Bassoon.

**Sassanides** were a dynasty of Persian rulers descended from Artaxerxes from 226 to 652.

**Satellites** are small planets revolving round the larger ones. The moon is the earth's only satellite. Jupiter has twelve; Saturn, nine; Uranus, five; Mars, two; and Neptune, two. A number of artificial earth satellites have been launched by America and Russia since Oct. 1957.

**Satin-Bird,** one of the bower birds of Australia; the male is silky blue-back and the female greyish green. See Bower Bird.

**Satinwood,** the timber of a tree plentiful in India and Ceylon, and valued for cabinet work. It is of fine grain and very hard. Varieties also exist in the West Indies, Florida, and Tasmania.

**Satrap,** the name given in ancient times to a Persian Governor of a Province.

**Saturday,** the seventh day of the week (the Jewish Sabbath), derived its name from Saturn, or, as some hold, is called after the Saxon idol, Saterne, which was worshipped on this day.

**Saturn,** a planet, the sixth from the sun, from which it is distant about 886 millions of miles, and around which it makes a revolution in about twenty-nine and a half years. It is about 71,500 miles in mean diameter, or nine times as large as the earth, and rotates on its axis in ten and a quarter hours. It is surrounded by a series of rings composed of myriads of tiny satellites. It has nine small satellites. See F7.

**Saturnalia,** festivals held in ancient Rome in honour of the god Saturnus. They were made the scene of the most boisterous festivities, and were continued for several days at the end of December.

**Sawfish,** a large marine ray found in tropical America and Guinea, whose snout often attains the length of several feet, and is provided with saw-like teeth. This "saw" is swung from side to side among a shoal of fish which form the food of this ray.

**Sawfly.** These insects are considered to be the most primitive members of the order (Hymenoptera) to which the bees and wasps belong. In appearance they resemble somewhat the latter, but there is no waist separating thorax and abdomen. The ovipositor is never used as a sting; usually it is saw-like so that the female can use it to make incisions into tissues of plants where the eggs are laid. The larvae look like caterpillars of butterflies and moths. One of the commonest species occurs on gooseberry bushes.

**Saxons,** a Teutonic race originally inhabiting what is now Holstein. By the 7th cent. they had, with the Angles and Jutes, conquered and colonised most of England.

**Scald,** the name of the Norse poets, who were

similar to the bards of Wales. They had to celebrate the achievements of their warriors and leaders.

**Scallop,** marine bivalve molluscs of the genus *Pecten*, which is widely distributed. The scalloped edge to the shell results from a pattern of radiating grooves. Related to the oyster.

**Scandium,** a metal element, symbol Sc. It was discovered in 1879 by Nilson, and occurs in small quantities in certain rarer minerals such as wolframite.

**Scapular,** a vestment hanging from the shoulder to the knees, worn by members of certain Roman Catholic orders. The name is also given to two small pieces of cloth worn over the shoulders by lay members of the Church in honour of the Virgin.

**Scarabaeidae,** a family of beetles (Scarabs) widely distributed through Africa and Asia and the inner parts of Europe. It is to this genus that the " Sacred Beetle " of the Egyptians belongs, and numerous representations of it are found on ancient monuments.

**Sceptre,** the staff or rod constituting the symbol of supreme authority. Tarquin, the elder, was the first Roman to assume the sceptre in 468 B.C. The French kings of the 5th cent. made a golden rod their sceptre.

**Schism,** an ecclesiastical term for division in a church. The Great Schism was the separation of the Greek Church from the Latin, finally established in 1054. The Western Schism was the division in the Roman Catholic Church from 1378 to 1417, when there were two lines of popes, one at Rome and one at Avignon, which arose over the election of Urban VI. and Clement VII. to the papacy and was more a matter of persons and politics than a question of faith.

**Schist,** the geological name of certain metamorphic rocks composed for the most part of minerals with thin plate-like crystals (*e.g.*, mica) so that the layers of a schist are closely parallel. Quartz occurs in schists, and where it preponderates the term " quartz schist " is applied.

**Scientific Units.** The International Bureau of Weights and Measures at Sèvres near Paris, is the custodian of accurate scientific measurement in terms of internationally agreed units. Methods of measurement are continually being improved and measurements of new kinds coming into use. In defining units certain principles have evolved which can be expressed as a statement of priorities:

(i) units should be so defined that measurements made in one laboratory should be reproducible in another with as much consistency as possible;

(ii) units of all kinds should, so far as practical, form an interrelated system based on as few fundamental units as possible;

(iii) the fundamental units adopted should have a natural basis, independent of particular man-made objects such as metal bars or weights. An invariable universal natural standard was achieved for the metre in 1958 when it was defined in terms of the wavelength of a line in the spectrum of krypton-86. *See* **S.I. Units.**

**Schoolmen,** the great scholastic philosophers of the Middle Ages who devoted themselves to the study and exposition of questions of religious inquiry, and attempted to reconcile the teaching of the Church with that of Aristotle. The chief Schoolmen were Archbishop Anselm, Albertus Magnus, Thomas Aquinas, Peter Lombard, Duns Scotus. *See also* **J39(2).**

**Scorpion.** The scorpions constitute an order of the arthropods. Distinctive features are the pair of powerful claws at the head and a " sting " at the tail, which curves over the back in attack or defence so that it points forwards. The poison injected by the sting is potent, causing instant death in spiders, centipedes, etc., and acute discomfort to humans. The idea that a cornered scorpion can sting itself to death is a myth; scorpions are immune to their own poison.

**Scorpion Fly.** The scorpion fly, of which there are less than 500 species, constitute a separate order of insects, the *Mecoptera*. They have 2 pairs of membranous wings, and gain their popular name because in some species the end of the abdomen is turned up, though it does not function as a sting.

**Scree** *or* **Talus,** the mass of loose, angular rock fragments which accumulate towards the bottom of hill-sides and mountain-sides. These fragments have been detached by weathering processes, in particular frost action.

**Scythians,** nomadic conquerors and skilled horsemen of ancient times (9th–3rd cent. B.C.) who inhabited much of Southern Europe and Asiatic Russia.

**Sea Anemones** *or* **Actinaria,** an order of marine animals of the coelenterate class *Anthozia*. They form a large and varied group of about 1,100 species and occur in many beautiful colours, flower-like in form.

**Sea Butterfly,** marine molluscs which propel themselves by two " wings," or side expansions of the foot. They constitute the order called *Pteropoda*.

**Sea Cow.** *See* Manatee.

**Sea Cucumbers** *or* **Holothurians.** These animals constitute the class of echinoderms called *Holothuroidea*. They are elongated and worm-like, with a ring of about twenty tentacles round the mouth. There are about 500 species.

**Sea Eagle,** a genus of flesh-eating birds related to the true eagles, kites, and other birds of prey. Examples are the Bald Eagle, emblem of the U.S.A., White-tailed Eagle (Grey Sea Eagle), and Steller's Sea Eagle of the Pacific coast of Asia. Last known in Britain in 1911.

**Sea Elephant** *or* **Elephant Seal,** a curious genus of seal, the males of which possess a proboscis a foot or more in length that suggests an elephant's trunk. They are found on the coast of California and in certain parts of the Southern Ocean; their blubber has a commercial value.

**Sea Gravimeter,** a new instrument to determine the density of the earth's crust beneath the oceans of the world. Designed by Dr. A. Graf of Munich and Dr. J. Lamar Worzel of Columbia University, it can detect changes of one-millionth of the value of gravity at the earth's surface and is being used in the oceanographical research programme of the I.G.Y.

**Sea Hare,** a genus of molluscs (*Aplysia*), so-called because of resemblance to a crouching hare. The shell is thin curved plate largely sunk in the animal's body. They have four tentacles, occur in Britain in the laminaria or ribbon-wrack zone, and discharge a purple fluid when molested.

**Sea Horse,** a sea-fish (*Hippocampus*), very numerous in the tropics and comprising some twenty species. Their bodies are ringed and they have prehensile tails. Their heads are horse-shaped, and they swim in a vertical position.

**Sea Lily.** A class of echinoderms, the sea lilies may be roughly described as " stalked star-fishes." There are about 400 living species, and several thousand extinct species are known. Otherwise called Crinoids.

**Sea Mouse,** a genus of marine worms called *Aphrodite*, oval in shape, 8 or 9 in. long, iridescent, covered with fine bristles.

**Sea Squirts** *or* **Tunicates.** These animals are placed in the sub-phylum called *Urochorda*; found growing in rounded, jelly-like masses on rocks near low-water level. They get their name through the water jets they discharge.

**Sea Urchin,** species forming the class *Echinoidae*. The body is globular and covered with spines which may be used for both defence and locomotion. The main organs of locomotion are, however, the tube feet, as in starfishes. Much has been learnt of recent years by marine biologists from experiments with the purple sea-urchin *Arbacia*.

**Seasons** comprise the four natural divisions of the year, and are due to the inclinations of the earth's axis to the plane of the ecliptic. *See* Equinox, *also* N25.

**Secondary Sexual Characters.** Characters of animals which are distinctive of sex, but have no direct connection with the reproductive process. Examples are: the mane of the lion and the antlers of some deer.

**Secretary Bird,** so called because of the quill-like plumes about its ears, is a bird of prey related to the eagles and vultures; common in Africa, and of considerable service as an exterminator of snakes. It is a large bird about 4 ft. in height.

**Sedimentary Rocks.** *See* F8(2).

**Seismology,** the branch of geophysics devoted to the study of earthquakes and other earth movements. The instruments used for the registration of earth tremors are termed seismographs and consist in principle of a pendulum system, the supporting framework following the ground movement and the bob remaining at rest, thus setting up a relative movement between two parts. In order to record the displacements completely, at one station, three seismographs are necessary to show the two horizontal and the vertical components of the motion. Apart from detection and study of waves from earthquakes, sensitive seismographs are now widely used in geophysical prospecting, particularly in the search for possible oilfields.

**Selenium,** a non-metallic element, symbol Se, related to sulphur, it is a dark red colour, and solid, found associated with sulphur, iron, pyrites, etc., though only in small quantities. It is a semiconductor (*q.v.*) and its special electrical properties have led to its use in photo-electric cells and rectifiers. Selenium is widely used in the chemical industry as a catalyst (*q.v.*) in producing aromatic hydrocarbons from less useful hydrocarbons. Also used in making some types of glass.

**Semiconductors,** substances with numerous special and useful electrical properties a few of which are:

(i) they conduct electricity much better than do insulators, but much less well than metals (hence their name);

(ii) their power to conduct depends strongly on their temperature—which makes them useful for temperature sensitive devices;

(iii) they are sensitive to light—hence their use in photoelectric cells and solar batteries;

(iv) when in contact with metals, or with other suitable semiconductors, they form a boundary layer which conducts electricity much better one way than the other—this is the basis of many rectifiers some of which, called crystal diodes, are an important component in radios and electronic devices;

(v) their electrical properties can be greatly influenced by putting in minute amounts of impurity, this enables semiconductor devices, especially transistors, to be made with carefully selected properties.

Semiconductors were known to Faraday, but the semiconductor age really arrived with the invention of the transistor (*q.v.*) in 1947. The ubiquitous transistor is only one of very many semiconductor devices which perform a variety of functions in technical apparatus of all kinds. Semiconductors used in technology are usually small crystals, frequently of germanium or silicon, and their robustness and small power consumption often make them superior to other devices, such as thermionic valves, which they often replace. Other semiconducting materials are cadmium sulphide, selenium, lead telluride, indium antimonide. *See also* F19.

**Senate,** the higher governing Assembly of a Legislature. The word, applied primarily to the Roman council, is also used to denote the upper chamber in the legislatures of France, the United States, and other countries. In certain universities the governing body is also called the Senate.

**Sensitive Plant.** A species of Mimosa (*Mimosa pudica*), whose leaves are extremely sensitive to touch, shaking, and burning.

**Sepia,** the " ink " of the cuttlefish. *See* Ink Sac.

**September,** the ninth month of the year, and the seventh of the old Roman calendar; hence the name, from Septimus. The designation was several times changed by the Emperors, but none of the new names survived for long.

**Septuagesima Sunday,** the third Sunday before Lent.

**Septuagint,** the Greek translation of the Old Testament made by Alexandrian Jews between 250 B.C. and 100 B.C. from Hebrew texts now lost. There are many differences between the Septuagint and the Massoretic version (A.D. 900), and therefore it is of great value for textual criticism. The symbol for the Septuagint is LXX.

**Serfs,** the name given to the slaves formerly existing in Russia, who answered to the condition of the feudal " villeins " of England. They were attached to the soil and were transferred with it in all sales or leases. Serfdom existed in Prussia until 1807 and in Russia until 1861.

**Serpentine,** a mineral; chemically a hydrous silicate of magnesium. Green serpentine is used as an ornament stone. Fibrous serpentine is called asbestos.

**Serval,** a small carnivorous animal of the lynx order, with black spots on a tawny ground. It is numerous in Africa, preys upon the smaller animals of the deer family, and is sometimes styled the " Tiger Cat."

**Set,** both in everyday speech (as in tea set, chess set) and in mathematics, a set is a collection of things. The members of the set can be specified by listing them or by describing the properties necessary for membership of the set, *e.g.*, the set of ginger-haired boxers. Set theory is a very important branch of mathematics founded by a great mathematician, Georg Cantor (1845–1918). Its development has influenced many other branches of mathematics. Perhaps one reflection of its fundamental nature is to be found in the fact that many schoolchildren, even of tender age, are now learning set theory and confounding parents who did not hear of it at school twenty years ago.

**Settlement, Act of,** passed in 1701, assigned the Crown to the House of Hanover in case of Anne's death without children. The decision represented the determination of the squires and the Anglican Church never again to trust themselves to a Roman Catholic king.

**Seven Champions of Christendom,** as set forth in mediæval literature, were St. George of England, St. Andrew of Scotland, St. Patrick of Ireland, St. David of Wales, St. James of Spain, St. Denis of France, and St. Anthony of Italy.

**Seven Churches of Asia,** referred to in the Revelation of St. John, were those of Ephesus, founded by St. Paul in 57, Smyrna, Pergamos, Thyatira, Sardis, Philadelphia (Lydia), and Laodicea (Phrygia), all in W. Asia Minor.

**Seven Wonders of the World** were: 1, the Pyramids of Egypt; 2, the tomb of Mausolus, King of Caria (hence the word mausoleum); 3, the Temple of Diana at Ephesus; 4, the Walls and Hanging Gardens of Babylon; 5, the Colossus at Rhodes; 6, the Ivory and Gold Statue of Jupiter Olympus; and 7, the Pharos, or Watch Tower, built at Alexandria by Ptolemy Philadelphus, King of Egypt.

**Seven Years' War** was waged by Frederick the Great and England against Austria, France, and Russia, from 1756 to 1763. It resulted in the secession of Silesia to Prussia, of Canada to England, and in the strengthening of our Indian Empire.

**Sexagesima Sunday** is the 2nd Sunday before Lent.

**Sextant,** an instrument which has superseded the quadrant as a measurer of angles between distant objects. It is of special importance in navigation and surveying, and contains 60 degrees described on a graduated arc. A small telescope is attached and there are also a couple of mirrors which reflect the distant objects so as to enable them to be accurately observed. The invention is attributed to John Hadley, and to Thomas Godfrey independently, about 1730. Even today it is still the best instrument for telling where you are at sea.

**Shad,** a marine fish belonging to the same genus as the herring. It is found along the Atlantic Coast of the U.S.A., and ascends rivers to spawn.

**Shagreen,** shark's skin: also untanned leather of peculiar grain made from skins of wild asses, camels, and horses.

**Shalloon,** a kind of cloth manufactured from wool and worsted, and used chiefly for women's dresses and coat linings. It gets its name from the fact that it was originally made at Chalons.

**Shamrock,** the three-leaved clover-like plant native to Ireland and its national emblem.

**Shark,** a large and powerful ocean fish, comprising many species, very widely distributed, but most numerous in tropical seas. They have formidable teeth and are the most carnivorous of all fishes. They usually attain a large size, the

**whale-shark** being often o a length of 50 ft. Commercially the shark yields shagreen from its skin, the fins are made into gelatine, and an oil is obtained from the liver.

**Sheep,** a well-known family of ruminants of great utility as wool-producers, and for food. From the earliest times sheep have been a source of wealth to England. So much were they valued in the 15th and 16th cent., that their exportation was frequently prohibited. Sheep are classified under (1) longwools; (2) shortwools; and (3) mountain breeds. Most of the longwools carry Leicester blood in their ancestry and the shortwooled Down breeds carry the blood of the Southdown. The Southdown produced the present Suffolk, one of the most popular breeds. Cheviot is an important mountain breed. Of the foreign breeds the most valued are the Merino sheep of Spain, which yield a fine long wool. Australia, U.S.S.R., Argentina, India, U.S.A., New Zealand, and S. Africa are the chief wool-producing countries in the world.

**Shelduck,** a handsome genus of surface-feeding ducks, one of which, the common shelduck, is an inhabitant of this country. It is a beautiful white-and-chestnut plumaged bird with darkgreen head and neck and red bill. Another species, the ruddy sheldrake, appears in Britain only occasionally.

**Shellac.** This resin is the secretion of the lac insect (*Coccus lacca*), which occurs in forests of Assam and Siam. It is used for making varnish and in the manufacture of gramophone records. *See also* Lac.

**Sherardizing.** Process for coating steel or iron parts with zinc to prevent corrosion; this is done by heating the parts in a closed rotating drum containing zinc dust.

**Shilling** has been an English coin from Saxon times, but it was not of the value of 12 pence until after the Conquest. It is interchangeable with the 5 new pence decimal piece which came into circulation in 1968.

**Ships** have existed from prehistoric times. There is mention of one that sailed from Egypt to Greece in 1485 B.C., and in 786 B.C. the Tyrians built a double-decked vessel. No doubledecked ship was known in England, however, before the *Royal Harry* was built by Henry VII., and it was not until the 17th cent. that shipbuilding was carried on in this country as a prominent industry.

**Ship-worm.** *See* Teredo.

**Shoddy,** the name given to a kind of cloth mainly composed of woollen or worsted rags, torn up and re-fabricated by powerful machinery. It was first made at Batley in Yorkshire about 1813, and became a very important industry employing many thousands of people at Batley and the neighbouring town of Dewsbury.

**Shot,** the name given to solid projectiles fired from guns. In the time of Henry V. stone shot was used, later leaden shot, then iron shot, and finally steel shot, introduced by Sir Joseph Whitworth.

**Shrike,** a large and varied family of birds of hawklike behaviour found in all continents except S. America. The Red-backed Shrike, which winters in Africa, is a beautiful visitor to England and Wales. It is commonly called the "Butcher Bird" from the way it impales its prey (small birds and insects) on thorn-twigs. The other species on the British list are the Great Grey Shrike, the Lesser Grey Shrike, the Woodchat Shrike, and the Masked Shrike.

**Shrove Tuesday,** the day before the first day of Lent, receiving its name from the old custom of shriving, or making confession, on that day. In England the day has always been associated with the making of pancakes.

**Sicilian Vespers,** the term applied to the terrible massacre of French people in Sicily in 1282. The French under Charles of Anjou were then in occupation of the island, and had been guilty of many cruelties. It began at Palermo on Easter Monday at the hour of vespers and resulted in the expulsion of the French king and the introduction of Spanish rule.

**Silence, Tower of,** or *dakhma,* a tower about 25 ft. high, built by the Parsees for their dead. The corpse is taken inside by professional corpsebearers and left to be consumed by vultures.

Parsees do not burn or bury their dead, and the *dakhma* is to protect the living and the elements from deflement.

**Silhouette,** a form of black profile portrait, invented by Etienne de Silhouette in 1759, and formed by an outline cutting made with scissors or other sharp instrument from cloth, paper, or other flat substance.

**Silicon,** an important non-metallic element, symbol Si, it is related to carbon. Next to oxygen, it is the most abundant constituent of the earth's crust (27% by weight). It occurs in many rocks, and its oxide occurs in many forms (*e.g.,* quartz, sand, flint, agate, chalcedony, opal, etc.). Coming into use as a semi-conducting material for making transistors and similar devices.

**Silicones** are synthetic organic derivatives of silicon which because of their high resistance to heat and moisture have special uses, *e.g.,* lubricants, heat-resistant resins and lacquers, and water-repellent finishes. Silicones are compounds in which the molecules consist of chains of atoms of silicon and oxygen alternately. Silicones were developed in the United States from discoveries first made by Prof. F. S. Kipping at Nottingham University. Manufacture began in Britain in 1950, and in the form of fluids, resins, rubbers, and greases they find wide use in industry. The largest plant in Europe is in Glamorgan.

**Silk,** the name given to a soft glossy fabric manufactured from the fine thread produced by the silkworm. It was known to, and highly prized by, the ancients, being at one time paid for, weight for weight, with gold. The manufacture of silk was carried on in Sicily in the 12th cent., later spreading to Italy, Spain, and the south of France. It was not manufactured in England before 1604; but when certain French refugees established themselves at Spitalfields in 1688, the industry was developed and became of importance. In the 18th cent. the Lombes of Derby achieved great success in this industry. Japan, China, Italy, Korea, and the Soviet Union are the chief silk-producing countries.

**Silkworm,** the larva of a species of moth, *Bombyx mori.* It is native to China, and has been cultivated with success in India, Persia, Turkey, and Italy. The silkworm of commerce feeds on mulberry leaves and produces a cocoon of silk varying in colour from white to orange. The cocoon is the silken habitation constructed by the worm for its entrance upon the pupal condition, and to obtain the silk the pupa is killed by immersion in hot-water.

**Sill,** a sheet-like mass of igneous rock which has been intruded parallel with the stratification of the country rock, cf. a dyke.

**Silurian.** This geological period is one of the major subdivisions of the Palaeozoic era. Its beginning is estimated at 440 million years ago, and the period lasted about 40 million years. Maximum thickness of the Silurian strata in Britain measures 15,000 ft. *See* F41.

**Silver,** a white precious metal, symbol Ag (Latin *argentum*), found in a free state, also in certain combinations, and in a variety of ores. The chief silver-producing regions are the Andes and Cordilleras. Peru, Bolivia, and Mexico have yielded vast supplies of the metal since the 16th century, and Colorado and Nevada in the United States have also been very prolific in silver yield. In England standard silver (that used for coinage) formerly contained 92½ per cent. fine silver and 7½ per cent. alloy, but when the price rose to 89½d. per oz. and the coins became worth more than face value, the Coinage Act of 1920 was passed, reducing the fineness to half. To provide silver bullion for industry and for a fund towards the redemption of our silver debt to America, it was decided in 1946 to replace the United Kingdom silver coinage by one made of cupro-nickel (75 per cent. copper, 25 per cent. nickel). Maundy money, however, is of the original silver standard. Silver chloride and bromide are light-sensitive compounds and are used in photography.

**Simony,** the offence of trading in church offices, has been contrary to English law since the time of Edward VI. Elizabeth also promulgated laws against simony. In 1879 a Royal Commission reported on the law and existing practice as to the sale, exchange, and resignation of benefices. The position is now controlled by the Benefices Act 1898, the Amendment Measure 1923, and the Benefices Rules 1926.

**Sinn Fein** (*Irish* = ourselves alone), an Irish nationalistic movement founded in 1905 which developed into a mass republican party and triumphed in the establishment of the Irish Free State. A small extremist group has survived which represents politically the outlawed I.R.A.

**Sins, The Seven Deadly or Capital Sins** are pride, avarice, lust, anger, gluttony, envy, sloth.

**Sirius,** the dog-star, so called because of its situation in the mouth of the Dog (Canis Major): it is the brightest of all the fixed stars, and is also one of the nearest to us.

**Sirocco,** a warm, southerly, often dust-laden, wind blowing across Mediterranean lands from the Sahara, in advance of an eastward-moving depression over the Mediterranean.

**Siskin,** a small bird of the finch family, common in Northern regions, nesting in Britain. The common Siskin has a yellow-green colour and is a lively, swift-flying bird with a stout bill.

**Sistine Chapel,** the chapel of the Pope in the Vatican, renowned for its frescoes by Michelangelo.

**S.I. Units** (Système International d'Unités) form an internationally recognised system of metric units for scientific and technical quantities. The basic units of length, time, mass, electric current, temperature, and luminous intensity are, respectively, the metre, second, kilogram, ampere, degree Kelvin (*see* Absolute Temperature), and candela. The S.I. was recommended for general adoption by a number of international organisations such as the General Conference on Weights and Measures (1960). Many countries have made or are making the S.I. the only legally recognised set of units. Gt. Britain's intention to " go metric " will bring widespread use of S.I. units in its train. These units command the widespread though not absolutely unanimous support of industrialists, technologists, and scientists. Many have urged that their adoption will be a triumph of commonsense and end the confusing multiplicity of units on the world scene. *See* **N13.**

**Six Articles, The Statute of the,** was passed in 1539 for compelling adhesion to the chief doctrines of Roman Catholic faith; transubstantiation, communion in one kind only for the laity, vows of chastity, celibacy of the clergy, private masses, and auricular confession: those who refused to subscribe to the Articles were treated as heretics. The Act was repealed in 1547.

**Skate,** a genus of sea-fishes related to the Rays.

**Skink.** The skinks constitute a large family of lizards with large smooth scales, under each of which is a bony plate. The largest species, found in Australia, is about 2 ft. long. Some skinks have adopted a burrowing habit and degeneration of the limbs is associated with this. The Common Skink is a small species about 5 in. long, living in the deserts of N. Africa.

**Skua,** falcon-like marine birds related to the gulls, found throughout the world. Known as " Robber Birds " because they steal not only the young and eggs of other birds (including penguins) but also their food, which they force them to disgorge in mid-air. The Arctic Skua breeds as far south as Scotland. The Great Skua breeds in both Antarctica and Arctica. Other species are the Pomarine, the Long-tailed, and McCormick's Skua.

**Skunk,** a North American mammal of the weasel family, with short legs and long bushy tail. All fifteen species are black and white, some being striped and the rest spotted. It secretes and ejects at will a foul-smelling fluid. Anything tainted with this retains the odour for days.

**Sky.** The blue colour of the sky on a summer's day is the result of the scattering of light waves by particles of dust and vapour in the earth's atmosphere. Blue light having almost the smallest wavelength in the visible spectrum (0·00004 cm.) is scattered laterally about 10 times as much as the red (0·00007 cm.).

**Skyscraper.** Owing to lack of ground space, increasing cost of land, and growth of modern cities, buildings are being made higher than broader; hence the name. The structures are constructed of a steel framework usually clothed in concrete or reinforced concrete. Among the highest New York skyscrapers are the Empire State Building (102 stories, 1,250 ft.), Chrysler (77 stories, 1,046 ft.), and the Rockefeller Center (70 stories, 850 ft.). The tallest building in Britain is the 580 ft. Post Office radio tower (basic diameter 52 ft.) near Tottenham Court Road, London. Japan's first skyscraper, the Kasumigaseki building (36 stories), in Tokyo, was due for completion in 1968.

**Slate,** fine-grained clayey rocks which have undergone metamorphism. They cleave easily, and it is this property of cleavage which makes them a valuable source of roofing material. Welsh slates are among the best, there being important quarries at Penrhyn, Llanberis, and Ffestiniog.

**Slavery.** In its earlier forms, as in the times of ancient Greece and Rome, in the feudal ages, when vassalage and villeinage existed, and in the serfdom of Russia and other northern nations, slavery was attended by many inhumanities and evils: but perhaps in the negro slavery system which prevailed in the British colonies for upwards of 200 years and in certain parts of the United States up to 1865, it attained its highest point of cruelty. In 1833 the Act of Emancipation was passed, emancipating all slaves in British territories, though slavery continued to be tolerated in northern Nigeria, Sierra Leone and in the Anglo-Egyptian Sudan long after that date. Even today slavery and forced labour are still prevalent in some parts of the world. *See* **C33.**

**Slide Rule,** an instrument which consists of two logarithmic scales sliding alongside each other. By its use multiplication, division, extraction of roots, etc., are speedily carried out.

**Sloth,** a curious family of mammals, only found in Central and South America. They dwell almost entirely in the trees, proceeding from branch to branch with their bodies hanging downwards, their weight being supported by their large hook-like claws. They eat foliage.

**Slow-Worm,** a species of lizard found in Britain which lacks legs. Silver with longitudinal brown stripes, it lives almost entirely on slugs.

**Smelting.** The process of heating an ore with a reducing agent to convert ore into metal, and with a flux to convert rocky impurities into a slag that will float on top of the molten metal. Slag and metal can then be tapped separately. An example is iron smelting; the reducing agent is coke, and limestone is added as the flux; the smelting is carried out in a blast furnace.

**Snake.** The snakes constitute the important reptilian order *Ophidia*. Snakes have a scaly, cylindrical, limbless body, lidless eyes, forked tongue, and the upper and lower jaws joined by an elastic ligament. Their locomotion is accomplished by means of the excessive mobility of their numerous ribs. All snakes have teeth used for seizing prey, and the poisonous varieties are furnished with poison fangs in the upper jaw. These fangs are hollow modified teeth and the venom passes into them from a special gland situated behind the angle of the mouth. Some 2,500 species of snakes are known, divided into 13 families. There are 3 British species—the grass-snake, smooth-snake and adder.

**Snipe,** a wading bird, long-legged, with long, slender, straight bill, brown plumage, and zigzag flight. The Common Snipe breeds locally throughout Britain; the Great Snipe and small Jack Snipe are occasional visitors. The close season is Feb. 1 to Aug. 11.

**Snort** (*Ger.* Schnorchel), a tubular device of modern invention used in submarines. It contains two pipes for the intake of air and outlet of gases, and can be maintained above the level of the surface of the water. When a submarine is submerging with snort at the surface it is said to be *snorting.*

**Snow.** When water vapour condenses at high levels at a temperature below freezing, a cloud of ice particles is formed. If these frozen droplets are small, they fall slowly and gradually assume a feathery crystalline structure, reaching the earth as snowflakes if the temperature remains below freezing.

**Socialism.** *See* **J40.**

**Soda,** carbonate of sodium, is now mainly obtained by certain processes of manufacture from common salt. It was formerly obtained from the ashes of plants. Bicarbonate of sodium is the primary product in the Solvay or Ammonia-soda method for commercial manufacture of soda; it is also formed when carbon dioxide is passed into strong soda solution. The bicarbonate is used in medicine and in the preparation of baking powder.

**Sodium,** a metallic element, symbol Na (Latin *Natrium*), first obtained by Sir Humphry Davy in 1807 from caustic soda by means of the electric battery. Its chloride is *common salt*; the deposits of salt (*e.g.*, in Cheshire and at Stassfurt) have come into existence through the drying up of inland seas. Salt occurs in sea-water to the extent of about 3 per cent.; the Dead Sea contains about 22 per cent. The blood of animals is maintained at a level of about 0·6% sodium chloride. That there is sodium in the sun's atmosphere was confirmed in 1859 by Kirchhoff from his spectroscopic observations. Liquid sodium metal has properties which make it suitable as a coolant in some nuclear reactors. A technique of handling this very reactive liquid has had to be developed.

**Soil,** the superficial covering of land areas composed mainly of disintegrated rock material and the remains of dead plants and animals (humus) and containing in varying amounts trace elements and other nutriments essential for plant growth.

**Solar Battery,** one of the innumerable devices made possible by the development of semiconducting materials, notably germanium and silicon. This device creates an electric current from light falling on it. The current can be put to use or stored in storage batteries. The energy of the current is derived from the sunlight, and the solar battery is thus an *energy converting* apparatus. Solar batteries have provided power for the instruments in satellites. In London in 1960 a car (developed in the U.S.A.) was demonstrated running on the power from sunlight and solar batteries.

**Solar Wind,** a continuous stream of electrically charged particles blowing outwards from the sun, supplemented from time to time by intense outbursts from particular regions of the sun's surface. These streams of protons and electrons on encountering the earth's magnetic field distort it and cause magnetic storms and aurorae.

**Soldering** is a means of joining together two pieces of material, usually metals, by melting a third metal (the solder) into the joint. The solder solidifies in the pores of the other metals and holds them together. The materials to be joined are not themselves melted so the technique requires less heat than welding. Solders are alloys; there are many kinds depending on the materials to be joined and the strength of joint desired. *See* Welding.

**Solstice,** an astronomical term indicating the point at which the sun is most distant from the equator. *See* N25.

**Soundings** at sea, to determine depth at any point, have been taken in all seas, and with considerable accuracy. A deep reading was that of the *Challenger* expedition in 1873, near St. Thomas's in the North Atlantic, when 3,875 fathoms were sounded. In 1851 H.M.S. *Challenger* recorded the then maximum ocean depth in the Marianas Trench (W. Pacific) by echo-sounding as between 5,882 and 5,940 fathoms. Another deep was located in the S. Pacific in 1952–53 of 5,814 fathoms in the Tonga Trench, 180 miles S. of Tonga Tabu. Since then even greater depths have been recorded, in the Marianas Trench and the Mindanao Deep. *See* Pacific Ocean.

**Southern Cross,** popular name of *Crux*, a constellation of the Southern hemisphere, consisting of four bright stars in the form of a Latin cross. It has been called the pole-star of the south and is indispensable to seafarers.

**South Sea Bubble,** the name given to a series of financial projects which began with the formation of the South Sea Company in 1711 and ended nine years later in disaster after a mania of speculation. The idea behind the parent scheme was that the state should sell certain trading monopolies in the South seas in return for a sum of money to pay off the National Debt (which stood at £51,300,000 in 1719 when the scheme started). The idea fascinated the public, fabulous profits being dreamt of, and the price of the stock rose out of all proportion to the earnings of the Company. Many dishonest speculative ventures sprang up in imitation with the inevitable result that thousands were ruined. All classes h..d joined in the gamble and a Committee of Secrecy set up by the House of Commons in Dec. 1720 to investigate the affairs of the Company proved that there had been fraud and corruption on a large scale in the affairs of the Company. Sir Robert Walpole who had been an opponent of the scheme from the outset dealt with the crisis.

**Soya Bean.** This is the bean of a leguminous plant (*Glycine soja*) found in Asia. The bean meal, which is rich in protein and oil, is familiar in Britain as "soya flour."

**Space Flight.** The Soviet Union was the first country to launch a man into space and bring him safely back to earth. This epoch-making event took place on April 12, 1961, when Yuri Gagarin, tragically killed in an air crash in 1968, circled the earth in a spaceship weighing about 4¾ tons. It was launched by rocket in an elliptical orbit with greatest height 187 miles and least 109 miles. The inclination of the orbit to the equator was 65 deg. 4 min. and the period of revolution was 89 min. 6 sec. Since then, the Russian *Vostok* cosmonauts Titov (17 orbits), Nikolayev (64 orbits), Popovich (48 orbits), Bykovsky (81 orbits), Tereshkova, the first woman space traveller (48 orbits), the *Voskhod* cosmonauts Komarov, Feoktistov and Yegorov (16 orbits), Belyaev and Leonov (17 orbits), the American *Mercury* astronauts Glenn (3 orbits), Carpenter (3 orbits), Schirra (6 orbits), Cooper (22 orbits), the *Gemini* astronauts Grissom and Young (3 orbits), McDivitt and White (62 orbits), Cooper and Conrad (120 orbits), Borman and Lovell (206 orbits), Schirra and Stafford (15 orbits), Armstrong and Scott (6·6 orbits), Stafford and Cernan (44 orbits), Young and Collins (43 orbits), Conrad and Gordon (44 orbits), Lovell and Aldrin (60 orbits) were among the first to complete successful missions in space. Leonov was the first to perform the extra-vehicular (EVA) experiment (1965), *i.e.*, to leave an orbiting spaceship and float freely in space. Russia was the first to achieve an automatic docking (link-up) between two unmanned orbiting satellites (Oct. 1967). The linking indicated their intention to build large space platforms—for astronomical and other scientific observations and eventually as part of the manned lunar enterprise. Russia again took the lead (Jan. 1969) with the successful docking in orbital flight of two manned spacecrafts (*Soyuz-4* and *Soyuz-5*). The flight of Borman, Lovell and Anders in *Apollo 8* during Christmas 1968 represented a great scientific and human achievement. They made the first manned flight to the moon, making 10 lunar orbits before returning to Earth. The second of the four-stage approach to "man on the moon" was accomplished with precision by McDivitt, Schweickart, and Scott in *Apollo 9* (March 1969). The plan to land on the moon in 1969 looked like being accomplished.

**Space Research.** By space research we mean scientific research work which can only be carried to otherwise inaccessible observing locations by rocket propulsion. Such propulsion does not rely on the presence of an atmosphere to provide oxygen so that it is capable in principle of conveying objects to unlimited distances. The subject of space research is, therefore, one which is concerned with scientific applications in various fields of a single highly specialised and powerful technique. It is not a single discipline, but can provide data of great importance for many, such as the physics of the earth, the sun, moon, and other bodies of the solar system, astronomy, geodesy, and the study of gravitation. The prospect of investigating the biological conditions on different planets such as Mars and Venus is also opened, as well as that of experimental biological studies under conditions of zero gravity. Although the results of many aspects of space research are vital for those concerned with the practical realisation of manned travel in space, space research is largely a branch of pure science, independent of any applications which may stem from it. The major technical problems involved in space research are:

(a) Launching of the instrument-containing vehicle with the necessary velocity.

(b) Guidance and control of the vehicle so it pursues the desired path.

(c) Tracking the vehicle to determine its actual path and the position on the path at any time.

(d) Transmission of the data, recorded by the instruments, back to the earth.

(e) Satisfactory operation of scientific instruments in the environment within the vehicle.

(f) Provision of adequate power supplies to operate the equipment within the vehicle for sufficiently long periods.

**Spanish Civil War, 1936 to 1939.** The war commenced by a revolt by the Fascist General Franco against the Republic which had succeeded the Monarchy in 1931. Germany and Italy aided the rebels who besieged Madrid for over 2 years. An International Brigade was formed to help the Republic, but the Spanish Government was faced by the greater part of the Army, and very effective assistance from Italy and Germany. Those powers seized the opportunity to have a curtain-raiser to the world conflict which they intended to precipitate. After a total loss of a million men the Fascists overpowered the Republic.

**Sparrow,** name given to finch-like birds found in most parts of the world, of which the House Sparrow. *Passer domesticus,* is the most familiar of British birds. Also native to Britain is the rural Tree Sparrow, distinguished from the male House Sparrow by its chestnut crown. Other European species are the Italian, Spanish and Rock Sparrows.

**Specific Gravity,** defined as the ratio of the mass of a particular volume of a substance to the mass of an equal volume of water at 4° C. *See* Hydrometer.

**Spectroscopy.** Newton's arrangement with the prism was the first spectroscope; its function was to separate out the colour components of a source of light. Two hundred years elapsed before this apparatus was developed into a precise scientific instrument, capable of measuring both the wavelength and intensity of each colour component. In this form it is called a spectrometer. All atoms and molecules have well defined characteristic spectra which can be used to recognise them. In order to produce emission spectra it is necessary to energise the material under investigation by some means, such as by heating in a flame. The resulting radiation then consists largely of sharp bright lines, characteristic of the material. Absorption spectra are produced by interposing the experimental material between a white light source and the spectrometer. Then dark lines are seen, corresponding to absorptions of energy, in exactly the same places as the bright lines are observed in the emission spectra. Spectroscopic techniques have now been developed to such an extent that accurate measurements of wavelength and intensity are possible not only in the visible region, but over almost the whole of the electromagnetic spectrum. Not only does spectroscopy play an important rôle in probing the structure of matter, but it can be applied in the field of astronomy. The use of radio wave spectroscopy has led to the discovery of several new types of stellar object, and this data is now producing a complete reappraisal of our understanding of the universe.

**Sphinx,** in Greek mythology, a winged creature with a woman's head and a lion's body. The sphinx of ancient Egypt represented the pharaoh in a divine form. The most famous is the Great Sphinx at Giza, sculptured out of natural rock.

**Spiritualism.** *See* J41.

**Spirituals,** negro melodies with religious inspiration and which are still spontaneously created, but have also passed into art-music.

**Sponge,** a marine organism consisting of a colony of cells organised in a more primitive way than most multi-cellular organisms without a nervous system. While the sponge lives a current of

water circulates through the main apertures. It is the dead skeleton of this mass that forms the sponge of commerce. *See* F33(1).

**Spoonbill,** a long-legged, marsh bird, closely related to the ibis and stork, remarkable for its snow-white plumage and broad, flat, spoon-shaped bill. The European species has not bred in England since the beginning of the 17th cent., but is still a regular summer visitor from Holland, where it nests in colonies in reed-beds and islets.

**Sputniks,** the name of the Russian earth satellites first launched during the period of the International Geophysical Year. *Sputnik I,* launched 4 Oct. 1957, became the first man-made earth satellite. *Sputnik II,* launched a month later, carried a dog as passenger. *Sputnik III,* launched in May 1958, and weighing well over 2 tons, became the first fully-equipped laboratory to operate in space. The father of space travel with rockets was a Russian—Konstantin Eduardovich Tsiolkovsky—the centenary of whose birth practically coincided with the launching of the first earth satellite.

**Squirting Cucumber,** *Ecballium elaterium,* so named from the fact that when ripe it breaks from the stalk and ejects its seeds and juice from the hole made by the breakage.

**Stainless Steel.** The development of stainless steel for cutlery manufacture, etc., began with the discovery of Harry Brearsley in 1912 that steel containing 12 per cent. of chromium is rust-proof.

**Stalactites** are deposits of calcium carbonate formed on the roofs and sides of limestone caves, and in tunnels, under bridges, and other places where the carbonic acid of rain-water percolates through and partly dissolves the limestone, resulting in the growth of icicle-like forms that often assume groupings. The water that drops from these may deposit further calcium carbonate, which accumulates and hardens into a series of sharp mounds or hillocks called stalagmites.

**Starch** is an organic compound occurring in granules in nearly all green plants, and especially in the seeds of dicotyledonous and cereal plants, potatoes, etc. In its pure form starch is a tasteless, odourless white powder, and is a carbohydrate consisting of carbon, hydrogen, and oxygen.

**Star Chamber,** an ancient tribunal of State in existence in 1487 and possibly earlier, charged with the duty of trying offences against the Government, unfettered by the ordinary rules of law. It was in effect a Privy Council entrusted with judicial functions. Under Charles I. the Star Chamber was used by the King and his party to persecute opponents; and in 1641 a Bill carried in both Houses abolished it.

**Starling** (*Sturnus vulgaris*), a well-known European bird now common in many parts of the world. It has handsome iridescent blackish plumage and nests in holes and crevices. Flocks of starlings are often seen wheeling in the air; thousands roost on buildings in the heart of London. Other European species are the Spotless and Rose-coloured starlings. The latter sometimes wanders to the British Isles.

**States-General,** national assembly in which the chief estates of the realm were represented as separate bodies. The name, though not the institution, has survived in the Netherlands, where the two houses of parliament are known as states-general. In France the states-general consisted of three orders, clergy, nobility, and commons. Philip IV. first summoned it in 1302 to support him in his quarrel with Pope Boniface VIII. While absolute monarchy was establishing itself it met rarely, and not at all from 1614 until 1789, when it was convoked as a last resort by Louis XVI. But when it met it declared itself the National Assembly which marked the beginning of the revolution.

**Statistics** is a science that deals with the collection of numerical facts and the evaluation of their significance. The word is also used to refer to the facts themselves as in " trade statistics." This important science gives precise meanings to words like " average " and to statements like " this set of data is significantly different from that." In a world in which more and more information is becoming available in numerical form (I.Q.s, examination results, tax yields, health records, road accidents, etc.) the proper—as opposed to the misleading—use of statistics cannot be over-emphasised. Many young people can now study statistics at school and college, and governments and industries employ many statisticians. *See* Average.

Statute of Westminster, 1931. An Act of parliament which gave a basis of equality to the British Dominions. The Dominions as well as the United Kingdom were defined by the Balfour Memorandum of 1926 as " autonomous communities within the British Empire, equal in status, in no way subordinate one to another in any aspect of their domestic or external affairs, though united by a common allegiance to the Crown, and freely associated as members of the British Commonwealth of Nations." The Statute was the sequel. The Dominions are sovereign States governed solely by their own Parliaments and Governments. *See also* K189.

Steam Engine, a machine whereby steam becomes the active agent of the working of machinery, and of very wide application. The leading types of steam engine are: (*a*) condensing, or low-pressure engines, where the steam is generated by a boiler; (*b*) non-condensing, in which the cylinder exhausts its steam into the open air. Engines of the latter type are used where portable engines are required.

Steam Hammer, invented by the Scottish engineer James Nasmyth (1808–90) in 1839, which proved of great utility in the development of the iron trade. The hammer itself, which is fixed to the end of a piston-rod passing through the bottom of an inverted cylinder, often weighs as much as 80 or 100 tons, and is so perfectly controlled by the steam power that its action can be so accurately gauged that it could be made to crack the glass of a watch without actually breaking it, or brought down upon a mass of molten iron with a force representing many hundreds of tons.

Stearin is the portion of fatty matters and oils which remains solid at an ordinary temperature, and is a compound of stearic acid with glycerine. It is largely used in the manufacture of candles and for other commercial purposes. With caustic soda stearin forms a soap (sodium stearate), which is present in most commercial soaps which contain sodium palmitate and oleate in addition.

Steel, an alloy of iron and carbon, with varying proportions of other minerals. The famous blades of Damascus and steels of Toledo were made by the cementation and crucible method. The metal produced by the " Bessemer process " (*q.v.*) is of the highest value for structural purposes, rails, etc. In recent years the technique known as continuous casting has been developed which bypasses some major steps in the conventional process of steel-making. *See also* Stainless Steel.

Stereophonic Broadcasting. A person having normal hearing is able to determine the direction from which a sound reaches him by virtue of the fact that he has two ears, and, therefore, the sound will reach one of them a fraction of a second before it reaches the other. This difference in arrival time allows the brain to calculate direction. It will, therefore, be apparent that if the same person listens to, say, an orchestral concert in a large hall he will be able to determine—even with his eyes shut—the approximate position of a particular instrument with respect to the rest of the orchestra. If, however, he listens at home to a broadcast of the same concert, then, due to the fact that he hears the music after it has been picked up by a single microphone located at one point and radiated over a single-channel transmission system, he will be unable to allocate a definite position to any instrument. The aim of stereophonic broadcasting or sound reproduction, therefore, is to restore the listener's ability to locate the position in space of the various sources of sound and to follow movement. To do this it is necessary to use two microphones in the studio—to simulate the two human ears—and to transmit their outputs, through two similar, but separate, chains of equipment, to two radio receivers and their two loudspeakers, which must be placed some distance apart, in the listener's home.

Stereotype, a metal cast taken from movable type

which has been set up in the ordinary way. The first to introduce the process in practical form in this country was William Ged, of Edinburgh, who made stereotype plates in 1730. An impression of the type matter is first taken by means of a mould of prepared plaster of Paris or moistened sheets of specially prepared paper, and when molten stereo metal is poured upon the mould and allowed to cool and harden, the stereo plate is formed, and can be printed from as a solid block for some time.

Steroids. A class of structurally related compounds, based on a system of condensed rings of carbon and hydrogen, which are widely distributed in animals and plants. Included in the steroid family are sterols, found in all animal cells, vitamin D, sex hormones, bile acids, and cortisone, a drug used in the treatment of rheumatic fever.

Stibnite, the chief ore of antimony; chemically it is antimony sulphide. Steely-grey in colour.

Stickleback, a family of small spiny-finned fish widely distributed in both fresh and salt water. Male constructs roofed nest held together by sticky secretion from glands near kidneys. Several females deposit eggs therein which he jealously guards until after young are hatched.

Stirrup, a loop of metal U-shaped strap suspended from the sides of the saddle, used for mounting and to support the horseman's foot. Some authorities allege their use as far back as the early Iron Age, and it is generally believed that they were used in battle in A.D. 378, when the Gothic cavalry defeated the legionaries of the Emperor Valens at Adrianople. Stirrups relieved the tension on the rider's knees and so enabled him to be armed from top to toe.

Stoat, a slender, carnivorous mammal with short legs, related to the weasels. The stoat is distinguished from the latter by its longer tail, which has a black tip. The black tip is retained even in the winter when the animal turns white, the fur then being known as " ermine." It is found in northern latitudes, and is abundant in Arctic America.

Stoma (pl. stomata), microscopic pores on the surfaces of leaves through which gaseous exchanges take place and water is lost. It has been estimated that a single maize plant bears 200 million stomata, usually closed at night.

Stone-Flies, comprise the order of insects called *Plecoptera*, which includes some 700 species, of which about thirty occur in Britain. The wings are membranous, and two long, threadlike feelers protrude at the tail end. The larvae are aquatic.

Stonehenge, a remarkable collection of Bronze Age monuments arranged in two circles, 340 ft. in diameter, standing on Salisbury Plain, Wiltshire. Modern archaeological research dates origin back to between 1860 and 1500 B.C. There is some evidence to suggest that the monument may have been built for astronomical purposes, providing a method of keeping a calendar for predicting the seasons and foretelling eclipses of sun and moon. *See also* J13(1).

Stork, a family of heron-like birds with long bills, freely distributed over Europe, Asia, Africa, and S. America. The White Stork is an occasional visitor to England, and, more rarely, the Black Stork; these are the only two European storks.

Stratosphere, a layer of the earth's atmosphere, which begins 6–7 miles above the earth. The attraction of the stratosphere as a medium for air travel rests upon the absence of storms; indeed weather phenomena as commonly understood do not occur, there being no vertical temperature gradient in the stratosphere and no convection currents.

Stratum (pl. strata), a bed or layer of rock.

Strontium. This silver-white metallic element was discovered by Hope and Klaproth in 1793, and isolated by Sir Humphry Davy in 1808. The chief strontium minerals are celestite (sulphate) and strontianite (carbonate). Compounds of strontium give a brilliant colour to fireworks and signal flares. Radioactive isotopes of strontium (strontium-90) are formed as fission products in nuclear explosions and tend to collect in bone on account of the chemical similarity of strontium and calcium (*q.v.*). This genetic hazard is a cause of great alarm. *See* Fall-out.

Sturgeon, a large fish found in northern seas and

rivers with five rows of bony plates along the back and sides and pointed mouth with four barbels. Caviare is prepared from sturgeon ova. Since the reign of Edward II. all sturgeon caught off the coasts of Britain, except in certain privileged places, have belonged to the Sovereign.

**Sublimation,** when a solid substance is heated and turns into vapour without passing through the liquid stage and then condenses as a solid on a cold surface, it is said to " sublime " and the process is called " sublimation ". Iodine behaves in this way, and sublimation is used as a method of purifying it. For the psychological meaning, *see* Mental Mechanisms, Q7.

**Submarine,** the first submarine, the *Nautilus*, was designed by Robert Fulton and tried out in the river Seine and in the sea off Brest in 1801. The idea was too revolutionary to find acceptance and it was not until electricity for under-water propulsion became available that the submarine underwent extensive development. Britain became interested about 1900 and the Germans developed it and made it into an instrument of warfare. The first voyage under the North Pole was made in 1958 by the American nuclear-powered submarine *Nautilus* (*q.v.*). The Royal Navy's nuclear submarine fleet includes 4 Polaris vessels—HMS *Resolution*, which became operational in 1968, *Renown* (1969), *Repulse* (1969), to be followed by *Revenge* in 1970—each armed with 16 Polaris nuclear missiles. Of the nuclear-powered Fleet submarines, *Dreadnaught, Valiant*, and *Warspite* are in service, *Churchill* has been launched, and four more have been ordered.

**Suez Canal,** connecting the Mediterranean and the Red Sea, was built by the French engineer Ferdinand de Lesseps and opened in 1869. An Egyptian company, *Canal Maritime de Suez*, was formed in 1866 with a capital of 200 million francs. The British Government acquired 176,602 shares out of a total of 400,000 for £4 million (value Mar. 31, 1956, £28,982,544). Its length is 101 statute miles, minimum width 196 ft. 10 in. (navigation channel). Under the Convention of 1888 all nations were granted freedom of navigation without discrimination in peace or war. The right was recognised by Egypt in the Anglo-Egyptian Agreement of 1954, under which Britain agreed to give up the Suez base. The Suez Canal Company was nationalised by the Egyptian Government without warning on July 26, 1956, since when it has been widened and deepened and the average time of transit reduced. The Canal has been barred to Israeli ships since the creation of the state of Israel in 1948, and to all shipping since the Middle East war of 1967. *See* C13(1).

**Suffragette,** member of the Women's Suffrage Movement who in the early part of this century agitated to obtain the parliamentary vote. The movement ended in 1918, when women of 30 were given the vote. In 1928 a Bill was passed which granted equal suffrage to men and women. The leaders of the Women's Suffrage Movement were Mrs. Pankhurst and her two daughters, Sylvia and Dame Christabel, Mrs. Fawcett, Nellie Kenny, and others.

**Sugar,** to the chemist the term is a generic one covering a group of carbohydrates, including cane sugar (sucrose), glucose, fructose, and maltose. In ordinary parlance sugar means sucrose, which is obtained from the sugar cane, sugar beet, or sugar maple.

**Sulphur,** an elementary, brittle, crystalline solid, symbol S, abounding in the vicinity of volcanoes. It is yellow in colour. It occurs in combination with other elements, as sulphates and sulphides, and allied with oxygen, hydrogen, chlorine, etc., is of great commercial utility. Used in its pure state it constitutes the inflammable element in gunpowder; it is also used for matches and for making sulphuric acid.

**Sulphuric Acid,** a compound of great commercial importance, used in a variety of manufactures, and composed of sulphur, oxygen, and hydrogen. Extremely corrosive.

**Sun,** one of the millions of stars in the universe, the centre of the solar system, estimated to be distant from the earth 93,004,000 miles, to have a diameter of 865,000 miles, and a volume

a million times that of the earth. It rotates on its axis from east to west, though not as a solid, the solar equator turning once in about $25\frac{1}{2}$ days and the poles in about 34 days. Large spots are observed on the sun—varying in size from 30,000 miles in diameter—which form and disappear at irregular intervals. The area of the disc covered by the spots, however, reaches a maximum roughly every 11 years, when the sun's heat seems rather greater than usual and magnetic storms more frequent (sunspot cycle). Spectrum analysis show that the sun is composed of many elements found in the earth. Its surface temperature is about 6,000° C. Observations made in 1964–65 (Year of the Quiet Sun) complemented those obtained during the International Geophysical Year 1957–58, when the sun was remarkably active. The earth is in the outer atmosphere of the sun and subject to its winds and storms. The apparently inexhaustible heat of the sun, which has maintained life on the earth for millions of years, is derived from the destruction of matter, involved in the transmutation of hydrogen nuclei into helium nuclei, in which process about four million tons of matter is destroyed every second. At this rate of conversion the sun will go on radiating for 30,000 million years. The Soviet space rocket *Lunik I*, fired on 2 Jan. 1959, became the first artificial planet of the sun. *See also* F7.

**Superconductor,** a metal in a state in which its electrical resistance has entirely vanished so that electric currents can flow indefinitely without generating heat or decreasing in strength. The superconducting state of metals was first discovered in mercury by Onnes in Leiden in 1911. There are many magnetic and thermal properties associated with superconductivity and the phenomenon as a whole has proved to be of great scientific interest; it resisted explanation till about 1957. In the meantime many metals and alloys were found to show the property but only at very low temperatures—below $c.-260°C$. There is a growing number of practical applications, *e.g.*, coils of superconducting wire (kept very cold by liquid helium) can be made to carry enough electric current to produce strong magnetic fields. Such fields are very constant and do not require the large supply of electrical power that ordinary electromagnets need.

**Supersonic Speed,** a speed greater than the speed of sound (in air at sea-level sound waves travel at about 760 m.p.h.). When a body travels at a speed which is greater than the speed at which disturbances themselves can travel, a mechanism exists for the generation of waves of enhanced intensity. Thus aircraft travelling at supersonic speeds produce shock waves in the air somewhat analogous to the bow waves of fast-moving ships. These shock waves are regions of intensely disturbed air which produce the sonic boom effect so distressing to people living near supersonic routes. *Supersonic* is not to be confused with *ultrasonic* (*q.v.*).

**Surface Tension.** The surfaces of fluids behave in some respects as though they were covered by a stretched elastic membrane. This property is called " surface tension." The action of detergents may be attributed in part to a reduction in the surface tension of water, allowing it to wet the surface of dirty articles.

**Surrealism.** The aim of the Surrealist school of painting and sculpture is to overcome the barriers between conscious and unconscious mind, the real and unreal worlds of waking and dreaming. As such it has a long and respectable ancestry, although the term was not in use until 1922 when it was picked by André Breton from Guillaume Apollinaire who had used it in connection with certain works by Chagall. However, Bosch in the 15th cent., Fuseli and Goya in the 18th, and many other purveyors of the weird and fantastic were the forerunners of modern Surrealism. The modern movement has broadly speaking taken two different directions: the first was towards complete fantasy and absurdity which took the form of "found objects" —*e.g.*, a bird-cage filled with sugar-cubes and a thermometer, a bottle-dryer, a bicycle wheel, or abstract works with strange and apparently irrelevant titles such as Paul Klee's *Twittering*

*Machine*; the second towards highly detailed and realistic paintings of objects placed in strange juxtapositions—*e.g.*, Salvator Dali's trees with limp watches drooping over their branches or Georgio de Chirico's deserted and classical-looking streets with long arcaded perspectives and a lone statue or a bunch of bananas in the foreground. On the whole Surrealism has spent its initial force and become almost respectable; its idea of strange juxtapositions, now widely commercialised, finds a place in advertisement illustrations and in the more sophisticated forms of window-dressing.

**Surtax,** an additional duty of income tax, chargeable on total income in excess of £2,000 (after deduction of certain allowances). The starting level on *earned* income is £5,000 or more depending on personal allowances. Payable on Jan. 1 following year of assessment, so that surtax for 1968–69 is payable on Jan. 1, 1970. The net sum is charged on a sliding scale. *See* Income Tax.

**Swans,** large, graceful birds which together with the ducks and geese form the family Anatidae. There are three European species with white plumage; the Mute Swan, distinguished by its orange bill with black knob, being the best known and a familiar sight on the rivers and ornamental lakes of this country. Two wild swans are winter visitors here, the Whooper and Bewick's Swan. The "pen" (female) and "cob" (male) mate for life and the young swans are called "cygnets."

**Swan-upping.** The annual marking of the Thames swans which takes place during the third week of July. This ancient ceremony dates back to the 15th cent. when all the Thames swans were declared to be Royal birds owned by the Crown. Two city guilds—the Vintners' and Dyers' Companies—own one third of the 600 swans now on the Thames. This privilege was granted to them by King Edward IV. in return for money grants. Vintners' birds are marked with a nick on each side of the bill, the Dyers' with a nick on the right side only. The Queen's birds are unmarked.

**Sweet Potato.** This plant (*Ipomoea batatas*), which is a climbing perennial belonging to the convolvulus family, has thick roots that are rich in starch, and are eaten like potatoes. A native of the W. Indies and Central America, new varieties of sweet potato have been bred which stand cooler climates and can be grown as far north as Cape Cod. The sweet potato of New Zealand is called the Kumara.

**Swift,** a bird so-called from the extreme speed of its flight, resembling a swallow but related to the humming-bird. It has long, scythe-like wings, sooty-black plumage and greyish-white chin. There are several species inhabiting most parts of the world, particularly the tropics. The British breeding bird is among the latest to return from Africa and the earliest to go. Swifts are the only birds to use saliva for their nests. One oriental species builds its nest entirely from saliva.

**Sword,** weapon used in personal combat, originally made of bronze. The Romans introduced the iron sword, 20 in. long. During the Middle Ages the most famous blades were those made by the Arabs at Damascus and those made at Toledo.

**Symbiosis.** When two organisms live together and both derive mutual benefit from the association, the partnership is known as symbiosis. An example is the symbiosis of an alga and a fungus in lichens; another is the ordinary pea plant and the bacteria which live in the nodules on the pea's roots.

**Synapse** is the point of association between one nerve cell and another. The nervous impulse travelling along one nerve has to be transmitted to the next across a minute gap. This is the synaptic gap. The mode of transmission is chemical though it was at first thought to be electrical. The impulse arriving at the synapse releases a chemical transmitter which diffuses across the gap and stimulates an impulse in the adjacent nerve cell.

**Syndicalism.** *See* J42.

**Synod,** an assembly of the clergy of a particular church, state, province, or diocese. The Synod of Whitby (663) settled the dispute between the Celtic and the Roman churches in the matter of Easter in favour of the Roman system of reckoning.

**Synoptic Charts.** These are meteorological charts used in forecasting on which weather conditions at a network of stations, at a standard hour of observation, are recorded, using symbols of the international weather code. Surface weather maps have been drawn regularly for more than a hundred years and the modern advance is the drawing of other maps showing conditions in the upper air.

# T

**Tabard,** a cloak or outer garment worn in mediæval days by the peasantry. The name was also applied to a garment worn by knights over their armour.

**Tailor-Bird,** name of a small group of warblers, familiar in India and China, and remarkable for their habit of sewing leaves together to enclose their nests. The bill is used as needle, vegetable fibre as thread, and a knot is tied to prevent it slipping.

**Taj Mahal,** the white marble mausoleum built at Agra by Shah Jehan in memory of his favourite wife who died in 1629. Over 20,000 men were occupied for over twenty years in its erection.

**Takahe or Notornis,** large New Zealand bird of the rail family which for many years was believed to be extinct. Small colony found in 1948 in remote valley of mountainous part of the S. Island. The bird is strictly protected.

**Take-over Bid** describes an offer made to all the shareholders of a company to purchase their shares at a named price and conditional upon acceptance by the holders of a named proportion of the total share issue. If accepted the purchaser thus gains control of the company.

**Tallage,** in Norman times, were taxes levied by the Crown upon lands of the royal demesnes. The levying of tallage was taken away by a statute of 1340 which required the consent of Parliament for all direct taxes.

**Tallow,** the more solid portions of animal fat, and prepared from beef, mutton, etc., by melting at a low temperature. Stearin is its chief constituent. Used for making candles, soap, etc.

**Tally Office,** in the Exchequer, was the department of the Government in which tallies were kept, representing the acknowledgment of moneys paid or lent; in 1834 the Houses of Parliament were burnt down through the overheating of a stove with discarded Exchequer tallies.

**Tambourine,** a light, small, single-headed drum with loose metal discs let into the side of the hoop so that they jingle when the tambourine is shaken. An older name for it is the timbrel.

**Tammany,** a New York democratic organisation, sprang out of an old benevolent society named after an Indian chief, and has exerted a powerful influence over political movements in New York. The leaders of the organisation have used their power when their party has been successful at the polls to appoint their nominees to every prominent office, and have exacted bribes for concessions and privileges, and generally Tammany rule has meant wholesale corruption. Of this there is ample evidence in the disclosures of the Tweed and other Tammany frauds, and in the fact that the "Boss" usually contrived to make himself wealthy.

**Tannins** are chemical substances obtained from a variety of plants and trees, from oak-bark, and from galls. They are used in the leather trade, the tanning process making the skins resistant to decay.

**Tantalum,** a scarce bluish metallic element, symbol Ta, discovered by Ekeberg in 1802. Chemically related to vanadium and niobium, it is usually associated with the latter in nature. For several purposes it can be used in place of platinum, and it finds application in the making of surgical instruments. Tantalum is very hard, and resistant to acids (other than hydrofluoric acid); it is used in alloys.

**Taoism.** *See* J42.

**Tapestry,** a fabric largely used in former times for wall decoration and hangings. It was known to the ancient Greeks, but in its modern form came into prominence in the 15th and 16th cent., when it was manufactured in a marked degree of excellence by the weavers of Flanders, especially those of Arras. The manufacture was introduced into England early in the 17th cent., and was attended by considerable success. At the present day the term is applied to worsted cloths for furniture coverings, and there are also various kinds of tapestry carpets now made. The most famous tapestries of olden times were the Aubusson Tapestry and the Savonnerie. The Gobelin Tapestry factory, originated in Paris in the reign of Francis I., is still a national establishment. *See also* Bayeux Tapestry.

**Tapirs.** The tapirs constitute a family close to the horse family and the rhinoceros in the Ungulate order. They have four toes on the front feet and three on the hind. The snout is drawn out into a short trunk. The largest tapir is the Malayan tapir, which stands 3½ ft. at the shoulder. Four species occur in Central and S. America.

**Tar** is a dark viscid product obtained from the destructive distillation of wood, coal, peat, etc. Wood tar is acid owing to the presence of acetic acid (" pyroligneous acid "). The highest proportion of coal tar goes into road making. Distillation of coal tar yields many valuable compounds, including benzene, phenol (carbolic acid), naphthalene, and creosote; the final residue after distillation is pitch. Based on the chemical manipulation of compounds from coal tar is the preparation of many perfumes, food essences, drugs, antiseptics, and plastics.

**Tarantula,** the name given to a large range of big hairy spiders. Music was supposed to cure their sting, hence the Tarantella dance.

**Tarpeian Rock** at Rome received its named from the tradition that Tarpeia, the daughter of the Governor of the Citadel who betrayed the fortress to the Sabines, was crushed to death by their shields and buried beneath the rock. From this height persons guilty of treason were hurled to death.

**Tartaric Acid** is prepared from tartar (potassium hydrogen tartrate) deposited in wine vats during fermentation. " Cream of tartar " is purified potassium hydrogen tartrate, which is incorporated in baking powder. Tartaric acid is also used in the manufacture of effervescent salts, and in medicine (*e.g.*, " tartar emetic ").

**Tate Gallery,** named after its founder, Sir Henry Tate, at Millbank, S.W., was opened in 1897; Sir Henry Tate bore the cost of the building (£80,000) and also contributed the nucleus of the present collection. " The Turner Wing," the gift of Sir Joseph Duveen, was added in 1910. The collection is thoroughly representative of British art and has been extended several times to include modern foreign art.

**Tay Bridge** spans the Tay at Dundee, opened for rail traffic on 20 June 1887. A previous bridge, completed in 1877, was blown down on 28 Dec. 1879, as a train was passing over it. A new bridge was opened on 18 August 1966 for road traffic, 7,356 ft. in length, the longest road bridge in Britain.

**Tea** was introduced into England about the middle of the 17th cent., when it was a great luxury, and fetched from £6 to £10 a pound. It is an Asiatic plant, native properly to China, Japan, and India. Up to about 1885 most of the tea imported into this country came from China; the bulk now comes from India and Ceylon.

**Teal,** the smallest of the European ducks and next to the Mallard the commonest British species. It is a handsome bird and a very swift flier, but not as swift as the Garganey or Summer Teal.

**Te Deum,** the song of praise (" Te Deum laudamus "—" We praise Thee, O God "), is supposed to have been the composition of St. Ambrose in the 4th cent. and is used in Roman Catholic and English Church services.

**Telecommunications.** The sending of messages over a distance. The term is generally applied to the sending of messages by telegraph, telephone, radio, television or radar. The first submarine telegraph cable between England and France was laid in 1850 and, following Hertz's investigations into electric waves, Marconi's invention led to Britain being linked with Europe by wireless telegraphy in 1899. The first permanently successful telegraph cable across the Atlantic was laid in 1866. The first telephone service between London and Paris was opened in 1891. The electro-magnetic telephone was invented by Alexander Graham Bell, a Scottishborn American, in 1876. The first submarine telephone cable to span the Atlantic was laid in 1956 connecting Britain with Canada and the United States, and many submarine telephone cables have since been laid, including the Commonwealth cable system completed in 1967. The spectacular advances in space research depended on the new tools of work provided by parallel developments in telecommunications, *e.g.*, long-range radio and television transmission, electronic computer control. The performance of *Telstar* in July 1962 and of *Early Bird* in April 1965 showed that intercontinental communication by satellites in space is practical. *See also* Radar, Radio, Television.

**Telemetry,** measurement at remote distances by means of a radio-link from the object (missile or satellite) to the ground. The third Russian sputnik, for instance, carried apparatus for measuring, among other things, the pressure and composition of the atmosphere, and the intensity of different kinds of radiation from the sun. Its radio transmitter, powered by solar-energy batteries, sent out the information in coded form by means of uninterrupted signals at 20·005 megacycles with a duration of 150–300 milli-seconds. Radio telemetry from inside the body is being increasingly used in medical and biological research; miniature radio transmitters can be swallowed or implanted in man or animal to detect various physiological conditions.

**Telepathy and Clairvoyance.** *See* J43.

**Teleprinter,** a telegraph transmitter with a typewriter keyboard, by which characters of a message are transmitted electrically in combinations of 5 units, being recorded similarly by the receiving instrument, which then translates the matter mechanically into printed characters. The telex or public teleprinter service provides direct person-to-person transmission of written messages.

**Telescope,** an optical instrument for viewing objects at a distance, " the astronomer's intelligencer." Lippershey is credited with construction of the first in 1608; Galileo constructed several from 1609 and Newton was the first to construct a reflecting telescope. The ordinary telescope consists of an object-glass and an eye-lens, with two intermediates to bring the object into an erect position. A lens brings it near to us, and the magnifier enlarges it for inspection. A refracting telescope gathers the rays together near the eye-piece and is necessarily limited as to size, but the reflecting telescope collects the rays on a larger mirror, and these are thrown back to the eye-piece. The world's largest reflectors are at Mount Palomar Observatory, California (200 in.), Mount Wilson Observatory, California (100 in.), the McDonald Observatory at Mount Locke, Texas (82 in.), and the Victoria B.C. Observatory (72 in.). At the Royal Observatory, formerly at Greenwich, now at Herstmonceux, Sussex, a 98 in. *Isaac Newton* telescope has been installed. The *Hale* 200 in. telescope at Mount Palomar is the largest ever made and has revealed objects never before photographed; it is able to probe space and photograph remote galaxies out to a limiting distance of 2,000 million light years. The *Schmidt* telescope at Mount Palomar has been used to make a huge photographic map of the universe. The giant steerable radio telescope built by Manchester University at Jodrell Park, Cheshire, has a 250 ft. reflector with a beam width of 12 minutes of arc. Early in its career it tracked the Russian earth satellites and the American lunar probes. Another instrument of radio astronomy is the interferometer which consists of two spaced aerials. *See also* Observatories.

**Television,** or the transmission of images of moving objects by radio. To understand the problems of television it is necessary to consider the action of the human eye. Basically the eye consists of a lens which projects an image of the scene before it upon the retina, a light-sensitive screen at the back of the eye. The retina is made up of several millions of tiny light-sensitive elements, each quite separate and distinct from its neighbours, and each separately connected to the brain by an individual fibre in the optic nerve. Thus the eye is a very complex organ, and it is able to pick out numbers of tiny details from a scene and convey each detail separately and simultaneously to the brain. It does not send a blend of different points of light and shade in the same way that the ear sends a blend of different sounds; if it did the brain would receive a completely unintelligible blur. From this it is clear that a television system which transmitted a mixture of detail would be useless; it must transmit all the details in a scene separately, yet almost simultaneously, and re-assemble them at such a speed that the eye cannot observe the building-up process. A means of doing this was provided by Nipkow in 1884, when he invented his famous scanning disc, and later Weiller invented the mirror drum for the same purpose. Such mechanical devices as these held the field for many years and in 1923 Baird in this country and Jenkins in America were both using them for the experiments which, in 1925, led to the successful transmission of shadows and simple outlines. It was not until 1926, however, that the first practical demonstration of television, as we understand it, took place when Baird transmitted by radio moving pictures of living human faces over a short distance. The B.B.C. began television broadcasts in 1930; the I.T.A. in 1955. The first television exchange across the Atlantic was made in July 1962 by way of the *Telstar* satellite.

Tellurium, a relatively scarce element, symbol Te, discovered in 1782 by Reichenstein. Chemically it behaves rather like sulphur; its salts are known as tellurides. It occurs chiefly combined with metals in ores of gold, silver, copper, and lead. It is a semiconductor, and some of its compounds (also semiconductors) are coming into use in technical devices.

Templars were soldier knights organised in the 12th cent. for the purpose of protecting pilgrims in their journeyings to and from Jerusalem, and obtained their name from having had granted to them by Baldwin II. a temple for their accommodation. At first they were non-military, and wore neither crests nor helmets, but a long wide mantle and a red cross on the left shoulder. They were established in England about 1180. During the crusades they rendered valuable service, showing great bravery and devotion. In the 12th cent. they founded numerous religious houses in various parts of Europe and became possessed of considerable wealth. It was this that caused their downfall. Kings and Popes alike grew jealous of their influence, and they were subjected to much persecution, and Pope Clement V. abolished the Order in 1312. Edward II. in 1308 seized all the property of the English Templars. The English possessions of the Order were transferred to the Hospitallers of St. John, afterwards called the Knights of Malta. *See also* Hospitallers, Knights, Teutonic Order.

Temple, a building dedicated to the worship of a deity or deities. Those built by the ancient Greeks at Olympia, Athens, and Delphi were the most famous. The Temple of Diana at Ephesus was another. The Temple of Solomon at Jerusalem was destroyed and rebuilt several times; Herod's Temple was destroyed by the Romans in A.D. 70.

Temple Bar, an historic gateway that until 1879 stood at the western entrance to Fleet Street near the bottom of Chancery Lane. In olden times it was the custom to impale the heads of traitors over this gateway. It has been at Theobald's Park, Cheshunt, since 1888.

Terbium, an element, symbol Tb, discovered in 1842 by Mosander, belonging to the group of rare-earth metals.

Teredo, the scientific name of the ship-worm, a peculiar bivalve mollusc, which lodges itself when young on the bottoms of wooden ships and bores its way inwards, causing much injury.

Termites, also known as *White Ants*, though they are not related to the true ants and are placed in an entirely different insect order (*Isoptera*). They abound in the tropics and also occur in temperate countries, though only two species are common in Europe. There is no British species. They live in colonies and their nests take the form of mounds of earth and

wood, cemented together with saliva, and up to 20 ft. in height. Five separate castes are recognised, three of them being capable of reproduction, and the other two are sterile.

Tern. This slender, gull-like bird has long pointed wings, a deeply-forked tail, pale grey and white plumage, black cap, and is a very graceful flier. There are several species, some of which are summer migrants to Britain. The Arctic tern winters in the Antarctic, returning to find a nesting place in the spring.

Terrapin, a kind of fresh-water tortoise. There are several species widely distributed in the Northern Hemisphere.

Tertiary Rocks, in geology the rocks formed during the Caenozoic era comprising the Eocene, Oligocene, Miocene, and Pliocene periods. *See* F41.

Teutonic Order, of German military knights, was founded in the Holy Land at the end of the 12th cent. for succouring the wounded of the Christian army before Acre. They were dispersed in the 15th cent. but the Order continued to exist until 1809, when Napoleon I. confiscated its properties. In 1840 the order was resuscitated in Austria as a semi-religious knighthood. *See also* Hospitallers, Knights, Templars.

Thallium, a blue-grey metallic element, symbol Tl, discovered by Crookes in 1861. It is obtained from the flue dust resulting from the burning of pyrites for sulphuric acid manufacture.

Thanksgiving Day, a national holiday in the United States, observed since 1864 on the last Thursday in November; instituted by the Pilgrim Fathers in 1621 to celebrate their first successful harvest.

Theodolite. The instrument used by surveyors for measuring angles in the horizontal and vertical planes; also used in meteorology for following balloons to measure the speed and direction of wind.

Therm. The charges for gas for lighting and heating (formerly reckoned at per cubic foot) are now based on the calorific, or heat, value of the gas, and the unit used is termed a therm. The therm is 100,000 British thermal units.

Thermionic Emission is the departure of charged particles from matter under the influence of heat. The higher the temperature the greater the flow of escaping particles. The most common example is the emission of electrons from red-hot electrodes—this is the basic phenomenon made use of in thermionic valves (*see* Valve). If the hot electrode (the cathode) is enclosed in an evacuated or gas-filled bulb, the emitted electrons can be collected at another electrode (the anode) and will flow through an external circuit back to the emitter. Thus an electric current has been generated by heat.

Thermodynamics, a term first applied by Joule to designate that branch of physical science which treats of the relations of heat to work. What is called the first law of thermodynamics is thus stated by Clerk Maxwell: "When work is transformed into heat, or heat into work, the quantity of work is mechanically equivalent to the quantity of heat." In one of its many formulations, the second law asserts that "the heat tends to flow from a body of hotter temperature to one that is colder, and will not naturally flow in any other way." *See* F17(1).

Thermo-electric Devices. If two wires of different materials are formed into a loop and if the two joins are kept at different temperatures a current flows in the loop. This was discovered by Seebeck in 1822, and the device is called a thermocouple. The electric current could in principle be made to drive some useful machine, and the energy comes from the heat that is absorbed by the thermocouple—if one part of the thermocouple is not hotter than the others it will not work. It has long been realised that this is a device that converts heat directly into electricity without raising steam and driving dynamos as in a power-station. However, until recently nobody has used thermocouples for much besides temperature measurement, for which they are exceedingly useful. The new development is the manufacture of semiconductors (q.v.); for the thermoelectric effects of these new materials are much greater than those of metals. A material much studied in this connection is a compound of bismuth and tellurium, bismuth telluride. It now seems practicable to generate useful electricity from suitably designed thermocouples. For example, the U.S.S.R. produces a thermoelectric device which uses the heat from the chimney of a domestic oil-lamp to produce enough electricity to work a radio. Presumably this is very useful in remote parts with no electricity supply. But the possibilities do not stop there. Indeed, an eminent Russian authority has stated that thermocouples could produce electricity direct from the warmth of sunlight on a scale and at a cost comparable with conventional fuel-burning power-stations. Even if solar energy cannot be so used, it might be possible to use the heat of nuclear reactors, but this means that the thermoelectric devices would have to stand up to very heavy radioactivity and still work. It is not surprising, however, that many firms are showing great interest in thermoelectricity these days.

**Thermometer,** an instrument by which the temperature of bodies is ascertained. The most familiar kind of thermometer consists of a glass tube with a very small bore, containing, in general, mercury or alcohol. This expands or contracts with variation in the temperature, and the length of the thread of mercury or alcohol gives the temperature reading on a scale graduated in degrees. Various forms of thermometer are used for particular purposes.

**Thermonuclear Reactions.** *See* Nuclear Fusion.

**Thirty-nine Articles.** *See* Articles.

**Thistle, Order of.** *See* Knighthood.

**Thorium,** a scarce, dark grey, metal element, symbol Th, discovered by Berzelius in 1828. All substances containing thorium are radioactive. Chief source of thorium is monazite sand, big deposits of which occur in Travancore (India), Brazil, and the U.S.A. Considered important as a potential source of atomic energy since the discovery that it can be transmuted into U233, which is capable of fission like U235.

**Thrush,** a large family of song-birds of the *Passeriform* order, distributed all over the world. The British species include the robin, redstart, nightingale, song-thrush (or mavis), blackbird, mistle-thrush, ring-ouzel of the mountains, and large numbers of migrant fieldfares and redwings from northern Europe are winter visitors.

**Thunder,** the sound heard after the occurrence of a lightning flash. It is due to vibrations of the air along the path of the flash, which are set up by the sudden heating (and expansion) followed by the rapid cooling (and contraction) to which the air is subjected. It is unusual for thunder to be heard more than 10 miles away, the distance being estimated roughly by allowing 1 mile for every 5 seconds which elapse between seeing the flash and hearing the thunder. Continued rolling of thunder results from the zig-zag nature of the flash and the multiple strokes of which it is composed, variations in the energy developed along the path, and echo effects. Thunderstorms are caused by powerful rising currents of air within towering cumulonimbus clouds and are most frequent during the afternoons and evenings of sunny summer days.

**Thursday,** the 5th day of the week, named after Thor, the Scandinavian deity. To the ancient Romans Thursday was *dies Jovis*, or Jupiter's day.

**Tidal Power.** The principle of exploiting the energy of the tides is similar to hydro-power since it involves the harnessing of falling water. A barrage across a bay or estuary is filled during flow tide and closed during ebb tide creating a difference in level. When the water is allowed to fall towards the lower side of the barrage it operates a turbine which drives a generator. More sophisticated schemes would incorporate pumped storage facilities. An essential requirement is a large tidal range in order to get a sufficient head of water. Although a 240MW scheme has recently been completed on the River Rance in France, it is believed that the economics of tidal power are generally insufficiently favourable for the method to be widely used. *See also* Hydroelectric Schemes.

**Tides,** the periodical rise and fall of the waters of the ocean and its arms, are due to the gravitational effect of the moon and sun. Newton was the first to give a general explanation of the phenomenon of the tides. He supposed the ocean to cover the whole earth, and to assume at each instant a figure of equilibrium, under the combined gravitational influence of earth, sun, and moon, thus making and controlling the tides. At most places there are two tides a day, and the times of high- and low-water vary according to the positions of the sun and moon relative to the earth. When earth, moon, and sun are in line (at full moon and new moon) the gravitational pull is greatest and we get "spring" tides. When sun and moon are at right angles (first and third quarters of the moon's phases) we get the smaller "neap" tides.

**Tiers Etat,** the lowest of the three estates of the realm as reckoned in France—nobility, clergy, and commons (*tiers état*)—prior to the Revolution.

**Tiger,** a powerful carnivorous animal of the cat family, which occurs in India and certain other parts of Asia. Its skin is of a tawny yellow, relieved by black stripings of great beauty of formation Some tigers attain a length of from 9 to 12 ft.

**Time.** The measurement of time has become of increasing importance to man with the advance of civilisation. It was at first almost inevitably based on the succession of night and day, the waxing and the waning of the moon, and on the changing seasons of the year, and the astronomical observation of these three periodic effects has served as the basis of time measurement until recent years. The precision of the observations has continually increased, and clocks have been developed for dividing the day into smaller units. The clocks were adjusted so as to keep in step with the rotation of the earth on its axis, but during recent years an atomic standard of time has been developed, and clocks are now adjusted so as to keep in step with the natural period of an atomic vibration. *See* Clocks, Greenwich Mean Time British Standard Time.

**Tin** is a white, metal element, symbol Sn (Latin *Stannum*), whose commonest ore is cassiterite (tin oxide), which occurs in Malaya, Indonesia, Bolivia, Congo, Nigeria, and Cornwall. It protects iron from rusting, and the tin coating on tinplate is applied by dipping the thin steel sheet in molten tin or by electrolysis. Tin alloys of importance include solder, bronze, pewter, and Britannia metal.

**Tit** *or* **Titmouse,** a small insectivorous bird of the woodlands and forests, bright of plumage and very active and agile, often seen hanging upside down searching for food. There are over fifty species, eight of which occur in Britain: the Great and Blue Tits, familiar in gardens and countryside, the Cole Tit, Marsh Tit, Willow Tit, Bearded Tit, Long-tailed or "Bottle" Tit, and the Scottish Crested Tit.

**Titanium,** a scarce metal, symbol Ti, difficult to extract from ores, found in association with oxygen in rutile, anatase, and brookite, as well as with certain magnetic iron ores. It combines with nitrogen at a high temperature. Discovered by the Rev. William Gregor in 1791. Titanium alloys, being very resistant to stress and corrosion, and combining strength with lightness, are finding wide application not only in marine and chemical engineering but in the building of aircraft, rockets, and the nuclear-energy field. Titanium dioxide is now widely used in making paints.

**Tithes,** an ecclesiastical tax consisting of a tenth part of the annual produce known to the ancient Jews, and first imposed by Christian authorities in the 4th cent., although not made compulsory in England before the 9th cent. Tithes derived from land are termed "praedial," those derived from cattle being styled "mixed," while others are personal. After the passing of the Tithes' Commutation Act of 1836, tithes were gradually converted into rent charges, and to-day the old form of tithes exists only to a small degree. Consult Tithe Act of 1936.

**T.N.T. (Trinitrotoluene).** A high explosive formed by the action of a mixture of nitric and sulphuric acids on toluene. Not highly sensitive to shock, it can be used in shells without danger, and is exploded by a time, or detonator, fuse. Apart from wartime applications, it is used in blasting in quarries and mines.

**Toad,** an amphibian, differing from the frog in having a dry, warty skin, a heavier, squat build and shorter limbs. It has a similar metamorphosis, is largely nocturnal, and will wander far from water after the breeding season. Two toads occur in Britain, the Common Toad and the Natterjack. The latter can be identified by the narrow light stripe running down the middle of the back.

**Tobacco** is made from the leaves of various narcotic plants of the *Nicotiana* family, which contain a volatile oil and an alkaloid called nicotine. Tobacco is largely grown in America, India, Japan, Turkey, Greece, Canada, Italy, Indonesia, Bulgaria, Philippines, France, Congo, China, Rhodesia, Zambia, S. Africa, S. America, and other countries of a warm climate. It undergoes various processes of preparation. The leaves are first dried, then cut into small pieces, moistened and compressed, and in this form it is known as cut or "shag" tobacco; when moistened with syrup or treacle and pressed into cakes, it is Cavendish; when twisted into string form, it is "twist" or "pig-tail." For cigars the midribs of the dry leaves are removed, and what is left is moistened and rolled into cylindrical shape. For snuff, the tobacco leaves are moistened and allowed to ferment, then dried, powdered and scented. *See* Section P (Respiratory System) for the connection between tobacco-smoking and lung cancer.

**Tolls.** Payments for privileges of passage were first exacted in respect of ships passing up rivers, tolls being demanded on the Elbe in 1109. Tolls for land passage are said to have originated in England in 1269, toll-bars being erected at certain distances on the high-roads in the 17th cent., where toll had to be paid for all vehicles passing to and fro. After about 1825 they began to disappear, but still linger on some country roads and bridges. Tolls on London river bridges ceased in 1878–79.

**Tonic Sol-Fa,** a system of musical notation in which monosyllables are substituted for notes. Thus the major diatonic scale is represented by Doh, Ray, Me, Fah, Soh, La, Te, Doh. The system was invented by a Miss Glover of Norwich in about 1840 and has proved of great assistance in the teaching of music in schools.

**Tonsure,** the shaven part of the head of a Roman Catholic ecclesiastic, dates from the 5th or 6th cent. In the Roman Catholic Churches only a circle, or a crown, is shaved, while in the Greek Church shaving is forbidden.

**Topaz,** a transparent mineral gem, being a silicate and fluoride of aluminium and generally found in granitic rocks. Its colour is yellow, but it also occurs in pink and blue shades. The best kinds come from Brazil.

**Topiary,** the art of clipping and trimming trees, shrubs, etc., into ornamental shapes. In Britain this art goes back before Elizabethan times when gardens were formal and the shapes simple and symmetrical. By the end of Queen Anne's reign topiary had become much more elaborate, and all kinds of fanciful shapes were produced. Pliny in his *Letters* tells how box hedges were clipped into different shapes in Roman times.

**Tornado,** a violent whirlwind, characterised by a black, funnel-shaped cloud hanging from heavy cumulonimbus. Usually tornadoes are only a few hundred feet in diameter and occur frequently in the Mississippi region of the U.S.A., where it has been estimated that the wind speeds within them may exceed 200 m.p.h. In West Africa the term is applied to thundery squalls.

**Tortoises and Turtles,** are cold-blooded reptiles, four-footed, and encased in a strong shell protection, the shells of some species being of beautifully horny substance and design, in much demand for combs, spectacle frames, and ornamental work. It is the custom to designate the land species as tortoises and the aquatic kinds as turtles. The green turtle, so called because its fat has a green tinge, is in great demand for soup. Together the tortoises and turtles make up the reptilian order called *Chelonia,* the biggest representatives of which

are the giant land tortoises of the Galapagos Islands, reaching a weight of 500 lb. and living a century. Some of these giant tortoises are even said to have reached 200 or 300 years of age.

**Toucan,** a South and Central American family of brilliantly coloured birds, remarkable for their huge bills. Toucans live on fruit, are of arboreal habits, and nest in holes. There are about 37 species.

**Touchstone,** a kind of jasper called by the ancients "Lydian stone," of economic value in testing the quality of metal alloys, especially gold alloys. The testing process is very simple. The alloy is drawn across the broken surface of the Touchstone, and from the nature of the mark or streak it makes the quality of the alloy can be ascertained.

**Tourmaline,** a mineral occurring in different colours in prismatic crystals. It is a well-known example of a pyro-electric crystal, *i.e.,* one that has a permanent electric polarisation. It is a double silicate of aluminium and boron, and occurs in Cornwall, Devon, South America, and Asia.

**Tournaments** were equestrian contests between military knights and others armed with lances, and frequent in the Middle Ages. The Normans introduced them to England.

**Tower of London** was built as a fortress by William the Conqueror. It was a royal palace in the Middle Ages and later used as a garrison and prison. Many distinguished prisoners were executed there, including Anne Boleyn, Catherine Howard, Lady Jane Grey, the 2nd Earl of Essex, and Sir Walter Raleigh. The Chapel Royal of St. Peter and Vincula in the Tower was built in 1105 and took its present shape in the reign of Henry VIII. The Crown Jewels are kept at the Tower, and in the Armoury a fine collection of armour is preserved. The attendant staff are called Yeomen Warders of the Tower. Their style of dress is of the Tudor period.

**Trade-Mark,** a mark used in relation to goods for the purpose of indicating a connection in the course of trade between the goods and some person having the right, either as a proprietor or registered user, to use the mark. Trade-marks can be registered, the registration holding good for 7 years and being renewable thereafter indefinitely for periods of 14 years. Infringement of a registered trade-mark renders the infringer liable to damages.

**Trade Winds** form part of the circulation of air round the great permanent anticyclones of the tropics and blow inwards from north-east and south-east towards the equatorial region of low pressure. Atlantic trades are more regular than those of the Pacific. The belts may extend over 1,500 miles of latitude and, together with the Doldrums, move north and south in sympathy with the seasonal changes in the sun's declination, the average annual range being about 5 degrees of latitude.

**Trafalgar, Battle of,** was fought off Cape Trafalgar on Oct. 21, 1805, between the British under Nelson and the French and Spanish under Villeneuve and Gravina. It was a complete victory for the British, but Nelson was killed.

**Trafalgar Square.** The site has often been referred to as the finest in Europe. It was conceived originally as a square by John Nash (1752–1835) when the project was considered of linking Whitehall with Bloomsbury and the British Museum. It was to be named after the new monarch as King William the Fourth's Square but on the suggestion of George Ledwell Taylor (a property owner near the site) alteration to the more popular name Trafalgar Square was agreed to by the King. On the north side the National Gallery was planned by Nash and erected by William Wilkins on the place of the Royal Mews—a work of William Kent a century before. The lay-out was the idea of Charles Barry but he did not approve the erection of the Nelson column (which see). His idea was for the square to have a grand flight of steps from the north side with sculptural figures of Wellington and Nelson but the Commons decided otherwise and the column as designed by William Railton was begun in 1840. The two fountains by Barry were supplanted in 1948 by ones designed (1938) by Sir Edwin Lutyens. Executed in Portland stone they are flanked by some bronze sculptures. In the same year memorial busts of Lords Jellicoe and Beatty were placed by the north wall.

**Transept,** the portion of a church which extends across the interior between the nave and the choir.

**Transistor.** An electronic device consisting of a small piece of semiconducting solid (usually germanium or silicon) to which contact is made at appropriate places by three wires. The three parts resemble in function (not construction or behaviour) the cathode, anode, and grid of a thermionic valve, and transistors can perform many of the operations that valves have hitherto been used for in radio, television, etc. They possess several advantages over valves since there is no need for evacuated glass bulbs nor for a heated emitter to give off electrons. This leads to much greater compactness and economy as well as to a much longer life. Nevertheless, there are certain limitations to their use, and they are not yet suitable as substitutes for valves in all cases. The device was invented by the Americans Bardeen, Brattain, and Shockley in 1948.

**Transubstantiation.** See J43.

**Treasure-Trove,** a legal term applying to treasure (coin, bullion, gold or silver articles) found hidden in the earth or other place, for which no owner can be discovered. The treasure legally belongs to the Crown, but it is the practice to return to the finder all articles not required for national museums and to reward him with the full market value of such as may be retained. It is the duty of the finder to report to the Coroner for the district in which the find is made who holds an inquest to find whether the discovery be treasure-trove or no. In England concealment is a criminal offence. See also Wreck.

**Tree Frog,** occurs most commonly in America and Australasia. The common European tree frog is a brilliant green animal, the adhesive discs at the tips of its fingers and toes enabling it to cling to trees, etc., wth ease.

**Tree Shrew,** an arboreal insectivorous mammal of Asia belonging to the family *Tupaiidae.* Tree shrews are related to the shrews, though in appearance they resemble squirrels except for their sharply pointed snout. They occur in Borneo, Siam, China, and Malaya. Some zoologists classify them as primitive primates.

**Trent, Council of,** the longest and one of the most important in the history of the Roman Catholic Church, was convened to combat the doctrines of Martin Luther. It first sat in 1545, the last sitting being in 1563. At this Council the general policy, principles, and dogmas of the Roman Catholic Church were authoritatively settled.

**Triassic** or **Trias,** the earliest geological period in the Mesozoic era, which began some 225 million years ago. Triassic formations 25,000 ft. thick occur in the Alps. Modern insects were appearing, and also small reptile-like mammals. Other important Triassic animals were: dinosaurs, ichthyosaurs (marine reptiles), and pterosaurs (flying reptiles). See F41.

**Tribunes,** name assigned to officers of different descriptions in ancient Rome. The original tribunes were the commanders of contingents of cavalry and infantry. The most important tribunes were the tribunes of the plebs, first elected in 494 B.C. as the outcome of the struggle between the patrician and the plebeian orders. They held the power of veto and their persons were sacred.

**Trichoptera.** This is the insect order comprising the Caddis-flies. These are moth-like insects, having hairs on the wings. They are usually found fluttering weakly near water. The larvae are aquatic and are remarkable for the cases (caddis cases) which they build out of sticks, small stones, sand grains, and shells.

**Tricolour,** the flag of the French Republic since 1789, consisting of three nearly equal vertical bands of blue, white, and red (ratio 90 : 99 : 111).

**Trilobites,** extinct marine arthropods, most abundant in the Cambrian and Ordovician systems. Their appearance may be roughly described as resembling that of a woodlouse,

and like that animal the trilobites were capable of rolling their bodies up into a ball.

**Trinity.** The Christian doctrine that God exists in three persons, all co-equal, and indivisible, of the same substance—God the Father, God the Son (who became incarnate as Jesus), begotten of the Father, and God the Holy Ghost, proceeding from Father and Son. The system denying the Trinity is Unitarianism (see J43).

**Trinity House,** on Tower Hill, London, was incorporated in 1514 as an association for piloting ships, and has ever since been entrusted with various matters connected with the regulation of British navigation. Since 1854 the lighthouses of the country have been under its supervision. The acting Elder Brethren act as Nautical Assessors in Marine causes which are tried by the High Court of Justice.

**Triptych,** a picture, carving, or other representation, with two swing doors, by which it could be closed in; frequently used as an altar-piece. Also a writing tablet in three parts, two of which folded over the one in the centre.

**Trireme,** an ancient vessel with three rows of oars of great effectuality in early naval warfare. Mentioned by Thucydides. It was a long, narrow vessel propelled by 170 rowers. The Romans copied it from the Greeks.

**Trisagion** ("thrice holy"), an ancient Jewish hymn, still regularly sung in the service of the Greek Church. A version of it—"Tersanctus"—also forms part of the Anglican Eucharistic service.

**Tritium,** a radioactive isotope of hydrogen which has three times the weight of the ordinary hydrogen atom. It is produced by bombarding an isotope of lithium with neutrons and has a half-life of $12\frac{1}{4}$ years, decaying with the emission of $\beta$-particles (electrons).

**Triumvirate,** a term used to denote a coalition of three persons in the exercise of supreme authority. The first Roman triumvirate was that of Pompey, Julius Caesar, and Crassus, 60 B.C.; the second was that of Mark Antony, Octavus, and Lepidus, 43 B.C.

**Tropic-Bird,** a long-tailed sea bird, of which there are 3 species (the Red-billed, the White-tailed, and the Red-tailed), frequenting the tropical regions of the Atlantic, Pacific, and Indian oceans. They are commonly called Bo'sun Birds.

**Troposphere.** The atmospheric layer which extends from the earth's surface to the stratosphere. As a general rule the temperature in the troposphere falls as altitude increases. See Atmosphere.

**Troubadours,** lyric poets who flourished from the 11th to the end of the 13th cent., chiefly in Provence and the north of Italy. They were often knightly amateurs, and cultivated a lyrical poetry intricate in metre and rhyme and usually of a romantic amatory strain. They did much to cultivate the romantic sentiment in days when society was somewhat barbaric and helped considerably in the formation of those unwritten codes of honour which served to mitigate the rudeness of mediaeval days. See also Jongleurs.

**Trouvère** or **Trouveur,** mediaeval poet of northern France, whose compositions were of a more elaborate character—epics, romances, fables, and chansons de geste—than those of the troubadour of the south. Flourished between the 11th and 14th cent.

**Truffles** are subterranean edible fungi much esteemed for seasoning purposes. There are many species, and they are found in considerable quantities in France and Italy, less commonly in Britain. They are often met with under beech or oak trees, and prefer calcareous soils, but there are no positive indications on the surface to show where they are, and they are not to be cultivated. Hogs, and sometimes dogs, are used to scent them out, the former, by reason of their rooting propensities, being the most successful in the work.

**Tsetse,** an African dipterous fly belonging to the same family as the house-fly. It is a serious economic pest as it transmits the protozoon causing African sleeping sickness when it pierces human skin in order to suck blood, which forms its food. See Gammexane.

**Tuatara** or *Sphenodon punctatum,* a primitive lizard found in New Zealand. It has a rudimentary third eye on the top of the head; this is called the pineal eye and corresponds to tissue which in mammals forms the pineal gland.

**Tube Foot,** the characteristic organ of locomotion of starfishes and kindred animals. They are arranged in pairs along the underside of the arms, and their sucker-like ends can grip a surface very tightly. The action of the suckers depends on hydraulic pressure.

**Tudor Period** extends from 1485 to 1603. The first Tudor sovereign was Henry VII., descended from Owen Tudor; then followed Henry VIII.,Edward VI., Mary, and Elizabeth, the last of the line.

**Tuesday,** the third day of the week, named from the Saxon deity Tuisto, Tiw, or Teusco. To the Romans it was the day of Mars.

**Tuileries,** a French royal and imperial palace dating from 1564. It was attacked by insurgents during the outbreaks of 1792, 1830, and 1848, and was burned down during the Commune of Paris in 1871.

**Tumulus,** a mound of earth raised over the bodies of the dead. The mound of Marathon, enclosing the bodies of the Athenians who were killed in the famous battle with the Persians, is a celebrated tumulus. Such mounds were commonly raised over the tombs of the distinguished dead in ancient times, and sometimes enclosed heavy structures of masonry. The Roman " barrows " were tumuli. Evidences of such mounds are frequent in prehistoric remains.

**Tuna** *or* **Tunny,** a large marine fish belonging to the mackerel family, frequenting the warm waters of the Atlantic, Pacific, and Mediterranean. Tuna fisheries are an important industry.

**Tundra,** the vast barren treeless plains with small lakes and morasses lying in the arctic regions of northern N. America and northern Russia where the winters are long and severe and the subsoil permanently frozen. Sparsely inhabited by nomadic peoples—Lapps, Samoyeds, and Eskimos—who support themselves by hunting and fishing. The reindeer is domesticated and supplies most of their needs.

**Tungsten,** a hard, brittle metal, symbol W (it was formerly called wolfram), silver to grey in colour. Its chief ores are wolframite (iron and manganese tungstate) and scheelite (calcium tungstate). Tungsten is alloyed in steel for the manufacture of cutting tools; also in the non-ferrous alloy stellite (*q.v.*). Electric lamp filaments are made from tungsten. Tungsten carbide is one of the hardest substances known and is used for tipping tools.

**Turbines** propelled by steam provide power for the propulsion of many ships, and on land steam turbines are a principal source of power, being used in large central electricity stations, for instance, to convert heat energy into electrical energy. Gas turbines have recently come into use in aeroplanes, and gas-turbine railway locomotives are being developed. The first gas-turbine ship had its trials in 1947, just half a century after the first steam-turbine ship.

**Turbot,** a large flat fish, highly valued as food. It often attains from 30 to 40 lb. in weight. Its flesh is white and firm. It is confined to European waters, and is caught by line or trawl.

**Turkey,** a fowl of American origin, brought to Europe from America soon after the discovery of that country. It was a domesticated bird in England in the first half of the 16th cent.

**Turpentine,** an oily substance obtained from coniferous trees, mostly pines and firs. It is widely used especially in making paints and varnishes, and also has medicinal properties.

**Turquoise,** formerly called Turkey-Stone, is a blue or greenish-blue precious stone, the earliest and best specimens of which came from Persia. It is composed of a phosphate of aluminium, with small proportions of copper and iron. India, Tibet, and Silesia yield turquoises, and a variety is found in New Mexico and Nevada. It derives its name from the fact that the first specimens were imported through Turkey.

**Turtle Dove,** a summer visitor from Africa to southern England. It is a small, slender bird with reddish-brown upper parts, pinkish throat, black tail with white edges, and a repeated purring note.

**Tweed.** A rough-surfaced fabric of the twilled type, usually all-wool, though cheaper kinds may include cotton. Of a soft, open, flexible texture,

it may have a check, twill, or herringbone pattern. Harris, Lewis, Bannockburn, and Donegal tweeds are well known. " Tweeds " is said to have been written in error by a clerk for " twills."

**Twelfth Night** is the eve of the feast of the Epiphany, and in olden times was made the occasion of many festivities. It was the most popular festival next to Christmas, but is now little observed.

**Twilight** is the light which is reflected from the upper portion of the earth's atmosphere when the sun is below the horizon (before sunrise or after sunset). The term is most usually understood to refer, however, to the evening light; the morning light we call dawn. The twilight varies in duration in different countries, according to the position of the sun. In tropical countries it is short; in the extreme north it continues through the night.

**Tyburn,** a former small tributary of the Thames, which gave its name to the district where now stands the Marble Arch, Hyde Park. Here public executions formerly took place.

**Tycoon,** the title by which the commander-in-chief of the Japanese army (virtually the ruler of Japan) was formerly described by foreigners. (In Japanese *taikun* means great lord or prince.) The term is now applied, usually in a derogatory sense, to an influential business magnate.

**Tympanum** is, in architectural phraseology, the triangular space at the back of a pediment, or, indeed, any space in a similar position, as over window or between the lintel and the arch of a doorway. In ecclesiastical edifices the tympanum is often utilised for sculptured ornamentation.

**Tynwald,** the title given to the Parliament of the Isle of Man, which includes the Governor and Council (the Upper House), and the House of Keys, the representative assembly. This practically constitutes Home Rule, the Acts passed by the Tynwald simply requiring the assent of the Sovereign.

**Typhoon.** The tropical cyclone of the China Seas which brings winds of hurricane strength and torrential rains, most frequently in late summer or early autumn.

# U

**Uhlan,** a light cavalry soldier armed with lance, pistol, and sabre and employed chiefly as skirmisher or scout. Marshal Saxe had a corps of them in the French Army; and in the Franco-German war of 1870 the Prussian Uhlans won fame.

**Ultramarine,** a sky-blue pigment obtained from *lapis lazuli,* a stone found in Tibet, Persia, Siberia, and some other countries. A cheaper ultramarine is now produced by grinding and heating a mixture of clay, sulphur, carbonate of soda, and resin.

**Ultrasonics,** sound waves of frequency so high as to be inaudible to humans, *i.e.,* about 12,000 cycles per sec. and upwards. Ultrasonic waves are commonly produced by causing a solid object to vibrate with a suitably high frequency and to impart its vibrations to the air or other fluid. The object may be a quartz or other crystal in which vibrations are excited electrically, or a nickel component which is magnetically energised. There are numerous technical applications, *e.g.* submarine echo sounding, flaw detection in castings, drilling glass and ceramics, emulsification. Ultrasonic waves are an important tool of research in physics.

**Ultra-Violet Rays.** These are invisible electromagnetic rays whose wavelengths are less than 3,900 A. (Angstrom = one-hundredth of a millionth of a centimetre). The sun's radiation is rich in ultra-violet light, but much of it never reaches the earth, being absorbed by molecules of atmospheric gases (in particular, ozone) as well as by soot and smoke particles. One beneficial effect of ultra-violet light on human beings is that it brings about synthesis of vitamin-D from certain fatty substances (called sterols) in the skin. The wave-lengths which effect this vitamin synthesis also cause sun tan and sun burn. Ultra-violet lamps (which are mercury-vapour discharge lamps) are also used for sterilising the air inside buildings, their rays being lethal to bacteria. Many substances fluoresce under ultra-violet light; for instance, zinc silicate glows green, while cadmium borate throws out red light. This phenomenon is applied practically in fluorescent lamps, the light of requisite hue being secured by judicious mixture of the fluorescent materials which coat the lamp. *See* Electric Light.

**Umbra,** the full shadow of the earth or moon during an eclipse; the half shadow is called penumbra.

**Uncials** were a form of written characters used in times prior to the 10th cent.; while smaller than capitals they were larger than the later minuscule. The term uncial was a misapplication of St. Jerome's *literae uniciales,* " inch-high " letters.

**Unction,** the act of anointing with oil, a symbol of consecration practised in the Roman Catholic, Greek, and other Churches, but not in the Protestant. *Extreme unction* is the rite of anointing a dying person with holy oil. This function consists in anointing the eyes, ears, nostrils, mouth, the palms of the hands, and the soles of the feet.

**Underdeveloped Countries** are countries in which primitive methods of production still largely prevail. Most of the population are peasants, carrying on agricultural pursuits on small-holdings without much use of capital, and the industrial production is largely in the hands of individual craftsmen working without expensive capital instruments. Many of these countries are now trying to carry through large plans of industrialisation, but are severely hampered by lack of capital resources, as they need to import capital goods for which they find it difficult to pay with exports, especially when the " terms of trade " (*see* G6) are unfavourable to primary producers. The need for capital imposes on such countries the necessity of a high rate of saving out of their national incomes; but this is difficult to enforce in view of the deep poverty of most of the people. They accordingly stand in need of help from the advanced countries, both with capital loans at low interest rates and gifts. *See* Section G, Part III.

**Unicorn,** a fabulous single-horned animal. In heraldry its form is horse-like, with the tail of a lion and pointed single horn growing out of the forehead. In the Middle Ages the unicorn was a symbol of virginity.

**Union of Great Britain and Ireland** was proposed in the Irish Parliament in Jan. 1799 after the 1798 Rebellion and came into force on Jan. 1, 1801. The troubled history of Ireland, associated with the question of self-government, nationalism, land, and religion, culminated in the Easter revolution of 1916. A treaty giving the 26 southern counties independence in 1921, as the Irish Free State, was followed by a period of internal dissention. In 1937 a new constitution was enacted in Eire in which no reference was made to the Crown. This, however, left in force the External Relations Act of 1936 and with its repeal in 1948, Eire separated itself from the British Crown and thus severed the last constitutional link with the Commonwealth, and became an independent Republic.

**Union, Treaty of,** was the treaty by which Scotland became formally united to England, the two countries being incorporated as the United Kingdom of Great Britain, the same Parliament to represent both, Scotland electing sixteen peers and forty-five members of the House of Commons. Uniformity of coins, weights, and measures was provided for, Scottish trade laws and customs were assimilated to those of England, and as regards religion and the practices of the law, Scotland was to continue as before. This Act was ratified on May 1, 1707.

**United Nations.** *See* Section C, Part II,

**Universe** in astronomy means not only the star system (of which the sun and planets are a small part) but all the countless star systems or nebulae which may be separated from each other by millions of light-years. *See* F3–7.

**Universities** are institutions of higher education whose principal objects are the increase of knowledge over a wide field through original thought and research and its extension by the teaching of students. Such societies existed in the ancient world, notably in Greece and India, but the origin of the University as we know it today lies in mediaeval Europe, the word *universitas* being a contraction of the Latin term for corporations of teachers and students organised for the promotion of higher learning. The earliest bodies to become recognised under this description were at Bologna and Paris in the first half of the 12th cent.; Oxford was founded by an early migration of scholars from Paris, and Cambridge began with a further migration from Oxford. Other Universities sprang up all over Europe, including three in Scotland—St. Andrews (1412), Glasgow (1451), and Aberdeen (1494)—which were followed by Edinburgh in 1582. These six bodies remained the only Universities in Great Britain until the foundation in 1826–29 of University and King's Colleges in London (resulting in the establishment of the University of London in 1836) and of the University of Durham in 1832. There are (1969) thirty-three Universities in England: Aston, Bath, Birmingham, Bradford, Bristol, Brunel, Cambridge, The City, Durham, East Anglia, Essex, Exeter, Hull, Keele, Kent, Lancaster, Leeds, Leicester, Liverpool, London, Loughborough, Manchester (including Manchester University Institute of Science and Technology), Newcastle, Nottingham, Oxford, Reading, Salford, Sheffield, Southampton, Surrey, Sussex, Warwick, York, in addition to the Royal College of Art, which under Royal Charter (1967) grants the degrees of Doctor, Master, and Bachelor of Art or Design (R.C.A.). Formed from colleges of technology, art and design, commerce, and other institutions, thirty polytechnics have been established in England and Wales as centres of higher education. Wales has one University (The University of Wales with Colleges at Aberystwyth, Bangor, Cardiff and Swansea) in addition to St. David's, Lampeter, which confers two degrees (in Arts and Theology), and the Welsh College of Advanced Technology, Cardiff, which is expected to be granted university status. Scotland now has eight (Aberdeen, Dundee (1967), Edinburgh, Glasgow, Heriot-Watt (1966), St. Andrews, Stirling (1967), and Strathclyde (1964), Britain's first technological University. Northern Ireland has two (Queen's University, Belfast, and the newly created University of Ulster). The number of students in the United Kingdom is expected to reach between 220,000 and 225,000 in 1971. The Government is establishing an Open University which will provide degree and other courses together with radio and television programmes. These are expected to be broadcast in 1971. The Republic of Ireland now has three Universities: Dublin, Cork, and Galway. The 19th cent. also saw a wide extension of the University movement throughout the British Empire, the early important foundations being McGill (1821), Toronto (1827), and Laval (1852) in Canada; Sydney (1850) and Melbourne (1853) in Australia; New Zealand (1870); South Africa (1873); Bombay, Calcutta, and Madras in 1857 in India; and the University of the Punjab (1882) in the present Pakistan. Since the war a number of Universities and University Colleges have been instituted in Commonwealth countries—in the West Indies, in East and West Africa and Rhodesia, in Malaysia, India, and Pakistan. In the U.S.A. the development of higher education has left the Universities less sharply defined than in Europe and the Commonwealth, the best-known being Harvard, Yale, Princeton, Columbia, and Chicago. In Britain, Universities receive aid from the State mainly in the form of direct grants from the Treasury made on the advice of the University Grants Committee. But they are self-governing institutions free from State control. In recent years students have increased their contributions to the formulation of university policy. *See also* N28–33.

**University Boat-race.** *See* U35.

**Uranium,** a metal, symbol U, discovered by Klaproth in 1789 in pitch-blende. It is a white metal which tarnishes readily in air. Great developments have followed the discovery that the nucleus of the uranium isotope $U^{235}$ undergoes fission, and uranium minerals have become very important since it was found that atomic energy could be released controllably by taking advantage of fission. Previous to the second world war the uranium content of all the uranium ores that were mined was estimated at 1,000 tons. Before atomic energy work began to take the major part of the world's output of uranium minerals, the chief users of uranium compounds were the ceramics and textile industries. *See also* Nuclear Reactors, Nuclear Fission, F12(1).

**Uranus.** This planet was discovered by Herschel in 1781. Its diameter is 32,000 miles and its average distance from the sun is 1,783 million miles. It has five small satellites.

**Urea,** the final product in mammals of the break-down of nitrogenous waste, *e.g.*, excess amino-acids. It is very soluble in water and is excreted in urine. In 1828 Wöhler synthesised urea from inorganic matter. This was the first laboratory synthesis of an organic substance and refuted the idea that living creatures or life force are necessary to create such substances.

**Ursa Major,** the Greater Bear, or "Charles's Wain," a constellation familiar to all observers because of the brilliance of the seven stars forming its outline. It never sets in these latitudes.

**Ursa Minor,** the Lesser Bear Constellation, has, like Ursa Major, seven prominent stars, of which the pole star is the brightest.

**Utopias.** *See* J43.

# V

**Vaccination,** a system of inoculation against small-pox discovered by Dr. Jenner in the 18th cent. In Great Britain it is usual for all infants at the age of three months to be vaccinated unless the parent conscientiously believes that it would be harmful to the infant's health. *See* P11(2).

**Valency.** A term used by chemists to describe the combining ability of an element with respect to hydrogen. Thus oxygen, which forms water, $H_2O$, with hydrogen is said to have a valency of two, nitrogen (forms ammonia, $NH_3$) three, and carbon (forms methane, $CH_4$) four. Chlorine forms hydrogen chloride, HCl, and is said to be monovalent. This empirical approach cannot account for valency in such compounds as carbon monoxide, CO, which appears to require both elements to have the same valency. With the discovery of the electron it was realised that the concept of valency and chemical bonds is intimately concerned with the electronic structure of atoms, and theories have been advanced to explain why the same element can have different valencies in different compounds. Iron, for example, can have a valency of two ($FeCl_2$, ferrous chloride) or three ($FeCl_3$, ferric chloride). *See* N34, F20(2).

**Valentine's Day,** the 14th Feb., is a festival in celebration of St. Valentine, one of the Christian martyrs of the 3rd cent. A sweetheart or Valentine is chosen on that day and letters or tokens sent secretly to the object of affection.

**Valhalla,** in Scandinavian mythology, is the special Paradise to which the souls of warriors slain in battle were transported. The term is also generally used to designate a burial place of great men.

**Valkyries,** the chosen handmaidens of Odin, appointed to serve at the Valhalla banquets. Their most important office, however, according to the Norse mythology, was to ride through the air at a time of battle and point out the heroes who were to fall. It is one of these Valkyries who is made the heroine of Wagner's opera " Die Walküre."

**Valve,** an electronic device consisting of two or more metal plates (electrodes) usually enclosed in an evacuated glass bulb. One of the electrodes is heated causing electrons to be emitted. If a positive voltage is applied to the other electrode, the electrons will move towards it and the valve must conduct electricity. The current will only flow in one direction as the electrons are emitted only from one electrode. A valve with two electrodes is called a diode, but by putting in one or more intermediate electrodes the flow of current can be sensitively controlled and the valves are then called triodes, pentodes, etc., according to the total number of electrodes in them. Valves have found extensive applications in amplifiers,

rectifiers, oscillators, and many electronic devices, but are now being superseded by transistors in many applications where it is advantageous to have greater reliability, smaller power consumption, and smaller size.

**Vampire** *or* **Werewolf,** according to ancient superstition, was a spectre in human form which rose from its grave in the night-time and preyed upon the living as they slept, sucking their blood, and then returning to the grave.

**Vampire-Bats,** blood-eating bats of tropical America. They puncture the skin with their incisor teeth, leaving a wound that bleeds profusely. The blood is lapped up by the bat, not sucked.

**Vanadium,** a scarce metallic element, symbol V, whose chief ores are carnotite and patronite. Some iron ores contain it. Most of the vanadium commercially produced finds its way into vanadium steels, which are used for tools and parts of vehicles, being hard, tough, and very resistant to shocks. The oxide is used as a catalyst in industry, especially in making sulphuric acid.

**Van Allen Belts.** One of the most remarkable discoveries made during the I.G.Y., 1957–58, was that the earth is surrounded by a great belt of radiation. Evidence came from *Sputnik II* (which carried the dog Laika) and from the American satellites, *Explorers I* and *III*. The American scientist, J. A. van Allen, was able to explain the puzzling data collected from these satellites. Subsequent observations with deep space-probes showed that there are in fact two zones of high intensity particle radiation surrounding the earth, one concentrated at a distance of about 1,000 miles, the other at about 15,000 miles. A close relation exists between the shapes of the zones and the earth's magnetic field. Recent evidence suggests that Jupiter also is surrounded by a dense belt of trapped energetic particles.

**Varnish** is of two leading kinds: spirit varnish, made from resinous substances dissolved in spirit; and oil varnish, in which the dissolving agent is linseed oil and turpentine.

**Vatican,** the Papal residence at Rome, a famous palace on the hill adjacent to St. Peter's. Its museum is a rich treasure-house of literary and artistic objects.

**Vauxhall Gardens,** a famous London pleasure resort from the early part of the 18th to the middle of the 19th cent. It was here that many great singers appeared, where the earliest balloon ascents were made, and where there were fine displays of fireworks.

**Vein.** *See* Lode.

**Venus,** the brightest of all the planets, whose orbit lies between that of Mercury and the earth, second in order from the sun (*see* F7). It can approach the earth to within 25 million miles. At wide intervals Venus passes across the sun's disc (" transit of Venus "). The first transit was recorded in 1639, since then four have occurred, in 1761, 1769, 1874, and 1882, and the next is due in 2004. In common with all the other planets it moves around the sun the same direction as the earth, but is the only one that rotates about its axis in the opposite direction. The planet takes just under 225 earth days to complete an orbit round the sun. In 1967 Russia succeeded in soft-landing an instrumented canister from their *Venus IV* research spacecraft. Measurements gave a picture of a very hostile environment—high surface temperature, a very high atmospheric pressure, an atmosphere 15 times denser than on earth of almost pure carbon dioxide. *See* Section F, Part VI.

**Venus Fly-trap,** a well-known insectivorous plant (*Dionaea muscipula*) occurring in Carolina in damp mossy places. It is related to the Sundew. The leaf is the organ that catches the insects. The leaf blade is in two halves, hinged along the centre line. Each half bears three sensitive hairs called " trigger hairs." When an insect touches a trigger, the two halves of the leaf clap together, trapping the insect between them, when it is digested by a secretion (digestive enzymes) from the leaf, which afterwards absorbs the soluble products.

**Vernalization.** Seeds which, after being exposed to a low temperature, produce plants that flower earlier than usual are said to have been " vernalized." This technique of seed treatment devised by Lysenko is called vernalization. It is claimed to have been widely used in Russia to obtain cereal crops in places where climatic conditions are favourable for only a short season.

**Versailles, Treaty of.** The Peace Treaty, 1919, ending the first world war. The first half was devoted to the organisation of the League of Nations. Among the territorial changes Germany ceded Alsace-Lorraine to France, Posen and the Corridor to Poland. Germany undertook to disarm, to abolish universal military service, to keep only a small army of 100,000 and a small navy. Her colonies were to be shared out among the Allies under League Mandates. Reparations were to be paid, but were gradually reduced and entirely ceased in 1932. Hitler took unilateral action against the Treaty especially in regard to rearmament and the annexation of Austria. Hitler's attempt to change the eastern frontiers was the immediate cause of the Second World War.

**Victoria and Albert Museum,** in Kensington, London, was begun in 1852 as the Museum of Ornamental Art at Marlborough House. The present building was completed in 1909, and has the following nine departments; Architecture and Sculpture; Ceramics; Engraving, Illustration and Design; Metalwork; Paintings; Woodwork; Textiles; Library (of books on art) and Book-production; and the Dept. of Circulation. The Bethnal Green Museum is a branch of the V. and A.

**Victoria Cross,** an order of merit for conspicuous valour, awarded to members of the Army, Navy, and Air Force, was established in 1856. In July 1959 it was announced that all holders of the V.C. for whom the British Government is responsible would receive a tax-free annuity of £100.

**Vienna Congress,** sat at Vienna from Sept. 1814 to June 1815, and settled the delimitation of the territories of the various European nations after the defeat of Napoleon. The Treaty of Vienna which resulted gave Ceylon, Mauritius, Cape Colony, Heligoland, Malta, and part of Guiana to England; France was not permitted to hold more territory than she had possessed at the outbreak of the Revolution in 1789; Austria took Northern Italy; Russia part of Poland; and Prussia, part of Saxony and the Rhenish province. Except for one or two changes the clauses of the treaty were maintained for over forty years.

**Viet-Minh,** the Indo-Chinese (Annamite) national movement led by Ho Chi-Minh which resisted French rule from 1945 to 1954, when Vietnam was partitioned as a result of the Geneva Conference. The National Liberation Front of South Vietnam is the political arm of the Viet Cong.

**Vikings.** Scandinavian pirates who from the 8th to the 10th cent. were the terror of northern waters. Sometimes the Viking raids reached south to the Mediterranean and east to the White Sea, and they ventured as far as Greenland and North America. Their leader Rurik founded the first Russian kingdom of Novgorod. They excelled in shipbuilding, were fine sailors and splendid craftsmen.

**Vinegar.** This condiment and preservative is a weak solution of acetic acid (3–9%) formed by the oxidation of ethyl alcohol by the action of bacteria on alcoholic liquor (wine, beer, cider, fermented fruit juices, or malted cereals). Wine vinegar is usually red; malt vinegar is brown. The name vinegar is derived from the latin *vinum aigre*, bad wine. *See also* Acetic Acid.

**Vinyl Plastics** are polymers made from derivatives of ethylene, examples are polyvinyl chloride (P.V.C.), which is used in making plastic pipes and kitchen utensils, among other things; polyvinyl acetate used in the paint industry and in bonding laminated articles like plywood; and polystyrene (poly vinyl benzene) used in making electrical fittings and for lenses.

**Viper,** a family of poisonous snakes of which there is one example in Britain, the common viper or adder, only found in very dry localities.

**Virus.** *See* P7, F26(2).

**Visibility** is defined by the distance at which the farthest of a series of objects, specially selected to show against the skyline or in good contrast with their background, can be distinguished. Visibility depends chiefly upon the concentration of water or dust particles suspended in the air. Instruments are available to measure the obscurity of the atmosphere more directly, including that at night. A large lapse rate of temperature and a strong wind are favourable to good visibility; a small lapse rate, calm or light wind favourable to bad visibility. Fog is when the visibility is less than 1,100 yds.; mist or haze when it is between 1,100 and 2,200 yds. *See* Pollution.

**Viscount,** a title of rank coming between that of Earl and Baron. The title originally stood for deputy-earl. The first English Viscount was Viscount Beaumont, created in 1440.

**Vitamins,** name of a group of organic substances found in relatively minute amounts in certain foodstuffs, essential for growth and the maintenance of normal bodily structure and function. The Hungarian biochemist Szen'-Györgyi, who first isolated vitamin C or ascorbic acid, defined the vitamin as " a substance that makes you ill if you don't eat it!" *See* P43, F27(1).

**Volcanoes** are vents through which magma reaches the surface as lava flows, or as the solid products, *e.g.*, ashes and bombs, of explosive eruption. The vent may be cylindrical or it may be a long fissure. The former type usually builds up cones, *e.g.*, Vesuvius. Notable active volcanoes are Etna, Vesuvius and Stromboli, in Italy; Hekla in Iceland; and Mont Pelée in Martinique. The last-named was in violent eruption in 1902, when the chief town of St. Pierre was completely destroyed. Volcanic eruptions are sometimes linked with brilliant sunset phenomena, *e.g.*, the Pacific island of Krakatoa (1883), whose atmospheric and tidal effects were recorded all over the world, and Agung on the island of Bali (1963), which had been dormant for 120 years. A new fissure volcano (Surtsey) developed off the coast of Iceland in 1963.

**Vole.** There are three species of British vole; the Field-vole, the Bank-vole, and the Water-vole.

**Volt,** the electromotive force unit, named after Alessandro Volta (1745–1827), and defined in terms of the coulomb, the second, and the joule.

**Vraic,** a name for seaweed in the Channel Islands, where it is extensively used as a manure.

**Vulgate,** a term used to designate the Latin version of the Scriptures sanctioned by the Council of Trent.

**Vulture,** a famous bird of prey of two distinctive groups; that of the Old World, whose nostrils are separated by a bony partition, and the New World vulture, which has no such division. Vultures feed on carrion and are the great scavengers of tropical regions. The European species are the Egyptian vulture, Griffon vulture, Black vulture, and Bearded vulture. Vultures have no feathers on the head and neck.

# W

**Wading Birds,** *Charadriiformes,* an order of migratory, long-legged, long-billed birds, frequenting marshes and shallow waters. They include the plovers, avocets, stilts, oystercatchers, curlews, phalaropes, godwits, dunlins, sandpipers, redshanks, greenshanks, snipe, woodcocks, the pratincole of the Mediterranean, and the sun bittern of tropical America. Many species breed in Britain.

**Wagtails,** familiar long-tailed small birds, the most common British species being the Pied or Water (with sub-species White) Grey and the Yellow (sub-species Blue.) Wagtails nest in holes and are active of habit.

**Walloons,** name given to the French-speaking population of the southern provinces of Belgium, in contrast to the Flemings or Dutch-speaking population of the northern provinces. The Walloon areas contain the mining and heavy industries of the country; the Flemish regions are more agricultural. Walloons number *c.* 3 million, Flemings *c.* 5 million. The *Mouvement Populaire Wallon* desires an autonomous Wallonia within the Belgian state.

**Walpurgis Night,** the night before May 1st, when witches and creatures of evil are supposed to have liberty to roam. Named after St. Walpurgis, an English nun, who went on a mission to Germany in the 8th cent.

**Walrus,** a very large marine mammal, related to the seals having in the upper jaw two large curved tusks, which average in length from 15 in. to 2 ft. It lives on bi-valve molluscs, and inhabits the Arctic seas. An adult walrus can exceed 12 ft. in length and weigh over a ton.

**Wapentake,** the ancient name given in the northern counties to territorial divisions corresponding to the Hundreds of southern counties.

**Warblers,** a family of small, lively song-birds closely related to the flycatchers and thrushes. Represented in Britain by about 36 species, including the chiffchaff, one of the earliest spring visitors, willow-wren, wood-warbler, blackcap, garden-warbler, whitethroats, sedge- and grasshopper-warbler.

**Water** is the simplest compound of hydrogen and oxygen. It is formed when an electric spark is passed through a mixture of the gases, and is a product of combustion of all hydrogen-containing compounds, e.g., petrol, coal, coal gas, and wood. Water is essential to living matter, and is the medium which carries food to animals and plants. Salts in hard water may be removed by distillation of the water or by a process known as ion-exchange (water softening). Pure water freezes at $0°$ C and boils at $100°$ C and is used as a standard of temperature on this scale. It has a maximum density at $4°$ C. Heating water above $100°$ C. converts it into steam, which is used under pressure to convert heat energy into useful work, as in electrical power stations and steam engines. Water gas is a mixture mainly of carbon monoxide and hydrogen formed by blowing steam and oxygen through red-hot coke: it is used as a fuel. Water is one of the very few compounds which freezes from the surface down rather than from the bulk of the liquid up. This property has important consequences on the preservation of life in rivers and lakes when they are frozen over. *See also* **F23.**

**Water Hyacinth** (*Eichhornia crassipes*), a beautiful aquatic plant native to Brazil which has spread to other favourable equatorial regions of the world causing havoc on account of its abnormal rate of reproduction away from its natural environment. In recent years it has invaded the Nile and the Congo, forming vast floating carpets which block the channels, clog the paddles of river craft and de-oxygenate the water, killing the fish. It is being held in check by spraying with the herbicide 2,4D.

**Waterloo, Battle of,** was fought on June 18th, 1815. The Allies (British, German, and Dutch) under Wellington and Blücher defeated the French under Napoleon. This ended Napoleon's career.

**Waterloo Bridge,** crossing the Thames, was built by Rennie, and opened in 1817. It had nine arches, each of 120 ft. span, was built of granite, and had a length (including approaches) of 2,456 ft. The present bridge, completed in 1942, and formally opened Dec. 10, 1945, is a fine example of reinforced concrete construction. (Architect, Sir Giles Gilbert-Scott.)

**Water-Spider,** an interesting little animal which spins a sac of silk on a water-plant, which it uses as a sort of diving bell. Into this bell it introduces bubbles of air, one at a time; thus the spider is enabled to remain below the surface a considerable time.

**Waterspout,** whirling tornado-like cloud, occurring at sea. It begins as a cone of cloud tapering slowly downwards, the sea surface becoming disturbed; on reaching the centre of the cloud of spray the spout takes on the appearance of a column of water. A number of these vortices may form fairly close together at about the same time, their duration ranging up to 30 minutes.

**Watling Street,** the name of the old Roman road which ran from the Channel ports by way of London to Shropshire. *See also* Roman Roads.

**Watt.** A unit of electrical power equivalent to 1 joule of work per second, named after James Watt (1736–1819). *See* **N14.**

**Wax,** the name applied to certain substances or mixtures which are solids having little crystalline form and may be regarded as solidified oils. They are used for various purposes, such as the making of wax candles, bleaching, and making artificial flowers and anatomical models, also in

pharmacy for blending in the composition of plasters, ointment, etc. The best-known natural wax is beeswax, and there are others, such sa spermaceti, obtained from the sperm whale, and Chinese wax, which is a cerotyl cerotate.

**Waxbill,** a small Oriental and African bird of the *Estrildidae* family, with wax-like bill and beautifully variegated plumage. The Java sparrow, and the Blue-breasted waxbill are attractive, and often find their way into cages.

**Wayz-Goose,** the name given to a festive gathering of people employed in printing and other works, so called from the fact that in earlier times a goose was the principal dish of the feast.

**Weasel.** A carnivore mammal found in Britain, smallest member of the group including the Stoat, Polecat, and Pine-marten, about 8 in. long. Its fur is reddish on the upper side of the animal, white on the under side; it may all turn white in winter with the exception of the tail.

**Weather,** the factors determining to-morrow's weather are so manifold, variable, and complex that the task of the meteorologist is no easy one. There are still people who cling to the idea that weather is determined by the phase of the moon, but their predictions have no scientific backing, and can be dismissed. Changes in temperature, humidity, and speed of air masses can best be measured by instruments designed for the purpose. By taking into account the peculiar character of any part of the country, whether coastal, high- or low-lying, industrial, sheltered, precise forecasts for that particular region can be made up to twenty-four hours ahead and sometimes longer. We need to know more about the heat exchange between oceans and the atmosphere before long-range forecasting is possible. The British Isles lie in the path of depressions moving north-eastward across the Atlantic. It is the frequency, intensity, and speed of these centres of low pressure, which give these islands such changeable weather. On the other hand, when an anti-cyclone builds up and embraces the British Isles, settled weather is fairly certain, the type of weather, whether dull or cloudless, warm or cold, depending mainly on the direction of the wind in the particular area concerned and the time of year. An American earth satellite, *Vanguard II*, was launched in Feb. 1959 to serve as the first "weather-eye" in space.

**Weather Lore.** Before instruments were invented to measure atmospheric conditions, man relied on his own observation of wind and sky, behaviour of birds and animals, and came to associate certain phenomena with types of weather. Many popular weather rhymes have survived the centuries, and as long as forecasting is confined to the next 24 hours there is perhaps something to be said for them, particularly those dealing with the winds. What is very unlikely is that next year's summer can be predicted from this year's winter, or that one month's weather is related to that of another. The study of past records reveals too many exceptions for such predictions to be of much use in forecasting.

**Weaver Bird,** the popular name for a large group of finch-like birds belonging to the family *Ploceidae*, found principally in Africa but also in Southern Asia, Australia, and Europe and remarkable for their habit of building nests formed of blades of grass dexterously interwoven and suspended from the boughs of trees.

**Weaving** has been practised since before any times of which we have record. The Egyptians credit the invention to Isis, the Grecians to Minerva. The main principle of the weaving loom is the same to-day as it was thousands of years ago; a warp extends lengthwise through the loom, the threads being held in separate regular order by being passed through a reed or "slay," while the weft is crossed through alternating threads of the warp by means of a shuttle which holds the weft. Thus the fabric is built up. Weaving was done by hand up to the early part of the 19th cent., when Cartwright's steam-power loom was introduced, and is now in universal use. The Jacquard loom for weaving figured designs dates from 1801.

**Wedding Anniversaries** are: first, Cotton; second, Paper; third, Leather; fourth, Fruit and Flower; fifth, Wooden; sixth, Sugar; seventh

Woollen; eighth, Salt; ninth, Copper; tenth, Tin; twelfth, Silk and Fine Linen; fifteenth, Crystal; twentieth, China; twenty-fifth, Silver; thirtieth, Pearl; thirty-fifth, Coral; fortieth, Ruby; fiftieth, Golden; sixtieth, Diamond; sixty-fifth, Blue Sapphire; seventieth, Platinum.

**Wednesday**, the 4th day of the week, derived its name from Woden or Odin, the Norse god of war.

**Weights and Measures.** *See* N12–14.

**Welding** is a means of joining together two pieces of material, often metals, by heating the joint until the substances melt locally, run together, and then solidify. The heating can be by burning gas (*e.g.*, oxy-acetylene welding) or electric current (electric arc welding). Techniques exist for welding anything from hair-like wires to massive steel plates. *See* Soldering.

**Werewolf**, a man or woman, who according to mediaeval belief, could be turned by witchcraft or magic into a wolf, eat human flesh or drink human blood, and turn into himself again. This belief was widely held in Europe, and similar superstitions prevail among most primitive peoples, *e.g.*, the " leopard man " of certain African tribes. Lycanthropy (from Gr. = wolfman) is a form of madness in which the patient imagines himself a beast.

**Westminster Abbey** stands on the site of an old church and Benedictine foundation of the 7th cent. It was rebuilt under Edward the Confessor, and again under Henry III., and important additions were made by Edward II., Edward III., Richard II., Richard III. and Henry VII., the latter erecting the beautiful eastern chapel in the perpendicular style which bears his name. The western towers and front were rebuilt by Wren in the 18th cent. It contains tombs of many sovereigns, of the Unknown Warrior, and many other illustrious men are commemorated by monuments.

**Westminster Cathedral**, seat of the Roman Catholic Archbishop of Westminster. It was designed by J. F. Bentley and built between 1895 and 1910. It is of red brick, in early Christian Byzantine style with a domed campanile, 283 ft. high, and a decorative interior.

**Westminster Hall**, adjoining the Houses of Parliament, was built as a Banqueting Hall by William Rufus, and many courtly festivals were held there in succeeding centuries. King John established the Law Courts there. It now forms a gigantic hallway, leading to the Houses of Parliament. Charles I., Sir Thomas More, and Warren Hastings were tried there.

**Whale**, a completely aquatic mammal; the fore-limbs are modified to form fin-like paddles and there is virtually no external trace of the hind-limbs. There are two major groups of whales—the *Toothed Whales*, including the Sperm-whale (Cachalot), Dolphins, Killer-whales, and Porpoises; and the *Whalebone Whales*. In the latter a series of whalebone plates grow down from the roof of the mouth, and, being frayed at their edges into a hairy fringe, together constitute a filtering mechanism. The animal takes in sea water containing minute organisms on which it feeds; the mouth is then closed and the tongue raised when the water is forced out through the filter, on which is left the food. As the tongue is lowered, the whalebone plates straighten up, flicking the food on to the tongue, which transfers it to the gut. Most whale oil is obtained from the thick layer of fat under the skin (blubber), but in the Sperm-whale there is a large reserve of oil in the head. The oil is used for making candles, margarine, and soap. Ambergris used in perfumery comes from the intestine of whales. The number of whales that may be killed in a season is limited by International Convention.

**Whimbrel**, a bird of the Curlew family, more common in Scotland than in England.

**Whinchat**, a small migratory bird, a breeding visitor to Britain (Apr. to Oct.); bright brown plumage, with prominent eye stripe.

**Whirlwind**, a sudden circular rush of opposing winds, which often causes much damage.

**Whiskers** in physics and materials science (*q.v.*) are tiny rods of crystal, thinner than human hair and perhaps half an inch long. Their importance lies in the fact that such crystals are free from the defects described on F18. They are

also free from surface cracks and steps. This means they are immensely strong because failures of strength in ordinary solids are due to imperfections and cracks of one kind or another. Large numbers of whiskers of strong solids like graphite, silicon, or silicon carbide embedded in a matrix of softer matter such as plastic or metal would make a very strong new material. Many laboratories are developing such substances.

**Whisky**, an ardent spirit distilled from malt or other grain, and containing a large percentage of alcohol. It has a greater consumption than any other spirit, and is of many kinds, Scotch and Irish whiskies being chiefly consumed in this country, and being of pot still or patent still production, or a blend of the two. Whisky is the most heavily taxed product; in 1661 a duty of 4d. a gallon was imposed, today the duty is £10 10s. 10d. on a proof gallon. American whiskies are mostly distilled from corn (maize), or rye. *See* Alcohol.

**White Elephant**, a term in common use to designate a gift that causes the recipient more trouble or cost than it is worth; derived from an old-time custom of the Kings of Siam who presented a white elephant to a courtier whom it was desired to ruin.

**Whitehall Palace**, built within sight of Westminster by Hubert de Burgh, Earl of Kent, round about 1240, was the residence of the Archbishops of York until Wolsey presented it to Henry VIII in 1530. Thence-forward to 1697, when it was burned down, it continued to be the favourite town residence of royalty, and to the Stuarts especially it was a great centre of court festivities. In those days, with its grounds, it extended from the Strand to the river. The only portion of Whitehall Palace now standing is the Banqueting Hall built by Inigo Jones, on a scaffold projected from the front of which Charles I was beheaded. A block of new government buildings has recently been built on part of the site of the old Palace.

**White House**, the official residence at Washington of the President of the United States.

**Whitsuntide**, the festival celebrating the descent of the Holy Ghost and occurring seven weeks after Easter.

**Whydah Bird**, the widow-bird of Equatorial Africa, The Paradise Whydah is remarkable for the long tail and handsome black-and-scarlet plumage of the male during mating season.

**Widow Bird**, certain species of African weaver birds with predominantly black plumage. In the breeding season the male birds are strikingly beautiful, with scarlet and buff markings and long tail feathers. They are social parasites and trick other birds into rearing their young.

**Wigeon**, a surface-feeding duck of northern Europe, known in Britain more as a winter visitor than a nesting bird. It feeds in flocks in the muddy estuaries and has a characteristic " whee-oo " call.

**Willow**, a water-side-loving tree of the genus *Salix*, to which the osiers belong. The best cricket-bat blades are made from a white willow, *S. alba* var. *caerulea*, a fine tree with bluish-green leaves, mostly found in Essex. Willow is also used for polo balls. Weeping willow, *S. babylonica*, is native to China and is the willow seen on Old China willow-pattern plates. It was introduced into England at the end of the 17th cent.

**Wind**, air set in motion by special atmospheric conditions, is of various degrees, from a slight rustling breeze to a hurricane. Winds are *constant*, as in trade winds or anti-trade winds; *periodic*, as in monsoons and other wind-visitations occurring according to influences of season; *cyclonic* and *anti-cyclonic*, when their motion is spiral; *whirlwinds*, *hurricanes*, and *tornados*, when high temperature and great density induce extreme agitation. Ordinarily, a wind is named from the point of the compass from which it blows, or it may be expressed in degrees from true north. The *sirocco*, the *mistral*, and the *simoom* are local forms of winds of great velocity. A *blizzard* is a biting blast of icy temperature. *See also* N33.

**Windmills** were in use in the East in ancient times. They were not much seen in Europe before the 13th cent. Wind sawmills were invented by a Dutchman in the 17th cent., and one was erected near the Strand in London in 1633. Great improvements have been made in these mills, especially in the United States, where, by the application of the windshaft principle, much space is saved and the mills can be used for pumping, grinding, and other purposes.

**Windows** (Old Norse *vindauga* = wind-eye), an opening in a wall of a building to admit light and air, and to afford a view of what is outside. In northern Europe windows, as the derivation of the word implies, were first used for ventilation and glass was not used in private houses before the end of the 12th cent. In early Gothic (12th cent.) windows were still small and narrow, with rounded heads. In Early English (13th cent.) they became longer and the heads pointed. In the Decorated period (14th cent.) windows were mullioned (divided by slender bars into panes) and the pointed heads often traceried. In Tudor times when the Renaissance had found its way to England, windows were larger and the bay-window (projecting from the wall) and the oriel window (*q.v.*) were much in vogue; in the late 18th cent. curved bays (called bow-windows) became fashionable. Sash windows (invented by the English) with wooden frames and divided into equal rectangular panes were used in Queen Anne and Georgian houses. Their design was influenced by a passion for symmetry; they were very efficient ventilators. The French window reaches to the floor and has double casements opening as doors. A Dormer window is a vertical window set on the sloping side of a roof. One of the main features of modern architecture is the large area devoted to windows, a development made possible by improved heating systems. Windows are now mass-produced in stock sizes and patterns.

**Windsor Castle,** the famous British royal residence on the banks of the Thames, as it now stands, was mainly built by Henry III., though a royal residence had existed there from the time of the Conqueror. Additions were made by Henry VIII., Elizabeth, and Charles II. Windsor Park and Forest comprise over 13,000 acres.

**Wine,** the fermented juice of the freshly-gathered grape. There are innumerable varieties, each obtaining its distinctive character from the species of wine producing the grape, the locality of the vineyard, method of cultivation, etc. Wines are of three main kinds: *sparkling*, as in champagne, due to their having been bottled before fermentation is complete; *beverage*, when the must has been fermented out before bottling. Such wines include the famous red and white wines of Burgundy, Bordeaux and the Rhone valley and the white wines of the Rhine Moselle and Loire valleys. Wines are *fortified* by the addition of alcohol either after fermentation is complete (*e.g.*, Sherry) or during fermentation (*e.g.*, Port). The principal wine-producing areas of the world are: France, Italy, Algeria, Spain, Portugal, Rumania, Argentine, Yugoslavia, U.S.S.R., Greece, Germany Hungary.

**Wirebird,** a species of plover confined to St. Helena where it is protected.

**Witan** *or* **Witenagemot,** the name given to the king's council of "wise men" in Anglo-Saxon times, composed of the archbishops, bishops, abbots of the greater abbeys, ealdormen, and influential thanes.

**Witchcraft.** *See* J45.

**Woad,** a plant (*Isastis tinctoria*) that in olden days was largely used in England for the blue dye obtained from the leaves. It is a biennial plant belonging to the same family (*Cruciferae*) as the wallflower and is still cultivated in some parts.

**Wolves,** well-known carnivorous animals still found in many parts of Europe, but not existing in Britain since the middle of the 17th cent. They usually hunt in packs.

**Woodcock,** a wading bird, greatly valued for its flesh. It is a member of the snipe family, and breeds in Britain. The parent bird is able to carry its young between its thigh and body when flying to and from the feeding spots. It is one of the birds protected by the Game Laws.

**Woodpecker,** a familiar tree-climbing, insectivorous bird of conspicuous plumage, of which three species are found in Britain, the green

woodpecker or yaffle (because of its harsh cry), the great and lesser spotted woodpeckers. They build in the hollows of trees. Yaffle has a long sticky tongue for licking up ground insects, especially ants. The other two obtain insects by digging into tree trunks with strong, chisel-like bills, spearing the insects with a sharp tongue. The metallic drumming sound made by the birds in spring is thought to be caused by their beaks hammering away at some hard resounding substance.

**Wood's Metal,** an alloy with a very low melting point (65° C., which is under 150° F.) so that a spoon made of it will melt when used to stir a cup of tea. Contains bismuth 4 parts, lead 2 parts, tin 1 part, cadmium 1 part. Its use as a heat exchanger has now been largely superseded by silicone oils, which have a wider temperature range.

**Woodworm.** Four beetles are mainly responsible for woodworm damage: common furniture beetle (*Anobium punctatum*), powder post beetle (*Lyctus brunneus*), death watch beetle (*Xestobium rufovillosum*), and house longhorn beetle (*Hylotrupes bajulus*). Particular attention should be paid to wood in damp, dark, and out-of-the-way places, and the backs and underneaths of furniture. The most frequent cause of woodworm damage is the common furniture beetle (*q.v.*).

**Wool** is a fibre, made up of very long protein molecules. It has been largely grown and used in the manufacture of cloth in England since before the Roman invasion. It is grown on the backs of sheep, and is of various kinds, according to the breed of sheep from which it is derived. Wool differs from hair in that it has a wavy, serrated fibre, its curl being a notable characteristic, whereas hair has a smooth surface comparatively free from serratures. Long wools are mostly used for the manufacture of worsted goods, and short wools for woollen cloths, though the improvements in machinery in recent years have enabled manufacturers to utilise short wools to a great extent for dress fabrics as well as for woollens. The finest wools are obtained from the fleece of the Spanish merino sheep. Australia, New Zealand, and the Argentine are the greatest wool-producing countries.

**Woolsack,** the name given to the seat occupied by the Lord Chancellor in the House of Lords. It is a large square bag of wool, without back or arms, covered with red cloth. At the time when it was first used, in the reign of Edward III., wool was the great staple commodity of the country and, it is said, chosen for the seat of judges as a constant reminder of the main source of the national wealth. The Lord Chancellor is said to be "appointed to the woolsack."

**World Council of Churches.** *See* J45.

**World Population.** According to the United Nations Statistical Yearbook (1967), the world's estimated population in 1966 was 3,356,000,000, an increase of 61 million since a year before. At this rate world population is likely to double by the year 2000. Nearly three-quarters live in the under-developed countries, half in Asia. Different countries are at different stages in a demographic transition from the stability provided by a combination of high birth rate and high death rate to that provided by a combination of low birth rate and low death rate. Their recent population history and current trend of growth, the age-structure of their population, and consequently their population potential for the near future are all widely different. By the beginning of the Christian era world population is believed to have been 200–300 million, rising to about 500 million by 1650, and it is estimated that about one in 25 of all human beings who have ever lived are alive today.

**Wreck,** the name given to trove found under water, usually from a maritime wreck. Finds must be brought to the notice of the Official Receiver of Wrecks, an officer of H.M. Customs and Excise.

**Wren,** a family of small passerine birds possessing upturned tails and most abundant in South America. The British species is an interesting singing bird with a surprisingly loud note for its size.

# X

**Xenon** a rare gaseous element, symbol Xe, occurring in minute quantities in the atmosphere, discovered by Sir William Ramsay and M. W. Travers in 1898. *See* Rare Gases.

**X-Rays** were discovered in 1895 by Professor Röntgen, of Wurzburg, while experimenting with a Crookes vacuum tube, when the fact was accidentally revealed that a photographic plate, contained in a dark box and exposed to its rays, was affected. X-ray photographs are now commonly taken to obtain information about objects enclosed within solid bodies; they enable bullets and any solid bodies of metal, as well as bones, etc., in the body to be perfectly located and investigated. The discovery has proved of great advantage in surgical operations. X-rays are used to determine the structure of matter; the atoms in a substance may be located and their relative positions determined by photographing reflections of the X-rays by the specimen. *See* F11(1).

**Xylem,** the woody tissue of higher plants whose function is to conduct water and mineral salts upwards, and to provide mechanical support.

# Y

**Yacht,** a light vessel now much used for pleasure trips and racing. The first yachting club was the Cork Harbour Club, started about 1720; and in 1812 the Royal Yacht Squadron was founded at Cowes. The Royal Thames Yacht Club dates from 1823. The most famous international yachting trophy is *The America's Cup* (*q.v.*). *See also* U32.

**Yak,** a curious, long-haired ox, found in Tibet, used as a beast of burden, and also kept for milk and meat.

**Yard,** a standard measure of 36 in., the word being derived from the Saxon gyrd, or rod. The yard and pound are now defined by reference to the metre and the kilogram: yard = 0·9144 of a metre; pound = 0·45359237 of a kilogram. By international agreement the metre is defined by reference to the wavelength of Krypton-86 light. *See* N12.

**Yellowhammer,** a common British bird of the bunting family, of lemon-yellow and brown plumage. Nests on or near the ground.

**Yeomen of the Guard** are a body of Foot Guards established in the reign of Henry VII. for the protection of the Royal Person. Yeomen are now about 100 in number, and their duties consist in being present on ceremonial State occasions, the yearly distribution of Maundy Money, and the searching of the vaults of the Houses of Parliament on Guy Fawkes' day. " Beefeater " is the nickname of both Yeomen of the Guard and Yeomen Warders of the Tower, and they both wear the style of dress of the Tudor period, but with one distinction, the Yeomen of the Guard wear a cross belt, the Warders do not.

**Yeti,** opinions differ as to whether this is a mythical inhabitant of the Himalayas, a primitive primate or bear. Evidence to date is inconclusive.

**Yoga.** *See* J45.

**York Minster,** one of the oldest and finest of English cathedrals, is 524 ft. long, its nave is 240 ft. broad, and the central tower is 216 ft. high. The present edifice, in parts, dates back to the 12th cent., but a church stood on the site in the 7th cent. In 1829 it was set on fire by a lunatic named Jonathan Martin, and the destruction that then took place cost £60,000 to restore.

**Ytterbium,** a chemical element discovered by Urbain in 1907; one of the group of rare earth metals.

**Yttrium,** a chemical element discovered by Mosander in 1842. It is found in a few rare minerals such as gadolinite, xenotine, fergusonite, and euxenite. One of the group of rare-earth metals.

# Z

**Zamboni Pile,** a dry galvanic battery, which can provide small amounts of high-voltage current over a very long time. At Oxford a couple of Zamboni piles have kept a bell ringing for over a hundred years. These piles in the second world war were perfected and produced in quantity, being the most convenient source of current for infra-red signalling devices.

**Zebra,** an African quadruped of whitish-grey colour, with regular black stripings, perhaps the most beautiful member of the Equine family. Rather larger than an ass and smaller than the horse, it has a tufted tail, is of light build, wild, and fleet of foot. The Zebra is threatened with extinction—already the fate of the Quagga species—because of its slaughter by man for its beautiful skin.

**Zen Buddhism.** *See* J46.

**Zenith,** the highest point in the heavens above an observer's head, the opposite pole to the Nadir.

**Zero,** the cypher signifying nothing. The West is indebted to the Arabs for it, who probably got it from the Hindus and passed it to European mathematicians towards the end of the Middle Ages. The zero has also been found in Babylonian cuneiform. The Greeks had no such symbol, which hindered the development of their mathematics. The use of zero led to the invention of decimal fractions and to the later developments in astronomy, physics and chemistry. For absolute zero on the temperature scale *see* L2.

**Zinc,** a familiar metallic element, symbol Zn, known to the ancients, and used by them in the making of brass. It occurs as the sulphide, carbonate, etc. The ores of zinc are crushed, roasted, and reduced with coal. In combination with copper it constitutes the familiar alloy called brass, and zinc itself is much used for roofing and other protective purposes. Zinc ores are mined in Canada, the U.S.A., Mexico, Poland, Australia, Russia, Italy, Spain, and many other parts of the world. Zinc smelting is carried on in most industrial countries, including Great Britain.

**Zionism.** *See* J46.

**Zirconium,** metallic element, symbol Zr, was discovered by Klaproth in the sand of the rivers of Ceylon in 1789. The crystalline metal is white, soft, and ductile; in its amorphous condition it is a blue-black powder. Zirconium is used in atomic reactors as containers for fuel elements, since it does not absorb neutrons.

**Zodiac,** an imaginary zone or belt of the sky enclosing the circuit over which the principal planets travel. It is divided into 12 equal spaces of 30 degrees each, comprising respectively the 12 signs of the zodiac—Aries, Taurus, Gemini, Cancer, Leo, Virgo, Libra, Scorpio, Sagittarius, Capricornus, Aquarius and Pisces. The idea of the zodiac originated with the Babylonians about 2000 B.C. and passed by way of the Greeks to the Western world.

**Zodiacal Light,** a faint cone of light occasionally seen stretching along the zodiac from the western horizon after evening twilight or the eastern horizon before morning twilight. It is believed to be due to the scattering of the sun's light by dust particles in orbit round the sun and extending beyond the earth. Recent observations at the high altitude station at Chacaltaya in the Andes suggest that the dust is travelling round the sun in regular planetary orbits.

**Zonda,** a warm moist wind in Argentina of great velocity blowing from the north or northwest, and, like the Sirocco in Southern Europe, causes much discomfort. It happens when a depression is moving across the pampas, bringing with it a mass of air from the humid tropics. It is followed by a refreshing wind from the southeast.

**Zoological Gardens** of London were opened in 1828, and belong to the Zoological Society of London. They contain one of the largest and most varied collections of living animals in the world. The Society maintains an open-air zoo at Whipsnade, on the edge of Dunstable Downs; this was opened in 1931.

**Zoology,** the science of animal biology, treating of the structure, classification, and distribution of the various members of the animal kingdom.

**Zoroastrianism.** *See* J46.

## NOBEL PRIZE WINNERS (1901–1968)

| YEAR. | PHYSICS. | CHEMISTRY. | PHYSIOLOGY AND MEDICINE. | LITERATURE. | PEACE. |
|---|---|---|---|---|---|
| 1901 | W. C. Röntgen (G). | J. H. van't Hoff (D). | E. v. Behring (G). | R. F. A. Sully Prudhomme (F). | H. Dunant (Sw), F. Passy (F). |
| 1902 | H. A. Lorentz (D), P. Zeeman (D). | E. Fischer (G). | R. Ross (B). | T. Mommsen (G). | E. Ducommun (Sw), A. Gobat (Sw). |
| 1903 | H. Becquerel (F), P. Curie (F), Marie Curie (F). | S. Arrhenius (S). | N. R. Finsen (Da). | B. Björnson (N). | Sir W. R. Cremer (B). |
| 1904 | Lord J. W. S. Rayleigh (B). | W. Ramsay (B). | I. P. Pavlov (R). | F. Mistral (F), J. Echegaray (Sp). | Institut de Droit International. |
| 1905 | P. Lenard (G). | A. v. Bayer (G). | R. Koch (G). | H. Sienkiewicz (P). | Bertha von Suttner (Au). |
| 1906 | J. J. Thomson (B). | H. Moissan (F). | C. Golgi (I), S. R. y Cajal (Sp). | G. Carducci (I). | T. Roosevelt (A). |
| 1907 | A. A. Michelson (A). | E. Buchner (G). | C. L. A. Laveran (F). | Rudyard Kipling (B). | E. T. Moneta (I), L. Renault (F). |
| 1908 | G. Lippmann (F). | E. Rutherford (B). | P. Ehrlich (G), E. Metchnikoff (R). | R. Eucken (G). | K. P. Arnoldson (S), F. Bajer (Da). |
| 1909 | F. Braun (G), G. Marconi (I). | W. Ostwald (G). | T. Kocher (Sw). | S. Lagerlöf (S). | A. M. F. Beernaert (Be), Baron d'Estournelles de Constant de Rebeque (F). |
| 1910 | J. D. van der Waals (D). | O. Wallach (G). | A. Kossel (G). | P. Heyse (G). | The Bureau International Permanent de la Paix, Berne. |
| 1911 | W. Wien (G). | Marie Curie (F). | A. Gullstrand (S). | M. Maeterlinck (Be). | T. M. C. Asser (D), A. H. Fried (Au). |
| 1912 | G. Dalén (S). | V. Grignard (F), P. Sabatier (F). | A. Carrel (A). | G. Hauptmann (G). | E. Root (A). |
| 1913 | H. Kamerlingh Onnes (D). | A. Werner (Sw). | C. Richet (F). | R. Tagore (In). | H. la Fontaine (Be). |
| 1914 | M. v. Laue (G). | T. W. Richards (A). | R. Bárány (Au). | — | — |
| 1915 | W. H. Bragg (B), W. L. Bragg (B). | R. Willstaetter (G). | — | R. Roland (F). | — |
| 1916 | — | — | — | V. von Heidenstam (S). | — |
| 1917 | C. G. Barkla (B). | — | — | K. Gjellerup (Da), H. Pontoppidan (Da). | Comité International de la Croix-Rouge, Geneva. |
| 1918 | M. Planck (G). | F. Haber (G). | | — | |
| 1919 | J. Stark (G). | | J. Bordet (Be). | C. Spitteler (Sw). | W. Wilson (A). |
| 1920 | C. E. Guillaume (F). | W. Nernst (G). | A. Krogh (Da). | K. Hamsun (N). | L. Bourgeois (F). |
| 1921 | A. Einstein (G). | F. Soddy (B). | | A. France (F). | K. H. Branting (S), C. L. Lange (N). |
| 1922 | N. Bohr (Da). | F. W. Aston (B). | A. Hill (B), O. Meyerhof (G). | J. Benavente (Sp). | F. Nansen (N). |
| 1923 | R. A. Millikan (A). | F. Pregl (Au). | F. G. Banting (C), J. R. Macleod (C). | W. B. Yeats (Ir). | |
| 1924 | M. Siegbahn (S). | | W. E. Einthoven (D). | W. Reymont (P). | |
| 1925 | J. Franck (G), G. Hertz (G). | R. Zsigmondy (G). | — | G. B. Shaw (B). | Sir A. Chamberlain (B), C. G. Dawes (A). |
| 1926 | J. Perrin (F). | T. Svedberg (S). | J. Fibiger (Da). | G. Deledda (I). | A. Briand (F), G. Streemann (G). |
| 1927 | A. H. Compton (A), C. T. R. Wilson (B). | H. Wieland (G). | J. Wagner-Jauregg (Au). | H. Bergson (F). | F. Buisson (F), L. Quidde (G). |

## NOBEL PRIZE WINNERS (1901–1968), *continued*

| Year. | Physics. | Chemistry. | Physiology and Medicine. | Literature. | Peace. |
|---|---|---|---|---|---|
| 1928 | O. W. Richardson (B). | A. Windaus (G). | C. Nicolle (F). | S. Undset (N). | — |
| 1929 | L. de Broglie (F). | H. v. Euler-Chelpin (S), A. Harden (B). | C. Eijkman (D), F. G. Hopkins (B). | T. Mann (G). | F. B. Kellogg (A). |
| 1930 | C. V. Raman (In). | H. Fischer (G). | K. Landsteiner (Au). | S. Lewis (A). | L. O. J. Söderblom (S). |
| 1931 | — | F. Bergius (G), K. Bosch (G). | O. Warburg (G). | E. A. Karlfeldt (S). | Jane Addams (A), N. M. Butler (A). |
| 1932 | W. Heisenberg (G). | I. Langmuir (A). | C. S. Sherrington (B), E. D. Adrian (B). | J. Galsworthy (B). | — |
| 1933 | P. A. M. Dirac (B), E. Schroedinger (Au). | — | T. H. Morgan (A). | Bunin (R). | Sir Norman Angell (B). |
| 1934 | — | H. C. Urey (A). | G. Minot (A), W. Murphy (A), G. Whipple (A). | L. Pirandello (I). | Arthur Henderson (B). |
| 1935 | J. Chadwick (B). | F. Joliot (F), I. Joliot-Curie (F). | H. Spemann (G). | — | C. von Ossietzky (G). |
| 1936 | V. F. Hess (Au), C. D. Anderson (A). | P. Debye (D). | Sir H. H. Dale (B), O. Loewi (G). | E. O'Neill (A). | C. de S. Lamas (Ar). |
| 1937 | C. J. Davisson (A), G. P. Thomson (B). | W. N. Haworth (B), P. Karrer (Swy). | A. v. Szent-Györgi (H). | R. Martin du Gard (F). | Viscount Cecil of Chelwood (B). |
| 1938 | E. Fermi (I). | R. Kuhn (G). | C. Heymans (Be). | Pearl S. Buck (A). | Office International Nansen pour les Réfugiés. |
| 1939 | E. O. Lawrence (A). | A. F. Butenandt (G), L. Ruzicka (Swy). | G. Domagk (G). | F. E. Sillanpää (Fi). | — |
| 1940–42 | — | | | — | — |
| 1943 | O. Stern (A). | G. Hevesy (H). | H. Dam (Da), E. A. Doisy (A). | — | — |
| 1944 | I. I. Rabi (A). | O. Hahn (G). | E. J. Erlanger (A), H. S. Gasser (A). | J. V. Jensen (Da). | Comité International de la Croix-Rouge, Geneva. |
| 1945 | W. Pauli (Au). | A. Virtanen (Fi). | Sir A. Fleming (B), Sir H. Florey (B), E. B. Chain (B). | G. Mistral (Ch). | Cordell Hull (A). |
| 1946 | P. W. Bridgman (A). | J. B. Sumner (A), J. H. Northrop (A), W. M. Stanley (A). | H. J. Muller (A). | H. Hesse (Sw). | Emily G. Balch (A), J. R. Mott (A). |
| 1947 | Sir Edward Appleton (B). | Sir Robert Robinson (B). | B. A. Houssay (Ar), C. F. Cori (A), G. T. Cori (A). | André Gide (F). | American and British Quaker Organisations. |
| 1948 | P. M. S. Blackett (B). | A. Tiselius (S). | P. Müller (Swy). | T. S. Eliot (B). | — |
| 1949 | H. Yukawa (J). | W. F. Giauque (A). | W. R. Hess (Sw), A. E. Moniz (Po). | W. Faulkner (A). | Lord Boyd-Orr (B). |
| 1950 | Cecil F. Powell (B). | Otto Diels (G), K. Alder (G). | E. C. Kendall (A), P. S. Hench (A), R. Reichstein (Sw). | Lord Russell (B). | Ralph Bunche (A). |
| 1951 | Sir J. Cockcroft (B), E. T. S. Walton (Ir). | E. M. MacMillan (A), G. T. Seaborg (A). | M. Theiler (A). | P. Lagerkvist (S). | Léon Jouhaux (F). |
| 1952 | E. Purcell (A), F. Bloch (A). | A. J. P. Martin (B), R. L. M. Synge (B). | S. Wakman (A). | F. Mauriac (F). | A. Schweitzer (F). |

## NOBEL PRIZE WINNERS (1901–1968), continued

| Year. | Physics. | Chemistry. | Physiology and Medicine. | Literature. | Peace. |
|---|---|---|---|---|---|
| 1953 | F. Zernike (D). | H. Staudinger (G). | H. A. Krebs (B), F. A. Lipmann (A). | Sir W. S. Churchill (B). | Gen. G. Marshall (A). |
| 1954 | M. Born (B), W. Bothe (G). | L. Pauling (A). | J. F. Enders (A), F. C. Robins (A), T. H. Weller (A). | E. Hemingway (A). | U.N. High Commission for Refugees. |
| 1955 | W. E. Lamb (A), P. Kusch (A). | Vicent du Vigneaud (A). | Hugo Theorell (S). | Halldór Laxness (Ic). | — |
| 1956 | W. Shockley (A), J. Bardeen (A), W. H. Brattain (A). | Sir Cyril Hinshelwood (B), N. Semenov (R). | A. F. Cournand (A), D. W. Richards (A), W. Forssmann (G). | J. Ramón Jiménez (Sp). | — |
| 1957 | T. Dao-lee (Chi), C. Ning-yang (Chi). | Sir Alexander Todd (B). | D. Bovet (I). | A. Camus (F). | L. B. Pearson (C). |
| 1958 | P. A. Cerenkov (R), I. M. Frank (R), I. Tamm (R). | F. Sanger (B). | G. W. Beadle (A), E. Tatum (A), J. Lederberg (A). | B. Pasternak (R). | Father George Pire (Be). |
| 1959 | E. Segrè (A), O. Chamberlain (A). | J. Heyrovsky (Cz). | S. Ochoa (A), A. Kornberg (A). | S. Quasimodo (I). | P. J. Noel-Baker (B). |
| 1960 | D. A. Glaser (A). | W. F. Libby (A). | P. B. Medawar (B), Sir M. Burnet (Aus). | A. St. Léger (F). | A. Lothuli (S.A.). |
| 1961 | R. Hofstadter (A), B. Mossbauer (G). | M. Calvin (A). | G. von Bekesy (H). | I. Andric (Y). | D. Hammarskjöld (S). |
| 1962 | L. Davidovich Landau (R). | M. F. Perutz (B), J. C. Kendrew (B). | F. H. C. Crick (B), M. H. F. Wilkins (B), J. D. Watson (A). | J. Steinbeck (A). | L. Pauling (A). |
| 1963 | Maria Goeppert-Mayer (A), J. H. D. Jensen (G), E. P. Wigner (A). | K. Ziegler (G), G. Natta (I). | A. L. Hodgkin (B), A. F. Huxley (B), Sir J. Eccles (B). | G. Seferis (Gr). | International Red Cross Committee and the International League of Red Cross Societies. |
| 1964 | C. H. Townes (A), N. G. Basov (R), A. M. Prokhorov (R). | Dorothy Hodgkin (B). | K. E. Bloch (A), F. Lynen (G). | Jean-Paul Sartre (F). | Martin Luther King (A). |
| 1965 | S. Tomonaga (J), J. Schwinger (A), P. Feynman (A). | A. B. Woodward (A). | F. Jacob (F), A. Lwoff (F), J. Monod (F). | M. Sholokhov (R). | UNICEF |
| 1966 | A. Kastler (F). | R. S. Mulliken (A). | F. P. Rous (A), C. A. Huggins (A). | S. Y. Agnon (Is), Nelly Sachs (Sw). | No award |
| 1967 | H. A. Bethe (A). | R. G. W. Norrish (B), G. Porter (B), M. Eigen (G). | R. Granit (S), H. K. Hartline (A), G. Wald (A). | M. A. Asturias (Gu). | No award |
| 1968 | L. W. Alvarez (A). | L. Onsager (A). | M. Nirenberg (A), H. G. Khorana (A), R. Holley (A). | Y. Kawabata (J). | R. Cassin (F). |

A = American
Ar = Argentine
Au = Austrian
Aus = Australian
B = British

Be = Belgian
O = Canadian
Ch = Chilean
Chi = Chinese
Cz = Czech

D = Dutch
Da = Danish
F = French
Fi = Finnish
G = German

Gr = Greek
Gu = Guatemalan
H = Hungarian
I = Italian
Ic = Icelandic

In = Indian
Ir = Irish
Is = Israeli
J = Japanese
N = Norwegian

P = Polish
Po = Portuguese
R = Russian
S = Swedish

S.A. = South African
Sp = Spanish
Sw = Swiss
Y = Yugoslav

Note: A new Nobel Prize for economics is to be awarded in 1969.

# LITERARY COMPANION

This section discusses the modern novel and suggests ways of approaching the poetry of the current century. It contains a guide to versification and to our figures of speech.

# TABLE OF CONTENTS

# I. THE CONTEMPORARY NOVEL

This section discusses novels written in English and published since 1945. It consists of two parts: I. Introduction; II. Directory of Novelists.

We are helped to appreciate the modern novel if we understand how it evolved from that of the nineteenth century. The Introduction that follows therefore summarises some of the important characteristics of English, American, and French novels of the nineteenth and early twentieth centuries and describes some of the literary and intellectual ideas that seem to have affected contemporary fiction.

It is important to remember that every worthwhile novel is an individual work of art that creates its own rules and however strange a writer's techniques or subject-matter may seem, we should try to suspend judgement until we have read his novel for a second or third time. Apart from the obvious difference that plays are written to be performed and novels to be read, the criteria of judgement suggested on 16 are as applicable to modern fiction as they are to contemporary drama.

## INTRODUCTION
### The Mid-Nineteenth Century
#### (a) English and American Novels.

At this time English novelists were members of a comparatively secure and stable society which possessed generally accepted social and moral standards, and the theme of almost all their writing is the interaction of the individual and the community. Novelists such as George Eliot, Dickens, Thackeray, and Trollope depict characters who progress towards self-knowledge as they learn to discriminate between the genuine and the false, the good and the evil in the people and institutions with which they are brought into contact. Since these writers were as much concerned with the presentation of society as of individuals, most of their work contains naturalistic descriptions of the life and manners of their day and, although the main characters of the Victorian novel are the focal points of its action, as Douglas Hewitt has remarked, they are not central to it in the way that the hero of a tragedy is central, the action is not " orientated towards them."

Most English novels of this period are comparatively loose and episodic in structure. Narrative is chronological and most writers place themselves between the reader and the story, standing apart from the characters, observing, commenting on and judging their actions, and, quite often, addressing the reader directly.

A notable exception to this general pattern is *Wuthering Heights.* In both its techniques and its view of life Emily Brontë's novel has more in common with mid-nineteenth-century American fiction than with the work of her compatriots and is unique among the English novels of its day in its disregard for society and of social and moral conventions.

American novelists, such as Twain, Hawthorne, and Melville, were interested in the presentation of individuals rather than of society. This was natural in a country inhabited by pioneers and exiles and their descendants, who had no common culture. Like the heroes of tragedies, the main characters of mid-nineteenth-century American novels are central to their action, isolated pioneers and exiles who create their own worlds.

American novelists used chronological narrative, but they generally wrote in the first person and their techniques were in other ways different from those of most of their English contemporaries and characterised by the use of allegory and symbolism.

In both countries novelists wrote for a middle-class public and, like their readers, they saw fiction as a mode of entertainment and, or, instruction. However, in France other ideas were being born which were to affect both the form and content of twentieth-century English and American fiction and lead many writers to think of novels as primarily works of art.

#### (b) French Novels.
##### Gautier and Æstheticism.

As early as 1825 Gautier had said that a writer must concern himself only with perfecting the style and form of his work and that this was impossible if he considered " the needs of society," " civilization," or " progress." Later, he wrote, " A beautiful form is a beautiful idea," implying that a novelist could treat any subject, no matter how sordid or painful, so long as he embodied it in a beautiful work of art.

##### Flaubert and Realism.

Flaubert, a leading member of the Realist school, felt that novelists must strive to be impersonal, adapting their style to their subject-matter, for only thus could they write " realistically." He believed that it helped novelists to be objective if they based their work on scientific documentation and said, " It is necessary to discuss the human soul with the [same] impersonality that one uses in [the study of] physical sciences." To the public, who were shocked by Flaubert's unconventional subject-matter, " realistic " became a term signifying moral disapproval.

" Realistic " is now used of (i) novels of working-class life, such as Sillitoe's *Saturday Night and Sunday Morning*; (ii) any frank treatment of the physical aspects of life, or of painful or sordid subjects, as in Mailer's *The Naked and the Dead.* Our use of the term has been influenced by Marxist theory and by the writing of the Naturalists.

##### Zola and Naturalism.

Zola and his followers called themselves Naturalists because, although they agreed with Flaubert that novelists should aim at objectivity, they wanted to produce " slices of life " rather than " works of art." Zola was stimulated by new scientific ideas and particularly interested in the effects of heredity and environment upon character. He inclined to the theory that character is largely determined by environment and wrote of the former in terms of the latter. Fascinated by the sordid side of nineteenth-century life, he tended to concentrate on it to the exclusion of all else and stimulated interest in the portrayal of moral degradation, brutality, and squalor. In England the National Vigilance Society waged a vigorous, and unsuccessful, campaign against the publication of translations of such " corrupt literature "!

### 1880–1910

This period introduced some of the most popular kinds of modern novel: inspired by the work of the Frenchman Verne, H. G. Wells began to write Science Fiction; Conrad's *Secret Agent* introduced the Spy Thriller; and Conan-Doyle developed the Detective Story, invented in 1868 by Wilkie Collins.

The work of the French Naturalists was influential throughout this period, but, although it helped to widen the scope of the novel it found few close adherents among English or American writers who were, and are, more interested in those idiosyncratic aspects of personality disregarded by the Naturalists. The influence of Gautier and, particularly, Flaubert was more important and was firstly apparent in the work of James and Conrad, both of whom saw themselves as artists, not teachers or entertainers. They have been called the first Modern English Novelists.

### (a) Henry James (1843–1916).

James admired the work of Gautier and was much impressed by Flaubert's theory of fiction. Like Flaubert, he strove towards an objective, detailed presentation of character and constantly sought to depict the naunces of feeling more delicately and precisely and to give his novels greater aesthetic unity. Many twentieth-century writers call James "The Master," for the scrupulous care with which he revised and polished the style of his novels and short-stories established an ideal of literary craftsmanship, and the artistry and poetic sensitivity of his writing have had a marked effect upon the work of writers such as Elizabeth Bowen and Hartley. James began the process of combining the social novel of the European tradition with the more poetic American novel, a process to be carried much farther by Conrad in *Nostromo*.

### (b) Joseph Conrad (1857–1926).

Conrad spent his youth in France and was well read in French literature. The sense of insecurity which permeates his writing is one of the first signs in English fiction of the break-up of the social and moral stability of the nineteenth century. This change appeared earlier on the Continent than in England and it is perhaps significant that Conrad was of Polish birth and always spoke French better than English, but his sense of insecurity was doubtless intensified by the hazards of his early naval career in the days of sailing-ships.

Like the novels of present-day writers such as Beckett, Lowry, and White, Conrad's books are essentially poetic and can be read on a number of different levels. They are as realistic as nineteenth-century French novels, but their every detail bears a significant relation to the plight of their central characters, and in his masterpiece, *Nostromo*, Conrad showed that a novel of great poetic intensity could yet encompass the life of a whole society.

James had been unable to banish the intrusive presence of the author from his novels; Conrad managed to, at times by using a narrator who is deeply involved in the action, at others by reviving an eighteenth-century technique of telling the story from shifting points of view. At the same time he abandoned chronological narrative for a shifting time sequence, which reinforces his themes by intensifying a feeling of insecurity. Narrative of this kind has been used with similar effect by a number of modern novelists, including Beckett, Bellow, and Naipaul, and, although the use of the shifting time sequence, which marks one of the most obvious differences between nineteenth- and twentieth-century fiction, has been influenced by the writing of Proust and Joyce and by new ideas in theoretical physics and psychology, Conrad was the first novelist to use this kind of narrative.

### The Early Twentieth Century

"On or about December 1910 human nature changed," said Virginia Woolf. She probably chose that date because it marked the opening of the first London exhibition of the paintings of the post-impressionists. The work of these artists expressed a new vision of reality which was characteristic of the intellectual and cultural revolution sweeping Western society in the early decades of the century. The stimulus of this new Renaissance was reflected not only in painting, but in the music of Stravinsky, the dance of the Diaghilev Ballet, the poetry of Pound and Eliot and the novels of Proust, Joyce, and Virginia Woolf herself. The sense of exhilaration felt at this time is vividly suggested in Leonard Woolf's autobiographical work *Beginning Again*.

The stability and formality of nineteenth-century life, which had already been undermined by the ideas of Darwin and Huxley, the growing literacy of the working-classes, and the accelerating technological revolution, was now shattered by the combined impact of psychological theories, the ideas of social anthropologists such as Sir James Frazer and the work of physicists like Planck, Einstein, and Rutherford (*see* F10–13). As a result, novelists could no longer assume that readers' attitudes and values would resemble their own and were obliged to reconsider the nature of the relationship between art and life. The exploration of this relationship becomes one of the major themes of twentieth-century fiction, and after the First World War it is accompanied by an increasing sense of the isolation and insecurity of the individual's life and the inadequacy of words as vehicles for communicating experience.

For most writers the nineteenth-century European novel now seemed inadequate to express the complex and fluid nature of consciousness revealed by psychologists, and narrative consisting of a simple chronological progression of events was felt to give a misleading impression of our experience of time. Novelists were therefore compelled to search for new techniques, and were encouraged to do so by the example of experiments already taking place in art and music and by the example of the French Symbolist poets.

### (a) The Influence of Psychological Theories.

The interest in the nature of perception revealed in the work of impressionist and post-impressionist painters had been growing since the turn of the century and was stimulated by the writings of the American William James and the Frenchman Henri Bergson.

In 1890, James, the brother of novelist Henry James, had published *Principles of Psychology*, in which he compared consciousness with a "river or a stream," implying that it carries within it submerged and floating memories and receives a fluid series of impressions of the exterior world. The term "stream of consciousness," derived from James's theory, was later applied to a new literary technique evolved by Joyce.

In *Matter and Memory* (1894), Bergson had suggested that perception is controlled by memory and said that our view of the world changes at every moment, "as though by a turn of a kaleidoscope," suggesting that perception involves an involuntary, creative readjustment of elements of past experience. This idea was to have a profound effect upon the work of Proust, to whom Bergson was related by marriage.

The writings of Freud, which began to be published in English in 1913, drew further attention to details of human experience, stimulating the growing interest in the subconscious mind, in dreams and the symbolic transformation of experience and combining with the influence of the Symbolist writers and the music of Wagner to give new impetus to the use of symbolism in fiction.

The influence of Freudian theory also extended the novel's potential subject-matter in two most important ways.

By emphasising the frail barrier between rational and irrational behaviour Freud made possible an imaginative discussion of neurosis and insanity, which had been regarded as shameful in the nineteenth century. The results of this more sympathetic attitude can be seen in the novels of writers such as Faulkner, Bellow, and White, while a novel like *The Ha-Ha-* (1961), Jennifer Dawson's imaginative study of a schizophrenic, is inconceivable as the work of any pre-Freudian writer.

Perhaps the most influential of all Freud's theories was his suggestion that our attitudes and behaviour are determined primarily by sexual needs and experience. Nineteenth-century novelists had been extremely reserved in their treatment of sexual life and although eighteenth-century writers had been uninhibited they had regarded erotic experience either as merely incidental to their characters' lives, or as a subject for ribald comedy and satire. Freudian theories have encouraged modern novelists to treat sexual experience more freely than it was in the nineteenth century and more imaginatively and seriously than it had been by earlier writers. Indeed it is now extremely rare for a novelist to treat sex humorously!

Freud's ideas on infantile sexuality also aroused enormous interest in childhood experience and relationships between parents and children, particularly in the ways that these might later affect the adult. Novelists whose work reflects this interest include Ivy Compton-Burnett, Hartley, Styron, and Wilson.

It is interesting to note that, despite the influence of Freud and later psychologists, and writers such as Kinsey, it is only within the last decade that English public opinion has allowed novelists to treat erotic love and sexual deviation as frankly as eighteenth-century writers could. An important date in the restriction of censorship came in 1960, when Penguin Books won their case for the publication of an unexpurgated edition of Lawrence's *Lady Chatterly's Lover*.

### (b) The Influence of the Symbolists. *See also* M23.

The work and ideas of the writers associated with this school, which arose in France in the last decades of the nineteenth century, and included the poets Rimbaud and Mallarmé, have had a far-reaching effect upon modern fiction.

The Symbolists' technical experiments in using verbal association, deliberate ambiguities of phrase and syntax, multiple analogies and esoteric allusion, in poetry, and interior monologue in fiction, suggested means by which modern novelists might attempt to express the subtleties of individual consciousness and to create new forms of novel. The Symbolists' feeling that artists are gifted with a mystical apprehension of Reality, and their consequent belief that, in order to express this apprehension, art should possess the evocative, lyrical qualities of music, not only helped novelists like Proust and Joyce to evolve new forms for the novel, but has had a less happy influence on some other writers, encouraging them to indulge in vague metaphysical musings. Two gifted novelists whose work seems to have suffered in this way are the Austrian Hermann Broch and a writer from Guyana, Wilson Harris, both of whose novels are at times highly evocative, but too often seem to degenerate into meaningless verbiage. (However, the eminent critic George Steiner suggests in *Language and Silence* that Broch's *Death of Virgil* (1945) is one of the greatest novels of the century, comparable only with Joyce's *Ulysses*. Its theme is similar to that of T. S. Eliot's *Four Quartets*, and, like Eliot's poem, it is constructed in the form of four "movements," each based on the "key" of one of the elements, earth, air, fire, and water.)

The Symbolists' dream of producing a "universal poem," an epic myth on the scale of Goethe's *Faust*, has been reflected in the work of many modern novelists, notably in Joyce's *Ulysses* and *Finnegans Wake*, the German Thomas Mann's *Joseph and His Brothers*, Broch's *Death of Virgil* and, more recently, in the novels of Beckett, Golding, Lowry, Styron, and White.

### (c) The Influence of Russian Literature.

A subsidiary, but nevertheless important influence upon the novel has come from the writing of the great nineteenth-century Russian authors. Turgenev has been available in English since the 1890s. Tolstoy, Dostoyevsky, and Chekhov began to be translated just before the First World War. Their writing heightened novelists' interest in conveying a more spiritual reality and the work of Turgenev and Chekhov particularly encouraged writers who were moving towards a more lyrical treatment of style and form, while the novels of Dostoyevsky stimulated the interest aroused by Freud in the imaginative presentation of mentally handicapped, neurotic, psychotic, and psychopathic characters. American and English novelists' attitudes to the work of these and other Russian authors can be studied in the anthology *Russian Literature and Modern English Fiction*, edited, D. Davie.

### (d) Innovators of Literary Techniques.

#### Marcel Proust (1871–1922).

In his huge novel *À la recherche du temps perdu* (1913–27) Proust evokes the kaleidoscopic patterns of involuntary memory as they float through his narrator's mind. His work has therefore been called a *roman fleuve*—a river novel. Its plot seems non-existent, but the novel is in fact constructed with the greatest artistry and, just as the Symbolist poets used evocative images with a multiplicity of associations, so Proust introduces the characters and events of his narrative, presenting them from different viewpoints and investing them with new significance each time they are recalled. Proust's work had a notable influence upon the writing of Virginia Woolf and Forster and among more recent novelists Powell is Proust's avowed disciple.

#### James Joyce (1882–1941).

Joyce, an Irishman, spent most of his life on the Continent and although his work, like that of all great artists, was highly individual, it owed much to the stimulus of the ideas of Flaubert and the work of the Symbolists. Like Flaubert, Joyce believed that a novel should be objective and rooted in experience of everyday life, and by developing the Symbolists' techniques he achieved an hitherto unparalleled impression of objectivity in his portrayal of character.

Joyce's name is particularly associated with the "stream of consciousness" technique, which he evolved from the Symbolist writer Dujardin's "interior monologue," in order to be able to express the mind's activity—not only the way we receive passive impressions of the exterior world and associate them with past experience, the subconscious distortion and imaginative control exercised by the mind, but also how our sensibility and imagination are involved in an active "dialogue" with the world as we apprehend it. Joyce's use of this technique therefore varies considerably, according to the kind of character he is presenting, and since he attempts to express non-verbal experience, as well as verbal thought, his sentences often have a poetic rather than a discursive logic. Stimulated by Joyce's example, later novelists, including Faulkner and Lowry, have evolved their own poetic forms of the stream of consciousness technique, but most later writers have preferred to use a less poetic version, more akin to the interior monologue, expressing the stream of thought, rather than of consciousness. A contemporary novelist who uses interior monologue in this way is Bellow.

It has been suggested that Joyce, having created a new kind of novel, himself used it in every possible way. In *Portrait of the Artist* (1916) he covered the childhood and adolescence of a writer. *Ulysses* (1922) shows a day in the life of Dublin through the eyes of three people and, at the same time, creates a universal image of man's experience of life. In *Finnegans Wake* (1939) Joyce attempted to express the history of the world by evoking the dreams of a Dublin publican, but, despite its occasional brilliance, *Finnegans Wake* is largely inaccessible to readers who have not spent years studying it. Joyce has, therefore, a twofold significance for later writers: he evolved a new kind of novel and, although he wrote with such skill that others have often despaired of emulating him, his achievements have encouraged novelists to experiment, while *Finnegans Wake* has provided a salutary warning of the dangers of indulging in esoteric mythmaking.

### (e) Heirs of the Victorian Tradition.

#### D. H. Lawrence (1885–1930).

Lawrence had a vivid appreciation of the beauty of the natural world and emphasised the importance of the instinctual, as opposed to the intellectual, life. He felt that it was only through basic human experience, particularly through the experience of unselfish erotic love, that we could attain the peaceful self-unity that comes from an apprehension of the sacramental quality of life.

Although he abhorred didactic literature, Lawrence was, therefore, a man with a message, the "flag-bearer of intuition in its interminable struggle against logic and reason"—a true heir of the Romantic movement (*see* J39). Lawrence's attitude to the novel was thus akin to that of Victorian writers and the form of his work has much in common with theirs, although, unlike most Victorians, he made deliberate use of poetic symbolism, which, as Walter Allen has said, "enabled him to render the felt quality of the immediate, instinctive self as it had never been before."

Although no later novelist has equalled Lawrence in the tender poetic expression of unselfish erotic love, his ideas have been widely influential. Doris Lessing is among those later novelists whose work, like Lawrence's, has emphasised the unhappiness and sterility of selfish relationships, and the American writer Baldwin also reflects his influence.

### E. M. Forster (b. 1879).

Like Lawrence, Forster is a moralist, primarily interested in relationships between people and uses techniques and a novel form that have much in common with those of the Victorians. A much more sophisticated novelist than Lawrence, Forster is, superficially, a writer of social comedy in the tradition of Jane Austen, but he is always aware of the numinous quality of life, and expresses it in his novels through complex symbols. His books explore individuals' attempts to "connect" with each other across "the divisions of daily life" in a mutual quest for truth. These themes, which are stated, rather than successfully conveyed in symbolic terms in his early novels, find poetic expression in his masterpiece, *A Passage to India* (1924).

Forster has published no novels since 1924, saying, "I had been accustomed to write about the old-fashioned world with its homes and its family life and its comparative peace. All that went, and though I can think about the new world I cannot write about it."

The "new world" is the theme of Kafka and Huxley.

### (f) Important Novelists of the 1930s.

### Franz Kafka (1883–1924).

A Czech by birth, Kafka wrote in German. His novels first became known to the English-speaking world on the appearance of a translation of *The Castle* in 1930. It was followed in 1935 by *The Trial*. These haunting parables of a man's nightmare life in a world where everything appears contingent, now seem prophetic, and their influence is apparent in works like Rex Warner's *The Aerodrome* (1941), Orwell's *1984*, Ellison's *The Invisible Man*, and the novels of Beckett. Surrealist techniques, giving an effect of confusion between the world of consciousness and that of dream, had been used before Kafka, but he gave them fresh significance.

His tragic short story, *Metamorphosis*, which tells of a man who wakes one day to find himself transformed into a huge insect, brought new dimensions to serious science fiction.

### Aldous Huxley (1894–1963).

Huxley was unique among the novelists of the inter-war years. He declared that nothing deserved to be taken seriously save the suffering men inflict upon themselves by their own crimes and follies, and he criticised both the traditional "social" novel of personal relationships and the more poetic individualism of Joyce, Virginia Woolf, *et al.*, as reflecting conventional values that create suffering and help to perpetuate misery. Although Huxley's highly intelligent satires are very different in style from those of any other twentieth-century writer, his themes look forward to those of some of the more important post-war novelists.

### John Dos Passos (b. 1896).

Dos Passos was a member of the group of Radical American novelists which also included Farrell and Steinbeck, all of whom were influenced by the work of the Naturalists. In his trilogy *U.S.A.* (1930–36), which is a panorama of American life between 1910 and 1927, Dos Passos developed the collage techniques he had evolved in *Manhattan Transfer* (1925). The trilogy is composed of short sections: some are written in interior monologue, others consist of extracts from newspaper headlines and articles and snatches of popular song, others are biographies of leading American personalities, written in a kind of "free verse" and yet others consist of extracts from the lives of fictional characters. *U.S.A.* does not form an imaginative whole and has nothing of the power of Proust and Joyce's novels, but Dos Passos's technical experiments have exerted considerable influence, not only on a number of later American novelists, particularly Mailer, but also on French writers such as Sartre.

### Recent Developments

Since 1945, the language of the novel has been invigorated by the work of writers from newly independent Commonwealth states. Outstanding among these novelists are the Nigerians Achebe and Soyinka, and Naipaul from Trinidad. Drawing on a long tradition of oral story-telling, African and Carribbean novelists are particularly skilful in their treatment of dialogue.

Meanwhile interesting technical experiments are being conducted in France by a heterogeneous group of novelists whose work is sometimes given the misleading collective title of *le nouveau roman*. The most interesting of these experimenters are Robbe-Grillet, Butor, and Nathalie Sarraute.

Robbe-Grillet's ideas have been influenced by Marxist theory and by his experience as a film-director, and his novels, like those of Butor, describe objects rather than people. He dispenses entirely with plot and conventional characters and recreates the vivid inconsequential images of a dream world. Nathalie Sarraute is attempting to give new depths and order to the novelist's study of "the wealth and complexity of the world of the psyche," of which she feels Proust only "skimmed the surface (survoler)." Although Christine Brooke-Rose is the only novelist writing in English whose work seems at all influenced by the *nouveau roman*, anyone interested in modern fiction should read the novels of these three writers—they are all available in English—and also, if possible, the criticism of Roland Barthes.

Contemporary novelists writing in English are experimenting with a variety of forms, continuing to use and adapt the techniques evolved by writers in the early part of the century, and in general their better work approaches more closely to that of the nineteenth-century American tradition than to that of the Victorian novel. This means that although the novel has gained in dramatic and poetic intensity its vision of the world has generally been restricted to that of one or a few characters. This may partly be a result of the interest in individual experience aroused by psychologists, but it seems more particularly a reflection of life in the contemporary world, in which many men feel exiles. Most modern art, not only fiction, expresses feelings of isolation, bewilderment, and suffering, and not only rebellious students, but eminent thinkers such as Tillich have suggested that life for many people in Western society is virtually little different from that under a totalitarian régime. It is significant that such a view of contemporary life was foreshadowed by Kafka and Huxley and is now reflected most impressively, because it is expressed poetically, in the grimly comic novels of Beckett.

1968 has, however, seen two developments which suggest new ways of expressing the dilemma of contemporary man. In *The Armies of the Night*, Mailer, following a pattern suggested by "Theatre of Fact" (*see* I5), has produced a fascinating documentary novel on the American anti-Vietnam War lobby, and from Russia have come the first part of *Cancer Ward* and *First Circle*, two painful, yet essentially hopeful novels by Alexander Solzhenitsyn.

## II. DIRECTORY OF NOVELISTS

In this part we discuss the work of some of the more important novelists who have published since 1945. It is inevitably selective. A more detailed treatment of the twentieth-century American and English novel may be found in Walter Allen's *Tradition and Dream* (P). Some helpful studies of individual authors are available in Oliver and Boyd's paperbacked series *Writers and Their Critics*.

Except for the later novels of Beckett, dates quoted are those of the first publication. The dates of the first English-language editions of Beckett's novels are given.

Paperback editions are referred to thus: C: Calder and Boyars. Co: Corgi. F: Faber and Faber. Fo: Fontana. FS: Four Square. M: Mayflower. P: Penguin. Pa: Panther. S: Signet Books.

### Chinua Achebe (b. 1930).

Achebe, the Nigerian author of four most elegantly written novels, was awarded the first *New Statesman* prize for African and Caribbean writers in 1965.

*Things Fall Apart*, 1958; *No Longer at Ease*, 1960; *Arrow of God*, 1964.

These novels are all concerned with the impact of Western society upon Ibo culture in the early years of the century. Achebe shows a vivid appreciation of the value and dignity of the Ibo's traditional ways of life, but his overriding theme is the need for men to have flexible, receptive minds. The hero of each of these novels comes to a tragic end because he cannot adapt to the demands of a new and unforeseen situation.

The three books are characterised by the grace and dignity of their language and are very different in tone from Achebe's latest novel.

*A Man of People*. 1966.

This is a fiercely ironic study of the career of Chief Nanga, leading demagogue in a newly independent African state. It has been suggested that the portrait of Nanga is modelled from Nkrumah. Although Achebe presents Nanga as an unscrupulous opportunist he also stresses the attractive qualities of his character and suggests that he is, ultimately, a victim of circumstances. It is interesting to compare this novel with Naipaul's *Mimic Men* (*q.v.*).

### James Baldwin (b. 1924). *See also* Section I.

Baldwin emphasises the harsh brutality of contemporary life, particularly for the American Negro. One of his dominant themes is the necessity for honesty about oneself; this includes a frank acceptance of one's sexual nature, whether heterosexual or homosexual. He suggests the brutality of modern life is due to the fact that many people, especially, though not only, White people, are afraid of themselves and therefore incapable of accepting or loving others, but fear them and sadistically exploit and attack them. He shows the tragic effects of such viciousness upon those who suffer it and also upon its perpetrators. Much of the distinction of Baldwin's work comes from the compassionate understanding with which he treats the latter. He acknowledges the discovery and acceptance of oneself may involve great suffering and always requires courage, and suggests it is only possible if one is willing to love others and accept the support of their love.

*Go Tell It on the Mountain*. 1954. Co.

The novel covers two days in the lives of a Negro family who belong to a strict fundamentalist sect, The Fire Baptised. The members of this fellowship identify themselves with the Israelites in captivity. Baldwin shows how this is a reaction to the harshness of their lives and compassionately reveals the mixture of genuine and deluded religious experience among the sect's members. The language of the novel is permeated by echoes of the Authorised Version of the Bible.

*Giovanni's Room*. 1956. Co.

This is a tragic story of a young American who fears his homosexual predilections and hideously ruins the lives of his Italian lover and of his own fiancée.

*Another Country*. 1962. Co.

The novel is centred on the lives of a mixed racial group of Greenwich Village artists and intellectuals. The brutality of New York life is reflected in the crude and obscene language the characters use so casually. At the end of the novel five of its central figures are, as the title suggests, on the verge of a new, though not necessarily easy, life, after their difficult and often bitter quest for love and self-knowledge.

*Tell Me How Long the Train's Been Gone*. 1968.

A star Negro actor looks back on a life dominated by fear and concludes that, for the majority of Black Americans, violence offers the only road to freedom. This is a disappointing novel when compared with Baldwin's earlier ones, for it is less objective and therefore less powerful than they. It is, nevertheless, an important expression of the growing bitterness of Black Americans and constitutes a vehement denunciation of the behaviour of the White community.

In each of these novels Baldwin uses a mixture of straightforward narrative and "flash-back" techniques.

### Samuel Beckett (b. 1906). *See also* Section I.

The form of Beckett's novels has been influenced by the work of his friend Joyce and also, and more particularly, by his study of Proust. An erudite man, Beckett delights to enrich his work with subtle allusions to the writings of other authors and those to whom he most often refers include St. Augustine and Dante. Belacqua, the hero of his first stories, who is often mentioned in the later novels, is a character from the fourth canto of Dante's *Il Purgatorio* (P).

Since Beckett's work becomes progressively more difficult and his later novels contain many references to his earlier ones, readers are advised to begin with *More Pricks Than Kicks*, 1934, and *Murphy*, 1938 (C). Beckett now writes in French, recreating his work in English. He is said to prefer French because that language is the more precise. This search for precision relates to one of the central themes of his novels, the agonising inadequacy of words to express the truth of the human condition, and links Beckett's work with that of other major twentieth-century writers like Kafka and Ionesco and the philosopher Wittgenstein. All Beckett's heroes are driven to feel that they can only tell lies, and they long to achieve the silence of truth, but since truth always eludes them they continue to tell their stories—" One must go on "—in the vain hope that they may at last *speak* the truth and so be released from the tyranny of words.

Beckett is a supreme exponent of the themes of isolation and bewilderment, imprisonment and suffering that are to be found in the work of so many contemporary writers and of artists like Francis Bacon. Poetic in structure and use of language his latest novels haunt the reader's imagination. Each is the monologue of a crippled old man imprisoned in a terrifying, incomprehensible world where life seems a grotesque, bitter farce directed by an elusive tyrant. Yet, harrowing as they are, these novels have their positive side and their bizarre humour has led one critic to call them " supremely entertaining." Beckett's heroes have the tragic gaiety of clowns and, although, as prisoners are said to, they fear to achieve their longed-for freedom, they never abandon their quest for it.

### Watt. 1953. C.

This transitional work is the last novel Beckett wrote in English and was composed between 1942–4 when he was in hiding as a member of the French Resistance.

Sam, a patient in a mental hospital, tells the story of his fellow inmate Watt, who has been a servant to the mysterious Mr. Knott. Watt's purpose in going to Knott's house is expressed in terms of a religious quest, but while he was there he discovered the impossibility of possessing any certain knowledge. The novel is comic in tone and its style recalls Sterne's *Tristram Shandy* (1760–67).

### The Trilogy—*Molloy*. Eng. pub. 1955, *Mallone Dies*, Eng. pub. 1956 (P), *The Unnamable*, Eng. pub. 1958.

In the first part of *Molloy* the bedridden speaker recounts his compulsive, futile quest for his mother; in the second, the tyrant Youdi sends a messenger, Gaber, to one Moran, ordering him to go and look for Molloy. Youdi's name, derived from the Arabic " Yahudi " (cf. Yahweh), is a French colloquialism for " Jew." " Gaber " suggests " Gabriel." Moran doubts Youdi's existence, but fears to disobey the order. He fails to discover Molloy. Molloy and Moran probably represent aspects of the same personality.

In *Mallone Dies* the bedridden Molloy-Moran-Mallone awaits death, " telling stories " about other personifications of himself.

The harrowing *The Unnamable* continues the hero's fruitless search for some understanding of his own identity.

### How It Is. 1964.

Arranged in short passages of unpunctuated prose-poetry, this extraordinary work has the effect of nightmare delirium. The speaker, who is at first anonymous, is, it seems, in the throes of a mortal illness, and imagines himself naked, dumb, crawling through mud with a sack of tinned fish suspended from his neck until he meets another, Pim, in a similar condition. He tortures Pim until the latter speaks. By now the narrator has a name, Bom. Pim deserts Bom, who, posing the idea of life as a circle, or procession, of torturers and victims, awaits his own torturer.

### Saul Bellow (b. 1915).

All the novels of this much praised American explore the question of how one may live a truly human life in the contemporary, urban society of " organisation man." Bellow feels that earlier answers to the question " What makes a good life? " are inadequate for the twentieth century. But the question remains, and he finds the answers of most modern writers unsatisfying and suggests novelists have retreated into ivory towers, concentrating on producing formally perfect works of art, and rejecting the vital concerns of modern life.

Bellow is keenly aware of the pressures society exerts upon us, but he remains unquenchably optimistic. " I do not believe the human capacity to feel or to do can really have dwindled, or that the quality of humanity has degenerated."

Bellow has published six novels: *Dangling Man*, 1944, *The Victim*, 1947, *The Adventures of Augie March*, 1953, *Seize the Day*, 1956, *Henderson the Rain King*, 1959, *Herzog*, 1964 (all P). Their heroes represent a variety of social types. Leventhal (*The Victim*) is a journalist who has known hardship and still feels insecure. Augie March, an illegitimate slum boy, has a variety of jobs, honest and dishonest, and ends as a dubious business representative. Wilhelm (*Seize the Day*) is a " broke," out-of-work salesman. The millionaire Henderson goes to Africa and inadvertently becomes Rain King of a primitive tribe. Herzog is a lecturer in the history of philosophy.

These men withdraw from society, which seems composed of " Machiavellians," " theorists," and " reality instructors " who believe only unpleasant facts are true. Each finds himself imprisoned by self-absorption, from which he longs to escape, though even in his worst moments he retains tenuous contact with people through his love of children, or, in Henderson's case, primitive people. The novels trace their heroes' progress towards an awareness of the brotherhood of man and a conviction that the significance of life is to be found " in the ranks with other people." Bellow never shows his heroes' attempts to put this belief into practice and none of his novels has a wholly convincing conclusion.

Refusing to give much attention to questions of form, he has yet to produce a novel that is a satisfying work of art, though his last book was more carefully constructed than his earlier ones.

Some of the finest parts of his novels are their realisations of the urban American scene and of the life of the Jewish immigrant community.

Though by no means an intellectual writer Bellow is a man of omnivorous learning which enriches all his work, and an exuberant, often highly comic novelist. Not infrequently verbose and undisciplined, occasionally overwhelming, his colourful, vernacular language has a vigour that at times recalls that of Nashe (1567–1601).

### Elizabeth Bowen (b. 1899).

A stylistic artist in the tradition of James, Elizabeth Bowen is famed for the beauty of her descriptive writing and for her sensitive analyses of feeling. Her finest novels are *To the North*, 1932, *The House in Paris*, 1935, *The Death of the Heart*, 1938 (P).

Of her later novels, the best is *The Heat of the Day*, 1949 (P), a love story set in war-time London.

### Ivy Compton-Burnett (b. 1892).

Miss Compton-Burnett is a highly conscious artist, who knows her limits and never exceeds them. Apart from an early, now rejected, work, she has published eighteen novels, the first, *Pastors and Masters*, in 1925, the last, *The Mighty and Their Fall*, in 1963. Written mainly in dialogue, each deals with the claustrophobic life of a well-to-do middle-class household at the turn of the century. Miss Compton-Burnett's themes are those of Greek tragedy; her formal, decorous language is reminiscent of Jane Austen. The combination can be disconcerting.

### Lawrence Durrell (b. 1912).

Durrell's shorter novels are *The Black Book*, *White Eagles Over Serbia*, and *The Dark Labyrinth*. His longer, baroque fantasies have had a mixed reception. Their most appreciative critic is G. S. Fraser.

### The Alexandria Quartet—*Justine*, 1956, *Balthazar*, 1958, *Mountolive*, 1958, *Clea*, 1960 (all F).

Some find the Quartet a most enjoyable novel, for others it is all but unreadable.

Its form, says Durrell, is based on the relativity proposition, the first three volumes, which give differing aspects and views of the characters' lives and motives, having a " spatial " relationship, the fourth, which continues the narrative more or less chronologically, representing time. The novel's construction thus resembles that of Faulkner's *The Sound and the Fury*, and has much in common too with works like Cary's Gulley Jimpson trilogy.

Durrell's apparent theme is erotic love, but his underlying interest is the relationship between art and life. He suggests life is significant only when interpreted by art. This attitude, rather than the form of his work, differentiates it from novels like Faulkner's and Cary's.

Durrell's volumes contain splendid passages, but too often in the novel as a whole his sensuous language seems merely florid and pretentious, his characters but flimsy inhabitants of a decadent fairyland.

*Tunc.* 1968.

The gifted inventor Charlock is captured by the all-powerful international firm of Merlin. *Tunc* is designed as the first half of a two-volume work.

## Ralph Ellison (b. 1914).

*The Invisible Man.* 1952. P.

Ellison is an American Negro and former musician. This, his only novel, is poetic in its complex symbolism and compelling language, and in the intensity of its feeling.

We learn from the prologue that Ellison's hero is not only " invisible," but an " underground man," living in a cellar. He has affinities with the narrator of Dostoyevsky's *Notes from the Underground.* The novel also recalls Kafka. Like Kafka's, its hero is anonymous, and his vividly recounted experiences have the quality of bewildering dreams, at times of nightmare. He tells of his life from the night he received a scholarship to the State Negro College, to the night of a terrifying Harlem race riot, when, fleeing from supporters of a deranged Black nationalist, Ras the Destroyer, he took refuge in the cellar.

One of the novel's central episodes is that in a paint factory hospital, where the hero is subjected to torturous experiments and there is talk of castrating him. Among other things, the episode signifies the way in which all the " scientists " he encounters exploit those in their power, attempting to force all life into rigid sterile patterns. " Life," he says, " is to be lived, not controlled." A free society is loving and infinitely various.

The hero realises the " scientists "—politicians, demagogues, and confidence men—are unaware of the limitations of their vision and cannot see they are destroying themselves as well as their dupes and victims. Images of blindness recur throughout the novel. The narrator calls himself " invisible " because he has come to feel people who look at him see only projections of their own imaginations. He realises he has been equally blind. One of the novel's themes is his gradual enlightenment as he learns to understand himself and others better—to see " reality."

## William Faulkner (1897–1965).

The American Faulkner received the Nobel Prize for Literature in 1950. Although his last novel was published only three years before his death, most of his best work appeared between 1929 and 1936: *The Sound and the Fury, As I Lay Dying, Light in August, Absalom, Absalom!* Together with the comic *The Hamlet,* 1940, these novels are his finest achievement.

Faulkner's post-war novels can be divided into three groups: (1) those which are simply enjoyable stories: *The Town,* 1957, *The Mansion,* 1959, which together with *The Hamlet* form the Snopes trilogy, and *The Reivers,* 1962; (2) *The Intruder in the Dust,* 1948 (P), which is too overtly didactic to be a successful novel, though of great interest to anyone concerned with the racial problems of the South; (3) two ritualistic novels: *Requiem for a Nun,* 1951 (P), and *A Fable,* 1954; the latter, set in France in early 1918, is constructed on an elaborate series of parallels with the events of Holy Week.

Faulkner's work is concerned almost exclusively with the Southern States and set in the mythological Yoknapatawpha County, Mississippi. A Southerner by birth, he is soaked in the history and legendary folklore of Mississippi. Although many of his most memorable characters are bizarre, tragic figures, subnormal poor-Whites, murderers, or other outcasts of society, his work reflects not only the grimness, the callousness and brutality of the South, but also the proud individualism, courage, humour, and vitality of its people. Thus one reads Faulkner with pleasure, despite the difficulties presented by his style.

These difficulties are at times inherent in his subject, as at the beginning of *The Sound and the Fury,* which is told from the viewpoint of a moron; in the touching episode in *The Hamlet,* when the idiot Ike Snopes steals a cow he loves; in the evocation of Charles Mallison's nightmare (*Intruder in the Dust*). Sometimes, however,

Faulkner seems needlessly obscure; he indulges in turgid rhetoric; his sentences are often three or four pages long, sparsely punctuated and containing innumerable parentheses, and parentheses within parentheses. The effect of such clumsy syntax is utterly bewildering, and one sympathises with the exasperated critic who declared Faulkner a " genius without talent." Such criticism, however, ignores the comic aspect of Faulkner's work, his gift for racy, vernacular humour.

## William Golding (b. 1911).

Golding's novels are poetic and, like all poems, cannot be fully appreciated on first reading. Essentially a religious novelist, he aims to write " total myths " illuminating contemporary life. To remarkable extent he has succeeded.

Golding has enormous technical virtuosity; no two of his works are alike, although they express the same vision—a vision of men without God as tragic figures who " seem unable to move without killing each other "; torture those they love; watch themselves becoming automata. But Golding suggests man can regain freedom and the state of grace in which " everything that lives is holy." Thus all his novels, except *Pincher Martin,* express not only the horror, but also the wonder and beauty of life.

*Lord of the Flies.* 1954. F. P.

Golding rewrites *Coral Island* in " realistic " terms, as an allegory of the Fall and an image of twentieth-century society that makes and drops atomic bombs.

*The Inheritors.* 1955. F.

This astonishing *tour de force* shows the advent of *Homo sapiens,* mainly through the eyes of the Neanderthal Lok. The measure of Golding's skill is not simply his brilliant evocation of the largely non-verbal world of Neanderthal Man, but his avoidance of sentimentality. He shows the inevitability of *Homo sapiens'* supremacy, and the tragedy in which it involves him, as well as Lok.

*Pincher Martin.* 1956. F. P.

This novel chronicles the struggles of a drowned sailor against God's overwhelming love. Made, like all men, in God's image, Martin is named Christopher. Alive he chose to " pinch " everything he could; dead, he refuses abnegation of himself, and therefore continues to exist, in a self-made Hell, on a rock he creates from the memory of a decaying tooth. Martin's struggles for " survival " are heroic, ghastly, futile.

*Free Fall.* 1959. F. P.

Sammy Mountjoy retraces his life, to discover when he lost his innocent delight in life and its beauty, and how he regained this. Containing fine passages, the novel is marred by the fact that Sammy interprets the significance of events, instead of the interpretation being left to us.

*The Spire.* 1964. F.

The narrative of this, Golding's masterpiece, centres on the building of the spire of Barchester (Salisbury) Cathedral. The cathedral symbolises three aspects of life: man suffering, crucified; man praying; erotic man.

Jocelyn, the Dean, believing himself divinely appointed to build the spire, presses for its completion with ruthless disregard of the suffering and death he causes. His motives are in fact mixed and largely unconscious. Gradually he recognises his hubris and the mixed motives behind his obsession, realising his wicked folly. Admitting on his deathbed he knows nothing about God, Jocelyn is granted a vision of His glory and the wonder of creation, as he gazes at the transfigured spire.

*The Pyramid.* 1967. F.

Set in Stilbourne, a small Wiltshire town, the novel is superficially a tragi-comedy of provincial life (its central episode is very funny) but on a deeper level *The Pyramid* is a searching exposure of materialism.

The novel's central images are musical ones. Various tastes in, and ways of performing, music signify various kinds of love and modes of life. The title suggests the social pyramid on which the townsfolk wish to rise, and also a metronome, to whose rhythm, that of a selfish, class-ridden society, they choose to move like robots.

### Nadine Gordimer (b. 1923).

The writing of Nadine Gordimer, a South African, is banned in her own country. She has published four volumes of stories and four novels. The last of the novels, *The Late Bourgeois World*, appeared in 1966. Nadine Gordimer is more successful as a short-story writer than as a novelist, for she seems to lack the power to develop character at any length. One is nevertheless compelled to admire her brave and outspoken criticism of the callousness of the South African régime, which makes the people of that country inhabitants of a " World of Strangers." The latter is the title and theme of her second novel.

### Graham Greene (b. 1904).

Greene's best work is *The Power and the Glory*, 1940 (P). Since the War he has published five novels, apart from " entertainments ": *The Heart of the Matter*, 1948, *The End of the Affair*, 1951, *The Quiet American*, 1955 (all P), *A Burntout Case*, 1961, *The Comedians*, 1966 (P). All have settings of topical interest: war-time London, the Congo, Vietnam, Haiti.

While Greene's work has been influenced by the thriller and the film, his literary master is Conrad and, although Greene's novels often seem rather superficial and, at times, he appears unable to treat his characters objectively, he nevertheless tells a good story and is skilled at evoking the discomfort and squalor of life in the tropics. In his first two post-war novels he failed to achieve artistic resolution between his religious beliefs and his feeling that life is a sordid struggle against impossible odds, but *The Quiet American* and *The Comedians*, which have no overtly religious themes, are more successful.

### L. P. Hartley (b. 1895).

Hartley is a professional novelist and craftsman in the tradition of James and Hawthorne, the latter his acknowledged master. Like Hawthorne's, Hartley's themes are moral, illuminated by skilful use of symbolism. In his best novels his style is humorous and gently ironical, but in others he lapses into sentimental melodrama.

Hartley seems at his happiest when writing of children and adolescents: a recurrent figure in his work is the delicate, overprotected, hypersensitive, and introspective boy, as in *Eustace and Hilda*, 1947, *The Go-Between*, 1953, *The Brickfield*, 1964. (The heroes of *The Boat*, 1950 (Co), and *The Betrayal*, 1966, are older, less successful versions of the same figure.) Hartley is skilled in evoking the atmosphere and scene of his characters' environment, particularly when the latter is East Anglia in the earlier years of the century, Oxford, or Venice.

Of the twelve novels he has published, the latest is *Poor Clare*, 1968. The best are:

The Eustace and Hilda trilogy—*The Shrimp and the Anemone*, *The Sixth Heaven*, *Eustace and Hilda*. F.

The novel's theme is symbolised in the opening chapter when Eustace and Hilda, playing on the beach at Anchorstone (Hunstanton) try to rescue a half-eaten shrimp from an anemone. The former is an image of the self-sacrificing Eustace, the latter of his beautiful, possessive sister. " The effort to qualify for Hilda's approval " is the " ruling force in Eustace's life."

Hartley presents his hero with sympathy and humour. The novel follows Eustace to Oxford and Venice and ends with his return to Anchorstone, to the now paralysed Hilda. Counter-

pointing their mutually destructive relationship is the vital life of their sister, Barbara, and her husband.

*The Go-Between.* P.

The innocent Leo, staying with the rich family of a school friend, acts as a messenger between the latter's sister and her farmer lover, who, like the rest of the characters, appear to him god-like figures.

*A Perfect Woman.* 1955.

Save for their children Isabel and Harold have little in common. She finds him dull, but, an ardent reader of novels, believes herself aware of the dangers of indulging in romantic daydreams. Her boredom and dissatisfaction become clear when the handsome novelist, Alec, enters their lives after a chance meeting with Harold. Both wish for Alec's approval and friendship and together scheme to procure for him the barmaid of the local pub.

The voice of Isabel's conscience, symbolised in her son's shouts to his sister, " Janice, go back! ", constantly interrupts her daydreams of Alec, and the children's game with the doll, Pamelia, gives symbolic warning of the dangers of their parents' wicked scheme.

The full irony of Hartley's title becomes clear at the end of the novel, when the publication of Alec's new book provides another comment on his relationship with Isabel and Harold.

Others of Hartley's novels, *The Boat*, *My Fellow Devils*, 1961, *The Brickfield*, and *The Betrayal*, have very similar themes to that of *A Perfect Woman*, but only in the treatment of Margaret, the heroine of *My Fellow Devils*, does he approach the objective sympathy which characterises his presentation of Isabel and Harold, and in none of these other novels does he make such subtle use of poetic imagery as he does in *A Perfect Woman*, *Eustace and Hilda* and *The Go-Between*.

### Ernest Hemingway (1898–1961).

This controversial American was awarded the Nobel Prize for Literature in 1954. Hemingway's language and syntax are of extreme, at times monotonous, simplicity. He writes best of physical activities like hunting and fishing. The theme of all his writing is personal honour and courage, but he tends to romanticise violence and suffering. His finest work is his earliest, the short stories *In Our Time*, 1924, and the novel *A Farewell to Arms*, 1929. Hemingway's last novel, *The Old Man and the Sea*, 1952, the story of an old man's struggle to catch and land an enormous fish, has immediate appeal, but on subsequent readings its language seems contrived and precious.

### Dan Jacobson (b. 1929).

The South African Jacobson has published five novels. The theme of *The Trap*, 1955 (P) and *A Dance in the Sun*, 1956 (P) is the tragic spiritual corruption of those who support apartheid. *The Price of Diamonds*, 1957 (P) is a fine comic study of two business partners. Jacobson's other novels are *The Evidence of Love*, 1959 and *The Beginners*, 1966 (P).

### Doris Lessing (b. 1919).

A Rhodesian by birth, Doris Lessing emigrated to England in 1949. She is probably best known as a novelist, but has also published poems, short stories, and plays.

Her novels explore ways in which people are affected by belonging to minority groups. Her subjects include white Rhodesians and South Africans, members of extreme left-wing political parties, and women who resent the fact that ours is still largely a man's world. The objective sympathy which is so distinguishing a feature of her treatment of the first two subjects occasionally deserts her when she writes about the third.

*The Grass is Singing.* 1950.

In this accomplished first novel, set in South Africa, Doris Lessing writes of the tortured lives of Dick and Mary Turner, isolated members of the White agricultural community, and of their relationships with their African servants.

**The Children of Violence**—*Martha Quest*, 1952, *A Proper Marriage*, 1954, *A Ripple from the Storm*, 1958, *Landlocked*, 1965 (all Pa), *The Four-Gated City*, 1969.

The first two books of this sequence constitute Doris Lessing's finest work to date. Reading them one is constantly reminded of George Eliot. Not only do both novelists employ similar techniques, but they share an intense concern with problems of morality and ethics.

Martha Quest, the novel's passionately idealistic heroine, recalls Dorothea Brooke and Maggie Tulliver, and is presented here with the same kind of objective, ironic sympathy that characterises George Eliot's treatment of Dorothea.

In the third and fourth books, however, the portrayal of Martha is almost overwhelmed in a detailed study of the social and political life of Rhodesia during the Second World War.

Fascinating as social documents, from a literary viewpoint these volumes are less satisfying than the first two books.

*The Golden Notebook.* 1962. P.

The content of this novel is most interesting but its form is awkward. The first part of each of its sections recounts incidents in the lives of the heroine, Anna, and her friends and acquaintances. The rest of the novel consists of extracts from notebooks, some diaries, some stories, in which Anna, a novelist, writes of her feelings about her work and her experiences as a disillusioned member of the Communist Party and as a divorcee who hopes to remarry.

Malcolm Lowry (1909–57).
*Under the Volcano.* 1947. P.

Readers of this complex novel, one of the century's finest, should see Lowry's own criticism of it in *Selected Letters*, edited: Breit & Lowry (Cape).

Set in Mexico in 1938 and '39, it relates the tragedy of the alcoholic Geoffrey Firmin and his wife, Yvonne, to the world tragedies of war and man's inhumanity to man.

In his neglected garden—a symbol both of his ruined marriage and of the mutilated world—Firmin stumbles on a broken notice-board. On it are the words:

    " Do you like this garden?
    Why is it yours?
    We evict those who destroy! "

words repeated at the end of the novel. They recall two of its central images: Eden, signifying the beauty man discovers in Nature and the beauty he creates in loving human relationships: Hell, signifying the agony he suffers and causes others when he rejects love. Lowry sees man as a splendid, noble creature who must struggle incessantly to control sado-masochistic impulses, which he can restrain only when he loves others and is able to accept their love. " Man cannot live without love," is the novel's main theme.

Firmin is a tragic hero in the tradition of Marlowe's Faustus, to whom the novel's imagery relates him. The objectivity of Lowry's portrayal of the tortured world of addiction is remarkable: Firmin always has our sympathy, rarely approval.

This book is not simply a good story, but a great poem, its themes expressed not only through the events of the narrative, the lives and feelings of the characters, but through vivid descriptions of Mexico and its people, through subtle, complex imagery.

Lowry intended *Under the Volcano* to form one volume of a sequence. The stories in *Hear Us O Lord From Heaven Thy Dwelling Place*, 1962, and the unfinished novel *Lunar Caustic*, 1968, were to have been incorporated in the other volumes.

Mary McCarthy (b. 1912).

The American journalist and critic Mary McCarthy has published five satirical novels on the lives of American artists and intellectuals: *The Company She Keeps*, 1942 (P); *The Oasis*, 1949 (S); *The Groves of Academe*, 1952 (S); *A Charmed Life*, 1955 (P); *The Group*, 1962 (P). Like Simone de Beauvoir and Doris Lessing, Miss McCarthy is particularly interested in the rôle of the educated woman in twentieth-century society. Parts of her novels are very amusing, but in general they seem too cerebral and anaemic.

Norman Mailer (b. 1923).

Mailer, an American, is a journalist and film-director and the author of one book of verse as well as six novels. He sees life as a battlefield between the forces of good and evil and the motive behind the sensationalism of much of his later work seems to be a desire to shock readers into an awareness of the nature of American society, which he feels is obscene and life-denying. Mailer suggests that the majority of Americans are either becoming cogs in the machines of a brutal, totalitarian " technology land," or taking selfish refuge in drugs and nihilism, instead of accepting the dangers of living adventurously and trying to establish creative relationships. Readers interested in Mailer's social philosophy should refer to *Advertisements for Myself*, 1959; *The Presidential Papers*, 1963; *Cannibals and Christians*, 1966; *Miami and the Siege of Chicago*, 1968.

*The Naked and the Dead.* 1948. Pa.

Many critics feel this novel constitutes Mailer's most successful expression of his view of the human condition. He regards it as " the work of a young engineer." Its subject is the American troops' capture of a Pacific island from the Japanese, but its interest lies in Mailer's treatment of the power structure within the American force, which is presented as a microcosm of society. The mass of the troops, represented by the soldiers of one platoon, are shown as the all but helpless victims of the men of power—the fascist General Cummings and the Platoon Sergeant, Croft. Between the two groups stands the ineffectual liberal, Lieutenant Hearn.

Mailer paints a remorseless picture of the agony of the ordinary soldier's life and of the absurdity of the war, and is very successful in his treatment of the characters of Cummings and Croft. The weakness of the book lies in his characterisation of the lower ranks. These soldiers are obviously intended to represent a cross-section of American society, but, although using techniques derived from Dos Passos, Mailer gives a biographical sketch of each man in the platoon, none of them is clearly differentiated from the others.

*Barbary Shore.* 1951.

This novel is now out of print in England.

*The Deer Park.* 1955. Co.

Mailer planned this novel as the first of eight, whose themes were to cover the whole of American life. This was the only one to be finished. Its theme is pleasure and its title comes from D'Angerville's *Vie privée de Louis XV*, which refers to " the Deer Park, that gorge of innocence and virtue in which were engulfed so many victims . . . ". Mailer's Deer Park is Desert D'Or, a fictional pleasure resort near Hollywood.

*An American Dream.* 1965. M.

Both the title and the wild improbability of this novel's action suggest that Mailer intends it to be read as an allegory, showing the narrator, Rojack, resisting the suicidal lure of nihilism presented by the moon and then escaping from the evil forces of American society, personified in his wife, her father, and her maid. The sexual relationships between the characters would thus have symbolic importance.

The novel has its comic moments, but its style is generally sensational and its language often highly obscene.

*Why Are We in Vietnam?* 1967.

Ostensibly this is a young Texan's account of a hunting expedition in Alaska. David Caut, who admires the book, has said, " The verbal texture of the novel is one of unrelieved obscenity."

*The Armies of the Night.* 1968.

Apparently Mailer's finest work since *The Naked and the Dead*, this is an absorbing and at times highly comic reconstruction of the events of the Peace March on the Pentagon in October 1967. It is written in two sections. In the first the protagonist is Mailer himself, described objectively in the third person. In the second part we are helped to understand the motives and feelings of other marchers and the fears of the police and troops who confronted them. The book is notable for its objectivity and humour.

Bernard Malamud (b. 1914).

Malamud's name is often coupled with that of his compatriot Bellow. They have a common Jewish heritage. Malamud's novels are similar in theme to those of Bellow, but his writing is less exuberant. Both men show a keen appreciation of natural beauty, rare in American novelists.

*The Natural.* 1952. P.

As Earl Wassermann has noted, the events of this novel have a factual basis and its theme is that of the Arthurian regeneration myth. However, this story of a baseball player lacks artistic unity and its hero is never fully convincing.

*The Assistant.* 1957. P.

Here Malamud found a much more fruitful subject, the quiet tragedy of Morris Bober, an unsuccessful Jewish grocer and, of his Gentile assistant, Frank Alpine. For the sake of Bober and of the latter's daughter, Helen, Alpine, who has made many " false starts " in life, gives up what may well be his last hope of achieving material success. The novel is written with beautiful restraint and Chekhovian irony.

*A New Life.* 1961. FS. P.

Levin, a reformed drunkard, obtains an English post at a small state college, but eventually sacrifices his hard-won chance of an academic career for the sake of the woman he has loved.

The novel is set in the early 1950s, the period of McCarthyism. Malamud criticises the hysteria pervading American life at this time, exemplified in the academic and social atmosphere of Cascadia College, where Levin, a man of liberal principles, suffers from his colleagues' fears and prejudices.

*A New Life* is less concentrated than *The Assistant.* It contains elements of picaresque comedy and is at times very amusing, though occasionally its tone seems frivolous and inappropriate.

*The Fixer.* 1966. P.

Yakov Bok is, like Levin, a victim of hysterical feelings of national insecurity. A Jewish odd-job-man—a fixer—he leaves the Pale Settlement for Kiev, hoping to begin a new, more fruitful life, but is arrested on a trumped-up charge and endures three terrible years' imprisonment awaiting trial.

The inspiration of the novel was the case of Mendel Beiliss, a Kiev labourer arrested in 1911, and falsely charged with the ritual murder of a Christian child. Malamud says the novel is intended to stand "rather as a myth than an isolated case-study." But it lacks the compelling force of myth.

Iris Murdoch (b. 1919).

A philosophy don, Iris Murdoch has published twelve novels, the latest being *Bruno's Dream,* 1968. A sympathetic study of her work has been written by A. S. Byatt.

All Miss Murdoch's novels have moments of poetic intensity, as in the descriptions of Rainborough gazing at a snail in *The Flight From the Enchanter,* 1956 (P), Dora releasing a butterfly in *The Bell,* 1958 (P), and the evocation of fog-bound east London in *Time of The Angels,* 1966 (P), but the majority of her novels seem little more than sophisticated versions of women's magazine fiction and belie the promise of her first tale, *Under the Net,* 1955 (P), an amusing exitentialist fantasy that recalls Beckett's *Murphy.*

V. S. Naipaul (b. 1932).

This distinguished Caribbean novelist was born in Trinidad of Indian parents. The heroes of all his novels are men who feel an urgent need to give their lives order and significance. Thus although most of his work has a Caribbean setting, its themes are of world-wide interest. Naipaul began as a writer of comedy and all his novels have a comic element although his work has become increasingly sombre in tone as it has increased in complexity.

*The Mystic Masseur.* 1957. P.

In this delightful comedy of Colonial politics, Naipaul shows the metamorphosis of Ganesh Ramsumair, an insignificant, semi-educated Indian, into G. Ramsey Muir, M.B.E., respected Colonial statesman.

*A House for Mr. Biswas.* 1961. Fo.

This sad story tells of Mr. Biswas's search for independence and security. Inveigled into early marriage, he finds he is expected to become a submissive appendage of his mother-in-law's enormous household. Biswas has no intention of playing this rôle, but he is not a practical man and has little formal education and no trade, so that his first two attempts to establish himself independently soon fail. At last, in his early forties, he manages to buy a house, but dies soon afterwards.

Naipaul makes us feel the dreadful tensions and frustrations of family life in overcrowded conditions where there is never any privacy, but despite its sad theme, the novel is often very funny, for Biswas is an imaginative man who delights in colourful language and has a flair for picturesque invective. His touching pride in his children's intelligence and his growing love and respect for his wife are most sensitively portrayed.

*Mr. Stone and the Knights Companion.* 1963. FS.

The elderly Mr. Stone is filled with despair at the prospect of his impending retirement. Then he suddenly conceives the idea that active pensioners of his firm should visit the disabled. Organising this scheme gives him new hope and vigour and although these fade the novel ends on a note of subdued confidence.

*The Mimic Men.* 1967.

Singh, the narrator of this fascinating novel, is an exiled politician from a newly independent Caribbean state. Singh analyses the events of his life, which he convincingly suggests is representative of those of all Colonial politicians. Thrust suddenly into power, they are compelled to destroy the former pattern of administration and, having no traditions to guide them, nor any experience of government, inevitably become " mimic-men."

Vladimir Nabokov (b. 1899).

A Russian by birth, Nabokov came to England during the Revolution, subsequently lived in Germany and France and emigrated to America in 1940.

Translations of his early novels are now becoming available. Those he has written in English include *Lolita,* 1955 (Co), *Pnin,* 1957, *Pale Fire,* 1962 (Co). The first of these gained notoriety among the ill-informed who imagined it was pornographic. Nothing could be further from the truth.

Nabokov is a learned writer. His humour, wit, and above all his masterly use of language, make his novels a constant source of delight.

## Flannery O'Connor (1925–64).

The work of this novelist and short-story writer from the Southern States of America has a growing reputation in her own country, although it is less well known in England and has until very recently been difficult to obtain.

Flannery O'Connor published two novels, *Wise Blood*, 1952, and *The Violent Bear it Away*, 1960. She writes in a poetic, ruthlessly comic style about isolated eccentrics afflicted with religious mania, who evolve their own grotesque, fundamentalist creeds.

## George Orwell (1903–50).

Orwell's post-war novels express feelings apparent in his earlier journalism.

### *Animal Farm.* 1945. P.

The theme of this satirical fable is the futility of popular revolutions. Led by the pigs, the animals of Manor Farm evict their brutal owners. However, one of the pigs, Napoleon, gains absolute power, establishing a police state. The animals are worse off than before.

### *1984.* 1949. P.

This grim nightmare, which Orwell wished to call *1948*—his publisher dissuaded him—develops the ideas of *Animal Farm* in a vision of a totalitarian world whose rulers exploit psychological and technological discoveries to retain and consolidate power.

As a novel it is less successful than *Animal Farm*. It has not the latter's occasional humour, and the presentation of its villain, O'Brien, is unconvincing. Raymond Williams's *Culture and Society* (P) sympathetically relates the novel to Orwell's paradoxical feelings about socialism.

## Anthony Powell (b. 1905).

Powell published five novels in the 1930s. The elegance of his style and the fact that he took a comic view of upper- and middle-class society led to his comparison with Waugh.

His sixth work, *A Dance to the Music of Time*, is planned in twelve volumes; nine have appeared: *A Question of Upbringing*, 1951, *A Buyer's Market*, 1952, *The Acceptance World*, 1955, *At Lady Molly's*, 1957 (all Fon), *Casanova's Chinese Restaurant*, 1960, *The Kindly Ones*, 1962 (both P), *The Valley of Bones*, 1964, *The Soldier's Art*, 1966, *The Military Philosophers*, 1968.

In this poetic novel Powell is clearly influenced by Proust. His narrator, Nicholas Jenkins, imagines the passage of time as a formal dance in which people appear and reappear unexpectedly and in surprising combinations. This is the novel's central image.

Jenkins, an extremely intelligent, thoughtful man, is a connoisseur of pictures and a novelist vividly aware of the limitations of our knowledge of others, even of our closest friends, and of the dangers of forming stereotyped ideas of people. He has an insatiable desire to understand what motivates human action, particularly how we are influenced by the thirst for power and by a love of adventure. Jenkin's gradual realisation of the complexity of life is expressed poetically through the references to paintings: as a young man he is usually drawn to Renaissance and Baroque works with classical subjects; as he becomes " less ascetic, intellectually speaking more corrupt perhaps," and recognises that " individuals live in different ways," that " all human beings . . . seen at close range are equally extraordinary," he refers increasingly to paintings of other periods.

The novel, which begins in the early 1920s, with a flashback to 1914, has now reached the end of the Second World War, and contains an enormous range and variety of characters. Each volume introduces new figures.

Powell has the most sensitive ear for nuances of speech. His novel, leisurely, but never dull, contains passages of brilliant comedy.

## Alan Sillitoe (b. 1928).

Sillitoe's first book, *Saturday Night and Sunday Morning*, 1958 (Pan) is among the better of a number of novels of working-class life which appeared in the late 1950s and early '60s. Others include Keith Waterhouse's *There is a Happy Land*, 1957 (P), *Billy Liar*, 1959 (P), Barstow's *A Kind of Loving*, 1960 (P), and David Storey's *Flight into Camden*, 1960 (P).

Arthur Seaton, the hero of Sillitoe's novel, is a belligerent young worker in a Nottingham bicycle factory. He sees life as a continual battle for survival and feels particular hostility towards the forces of " the Establishment ". Seaton's hero is Boris Karloff, but his deepest satisfaction comes from a quiet day's fishing and a country walk with his girl friend.

The novel is uneven in quality, but its occasionally cheap and sensational language appropriately suggests the influence of Seaton's favourite films, and much of the dialogue is vigorously realistic. The rural scenes reflect the influence of Lawrence, who also came from Nottinghamshire.

*Saturday Night and Sunday Morning* was followed in 1959 by a volume of stories containing a fine nouvelle, *The Loneliness of the Long-Distance Runner*, which gives the book its title. Sillitoe's later novels, which have been generally less favourably received by critics, include *The General*, 1960 (Pan), *The Death of William Posters* (1965) and *A Tree on Fire* (1967). The two latter are the first volumes of a projected trilogy.

## C. P. Snow (b. 1905).

*Strangers and Brothers*—10 vols. 1940–68. P.

In the course of this sequence the narrator, Lewis Eliot, rises from humble beginnings to success at the Bar, at Cambridge, and in the Administrative Civil Service. While this is clearly not an autobiographical work, the course of Snow's own career as a scientist, don, and civil servant has followed a similar pattern.

One of the strengths of these volumes derives from the fact that Eliot is an unprejudiced observer of his friends' and colleagues' behaviour. We feel he prefers some men to others, but rarely does he judge any of them.

The volumes follow no strict chronology and only two, *A Time of Hope* and *Homecomings*, are concerned directly with Eliot's personal life. The other books of the sequence are each centred on the life of one of Eliot's friends or acquaintances. The best of them all is *The Masters*, where an account of the election of the Master of a Cambridge college becomes an image of political life. The other volumes have a less perfect form and vary in quality, but all are of documentary interest in that they deal with such subjects as the making of the first atomic bomb and the painful decisions in which scientists and civil servants were involved at that time.

## Wole Soyinka (b. 1934). *See also* Section I.

The Yoruba poet and dramatist Soyinka has published one novel, which has lately been awarded the *New Statesman's* triennial prize for African and Caribbean fiction.

### *The Interpreters.* 1965. Pa.

In this original, highly enjoyable novel, Soyinka writes about a group of young Nigerian artists and intellectuals. The narrative is arranged in " solo " and " choral " sections, now reflecting the experience of individuals, now that of the group. The work has two main themes, which are expressed through complex symbols. The first is the characters' struggle to discover and express the relationship between their traditional culture and contemporary Nigerian society. The second is the need for a fearless commitment to the search for truth. Soyinka includes some highly comic episodes and sketches of dishonest and selfish people. Particularly memorable are an encounter with a German reporter, who likes to pretend he is American, a party given by the Oguazors, an ignorant, snobbish Nigerian don and his wife, and the ridiculous behaviour of

Faseyi, who accuses his charming wife of behaving like " a bush-girl from a London slum." Soyinka takes a poet's delight in vivid and inventive use of words and is particularly skilful in his treatment of comic dialogue.

### Muriel Spark (b. 1918).

Since the appearance of her first nouvelle *The Comforters* (P), in 1957, Mrs. Sparke has published seven others, the latest being *The Public Image*, 1968. She has also written one full-length novel *The Mandelbaum Gate*, 1965 (P), short stories, a play, verse, and critical works.

Mrs. Sparke is an entertaining writer likely to be enjoyed particularly for the tart economy of her language and for her keen observation of absurd and grotesque behaviour and speech, but most of her work is slight and *The Mandelbaum Gate* suggests that she is indeed unable to treat characters or themes in depth or at any length.

Her early nouvelles are strange mixtures of comedy of manners and surrealist fantasy, her later tales melodramatic rather than surrealist. Most of them illustrate Mrs. Sparke's interest in violent death, a subject she sometimes treats with naïve callousness. Her most satisfying work to date seems *Memento Mori*, 1957 (P), which chronicles the reactions of a group of elderly people to mysterious telephone calls telling them to " remember you must die." Only in this book and, to a lesser extent, in *The Prime of Miss Jean Brodie*, 1961 (P), does Mrs. Sparke show much imaginative sympathy for human weakness. However, Professor Kermode has suggested that her three books *The Prime of Miss Jean Brodie*, *The Girls of Slender Means*, 1963 (P), and *The Mandelbaum Gate*, " add up to the most distinguished achievement of any British novelist since the war," and perhaps those of us who would question this opinion have not yet learnt to appreciate Mrs. Sparke's techniques.

### William Styron (b. 1925).

A native of Virginia, one of the former slave states, Styron is particularly concerned with the theme of slavery as an emotional or spiritual condition. He implies that it is responsible for the immaturity, brutality, and ugliness of much American life and suggests that it stems primarily from the Americans' heritage of militant, repressive, and self-righteous Puritanism.

Styron's weakness is his tendency to illustrate rather than to explore his novels' themes and many of his characters are too cerebrally conceived, yet even in *Set This House on Fire*, his least successful work, Styron remains an impressive novelist. The architecture of his books, three of which are very long, is most skilful and all his work is illumined by a poetic gift for capturing the atmosphere of an event or scene and embodying fleeting visual impressions in vivid, precise images.

### Lie Down in Darkness. 1948. Co.

The events of this novel take place on the day of Peyton Loftis's funeral, but most of the book consists of long flashbacks through which we learn about the lives of Peyton and her unhappy parents and come to understand why she committed suicide.

Styron implies that the Loftises' story is symbolic of life in the southern States and that the latter is itself a paradigm of American life in general. However, the novel does not sustain the weight of this interpretation, for although the characters arouse our pity they never attain the stature of representative tragic figures that such a theme demands. Nevertheless, this is a remarkable novel to have been produced by a writer of twenty-three. Its strength comes from Styron's gift for presenting individual scenes, illustrated in the novel's brilliant opening paragraphs and in episodes such as the account of Peyton's wedding.

### The Long March. 1952.

The narrative of this very short book gives an account of the relationships between two Marines,

recalled for service during the Korean war, with which they have no sympathy, and their Colonel, a regular officer, whose avoidance of any sign of emotion has earned him the sobriquet of Old Rocky. Here Styron writes of the slavery of military life and the corruption and brutality it engenders, but his underlying theme is the dilemma of liberals, who " born into a generation of conformists " are thus " trapped in a predicament which personal insurrection could, if anything, only make worse," and yet to acquiesce in it would be to become, " like cannibals, hardly men at all." The passion with which Styron expresses this dilemma makes *The Long March* his masterpiece.

### Set This House on Fire. 1960

Themes from the previous books are here combined with a sweeping condemnation of the " moral and spiritual anarchy " of contemporary American life, but the novel remains essentially a *roman a thèse* and of the three main characters only Kinsolving, a drunken artist and ex-soldier, becomes more than a blueprint, and even so the parallels Styron suggests between him and Oedipus seem grotesquely inappropriate. Nevertheless, the novel is well worth reading for its incidental poetry. It contains brilliant evocations of the beauty of the Italian countryside and of rural Virginia, the hideousness of American cities and the langour of New York on a Spring Sunday.

### The Confessions of Nat Turner. 1967.

This is an imaginative reconstruction of the life of the leader of an abortive slave rebellion. The story is told in the first person as Nat, awaiting trial, looks back over the events of his life and explains why he decided to murder his White masters. Nat himself is not a fully convincing figure, but minor characters are, and Styron is particularly successful in his portrayal of the liberal Judge Cobb, whose predicament recalls that of the marines in *The Long March*.

### Evelyn Waugh (1902–66).

Waugh's style is elegant and his novels are often amusing, but they are generally superficial and marred by cruelty and distasteful snobbery. A popular writer of the 1930s, he has published nine novels since the War.

### The Sword of Honour trilogy (pub. in 3 vols. 1952–62, revised and reissued as one book 1965).

Waugh's best novel, this chronicles the experiences of Guy Crouchback during the Second World War. Crouchback welcomes the War, which he feels will give his life the direction and purpose it has lacked since his wife deserted him. The first two volumes of the trilogy give a convincing impression of administrative incompetence during the early stages of the War and are occasionally very funny, but they share the cruelty and snobbery of Waugh's other writing.

The third volume is much better. Crouchback, a cardboard figure until now, comes alive and, in a moving encounter with a refugee woman, is forced to admit he became a soldier in order to evade the difficulties of his personal life, and that he, and others like him, were as responsible as the " enemy " for the horrors of the War.

### Patrick White (b. 1912).

White, an Australian, was educated in England, where he took a degree in Modern Languages, and has travelled widely in Europe and America. Five of his seven novels have appeared since the War: *The Aunt's Story*, 1948, *The Tree of Man*, 1955, *Voss*, 1957, *Riders in the Chariot*, 1961 (all P), *The Solid Mandala*, 1966. He has also published plays and short stories.

Like Golding's, White's novels are, essentially religious poems, but whereas Golding, except in *The Spire*, concentrates on man's loss of grace, White is more concerned with his experience of an awareness of " the God above God," who is both immanent and mysteriously transcendent, and with man's struggle towards some understanding of the purpose of life, and of the nature of good and evil.

White's vision of life, as reflected in these novels, is similar to that of the existentialist theologian Tillich (see his *The Courage to Be*, Fo). He suggests that the "conformism" of "civilised" life is inimical to goodness, and exemplifies this in his treatment of the suburb Sarsaparilla, the setting of *The Solid Mandala*, and of parts of all the other novels (though it does not acquire the name until *Riders in the Chariot*). The everyday life of Sarsaparilla is presented variously, as comic, sterile, hypocritical, cruel, and evil. It is almost always hideous and invariably pitiful. White's creation of Sarsaparilla, which is also the setting of one of his plays and of several stories, invites comparison with Faulkner's creation of Yoknapatawpha County.

In each of the three middle novels, White creates a wide range of characters. In *The Aunt's Story* and *The Solid Mandala* he limits himself to a few. All his main characters are regarded by most of their acquaintances as odd, or stupid, or mad. They are generally avoided, and often feared and attacked, because their essential innocence presents an intolerable challenge to the self-protective conformism of "normal" people. Notable exceptions are the tragic Nietzschian "superman," Voss, and Waldo, one of the main characters of *The Solid Mandala*. Both are isolated by their own colossal arrogance. All White's heroes and heroines suffer greatly, and some die, but, except in *Voss*, he does not imply that suffering is a necessary condition of goodness, but rather that it is its inevitable concomitant. Joy returns to those who survive, for, all these novels emphasise, though good must endure evil, it never yields to it.

Another of the novels' recurrent themes is the difficulty of communication. Even the most educated of White's characters find it almost impossible to articulate their experiences of joy and suffering. Many of them try to express themselves in other ways, in painting, music, dance, and increasingly, through a selfless love for others.

Like that of all major writers, White's style is highly individual and makes challenging demands upon his readers. His idiosyncratic punctuation and, in *The Tree of Man*, his frequent use of "verbless sentences," seem attempts to reflect his characters' fumbling for understanding and expression of their experiences. Sometimes White makes no obvious distinction between his characters' expression of feeling and his own comment upon that expression. In *The Aunt's Story*, such interplay between his own and his character's viewpoint is at times confusing, but in subsequent novels his increasing mastery of technique adds to the subtle, allusive qualities of his style. White takes a poet's delight in the metaphorical ambiguity of words. He is a master of ironic bathos and epigrammatic wit.

His work is by no means faultless. Occasionally the style of *The Tree of Man* seems self-conscious, the symbolism clumsy. Passages of *Riders in the Chariot* are empty rhetoric, and in this novel we never discover, as we need to, how far, if at all, Miss Hare is responsible for her father's death. In *Voss*, when he describes Laura's feelings during Rose's terrible confinement, White does not seem in full control of his material.

Despite faults like these, White remains one of the most rewarding, if also one of the most demanding, of contemporary novelists. Each of these five works is extremely complex. To write of them so briefly is to deal summary justice. They are often highly comic, and all express a joy and wonder in the glory of Creation that recall the magnificent sections 29–38 of the first of Thomas Traherne's (d. 1674) *Centuries of Meditation*.

**Angus Wilson (b. 1913).**

Although now best known as a novelist, Wilson first made his name with a volume of short stories, *The Wrong Set*, 1949 (P). He has since published two other collections of stories and a play, as well as six novels.

He is an admirer of Jane Austen, whom his style occasionally recalls, and of the great nineteenth-century French and English novelists. Like theirs, his work reads aloud extraordinarily well.

A serious comic novelist, Wilson is merciless in exposing snobbery, hypocrisy, and self-deception. However, he does not always achieve artistic transformation of his material. Thus, although some of the finest parts of his work are in dialogue, some of his virtual conversations are as painful to read as they would be to endure in reality. Horrified, yet fascinated by cruelty and vulgarity, Wilson has been called "morbid" by some critics. There are certainly times, especially in *The Old Men at the Zoo* and *No Laughing Matter* when the charge seems justified. But Wilson can also be deliciously funny, as in his account of the Historical Association meeting (*Anglo-Saxon Attitudes*).

His chief technical fault is a tendency to overload his novels with characters he has no time to develop. His best works seem to be *The Middle Age of Mrs. Eliot* and *Late Call*; in both his cast is limited. Some of the minor characters, particularly working-class ones, appear caricatures, and variations of the same types recur from one book to another. Wilson is, nevertheless, a writer of immense vitality. Each of his novels is quite unlike the others, although they have certain common themes.

Obviously aware of the stresses imposed by the political and social problems of our century, Wilson was the first contemporary English novelist to write frankly of the homosexual "underworld."

*Hemlock and After*, 1953 (P), *Anglo-Saxon Attitudes*, 1956 (P), *The Middle Age of Mrs. Eliot*, 1958 (P), *Late Call*, 1964.

Each of these novels opens with the hero or heroine facing a crisis which compels him (her) to reassess his (her) adequacy as a person and in relation to others. Each endures considerable mental suffering. Bernard Sands, the novelist hero of the first book, dies before he can rebuild his life. Geoffrey Middleton, historian, connoisseur of pictures (*Anglo-Saxon Attitudes*), Meg Eliot, widow of a successful barrister, and Sylvia Calvert, retired hotel manageress (*Late Call*), each, in quite different ways, comes to find purpose and meaning in life.

Conversely, Meg's brother, David, who has also suffered bereavement, withdraws to the "petty isolation" of his market garden. David is the most fully drawn of the several figures in Wilson's novels who indulge in ritual self-denial, instead of facing facts (cf. Inge, *Anglo-Saxon Attitudes*; Susan, *No Laughing Matter*).

*The Old Men at the Zoo.* 1961. P.

A political satire, the novel abounds in images of brutality and sadism. At the beginning of the book, the narrator, Simon Carter, Administrator of the London Zoo, seems more imaginative and sensitive than his colleagues, but he becomes increasingly cold-blooded. The novel is an exploration of megalomania. Each of the Zoo's successive Directors is obsessed with putting his own pet schemes into practice and ruthlessly exploits his colleagues and the animals in his care, all of whom he regards as objects to be manipulated. The book closes, at the end of a British–European war, with Simon's canvassing his own appointment to the Directorship.

*No Laughing Matter.* 1967.

This ambitious, extremely long novel, written in a variety of styles and containing a short story and several plays, presents a panorama of twentieth-century life. Ultimately, it seems to fail, because, since the narrative is divided among the lives of the six Matthews children and their parents, constantly shifting from one to another, none of the characters is fully realised.

# II. TWENTIETH CENTURY POETRY

This section does not profess to be a full account of the poetry of the current century, as that would not be possible within the present compass. The aim is rather to touch upon some aspects of the poetry and to suggest ways of approaching it.

## I. INTRODUCTION

**The Poem as an Art Form expressive of Feeling.**

There is no short cut to the enjoyment of poetry. The only approach is an attentive reading, poem by poem, remembering always that the poet is attempting to express personal *feeling* through a pattern of words, in which their order, their associations, and their verbal music are all of the utmost significance.

Coleridge described poetry as a more than usual feeling with more than usual order, and the reader may like to turn to the paragraph on the function of dramatic art (I2) where reference is made to Susanne Langer's thesis that art gives form to our feeling response to life. By this is meant not only emotion as distinct from reason, but the whole gamut of our response to life as human beings—what it *feels* like to use the senses, to have emotions, even what it feels like to think.

Such feeling response cannot adequately be conveyed by logical discourse. How often we hear the phrases " I mean ", " You know," from speakers who implicitly acknowledge that they are incapable of " expressing the inexpressible ", through the medium of prose discourse and must rely on the sensitivity of their hearer to interpret their feeling. The artist's task is to translate the inarticulate cry into significant images, patterns and forms which convey their import with precision and beauty.

It is perhaps easier for us to see how the painter, the sculptor, or the musician can do this, and how, like Henry Moore, they may resolutely refuse to say what their work " means," for to limit it to " meaning " is to divert attention from its " unique value, its numinous feeling quality. But the poet in his subtle and difficult art uses as his material words and grammatical structures which themselves have meaning from which they cannot be divorced. Although possible meanings of individual phrases must be established, the modern literary critic eschews any attempt to state what the poem as a whole " means." He attempts rather to " explicate " the poem, to unfold its hidden implications, to make clear its significance as a whole. The best approach is first to read the poem as a whole and then to re-read it with particular attention for the special import of the individual figures of speech.

**Special Difficulties of Twentieth-Century Poetry.**

Poetry of the current century presents the reader with special difficulties. Hitherto, however strange or elaborate the imagery, in most poems prosaic statements and a rational framework could be discerned, but from about 1910 even these were often discarded, so that an even greater receptivity is demanded of the reader.

*Drastic Social Changes in the Era between the Wars.*

For a fuller understanding of modern poetry we should return to the vital period between the wars, when the masters, Yeats and Eliot, were developing new insights and techniques and setting standards which have not since been equalled.

Inevitably the poetry of the time reflected contemporary changes in society. The Georgian Books of Verse, 1911–22, illustrate how the familiar rural tradition was becoming outworn and it was now to be maintained by only a few poets, Hardy being the most distinguished and influential. For England was fast becoming a predomi-

nantly urban society and the imagery of the countryside, inevitably used by Shakespeare, Wordsworth, and Keats, was becoming no longer relevant, sometimes incomprehensible to the town-dweller.

In France, fifty years earlier, Baudelaire (1821–67) had drawn inspiration from the city, both in his preoccupations and in his imagery. In England it was the genius and originality of Ezra Pound (b. 1885) and T. S. Eliot (1888–1965), with their highly original experiments in theme and style, who now gave direction to a new kind of poetry, urban, sophisticated, and cosmopolitan.

Other social factors had their influence. The horror and futility of the First World War, the Communist revolution, the economic slump, the decline in religious faith, the discoveries of Freud, all contributed to the collapse of the old stable sureties and left poets profoundly shaken and searching for new values and effective modes of expression.

Pound, Eliot, and W. B. Yeats (1865–1939) all repudiated the current bourgeois values of wealth and worldly success, which with the rapid growth of industry, commerce and advertising were becoming ever more deeply entrenched. Stigmatised by Matthew Arnold as " Philistine " in 1869, they are the corrosives of art and cause the poet to feel out of sympathy with society.

Pound and Eliot, and later William Empson (b. 1906) consciously directed their poetry to a select minority. Intellectual and satirical, it makes no appeal to facile emotion. The familiar metres and rhymes have been discarded. The elliptical syntax, the complex organisation of the imagery, the erudite references to other cultures, all make demands. A phrase like Pound's " His Penelope was Flaubert " is not immediately clear. Such poetry is not intended to be lapped up by a complacent bourgeoisie.

Another aspect of the new style was indifference to accepted canons of " respectability ", in subject and in diction, a candour about sex (encouraged by the work of Freud), and the use of vernacular and slang, which in the Sixties sometimes degenerated into scurrility.

*Aesthetic influences.*

(a) *The development of the romantic aesthetic*

One of the prime causes of the change in poetic method is not social but aesthetic, the clarification and evolution of the Romantic concept of poetry.

In *Romantic Image*, Frank Kermode has pointed out that from the time of Coleridge there has been a growing conviction in writers such as Keats, Blake, Pater, and Yeats that the artist, with his passionate sensibility and powers of creative imagination, has a different quality of sensibility and apprehension than other men. His work of art is utterly original and unique, essentially whole in itself, an " aesthetic monad " and resists analysis into form and content. Without ulterior purpose or utility, its only *raison d'être* is " to be." The image, Coleridge insisted, is essentially " vital," not mechanistic but organic, and it has itself been presented by organic images, notably that of the tree and the dancer.

(b) *The French Symbolists*

In his *Axel's Castle*, 1931, Edmund Wilson discussed the aims of the French Symbolists and their stimulus to English writers, including Yeats and Eliot.

The Symbolist leader, Stephane Mallarmé, attempted to create a new idiom for poetry. Supremely disinterested, a " saint of literature," he wrote little himself, but at his modest weekly receptions he gently expounded his influential views to such visitors as Whistler, Degas, Laforgue, Valéry, Claudel, Gide, Wilde, George Moore, Yeats, and Debussy.

Influenced by Poe, Mallarmé cultivated in his poetry a suggestive indefiniteness, blurring the distinctions between the actual world and that of dream and reverie. Debussy's well-known translation into music of his *L'Après-midi d'un Faune* wonderfully conveys his evocative and amorphous imagery.

Like Poe, the Symbolists were much concerned to reproduce in their poetry the flow of music and they were much influenced by Wagner. They came even to discard the classical Alexandrine and to develop *vers libre*. In the cult of indefiniteness they would, like Poe, confuse the perceptions of the senses. Poe, for instance, " hears " the oncoming of darkness.

What was the purpose of these experiments in poetic language? The Symbolists were so much preoccupied with the unique quality of individual experience, and with the complex and evanescent nature of consciousness, that they eschewed anything so commonplace as a description or statement as a falsification of experience and endeavoured, instead, to express unique and transitory feelings by suggestive images and symbols fastidiously chosen and patterned with exquisite care. The time-honoured rational framework of poetry was being scrapped so that it was becoming irrelevant to speak of the " meaning " of a poem.

(c) *The problem of objective validity in symbolist art*

The symbolism was not of the commonly accepted kind, such as the dove with the olive branch. Each poet deployed a highly idiosyncratic symbolism peculiar to himself in order to express his own intensely personal feelings. Such symbols were, says Wilson, really " metaphors detached from their subjects." Inevitably such poetry is not easy to interpret. An example easily available in English is Valéry's *Le Cimitière Marin*, translated by our Poet Laureate, Day Lewis, as " The Graveyard by the Sea."

The basic problem for the Symbolist poet is to find an imagery both true to his own unique experience and also in some way significant and communicable. That is the supreme test.

It is fascinating to see how English poets, such as Yeats, Eliot, and Sitwell, stimulated by the French experiments, tackle this problem and give objective validity to an intensely subjective vision.

## II. SOME INDIVIDUAL POETS

1. The Masters of the Decade between the Wars.

### W. B. Yeats (1865–1939).

References are to the *Collected Poems* (Macmillan).

Yeats's influence is exerted not by the limp romantic Celtic twilight verses between 1889 and 1904 but by the complex, sinewy poems appearing between 1910 and 1939. Although in traditional verse forms they establish Yeats as a great master of the modern symbolic image.

Brought up by a sceptic father, Yeats had sought from early youth for some significance in life in " heterodox mysticism," such as theosophy and the Kabbala, and above all in Blake. Their highly developed systems of symbols stimulated his innate sensitiveness to this intuitive form of insight and expression and encouraged him to develop his gift for waiting on images as they arose from the deeper regions of his mind. Arthur Symons, whose *The Symbolist Movement in Literature* was published in 1899, introduced him to the work of Mallarmé and other French symbolists, and confirmed him in his poetic approach which he now realised was part of a European movement.

To give objective validity to highly subjective images he used several techniques. Following Shelley's example, he would repeat the same symbol throughout the body of his work, so that one poem illuminates another. The symbol thus seen in perspective reveals new facets of its significance, sometimes even contradictory aspects.

For example, in early poems the rose signifies not only love and, in its Rosicrucian form, a mystic union, but also Ireland, beauty both sensuous and intellectual, and the beauty of Maud Gonne, with whom Yeats remained hopelessly in love.

A ruined Norman tower which Yeats had converted into a dwelling recurs from 1919 in many poems. Its basic significance is the artist's isolation, but it also suggests Milton's Platonist, Shelley's " visionary prince," Samuel Palmer's " lonely light," and Yeats's own Anglo-Irish heritage. He was greatly concerned to give the symbol solidity and firm outline and stresses the tower's emblematic " winding, gyring, spiring, treadmill of a stair " and the " grey stone fireplace with an open hearth " and the " fire of turf " of simple hospitality.

He juxtaposed exalted symbols with the singularly down-to-earth motifs which he deployed with increasing frequency. The indignity of age is " a sort of battered kettle at the heel," or " a tattered coat upon a stick " until in his emblematic protagonist, " Crazy Jane," he presents the ultimate in physical destitution inspired by poetic frenzy.

Yeats also relied on archetypal images from the " Great Memory," to which we respond unconsciously. In *The Two Trees* (p. 54), he follows Blake in his use of the image of the tree, which develops from the Kabbala and the Biblical Tree of Life. To Yeats it came to embody the organic nature both of all life and of the imagination, or reality intuitively perceived by the artist as whole and vital. Yeats, like Blake, contrasted this imaginative vision with the abstractions of the discursive intellect and his most perfect expression of the work of art as an organic and indissoluble unit occurs at the climax of *Among School Children*. Here in a passage of multiple import he marries the image of the tree to that of the dance.

" O chestnut-tree, great-rooted blossomer,
   Are you the leaf, the blossom or the bole?
   O body swayed to music, O brightening glance,
   How can we know the dancer from the dance? "

Yeats's poetry was also supported by a framework of mythology, whether of Gaelic legend, Greek mythology, as in *Leda and the Swan*, or, as in much of his more mature work, that of his own private system, which he expounded in his prose *A Vision*, 1926. For instance, he saw history as opposing cycles of 2000 years, each cycle being a reversal of the previous one. He represented this diagramatically by opposing " gyres," his gyre being the spiral traced on a cone.

But Yeats's finest poems, even when the meaning depends on his private hinterland, are still valid and intelligible in themselves. *The Second Coming* affects us through the singular clarity and force of the metaphors and the controlled energy of the rhythm.

Yeats is the poet of paradox and often quoted Blake, " Without contraries there is no progression." His own life was one of manifold tensions, especially between contemplation and his active participation in Irish politics and art. (He was Production Manager of the Abbey Theatre and was made Senator.)

A dominant theme is the dichotomy between sensuous living and the creation of immortal works of art, the latter symbolised by Byzantium in two splendid poems. Here he rejects the " sensual music " of " whatever is begotten, born, and dies " or " the fury and the mire of human veins " for " monuments of unageing intellect," symbolised by Byzantium, with its gold mosaic, the starlit or the moonlit dome and the golden singing bird, a miracle, " in glory of changeless metal," (pp. 217, 280).

Yet in the contemporary *Dialogue of Self and Soul*, p. 265, the poet opts for life, however sordid.

" I am content to live it all again
And yet again, if it be life to pitch
Into the frog-spawn of a blind man's ditch,"

Paradoxically the splendour of Yeats is the unresolved conflict. In poem after poem he passionately faces his dilemmas, personal, political, artistic, metaphysical, never to rest in a complacent final solution but forging instead enigmatic and arresting images of universal experience.


### T. S. Eliot (1888–1965).

The poems referred to are contained in *Collected Poems 1909–1962* (Faber).

Thomas Stearns Eliot is a poet who makes considerable demands on his readers. To some extent these may be met by using critical works such as George Williamson's *A Reader's Guide to T. S. Eliot*; but a poet who apparently needs to be read with a key is a little daunting, so it is perhaps as well to decide what these demands are and whether they are much heavier than or very different from those made by other poets.

Eliot studied philosophy at Harvard (1906–10) and continued his studies abroad at Munich, the Sorbonne, and later (1914) Oxford. He had been interested for a time in Eastern philosophy but chose not to indulge his inclination as he considered it might hinder his participation in Western culture, and in Western culture from the Greeks onward he was steeped. One must expect from a writer who read so widely in Greek, Latin, French, Italian, and German, as well as English, a range of references beyond what is usually expected of the well-educated arts graduate, and from a poet trained in philosophical disciplines one should further expect subtlety and precision. These expectations are met and the poetry, most of it at least, well repays the effort of the reader, who must follow a technique in which unity is achieved not by a framework of narrative or sensory description or even a logical sequence of thought, but by imaginative association where several layers of thought and feeling are fused.

Eliot's first book of verse, *Prufrock and Other Observations*, was published in 1917, although the title poem *The Love Song of J. Alfred Prufrock* had been published separately in 1915 in America, apparently at Ezra Pound's instigation. This poem is probably one of the easiest to begin with and yet touches on ideas and experiences with which Eliot was continually concerned.

At the head of the poem is a quotation from Dante's *L'Inferno*; it is relevant to the poem in that its speaker says that he has answered Dante only because he believes that his answer cannot be taken back to earth, since no one ever leaves the deep abyss alive. Eliot's character is first seen making his way through a maze of streets, a scene which reflects Prufrock's state of mind. The correlation between the exterior situation and the interior state is suggested clearly:

" Streets that follow like a tedious argument."

He arrives at a party; we hear, at a distance as it were, the sounds made by the guests, but in the foreground are Prufrock's thoughts. He is sadly aware of the impression he makes, the figure he cuts, and this inhibits him so that for fear of being misunderstood he withdraws and does not ask his question. This much is achieved with great delicacy. His fear of being ridiculous, misunderstood, and becoming old, together with the wry mockery of self-depreciation

" Though I have seen my head [grown slightly bald]
brought in upon a platter,
I am no prophet—and here's no great matter; "

makes him a sympathetic character. But there is more to the poem than the failure of a middle-aged man. Prufrock's city is characterised by fog, smoke, drains, restlessness; its citizens use prepared faces and formulated phrases, perhaps to defend themselves against any contact with reality which might disturb their pleasant but futile lives, measured out with coffee spoons. In this society people may talk of culture but it is the culture of the past; the present remains unproductive and people remain isolated and unable to communicate. The sea images which replace the fog are less picturesque but possibly more emotive; the fog may be understood, as Baudelaire used it, to represent the Unreal City, half dead, but the sea image comes from the English tradition and the Mermaids may recall Donne's satirical love poem *Go and Catch a Falling Star*, while the last three lines remind us of Keats's concluding lines in *Ode to Melancholy*. It is these two recurrent images of fog and sea which form the " framework " of the poem and which suggest the breadth of the poet's intention.

The same loneliness and sense not only of failure but of there being nothing worth succeeding in, is expressed in *Gerontion* perhaps more bitterly. This meditation on approaching death is inconclusive,

" I would meet you upon this honestly,"

but if the speaker is not sure what death means he is even less sure of the meaning or value of human life. The references to " windy spaces " (line 15) and

" Gull against the wind, in the windy straits "

suggest Claudio's speech on the terrifying prospect of existence after life has ended, in *Measure for Measure*. The quotation at the head of *Gerontion* comes from the Duke's speech in that play when he tries to steel Claudio's nerve for his coming execution by proving that life is not worth having. Eliot's Old Man seems to agree, but the Duke's Christian assurance, for he is disguised as a friar, evokes no response in him for Christ, the Word, cannot communicate through the swaddling darkness. Whatever the crucifixion may have once meant has been adulterated beyond recognition and there is nothing to replace it.

The *Waste Land*, published in 1922, established Eliot as a major figure on the contemporary scene. Some reviewers thought it a literary hoax because of the elaborate use of allusion and quotation (in several languages) as well as the lack of any formal structure. Charles Powell in *The Manchester Guardian* dismissed most of it as " so much waste paper." F. L. Lucas thought the " unhappy composition should have been left to sink itself; but it is not easy to dismiss in three lines what is being written about as a new masterpiece." Those who thought it a masterpiece praised its honesty, its emotional unity and above all its projection of twentieth-century malaise " the plight of a whole generation." At all events Eliot's reputation as a poet increased, though controversy may be raised again in a different form now that Eliot's original notebooks are being studied. It has been known for some time that Ezra Pound, to whom *The Waste Land* is dedicated, recommended considerable revisions mostly in the form of cuts which Eliot accepted, but the extent was not known until the John Quinn papers were made public in 1968.

However, the version published in 1922 certainly impresses one with a sense of disillusion and anti-climax. The old pre-war Edwardian world has been destroyed, perhaps it was never very satisfactory, but there seems to be nothing to replace it. The theme is repeated at intervals throughout, in different ways; sometimes as a dead land where the sun beats, a place where the cisterns are empty, the wells exhausted, an empty chapel with dry bones. The crowds on London Bridge walking through the fog are dead, for each is locked within himself. The modern Cleopatra seated in her burnished chair is surrounded by erotic symbols, but the romantic suggestion of the gold Cupidon is disturbed by *synthetic* perfume and destroyed by recollection of the rape of Philomel. This " Cleopatra's " life is pointless and unreal; she can only look forward to a game of chess. At the other end of the social scale there is the prostitution of personal relationship to the level of having a " good time " and instead of new life, abortion. " The nymphs are departed " indeed.

But at the end there is perhaps some hope in

" The awful daring of a moment's surrender
   Which an age of prudence can never retract."

At all events it seems particularly relevant to this half of the twentieth century when the possibilities of our producing a waste land seem even greater.

In 1927 Eliot became an Anglican. His poems, *Ash Wednesday, Journey of the Magi, A Song for Simeon*, reflect his new belief and his gift for using allusion is directed towards Christian sources. Thus in *Ash Wednesday* single lines from well-known prayers and responses from the Ave Maria and The Reproaches of the Catholic Good Friday service are used technically in the same way that the repeated and echoed phrases in earlier poems are used to give unity; but as the phrases that Eliot uses are ones that are frequently repeated in the liturgy of the church, the poem provides, for some readers, a kind of ceremony.

His major work after this is *Four Quartets*, where he is concerned with the Christian philosopher's interpretation of time, meaning as expressed through words, and salvation. They are full of paradoxes and though a progression of thought may be traced in the four, each Quartet may be read as a unity in itself. The mood of the second Quartet, *East Coker*, is sombre and the fear of nothingness, the dissatisfaction with the " shabby equipment " of contemporary language recalls parts of *The Waste Land*; but the fourth, *Little Gidding*, named after the home of a seventeenth-century community of Anglican mystics, is more hopeful

   " All manner of thing shall be well."

Considerable time needs to be spent on these poems if the complexity of the thought is to be appreciated, but the pattern of the verses, the delicate manipulation of the metre may be enjoyed by the reader who is prepared to listen carefully.

## 2. Edith Sitwell (1887–1964).

Edith Sitwell's work is in some ways similar to Eliot's. She shares his deep interest in the Elizabethan writers, especially their use of images. Like Eliot, she experimented with verse forms, sound patterns and, in common with James Joyce and Virginia Woolf, in the novel, creating a structure based on association of ideas and feelings as they appear to the subconscious or in dreams. She says that " the poems in *Façade* are *abstract* poems—that is they are patterns in sound " and she compares them to " certain studies by Liszt." A certain degree of pleasure may be derived from reading aloud these poems which seem to provide for adults what " nursery rhymes " provide now for children.

*Gold Coast Customs*, written in 1929, should be seen as the finished product of these early experiments. Like *The Waste Land* this is the poet's vision of a world where activity has become meaningless, but here the similarity ends. The heat in *The Waste Land* is associated with dryness, sterility, emptiness; here it is associated with feverish activity, uncontrolled passion, violent destruction. The poem's weakness lies in its length; it is not possible to maintain this pitch of emotion without some contrast to act as a control. A nightmare must be tightly controlled if it is to become an artefact.

Of her later poems *Still Falls the Rain* is probably best known. It was written during the London air raids and has lyrical quality made the more poignant by its subject. Similarly the poem written on the dropping of the atomic bomb, *Dirge for the New Sunrise*, is effective because one senses the writer is in command of her revulsion.

On the whole she succeeds where the effects are not so obviously strained after. If Eliot is castigated for being too intellectual one can see in some of Sitwell's verse the danger of a highly imaginative and emotive use of words which is not sufficiently subjected to intellectual scrutiny. Where Eliot may be idiosyncratic, Sitwell sometimes becomes eccentric.

## 3. Some Poets of the Thirties.

### Wystan Hugh Auden (b. 1907).

Auden was educated in a small public school, Gresham's, and later went to Oxford. Here he met Stephen Spender, Louis MacNeice, and others who formed temporarily a group of " political " poets most of whom were involved in the Spanish Civil War.

His first book of poems appeared in 1930 and was well received. After the publication of *The Ascent of F6*, a play which he wrote in collaboration with Christopher Isherwood, he was expected to become a major figure in English poetry. However, later books of verse were less well reviewed and in the mid-thirties the *Scrutiny* critics complained of his triviality, irresponsibility, and lack of maturity. He left England in 1939 and has since lived in America and Austria. As Eliot took out British citizenship Auden took out American, and, again, like Eliot, he accepted Christianity though perhaps in a less orthodox form.

Auden's interest in politics and the violence of political struggle is reflected in much of the imagery he uses as well as more directly in such different poems as *The Shield of Achilles* and *Alsono to Ferdinand*. *Let History be my Judge* is an early example of his political verse. Russia's forced collectivisation policy is the event which roused the feeling expressed here, but it is not directly referred to so that, if it were not for the date, the reader would not necessarily associate the poem with that particular policy, but with the harsh repression of any uprising or with the invasion of a weak country: the tragedy of the imposition of impersonal policy on the ignorant and defenceless is suggested and the callous self-justification of the powerful, ironically revealed. A later poem, *The Unknown Citizen*, satirises the omnipresence of the bureaucratic state and possibly the twentieth-century obsession with statistics. It begins with particular people, as in the dramatic monologues and some of the elegies, or poems for Auden's friends. In his less successful poems he tends to be either too clever (like Gratiano's in *The Merchant of Venice*, his reasons are like " two grains of wheat hid in two bushels of chaff ") or too anxious for effect. In the same way his dry humour and use of anti-climax is very effective at times, but sometimes the very ease with which he seems to do it betrays him and the joke becomes irritating.

Apart from anthologies, in some of which he is fairly well represented, the Penguin edition, which is the poet's own selection of verse, makes a good introduction to his work. There is one collected edition of *Collected Shorter Poems 1927–1957* (Faber). Otherwise his large production of verse is to be found in about ten small editions (all Faber). A recording of the poet's reading of his own poems has been made by Caedmon and is well worth listening to.

### Stephen Spender (b. 1909).

*Collected Poems 1928–1953* (Faber).

Spender's first poems, up to 1933, are mainly concerned with or derived from the ideas of Marxism and Freud. There are the stormy calls

" Oh, comrades, let not those who follow after
   —The beautiful generation that will spring from
      our sides
   Let them not wonder after the failure of banks
   The failure of cathedrals, the declared insanity
      of our rulers,
   We lacked the Spring-like resource of the
      tiger— "

but what the comrades are to do is not clear. One does not expect a political manifesto in a poem, but the vagueness of the sentiment of " equal like the shine from the snow " is irritating. It is difficult to take the optimism of such a poem as *The Funeral* seriously, yet if it is meant to be ironic the wit needs clarifying. Spender's early impact and placing in literature doubtless derived from his political and psychological idiom, but the poems which have stood the test of time are those which are more personal, *e.g.*, *My parents kept me from children who were rough*, which strike a more convincing note.

From 1936 onwards his poems are often about war, first the Spanish Civil War and then the Second World War. He is moved by the fate of the ordinary civilian, particularly the young who became involved in battles they do not understand. The defencelessness of the young soldier is poignantly conveyed and in poems such as *Ultima Ratio Regum* he links the greed of society, particularly the middle classes, with the slaughter of the innocent.

The belief in socialism and the brotherhood of man, rather glibly expressed in the earlier poems, is still present, but the tone of poems from this later period is compassionate. Spender rejects the easy, outright condemnation of either war or the enemy and refuses to glorify war by celebrating heroism. In fact there are no easy answers to the questions proposed in these exploratory poems. In the introduction to his collected volume Spender speaks of them as being " malleable " and possibly this unfinished sense is both their weakness and strength.

### C. Day Lewis (b. 1904).

*Collected Poems 1954* (Cape) and various short, later volumes.

Of this group of poets, C. Day Lewis is probably the most prolific. He began to publish in 1925 and was associated with Auden and Spender up to the outbreak of the Second World War. His early poems show Auden's influence—the use of colloquialism, the experiment with verse form and the concern with politics. How alien this type of verse was from his own vein may be seen from the symphonic poem *A Time to Dance*, 1935, where, in one section, he parodies the Apocalypse to describe the division of society into the exploiters and the exploited:

" I saw . . .
    The director placing explosives under the
        infant's cradle, the editor keeping a nursery
        for snakes:
    The scientist madly driving against traffic lights,
        the artist studying his acne in a pocket
        mirror: "

Later he imitates the rhythm of popular songs.

As his expectation of a Marxist solution faded and involvement in politics lessened, due at least in part to the Spanish Civil War and then the World War, he developed a quieter tone and used the more traditional verse forms. His work is generally polished, if not particularly vigorous. His translation of Virgil's *Aeneid* in 1952 was generally well received and in addition he has written several books of criticism, as well as detective stories under the pseudonym Nicholas Blake.

### Louis MacNeice (1907–63).

*The Collected Poems of Louis MacNeice*, edited E. R. Dodds, 1967 (Faber).

Louis MacNeice was born in the same year as Auden, published his first book of poems in 1929, and continued writing fairly steadily until 1963. He was actively interested in politics of an idealist, left-wing type and was influenced by the contemporary interest in psychology. In 1937 he joined with Auden in publishing *Letters from Iceland*, but after Auden's departure for America in 1939 the partnership, if so it may be called, dissipated itself. MacNeice continued his work as a lecturer in classics and also wrote several radio scripts for the B.B.C., including the verse drama, *The Dark Tower*.

His longest non-dramatic poem is *Autumn Journal*, which covers events from August to December 1938. Apart from its obvious historical interest—he clearly records his impressions of and fears about the political events of that period —it is an unusually convincing poem. It has

an authenticity as of Pepys's diary, but it is pervaded by a philosophical tone which brings details into focus. The verse flows smoothly most of the time, but the metre is not intrusive; in fact as an example of the " art to hide art " it is of its kind hardly bettered.

Observation of significant detail, personal reflection on the political situation as it affects society as a whole, reminiscence and a private transitory reaction are skilfully interwoven. For instance, he has spent most of the night anxiously assessing the possibilities of war breaking out and at six o'clock hears various sounds of people going to work—

" And I notice feathers sprouting from the rotten
        Silk of my black
    Double eiderdown which was a wedding
        Present eight years back.
    And the linen which I lie on came from Ireland
        In the easy days
    . . . . . . . . . . . . . . . . . .
        . . . and I wonder what the morning
        Papers will say,
    And decide to go quickly to sleep for the morning
                                                already
    Is with us, the day is to-day."

Humour, often directed at himself, gives his poetry a sharpness which it might otherwise lack since he seldom seems driven by an overpowering inspiration. His use of colloquialisms and cliché is less frequent than Auden's and, possibly because of this, more effective. The opening to his tribute to his friend in *The Casualty* is a good example of this, and the rest of the poem illustrates MacNeice's gift for characterisation, for expressing admiration and regret without sentimentality.

In spite of disappointments and disillusionments MacNeice remained liberal in outlook, and sympathetic to many views (see, for example, *Bottleneck* and *The Conscript*). He may not be a major poet but he has integrity and a respect of poetry, reflected in his skilful handling of metre, which makes him an honest poet rather than a brilliant dilletante.

### 5. Dylan Thomas (1914–53).

*Collected Poems*, 1952 (Dent).

In many ways his poetry could hardly be more different from that of the previous group. Dylan Thomas, as a poet at least, was hardly touched by social concerns, and was uncommitted politically. His poems do not exhibit the intellectual force which Auden's and Eliot's do. If these lastmentioned poets derived their inspiration from metaphysical poets like Donne, then Dylan Thomas may be said to derive his from poets such as Southwell or the visionary Blake.

The theme of much of his poetry is the oneness of all creation, the unity of experience: the human is intermingled with the divine, flesh and spirit are indivisible, and the world we inhabit is not essentially different from us.

" The force that through the green fuse drives
                                            the flower
    Drives my green age; that blasts the roots of
                                                trees
    Is my destroyer."

Death is incipient in birth and so in love—

" The word flowed up, translating to the heart
    First characters of birth and death."

Sometimes death is accepted as in *And death shall have no dominion* and in *A Refusal to Mourn*; at other times Thomas seeks to defy death by protest:

" Go not gentle into that good night
    Old age should burn and rave at close of day."

The condensed language, particularly the use of verbal nouns and adjectives, reflects, sometimes not very clearly, this sense of the unity of creation.

His use of language though much imitated, remains recognisably his own. He uses cosmic symbols: sun, heaven, stars, sea, fire, and wind; images such as womb, bird, blood, and tomb; colours: green, gold, red, blue, and black. Much of his verse—that is when it is not overloaded with images—evokes kaleidoscopic pictures and the rhythmic metrical pattern is generally strong, which is possibly why he was in his own lifetime a popular poet. He draws too a great deal on biblical symbols and this coupled with the use of formal sound patterns, assonance, rhyme, and alliteration gives his verse an incantatory sound which is quite impressive. Finally he has resuscitated the " transferred epithet technique."

At his best he has produced moving but unsentimental celebrations of childhood, *Fern Hill*, *Poem in October*, *Over Sir John Hill*; some religious poems, for example, the unusual pattern poem *Vision and Prayer* and some " occasional " poems.

Very good recordings of Thomas's readings of his poems have been made by the Caedmon group.

### 6. The English " Movement " Poets.

Robert Conquest's anthology *New Lines*, 1956 (Macmillan), marks the next stage—sometimes called the " Movement "—in English poetry. In his introduction Conquest remarks that groups of poets typical of their decade were " presented to public fire by anthologies which took up definite positions." His anthology was prepared in the belief that " a genuine and healthy poetry of the new period has established itself." The main objections he makes to criticism published from the beginning of the Second World War is that it encouraged poets " to produce diffuse and sentimental verbiage or hollow technical pirouettes." The poets he chose, apart from being contemporary, have in common only the acceptance that " poetry is written by and for the whole man, intellect, emotions, senses and all," and on the technical side a " refusal to abandon rational structure and comprehensible language."

The collection aroused considerable controversy and, according to Conquest's Introduction to the second edition, " absurd misrepresentation," though it is difficult to see why. The poems collected are low-pitched, conversational in tone; the superlatives are avoided and wit is more apparent than emotion, but this does not mean that feeling is absent or undervalued.

### Philip Larkin (b. 1922).

*The North Ship*, 1945; *The Less Deceived*, 1955; *The Whitsun Weddings*, 1964 (all Faber).

Larkin is one of the poets represented in *New Lines*. Like Dylan Thomas, he recalls his childhood, but he refuses to romanticise it. In *I Remember, I Remember*, he speaks of Coventry where he was born as a place where his childhood was " unspent " and he lists the crises commonly associated with precocious youth which did not occur. So far the poem is mildly ironic, but its end is disturbing:

" ' You look as if you wished the place in Hell,'
    My friend said, ' judging from your face.' ' Oh
                                                well,
    I suppose it's not the place's fault,' I said.
' Nothing, like something, happens anywhere.' "

The sense of emptiness, of opportunities untaken, of flatness, is a theme of much of Larkin's verse, *e.g.*, *Work, Departures, Triple Time*, but the self-mockery and irony give the work a pointedness which most elegaic verse lacks; when he reflects on the past he is neither nostalgic nor resentful. A conversational tone is used to attract attention, but the language is a " *selection* of the language really used by men "; he does not indulge in the vague slipshod phrasing of what passes for the conversation of " ordinary people." A good example of his style is *Church Going*, a reflection on the future of churches when they " fall completely out of use," which raises the whole question of belief (in values neither immediate nor material).

### 7. The American " Confessional " Poets.

The poets associated with this movement are for the most part those who concentrate on the inner, private world, whose poetry seems to be an exorcism of personal fears, anxieties, and guilts. This is not to say that most poets do not, at times anyway, draw on these sources, but usually the " material " is transformed in the process of composition into something more general and less personal. Allen Ginsburg, a selection of whose work may be found in *Penguin Modern Poets 5*, has probably gone as far (or further) in this " confessional " direction as anyone can without becoming completely unintelligible, but the leading spirit of the movement is Lowell.

### Robert Lowell (b. 1917). *See also* Section I.

*Poems 1938–1949*; *Selected Poems 1938–1964*; *Life Studies*, 1960; *For the Union Dead*, 1964; *Imitations* (all Faber).

Lowell's poetry is generally highly wrought. The contrast between the conventional appearance of the poem and its barely contained emotion within is one way of indicating the personal Waste Land only just below the consciousness of the individual. Thus in *The Drinker* the picture of the man who has thrown his fifth bottle, who is alienated from himself, his neighbours, and his wife, is recognisable, even acceptable. What is less easily accepted is the suggestion that he may be becoming what he sees:

" His despair has the galvanized color
    of the mop and water in the galvanized bucket."

Still less reassuring is the voice of Eve and the last stanza which hints that the suicidal tendency is endemic in a society bound to such trivia as parking meters.

Suggestions of schizophrenia, dissolution and failure underlie most of Lowell's work; fish seem to symbolise the destruction of civilisation and of the poet himself, as if we are all on the verge of, or perhaps are, actually reversing the evolutionary process and thus losing our identity as human beings. The poem *For the Union Dead* clearly seems to imply this.

### Sylvia Plath (1932–63).

*The Colossus*; *Ariel* (both Faber).

Sylvia Plath, also an American, but married to the English Ted Hughes, writes on similar themes to those of Lowell and uses similar images suggestive of horror and terror. In her earlier book, *The Colossus*, 1960, the irrational forces are not far away, but are more or less under control, except perhaps in *Poem for a Birthday*. The second book, *Ariel*, is more painful. Probably A. R. Jones is right when he says, " In some ways the most impressive and horrifying fact about these last poems is that they were written at all, that the creative mind could articulate and organise mental conflicts of such intensity."

### Anne Sexton (b. 1928).

Anne Sexton began writing in 1957. *Selected Poems*, 1964, has been published in England by the Oxford University Press. She acknowledges a debt to Lowell and deals with the same kind of subject as Sylvia Plath.

### 8. Other Notable Poets.

### Thom Gunn (b. 1929).

*Fighting Terms*, 1954; *The Sense of Movement*, 1957; *My Sad Captains*, 1961 (all Faber).

At first glance Gunn's poetry seems as contemporary as the morning paper. Titles such as *On the Move*, subtitled *Man you gotta Go*, *Black Jackets, Elvis Presley*, suggest, rightly, that his poetry is rooted in the present, but not in such a way that it will be incomprehensible when the present has become the past. He is concerned with violence in the classical world in *The Wound* and *Helen's Rape*, in the sixteenth century in *A Mirror for Poets*, and in the twentieth century in *Claus von Stauffenberg*, in personal relationships as well as public, but it is not an unthinking surrender to mere excitement or admiration of brutality, but a recognition of its necessity:

> " In this society the boundaries met
> Of living, danger, death, leaving no space
> Between, . . .
> . . . Yet at this point they found
> Arcadia, a fruitful permanent land."
> (A Mirror for Poets)

In Saint Martin and the Beggar, Martin, the saint of man, must learn to fight before he can " grow " and then without hesitating he halves his cloak to cover the beggar. He is justified because his action was natural. The tragedy of modern man lies in his inability to marry instinct, intention, and action:

> " One joins the movement in a valueless world,
> . . . . . . . . . . . . . . . . . . . .
> At worst, one is in motion; and at best,
> Reaching no absolute, in which to rest,
> One is always nearer by not keeping still."
> (On the Move)

Ted Hughes (b. 1930).

The Hawk in the Rain, 1957; Lupercal, 1960; Wodwo, 1967 (all Faber). There is also a small book of Selections from Hughes and Gunn (Faber).

There is some similarity between these two poets. Both have worked in America; both have developed a concise style which mirrors the toughness of their attitude to experience, their refusal to make the rough places smooth.

This said, the differences become more apparent as their individuality becomes clearer. Hughes, for example, uses animal imagery far more than Gunn. He approaches the human dilemma through the animal, but the animal is not a mere cipher. In Pike, for instance, the pike exists in its own right and, since Hughes did collect animals in his boyhood, the incident

> " Suddenly there were two. Finally one
> With a sag belly and the grin it was born with "

is probably true. But the recollected " nightmare " at the end of the poem goes beyond a boy's terror. The pond he fished, the eye, the dream darkness are symbolic both of the violence which lay in his own subconscious and that of the human race. The human being too is potentially a killer from the egg.

In other poems Hughes is searching for an identity. In An Otter, the otter

> " Gallops along land he no longer belongs to;
> Re-enters the water by melting."

At one level we have the hunt which loses and then finally catches the otter, but at another level there is the self, " attendant and withdrawn," the individual who " does not take root."

Hughes's descriptive powers are certainly strong and sensuous and, as a bonus, perhaps, there are in his verses for children, Meet my Folks and The Earth Owl, descriptions of people and creatures some of which are as strange and amusing as those of Edward Lear or Lewis Carrol.

Conclusion.

The above list is not of course intended to be a guide to the Best Modern Poets. Some, like Robert Graves and D. H. Lawrence, have been omitted because their contribution to literature has been relatively more important in other fields. The selection has not been made on a vague merit basis, but most of the poets mentioned do illustrate some of the ways in which twentieth-century poetry differs from the poetry of previous ages.

Apart from the collections mentioned, there are several good anthologies, for example, The New Poetry, edited by A. Alvarez; Contemporary American Poetry, edited by D. Hall (both Penguin); and Contemporary Poetry 1944–1960, edited by G. C. Rosser (University of London Press).

# III. TRADITIONAL VERSE PATTERNS

The poet's intensely individual music is played on the age-old instrument of metre and rhyme, and the better we understand the instrument, the keener will be our enjoyment of the poet's skill and genius.

Even verse that cannot be called poetry—verse that is mechanical, uninspired, lacking that intensity of insight and expression that we recognise as poetic—even this mediocre verse can teach us something of the poet's instrument. A homely nursery rhyme like " Humpty Dumpty " can help us to appreciate the metre of Ariel's unearthly song, " Where the bee sucks."

It is for this reason that the following guide to versification throws its net wide, gathering together for our consideration patterns as diverse as those of the mediæval ballad and the modern Frenchified triolet, of the flippant clerihew, and the grave blank verse of Wordsworth's " Prelude."

The following account of English verse is illustrated by quotations and by constant reference to the numbered poems in the new edition of " The Oxford Book of English Verse," 1939.

Thus " OBEV 16 " means " Oxford Book of English Verse," New Edition, Poem No. 16.

## I. INTRODUCTION. STRESS, METRE, AND RHYME.

If we listen carefully to spoken English, we shall observe that there is a natural tendency to stress some syllables more than others. In the following sentence, for example, the greater stress normally falls on the syllables whose vowels are marked with an acute accent, which is the usual way of indicating stress.

> " The exprés léft Mánchester at séven."

It is obvious that in this sentence the stress falls in a quite haphazard way, and it is for this reason that we recognise the sentence as prose, for the essential difference between English prose and verse is that in prose the stress falls at random, while in verse the stressed syllables occur according to some regular pattern.

If we mark the stressed syllables in the following line from Wordsworth,

> " And lóud hallóos and scréams and échoes lóud,"

it is immediately clear that the stress occurs regularly. The line is in fact, composed of a simple stress pattern of an unstressed syllable followed by a stressed (e.g., and lóud) which is repeated throughout.

It is a regular pattern of stress, such as this, that in English verse constitutes what we call " metre." Metre in Greek means simply " measure," and it is always by stress that we measure our verse.

Another feature that distinguishes our verse from prose is the use of rhyme, although rhyme, unlike metre, is not essential to verse.

## II. METRE.

### Different Kinds of Feet.

In English verse the unit of stress pattern constitutes a foot, the foot of verse being comparable to the bar of music.

English verse uses several kinds of feet, some of two syllables, or disyllabic, some of three syllables or trisyllabic, and occasionally a foot of four syllables.

*Disyllabic feet are of four kinds:*

The Iamb, consisting of an unstressed syllable followed by a stressed, *e.g.* " retúrn."

The Trochee, consisting of a stressed syllable followed by an unstressed, *e.g.*, " ríver."

The Spondee, consisting of two stressed syllables, *e.g.*, " dóor mát."

The Pyrrhic, consisting of two unstressed syllables, *e.g.*, in the phrase " into tówn," " into " is a pyrrhic.

*Trisyllabic feet are of four kinds:*

The Anapæst, consisting of two unstressed syllables followed by a stressed, *e.g.*, " as you wish."

The Dactyl, consisting of a stressed syllable followed by two unstressed, *e.g.*, " árchery."

The Amphibrach, very rarely used, consisting of a stressed syllable between two unstressed, *e.g.*, " delíghted."

The Tribrach, still more rare, consisting of three unstressed syllables, *e.g.*, last three syllables of " incommúnicable."

*A four-syllabled foot is very occasionally found:*

The Choriambus, which may be thought of as a trochee followed by an iamb, *e.g.*, " Tóll for the bráve."

### Different Kinds of Metrical Line.

Based on the different kinds of feet are the different kinds of English metre, which may be compared with the " time " in music.

Disyllabic metres may be either iambic or trochaic, for it is impossible to speak at any length using only pyrrhic or spondees, and the most common trisyllabic metres are anapæstic or dactyllic. Examples of different kinds of metrical line follow.

### Iambic Line.

" I stróve with nóne for nóne was wórth my strífe."
[OBEV 584]

### Trochaic Line.

" Hóme art góne and tá'en thy wáges."
[OBEV 150]

### Anapæstic Line.

" With a héy and a hó and a héy noninó."
[OBEV 147]

### Dactylic Lines.

" Wit with his wántonness,
Tásteth death's bitterness."
[OBEV 177]

### Amphibrach Lines.

" Most friendship is feigning, most lóving mere fólly
Then héigh ho, the hólly!
This life is most jólly."          [OBEV 146]

### Choriambic Line.

" Kéntish Sir Býng stóod for his Kíng."

### Variations in Metre.

Satisfying poetry is rarely entirely regular. Mechanical regularity is soon wearisome to the ear and is a characteristic of doggerel. The poet satisfies our love of rhythm in a more interesting and subtle way by introducing all kinds of variations and inversions, while at the same time maintaining the throb of the basic metre. An account of the chief variations follows.

### Elision.

Elision is the suppression in pronunciation of a vowel or a syllable.
In the anapæstic line,

" The Assýrian came dówn like a wólf on the fóld "

the second foot appears to have four syllables, but in fact the " i " in " Assýrian " is elided or dropped before the " a " as shown by the little bracket. The elision of " i," which is pronounced " y " and known as " consonantal y," is especially common, and occurs in such words as " familiar," " opinion." Elision is often shown by the use of the apostrophe as in " heav'n." In " heav'n " we see one of the many conventional elisions of poetry, like " 'tis," " 'twas," " did'st," " o'er," " e'er," " 'gainst," and many more.

### Substitution.

Substitution is the use of a foot different from that of the metre in which the poem is written. In the following examples we can see the effect on iambic verse of some common substitutions.

*Of a Trochee.*

" Stíffen the sínews, súmmon úp the blóod."
Shakespeare, " Henry V."
Here the initial trochee gives force and emphasis.

*Of a Spondee.*

" Rócks cáves, lákes féns, bógs déns and shádes of déath."
In this extraordinary line of Milton's the spondees slow down and weight the verse.

*Of a Pyrrhic.*

" They flý forgótten as a dréam "
Here the pyrrhic in the third foot gives lightness to the line.

*Of a Dactyl.*

" Cháttering his téeth for cóld that díd him chíll."
When a dactyl replaces an iamb it is usually in the first foot as in this typical instance from Spenser, where the dactyl gives emphasis and variety to the line.

*Of Anapæsts.*

" And the cóming wind did róar more lóud
And the sáils did sígh like sédge."
[OBEV 562]

The initial anapæsts in these two lines from " The Ancient Mariner " give an effect of hurry and speed.

### Additional Syllable.

An additional syllable may be added to either the beginning or end of a line.

### *Feminine Ending.*

A feminine ending is an extra unstressed syllable that is added after the final stressed syllable of a line, giving a gentle falling inflexion. It is often used in blank verse and is a marked characteristic of Shakespeare's later plays, *e.g.*,

"Be not afear'd; the isle is full of noises,
  Sounds and sweet airs that give delight and hurt
    not."

### *Anacrusis.*

Anacrusis is the use of an extra syllable before the first regular foot of the line.

### Dropped Syllable.

It sometimes appears that a line is a syllable, or syllables, short, until we realise that a suspense or pause occupies the time that would have been taken by the missing syllable. The dropped syllable can be indicated by the "caret" mark, thus ʌ. The following technical terms are used for lines that are short of syllables.

### *Catalectic Line.*

This leaves off in the middle of the last foot, as in the trochaic line

"Éver lét the fáncy róam,"

or the dactylic line,

"Ríngs on her fíngers and bélls on her tóes."

The catalectic line is common in trochaic and dactylic verse, for it is in keeping with the tendency of English verse to end on a stressed syllable.

### *Acephalous Line.*

This omits the first syllable of the line, as in the anapæstic line,

"That hóst with their bánners at súnset were
    séen."

### The Cæsura.

The cæsura is a special kind of pause, quite different from that which indicates a dropped syllable. It is a pause about the middle of a line and is usually indicated by a pause in the sense, *e.g.*,

"Both hungered after death; both chose to win
  or die."

### Two Ways of Describing Metre.

### The Classical.

The actual names that we have been using for the different kinds of feet and metres are derived from Greek. It is most important, however, to realise that in the classical languages they had a different meaning, for Greek and Latin verse was written on a quite different principle from ours, and was scanned according to the "quantity" or length of the syllable, and not according to stress. Thus an iamb in Greek and Latin consisted of a short syllable followed by a long, marked thus, ᴜ –, and a trochee of a long syllable followed by a short, marked – ᴜ.

In English verse the length of the syllable is totally irrelevant. For instance, the line,

"Pólly pút the kéttle ón and léts have téa"

begins with five trochees, all consisting of two *short* syllables.

The application of Greek words to English metres is confusing only if we forget that in English verse the criterion is stress.

### The Modern.

Some writers, however, prefer new ways of describing our verse, and the most popular method is set out below:

  A foot is called a period.
  A disyllabic metre is called duple or double time.
  A trisyllabic metre is called triple time.
  A period with the stress on the first syllable is said to be falling.
  A period with the stress on a second or third syllable is said to be rising.

### III. RHYME.

Another thing that gives a formal pattern to English verse, and distinguishes it from prose, is rhyme. It is not essential to our verse, much of our verse being rhymeless.

Rhyme is a similarity in sound in words occurring normally at the ends of lines. In true rhyme the last stressed syllable and consonants following it are the same, while the sounds preceding the stressed vowel are different, *e.g.*, "cage/page," "pleasure/treasure."

### The Types of Rhyme.

The most familiar division of rhyme is into masculine, feminine, and triple rhyme, but we also distinguish broken and Leonine rhyme.

### Masculine, Male, or Single Rhyme.

The final syllable is stressed, *e.g.*, "cage/page," "joy/boy."

### Feminine, Female, or Two-syllabled Rhyme.

The syllable before the last is stressed, and the final syllable unstressed, *e.g.*, "pleasure/treasure," "bending/lending."

### Triple or Tumbling or Three-syllabled Rhyme.

The antepenultimate syllable is stressed. Triple rhyme is normally found in light or comic verse, like that of W. S. Gilbert. This punning "Epitaph on a Dentist" employs it:

"Stranger! Approach this spot with gravity!
  John Brown is filling his last cavity."

In "The Bridge of Sighs" [OBEV 662] Hood dares to use it in a serious poem with such rhymes as "scrútiny/mútiny."

### Broken Rhyme.

Broken rhyme, where more than one word is needed to complete the rhyme, is occasionally used, *e.g.*, "estate/their gate."

### Leonine Rhyme.

Although rhyme normally occurs at the end of the line, we also find verse where the first half of the line rhymes with the second. This device, known as Leonine rhyme, is frequently used in Coleridge's "Ancient Mariner" [OBEV 562], *e.g.*,

"The ice did split, with a thunder-fit."

### Poetic Licence in Rhyme.

The difficulty of rhyming in English is considerable, for many words have not a single rhyming word, some have only one, others very few. Certain licences are therefore allowed to the poet in the following ways:

### Eye Rhyme or Printers' Rhyme.

Here words rhyme only to the eye, as "love/move." Keats in "Meg Merrilies" uses "rushes/bushes."

### Identical Rhyme.

Here the same syllable or word is used twice so that the line rhymes with itself, e.g., " part/impart " [OBEV 562], " universe/this verse " [OBEV 617]. The use of rhyming words spelt differently but pronounced identically is also a poetic licence, e.g., " wright, write, right."

### Cockney Rhyme.

Keats' use of Cockney rhymes has been much criticised, e.g., " mourn/torn," " faces/vases," " briar/attire." There is still considerable difference between Northern and Southern pronunciation of English, and many eminent poets have availed themselves of a Southern pronunciation in rhyming " dawn/morn," although in the North of England the "r" of "morn" would be sounded.

### Assonance.

Assonance is sometimes used instead of rhyme, and occurs frequently in early folk poetry and less formal verse. It consists in a similarity in the accented vowels and those which follow, but not in the consonants, e.g., " feet/creep," " skin/swim."

### Perversion of Rhyme.

Modern poets, following Wilfrid Owen, have sometimes used a deliberate perversion of rhyme, which should not be confused with assonance. Wilfrid Owen opens his bitter poem " A Terre " with the following stanza:

" Sit on the bed. I'm blind and three parts shell.
Be careful; can't shake hands now; never shall.
Both arms have mutinied against me,—brutes.
My fingers fidget like ten idle brats."

The deliberate falsity of rhymes like " shall/shell," and " brutes/brats " conveys Owen's horror at the disintegration and collapse of the First World War.

### Recording of Rhyme Schemes.

The conventional way of noting rhyme schemes is to call the first series a, the second b, and so on. Normally each new series is indented, e.g.,

| | |
|---|---|
| " Joyful, joyful! | a |
| When virginity | b |
| Seeks all coyful | a |
| Man's affinity. | b |
| Fate all flowery, | c |
| Bright and bowery | c |
| Is her dowery! | c |
| Joyful, joyful." | a |

W. S. Gilbert, " Yeomen of the Guard."

## IV. THE STANZA.

Some poems are divided into groups of lines, which strictly speaking are called " stanzas," though in popular language they are often known as " verses." Generally the stanzas of a poem are uniform, but sometimes they are varied as in Milton's " Lycidas " [OBEV 325].

## V. ENGLISH VERSE FORMS.

English poetry uses an immense wealth of verse forms, distinguishable from each other by the predominating metre and also by the pattern of rhyme and the kind of stanza—or by the absence of rhyme and stanza. An account of these follows.

### Iambic Metres.

The metre most natural to the English language is undoubtedly the iambic.

### With Iambic Pentameter as Basis.

The iambic pentameter of five stresses and ten syllables, also called the iambic decasyllabic line, is more used than any other, and is the basis of the following forms.

### Blank Verse.

Blank verse, consisting of unrhymed iambic pentameters, is the metre of Shakespeare's plays, Milton's " Paradise Lost," Wordsworth's " Prelude," and Tennyson's " Idylls of the King." In the hands of such masters it is a most flexible instrument, especially when diversified with the eleven-syllabled line with a feminine ending. Shakespeare used the metre with increasing freedom, though it must be remembered that some apparent variations are due to the different pronunciation of Elizabethan times.

The following lines of blank verse occur in Wordsworth's " Prelude," Book III. He is describing his rooms in St. John's College, Cambridge.

" And from my pillow, looking forth by light
Of moon or favouring stars, I could behold
The antechapel where the statue stood
Of Newton with his prism and silent face,
The marble index of a mind for ever
Voyaging through strange seas of Thought, alone."

### Heroic Couplet.

The heroic couplet, consisting of iambic pentameters rhyming in pairs, was in Elizabethan times called " riding rhyme," possibly because it is the metre of The Prologue of Chaucer's " Canterbury Tales," and of many of the tales themselves. It became the most fashionable metre of the eighteenth century when it was used by Pope, Goldsmith, and Johnson. Keats later employed it in " Lamia."

The Closed Couplet was, in the heyday of the couplet's vogue, considered the most polished and correct. Here the sentence form exactly coincides with the couplet and the rhyme has a clinching effect, e.g.,

" True ease in writing comes from art, not chance,
As they move easiest who have learned to dance."

Pope was the supreme master of the closed couplet, and eschewed variations such as enjambement, or the Alexandrine.

Enjambement is a variation used by poets before Pope's time and revived by the Romantic poets. In enjambement the sentence flows over from one line or couplet to the next, and the click of the rhyme is submerged, e.g., Keats' description of Lamia in her serpent form with skin of " dazzling hue."

" And full of silver moons, that, as she breathed,
Dissolv'd or brighter shone, or interwreathed
Their lustres with the gloomier tapestries."
Keats, " Lamia."

The Alexandrine, another variation, is a line of six iambic feet. Dryden made frequent use of the Alexandrine but Pope parodied it in the brilliant line that serves as a mnemonic.

" A needless Alexandrine ends the song,
That, like a wounded snake, drags its slow length along."

The triplet, another variation, consists of three lines rhyming together. The third line is frequently an Alexandrine.

### Rhyme Royal.

Rhyme royal has seven iambic pentameters, rhyming ABABBCC. Used by Chaucer in " Troilus and Cressida " [OBEV 14 and 15] and Shakespeare in " Lucrece," it was revived by Masefield in such poems as " Dauber."

### Spenserian Stanza.

The Spenserian stanza has eight iambic pentameters followed by an Alexandrine, rhyming ABABBCBCC. Invented by Spenser in " The Faerie Queene," it was used by Byron in " Childe Harold," Keats in " The Eve of St. Agnes," and Shelley in " Adonais."

**Elegaic Stanza.** The Elegaic stanza has four iambic pentameters, rhyming ABAB. It is also called the "heroic quatrain," quatrain meaning a four-lined stanza. This form is best known through Gray's "Elegy" [OBEV 465].

**"Omar Khayyám" Stanza.**

The "Omar Khayyám" stanza receives its name from its use by Fitzgerald in his translation of the "Rubaiyat." It has four iambic pentameters, rhyming AABA.

**Ottava Rima.** Ottava rima, also called the octave stanza, has eight iambic pentameters, rhyming ABABABCC. It was used by Byron in "Don Juan," and by Keats in "Isabella."

**Terza Rima.** Terza rima has stanzas of three iambic pentameters with a linking rhyme scheme: ABA, BCB, CDC, etc. The concluding stanza is rounded of with an extra line rhyming with its central line, e.g., DEDE, constituting, in effect, a heroic quatrain. Used by Dante, the verse has been adapted by English poets. Shelley's "Ode to the West Wind" [OBEV 617] uses modified terza rima, the final rhymes being DEDEE.

**The Sonnet.** A sonnet has fourteen iambic pentameters. Perfected in Italy by Petrarch, who died in 1374, it was introduced into England in the sixteenth century. There are two chief types of sonnet.

*The Petrarchan, or Italian, sonnet* has an "octave" of eight lines, rhyming ABBAABBA, followed by a "sestet" of six lines, where some variety of rhyme schemes is found. The strictest Petrarchan sonnets have either two "tercets" of three lines each, with rhymes CDECDE, or else three pairs of lines rhyming CDCDCD.

An example of sestet rhyming CDECDE is Milton's "On His Blindness" [OBEV 327].

Examples of sestets CDCDCD are Wordsworth's "Upon Westminster Bridge" [OBEV 534] and Keats' "On First Looking into Chapman's Homer" [OBEV 641].

Not all of these examples observe the natural pause between octave and sestet which is characteristic of the strict Italian form, and many of our finest sonnets depart from the original rhyme scheme in both octave and sestet.

A lesser-known Petrarchan sonnet by Keats:

"To one, who has been long in city pent,
 'Tis very sweet to look into the fair
 And open face of heaven,—to breathe a
   prayer
Full in the smile of the blue firmament.
Who is more happy, when, with heart's content,
 Fatigued he sinks into some pleasant lair
 Of wavy grass, and reads a debonair
And gentle tale of love and languishment?
Returning home at evening with an ear
 Catching the notes of Philomel,—an eye
Watching the sailing cloudlet's bright career,
 He mourns that day so soon has glided by:
E'en like the passage of an angel's tear
 That falls through the clear ether silently."

The *Elizabethan, or Shakespearean,* sonnet consists of three quatrains with the rhymes ABAB/CDCD/EFEF/ concluded by a couplet rhyming GG. The couplet often clinches the thought.

Examples are Shakespeare's sonnets [OBEV 155–174], and Keats' last sonnet [OBEV 644].

**Other Iambic Metres.**

Many of our iambic verse forms use a shorter or longer line than the pentameter.

**The Octosyllabic Couplet.** The octosyllabic couplet consists of lines of four stresses and eight syllables, and the lines rhyme in pairs. English poets like Marvell have used this metre effectively, e.g., "A Garden" [OBEV 365, see also OBEV 367, 370]. It is the metre of Masefield's "Everlasting Mercy" and "Reynard the Fox."

**The Ballad.** There are two chief kinds of ballad metre.

(a) *Strict Ballad Form* consists of stanzas of four iambic lines, the first and third with four stresses, and the second and fourth with three, with the rhyme scheme ABCB. The fine old ballads "Sir Patrick Spens" [OBEV 381] and "The Wife of Usher's Well" [OBEV 388] are in this metre. Coleridge, in "The Ancient Mariner" [OBEV 562] shows how many varieties of stanza can be based on the simple ballad stanza.

"*Fourteeners*" is the name given to a form which is simply a re-arrangement of the ballad quatrain as a rhyming couplet of two iambic lines with seven stresses, as in Macaulay's "The Armada."

(b) *Less Strict Ballad Form, or Long Metre,* consists of stanzas of four iambic lines each with four stresses, the rhyme scheme being ABCB or ABAB. Many ancient ballads, such as "Thomas the Rhymer" [OBEV 379], are of this type.

**"In Memoriam" Metre.** This, the metre of Tennyson's "In Memoriam," is like the less strict ballad metre in having four iambic lines, each with four stresses, but its rhyme scheme is ABBA.

**Short Metre.** Short metre, rarely used, consists of iambic quatrains, each line having three stresses and the rhyme scheme being ABCB.

**English Hymn Metres.** Most English hymns are written in short iambic lines, and English hymnology names them according to the number of syllables. The most common are:

*Common Metre,* or 8686, with rhymes ABAB, e.g., "O for a thousand tongues to sing" ["Songs of Praise" 595].

*Long Metre,* or 8888, with rhymes ABAB, e.g., "When I survey the wondrous cross" ["Songs of Praise" 133].

*Short Metre,* or 6686, with rhymes ABCB, e.g., "Blest are the pure in heart" ["Songs of Praise" 455].

**Double Iambic Metre.** When we are accustomed to hearing verse we come to realise that stresses are not always of equal weight. It is possible to distinguish in these "fourteeners" of Masefield a major stress, marked ´ and a minor stress marked ˘.

"Oh sŏme are fŏnd of Spănish wine, and sŏme are
   fŏnd of Frĕnch,
And sŏme'll swăllow tăy and stŭff fĭt ŏnly fŏr a
   wĕnch."
                Masefield's "Captain Stratton's Fancy"
                                   [OBEV 939]

The lines have in fact four major stresses, and between the major stresses intervene three syllables, of which the middle has a minor stress. It is this alternation in the weight of the stress which gives its characteristic swing to such a poem as Chesterton's "The Rolling English Road" [OBEV 930].

**Trochaic Metres.**

**Pure Trochaic Metre.**

English poets seldom use a pure trochaic metre, partly because of the difficulty of rhyming, and partly because the continual feminine ending that it involves is not pleasing to the English ear. A few very short lyrics in this metre can be found, as Browne's Song "For her gait, if she be walking" [OBEV 251], but the only poem of any length is Longfellow's "Hiawatha," and the metre of this *tour de force* tends to sound monotonous. It consists of unrhymed lines, each of four stresses, *e.g.*,

> " Like a yéllow léaf in áutumn
> Like a yéllow wáter-lily."

## Modified Trochaic Metre.

Ever since the Middle Ages our poets have contrived to combine the advantages of a trochaic metre and of a masculine ending by the simple expedient of shortening the last foot of the line to a stressed monosyllable. This catalectic, or shortened, trochaic line is found both in couplets and in stanza forms. *The seven-syllabled trochaic couplet, also called the trochaic tetrameter,* consists of these catalectic, or shortened, lines rhyming in pairs, and is a gay, tripping measure, as in some passages of Milton's " L'Allegro " [OBEV 318].

> " Háste thee nýmph and bring with thée
> Jést and yóuthful Jóllity."

Keats uses the metre in " Bards of Passion," and " Fancy " [OBEV 637 and 638].

*Lyrics in modified trochaic metre* are often found. Herrick uses the seven-syllabled lines rhyming in pairs in " Cherry Ripe " and other lyrics [OBEV 264, 279, 280, 281]. Edmund Blunden, in " Forefathers " [OBEV 965], uses it in a stanza rhyming ABABCC. George Herbert in his lyric " Discipline " [OBEV 291] brilliantly combines five- and three-syllabled lines rhyming ABAB, *e.g.*,

> " Thrów awáy Thy ród,
> Thrów awáy Thy wráth;
> Ó my Gód,
> Táke the géntle páth."

## Further Variations in Modified Trochaic Metre.

The modified trochaic line is especially subject to further variation.

(*a*) It is often combined with a pure trochaic line, *e.g.*, in Hunt's poem " Jenny Kiss'd Me " [OBEV 600] where the catalectic and the complete trochaic line alternate regularly.

(*b*) It often has an extra unstressed syllable preceding it (anacrusis), as in the second of these lines from Keats' poem " Fancy " [OBEV 638].

> " Ín a dárk conspíracy
> To | bánish Éven fróm her ský."

The line that results might well be taken for iambic, and there are some passages in English poetry, such as lines in Milton's " L'Allegro " [OBEV 318], which can be described either as irregular trochaic or irregular iambic lines! It depends on what the hearer judges to be the *basic* stress.

## Double Trochaic Metre.

Corresponding to double iambic metre there is a double trochaic metre. W. S. Gilbert effectively uses it in many of his patter songs, as in " Ferdinando and Elvira," *e.g.*,

> " Thén we lét off páper cráckers, eách of which
>   contáined a mótto,
> And she lístened while I réad them, till her
>   móther tóld her nót to."

These lines, like those in double iambic metre, have four major stresses (marked ″), and between the major stresses three syllables, of which the middle carries a minor stress.

A modified double trochaic metre, where the last foot is shortened to a stressed monosyllable, can be recognised in Tennyson's " Locksley Hall," or in Lewis Carroll's verses in " Alice in Wonderland ":

> " ' Will you wálk a little fáster? ' sáid a whíting
>   tó a snáil."

## Trisyllabic Metres Generally.

Because of the irregularities incident to verse in anapæsts, dactyls, and amphibrachs, it is not easy to distinguish one trisyllabic metre from another. Swinburne, the past master of trisyllabic metres, often passes with great freedom from anapæstic to dactylic lines within the same stanza.

## Anapæstic Metres.

### Pure Anapæstic.

Anapæstic metre is used only in short poems, and often conveys a sense of speed and urgency. The chief variation is the omission of one or two of the unstressed syllables at the beginning of a line. Some of the best-known examples of anapæstic verse are Byron's " Sennacherib," Flecker's " The War Song of the Saracens," and Lewis Carroll's parodies, " 'Tis the voice of the lobster " and " You are old, Father William," from " Alice in Wonderland."

### The Limerick.

The limerick may be defined as a single anapæstic stanza, having the first two lines of three feet, the next two lines of two feet and a concluding line of three feet, with the rhyme scheme AABBA.

The origin of the limerick is uncertain, but it became popular after the appearance in 1846 of Edward Lear's " Book of Nonsense." Lear's limericks differ from the contemporary type in that his final line is normally a repetition, adding nothing to the sense and repeating one of the previous rhyme words.

Most of our modern limericks are passed on by word of mouth, but some that concisely express some intellectual attitudes have appeared in print, as the following, on " Determinism "—

> " There wás a young mán who said ' Dámn!
> It appéars to me nów that I ám
>   Just a béing that móves
>   In predéstinate gróoves,
> Not a táxi or bús, but a trám.' "

### Dactylic Metres.

#### Pure Dactylic.

Like pure trochaic metre, pure dactylic metre has a feminine ending to the line, which makes rhyming difficult and does not satisfy the English ear. Very few serious poems keep consistently to a pure dactylic verse, and Robert Graves' " In the Wilderness " is most unusual in this respect, *e.g.*,

> " Christ of His géntleness
> Thirsting and húngering
> Wálked in the wilderness."

### Modified Dactylic Metre.

Normally dactylic metre is modified in that a catalectic line is frequently used, where the final foot is shortened to a trochee or a stressed monosyllable, as in Hood's " Bridge of Sighs " [OBEV 662], the most remarkable dactylic poem in the language, *e.g.*,

> " Óne more unfórtunate
> Wéary of bréath
> Ráshly impórtunate
> Góne to her déath."

Shakespeare also uses the catalectic line in the refrain to " Where the bee sucks " [OBEV 140]—

> " Mérrily mérrily sháll I live nów
> Únder the blóssom that hángs on the bóugh."

It is interesting to note how the catalectic dactylic line of the refrain is matched by the catalectic trochaic line of the verse.

### Amphibrach Metres.

#### Pure Amphibrach Metre.

The amphibrach metre is extremely rare in English, although it occurs occasionally in a few lines, or a refrain, like that to " Blow, blow thou Winter Wind " [OBEV 146]. Laurence Binyon's

" Bablock Hythe " is one of the few poems to use amphibrachs continuously, *e.g.*,

> " Till súnset was rímming
> The Wést with pale flúshes;
> Behind the black rúshes
> The lást light was dímming."

### Modified Amphibrach Metre.

The pure amphibrach line can be used alternating with a catalectic line, shorn of its last syllable, as in Goldsmith's drinking song in " She Stoops to Conquer," Act I, Scene 2, *e.g.*,

> " Let schóol-masters púzzle their bráin
> With grámmar and nónsense and léarning."

### Choriambic Metre.

There are few poems in pure choriambic metre. Ruskin's quatrain " Trust Thou thy Love " [OBEV 753] is one of the few examples, *e.g.*,

> " Trúst thou thy Lóve; if she be próud, is she not swéet? "

Choriambic effects are often obtained incidentally, especially in blank verse, when the first foot of a line is a trochee.

Lionel Johnson frequently achieves the same kind of effect in lyric verses by substituting a choriamb for two iambs, as in the poem " By the Statue of King Charles " [OBEV 909], *e.g.*,

> " Cómely and cálm, he rídes
> Hárd by his ówn Whitehall."

### Sprung Rhythm.

Sprung rhythm was practised by Gerard Manley Hopkins and his followers.

Its distinction lies in the fact that in a foot of verse the first syllable is always stressed, and this stressed syllable may be followed by any number of unstressed syllables from none to three, or even more, as the occasion demands. Hopkins has described sprung rhythm in the Preface to his "Poems."

### Quantitative Classical Metres.

Since the Renaissance poets such as Spenser, Coleridge, and Tennyson have from time to time endeavoured to reproduce in English verse the complicated quantitative metres of Greek and Latin verse. The difficulty, if not impossibility, of putting the stress on the long vowel in English has for the most past rendered such experiments interesting only to the scholar.

It should always be remembered that the technical names, such as iamb and trochee, although borrowed from the classics, have in English verse a quite different meaning, referring never to quantity but always to stress.

### Metrical Forms of French Origin.

It became fashionable during the last years of the nineteenth century for poets to imitate certain verse forms which had long been practised in France, some of them from the time of the troubadours.

Chaucer and Gower had in the fourteenth century used some of these forms, later English poets had occasionally experimented with some of them, and Swinburne, Austin Dobson, Edmund Gosse, and others did much to adapt and naturalise them, although their intricate rhyming patterns are very difficult to construct in a language so short of rhymes as English. The most popular were the triolet, villanelle, rondeau, ballade, and sestina.

*Characteristic of the Anglicised versions are:*

1. Freedom as regards metre and length of line.

2. Complicated and exacting rhyme schemes, which permit of no such poetic licence as identical rhyme.

3. A refrain line which recurs in certain stereotyped positions without any alteration of sound, although there may be significant alteration of meaning. Only the sestina is without a refrain.

### Triolet.

A triolet is a single stanza of eight short lines. The first line is repeated as the fourth, and the first and second appear again as seventh and eighth. Only two rhymes are used, the scheme being: ABAAABAB.

The triolet was re-introduced into England by Bridges in 1873. Austin Dobson's " A Kiss " is a good example of the form.

> " Rose kissed me today.
> Will she kiss me tomorrow?
> Let it be as it may,
> Rose kissed me today,
> But the pleasure gives way
> To a savour of sorrow;—
> Rose kissed me today,—
> Will she kiss me tomorrow ? "

See also Dobson's triolet " I intended an Ode " [OBEV 828].

### Villanelle.

The villanelle has five stanzas, each of three lines, followed by one stanza of four lines. It has a refrain which consists of the first and third lines of the first stanza. These lines alternately form the last lines of the four middle stanzas, and reappear as a concluding couplet to the poem. Only two rhymes are employed throughout. Stanzas one to five rhyme ABA and stanza six ABAA.

Austin Dobson wrote several villanelles including the well-known " On a Nankin Plate." The following of Henley's is both a good example and description of the form.

*Villanelle by W. E. Henley:*

> A dainty thing's the Villanelle
> Shy, musical, a jewel in rhyme,
> It serves its purpose passing well.
>
> A double-clappered silver bell
> That must be made to clink in chime,
> A dainty thing's the Villanelle;
>
> And if you wish to flute a spell,
> Or ask a meeting 'neath the lime,
> It serves its purpose passing well.
>
> You must not ask of it the swell
> Of organs grandiose and sublime—
> A dainty thing's the Villanelle;
>
> And, filled with sweetness, as a shell
> Is filled with sound, and launched in time,
> It serves its purpose passing well.
>
> Still fair to see and good to smell
> As in the quaintness of its prime,
> A dainty thing's the Villanelle.
> It serves its purpose passing well.

### Rondeau.

A rondeau is a short and compact verse form. It has thirteen lines, usually of eight syllables, which use only two rhymes, and in addition a refrain, usually of four syllables, which introduces a third rhyme. This refrain consists of the first half of the opening line and is twice repeated, thus giving the rondeau fifteen lines all told. The rondeau is divided into three stanzas with the following rhyme scheme: AABBA: AAB + refrain, C: AABBA + refrain C.

Austin Dobson wrote many rondeaus to this exacting plan, including the ingenious " You bid me try " and " In After Days " [OBEV 830].

*A Rondeau by Austin Dobson:*

> *You bid me try.*
>
> You bid me try, Blue-Eyes, to write
> A Rondeau. What!—forthwith?—to-night?
>    Reflect. Some skill I have, 'tis true:—
>    But thirteen lines!—and rhymed on two!
> " Refrain," as well. Ah, hapless plight!
>
> Still, there are five lines,—ranged aright.
> These Gallic bonds, I feared, would fright
>    My easy Muse. They did, till you—
>       *You* bid me try!
>
> That makes them eight. The port's in sight:—
> 'Tis all because your eyes are bright!
>    Now just a pair to end in ' oo '—
>    When maids command, what can't we do.
> Behold!—the RONDEAU, tasteful, light,
>       You bid me try!
>
>                                   1876

### Roundel.

The roundel is a variation of the rondeau. Swinburne in his " Century of Roundels " wrote a hundred, and his pattern is usually followed. It consists of nine full lines, plus the refrain (consisting of the opening half of the first line), which is twice repeated, giving eleven lines all told. Only two rhymes are used throughout. The roundel is divided into three stanzas with the following rhyme scheme: ABA + refrain B; BAB; ABA + refrain B.

Swinburne's roundel called " The Roundel " is especially interesting.

### Rondel.

The rondel is a form of verse similar to the rondeau. The modern English version consists of fourteen lines all told. Only two rhymes are used, and the initial two lines are repeated as lines 7 and 8 and again as lines 13 and 14. The rondel is frequently arranged in three stanzas with a rhyme scheme as follows: ABBA; ABAB; ABBAAB.

The rondel was revived in the nineteenth century by Bridges, Dobson, Gosse and Henley, and Dobson's " Love comes back to his vacant dwelling " is one of the best known.

### Ballade.

There are several kinds of ballade, but the most popular modern form consists of three eight-lined stanzas followed by an envoy of four lines. Each of the stanzas and the envoy end with a refrain. The rhymes of the eight-lined stanzas are ABABBCBC, and of the envoy BCBC.

Austin Dobson wrote several ballades of this kind, the best known being, " This was the Pompadour's fan," and " And where are the galleons of Spain? "

Chaucer's " Balade," " Hyd, Absolon, thy gilte tresses clere," is of an earlier seven-lined type without an envoy.

*A ballade by Austin Dobson:*

> *The Ballad of the Thrush.*
>
> Across the noisy street
>    I hear him careless throw
> One warning utterance sweet;
>    This faint at first, and low
>    The full notes closer grow;
> Hark! What a torrent gush!
>    They pour, they overflow—
> Sing on, sing on, O Thrush!
>
> What trick, what dream's deceit
>    Has fooled his fancy so
> To scorn of dust and heat?
>    I, prisoned here below,
>    Feel the fresh breezes blow;
> And see, thro' flag and rush,
>    Cool water sliding slow—
> Sing on, sing on, O Thrush!

> Sing on. What though thou beat
>    On that dull bar, thy foe!
> Somewhere the green boughs meet
>    Beyond the roofs a-row;
>    Somewhere the blue skies show,
> Somewhere no black walls crush
>    Poor hearts with hopeless woe—
> Sing on, sing on, O Thrush!
>
>       Envoy.
> Bird, though they come, we know,
>    The empty cage, the hush;
> Still, ere the brief day go,
>    Sing on, sing on, O Thrush!
>                                   1883

### The Chant Royal.

The chant royal is a longer form of ballade. It has five stanzas of eleven lines and an envoy of five lines.

The rhyme scheme is ABABCCDDEDE, and the envoy has rhyme DDEDE.

### The Sestina.

The sestina has six stanzas, each of six lines. The end words to the lines of the first stanza are repeated as end words in the other five stanzas, but in a different and stereotyped order. The poem concludes with an envoy.

The first sestina published in English was in Spenser's " Shepheardes Calender " (1579). Swinburne wrote many, including " I saw my soul at rest upon a day."

### The Clerihew.

The clerihew is an amusing quatrain, so called after its inventor Edmund Clerihew Bentley. It disdains regular metre and depends on the simple rhyme scheme AABB. The distinctive characteristic of the clerihew is that it is concerned with some eminent person, who is named in the first line and then described in a wilfully fanciful way, the matter being dictated by the exigencies of the rhyme, as in Bentley's clerihew on J.S. Mill.

> " John Stuart Mill,
> By a mighty effort of will,
> Overcame his natural bonhomie
> And wrote ' Principles of Political Economy.' "

We might invent a clerihew for Pears Cyclopædia, and say

> " You will find *Pears Cyclopædia*
> A simpler and speedier
> Aid in your search for verity
> If you do not use it with levity."

### Free Verse or Vers Libre.

It is hardly possible to define anything so vague as Free Verse. It is characterised by a greater intensity of feeling and a more elevated language than is usual in prose, and has a rhythm that is different from that of poetry in that it is irregular; it has rhythm but not metre.

Free Verse is arranged in lines, but these lines have an indefinite number of syllables. They have balance but no regularly recurring pattern of stress, and no rhyme.

The best-known writer of Free Verse is Walt Whitman, whose " Leaves of Grass " was published in 1855.

### VI. CONCLUSION.

The foregoing account is no more than a description of our traditional verse forms. It in no way implies that verse is written according to rules.

We have only to look at Shakespeare's lyrics [OBEV 133–174] to realise how brilliantly free and inventive the poet can be in devising new and delightful patterns of verse—many of them so subtle as to be very difficult to define All that the students and critics can do is to follow in the poets' wake, endeavouring to understand and elucidate the forms that the maker has created.

# IV.  FIGURES OF SPEECH

We constantly use figurative language without realising it.  When we say that we are " browned off," " fed up," " at the end of our tether," we do not expect to be taken literally.  We are in fact employing metaphors.

An understanding of metaphors and other figurative expressions enables us to use our language with greater confidence and effectiveness.  It also helps us to understand more fully what others have written.  Especially is it valuable when we read a good novel, play, or poem, for to the creative writer figurative language is as natural as the air he breathes.

The following guide to our figures of speech is arranged alphabetically for ease of reference.

**Alliteration.**  A kind of repetition.  Two or more words in close succession begin with the same letter, or sound, usually a consonant.  Up to the fourteenth century much English verse was written according to an alliterative principle, as in this modernised quotation from " Piers Plowman."

" I had *wandered* me *weary* so *weary* I rested me
On a *broad bank* by a merry-sounding *burn*."

A strong tendency to alliteration still survives in our poetry.  Shakespeare ridicules it in the mechanical's play in " A Midsummer Night's Dream " (Act V, Scene 1) in such lines as—

" Whereat, with blade, with bloody blameful blade,
He bravely broach'd his boiling bloody breast."

**Anti-climax.**  See Bathos.

**Antithesis.**  A figure of speech where ideas are so set out that they are in sharp contrast to each other, *e.g.*,

" Better to reign in Hell than serve in Heav'n."
                              Milton.

" To err is human, to forgive divine."
                              Pope.

**Apostrophe.**  A figure of speech where the speaker or writer suddenly breaks off and directly addresses some other person who may be present either in the flesh or only in the imagination.  Often it is not a person but a thing, abstraction, or personification that is addressed, as in Milton's famous apostrophe, " Hail, holy light " in " Paradise Lost," Book III, line 1.  Apostrophe can be used with comic effect, *e.g.*,

" She turns, O guardian angels stop her
From doing anything improper."

(This couplet is also, incidentally, an example of bathos.)

**Assonance.**  (1) Assonance is correspondence of vowel sounds.  For instance, in the opening lines of the " fairy song " in " A Midsummer Night's Dream " (Act II, Scene 3) there is a play on only three vowels, and this repetition helps towards the effect of a magic charm, *e.g.*,

" Philomel, with melody, Sing."

In Tennyson's poem " Break, break, break " the repetition of the " o " sound in the second line is like an outcry of grief, *e.g.*,

" On thy cold grey stones, O sea."

(2) Assonance is sometimes used instead of rhyme, especially in early folk poetry.  Here there is correspondence of one word with another in the accented vowel and any vowels which follow, but not in the consonants, *e.g.*, in " King Estmere," " Spain " is rhymed with " same," and " barone " with " home."

**Bathos or Anti-climax.**  A figure of speech that consists of a sudden and ludicrous descent from lofty to trivial things.  In " The Rape of the Lock " Pope wittily used bathos to satirise the frivolity of the woman of fashion, who lacking all sense of proper feeling, casts the same " screams of horror," and " shrieks to pitying heav'n,"

" When *husbands* or when *lapdogs* breathe their last."

The careless writer may fall to bathos which is unintentionally comic in its effect.  The word " bathos " in Greek means " depth."

**Climax.**  A figure of speech where ideas are set out in such a way that each rises above its predecessor in fable.  In Greek the word " climax " means a ladder.  One of the finest examples is in Shakespeare's " The Tempest " (Act IV, Scene 1) when Prospero says,

" And like the baseless fabric of this vision
The cloud-capp'd towers, the gorgeous palaces,
The solemn temples, the great globe itself,
Yea, all which it inherit, shall dissolve."

**Epigram.**  A concise and pointed saying, effective by its wit and ingenuity.  It often uses antithesis.  S. T. Coleridge's definition of this form is in itself an epigram, *e.g.*,

" What is an epigram?  a dwarfish whole:
Its body brevity, and wit its soul."

**Euphemism.**  A figure of speech where a harsh or distressing expression is replaced by one that is gentler, if less accurate.  Thus we may call a lie a " flight of fancy," or a " terminological inexactitude."  There is a striking instance of euphemism in " Macbeth " (Act I, Scene 5), when Lady Macbeth, planning the murder of her guest, Duncan, says, " He that's coming must be provided for."

**Hypallage** or " Transferred Epithet."  A figure of speech where an adjective, or adverb, is separated from the word to which it belongs grammatically, and is transferred to some other word in the sentence, its unusual position giving it a kind of emphasis.  The word " obsequious " is thus transferred in the sentence " A lacquey presented an obsequious cup of coffee."

**Hyperbole.**  A figure of speech where there is a deliberate use of exaggeration for the sake of effect as in the phrase " tons of money."  Lady Macbeth uses hyperbole when she says, " Here's the smell of blood still; all the perfumes of Arabia will not sweeten this little hand " (Act V, Scene 1).

Writers of film trailers frequently indulge in hyperbole.

**Innuendo.**  A figure of speech where something is hinted at, or suggested, but not openly stated.  Dickens uses innuendo to suggest Scrooge's stinginess by saying, " Darkness was cheap, and Scrooge liked it."

**Irony.**  (1) A figure of speech where the speaker says one thing but intends the opposite to be understood.  Shylock uses the word " courtesies " ironically when he says,

" Fair sir, you spit on me on Wednesday last,
You spurn'd me such a day; another time
You call'd me dog; and for these courtesies
I'll lend you thus much moneys."
                              " Merchant of Venice " (Act I, Scene 3).

The use of irony can clearly be seen in Shakespeare's " Julius Cæsar " in Antony's well-known speech to the citizens.  They gradually realise that when Antony repeats that Brutus and the rest are "honourable men," he is speaking ironically, and intends the opposite. When they fully perceive this they cry, "They were traitors . . . villains, murderers." ("Julius Cæsar," Act III, Scene 2.)

(2) *Dramatic irony* is the use of words which have a second inner significance that is not realised by some of the actors in a scene. For instance, in Sheridan's "School for Scandal," Act IV, Scene 3, Sir Peter admires Joseph Surface's useful screen, and Surface replies, " Oh yes, I find great use in that screen." He and the audience know, but Sir Peter does not, that at that very moment the screen is concealing Peter's own wife who had rashly visited Joseph.

It is helpful to remember that in Greek the word "irony" means "dissimulation."

**Litotes.** A figure of speech which is really a special kind of understatement (or Meiosis). Instead of making a positive statement (*e.g.*, "This is a difficult task") we might use Litotes, and say " This is no easy task," thus expressing a positive by the negative of its opposite.

**Malapropism.** An amusing inaccuracy in vocabulary. Words that have an accidental similarity in sound may become confused in the speaker's mind and the wrong word may come uppermost. Thus Mrs. Malaprop complains that the disobedience of her niece gives her, not "hysterics," but " hydrostatics." It is not surprising that Mrs. Malaprop, of Sheridan's " The Rivals," has given her name to this kind of verbal confusion, though many before her time, including humble folk in Shakespeare's plays, have uttered malapropism. Bottom, in "A Midsummer Night's Dream," says that in the wood they " may rehearse more obscenely " when he means " obscurely."

**Meiosis.** A figure of speech where a deliberate understatement is made for the sake of effect. English people are especially fond of Meiosis and often use it colloquially, in such an expression as " He made a very ' decent ' contribution," meaning a very " generous " contribution. The full meaning of what we intend is often conveyed by the tone of voice, *e.g.*,

" This is *some* war."

**Metaphor.** It is helpful to think of the figure of speech, metaphor, as a condensed simile. In metaphor one thing is not merely *compared* to another, as in simile, but is boldly spoken of as if it actually *were* that other. Thus Bacon, in the following metaphor, does not say books are *like* food, but speaks of them as if they actually *were* food, *e.g.*, " Some books are to be tasted, others to be swallowed, and some few to be chewed and digested."

Metaphor is usually defined as the transfer of a name, or descriptive term, to some object to which it is not properly applicable, thus making an implicit comparison. Shakespeare uses nautical terms to describe our human situation when Brutus says,

" There is a tide in the affairs of men which, taken at the flood, leads on to fortune " ("Julius Cæsar," Act IV, Scene 3).

In *Mixed Metaphor* two or more inconsistent metaphors are used of the same object, as when, speaking of a suspicion, someone said, " I smell a rat; I see it in the air; but I will nip it in the bud."

**Metonymy.** A figure of speech where a person or thing is not named directly, but by some associated thing. Instead of saying, " The prisoner addressed the magistrate," we might use metonymy and say, " The prisoner addressed the bench." Similarly, "a speech from the Lord

Chancellor " is sometimes called " a speech from the Woolsack."

**Onomatopœia.** The use of words which imitate or echo the sounds they suggest, *e.g.*,

" Seas half-frozen slushed the deck with slime."
　　　　　　　　　　　　　　　　　　Masefield.

**Oxymoron.** A figure of speech where words that are usually contradictory are combined in one expression, *e.g.*, " bitter-sweet."

" I know this is a joyful trouble to you."
　　　　　　　　　　　　"Macbeth," Act II, Scene 3.

**Paradox.** A figure of speech where a statement is made that at first sight seems contradictory, or absurd, *e.g.*,

" The rule of the road is a paradox quite:
If you keep to the left, you are sure to be right."
and

" The child is father of the man."
　　　　　　　　　　　　　　　　Wordsworth.

**Pathetic Fallacy.** A figure of speech where it is assumed that things of nature have feelings like those of human beings, *e.g.*,

" And daffadillies fill their cups with tears."
　　　　　　　　　　　　　　　　　Milton.

In Greek " pathos " means " feeling."

**Personification.** A figure of speech where some abstraction, or some inanimate thing is represented as a person, *e.g.*,

" Rule, Britannia."

" But look the dawn in russet mantle clad
Walks o'er the dew of yon high eastern hill."
　　　　　　　　　　　*Hamlet*, Act I, Scene 1.

Personification is really a special kind of metaphor.

**Pun.** The use of words so as to convey a double meaning, as in Belloc's couplet

" When I am dead, I hope it may be said
" His sins were scarlet, but his books were read.' "

In the three puns that follow there is a suggestion of a banking transaction! " The Egyptians received a check on the bank of the Red Sea which was crossed by Moses." Puns, which were popular in the nineteenth century, especially with Lamb and Hood, are now out of favour.

**Simile.** A figure of speech which makes a comparison pointing out a similarity between things otherwise unlike. It is usually introduced by " like " or " as," *e.g.*,

" Men fear death as children fear to go in the dark."　　　　　　　　　　　　Bacon.

" His own thought drove him like a goad."
　　　　　　　　　　　　　　　　Tennyson.

**Spoonerism.** An accidental transposition of the sound of two words, so called after Rev. W. A. Spooner, warden of New College, Oxford, *e.g.*, " You have hissed all my mystery lectures " for " You have missed all my history lectures."

**Synecdoche.** A figure of speech where the name of a part is used for the whole, or the whole for the part, *e.g.*,

" A fleet of a hundred sail ",

meaning of a hundred ships.

Synecdoche is really a special kind of Metonymy.

**Transferred Epithet.** See Hypallage.

# V.  LITERARY FORMS

**Allegory.** A description or story which has a second and deeper significance below the surface. The characters are really personifications, usually representing some vice or virtue. Allegory flourished in the Middle Ages, but the best-known allegory in the world is Bunyan's " Pilgrim's Progress " (1678), which has been translated into over a hundred different languages and dialects. On the surface " The Pilgrim's Progress " is the story of a journey in which the hero encounters many difficulties but at last reaches his destination. Its inner meaning is the progress of the Christian soul through life on earth. Spenser's " Faerie Queene " (1589 and 1596) is a more subtle and complex allegory, capable of several interpretations, religious, ethical, and political. Allegory has been described as extended metaphor. *See* M31.

**Autobiography.** The story of a man's (or woman's) own life, written by himself. The autobiography is becoming increasingly popular, recent excellent examples being Stephen Spender's *World within World*, Richard Church's *Over the Bridge* and Laurie Lee's *Cider with Rosie*.

**Ballad.** There are two chief types of ballad:

1. A light song, often sentimental, as was the Victorian ballad, or a popular song, often of a personal kind, praising or attacking some notability.

2. A traditional poem, passed on by word of mouth. Many of our traditional ballads date from the 15th century. They tell some stirring tale, as do the many ballads about Robin Hood. Sometimes they record an actual occurrence, like the ballad " The Battle of Otterbourne," which tells of a Border skirmish, fought in 1388. Such ballads are enlivened by lively dialogue, and they use a special kind of stanza, which is described on M25.

**Ballade.** A short highly stylised poem, with a strict verse form. *See* M29.

**Biography.** A narrative telling the life story of some actual person, usually a well known figure. The most famous biographer of classical times was Plutarch, who in the 1st century A.D. wrote his series of parallel " Lives " of twenty-three Greeks and twenty-three Romans. The English translation of this provided Shakespeare with some of the plots of his plays. Boswell's *Life of Samuel Johnson* (1791) is our best-known English biography.

**Burlesque.** The aim of burlesque is to make us laugh by ridiculing the work of some other writer. Sometimes it treats his serious subject in a mocking way. Sometimes it takes the form of an absurd imitation or caricature of his style. Some of our most successful burlesques are dramatic in form, like Sheridan's " The Critic," produced in 1779. This has a play within a play, called "A Tragedy Rehears'd," a brilliant burlesque of the sentimental, historical plays so popular in his time. Danny Kaye's film, " The King's Jester," is a burlesque of pseudo-historical films.

**Chant Royal.** A poem of a strictly formal kind, French in origin. *See* M29.

**Clerihew.** A single-stanza verse form, four lines long. *See* M29.

**Comedy.** A play which is happy and amusing in tone, but not necessarily light or superficial. A comedy always has a fortunate conclusion. Shakespeare's " Twelfth Night " and Oscar Wilde's " The Importance of being Earnest " are typical examples.

**Drama.** A play in verse or prose, where the story is unfolded and the characters represented through the actions and speeches of actors on a stage. It is essential to good drama that there should be some kind of dynamic action and some conflict between the characters. In comedy the conflict is usually open and external. "As You Like It," for instance, begins with a quarrel between Orlando and Oliver. But most of the world's finest tragedies reveal also an inner conflict in the soul of man. In " Hamlet " the hero is at odds with many people, including his mother, the king, Ophelia, Polonius, and Laertes, but all these struggles are of secondary significance, compared with the conflict in his own mind. Even a play like " Waiting for Godot," which reduces incident and conflict to a minimum, must make some concession to the demand of the audience for the dynamic. Drama cannot be static. Occasionally poets have written dramas which they knew were not practicable for the stage. Shelley's lyrical dramas, " Prometheus Unbound " and " Hellas," are of this kind. *See* Section I.

**Eclogue.** In classical literature a brief poem, usually in the form of a dialogue between shepherds. It was a popular form in the time of the Renaissance; Spenser's " Shepheardes Calendar " (1579) consists of twelve eclogues, one for each month of the year.

**Elegy.** A lyric poem of lamentation for the dead. Gray's " Elegy in a Country Church-yard " (1750) is the best-known English elegy. It reflects in a general way on the " destiny obscure " of the humble folk who are buried in a quiet church-yard, probably that of Stoke Poges, but most elegies mourn the death of only one person. Such are Shelley's " Adonais " (1821), on the death of Keats, and Matthew Arnold's " Thyrsis " (1867), commemorating his friend Arthur Hugh Clough. Tennyson's " In Memoriam " (1850) is unusual, in that it is not a single elegy, but a series of elegiac poems, inspired by the poet's grief for the death in 1833 of his friend Arthur Hallam.

**Epic.** A very long narrative poem, usually consisting of several books. The epic tells of the splendid deeds of some hero of history or legend and is frequently concerned with war. Some of the world's greatest epics are the Greek " Iliad " and " Odyssey," ascribed to Homer, the Latin " Aeneid " of Virgil, the Hindu " Mahabharata," and Milton's " Paradise Lost," whose hero is God himself. The epic is distinguished by its sustained dignity of style.

**Epilogue.** *See* Prologue.

**Essay.** The word essay, derived from the French, means literally an " attempt " or " endeavour," and as a literary term it applies to a short prose composition which attempts to present the author's reflections on any subject he chooses. As a literary form the essay derives from the French " Essais " of Montaigne, first translated into English by Florio in 1603. Our first English essayist was Francis Bacon, who published between 1597 and 1625 three volumes of his essays, brief, pithy, and objective in character. In course of time the essay has become more subjective and personal, especially in the hands of Lamb, Hazlitt, and contemporary writers.

**Extravaganza.** A composition, musical or literary, which uses improbable and fantastic elements and incidents. A good example of narrative extravaganza is Thackeray's *Rose and the Ring* (1855), in which, for instance, Gruffanuff's husband, the footman, is, because of his rudeness, turned into a door-knocker. Extravaganzas are frequently dramatic in form, and most pantomimes may be regarded as such.

**Fable.** A very brief story designed to teach some lesson or moral. The characters of the story are often animals, birds, or insects, which converse like human beings. The most famous of all fables are those attributed to Aesop, and those of La Fontaine, the French writer of the 17th century.

**Farce.** A species of dramatic comedy whose whole aim is to excite laughter. It does not scruple to use improbable characters and incidents and absurd situations. " Charley's Aunt " is a typical farce.

**Lampoon.** A coarse satire (q.v.) attacking an individual. Lampoons are usually short. The word itself is derived from a French word meaning " drinking song."

**Limerick.** A single-stanza verse form, 5 lines long and with a formal metre and rhyme scheme. *See* M27.

**Lyric.** In ancient Greece a lyric was originally a poem meant to be sung to the accompaniment of the lyre, a stringed musical instrument rather like a small harp. Later the word was used for a poem with song-like qualities; short, usually divided into verses, and expressing the feelings of the poet. The lyric flourished in England in the Elizabethan age, as witnessed by the lovely lyrics scattered through Shakespeare's plays. Neglected in the 18th century, it became popular again with the Romantic poets of the 19th century. Odes, elegies, and sonnets are all species of lyrics.

**Mask or Masque.** A dramatic entertainment performed by amateurs and originating in the court masquerade. The action or plot of the masque is of the slightest and there is little concern with portrayal of character, for the masque gives pleasure by means of its verse, music, and dancing, and its elegant costume and scenery. It was very popular in the 16th and 17th centuries, and from 1605 Ben Jonson wrote many court masques, for which Inigo Jones designed original costumes and settings. Our best-known examples are Shakespeare's masque in Act IV of " The Tempest " and Milton's " Comus."

**Melodrama.** There are two meanings of the word melodrama.

1. In the early 19th century a melodrama meant a play, usually of a romantic and sensational kind, in which songs were inserted, and where an orchestra accompanied the action. The musical comedy of today might be regarded as its modern counterpart.

2. Today the word melodrama is used of an inferior kind of play, which deliberately excites the emotions by its sensational and violent happenings, but which has a happy ending. We should be careful to distinguish melodrama, which uses violence for its own sake, from serious plays, like " Hamlet " or " King Lear,'' where violent acts are only incidents necessary to a profound interpretation of human conduct.

**Memoirs.** The word is normally used of a record of events of which the author has some personal experience or special source of information.

**Miracle Plays.** Mediæval verse plays produced from the late 14th to 16th centuries by the town guilds and performed in the market-place, or other suitable open space. They consisted of a series of dramatised stories from the Bible or Lives of Saints. Each scene would be allotted to one of the guilds, which was then responsible for its production on a wheeled stage. As soon as the actors of one guild had completed their scene, their stage would be trundled off, sometimes to another rendezvous, and would itself be succeeded by another stage with its scene, until a whole cycle of episodes had been performed. Four great cycles of miracle plays are still extant, called after the towns where they were probably performed, York, Coventry, Chester, and Wakefield. The Wakefield cycle is often called the Towneley cycle. The plays have not only a strong religious sense but also a lively comic spirit. The Towneley cycle has some especially racy comic scenes. One popular incident shows the noisy quarrel that results when Noah's wife refuses to go into the ark.

**Mock Heroic.** A species of parody (q.v.), caricaturing some play or poem written in a lofty and high-flown style. " The Rehearsal " (1672), by Villiers, is typical. It is an absurd imitation ridiculing the artificial and high falutin' heroic plays which were then in vogue.

**Monody.** In Greek literature an ode sung by a single voice, like our solo in music. In English literature it signifies a poem of mourning for someone's death. The elegies " Lycidas," by Milton, and " Thyrsis," by Matthew Arnold, were both called monodies by their authors.

**Monologue.** Originally a scene where one person of the drama spoke alone. Today it usually means a dramatic composition for a single actor, such as the well-known Lancashire monologues presented by Stanley Holloway. The word is also sometimes used as meaning soliloquy.

**Moralities or Morality Plays.** Mediæval verse plays of an allegorical kind, which attempted to teach lessons of virtue, the persons of the drama usually being not real people, but personifications. Most Moralities date from the 15th century, the best known being " Everyman," which is Dutch in origin. The hero, Everyman, is summoned by Death, and vainly appeals for help to his friends, Fellowship, Kindred, Goods, Knowledge, Beauty, and Strength, but all fail him. Only his own Good Deeds will consent to accompany him on his last journey.

**Mysteries or Mystery Plays.** Some modern writers use the term " Mystery play " instead of " Miracle play " (q.v.). It is really an alternative title. One critic tried to distinguish between " Mystery plays," as concerned with stories from the Gospels, and " Miracle plays," as concerned with the lives and deeds of Saints, but this distinction is not usually followed.

**Novel.** A lengthy prose fiction in narrative form, telling a realistic story of people and their doings. Its chief interest is in character and incident. The first English novelist was Samuel Richardson, whose novels, especially *Pamela* (1740–41) and *Clarissa Harlowe* (1747–48), had a European reputation. In the present century writers like James Joyce, and Virginia Woolf have written what have been called novels of the " stream of consciousness," where the interest lies not so much in the incidents as in the mind's response to events, and reflections. *See* M3–15.

**Ode.** In classical literature an ode was a poem to be sung. In English literature it signifies a lyric poem, usually in rhyme, and is seldom longer than 150 lines. It is usually in the form of an address, and lofty in its feeling and style. The ode was popular with the romantic poets. Some of our best known are Shelley's " Ode to the West Wind," and Keats' " Ode to a Nightingale," " Ode on a Grecian Urn," and " To Autumn," all of them published in 1820.

**Parable.** A parable is an arresting simile or metaphor from nature or common life, which may be elaborated into a life-like story. It presents a situation which at a certain point implies some correspondence with ethical or religious principle. *See* C. H. Dodd's *The Parables of the Kingdom.*

**Parody.** A literary caricature, which mimics the themes and style of some other author in such a way as to make his faults seem absurd and laughable. J. C. Squire's *Tricks of the Trade* is an amusing collection of his skilful parodies of such writers as Byron, Wordsworth, and Masefield.

**Pastoral.** A pastoral poem, romance, or play is one in which the life of shepherds or of simple rustic folk is portrayed in an idealised way. Originating in Greek literature, the pastoral was revived at the time of the Renaissance. Spenser's " Shepheardes Calendar " consists of twelve pastoral eclogues. Shakespeare's " As You Like It " is a pastoral play, Milton's " Lycidas " is a pastoral elegy and his " Comus " a pastoral masque. There is usually in the pastoral a deeper meaning below the surface. A critic has said, " The shepherd's cloak was the acknowledged disguise of the lover, the poet, the courtier, the pastor of souls, the critic of contemporary life." In the pastoral form the charm of a simple setting and deeper significance are combined.

**Prologue and Epilogue.** Generally speaking, a prologue means a foreword, or preface, and an epilogue an appendix to a literary work, but the terms are often used more specifically when referring to a play. Here the prologue is a short speech in verse or prose spoken to the audience by one of the actors before the play begins, the epilogue a similar speech after its conclusion. The prologue endeavours to put the audience into a receptive state of mind, the epilogue to ask for a kind reception to the play. Shakespeare's " Romeo and Juliet " has a prologue, his " As You Like It " an epilogue, spoken by Rosalind, who says, " Good plays prove the better by the help of a good epilogue." In the 18th century it was customary for a leading actor to speak the prologue and for a leading actress to make a plea for the play in the epilogue.

**Romance.** The romance of the early Middle Ages was a fictitious tale in verse, telling the adventures of some hero of chivalry, the interest being in the incidents, sometimes of a supernatural kind, rather than in character. The most famous of these early romances is the French " Chanson de Roland " of the early 12th century. In the later Middle Ages a romance might be written in prose. In the 16th and 17th centuries a romance meant a tale in either prose or verse in which the scenes and incidents were remote from those of real life. Sir Philip Sidney's " Arcadia " (1590), written to entertain his sister, is of this type. Today the word romance is rather vaguely used of a tale of somewhat improbable events. Sir Henry Rider Haggard wrote several such romances, including *King Solomon's Mines* (1886) and *She* (1887).

**Rondeau.** A poem of a strictly formal kind, French in origin. *See* M28.

**Rondel.** A poem similar in form to the rondeau. *See* M29.

**Roundel.** A variation of the Rondeau. *See* M29.

**Saga.** The word saga, which is of Norse origin and means story, is applied to the mediæval prose narratives of Iceland and Norway, especially those concerned with the traditions of Icelandic families and Norwegian kings. William Morris, in his " Earthly Paradise," gives in " The Lovers of Gudrun " a version of the Icelandic Laxdæla Saga.

**Satire.** A work in either verse or prose attacking folly and vice. Pope's " Dunciad," in verse, published between 1728 and 1743, ridicules contemporary authors and literary follies in a massive attack on dullness and literary hacks. Swift's *Gulliver's Travels* (1726), which on the surface is a series of prose tales of travel to imaginary countries, is actually a comprehensive satire. It begins, in the first book on " Lilliput," with incisive ridicule of the squabbles between English political parties and religious sects, and culminates, in the final book on the Houyhnhnms, in a devastating attack on all that is bestial in human nature. Samuel Butler's *Erewhon* (an anagram of Nowhere), published in 1872, also uses a prose travel tale in his satirical exposure of Victorian convention and hypocrisy. Although not precisely satires, many of Shaw's plays are satirical in spirit. " Arms and the Man " may be considered in one of its aspects as a satire on war.

**Sestina.** A poem of a strictly formal kind, French in origin. *See* M29.

**Skit.** A light satire, often in the form of parody.

**Soliloquy.** In a soliloquy a man talks to himself, or utters his thoughts aloud regardless of the presence of others who may hear him. The word is usually applied to such utterances by a character in a play. The most famous soliloquies in literature are those of Hamlet.

**Sonnet.** A lyric poem of fourteen lines, with an intricate rhyme scheme. *See* M26.

**Squib.** A brief, sharp satire (*q.v.*) attacking an individual.

**Threnody.** A term from the Greek, seldom used today. It means a song of mourning, especially a lament for the dead.

**Tragedy.** A play, or other literary work, which is preoccupied with the serious and unhappy aspects of life. It is sombre in tone and ends with misfortune. Shakespeare's " Macbeth " and Ibsen's " Ghosts " are typical tragedies.

**Tragi-Comedy.** The word is used in two different ways:

(a) It may denote a play (or very occasionally a story) which combines both tragic and comic elements. Chekhov's " The Cherry Orchard " is a tragi-comedy of this type.

(b) It may also mean a play which is for the most part sombre in theme and tone, but which has a happy conclusion, like Shakespeare's " The Winter's Tale."

**Trilogy.** In Greek literature a series of three tragedies, like Aeschylus' trilogy, the " Oresteia," written when he was nearly seventy, in the 5th century B.C. In modern times the word trilogy is applied to any sequence of three literary works which are related to each other in subject and theme.

**Triolet.** A single-stanza verse form, eight lines long, and with a very formal pattern, French in origin. *See* M28.

**Villanelle.** A poem of a strictly formal kind, French in origin. *See* M28.

# VI. LANGUAGES

The number of known, living languages exceeds 3,000, the great majority of which can be ascribed to about a dozen main language families. More than half the world's population of 3,356,000,000, however, can be reached by as few as 13 languages.

Languages are related in a distinct group if their ancestry can either be traced back to the same mother tongue or be inferred to derive from an assumed parent language (through comparative linguistic methods, historical records, etc.). The term "family" is used for the largest possible such grouping. Contrary to common belief related languages need not be alike phonetically or grammatically, nor need speakers of related languages have racial or cultural characteristics in common.

The scientific study of the structure and mechanics of language in general is the domain of *general linguistics*, various branches of which connect with other sciences, such as, for example, communication theory. *Comparative linguistics* denotes the study of the history and relationships of individual languages and language groups, and has connections therefore with social studies such as ethnology and historical geography. Modern linguistic study has developed from the study of comparative philology, which dates from the end of the 18th cent. It achieved greater scientific objectivity and exactitude in the last decades of the 19th cent., since when the term *philology* has reverted to its original significance, denoting the study chiefly of written texts: its connections lie therefore rather with literary history and criticism.

Chinese has the greatest number of speakers, followed by English, Hindi, Russian, Spanish, Japanese, German, French, Italian, Malay, Bengali, and Portuguese.

The oldest recorded language is Sumerian, which was spoken by a non-Semitic people who lived in the southern part of ancient Mesopotamia, c. 3,500 B.C. It was a language conveyed in cuneiform script with a structure and vocabulary unrelated to any other known language. It lost ground to the Akkadian Semitic language and began to die out in Hammurabi's time.

The oldest living language is Chinese, with a progressive history of 4,000 years during which it has maintained its identity and given shape to ideas. It is not phonetic, *i.e.*, it is not written in groups of letters which represent sounds, but each word is represented as a character. Coptic, a direct descendant of the ancient Egyptian language, has also survived but only as the liturgical language of the Christian Coptic Church. (Modern Egyptian is a dialect of Arabic.)

In grammar and phonetics, the most complex languages are those of the Caucasus, together with North American Indian tongues (including Eskimo), while the simplest is said to be Malay. The native languages of Britain, besides English, are Welsh (with an unbroken literary history since the 6th cent. A.D.), Irish Gaelic (the native tongue of Ireland with a literary history dating back to the 9th cent. A.D.), and Scots Gaelic (which became separate from Irish Gaelic in the 13th cent., though for literary purposes classical (Irish) Gaelic was employed in Scotland until the 18th cent.). Manx Gaelic is on the point of extinction. Cornish survived until the 18th cent.

A *lingua franca* is a language which acts as a medium of communication over a large multilingual area, such as Hindi in India, Swahili in southern Africa, Malay in the southwestern Pacific areas.

A *hybrid* language arises when foreign speakers adopt the basic vocabulary of a second language, usually as a commercial medium, and adapt it to their own phonetic and grammatical patterns: *Pidgin English* is English–Cantonese, *Beach-la-Mar* is English–Polynesian, *Papiamento* is Negro–Spanish of Curaçao.

An *artificial* language is one that has been deliberately constructed to act as a universal medium of communication; the best known is Esperanto.

A *standard* language is one recognised by a state as its national language and used for administration, national communications (*e.g.*, radio), and education. It may be one of several languages actually spoken in a particular country; or a particular form or dialect in a state where dialectal differences are acute, *e.g.*, standard Italian is the Tuscan dialect; or a purely written standard, *e.g.*, most Arabic-speaking nations, despite vernacular dialectal differences, employ classical Arabic in books and newspapers. A standard language thus tends to act as a *lingua franca*.

Nine major language-families and 11 major individual languages are listed below:

African Languages. Two linguistic pictures of Africa could be drawn, one showing the native languages and dialects, the other showing a patchwork cover of European languages of colonisation; yet neither would be complete without the other, for the two groups are everywhere in close contact. Many states recognise two or more official languages, both native and colonial in origin.

The principal colonial languages are French, English, Spanish, Portuguese, Italian, German, and Flemish. Dutch is of particular interest, since it has developed into what is virtually a new language, Afrikaans, the standard form of which differs in many respects from the European Dutch standard.

The native languages of North Africa, and of East Africa down to the equator, belong to the Semito-Hamitic family (*q.v.*). The true Negro-African languages number many hundreds, with a profusion of dialects. The southern half of the continent is almost exclusively the domain of the Bantu languages. Of these, the chief representative is Swahili: it boasts a considerable body of literature, has long had currency as a medium of trade and commerce, and is fast thriving as a native *lingua franca* over the whole region. It may have as many as 10 million speakers. The Khoin, or Bushman–Hottentot languages, are spoken in parts of Angola, South West Africa and Botswana. The remaining languages, from Senegal to the Sudan, are roughly described as Sudanic, but they have not been satisfactorily classified and probably include many separate language families. The most significant of these is Hausa: originating in northern Nigeria, it has become, like Swahili in the south, an extensive *lingua franca*, with some 15 million speakers.

**Altaic.** A family of languages extending from Turkey to Mongolia and to northern Siberia, consisting of three main groups: (1) the Turkic languages, the most important member being Turkish, with about 26 million speakers; (2) Mongolian; (3) Tungusic languages of northern Asia, chiefly represented by the Manchu literary language.

**Arabic.** The language has a great history—as the evangelising medium of Islam, as the vehicle of a rich imaginative literature, and as the repository of science and philosophy during Europe's "dark ages." Spoken by some 75 million inhabitants of countries south and east of the Mediterranean, it remains one of the great languages of the present day. Countries in which it occupies official status include Algeria, Iraq, Israel, Jordan, Kuwait, Lebanon, Libya, Morocco, Saudi Arabia, Syria, and the United Arab Republic. *See also* **Semito-Hamitic.**

**Austro-Asiatic.** Family of languages in southern Asia. They include (1) the Mon–Khmer languages, chief representative Cambodian or Khmer, and (2) the Munda or Kolarian languages of Bihar and Orissa in north-east India. Some linguists ascribe to this group the Annamese and Mu'ong languages of Vietnam.

**Chinese.** As the national language of China's estimated 710 million inhabitants, Chinese is spoken by over twice the number who speak English, the second most widely spoken language in the world. Unlike India, China is not divided linguistically except in the south-eastern maritime provinces where several differing and mutually unintelligible dialects are found, including Cantonese, Wu, Min, and Hakka. In most of the rest of the country the language known in the West as Mandarin is spoken.

Mandarin, as spoken in Peking, is now the standard form of Chinese. This national language is called *p'u-t'ung-hua* (common speech). Mandarin is also the official standard of Taiwan, although the local dialect is Amoy, a variety of Min. The majority of the Chinese people who have settled in the United Kingdom speak Cantonese.

The traditional Chinese script is ideographic, *i.e.*, each character represents the meaning of a word, not its pronunciation, so that speakers of otherwise divergent dialects have always been able to follow the written language. The Chinese Government have recently introduced a system of romanisation, a language reform which will facilitate writing and printing through the replacement of the 4,000 essential characters by the relatively few letters of the Roman alphabet. Chinese has an attested history of over 4,000 years. *See also* Sinitic.

**Dravidian.** Family of languages found in southern India. Chief representatives: Telugu (spoken by some 35 million in Andhra Pradesh), Tamil (over 30 million in Madras and eastern Ceylon), Canarese or Kannada (16 million in Mysore) and Malayalam (15 million in Kerala). These are the only four Dravidian languages officially recognised in the Indian Union (*see* Indian languages). They are written in native alphabets which, while ultimately related to the Devanagari script, are so modified as to appear totally different. Tamil and Canarese are well established literary languages.

**English.** The English language belongs to the Germanic branch of the great Indo-European family of languages. Its closest relatives are Frisian and Dutch. It originated in the various Saxon dialects carried across by invaders during the 4th and 5th cent. A.D. Old English, as it is now known, was essentially a spoken language, but with the rise of Christianity and the influence of Latin writers, it emerged as a literary language. Other influences came from Scandinavian sources (Viking invasions) and French (Norman conquest). Modern English dates from the emergence of Mercian as the dominant dialect during the 14th century. As the major language, through former colonisation of countries in all five continents, and as a world-wide cultural, scientific, and commercial medium, English may have up to 300 million speakers.

**French.** The official language of France's 48 million inhabitants. It is also one of the two official languages of Belgium (spoken mainly in Brussels and the south by about 4 million), and one of the three official languages of Switzerland, with over 1 million speakers in the western cantons (Geneva, Neuchatel, Fribourg, Valais, Vaud). With French-speaking peoples in many parts of the world, in Canada (Quebec and Ontario) and in countries belonging to the French Community, it may have a total of 80 million speakers. Its derivation from Latin classes it as a Romance language, and it is thus related to Portuguese, Spanish, Italian and Rumanian.

**German.** The language spoken by over 75 million people in East and West Germany, by 7 million in Austria, and as an official language of Switzerland, by nearly 4 million in 19 of the 25 cantons. In addition there are German-speaking peoples in Hungary, Czechoslovakia, Poland, and other smaller areas of Europe, and in former colonial regions (in Africa and some of the Pacific islands), bringing the total to between 95 and 100 million. The standard, High German, is distinct from the Low German or *Plattdeutsch* colloquial dialects spoken in the lowlands of northern Germany. German and English are the chief representatives of the Germanic group of languages, which also include Dutch and the Scandinavian languages.

**Hindi.** The official language of India, as laid down in the 1950 Constitution. English also continued as the official language until 1965 and under the Official Language Act, 1963, may still be used in addition to Hindi. Technically, Hindi denotes a group of dialects of which Hindustani is the principal member. It is written in the Devanagari script, but has a variant Urdu, written in Arabic script and considerably influenced by Arabic and Persian vocabularies. There are close on 170 million speakers of Hindi/Urdu. The necessity of establishing an official medium was emphasised by the fact that, according to the 1961 census, the number of languages and dialects spoken in India amounted to 1,652. Hindi is an Indo-Aryan language of the Indo-European family related to Persian and more distantly to the majority of European languages. It is a modern descendant of Sanskrit, the literary language of the Vedic scriptures.

Urdu and Bengali are the two state languages of Pakistan. English continues to be the official language until 1970.

Indian Languages. *See* Hindi, Indo-European, Dravidian, Austro-Asiatic.

Indo-European. Most of the languages of Europe and of a large part of southwestern Asia belong to the Indo-European family. The notable exceptions are Hungarian, Basque, Finnish, Lappish, Turkish, and the Caucasian languages. The major branches and languages are: Germanic (English, German, Dutch, Flemish, Danish, Swedish, Norwegian, Icelandic), Romance (French, Portuguese, Spanish, Italian, Rumanian—all derived from Latin), Celtic (Gaelic, Welsh, Breton), Slavonic (Russian, Polish, Czech, Serbo-Croat, Bulgarian), Baltic (Lithuanian, Latvian), Greek, Albanian, Armenian, Iranian (Persian, Afghan) and Indo-Aryan (Hindi, Rajasthani, Punjabi, Bengali).

Italian. The official language of Italy's 50 million people, and spoken by about half a million in the Ticino canton of Switzerland. With emigrant speakers exceeding 10 million, and as a language of former colonisation in Africa (principally in Libya and Ethiopia), the language is probably spoken by as many as 65 million. Italian is the most direct descendant of Latin and is thus related to French and Spanish.

Japanese. The language spoken by Japan's 95 million people and by some speakers in Korea and Hawaii. Known from the 5th cent. A.D., it has been considerably influenced throughout its history by Chinese, both in speech and script. Nevertheless, it differs markedly in structure and vocabulary from its neighbour, and is more likely to be related to Korean, although such a relationship has not been proved.

Malayo-Polynesian. Family of languages native to the southwestern Pacific area, with the following groups: Indonesian (including Malay, Javanese, Tagalog, and Malagasy, totalling over 120 million speakers), Melanesian (which includes Austromelanesian and Micronesian languages, with just over 1 million speakers), and Polynesian (including Tahitian, Hawaiian, Maori, totalling less than half a million). Malay, with over 65 million speakers, is the official language of Indonesia, and is widespread as a *lingua franca* throughout the eastern archipelago. In Indonesia it is called *Bahasa Indonesia*.

Palaeo-Siberian. Family of languages, now considerably on the decline, spoken in north-eastern Siberia and including Chukchee, Koryak, and Gilyak. Ainu, of the southern Sakhalin, may belong to this group, which shows some similarities to native languages of North America.

Russian. The major language of the U.S.S.R. is the mother tongue of over 80 per cent of the R.S.F.S.R.'s 125 million inhabitants. It is the official language throughout the Soviet Union, and, as such, is extensively propagated at all levels of education, although the native languages of most minority groups are also legally recognised. Discounting Byelo-Russian and Ukrainian, which are distinct languages, speakers of Russian number at least 160 million. Russian proper may be said to date from the 11th cent. The standard is Muscovite, and the language is written in Cyrillic script.

Semito-Hamitic. Family of languages chiefly represented by Arabic. Hamitic includes the Berber languages of desert nomads of northern Africa, and the Cushitic tongues of coastal Ethiopia and Somalia (the ancient Egyptian language was also a member of this group). The Semitic languages include Arabic (*q.v.*), Hebrew (official language of Israel and widely used by Jews all over the world), and Amharic (the official language of Ethiopia, spoken by some 5 million). Aramaic, the language spoken by Christ, is still spoken in parts of West Syria.

Akkadian, one of the oldest recorded languages and current throughout the Babylonian Empire, was spoken by the Semitic people who came to Mesopotamia *c.* 2,500 B.C. from the Arabian peninsula. They took over the cuneiform script of the non-Semitic Sumerians, although the two languages had no affinities. Akkadian was gradually replaced by the Aramaic language and alphabet.

Most of the Semitic languages have proved important languages of civilisation during their history, and have a rich literature.

Sinitic. Family of languages of southeastern Asia. The main languages and groups are: Chinese (*q.v.*), Tibetan-Burmese, and Thai. The last-named includes Siamese and Laotian. These and other languages of Thailand are very similar to one another, but the official language is Lao (Laotian). The Annamese language of Vietnam may also belong to the Thai group.

Spanish. The official language of Spain, Mexico and most of the Central American states (except Brazil, Guyana, Surinam, French Guiana) as well as of the Greater Antilles, and widespread as a former colonial medium and an important language of trade, with a total of at least 115 million speakers. Modern Spanish may be said to date from the 10th cent. It is very closely related to Portuguese (Portugal, Brazil, and colonial territories).

Uralian. Family of languages including Finnish (4 million in addition to 90,000 speakers of Finnish in the Soviet Union), Hungarian (over 10 million), Lappish (30,000, mainly nomadic) and Samoyedic languages of the northern coastal regions of the U.S.S.R.

# VII.  FOREIGN PHRASES

Fr., French.　Gr., Greek.　Ger., German.　It., Italian.　L., Latin.　Sp., Spanish.

*à bas* (Fr.), down, down with.

*ab extra* (L.), from without.

*ab incunabilis* (L.), from the cradle.

*ab initio* (L.), from the beginning.

*ab intra* (L.), from within.

*à bon chat, bon rat* (Fr.), to a good cat, a good rat; well attacked and defended; tit for tat; a Rowland for an Oliver.

*à bon marché* (Fr.), cheap, a good bargain.

*à bras ouverts* (Fr.), with open arms.

*absente reo* (L.), the accused being absent.

*absit invidia* (L.), let there be no ill-will; envy apart.

*ab uno disce omnes* (L.), from one specimen judge of all the rest; from a single instance infer the whole.

*ab urbe conditâ* (L.), from the building of the city; i.e., Rome.

*a capite ad calcem* (L.), from head to heel.

*à chaque saint sa chandelle* (Fr.), to each saint his candle; honour where honour is due.

*à cheval* (Fr.), on horseback.

*à compte* (Fr.), on account; in part payment.

*à corps perdu* (Fr.), with might and main.

*à couvert* (Fr.), under cover; protected; sheltered.

*ad astra* (L.), to the stars.

*ad calendas Græcas* (L.), at the Greek calends; i.e., never, as the Greeks had no calends in their mode of reckoning.

*à demi* (Fr.), by halves; half-way.

*a Deo et rege* (L.), from God and the king.

*ad hoc* (L.), arranged for this purpose; special.

*ad hominem* (L.), to the man; to an individual's interests or passions; personal.

*adhuc sub judice lis est* (L.), the case has not yet been decided.

*a die* (L.), from that day.

*ad infinitum* (L.), to infinity

*ad interim* (L.), in the meantime.

*ad libitum* (L.), at pleasure.

*ad modum* (L.), after the manner of.

*ad nauseam* (L.), to disgust or satiety.

*ad referendum* (L.), for further consideration.

*ad rem* (L.), to the purpose; to the point.

*ad valorem* (L.), according to the value.

*affaire d'amour* (Fr.), a love affair.

*affaire d'honneur* (Fr.), an affair of honour; a duel.

*affaire de cœur* (Fr.), an affair of the heart.

*a fortiori* (L.), with stronger reason.

*à gauche* (Fr.), to the left.

*à genoux* (Fr.), on the knees.

*à haute voix* (Fr.), aloud.

*à huis clos* (Fr.), with closed doors; secretly.

*à la belle étoile* (Fr.), under the stars; in the open air.

*à la bonne heure* (Fr.), well timed; all right; very well; as you please.

*à l'abri* (Fr.), under shelter.

*à la mode* (Fr.), according to the custom or fashion.

*à la Tartufe* (Fr.), like Tartuffe, the hero of a celebrated comedy by Molière; hypocritically.

*al fresco* (It.), in the open air; out-of-doors.

*al più* (It.), at most.

*alter ego* (L.), another self.

*à merveille* (Fr.), to a wonder; marvellously.

*amor patriæ* (L.), love of country.

*amour-propre* (Fr.), self-love; vanity.

*ancien régime* (Fr.), the ancient or former order of things.

*anguis in herba* (L.), a snake in the grass.

*anno Christi* (L.), in the year of Christ.

*anno Domini* (L.), in the year of our Lord.

*anno mundi* (L.), in the year of the world.

*annus mirabilis* (L.), year of wonders; wonderful year.

*ante bellum* (L.), before the war.

*ante lucem* (L.), before light.

*ante meridiem* (L.), before noon.

*à outrance* (Fr.), to the utmost; to extremities; without sparing.

*à pied* (Fr.), on foot.

*à point* (Fr.), to a point, just in time, exactly right.

*a posse ad esse* (L.), from possibility to reality.

*ariston metron* (Gr.), the middle course is the best; the golden mean.

*arrière-pensée* (Fr.), hidden thought; mental reservation.

*au courant* (Fr.), fully acquainted with.

*audi alteram partem* (L.), hear the other side.

*au fait* (Fr.), well acquainted with; expert.

*au fond* (Fr.), at bottom.

*auf Wiedersehen !* (Ger.), till we meet again.

*au pis aller* (Fr.), at the worst.

*au revoir* (Fr.), adieu till we meet again.

*aut vincere aut mori* (L.), either to conquer or to die; death or victory.

*a verbis ad verbera* (L.), from words to blows.

*a vinculo matrimonii* (L.), from the bond of matrimony.

*à volonté* (Fr.), at pleasure.

*a vostra salute* (It.)
*à votre santé* (Fr.) } to your health.
*a vuestra salud* (Sp.)

*bas bleu* (Fr.), a blue-stocking; a literary woman.

*beau monde* (Fr.), the world of fashion.

*beaux esprits* (Fr.), men of wit; gay spirits.

*beaux yeux* (Fr.), fine eyes; good looks.

*ben trovato* (It.), well or cleverly invented.

*bête noire* (Fr.), a black beast; a bugbear.

*bon gré mal gré* (Fr.), with good or ill grace; willing or unwilling.

*bonhomie* (Fr.), good-nature; artlessness.

*bonne bouche* (Fr.), a delicate or tasty morsel.

*bon vivant* (Fr.), a good liver; a gourmand.

*brutum fulmen* (L.), a harmless thunderbolt.

*canaille* (Fr.), rabble.

*candida Pax* (L.), white-robed Peace.

*casus belli* (L.), that which causes or justifies war.

*causa sine qua non* (L.), an indispensable cause or condition.

*caveat emptor* (L.), let the buyer beware (or look after his own interest).

*cela va sans dire* (Fr.), that goes without saying; needless to say.

*ceteris paribus* (L.), other things being equal.

*chacun son goût* (Fr.), every one to his taste.

*cogito, ergo sum* (L.), I think, therefore I exist.

*comme il faut* (Fr.), as it should be.

*compos mentis* (L.), sound of mind; quite sane.

*compte rendu* (Fr.), an account rendered; a report or statement drawn up.

*conditio sine qua non* (L.), a necessary condition.

*conseil de famille* (Fr.), a family consultation.

*consensus facit legem* (L.), consent makes the law.

*consilio et animis* (L.), by wisdom and courage.

*consilio et prudentia* (L.), by wisdom and prudence.

*constantia et virtute* (L.), by constancy and virtue.

*contra bonos mores* (L.), against good manners.

*contretemps* (Fr.), an unlucky accident; a hitch.

*cordon bleu* (Fr.), blue ribbon; a cook of the highest class.

*cordon sanitaire* (Fr.), a line of guards to prevent the spreading of contagion or pestilence.

*corpus delicti* (L.), the body or substance of a crime or offence.

*corrigenda* (L.), things to be corrected.

*coup de grâce* (Fr.), a finishing stroke.

*coup d'état* (Fr.), a sudden decisive blow in politics; a stroke of policy.

*coup de soleil* (Fr.), sunstroke.

*credat Judæus Apella* (L.), let Apella, the superstitious Jew, believe it (I won't); tell that to the marines.

*cucullus non facit monachum* (L.), the cowl does not make the friar.

*cui bono ?* (L.), For whose advantage is it? to what end?

*culpam pœna premit comes* (L.), punishment follows hard upon crime.

*cum grano salis* (L.), with a grain of salt; with some allowance.

*cum privilegio* (L.), with privilege.

*currente calamo* (L.), with a fluent pen.

*da locum melioribus* (L.), give place to your betters.

*damnant quod non intelligunt* (L.), they condemn what they do not comprehend.

*data et accepta* (L.), expenditures and receipts.

*de bon augure* (L.), of good augury or omen.

*de bonne grâce* (Fr.), with good grace; willingly.

*de die in diem* (L.), from day to day.
*de facto* (L.), in point of fact; actual or actually.
*dei gratia* (L.), by God's grace.
*de jure* (L.), from the law; by right.
*de mal en pis* (Fr.), from bad to worse.
*de novo* (L.), anew.
*deo volente* (L.), God willing; by God's will.
*de profundis* (L.), out of the depths.
*dernier ressort* (Fr.), a last resource.
*deus ex machina* (L.), one who puts matters right at a critical moment; providential intervention.
*dies non* (L.), a day on which judges do not sit.
*distingué* (Fr.), distinguished; of genteel or elegant appearance. [idleness.
*dolce far niente* (It.), sweet doing-nothing; sweet
*double entente* (Fr.), a double meaning; a play on words.
*dramatis personæ* (L.), characters of the drama or play.
*dum spiro, spero* (L.), while I breathe, I hope.
*ecce homo !* (L.), behold the man !
*eheu ! fugaces labuntur anni* (L.), alas ! the fleeting years glide by.
*einmal ist keinmal* (Ger.), just once doesn't count.
*en avant* (Fr.), forward.
*en badinant* (Fr.), in sport; in jest.
*en déshabillé* (Fr.), in undress.
*en famille* (Fr.), with one's family; in a domestic state.
*enfant terrible* (Fr.), a terrible child, or one that makes disconcerting remarks.
*enfin* (Fr.), in short; at last; finally.
*en passant* (Fr.), in passing; by the way.
*en plein jour* (Fr.), in broad day.
*en rapport* (Fr.), in harmony; in agreement; in relation.
*en règle* (Fr.), according to rules; in order.
*entente cordiale* (Fr.), cordial understanding, especially between two states.
*entre nous* (Fr.), between ourselves.
*en vérité* (Fr.), in truth; verily.
*e pluribus unum* (L.), one out of many; one composed of many.
*esprit de corps* (Fr.), the animating spirit of a collective body, as a regiment, learned profession or the like.
*et sequentes, et sequentia* (L.), and those that follow.
*et tu, Brute !* (L.), and thou also, Brutus !
*ex animo* (L.), heartily; sincerely.
*ex capite* (L.), from the head; from memory.
*ex cathedra* (L.), from the chair or seat of authority, with high authority.
*exceptio probat regulam* (L.), the exception proves the rule.
*ex curia* (L.), out of court.
*ex dono* (L.), by the gift.
*exeunt omnes* (L.), all go out or retire.
*exit* (L.), he goes out.
*ex mero motu* (L.), from his own impulse, from his own free will.
*ex nihilo nihil fit* (L.), out of nothing, nothing comes; nothing produces nothing. [spective.
*ex officio* (L.), in virtue of his office.
*ex post facto* (L.), after the deed is done; retroface à face* (Fr.), face to face.
*façon de parler* (Fr.), manner of speaking.
*faire bonne mine* (Fr.), to put a good face upon the matter.
*fait accompli* (Fr.), a thing already done.
*fama clamosa* (L.), a current scandal; a prevailing report.
*faute de mieux* (Fr.), for want of better.
*faux pas* (Fr.), a false step; a slip in behaviour.
*festina lente* (L.), hasten slowly.
*fiat justitia, ruat cœlum* (L.), let justice be done though the heavens should fall.
*fiat lux* (L.), let there be light.
*fide et amore* (L.), by faith and love.
*fide et fiduciâ* (L.), by fidelity and confidence.
*fide et fortitudine* (L.), with faith and fortitude.
*fidei defensor* (L.), defender of the faith.
*fide non armis* (L.), by faith, not by arms.
*fide, sed cui vide* (L.), trust, but see whom.
*fides et justitia* (L.), fidelity and justice.
*fides Punica* (L.), Punic faith; treachery.
*filius nullius* (L.), a son of nobody; a bastard.
*finis coronat opus* (L.), the end crowns the work.
*flagrante bello* (L.), during hostilities.
*flagrante delicto* (L.), in the commission of the crime.
*floreat* (L.), let it flourish.
*fons et origo* (L.), the source and origin.

*force majeure* (Fr.), irresistible compulsion; war, strike, Act of God, etc.
*forensis strepitus* (L.), the clamour of the forum.
*fortuna favet fortuus* (L.), fortune favours the bold.
*functus officio* (L.), having performed one's office or duty; hence, out of office.
*gaudeamus igitur* (L.), so let us be joyful !
*genius loci* (L.), the genius or guardian spirit of a place.
*gradu diverso, via una* (L.), the same road by different steps.
*grande parure* (Fr.), full dress.
*grande toilette*
*guerra al cuchillo* (Sp.), war to the knife.
*Hannibal ante portas* (L.), Hannibal before the gates; the enemy close at hand.
*hiatus valde deflendus* (L.), a chasm or deficiency much to be regretted.
*hic et nunc* (L.), here and now.
*hic et ubique* (L.), here and everywhere.
*hic jacet* (L.), here lies.
*hic labor, hoc opus est* (L.), this is a labour, this is a toil.
*hic sepultus* (L.), here buried.
*hoc genus omne* (L.), all of this sort or class.
*hoi polloi* (Gr.), the many; the vulgar; the rabble.
*hominis est errare* (L.), to err is human.
*homme de robe* (Fr.), a man in civil office.
*homme d'affaires* (Fr.), a man of business.
*homme d'esprit* (Fr.), a man of wit or genius.
*honi soit qui mal y pense* (O. Fr.), evil to him who evil thinks.
*honores mutant mores* (L.), honours change men's manners or characters.
*hors de combat* (Fr.), out of condition to fight.
*hors de propos* (Fr.), not to the point or purpose.
*hors-d'œuvre* (Fr.), out of course; out of order.
*ich dien* (Ger.), I serve.
*idée fixe* (Fr.), a fixed idea.
*id est* (L.), that is.
*il a le diable au corps* (Fr.), the devil is in him.
*Ilias malorum* (L.), an Iliad of ills; a host of evils.
*il penseroso* (It.), the pensive man.
*il sent le fagot* (Fr.), he smells of the faggot; he is suspected of heresy.
*imperium in imperio* (L.), a state within a state; a government within another.
*in actu* (L.), in act or reality. [last struggle.
*in articulo mortis* (L.), at the point of death; in the
*in capite* (L.), in chief.
*in curia* (L.), in court.
*index expurgatorius* ) (L.), a list of books prohibited
*index prohibitorius* ) to Roman Catholics.
*in esse* (L.), in being; in actuality.
*in extenso* (L.), at full length.
*in extremis* (L.), at the point of death.
*in memoriam* (L.), to the memory of; in memory.
*in nubibus* (L.), in the clouds.
*in petto* (It.), in (my) breast; to one's self.
*in re* (L.), in the matter of.
*in sano sensu* (L.), in a proper sense.
*in situ* (L.), in its original situation.
*in vino veritas* (L.), there is truth in wine; truth is told under the influence of intoxicants.
*ipse dixit* (L.), he himself said it; a dogmatic saying or assertion.
*ipsissima verba* (L.), the very words.
*ipso facto* (L.), in the fact itself.
*ipso jure* (L.), by the law itself.
*jacta est alea* (L.), the die is cast.
*je ne sais quoi* (Fr.), I know not what.
*joci causa* (L.), for the sake of a joke.
*labor omnia vincit* (L.), labour conquers everything.
*l'allegro* (It.), the merry man.
*lapsus linguæ* (L.), a slip of the tongue.
*lares et penates* (L.), household gods.
*laus Deo* (L.), praise to God.
*le beau monde* (Fr.), the fashionable world.
*lector benevole* (L.), kind or gentle reader.
*le jeu n'en vaut pas la chandelle* (Fr.), the game is not worth the candle; the object is not worth the trouble.
*le mot de l'énigme* (Fr.), the key to the mystery.
*le point du jour* (Fr.), daybreak.
*lèse-majesté* (Fr.), high-treason.
*lettre de cachet* (Fr.), a sealed letter containing private orders; a royal warrant.
*lex loci* (L.), the law or custom of the place.
*lex non scripta* (L.), unwritten law; common law.
*lex scripta* (L.), written law; statute law.
*locum tenens* (L.), a deputy.

*lucri causa* (L.), for the sake of gain.

*magnum opus* (L.), a great work.

*mala fide* (L.), with bad faith; treacherously.

*mal à propos* (Fr.), ill-timed; out of place.

*malgré nous* (Fr.), in spite of us.

*malheur ne vient jamais seul* (Fr.), misfortunes never come singly.

*malum in se* (L.), evil or an evil in itself.

*mardi gras* (Fr.), Shrove-Tuesday.

*mariage de convenance* (Fr.), marriage from motives of interest rather than of love.

*mauvaise honte* (Fr.), false modesty.

*mauvais goût* (Fr.), bad taste.

*mea culpa* (L.), my fault; by my fault.

*me judice* (L.), I being judge; in my opinion.

*mens agitat molem* (L.), mind moves matter.

*mens legis* (L.), the spirit of the law.

*mens sana in corpore sano* (L.), a sound mind in a sound body.

*meo periculo* (L.), at my own risk.

*meo voto* (L.), according to my wish.

*mise en scène* (Fr.), the getting up for the stage, or the putting on the stage.

*modus operandi* (L.), manner of working.

*more suo* (L.), in his own way.

*motu proprio* (L.), of his own accord.

*multum in parvo* (L.), much in little.

*mutatis mutandis* (L.), with suitable or necessary alteration.

*nervus probandi* (L.), the sinews of the argument.

*nihil ad rem* (L.), irrelevant.

*nil desperandum* (L.), there is no reason to despair.

*noblesse oblige* (Fr.), rank imposes obligations; much is expected from one in good position.

*nolens volens* (L.), willing or unwilling.

*nom de guerre* (Fr.), a false or assumed name.

*non compos mentis* (L.), not of sound mind.

*non sequitur* (L.), it does not follow.

*nosce te ipsum* (L.), know thyself.

*nota bene* (L.), mark well.

*nudis verbis* (L.), in plain words.

*obiter dictum* (L.), a thing said by the way.

*omnia vincit amor* (L.), love conquers all things.

*ora pro nobis* (L.), pray for us.

*O tempora! O mores!* (L.), O the times! O the manners (or morals)!

*ouï-dire* (Fr.), hearsay.

*padrone* (It.), a master; a landlord.

*par excellence* (Fr.), by way of eminence.

*pari passu* (L.), at an equal pace or rate of progress.

*particeps criminis* (L.), an accomplice in a crime.

*pas de quoi* (Fr. abbrev. Il n'y a pas de quoi), don't mention it.

*passim* (L.), everywhere; in all parts of the book, chapter, etc.

*pâté de foie gras* (Fr.), goose-liver pie.

*pater patriæ* (L.), father of his country.

*patres conscripti* (L.), the conscript fathers; Roman senators.

*pax vobiscum* (L.), peace be with you.

*per ardua ad astra* (L.), through rough ways to the stars; through suffering to renown.

*per capita* (L.), by the head or poll.

*per contra* (It.), contrariwise.

*per diem* (L.), by the day; daily.

*per se* (L.), by itself; considered apart.

*pied-à-terre* (Fr.), a resting-place; a temporary lodging.

*pis aller* (Fr.), the worst or last shift.

*plebs* (L.), the common people.

*poco a poco* (It.), little by little. [called for.

*poste restante* (Fr.), to remain in the post-office till sent.

*prima facie* (L.), at first view or consideration.

*primus inter pares* (L.), first among equals.

*pro forma* (L.), for the sake of form.

*pro patria* (L.), for our country.

*pro tanto* (L.), for so much; for as far as it goes.

*pro tempore* (L.), for the time being.

*quid pro quo* (L.), one thing for another; tit for tat; an equivalent.

*qui m'aime, aime mon chien* (Fr.), love me, love my dog. [sent.

*qui tacet consentit* (L.), he who is silent gives consent.

*quod erat demonstrandum* (L.), which was to be proved or demonstrated.

*quod erat faciendum* (L.), which was to be done.

*quod vide* (L.), which see; refer to the word just mentioned.

*quo jure?* (L.), by what right? [tence.

*raison d'être* (Fr.), the reason for a thing's existence (L.), in the matter or affair of.

*reculer pour mieux sauter* (Fr.), to draw back in order to make a better spring.

*reductio ad adsurdum* (L.), the reducing of a position to a logical absurdity.

*requiescat in pace* (L.), may he (or she) rest in peace.

*respice finem* (L.), look to the end.

*respublica* (L.), the commonwealth.

*revenons à nos moutons* (Fr.), let us return to our sheep; let us return to our subject.

*re vera* (L.), in truth.

*sans peur et sans reproche* (Fr.), without fear and without reproach.

*sans rime ni raison* (Fr.), without rhyme or reason.

*sans souci* (Fr.), without care.

*sartor resartus* (L.), the botcher repatched; the tailor patched or mended.

*sauve qui peut* (Fr.), let him save himself who can.

*savoir-faire* (Fr.), the knowing how to act; tact.

*savoir-vivre* (Fr.), good-breeding; refined manners.

*semper idem* (L.), always the same.

*seriatim* (L.), in a series; one by one.

*sic passim* (L.), so here and there throughout; so everywhere.

*sicut ante* (L.), as before.

*sine die* (L.), without a day being appointed.

*sine mora* (L.), without delay.

*sine qua non* (L.), without which, not; indispensable condition.

*sotto voce* (It.), in an undertone.

*spirituel* (Fr.), intellectual; witty.

*stet* (L.), let it stand; do not delete.

*sub judice* (L.), under consideration.

*sub pœna* (L.), under a penalty

*sub rosa* (L.), under the rose; privately.

*sub voce* (L.), under such or such a word.

*sui generis* (L.), of its own or of a peculiar kind.

*summum bonum* (L.), the chief good.

*tableau vivant* (Fr.), a living picture; the representation of some scene by a group of persons.

*tant mieux* (Fr.), so much the better.

*tant pis* (Fr.), so much the worse.

*tempora mutantur, nos et mutamur in illis* (L.), the times are changing and we with them.

*tempus fugit* (L.), time flies.

*tête-à-tête* (Fr.), together in private.

*tiers état* (Fr.), the third estate; the commons.

*to kalon* (Gr.), the beautiful; the chief good.

*to prepon* (Gr.), the becoming or proper.

*tour de force* (Fr.), a feat of strength or skill.

*tout à fait* (Fr.), wholly; entirely.

*tout à l'heure* (Fr.), instantly.

*tout de suite* (Fr.), immediately.

*tu quoque* (L.), thou also.

*ubique* (L.), everywhere.

*ubi supra* (L.), where above mentioned.

*ultra licitum* (L.), beyond what is allowable.

*ultra vires* (L.), beyond powers or rights conferred by law.

*urbi et orbi* (L.), to the city (Rome) and the world.

*utile dulci* (L.), the useful with the pleasant.

*ut infra* (L.), as below.

*ut supra* (L.), as above stated.

*vade in pace* (L.), go in peace.

*variæ lectiones* (L.), various readings.

*variorum notæ* (L.), the notes of various commentators.

*vede et crede* (L.), see and believe.

*veni, vidi, vici* (L.), I came, I saw, I conquered.

*verbatim et literatim* (L.), word for word and letter for letter.

*verbum sat sapienti* (L.), a word is enough for a wise man.

*ver non semper viret* (L.), spring is not always green.

*vexata quæstio* (L.), a disputed question.

*via media* (L.), a middle course.

*via trita, via tuta* (L.), the beaten path is the safe path.

*vice versâ* (L.), the terms of the case being reversed.

*videlicet* (L.), that is to say; namely.

*vi et armis* (L.), by force of arms; by main force; by violence.

*vigilate et orate* (L.), watch and pray.

*vita brevis, ars longa* (L.), life is short; art is long.

*vivat regina!* (L.), long live the queen!

*vivat rex!* (L.), long live the king!

*viva voce* (L.), by the living voice; orally.

*voilà* (Fr.), behold; there is; there are.

*voilà tout* (Fr.), that's all.

*volo, non valeo* (L.), I am willing, but unable.

*vox populi, vox Dei* (L.), the voice of the people is the voice of God.

# VIII. ABBREVIATIONS IN COMMON USE

## A

a. = area; acre(s); are (100 sq. metres).
A.A. = Automobile Association; Alcoholics Anonymous.
A.A.C.C.A. = Associate of the Association of Certified and Corporate Accountants.
A.A.I. = Associate of the Chartered Auctioneers' and Estate Agents' Institute.
A.A.L.P.A. = Associate of the Incorporated Society of Auctioneers and Landed Property Agents.
A. and M. = Ancient and Modern (Hymns).
A.B. = able-bodied seaman; *Artium Baccalaureus* (Bachelor of Arts).
A.B.A. = Amateur Boxing Association.
A.B.I.C.C. = Associate of the British Institute of Certified Carpenters.
ABM = anti-ballistics missile defence system.
Abp. = Archbishop.
abr. = abridged.
abs. = absolute
a.c. (*or* A.C.) = alternating current.
A.C.A. = Associate of the Institute of Chartered Accountants.
A.C.C.S. = Associate of the Corporation of Certified Secretaries.
A.C.I.S. = Associate of the Chartered Institute of Secretaries.
A.Comm.A. = Associate of the Society of Commercial Accountants.
A.C.P. = Associate of the College of Preceptors.
ACT = Advisory Council on Technology.
ACTH = adreno-cortico-trophic hormone.
A.C.W.A. = Associate of the Institute of Cost and Works Accountants.
A.D. = *anno domini* (in the year of our Lord).
A.D.C. = Aide-de-Camp.
Adm. = Admiral.
advt. (*or* adv.) = advertisement.
A.F.A.S. = Associate of the Faculty of Architects and Surveyors.
AEA = Atomic Energy Authority (UK).
AEC = Atomic Energy Commission (US).
AERE =[Atomic Energy Research Establishment.
aet. (*or* aetat.) = *aetatis* (of age).
A.F.C. = Air Force Cross.
A.F.L. = American Federation of Labour.
A.F.M. = Air Force Medal.
AFRASEC = Afro-Asian Organisation for Economic Cooperation.
A.G. = Adjutant-General.
AGR = Advanced Gas-cooled Reactor.
A.H. = *anno Hegirae* (in the year of the Hegira).
A.I.A. = Associate of the Institute of Actuaries.
A.I.A.C. = Associate of the Institute of Company Accountants.
A.I.B. = Associate of the Institute of Bankers.
A.I.B.P. = Associate of the Institute of British Photographers.
A.I.C.E. = Associate of the Institution of Civil Engineers.
A.I.C.S. = Associate of the Institute of Chartered Shipbrokers.
AID = Agency for International Development (U.S.).
A.I.I.A. = Associate of the Institute of Industrial Administration.
A.I.M.E. = Associate of the Institution of Mining Engineers.
A.I.Mech.E. = Associate of the Institution of Mechanical Engineers.
A.I.N.A. = Associate of the Institution of Naval Architects.
A.Inst.P. = Associate of the Institute of Physics.
A.I.Q.S. = Associate of the Institute of Quantity Surveyors.
A.I.R.I. = Associate of the Institution of Rubber Industry.
A.L.A. = Associate of the Library Association.
A.L.S. = Associate of the Linnean Society.

alt. = altitude.
A.M. = *anno mundi* (in the year of the world); *Artium Magister* (Master of Arts); amplitude modulation.
a.m. = *ante meridiem* (before noon).
A.M.D.G. = *ad majorem Dei glorium* (to the greater glory of God).
AMM = anti-missile-missile.
amp. = ampere(s).
A.M.I.C.E. = Associate Member of the Institution of Civil Engineers.
A.M.I.Chem.E. = Associate Member of the Institution of Chemical Engineers.
A.M.I.E.E. = Associate Member of the Institution of Electrical Engineers.
A.M.I.Mech.E. = Associate Member of the Institution of Mechanical Engineers.
A.M.I.Mun.E. = Associate Member of the Institution of Municipal Engineers.
A.M.T.P.I. = Associate Member of the Town Planning Institute.
A.N.A.R.E. = Australian National Antarctic Research Expeditions.
ANC = African National Congress.
anc. = ancient.
ANF = Atlantic Nuclear Force.
anhyd. = anhydrous.
anon. = anonymous.
ANZAC = Australian and New Zealand Army Corps.
ANZUS = Australian, New Zealand and U.S. Defence Pact (Pacific Security Treaty).
A.O.C. = Air Officer Commanding.
A.P. = Associated Press.
aq. = aqueous.
A.R.A. = Associate of the Royal Academy.
A.R.A.D. = Associate of the Royal Academy of Dancing.
A.R.A.M. = Associate of the Royal Academy of Music.
A.R.B.S. = Associate of the Royal Society of British Sculptors.
ARC = Agricultural Research Council.
A.R.C.A. = Associate of the Royal College of Arts.
A.R.C.M. = Associate of the Royal College of Music.
arch. = archipelago.
A.R.C.O. = Associate of the Royal College of Organists.
A.R.C.Sc. = Associate of the Royal College of Science.
A.R.I.B.A. = Associate of the Royal Institute of British Architects.
A.R.I.C. = Associate of the Royal Institute of Chemistry.
A.R.I.C.S. = Associate of the Royal Institution of Chartered Surveyors.
A.R.P.S. = Associate of the Royal Photographic Society.
A.R.W.S. = Associate of the Royal Society of Painters in Water Colours.
A.S. (*or* AS) = Anglo-Saxon.
A.S.A. = Amateur Swimming Association.
ASDIC = Anti-submarine detector indicator
ASEAN = Association of South-East Asian Nations (Indonesia, Malaysia, Philippines, Singapore, Thailand.)
ASLIB = Association of Special Libraries and Information Bureaux.
A.T.C. = Air Training Corps.
atm. = atmospheric pressure.
ATP = adenosine triphosphate.
A.T.S. = Auxiliary Territorial Service.
ATV = Associated Television Authority.
at.wt. = atomic weight.
A.U.C. = *ab urbe condita* (from the founding of the City (Rome)), *or*, *anno urbis conditae* (in the year of the founding of the City).
av. = average.
AV = Authorized Version.
A.W.O.L. = Absent Without Leave.

# B

b. = born; bowled.
B.A. = Bachelor of Arts.
B.A.A. = British Astronomical Association.
BAF = British Athletic Federation.
B.A.O. = Bachelor in the Art of Obstetrics.
BAOR = British Army of the Rhine.
B.Arch. = Bachelor of Architecture.
Bart. (or Bt.) = Baronet.
B.B. = Boys' Brigade.
B.B.C. = British Broadcasting Corporation.
B.C. = before Christ; British Columbia.
B.Ch. (or Ch.B.) = Bachelor in Surgery.
B.C.L. = Bachelor in Civil Law.
B.Com. = Bachelor of Commerce.
B.D. = Bachelor in Divinity.
B.D.A. = British Dental Association.
Bde. = Brigade.
B.D.S. (or B.Ch.D.) = Bachelor in Dental Surgery.
BEA = British European Airways Corporation.
B.E.C. = British Employers' Confederation.
B.Ed. = Bachelor of Education.
B.E.M. = British Empire Medal.
B.Eng. = Bachelor of Engineering.
BIM = British Institute of Management.
BIS = Bank for International Settlements.
BISRA = British Iron and Steel Research Association.
B.Litt. = Bachelor in Letters.
B.M. = Bachelor in Medicine; British Museum.
B.M.A. = British Medical Association.
B.M.C. = British Motor Corporation.
B.Mus. = Bachelor in Music.
B.N.C. = Brasenose College, Oxford.
BNEC = British National Export Council
BOAC = British Overseas Airways Corporation.
bor. = borough.
B.O.T. = Board of Trade.
b.p. = boiling point.
Bp. = Bishop.
B.Phil. = Bachelor of Philosophy.
Br. (or Brit.) = British.
Brit.Ass. = British Association for the Advancement of Science.
B.R. = British Railways; British Rail.
B.R.B. = British Rail Board.
B.R.C.S. = British Red Cross Society.
B.R.S. = British Road Services.
B.Sc. = Bachelor of Science.
BSC = British Steel Corporation.
B.S.I. = British Standards Institution.
BST = British summer time.
Bt. = Baronet; Brevet.
B.T.H.A. = British Travel and Holidays Association.
B.Th. = Bachelor in Theology.
Btu = British thermal unit.
B.U.A. = British United Airways.
B.V.M. = Blessed Virgin Mary.
B.V.M.S. = Bachelor in Veterinary Medicine and Surgery.
B.W.B. = British Waterways Board.

# C

C. = Centigrade; Conservative.
c. = circa (about); centi- (10⁻²).
C.A. = Chartered Accountant (Scottish Institute).
CABs = Citizens' Advice Bureaux.
Cal. = Calorie (nutritional kilogram-calorie).
cal. = calorie (gram-calorie used in physics and chemistry).
calc. = calculated.
Cantab. = of Cambridge.
Cantuar. = of Canterbury.
cap. = capital letter; capitulum (chapter).
CARD = Campaign Against Racial Discrimination.
CARIFTA = Caribbean Free Trade Area.
CATs = Colleges of Advanced Technology.
C.B. = Companion of the Order of the Bath.
C.B.E. = Commander of the Order of the British Empire.
CBI = Confederation of British Industry (replaces BEC, FBI and NABM).
C.C. = County Council; County Councillor; Chamber of Commerce.
cc = cubic centimetre(s).
CCPR = Central Council of Physical Recreation.

C.D. = Civil Defence.
C.D.C. = Commonwealth Development Corporation.
C.D.S. = Chief of Defence Staff; Campaign for Democratic Socialism.
CDU = Christian Democratic Union (W. Ger.).
C.E. = Civil Engineer; Christian Era.
CEGB = Central Electricity Generating Board.
CENTO = Central Treaty Organisation.
centi = one-hundreth part (10⁻²)
CERN = European Organisation for Nuclear Research.
CET = Central European Time.
C.F. = Chaplain to the Forces.
cf. = confer (compare).
C.G.M. = Conspicuous Gallantry Medal.
C.G.S. = Chief of General Staff.
cgs = centimetre-gram-second.
CGT = Confédération Générale du Travail (French TUC).
C.H. = Companion of Honour.
Ch.Ch. = Christ Church.
Ch.M. = Master in Surgery.
C.I. = Lady of Imperial Order of the Crown of India; Channel Islands.
CIA = Central Intelligence Agency (US).
CID = Criminal Investigation Department.
C.I.E. = Companion of the Order of the Indian Empire.
Cie = Compagnie (Company).
c.i.f. = cost, insurance and freight.
C.-in-C. = Commander-in-Chief.
CIO = Congress of Industrial Organisations (US).
CIR = Commission on Industrial Relations.
C.L. = Companion of Literature.
C.L.B. = Church Lads' Brigade.
cm = centimetre(s).
C.M.G. = Companion of the Order of St. Michael and St. George.
C.M.S. = Church Missionary Society.
CNAA = Council for National Academic Awards.
CND = Campaign for Nuclear Disarmament.
C.O. = Commanding Officer; Colonial Office; Conscientious Objector.
Co. = County; Company.
c/o = care of.
C.O.D. = Cash on Delivery.
C. of E. = Church of England.
COI = Central Office of Information.
CoID = Council of Industrial Design.
COMECON = Council for Mutual Economic Assistance (East European).
Con. (or C.) = Conservative.
conc. = concentrated.
const. = constant.
corr. = corrected.
COSPAR = Committee on Space Research.
CP = Communist Party.
CPC = Communist Party of China.
C.P.R.E. = Council for the Preservation of Rural England.
CPSU = Communist Party of the Soviet Union.
crit. = critical.
C.R.O. = Commonwealth Relations Office.
crystl. = crystalline.
C.S.C. = Conspicuous Service Cross.
C.S.E. = Certificate of Secondary Education.
C.S.I. = Companion of the Order of the Star of India.
CSP = Council on Scientific Policy.
C.T. = Civic Trust.
C.T.C. = Cyclists' Touring Club.
CTR = Controlled thermonuclear research.
cu. = cubic.
C.V.O. = Commander of the Royal Victorian Order.
cwt. = hundredweight.

# D

d. = denarius (penny), denarii (pence); died; daughter.
D.A.R. = Daughters of the American Revolution.
dB = decibel(s).
D.B.E. = Dame Commander of Order of British Empire.
D.C. = District of Columbia.
d.c. (or D.C.) = direct current.
D.C.L. = Doctor in Civil Law.

D.C.M. = Distinguished Conduct Medal.
D.C.M.G. = Dame Commander, Order of St. Michael and St. George.
D.C.V.O. = Dame Commander of the Royal Victorian Order.
D.D. = Doctor in Divinity.
D.D.R. = German Democratic Republic (E. Ger.).
D.D.S. = Doctor in Dental Surgery.
DDT = Dichloro-diphenyl-trichloro-ethane.
DEA = Department of Economic Affairs.
deca = ten times
deci = one-tenth (10⁻¹)
del. = *delineavit* (he drew it).
DEP = Department of Employment and Productivity.
D.ès L. = Docteur ès Lettres.
D.ès Sc. = Docteur ès Sciences.
D.F.C. = Distinguished Flying Cross.
D.F.M. = Distinguished Flying Medal.
D.G. = *dei gratie* (by the grace of God).
DIA = Design and Industries Association.
dil. = dilute.
Dip.Tech. = Diploma in Technology.
D.L. = Deputy-Lieutenant.
D.Lit. (*or* D. Litt) = Doctor of Literature.
D.M. = Doctor in Medicine (Oxford).
DM = Deutschemark.
D.Mus. = Doctor of Music.
DNA = deoxyribonucleic acid.
D.N.B. = Dictionary of National Biography.
do. = *ditto* (the same).
D.O.M. = *dominus optimo maximo* (To God, the best, the greatest).
D.P. = Displaced Person(s).
D.P.H. = Diploma in Public Health.
D.Phil. = Dictor of Philosophy.
D.P.M. = Diploma in Psychological Medicine.
Dr. = Doctor; debtor.
dr. = drachm.
D.Sc. = Doctor of Science.
D.S.C. = Distinguished Service Cross.
DSIR = Department of Scientific and Industrial Research (to be abolished and replaced by SRC, IRDA, and NERC).
D.S.M. = Distinguished Service Medal.
D.S.O. = Companion of the Distinguished Service Order.
D.Th. = Doctor in Theology.
D.T.M. = Diploma in Tropical Medicine.
D.V. = *Deo volente* (God willing).
dwt. = pennyweight.

# E

EAAFRO = East African Agriculture and Foresty Research.
E. and O.E. = Errors and omissions excepted.
Ebor. = of York.
EC = Electricity Council.
ECA = Economic Commission for Africa (UN).
ECAFE = Economic Commission for Asia and the Far East (UN).
ECE = Economic Commission for Europe (UN).
ECG = electro-cardiograph.
ECGD = Export Credits Guarantee Department.
ECLA = Economic Commission for Latin America (UN).
ECSC = European Coal and Steel Community.
EDC = European Defence Community.
EEC = European Economic Community (Common Market).
EEG = electro-encephalogram.
EFTA = European Free Trade Association.
e.g. = *exempli gratio* (for example).
ELDO = European Launcher and Development Organisation.
EMA = European Monetary Agreement.
EMBO = European Molecular Biology Organisation.
emf = electromotive force.
e.m.u. = electromagnetic unit.
ENEA = European Nuclear Energy Agency.
EPU = European Political Union.
E.R. = Elizabetha Regina, *or* Edwardus Rex.
E.R.A. = Electrical Research Association.
ERNIE = electronic random number indicating equipment.
ERP = European Recovery Programme.
ESC = Economic and Social Council (UN).
ESRO = European Space Research Organisation.

et al. = *et alibi* (and elsewhere); *et alii* (and others).
etc. = *et cetera* (others; and so forth).
et seq. = *et sequens* (and the following).
et sqq. = *et sequentes, et sequentia* (and those following).
E.T.U. = Electrical Trades Union.
Euratom = European Atomic Energy Community.
ex lib. = *ex libris* (from the books of).

# F

F. = Fahrenheit; Fellow.
f. = and the following page; ff. = and the following pages.
F.A. = Football Association.
F.A.C.C.A. = Fellow of the Association of Certified and Corporate Accountants.
F.A.I. = Fellow of the Chartered Auctioneers' and Estate Agents' Institute.
F.A.L.P.A. = Fellow of the Incorporated Society of Auctioneers and Landed Property Agents.
F.A.N.Y. = First Aid Nursing Yeomanry.
FAO = Food and Agriculture Organisation of the United Nations.
f.a.s. = free alongside.
F.B.A. = Fellow of the British Academy.
FBI = Federal Bureau of Investigation (U.S.).
F.B.I.M. = Fellow of the British Institute of Management.
F.B.O.A. = Fellow of the British Optical Association.
F.B.S. = Fellow of the Botanical Society.
F.C.A. = Fellow of the Institute of Chartered Accountants.
F.C.C.S. = Fellow of the Corporation of Secretaries.
F.C.G.I. = Fellow of City and Guilds Institute.
F.C.I.A. = Fellow of Corporation of Insurance Agents.
F.C.I.B. = Fellow of Corporation of Insurance Brokers.
F.C.I.I. = Fellow of Chartered Insurance Institute.
F.C.I.S. = Fellow of the Chartered Institute of Secretaries.
F.C.P. = Fellow of the College of Preceptors.
F.C.W.A. = Fellow of the Chartered Institute of Cost and Works Accountants.
F.D. = *Fidei Defensor* (Defender of the Faith).
Fed. = Federation; Federal.
ff. = folios; and the following pages; fortissimo.
F.F.A.R.C.S. = Fellow of the Faculty of Anaesthetics, Royal College of Surgeons.
F.F.R. = Fellow of the Faculty of Radiologists.
F.G.S. = Fellow of the Geological Society.
F.H. = Fire Hydrant.
F.H.S. = Fellow of the Heraldry Society.
F.I.A. = Fellow of the Institute of Actuaries.
F.I.B. = Fellow of the Institute of Bankers.
F.I.B.P. = Fellow of the Institute of British Photographers.
F.I.C.S. = Fellow of the Institute of Chartered Shipbrokers.
F. Inst.F. = Fellow of the Institute of Fuel.
F.I.I.A. = Fellow of the Institute of Industrial Administration.
F.Inst.P. = Fellow of the Institute of Physics.
F.Inst.Pet. = Fellow of the Institute of Petroleum.
F.I.Q.S. = Fellow of the Institute of Quantity Surveyors.
F.I.R.E. = Fellow of the Institute of Radio Engineers.
F.J.I. = Fellow of the Institute of Journalists.
F.K.C. = Fellow of King's College (London).
fl. = *floruit* (flourished).
F.L.A. = Fellow of the Library Association.
F.L.A.S. = Fellow of the Land Agents' Society.
F.L.N. = (Algerian) National Liberation Front.
F.L.S. = Fellow of the Linnean Society.
FM = Frequency modulation.
FMC = Federal Maritime Commission (US).
F.N.S. = Fellow of the Newtonian Society.
F.O. = Foreign Office.
fo. = folio.
f.o.b. = free on board.
F.O.P. = Friendship Oil Pipeline (E.Europe).
f.p. = freezing point.

F.P.S. = Fellow of the Pharmaceutical Society.
F.Ph.S. = Fellow of the Philosophical Society.
F.R.A.D. = Fellow of the Royal Academy of Dancing.
F.R.A.I. = Fellow of the Royal Anthropological Institute.
F.R.A.M. = Fellow of the Royal Academy of Music.
F.R.A.S. = Fellow of the Royal Astronomical Society.
F.R.Ae.S. = Fellow of the Royal Aeronautical Society.
F.R.B.S. = Fellow of the Royal Society of British Sculptors.
F.R.C.M. = Fellow of the Royal College of Music.
F.R.C.O. = Fellow of the Royal College of Organists.
F.R.C.O.G. = Fellow of the Royal College of Obstetricians and Gynaecologists.
F.R.C.P. = Fellow of the Royal College of Physicians of London.
F.R.C.P.Ed. = Fellow of the Royal College of Physicians of Edinburgh.
F.R.C.S. = Fellow of the Royal College of Surgeons of England.
F.R.C.S.Ed. = Fellow of the Royal College of Surgeons of Edinburgh.
F.R.C.V.S. = Fellow of the Royal College of Veterinary Surgeons.
F.R.E.S. = Fellow of the Royal Empire Society.
F.R.Econ.S. = Fellow of the Royal Economic Society.
F.R.F.P.S. = Fellow of the Royal Faculty of Physicians and Surgeons (Glas.).
F.R.G.S. = Fellow of the Royal Geographical Society.
F.R.H.S. = Fellow of the Royal Horticultural Society.
F.R.Hist.S. = Fellow of the Royal Historical Society.
F.R.I.B.A. = Fellow of the Royal Institute of British Architects.
F.R.I.C. = Fellow of the Royal Institute of Chemistry.
F.R.I.C.S. = Fellow of the Royal Institution of Chartered Surveyors.
F.R.M.S. = Fellow of the Royal Microscopical Society.
F.R.Met.S. = Fellow of the Royal Meteorological Society.
F.R.N.S. = Fellow of Royal Numismatic Society.
F.R.P.S. = Fellow of the Royal Photographic Society.
F.R.S. = Fellow of the Royal Society.
F.R.S.A. = Fellow of the Royal Society of Arts.
F.R.S.C. = Fellow of the Royal Society of Canada.
F.R.S.E. = Fellow of the Royal Society of Edinburgh.
F.R.S.L. = Fellow of the Royal Society of Literature.
F.S.A. = Fellow of the Society of Antiquaries.
F.S.A.A. = Fellow of the Society of Incorporated Accountants and Auditors.
F.S.M.C. = Fellow of the Spectacle Makers Company.
F.S.S. = Fellow of the Statistical Society.
F.T.I. = Fellow of the Textile Institute.
F.Z.S. = Fellow of the Zoological Society.

# G

g. = gram(s).
GATT = General Agreement on Tariffs and Trade.
G.B.E. = Knight (or Dame) Grand Cross of the Order of the British Empire.
G.C. = George Cross; Gas Council.
G.C.A. = Ground Control Approach.
G.C.E. = General Certificate of Education.
G.C.B. = Knight Grand Cross of the Order of the Bath.
G.C.I.E. = Knight Grand Commander of the Indian Empire.
G.C.M.G. = Knight Grand Cross of the Order of St. Michael and St. George.
G.C.S.I. = Knight Grand Commander of the Star of India.
G.C.V.O. = Knight (or Dame) Grand Cross of the Royal Victorian Order.

GDP = gross domestic product.
Gen. = General; Genesis.
GeV = thousand million electron-volts.
G.H.Q. = General Headquarters.
G.I. = American soldier (from army term "Government Issue" applied to kit and equipment).
GLC = Greater London Council.
G.M. = George Medal.
G.M.C. = General Medical Council.
G.M.T. = Greenwich mean time.
GNP = gross national product.
G.O.C. = General Officer Commanding.
G.O.P. = Grand Old Party (US Republican Party).
G.P. = General Practitioner.
G.P.O. = General Post Office.
gr. = grain(s).
G.R.C.M. = Graduate of the Royal College of Music.
G.R.S.M. = Graduate of the Royal Schools of Music (Royal Academy and Royal College).
G.S.O. = General Staff Officer.
GYP = gross domestic income.

# H

ha = hectare (100 ares).
H.E. = His Excellency; His Eminence; high explosive.
hecto = one hundred times ($10^2$).
H.H. = His (or Her) Highness.
hhd. = hogshead.
H.I.M. = His Imperial Majesty.
H.J.S. = Hic jacet sepultus (Here lies buried).
H.M. = His (or Her) Majesty.
H.M.A.S. = Her Majesty's Australian Ship.
H.M.I. = Her Majesty's Inspector.
H.M.L. = Her Majesty's Lieutenant.
H.M.S = Her Majesty's Ship; Her Majesty's Service.
H.M.S.O. = Her Majesty's Stationery Office.
H. of C. = House of Commons.
H. of L. = House of Lords.
Hon. = Honourable; Honorary.
hp = horsepower.
H.P. = Hire purchase.
H.R. = House of Representatives (US).
H.R.H. = His (or Her) Royal Highness.
H.S.E. = Hic sepultus est (Here lies buried).
H.T. = high tension.
H.V. = health visitor.
H.W.M. = high water mark.

# I

IADB = Inter-American Development Bank.
IAEA = International Atomic Energy Agency (UN).
IATA = International Air Transport Association.
ib. (or ibid.) = ibidem (in the same place).
IBERLANT = Iberian Atlantic Command (NATO).
IBRD = International Bank for Reconstruction and Development (World Bank).
ICAO = International Civil Aviation Organisation (UN).
ICBM = Intercontinental ballistic missile.
ICFC = Industrial and Commercial Finance Corporation.
ICFTU = International Confederation of Free Trade Unions.
ICI = Imperial Chemical Industries.
ICJ = International Court of Justice (UN).
ICSU = International Council of Scientific Unions.
ICT = International Computers and Tabulators.
ICY = International Co-operation Year (1965).
Id. = idem (the same).
IDA = International Development Association.
i.e. = id est (that is)
IFC = International Finance Corporation (UN).
Ign. = ignotus (unknown).
IGY = International Geophysical Year (1957–8).
IHS = Iesus Hominum Salvator (Jesus Saviour of men)—repr. a Greek abbrev. of the word Jesus.

ILEA = Inner London Education Authority.
ILO = International Labour Organisation (UN).
I.L.S. = Instrument Landing System.
IMCO = Inter-Governmental Maritime Consultative Organisation (UN).
IMF = International Monetary Fund (UN).
Inc. = Incorporated.
Incog. = *incognito* (unknown, unrecognised).
inf. = infinitive; *infra* (below).
*in loc.* (*in loco*) = in its place.
I.N.R.I. = *Iesus Nazarenus, Rex Iudaeorum* (Jesus of Nazareth, King of the Jews).
Inst. = Institute; Institution.
inst. = instant (the present month).
Interpol = International Criminal Police Commission (HQ in Paris).
I.O.M. = Isle of Man.
I.O.W. = Isle of Wight.
IOU = I owe you.
IQ = intelligence quotient.
IQSY = International Years of the Quiet Sun.
I.R. = Inland Revenue.
I.R.A. = Irish Republican Army.
IRBM = Intermediate-range ballistic missile.
IRC = International Red Cross; Industrial Reorganisation Corporation.
IRDA = Industrial Research and Development Authority.
I.S.O. = Imperial Service Order; International Standardisation Organisation.
I.T.A. = Independent Television Authority; Institute of Travel Agents; Industrial Transport Association; Invalid Tricycle Association.
I.T.O. = International Trade Organisation.
I.T.U. = International Telecommunication Union.
ITV = Independent Television.

# J

J. = Judge; Jet (aircraft).
J.P. = Justice of the Peace.

# K

K = Kelvin.
K. = Köchel numeration (of Mozart's works).
KANU = Kenya African National Union.
k = kilo = thousand.
K.B.E. = Knight Commander of the Order of the British Empire.
K.C. = King's Counsel.
kc. = kilocycle(s).
K.C.B. = Knight Commander of the Order of the Bath.
K.C.I.E. = Knight Commander of the Order of the Indian Empire.
K.C.M.G. = Knight Commander of the Order of St. Michael and St. George.
K.C.S.I. = Knight Commander of the Star of India.
K.C.V.O. = Knight Commander of the Royal Victorian Order.
K.G. = Knight of the Order of the Garter.
KGB = Soviet State Security Service.
kg = kilogram(s).
kilo = one thousand times ($10^3$).
KJV = King James Version.
K.K.K. = Ku Klux Klan.
km = kilometre(s).
k.o. = knock out (boxing).
K.P. = Knight of the Order of St. Patrick.
K.T. = Knight of the Order of the Thistle.
Kt. = knight.
kV = kilovolt(s).
kW = kilowatt(s).
kWh = kilowatt hour(s).

# L

L. (*or* Lib.) = Liberal.
L.A. = Local Authority.
Lab. = Labour.
L.A.C. = London Athletic Club.

LAFTA = Latin American Free Trade Association.
LAMDA = London Academy of Music and Dramatic Art.
lat. = latitude.
lb. = *libra* (pound). *librae* (pounds).
lbf = pound-force.
l.b.w. = leg before wicket.
l.c. = lower case (small letter(s)).
LCC = London County Council.
L.C.J. = Lord Chief Justice.
L.C.P. = Licentiate of the College of Preceptors.
L.D.S. = Licentiate in Dental Surgery.
L.ès L. = Licencié ès Lettres.
L.F.B. = London Fire Brigade.
L.H.D. = *Litterarum Humaniorum Doctor* (Doctor of Humane Letters).
Lic.Med. = Licentiate in Medicine.
Lic.S. = Licentiate in Surgery.
Lit.Hum. = *Literae Humaniores* (Study of the Classics).
Litt.D. = *Litterarum Doctor* (Doctor of Letters; Doctor in Letters (Camb.)).
LL.B. = *Legum Baccalaureus* (Bachelor of Laws).
LL.D. = *Legum Doctor* (Doctor of Laws; Doctor in Law (Camb.)).
L.M. = Licentiate in Midwifery.
loc.cit. = *loco citato* (in the place sited).
log. = logarithm.
long. = longitude.
L.R.A.D. = Licentiate of the Royal Academy of Dancing.
L.R.A.M. = Licentiate of the Royal Academy of Music.
L.R.C.M. = Licentiate of the Royal College of Music.
L.R.C.P. = Licentiate of the Royal College of Physicians.
L.R.C.S. = Licentiate of the Royal College of Surgeons.
L.R.C.V.S. = Licentiate of the Royal College of Veterinary Surgeons.
L.S. = *loco sigilli* (place of the seal).
L.S.A. = Licentiate of the Society of Apothecaries.
L.s.d. = *Librae, solidi, denarii* (Pounds, shillings, pence).
LSD = Lysergic acid diethylamide
L.S.E. = London School of Economics.
L.S.O. = London Symphony Orchestra.
L.T.A. = Lawn Tennis Association.
LTB = London Transport Board.
L.Th. = Licentiate in Theology.
Lt.-Gen. = Lieutenant-General.
L.W.M. = lower-water mark.
LXX = Septuagint.

# M

M. = Member; Monsieur; mark (German coin); *meridies* (noon); mega (million times).
m = metre(s).
m. = married; masculine; million.
M.A. = Master of Arts.
MAOT = Member of the Association of Occupational Therapists.
M.A.O. = Master in the Art of Obstetrics.
max. = maximum.
M.B. = Bachelor in Medicine.
M.B.A. = Master of Business Administration.
M.B.E. = Member of the Order of the British Empire.
M.C. = Military Cross; Master of Ceremonies.
Mc = million cycles, *or* megacycle.
M.C.C. = Marylebone Cricket Club.
M.Ch. = Master in Surgery.
M.Ch.D. = Master in Dental Surgery.
M.Ch.Orth. = Master in Orthopaedic Surgery.
M.Com. = Master of Commerce.
M.C.S.P. = Member of the Chartered Society of Physiotherapy.
M.C.T. = Member of the College of Technologists.
M.D. = *Medicineae Doctor* (Doctor in Medicine).
M.D.S. = Master in Dental Surgery.
M.E. = Middle English.
mega = one million times ($10^6$).
MeV = megaelectronvolt(s)
M.F.H. = Master of Foxhounds.
mg = milligram(s).

Mgr. = Monsignor.

MHD = magnetohydrodynamics.

micro = one-millionth part ($10^{-6}$).

M.I. = Military Intelligence.

M.I.C.E. = Member of the Institution of Civil Engineers.

M.I.Chem.E. = Member of the Institution of Chemical Engineers.

M.I.E.E. = Member of the Institution of Electrical Engineers.

milli = one-thousandth part ($10^{-3}$).

M.I.Mar.E. = Member of the Institute of Marine Engineers.

M.I.Mech.E. = Member of the Institution of Mechanical Engineers.

M.I.Min.E. = Member of the Institution of Mining Engineers.

min. = minimum.

M.I.N.A. = Member of the Institution of Naval Architects.

M.Inst.Met. = Member of the Institute of Metals.

Min. Plenip. = Minister Plenipotentiary.

Mintech = Ministry of Technology.

M.I.Mun.E. = Member of the Institution of Municipal Engineers.

M.Inst.T. = Member of the Institute of Transport.

M.I.T. = Massachusetts Institute of Technology.

M.I.T.M.A. = Member of the Institute of Trade Mark Agents.

M.I.W.M. = Member of the Institution of Works Managers.

M.J.I. = Member of the Institute of Journalists.

MKS = metre-kilogram-second system

MKSA = metre-kilogram-second-ampere (Giorgi) system

MLF = Multilateral Force.

Mlle. = Mademoiselle.

MM. = Messieurs.

mm = millimetre(s).

Mme = Madame.

m.m.f. = magnetomotive force.

mmHg = millimetre(s) of mercury.

M.N. = Merchant Navy.

Mods. = Moderations (Oxford).

M.O.H. = Medical Officer of Health; Ministry of Health.

m.p. = melting point.

M.P. = Member of Parliament; Military Police.

m.p.h. = miles per hour.

M.P.S. = Member of the Pharmaceutical Society; Member of the Philological Society; Member of the Physical Society.

M.R. = Master of the Rolls.

M.R.A.S. = Member of the Royal Asiatic Society; Member of the Royal Academy of Science.

M.R.Ae.S. = Member of the Royal Aeronautical Society.

M.R.C. = Medical Research Council.

M.R.C.O.G. = Member of the Royal College of Obstetricians and Gynaecologists.

M.R.C.P. = Member of the Royal College of Physicians.

M.R.C.P.(E.) = Member of the Royal College of Physicians (Edinburgh).

M.R.C.S. = Member of the Royal College of Surgeons.

M.R.C.V.S. = Member of the Royal College of Veterinary Surgeons.

M.R.I. = Member of the Royal Institution.

M.S. = Master in Surgery.

Ms., Mss. = Manuscript, Manuscripts.

M.S.A. = Mutual Security Agency.

M.Sc. = Master of Science.

M.T.B. = Motor Torpedo Boat.

M.T.P.I. = Member of the Town Planning Institute.

Mus.B. = *Musicae Baccalaureus* (Bachelor in Music).

Mus.D. = *Musicae Doctor* (Doctor in Music).

MV = million volts *or* megavolt.

M.V.O. = Member of the Royal Victorian Order.

MW = million watts *or* megawatt.

M.W.B. = Metropolitan Water Board.


## N

NAAFI = Navy, Army and Air Force Institutes.

N.A.B.M. = National Association of British Manufacturers.

NADGE = Nato Air Defence Ground Environment Organisation.

nano = one-thousand-millionth part ($10^{-9}$)

NASA = National Aeronautics and Space Administration (US).

NATO = North Atlantic Treaty Organisation.

NATSOPA = National Society of Operative Printers and Assistants.

N.B. = *nota bene* (note well).

NBS = National Bureau of Standards (US).

N.C. = Nature Conservancy.

N.C.B. = National Coal Board.

N.C.L.C. = National Council of Labour Colleges.

N.C.O. = Non-commissioned Officer.

N.C.U. = National Cyclists' Union.

n.d. = no date (of books).

NEDC = National Economic Development Council.

NEL = National Engineering Laboratory.

Nem.con. = *Nemine contradicente* (no one contradicting = unanimously).

Nem.diss. = *Nemine dissentiente* (no one dissenting = unanimously).

NERC = Natural Environment Research Council.

Net. (*or* Nett.) = free from, or not subject to, any deductions.

NHS = National Health Service.

NIBMR = no independence before majority rule.

NIC = National Incomes Commission.

NIRNS = National Institute for Research in Nuclear Science.

NLF = National Liberation Front (political arm of Vietcong in S. Vietnam).

NLL = National Lending Library for Science and Technology.

No. = *numero* (number).

*non.seq.* = *non sequitur* (it does not follow).

N.P. = Notary Public.

N.P.C. = National Parks Commission.

NPD = National Democratic Party (W. Ger.).

N.P.F.A. = National Playing Fields Association.

NPL = National Physical Laboratory.

N.R.A. = National Rifle Association.

NRDC = National Research Development Corporation.

N.S. = New Style in the calendar (in Gt. Britain since 1752).

N.S.P.C.C. = National Society for the Prevention of Cruelty to Children.

N.T. = New Testament; National Trust.

N.U.R. = National Union of Railwaymen.

N.U.T. = National Union of Teachers.

N.Y. = New York.

N.Z. = New Zealand.


## O

OAS = Organisation of American States; Organisation de l'Armée Secrète (the clandestine army of the French colonists in Algeria).

OAU = Organisation of African Unity.

ob. = *obit* (died).

obs. = observed.

O.B.E. = Officer of the Order of the British Empire.

OCAM = Joint African and Malagasy Organisation

OCTU = Officer Cadets' Training Unit.

ODECA = Organisation of Central American States.

OECD = Organisation for Economic Co-operation and Development.

O.E.D. = Oxford English Dictionary.

O.F.M. = *Ordo Fratrum Minorum* (Order of Friars Minor = Franciscan).

O.H.M.S. = On Her Majesty's Service.

O.M. = Member of the Order of Merit.

O.P. = *Ordinis Praedicatorum* (Order of Preachers = Dominicans); opposite to prompter (stage term); out of print.

op. = *opus* (work).

op cit. = *opere citato* (in the work cited).

ORC = Overseas Research Council.

ORGEL = Organique et Eau Lourde (organic liquid and heavy water nuclear reactor).

O.S. = Old Style in calendar.

O.S.B. = *Ordo Sancti Benedicti* (Order of St. Benedict = Benedictines).

O.T. = Old Testament.

O.T.C. = Officers' Training Corps.
Oxon. = of Oxford.
oz. = ounce(s).

# P

p = penny, pence (decimal system).
P.A. = Press Association.
PAYE = Pay as you earn (income tax scheme).
P.C. = Privy Councillor; Police Constable.
P.C.C. = People's Caretakers' Council (Nat. movement in Rhodesia).
p.c. = per cent.; postcard.
p.d. = potential difference.
pdl = poundal.
P.D.S.A. = People's Dispensary for Sick Animals.
P.E.N. = Poets, Playwrights, Essayists, Editors and Novelists (Club).
P.E.P. = Political and Economic Planning (Society).
per pro (or p.p.) = *per procurationem* (by proxy).
Ph.D. = *Philosophiae Doctor* (Doctor of Philosophy).
PIB = Prices and Incomes Board.
pinx = *pinxit* (he painted).
P.L.A. = Port of London Authority.
PLUTO = Pipe-line under the ocean.
P.M. = Prime Minister; Post master; *post meridiem* (afternoon).
P.M.G. = Postmaster General.
P.M.O. = Principal Medical Officer.
P.N.E.U. = Parents' National Education Union.
P.O. = Post Office; postal order; Petty Officer.
P. & O. = Peninsular and Oriental Steamship Co.
P.O.W. = prisoner of war.
pp. = pages.
P.P.C. = pour prendre congé (to take leave).
P.Q. = Parliamentary Question.
P.P.S. = Parliamentary Private Secretary.
P.R. = Proportional Representation.
P.R.A. = President of the Royal Academy.
P.R.B. = Pre-Raphaelite Brotherhood.
Pro tem. = *pro tempore* (for the time being).
Prox = *proximo* (of the next month).
P.R.S. = President of the Royal Society.
P.S. = *post scriptum* (postscript).
Ps. = Psalm.
Pss. = Psalms.
P.S.W. = Psychiatric Social Worker.
P.T. = Physical Training.
Pte. = Private.
P.T.O. = please turn over.

# Q

Q. = Queen.
Q = $10^{18}$ British Thermal Units ($1.05 \times 10^{21}$ joules).
Q.B. = Queen's Bench.
Q.C. = Queen's Counsel.
Q.E.D. = *quod erat demonstrandum* (which was to be demonstrated).
Q.E.F. = *quod erat faciendum* (which was to be done).
Q.E.I. = *quod erat inveniendum* (which was to be found).
q.l. (or q.pl) = *quantum libet* (or *quantum placet*) (as much as one pleases).
Q.M. = Quartermaster.
Q.M.C. = Queen Mary College.
q.s. = *quantum suficit* (a sufficient quantity).
Q.S. = Quarter Sessions.
QSEs = Qualified Scientists and Engineers (*i.e.,* skilled manpower).
QSSs = Quasars (quasi stellar radio sources).
Q.T. = quiet (slang).
Qto. = quarto (folded in four).
q.v. = *quod vide* (which see).

# R

R. = Réaumur; *Rex* (King); *Regina* (Queen); Right (stage direction).
R.A. = Rear Admiral; Royal Academy; Royal Academician; Research Association; Right Ascension (astron.).

R.A.C. = Royal Automobile Club.
RAE = Royal Aircraft Establishment.
R.Ae.S. = Royal Aeronautical Society.
R.A.E. = Royal Aircraft Establishment.
R.A.F. = Royal Air Force.
R.A.M. = Royal Academy of Music.
R.C. = Red Cross; Roman Catholic.
R.D. = Rural Dean; Royal Naval Reserve Decoration; Refer to Drawer.
R.D.C. = Rural District Council
R.D.I. = Designer for Industry of the Royal Society of Arts.
R.E. = Royal Engineers.
Reg. Prof. = Regius Professor.
R.E.M.E. = Royal Electrical and Mechanical Engineers.
Rep. = Representative; Republican.
R.G.S. = Royal Geographical Society.
r.h. = relative humidity.
R.H.S. = Royal Humane Society; Royal Horticultural Society.
R.Hist.S. = Royal Historical Society.
R.I. = Royal Institution; Royal Institute of Painters in Water Colours; Rhode Island; Religious Instruction.
R.I.B.A. = Royal Institution of British Architects.
R.I.I.A. = Royal Institute of International Affairs (Chatham House, London).
R.I.P. = *requiescat in pace* (may he rest in peace).
R.L.O. = Returned Letter Office.
R.M. = Royal Marines; Resident Magistrate.
R.M.C. = Royal Military College, Sandhurst.
r.m.s. = root mean square.
R.N. = Royal Navy.
RNA = ribonucleic acid.
R.N.L.I. = Royal National Lifeboat Institution.
Ro. = *recto* (on the right-hand page).
R.P. = Member of the Royal Society of Portrait Painters.
RRE = Royal Radar Establishment.
rpm = revolutions per minute.
R.S.A. = Royal Society of Arts; Royal Scottish Academician.
R.S.M. = Regimental Sergeant Major.
R.S.P.C.A. = Royal Society for the Prevention of Cruelty to Animals.
R.S.V.P. = *Répondez, s'il vous plaît* (An answer is requested).
R.S.W. = Royal Scottish Society of Painters in Water Colours.
Rt. Hon. = Right Honourable.
Rt. Rev. = Right Reverend (of a Bishop).
R.U. = Rugby Union.
RV = Revised Version.
R.W.S. = Royal Society of Painters in Water Colours.
R.Y.S. = Royal Yacht Squadron.

# S

S. = *San, Santa, Santo,* or *São* (Saint); SS. = Saints.
s. = *solidus* (shilling), *solidi* (shillings).
S.A. = Salvation Army; Sex Appeal; South America; South Australia; South Africa; Société Anonyme (Limited).
SACEUR = Supreme Allied Commander Europe.
SACLANT = Supreme Allied Commander Atlantic.
Sarum = of Salisbury.
S.C. = qualified to admission to Staff College.
sc. = *scilicet* (namely).
Sc.D. = *Scientiae Doctor* (Doctor in Science).
S.C.F. = Senior Chaplain to the Forces.
S.C.M. = State Certified Midwife; Student Christian Movement.
SEATO = South-East Asia Treaty Organisation.
S.G. = Solicitor-General; Scots Guards.
SHAPE = Supreme Headquarters, Allied Powers, Europe.
SI = Système International d'Unités (International System of Units).
sic. = so written.
SINS = Ships Inertial Navigation System.
SISTER = Special Institution for Scientific and Technical Education and Research.
SOS = distress signal (wireless code signal, used especially by ships at sea).

s.p. = *sine prole* (without issue).
S.P.C.K. = Society for the Promotion of Christian Knowledge.
SPD = Social Democratic Party (W. Ger.).
S.P.G. = Society for the Propagation of the Gospel.
sp. gr. = specific gravity.
sq. = square; *sequens* (the following).
sqq. = *sequentes, sequentia* (those following).
SRC = Science Research Council.
S.R.N. = State Registered Nurse.
SS. = Saints.
S.S. = Steamship.
S.S.C. = Solicitor before Supreme Court (Scotland).
SSCR = Social Science Research Council.
S.T.D. = *Sacrae Theologiae Doctor* (Doctor of Theology); Subscriber Trunk Dialling.
St. = Saint; Street.
Ste = *Sainte* (Saint, feminine).
Stet = Let it stand (printing term).
s.t.p. = standard temperature and pressure.
S.T.P. = *Sacrae Theologiae Professor* (Professor of Divinity, old form of D.D.)
s.v. = *sub verbo* (under the entry).

# T

TAB = Technical Assistance Board (UN).
TAVR = Territorial and Army Volunteer Reserve
T.B. = Tubercule bacillus (tuberculosis).
t.b. = torpedo boat.
T.C.D. = Trinity College, Dublin.
T.C.C.B. = Test and County Cricket Board.
T.D. = Territorial Decoration; Teachta Dála (Representative of the Dáil).
temp. = temperature.
T.F. = Territorial Force.
T.H. = Trinity House.
TNT = trinitrotoluene (high explosive).
Toc.H. = Talbot House.
tr. = transpose.
T.R.C. = Thames Rowing Club; Tithes Rent Charge.
T.T. = tubercular tested; teetotal.
TUC = Trades Union Congress.
TV = Television.
TVA = Tennessee Valley Authority.
T.V.W.B. = Thames Valley Water Board.
TWI = Training Within Industry for Supervisors.
T.Y.C. = Thames Yacht Club; Two-year Old (*or* Thousand Yards) Course.

# U

U.A.M. = Afro-Malagasy Union.
U-boat = German submarine.
UAR = United Arab Republic.
UCL = University College, London.
U.D.C. = Urban District Council.
UDEAC = Central African Economic and Customs Union.
UEAC = Union of Central African States.
UGC = University Grants Committee.
UHF = ultra-high frequency.
U.K. (*or* UK) = United Kingdom.
UKAEA = UK Atomic Energy Authority.
ult. = *ultimo* (of the last month).
U.N. (*or* UN) = United Nations.
UNCTAD = United Conference on Trade and Development (UN).
UNEF = United Nations Emergency Force(s).
UNESCO = United Nations Education, Scientific, and Cultural Organisation.
UNICEF = United Nations Children's Fund.
UNRWA = United Nations Relief and Works Agency for Palestine Refugees.
UNTSO = UN Truce Supervision Organisation (Palestine).
U.P. = United Press.
U.P.U. = Universal Postal Union (UN).
U.S. (*or* US) United States.
U.S.A. (*or* USA) = United States of America.

USAEC = US Atomic Energy Commission.
U.S.S.R. (*or* USSR) = Union of Soviet Socialist Republics (Russia).

# V

V = volt(s).
v. = *vide* (see); *versus* (against).
V.A. = Vicar-Apostolic.
V. & A. = Victoria and Albert Museum, S. Kensington.
V.C. = Victoria Cross.
V.C.H. = Victoria County Histories.
V.D. = venereal disease; Volunteer Officers' Decoration.
v.d. = various dates.
V.E. Day = Victory in Europe Day, 8 May 1945.
Ven. = Venerable (of an Archdeacon).
*verb. sap.* = *verbum sapienti sat est* (a word to the wise is enough).
Very Rev. = Very Reverend (of a Dean or a Provost).
v.g. = very good.
v.h.c. = very highly commended.
V.H.F. = very high frequency.
V.I.P. = very important person.
viz. = *videlicet* (namely).
V.J. Day = Victory over Japan Day, 15 August 1945.
V.L. = Vice-Lieutenant (of a County).
V.M. = Virgin Mary.
V.M.H. = Victoria Medal of Honour (Royal Horticultural Society).
Vo. = *verso* (on the left-hand page).
V.P. = Vice-President.
V.R. = *Victoria Regina* (Queen Victoria).
v.r. = variant, *or* various reading.
V.S. = veterinary surgeon; vital statistics.
VTOL = vertical take-off and landing (aircraft).

# W

W = watt(s).
W.A. = Western Australia.
Wasps = White Anglo-Saxon Protestants.
WCC = World Council of Churches.
W.E.A. = Workers' Educational Association.
WEU = Western European Union.
WFTU = World Federation of Trade Unions.
WHO = World Health Organisation (UN).
WMO = World Meteorological Organisation (UN).
W.O. = Warrant Officer.
W.R.A.C. = Women's Royal Army Corps.
W.R.A.F. = Women's Royal Air Force.
W.R.N.S. = Women's Royal Naval Service.
W.S. = Writer to the Signet.
W.V.S. = Women's Voluntary Services.

# X

X = Christ (X repr. first letter of the Greek word).
X's = expenses (slang).
xd = ex dividend.
Xmas = Christmas.

# Y

y. = year(s).
yd = yard(s).
Y.M.C.A. = Young Men's Christian Association.
Y.W.C.A. = Young Women's Christian Association.

# Z

ZANU = Zimbabwe African National Union (Nat. movement in Rhodesia).
ZAPU = Zimbabwe African People's Union (Nat. movement in Rhodesia)

# GENERAL COMPENDIUM

A collection of useful tables and data on a variety of unrelated subjects, including silver and china marks, the colours of academical hoods, and foreign currencies in relation to the £.

## TABLE OF CONTENTS

# GENERAL COMPENDIUM

## ENGLISH MONARCHS
### (A.D. 827–1603)

| Monarch | Accession | Died | Age | Reigned |
|---|---|---|---|---|

### I.—BEFORE THE CONQUEST.

#### SAXONS AND DANES

| Monarch | Accession | Died | Age | Reigned |
|---|---|---|---|---|
| Egbert | 827 | 839 | — | 12 |
| Ethelwulf | 839 | 858 | — | 19 |
| Ethelbald | 858 | 860 | — | 2 |
| Ethelbert | 858 | 865 | — | 7 |
| Ethelred | 865 | 871 | — | 6 |
| Alfred the Great | 871 | 899 | 50 | 28 |
| Edward the Elder | 899 | 924 | 54 | 25 |
| Athelstan | 924 | 939 | 45 | 15 |
| Edmund | 939 | 946 | 25 | 7 |
| Eadred | 946 | 955 | 32 | 9 |
| Eadwig | 955 | 959 | 18 | 3 |
| Edgar | 959 | 975 | 32 | 17 |
| Edward the Martyr | 975 | 978 | 17 | 3 |
| Ethelred II (" the Unready ") | 978 | 1016 | 48 | 37 |
| Edmund Ironside | 1016 | 1016 | 27 | Apr.–Nov. |
| Canute the Dane | 1017 | 1035 | 40 | 18 |
| Harold I | 1035 | 1040 | — | 5 |
| Hardicanute | 1040 | 1042 | 24 | 2 |
| Edward the Confessor | 1042 | 1066 | 62 | 24 |
| Harold II | 1066 | 1066 | 44 | Jan.–Oct. |

### II.—FROM THE CONQUEST TO THE PRESENT DAY.

#### NORMANS

| Monarch | Accession | Died | Age | Reigned |
|---|---|---|---|---|
| William I | 1066 | 1087 | 60 | 21 |
| William II | 1087 | 1100 | 43 | 13 |
| Henry I | 1100 | 1135 | 67 | 35 |
| Stephen, Count of Blois | 1135 | 1154 | 50 | 19 |

#### PLANTAGENETS

| Monarch | | Accession | Died | Age | Reigned |
|---|---|---|---|---|---|
| Henry II | | 1154 | 1189 | 56 | 35 |
| Richard I | | 1189 | 1199 | 42 | 10 |
| John | | 1199 | 1216 | 50 | 17 |
| Henry III | | 1216 | 1272 | 65 | 56 |
| Edward I | | 1272 | 1307 | 68 | 35 |
| Edward II | | 1307 | dep. 1327 | 43 | 20 |
| Edward III | | 1327 | 1377 | 65 | 50 |
| Richard II | | 1377 | dep. 1399 | 34 | 22 |
| Henry IV | Lancaster | 1399 | 1413 | 47 | 13 |
| Henry V | Lancaster | 1413 | 1422 | 34 | 9 |
| Henry VI | Lancaster | 1422 | dep. 1461 | 49 | 39 |
| Edward IV | York | 1461 | 1483 | 41 | 22 |
| Edward V | York | 1483 | 1483 | 13 | Apr.–June |
| Richard III | York | 1483 | 1485 | 32 | 2 |

#### TUDORS

| Monarch | Accession | Died | Age | Reigned |
|---|---|---|---|---|
| Henry VII | 1485 | 1509 | 53 | 24 |
| Henry VIII | 1509 | 1547 | 56 | 38 |
| Edward VI | 1547 | 1553 | 16 | 6 |
| Jane | 1553 | 1554 | 17 | 9 days |
| Mary I | 1553 | 1558 | 43 | 5 |
| Elizabeth I | 1558 | 1603 | 69 | 44 |

# BRITISH MONARCHS
## (1603 to the Present day)

| Monarch | Accession | Died | Age | Reigned |
|---|---|---|---|---|
| **STUARTS** | | | | |
| James I (VI of Scotland) . . . . . | 1603 | 1625 | 59 | 22 |
| Charles I . . . . . . . . . | 1625 | beh. 1649 | 48 | 24 |
| **COMMONWEALTH DECLARED, MAY 19, 1649** | | | | |
| Oliver Cromwell, Lord Protector . . . | 1653–8 | — | — | — |
| Richard Cromwell, Lord Protector . . | 1658–9 | — | — | — |
| **STUARTS (RESTORATION)** | | | | |
| Charles II . . . . . . . . | 1660 | 1685 | 55 | 25 |
| James II (VII of Scotland) . . . . | 1685 | dep. 1688 | 68 | 3 |
| *Interregnum Dec. 11, 1688 to Feb. 13, 1689* | | | | |
| William III and Mary II . . . . . | 1689 | 1702 | 51 | 13 |
| | | 1694 | 33 | 6 |
| Anne . . . . . . . . . . | 1702 | 1714 | 49 | 12 |
| **HOUSE OF HANOVER** | | | | |
| George I . . . . . . . . . . | 1714 | 1727 | 67 | 13 |
| George II . . . . . . . . . . | 1727 | 1760 | 77 | 33 |
| George III . . . . . . . . . | 1760 | 1820 | 81 | 59 |
| George IV . . . . . . . . . | 1820 | 1830 | 67 | 10 |
| William IV . . . . . . . . . | 1830 | 1837 | 71 | 7 |
| Victoria. . . . . . . . . . | 1837 | 1901 | 81 | 63 |
| **HOUSE OF SAXE-COBURG** | | | | |
| Edward VII . . . . . . . . . | 1901 | 1910 | 68 | 9 |
| **HOUSE OF WINDSOR** | | | | |
| George V . . . . . . . . . | 1910 | 1936 | 70 | 25 |
| Edward VIII . . . . . . . . . | 1936 | Abd. 1936 | — | 325 days |
| George VI . . . . . . . . . | 1936 | 1952 | 56 | 15 |
| Elizabeth II . . . . . . . . | 1952 | | | |

# SCOTTISH MONARCHS
## (1057–1603)

| Monarch | | Accession | Died |
|---|---|---|---|
| Malcolm III (Canmore) | Son of Duncan I (slain by Macbeth) | 1058 | 1093 |
| Donald Ban | Brother of Malcolm Canmore | 1093 | — |
| Duncan II | Son of Malcolm Canmore, by first marriage | 1094 | 1094 |
| Donald Ban | Restored | 1094 | 1097 |
| Edgar | Son of Malcolm Canmore, by second marriage | 1097 | 1107 |
| Alexander I | Son of Malcolm Canmore | 1107 | 1124 |
| David I | Son of Malcolm Canmore | 1124 | 1153 |
| Malcolm IV (the Maiden) | Son of Henry, eldest son of David I | 1153 | 1165 |
| William I (the Lion) | Brother of Malcolm the Maiden | 1165 | 1214 |
| Alexander II | Son of William the Lion | 1214 | 1249 |
| Alexander III | Son of Alexander II, by second marriage | 1249 | 1286 |
| Margaret, Maid of Norway | Daughter of Eric II of Norway, granddaughter of Alexander III | 1286 | 1290 |
| John Baliol | Grandson of eldest daughter of David, Earl of Huntingdon, brother of William the Lion | 1292 | 1296 |
| Robert I (Bruce) | Great-grandson of 2nd daughter of David, Earl of Huntingdon, brother of William the Lion | 1306 | 1329 |
| David II | Son of Robert I, by second marriage | 1329 | 1371 |
| Robert II (Stewart) | Son of Marjorie, daughter of Robert I by first marriage, and Walter the Steward | 1371 | 1390 |
| Robert III | (John, Earl of Carrick) son of Robert II | 1390 | 1406 |
| James I | Son of Robert III | 1406 | 1437 |
| James II | Son of James I | 1437 | 1460 |
| James III | Eldest son of James II | 1460 | 1488 |
| James IV | Eldest son of James III | 1488 | 1513 |
| James V | Son of James IV | 1513 | 1542 |
| Mary | Daughter of James V, by second marriage | 1542 | 1587 |
| James VI (ascended the Throne of England 1603) | Son of Mary, by second marriage | 1567 | 1625 |

# THE ROYAL FAMILY

Showing the common descent of Queen Elizabeth and The Duke of Edinburgh from Queen Victoria and from Christian IX of Denmark.

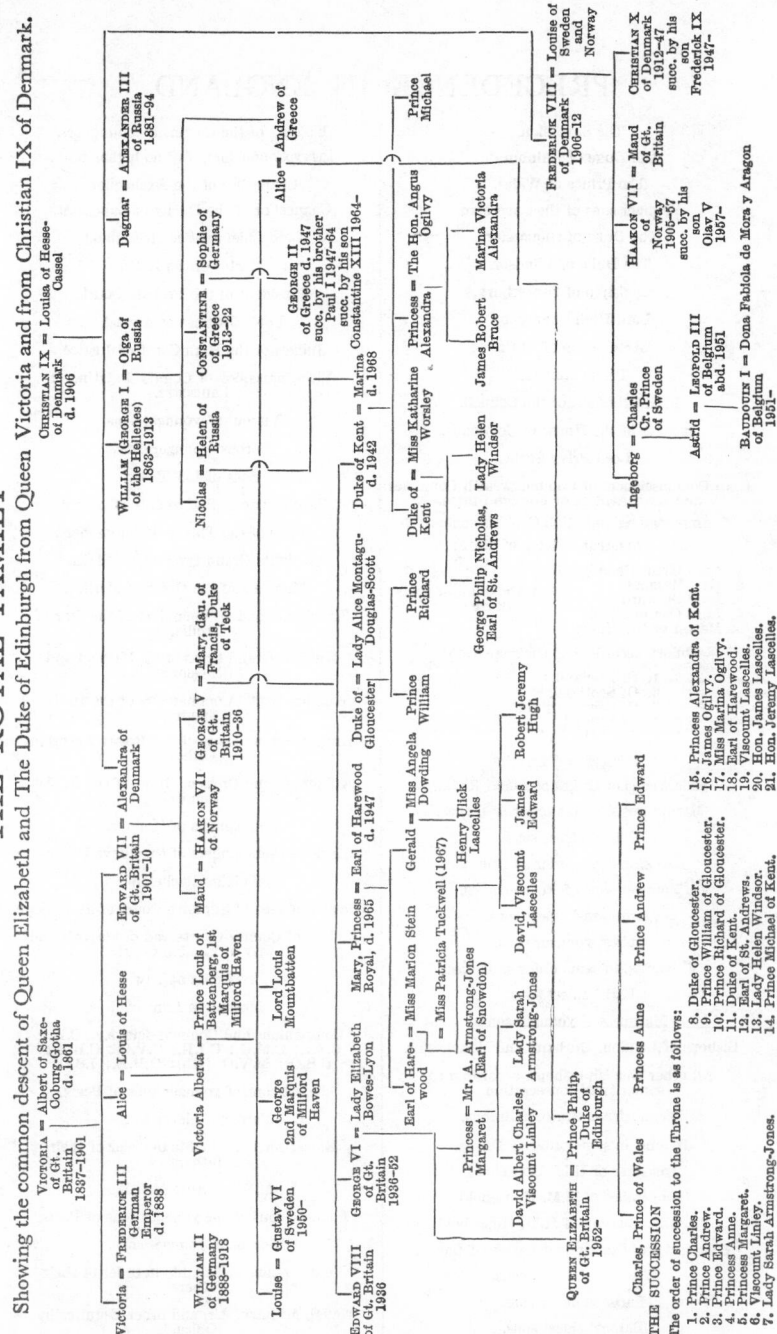

THE SUCCESSION

The order of succession to the Throne is as follows:

1. Prince Charles.
2. Prince Andrew.
3. Prince Edward.
4. Princess Anne.
5. Princess Margaret.
6. Viscount Linley.
7. Lady Sarah Armstrong-Jones.
8. Duke of Gloucester.
9. Prince William of Gloucester.
10. Prince Richard of Gloucester.
11. Duke of Kent.
12. Earl of St. Andrews.
13. Lady Helen Windsor.
14. Prince Michael of Kent.
15. Princess Alexandra of Kent.
16. James Ogilvy.
17. Miss Marina Ogilvy.
18. Earl of Harewood.
19. Viscount Lascelles.
20. Hon. James Lascelles.
21. Hon. Jeremy Lascelles.

# PRECEDENCE IN ENGLAND

The Sovereign.

The Duke of Edinburgh.

The Prince of Wales.

Younger sons of the Sovereign.

The Duke of Gloucester.

The Duke of Windsor.

Archbishop of Canterbury.

Lord High Chancellor.

Archbishop of York.

Prime Minister.

Lord President of the Council.

Speaker of the House of Commons.

Lord Privy Seal.

High Commissioners of Commonwealth Countries and Ambassadors of Foreign States.

Ambassadors and High Commissioners.

The five Great Officers of State:

1. Lord Great Chamberlain
2. Earl Marshal
3. Lord Steward          } Above all of their degree.
4. Lord Chamberlain
5. Master of the Horse

Dukes, according to their creation:

1. Of England.
2. Of Scotland.
3. Of Great Britain.
4. Of Ireland.
5. Since the Union.

Ministers and Envoys.

Eldest sons of Dukes of Blood Royal.

Marquesses, in same order as Dukes.

Dukes' eldest sons.

Earls, in same order as Dukes.

Younger sons of Royal Dukes.

Marquesses' eldest sons.

Dukes' younger sons.

Viscounts, in same order as Dukes.

Earls' eldest sons.

Marquesses' younger sons.

Bishops of London, Durham, and Winchester.

All other English bishops, according to seniority of consecration.

Secretaries of State, if Barons.

Barons, in same order as Dukes.

Treasurer of H.M. Household.

Comptroller of H.M. Household.

Vice-Chamberlain of H.M. Household.

Secretaries of State under degree of Baron.

Viscounts' eldest sons.

Earls' younger sons.

Barons' eldest sons.

Knights of the Garter, if commoners.

Privy Councillors, if of no higher rank.

Chancellor of the Exchequer.

Chancellor of the Duchy of Lancaster.

Lord Chief Justice of England.

Master of the Rolls.

President of the Probate Court.

Lords Justices of Appeal.

Judges of the High Court of Justice.

Vice-Chancellor of County Palatine of Lancaster.

Viscounts' younger sons.

Barons' younger sons.

Sons of Life Peers.

Baronets according to date of patent.

Knights of the Thistle, if commoners.

Knights Grand Cross of the Bath.

Members of the Order of Merit.

Knights Grand Commanders of the Star of India.

Knights Grand Cross of St. Michael and St. George.

Knights Grand Commanders of the Indian Empire.

Knights Grand Cross of the Royal Victorian Order.

Knights Grand Cross of Order of the British Empire.

Companions of Honour.

Knights Commanders of the above Orders.

Knights Bachelors.

Official Referees of Supreme Court of Judicature.

Judges of County Courts and of Mayor's and City of London Court.

Serjeants at Law.

Masters in Lunacy.

Companions and Commanders, e.g., C.B.; C.S.I.; C.M.G.; C.I.E.; C.V.O.; C.B.E.; D.S.O.; M.V.O. (4th); O.B.E.; I.S.O.

Eldest sons of younger sons of Peers.

Baronets' eldest sons.

Eldest sons of Knights in order of their fathers.

M.V.O. (5th); M.B.E.

Younger sons of the younger sons of Peers.

Baronets' younger sons.

Younger sons of Knights in order of their fathers.

Naval, Military, Air, and other Esquires by Office.

Women take the same rank as their husbands or as their eldest brothers; but the daughter of a Peer marrying a Commoner retains her title as Lady or Honourable. Daughters of Peers rank next immediately after the wives of their elder brothers, and before their younger brothers' wives. Daughters of Peers marrying Peers of lower degree take the same order of precedency as that of their husbands; thus the daughter of a Duke marrying a Baron becomes of the rank of Baroness only, while her sisters married to commoners retain their rank and take precedence of the Baroness. Merely official rank on the husband's part does not give any similar precedence to the wife. Dames Grand Cross (G.C.V.O. or G.B.E.) rank after wives of Baronets and before wives of Knights Grand Cross. Dames Commanders (D.C.V.O. or D.B.E.) rank after wives of Knights Grand Cross and before wives of Knights Commanders.

Precedence is formed by statute, patent, or usage, but the chief regulations regarding the order of precedence were settled by Parliament in the reign of Henry VIII.

Precedence locally, in county or city, has not been promulgated by written code, but in Counties the Lord Lieutenant stands first, and secondly the Sheriff, and therefore in Cities and Boroughs the Lord Lieutenant has social precedence over the Mayor; but at City or Borough functions the Lord Mayor or Mayor will preside. At Oxford and Cambridge the High Sheriff takes precedence of the Vice-Chancellor.

# PRECEDENCE IN SCOTLAND

The Sovereign.

The Duke of Edinburgh.

The Lord High Commissioner to the General Assembly (while that Assembly is sitting).

The Duke of Rothesay (eldest son of the Sovereign).

Younger sons of the Sovereign.

The Duke of Gloucester, the Duke of Windsor, uncles of the Sovereign.

Lords Lieutenant of counties, Lords Provost of cities being ex-officio Lords Lieutenant of counties of cities, and Sheriffs Principal, when within their localities, in the order named.

Lord Chancellor of Great Britain.

Moderator of the Assembly of the Church of Scotland.

The Prime Minister.

Keeper of the Great Seal of Scotland (Secretary for Scotland), if a peer.

Keeper of the Privy Seal of Scotland, if a peer.

Hereditary Lord High Constable of Scotland.

Hereditary Master of the Household in Scotland.

Dukes, as in English precedence.

Eldest sons of Dukes of Blood Royal.

Marquesses, as in England.

Eldest sons of Dukes.

Earls as in England.

Younger sons of Royal Dukes.

Eldest sons of Marquesses.

Younger sons of Dukes.

Keeper of the Great Seal of Scotland (Secretary for Scotland), if not a peer.

Keeper of the Privy Purse, if not a peer.

Lord Justice-General.

Lord Clerk-register.

Lord Advocate.

Lord Justice Clerk.

Viscounts, as in England.

Eldest sons of Earls.

Younger sons of Marquesses.

Barons, as in England.

Eldest sons of Viscounts.

Younger sons of Earls.

Eldest sons of Barons.

Knights of the Garter.

Privy Councillors not included in above ranks.

Lords of Session (by date of appointment).

Younger sons of Viscounts.

Younger sons of Barons.

Sons of Life Peers.

Baronets.

Knights of the Thistle.

Knights of other Orders as in England.

Solicitor-general for Scotland.

Lord Lyon King of Arms.

Sheriffs Principal (except as shown above).

Knights Bachelor.

Sheriffs Substitute.

Companions of Orders as in England.

Commanders of Royal Victorian Order.

Commanders of the British Empire Order.

Eldest sons of younger sons of Peers.

Companions of Distinguished Service Order.

Member of Fourth Class of Royal Victorian Order.

Officers of British Empire Order.

Eldest sons of Baronets.

Eldest sons of Knights of the Garter, and of the Thistle.

Eldest sons of Knights.

Members of Fifth Class of Royal Victorian Order.

Members of British Empire Order.

Younger sons of Baronets.

Younger sons of Knights.

Queen's Counsel.

Barons-feudal.

Esquires.

Gentlemen.

# MODES OF ADDRESS TO PERSONS OF RANK

## ROYALTY.

QUEEN.
*Begin:* Madam, *or* May it please Your Majesty, *or* Lord ——— presents his duty to Your Majesty.
*Address:* The Queen's Most Excellent Majesty.
*Speak to as:* Your Majesty.

PRINCES AND PRINCESSES, DUKES AND DUCHESSES OF THE BLOOD ROYAL.
*Begin:* Sir (*or* Madam).
*Address:* His (*or* Her) Royal Highness the Prince (*or* Princess) ———.
　　　 His (*or* Her) Royal Highness the Duke (*or* Duchess) of ———.
*Speak to as:* Your Royal Highness.

## NOBILITY.

DUKES AND DUCHESSES.
*Begin:* My Lord Duke.
*Address:* His Grace the Duke of ———, K.G., etc.
*Speak to as:* Your Grace.

*Begin:* Madam.
*Address:* Her Grace the Duchess of ———.
*Speak to as:* Your Grace.

MARQUESSES AND MARCHIONESSES.
*Begin:* My Lord Marquess, *or* My Lord.
*Address:* The Most Hon. the Marquess of ———.
*Speak to as:* Your Lordship.

*Begin:* Madam.
*Address:* The Most Hon. the Marchioness of ———.
*Speak to as:* Your Ladyship.

EARLS AND COUNTESSES.
*Begin:* My Lord.
*Address:* The Right Hon. the Earl of ———, *or* The Earl ———.
*Speak to as:* Your Lordship.

*Begin:* Madam.
*Address:* The Right Hon. the Countess of ———, *or* The Countess ———.
*Speak to as:* Your Ladyship.

VISCOUNTS AND VISCOUNTESSES.
*Begin:* My Lord.
*Address:* The Right Hon. Viscount, *or* Viscount ———.
*Speak to as:* Your Lordship.

*Begin:* Madam.
*Address:* The Right Hon. the Viscountess ———.
*Speak to as:* Your Ladyship.

BARONS AND BARONESSES.
*Begin:* My Lord.
*Address:* The Right Hon. Lord ———.
*Speak to as:* Your Lordship.

*Begin:* My Lady.
*Address:* The Right Hon. Lady ———.
*Speak to as:* Your Ladyship.

BARONETS.
*Begin:* Sir.
*Address:* Sir (Christian name and surname), Bt.

KNIGHTS BACHELOR.
As Baronet, except that the word Bt. is omitted.

## THE CHURCH.

ARCHBISHOPS.
*Begin:* My Lord Archbishop, *or* Your Grace.
*Address:* His Grace the Lord Archbishop of ———.
*Speak to as:* Your Grace.
A retired archbishop is addressed as The Most Rev. Archbishop ———.

BISHOPS.
All Bishops, whether Diocesan or Suffragan, are addressed by the spiritual title "Lord."
*Begin:* My Lord Bishop.
*Address:* The Right Rev. the Lord Bishop of ———.
*Speak to as:* Your Lordship.
It is usual to accord to Colonial Bishops the courtesy title of "Lord Bishop," and they are addressed in the same manner as English Bishops. Assistant and retired Bishops are not addressed as "Lord Bishop" but as The Right Rev. Bishop ———, *or* The Right Rev. (surname), D.D.
*Begin:* Right Rev. Sir.

DEANS.
*Begin:* Very Reverend Sir.
*Address:* The Very Rev. the Dean of ———.

ARCHDEACONS.
*Begin:* Venerable Sir.
*Address:* The Venerable the Archdeacon of ———.

CANONS.
*Begin:* Reverend Sir.
*Address:* The Reverend Canon ———.
*Speak to as:* Canon ———.

THE POPE.
*Begin:* Your Holiness *or* Most Holy Father.
*Address:* To His Holiness the Pope.

CARDINALS.
*Begin:* My Lord Cardinal *or* My Lord.
*Address:* To His Eminence Cardinal ———.

THE CHIEF RABBI.
*Begin:* Very Rev. and Dear Sir.
*Address:* To the Very Rev. the Chief Rabbi *or* To the Very Rev. (Dr.) ———

RABBIS.
*Begin:* Rev. and Dear Sir.
*Address:* To the Rev. Rabbi (Dr.) ———.

## THE LAW.

LORD CHANCELLOR.
*Begin:* According to rank.
*Address:* The Right Hon. the Lord High Chancellor.
*Speak to:* According to rank.

LORD CHIEF JUSTICE.
*Begin:* According to rank, if a peer, otherwise as a Judge.
*Address:* The Right Hon. the Lord Chief Justice of England.

LORD JUSTICE OF APPEAL.
*Begin:* Sir.
*Address:* The Right Hon. the Lord Justice ———
*Speak to as:* Your Lordship (addressed on the Bench as "My Lord").

LORD OF APPEAL IN ORDINARY AND HIS WIFE.
As Baron and Baroness.

JUDGES.
*Begin:* Sir (*or* Madam)
*Address:* The Hon. Mr. Justice ——— *or* The Hon. Sir ——— (if a Knight).
*Speak to as:* Your Lordship (*or* Ladyship) (addressed on the Bench as "My Lord" (*or* "My Lady").

JUDGES OF COUNTY COURT.
*Begin:* Dear Judge ———.
*Address:* His Honour Judge ——— (addressed on the Bench as "Your Honour").

JUSTICES OF THE PEACE.
*Address:* The Right Worshipful ———, J.P. (addressed on the Bench as "Your Worship").

LORD MAYORS.
*Begin:* My Lord.
*Address:* The Right Hon. the Lord Mayor of —— (London, York, Dublin, Belfast, Adelaide, Sydney, Melbourne, Perth (Aust.), Brisbane and Hobart).
*Speak to as:* Your Lordship.

MAYORS.
*Begin:* Sir.
*Address:* The Right Worshipful the Mayor of —— (Mayor of a City). The Worshipful the Mayor of —— (Mayor of a Borough).
*Speak to as:* Your Worship.

LORD PROVOSTS.
*Begin:* My Lord Provost, *or* My Lord.
*Address:* The Right Hon. the Lord Provost of —— (Edinburgh and Glasgow). The Lord Provost of —— (Aberdeen, Dundee, Elgin, and Perth).
*Speak to:* Your Lordship.
(The Lord Provost's wife is called Lady Provost.)

DIPLOMATIC SERVICE.

AMBASSADORS (in charge of Embassies).
*Begin:* Sir, My Lord, etc., according to rank.
*Address:* His Excellency (in other respects according to rank) H.B.M. Embassy.
*Speak to as:* Your Excellency.

MINISTERS (in charge of Legations).
Rules as for ambassadors, except in the case of commoners when the envelope should be addressed:

(Christian name and surname), Esq., H.M.B. Legation, ——.

CONSULS.
*Begin:* Sir.
*Address:* (Christian name and surname), Esq., H.B.M. Agent and Consul-General, *or* H.B.M. Consul-General, *or* H.B.M. Consul, *or* H.B.M. Vice-Consul.

GOVERNORS-GENERAL.
*Begin:* According to rank.
*Address:* His Excellency (ordinary designation), Governor of——.
*Speak to as:* Your Excellency.

PRIVY COUNCILLORS.
The courtesy title of " Right Honourable " is accorded all Privy Councillors (all members of the Cabinet are privy councillors, and the office is conferred for life). In the case of peers below the rank of Marquess, who already have a right to it in virtue of their peerage, the rank of Privy Councillor is indicated by the letters " P.C." after the name. Wives do not share the title.
*Address:* The Right Hon. ——.
Admiral the Right Hon. Sir ——.
The Right Rev. the Right Hon. the Lord Bishop of ——.
The Most Hon. the Marquess of ——, P.C.

BUSINESS LETTERS.
Business letters to persons of rank can either be written in the third person (grammatical pitfalls must be guarded against), in which case they are not signed, or in the first person plural.

# ORDERS OF CHIVALRY

**Garter**
K.G.

The Most Noble Order of the Garter (1348). *Ribbon:* Garter blue, not worn in undress uniform. *Motto:* Honi soit qui mal y pense (*Evil to him who evil thinks*).

**Thistle**
K.T.

The Most Noble and Most Ancient Order of the Thistle (1687). *Ribbon:* Green, not worn in undress uniform. *Motto:* Nemo me impune lacessit (*No one provokes me with impunity*).

**Saint Patrick**
K.P.

The Most Illustrious Order of St. Patrick (1783). *Ribbon:* Sky blue, not worn in undress uniform. *Motto:* Quis separabit? (*Who shall separate ?*).

**Bath**
G.C.B. (Knight Grand Cross), (Mil.& Civ).
K.C.B. (Knight Commander), (Mil. & Civ).
C.B. (Companion), (Mil.).

The Most Honourable Order of the Bath (1399). *Ribbon:* Crimson. *Motto:* Tria juncta in uno (*Three joined in one*). (Remodelled 1725 and 1815, and enlarged 13 times since.)

**Order of Merit.**
O.M. (Mil. & Civ.)

The Order of Merit (1902). *Ribbon:* Blue and crimson. Ranks after G.C.B. before K.C.B.

**tar of India**
G.C.S.I. (Knight Grand Commander).
K.C.S.I. (Knight Commander).
C.S.I. (Companion).

The Most Exalted Order of the Star of India (1861). (Since enlarged 8 times.) *Ribbon:* Light blue, with white edges. *Motto:* Heaven's Light our Guide.

**Saint Michael and Saint George**
G.C.M.G. (Knight Grand Cross).
K.C.M.G. (Knight Commander).
C.M.G. (Companion).

The Most Distinguished Order of St. Michael and St. George (1818). *Ribbon:* Saxon blue, with scarlet centre. *Motto:* Auspicium melioris aevi (*Token of a better age*).

**Indian Empire**
G.C.I.E. (Knight Grand Commander).
K.C.I.E. (Knight Commander).
C.I.E. (Companion).

The Most Eminent Order of the Indian Empire (1877). (Since enlarged 8 times.) *Ribbon:* Imperial purple. *Motto:* Imperatricis auspiciis (*Under the auspices of the Empress*).

**Victorian Order**
G.C.V.O. (Knight or Dame Grand Cross).
K.C.V.O. (Knight Commander).
D.C.V.O. (Dame Commander)
C.V.O. (Commander).
M.V.O. (Member).

The Royal Victorian Order (1896). *Ribbon:* Blue, with red and white edges. *Motto:* Victoria.

**British Empire**
G.B.E. (Knight or Dame Grand Cross).
K.B.E. (Knight Commander).
D.B.E. (Dame Commander).
C.B.E. (Commander).
O.B.E. (Officer).
M.B.E. (Member).

The Most Excellent Order of the British Empire (1917). *Ribbon:* Rose pink edged with pearl grey with vertical pearl stripe in centre (Mil. Div.); without vertical stripe (Civ. Div.). *Motto:* For God and the Empire.

**Companions of Honour**
C.H.

Order of the Companions of Honour (1917). *Ribbon:* Carmine, with gold edges. Ranks after G.B.E. and before K.B.E.

**Victoria and Albert**
V.A.

The Royal Order of Victoria and Albert (for Ladies) (1862). (Since enlarged 3 times.)

**Crown of India**
C.I.

The Imperial Order of the Crown of India (for Ladies) (1878). *Ribbon:* Light blue watered edged white, worn as bow on left shoulder.

# BRITISH PRIME MINISTERS

| | Party | Served | | Party | Served |
|---|---|---|---|---|---|
| **George I, 1714–27** | | | Viscount Palmerston | Liberal | 1859–65 |
| | | | Earl Russell | Liberal | 1865–6 |
| **George II, 1727–60** | | | Earl of Derby | Conservative | 1866–8 |
| Sir Robert Walpole | Whig | 1721–42 | B. Disraeli | Conservative | 1868 |
| Earl of Wilmington | Whig | 1742–3 | W. E. Gladstone | Liberal | 1868–74 |
| Henry Pelham | Whig | 1743–54 | B. Disraeli | Conservative | 1874–80 |
| Duke of Newcastle | Whig | 1754–6 | W. E. Gladstone | Liberal | 1880–5 |
| Duke of Devonshire | Whig | 1756–7 | Marquis of Salisbury | Conservative | 1885–6 |
| Duke of Newcastle | Whig | 1757–60 | W. E. Gladstone | Liberal | 1886 |
| | | | Marquis of Salisbury | Conservative | 1886–92 |
| **George III, 1760–1820** | | | W. E. Gladstone | Liberal | 1892–4 |
| Duke of Newcastle | Whig | 1760–2 | Earl of Rosebery | Liberal | 1894–5 |
| Earl of Bute | Tory | 1762–3 | Marquis of Salisbury | Conservative | 1895–1901 |
| George Grenville | Whig | 1763–5 | | | |
| Marquis of Rocking-<br>ham | Whig | 1766 | **Edward VII, 1901–10** | | |
| | | | Marquis of Salisbury | Conservative | 1901–2 |
| Duke of Grafton | Whig | 1766–9 | A. J. Balfour | Conservative | 1902–5 |
| Lord North | Tory | 1770–82 | Sir H. Campbell-<br>Bannerman | Liberal | 1905–8 |
| Marquis of Rocking-<br>ham | Whig | 1782 | H. H. Asquith | Liberal | 1908–10 |
| Earl of Shelburne | Whig | 1782–3 | | | |
| Duke of Portland | Coalition | 1783 | **George V, 1910–36** | | |
| William Pitt | Tory | 1783–1801 | H. H. Asquith | Liberal | 1910–15 |
| Viscount Sidmouth | Tory | 1801–4 | H. H. Asquith | Coalition | 1915–16 |
| William Pitt | Tory | 1804–6 | D. Lloyd George | Coalition | 1916–22 |
| Lord Grenville | Whig | 1806–7 | A. Bonar Law | Conservative | 1922–3 |
| Duke of Portland | Tory | 1807–9 | S. Baldwin | Conservative | 1923–4 |
| Spencer Perceval<br>(assassinated) | Tory | 1809–12 | J. R. MacDonald | Labour | 1924 |
| | | | S. Baldwin | Conservative | 1924–9 |
| **George IV, 1820–30** | | | J. R. MacDonald | Labour | 1929–31 |
| Earl of Liverpool | Tory | 1812–27 | J. R. MacDonald | National | 1931–5 |
| George Canning | Tory | 1827 | S. Baldwin | National | 1935–6 |
| Viscount Goderich | Tory | 1827 | | | |
| Duke of Wellington | Tory | 1827–30 | **Edward VIII, 1936** | | |
| | | | **George VI, 1936–52** | | |
| **William IV, 1830–7** | | | S. Baldwin | National | 1936–7 |
| Earl Grey | Whig | 1830–4 | N. Chamberlain | National | 1937–39 |
| Viscount Melbourne | Whig | 1834 | N. Chamberlain | War Cabinet | 1939 |
| Sir Robert Peel | Tory | 1834–5 | W. S. Churchill | War Cabinet | 1940–45 |
| Viscount Melbourne | Whig | 1835–7 | W. S. Churchill | Caretaker | 1945 |
| | | | C. R. Atlee | Labour | 1945–51 |
| **Victoria, 1837–1901** | | | Sir W. S. Churchill | Conservative | 1951–2 |
| Viscount Melbourne | Whig | 1837–41 | | | |
| Sir Robert Peel | Tory | 1841–6 | **Elizabeth II, 1952–** | | |
| Lord John Russell | Whig | 1846–52 | Sir W. S. Churchill | Conservative | 1952–5 |
| Earl of Derby | Tory | 1852 | Sir A. Eden | Conservative | 1955–7 |
| Earl of Aberdeen | Peelite | 1852–5 | H. Macmillan | Conservative | 1957–63 |
| Viscount Palmerston | Liberal | 1855–8 | Sir A. Douglas-Home | Conservative | 1963–4 |
| Earl of Derby | Tory | 1858–9 | H. Wilson | Labour | 1964– |

# PRESIDENTS OF THE UNITED STATES

The terms are for four years; only President F. D. Roosevelt
has served more than two terms.

| | Party | Served | | | Party | Served |
|---|---|---|---|---|---|---|
| 1. George Washington | Fed. | 1789–97 | | 21. Chester A. Arthur | Rep. | 1881–5 |
| 2. John Adams | Fed. | 1797–1801 | | 22. Grover Cleveland | Dem. | 1885–9 |
| 3. Thomas Jefferson | Rep. | 1801–9 | | 23. Benjamin Harrison | Rep. | 1889–93 |
| 4. James Madison | Rep. | 1809–17 | | 24. Grover Cleveland | Dem. | 1893–7 |
| 5. James Monroe | Rep. | 1817–25 | | 25. William McKinley | Rep. | 1897–1901 |
| 6. John Quincey Adams | Rep. | 1825–9 | | (assassinated) | | |
| 7. Andrew Jackson | Dem. | 1829–37 | | 26. Theodore Roosevelt | Rep. | 1901–9 |
| 8. Martin Van Buren | Dem. | 1837–41 | | 27. William Howard Taft | Rep. | 1909–13 |
| 9. William H. Harrison<br>(died in office) | Whig | 1841 | | 28. Woodrow Wilson | Dem. | 1913–21 |
| | | | | 29. Warren G. Harding<br>(died in office) | Rep. | 1921–3 |
| 10. John Tyler | Whig | 1841–5 | | 30. Calvin Coolidge | Rep. | 1923–9 |
| 11. James K. Polk | Dem. | 1845–9 | | 31. Herbert C. Hoover | Rep. | 1929–33 |
| 12. Zachary Taylor<br>(died in office) | Whig | 1849–50 | | 32. Franklin D. Roosevelt<br>(died in office) | Dem. | 1933–45 |
| 13. Millard Fillmore | Whig | 1850–3 | | 33. Harry S. Truman | Dem. | 1945–53 |
| 14. Franklin Pierce | Dem. | 1853–7 | | 34. Dwight D. Eisenhower | Rep. | 1953–61 |
| 15. James Buchanan | Dem. | 1857–61 | | 35. John F. Kennedy | Dem. | 1961–3 |
| 16. Abraham Lincoln<br>(assassinated) | Rep. | 1861–5 | | (assassinated) | | |
| 17. Andrew Johnson | Rep. | 1865–9 | | 36. Lyndon B. Johnson | Dem. | 1963–69 |
| 18. Ulysses S. Grant | Rep. | 1869–77 | | 37. Richard N. Nixon | Rep. | 1969– |
| 19. Rutherford B. Hayes | Rep. | 1877–81 | | | | |
| 20. James A. Garfield<br>(assassinated) | Rep. | 1881 | | | | |

# UNITED KINGDOM COINAGE

The Royal Mint is authorised to issue coins of the following denominations and specifications :—

| Denomination. | Standard Weight. |
|---|---|
| | Grains. |
| **Gold:** | |
| Five Pound Piece . . . . | 616·37239 |
| Two Pound Piece . . . . | 246·54895 |
| Sovereign . . . . . | 123·27447 |
| Half Sovereign . . . . | 61·63723 |
| **Cupro-Nickel:** | |
| Crown . . . . . . | 436·36363 |
| Half-Crown . . . . . | 218·18181 |
| Florin . . . . . . | 174·54545 |
| Shilling . . . . . . | 87·27272 |
| Sixpence . . . . . | 43·63636 |
| **Silver:** | |
| Maundy Fourpence . . . | 29·09090 |
| Maundy Threepence . . . | 21·81818 |
| Maundy Twopence . . . | 14·54545 |
| Maundy Penny . . . | 7·27272 |
| **Nickel Brass:** | |
| Threepence . . . . . | 105·00000 |
| **Bronze:** | |
| Penny | 145·83333 |

*See also* **Decimal Currency.**

**Gold Coinage.** Under the Exchange Control laws it is illegal for a resident in the U.K. to hold gold coin other than collectors' pieces, and collectors must apply for official permission if their collection contains more than four gold coins minted after 1837. A new collector must obtain permission to hold even one such coin. The English sovereign, however, is still used as currency in certain Middle East countries.

**Cupro-Nickel.** Since 1 January 1947 all " silver " coins have been struck from cupro-nickel, composed of 75% copper and 25% nickel. Maundy money is, however, made of silver, at the standard of 925 parts per 1000.

**Bronze,** introduced in 1860 to replace copper, varies slightly in composition from time to time. At present it consists of 97% copper, $\frac{1}{2}$% tin, and 2$\frac{1}{2}$% zinc.

**Nickel Brass.** The twelve-sided threepenny piece is composed of copper 79%, zinc 20%, and nickel 1%.

**Bank of England Notes** are issued in denominations of 10s., £1, £5, and £10. Scottish banks issue £1, £5, £10, £20, £50, and £100 notes which are generally accepted in Scotland and in some other parts of the U.K. Northern Ireland banks issue £1, £5, £10, £50 and £100 notes.

**Legal Tender of Coin.** Gold coins, dated 1838 onwards, if not below the minimum current weight, are legal tender (but see above). Silver from 1816 onwards, and cupro-nickel coins are legal tender for sums up to £2, nickel-brass threepenny pieces up to 2s., and bronze up to 1s. The farthing ceased to be legal tender from 1 January 1961 and the halfpenny from 1 August 1969. The half-crown will cease to be legal tender from 1 January 1970.

**Decimal Currency.** The Decimal Currency Act, 1967, provides for the adoption in 1971 of a currency system based on the pound sterling divided into one hundred new pence. The coins authorised for issue by the Act are:

| Denomination. | Standard weight. | Standard diameter. |
|---|---|---|
| | grams | cm |
| **Cupro-Nickel:** | | |
| 50 New Pence . | 13·5 | 3·0 |
| 10 New Pence . | 11·31036 | 2·8500 |
| 5 New Pence . | 5·65518 | 2·3595 |
| **Bronze:** | | |
| 2 New Pence . | 7·12800 | 2·5910 |
| 1 New Penny . | 3·56400 | 2·0320 |
| $\frac{1}{2}$ New Penny . | 1·78200 | 1·7145 |

**Decimal Coin Designs.** The portrait of the Queen that appears on the obverse of all the new coins is the work of Mr. Arnold Machin,

O.B.E., R.A., and is already in use on the coinages of a number of other Commonwealth countries including Canada, Australia and New Zealand.

The reverse designs, which are the work of Mr. Christopher Ironside, are as follows:

*Fifty New Pence.* 50p (10s.): Figure of Britannia seated beside a lion with a shield resting against her right side, holding a trident in her right hand and an olive branch in her left hand.

*Ten New Pence.* 10p (2s.): Part of the crest of England. A lion passant guardent royally crowned. This design may also be described as part of the crest of the United Kingdom of Great Britain and Northern Ireland.

*Five New Pence.* 5p (1s.): The badge of Scotland. A thistle royally crowned.

*Two New Pence.* 2p (4·8d.): The badge of The Prince of Wales. Three ostrich feathers enfiling a coronet of crosses pattee and fleurs de lys with the motto ICH DIEN.

*One New Penny.* 1p (2·4d.): A portcullis with chains royally crowned, originally a badge of King Henry VII. In modern times it has been particularly associated with the Palace of Westminster and is used extensively as a badge connected with Parliament.

*New Halfpenny.* $\frac{1}{2}$p (1·2d.): The Royal Crown.

*Notes:*

(1) The United Kingdom will change over to decimal currency on Monday, 15 February 1971— Decimal Day or D Day.

(2) The pound (£) is unchanged. It will be divided into 100 new pence (100p) so each will be worth 2·4 of our present pence.

(3) The symbol for the pound will remain £; the new penny will be abbreviated to p and the halfpenny will be written as $\frac{1}{2}$p.

(4) Our seven £sd coins and the 10s note will be replaced over a period by six decimal coins; the £1, £5, and £10 notes need not be changed.

(5) Cupro-nickel (silver) coins of 5p and 10p came into circulation on 23 April 1968. Except for designs they are identical with the shilling and two-shilling coins and are completely interchangeable with them.

(6) A seven-sided cupro-nickel (silver) 50p coin will start to replace the 10s note from mid-October 1969. It will have a smooth, non-milled edge and in size and weight will be about half-way between a two-shilling piece and a half-crown. Its shape is technically known as an equilateral curve heptagon.

(7) The bronze 2p, 1p and $\frac{1}{2}$p coins will not be legal tender until D Day. But souvenir coin sets are available from banks.

(8) D Day will be followed by a changeover period not exceeding 18 months, during which, for most purposes except banking, both £sd and £p will remain legally in use together. At the end of this period the pennies, threepenny bits, and sixpences will cease to be legal tender.

(9) On and from D Day the Banks will work in decimals and all cheques will then have to be written in decimals.

(10) Two conversion tables have been accepted by the Government: a " shoppers' table " which gives equivalents to the nearest half new penny, and a banking and accounting table which takes them to the nearest whole new penny.—Here we give the shoppers' or new halfpence table:

### Shoppers' Table

| £sd | £p | £sd | £p |
|---|---|---|---|
| 1d. | $\frac{1}{2}$p | 7d. | 3p |
| 2d. | 1p | 8d. | 3$\frac{1}{2}$p |
| 3d. | 1p | 9d. | 4p |
| 4d. | 1$\frac{1}{2}$p | 10d. | 4p |
| 5d. | 2p | 11d. | 4$\frac{1}{2}$p |
| 6d. | 2$\frac{1}{2}$p | 1s. | 5p |

*Note.*—Only those £sd amounts which end in sixpence or multiples of sixpence convert exactly into £p. Thus to convert shillings to new pence one has simply to multiply by five. The pence should then be converted by using the table and the two amounts added together.

# WEIGHTS AND MEASURES

## I. IMPERIAL WEIGHTS AND MEASURES.

### AVOIRDUPOIS.

| | |
|---|---|
| 1 dram (dr.) | 27·34375 grains (gr.) |
| 16 drams | 1 ounce (oz.) = 437·5 gr. |
| 16 ounces | 1 pound (lb.) = 7000 gr. |
| 14 pounds | 1 stone |
| 28 pounds | 1 quarter |
| 4 quarters | 1 hundredweight (cwt.) = 112 lb. |
| 20 hundredweight | 1 ton = (2240 lb.) |

### TROY WEIGHT.

| | |
|---|---|
| 1 pennyweight (dwt.) | 24 grains |
| 480 grains | 1 ounce |

The only unit of troy weight which is now legal for use in trade in this country is the ounce Troy, and weighings of precious metals are made in multiples and decimals of this unit.

The term *carat* is not a unit of weight for precious metals, but is used to denote the quality of gold plate, etc., and is a figure indicating the number of 24ths of pure gold in the alloy, *e.g.*, a 9 carat gold ring consists of nine parts of pure gold and fifteen parts of base metals.

### CAPACITY MEASURE.

| | |
|---|---|
| 4 gills | 1 pint |
| 2 pints | 1 quart |
| 4 quarts | 1 gallon |
| 2 gallons | 1 peck |
| 4 pecks | 1 bushel |
| 8 bushels | 1 quarter |
| 36 bushels | 1 chaldron |

The gallon, as the capacity standard, is based upon the pound.

1 gallon = 277·274 cubic inches.

*Note.*—The British Pharmaceutical Code and the British National Formulary—the official works of medicinal reference—no longer contain the apothecaries' units of measurement, for since 3 March 1969 medicine has been measured in metric units. Prescriptions are in 5 millilitre units; medicine bottles are in six sizes from 50 to 500 millilitres. The metric equivalents of the old apothecaries' units are given below.

The metric system (with apothecaries' equivalents) is used for formulae and prescriptions in the *British Pharmacopœia*.

### LINEAR MEASURE.

| | |
|---|---|
| 1 nail | 1/16 yard |
| 1 link | 7·92 inches |
| 12 inches | 1 foot |
| 3 feet | 1 yard |
| 22 yards | 1 chain |
| 10 chains | 1 furlong |
| 8 furlongs | 1 mile = 1760 yards |

### SQUARE MEASURE.

| | |
|---|---|
| 144 sq. inches | 1 sq. foot |
| 9 sq. feet | 1 sq. yard = 1296 sq. inches |
| 484 sq. yards | 1 sq. chain |
| 1210 sq. yards | 1 rood |
| 10 sq. chains | 1 acre |
| 4 roods | 1 acre |
| 4840 sq. yards | 1 acre |
| 640 acres | 1 sq. mile |

### CUBIC OR SOLID MEASURE.

| | |
|---|---|
| 1728 cu. inches | 1 cu. foot |
| 27 cu. feet | 1 cu. yard |

The primary standards are the yard, pound, metre and kilogram.

The international yard = 0·9144 metre (and so defined under the Weights and Measures Act 1963).

The international pound = 0·45359237 kilogram.

*Note.*—The Government announced in 1965 that it was encouraging the adoption of the metric system of weights and measures and by 1975 the greater part of British industry should have effected the change.

## 2. METRIC WEIGHTS AND MEASURES.

### LINEAR MEASURE.

| | |
|---|---|
| 10 millimetres (mm.) | 1 centimetre (cm.) |
| 10 centimetres | 1 decimetre (dm.) |
| 10 decimetres | 1 METRE (m.) |
| 10 metres | 1 dekametre (dam.) |
| 10 dekametres | 1 hectometre (hm.) |
| 10 hectometres | 1 kilometre (km.) |

### SURFACE OR SQUARE MEASURE.

| | |
|---|---|
| 100 centiares | 1 are = 100 sq. metres |
| 100 ares | 1 hectare = 10,000 sq. metres |

### CAPACITY.

| | |
|---|---|
| 10 millilitres (ml.) | 1 centilitre (cl.) = 10 c.c. |
| 10 centilitres | 1 decilitre (dl.) = 100 c.c. |

### CAPACITY (*cont.*).

| | |
|---|---|
| 10 decilitres | 1 LITRE (lit.) = 1000 c.c. |
| 10 litres | 1 dekalitre (dal.) |
| 10 dekalitres | 1 hectolitre (hl.) |
| 10 hectolitres | 1 kilolitre (kl.) = 1 cu. metre |

### WEIGHT.

| | |
|---|---|
| 1000 micrograms | 1 milligram (mg.) |
| 10 milligrams | 1 centigram (cg.) |
| 10 centigrams | 1 decigram (dg.) |
| 10 decigrams | 1 GRAM (gm.) |
| 10 grams | 1 dekagram (dag.) |
| 10 dekagrams | 1 hectogram (hg.) |
| 10 hectograms | 1 kilogram (kg.) |
| The metric carat | 0·2 gram |

## 3. IMPERIAL AND METRIC EQUIVALENTS.

### LINEAR MEASURE.

| IMPERIAL TO METRIC | |
|---|---|
| 1 inch | 2·54 centimetres |
| 1 foot | 30·48 centimetres |
| 1 yard | 0·9144 metre |
| 1 chain (22 yards) | 20·1168 metres |
| 1 furlong (220 yards) | 201·168 metres |
| 1 mile (8 furlongs) | 1·6093 kilometres |

*Note.*—The physical metre, the platinum–iridium bar kept at Sèvres, was rendered obsolete when in 1960 the metre was re-defined in terms of a wavelength of light.

| METRIC TO IMPERIAL | |
|---|---|
| 1 millimetre | 0·039 37 inch |
| 1 centimetre | 0·3937 inch |
| 1 decimetre | 3·937 inches |
| 1 metre | 39·370 078 740 16 inches |
| 1 metre | 3·280 839 895 feet |
| 1 metre | 1·093 613 198 yards |
| 1 dekametre | 10·936 yards |
| 1 hectometre | 109·36 yards |
| 1 kilometre | 0·621 37 mile |

## SQUARE MEASURE

| IMPERIAL TO METRIC. | | METRIC TO IMPERIAL. | |
|---|---|---|---|
| 1 sq. inch | 6·4516 sq. cm. | 1 sq. cm. | 0·15500 sq. inch |
| 1 sq. foot | 9·2903 sq. decimetres | 1 sq. metre | 10·7639 sq. feet |
| 1 sq. yard | 0·836127 sq. metre | 1 sq. metre | 1·1960 sq. yards |
| 1 rood (1210 sq. yd.) | 10·117 ares | 1 are (100 sq. metres) | 119·60 sq. yards |
| 1 acre (4840 sq. yd.) | 0·40468 hectare | 1 hectare (100 ares or | |
| 1 sq. mile (640 acres) | 258·999 hectares | 10,000 sq. metres) | 2·4711 acres |

## CUBIC MEASURE

| IMPERIAL TO METRIC. | | METRIC TO IMPERIAL. | |
|---|---|---|---|
| 1 cu. inch | 16·387 cu. cm. | 1 cu. centimetre | 0·0610 cu. inch |
| 1 cu. foot (1728 cu. in.) | 0·028317 cu. metre | 1 cu. decimetre (1000 | |
| 1 cu. yard (27 cu. ft.) | 0·764553 cu. metre | cu. cm.) | 61·024 cu. inches |
| | | 1 cu. metre | 35·3148 cu. feet |
| | | 1 cu. metre | 1·307954 cu. yards |

## CAPACITY MEASURE

| IMPERIAL TO METRIC. | | METRIC TO IMPERIAL. | |
|---|---|---|---|
| 1 gill | 1·42 decilitres | 1 centilitre | 0·070 gill |
| 1 pint | 0·568 litre | 1 decilitre | 0·176 pint |
| 1 quart | 1·136 litres | 1 litre | 1·75980 pints |
| 1 gallon | 4·546 litres | 1 dekalitre | 2·200 gallons |
| 1 peck (2 gallons) | 9·092 litres | 1 hectolitre | 2·75 bushels |
| 1 bushel (8 gallons) | 3·637 dekalitres | | |
| 1 quarter (8 bushels) | 2·909 hectolitres | | |

## APOTHECARIES' MEASURE

| IMPERIAL TO METRIC. | | IMPERIAL TO METRIC. | |
|---|---|---|---|
| 1 minim | 0·059 millilitre | 1 pint | 0·568 litre |
| 1 fluid scruple | 1·184 millilitres | 1 gallon (8 pints or 160 fluid | |
| 1 fluid drachm (60 minims) | 3·552 millilitres | ounces) | 4·546 litres |
| 1 fluid ounce (8 drachms) | 2·84123 centilitres | | |

## AVOIRDUPOIS WEIGHT

| IMPERIAL TO METRIC. | | METRIC TO IMPERIAL. | |
|---|---|---|---|
| 1 grain | 0·0648 gram | 1 milligram | 0·015 grain |
| 1 dram | 1·772 grams | 1 centigram | 0·154 grain |
| 1 ounce (16 drams) | 28·350 grams | 1 decigram | 1·543 grains |
| 1 pound (16 ounces or | | 1 gram | 15·432 grains |
| 7000 grains) | 0·453592 kilogram | 1 dekagram | 5·644 drams |
| 1 stone (14 lb.) | 6·350 kilograms | 1 hectogram | 3·527 ounces |
| 1 quarter (28 lb.) | 12·70 kilograms | 1 kilogram (1000 gm.) | 2·20462 lb. |
| 1 cwt. (112 lb.) | 50·80 kilograms = | 1 myriagram (10 kg.) | 22·046 lb. |
| | 0·5080 quintal | 1 quintal (100 kg.) | 1·968 cwt. |
| 1 ton (20 cwt.) | 1·0160 tonnes or 1016 | 1 tonne (1000 kg.) | 0·9842 ton |
| | kilograms | | |

## TROY WEIGHT

| IMPERIAL TO METRIC. | | METRIC TO IMPERIAL. | |
|---|---|---|---|
| 1 grain | 0·0648 gram | 1 gram | 0·03215 ounce troy |
| 1 pennyweight (24 grains) | 1·552 grams | 1 gram | 15·432 grains |
| 1 troy ounce (20 pennyweights) | 31·1035 grams | | |

## APOTHECARIES' WEIGHT

| IMPERIAL TO METRIC. | | METRIC TO IMPERIAL. | |
|---|---|---|---|
| 1 grain | 0·0648 gram | 1 gram | 0·2572 drachm |
| 1 scruple (20 grains) | 1·296 grams | 1 gram | 0·7716 scruple |
| 1 drachm (3 scruples) | 3·888 grams | 1 gram | 15·432 grains |
| 1 ounce (8 drachms) | 31·1035 grams | | |

# SI UNITS

The system based on the following six basic units is called the International System of Units (SI). It is replacing older systems in several branches of science and technology. There are, at present, differences in metric practice between the various metric countries but SI units will become, in time, the only acceptable international system.

| | SI Unit | Symbol |
|---|---|---|
| Length | metre | m |
| Mass | kilogram | kg |
| Time | second | s |
| Electric current | ampere | A |
| Thermodynamic temperature | degree Kelvin | K |
| Luminous intensity | candela | cd |

Some Derived SI Units.

| | SI Unit | Symbol |
|---|---|---|
| Force | newton | $N = kg\ m/s^2$ |
| Work, energy, quantity of heat | joule | $J = N\ m$ |
| Power | watt | $W = J/s$ |
| Electric charge | coulomb | $C = A\ s$ |
| Electrical potential | volt | $V = W/A$ |
| Electric capacitance | farad | $F = A\ s/V$ |
| Electric resistance | ohm | $\Omega = V/A$ |
| Magnetic flux | weber | $Wb = V\ s$ |
| Inductance | henry | $H = V\ s/A$ |
| Luminous flux | lumen | $lm = cd\ sr$ |
| Illumination | lux | $lx = lm/m^2$ |

Some Derived SI Units (cont.)

| | SI Unit | Symbol |
|---|---|---|
| Frequency . . | cycle per second | c/s |
| Angular velocity | radian per second | rad/s |
| Pressure . . | newton per sq. metre | N/m² |
| Surface tension. | newton per metre | N/m |
| Thermal con- | watt per metre | |
| ductivity . | degree Kelvin | W/(m°K) |
| Electric field | | |
| strength . . | volt per metre | V/m |
| Magnetic flux | | |
| density . . | weber per sq. metre | Wb/m² |
| Magnetic field | | |
| strength . . | ampere per metre | A/m |
| Luminance . . | candela per sq. metre | cd/m² |

*Note.*—In Continental literature the frequency unit is the hertz (symbol Hz), the weber unit, the tesla (symbol T).

Prefixes for decimal multiples and sub-multiples of units are indicated thus:

| | | Multiple | Symbol |
|---|---|---|---|
| × 10¹² | . . . . | tera | T |
| × 10⁹ | . . . . | giga | G |
| × 10⁶ | . . . . | mega | M |
| × 10³ | . . . . | kilo | k |
| × 10² | . . . . | hecto | h |
| × 10 | . . . . | deca | da |
| | | *Sub-multiple* | |
| × 10⁻¹ | . . . . | deci | d |
| × 10⁻² | . . . . | centi | c |
| × 10⁻³ | . . . . | milli | m |
| × 10⁻⁶ | . . . . | micro | μ |
| × 10⁻⁹ | . . . . | nano | n |
| × 10⁻¹² | . . . . | pico | p |
| × 10⁻¹⁵ | . . . . | femto | f |
| × 10⁻¹⁸ | . . . . | atto | a |

*Note.*—The prefixes carry no hyphen, *e.g.*, megaelectronvolt.

# CONVERSION FACTORS FOR SI AND UK UNITS

| | Dimension | SI Unit (symbol) | UK Unit (symbol) | Ratio (UK unit/SI unit) |
|---|---|---|---|---|
| Length . . . . . . . | L | m | in | 0·0254 |
| | | | ft | 0·3048 |
| | | | yd | 0·9144 |
| | | | mile | 1609·344 |
| Velocity . . . . . | LT⁻¹ | m/s | ft/s | 0·3048 |
| | | | mile/h | 0·447 04 |
| Mass . . . . . . | M | kg | lb | 0·453 592 37 |
| Density. . . . . . | ML⁻³ | kg/m³ | lb/in³ | 2·767 99 × 10⁴ |
| | | | lb/ft³ | 16·0185 |
| Force . . . . . . | MLT⁻² | N | lb/Ukgal | 99·7764 |
| | | | pdl | 0·138 255 |
| | | | lbf | 4·448 22 |
| Pressure . . . . . | ML⁻¹T⁻² | N/m² | lbf/in² | 6894·76 |
| Energy (work, heat) . . . | ML²T⁻² | J | ft pdl | 0·042 140 1 |
| | | | ft lbf | 1·355 82 |
| | | | cal | 4·1868 |
| | | | Btu | 1055·06 |
| Power . . . . . . | ML²T⁻³ | W | hp | 745·700 |

*Note.*—Figures printed in bold type are exact. Unit symbols are the same in the singular and the plural and do not carry a full point (as a mark of an abbreviation). The symbol for the poundal is pdl and for the pound-force lbf. N = 10⁵ dynes, J = 10⁷ ergs (in c.g.s. system).

# INTERNATIONAL PAPER SIZES

Trimmed or finished sizes

"A" Series

(Books and Magazines)

| Designation | Size | |
|---|---|---|
| | mm | in |
| A0 | 841 × 1189 | 33·11 × 46·81 |
| A1 | 594 × 841 | 23·39 × 33·11 |
| A2 | 420 × 594 | 16·54 × 23·39 |
| A3 | 297 × 420 | 11·69 × 16·54 |
| A4 | 210 × 297 | 8·27 × 11·69 |
| A5 | 148 × 210 | 5·83 × 8·27 |
| A6 | 105 × 148 | 4·13 × 5·83 |
| A7 | 74 × 105 | 2·91 × 4·13 |
| A8 | 52 × 74 | 2·05 × 2·91 |
| A9 | 37 × 52 | 1·46 × 2·05 |
| A10 | 26 × 37 | 1·02 × 1·46 |

*Note.*—The basis of the international series of paper sizes is a rectangle having an area of 1 sq. metre, the sides of which are in the proportion of 1 : √2 (a geometrical relationship, the side and diagonal of a square being in that proportion). In addition there is a series of "B" sizes intermediate between any two adjacent sizes of the "A" series (for posters, etc.) and of "C" sizes (for envelopes).

# SIZES OF BOUND BOOKS

| Name | Size of untrimmed page | |
|---|---|---|
| | in | mm |
| Foolscap octavo . | 6⅝ × 4¼ | 170 × 110 |
| Crown octavo . . | 7½ × 5 | 190 × 125 |
| Large crown octavo | 8 × 5¼ | 205 × 135 |
| Small demy octavo. | 8½ × 5⅝ | 215 × 145 |
| Demy octavo . . | 8¾ × 5⅝ | 220 × 145 |
| Medium octavo . . | 9 × 5¾ | 230 × 145 |
| Small royal octavo. | 9¼ × 6¼ | 235 × 155 |
| Royal octavo . . | 10 × 6¼ | 255 × 160 |

*Note.*—The standard for paperbacks is a trimmed page size of 7⅛ in × 4¾ in (180 mm × 110 mm).

# HOW TO CORRECT PRINTERS' PROOFS

| Marginal mark | Meaning | Corresponding mark in text |
|---|---|---|
| ƌ̵ | Delete (take out) | Cross through |
| ƌ̲ | Delete and close-up | ⟋ Above and below letters to be taken out |
| *stet* | Leave as printed (when words have been crossed out by mistake) | . . . . Under letters or words to remain |
| *caps* | Change to capital letters | ≡ Under letters or words to be altered |
| *s.c.* | Change to small capitals | ≡ Under letters or words to be altered |
| *caps & s.c.* | Use capital letters for initial letters and small capitals for rest of words | ≡ Under initial letters and ═ under the rest of the words |
| *l.c.* | Change from capitals to lower case | Encircle letters to be altered |
| *bold* | Change to bold type | ∿ Under letters or words to be altered |
| *ital.* | Change to italics | ── Under letters or words to be altered |
| *rom.* | Change to roman type | Encircle words to be altered |
| *w.f.* | (Wrong fount.) Replace by letter of correct fount | Encircle letter to be altered |
| ∽ | Invert type | Encircle letter to be altered |
| × | Replace by similar but undamaged character | Encircle letter to be altered |
| ⅄ | Insert (or substitute) superior figure or sign | ⋏ (Or encircle letters or signs to be altered) |
| ⅄ | Insert (or substitute) inferior figure or sign | ⋏ (Or encircle letters or signs to be altered) |
| ⌒ | Close-up—delete space between letters | ⌒ Linking words or letters |
| # | Insert space | ⋏ |
| *eq.#* | Make spacing equal | ⌐ Between words |
| *less#* | Reduce space | ⌐ Between words |
| *trs.* | Transpose | ⌐⌐ Between letters or words, numbered when necessary |
| *centre* | Place in centre of line | Indicate position with ⌐ ⌐ |
| ⌐ | Move to the left | ⊐⌐ |
| ⌐ | Move to the right | ⊏⌐ |
| *n.p.* | Begin a new paragraph | ⌐ Before first word of new paragraph |
| *run on* | No fresh paragraph here | ⟶ Between paragraphs |
| *spell out* | The abbreviation or figure to be spelt out in full | Encircle words or figures to be altered |
| ⋏ | (Caret mark.) Insert matter indicated in margin | ⋏ |
| ⅋⅋ | Insert single quotation marks | ⋏ ⋏ |
| ⅋⅋ | Insert double quotation marks | ⋏ ⋏ |

# THE LONDON

| Letter | Year | Letter | Year | Letter | Year | Letter | Year | Letter | Year | Letter | Year |
|---|---|---|---|---|---|---|---|---|---|---|---|
| A | 1598 | a | 1618 | B | 1638 | a | 1658 | a | 1678 | a | 1697 |
| B | 9 | b | 19 | b | 39 | B | 59 | b | 79 | b | 97 |
| C | 1600 | C | 20 | C | 40 | C | Chas. II. 60 | C | 80 | c | 98 |
| D | 1 | d | 21 | D | 41 | D | 61 | D | 81 | d | 99 |
| E | 2 | e | 22 | E | 42 | E | 62 | E | 82 | e | 1700 |
| F | Jas. I. 3 | f | 23 | F | 43 | F | 63 | F | 83 | ff | 1 |
| G | 4 | g | 24 | G | 44 | G | 64 | g | 84 | g | Anne. 2 |
| h | 5 | h | Chas. I. 25 | K | 45 | H | 65 | h | Jas. II. 85 | h | 3 |
| I | 6 | i | 26 | J | 46 | I | 66 | I | 86 | i | 4 |
| K | 7 | k | 27 | B | 47 | R | 67 | k | 87 | k | 5 |
| L | 8 | l | 28 | E | 48 | L | 68 | l | 88 | l | 6 |
| m | 9 | m | 29 | S | Cmwth. 49 | M | 69 | m | W. & M. 89 | m | 7 |
| n | 10 | n | 30 | N | 50 | N | 70 | n | 90 | n | 8 |
| O | 11 | O | 31 | O | 51 | O | 71 | O | 91 | o | 9 |
| P | 12 | P | 32 | P | 52 | P | 72 | p | 92 | p | 10 |
| Q | 13 | q | 33 | q | 53 | Q | 73 | q | 93 | q | 11 |
| R | 14 | r | 34 | C | 54 | R | 74 | r | 94 | r | 12 |
| S | 15 | s | 35 | S | 55 | S | 75 | s | Wm III. 95 | s | 13 |
| T | 16 | t | 36 | t | 56 | Z | 76 | t | 96 | t | Geo. I. 14 |
| V | 17 | V | 37 | B | 57 | U | 77 | | | V | 15 |

## PROVINCIAL SILVER MARKS

| City | | Year | Marks | Year | Marks |
|---|---|---|---|---|---|
| BIRMINGHAM | . . | 1800 | | 1900 | |
| CHESTER | . . | 1701 | | 1800 | |
| EXETER | . . | 1601 | | 1800 | |

*See also* Hall-mark, Gen. Information.

# SILVER MARKS

| Col 1 | | Col 2 | | Col 3 | | Col 4 | | Col 5 | | Col 6 | |
|---|---|---|---|---|---|---|---|---|---|---|---|
| A | Geo. I. 1716 | a | 1736 | A | 1756 | a | 1776 | A | 1796 | a | 1816 |
| B | 17 | b | 37 | B | 57 | b | 77 | B | 97 | b | 17 |
| C | 18 | C | 38 | C | 58 | c | 78 | C | 98 | c | 18 |
| D | 19 | dd | 39 | D | 59 | d | 79 | D | 99 | d | 19 |
| E | 20 | e | 40 | E | Geo.III 60 | e | 80 | E | 1800 | e | Geo. IV. 20 |
| F | 21 | f | 41 | f | 61 | f | 81 | F | 1 | f | 21 |
| G | 22 | g | 42 | G | 62 | g | 82 | G | 2 | g | 22 |
| H | 23 | h | 43 | H | 63 | h | 83 | H | 3 | h | 23 |
| I | 24 | i | 44 | I | 64 | i | 84 | I | 4 | i | 24 |
| K | 25 | k | 45 | K | 65 | k | 85 | K | 5 | k | 25 |
| L | 26 | l | 46 | L | 66 | l | 86 | L | 6 | l | 26 |
| M | Geo. II. 27 | m | 47 | M | 67 | m | 87 | M | 7 | m | 27 |
| N | 28 | n | 48 | N | 68 | n | 88 | N | 8 | n | 28 |
| O | 29 | o | 49 | O | 69 | o | 89 | O | 9 | o | 29 |
| P | 30 | p | 50 | P | 70 | p | 90 | P | 10 | p | Will.IV. 30 |
| Q | 31 | q | 51 | Q | 71 | q | 91 | Q | 11 | q | 31 |
| R | 32 | r | 52 | R | 72 | r | 92 | R | 12 | r | 32 |
| S | 33 | s | 53 | S | 73 | s | 93 | S | 13 | s | 33 |
| T | 34 | t | 54 | T | 74 | t | 94 | T | 14 | t | 34 |
| V | 35 | u | 55 | U | 75 | u | 95 | U | 15 | u | 35 |

## PROVINCIAL SILVER MARKS

| | | | |
|---|---|---|---|
| NEWCASTLE | 1702 | | 1800 |
| SHEFFIELD | 1800 | | 1900 |
| YORK     . | 1700 | | 1800 |

# THE LONDON SILVER MARKS

| | | | | | | | | | | | |
|---|---|---|---|---|---|---|---|---|---|---|---|
| A | 1836 | R | 1856 | A | 1876 | a | 1896 | a | 1916 | A | Ed. VIII. 1936 |
| B | Vic. 37 | b | 57 | B | 77 | b | 97 | b | 17 | B | Geo. VI 37 |
| C | 38 | c | 58 | C | 78 | c | 98 | c | 18 | C | 38 |
| D | 39 | d | 59 | D | 79 | d | 99 | d | 19 | D | 39 |
| E | 40 | e | 60 | E | 80 | e | 1900 | e | 20 | E | 40 |
| F | 41 | f | 61 | F | 81 | f | Ed. VII. 1 | f | 21 | F | 41 |
| G | 42 | g | 62 | G | 82 | g | 2 | g | 22 | G | 42 |
| H | 43 | h | 63 | H | 83 | h | 3 | h | 23 | H | 43 |
| J | 44 | i | 64 | I | 84 | i | 4 | i | 24 | I | 44 |
| K | 45 | k | 65 | K | 85 | k | 5 | k | 25 | K | 45 |
| L | 46 | l | 66 | L | 86 | l | 6 | l | 26 | L | 46 |
| M | 47 | m | 67 | M | 87 | m | 7 | m | 27 | M | 47 |
| N | 48 | n | 68 | N | 88 | n | 8 | n | 28 | N | 48 |
| O | 49 | o | 69 | O | 89 | o | 9 | o | 29 | O | 49 |
| P | 50 | p | 70 | P | 90 | p | Geo. V. 10 | p | 30 | P | 50 |
| Q | 51 | q | 71 | Q | 91 | q | 11 | q | 31 | Q | 51 |
| R | 52 | r | 72 | R | 92 | r | 12 | r | 32 | R | Eliz. II. 52 |
| S | 53 | s | 73 | S | 93 | s | 13 | s | 33 | S | 53 |
| T | 54 | t | 74 | T | 94 | t | 14 | t | 34 | T | 54 |
| U | 55 | v | 75 | U | 95 | u | 15 | u | 35 | U | 55 |

# SCOTTISH AND IRISH SILVER MARKS

| | | | | | | |
|---|---|---|---|---|---|---|
| EDINBURGH | . . | 1700 | | 1800 | |
| GLASGOW | . . | 1700 | | 1800 | |
| DUBLIN | . . | 1700 | | 1800 | |

# MARKS ON ENGLISH POTTERY AND PORCELAIN

Many of the marks found on ceramics are merely the marks of painters and workman. Even when identified, they are not a sure guide to the place of manufacture, as these people would work in many different factories in the course of their careers. The throwers or "repairers" (the workers who assembled the various parts of figures, etc.) invariably used a mark scratched in the body of the ware prior to the biscuit-firing. These marks when *under* the glaze can safely be treated as genuine. A mark which has been ground in after firing, in order to deceive, will not have the characteristic burr or raised edge produced when soft clay is scratched.

Painters and gilders would generally use one of the colours in their palette or gilt to mark the wares upon which they worked. This was probably for the benefit of the management as payment was often on a piecework basis.

The marks used on English wares were applied in several different ways—by incising, impressing, painting, or by transfer-printing *under* the glaze in blue (also in green after 1850). Marking by painting, transfer-printing, or stencilling over the glaze in enamel colours is always liable to be fraudulent as these types of mark can be added at any time after the piece has been made.

From 1842–83 many manufacturers' wares were marked with the " diamond-mark ", illustrated above. This was an indication that the design had been registered with the British Patent Office. Ceramics was Class IV, indicated in the topmost section of the mark. This gave copyright protection for three years. After 1883 the mark was written as a number, e.g., Rd. No. 12345.

A further indication of late wares is the inclusion of the word " England " in the mark. This was necessary to comply with the American McKinley Tariff Act of 1891. The full term " Made in England " is an indication of 20th century manufacture.

# MARKS ON CONTINENTAL POTTERY AND PORCELAIN

## FRANCE

### Saint-Cloud
c.1678 ~ 1766

early incised mark

St.C
T
c.1722-66
in blue

### Chantilly
1725 ~ 1800

'hunting-horn' mark

red on early wares

blue & other colours from c.1750

### Mennecy
1734-1806

'D.V' mark for duc de Villeroy

·D·V· in red

in black D·V

D.V. incised.

### Sceaux
c.1763 ~ 94

S·X incised

c.1775 ~

### Lille 1784-1817

stencilled in red

## Sèvres
First established at Vincennes c.1738, moved to Sèvres c.1756 ~

early Vincennes marks

mark with date-letter for 1753

letters were used from 1753 until 17th July 1793 to show year of manufacture

| | | | |
|---|---|---|---|
| A ~ 1753 | | V ~ 1774 | |
| B ~ 1754 | | X ~ 1775 | |
| C ~ 1755 | | Y ~ 1776 | |
| D ~ 1756 | | Z ~ 1777 | |
| E ~ 1757 | | AA ~ 1778 | |
| F ~ 1758 | | BB ~ 1779 | |
| G ~ 1759 | | CC ~ 1780 | |
| H ~ 1760 | | DD ~ 1781 | |
| I ~ 1761 | | EE ~ 1782 | |
| J ~ 1762 | | FF ~ 1783 | |
| K ~ 1763 | | GG ~ 1784 | |
| L ~ 1764 | | HH ~ 1785 | |
| M ~ 1765 | | II ~ 1786 | |
| N ~ 1766 | | JJ ~ 1787 | |
| O ~ 1767 | | KK ~ 1788 | |
| P ~ 1768 | | LL ~ 1789 | |
| Q ~ 1769 | | MM ~ 1790 | |
| R ~ 1770 | | NN ~ 1791 | |
| S ~ 1771 | | OO ~ 1792 | |
| T ~ 1772 | | PP ~ 1793 | |
| U ~ 1773 | | (until 17th July) | |

in blue
1793-1804

jévres

M.N.le in red

Sèvres 1803
—11—    1804
Consular period

## Paris factories

### rue Thiroux
c.1775 ~ 19th. Cent.

blue    red

red

LEVEILLE
Rue THIROUX

### rue de Crussol
1789 ~ 19th.Cent.
Christopher Potter

B
Potter
4-2
EB    PB
all in blue

### rue de Charonne
1795 ~ c.1840

DARTE    in
FRERES    red
A PARIS

### rue de Bondy

1780-1829
gold

### Pont-aux-Choux
1743 ~ c.1785
gold

### La Courtille 1771 ~ c.1840

in blue

incised.

### Clignacourt
1771 ~ c.1798

in gold

stencilled in red.

marks on reproductions made by:-

### Samson & Co.
1845 ~

on so-called ('Chinese-Lowestoft')

Japanese and Chinese wares

Persian and Hispano-Moresque.

Limousin enamels, Italian wares

Sèvres and terra-cotta.

Meissen

French, Italian, Spanish, English porcelain, European enamels

---

It was not until the adoption on Meissen porcelain in 1723 of the "K.P.M." and in 1724 of the cross-swords (from the arms of Saxony) that marks began to be used at all regularly in Europe. The placing of the mark underneath and the use of blue are clear indications that the Chinese model was being followed. The Meissen practice was then adopted by other German and, indeed, by most porcelain factories of repute.

Throughout the 18th century the practice was never regularised, and except for a brief period in France from 1766, and two years later in the Dutch town of Delft, there was no compulsory marking of wares. The factories of repute, proud of their productions, added a recognised mark and even used it, as at Nymphenburg, as part of the decoration. Their imitators left their wares unmarked or employed a mark likely to be mistaken for a more famous one: Weesp and Tournay both adopted a version of the Meissen crossed-swords;

## MARKS ON CONTINENTAL POTTERY AND PORCELAIN

### GERMANY
#### Meissen 1710~

**K. P. M**

'Königliche Porzellan Manufaktur' 1723–24.

'caduceus-mark' c. 1723

blue

cipher (for 'Augustus Rex') of King of Poland, generally 1725–1730. Common on forgeries

c. 1724~

'Dot period' c. 1763–1774

'Marcolini Period' 1774–1814

19th Cent all in blue

#### Vienna 1719–1864

Du Paquier period (1719–1744)

in blue c. 1720–30

State period (1744–1784)

---

red and other colours

impressed

blue

#### Sorgenthal period (1784–1864)

blue, 1820–27

blue, c. 1850–64

#### Höchst c. 1750–96

1750–c. 1765 red

1762–96 blue

c. 1765–1774 blue

#### Fürstenberg 1753~ present

all in blue

#### Frankenthal 1755–99

**PH**

**PHF** impressed marks of Paul Hannong. c. 1755–c. 59.

in blue c. 1756.

---

c. 1756–59 in blue

#### Nymphenburg 1753~ present

impressed 1754–65

impressed c. 1850–62

1763~67 'hexagram mark'

#### Ludwigsburg 1756–1824

in blue 1758–93

in blue c. 1775–1810

marks of factories in imitation of Meissen

Freiwaldau H. Schmidt 1842~

Gräfenroda Dornheim, Koch & Fischer 1860~

**DKF**

Kloster-Veilsdorf modern mark

Limbach 1772–88

Plaue-on-Havel Schierholz 1817~

---

### ITALY Florence
Medici porcelain 1575–87

in blue.

#### Venice
Vezzi factory c. 1719–1727

incised

red green or blue

Cozzi factory c. 1764–1812

in red.

#### Capodimonte 1743–59

impressed

gold    blue

similar marks on Buen Retiro of Spain 1760–1808

#### Naples 1771–1806
in blue

1772

in blue or incised

#### Doccia, 1735~

in blue    impressed

---

the torches of La Courtille, the hooks of Rauenstein, the hayforks of Rudolstadt, the "L"'s of Limbach, and the "W" of Wallendorf, were all drawn in such a way as to resemble the Meissen mark.

The firm of Samson & Co. was established in Paris in 1845, claiming to make "Reproductions of Ancient Works emanating from the Museums and from Private Collections". When imitating the true hard-paste porcelain of the Far East or the Continent, Samson's wares are difficult to detect, due to their being made from similar materials, whereas his reproductions of such English factories as Bow, Chelsea, and Derby are more easily recognised as fakes. Unfortunately the range of Samson's marks, illustrated above, do not appear to have been regularly used, or, as is sometimes the case, the original mark has been removed by grinding or by etching away with acid, and a replica of a known genuine mark added.

## CHINESE REIGN MARKS    MING DYNASTY

年洪
製武

Hung Wu
(1368~1398)

建文

Chien Wên
(1399~1402)

Yung Lo
(1403~1424)
In archaic script

年永
製樂

Yung Lo
(1403~1424)

洪 熙
Hung Hsi ( 1425)

德 大
年 明
製 宣

Hsüan Tê
(1426-1435)

In seal
characters

正統
Chêng T'ung
(1436~1449)

景泰
Ching T'ai
(1450~1457)

天順
T'ien Shun
(1457~1464)

化 大
年 明
製 成

Chêng Hua
(1465~1487)

In seal
characters

治 大
年 明
製 弘

Hung Chih
(1488~1505)

德 大
年 明
製 正

Chêng Tê
(1506~1521)

靖 大
年 明
製 嘉

Chia Ching
(1522~1566)

慶 大
年 明
製 隆

Lung Ch'ing
(1567~1572)

曆 大
年 明
製 萬

Wan Li
(1573~1619)

泰昌
T'ai Ch'ang (1620)

啟 大
年 明
製 天

T'ien Ch'i
(1621~1627)

年 崇
製 禎

Ch'ung Chêng
(1628~1643)

Factory marks in the Western sense are practically unknown on Chinese porcelain wares, while those purporting to record the period of manufacture are so liable to be " commemorative ", or even deliberately fraudulent, as to be a frequent cause of dispute among students. Marks of the Ming Chinese Emperors, Hsüan Tê, Ch'êng Hua and Chia Ching are commonly found on wares of the reign of the Ch'ing Emperor K'ang Hsi, while the reign name of K'ang Hsi himself, rare on the abundant porcelain of his period, is chiefly found on 19th- and 20th-century wares.

Under the rule of the Ming Emperors (1368–1644) the Sung ideals in pottery were largely rejected in favour of the vogue for fine-grained white porcelain heralding the beginning of a new period in Chinese ceramic history with its centre in the town of Ching-tê Chên in Kiangsi province where a new Imperial factory was started in 1369 with a prolific output of early Ming blue-and-white

# CHINESE REIGN MARKS    CH'ING DYNASTY

Shun Chih (1644~1661)

In seal characters

In seal characters

Ch'ien Lung (1736-1795)

K'ang Hsi (1662-1722)

In seal characters

Chia Ch'ing (1796~1821)

Yung Chêng (1723~1735)

In seal characters

Tao Kuang (1821~1850)

In seal characters

Hsien Fêng (1851~1861)

In seal characters

T'ung Chih (1862~1873)

In seal characters

Kuang Hsü (1874~1908)

In seal characters

Hsüan T'ung (1909~1912)

Hung Hsien (1916) (Yüan Shih-kai)

*Drawn by J. P. Cushion, Victoria and Albert Museum.*

and fine enamel-painted porcelain both for the court and later for general use and export.

Following the fall of the Ming Dynasty in 1644 their declining culture was revived by the Ch'ing Emperor K'ang Hsi (1662—1722) who was a great patron of the arts. The European influence of the French and Netherlandish Jesuits at his courts is seen in the Baroque character of the early Ch'ing porcelain.

There was a backward-looking tendency during the reigns of Yung-Chêng (1723–35) and Ch'ien Lung (1736–95) when exact copies of the classical Sung wares and the early Ming painted porcelain were made.

The Imperial porcelain of the 19th century was as a rule carefully and weakly correct in following earlier styles and models. The factory was burnt in 1853 by the T'ai-ping rebels and hardly recovered before the 1911 revolution ended the Dynasty.

# BANK AND PUBLIC HOLIDAYS

In addition to Good Friday and Christmas Day, there are Bank holidays in most parts of England, Wales and the Channel Islands on Easter Monday, in late Spring and late Summer (see below), and on the first weekday after Christmas (Boxing Day). The Channel Islands also observe New Year's Day and Liberation Day, May 9. Scotland observes New Year's Day, Good Friday, a late Spring and a late Summer holiday (see below) and Christmas Day. In addition most towns in

Scotland have locally determined holidays in the Spring and Autumn. Northern Ireland observes all the English holidays and, in addition, has a holiday on St. Patrick's Day, 17 March, and on 12 July, commemorating the Battle of the Boyne (1690). Easter Tuesday is also a customary holiday for industry and trade.

The Queen's birthday (when decreed) is observed in the Customs and certain other Government establishments as a holiday.

| 1969 | Easter Monday | Apr. 7 | *Late Spring | May 26 | *Late Summer | Sept. 1 |
| 1970 | " | Mar. 30 | " | May 25 | " | Aug. 31 |
| 1971 | " | Apr. 12 | " | May 31 | " | Aug. 30 |

*Note.—In Scotland: May 26; Aug. 4 (1969)   May 25; Aug. 3 (1970)   May 3; Aug. 2 (1971)

## THE SEASONS

| | 1970 | 1971 |
|---|---|---|
| Vernal Equinox—Spring begins | Mar. 21, 1.57 a.m. | Mar. 21, 7.38 a.m. |
| Summer Solstice—Summer begins | June 21, 8.43 p.m. | June 22, 2.20 a.m. |
| Autumnal Equinox—Autumn begins | Sept. 23, 11.59 a.m. | Sept. 23, 5.45 p.m. |
| Winter Solstice—Winter begins | Dec. 22, 7.36 a.m. | Dec. 22, 1.24 p.m. |

(These times are in B.S.T.)

## QUARTER DAYS

### ENGLAND, WALES, AND N. IRELAND.

| Lady Day | March 25 | Michaelmas | September 29 |
| Midsummer | June 24 | Christmas | December 25 |

### SCOTLAND.

| Candlemas | February 2 | Lammas | August 1 |
| Whitsun | May 15 | Martinmas | November 11 |

## HALF QUARTER DAYS

### ENGLAND

| February 8. | May 9. | August 11. | November 11. |

## GAME

Game is defined under the game laws as including hares, pheasants, partridges, grouse, heath or moor game, black game, deer, rabbits and (in Scotland) ptarmigan. The close times for game are as follows (the dates given are inclusive).

Black (or Heath) Game   Dec. 11 to Aug. 19 (Aug. 31 in Somerset, Devon, and New Forest).

Grouse (or Moor Game) and (in Scotland) Ptarmigan . . . Dec. 11 to Aug. 11.
Partridge . . . . Feb. 2 to Aug. 31.
Pheasant . . . . Feb. 2 to Sept. 30.

Deer, hares and rabbits are also protected to a limited extent.

CLOSE TIMES FOR SPORTING BIRDS

Birds for which the close season is Feb. 1 to Aug. 31 (inclusive) :—

| Godwit, bar-tailed | Plover, grey | Coot | Redshank, common |

Curlew (other than stone curlew)   Moorhen   Whimbrel   Plover, golden

Birds for which the close season is Feb. 1 to Aug. 31 (inclusive) (except below high water mark when it is Feb. 21 to Aug. 31 (inclusive) :

Wild duck of the following species :—

| Common pochard | Long-tailed duck | Teal |
| Common scoter | Mallard | Tufted duck |
| Gadwall | Pintail | Velvet |
| Garganey teal | Scaup-duck | scoter |
| Goldeneye | Shoveler | Wigeon |

Wild geese of the following species :—

| Bean-goose | Grey lag goose | White-fronted |
| Canada goose | Pink-footed goose | goose |

Birds for which the close season is Sept. 30 (inclusive) :—

Capercaillie   Woodcock (in Scotland Feb. 1 to Aug. 31).

Birds for which the close season is Feb. 1 to Aug. 11 (inclusive) :—

Snipe, common   Snipe, jack.

## THE COUNTRY CODE

**GUARD AGAINST THE RISK OF FIRE.** Great damage is done every year to crops, plantations, woodlands, and heaths. A match or cigarette thrown away or a pipe carelessly knocked out, picnic fires not properly put out or lighted near dry crops, can quickly start a blaze.

**FASTEN ALL GATES.** If animals get out of a field they stray. As a result they may do serious damage to crops, suffer injury on the roads, or eat food that is harmful.

**KEEP DOGS UNDER CONTROL.** Animals are easily frightened, even by small, playful dogs. Stillbirths may be the result.

**KEEP TO THE PATHS ACROSS FARM LAND.** Crops are damaged by treading; flattened crops are difficult to harvest. Grass is a valuable crop.

**AVOID DAMAGING FENCES, HEDGES, AND WALLS.** If these are damaged, gaps will be caused. Where a man goes, an animal may follow.

**LEAVE NO LITTER.** Litter is not just unsightly, but often a danger as well. Broken glass and tins may injure animals and harm machinery.

**SAFEGUARD WATER SUPPLIES.** Countrymen often depend on wells and streams for water for themselves and for their animals.

**PROTECT WILD LIFE, PLANTS, AND TREES.** Wild animals should not be disturbed, plants uprooted, or trees treated roughly.

**GO CAREFULLY ON COUNTRY ROADS.** If there is no footpath, walkers are generally safer on the right, facing on-coming traffic. Care and patience are needed by motorists when passing farm animals.

**RESPECT THE LIFE OF THE COUNTRYSIDE.** Many of the machines and much of the business stock on which the farmer depends for his livelihood have to be kept in the open. Take care not to damage them.

# SUNRISE AND SUNSET, LONDON 1969–70

(These times are given in B.S.T. throughout.)

| Sundays, 1969 Date | Sunrise a.m. | Sunset p.m. | Sundays, 1970 Date | Sunrise a.m. | Sunset p.m. | Sundays, 1970 Date | Sunrise a.m. | Sunset p.m. |
|---|---|---|---|---|---|---|---|---|
| July 6 | 4.51 | 9.18 | January 4 | 9.05 | 5.05 | July 5 | 4.50 | 9.18 |
| 13 | 4.58 | 9.13 | 11 | 9.02 | 5.13 | 12 | 4.57 | 9.14 |
| 20 | 5.06 | 9.06 | 18 | 8.57 | 5.24 | 19 | 5.04 | 9.07 |
| 27 | 5.15 | 8.57 | 25 | 8.49 | 5.36 | 26 | 5.14 | 8.58 |
| August 3 | 5.26 | 8.45 | February 1 | 8.39 | 5.49 | August 2 | 5.24 | 8.47 |
| 10 | 5.37 | 8.33 | 8 | 8.27 | 6.02 | 9 | 5.35 | 8.35 |
| 17 | 5.48 | 8.19 | 15 | 8.15 | 6.14 | 16 | 5.46 | 8.21 |
| 24 | 5.59 | 8.05 | 22 | 8.01 | 6.27 | 23 | 5.57 | 8.07 |
| 31 | 6.10 | 7.50 | March 1 | 7.46 | 6.40 | 30 | 6.08 | 7.52 |
| September 7 | 6.21 | 7.34 | 8 | 7.31 | 6.52 | September 6 | 6.20 | 7.36 |
| 14 | 6.32 | 7.18 | 15 | 7.15 | 7.04 | 13 | 6.31 | 7.20 |
| 21 | 6.43 | 7.02 | 22 | 6.59 | 7.16 | 20 | 6.42 | 7.04 |
| 28 | 6.55 | 6.46 | 29 | 6.44 | 7.27 | 27 | 6.53 | 6.48 |
| October 5 | 7.06 | 6.30 | April 5 | 6.28 | 7.39 | October 4 | 7.05 | 6.32 |
| 12 | 7.18 | 6.15 | 12 | 6.12 | 7.51 | 11 | 7.16 | 6.17 |
| 19 | 7.30 | 6.00 | 19 | 5.57 | 8.03 | 18 | 7.28 | 6.02 |
| 26 | 7.42 | 5.45 | 26 | 5.43 | 8.14 | 25 | 7.40 | 5.47 |
| November 2 | 7.54 | 5.32 | May 3 | 5.29 | 8.25 | November 1 | 7.53 | 5.34 |
| 9 | 8.06 | 5.21 | 10 | 5.17 | 8.37 | 8 | 8.05 | 5.22 |
| 16 | 8.19 | 5.10 | 17 | 5.06 | 8.48 | 15 | 8.17 | 5.12 |
| 23 | 8.31 | 5.02 | 24 | 4.57 | 8.58 | 22 | 8.29 | 5.03 |
| 30 | 8.41 | 4.55 | 31 | 4.50 | 9.06 | 29 | 8.40 | 4.56 |
| December 7 | 8.50 | 4.52 | June 7 | 4.45 | 9.13 | December 6 | 8.49 | 4.52 |
| 14 | 8.57 | 4.51 | 14 | 4.43 | 9.18 | 13 | 8.57 | 4.51 |
| 21 | 9.02 | 4.53 | 21 | 4.43 | 9.21 | 20 | 9.02 | 4.53 |
| 28 | 9.05 | 4.58 | 28 | 4.45 | 9.21 | 27 | 9.05 | 4.57 |

# MOON'S PHASES, 1969–70

(These times are given in B.S.T. thoughout.)

**1969**

| | | | |
|---|---|---|---|
| New Moon | June | 14 | 12.09 a.m. |
| First Quarter | | 23 | 2.44 a.m. |
| Full Moon | | 29 | 9.04 p.m. |
| Last Quarter | July | 6 | 2.17 p.m. |
| New Moon | | 14 | 3.11 p.m. |
| First Quarter | | 22 | 1.10 p.m. |
| Full Moon | | 29 | 3.45 a.m. |
| Last Quarter | August | 5 | 2.38 a.m. |
| New Moon | | 13 | 6.17 a.m. |
| First Quarter | | 20 | 9.03 p.m. |
| Full Moon | | 27 | 11.32 a.m. |
| Last Quarter | September | 3 | 5.58 p.m. |
| New Moon | | 11 | 8.56 p.m. |
| First Quarter | | 19 | 3.25 a.m. |
| Full Moon | | 25 | 9.21 p.m. |
| Last Quarter | October | 3 | 12.05 p.m. |
| New Moon | | 11 | 10.39 a.m. |
| First Quarter | | 18 | 9.32 a.m. |
| Full Moon | | 25 | 9.44 a.m. |
| Last Quarter | November | 2 | 8.14 a.m. |
| New Moon | | 9 | 11.11 p.m. |
| First Quarter | | 16 | 4.45 p.m. |
| Full Moon | | 23 | 12.54 a.m. |
| Last Quarter | December | 2 | 4.50 p.m. |
| New Moon | | 9 | 10.42 a.m. |
| First Quarter | | 16 | 2.09 a.m. |
| Full Moon | | 23 | 6.35 p.m. |
| Last Quarter | | 31 | 11.52 p.m. |

**1970**

| | | | |
|---|---|---|---|
| New Moon | January | 7 | 9.36 p.m. |
| First Quarter | | 14 | 2.18 p.m. |
| Full Moon | | 22 | 1.55 p.m. |
| Last Quarter | | 30 | 3.39 p.m. |
| New Moon | February | 6 | 8.13 a.m. |
| First Quarter | | 13 | 5.10 a.m. |
| Full Moon | | 21 | 9.19 a.m. |
| Last Quarter | March | 1 | 3.33 a.m. |
| New Moon | | 7 | 6.43 a.m. |

| | | | |
|---|---|---|---|
| First Quarter | | 14 | 10.16 p.m. |
| Full Moon | | 23 | 2.53 a.m. |
| Last Quarter | | 30 | 12.05 p.m. |
| New Moon | April | 6 | 5.09 a.m. |
| First Quarter | | 13 | 4.44 p.m. |
| Full Moon | | 21 | 5.21 p.m. |
| Last Quarter | | 28 | 6.18 p.m. |
| New Moon | May | 5 | 3.51 p.m. |
| First Quarter | | 13 | 11.26 a.m. |
| Full Moon | | 21 | 4.38 a.m. |
| Last Quarter | | 27 | 11.32 p.m. |
| New Moon | June | 4 | 3.21 a.m. |
| First Quarter | | 12 | 5.07 a.m. |
| Full Moon | | 19 | 1.28 p.m. |
| Last Quarter | | 26 | 5.01 a.m. |
| New Moon | July | 3 | 4.18 p.m. |
| First Quarter | | 11 | 8.43 p.m. |
| Full Moon | | 18 | 8.59 p.m. |
| Last Quarter | | 25 | 12.00 noon |
| New Moon | August | 2 | 6.58 a.m. |
| First Quarter | | 10 | 9.50 a.m. |
| Full Moon | | 17 | 4.15 a.m. |
| Last Quarter | | 23 | 9.34 p.m. |
| New Moon | | 31 | 11.01 p.m. |
| First Quarter | September | 8 | 8.38 p.m. |
| Full Moon | | 15 | 12.10 p.m. |
| Last Quarter | | 22 | 10.42 a.m. |
| New Moon | | 30 | 3.32 p.m. |
| First Quarter | October | 8 | 5.43 a.m. |
| Full Moon | | 14 | 9.21 p.m. |
| Last Quarter | | 22 | 3.47 a.m. |
| New Moon | | 30 | 7.28 a.m. |
| First Quarter | November | 6 | 1.47 p.m. |
| Full Moon | | 13 | 8.28 a.m. |
| Last Quarter | | 20 | 12.13 p.m. |
| New Moon | | 28 | 10.14 p.m. |
| First Quarter | December | 5 | 9.36 p.m. |
| Full Moon | | 12 | 10.03 p.m. |
| Last Quarter | | 20 | 10.09 p.m. |

*Reproduced, with permission, from data supplied by H.M. Nautical Almanac Office.*

Since 18 February 1968 Clocks in Britain have been set one hour fast on G.M.T.

LIGHTING-UP TIME is from half an hour after local sunset to half an hour before local sunrise throughout the year.

## FOREIGN CURRENCIES IN RELATION TO STERLING

| Country | Currency | Parity[1] value to £ at 16.1.69 | Approximate rate at 11.3.69 or latest date available |
|---|---|---|---|
| Argentina | Peso | | 834·00 |
| Australia | Dollar | 2·143 | 2·147 |
| Austria | Schilling | 62·40 | 61·87 |
| Belgium/Lux. | Franc | 120·00 | 120·05 |
| Bolivia | Peso Boliviano | | 28·50 |
| Brazil | Cruzeiro | | 9·32½ [3] |
| British Honduras | Dollar | 4·00 | 4·00 |
| Burma | Kyat | 11·429 | 11·429 |
| Canada | Dollar | 2·595 | 2·573 |
| Ceylon | Rupee | 14·286 | 14·249 |
| Chile | Escudo | | 21·95 [3][4] |
| China | Peoples Bank Dollar | | 5·909 |
| Colombia | Peso | | 40·50 [3][4] |
| Congo (Kinshasa) | Zaire | | 1·199 [2] |
| Costa Rica | Colon | 15·90 | 15·924 |
| Cuba | Peso | | 2·39 |
| Czechoslovakia | Koruna | | 17·28 [2] |
| Denmark | Krone | 18·00 | 17·953 |
| Dominican Republic | Peso | 2·40 | 2·39 |
| Ecuador | Sucre | 43·20 | 54·50 [3] |
| Egypt (U.A.R.) | Pound | 0·836 | 1·04 |
| El Salvador | Colon | 6·00 | 5·98 |
| Ethiopia | Dollar | 6·00 | 6·00 |
| Finland | Markka | 10·08 | 9·986 |
| France | Franc | 11·849 | 11·85 |
| French monetary a. terrs. in C. and W. Africa and Malagasy Republic | C.F.A. Franc | | 592·50 |
| Germany (Fed. Rep.) | D. Mark | 9·60 | 9·593 |
| Greece | Drachma | 72·00 | 71·375 |
| Guatemala | Quetzal | 2·40 | 2·39 |
| Guyana | Dollar | 4·80 | 4·80 |
| Haiti | Gourde | 12·00 | 11·95 |
| Honduras Rep. | Lempira | 4·80 | 4·78 |
| Hong Kong | Dollar | 14·545 | 14·628 |
| Iceland | Krona | 211·20 | 210·00 |
| India | Rupee | 18·00 | 18·04 |
| Indonesia | New Rupiah | | 974·4 [3][4] |
| Iran | Rial | 181·80 | 179·824 |
| Iraq | Dinar | 0·857 | 0·857 |
| Israel | Pound | 8·40 | 8·40 |
| Italy | Lire | 1,500·00 | 1,503·00 |
| Jamaica | Pound | 1·00 | 1·00 |
| Japan | Yen | 864·00 | 855·50 |
| Jordan | Dinar | 0·857 | 0·858 |
| Lebanon | Pound | 5·26 | 7·735 [3] |
| Malaysia | Dollar | 7·347 | 7·319 |
| Morocco | Dirham | 12·145 | 12·125 |
| Mexico | Peso | 30·00 | 29·99 |
| Netherlands | Guilder | 8·688 | 8·653 |
| Netherlands W.I. | Guilder | 4·526 | 4·50 |
| New Zealand | Dollar | 2·143 | 2·143 |
| Nicaragua | Cordoba | 16·80 | 16·75 [3] |
| Norway | Kroner | 17·143 | 17·065 |
| Pakistan | Rupee | 11·429 | 11·437 |
| Panama | Balboa | 2·40 | 2·39 |
| Paraguay | Guarani | | 297·50 |
| Peru | Sol | | 102·50 |
| Philippines | Peso | 9·36 | 9·363 |
| Poland | Zloty | | 9·60 [5] |
| Portugal | Escudo | 69·00 | 68·10 |
| Rwanda | Franc | 240·00 | 240·00 [2] |
| South Africa | Rand | 1·714 | 1·716 |
| Spain | Peseta | 168·00 | 166·60 |
| Sweden | Kronor | 12·416 | 12·368 |
| Switzerland | Franc | | 10·265 |
| Syria | Pound | 5·26 | 10·00 |
| Thailand | Baht | 49·92 | 49·67 |
| Trinidad and Tobago | T.T. Dollar | 4·80 | 4·80 |
| Tunisia | Dinar | 1·26 | 1·262 |
| Turkey | Pound (Lira) | 21·60 | 21·60 |
| U.S.A. | Dollar | 2·40 | 2·39 |
| Uruguay | Peso | 17·76 | 593·00 [3] |
| Venezuela | Bolivar | | 10·73 [3][4] |
| Yugoslavia | Dinar | 30·00 | 30·00 |

[1] Established under agreement with the International Monetary Fund which requires that the par value of the currency of each member be expressed in terms of gold or U.S. Dollars.
[2] Official rate.
[3] Free market rate.
[4] Not necessarily the effective rate for all transfers.
[5] Basic rate.

## THERMOMETER COMPARISONS

| Centigrade 100° | Fahrenheit 212° | Centigrade 100° | Fahrenheit 212° |
|---|---|---|---|
| 95 | 203 | 20 | 68 |
| 90 | 194 | 15·5 | 60 |
| 85 | 185 | 12·8 | 55 |
| 78·9 | 174 | 10 | 50 |
| 75 | 167 | 7·2 | 45 |
| 70 | 158 | 5 | 41 |
| 65 | 149 | 1·7 | 35 |
| 60 | 140 | 0 | 32 |
| 55 | 131 | − 1·1 | 30 |
| 52·8 | 127 | − 5 | 23 |
| 50 | 122 | − 6·7 | 20 |
| 45 | 113 | − 10 | 14 |
| 42·2 | 108 | − 12·2 | 10 |
| 40 | 104 | − 15 | 5 |
| 36·7 | 98 | − 17·8 | 0 |
| 35 | 95 | − 20 | − 4 |
| 32·2 | 90 | − 25 | − 13 |
| 30 | 86 | − 30 | − 22 |
| 26·7 | 80 | − 35 | − 31 |
| 25 | 77 | − 40 | − 40 |

To reduce Fahrenheit to Centigrade, subtract 32 degrees and multiply by 5/9; to reduce Centigrade to Fahrenheit, multiply by 9/5 and add 32 degrees.

An alternative method, perhaps easier to remember, is to add 40 to the given figure, multiply by 5/9 (°F to °C) or 9/5 (°C to °F) and subtract 40.

## ROMAN NUMERALS

| | | | |
|---|---|---|---|
| I | 1 | LXX | 70 |
| II | 2 | LXXX | 80 |
| III | 3 | LXXXVIII | 88 |
| IV | 4 | XC | 90 |
| V | 5 | XCIX | 99 |
| VI | 6 | C | 100 |
| VII | 7 | CX | 110 |
| VIII | 8 | CXI | 111 |
| IX | 9 | CXC | 190 |
| X | 10 | CC | 200 |
| XI | 11 | CCXX | 220 |
| XII | 12 | CCC | 300 |
| XIII | 13 | CCCXX | 320 |
| XIV | 14 | CD | 400 |
| XV | 15 | D | 500 |
| XVI | 16 | DC | 600 |
| XVII | 17 | DCC | 700 |
| XVIII | 18 | DCCC | 800 |
| XIX | 19 | CM | 900 |
| XX | 20 | XM | 990 |
| XXX | 30 | M | 1000 |
| XL | 40 | MD | 1500 |
| L | 50 | MDCCC | 1800 |
| LV | 55 | MCMLXX | 1970 |
| LX | 60 | MM | 2000 |

## GREEK ALPHABET

| | | | | | |
|---|---|---|---|---|---|
| A | α | Alpha | N | ν | nu |
| B | β | beta | Ξ | ξ | xi |
| Γ | γ | gamma | O | o | omicron |
| Δ | δ | delta | Π | π | pi |
| E | ε | epsilon | P | ρ | rho |
| Z | ζ | zeta | Σ | σ | sigma |
| H | η | eta | T | τ | tau |
| Θ | θ | theta | Υ | υ | upsilon |
| I | ι | iota | Φ | φ | phi |
| K | κ | kappa | X | χ | chi |
| Λ | λ | lambda | Ψ | ψ | psi |
| M | μ | mu | Ω | ω | omega |

# UNIVERSITY DEGREES—COLOURS OF HOODS

## Aberdeen

| | |
|---|---|
| M.A. | Black silk, lined with white silk. |
| M.Litt. | White silk, lined with violet silk. |
| D.Litt. | Scarlet cloth, lined with white silk. |
| Ph.D. | Scarlet cloth lined with black ribbed silk the ribs running horizontally. |
| B.Ed. | Black silk, lined with orange silk. |
| M.Ed. | White silk, lined with orange silk. |
| B.Sc. | Black silk, lined with green silk. |
| B.Sc.Agr. | Black silk, edged with green silk. |
| B.Sc.For. | Black silk, lined with waved green silk. |
| BSc.Eng. | Black silk, edged with green silk and bordered inside, within the green edging, with white cloth ($\frac{1}{4}$") |
| M.Sc. | White silk, lined with green silk. |
| D.Sc. | Scarlet cloth, lined with green silk. |
| B.D. | Black silk, lined with purple silk, and bordered inside with white silk (1"). |
| M.Th. | White silk, lined with purple silk. |
| D.D. | Scarlet cloth, lined with purple silk. |
| LL.B. | Black silk, lined with pale blue silk. |
| LL.D. | Scarlet cloth, lined with pale blue silk. |
| M.B., Ch.B. | Black silk, lined with crimson silk. |
| M.D. | Scarlet cloth, lined with crimson silk. |
| Ch.M. | White silk, lined with crimson silk. |

*Note.*—All the hoods of this University are of uniform pear shape of a cloth or silk foundation and lined or edged with the colour peculiar to the Faculty or Degree.

## Aston

| | |
|---|---|
| B.Sc. | Black, faced with 3" red silk interwoven with University crest. |
| M.Sc. | Like B.Sc. but fully lined. |
| Ph.D. | University red, faced as for B.Sc. |
| D.Sc. | Like Ph.D. but fully lined. |

## Bath

| | |
|---|---|
| B.Sc. B.Pharm. B.Arch. } | Old-gold lined olive-green taffeta. |
| | Old-gold lined olive-green taffeta with $\frac{3}{4}$" dark red edging. |
| M.Sc. M.Pharm. } | Old-gold lined pale-blue taffeta. |
| M.Arch. | Old-gold lined pale-blue taffeta with $\frac{3}{4}$" dark red edging. |
| Ph.D. | Old-gold lined medium-crimson taffeta. |
| D.Sc. | Old-gold lined scarlet taffeta. |
| LL.D. | Old-gold lined scarlet taffeta with $\frac{3}{4}$" white edging. |

## Belfast, The Queen's University

| | |
|---|---|
| B.A. | Black ribbed silk edged with white fur and the neck edged with blue watered silk. |
| M.A. | Black ribbed silk lined with blue silk and edged with blue watered silk. |
| D.Lit. | Scarlet superfine cloth lined with white silk and edged with blue watered silk. |
| B.D. | Black ribbed silk lined with white silk and edged with blue watered silk. |
| M.Th. | Red silk lined with black silk and edged with blue watered silk. |
| D.D. | Scarlet superfine cloth lined with black silk and edged with blue watered silk. |
| LL.B. | Black ribbed silk lined with pink silk and edged with blue watered silk. |
| LL.M. | Royal blue ribbed silk, lined with pink silk and edged with blue watered silk. |
| LL.D. | Scarlet superfine cloth lined with pink silk and edged with blue watered silk. |
| M.B., B.Ch., B.A.O. } | Black ribbed silk lined with scarlet silk and edged with blue watered silk. |
| M.Ch. | Red ribbed silk lined with white silk and edged with blue watered silk. |
| M.D. | Scarlet superfine cloth lined with scarlet silk and edged with blue watered silk. |
| M.A.O. | Black ribbed silk lined with purple silk and edged with blue watered silk |
| B.Ed. | Black ribbed silk lined with mauve silk and edged with blue watered silk. |
| B.Mus. | Blue silk lined with white silk and edged with blue watered silk. |
| D.Mus. | Scarlet superfine cloth lined with blue silk and edged with blue watered silk. |
| Ph.D. | Scarlet superfine cloth lined with violet silk and edged with blue watered silk. |
| B.Sc. | Black ribbed silk lined with green silk and edged with blue watered silk. |
| M.Sc. | Red ribbed silk lined with green silk and edged with blue watered silk. |
| D.Sc. | Scarlet superfine cloth lined with green silk and edged with blue watered silk. |
| B.Sc.(Econ.) | Black ribbed silk lined with rose pink silk and edged with blue watered silk. |
| M.Sc.(Econ.) | Rose pink silk lined with white silk and edged with blue watered silk. |
| B.D.S. | Black ribbed silk lined with dove-grey silk and edged with blue watered silk. |
| M.D.S. | Scarlet ribbed silk lined with dove-grey silk and edged with blue watered silk. |
| B.Agr. | Black ribbed silk lined with primrose silk and edged with blue watered silk. |
| M.Agr. | Red ribbed silk lined with primrose silk and edged with blue watered silk. |

*Note:*—Bachelors' and Masters' hoods are of the simple shape and Doctors' of the full shape. All the hoods have the neck portion at least edged with the pale blue watered silk peculiar to this University.

## Birmingham

| | |
|---|---|
| B.Sc. | Black, edged with silver-grey watered silk |
| M.Sc. | Black, lined with silver-grey watered silk |
| D.Sc. | Scarlet, lined with silver-grey watered silk |
| Ph.D. | Crimson, lined with silver-grey watered silk. |
| B.A. | Black, edged with electric-blue watered silk. |
| M.A. | Black, lined with electric-blue watered silk. |
| B.Ed. | Black, edged with primrose yellow watered silk. |
| D.Litt. | Scarlet, lined with electric-blue watered silk. |
| Ph.D. | Crimson, lined with electric-blue watered silk. |
| B.Mus. | Black, edged with tangerine watered silk. |
| M.Mus. | Black, lined with tangerine watered silk. |
| D.Mus. | Scarlet, lined with tangerine watered silk. |
| B.D. | Black, edged with cobalt-blue watered silk. |
| D.D. | Scarlet, lined with cobalt-blue watered silk. |
| M.B., Ch.B. | Black, edged with cardinal watered silk. |
| Ch.M. | Black, lined with cardinal watered silk. |
| M.D. | Scarlet, lined with cardinal watered silk. |
| Ph.D. | Crimson, lined with cardinal watered silk. |
| B.D.S. | Black, edged with dark-red (Grenat) watered silk. |
| M.D.S. | Black, lined with dark-red (Grenat) watered silk. |
| B.Com. | Black, edged with terracotta watered silk. |
| B.Soc.Sc. | Black, edged with terracotta watered silk and bound with grey silk at top edge. |
| M.Com. | Black, lined with terracotta watered silk edged with grey watered silk. |
| Ph.D. | Crimson, lined with terracotta watered silk. |
| D.Soc.Sc. | Scarlet, lined with terracotta watered silk and bound with grey silk at top edge. |
| LL.B. | Black, edged with bronze-green watered silk. |
| LL.M. | Black, lined with bronze-green watered silk. |
| Ph.D. | Crimson, lined with bronze-green watered silk. |
| LL.D. | Scarlet, lined with bronze-green watered silk. |

*Note:*—All hoods are of the full shape and all capes have well-rounded corners.

## Bradford

| | |
|---|---|
| Bachelors (B.A., B.Sc., B. Tech.) | Black, edged 3" saffron. |
| Masters | Black, edged and fully lined saffron. |
| Ph.D. | Scarlet, fully lined saffron. |
| Higher Doctorates: | |
| Technology | Scarlet, fully lined saffron, edged on inside 1$\frac{1}{2}$" violet. |
| Science | Scarlet, fully lined saffron, edged on inside 1$\frac{1}{2}$" blue. |
| Literature | Scarlet, fully lined saffron, edged on inside 1$\frac{1}{2}$" white. |

*Note:*—All hoods of this University are of the full shape.

## Bristol

| | |
|---|---|
| B.Ed. | All hoods are of the full shape, similar to Cambridge. Hoods are made of the University's special red stuff or silk. Bachelor's hoods are partly lined with a silk of a somewhat lighter shade of University red. Master' hoods are full lined with white silk, and Doctors' are fully lined with salmon-coloured silk. The M.B., Ch.B. hood is fully lined with light red silk and edged inside the hood proper with $\frac{3}{4}$" of white silk. The LL.B. hood is |
| B.A. | |
| M.A. | |
| M.Ed. | |
| M.Mus. | |
| LL.B. | |
| LL.M. | |
| LL.D. | |
| M.B., Ch.B. | |
| Ch.M. | |
| M.D. | |

| D.Mus | fully lined with the lighter shade of University red and edged with ⅞" violet silk. |
| Ph.D. | |
| B.Sc. | The Ph.D. hood is of red silk fully lined with dark violet silk. |
| M.Sc. | |
| D.Sc. | |
| M.Litt. | |
| D.Litt. | [This is an unconventional system.] |
| B.D.S. | |
| M.D.S. | |
| B.Sc.(Dom.Sc.) | |
| B.V.Sc. | |

## Brunel

| B.Sc. | Black, lined white and faced inside 1½" with Brunel blue velvet, reversed band showing blue in front. |
| M.Sc. | Brunel blue, lined silver and faced inside 2¼" with Brunel blue velvet. |
| Ph.D. | Mushroom, lined and edged Cardinal red, faced inside 3½" with Brunel blue velvet. |
| D.Sc. | Cardinal red, lined and edged gold and faced 4½" with Brunel blue velvet. |

*Note:*—Bachelors' hoods are of a special simple shape, Masters' and Doctors' of the Cambridge shape.

## Cambridge

| D.D. | Scarlet cloth lined with dove-coloured silk, that is silk of a turquoise-blue shot with rose-pink. |
| LL.D. | Scarlet cloth lined with light-cherry silk. |
| M.D. | Scarlet cloth lined with mid-cherry silk. |
| Sc.D. | Scarlet cloth lined with pink silk shot with light blue. |
| Litt.D. | Scarlet cloth lined with scarlet silk to match the cloth. |
| Mus.D. | Cream damask lined with dark-cherry satin. |
| B.D. | Black corded silk lined with black silk. |
| Ph.D. | Black corded silk lined with scarlet cloth. |
| M.Chir. | Black corded silk lined mid-cherry silk. |
| M.A. | Black corded silk lined with white silk. |
| LL.M. | Black corded silk lined light-cherry silk. |
| Mus.M. | Black corded silk lined dark-cherry satin. |
| M.Sc. | Black cloth lined pink silk shot light blue. |
| M.Litt. | Black cloth lined with scarlet silk. |
| M.B. | Mid-cherry silk part-lined with white fur, the tippet edged with white fur. |
| B.Chir. | Mid-cherry silk part-lined with white fur but with no fur edging to the tippet. |
| B.A. | Black stuff, part-lined with white fur, the tippet edged with white fur (or black stuff, part-lined with white, the tippet edged with white). |
| LL.B. | Light-cherry silk part-lined with white fur, the tippet edged with white fur. |
| Mus.B. | Dark-cherry satin part-lined with white fur, the tippet edged with white fur. |
| Vet.M.B. | Mid-cherry silk part-lined with white fur, with white fur edging (2") to the tippet. |

*Note:*—The neck band of the hood is of the outer colour, with no edging of the lining material. The corners of tippets are square. All hoods are of the full shape.

## The City

| B.Sc. | Maroon cloth, lined gold taffeta with " discipline " colour neck band. |
| M.Sc. | Maroon silk, lined and cape edged with gold taffeta, with " discipline " colour neck band. |
| Ph.D. | Maroon cloth, lined half maroon and half gold taffeta, with " discipline " colour neck band. |
| D.Sc. | Cardinal red cloth, lined half maroon and half gold taffeta with " discipline " colour neck band. |
| Disciplines: | Engineering   Blue. |
| | Science   Grey. |
| | Management  }Green. |
| | Social Science  } |

*Note:*—Bachelors' hoods are of the simple shape, Masters' and Doctors' of the full shape.

## Dundee

| M.D. | Stewart blue, cherry lining. |
| Ch.M. | Black, imperial purple lining. |
| M.B., Ch.B. | Black, cherry lining, white fur edging. |
| D.D.Sc. | Stewart blue, ruby lining. |
| M.D.S. | Black, ruby lining. |
| B.D.S. | Black, ruby lining, white fur edging. |
| D.Sc. | Stewart blue, buttercup-yellow lining. |
| M.Sc. | Black, buttercup-yellow lining. |
| B.Sc. | Black, buttercup-yellow lining, white fur edging. |
| LL.D. | Stewart blue, old-gold lining. |
| LL.B. | Black, old-gold lining, white fur edging. |
| D.Sc. (Eng. & App. Sc.) | Stewart blue, powder-blue lining. |

| M.Sc. (Eng. & App. Sc.) | Black, powder-blue lining. |
| B.Sc. (Eng. & App. Sc.) | Black, powder-blue lining, white fur edging. |
| D.Litt. | Stewart blue, smalt-blue lining. |
| M.A. (Soc.Sc. & Letters). | Black, tartan-green lining. |
| Ph.D. | Stewart blue, eggshell-blue lining. |
| B.Phil. | Black, eggshell-blue lining, white fur edging. |
| M.Ed. | Black, tuscan-yellow lining. |
| B.Ed. | Black, tuscan-yellow lining, white fur edging. |

*Note:*—Hoods have a cowl without liripipe, the cape being oblong with rounded bottom corners. All are in silk ottoman.

## Durham

| B.A. | Black and white fur lining. |
| M.A. | Black and Palatinate purple. |
| B.D. | Black and black. |
| D.D. | Scarlet and Palatinate purple. |
| B.C.L. | Palatinate purple and white fur. |
| D.C.L. | Scarlet and white. |
| B.Mus. | Palatinate purple and brocaded satin. |
| D.Mus. | Brocaded satin and Palatinate purple. |
| Ph.D. | Scarlet, scarlet and Palatinate purple silk edging 1". |
| B.Sc. | Palatinate purple, fur, edged scarlet silk (½") |
| M.Sc. | Black, Palatinate purple, edged scarlet (½") |
| D.Sc. | Palatinate purple and scarlet. |
| D.Litt. | Scarlet and gold. |
| M.D.S. | Rose and ivory. |
| B.Com. | Black and cerise and white fur edging. |
| M.Com. | Black and cerise silk lining. |

and 1 Diploma (*not* Degree):—L.Th.

*Note:*—Palatinate purple silk, cloth, or cassimere is peculiar to this University: it is in fact a soft lilac shade.

## East Anglia

| B.A. | Blue with 6" coral outside lining in one fold. |
| B.Sc. | Blue with 6" spectrum-green outside lining in one fold. |
| M.A. | Blue with coral outside lining in folds. |
| M.Sc. | Blue with spectrum-green outside lining in folds. |
| Ph.D. | Guardsman red with facings same colour. |
| D.Litt. | Blue with coral outside lining, draped. |
| D.Mus. | Blue with Beaton-pink outside lining, draped. |
| D.Sc. | Blue with spectrum-green outside lining, draped. |
| D.C.L. | Blue with crocus outside lining, draped. |

## Edinburgh

| B.Arch. | Black silk, lined with orange-brown silk, and edged with white fur. |
| B.Com. | Black silk, lined with pale primrose yellow silk, and edged with white fur. |
| B.D. | Black silk, lined with purple silk, and bordered with white fur. |
| B.D.S. | Black stuff, lined crimson silk bordered ivory poplin 3" broad, edged white fur showing 3" crimson silk at front of neck-band. |
| B.Ed. | Black silk, lined with pale blue silk, and edged with white fur. |
| B.Mus. | Scarlet silk, with white silk lining, and edged with white fur. |
| B.Sc. | Black silk, lined with green silk, and bordered with white fur. |
| B.Sc.(Med.Sc.) | As B.Sc. |
| B.Sc.(Soc.Sc.). | Black silk, lined with deep turquoise silk and edged with white fur. |
| B.V.M. & S. | Black silk, lined maroon silk bordered golden yellow 3" broad, edged white fur. |
| Ch.M. | Black velvet, lined with golden silk. |
| D.D. | Black cloth, with appended cape, lined and faced with purple silk. |
| D.D.S. | Black silk, lined with crimson silk bordered with white silk 3" broad. |
| D.Litt. | Black cloth, lined with royal blue silk shot with maize-colour. |
| D.Mus. | Rich scarlet cloth, lined with rich white corded silk. |
| D.Sc. | Black cloth, lined with green silk. |
| D.V.M. & S. | Black silk, lined with maroon silk bordered with golden yellow 3" broad. |
| LL.B. | Black silk, lined with blue silk, and bordered with white fur. |
| LL.M. | Black silk, lined with blue silk. |
| LL.D. | Black cloth, with appended cape, lined and faced with blue silk. |
| M.A. | Black silk, lined with white silk. |

| | |
|---|---|
| M.Arch. | Black silk, lined with orange-brown silk. |
| M.B., Ch.B. | Black silk, lined with crimson silk bordered with white fur. |
| M.D. | Black silk, with appended cape, lined and faced with crimson silk. |
| M.Litt. | Black silk, lined with royal blue silk shot with maize colour bordered with ivory poplin 3″ broad and showing 3″ of royal blue silk. |
| M.Sc. | Black silk, lined white silk bordered green silk 3″ broad, showing 3″ green silk at front of neckband. |
| M.Sc.(Soc.Sc.) | Black silk, lined with deep turquoise silk bordered with 3″ ivory poplin and showing 3″ of turquoise silk. |
| M.Theol. | Black silk, lined with purple silk bordered with ivory poplin 3″ broad and showing 3″ of purple silk at front of neck band. |
| M.Ed. | Black silk, lined with pale blue silk. |
| Ph.D. | Black cloth, lined blue silk shot brown. |

*Note:*—Bachelor hood of the simple shape (as Oxford); Master of full shape (as Cambridge); Ph.D. of full shape (as Oxford Doctors); Doctor and Hon. Doctor of full shape (as Cambridge).

## Exeter

| | |
|---|---|
| B.A. | Dove grey cloth edged Faculty colour silk. |
| M.A. | Dove grey cloth lined Faculty colour silk. |
| D.Litt. | Scarlet superfine cloth lined dove grey cloth, edged with Faculty colour. |
| LL.B. | Dove grey cloth edged Faculty colour silk. |
| LL.M. | Dove grey cloth lined Faculty colour silk. |
| LL.D. | Scarlet superfine cloth lined dove grey, edged with Faculty colour. |
| B.Sc. | Dove grey cloth edged Faculty colour silk. |
| M.Sc. | Dove grey cloth lined Faculty colour silk. |
| D.Sc. | Scarlet superfine cloth lined dove grey, edged with Faculty colour. |
| B.A. (Social Studies). | Dove grey cloth edged Faculty colour silk. |
| M.A. (Social Studies). | Dove grey cloth lined Faculty colour silk. |
| Ph.D. (all Faculties). | Dove grey cloth lined with scarlet. |

The Faculty colours are:—

| | | |
|---|---|---|
| Arts | Kingfisher blue. | Science　Turquoise blue. |
| Law | Purple. | Social Studies　Dark blue. |

*Note:*—All bachelors have theological college style hoods unlined, all the seams show, and the hood proper is merely edged with the Faculty colour 2″ both inside and outside the cowl portion. All Doctors' hoods (incl. Ph.D.) are very heavy, being made of cloth and fully lined with cloth—no silk. All hoods are of the full shape similar to Cambridge.

## Glasgow

| | |
|---|---|
| M.A. | Black lined and edged with purple silk. |
| B.D. | Black, lined with cherry silk, cherry, and scarlet cloth border. |
| M.Th. | Black silk, lined with light cherry silk. |
| D.D. | Scarlet, lined with white silk. |
| B.L. | Black and red (Venetian red silk). |
| LL.B. | Black, lined with Venetian red silk, and scarlet cloth border. |
| LL.D. | Scarlet lined with red (Venetian red silk). |
| M.B., Ch.B. | Black, lined with scarlet silk and scarlet cord border. |
| Ch.M. | Black silk lined and edged with scarlet silk. |
| M.D. | Scarlet cloth lined with scarlet silk. |
| B.Mus. | Black, lined with azure blue silk, with scarlet cord border. |
| D.Mus. | Scarlet, lined with azure blue silk. |
| Ph.D. | Black, lined and edged with crimson silk. |
| B.Sc. | Black, lined with gold silk, scarlet cloth border. |
| D.Sc. | Scarlet, lined with gold silk. |
| B.Litt. | Black, lined with white silk, scarlet cloth border. |
| D.Litt. | Scarlet, lined with purple silk. |
| B.D.S. | Black, lined with emerald green silk, scarlet cloth border. |
| M.D.S. | Black, lined and edged with emerald green silk. |
| B.V.M.S. | Black, lined with terra-cotta silk, scarlet cloth border. |
| M.V.S. | Black, lined and edged with terra-cotta silk. |
| D.V.M. | Scarlet, lined with terra-cotta silk. |

| | |
|---|---|
| B.Ed. | Black, lined with blue silk with scarlet cloth border. |
| M.Ed. | Black, lined and edged with blue silk. |
| M.Sc. | Black, lined and edged with gold silk. |

*Note:*—All hoods are of the full shape with well-rounded capes.

## Heriot-Watt

| | |
|---|---|
| B.Sc. | Black, lined light blue with gold edging. |
| M.Sc. | Black, lined light blue. |
| D.Sc. | Light blue, lined white. |
| B.Sc.(Eng.). | Black, lined dark blue with gold edging. |
| M.Sc.(Eng.). | Black, lined dark blue. |
| D.Sc.(Eng.). | Dark blue, lined white. |
| B.A. | Black, lined purple with gold edging. |
| M.Litt. | Black, lined purple. |
| D.Litt. | Purple, lined white. |
| Ph.D. | Magenta with white lining. |

## Hull

| | |
|---|---|
| B.A. | *All* hoods are lined throughout with the |
| M.A. | University silk, a turquoise blue taffeta. |
| D.Litt. | All Bachelors' hoods (other than B.D. and |
| B.D. | B.Mus.) are of black ribbed rayon, of the |
| D.D. | improved Oxford Burgon shape. The |
| LL.B. | B.D. is of black superfine cloth of the same |
| LL.M. | shape as the Doctors'. The B.Mus. is of |
| LL.D. | the same shape as the B.A., LL.B. and |
| B.Mus. | B.Sc., but is of cream figured damask silk. |
| D.Mus. | The Doctors' hoods are of the improved |
| B.Sc. | Oxford Doctors' shape with semi-circular |
| M.Sc. | cape. The Ph.D. is of claret coloured |
| D.Sc. | cloth and the D.Mus. of cream figured |
| B.Sc.(Econ.) | damask silk; all the other Doctors' hoods |
| M.Sc.(Econ.) | are of scarlet superfine cloth. The necks |
| D.Sc.(Econ.) | of all hoods are cut in one piece with a |
| B.Ed. | single central seam and no neck bands are |
| M.Ed. | let in. Edging of all hoods is forbidden |
| Ph.D. | except that Masters' hoods are ordered to |
| (in all Faculties) | be edged ⅜″ with the lining silk (turquoise blue) round the cape portion only: all Masters' hoods are of the London shape, with well-rounded cape. |

## Keele

| | |
|---|---|
| Bachelors | Black, faced inside w th gold, top edge piped University red. |
| Masters | Black, lined University red and piped gold. |
| Doctors of Philosophy | Gold, lined University red. |
| Doctors | Purple lined University red, piped gold. |

*Note:*—All hoods are of the full shape.

## Kent at Canterbury

| | |
|---|---|
| Bachelors | Silver. |
| Masters | Gold. |
| Ph.D. | Cardinal red. |
| Higher Doctorates | Scarlet. |
| D.C.L. | Scarlet. |
| Faculty Colours: | Natural Sciences—Purple<br>Social Sciences—Grey<br>Humanities—Green<br>D.C.L.—Black |

*Note:*—Al hoods are of the special University shape *i.e.,* flat cape effect, with the faculty denoted by a centre " V " shape panel of velvet.

## Lancaster

| | |
|---|---|
| B.A. | Black, lined with grey taffeta with ½″ in side edging of red taffeta. |
| M.A. | Black, lined with red taffeta with 1½″ grey border. |
| M. Litt. | Black, lined with red taffeta with 1½″ blue taffeta border. |
| M.Sc. | Black, lined with red taffeta with 1½″ gold taffeta border. |
| Ph.D. | Red, lined with red taffeta. |
| D.Litt | Red, lined with blue taffeta. |
| D.Sc. | Red, lined with gold taffeta. |
| LL.D. | Red, lined with grey taffeta. |

*Note:*—The B.A. hood is of the simple shape; a ll other hoods are of the full shape.

## Leeds

| | |
|---|---|
| B.A. | Dark green. |
| M.A. | Dark green and white. |
| B.D. | Dark green, scarlet and white. |
| D.D. | Scarlet, dark green and white. |

| | |
|---|---|
| LL.B. | Light green. |
| LL.M. | Light green and white. |
| LL.D. | Scarlet and light green. |
| M.B., Ch.B. | Dark green and light green. |
| Ch.M. | Dark green, white and light green. |
| M.D. | Scarlet, dark green and light green. |
| B.Mus. | Dark green and white. |
| Ph.D. | Green and scarlet. |
| B.Ch.D. | Dark green and middle green. |
| M.Ch.D. | Dark green, white and middle green. |
| B.Sc. | Middle green. |
| M.Sc. | Middle green and white. |
| D.Sc. | Scarlet and middle green. |
| D.Litt. | Scarlet and dark green. |
| M.Ed. | Dark green, white and middle green 1″ laid on the lining. |
| B.Com. | Light green and dark green. |
| M.Com. | Light green, white and dark green. |

*Note:*—Bachelors' and Masters' hoods are of the simple shape and Doctors' hoods are of the full shape.

## Leicester

| | |
|---|---|
| B.A. | Red, lined with silver grey. |
| B.Sc. | Red, lined with royal blue. |
| LL.B. | Red, lined with black. |
| M.A. | Red, lined with silver grey. |
| M.Sc. | Red, lined with royal blue. |
| M.Ed. | Red, lined with red. |
| Ph.D. | Red, lined with a watered taffeta of lighter shade. |
| D.Litt. | Silver grey, lined red. |
| D.Sc. | Royal blue, lined red. |
| LL.D. | Black, lined red. |

*Note:*—Bachelors' hoods are of a special simple shape, and all other hoods are of a specific small full shape.

## Liverpool

| | |
|---|---|
| B.A. | Black cloth, lined with apple-blossom silk, and bordered with white fur. |
| B.Com. | Black cloth, lined with citron silk, and bordered with white fur. |
| B.Arch. | Black cloth, lined with white silk, edged with two narrow lines of black velvet, and bordered with white fur. |
| B.Ed. | Black cloth, lined with green silk, and bordered with white fur. |
| B.Phil. | Black cloth, lined with yellow silk, and bordered with white fur. |
| M.A. | Black silk or cloth, lined with apple-blossom silk. |
| M.Ed. | Black silk or cloth, lined with green silk. |
| M.Arch. | Black silk or cloth, lined with white silk, edged with two narrow lines of black velvet. |
| M.C.D. | Black silk or cloth, lined with white silk, edged with one broad line of black velvet. |
| M.Com. | Black silk or cloth, lined with citron silk. |
| Litt.D. | Scarlet cloth, lined with apple-blossom silk. |
| B.Sc. | Black cloth, lined with slate-blue silk, and bordered with white fur. |
| M.Sc. | Black silk or cloth, lined with slate-blue silk. |
| D.Sc. | Scarlet cloth, lined with slate-blue silk. |
| M.B., Ch.B. | Black cloth, lined with lavender silk, and bordered with white fur. |
| Ch.M. M.Ch.Orth. M.Rad. M.Ch.O to M.D. | } Black silk or cloth, lined with lavender silk. |
| B.D.S. | Scarlet cloth, lined with lavender silk. Black cloth, lined with dark red silk, and bordered with white fur. |
| M.D.S. | Black silk or cloth, lined with dark red silk. |
| LL.B. | Black cloth, lined with bronze silk, and bordered with white fur. |
| LL.M. | Black silk or cloth, lined with bronze silk. |
| LL.D. | Scarlet cloth, lined with bronze silk. |
| B.Eng. | Black cloth, lined with orange silk, and bordered with white fur. |
| M.Eng. | Black silk or cloth, lined with orange silk. |
| D.Eng. | Scarlet cloth, lined with orange silk. |
| B.V.Sc. | Black cloth, lined with grey silk, and bordered with white fur. |
| M.V.Sc. | Black silk or cloth, lined with grey silk. |
| D.V.Sc. | Scarlet cloth, lined with grey silk. |
| Ph.D. | Scarlet cloth or cord, lined with black silk, and trimmed with scarlet velvet. |

*Note:*—All hoods of this University are of the simple shape.

## London

| | |
|---|---|
| B.D. M.Th. D.D. | } Sarum red. |

---

| | |
|---|---|
| B.A. M.A. D.Litt. | } Russet-brown. |
| LL.B. LL.M. LL.D. | } Blue. |
| B.Mus. M.Mus. D.Mus. | } White (watered silk). |
| M.B., B.S. M.S. M.D. | } Violet. |
| B.D.S. M.D.S. | } Olive green (corded). |
| B.Pharm. M.Pharm. | } Old gold. |
| B.Vet.Med. M.Vet.Med. D.Vet.Med. | } Lilac. |
| B.Sc. M.Sc. D.Sc. | } Gold. |
| B.Sc.(Eng.) M.Sc.(Eng.) D.Sc.(Eng.) | } Gold. |
| B.Sc.(Econ.) M.Sc.(Econ.) D.Sc.(Econ.) | } Gold. |
| B.Sc.(Est.Man.) M.Sc.(Est.Man.) | } Gold. |
| B.Ed. | Eau-de-nil green. |

*Note.*—All London hoods are of identical shape (full shape with rounded cape). With the exception of B.Mus., for whom the hood is of light blue corded silk, Bachelors' hoods are of black silk or stuff faced and edged with silk of the faculty colour 3″ only. Bachelors who are members of Convocation are entitled to wear hoods lined with white silk and edged with silk of the faculty colour. With the exception of M.Mus., for whom the hood is of medium blue corded silk, Masters' hoods are of black corded silk, with a silk lining and edging of the faculty colour. For M.Phil. the lining is of claret colour with an edging of the colour of the faculty. Masters who are members of Convocation are entitled to wear hoods with a facing, 1½″ wide, of white silk. The Ph.D. hood is of claret-coloured cloth lined with silk of a lighter shade of claret, with an edging of the faculty colour about ¾″ wide. Doctors' hoods are of scarlet cloth lined with silk of the faculty colour.

## Loughborough

| | |
|---|---|
| Bachelors | Purple, lined grey (science) or yellow (technology). |
| Masters | Purple, lined grey (science) or yellow (technology), with ¼″ edging of grey (science) or yellow (technology). |
| Doctors of Philosophy | Purple lined and edged 1″ maroon taffeta. |
| Doctors | Grey (science) or yellow (technology), lined and edged scarlet taffeta. |

*Note:*—All hoods of the full shape.

## Manchester (Victoria University)

| | |
|---|---|
| B.A. | Back, pale blue and fur. |
| M.A. | Black and pale blue. |
| B.D. | Black, heliotrope and fur. |
| D.D. | Gold and gold. |
| LL.B. | Black and violet. |
| LL.M. | Black and violet. |
| LL.D. | Gold and gold. |
| M.B., Ch.B. | Black and red. |
| Ch.M. | Black and red. |
| M.D. | Gold and gold. |
| Mus.B. | Dark and light blue. |
| Mus.D. | Gold and gold. |
| Ph.D. | Gold and gold. |
| B.Sc. | Black, salmon and fur. |
| M.Sc. | Black and salmon. |
| D.Sc. | Gold and gold. |
| D.Litt. | Gold and gold. |
| B.D.S. | Black, fawn and fur. |
| M.D.S. | Black and fawn. |
| D.D.S. | Gold and gold. |
| B.A.(Theol.) * | Black, heliotrope and fur. |
| B.A.(Mus.) | Black, pale blue and fur. |
| B.A.(Econ.) B.A.(Admin.) B.A.(Com.) | } Black, orange and fur. |
| M.A.(Econ.) M.A.(Admin.) M.A.(Com.) | } Black and orange. |
| B.Sc. Tech. | Black, terra-cotta and fur. |
| M.Sc. Tech. | Black and terra-cotta. |
| M.Ed. | Black and bluish-green. |

\* B.A.(Theol.) who have graduated before 1967 are allowed if they wish to use a hood with an edging of pale blue silk and white fur lining inside the edging.

*Note:*—All hoods are of the simple shape and are worn back to front with the tippet or liripipe outwards.

## Newcastle upon Tyne

| | |
|---|---|
| M.B., B.S. | Scarlet, Palatinate purple and white fur edging. |
| M.D. | Scarlet, scarlet and Palatinate purple. |
| M.S. | Rose and Palatinate purple. |
| D.Hy. | Scarlet, scarlet, Palatinate purple and white. |
| D.Ch. | Scarlet, rose and Palatinate purple. |
| B.D.S. | Rose, ivory and white fur edging. |
| M.D.S. | Rose and ivory. |
| D.D.Sc. | Scarlet, rose and ivory white edging. |
| B.A. | Black, white fur, old gold edging. |
| B.Arch. | Same as B.A. |
| M.A. | Black and old gold. |
| M.Phil. | Same as M.A. |
| B.Ed. | Same as M.A. |
| M.Ed. | Same as M.A. |
| M.Litt. | Scarlet, white and old gold edging. |
| D.Litt. | Same as M.A. |
| M.Mus. | Maroon, Palatinate purple and white fur edging. |
| LL.B. | Maroon, Palatinate purple and white fur edging. |
| LL.M. | Maroon and Palatinate purple. |
| LL.D. | Scarlet and maroon. |
| D.C.L. | Scarlet and white. |
| B.Sc. | Black, white fur, royal blue edging. |
| M.Sc. | Black and royal blue. |
| D.Sc. | Scarlet, white and royal blue edging. |
| Ph.D. | Scarlet and scarlet. |

## Nottingham

| | |
|---|---|
| B.A. | Light blue and cherry and black. |
| M.A. | Light blue and cherry and black. |
| B.D. | Light blue and purple and black. |
| D.D. | Light blue and purple and scarlet. |
| LL.B. | Light blue and maroon and black. |
| LL.M | Light blue and maroon and scarlet. |
| LL.D. | Light blue and maroon and scarlet. |
| D.Mus. | Light blue, pink and scarlet. |
| D.Litt. | Light blue and cherry and scarlet. |
| B.Sc. | Light blue and royal blue and black. |
| M.Sc. | Light blue and royal blue and black. |
| D.Sc. | Light blue and royal blue and scarlet. |
| Ph.D. | Light blue and Faculty colour and claret. |
| B.Sc.(Agric.) | Light blue and green and black. |
| M.Sc.(Agric.) | Light blue and green and black. |
| D.Sc.(Agric.) | Light blue and green and scarlet. |
| B.Sc.(Eng.) | Light blue and light navy and black. |
| M.Sc.(App.Sc.) | Light blue and light navy and black. |
| D.Sc.(App.Sc.) | Light blue and light navy and scarlet. |
| B.Pharm. | Light blue and grey and black. |
| M.Pharm. | Black, light blue and grey. |
| M.Ed. | Light blue and lilac and black. |

*Note:*—All hoods of this University are of the full, Cambridge shape. All Bachelors' hoods are of black stuff, lined for 3" only with light blue silk. The hoods of all Masters and of Bachelors in Divinity are of black silk, and lined throughout with light blue silk.

The hoods of Doctors in Philosophy are of claret coloured silk or cloth lined throughout with light blue silk. The hoods of the Higher Doctors are of scarlet superfine cloth lined throughout with light blue silk.

All hoods of this University are bound (cowl portion only) with a ribbon of the appropriate colour. The colours are:—

| | | | |
|---|---|---|---|
| Arts | Cherry red. | Pharmacy | Dove grey. |
| Theology | Purple. | Agriculture and | Green |
| Law | Maroon. | Horticulture | |
| Music | Pink. | Applied | Light navy |
| Education | Lilac. | Sciences | blue. |
| Science | Royal blue. | | |

## Oxford

| | |
|---|---|
| B.A. | Black, half-lined and edged with white fur. |
| M.A. | Black silk, lined crimson or shot crimson silk. |
| B.D. | Black, lined fine ribbed black silk. |
| D.D. | Scarlet superfine cloth, lined fine ribbed black silk. |
| B.C.L. | Medium blue silk, half-lined and edged with white fur. |
| D.C.L. | Scarlet superfine cloth, lined crimson silk. |
| BM., B.Ch. | Medium blue silk, half-lined and edged with white fur. |
| M.Ch. | Black silk, lined and edged with blue silk. |
| D.M. | Scarlet superfine cloth, lined crimson silk. |
| B.Mus. | Lilac silk, half-lined and edged white fur. |
| D.Mus. | Cream silk brocade, with apple-blossom embroidery, lined cherry crimson silk. |
| D.Litt. | Scarlet superfine cloth, lined with grey silk. |
| D.Sc. | Scarlet superfine cloth, lined with grey silk. |
| B.Litt. | Light blue, half-lined and edged white fur. |
| B.Sc. | Same as B.Litt. |
| B.Phil. | Dark blue silk, lined with white silk. |
| D.Phil. | Scarlet superfine cloth, lined navy-blue silk. |

*Note:*—The Oxford Bachelors' hoods (except B.D. & B.Phil.) and the M.A. hood are either of Burgon or Oxford shape. The B.Phil. and M.Ch. hoods are always of Oxford shape. The B.D. and all Doctors' hoods are of the correct full apron shape. B.A., M.A., M.Ch., and B.D. hoods are of corded black silk; the other Bachelors' hoods are of corded or ribbed silk of the colour shown, lined or trimmed with white fur. When the Burgon shape is used the hood is half-lined and edged with fur, but for the Oxford shape only an edging of fur is used.

## Reading

| | |
|---|---|
| B.A. | All Reading hoods are lined with cream coloured silk. Bachelors' hoods are of dark blue lined with cream silk to a depth of 3". All hoods are full shape. All Doctors' hoods are of scarlet superfine cloth fully lined with cream silk, of the full shape, except Ph.D., which is of crimson cloth lined with cream silk (maroon Russell-Cord is generally used). |
| B.Ed. | |
| B.Mus. | |
| M.A. | |
| M.Ed. | |
| M.F.A. | |
| M.Phil. | |
| D.Litt. | |
| B.Sc. | |
| M.Sc. | |
| M.Agr.Sc. | |
| D.Sc. | |
| Ph.D. | |

## St. Andrews

| | |
|---|---|
| M.A. | Black, cherry lining. |
| B.D. | Wood violet, white fur edging. |
| B.L. | Pimento, white edging. |
| LL.B. | Pimento, white fur edging. |
| LL.D. | Pimento, white lining (satin). |
| Mus.D. | Cerulean blue silk or cloth with a white lining (satin). |
| Ph.D. | Nanking blue, white lining (satin). |
| B.Sc. | Purple lilac, white fur edging. |
| M.Sc. | Black, purple-lilac lining. |
| D.Sc. | Purple lilac, white lining (satin). |
| B.Litt. | Saffron yellow, white fur edging. |
| D.Litt. | Saffron yellow, white lining (silk). |

*Note:*—All hoods of this University are of the full shape with well-rounded capes.

## Salford

| | |
|---|---|
| Bachelors | Light "university-blue," lined gold and faced 2" faculty colour. |
| Masters | Light "university-blue," lined gold and faced 3" faculty colour. |
| Ph.D. | Light blue, lined and edged scarlet. |
| Doctors | Dark blue, lined and edged gold. |

*Note:*—All the hoods are of the special full shape (as Aberdeen). Faculty colours had not been chosen at the time of going to press.

## Sheffield

| | |
|---|---|
| B.A. | Green, white fur and crushed strawberry. |
| M.A. | Green and crushed strawberry. |
| Litt.D. | Red and crushed strawberry. |
| B.Mus. | Green, white fur and cream (brocade). |
| D.Mus. | Red and cream (brocade). |
| B.Ed. | Green, white fur and crushed strawberry (Arts) or apricot (Pure Science). |
| B.Sc. | Green, white fur and apricot. |
| M.Sc. | Green and apricot. |
| D.Sc. | Red and apricot. |
| M.B., Ch.B. | Green, white fur and red. |
| Ch.M. | Green and red. |
| M.D. | Red and red. |
| B.D.S. | Green, white fur and pale rose pink. |
| M.D.S. | Green and pale rose pink. |
| LL.B. | Green, white fur and pale green. |
| LL.M. | Green and pale green. |
| LL.D. | Red and pale green. |
| B.Jur. | Green, white fur and olive green. |
| B.Eng. | Green, white fur and purple. |
| M.Eng. | Green and purple. |
| D.Eng. | Red and purple. |
| B.Met. | Green, white fur and steel grey. |
| M.Met. | Green and steel grey. |
| D.Met. | Red and steel grey. |
| B.Sc.Tech. | Green, white fur and lilac. |
| M.Sc.Tech. | Green and lilac. |
| D.Sc.Tech. | Red and lilac. |
| B.A.Econ. | Green, white fur and lemon yellow. |
| M.A.Econ. | Green and lemon yellow. |
| Litt.D.Econ. | Red and lemon yellow. |
| | (Arch. Studies) Green, white fur and old gold. |
| M.A. | (Arch. Studies) Green and old gold. |
| Ph.D. | Red and dark green. |

*Note:*—All hoods of this University are of the full shape.

## Southampton

Faculty colours:—

| | | | |
|---|---|---|---|
| Arts | Mid-cerise | Engineering | Orange |
| Law | Blue(Univ. silk) | Social Sciences | Light green |
| Science | Rich gold | Education | White |

| | |
|---|---|
| B.A. | All hoods are lined throughout with the University silk, a peacock blue. The neck portion must be cut on the curve with a |
| M.A. | |
| D.Litt. | |

| | |
|---|---|
| LL.B. | single central seam, no neckband must be |
| LL.M. | let in and the neck must not be edged. All |
| LL.D. | Bachelors' hoods are of black ribbed rayon |
| B.Sc. | of the improved Oxford Burgon shape. |
| M.Sc. | The cowl portion only is edged inside and |
| D.Sc. | outside with ⅜" of the Faculty colour, ex- |
| B.Sc.(Eng.) | cept in Law, in which case the lining is |
| M.Sc.(Eng.) | turned over ⅜" on to the outside to form |
| D.Sc.(Eng.) | the edging. All Masters' hoods are of the |
| B.Sc. (Social | London shape, but with well rounded cape, |
| Sciences) | the cowl portion is edged ⅜" inside and |
| M.Sc. (Social | outside with the Faculty colour except |
| Sciences) | LL.M., in which case the lining silk is |
| D.Sc. (Social | turned over ⅜" on the outside to make the |
| Sciences) | edging, and M.Phil. where the ⅜" edging |
| B.Ed. | to the cowl portion is of claret-coloured |
| M.Phil. (in all | silk. The cape of Masters' hoods is edged |
| faculties) | ⅜" with the peacock-blue lining silk. All |
| Ph.D. (in all | Ph.D. hoods are of claret-coloured cloth |
| Faculties) | fully lined with peacock-blue silk. All the |
| | Higher Doctors' hoods are of scarlet super- |
| | fine cloth fully lined with peacock-blue |
| | silk. All Doctors' hoods (inc. Ph.D.) are |
| | of the improved Oxford D.D. shape. |

## Strathclyde

| | |
|---|---|
| B.A. | Blue, lined with white silk. |
| B.Sc. | Blue, lined with gold silk. |
| B.Arch. | Blue, lined with gold silk, bound with scar- |
| | let cord. |
| M.B.A. | Blue, lined and edged with white silk |
| | bound with black cord. |
| M.A. | Blue, lined with white silk with a ¾" edging |
| | of white silk. |
| M.Sc. | Blue, lined with gold silk with a ¾" edging |
| | of gold silk |
| M.Litt. | Blue, lined and edged with white silk, |
| | bound with scarlet cord. |
| M.Arch. | Blue, lined with white silk with a ¾" edging |
| | of gold silk. |
| Ph.D. | As for B.A., B.Sc., B.Arch. (as appro- |
| | priate). |
| D.Sc. | As for B.Sc., B.Arch. (as appropriate). |
| D.Litt. | As for B.A. |
| LL.D. | (honoris causa only) Blue, lined with white |
| | silk, bound with scarlet cord. |

*Note:*—All hoods are of the full shape, of saltire blue (*i.e.*, the blue of the St. Andrew flag).

## Surrey

| | |
|---|---|
| B.Sc. | Black cloth. |
| M.Sc. | Black cloth. |
| M.Phil. | Black cloth with blue rayon damask |
| | edging. |
| Ph.D. | Cardinal red cloth. |
| D.Sc. | Gold rayon satin. |

*Note:*—All the hoods of this University are fully lined with blue rayon damask and except for the B.Sc. hood, which is modified similar to simple Oxford, are all of uniform parabolic shape.

## Sussex

| | |
|---|---|
| B.A. | Black cloth lined with grey fur in squares |
| B.Sc. | and edged with 1" band of silk in school colour. |
| M.A. | Black alpaca lined with dove grey silk |
| M.Sc. | with edge bound in school colour. |
| M.Phil. | Black alpaca lined with dove grey silk |
| | with 1" band of scarlet silk over lining |
| | set in ¼" from edge. |
| D.Phil. | |
| LL.D. | No hood but a distinctive gown is pre- |
| D.Sc. | scribed. |
| D.Litt. | |

## Wales

| | |
|---|---|
| B.A. | Black and green shot blue (3"). |
| M.A. | Black and green shot blue. |
| LL.B. | Black and purple shot red (3"). |
| LL.M. | Black silk lined with red silk shot with purple. |
| LL.D. | Scarlet and purple shot red. |
| M.B., B.Ch. | Black and black shot green and white. |
| M.Ch. | Black and black shot green edged white. |
| M.D. | Scarlet and black shot green and white. |
| B.Mus. | Blue and pearl silk lining to a depth of 3". |
| M.Mus. | Blue silk fully lined with pearl-coloured silk. |
| B.D.S. | Black and shot saxe blue edged purple. |
| M.D.S. | |
| B.Pharm. | Black and shot saxe blue. |
| M.Pharm. | |
| D.Mus. | Scarlet and pearl. |
| B.Sc. | Black and black shot yellow. |
| M.Sc. | Black and black shot yellow (3"). |
| D.Sc. | Scarlet and black shot yellow. |
| Ph.D. | Crimson and Faculty colour. |
| D.Litt. | Scarlet and green shot blue. |

*Note:*—Bachelors' hoods are of the simple shape, Masters' and Doctors' hoods are of the full shape.

## St. David's College, Lampeter.

| | |
|---|---|
| B.D. | Black silk, lined with violet and edged with white silk. |
| B.A. | Black stuff or silk, edged on inside and bound with miniver. |

*Note:*—Both of Cambridge pattern.

## York

| | |
|---|---|
| B.A. | Grey with white edging. |
| B.Phil. | Grey with red edging. |
| M.Phil. | Red with grey edging. |
| D.Phil. | Red with grey lining. |
| D.Univ. | Red with grey lining. |
| | (hon. degree) |

## THE BEAUFORT SCALE OF WIND FORCE

| Beaufort number | Wind | Effect on land | Speed | |
|---|---|---|---|---|
| | | | M.p.h. | Knots |
| 0 | Calm | Smoke rises vertically | Less than 1 | Less than 1 |
| 1 | Light air | Direction shown by smoke but not by wind vanes | 1–3 | 1–3 |
| 2 | Light breeze | Wind felt on face; leaves rustle; wind vanes move | 4–7 | 4–6 |
| 3 | Gentle breeze | Leaves and twigs in motion; wind extends light flag | 8–12 | 7–10 |
| 4 | Moderate breeze | Raises dust, loose paper and moves small branches | 13–18 | 11–16 |
| 5 | Fresh breeze | Small trees in leaf begin to sway | 19–24 | 17–21 |
| 6 | Strong breeze | Large branches in motion; whistling in telegraph wires; difficulty with umbrellas | 25–31 | 22–27 |
| 7 | Moderate gale | Whole trees in motion; difficult to walk against wind | 32–38 | 28–33 |
| 8 | Fresh gale | Twigs break off trees; progress impeded | 39–46 | 34–40 |
| 9 | Strong gale | Slight structural damage occurs; chimney pots and slates blown off | 47–54 | 41–47 |
| 10 | Whole gale | Trees uprooted and considerable structural damage | 55–63 | 48–56 |
| 11 | Storm | Widespread damage, seldom experienced in England | 64–75 | 57–65 |
| 12 | Hurricane | Winds of this force only encountered in tropical revolving storms | Above 75 | Above 65 |

# ELEMENTS

| Element (Symbol) | Atomic Number | Atomic Weight | Valency | Element (Symbol) | Atomic Number | Atomic Weight | Valency |
|---|---|---|---|---|---|---|---|
| actinium (Ac)* | 89 | 227 | | molybdenum (Mo) | 42 | 95·94 | 3, 4, 6 |
| aluminium (Al) | 13 | 26·9815 | 3 | | | | |
| americium (Am)* | 95 | 243 | 3, 4, 5, 6 | neodymium (Nd) | 60 | 144·24 | 3 |
| antimony (Sb) | 51 | 121·75 | 3, 5 | neon (Ne) | 10 | 20·183 | 0 |
| argon (A) | 18 | 39·948 | 0 | neptunium (Np)* | 93 | 237 | 4, 5, 6 |
| arsenic (As) | 33 | 74·9216 | 3, 5 | nickel (Ni) | 28 | 58·71 | 2, 3 |
| astatine (At)* | 85 | 210 | 1, 3, 5, 7 | niobium (Nb) | 41 | 92·906 | 3, 5 |
| | | | | nitrogen (N) | 7 | 14·0067 | 3, 5 |
| barium (Ba) | 56 | 137·34 | 2 | nobelium (No)* | 102 | 254 | |
| berkelium (Bk)* | 97 | 249 | 3, 4 | | | | |
| beryllium (Be) | 4 | 9·0122 | 2 | osmium (Os) | 76 | 190·2 | 2, 3, 4, 8 |
| bismuth (Bi) | 83 | 208·980 | 3, 5 | oxygen (O) | 8 | 15·9994 | 2 |
| boron (B) | 5 | 10·811 | 3 | | | | |
| bromine (Br) | 35 | 79·909 | 1, 3, 5, 7 | palladium (Pd) | 46 | 106·4 | 2, 4, 6 |
| | | | | phosphorus (P) | 15 | 30·9738 | 3, 5 |
| cadmium (Cd) | 48 | 112·40 | 2 | platinum (Pt) | 78 | 195·09 | 2, 4 |
| calcium (Ca) | 20 | 40·08 | 2 | plutonium (Pu)* | 94 | 242 | 3, 4, 5, 6 |
| californium (Cf)* | 98 | 249 | | polonium (Po)* | 84 | 242 | |
| carbon (C) | 6 | 12·01115 | 2, 4 | potassium (K) | 19 | 39·102 | 1 |
| cerium (Ce) | 58 | 140·12 | 3, 4 | praseodymium (Pr) | 59 | 140·907 | 3 |
| caesium (Cs) | 55 | 132·905 | 1 | | | | |
| chlorine (Cl) | 17 | 35·453 | 1, 3, 5, 7 | promethium (Pm)* | 61 | 145 | 3 |
| chromium (Cr) | 24 | 51·996 | 2, 3, 6 | | | | |
| cobalt (Co) | 27 | 58·9332 | 2, 3 | protactinium (Pa)* | 91 | 231 | |
| copper (Cu) | 29 | 63·54 | 1, 2 | | | | |
| curium (Cm)* | 96 | 245 | 3 | radium (Ra)* | 88 | 226 | 2 |
| | | | | radon (Rn)* | 86 | 222 | 0 |
| dysprosium (Dy) | 66 | 162·50 | 3 | rhenium (Re) | 75 | 186·2 | |
| | | | | rhodium (Rh) | 45 | 102·905 | 3 |
| einsteinium (Es)* | 99 | 254 | | rubidium (Rb) | 37 | 85·47 | 1 |
| erbium (Er) | 68 | 167·26 | 3 | ruthenium (Ru) | 44 | 101·07 | 3, 4, 6, 8 |
| europium (Eu) | 63 | 151·96 | 2, 3 | | | | |
| | | | | samarium (Sm) | 62 | 150·35 | 2, 3 |
| fermium (Fm)* | 100 | 252 | | scandium (Sc) | 21 | 44·956 | 3 |
| fluorine (F) | 9 | 18·9984 | 1 | selenium (Se) | 34 | 78·96 | 2, 4, 6 |
| francium (Fr)* | 87 | 223 | 1 | silicon (Si) | 14 | 28·086 | 4 |
| | | | | silver (Ag) | 47 | 107·870 | 1 |
| gadolinium (Gd) | 64 | 157·25 | 3 | sodium (Na) | 11 | 22·9898 | 1 |
| gallium (Ga) | 31 | 69·72 | 2, 3 | strontium (Sr) | 38 | 87·62 | 2 |
| germanium (Ge) | 32 | 72·59 | 4 | sulphur (S) | 16 | 32·064 | 2, 4, 6 |
| gold (Au) | 79 | 196·967 | 1, 3 | | | | |
| | | | | tantalum (Ta) | 73 | 180·948 | 5 |
| hafnium (Hf) | 72 | 178·49 | 4 | technetium (Tc)* | 43 | 99 | 6, 7 |
| helium (He) | 2 | 4·0026 | 0 | tellurium (Te) | 52 | 127·60 | 2, 4, 6 |
| holmium (Ho) | 67 | 164·930 | 3 | terbium (Tb) | 65 | 158·924 | 3 |
| hydrogen (H) | 1 | 1·00797 | 1 | thallium (Tl) | 81 | 204·37 | 1, 3 |
| | | | | thorium (Th) | 90 | 232·038 | 4 |
| indium (In) | 49 | 114·82 | 3 | thulium (Tm) | 69 | 168·934 | 3 |
| iodine (I) | 53 | 126·9044 | 1, 3, 5, 7 | tin (Sn) | 50 | 118·69 | 2, 4 |
| iridium (Ir) | 77 | 192·2 | 3, 4 | titanium (Ti) | 22 | 47·90 | 3, 4 |
| iron (Fe) | 26 | 55·847 | 2, 3 | tungsten (see wolfram) | | | |
| krypton (Kr) | 36 | 83·8 | 0 | | | | |
| | | | | uranium (U) | 92 | 238·03 | 4, 6 |
| lanthanum (La) | 57 | 138·91 | 3 | | | | |
| lawrencium (Lw)* | 103 | 257 | | vanadium (V) | 23 | 50·942 | 3, 5 |
| lead (Pb) | 82 | 207·19 | 2, 4 | | | | |
| lithium (Li) | 3 | 6·939 | 1 | wolfram (W) | 74 | 183·85 | 6 |
| lutetium (Lu) | 71 | 174·97 | 3 | | | | |
| | | | | xenon (Xe) | 54 | 131·30 | 0 |
| magnesium (Mg) | 12 | 24·312 | 2 | | | | |
| manganese (Mn) | 25 | 54·9380 | 2, 3, 4, 6, 7 | ytterbium (Yb) | 70 | 173·04 | 2, 3 |
| mendeleevium (Mv)* | 101 | 256 | | yttrium (Y) | 39 | 88·905 | 3 |
| mercury (Hg) | 80 | 200·59 | 1, 2 | zinc (Zn) | 30 | 65·37 | 2 |
| | | | | zirconium (Zr) | 40 | 91·22 | 4 |

* In the cases of these elements, which are very rare or not found in nature, but have been artificially prepared, atomic weight in the chemical sense is meaningless; the integral mass of the most stable isotope known is given.

*Note:* In 1961 the isotope of Carbon-12 replaced Oxygen as a standard, the weight of its atom being taken as exactly 12. This change of standard has meant a slight adjustment in atomic weights from the old chemical scale.

The new elements with an atomic number higher than that of uranium 238 (element 92) are termed Transuranics.

# GAS LAWS

Boyle's Law (1662) $pV$ = constant.

Charles' Law (1787) $\dfrac{pV}{T}$ = constant.

Van der Waal's equation $\left(p + \dfrac{a}{V^2}\right)(V - b) = RT$ where $a$ and $b$ are constants.

Adiabatic expansion of a gas $pV^\gamma$ = constant where $\gamma = \dfrac{C_p}{C_v}$.

# MEDICAL
# MATTERS

Here we give a brief summary of up-to-date medical knowledge, including some recent developments. It must not be allowed to replace your doctor, who should be consulted immediately if you are worried. An index ensures easy reference.

# TABLE OF CONTENTS

    An alphabetical index of diseases mentioned in the text of Part II, referring
the reader to the appropriate page and column.

# MEDICAL MATTERS

## PART I. INTRODUCTION.

### (a) HOW TO USE THE SECTION.

Diseases do not exist in watertight compartments, but doctors arrange them according either to their cause or the area of the body affected. This plan has been followed here, and at the beginning of each part an account of the group of diseases under discussion is given. Unless you know enough already, you would be wise to read it.

Here is some advice about your attitude to disease in general, and your use of this section in particular.

First of all, and obviously, no book is a substitute for the doctor, and when you are ill you must see him. There are good and bad doctors, competent and incompetent ones, just as in any other profession or trade; so choose a doctor you can trust, *and then believe what he tells you and carry out his advice.* There is no use complaining about the whole medical profession just because you are dissatisfied with your own G.P. If you are, you should change him.

Secondly, *never* believe what you hear from non-medical sources. Literally millions of people are made miserable every year by taking to heart nonsense told them by others, who may well be quite unaware of the harm they do, or even have the very best intentions. In any medical matter ask your doctor, and ignore your next-door neighbour's asked-for or unasked-for advice. Doctors are sometimes wrong, but they are much less likely to be wrong than someone without a medical education. Remember, too, that the statement that there is no cure for a disease does not necessarily mean that it is deadly: and it never means that nothing can be done to make it more tolerable. There is much more to modern doctoring than simply curing the curable.

Thirdly, don't try to diagnose your own trouble or decide what treatment you think you should have. This section will have failed completely in its intentions if it puts you in the position of a character described by an English humourist, who, from a medical dictionary, discovered that he had every disease listed in it with the solitary exception of housemaid's knee. Diseases which appear to the layman to have the "same" symptoms may be vastly different in seriousness: influenza and poliomyelitis, for example, may in, the initial stages, appear very similar. So also may stomach ulcer and cancer of the stomach. No human being is infallible, but it is most important that you should go to the person who is best fitted to know—your doctor.

Lastly, you should not be misled into thinking that you can always tell the seriousness of a disease by the general appearance of the patient. Children, in particular, may have a high temperature, or even be delirious, on one day, and the next be out of bed and wanting to get back to school. On the other hand, many of the most dangerous fevers (as we shall see later) are accompanied by a low temperature and do not appear particularly dramatic in the initial stages. Thus a young woman who may be aware of nothing wrong but lack of energy and getting easily tired may be dangerously ill with tuberculosis of the lungs.

The best rule is to seek medical advice either when you have suddenly become ill with symptoms you don't understand or (and this is equally important) if you have gradually been feeling less fit over a period of time. Perhaps, too, it is wise to call your doctor if you have been ill with *anything* for more than three days. You should *not* call in a specialist before seeing your G.P., as is so often done in America and on the Continent. Specialists are very clever, but are naturally prejudiced in favour of their own subject; for example, an eye specialist will be predisposed to think of your headache in terms of eyestrain, an ear, nose, and throat specialist in terms of sinus trouble, and a psychiatrist in terms of mother-in-law trouble. Therefore you should first have a check from your G.P., who knows a little of all these things and probably a great deal about you and your past history. He will then advise you about a specialist if necessary.

### (b) NEW VIEWS ON MEDICINE

(1) Body and Mind. In former times, or, at least during the nineteenth century, the body was regarded as a sort of machine belonging to you in much the same way that you own your watch. You went to your doctor and, in effect, said: "Now what on earth are you going to do about my stomach?"—and you spoke as if, somehow, your stomach didn't have anything to do with the *real* you—it was just an awkward thing that happened to be annoying you. But we know now that this is not so—that your body *is* you, that it is a fort fighting against such enemies as poisons, parasites, germs, cancer, and injuries. The defences are seriously weakened by not enough of the right kind of food, insufficient sleep, or by anxiety. Your anxieties and worries can kill you just as surely as the other agents, and can prevent recovery or retard it when you are already ill.

A stomach ulcer therefore is not just something that is happening to you, you are happening to it. Your fears, your jealousies, your hatreds, your inability to get on in life, can be (in some cases) just as harmful as germs or poisons—in fact, they act by setting free glandular poisons in your blood-stream. Scientists have discovered a reaction which they call the "stress response," and we now know that stress can ultimately lead to sickness or death without any bodily injury at all. Thus, Dr. L. J. Saul, a leading American doctor, writes: "Emotional stress in which there is no physical damage can produce responses which lead to actual damage and even to death." Rats in the laboratory can be killed through long exposure to fear caused by loud noises or other forms of shock without even being touched.

This stress factor is emphasised not because it is more important that the other enemies of the body or mind (it would be better to say body-mind), but because, as we shall see later, it does cause serious diseases, and, secondly, as mentioned already, it influences the process of recovery. A person who is afraid or has no hope is less likely to recover from pneumonia or another disease than one who is hopeful, who has peace of mind and confidence.

(2) New Views about Health. A great deal of nonsense has been talked about the healthy life; at one time we were told to take eighteen chews to each bite, to do deep breathing, to take plenty of exercise, to get lots of fresh air, to eat regularly (or to indulge in peculiar diets). But more recently,

eminent doctors have cast doubt on most of these fancies. Moderate exercise is necessary to health, but athletes who indulge in violent exercise have not always been noted for longevity. Fresh air is pleasant and stimulating, but, where actual breathing is concerned, it is no better than the air in most rooms. Certainly, one of the problems of our time is air pollution by smoke and Diesel fumes, which are highly dangerous, but at present we are considering ordinary fresh air in comparison with the air indoors, and, in this case, the experts say there is little difference so far as health is concerned.

A balanced diet containing correct amounts of the basic food substances is essential, but there is no evidence that when, or at what intervals, you eat makes the slightest difference—unless you are a sufferer from stomach ulcer, in which case it is necessary that the intervals between meals should not be too long. The whole business of having meals at fixed intervals is nothing but a social convention, and in modern life obviously a matter of convenience.

Sleep, too, is a necessity. But different people require vastly different amounts of sleep. Some manage on as little as three hours, others seem to believe that they need ten or more, and there are well-authenticated records of people who never sleep at all. For example, a certain Dr. Pavoni in Northern Italy did not sleep for sixty years and made a virtue of necessity by specialising in night calls! Insomnia is unpleasant, but its only harmful effect results not from sleeplessness itself but from worry about it; for many people seem to believe that if they do not sleep they will go mad or at least become seriously ill. This is quite untrue.

In a number of studies of men and women who lived to a ripe old age it was found that the only factors in common between them were that they had a good balanced diet of healthy food, that they had contented minds, and that they were interested in something which gave them an aim in life. They also came of long-lived families—for living a long and healthy life depends partly upon heredity.

So the main rules of health are: do not think too much about your health unless it gives you trouble; have an interest in life and be prepared to sacrifice a lot for it (nothing useful has ever been done by those who are always " taking care " and being over-cautious); eat a good balanced diet; do not worry, and have a contented mind.

(3) New Drugs. A great surgeon, the first of the moderns, was Ambrose Paré, who died in 1590, and one of his best known sayings was: " I apply the dressing, but God heals the wound." He was quite right; for until about forty years ago, or even less, all the physician could do was to put the patient in as favourable a state as possible to enable his body to cure itself. That is to say, there were hardly any specific drugs—drugs that had a direct effect on the disease. There was quinine, discovered by the Spaniards in America, which was specific for malaria, and there were iron (specific for anæmia) and digitalis (specific for certain types of heart disease), but otherwise nothing until the nineteenth century, when Paul Ehrlich discovered salvarsan, which is specific for syphilis. Ehrlich died in 1914, having conceived the brilliant idea of drugs which he described as " magic bullets "—i.e., drugs which, like bullets, would be aimed at the real cause of the disease. They would, that is to say, be specific.

Since then a large number of such drugs have been discovered. For example, the antibiotics, such as penicillin, discovered in 1928 by Fleming at St. Mary's Hospital, Paddington. Later, Florey and Chain in Oxford, helped in the war years by the vast resources of the American pharmaceutical industry, were able to make penicillin available to the public in sufficient quantities by new techniques of production. Penicillin is practically non-poisonous (although it is possible to become allergic to it, sometimes with

serious results). It can kill some germs in a dilution of one part of penicillin to one hundred million parts of water; it is effective against streptococci, the cause of blood-poisoning, sepsis in wounds, and many other diseases; and also against the germs of anthrax, gonorrhœa, meningitis of some types, syphilis—a whole list of plagues which have troubled man for centuries. Blood-poisoning, whether from wounds or childbirth, used to be almost incurable—now the rate of cure is 80–90 per cent.; anthrax and gonorrhœa have an almost 100 per cent. rate of cure. In pneumonia the rate is about 90 per cent., and early syphilis can be cured in a week, instead of the previous two to three years.

But this was only the beginning. Other antibiotics—streptomycin, tetracycline, erythromycin, and many others—are helping to wipe out the terrible scourges of the human race, in particular, in the case of streptomycin, tuberculosis. The sulpha group of drugs—sulphadiazine, sulphadimidine, etc.—have also proved a great boon. Then there are the new drugs which have created a revolution in psychiatry—the tranquillisers which relieve anxiety, the drugs which clear up certain types of depression, and substances such as chlorpromazine which make it possible to nurse formerly violent patients in the wards of a general hospital. The antihistamine drugs help in many cases of allergy, the anticoagulants prevent further attacks of coronary thrombosis, and every year new and powerful aids in the fight against disease are discovered.

Of course, these potent new drugs are not without their concomitant risks. The doctor is trained to weigh the harm they can do against the disadvantages of not using them in any particular case. He should not use them for every trivial illness in which their only effect may be to shorten slightly the course of a condition which, left alone, would recover of itself. Yet in Britain and other technically-advanced countries indiscriminate prescribing is common, largely because of pressure on the doctor from his patients and the drug firms. The busy mother whose child has a mild sore throat is not going to see the child sweat it out when she knows from past experience that a dose of penicillin can remove the fever and most of the symptoms within twenty-four hours. She is unlikely to listen to the argument that the slower process is capable of increasing the body's resistance to future attacks, or that repeated administration of penicillin may create germs which are insensitive to it in a future emergency, or, worse still, produce an allergy to the drug. The thalidomide tragedy of 1962–3, when a new sedative, hailed as being both effective and safe (cases were quoted of would-be suicides who had taken up to 100 of the tablets without loss of life), resulted in the birth of children with undeveloped arms and legs to mothers who had used the drug in early pregnancy, and prolonged neuritis in some adults, has been quoted against the drug industry as an example of cut-throat competition allowing new preparations on the market before they had been exhaustively tested. But the truth is not quite so simple. There can be no reasonable question that the drug industry needs to be under stricter control; that its methods of advertising its wares to the doctor are wasteful, importunate, and often in bad taste; that different firms put out what is virtually the same drug under various trade names which merely leads to confusion; that the " authorities " quoted in the advertising of some drugs are often obscure individuals in countries not noted for the high standard of their practice of medicine writing in equally obscure journals; and that many drug firms make grossly inflated profits at the expense of our National Health Service. On the other hand, it must be remembered that some of the best drug firms have played a major part in medical progress. But they must constantly check their commercial instincts where these conflict (as they sometimes do) with your interests as the patient-consumer. To be fair about thalidomide, the fact is that nobody previously had seriously considered the possibility of a drug capable of causing deformity in the unborn child, and, if they had done, it is quite likely that the danger would still have been undiscovered, since only certain laboratory animals respond to thalidomide in a similar way to man. The drug had been exhaustively tested by all ordinary methods before being put on the market, and for a number of years (during which, in Germany, it was on sale to the public without prescription because of its apparent safety), millions of people took it without any ill-effects either immediately or subsequently. Its terrible side-effects were, in fact, limited to those mothers who used it in early, not later, pregnancy, and in a lesser degree to a small proportion of adults who developed unpleasant, but not dangerous, symptoms of neuritis.

The taking of any effective drug is always a calculated risk. We have mentioned that the use of penicillin—a drug which is almost completely non-poisonous—may nevertheless cause other germs and fungi to multiply in the body with unpleasant results. This is because penicillin wipes out, not only the disease-producing germs it is being used to destroy, but the penicillin-sensitive harmless germs which hold the other potentially harmful germs at bay. Thus those who keep on sucking penicillin lozenges for a real or imaginary sore throat may develop a black tongue due to the spread of a fungus normally present but kept under control. Other antibiotics, described as "wide spectrum" because they wipe out an even greater variety of germs than penicillin, also kill the organisms responsible for the absorption and possibly the creation of vitamin B in the body, thus causing severe vitamin deficiency. Tranquillisers made by various firms vary from the wholly useless to the very useful, but both can have unpleasant side-effects. One type is prone to lead in a small number of cases to severe depression, others may lower the blood-pressure to a degree that causes fainting attacks, and serious blood and liver diseases are not unknown if not common. Both tranquillisers and the antihistamine drugs can cause some people to become extremely drowsy—an obvious danger if one drives a car or works on heights. Even aspirin causes gastric haemorrhages which have sometimes been very severe and even lethal, particularly in those with peptic ulceration of the stomach and duodenum. Aspirin, one of the most useful and safest of drugs should never be taken for an "upset stomach", or by people with known stomach trouble. Such patients should be warned that about 150 preparations including some hang-over remedies widely advertised for "upset stomach", contain large quantities of aspirin (acetyl salicylic acid).

None of this should deter the patient from being advised by a doctor he trusts to use whatever drugs are prescribed; it *should* deter him from putting emotional pressure on his doctor to obtain drugs unwillingly given. It is high time that we gave up the notion that no patient should leave the consulting-room without a prescription for some pill or potion; for something like 40 per cent. of patients simply require advice about the conduct of their life from their diet to their relationships with others rather than medicine of any kind. The housing shortage, a bullying boss, or a nagging mother-in-law cannot be removed by a tranquilliser—in fact, a tranquilliser, by making a man or woman feel better, may prevent them from constructively solving problems which exist in the real world. We should all learn to rely as little on drugs as possible: stop taking tranquillisers or pep pills when we are merely worried about something that any normal person would worry about, or because we are just "fed-up"; stop using antibiotics (which are badly needed elsewhere in the world) for trivial infections in which they are anyhow useless; stop swallowing vitamin pills which do not relieve tiredness and are merely wasted on this overfed nation; stop buying any patent medicine whatever. Modern drugs are potent and effective; they are a dagger to destroy the enemy of disease. But, like a dagger, those who play about with them incompetently and unnecessarily are liable to get badly hurt.

**(4) New Methods in Surgery.** Only a few years before the Second World War many surgeons were saying that surgery had reached its extreme limits. It was impossible, they believed, to improve on the delicate techniques then reached. But events have proved them wrong. Operations on the heart, for example, which would have been inconceivable a short time ago are now carried out daily—the heart can be opened and defects of the all-important valves made good. "Blue-Babies" or adults with a heart disease which might have led to their death in a few years are now cured by surgery, and it is possible during such operations to cut off all the blood from the heart by deflecting it through tubes to an artificial heart outside the body—a machine which pumps the blood round the body whilst the real heart is at rest.

This however, will be described in more detail later.

Then there are the new anaesthetics, such as Pentothal, which are injected into a vein in the arm instead of being breathed in through a mask, as were ether and chloroform or ethyl chloride. Pentothal is much safer, and avoids the unpleasant after-effects of vomiting and nausea, which usually followed the old type of anaesthetic. Most curious of all anaesthetists use the poison curare, used by South American Indians to poison their arrow-heads. Curare produces paralysis, but in small doses merely gives the degree of muscle relaxation which is so important to the surgeon when he is operating.

Lastly, we might mention the new techniques of plastic surgery. Thus large areas of skin which have been destroyed by severe burns can be replaced by shaving off thin layers from another part of the body. These do not need to cover completely the whole damaged area: small pieces are scattered over the wound and gradually grow together. Corneal disease (the cornea is part of the "window" of the eye, and when it becomes opaque the patient cannot see) is treated by removing the diseased cornea and replacing it by a cornea removed from a dead body, or sometimes from an eye which has had to be removed from a live patient for other reasons. There are, in fact "cornea banks" where corneas are kept in refrigeration for future use, just as there are "blood banks" for use in blood transfusions. Other advances in surgery will be described elsewhere in the section.

**(5) New Approaches in Social Medicine.** Medicine has passed through many phases from the time when disease was regarded as a punishment from the gods or a sign of devil possession to the present era, when increasingly there is a tendency to look on society as the patient. Indeed, one commonly hears doctors and sociologists nowadays talking about "the sick society."

The early primitive stage came to an end—at least in one part of the world—when in Greece, five centuries before Christ, Hippocrates and others began to teach that all diseases were due to natural causes. But after the first ray of hope the outlook began to deteriorate when, during the Middle and Dark Ages (that is, from the fall of the Roman Empire right up to the fifteenth century), there was a return to the belief in devil possession and supernatural causes.

Eighteenth-century medicine in Europe was materialistic, regarding the body as a machine. It was founded upon a sort of pseudo-science—although, of course, there were always physicians in exceptions, physicians such as Sydenham in England, who, avoiding all theories, based their work on observation of the patient. This mechanistic approach persisted right through the nineteenth century, but medicine became more and more truly scientific, and the century saw the most rapid advances in the field ever known until our own times: the discovery of germs by Pasteur, of antiseptics to combat them by Lister, of vaccination by Jenner and anaesthetics by the American Wells and the Scot Simpson. The use of the microscope by Virchow, who was a German, brought great advances in the understanding of disease and Ehrlich, another German, conceived, as we have already seen, the idea of "magic bullets" which would attack the germs at the root of a disease without harming the patient. But one of the greatest of all these great men is perhaps the least known. His name was Edwin Chadwick.

From the earliest period of recorded history human communities had been constantly ravaged by great plagues which swept over their lands year after year, killing untold millions. Such plagues are recorded in the Bible and other ancient books, but, when town life became more and more common, as during the Roman Empire and the Middle Ages in Europe, the overcrowded conditions were even more favourable to the spread of disease. The Black Death of 1348-9 wiped out almost half the population of Europe. But, even in the first quarter of the nineteenth century in London, tens of thousands died from typhus, typhoid, and smallpox—and not only these, for periodically cholera would be brought into the country by travellers from abroad.

In the face of these terrible visitations the individual physician was helpless. He could not treat each one of the many sick even had he known how, and Chadwick's claim to fame rests on the fact that he was the first man to think in terms of *social* control of diseases, by so dealing with their causes that they were prevented from arising at all. In order to wipe out typhoid and cholera, he argued, we must ensure clean water supplies; for these diseases are caused by germs carried in polluted water. In order to attack typhus and plague, one must get rid of the lice which carry the germs of typhus and the rat-fleas which carry the germs of plague (including, of course, the rats, which, in turn, carry the fleas).

In the past, some attempts had been made to segregate the sick to prevent the spread of disease—for example, in the case of leprosy (which, strangely enough, we now know to be less infectious than most germ-borne diseases). But segregating those who are sick with typhoid or cholera is of little use if others are still drinking polluted water, just as it is of little use segregating plague cases if rats with their infected fleas are allowed to run at large. So these early attempts met with little success, due to lack of understanding of how the infections were passed on.

Chadwick was born in a Lancashire farmhouse where the children were washed every day all over, and he ruthlessly drove an obsession with cleanliness into the heads of his countrymen until, later in the century, it was possible for the German philosopher Treitschke to tell his class in Berlin: "The English think soap is civilisation." Although this remark was meant cynically, there is little doubt that soap, if it is not civilisation in itself, has played a greater part in making civilisation possible than many more elaborate remedies. A population riddled with chronic infectious illness has neither the time nor the energy to apply to the arts or sciences, and soap did a great deal to reduce infection.

One of the first Public Health measures was introduced by Chadwick and others when they brought in legislation to purify the water supply of London. Previously, the citizens had used water from the Thames (they still do, but only after it has been filtered and sterilised at the waterworks!), and from filthy, refuse-laden ponds and springs. Later, Chadwick helped to found the Poor Law Commission, and produced a Report in 1842, the principal suggestions of which were: a municipal water supply for all towns; scientific drainage both in town and country; and an independent health service with large powers for dealing with those who endangered the lives of others by polluting water or causing nuisances. He also proposed a national service for interment of the dead; for in those days bodies often remained for days in the overcrowded homes of the poor without burial.

What has the twentieth century contributed to the concept of social health? Well, of course, there has been a great deal of legislation along the lines initiated by Chadwick to control disease, and a great many other measures have been introduced concerned with the idea of positive health—not merely preventing bad health, but trying to bring about the highest possible state of good health. Orange juice, milk, and good meals for school-children have brought about a transformation in child health which has become apparent to the least observant in the last ten or fifteen years. And the National Health Service is in the direct line of descent from early nineteenth-century legislation.

But in future years it is probable that the main achievement of the twentieth century in social medicine will prove to be its extension of the term "social health" to cover every aspect of community life, not only in such subjects as bodily health and its control of social means, but also such problems as mental illness, crime, delinquency, drug addiction, and so on. What we are now asking ourselves is: how far are these problems produced by society itself, and if this is the case, how far can we go in preventing them by social means?

Social medicine takes the view that these problems can never be dealt with solely by moralising and retribution, but only by dispassionately analysing causes and dealing with them. In this century we have developed a social conscience. Not always, it is true, a very well-informed social conscience, but at least this is a good beginning. There are organisations for dealing scientifically with delinquency, for dealing with problem children, for spreading knowledge about cancer in order to show people that it can be successfully treated if taken in time. The organisation known as "Alcoholics Anonymous" has, on the whole, been more successful in treating alcoholics by social means than have any of the individual medical methods. Mental illness is also treated by group methods, which, together with the new drugs, have revolutionised the position in mental hospitals. We can well say with John Donne, who died in 1631, that "no man is an island . . . every man's death diminisheth me; for I am involved in mankind." This is the attitude of twentieth-century social medicine.

Summary. Perhaps we can sum up our progress in the past hundred years more dramatically in terms of hard facts.

*One hundred years ago,* a surgical operation was never undertaken except under the gravest circumstances. There were no anæsthetics and no antiseptics, and the operation was carried out by a surgeon in a filthy tail-coat, stained with the congealed blood of countless operations (indeed the surgeons of that time took pride in the dirty condition of their coat as showing how much experience they had previously had). Germs and the part they play in producing disease were unknown, and Paul Ehrlich had not yet been born, so there were no "magic bullets" to attack syphilis, or sera for diphtheria and other diseases. The mentally ill were simply locked up with little treatment and subjected to such indignities as the strait-jacket and the padded cell; now they are given treatment which becomes more effective each year, the padded cell and strait-jacket have gone, and in the more progressive hospitals even the ward doors are not locked.

*Only thirty years ago* you would very likely have died if you had developed pneumonia, "childbed fever" after the birth of a child, meningitis, dysentery, typhoid, or tuberculosis. With such infections as blood-poisoning you would have had practically no chance at all. Today, the sulpha drugs and the antibiotics have changed all that. Syphilis and gonorrhœa were lifelong tragedies both to the patient and his family, but now they, too, can be conquered.

The National Health Service has brought the possibility of good treatment equally to all, and other bodies—some of them privately run—deal with alcoholism and neurosis, with rehabilitation of the mentally and physically ill, with spastics, birth control, and marriage guidance. It is up to us to see that all these facilities are used to the full by all who need them.

## PART II. DISEASES ARRANGED ACCORDING EITHER TO THEIR CAUSE OR THE AREA OF THE BODY AFFECTED.

## THE INFECTIOUS DISEASES
### INTRODUCTION.

INFECTIOUS diseases are those which are caused by an invasion of the body by organisms from outside (the word " organism " simply means other living things, and we are using this word because, as will be seen later, it is not only what are known as " germs " which can cause infection. We know, too, that what is generally typical about this group is: (a) that the disease can be passed on from one person to another, and (b) that it is usually accompanied by a raised temperature or fever. Now (a), of course, is always true, because the definition of an infectious disease is one that can be passed on to others, but (b) is not always true, because a few infections produce little or no temperature, and also because it is possible to have a raised temperature (again in only a few cases) without any infection. For example, certain types of brain injury, tumour, or hæmorrhage can produce a raised—or lowered—temperature, and so can the injection of some foreign substance such as milk into the muscles. This is known as " protein shock," and was at one time used in the treatment of certain illnesses. Finally, solutions of dead germs, such as the antityphoid vaccine given to protect troops during the War, may lead when injected to very high temperatures. But, by and large, we are entitled to suppose that the patient with a raised temperature is probably suffering from an infection.

### Types of Infection.

As we have seen, it is not only germs which cause infections—so from now on we shall give germs their proper name of " bacteria." Here is a list of the chief offenders which are liable to attack our bodies: bacteria, spirochætes, viruses, fungi, amœbæ, worms and other parasites. Of these, bacteria and viruses are by far the most important, but let us look at them all more closely.

*Bacteria* are tiny living things which can be seen only under a fairly powerful microscope. Some are grouped like bunches of grapes (staphylococci) or in strings or chains (streptococci). They are given these names because " staphylos " is the Greek word for a bunch of grapes, and " streptos " means a chain. Yet others are comma-shaped (such as the cholera vibrio), or shaped like a drumstick—a rod with a small knob at the end (the tetanus bacillus, which causes lockjaw).

It would be a mistake to think that all bacteria are harmful; for without some species we could not survive for long. Bacteriologists divide them according to their behaviour in the human body into three groups: saprophytic, parasitic or pathogenic, and symbiotic. The *saprophytic* organisms are the bacteria normally found in the skin, mouth, and intestines; they do us neither harm nor good. The *parasitic*, or as they are more usually called, pathogenic (i.e., disease-producing) organisms, are the harmful ones with which we are naturally more concerned. Lastly, there are the *symbiotic* organisms, which, whilst taking something from the body, give something in return. For example, cattle would not be able to digest the cellulose of the grass they eat were it not for helpful bacteria in the lower parts of the intestines, and there are certain bacteria in the large intestine of man which build up vitamin B2.

Bacteria have two peculiar characteristics: each reproduces by splitting into two separate individuals as often as every twenty minutes in favourable circumstances like an open wound. If no bacterium were destroyed, one individual could produce a mass of bacteria larger than the whole world in a matter of a few weeks (since each of the offspring also divides into two, which in turn divide again—the progression goes: one gives birth to two, these two to four, the four to eight, eight to sixteen, sixteen to thirty-two, and so on—you will see, if you work it out, that in a short period the figure becomes astronomical). Fortunately, many bacteria have accidents, so for the present the world is safe! The other curious thing about bacteria is that, barring accidents, they are potentially immortal. Under ideal conditions in which no bacteria were killed, none would die; for a bacterium there is no death from old age, no corpse except when it is actively destroyed. It simply goes on dividing, dividing, and subdividing for ever.

How, then, are bacteria destroyed? Briefly, the answer is that most are destroyed by the natural defences of the body of whatever host they are preying on; others are destroyed by antiseptics and the new drugs; and many are destroyed when they are excreted from the body in the sputum or through the bowels and land in places where they are dried up and cannot survive —although some bacteria in such circumstances can form what are called " spores," rather like the seed of plants, so making it possible for them to survive in a state of suspended animation for months on end until picked up accidentally by another unfortunate host. Finally, bacteria, in addition to all these possibilities, face another danger: they may themselves develop disease. This disease is caused by even more minute organisms known as bacteriophages (viruses which affect bacteria), discovered by the French bacteriologist d'Hérelle a good many years ago. Attack by bacteriophage causes whole groups of bacteria (known as " colonies ") to disintegrate and become harmless.

Although bacteriophage has been used in the treatment of some diseases in human beings, this method has now been largely given up, since the new drugs are infinitely more effective.

*Spirochaetes.* Spirochætes, like bacteria, are minute organisms, but differ in being shaped somewhat like a corkscrew and in being able to move (which many bacteria cannot do). Their progress is produced by a sideways wriggling motion. The two main diseases caused by spirochætes are syphilis and spirochætal jaundice. Spirochætal jaundice is carried by rats, and is common in those who work in mines. It is now rare in Britain, but still occurs in Japan, Egypt, and Malaya; the infection is passed through the skin where the excreta of infected rats mingles with water on damp ground in the mine where miners kneel. Infection may also occur through eating infected food.

*Viruses.* Unlike bacteria, viruses are too small to be seen under an ordinary microscope. They can, however, be photographed in some cases under an electron microscope, which uses a magnetic field instead of a glass lens and a stream of electrons in place of a beam of light. Viruses cause such diseases as typhus, measles, mumps, poliomyelitis, smallpox, and chickenpox—not to mention such plant and animal diseases as tobacco mosaic disease and foot-and-mouth disease, which often have serious economic consequences. Other virus diseases are psittacosis (an infection of parrots and similar birds which can be transmitted to Man), swine fever in pigs, influenza in Man, and myxomatosis in rabbits. They also cause, it is believed, the common cold.

The main characteristics of viruses are, first, that they can only grow in living cells—unlike bacteria, which readily grow in the laboratory on plates containing a jelly made from meat broth, gelatin, milk, and other delicacies. The scientist, therefore, must keep them in portions of living tissue kept alive outside the body. Secondly, they are so small that they pass through the pores of the finest filter. Thirdly, a first attack usually produces immunity for life. Second attacks of the common virus diseases mentioned above are very rare; but unfortunately, this rule does not apply to influenza or the common cold. Fourthly, there is reason to believe that viruses represent an extraordinary intermediate stage between the living and non-living; they can, for instance, be produced in crystalline form and yet are just as dangerous when " thawed out." Lastly, the virus diseases have proved for the most part to be little affected by the new antibiotics and other drugs, although vaccination in smallpox and the injection of sera from infected patients in other infections may give immunity for longer or shorter periods.

The two great practical problems that doctors face with viruses are: (i) many viruses are unknown because of the difficulty of growing them outside the body in suitable tissue culture. They cannot therefore be conveniently identified in specimens from the patient, as bacteria can; and (ii) they are unaffected by antibiotics like penicillin. It has been a great step forward to grow viruses artificially in tissue culture, in which they are identified indirectly by the effects they have on the cultured *cells*. But since we do not know exactly how to grow some viruses (like those of infective hepatitis) they have still not been seen.

When we recover from a viral illness like chickenpox, we probably do so by producing virus-killing substances inside our own cells. Scientists are currently searching for these substances in case they can be used, like penicillin, to cure viral disease.

*Fungi.* Some infections are caused by fungi—that is to say organisms belonging to the same group as moulds, mushrooms, and toadstools. Penicillin and some other antibiotics are produced from moulds, so, as in the case of bacteria, some fungi are helpful; they even help to destroy each other, as bacteria do. For example actinomyces, which can cause infection of the jaw and other tissues, is destroyed by other tissues.

Most fungal infections are trivial and limited to the skin. But, although trivial, they can be unsightly and uncomfortable. Ringworm of the scalp, dhobie itch—an infection of the groin spread by infected underclothing—and so-called " athlete's foot " are caused by a fungus.

*Amœbae.* Amœbæ are small, single-cell organisms, the largest of which (a harmless type found in stagnant ponds in Britain and elsewhere) is just visible to the naked eye. It is about the size of the head of a pin. Amœbæ move, in the species which are capable of moving, by pushing forward a part of the cell in the appropriate direction and causing the rest to flow into the advancing portion. Like bacteria, they reproduce by dividing into halves, each of which becomes a new amœba.

The main human disease caused by amœbæ is amœbic dysentery (not to be confused with bacillary dysentery).

*Parasites.* These may live on the skin like lice (which can carry typhus) or fleas (carriers of plague), or the parasites of scabies which burrow into the skin, or they may live part of their time in the blood or other tissues, like malaria. They often have complicated life-cycles involving other hosts (like mosquitoes) at certain stages of development.

*Worms.* Worms are intestinal parasites, but the only common types found in Britain are threadworms, the tiny thread-like worms which cause irritability and itching in the skin of children, less often in adults; round-worms, somewhat resembling the ordinary garden earthworm, which seldom lead to symptoms; and tapeworms, which may reach a length of 10 or even 20 ft. Many parasitic worms (like parasites elsewhere) lead a double life—they spend part of their life in the human intestine and the other part in the muscles of another animal. The tapeworm, for example, whilst in the human intestine, lays eggs which pass out of the body in the excreta, and are then swallowed by pigs, especially in those parts of the world where human excreta are used as manure in the fields. In the pig, the eggs form cysts in the muscles—meat infected in this way is known as " measly pork "—and when, in turn, the meat is eaten by man, the process in the intestine begins all over again.

Less common types, from our point of view, are the Russian tape-worm (which, as befits a Russian, grows to nearly 30 ft.!); this type is spread by caviare or undercooked infected fish. The small, leaf-shaped liver fluke, lays eggs which are passed into canals or pools in tropical countries in the urine of infected people, hatch out and enter a water snail, and finally leave the snail in the form of small parasites which pierce the skin of bathers, whence they pass to the liver and subsequently the bladder and rectum. This is a serious condition, as is also filariasis (another

tropical disease), for which, unlike bilharzia—caused by the liver fluke—no cure is known. The tropical disease known as loa-loa is caused by a variety of filaria.

## How the Infection is Spread.

Infection is spread in many ways, some of which have already been mentioned. In the common fevers found in Europe and elsewhere one of the most frequent ways is by *droplet infection*—that is to say, by minute drops carrying the germs which are coughed or sneezed into the air by someone already suffering from the disease. Such droplets can be projected into the air for 10 ft. or more, and when breathed in by someone within range infection may result. Next commonest mode of spread is perhaps by *infected food, water,* and the dirty hands of those who prepare food: cholera, dysentery, food-poisoning, and typhoid are spread in this way. Spread by *direct contact* is found in the venereal diseases (usually, but not always, spread by sexual intercourse with someone who already has the disease), and, of course, lice, fleas, and other parasites, including the scabies mite, are spread by contact with the infested individual—or sometimes with his clothes or bed linen. Spread through an *intermediary host,* whether it be lice, fleas, or mosquitoes carrying infection, or the various means adopted by worms, has already been described above, so no more need be said. Lastly, the infection may result from *bacteria already within the body;* for example, the bacillus coli which lives in the large intestine is there harmless, but if it gets into the bladder or the ureters (the tubes leading from kidney to bladder) a quite unpleasant result may follow in the form of cystitis or pyelitis.

## How the Body Deals with Infection.

The body has many mechanisms of defence against intruders, but suffice it to say here that there are two main ones. First, substances known as antibodies and antitoxins are produced in the blood—the antitoxins to neutralise the poisons produced by the invaders, the antibodies to render them helpless, for example, by causing them to clump together so that they can more easily be dealt with by the second defence mechanism. This second mechanism is provided by the white cells in the blood, some of which (the phagocytes) act like amœbæ and swallow up and destroy the germs. Antibodies and antitoxins can be transferred from one individual to another and are used in medicine both to prevent infection and to cure it. This is known as immunisation, and can be active or passive. Active immunisation is produced by injecting either a solution of dead bacteria, as in the case of antityphoid injections, or by injecting live, but weakened, strains of the organism, as in the case of smallpox vaccination. In both cases the body is stimulated to produce its own immune substances. Passive immunisation is used either for people who have been in recent contact with infection or who are already ill, and in this case the antitoxins produced in another person who has had the illness are injected in the form of serum—*i.e.,* the liquid part of the blood without the blood cells. All these natural defences are inefficient in the ill, the underfed, the very young, and the very old.

## Antiseptics.

We have already discussed the other ways in which bacteria are destroyed and now need only make brief mention of antiseptics, and antibiotics. The earliest antiseptic was carbolic acid, used by Lister in his operating-theatre in the form of a fine spray directed throughout the operation on the wound, or sometimes in the form of steam from a kettle containing a solution of carbolic. But carbolic is dangerous, and since Lister's time many more useful antiseptics have been discovered. Acriflavine, thymol, and other old favourites have been discarded too. The various forms of carbolic are still used to disinfect drains, but, to tell the truth, the use of antiseptics nowadays is very limited. In surgery the *antiseptic* method has given way to the *aseptic* method—instead of fighting sepsis we see to it that no possibility of sepsis is present before operating: all instruments, the surgeons' and nurses' hands, the skin, are sterilised—the instruments by boiling, the dressings by dry heat, the hands by soap and water, and almost the only antiseptic used is to clean the patient's skin in the area to be operated on.

Antiseptics are used as first-aid treatment for cuts and wounds, but should be applied only once as a general rule—that is, when the wound is first received. The trouble with antiseptics is that as well as killing germs they also kill the surrounding tissues, which antibiotics never do.

Antiseptic sprays to purify the air of a room or to destroy germs lurking in the dust on the sick-room floor—or any other floor—are practically useless. To quote the *British Medical Journal*: " There is no good scientific evidence that any of the chemical air-disinfectants can control the spread of infection in places such as schools, offices, or cinemas. Nor is there good evidence that any substantial effect on the spread of illness can be obtained by disinfection of dust."

Neither is there any good reason to believe that mouth-washes and gargles have any effect other than making the mouth feel fresher and (temporarily) removing mouth odour—by covering it up with the scent of the antiseptic. Mouth-washes are in contact with the bacteria for far too short a time to have any damaging result, and, in the case of tonsillitis and other diseases, all the important bacteria are hidden far out of any danger from gargles.

### Antibiotics.

The antibiotics—penicillin, streptomycin, erythromycin, terramycin, aureomycin, and chloramphenicol—have already been dealt with, and only two important practical points need to be mentioned. These are that although most of such drugs are entirely safe under ordinary conditions, it is extremely dangerous for the layman to use them without medical guidance. If, for example, people get into the undesirable habit of sucking penicillin lozenges for sore throat and keep on doing this every time the sore throat returns, they may become sensitised to penicillin so that, when they become really ill—say, with pneumonia—the serious illness no longer responds to the drug. Or the same habit may make them allergic or hypersensitive to penicillin, and an injection given later may have serious and even fatal results.

Doctors no longer use the lozenges anyway, because of this danger and another one which is that excessive use of antibiotics may kill not only the dangerous bacteria, but also the ones which are helpful to the body. When this happens, other types of organism which are not affected by antibiotics will multiply in the absence of the bacteria which normally keep them under control. Thus chloramphenicol or aureomycin, by killing useful germs in the large intestine, may cause vitamin B deficiency, and when the non-sensitive organisms have their natural enemies removed they may step in and multiply, causing inflammation of the mouth, diarrhœa, and occasionally a fatal bowel infection. Chloramphenicol is too dangerous for general use.

### General Treatment of Fevers.

Fevers are ordinarily heralded in by a rise in temperature which is noticeable either by a flushed face or by alternate sensations of heat and cold. A patient with a high temperature may have shivering attacks known as " rigors." Tell the doctor.

A high temperature does not necessarily (especially in a child) mean that the trouble is serious but the lay person should always treat it as such and certainly call a doctor if the patient is a child or an elderly person.

Even the trained physician finds it difficult to tell one fever from another in the early days; for most of the common fevers begin in more or less the same way. It is only when a rash or some other more definite sign becomes evident that a certain diagnosis can be made, and these may not show themselves until the patient has been feeling " run-down " and fevered for some days. Incidentally, although a clinical thermometer is a very useful thing when properly used, many a

doctor must feel that, in unskilled hands, it is a menace. The " fussy " type of mother who is constantly taking her child's temperature whenever it looks in the slightest degree different from usual (probably it is simply feeling justifiably bored with its parents), not only causes anxiety to herself but also gives the habit of anxiety to her child. The child is made to feel that the world is a dangerous place, full of germs and all sorts of causes for fear—as indeed it is, but one needs a sense of proportion, and other dangers which we think much less about are at least as frightening and twice as deadly as most germs. Whatever you do, don't get the thermometer habit; your child, so far as fevers are concerned, is a good deal tougher than you.

Briefly, then, the way to treat a fever in the early stages before the doctor comes, and before one knows exactly what is wrong, is as follows:

(1) Put the patient to bed.

(2) Give little, and easily digested, food; if the patient wants none, give none.

(3) Give plenty to drink—the proprietary preparations containing lemonade and glucose are excellent, but water, weak tea with sugar, or home-made lemonade with squeezed-out lemon juice and sugar, whichever the patient likes best, are at least as good.

(4) Aspirin is useful to relieve headache or other pains and will reduce fever for two or three hours. But it will cure nothing. The patient will be more comfortable, but his illness will not be cured by aspirin except in certain very special cases. Soluble aspirin is best. Do not have special children's aspirins in the house. They are often nicely flavoured, the children are tempted to eat them like sweets, and there have been serious cases of poisoning. For small children, use suitably small quantities of ordinary adult soluble aspirin, having checked the dose with your doctor. Other methods of cooling seriously fevered patients such as bathing, tepid sponging, etc., are strictly for the doctor to prescribe. A patient as hot as that should be in a doctor's hands anyway.

### THE INFECTIOUS FEVERS.

The remarks made above apply to the management of *any* fever, and we are now going to discuss particular infectious diseases, beginning with the common childhood fevers, then passing on to less common ones, tropical diseases, and worm and parasitic infestations.

The common infectious fevers are caused by bacteria or viruses, and it is useful to know the meaning of the following terms: *incubation period* is the time which elapses between being infected and developing symptoms; *prodromal period* is the time which elapses between the end of the incubation period and the appearance of a rash; *quarantine period*, the maximum time during which a person who has been in contact with the infection may develop the disease—it is usually two days more than the incubation period; *isolation period*, the time a patient is supposed to be isolated.

Views regarding the common infectious fevers have changed a good deal in recent years. Disinfection of rooms is now regarded as almost useless, and more cases are treated at home. Quarantine in the case of the common fevers is thought by a good many doctors to be a waste of time, since all it can do is to postpone infection from early childhood to early adult life, when it is likely to be more serious. For it is a characteristic of these fevers that they affect the adult much more violently than they do the child. However, on this, and all other points, you will have to be guided by the opinion of your family doctor.

### Virus Diseases.

First, we shall take the common virus diseases, measles, chickenpox, and rubella or German measles, then the other virus diseases, mumps, infective hepatitis, virus pneumonia, and some less common conditions which do not always produce a typical rash as in the case of the first three.

In nearly all of these fevers there is a long incubation period, and one infection gives immunity for life.

*Measles.* The incubation period is 10–11 days. The first sign is the appearance of symptoms rather like a severe cold. The eyes become red, and exposure to light is unpleasant, the nose runs, the throat becomes inflamed, and a dry, harsh cough develops. There may be headache, and the temperature rises to 102° or more. Usually the patient is a child, and especially typical is the development of so-called Koplik's spots, which are small, bluish-white, raised spots seen on the inside of the cheek at the back of the mouth. The rash begins on the fourth day of the prodomal period, *i.e.*, 14 days after the initial infection. It shows on the forehead and behind the ears, spreading within a day downwards over the whole body; in another two days it starts to disappear, but often leaves behind a sort of brownish staining which may last for one to two weeks.

Measles can be serious, especially in very young children because of its complications, such as bronchopneumonia and infection of the ear, which can now be treated with antibiotics. These drugs have no effect on the measles virus, but only on the secondarily invading bacteria which have invaded the lungs and ear during the illness. The illness can be attenuated or lessened by injection of antibodies (gamma globulin) from an immune adult, and this is often worth while in the very young.

*Rubella or German Measles.* Incubation period 14–19 days. A mild fever, similar to measles except that the rash is usually the first sign that anything is wrong, and the temperature is rarely above 100°. The eyes may be pink, and there are enlarged glands at the back of the neck. The rash disappears completely in thirty-six hours. There are no complications.

German measles, in itself, is harmless, but if a woman gets the disease in the early months of pregnancy malformations in the child may appear at birth. Hence some doctors believe that girls particularly should have the opportunity of contracting German measles before they grow up. There is no special treatment, except the general rules for fevers given above.

*Chickenpox.* Incubation period 14–15 days, but may be more variable. In children chickenpox is a mild fever which begins with the appearance of tiny blisters on the chest and back. These later spread outwards to the legs, arms and face, and cause itching. Treatment is the general one for fevers already described. Calamine lotion or dusting powder will be helpful for the irritation, and the child's nails should be cut short to prevent scratching and infection of the spots. Whereas children are usually little bothered by chickenpox, young adults may be much more drastically affected—a temperature of 104° is not uncommon, and there may be severe headache.

*Mumps.* Incubation period 17–18 days. Everyone knows the typical appearance of the patient with mumps—the swelling in the salivary glands in front of the ears which makes the face look full. This causes pain later on, and it may be difficult to open the mouth. Temperature is not usually high (about 101°). Although uncomfortable, mumps is rarely dangerous, but orchitis—swelling of the testicles—is sometimes a complication. Fluid diet should be given if eating is painful, with mouth-washes, and rest in bed.

*Infective Hepatitis.* "Hepatitis" means inflammation of the liver, and infective hepatitis, which is much the commonest cause of jaundice in young adults, is a virus infection of the liver. In fact, this disease caused serious difficulties during the Italian campaign of 1943, and has probably become more frequent (or, at any rate, more frequently recognised) in this country since the War. The main symptoms are fever, followed by jaundice, which is first noticed in the whites of the eyes as yellow staining, then in the skin. The urine becomes coloured also, and this is most easily noticed if, on shaking in a bottle, the froth shows coloration. If the froth remains white, no jaundice is present. Treatment is a matter for the doctor, but great care should be taken, both by the patient and those in contact with him, to wash the hands thoroughly after urinating or defecating, after handling utensils from the sickroom, and both before and after eating; for the disease is very infectious.

*Virus Pneumonia.* Pneumonia is usually caused by bacteria, and when we speak of pneumonia, that is the type we ordinarily refer to. Virus pneumonia is known by doctors as " pneumonitis," and is believed to be closely related to influenza. There is no specific treatment so far, and since diagnosis is a specialist matter, little more need be said except that the symptoms in general resemble those of ordinary pneumonia. Psittacosis, another virus disease, can also lead to pneumonia, and although there is no specific treatment for virus infections of the lungs, it is always worth while trying the antibiotics or sulpha drugs in view of the possibility that the lung condition may be caused by a secondary invasion by bacteria.

*Influenza.* While serious epidemics of influenza take the form of a very dramatic and often fatal disease—for example, the epidemic of " Spanish 'flu " which followed the First World War killed more people than the actual fighting—the milder type more usually seen is difficult to distinguish from the common cold. In fact, many people who complain of " a dose of the 'flu " are suffering from simple colds.

However, a sudden onset, aching in the muscles of the back and legs, and redness of the eyes, would suggest influenza, and especially typical is the depression and weakness which follow influenza but not a cold. The measures suggested above for the general treatment of fever should be applied; but the depression and weakness which follow influenza may need special treatment by the doctor.

*Colds.* Although everyone thinks he, or she, knows what a " cold " is, the issue is not so simple; for the symptoms of fever, running nose, and a run-down, " headachy " feeling are found in many illnesses. They may be observed, as we have seen, in the early stages of measles before the arrival of the rash, or in a number of other fevers, such as whooping cough. Mild attacks of influenza (see above) may resemble the common cold, and blocking of the nose with discharge and fever may be due to sinusitis—although here there is usually pain above, between, or below the eyes. Colds can be caused by any one of thirty different viruses known as " rhinoviruses " as well as by others which cause influenza, or infect glands (adenoviruses). This is why a single cold does not confer immunity on the sufferer. It is probable that you will not catch a cold from the same virus, at least for the rest of the year, but there are all those others waiting to infect you with other colds in buses, tubes, and other crowded places. Like all infections, do not forget that the best way to avoid them is to keep generally well, and in a good nutritional state. Do not spend money on injections or other vaccines. They do not work, probably because of the multiplicity of viruses involved. It is also unlikely that added vitamins or other expensive additions to the normal diet will do any good at all provided you are eating sensibly. There has recently been a vogue for treating colds with massive doses of Vitamin C. This doesn't work either, as has recently been proved.

*Poliomyelitis.* "Polio," or infantile paralysis as it used to be called, is a virus infection of the motor nerves—the nerves of movement—at the point where they leave the spinal cord. Fortunately, all the nerves are never affected, but only a few controlling one or more muscle groups.

If these groups happen to be the ones controlling breathing or swallowing (which, fortunately, is not very common) the results may be serious, but ordinarily the muscles affected are those of the legs or arms. Poliomyelitis is almost as common now in adults as in children. Usually it occurs in small epidemics after hot weather, that is in Summer or Autumn, and it often seems to strike at fairly healthy normal people. This, however, is not because healthy people are specially prone as such, but because those living under less hygienic conditions are more likely to have developed immunity. In point of fact, the majority of cases of polio are so mild that they are never discovered at all, and paralysis does not develop; such people are specially dangerous, precisely because they pass unnoticed and spread the disease to others.

Like many other infections, polio begins with sore throat, fever, and sometimes vomiting five to ten days after contact. There may be severe headache and rigidity of the neck muscles. Paralysis is noted about the second or third day after this, and is usually at its maximum from the start, although this is not always the case. This stage lasts two or three weeks, by which time the temperature is down and the paralysis greatly improved, although further improvement may go on up to eighteen months after the acute stage.

This is another disease which has been dramatically reduced and even wiped out in many areas by the widespread use of vaccine. However, when the illness is already present attention is directed to relief of discomfort, resting and splinting the affected limbs, and preventing spread of infection to others. The Kenny method, devised by Nurse Kenny, and much publicised as a means of reducing permanent paralysis, is not believed by most doctors to be any improvement upon orthodox methods. The use of the iron lung is restricted to cases where the muscles controlling breathing are attacked, and any permanent paralysis of the limbs can often be helped by surgical operation.

*Encephalitis.* This is an infection of the brain caused by a virus, first noted in Vienna in 1916. There was an epidemic in London in 1918, but it is not very common today.

*Smallpox.* Smallpox was once common in Western Europe, and, as late as the early nineteenth century, was not unknown in Britain. Now, since the introduction of vaccination, it is comparatively rare in industrialised countries, although minor epidemics have occurred here recently. Jenner, who introduced vaccination, noted that dairy-maids who had suffered from the mild disease known as " cow-pox," contracted from the udders of infected cows, and transmitted to the hand of the dairy-maid, did not develop smallpox. In fact, cow-pox is a mild form of smallpox modified by transmission through cattle. Vaccination should be carried out at the age of three months, and repeated at the ages of seven, fourteen, and twenty-one years—also at any time when an epidemic occurs, or when travelling to any part of the world where smallpox is prevalent, or where immigration laws stipulate that it must be done. Many countries insist on an international certificate of recent vaccination before landing. Your family doctor will make out the certificate (he is entitled to charge you for it) and your local Medical Officer of Health will countersign it. Smallpox is one of the diseases which can very readily be spread from countries where it is prevalent because of the great increase in numbers of people travelling about the world by air.

Smallpox attacks people of all ages and is carried by excreta and droplet infection, but particularly by the dried scales on the skins of convalescent patients; it is now most common in the tropics.

Smallpox is similar in many ways to chickenpox. Typical cases are easy for the qualified doctor to distinguish from one another, but one of the difficulties of vaccination (as with Typhoid, and other artificially conferred immunities) is that the typical signs are often modified. Differential diagnosis is a job for the expert, and if your own doctor is in any doubt, he will consult with the local health authorities. The disease begins with

shivering, headache, and backache, and the temperature is raised to 102–104°. On the third day a rash appears, which turns into small blisters on the sixth day, and the blisters become filled with pus by the ninth day. On the twelfth day they burst and form crusts. Unlike chickenpox, in which the rash starts in the middle of the body and works towards the outer parts, smallpox produces a rash which begins in the scalp, forehead, wrists, and feet and then moves towards the middle.

Smallpox is a serious disease, and the result depends largely upon whether the patient has been vaccinated within seven years of the attack. Contacts should be vaccinated and kept under observation for sixteen days; the patient must be isolated until all the scabs have separated and the skin healed. An effective drug has recently been announced.

*Glandular Fever.* This is sometimes called infective mononucleosis, since one of its features is an increase in certain mononuclear white cells and an alteration in their appearance. Another feature is an apparent infectivity. Beyond this the disease is a great mystery, and although it is probably caused by a virus, it may even be related to other (malignant) diseases of white cells. This one, however, is not dangerous although it often causes a lot of trouble by dragging on for many weeks. The main symptoms are fever, enlargement of lymph glands and sore throat. The patient feels very debilitated and often very depressed. Diagnosis is often very difficult, but there is a blood test known as the " Paul-Bunnell " test which is almost specific for the disease. The patient is usually presented as a case known to doctors as " P.U.O.," meaning Pyrexia (fever) of Unknown Origin. He has often been treated with several antibiotics, one after another, without effect, because the causal agent is not affected by these drugs. He is only very mildly infective, and it is unusual to insist on isolation or quarantine.

*Typhus.* This disease used to be known as " jail fever," because it was frequent in prisons; but overcrowding, poverty, and bad hygienic surroundings anywhere are suitable conditions for epidemics of typhus. Improved conditions in industrialised countries have made it unusual, since typhus is carried by a virus carried from one person to another by lice, and where lice are absent the virus is powerless to enter the human body.

Typhus comes on suddenly with a rise in temperature of about 102°, but within four days it may be as high as 107°. There may, or may not, be a rash at this time, and in the second week, when the temperature is at its highest, there is delirium, weakness, and a feeble pulse. The typical typhus rash appears about the fifth day as reddish blotches on the chest, abdomen, and wrists.

Typhus is, needless to say, very serious but responds to such modern antibiotics as chloramphenicol, aureomycin, and terramycin. Preventive measures are directed towards destroying all lice with D.D.T.

*Rabies.* Finally, we shall deal very briefly with a number of less common virus diseases, beginning, as is appropriate, with *hydrophobia or rabies*, since it was in this infection that the great French scientist Louis Pasteur (1822–95) showed the possibility of prevention by vaccination. Unlike Jenner, with his ready-made cowpox virus, which we have seen to be the virus of smallpox weakened by natural passage through cows, Pasteur had to weaken the rabies virus by passing it through rabbits. The rabbits were infected, and after death the spinal cord was dried and powdered, a solution passed through another rabbit, and so on until the virus was sufficiently weakened.

Rabies is spread by the bite of infected animals, usually dogs, cats, or wolves, who are driven mad by the disease; in Trinidad, however, it has been spread by vampire bats. Those who are bitten usually show no symptoms for six weeks or more, but sooner or later convulsions and delirium arise, which within four to five days are fatal.

There is no cure once the symptoms have developed, but Pasteur's serum, if given soon after the bite, prevents illness in the vast majority of cases—the sooner after the bite, the better the outlook. Dogs should be muzzled in areas where the disease is common, but quarantining imported dogs has made the infection almost unknown here.

*Psittacosis.* This is another virus disease which is of interest mainly in that it is spread by birds of the parrot group, such as parrots, love-birds, macaws, and the rest. It occasionally occurs here in people who have been in contact with birds of this type, and is serious both to the bird and its owner. As in the case of rabies, quarantine regulations have greatly reduced the likelihood of infection in Britain.

The symptoms of psittacosis are fever, cough, and bronchitis. The disease is especially danger-ous to old people, but it responds to the same anti-biotics as typhus.

*Sandfly Fever,* or phlebotomus fever, *Dengue,* or breakbone fever, and *Trench Fever* are all some-what similar conditions in that they resemble influenza and are rarely fatal. They are all due to viruses, spread in the first case by sandflies in tropical climates; in the second by mosquitoes in tropical climates; and in the third by lice in temperate climates. They are all typical " soldiers' diseases "; the first two were common in the Middle East and Far East during the last War, the third during the First World War in France.

*Yellow Fever.* Of all the virus diseases, only four can be prevented by vaccination—smallpox, hydrophobia, yellow fever, and poliomyelitis. Yellow fever is carried by a mosquito known as Stegomyia, common in South and Central America and in African ports. For its spread, it therefore needs: a hot climate, the stegomyia mosquito, and an infected person.

In 1898 the United States was at war with Spain in Central America, where yellow fever was a serious problem. Following this war the United States, by this time acutely aware of this terrible disease, asked a Dr. G. E. Waring to deal with it in Havana, where it was rife. But Waring died of yellow fever, as had many millions before him, without knowing its cause, and it was left to Walter Reed, who died in 1902, to prove the con-nection between the mosquito and yellow fever. By a vigorous war on the mosquito, the disease has been eradicated from Havana and the West In-dian islands, and Reed's discovery made possible the building of the Panama Canal (Ferdinand de Lesseps, the builder of the Suez Canal, had made a similar attempt in Panama, but had been beaten, amongst other factors, by yellow fever).

In yellow fever there is a sudden high tempera-ture, aching of limbs and head, jaundice, and black vomit; the pulse-rate falls as the fever rises. Previous vaccination seems to be preven-tive if undertaken in time.

Conclusion.

All these virus diseases have this in common: that for many there is no specific cure, although smallpox, rabies, yellow fever, and poliomyelitis can be prevented by vaccination, or by the social control of the creatures carrying the virus. Some of the larger viruses (psittacosis, whooping cough) are destroyed by certain antibiotics. There is usually a long incubation period. Finally the question will sometimes arise of protecting some people from German measles or measles with gamma globulin containing another person's anti-bodies to the disease. This may be considered for measles in very young patients or to protect the foetus in pregnant mothers in contact with German measles.

Bacterial Diseases.

Bacterial diseases differ from virus infections in a number of respects: their incubation period tends to be shorter; having the disease once does not often confer lifelong protection; and unlike virus diseases, most bacterial diseases respond to one of the antibiotics or sulphonamides. In many cases it is possible to inoculate against the disease to prevent it occurring, as we have seen is possible with only a few of the virus diseases.

*Scarlet Fever and Other Streptococcal Infections.* In the days, not so long ago, before the arrival of chemotherapy (sulphonamides) and antibiotics, streptococci were very much feared and even caused a high mortality, particularly in such susceptible groups as children, and mothers and babies in maternity hospitals. They are still taken very seriously in the latter and rightly so, although one wonders how much of the mystique is simply a hang over from the days, thirty years ago, when many mothers died from " childbed fever." All signs of infection, such as fever, during the puerperium (the period following child-birth) must be promptly dealt with by a doctor, and only occasionally now is there real cause for anxiety provided treatment is prompt and rigorous.

Scarlet fever is much less common and very much less serious an illness than it used to be, partly because of the effective treatments avail-able today, but also because of a definite but un-explained reduction in its severity. Perhaps the streptococcus has changed, and certainly the im-proved physical condition of people who are now much better fed and housed than they were, has helped to ward off the terrors of this disease as of so many other infections. The classical picture of signs and symptoms is now so rarely seen that it will not be further described.

The importance of streptococcal infections has shifted from the initial infection, such as a sore throat, to some serious conditions which occa-sionally arise as a result of some form of delayed sensitivity to the bacteria. Acute rheumatism or rheumatic fever (not to be confused with ordinary aches and pains nor with rheumatoid arthritis) occasionally arise in people who have had a sore throat a few weeks before. Since the strepto-coccus is not the direct cause of the damage which may consequently occur in the heart or kidney, the antibiotics are no answer except sometimes to keep off further streptococcal invasions.

*Diphtheria.* This used to be an extremely serious disease, but immunisation has made it almost unknown; it is important, therefore, that all children should be immunised. There are many modern and up-to-date doctors who have qualified since the war who have never seen a case because it has become so rare, and in spite of the propaganda of certain ill-informed people this saving of children's lives is entirely the result of nationwide inoculation during the war and since. The following description is of historic interest only, and will remain so if a high level of inocula-tion is kept up by parents.

In a typical case of diphtheria the incubation period is about three days; the patient is a child who becomes ill and pale-looking (*i.e.,* the onset is not sudden, as in many fevers, but insidious); the temperature is only slightly raised to, perhaps, 99° or 101°, and although there may be no com-plaint of sore throat, examination will reveal in-flammation with—and this is typical of diphtheria —a grey membrane spread over the tonsils, the palate, and the back of the mouth generally. The diphtheria germ does not spread within the body. It stays at the place where it entered (in this case the throat) and sends its toxins through-out the body.

Even after the acute phase is over the patient must not be allowed to walk, because the diphtheria toxin is particularly poisonous to the heart. The ordinary rule is at least one or two months in bed.

Diphtheria also occurs in the larynx—in pre-inoculation days many children choked to death with this form of the infection; in the nose; and, although this is not generally known, wounds can be infected. The so-called " Desert sores " of the North African campaign seem to have been caused by diphtheria-like organisms.

Diphtheria may lead to paralysis of the throat, with difficulty in speaking or swallowing, and paralysis of the eyes or limbs; these are due to neuritis caused by the influence of the toxin on the nerves.

*Whooping Cough.* For many years whooping cough has been regarded merely as a bother to the patient and a nuisance to others, as, in fact, a trivial disease. Unfortunately, this is not so: because statistics show that it causes more deaths than polio, diphtheria, scarlet fever, and measles all put together.

Whooping cough begins in a child as an ordinary cold with cough and slight fever, and this stage lasts for a week or ten days. Then the " paroxysmal stage " begins as a series of coughs following in rapid succession, during which time the patient is unable to breathe. The " whoop " is caused by the noisy indrawing of breath when the fit stops. The face may become blue and congested. Bronchitis is usually present, and bronchopneumonia may result as a complication, so inoculation of all children before the disease has a chance to strike them is most important.

Once whooping cough has begun, there is no specific treatment, although modern drugs can reduce the frequency of the fits of coughing. The antibiotic chloramphenicol has been used for this disease, but the general opinion is that it is ordinarily of little benefit. Chinese physicians once described whooping cough as the " hundred-days cough," and the cough may, indeed, continue for at least a hundred days.

### Food Poisoning Diseases.

Strictly speaking, there is no such thing as " food poisoning " if one is thinking of " poison ing " in terms of anything apart from germs. But not so long ago it used to be thought that decomposition of food in itself produced poisons known as " ptomaines " which were deadly to those who swallowed them. All food poisoning is caused by infection of food with bacteria and by no other cause—unless, of course, we are thinking of the kind of poisoning which is the concern of the lawyer rather than the medical man.

Here we are considering those diseases which are commonly spread by contaminated food or drink. The classification is not scientific, but then no scientific classification has as yet been devised. First, we shall deal with typhoid, paratyphoid, and dysentery—uncommon here in Britain, although Sonné dysentery is fairly frequent. Then there is gastro-enteritis (which means irritation of the stomach and intestines), which is caused by staphylococci and the germs of the salmonella group, and lastly, botulism, which is rare.

*Typhoid and Paratyphoid.* These diseases are spread by infected water, food, or hands—especially uncooked food, such as milk, salads, oysters, and shellfish. Flies, too, play some part in spreading the disease. Some people are " carriers " and carry and excrete the germs without being themselves affected; for example, " Typhoid Mary," a carrier in the United States in the early years of this century, spent a large part of her life in custody as a public danger, although she did not show any symptoms of typhoid. Nevertheless, this woman caused a great deal of illness in others in her chosen profession of cook.

The influence of Chadwick's propaganda for pure water supplies is shown by the fact that deaths from typhoid, still 332 per 1,000,000 in 1870, fell to 198 per 1,000,000 at the beginning of this century. In the 1920s the death-rate was only 25 per 1,000,000, and now it is even less.

Typhoid fever begins like most fevers with headache, raised temperature, and general feeling of unwellness. This stage lasts about a week, and then the rash appears in the form of rose-red spots on the front of the chest and abdomen and on the back. In the second week there is great weakness, sometimes diarrhœa, flatulence, and mental dullness, together with dry and cracked lips and tongue. The third week is the week, in hopeful cases, of gradual decrease in temperature and other symptoms, and the fourth week is the week of convalescence.

Complications are perforation of the intestine (which needs surgical treatment), delirium, and bronchitis.

Paratyphoid fever is a milder form of typhoid (there are two forms, A and B); ordinarily it can be diagnosed only by scientific tests. The main thing is to inoculate contacts with T.A.B. vaccine and to protect food supplies; treatment is with chloramphenicol.

*Dysentery.* Dysentery may be caused *either* by a bacterium or an amœba; the first type is known as bacillary dysentery, the latter as amœbic dysentery (which is dealt with under tropical diseases). Infection is spread in much the same way as in typhoid. There is high fever, abdominal pain, and diarrhœa, at first consisting of fæcal matter, then blood and mucus. In severe cases the death-rate used to be over 20 per cent.

Various bacilli cause dysentery. The common tropical types are the Shiga and Flexner groups, but in this country most epidemics are due to the milder Sonné group.

However, in all these infections sulphaguanidine, one of the sulpha drugs, brings rapid relief, but care must be taken to avoid infection of other people.

*Diarrhœa and Vomiting.* Leaving out typhoid and paratyphoid fevers and dysentery, there is a group of infections known as " D. & V."—diarrhœa and vomiting. In Britain D. & V. is mostly due to:

(1) Salmonella infection.
(2) Staphylococcal infections.
(3) Other bacteria, ordinarily harmless, such as bacillus coli, when present in sufficient quantity.

*Salmonella Infections* are the most serious of this group; they affect the small intestine and produce vomiting, severe abdominal pain, and diarrhœa. These symptoms occur about one day after eating infected food and usually clear up within about two weeks, but occasionally death results. Salmonella bacteria are most likely to be found in meat, egg powder, vegetables, and ducks' eggs, but staphylococci are liable to grow in milk products, such as ice-cream and cream buns. Food poisoning from staphylococci is seldom severe, and recovery takes place in about a week. Nevertheless, it is extremely infectious, and causes a great deal of lost time in industry and temporary illness in institutions; for it is in such situations that it is most likely to occur.

*Staphylococcal Food Poisoning* has greatly increased in recent years, so it is important to know what circumstances are likely to cause it. The reason for its increase has nothing to do, as many people suppose, with the greater use of canned foods, but it has much to do with the greater use of communal feeding and canteen meals. It is *possible* for bacterial toxins in infected food to bring about illness even when the canning process has killed the bacteria, but it is certainly extremely rare. Canned foods, in fact, are much safer than so-called " fresh " foods in this respect—except when they have been opened, left about, and then re-heated. The same applies to the re-heating of any kind of food.

The real enemy is the canteen worker with a boil, a discharging nose, dirty hands, or a septic finger. Occasionally food may be infected in the larder by rats or mice, but the sort of canteen or restaurant where this can happen has little to commend it! Frankly, these infections are caused by dirty or stupid people who do not realise that their sore finger or boil can become someone else's diarrhœa and vomiting. Where children are concerned, the outlook is potentially more serious, and in the early part of this century the Summer-time " procession of baby coffins " was all too familiar. Infection is much more common in artificially fed babies or in older children who eat infected ice-cream. However trivial the condition may seem, diarrhœa and vomiting with fever in a child should never be ignored. Those in charge of canteens or restaurants must ensure that staff is supervised, that anyone with a septic infection is put off duty, and that all know about washing after visiting the lavatory and absolute cleanliness.

Bacilli normally present in the intestine, such

as bacillus coli, can cause infections if absorbed in large amounts, or if of a different strain from those in the patient's intestine. They are not usually serious.

*Botulism.* Now uncommon, this is the disease which used to be known as "ptomaine poisoning" on the theory that it was caused by poisons produced by bad food apart from germs. In the 1920s a party of picnickers at Loch Maree in the Scottish Highlands developed botulism and a number died, with the result that the disease attracted much public attention. Botulism is caused by a germ, the bacillus botulinus, which is peculiar in that, like tetanus, its poison attacks the nervous system rather than the intestines, resulting in fits, double vision, paralysis beginning in the face and spreading downwards, and difficulty in swallowing. It is found in tinned fruits or vegetables containing the toxin even when the germ has been killed, but, as we have already seen, the toxin comes from the bacilli, not from decomposition of food as such (in fact, food does not decompose in the absence of germs). Death is common in botulism, but an antitoxin is now available which, if used in time, can cure the disease.

*Tuberculosis.* No disease causes more public concern, and no disease is more difficult to describe, than tuberculosis; for, like the streptococcus or the staphylococcus, the tubercle germ can attack many different parts of the body and manifest itself in many ways. Furthermore, it is a widely spread disease, infecting not only humans but also cattle, birds, and reptiles. But here we shall be concerned with those types common to Man—the human and bovine (*i.e.*, the type occurring in cattle which can be spread to man by infected milk).

The tubercle bacillus is particularly hardy, so that when coughed or spat out on the ground it continues to be infectious for a long time. Infection is therefore caused by: (a) drinking infected milk; (b) droplet infection through having germs coughed in the face; (c) breathing in infected dust. In other words, tuberculosis is caused by absorption through either the lungs or the intestines; the former is common in adults, the latter in children.

But there is a good deal more to the problem than this; we know, for example, that over 90 per cent. of people in industrialised countries have been infected with T.B. in early life and have conquered the infection. So the question arises: what conditions predispose to T.B.—why do some people get over the early infection and others not? There are two answers to this question: one is certain—that those who are impoverished and do not get enough food are liable to T.B.; the second is not so certain—that mental stress plays some part. Yet there is reasonably good evidence that such stress as a broken love-affair can cause lowered resistance to breakdown so that when germs are encountered infection will occur.

In children, lung tuberculosis is not common, but tuberculosis of the bones and glands is, as is also infection in the abdomen, the kidney or spine, and, worst of all, tuberculous meningitis. These are often of the bovine type from infected milk. Ordinarily, T.B. in children is less serious than adult infections; but tuberculous meningitis used to be almost invariably fatal until streptomycin was discovered.

Adult tuberculosis usually occurs in the lungs or the pleura—the thin membrane surrounding the lungs. In younger people miliary tuberculosis, which is a form of T.B. blood-poisoning or septicæmia, is a very serious condition, and the infection spreads throughout the whole body in a few weeks.

Lung infection begins gradually in someone who has previously felt unwell. There may be cough, and later blood-stained sputum (although blood which is coughed up does not necessarily prove that T.B. is present). Whatever means of treatment are used, the struggle between disease and patient is likely to be fairly long, but the outlook is now good. The closure of the Swiss sanatoria is due partly to modern disbelief that air in one place is better than that in another, but mainly to improved treatment.

Prevention depends on legal action ensuring

tuberculosis-free herds of cattle; on control of spread of the disease by those "open" cases who carry germs in their sputum; on the use of vaccination in childhood with B.C.G. vaccine (which you can ask your doctor about).

Many methods are used in treatment: new drugs, such as streptomycin, isoniazid, and P.A.S., lung surgery, rest, and so on. At any rate, tuberculosis is being got under control, but anyone who is worried can get a free X-ray at the nearest Mass Radiography Centre. For children, there are skin tests to show whether there is suceptibility to T.B.

*Septicæmia.* Commonly known as "blood-poisoning," is one of those diseases of which text-books prior to the Second World war used to say: "death usually occurs."

Blood-poisoning occurs generally by spread from some septic area such as a wound (or even a small prick), after childbirth, or any place where certain germs have got admission to the body. The most usual germ is the streptococcus, although the pneumococcus—which ordinarily causes pneumonia—and the staphylococcus may also cause septicæmia.

Fever comes on suddenly and rises rapidly with headaches, sweating, and shivering. The patient is obviously very ill, and later there is wasting and delirium. The white blood cells increase in number. Septicæmia sometimes occurs without any apparent local infection in those who are weak and debilitated.

*Pyæmia* is a type of septicæmia which leads to the formation of numerous abscesses throughout the body. Its symptoms are the same as described above, except that the causative germ is usually the staphylococcus, and abscesses are found which may need surgical treatment.

However, in both conditions the state of affairs has been revolutionised by the use of the sulpha drugs and antibiotics; cure is now the rule rather than the exception.

Septicæmia should be suspected when any small wound or cut is followed by high temperature and the symptoms described above.

The word "*Toxaemia*" is used when the germs stay in their original position and produce symptoms by spreading their toxins throughout the body. Tetanus, diphtheria, and some kinds of childbirth infection come into this category; the symptoms may vary from mild disturbance to severe illness.

*Meningitis* means inflammation of the meninges, the covering which, like a layer of plastic, lies over the brain and spinal cord, just as the pleura covers the lungs and the peritoneum covers internal organs in the abdomen. (Hence inflammation of the pleura is known as pleurisy, and inflammation of the peritoneum as peritonitis.)

Various germs may cause meningitis, for example, the bacillus of tuberculosis, the pneumococcus, which ordinarily causes pneumonia, and the streptococcus or staphylococcus, but ordinarily the word refers to *Cerebrospinal Meningitis* or "spotted fever" caused by the meningococcus and occurring at times as an epidemic. It is commonest in the years from infancy to the early twenties, and begins suddenly with headache, vomiting, and fever. The temperature rises quickly, and pain develops in the back and legs; on the second or third day a rash appears on the body, and particularly on the inside of the thighs. Later there is stiffness of the neck, the head may be drawn back, vomiting persists, and the headache can be so severe as to cause the patient to scream with pain.

Fortunately, this type of meningitis (and most of the others) respond to treatment with antibiotics or the sulpha drugs, so the risks are very much less than formerly.

*Pneumococcal Meningitis* is an unusual complication of pneumonia, and the septic types (*streptococcal* or *staphylococcal*) arise either following an infected fracture of the skull or from infection of the ear or mastoid.

*Tuberculous Meningitis* has already been mentioned; originally always fatal, it is now treatable with streptomycin.

All these diseases are very much a matter for

specialist and hospital treatment, but it is worth while mentioning *benign lymphocytic meningitis*, in which, although all the smyptoms of meningitis are present, recovery without specific treatment is invariable. Meningitis, which was during the First World War and after what polio is to us now, is no longer common, and when taken in time is easily treated.

*Tetanus* is usually known as " lockjaw " because there may be difficulty in opening the mouth, although this is simply part of a spasm of all the muscles of the body. The tetanus bacillus is found in rich soil—hence the disease is less common in desert areas—and tetanus resembles rabies in that: (*a*) it enters at a wound; (*b*) it affects the nervous system; (*c*) it results in fits and ultimately death.

However, active immunisation with T.T. (tetanus toxoid) has resulted in the disease becoming uncommon, and even when developed, treatment with antitoxin, anæsthetics, and curare may lead to cure.

The bacillus is anærobic (*i.e.*, does not use oxygen) and is most likely to occur in such situations as when a man digging manure or working in his garden sticks a fork through his foot, or, in war-time, when he is wounded in soil contaminated with manure.

*Undulant fever*, also known as Malta fever or abortus fever, falls into two types: melitensis, which infects goats, and abortus, cattle and pigs. Man gets the disease by reason of close contact with or drinking the milk of infected animals. (The name abortus is given because abortion is produced in cattle and sows.)

In Undulant Fever, as one would suppose, the fever goes up and down for two to three weeks; it may then go down and rise again, persisting for many months. The disease may occur in Britain, but modern drugs are on the whole successful in dealing with it. A striking feature of the disease is the combination of a high termperature with an appearance of relative well-being.

Another disease carried by mammals is *Glanders* or *Farcy*, spread by horses. In glanders there is discharge from the nose and sometimes pneumonia. Occasionally the disease is fatal. In farcy abscesses form, usually along the lymph vessels. Both conditions are very contagious, and treatment is a matter for a specialist; infected horses should be destroyed.

*Cholera.* Cholera could be classified under the head of food-poisoning, because it is mainly spread by infected water (however, like typhoid, it can also be spread by flies, infected food, and carriers); it could also be classified as a tropical disease, since, although it used to be found in Europe, it is now mainly rife in India.

Also like typhoid, cholera is caused by a bacillus, and can be prevented by early inoculation and care over food supplies—boiling water and milk, washing uncooked foods in chlorinated water, and keeping flies away.

The fever begins in the usual way with a short incubation period, followed by abdominal pain, severe vomiting, and diarrhœa. Later with the loss of fluid from the body there may be cramps in the muscles, diarrhœa increases, and the motions become of the typical " rice-water " type —*i.e.*, there is no solid matter, and the appearance is that of water to which a little milk has been added. This stage is followed by collapse, with low pulse and cold hands and feet. Death, if adequate treatment is not available, results in about 70 per cent. of cases.

*Anthrax.* The bacillus of anthrax, like that of tuberculosis, can exist outside the body for long periods, and, like that of tetanus, then takes the form of spores or seed-like bodies. It is spread by infected cattle and horses, which get the disease from eating grass containing spores.

In human beings the form the disease takes depends on where the germ alights; sometimes it comes from infected shaving-brushes, when it causes a large sore, like a boil, on the face, known as " malignant pustule "; sometimes it develops in those who inhale the dust from infected hides or wool (hence the name " wool-sorters' disease," which is a form of bronchitis with blood-stained

sputum); lastly it may arise through eating infected meat, when the result is intestinal anthrax.

In all cases the outlook is serious. Death is common, preceded by a high temperature, skin symptoms in the first instance, lung symptoms in the second, and food-poisoning symptoms in the third. Serum and arsenical preparations were formerly used, but now the suplha drugs seem to offer more promise.

## Diseases Caused by Fungi.

There are only two important groups of disease caused by fungus: the serious *actinomycosis* and the relatively harmless, if unpleasant, *ringworm.* Ringworm or tinea will be dealt with later; it affects the hair, the body, the groin (dhobie itch, already referred to), and the feet (athlete's foot). Actinomycosis is spread by a fungus in barley and grasses which may reach the human mouth, settle around bad teeth, and thence pass to the lungs, the bone of the jaw, and even to the intestines or brain. Fortunately, this unpleasant fungus, which was once difficult to eradicate, has proved susceptible to penicillin.

## The Venereal Diseases.

The venereal diseases are those caused—or at least that is what the name means—by the goddess of love, Venus. Venus, of course, causes a great deal of trouble, but venereal disease is not necessarily the worst she can do. Venereal disease is spread by sexual intercourse with an infected person.

*Gonorrhoea* is the result of an infection by the gonococ_us (*Neisseria gonorrhoea*) and ordinarily comes on after an incubation period of three to seven days. However, babies can get an infection of the eyes, known as ophthalmia, from their mother if she is infected, and gonorrhoea in young children is often the result of being in contact with infected towels or clothes. The disease in adults is evident when there is a thick, creamy discharge from the sexual organs and sometimes pain on passing water; in infants ophthalmia is prevented by the use of silver nitrate eye-drops at birth. Gonorrhoea is fairly easily cured by the use of sulpha drugs or penicillin; but unfortunately venereal disease is increasing in recent years and drug-resistant forms are becoming more common.

*Syphilis* is a serious venereal disease caused by a spirochete (*Treponema pallidum*). Stories about lavatory seats are simply stories, although it is occasionally possible to get syphilis by other than sexual means: for example, it has happened that a man playing football has been infected through his hand being grazed by the teeth of someone with syphilis. But this is very unusual, although kissing can spread the disease. Children, too, can be born with syphilis (the so-called congenital syphilis).

Adult syphilis begins with a sore, known as a hard chancre, at the point where the sporochæte of syphilis has entered; this may be on the lips, through kissing; on the sexual organs, through intercourse; and very rarely, as explained above, elsewhere. In a short time the chancre disappears and all may seem to be well, but this primary stage is followed by a secondary stage with sore throat, a rash, headache, and enlargement of glands. This, if left alone, also clears up, but is followed by the tertiary stage, in which a chronic infection develops in some part of the body which, presumably, is most susceptible in the particular individual. Thus there may be chronic syphilis of the skin, the bones, the heart, liver, or nervous system.

In the nervous system, the commonest forms are the two diseases of *tabes dorsalis*, in which the spinal cord is infected, and G.P.I. (general paralysis of the insane), in which the brain and mind are affected. These will be discussed under Nervous Diseases.

In congenital syphilis the pregnant mother gives her child syphilis. Such infants are often stillborn or premature, they look wizened, like a little old man, and amongst other symptoms are eye disease, " snuffles," a flattened nose, and when the adult teeth appear the front ones may be notched at the biting surface.

The treatment, of course, is very much a matter for a specialist, but diagnosis is usually made through the Wassermann blood test. It was for syphilis that Ehrlich produced his " magic bullet "—an arsenical drug, known as salvarsan, which could attack the organism selectively without harming the body and was the first of the modern specific drugs. Present-day treatment is with penicillin. G.P.I., once hopeless, is now dealt with by malarial therapy with a good deal of success. Penicillin alone is often adequate.

It is important to understand about venereal disease in general: (1) that it happens to many people who are no worse than anyone else; (2) that many patients believe themselves to have V.D. when, in fact, they have not; (3) that the best thing to do is to see your doctor as soon as possible—he is not concerned with your morals, and the sooner you go, the sooner you will get well; (4) every sore in the sexual area need not be V.D. There are other diseases which may be contracted as venereal infections.

*Chancroid* produces small septic ulcers around the sex organs, with swelling of the local glands in the groin, which may suppurate. It is caused by a bacillus, and can usually be cleared up by sulpha drugs within a week. Scabies and lice often pass from one body to another during sexual intercourse, but are not usually thought of as venereal in origin, although in many cases they are.

### Tropical Diseases.

Nothing is more difficult than to define the term " tropical diseases." One might define them as the diseases which occur in tropical climates—but then measles occurs there too; and if they are defined as those diseases which are found *only* in the tropics, the solution is no easier, since leprosy, cholera, smallpox, and typhus are usually listed as tropical diseases, yet were found in this country until fairly recently—and the odd case still is.

But what a story could be told about the conquest of those infections which were—and many still are—the scourge of humanity! One day when generals and dictators are forgotten we shall remember that great international army of physicians and bacteriologists who have saved millions of lives and infinitely reduced human suffering: Koch and Ehrlich of Germany, Pasteur and Roux of France, Ross and Jenner of Britain, Reed of America, Noguchi of Japan, and many others. We shall remember how the Jesuit priests brought quinine from Peru to Europe in 1638, the first drug to save people from malaria; how in tropical heat Ronald Ross (1857–1932) peered for hours through his microscope to discover the connection between malaria and the mosquito until the sweat running from his brow rusted the instrument; how Major Walter Reed's work in Havana (1851–1902) made possible the building of the Panama Canal, and think, too, of the American soldiers who died in helping him to find the cause of yellow fever. In mentioning Jenner once more, we should recall Lady Mary Montagu (1689–1762), who brought the practice of vaccination to England from Turkey—or, rather, the practice of " variolation," which meant inoculating with the pus from smallpox cases. This was, of course, a dangerous practice, but the idea was there. Noguchi, one of the great bacteriologists of the nineteenth century, was the son of a poor peasant. He often had to steal to get enough bread even to keep alive, but was later to help in our understanding of syphilis and many tropical diseases.

Yet there is still much to do. Take, for example, the case of Egypt, one of the world's poorest countries, supporting with the help of water from the Nile about 24 million people. But if the river gives food and drink it does other things; for it carries the disease of bilharzia, which kills thousands of peasants yearly. In the villages of Egypt as many as 90–100 per cent. of the population suffer from this terrible disease. The infantile mortality rate is the second highest in the world—29·5 per cent.—seven times higher than that of Holland; the average expectation of life amongst the lower classes is thirty-one years

of the upper classes fifty to sixty years. The country is ridden with bilharzia, ankylostomiasis, malaria, plague, amœbic dysentry, typhus, tuberculosis, and pellagra. Blindness, due to trachoma and other diseases, affects tens of thousands. Such a situation cannot be treated simply by pouring drugs into the country; what is necessary is social control, to enforce purification of the water supplies, the use of insecticides such as D.D.T. to kill the disease-bearing pests, and removal of the causes of extreme poverty (tuberculosis and vitamin deficiencies which are common in Egypt are diseases of malnutrition).

*Relapsing Fever*, common in India and Africa, is caused by bad hygiene (rubbing infected lice into the skin; the germ is a spirochæte, similar to that of syphilis, but the disease is non-venereal. Relapsing fever gets its name from the fact that the temperature remains high (103–106°) for about a week, returns to normal for a week, and rises again. There may be three to five relapses of this sort. Cure can be brought about by the arseno-benzol drugs used in syphilis. Lice, of course, should be dealt with.

*Epidemic Jaundice* (also known as Weil's disease or—if you prefer it—ictero-hæmorrhagica spirochætosis), is also caused by a spirochæte, and spread by rats. Now it is rarely found in Europe, although it occurred in the trenches during the First World War, in men working in sewers, and in the women who worked in the fish market of Aberdeen, which at one time was rat-infested. It is rarely fatal, but leads to high fever and jaundice. Anti-syphilitic drugs are useless, but some of the new antibiotics may help.

*Yaws* is also a spirochætal disease, common in the tropics and particularly in children. It is unpleasant, but not serious, and tends to clear up in a year or so. There are raspberry-like growths on the skin, which disappear with the drugs used in syphilis (although the condition is non-venereal). The Wassermann reaction, positive in syphilis, is also positive in yaws.

*Leprosy.* Whereas syphilis, relapsing fever, epidemic jaundice, and yaws are caused by spirochætes, leprosy is caused by a bacillus resembling the bacillus of tuberculosis. Leprosy, in fact, should not be included here at all, for it is non-spirochætal, and not necessarily a tropical infection. Apart from the difficulty of classification, many popular beliefs about the disease are untrue. It is *not* the oldest disease afflicting man; *not* a disease confined to tropical countries; it is *not* very catching; *not* hereditary, *not* incurable; in leprosy the fingers and toes do *not* drop off; it is *not* a divine punishment for wrongdoing. So there are many misunderstandings about this disease, and placing it in the wrong part of the medical section is probably the least.

Leprosy is a serious disease not because of disfiguring light-coloured skin patches and lumps, but because it destroys peripheral nerves. Leprosy may disappear spontaneously, or it may progress until the face is lion-like and the hands and feet wasted and ulcerated. The disease rarely kills, but it is the world's greatest crippler.

Leprosy was once fairly common in colder Western countries, though its extent was exaggerated. The great majority of the 15 million people who suffer from leprosy live in tropical countries, but it still exists in Iceland, Japan, Korea and some of the southern states of the United States. Prolonged and intimate contact with an " open " case is said to be the main mode of infection, but only one infected husband in twenty passes leprosy to his wife.

The sulphone drugs have revolutionised the treatment of leprosy. Given early diagnosis and adequate treatment, the great majority of sufferers could be cured. Established deformity (such as claw hand, drop foot, paralysed eyelids) can be mitigated by reconstructive surgery, although lost sensation cannot be restored.

In the past, only Christian missions were concerned with the plight of the leprosy sufferer. Now, non-sectarian voluntary agencies, Governments and the World Health Organisation have joined in the fight against the disease. Enough is known to control the disease, but not enough is being done, as only one victim in five is at present getting treatment.

*Plague* is another disease caused by bacteria, common in Europe at one time, but now largely restricted to Asia. Nevertheless, it caused millions of deaths in Europe during the years 1348–49 and 1665 and was the " Black Death," which, indeed, changed the course of history. Interested readers may read Hans Zinnser's *Rats, Lice, and History* about this aspect of the disease. Plague is carried by the bite of the rat flea, but, once people become infected, spread may occur from one to the other by droplet infection—*i.e.*, by coughing and sneezing. After an incubation period of two to ten days, fever develops, rather like severe influenza, and in a day or two the glands in the groin begin to swell, followed perhaps by swelling of the glands elsewhere. This is the usual type of plague, but it is also possible to get disease of the lungs from droplet infection and blood-poisoning from infection of the blood-stream. Both the latter types are almost invariably fatal, and even the glandular type (bubonic plague) has a mortality of about 80 per cent. The vaccine has given place to streptomycin and sulpha drugs which are also used on contacts.

Although we have little space to discuss the subject of plagues and epidemics in general, it is worth noting that serious epidemics have almost always followed wars, revolutions, and economic and political collapse. Thus the Black Death followed the break-up of the Roman Empire, and, in the fourteenth century, accompanied the end of mediæval civilisation. The Napoleonic wars were followed by other epidemics, and the wars of the 1830s in Europe were followed by influenza. In the most widespread outburst of influenza after the First World War, more people were killed by the disease than in all the fighting of four years. It is a reflection on the peculiar mentality of Man that this devastating epidemic, which affected almost the whole world, occupies little space in his history books—we still, with few exceptions, regard history as the doings of kings, queens, and generals. Yet, in 1918, 20 million men, and women, and children died from influenza, and no cure has, as yet, been found! Later we shall see that many millions of people die yearly from starvation or vitamin deficiencies But these facts—the real facts of life—we rarely hear about.

## Protozoal Diseases.

Nearly all the diseases caused by protozoa are tropical diseases, although one of the best-known protozoans is the harmless amœba found in British ponds. Protozoal diseases are caused by these organisms, large in comparison with bacteria which are really one-celled plants. Viruses are neither animals nor plants, are much smaller than the other two groups, and have some distinctive characteristics described elsewhere.

The only important diseases caused by protozoa are sleeping sickness or tryanosomiasis, malaria, and amœbic dysentery (as contrasted with bacillary dysentery), another disease, leishmaniasis—also known by the numerous names of kala-azar, dum-dum fever, and, in milder form, Delhi boil, Oriental sore, or Bagdad sore—will also be mentioned briefly. These infections are few, but important in their influence on Man; for, as Dr. Clark-Kennedy has pointed out, malaria until recently was responsible for one-fifth of all human sickness, sleeping sickness not so long ago caused a large part of Central Africa to be uninhabitable, and in some areas of the tropics there are probably more people with, than without, amœbic dysentery.

*Malaria.* The word, of course, means " bad air," just as " influenza " means " influence "—in Italian *influenza di freddo*—the influence of cold. Human beings have a natural tendency to suppose that, when two events occur together, then one must be caused by the other. Yet, although malaria and " bad air " may often go together, and influenza and cold, it does not follow that bad air (whatever that may be) causes malaria nor that cold causes influenza. In fact,

the anopheles mosquito carries the amœba of malaria, and the mosquito prefers climates which some people might describe as " bad," but it is the amœba, not the air, which causes the disease. Anyhow, the unfortunate mosquito might well use the phrase honoured by many generations of schoolmasters: " It hurts me more than it hurts you!" For the mosquito, too, is sick, and passes on its sickness to the person it bites.

There are several types of plasmodium—which is the scientific name for this amœba—producing attacks of fever varying in severity and frequency: benign tertian, quartan, and malignant quartan. Entering the body from the mosquito bite, the parasites penetrate the blood cells, multiply there, and finally burst into the blood stream. When this happens the temperature rises, and then they return to the cells to carry out once more the same procedure. Depending on the type, the attacks of fever may be at intervals of three or four days, severe or milder. When someone with malaria is bitten by a mosquito the infection can be transmitted to the next person it meets, but malaria is not infectious from one person to another directly. Quinine, of course, is the time-honoured remedy, but many other drugs are now available: mepacrine, palmaquine, atebrin, and even a sulphonamide derivative known as promin have been tried. The drug must be taken long enough for the infection to die out, otherwise relapses can occur even after leaving a malarial country (but it is only fair to say that, just as some people continue to give themselves the title of " Major " when they have left the Army, so others long in Britain continue to describe attacks of cold or 'flu as " my old malaria again," when, to say the least of it, they are exaggerating).

Important as are the drugs used in the treatment of malaria, even more so is the control of the parasite-bearing mosquito. The eggs of mosquitoes hatch in water, and there the young or larval forms can be attacked by pouring oil on the surface of pools so that they are unable to breathe, or by introducing small fish which have a partiality for them. Adult mosquitoes can be killed by D.D.T. and other insecticides or kept away by nets over beds and skin creams. Finally, anti-malarial drugs can be taken in dangerous areas. Whereas anopheline mosquitoes were once well on the way to getting rid of Man, now Man is well on the way to getting rid of mosquitoes.

*Blackwater Fever* is a sequel to malaria in tropical Africa and some parts of India. Rather illogically, it is described as " Blackwater," although the urine is red and the skin is yellow but the result is due to breaking down of the red blood cells by some malarial toxin. Possibly too much quinine may help in producing the illness. Treatment is to give plenty of fluids and no quinine or any other anti-malarial drugs in the early stages. The death-rate is about 25 per cent.

*Trypanosomiasis* or sleeping sickness—not to be confused with *sleepy* sickness, which has already been dealt with under the name of encephalitis lethargica—is essentially an African disease (although also found in tropical America) spread by the tsetse fly. Its cause is the type of protozoan known as a trypanosome, almond-shaped with vibrating membranes at the sides which enable it to move through the blood-stream, rather like a flat fish in the water.

There are three stages of the disease: first, the stage of fever with enlarged glands and a rapid pulse, which may continue off and on for three years; secondly, the stage of trembling hands, legs, and tongue, vacant expression, and slow and stumbling speech; thirdly, and lastly, the stage of low temperature, apathy, wasting of the muscles, and possibly death.

Treatment is with arsenical drugs—such as tryparsamide or Bayer 205—which give good results in early cases. Preventive measures in infected areas include the destruction of tsetse flies by insecticide, the cutting down of forests near rivers which are inhabited by tsetse flies, and some authorities have suggested the shooting of big game which may form a " reservoir " of the parasites, whence tsetse flies can carry them to human beings. For similar reasons infected people should not be allowed to move to non-infected areas.

*Amœbic Dysentery*, also known as *Amœbiasis*, is caused by the *Entamœba histolytica*, an amœba whose cysts are found in food, water, or spread by infected fingers or flies. There is mild fever and diarrhœa which contains blood. The disease may become chronic, and can cause abscesses, usually in the liver but sometimes in the lungs. Amœbiasis is treated and usually cured by injections of emetine hydrochloride, but in the chronic phase the drug known as Yatren is used in the form of an enema.

*Leishmaniasis*, kala-azar, or dum-dum fever, is another amœbic disease, probably spread in this instance by the bite of sandflies. It is also known as tropical splenomegaly—enlargement of the spleen in ordinary language—since infection results in enlargement of the spleen and liver, low, irregular fever, and death within a year or so. A milder form, affecting the skin, is known as Delhi boil, Oriental sore, or Bagdad sore, does not lead to kala-azar, and is fairly readily cured. The cure for both conditions is to give injections of tartar emetic, which reduces the death-rate from kala-azar from 80 per cent. to about 5 per cent.

### Diseases Caused by Parasitic Worms.

Many types of worms infest human beings and other animals. They are interesting for such reasons as their size (which may range from the almost invisible to 30 ft. or more), their life histories, and their serious or trivial consequences on their hosts. We shall mention only a few groups here, and mainly the ones likely to be met with in Europe—the tapeworms, the roundworms, and the threadworms—although some tropical types will be described briefly.

*Tapeworms*, as we have seen earlier, like many other types of intestinal worm, lead a double life. What usually happens is that the worm breeds in the human intestine, the eggs pass out in the fæces, and are then swallowed by animals eating contaminated material. In the animal the eggs hatch out into larvæ—primitive forms which penetrate the muscle, forming cysts—and Man is infected in turn by eating its meat. Thus *taenia solium* gets into the flesh of pigs, which, if imperfectly cooked (measly pork), causes infestation of the intestine in Man. It reaches a length of about 10 ft. *taenia saginata*, which reaches a length of about 20 ft., is spread in imperfectly cooked beef, and in Baltic countries *dibothriocephalus latus* gets into the human intestine from caviare or undercooked fish. It reaches the awesome length of 30 ft.

Now all the worms we have mentioned so far are found in the human intestine, and the cysts, which are much more dangerous and unpleasant, in the animal's muscles. But in some worms the reverse happens, with the adult in the animal's intestines and the cysts in Man. Thus in Australia the dog tapeworm (*taenia echinococcus*) produces cysts in both sheep and Man. This is known as hydatid disease, and may remain unsuspected until cysts in the lungs, liver, or elsewhere become infected or rupture. *Trichinella spiralis* is similar in action, being found in the intestines of pigs and getting into the muscles or other organs of Man. The main difference is that this worm migrates from the pig's intestines into its muscles, whence it reaches Man in undercooked pork meat or sausages. The muscular cysts cause swellings and sometimes pain. There are changes in the blood, swelling of the face and leg in the early stages, and fever. A minor epidemic occurred in England in 1941. *Taenia echinococcus* and *trichinella spiralis* are small—not more than ¼ in. in length—but are more serious in their consequences than the large worms. Treatment is very difficult, and ordinarily all that can be done is to deal with individual cysts when they make themselves apparent.

The large tapeworms, *taenia solium* and *saginata* and *dibothriocephalus latus*, produce varying symptoms or none at all. Usually they are not discovered until some segments of the worm are excreted, but there may be mild indigestion, excessive hunger, and occasionally anæmia. However, when the worm is discovered the patient, not unnaturally, is likely to become anxious and uncomfortable at the thought of " having " a tapeworm; these symptoms are caused by the worry rather than the worm.

Treatment is, of course, a matter for a doctor, but purging followed by extract of male fern is usually successful. One has to make sure that the head of the worm has been removed, otherwise it will continue to grow.

*Roundworms* are similar both in appearance and size to ordinary earth-worms, and the eggs reach Man, not from an animal, but from the contaminated fingers of someone else who handles food. They give rise to no symptoms, and are noticed only when discharged in the fæces or occasionally vomited up. They can be removed by the use of santonin.

*Threadworms*, as the name suggests, are like small ⅓-½-inch-long pieces of white thread. They are very common in children, and live mainly in the cæcum—*i.e.*, the part of the large intestine near the appendix. The males, which are the smaller ones, remain there, but the females pass down towards the rectum at night-time and lay their eggs in the area around the anus. Infection is by contaminated hands handling food—especially uncooked food—and water. Threadworms are not serious, and cause few symptoms other than itching around the anus and between the legs, but heavily infected children may show symptoms of anæmia. The nervousness often shown by such children is usually the result of the irritation produced by the worms in the anal region. Infection is not common in adults, and in children tends to disappear at puberty.

Treatment is, in theory, simple; for the worms are easily destroyed by a number of drugs, such as gentian violet, thymol, or one of the proprietary remedies. Ointment is applied to the itching area, and the child should be prevented from scratching. However, since the eggs may lie about the house for some time, reinfection often happens, especially if there are several small children in the home who may pass the disease from one to another.

The idea that intestinal worms in general are likely to cause loss of weight by absorbing food eaten by the patient is largely mistaken: for, although it is true that they do live on this food, the amount taken is certainly not enough to be significant.

*Tropical Worms. Bilharzia* has been mentioned before in connection with its frequency in Egypt, although it is also found in other parts of Africa, Arabia, and Iraq. There are two main types: one infecting the bladder (*schistosomum haematobium*), the other the rectum (*schistosomum mansoni*). Bilharzia is more correctly known as schistosomiasis.

The parasite's fantastic life-history begins when a man bathes in infected water, and the small swimming forms known as cercariæ pierce and enter his skin—or they may enter the body by drinking infected water. From the skin they pass to the portal vein below the liver, remain there six weeks until they become adult and then swim against the blood-stream down to the pelvis, where the female lays eggs which have a sharp spine. The eggs penetrate into the bladder or rectum—depending on the type of fluke—and pass out in the fæces or urine. If they enter water they hatch out into small moving forms which seek out a water-snail, develop further in its body, and leave it in the form of cercariæ ready to find a new human victim. The female fluke is slender and round, about 1 in. in length, the male, flat and leaf-shaped, is about ¾ in. long, and, as we have seen, their grisly courting takes place in the portal vein, whence the impregnated female passes to the bladder (hæmatobium) or rectum (mansoni) to lay her eggs.

Infection results in raised temperature and, in the urinary type, blood in the urine; in the intestinal type blood is found in the fæces, and there are symptoms resembling dysentery—e.g., diarrhœa. Treatment in both cases is by injections of antimony tartrate. Needless to say, attempts should be made at prevention by telling people to avoid infected canals (usually easier said than done), and by periodically cutting off the water supply to the canals to kill the snails.

*Hookworm Disease*, or ankylostomiasis, is found in many parts of the world, especially in miners who work on damp ground. The tiny worm enters the body usually through the feet, passes through the blood-stream to the lungs, eats through into one of the bronchial tubes, climbs the windpipe, and passes down the œsophagus into the stomach to end up in the duodenum. It causes anæmia, can be fairly readily cured, but is occasionally fatal.

*Elephantiasis.* Some types of parasitic worm are spread by insects. Thus in *Filiariasis* mosquitoes inject by their bites the infantile forms of a tiny worm which enters the lymphatic channels; there the blockade they cause leads to the swelling of the legs and the lower part of the body, known as elephantiasis.

## PHYSICAL INJURIES

### INTRODUCTION.

In this section we shall inevitably discuss much that could be described as Principles of First Aid. You cannot learn First Aid from a book, even if you read one of the excellent first aid manuals, like those published by the St. John Ambulance Association. The only way is to join one of their many classes of practical and theoretical instruction which are held in all parts of this country and many others. There is much to be said for many more people receiving instruction, to judge by the level of general ignorance and ineffectiveness to be witnessed at most road accidents before the ambulance comes.

The most difficult thing to learn is what *not* to do. When a patient is knocked down in the road, people instinctively seem to want to drag him immediately to his feet, or otherwise pull him on to the pavement away from the traffic. Someone will have entered the nearest shop and be emerging with a chair so that the casualty can sit down. Before long a hot strong sweet cup of tea has arrived, and this or some other beverage is being poured into him. All this is instinctive, and all of it is wrong. Do *not* move the patient until you are sure he has no fracture which will be further aggravated by movement. To take an extreme case, a fractured spine clumsily moved may result in permanent widespread paralysis. Guard your patient from the traffic but only move him when you are certain it is safe to do so. If he has any injury which is likely to require a general anaesthetic on arrival in hospital (and this applies to most fractures) do not give anything at all by mouth. No anaesthetic can be given to a patient who has eaten or drunk anything in the previous three hours, in case he vomits while unconscious and dies of obstruction of his airway. Keep your patient warm (do *not* warm him up artificially) keep his head low, and unless he is bleeding severely or has stopped breathing, do nothing but protect him from the ministrations of the uninstructed until the ambulance comes.

### Injuries to the Head and Back.

The head contains the brain, an organ with a number of inconvenient properties from the point of view of injury. Its very great importance is matched by its very great vulnerability as a tissue. Its consistency is that of stiff junket. It is quite incapable of repair once damaged and cannot heal by growing new parts in the way that skin and bone can. So it has to be totally enclosed by protective bone which means it cannot swell without compressing itself dangerously within its box—and this not infrequently happens after injury. Furthermore, any bleeding into the interior of the skull can only occur at the expense of compressing the brain, since the brain box is already fully occupied by the brain. There is a story in first aid known as " Concussion and Compression." It begins with a knock-out blow to the head and this is known as concussion. The patient struck a hard enough blow to the head will lose consciousness, if only for a short time, due to the brain being shaken up. Even slight knocks would do this if the brain were not cushioned by a thin layer of cerebrospinal fluid. Most concussed patients quickly regain consciousness, and for the great majority that is the end of the affair except for a sore head and a headache for a few days. Unfortunately for a minority, even though there may have been no fracture, the blow that knocked them out will also have damaged a small blood vessel on the surface of the brain. These patients may be indistinguishable from the luckier ones at first. They may have regained consciousness and will be just as anxious to go home. They will often be quite lucid for some hours. Surgeons call this the "lucid interval." However, when more than a certain amount of blood has accumulated in the head, and the brain is sufficiently compressed by it the patient loses consciousness slowly, for a second time, and from this phase of " compression " he will not recover unless something is done. The lucid interval can last some hours. Brain surgeons can relieve the compression and save the life of the patient only if they have him in their care when it occurs. This is why *all* cases of head injury who have once lost consciousness (concussion), for however short a period of time, and however lucid they may subsequently appear, *all* must be seen by a doctor and, if thought necessary, observed overnight in hospital, in case they are bleeding and proceeding to compression. There is no way of saving these avoidable fatalities other than by treating all cases of concussion seriously. Fractured skull is potentially even more serious, because the blow will have been harder and, the brain is therefore more seriously at risk.

The spinal cord can be regarded as an extension of the brain which runs down the middle of the spinal bones of the vertebral column. It has the same delicate consistency, and the same inability to recover from injury as the brain. Injury is usually the result of a fracture-dislocation of the spine. The consequences of injury are due to a permanent interruption of its two main functions. All movements of the voluntary muscles are only possible if they are connected by nerves to the brain. Except for muscles in the head, all these "motor" nerves run in the spinal cord. The nerve pathways leave the skull through a large hole in its base and run down in the spinal cord to the required level. They then emerge between the spinal bones and travel in bundles to reach the muscles. Motor nerves for the arm leave the cord between the vertebrae of the neck. Those for the leg leave the cord in the lumbar region in the small of the back. If the nerve supply is damaged in any part of its course, the muscles being supplied become paralysed and are unable to move. It follows that if the spinal cord is damaged, all muscles below the point of damage have been cut off from the brain, and will be paralysed, and this will be permanent because the cord cannot be repaired. Damage to the nerve pathway *after* it has left the cord can often be repaired. Permanent paralysis is only one of the consequences of cord damage, since there is another whole series of nerves running in the cord which carry sensations from all parts of the body to the brain. Therefore there will be loss of sensation as well as paralysis below the point of injury.

It is emphasised that fracture of the spinal bones can occur without damage to the cord taking place. It is when these bones move one over the other, or "dislocate," that permanent cord damage occurs. It is therefore extremely important that cases of back injury be moved very carefully indeed in order to avoid such a disaster, and special ways of moving such patients are taught in First Aid classes.

## Haemorrhage and Shock.

Every part of the body must have a blood supply, or else it will die. It is possible to stop the blood supply to a leg, for example, by fastening a wide rubber bandage tightly around the top of the thigh. This so-called " constrictive bandage " is still mentioned in First Aid books as a desperate means of controlling haemorrhage in a limb. It should hardly ever be used, because by stopping all circulation of blood, the entire limb will die in the course of time. Besides, most haemorrhage can be stemmed by direct pressure on the bleeding point. The tissues of the leg, such as its muscle and skin and bone will begin to die in a little more than half an hour after cutting off the blood supply. The brain, however, will begin to suffer within three *seconds* of its blood supply being cut off, and will die in about three minutes. Thus it can be seen that some parts of the body are more susceptible than others to a failure of the blood supply and the brain suffers earliest of all. Since the brain is where most of the vital functions of the body are controlled, it follows that a shortage of blood to the brain is likely to lead to a " depression of the vital functions "—a state of affairs known to First Aiders as "'shock."

Shock occurs in a number of conditions, but is always due to a failure of the supply of blood to the vital functions of the brain for one reason or another. Its usual causes are:

(1) haemorrhage, when there is a general shortage, but the brain feels it most;

(2) severe burns, in which much fluid is lost from the blood as will be seen later; and

(3) certain medical conditions causing acute heart failure in which there is a failure to pump blood to the brain because the pump has failed.

The treatment for shock consists basically of restoring the blood supply to the brain, and where it is caused by loss of blood or other fluid, the treatment is transfusion. Finally, it must be emphasised that treatment is always urgent, since the brain cannot function for long without its blood supply, and once damaged by the shortage, can never be repaired. No attempt is made here to describe such treatment completely, but the most important things are to keep the head low so as to reduce the work the heart must do to drive blood to the brain; and to avoid artificial heating of the body by hot water bottles, etc., which only diverts blood away from the brain where it is needed, into the skin where it is not.

The treatment of severe haemorrhage is to stop the bleeding, usually by firm, direct pressure, and then to remember above all things that even though the bleeding has stopped, there may be a dangerous state of shock from which the patient could die. This can only be prevented by restoring the circulation to the brain, usually by transfusion; so, having stopped the bleeding drive him fast to hospital for the second part of the treatment which may be as necessary to save his life as the first.

There is great confusion over the use of the word " shock." In the lay mind it is a shake-up of the nervous system caused by a fright, or some bad news, or the sight of something nasty in the woodshed. Even in the medical mind it is sometimes confused, and some of the First Aid books confuse it still further. Too frequently they give the treatment as " loosen all tight clothing from neck, chest, and waist; reassure the casualty and ensure a good supply of air." All this, together with grandmother's hot strong sweet tea is perfectly good enough if the patient is only " shaken-up " by a fright or a fall, but it will be dangerously negligent and time-wasting if he is suffering from true shock due to a failure of blood supply to the brain.

Fainting is a special case which can be prevented by keeping the head low in those who feel faint. It is usually self-curing due to the patient automatically falling into a position in which the head is low. If the faint, however, is due to severe blood loss, this is the same as shock in our proper meaning of the word and must be treated accordingly.

Haemorrhage can therefore be a difficult problem. It is even more so when it is internal. This may be in *medical* cases such as in occasional cases of peptic ulceration in which the blood will be vomited and also passed in the stool. Or it may be *surgical*, in the sense of being caused by injury to internal organs. The blood may emerge from one or other of the various orifices of the body, or it may be entirely concealed within the body. Rupture of internal abdominal organs such as the spleen, kidney and liver can occur with surprisingly little to show in the way of external injury. A fractured thigh bone can pierce the main artery of the leg and cause lethal internal haemorrhage without a drop of blood being visible. In all these cases diagnosis is urgent, followed by emergency blood transfusion if the brain, and hence the patient's life, is to be saved.

Means of detecting the presence of severe haemorrhage without seeing any blood are taught in First Aid Classes as the Signs of Haemorrhage. They are in fact manifestations of the reactions of the body in its attempts to save the failing brain, and are therefore the same as the signs of shock. The main ones are a rapid, feeble pulse, getting more rapid and more feeble as time goes on in a desperate attempt to get the remaining blood to the brain; skin pallor caused by constriction of blood vessels near the surface so that the blood which remains is shunted to the brain away from the less vulnerable skin; and finally, just before death, restlessness and air hunger.

A word of warning about the First Aid treatment of shock due to heart attack (coronary thrombosis). These patients must be transported at complete rest, but many of them react very badly to being made to lie down, since they have great difficulty in breathing in this position. Transport them relaxed, in a sitting position, supported by a large comfortable back rest.

It cannot be too strongly emphasised that with haemorrhage and shock, as with so many First Aid emergencies, the importance of protecting the brain is paramount.

## Asphyxia.

The previous section was concerned with maintaining an adequate supply of blood to the brain. This is needed in order to supply the brain's only possible fuel—glucose—and the oxygen with which to burn it. Many different circumstances can conspire to reduce the oxygen content of the blood, and the result in each case is asphyxia. Normally, air is taken into the lungs through the air passages and brought into contact with all the circulating blood. It diffuses from the lungs into the blood, where it enters into a special relationship with the pigment of the red cells—haemoglobin. At the same time, the waste gas carbon dioxide enters the lungs from the blood and is breathed out. The revitalised blood is passed through the heart to build up sufficient pressure to drive it into all the tissues of the body, and in particular into the brain. A special system in the brain—the respiratory centre—controls the complicated machinery of respiration and is itself, of course, kept alive by the products of the very mechanism it controls. This mechanism consists of all the muscles of respiration—those which lift the ribs, the diaphragm and many other so-called accessory muscles. They all have to be finely co-ordinated by means of nerve impulses which begin in the brain, pass down the spinal cord and out to the muscles. Information of many kinds comes along sensory nerve pathways to the respiratory centre so that breathing can be automatically adjusted to the changing needs of the moment. In order that life may continue there must be:

(1) a functioning breathing mechanism to revitalise the blood; and

(2) a circulation to carry the revitalised blood to the brain and other tissues.

In many cases when breathing stops and unconsciousness supervenes as brain function is depressed, the heart will go on beating for some time longer. The aim of First Aid is to restore the breathing by artificial respiration *before the heart stops*. Once the heart stops—and it eventually does so abruptly and without warning—the brain is dead within the usual few minutes unless *both* the heart and the breathing are restarted; and this is a very much more difficult proposition than artificial respiration alone.

For these reasons, a patient whose breathing has stopped must have it started again without any delay. Here, as in the case of severe haemorrhage, it is no use telephoning the doctor or even putting the patient in an ambulance. The First Aider must act himself, because he is on the spot and the only one in a position to save life. Both actions require elementary First Aid training, and even school children can accomplish them if they have been well taught.

Asphyxia is the name given to a failure of the oxygen supply to the brain and is due to a breakdown in some part of the complicated breathing mechanism outlined above. One of its chief causes is a blockage of the airway by (a) solids or (b) liquids. Any foreign body of the right shape and size will block the airway, as also will the tongue in the unconscious patient. Remember how much more easily the child's airway can become blocked because it is so much smaller. Blockage by a liquid, is of course, drowning. Remember that if a patient drowns in the entire ocean, it is only about half a cupful which is doing him any harm—as it only takes this amount to fill the airway. The same goes for the amount of tea, or vomit, required to kill an unconscious patient if it gets down the " wrong way "—as it will unless someone prevents it.

Another very common cause of asphyxia is carbon monoxide poisoning. Carbon monoxide is a lethal component of car exhaust fumes, incompletely burning and badly ventilated fires and stoves, and domestic coal gas. One of the inconvenient properties of haemoglobin is that it combines with carbon monoxide very much more eagerly than with oxygen. Prolonged contact with even a very slightly contaminated atmosphere can build up a concentration of carbon monoxide in the blood which will prevent the blood from carrying sufficient oxygen—and this is in fact how it kills. It takes a very short time for this to happen if the atmosphere is heavily contaminated. Remember the danger of even a very slight leak of the gas either in the kitchen, or into a car from a faulty exhaust pipe or silencer. Many elderly people die of coal gas poisoning every day because their sense of smell is poor and they do not detect the leak.

Other causes of asphyxia are lack of oxygen in the atmosphere, as occurs at high altitudes; crushing of the chest so that the ribs cannot move; paralysis of the muscles of breathing by interference with their nerve supply, usually in First Aid, as a result of a broken neck and consequent damage to the spinal cord (poliomyelitis can occasionally produce the same effect by attacking the nerves just before they leave the spine); and depressing the respiratory centre in the brain, most commonly nowadays by barbiturate poisoning.

The only really effective method of artificial respiration, which all members of any civilised community should be able to carry out, can be learned in half an hour at a good First Aid class. This is the direct, mouth-to-mouth method, sometimes dramatised by journalists as the " kiss of life." The method is taught with the aid of models and cannot be satisfactorily learned by only reading about it.

In discussing asphyxia, we have again had to consider the particularly vulnerable situation of the brain.

### Fractures.

Broken bones are not the most serious possible consequences of injuries causing fractures. It is usually more to be feared that further damage will be done by the broken ends of the bones to tissues and organs in the neighbourhood of the fracture. The First Aid treatment of immobilising the part before transporting the casualty is designed to avoid this.

Six types of fracture are commonly taught, but some of them may co-exist in the same injury and the division is only for descriptive purposes. In addition there are two special fractures of the skull.

A " simple " or " closed " fracture is where only the bone is broken, without damage to surrounding tissues and without a wound. A " compound " or " open " fracture is one in which air, and hence germs, can get at the broken bone. This may be through a wound, in whose depths lies the broken bone; or the bone may have been pushed out through the skin; or a bullet track may lead down to the fracture. All these are examples of compound fracture and the great danger is that the bone will become infected. Even now that infections are less feared than before the days of antibiotics, it is still a grave matter for bone to get infected. However the antibiotic is given, we rely on the blood supply to carry it into the infected tissue, and bone has only a very small blood supply. If the infection is not successfully treated it can smoulder for a long time and become a " chronic osteomyelitis " which might ultimately necessitate amputation of the limb—and all because the original fracture was compound or open.

A " complicated " fracture is one in which the broken ends of the bone have damaged some important organ or tissue in the region. For example, a complicated fracture of the ribs is one in which the lung tissue, close behind the inner surface of the rib, has been pierced, and the patient will be coughing up small amounts of bright red, frothy blood. A " comminuted " fracture is one where the bone is broken into several pieces, and an " impacted " fracture is one in which the broken ends have been driven into each other and are firmly impacted. Finally a " greenstick " fracture occurs sometimes in children because their bones are not brittle and do not always break clean across. They partly break like a green stick.

" Depressed " fracture of the skull is where the vault of the skull has been struck and dinted. Many problems arise, since the brain is inevitably compressed and no dressing of the accompanying wound should be allowed to press on the brain. The dangers of infection here are not only to the broken bone, but to the meninges covering the brain, causing meningitis.

Fractured base of skull often passes through that part of the base through which the internal ear channel runs. Thus it frequently results in blood, or cerebrospinal fluid, or a mixture of both, emerging from the ear. The gravity of this fracture lies in the severity of the impact necessary to produce it, which will probably have also caused great destruction of delicate brain tissue. The outlook is usually very poor.

Remember that most casualties with fractures will require a general anaesthetic on arrival in hospital so that their fracture can be set in plaster or otherwise treated. Avoid giving them things by mouth such as drinks, which will mean a three-hour wait before anaesthetic can be administered.

### Burns and Scalds.

The severity of a burn or scald depends largely on its surface area. If a patient dies of a burn, the cause of death is either infection or shock, the latter being due to fluid loss from the surface. Both hazards depend on surface area, since the bigger the surface the more germs are able to enter, and the more fluid can be lost. It follows that the small burn on the hand or arm is seldom a threat to life, however deep the injury; and we shall therefore confine our attention to the larger burns of the whole surface of the limb or trunk. Smaller bodies have a relatively larger surface area, and so a burn of the surface of a child's limb or trunk represents an even greater risk from fluid loss than a corresponding burn in the adult. Everyone has seen the fluid form in the blister of an ordinary small burn. It comes from the fluid part or "plasma" of the blood stream and the loss into such a blister may amount to a thimbleful. This will not hurt anyone. But the loss of similar fluid from the surface of a large burn may amount to many pints. The resultant shock will be partly due to this fluid loss from the blood stream resulting in a reduction in blood supply to the brain. Thus shock from burns has common features with shock from haemorrhage, and it is treated similarly, by transfusion. This time it is not a transfusion of blood but of plasma or some plasma substitute. In practice it is not only water that has been lost but a number of important chemicals dissolved in it as well, so that transfusion solutions have to contain sufficient of each individual substance to restore the deficit. The arrangements for replacing the lost materials are complex and urgent; every bit as urgent as after a haemorrhage and for the same reason. The brain cannot be left too long in need. In general, the First Aid treatment of burns of large surface area is to keep them clean with a dry dressing and get them very quickly to hospital. Life-saving treatment by transfusion cannot start until they arrive. The only permissible delay is in the case of burns caused by corrosive chemicals which must be thoroughly washed off before transport, so that they do not continue to burn the patient on the way.

## Unconsciousness.

It is not sufficiently appreciated that the dangers of being unconscious can often far outweigh the dangers from the cause of the unconsciousness. For example it is known that as many as half the deaths from head injuries are due to the airway becoming obstructed and not to the injury itself. The most important thing in managing the unconscious patient from any cause is to preserve an airway. Particularly if the patient is lying on his back it is likely to get blocked:

(a) by his own tongue as the lower jaw sags backwards;

(b) by his dentures (so remove them);

(c) by vomit; and

(d) by anything anyone may be tempted to give him by mouth.

Nothing whatever should be given by mouth in any circumstances to the unconscious patient, since he cannot swallow and it will inevitably go into his lungs.

Many of these dangers can be very much reduced by not having him on his back. Place him instead in the semi-prone position: half on his side, half on his front, with the upper leg drawn up to prevent him from rolling about. In this position the head will be inclined downwards. The jaw will tend to sag forwards and the tongue with it, away from the back of the throat. Any vomit will also come forwards. If the tongue does get in the way of the breathing the airway can usually be cleared by bending the head backwards as far as it will go and pushing the whole lower jaw forwards, by pushing from behind the angle of the jaw on both sides.

## DRUG ABUSE AND DRUG DEPENDENCE.

This section of earlier editions of *Pears* was simply called "Addiction." This word is still much used, but is gradually being replaced by the terms in the present title, because ideas about the nature of the problem and methods of dealing with it are changing. Addiction is a word that conjures up rather 19th century ideas in the minds of readers: opium dens, inscrutable orientals, Sherlock Holmes injecting himself with cocaine—basically a phenomenon of foreign origin, rather frightening if its implications were not literary rather than factual, and not of great significance in Great Britain.

## Drug Abuse.

It is now realised by doctors, research scientists, social workers, and the police—if still not by society as a whole—that the truth is quite different. The *abuse* of drugs in this country is of large proportions, increasing rapidly and showing no signs of diminishing. It is responsible each year for thousands of deaths by suicide and by accidental overdosage; for an enormous but virtually unmeasurable amount of private suffering; and for the loss to society, in terms of reduced working efficiency, of millions of man-hours every year. It has nothing to do with opium smoking which was never in any case more than the eccentricity of the few. Opium is virtually unused in medicine these days and the amount of smuggling, always small, is now negligible. The problems today arise chiefly from the misuse of drugs given by doctors for their effects on the central nervous system—the pain-killers, sleeping pills, "stimulants," and "tranquillisers."

## Drugs and Medicines.

To the doctor, any substance is a drug that can be introduced into the body from outside, and that is capable of producing some detectable effect. Most such substances have a beneficial use. They are "medicines," and as such are given by doctors in suitable cases. Others, for example, nicotine (in cigarettes), alcohol (in beer, wine, or spirits), and carbon monoxide (in coal gas), are of doubtful benefit and of certain harm and are used by doctors, if at all, only under certain very special and usually experimental conditions.

Medicines may be classified under four main headings. First, there are those like quinine, or penicillin and other so-called antibiotics, that actually cure diseases by eradicating the organism (bacteria or other parasites) that cause disturbance of normal bodily function. Second, drugs such as insulin or the steroids overcome in the unhealthy the lack of some necessary substance a healthy body manufactures for itself: they must usually continue to be given for life. Third are the drugs which relieve the signs of disease—for example, there are many new drugs that lower the blood pressure or increase the output of urine—without being able to put right the disturbed basic situation which is the cause of the trouble. Fourth are drugs to relieve the patient's symptoms—which make him feel better, less breathless, take away his pain, help him to sleep, and so on—although we seldom know why they are able to do this. Indeed, in many cases we suspect that they are acting mainly as a token of help from doctor to patient, and so encouraging his body to fight a more successful battle on its own behalf. (There is in fact a fifth class of drugs, which includes the majority of those on the market at any time, the members of which are devoid of any action whatsoever except that of enriching those who manufacture and sell them; but we are not concerned with these at the moment. They constitute a related, but different, kind of problem.)

There is no doubt that the genuine advances in beneficial drugs during the last thirty years have been enormous; but the very successes of the penicillins, tetracyclines, antimalarials, hormones, and so on have bred in the public and in the medical profession itself an attitude of uncritical wonder. There have been relatively few drugs in the first and second categories mentioned above; and in the field of mental health, the importance of which is now so rightly emphasised, there are virtually none. Yet drugs which act upon the brain are often received as if they were curative although they may pose fresh problems rather than solve the old. Thus, although there are many drugs which act upon the mind, few do this in any fundamental sense: they relieve pain and anxiety, bring sleep and lessening of stress, and may allow the patient to recuperate himself during the relief they provide. But often this deeper change does not occur—sometimes because the doctor has not clearly seen his part in helping to bring it about—and then the symptomatic relief may come to be sought for its own sake.

New and old drugs are still prescribed for their effects upon the mind—less so now than even a few years ago, before the thalidomide disaster—without sufficient attention to possible long-term dangers, of which there are in effect four.

## Dangers of Long-term Medication with Drugs acting on the Brain.

1. *Toxic effects.* Drugs which act upon the nervous system, like any others, have characteristic toxic or unwanted effects of their own (incidentally, these may become apparent rapidly; even, on rare occasions, after only a single dose). Such effects may have little or nothing to do with the desired effects for which they are being prescribed and taken. For example, it has only come to be realised quite recently that aspirin is liable to cause bleeding, which is occasionally serious, from the lining of the stomach in a large proportion of people who take aspirin regularly; or that phenacetin, another substance very frequently present in pain-killers that can be bought from chemists without prescription, leads (after prolonged use) to kidney damage. Some drugs may cause rashes and other allergic reactions in susceptible subjects; and jaundice, fainting, tremors, and motor disorders are known to occur in some patients taking a variety of other drugs.

2. " *Rebound.*" The body works in such a way, over a variety of its activities, that it tends to return to a "neutral" position after it has departed from this for any reason. For example, over-eating tends to be followed by a lessening of appetite, at least for a time; the runner makes up for his air-deficit during the race by breathing more deeply thereafter; and if, at rest, you breathe for a time more rapidly and deeply than you need, this period will be followed by one in which you breathe *less* often than usual until the balance is restored. These illustrations—and there are others—have nothing to do with drugs: but in a similar way, it seems that if a continued pain, or an unpleasant emotional state such as anxiety or depression is changed into its opposite, or removed altogether by the use of a drug, the prior state may return with increased force when the drug is no longer taken. The "rebound" phenomenon, naturally, encourages the patient to take another dose, and so on.

3. *Habit formation.* This alternation of mood-changed-by-drug with the disturbed mood itself leads to the habit of taking the drug. The patient comes to rely upon it and to take it anyway, even before the unpleasant state has returned. At this stage he is said to be "habituated": he has a psychological need for the drug, and later may become disturbed at the possibility that it will not be available when he needs it. This might not matter so greatly, if it were not that continued use of drugs in this way has physical consequences as well.

4. *Tolerance and habituation.* The body also tends to restore its own balance when drugs are given, too. It "learns" surprisingly quickly how to deal with substances with which it has never before been confronted, so that it eliminates subsequent doses more and more quickly and completely. Thus the effect of each successive dose is smaller and lasts for progressively shorter periods of time. To counter this, the patient

tends to increase the dose: and the vicious circle continues. At this point he has become physically dependent upon the drug: and he may suffer physically—sometimes so severely that he dies—if supplies are not continued.

As he increases the dose in this way, so his tolerance of its effects increases, to such an extent that after prolonged use he may be taking doses of a drug that are five or ten times greater than those which will kill somebody not dependent upon them in this way. It sometimes happens that a patient develops a renewed craving at some point after a course of treatment, in which the dose of drug has been reduced without removing the underlying cause of his dependence. He may then obtain and use the dose he habitually took before treatment, not knowing that his body will have lost its tolerance of such doses. That dose is now as high for him as for any other person and so may be lethal. There has been a number of deaths for this reason.

## Factors in the Causation of Dependence.

The risk of becoming dependent upon a drug is governed by three main factors: the drug itself, the personality of the individual who takes it, and the circumstances in which it is taken. Most adults have taken alcohol at one time or another, unless it is against their code to do so; yet *relatively* few are dependent upon it (relatively few, but many too many: perhaps half a million in the United Kingdom alone). Many of us have had morphine or some other strong pain-killer for medical reasons, without becoming dependent upon it (whatever so-called addicts say, it is extremely rare for anyone to become dependent on an opiate because he was introduced to it in a medical setting). On the other hand, if we start to take such a drug "for kicks"—as more and more people, particularly teen-agers and young adults are doing—it is extremely probable that we shall become dependent upon it, and sooner rather than later at that. It is also probable that each one of us would become dependent, were he obliged to take it regularly, for long enough, and in sufficient dosage. Thus, although there are personalities—psychopathic, immature, or unstable—that are more prone than others to become dependent if they are exposed to the drug, there are also drugs that are more likely than others to cause such dependence no matter to whom they are given. The extent of the dependence will vary: with some, it is never physiological but remains psychological (but not the less real or disturbing for that). Also, the rate at which dependence develops may vary; and the picture presented by the dependent subject—the extent to which his normal life is impaired, or to which he becomes dangerous to himself or others—varies as well. In a very much oversimplified way, some of these relationships will now be summarised for certain substances.

Heroin, morphine and cocaine are usually injected. Barbiturates (sleeping pills) and Amphetamine ("Benzedrine") are tablets or capsules, and Marihuana ("reefers," hashish) is smoked in cigarettes. Heroin and cocaine are now usually taken together. Combinations of drugs often act differently from their individual constituents and patients dependent upon them are even more difficult to treat. Barbiturate and amphetamine, also, are often mixed (as in "purple hearts"). There is considerable *psychological* dependence on heroin, morphine, cocaine, and amphetamine, but much less with marihuana. *Physiological* dependence is great with heroin and morphine, less with barbiturates, alcohol, and amphetamine in that order, and virtually nil with cocaine and marihuana. Personality plays a greater part in initiating dependence on alcohol, marihuana, and barbiturates than with the others. Heroin, cocaine, and morphine are the cause of more antisocial tendencies in dependent people than alcohol, barbiturates, and amphetamine. The chief danger of marihuana (mere possession of which is illegal) seems to be that the search for it will lead the searcher into localities where his risk of exposure to even more dangerous influences is greatly increased. It is thus sometimes argued that if it were legal to consume marihuana, the number of young people who yearly become dependent upon the other more dangerous drugs would in fact decrease. There is as yet no evidence for or against this proposition. The number of drug dependent people in U.K. is rising fast for heroin and cocaine. This number is very large for alcohol, and is increasing in the case of barbiturates and marihuana. Very few people are dependent on morphine, and the number is not growing.

### Treatment.

Exhortations, imprisonment, and other moralistic or legalistic approaches are useless. Treatment of any person dependent upon a drug is a matter for a qualified psychotherapist. It is liable to be time-consuming and frustrating for patient and doctor, and it is frequently unsuccessful. At present, there are too few specialists or centres where treatment can be obtained, although it is to be hoped that this situation will change as the problem is increasingly seen by our society to be of exceptional gravity.

When there is little or no chance of cure, prevention is certainly the best treatment. Drugs should only be taken on the prescription of a doctor: and the patient should remind him from time to time, if this be necessary, that he would like to dispense with his drugs as soon as the doctor thinks it possible. It should also be remembered that there is often no need to reach for the aspirin (or any other drug that anyone can buy from the chemist without prescription) at the first sign of a headache—or to reach for it at all to help one sleep or relax, for which purpose such drugs are in any case pharmacologically useless. A wait for ten minutes is good discipline, and will frequently resolve the problem to an extent that makes a drug unnecessary.

## DISEASES OF THE BLOOD
### INTRODUCTION.

There are about eight or ten pints of blood in the adult human body. Its main function is to transport nutrient materials to all the various tissues and to carry waste products of tissue activity to organs such as the lungs, kidneys, and liver for disposal. It also helps to maintain a constant chemical environment for the body cells, some of which would be very disturbed in their function if the correct balance of organic and inorganic chemicals were not maintained. The blood also serves a protective function in fighting disease, either with certain of the white cells, or by means of immune antibodies dissolved and carried in the plasma.

A little more than half the volume of blood is the fluid plasma, in which are dissolved all the nutrient materials, organic and inorganic chemicals, hormones and large quantities of protein. The remainder consists of red cells, white cells, and some particles which are not really cells, called platelets. In every cubic millimetre of whole blood, or in every droplet the size of a pin head, there are about 5 million red cells, between 5,000 and 10,000 white cells, and 200,000 platelets as well as half a cubic millilitre of plasma. The red cells suffer a great deal of wear and tear as they are hurled round the circulation, and they only survive for three or four months. There is a red cell factory in the bone marrow which replaces them at exactly the rate they are destroyed, and you have made very many millions of new ones while you have been reading this single paragraph. The function of the red cells is to carry the oxygen from the lungs to the tissues, and to play an important part in carrying the waste gas, carbon dioxide, in the reverse direction. A shortage of red cells, and hence of their oxygen-carrying pigment, hæmoglobin, is called anæmia; an excess is called polycythæmia.

There are five kinds of white cells or leucocytes: neutrophils (or polymorphonuclear leucocytes), eosinophils, basophils, lymphocytes, and mono-cytes. The first three are quite actively motile, like amœbæ, and are capable of ingesting bacteria and other particles by "phagocytosis." There is a great increase in the number of neutrophils (a leucocytosis) during bacterial infections and other inflammatory conditions like appendicitis. Eosinophils are found in larger numbers than usual in allergic conditions like asthma, and in infestations by worms and other parasites, but we do not know why this should be. Lymphocytes are concerned with the manufacture of antibodies. In some infections, particularly tuberculosis and viral infections, there are fewer white cells than usual (leucopenia). Pus consists of the dissolved remnants of inflamed tissue and many dead neutrophils which have become casualties in the battle against infection. It also contains surviving bacteria, and as such is a source of further infection.

Platelets are curious particles, smaller than any of the cells. They are little pieces broken off certain special bone-marrow cells which produce them. They have a role in the stemming of blood loss after injury, partly because they are sticky and adhere to one another and to broken blood vessels and help to plug the open ends of damaged vessels; and partly because they contain a great deal of a substance (thrombokinase) which is necessary to the clotting mechanism of the blood.

Hæmatology, as the study of blood and its diseases is called, is a very complicated subject and only a brief general account will be given here. Diagnosis is usually made by taking small samples of blood (or of the bone marrow where blood cells are made), counting the numbers of the different cells and examining their appearance under the microscope. We shall briefly consider the main diseases involving red cells, white cells, and platelets.

### Red Cell Diseases.

These are of two main groups leading to a shortage of red cells (anæmia), or an excess (polycythæmia). The former is much the more common and there are many different kinds. In all of them the shortage of red cells results in a depletion of the capacity of the blood to carry oxygen. This means that the heart must work harder to send more blood than usual to the tissues, and even so the tissues will often go short. The patient will be persistently tired and listless, and if the anæmia is severe the action of the brain and heart will be seriously impeded, even leading to fainting, cardiac pain, and breathlessness on exertion. All these symptoms, however, can be caused by many other conditions. The only way to be sure they are due to anæmia is by a proper examination of the blood, and even this will not lead to the truth if the picture has been spoilt by the patient taking iron tonics and other remedies of his own accord. Therefore do not dose yourself with tonics, in case you really have anæmia. You may make it impossible to arrive at a proper diagnosis later.

*Hæmorrhagic Anæmia.* Anæmia, a shortage of red cells, may be due to a variety of causes, singly or in combination. One very obvious cause is loss of blood, or hæmorrhage. Following the sudden loss of a pint or two of blood or more, the red-cell-producing bone marrow "factory" will step up its production; but even if it is adequately supplied with all the raw materials such as iron, it may well take many weeks to build up the numbers to normal. A very severe degree of hæmorrhagic anæmia is usually treated by blood transfusion. Milder degrees can be treated by taking extra iron, often over a long period of time. The supply of iron for making new red-cell pigment is nearly always the bottle-neck which limits production. Hæmorrhagic anæmia can commonly occur, however, without a sudden severe hæmorrhage. From what has been said about the constant replacement of red cells as they wear out, it must be obvious that even if there is only a slight failure to keep pace with the numbers lost, several months of such a failure can eventually deplete the numbers to the level of very severe anæmia. This situation is common when small amounts of blood are being continuously or repeatedly lost, and here again it is a shortage of dietary iron which is the usual cause of the failure to replace the lost red cells. Normal menstrual loss in women and girls whose diet is on the border-line of iron deficiency is a common cause of progressive tiredness and lack of energy. Where the menstrual flow is heavier than usual, or where it is frankly excessive in older women due to the various common gynæcological disorders, serious anæmia is surprisingly common. During pregnancy a great deal of iron is lost by the mother to the baby, and this, together with the inevitable blood loss at delivery, often makes for a very tired mother indeed, just at the time when there is an enormous amount of work to be done to manufacture milk and attend to all the extra household tasks of baby care. For these reasons it is almost routinely advisable to build up stocks of iron throughout the pregnancy by remembering to take the pills provided. Men as well as women can lose small amounts of blood continuously in later life from gastro-intestinal conditions such as piles, ulcers, and tropical infestations such as hookworm; and here again the anæmia may be just as severe in the long run as that which inevitably follows a sudden, massive hæmorrhage. One extra word of warning. Do not assume because you are pale that you are anæmic. Pallor is a very poor guide, because it is dependent on so many other things, like the blood vessels in your skin, and its thickness and translucency. Nothing but a blood test (which is so easy for your doctor to do) can really tell you if you are anæmic. And if your anæmia is due to a blood-losing condition, then that too must be treated. So do not be tempted to treat yourself, and never delay seeing your doctor about any excessive or unexplained bleeding, from any source.

*Hæmolytic Anæmia* occurs when for any reason, there are more blood cells than usual being destroyed in the body. This may be because the cells are abnormally fragile, or because normal cells have been attacked by something to which you are allergic, or rarely because you have become sensitive to your own red cells. Sometimes unborn babies have severe hæmolytic anæmia, due to an incompatability of blood group (Rh factor) between the mother and the baby, and the same sort of thing happens if incompatible blood is given by mistake in blood transfusion. Up to a point, in mild hæmolytic anæmia, the bone marrow can keep pace with the increased loss of cells, but beyond this point anæmia develops. After incompatible blood transfusions a very dangerous situation results from the effects of the destruction of red cells and the liberation of their products into the blood. One form of jaundice is often produced in hæmolytic anæmia, the patient becoming yellow because of the breakdown products of red cells circulating in excess as bile pigments. These latter are normally always present to a small extent due to the normal, comparatively small, rate of destruction of effete red cells

*Aplastic Anæmia* is the term given to anæmia due to a virtually total failure of the bone marrow red-cell factory. Sometimes this occurs for no obvious reason. It is sometimes due to a heavy dose of radioactivity or X-rays knocking out the cells of the " factory." It may even be due to cancer cells growing in the bone marrow cavity and not leaving sufficient room for the red marrow cells. It is fortunate that aplastic anæmia is very rare, because it can only be treated by blood transfusions every few weeks for the rest of the patient's life. Very occasionally there have been exceptions to this rule, when the patient's marrow has re-awakened for no apparent reason and suddenly begins to make red cells again.

*Pernicious Anæmia.* This is a fairly uncommon anæmia, which has a very interesting story. The processes by which red cells are manufactured are many and complex, and depend, like so many other bodily activities, on the supply of a vitamin containing cobalt, called vitamin $B_{12}$. This is nearly always present in more than adequate quantities in the diet, but in order for it to be absorbed from the intestine, there must also be a substance called " intrinsic factor " which is normally made by the lining of the stomach. People with pernicious anæmia have suffered a degeneration of the lining of their stomachs, probably because, for some reason, they have become " sensitive " to this part of their own tissue. This kind of civil war within the body is known as an " auto-immune " disease, and is comparable in type with some other forms of hæmolytic anæmia. In other words they destroy their own stomach lining, fail to produce " intrinsic factor," and as a result fail to absorb vitamin $B_{12}$ into the body. Faced with a failure in the supply of this essential substance, the bone marrow produces too few red cells, and the few that are produced are deformed, much too large, and very fragile. In addition to its role in blood formation, vitamin $B_{12}$ is essential to the normal functioning of the spinal cord, and in long-standing cases of untreated pernicious anæmia, there is often a resulting neurological disability.

The cure for pernicious anæmia was discovered about forty years ago, and is a triumph for the scientific investigation of the causes of disease. While treating anæmic dogs, an American scientist named Minot discovered that eating raw liver in large quantities produced a tremendous improvement. Patients with pernicious anæmia were then made to eat vast quantities of raw liver—about one or two pounds a day—and were found to get better, whereas previously they had inevitably died. Raw liver is, of course, very unpleasant to eat, and after a few years it was found possible to prepare crude extracts for injection. Injection had the great advantage that no absorption difficulties arose, and much less liver could be used. Biochemists then began the enormous task of trying to find which of the thousands of substances in liver was the vital factor, and after many years of painstaking chemical fractionation of liver and trying out the various fractions as a cure for the disease, vitamin $B_{12}$ was discovered. The pure substance is one of the most powerful substances known, being active in amounts as small as millionths of a gram. Nowadays pernicious anæmia is treated by small occasional injections of the vitamin, whose other name is cyanocobalamin.

*Polycythæmia.* Too many red cells per cubic millilitre of blood can be found without there being an increase of the total number of red cells in the body. This occurs in dehydration, when there is a loss of plasma without a comparable loss of cells, and is called hæmo-concentration. Alternatively, the bone marrow can manufacture more cells than usual as a response to living for long periods at high altitudes. The beneficial result can be that the blood can carry normal amounts of oxygen, even though the supply (in the rarefied air) is reduced. Finally there is a red cell disease, analogous to leukæmia (*q.v.*) in which the bone marrow factory gets out of control and produces too many cells with no beneficial results. The number in the blood can be double the normal and the blood becomes so thick that the heart has difficulty pumping it round the body. This disease (*polycythæmia rubra vera*) used to be treated by repeatedly bleeding the patient to reduce the numbers. It is now treated very successfully with carefully judged amounts of radioactive phosphorus or certain other " antimitotic " chemicals which reduce the rate of multiplication of bone marrow cells. Care has to be taken not to knock them out altogether, in which case aplastic anæmia or agranulocytosis (*q.v*) could result.

### White Cell Diseases.

These are fortunately much rarer than diseases involving red cells, and are usually much more to be feared.

*Agranulocytosis.* In this condition the number of those white cells which are responsible for phagocytosis of bacteria falls precipitously. The result is that one of the main bodily defences against infection fails, and the patient may die from an overwhelming invasion of germs and the accompanying high fever. The usual cause is abnormal sensitivity to certain drugs, often those which are in widespread use and only give trouble in the occasional case. One example among hundreds is the antibiotic chloramphenicol which specifically kills typhoid bacteria and is used for that purpose. It is believed that about one case in 60,000 becomes sensitive to it and agranulocytosis often fatally follows. The fact that almost any drug *can* do this to some people and yet be quite safe for the majority, is one good reason not to dose yourself unnecessarily with over-the-counter medicines.

*Leukæmia.* This is a cancer of the white cells, in which the normal rate of production of any of the white cells gets out of control, leading to a pile-up of abnormal cells at the site of production (bone marrow, lymph nodes, and spleen) or in the blood, or both. In spite of an increase in their numbers, their abnormality renders them unable to combat infection; sepsis and fever result. It is known that this kind of cancer can be caused by the effects of ionizing radiation on the white-cell factory, and it is certain at least in animals, that viruses can also be responsible. Survivors from the atomic explosions in Japan have subsequently suffered from leukæmia far more commonly than the rest of us, as have doctors, nurses, and patients who have been over-exposed to X-rays. At the time of writing, leukæmia is still a uniformly fatal disease, although patients may sometimes survive many years. Their remaining time can nearly always be made more comfortable by various forms of treatment, and one day a cure will be found by the research workers devoting their time to its study. It is difficult not to get very impatient with the slow rate of progress of these studies, particularly when caring for children and young people whose lives are inevitably ended by the disease. The solution, however, as with other forms of cancer, probably depends on the understanding of the nature of life itself, and as long as biological research remains short of the relatively small amounts of money required to tackle these problems at reasonable speed, we have no right to be impatient, except with our elected leaders who spend far more than is needed on less important things.

*Hodgkin's Disease, Lymphosarcoma, and Reticulosarcoma.* These are cancerous diseases in many ways similar to leukæmia, in which the cancer process involves cells of the so-called reticulo-endothelial system. Such cells are principally in lymph nodes (which used to be called lymph glands) and the spleen. Hodgkin's disease is named after one of the more illustrious pathologists at Guy's Hospital who first described it nearly a hundred years ago, and whose early specimens of affected lymph nodes are still preserved there; is an even greater puzzle than leukæmia. There are all grades of severity, and although many patients die within six months, many survive much longer, even for twenty years in some cases.

**Hæmorrhagic or Bleeding Diseases.**

Whenever blood vessels are damaged by injury, there is a remarkable series of mechanisms which automatically come into operation to stem the flow of blood. There is a constriction of all the smaller vessels in the locality. Platelets stick together and release substances which help the vessels to stay constricted as well as others necessary to blood clotting, and yet others which help to bind the clot tightly together. Later, materials appear to prevent too much clotting, and eventually the clot is removed altogether as healing proceeds. There are some very complicated diseases of this blood-conserving mechanism which can lead to abnormal bleeding, sometimes beneath

the skin to produce bruising or even smaller leaks; sometimes leading to a greater loss of blood, particularly following a wound. In some kinds of *purpura* (bleeding tendency) the blood vessels are the cause of the trouble, having become fragile and leaky for a number of reasons. This happens in old age (*senile purpura*), in scurvy, or vitamin C deficiency, as an occasional accompaniment to infective diseases, or as an immunological effect on the lining of blood vessels when the patient becomes sensitised to certain substances (*Schönlein-Henoch* or *anaphylactoid purpura*). The latter often follows a streptococcal sore throat, just as rheumatic fever and acute nephritis do; and as well as the purpura there may be joint pains and nephritis. Just as almost any drug or chemical will cause agranulocytosis in some people, so it can also cause anaphylactoid purpura.

*Purpura* may also be due to a lack of platelets, known as thrombocytopenia (a shortage of thrombocytes or platelets). This can happen if the bone marrow factory is depressed, since this is where platelets too are made. It is therefore a common accompaniment of leukæmia or aplastic anæmia. Or there can be increased destruction of platelets in some diseases of the spleen. Platelets normally last eight to ten days, but their life-span can be shortened in heart failure, and following massive transfusions, or often for no apparent reason ("idiopathic" thrombocytopenia), when removal of the spleen can sometimes help.

Finally, defects of the *clotting mechanism* will lead to a bleeding tendency, and since the mechanism itself is very complex, so is the variety of things which can upset it. The liver provides the blood with many of the substances required for clotting, so it is not surprising that a clotting defect commonly accompanies liver disease. One necessary substance for blood clotting is called "antihæmophilic factor" and is missing from people who have inherited the disease *hæmophilia*. These unfortunate people may die of hæmorrhage from quite small cuts or minor surgical procedures like tooth-extraction, and although it is possible to prepare antihæmophilic factor, it is not yet possible to give continuous, life-long treatment with it. In emergencies a transfusion of fresh blood (the factor is destroyed by storing) is sometimes used.

## DISEASES OF THE HEART AND BLOOD-VESSELS.

### INTRODUCTION.

The heart consists of about three-quarters of a pound of muscle, which makes up the walls of its four chambers. Anatomically the human heart closely resembles the sheep's hearts to be found in a butcher's shop. Indeed it would be an instructive exercise to dissect one of these in the order described below, since there is no other way of properly appreciating what the chambers, valves, etc., are really like. There are two quite separate pumps in the heart—one on the owner's right (or on your *left* if you are looking at the front of someone else), and one on his left. The right heart collects spent, deoxygenated, "venous" blood which returns there from the whole of the body, and gives it the comparatively small push required to drive it through the adjacent lungs. The left heart collects the revitalised, oxygenated "arterial" blood as it trickles away from the lungs, and gives it the enormous push required to build up the arterial blood-pressure, so that it can be forced through all the tissues of the body. As may be expected, the right heart chambers have much thinner walls than the left, since their muscle has much less work to do. This will help you get your bearings with the sheep's heart. The tip, or apex, is the lowest part. The thick-feeling side is the left, the thin the right; and the great vessels are at the top.

The upper chamber on the right, or right atrium, has two large openings into it through which all the spent blood arrives from the upper and lower great veins (the superior and inferior venae cavae). Cut open the thin wall of the right atrium with scissors between these two holes to lay open the interior of the chamber, noting the "auricle" or "dog's ear" that forms a small cul-de-sac. The whole chamber is sometimes, inaccurately, called the auricle. You should be able to push a finger downwards into the lower chamber—the right ventricle—through a communicating hole guarded by the three thin cusps of the *tricuspid valve*. These will not obstruct your finger, since they are designed to permit blood flow in the same direction. When the atrium is full of blood, it squeezes its contents through the tricuspid valve into the right ventricle; and when, a split second later, the ventricle is full and contracts, the three cusps come together to prevent the blood from flowing backwards into the atrium again. Instead the spent blood is driven onwards through the *pulmonary valve* (in the upper part of the right ventricle), through the pulmonary artery, to be delivered to the lungs. The pulmonary valve has three very well-defined cusps which prevent blood from coming back into the ventricle as it relaxes to receive more blood from the atrium before the next contraction or beat. It is possible to pass a blade of the scissors from the opened-out right atrium, through the tricuspid valve towards the tip of the heart, and cut along the right border of the heart through the thickness of the ventricular muscle. Then cut upwards again, passing the scissors blade through the pulmonary valve and open up the *pulmonary artery*. If you have done this successfully you will have followed the path taken by the spent blood through the right heart to the lungs. Notice the thick round bands of muscle lining the ventricle, and notice too that you have not entered the left heart, which has no connection with the right except in some congenital malformations (see later). The same dissection can now be made of the left heart. Open up the *left atrium*, noting its "dog's ear" or "auricle," pass the scissors down into the *left ventricle* through the two rather flimsy cusps of the *mitral valve*. Notice how much thicker is the muscle of the left ventricle, and cut upwards through the three well-formed cusps of the *aortic valve* into the main artery of the body—the *aorta*. The aorta as it leaves the left heart is distinguishable from the pulmonary artery as it leaves the right, partly by the extreme toughness of the aortic wall (it has to withstand so much more blood-pressure); and partly by the entrances or orifices of the two small branches given off by the aorta, just beyond the valve cusps, which go to supply the heart muscle itself with blood. These are the *coronary arteries* which are so necessary for the heart's own survival.

The amount of blood pumped in unit time, or the *cardiac output*, can be varied a great deal, according to the needs of the moment. This is accomplished by altering both the heart rate and the stroke volume, the amount expelled per beat. Every minute, the healthy adult man at rest shifts about ten pints of blood through the heart— an amount equivalent to all the blood he possesses. When exercise is taken, or in response to anxiety or fear, this is stepped up many times, so that the muscles can receive a greatly augmented supply of the materials required for action. The controlling mechanisms which allow these changes to be made automatically are partly organised in the brain by the so-called *cardiac centre*; and partly by local mechanical and chemical stimuli to the heart muscle itself. The cardiac centre is continuously receiving information through nerves about the physical and chemical state of the circulation, and also from the mind; which is partly how certain emotions make the heart beat faster. All the information is integrated, and a cardiac output continuously arranged which is appropriate for current demands.

*Cardiac Neurosis.* In ordinary circumstances at rest, most healthy people are not conscious of their heart-beat. However, there are many perfectly healthy people whose hearts slip in an extra beat occasionally. Sometimes their owners are aware of this, and become unnecessarily alarmed.

Their fear causes palpitations (a pounding of the heart) and the tension mounts. An undue anxiety about the tricks played by a healthy heart sometimes leads people to interpret minor pains in the chest, or even indigestion, as grave symptoms of heart disease, and the consequent anxiety leads to still worse symptoms. If you are one of these worried people, take your worries to your doctor, and let him decide for you whether there is anything wrong. A hundred to one there isn't, and then you will have to find something else to worry about, or better still give up the habit altogether. Many people secretly worry about heart disease and high blood-pressure for years, when very often they are worrying unnecessarily. Even if there is cause for worry, so much can be done for these conditions (as it can for cancer) provided medical advice is taken early in the course of the disease. Remember, too, that the slight feeling of giddiness when you get up suddenly from having been lying down, is often experienced by most normal people; but if you get frightened by it you will begin to breath more quickly and deeply: and this in itself will make you feel even more faint— and so on.

*Heart Failure.* When the cardiac output of blood is too little for the requirements of the body, a state of *circulatory failure* has arisen, and when this is due primarily to the heart itself being at fault, it is more properly called *heart failure*. As will be seen, heart failure is not a disease, but the common result of a large number of different diseases. The signs and symptoms produced are caused by two sorts of process: (*a*) tissues of the body have too little blood flow through them and are therefore undersupplied; (*b*) blood accumulates and stagnates in tissues, causing congestion, since the failing heart cannot move forward the amount of blood presented to it in the great veins. Often the left or right side of the heart fails disproportionately. In *left heart failure* the lungs are congested because they are the territory from which the left heart is failing to move blood. The patient has great difficulty with his breathing, and in advanced cases may not be able to breathe when he lies down horizontally, because the lungs become so congested and waterlogged. In *right heart failure* the main veins are congested and other parts of the body become swollen with excess tissue fluid, mainly in the lower parts such as the legs and ankles. This swelling with fluid is called œdema, and in heart failure is only partly due to the mechanics of the failing heart. It is mainly due to a poorly understood retention of sodium in the body, a situation in which excess water is also retained. Whatever the type of heart failure, it is always likely to be a changing condition, since the amount of failure will depend as much on the demands being made as on the state of the heart. For instance, in mild cases at rest when the required cardiac output is small, there may be no signs or symptoms. These may only appear on exertion. Heart failure will be referred to again later under the various conditions which cause it.

Treatment of heart failure is quite logical. It is aimed at correcting the imbalance between supply and demand of blood, and at the removal of the accumulated excess fluid. We can therefore (*a*) reduce the body's demand for blood; (*b*) increase the supply or cardiac output; and (*c*) promote the excretion of sodium and fluid. Demand for blood is reduced by rest, both physical and mental, and by reduction of weight, since obesity (being overweight) is an additional demand on the cardiovascular system. The cardiac output can be increased by administering a "tonic" to the heart muscle in the form of *digitalis*, which is a powerful heart stimulant derived from foxglove leaf. Fluid (and hence salt) accumulation can be helped by restricting the intake of salt and by giving drugs which promote its excretion by the kidneys (diuretics). Very occasionally, very large accumulations of fluid in the legs, abdomen, or thorax, are tapped and drained physically, with needles. These remarks on treatment, as elsewhere in the Medical Section, are of course very general and must not encourage anyone to treat themselves for such a potentially serious condition as heart failure. Even such a simple measure as doing without salt can be practised quite unnecessarily by many people for years, simply as a result of reading a paragraph like the above. The most they accomplish is to make their food taste horribly dull. If you need to reduce salt intake you should be in your doctor's care, and so please let him decide.

*Congenital Heart Disease.* It has been estimated that of all the babies born who survive at least one month, there will be about one in every two hundred with some form of congenital heart disease; that is to say that the heart will have failed to develop properly in embryonic life. In some cases this is associated with a virus disease of the mother (commonly rubella, or German measles) or with certain drugs taken by the mother (e.g. thalidomide) at a time, very early in pregnancy, when organs are assuming their adult shape. Parents should see to it that their daughters get German measles before they grow up; and drugs of all kinds should be avoided where possible during early pregnancy. In most cases of congenital heart disease, however, there is no known cause, and it seems that the manner of formation of the embryonic heart is so delicate that it can be thrown out of gear very easily, perhaps even by chance. Scores of different types of defect occur, singly and in combination. Any of the valves may be anatomically defective—either failing to close properly (*incompetence*) or being too tight (*stenosis*); the great vessels (pulmonary artery and aorta) may be switched round, or *transposed*, so that they emerge from the wrong ventricle; there may be defects in the wall (*septum*) which separates the atria or the ventricles on each side (*septal defect*, or " hole in the heart "); or there may be a persistence of the vessel which in the fœtus normally by-passes the lungs by joining the pulmonary artery to the aorta (*patent ductus arteriosus*). This vessel normally closes at the time of birth when the first breaths are taken, and subsequently disappears, so that the whole output of the heart is then sent round the lungs. Detecting congenital heart disease early is one of the purposes of routine post-natal check-up examinations of the baby. Exact diagnosis requires very complicated techniques, and sometimes the structural defect can be corrected by surgery, with almost miraculous results.

*Rheumatic Heart Disease.* Acute rheumatic fever is not to be confused with other forms of rheumatism. Many tissues of the body (particularly the heart) are attacked, as well as the joints, and the trouble is due to a sensitivity which has developed to certain bacteria (*haemolytic streptococci*) which have probably caused a sore throat about three weeks before the onset of the disease. Why acute rheumatism only rarely follows streptococcal sore throat is poorly understood, but this is no consolation to the one per cent or so of the population whose hearts bear its scars. During the acute phase of the illness which usually occurs before the age of fifteen, inflammatory damage occurs to the valves, the heart muscle, and the sac in which the heart lives, the *pericardium*. So there is a *valvulitis* or *endocarditis*, a *myocarditis* and a *pericarditis*. There may be acute heart failure at this stage if the heart is severely affected. The better-known results of rheumatic heart disease, however, are caused in the ensuing years by scarring of the healed valves. The valves are thickened and deformed. They may have lost their elasticity and stretch, so that they do not close properly (*incompetence*); or they may contract and tighten (*stenosis*). In both cases the heart chamber situated next to the affected valve has to work progressively harder, either because it gets no rest in between beats (in *incompetence*); or it has to force the blood through too narrow a hole (in *stenosis*). The end result is some variety of heart failure (P27). Although there are other causes of valvular heart disease which will now be mentioned, rheumatic fever is much the commonest, and much valve trouble can be blamed on rheumatic fever even when the patient has no recollection of ever having suffered

from it. The other, much rarer, causes may be syphilis, congenital valvular anomaly, healed bacterial endocarditis, atherosclerosis, and mechanical injury.

The most commonly affected valve is the mitral, usually causing *mitral stenosis*, in which the opening between the left atrium and left ventricle will sometimes only admit one finger-tip instead of three fingers as it should. In time the left atrium becomes much enlarged as it overworks to force blood through this narrow orifice. Later still a back pressure develops in the lungs causing congestion and breathlessness; and even later the right ventricle is strained as it tries to force blood into the already congested lung. This is a classic example of the march of trouble backwards from the site of the damaged valve involving first the chamber " behind " it (the left atrium), then the territory " behind " that (the lungs), then the pulmonary arteries taking blood to the lungs, and finally the right ventricle trying to send blood to the pulmonary artery. This steady march of events is usually very slow, and can commonly take twenty years or longer from the initial attack of acute rheumatism to the severer symptoms of advanced mitral stenosis. Treatment is both medical and surgical. The heart failure is treated medically as already described. These days surgical reopening of the valve is almost commonplace, either by inserting a finger through the left auricle and breaking down the constriction, or by opening up the heart and re-shaping the valve under direct vision. The latter involves the additional problem of by-passing the heart by the use of some sort of external pump and poses additional problems, even though from other points of view it is obviously more convenient. As always with major surgical procedures much of the problem is in selecting the patients who will benefit from the operation and in whom it is feasible. Quite often there are other valves involved, mainly the aortic or tricuspid or both, and the hydrostatic or " plumbing " problems can be extremely complex. With luck, however, combined with good judgement and good surgery, the lives of incapacitated patients can be transformed by mitral, and other valvular, surgery. The *aortic valve* is stenosed or narrowed by other degenerative processes besides rheumatism. *Tricuspid stenosis* is nearly always rheumatic in origin.

*Coronary Heart Disease.* This is the term used whenever the blood supply to the heart muscle (through the coronary arteries) is reduced to such an extent that the heart muscle suffers from a lack of supplies. It has a number of causes, but the only really common one is partial obstruction of the coronary arteries by a condition known as *atheroma* or *atherosclerosis*, and sometimes inaccurately called *arteriosclerosis*. This arterial disease is described later (P30). It takes the form of swellings or lumps on the lining of the artery which, if they become large enough to interfere seriously with the flow of blood, produce a blood starvation or *ischaemia* of the tissue being supplied. Obviously, the smaller the artery, the more easily will a lump of given size impede the flow. Equally obviously, the greater the demand for blood, as in exercise, the more blood " starvation " there will be. There are two degrees of coronary artery disease: one in which the blood flow is reduced to the point where the increased demands of hard work cannot be met, and this results in *angina pectoris* due to *coronary insufficiency*; the other is when the coronary artery becomes completely blocked, preventing the flow of blood altogether, usually by a *thrombus* or clot of blood, and this is *coronary thrombosis*.

*Angina Pectoris.* Whenever activity is increased in any muscle, the demands for oxygen and nutriments from the blood-stream increase, and as these are used up there is an increased production of waste products known as metabolites. To meet these demands for a greater supply and a more efficient waste-disposal, the blood flow through the exercising muscle must always be increased. If sufficient increase does not occur, not only will there be a shortage of supplies, but there will also be a pile-up of metabolites in the muscle which cannot be carried away. It is mainly because of these latter that pain is caused in ischæmic, or blood-starved muscle, and pain is one of the chief symptoms when heart muscle becomes ischæmic. One important mechanism for increasing blood flow normally to exercising muscle is by automatically dilating the vessels concerned. Diseased vessels, such as coronary arteries when they are affected by atheroma, are not so easily dilated, although certain drugs which are powerful dilators of arterioles can accomplish a great deal, albeit temporarily. The measures taken to relieve the pain and blood-starvation of angina are two-fold. The patient can reduce the demands of the heart by a few minutes' rest, and a drug (usually nitroglycerin) can be taken to dilate the coronary vessels of supply. Another obvious long-term way to reduce demands is for the overweight patient to eat less, and reduce the load of extra body weight on his circulation. It is very frustrating, to say the least, that such an incapacitating and often lethal condition should be caused by the narrowing or blockage of only two or three inches of narrow piping about one-eighth of an inch wide. One obvious form of treatment in theory would be surgical replacement of the piping (many larger arteries than these in other parts of the body are commonly replaced already); or surgical removal of the obstruction inside it. It is very likely that surgeons will one day overcome the technical difficulties involved.

*Heart Attack* or *Coronary Thrombosis.* It should readily be understood from the above description that heart attacks will vary in their severity according to the amount of heart muscle deprived of blood; and this in turn will depend on where in the coronary artery the obstruction occurs. Most usually it is the left ventricular muscle which is cut off from supplies and dies, either in part or in all of its thickness. Since it is the left ventricle which does most of the work of pumping blood to the body, serious heart failure (P27) is to be expected. If too much muscle is killed, the heart will simply stop, and the patient will suddenly die. It is much more usual, however, for enough muscle to be left for survival, albeit with a greatly reduced cardiac efficiency. A heart attack is usually accompanied by severe pain, similar to the pain of angina but more severe, and unrelieved by rest or by the patient's usual drugs. Very occasionally the event occurs apparently without pain, or with so little that it is ignored. These so-called "silent" coronary attacks can make diagnosis extremely difficult. Since the doctor depends very considerably with heart attacks on an exact, spontaneous description of symptoms for his diagnosis, no description will be given here. There are many over-anxious people who will read these words and could be misled into an unspontaneous description of their own symptoms, and this could make the task of treating them such a problem that they could even be mis-diagnosed as a result. If you have the smallest worry that your chest pain is due to your heart, take your anxiety to your doctor without delay. He will almost certainly be able to reassure you; and if it happens to be your heart after all, you will have taken the first sensible step towards proper treatment. Dangerous as heart attacks are, they are by no means the death warrant that many lay people think, any more than cancer is. The treatment for a true heart attack is urgent and prolonged. Patients must be at complete rest and their pain relieved quickly. The area of heart muscle they have lost must be allowed to heal with a good, firm scar, and this can take three months of rest often in hospital.

*Blood-pressure.* The blood is normally under great pressure in the arterial system, since it is this which forces it into all the tissues of the body. It is therefore no more meaningful to say you have "blood-pressure" than to say you have a temperature. You would be very badly off without. Blood-pressure which is too high, however, can give rise to problems, though not always. It is

another of those conditions like angina and cancer, which engender much anxiety among people even when they do not suffer from them. For this reason doctors are often unwilling to disclose a patient's blood-pressure and because of this they unjustifiably earn a reputation for unreasonable secrecy. They are themselves to blame for the general public anxiety as the following true story shows. Twenty years ago a lady in her fifties wished to accompany her husband to a post abroad which was to last four years. All arrangements had been made—the husband resigned his previous job, sold the house, etc.—when it was discovered at a routine medical examination that she had a high blood-pressure, and she was very solemnly advised by the rather elderly doctor not to go. There was great consternation and emotional upheaval, not least because of the inconvenience involved. Eventually she was allowed to go at her own risk. The husband's job lasted eight years instead of four, during which the lady was in no way inconvenienced by her blood-pressure; except that she worried interminably about it. On returning home to retire she began to think she had angina, and elaborate hospital investigation revealed that, as might be expected, her arteries were not as young as they used to be. She was undoubtedly suffering from mild angina, but not as badly as she thought. The opportunity then arose, in her late sixties, to go abroad yet again, and this she did, living a quite strenuous life, and one which she enjoyed. At the time of writing she has returned home and, twenty years later, at the age of seventy three is running a home very actively, still with very little inconvenience from her blood-pressure. There is no doubt that it has been very high all this time, and it is also certain that she will die one day, although it may well not be of her blood-pressure. How much better it would have been for her not to have been told it was high twenty years ago and to have avoided all these years of anxiety. It is not being suggested here that high blood-pressure is a trivial condition, but that it is for doctors to worry about rather than patients! If you ever find out your own blood-pressure, never try to work out for yourself what the figures mean. It is much too complicated. Finally, it should be mentioned that high blood-pressure may occasionally be associated with, or "secondary to," certain kidney diseases (*nephritis*) including a strange condition known as *toxaemia of pregnancy*, which lasts only as long as the pregnancy, provided great care is taken. Most high blood-pressure is, however, "primary", and without any known association or cause.

*Low Blood-pressure.* Some people seem normally to have surprisingly low blood-pressure all the time. There is nothing whatever wrong with this; indeed it may even be beneficial. At least they are unlikely ever to suffer the effects of high blood-pressure. The sudden low blood-pressure of circulatory failure or shock (P27) is another matter and must be urgently treated.

*Irregularities of the Heart-beat.* How quickly or how slowly the heart beats is largely under the control of the cardiac centre in the brain and the level of certain hormones in the blood. The *regularity* of the beat, however, is controlled by the so-called pace-maker in the wall of the right atrium, and by the way impulses from the pace-maker travel through specialised conducting heart cells (the bundle of His and its branches) to the ventricles. When any part of this elaborate mechanism is upset, either by altering the biochemical or electrical conditions of these specialised tissues, or by killing some of them off by deprivation of blood supply in the course of a heart attack, disordered rhythm can result. Increase (*tachycardia*) or decrease (*bradycardia*) in rate is nearly always a normal response to exercise, or anxiety. Very occasional irregularity, such as the mis-timing of an occasional beat is also quite normal in some people, although many are alarmed by it. Persistent irregularity, however, is abnormal. Its true nature can usually be elucidated by making an electrical record of the heart-beat— an electro-cardiogram. The commonest causes are varieties of coronary artery diseases or rheumatic heart disease.

*Pericarditis.* The heart beats inside a bag or sac. At every beat its outer surface slides against the lining of the sac, lubricated by a small amount of fluid. This is the pericardial sac, the *pericardium* being strictly the lubricated membrane which lines the sac and which also covers the outer surface of the heart. Sometimes inflammation occurs—*pericarditis*—and the sliding surfaces become roughened and even separated by a fluid effusion. Very occasionally, so much fluid accumulates that the heart's action is seriously impeded. Pericarditis may be due to infection or to rheumatic fever, and it usually overlies the area of damaged muscle after a heart attack. This illustrates something which people rarely appreciate—that inflammation is not by any means always due to infection by bacteria. The last two varieties of pericarditis are quite free from germs (sterile).

*Myocarditis.* A term loosely applied to disorders affecting the heart muscle. There are lots of very rare causes. The really common ones are due to acute or chronic rheumatic causes or to coronary artery disease, both of which are described above.

*Endocarditis* or inflammation of the lining of the heart is a term loosely applied to any disorder of the valves or heart lining. All varieties of rheumatic valvular disease (P28) are included. Bacterial endocarditis in its several forms usually involves valves already damaged by rheumatic disease. It is a complication which is still much to be feared, though somewhat less so now that antibiotic drugs are available.

*Atheroma or Atherosclerosis.* This is the condition referred to above in which lumps arise on the lining of arterial blood-vessels. Although it is therefore a disease of the arteries, its importance lies in the way blood flow is held up, either by the lumps themselves, or by thrombosis ultimately blocking the narrowed portion of the pipework. The effects on the body are therefore those of depriving the tissues of blood. It is an astonishing fact that in England and America, more people die of the consequences of atheroma than of any other single disease, including all forms of cancer put together. Furthermore, cancer is mainly a disease of old age, whereas many of the effects of atheroma on men occur in early middle age. If narrowing of the artery is going to do significant harm it is easy to see that it will be of more consequence in those parts of the body where small-bore vessels are supplying tissues whose functions are necessary for life. Exactly such a situation exists in the heart and in the brain. An additional factor is that the arrangement of the blood supply in these tissues is such that any particular area has only one vessel leading to it. This is unusual among the tissues generally, where several alternative, or "collateral" vessels usually supply an area, and where others can take over if one becomes obstructed. We have, therefore, a situation in which perhaps the most important tissues —the heart and the brain—run the greatest risk of deprivation, and this leads to angina and coronary thrombosis on the one hand, and cerebral thrombosis on the other, accounting jointly for about one death in every five. In addition, the effects of atheromatous narrowing are often felt in the legs, where the blood supply to the muscles is inadequate for exercise, leading to intermittent pain comparable with that in the heart in similar circumstances. This is called *intermittent claudication,* or intermittent closing of the leg arteries. In its most severe forms, it leads to the need for amputation, although in most cases early treatment can avoid this. It is small wonder that there is intensive research into the causes of atheroma, as with cancer, but it is probably true to say that we still know rather more about cancer.

A lot of attention has been given to the amounts of certain fats in the circulating blood, particularly cholesterol. This fat is found in larger amounts in the blood of sufferers from atheroma, and is also found in the arterial lumps themselves. Efforts have therefore been made to reduce blood cholesterol by modifications of the diet, but it has been extremely difficult to prove that this has done any good. Many other factors are known to contribute to atheroma, and hence to heart attacks and strokes, some of which can be reduced and others not. Such factors are age, obesity, high blood-pressure, and smoking cigarettes. People who lead an active life, like bus conductors, seem to have less trouble than others who are less active, like bus drivers. Sudden severe exercise, however, is bad if you are not used to it. It is better, and life saving, to take regular, moderate exercise. Women have less atheroma than men, until the menopause when they begin to catch up, so that hormones have something to do with it. Serious starvation, such as occurred in the German-occupied territories of Holland and Scandinavia and in the concentration camps conferred one benefit—a freedom from atheroma, but obviously we cannot all starve, and the puzzle remains. Like many of the more important outstanding medical puzzles, there is no single factor responsible, and this is what makes it difficult to solve.

*Aortic Disease.* The aorta, the main artery of the body, running from the left ventricle down through the chest and abdomen, also suffers from atheroma, but is too wide (about an inch across) to become obstructed. However, weaknesses occur in the thickness of its wall, sometimes due to syphilis but nowadays much more usually due to atheroma, which results in a ballooning out of a part of the vessel, rather like you sometimes see in an old bicycle inner tube. In days gone by these *aneurysms,* as the dilations are called, reached an enormous size, and would wear away the breastbone and ribs, to appear as large pulsating masses on the chest. Now that advanced syphilis is less common, atheromatous aneurysm, with a predilection for the abdominal aorta, is the one most commonly seen; and these days it is treated by replacement of the diseased portion of vessel. *Dissecting aneurysms* of the aorta are another variety in which the blood, under high pressure, somehow finds its way in between the layers of the aortic wall and then suddenly rips up and down the whole length of the vessel, separating (or dissecting) one layer from another in its path. Sometimes it tracks back towards the heart and suddenly fills the pericardium with blood to stop the heart's action altogether.

*Embolism.* This term refers to any foreign object travelling in the circulation and becoming impacted when it reaches a vessel too small for it to pass through. It may be a thrombus (P31) a collection of cancer cells, a group of bacteria, a chunk of infected pus from an abscess, a collection of fat droplets or even a bubble of air. If it originates in a vein it travels to the right heart and to the lungs. If it comes from the left heart or an artery, it will impact in any part of the arterial tree. Reasonably enough an arterial embolus will commonly end up in those parts of the body with the richest blood supply, like the brain, the kidneys, the liver or the bone marrow. A thrombotic embolus will cause death of the tissue in the area previously supplied by the blocked vessel, a condition known as *infarction.* Perhaps the commonest source of thrombotic embolism is the lining of the heart chambers where a thrombus has occurred at the site of muscle damaged by a heart attack. Massive pulmonary (lung) embolism is usually the result of thrombosis of the leg veins in people kept immobile following surgery or childbirth. That is why postoperative patients are got out of bed for a while as soon as the first day after the operation. The cells of a cancer embolus usually die; but if they survive, a new cancer deposit begins to grow where the embolus impacts, and this is one of the ways cancer may spread. An infected embolus may infect the vessel wall when it impacts, producing a weakness which may give way. Air embolism, if enough insoluble gas enters the circulation, can kill by making so much froth in the heart chambers as to impede the normal pumping action. If bubbles pass the lungs and enter the brain, all sorts of neurological disorders like scores of tiny strokes arise. The same sort of thing happens all over the body in the "*bends*" or "*caisson*" *disease*, in which the blood literally boils. It is due to a too rapid return to normal pressure from regions of high pressure at great depths or from pressurised chambers. Fat embolism sometimes occurs after fractures due to marrow fat entering damaged veins and being carried away to the lungs.

*Thrombosis.* This is not quite the same as clotting. It is the mass which arises when platelets adhere to the lining of blood-vessels or heart chambers. Blood clot accumulates among layers of deposited platelets and the thrombus therefore has structure, unlike pure blood clot. Thrombosis usually occurs when the lining of the vessel or chamber is damaged by atheroma or inflammation, or when the circulation becomes very stagnant. One danger is that it will become dislodged and travel as an embolus during the first week or ten days of its existence. After this time it is usually firmly incorporated into the vessel walls by cells which migrate into it from the surrounding tissue. The other danger is, of course, that the tissue previously supplied by the blocked vessel will die before a collateral circulation can be established. As previously explained, this is called infarction. All the technical terms in this section are used elsewhere and can be looked up.

*Buerger's Disease* or *thromboangiitis obliterans.* This is an inflammation of the arterial wall which leads to blockage by thrombosis. The leg arteries of comparatively young men are most commonly affected, leading to amputation in some cases. Unlike lung cancer, coronary heart disease, and bronchitis, which are known to be associated with smoking, Buerger's disease is only thought to be. There is a horrible tale of a young man who had lost all his four limbs one after another, sitting on the hospital steps begging passers-by to light his cigarette for him.

*Reynaud's Disease.* This is a strange condition in which the finger tips and in severe cases all the fingers or the whole hand respond in an exaggerated way to cold. The vessels supplying the hand are constricted and the fingers go white as the blood drains from them. Then the capillaries dilate and become distended and filled with blood. But owing to stagnation it is venous and blue, and the fingers are therefore blue. Now we have all experienced this in very cold weather, but sufferers from Reynaud's disease, nearly always women, respond even to very slight cold, like putting their hands into cold water. Even emotional stress will start the process off. In very severe cases the fingers will be so deprived of blood for so long, that sores will develop and fingers can even be lost, but this is very rare, and can be avoided by an operation to cut the nerves which supply the circular muscle of the vessels concerned. In most cases it is sufficient to avoid getting the hands cold.

*Frostbite.* Strictly speaking, this is literally a freezing of the tissues. Although their freezing point might be expected to be close to that of water, it usually only occurs at temperatures below $-13°$ C ($8°$ F). The patient may feel a pricking feeling at first, and feel an area of firmer, pale skin on the cheeks, nose, ears, fingers, or toes. If these parts are numb with cold, the onset of frostbite may not be felt, and will often only be noticed by others. In countries where extreme cold is prevalent, it is usual for complete strangers to stop each other in the street and point it out when they see it. It is important not to rub the affected part, but contrary to popular belief it must be warmed as *rapidly* as possible. Fingers should be immersed in water as hot as the normal hand can bear ($110°$ F). Many First Aid books still quite wrongly teach that return to warmth must be gradual.

# DISEASES OF THE RESPIRATORY SYSTEM

## INTRODUCTION.

When air is drawn in during the process of breathing, it is brought into very close contact with the blood passing through the lungs. In this way the air we breathe in, which contains 20 per cent oxygen, is confronted with " spent " blood returning from the tissues which contains much less, and oxygen therefore diffuses into the blood from the air. At the same time, the waste gas, carbon dioxide, passes by diffusion in the reverse direction from the blood into the air, because there is much more carbon dioxide in the returning " spent " blood than the tiny amount in the air we breathe. The blood is therefore continually circulating through the lungs and exchanging carbon dioxide for oxygen from the air we breathe in. When we breathe out, we disperse the carbon dioxide into the atmosphere.

When the air enters the nose or mouth, it passes into the windpipe or *trachea*, through the vocal cords in the pharynx. The trachea is held open all the time by rings of cartilage and is lined by a mucus-secreting membrane covered by millions of tiny " hairs " or cilia. These continuously waft a sheet of sticky mucus upwards, which traps any dust or other small particles we may have inhaled, until a collection of this material in the pharynx stimulates us to cough and expel the phlegm, usually to be swallowed. At its lower end, the trachea or windpipe divides into two, the right and left main *bronchus*. Each main bronchial tube enters a lung, one on each side, and proceeds to divide repeatedly within the lung until the air is being carried by more and more smaller and ever smaller tubes called *bronchioles*. There are many millions of these on each side, and each one ends in a collection of very small balloon-like structures —the air sacs or *alveoli*. If you were to cut across a lung and examine the cut surface in a good light, you would see that it is a spongy tissue, with many millions of tiny holes, each one just visible to the naked eye. These are the air sacs. In their walls run the blood capillaries, each one of which is a branch of the vessels carrying " spent " blood from the right side of the heart. At this stage, the blood is only separated from the air in the sacs by the walls of the capillaries and of the air sacs themselves. Both structures are extremely thin, making for easy diffusion of the gases between blood and air.

The action of breathing is accomplished by two muscular mechanisms. One is by the muscles which move the ribs, and the other by the diaphragm, a sheet of muscle which runs across the body, separating the chest cavity from the abdominal cavity. These muscles are all actuated by nerves, just as all other muscles are. Those running to the muscles of breathing are organised by a mechanism in the brain known as the *respiratory centre*. It is this centre—one of the so-called vital centres of the brain—which receives information from many different sources, and translates it into instructions for the breathing mechanism. Thus, when you run for a bus, you will automatically breathe more deeply and more quickly because the respiratory centre has been informed about all the extra carbon dioxide in your blood which has been produced by the exercising leg muscles. Even the conscious instructions involved when you blow a trumpet, inflate a balloon, or during speaking, all pass first to the respiratory centre. It is the death of the cells of this and other vital centres of the brain that is the ultimate cause of death in everyone who dies.

*Bronchitis* may be acute or chronic. It is an inflammation of the lining mucous membrane of the larger air passages or bronchi, and results in much more secretion than the amount normally produced, mixed with some pus. The acute form is often caused by viruses, with " secondary " infection from bacteria. It may sometimes be caused by irritant gases, like the sulphur dioxide in smog. The chronic, or long-standing form of bronchitis is often associated with *emphysema*, in which the small air sacs of the lung architecture are destroyed or distorted, leaving larger spaces than normal, often surrounded by fibrous scar tissue. Such an arrangement makes the normal gaseous exchange difficult between air and blood. While the exact cause of chronic bronchitis is difficult to discover, because it is such a mixture of causes, it is mainly associated with older age groups, particularly men, in damp foggy climates like ours in Britain, with polluted town air and especially with smoking. Smoking also makes any existing bronchitis much worse. Patients cough, and produce varying amounts of sputum, or phlegm. They often wheeze like asthmatics. This may go on for many years before the right side of the heart begins to fail (P27). Gradually, during this time, the chest tends to become barrel-shaped. Treatment consists of getting the patient to stop smoking or otherwise contaminating his lungs, preventing infection, particularly during winter months, with germ-killing antibiotics, and breathing exercises. The outlook for chronic bronchitis and emphysema is nevertheless not good, although many patients continue with their disease for many years, provided they take constant care to obey instructions and stop smoking.

*Bronchial Asthma* (not to be confused with *cardiac asthma*) is a condition in which the finer air passages become constricted due to an allergic response. In addition, an increased secretion tends to obstruct them and the patient wheezes. In many cases it can be shown that he is allergic to a particular component of dust, or, less commonly, a foodstuff. This is the same sort of thing as occurs in the upper respiratory passages in hay fever, but the effect is on a different, lower part of the respiratory system. Many other cases are due to respiratory infection of some sort, probably combined with an allergy to the bacteria causing it. A predisposition to asthma is often inherited. Once a patient has become asthmatic, his attacks will be triggered off by such additional things as emotional stress, changes in temperature (particularly sudden cold), irritating fumes or smoke, and physical exertion. These are secondary factors, and although much of the treatment is concerned with them, it is unlikely that any of them are a sole cause of the condition. Treatment is directed at the relief of the breathing difficulty and of the wheezing, as well as the control of the causative factors. Many useful drugs are available to dilate the contracted air passages and reduce the obstructing secretions. Asthma in children often gets better as the patient grows up. Asthma is another condition made much worse by smoking. Patients should avoid extremes of cold and humidity, particularly outdoor exertion in cold, damp weather. They should also avoid exposure to respiratory infection.

*Bronchiectasis.* In this condition the bronchial air passages are abnormally and permanently dilated, and the normal structure of the walls destroyed. It is thought to be caused by obstructions of the tubes which lead to dilatation of the parts beyond. Secretions accumulate, and since they cannot easily drain away, they become infected. The infection helps to complete the process of destruction of structures in the bronchial wall. The patient has a chronic cough which often produces large quantities of purulent sputum, and there are often recurrent episodes of pneumonia. Diagnosis is made by a special X-ray examination—a bronchogram—in which a material, opaque to X-rays, is dropped into the air passages. This shows up the dilated and distorted tubes. In some cases, where the disease is localised to one part of the lung, it is often a good idea to cut out that portion, and this is particularly true in young people. Vigorous physiotherapy, involving drainage of the lungs by placing the patient in a suitable posture, together with antibiotic drugs for the infection, are other forms of treatment.

*Cystic Fibrosis* is an inborn disease which affects chiefly the lungs and the digestive system. It is sometimes called *Fibrocystic disease of the Pancreas*, and sometimes "Mucoviscidosis." Until it was medically recognised twenty-five years ago,

children affected usually died from pneumonia in the first year of life. This, of course, was before antibiotics were available for the treatment of infections. Today, cystic fibrosis is known to be the commonest genetically determined disorder affecting children in Britain. One child in 2,000 receives one of the abnormal genes from each parent. Such a child therefore has a double dose of the harmful gene, and will have the disease from birth. One person in 25 of the general population carries only one of these abnormal genes, and such an individual will not have the disease, but will be a carrier of the abnormal gene. If such a seemingly normal carrier marries another carrier, there is a one in four chance of each of their children being affected. The children, therefore, who actually develop cystic fibrosis, have inherited the disease *equally* from both parents, who are carriers, but are themselves unaffected by the disease. Although much has been learned about cystic fibrosis in the past twenty-five years, there remain many unsolved problems, and we still cannot define precisely the biochemical fault which causes it. The prospects for survival into reasonably healthy adult life are steadily improving, but they depend upon early diagnosis and careful management through childhood. In cystic fibrosis most of the damage is caused by the excessive viscidity, or stickiness, of the mucus which is produced in the breathing tubes as a lubricant, and also in the ducts of the pancreatic gland which provides enzymes to help digestion. Being thick and sticky, instead of thin and slimy as in the normal, this mucus tends to block the passages instead of keeping them clear. The pancreatic cells are permanently destroyed. The gland cannot secrete pancreatic enzymes, and the food, especially protein and fat, is not properly absorbed. This deficiency can be compensated fairly well by giving pancreatic extract by mouth with every meal, and by dietary care.

The major clinical problem is in the lungs. The lung passages normally have a thin coating of mucus which is propelled steadily upwards, and is completely renewed in less than one hour. It moves more suddenly on coughing. In cystic fibrosis this upward movement is slowed down and interrupted. There is difficulty in keeping the passages clear, especially when infection with bacteria or viruses greatly increases the amount of mucus. This results in intermittent blocking of the air passages, difficulty in breathing, incomplete use of the lungs, and persistent local pockets of infection. If such infectious processes are not controlled, areas of lung will be destroyed, chronic infection will persist, and multiple lung cavities will develop. These predispose to further infection, interfering with the natural development of the lung—a process not normally complete until halfway through childhood—thus adding to the respiratory problems which the child will face in later life. Unless a correct diagnosis is made, and proper treatment instituted before the first serious lung infection has occurred, the resulting lung damage may well be permanent. The Cystic Fibrosis Research Foundation Trust of Stuart House, 1 Tudor Street, London, E.C.4., was founded in 1964 to raise funds to finance research, and to help and advise parents with everyday problems in caring for these children.

*Pneumonia.* This is an infection of the lung tissue, rather than of the air passages. The lung is the only internal organ which is directly exposed to the air, and since there are germs of all kinds in the air, it is a source of surprise that pneumonia is not a much more common event in all of us. The answer lies, as with all infections, in the fact that it is not simply (or even mainly) bacteria which cause disease, but our own lack of resistance to them. If we allow germs to thrive and multiply by being unhealthy or run down or undernourished, infective disease will occur. If we are fit, the entry of those same harmful germs into the body causes us no inconvenience, unless we are very young, or very old, or unless the invasion of germs is abnormally overwhelming. This helps to explain why pneumonia is so often quoted as a cause of death. In most cases it is merely a terminal event occurring in the elderly sick, whose normal resistance is so far reduced by their illness that they succomb to an invasion which they would normally not notice. There are two main kinds of pneumonia, and in both the air sacs become filled with inflammatory secretions, making the normally porous lung tissue as solid as liver. In *lobar pneumonia*, a whole segment (or lobe) of the lung becomes solid. In *broncho-pneumonia*, areas of lung tissue surrounding the smaller bronchioles become consolidated, leaving normal porous lung tissue in between. Broncho-pneumonia is the one which occurs in the rather stagnant lungs of people who are already ill or bedridden. Both forms respond to treatment with the appropriate antibiotics, provided any underlying debility does not interfere with the patient's own resistance. In the terminal bronchopneumonia of fatal illness, it is sometimes considered kinder not to treat the additional pneumonia. *Pleurisy* is a natural complication, and before the days of antibiotic drugs *lung abscess* was very much feared. Another form of pneu-monia—*virus pneumonia*—has been referred to on P10(2).

*Pneumoconiosis.* This is a term which refers to a large group of different diseases, all of which are caused by breathing in some form of dust over a very long period of time. It is therefore an occupational hazard of certain trades. We have already mentioned the mechanisms of mucus secretion in the air passages which normally trap small particles from the air, and prevent them reaching the lung. However, in some occupations there is so much dust breathed in over the months and years that these normal barriers are defeated. About a quarter of the earth's crust consists of silicon, in quartz, flint, or sand. *Silicosis* occurs in people who have worked for many years in trades like mining, stone crushing, sandblasting, or metal grinding, who are often breathing silicon dust in high concentration. When the particles arrive in the air sacs, they set up an irritant chemical reaction which produces nodules of scar tissue. Silicosis for some reason predisposes to tuberculosis (P14(1). Emphysema also occurs and there is a general impairment of respiratory function. Coalminer's pneumoconiosis is similar to silicosis but not identical with it. It is more prevalent in some coalfields than others, owing to the different composition of the dust to which these unfortunate men are daily exposed. It is hoped that modern mining methods will help to reduce this dread disease. Asbestos is a complex silicate of magnesium, calcium, and iron. *Asbes-tosis* is caused by inhaling its fine fibres. *Beryl-liosis* is caused by compounds of beryllium, used in the manufacture of fluorescent lamps. *Farmers lung* is a pneumoconiosis caused by inhaling hay and grain dust, and is similar to *bagassosis* and *byssinosis* caused by sugar cane and cotton dust respectively. The newest pneumoconiosis to be reported is *mushroom worker's lung*, caused by something in the compost in which mushrooms are commercially grown.

*Pulmonary Embolism.* This catastrophic, yet quite common condition has already been briefly referred to (P30(2)). It is a cause of tragic, sudden death in people who have had operations or have given birth to babies some days previously, or who have been bedridden for any other cause. The first event is that the blood in the veins of the legs becomes stagnant, due to the lack of exercise; and together with the tendency to clot which often follows surgery or childbirth, the whole length of a leg vein may be obstructed for twelve inches or more by an elongated clot of blood. This does little harm to the circulation of the leg, since there are plenty of other veins for returning blood to the heart. The danger is that the clot will become dislodged and be swept upwards towards the heart by the flow of returning blood. When this happens it is carried by way of the right auricle and ventricle into the pulmonary vessels which normally carry spent blood to the lungs. Here, for the first time, it enters vessels which are getting smaller as they divide, and it then impacts in the main pulmonary artery. The patient, who may have been recovering very well, suddenly collapses and not unusually dies there and then. At autopsy a long coiled-up mass of clot is found

obstructing the pulmonary vessels. It often can be seen to form a cast of the leg vein and even bears the marks of the small venous valves which are present at its site of origin. With the dramatic advances being made in chest surgery, it is now sometimes possible in selected cases to operate to remove the clot. Success clearly depends on the patient's surviving long enough to be taken to the operating theatre for the major operation of *pulmonary embolectomy*. Three quarters of all cases of pulmonary embolism die within two hours, and therefore the best hope would be to prevent the occurrence altogether. This is not at present possible, but clotting in leg veins can be dis-couraged by early exercise following surgery and childbirth. Patients often resent having to get up the next day because it is so uncomfortable. Herein, however, lies their best hope of avoiding pulmonary embolism.

*Haemoptysis.* This means coughing up blood or blood-stained material. It must be distin-guished from *haematemesis*, in which the blood is vomited from the stomach. It must always be taken seriously because of the underlying lung disease which may be present. No one who coughs up blood, in however small a quantity, should neglect to inform their doctor so that its source can be determined. Hæmoptysis occurs in a variety of lung disease, some of which is not serious but much of which must be treated im-mediately if it is not to become so. This is a suitable place to repeat our general rule that you should see your doctor without delay if you have any unexplained bleeding from any part of the body, however well you feel. And this includes hæmoptysis.

*Fat Embolism.* Liquid fat sometimes enters the bloodstream following extensive crush injuries to soft tissue and bone. It splits up into millions of small globules which are carried to the lungs, and impact in small blood vessels there, producing obstruction of the lung circulation and consequent difficulties in breathing.

*Lung Cancer.* This is one of the nastiest and most incurable forms of cancer which can occur. It is also probably the easiest to prevent. There has been no reasonable doubt for several years now that it is associated with cigarette smoking, and the evidence is overwhelming. However, in spite of this certain knowledge, smoking continues to increase, and every year there are more and more people dying unpleasantly of lung cancer. It seems that nothing the health authorities can do is able to stop it. Intensive campaigns of public advertising of the dangers, and well organ-ised instruction in schools have so far made no impression whatever on the smoking habits even of people who accept the evidence. The only group of people who are known to have stopped smoking are British doctors, very many of whom have given it up, and it is easy to show that giving it up has saved them from the disease. Their colleagues who have not done so have continued to die. Undoubtedly a large factor contributing to the failure of anti-smoking propaganda is the enor-mous expenditure by the tobacco manufacturers on very clever advertising, amounting to many millions of pounds each year. Moreover they spend a pitiful fraction of this amount on their own research into the harmful effects of their own product, which has so far discovered nothing which was not already known by research doctors many years ago. Another problem is that it takes a number of years to get cancer. It is not like an infectious disease which is caught a few days after exposure to the bacteria concerned. It may be fifteen or twenty years before the cancer begins, and many smokers are apparently un-willing to look so far ahead. Furthermore, not everyone who smokes dies this way; and so a smoker can gamble with his life and hope it will not be him. The present writer once had to perform a series of post-mortem examinations on people who died of lung cancer, and this helped him to stop smoking completely, having smoked more than twenty cigarettes a day for several years. Not everyone can have this incentive. The main encouragement to smoke probably comes from other people. Schoolboys are easily impressed when their teachers and parents stop smoking. They are not likely to fear the habit when these same people smoke openly. The smoking doctor is also a powerful stimulus to people to carry on smoking.

Lung cancer grows in the wall of a main bronchial air passage. If it grows inwards it can obstruct the air way, choking that part of the lung it is supplying with air. This causes collapse and infection of the lung and may lead to *lung abscess*. The patient will then cough up blood-stained infected and purulent material. Such a case is comparatively lucky, since the disease declares itself early by producing symptoms. In others, the lump may grow outwards into the surrounding lung and produce no symptoms at all in the early stages. Indeed, it may spread to other parts of the body, like brain or bone or liver before causing any trouble to the patient. If this happens he may go to his doctor because of fits, changes of personality, or fracture, only to discover that the origin of the trouble is in the lung.

The chances of cure are negligible, although much can be done to relieve the pain and suffering of the last stages of the illness. Not more than one in twenty cases is alive two years after it is first diagnosed. Surgery, by removing the lung, and irradiation of the growth are the standard palliative treatment. It is not the practice of the Medical Section to alarm the reader unnecessarily, but if only a few are induced to stop giving themselves such a horrible disease, then writing in this way will have been justified.

*Secondary Cancer of the Lung.* In nearly all forms of cancer, the big problem is that it spreads to other parts of the body. If this were not so it could be eradicated by surgical removal more often than it is. One common way in which it spreads from any part of the body is by entering the bloodstream and being carried as clumps of living cancer cells to distant parts. When these come to rest in smaller blood vessels, they begin to grow and colonise the new environment. Such new colonies are called *secondary deposits* or *metastases*. It so happens that all veins (except portal veins of the liver) lead to the right heart and thence directly to the lungs, and for this reason the lungs are a very common site of *secondary* cancer, which may have begun in the bowel, or breast, or indeed anywhere else in the body. Other common sites of secondary, blood-borne cancer are the brain, liver, bone marrow, and kidney, since all of them have an abundant blood supply, and there is therefore a high chance of the travelling cells arriving there. Secondary cancer of the lung usually consists of several lumps scattered throughout the lung. Lung cancer itself is usually only one growth. One of the main reasons for the success of early diagnosis is that treatment may be possible before blood-borne and other means of spread have occurred. Unfortunately, in the case of primary cancer of the lung, even early diagnosis is of little avail, but in many other common cancers permanent cure is possible if treatment is begun early enough.

*Pleurisy.* The chest is lined by one layer of a thin membrane called the *pleura.* The lungs are covered and enclosed by a second, continuous layer of this same membrane. When the lungs move during respiration, the pleura covering the lungs rubs against the pleura lining the chest, lubricated by a very thin layer of pleural fluid separating the two pleura. Whenever the pleural surface becomes inflamed, this is known as *pleurisy.* It is nearly always due to inflammatory disease of the adjoining lung, and is therefore not strictly a disease in its own right. For example, pneumonia, tuberculosis, lung cancer, or a lung infarct (P30(2)) will produce a pleurisy if the area of diseased lung adjoins the lung surface. Sometimes the area of inflamed inner pleura will tend to stick to its outer layer or rub painfully against it, producing a sharp pain when the patient breathes. Sometimes a large effusion of fluid is produced which separates the two layers and collapses the

lung by occupying space in the chest which the lung should be occupying. This latter is more usual in tuberculosis or cancer.

The lung can be collapsed by the entry of anything between the normally adjacent layers of pleura. For example, air can be introduced, either deliberately to rest the lung in tuberculosis, or by accidental penetrating wounds of the chest wall, or by accidental rupture of the emphysematous lung (*q.v.*). This condition is called *pneumothorax* or " air in the chest." Bleeding into the cavity between the pleura is called *haemothorax.*

## DISEASES OF THE DIGESTIVE TRACT AND LARGE INTESTINE.

### INTRODUCTION.

The digestive tract consists of the mouth, pharynx, oesophagus (or gullet), stomach, small intestine, large intestine (or colon), rectum, and anus. The small intestine is very long, and is subdivided into the duodenum, jejunum, and ileum. It ends at the junction of the ileum with the cæcum, where there is a small blind side-tube, the appendix. The cæcum leads into the colon. The whole tract has two main mechanical functions and two main biochemical ones. Mechanically, food has to be chewed in the mouth and further minced up by muscular squeezing, mainly by the stomach. It has also to be propelled along by an orderly series of squeezing movements known as *peristalsis.* While it is still in the digestive tract, food has to be digested. That is to say, it has to be broken down chemically into suitable materials for absorption into the system, and secondly, it has to be absorbed across the wall of the intestine into the blood stream, itself a highly complex biochemical process. The blood stream it now enters is a special part of the circulation, the " portal " system, which travels directly to the liver without first passing to the heart. In the liver the broken-down foods are processed and issued in their new form into the general, or " systemic " circulation, by which they are finally carried to all the tissues of the body.

As the food passes along the digestive tract (or, as it is sometimes called, the alimentary canal), it is mixed with various secretions which are either made in the wall of the tract, or by organs outside the wall connected to the main pathway by small tubes. Examples of the latter are bile, manufactured by the liver and sent into the duodenum through the bile ducts. Also pancreatic juice comes from the pancreas down the pancreatic ducts, also into the duodenum. These secretions are either digestive juices concerned with splitting up the foodstuffs so that they can be absorbed, or they have a lubricant function so that the gut contents slide along easily under the influence of peristalsis. Roughly speaking, it may be said that digestive juices give place to lubricant secretions at the junction between the small and large intestine.

The constituents of the diet are dealt with in a later section. The principle classes with whose digestion we are now concerned are carbohydrates, proteins, and fats.

*Carbohydrates* are sugars and starches. There are many sugars, which may exist alone, in pairs, or with lots of them stuck together. Alone they are such things as glucose or fructose. Common table sugar is a substance called sucrose, formed by sticking one glucose molecule to one fructose molecule. Starch is lots of glucose molecules all stuck together. Digestion of carbohydrates consists of splitting up sugars and starch into single sugars like glucose, since only single sugars can be absorbed into the system. The splitting is done by digestive *enzymes* which are found in the juices secreted into the digestive tract. Sugar-splitters are found in the saliva of the mouth, in the pancreatic juice of the duodenum, and in the duodenum's own juice from its own wall. On the face of it, you might think it would be better to eat glucose which needs no digestion and can be absorbed in this form, than to eat starch which has first to be split; and so a lot of money has been made out of a gullible public by the sale of glucose drinks and powder. In fact digesting starch is no problem whatever, even for the sick, who can obtain their carbohydrate energy just as easily (and much more cheaply) from potatoes as from expensive glucose. The end result of eating both is the same. The starch-splitting enzyme in saliva is mixed with the food as it is chewed, and it is therefore probably a good idea to chew it well. However, even if the food is bolted it does not seem to matter very much. People without teeth (neither their own nor dentures) seem to digest their carbohydrate quite well, presumably by means of their pancreatic juice at a later stage.

*Proteins*, which are found in meat, cheese, and eggs, have very large molecules consisting of lots of small ones strung together. Unlike starch, in which all the component glucose molecules are identical, the amino acids of which proteins are composed come in many different types. They all contain nitrogen, and there are about twenty-seven varieties. One protein differs from another in the proportions of the mixture and the order in which they are stuck together. Only single amino acids can be absorbed from the food, and so protein digestion again consists of splitting the material down into its building bricks. There is a strong protein splitting enzyme in the gastric (or stomach) juice called pepsin, whose job it is to split the long amino-acid chains into shorter chains. Several other protein-splitters in the duodenal and pancreatic juice contrive to break the smaller chains into individual amino acids which are then absorbed and sent to the liver for processing.

*Fats* mainly consist of glycerol to which are attached three fatty acid molecules for each molecule of glycerol. An enzyme in pancreatic juice splits the fatty acids off the glycerol, but would have some difficulty penetrating the globules of fat without the help of bile. One of the constituents of bile (bile salts) has detergent properties like washing-up powder and breaks the fat globules up into a very fine suspension so that the enzyme can get at the fat. Some fat particles of this size can even be absorbed as such, without preliminary splitting.

The processes by which all these enzymic secretions are produced are very finely controlled. They are very expensive to make in terms of energy and raw materials, and so it would be very wasteful to produce them all the time, even when there was no food to digest. And so the body has some very well designed automatic arrangements for sampling the foods as they are eaten and passed on, which ensure that exactly the right kind of juice is waiting in every part of the digestive tract for whatever food arrives. As soon as the food is digested the supply of enzymes is automatically switched off, so that there is very little waste of precious materials. It is, of course, beyond the scope of this account to describe the control mechanisms. Suffice it to say that they are operated partly by nerve reflexes which signal the imminent arrival of food, and partly by special hormones produced in various parts of the gut wall. The best secretion is affected even by psychological factors, so that pleasant company and surroundings, attractive appearance of the food, and an eager anticipation of it all make for good digestion and good health. These psychological factors are all capable of proper scientific investigation and proof. The poor health of those who habitually and irregularly bolt unpalatable food is probably due to such factors as these. So is the failure of appetite in the depressed, the anxious adult, or the scolded child.

Nearly all the digestion which has been described occurs in the stomach and upper part of the small intestine (the duodenum, jejunum, and upper ileum). Almost all absorption of the products of digestion occurs in the small intestine which is long and intricately folded to give it a large surface area for this purpose. The colon, or large intestine, is adapted for conserving water, by removing it from the residual waste material. This has then to be eliminated, and being rather dry its passage has to be lubricated by suitable secretions of mucus.

*Constipation.* Here, perhaps we had better mention the morbid question of constipation, about which so many people are obsessed and hold such pronounced views. First of all, what is it? For some people it is entirely normal only to pass motions about once or twice a week. For others the normal frequency is once or twice a day. What is abnormal? The answer is that the only thing worth worrying about is any pronounced change of bowel habit, particularly in middle-aged and older people. By a change is meant a change from that individual person's normal routine. Such a pronounced change—either in the direction of constipation or diarrhœa is worth consulting your doctor about if it persists for more than a week or two. Otherwise, forget your bowels and leave them to work naturally as they know best. Many believe that constipation is the root of all evil, that it causes a mysterious condition known to them (although, alas, not to doctors) as " auto-intoxication." Sedulously fostered by the manufacturers of patent medicines, their beliefs range from the notion that headaches, spotty skin, muddy skin, and tiredness are caused by constipation, to the more extreme idea that the whole system is being poisoned and that, if the bowels do not work, the individual will shortly die. Of course, all this is the merest rubbish; for, as Professor Samson Wright, whose *Applied Physiology* is one of the most famous of medical text-books, has pointed out, there is no such thing as absorption of poisonous products from the bowel. There is no such thing as " auto-intoxication." " The symptoms of constipation," he writes, " are largely due to distension and mechanical irritation of the rectum." It has been shown that an enema removes these symptoms *immediately*, which would not be the case if they were due to poisons in the blood, and exactly the same symptoms can be produced by packing the rectum with cotton-wool. Wright mentions the case of a man who went for just over a year without a bowel motion, and at the end of that time, although his abdomen was distended and he felt some discomfort, he was not noticeably ill. Needless to say, telling these facts to the purgative addict will only make him annoyed, but it is as well to note that if no known diseases are due to constipation (although constipation may be a symptom of another disease), the regular use of purgatives *can* cause disease.

Constipation should be treated first by diet containing plenty of roughage—bran and oatmeal are excellent—plenty of stewed and fresh fruits, and at least three pints of fluid should be taken daily. Failing that, one of the best things to take is a proprietary product prepared from senna pods. Never to be taken regularly are liquid paraffin, castor oil, preparations of aloes, Epsom salts, and all the other dreadful stuff that people swill down.

**Œsophagus.**

The œsophagus, or gullet, is more than a simple tube for taking the food from the mouth to the stomach. It is normally closed except when swallowing, and the act of swallowing is very complicated. When the material to be swallowed arrives in the back of the throat there is an automatic mechanism which opens the top end of the œsophagus to receive it, and from then onwards everything happens automatically. The next portion of the tube opens and the top closes strongly, so that the food (or drink) is propelled forcibly down the next segment. Then the part below this relaxes and the material is squeezed further downwards and so on until it arrives in the stomach. This squeezing (or milking) action is akin to the action known as peristalsis which propels contents in other parts of the gut. Thus when you see someone swallowing a glass of beer very quickly in warm weather, it is not going "down the hatch" under the influence of gravity, however much it may look like it. It is perfectly possible to swallow the same, or any other liquid, standing on your head. Getting into that position is the only difficult part. Sometimes this complicated swallowing mechanism gets out of order, leading to difficulties of swallowing, or *dysphagia*. Another disorder known as *hiatus hernia* occurs at the lower end of the oesophagus as it meets the stomach. At this point the oesophagus has to pass through the diaphragm, the sheet of muscle which separates the chest from the abdomen. The muscular fibres of the diaphragm are normally arranged in a ring around the oesophagus. These help to keep the lower end shut, so that the acid contents of the stomach do not regurgitate upwards, causing inflammation (*oesophagitis*) or heartburn. A hiatus hernia is when muscle fibres get slack, and the upper end of the stomach can even slide upwards into the chest. People with hiatus hernia get heartburn after meals, and particularly when they bend down or lie down. Except for very severe forms, which need surgical repair, the treatment is to eat less at a time, reduce the acidity with a suitable antacid and reduce weight, so that the weight of the abdomen does not press upwards so much. The other disease of the oesophagus, quite unrelated to the above, is *cancer of the oesophagus*, the cause of which is still unknown in most cases. When cancer occurs in the wall of any tube, it will often encircle the tube and gradually narrow the way through. This is what happens in the oesophagus, leading to difficulty in swallowing, particularly solids. It is a condition, usually, of rather elderly men, although it is sometimes associated with a special form of severe anæmia in women. Treatment is in some way to keep the passage open, either by transplanting a new tube, or more usually, by removing the constricted piece and joining up the remainder.

### The Stomach and Duodenum.

By far the commonest diseases of the stomach and duodenum are *gastric ulcer* and *duodenal ulcer*. They are actually the same condition in two different sites and are often classed together as *peptic ulcer* or *acid-peptic disease*. The ulcers, which are rather like sores on the lining of the stomach or duodenum, may be " acute " or " chronic." Acute ulcers tend to be small and there are often several of them. Chronic ulcers are usually single. They may be small, or they may be several centimetres across. Chronic ulcers smoulder for months and even years, like a sore which will not heal, and a great deal of scar tissue forms in their depths. Thus they may in time erode their way right through the wall of the stomach, destroying all its layers, and begin to eat into surrounding structures like the pancreas or liver. The fact that they do not perforate more frequently is due to all the fibrous scar tissue which is formed during the slow eroding process. Healing of such a destructive ulcer is nevertheless common, and the great problem is how to help the natural healing process to win against the ulcer's tendency to erode. Better still would be to discover the cause, and prevent it happening in the first place. This extremely common affliction is confined to the human species and has been known since the earliest times. It does not vary very much with diet or with social class. Although occurring at all ages, it usually begins between the ages of twenty and forty, and is most commonly found in men between forty-five and fifty-five. Gastric ulcer is four times, and duodenal ulcer ten times more common in men than in women. It is always due to an inability of the lining to stand up to the normal digestive activity of the stomach contents. These are normally acid and contain a powerful enzyme for digesting proteins. Again it is perhaps more surprising that we all do not digest our own stomachs, rather than that some unfortunate people do digest small areas slowly. In certain abnormal conditions when the stomach stops making acid, ulcers always heal. However, some ulcers occur without excessive secretion of acid and many heal without the acid being neutralised with antacids. All this points to the main trouble being in the response of the lining to acid, rather than to the acid itself. Nevertheless, the most effective treatment at present known involves regulating gastric secretion, and particularly its acidity. It is also known that peptic

ulcers are more common in people whose occupations involve administrative and professional responsibility, competitive effort and nervous tension, long periods of anxiety or frustration. Presumably the higher nervous system influences these events by the same nerves, which normally help to control secretion.

The main symptom of peptic ulcer is pain, and this usually responds well to proper doses of antacids. Many different varieties are available and a lot of money is made from selling them. When indigestion persists for longer than a few days it is always better to see your doctor so that a proper diagnosis can be made and the best remedies begun. Many other causes exist for similar pains, and you should not try to make the diagnosis yourself. It may be necessary to analyse your gastric secretions in the hospital laboratory. Almost certainly you will have a special X-ray examination, and since the stomach cannot easily be seen on a normal X-ray, they will have to show it up by making you drink a white material containing barium. This will be seen as a silhouette of the stomach and duodenal contents. Searching for an ulcer this way is a highly skilled matter and is performed by doctors specially trained in radiology.

Treatment of peptic ulcer is designed to relieve symptoms, heal the ulcer, and prevent complications (see later). Some rest and sedation may help to deal with the psychological influences at work. A special diet may be required. If certain foods cause discomfort they will naturally be avoided, but there is no evidence that any particular foods, like coarse or highly seasoned things retard, or that a soft, bland diet enhances healing. The era of sloppy, milky diets is almost over, for which countless ulcer sufferers will be profoundly thankful. Suitable antacids will be prescribed. Once an ulcer is diagnosed, the time has come to stop treating yourself with antacids from the chemist's counter, and to take the ones your doctor decides are best. Smoking should be stopped by ulcer patients (as, indeed, by everyone else, but that is another matter) because it inhibits healing. Alcohol tends to increase acid secretion and should be avoided. It is also *extremely important* to avoid taking any form of aspirin, even in quite small amounts, since this can lead to very serious bleeding from the ulcer. The ulcer patient should be warned that hundreds of proprietary preparations contain aspirin and all of them are dangerous for him. Search for the formula in the small print on the label before taking any remedy, looking particularly for acetyl salicylic acid—the correct name for aspirin. Doctors have been pressing for years for a law which would make it obligatory for patent medicine manufacturers to label aspirin-containing drugs clearly. There is still no such regulation, so that even some widely sold " hang-over " remedies which are sold for " upset-stomach " contain large quantities of aspirin. Some of the patients with " upset stomach " are, of course, ulcer patients, and some even die of haemorrhage following the ingestion of aspirin.

The main complication of peptic ulcer are bleeding, perforation, and a narrowing of the pylorus, or lower part, known as *pyloric stenosis*. Bleeding is caused by the eroding ulcer eating away at one of the many blood vessels in the stomach or duodenal wall. It leads to the passing of " altered " blood in the stool (*melaena*), or to the vomiting of blood (*haematemesis*). When the initial bleeding occurs, the patient may feel suddenly faint, and a little later will notice the black, tarry colour of his stool. This is sometimes confused with a similiar colour when the patient is taking iron. Peptic ulcer is not the only cause of this very serious hæmorrhage, which constitutes a hospital emergency whatever its cause. The treatment, like that of every large hæmorrhage, is blood transfusion which must be continued until the bleeding stops, or until the patient is sufficiently fit for surgery, should that be deemed necessary. Perforation is perhaps the most serious complication of peptic ulcer, leading to the spilling of stomach contents within the abdominal cavity. Treatment is invariably surgical, either the closure of the perforation or the partial removal of the stomach.

Surgical removal of part of the stomach is often the only way to treat a peptic ulcer which has had its chance to heal in other ways. It is tempting for the patient to " have it out and done with ", but the time for surgery is a matter of fine judgment. So many ulcers heal by medical means if you give them a chance, and operations are for those which persistently refuse, or which become complicated.

*Stomach Cancer.* The stomach is a fairly common site for primary cancer. There is no known reason for this, and it is particularly important to stress that we know of no connection whatever between the peptic ulcers which have just been discussed and cancer. Stomach cancer used to be the commonest cancer of men, but the current rise of lung cancer has pushed it into second place. There are some strange geographical differences in its distribution. For example, it is much commoner in Japan and Scandinavia than in England or the U.S.A. It is difficult to see any reason for this in dietary habits. In Wales it causes three times as many deaths as in South-East England. All this is very puzzling, as is so much of our information about cancer generally. One of the main problems with stomach cancer is that it often causes the patient no inconvenience and thus produces no symptoms of note until the disease is far advanced and it is difficult to do much. Treatment is by surgical removal of the growth, and even in the most advanced cases a great deal can often be done to make the patient more comfortable.

**The Small Intestine.**

The small intestine runs from the stomach to the cæcum and comprises the duodenum, jejunum, and ileum in that order. On a more cheerful note it may be remarked that it is very rarely the site of cancer. Its main problems arise in connection with defects in absorption mechanisms, with obstructions, and with a strange inflammatory condition known as *regional enteritis*. Most obstructions are due not to blockages of the tube, but to failures of peristaltic propulsion, the process which is briefly described above under " œsophagus." Such a failure is called *ileus*. When peristalsis stops for any reason, the result is severe dehydration and loss of important chemicals like sodium and chloride from the body. This is because about two gallons of fluid enter the small intestine each day in the form of digestive juices, and all of this has to be pushed onwards to be reabsorbed into the system at lower levels. If peristalsis fails, this bulk of fluid remains in the small intestine, or is vomited. In both cases it is lost to the body itself, leading to serious dehydration and illness. Treatment is by very careful replacement by transfusion of the fluid and the chemicals lost, and by removal of the trapped fluid within the intestine through a tube threaded down through the mouth.

*Regional enteritis* or *ileitis* is sometimes known as *Crohn's disease.* It is a very mysterious condition in which the normally supple wall of the small intestine becomes inflamed and gradually replaced by thick fibrous scar tissue, so that it looks and feels like a thick garden hose. Loops of inflamed gut stick together, and channels open between them, and if the disease progresses a mass of adherent, thickened intestine results to which everything in the neighbourhood also adheres. However, for some unknown reason some cases do not progress downhill in this way and get better spontaneously. Surgical treatment is necessary for the majority, however, particularly those with advanced disease leading to complications such as obstruction or perforation. Sometimes an early case can be resolved by cutting out the length of affected gut, although recurrences are unfortunately common.

*Appendicitis.* This must be one of the best known surgical diseases of the intestinal tract.

The appendix is a narrow, blind-ended side tube attached to the cæcum near the end of the small intestine. Appendicitis is when it becomes obstructed, or infected, or both. From its position it is almost predictable that it will get obstructed sooner or later by pieces of fæcal matter which pass its entrance and which are normally infected. The surprising thing is that it does not happen more often. Once this has occurred, however, a closed abscess forms, and as the abscess distends the appendix, it first weakens its wall, making it gangrenous, and then bursts into the abdominal cavity causing *peritonitis* (see later). It would be useless and misleading to describe the symptoms of acute appendicitis in detail, since it is difficult even for experienced doctors to distinguish them from those of several other conditions. Suffice it to say that any severe, persisting pain in the abdomen, whether continuous or intermittent, whether associated with diarrhœa or not, should lead the sufferer to a doctor for a quick diagnosis. Germ-killing antibiotics are useless against appendicitis, and any laxative is extremely dangerous as it may cause an acutely inflamed appendix to perforate.

**The Large Intestine or Colon.**

The two main serious diseases of the colon are ulcerative colitis and cancer in its various forms. *Ulcerative colitis* is yet another mysterious disease in which severe ulceration of the lining of the colon gives rise most frequently to diarrhœa with the passage of blood and mucus. In fact it can be like dysentery, and it has often been considered to be due to some form of infection. Unfortunately no particular germ can routinely be found in these cases, and the situation is endlessly confused by the presence in the normal bowel of lots of different germs anyway. Nevertheless the ulcerated lining of the bowel certainly does get infected by the germs normally present, and this makes the disease worse. Therefore germ-killing antibiotics are often helpful in alleviating symptoms and can lead to an earlier settling down of the condition, although not to a cure. It has long been known that certain kinds of psychological upset are often associated, but here again the disease is so unpleasant for the sufferer that he is to be forgiven some despondency as a result of, rather than as a cause of, his troubles. It is also suspected that ulcerative colitis may be an auto-immune disease; that is it may represent rejection by the patient of his own colonic lining in a manner somewhat comparable to the tissue rejection which often follows organ transplantation. Some of the more alarming complications are perforation through the wall of the ulcerated bowel, and sometimes massive hæmorrhage occurs. Medical treatment takes the form of keeping the patient in good physical condition in spite of his fluid and blood loss and his frequent lack of appetite. Surgery is often required to relieve obstruction, deal with perforation, remove chronically affected parts of the bowel, etc.

*Cancer of the Colon and Rectum.* This is another very common form of cancer, which can often be completely cured by surgical removal of the growth provided it is caught in the early stages before it has spread. The commonest symptom is a change in bowel habit, either towards constipation or, more often, towards diarrhœa, in the second half of life. There may be rectal bleeding, or the passage of mucus, and there may be abdominal pain. We cannot too often repeat that any such change of bowel habit, or any unexplained bleeding from any site should lead the patient promptly to his doctor.

*Diverticulitis.* Some people have small pockets or sacs in the wall of the colon known as diverticula. A minority of these sometimes get inflamed, and this is *diverticulitis*. Occasionally perforation occurs.

*Hernia or Rupture.* This is a condition in which abdominal contents, usually a loop of intestine, protrude forwards through the muscular wall of the abdomen. The wall consists of a sheet of muscle fibres running in several directions. They normally become tense when we cough, or strain, or in getting up from a recumbent position. There are places in the groin on each side where there is a way through the muscle for the spermatic cord in the male. In many men a weakness can arise at this point, and if it persists, the way through may enlarge and allow loops of bowel to emerge from behind the muscle sheet to appear as a lump under the skin of the groin. On relaxation the lump can be made to disappear by pushing the contents back the way they came; and they will re-emerge when the patient strains. This is an extremely common complaint in men, and it should be treated by an operation in which the muscle wall is repaired. Some men, however, neglect to have their rupture treated until one day it proceeds to "strangulate." This is the term used when the muscle tightens around the neck of the protruding loop of bowel, cutting off its blood supply. From then onwards the loop becomes gangrenous and the intestine is obstructed by having a part of itself nipped outside the abdominal wall. The patient is in severe pain, vomits continuously, and quickly is liable to get into such a poor condition that surgical relief is difficult. It is therefore a surgical emergency, and it would have been better to have had the relatively simple repair operation earlier and at leisure. Hernia in the region of the groin is of two types: *inguinal hernia* and *femoral hernia*, the difference between them being technical and of no consequence to the patient. They nearly always occur in men. Other types of hernia less frequently occur in both sexes. *Incisional hernia* is when the muscle wall has been weakened at the site of an old abdominal operation and has failed to heal properly. *Umbilical hernia* occurs owing to the natural weakness of the abdominal wall at the navel, and is so common in babies as to be almost normal. When a baby cries and thereby puts a strain on his abdominal wall, a lump often appears in the region of the navel, and this can be very alarming for the parents. They should of course show it to their doctor who will nearly always be able to reassure them. It is self-healing without operation in the majority of cases.

*Peritonitis.* The cavity of the abdomen in which the intestines and other organs lie is called the peritoneal cavity, and it is lined by a thin membrane called the peritoneum. When this becomes inflamed the condition is a serious one and is called *peritonitis*. Inflammation may be bacterial, as occurs following a burst appendix and the spillage of bacteria and pus in the cavity. It may be a sterile peritonitis as often follows perforation of a peptic ulcer, when the inflammation is caused by the acid contents of the stomach. It is always very dangerous, probably because of the large surface area afforded by the peritoneum for the absorption of inflammatory toxins.

*Hæmorrhoids* are simply varicose veins in the rectal and anal regions. They are very common, and are caused probably in about equal degrees by inherited weakness of the veins, strain such as heavy lifting, and constipation (this is one of the very few conditions in which constipation may do some damage, due to the mechanical pressure of hardened fæces in the rectum on the veins). Pregnant women are liable to develop hæmorrhoids or "*piles,*" as they are commonly called, owing to the pressure of the baby's head in the pelvis. Hæmorrhoids may be external or internal, the former being in the anal region below the sphincter, the latter in the rectum; the two usually go together. There may be no symptoms, but the veins are liable to bleed, to get thrombosed (*i.e.,* a clot forms within) or to become infected. When clotting or infection occurs the piles enlarge and tend to be pushed out through the anus during defæcation, when they form extremely painful external swellings. Treatment in simple cases may be by the use of suppositories—cones of a firm grease containing suitable medicaments which are inserted in the rectum—in other cases the veins may be injected, as with varicose veins of the leg, in order to close them, but when there is

much bleeding, thrombosis, infection, or interference with bowel movements they should be removed surgically.

## DISEASES OF THE LIVER

The liver is the largest organ and has such a wide variety of known functions (to say nothing of the unknown) that it is also one of the most complicated. Nearly all of its functions are biochemical, and it is often called the laboratory of the body. Medical students, when asked to enumerate the functions of the liver, usually stick at about twenty-five, nearly all of them to do with general metabolism: that is the biochemical processing of substances taking part in structure or as body fuel. For example, the liver makes proteins from the amino-acids absorbed from the gut, and breaks down amino-acids and manufactures a waste product (urea) from them. It stores carbohydrates as glycogen, and conducts many of the processes necessary to turn carbohydrates into energy. It manufactures prothrombin with the help of vitamin K, and this is essential for blood clotting. It makes bile and secretes it into the gall bladder and bile ducts (*see later*). The three main constituents of bile (cholesterol, bile pigment or bilirubin, and bile acids) all have to be processed, or metabolised, in the liver during the production of bile. Vitamin $B_{12}$ and iron is also stored and dealt with there, and these are involved in preventing various forms of anaemia (*q.v.*); and in addition to all these things the liver is the place where harmful substances, both from within the body and from outside it, are dealt with and rendered harmless. This last function of "detoxication" is often accomplished by making the offending molecules suitable for rapid excretion by the kidneys, or by altering their chemical shape to make them harmless.

Nearly all of these very different things are done by one single type of cell: the liver cell, and it is one of the remarkable features of the design that this cell can be so versatile. There also have to be some very efficient transport systems in the liver, in addition to the usual blood supply and venous drainage possessed by all other tissues.

One of these is the "portal venous system." Whenever a substance is absorbed across the gut wall from any part of the intestine into the interior of the body it enters the special draining blood vessels of the portal system, which are arranged throughout the length of the digestive tract. All these veins eventually unite in the main portal vein which enters the liver. Everything absorbed from the gut is therefore taken first to the liver to be processed. After this the products are carried away from the liver in the ordinary veins to the heart, and are distributed to the rest of the body by the arterial system. The liver has arteries of its own by which it receives oxygen and nutriment like any other tissue. The fourth transport system collects the bile as it is formed within the liver and delivers it to the gall bladder and bile ducts, which eventually drain it into the diodemim.

*Portal Hypertension* means high blood pressure in the portal venous system, and is the usual accompaniment to *cirrhosis* (*see later*). When the terminations of the portal veins in the liver are strangled and obstructed by cirrhotic disease, this tends to blow them up, or dilate them with blood. There is a natural escape route for the portal blood where the lower end of the oesophagus or gullet joins the upper end of the stomach. At this place some of the portal veins draining the stomach are connected with the ordinary veins draining the oesophagus so that when pressure rises in the portal system, blood tends to be diverted into these connecting veins, and they in turn become dilated, or varicose. Trouble begins when these dilated connecting veins, which bulge inwards into the oesophagus, are damaged by food particles passing across them and bleed severely into the stomach. The patient vomits large quantities of blood (*haematemesis*) or passes tarry altered blood in the stool (*melaena*). The other main cause of these are the bleeding which occasionally accompanies peptic ulcer (*q.v.*).

A second complication of portal hypertension (and hence of cirrhosis) is *ascites*, in which large amounts of a lymph-like fluid accumulate in the abdominal cavity. The fluid contains a great deal of precious protein and salt which is lost to the body economy. Ascites also sometimes accompanies cancerous deposits in the abdomen.

*Jaundice* means being yellow because there is too much yellow bile pigment circulating in the blood, and there are three main possible causes for this. The term "yellow jaundice," like "gastric stomach" is therefore unnecessarily redundant: there is no other kind.

Bile pigment comes from broken-down red blood cells, which normally come to the end of their time after existing for about 120 days. The breakdown products of red cells can always be found in the blood of normal people, but there is normally insufficient colour to show. Abnormal amounts of colour build up quite logically in any of the following three circumstances:

(1) If too many red cells are being destroyed and even the normal liver cannot deal with the amount of bile pigment produced, it piles up in the blood, and *haemolytic jaundice* is the result. The expression simply means jaundice due to (abnormally large) red-cell destruction.

(2) If the liver cells are themselves sick and unable to cope even with the normal amounts of pigment from normal red-cell destruction. Here too the pigment will pile up and cause *hepatocellular jaundice*, or liver-cell jaundice.

(3) If the bile ducts carrying bile away from the liver are blocked, then bile will pile up behind the blockage and re-enter the blood stream, causing *obstructive jaundice*. In this case the rate of red-cell breakdown is normal, and the liver cells are normal: at least for a time.

It is enormously important for the treatment of jaundice for the doctor to diagnose its type correctly, since the treatment varies from surgical relief of obstruction to the medical treatment of viral infection or of excess red-cell destruction.

The so-called differential diagnosis of jaundice is often exceptionally difficult, and sometimes requires some very sophisticated laboratory tests and X-rays. At other times it is extremely easy and is obvious from a cursory glance at the urine and the stool. In any case all jaundice is a highly technical matter for the doctor who must be consulted early.

There is a special jaundice of newborn babies which resembles haemolytic jaundice and can occasionally have serious consequences for the developing brain (*kernicterus*) if it is allowed to become too severe. When this is threatened, steps are taken to reduce the level of circulating bile pigment by replacement of the baby's blood or by other means.

The commonest cause of hepatocellular jaundice is infective or viral hepatitis. Obstructive jaundice is usually due either to blockage by gallstones (*q.v.*) or by a lump pressing on the bile ducts from an adjacent cancer. This can often be quite satisfactorily relieved by surgery.

*Infective Hepatitis.* There is a group of disorders affecting the liver which are caused by viruses. The incubation period is often very long, and the sickness and other debility caused is often quite severe and prolonged. One variety, known as serum sickness, is now much less common than a few years ago. It used to be transmitted by using the same needle for injections into several different people, or from transfusing contaminated blood. A greater awareness of the problem, and the use of disposable needles and syringes has cut down the incidence.

*Cirrhosis.* There are many different kinds of cirrhosis, the commonest of which has already been mentioned under *portal hypertension* above. In all cases, liver cells are slowly poisoned and are killed off over a long period of time. In response to this, the surviving liver cells undergo cell division, trying to make good the numbers lost, and at the same time fibrous scar tissue replaces the damaged tissue throughout the organ. The result is a hard, knobbly liver. The many "knobs" are spherical areas of regenerated new cells, and they are separated by thickened bands of scar tissue. All of this destroys the normal architecture and leads to the portal hypertension and ascites mentioned above. In some countries (*e.g.*, France and the United States) excessive alcohol is the main cause of the original liver damage which starts it all off. In others (*e.g.*, Bantu South Africa) it seems to be nutritional starvation of the liver. In England much less than half the cases are due to alcohol, and many are thought to be due to a previous episode of infective hepatitis (*q.v.*), but this is not certain. Infective hepatitis is quite common but cirrhosis is comparatively rare. So that the great majority of people do not progress from one to the other. One day soon the treatment for advanced cirrhosis will be to replace the liver by transplantation, but there are still many problems to overcome before this can become routine.

*Cancer of the Liver.* Cancer of the liver is quite common, but it is nearly always cancer which has spread in the blood stream from other parts of the body. The liver is a favourite site for such secondary deposits, since it has a large blood supply and will receive a generous helping of anything being carried. It is also a very "fertile soil" for the cancer seedlings to grow in. Primary cancer of the liver is uncommon, and only occurs in a few cases of pre-existing cirrhosis.

*Gallstones.* These are "stones" formed by some of the major constituents of bile coming out of solution and forming solid bodies. They are very common, and often cause no trouble at all. When they do, it is usually a cholicky intermittent severe pain. This is due to the muscular walls of the bile passages contracting in an effort to expel an obstructing stone into the duodenum. The second common trouble arising from gallstones is obstructive jaundice, described above. It is small consolation to gallstone sufferers that the stones are often very pretty, often being composed of beautiful cholesterol crystals coloured by varying shades of bile. If they contain calcium they will be visible on an X-ray. Otherwise they are not seen. There is a persisting myth in the textbooks that sufferers are usually Females who are Fair, Fat, Forty and Fecund. It is not true. Stones often occur in conjunction with inflammation of the gall bladder, known as *cholecystitis*. The treatment for gallstones is to remove them surgically together with the gall bladder if they are causing persistent symptoms.

## The Pancreas

This is a soft, elongated gland lying behind the stomach; it is about 5 in. long and 2 in. wide. Within its tissues lies the duct, which, when it leaves the pancreas, passes into the duodenum near the point of entry of the bile-duct. This duct transmits the juices containing enzymes which aid in the digestion in the small intestine. The pancreas, however, has two main functions: not only does it manufacture these important digestive juices, but in certain specialised areas, known as the islets of Langerhans, it manufactures insulin.

*Diabetes.* Although we know so much about diabetes, we still have not the faintest notion as to what causes it. Its immediate cause is a failure in varying degrees of the pancreas to produce insulin, but examination of the pancreas rarely reveals any significant changes. The disease is commonest between thirty and sixty years, but may occur even in children. Now, insulin is the substance which makes it possible for the body to make use of sugar—the glucose which is the end-product of carbohydrate digestion. So in its absence the glucose, although there to be used, is useless to the body and accumulates in the blood, finally passing out in the urine. (The fundamental test for diabetes is the discovery of sugar in the urine by the use of certain simple procedures.) The diabetic, then, is being starved of sugar no matter how much he takes in, and the excess sugar in the blood which cannot be used acts as a poison, which, in extreme cases, sends the patient into coma and may—indeed, in former times, usually did—result in death. The symptoms of diabetes vary, of course, with its severity, but in the main they are: increasing appetite in an attempt on the part of the body to supply the sugar which is there but so tantalisingly unavailable, great thirst, because this useless sugar has to be excreted, and the production of urine demands water, frequency in passing urine, and increasing loss of weight in spite of all that is taken in. In severe and untreated cases boils, itching of the skin, gangrene of the limbs, and finally coma and death may occur.

Although mild cases of diabetes could, and still can, be treated by dieting alone, by reducing the intake of carbohydrate, the diagnosis of diabetes prior to 1922 amounted almost to a death-warrant. In that year, however, the Canadian physicians Banting and Best separated out the secretion of the islets of Langerhans and named it " insulin "; they showed that insulin taken from the pancreas of animals and injected into the diabetic patient was just as effective as the home-made article.

Since a diabetic regime has to be decided on by the doctor according to the severity of the disease, no useful purpose would be served by discussing the details of diet or dosage of insulin, which vary from one person to another. On the whole, diabetes is more severe in young people than in the elderly, but with correct treatment it is possible for all cases to lead a perfectly normal life except in so far as dietary restrictions and insulin injections are concerned.

Whereas the type of diabetes we have been describing, the disease ordinarily known by that name, is properly known as *diabetes mellitus*, there is another disease known as *diabetes insipidus*, which, in fact, has no real relation to the other at all. In this disease there is no sugar in the urine, nor has it anything to do with the pancreas. Diabetes insipidus is a rare disease characterised by the passage of large amounts of dilute urine and appears to be due to deficiency of the secretion of the posterior part of the pituitary gland at the base of the brain. It can be partially controlled by the use of pituitrin.

### DIET.

Food, like alcohol, tobacco, and constipation, is one of those subjects which people tend to have a " thing " about. In point of fact, what we know at present about this subject may be summarised as follows: Any diet to be adequate must first of all provide enough energy, and energy is measured in terms of Calories (for definition of a Calorie see Gen. Inf.). Thus a ten-stone man leading a moderately active life will require about 3,000 Calories daily; that is the amount of energy he requires in order to carry out his work and avoid living on himself, on his stored-up food. The amount of Calories required varies with age, size, and the amount of work done, from 1,500 Calories for the light-weight sedentary worker to three or more times this amount for the heavy manual worker.

Now, in theory, the adequate amount of Calories could be supplied from carbohydrate and fats alone, since, as we have seen, Calories are merely a measure of energy and can be supplied by any food. But in this case the individual would not live long, because he needs for body maintenance certain kinds of food in adequate proportions. Just as you cannot run a car for long simply by putting in petrol and ignoring lubricating oil and maintenance of the engine, so you cannot run your body simply by taking in enough Calories.

There must be adequate proportions of the three basic foodstuffs: carbohydrates (the fuel), fats (for insulation and other purposes), and proteins (for body-building purposes). Proteins are necessary to replace the parts of the body, which is largely a protein structure, when they become run-down In addition to being a ready source of energy, carbohydrate is converted into fat within the body, a fact within the knowledge of everyone, for it is by reducing the consumption of sweets, potatoes, and bread, which are starch and sugar-containing foods, that a tendency to put on weight is reduced. Proteins cannot be manufactured from carbohydrates or fats since proteins contain nitrogen and the others do not. One could even live on a diet of nothing but protein, but not on a diet of fat or sugar; proteins are a biological necessity. It is generally agreed that a well-balanced diet should provide 25 per cent of its energy from fats, 10–15 per cent from proteins, and the remainder, 60–65 per cent, from carbohydrates.

Here are some foods classified according to the predominating basic foodstuff they contain:

    (1) *Carbohydrates:* bread, sugar, and all starchy foods or sweet things such as confectionery, puddings, and cakes.

    (2) *Fats*: animal fats, such as dripping, fat meat, fried foods, butter, margarine, and vegetable oils, such as olive oil, or fish oils, which are found more in some fish than others —*e.g.*, herring.

    (3) *Proteins:* lean meat, cheese, non-fatty fish, nuts, oatmeal.

In addition to these basic foods, the body must also have adequate supplies of vitamins (P42, 43) and certain minerals, such as iron, manganese, calcium, copper, sodium, potassium, iodine, and phosphate.

*Obesity.* Many people worry because they are overweight, and statistics show that the expectation of life is shorter in fat people than in thin ones. This, however, is a statistical view, and need not apply to any single person.

Being overweight is due to one cause—eating too much, and especially eating too much of the wrong kinds of food. There are, obviously, some people who can eat to their heart's content without becoming fat, perhaps because their bodies burn up the food more quickly. Their *basal metabolic rate*, which is the measure of the speed at which their body cells work, is higher than normal, and the basal metabolic rate is largely dependent on the functioning of the glands—in particular, the thyroid. Nevertheless, being overweight means that you are eating too much for you; that your intake of Calories is greater than your output.

Reducing is not difficult, but it does require an effort of will. Basically it depends on: (*a*) taking less food, and (*b*) taking food which is not fat-producing. In practice, this means taking a high-protein diet, little fat, and no sugars or starches. The basic principles are obvious: plenty of lean meat, non-fatty fish, eggs, cheese, fruit, Energen rools or crispbread (the ordinary crispbread is just as fattening as bread itself), but no fried foods, fat meat of fish, bread, potatoes, sweets, or cakes. However, small amounts of butter and quite a lot of milk are permissible, and the monder tendency is to ignore fat intake which, by reason of its nature, is self-limiting.

Obesity may have a psychological basis, and excessive eating is often a substitute for affection in individuals who have been spoilt as children. But, however this may be, most people find it as difficult to stick to a reducing diet as they do to give up smoking. For such people there are certain drugs which may help. Thyroid tablets, once generally used for reducing, are little used now, and should be used only when the thyroid gland is underactive; otherwise they simply increase appetite, and although they speed up the combustion in the body (the basal metabolic rate), the effect is cancelled out by the increased appetite. Dexedrene, one of the derivatives of benzedrene or amphetamine, acts by reducing the appetite, but in some people of a nervous disposition it may have the effect of causing a feeling of tenseness, and they may even have difficulty in sleeping. Finally, there is a substance obtainable at chemists' shops without prescription either in the form of granules or biscuits which does not exercise any chemical effect on the body; what it does is to swell up into a gelatinous mass within the stomach under the influence of water, which is drunk later, and this gives the impression of a "full stomach" and allays the pangs of hunger.

There are, as has already been mentioned, many fads about food, although one is treading on dangerous ground when one mentions them; for every faddist is a fanatic, and every argument one may put before him is seen as an attack on himself. For example, there was the "Hay diet," now, it appears, largely forgotten; then the "Gaylord Hauser diet" much favoured by Americans, which seems to be based largely on large quantities of molasses and brewer's yeast; and there was not so long ago a gentleman who lived on grass freshly clipped each morning from Hyde Park—it would be interesting to know whether he has survived his self-imposed ordeal. However, few doctors would deny that, although diet in some cases is an adjunct to the cure of disease (for example, peptic ulcer, diabetes, sprue), it is not a cure for disease, and those who make such claims are claiming a great deal too much. It must be repeated that, so long as a diet contains adequate amounts of the basic foodstuffs, adequate amounts of vitamins and the necessary minerals, and so long as it supplies adequate Calories for the build of the individual and the amount of work he does, it matters very little how these needs are supplied.

## Vegetarianism.

This can hardly be called a fad, although it cannot be denied that many of its adherents are faddists. It apparently has two main sources. There are those who abstain from animal food for moral reasons because they believe that killing is wrong, even for food; and there are others who believe that vegetable food is more healthy than animal food. Some vegetarians live almost entirely on vegetables and fruits, whilst others allow themselves milk, eggs, and cheese. The moral issue cannot be argued here, although it must be admitted that few people who have visited a slaughter-house for the first time have as much appetite for their steak the day after, so we shall only discuss the health aspects of vegetarianism. On the negative side, it must be said that, in general, vegetable foods are much less rich in protein than animal foods, so one has to eat a great deal more in order to get an adequate amount. If, however, one includes in a vegetarian diet cheese, milk, and nuts or eggs this difficulty is largely obviated. Cows and other animals living on grass or vegetable matter have to spend practically their whole lives eating, precisely because they would not otherwise get sufficient protein. On the positive side we have the as yet unconfirmed assumption that, in predisposed people over forty, excess of animal fats can lead to cholesterol being deposited in the blood-vessels, notably the coronary vessels in the heart, and thus to coronary thrombosis. Vegetable and fish oils do not seem to have this effect, hence the infrequency of thrombosis amongst those peasants in Europe who are too poor to afford much meat and amongst the Eskimos who eat fish. From the point of view of evolution it would seem that Man is designed to be both carnivorous and vegetarian; for he has sharp, cutting teeth in the front for tearing meat and flat, grinding teeth at the back for dealing with grains. We must conclude that those who are vegetarians for moral reasons should have all our respect; for killing is not a pleasant thing, and we have already too much of it. From the merely medical point of view vegetarianism has both advantages and disadvantages. Nobody will suffer from being vegetarian, but, apart from the exceptions mentioned, there is little reason to suppose that their health will be any better than that of meat-eaters. We are less able to influence our fates than we often suppose, since longevity and good health are much more a matter of heredity than is ordinarily believed.

## THE DEFICIENCY AND METABOLIC DISEASES

### INTRODUCTION.

If you have read earlier parts of this section you will know that there can be two types of malnutrition: the first, of course, is the type we ordinarily think of when the word is mentioned, and in this case the individual is simply not getting enough food or enough of the right kind of food. The second type might well not be regarded by most people as malnutrition: for here we are referring to diseases such as diabetes and sprue, in which, although there is adequate supply of certain foods, the body, owing to some deficiency, is unable to make use of them. The patient with diabetes cannot make use of sugar, the patient with sprue of fat—they are starving in the midst of plenty, as is shown by the fact that in both cases one of the prominent symptoms is wasting.

We shall deal first with the ordinary type of malnutrition and later with the second. Since diabetes and sprue have already been mentioned, we shall be looking at some other conditions in which something or other is missing or is present in the wrong amounts, as in the diseases of the endocrine glands.

Two-thirds of the population of the entire world are undernourished, and particularly in Asia famines are common—famines like the one in Bengal in 1943, in which 3 million people died of starvation. In Europe such conditions exist only when war dislocates food supplies, but nevertheless individual cases of malnutrition can occur. For example, the lazy or ignorant mother of a large family may feed them largely on bread and margarine, with no fresh fruit or vegetables and only tinned meat because she "can't be bothered" cooking. Or the self-sacrificing mother of a large family may give all the meat and protein food to her working husband (somehow or other many men fail to notice that a housewife works!) and her children. Then old people or people living alone are liable to neglect their food, either because they have lost heart, because they are too frail, or because they cannot afford to buy enough good food. Lastly, those who are addicted to alcohol neglect their food and, drinking on an empty stomach, soon get such a degree of gastritis that they find it difficult to eat even when they need to.

A human being can live about six weeks without food, and a much shorter time—a week or ten days—without water. Naturally, human nature being as it is, there have been many claims to longer periods of starvation, and some of the more enthusiastic claim not to eat at all! Thus, in the sixteenth century Eve Fliegen of Brabant appears to have lived for fourteen years solely on the smell of a rose, and, coming nearer our own time, Mollie Fancher of Brooklyn, who died in 1916, similarly lived for fourteen years without eating, and in 1864 even stopped breathing. However, presumably becoming bored with this, she resumed her respirations after only fourteen weeks.

These people, needless to say, were humbugs, as is revealed by the grim case of Sarah Jacob "the Welsh Fasting Girl," who towards the end of last century allegedly took no nourishment whatever for two years, two months, and one week. The one week, at any rate, is certain; for, at the invitation of the local vicar, who was convinced of her genuineness, a number of doctors from London came to observe her. They put relays of nurses to sit by her bed day and night to note whether she ate, but in a few days she began to decline so alarmingly that the doctors begged the parents to feed her. This refused to do, and Sarah would not ask for food. She died within a week on December 17th. The most famous non-eater of today is Theresa Neumann, who lives in Bavaria and claims that nothing but the wafer, the Eucharist, at Holy Communion has passed her lips since 1927. The Roman Catholic Church, however, has been careful never officially to recognise her claims as true. So we shall still assert that six weeks, more or less, is the longest period a human being can go without eating.

### DEFICIENCY DISEASES.

The materials which are necessary to the body have been mentioned elsewhere, and we can now look at some of the diseases (other than those already discussed) which result from their lack.

Lack of iron leads to anæmia, but less well known is the type of deficiency caused by lack of iodine. Iodine is found in large amounts in seaweed, which obtains it from the sea surrounding it and concentrates it in its fronds. But ordinary water contains enough for our needs. In some districts, however, especially where the main rock is limestone—Derbyshire and some valleys in Switzerland and the Himalayas—the water contains very little iodine, and there the inhabitants are prone to develop goitre. There are several types of goitre, but this type is caused by lack of the iodine which is necessary to build up thyroxin, the secretion of the thyroid gland. It is a deficiency goitre known in adults as myxœdema, but in those parts where iodine is lacking in the water supplies the disease develops in childhood and the children become, although perfectly normal when born, dull, gross, and stupid—they become idiots or, as they are more correctly described, cretins. This is one of the commonest types of mental deficiency in children, and, if noted in time, they can become completely normal by the use of thyroxin or thyroid tablets. But prevention is better than cure, and this terrible disease has now been almost eliminated in the districts where it used to be prevalent by adding iodine to the water supply of towns and villages, by giving iodised chocolate at schools, or otherwise supplying the missing element.

In this country cretinism and myxœdema are found in individual cases for reasons other than lack of iodine: in children, cretinism may be due to congenital lack of the thyroid gland or early failure, in adults myxœdema may occur when the gland, usually in the middle period of life, runs down. Both conditions can be treated by thyroid tablets, which, like insulin, have to be taken for the rest of the patient's life.

Lack of calcium is less common in this country than it once was. Calcium is necessary for building the bones: it is calcium, in fact, that makes the bones hard. Actual lack of calcium in the diet is very rare, because calcium is one of the commonest elements in Nature, and what usually happens is that lack of vitamin D or calciferol, without which calcium cannot be utilised or absorbed, causes the deficiency.

The two main diseases caused by calcium, or rather vitamin D, deficiency are rickets and osteomalacia. Vitamin D is found in fats—but only animal fats such as are found in meat, fish, and milk; it is not found in vegetables, plants, or fruit. A second source of the vitamin is sunshine or ultra-violet light, which manufactures it in the skin; hence, in spite of inferior diet, rickets and osteomalacia are perhaps less common in sunny countries. In *rickets*, a child during the period when its bones are developing does not get enough vitamin D and cannot make use of the calcium taken in. Its bones become soft and are liable to bend, producing defects such as bow legs, curvature of the spine, and deformities of the chest (pigeon chest, funnel chest). In bad cases the skull is deformed and assumes a square shape. Rickets is rare today, at least in Britain; it is prevented by taking vitamin-D-rich oils, such as cod- or halibut-liver oil, or the vitamin can be taken in a more or less pure form in capsules.

In these days when diets are adequate, when children get cod-liver oil at home or school, and when they are much more often in the sunshine than used to be the case, it is not always realised that *overdosage* of vitamins, especially vitamin D, is possible. In its extreme form this is a rare condition, but children have died from overdoses which caused calcium to be laid down where it did not belong—in the kidneys and elsewhere. It is possible to have too much of anything.

Rickets is uncommon in adult life because the demand for calcium is less than in the growing child. But in pregnancy the demand increases, and especially in Eastern lands, where famine is frequent and where, although there is plenty of sunshine, the women are veiled from any of the sun's rays, there may occur the disease of *osteomalacia*. In this disease the bones soften and deformities occur which are particularly important in the case of women, in whom the pelvis becomes deformed, with resultant difficulties in child-birth. Osteo-

malacia is a main cause of the high maternal and infant mortality in such countries as India.

In old people who do not get enough food, lack of vitamin D causes no deformity, but leads to the condition known as *osteoporosis*, in which the bones, through lack of available calcium, become brittle and break easily.

*Scurvy* is another once-common deficiency disease which is now rare except under such unusual conditions (or perhaps not so unusual in these days) as life in concentration camps or amongst prisoners-of-war. It is due to lack of vitamin C, which is found in fruits and vegetables, particularly in lemons, oranges, tomatoes, and turnips. In scurvy the gums swell and bleed, there is increasing anæmia, and spontaneous bruises, due to hæmorrhage under the skin, occur. In former times the disease was the bugbear of sailors and travellers, because on long journeys or voyages before means of preserving food were known other than drying or salting no fresh fruit was available. It was no less a personality than Captain Cook who on his long voyages found that the simple use of lemons or limes would prevent the disease. Hence the almost international description of Englishmen as " Limeys "—a name which is not always used flatteringly, but of which we have every reason to be proud. Minor degrees of scurvy may occur in British children even today through faulty diet, but this is much less common since orange, blackcurrant, or rose-hips syrups became available to all.

We now come to the B group of vitamins. There are, regrettably, many members of the vitamin B family, but we shall mainly deal with vitamins B1 and B2.

*Beri-beri* is caused by lack of vitamin B1, which is found in most grains, principally in the embryo and the outer covering. Now, since many people are snobs, who prefer white bread to wholemeal and polished rice to the crude article, it has become the habit to remove the precious outer covering of the grain and its embryo which contain the vitamin: white bread and polished rice *look* so much better. Thus, in those parts of Asia where rice is the staple diet, it was frequently machine milled, with loss of the vitamin, and the result was the serious form of neuritis known as beri-beri. Just as Captain Cook eradicated scurvy from his men by the use of citrus fruits, so, in 1882, Takaki eliminated beri-beri from the Japanese Navy by giving a good mixed diet. This led two Dutchmen, Eijkman and Grijns, to study the disease experimentally. They found that fowls fed on polished rice developed the disease, whereas those fed on rice with the husk did not. In this country we are still in the rather foolish position of carefully removing the vitamin by " refining " the flour and then replacing it chemically. However, although wholemeal bread is probably better, there is really little risk of any European diet lacking vitamin B1.

The symptoms of beri-beri are neuritis (*i.e.*, degeneration of the nerves), which leads to weakness of the muscles, wasting, and sensations of " pins and needles "; the heart muscle is also affected and œdema—swelling of the limbs—or ascites (fluid in the abdomen) occurs.

*Pellagra.* Vitamin B2, or rather the vitamins of the B2 group, of which the main ones are riboflavin and nicotinic acid, is another substance deficiency of which in this case leads to pellagra. Pellagra is found in those parts of the world where maize is a staple diet, that is in parts of America and the Far East and round the Mediterranean. Maize does not contain the vitamin which, like vitamin B1, is found in most other grains and vegetables, but since vitamin B2 is also normally produced by the action of bacteria in the human colon, it would appear that there is some other factor than the mere absence of the substance from the diet. Probably maize contains a substance which prevents the absorption of the vitamin from the colon.

In pellagra there is wasting, soreness of the mouth, diarrhœa, skin rashes on the hands, forearms, face, and neck. In severe cases insanity may occur. The disease does not occur in this country in its full-blown form, but minor degrees may develop with the use of certain antibiotics, such as chloramphenicol and aureomycin, which kill the "good" vitamin-producing bacteria in the intestine as well as the disease-producing ones.

### Vitamins.

Whereas vitamins B and C are found mainly in vegetables and fruits, vitamins A and D are found in oils and fats. Vitamin A is, indeed, found in the form of carotene in all green vegetables, but it is not much use to us until it has become concentrated in the fat and milk of the animals who eat the vegetables. Lack of the vitamin leads to *night-blindness*, to difficulty in seeing in the dusk. This is because the retina, the "mirror" at the back of the eye, requires adequate amounts of a substance known as visual purple for its full efficiency, and visual purple is manufactured from vitamin A. (It must be noted, however, that not all cases of night-blindness are due to lack of vitamin A—there is often a very large neurotic element, and it was frequently found during the War that men who on this account pleaded their inability to carry out sentry duties at night might show a very considerable talent for seeing their girl-friend at the camp gate even in pitch darkness.) Vitamin A is also connected with the health of the skin and the ability of the body to resist diseases of the respiratory tract such as bronchitis. Like vitamin D, it is most easily obtained from fish oils, such as halibut-liver oil.

Lesser-known vitamins are vitamins E and K. The former, found in wheat-germ oil, influences fertility; the latter influences the clotting power of the blood and the healing of wounds. Most vitamins can now be produced in the laboratory synthetically; in the case of vitamin B1 from coal-tar.

It is important to realise that vitamins, although necessary to health, are not cure-alls. There are few sights more ridiculous than the fad of over-fed individuals taking vitamin pills as a tonic to keep themselves up to scratch. Any vitamins taken in excess of requirements may either cause damage —as in the case of vitamin D—or else are simply excreted from the body. Extra vitamins are not a tonic, those who take them in excess are simply wasting their money, and if one eats a good mixed diet they are totally unnecessary.

### GLANDULAR DISEASES.

#### The Endocrine Glands.

The workings of the body are regulated in all sorts of different ways—by the nervous system, the circulation, and by the endocrine glands or ductless glands, as they are sometimes called. We have already seen that there are glands, such as the liver (the largest gland in the body) and the pancreas, which manufacture substances and pass them through a duct or tube to their destination. But the ductless glands, as their name implies, have no duct and pass their secretion directly into the blood; the pancreas, for example, discharges the pancreatic fluid down a duct, but it also produces insulin, which is secreted directly into the blood. It is thus partly an endocrine gland and partly an ordinary one. The other endocrine glands are particularly important in that they produce hormones (the word means "chemical messenger"), which have a great deal to do with personality and health.

*Myxœdema*, we saw, is due to lack of thyroid hormone either because the gland, which is at the base of the neck astride the windpipe, has failed or because it has insufficient iodine to manufacture its product. The opposite effect occurs when the gland becomes overactive, and then we get a quite different state of affairs: instead of being dull, slow-witted, and flabby-looking, the patient with an overactive gland—*exophthalmic goitre* or *thyrotoxicosis* is excitable, nervous, flushed and thin. The eyes become prominent and bulge forward, giving a staring,

scared look. The disease is commonest in young adults, mostly women, and its origin is often associated with an emotional shock. Thyrotoxicosis is not primarily a disorder of the thyroid gland, and it is likely that the sequence of events is: emotional shock, which influences the nerves supplying the pituitary gland at the base of the brain, overactivity of the pituitary with over-production of the hormones, which in turn affect the thyroid. (The pituitary is the main endocrine gland in the body and gives off hormones which control all the other glands—it has been called the "conductor of the endocrine orchestra.") All the body processes—the basal metabolism—are speeded up in this disease, which, however, cannot be treated at its roots in the pituitary. Sometimes it can be treated medically by the drug thiouracil, which damps down the activity of the thyroid, but more usually an operation is necessary to remove part of the gland. It is also possible in suitable cases to give the patient radioactive iodine—a radio-isotope which is carried, as all iodine is, to the gland, where it destroys some of the overactive tissues. The results of these procedures are good, but any exophthalmos, the prominence of the eyes, which may be present always remains.

A similar condition appearing in the middle age, may result, not from shock or from an overall enlargement of the gland, but from a *toxic adenoma*, which is a simple, non-malignant tumour. In this case exophthalmos does not occur, but the tumour should be removed. Malignant tumours also occur.

#### The Parathyroid Glands.

We have already discussed the importance of calcium in the body and seen how vitamin D is necessary for its utilisation. But the calcium content of the body is controlled by another factor, the parathyroid glands—two pairs of small glands lying behind the thyroid. Now calcium, in addition to building the hard structure of bones, has another function in that it acts as a kind of sedative, damping down nerves and preventing overexcitability. When the para-thyroid glands do not work properly, or when they have been partially removed during a thyroid operation, *tetany* (not to be confused with tetanus) arises. The hands and feet go into spasm and there may be generalised convulsions. Tetany can be produced in a number of other ways which influence the amount of calcium in the blood: for example, alkalosis when people have taken too much alkali for stomach disease, or when they have lost acid through persistent vomiting, or even by overbreathing—*i.e.*, persistent deep and rapid breathing, which causes the body to lose carbon dioxide—a condition which may occur in hysterical or neurotic patients. The treatment is to give large amounts of calcium and vitamin D.

Overactivity of the parathyroid glands, usually due to a tumour, causes the reverse effects. The blood calcium is high, but this calcium has been withdrawn from bones, and a disease known as *generalised osteitis fibrosa* arises, in which the bones become soft and there is pain, fractures, and deformities. Sometimes cysts form in the bones. The treatment is operative removal of the tumour.

Salt is very important in the running of our bodies. Indeed our blood has been described as an "inner sea"; for, whereas primitive creatures in the ocean, such as sea-anemones and sponges, get their sustenance from the sea surrounding them and do not need a blood-stream within, in the course of evolution the situation gradually changed. As sea-animals grew bigger, the water outside did not suffice, and they had to develop some sort of circulation within; even more so, when they developed into land animals they had to carry their sea about with them. Loss of the salt in this inner ocean is occurring all the time, both through the urine and through sweating. Workers who do heavy jobs in a hot atmosphere lose a great deal of salt through sweating, and if afterwards they drink a great deal of water the remaining salt in the body becomes even more diluted, with the result that they will get painful cramps. Similarly, diarrhœa or prolonged vomiting can bring about the same result through loss of salt from the body. After long periods of exercise it is much more refreshing to take water with added salt than to take pure water, which will increase rather than diminish our fatigue.

### Suprarenal Glands.

A glandular disease which influences the balance of salt in the body is *Addison's disease*, named after the famous English physician who first described it. This disease is characterised by great weakness of the muscles, tiredness, loss of weight, low blood-pressure, and a brown pigmentation of the skin. Until recently it was always fatal. Addison's disease is caused by damage to the suprarenal glands, two small glands which sit one on top of each kidney like little cocked hats. These glands produce a number of hormones, one of which controls the excretion of salt from the body; if it is lacking, too much salt escapes, with the results described above. The disease is now treatable by the use of cortisone, one of the suprarenal hormones.

These glands consist of an inner part or medulla which secretes a hormone known as adrenalin—the substance which, when released into the blood, prepares us for states of emergency. It reinforces states of anger or fear, and aids in the process of fighting back or running away. The cortex (the word means " bark of a tree "), on the other hand, secretes a number of hormones, one of which, as we have seen, is connected with the salt content of the body and another which plays some part in sexual development. Thus a tumour of this area may bring about a state of *hyperadrenia*, in which excessive secretion leads to premature or excessive development of masculine sexual traits. Boys show precocious sexual development, their voice breaks, and their muscular development increases. Girls assume male characteristics. This is known as the *adreno-genital syndrome*.

### The Pituitary Gland.

The pituitary gland, lying at the base of the brain, is only about the size of a small cherry, yet it not only regulates the behaviour of all the other glands but is responsible for sexual development and growth. It consists of two parts, the anterior (which does all the interesting things), and the posterior, which secretes a hormone known as pituitrin, thus raising the blood-pressure and causing the muscle of the uterus to contract. Many conditions are described in which the anterior part of the gland either produces too much or too little of its hormones. For example, when this part overacts in early life the result is a giant—*i.e.*, anyone over 6 ft. 8 in. In later life, when the bones are set, the result of overaction is *acromegaly*, in which the face is elongated, the hands are relatively huge, as also are the feet. The head, too, is large, and the patient gives a somewhat gorilla-like impression.

When the anterior part of the pituitary underacts there are many unpleasant possibilities: the individual may develop into a fat boy, like the one in *Pickwick Papers*, sleepy, greedy, and monstrously fat; or into a human skeleton who appears to have hardly any flesh at all; or there may develop painful masses of fat in the wrong places, a condition described as *adiposis dolorosa*; or again, dwarfism may result and the individual retain the appearance and size of a child with normal adult mentality. These conditions are known by the various names of *Frölich's syndrome* in the fat-boy type, *Simmond's disease* in the human skeleton, *Dercum's disease* in the case of adiposis dolorosa, and *Lorrain's disease* in the case of dwarfism.

### The Sex Glands.

In women these are the ovaries, and in man the testes. The ovaries produce two hormones, one of which, œstrin, brings about, under the influence of the pituitary, the normal sex changes at puberty, controls the release of the ovum from the ovary, and, in animals, produces sexual excitement. The other, also controlled by the pituitary, is progesterone, which in general has a sedative effect: it prepares the uterus for pregnancy, and, when a pregnancy exists, maintains it.

The internal secretion of the male sex glands is testosterone, and it, like œstrin, produces the sex changes at puberty. The problems of sex, however, will be discussed later.

### DISEASES OF THE URINARY SYSTEM.

Everyone knows what kidneys look like—in fact, the term " kidney-shaped " is used to describe other objects. Within the kidneys the blood-vessels carrying waste materials subdivide and finally end up in little coils or glomeruli through which waste products are filtered into the other system, the system of tubes which, beginning as tiny cups around the glomeruli, become larger and larger until they join the ureter passing out at the root of the kidney, the hilum, a point at which both the veins and tubes enter and leave. The kidneys, of course, lie one on each side in the loins, so that if one puts one's hands on the hips and then slides them farther back they will cover the area over the left and right kidney. The ureters pass down on each side to the bladder, which is the storage tank of the products excreted by the kidneys, and lies in the mid-line down low in the abdomen; it is somewhat pear-shaped, and at its base in men there lies the prostate gland—a gland which apparently has few functions but can be a nuisance. Its only known function is that it adds something to the semen from the testes without which the semen would be sterile. Then, from the base of the bladder a single tube, the urethra, passes to the outside. One can, in fact, visualise the urinary system as a capital Y, in which the two upper limbs are the ureters, the place where they meet is the bladder, and the single limb at the foot is the urethra. Clearly, then, there may be diseases of the kidneys, of the ureters, of the bladder, of the prostate gland, or of the urethra.

The amount of urine may be increased or diminished. It is *increased* in the following conditions: after drinking excess of fluids; after taking drugs (known as *diuretics*) which are given to increase the flow; in diabetes of both types—mellitus and insipidus; in some types of chronic kidney disease; and finally, in emotional states of excitement. It is *decreased* in the following conditions: acute nephritis; any disease in which fluid is being lost in other ways, such as diarrhœa or sweating in fevers; when the fluid intake is small; and when both ureters are blocked by stones. Passing a great deal of urine is known as *polyuria*, passing very little as *oliguria*, passing frequent small amounts is simply called *frequency*. Normally, the urine is acid, but in infections of the bladder it may become alkaline owing to decomposition by bacteria. Abnormal substances, or normal substances in abnormal quantities, may occur in the urine and give the doctor an indication of what is wrong. In fact. urine analysis is a very important part of medical diagnosis. Thus urea is a normal content of urine which is increased in fevers, wasting diseases, or diabetes; the amount of urea is to some extent a measure of the degree of tissue breakdown. Uric acid is found in small quantities in normal urine, but the amount is increased in fevers and after an attack of gout (uric acid is important in the causation of gout, but has nothing at all to do with rheumatism in general, so one may disregard the advertisements in the popular Press showing unpleasant pictures of joints with sharp crystals of uric acid which are alleged to cause the pain of rheumatic disease). Oxalates are not ordinarily found in urine, but, since they occur in such foods as rhubarb and strawberries, and some people are unable to deal with them, such individuals may develop stones or have pain on passing urine after eating oxalate-containing fruits.

Two very important substances which ought not to be in normal urine are albumen and sugar. Albumen is a protein, and its presence in the urine indicates that the filters of the kidney are leaking —they are allowing protein to pass out which ought to remain in the body. Albumen is easily tested for, and its presence may indicate kidney disease or nephritis as it is usually called by doctors. On the other hand, small amounts of albumen occur in fevers and in nervous conditions —*functional albuminuria*. Sugar, too, should not be present, but its presence does not necessarily indicate diabetes; for small amounts may occur in nervous conditions or in some people after taking large quantities of carbohydrate.

Blood in the urine may give it an appearance which varies from bright red to a dark, smoky colour. It is found in many diseases: acute nephritis, stone, tumours, poisoning by certain drugs, infections such as bilharzia or malaria, papilloma (*i.e.*, non-malignant tumour of the bladder), after injury, in high blood-pressure, scurvy, and blood diseases. Sometimes it occurs for no known reason at all.

It will be remembered (or if it is not, you can look it up on p. 28 (1)) that streptococcal infection of the throat may cause in some people disease of the valves in the heart or endocarditis. In such cases, although the germ is found in the throat, it is not found in the heart or indeed anywhere else in the body. *Acute nephritis* occurs in the same circumstances, with the sole difference that the kidneys instead of the heart are affected. The disease appears to be an allergic reaction to the toxins of the streptococcus. The patient, often a child, has a sore throat (and even this may be absent or fail to be noticed) or sometimes the infection may arise in other sites: after scarlet fever, erysipelas, burns, and disease of the ear. A few days later there is headache, vomiting, pain in the loins, slight rise in temperature, and especially typical is *dropsy* or œdema. This begins in the face, first around the eyelids, and then affects the ankles; later it may become more general and affect the rest of the body. Blood and albumen are found in the urine, and the blood-pressure is slightly raised. The outlook is usually good if the kidneys are rested by reducing the amount of protein taken in and also the amounts of salt and water. When this is done, the inflammation soon goes and no permanent harm results. In other cases, however, if treatment is inadequate or the condition severe, the symptoms may go, but the albumen found in the urine persists. This means that permanent damage has been done, and although there may be nothing else to show for many years, *chronic nephritis* develops. In this case, the blood-pressure continues to rise, and since the filters of the kidneys no longer work efficiently, urea, the principal waste-product of the body to be excreted in the urine, is retained in the blood and only small amounts escape from the system. Hence chronic nephritis sooner or later leads to heart failure or hæmorrhage in the brain from the rising blood-pressure, or to the form of poisoning known as *uræmia* which results from the retention of urea in the blood. Uræmia may come on suddenly or gradually, but ends in progressive coma, drowsiness, and unconsciousness. There may be convulsions similar to those of epilepsy, high fever, and difficulty in breathing to complicate the picture.

Another type of nephritis which seems to have nothing at all to do with streptococcal infections, and the cause of which is completely unknown, is *nephrosis*. Developing in early adult life, its onset is insidious, and the patient first shows signs of œdema in his white and puffy face and the swelling of his legs. (It should be said here that if you have swelling of the ankles or elsewhere, you would be foolish to jump to conclusions; for such swelling is common in many diseases—in heart disease, in allergic conditions, in neurotic illness, and even just from hot weather.) When the urine is examined in a case of nephrosis it is found to be full of albumen and, as in chronic nephritis, the blood urea starts to rise. The end-results of nephrosis are the same as those of chronic nephritis and depend upon the damage originally done.

The modern diuretics of the chlorothiazide group help to control the œdema and, provided enough healthy tissue remains, remove both the fluid and the waste-products. In advanced or more serious cases artificial kidneys can be used, but as yet the transplantation of a kidney is largely in the experimental stage.

*Pyelitis* is an infection of the pelvis of the kidney, that is to say, of the part where the ureter leaves the kidney. It is usually caused by the bacillus coli, which is normally present in the body, or by the streptococcus. These germs may reach the ureter through the blood-stream or may pass upwards from the bladder. Obstruction anywhere in the urinary tract which causes the urine to stagnate is liable to cause pyelitis. Symptoms come on suddenly, with high fever, pain in the loin (the infection is usually on one side only, and is commoner in women), and pain in the abdomen. When urine is passed there is a burning sensation, and it is passed frequently and in small amounts. On examination, the urine is found to be highly acid and full of bacillus coli or whatever the causative germ may be. Pyelitis is fairly readily treated by the antibiotics or sulpha drugs. Plenty of fluids should be given and the urine made alkaline by administration of alkalis.

*Cystitis* means inflammation of the bladder, either acute or chronic, and its causes are much the same as in the case of pyelitis. There is pain over the lower abdomen, frequency, and sometimes slight fever. The treatment is as for pyelitis. *Urethritis* is an inflammation of the urethra, with burning pain on passing water and frequency. The most serious cause (although it can usually be easily dealt with now) is gonorrhœa. But non-specific urethritis is common, and in this case various germs or none may bring about pain and frequency; there is often a large neurotic element. Urethritis should be regarded as probably due to gonorrhœa, which has already been discussed elsewhere, when there is a thick, creamy discharge from the penis or discharge in women following sexual intercourse with an infected person.

*Kidney stones or Renal calculi* sometimes form, and, as in the case of gall-stones, what causes them is not certain. They may be caused by disorders of metabolism—that is, in the inability of the body to deal with calcium, proteins, uric acid, and other products; or by vitamin deficiency obstruction in the urinary tract, and urinary infections. But when a stone or stones are formed various events may occur: thus it may remain in the kidney and cause no symptoms; or it may cause repeated attacks of pain, infection, and blood in the urine (hæmaturia); or it may completely block the passage of urine from the kidney to such a degree that it degenerates and becomes useless; or, lastly, it may pass into the ureter, and when this occurs very severe pain, known as *renal colic*, will occur. A stone passing down the ureter into the bladder may become stuck in the urethra, although this is uncommon, since a stone small enough to get down the ureters is likely to be capable of manoeuvring through the rest of the tract. In fact, about 80–90 per cent. of stones are passed spontaneously. Stones not passed spontaneously may have to be removed by operation, but whether this is undertaken or not depends on various factors, such as the general health of the patient, the amount of trouble caused by the stone, and the health of the other kidney —for it is dangerous to operate on one kidney unless one is sure that the other is functioning efficiently.

If a stone blocks the passage of urine on one side for any length of time *hydronephrosis* may result, in which the part where the ureter enters the kidney swells with the retained urine. Ultimately much of the kidney may be destroyed by the back-pressure. The same effect may be produced by kinking of the ureter or anything else which causes obstruction. Sometimes children are born with hydronephrosis, and when the dilation is due to kinking of the tube the condition may be intermittent, with attacks of renal colic during which only small amounts of urine are passed; this is followed with relief and the passage of large quantities.

*Tumours and Cysts.* The kidney may also be the site of tumours and cysts which produce pain in the loins, sometimes a lump over the kidney which can be felt, and blood in the urine. Cancer of the bladder is a serious condition in which the bladder may have to be removed, so the urinary flow has then to be directed elsewhere. Either the ureters are brought out on to the skin surface, a procedure known as *cutaneous ureterostomy*, or they are implanted in the large bowel, so that the urine flows out with the fæces. This is described as *uretero-colostomy.*

There may also be benign tumours of the bladder or *papillomas*, which are soft and bleed easily; a great deal of blood is passed, but there is usually little or no pain. In this, and similar, diseases of the bladder examination of the inside of the organ is carried out by means of a cystoscope, a thin tube which is passed up the urethra and has a small electric light at the end which enables the surgeon to see what is going on. Instruments may also be passed through the tube, and simple papillomas can be cauterised. Similar instruments are used in the examination of the stomach (gastroscope) and the bronchial tubes (bronchoscope). When some obstruction in the outlet of the bladder or in the urethra occurs the bladder, of course, fills with urine, which cannot be passed, and very painful dilation occurs. In this case an attempt may be made to pass a catheter, a thin rubber tube, into the bladder to relieve the tension, or if this fails a *suprapubic cystomy* is performed—an incision is made in the abdomen over the bladder and a tube inserted into it, through which the urine escapes. This is ordinarily a temporary expedient, and later when the patient's health has improved an attempt will be made to remove the cause of obstruction. The most common cause of such obstruction is *enlargement of the prostate gland* at the base of the bladder, which surrounds this area and the beginning of the ureter. About 40 per cent. of men over sixty have some degree of obstruction due to this cause, and about 20 per cent. of these require operation. The gland is about the size of a walnut, and, as we have seen, its function is to supply part of the fluid which makes up the semen, the male sex secretion. Enlargement of the prostate may be benign or malignant, and, although nobody knows just why, such benign enlargement tends to occur in most men in later life. There may be no symptoms, but characteristically there is frequency during the day and the need to get up at night to pass water. The flow of urine being impeded by constriction of the urethra, the passage is less forceful than normal, and there is a tendency for dribbling to occur. If the obstruction is severe and not relieved the back-pressure may be transmitted to the ureters and kidneys, resulting finally in kidney failure and uræmia. The prostate, except in cases of very mild enlargement, has to be removed either through the abdomen or through the perineum (the part of the body lying between the sex organs and the anus). Sometimes, in less serious cases, it is possible without an incision to cut away the obstructing part by an electrocautery inserted, as is a cyst scope, through the urethra. Prostatectomy was once a serious operation, all the more so because the patient was usually elderly and not in good condition, but new techniques and the use of antibiotics have greatly improved the outlook.

*Cancer of the Prostate* is always serious, but if discovered in time it can be operated on successfully. The gland, of course, has to be completely removed; in inoperable cases, or in patients unfit to stand operation, the tumour may be treated by means of female sex hormones, which cause it to shrink and may prolong life by some years.

## DISEASES OF THE NERVOUS SYSTEM.

The brain and nervous system are like a telephone exchange which sends out and receives messages from the rest of the body. Essentially it consists of two levels, the lower centres, where primitive emotions are felt, the viscera controlled, and simple actions initiated, and the true brain, which holds the lower centres under control. When, for example, one is pricked with a pin, a message is passed up the nerves (the sensory nerves or nerves of feeling) to the lower centres in the spinal cord, which return a message through the motor nerves (the nerves dealing with movement), causing the hand to jerk away. All this takes place without any conscious interference, and can, in fact, happen even when the true brain has been removed. It is, of course, possible for the movement which jerks the hand away to be inhibited, because in this case the brain intervenes; all mental life is a constant interaction between the lower and higher centres.

When we become angry, for instance, the anger originates in the lower centres, but may be inhibited by the higher ones. To some extent, the former correspond to what a psychologist would describe as the unconscious mind, the latter to the conscious mind.

The nervous system is made up of nerve cells which are smaller than the head of a pin but end in a long, thin fibre, which may be several feet long. These fibres form the nerves of the body, and they end in the motor nerves, which bring about muscular movement, or in the skin, where there are separate nerve-endings dealing with pressure, heat, cold, pain, and so on. It used to be supposed that there were areas in the brain dealing with such mental faculties as acquisitiveness, conscientiousness, and other abilities; but this is known to be quite untrue. There are, indeed, areas dealing with movement, sight, hearing, speech, feeling, and thought, but certainly none dealing specifically with the more complex mental faculties. Nor is it correct to suppose that each nerve cell carries some particular thought or feeling; for it appears that thinking and feeling are represented by nervous circuits in the brain and are not isolated in any special area. Thus large parts of the brain can be removed without interfering with mental activity.

The most primitive part of the nervous system is the autonomic nervous system, which has its "brain" in the hypothalamus at the base of the true brain. It is divided into two parts: the sympathetic nervous system, which supplies the viscera with impulses which prepare the body for flight or fight (causing the heart to beat faster, the muscles to become congested with blood, the skin to become pale, and the blood-sugar to rise whilst the intestines become less active), and the parasympathetic nervous system, which, in general, produces relaxation. When the parasympathetic system acts, the heart beats more slowly, the skin becomes flushed, the intestines digest food, and the body is prepared for rest. Since, as we have seen, the lower centres are the centres controlling both emotion and the internal organs, it is clear that emotional states will influence the action of the body. This is the basis of psychosomatic medicine.

The brain and the spinal cord, which passes down the bony canal within the spine, are covered with a thin layer of tissue known as the meninges and surrounded with cerebro-spinal fluid, which is also found in the cavities of the brain known as ventricles. A specimen of cerebro-spinal fluid, or C.S.F., may be removed by pushing a hollow needle between the vertebrae in the lumbar region, and such specimens can give a great deal of information about what is going on in the nervous system.

The diseases of the nervous system can be divided into various groups: there are those due to injuries, such as fractures of the skull or divided nerves; the infectious diseases, most of which have been discussed already; the diseases due to hæmorrhage or embolism; tumours; and, perhaps the biggest group, the degenerative diseases.

The blood-vessels of the brain are one of the common sites of *aneurisms*, bulges like small berries, often at the base of the brain, caused by weakness of the vessel wall. This is sometimes the result of arteriosclerosis, syphilitis infection, or injury, but perhaps most often the aneurisms are congenital—*i.e.*, the individual is born with them. There are usually no symptoms, although if the aneurism is large enough it may press upon other structures and cause symptoms recognisable by the specialist. In most cases the diagnosis is apparent only when the aneurism, as may occur, ruptures. When this happens the symptoms are those of brain hæmorrhage. There is severe headache, vomiting, and loss of consciousness, the patient breathes heavily, and when the doctor does a lumbar puncture the C.S.F. is stained with blood. Such an event is very serious, and ordinarily all that can be done is to rest the patient; nevertheless, over 60 per cent. of cases are fatal.

When in the few cases in which symptoms occur *before* hæmorrhage, the presence of an aneurism is suspected, this may be confirmed by X-ray. Since soft tissues are not seen in X-ray pictures, it is necessary (for example, in the gallbladder, the kidneys, the bronchi, or the blood-vessels of the brain) to inject some radio-opaque substance which outlines them. In the brain this is known as arteriography, and when by this means aneurisms or other abnormalities are found surgery is sometimes possible. Hæmorrhage into the brain substance produces what is generally known as a *stroke*. The artery affected is usually the middle cerebral, when in later adult life it has been strained and weakened by high blood-pressure or arteriosclerosis. It can, however, be caused by bleeding from a tumour, or in children by birth injuries. Hæmorrhages may also result in the small veins from the strain of coughing in whooping cough.

A stroke comes on suddenly, and the patient is flushed with a bluish tinge. He breathes heavily and, as he breathes, the cheek on the affected side may be blown in and out. Since the left side of the brain supplies the right side of the body, and *vice versa*, the side of the body on the opposite side from hæmorrhage is paralysed. The limbs and face right down the affected area are flaccid and useless, but if the patient survives they will at a later stage become spastic. There are, therefore, two types of paralysis: flaccid and spastic. In the first, the limb is incapable of movement, and when lifted it falls back like a dead weight; there are no reflexes, so that when the knee-cap is tapped to elicit the knee-jerk there is no response. Flaccid paralysis is typical of injury to the lower parts of the nervous system, and it means that no impulses are getting through. Spastic paralysis, on the contrary, is characterised by rigidity of the limb, overactive reflexes, and even when movement is possible it is out of control. This, in fact, is what has occurred; for spastic paralysis indicates that, although the lower nerves are undamaged, the controlling centre in the brain has been affected.

If the patient survives, there may be varying degrees of improvement in the paralysis, which is always at its greatest in the beginning.

When such an emergency occurs it is best to leave the patient where he is, keep him warm, take out his dentures if any, call the doctor, and on no account to give him any fluids or alcohol. No patient in coma should ever have fluids poured down his throat. Other causes of coma are diabetes, alcohol, uræmia, acute hypertensive (high blood-pressure) attacks, and thrombosis or embolism.

In thrombosis and embolism a similar picture to that of hæmorrhage occurs. Embolism comes on suddenly like a hæmorrhage, but in thrombosis or clotting the onset may be more gradual, with premonitory symptoms of headache, giddiness, and numbness or pins and needles in the limbs. There may be difficulty in speaking.

*Tumours and Abscesses.* The brain is soft, greyish white in colour, and from the upper surface closely resembles a huge walnut in that it has two sides joined across the middle by a smaller part known, in the brain, as the corpus callosum. It resembles a walnut, too, in that its surface is crumpled up into convolutions. Investigation of the brain has become more and more refined in recent years, the following being some of the techniques employed:

(1) Straight X-rays.
(2) Arteriograms, which have already been described.
(3) Encephalograms or ventriculograms, in which some of the fluid, the C.S.F. sur-rounding the brain or in the cavities known as ventricles within the brain substance, is removed and replaced by gas. The gas may be helium or oxygen, and it has the effect in an X-ray picture of outlining the brain and ventricles so that any distortion of shape due to a tumour or abscess is outlined.
(4) Electroencephalograms are pictures made of the electrical brain waves produced by the brain, just as the electrocardiograph takes pictures of the similar waves pro-duced by the heart. Electrodes attached to the scalp may show abnormal waves over the site of a tumour or abscess.
(5) Still more recently, radioisotopes have been used to locate tumours, since radio-

active substance become concentrated in the area of the abnormal tissues.

The main symptoms of brain tumour are severe headache, vomiting, and disturbances of vision; such symptoms must be referred to a doctor at once. The pulse-rate is usually slow. All these symptoms are caused by increasing pressure within the brain because of the space taken up by the tumour.

The popular belief that a brain tumour is tantamount to a death warrant is simply untrue; for at least 80–90 per cent. of cases recover. The main types of tumour are meningiomas (*i.e.*, tumours of the brain coverings or meninges); tumours of the nerve fibres within the brain or neurofibromas; tumours of the pituitary gland; and gliomas, which are tumours of the background substance. The outlook for all of these is good, except in the case of the glioma, which is a type of tumour which tends to infiltrate into the rest of the brain fairly rapidly. It is not localised, and therefore complete removal is not always possible.

Brain abscesses may be spread from the blood-stream in people with bronchiectasis, osteomy-elitis, infected sinuses, or chronic ear disease. The symptoms are similar to those of tumour, but there is also fever and drowsiness.

*Aphasia* is a disturbance of the ability to speak, write, or to understand spoken or written words. It is usually due to a tumour, abscess, throm-bosis, or embolism of the speech area in the brain. In motor aphasia the muscles of speech are normal, but the patient is unable to speak in-telligibly. In nominal aphasia the patient cannot name objects, which he nevertheless is able to recognise. In agraphia the patient cannot write, although his muscles are normal. In word-blindness and word-deafness the patient cannot understand written or spoken words respectively. Treatment depends upon the cause, but in hopeful cases re-education is sometimes possible.

*Headaches.* This seems a convenient point to say something about headache, which must surely be one of the commonest symptoms suffered by the human race. We shall begin by noting that at least 90 per cent. of all headaches are nervous in origin or the result of such other minor troubles as gastric upset. It is doubtful whether headache is as frequently brought about by eye-strain as is often supposed, but there is certainly no harm in having one's eyes tested if frequent headaches are present.

A doctor will first try to distinguish between headaches due to mental causes and those due to organic or physical ones. When the cause is physical the headache is often very severe, usually located sharply in one area (for example, on one side of the head), and it is likely to be accompanied by other symptoms, such as vomiting and eye-disturbances. The person with this type of pain often tries to minimise the pain he suffers, but his behaviour—for example, his obvious fear of moving his head—belies him. The neurotic person, on the other hand, suffers from headaches which are "terrible," "awful," "unbearable," vague in their location (they are "all over"), and, if they are accompanied by other nervous symptoms, the diagnosis is clear. Apart from the neurotic type, headaches are caused by migraine, increased pressure within the skull, as in brain tumour or abscess, sinus disease, and eye diseases. Treatment obviously depends on the cause, and the sensible thing to do is to go to a doctor, believe what he says, and take his advice. Neurotic headaches may be dealt with by in-vestigation of the sources of worry, frustration, and so on which cause the pain, or by taking aspirin or other pain-relieving drugs. (Pain, in fact, is one of the very few things aspirin is good for, and as has already been said elsewhere, those who believe that it is good for "nerves," insomnia, and all the various conditions which make aspirin an almost universal cure in the minds of many, are deluding themselves.)

*Migraine* is a disorder which many claim to possess and not so many really do; for if all the people who claim this dubious honour—often those who have little better to do than be bored with themselves—if all these were put end to end, or even stood upright in a line, they would surely encircle the Earth. True migraine, however, is a very clear-cut disease, and happens in a very definite type of person. The owner of the migraine tends to be a highly intelligent and conscientious—even over-conscientious—individual (not at all like Mrs. Jones, who says she suffers from it and could by no stretch of the imagination be described either as intelligent or over-conscientious). The headaches are severe, usually on one side of the head only, occur in periodic attacks, and are not, like the headaches suffered by Mrs. Jones, "there all the time." Vision is affected so that there may be hemianopia (i.e., half-vision), flashes of light before the eyes, and the so-called fortification spectra (i.e., zig-zag patterns in the field of vision). The pain is often prostrating, and is usually followed by attacks of vomiting. Migraine is a mystery disease which apparently has something to do with the personality, with emotional stresses, and conceivably in some cases with allergy; the actual pain appears to be caused by spasm of the blood-vessels in the brain. The usual treatment is with tablets of ergotamine (Fermergin), but other remedies are also helpful in different cases.

There are a number of other nervous diseases the cause of which remains a mystery, and of these we shall mention epilepsy, chorea, and pink disease.

*Epilepsy* is a symptom, not a disease, which is common at all ages but especially children. It has been attributed to St. Paul, Julius Caesar, Napoleon, and (with more justice perhaps) to Dostoievsky. Many varieties of attack occur often in the same patient, the commonest and best known being the *grand mal* or major seizure. In this the patient falls down unconscious and rigid and the jaw is clenched, so that there is danger of the tongue being bitten. This so-called tonic phase is followed, within a minute or so, by a clonic phase in which the limbs contract rhythmically. The attack ends with the patient going limp and gradually recovering consciousness, a process which may take up to an hour. Occasionally the patient has a brief warning, most often an indescribable feeling in the stomach. There are two common forms of minor seizure, one occurring mainly in children and the other more often in adults. The common minor attacks in children are often called *petit mal* or *absence*, which well describes the instantaneous and brief loss of consciousness often unaccompanied by any change in posture. Recovery is equally instantaneous. On the other hand, in the other forms of epilepsy which arise from various parts of the brain, but especially from the lobe under the temporal region, there is often a warning similar to that which may precede a major seizure. In these cases the patient shows only confusion, no definite loss of posture, but automatic activity such as fumbling with buttons, muttering, and grimacing. Following these attacks there may be a quite prolonged period of confusion in which the patient may wander away and occasionally may be violent. Criminal acts are very rarely carried out in this state.

A large number of people have had one or two fits in their lives, particularly at times of physical or psychological stress. "Fever" or "Febrile" convulsions (often called teething fits in the past) are extremely common in young children and are often thought of as something different from epilepsy since the attacks rarely continue in later years. This form of epilepsy and some cases of *petit mal* are the only forms in which hereditary factors are important in the causation, and these are the least serious forms of epilepsy. They are very rarely associated with serious physical or psychological disturbances. Most other forms of epilepsy are due to a scar or other area of brain damage. It is a proportion of these cases which develop the psychological disturbances that are occasionally very serious.

Not every patient who has had one or two fits need necessarily take regular anticonvulsant drugs; that is drugs which damp down the abnormal excessive activity of the brain that leads to the attacks. Many drugs are available of which the most important are phenobarbitone, phenytoin, succinimides, and troxidones, the last two

being effective only against minor seizures. Which one to use and whether to use one at all is, of course, quite a complicated judgment, and must be left to the doctor. Epileptics often find it difficult to get work because of the reluctance of employers to take on someone who may be more prone to accidents and whose fits may distress other workers. Obviously there are some jobs which epileptics should not do because of the danger involved, (from, for example, moving machinery), and they should not drive a car. A few cases are so severe that work is almost impossible, but employers have a duty whenever possible to employ these people whose mental health may suffer greatly if they are made to feel outcasts and who ordinarily are as efficient, or even more so, as the next man. It is also hoped that employees will become less prejudiced about epilepsy as the general public become less ignorant about medical matters. In this way epileptics will come to be accepted in all those kinds of employment for which they are well suited. If some of the famous men who have suffered from this disease had had to rely on the charity of some employers today the world would have been much the poorer, although possibly we could have managed without the generals.

The British Epilepsy Association exists to give guidance to people with epilepsy, their families, and friends. It provides a full-time welfare service and a chain of social clubs. It is concerned by means of books, films, courses, and lectures to make known the true facts about epilepsy. It seeks to share its knowledge with organisations in other countries. Its offices are at 3–6 Alfred Place, London, W.C.1. Tel. LAN 2704/5.

*Chorea*, or St. Vitus' Dance, is connected in some way with rheumatism, especially with rheumatic fever. It is much less common than formerly, and is also known as Sydenham's chorea, after the English physician who first described it and to distinguish it from Huntington's chorea, a serious hereditary and incurable degenerative disease which leads to progressive mental deterioration. Fortunately, Huntington's chorea is rather rare. The patient with Sydenham's chorea is a child, most often a girl, and one who has been rather delicate and nervous. She shows an inability to keep still and makes purposeless movements, such as writhing and twitching of the limbs and grimaces of the face. The speech may be affected, and the muscular inco-ordination may be so pronounced that dishes or other objects fall from the hands when lifted. The treatment for chorea is that for acute rheumatism with the addition of sedatives. The heart may be affected.

*Pink Disease* is a disease of young children between the ages of six months and three years. Why it should be included here is not certain: for its cause is unknown, and the theories to explain its origin range from the supposition that it is a vitamin-deficiency disorder, an infection, or the result of poisoning by mercury in teething powders, to the more probable theory that it is a vasomotor disorder like chilblains brought about by the nerves which control the diameter of the arteries. (Here it should be said that "teething powders," whether or not they play any part in causing this disease, should never be used anyhow, since in the first place—doubtless to the great indignation of mothers who, of course, always know best—one must say that it is extremely uncertain whether the many disturbances allegedly due to teething have anything to do with teeth at all, and secondly, that whether or not teething causes anything, it is certain that the numerous powders available in the shops can do nothing about it.) Pink disease was first described in Australia in 1914, and the general picture is that of a child in acute misery with itching or burning of the hands and feet, which are swollen and pink in appearance. Sometimes the face, ears, and nose are affected, there is loss of appetite, sweating, insomnia, and thirst. The treatment of the condition, which may last many months but with an ultimately good outlook, is injection of the B vitamins, especially B12, rest, and sedatives.

*Angio-neurotic œdema.* Another mysterious disease, common to both children and adults, and mentioned here because it, too, seems to be caused by malfunctioning of the nerves controlling the blood-vessels, is angio-neurotic œdema in which attacks of œdema (swelling) occur in various parts of the body, but are most apparent in the face. Undoubtedly allergy to various foodstuffs can play some part, but emotional factors are at least equally important. Very frequently, without any warning at all—but often after an emotional outburst—the face within a short time swells so that the patient is almost literally unrecognisable. Sometimes the swelling is so severe that breathing is endangered by œdema of the glottis, the entry to the windpipe. An immediate injection of adrenalin usually starts to clear up the condition, and for later use the antihistamine drugs have proved helpful.

## THE DEGENERATIVE DISEASES.

There are very many conditions coming into this category, and they are given different names according to the parts of the nervous system affected. However, they all have this in common, that they are the result of a degeneration of groups of nerve cells, usually for no known reason, and, since nerve cells once destroyed can never regenerate, the diseases are usually irreversible and progressive. In a few cases, however, they can be arrested or simply die out.

It would be impossible to deal even briefly with all these diseases, so here only a few of the more common ones will be discussed. The ones we shall mention are: muscular atrophy, amyotrophic lateral sclerosis, disseminated sclerosis, syringomyelia, and subacute combined degeneration.

Muscular atrophy is, in fact, a whole group of diseases in which there is some damage to the lower parts of the nervous system, usually in the nerve cells at the point where they leave the spinal cord. The common type, *progressive muscular atrophy,* occurs in middle age or over, and the patient begins to note wasting of the muscles in first one hand and then the other. Ultimately, the hand becomes claw-shaped, and some wasting may spread up the forearm. It may finally spread up to the base of the brain, with fatal results. There is no known cure. In children a similar condition is *peroneal muscular atrophy,* in which degeneration of the nerve cells in the spinal cord leads to wasting both of the hands and legs. In this case the disease may stop of itself after several years.

*Amyotrophic lateral sclerosis* affects both the lower and higher nerve cells. There is wasting of the hands and arms, with increasing weakness, and the legs show a spastic type of paralysis, *i.e.,* they do not waste, but the muscles are in varying degrees of spasm and the knee-jerk and other reflexes are increased. The disease has been treated with concentrated vitamin E, but the results are uncertain. It should be noted that to say that a disease is incurable is not at all the same thing as saying that the patient is going to die from it. Some of these diseases progress very slowly, or may stop of themselves, and any disease process tends to go slower as one gets older. For example, many old people with cancer die of old age long before they are in danger of dying from the disease.

*Disseminated sclerosis*—sclerosis means hardening of the affected parts of the nervous system —is a progressive condition which goes on with periodic intermissions of improvement. Often the first symptom is double vision or sudden weakness in a limb, but the later symptoms are largely those resulting from loss of muscular co-ordination; thus, when the patient is asked to shut the eyes, stretch out the arm at right-angles to the body and then touch the tip of his nose, he manages the first part of the movement fairly adequately, but as the finger nears the nose it starts to wobble and fails to reach its goal. There is thus some loss of sense of position and difficulty in carrying out such actions as drinking tea from a cup. Another typical symptom is nystagmus, in which, when he is asked to look to one side, the patient's eyes jerk back and forth (this condition is, of course, also a feature of so-called " miner's nystagmus," which appears to have a large psychological element and certainly has nothing to do with disseminated sclerosis). In later stages the spinal cord becomes affected and there are varying degrees of paralysis in the lower half of the body so that the legs are useless and there is loss of control of bladder and bowels. Thus, although disseminated sclerosis is not by itself a fatal disease, it does result in the long run in the patient becoming increasingly bed-ridden. Examination of the nervous system reveals that the covering of the nerve fibres—which have a sort of insulating layer much the same as in the case of electric wires—has been damaged and the underlying fibres have degenerated themselves. Where this damage occurs, and this appears to be completely fortuitous, determines the nature of the symptoms and where they occur. Many treatments have been tried, but their number only emphasises how little we know. The disease may be the result of inborn weakness in the fibres, of allergy, or of a virus infection with a so far undiscovered virus, but since it occurs in young adults in the prime of their life it is a particularly tragic disorder. Strangely enough, it is confined almost entirely to Europeans, and is rare elsewhere in the world.

*Syringomyelia,* another degenerative disease, is caused by the formation of small cavities in the upper parts of the spinal cord in the neck and chest regions. These cavities become surrounded with scar tissue, and hence interfere with nerve impulses passing down the areas where they occur. The patient may be any age between ten and thirty, and suffers from both sensory and motor symptoms. There is wasting of the muscles of the hand, and sometimes of the arm and shoulder, and specially typical is loss of the sense of pain with retention of the sense of touch. Because of this, the patient may burn or cut his fingers without noticing anything. The disease is slowly progressive over a long period of time, and there is no known effective treatment.

One of the few degenerative diseases which can be treated is *subacute combined degeneration,* which is invariably associated with pernicious anæmia. A middle-aged patient notices numbness, pins and needles, and so-called lightning pains in the fingers and toes and later in the limbs. The muscles are weak, and the tongue is smooth and glossy. On examination, the symptoms of pernicious anæmia are found. Treatment for the anæmia puts a stop to the disease, although damage already done may remain.

## INFLAMMATORY DISEASES.

These are those, such as shingles or neuritis, which may be due, as is shingles, to virus infection, or to various causes, as is neuritis. The virus causing *shingles* is apparently the same as that causing chickenpox. Shingles, or to give it its proper title *herpes zoster* (it must not be confused with *herpes labialis* or cold sore of the lips, with which it has no connection whatever), shows itself in the form of a band of pain surrounding the upper abdomen or chest, which is then followed by an eruption with blisters in the affected area. There is no specific treatment; aspirin may be given for the pain and the reuption painted collodion or " New Skin." Ordinarily the condition clears up fairly quickly, but the pain may persist for a long time. Injections of vitamin B12 are sometimes helpful.

The word " neuritis," meaning inflammation of a nerve, covers many different types of illness: polyneuritis, simple neuritis, neuralgia, sciatica, prolapsed vertebral disc, and other conditions. All they have in common is nerve pain; for, as in the case of " colds," one cannot assume that because a condition has one name it represents one disease or has even one cause.

*Multiple, peripheral,* or *polyneuritis* is, as the name indicates, a condition in which numerous of the peripheral nerves, mainly in the limbs, are affected. The symptoms will vary according to whether motor or sensory nerves are attacked. The causes are various: poisons, such as lead, arsenic, or alcohol; bacterial toxins, such as those of diphtheria, typhoid, or gonorrhœa; vitamin deficiencies, as in beri-beri; and, finally diseases of metabolism, such as diabetes. Rarely, an infection known as acute infective polyneuritis causes the symptoms. The parts affected depend to some extent on the cause. Thus alcohol brings about, when taken in excess, pain in the calves and foot-drop (*i.e.*, the foot hangs down and cannot be raised to its normal position); neuritis due to diabetes and arsenic shows similar symptoms, whereas in lead poisoning not only the foot but also the wrist may be affected. Diphtheria tends to attack the palate and the eyes, causing difficulty in swallowing and in vision.

The ordinary type of neuritis, however, is localised—and here it should be said that many pains described as neuritic are nothing of the sort, being probably caused by fibrositis or muscle and joint disorders. Typical of localised neuritis is *Bell's palsy*, neuritis of the facial nerve, in which one side of the face is paralysed so that the eye on the affected side will not shut, and the mouth droops down. Asked to whistle or blow out his cheeks, the patient with facial paralysis is unable to do so. The usual cause of Bell's palsy is cold—for example, it is common to find that the patient has been driving with the car window open in cold weather. But facial paralysis may also be caused by infection in the middle ear. Most cases clear up in a fairly short time, but in a few instances the palsy is permanent. There is very little evidence that the treatments usually employed, such as electrical stimulation, have any effect, but injections of concentrated vitamins B may be used.

Other familiar types of neuritis are *sciatica* and neuritis in the arm. They can be caused by fractures, or pressure from tumours, or the callus (excess bone) in badly healed fractures; cold, too, is said to be a factor, and then there is always " idiopathic neuritis "—which, in everyday language, means that one does not know the cause. Most cases, regrettably, are idiopathic. In sciatica, we have a condition which is not a disease but rather a symptom. The familiar pain down the back of the leg may be caused by alcohol, rheumatism, diabetes, tumour, fibrositis, " slipped disc," arthritis of the hip joint, dislocated sacro-iliac joint, infection such as tonsillitis, and so on. Treatment depends on the cause, which frequently is never found.

*Prolapsed Intervertebral disc* is a popular disease in these days. It causes a sciatica-like type of pain, and is brought about by the bulging of an intervertebral disc (the shock-absorbers, which lie between the vertebræ of the spinal column) into the area where it can press upon the nerve root. Treatment is first by rest and pain-relieving drugs; if this is not enough laminectomy is performed and the protruding part of the disc removed.

*Paralysis agitans* or *Parkinson's disease* may result in young adults following an attack of encephalitis, or in older people, in whom the part of the brain concerned simply deteriorates. The face becomes expressionless, the movements stiff and slow, the gait shows a shuffling tendency, in which the patient bends forward and seems to be running to catch up with himself. There is tremor of the fingers and the so-called " pill-rolling " movements, in which the thumb and fingers are constantly moving against each other. Treatment is by drugs, such as hyoscine or more modern proprietary ones; in some cases surgical operation has been used with varying degrees of success. The disease is also known as " shaking palsy."

## MENTAL DISEASES.

### Psychosis.

Mental diseases are divided into psychoses (*i.e.*, insanity) and neuroses (*i.e.*, what is ordinarily known as " nerves "). Psychoses, in their turn, are divided into organic and functional—those due to physical disease and those in which no physical cause has been discovered. In point of fact, the distinction into organic and functional is rather meaningless; for if we accept the modern view of psychosomatic medicine which regards the body and mind as a single unit it is clear that organic disease brings out psychological defects which were already there and that functional disease must, in the final analysis, be the result of physicochemical causes, even if this is brought about by mental stress.

Organic disease results from poisoning of the nervous system by such poisons as alcohol, carbon monoxide, or lead; vitamin deficiencies, as in pellagra; infections such as syphilis; and degeneration of the brain, either primary or as a result of poor blood supply. In all cases its main symptoms are confusion, signs of other disease, and loss of memory. Alcohol leads to various conditions: in *delirium tremens* heavy bouts of drinking end in delirium (" D.T.s "), confusion, hallucination—although not necessarily of pink elephants or rats. It is a serious disease, but the outlook is much improved since it was discovered that injections of concentrated vitamins B and C in the form of " Parentrovite " can help. In more chronic cases *Korsakov's syndrome* manifests itself in the form of mental deterioration and memory defects. There can be little doubt that previously existing mental instability is a predisposing factor in these conditions. The same may be said of *general paralysis of the insane* or G.P.I., and in this case the immediate cause is syphilitic infection of the nervous system. Nevertheless, of all the patients with chronic syphilis, only a small number get syphilis of the nervous system. G.P.I. is typically associated with the usual symptoms of organic disease and delusions of grandeur; for example, a man with this disease may go out and buy several expensive cars in one day. However, it is not uncommon to find G.P.I. associated with severe depression—again the picture depends on the previous personality. At one time G.P.I. was considered hopeless, but treatment by malaria (that is, deliberate injection of malarial germs) was found to be helpful. Today, although in some places the treatment is still used, penicillin is found to be adequate. The association of the above symptoms with a positive Wasserman test—which proves the presence of the spirochæte in the blood—indicates neurosyphilis. When the lower centres of the nervous system are affected the disease is known as *tabes dorsalis*, in which there is difficulty in passing urine, limb pains, inability to stand when the eyes are closed, and finally difficulty in walking. The patient becomes paralysed and ultimately bedridden. Treatment is with penicillin.

People age at varying rates, so that some are hale and hearty at eighty or ninety whereas others are old at sixty or seventy. They present the typical picture of old age: " second childishness and mere oblivion, sans eyes, sans teeth, sans everything." When this condition, which is caused by degenerative changes in the brain or by defective blood-supply resulting from arteriosclerosis, is pronounced we speak of *senile psychosis*. There is mental confusion, forgetfulness, and delusions, in which the previous personality defects which we all have are accentuated. Such patients may have to be put under special care, but the process is largely irreversible.

The functional psychoses are two in number: schizophrenia and manic-depressive insanity. In *schizophrenia*, which, when it occurs in early adult life, is known (or used to be known) as *dementia præcox*, the symptoms are bizarre. There are delusions and hallucinations, so that the patient often believes himself to be persecuted and hears voices which say objectionable things to him. Sometimes the schizophrenic is wildly excited, and in other cases he goes into a state of stupor which is described as a catatonic state. Although the disease is described as functional, recent discoveries seem to suggest that there is some derangement of the blood chemistry. Treatment by insulin and the new tranquillising drugs has revolutionised the outlook in this admittedly serious disease. Indeed, some cases of psychosis are more easily treated than neurotic patients, since the former respond to physical methods, whereas the latter may require fairly prolonged psychotherapy (psychological treatment) and are less responsive to drugs.

In cases which do not respond to other methods, the brain operation known as *leucotomy* may be performed. Leucotomy is also performed to alleviate intractable pain, as in incurable cancer, but some of the ataraxic drugs (tranquillisers) are probably equally useful for this purpose. Leucotomy involves the severing of the connecting nerve fibres between certain areas of the brain, and the results are often favourable, but in fact the operation should be performed only in cases where the outlook is otherwise very poor; chronic severe neuroses, frequent attacks of manic depressive psychosis, severe chronic depression, and schizophrenia which has not responded to other forms of treatment. The operation reduces anxiety, fear, aggressiveness, and agitation, but may result in the less-desirable symptoms of apathy, impaired judgment, lack of self-control, and loss of initiative.

Schizophrenia developing in later life is likely to be less dramatic in origin, and the delusions tend to be more systematised—that is, they take a persistent form, which does not change from day to day. This type of the disease is known as *paraphrenia*. In those beyond middle age the rare but dangerous condition described as *paranoia* may develop in which there are no hallucinations and the only symptom is a completely systematised collection of persecutory delusions, which on recital may sound entirely convincing even to the ordinary doctor. Such people are dangerous precisely because they are so plausible, and they fill the ranks of the litigious, the troublemakers, and the political and religious eccentrics. One such patient known to the writer spent his life in a mental hospital from which he had parole, employing this to form a society propagating highly eccentric sexual and political beliefs. It says little for the intelligence of the general population that his meetings were invariably crowded out (although, of course, when one reads of the people who apparently believe that the various fictitious families on radio or television—the Groves, the Archers, and the like—really exist, one need not be surprised at such examples of communal dottiness, even if one may despair of democracy).

*Manic-depressive insanity* is characterised by mood swings in which the emotions alternate between wild elation without obvious cause and equally causeless depression. However, the picture is not quite as simple as this; for phases of mania or excitement may occur without depression obviously following, or there may be a single attack of depression with no manic phases. The disease may be absolutely incapacitating, or there may be periods of relative normality; typically, then, manic-depressive insanity is a disease of alternating moods. The depression responds to electroconvulsive therapy or E.C.T., but mania is less responsive to treatment. However, it ordinarily remits of itself. Sometimes in middle age *involutional depression* occurs, and this in the vast majority of cases is cured by E.C.T. As in the case of schizophrenia drugs are increasingly used for depression. Chlorpromazine in the former case and in depression Nardil or Tofranil, etc. The ever-present risk in depression is suicide.

### Neurosis.

The main neuroses are anxiety neurosis, hysteria, and obsessional neurosis. *Anxiety neurosis* is an illness in which the main symptom (as the name implies) is anxiety. There is fear which rationally the patient knows to be groundless; there may be anxiety attacks, in which the heart pounds, the patient feels he is going mad, is unable to sleep, and worries " for no reason at all." In hysteria, anxiety is largely absent, but there may be apparently physical symptoms ranging from paralysis of the limbs to blindness, deafness, inability to write, and lapses of memory (the so-called hysterical fugues or loss of memory). Typical of *hysteria* is the fact that the patient is less worried by his symptoms than would be expected from their apparent seriousness; this is what the early psychiatrists described as "la belle indifférence." The reason for the indifference is simple—it is that the paralysed individual *wants* to be paralysed, the blind *want* to be blind, the deaf to be deaf (there are none so blind—or deaf—as those who don't want to see, or hear), and the person who doesn't want to write conveniently finds that he cannot.

Generally speaking, neurotic people are suffering from a failure to face up to reality. They are not physically ill and are largely the end result of a faulty upbringing. It is wrong to suppose that the only bad families are those in which the children are ill-treated; much the worst ones are those in which children are spoilt, the parents possessive, and the wrong kind of love is dispensed. Neuroses are the result of a conflict between primitive desires and what the individual has been brought up to believe he should be. For example, before an examination a student may develop a nervous breakdown because he fears failure when he has been brought up to expect success. The excuse, of course, is " overwork " —an entirely non-existent condition. With his breakdown he solves his problem, he avoids the fear of failing and preserves his self-respect: he has been ill. Similarly, the soldier with " shell shock " (another non-existent condition) has a conflict between his sense of duty and his fear of death, which again is solved by becoming ill. Or, to take a final example, a woman feels the duty to look after her ageing mother. But she also wants to get married. So she unconsciously develops a neurosis which says, in effect, " I should like to do my duty in looking after my mother, but unfortunately I am unable to." There is an unconscious rebellion on the part of the mind.

Neurosis, in effect, is not a disease—it is a self-inflicted injury, a form of maladaptation to life. The neurotic, no matter how much he suffers, does not want to get well; he has found some way of getting along, even if a foolish way, and he intends to keep it. Often his symptoms are the sort of excuse that say: " If only I wasn't ill what wouldn't I be able to do! " The neurotic is a person who is different and is afraid to be himself; his problem is a conflict between being " ordinary," " like other people," and being what he was supposed to be. You will find some further references to neurosis in Section Q, Part II.

*Obsessional Neurosis* is a more severe type of neurotic illness; for although in anxiety neurosis we find such symptoms as phobias—irrational fears of open spaces, closed spaces, animals, and so on—obsessional states are characterised by compulsive feelings that certain acts must be performed or certain thoughts thought. In a mild form we all have obsessions: we feel that we must walk on the spaces between paving-stones, that we must touch lamp-posts, and so on. But when this type of compulsion gets to the stage when we must go back several times to make sure the lights have been put out, when we feel the need to wash our hands every few minutes, become obsessed with numbers on cars or dates on coins, then it becomes a nuisance and requires treatment. Usually the treatment is psychotherapy—whether psychoanalysis according to the method of Freud or shorter methods—and, in serious cases, physical methods such as L.S.D. (lysergic acid) or leucotomy. The obsessional neurotic is a person who feels that life must be controlled; he is " a creature who moves in predestinate grooves—he's not even a bus but a tram." His symptoms are an attempt to devise self-imposed rules which will control the unconscious desires of which he is so afraid.

*Neurasthenia* is an entirely imaginary condition allegedly due to exhaustion of the nervous system. Since no such condition exists, we need not bother with it. Neuroses cannot be treated by feeding the nerves (which are perfectly normal). They can be helped by such things as sedatives, but not cured. *Neurosis has nothing at all to do with disease of the physical nerves, so nerve tonics do not exist, and anyone who asserts that they do is a humbug.* Glycerophosphates and the usual contents of tonics are excreted almost as soon as they are taken in, and tonic wines are one of the best ways of becoming an alcoholic. The one reason for not taking alcohol is when one craves it, and many a " respectable " old lady has required several dust-carts to carry away the store of empty bottles left behind when she died.

*Psychopathic Personality* is the term given to anyone who has different standards of behaviour from those generally accepted by society. Some of these unfortunates may be *inadequate*, that is to say, although perfectly intelligent, unable to earn their own living. Others are the *creative* people, who, as in the case of Van Gogh did many eccentric things but also many productive things—Van Gogh was gifted, or cursed, with an intense sensitivity. Lastly, there are those who have what others regard as peculiar sexual habits. Of the first two classes nothing more need be said, and all that is necessary is to mention certain of the so-called sexual perversions. (When we say so-called the implication is not that none of these forms of behaviour is perverse but that some of them are carried out by otherwise quite ordinary people.) *Sadism* and *Masochism* refer to, in the first place, pleasure in inflicting pain and, in the second, to receiving pain. The pleasure is sexual, and it is incorrect to talk of cruelty in itself as sadism. Sadism is named after the Marquis de Sade, who suffered from this perversion, although he certainly did much less harm in his small way than numerous politicians or generals of our time, and masochism is named after the Austrian novelist Sacher-Masoch, who wrote books which, although unpleasant, were not notably more so than certain Sunday newspapers of today.

*Masturbation* is sexual self-stimulation. Needless to say, it produces no more *physical* harm than ordinary sexual intercourse—that is to say, none at all, although some people have the strange belief that every act of intercourse weakens the body and it has even been believed that each act shortens life by a specific length of time. This is rather illogical in view of the fact that most of the famous rakes have been noted for their longevity! Masturbation is almost universal in infancy, adolescence, or even in later life when other outlets are not available. It need only be a matter of concern: (a) when it is chosen in preference to normal sexual activity, or (b) when it is compulsive and excessive, since then it is a sign, not of sexual desire, but of severe underlying anxiety.

*Homosexuality* is, as presumably most people now know, an attraction between individuals of the same sex. Most people pass through a brief homosexual stage. Ordinarily this comes just before puberty when schoolgirls get " crushes " on older girls or teachers and schoolboys have similar feelings towards their heroes. The disposition, however, may be retained into adult life. Nowadays people take a much more tolerant view of homosexuality, accepting that what adults do (with consent) is their own business and that a male homosexual who seduces a boy under age should be treated in no way differently from the man who seduces an under-age girl. Male homosexual practices are no longer an offence if committed in private between consenting adults. Female homosexual practices have never been an offence. *See* D42.

All that remains to be said is that many of these conditions are treatable or, if not treatable so far as cure is concerned, they can at least be relieved. The world is full of people who are " different "; there are those who are different in the right way, who should take satisfaction from their achievements, and those who are different in the wrong way, who should seek expert advice. Since psychological treatment is time-consuming, it is not very easy to obtain it within the National Health Service, although group treatment has simplified the problem. However, any person with such difficulties would probably benefit from a discussion with his family doctor.

## DISEASES OF THE SKIN.

The skin in the course of development before birth is particularly closely associated with the nervous system. It is therefore not surprising that so many skin diseases are influenced by emotional states. Other causes of skin disease are infections, glandular disorders, vitamin deficiencies, and the numerous conditions for which no cause has been discovered, but which presumably are due to metabolic disorders.

One of the commonest skin symptoms is *itching or pruritus.* It may accompany many different general diseases, for example diabetes and jaundice. It may also be troublesome during the menopause (the change of life in women), in old age, or in nervous conditions. Sedatives and sex hormones sometimes help the itching during the menopause, and there are ointments which may be useful.

Itching in the region of the anus and genital organs is relatively common. It may be caused by worms, by irritating vaginal discharge, or by sugar in the urine, as in diabetes. The alteration in the normal bacteria of the bowel which follows treatment with various antibiotics also often causes anal pruritus and soreness. In many cases however the itching has some psychological cause. In treatment it is important to avoid ointments and creams which contain a local anæsthetic, because these substances can cause severe allergic reactions if used for longer than a few days, and may thus make the condition much worse. Treatment with a local corticosteroid application is more effective and safer.

Parasites, such as the *scabies* mite or *lice* can cause severe and persistent itching. The scabies mite is very small, and since it burrows under the skin surface, is unlikely to be seen; it is the cause of itching most commonly between the fingers and on the front of the wrists. The itching is worst when the body becomes heated, as in bed. Treatment consists of painting the body from head to foot with benzyl benzoate application, followed the next day by a hot bath. Since scabies is contracted through close personal contact with an infested person it is often desirable for several or all members of a family to be treated at the same time, even though only one of them may be affected. Lice are specialists, one type of which affects the scalp, another the body, and a third the genital area. Head lice are destroyed by lethane, body lice by D.D.T (dicophane) powder, and genital (pubic) lice by shaving off hair and washing. Obviously, the clothes, especially in the case of body lice, should be disinfested, either by the use of D.D.T. or, if this is not available, by using a hot iron over the seams, which lice (for some inexplicable reason) seem to favour. Apart from the discomfort they cause, lice are dangerous as potential carriers of typhus fever.

*Baldness, or Alopecia,* is a very common condition, as is manifested by the extraordinary number of preparations advertised as curing it. When many preparations are offered for the treatment of one condition it is a fair judgment to assume that none of them is likely to be effective. There are, in fact, two types of baldness; one, which is much the commoner, is hereditary, and cannot be influenced in the slightest by any treatment, the other, *alopecia areata*, is caused by nervous stress, and would recover in most cases by itself, whether one used a solution of soot and water or the most expensive " hair food." There is no such thing as a hair food, any more than there is such a thing as a nerve food, and although it is probable that hair hygiene may delay baldness, it certainly cannot prevent it. All hair tonics and " foods " are useless, and their uselessness is only equalled by their costliness. Those who have lost their hair and find it growing again after using some alleged tonic are people who have had *alopecia areata* and whose hair would have grown back anyhow. In women the hair often thins out soon after a pregnancy, but a few months later it usually returns to normal.

*Seborrhœa* is a condition in which there is over-activity of the sebaceous glands. The most usual form it takes is *dandruff*. However, it takes other forms, and those who have dandruff may also have rashes on the face, shoulders, and chest. In these areas there is a patchy, greasy, and often itchy, rash which does not clear up until the primary condition in the scalp is dealt with. The scalp should be washed with one of the modern sulphur-containing shampoos at least twice a week, and the affected parts on the face and chest can be dealt with by the use of a sulphur lotion (*not* on any account by greasy ointments). Seborrhœa is not in itself difficult to treat, but, since the condition depends on over-secretion of sebum, the skin lubricant, treatment may have to be persisted in during the years of early adulthood, when it is most active.

*Erythema Intertrigo* is, quite simply, the sort of irritation which occurs usually from excessive sweating under the armpits, between the legs, and under the breasts in women. All that need be done is to wash frequently and to dust the affected areas after washing with powder. This is the condition which, in the tropics, is known as " prickly heat " and elswhere as a " sweat rash." In some people *hyperidrosis* or *excessive sweating* is a problem, especially when the sweating is accompanied with body odour—the sort of thing that, according to the advertisements, " even your best friends won't tell you." There is little need for anyone in these days to suffer in this way: for the cosmetic firms have produced many highly efficient deodorants which not only control odour but also control the amount of sweating. Chlorophyll, which has been much advertised as removing odours, is effective when applied directly to surfaces which give off an unpleasant smell. It is however ineffective when taken by mouth, and does not prevent body odours. Stale sweat smells bad because it is decomposed by bacteria, and this type of body odour can be largely prevented by preparations containing a harmless antiseptic such as hexachlorophane and an antiperspirant such as aluminium chloride (see *Which*, February 1960).

*Erysipelas* is an infection of the skin caused by the hæmolytic streptococcus. It begins as a red, raised area anywhere on the body where the germs have been able to enter through a small crack or cut in the skin. The red area advances and spreads over the body until the disease is got under control. Erysipelas is very infectious, and those who look after the patient should wash their hands throughly after contact. At one time the disease used to spread as an epidemic throughout the hospital wards, but this is very rare nowadays. Treatment is, of course, a matter for the doctor.

*Chilblains* are common in cold weather, especially in those with poor circulation. Ordinarily they occur in the toes and fingers, but may appear on the nose and ears. The part affected becomes swollen, dusky, and there is pain and itching, sometimes leading to ulceration. Protection of the body, especially the hands and feet, from cold is the best and the only really effective way of preventing chilblains. Warm lined gloves and footwear, and warm stockings or trousers should be worn outdoors. Adequate heating of rooms is essential: a temperature between 18° and 21°C is recommended (65°–78°F). Most tablets, medicines, ointments, or creams for chilblains are useless. A skin affection caused by heat is rather grandiosely described as *erythema ab igne*, and is frequently seen on the legs of ladies addicted to roasting their legs before the fire. It takes the form of red patches on the front of the legs, and can be removed only by avoiding the cause.

*Dermatitis* means " inflammation of the skin," and therefore the word could be, strictly speaking, applied to any skin disease. In fact the term is used almost interchangeably with the term *eczema*. There are three main types of dermatitis or eczema. The first, *primary irritant dermatitis* results from injury of the skin by some powerful chemical, such as strong alkali or turpentine. The second, *contact dermatitis* is due to sensitisation of the skin to some substance which is normally liable to cause this type of allergic sensitivity; examples are nickel (in jewellery and suspender buckles), epoxy resins, rubber additives, primulas and chrysanthemums, and even ingredients of cosmetics. Contact dermatitis may continue for a long time, even after the patient is no longer in contact with the offending material. The third type is often called *constitutional eczema*. Although the skin is apt to react adversely to various irritants and sensitisers the major part is played by the personality, and there is often a history of eczema, hay fever or asthma in the family. Treatment is more difficult, but local corticosteroids and tar, sedatives and psychological treatment can be of great help. Infantile eczema also belongs in this category, but in most patients it disappears as the child grows up.

*Impetigo* is an infectious skin disease caused primarily by the streptococcus, but later often infected with staphylococci. It usually occurs on the face, and takes the form of blisters filled with pus on a red base; when the blisters burst their place is taken by yellow crusts. Impetigo is very infectious and easily spread by the fingers, dirty towels, or cloths; therefore, one of the first necessities is to prevent infection of others or reinfection of oneself by avoiding scratching and using a different towel each day, which must on no account be used by anyone else. Treatment is simple with an antibacterial ointment, so the main issue is prevention of contamination.

*Sycosis* or " Barber's Rash " occurs in men, and is similarly treated.

*Urticaria* or *Nettlerash* is a familiar skin disease in which itching weals appear on the skin, usually for no obvious reason. It is not infectious, and can be caused by nervous stress, certain drugs, allergy to some foods, or even exposure of the skin to cold. In some people it is possible to write on the skin with a fingernail: the " writing " appears in the form of weals. This is known as *dermographism*; it occurs in many normal persons as well as in many patients with urticaria. The antihistamine drugs are the most useful in the treatment of urticaria. Urticarial swelling of the tongue or throat must however be relieved at once and is treated by an injection of adrenaline.

*Acne*, or " *Blackheads*," is a condition found on the face and shoulders; its appearance is so familiar that no description is necessary. Acne is one of those conditions which is the end result of many factors. There is, first, a greasy skin, the result of glandular upset (which is why the disease usually occurs in adolescence); secondly, there is infection of the skin; and thirdly, there is blockage of the sebaceous ducts, which ordinarily allow the grease from the skin to pass out on to the surface. Since the condition starts with excess secretion of grease, ointments should never be used, and probably the best applications are drying lotions containing some sulphur preparation which inhibits secretion of grease. The face should be frequently washed, and it is possible now to obtain detergent solutions which are both antiseptic and prevent grease formation. In severe cases ultraviolet ray treatment may be necessary.

*Rosacea.* As has already been implied elsewhere, although the wages of sin may be extremely unpleasant, the wages of extreme virtue may be no less troublesome. Thus *rosacea*, in which the nose and cheeks become red and greasy and the skin coarsened, occurs alike in chronic alcoholics and elderly ladies with no vices other than a preference for strong tea. Both cases are associated with indigestion, since, regrettable as it may seem, strong tea and alcohol are about equally liable to cause the gastritis which may be at the root of this complaint. However, in many patients the chronic flushing is caused in other ways and psychological factors are important.

*Lichen Planus* is one of the numerous skin diseases which seem to be due to nervous states of tension. It may occur on any part of the body, but is most common on the front of the forearms and legs. The rash takes the form of nodules which are lilac in colour and have a dent on the top; when these disappear a stain is left behind. There is severe itching. Treatment is a matter for a doctor, as it also is in the case of *psoriasis*, a very common disease of largely unknown origin, which is extremely resistant to treatment. It tends to run in families. It takes the form of slightly raised papules, usually on the elbows and knees; typically the papules are covered with dry, silvery-looking scales. Apart from the rash, the patient is usually in perfectly good health and there is no itching. Many drugs have been used in psoriasis, notably chrysarobin, and while it is not difficult to cause the rash (which may occur anywhere on the body) to disappear in one area or even in all areas for a time it has a strong tendency to return.

*Warts,* or *Verrucae* are familiar enough. They are caused by a virus, and are, theoretically at least, contagious (although having removed many warts, the writer has never found them contagious). Most frequently they are found on the hands, but may occur elsewhere. Treatment is best carried out by a doctor, who will use a cautery, a caustic carbon dioxide frozen into " snow ". A curious feature of the common wart is that it can sometimes be caused to disappear by suggestion, which is presumably why so many old wives charms are not necessarily without effect. Different altogether from the common wart is the *plantar wart,* which occurs on the soles of the feet and often causes a good deal of discomfort. It is best dealt with by a chiropodist or in bad cases by a skin specialist since it is highly infectious.

*Icthyosis* is a disorder of horn formation with which some unfortunate people are born. The oil and sweat-producing glands do not function well and the skin is dry and scaly like the skin of a fish. It is, however, possible to help the condition, which does not affect the general health, by frequent alkaline baths to wash off the scales, and the subsequent use of lanolin to replace the lacking oil. Large doses of vitamin A seem to help in some cases, and there have been reports in the medical Press of cases being helped by hypnosis; this, however, is very much a matter for speculation.

*Cancer, Rodent Ulcer, and Cysts.* Cancer of the skin occurs mostly in old people, and takes the form of what is described as an *epithelioma.* It is most common on the face or hands, and usually appears as a nodule which breaks down and produces an ulcer. The glands may later be affected, but such cancers can almost invariably be cured unless a considerable time has elapsed during which they have been neglected. *Rodent ulcer* is a form of ulcer which appears on the inner corner of the eye or the side of the nose in old people. It does not spread over the body, but acts by eating into the tissues in the area where it has started. X-ray or operation is necessary, but the outlook is good. *Cysts* on the skin are due to blockage of the sebaceous glands. They may become very large, and are best removed, as they may become infected. They do not turn into cancer, and there is no such thing as " male " and " female " cysts. It does sometimes happen that *moles,* especially of the bluish-black type, may become malignant, so it is perhaps best to have them removed surgically when they exist. *All moles which change in appearance or size should be at once referred to a doctor.*

Skin Grafts.

These are a very complex subject which can be only briefly discussed here. They are used basically for a number of conditions in which large areas of skin have been removed from the body, as in burns or serious accidents. In other cases, as in plastic surgery, grafts may be used to make a new nose, eyelids, and so on. The following are the main types:

*Pinch Grafts* are small, circular pieces of skin cut from some other part of the body. (The former method of using grafts from another person has been given up almost completely, since such grafts—except in the case of identical twins—never " take.") The small pieces are laid on the area without skin and gradually grow together. *Split-thickness grafts* are grafts removed from another part of the body by an instrument known as a dermatome, which cuts sections about 4 in. by 8 in. containing part of the deep layers of the skin.

In *Full-thickness Grafts,* on the other hand, the whole thickness of the skin is removed from elsewhere and applied to an area which has to bear friction or heavy weights, such as the hand or the foot. Lastly, and this is largely used in plastic surgery, there is the *Pedicle graft,* which, unfortunately, although it is certainly the most exciting type, is rather difficult to describe. Briefly, if one, for example, wants to make a new nose, one cuts an area of skin and underlying fat about 2 in. wide and 5 or 6 in. long in the abdomen. One end, however, remains attached so that it gets adequate blood-supply. The problem is how to get this tissue to the nose, and this is done by a complicated process of leap-frog. First, the free end of the graft is attached to the forearm, whilst its " root " remains in the original site, and when it begins to grow and get its blood-supply from the arm, the original " root " is cut. So we now have a " sausage " of tissue attached to the arm. The arm is then lifted to the face and kept firmly in position there until the new free part becomes attached. It is then detached from the arm, modelled to the correct shape, and grows where the nose used to be!

## THE RHEUMATIC DISEASES.

The main rheumatic diseases (or so they are described, although they seem to have little relationship one with the other), are *rheumatic fever,* the acute form, which has already been dealt with (**P28**); *chorea,* or rheumatism of the nervous system, also mentioned (**P49**); *rheumatoid arthritis; osteoarthritis;* and *gout.* The only thing these diseases seem to have in common is that most seem to be associated with the connective tissues, muscles or joints—this, of course, with the single exception of chorea. Apart from this, there is very little similarity.

*Rheumatoid arthritis* often starts without evident cause in early adult life, and affects the small joints of the fingers and toes, causing swelling and pain. No infective process has been discovered, yet the disease goes on and on, sometimes better, sometimes worse. It is (and this is all one can say) a disease commoner in women, commoner in temperate climates, commoner following emotional stress. Although, as we have seen, rheumatoid arthritis is a disease characterised by frequent remissions, it takes a considerable time to burn itself out. The most likely explanation for its occurrence is that stress reactions act on the suprarenal glands and the secretion of cortisone is inadequate to play its usual part in preventing the body from responding too severely to injury. However, the injection of cortisone has proved, on the whole, less useful than might have been expected, and there is little reason to suppose that in most cases it is any better than aspirin.

*Osteoarthritis* is essentially a degenerative disease of old people. The bones affected are ordinarily the larger joints: the shoulders, the hips, or the spine. There is no disease in the ordinary sense, and essentially what has happened is that these joints have got " old " and the bone has overgrown so that movement is less simple than it once was. Osteoarthritis is not curable, but can be relieved by drugs and physiotherapy.

*Gout*, so far as one knows, has nothing at all to do with rheumatism. It is a metabolic disease caused by the inability of the body to deal with certain protein breakdown substances, such as uric acid. Typically, the pain develops in the big toe, and the foods concerned are such luscious products as wines, spirits, liver, sweetbreads. Although drugs such as cinchophen can help, the plain fact is that those liable to gout cannot have sweetbreads and wine, liver and spirits, without having gout as well. Most people, perhaps, would prefer the food and wine, but those who dislike gout must abstain.

## DISEASES OF THE EYE.

### The Eye.

The eye is frequently compared to a camera, and in a general sort of way there is some resemblance. The eyeball consists of 3 coats within which are contained the refraction media: (1) The outermost layer, the main support of the eyeball, comprising the sclera (opaque) and the cornea (transparent, covering the front of the eyeball). The conjunctiva (the part which gets inflamed when you get germs or dust on the surface of the eye) is a thin protective membrane covering the sclera and doubles back to line the inside of the upper and lower lids. It stops at the junction of the sclera and cornea. (2) The middle layer containing many blood vessels which forms the choroid and, in front, the iris (the coloured part of the eye). The muscle in the iris enables its central aperture, the pupil, to contract in bright light, and to dilate in dim light. (3) The innermost layer of nervous tissue, the retina. The retina contains the expanded termination of the optic nerve which is part of the brain. Behind the iris is the lens, which is controlled by a series of muscles which increase or diminish its curvature, and thus produce, according to the nearness or distance of the object, a clear picture on the retina. Some of these parts may, of course, be affected by disease. Here we shall deal only with a few of the more common diseases.

*Blepharitis* is an infection of the eyelids which is easily recognisable from the red, sore appearance at the margins, the formation of crusts, and the falling-out of the eyelashes. If it has just developed, an attempt may be made to treat it at home with hot bathing and the so-called Golden Eye Ointment, but *blepharitis* is liable to become a chronic disease, and it is wiser to see a doctor. Penicillin cream or ointment can cure the disease, but must *never* be used save under medical advice; allergy to penicillin is commoner in the eyes than anywhere else, and in some cases patients have lost their sight through its use in this way.

*Conjunctivitis* is the result of infection of the conjunctiva, and the symptoms are the familiar ones of a feeling as if some grit had got into the eye, running from the eye, and frequently gummed-together eyelids in the morning. In some cases it can be treated by hot bathing and eye-baths with one of the proprietary lotions on the market, but it is much wiser to see your doctor, who can supply much more effective remedies and may save you a lot of unnecessary discomfort.

*Other Eye Diseases.* We can only mention briefly *keratis*, inflammation of the cornea; *iritis*, inflammation of the iris; and *glaucoma*. These are all potentially serious diseases, and should not be diagnosed or treated by the layman. Glaucoma, in particular, may lead to blindness if help is not sought in time. If there is redness and congestion over the eye, dimness of vision, *severe* pain (as contrasted with the irritation caused by conjunctivitis), and perhaps even vomiting, the doctor must be called immediately.

The main disease of the lens is *cataract*, in which the lens becomes opaque and varying degrees of blindness result. Ordinarily, cararact is a condition found in people after middle age, but sometimes it is found in children at birth. The treatment is by operation—one which has been carried out for centuries—in which the opaque lens is removed. The patient thereafter has to wear glasses, but the vast majority of patients obtain good vision.

In *retinitis*, however, where the "screen" at the back of the eye is affected, the general outlook is more serious. This is because, whereas cataract is a localised disease, retinitis often signifies some bodily illness: infection, hardening of the arteries leading to hæmorrhage, diabetes, or kidney disorders. Sometimes the retina becomes detached, leading to blindness. As has been suggested above, except in very minor conditions such as styes (a localised infection treated in the same way as blepharitis), or conjunctivitis, the doctor should always be consulted. He should be consulted, too, when a foreign body gets into the eye unless it can be removed by very gentle manipulation with a handkerchief, for it must be remembered that such " poking about " on the surface of the eye may do much more harm than the original condition. So, if a couple of minutes fail to remove the grit, give up, and go to the surgery.

## DISEASES OF WOMEN.

The *internal sexual organs* of a woman, like the urinary system, can best be described as shaped like a capital Y. At the tips of the arms of the Y are the female sex glands, the ovaries: the two arms running downwards are the Fallopian tubes: the point where the arms meet is the womb or uterus: the single leg of the Y is the vagina. These are the *primary sexual organs* of a woman and they undergo regular cyclical changes in response to the control exercised over them by the pituitary gland, situated in the base of the skull. This control is mediated by chemical messengers (hormones) secreted into the circulation. The ovaries also secrete hormones, œstrogen, and progesterone, and a delicate hormonal balance is maintained between the pituitary gland and the ovaries. Each month an egg cell (ovum) matures and is released from the ovary, usually midway between two menstrual periods: the ovum is wafted along the Fallopian tubes by waves of contraction and if fertilised embeds in the lining of the uterus which has been conditioned to nourish it by the ovarian hormones. If it is not fertilised the ovum escapes from the uterus, altered hormone levels then cause the lining of the uterus to be shed (this is menstruation), usually about 14 days after ovulation. After menstruation a new cycle begins: another ovum matures and a fresh lining grows in the uterus. These cyclical changes recur from puberty to the menopause. Menstruation does not occur during pregnancy, of which a missed period is often the first sign. However, women do miss periods even though they are not pregnant, and this usually means that some minor and temporary change has occurred in the hormone balance. If three consecutive periods are missed it is wise to consult a doctor.

The *breasts* are called *secondary sexual organs* and are also under the influence of the ovarian hormones. Women are sometimes worried because they believe that their breasts are either too small or too large. However, small breasts cannot be made larger and are just as efficient for feeding babies as large ones, which are not always as effective as they appear. If breasts become too large they can be dealt with by plastic surgery. Two conditions which do need treatment are *mastitis* and *cancer of the breast*, both of which are characterised by lumps within the breast tissue. Mastitis may be uncomfortable but is not dangerous and can be treated medically, whereas cancer is more serious. The distinction between mastitis and cancer can only be made by a doctor and any woman who discovers a lump in her breast must seek medical aid *at once*.

*Abscesses* also occur in the breast, nearly always when the mother is feeding her child. Here again, a lump appears, the breast becomes red and very tender, and the woman may be feverish.

Treatment with antibiotics is sometimes successful, especially if the mother consults her doctor quickly, otherwise treatment is by a small operation.

*The Ovaries.* The two commonest diseases of the ovaries are cysts and disorders arising from hormonal imbalance. The symptoms of ovarian disease are usually abdominal or low back pains, and heavy and painful loss during the periods, which may become irregular. These signs should be taken as a warning to consult a doctor.

*The Fallopian Tubes.* Infection of the Fallopian tubes is called salpingitis. The membrane lining the tubes is continuous with the lining of the uterus, hence an infection is rarely confined to a circumscribed area in either the tubes or the uterus, and pelvic inflammatory disease is a better name for this condition. Pelvic inflammatory disease often follows an abortion, or childbirth where part of the afterbirth (placenta) has been retained, or can spread from an infection in a nearby organ, for example the appendix. Infection is sometimes conveyed by the blood from another septic source in the body. The gonococcus is another cause of infection. The disease is characterised by pain and tenderness in the lower part of the abdomen, accompanied by fever, general malaise and frequently (but not invariably) a vaginal discharge. The treatment of pelvic inflammatory disease is usually medical and is the same irrespective of the primary site of infection. Before the introduction of antibiotics the disease often became chronic and the Fallopian tubes were frequently blocked by a cicatrising scar, a cause of subsequent sterility.

*The Uterus.* This is a hollow muscular organ and both its musculature and its lining membrane can be the site of disease. *Fibroids* are non-malignant muscular tumours which develop in many women. The main symptom is a heavy menstrual loss and surgical removal of the uterus (hysterectomy) is often necessary. This is a major operation, but modern anæsthesia and operative techniques minimise the discomfort. Hysterectomy does not impair sexual pleasure, but no more babies can be conceived. Infection of the lining of the uterus is usually part of a generalised pelvic inflammatory disease (*see* Fallopian tubes).

*Cancer of the Uterus and Cervical Smears.* The uterus is pear-shaped and consists of a body and neck. The wide end is uppermost (the body) and the narrow neck (cervix) projects into the top of the vagina. Cancer of the cervix is commonest in middle-aged women who have married young and have had a large family; cancer of the body of the uterus usually occurs after the menopause and is most common in childless women. The symptoms are variable and it is sufficient to emphasise that any woman who has unexpected bleeding, especially after intercourse, whether her periods have stopped or not, *must* see her doctor at once. The treatment depends on individual circumstances, but is usually by operation. It is now possible to detect cancer of the cervix long before symptoms develop and at a stage when the disease can be eradicated by a relatively small operation. This early detection has been made possible by the development of exfoliative cytology. Cells taken from the cervix (without discomfort to the woman) are examined under a microscope. This test is popularly known as the " cancer test " or " cervical smear." A cervical smear is often taken as part of the routine gynæcological examination by consultants, general practitioners, and family planning doctors, and is also being included in some population screening programmes. It is a big step forward in preventive medicine and may ultimately solve the problem of cancer of the cervix. Every woman between the ages of 25 and 60 should seize any chance to have this test done.

*Prolapse* means a sagging down of the uterus into the vagina and the cervix may even appear at the outside. It is a result of frequent childbirth and laxness of the ligaments which support the uterus: weakness of the vaginal walls often occurs at the same time. The symptoms of uterine prolapse are low back pain and a heavy dragging feeling in the lower abdomen: these are often overshadowed by the distressingly embarrassing incontinence which results from lax vaginal walls. The stress of only a sneeze, a cough, or a giggle often causes the involuntary escape of urine. The cure is operative and very rewarding.

*Discharge (Leucorrhœa).* A white discharge is called leucorrhœa. It is normal for a woman to have a white odourless discharge: medical help should be sought if a discharge becomes offensive, is unduly watery, is bloodstained or causes irritation. A discharge can originate in the Fallopian tubes and uterus, for example in pelvic inflammatory disease, but is more commonly due to an infection of the vagina by bacteria or fungi. A vaginal discharge causes the patient a great deal of discomfort and misery but as soon as the exact cause has been found treatment is speedily followed by cure.

The change of life or *Menopause* is the outward manifestation of a change in the hormonal balance in a woman's body: the periods stop and she can no longer conceive. Many women are very troubled at the prospect of the menopause, and this is not unnatural for nobody likes growing older. This natural apprehension is overlaid with all sorts of irrational fears largely based on " old wives' tales." Heavy losses of blood, growth of facial hair, depression, loss of sexual pleasure, and frequent hot flushes are not an inevitable burden. The commonest symptoms are hot flushes and depression, but both are usually rapidly relieved by small doses of hormones, especially if the woman consults her doctor when her symptoms first appear. At the menopause periods may stop rapidly or become irregular and finally cease: sometimes a woman misses one or more periods, then periods re-start and this cycle may be repeated several times before menstruation finally stops. The pattern at the menopause is as varied as woman herself—but if a woman has had no period for two years and then notices spotting or bleeding she should consult her doctor to make sure that all is well. The menopause has no influence whatever on sexual life (although naturally it has on fertility) and desire is not affected. It is recounted that a famous courtesan, at the age of 80, on being asked by Voltaire when women ceased to feel desire, replied, " I don't know—I haven't lived long enough."

*Dysmenorrhœa* or pain with the periods, is very common and most women experience this symptom at some time or another. Very often a girl's first periods are troublefree, but dysmenorrhœa develops after a year or two: this suggests that a psychological element is involved. Dysmenorrhœa is a symptom which has many varying causes, and the sensible thing to do, if pain is troublesome, is to see a doctor.

*Amenorrhœa* means stopping of the periods in a young woman. It may signify pregnancy or glandular disease or it can be purely psychological.

*Abortion,* or its more acceptable name, miscarriage, describes the spontaneous or induced termination of a pregnancy before the fœtus (baby) is able to survive. A baby cannot live unless it is born after the twenty-eighth week of pregnancy, though many infants born at this time die. The two main symptoms of abortion are bleeding and abdominal pain. Any bleeding occurring during pregnancy ought to be reported at once. Pain starts in the back and lower abdomen and is usually spasmodic in character, and like colic it works up to a peak and then temporarily passes off. Any pregnant woman with pain and bleeding should go to bed at once and send for her doctor. When doctors are convinced that a pregnancy should be terminated then an abortion by safe surgical means may be performed in hospital. *See* D42 (2).

## CONTRACEPTION.

If a couple intends to practice birth control expert advice should be obtained from their family doctor or family planning clinic. The matter of whether or not a baby is born is too important to leave to chance. The method chosen must be effective as well as acceptable to the couple concerned, and the extent of the choice only emphasises the fact that the ideal contraceptive which is best for every couple at all times has yet to be discovered. The only method which is 100 per cent. reliable is abstinence. If the male seed (sperm) fertilises the female seed (ovum) then pregnancy results. Contraception is only effective if this union is prevented. A couple can achieve a measure of contraception without the help of pills or appliances if the husband practises *coitus interruptus* or they rely on the wife's " safe period." *Coitus interruptus* (when the man withdraws before emission occurs) is a thoroughly unreliable method which often leads to psychological difficulties in both partners. The " rhythm " or " safe period " method relies on estimating the time of ovulation and abstaining from intercourse during this time. This is at best unreliable, though its effectiveness can be improved by keeping careful records of the body temperature on waking each morning as the temperature rises once ovulation has occurred. The interpretation of these temperature records needs care and couples who must rely on this method can obtain expert advice from, for example, The Catholic Marriage Advisory Council, or a family planning clinic. *Barrier methods* prevent the sperms from reaching the ovum and can be used by the man (sheath or condom) or woman (cap or diaphragm): the reliability of the barrier is greatly increased if it is used in conjunc-tion with a spermicidal cream, jelly, or pessary. A great many women have found that the *oral contraceptive pill* is ideal for their needs: it is the most aesthetic means of contraception and offers the most complete protection against pregnancy. Oral contraceptive pills contain chemical substances (oestrogen and progestagen) which replace the hormones normally released from the ovary while an ovum is developing. Ovulation does not occur, and without an ovum there can be no pregnancy. Pills must be taken strictly as directed as the dose is the lowest that will provide effective contraception and missing a tablet may result in pregnancy. Side effects sometimes occur (for example, nausea, breast discomfort, headaches,) but usually decrease after a few cycles of medication. Newspaper reports of the deaths of young women taking the pill have caused widespread concern. These tragedies have followed blockage of a blood vessel (by thrombosis or embolism) and have been carefully investigated, and the conclusions are that the number of such deaths is small and does not differ from the number which would probably have occurred in any case. No satisfactory pill for a man has yet been developed. In the newest method of contraception a small plastic *intra-uterine device* (loop, bow, or coil) is inserted into the womb. Once inserted it can be forgotten: a tremendous advantage to many different peoples and societies. It is not as effective as the pill but is more satisfactory than barrier methods. This intra-uterine device is not suitable for all women and is usually not recommended to women who have borne no children or who have very heavy periods. However, careful selection of suitable women has resulted in a high proportion of satisfied users. The search for the ideal contraceptive continues.

# PART III.  SPECIAL TOPICS

## SPARE-PART SURGERY.

SPARE-PART surgery began when the first pre-historic man to survive a traumatic amputation of a limb attached a piece of wood to the remaining stump to help himself walk or grasp. It remained in this phase, with a few exceptions, until the present century, when the combined advances of many different aspects of medicine made possible the insertion of artificial materials and living tissues *into* rather than on to the body.

A notable exception to this recent development is the ancient use of skin grafts. It is often quoted that as long ago as the 6th cent. B.C. Indian surgeons were moving flaps of skin from the fore-head to the nose to repair severe nasal defects (usually a result of the punishment of " cutting off the nose "). The Italian, Tagliacozzi, gives a description of nose-repairing using grafts from the arm in a work published in 1597, and the *Madras Gazette* of 1792 describes in detail the rotation of a forehead flap to the nose. The old maxim " there is nothing new in medicine " comes to mind yet again.

Spare-part surgery can be divided into three sections:

(1) the attachment of devices to the outside of the body to replace missing parts (*external spare parts*);

(2) the insertion of parts made of foreign dead material into the body; and

(3) the insertion of foreign, living, function-ing tissue into the body (*internal spare parts*).

Each presents its own problems, the last being by far the most complex.

## 1. EXTERNAL SPARE PARTS.

It is not intended to discuss the tremendous advances that have been made in this field. Artificial limbs are being improved continually. For example, it is possible to make a power-driven upper limb that can be controlled by the patient from the electrical potentials developed in the muscles of the stump. Although such complex spares are seldom required by adults, they may be valuable to children, and the cripples of the thalidomide disaster have been a great stimulus and challenge to the limb-makers. One must not forget that spectacles, hearing aids, false teeth, and even wigs can be defined as external spare-parts. The benefit to mankind of this type of spare-part medicine is incalculable.

For the future this branch of spare-part medicine holds promise of the development of other artifi-cial sense organs. Many years hence we may see an artificial eye relaying its message to the brain, for preliminary experiments have already been performed with this object in mind. Such progress will be especially important in the re-placement and bypassing of organs incapable of repair, such as the nerves from the eye and ear.

## 2. INTERNAL SPARE PARTS.

### Dead and Inert Foreign Materials.

Artificial spare parts of metal, plastic, or dead tissues have been of most value in the replacement of those parts of the body that have a simple, relatively inert, mechanical function, such as arteries and joints. Three problems face the surgeon. The first is to insert the spare part with-out infection, for infection around a foreign body almost always results in its extrusion from the host. Secondly, the material inserted must be acceptable to the tissues. The chemical and the physical properties of a spare part are important. Vitallium and stainless steel evoke little tissue reaction, and most of the newer plastic materials based on nylon, Terylene, or polyethylene none at all. Nevertheless, even an inert material if it is porous will evoke a foreign-body reaction in response to the changes of tissue and surface tension in and around the pores, and any constitu-ent that is at all water-soluble may cause inflam-mation. Thirdly, but by no means least, the material must be strong enough to withstand the enormous stresses of daily life. The strains placed on an artificial hip joint by a few years' weight-bearing are far in excess of the stresses and strains that we expect our motor-car engines to withstand. Fortunately the newer metals and plastics are both inert and strong; indeed, much of this field of spare-part surgery could not have developed without the brilliant discoveries of the chemical and other industries.

### Artificial Joints.

Since 1938, when Smith-Petersen found Vitallium to be a suitable metal for inserting into the body, many types of spare hip have been made. Metal cups have been inserted between the joint surfaces; the head of the femur (thigh bone) has been replaced; and in recent years complete joints have been inserted. The problem of wear due to friction, not so serious in the older operations where one surface was living and capable of self-repair, has not been completely solved and at the moment these spare parts are being inserted only in elderly patients. Time will tell how successful such operations can be. The production of a " frictionless " joint is now being pursued by many workers, and the complete replacement of the hip joint will probably soon be a common routine procedure.

Apart from the problem of wear at the joint surfaces the orthopædic surgeon (who deals with bones and joints) has also to solve the problem of making a permanent joint between the spare part and the bone. Occasionally the metal wears right through the bone or, more often, just becomes loose. Much work will have to be done before we have a spare part that the skeleton will accept without complaint. Probably this aim will not be achieved until the growth and metabolism of the host bone around the spare part can be controlled, and the stresses can be transmitted from it to the host in a more physiological manner.

Many other joints have been replaced, the finger joints in patients with severe rheumatoid arthritis, the elbow, and the knee. The problems are similar but greater than those of spare hips; fixing metal to bone becomes more difficult as the bones get smaller and the mechanics of the joint more complex.

### Artificial Arteries

The replacement of arteries with artificial tubes has developed over the last 15 years. The techniques of joining vessels have been understood since the beginning of the century, but suitable materials with which to make artificial arteries have become available only recently. Fifteen years ago the enterprising surgeon simply sewed together two strips of man-made fibre cut almost literally from his shirt-tails, but now we have a vast array of vessel substitutes. Many are made of Dacron (Terylene). One difficulty with these tubes is that they kink when bent, and we still hope to develop a more flexible elastic graft. With such substitutes one can replace a segment of vessel knowing that the holes in it will be effectively stopped by blood clot; that a firm fibrous reaction will develop at the line of stitches to bind it to the host vessel; and that, provided there is enough blood flowing through, it will not become occluded by blood clot.

These grafts are not perfect. Thus, though the material is strong enough to withstand the arterial blood pressure for many years, it does not conduct blood as well as a normal vessel and thrombosis is a hazard. Partial replacement of an organ may fail because of the progression of the primary disease. As total replacement of all the vessels is impossible, we will continue to have late failures until we can also cure or arrest the underlying disease. It follows, therefore, that the aim of spare-part surgery should be the complete removal and total replacement of a diseased organ or system.

### Artificial Heart Valves.

The aortic valve (see P27) is often so extensively destroyed by disease that repair is impossible. In such circumstances the damaged valve must be replaced with an artificial one or one from another person. The valve most commonly used is the Starr valve, made entirely of metal and plastic, but freeze-dried aortic valve homografts, taken soon after death, are also used. Both may be considered as inert foreign material, for the cells of the freeze-dried valve are dead and disorganised and do not cause an immune response.

Sometimes patients can be given three artificial valves—aortic, mitral, and tricuspid (see P27). This is as near as we can go at present towards giving them an artificial heart, but it is unlikely to be long before an artificial pump will be inserted as a long-term replacement for the myocardium.

The heart valve presents another complication of spare-part surgery. The materials of which it is made are inert when placed in soft tissues, but not when placed in a continuous stream of blood. Whereas the normal valve falls back away from the mainstream, when blood is ejected from the ventricle, the ball of the Starr valve lies right in the middle of the stream. Turbulent flow around the valve may cause sufficient destruction of red blood cells to produce anæmia, and if the thrombus around the valve becomes infected, endocarditis (see P30) will develop, which may be fatal.

It is in many ways surprising that either artificial or freeze-dried valves function so well; some Starr valves have been in position for as long as 5 years and the one-year success rate for these operations is now well above 70 per cent.

### Artificial Hearts.

The " heart–lung " machine is both an artificial heart and an artificial lung, and is used extensively during cardiac surgery. It is only recently that very small pumps have been devised that can be left connected to the conscious patient to replace or aid the heart muscle for long periods.

When perfected these devices will be used when the muscle is so weak that it is unable to function properly following the repair or replacement of chronically diseased valves, or after infarction (P30) of the heart muscle. Thus such a device is not an artificial heart, just a temporary artificial left ventricle—though it represents the beginning of another new field of spare-part surgery.

### Artificial Nerves.

For the Heart. The commonest conducting system to be replaced with an artificial device is the conducting system of the heart. Failure of ventricular contraction due to a permanent or transient heart block results in a fall in blood-pressure and collapse. Conversely, the same result will occur if the heart-beat becomes excessively fast. In either case, whatever the cause, it is necessary to control the heart rate to maintain life. An artificial pacemaker takes over from the natural one. The battery and timing device replace the natural pacemaker (sino-auricular node) and wires replace the special conducting fibres of the normal heart, the ends of the wires being placed on that portion of the heart that one wishes to control—usually the ventricle.

The problems of implanting wires and fixing them to the heart are no different from those already discussed, but a new problem arises—the source of power. Early models had the wires coming to an external electrical source, and temporary pacing is still done in this way. This is unsuitable as a permanent method, as the site at which the wires come through the skin is extremely susceptible to infection. Permanent pacing is therefore achieved with either long-life implanted batteries (needing regular renewal) or by induction. In the latter system the wires from the heart are brought to a coil beneath the skin and current is induced therein from an overlying primary circuit. The source of power is then external, removable, and without any direct connections with the internal secondary circuit (Fig. 1). This overcomes the problems of sepsis, breakage of wires, and renewal of power supply. Recently attempts have been made to harness electric current produced within the body as a source of power.

Fig. 1. Diagram of the electrical circuit of an inductive cardiac pacemaker.

Perhaps we are not far from the day when a patient may have three artificial heart valves and an artificial left ventricle paced by a pacemaker, which is in turn fired from the electrical activity of the right ventricle. This may be as near as we will get to a truly artificial heart, at least for the next 50 years.

*Other Sites.* The development of the cardiac pacemaker is far ahead of all other artificial nerve implants. Electrodes have been implanted on the bladder to stimulate micturition in paraplegics, and attempts have been made to control the sphincter of the bladder to prevent incontinence of urine. Anal incontinence has also been studied, and the most promising approach is the stimulation of the sphincter from the outside with a dumb-bell-shaped electrode fitted into the anal canal. These efforts will no doubt lead to the development of permanently implanted electrodes with external inductive power circuits to maintain sphincter competence but which allow it to relax on demand.

A final example of the way in which man is attempting to take over the nervous control of the body is the study of methods of pacing the nerve to the carotid sinus. The carotid sinus is a " baroreceptor " which monitors the blood-pressure and transmits information to all the various mechanisms which help to avoid unwanted changes in pressure. By pacing the nerve transmitting such information, the aim is to regulate blood-pressure artificially.

### 3. INTERNAL SPARE PARTS.
#### Living Tissues.

In many instances we have within ourselves the tissues required to fashion a spare part. Flaps of skin can be fashioned into new noses, the ileum can be made into a bladder, the colon can become an œsophagus.

The use of host tissues depends to a large extent in the ingenuity and technical skill of the surgeon. Provided the blood supply of the part remains intact or is re-established, the tissue will live, and often shows a remarkable degree of adaptation to its new function.

#### Living Foreign Tissue.

The problems of placing living foreign tissue into the body are those outlined for inert materials, with the addition of several greater ones, all yet to be fully resolved. Thus, first, one must obtain suitable material. Second, the latter must be kept alive during transit from donor to host. Third, it must be kept alive within the host. These problems are best discussed in the context of renal (kidney) transplantation.

#### Source of Materials.

Organs for transplantation must be living and healthy. The obvious source is another living person, as tests of function can be performed preoperatively and the organ removed at leisure and at a time most suited to the well-being of the donor, recipient, and surgeon. Is it morally and ethically right to ask or expect a healthy subject to donate a kidney? This problem does not arise with other organs such as the liver, heart, or lungs, for the living have none to spare; but, as it is well known that man can live a normal life with one kidney, relatives are often eager to volunteer as donors. Donation is not, however, free from risk. Nephrectomy (removal of the kidney) has its hazards, such as hæmorrhage, in addition to those associated with all operations, such as pneumonia and pulmonary embolism. After the donor has survived the operation there is still the possibility of an accident or disease process affecting the function of the remaining kidney. Against these problems must be set the undoubted fact that transplants from live, related donors do better than those from dead, unrelated donors. The problem is one for the individual surgeon concerned. Obtaining kidneys from dead bodies has its problems. The best source is the recently dead young person, but there are legal problems concerning the rights of the relatives. Most relatives, however, agree to the removal of a kidney.

#### Preservation of Organs.

Whatever organ is used, and whatever its source, it inevitably undergoes a period of ischæmia (being without blood) between removal and insertion. The effects of this ischæmia are minimised by keeping it as short as possible and by keeping the organ cool. A cold kidney (4°C) can survive six hours or more of total ischæmia and function. A warm kidney is severely damaged after 30 minutes, but may still recover after one and a half hours of ischæmia.

Any organ must of course be removed in aseptic conditions, and if the donor is alive this is done as an elective procedure in an operating-theatre adjoining that in which the recipient is being prepared. The kidney is then carried from one room to the next, and the ischæmia time is that which is needed to make joints in two blood vessels (10–20 minutes). With cadaveric donors the preparation of the recipient takes longer, as it is begun as an emergency after the donor has died. The kidney is therefore washed through with cold saline solution and kept in ice until the recipient is ready.

In ideal conditions a transplanted kidney will produce urine as soon as the clamps are removed from the blood vessels. There may follow a diuretic (high output) or anuric (low output) phase, depending upon the degree of tubular death in the kidney.

#### Preparation of the Recipient.

Surgeons like to operate on a fit patient, for an ill one is more susceptible to all the common postoperative complications. Patients in kidney or liver failure are not usually subjected to operation.

but in transplantation these are the very subjects with whom the surgeon has to deal. The immediate success of kidney transplantation is entirely dependent upon the efficiency with which an artificial kidney can bring the patient back to a normal condition before operation. Careful use of the artificial kidney gives a fit patient who can withstand surgery and the necessary postoperative medication. Without such preparation the mortality rate is high.

There is no machine to replace liver function, and hence liver transplantation is performed on sick patients. Passing the patient's blood through a pig or human cadaveric liver has not been outstandingly successful in the treatment of liver coma. Once an artificial liver is available to prepare the patient, liver transplantation will become a practical proposition.

## Surgical Techniques.

Joining the vessels of the graft to those of the host is a fairly simple procedure requiring the basic skills of vascular surgery. In the case of the kidney, there are three large tubes to join: the renal artery, renal vein, and the ureter. Each is joined to its counterpart in the host, except that in the case of the blood vessels, any suitable sized vessel will do, and the *internal* or *common iliac* vessels are more convenient than the patient's renal vessels.

The transplantation of other organs, such as the liver or the lungs, is more difficult, as there are more (usually smaller) vessels to join.

The development of the techniques of transplantation have depended upon work in animals. Many thousands of renal, liver, heart, and lung transplants have been performed in dogs and kidney and liver techniques perfected, so that the practical problems of inserting the graft into the recipient are now the least of the transplanter's worries.

## Prevention of Rejection.

Once inside the recipient, perfused with recipient blood, the transplanted organ is subjected to the major hazard of this whole problem—namely, that of host rejection.

From a very early stage in interuterine growth special cells develop, particularly in the thymus, which are capable of recognizing any protein which is foreign to the body. They then migrate to populate the so-called reticuloendothelial system. These "self-recognising" cells can initiate a series of responses by which any "nonself" material is destroyed. This, in very simple terms, is the basis of immunity (*see* P63). Any cell capable of initiating an immune response is called an immunologically competent cell.

Foreign tissue is destroyed either by antibody production or a local cellular reaction. It is thought that the local cellular response is the most important line of defence. Circulating antigens are released by implanted tissues, but in small amounts, so that there are probably only low levels of circulating antibody.

If one accepts this mechanism of graft rejection then a number of methods of preventing this response become apparent. Only two are of practical value today.

*Make the Graft Non-antigenic.* Homozygous (identical) twins have an identical genetic make-up. Tissue grafted from one to the other is totally accepted. The results of kidney transplants between identical twins are excellent, some functioning 6–8 years after transplantation. Such good results justify the use of a living donor, but regrettably few patients with kidney failure have an identical twin.

Attempts are being focused on ways of typing the tissues of both donor and recipient to get the best degree of immunological compatibility.

These studies are in their infancy and involve many sophisticated techniques.

Recipient and donor should have the same blood group. White blood cells can also be "typed" in the same way as red cells, but this is a much more difficult procedure.

A host-versus-graft reaction can be detected before transplantation by injecting the recipient's lymphocytes (P24) into the skin of the donor and observing the local reaction. This test can be used only with living donors.

*Prevent the Host Recognising "Non-self" Material.* Once a foreign tissue is in the body and has acquired a blood supply from the heart, there is only one way to stop the host recognising and starting an immune reaction against it—to destroy those cells involved in the recognition process. This is known as immunosuppression. The small lymphocytes are the target cells and there are three possible methods of attack.

*Irradiation.* Total body irradiation was the first method to be tried, but was given up when it was found that the dose required to achieve effective immunosuppression invariably killed the host. Local irradiation of the graft is used occasionally—but to help suppress a severe rejection phase.

*Cytotoxic Drugs.* Many drugs have been studied, but by far the most successful is azathioprine (Imuran). Imuran will destroy all types of white cell, and complete depression of marrow and lymph-node activity can occur if the dose is not carefully controlled. Cortisone has an inhibitory effect on the reticuloendothelial system and is used in combination with azathioprine. The other cytotoxic drug in common use is actinomycin C.

The present-day successes of kidney transplantation are due either to chance tissue compatibility or the control of rejection by azathioprine and cortisone, but better substances are needed.

*Antilymphocyte Serum.* The wholesale destruction of bone marrow and lymphoid tissue is a blunderbuss approach. Antilymphocyte serum can specifically destroy those cells believed to be responsible for graft rejection. It is made by injecting human white cells into the horse and then preparing the anti-serum in just the same way that the antisera against many bacteria are made. Preparations can now be made of pure antilymphocyte globulin. As white cells from many different subjects have to be pooled to get enough for an adequate antigenic stimulus, the antiserum is species—but not individual—specific.

Studies with this substance in man are just beginning; those experiments that have been performed show great promise. Antilymphocyte serum is the only specific immunosuppressive agent yet developed and those patients who have received it both preoperatively and post operatively have shown a worthwhile improvement in their tolerance to the grafted kidney.

The one-year survival rate of the graft is continually improving. Figures of 80 and 90 per cent have been claimed, while the overall world figure for living related donors is about 70 per cent—for unrelated cadaveric donors the figure is about 50 per cent.

## Liver Transplantation.

A few livers have been transplanted between humans and many have been exchanged between dogs. The latter work has shown the procedure to be technically possible and that the problems of rejection can be met in the same way as kidney transplants. Many animals have survived six months, some as long as a year and a half, but there are no long-term survivors in man.

The functions of the liver are more complex than those of the kidney and certainly less well understood. Thus, though the blood of a man n hepatic coma (unconsciousness due to liver failure) can be passed through another human or pig liver to lower the concentration of bile pigment and ammonia, there is often no change in the level of coma. A fully functioning transplanted liver would presumably restore a patient in liver failure to normal, but this has rarely been achieved for even a short term.

At present anyone attempting liver transplantation for hepatic failure must work with a very ill recipient, and the chances of success are slight. With the kidney this problem was overcome by the development of the artificial kidney; little progress can be expected with liver transplantation until we have an effective artificial liver. It would help in the making of such a machine if the biochemistry of hepatic coma were more fully understood.

Liver transplantation will become a practicable procedure when the problems of temporary support for the patient in liver failure and the rapid collection and perfusion of the cadaveric donor liver have been solved.

## Other Organs.

The transplantation of the heart, lung, pancreas, gut, and endocrine glands are all technically feasible procedures. At the time this edition was going to press in the spring of 1969, the second human heart transplant carried out by South African surgeons was reported to be functioning more than a year after operation. One patient has had a successful pancreas transplant. So continued progress is being made. Any organ that can withstand being without a blood supply for 30 minutes may be transplanted, and as our knowledge of the immune reactions increases so these transplants can be kept alive for longer periods.

## Other Tissues.

Perhaps the most important body tissue to be transplanted, and certainly the one that has made all the recent developments of transplantation possible, is blood. Blood transfusion is a form of tissue transplantation, the value of which is inestimable. A major part of modern surgery could not be done without it. The transfer of blood-cell-producing tissues, the bone marrow, has not been so easy. It is beset with all the problems of organ transplantation. Experiments have shown that antilymphocyte serum will improve the results of bone-marrow exchange. If a diseased blood-forming system could be completely destroyed and replaced with a healthy one a great number of diseases such as aplastic anæmia (P25) and leukæmia (P26) might become curable.

The future of transplantation is bright. Solving the problems of immunity will solve many of the fundamental problems of cellular biology. Transplanting organs successfully will give life to many. All this will repay the singlemindedness and courage of the few who have pressed on in this field during the last twenty years in the face of failures, discouragement, and seemingly insurmountable barriers.

(Reprinted with modifications from the *British Medical Journal*, 1967, 4: 157–161, with the kind permission of the author and the publishers).

## CONGENITAL MALFORMATIONS (TERATOLOGY).

At the end of 1961, reports began to appear in medical journals of malformed children, born to mothers who had taken the drug " thalidomide " during their pregnancy. These reports, and those which followed in the next two years, demonstrated yet another hazard to which the developing fœtus might be exposed—substances taken by pregnant women which were active teratogenic agents, *i.e.*, substances inducing abnormal formation of organs and tissues. These tragic events

drew renewed attention to a subject that had been studied for many centuries: the origin of abnormally developed children. Various collections of malformations had been made from the 16th cent. onward culminating in Taruffi's *Teratology* in 8 volumes (1881–1895), but it was between 1880 and 1900 that the Leipzig anatomist, Wilhelm His, described a number of abnormal young embryos, in order to investigate the possible mechanisms of development of various abnormalities. Others extended this work and noted that many early embryos showed defects also seen in deformed still-born or live-born infants (for example, deformities of the extremities or of the brain and spinal cord, such as *spina bifida, anencephaly*, etc.). It was realised that early disturbances of fœtal growth might cause similar abnormalities to those found in abnormal individuals, and that the death of the embryo in instances of severe interference with growth was a change different only in degree from that which might cause a malformation. Almost a hundred years before these observations were made, G. St. Hilare had produced abnormal chick embryos by pricking them with needles introduced through holes in the shell, or by varnishing the egg to exclude oxygen. These early experiments and those of Driesch, who induced the formation of " twins " in sea urchin eggs by placing them in warm water, represented the beginnings of the science of experimental teratology which has, in recent years, made a considerable contribution to our knowledge of early mammalian development.

The factors that cause malformations may be divided into those which act *via* the genetic constitution of the embryo, and those which are a result of changes in the intra-uterine environment. While it is with these latter factors that this discussion is concerned, it should be pointed out that abnormalities of the $x$ and $y$ chromosomes (sex chromosomes) or of the other 22 pairs of chromosomes (autosomes) may give rise to characteristic syndromes or malformations. These abnormalities will not be further considered except to say that the majority of autosomal abnormalities are probably lethal, and that relatively few embryos which are abnormal in this respect survive to give rise to abnormal infants. The large list of agents potentially harmful to the fœtus is growing, as more information is obtained from experimental work. Virus infections, radiation, drugs, chemicals, hormones, malnutrition, and physical injury have all been shown to be capable of producing abnormalities of development under appropriate circumstances. A number of agents of this kind will now be considered and their possible mode of action described where it is known. It must be emphasised that although many teratogens have been described, very little is known about their method of action.

## Virus Infections.

An Australian opthalmologist (Gregg, 1941) was the first to realise that an epidemic of German measles (rubella) had resulted in the production of an abnormally large number of infants with eye defects, born to mothers infected with the causative virus in the early stages of pregnancy. These findings, and the association of German measles with other malformations, notably of the heart and ears, have since been amply confirmed and extended. Many other viruses have been shown to pass from mother to fœtus, but evidence incriminating any other virus in teratogenesis in man is lacking. Although virus infection during pregnancy may be associated with the birth of an abnormal child, these infections are so common, and high fever, drug administration and metabolic disturbance such common features of the accompanying illness, that a number of " red herrings " are introduced into any study of viral teratogenesis.

In an effort to overcome these difficulties, prospective studies of large numbers of women during pregnancy are being carried out. In these studies, the large number of individuals who are infected without any evidence of clinical illness are also detected. The method used is to take blood samples in the early and late stages of pregnancy and to test for the presence of antibodies to infective agents in both samples. Any change, either the development of an antibody not present in the first sample, or a significant increase in antibodies already present, may thus be observed and provides evidence of infection. In this way, a recent study in the United States of America has provided some evidence of a possible relationship between Coxsackie B₄ virus infections (" Flu "-like illnesses with sore throats) and the occurrence of congenital heart disease, but the relationship is not yet proved.

### Radiation.

Ionising radiation is a normal part of our life in the form of isotopic sources in the earth, irradiation from outer space and the small doses to which we are exposed during chest and dental X-ray procedures, etc. Very extensive studies of the effects of radiation on embryonic development have been made in animals. All stages have been examined and the effects of radiation on sperm and ova also observed. Some important points have been demonstrated in these experiments. In general it may be said that so-called " harmless " doses are probably not without biological effect, and may act by potentiating genetic factors associated with malformation. This has been shown to occur in the mouse by L. B. Russell, who found that a strain of mice occasionally showing skeletal abnormalities, produced rather more abnormal offspring after low dosage irradiation. Direct effects of larger doses have unfortunately been studied in man. Japanese children *in utero* at the time of atomic explosions who were exposed to varying doses of irradiation, showed evidence of impaired growth, small head size and occasionally mental retardation. Other reports have shown an association between irradiation *in utero* and cerebral abnormalities at high dose levels. Intra-uterine irradiation associated with diagnostic X-rays has also been found to be dangerous to the fœtus, although in a less direct way. There is evidence showing that children irradiated during pregnancy are more likely to develop a malignant tumour in childhood than are normal controls. Although all of these facts point to the obvious precautions necessary with regard to irradiation and pregnancy, it should be emphasised that direct irradiation probably plays a small part in teratogenesis in man. More important is the effect of " background " radiation in potentiating other biological factors.

### Drugs and Malformations.

Thalidomide: The abnormalities induced by thalidomide include absence of limbs, gross shortening, and absence of bones of the forearm. The malformations are generally bilateral and symmetrical, and the arms are involved more often than the legs. Heart disease, abnormalities of the eyes and external ears, and kidney malformations may also be produced by this drug. Very small doses of the drug are teratogenic; a case is reported in which a woman took two 100 mgm. tablets on the fortieth day of her pregnancy and later gave birth to a child with deformities of all four limbs. This extreme sensitivity to the drug has been confirmed by other case reports. It is also true that administration of the drug produces abnormalities in almost 100 per cent of the fœtuses exposed, provided it is given at the critical period of development. From a number of careful studies it is apparent that this danger period in man is from the 34th to 50th days after the last menstrual period. Early dosage causes ear and cranial nerve abnormalities (days 34–38); upper limb malformations occur later (39–44 days), followed by lower limb anomalies (42–48 days). At about this time (40–45 days), most heart defects probably occur. How the drug works on the embryo is uncertain, but in experimental work this compound has been shown to inhibit cell growth and division. Perhaps one of the most disturbing facts about the entire thalidomide disaster is that the drug was developed as a " harmless " sleeping tablet which was non-addictive and which, even if accidentally taken in enormous quantities, did not kill. These virtues led to the widespread use of the compound, thus adding to the size of the disaster. Since these

events, all new drugs are now examined routinely for possible teratogenic effects. The only really safe course, however, is to avoid drugs of all kinds during pregnancy, unless they are absolutely necessary.

### Other Compounds.

*Hormones.*

1. *Insulin:* The children of diabetic mothers are a special group in several respects. Recently, however, a characteristic bony deformity of the leg has been described which is possibly related to the administration of insulin to the mother. This association cannot yet be considered proved but it is certain that insulin has allowed many diabetic women to have normal children who would otherwise not have been well enough to undertake pregnancy.

2. *Cortisone and Related Compounds:* Although these hormones are capable of producing cleft palate in rodents, there is no evidence to implicate the drugs in teratogenesis in man. In general, just as in diabetes, the conditions for which these compounds are given have a greater immediate relevance for the continued survival of mother and baby.

3. *Anti-thyroid Drugs:* These drugs, given for overactivity of the maternal thyroid gland, are able to cross the placenta and may thus act against the fœtal thyroid, causing a diminution in the output of thyroid hormone. After this, the pituitary gland of the fœtus produces more thyroid stimulating hormone and the thyroid is thus forced to grow excessively, often producing a goitre (which may even affect the normal process of delivery). This effect cannot be regarded as truly " teratogenic " but indicates an alternative mode of action for some compounds, *i.e.*, indirectly via the developing glands of the embryo.

4. *Sex Hormones:* In the same way, these compounds, sometimes given to prevent abortion in early pregnancy, may produce masculinisation or femininisation, depending on the compound and the sex of the child.

Cytotoxic Drugs (substances inhibiting cell growth and division): These are used primarily in the treatment of malignant disease but are also used to suppress the immune response in diseases of " auto-immune " origin, such as some kinds of kidney disease. All compounds which are effective in treating malignant diseases are capable of disturbing the division and growth of primitive cells. Thus, they will affect fœtal tissues as well as those of a malignant tumour. Many species of animals have been used in experiments with these drugs and most major malformations may be produced. There have been several reports of abnormal children born to mothers treated with cytotoxic drugs for malignant disease.

Antibiotics: Although sulphonamides, streptomycin and penicillin, and tetracycline have all been shown to be teratogenic in animals, there is no evidence of teratogenesis in man. Tetracyclines, however, must be considered as potentially dangerous drugs in pregnancy. Tetracycline crosses the placenta and may discolour fœtal teeth and inhibit bone growth. Its effect in man should be more closely watched.

### Other Compounds.

Some naturally occurring agents may be shown to be teratogenic in animals. 5-hydroxytryptamine is a compound which, in man, is important in the control of small blood vessels. If given to rats during pregnancy, the changes in vessel tone in the uterus reduces blood flow to the placenta, and malformations may result. It is easy to speculate that this type of change is responsible for many anomalies in man, but it is not, at present, possible to test this hypothesis.

## Experimental Teratogens.

A number of compounds, never administered to man, are teratogens. Despite the apparent lack of relevance of these compounds to human malformations, a great deal of valuable information has been obtained by using them experimentally. The dye, trypan blue, has been found to produce heart defects in rats which resemble those seen in man. These defects are found to be due to improper folding of the heart tube. Early in development, the heart is a straight, contractile tube which gradually folds and divides into four chambers. If this folding is imperfect, the relative positions of the chambers change and the vessels which enter or leave them may thus be forced to take up abnormal relationships with surrounding tissues. By studying this abnormal situation in animals, much may be discovered about the mechanical production of defects in man.

Another example of this kind, relating to kidney malformations, has been investigated by Monie. He found that a certain cytotoxic drug prevented proper development of the vertebral column. This resulted in failure of certain vessels to develop normally, and the kidney, which normally develops in the pelvis and moves up the posterior abdominal wall in later development, remained in the pelvis resulting in " ectopic kidneys ", i.e., those in abnormal situations. These are most often situated in the pelvis in man.

An important general point can be made from experimental work. Identical malformations may be caused by the administration of many different compounds, or as a result of several different pathological processes. In other words, not all similar malformations need necessarily have a common cause. Elimination of a particular teratogen (e.g., Rubella virus, by the development of a vaccine), may reveal the existence of other dangerous agents. Only constant attention to the prevalence and type of malformation seen in a given population will allow early recognition of any new factor, and this can only be done by keeping careful registers of cases, much in the way that epidemiologists study the spread of infections.

## Immunological Aspects of Intra-uterine Life.

One of the most rapidly expanding areas of medical knowledge is that of immunology (see below). This science, which deals with the ability of the body to defend itself against infection, has an immediate relevance to teratology, since many of the mechanisms involved in immune responses are probably important in development.

If an organ, or part of a tissue, is transplanted from any individual to another, it will be " rejected " by the recipient unless the two individuals concerned are identical twins. This phenomenon (Homograft rejection), although capable of modification by various measures, holds true for all tissues which depend on cellular activity for their continuing existence. The cornea of the eye is an example of a tissue which does not depend on living cells in this way, and therefore may usually be transplanted without rejection. However, although the success of corneal grafts and some bone grafts are explained by this qualification, no such mechanism explains the tolerance of the fœtus by the mother. Here the fœtus represents a graft and the mother the host. Various research workers have demonstrated that fœtal cells, which are composed of genetic material from father and mother, are capable of exhibiting " histocompatibility antigens ", i.e., recognition markers that allow the body to distinguish " self " and " non-self " components. Despite this, and the ability of the mother to " reject " homografts, the fœtus is tolerated. The reason for this protection is not certain but is probably related to the ability of the cells forming the placenta—i.e., those in contact with maternal tissues—to " mask " their antigenic determinants by a surface layer of mucoprotein. This type of cell recognition mechanism is of great interest to researchers in experimental teratology. Much of the process of development of tissues might be explained on the basis of an increased tendency of

cells with a similar " identification " pattern to associate together. In this context it has been shown that if fœtal liver cells and heart cells are separated to form collections of single cells, they will aggregate into groups of " liver " and " heart " cells, rather than at random. Further, when mixed antigens from several organs are injected intravenously, they have been shown to be more likely to go to the organ from which they were derived. It is possible that these effects are the result rather than the cause of differentiation, and are thus in no way responsible for the changes that take place. Another alternative is that the sites on the cell surface responsible for antigenic markers are different from those involved in recognition by cell to cell contact. It is along these lines that much recent work in teratogenesis is directed. The results have an obvious relevance in other diseases of man, notably the malignant transformation of tissues to form tumours, for in these tissues a population of cells has escaped from the normal control mechanisms that prevent unrestrained growth. It is essentially the normal inter-relationships of cells that must be maintained for the normal development, growth, and continued existence of man.

In summary, a great many substances have been shown to be potentially teratogenic, but the mode of action of the majority is not understood. It is evident from the information available to date that no drug should be taken during pregnancy unless it has been specifically prescribed for the individual concerned. In this way, unnecessary self-administration of potentially dangerous compounds will be reduced.

## IMMUNOLOGY.

The mechanisms of the response of the animal body to infection is the broad field of study of the immunologist. For centuries it has been well understood that a second attack of some diseases is unknown or at least exceedingly rare. Those recovering from the plague could nurse fellow sufferers with impunity. Similarly those who recovered from quite mild smallpox were immune to even the most severe form occurring in devastating epidemics.

The basis for understanding, and therefore of utilising beneficially, this interesting phenomenon developed during the later years of the last century. First came the recognition under the microscope of specific " germs " or organisms responsible for many of the infectious diseases, then the demonstration in 1890 by von Behring and Kitasato of specific " antibodies " (to tetanus toxin).

### Antibodies.

Following survival of almost any infection natural or experimental, substances can be demonstrated to have appeared in the bloodstream which act in some way against (anti-) the infecting organism. The techniques to demonstrate the existence of these antibodies are often complex as they are of many different types. For example, the serum of a patient who has suffered from typhoid fever will contain an antibody capable of agglutinating (clumping together) a suspension of the specific organism grown on artificial media—even a suspension killed by heat or chemicals. Depending upon the severity of the infection and the individual this agglutination may occur even when the patient's serum is diluted 1:1,000 or more. Again, some organisms produce toxins (poisonous substances specific to the organism) often acting specifically on heart, muscle, or nervous system. Tetanus or lockjaw (due to infection of a wound with Clostridium tetani) is a very serious, often fatal, illness caused by a powerful toxin elaborated by a relatively small number of organisms. An antibody (in this case specifically an antitoxin) can be produced artificially in an animal, and if its serum, after suitable purification, is injected into the human sufferer it will prevent or cure the illness provided, of course, the necessary surgery is carried out on the wound.

### Antigens.

Typhoid infection or injection of the causative organism Salmonella typhi causes the generation of antibodies; the organism is said to be antigenic, *i.e.*, to have stimulated antibody response. A rather milder disease is paratyphoid (caused by *S. paratyphi*) and the antibodies produced in this disease are different and do *not* react with *S. typhi*. Furthermore it was soon discovered that there is not one but three types of *S. paratyphi* designated A, B, and C! This is in some ways a help and in some ways a hindrance. It may aid the epidemiologist studying an outbreak to track down the source and to exclude from his considerations sporadic cases of different types. But at the same time it complicates the production of vaccines (*see below*).

Again there are many other species of the *Salmonella* group of organisms causing " food poisoning " of varying severity. All these species have antigenic differences and can be separately identified using suitable prepared sera and this provides further help for the epidemiologist tracing the source of an outbreak. (*See also* Other Antigenic Substances, P65).

### Immunisation.

Experiments show that if a group of animals or humans is given small doses of an organism and thus caused to produce antibodies, then " challenged " with a much larger dose of the same organism there is a highly significant difference in the degree of illness between the pre-treated and the untreated group. In the pre-treated group there may be a much milder illness or a high proportion of the group may not develop an illness at all (depending on which particular group of organisms is being investigated). The performance of this pre-treatment—safely— is the basis of modern immunisation procedures.

(1) *Killed Vaccines.* The safest way is to inject beneath the skin a suspension of the dead organism. Such a *killed vaccine* for typhoid was employed by Almroth Wright in 1897 at a time when large numbers of soldiers were dying of the disease in the war in South Africa. His vaccine was killed by heat and preserved with 0·5 per cent phenol. The modern vaccines are prepared by killing with 70 per cent alcohol and preserving in 25 per cent alcohol. The final concentration of organisms is about 1,000 million *S. typhi* and about 500 million each of *S. paratyphi* A, B, and C per c.c. The vaccine is given in two doses, the second twice the size of the first, with a month's interval between. The injections often produce temporary malaise but not illness, certainly no intestinal illness. The degree of protection is good and can be maintained by " booster doses " at intervals of 1-3 years. Similar vaccines can be prepared against plague and cholera and, using different methods for killing the organisms, many other diseases.

(2) *Attenuated Vaccines.*—With some organisms even the most careful and gentle technique of killing them in some way alters their antigenicity. In the case of some of these it has been possible to use an " attenuated " organism, *i.e.*, an organism which for some reason has lost the power of producing severe disease. Edward Jenner published in 1798 his observations on the protection against smallpox given by either inoculation with, or infection by, cowpox. In earlier centuries and other countrieswhere the disease was a permanent feature of life and epidemics often reached devastating proportions, children were inoculated with material from an actual pustule from a mild case of smallpox. Jenner's method was infinitely safer and after initial fierce opposition gained wide acceptance. With a modified vaccine and technique it is in use to this day. Pasteur was a very great experimentalist but he discovered the first method of *artificial attenuation* in much the same way as Fleming discovered Penicillin—by accident. A culture of chicken cholera bacillus was left on the bench during a summer holiday instead of being regularly sub-cultured and incubated. It failed to produce cholera on inoculation into chickens but at the same time caused them to develop an immunity which protected them completely from a fully virulent organism—one which killed other chickens. Pasteur was then spurred on to search for other methods of attenuation. Culture of organisms at higher than usual tem-

perature succeeded with anthrax—a very fatal disease of sheep and cattle. Of recent years similar attenuation has been attained by rearing viruses (infective agents very considerably smaller than bacteria) in cultures of living cells for many generations. The strain of yellow fever virus (called 17D) grown in chick embryo tissue cultures is in worldwide use as a vaccine. It is immensely effective, immunity lasting for at least 6 years after a single dose. Yellow fever caused the deaths of many thousands of workers during the building of the Panama Canal; all this loss of life could have been prevented if the vaccine had been available then.

Pasteur developed a technique for attenuating the virus of rabies (hydrophobia), a widespread, very horrible, and usually fatal disease in France and indeed all Europe at that time. The disease results from the bite of a mad dog or wolf, the bite inoculating the virus which is in the animal's saliva. Pasteur could not demonstrate the organism, it was far too small to see, but he could demonstrate the *infectivity* of the saliva. Furthermore he appreciated that, although the saliva was infective, the main brunt of the disease was borne by the spinal cord. He therefore dried the spinal cords of infected rabbits in air for varying periods. By injecting an emulsion made from these cords, first those dried for a long period and then those for less and less time he was able to protect dogs from fully virulent virus—" street virus." Just think of the difficulty of catching mad dogs off the street and collecting their saliva at a time when no treatment was available if you were bitten! Such bravery was rewarded when in July 1885 the boy Joseph Meister was brought to Pasteur having been bitten many times by an undoubtedly rabid dog. The boy was injected with 13 graded doses of the spinal cord emulsion over the succeeding days and survived to serve as gate porter at the Pasteur Institute for many years in later life. An important feature of this disease in this context is the long incubation period—1-3 months between being bitten and developing the illness. This long period allows time for the serial injections necessary with Pasteur's method. With most infectious diseases the immunity must be raised *before* the date of infection.

The search for attenuated viruses and methods of artificially attenuating viruses is now very " big business " indeed. The current poliomyelitis (infantile paralysis) vaccine is a live attenuated vaccine and has the enormous advantage that it can be given by mouth—on a lump of sugar. The formol-killed vaccine formerly used cannot be given by mouth because its antigenicity is destroyed by the digestive processes. However, the living virus can survive because indeed this is its natural route of entry into the body— through the wall of the intestinal tract. This search has also yielded strains of measles virus which are antigenic but produce only minor illness. Measles itself is to us a mild disease and you may think it strange to bother about a vaccine, but in some undeveloped regions measles can cause very severe epidemics with a high mortality rate.

(3) *Passive Immunisation.*—The third method of immunisation, formerly very important, is *passive* immunisation. By passive immunisation is meant the transfer to a patient of an immune antibody from another person already immunised or indeed from an immunised animal. It is passive in that the patient does not have to produce actively his own antibodies which takes time, and could mean a delay of days or weeks. The immense advantage is that the treatment is immediately effective. Antitoxins are extremely effective in this way; in particular diphtheria and tetanus antitoxins have saved thousands of lives over the years. The effect is immediate but only short-lived and this is the first disadvantage; the dose must be repeated quite frequently. Second, as it is only an antitoxin it neutralises the effect of the toxin but does not affect the diphtheria, tetanus, or other organisms themselves—they must be eradicated by other means. Third, the antitoxins are very specific; it is simple enough to know whether to use anti-diphtheria or anti-tetanus serum from the clinical findings but the case of pneumococcal

pneumonia it is not such a simple matter. A large number of antigenically different types are found and even though group polyvalent antisera can be made the group of the organism isolated from the sputum or phlegm must be known before effective treatment can be started (*see also later*). This brings us to our fourth disadvantage—to have sufficient quantities of these antisera they must be produced in animals, commonly horses. Hence a " foreign " protein is introduced into the patient and this in itself acts as an antigen (*see below*).

With a few exceptions antitoxins are less important now that antibiotics such as Penicillin and Streptomycin are available and can rapidly eliminate the organisms themselves. However, convalescent serum can be used, that is serum from a patient who has recently had the disease or in fact has recently been actively immunised and shown, by laboratory testing, to have given a good response. This can be valuable in aborting an attack of measles, for instance, when an epidemic breaks out among children already suffering from some other disease, as perhaps in hospital. Similarly some people cannot be vaccinated due to a skin condition such as eczema but in a small-pox epidemic they can be protected. However, this protection is brief and the serum always in short supply, so that the indications for its use have to be very strong indeed. Modern methods of protein fractionation can provide an even more potent and pure protective agent—immune $\gamma$ globulin—to be discussed later under Antibody Detection. This is difficult and expensive to produce and therefore also in short supply.

There is one stage at which we are all largely dependent upon passive immunity and that is during the first few months of life. Antibodies transferred from the mother across the placenta to the infant, perhaps reinforced by antibodies taken in with the mother's milk, render the infant relatively immune during the first six months of life to the acute infectious fevers and other diseases to which the mother had a strong immunity.

### Other Antigenic Substances.

So far we have only discussed antibodies to *whole organisms*, living or dead, and their products, such as toxins. In fact almost any protein, strange to the animal into which it is injected, will cause production of an antibody. For instance, rabbit blood injected into a goat will cause the production by the goat of an " anti-rabbit " antibody. This is the basic fact preventing the easy grafting of organs from animals to humans. It is the basic difficulty in the extension of the utilisation of passive immunity in treatment and it is also a major difficulty in blood transfusion (*see below*).

When investigated in detail quite small molecules can be shown to be antigenic. Thus purified insulin (molecular weight about 6,000) prepared from the pancreas of one animal is antigenic when suitably injected into a different species. Furthermore, very small variations in molecules can cause the production of specific and different antibodies. By coupling certain glucoside and galactoside molecules to proteins Avery and Goebel were able to produce specific antibodies although the antigens differ only in the attachment of *one* H atom and *one* OH group to one Carbon atom. In many instances the action of quite a simple chemical (for instance formaldehyde) can alter the specificity of an antigen but fortunately this is not universally so. Apart from proteins, polysaccharides (*i.e.*, quite large molecules made up by the polymerisation or linking together of glucose and similar small carbohydrate molecules) are antigenic in many animals. This has been closely investigated in the case of dextran (a polymer of glucose alone) where in man molecules with a molecular weight less than about 100,000 are not antigenic whereas polymers with molecular weights over 600,000 certainly can be. Dextran is widely used in medicine where blood for transfusion is not available. The larger molecule material would be valuable in that it remains

in the circulation longer but unfortunately it cannot be used owing to its antigenicity.

The various serological types of *Str. pneumoniae* causing pneumococcal pneumonia have been mentioned above. It was quickly appreciated that the organisms when first isolated were surrounded by an individual capsule, that this capsule was related to the specific serological type and that the capsule consists of polysaccharide substance. Curiously enough, the polysaccharide substance itself is antigenic in man and mice but in rabbits the whole organism has to be used although the antibody produced only reacts with the capsular substance.

### Blood Groups.

*The ABO System.*—It was mentioned above that *species specific antibodies* can be prepared by the repeated injection of the blood of one species into another. Apart from induced antibodies there are in humans antibodies quite normally in circulation. These are called *agglutinins* because they agglutinate or clump together corpuscles foreign to them. The whole human race can be divided into four groups named from the agglutinogens (antigens) present in their red corpuscles— A, B, AB, and O. Everybody of group A will have agglutinins against B cells in his or her blood, and everybody of group B agglutinins against A cells. The AB person has neither, and the O person has both agglutinins in his or her serum. More recently it has been appreciated that group A is not homogeneous but can be divided into sub-groups $A_1$ and $A_2$ and other subdivisions. The recognition of these groups is of course the first step in the selection of blood for transfusion.

*The Rh System.*—In 1939 arising out of work with Rhesus monkeys it was suddenly appreciated that there was a whole new blood group system (designated the Rh system or rhesus system) and everybody was either Rh-positive or Rh-negative. Mathematical examination of the experimental results led Fisher to state that three allelomorphic (Greek roots: *allelo-* = other, *morph-* = form) pairs of factors were involved and he designated the Rh+ factors C, D, E, the Rh— factors c, d, e. It is important to realise that (1) this system is inherited separately from the ABO group so that one may be Group A Rh+ or Group A Rh—, etc.; (2) both the factors CDE and cde are antigenic although there is a great difference in their respective degrees of antigenicity; for instance, anti-D antibodies develop very readily with a small stimulating dose, anti-c antibodies less readily, and anti-d antibody has not yet been definitely identified; (3) there are *no* circulating antibodies of the Rh system in normal people corresponding to the agglutinins of the ABO system normally present.

*Inheritance of Rh Factors.*—We inherit some factors from each parent. Thus to take a specific example, a man might be cDE/CDe and his wife cde/cde; thus their children would be either cDE/cde or CDe/cde—in both cases Rh+ born of an Rh— mother. Unfortunately it is possible, indeed very usual, for some of a baby's red cells to obtain access to its mother's circulation and stimulate her to form antibodies to the baby's red corpuscles. In general it is only in the type of situation exampled above (*i.e.*, an Rh+ baby carried by an Rh— mother) that serious consequences arise. As mentioned previously, the D factor is highly antigenic; the mother may have an antibody titre of 1:1,000 or even more and these antibodies leak back across the placenta into the baby's bloodstream causing destruction of the red corpuscles, and at the same time jaundice (yellowness due to accumulation of bile pigments). The diseases produced, *Hydrops oetalis* and *Icterus gravis neonatorum*, and many puzzling facts about them, had been known for a long time but only became explicable with the discovery of the Rh system. Thus first babies are rarely affected and never seriously; the mother has not produced sufficient antibody. Subsequent pregnancies are more and more seriously affected until about the fifth or sixth when the baby may be so seriously affected as to be born dead. But yet again in some families some of the children are born perfectly healthy, neither jaundiced nor anaemic. To understand this let us imagine a father CDE/cde; he will react as and be called Rh+ but in fact he is heterozygous (Greek roots: *hetero-* = different; *zygo-* = join) meaning his reproductive condition is "mixed". Suppose he marries an Rh− woman cde/cde; half of their children will be CDe/cde and the other half cde/cde. The latter children are Rh− and cannot be affected even if the mother has been sensitised by a previous Rh+ infant.

### Antibody Detection.

There are many fascinating technical tricks used for detecting and estimating quantitatively the presence of antibodies. Quantitation is usually done by using serial doubling dilutions of the patient's serum (or unknown serum) in the test and the greatest dilution in which a positive result is detected is recorded as the *titre* (thus 1:256 or 1:10,000, etc.). For some antibodies, particularly antitoxins of therapeutic value, international standards have been laid down and these are available to manufacturers to compare with their own products so that they can mark them as "containing not less than 100,000 i.u./ml", etc., etc.

(1) *Protection.*—The earliest methods assessed the actual protection given to experimental animals. Thus groups of 50 or more animals would be given different amounts of the antitoxin, etc., being assayed and then challenged with a standard amount of toxin of known potency. In some groups all the animals would die, in one group about half and in the other groups all would survive. This method has been replaced as far as possible by methods not using animals as the test system.

(2) *Agglutination.*—Rh antibodies and some antibacterial antibodies cause clumping or agglutination of Rh+ corpuscles (or the bacteria as the case may be) and all that is necessary is to incubate tubes containing serial doubling dilutions of the unknown serum in a standard volume with a standardised suspension at 37° C (98·4° F) and then read the tubes with hand lens or microscope. There may be one doubtful tube but above this dilution the suspension will remain milky and below this dilution the corpuscles (or bacteria) will have clumped together and fallen in a mass to the bottom of the tube so that the liquid is clear.

(3) *"Complement Fixation".*—The above is a valuable technique but in many antigen-antibody reations there is no visible change. In many of these, fortunately, *complement* is used up. Complement is a heat labile protein present in fresh blood and vitally necessary for some antigen-antibody reactions to occur at all. It is a very complex test to describe but systems can be devised where the quantity of complement is sufficient for one reaction only. Thus if there *is* antibody in the unknown serum the complement will be used up and the second reaction (usually a lysis or destruction of red cells) cannot occur. Thus the tubes without antibody go clear bright red, the tubes with antibody remain smoky pink with intact red corpuscles. Again the titre can be read.

(4) *Precipitin Test.*—Another large group of antibodies fortunately produce a precipitate which can be shown by techniques developed by Ochterlony and others. A gel of gelatine, agar or some such material is formed in a shallow sheet; a number of holes are cut vertically into it—one in the centre and a ring at suitable intervals round the outside—usually about six or seven holes in all forming little "wells." The known antigen is placed in the centre well and the unknowns, with a suitable control, are placed in those round the outside. The preparation is kept moist and within a few hours the protein solutions have diffused through the gel and a line of precipitate is produced where antigen and antibody meet. The precipitate is often visible by direct oblique lighting but may need staining with a dye. This is an over-simplified description and there are many difficulties; for instance left too long the precipitate will re-dissolve in excess of antigen. However, the technique is immensely valuable for many applications and can be used quantitatively. Also working with an unknown serum in the centre and a series of known antigens around the outside a great deal of information about the antibodies present can be obtained from one test.

(5) *Immunoelectrophoresis.*—The method can be further extended by utilising *Immunoelectrophoresis.* If we pass an electric current through serum under suitable conditions (say 100 m.a. at 300 v.D.C.), overnight the proteins in the serum separate into zones or bands according to the size of the molecule. Thus separate bands represent the globulins and the albumins. The globulins can be further divided into $\alpha$, $\beta$, and $\gamma$ globulins. Now if this technique is performed in an agar gel and a narrow trough cut along the length of the direction of passage of current, multiple precipitin bands can then be produced by filling this little trough with potent but dilute antiserum. Curiously this technique has proved of more value for the recognition of unusual protein fractions than for the separation of antibodies but it is primarily an immunologist's technique. In passing we may mention that it is in the $\gamma$-fraction of the globulin that the majority of the antibodies occur and it is this fraction, when obtained in bulk from suitable subjects and purified, which is available for use in treatment (*see earlier*).

(6) *Fluorescence.*—Another technique which has recently come to the fore and proved immensely valuable is *immunofluorescence.* Certain dyestuffs fluoresce very brilliantly (i.e., when illuminated with light of short wavelength—either blue or ultra-violet—they give out golden-yellow, orange, or red, etc., light). This is sufficiently brilliant, when a suitably bright source of illumination is available (now the H.P. mercury vapour lamp), and of sufficiently different colour from the tissue auto-fluorescence that it can be applied to thin tissue sections under the microscope. The first technique is to "conjugate" the antibody with the dye (commonly Fluorescein) and remove the excess dye. This is technically complicated and needs care or the antibody loses its potency. However, it is a routine procedure these days. The technique can be used in many ways: for example (1) supposing the antibody is of known specificity it can be used to identify in tissues or to smear the virus, bacterium, fungus, or protozoan against which it is specific; or (2) using known antigens, the conjugated unknown antibody can be identified.

The second technique of very much wider application is the *indirect* or *sandwich technique.* It has the advantage that only one fluorescent antibody need be prepared instead of one for each patient. It is best explained by a specific example. In cases of the anaemia called *pernicious anaemia* there is an antibody circulating in the blood which reacts with the lining cells of the stomach. So to provide a routine test for these antibodies one needs fresh frozen sections of stomach (usually rat stomach). The patients' sera are then applied to these sections, one section per patient and suitable controls. The antibody, if present, attaches itself to the antigen—the stomach cells. Remember this is *human* antibody attaching itself to *rat* cells. The sections are then washed so that the only remaining protein of human origin will be the antibody, if present. Then the reagent required to demonstrate this is an anti-human antiserum to which Fluorescein has been conjugated, an antiserum commercially available and usually from rabbit. Under the microscope a positive result is shown by a striking and beautiful yellow-green fluorescence of the lining cells whereas the muscle and blood vessels, etc., will only show the pale blue and silver auto-fluorescence of all biological tissues.

One very exciting use of these fluorescent techniques is to track down the cells actually manufacturing the antibody, this seems in general to be in cells of the lymphoid series (*see below*).

### Tissues as Antigens.

Most tissues ground up and injected into animals cause the production of specific antibodies; kidney produces specific anti-kidney antibody and so on. A few tissues contain several antigens; for instance with thyroid gland there may be anti-thyroglobulins reacting with the secretory material and also antibodies reacting with the epithelium (the sheets of cells which cover such surfaces as the skin and lining membranes). There are two exceptions to this general rule; fortunately and very importantly the cornea of the eye, the tissue forming the transparent window at the front of the eye, is non-antigenic. Hence any healthy cornea can be grafted into any other human related or not, of the same blood group or not. Second, it has been claimed that the material of heart valves, provided they are completely free of blood and of all other tissues, is non-antigenic. This has led to attempts to transplant pig valves into humans but at present artificial valves of plastic have proved more reliable

An animal does not usually manufacture antibodies to its own tissues. This was recognised and commented upon by Ehrlich ("autotoxicus horrificus"). The mechanism for this has only recently been discovered through experimental grafting of skin into new-born animals. At birth the skin will, in some species, "take" (i.e., survive) even if grafted from an unrelated individual of the same species. Yet if grafted only a few days after birth the graft will not take. During this short period immunologically potent cells (i.e., cells capable of producing antibodies when stimulated) have spread to all parts of the body, it is now believed from the thymus (a hitherto enigmatic structure, largely of lymphoid tissue, found above and in front of the pericardial sac (enclosing the heart) in young animals, in humans practically disappearing by the late 'teens). These cells are capable of "recognising" all the constituents of the owner's body and yet reacting to almost any protein and many other substances as "foreign."

Just occasionally this mechanism fails and patients develop antibodies against their own tissues. This was first appreciated in regard to a rather uncommon thyroid disorder but every year an immune aspect to the development of some other disease is brought to light (as, for instance, in pernicious anaemia mentioned above). These anti-tissue antibodies are detected by the fluorescent methods discussed above but their rôle in the production of disease is as yet poorly understood, and the reason for the breakdown in the protective mechanism even less well.

### Depression of the Immune Response.

It is well known that starvation, malnutrition, old age, and some disease states lower the ability to produce an immune response. More recently, some drugs and also full body irradiation (with X-rays) have been used to produce deliberately a reduction in immune response particularly when grafting kidneys or bone marrow. The X-rays cause an almost total disappearance of circulating lymphocytes (one of the several types of white cell in the blood, numbering in humans about 1,500 per cubic mm.) Of course during the period of lymphocyte depression the patient is unable to respond to infection of any sort so that immense care has to be taken to completely isolate the patient, sterilise the air he breathes and everything with which he comes in contact. If the lymphocytes are not sufficiently depressed they will react to the grafted tissue, spread into it and produce changes which prevent it surviving. In animals it has been shown that, with bone marrow transplants, the graft can reject the host. The animal ceases to put on weight and eventually dies. This may be a bar to the more widespread application of bone marrow transplantation in humans.

### Hypersensitivity.

Animals, particularly guinea pigs, sensitised with protein such as horse serum and given, after a suitable interval, another very small dose intravenously go into a state of shock and frequently die—a reaction called anaphylaxis. A similar reaction, fortunately usually less dramatic and readily treated, occasionally occurs in humans. Depending on the traits of the person concerned the attack may take the form of severe asthma or of severe urticaria (large fluid-filled "blisters," painful and itching, occuring in the skin of the whole body). This is called "serum sickness" and is a major difficulty in the application of the methods of passive immunity.

Similarly some people become readily sensitised to other foreign materials, inhaled or injected. Among such substances may be mentioned grass and tree pollens (asthma and hay fever), flour and pollens such as Primula obconica (dermatitis) and less commonly foodstuffs such as egg protein (producing immediate vomiting probably followed by diarrhoea). However, this is the field of the allergist not the immunologist and so will not be further discussed.

### Delayed Sensitivity and Transferable Sensitivity.

With some immune reactions no detectable antibody appears in the blood. For instance, a skin graft from an unrelated animal of the same species survives perhaps for 7–10 days and then dies and is rejected. This seems clearly an immune response and yet there are apparently no circulating antibodies. From fluorescence microscopy it now seems clear that lymphocytes do respond to this stimulus but only locally. However, the induced sensitivity is retained, a second graft is rejected more quickly, and a third graft even more quickly. Furthermore, this sensitivity can be transferred by transferring the lymphocytes. This has to be done with highly in-bred strains of animals but if lymphocytes collected from the thoracic duct of a rat that has rejected a graft are transferred to another closely related rat, the second rat will reject a skin graft as quickly as if it had been previously sensitised by a graft itself. Some other sensitivity reactions have been similarly transferred just by transferring lymphocytes (for instance, allergic encephalomyelitis in rabbits).

### DRUGS ACTING ON THE BRAIN.

Drugs which act primarily on the brain can be classified into four main groups:

| | |
|---|---|
| (1) Depressant (Anæsthetics and sedatives) | Ether Barbiturates |
| (2) Stimulant | Caffeine Amphetamine (Benzedrine) |
| (3) Tranquillisers | Chloropromazine (Largactil) Reserpine |
| (4) Hallucinogenic | Mescaline d-Lysergic acid diethylamide (LSD 25) |
| (5) Miscellaneous Analgesic Anti-convulsant | Morphine, Heroin Trimethadione |

There are those which depress the central nervous system and cause loss of consciousness, such as anæsthetics and sedative drugs, and those which stimulate the brain, retarding sleep and lethargy and causing increased wakefulness; then there are drugs which have a depressant action on certain types of behaviour such as the hyperactivity which is present in some psychiatric conditions, but without affecting consciousness, i.e., tranquillisers. Finally, we have a group of drugs which mimic symptoms normally associated with psychiatric disturbances, producing sensory illusions and hallucinations, the hallucinogenic drugs.

These are not, of course, the only types of drugs which have actions on the brain; there are also analgesic or pain-relieving drugs such as morphine and heroin, anti-convulsant drugs which are used in the treatment of epilepsy and which are not simply depressant, and many others used for specific purposes such as the relief of tremor and rigidity, the prevention of vomiting, temperature lowering, etc. In addition, there are some newer types of drugs which appear to act specifically on certain mental states. Examples here are the "antidepressant" drugs which do not simply produce increased alertness but elevate mood and relieve psychiatric depression.

Thus, it can be seen that the classification of drugs acting on the brain is at present mainly based on their clinical effects rather than on their pharmacological mechanisms of action. This is largely because most of these drugs have been developed to treat certain clinical conditions and their precise mechanisms of action are not yet fully understood. In addition, it must be mentioned that many drugs do not have a single action but often multiple actions. Thus, some barbiturates are not only sedatives but can be used as anti-convulsants and the phenothiazine tranquillisers can be used as anti-emetics. Furthermore, many drugs which act on the brain also have effects in other parts of the body. It is therefore sometimes difficult to distinguish between the effects produced by a drug due to its direct action on the central nervous system and those which are produced indirectly.

### Investigating the Brain.

The brain is a very complex organ, perhaps the most complex in the body, and the study of its function has been largely neglected until recent years, mainly because of the lack of suitable techniques for investigation. The present techniques for researching into the functioning of the central nervous system have come from different fields. The brain is made up of many nerve cells, the human brain containing more than ten thousand million. One way in which we can study the brain is to examine its structure or anatomy in order to determine how the nerves from the various parts of the body are connected to it and also follow connections within the brain itself. However, this does not help us to understand how it functions. Another way is to look at the chemical constitution of the brain and especially to see how chemical changes may be associated with changes in function. The use of biochemical techniques in this way is becoming of increasing importance, especially in studying some psychiatric disturbances. A third method is to study the electrical properties of nerve cells. It has been found that all nerve cells are electrically excitable and when stimulated they produce a characteristic change in electrical potential which is called the *action potential*. This travels along the nerve and is believed to be responsible for the conduction of messages from the brain to other parts of the body and also from the sense organs to the brain. In the brain where we have many thousands of nerve cells aggregated together, they not only produce individual action potentials, but other electrical patterns which appear as waves and can be recorded from the surface of the brain (the cerebral cortex) or from the scalp. These "brain waves" are normally recorded on a moving chart or strip of paper and form a graph: the electroencephalogram or EEG. Studies of the EEG and other electrophysiological potentials of the brain have yielded important information about the actions of some of the drugs mentioned above.

One characteristic feature of the EEG is that it shows pronounced changes during the transition from sleep to wakefulness and *vice versa* and the patterns which are recorded in different states of wakefulness and sleep are well-defined. This is true not only in man but also for many species of animals. While the electrical patterns recorded from the cerebral cortex reflect different levels of somnolence or vigilance, it has been found that the control of sleep and wakefulness is exerted by a structure known as the *reticular formation of the brain stem* lying deep within the brain. This structure produces widespread effects on the higher centres of the brain and normally provides an influence which keeps the rest of the brain awake. Removal of this influence results in sleep or loss of consciousness. The reticular formation is itself influenced by other regions of the brain, particularly the sensory pathways conveying information from the sense organs. Thus, impulses in sensory nerves corresponding to particular sensory stimuli are conveyed not only to that region of the brain (the sensory area of the cerebral cortex) responsible for their perception but also into the reticular formation where they produce a change in the level of activity and, ultimately, increased alertness. This influence from the sensory pathway is known as the *collateral sensory input*. Changes in the level of activity in the reticular formation may also occur spontaneously and in response to other influences, *e.g.*, humoral, blood pressure, drugs, etc. The reticular formation is concerned with other functions in the central nervous system, for example, the control of respiration and blood pressure, and it has influences on spinal reflexes.

### Drugs, Wakefulness, and Sleep.

There are two groups of drugs (*see above*) which produce profound changes in levels of wakefulness and sleep. Since the brain stem reticular formation is the region responsible for the maintenance of wakefulness, it would seem likely that these drugs might have actions on this structure and this has, in fact, been found to be the case for many drugs which depress wakefulness and others which stimulate it. Thus, barbiturates such as pentobarbitone and pentothal, which are used to induce anæsthesia, produce their depressant effects by direct action on the mechanisms located in the reticular formation which are concerned with the maintenance of wakefulness. It seems likely that these drugs block the conduction of nerve impulses in the reticular formation and so prevent the latter from maintaining its influence on other higher brain structures, particularly the cerebral cortex. Sleep or loss of consciousness therefore ensues, the degree of the effect depending upon the potency of the substance and the amount which has been given. Thus, some barbiturate drugs given in large enough quantities cause loss of consciousness and a loss of responses to sensory stimuli, including pain, therefore producing anæsthesia. Other barbiturates cause only sedation and can be used to relieve insomnia. The central stimulant drugs, on the other hand, produce opposite effects and the increased wakefulness and alertness which they induce appears to be related to a facilitatory action on the reticular formation of the brain stem. This action is probably related to an increase in the spontaneous activity of the neurones (nerve cells) in the reticular formation which has been observed following administration of amphetamine. Similar effects have been observed with a number of centrally stimulating drugs and are in all probability responsible for the more mild stimulation produced by caffeine. These two groups of drugs therefore, the central depressants and central stimulants which have opposite effects on behaviour, also have opposite actions on the nervous mechanisms concerned with sleep and the maintenance of wakefulness. We conclude that these actions are probably responsible for their effects on levels of consciousness.

### Tranquillisers.

The drugs of groups (3) and (4) (*see above*) do not produce appreciable changes in conscious states, but appear to have more subtle actions on brain function. For this reason, therefore, they are rather more interesting. There are now a large number of drugs which have a tranquillising action on the brain. Some of the most potent of these are derivatives of phenothiazine and one of these, chlorpromazine (or Largactil), is the oldest of this group of drugs and is still extensively used. Administration of this drug in both animals and man produces a state of unresponsiveness and non-reactivity and it is particularly useful in the treatment of certain mental disorders, especially where hyperactivity is prevalent, *i.e.*, in manic states. Investigations of the actions of the phenothiazine tranquillisers using electrophysiological techniques have shown that they act at the level of the reticular formation of the brain stem but do not directly depress the arousal mechanisms as do the barbiturates. Their depressant action appears to be more closely linked to the collateral influences from sensory pathways entering the reticular formation. Thus, chlorpromazine depresses sensory influences on arousal mechanism without preventing the conduction of impulses through the main sensory pathways and also without depressing the arousal mechanisms located in the reticular formation. This drug therefore has a selective depressant action related to the collateral sensory input to the arousal system. Such an action can also explain many of the other effects produced by the drug, *e.g.*, effects on temperature regulation, anti-vomiting action, potentiation of anæsthesia, etc.

## LSD.

Of the hallucinogenic drugs, the synthetic substance d-lysergic acid diethylamide (LSD 25), which was discovered accidentally, has been the most widely studied of this group of compounds because of its extreme potency. A dose as small as 50 micrograms or 50 millionth parts of a gram can cause marked disturbances of mental function in man. The substance has little or no therapeutic value, but since the symptoms which it produces closely resemble those observed in naturally occuring mental disorders, it provides a means for making a model of these diseases. By studying the mechanism of action of this drug on the brain we may learn more about the kind of mechanisms which may be responsible for such naturally occurring disorders as schizophrenia. Electrophysiological experiments with LSD 25 have shown that its site of action in the brain is closely related to that of the tranquillisers, *i.e.*, it has effects related to sensory influences on the reticular formation. However, the action of LSD 25 is opposite to that of chlorpromazine and is facilitatory instead of depressant. The effect of a given sensory stimulus on the level of wakefulness is therefore enhanced by administration of LSD 25. This means that behavioural effects observed with this drug are very dependent upon the degree of sensory stimulation and therefore upon environmental conditions. This factor is important in observations of the effects of drugs in which changes in behaviour are used to define their actions and illustrates the need for careful control of environmental conditions in such experiments. The action of LSD 25 in facilitating the influence of sensory stimuli on the reticular formation of the brain stem can easily explain the effects of this drug on sensory experience if we remember that the brain stem controls the level of vigilance at the cerebral cortex.

Other experiments with tranquillisers and hallucinogenic drugs have been carried out in animals using conditioning techniques and have shown that the actions of both of these groups of drugs are very closely linked to the neurophysiological mechanisms in the central nervous system which are concerned with the way in which the brain handles sensory information—with the filtering and integration of such information. These experiments have also shown that while chlorpromazine potentiates the process of habituation in which the organism learns not to respond to a repeated stimulus of low biological significance, LSD 25 acts in the opposite manner, retarding the process of habituation and increasing the apparent " significance " of such stimuli. These observations are again consistent with the observed effects of these drugs in man. However, very little is as yet known about the detailed mechanisms involved in these processes and this places a limitation on the degree of precision with which the effects of these drugs can be defined in such terms.

### Investigation of Individual Nerve Cells.

A recent further development in the analysis of drugs on the brain consists of recording the electrical activity of the individual cells of the brain with micro-electrodes and applying drugs directly to the surface of the nerve cell. This is done by means of small glass pipettes fused into four or five barrels, which are drawn out to a very fine tip. One barrel is used for recording the action potential (*see* **F68(1)**) of the cell while the others contain aqueous solutions of the substances to be tested. By passing a small electric current through the appropriate barrel of the pipette, ions of the active substance are ejected from the tip in the vicinity of the cell. If the cell is sensitive to this particular substance, then a change in its activity will be observed. This method, which is known as " iontophoretic " application, is enabling the actions of drugs to be studied in more detail in order to determine whether they are producing effects by direct actions on the nerve cells of the brain or by indirect actions. In addition, the effects of various substances which are thought to be chemical transmitters in the brain, *i.e.*, are responsible for the conduction of nerve impulses from one cell to another, can be examined by this technique. Substances in the latter category are acetylcholine, noradrenaline and 5-hydroxytryptamine, all of which naturally occur in the brain. Furthermore, acetylcholine is the transmitter substance at the neuromuscular junction, *i.e.*, the junction between motor nerves and muscle fibres in the body and both acetylcholine and adrenaline are concerned with transmission at certain ganglia (nerve centres).

In studies of the pharmacological properties of neurones in the brain stem reticular formation, using the method of iontophoresis, it has been found that all three of these substances are effective in modifying the activity of certain cells, and that each substance can have either an excitatory or depressant effect. Thus, there are some cells whose activity is increased by application of acetylcholine, others whose activity is depressed, and some which are unaffected by iontophoretic application of this substance, and the same is true for noradrenaline and 5-hydroxytryptamine although the proportions excited, depressed, or unaffected vary. Furthermore, it has been found that when the actions of all three substances are tested on the same neurone, mixed effects can occur. Thus, some cells may be excited by all three substances, others depressed by all three; some excited by one and inhibited by the other two, and others excited by two and inhibited by one and various combinations of excitation, inhibition, or lack of effect, occur. The situation is therefore somewhat complex and it appears that there is a considerable variety of pharmacological properties in the neurones of the brain stem reticular formation. At this stage it is not possible to relate these properties of the neurones to their functional rôle.

### Some Preliminary Results.

This work is still in its infancy and while it is not yet possible to explain the actions of drugs fully in terms of their effects on individual neurones, some of the preliminary findings give tentative indications. For example, when the effects of barbiturate drugs were examined iontophoretically on single neurones, it was found that depression of activity almost always occurred, although the sensitivity of the neurones to the substances appeared to vary. Further studies of this kind should yield important information about the nature of the depressant action of the barbiturates on the neurones of the brain stem reticular formation. Similarly, it has been found that while chlorpromazine has a depressant action on many neurones in this region, it seems to affect only neurones which are also affected by application of noradrenaline. Furthermore, chlorpromazine antagonises the excitatory actions of noradrenaline but not its inhibitory actions; nor does it modify the actions of acetylcholine or 5-hydroxytryptamine. This drug may therefore be acting as a selective antagonist at sites in the brain where noradrenaline is an excitatory transmitter substance and if this proved to be true, it provides an important clue to its mode of action in the brain.

It can be seen that electrophysiological investigation of drug action in the central nervous system can provide useful information on their sites and mode of action. Investigations at the level of the single cell with local application of drugs will carry this a stage further and provide us with information of a more precise nature.

## PART IV. INDEX AND GLOSSARY

**Abdomen.** The part of the body below the chest and above the thighs.

**Abortion.** The termination of pregnancy, from whatever cause, before the child is capable of independent existence, 56 (2).

**Abortus fever.** An infectious disease known as undulant fever, 15 (1).

**Abrasion.** Any injury which rubs off the surface skin.

**Abscess.** A collection of pus enclosed anywhere in the body.

**Acidity.** *See under* Peptic ulcer, 36 (1).

**Acne,** 53 (2).

**Acromegaly.** A state of excessive growth of the body caused by overaction of the pituitary gland in the base of the brain, 44 (1).

**ACTH.** An abbreviation for adreno-cortico-trophic-hormone, a drug related to cortisone.

**Actinomycosis,** 15 (1).

**Acute nephritis,** 45 (1).

**Addiction to drugs.** *See* Drug abuse, 22.

**Addison's disease,** 44 (1).

**Adenoids,** 32 (1).

**Adhesions.** An occasional cause of pain after operations when abraded areas adhere to each other.

**Adreno-genital syndrome,** 44 (1).

**Air we breathe,** 4 (1).

**Agranulocytosis,** 26(1).

**Alcoholics Anonymous,** 6 (2).

**Allergy.** Abnormal sensitivity to any substance which does not affect normal people.

**Alopecia,** 52 (2).

**Amenorrhœa,** 56 (2).

**Amnesia.** Loss of memory, *see under* Neurosis, 51 (1).

**Amœbæ,** 8 (1).

**Amœbic dysentery,** 17 (2).

**Amphetamine,** 23 (2), 67 (2).

**Amyotrophic lateral sclerosis,** 49 (1).

**Anæmias,** 24–25.

**Anæsthetic.** Any drug used by surgeons to remove pain during an operation.

**Aneurism,** 30 (2), 46 (2).

**Angina pectoris,** 28 (2).

**Angio-neurotic œdema,** 49 (1).

**Ankylosis.** Partial or complete fixation of a joint as after some types of arthritis. In other cases deliberately produced by surgery.

**Ankylostomiasis,** 16 (2).

**Anorexia.** Loss of appetite.

**Anthrax,** 15 (1), 9 (1), 4 (2).

**Antibiotics** are drugs which act directly against the organism causing the illness by interfering with its growth or some other aspect of its living mechanisms. Of all drugs which are used against bacteria, antibiotics do least harm to the patient's own tissues; some do have unwanted side-effect, but many have none at all. *See* 4, 9, 22.

**Antihistamine drugs,** 4 (2), 5 (1).

**Antiseptics,** 8 (2).

**Antibodies,** 63 (2).

**Antigens,** 63 (2).

**Anxiety neurosis,** 51 (1).

**Aortic diseases,** 30 (2).

**Aphasia,** 47 (2).

**Aplastic anæmia,** 25 (1).

**Appendicitis,** 37 (1).

**Arthritis,** 54 (2).

**Artificial respiration (kiss of life),** 21 (1).

**Ascites,** 39 (1).

**Asphyxia,** 20 (2).

**Aspirin and " upset stomach ",** 5 (1), 23 (1), 36(2).

**Asthma,** 32 (1).

**Atheroma or Atherosclerosis,** 30 (1).

**Athlete's foot,** 8 (1), 15 (2).

**Auscultation.** The method used by a doctor when he listens for signs of disease inside the body by means of a stethoscope.

**Autonomic Nervous System,** 46 (2).

**Backache.** A symptom which may be caused by many different diseases—sometimes disease of the vertebræ themselves, sometimes strain of the ligaments, and sometimes inflammation or spasm of the surrounding muscles. " Lumbago " is usually due to inflammation of the muscles in the small of the back. Backache from purely local causes may be treated temporarily by applying heat in the form of a kaolin poultice or a rubber hot-water bottle and taking two aspirin tablets a day. On the other hand, many cases of backache are due to disease elsewhere. The most important thing is to find out the cause, and therefore a doctor should be consulted.

**Bacteria,** 7 (1). Bacterial diseases, 12–15.

**Bacteriophage,** 7 (2).

**Baldness,** 52 (2).

**Barber's rash,** 53 (2).

**Barbiturates,** 23 (2), 67 (2).

**Bell's palsy,** 50 (1).

**Benzedrine.** The proprietary name of a drug known as amphetamine. *See* 23 (2), 67 (2).

**Beri-beri,** 42 (2).

**Bilharzia,** 18 (2), 16 (1).

**Birth control,** 57.

**Blackwater fever,** 17 (2).

**Bladder.** *See under* Urinary diseases, 44 (2).

**Bleeding diseases,** 26 (1).

**Blepharitis,** 55 (1).

**Blood, function of the,** 24.

**Blood, diseases of the,** 24.

**Blood Groups.** Human blood plasma contains factors which clump, or agglutinate, the red cells of some other people's blood. The main blood groups are called A, B, AB, and O. The plasma of group A blood contains an anti-B factor and *vice versa*, so that people of groups A and B cannot accept each other's blood. Group AB contains neither anti-A not anti-B factor and people with this group can therefore receive transfusions from both but can give to neither. Group O contains both anti-A and anti-B, and can therefore receive blood only from group O but can donate blood to all groups. It is important that transfused cells should not be agglutinated by the factors in the recipient's plasma. Apart from the so-called ABO system, there are several other blood groupings, one of which is mentioned under Rhesus Factor. *See also* 65 (2).

**Blood poisoning (septicæmia),** 14 (2).

**Blood-pressure,** 30.

**Blood-vessels, diseases of the,** 30.

**Blue babies,** 5 (2).

**Botulism,** 14 (1).

**Brain.** *See under* Nervous system, 46, Physical injuries, 19, Drug effects, 68.

**Brain abscess,** 47 (1).

**Brain tumour,** 47 (1).

**Breasts,** 55 (2).

**Bronchial asthma** 32 (1)

**Bronchiectasis,** 32 (1).

**Bronchitis,** 31(2).

**Bruises and abrasions,** 19 (2).

**Bürger's disease,** 31 (1).

**Burns and scalds,** 21 (2).

Meningitis, 14 (2).

Menopause, 56 (2).

Mental diseases, 49.

Migraine, 47 (2).

Minot, George Richards (1885–1950) American physician and pathologist, specialised in diseases of the blood, 25 (2).

Mitral stenosis, 28 (2).

Moles, 54 (1).

Montagu, Lady Mary (1689–1762). English wit and letter writer, 16 (1).

Morphine, 23 (2).

Mumps, 10 (1).

Myxœdema, 42 (1), 43 (1).


National Health Service, 6.

Nephritis, acute and chronic, 45 (1).

Nephrosis, 45 (1).

Nettle rash, 53 (2).

Neurasthenia, 51 (2).

Neuritis, 49 (2).

Nephrosis, 45 (1).

Neurosis, 51 (1).

Nervous system, diseases of the, 46.

Night-blindness. See under Vitamins, 43 (1).

Noguchi, Hideyo (1876–1928). Japanese bacteriologist, 16 (1).


Œdema (dropsy), 45 (1), 27 (2).

Obesity, 40 (2).

Obsessional neurosis, 51 (2).

Œsophagitis, 36 (1).

Olfactory. To do with the sense of smell.

Ophthalmia, 15 (2).

Orthopædics. A branch of medicine dealing with the surgery of bones and joints.

Osteoarthritis, 54 (2).

Osteomalacia, 42 (1).

Osteomyelitis. An inflammatory disease of bone caused by infection with the streptococcus or staphylococcus. The germ is carried by the blood, but the part where it settles depends on local weakness or such factors as blows and injuries. The first sign is severe pain in the infected bone and fever. Usually the site affected is in the long bones of the arm or leg. Later, a chronic state may develop in which a small sinus, or hole in the limb, discharges large amounts of pus which comes from the inside of the bone. Operation may be necessary, but if caught in an early stage, the disease may be treated with penicillin or sulphonamide drugs. The main danger of osteomyelitis is that absorption of the bacterial poisons into the system leads to damage to the other organs of the body.

Osteoporosis, 42 (2).

Ovaries, 56 (1).


Palpitation. See Tachycardia, 29 (2).

Pancreas, 39 (2).

Papilloma, 45 (1).

Paralysis (flaccid and spastic), 47 (1).

Paralysis agitans, 50 (1).

Paraphrenia, 51 (1).

Parasites, 8 (1), 52 (2).

Parasitic worms: diseases, 18 (1).

Parathyroid glands, 43 (2).

Paré Ambroise (c. 1510–90). French army surgeon, 4 (1).

Parkinson's disease, 50 (1).

Pasteur, Louis (1822–95). French chemist, 5 (2), 16 (1).

Pediatrics. The study of the diseases of children.

Pellagra, 42 (2).

Penicillin, 4 (1), 9 (1), 22 (2), 55 (1).

Peptic ulcer, 36 (1).

Pericarditis, 30 (1).

Peritonitis, 38 (1).

Pernicious anæmia, 25 (1).

Peroneal muscular atrophy, 49 (1).

Petit mal. See Epilepsy, 48 (1).

Physical injuries, 19–22.

Piles. See Hæmorrhoids, 38 (1).

Pink disease, 48 (2).

Pituitary gland, 44 (1).

Plague, 17.

Plastic surgery, 5 (2), 54 (2).

Pleurisy, 34 (1).

Pneumonia, 32 (2).

Pneumoconiosis, 33 (1).

Poliomyelitis, 10 (2).

Polycythæmia, 25 (2).

Polyneuritis, 49 (2).

Portal hypertension, 38 (2).

Prognosis. The medical name for the outlook of a disease.

Progressive muscular atrophy, 49 (1).

Prolapsed intervertebral disc, 50 (1).

Prolapse of uterus, 56 (1).

Prostate disease, 46 (1).

Proteins, 35 (1), 40 (2).

Protozoal diseases, 17–18.

Pruritus, 52 (2).

Psittacosis, 12 (1).

Psychosis, 50.

Psychosomatic diseases. Psychosomatic diseases are those physical ailments due to emotional causes. They include such complaints as high blood-pressure, gastric ulcer, certain skin diseases, and certain glandular diseases (e.g., exophthalmic goitre). Most physicians nowadays believe that all diseases may show a greater or less degree of emotional causation; that physical and mental factors are both present in all illness. Even in psychosomatic illnesses, heredity and other factors play a large part. Briefly, the main cause of these diseases is worry. The importance of this lies in the fact that they cannot be cured without dealing with the fundamental cause. See also New Views on Medicine, 3 (2).

Psychopathic personality, 52 (1).

Pulmonary embolism, 33 (1).

Purpura, 26 (2).

Pyæmia, 14 (2).

Pyelitis, 45 (1).

Pyloric stenosis, 36 (2).

Pyorrhœa. An infection of the gums which causes the edges of the tooth sockets to bleed easily when the teeth are being brushed. There is a constant discharge of pus, which causes the breath to smell and may lead to arthritis and other diseases. Treatment should be carried out by a dentist.


Quarantine period. See Infectious Fevers, 9 (2).


Rabies, 11 (2).

Raynaud's disease, 31 (1).

Rectum, cancer of the, 37 (2).

Reducing weight, 40.

Reed, Major Walter (1851–1902). American army surgeon, 12 (1), 16 (1).

Regional enteritis, 37 (1).

Relapsing fever, 16 (2).

Renal colic, 45 (2).

Respiratory system, diseases of the, 31.

Reticulosarcoma, 26 (1).

Retinitis, 55 (2).

Reynaud's disease, 31 (1).

Rhesus Factor. Apart from the ABO blood group system (see Blood Groups) there is another blood group system (designated the Rh-system or Rhesus system). Everybody is either Rh-positive or Rh-negative. Three positive factors (denoted C, D, E) and three negative factors (denoted c, d, e) are involved. This system of blood factors is inherited

# HUMAN RELATIONS

An introduction to the study of
personality and interpersonal relations, touching upon some of the
psychological and sociological problems raised by our industrial society.

# TABLE OF CONTENTS

Introduction

# HUMAN RELATIONS

In this section we have tried to give the reader an understanding of modern society and of the forces that motivate behaviour so that he can interpret what is going on around him and in his own mind. An effort has also been made to provide that help which understanding alone can give not only in the working out of one's own problems but in extending tolerance towards the shortcomings of others.

The section is in three parts:

    I. The Self (i.e., the individual and his development and the way he meets the problems of life in the process of growing up).

    II. Society (i.e., our relationships with other people from the family to the larger social groups and the problems created by changing social patterns).

    III. Work (i.e., all the many factors that affect the worker in an industrial society).

These categories overlap to some extent since we are not isolated individuals but involved with people from the earliest days, and work is an integral part of everyone's life, so each part flows into the next, occasionally making a little repetition inevitable.

Before we enter this field of human relations, let us remember the words of that great teacher and writer, R. H. Tawney: " Everyone, whether he intends it or not, adopts some attitude to the world of human beings in which his lot is cast; and, as that attitude is, so in large measure will be both his personal happiness and his utility to his fellows. It may be one of sympathy and co-operation, or of antagonism and suspicion."

## INTRODUCTION.

All societies have had their problems and their times of crisis and modern society is no exception. What is special about our problems is that they are of an entirely different nature from those which faced our forefathers. For them, as over vast areas of the earth even today, the main hazards came from an untamed natural environment in which plagues were rampant and malnutrition the rule, in which crops and livestock could be ravaged by adverse weather or disease, bringing starvation and death just as surely as the plagues afflicting man himself. This is still the state of affairs in many of the technically under-developed countries of the world where epidemic diseases, chronic infections such as malaria and tuberculosis, hunger, poverty, and malnutrition still need immediate action. To improve the human environment calls for efforts by the community as a whole which these poorer countries are, as yet, incapable of making by themselves, for their people have neither the necessary knowledge, wealth, nor organisation to do so, and, most difficult of all, they need to change long-established habits and attitudes.

The peoples of the Western countries have so modified their environment that they have succeeded in adding many years to their average expectation of life, yet it is not so long ago that they had to face similar problems. For example, it is little more than a hundred years ago (1848), when the appalling living conditions resulting from the industrial revolution threatened to spread disease throughout Britain, that the first public health measures were taken to deal with the fearful cholera and smallpox epidemics which were then prevalent. In Ireland, failure of the potato crop led to the great famine of the 1840s when a million people died of starvation and a million and a quarter were forced to emigrate. During the influenza epidemic which followed the First World War more people died in a single year than were killed on all the fronts in four years of devastating war. During the last 50 years new discoveries and increased medical skill have combined to reduce the death rate of children in Britain in the first year of their lives from 120 per thousand to 22 per thousand (boys) and from 98 to 17 (girls), so that a baby boy may now expect to live to 68 years and a girl to 74. By a process which began gradually about a hundred years ago and accelerated in recent times until it has become an explosion, our circumstances have radically changed as technology has advanced and along with the truly wonderful scientific achievements of our civilisation have come new and unheralded dangers. We are living largely in a synthetic environment created by our own technology and our most serious problems today are caused not by nature but by ourselves. This is perhaps a depressing fact, but it is also a hopeful one: for we are now at little risk from the physical world around us and it might be thought that the minds which created the new environment are surely capable of solving the problems which come in its wake.

Unfortunately the situation is not quite so simple because, though we know a good deal about the physical universe and how to bring it under control, we know rather less about ourselves and what information is available does not suggest that human problems are as easy to solve as technical ones. Most of us are able to handle things with some measure of efficiency, but we are likely to be much less skilled when it comes to human relationships and, in the long run, even things become tied up with personal emotions. Thus there are not *two* sets of problems, the one concerned with science and technology and the other with mental life, because science and technology *in themselves* create no problems at all—there is really only one problem and that is the uses to which we put our knowledge. Man uses his reason to find out about the physical universe but all too often what he does with his discoveries is determined not by reason but by false beliefs, old traditions, and emotional prejudice.

Among the major problems in the world today are racial and national hatred, undernourishment, over-population, disease in impoverished countries, the threat of nuclear war, failure to adjust to change, superstition, illiteracy and poor educational standards. Most of the causes of these are already known and in many cases the remedies are not only known but capable of being put into practice immediately. What stops them from being effectively dealt with is not lack of knowledge but the fact that we are unable to understand or control ourselves; the problems are not outside but inside man—his stupidity, greed, aggressiveness, suspicions and prejudices. These are the concern of the psychologist, because psychology is the scientific study of human behaviour, emotions, and thoughts. In the pages that follow we shall be dealing mainly with those aspects of the subject which are most relevant to the individual citizen in the Western world today but it is hoped that the reader will gain some insight into the forces which motivate all men irrespective of politics, race, or creed.

**Adjusting to Inevitable Change.**

Broadly speaking, the problems of the West are those of the Welfare State or what has been described as the Affluent Society (the two are not quite the same because, though a welfare state may be affluent, an affluent society like America is certainly not a welfare state). Along with very real benefits such as comparative economic security, improved material well-being, freedom from many of the killing diseases which once plagued us, greater social mobility, and better opportunities for higher education, have come other features which cannot be cured by more affluence. Many people are bored, rebellious, perplexed, and downright unhappy, and some would ascribe this to the 'spiritual sickness of our time' brought about by the loss of traditional values. Perhaps they are right. The only trouble about this analysis is that it is not a very helpful approach because traditional values cannot be brought back by legislation, nor is it desirable that they should be brought back at all. Our real problem is that we have failed to adjust to a rapidly-changing technological environment, which demands a new set of values and fresh attitudes. More than a century and a half ago a famous philosopher wrote that " man, insofar as he acts to change his environment, acts to change himself," and herein lies our failure; we have created a new environment but have failed to make new adjustments to it though the essence of normality is the ability to see and react appropriately to life as it is. The authoritarian family has gone, woman's place in relation to home and work has changed, traditional attitudes in industry are dying, and the gulf in understanding between parents and children has increased because the pre-war world is not the world of today. All these issues will be discussed here.

# I.  THE SELF

## 1. THE FOUNDATIONS.

### What is Personality?

Personality may be defined as that arrangement of traits which are relatively consistent and enduring attributes of an individual's behaviour. Thus if one man is aggressive in any and every situation and another gentle and thoughtful towards everyone he meets, then we are entitled to assume that these are fundamental and relatively fixed aspects of their personalities.

On the other hand, it is easy to see that whilst some aspects of behaviour are comparatively stable, people's actions are also variable—they may be shy in one set of circumstances and not in another, dominating within one group and submissive elsewhere. This is because these traits are not something *in* the individual, but are simply a response to the social circumstances he is facing at the moment. In more technical terms, they are not a function of his personality but rather a function of the role he is playing as a member of a group facing a specific situation. So it often happens that we attribute certain characteristics of a person to his innate traits when, in fact, they only appear to be fixed because we always meet him in the same social surroundings. For example, a supervisor in a factory who finds that one of his workers is always resentful is liable to suppose that he is just resentful by nature, whereas, if he saw the man at home he might be surprised to discover that his family and neighbours regard him as kindly and generous to a fault. The reason is, of course, that the worker is resentful in response to the factory situation which, being the kind of person he is, he finds frustrating because it does not permit free expression to his real abilities. Thus what might be described as the ' core ' personality is rigid in structure and resists change, whilst the more superficial aspects of personality, of which the above is an instance, change very rapidly as the individual moves from one group to another, and these aspects are described as relating to the ' peripheral ', ' public ', or ' social ' personality. The practical significance of this distinction will be seen later, but it is obvious that if we are dealing with a social problem such as juvenile delinquency it is absolutely necessary to know whether, in a given case, we are faced with an attitude which is firmly ingrained in the youth or whether he is simply responding to a frustrating environment.

Some aspects of personality are therefore relatively fixed whilst others merely reflect responses to a particular environment, but the two cannot be entirely separated because most of the time people tend to respond, not to the environment as it really is but *to the environment as they interpret it* and this naturally depends upon the nature of their core personality. In the example of the worker quoted above, it is obvious that he was suspicious, not merely because of the objective situation (which of course first aroused his suspicions) but because he was the sort of person who might be expected to feel that way in those circumstances. Perhaps his innate intelligence and the fact that he had been brought up with the ambition to better himself made the situation more intolerable to him than to his mates (though in some factories things may be so bad that nearly everyone feels dissatisfied). But this does not alter the fact that a change to a more satisfying job would change the behaviour of this particular man, whilst, in other cases, suspiciousness may be an ingrained trait which appears in any situation.

### How is Personality Fashioned?

Where, then, do these fixed traits come from? Broadly speaking, they arise from three distinct but interacting sources: temperament, the childrearing patterns of the first five or six years of life, and the culture in which the individual is brought up. Temperament is what we inherit, and childrearing patterns are based on the way in which the parents attempt to pass on the culture to which they and their children belong. The family, it has been said, is the personality-factory of society which attempts with greater or lesser success to inculcate the ideals of a particular group into each new generation. To use another metaphor, we come into the world as an undifferentiated lump of clay which nevertheless has its own particular properties, the family is the potter, and culture supplies the design. If our society values conquest, we shall be brought up to admire and try to emulate war-like men; if it measures success in terms of money we shall see acquisitiveness and wealth as our goal; and, in a caste society, we must learn to behave in all ways according to the position into which we are born. This ideal pattern is the *basic personality structure* and represents those aspects of personality which distinguish the members of one cultural group from another and defines what is considered as ' normal ' in a given society. The variations on this common theme which differentiate one member of the group from any other member making him, to some extent, a unique individual, are what is described as ' character '. Since the interplay between these various factors is very subtle, it is necessary to discuss them in more detail.

### Temperament.

Just a century ago the Austrian monk Gregor Mendel was able to show that the physical characteristics of plants are passed on from one generation to the next according to certain definite laws (*see* Section F, Part IV). It is known that such factors as body-build, hair and eye colour, height, and the rest are inherited in this way, and there are a few diseases (probably not more than can be counted on the fingers of one hand) such as haemophilia, which are also known to be hereditary. But when it comes to mental traits, we are on much less secure ground, largely because it is difficult to distinguish between what has been inherited and what has been learnt. Nearly all psychologists believe that if a son is fussy and punctilious like his father this is because he has been taught to behave in this way or has learned it by imitation, and whilst many psychiatrists (i.e., physicians who specialise in treating mental disorders) believe that a *tendency* to certain forms of insanity is inherited, few would accept that this is true of the minor forms of neurosis. It is known for certain that general intelligence is determined at the moment of conception, and quite likely that the traits collectively described as ' temperament ' are largely inherited because they seem to be correlated with body-build. The short stocky individual with a tendency to run to fat is usually cheerful and outgoing—one of those described by Shakespeare when he referred to " men that are fat, sleek-headed men and such as sleep o'nights " and compared them to Cassius with his " lean and hungry look " who " thinks too much— such men are dangerous ". The former type of body-build is the ' pyknic ' and his temperament is ' cyclothyme ' or ' extraverted ', the latter has an ' æsthenic ' build associated with a ' schizoid ' or ' introverted ' temperament. (*See also* Characterology, J8.)

### The Interplay of Heredity and Environment.

But all this has to be modified because the introvert and extravert are obviously at the extreme ends of a normal curve of distribution so most people fall in between the two and both attitudes can be considerably modified by cultural factors. An extravert, who would naturally be given to talkativeness and the strong expression of his emotions, if born into a Red Indian tribe, where the approved basic personality structure is the impassive and silent man, would become just as impassive as the rest. Even intelligence, the only mental trait which we know *for certain* to be inherited, can be considerably modified by environmental factors which encourage or discourage its full development. Furthermore, there are two other considerations to be taken into account: first, not every trait that a child is born with is inherited, and second, heredity may have an indirect as well as a direct effect on character. What a child is born with is congenital, but congenital traits are not always inherited or determined at the moment of conception; for we know that what takes place whilst the child is developing within the womb also has a potent influence on its future life, usually for the worse. Thus German measles in the mother, birth injury, and drugs such as thalidomide taken in the early weeks of pregnancy (*see* P4) can cause severe mental defect or physical deformity. Again, the effect of inherited characteristics may be indirect depending upon how they are regarded by the society into which the child is born and the way the child reacts to the views of his society. For example, a mentally-retarded or brain-damaged person may be regarded with contempt or pity in one group or be thrust into a position of high status as a witch-doctor or sorcerer in another. A boy who is short in stature may become neurotic and a failure when he is teased by his associates or, on the other hand, may compensate by becoming powerful and dominating to cover up his deficiency. The influence of heredity is therefore very complex and even the most fixed traits may be considerably modified by environment; stature is inherited, but without adequate diet the full stature will not be reached, whereas given better nourishment it will. The youth of Britain today are on the average considerably taller than their grandparents, and the Japanese who were always regarded as ' naturally ' small are becoming taller as the economic position of their country improves. Heredity, by and large, does not determine the details—it merely sets the limits.

### Child-rearing Patterns.

It follows that, though we are prone to think of the child as a pre-fabricated structure waiting at birth to be erected, for better or worse, by the adults who look after it, this is a wholly mistaken belief, because *prior to an infant's earliest contacts with other human beings it simply does not exist as a ' person ' at all.* All we have is a living thing with certain physical characteristics, a *potential* intellectual level which, again, without the intervention of people could not raise him above the

level of an idiot or a chimpanzee, and a bundle of biological drives such as hunger, thirst, sex, and the needs for sleep and warmth which only others can satisfy. Human beings are unlike animals in their prolonged period of helplessness, in their ability to communicate by speech, in the possession of an opposable thumb which makes it possible to carry out delicate manipulations, in the fact that they alone can hand on knowledge or culture from one generation to the next and, above all, in having no instincts. Correctly used, the word ' instinct ' refers to behaviour inherited in the structure of the nervous system, unlearned, and relatively unmodifiable; it is typical of the lower animals which automatically carry out quite complicated actions such as nest-building, yearly migrations, courting behaviour, and so on, without having been taught how to do so. In the higher animals such as apes this is already a disappearing category and, so far as human beings are concerned, it has disappeared altogether, being replaced by undifferentiated drives or needs that are inherited, but require the help of a family before they develop into the patterns for satisfying them approved in a given society.

### The Sense of Self.

The need for food like the need for sleep, is innate but from a very early age the child learns not merely to demand food or sleep as such, but certain kinds of food and certain hours of sleep which it has been taught are ' right ' and ' good '. The basic psychological process occurs in a particular direction: the infant has physical needs which demand satisfaction, it becomes aware of the world around it, interprets it, responds to it, finally responds to the results of its own response. It feels sensations of hunger, becomes aware of the breast, interprets it as a source of food, sucks it, and depending upon whether its experience is satisfying or not, feels pleasure, anger, or anxiety. Because the way in which people or things respond to our approaches to them influences our attitude towards ourselves, it has been said that the self is based on " the reflected appraisal of other people ", or more dramatically by an Italian novelist, that " the self is the meeting-place of all relationships ". In other words, we do not just *have* experiences, we *are* our experiences and in later life we treat others as we interpret the way they treated us during the formative years, and value or dislike ourselves as we believe we were valued or otherwise. This too is important in understanding certain types of delinquency, because one can only give as much love as one has received, and a delinquent who has suffered from parental neglect may become what is known as a ' loveless character ' because he literally has no love to give and can only respond with hate. The selfish person does not care for others, but he does not care for himself either.

## 2. THE FORMATIVE YEARS.

### The Fundamental Need for Love and Protection.

The biological needs of hunger, thirst, and the rest, by reason of the utter helplessness of the human infant, cannot be satisfied unaided, so there arises very early in life the most fundamental of psychological needs—the need to be loved, protected, and cared for. Love is not something we are born with; it develops through a series of stages from mere cupboard love to a mature and disinterested affection for other people. Hate is an emotion which arises when certain needs are frustrated—in fact, it might almost be said to be a derivative of love since, together with anxiety, it is initially aroused by fear of loss of love. This need to be cared for leads in later life to the need for personal affection and subsequently to a desire for the approval of society so, as one psychologist puts it, love forms " the underpinning on which all the later motives and the cultural imperatives are constructed ".

### The Formation of Basic Attitudes.

During the first five years of life the child begins to learn, not only by the process of conditioning whereby it comes to associate two quite different stimuli together as a dog learns to associate the the sound of a whistle with food because one has always followed the other, whilst ignoring the sound of a bell which has been unrelated to food but also by a process of trial and error and by imitating its parents. Habits are established by differential reward and punishment, indulgence and deprivation, or the implied threat of deprivation of affection on the part of the parents who make use of the infant's needs to avoid harm and obtain approval and the satisfaction of its biological drives to this end. The habits acquired at this stage relate to sleeping and feeding, bowel and bladder control and the child's early loves and hates (Œdipus complex) within the family circle. Throughout this period it develops attitudes towards its father and mother, brothers and sisters, which becomes the model of its attitudes towards all the people it meets subsequently. So, whilst the core personality is being laid down, the child is not only learning control of its excretory and feeding functions but also how to deal with people; if it is not given affection freely, consistently, and unconditionally, it will soon discover more devious ways of getting attention. If being sick produces the required results, the child will grow up into the sort of person who tries to get affection by taking refuge in real or imaginary illnesses when trouble threatens. If keeping to oneself works (" If I leave people alone they won't harm me "), he will be unsociable, and if a domineering or aggressive attitude works that is what he will become. Naughty and ultimately delinquent behaviour sometimes arises from the child's feeling that he is not cared for (" All right, if you don't love me, at least I'll see to it that you have to give me *some* sort of attention ")

The important point is that all our most basic attitudes arise because at one time they demonstrably worked. As a child psychiatrist expresses it: " We become acceptable or non-acceptable, helpless or capable, important or insignificant, passive or aggressive, busy or lazy, resourceful, or cautious, or sweet, or clever, or polite, or thoughtful, or obedient, or demanding, or a thousand and one other characteristics. These are the traits which are produced by the child and structuralised into his very self because of their *functional* value to him in the earliest years of life. Each one was the trait that worked best and got the best results in the particular setting in which he was placed."

### How the Personality Develops.

Parents usually think of child-rearing as a simple—or at least theoretically simple—and direct process whereby ' good ' behaviour is inculcated and ' bad ' behaviour discouraged by reward and punishment, personal example, and later by speech. Unfortunately this is not the case because, though these are important, other facts must be taken into consideration. To begin with, character formation starts from the very earliest weeks and those traits which are learned then are the most potent by reason of the Law of Primacy which states that the earlier an experience the greater its effect. This is because from birth onwards the way we interpret a new experience depends on our previous mental state; for example, though a child will certainly have no conscious memory of satisfying or unsatisfying emotions at the breast, these are nevertheless built into its brain structure and cause it to see later events in a hopeful or depressing light.

### Early Infancy.

There is very good evidence that in the first six months of infancy we have already acquired basic traits which make for an authoritarian or humanitarian outlook and, in fact, the words of the song by Gilbert and Sullivan to the effect that " every boy and every girl that's born into this world alive is either a little Liberal or else a little Conservative " are quite literally true with the single modification that we are not born that way but learn these attitudes at the breast.

Of course, like the introvert–extravert scale and the level of intelligence, these attitudes are distributed over a normal curve so that most people fall somewhere about the middle, and the radical-conservative scale is not meant to refer to any political party, though it will clearly influence later political beliefs.

Again, it is almost certain that such traits as fussiness, punctuality, belief in discipline, excessive concern with cleanliness, and extreme (but repressed) aggressiveness are learned, not by direct example, but are intercorrelated attitudes associated with an over-strict emphasis on bowel training. Those nations which value punctiliousness, obedience, and strict hygiene (*e.g.*, the Teutonic nations) are also likely to be aggressive, obsessed with bowel functions (*c.f.*, Martin Luther), and to make jokes, not as in other countries about sex, but about lavatories.

### The Beginnings of Conscience.

At a later stage, about the age of five or six, the child normally passes through what is known as the Œdipus complex when it loves the parent of the opposite sex and feels correspondingly jealous of the parent of the same sex as a rival and this influences its attitudes towards the opposite sex throughout life. But quite soon it begins to realise the futility of this state of affairs and from then on two important things happen. First, the child leaves behind the stage when its moral controls came from outside, from the orders of its parents, and by a process known as ' introjection ' takes the parent's moral attitudes inside itself. This is the earliest beginnings of the adult conscience which initially starts as an ' internalised parent ' exercising control from within instead of having it superimposed from without. Second, the child now begins to imitate the parent of the *same* sex, and in this way the boy learns how to play the masculine role as defined in his society, the girl to play the feminine role. This is a very important stage and in households where the father is absent, badly behaved, or a weakling, the boy may imitate his mother and develop homosexual tendencies in later life.

### Child–Parent Relationship.

There are therefore two parallel processes involved in child-rearing, the one conscious and deliberate in which the child is taught to behave according to the rules of its society and also learns in the academic sense, but the more significant one is an unconscious process because, as we have seen, many of our most deep-rooted traits arise during the period when the child cannot understand speech and are the result of an interaction between parent and child at a time when the parent is unlikely to realise the values he or she is actually inculcating. In short, the child is responding more to what his parents *are* than to what they *say*, and therefore *the basic rule in bringing up a child is to give it unconditional, secure, and consistent affection.* But it is only the normal parent who is able to do this and, since not many of us have reached full emotional maturity, our children may appear to be getting plenty of affection, but the true reasons for the mother's behaviour may be guilt at not feeling enough love or, if she is unhappy with her husband, she may be displacing her frustrated affections on her son— in neither case is the love healthy or genuine and the child will suffer.

Even the formal educational process is influenced by these emotional undercurrents which the parents neither understand nor are capable of controlling, and the child will accept or reject what it is deliberately taught, not in terms of its truth or real value, but rather in terms of his unconscious (or sometimes conscious) feelings towards the parent who tries to inculcate them. The boy who either unconsciously resents his father or is striving to become independent of unduly possessive parents (or even, as sometimes happens, trying to avoid being overwhelmed by the reputation of a well-loved but very famous father) is more likely to reject his father's religious, philosophical, or political views than to accept them. One little boy whose very tolerant parents had never uttered a word of condemnation against his lack of interest in books were distressed to hear him say when he thought they were not listening, "Of course, I'm the idiot of the family" —they had *said* nothing, but the walls of their home covered with bookshelves filled with books, many of which they themselves had written, had said a great deal. The boy excelled at getting on with his schoolmates and at sport, but until the reasons for his attitude against learning were pointed out to him, he did not do well academically. Once he had learned what was going on in his unconscious, he became one of the best scholars in his college.

## 3. THE UNCONSCIOUS PROCESSES SHAPING PERSONALITY

### The Repression of Emotions.

In general, we only pay attention to those elements of our environment which (*a*) fit in with the rest of our beliefs, and (*b*) help to further the action in hand at the moment. Freud, the founder of psychoanalysis, pointed out that all those emotions and thoughts which are repugnant to the individual are either pushed into his unconscious or never allowed to leave it. They are, as Freud said, "repressed"—a term which does not mean the conscious *suppression* of antisocial desires, but the refusal even to recognise their existence. However, as others have pointed out since, it is not only those aspects of personality which are regarded as morally objectionable that come to be repressed, but traits which, whilst not necessarily ' bad ' in themselves, do not fit in with conscious attitudes. Charles Darwin, for example, admitted that, as he became more and more absorbed in reasoning and scientific pursuits, he lost the ability to enjoy, as he once had done, the pleasures of poetry and literature. We shall see later that one of the great barriers to changing attitudes from whatever motive is the fact that, after they have grown up, people do not tend to seek new experiences but rather to reinforce existing prejudices.

For the moment, however, we are concerned with those emotions and desires which are repressed in the original Freudian sense. When such emotions are repressed they do not cease to exist and sometimes have quite devastating effects on the individual and his associates. Thus those who have been brought up to refuse to recognise their aggressiveness may repress it and, by the process known as ' reaction-formation', become compulsively ' gentle '. Their assumed ' gentleness ' is adopted in order to fight their ' bad ' aggressive side; and so we often find (and this is the tragedy of these movements) that those who are pacifists, vegetarians, and against cruelty to animals or children cannot help their latent aggressiveness from leaking out. This leads to such unpleasant phenomena as the obvious tendency to fragmentation and quarrelsomeness within pacifist movements, an unhealthy absorption in cruelty quite frequently in situations where others see none, and extreme intolerance. Jung described this unrecognised aspect of a man's nature as his " shadow ", giving as an example a man he had once met, a Quaker, who could not imagine that he had ever done anything wrong in his life. "And do you know what happened to his children? " Jung asked. " The son became a thief, and the daughter a prostitute. Because the father would not take on his shadow, his share in the imperfection of human nature, his children were compelled to live out the dark side which he had ignored." Thus unconscious attitudes in the parents are sometimes more potent in influencing their children than the respectable conscious ones.

### Mental Mechanisms to Guard Our Self-Esteem.

Freud describes various mental mechanisms which even those who do not accept Freudian theory in its entirety have found valuable in understanding human behaviour. The chief protective strategies we employ in order to guard our self-esteem are: (1) repression—denying conscious outlet to unwelcome wishes and thought; (2) denial—

denying the existence of unwelcome facts; (3) rationalisation—giving bad reasons to justify our misdeeds; (4) projection—ascribing our own wishes or shortcomings to another; (5) displacement—directing " bottled-up " emotion against an innocent party (finding a scapegoat); (6) fixation and regression—avoiding being one's true age in order to get out of responsibilities; (7) reaction-formation—vigorously pretending the exact opposite to what one feels in order to hide the source of conflict; (8) sublimation—consciously expressing repressed impulses in socially and personally accepted channels; (9) compensation—taking counteractive measures against feelings of inferiority (this is an Adlerian concept).

### The Nature of Aggression.

Hardly any subject in the whole field of psychology is more important than the problem of aggression, and it is doubtful if any is less understood by the layman. This is little short of tragic since it is obvious that what is generally comprehended under the name of aggression is responsible for many of the issues facing us today: for example, warfare between nations, crimes of violence, race prejudice, and the concern felt by many-about violence on television or in children's ' comics ', all reflect the necessity for taking the matter seriously. What stands in the way of genuine understanding is the fact that, as is so often the case in psychology, most people are not only convinced that they already know all that needs to be known but, worse still, they are confident that they know the solutions. What could be more apparent than that war is caused by the ' instinct ' of aggression, that violent crimes can be cured by violence, or that horror scenes in comics or on television are a cause of juvenile delinquency which can therefore be reduced by preventing children from being exposed to them? Naturally enough, anyone who is rash enough to attempt to show that these are dangerous delusions or that, to say the least, the problem is much more complex than is often supposed, is immediately suspect of blinding himself to realities or of being ' soft ' when the correct attitude is to be ' hard ' and ' objective '. However, the reader is invited to try to see the other side of the picture.

### Life Energy or Drive.

In the first place, ' aggression ' is not a simple entity synonymous with ' hate ', and this confusion leads to the belief that what is a perfectly natural and inborn tendency is, without qualification, evil. Actually, as Dr. D. W. Winnicott, who is one of the most eminent British psychoanalysts (*i.e.*, those who treat patients by the methods based on the theories of Freud) has pointed out, " at origin aggressiveness is almost synonymous with activity ". It is not an ' instinct ' nor even a specific drive but the natural tendency to overcome obstacles to the attainment of goals without which life itself could not exist; thus we talk about ' attacking ' a problem, ' struggling with ' and ' overcoming ' a difficulty, ' mastering ' a subject or ' getting one's teeth into it '.

### Hate or Anger.

In this sense aggressiveness is simply life-energy which, when it meets a barrier to satisfaction (whether the need for satisfaction involves solving a mental problem or looking for one's next meal) accumulates in order to summon up enough power to overcome it. This sort of behaviour is happening to everybody at every hour of the day and usually the barrier is successfully overcome and the organism returns briefly to the original resting state. But if it proves insurmountable, a state of frustration develops which leads to emotions which can be described as ' aggression ' in the more limited sense of the word implying anger, anxiety, and hate. Hate arises in interpersonal situations, that is to say, it is something we feel towards *people*, arising originally from fear of loss of love which threatened our security in infancy because an unloving mother could not be relied upon to satisfy our physical needs, and subsequently it arises in situations where security is threatened either in the emotional sense or when there exists a real or imagined physical danger to status, life, or property. For example, rejection in love threatens our self-image by damaging that personal esteem which is the badge of psychological security, and the fear of attack from other individuals, groups, or nations threatens our physical security, so both are prone to lead to hate. *Since hatred is so closely linked with anxiety, anxious and insecure people are particularly prone to irrational hatred.* Thus revolutions are not made by the secure ruling classes who have nothing to gain, nor (as the Communists have learned to their cost) by the very poor who have nothing to lose, but by the insecure lower middle classes; those who incite race riots in the southern states of America are not the well-to-do or the old 'aristocracy' who are often, in private, quite liberal in their views, but the 'poor whites' whose only claim to superiority rests on their colour. Anger, though often directed against people, is also aroused by situations or things which frustrate the individual, such as the car that fails to start; hate always involves people, anger does not.

### How Aggression is Dealt With.

When a great deal of anger or hatred (*i.e.*, aggression in the narrower sense of the word) has been aroused, various possibilities of handling it arise. The normal reaction is to assess the situation rationally and consciously recognise one's feelings for what they are; from this point one may feel that by an increased effort the barrier to satisfaction may be overcome and decide to carry on, or that the barrier is genuinely insuperable so that further effort would be wasted and that, failure being no disgrace in the circumstances, one can without loss of self-respect redirect one's efforts elsewhere. Unfortunately, in our own culture children are often brought up to believe that anger, aggression, or even normal self-assertion are 'bad' emotions to be suppressed just as much as 'evil' sexual desires. When this happens, what was once consciously suppressed by the threat of punishment or loss of love in childhood soon comes to be automatically and unconsciously repressed in later life. In this case our aggressive feelings (which, as mentioned above, may sometimes extend to what is merely self-assertiveness or the right to develop oneself as an independent individual) are dealt with by *denial*—we deny that they exist at all, or assert that they exist in other people but not in ourselves, or direct them against a socially-accepted scapegoat. That is to say, they are repressed, projected, or displaced, and this is the cause of most of the troubles facing the modern world. Those who lead campaigns for peace, if in many cases genuinely gentle people or motivated by a commonsense realisation that the human race must choose between international peace or total destruction, are all too frequently individuals who are compulsively 'gentle' in a neurotic attempt to deny their own destructive tendencies. But the denial of such tendencies does not prevent their manifesting themselves in such a way as to frustrate the achievement of the avowed goals of the movement and, to quote Dr. Winnicott once more: "*If society is in danger, it is not because of man's aggressiveness, but because of the repression of personal aggressiveness in individuals.*"

### The Effects of Repressing Aggressive Feelings.

Normal sexual or aggressive feelings when denied give rise to those horrible sexual and aggressive fantasies which, when projected upon the outer world, lead to that race hatred when the victim of what is in fact a diseased imagination pictures his womenfolk being raped by Negroes or himself being dominated by designing Jews. The problem of war will be discussed elsewhere, but it is worth while noting here that one of the main reasons why warfare occurs is that for masses of frustrated people it is the most obvious way out of their frustrations; in fact, if we do not exactly *want* wars there are millions who *need* them. Freud pointed out the apparent paradox that a nation is never so much at peace within itself as when it is fighting an external enemy, from which it follows that countries which have long been living peacefully with their neighbours will have more aggression to direct inwardly. That this contains more than a grain of truth is evinced by the high suicide rate in such countries as Sweden and Switzerland, and Jung, himself a Swiss, referring to the peculiar bitterness of Swiss internal politics, made the remark that his people had " introverted war ".

But there are some people in whom any self-assertive or aggressive manifestations have been so thoroughly repressed that they are permitted hardly any expression even in the forms described above; such individuals are as embarrassed and anxious at the least sign of anger or self-assertion in quite normal circumstances as the prude is upset by things with a sexual connotation which the ordinary person simply does not notice. When this occurs the only possible solution is to *introject* the aggression (*i.e.*, turn it against the self), and this leads to severe states of depression—which is really self-hatred—to actual suicide, or to psychosomatic disorders such as high blood-pressure brought about by prolonged stress. Finally, it must be remembered that suicide is not the only form of self-destruction, that chronic alcoholism, drug addiction, accident-proneness, and other conditions are often unconscious attempts to walk slowly or rapidly along the road to death and failure, resulting from inwardly-directed aggression. These are, of course, states that *may* be brought about by introjection, though since different people have different levels of tolerance and stamina they do not invariably occur; what we can safely say is that, as aggression in its original aspect is a manifestation of the drive towards self-assertion and self-realisation, its repression will *inevitably* lead to impoverishment and inadequacy of the personality.

### 4. THE FIVE AGES OF MAN.

Disregarding Shakespeare's account of the seven ages of man, we shall describe for the sake of convenience a mere five: childhood, adolescence, the period during which we can still hopefully expect to be described as a young bachelor or married couple, middle age, and old age. Each of these age groups has its own special problems, so it is necessary to observe the process of development and the satisfactions and difficulties arising at each stage whilst remembering that many, if not most, of these difficulties arise in a social context and cannot be usefully considered in terms of the non-existent isolated individual. For example, though we in the West commonly (and not without justice) regard adolescence as a period of ' storm and stress ', this is not the case in other societies, and therefore must be regarded as a socially-conditioned phenomenon. But since most people tend to regard their particular problems as unique and ' inside ' themselves, some of these will be mentioned here, whilst in Part II other problems will be discussed and it will become evident that, in fact, *all personal problems are also social problems.*

The childhood years are the formative years and what we later become can only be discussed in their light; furthermore, the child only experiences society indirectly through the medium of the family and, initially at least, is the only true individualist until moulded into the image of society. What we have so far been discussing are the basic principles of dynamic psychology without which none of the rest of this section could be understood. Whilst the problems of the child are to some extent peculiar to the particular family even when it acts under social pressures, those of the other age groups result from interaction at first hand with society. The difficulties of the other age groups are not *related* to society, but in large measure *created* by society. So, whilst adolescence, young married life or bachelorhood, and old age have their problems, they cannot usefully be discussed outside their social context and properly belong to Part II. How true this is will be shown in what follows.

### THE CHILD.

A child is described as an *infant* from one month until he is able to walk at fifteen or sixteen months, a *toddler* from fifteen months to the age of 2½, a *preschool* child from 2½ years to 5 or 6 years, and a *child in middle years* from 6 to about 12 years. About the latter period he has, with fairly wide variation, reached *physical* maturity, but it is not until the end of adolescence that he has reached *social* maturity. He can follow a moving object with his eyes at about 4 weeks, control his head about 16, grasp and manipulate objects at about 28, crawl and sit about 40, and stand and move around at 52 weeks or slightly later. But it is important for parents to recognise that although all children grow up in the same way, they do so at different rates. You cannot *teach* a child to walk; it will do so when it is ready, *i.e.*, when it has reached that stage of controlled movement.

## Parental Behaviour and its Effects on the Personality of the Child.

Something has already been said about the way in which the personality develops and there is good evidence that important traits have arisen long before the child is able to speak or understand speech; whether he tends to be tolerant of himself and others is probably determined in the first six months of life. Then, and even after acquiring speech, he responds more to what the parent is than to what she (because at that time it is the mother who is the important person) deliberately tries to inculcate. For example, a nervous and tense mother or one who secretly dislikes the process of breast-feeding cannot help but convey these impressions to the child through body tensions and the adequacy or otherwise of the flow of milk. The two problems facing the infant at the breast are, first, that it is unable to foresee the future and so it takes some time before it comes to learn that its hunger and thirst will sooner or later be reliably appeased; second, that its emotions are of the all-or-none type which it is not yet able to deal with and therefore even momentary frustration of its needs brings about outbursts of uncontrollable rage. In short, it alternates between states of satisfaction and fury, and the latter are so frightening that it may *introject* them (in which case it feels that there is something ' bad ' inside itself) or *project* them against the frustrating breast or mother (in which case it will feel that mother is ' bad ').

## The Mature Personality.

All of us employ both of these mechanisms to deal with infantile aggression and what we later become is influenced by which one predominated; there is at one extreme the type of person who, when things go wrong, tends to feel ' I am bad ' and at the other the type who will tend to blame others. The former will develop the sort of conscience based upon fear of having disappointed or hurt something that is loved (*i.e.*, will have humanitarian attitudes), the latter will have the sort of conscience based upon fear of punishment (*i.e.*, he will have authoritarian attitudes). As we shall see in more detail later, both of these extremes are undesirable; for it cannot be too often emphasised that the fully mature personality is one whose relationships are neither self-denying nor denying the rights of others but one *based on mutual acceptance and respect*. The man or woman who denies his or her own rights as an individual and becomes dedicated to ' helping ' others merely in order to assuage personal guilt-feelings is just as abnormal as the one who projects his ' bad ' emotions into the outer world; neither is motivated by anything better than a neurotic attempt to solve personal tensions. Genuinely helpful people are motivated by that overflow of love for humanity which can only arise from love and respect for themselves and that, as we have seen, comes from the experience of deep and satisfying parental affection in childhood.

## The Neurotic Personality.

The effects upon the personality of over-strict bowel control have already been mentioned and this sort of parental behaviour leads to the obsessional type of basic personality structure

shown in some of the peoples of northern Europe where the approved attitudes are seriousness, hard work, punctuality, acquisitiveness, authoritarian-submissiveness (*i.e.*, a heirachy in which one does not mind being kicked so long as there is an inferior who can be kicked in return), and repressed aggression manifesting itself in a superficial sentimentality or the search for a scapegoat. Heinrich Himmler, whilst responsible for the murder of six million Jews, was also a leader in the society for prevention of cruelty to animals in Germany. In southern Europe, on the other hand, where parents are more lenient in this respect, the general attitude is easy-going, impulsive, warm, and not over-concerned about the passage of time. It is true that many Latins are indifferent to animals, but they have no need (as in some other countries) for a society for the prevention of cruelty to children. It should hardly be necessary to repeat that nobody asserts (*a*) that all people who are kind to animals are necessarily motivated by a ' gentleness ' which is merely a cover-up for concealed sadism, since many of them are just naturally gentle people to man and beast alike; nor (*b*) is it asserted that there is necessarily an inverse relationship between the degree of affection shown to animals and that shown to people. Obviously the ideal is to be kind to both. But nobody who uses his eyes can fail to see that some people love animals to the exclusion of human beings and that many gentlewomen who are good to their cats are very vocal in informing us that they would " beat a man to death " for whipping a horse, and regular in their attendance at conferences where motions are proposed for bringing back the birch and re-imposing capital punishment. Of course, they are perfectly entitled to these views; but they are certainly not entitled to regard themselves as kind and loving or opposed to aggression. Such people are merely displacing the affection normally felt for their fellow men on to animals as a substitute object, or displacing their aggression from its true cause in their personal frustrations towards other substitute objects which happen to be the socially accepted scapegoats of society.

## Sexual Development.

Just as ' aggression ' has a general application signifying life-energy or drive and the narrower and more common application meaning hatred or anger, so the word ' sex ' has a general and a particular meaning. The former is more or less synonymous with ' desire ' and this type of sexuality is present from birth, manifesting itself first in the pleasure of sucking where the source of pleasure is the mouth, later in the interest in bowel motions which children experience during the ' house-training ' period, and subsequently in the more overtly sexual feelings of the young boy towards his mother and the young girl towards her father at the Œdipus stage. At this stage, about the age of five or six years, the child becomes interested in its sexual organs—though even quite young babies often show a similar interest. All these stages of immature sexuality are described as ' autoerotic ' because the main object of love is the self and other people are seen in terms of the degree to which they satisfy or frustrate the child's self-love. Masturbation is natural at this time and later attitudes to sex will be strongly influenced by parental attitudes of permissiveness or severe prohibition since the latter may cause the individual throughout life to feel that sex is something ' dirty ' and ' sinful '—a belief which has ruined many a married life. The question of masturbation in later life will be dealt with when adolescence is discussed.

With the passing of the Œdipus stage, the adult conscience begins to develop on the foundations already laid in the early months of life and the parents' values are internalised as the ' still small voice '. However, it must not be thought that this is the whole of conscience because it is still primitive and in later life continues to develop with the formation of an ' ego-ideal ' when we consciously try to imitate the behaviour of those we admire and respect. With puberty the sexual drive becomes directed towards the other sex and the child is physically mature, but this level is preceded by a homosexual phase in which the object of love belongs to the same sex. This does not mean that overt homosexual behaviour necessarily occurs, though it is not infrequent, and according to the Kinsey report, the majority of American males reported such experiences, but in this country its most obvious manifestation is the 'crushes' felt by schoolgirls towards attractive teachers or senior girls and the similar behaviour among boys when they admire other schoolboy friends and think girls silly. However, what actually happens depends upon social factors; homosexuality is common in public schools whether overtly or in a more sublimated form, and much less frequent among those who have been lucky enough to be reared in a more natural environment where extreme segregation of the sexes does not occur.

Thus the course of sexual development is a gradually moving away from self-love (autoerotic), by way of love of someone of the same sex (homosexual), towards the wholly other (heterosexual). But since nobody completely leaves behind all the manifestations of the various stages through which he has passed, everyone has homosexual and autoerotic elements in his or her personality.

### The Subjective Life of the Child: Fantasies.

No child can avoid the various conflicting situations which are part of the process of growing up from infancy to puberty and after; for, to take the more superficial difficulties first, every child must feel small and helpless in the great world of adults, feel jealous of older brothers or sisters, and even more so of the new baby who intrudes upon his supremacy in his parents' attention, just as the new baby will later feel a particular need to clamour for attention in face of the existing competition.

Now these are some of the situations that are dramatised in fairy-tales and the ancient myths (which have been described as the "dreams of a people"), and form part of much great literature and art. Whilst an obvious function of art is its aesthetic aspect when the artist creates something of beauty, it has another function which Aristotle describes as 'catharsis' (*see also* I6)—that is, by moving people to pity, love, or terror, it helps them to discharge emotional tensions and even to resolve their conflicts by enabling them to see that their individual problem is part of the whole human situation, and by pointing out reassuring solutions. Thus art is a form of psychotherapy and, of course, is often deliberately used to that end in the treatment of mental illness. Keeping at the superficial level, it is easy to see that two very pervasive and readily interpreted themes in fairy-tales are the giant-killer theme which reassures the child that the frequently awe-inspiring 'giants' of the adult world are capable of being dealt with and have their weaknesses, and the theme which pictures the youngest son as the 'hero' who accomplishes all the tasks the older brothers have failed in and wins the hand of the fairy princess. But at a much deeper level there lies a darker and more sinister set of fantasies shared by all of us in a world peopled by demons, witches with iron teeth who devour children, the wicked stepmother who wishes to poison her lovely stepdaughter, all of which are depicted in such tales as 'Hansel and Gretel', 'Snow-white', 'Rumplestiltskin', and the rest. The great Greek plays centre around such incredible plots as that of King Œdipus who kills his father and marries his mother, or Princess Electra who connives at the death of her mother who had murdered her father Agamemnon (*see* H24), and the myths of all countries tell of infants born out of the mouth or navel, of castration, incest, and milder stories such as that of the unknown child reared by simple folk who turns out to be of royal blood.

These horror-comic themes, in short, are universal not because some eccentric invented them but *because we have all experienced them in real life.* The child unsatisfied at the breast has fantasies of devouring the breast and, when these are projected, they reappear as the mother who wishes to devour the child; the mother in one stage of infancy is divided into the good satisfying mother and the bad devouring one, the former becoming the 'fairy godmother' and the latter the witch or

evil 'stepmother'. Shakespeare's *Hamlet*, incidentally, is a good example of this mechanism father's possession of his mother but, being unable to accept that the father he also loved could be hated, the wicked uncle-stepfather is made to bear the hated side; psychologically speaking, the bad stepfather and the good murdered father are different aspects of the same person and Hamlet has projected his own incestuous desires for his mother upon the stepfather. Many children quite consciously have the feeling that their mother is not their true parent and that they have more exalted origins. This necessity to think in terms of a good parent and a bad one is later replaced by the realisation that there is simply one individual who is sometimes lovable and sometimes hateful and this ambivalence, *i.e.*, having mixed feelings for the same person, is a step towards maturity though later it will be replaced by a more discriminating picture of goodness and badness based, not on how people react to us in satisfying or unsatisfying terms, but on more objective standards.

There are two main conclusions to be drawn from this analysis of the fantasies of the child:

(1) that children are far from 'innocent' in the Victorian sense and have experienced far greater horrors in their own minds than can be introduced from outside. They enjoy, for example, Grimm's fairy-tales because *in an atmosphere of security* at the mother's knee or by the nursery fireside, their conflicts are objectified and the story has a satisfying ending which helps to resolve them.

(2) that the normal child is the ambivalent child who has received enough sense of security from its parents to be able to express openly its alternate affection and resentment which, beginning at an early age, becomes increasingly evident as it grows older when a conflict arises between the need for dependency and its ever-increasing need for independence and self-realisation. Large-scale studies have shown beyond shadow of doubt that ambivalence is characteristic of the normal child; obedience, dependence, and unnatural 'goodness' or compliance are characteristic of the neurotic child; and complete lack of feeling is typical of the potential delinquent.

### ADOLESCENCE.

Adolescence is manifestly brought about by physical changes in the body due to changes in the sex and other glands such as the pituitary and the adrenal glands on top of the kidneys. Obvious bodily developments begin to take place: menstruation, the development of the breasts, and the increasingly rounded contours of the figure in girls, the breaking of the voice, development of the muscles, and the production of semen in boys, together with the growth of the beard in boys and growth of hair under the armpits and in the genital region in both sexes. But even these manifestly organic changes are influenced by social factors, both psychological and nutritional, and within the present century the average height of each younger generation has increased and sexual maturity, particularly in girls, begins at an earlier age. Therefore, though these physiological reactions *started* the process, it is very important to avoid ascribing to adolescents in general features which are merely typical of our own and a few other societies. On the other hand, once they have been recognised as non-universal, it is still necessary to consider the characteristics of adolescence in the technologically advanced countries and try to discover their social causes.

### The Characteristics of Adolescence in the Technically Advanced Countries.

We can begin by taking two accounts of the traits said to be typical of the adolescent in America, one dating back to G. Stanley Hall in 1908, the other to E. B. Hurlock in 1953. Stanley

Hall's list includes (with particular reference to the immediately post-pubertal period): inner absorption and reverie; the birth of imagination, illusions, dreams, etc.; self-criticism, scruples; the over-assertion of individuality; a strong tendency to imitation; the assumption of dramatic poses, roles, affectations; folly, absurdities, freakishness; new speech consciousness; absorption in friendship; intense fluctuations in energy and emotional and intellectual plasticity. Hall likened the manifestations of adolescence to the symptoms of hysteria and insanity, and considered it a period particularly prone to religious conversion and other violent personality changes. Hurlock describes the emotional life of the adolescent as characterised by intensity, lack of control, inconsistency, prevalence of long-drawn-out emotions or moods, and the growth of such sentiments as patriotism, loyalty, and reverence.

## Comparison with Other Cultures.

Unfortunately both these catalogues of traits, and particularly that of Hall, show by the very language in which they are expressed the lack of sympathy which, in part, makes the adolescent what he or she is: freakish, given to absurdities, self-conscious about his speech, too individualistic and yet given to self-criticism, lack of control, and the rest. Yet, if some of the features mentioned are dated (e.g., proneness to religious conversion and patriotism are less common than they used to be) and others are obviously more typical of the middle- than the working-class adolescent, as a whole they are recognisably true of our society. That they are far from being true of all, or even many, societies is shown by Margaret Mead's study of Samoa where adolescence brings about no conflict or revolt and no neurotic worries; all children from the earliest age have freely engaged in sexual play and, on the arrival of puberty, the girl engages in a series of affairs with the boys of the community each of which is short-lasting. There are no rules which allow members of certain age-groups definite rights and privileges and in this respect nobody may progress faster than anybody else. So far as sex is concerned, the adults are perfectly well aware of what is going on and make no criticisms nor attempt to interfere in any way.

If one looks behind the lists of traits supposedly typical of the adolescent in our society, it will be found that they can all be compressed into a few fundamental problems or conflicts: there is the quest for identity, the answer to the question, " Who am I? "; the exaggeration of the conflict between dependency and self-sufficiency; and, if frequently the subject of prurient interest on the part of certain adults, the rather less significant sexual problems which do not actually arise at this time, though there is more opportunity to accept or refuse approaches from the other sex, to engage or not to engage in overtly sexual affairs.

## No Fixed Rules.

The adolescent in our society is in a confused and precarious position. His childish behaviours are no longer adequate or tolerated and the apparently secure and settled ways of the adult have not yet been learned—in short, he is playing a game with no fixed rules. Now this is not so elsewhere, nor was it always so here; in mediæval society everyone had a fixed role to play according to age, sex, and social status just as in Samoa, and even just prior to the last war few problems of this sort bothered the middle-class child. A girl was a girl until she left school, possibly at the age of eighteen or more; a boy was a boy until he went to university or started in a job. This, indeed, is still the case in less sophisticated societies where a boy becomes a man at a specific age and the occasion is marked by initiation rites following which he *knows* that he is a man with full adult rights. In many European peasant communities one can tell an individual's position from his (or her) dress: the unmarried girl, the widow, the bachelor, the married couple, all have sartorial indications of their state. Today none of this exists in the technically developed countries: according to traditional morality, sexual intercourse is forbidden before marriage (at least to girls) and yet the period between the attainment of sexual maturity and the possibility of marriage increases for those who wish to advance themselves. There are no fixed rules regarding the age at which certain privileges are automatically obtained; for example, one piece of research showed that in a suburb in a large American city the age at which parents permitted their daughters to go out unaccompanied varied from fourteen to twenty. The law decides when children may buy cigarettes, parents make their own widely differing regulations and it is understandable that those who see this behaviour permitted in others of their own age-group will feel deprived and embarrassed if it is forbidden to themselves.

## Moral Standards,

The period at which an adolescent ceases to be a child and becomes an adult not only varies widely in general but even varies in relation to specific activities; it is possible to be a ' child ' in one field and an ' adult ' in others. Hence the adolescent's search for identity, role-playing, imitation of heroes or pop-singers of his own age, self-searching, and resentment of adults. The latter is increased by the ardent moving away from childhood status towards self-realisation as the individual interprets it, and both lead to adolescent assertion, aggressiveness, and the feeling that he is not ' understood '. Nor is he understood, because technical progress and the changes it has brought about in social patterns make even the young parent useless as a model for youth to follow—there is an ever-increasing gap between the generations who cannot understand that each is literally living in a different world and the old rules of even twenty years ago are not always applicable now. Sexual behaviour is as much a sign of revolt and defiance as of genuine sexuality, and having a sexual affair is often regarded as a status-symbol just as smoking in school was a status-symbol before the war. Modern youth is much more knowledgeable about sex than formerly (though still not sufficiently instructed) and therefore less prone to genuinely sexual conflicts than previous generations. Few indeed worry about masturbation, that object of baseless terror to their parents; for they know that it is largely universal and entirely harmless. Of course, many moralists regard it as wicked as they are perfectly entitled to do, but that it is harmless is a medical *fact* which they are not entitled to query. Indeed, the main cause of excessive masturbation is not overdeveloped sexuality but anxiety brought about by threats of this sort.

## Good Morals begin with Right Attitudes to Others.

The trouble about sexual morality is that, though some may believe that there are certain fixed standards which determine what is ' right ' or ' wrong ' in this field—and it is impossible to contradict them because this is not a matter science can usefully discuss—in reality all moral standards have varied widely from one place or time to another. It is clear that the basic revolution brought about by Jesus Christ was a realisation that good morals begin with right *attitudes* to other people and cannot be codified in a fixed set of rules that tell people what they must *not* do, and we have given numerous examples from modern psychology to show that when people do the ' right ' thing for the wrong reason they are not likely to be successful in achieving their goal. Saint Augustine put it even more bluntly when he said: " Love God and do what you like "—or as some might say, " If you genuinely care for other people in their own right you can't go far wrong."

## ADULTHOOD AND MATURITY.

### Psychological Maturity.

It is evident that society decides when a person shall be regarded as adult and that, on the whole, this bears little relationship to biological maturity —much less to psychological maturity which is achieved by few. Among the qualities which are the signs of psychological maturity one must take into account:

(1) Emotional control, which implies that the truly adult person has to learn to defer immediate gratification of his wishes or expressions of his feelings which must become subject to his total way of life—he will learn that it is not worth while giving way momentarily to a form of behaviour which will only be followed by shame or is likely to ruin all that he has regarded as his highest ideals.

(2) The appropriateness of his emotions—that is to say that, broadly speaking, a mature person's emotional responses are objectively relevant to the actual situation facing him and his expression of feelings shows an awareness of those of others. The problem of achieving emotional maturity is not solved by stamping out or denying emotions, however strong or unpleasant they may be; it is a problem of learning to live with emotions, keeping them within reasonable bounds, and of turning them, whenever possible, to the ends of survival of ourselves and others in this complicated world.

(3) The richness and variety of experience, whereby the all-or-none emotions of the infant become highly differentiated, varying from righteous anger or disgust, to wry amusement and the most subtle æsthetic pleasures. Unfortunately most of us, partly from psychological distortions arising in childhood and partly from lack of stimulation from the environment such as inadequate education, never wholly reach this stage and it is obvious that some of the greatest geniuses, whilst adding to our own capacity for æsthetic pleasures, still remained emotionally childish —not with the *child-like* simplicity of a poet such as Blake, but often with the vicious childishness of the antisemitic Wagner or the woman-obsessed yet woman-terrified Strindberg.

Most people are immature in various ways and must simply try to make the best of things and it is probably true to say that many lives of quiet desperation. Marriage takes place for the wrong reasons because of modern society's obsession with sex and its failure to see that sex without comradeship, compatibility of temperament, and the appreciation and respect due to a partner who is a human being in his or her own right, is bound to fail. Men marry women sometimes as lovely status-symbols, sometimes as mother-substitutes, and sometimes as someone to boss for the lack of any other means of expressing their power obsessions—yet, strangely enough, marriage survives and perhaps has never been in a stronger position as a social institution. But, again, society determines the form of marriage and the structure of the family and exerts pressures upon it for good or ill that must be considered later. Even when the change of life, which is biologically conditioned, makes its appearance in the course of time how it is experienced is socially influenced. Like adolescence, it may become a period of storm and stress, or, on the other hand, the prelude to a contented retirement with enhanced powers of enjoyment both sexual and æsthetic; its connection with cultural factors is demonstrated even within the bounds of our own country where serious depressive states in middle age are much commoner in the more puritanical north than in the more permissive south.

## OLD AGE.

### Biological Factors.

Anyone can see that not only do the signs of old age come on at very varying times, being sometimes relatively early and in other cases hardly apparent at all even in advanced years, but also that, when the signs do come, they assume a form which is the same for all peoples and at all places. This is because old age, like puberty and the change of life but even more so, is brought about by basically biological factors. These include glandular changes, though the most obvious results of senility arise from a deterioration of the substance of the brain caused either by a primary degeneration of the cells in the nervous tissues or a secondary degeneration which produces the same result by reducing their blood supply when ageing arteries become hardened and narrow. The effects of these changes can be summarised by saying that senile deterioration leads in varying degrees to memory changes such that memory for recent events is poor whilst that for long past events is usually retained or even emphasised and dwelt on; that the individual tends to become emotionally unstable and, for example, more easily moved to tears; and that there may be apparent changes in personality.

### Social Influences.

These changes are more apparent than real, for what actually happens is that, with the deterioration of the higher centres of control, features such as jealousy, greed, or meanness, which have hitherto been kept under control, are released. In other words, the senile person ' becomes himself, only more so'. But even in the presence of such changes as are clearly due to biological factors, social influences are very much in evidence —for example, in our form of society where old people are often regarded as a problem or a nuisance, it is hardly surprising that they tend to become suspicious, irritable, and self-centred.

Technical change has brought a situation in which, unlike that in the old peasant or agrarian community, old people and schoolchildren, up to quite a later age, are unproductive. Whereas in the changing rural communities of today and even in the old East End of London, the grandparents played an important part in the life of the community, looking after the grandchildren whilst their mother and father were at work, advising their own children about matters in which their long life had given them the experience to guide, and acting as the respected elders of the village or suburban group, they now find themselves unwanted. The younger generation is moved out to satellite towns whilst the old people are left behind, alone and lost in a world they no longer understand. What seemed to be eternal verities have gone, and these are needs that even the best treatment in an old people's home cannot satisfy.

Here is another clear example of a biological problem which is also a personal one and at the same time very much a social one to be solved not by charity and misplaced sympathy but by the understanding that comes from a combination of science and caring which are more closely related than is always realised. As Leonardo da Vinci wrote in his ' Treatise on Painting ': " In truth great love springs from great knowledge of the beloved object, and if you know it but little you will be able to love it only a little or not at all." Or in the language of Freud, even the most abstract study of the universe requires that the object of our study should be invested with the love we have projected upon it; when hate is projected hate is what is reflected back and we understand nothing.

# II. SOCIETY

In past editions this section gave information on some aspects of social anthropology. In this edition Section F has been expanded to include a new chapter on the Sciences of Man, covering both physical and social anthropology. The reader is therefore asked to turn first to Section F, Part V.

## 1. SOCIETY AND CULTURE.

A society is a more or less permanent group of people living together and sharing a common way of life and common attitudes and beliefs. Its culture is the name given to this way of life. The people who make a special study of different cultures are known as social anthropologists and when they first began to take their work seriously and carry out field studies by living among the people they were studying, it was natural that they should choose primitive tribes as being the most convenient because (at any rate at that time, from the beginning of the present century to just before the last war) there were many of these primitive groups which had lived in comparative isolation and therefore showed the culture in an almost unadulterated form. The culture had remained unchanged for many centuries, and among these people the social structure was much more rigid and easily defined than in the larger and more complex industrial societies. Nowadays, however, a social anthropologist may study any sort of culture, for example, a Yorkshire mining community, or a working-class community such as Dagenham.

## Basic Personality Structure of a Society.

Enough has already been said to show that there are great variations among different cultures as to what people consider ' normal ' behaviour and the different roles its members ought to play in relation to the rest. Culture not only imposes general beliefs which are expected to be shared by all members of a society (for example, its religion and mythology, or its economic and political system) but defines the part men and women must take in the division of labour or rearing the family together with accepted methods of doing so, and the rules children must follow in dealing with each other and their parents or elders. This results in what has been described as the ' basic personality structure ' of a society, the blueprint for parents to adopt when bringing up their children.

## Cultural Change.

Two important questions arise, the first is how the various cultures arose and took the particular form they did, the second is the problem of what makes cultures change. The answer to the first question is fairly simple; it is that each culture is a way of life suited to a particular group with certain historical traditions and adapted to a specific physical environment. It is both unconsciously and deliberately passed on from one generation to the next by specific methods of child rearing. " Systems of child training ", writes Erikson, " represent unconscious attempts at creating out of human raw material that configuration of attitudes which is (or once was) the optimum under the tribe's particular natural conditions and economic-historic necessities."

As will be seen in more detail later, the basic personality structure of Western Europe completely changed about the time of the Renaissance from a state of affairs in which conformity and a static social structure was the ideal to one which valued the most extreme expressions of individualism, personal aggrandisement, acquisitiveness, and social mobility. No living things are so variable as human beings and, though the existence of their innate needs explains why they *initiate* certain actions (*e.g.*, why they want to eat, drink, or obtain sexual satisfaction), it does not in any way explain *how* they do these things, why they sometimes do them when they do not wish to, or do not do them when they do wish to; biology becomes subservient to culture and even the most pressing physical needs may become secondary to social needs. Thus in an American town during the depression of the early 1930s, purchases of food declined markedly whilst petrol sales remained at the normal level—obviously the social prestige associated with running a car was more important to many impoverished citizens than having regular and satisfying meals.

## Technological Change.

Primarily, says W. F. Ogburn of Chicago, " the cause of social change is the making of inventions mechanical or otherwise, and secondarily, the diffusion of inventions already made." Whilst new *discoveries* are by their very nature quite original, *e.g.*, the discovery of how to make bronze (the first alloy known to man) from its constituent metals of copper and tin, was something entirely novel in man's history, new *inventions* are for the most part a combination of old elements—that is, they are dependent upon already-known principles. It follows that the more of such elements or principles existing in a particular culture the greater will be the number of possible new in-

ventions. So although a simple kind of steam-engine was devised by Hero of Alexandria (*fl.* A.D. 62) nearly two thousand years ago, it was of no practical use because before the steam-engine of the eighteenth century could be produced it was necessary to know about new ways of treating iron to make it harder, the principle of transmitting power from shaft to shaft and from one direction to another which involves knowledge of the toothed wheel or gear, the idea of vehicles travelling on rails, and many other elements. Today, even a complicated piece of machinery such as the electronic computer was readily put together by utilising and recombining a large number of elements and principles already known. Technical progress moves at an ever-increasing rate for just this reason, and as Ogburn has pointed out material culture grows according to the exponential principle, *i.e.*, like compound interest.

## The Social Effects of Technical Change.

Since culture is an attempt to adjust to a particular environment which is now almost entirely of our own making, it follows that the culture of modern society is an attempt to adjust to our man-made environment and reflects this material background, and also that, since the pace of development is rapidly increasing, adjustment becomes ever more difficult. This has been noted already in the gulf of understanding between generations; for even the most modern youth is barely adjusting to the changes of ten years earlier. The situation is very similar to that described by Karl Marx, who whatever one may think of his economic theories, was one of the greatest sociologists who ever lived. Marx described a substructure or *Unterbau* which he believed to be the economic system of a society, and pointed out that upon this is built the religious attitudes, ethics, laws, and institutions which form the *Oberbau* or superstructure of society. (*See* J27). In fact, the less a body of thought is subject to objective verification, the more is it likely to reflect the substructure of society which modern sociologists regard as its technology. Whilst science is comparatively culture-free, existing religious attitudes or philosophical systems or ethical beliefs are very strongly influenced in this way; for example, the Reformation (J38) was not brought about by Luther's distaste for the corruption of Rome, since movements dating back to the thirteenth century or earlier (the Waldenses (J45), the Albigenses (J2), and that led by Wyclif in England) had felt just the same—it happened *at that time* because Luther's ideas fitted in very well with new individualist attitudes resulting from the early stirrings of the industrial revolution and German nationalism. Again, slavery would have been abolished in America even if William Lloyd Garrison had never been born and *Uncle Tom's Cabin* had never been written; slavery disappeared because it was becoming useless as a means of production, just as it had previously been supported by moralists so long as it was useful. Reformers need to learn that one can rarely start a trend without pre-existing foundations, frequently accelerate one that already exists, but never reverse trends already moving in a particular direction in response to environmental pressures.

## The Stages of Cultural Change.

The development from technical changes to changes in the ideological superstructure takes place in four stages:

(1) The material invention or discovery.

(2) Changes in the economic and social structure.

(3) Changes in the other parts of the social structure.

(4) Change in cultural attitudes and popular ideology.

Let us take as an example the influence of the steam-engine on woman's position in society. First, the various types of steam-engine led to the development of more efficient and specialised power-driven machinery on the railroads, in the factory, and ultimately in the home; transport is made easier and therefore cities grow larger, industrial work is made lighter, and house-work less onerous. As a result of this the greater physical strength of men becomes less important in many forms of work and women become as efficient as men over a wider field; they are increasingly employed in industry, work becomes separated from home, and gradually there arises an improved standard of living, increased consumption, and a more easy-going attitude to life.

Changes in other parts of the social structure develop more slowly: the modern family is no longer an economic unit as in the agrarian society, and it is losing its rigid social control over its individual members whilst, as Folsom puts it, "elaborating other functions, most important of which is the more complete satisfaction of the love-wish, both with regard to marital and parent–child love". There is no longer one single accepted family-pattern, the patriarchal family, but wide variations from the mother-centred family to the egalitarian family and even the filiocentric family, so that power is no longer centred exclusively upon the father and the family is becoming more democratic. Of course, all these developments arose not from any single cause but were helped along by such other technical inventions as gas and subsequently electric lighting in the streets and home, the wider knowledge and use of contraceptives, and the mass media which (in one of their aspects) led to a wider and faster spreading of knowledge and a levelling in cultural standards.

### Cultural Lag.

Traditional attitudes and old ways of thinking, however, tend to persist much longer, largely because they are identified with values which are very deep-seated and any attempt to modify these is likely to be described as "a lowering of moral standards" or in such terms as "the moral crisis of our time". Of course, there is a moral crisis, but it is due not to change but precisely to the failure to change; it is caused by the 'cultural lag' between old attitudes and a new environment. Thus the so-called 'equality of the sexes' to which all but the least-enlightened pay lip-service is more nominal than real; for what has happened is that, whilst women have gained many new functions, they have lost few of their old ones. The girl who comes back from work at the factory is still expected to do some of the housework whilst her brother is not. There is even an attempt to drag women back to their more 'feminine' role with the appeal of cosmetic, fashion, and home-decoration advertising; papers of good standing intended for both sexes nevertheless have a special section for women as though they were social oddities in a way that men are not; and there is the tremendous number of women's magazines catering for all that is most infantile and written in a kind of baby-talk, stories of how the heroine succeeds in marrying her boss, columns dealing with how to dress, solving one's love-problems, and the rest. As Dr. Viola Klein says, the state of women at the present time is characterised by a dilemma, which is another of the many conflicts inherent in our present cultural situation. "It results from the contrast between a materially changed situation and the simultaneous survival of traditional ideologies and attitudes." One has only to think of the fuss made by many men teachers at any suggestion that women should get equal pay for equal work, to see how true this statement is.

### Cultural Change in the Underdeveloped Countries.

In the more technically backward societies, the impact of industrialisation and new mass-production techniques has been even more dramatic. Drucker has shown how "the sweep of mass-production technology is undermining and exploding societies and civilisations which have no resistance to the new forces, no background or habit-pattern of industrial life to cushion the shock. In China the mass-production principle, swept into the hinterland from the coastal cities by the forced migration of industries during the Japanese invasion, is destroying the world's oldest and hither-

to its stablest institution: the Chinese family. In India industrialisation has begun to corrode the Hindu caste system: ritual restrictions on proximity and intercourse between castes simply cannot be maintained under factory conditions. In America the Old South, hitherto least touched by industry and still living in the ruins of its ante-bellum order is speedily being 'tractored off'. Indeed, conversion of the Southern farm into a rural assembly-line seems on the verge of 'solving' the Southern race problem in a manner never dreamed of by either Southern Liberal or Southern Reactionary: by pushing the Negro off the land into the industrial cities."

Whilst we in Britain have had ample time to adjust to the results of the industrial revolution and have not yet succeeded in completely doing so, the danger in these new societies is that what took more than two centuries here is being compressed into a matter of a few years with a consequent risk of serious conflict and the uprooting of old values with nothing to take their place. Unless social scientists work alongside technicians to ensure that social change is smooth, the persistence of traditional attitudes against a new material background may have dangerous results.

Since the end of the last war the introduction of modern medicine to Ceylon has halved the death-rate, largely by virtually wiping out malaria with drugs and DDT; it was reduced from 22 to 11 per thousand in less than ten years—but the birth-rate remains the same and, at the present rate, the population will more than double every 25 years. The failure to make psychological adjustments to situations of this sort has resulted in the great benefits made possible by science in the form of better health, better nutrition and higher standards of living being nullified as quickly as they are being developed.

All over the world man's greed has led, in the words of Julian Huxley, to the despoiling of nature at an appalling rate. "Wildlife is being exterminated; forests are being cut down, mountains gashed by hydroelectric projects, wildernesses plastered with mine shafts and tourist camps, fields and meadows stripped away for roads and airports." Processes such as these are not planned with a view to the greater benefit of people in general but motivated by a blind and stupid acquisitiveness. *See also* G25.

## 2. THE MODERN SOCIETY.

The large-scale modern society differs from the primitive societies in some important respects which will now be discussed.

### The Social Structure: Sub-cultures.

The social structure of modern society is much more complex due to the existence of class differences, regional groupings, and different racial and religious or political groups within the national boundaries. These are described as sub-cultures and require to be considered separately against the overall culture of the state. Thus, though all Britons share some attitudes in common which can be described as the national character, a Roman Catholic Briton does not share all the values of a Protestant one; a middle-class Briton has very different attitudes to many things compared with a working-class one; and a Yorkshireman differs culturally from a Welshman. It is necessary to understand this when we are trying to unravel the causes of racial disturbances, industrial unrest, and other problems in which there are two opposed groups failing to communicate because they are simply not talking the same language and see the same events in a totally different light. We must repeat, too, that national character is not fixed nor is it innate, but like other constellations of traits has social and historical roots.

### Rapid Social Change and Social Status.

Another respect in which modern society differs from primitive societies is the rapidity of social change which leads to the discrepancy between old traditions and present realities with results which have already been discussed. In a society of rapid change social status is not only subject to fluctuation as the individual moves up or down a scale created by extreme social mobility, but quite often status is not (as it is in more primitive groups) very clearly defined, and this leads to feelings of insecurity. Since social status is a kind of transference of the child's need for maternal approval towards the need for the approval of society in later life, we can say that the desire for status is one of the most fundamental of human drives and its absence or loss is a common precipitating factor in neurosis.

In the first part of this section we saw how many of the individual's attitudes are derived from the groups to which he belongs, and it is these which are his main source of status, from the small, primary, informal groups such as the family, the play-group, the work-group, the group of village elders, the group of housewives who regularly meet for a cup of coffee, to the large and more impersonal secondary institutions which confer formal status, e.g., the army, the professions, industry, the churches, and so on. If the primary groups break up, status is in peril.

## The Sick Society Concept.

Now, in the view of some authorities, this is just what is happening. The old primary groupings are allegedly disintegrating in what has become a mass society, and the family, the working group, the village council, are being replaced by huge anonymous bodies in relation to which personal status, useful function, and individual significance are lost. It is further claimed that more than any previous society ours is one which persistently stimulates people's desires without being able to satisfy them, and that it is based on conflicting ideals which the individual finds it impossible to reconcile. Whilst accepting the two latter statements with reservations, the present writer, for reasons to be discussed elsewhere, does not wholly accept the first. Nevertheless it is obvious that many supposedly personal conflicts are really imposed upon us by society, and the psychoanalyst Karen Horney believed that the conflicts found in the neuroses are simply a microcosm of social conflicts. From such considerations as these has arisen the concept of the 'sick society', elaborated on by Halliday in this country and Frank in America, which suggests that since all our most pressing problems are simply facets of a more fundamental problem lying at the very heart of modern society, they can be dealt with constructively only at the social level. Certainly we are made what we are by social pressures, but as individuals we have to learn to live with these pressures and in what follows an attempt will be made to show that individual responsibility must still play a part and that we personally can do something to help ourselves.

The sick society concept is both true and useful and, practically speaking, it does three things:

(1) It makes us realise that it is not profitable to try to help people by blaming them and that an additional reason for not doing so is that society (which is another name for ourselves) has played some part in making them what they are. One has only to think of the many moralists who have supported prostitution in the past because it upheld the 'sanctity' of the family, maintained the 'purity' of the middle-class girl, and reduced what might otherwise have resulted in emotional tensions.

(2) It makes us realise that our own problems, if often peculiar, are never unique.

(3) It helps not only in discovering what these problems are but, by revealing their social background, enables us to see them more constructively, less uncharitably, and points to possible solutions.

If we recall Jung's case of the Quaker who could not imagine that he had ever done anything wrong, yet whose son became a thief and his daughter a prostitute, we may see therein a parable showing how the respectable members of society are not guiltless of creating juvenile delinquency and prostitution because those who engage in these

activities represent the dark aspects of society and act as our scapegoats. In a perfectly real sense, we are enabled to remain ' good ' because they are ' bad '.

## 3. THE FAMILY.

### Family Conflicts.

The original family was the extended family of agrarian communities which included not only both pairs of grandparents but also various uncles and aunts and assorted relatives. It was an economic unit in which throughout life each member had a useful part to play; moreover being large, family tensions were less prolonged if often no less acute than in the family of today.

The modern family is usually small because children, until they go to work, and the old who have finished working, are economic liabilities, but this very smallness leads to more intense and chronic disagreements. In his 1967 Reith Lectures, *A Runaway World*, Dr. Edmund Leach, social anthropologist and Provost of King's College, Cambridge, said the modern family looked inward upon itself. There was an intensification of emotional stress between husband and wife, parents and children. " The strain is greater than most of us can bear. Far from being the basis of the good society, the ' family,' with its narrow privacy and tawdry secrets is the source of all our discontents." Children, he said, need to grow up in larger, more relaxed domestic groups centred on the community rather than on the mother's kitchen. Other sources of difficulty arising from without the family are modern society's obsession with commercial sex which incessantly stimulates desire whilst conventional morals deny it outlet, and the no less stupid obsession with the achievement of complete sexual satisfaction as a necessity for a happy marriage. Working mothers in addition to their other worries are told by reputable psychiatrists that by going out to work they are turning their children into potential delinquents; many men still refuse to recognise the changing role of women in society and attempt to reverse the trend by reverting to the ' baby doll ' image of womanhood; the ' housebound housewife ' feels the boredom that only increases with affluence. All these are real problems yet it is undoubtedly true that at no time has the British family been so stable and so mature in its relationships. We hear about the failures because they are newsworthy and most widely discussed by experts and, as Michael Young and Peter Willmott have shown in their study of the family in Bethnal Green, all that is written about broken marriages, juvenile delinquency, child neglect, and problem families has " created an impression that working-class families are disunited, unsocial, and unhappy ".

### The Present Status of the Family.

We have no space to discuss the fallacies involved in this belief, but perhaps this is best done by quoting from two of the most detailed accounts of current attitudes towards the family: the study mentioned above on working-class attitudes, *Family and Kinship in East London*, and Gorer's more inclusive book, *Exploring English Character*. Of the modern working-class family Young and Willmott write: " (Our) impressions suggest that the old style of working-class family is fast disappearing . . . in place of the old comes a new kind of companionship between man and woman, reflecting the rise in status of the young wife and children which is one of the great transformations of our time. There is now a nearer approach to equality between the sexes and, though each has a peculiar role, its boundaries are no longer so rigidly defined nor is it performed without consultation."

In a survey which covered all classes in England, Gorer discovered that half the married population of the country have had no sexual relationships either before or after marriage with anyone else but their spouse, and continues: " What seems to me most noteworthy is the high seriousness with which the great majority of English people approach and regard marriage. Whether premarital experience is advocated or reprobated, the effect on the future marriage is the preponderating consideration. Secondly, the high valuation put on virginity for both sexes is remarkable and I should suspect specifically English." Neither sex pays any appreciable heed to the aesthetic qualities of the other, and when asked to give their opinions on the factors making for happiness in marriage most people mentioned " give and take, understanding, love, mutual trust, equanimity, sexual compatibility, comradeship, a decent income, mutual interests, happy home life, and no money difficulties." One of the biggest surprises in this study was the small number of people who thought that infidelity was a significant cause of marital unhappiness, and most believed that adultery " should not terminate the marriage (if that can possibly be avoided) and does not justify the wronged spouse in adopting violent or aggressive behaviour". This view was accepted by more than half the men and nearly three-quarters of the women. Furthermore, as Gorer says, " there is at least as much tendency to blame oneself for a spouse's dereliction as to blame or punish the offending spouse." He suggests that such attitudes imply a relatively low valuation of ' love' and a very high estimation of the institution of marriage, and concludes: " (I) have I hope illustrated the great importance for English men and women of the institution of marriage and the seriousness with which they consider it. It is marriage itself which is important, not, I think, love or sexual gratification; and marriage is living together, making a home together, making a life together, and raising children. Perhaps even more for Englishmen than for English women, parenthood is the greatest joy and greatest responsibility of adult life."

## The Married Couple.

There is therefore ample reason to suppose that most married couples in this country are reasonably satisfied with their own lot even if the new society has also given rise to problems. Here we are going to discuss some of those involved in the husband–wife relationship, and it is convenient to do so under the three headings of personal relationships, sex, and work. But before going into details, it is important to consider what exactly is meant by ' happiness ', the goal towards which most people seem to be so fervently striving. Indeed, the word ' striving' sums up very clearly what ' happiness' implies; it is, as one psychologist has said, " the state of going someplace ". A person is happy when he or she has certain goals which they are on the way towards achieving, no matter how slowly or with what difficulty. Happiness means movement towards, and the pleasure is in the moving rather than in the achieving—which sometimes comes as rather a disappointment. When the philosopher Schopenhauer said that the lot of man must inevitably be a wretched one because he could only be happy in relation to a previous state of comparative unhappiness, he was perhaps being unduly pessimistic but at the same time he was expressing a profound truth: that there is no absolute happiness, but only happiness *in relation to how we felt before*. Thus a crust to a starving man provides more pleasure than another million pounds to a millionaire.

This was strikingly illustrated in a social survey in the United States where many people of all income-groups were asked by what percentage their annual income would require to be increased in order to make them entirely satisfied. The result showed that *all* income-groups produced practically the same figure; both the fifty-dollar-a-week man and the five-hundred-a-week man agreed that an increase of 25 per cent would be adequate. People talk glibly of the ' essentials of life' or the ' basic essentials ', but there is, of course, no such thing; what we already have are the basic essentials for us and we usually want a little more. No amount of affluence can make us happy because happiness is a state of striving for more—it may be more money, more household appliances, more children, more rooms and space or more knowledge and virtue, but it is always more of something. Happiness is quite different from contentment which is a state of not wanting, of being satisfied with what we already have, and it is probable that static communities such as

the so-called ' backward' countries or the Europe of the Middle Ages contain more contented people because they can move neither up nor down the social scale nor very easily change their position geographically. Doctors and psychiatrists see plenty of people who ' only ' want happiness when what they really mean is that they want peace of mind (which is contentment) or that they want happiness but are not prepared to accept that, since this involves striving, it also means the acceptance of much pain and frustration and hard work. Those who think that happiness is something they are *entitled* to—as the Welfare State or the Affluent Society often leads them to believe— had better think again; the *means* to contentment, yes, the *right* to happiness, no. Men or women who set their aim far above what they are humanly likely to achieve should remember the equation which reads: expectation minus realisation equals neurosis.

## Personal Relationships in Marriage.

Now this applies with particular force to marriage; for those who have been dazzled by silly romantic stories or commercial advertising into thinking that they are entering a state of undiluted bliss, and, if that fails, there is always a new washing machine to create happiness by lightening their labour, are living in a fool's paradise. Marriage is a constant struggle throughout life to become more mature, better adjusted to one's partner, more tolerant, but above all it is a constant process of education in human relationships. Maturity has already been defined as a state in which relationships are neither self-denying nor denying the rights of others but based on mutual acceptance and respect, and this is the key to satisfaction in marriage. Nobody is more pathetic and in the end, more distasteful, than the mother who is continually telling her husband or her children or her own mother how she has ' sacrificed herself ' for them; for in doing so she is either demonstrating her own insincerity (since what one gives up *willingly* for the sake of others is not a sacrifice any more than it is a sacrifice for a man to give up his game of darts at the local in order to give more attention to his pigeons or the new baby which he finds much more interesting), or revealing her masochism, her stupidity, and, almost always, her malice. What she really wants is to make the others feel dependent on her, to inflate her own ego, show her spite, or cause them to feel guilty. Nobody can usefully help by relinquishing personal rights *unwillingly and unnecessarily* for the supposed rights of others, *because love for humanity begins with genuine self-love and self-respect*. In other words, whilst situations frequently arise in which one must consciously and deliberately give up some personal rights, this is totally different from the case of the mother who keeps on harping about her total self-sacrifice because, as we have seen, her action is not motivated by the desire to be helpful but rather by a neurotic compulsion to feel ' put upon '. Now this kind of behaviour leads to a vicious circle; for the woman's self-induced limitation of her rights as a person naturally makes her increasingly resentful of those who are felt to be responsible for her frustrations and since this resentment must remain unconscious (because it would clash with her self-picture of martyrdom), she can only respond by making herself even more of a martyr in ways which other people will easily recognise to be motivated by malice and spite. She is not only tormenting herself, but everybody else in her family.

## The Housebound Housewife.

In order to distinguish between the normal and the neurotic giving up of individual rights, let us take an example from the so-called ' housebound housewife '. Here is a woman who feels lonely and depressed for various reasons discussed elsewhere but, in general, because she has been used to company before marriage and feels isolated when tied to the home looking after young children, or perhaps because she is ambitious and feels that her present position does not give sufficient scope for her abilities. There is nothing surprising or reprehensible about feeling this way in the circumstances, and the normal approach is that she should begin by being fully aware of the total situation and honest about her feelings in relation to it, subsequently doing something practical to alter the actual situation or herself. Three solutions immediately present themselves:

   (1) After discussion with the other members of the family, and having made suitable arrangements for the children, decide that a part- or full-time job is the answer.

   (2) To look around for work, studies, interests, or hobbies that can be carried out in the home to alleviate boredom and possibly prepare the path for more interesting work in the future.

   (3) To accept the situation and, after careful thought, change her own attitude towards it, arguing, for example, that looking after the home and her young family should be a rewarding and important period of life which will all too soon be over leaving her free to do as she pleases.

At the other extreme is the neurotic solution which occurs with the type of woman who refuses to face the situation constructively and thinks of it in 'moral' terms, denying that she wants to leave the home at all or that the children tie her down and limit her freedom of movement; she is so 'self-sacrificing' that she does not realise that normal love is always ambivalent in which love and anger and hate are parts of the mixture. Her world is composed of black and white, not as in the real world of varying shades of grey. This may lead to the not uncommon type of neurosis which has as its main symptom the fear of leaving the house even for a single moment, because as was seen earlier a conscious fear is often the expression of an unconscious wish. Immediately she puts her foot outside the door or attempts to cross the street, she is suddenly overwhelmed by attacks of sheer panic. What are the consequences of this 'solution'? First, her neurosis prevents her doing what she really wants but refuses to admit to wanting; second, she is punishing herself for her 'wicked' desires but, being frustrated, her unconscious resentment increases and with it her conscious anxiety; third, she is punishing the rest of the family by being 'ill', becoming a professional martyr probably requiring psychiatric treatment, and fills them with guilt both by snide remarks inferring that her condition is caused by overwork, and by coldness towards them, or perhaps by outbursts of irrational and uncontrollable rage. Certainly she is frustrated, but the cause of the frustration lies not in her objective surroundings but in the way she interprets them.

### Truth and Honesty.

Normality in personal relationships can be judged by the degree to which one is aware of the objective situation and able to appreciate the nature of unconscious factors motivating behaviour. So far as humanly possible, one is true to one's own nature and truthful in most circumstances. The more mature a married couple are, the more will it be possible for them to be completely truthful with each other but, since no one is completely mature, it is not always wise to tell the truth regardless of circumstances because those who do so are not always motivated by a desire for truth but by unconscious motives ranging from the need to purge personal feelings of guilt without the least regard for the feelings of others to the desire to wound. One of the commonest questions appearing in the personal problems columns of women's magazines is whether some sexual peccadillo in the individual's past should be revealed to the husband, to which (unless the act had repercussions which are still having an effect) the simple answer is: certainly not. Assuming that the person is moved to tell because of continuing feelings of guilt or shame, then one can only say:

   (1) that such feelings, like those of so-called self-sacrifice, are very often a sign of a concealed but overweening conceit demonstrating to the individual's own satisfaction what a tender conscience he (or she) must possess;

   (2) that the correct solution to guilt is surely not to permit what cannot be undone to spoil the present—which is a much more practical reason for feeling guilty—but to resolve to learn from experience and employ it in avoiding similar mistakes in the future;

   (3) that if the act must be confessed, then the best person to confess to is someone who is not emotionally involved, such as a priest, physician, psychiatrist or even a sympathetic, reliable and impartial friend;

   (4) that the woman (or man) concerned should consider very seriously what the *real* motives lying beneath the need to confess, which, as suggested above, are not infrequently the desire to attract attention or even to wound the other partner.

The only circumstances in which these rules would not always apply are those in which the wrong can still be undone or partly undone in which case the individual's duty is clear, or those in which news of the act is likely to reach the ears of the partner sooner or later from some other source, when it is usually wisest to consider making a clean breast of it (though, even then, it would be wise to be sure of one's correct estimation of the objective situation and the probable response of the other).

### Knowing Oneself.

The fundamental rules for close personal relationships within or without marriage are: mature affection (which has already been defined), sincerity, as much honesty as is wise judged by the criteria above and, most of all, self-knowledge. One of the ways in which we can become more self-aware is by observing not merely what we believe to be our conscious motives, but the consequences of our actions. If a husband or wife resolves to be pleasant and friendly when the other returns from work yet every time the evening is spent in constant bickering, then there must be some underlying resentment which it would be more helpful to bring out into the open and discuss frankly, than to continue making futile resolutions that are never kept. If a particular emotion or type of event always seems to keep on recurring; for example, if in all our relationships we invariably end up by feeling 'put upon', if we can never maintain a friendship for long, if a woman says that her dearest wish is to get married yet she fails to do so, if one allegedly loves a child yet is constantly losing one's temper with it, if other people always seem unfriendly and shop assistants rude, if we are frequently depressed or anxious without apparent cause, then the causes must be sought inside ourselves, since it is impossible that the environment is always to blame. The woman who believes that she wants to get married yet never finds the 'right' man, has affairs which invariably come to an end, or somehow inevitably seems to fall in love with unsuitable people—married men, confirmed bachelors, or those with latent homosexual tendencies, is obviously not being quite truthful with herself. Perhaps she wants to marry but fears the loss of her independence, perhaps she feels incapable of any close relationship with another, or perhaps she is afraid of sex and motherhood; for the fact is that even the plainest woman can get married if she wishes, and whether one falls in love or not depends less on that person's objective qualities than on our own deepest needs. In other words, a person who really wants love and marriage can't help falling in love. If we are constantly quarrelling with a loved one, it is because we refuse to admit that in certain respects we also resent him, and it is sensible to recall Dr. Winnicott's dictum that the danger arises, not from aggressiveness in itself, but from the repression of personal aggressiveness in individuals. Or, as the poet Blake expressed it:

   " I was angry with my friend,
   I told my wrath, the wrath did end;
   I was angry with my foe,
   I told it not, the wrath did grow."

Indeed, as the poem continues, the wrath was lovingly nurtured and increased until it finally ended in murder. Anger and aggression must often be consciously suppressed in ordinary social situations in which emotion would be inappropriate, but in personal relationships it should never be repressed but admitted and talked out.

### Sexual Relationships.

The belief so assiduously spread by specialists during the 1930s that complete sexual satisfaction in both partners is not only necessary but inevitably results in a happy married life turned the truth upside down; for the fact is that, in general, a happy married life based on love and respect is the cause rather than the effect of good sexual relations. Every psychiatrist has seen many cases of marriages in which physical relations were perfect and yet the marriage ended in divorce, and even more in which the sexual life was not wholly satisfactory but the marriage as a whole was.

The causes of sexual difficulties are rarely anatomical but have their origin in unconscious fears, guilt, and sometimes in ignorance. But ignorance is not as common a cause as used to be thought, not because it does not exist, but because a genuinely loving couple will find it easy in the course of time to make adjustments and discover for themselves. The bogey set up by these foolish 'experts' that women who do not always achieve complete satisfaction are in some way abnormal may have some sort of theoretical background, but it has very little relationship to the real state of affairs in which a majority of women may achieve orgasm fairly frequently, only occasionally, or not at all throughout their married life. Men who are always impotent are not very common and need medical or psychiatric help, but for women the state of affairs is quite different. Most men experience sexual desire initially as a physical need like hunger, whilst women for obvious biological reasons experience desire in a much more complex form which cannot be separated from emotional security; for a man sex begins and ends with the act, for a woman it only begins with the act since she has to think of (and normally look forward to) future consequences. Of course, this is not true of all women, and as contraceptive measures become more efficient and women more socially independent, many regard sex in pretty much the same light as men. But women even more than men have been brought up to feel that sex is unpleasant or dirty, and many people of both sexes are afraid to give themselves completely in love (the childhood mechanism: "If I don't give all of myself to others, then they can't hurt me"), so it is hardly surprising that comparatively few lead a completely satisfying sexual life. In any case, mutual adjustment usually takes some time and many men and women may take years to accomplish this. However, with or without complete sexual satisfaction most couples as we have seen lead reasonably happy lives together because their goal is not sex alone but the maintenance of a marriage and a home.

There are some cases in which this is not so and the help of a psychiatrist or Marriage Guidance Counsellor is required: if intercourse is completely impossible, if one of the partners finds it totally repulsive, if the couple desire to have children and fail to do so, or if, as sometimes happens in women, the act by arousing desires which they are ashamed of leads not only to non-completion but to anxiety and emotional tension. When this happens, the wife may find that following intercourse her nervous tension brings about irritability and this in turn may lead to constant bickering that may threaten to wreck the marriage. All these cases require skilled advice though, of course, they are no ground for worry on physical grounds alone nor are they anything to feel ashamed about. Everybody fails from time to time in some aspect of their lives and, if it cannot be dealt with by ordinary means, the sensible thing to do is to seek expert advice; there is no more need to feel embarrassed about seeking help from a psychiatrist in these circumstances than in seeking help from a lawyer or house-surveyor in others.

### The Goal of Self-Realisation.

Gordon Allport, a leading American psychologist, has emphasised that every living being is trying to complete his own nature—in the terms already used here, he is striving towards self-realisation. But his search, depending upon parental attitudes, may take one of two roads. One road seeks safety through exclusion, through a restrictive and rejective equilibrium employing the mechanism of repression and denial, yet, because the more we repress the more we must continue to repress, the personality inevitably becomes impoverished and incapable of free self-expression. The person clings to a narrow island, restricts his circle, sharply selects what reassures him and rejects what seems to threaten him. The other road is one of relaxation, self-trust, and therefore trust of others. "There is no need to exclude strangers from one's gathering. Self-love is compatible with love of others. This tolerant orientation is possible because security has been experienced in the realistic handling of inner conflicts and social transactions. Unlike the authoritarian and prejudiced person, the tolerant person does not perceive the world as a jungle where men are basically evil and dangerous."

### Teaching Morals.

The disasters arising from a restrictive upbringing have to do with the child's early failure to live with his own impulses; he is made to feel guilty and punished whenever he soils himself or is found handling his own genitals. (Incidentally, research has demonstrated that mothers of prejudiced children are mostly likely to punish the child for this offence.) He is punished or made to feel guilty too—and only a child can tell what guilt and pain can be aroused by the hurt and suffering expression on a mother's face which is much worse than a physical blow—whenever he has a tantrum or strikes a parent or other relative. A child who finds his every impulse, even his desire to self-expression, wicked, and feels that he is unloved when he gives way to it—is likely to grow up hating himself for his many transgressions. Says Allport: "He carries a burden of infantile guilt. As a consequence, when he sees any lapses from the conventional code in others he grows anxious. He wishes to punish the transgressor, just as he himself was punished. He develops a dread of the very impulses that trouble him. When a person grows overconcerned with sin in others, the tendency may be viewed as a 'reaction formation'. Having had to fight unholy impulses in himself, he cannot be permissive and lenient toward others. (This) moralism is only surface compliance; it does not solve the conflicts within. It is tense, compulsive, projective. True morality is more relaxed, integral, and congruent with the life pattern as a whole."

### The Development of Normality and True Morality.

The way to avoid these developments is obvious. In addition to the fundamental parental attitudes already mentioned, the basic rule is *never to apply prohibitions to a child until it is capable of carrying them out and understanding them.* For example, the senseless attempt to 'train' a child in potting habits before the muscle controlling bowel movements has even been developed is something which is carried out to suit the parents' convenience rather than for the child's own benefit as, alas, in many cases are the sleeping habits and regular feeding habits imposed upon the infant. What parents should realise is that to a considerable extent normality and genuine moral attitudes are developed by a process of internal maturation rather than by any sort of direct intervention on the part of the father or mother whose real job in the early years is to provide the right emotional background. The child who is fed 'on demand', that is, whenever it wants, does not become an anarchist but in a few weeks develops as regular a rhythm as the unfortunate who has regular feeding imposed upon it; the child who is left alone so far as bowel-training is concerned learns control by itself in the course of time.

Young children naturally play with their genitals which, after all, are an interesting part of the body and, quite apart from sex, an obvious object for attention; they should be left alone to do so unless the parents prefer that the child should learn to do the same thing in secret or, worse still, that it should learn that sex is dirty and sinful and therefore to be repressed. In fact the young child's genital play is not initially sexual at all but merely natural curiosity, and it is only the guilt-ridden adult who interprets it in this way.

### The Good Parent.

A permissive attitude on the part of parents is the only sensible one because it is impossible to destroy a desire but only to drive it underground when it will reappear in far less desirable forms. Aggression, even more than sex, is dangerous if not permitted free expression in the early years; the child with a temper-tantrum should be hugged and reassured because it is frightened by its inability to control this terrifying emotion. Training, until the child has acquired the ability to understand what he is told, is a matter of living and leaving well alone. (Obviously, this does not apply to situations where the child is in physical danger of falling or touching dangerous objects, but even then the minor accident should be minimised as far as possible because the mother who shows her excessive anxiety infects her child with it and causes it to feel that the world is a dangerous place. It is, but one can handle it better when unafraid.) Thus the good parent must strike a useful balance between sincere love and concern for the child and the avoidance of inducing too much anxiety by undue fussing about risks and illness. So far as dangerous situations are concerned, the sensible thing to do is to remove or guard against any potential source of danger rather than worry the child about it.

### Sex Education.

Sex education has often been conceived as a process whereby the child—hitherto assumed to be totally ignorant of sex—is, at a certain age (usually puberty), taken aside and given a serious talk either by the parent, or (as some seem to suppose) by the biology teacher at school whose duty it is naïvely believed to be. This, of course, is simply nonsense. Sex education begins at birth by supplying the child's physical needs, its psychological need for love, and otherwise leaving it alone to explore its body as it pleases. Later, when it acquires speech, the child who trusts its parents and has not been made to feel that there is anything ' bad ' about its natural processes, will start to ask questions. The rules which should be followed by the parents at this stage are clear:

(1) Every question should be answered *honestly* in a way the child at that age can comprehend;

(2) The answer should be a simple and *brief* reply to what has actually been asked;

(3) Formal sex education, in the sense of a more detailed and scientific account, belongs only to the later years of childhood when the parents should continue to answer all questions honestly and in the greater detail the child now requires, discussing the *social* implications of sex insofar as they are capable of doing so;

(4) Sex will finally become something to be taught by the teacher as part of a course in general biology.

The reasons for this approach are clear: we have seen that in the early months it is useless—and worse than useless—to apply prohibitions which the child is unable to understand. When it acquires speech and subsequently goes to school, it will inevitably obtain some sort of sexual information anyhow, so the parents' choice is not between some knowledge and none at all but between garbled and often nasty information and that which is decent and honest. In fact, the child whose questions have been answered briefly and truthfully becomes *less* interested in sex except

as one feature of life as a whole than the one who has been told nothing, to whom the secret and forbidden knowledge becomes both a private obsession and a status symbol.

Everybody has a particular desire to acquire knowledge which he or she knows to exist, but which has clearly been withheld because it is supposedly ' naughty ' and ' dirty '. Thus sex education is a continual process, inseparable from education in general; it is, in fact, merely one aspect of personal relationships and should be taught as such. What the child should learn is that, since no form of sex is harmful *in itself*, the only practical considerations to be taken into account are whether any given sex act is hurtful to either person involved, a breach of their self-respect, or a risk to their future happiness—as, for example, an unwanted pregnancy. It would be wrong therefore to encourage someone to engage in any sort of behaviour which their religion teaches them to be evil, even if we ourselves believe it to be harmless or even good.

### Pre-marital Relationships.

There are social reasons already mentioned why pre-marital relationships *may* be more frequent, and it seems likely that this trend may continue to increase. But we might well wonder whether those who are so alarmed about it (and no decision as to its moral desirability can be made here, since this must be left to the reader) are fully aware of its background. It is usually assumed that morals are becoming more lax in this respect, whereas a large part of the truth is that people are simply more frank and at less pains to conceal what they do. Again, the kind of behaviour condemned by the moralists is very far from being new: for instance, in the heyday of the Church during the Middle Ages what was then more kindly described as the ' natural ' child was not only as well treated as the child born in wedlock, but the term ' bastard ' was applied to many exalted people as an honourable title. In agricultural societies—including our own—when children were regarded as an important asset, engaged couples deliberately sought pregnancy because the man wanted to make sure that the woman was fertile before marriage. Another obvious reason for the apparent increase in illegitimacy is that the ' shot-gun ' marriage is less frequent, and a woman who has become pregnant will not marry her lover if she subsequently decides that he is unsuitable; this is surely a tendency in the right direction since no good can come of an enforced marriage and, in view of the stigma still attached to illegitimacy, shows that the young take these matters more seriously today.

## 4. SOCIAL PATHOLOGY.

We are now going to glance very briefly at certain aspects of what are regarded as some of the more important problems of our day and, since it is only possible to select a few, those chosen are juvenile delinquency, neurosis and the stress diseases, and what appears to be an increase in boredom and discontent.

### Changing Social Attitudes.

Take first of all the background. There is a tremendous technical revolution going on in which there exists a lag between the actual environment in which we live and our ability to adjust to it; the real enemy, however, is not so much lack of ability as ignorance and superstition. For example, it is indeed true that malnutrition is a world-wide problem, but it is necessary to realise that the causes of hunger are just as often political and religious as the result of any lack in foodstuff. In Asia, one of the main drawbacks to an adequate diet is the caste system of India which prevents certain foods from being eaten and in communities in both Asia and Africa, as people earn more money, they frequently spend it, not on food, but on clothes and bicycles. Attitudes require changing at least as much as the agricultural system; *for all the attitudes which we regard as special problems are common to every country in* which industrialisation and democratisation are taking place and the mass media are not the cause but merely a single symptom of this total process. Rebellious youth, for instance, and the search for more possessions and affluence is as much in evidence in the Communist countries where the media have been used not only to indoctrinate but also to improve, and they are just as common in the new countries where the mass media hardly exist. In our own country the working class are doing exactly what the middle class were doing when they first got into power, only more obviously so because of the narrowed time-scale within which social change takes place: gambling, buying rather tasteless objects, building rather ghastly houses and fitting them with equally ghastly furniture, reading bad books (the women's magazines of today are really no worse than the writings of Ethel M. Dell and Ouida) and horror comics (which were invented in the late eighteenth century, and the most famous, *Frankenstein*, was written by the wife of Shelley). Of course, the middle class to a considerable extent are still doing these things—but they dislike the working class having the same freedom. Just as one can well imagine the first time that the well-to-do on the Riviera looked with distaste on the newly affluent grocers and ' tradesmen ' who were beginning to flood into ' their ' preserve, so today the descendants of the grocers and tradesmen view with the same distaste each favourite resort as it becomes flooded with newly affluent workers.

### The Cost of Affluence.

But affluence is a state for which a price has to be paid, particularly by youth. In modern society teenagers for the first time have money to spare, are socially emancipated, reach puberty earlier, and have far greater possibilities for success (and failure) than their forebears ever had. A society based on the concept of social mobility, whether the goal is wealth, affluence, or status, must necessarily be associated with striving and the more sensitive members will feel more strongly than others the pressure to achieve, to avoid failure, or even to maintain their present position. In addition, if one has been indoctrinated with the belief that success is essential to self-respect and that affluence is ' normal ', it is not surprising that the failures will try to walk round the ladder if they are unable to climb it, *i.e.*, they may attempt the devious way of criminality. Whereas in former times people stole because in some sense they were genuinely deprived, today they do so because they feel relatively deprived. Since happiness is not an absolute, the affluent society aided by the power of commercial advertising ensures a state of affairs in which there is always a gulf between what people have and what they think they are entitled to. Crime and neurosis are the two sides of this single penny; for, as Freud pointed out, whilst the criminal is in open rebellion against his society, the neurotic is in a state of unconscious rebellion. Which ' solution ' is selected depends upon a number of factors, one of the most important being social class; for the unsatisfactory upbringing will tend to make the middle-class boy neurotic will tend to make the working-class boy *living in an area where delinquency is a socially-accepted pattern, or at least not a wholly condemned one*, into a delinquent. Here, of course, we are referring, not to the whole working class, but to specifically delinquent areas.

### The Delinquent.

Among the most striking facts about crime are (a) that it is predominantly a male, adolescent, and working-class activity; (b) that it is at its height in the 14–17 age-group; and (c) that, not only do crimes become less violent after the age of 30, but they tend to cease altogether in the majority of cases. An obviously important conclusion of (c) is that the majority of delinquents would stop their behaviour regardless of what was done whether by way of punishment or ' treatment '.

It is completely fallacious to suppose that a large majority of criminals of all categories are suffering from some form of mental disturbance,

and for the sake of convenience it is useful to consider the following categories: mere wildness and ' proving offences ', the disturbed and violent delinquent, the sexual offender, and the professional criminal or old lag. Of course, there are other groups such as those who habitually engage in fraud, blackmail, and shady financial transactions, but these can be fitted into the last of the above categories.

The first type of case is very often a perfectly normal boy who is simply engaged in ' working off steam ' and doing the sort of things most of the rest of us have done, since aggressiveness and a certain amount of destructiveness are usual accompaniments of adolescence, or, in the case of the ' proving ' offence, he feels the need to demonstrate his toughness or lack of fear by engaging in crimes which are clearly not carried out primarily for personal gain. Typical of these are those who smash street lamps, steal apples or other goods, damage railway property, and so on, or the group of boys who break and enter an office yet, whilst smashing up some of the furniture, steal nothing but a few pencils or other worthless objects. These form the vast majority of all cases and the act, as a German criminologist puts it, is " an episode rather than a symptom ", *i.e.*, most of these cases are normal and will develop into perfectly good citizens. More dangerous is the delinquent who takes crime seriously and is often violent towards his victim. Whilst the first group can belong to any class, this group usually comes from a disturbed home and a delinquency area—which is not at all the same thing as saying that he is necessarily abnormal though he may need help: nevertheless, except in grave cases, even this type tends to outgrow his criminal tendencies or, at least, to become less violent after the late twenties. In other instances he may develop into the old lag.

Sexual perversions are, of course, the concern of the psychiatrist and need not be discussed here, but it should be noted that most perverts are suffering from a lack of sexual drive rather than, as popular belief would have it, a state of being ' oversexed '. They are rarely dangerous and most are sexually impotent in normal relationships, but even those who murder with a sexual motive tend to have the same incapacity and a surprising number (*e.g.*, Christie and Haigh) have been brought up in oppressively religious households. The professional criminal is frequently just that, and those who seek complicated psychiatric explanations for his behaviour are usually wasting their time: few people seem to realise that there are those who take to crime as a ' career ' just as others become doctors or carpenters. In many instances they are merely ' following the dear old dad '. The old lags or recidivists who form such a large proportion of our prison population are commonly dullards but it is doubtful if many are in the clinical sense mentally ill. As the late Sir Norwood East, one of Britain's leading criminologists, said: " As the result of more than fifty years' practical experience of crime I am unable to regard crime as a disease, although sometimes the result of it."

### Crime and Punishment.

Since the great majority of offenders who show early delinquent tendencies simply grow out of them, it is doubtful whether punishment (or for that matter, psychiatric treatment) has any great influence upon the course of events, though detention may often be necessary. But it is really more than doubtful whether punishment has any preventive effect at all. On the contrary, we know that severe corporal punishment can often arouse such a store of resentment as to last through a lifetime of violence and it is also well known that many people commit crimes in order to be found out because they are unconsciously seeking punishment.

Murder is very unlike any other form of crime in that its incidence hardly changes from year to year, the number of mentally disturbed cases is large, the vast majority of murders are due to family or intimate quarrels where gain is seldom the motive, and (except for the occasional psychopathic murderer) the crime is unlikely to be committed again.

## Stress and Mental Illness.

Before discussing this problem we must say something about the nature of mental illness, and the first point to note is that, apart from the fact that all cases of mental illness show symptoms of disturbance in thought, emotion, or behaviour, this is the only factor that they do have in common. Without encroaching too far on the material presented by the writer of the Medical Section, mental disorders can be roughly classified as psychoses (i.e., the insanities); the neuroses, which are minor if very uncomfortable conditions differing from the psychoses mainly in that the psychotic person adjusts as well as he can to his inner conflicts but little if at all to his social milieu, whereas the neurotic's methods of adjustment are rigid and stereotyped; the psychopathic personalities who are people that are more of a trouble to society than to themselves; the mental defectives suffering from a defect of intelligence; and the psychosomatic diseases in which actual physical disease has been brought about by mental stress.

The causes of these conditions are very various, some like the so-called organic psychoses being really physical diseases with mental symptoms brought about by infections such as syphilis or toxins such as alcohol, others such as mental defect being either inherited or caused by damage to the child before birth. The functional psychoses, such as schizophrenia or manic-depressive insanity, have no known physical cause though some authorities believe that they have discovered abnormal substances in the body fluids of schizophrenics. But with these exceptions (and possibly a few cases of so-called psychopathic personality), we have to realise that 'mental diseases' are not in any meaningful sense diseases at all but cases of social maladjustments. From this fact the following important conclusions can be drawn:

(1) that the neuroses and the psychopathic conditions—insofar as the latter term has any meaning at all—are really the result of a faulty upbringing resulting in a basic defect in interpersonal relations and the symptoms are usually brought on by a precipitating cause when the individual is confronted by a problem which, by reason of his early experiences, he is unable to face;

(2) that, unlike ordinary diseases, a neurosis is not something that one 'has' but something that one 'is';

(3) that, since nobody has had a completely perfect upbringing, everybody is in some degree neurotic and it is therefore meaningless to suggest that a person is either neurotic or not—what we usually mean is that he (or she) is neurotic to a degree which troubles him (or her) or troubles others.

The latter is the criterion upon which the person is declared to be suffering from a neurosis and, since this is obviously a matter of individual judgment, it follows that all statistics purporting to tell us the incidence of neurosis in a given community are to a large extent based on value judgments and of very dubious validity.

Perhaps the sort of neurosis that does most harm is the sort of behaviour described earlier when we were discussing harmful influences on children: the possessive and jealous, the mother-in-law who cannot leave well alone, the suspicious wife or husband, those with a profound sense of guilt with which they may infect others. All these are suffering from behaviour disorders but few indeed see a psychiatrist.

## The Structure of a Neurosis.

We must distinguish between the early roots of neurosis which are laid in childhood, e.g., the unsatisfied need for love and security, resentment against authority, and other undesirable patterns of behaviour which, being unsatisfied, continue to repeat themselves throughout life, and the immediate cause of a breakdown which is the result of the individual's applying these outdated patterns to new situations. The main difference between the relatively neurotic and the relatively normal is that the neurotic tries to apply old solutions to new situations whereas the normal person takes every new situation on its own merits. Thus the man who has had a conflict between his desire for self-realisation and the authority of a repressive father does not distinguish between different authorities in later life, continues to act on the belief that all authority is bad, and naturally frequently finds himself in trouble. The man or woman who has felt some denial of love in childhood, continues to seek the symbols of love throughout life in stereotyped ways even if these take many different forms. The individual may become promiscuous, feel victimised, become parasitic upon others, overeat, or constantly strive for more goods or status. It is not that all these forms of self-expression are necessarily bad in themselves: what makes them neurotic is that they are compulsive. Broadly speaking, then, there are two main types of conflict, that which shows itself in the search for approval, love, status, and goods, and the other type which is a crisis of self-expression, the freedom to assert oneself. The one is shown in the person who looks for affluence, the other in the person who seeks for power, even if both have a common root, the search for security.

## Boredom and Anomie.

Many people are bored today because, instead of seeking contentment within, they are in the position of a spoilt child who has been offered so many things that he does not know what to do with them since none is a substitute for love. Whatever point he reaches, there is always something more to desire and each goal as it is reached is less satisfactory than the last. Not only is success less satisfying than it once appeared, there is also the danger of falling from the position achieved, and those who want what they cannot have may become no less neurotic than those who have got what they wanted and are afraid of losing it. It is not only people who want who develop a neurosis but those who have achieved their dreams: the East End family moved to a new town is often troubled by the idea that they will be unable to keep up with the higher standard set by others—there is a 'success' no less than a 'failure' neurosis.

A feature of modern society was described by the French sociologist Durkheim as anomie, the feeling of futility and not-belonging as old groups are broken up and the mass becomes the 'lonely crowd'. Social mobility has introduced the working-class student to new ways of life which often arouse a conflict between his attitudes towards his family and the atmosphere of Oxbridge; the worker's new desire to get on often alienates him from his mates; and the housewife stranded at home knows, unlike her predecessors, what she is missing—life is passing her by. There is a gulf between what we want and what we can have, between what we are and what we want to be; our society is characterised by a never-ending search for the end of the rainbow and for security that will never be ours. The only solution is to learn to live with conflict by seeing our own personal problems as problems to be shared and understood together.

# III. WORK

## 1. THE SATISFACTIONS OF WORK.

Work, no matter how we define it, is not simply something that we have to do in order to make money to do something else; it is the main source in modern society of status—the sign of approval of other people. In the words of an industrial psychologist: "Work is the source of man's most basic satisfactions, it is his social catalyst—the purveyor par excellence of his status and prestige among his fellows." In former times, status came from one's social position, rank, position in the church, craftsmanship, or some special ability; but few of us today are lords, churchmen, or craftsmen and it is our job that tells others what we are. Even from the psychological point of view, it is desirable that our aggressive or creative drives should find expression in doing the sort of work that fulfils and helps towards the goal of self-realisation. Of course, many people are actively dissatisfied in their work, many more satisfied, and others feel that, however well they have done, they might have done better. So it is worth discussing, first, what is satisfying about work, and second, the process of education and selection for work.

Work and boredom are not necessarily related, because from the earliest times work has often been objectively boring but subjectively interesting. To the woman washing clothes in the stream, or to the man planting rice-shoots, boredom was unknown because what they were doing made sense to them. The craftsman in mediæval times took pride in producing a good and useful article. One unfortunate result of the industrial revolution was that, while in the long run it created more wealth and goods and benefited more people than any comparable period in history, it was a first step for the majority of workers in the direction of taking the meaning out of work. As Christopher Salmon has said: " Because the Victorians regarded work in industry as necessarily hard and disagreeable they made little effort to introduce tolerable conditions into mines and mills, and foundries, and were content to think of industry itself as an economic necessity instead of as an element in society."

For work to be agreeable it should be meaningful, and, since most people are sociable to a greater or less degree, the company of one's workmates is important. These are two of the factors which, apart from material rewards, the manager or the industrial psychologist has to consider, and some of the modern views on the subject of incentives will be mentioned later. It will become evident that conditions have much improved in the course of this century, but there is no doubt that they might be very considerably better. The fact that work is not only necessary to man but necessary to most people's mental health as well as being an activity that it is normal to like, stands out in odd contrast to a background of industrial unrest. We shall have to ask ourselves what it is that transforms a necessary and ordinarily pleasant activity into a source of strife.

## 2. EDUCATION AND SELECTION.

### The Past.

In former times education was a privilege of the few and compulsory education was not introduced into this country until as late as 1870. The sort of training given by well-to-do parents to their boys was based on the classics and its intention was to create the cultured gentleman at ease in company and able to discourse intelligently on as many subjects as possible without appearing to be too uncomfortably intelligent. Since science was not regarded as a very cultural pursuit and, until the seventeenth and eighteenth centuries, chemistry and physics were still ' natural philosophy ' and hardly existed as sciences in the modern sense, it was little taught at school. Those who practised it were comfortably-off gentlemen who, living more or less in isolation, became interested in it as a hobby. It was only the founding of the Royal Society in 1660 that began to bring these people together to exchange ideas and, since the Society was given a Royal Charter by Charles II, science began to be respectable. Its respectability, however, was conditional and the condition was that it should remain theoretical because gentlemen were not expected to work towards practical ends.

From this attitude there arose the unfortunate distinction between pure science and technology which bedevilled British science and caused parents to feel that technical schools and colleges were somehow inferior to the universities and grammar schools. Of course, another unfortunate result has been that, whereas Britain has never been short of ideas, their serious application has often been carried out in other countries: obvious examples are the jet engine and penicillin. Until much more recently girls, apart from a smattering of languages, music, and drawing, were taught almost entirely such crafts as might be expected to make them good housewives, and the daughters of wealthy parents were not even taught the domestic arts—indeed, since it was believed that any sign of intelligence was likely to put off a prospective suitor, many manuals of instruction suggested that they should actively conceal what intelligence they had.

### The Modern Educational Outlook.

Much of this has changed with the acceptance, at least in theory, of the equality of the sexes and the realisation that, as a nation, we cannot afford to waste our human resources. Children are carefully selected at an early age in terms of their abilities and the intelligent child, regardless of his origins, has the opportunity to reach a position consonant with his gifts. But, just as the science-technology dichotomy still persists, whatever governments may say, so other traces of past attitudes make freedom of opportunity less real than might at first appear. Women have not yet gained full equality and we have already seen that what they have gained is more by way of an addition to their traditional tasks than a release from them. One of the greatest barriers to social equality is less any sort of physical barrier confronting the working-class child than the traditional attitudes of his class. It is easy to see why history has made solidarity a traditional working-class virtue and why the boy who tries to better himself is often regarded as a traitor to his class, nor is it unnatural that many workers regard education as synonymous with childhood as work is synonymous with manhood. High culture is still regarded with suspicion as the special province of the ruling class in spite of the fact that, at least since Elizabethan times, most of our great writers and artists have been of comparatively humble origin. These intangible attitudes are obviously a serious barrier to working-class children, as are also the difficulty of finding sufficient privacy to study, the pressures of the affluent society which cause them to want as much money as possible as soon as possible, and the not infrequent family problems centering around the cultural gulf between the university-trained youth and his relatively uneducated parents. Physical barriers exist, too, because the smaller classes, sometimes the better quality of the teaching, and the limited number of university places in some areas favour the public school child and it is well known that certain universities or colleges prefer the products of particular schools.

### The Comprehensive Principle.

The doubts of the value of attaching too much importance to the results of intelligence tests and early progress at school has brought about a movement in favour of abolishing the 11-plus examination and making more use of the comprehensive secondary school. Some people argue that comprehensive schools penalise the able but the 11-plus already does that. Any sort of single test which determines what form a child's future education shall take is highly fallible. Parents are often very upset when their child fails to obtain a grammar-school place and this puts a great deal of tension upon family relationships when both parents and children become obsessed with school marks and examinations. Outmoded ideas are rapidly being broken down throughout the country despite the failure of some authorities to co-operate on the comprehensive principle.

### Selection Procedures.

Some fortunate people are able to select freely the sort of work they would like to do—writers and artists, for example—and others simply slide in and out of unskilled jobs, going where the pay is best but the prospects less satisfactory. Today, however, the vast majority of people, including those who are going to fall into the above categories, have to go through at some time or another in their lives various tests to discover their abilities. The justification for these tests is (a) the present need for able people with particular qualifications; (b) the need to avoid wastage by attempting to train people who cannot be trained to the necessary level; and (c) the obvious fact that it is a good idea to have a square peg in a square hole and a worker who is not only suited to his job but satisfied with it.

There are three aspects of personality which can be tested in this way: general intelligence, special abilities such as manual dexterity, engineering ability, speed of reaction, the absence of colour blindness, and so on, and tests of personality itself —that is to say, the individual's attitudes.

There can be no doubt that intelligence tests are valuable in predicting which people are *not* capable of doing certain jobs or following certain careers. What they cannot predict is what they *are*—for example, a very intelligent man may be emotionally or temperamentally unsuited for industrial management. Nor does anyone now believe that what the tests measure is some absolute intelligence which appears in all that a man does; they simply test those abilities which are useful in industrial society. Aptitude tests are less likely to be met with by the average citizen, being mainly employed where a specific job requires specific abilities (*i.e.*, in situations where we know that before the individual is taken into the job he requires a certain minimum of quality x unless time is to be wasted, efficiency diminished, or danger incurred.) Obviously an air pilot must be able to react quickly, an engine driver capable of distinguishing between green and red signals, a musician possess a good ear for tone, and so on. Most of these tests are very accurate and nobody who fails them need feel ' let down ' because they are in his or her own interests as well as those of others.

### Personality Tests.

The personality test is a procedure which, when applied outside its original field of psychiatry, has given rise to a good deal of controversy. One of its earliest forms, still used in conjunction with the lie-detector employed in criminology, was the word-association test devised by Jung at the beginning of the century to discover hidden complexes. In this a list of words, some neutral and others which are believed to have special significance for the patient, is slowly read out and the testee is asked to respond as quickly as possible with the first word that comes into his head. His reaction-time is measured with a stop-watch, and any delay or hesitation or any unusual responses noted. These give clues to unconscious problems.

Today, however, the usual form of personality test is what is known as a projection test, now widely employed in industry as well as in psychiatry to discover much more accurately personality traits of which the individual is probably totally unaware himself—indeed, his unconsciousness of the traits is almost a necessity for the use of the test. The three tests of this sort which the reader is most likely to come across are the Rorschach or ' inkblot ' test, the Szondi test with its photographs of oddly-assorted individuals, and the TAT or thematic apperception test in which the outlines of vague human figures in various postures in relation to each other are shown. In the first, the testee is asked to say what he imagines himself to ' see ' in the multicoloured inkblot, in the second, he is asked to say which of the people in the photograph he would prefer to sit with in a railway carriage and which he would most dislike in these circumstances, and in the third he is asked to write a story about the shadowy figures. As the name indicates, all three tests are based on the same idea—that, presented with a vague situation to which he has no outward clues, the testee will project upon the figures or shapes his own attitudes. When a picture of an apple is presented to anyone, he has no choice but to recognise it for what it is, but when he is presented with a Rorschach inkblot what he ' sees ' in it must come from himself. In this way, such traits as introversion or extraversion, authoritarianism or humanitarianism, latent homosexuality, sado-masochistic trends, and the degree of integration or otherwise of the mind can be fairly reliably assessed.

### Criticisms of Personality Tests.

These procedures are widely used in the selection of management in America and have been severely criticised. The most cogent of these criticisms are: (*a*) the moral one that it is an invasion of privacy and that no one at a man's place of work has any right to knowledge of the most intimate type about himself which, if he knew, he would not wish to be communicated; (*b*) the factual one that, although the tests are probably scientific, the uses to which they are put in industry are not, since nobody knows what makes a good manager good (in other words, unlike aptitude tests in which one knows what one is looking for, projection tests reveal material which is only of interest to the psychiatrist); (*c*) the fact that, given knowledge of the technique of the tests, it is very easy to cheat at them. (Those who wish to learn how to do so should consult W. H. Whyte's book *The Organisation Man.*) All that is necessary is to imagine that one is moderate in all things, has no unduly strong feelings either for or against parents and relatives, has conservative views on politics and religion, and has been good—but not too good—at all the tasks one has been presented with throughout life. That, to sum up, one is an insufferable prig and a complete bore.

### Group Tests.

Another type of test, or rather group of tests, is that carried out in management selection and at officer selection boards for the army. Here a group of about ten applicants are asked to spend a week-end at a country house (in the case of industry); they are given batteries of tests from intelligence tests to TAT personality tests, are in some cases seen by a psychiatrist who has the test results, and are carefully observed as unobtrusively as possible by trained observers as they interact with each other. The fundamental part of the programme is the group task in which various assignments are given to the group as a whole and, in the course of time, it will be found that, in the discussions as to how these tasks are to be accomplished, those who have superior organising abilities and other useful qualities come to be recognised by the group as its informal leader. Thus in this type of test, it is the group itself which chooses (consciously or unconsciously) the most suitable applicant—not, of course, by votes or words but by behaviour. He is the person who is most frequently turned to for advice during the carrying out of the task, which naturally is related to the activities for which the group is being tested. In the case of industry, for example, it will be the solving of an imaginary business problem, in the army it is usually a problem involving doing things of a para-military nature. All that one can say of this method is that it gives the candidate a better opportunity than the individual interview, since he is checked by a fair number of people and this eliminates the prejudices of selection by one person.

### 3. THE PROBLEM OF LEADERSHIP IN MODERN SOCIETY.

What has been said above leads us directly to the question of leadership, not necessarily in industry, but in modern society as a whole. We have seen that in many cases there still exists the belief that ' leadership ' is a psychological trait which is somehow situated inside a person, being either there or not. Oddly enough, so far as industry and the services are concerned, this innate quality is most frequently found in those who have had a public school education—indeed, one of the mainstays of the argument for retaining public schools is that they train the ' character ' and produce qualities of ' leadership ' denied to lesser breeds. Scientifically speaking, this is the merest nonsense (*a*) because one can no more train character in a public school than in a borstal or any other place—that has, for better or worse, occurred in the home in the early years of life, and (*b*) because there is no such quality as leadership within a particular man or woman, only the ability possessed by nearly everyone to be a leader in a given situation. Many pieces of psychological research have shown that the only common factor found in those who become leaders in a particular field is their superior competence or knowledge in that area. Of course, many people are thrust into positions of leadership by reason of their social position, their wealth, their education (not what they have *done*, but *where* they have *been*), but these are leaders only in the formal sense and, if many products of our public schools have made good army officers, that is first because they have supreme self-confidence and, second, because they were acting within an authoritarian network in which even the less competent had the full backing of authority behind them. Even the self-assurance is more likely to have been derived from the social background of which their school is only one aspect than from any training within the school itself. This sort of leadership is all very well for the army which of its very nature must be authoritarian, but it is of no use at all in a modern democracy in which a leader must be chosen because he represents the feelings and views of the group he leads. The reason for saying this is not a sentimental one or based on political faith in democracy; it is simply that, in a society which is not authoritarian and where there is more or less full employment, there are no means open to a leader to get his subordinates to work effectively or even to stay with him than by possessing their confidence and respect.

### Leadership as a Function of the Working Environment.

We have seen that leadership is a function of the situation confronting the group, so it follows that if the situation changes the leader may have to change too. This is well illustrated in the following case: a factory manager who had been well liked and respected retired and his place was taken by a bumptious, self-assertive man who did not believe in consulting his subordinates. Hitherto, the supervisors had formed their own group which elected one of their members to deal with their interests or problems when he took them to the factory manager for advice, help, or information. Throughout the period of office of the first manager, the supervisors' leader was a quiet, sensible man and the two got on very well together and with the rest of the men. But when it was seen what the new manager was like, resentment began to grow and, at the next election, the old leader was ousted and the man put in his place was an agitator who had up till then been regarded by most of the supervisors as aggressive, unpleasant, and even a little ' cracked '. Year after year the same man continued to be elected in spite of the fact that each member of the group still continued to dislike him, and when they were asked why the answer was: " Well, you see, he's the only man amongst us who is capable of dealing with that (unmentionable) manager."

A Taoist philosopher, about five or six hundred years B.C., made the observation that the great ruler is one whose people do not even notice his existence, the lesser one is feared, and the still lesser one despised. This is confirmed by the leading American authority on management, C. I. Barnard, who wrote that the good leader in industry in a democratic society may sometimes give the impression that he is a " rather stupid fellow, a mere channel of communications, and a filcher of ideas. In a measure this is correct. He has to be stupid enough to listen a great deal, he certainly must arbitrate to maintain order, but he has at times to be a mere centre of communication. If he used only his own ideas he would be somewhat like a one-man orchestra, rather than a good conductor, who is a very high type of leader." Or, as the same Chinese philosopher wrote:

The best employer of men keeps himself below them.
This is called the virtue of not contending;
This is called the ability of using men.

In a democracy politics is ' the practice of the possible ' because the leader can never be too far ahead of the desires and attitudes of the people.

### The Nature of Democratic Society.

A democratic society is, of course, in one of its aspects a society which elects its leaders by secret and universal voting; but this is not the only, or even the most important part of democracy. In modern societies it is often necessary to put people in high positions because of their specialist knowledge—government by amateurs is now no longer possible in all fields, and in industry and other spheres such as the armed forces it is not always possible to elect leaders. What is much more important is (a) that the leaders at all levels even when they have been chosen primarily because of their technical qualifications should be able to make themselves acceptable to those under them, and (b) that there should be free flow of information both up and down the channels of communication. This is not achieved by manipulating others on the model of Dale Carnegie's book *How to Make Friends and Influence People*— which is often used as a means of influencing people without necessarily making friends of them —but by being the sort of leader described by Barnard who acts, not on his own decisions taken in isolation, but with regard to the feelings of others and an ear to their opinions. There would be far fewer strikes if management employed genuine joint consultation in which no major decisions were taken on matters affecting the workers without consulting them about the decisions beforehand, seeking their cooperation and advice as to how they should be carried out— and this not because of common decency alone but because management *in fact* cannot act without the cooperation of their employees. Indeed, many strikes happen not because the workers object to the decisions as such, but because their human dignity is affronted by not being told about them. Sometimes it is necessary to make decisions, for example, about redundancy, which on the one hand may be inevitable and on the other hardly likely to be pleasant to the workers, but in these cases there is all the more reason why they should be kept informed from the earliest stages and allowed, at least, to express their views as to how the process can be carried out with least hardship.

### An Effective Communication System.

One of the secrets of good management is an effective communication system; for workers will do their job efficiently only when they are able to identify themselves with their firm and feel that they are taking part in joint enterprise rather than being used as mere tools. Thus it must be possible for all grievances to be dealt with openly at the earliest moment and everybody in a factory ought to know what he is doing, for whom he is doing it, and why—the days of ' You're not paid to think: do what you're damn well told,' are, or should be, long past. The widest publicity must be given to the firm's finances, its future projects, its exports, and sales within the country because, as we have seen, nobody works satisfactorily unless he can feel that his work is meaningful. The real essence of democracy is not any special technique but the confidence of the ruled that they can influence their rulers, trust them and receive justice at their hands. Much the same might be said about the discontent of students for there is a close analogy between industrial and student disputes.

### Social Mobility.

Social mobility is another characteristic of a democracy, and we have seen that in England the barriers to the right man finding the right job and attaining the highest status of which he is capable are psychological and based on traditions rather than the result of any legal or physical hindrances. Indeed, it is surprising to note that social mobility in Britain is freer than in the United States in spite of the latter country's tradition of ' from log cabin to White House '. Probably the main reason for this, as Vance Packard has suggested, is that the American manager has little chance of success unless he is a WASP (White, Anglo-Saxon, Protestant) and, of course, industry is the main field controlling social mobility and status. In Britain the main obstacles for a man are the dying ' old boy ' tradition and the worker's fear of leaving his class, but for a woman the sole obstacle is simply the fact of being a woman.

## 4. THE DEVELOPMENT OF INDUSTRIAL PSYCHOLOGY.

We turn now to a brief account of the discoveries in the field of industrial psychology which had its beginnings in the United States at the turn of the century. One of its first exponents was a man known as Frederick Winslow Taylor who was to become famous—and, in the eyes of some, notorious—as the founder of the system described as ' Taylorism '. The principles of this system were simple:

(1) to select the best man for the job;

(2) to instruct him in the most efficient methods and the most effective movements to employ in his job;

(3) to give incentives in the form of higher wages to the best workers.

By applying these principles—which, in a more humane form, were to develop into modern Time and Motion Study—Taylor was able to reduce the number of workers needed to load wagons at his firm, the Bethlehem Steel Company, from 500 to 140, increase daily earnings of those who remained by 60 per cent, and save his bosses about 75,000 dollars a year. He was, not unnaturally, unpopular with the workers who, to this day, have always tended to dislike the man with the stop-watch and if Taylor as a sincere Quaker was basically a humane man and hoped that his system would benefit all, he nevertheless held the very odd philosophy that " all employees should bear in mind that each shop exists first, last, and all the time, for the purpose of paying dividends to its owners ".

About the same time Frank B. Gilbreth was encouraging the fragmentation of work which, as we have seen, was already an increasing tendency throughout the middle period of the industrial revolution in an attempt to increase efficiency and, to be fair, decrease the amount of hard work necessary. Like Taylor, his ideal was to make work so simple that " it could be carried out by a trained chimpanzee ". Neither of these two men was a trained psychologist; they only entered the field about the time of the First World War and concerned themselves mainly with experimenting on such environmental factors as the influence of temperature, humidity, noise and so on, on efficiency, but the total effect of all this early work was to increase the meaninglessness of the job, arouse resentments in many cases, and cause the workers to feel that they were being exploited. Since it is necessary to most workers to feel that what they are doing is meaningful and worthwhile, it is now generally admitted that if, from the economic point of view, many of these researches were really successful, the early investigators took a far too simple and mechanistic view of the nature of the problem. The philosophy lying behind them implied the beliefs (a) that man was a machine or, at any rate, that his mind could be ignored since the real problem lay in adjusting the physical environment or the way of doing the job; (b) that the only incentives were ' the carrot or the stick '—that is money or the negative incentive of fear of losing one's job; (c) that these propositions were self-evident because only a privileged few ever learn to like their work.

### The Importance of Status.

These assumptions were to receive a rude shock with the so-called researches carried out in the early 1930s by Elton Mayo and others at the works of the Western Electric Company in the United States. Mayo was an Australian working at Harvard University who initially started off with the same assumptions as his predecessors and contemporaries—basically, that the main factors in improving output were the conditions in the physical environment of the work-room and, when Western Electric called on him because they were having labour problems, he proceeded to put them into force. However, as a good scientist, Mayo found by accident that other factors than those of the physical environment were the most important in determining the worker's attitude to his work. These were his relationship to his working group, the attitude of his management, his knowledge of what he was doing and why he was doing it, and

above all his status. Everyone, in however modest a way, has to feel that what he is doing is of some value and is regarded as such by others. Psychiatrists, too, have pointed out that many neuroses have as their *immediate* cause conflicts over status which, when it is felt to be absolutely or relatively lowered, leads to a reduction of self-esteem, one of man's most potent drives. This is perhaps the most obvious connection between neurosis and unhappiness in a society which continues to stimulate ambition in a situation where ambitions are ever less easily attained.

### Incentives.

Social surveys carried out by numerous workers in this country and the United States under the influence of Mayo showed that *in all cases money was one of the least powerful incentives*. Of course, it has to be remembered that this may not be so when inflation occurs and prices rise and it may even be the case that, in an affluent society, workers may want more money as an aim in itself, but generally speaking the demand for higher wages is more likely to reflect either dissatisfaction with the firm or a concern with ' differentials '. That is to say, since the workers have their own informal status hierarchy, one group may feel aggrieved if those of a lower status have their wages increased in such a way as to lower the relative prestige of the other—it is the prestige rather than the money that matters, *e.g.*, when the very low wages of the lower grades of railway workers were raised, the engine drivers demanded correspondingly more, not because they begrudged their work-mates their increase affluence, but because their self-esteem had been hurt. The following are some of the relevant facts about incentives in general:

(1) There is no single ideal incentive, because incentives vary greatly from one culture to another (we have seen elsewhere that one of the difficulties in motivating workers in South America and the Afro-Asian countries is their lack of interest in bettering their material conditions), and from one individual to another (*e.g.*, one man may value money whilst another may find more leisure or opportunity for promotion a stronger stimulus to work);

(2) The law of diminishing returns applies to all material incentives, *i.e.*, as the reward increases the desire for further reward decreases until it reaches vanishing-point. Thus the miners, when given higher wages, increased their absenteeism, because the point had been reached at which the need for more money had become secondary to the need for more leisure;

(3) Incentives may conflict with each other; for the worker may ignore financial incentives if he fears that the rate for the job may be cut or that he may work himself out of a job;

(4) It is necessary to realise that in our own culture all motives tend to become ' monetised ' since people have subconsciously been taught to believe that money is the key to satisfaction and, when they feel that something is wrong, naturally ask for more money—as Gordon Rattray Taylor has noted " a demand for money undoubtedly indicates that they want *something*, but it does not tell us what ".

### Restrictive Practices.

We have already seen that incentives can conflict with each other, and one of Mayo's researches demonstrated very clearly the phenomenon of restrictive practices arising from such conflicts. In what was known as the ' bank-wiring room ' of the Western Electric Company, he found a group of male workers who completely disregarded all financial incentives and, though the incentive plan provided that the more work a worker did the more money he received, productivity remained at

6,000 units a day in spite of the fact that without the least difficulty the group could have produced 7,000. Here Mayo found that the informal group, which he believed to be the basic unit in industry (it has been described elsewhere as the ' primary group '), had selected an informal leader who was not the same person as the official one. There was an unofficial code of behaviour which exerted a strong influence over group members and impressed upon them the following rules: " You should not turn out too much work, otherwise you will be a ' chiseller '." " You should not tell a supervisor anything to the detriment of a work-mate, otherwise you will be a ' squealer '." " You should not ' act officious '—if you are an inspector, for example, you should not act like one." These are, of course, as Sargant Florence points out, the same sort of principles as are found in the English public school: " Rate-busters have been called ' swots ', chisellers, ' slackers ', squealers, ' sneaks '. Americans apparently had no name for the form of behaviour described as ' acting officious ', but familiar English slang is ' swank '." These form the basis for restrictive practices in industry though here the need to maintain status and avoid the traditional fear of insecurity plays a greater part.

## Summary of Mayo's Researches.

Mayo's important conclusions can be summarised as follows:

(1) Work is a social activity in the sense that, even when working in physical isolation as in the case of the artist, what is done is carried out either in society or for society.

(2) The social world of the adult is primarily patterned around work activity.

(3) The need for recognition, security, and sense of belonging is more important in determining workers' morale and productivity than the physical conditions under which the work is carried out.

(4) A complaint is not necessarily an objective recital of facts; it is commonly a *symptom* manifesting disturbance of an individual's status position. Contrary to general belief, the majority of strikes are not about wage claims, but about matters in which the workers feel their status or self-respect to be threatened.

(5) The worker is a person whose attitudes and effectiveness are conditioned by social demands from both inside and outside the work plant.

(6) The change from an established to an adaptive society—*i.e.*, one in which there is great social and geographical mobility, and where a traditionally static society has given way to mass democracy—tends continually to disrupt the social organisation of factories and industry generally.

Two of the dangers of high geographical mobility are (a) that a constantly mobile population never has the time to develop loyalty to individual members or individual firms—as one supervisor said, his department was more like a procession than a work-room because its members were continually changing; (b) since social control by the superego or conscience is less effective in many fields than control by group-membership, those who never stay in a community long enough are apt to become ' rootless ' with a subsequent weakening in moral control. This, of course, is one of the reasons why immigrants are peculiarly liable to get into trouble. It is not their innate wickedness, but the fact that they have left the community which originally supported their moral beliefs, their old cultural imperatives have weakened, and they have not become sufficiently identified with their new surroundings to accept the current mores. Hence the social phenomenon of gangsterism during the 1930s in America was almost exclusively an Italian or Irish one—in fact, even now, the old secret society founded in Sicily and known as the Mafia, virtually rules a large sector of modern gangsterism.

(7) Group collaboration does not occur by accident; it must be planned for and developed. If group collaboration is achieved, a cohesion may result which resists the disrupting effects of the mass society.

## CONCLUSIONS.

What we have found in this brief survey is that society is constantly changing in order to adapt itself to a new environment which itself alters with disconcerting and ever-accelerating speed. It follows that it is incorrect to say that ' human nature ' is always the same and that moral standards never change—on the contrary, it should be evident by now that changes in these fields are not only inevitable but desirable. Of course, there are a few basic laws which are ' absolute ' in the sense that they are firmly based on the nature of society—*e.g.*, " Love thy neighbour as thyself " is a fundamental rule simply because society, by definition, is a state of affairs in which most people are neighbourly, and Stuart Chase has said that if more than 10 per cent of any community failed to cooperate, the community would simply collapse.

' Free competition ' may well have been in the interests of society as a whole in a developing economy, but it is neither possible nor desirable now—in fact, it was brought to an end some time ago, not by the machinations of wicked socialists, but because capitalists could not keep up with the pace and began to combine to protect their own interests.

Again, though we have not presumed to prescribe in what direction sexual morality should change, there is not the slightest doubt that it is changing and will continue to do so. What we have suggested is that sexual relations must be based on mutual respect and, when that is done, nothing serious is likely to go wrong. This was the fundamental meaning of the teachings of Christ when he shifted the emphasis from the externally applied laws of the Ten Commandments to inward intentions and motives. However, no matter how important sexual morality may be, it is very far from being the whole of morality and we might guess that one of the reasons for the general decline of interest in the churches has been their tendency to equate sex with sin to the exclusion of the social injustices which people feel to be among the major issues of our times. If this does not always apply to individual churchmen, it does in general apply to their churches. Very often their influence has been on the side of reaction as in Spain, and it was an Anglican clergyman who described his church as " the Tory party at prayer " but, again, there are many exceptions, such as the attitude of the Church of Scotland to African affairs and the last Encyclical of Pope John.

In the field of industry what has been said here may be summarised in the words of Goronwy Rees: " It seems sometimes, today, as if the grand committee of management which has for so long conducted the affairs of the country has at last become conscious of its failure and seeks desperately for a cure. Hence the ' lofty symbols ', the ' admonitions ', the ' signals for a change of heart ', which we are offered daily. But how are our managers to cure themselves, and where, in the short time that may be left to us, are they to discover either the knowledge and competence, or the powers of will, energy, and creativeness, which today so many of them conspicuously lack? " Much the same might be said of some of the workers' leaders who cannot divest themselves of wholly outdated notions and superstitions.

We have tried to show that there is a more hopeful side to the picture presented, notably in the field of education; but what is clear is that radical changes in attitudes are needed on all fronts. What mainly hinders this is not only the backward-looking traditionalist mentality but, oddly enough, the ' affluent society ' which, along with its many benefits, has brought about the state of affairs described by J. K. Galbraith, the eminent economist, and lately American Ambassador to India, when he pointed out that " in a country where well-being is general, the astute politician will be the one who stalwartly promises to defend the *status quo.*"

# MODERN GARDENING

A guide for the gardener on all aspects of horticulture particularly in the control of pests and diseases and the eradication of weeds by the latest means.

## TABLE OF CONTENTS

# MODERN GARDENING

## CULTIVATION OF FLOWERS.

Throughout this section the notes must be taken to refer to cultural conditions in the British Isles, although in many cases the information can be adopted to suit the necessity of readers living abroad. Undoubtedly, in many temperate parts of the world interest in gardening has increased enormously during the past decade or so, despite the fact that numbers of large gardens have ceased to exist and that few people can afford to pay for full-time help in their gardens. To counteract this, the all important labour-saving garden has come into its own; shrubby plants have replaced annual bedding schemes and large lawns put down instead of herbaceous borders or beds of particular plants.

In addition, the owner-gardener is anxious to avail himself of the excellent selection of modern tools; thus the conventional hoe is being replaced by the " Swoe " or the Wolf pattern of Dutch weeder, both of which are very easy to use, and digging can be done quickly—and with much less effort—by using a German digger called a " Terrex " spade. For grass mowing, the work is easily done with motor mowers like any of the new battery-driven patterns.

For greenhouse work, smaller houses are being used and one, say, 12 ft. by 8 ft., can be run economically with a minimum winter temperature of 40° Fahrenheit by the introduction of trouble-free, thermostatic heaters or the turbo-heaters. At the moment, besides automatic heating, the prototypes for automatic ventilation and watering are making an appearance.

While advocating the use of such appliances, it must be pointed out that there are also to be found tools, sundries, and fertilisers of little value, and many of which have never been properly tested prior to being put on the market. It is, therefore, a good plan to discuss the comparative merits of any appliance or horticultural sundry with a competent horticulturist or to contact a public authority. In particular, many local horticultural societies have special trading facilities, and the merits of most garden things are generally known and discussed among members.

Throughout this Guide the vexed question of change in scientific name has been dealt with as liberally as possible and, whenever necessary, synonyms and cross references are given. In dealing with cultivar names, that is, varietal names like rose ' Peace,' reference is made as recommended in *The International Code of Nomenclature for Cultivated Plants* (1961). By so doing, the references are right up to date and further information on any particular plant or subject is easy to find. For the purpose, a few standard works of reference are given after each section. Normally, all the plants mentioned in the text are available through the usual trade channels.

After each plant listed there is a note on its propagation. Generally, this is the easiest or most efficient way of doing so, but it is not necessarily the only means. Details of the various methods employed are as follows:

**Seed.** Generally speaking, the early spring is the most suitable time for sowing seeds of trees and shrubs besides those of herbaceous plants and alpines. Where only a few plants are needed, the seed can be sown in pots and a suitable compost made up with 2 parts of soil, 1 part of peat, and 1 part of coarse sand. Before sowing, the pot should be stood up to its rim in water so that the soil is soaked. Then the seed can be sown thinly and covered with a light sprinkling of sifted compost.

For very fine seed, like begonias or azaleas, the seed must have only the merest " sugaring " of sand just sufficient to anchor it. When sown, the pots should be covered with a pane

of glass (to prevent evaporation) and kept, if possible, in a warm greenhouse or frame. With this method of propagation it is important to remember that failure will result if the seed is sown too deeply, if the temperature is too low, or if the soil is too dry.

CORRECT PREPARATION OF SEED POTS AND PANS—Note provision for ample drainage and compost to rim of its container. After sowing, the containers are covered with a sheet of glass.

**Cuttings.** There are two main types of cutting: soft-wood cuttings made from fresh, green shoots in the spring and summer and hard-wood cuttings made of mature or semi-mature woody shoots in the autumn. A soft cutting is taken about 3 in. long, the lower leaves removed and a clean cut made through a node in the stem. These are then inserted in pots containing a light, sandy soil or a rooting medium such as horticultural vermiculite, well watered, and covered with a bell jar or plastic bag. Delphiniums, hydrangeas, and lupins are all propagated in this way.

Hard-wood cuttings are taken in the autumn and made from shoots about 8–12 in. long. These are inserted in a sandy soil out of doors or in a cold frame, and left to develop for a year. Blackcurrants, forsythia, and roses can be propagated by this means.

**Layering.** This is one of the easiest ways of propagating the majority of woody plants, and is used to increase stocks of plants like clematis, lilacs, and rhododendrons. Normally, layering is done in the autumn or spring when suitable branches are pegged down. On each of these the young shoots are, in turn, pegged down and tips turned upwards and tied in position. To encourage rooting, gritty sand and peat should be worked around each layer, and usually the young plant can be severed from the parent after about eighteen months.

**Division.** By this method it is easy to propagate the majority of herbaceous plants, some rock-garden plants, and a few shrubs. A few herbaceous plants, like delphinium and paeony, are slow to get established after moving, and here the method should not be employed. In any case, old plants should not be split up in a wholesale manner; instead, it is far better to select a few young healthy plants, divide these, and replant the best of the young shoots, in the autumn.

## ALPHABETICAL LIST OF ORNAMENTAL PLANTS.

**Abutilon.**—The greenhouse species is often used in public parks for bedding schemes. *A. vitifolium*, with white, mauve, or blue flowers makes a fine wall shrub for warm gardens. If given full sun it will quickly reach 10–15 ft., but is sometimes short-lived. *Prop.*—Easily raised from seed sown in March in a warm greenhouse or frame.

**Acer (Maple).**—Hardy, ornamental trees; the Norway maple is often planted for its magnificent autumn colour and as a lawn tree. *A. palmatum* and vars. constitute the Japanese maples; all colour brilliantly in the autumn but do not grow freely unless given some shade and a light soil rich in humus. *Prop.*—Seed, layering, or budding.

**Achillea (Yarrow).**—Grey-leaved perennials for open border or, dwarf species, for rock garden. Valued as a cut flower, particularly *A. ptarmica* 'Perry's White,' with double, white flowers and *A. eupatorium* 'Gold Plate,' with large, flat, yellow flower heads. *A. millefolium* is a pernicious weed of turf (T34). *Prop.*—Division in autumn.

**Acidanthera.**—Scented, bulbous plant introduced from Abyssinia. It is not difficult to grow if the corms are planted in the spring and lifted in the autumn for storing in a frost-proof shed. It requires a sunny position and plenty of water in the summer. *Prop.*—Offsets removed when the old crop of bulbs is lifted.

**Aconitum (Monkshood).**—Blue-flowered perennial plants particularly useful for lightly shaded positions or full sun; flowers from May to July, height 3-5 ft.; roots poisonous. *Prop.*—Seed or division.

**Adiantum.**—*See* Ferns.

A WELL-GROWN AGAPANTHUS—In winter the pot should be kept in a cold greenhouse or some protected place; in summer afforded full sun.

**Agapanthus.**—A bulbous plant, native of South Africa, usually found in seaside gardens and sometimes grown in tubs; flowers blue, violet, or white. It needs winter protection in the form of a covering of bracken or straw and a light soil heavily enriched with manure. Worthy of wider cultivation. *Prop.*—Seed or division in March.

**Ageratum.**—Blue-flowered carpeting plant. *See* Annuals.

**Allium (Flowering Onion).**—A genus of nearly 300 species of bulbous plants widely distributed over the Northern Hemisphere. The foliage has the distinctive smell of garlic, but some species are grown for garden ornamentation; in particular *A. roseum*, valuable late-flowering rock plant for dry positions. *Prop.*—Offsets, taken from parent bulbs in the spring.

**Alstroemeria aurantiaca (Peruvian Lily).**—This tuberous-rooted, herbaceous plant is often grown for cutting. Flowers orange-red and height 2-3 ft.; of easy culture if afforded a sunny position and left undisturbed. For best results apply liquid manure or soot water when growth starts. *Prop.*—Seed or division.

**Althaea (Hollyhock).**—A truly delightful, old-world plant, but not often seen, as modern hybrids

have given way to rust disease. Best grown in a rich, heavy loam. Mulch with manure of any sort and stake as necessary. *Prop.*—Seed in June, thin out, and transfer to flowering position in September. Although a perennial, in some localities the best results are obtained by treating it as a biennial and raising a small supply annually.

**Alyssum.**—Low-growing annuals and perennials for rock garden and sunny border. The perennial, *A. saxatile*, is deservedly popular by reason of its bright, spring flowers and value as a wall plant. The variety 'Citrinum' is bright yellow and 'Dudley Neville' biscuit-yellow. *Prop.*—Perennial sorts by cuttings in June.

**Amaryllis belladonna.**—Often this plant is confused with the greenhouse, bulbous plant, *Hippeastrum*. The true amaryllis is a half-hardy bulb for planting at the foot of a warm wall; it has white to pinkish-red flowers. When planting, cover neck of bulb with an inch of soil and leave undisturbed, as the plant resents moving and is slow to get established. Lack of flowering is generally due to planting too deep. Established clumps may be fed with hoof and horn meal at 2 oz. per sq. yd. in July. *Prop.*—Divide and replant clumps in early July.

**Amelanchier canadensis.**—A large shrub or small tree; valuable for its spring flowers and autumn colour. As it will grow almost anywhere in sun or shade, it makes a good plant for informal screening. *Prop.*—Seed or layers.

**Amepelopsis.**—*See* Parthenocissus.

**Anchusa italica.**—A blue-flowered perennial with fleshy roots, growing to a height of about 3 ft. Responds to feeding and needs a position in full sun. *Prop.*—Root cuttings in the spring; division in the autumn.

**Anemone.**—The tuberous-rooted section includes the 'Caen' and 'St. Brigid' strains. These are best grown in an open position in light, rich soil; plant in October, lift and store when foliage dies. The hardy, fibrous-rooted perennials are varieties of *A. hybrida* (syn. *japonica*) and constitute one of the most accommodating of perennials, being particularly useful for damp, shady positions. Worthy of wider attention from gardeners. *Prop.*—Perennial sorts by division in autumn.

**Annuals.**—These are plants which develop from seed, flower, fruit, and die within a year. Additionally, some perennials, like antirrhinums, may be treated as annuals for the convenience of their cultivation. Sunny borders may be planted solely with annuals, they may be interplanted with perennials, used for window boxes, or, occasionally, in the rock garden. All sorts do best in well-worked, light loam enriched each year with a dressing of fish meal at 3 oz. per sq. yd., ten days before sowing or planting.

In the division of the group Hardy Annuals may be sown in the open ground as soon as conditions permit during March or April where the plants are to flower. Wet or cold soils will give many failures, and fine seed should be covered only with the lightest sugaring of soil. Often surprising—but delightful—results may be obtained by sowing broadcast mixed seed of annuals specially offered by some trade houses.

To raise Half Hardy Annuals, seed may be sown in early March in a warm greenhouse and the seedlings pricked out into boxes. Subsequently, the plants are grown on in a cold frame, gradually hardened off, and then transferred to their flowering positions towards the end of May.

**Anthemis tinctoria.**—Hardy perennial with feathery, grey foliage and flowers in varying shades of yellow. Height 2-3 ft., needs full sun and good for cutting. *Prop.*—Division in the autumn. *Anthemis nobilis* is the chamomile sometimes unwisely used to make lawns.

**Antirrhinum (Snapdragon).**—The popular bedding plant requiring a good soil and position in full sun now largely in disfavour owing to rust disease; planting should be restricted to rust-resistant varieties. *See* Annuals.

**Aphelandra squarrosa.**—An evergreen, perennial plant introduced from Brazil. Often sold as a house plant, albeit a warm temperature and a high humidity are necessary for its cultivation. When grown indoors it is best discarded when the flowers fade and the foliage starts to wither, as it cannot be successfully grown on from year to year under normal conditions indoors.

**Aquilegia.**—The modern race of hybrids are the result of much interbreeding with wild forms to give a wide range of colours. Best when planted in light shade where soil is naturally moist. *Prop.*—Seed in late spring; transplant to flowering position for following year.

**Arabis caucasica.**—Once known as *A. albida*, this common rock plant is often used on dry walls. The double-flowered form is particularly good. *Prop.*—Cuttings in July; a fresh stock should be raised regularly as the special forms tend to die out.

**Araucaria (Monkey Puzzle).**—This tree was introduced from Chile, where it forms large natural forests, and widely planted in Victorian days. Browning of foliage suggests lack of water in the summer or, occasionally, effects of very cold weather. It should be planted in a position protected from the prevailing wind. *Prop.*—Seed in a warm greenhouse.

**Armeria maritima.**—A hardy perennial with pink or red flowers in the spring; must be grown in full sun where the soil is dry. *Prop.*—Division after flowering.

**Artemisia.**—A genus of shrubs and perennials suitable for sunny borders or rockeries. *A. lactiflora* is among the best of the herbaceous species, having grey foliage and creamy-white flowers. *A. abrotanum* (lad's love) in the shrubby section has grey, fragrant foliage. *Prop.*—Herbaceous section by division; shrubs by cuttings in the early summer.

**Arundinaria.**—*See* Bamboo.

**Aster (Michaelmas Daisy).**—By careful breeding this plant has been improved out of all recognition, and many first-class varieties are available in the trade. Responsive to good cultivation, it is used for its colour late in season and properties as a cut flower, particularly *A. yunnanensis* ' Napsbury' and *A.* ' Barr's Pink.' A wide range of colours are available besides some fine, low-growing forms. In the border one pleasing combination can be made with *A.* ' Harrington's Pink' and *Scabious* ' Dinkie.' *Prop.*—The clumps should be split up *annually* in the spring, and only the plumpest pieces of outer root replanted.

**Aster, China or Common.**—*See* Callistephus.

**Astilbe.**—Allied to the *Spiraea* and useful for planting in moist, rich soils; flowers white, pink, and crimson; height 2 ft. *Prop.*—Division of clumps.

**Aubrieta.**—A name often misspelt. Throughout the country it is used as edging or for dry walls. Many lovely sorts available apart from the commonly found, pale-blue variety. It is a lime lover. *Prop.*—After flowering the plants should be severely trimmed and, as necessary, stock increased by division.

**Aucuba japonica.**—Much maligned and over-planted shrub, but one tolerant of neglect and sunless or smoky conditions. Interesting variants of the type, like ' Crotonifolia,' may be found in trade lists. *Prop.*—Cuttings rooted in the open in July.

**Auricula.**—Correctly known botanically as *Primula auricula*. Flowers of alpine auriculas are white or yellow, while in those of florists' auriculas are to be found some of the most delicate colourings among hardy plants Choice varieties are grown in pots under glass; others in moist,

shady borders. *Prop.*—Seed or division in the spring.

**Azalea.**—*See* Rhododendron.

**Bamboo.**—The common name for the large group of woody grasses, reference to which is difficult owing to the confusion in their nomenclature. Often grown for screening and wind breaks, and is a favourite shelter for small birds; the best for home-grown canes are *Phyllostachys viridiglaucescens* and *Sinarundinaria nitida*. An interesting account of bamboo growing is found in the *Jour. Roy. Hort. Soc.* (June 1957). Growth can be encouraged by feeding with sulphate of ammonia and mulching with leaf-mould in the spring. *Prop.*—Division of clumps in late spring; transplants must be kept watered until established.

**Begonia.**—A genus showing wide diversity of form and much horticultural value. Of particular interest is the tuberous-rooted section, of which many of the loveliest varieties have originated in the nurseries of Messrs. Blackmore and Landon at Bath. For bedding schemes, the tubers are started in boxes of rich soil under glass in late March and planted out 9 in. apart in June. During the summer feed with liquid manure of any sort and keep moist in dry periods. *Prop.*—Cuttings in early spring in a warm case.

**Berberis.**—An extensive genus of beautiful and easily grown shrubs, evergreen and deciduous; the former used mainly for beauty of flower, and the latter for autumn colouring and ornamental fruits. *B. stenophylla* makes a fine evergreen hedge; invaluable for preventing illicit entry by dogs and, even, unruly children. *B. aggregata* and *B. jamesiana* are among the best berrying kinds. Prune in the winter by removing old wood. *Prop.*—Seed in spring or layering in autumn.

**Buddleia.**—Deciduous shrubs of easy culture for sunny positions. Varieties of *B. davidii* available in range of colours from purple to white; best when pruned hard by cutting all previous year's growth back to main stems in February. The weeping species, *B. alternifolia*, often grown as a standard; good specimens at R.H.S. Gardens, Wisley. This sort must be pruned in the summer by cutting off the dead flowering stems. *Prop.*—Cuttings in July–August in cold frame.

**Cactus.**—In the main grown in cool greenhouses or as house plants and, if cultivated well, many will flower every year. As a general guide, plants should be watered fairly freely in the summer and little in the winter, but there are exceptions. A detailed account of growing these fascinating plants will be found in *The Cactus Grower's Guide*, by Vera Higgins (Latimer House), 1946.

**Calceolaria.**—Seed of the greenhouse biennials sown in June or July for flowering in the following year. Mixed seed provides a wide range of colour. *C. integrifolia* is a half-hardy perennial, raised by cuttings or seed, for greenhouse or bedding work.

**Calendula (Marigold).**—This common hardy annual is freely raised from seed sown in August. Of easy culture in any sort of soil, although it is worth getting seed of new varieties now available. *See* Annuals.

**Callistephus.**—The China asters are among the best half-hardy annuals for garden and indoor decoration, but good soil and full sun are necessary for best results. *See* Annuals.

**Camellia japonica.**—Hardy, evergreen shrub rightly beloved by connoisseurs and cultivated in gardens for many centuries. May be grown in cold greenhouses, woodland gardens, and against north- and west-facing walls; under all conditions camellias must have a moist, acid soil. Best varieties for outdoors are ' Althaeaflora' (dark red), ' Donckelarii' (red, white marbling), and ' C. M. Wilson' (pink). Of recent introduction is the desirable *C. williamsii* bred from *C. japonica* in part; often the subject of television and gardening notes. The dropping of buds is thought due to dryness at the roots at some time or sharp fluctuation in temperature. *Prop.*—Named varieties by cuttings under glass in early July. Otherwise plants easily raised from seeds if sown in the autumn immediately they are ripe, in acidic peat and kept moist.

**Campsis grandiflora.**—Sometimes found listed as *Bignonia* or *Tecoma*; choice deciduous climber for warm wall, large reddish-orange flowers in autumn. To encourage flowering growth, prune hard back to old growth in spring. *Prop.*—Cuttings in April struck in a warm case.

**Canary Creeper.**—*See* Tropaeolum.

**Candytuft.**—Hardy annual (*q.v.*) and perennials with white, crimson, blue, or purple flowers. The perennial—*Iberis sempervirens*—is a fine plant for a rock wall. *Prop.*—Seed or, perennials, from cuttings.

**Carnation.**—*See* Dianthus.

**Centaurea (Cornflower).**—The perennial species are valuable for cutting and border use, and may be found in such colours as pink, crimson, and yellow. *Prop.*—Lift and divide every third or fourth year. The hardy annual, *C. cyanus*, is often sold as a cut flower. *See* Annuals.

**Chaenomeles speciosa.**—This is the correct botanical name for japonica. The species commonly grown is a wide-spreading, rounded shrub, 6–10 ft. in height, and often used against walls. It is a plant of easy culture with best results being achieved by the annual spurring back of the current season's growth in the same way as an apple tree is pruned. All japonicas can be used for making jelly but, for this purpose, the best one is *Chaenomeles cathayensis*, a gaunt shrub about 10 ft. in height which bears fruit up to 8 oz. in weight. To obtain a crop within a reasonable time, two or three plants may be set in a group about 5 ft. apart. If growth or flowering is below par all japonicas should be fed with " Growmore " and mulched with compost.

**Cheiranthus cheiri (Wallflower).**—Among the finest displays of this biennial are those found each year in the public gardens of Southend-on-Sea, where it is used in conjunction with bulbs and forget-me-nots. *Prop.*—Seed sown thinly in rows in May and seedlings thinned or lined out and then transplanted in late autumn. The so-called Siberian wallflower, *Erysimun asperum*, which has bright orange flowers, is grown in the same way, but it is intolerant of wet soils. Both sorts are lime lovers, and on acid soils plants may receive treatment with 1 oz. of lime in a gallon of water.

**Chimonanthus (Winter Sweet).**—Hardy, winter-flowering shrub with heavily scented flowers. Although brought to this country from the Far East in the mid-eighteenth century, its garden value is not widely appreciated. The large-flowered, yellow sort, *C. praecox*, is particularly fine, but like all the varieties, it is best grown against a sunny wall and where the soil tends to be poor. If growth is excessive and flowering poor, trim back young growth severely in March to encourage short, spur-like shoots. *Prop.*—Easily raised from seed or layers.

**Christmas Rose.**—*See* Helleborus.

**Chrysanthemum.**—Hardy annual sorts are available in a wide range of colours and give a fine display in the summer months. *See* Annuals. There are also a number of perennials such as the shasta daisy and the oxeye daisy for sunny, herbaceous borders; all do well in ordinary soil, but should be lifted and split up about every three years. The plant sold by florists in the autumn is the Japanese chrysanthemum. Many are hardy out-of-doors, but no plant is more responsive to good cultivation and normally is best left to the specialist grower. For ordinary garden work, the best sorts are the Korean and Otley types. Under a brief reference the interesting details of cultivation cannot be dealt with fairly, and reference to specialist books is recommended.

**Clematis.**—A hardy climber for walls, screens, pergolas, and the like. Best kinds are to be found among named varieties in nurserymen's lists. A light, well-drained soil is necessary and if fed annually with a bucketful of manure or compost the plant will thrive for many years. Occasionally plants will be found on north walls, and if grown in full sun some light protection from the sun is desirable for the roots. Varieties which flower on the *current* season's growth, like *C. jackmanii*, should be pruned in late February to within a foot of the ground; other sorts should have sufficient old growth removed, after flowering, to keep them within bounds.

Unfortunately, the climber is sometimes killed by clematis wilt, a disease about which very little is known, and the premature death of young plants should not be blamed automatically on the supplier. *Prop.*—Layering, by which means one shoot will often give three or four plants.

**Convallaria majalis (Lily of the Valley).**—Well-known perennial that will thrive in any damp, shady position. For best results lift every four or five years and mulch annually with old manure. *Prop.*—Division when foliage fades.

**Coreopsis.**—The hardy annuals are found in catalogues under " Callipsis," and all will thrive in ordinary soil. The flowers are mainly bright yellow, and many are good for cutting. *See* Annuals. Similarly, the perennials have the same predominant colour and are useful because of their long flowering season and abundance of flower. *Prop.*—Division.

**Cornflower.**—*See* Centaurea.

**Cosmos.**—Tall-growing, half-hardy annuals that are best grown in full sun in a dryish border. The large, daisy-like flowers can be had in a variety of colours, including white, yellow, pink, and crimson. *See* Annuals.

**Cotoneaster.**—Hardy evergreen and deciduous shrubs or small trees bearing scarlet or sometimes yellow berries in the autumn. All may be grown in ordinary or poor soil and planted in open or shady shrubberies and trailing species used against walls, over banks, or as ground cover. For shrub-berries *C. lacteus* and *C.* ' Cornubia ' with red berries and *C. rothchildianus* with yellow berries are among the best sorts; *C. conspicuus* ' Decora ' is a strong grower for banks, while *C. horizontalis* is an excellent cover for any wall. Planting may be done in the autumn or spring, and no pruning, apart from occasional shaping, is required. *Prop.*—Seeds and layering.

**Crataegus (Hawthorn).**—There are many good varieties of our British hawthorn, *C. oxyacantha*, worthy of attention, particularly ' Coccinea,' (crimson) and ' Paulii ' (double, red). All will do well on poor soils, and no pruning is required. The common hawthorn makes a stout, impenetrable hedge planted 9 in. apart in a double row 9 in. asunder. *Prop.*—Common sort by seed; choice varieties by budding.

**Crocus.**—A hardy bulb of great beauty which was studied for many years by one of the greatest horticulturists of the twentieth century, the late E. A. Bowles. Does best in rich soil planted in bold groups around margins of beds or borders and naturalised in grass. When required, feed in early spring with bone meal at 2 oz. per sq. yd. *C. sieberi* and *C. tomasinianus* very early flowering; large-flowered, garden forms about three weeks later. *C. zonatus* flowers in the autumn and is often naturalised in grass. *Prop.*—Clumps may be lifted and divided about every five years, in July. The so-called autumn crocus is *Colchicum autumnale*. This bears large, lustrous leaves in the summer, followed by mauve or white flowers—of fleeting duration—in the autumn.

**Crown Imperial.**—*See* Fritillaria.

**Cyclamen.**—*See* House plants.

**Cytisus (Broom).**—Only does really well in dry, poor soils in full sun; choice, procumbent sorts, like *C. kewensis*, used in rock gardens and tall ones in open shrubberies. Pruning is important; shoots should be shortened after flowering, but old wood must never be cut. *Prop.*—Seed and cuttings in August in a sandy soil.

**Daffodil.**—*See* Narcissus.

**Dahlia.**—The cultivation of this plant is a special study, and there are probably more garden varieties of it than any other plant. Ordinary soil enriched with manure and an open position is required. Tubers may be planted 3 in. deep in April or young plants in late May. During the summer feed with soot water and liquid manure. After the first frosts lift, dry, and then store tubers in peat or straw in frost-proof place. Many stocks of dahlia are affected by virus (T30), and purchasers should be careful to check source of supply.

**Daphne.**—Shrubby plants, giving some of the most richly scented of all flowers. In particular, there is *D. mezereum*, which requires a damp soil; failure with the shrub is due usually to root disturbance or virus disease (T31) *D. odora* is one of the evergreen, fragrant species. Some references have suggested that this lovely shrub is not hardy, but there is no evidence to support the supposition. *Prop.*—Seed or layering.

**Delphinium.**—Hardy annuals and perennials. The latter sorts have gained popularity enormously since the War, due in the main to the activities of the Delphinium Society but also to the introduction of many very fine new varieties. American hybrids, like the 'Pacific Strain,' are very large but tend to die out and, consequently, lack the true, perennial habit of European sorts, albeit some of these have been weakened by the introduction of poor lines. It is important therefore to select stocks of strong constitution. Delphiniums need a deep, rich soil and a sunny position protected from wind. Plant in autumn 3 ft. apart, feed in the summer with liquid soot water, and mulch with decayed compost or manure in the spring. When growth starts, thin out weak growths to leave not more than five stems per plant. In winter take steps against possible slug damage (T29), and on this point it is beneficial to protect crowns with a covering of ashes. *Prop.*—Cuttings in the spring or seed; division of clumps is a poor alternative.

The hardy annual sorts are the well-known larkspurs, which grow to a height of 18 in. to 2 ft. and may be found in a range of colours including pink, red, white, and shades of blue. *See* Annuals.

**Deutzia.**—Hardy deciduous shrubs thriving in any soil and valuable for their summer flowers of white or whitish-pink shade. To keep the plants vigorous, shoots should be shortened after flowering and old or weak wood cut out. *D. scabra* is of robust habit, reaching about 7 ft., and *D. elegantissima* 'Fasciculata' proves a graceful shrub some 5 ft. tall with clusters of about twenty flowers coloured rosy-pink and each nearly an inch across. *Prop.*—Cuttings made from firm young growths about 10 in. long in sandy soil out-of-doors.

**Dianthus.**—This name covers a wide range of annual, biennial, and perennial plants. At one time often grown for their fragrance, but to a large extent this has been lost with the introduction of wider ranges of colour. Border carnations and picotees grown out-of-doors need a limy, fairly rich soil in full sun. Plant in the autumn or spring and, as the buds appear, feed with soot water or liquid animal manure, if necessary. These groups are *not* of good perennial habit and should be propagated annually to ensure continuation of stock.

The common pink requires the same soil conditions, and should be propagated when the stock gets weak; good scented varieties should be sought, and include the 'Imperial Pinks,' 'Mrs. Simkins,' and 'White Ladies.' *Prop.*—The best method is by layering in July so that the new plants can be put in their flowering position by mid-September. The lower leaves are pulled off selected shoots and a slit passing through a joint is made in the stem. Each layer is then pegged down with a hair-pin, the pin being placed above the cut. The layers are then covered with an inch of sandy compost and well watered.

In this genus is the sweet william; although truly a perennial, it is generally grown as a biennial and, consequently, the plant is raised from seed in May out-of-doors. In gardens where it is prone to rust disease control is most difficult and it is not worth a place.

LAYERING CARNATIONS—This is a typical example of how many plants can be propagated. A strong, new growth is pegged down into sandy soil after a cut has been made in the stem, at the point of pegging. Once rooted the layer can be severed from the parent and transplanted a week or two later.

**Digitalis.**—The biennial sort generally found in gardens is the common foxglove, which is grown in light shade in fairly rich, moist soil. In the past many named forms have been offered in the trade, but undoubtedly the best one is *D.* 'Sutton's Excelsior.' *Prop.*—Seed sown in May out-of-doors.

**Doronicum.**—Hardy perennials with yellow flowers; warrants wider planting, as they are among the earliest perennials to bloom and will thrive in poor soil or in some shade. The best is *D. austriacum* flowering in March, height 9 in. *Prop.*—Division after flowering.

**Echinops.**—Name appropriately derived from *echinos*, a hedgehog, in reference to the spiny, long scales of the flowers. The plant does well in an open position, where the globular heads of steely-blue flowers can be seen to advantage. *Prop.*—Division in March, but best left undisturbed as long as possible, as it must be moved with care.

**Elaeagnus.**—Hardy deciduous and evergreen shrubs generally grown in rather dry positions as foliage plants. Of the evergreen sort, *E. pungens* 'Aureo-Variegata' has bright golden variegation, and is therefore valuable for indoor decoration during the winter. *Prop.*—Layering in late summer.

**Erica.**—The heathers are native plants to Britain, and many variants found in the wild have been introduced into gardens to good purpose. Indeed, heathers have become so popular that special Heather Gardens have been made, and two fine examples may be found in the Royal Gardens, Windsor, where the planting is new and the Royal Horticultural Society's Gardens, Wisley. Here, different sorts reaching the dimensions of small trees, dwarf kinds, and many scores of interesting variants, to supply flower throughout the year, will be found.

The Scottish heather is, botanically, *Calluna vulgaris*, and, like all British heathers, it is intolerant of lime or chalk. Where alkaline conditions exist, planters can try *E. carnea*—a winter-flowering heather—or *E. darleyensis*, but the results are usually disappointing. When planting all heathers, clumps must be well firmed and after.

wards kept moist; subsequently, mulch all types annually with peat. *Prop.*—Division and layering.

**Erigeron.**—Hardy perennial for sunny borders; daisy-like flowers freely develop and are good for cutting. *Prop.*—Division in the autumn.

**Escallonia.**—Slightly tender evergreen and deciduous shrubs. In the Midlands protection of a south wall is necessary; suitable for open shrubbery in the South. Ideal for maritime conditions, and here may be used to good effect as hedges. Many of the best varieties originated in the nursery of Messrs. The Slieve Donard Co. in County Down. *Prop.*—Cuttings under a glass jar in summer; layers in September.

**Eschscholzia californica.**—A hardy annual of easy culture; height 18 in., flowers mainly shades of orange. *See* Annuals.

**Everlasting Flowers.**—*See* Helichrysum.

**Ferns.**—A large number of plants are included under this name and, as they grow wild in many parts of the world, some need hothouse conditions. They are distinguished from flowering plants by their method of reproduction; instead of producing seeds, ferns develop spores, usually on the back of their leaves. The hardy kinds may be grown in equal parts of leaf-mould and soil, and the fronds of leaf-losing kinds should not be removed until the spring, as they offer some protection from the cold. Tender ferns should be repotted when new growth starts in the spring in a compost of equal parts soil, leaf-mould, and sand, using a pot just large enough for the purpose. During the growing season, in particular, keep the roots moist and plants free from a dry or smokey atmosphere. *Prop.*—Division of clumps when growth starts in the spring.

**Forget-me-nots.**—*See* Myosotis.

**Forsythia.**—Commonly found in many gardens, as it is of easy culture in any soil. Flowers bright yellow in early spring. To keep in good shape prune directly after flowering by cutting out old wood. *F. intermedia* 'Lynwood' is upright in growth and *F. suspensa* of weeping habit; both types make good wall plants for North aspects. *Prop.*—Cuttings in the autumn.

**Foxglove.**—*See* Digitalis.

**Freesia.**—Greenhouse bulbous plant and, if grown for scent, care must be taken to select fragrant varieties. Pot in the autumn in a fairly rich compost and keep as cold as possible until growth is seen. Then bring into a frost-free greenhouse and water freely. When flower stems appear, feed with liquid manure; after flowering, gradually dry-off until time for repotting. Failures almost invariably traced to premature forcing before root growth has been made or growing in excessively high temperature. *Prop.*—Offsets at potting time.

**Fritillaria.**—The one mainly used in gardens is *F. imperialis*, a handsome, spring-flowering bulb. To grow it *really* well, this species must be given a deep, rich soil and, contrary to some views, it is best lifted every year as soon as the foliage fades. If growth is poor or plants do not flower, feed when growth starts in the following spring with equal parts of bone meal and superphosphate at 3 oz. per sq. yd. *Prop.*—Offsets removed from parent bulb at lifting time. The old bulb should then be replanted at once and any offsets lined out in a nursery row.

**Fuchsia.**—Greenhouse and tender flowering shrubs. The outdoor sorts (of which *F. riccartonii* is the best) may be grown in light soil in full sun. In the spring prune all growth down to ground level; protect, if necessary, in winter with covering of cut bracken or dry straw. Greenhouse varieties are potted firmly before growth starts in the spring and, when buds burst, all the previous year's growth can be cut back hard. To encourage flowering, feed with a liquid manure, such as dried blood, and syringe foliage in hot weather. During the winter keep plants dry and house in a cool

greenhouse. *Prop.*—Cuttings of new growth taken about 1 in. long and inserted in sand under a bell jar.

**Gaillardia.**—Hardy annuals and perennials 18 in. to 3 ft. high which bear large, richly coloured flowers invaluable for cutting in mid- and late-summer. Unfortunately, on heavy soil the perennials are liable to die after flowering, and even on well-drained soils they cannot be considered long-lived plants. *Prop.*—Normally it is necessary to raise a fresh stock in alternate years; seed is sown in May in a cold frame and the young plants lined out in a reserve border prior to planting in the autumn.

**Galanthus (Snowdrop).**—Hardy bulbs well worth growing if given a moist, shady position where stock can be left undisturbed. Planting should be done in fairly bold clumps; bulbs are not expensive, and many variants, like double-flowered and tall-stemmed ones, are well worth a trial. *Prop.*—Lift and divide clumps in August.

**Gentiana.**—The gentians comprise some of the most fascinating of all rock-garden plants partly, perhaps, because some are difficult to manage. In particular, *G. acaulis*—which has true "gentian blue" flowers—is exacting in its requirements, and in many gardens flowering can never be induced. What controls flowering has not been discovered, and the plant can be grown well in acid or limy soils. On the other hand, *G. sino-ornata* must have an acid soil and is best in a position out of the direct sun. Beginners with the genus are advised to start with easily grown sorts, like *G. lagodechina* and *G. septemfida*. *Prop.*—Seed sown in cold frame in March or division in early spring.

**Geranium.**—The true geranium or cranesbill is a hardy floriferous perennial for rock garden or open border. In the latter case *G. ibericum* (blue flowers) and *G. sanguineum* 'Lancastriense' (rosy-pink flowers) are exceptionally good, and both do well in dry, sunny positions. The so-called "bedding" or "greenhouse" geranium is a pelargonium (*q.v.*). *Prop.*—Seed in March.

**Gladiolus.**—Dutch hybridists have done much work on this bulbous plant, and many new and lovely varieties are now available. The plant is responsive to good cultivation, and corms may be planted 4 in. deep and 6 in. apart during the spring in well-prepared ground. When the blooms fade remove the dead spikes of flower and lift the corms in September. After a month—and this point is important—pull off the old shrivelled corm and clean the new one. By doing this there is less likelihood of spores of diseases overwintering on the new stock. Finally, the corms should be stored in a dry, frost-free shed, and if given proper attention can be kept for a number of years. *Prop.*—Bulbils, removed when the corms are cleaned, can be sown in the spring in nursery rows and will flower within two years.

**Godetia.**—Hardy annual of easy culture and tolerant of poor soil conditions and even some shade. There are many varieties, mainly with bright flowers of rosy-pink and crimson. *See* Annuals.

**Guernsey Lily.**—*See* Nerine.

**Gypsophila.**—The favourite sort is *G. paniculata*, which is often grown for cutting, together with its double-flowered form, 'Bristol Fairy.' To do well gypsophila must be given a dryish soil which the roots can penetrate undisturbed; if growth is poor mulch in the spring with animal manure. *Prop.*—Generally done by seed in spring; special forms by grafting.

**Hamamelis.**—A lovely, but little grown, winter-flowering, heavily-scented shrub. The delicate, lemon-coloured flowers appear interminably from December to February. Although it flowers in its young stage, hamamelis is slow to get established and must be left free of root disturbance. The best sort is *H. mollis* introduced from China in 1879. *Prop.*—Usually by grafting; can be layered.

**Heather.**—*See* Erica.

**Hedera.**—Although ivy is seldom planted nowadays, there are a few evergreens to equal it for covering buildings. The large-leaved ivy with golden variegation, *H. colchica* 'Dentato-Variegata,' is invaluable for cold or shady walls. *Prop.*—Cuttings in August in shady border out-of-doors.

**Helianthus.**—The perennial sunflowers are tall, yellow-flowered plants of vigorous habit. They spread quickly and become a nuisance, and therefore clumps should be lifted and single, rooted pieces replanted every other year. The annual sunflower may reach a height of 10 ft. or so; seed is sown out-of-doors in April or seedlings raised under glass in the spring. When the flower bud appears, feed with soot water. The seed may be used as food for large birds like parrots.

**Helichrysum.**—Although this is a large group of plants, the most interesting is the half-hardy annual, *H. bracteatum*, the everlasting flower. When the flowers are fully developed they are cut with long stems and hung up to dry for winter decoration. *See* Annuals.

**Heliotropium peruvianum (Cherry Pie).**—Scented, shrubby plants used for greenhouse decoration or summer bedding. *H.* 'Sir Edward Fry' is among the scented varieties and *H.* 'Princess Marina' is the best dark-purple variety. For really good results, heliotropes need a rich soil and plenty of water in summer. *Prop.*—Cuttings 2–3 in. long in early autumn or spring, struck in sandy loam in a warm greenhouse.

**Helleborus.**—The Christmas rose, *H. niger*, should be planted out of the direct sun in a moist soil which has been liberally enriched with leaf-mould and old manure and here left free from root disturbance. Its large, white flowers appear irregularly from December to February with early flowering encouraged by protection with cloches. The Lenten rose, *H. orientalis*, flowers from February to April, and it is well worth searching nurserymens' lists for varieties with a wide range of colours. *Prop.*—Division of clumps in the spring, with each piece having four or five growth buds; the clumps should not be split into small pieces.

**Hemerocallis.**—Hardy perennial for moist border either open or slightly shaded. Mulch established clumps in the spring with compost or manure. Many new varieties are coming on the market as a result of introductions from America, where the plant is popular. *Prop.*—Division.

**Hibiscus.**—The evergreen, shrubby sorts with large exotic flowers are widely grown in the tropics and can be seen under glass in botanic gardens in Britain. *H. syriacus* is a deciduous, hardy species; little pruning is required, and in full sun it will reach 8–10 ft. Normally, it is a free-flowering plant of great beauty and, in cases where the flowers fail to develop, the stock is best replaced with good varieties, like 'Coeleste' (single, blue) and 'Woodbridge' (single, red). *Prop.*—Cuttings under glass; grafting.

**Holly.**—*See* Ilex.

**Hollyhock.**—*See* Althaea.

**Honeysuckle.**—*See* Lonicera.

**House Leek.**—*See* Sempervivum.

**Hyacinth.**—Bulbs generally used for bowl culture; often results are disappointing, but responsibility does not necessarily rest with the nurseryman, as poor cultivation is the most probable cause. Plant in September–early October (not later) in peat, loam, and sand, and keep as cool as possible until growth starts, when bowls may be brought into a warm room. Care must be taken with watering, as the bulbs must not dry out nor the compost allowed to become wet and soggy. After flowering, plant out-of-doors and lift annually in June for replanting in the autumn; for bowls a fresh stock is required every year.

Failures are mostly due to late planting or faulty watering.

**Hydrangea.**—A favourite shrub introduced from the Far East. Of the many forms, the one offered by florists, *H. macrophylla*, is the most popular. This can be bought in a wide range of shades, from white and pink through to crimson and blue. The colour will depend on soil reaction; in alkaline or neutral soils *only* white and pink shades can be grown, and blue flowers will be found *only* on acid soil. The intensity of colour can be improved by adding lime in the first instance and flowers of sulphur in the second, but it is not possible to make an alkaline garden soil acid in reaction. Lack of flower is generally the result of buds being killed by cold weather. For this reason, hydrangeas are best not pruned until the late spring; then old flower-heads and any weak or unwanted growth can be cut out. During the summer the plants must not suffer from lack of water.

Among the many other sorts are *H. paniculata*, with large, cone-shaped panicles of flower and *H. petiolaris*. The latter plant is a vigorous climber, well suited to cover cold walls or for climbing over dead trees. *Prop.*—Cuttings in July–August in a cold frame.

**Iberis (Candytuft).**—The hardy annual sorts will thrive in any soil, and may be had in a range of colours. *See* Annuals. The perennial candytuft (*I. sempervirens*) is a good plant for a rock wall and has white flowers in early spring. *Prop.*—Seeds in spring and cuttings in summer.

**Ilex.**—The ornamental value of our native holly is rarely fully appreciated, bearing in mind that, on good varieties, the berries sometimes persist until March. The greenish flowers are sometimes bisexual, and sometimes male and female flowers are on *separate* plants. For this reason hollies should be planted in groups, and at least one plant of good berrying habit, like *I. aquifolium* 'Pyramidalis,' grown. Some varieties have yellow berries and gold or silver variegations on their leaves. *Prop.*—Seed; special forms by budding.

**Iris.**—This plant is divided into two main sections: those types which grow from bulbs and those which grow from fleshy rhizomes, with many subdivisions in each of them. Of the latter type, there are the commonly grown bearded flag irises, which, owing to their ease of cultivation and wide range of colours, are appropriately known as the poor man's orchid. Notwithstanding, these irises respond to good treatment, doing best in well-dug soil to which a little manure has been added and a dressing of rough chalk forked into the surface. The site should be in full sun for preference and one that never lies wet in winter. Planting or division of established clumps is done in July, setting the rhizome on the surface of the soil but firming the roots well. To maintain growth and flower, feed annually in the spring with equal parts of superphosphate and bone meal at 3–4 oz. per sq. yd. Iris gardens are not often seen nowadays, but the fine example still maintained at Kew is well worth close inspection.

In the bulbous section the Siberian iris is a graceful plant with delicate foliage, though much smaller-flowered than the flags. They make a fine waterside planting or may be grown in the herbaceous border. The Japanese iris is another water lover, and this has delicate-coloured, clematis-like flowers. On the other hand, for dry, poor, stony soils in full sun the lovely, winter-flowering, Algerian iris, *I. unguicularis (stylosa)*, is an ideal plant, flowering as it does in December and January. This is a plant which must be left undisturbed after planting in June and if leafy growth is excessive the foliage can be cut back by half in August. Spanish, Dutch, and English types of bulbous iris are often used as cut flowers. These may be planted in ordinary garden soil in the autumn and left undisturbed until signs of deterioration are found.

**Japonica.**—Common misnomer of *Chaenomeles.* (*q.v.*).

**Jasminum.**—The yellow-flowered, sweetly scented winter jasmine blooms intermittently from November to February. It grows in any soil, and is best trained up a wall or grown on a trellis. Pruning consists of cutting out the flowering shoots as soon as the blossoms fade. The summer jasmine is a vigorous climbing plant with white, scented flowers. It needs a sunny position and should be well thinned after flowering. *Prop.*—Layering in summer.

**Kalmia.**—Hardy American shrubs with clusters of waxy, rose or pink blossoms in early summer. Although slow to get established and requiring a damp, acid soil, the plant is well worth growing. It constitutes a feature of the gardens of the National Trust at Sheffield Park, Sussex. *Prop.*—Seed or layering.

**Kerria japonica.**—A hardy shrub which will thrive in any garden but is best fed with manure to encourage strong growth. When the yellow flowers fade, the stock should be kept vigorous by cutting out old or weak growth. The plant is named after William Kerr, a young man despatched from Kew to collect plants in China. *Prop.*—Division in autumn.

**Kniphofia (Red-hot Poker).**—Although these plants are so commonly seen, their full value as late-flowering subjects is not often fully explored. There are a number of good varieties worth growing, such as ' Maid of Orleans ' (white, 4 ft.), ' Mount Etna ' (scarlet, 5 ft.), and ' Royal Standard ' (gold and scarlet, 4 ft.). Of equal value is the dwarf variety with grass-like foliage, *K. nelsonii. Prop.*—Division in March; easily raised from seed if so desired.

**Laburnum.**—Handsome trees with long racemes of yellow flowers the seeds of which are very poisonous. It is not advisable to remove branches, as wounds do not heal well or quickly, and once a specimen shows signs of deterioration it is best replaced with little delay. *Prop.*—Seed or grafting.

**Larkspur.**—*See* Delphinium.

**Lathyrus (Sweet Pea).**—For general garden decoration, seed may be sown in pots in a warm greenhouse in early February prior to transplanting out-of-doors in April. When heat is not available sowing can be done in the open in October, setting the seed 4–6 in. apart and 2 in. deep where the plants are to grow. In this case the rows are best protected with cloches. As the plants flower with great freedom and make strong growth, a rich, deep soil is required. During the summer water should be given freely and liquid animal manure or soot water applied weekly when flowering starts. When raised for exhibition, special cultural treatment is necessary. The cause of the condition referred to as bud drop is not known, but it is thought to be connected with low temperature and faulty root action.

There is also the hardy, perennial sweet pea, an old-world plant usually seen at its best in cottage gardens. This plant requires the same cultural conditions, except that the old stems are cut down in the autumn. Three or four different species are available, and all are easily raised from seed sown in the spring.

**Lavandula.**—The lavender is one of the best known of garden plants. It thrives in full sun in a light soil; old flower heads should be clipped off in the summer, but any cutting back into old growth must be left until the spring. The best garden form is *L. spica* ' Nana Atropurpurea '; it has a neat, dwarf habit, with deep purple flowers, and is available from leading nurserymen. *Prop.*—Cuttings out-of-doors in August-September.

**Leucojum.**—The spring snowflake flowers in February and is a charming plant for any damp, shady border. Although it has a large flower, it has never become as popular as the snowdrop, despite its ease of culture. It should be grown by everyone who values early spring flowers. *Prop.*—Lift clumps and replant after removing offsets in August.

**Lilac.**—*See* Syringa.

**Lilium.**—The lilies constitute a large genus of plants, some of easy culture, some demanding the most exacting of conditions. For a soil containing chalk two of the best lilies are *L. candidum*, the Madonna lily, and *L. regale*. The former is a feature of many gardens in South Wales, where bulbs are planted near the surface of the soil and the clumps eventually left to develop undisturbed. Only the easiest-grown lilies are suitable for the herbaceous border and, here, apart from the Madonna lily, the tiger and martagon lilies should be first choices for beginners in the cultivation of this genus. *Prop.*—Those referred to above may all be raised from seed sown out-of-doors (or in deep boxes in a cold frame) in the spring. In the following April line out into nursery rows prior to transplanting to flowering positions. Also propagated by offsets and bulbils.

**Lily of the Valley.**—*See* Convallaria.

**Lobelia.**—The bedding lobelias are perennial plants best raised as annuals (*q.v.*). They do well in a light soil, but should be firmed at planting time to prevent plants dying off during a hot spell. The handsome, tall-growing lobelias with scarlet flowers, like *L. fulgens* ' Huntsman,' may be used in herbaceous borders with great effect, but the roots must be lifted and overwintered in a cold frame. These sorts grow to a height of 2–3 ft. and will do well only on a wet, heavily manured soil.

**Lonicera.**—The honeysuckles make effective climbing plants if grown on the shady side of arches or tree stumps or against north or west walls. Care should be taken to train young growth before it becomes hard. Old shoots may be cut out each spring to keep the plant within bounds, although space must be available for free development. If growth and flowering is poor mulch the roots in the spring with old manure. *Prop.*—Easily done by layering in late summer.

**Lupins.**—There are two sorts of lupins, perennial and annual. The herbaceous perennials are among the most colourful of plants as a result of the famous ' Russell ' strain being introduced. Of late years, however, the constitution of the plant has been weakened through, perhaps, breeding and virus diseases, and it should be taken for granted that most stocks have to be replaced every two years or even annually in some cases. The plant requires a rich soil and is best in ground free of lime. Conversely, in poor soil the tree lupin thrives and will reach a height of 7–9 ft.; plant in full sun and lightly prune into shape after flowering. *Prop.*—Both sorts are best raised from seed sown in May out-of-doors and transferred to flowering positions in October. The annual lupin may be obtained in a range of colours, and should be grown in full sun. *See* Annuals.

**Magnolia.**—Rightly said to be one of the most beautiful of all flowering plants. Contrary to popular belief, some kinds are of easy culture, flowering when young and suitable for small gardens. Of course, careful selection is necessary and for a specimen on a lawn *M.* ' Soulangeana ' (large, white or white, purple-stained flowers) is ideal. *M. stellata* freely flowers in the young stage, and may be planted in an ordinary border if the soil is lime free. To encourage growth, mulch annually with peat or leaf mould, but never dig near the roots. The evergreen magnolia is often seen as a fine wall plant in old gardens. This is the only species which may be pruned, and long shoots can be cut back hard in April. There are a number of non-flowering strains of the evergreen one, and unsatisfactory plants are best destroyed, as flowering cannot be induced; in buying a replacement care is necessary in order to avoid *another* dud. *Prop.*—Seed sown as soon as it is ripe in October; layering.

**Mahonia.**—Hardy evergreen shrub. *M. aquifolium* is useful as ground cover, and will thrive in any soil and in any cold, shady position providing the soil is not waterlogged. *M. japonica* has long racemes of lemon-scented flowers in the winter; inferior sorts are often offered by nurserymen under this name. *Prop.*—Seed, suckers, and layers.

**Marigold.**—*See* Calandula.

**Mathiola.**—The night-scented stock is a hardy annual with insignificant purplish flowers which open at dusk; grown primarily for its perfume. Conversely, the so-called Ten-Week stocks and a selection of these, the East Lothian stocks, have a wide range of colours. If sown in March they may be used for summer bedding or if sown in August overwintered in a sunny frame and grown as a biennial.

Brompton stocks flower earlier than the other sorts, and are grown as a biennial by sowing seed in June or early July and, after pricking out into boxes, are overwintered in a sunny frame. In mild districts, if the soil is well drained, stocks may as by careful selection of varieties a long season of flower can be obtained when they are grown in formal borders or naturalised. Thus, a season may be extended with 'Peeping Tom' and 'Covent Garden' (early) and 'Geranium' and 'Buttermilk' (late). The bulbs can be left undisturbed until flowering is affected by over-crowding; the clumps should then be lifted and be divided in the late summer. To maintain vigour, feed annually in February with 2 parts bone meal, 1 part hoof and horn meal, and 1 part sulphate of potash at 2 oz. per sq. yd. The chief troubles with narcissi are due to eelworm (T29) and the narcissus bulb fly (T28). For indoor work, plant in bowls in October and keep in cold place until growth is an inch high; failure is invariably due to premature forcing or faulty watering.

**Nasturtium.**—*See* Tropaeolum.

WATER LILIES IN TUBS—Drawing (A) shows a cross-section with correct percentage of water and soil together with water lilies and fish. Drawing (B) illustrates marginal planting with primulas, Japanese irises, and a dwarf coniferous tree.

be planted out-of-doors in the autumn, but a reserve should be kept for filling up gaps in the spring.

**Meconopsis.**—This genus includes the famous "blue poppy," introduced from the Himalayas. It is not a plant of easy culture, albeit large groups are grown in many woodland gardens where soil conditions permit. After flowering the plants generally die, although an occasional plant may persist. *Prop.*—Seed sown in March.

**Michaelmas Daisy.**—*See* Aster.

**Montbretia.**—This bulbous plant is of easy culture and has a long season of flowering. Many new varieties with large flowers are now available, and growth can be kept vigorous by lifting and dividing the clumps every three or four years. Plant in early spring 4 in. deep and 6 in. apart and in cold gardens protect clumps in winter with a covering of ashes.

**Myosotis.**—The forget-me-not is grown as a biennial by sowing seed in May and planting out in the autumn in conjunction with spring-flowering bulbs and wallflowers. Poor varieties freely establish themselves, and these should be destroyed before planting any of the really good sorts offered by seedsmen.

**Narcissus.**—This botanical name includes plants commonly known as "daffodil" and "narcissus." Although often grown, the wide garden value of these spring-flowering bulbs is not fully realised,

**Nepeta (Catmint).**—In recent years this edging plant with silvery foliage and mauve flowers has become increasingly popular. When flowering in mid-summer there is no finer display of colour. It grows freely on any light, well-drained soil in full sun. The best sort is *N. faassenii*. *Prop.*—Division of clumps in March.

**Nerine.**—Lately this lovely bulbous plant has increased in popularity mainly through the varieties introduced from the late Lionel de Rothschild's garden at Exbury. The hardy sort *N. bowdenii* flowers in the autumn and should be planted at the foot of a warm wall in August or September and left undisturbed for many years. As the bulbs gradually multiply and work to the surface, a light dressing of sandy compost, to which has been added a little bone meal, can be applied. *Prop.*—Separation of bulbs in August.

**Nicotiana (Tobacco Plant).**—This half-hardy annual is grown mainly for its heavily scented flowers, which open in the evening. It is worth remembering that the white-flowered sorts are the best in this respect; scarlets and pinks are very much inferior. *See* Annuals. The tobacco of commerce is a different plant, namely, *N. tabacum*.

**Nymphaea.**—No branch of gardening is more fascinating than the water garden, and for it the chief plant must be the water lily. Basically, the main reason for failure is in the fact that in most pools the *average* depth of water is less than 18 in.; this means that the water is liable to be adversely affected by extremes of temperature. All nymphaeas should be grown in full sun and where the water is still; in streams it is necessary to utilise a little backwater out of the current. Water lilies are planted in May in large wicker baskets with a compost of three-quarters of loam and a quarter of peat; alternatively, planting sites can be built up with bricks to the desired height. If growth is poor, mould Clay's Fertiliser into the size of pigeons' eggs and drop one around each clump. To maintain a healthy condition in the water, fish should be introduced as soon as the plants are established. *Prop.*—Division of tuberous roots in late May.

**Orchids.**—In the main, this large group of plants needs greenhouse conditions and specialised knowledge. Their cultivation has attracted the attention of some of the greatest of horticulturists, and detailed references may be found in books like *Orchids, their Description and Cultivation*, by C. H. Curtis (Putnam), 1950.

**Paeonia.**—There are two sorts of paeony, the tree paeony and the herbaceous paeony. The former needs a sheltered, warm position and takes about three years to flower from planting time. The latter sort needs a moist, rich soil, and should be mulched annually in the spring with well-rotted manure; some are known not to flower, and as such plants cannot be induced to do so they should be destroyed. The old-fashioned variety of paeony has been superseded by many fine new varieties found listed by specialists. *Prop.*—Tree paeonies by layering or seed sown in the autumn; herbaceous sorts by seed or division.

**Pansy.**—*See* Viola.

**Papaver (Poppy).**—The oriental poppy is a hardy herbaceous perennial with striking flowers, intolerant of shade and root disturbance. As it blooms early, it should be set near the back of a border, as the large leaves look untidy later in the year. Apart from the commonly grown, red-flowered sort there are others in shades of crimson, pink, and lavender. *Prop.*—A wide range of colours can be obtained by sowing mixed seeds in May. This is a better method than division. The Shirley poppy is a hardy annual (*q.v.*), while *P. nudicale* is a biennial needing a warm, sheltered position.

**Parthenocissus (Virginia Creeper).**—This climber, with its brilliantly-coloured leaves, makes a fine sight in the autumn, and there is no better plant for covering brickwork or unsightly buildings with a south or west aspect. It has been suggested (mainly by builders) that the plant will damage stonework or cause dampness. There is little evidence to support these suppositions, and reasons for damage can usually be traced—often without difficulty—to other sources. The plant has had a number of names—*Ampelopsis veitchii* is one—but up-to-date nurserymen are listing it correctly as *P. tricuspidata*. *Prop.*—Cuttings out-of-doors in the late summer; layering.

**Passiflora caerulea (Passion Flower).**—A south wall in favoured gardens is needed to grow this plant. It is of vigorous habit and, once the framework of branches has been produced, it should be pruned annually in the early spring, by cutting back all the previous season's growth to 2–3 in. of the main stem. *Prop.*—Layering.

**Pelargonium (Geranium).**—So-called " bedding geraniums," such as ' Paul Crampel,' are really zonal pelargoniums. To maintain a stock, take cuttings in early August and insert in sandy soil around the edge of a pot and overwinter in a frost-free greenhouse. In the spring pot-up singly and use for bedding. Otherwise pot-on after two months and, if early buds are nipped off, plants can be adopted for late flowering indoors. Pelargoniums are easy to grow, but for best results a position in full sun is necessary, and cuttings should be rooted *before* the autumn so that overwintering constitutes no great difficulty.

**Petunia.**—Although really perennials, these plants, native of South America, are treated as annuals (*q.v.*). They are sun lovers and do best

on light soils. Petunias make fine plants for sunny window boxes, and particularly happy combinations can be made by planting together varieties such as ' Violacea ' (deep violet) and ' Cheerful ' (pale pink) or ' Flaming Velvet ' (crimson) and ' Cream Star ' (pale cream). The violet-flowered sorts are faintly scented.

**Philadelphus (Mock Orange).**—Although some fine varieties of this shrub are available in the trade, it is not grown as widely as its merit deserves. As a scented shrub it has few equals, while it is tolerant of poor soil conditions and shade. Particularly good sorts worth searching for are ' Albatre ' (double), ' Beauclerk ' (single), and ' Sybille,' which, at 3 ft., is about half the height of the others. After flowering, prune annually by removing as much old flowering wood as possible. *Prop.*—Hard-wood cuttings out-of-doors in November.

**Phlox.**—A wide range of varieties of the border phlox are offered to make an impressive display late in the season. If grown on light soils some shade is desirable, as phloxes do well where only the soil is damp. For this reason, mulching should be done annually in the spring with compost or animal manure. Failures are usually due to eelworm (T30). *Prop.*—Seeds in autumn; division.

**Poppy.**—*See* Papaver.

**Polyanthus.**—*See* Primula.

**Polygonum.**—In the main these plants are weeds of gardens, although originally they were introduced from the Orient for ornamental purposes at a time when their invasive habits were not fully appreciated. The one woody climber in the genus, *P. baldschuanicum*, makes an admirable cover where a very vigorous plant is wanted. Rampant and unwanted species may be eradicated by hormone treatment (T34).

**Primula.**—Polyanthuses, primroses, greenhouse primulas, and the hardy primulas all belong in this genus. The first two are the most popular; both will do well only in damp soil and respond to generous manurial treatment; both are available in a wide range of colours. *Prop.*—The Blackmore and Langdon strains of seed will give a magnificent display of mixed colours. Sow in warm greenhouse in early March or cold frame in April; prick out into boxes and transfer to flowering positions in the autumn.

**Prunus.**—A large genus which includes the flowering peaches, Japanese cherries, and flowering almonds. All of them are best left to develop

REMOVAL OF SUCKERS—As illustrated, these must be sawn off into the root or pulled off the root with a sharp tug and never so removed that dormant buds are left.

naturally and are not responsive to pruning or cutting back in any way. A few sorts are over-planted in gardens and as street trees (by Park Superintendents), but anybody wishing to be a little out of the ordinary would do well to see the wide range of some of these lovely trees flowering in April and May in our botanic gardens and many of the large gardens now under the jurisdiction of the National Trust. The selection offered by nurserymen is often strictly along conventional lines. Lack of flower in some seasons can often be traced to bird damage.

**Red-hot Poker.**—*See* Kniphofia.

Rhododendron.—Greenhouse and hardy, evergreen and deciduous shrubs, including *Azalea*. With something like ten thousand different sorts, it is impossible to deal with individual requirements. General cultivation; an acidic soil is essential, with adequate moisture in summer. If growth is poor on established plants, mulch liberally with animal manure. Beginners should plant from the accepted list of hardy garden hybrids. Since the turn of the century widely planted and fine examples are to be found, for instance, in many gardens of the National Trust. *Prop.*—Seed and layering.

Romneya.—Since its introduction from California in about 1850 the plant has proved a fascination to gardeners, as sometimes it fails completely

lished, spray with "Captan." For a manurial programme, an application of 2 parts of superphosphate and 1 part of sulphate of potash can be applied at 3 oz. per sq. yd. after pruning. Following this, a surface mulch of animal manure, compost, peat, or leaf-mould or a mixture of all of them is given about 2–3 in. thick. Subsequently, if growth is poor, a dressing of nitro-chalk can be made at 1 oz. per sq. yd. Some other manurial treatments, like the so-called "Foliar Feeding" and use of "special" (and often expensive) compounds, have little to commend them.

Where soil conditions are poor and disease prevalent, it is important to buy plants only from nurserymen who take special precautions to ensure that their customers have disease-free stock. Likewise, varieties of robust constitution are

PRUNING ROSES—(A) A vigorous unpruned plant.   (B) The same plant pruned for the production of exhibition blooms, (C) and pruned for garden decoration.

or does exceedingly well. It appears to require a light soil and a sheltered position, preferably against a sunny wall, and there is no point in trying to grow a romneya on a heavy, wet soil. Usually the annual stems die off in the winter and may be cut down at ground level in the early spring; if persistent the stems can be cut back to sound growth. The new growth is susceptible to slug damage, and appropriate steps must be taken (T29). *Prop.*—Seed or suckers taken off in the spring.

Rosa (Rose).—Undoubtedly the rose is the most popular of all garden flowers, and it may be found in a multitude of forms. The dwarf roses for bedding may be grown on most soils, but are best on a rich, heavy loam. Planting is done from early November onwards when soil conditions permit and the first pruning carried out in the following spring, when the extent of any winter damage can be seen. Opinions differ sharply on pruning; a sound, general rule is to do the work in March and—unless there are special circumstances—to prune on the light side. Thus, for Hybrid Teas and the like, reduce strong stems by about one-third of their length, medium ones by a half, and weak ones to within two or three buds of the main stem.

Whatever sorts of soil roses are grown in, feeding is important, but, of course, it is particularly so on poor ones. It is in soils of *low* fertility that diseases such as rust and black spot are most prevalent and, in some measure, persistence of the disease is due to bad cultivation and lack of treatment with fertilisers. Where black spot is estab-

essential, and a selection list may include: *Hybrid Teas:* 'Christopher Stone' (crimson), 'Dame Edith Helen' (pink), 'Eden Rose' (magenta pink), 'Granmere Jenny' (yellow, rose-pink flush), 'Madam Henri Guillot' (salmon pink), 'Quebec' (yellow), and 'Tzigane' (bicolor: vermilion and yellow). *Floribundas:* 'Dainty Maid' (rose pink), 'Dusky Maiden' (dark red), 'Tantau's Surprise' (deep crimson), and 'Yellow Holstein' (yellow).

In most of the modern hybrids scent is almost absent. The true rose perfume is found only in the Old Fashion or shrub roses and, normally, these are planted in a mixed shrub border. For the richest perfume varieties like 'Mrs. John Laing' and 'Conrad F. Meyer' should be sought. *Prop.*—Nurserymen's plants are budded; many varieties are easily raised from cuttings taken in the autumn and struck in sandy soil out-of-doors.

Salvia.—Annuals, perennials, and tender shrubs. The most popular one is the scarlet sort used for bedding. It requires careful attention, and seed should be sown in February in a temperature of 60° Fahrenheit and seedlings put into single pots when large enough. Gradually the young plants are hardened off and finally planted out in rich soil in a sunny bed.

Saxifraga.—A large genus of plants suitable for the rock garden and valued for their bright flowers in the spring. The encrusted saxifrages are cushion-forming plants requiring sharp, surface drainage and an open position out of the direct sun. The mossy saxifrages are mat-forming in growth and of easy culture. In time old clumps develop brown patches and then require splitting up and replanting in the spring.

**Scabiosa.**—The commonly grown perennial sort is *S. caucasica* and is invaluable as a cut flower. It is not at home on all soils, and only does really well in a deep, rich loam containing plenty of chalk. In addition, it must be grown in full sun and particular care taken against slugs. *Prop.*—Old plants divided in the spring and rooted pieces replanted in their flowering positions. A wide range of shades in white, blue, and purple can be had normally from sowing mixed seed in April.

**Sedum.**—The stonecrops make up a large group of hardy and tender plants, but comparatively few are of horticultural value. Notwithstanding, *Sedum spectabile* is to be found in most herbaceous borders, where its fine, flat heads of pink flowers are a feature for many weeks. It is beloved by bees and butterflies. *S. sieboldii* was introduced from Japan about 100 years ago and, although hardy, it is usually grown as a house plant. In the winter it can be stood out-of-doors, and every two or three years repotted in the spring; keep well watered during the summer and feed with liquid manure occasionally. *Prop.*—Division in the spring.

**Sempervivum (House leek).**—These hardy plants with succulent leaves often decorate the crevices of old walls and are regular features of trough or sink gardens. If given a light, poor soil and a position in full sun a fascinating collection of house leeks can be built up. The species which gives the plant its common name can be established easily on a sunny roof by planting in a mixture of cow manure and clay during the spring. *Prop.*—Division in the spring.

**Skimmia.**—A hardy evergreen 2–3 ft. tall which is tolerant of shade and some degree of dryness. If growth is poor water with a liquid manure and mulch with peat or leaf mould. Some forms bear only male flowers and to ensure a good crop of berries plant an hermaphrodite like *S. foremanii*. *Prop.*—Layering in the autumn.

**Snowdrop.**—*See* Galanthus.

**Snowflake.**—*See* Leucojum.

**Solanum capsicastrum (Winter Cherry).**—A berrying plant with bright-red fruits which is often used for house decoration. To maintain the plant in a healthy condition it should be clear of draughts and fumes of gas fires and the foliage kept fresh and free of dust by vigorous syringing. If the stock is to be kept for more than one season water should be given only sparingly in the New Year, and in early March all the side shoots pruned back hard to within a bud or two of the main stems. As new growth develops, water can be given more freely and syringing started when the flowers first appear; liquid manure will prove beneficial when berries develop.

**Spiraea.**—Hardy deciduous shrubs for open borders; tolerant of poor soil conditions. The commonly grown one is *Spiraea bumalda* (syn. *japonica*). After flowering, a percentage of the old wood should be removed together with any weak growth, and development of new shoots encouraged by mulching with compost or animal manure. *Prop.*—Cuttings rooted in sandy soil under a hand light in summer; suckers thinned out in winter.

**Stocks.**—*See* Mathiola.

**Sunflower.**—*See* Helianthus.

**Sweet William.**—*See* Dianthus.

**Symphoricarpos (Snowberry).**—Often found existing in deep shade and in competition with roots of overhanging trees, presumably as a result of the generalisation that the shrub is a shade lover. Certainly a useful one in this respect, but it is responsive to good treatment. Given an average soil and if growth is thinned annually in

the early spring, then *S. albus* 'Laevigatus' is well worth having. Its large white fruits are untouched by birds and hang well into the winter, and are thus beloved by the floral decorator. *Prop.*—Suckers removed in the winter.

**Syringa (Lilac).**—The botanical name of *Syringa* is often erroneously applied to the Mock Orange, correctly named *Philadelphus* (*q.v.*). A wide selection of first-class varieties are available in nurserymen's lists. To obtain heavy crops of flowers nip off all dead flower-heads as the blossom fades, but do *not* cut back into the old stem, as this will prevent flowering. At the same time any branches causing overcrowding can be removed. Annually feed with "National Growmore" at 2 oz. per sq. yd. and on poor soils mulch with any sort of manure or compost. *Prop.*—Layering in the autumn.

**Tagetes (African and French Marigolds).**—Half-hardy annuals of free-flowering habit and easiest culture. Best if fed generously with soot water or other nitrogenous manure during growing season. *See* Annuals.

**Tropaeolum.**—The common nasturtium and the flame flower (*T. speciosum*) belong to this genus. The former is easily grown from seed sown in May in a sunny position. The latter is a very difficult plant to grow outside the conditions which it demands. To be successful, this perennial climber must be planted in acid soil which is naturally damp and lightly shaded but yet where the new growth can reach full sun. Much disappointment often results from planting it in eastern England, for instance, after seeing it flourishing almost as a weed where the rainfall is high in Ireland and the west of Scotland.

In the genus will also be found the canary creeper, which can be used for screening purposes and will thrive in full sun or shade. Seed is sown in May in open ground and light supports supplied by way of pea sticks or strings; failure is normally due to nothing more than lack of moisture.

**Tulipa (Tulip).**—Thrives in a deep, rich loam, but will do well for one season in ordinary garden soil. When used for bedding, bulbs must be lifted after flowering, replanted in a trench, and thoroughly watered. Sometimes tulips may be left in the ground *if* conditions are favourable, and then the stock only needs lifting and replanting every three years. To check the incidence of tulip fire plant in late November or early December, covering the bulbs with 4–5 in. of soil and treat the ground with a fungicide like "Botrilex." Before doing so rake in a dressing of 2 oz. superphosphate and 1 oz. sulphate of potash per square yard. A small collection of wild tulips is being got together at Cambridge and grown there in the University Botanic Garden.

**Viola.**—This name embraces pansies, violas, and violets. Although the viola has not got the rich colours of the pansy (or its attractive markings), it has got a remarkably long season of flower, and for this reason it is invaluable as an edging plant or as ground cover for roses. *Prop.*—Both plants are easily raised from seed sown in a frame in the spring, pricked out, and then transferred to their flowering positions in late May. Alternatively, seed may be sown in July for planting out in October. Named varieties increased by cuttings in a frame in late summer.

**Virginia creeper.**—*See* Parthenocissus.

**Wallflower.**—*See* Cheiranthus.

**Water Lily.**—*See* Nymphaea.

**Winter Sweet.**—*See* Chimonanthus.

**Wistaria.**—One of the finest of all climbing plants for south or west walls or stout pergolas. Plants which do not flower, or only do so poorly, are probably seedlings and the true flowering habit cannot be induced; the only solution is to replace with a *grafted* plant of known flowering capacity from a reliable nurseryman. All young shoots not required for the extension of branches should be shortened to within 3 in. of the old stem in the autumn. Wistarias growing over trees do not require pruning. *Prop.*—Layer shoots of current season's growth in the autumn.

Zinnia.—Half-hardy annual, ideally grown on moist, deep loam liberally enriched with well-decayed manure. Mulch with manure after planting and apply liquid fertiliser as buds appear; plants must not suffer from lack of water. *See* Annuals.

Standard References.

*Chrysanthemums*, by E. T. Thistlewaite (Penguin) 1960 (6s.).

*Collins Guide to Roses*, by Bertram Park (Collins), 1962 (25s.).

*Hortus Second*, by L. H. Bailey and Ethel Zoe Bailey (Macmillan), 1947 (40s.).

R.H.S. *Dictionary of Gardening*, edited by F. J. Chittenden (Oxford), 1956 (14 guineas).

Sanders' *Encyclopaedia of Gardening*, revised by A. G. L. Hellyer (Collingridge), 1952 (21s.).

## MAKING A LAWN

In almost every garden the most prominent feature is the lawn, and often a lot of work is put into making one without any great measure of success. Usually, the reason for failure may be found in faulty preparation of the soil or premature sowing, albeit the blame is often placed on bird damage or poor seed.

For anything like a reasonable turf, the site must be thoroughly dug and the content of organic matter increased by incorporating generous quantities of materials like peat, leaf-mould, compost, sewage sludge, and animal manure. A dressing of these ingredients can be applied in a layer 3–4 in. thick and buried in the bottom of the top spit of soil. As the ground is dug to incorporate the organic matter, roots of perennial weeds should be removed.

If the site is one on which water tends to lie or if the soil is heavy, then surface drainage should be sharpened by forking into the top 2 or 3 in. a liberal application of some coarse material such as builders' rubble, road grit, screened ashes, or coarse sand. In some cases this treatment will not be sufficient, and then the installation of land drains must be resorted to. This particular task is not as difficult as is sometimes imagined, but, before a start is made, it is always a good plan to discuss the matter with an experienced man.

After the initial work a fine tilth on the soil may be obtained by thoroughly raking and cross-raking and at the same time establishing a level surface. On this point, it should be remembered that good lawns can be made on undulating ground or on natural slopes, but the things to avoid are the shallow depressions where water will naturally tend to lie. Finally, ten to fourteen days before sowing the subsequent growth of grass can be encouraged by making an application of " National Growmore " at 2 oz. per sq. yd.

Sowing is best done in the late summer at a time when the soil is moist For the purpose, a good mixture of seed should be obtained from a reliable seedsman, and it is worth paying a reasonable price for it, as, by and large, the coarsest and roughest grasses have the largest and heaviest seeds. Opinions differ on rates of sowing, but, with care and in a well-prepared soil, 1 oz. per sq. yd. is ample; heavier rates may give quicker results, but the density of seedlings in such cases often leads to the finer grasses being choked by the coarser ones.

After sowing, the ground should be lightly raked, but not rolled. At this stage the important point is to protect the seed bed from birds by the use of hazel sticks, strings of papers tied to stakes after they have been dipped in lime-wash, and strands of black cotton. Subsequently, annual weeds may appear in quantity; these are of no consequence, and they will be eliminated once the grass is cut regularly. Until a good turf is formed —usually about twelve months after sowing—it s not desirable (or probably necessary) to use hormone weed-killers. *See* T33.

Care of Established Lawns.

Most turf is never manured from year to year, and the soil may seriously lack plant foods. In the first place this can be corrected by making an application annually in the spring of " National Growmore " at 1 oz. per sq. yd. Subsequently, if growth is below par in the early part of the year an application of sulphate of ammonia can be made at the same rate. To avoid scorching or blackening of the foliage, each fertiliser can be mixed with equal parts of dry soil or sand as a carrier to ensure even distribution and, what is most important, each one should be applied only when the turf is wet and there is the prospect of rain to follow. Linked with this treatment, turf is always responsive to top dressings. A compost for the purpose can be made up with:

2 parts of loam;
1 part of sieved compost;
1 part of fine peat or leaf soil.

This may be used in the spring at 3–5 lb. per sq. yd. and if the soil is heavy 1–2 parts of gritty sand may be added.

With the introduction of new designs in motor mowers, most lawns are seriously overcut, and this has led to a sharp decline in the quality of the grass and the appearance of one or two pernicious weeds. It is appreciated that special turf, such as that found on a bowling green, may be shaved off to $\frac{1}{8}$ in., but if a utility lawn is cut below half to 1 in., then the quality of the grass will deteriorate. Of course, it is a good thing to occasionally cut the grass very short, but, conversely, if the blades of the mower are set as low as possible and left like it throughout the season nothing but harm can result. The reason for this hard fact is that when the turf is cut very close the grasses simply cannot develop and spread, and weeds will gradually establish themselves. Eventually the cultivator will be faced with the difficult problem of trying to deal with such plants as pearlwort, yarrow, and various mosses, all of which are resistant to hormones.

As for the vexed question of whether or not to remove the mowings, there is no doubt that the best turf is found where the mowings are collected up, although in very dry weather they can be left on the surface. If the clippings are not removed the surface of the turf tends to become choked with semi-decayed organic matter, and conditions are brought about which are inducive to the spread of moss.

Finally, it is worth noting that the finest turf is found on acidic—not alkaline—soils. For this reason, lime should not be applied as a general rule, for apart from helping the development of coarse grasses, it encourages the growth of clover. Of course, there are times when lime is necessary, but the occasions are rare and before it is used it is a good plan to test the soil by chemical means.

## THE FRUIT GARDEN.

The guidance of an expert is probably more important in the growing of fruit than for most of the commoner vegetables and ornamentals. This is primarily because the majority of fruit trees and bushes are long-lived, and only in the case of strawberries can a change of site or variety be made easily and inexpensively.

Gardens which are low-lying are very prone to damage from spring frosts, and should not have too much space devoted to fruit, as returns may well prove unprofitable. Here, as with the selection of varieties, advice of a local expert is invaluable. Some varieties do better in certain localities and on certain soils than others, although personal preferences will naturally be met where possible. Varieties chosen should cover as long a season as is practicable so that the fruit can be used and enjoyed to the full.

Tree fruits are grown on a rootstock, and for apples and pears special dwarfing stocks make these a possibility for the small garden. It is therefore important to explain to the nurseryman what type of tree is required. As a general rule, however, the smaller gardens will gain by concentrating on currants, gooseberries, raspberries, and strawberries. Plums and cherries have no dwarfing stocks, and should be included only where sufficient room is available.

Adequate preparation of the ground is important, and this, followed by good management, can result in worth-while crops from most soils, providing they are reasonably free of frost, well-drained, and sufficiently sunny.

**Apples.**—Can be grown on most soils. Manure should not be used when planting, except in sandy and chalky gardens. Obtain trees on dwarfing rootstocks, such as M.IX, M.VII, or MM.106. Always stake trees on M.IX, otherwise this practice is necessary only in exposed sites. The tie must be rigid, with a " cushion " between tree and stake to avoid chafing, and must be renewed annually to avoid constriction. Plant between late October and early March, preferably before Christmas if soil and weather allow. Make the hole large enough to spread the roots evenly; firm thoroughly while filling in and plant level with the nursery soil mark already on the tree. Mulch around each tree with manure or compost, mainly to avoid drying out, and supplement with watering during the summer when necessary.

In the first year any flowers produced are best pinched out to encourage root and shoot development. For walls or fences use oblique cordons or espaliers; these are also useful for flanking paths and lawns. Plant cordons 2¼ ft. apart with 6 ft. between rows, and espaliers 12–15 ft. apart. For larger areas use bush trees 12–15 ft. apart.

Manuring for cropping trees should be varied according to growth. Generally apply 1 oz. sulphate of ammonia (or nitro chalk on acid soils) in early March, repeating this in early April if trees are growing in grass. Give ½ oz. sulphate of potash in February and add 3 oz. of superphosphate every third year. The above rates are per square yard, and a complete fertiliser can be used in lieu if preferred.

Young bush trees should have main shoots reduced by half in early years to produce strong branches. Thereafter prune side shoots to three to six buds. For weak growers prune harder, and for strong growers prune less. It is wiser to leave a strong tree unpruned than to prune it too severely, the latter merely encouraging even stronger growth. A few varieties (e.g., ' Bramley's Seedling,' ' Worcester Pearmain ') fruit at shoot tips, and here a proportion of side shoots should be left unpruned. Summer pruning is advisable on restricted trees, such as cordons; for details see pears. Very few varieties are self-fertile, and at least two sorts should be planted to ensure satisfactory crops. Good combinations are ' Cox's Orange Pippin' with ' Laxton's Fortune ' and ' Winston ' with the cooker ' Lord Derby.' Seek expert advice on pairings if in doubt.

**Apricots.**—These are often an unreliable fruit to grow, needing a well-drained, calcareous loam and a warm wall for success. Train the tree as a fan, and once established pinch unwanted side shoots to four leaves in summer. Thin fruits when young, these developing mainly on spurs on older wood. ' Moor Park ' and ' Hemskirk ' are good varieties.

**Blackberries.**—Allow plenty of room and train against fences or wires. Autumn planting is preferable, using good, well-manured soil and cutting back the cane to 9 in. from the ground. Mulch with manure each spring, water freely in drought, and cut out old canes as soon as they have fruited. Good varieties are ' Himalaya,' ' Merton Thornless,' and the parsley-leaved blackberry. Increase by tip layering.

**Cherries.**—Sweet cherries are unsuited to most gardens. The trees become too large, and *must* be planted in selected pairs to fruit satisfactorily, as all varieties are self-sterile. Large wall spaces are ideal for fan trees, as the fruit can then be protected from birds by the use of nets. Pinch side shoots on fans to four leaves in July; further pruning details being as for plums. Expert advice is essential to ensure that suitable varieties are grown together, the factors involved being complicated. ' Early Rivers ' with ' Bigarreau Schrecken ' and ' Merton Heart ' with ' Waterloo' are good combinations.

For the small garden the dwarf-growing, acid ' Morello ' cherry is more useful, being infinitely superior for preserves as well as self-fertile. It also succeeds on a north wall, but unlike sweet varieties, fruits *only* on one-year-old wood.

**Currants, Black.**—These are perhaps the most valuable of all hardy fruits, and bushes will give up to 10 lb. and more of currants with correct treatment. Plant from November to February, preferably autumn, at 5 ft. square on clean, heavily manured ground. Then cut all shoots to one bud above soil level. Mulch each spring with well-rotted manure and supplement with fertilisers if necessary. The mulch is essential as much for keeping the soil moist as for a general feed.

On established bushes prune preferably after fruiting or in winter, retaining strong young wood and cutting out older shoots, where possible from ground level. If necessary, alternate bushes can be cut down completely every other year to maintain vigour, as the bulk of the crop is always borne on young wood. Increase by 8-in. cuttings of one-year-old wood taken in late September from healthy bushes. Remove lower leaves and insert firmly with one bud above ground. Good varieties: ' Boskoop Giant,' ' Wellington XXX,' ' Baldwin.'

**Currants, Red and White.**—One or two well-grown bushes are usually sufficient for the average household. Plant between November and March at a minimum of 5 ft. square on well-manured ground and mulch each spring. Supplement with fertilisers if necessary, potash being particularly important in the form of sulphate of potash at 1 oz. per sq. yd. in February. Can be grown as cordons or fans against walls or fences, on which the pinching of young side shoots to four leaves in mid-June is essential. Winter pruning of all types simply involves cutting side shoots to one bud and tip pruning branch leaders. Propagate by 12-in. cuttings of young shoots in late September inserted to half their length with all buds removed except the top four. This enables the bush to be grown on a " leg." A permanent framework of branches is then developed, as, in contrast to the black currant, fruit is borne on spurs on the old wood. Good varieties: ' Laxton's No. 1,' ' Red Lake,' ' White Grape.'

**Damson.**—*See* Plums.

**Figs.**—A warm south wall is usually essential, ' Brown Turkey ' being one of the few reliable outdoor varieties. Plant in a brick or concrete trough (with drainage holes) about 2½ ft. wide, 5 ft. long, and 2½ ft. deep so that the root run is restricted. This will curb excessive growth (which otherwise is difficult to control) and encourage fruiting. Plant in March for preference, to avoid frost injury to young shoots, and then train fan-wise. A rich soil is not essential. Figs visible as such in the autumn will never over-winter, and should be rubbed out. Those the size of a pea and less at the tips of short, well-ripened shoots, on the other hand, are the potential crop for the following year, and should be covered in severe weather to avoid frost damage. To encourage the formation of these embryo fruits pinch young shoots back to the fifth leaf in late August. Winter prune in March, removing any wood that is frosted, overcrowded, or worn out; growths should be spaced at about 1 ft. Apply a spring mulch and water freely when required to avoid premature fruit drop.

**Gooseberries.**—Need conditions and spacing very similar to red currants, but with rather more moisture to ensure ample new wood, as this bears fruit as well as the older wood. Apply sulphate of ammonia and sulphate of potash annually in late February at up to 1 oz. per sq. yd. of each in addition to mulching. Can also be grown as cordons, etc., as for red currants. Pruning is also similar, though not quite so severe, as the young wood is productive of fruit. Cuttings are more difficult to root, and for best results should be taken in mid-September, again as for red currants. Good varieties: 'Lancer,' 'Leveller,' 'Whinham's Industry.'

**Grapes.**—Outdoor vines should be grown against a warm south- or south-west-facing wall. With good cultivation, the grapes should then ripen successfully providing suitable varieties are chosen. In preparing the site ensure that it is well drained and break up the soil to a depth of about 2 ft. Add bone meal to the top few inches at 4 oz. per sq. yd. and incorporate mortar rubble, particularly on the heavier soils. Do not dig in any manure except on poor, light soils, but always apply some as a mulch after planting, repeating this every spring. On poor, hungry soils the importation of some fibrous loam is advisable where possible.

Plant in November or, failing this, before early March, with the stem about 6–9 in. away from the wall. Firm well and then wait a further two months before tying to any wires or stakes, in case of soil sinkage. Cut the vine back in winter to well-ripened wood and to just above a bud. The training of subsequent growth will then depend on the space available, single and double cordons being the most convenient. Unwanted shoots should be pinched at about 2 ft. in summer and leading shoots carefully tied in to wire or bamboo supports. The following winter (December) prune leading shoots back to well-ripened wood so as to leave 3–4 ft. of new growth. Then cut all laterals hard back to one bud. In spring reduce young side shoots to one at each bud, stop laterals at about 12 in., and pinch any sub-laterals that may develop to the first leaf. Do not allow any crop to develop, except perhaps one bunch if growth is adequate; others should be pinched off. As fruit develops, thinning should be done as required. Winter prune as before, and then in the third summer four or five bunches of grapes can be allowed if the vine is healthy, the crop then increasing annually. Shoots carrying bunches should be pinched to two leaves beyond the bunch. Winter pruning is repeated each year as already described. Sour top-soil should be carefully removed when necessary and replaced with good loam while the vine is dormant. Good varieties: 'Black Hamburgh' and 'Foster's Seedling.'

**Loganberries.**—A very popular hybrid berry which should be treated as for blackberries. A thornless form is now available. Suitable for a north wall.

**Medlars.**—A tree of spreading habit, the peculiar fruits of which are best used for jelly before they are fully ripened. Most soils are suitable, and no pruning is needed except to keep in shape.

**Nectarines.**—A fruit very closely allied to the peach but with a richer flavour and needing rather more warmth. The skin is smooth, as distinct from the hairiness of the peach. For full details see Peach.

**Nuts.**—The most important kinds grown are cobnuts, the closely related filberts, and walnuts, but none of these is cultivated to any great extent. The two former kinds flower very early in February, and are therefore predisposed to frost damage; similarly, the young shoots of walnuts are easily injured by spring frosts, and all are therefore inadvisable for frosty areas.

*Cobnuts and filberts.*—Highly developed forms of the ordinary hazel nut. The nut of a cob is only partially covered by the husk, whereas a filbert is completely enclosed by it, this being the essential difference between the two. Will grow on most soils, including the poorer ones, and spacing should be about 15 ft., choosing sites sheltered from the colder winds. Plant during the autumn. Prune established bushes in March, cutting back shoots that have borne nuts to two or three buds; strong young shoots are cut back to a catkin near their base, and the weaker ones are left untouched. In August any strong new side growths are " brutted "—that is, broken off—and left hanging until the March pruning. Gather the nuts as they fall and allow to dry. Then store

in jars for Christmas use, packing salt and coconut fibre between each layer of nuts.

*Walnuts.*—Special, grafted varieties are now available which produce early crops compared with the unreliable seedling trees that used to be planted. Plant between October and March and water well in spring and summer. Do not prune, as walnuts bleed badly. Gather nuts in mid-July for pickling. For storing allow to drop naturally and remove outer husk immediately, scrubbing the shell clean and then drying thoroughly. The shells can be bleached if necessary before storing the nuts as for cobs above.

**Peaches.**—This fruit along with its close ally, the nectarine, is best grown against a warm south or south-west wall, but two varieties of peach, 'Peregrine' and more particularly 'Rochester,' will succeed as bushes in the open in southern England. The fan-trained peach is one of the most difficult trees to keep in order, as sufficient new shoots must be retained annually to replace old wood. This is essential, as it is only the previous year's shoots which bear fruit. Badly placed shoots are rubbed out when only an inch long, and the principle is to allow one young replacement shoot to develop near the base of each fruiting shoot, pruning back to the former and tying it in as soon as all fruit has been picked. Other shoots may be used to extend the fan where space allows or to replace any branches or parts of them which may have become worn out. Other unwanted shoots are bound to arise during each summer, and these are either removed immediately or pinched to three leaves and then removed when pruning in late summer. Those shoots retained are spaced at about 4 in. apart.

Most peaches are self-fertile, but hand-pollinating on sunny days can improve the set. Excessive feeding should be avoided, varying this according to each tree's performance, but as a general rule a surface mulch of well-rotted manure or compost should always be given each spring, together with sulphate of potash at ½ oz. per sq. yd. Prick over and rake off top-soil and replace with good loam every few years. Never allow the sub-soil to dry out—this can quickly occur against warm walls—and water thoroughly when doing so to ensure an even distribution of moisture. On the other hand, drainage must be satisfactory to avoid waterlogging.

There are numerous other essential operations in the growing of trained peach trees (for example, fruit thinning), and it is impossible to deal with these adequately in brief notes. Would-be growers should therefore seek expert advice and obtain literature dealing specifically with the crop rather than risk disappointment. Good varieties for outside wall training include: *Peaches:* 'Peregrine,' 'Bellegarde.' *Nectarines:* 'Early Rivers,' 'Lord Napier.'

**Pears.**—The requirements for pears are similar to those for apples, but the necessity for adequate summer and autumn warmth rules out many varieties for northern areas. In these less-favoured localities enquire which varieties do succeed, and where possible make use of a warm, south-facing wall. Protection from wind is very important, particularly from the cold easterlies of spring. Many soil types grow pears satisfactorily, providing drainage is good and the trees are looked after. Plant as for apples. Fertiliser requirements are also similar once cropping commences, except that pears may require a little more nitrogen.

Pruning (winter) is comparatively simple, the spur pruning given for apples suiting all except a very few pears. Initial shaping is essential, cutting the stronger shoots selected to form branches by about half their length and keeping the centre of the tree open. For cordons and other restricted forms of tree, to which pears lend themselves particularly well, summer pruning is advisable. This involves shortening all young shoots more than 10 in. in length to about 5 in. from the base. Do this when the base of such shoots is hardening and turning brown in colour, usually late July–early August. Pruned shoots may then be further reduced in winter. Such summer treatment may also be given to trained apple trees with advantage during August.

Only a few pears are self-fertile and 'Conference' is the most reliable if only one tree can be planted. Good pollinating pairings include 'Laxton's Superb' with 'Doyenné du Comice' and 'Conference' with 'Williams' Bon Chrétien.' Early varieties should be picked a little before ripening and used quickly.

**Plums.**—This general term includes gages and damsons. Numerous varieties are easy to grow but are unsuited to small gardens because of the amount of space required. Unlike apples and pears, there are no dwarfing rootstocks, and a minimum spacing of 14 ft. should be allowed for, growing the trees as half standards, or fan-trained against a south or west wall. Flowering is during April, and frost damage can be serious in some seasons. Plant preferably in the autumn, and by early March at the latest, using no manure unless soil is distinctly poor. Young trees should be staked during their early years, and must not be allowed to rub against the support.

Pruning should be reduced to a minimum, as the spores of silver leaf disease gain entry through wounds such as pruning cuts and stake rubs. Shorten branch leaders on young trees just as buds are bursting, but on older trees prune only when bianches become overcrowded. Do this between June and August, when the risk of silver leaf is at a minimum. Cut cleanly and coat the wounds thoroughly with a bituminous paint; treat broken branches similarly immediately they are noticed. Trees fruiting heavily should have the branches supported and the fruit thinned in late June. Side shoots on fans must be cut to four to five leaves in late June and reduced still further following picking if necessary. Feed cropping trees regularly to encourage new growth, using well-rotted manure or sulphate of ammonia at 1 oz. per sq. yd. in early spring. Some varieties are self-fertile, including 'Victoria,' 'Oullin's Golden Gage,' and 'Merryweather Damson.'

A WELL-PLANTED TREE, illustrating (A) a good method of tying and (B) sapling firmly secured with sacking around the trunk and held with stout cord.

**Raspberries.**—These are an ideal fruit for the small garden, but because of virus disease always buy certified canes from a fruit nursery. Plant between November and March on clean, well-manured ground, allowing 18 in. between canes and 6 ft. between rows. After planting prune each cane back to 12 in. Do not attempt to crop them in their first year, or the production of young canes for the following year's fruit will suffer.

A semi-shaded position will answer, but full sun is preferable for quality fruit. New canes should be looped with string to a post-and-wire fence and later tied individually to each wire when fully hardened. Space them at about 4 in. and remove any weak or diseased canes at ground level. In late February cut each cane to just above the top wire, which is usually 5–6 ft. high. This removes any damaged tips and may encourage fruiting over a longer length of cane. In the second summer a fair crop should result, and netting against birds is essential. Regular watering is imperative in dry weather, and spring and summer mulches of well-rotted manure or compost should always be applied. Supplement this in March with nitrogen and potash (fertilisers) if required, this depending on how well the ground was manured before planting. After fruiting cut out all old canes and tie in the new ones as already described. 'Malling Promise' and 'Lloyd George' are good varieties.

For autumn-fruiting varieties prune all canes to the ground in late February and tie in the best during the summer for cropping in September–October. 'September' is a good variety, and 'Lloyd George' can also be used.

**Strawberries.**—This is the one fruit that should be included in the vegetable garden. Fresh ground can then be used regularly for establishing new beds. Plants more than two years old are seldom profitable, and the best fruit is always picked from healthy one-year-olds planted the previous August or September. Runners put in later than early October should be deblossomed the following spring, the reward being a much heavier crop in the second year. This wastes ground, however, and early planting is preferable on all counts. Prepare the ground well in advance of planting and dig in plenty of well-rotted manure or compost or both, as this is the key to success.

Because of virus diseases order certified plants from a fruit nursery and burn any unhealthy ones in old beds before planting. Insert firmly with the base of the crown of each plant just at soil level and refirm after winter frosts; space at 20 in. in rows and 2 ft. 6 in. between rows (3 ft. if possible). A mulch of rotted manure or compost is beneficial each autumn, and if this is lacking apply sulphate of potash at 1 oz. per sq. yd. instead. Bonemeal is also advisable in spring and again in July, but quick-acting *nitrogenous* fertilisers should normally be avoided.

During flowering cover the plants where possible to guard against frost damage reducing the crop. Keep the ground weed-free and remove runners regularly; a few plants should always be grown away from the main bed, deblossomed and kept purely for runner production, as this then helps to reduce the spread of virus. Ruthlessly burn any plant that remains stunted, including its runners, as this is usually a symptom of virus disease. When the young fruits are just forming spread clean straw underneath them to avoid splashing from the soil; it is a mistake to do this too early, as it increases the risk of frost damage. Net the fruit against birds and remove any rotting specimens when picking.

After fruiting remove and burn all old foliage, weeds, and straw, and feed as already described. Plant a percentage of new, vigorous runners each year on fresh ground, at the same time burning the old ones they are replacing. For flavour, the best variety is still 'Royal Sovereign' of which healthy stocks are available.

Alpine strawberries require similar treatment, preferably with a semi-shaded position, and should be raised from seed. Perpetual fruiting types continue fruiting on and off well into the autumn, and should be treated as for ordinary varieties. In all cases cloches can be used from late February onwards to obtain early fruit.

Standard References:

*Tree Fruit Growing*, by Raymond Bush, revised by E. G. Gilbert, N.D.H. (Penguin) 1962 (12s. 6d.)
*The Fruit Garden Displayed* (R.H.S.) Revised Ed. 1965 (7s. 6d.)

## THE VEGETABLE GARDEN.

The vegetable garden is, or should be, an integral part of home economy nowadays. Home-grown vegetables, although requiring considerable labour, are cheaper and fresher than most shop supplies. The ideal site is in an open, sunny position sheltered from cold winds with the soil a deep, rich loam well supplied with humus; quite obviously very few gardens have the ideal site, and we have to do the best we can with the ground available. In laying out the vegetable plot, ease of working should be considered; the lines of vegetables should go from north to south, and paths should be wide enough for a barrow to pass. The vegetable lines should not be too long, or the soil will be trodden down too much.

Each individual will have to decide the size of his plot according to the amount and types of vegetables required, and the land available. Shelter from a hedge or wall is desirable, and a plot about 90 ft. by 30 ft. can be made to produce a succession of vegetables to feed an average family over the year. Land preparation is important;

the carry-over of some pests and diseases and providing for a full use of the manures in the soil, as different groups of vegetables need more of some nutrients than others. It also allows the clearance of one section to enable winter digging and manuring to be carried out. On this freshly manured plot peas, beans, onions, leeks, and lettuces, all revelling in rich ground, should be grown. The next plot, manured for the *previous* crop, can be used for root crops—early potatoes, carrots, parsnip, and beet. A light dressing of artificial fertiliser such as " National Growmore " should be applied before sowing. On the third plot the green vegetables should be grown; a dressing of fertilisers is desirable, and lime should also be applied.

In the following season the root crops can be grown on the plot which was manured the previous year, and the brassicas grown on the land vacated by the root crops. The plot on which the brassicas were growing is double dug and manured ready for the peas, beans, and onions. A system of this type proves very satisfactory, but numerous variations can be devised, and it is really a matter for

DOUBLE DIGGING—A sound cultural practice. A trench 2 ft. wide and the depth of a spade is taken out at A and placed as shown. The bottom of trench A is then forked up and filled in with soil from B and the process repeated with C and D, etc. In double digging the sub-soil is *always* left on the bottom and never brought to the surface.

on a new site the weeds should be cut down and removed, but any turf can be left and dug in. The land should be dug two spits deep (" double digging ") in winter, and for this the plot is divided into two longitudinally and a trench 2 ft. wide and 10 in. deep is dug out at one end, as shown on the accompanying diagram. The sub-soil below the trench is then broken up and manure or compost incorporated (or turf if grassland is being dug). The next strip is then dealt with in a similar manner, and this continues down the plot until the last trench, which is then filled with the loose soil from the first trench.

Clay soils which are sticky are much improved by humus and constant working, but should not be dug in wet weather. Sandy soils also require plenty of humus to conserve moisture, but are less fertile, though often warmer and earlier. For the majority of vegetables a slightly acid soil is best, and a dressing of lime is only desirable if the soil is too acid. Double digging is not necessary each year, and single digging, carried out in a similar manner without breaking up the second spit, or a light forking over is sufficient for some crops, provided the ground has been well cultivated previously.

The lay-out with vegetables must be designed to provide a succession through the year and to utilise the full capacity of the ground by catch crops and a suitable succession. The land can be divided into four plots; one is used for the more or less permanent crops, such as asparagus, rhubarb, and globe artichokes, and the other three will provide a rotation. This is used to stop any group of vegetables being grown on the same land more than once in every three years, so preventing

the gardener to decide his best method. The growing of maincrop potatoes will complicate the system, as a large area is usually required. They are better grown separately in another part of the vegetable garden.

Usually it is wise to have a small piece of ground available for a nursery bed. This should be of good, fine soil in which seeds can be sown to supply the main plot. In all cases seed should be sown very thinly to prevent the necessity for much pricking out, and a slug-killer is often a wise precaution to use before sowing. Sowing dates, as given, are mainly for growers in the South. In the North sowing dates in spring will be generally two weeks or more later and autumn operations the same amount earlier. Any gardener must adjust his work to suit local conditions of soil and climate, and this knowledge is only gained by experience of the particular area.

General cleanliness in the vegetable garden is at all times desirable; weeds and rubbish only harbour pests and diseases, and the hoe should be busy whenever possible. Waste material can be utilised in that essential of the modern garden— the compost heap. *See* Manures and Fertilisers for description.

**Frames and Cloches.**—The gardener is able to extend the season of many crops by protecting them under frames and cloches; this is particularly useful where spring or early autumn frosts are prevalent. The use of frames is limited, as they are in a fixed position, but nevertheless they are very useful for obtaining out-of-season salad crops, especially if they are heated by electricity or a hot bed.

Cloches have the advantage of mobility and can be used on a number of crops in succession. Essentially, each is a number of pieces of glass in a tent or barn shape held together by wire. Pattern, size, and height vary according to the crop to be covered and the manufacturer's design. A good cloche should be of simple design, rigid and capable of standing up to ordinary winds, easily transported, and well ventilated.

The low barn cloche is probably the most economical type. This is 23 in. wide and 13 in. high when erected, and will allow two rows of lettuce to be grown, with an intercrop of another vegetable. The large barn or barn cloche of similar design, but with 12-in. side is 19 in. high in the centre, enabling taller crops, e.g., peas and dwarf beans, to be grown on, almost to maturity.

Dwarf varieties should be used for growing under cloches, although methods of raising the cloches another foot or so have been devised and are on the market, which allow the use of taller growing varieties. Many different vegetables can be helped to some extent in the early stages, besides those crops which can be grown entirely under cloches; the grower must decide what crops he needs and fit a rotation to cover as many crops as possible with the cloches available. This is mainly a matter of experience, but books on the subject will suggest many variations that can be tried. Intercropping with quick-maturing crops can also be practised. As instances, radish or mustard and cress can be cropped between two rows of lettuce, or a row of cos lettuce can be grown between two rows of cabbage lettuce.

BARN                    LOW BARN

PLASTIC

TYPES OF CLOCHES—The most popular is the barn cloche; with 12-in. sides it will cover strawberries and peas and beans in their early stages. The low barn will accommodate three rows of lettuce in winter and cucumbers in the summer. Plastic cloches are growing in popularity, especially those patterns using toughened plastic, and have some decided advantages over glass ones.

The tomato cloche has sides 24 in. square and a basal width of 26 in. Many others of various shapes and sizes are offered; the amateur should buy to suit his own requirements. Other materials have been tried instead of glass with varying success. Plastic cloches are on the market, but their lightness entails very safe anchoring, and at the moment glass still seems to be the best material in most instances.

Gardening under cloches obviously is a subject too large to be dealt with in a few sentences, and the reader would be well advised to refer to one of the books mentioned in the bibliography for fuller information. A few of the main points are mentioned here and also under the individual crops.

Cloche cultivation is an intensive method of production, and this means that the land must be well cultivated and manured to ensure good-quality crops at all times. About ten days before crops are sown or planted the cloches should be put in the position where they are to be used, to warm the soil. The crop is sometimes sown a month before the normal date, and this prewarming ensures that the soil can be cultivated to a good tilth, as well as giving the plants a good start. Watering is a problem that often bothers the amateur. Provided the soil is well watered at sowing time, there should be no need to decloche to water. Rain seeping under the cloches and a spray directed over them occasionally will provide enough for the crop in normal weather; on dry, sandy soils it may be necessary to spray over the cloches more often. A mulch of compost is also very useful to help retain water.

It must be remembered that the glass of cloches will need cleaning from time to time; the crop still needs the maximum light available, although shading of certain crops may be necessary in hot sun.

Artichokes.—Two different plants are grown as artichokes. One, the Jerusalem artichoke (*Helianthus tuberosus*), is related to the sunflower and is grown for its tuberous roots, which are second in food value only to the potato. It will grow in poor soil, but amply repays good cultivation, and may be placed at the more exposed end of the vegetable plot as a windbreak and screen. Tubers should be planted during February or March, on well-manured ground in drills 4–6 in. deep, and 2 ft. 6 in. apart, with 15 in. between the tubers. Hoe frequently during the summer and cut the stalks down in early winter. The tubers may then be lifted and stored, or better dug as required, reserving a number for replanting the following February.

The other type, the globe artichoke (*Cynara scolymus*), is often grown as an ornamental plant, but is esteemed as a vegetable for its young, fleshy flower-heads, which must be cut before the scales begin to open, after which they become hard and unpalatable. A deep, rich, well-manured soil is required, and after planting in early spring in rows 4 ft. apart, with 2 ft. between the plants, a compost or manure mulch is beneficial. A good crop may be expected for five or six years provided an annual dressing of manure is applied. After this time they should be replaced by young suckers, planted in a fresh position. A covering of straw or bracken on the crowns is advisable during winter.

**Asparagus.**—This will grow on most types of soil provided that drainage is good and that plenty of organic matter is available. The site for the asparagus bed should be double dug in the autumn prior to planting, and a generous dressing of about half a barrow load of manure per square yard incorporated. Crowns up to three years old may be bought, but it is found that one-year-old crowns give the best results. Plants may be obtained cheaply by sowing seed in late March in drills 1½ in. deep and 18 in. apart and thinning the seedlings to 4 in. apart. It is thought that male plants produce more stalks of better quality than female plants, but at present no supplies of male crowns alone are available.

Planting may be on the single-row system or the wide-bed system. In the single-row system crowns are planted 18 in. apart in rows 4½ ft. apart; the wide-bed system consists of 5-ft. beds, with three rows of crowns 15 in. apart each way, and 2 ft. between each bed. Planting is best done during April and the plants are placed in a trench 8 in. deep and 1 ft. wide, with a slight ridge at the base, and covered with 3 in. of soil. The remaining soil is worked in during the summer. The roots should never be allowed to dry out.

The following March 2 oz. per sq. yd. of sulphate of ammonia should be applied; in subsequent years 3 oz. per sq. yd. of " National Growmore " applied at the same time, followed by 2 oz. per sq. yd. of sulphate of ammonia in June, after cutting, can be used. Salt, as a fertiliser, is not recommended nowadays. An annual dressing of manure or compost in November is desirable.

No cutting should be done for the first two years after planting and only a light cut taken in the third year. After this a six-to-eight-week season beginning in early May is usual. The spears should be cut when about 4 in. above soil level and severed about 2 or 3 in. below the soil, giving an overall length of 6–7 in. The fronds should be cut in October before the seeds drop, but not during the summer, as the plant is weakened. Weeds should be kept down and in the autumn the plant may be earthed up.

Varieties: 'Connover's Colossal' and 'Kidner's Pedigree.'

**Beans.** Three types are commonly grown, as follows:

**Broad Beans** are the hardiest and can, in warm gardens, be sown during autumn to obtain an early crop. Little is gained by this as a rule, and sowing in well-manured ground in February, when the soil is frost free, with successional sowings during March and April, is generally better in most gardens. The soil is broken down, finely raked, and the seed sown 9 in. apart in drills 3 in. deep, with 18 in. between each row. If double rows are sown 10 in. should be left between the rows, and 2 ft. between each pair of rows. Staking may be necessary. Plants from sowings under glass or under cloches in January may be used to obtain an earlier crop; the cloches should be removed in March and a further crop sown, and recloched.

Black aphis was a serious pest, but is now easily checked by pinching out the young tips and applying malathion or lindane as soon as any are seen. The pods may be used before the beans are fully developed and sliced as are runner beans, but normally they are picked when the beans are well formed but not tough.

Varieties: 'Aquadulce' and 'Green Masterpiece.'

**Dwarf Beans** (which include French, Kidney, and Haricot Beans) may be either used as young pods in a similar manner to runner beans or ripened in the pod for winter use. A rich well-manured soil gives the best results, and seeds sown during the first week in May, 2 in. deep and 6 in. apart, in drills 18 in. apart, may be followed by a second sowing at the end of May. The young plants should be thinned out to 1 ft. apart and small twigs used to stake them. If sown earlier, frost damage may occur. Seeds may also be sown in the greenhouse and the seedlings trans-

planted, or sown under cloches in the last week in March, provided the soil has been prewarmed.

The plants, as long as the pods are picked over frequently, will continue to bear until the frosts; a little liquid manure will be beneficial during the summer. A late sowing in July, cloched in September, will continue the season into the autumn.

If required for winter use (Haricot varieties) certain plants should be left unpicked and the pods allowed to ripen on the plants. They should not be picked green; if unripe when frosts come, the plants should be pulled up and dried in a shed.

Varieties: 'The Prince' (Cloche), 'Masterpiece,' and 'Comtesse de Chambord' (Haricot).

Runner Beans are the most popular type, and can be grown in two ways: either without stakes, in which case the tips of main and side shoots are regularly pinched out to make a bushy, dwarf plant, a method often used by farmers, or staked, with cross poles, allowing the plants to climb to the tops of the poles before pinching. Seed is sown from early May (mid-April under cloches) until late June, depending on the danger of frost, usually in a double row with drills 15 in. apart, and with seeds 3 in. deep and 6 in. apart in the rows, alternate plants being removed later.

Staking should be done as soon as the first pair of leaves unfolds, and a surface mulch is then applied. If the beans are to be dwarfed the rows should be about 18 in. or 2 ft. apart, and pinching may be required about once a week. A good, well-manured soil is essential, and plenty of moisture is required. The flowers may fail to set in dry weather, and an evening spray of water is helpful in preventing this " running off." Harvesting should be carried out regularly while the pods are young, before the seeds swell; older pods are stringy and seldom worth eating.

Varieties: 'White Czar' (white-flowered, heavy cropper) and ' Streamline.'

**Beetroot.**—From mid-April onwards varieties of beet may be sown on soil that has not recently been manured but is in good heart; on freshly manured soils coarse, forked roots subject to cracking occur. If in poor condition a light dressing of a complete fertiliser should be given before sowing. Sow in drills 1 in. deep and 12 in. apart and make a first thinning to 4 in. apart when the first rough leaf appears, and a second later, leaving 9 in. between the plants. Transplanting is inadvisable. Early roots for summer pulling may be obtained from a sowing of a Globe type in mid-April, and the main sowing should be made during May or early June for the winter supply. A sowing under cloches in late February will provide roots for pulling in late May.

On a heavy soil the oval-rooted types are best, but on a lighter soil the long-rooted types may be used. A sowing in late July of the Globe type will provide beet for use at the end of winter. Salad beet from early sowings may be pulled as required; the main crop should be allowed to mature and is lifted in October before the roots become woody and tough. Any damaged roots should not be stored. Twist off the tops just above the roots, shake the soil from the roots, and store in boxes of sand or peat in a frost-free shed. If clamped outside, straw and a thick layer of soil should be used; if frost reaches them they are spoilt.

Varieties: globe—'Detroit Red,' 'Red Globe,' and 'Crimson Globe '; oval—'Cobham Early '; long—'Cheltenham Green Top.'

Sugar beet is similar but is white, not red-fleshed, and is mainly a farm crop; if desired it may be grown in a similar manner. Care should be taken in hoeing all beet crops to avoid damage to the small surface roots which feed the swollen rootstock.

**Borecole.**—See Kale.

**Brassica.**—A generic name of vegetables usually known to gardeners as " greens." This group includes brussels sprouts, cabbages, cauliflowers, kale, turnips, kohl-rabi, broccoli, and couve tronchuda. As they are all related, similar soil and cultural treatment is needed, and many pests and diseases are common to them. Each is dealt with under a separate heading.

**Broccoli.**—*See* Cauliflower.

**Brussels Sprouts.**—Young plants from seed sown thinly in a nursery seed bed during mid-March can be transplanted during May or June. The soil should be firm, well drained, in good heart, and contain adequate lime, some manure preferably having been dug in during the winter; a supplementary dressing of 2 oz. superphosphate and 1 oz. of sulphate of potash per square yard is given before planting. The young plants should be set out 3 ft. apart both ways, planted firmly, and watered in thoroughly. Regular hoeing is necessary, and about a month after planting a little soil should be drawn round the stems.

If growth seems weak a top dressing of nitro-chalk should be given and this repeated in early September. As the lower leaves yellow, cut them off and gather the sprouts as they mature, picking from the bottom of the stem. Where space is available a succession of sowings from March to June can be made to lengthen the cropping period.

Club root, the worst disease of brassicas, is kept in check by only using well-limed, well-drained soil, and dipping the roots in 4% calomel before planting, and cabbage root fly, a frequent insect pest, by using dieldrin.

Varieties: early—' Cambridge No. 1 '; midseason—' Rous Lench ' and ' Triumph ' (dark foliage, distinct).

**Cabbage.**—Sowings in March and April for summer use, in May or June for winter use, and in late July or August for spring use will give a succession of cabbages all the year round. Seed is sown thinly in a nursery bed of well-firmed, limed soil, clear of weeds, in drills ¾ in. deep and 6 in. apart, and the seedlings are dusted with D.D.T. to check flea beetle attack (prevalent with all *brassica* seedlings). All cabbages are gross feeders, and a well-drained soil in good heart, with adequate lime, is required.

" Spring cabbage " should be sown during late July (north) and August (south). If sown too early the plants may " bolt " without making a heart. The young plants are set out in mid-September 18 in. apart and with 18 in. between the rows if for hearting, or 9 in. apart with 18 in. between the rows, in which case the alternate plants are cut for " spring greens." On a heavy soil ridging along the rows of plants keeps the soil round the roots drained and helps to prevent loosening by frosts. In cold districts cloches may be used with advantage to help plants through the winter. In early March a dressing of 1 oz. per sq. yd. of sulphate of ammonia or nitro-chalk is a good stimulant.

Seed of " summer " and " autumn cabbage " is sown in March and April and planted during late May and June, 18 in. to 2 ft. each way between the plants, depending on the variety. The plants should be thoroughly watered, both before and after transplanting. A top dressing of 1 oz. per sq. yd. nitro-chalk may be given if required.

" Winter cabbage," maturing from October to February from sowings during May and early June, are set out 2 ft. apart each way in July or early August, usually on ground which has been cropped with early potatoes or peas. No nitrogen fertiliser should be given late in the season, as soft growth, liable to frost damage, is encouraged. A balanced fertiliser, such as " National Growmore," may be used if needed. When the stalks of cabbage are left standing over winter a common practice is to cut across the tops to obtain bunches of leaves, for use as greens during early spring.

" Savoy cabbages " mature during winter and early spring from seed sown in May. Seedlings are transplanted in late July and early August on to land manured for the previous crop, to which a dressing of 2 oz. superphosphate and 1 oz. sulphate of potash per square yard has been given. The young plants should be set out 2 ft. apart each way; they are exceptionally hardy, and should be grown in every garden in case of a hard winter.

Varieties: Spring sowing—autumn cutting, Greyhound ' (early), ' Winningstradt.' Autumn

sowing—spring cutting, ' April,' ' Wheeler's Imperial.' Savoy ' Ormskirk Late Green.'

Red Cabbage is slow to mature; plants from sowings in August are transplanted 6 in. each way in autumn and set out in early spring 18 in. each way. They are ready to cut in late summer.

**Cardoon (Cynara cardunculus).**—Closely related to the globe artichoke and grown for the blanched hearts. Seed is sown in trenches 18 in. wide and 1 ft. deep; 3 in. of manure is worked into the bottom soil and covered with 3 in. of fine soil. Three or four seeds are dibbled in every 18 in. and covered with a flower pot till visible, and then thinned out, leaving one strong seedling at each station. Protection from sun and late frosts is provided by twigs over the trench, and copious watering is given during the summer. On a fine day in September the plants are blanched by tieing the leaves together and covering with dry hay, 3 in. thick, kept in position by raffia, and earthed up in the same way as celery. Blanching is completed in about a month. Litter over the top protects them from frost.

**Carrots.**—A light, well-drained soil, enriched with decayed organic matter, is suitable for carrots. No fresh manure should be given, but a light dressing of " National Growmore " fertiliser can be applied prior to sowing. The surface is left rough until sowing time and then broken down to a fine tilth. The first sowing is made in early April in drills ¾ in. deep and 12 in. apart, and a succession is obtained by sowing at intervals of a month until the end of July.

On heavy, unfavourable soils stump-rooted varieties are best grown, long-rooted varieties needing a light soil. Thin out the stump-rooted varieties to 4 in. apart and the longer varieties to 6 in. Thinnings should be removed and the soil pressed firmly back to minimise damage by carrot fly. The early sowings are pulled as required, but the later sowings for winter use should be lifted in October and stored in slightly damp sand in a frost-proof shed or clamped in the open.

Frames and cloches are sometimes used to obtain early and late carrots. Seed of a quick-growing variety, such as ' Amsterdam Forcing ' or ' Early Nantes,' sown in late January under cloches or in frames will provide an early crop; the same varieties sown in frames or cloches in early August will provide young carrots for the autumn. Carrot fly is a bad pest, especially on light soils; the seedlings should be dusted with lindane or dieldrin when 2–4 in. high to prevent the flies from egg laying.

Varieties: globular—' Early Gem '; stump-rooted—' French Short Horn '; intermediate—' Amsterdam Forcing ' and ' Early Nantes '; long—' St. Valery ' and ' Long Red Surrey.'

**Catch Crops.**—A term used for quick-growing crops interplanted between rows of other crops. Radishes between rows of broad beans, and lettuce between celery rows provide examples. In this way the best use of a limited amount of land can be made.

**Cauliflower.**—Broccoli is for all practical purposes a hardy winter cauliflower. Seed is sown ¾ in. deep in a nursery bed from mid-April to mid-May, depending on the variety, and transplanted during June and July on to firm soil, well manured for the previous crop. The plants are set out 2 ft. apart each way; 2 oz. superphosphate and ¾ oz. of sulphate of potash per square yard may be hoed in before transplanting. No nitrogenous manure should be given late in the year.

Varieties: cauliflower—' Snowball ' (summer), ' Majestic ' (autumn). Broccoli—' Snow's Winter White ' (winter), ' St. George ' (early spring). Sprouting broccoli—' Nine Star Perennial ' (a many-headed sort).

Sprouting broccoli is very hardy, has a more leafy head, and is cultivated in the same way. Purple- and green-sprouting varieties are grown.

Summer cauliflowers require a soil which has been limed and manured during the winter; 1–2 oz. per sq. yd. of superphosphate should be given before transplanting. An early sowing in frames in February or March will provide plants for cropping in June. These should be hardened off and planted in March or April from 18 to 24 in. square, depending on the variety. Seed sown outdoors in April in drills ¾ in. deep will give plants for transplanting in May or June, for cropping from late July onwards. If growth is slow a dressing of 1 oz. per sq. yd. of sulphate of ammonia should be given. Leaves broken over the curds will help to prevent any damage from early frosts. Varieties given in previous paragraph.

**Celeriac.**—A plant allied to celery grown for its edible root, which resembles a turnip but has the flavour of celery; the stems are bitter to the taste and are not eaten. It is used in salads or boiled as other root crops. Seed is sown in gentle heat in March and seedlings pricked out into seed-boxes, 2 in. apart each way. In June, after hardening off, the seedlings are planted out in shallow drills 18 in. apart, leaving 12 in. between each plant in the row. Water freely during the summer and remove side shoots as they appear. Lift the roots in October or November and store in a frost-free shed.

**Celery.**—Richly prepared ground is required. A trench 15 in. wide and 1 ft. deep is taken out and manure worked into the bottom of the trench. The soil is then returned to within 3 in. of the ground level. Seed should be sown in early March at about 60° Fahrenheit and the seedlings pricked out in deep boxes 3 in. each way and gradually hardened off. Celery seed is very fine, and care should be taken to cover it with only a fine layer of soil; if covered too deeply it may not germinate.

In late May or June set the plants out in staggered double rows 1 ft. apart, with 10 in. between the plants, and water them in. Frequent watering during the summer is required, and a light dressing of nitrate of soda will stimulate them if growth is poor. Before earthing up to blanch the plants, tie the stems loosely below the leaves and remove any suckers. Earthing up begins when the plants are about 15 in. high; the ground should be moist, and the first earthing should only be slight. The second and third earthings, at intervals of about three weeks, should be more generous, but should never reach higher than the base of the leaves, and no earth should fall into the heart. For exhibition purposes brown-paper collars may be tied round the stalks before earthing. The final earthing should cover all the stems right up to the leaves, and the soil should slope away neatly. In winter litter or bracken spread over the plants will help protect them from frost.

Celery fly is a serious pest, and the brown leaf-blisters should be pinched to kill the maggot inside and lindane applied two or three times at fortnightly intervals. Slugs should be discouraged with a good slug killer. Leaf spot, a seed-borne disease, can be prevented by spraying with Bordeaux mixture.

Varieties: white—'Solid White'; pink—'Clayworth Prize Pink'; red—'Standard Bearer' self-blanching—'Golden Self-Blanching.'

**Chervil.**—An annual herb sown during March in drills 10 in. apart, and thinned to 6 in. in the rows. Further sowings can be made during the summer. Used in salads and soups.

**Chicory.**—The young, blanched growths are used in winter salads. Seeds are sown in drills 1 ft. apart in May; the young seedlings are thinned to 8 in. apart and grown on until October or November, when they are lifted and the roots trimmed to 8 or 10 in. long. They are then planted in deep boxes in a moist, sandy soil 5 in. apart each way, leaving 1 in. above the soil surface, and the boxes put in a warm greenhouse or cellar. No light must reach the crowns; one method sometimes used is to cover the crowns with 6 in. of sand. When the blanched growths show through they are about 6 in. high and ready for cutting.

**Chives.**—These are like small onions, and the leaves are used for flavouring salads and soups.

They are easily grown in window boxes and town gardens. Bulbs can be planted in March 6 in. apart and divided when the clusters become too large.

**Corn Salad or Lamb's Lettuce.**—Occasionally grown for the leaves, which are used in early spring salads. Seed sown from August to October will provide plants for winter and spring use.

**Couve Tronchuda.**—A large brassica known as "Portugal cabbage," not generally suitable for smaller gardens. Seed is sown in March and the plants set out 2–3 ft. apart each way. The hearts may be cooked in the same way as cabbage.

**Cress.**—An annual growing rapidly from seed and used as a salad when only the seed leaves have developed. Seed sown as required, in boxes of light, moist soil and covered with brown paper until germination, when it is removed, will provide salad all the year round. The seed is merely pressed into the soil and the boxes kept moist. Cress may even be grown on damp flannel in a window.

**Cucumber.**—The cucumber of the shops is grown as a specialist crop under glass. Temperatures of 85° Fahrenheit or more may be required, and only occasionally are they grown by the amateur, although cloche and frame culture is now popular.

Ridge cucumbers, which are smaller and prickly outside, may be grown outdoors in summer. Plants from seed sown singly in pots under glass can be planted during late May on ridges of good, well-manured soil or, alternatively, sown on the ridges 1 in. deep at the same date. Water freely during the summer and cut the cucumbers while young to encourage further production.

If cloches are available greenhouse-raised cucumbers can be planted under them, in mid-April. Frame cucumbers are less hardy, but young plants raised under glass can be planted under cloches in early May.

Varieties: ridge—'King of the Ridge' and 'Stockwood Ridge'; frame—'Conqueror' and 'Telegraph.'

**Endive.**—Used in winter or autumn salads. Seed is sown during April in drills 18 in. apart and the seedlings thinned to 12–15 in. apart. Sowings in June and August will provide a succession. A rich soil and plenty of moisture are the main requirements; before eating blanching is necessary, as the leaves are very bitter. This is achieved by tieing the leaves loosely together and covering the plants with inverted flower pots (with the holes blocked) to exclude the light; frost should be kept out by piling litter over the pots in winter. If cloches are used they can be coated inside with lime-wash to achieve the same effect. Alternatively, plants may be lifted in October and blanched in darkened frames.

Varieties: summer—'Green Curled'; winter—'Batavian Broad Leaved.'

**Fennel.**—A perennial culinary herb used in fish sauces and salads. Blanched stems may also be cooked in the same way as celery. Seed is sown in drills 2 ft. apart in rich soil and the seedlings thinned to 18 in.

**French Beans.**—*See* Dwarf Beans.

**Garlic.**—One or two "cloves" planted in February, 9 in. apart, will provide ample garlic for salads, as only a little is required. After growth is complete in summer the bulbs can be lifted, dried, and stored and some saved for replanting.

**Haricot Beans.**—*See* Dwarf Beans.

**Herbs.**—Many herbs are useful in small quantities for flavouring and garnishing, as well as being decorative. If possible, a separate herb garden should be made as a feature in the garden, or they may be used as edging plants. Perennial herbs, of which borage, caraway, chamomile, chives, fennel, garlic, horseradish, lavender, mint, penny-royal, marjoram, rosemary, rue, sage, tansy, tarragon, and thymes are the main types grown, should be given a permanent position. Those grown as annuals—anise, basil, coriander, dill, parsley, purslane, and summer savory—can be used as " fill-ins " on the vegetable garden. Brick and cobble paths associate well with herbs, imparting something of the character of the gardens of bygone days, when herb gardens were considered one of the most important features.

**Horseradish.**—A deep-rooting perennial herb which appreciates a well-manured, moist soil. It is easily propagated from root cuttings and can become a nuisance, as pieces of root left in the soil will make a new plant; care should be taken to lift the complete root when digging it for use. Straight roots planted in spring with the crowns 6 in. below soil level and 1 ft. apart can be lifted for use in autumn; no further treatment is required, apart from keeping weeds in check. Some of the roots should be kept for planting the following spring.

**Kale.**—Very useful during a cold winter, when other green vegetables are scarce, because of its hardiness. Seed sown in April or May will provide young plants for transplanting 18 in. apart each way in July or early August, on to a site used for peas or early potatoes, in good heart. A catch crop of lettuce can usually be taken from between the rows. The variety 'Hungry Gap' is usually sown in rows 18 in. apart where it is to mature and thinned, leaving 18 in. between the plants. There are many varieties; which types are grown is a matter of personal preference.
Varieties: ' Cottager's ' and ' Hungry Gap.'

**Kidney Beans.**—*See* **Dwarf Beans.**

**Kohl Rabi.**—A brassica with a swollen stem base, in flavour and appearance something between a turnip and a cabbage. Seeds sown in April in rows 1 ft. apart are thinned to 1 ft. apart in the rows, and the swollen stem harvested when about the size of a tennis ball. If left to grow it becomes coarse.

**Lamb's Lettuce.**—*See* **Corn Salad.**

**Leeks.**—A vegetable which repays planting on a well-manured soil. If they are to follow winter greens, then manure or compost should be dug in after the previous crop is cleared. Leeks may be sown from early March to April in lines 8 in. apart on a prepared seed bed, and the seedlings transplanted as land becomes available during June and July, when about 6 in. high. Thinning in the seed bed should be unnecessary provided the sowing has been correct. The seedlings are set out 9 in. apart in rows 15 in. apart; a hole is made with a dibber, and each seedling dropped in and watered thoroughly. No firming is needed, the watering should tighten the plants sufficiently. Alternatively, drills 4 in. deep and 15 in. apart can be drawn out with a hoe and the plants put in 9 in. apart in the drills.
Regular hoeing is required, and a feed of sulphate of ammonia (1 oz. per gallon of water) can be applied if in poor growth. In September a little earth should be drawn up around the roots, which should, by then, be almost full grown. Leeks are very hardy and can be left in the soil until required for use.
Varieties: ' Lyon ' and ' Musselburgh.'

**Lettuce.**—Two main types are grown: cos lettuce, a summer crop with long, straight leaves that curl inwards naturally or are tied in so that the heart is more or less blanched; and cabbage lettuce, which are broad and spreading, with round cabbage-like hearts, and are grown to supply salad all the year round. Lettuce should be grown on ground manured during autumn or winter, dug and left rough till planting time, when it is broken down and raked to a fine tilth.

Seed, sown in January in frames and cloches, or outdoors in March and at fortnightly intervals thereafter, a little at a time, until September outdoors, or October in frames and cloches will provide lettuce for most of the year. Sow thinly in drills ½ in. deep, in rows 1 ft. apart, and thin out or transplant young seedlings so that they are 9–12 in. apart, depending on the variety. Quick, unchecked growth with adequate moisture is required; a dressing of bonemeal worked into the soil before planting and a light dressing of sulphate of ammonia in water on poor soils will help growth considerably. Aphids may be troublesome, and should be checked by using lindane or malathion.
Varieties: summer—'All the Year Round' and 'Continuity'; early spring—'Arctic King' and ' Cobham Green.'

**Maize.**—*See* **Sweet Corn.**

**Marrows.**—Pumpkins, gourds, bush, and trailing marrows all require similar treatment; plenty of sun and water and a rich soil, such as an old hot-bed or compost heap, which will provide a porous medium of humus. Seed can be sown singly in pots under glass in March, or outdoors on the site in May. For cloches a bush variety must be used, and greenhouse-raised plants are clocked in mid-April. Plant four or five seeds in groups about 6 in. apart and 1 in. deep and finally thin to two plants 15 in. apart. Protection from late frosts may be necessary. Water copiously and hoe regularly. Cut marrows when about 12 in. long to encourage further fruits. Some can be left until they are full size and cut before the frosts, for storing in a dry, frost-proof place.
Varieties: bush—' Green Bush ' and ' White Bush '; trailing—' Long Green Trailing.'

**Melons.**—Although usually a glasshouse crop, melons can be grown outdoors under cloches and in frames. Seed is sown under glass in April at 60° Fahrenheit, and seedlings can be set out 3 ft. apart in early May. The soil should be manured generously and the seedlings planted on a mound of compost mixed with soil. The plants must be stopped at the fourth or fifth leaf to encourage laterals. Two can be selected to grow on and, when 18 in. long, pinched out to obtain sub-laterals, which will bear the fruit. The female flowers may require pollinating, and on a sunny day a male flower or rabbit's tail can be used to transfer the pollen; as soon as the young fruits swell, remove all but two or three per plant and pinch back the laterals bearing fruit to two leaves from the melon. A feed of dried blood once a week, with plenty of watering (though not saturation!) will help the developing fruits. Light shading may be necessary.
Varieties: ' Dutch Net ' and ' Tiger.'

**Mint.**—Easily grown from suckers in any soil. For winter use a few pieces can be planted in a frame. A number of varieties—'Apple Mint,' ' Peppermint,' and ' Spearmint '—can be grown besides common mint.

**Mushrooms.**—Growing mushrooms is really a specialist occupation. For the experimental amateur, beds of composted stable-manure are made up in a warm, damp cellar or disused air-raid shelter. Pieces of spawn are inserted when the temperature of the compost has dropped to about 70° Fahrenheit and the whole bed covered with an inch of inert sub-soil. The air temperature should be from 60° to 70° Fahrenheit, and in a few weeks mushrooms may appear. Full instructions will be given with the spawn, but it is advisable to consult a text-book dealing with the culture, as even for professional growers a crop is never certain.

**Mustard.**—Grown exactly in the same way as cress, but is ready two or three days earlier. If used together, mustard seed should be sown two or three days after cress. Again it is the seed leaves which are eaten.

**Onions.**—These respond well to good cultivation. The site is dug deeply in winter, manure incorporated, and left rough until February, when it is broken down to a fine tilth and firmed well. Seed can be sown ½ in. deep in drills during August and planted in March for exhibition onions, but the usual practice is to sow seed in late February outdoors or under glass in January and transplant during April in rows 12 in. apart with 6 in. between the onions, taking care to keep the bases about ¼ in. below the surface. If sown outdoors and thinned the thinnings may be used in salads. Autumn-sown onions are liable to bolt, but less liable to attack by onion fly than spring-sown plants.

Dressings of sulphate of ammonia or nitrate of potash may be given during the growing season, but not later than July. In August the tops are bent over to hasten ripening and the bulbs harvested in a dry spell at the end of the month, first laying them on the ground for a day or two to dry off. They should be stored in a dry, airy place. The chief pest is onion fly, controlled by dusting the seedlings with aldrin at the loop stage. Onion sets are small onions produced the previous summer, stored and replanted in spring to obtain very large bulbs. They are particularly valuable on poor soils.

Varieties: spring sowing—'Bedfordshire Champion,' 'Best of All,' and 'White Silverskin' (pickling); autumn sowing—'Giant Zittau,' 'Sutton's Solidity,' and 'White Lisbon' (salad onions); sets—'Ebenezer' and 'Stuttgarter Reisen.'

**Parsley.**—Sow thinly in rows 8 in. apart during March and again in July for a succession of young foliage; thin to 4 in. between plants.

**Parsnip.**—Grow parsnips on ground manured for a previous crop; if given fresh manure splitting and forked roots occur. Dig the soil deeply, and at sowing time in March, work the soil to a fine tilth. On a soil unsuitable for deep-rooted crops special holes 10–12 in. apart, filled with sifted soil, may be prepared. If this method has to be used four or five seeds are sown per hole; normally drills 15 in. apart and 1 in. deep are made and four or five seeds sown every 9 in. The seedlings are thinned, leaving one at each station. Parsnips should be left in the ground until needed; litter over the rows will ease lifting in frosty weather.

Varieties: 'Evesham' and 'Student.'

**Peas.**—Dig the ground well in autumn and add a generous amount of manure or compost. Seed sowing begins at the end of February, and can be continued at three-weekly intervals until early July. Under cloches sowings in January and October will lengthen the season. Both early and late sowings should be of a quick-maturing variety. Seed is sown in drills 6–8 in. wide and 3 in. deep, with 2 ft. between drills; the seeds can be scattered thinly in the drill or spaced 3 in. apart in a treble row. Cover with 2 or 3 in. of soil and as soon as the peas are about 2 in. high stake with twigs.

Failures are often due to attacks by birds and field-mice. The former should be discouraged by netting and the latter by trapping. Pea-sticks will be necessary for the taller varieties which should have 3–4 ft. between the rows. With limited space only the dwarf quick-maturing varieties should be used. A summer mulch will keep the soil moist, and picking should be done regularly.

Varieties: 1½–2 ft.—'Kelvedon Wonder,' 'Kelvedon Triumph,' and 'Meteor' (cloches); 2¼ ft.—'Onward'; 3½–4 ft.—'Gladstone.'

**Potatoes.**—In general, it is only economic for the amateur to produce an early crop; the main winter supply can be grown if room and labour are available. They should be grown on land well manured the previous season, dressed at planting time with a mixed fertiliser, such as "National Growmore," at a rate of 1½ lb. to a 30-yd. row. The soil should not contain too much lime, as the damage of scab disease is increased.

"Seed" tubers about the size of a large egg are best used, and these can be bought or saved from the previous season's crop. Large potatoes may be cut leaving about three eyes to each part. New stocks should be bought occasionally if the "seed" is home saved to obviate risk of virus. "Seed" should be put in trays during February in a frost-proof shed to sprout, and in early April the "first-earlies" can be planted.

Drills 2 ft. apart and 4–5 in. deep are taken out and the sprouting "seed" planted 12 in. apart in the rows. Maincrop varieties are planted in early May 15 in. apart. The young growths should be protected from frost by earthing up slightly, and a further earthing is done as the potatoes mature. This practice of earthing prevents the tubers near the surface from becoming green when exposed to light, keeps weeds down, and protects the tubers from spores of potato blight, which are washed into the gullies. If growth is poor sulphate of ammonia can be applied at a rate of ½ lb. per 30-yd. row. Early varieties should mature in late July and later varieties in September and October; when the tops (haulm) turn yellow the crop can be lifted, dried for a few hours (too much light will turn them green), and stored in boxes in a frost-proof shed or clamps.

SEED POTATOES—Good seed is essential for first-rate crops. Illustration shows (left) a well-sprouted tuber, (centre) a large well-sprouted tuber suitable for cutting, and (right) a poor, badly sprouted tuber.

Potato blight is a common disease, and control by spraying with "Bouisol" before the leaves touch in the rows is effective. Virus diseases, spread by greenfly, are checked by using "seed" from Scotland, where greenfly is less troublesome because of the lower temperatures. Colorado beetle should be watched for, and if found notified to the Ministry of Agriculture.

Varieties: Discerning growers will find the following well worth growing: 'Edzell Blue' (violet-coloured skin; excellent cooker), 'Pentland Dell' (white-fleshed; heavy cropper), 'Red Craigs Royal' (red-fleshed; heavy cropper), 'Ulster Chieftain' (white-fleshed, good early variety). Epicureans seeking a first-class potato should grow 'Maris Peer', a sort understandably gaining in popularity in Scotland, since its introduction. Another interesting sort is the Dutch-raised 'Record', a yellow-fleshed variety which has a trace of sweetness in its flavour.

**Pumpkin.**—See Melon.

**Radish.**—Most cultivated ground is suitable for growing radishes; successional sowings at fortnightly intervals from early March until May in drills ½ in. deep should be made. Summer-sown radishes bolt and are hot and tough, but autumn sowings for late salads can be made. As radishes germinate very quickly, they can be sown together with another crop and used quickly, and also enable the rows to be seen and hoed early.

Varieties: 'French Breakfast' and 'Scarlet Globe.'

**Rhubarb.**—Before planting the ground should be generously manured and deeply dug. Crowns are planted in March, 3–4 ft. apart each way and mulched, but no rhubarb should be pulled until the following year, when a light pull can be taken. Remove any flowering shoots and give a dressing of sulphate of ammonia if growth is weak. Manure well each winter; if early supplies are needed, some of the crowns can be covered with inverted boxes or barrels and a packing of loose straw or bracken. An established, well-cultivated bed will continue almost indefinitely.

Sage.—A hardy shrub for the herb garden easily raised from cuttings. The leaves are harvested and dried in summer.

Salsify (Oyster Plant).—A winter root rather like a parsnip which requires similar growing conditions.

Savoy.—See Cabbage.

Scorzonera.—A winter root cultivated in the same way as salsify. It has a purplish root instead of the yellow-green one of salsify.

Sea-kale.—A perennial plant native to our sea-shores, which can be either grown from seed sown in March and left for two years to produce forcing crowns or from bought thongs, which are planted during March, 9 in. apart in groups of three, leaving 3 ft. between groups. During summer a manure mulch and nitrogenous fertiliser can be applied. When the tops die down in autumn the crowns are covered with boxes to force and blanch the new growths. Crowns can be covered in succession to keep a supply. Earlier sea-kale can be obtained by lifting crowns in November. These are planted in batches five or six to a pot, watered well, and a second pot, with the hole blocked, placed over them. In a warm green-house or similar position they should develop sufficiently for cutting in about three weeks. Slugs are the chief pest outside, and should be kept in check by a proprietary slug-killer.

Shallots.—A popular crop for the small garden. Shallots are purchased as bulbs, like small onions. A deep, well-manured soil is required, as for onions, and they are planted during February, the bulbs being pressed about half their length into soft soil, 6 in. apart in the rows, leaving 1 ft. between rows. In mid-July the little bunches of bulbs can be lifted. Leave them on the surface to dry for a few days and then store in a dry, frost-proof shed. Some, about the size of a shilling, should be kept for planting the following year.

Spinach.—Sowings in February to April on a well-manured soil will provide a succession during the summer. Sow in drills 1 in. deep and 12 in. apart and thin the young plants to 3 in., and then to 6 in., using the second thinning to eat. A sowing of the prickly variety in August at the same distances will provide a winter crop. When picking gather a few leaves from each plant in the row.

Varieties: 'America' and 'Giant Prickly.'

Sprouting Broccoli.—See Cauliflower.

Sugar Beet.—See Beetroot.

Swede.—See Turnip.

Sweet Corn (Maize).—Gardeners should distinguish between the types of maize used for poultry food and those which supply sweet corn for human consumption. It is wise to use cloches for growing sweet corn, as it is only half-hardy and resents transplanting. Seeds sown under cloches in mid-April in two drills 12 in. apart and 1½ in. deep should be placed 1 ft. apart in staggered positions in the rows. More robust varieties may need 15 in. from plant to plant. A soil well manured for the previous crop is best used, and a mulch can be given as soon as the plants are a few inches high. The first cobs should be ready by mid-July, and should be eaten when the cob is milky.

Variety recommended: 'John Innes Hybrid.'

Tarragon.—A herb used for flavouring vinegar. Raised by root division in spring. Cut down and dried for use in winter.

Tomato.—A sunny, sheltered site is required, otherwise ripening outdoors in our climate is uncertain. Sow seeds under glass in late March and

harden off the plants in a cold frame or buy plants for setting out in late May or early June. The soil should be thoroughly dug and some artificial manure applied before planting. Allow 18 in. between plants and 2½ ft. between rows, and put in a strong stake with each plant. Keep to a single stem, pinching out side shoots regularly. When four or five trusses are set pinch out the top of the main shoot.

Feed with a liquid manure during summer. Fruit which fails to ripen outdoors can be gathered and stored at about 50° Fahrenheit or the plants laid flat on the ground and covered with cloches, when the tomatoes should ripen. Under cloches plants can be planted out in mid-April instead of late May, gaining six weeks growing time, and the cloches removed when they become too large.

Potato blight attacks tomatoes, and a spray of "Bouisol" during the first week in August and repeated after fourteen days will give a control.

Varieties: 'Market King' and 'Money-maker'; some heavy-cropping sorts have little or no flavour and a thick skin.

Turnips.—Ground manured the previous season should be dug well and dressed with 2 oz. super-phosphate per square yard. An early variety can be sown during April in drills ¾ in. deep and 15 in. apart, followed by successional sowings at three-week intervals as required. The main crop for storage is sown in July and August, and seedlings should be thinned gradually to 10 in. apart. Use when about the size of tennis balls. A sowing can be made in September, left almost unthinned and the tops used as "greens" in spring. In autumn the storage crop is lifted and all un-damaged roots put in sand in a shed or clamped. Flea beetle and turnip fly can be checked by D.D.T. at the seedling stage.

Swedes are grown in a similar manner.

Varieties: turnips—'Early Milan' (summer) and 'Green Top Stone' (winter storage); swedes—'Purple Top.'

Standard References.

*Cloche Cultivation* by G. B. Walkden (Colling-ridge) 1955 (9s. 6d.)

*Gardening with Cloches*, by Louis Flawn (Gifford) 1957 (16s.).

*The Vegetable Garden Displayed* (R.H.S.) 1961 (6s.).

*Vegetables for Garden and Exhibition*, by S. M. Gault (Collingridge) 1956 (50s.).

## FERTILISERS AND ORGANIC MANURES.

The elements essential for healthy plant growth may be roughly grouped into classes—first, those required in some quantity, the major elements, nitrogen, potassium, and phosphorus; secondly, calcium, magnesium, and sulphur, which are required in lesser quantities; and thirdly, the trace elements, boron, manganese, iron, zinc, copper, and molybdenum, of which only minute quantities are needed. As well as the elements mentioned, others, such as silicon, aluminium, chlorine, nickel, and sodium, are often found on plant analysis, but the evidence that these are essential is inconclusive, though they may be beneficial to certain crops.

It is important to remember, when adding fertilisers to the soil, that different crops may require relatively more of one element than another, but a balance between all the elements is essential. As an instance, brassicas (the cabbage family) are gross nitrogen feeders, while root crops (e.g., carrots) require far less nitrogen, and an excess may be harmful. A further point to notice is that although an element may be present in the soil the plant may be unable to absorb any because it is being kept in an insoluble state by excess of another element. An instance of this is the frequent yellow and sickly appearance of plants on very chalky soils due to lack of iron, which is present, but locked in an insoluble state by too much calcium.

The elements needed by the plant are in the form of various compounds, such as nitrates and phosphates, and may be applied as artificial fertilisers, which are manufactured, or as humus, which contains most of the foods required and also provides the essential soil micro-organisms or bacteria, without which the soil would be inert and no plants would grow. Bacteria break down the complicated animal and vegetable matter of which humus is composed to soluble compounds which plants can absorb. Humus can be supplied as farmyard and poultry manure, leaf mould, compost, sewage sludge, spent hops, and from animal by-products like hoof and horn, dried blood, meat and bone meal, and many others.

Nitrogen is mainly concerned with vegetative growth, encouraging leaf and stem formation. It is also contained in chlorophyll, the green colouring matter of the plant, and one of the symptoms of nitrogen starvation is a pale-green colour to the leaf, indicating a lack of chlorophyll. Most of the nitrogen compounds used are soluble, and it is a wise maxim to apply "little and often"; if given in large doses much is washed through the soil and wasted.

Nitrogenous fertiliser should not be given to any plant late in the season, as sappy growth, easily damaged by winter cold and frosts, is encouraged. Similarly, at no time should large quantities be given to any plant, as this results in an excess of leafy growth, which is very susceptible to disease and adverse conditions of drought and cold; also plants tend to be later flowering.

Sulphate of ammonia is the most used inorganic nitrogenous fertiliser, and is excellent for spring use on seed beds, lawns, and early crops, and it is contained in most fertiliser mixtures. It makes soils acid in reaction, and if both lime and nitrogen are required, nitro-chalk should be used instead. Other nitrogen fertilisers used are potassium nitrate, which has the advantage of supplying two major elements at once, and is very soluble, and nitrate of soda, often used on beet and mangolds. The latter chemical should not be applied in excess, as too much sodium has a bad effect on soil structure. These inorganic fertilisers are all soluble and quick acting. As a general guide, 1 oz. of the fertiliser to a gallon of water, applied at 1 oz. to a square yard, is a good general summer dressing, given at intervals of two or three weeks. It should always be given after rain or watering, and should be applied to the soil and not to the foliage.

Among organic fertilisers containing a percentage of easily available nitrogen are dried blood, soot, and meat and fish meals. Slower to decompose, and so having a more lasting effect, are shoddy (wool waste) and hoof and horn.

Phosphorus is concerned in the plant with the production of young cells of the root and shoot, and also encourages flower and fruit production and early ripening. Most of the compounds are relatively insoluble (rendering absorption by the plant difficult), and so large amounts can be supplied without deleterious effects, especially on acid soils, where the availability is less than on alkaline soils.

Phosphorus is generally applied to the soil in the form of phosphates, and among these superphosphate of lime is quick acting, and is usually applied at 2–3 oz. per sq. yd. in spring and summer, when the need is greatest. More slow acting is basic slag, a by-product of the steel industry, sold as a fine black powder and containing, besides phosphates, many of the trace elements, as well as a considerable percentage of lime. This is good for application to acid, wet soils, but should not be applied to potatoes owing to the risk of scab disease with the increase in the content of lime. It should not be applied with sulphate of ammonia. Bonemeal is also slow acting and also contains some nitrogen. It is excellent for crops like tomatoes, and is also used extensively for ornamental and pot plants.

Potassium, the third major element, is essential for good flower colour and ripeness in fruits. Dessert apples, potatoes, cereals, and root crops all need potash in some quantity, and if excess nitrogen has been applied a dressing of potash may counterbalance the effect. Sulphate of potash is the main inorganic compound in use. Muriate of potash (potassium chloride), to which some crops are sensitive, is much less used; it should be

applied as a winter dressing before the crop is sown to lose the impurities by weathering. Sulphate of potash is purer, and may be applied during the growing season at 1 oz. per sq. yd. on the vegetable plot, and is used in many proprietary fertiliser mixtures.

Wood ash contains variable quantities of potassium, and provided that the ash has not been washed by rain and the potassium leached out, is a useful addition to the soil; bracken, cut during June and July, when large amounts of potassium are present in the foliage, can be composted when green to provide a good supply of the element.

Elements Required in Lesser Quantity.—Calcium, although required in small quantities in the plant, has profound effects on the soil. Its main function in the plant is in the production of cell walls, but in the soil it helps to bind light soils together and to make the structure of sticky clay soils finer and more workable. Also soils without calcium are acid and tend to lock up some elements in an insoluble form. Addition of calcium changes the acidity, making it slightly alkaline or neutral, and releases the locked elements.

Calcium is applied as some form or derivative of calcium carbonate, commonly known as lime, which can be obtained in various forms. Hydrated or slaked lime (calcium hydroxide) is commonly used on clay soils, and chalk or ground limestone on lighter soils. Calcium is gradually leached from the soil, and it is necessary to replace it, or the soil becomes too acid and many crops will fail to grow. A normal dressing of lime for a vegetable garden is about 4 oz. lime or ½ lb. chalk per square yard every two or three years, and is best applied in autumn as a surface dressing after digging. It should not be applied together with other fertilisers. The amount of lime will depend on the type of soil, but it must be remembered that most vegetables grow best on a slightly acid soil.

Gypsum, or calcium sulphate, is sometimes recommended to supply calcium, but its solubility is negligible, and it is preferable to chalk or limestone only on soils containing salt due to sea flooding. It has been used to help reclaim parts of East Anglia flooded by sea-water during the storm surge of January 1953 by improving the soil structure. Sulphur, as sulphates, and magnesium, as an impurity in limestone, are usually present in sufficient quantities for the plants' needs.

Trace Elements.—In the case of the trace elements most soils contain enough for the plant, but in certain circumstances deficiencies occur. Iron on very alkaline soils is insoluble and, as it is essential for the production of chlorophyll, deficiency results in the chlorosis of the leaves. It can be rectified by spraying the leaves with "Sequestrene Plus," as can the lack of magnesium and manganese, which may also be deficient on acid soils.

Chlorosis in brassicas and marsh spot of peas are due to magnesium deficiency. Boron deficiency, often occurring on light, calcareous soils, is responsible for brown heart of cauliflower and several other "diseases," mainly affecting the growing point. It can be rectified by applying borax to the soil at about 1 oz. per 15 sq. yd. Zinc and copper deficiencies are unusual in England, but lack of molybdenum has caused whiptail disease of cauliflower. Only minute quantities of the last three are required; more may be poisonous to plants and animals.

Organic Manures.—It should be noted that most of the deficiencies will not concern the amateur, especially if he keeps the ground in good heart with ample organic manure, which contains all the plant foods necessary. Well-rotted farmyard manure from cows and pigs is by far the best organic food, but is scarce now, good farmers returning it to their own land, and generally the material offered is low in nutrients. Poultry manure, which is rich in soluble nitrogen salts, is excellent either applied direct to the soil (not to the growing crop for fear of damage) or composted with straw.

Many substitutes have been devised to use in place of manure, among them sewage sludge, best applied some time before growing the crop, spent hops from breweries, dried seaweed, excellent for potatoes when supplemented by superphosphate, soot, rich in nitrogen, composted town refuse, and the waste organic animal products mentioned earlier. The organic matter in all these materials is essential for maintaining the soil structure and cannot be replaced simply by artificial fertilisers.

Liquid manure, produced by suspending an old sack of animal manure or soot in water for a few days, is useful for the amateur to apply to pot plants and to individual crops like sweet peas, tomatoes, and chrysanthemums. Leaf mould and peat can be used as a mulch and also to supply organic matter to the soil. Sawdust in a well-rotted condition is also useful for inclusion in compost and as a mulch. It is emphasised that it must be well-rotted, and it is advisable to apply a nitrogen fertiliser, such as sulphate of ammonia, at the same time.

Composting of organic refuse from house and garden is much practised by the amateur nowadays.

**Compost-making.**—The methods developed for making compost heaps are many and various; they depend on three basic principles, good aeration, plenty of moisture, and a nitrogen supply for the decomposition bacteria. A fairly simple method by which much garden and house refuse can be utilised is as follows. An area about 9 ft. by 4 ft. is marked out and all waste vegetable matter—weeds, lawn mowings, cabbage leaves, pea haulm, straw, dead leaves, and hedge clippings—are put in this area and trodden down. Care should be taken not to use diseased material but grass clippings and weeds which have been recently treated with hormone weed-killers may be applied. When the heap is about 9 in. thick it is sprinkled with sulphate of ammonia and superphosphate, at ½ oz. of each per square yard (2 oz. of each for a 9-ft. by 4-ft. plot) and any wood ash available, and then sprinkled with 4 gallons of water and covered with an inch of soil. This process is repeated with 9-in. layers of rubbish until the heap is about 4 ft. high, when it is better to begin a second heap. A sprinkling of ground lime may be given as each layer is added, but should not be applied until after watering to avoid reaction with the sulphate of ammonia.

The completed heap should be watered occasionally, and after about a month or six weeks, if time permits, it can be turned completely over, watered again, and re-covered with soil. The heap may then be left until rotted, and the compost can be dug in as required; any unrotted material can be used as a basis for a new heap. The time taken for rotting will vary with the time of year and material used, but generally a compost heap made during the summer should be available for autumn use, and one made during the autumn ready for spring use.

There are a number of compounds on the market, known as compost makers, which are said to accelerate the decomposition, but in general a heap made in the way described is eminently satisfactory, and although requiring a certain amount of labour, is the least expensive way of obtaining humus for the garden. This latter point is extremely important nowadays with the scarcity of animal manure and the high costs of both inorganic and organic fertilisers. Prices are, of course, not static, but comparatively the organic manures, such as dried blood, hoof and horn, and guano, are more expensive than the inorganic salts, but these lack humus, which is an essential of a well-cultivated soil.

**General Fertiliser.**—Many firms supply compound fertilisers containing given amounts of the main nutrients needed, in either liquid or powder form, and some are made up with quantities of nitrogen, potassium, and phosphorus suitable for specific crops like roses, tomatoes, and chrysanthemums. A general fertiliser which can be made up by the amateur is as follows:

7 parts by weight superphosphate.
5 parts by weight sulphate of ammonia.
2 parts by weight sulphate of potash.

All the ingredients are easily obtained from local sundriesmen, and a mixture of this sort will supply a good general feed.

**Green Manuring.**—Another method of enriching the soil with organic matter is green manuring, which has been practised for some time by farmers and can no doubt be adapted to the gardener's purpose. Green manuring consists of planting a fast-growing catch-crop and ploughing the mature crop back into the soil. Legumes are especially good for this, as certain bacteria in their roots can " fix " the nitrogen in the air. Field peas, sown at 4 oz. per sq. yd. and Italian rye grass at 2 oz. per sq. yd. are commonly used, and clover and annual lupins are also suitable.

If sown after an early crop on land needing organic matter the green manure may be dug in during late summer. Alternatively, if the land is not being cropped at all during the year two green-manure crops may be grown; an early sowing of field peas in April may be dug in during July, and a further sowing of field peas or Italian rye grass sown immediately after may be dug in following the first few frosts.

New chemicals often appear on the market at exorbitant prices and with fantastic claims as to their value as " soil conditioners " and the like. Contrary to this generalisation, in recent years a chemical known as " Gibberellin " has been used to increase the growth of certain plants. It is now available to the amateur, but should be used with care and mainly in a spirit of experimentation, as no conclusive proof of its efficacy has yet been put forward.

Standard References.

*Fertilizers and Manures* by Keith Paisley (Collingridge) 1960 (30s.).
*Seed and Potting Composts*, by Lawrence and Newell (Allen and Unwin) (9s. 6d.).

## GARDEN PESTS.

Every garden abounds in insects and other small creatures, but comparatively few species are pests which feed on plants. The great majority are quite harmless, while many are positively beneficial and help to keep the number of pests under control by catching and eating them. Every good gardener should make it his business to be able to differentiate between friend and foe. This is not always easy, but the speed of a creature's movements may often provide a clue. Fast-running, active creatures, such as the black ground-beetle or the centipede, are usually beneficial, while the slow-moving and sluggish ones, *e.g.*, wireworms, aphids and caterpillars, are usually pests. This is by no means an infallible rule, but it is handy to remember when in doubt.

The good gardener should also get to know the pests which are most prevalent in his district and which can be expected to crop up year after year. The first principle of good control measures is to act while an infestation is still in its early stages and before a great deal of damage is done. When one knows what to expect, steps can be taken to prevent an attack or to stop it developing to serious proportions.

Also, from the experience of past years one can often forecast whether a pest is likely to become numerous enough to make chemical treatment worthwhile. Remember, insecticides can become an expensive item, and there is little point in using them if the damage is negligible. In these circumstances insecticides may eventually increase the numbers of pests, since the treatment will also have killed off many of their natural enemies which had hitherto kept the pests under adequate control. In addition, good cultivation and general garden hygiene helps to reduce the numbers of pests.

The common pests of garden plants can be roughly divided into four main groups.

I. **Root Pests.**—These destroy the feeding mechanism of plants or tunnel into fleshy tap roots, tubers, and bulbs. Attacked plants make poor growth, and may eventually wilt and die.

Some insects are general root-feeders. These include (a) **Swift Moth Caterpillars**, soft, white caterpillars with reddish-brown heads; (b) **Chafer Grubs**, large, C-shaped, whitish grubs with chestnut-brown heads; (c) **Wireworms**, long, cylindrical, yellowish-brown grubs with a hard shiny skin; and (d) **Leatherjackets**, greyish-black grubs with a wrinkled, leathery skin. These are particularly prevalent in recently cultivated grassland or in gardens surrounded by fields, and will attack the roots of a wide range of plants. Chafer grubs, however, are particularly fond of the roots of shrubs, and wireworms will often tunnel in potato tubers and other fleshy roots, whereas leatherjackets prefer the roots of grasses, and may cause browning on large patches of lawn.

Badly infested ground should be dressed with lindane dust when cultivating, working the dust into the top 4 in. of soil. Where this is not possible, i.e., on lawns or around established shrubs, the liquid form of the insecticide should be watered into the soil.

**Cutworms** are stout, fleshy caterpillars, varying in colour from greyish-brown to dingy green. They feed on roots during the day, but at night come to the surface and feed at the base of the stems of plants, causing them suddenly to collapse and wither. Brassicas and lettuce are commonly damaged in this way. Infested ground should be dusted with D.D.T.

**Millepedes** are hard-skinned, cylindrical creatures, brown or black, with numerous short, hair-like legs. They are slow-moving and curl up when disturbed. They should not be confused with the active, long-legged centipedes, which are beneficial. Millepedes commonly extend the damage made by other pests, such as slugs and wireworms. They also bore into the sown seeds of peas and beans. During the day they hide in dark, damp places, such as long vegetation or under stones and pieces of wood. Such hiding-places should be removed or dusted with lindane. Drills for pea and bean seed should also be dusted before covering.

**Weevil Grubs**, small, curved, white grubs, may infest the roots of pot plants and plants in rockeries. Such plants should be removed, the roots cleaned, and replanted in soil which has been dressed or mixed with lindane dust. Where it is not practicable to remove the plants they should be watered copiously with a liquid form of these insecticides and soil dressed properly at the earliest opportunity.

**Slugs** need no description. They vary greatly in colour. The most destructive are the underground keeled slugs, small, grey-black in colour, which tunnel in roots, tubers, and bulbs. There are also several foliage-feeding species which rasp holes in the top parts of plants. Slugs like wet conditions, and much can be done to control them by ensuring that the soil is well-drained and that long, tangled vegetation is removed.

Poison baits can be bought or made by mixing 1 oz. metaldehyde with 3 lb. bran (or bonemeal for keeled slugs). The bait is sprinkled over the infested ground or distributed in small heaps and protected from the rain. There is also available on the market a metaldehyde spray for dealing with the foliage-feeding types.

**Cabbage Root Fly** attacks brassicas and wall-flowers. The small white maggot eats away the side roots and tunnels in the main root, causing the plant to wilt and collapse. The roots of young seedlings should be dipped in lindane before planting out. Alternatively, the plants can be given a drench of lindane within four days of planting out.

The maggots also tunnel in radishes and turnips, and this can be avoided by dusting the seed drills with lindane.

**Carrot Fly.**—The maggot of this fly tunnels in carrots and parsnips. Where the pest is serious it is best to delay sowing until the end of May. If possible, seeds should be sown in exposed, windy places, which are avoided by the egg-laying flies. Seedlings should be dusted or sprayed with lindane when 2–4 in. high, particularly in late May or early August, the peak periods for egg-laying.

**Onion Fly** maggots tunnel into the bulbs of onions, leeks, and shallots, causing the foliage to collapse. Dig out attacked plants carefully, ensuring that parts of them are not left in the soil, and burn them. To prevent attacks dust around the seedlings with lindane when they are at the " loop " stage, i.e., about 1 in. high, and again ten days later.

**Narcissus Bulb Flies** are serious pests of narcissi and also snowdrops and other bulbous plants. The maggots burrow in the centre of the bulbs, causing them to rot. All soft bulbs should be burned and the remainder immersed for three hours in a solution of lindane containing a wetter. To prevent future attacks and a reinfestation, dust around the necks of growing bulbs with lindane at fortnightly intervals from the end of April until the end of June.

Insects which feed above ground include:

**II. Sucking Pests** pierce the tissues of plants with needle-like mouth parts and suck the sap. This devitalises the plant, checks growth, and causes wilting. Some species cause distortion of leaves and young shoots, and aphids, suckers, scale insects, and mealy bugs excrete a sugary fluid which disfigures the foliage, attracts ants, and allows the growth of sooty moulds.

**Aphids**, i.e., blackfly, greenfly, etc., are serious pests which attack almost all plants and multiply rapidly in warm weather. They feed on the shoots and undersides of the leaves, and many species are responsible for the transmission of virus diseases. Infestations should be treated as early as possible. Malathion, lindane, D.D.T emulsion, and nicotine are all good sprays to use, and should be applied to the undersides of the leaves. With the advent of these sprays the control of aphids on roses and broad beans, for example, is no longer a serious problem.

Tree fruits should be sprayed when the buds are bursting and again when the flower buds are still green. Currants should be treated at the " grape " stage, but lindane should not be used on this fruit. Tar oil, applied to deciduous woody plants while they are completely dormant, will kill the over-wintering stages of these and many other pests. It does not, however, give a good winter control for Woolly Aphid on apples. This pest is best controlled by spraying at the pink-bud stage with B.H.C. with a succinate spreader added. Small colonies on the bark can be eradicated by painting with 10% tar oil.

Some aphids feed underground on roots, particularly of lettuces, currants, and cacti. Where practicable, infested plants should be lifted and the roots cleaned and sprayed before replanting in clean soil. Otherwise water them copiously with malathion or lindane.

**Scale Insects** are often found in greenhouses, but also occur out-of-doors on trees and shrubs. Flat or dome-shaped, these creatures spend most of their lives immobile, and they do not at all resemble insects, or even appear to be alive. Again tar oil is useful for killing the overwintering stages on deciduous woody shrubs which are dormant. Plants which are in leaf should be sprayed with malathion or nicotine/white oil emulsion two or three times at fortnightly intervals. These substances are more effective if as much as possible of the scale is first removed by means of a sponge, brush, or scraper with water in which soft soap has been dissolved. **Mealy Bugs** are common pests of greenhouse plants, and should be given the same treatment as scale insects.

**Capsid Bugs** are very active insects which cause considerable damage to fruit trees and bushes and also to various ornamental plants, principally chrysanthemums and dahlias. They feed on the young leaves, causing distortion and raggedness, and on the buds, which later produce misshapen blooms. These insects, green or reddish in colour, can be controlled by spraying with lindane or D.D.T. when the flower buds are still green (tree fruit) or with D.D.T. at the " grape " stage (currants). Herbaceous plants should be sprayed two or three times at three-weekly intervals, starting when the plants are young and before the damage is seen. The ground under the plants should also be sprayed to kill those insects which fall off during treatment.

Leafhoppers are small, yellowish-green insects like aphids but much more active. They feed on the undersides of the leaves of a variety of plants, causing them to become speckled with yellow. Roses are commonly attacked. The treatment given to capsids on herbaceous plants will control these also, the sprays being directed to the undersides of the leaves.

Whiteflies are serious pests in greenhouses, and also occur out-of-doors on rhododendrons and other evergreen shrubs. The adults are like miniature moths with white wings, and the young are small, scale-like creatures, generally greenish in colour, which feed without movement on the undersides of the leaves. To control this pest D.D.T., lindane, or malathion should be used as a spray or smoke, two to three applications being given at fortnightly intervals.

Red Spider Mites are extremely small creatures, red or greenish in colour and just visible with the naked eye. They feed on the undersides of the leaves of many greenhouse and outdoor plants, including fruit, causing the leaves to turn sickly yellow. Control is difficult, the most effective materials being malathion, derris, summer ovicides, or azobenzene smoke. The directions on the labels of these products should be followed carefully.

III. Biting Insects have chewing and biting mouth parts which are used to cut away pieces of plants.

Caterpillars (the young stages of moths and butterflies) are the best-known pests in this group. They vary in size and colour according to the species, and most plants are liable to be attacked. These should be sprayed or dusted with D.D.T. or derris as soon as damage is seen. On fruit trees D.D.T. should be used when the fruit buds are still green, and again at the pink-bud stage if the infestation is serious.

The Codling Caterpillar, which tunnels in apples, is controlled by spraying with D.D.T. at the end of June and again three weeks later. Since this latter treatment tends to encourage red spider mites, it is advisable to add to the D.D.T. one of the materials recommended for these pests.

Sawfly Caterpillars are very similar to those above, and commonly attack gooseberry and rose foliage. They can be controlled by spraying with D.D.T., derris, or lindane. Attacks by the Apple Sawfly, which burrows in young apples and forms ribbon-like scars on the skin, can be prevented by spraying with lindane seven days after 80% of the blossom has fallen.

Beetles and Weevils which feed on foliage are usually best controlled by spraying or dusting with D.D.T. To kill the tiny Flea-beetles which eat small holes in the seedlings of brassicas and turnips, treat the plants at fourteen-day intervals until they reach the " rough-leaf " stage.

The golden-brown Raspberry Beetle, which feeds on the flowers and whose grub tunnels in the fruit, is eradicated by D.D.T. or derris applied ten days after full bloom and again ten days later. For other common pests in this group, e.g., Vine Weevil, Clay-coloured Weevil, Pea and Bean Weevil, etc., apply the D.D.T. as soon as the damage is first seen.

Earwigs feed at night on the foliage and flower petals of many plants. They hide by day inside flowers, in the folds of leaves, and in nooks and crannies on the ground, under flat stones, etc. These pests are killed by D.D.T., applied to the plants (but not to open flowers) and to their hiding-places.

Leaf Miners are very small grubs which tunnel between the upper and lower surfaces of leaves, forming pale blisters, as on lilac, holly, celery, etc., or long, twisting galleries, as on chrysanthemum, pea, and tomato. In small infestations the affected leaves should be picked off and burned. Otherwise spray with lindane as soon as the damage starts, giving three applications at fourteen-day intervals.

IV. Eelworms are microscopic pests which are invisible to the naked eye. They are able to live for very long periods without food and are extremely difficult to eradicate. The most common species are:

Stem and Bulb Eelworm, which infests narcissus, phlox, strawberry, hyacinth, onion, and other plants. Infested plants show distorted foliage and dwarfing and gradually deteriorate. They can only be sterilised by immersion in hot water kept at well-defined temperatures for one to three hours, but expert diagnosis and advice should be obtained before this or any other control is attempted. Infested ground must be kept clear of any host plants for at least three years to starve out the eelworms.

Chrysanthemum Eelworm causes the formation of yellowish blotches between the veins of chrysanthemum leaves, which later turn black and drop off. In severe infestations the blooms are undersized and malformed. Expert advice should be obtained before control measures are attempted.

Potato Root Eelworm is a serious and widespread pest of potatoes, causing the plants to become stunted and sickly, giving very poor yields. The pest can only be kept in check by crop rotation, potatoes being grown on the same ground only once in four years. This is difficult in small gardens, and where land becomes heavily infested the only remedy is to rest it from potatoes for at least five years.

The Purchase and Use of Insecticides.—To ensure that an insecticide will do what the maker claims, it is advisable only to buy brands which have been tested and approved by the Ministry of Agriculture. This can be ascertained from the Approval Mark (T31) on the label. Read the directions and follow them carefully. Over-strength insecticides can cause damage to plants, and certain plants (usually listed) can be injured by some insecticides at any concentration, e.g., cucumbers, marrows, etc., by D.D.T. and lindane. Never apply insecticides to flowers in full bloom, otherwise many valuable pollinating insects will be killed.

Standard References.

*Encyclopaedia of Garden Pests and Diseases*, by van Konynenburg and Lawfield (Collingridge), 1958 (42s.).

*Horticultural Pests: Detection and Control*, by G. Fox Wilson, revised by P. Becker (Crosby Lockwood), 1960 (25s.).

## DISEASES OF PLANTS.

Plant diseases are important because they can cause great loss not only in growing crops but also in the produce after it has been harvested and stored. The skill in growing crops is wasted if they are destroyed by disease, and many people know the wastage of potatoes through blight disease in winter stores and rotting of onions when they decay through neck rot disease. For these reasons the keen gardener must take notice of diseases and use the knowledge available to him in checking them wherever possible.

The most important point to remember about plant diseases is to recognise the first signs so that the remedy can be applied at once. In greenhouses this is of great importance because the atmosphere is warm and moist, and in such conditions diseases flourish. It must also be remembered that the same crop is often grown in the same soil in a greenhouse so that we get a build-up of disease, and this causes the well-known " soil sickness." This means that new soil must be brought in or the old soil enriched and also sterilised by steam or by chemicals. Even frames and propagating pits require periodic cleaning up by a disinfection treatment.

Unlike insect pests, the actual cause of a plant disease cannot be seen with the naked eye, and microscopic examination is required for its detection. The scientists who study diseases are called plant pathologists, and these are stationed

THE APPROVAL MARK—An officially approved crop-protection product shows on its label this design.

at universities and other institutes throughout the country, where they carry out research on various plant troubles and advise on suitable remedies for checking them. It is obviously necessary to understand the exact cause of a disease and how that cause operates before a means of checking the trouble can be devised. The advice can then be passed on to growers, farmers, and the gardening public.

The presence of disease in most cases can only be detected by the symptoms shown by the affected plant, which is called the " host " plant. The actual cause must then be determined by careful examination in the laboratory, which is done by the pathologist.

Plant diseases in general are divided into three classes as follows: 1. Fungus and Bacterial. 2. Virus. 3. Functional Disorders.

**1. Fungus and Bacterial Diseases.**—The first kind called fungus diseases are caused by the attack of fungus parasites; examples being the well-known club root of cabbages, potato scab, apple scab, and plum brown rot. These parasitic fungi are microscopic and composed of fine threads, but they attack plants and penetrate them either through wounds (insect bites, hail damage, pruning cuts) or directly through the surface cells (epidermis). The threads grow into the plant, killing the cells and absorbing their contents. There is usually some discoloration or even decay of the tissues around the point of infection, but it is possible for the plant to show distress in one part although the parasite is at work some distance away. Examples are silver leaf in plums and the honey fungus, which kills trees by attacking the roots.

The fungus spreads by means of spores which are equivalent to seeds in flowering plants but which are microscopic in size. These spores are produced on the surface of the plant in enormous numbers and are blown (wind), splashed (rain), or carried (insects, etc.) in all directions to alight on other healthy plants, where they germinate and spread the disease. This occurs in the growing season, but when winter approaches, the parasite forms tough, resting bodies of one kind or another, and these are resistant to extreme cold.

They overwinter in the soil or in the surface of tree bark, etc., so that in the following spring they can germinate and cause disease again. So we get the reappearance of such troubles as damping off in seedlings, scab in apples, brown rot in apples and plums, foot rot in peas, wart disease in potatoes, mildews on all kinds of plants, and so on. This question of soil contamination by overwintering spores is one of the most serious in the fight against plant disease.

The signs of fungus and bacterial diseases are varied, and may show as yellowing, silvering, brown spotting, or blackening of leaves (potato blight, rose black spot, celery leaf spot, antirrhinum rust), as stunting (cabbage wire stem), as pustules and cankers in stems (coral spot, apple canker), as gumming or dieback in branches (rose canker, plum dieback), as galls, warts, witches brooms, or other malformation (club root in cabbages, crown gall, leafy gall, peach leaf curl), as dry or soft rots of fruits, tubers, vegetable bulbs, and corms (gladiolus dry rot, potato dry rot, iris rhizome rot, celery heart rot), and many other abnormal conditions. Sometimes only a part of the plant is affected and can be removed, *e.g.*, branches showing attack by coral spot or one of the large bracket fungi seen on trees, these having gained entrance through a wound.

**2. Virus Diseases.**—This class of disease is becoming increasingly important as more is discovered about them, although research on them is a comparatively recent development. A virus disease is caused by infection with a virus, and the exact nature of this is not yet clearly understood, but it is so small that it cannot be seen with ordinary microscopes. Its detection is therefore not easy, but when the sap of a virus-diseased plant is injected into a healthy one it causes the disease.

In nature this spread is brought about by biting and sucking insects, which are referred to as Vectors. They transmit the virus by feeding on infected plants and then travelling to healthy ones, on which they feed and so spread the disease. Most viruses are transmitted by aphids (greenflies).

In the garden and nursery they can be carried from plant to plant by pruning knives or by the fingers in the process of trimming plants such as tomatoes, melons, and cucumbers or by the use of the knife in taking cuttings. In general, the virus does not kill a plant quickly but tends to cripple it and cause a slow deterioration. Infected plants cannot recover but remain, sometimes for years, as sources of infection on which insects feed and carry on the disease. So viruses may increase in lily stocks, strawberry beds, and raspberry plantations unless virus-infected plants are removed and aphids strictly suppressed.

The signs of virus disease are of different kinds, but the commonest are those of the type called mosaic, in which the leaves show a mottling with light-green or yellow patches scattered in irregular fashion on the darker green of the leaf. There may be also some reduction in the leaf blades. These symptoms can be seen in the mosaic of cucumber, vegetable marrow, lettuce, cabbage, turnip, tomato, delphinium, primula, dahlia, apple, raspberry, and many other common plants. In some, such as lilies, daffodils, and onions, the mosaic is more in the form of stripes down the leaf blades.

Another virus symptom is flower " breaking," where the normal colour of the petals is broken by streaks and spots of white, and this can be seen in tulip, wallflower, pansy, stocks, or carnations affected by the mosaic virus. Other viruses cause bronzing of the top leaves (as in tomato spotted wilt) or small light-coloured rings arranged in concentric circles (as in dahlia ring spot) or even reduction of leaves until they are tendril like (as in tomato fern leaf). Sometimes there is malformation or even proliferation, producing innumerable stunted shoots, as in blackberry dwarf disease.

The important point to note about these virus diseases is that every part of the plant is quickly infected, so that the sap is infectious to other plants of the same kind. The virus is present in all parts, and for this reason it is useless to propagate from a virus-infected plant. This means that all the scales and offsets from bulbs such as lilies and tulips, all the tubers from potatoes, and all cuttings from herbaceous plants which are taken from a virus-infected plant are useless, because they will carry the virus. They should be destroyed, and the only exception is where the plant is greatly valued, in which case seed can be taken from it before it is destroyed. In general, viruses do not travel in the seed, and only in one or two cases is seed infected, and this only in negligible quantity.

**3. Functional Disorders.**—This third class of disease is often called non-parasitic, because unlike the previous two kinds there is no parasite involved, and these troubles are therefore not infectious. They are due to faulty cultivation or unsuitable environment, in which soil conditions or climate affect the plants adversely. In this group we include cases of unsatisfactory growth due to waterlogging, drought, frost, high temperature, damage by fumes or atmospheric pollution, or even excess lime.

Perhaps the most important kinds of trouble in this class are the so called Deficiency Diseases, where the plants suffer from shortage of some important food. This may be one of the common food substances, such as nitrogen, potash, or phosphate, and details will be found under the section on manures and fertilisers (T26).

## CONTROL OF DISEASES.

**1. Garden Hygiene.**—The control of plant diseases can be dealt with only briefly, but to begin with we must emphasise the value of good cultivation as an insurance against losses from disease. Robust plants are better able to stand up to disease than sickly ones, and everything in the way of proper drainage, soil aeration, proper spacing, sensible feeding, and so on, will help to keep the plants vigorous, and this is the first line of defence against diseases. Garden hygiene is important, weeds need to be kept down, wounds in trees and shrubs covered with a good paint against infection, new stocks examined carefully, seed bought only from reliable sources, diseased plants burnt, and dead material regularly removed from plants, especially in greenhouses.

**2. Soil Sterilisation.**—There are other precautions, among which the sterilisation of the soil in greenhouses by means of steam or chemicals is of some importance. Outdoors this is not possible, but rotation of crops is a most useful system in helping to avoid disease. Disinfection of frames, propagating pits, and seed boxes by formalin or cresylic acid are other useful measures.

All these operations aim at destroying the resting spores of fungus parasites responsible for such diseases as tomato leaf mould, gladiolus dry rot, damping off in seedlings, root rots, and downy mildews of many kinds in young plants such as stocks, cheiranthus, cineraria, tomato, aster, and calceolaria when grown in boxes or pots.

**3. Disease Resistant Plants.**—The use of disease-resistant varieties of plants is very desirable, but there are not many kinds available, and often the resistant kind does not possess flowers or fruit of such fine quality or flavour as the more susceptible kind. The outstanding success of this kind is that of potatoes immune to the dreaded wart disease, and these can be grown safely in the most heavily infected land. There are antirrhinums resistant to rust disease, and there is resistance in some degree in the case of delphinium mildew, potato blight, tomato leaf mould, and some others. Research goes on to discover still more, because any such plants are always worth a trial.

**4. Treatment of Seeds and Bulbs.**—For seed-borne diseases seed treatments may be done with an organo-mercurial seed dressing, or even by immersion of the infected seed in warm water.

In some diseases, for example, tulip fire, we can protect the bulbs from the danger of infected soil by raking in a powder such as " Botrolex " when planting the bulbs, and a similar treatment is done with calomel dust against club root in beds intended for sowing brassica seeds.

**5. Fungicides.**—Even after all this, a disease may still appear in the crop, and more direct action must be taken. It is then necessary to protect the plants by means of a Fungicide. This is a chemical which is poisonous to fungus parasites but which will not harm the crop plant (host). Fungicides are used as wet sprays or in powder form as dusts, and they are sprayed or dusted all over the plants to protect them from infection by diseases.

The object of the treatment is to cover the plants with a film of the fungicide so as to protect the still healthy ones. To help the spray fluid to spread over and adhere to the foliage another substance, called a wetter, spreader, or sticker, is added to the spray, but sometimes this is already included by the manufacturer.

**5. (a) Sprays.**—Sprays are applied by means of machines called sprayers which vary from small, hand-syringe types giving a continuous jet of spray to those pumped up to a pressure and carried on the back (knapsack machines), and so on to the large machines driven by a petrol engine, which deliver the spray at a high pressure. It is necessary to have a suitable nozzle giving a fine mist-like cone of spray which settles on the foliage and is not wasted.

**5. (b) Dusts.**—Dusts are similar chemicals produced in such finely divided form that the powder can be blown over and on the foliage almost like a fog. This is best done after a shower of rain or after a heavy dew. The machines used are far more varied in design than spraying machines. There are small hand dusters worked either like a small pump or like a bellows, of which the " Acme " is a good example, and there are those which are carried on the back and worked as a double-bellows action or on the front of the body with a rotary-fan action. It is important in gardens to clean and dry the machines after use, and small sprayers may be best put upside down to drain for a time after use.

The substances used as sprays and dusts against plant diseases for many years have been copper and sulphur and their compounds. Perhaps the best known copper-containing spray is " Bordeaux Mixture," which is still a good spray, but which has been largely replaced by colloidal copper available under trade names like " Coppicide " for such diseases as tomato blight, etc. Sulphur is used extensively as lime-sulphur against apple scab and as colloidal sulphur against the powdery mildew diseases. As dusts, copper is mixed with lime to give copper-lime dust and sulphur is used alone either as flowers of sulphur or green sulphur.

**5. (c) The Newer Fungicides.**—In recent years much research has been carried out in tests to see whether other chemicals have value as fungicides, and the search has been in the field of organic chemistry and among all kinds of these chemicals. Tests of this kind take a long time, but a few substances have already been picked out as showing great promise, and we can mention " Captan," which is so good against apple and pear scab, " Zineb " aginst tomato leaf mould, onion mildew, and tulip fire, " Karathane " against any of the powdery mildews, such as american gooseberry mildew, strawberry mildew, vine and peach mildews, as well as the same diseases on ornamental roses, delphiniums, michaelmas daisies, and the like.

**6. Control of Viruses.**—The control of virus diseases is very different, because in this case the only spray treatments likely to be of use are those designed to keep down insects. The other necessary control measure is to remove and destroy the virus-infected plants, which are a danger as sources of infection.

This is best done when the plants are young, so that any young marrows, cucumbers, dahlias, delphiniums, sweet peas, lupins, lilies, etc., which show virus symptoms as commonly revealed in leaf mottling and poor growth should be removed as soon as detected. Propagation should be done carefully, so that young stock is not propagated from stocks of strawberries, raspberries, and all kinds of herbaceous perennials which show signs of virus infection. Even the knife used for taking cuttings should be wiped occasionally on a rag dipped in a good disinfectant.

**7. Prevention of Functional Disorders.**—In the case of Functional Disorders (non-parasitic diseases) it is not always easy to advise remedies. Where the soil conditions are faulty attention can be directed to improving drainage if necessary or counteracting dryness by digging in humus, irrigating, and general mulching. Dryness at the roots of tomatoes causes loss of fruit, and so does extreme dryness in the air of the greenhouse, but these should be adjusted fairly easily.

Hail damage can spoil many crops, but robust foliage may help a little to lessen the damage. Late frost damage to fruit in some areas can be lessened by various methods of cultivation and planting. The effects of drought can be aggravated by shortage of certain foods, especially potash, so that even here some attempt can be made to avoid loss. Excess liming may cause food shortages by causing the appearance, in the leaves, of a yellowish or even whitish colour, which is known as lime-induced chlorosis. The real reason may be lack of iron or manganese due to the excess lime in the soil, but recently very good results at counteracting this condition have been obtained by using the substance known as "Sequestrene Plus."

Another method of treating these food shortages is to spray the young foliage in early summer with the required element in a very weak solution. They can even be included in sprays used for keeping down diseases or pests. It must not be forgotten that even the ordinary foods, such as nitrogen, potash, and phosphate, may sometimes be in short supply, and the effect can be seen by the trained plant pathologist. In these cases the effect may not always show clearly in the growing crop, but may appear long afterwards in the stored fruits and vegetables, which as a result deteriorate and break down long before they are required for use.

The present-day methods of cultivating large numbers of the same plant in one spot tend to increase the risk of large-scale disease attacks. Modern plants may be highly bred and selected for great purity of strain. Indeed, they have often been chosen for fine quality and flavour, with little regard to their ability to resist disease, so that the gardener must always be ready to give them the protection they may need.

**Standard References.**

*Diseases of Vegetables,* by Donald E. Green (Macmillan), 1946 (8s. 6d.).

*Plant Diseases,* by F. T. Brooks (Oxford), 1953 (38s.).

*Insecticide and Fungicide Handbook* Ed. Hubert Martin (Blackwell) 1965 (32s. 6d.).

## USES OF MODERN WEEDKILLERS

The eradication of weeds by chemical means is one of the greatest advances of recent years albeit the value of herbicides is still unappreciated by most gardeners. With a planned programme, all cultivated ground and lawns can be kept free of weeds without hoeing or any other sort of manual cultivation.

Occasionally troubles have arisen in not following makers' instructions. Sometimes the damage has been most unfortunate, as the majority of herbicides are toxic, in varying degrees, to a wide range of plant life. In the main, controls are determined by circumstance, as typified in the following cases:

**Asparagus Beds.**—Annuals and top growth of perennial weeds can be controlled with cresylic acid in the autumn and before the asparagus appears in the spring. In beds free of perennials, a first-class control of weeds can be maintained with Simazine applied in the early spring.

Where annual and perennial grasses predominate, Dalapon or Diquat will give good control. As for bindweed, this may be eradicated by watering the foliage with 2,4-D in late July or August taking care to avoid contact with the asparagus stems and particularly the fern.

**Fruit Garden.**—Around blackcurrants, gooseberries, raspberries, apples, and pears, grasses can be killed with Dalapon. Once clear of perennial weeds, annuals may be controlled effectively with Simazine. Alternatively, weeds may be killed with Diquat, making applications as necessary throughout the season.

**Garden Paths.**—On any surfaced path or drive a first-rate control of weeds can be maintained by watering with a residual herbicide such as Simazine. As this preparation is virtually insoluble in water, it does not seep through the soil as sodium chlorate would, and therefore it can be used near garden crops and grass edgings. Further to this, it is not easily washed from the soil and remains active near the surface for up to twelve months. Notwithstanding, the herbicide must be used with proper care.

A dilute solution of sodium chlorate with 4–6 ozs. to a gallon of water may be applied, but it is liable to affect plants near by and, for this reason, application should be confined to the centre of the path, thereby leaving room for the chlorate to seep through the soil.

**Lawns.**—The majority of weeds in turf can be eradicated easily with formulations of 2,4-D or M.C.P.A. (*see* Finding List). In particular, daisies, dandelions, plantains, and most broad-leaved weeds are susceptible although it may be necessary to repeat the dose after 10 days. The best time to do the work is on a warm, fine day in the spring when the plants are growing actively and there is the prospect of fine weather to follow for twenty-four hours. The action of the herbicides is rapid, and grass may be cut after a couple of days, composting with mowings in the normal way. It appears that the hormones are not injurious to bacterial life in the soil and in a few weeks break down into harmless substances.

Where bulbs are naturalised in grass, steps to control weeds should not be taken until the foliage of the bulbs has died down and the bulbs are dormant. Thus, as a general rule, control measures are best applied throughout July.

To deal with weeds in turf where there arises the danger of the spray—or even a drift from it—touching cultivated plants near by, as, for instance, on grass paths in a rose garden, then a wax bar impregnated with a hormone can be lightly drawn over the turf. Such bars are available at a reasonable price under trade names like "Supplex Touchweeder."

Some weeds are resistant to normal doses of hormones and need special treatment. These are mostly mat-forming plants of low-growing habit which are not cut off by mowing. Typical examples include mosses of all sorts, pearlwort, speedwell or veronica, yarrow, and yellow-flowered clover. Here, the main control must be in the use of lawn sand, a good mixture of which can be made up with:

2 parts by weight sulphate of ammonia.
1 part by weight sulphate of iron.
13 parts by weight LIME-FREE sand.

Where moss is the most prevalent weed, to the mixture should be added sufficient superphosphate to give 1 oz. of it per sq. yd. for the area to be treated. A hundredweight of the lawn sand plus superphosphate can be made up for about 17s. and is sufficient to treat about 450 sq. yds. at 4 oz. per sq. yd.

Applications to patches of the weeds should be made when the turf is damp and there is the prospect of fine weather; if a period of drought follows an application, then water should be applied to avoid serious scorching. Repeat the treatment as necessary throughout the growing season. Linked with this "spot" treatment, the growth of grass must be encouraged, as this will tend to smother low-growing weeds. Thus, in the early spring when the turf is wet, feed with a mixture of equal parts of superphosphate, sulphate of ammonia and dry soil at 2 oz. per sq. yd. over the whole area and repeat after a month, if desirable. In addition, do *not* shave off the grass by close cutting; instead, the blades of the mower should be set reasonably high for a whole season.

Where fertility is low, clovers often predominate in turf. The Dutch clovers with white—or pink—flowers and a white-angled band towards the base of each leaflet, can be eradicated with Mecoprop. Afterwards the turf should be fed with nitrogenous fertilisers like soot and sulphate of ammonia, to discourage reinfestation. Other types of clover found in turf are species of *Trifolium*. Compared to the Dutch clover, these have a tight, bunched habit of growth and yellow flowers. All of them are resistant to hormones and, in addition to manurial treatment, should be treated with lawn sand.

**Lakes.**—It sometimes happens that aquatic plants with large floating leaves, such as water lilies, get out of hand. Here, control can be established by cutting off the foliage with a long-handled appliance like the "Corypu Water Scythe." The work should be done early in June and repeated as often as any fresh growth is seen.

Bulrushes are difficult to eliminate, but can be destroyed by digging out the roots when the level of the water permits. Dalapon has been found to give a control; applications should be made, with a wetting agent added, when the rushes reach maturity.

**Ponds.**—Problems of weed control in ornamental ponds are often not easy to solve. Where duckweed is prevalent this small floating plant can be eliminated by sweeping the surface of the water at regular intervals. If this practice is carried out thoroughly much of the vegetative growth will be eliminated, and the plant will not be able to form resting bodies whereby it overwinters. Once a control has been established, further spread of the plant can be prevented by introducing a few moorhens or ornamental ducks.

The most common of unwanted plants in pools is blanket weed. There is no single means of dealing with this plant, for its spread is governed, to a certain extent, by unbalanced plant and anima life in the water. With this fact in mind, water lilies should be established so that their foliage shades about 25 per cent of the water. In addition, a few oxygenating plants should be introduced from local ponds or streams and a supply of goldfish added. Blanket weed is usually found in pools where the water gets overheated in summer; for this reason, the average depth of garden ponds should be a minimum of 2 ft. and preferably a minimum of 3 ft.

**Rose Beds.**—A complete control of annual weeds among roses can be obtained with Simazine. Here, the salient point is to apply the herbicide immediately after pruning in March *before* any weed growth starts. Alternatively, Diquat can be used in April or early May and the application repeated as necessary.

**Shrubberies.**—With a shortage of labour, beds of shrubs are often weed infested. Perennials can be eradicated with Diquat and annuals controlled by this treatment as they appear. Alternatively, once the perennials are removed, the ground can be kept clear with Simazine used in the early spring. Much to check weeds in shrubberies can be done by mulching the surface of the soil with heavy dressings of peat, fallen leaves, or sawdust; if the weeds push through the mulch, a second application should be made at once.

**Vacant Ground.**—On land free of crops all plants can be killed by watering the herbage with sodium chlorate at 1 lb. to a gallon of water. In some cases repetition may be necessary. When using this method it should be remembered that treated ground will remain toxic to plant life for a period of up to six months; if doubt exists about the persistence of the chlorate in the soil, then it is advisable to wait for the appearance of annual weeds before planting.

Apart from its persistence, sodium chlorate is prone to seep through soil and affect plants for some distance away. To avoid danger of fire from clothes being soaked in a solution of the chlorate and then dried, it is prudent to use a formulation with an additive to reduce the risk of fire. (*See* Finding List.) Where couch grass is predominant then the best control is to be obtained with Dalapon.

## SPECIAL PROBLEMS OF WEED CONTROL

**Bindweed.**—Probably the most ubiquitous of all garden weeds. Up to the present time the main control has been to carefully fork out the roots as new growth is seen; if this is done methodically the plant can be eliminated within a reasonable time.

Lately, chemicals have come to the fore, and bindweed may now be eliminated by watering or painting the foliage with a formulation of 2,4-D when the annual growth has nearly reached maturity. Thus, first applications can be applied in July and the treatment repeated, if necessary, to good effect. Where the weed is among cultivated plants, the herbicides must be applied with a paint brush or the foliage rubbed with a cloth damped in a solution. When doing this rubber gloves should be worn.

**Blanket Weed.**—*See* Ponds.

**Bracken.**—Horticulturally, control is not a big problem, and in limited areas it is easily dealt with by repeatedly cutting the aerial stems with a grass hook as the first fronds open. This practice will exhaust the underground food supply of the plant, and gradually it will die out. The young fronds are rich in plant food and, while still green and fresh, they should be composted. No chemicals will offer a reasonable control of this plant and, indeed, it is best dealt with by cutting and final digging out of the roots.

**Couch Grass.**—Where the soil is light and tends to be low in fertility, it is often found that this is a difficult plant to eradicate by cultural means. If the long, underground stems are forked out in the conventional manner and left on the surface to dry, the roots may be composted to advantage and a good control established. To prevent reinfestation, manures and fertilisers should be applied generously and the ground kept hoed regularly.

Chemically, couch grass can be killed easily by watering the foliage with Dalapon.

**Ground Elder.**—Without question this is one of the worst garden weeds and, whether or not the fact is pleasant or acceptable, it is indubitably a weed of neglected ground. In varying degrees it is resistant to hormone weed-killers of all sorts. On ground free of crops it may be reduced by an application of sodium chlorate, as explained in the paragraph **Vacant Ground**. The first treatment should be made as soon as growth starts in the spring and repeated if the desired effect is not abundantly clear. When ground elder is to be found among herbaceous plants the cultivated plants must be lifted out and the weed removed by repeated hand-forking.

In shrubberies reasonable control can be had by smothering the young growth in the spring with a thick dressing of peat, leaf mould, baled straw, or sawdust. If growth penetrates the surface dressing it will be found that the etiolated shoots are not difficult to remove by hand, or a second layer can be applied to complete the treatment.

Alternatively, the foliage of ground elder can be watered with Diquat and the treatment repeated once or twice during the growing season.

**Horsetail.**—This is sometimes erroneously called marestail and on poor, sandy soils it is often a common weed. Fortunately, recent experiments have proved that it can be easily controlled by spraying or painting the *mature* growths with a formulation of 2,4-D, taking care, of course, to keep the spray off cultivated plants near by. As the appearance of horsetail is symptomatic of low fertility, manurial treatment should be carried out on a generous scale. Where the weed is growing among cultivated crops, individual stems must be treated separately as recommended for bindweed.

**Marestail.**—*See* Horsetail.

Moss.—*See* Lawns (T33).

Nettles.—It is difficult to understand why the perennial nettle is so abundant as it is immediately responsive to applications of 2,4-D and 2,4,5-T made any time during the growing season.

The annual nettle is usually proved a denizen of rich, light soils and may be eradicated with cresylic acid, Diquat or 2,4-D.

Oxalis.—Of all weeds this is probably the most difficult to destroy. It is easily identified by its large, trifoliolate leaves like that of clover. Unlike other weeds, oxalis cannot be efficiently removed by hand, as this disturbs the bulbils clustered around the base of the stem of mature plants. On ground free of crops, sodium chlorate can be applied in March (*see* Vacant Ground). Perhaps a second application may be necessary, but, even so, control may not be complete. Among shrubby plants, it may be possible to eradicate the weed by smothering, as suggested in the paragraph on ground elder.

The foliage can be killed with Diquat and, by repeated applications, this may constitute the best means of control.

Speedwell.—*See* Veronica.

Veronica.—This procumbent, blue-flowered weed of turf is sometimes know as speedwell. Being resistant to hormones, its control may only be established with lawn sand. *See also* Lawns.

Woody Plants.—With or without the addition of 2,4-D, these may be killed with 2,4,5-T. This hormone is particularly useful on bramble, gorse, ivy, and other unwanted shrubby plants. It is necessary to thoroughly saturate the foliage of deciduous trees, and the best results are obtainable when the leaves are fully mature but not starting to die off. In the case of ivy, the dormant shoots should be generously sprayed for the best results.

Yarrow.—A weed found in many lawns where its presence often signifies low fertility. Control is with lawn sand. *See* Lawns (T33).

Summary.—From these notes it will be seen that there are many aids for dealing with weeds. The salient point is to get the *right* method for *each* plant. Equally important is to check the reason why certain weeds grow profusely under some conditions. Very often this natural tendency can be counteracted as in the case of phosphatic fertilisers against moss and in the application of organic manures and chemical fertilizers where horsetail and yarrow are concerned. *See* T35.

Standard References.

*Chemicals for the Gardener*, H.M. Stationery Office, 1965 (1s. 7d. incl. postage).

*List of Approved Products for Farmers and Growers* (published annually), copies free from Ministry of Agriculture, Fisheries, and Food (Publications), Tolcarne Drive, Pinner, Middlesex.

*Weed Control Handbook*, issued by the British Weed Control Council (Blackwell), 1965 (32s. 6d.).

## HORTICULTURAL SOCIETIES.

There are many specialist societies in Britain. Detailed information on particular plants is normally available from them, and membership is open to all wishing to join. The most prominent societies are:

Alpine Garden Society
   *Sec.* Michael Upward, 58 Denison House, 296 Vauxhall Bridge Road, S.W.1.

Auricula and Primula Society, The National
   *Sec.* A. Marlow, 2 Glebe Close, Thornford, Sherborne, Dorset.

Begonia Society, The National Society of England and Wales
   *Sec.* F. J. Martin, 50 Woodlands Farm Road, Erdington, Birmingham 24.

Cactus and Succulent Society of Great Britain
   *Sec.* D. V. Brewerton, 26 Chester Road, Ilford, Essex.

Camellia Society, The International
   *Sec.* Charles E. Puddle, V.M.H., Bodnant, Tal-y-Cafn, Denbighshire.

Carnation Society, The British National
   *Sec.* E. G. Cook, 1 Evelyn Rd., Worthing, Sussex.

Chrysanthemum Society, The National
   *Sec.* S. G. Gosling, 65 St. Margaret's Avenue, Whetstone, N.20.

Daffodil Society
   *Sec.* D. J. Pearce, College of Ascension, Selly Oak, Birmingham, 29.

Dahlia Society, The National
   *Sec.* P. Damp, 26 Burns Road, Lillington, Leamington Spa, Warwickshire.

Delphinium Society, The
   *Sec.* C. J. H. Topping, B.A., Ph.D., 5 Park Lane, Sevenoaks, Kent.

Floral Arrangement Societies of Great Britain National Association of
   *Sec.* Mrs. F. C. Dobson, 21A Denbigh Street, London, S.W.1.

Fuchsia Society, The British
   *Sec.* W. G. Sharp, Rydal, The Green, Gt. Bentley, Colchester, Essex.

Gladiolus Society, The British
   *Sec.* J. G. Lord, 25 Kimpton Avenue, Brentwood, Essex.

Hardy Plant Society
   *Sec.* Miss B. White, 10 St. Barnabas Rd., Emmer Green, Reading, Berks.

Heather Society, The
   *Sec.* Mrs. C. I. MacLeod, Yew Trees, Horley Row, Horley, Surrey.

Iris Society, The British
   *Sec.* Mrs. D. J. Waters, 87, Roglan Gardens, Oxley, Watford, Herts.

Pansy and Viola Society, The North of England
   *Sec.* F. C. Marshland, 2 Jubilee Mount, West Lillands, Brighouse, Yorks.

Pansy and Viola Association, The Scottish
   *Sec.* Hugh Campbell, O.B.E., 960 Dumbarton Road, Dalmuir, Glasgow.

Pelargonium and Geranium Society, The British
   *Sec.* Mrs. G. M. Weller, 85 Sparrow Farm Road, Ewell, Surrey.

Pteridological Society, The British
   *Sec.* J. W. Dyce, 46 Sedley Rise, Loughton, Essex.

Rose Society, The Royal National
   *Sec.* L. G. Turner, Chiswell Green Lane, St. Albans, Herts.

Royal Horticultural Society
   *Sec.* John Hamer, M.B.E., B.A., Royal Horticultural Society's Offices, Vincent Square, S.W.1.

Royal Caledonian Horticultural Society
   *Sec.* John Turnbull, D.S.O., D.F.C., C.A., Royal Caledonian Horticultural Society, 44 Melville Street, Edinburgh 3.

Saintpaulia and Houseplant Society
   *Sec.* Mrs. E. A. Robbins, 296 Perth Road, Ilford, Essex.

Scottish Rock Garden Club
   *Sec.* Mrs. L. C. Boyd-Harvey, Boonslie, Dirleton, East Lothian.

Sweet Pea Society, The National
   *Sec.* R. J. Huntley, 431 Wokingham Road, Earley, Reading, Berks.

Vegetable Society, The National
   *Sec.* 288 Northumberland Avenue, Welling, Kent.

## FINDING LIST FOR WEEDKILLERS

All the herbicides in this list are first-class chemicals which have been approved by the Ministry of Agriculture and are available in small packs designed for use by amateur gardeners. In case of difficulty in obtaining any of them, the manufacturers should be contacted.

The list may appear unnecessarily long but the pipe dream of multipurpose herbicides is not a reality and the full extent and value of chemical weed controls are only obtained by using herbicides for their specific purposes; as such, they constitute an efficient and economic method of eradicating unwanted plants of all sorts.

| Trade names | Chemicals | Manufacturers | Type of action | Plants controlled | Notes and precautions |
|---|---|---|---|---|---|
| | | WEED KILLERS FOR USE ON TURF | | | |
| "Bugges 2,4-D" "Dicotox" "Shell Weed-kill" | 2,4-D | Bugges Insecticides Ltd., London Rd., Sittingbourne, Kent. May and Baker Ltd., Dagenham, Essex Shell Chemical Co. Ltd., 15–17 Gt. Marlborough St., W.1. | Hormone growth regulator translocated throughout the plant. | Many broad-leafed weeds and some perennial ones. Best hormone type for killing daisies, dandelions and plantains. | Primarily for use on lawns Beware of drift. |
| "Bugges M.C.P.A." "Weed-a-Lawn" and "Spot" (in powder form) | M.C.P.A. | Bugges Insecticides Ltd., London Rd., Sittingbourne, Kent. Pan Britannia Industries Ltd., Britannia House, Waltham Cross, Herts. | Hormone growth regulator translocated throughout the plant. | Many broad-leafed weeds and some perennial ones. Best hormone type for killing creeping buttercup. Useful against pearlwort with repeated applications. | Primarily for use on lawns Beware of drift; on small areas the powdered formulation in puffer pack can be used. |
| "Clovotox" "Lawn Clover Killer" | Mecoprop | May and Baker Ltd., Dagenham, Essex. Pan Britannia Industries Ltd., Britannia House, Waltham Cross, Herts. | Hormone growth regulator translocated throughout the plant. | Best control for white-flowered clover, chickweeds and field woodrush. Useful against pearlwort with repeated applications. | Primarily for use on lawns Beware of drift. |
| Lawn sand "Velves Lawn Sand" "pbi Calomel Dust" | See T33(2). | Usually home made. Pan Britannia Industries Ltd., Britannia House, Waltham Cross, Herts. | Scorching of annual growth. Of herbicidal and manurial value, in most cases. | Invaluable against weeds resistant or semi-resistant to hormones, like pearlwort, moss, veronica (speedwell), yellow-flowered clover, and yarrow. | See Lawns (T33(2)) for detailed information. The use of calomel dusts should be confined to mosses; of no manurial value. |
| | | WEEDKILLERS FOR GARDEN USE | | | |
| 'Nova Soil Steriliser" | Cresylic Acid | The Murphy Chemical Co. Ltd., Wheathampstead, St. Albans, Herts. | Contact herbicide. | For destruction of growth of annual weeds and top growth of perennials. | Particularly valuable on asparagus beds and where annual weeds have to be controlled. Also used as a soil sterilant. |
| "Bugges Dalapon" | Dalapon | Bugges Insecticides Ltd., London Rd., Sittingbourne, Kent. | Translocated throughout the plant, killing vegetation by movement from leaves to roots. | Annual grasses, couch grass, sedges, reeds, and bulrushes. | Delay planting for 40 days after application. May be used, upon makers' instructions as a selective herbicide on asparagus, shrubberies, fruit gardens, etc. |
| "Weedol" | Diquat Salt | Plant Protection Ltd., Yalding, Kent. | Translocated throughout the plant but with scorching effect similar to contact herbicides. | Kills annual weeds and top growth of perennials. One of the few herbicides to give a good control of ground elder. Selective only by application, i.e., kills all foliage it contacts. | Undoubtedly one of the most valuable and interesting herbicides to be introduced. Inactivated upon contact with soil; no residual effects. Available in small packs. Can be stored from season to season. |
| "Weedex" | Simazine | Fisons Horticultural Ltd., Harvest House, Felixstowe, Suffolk. | Soil acting, killing seedling vegetation by uptake through roots. | Controls germinating seeds of many weeds over a long period. | Apply when ground is wet in early spring on asparagus, apples, pears (not plums), soft fruit, ornamental trees, and shrubs including roses. Slow acting. |
| "Polybor-Chlorate" | Sodium Chlorate | Borax Consolidated Ltd., Borax House, Carlisle Place, S.W.1. | Translocated throughout the plant and soil acting. | Toxic in varying degrees to all plants except mosses. The best chemical for killing tree stumps. | To a large extent superseded by other chemicals. Can be used on paths, drives, and vacant ground. |
| "Boots Bramble, Brushwood and Nettle Killer" | 2,4,5-T | Boots Pure Drug Co. Ltd., Station Street, Nottingham. | Hormone growth regulator translocated throughout the plant. | Special value in control of woody plants like brambles, brushwood, and ivy. Also good against nettles. | Beware of drift. |

## THE GARDEN CALENDAR.

**January.**—All digging should be finished this month. As the work is done, so generous applications of organic matter such as peat, compost, sewage sludge, leaf mould, animal manure, or a mixture of any of them, should be incorporated into the ground. On clay soils the physical condition can be improved by raking into the surface dressings of rough materials like screened ashes, road grit, or coarse sand.

Fork over ground between rows of fruit trees and in shrubberies and bury annual weeds; if land is not free of weeds in January it is unlikely to be so throughout the year.

A trench for runner beans can be made, the bottom forked over, a thick dressing of compost or kitchen waste added, and the soil replaced.

Rhubarb will require protection with compost or straw and early growth forced by covering with small tubs.

GROUND ELDER—A pernicious weed of neglected land. Eradicated by hand-forking early in the year or by chemicals (*see* T34).

Pruning of orchard trees and fruit bushes should be completed. When bird damage is severe gooseberries can be left until bud burst.

Autumn-planted shrubs and trees should be checked over, and any which have worked loose through the action of frost or wind should be firmed by thoroughly stamping over the soil.

**February.**—Broad beans can be sown if conditions are favourable and shallots planted by pressing the bulbs into the soil until only the tips show.

Jerusalem artichokes are an unusual crop well worth growing; plant tubers as early as possible to give a long season for maturity.

Parsnips should be lifted to check new growth and stored on the north side of a wall or fence.

" Seed " potatoes can be arranged in boxes and kept in a frost-proof shed; a light, airy position will encourage short, sturdy shoots.

Protective covering on half-hardy shrubs, like fuchsias and mimosa, should be removed as early as possible.

Herbaceous plants which do not over winter easily, such as delphiniums and gaillardias, may be planted at the end of the month.

Turf may be laid in February so that the grass can be established before the ground starts to dry out in the spring. Before laying, rake in a dressing of " National Growmore " at 1½ oz. per sq. yd. to encourage root action.

Vines under glass should still be kept as *cold* as possible to maintain the dormant period. As the buds swell the temperature can be higher, but ventilation must be increased if it reaches 45° Fahrenheit.

Fuchsias grown under glass should be pruned hard by cutting back all of last season's growth to within a bud or two of the old stems. Later, as new growth appears, take cuttings which will root easily in sand under a plastic bag.

Shrubby plants like the india-rubber plant and most pot plants grown indoors or under glass should be repotted or top dressed with fresh potting compost.

Early strawberries can be obtained by clocking rows at the beginning of the month.

**March.**—Sow round-seeded spinach and broad beans for a succession in cropping.

Brussels sprouts, cabbage, lettuce, leeks, onions, parsley, parsnips, peas, and radish should all be sown as the soil gradually warms up

Asparagus is easily raised from seed sown this month. Sow the seeds individually 1 in. apart and mark the rows by sowing a pinch or two of radish seed at intervals, as the asparagus is slow to germinate.

Onion sets can be planted as early as possible on well-manured ground.

Spring cabbage will respond in the spring to an application of nitrate of soda at 1 oz. per sq. yd.

Tomato seed may be sown in a warm greenhouse at the end of the month. It is a mistake to sow early in the year, as then seedlings get drawn and weak before it is time for planting outdoors.

Seed of half-hardy annuals, such as antirrhinums, China asters and *Phlox drummondii*, may all be sown in a greenhouse or frame. Remember the seed should only be covered with a sugaring of fine soil sufficient to " anchor " the seedlings and to sow thinly.

Hedges, and particularly evergreen sorts which have outgrown their stations, should be cut back, and this is the *best* month for doing so. Often drastic reduction is necessary, and such treatment will save endless, unnecessary work in trimming later on in the year. As an example, privet may be safely reduced to a width of 9 in. and a height of 4–5 ft.

Evergreen shrubs, like some daphnes, rhododendrons, and hollies, may be planted and—what is most important—kept moist until growing freely.

Over-grown lavender may be reduced in size by cutting back into old wood.

Lawns should be fed with fertilisers to encourage new, strong growth when the turf is damp.

As buds burst on roses, so pruning and manuring can be started.

Planting time for all fruit trees is nearly over, and should be completed without delay.

As buds burst on early planted raspberries, so the already shortened canes can be cut down to just above the lowest bud in growth; as further growth develops so the old stems can be shortened further until, finally, cut to ground level.

**April.**—Potato planting for an early crop is done this month using well-sprouted " seed." Protect from late frosts by covering the first shoots with earth and, if necessary, applying a coating of straw or sacking.

Onions raised under glass in boxes can be planted outdoors.

Watch for germination of asparagus seed; as the fern-like growths appear, hand weed the rows with great care and thin seedlings to 2–3 in. apart.

Hardy annuals can be sown outdoors when soil conditions are right; lightly cover and protect from birds. Half-hardy sorts must be grown-on in frames.

New stocks of carnations, chrysanthemums, and violas may be planted outdoors.

Transplant autumn-raised sweet peas to open garden early in the month.

Lawns may be sown as the soil warms up, and a good surface tilth can be obtained by raking; *prior* to sowing, make arrangements to protect the seed bed from birds by use of pea sticks, wire netting, strips of newspaper dipped into lime-wash, or " Glitterbangs " or a combination of these scarers.

Evergreen shrubs, like bamboos, hollies, and rhododendrons, should be planted and kept moist until well established.

Gladioli and montbretias can be planted in sunny positions where soil is in good heart.

Prune winter-flowering shrubs, such as winter jasmine and forsythia, by cutting off the old flowering stems.

Weeds will be appearing on garden paths and drives; establish an early and efficient control by watering with " Weedex."

Early planted fruit trees should be mulched with organic matter to conserve moisture in the soil.

May.—Brussels sprouts should be planted early in the month and also late potatoes. Watch out for blackfly on broad beans, as the first infestations are the important ones to deal with promptly.

Encourage growth on leafy vegetables, like lettuce and spinach, by a dressing of nitrate of soda at 1 oz. per sq. yd.

Towards the end of month plant out tomatoes, or in the first week if cloches are available.

Sow sweet corn and vegetable marrows in the open. Bedding plants and half-hardy annuals may all be planted outdoors.

Roses should be checked over for first signs of greenfly infestation; spray with nicotine if necessary.

Garden pools in need of cleaning should be dealt with thoroughly. At the same time water lilies may be lifted and divided when growth in the previous year was excessive.

Delphiniums now develop rapidly; for best results cut out thin shoots to leave five to seven strong growths to each plant. Stake and tie each one and encourage healthy growth by feeding with liquid animal manure or soot water on one or two occasions.

Faded blooms on azaleas, lilacs, and rhododendrons should be removed.

Agapanthuses and hydrangeas grown in tubs can be brought into a sunny position. If repotting has not been necessary remove top 2 in. of soil and replace with fresh compost. Encourage new growth with applications of liquid animal manure.

Window boxes should be repaired, filled with fresh compost, and replanted. Remember a generous layer of peat or leaf soil placed in the bottom will do much to conserve moisture.

Lawns will need attention, and broad-leaved weeds can be eliminated by treatment with hormone weed-killers.

Small greenhouses are liable to get very hot and plants suffer accordingly especially if short of water; therefore keep staging and floors well damped. Conversely, sharp falls in temperature may be experienced and every day the ventilators should be shut down in the late afternoon in order to conserve the heat from the sun.

June.—Plant cabbages, cauliflower, celery, marrows, and tomatoes.

Sow seed of garden swedes.

After thinning beet, carrots, onions, and parsnips, feed with nitrate of soda at ½ oz. per yd. run.

Asparagus raised from seed must be kept clear of weeds and watered thoroughly at the least sign of being dry. Beds cropping in their third season should not be cut after June 1st; on old beds cutting may continue until the third week of June.

Sweet corn should be thinned and a surface dressing of compost applied.

Aubrietas now past their best should be clipped back hard to the old stems, with a pair of shears.

Seed of delphiniums, hollyhocks, lupins, and wallflowers may be sown.

Phloxes, especially if grown on light soil, should be mulched with compost and watered when necessary.

Herbaceous plants of all sorts respond to feeding if growth is below par; individual species may be fed with soot water or large beds given an application of sulphate of ammonia at 1 oz. per sq. yd., taking care to keep the crystals off the foliage of plants.

Old flower-heads on roses should be removed regularly by cutting back old flowering stems to within 4 or 5 in. of the mature wood.

Raspberries and similar berries should be mulched with compost or old manure to encourage new growth.

Strawberries may be layered if the stock is healthy and growth vigorous.

July.—Plant winter cabbage, leeks, sprouting broccoli, and kales as ground becomes available.

Sow prickly spinach and turnips for autumn and winter use.

Water celery, marrows, and runner beans at first sign of dryness. If setting is poor, beans should be sprayed vigorously with water from a hose.

Shallots may be lifted and dried off as foliage gradually yellows.

Carnations may be layered as sturdy young shoots develop; remove sufficient leaves to make a horizontal cut up the stem passing through a joint, and peg down.

Flag irises can be lifted and divided as flowering finishes. After replanting, the tubers should be showing above ground but, nevertheless, firmly in the soil.

Wallflowers may be lined out in nursery rows. To avoid sappy, lush growth do not plant on rich soil. Where ground is acid water plants with lime-water (a large handful to a gallon).

Hydrangeas can be easily propagated in July by cuttings of short flowerless shoots. These should be inserted in pots in a sandy compost and kept under a plastic bag or hand light until rooted.

Transplant into nursery rows, seedlings of biennials and perennials sown earlier in the year.

Order supplies of daffodils, hyacinths, and other bulbous plants for delivering in September. Stocks in good trade houses are often soon exhausted.

Late in the month hedges of beech, holly, hornbeam, and yew can be clipped.

**August.**—Runner beans are now in full bearing, and the pods should be gathered while still young, to encourage further croppings; often beans are picked much too old. Water and feed with nitro-chalk at 2 oz. per yd. run if necessary. If properly grown this is one of the most profitable of *all* crops.

Marrows should also be gathered while still young and fresh; early development of seeds checks fruiting.

Strawberries layered in pots earlier in the year may be planted when the soil conditions are right. Use a well-manured site and plant at approved distances.

Raspberries and loganberries will now have finished cropping, and all the old fruiting canes may be cut out at ground level.

**September.**—Tomatoes can be gathered while still green and ripened easily and quickly by storing in open boxes, out of the direct sun, in a warm kitchen. Such a practice is better than putting the fruit in a dark, airless cupboard.

Ground recently cleared of onions and potatoes is admirable for planting out cabbages for spring cutting. Apart from removing any weeds, no preparation is desirable.

CORRECTLY PLANTED SHRUB, showing planting hole and bush in position. The loosened sub-soil must be firmed prior to planting, and any tree or shrub must never be planted deeper than it was in its previous position or nursery row.

Seed of prickly spinach—a valuable winter crop—may be sown. As seedlings develop, thin out and on acid soils apply lime-water.

Tomatoes should be sprayed with " Bouisol " at fortnightly intervals to prevent potato blight.

Winter greens, if not already planted, should be put in as soon as possible.

Pelargoniums (" Geraniums ") should be propagated by cuttings taken throughout the month as young, short side-shoots develop. Rooting soon starts if the cuttings are inserted in sand or a mixture of sand and peat.

Border carnations may be layered; encourage rooting by not allowing the plants to suffer from a lack of water.

Madonna lilies may be planted this month in an open position where they will not be disturbed.

Flowering shrubs of a wide range may be propagated in August. Short side-shoots of the current season's growth should be taken off with a heel when the wood is still young but starting to harden at the base. Insert in sand and cover with a plastic bag.

Grass seed is best sown this month whenever the soil is moist but not wet, as in the notes for April. Before sowing, any perennial weeds must be removed by hand forking.

Brussel sprouts are heavy feeders and growth should be encouraged by an application of nitro-chalk at 1 oz. per sq. yd. early in the month.

Carnation layers will now be rooted and the young plants may be severed from the parents and transferred to their flowering positions.

Crocuses, daffodils, and snowdrops are often planted too late; September is the time for the job. Similarly, these, together with hyacinths, may all be planted in bowls for indoor decoration before the end of the month.

Lavender bushes can be trimmed when the flowers fade; do not, however, trim or cut back in any way the old stems or foliage.

Grass seed not sown last month should be put in without delay.

Roses of nearly every sort can be propagated by inserting cuttings 8–10 in. long in a shallow trench outdoors. A sprinkling of sand should be put in the bottom of the trench and the cuttings firmed well.

Brown rot is often prevalent on fruit. There is no remedy for the disease, and brown, rotten fruit on apple and other trees should be picked off and burnt.

**October.**—Jerusalem artichokes are safe left in the ground, but the stems should be cut down.

If a regular supply is wanted, then a store of tubers may be lifted to ensure against hard frost.

Parsnips may, similarly, be left in the ground until needed.

Asparagus stems should be cut down before the seeds drop. If " fern " is cut during the summer for indoor decoration, subsequent cropping is affected.

Lettuce for early cutting next spring should be sown, late in the month, under cloches.

Virgin ground which is to be taken into cultivation should be dug as soon as possible in order that it may be exposed to a *full* season of winter frosts. There is no doubt that the maximum value in digging virgin land can only be had if the work is completed well before Christmas.

Evergreen shrubs should be planted before the weather turns severely cold.

Lily-of-the-valley will respond to a top dressing of old animal manure or an application of bone meal at 2 oz. per sq. yd. followed by a mulch of leaf soil.

Clematis grown in pots may be planted in their permanent positions.

Lilies of various sorts can be planted early in the month.

Gladioli should be lifted, cleaned, and stored in a dry, frost-proof shed.

Polyanthuses and all sorts of primroses may be planted in moist, rich soil for flowering in the spring.

Sweet Williams and pansies may be transferred from nursery rows to their flowering positions.

Wallflowers should be planted without delay, firming the plants well. Forget-me-nots and daffodils may be used in conjunction with them and planted at the same time.

Most plants grown indoors have been watered freely during the summer; from now on care must be taken in applying water, as soil only dries out slowly in winter, and growth has virtually stopped.

Bulbs in bowls must be kept as cold as possible, and up to early November not more than about ½ in. of growth should be showing. Damp the peat as it shows signs of drying out.

Black and red currants and gooseberries may all be propagated by cuttings.

**November.**—Runner beans can be cleared and the haulms used for compost; the old roots can be left in the ground and later dug-in. If the sticks are pulled up early and stored they will last for some years.

Broad beans may be sown outdoors in districts where they are known to succeed; an allowance for losses should be made by sowing 3 in. apart.

Asparagus responds well to a top dressing of animal manure or compost; if supplies are short, aim to apply once in three years.

Lettuce sown last month under cloches can be transplanted and, under wide barn cloches, three rows can be grown easily for cutting in the spring. Slugs may cause serious losses, so water with " Slugit " at planting time and keep a few spare seedlings to fill any gaps.

Tulips may be planted throughout November.

Heaths and heathers of all sorts can be planted in peaty soils. Large clumps may be split up and replanted.

Roses and all deciduous shrubs and trees, including fruit trees of all sorts, should be planted as soon as possible. Always firm the soil well, but do not plant too deeply.

Where necessary, herbaceous borders can be replanted. Large clumps of perennials can be split up and the strong pieces from outside of the clump replanted; the centre of the clump should be discarded.

Continue to keep indoor bulbs as cold as possible. By the second week in November, growth should be about an inch high. Towards the end of the month, transfer to a cool, light position.

Throughout the winter continue digging and incorporating organic matter like compost, spent hops, and coffee grounds.

Vines grown in a cold greenhouse should be given full ventilation night and day. After leaf fall cut back annual growth to one bud.

WATER LEVEL ⟶

CHARCOAL ⟶

**BULBS INDOORS**—Note strong root development before leaves appear. This factor can only be brought about by early planting (*see* September notes). In both bowl (A) and glass (B) a little bonfire charcoal is necessary for healthy growth.

**December.**—Decaying leaves on winter greens should be removed to give free circulation of air around the plants.

Bird damage may be prevalent on spring cabbages because of pigeons. In serious cases it is worthwhile to erect fish netting.

When frost makes cultivations impossible, pruning of fruit trees should be done. The only exception may be red currants and gooseberries, because in districts where bird damage is serious any pruning is best left until the spring.

Deciduous hedges of beech, hawthorn, and the like can all be cut back hard where the plants have got out of hand, with a view to reducing work of trimming during the growing season.

Well-berried holly is always in demand, and a variety of regular fruiting habit to fulfil the requirement is *Ilex aquifolium* ' Pyramidalis.'

For those wanting mistletoe, the seed should be planted on apple trees in the spring—not in December.

Early in the month, hyacinths can be brought into full light and warmth for Christmas flowering. If growth is a little stunted cover plants with a sheet of newspaper and give more warmth; if growth is poor look to the cultivator not the supplier.

Christmas trees to be brought indoors in pots should be thoroughly watered first, to check the needles falling through lack of moisture in hot, stuffy rooms.

# GAMES &
# RECREATIONS

---

Indoor and outdoor games and
leisure activities, alphabetically
arranged, together with 4 pages
of records, including the 1968
Olympic Games.

# GAMES AND RECREATIONS

PEOPLE have always been fond of playing games and of thinking out ways of spending their leisure time and of celebrating special occasions. The result is a long history of games, recreations, and customs, some of which are described in this section. The arrangement is alphabetical.

One problem that confronts those keen to try some game or recreation is how to set about it. In many cases, the simplest way of finding out what facilities exist in a particular area is to enquire at a local newspaper office, which will have particulars of all sports clubs, dramatic societies, and other recreational bodies in the area. A few addresses that might be useful to those with certain specialised interests appear at the appropriate places in the text, and a valuable source of helpful information on many games and recreations is the Central Council of Physical Recreation, which has English, Scottish, Welsh, and Northern Irish addresses as follows: England, 6 Bedford Square, London, W.C.1; Scotland, 4 Queensferry Street, Edinburgh, 2; Wales, 18 Windsor Place, Cardiff; and Northern Ireland, 45 Arthur Street, Belfast. Those keen on touring the country at moderate cost might appreciate the services provided by the Youth Hostels Association, which has addresses as follows: England and Wales, Trevelyan House, St. Albans, Herts, with a London office at 29 John Adam Street, W.C.1; Scotland, 7 Bruntsfield Crescent, Edinburgh, 10; Northern Ireland, 28 Bedford Street, Belfast; and the Irish Republic, 39 Mountjoy Square, Dublin.

## American Football.

American Football is played eleven-aside on a pitch marked by a line across it every 5 yards, and with goals and a ball resembling those used in Rugby Football (q.v.), though the ball is smaller. Scoring is by "touchdowns," which are like Rugby tries, but count six; goals after touchdowns, which count one; field goals during play, which count three; and "safeties," which give the attacking side two points if the defenders carry the ball over their own goal-line and touch it down. The ball is advanced by carrying it, forward passing, and kicking. The game consists of a series of "plays" or "downs," the ball becoming dead when the ball-carrier is tackled. A team must advance 10 yards in four downs or give up the ball to their opponents. Players can run ahead of the ball-carrier to protect him by "blocking" opponents. Penalties take the form of distance, usually 5 or 15 yards, lost. A game lasts 60 minutes, divided into four 15-minute quarters.

## Angling.

Angling, which is catching fish with rod, line, and hook, goes back to beyond the beginning of history, for it was known to the Greeks and Romans. It is now a recreation, for, though the catch may subsequently be used, it is not primarily fishing for the pot. It has its competitive side, with competitions offering prizes for the biggest catch, and there are angling clubs, but many people prefer to use it as a recreation to be enjoyed alone in quiet surroundings. It is actually not so much a recreation as many recreations, for fishing can take place in the sea, rivers, lakes, ponds, and even canals, and there are several entirely different kinds of angling. The most obvious divisions are fresh-water fishing, including coarse and fly-fishing, and sea angling, including fishing from piers and the shore and big-game fishing.

The biggest branch of angling is fresh-water fishing for general or "coarse" fish, which are so called to distinguish them from "game" fish like salmon. Coarse fishing is bait fishing, or, in the case of pike, spinning, groundbait also being thrown in before and during fishing. It covers many varieties of fish, and the bag may be a very mixed one. Certain fish, of course, are known to frequent certain localities or types of locality, but, though the angler may know exactly the kind of fish he is after, he rarely knows if his catch will consist entirely of that kind of fish, or even if it will include any of that kind. Coarse fish do not generally make good eating.

Fly-fishing for salmon and trout differ widely from coarse fishing, and from each other. As the name implies, artificial flies are used, but those used for trout are quite different from those that attract salmon. In the case of trout, a fly is made to resemble a real insect as closely as possible, but, with salmon, this is not necessary. Salmon rarely, if ever, feed in fresh water, and, when in that type of water, they are usually irritable. They will dart wildly at any objects that attract their attention, so salmon flies are simply bright objects designed to draw them on. Fly-fishing is rather an expensive sport, for it means hiring beats on private water. In both coarse and fly-fishing the angler would be well advised to keep out of sight of the quarry as much as possible.

Sea angling is now the most competitive form of angling, with sea-angling festivals and competitions plentiful during the holiday season. It has what might be called its equivalent of fly-fishing with feathers, which attract several kinds of fish.

Big-game fishing takes place from a motor-launch, which is not towed by the hooked fish, but follows it, so that the ensuing fight is between man and fish, and not between the fish and the dead weight of the boat. Such a fight could last for 12 hours, and it is never certain that the angler will win it. Tunny is the only big game found off the British coasts.

Archery. *See* Old English Games and Customs.

## Association Football.

Games that may have resembled football were played by very ancient races, and games that certainly were football of a kind were played in the England of several centuries ago, but the Association Football that is the most popular game in Britain, and perhaps the world, to-day had its origins in the games played at English Public Schools in the days before sport became organised.

It was not surprising that some of those who had played football of one kind or another at school should want to go on playing after they left, but, before they could do so, it was necessary to work out a set of rules that would be universally understood and accepted. Meetings were organised by those interested, and, as the universities were natural meeting-places for boys from many schools, it was there, particularly Cambridge, that these took place.

It was soon evident that there was a major difference of opinion between those who wanted handling permitted and those who opposed this. The rival factions proved irreconcilable, so they went their separate ways. The handling enthusiasts based their rules on those in force at Rugby School, and thus pioneered Rugby Football (q.v.). Those who felt that football should be played primarily with the foot brought into being the game that was to take its name from the Association that was formed, in 1863, to govern it.

and became Association Football, often called by the abbreviation, " Soccer."

Soccer is played with a round, leather-covered ball weighing from 14 to 16 ounces, and with a circumference of from 27 to 28 inches, on a pitch marked out as in the accompanying diagram. It is played eleven-aside, the positions being goalkeeper; right and left full-backs; right, centre, and left half-backs; and five forwards, playing at outside-right, inside-right, centre-forward, inside-left, and outside-left. The object is to score goals by putting the ball between uprights 8 yards apart and under a crossbar 8 feet high. The ball is advanced by kicking or heading, but only the goalkeeper when in his own penalty area may handle it, and he may not carry it. A game lasts for 90 minutes, divided into two halves.

The game is started by a kick-off from the centre, with all the opposing players outside the

his own half, from a corner kick, or from a throw-in. If a player in an offside position interferes with the game, a free kick is awarded.

A game is controlled by a referee, who has the assistance of two linesmen. These may signal infringements, but the referee is not bound to act on such signals.

In Britain, soccer is a winter game, the season lasting from August until May, though, in Scotland, it continues even during the short summer season in the form of five-aside football, known as the " short " game. British soccer is highly organised, ranging from the fully professional Football League of four divisions and the equivalent, though slightly smaller, Scottish League through minor professional leagues to amateur leagues. There are also many cup competitions, from the Football Association Challenge Cup and the Scottish Cup downwards.

centre circle and in their own half. The ball must travel at least its own circumference into the opponents' half, and the kicker may not play it again until someone else has done so. The right to kick-off is decided by a toss that gives the winner the option of kicking or choosing which goal he will defend. Ends are changed at half-time, after which the ball is kicked-off by the side that did not do so at the start. The game is restarted in this way after each goal, the non-scorers kicking-off.

If the ball crosses the touch-line it is thrown in by a player of the side that did not put it out, the throw being two-handed. If it crosses the goal-line wide of the goal it is kicked-off by a defender from the 6-yards line if the attackers were responsible, and by an attacker from the intersection of the goal-line and the touch-line if the defenders were responsible.

Infringements are penalised by free kicks, which may be " direct " or " indirect." Direct free kicks, from which a goal may be scored, follow deliberate infringements, indirect free kicks, from which a goal cannot be scored, being for more technical offences. Offences by defenders in the penalty area are generally penalised by a penalty kick, which is a shot from a spot 12 yards out from the centre of the goal, with only the kicker and the goalkeeper in the penalty area, and the goalkeeper barred from moving until the ball has been kicked. However, certain offences in the penalty area, such as carrying by the goalkeeper and obstruction, are penalised only by an indirect free kick.

A player is " offside "—called " sneaking " in the school games from which the rule came—if he is nearer the opponents' goal-line than is the ball unless there are two opponents between him and the goal-line, or unless the ball was last played by an opponent. He cannot, however, be offside in

The game has also spread almost all over the world, being extraordinarily popular all over Europe and in South America, and played to some extent in the United States, Canada, South Africa, Australia, and other areas. There is a World Cup competition that is played for every four years, a European Nations Cup, played for every two years, and an annual European Champion Clubs Cup competition played for by the top club of almost every European country. Soccer is also included in the Olympic Games.

## Athletics.

The sport of Athletics, which includes running, walking, jumping, and throwing, is probably the most natural of all sports, and certainly one of the oldest.

Modern Athletics can be said to have begun in 1849, when the Royal Military Academy instituted a meeting that was followed by a similar meeting at Exeter College, Oxford, and, subsequently, at other Oxford and Cambridge Colleges. The Civil Service were also early in the field; and the first athletic club was the Mincing Lane Athletic Club, now the London Athletic Club. There was also the Amateur Athletic Club, which organised an annual championship meeting, and acted as a governing body for both athletics and amateur boxing.

In 1880 the Amateur Athletic Association was formed as a governing body. Other countries, particularly the United States, took to the sports and in 1896 the first modern Olympic Games were held at Athens. Other international meetings and matches followed, and championships and competitions of all standards were started in many countries. Women came into the sport in the early 1920s, and were included in the Olympic Games in 1928. There is now a long list of internationally agreed standard events, including distances measured in yards and miles, and also their metric equivalents; and including also a major all-round test, the ten-event Decathlon.

The longest strictly standard distances are the Marathon of 26 miles 385 yards for runners, and 50,000 metres for walkers, but there are regularly held longer events. For runners, the longest annual race is between Durban and Maritzburg, about 55 miles, the longest in Britain being from London to Brighton, about 53 miles; but there are occasional 100-mile and 24-hour events. For walkers, there are annual 100-mile races and fairly regular 24-hour ones.

The Marathon commemorates the run of the

## Australian Rules Football.

Australian Rules Football is played 18 aside on large oval grounds. At each end, there are four posts seven yards apart; and scoring, which is high, is by goals, counting six points, when the ball is kicked between the two inner posts, and behinds, counting one point, when it is kicked between the outer ones. The ball resembles a Rugby ball, but is less pointed. Players must not run more than 10 yards with the ball without bouncing it or touching it on the ground. The ball must not be thrown, but it can be passed by holding it with one hand and punching it with the other, or by kicking. Players in possession can be tackled between the shoulder and the knee or

DOUBLES COURT.                    SINGLES COURT.

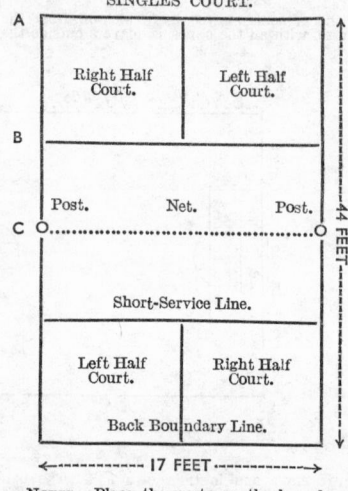

NOTE.—If it is practicable place the posts on the side boundary lines; failing this, place them at any distance not more than 2 ft. outside these lines.

A to B 2 ft. 6 in.  A to C 15 ft. 6 in.
A to D 22 ft.

NOTES.—Place the posts on the boundary lines or not more than 2 ft. outside these lines.

The back boundary lines become the long-service lines.

A to B 15 ft. 6 in.  B to C 6 ft. 6 in.

Top of net 5 ft. from ground at centre and 5 ft. 1 in. at posts.

*Diagram of Ground as marked out for Badminton.*

courier Pheidippides from the battlefield at Marathon to Athens, carrying the news of victory over the Persians (490 B.C.). This run covered about 25 miles but the distance was standardised at 26 miles 385 yards in the 1908 Olympic Marathon from Windsor to the White City, London. All Marathons commemorate the Battle of Marathon, but the oldest annual Marathon, the Boston Marathon, also commemorates the Battle of Lexington (the first battle of the American Revolution), and, more particularly, the ride by Paul Revere that preceded it.

*Cross-Country.* Athletics is mainly a summer sport, but in cross-country running it has an extremely popular winter branch.

Cross-country originated in the traditional runs at various English Public Schools, particularly Rugby and Shrewsbury; and came into wider prominence when it was adopted by the Thames Rowing Club as winter training. It is still used as training by many sportsmen of all kinds, but it is now also a thriving competitive sport in its own right. There is an International Championship, but this is not yet fully representative, being virtually confined to Western European nations. Major cross-country championships are over courses of 9 or 10 miles.

charged. There is no offside and no scrummaging. A game consists of four 25-minute quarters. The game has existed since 1858, and is played to the practical exclusion of all other forms of football in the southern half of Australia and in Western Australia. There are over 3,000 clubs.

## Badminton.

Badminton might be described as an indoor version of Lawn Tennis (q.v.) in that it is played over a net, and can consist of either singles or doubles. There, however, the resemblance ceases. Only the serving side can score. If the server wins the rally only one point is scored; if he loses the next player serves. A game is won by the side first making 15 points. Three games make a set. The shuttlecock or " bird " is a small cork hemisphere in which feathers are fixed. All shots are volleys.

Bandy. *See* Skating.

## Baseball.

The invention of Baseball, a summer game played from April until October, and the national game of the United States, is generally credited to an Army officer, its origins being old country games called " One Old Cat " and " Two Old Cat."

Teams are nine-aside, and bat and field in turn. The main part of the ground, the " diamond," has a " base," marked by a sack, at each corner, the lines from sack to sack being the " base paths." One base is " home," and there the batter stands, by a square of rubber on the ground, called the " plate." The base forward and to the right of a right-handed batter is " first," the one straight ahead of him is " second," and the one forward and to his left is " third," the distance from one base to the next being 30 yards. 20 yards out straight in front of the plate is the pitcher's " mound." The lines from home to first and from home to third are continued beyond these bases, and are the " foul lines."

It is the object of the batting side, using a bat which resembles a long, heavy Indian club with which to hit a hard, white ball weighing 5 ounces, to score runs, one being scored each time a player completes a circuit of the bases, not necessarily from one hit. When a batter leaves the plate, either " out " or to proceed along the base paths, the next man comes in, the team's innings lasting until three men are out. Nine such innings complete the game, and, in each innings, the batting side carries on at the point in the batting order reached in the previous innings. There is no toss for first innings, the visiting side always batting first.

The pitched ball reaches the batter without touching the ground, and, if not hit, it should pass over the plate between the batter's shoulders and knees. If it does so, it is a " strike," and three such strikes dismiss the batter. If it does not, it is a strike only if the batter swings at it; otherwise it is a " ball," and four balls give the batter a free passage to first base, called a " walk." A batter also walks if he is hit by a pitched ball. Other ways in which the batter can be dismissed are by being caught, and by being " put out " while on the base paths by failing to reach the base to which he is running before the ball. When an out is made, the ball does not become " dead." If there is more than one runner on the base paths, then, if the ball can be relayed quickly enough, two, or even three, men can be put out on the same " play."

If the batter hits fairly, he must run, but, to be fair, the hit must be in front of him and between the foul lines. A " foul hit " counts as a strike against him, except that the third strike, which actually dismisses him, must be a clean one across the plate. If a foul is caught, he is out.

The fielding side is divided into three sections, the " battery," the " infield," and the " outfield." The battery consists of the pitcher and the catcher, who stands behind the plate and gives signals indicating the kind of ball he thinks the pitcher should deliver: for, though the pitched ball does not touch the ground, pitchers can produce a wide variety of deliveries, including various kinds of curve. The infield consists of the first baseman, at or near first; the second baseman, between first and second; the short-stop, between second and third; and the third baseman, at or near third. The outfield covers the ground beyond the infield, three remaining fielders taking the right, centre, and left sections of it. Catchers wear a large glove on the non-throwing hand, a mask, a chest protector, and leg-guards. All the other fielders wear a glove on the non-throwing hand, the first baseman's being larger than the others. The batter wears no protective gear.

Substitutes are permitted, pitchers frequently being changed if they are being hit, and " pinch hitters " being sent in instead of weak batters if a hit is desperately needed. If this happens, the man replaced, often the pitcher, cannot return when his side fields again, though his field replacement need not be the man who batted for him.

As with Cricket (q.v.) batting averages are recorded, these being calculated by dividing the number of times at bat into the number of hits. An average of 0·400, referred to as " four hundred," would be exceptionally good. " Hits " mean safe hits on which the batter achieved one or more bases without giving a chance. If he reaches base because a catch was dropped or a ball mis-fielded, he plays on from there in the usual way, but is not credited with a hit. Pitchers are graded according to the number of games won and lost. Recorded fielding statistics include each man's " put outs," " assists," which are throws from which a team-mate made a put out, and " errors."

In the United States there are clubs and leagues of all standards, from professionals of various classes through semi-professionals to amateurs, called " sandlotters," and boys. The top class of all consists of two major leagues, the National and the American, each with eight clubs. The champions of these two leagues meet in a best-of-seven-games series for the " Championship of the World," always known as the World Series.

Baseball is also the chief summer game of Canada, and it is quite widely played in some other countries, including Australia, Britain, and Japan.

*Softball.* Similar to Baseball is Softball, which is popular in the United States with girls as well as men, and which was demonstrated in Britain during the War by American and Canadian servicemen. The ball is not particularly soft, but it is larger than a baseball, and pitching is under-arm. Distances between bases, and between the plate and the mound, are shorter than in the parent game.

### Basketball.

Basketball was invented by an American Y.M.C.A. official at Springfield, Massachusetts, as a winter team game that could be played indoors. It can be played in almost any gymnasium or hall, and it can also be played outdoors on an asphalt court. In America it is played by teams of all standards from schoolboys to professionals, and it is watched by more spectators than any other game. It has also spread to almost as many other countries as has Association Football (q.v), and it is included in the Olympic Games. It has been established for some years in Britain, where it has been encouraged by the Services and the Y.M.C.A.

Basketball is played five-aside, substitutes being permitted, with a ball resembling that used in Association Football, and goals consisting of posts that have iron rings with short nets attached to them and backboards. It is purely a handling game, and the ball is advanced by dribbling, which means bouncing, and by passing. Deliberate bodily contact is not allowed. Goals thrown during play count two points, and goals thrown from free throws after infringements one point. Height is an asset in the game, which demands stamina and agility, and which has been highly recommended as an ideal training activity by coaches of other sports, particularly Athletics (q.v.).

Girls also play Basketball, and, in Britain, there are national championships for clubs and schools, and international matches between England and Scotland.

### Biathlon. *See* Winter Sports.

### Billiards.

Billiards, which originated in France, is a game of angles, and of very great skill. It is played on a table measuring 12 feet by 6 feet 1½ inches, having six pockets, one at each corner, and one in the middle of each side. The table is covered with green baize, the edges being of cloth-covered rubber, called " cushions." Across the table, 2 feet 5 inches from the bottom edge, is a line, called the " baulk " line, the space between the line and the bottom of the table being " baulk." On the baulk side of the line there is a semi-circle with a radius of 11½ inches from the centre of the line. Down the centre of the table are four "spots," one 12¾ inches from the top, one midway between the top and the centre, one in the centre, and one in the middle of the baulk line. Two white balls, one with a spot for identification purposes, and one red one, are used, the balls being played with " cues " that taper down to a striking tip. The remaining equipment includes a long, cue-like stick with a metal cross fixed diagonally on the end, called a " rest " or " jigger," and a special long cue, these being used when the player cannot reach his ball in the ordinary way. Most games are " singles," though " doubles " can be played, the object of the game being to score points according to fixed rules, an agreed number of points making the game.

To decide who is to start, players " string " by playing their balls simultaneously from baulk up to the top cushion, the ball which returns nearer to the bottom cushion winning. At the start, the red ball is " spotted " on the top spot, and players start from the baulk circle. Scoring is three for pocketing, or " potting," the red or going in off the red; two for potting the white, which is, of course, the opponent's ball, or going in off the white; and two for a cannon, which is hitting both the other balls. A player whose shot hits no other balls at all gives one point to his opponent, unless his ball goes into a pocket, when he forfeits three. A player's turn, called a " break," continues as long as he is actually scoring. When the red is potted, it is immediately respotted.

*Snooker.* Also played on a billiard table, and perhaps even more popular, is Snooker, which uses 22 balls, positioned as follows: 15 reds in the form of a triangle with its apex on the second spot from the top, and its base at the top end; a black on the top spot; a pink touching the apex ball of the triangle; a blue on the centre spot; a brown in the middle of the baulk line, with a green beside it on the left end of the baulk circle, and a yellow on the right end; and a white, which is the cue-ball to be played. The points values of the balls are from one for red, through yellow, green, brown, blue, and pink, to seven for black. A player's turn continues as long as he scores, his first shot being at a red, when, if he pots one, he plays at one of the other colours, play being at reds and colours alternately as lon as balls are being potted, and as long as there are reds on the table, after which the remaining colours are played in ascending order of value.

A variation of Snooker is Snooker Plus. This uses two additional balls, an orange, placed between the pink and the blue and valued at eight points, and a purple, placed between the blue and the brown and valued at ten points.

*Pool, Russian Pool, and Pyramids.* Other games played on a billiard table include Pool, Russian Pool, and Pyramids. In Pool each player has a ball of a different colour, the order of play being white, red, yellow, green, brown, blue, pink, black. Each player plays at the ball of his predecessor, and tries to pot it, the game starting with white spotting his ball on the top spot, so that red is actually the first to play. A player whose ball is potted loses a life, players losing three lives dropping out of the game. A turn continues as long as a player is potting balls, and if he clears all the balls on the table he then spots his own ball for the next player.

Russian Pool uses the yellow, green, blue, and black balls, with the white as cue-ball, the black being placed on the top spot, the blue on the centre spot, the green on the left side of the baulk circle, and the yellow on the right side. A player's first shot must hit the black, after which he can play at will. Scoring is by potting balls, by going in off balls, and by cannons, but the black can be used only for the top pockets, the blue for the middle pockets, and the green and the yellow for the bottom pockets. Cannons count two, potting or going in off counting nine for the black, seven for the blue, five for the green, and three for the yellow. A player's turn continues as long as he is scoring, but consecutive cannons on the same balls are limited to 25, and the same ball must not be potted from the same spot more than three times in succession. A complete miss forfeits

three points. A variation of Russian Pool adds the pink ball, which is spotted on the second spot from the top, counts six, and can be used with any pocket.

Pyramids uses the 15 reds, starting in their triangle, and a white cue-ball, the object being to pot the reds. A turn continues while a player is scoring, 8 balls potted ending the game.

Bird-watching. *See* Natural History and Field Studies.

Boat Races.

Race rowing is a strenuous sport that makes no pretence of attracting as many active participants as some other sports and games; yet its long history includes races with unusual stories about them; races that are amongst the greatest annual international sporting events; and one race that provides what is probably the most enthusiastically supported free sporting spectacle in the world.

That, of course, is the Oxford and Cambridge University boat race, rowed on the Thames from Putney to Mortlake. First rowed in 1829, it has offered its excited public, which includes thousands of people with no connection of any kind with either university, everything, including runaway victories, dead heats, and even sinking boats. To all intents and purposes, this is a regular annual event, and has been so since 1856; but, in actual fact, every race is the result of a separate special challenge from the losers of the previous race to the winners of it. The race has an interesting parallel in the United States, where Yale University, whose colours are dark blue, annually meet Harvard University, which is at Cambridge, on a river called the Thames.

The Oxford and Cambridge race is the best-known annual race on the Putney–Mortlake stretch of the Thames, but it is by no means the only one. There are other races that attract entries sometimes numbered in hundreds: entries that are far too big to race abreast on the Thames, and so race in single file, with crews following each other at fixed intervals in what are known as the Head of the River races. The biggest of these is for crews of eight, but there are other Head of the River races for women's crews, who cover only part of this famous stretch of water, and for single scullers. Single scullers also cover this course in a straightforward race in the Wingfield Sculls event, which ranks as the English Amateur Championship, and which was first held one year after the first Oxford and Cambridge race, in 1830.

Head of the River races, but with a difference, are also held between the colleges of Oxford and Cambridge, where the Isis and the Cam, respectively, are much too narrow to permit straightforward racing. These are the Bump Races, in which each crew endeavours to catch and bump the crew ahead of it, except for the leading crew, which can concentrate on staying in front. When a bump is achieved, the two crews pull into the bank, and change places for the next day's racing. The racing goes on for four days, and it is, of course, the ambition of each crew, apart from the leaders, to register a bump on each day.

Back on the Thames, but farther down it towards the port and docks of London, is the scene of a race that makes the Oxford and Cambridge race and the Wingfield Sculls look like recent innovations. This is the annual race from London Bridge to Chelsea for the Doggett's Coat and Badge, a single sculling event open only to young watermen who are within twelve months of completing their apprenticeship. It was founded in 1715 in honour of the House of Hanover and to commemorate the anniversary of " King George I's happy accession to the throne of Great Britain," by Thomas Doggett, a Dublin-born actor connected with the Drury Lane and Haymarket theatres, who regularly travelled on the Thames in preference to using the roads, and who left a sum of money to perpetuate the race, which is now controlled by the Fishmongers' Company.

This race is more truly an annual one than almost any other event; for, while most so-called annual races have been subjected to long interruptions because of the two World Wars, those qualified for the Doggett races during those years were subsequently traced, and the races duly decided after the wars. The event is a colourful one, always followed by a barge carrying a batch of past winners wearing the Coat and Badge, and also the cap, breeches, silk stockings, and buckled shoes that go with them. The scarlet, pleated, quilted Coat, with its silver buttons and the large silver arm Badge bearing the White Horse of Hanover and the word " Liberty ", are presented at the Fishmongers' Hall, where the winner is greeted with a salute of trumpets and the tune, " See the Conquering Hero Comes."

For a rowing event of a very different kind, dating back " only " to 1839, one must go up the Thames, far beyond the end of the Tideway, to Henley, for the annual Royal Regatta. This consists of events open to the world and others closed to English colleges and schools for eights, fours, pairs, double sculls, and single sculls, the most famous of its races being the Grand Challenge Cup for eights and the Diamond Sculls.

A journey far from the Thames will bring to light the story of a rowing trophy that first appeared sixteen years before Oxford first met Cambridge. The Carrow Cup was awarded for a four-oared race on the River Yare, in Norfolk, from Carrow Bridge to Whitlingham and back in 1813. Sometime during the 1840s that cup disappeared: to reappear in 1890—in Australia. In 1947 it came into the possession of the Victoria Rowing Association, which made it the trophy for a pair-oared race, but sent it to England for exhibition in the 1948 Olympic rowing museum. There it was recognised as a Norfolk trophy, and, though it returned to Victoria, it came home again in 1950, when the Melbourne club gave it to the Norwich Rowing Committee, which now annually awards it to " the Norwich club whose general performance, judged by a points system in Regattas, shall be best."

Boats. *See* Canoeing, Cruising, Sailing, Yachting.

Bobsleigh Riding. *See* Winter Sports.

Bowling. *See* Skittles.

Bowls.

Bowls, one of the oldest of all games, was once regarded as " an old man's game," but it actually has many devotees of all ages and both sexes, and is played indoors as well as outdoors. It certainly goes back to the thirteenth century, when its popularity made it one of the games legislated against as likely to draw people away from archery. Henry VIII played; and the famous game on Plymouth Hoe, in which Sir John Hawkins stayed to beat Sir Francis Drake even after the Armada had been sighted, if not definitely authenticated, is accepted as fact by several historians. It is interesting to note that, if this game was played, it would have been almost identical with a game of to-day, for it was in that century that the " bias " that is a leading feature of the bowls or " woods " was introduced. A century later, however, Bowls, which was largely played on greens attached to taverns, acquired a reputation as being merely an adjunct to pot-house revelry, but it was revived on a higher level in Scotland, and never again came so near to oblivion.

There are actually two games of Bowls, the Rink or Level Green game and the Crown Green game, and it is the rinks rather than the objectives that differ. The Level Green game is the more widely played, and it takes place on a perfectly flat piece of well-cared-for turf. The Crown Green game, which is popular in the North and Midlands, is played on a green of which the centre is 6 inches or more higher than the corners. The games differ—for instance, in the putting into play of the object ball—but only slightly, so it will be appreciated that the Crown Green game demands a good deal of experience and skill. It is mainly a singles game, whereas the Level Green game is played between sides consisting of one, two, three, or four players.

Bowls looks a simple game, the object being simply to place the bowls as near as possible to the object ball, or " jack." The bowls, however, are " biased," and the game is actually one of considerable skill. When bias was introduced, it took the form of weighting with lead, but it is now achieved by turning one side of the bowl less round than the other. Level Green bowls weigh up to 3½ lb., but Crown Green bowls are smaller and less biased. On the Crown Green, however, the jack, which is played into position by the first player, is also biased.

Players normally use two bowls in a game, or four in singles, and the side with the best record of bowls near the jack wins the " end," and the best record of shots in an agreed number of ends the game.

A Bowls green is such a perfect piece of grass that it might be thought that the expression " rub of the green," used to describe an unavoidable piece of bad luck, comes from this game. In actual fact, though, it would probably be more correct to attribute this phrase to Golf (*q.v.*).

Boxing.

Boxing, sometimes called " The Noble Art of Self Defence," though actually aggression is its keynote and defence an incidental, is a modern continuation of the old sport of prize-fighting, which, though always illegal, was popular from the time of the Regency until it was succeeded by the present-day glove-fighting at the end of the nineteenth century.

In prize-fighting bare fists were used, and wrestling holds were allowed. Rounds ended when a fighter went down, and fights continued until, following a knockdown, a man failed to come up to the scratch line in 30 seconds.

In modern boxing, gloves are worn, and no wrestling is allowed. Rounds last for a fixed time, generally 3 minutes with 1 minute between rounds, and fights last only for a fixed number of rounds, never more than fifteen. A knockdown does not end a round, the man who is down having 10 seconds in which to rise. If he fails to do so, his opponent wins by a knock-out. If a man fails to come up at the beginning of a round or if the fight is stopped to save a man from further injury, the victory is by a technical knock-out. If, however, both men are still on their feet at the end of the stipulated number of rounds, a decision is given on points. Boxing is therefore technically a contest of skill for points, and, as such, far removed from prize-fights to a finish.

Fights are controlled by a referee, and, in British professional boxing, he is solely responsible for any points decision. In amateur boxing the decision is given by several judges, who sit apart from each other. The difference between a good professional and a good amateur is probably more marked in boxing than in any other sport.

Boxing contests are arranged in classes according to weight, the divisions being: fly-weight, up to 8 stone; bantam-weight, up to 8 stone 6 lb.; feather-weight, up to 9 stone; light-weight, up to 9 stone 9 lb.; welter-weight, up to 10 stone 7 lb.; middle-weight, up to 11 stone 6 lb.; light-heavy or cruiser-weight, up to 12 stone 7 lb.; and heavy-weight, any weight. In amateur boxing some of these weights are slightly different, and there are two additional classes, light-welter-weight, up to 10 stone, and light-middle-weight, up to 11 stone.

Prize-fighting was governed successively by " Broughton's Code," the " New Rules of the Ring," and the " London Rules." Then, in 1867, the eighth Marquess of Queensberry and Mr. J. G. Chambers drew up the rules that have been the basis of boxing ever since. British professional boxing has been controlled since 1929 by the British Boxing Board of Control. The Amateur

Boxing Association has governed amateur boxing since 1884, when it took over from the Amateur Athletic Club, which had looked after both boxing and athletics.

Prize-fighting is finished, but it has left a legacy, not only in modern boxing, but through an expression that has become part of the language, for the phrase " come up to scratch " originally referred to a prize-fighter stepping up for a new round.

### Bridge.

Bridge is probably about one hundred years old, but though it clearly developed from Whist, its exact origin is unknown. Similar games were played in Denmark, Turkey, Egypt, and Russia, and it first appeared in Britain as Dutch Whist in 1884. It was subsequently known as Russian Whist and Biritch. Then in 1895 the first Bridge rules appeared, followed in 1908 by rules for a new version, Auction Bridge. A third version, Contract Bridge, was known before the First World War, reached Britain just after it, and acquired international rules in 1929. During the 1930s all three forms were played. The object of each succeeding version was to make the game less one of chance and more one of skill. Contract now supplanted them all and this is the game we shall describe.

Two partnerships of two oppose each other, and as the names Auction and Contract imply, the playing of each hand is preceded by an auction in which players bid, or refrain from bidding, on the value of their hands to decide which pair will attempt to make how many tricks with what trumps, or with no trumps.

The suits have different values, the order being spades, hearts (known as major suits), diamonds, clubs (minor suits), but no trumps takes absolute precedence.

Originally, spades were the lowest suit, and when spades bids prevailed players took to throwing in their cards and giving the caller the points rather than play such a low scoring hand. To prevent this, spades were given a value which made them the top suit.

A feature of the actual play is that the member of the pair whose bid prevails who first named the successful suit plays the hand alone, playing both his own cards and his partner's, which are placed face upwards on the table after the first card has been played.

Bridge terms the beginner should know include: *bid*, an offer to make so many tricks in a particular suit or with no trumps; *auction*, the bidding process; *contract*, the last and prevailing bid; *forcing bid*, a bid which forces the player's partner to bid and keep the auction open; *take out*, a bid in a suit other than that bid by the player's partner; *system* or *convention*, the bidding system used by a pair; *the book*, the first six tricks won by a pair, which do not count towards the contract—a bid of one means, in fact, seven; *declarer*, the player of the pair whose bid prevails who first named the successful suit; *dummy*, declarer's partner; *defender*, during the auction, a member of the pair which did not open the bidding, during play, an opponent of the declarer; *game*, 100 points; *rubber*, two games won by a pair; *vulnerable*, a partnership which has won a game becomes vulnerable; *overtrick*, a trick won in excess of the contract; *undertrick*, a trick by which the contract fails; *grand slam*, 13 tricks bid and won; *small slam*, 12 tricks bid and won; *trump*, a card of the contract suit; *ruff*, to trump; *tenace*, two cards not in sequence which may win two tricks, but may win only one. Other terms, not peculiar to Bridge, include: *void*, no cards of a suit; *singleton*, one card of a suit; *doubleton*, two cards of a suit; *honour*, ace, king, queen, knave, or ten; *yarborough*, a hand with no honours; *revoke*, failure to follow suit when able to do so.

A Bridge score-sheet has a line across it, and points are scored above or below the line. Only points towards game go below the line, these being points for contracts made. Diamonds and clubs count 20 per trick (over six), spades and hearts 30, and no trumps 40 for the first trick and 30 for each subsequent one. When a game is won, points below the line revert to nothing. Above the line go points for tricks won in excess of the contract; for tricks by which opponents fail to make contracts; for winning a rubber; for slams (if bid); and for holding four aces in no trumps or four or five honours in a trump suit in one hand. Being vulnerable affects the points, as does the fact that bids may be doubled by opponents, then redoubled by the bidding pair. It might seem that points for honours in a hand are a gift for a piece of pure luck, but there is more to it than that. A player holding four honours might be tempted to go to almost any lengths to have the hand played in that suit, when, in fact, it might pay him better to play in, or against, another suit and forego the honours bonus.

In addition to rubber Bridge, there is duplicate Bridge, in which several pairs play the same hands. For those who have reached a certain standard, this is excellent for spotlighting weaknesses in one's play. As there are no rubbers, points are scored for games. Rubber Bridge is generally played for money, though the stakes can be quite small, duplicate Bridge is not.

Bridge suffers from a certain " mystique " which frightens some people. They hear of " card sense " and fear they might not have it. Actually, the only qualities required are commonsense and concentration; and card sense comes from playing cards. It is fairly widely believed that women make better players than men at all levels up to the very top, where the men take over. The bidding systems or conventions by which players give or request information also frighten people; and, in earlier days, these made supporters of the older versions describe Contract as a game for cheats, though, of course, it is not. In addition to the actual laws, there are a number of proprieties which must be observed. Regular partners must not devise their own private bidding system. Only recognised systems may be used, and these must be communicated to the opponents. Unorthodox bids may be made, but not by prior arrangement with one's partner. There are almost countless conventions, and, in the very top class, players have an imposing list beside them. Beginners will soon learn those used in their own circles.

There are professional Bridge teachers, and it is also possible (though not easy) to learn from books. Most people, though, learn at home, having a few lessons from friends and then learning by playing. The first thing to learn is how to value a hand, and this is done either by allocating points to cards or, more effectively, by assessing the tricks. Some players assess only honour tricks, but, as honours take, on average, only eight of the 13 tricks, this is not really sufficient. The value given to the hand may have to be readjusted on hearing the partner's bids. It is important to bid up to the full value of the combined hands.

There are countless Bridge clubs, many quite small and informal, and some limiting novices to very small stakes until a certain standard has been reached. Eventually, more people will probably learn at school for unlike most card games Bridge is encouraged in many schools, and the English Bridge Union runs an annual schools' tournament.

### Bumping Races. *See* Boat Races.

### Camping.

Camping expresses the townsman's desire to get away from cities and fend for himself in quiet. But some organisation is necessary to provide camping facilities and to maintain high standards. The Camping Club of Great Britain has a membership of over 50,000. Its work is twofold: it selects sites suitable for mobile campers and caravanners; and establishes and maintains well-equipped permanent camping grounds. A *Sites List* published annually contains details of 2,000 camp sites. Members agree to abide by the Club's Code of Campers, which stresses the need of the camper to pay full regard to the countryman's way of life and to maintain by country courtesy the goodwill of those among whom he camps. The Club's address is 35 Old Kent Road, London, S.E.1.

## Canadian Football.

Canadian Football resembles American (*q.v.*), but is twelve-aside, uses only three downs, and limits blocking.

## Canoeing.

Canoeing is both a recreation and an organised competitive sport.

As a recreation, it can take the form either of simply taking a canoe out and "paddling about" for a short period or, by combining it with Camping (*q.v.*), of a lengthy and interesting river trip, the canoe-camper proceeding, of course, at his own pace, and giving as much time as he wishes to sightseeing.

As a sport, Canoeing has Olympic Games status. In Britain it has its headquarters on the Thames at Teddington in Middlesex, the governing body being the British Canoe Union. There are races for singles and pairs, including events for women. There is also one long annual race for pairs that really combines Canoeing with Camping. The course is from Devizes in Wiltshire to London, and the competitors have to negotiate a long series of locks.

There are two types of canoe: Canadian canoes, like those used for many years by Red Indians, and kayaks, the very light Eskimo-type canoes, in which an expert, but not a beginner, can turn a complete circle into the water and out again without losing his seat in his craft. Both types are catered for in the Olympic Games, but most of the Canoeing in Britain is in kayaks.

Card Games. *See* Bridge; Patience; Solo Whist; Whist.

## Chess.

Chess, greatest of all board games and a game of pure skill, has a known history of some 1500 years. Eastern players, who originated it, reached a high standard, but the game's greatest advances were made in Italy in the fifteenth and sixteenth centuries. In the early days the value of the pieces and their moves underwent periodical changes, but the game we know to-day dates from the sixteenth century.

The board has 64 squares in eight rows of eight, and each player has 16 pieces, one set being white and the other black or red, but always referred to as black. A toss decides possession of white, which always starts. The object is the capture of the opponent's King, no matter how many pieces are lost in doing so, nor how many opposing pieces remain untaken. If the King could be captured on the next move, it is in "check." It must be released from check (by moving, by covering, or by capture of the checking piece), otherwise it is "checkmate" and the game is over. If the King is not in check, but cannot move except into check, and the player has no other pieces he can move, it is "stalemate," and a draw. Games may also be drawn if neither player has sufficient pieces to force a win.

In addition to the King, each player has a Queen, two Bishops, two Rooks—sometimes wrongly called Castles—two Knights, and eight Pawns, and all these move in accordance with rigid rules. The following diagram shows the pieces at the start of a game:

BLACK

(The initial position as seen by White)

Each line of squares across the board is a "rank," and each line up and down the board is a "file."

The permitted moves are as follows:—

The King can move one square at a time in any direction.

The Queen can move in accordance with the powers described below for both Bishops and Rooks.

The Bishops move diagonally as many squares as desired.

The Rooks move straight along the ranks or files as far as desired.

The Knights move as shown in the following diagram:—

(The Knight's Move)

Stationed away from the side of the board, and on a black square, the Knight illustrated can move to any of the numbered white squares. The move is one square along rank or file in the desired direction, and one square diagonally. The

Pawns move straight forward, one square at a time, but may move two squares when moved for the first time. They capture by moving one square diagonally forwards. A Pawn reaching the eighth rank may be replaced by any other piece.

Once during a game, a player may "Castle," by moving the King two squares towards the Rook, which is placed on the last square passed over by the King. This move cannot be made if either the King or any of the squares he would pass over are in check. Neither King nor Rook must have moved previously.

Games of Chess can be recorded, so players can play over great "Masters" games, and record their own games.

*Draughts.* Draughts—called Checkers in America—is also played on a chess board. Possibly older even than Chess, it is much simpler, but not devoid of skill.

Each player has twelve pieces or "men," all alike. Squares of one colour only are used, the men starting on the first three rows on the board. The move is one square diagonally forward, but a man reaching the eighth row becomes a "King," and may then move forward or backward. The object is the capture of all the opposing men by jumping over them. If the arrangement of the men permits it, more than one man may be captured in a single move. A man which can effect a capture but does not do so is removed from the board, or "huffed."

### Cricket.

Cricket, traditionally England's national game, has a longer history than most team games. There have been attempts to trace its origin in various games played by ancient races; and, even if some of these derivations are a little far-fetched, it certainly developed from very old country games, and has been played in a form not so very dissimilar from that of to-day for over 250 years. The men of Hampshire, particularly the village of Hambledon, Surrey and Kent were the real pioneers of the cricket of to-day.

Cricket is played by two teams of eleven players, which bat and field in turn. In the centre of the ground are two "wickets," 22 yards apart, and each consisting of three "stumps," joined at the top by two "bails." The bats used have a flat striking surface, and the ball is a hard red one weighing 5 ounces.

There is a batsman at each wicket, and their object is the scoring of runs by hitting the ball away, and running before it can be returned, each time the two batsmen cover the length of the pitch counting as one run. Should the ball be hit beyond the boundary line round the ground, it counts four or, if it crosses the line without touching the ground, six.

The ball is "bowled" from one wicket to the batsman at the other, six balls, or, in some cases, eight, which comprise an "over," being bowled from each end in turn. The object of the fielding side is to get the batsmen "out," ten dismissals completing the "innings" as the eleventh man is left without a partner.

A batsman can be dismissed in several ways. If he misses the ball and it hits the wicket, or if he plays it on to the wicket, he is out "bowled." If he leaves his ground, indicated by a line in front of the wicket, misses the ball, and has the wicket "broken" by the wicket-keeper he is out "stumped." If he hits the wicket with his bat he is out "hit wicket." If his hit is caught he is out "caught." If, when running, he fails to reach his ground before the wicket is "broken" he is out "run out." If a ball, when bowled, would have hit his wicket, but hits his leg instead, then, subject to certain provisions regarding where the ball actually pitched, he is out "leg-before-wicket." A batsman may also be given out if he handles the ball or obstructs the fielding side, but these are rare occurrences.

In addition to runs hit by the batsmen, there are certain "extras." If the ball passes the bat, misses the wicket, and goes far enough for the batsmen to run, it is a "bye." If, however, it goes off the batsman's leg it is a "leg-bye," but leg-byes cannot be run unless the batsman was definitely attempting a stroke. If it is bowled so wide that the batsman cannot reach it, it is a "wide." If the bowler comes in front of his wicket before releasing the ball, or if he throws it,

it is a "no-ball," in which case the umpire calls it as quickly as he can, for the batsman can hit such a ball, but he cannot be out to it, unless he is run out. If he does not score, one extra is added.

Of the fielding side, one, of course, is the bowler, and another, placed behind the batsman's wicket, is the wicket-keeper. The others will be placed as the bowler and his captain decide, for there are far more recognised positions than can be occupied at one time. To gain some idea of these positions, imagine a right-handed batsman at the wicket, his left side towards the bowler. The side of the wicket in front of him, nearer to his bat than to his body, is the "off" side; the side behind him, nearer to his body than to his bat, the "leg" side. On the off, behind the wicket and close to it, are the "slips," and, behind them, "third man." Farther round, but still behind the bat and close to it, is "gully." Level with the bat is "point" or, if he is some way from the bat, "deep point." In front of the bat, but in front also of the bowler's wicket, is "cover" and "extra cover." Roughly level with the bowler's wicket is "mid-off," with, behind him, "long off." Similarly on the leg side, where "long on" is the equivalent of "long off," "mid-on" of "mid-off," "mid-wicket" and "deep mid-wicket" of "cover" and "extra cover," "square leg" and "deep square leg" of "point" and "deep point," "short leg" of "gully," "long leg" of "third man," and "leg slip" of "slip."

First-class cricket matches last for three six-hour days or longer, but there are also two-day, one-day, and half-day matches. Matches of two days or more are two-innings games; of one day or half a day, one innings. If the side batting first, which is decided by a toss that gives the winner the choice of batting or fielding first, dismisses the opposing side for a smaller score, the victory is by the number of runs by which the smaller score was exceeded. If the side batting second pass the other total, the game ends, and the victory is by the number of wickets the second side still have standing. In a two-innings match, should the side batting first gain a first-innings lead of a certain size, normally 150 runs in a three-day match, it can require the other side to follow straight on with its second innings, the leading team keeping its second innings in reserve, to be played if needed. If a batting side has sufficient runs, and is anxious to see the other side batting while there is still plenty of time to dismiss it, it can declare its innings closed. In this case, should the second team score enough runs to win, it does, in fact, win, even though it may have lost more wickets than had the declaring side.

Cricket is not a fast-moving game, and for years views have been expressed to the effect that it must be "brightened up" if it is not to die out. Periodically, small changes in the rules are made; but, for the most part, the game just goes steadily on, easily retaining a large following that is satisfied with it as it is, and still able, when big international matches take place, to command a place, not only on the sports pages, but on the front pages of the Press.

The game is unusual in that it has no really official governing body. It is ruled by the M.C.C., which stands simply for Marylebone Cricket Club, from its headquarters at Lord's ground in London; and the M.C.C.'s pronouncements are accepted almost without question.

Outside England, the development of cricket has been peculiar. Even as near at hand as Scotland and Ireland, the game has never aroused much enthusiasm; and in Continental Europe, where many British games have won great acclaim, cricket has gained a real foothold only in the Netherlands and Denmark. In the United States and Canada it is played, but only to a small extent. However, in Australia, South Africa, New Zealand, the West Indies, India, and Pakistan, it is extremely popular; and the national teams of these countries, together with England, provide the top-class international sides of the game. They meet regularly in "Test Matches," a "rubber" normally being decided in a series of five Tests. *See* U34.

Cricket is rich in technical terms and expressions, which are seen and heard frequently through newspapers, television, and radio when a Test series is in progress. Many of these are almost self-explanatory, but a few never fail to puzzle less-experienced readers, viewers, and listeners. Prominent amongst these are three types of ball used by bowlers, the " yorker," the " googly," and the " chinaman."

A yorker is a fast ball that pitches just in the batsman's block-hole, and often passes under his defensive stroke. The term is believed to have originated in Yorkshire, but the only known explanation of it is that attributed to a Yorkshire cricketer, who, asked why a yorker was so called, replied simply, " Well, what else would you call it? " There is an answer to that, for the yorker was originally known as a " tice." A googly is an off-break or a leg-break which is disguised, because the bowler has delivered the one with the action of the other. A chinaman is an off-break bowled by a left-handed bowler to a right-handed batsman. These words also lack an authentic derivation.

Cricket has provided one expression that is now heard in many connections. That is " hat-trick," which dates back to the days when cricketers wore top-hats, and any player who took three wickets with three successive balls was presented with a white top-hat. Now, he is usually given the ball.

### Croquet.

Croquet originated in France, and has been played in Britain for about a century. The governing body, the All-England Croquet Club, was founded in 1868, with headquarters at Wimbledon. Soon afterwards, this also became the head-

STANDARD SETTING.

*Only those portions indicated by a continuous line need be marked on the court.*
*The order of making the points is indicated by the arrows.*

quarters of Lawn Tennis (q.v.), and it is probable that the rapid growth of that game was a factor that restricted the development of Croquet. Croquet, however, still retains a following, and, in addition to Championships and tournaments, it is widely played on private lawns.

The equipment consists of four balls, coloured blue, black, yellow, and red; four mallets, usually marked with the same colours; six hoops; and a peg. The playing area is 35 yards by 28 yards, but this can be reduced, provided that the proportion remains 5 to 4. The hoops, which stand 1 foot out of the ground, and the peg are placed as shown in the diagram. Generally two players, taking the blue and black balls, oppose two using the yellow and red, but singles can be played, each player using two balls, blue being paired with

black, and yellow with red. Each player completes the circuit of hoops twice, finishing by hitting the peg.

Croquet is a game of skill, and players can earn extra turns in various ways, such as hitting another ball with their own or passing through hoops. While making their own circuits, players also concentrate on leaving their opponents at a disadvantage. Handicap matches are possible through the giving of extra turns, or " bisques." A " half-bisque " is an extra turn in which no hoop may be scored.

Croquet can, perhaps, claim some credit for a phrase used in everyday life. " Pegging out " has the rather sinister meaning of " dying " or " finishing," but it is actually the term used for finishing a Croquet round by hitting the peg.

### Cross-country. *See Athletics.*

### Cruising on Inland Waterways.

For those who want a touring holiday in Britain away from crowded roads, but who do not want to walk or ride, cruising on inland waterways offers a pleasant and interesting alternative. Facilities are available on a number of canals, rivers, and, of course, the Norfolk Broads; and motor-cruisers can be hired, complete with sleeping accommodation, bed linen, and cooking utensils. At some places, for example, the upper reaches of the Thames, those who prefer to do so can hire cruisers without sleeping accommodation, and spend the nights at riverside inns. The Inland Waterways Association exists to keep the waterways open and, where possible, to re-open others. Particulars of available facilities can be obtained from the Association at 114 Regent's Park Road, London, N.W.1.

### Cycling.

As a pleasant recreation, cycling offers a wide range of possibilities. Outings can be for a day or part of a day, or they can be tours of any length the rider wishes, with the overnight halts spent in hotels or hostels or Camping (q.v.), which can easily be combined with cycling.

As a competitive sport, cycling offers a remarkable variety, for no other form of racing provides events of so many different types. On the Continent, cycle racing is by far the most popular sport, and the leading riders are national heroes. The sport, which caters for both amateurs and professionals, also has a large following in Britain, where it would soon make progress still farther if there were more tracks suitable for big events available.

Cycle races are held on banked tracks rather like motor-racing tracks, on flat grass tracks, on cinder tracks, on indoor banked board tracks, on roads, and even across country. There are races at all distances, from short sprints to road tours divided into daily stages lasting for several weeks. There are massed-start races, in which all the competitors start together; races in which competitors are drawn in twos or threes through several rounds up to a final; and time trials, in which each rider starts alone. Track races may be straightforward races or time trials; or motor-paced, with the riders behind motor-cycles; or tandem-paced; or pursuit races, with riders or teams of riders starting on opposite sides of or spaced round the track; or point-to-point, with points awarded to the leaders at the end of each lap; or courses des primes, with a prize for the leader at the end of each lap; or Madison races, for teams of two, and occasionally three, riding one at a time, and relieving each other at will. There are also races for tandems and tricycles; and the sport includes races on both track and road for women as well as men.

In the cross-country side of cycle racing, called Cyclo-Cross, riders cover a cross-country course of perhaps 10 miles, riding when they can and carrying their machines where riding is impossible. Still another form of cycle racing is roller racing. In this, the cycles are fixed on rollers, and do not move at all, the distance the riders pedal being registered on large dials. There is also cycle speedway, a sport devised by youths, and practised only by youths. Events take the form of team matches, generally on rough cinder tracks constructed on waste ground by the youths themselves, with pairs of riders opposing rival pairs in a series of races, and points awarded to the leaders in each race. Corners have to be "skidded" round, as they sometimes are in ordinary grass-track cycle racing. Very different, but still competitive in a way, is a form of event that provides a link between the sporting side of cycling and the more purely recreational side, the reliability trial or attempt to achieve a fixed standard.

Cycling also has its team game in Bicycle Polo, a hard game requiring a high level of cycling skill and considerable nerve.

There is also an organisation that caters especially for the distance tourist in the Cyclists' Touring Club, which keeps a check on premises offering accommodation to cycle tourists, and provides a sign for use on approved accommodation. It is interesting to note that the Automobile Association, which offers similar services to motorists, but which is not as long-established as the C.T.C., originally based its methods on those of the C.T.C. The address of the C.T.C. national headquarters is Cotterell House, 69 Meadow, Godalming, Surrey. The office for travel facilities is C.T.C. Travel Ltd., 13 Spring Street, Paddington, London, W.2.

## Darts.

Originally just a casual amusement confined almost entirely to public-houses, the game of Darts is now one of Britain's most popular pastimes. Public-houses still provide facilities for it, but to-day clubs, canteens, factories, offices, and private houses also have their boards, and there are numerous team and individual competitions, including a National Championship. The prizes rival those of any other game for value, matches are widely reported, and the attendance for the bigger contests is limited only by the size of the hall. This enthusiasm is not misplaced, for the game is a test of skill, and luck plays little part in it.

The circular board has a diameter of 18 inches, and is divided into segments numbered from 1 to 20, but not consecutively. In addition, there are two rings, each ⅜ inch wide, that go right round the board and through each segment. These are the "double" ring, at the extremity of the board, and the "treble" ring, near the centre of the board, darts in these rings counting double or treble the value of the segment. In the centre of the board there are two small rings, the "bull" or "dosser," counting 50, and the "outer," counting 25. The bull is 5 feet 8 inches from the ground, and the wooden or metal feathered darts are thrown from a line, called the "hockey," 9 feet away.

Matches may be singles, doubles, or between teams of four or eight players. Games are for a certain number of points, usually 101, 201, 301, 501, 801 or 1001, the lower totals being used for individual, and the higher for team contests, and matches are generally the best two out of three games or "legs." Conditions for matches vary, but normally stipulate either "straight start and finish on a double" or "start and finish on a double." In the first case players score from the start, but in the second they do not score until one double has been registered. In both cases they must finish on a double, and they must finish with the exact number they require. Scores are counted downwards, players being told how many they need, rather than how many they have scored.

In addition to the straightforward game, there are many Darts variations. In one, "Round the Clock," a player has to throw one dart into each segment from 1 to either 20 or the bull, his turn continuing until he throws three darts unsuccessfully. In "Shanghai," players start with a complete throw of three darts at number 1, and continue with a throw at every number up to 9, but players who fail to score at number 5 drop out. In "Cricket," one player "bats," throwing normally, and counting everything over 40, while the other "bowls," throwing only at the bull, and counting one wicket for every "outer" and two for every "bull," five wickets ending his opponent's "innings." In a Darts version of Shove-Ha'penny players have to get three darts in each segment from 1 to 9, and three in the centre. In "Fives," players score only if their total is divisible by five.

## Diving. *See* Swimming.

## Dominoes.

Dominoes are similar in many ways to cards, in that many games can be played with them with varying degrees of skill. Players play (or *pose* or *down*) in turn from hands. The game was introduced in Europe by way of Italy in the 18th century, though the actual games as they are played today, and also the scoring methods, are of French origin.

The domino itself (called a *card* or *stone*) is oblong with its face divided by a centre line and marked in each half by indented dots. A set normally consists of 28 pieces, respectively marked 6–6 (double six), 6–5, 6–4, 6–3, 6–2, 6–1, 6–0, 5–5, 5–4, 5–3, 5–2, 5–1, 5–0, 4–4, 4–3, 4–2, 4–1, 4–0, 3–3, 3–2, 3–1, 3–0, 2–2, 2–1, 2–0, 1–1, 1–0, 0–0 (double blank). (There are special sets for games consisting of 55 pieces, running up to 9–9, and 85 pieces, running as high as 12–12).

In the common form of the game, using 28 pieces, the dominoes are laid face downwards on the table, each player taking seven, the rest being left as a reserve. A player stands his hand so that the faces of his pieces are visible to him but not to his opponents. The idea of the game is to match the number on one domino-half to that of the free half of a piece already played on the table. Pieces are laid end to end but double pieces are laid transversely and allow the player an extra turn. The winner is the one who plays all his pieces.

Variations include playing a piece that is not the same as the one to which it is fitted, but that, with it, adds up to seven, or one that will make the two ends of the line add up five or a multiple of five, or three or a multiple of three. Another variation makes the double-blank and any piece on which the two halves add up to seven *matadors*. These are the equivalent of the card player's *wild* cards, and may be played at any time.

In some games, a player who cannot play simply misses the turn, while, in others, he may draw from the reserve, having, of course, to retain the domino in his hand if he still cannot play.

Games are for two, three, four or more players; and, in some of those for four players, two play together against the other two, each player trying to block his opponents, but to assist his partner.

As with cards, solitary players can play Patience, and this is a good way for a beginner to learn how to play a hand. The player picks five dominoes from a shuffled set, starts with any piece he chooses, and then continues to play in the normal way. When he cannot play, he draws enough pieces from the reserve to make his hand up to five and carries on, continuing until either he can play out or cannot play at all from the pieces left.

In the more skilful games, as in the more skilful games of cards, a good memory is an asset, as it is essential to remember which player played which piece. Despite the claims of many more modern pastimes, dominoes is gaining in popularity, particularly in such places as works' canteens.

## Drama.

Few countries can boast so eager an interest in amateur drama as Britain, and it is estimated that there are some 20,000 groups in the British Isles with half a million membership. The cardinal influence in this enormous movement is the British Drama League, to which some 3,500 groups belong besides nearly 2,000 private individuals.

The league's influence on drama is exercised in two ways. Its members have the use of the library, which possesses the largest collection of plays and books on the threatre in Great Britain and of its information services, which give help and advice on every conceivable dramatic topic. They can, of course, hire sets of plays (one copy for each character up to twelve.) Then there are the league's training schemes. Courses in production, acting, and décor take place in London all the year round, and there are summer courses in the country. The address of B.D.L. is 9–10 Fitzroy Square, London, W.1.

It was not until the great International Theatre Exhibition at the Victoria and Albert Museum in 1922 that the English public became fully aware of the " new man " who had arrived in the theatre —the " producer " or " director," as the Americans call him. It is the producer who decides how the play is to be produced and sets his signature upon it, very much like the conductor of an orchestra. In this task he unifies the work of the author, actors, designers, and craftsmen of various kinds. The technical side of staging a play is a fascinating one involving problems of the framework (the stage, sight lines, auditorium); curtain settings, lighting, skycloths; the construction of scenery; designing the scenery and the making of scale plans and models; painting the scenery; lighting, and so on.

Television offers new opportunities for the playwriting aspirant, with its need for new methods. In the theatre the playwright and actor must make all things plain to distant members of an audience—whereas the television actor's slightest change of expression is clear to the person sitting within a couple of yards of him. A wink, a nod, a shrug on the television screen suffice for the implications which would be lost in the theatre. The gearing, so to speak, between text and meaning is different. A new field opens, therefore, for the writer for television drama.

**Draughts.** *See* Chess.

**Eton Fives.** *See* Fives.

**Fencing.**

Fencing can claim a longer history than most sports, for it is the modern equivalent of duelling. In mediæval tournaments mounted knights fought with lances, and, in addition to actual fights to the death, they also met with special, less lethal lances purely for sport. Later, duels were fought dismounted, and with different weapons. In Elizabethan days duellists used a sword, for attacking, in the right hand, and a dagger, for defence, in the left. Later still, the dagger was discarded, and duels were fought, as are fencing bouts to-day, with a sword only.

Duelling declined in Britain during the Regency period, when it became fashionable for gentlemen to learn to fight with their fists, but they continued to learn swordsmanship, and to fence with the practice weapon, the foil. Eventually, duelling became illegal almost throughout the world, but swordsmen of other countries similarly continued to fence with the foil. Even before Britain took to fist-fighting, most of the advances in fencing technique had been made in France and Italy, and the fencers of these and other Continental countries are still the best in the world, countries like Britain and the United States relying largely on fencers of Continental European descent.

Duelling was restricted to " gentlemen," and something of this restricted atmosphere pervaded the early days of fencing as a sport, clubs being few, expensive, and rather exclusive. Now, however, that has changed, and widespread class tuition in fencing has opened the sport to anyone.

Modern fencing includes contests with three weapons: the foil, which is the only one used by women; the épée, the real duelling sword; and the sabre, which cuts as well as thrusts. These weapons have " buttons " on the points, but fencers wear a special glove, a padded jacket, and a mask. Fencing requires grace of movement,

lightness of foot, agility, strength of wrist and forearm, quick mental reactions, and good eyesight; and it will do much to develop these qualities, including the eyesight. As masks are worn, it is perfectly practicable to fence wearing glasses.

**Figure Skating.** *See* Skating.

**Fives.**

There are two games of Fives, Eton Fives and Rugby Fives. They are court games using walls, but an Eton Fives court has the addition of a buttress or " pepper " jutting out from one side wall. The striking implement is the gloved hand. Eton Fives is a doubles game, but both singles and doubles are played in Rugby Fives.

**Folk Song and Dance.**

Whether or not you play, sing, or dance yourself, you can enjoy the heritage of English folk music, song, and dance. To enable you to enjoy it to the full the story of Cecil Sharp House will be useful. Cecil Sharp went out to collect the folk songs of England in the fields and cottages, in almshouses, and by the roadside. He systematically combed some counties like Somerset. Cecil Sharp and Vaughan Williams joined the English Song Society, which had had Elgar and Parry among its first members. Sharp went on to note down folk dances and to publish details of the steps and figures. In course of time he founded the English Folk Dance Society to restore their traditional dances to the people of England. The two Societies amalgamated in 1932 and, today, Cecil Sharp House (2 Regents Park Road, London, N.W.1) is the home of the English Folk Dance and Song Society, with over 12,000 members.

Scottish Dancing and singing are the primary objectives of special holidays by the Holiday Fellowship at Scottish centres; and Old Time Dancing is enjoyed at an English Centre. Folk dancing is also the feature of special holidays by the Cooperative Holidays Association.

**Football.** *See* American Football; Association Football; Australian Rules Football; Canadian Football; Gaelic Football; Public-School Football; Rugby Football.

**Gaelic Football.**

Gaelic Football is seldom played by anyone who is not Irish, but it is frequently played outside Ireland, for Irishmen have taken it with them to Britain, the United States, Australia, and South Africa.

Played fifteen-aside, it is a blend of Association and Rugby Football (*q.v.*), the goals having the uprights, cross-bar, and net, exactly as in Association, but having the uprights extended above the cross-bar, as in Rugby. If the ball goes under the cross-bar it is a goal, and if it goes over it is a point, a goal equalling three points. The ball is round, and it may be kicked or caught, but not thrown forward, nor carried, though it may be dribbled by bouncing it. In its essentials, it is probably simpler than most other forms of football, but it is fast and involves frequent hard bodily contact. Substitutes are permitted in case of injury.

Gaelic Football joins with Hurling (*q.v.*) in coming under the old-established Gaelic Athletic Association.

**Gliding.**

The first serious efforts to develop Gliding which is flying in engineless aircraft or sailplanes making use of natural air currents, took place in Germany in 1919, and were successful enough to lead to experiments in France and England, where it arrived in 1922. At that time, however, it failed to gain much support, and the real history of gliding in Britain dates from a second attempt to encourage it in 1929. Little more than ten years later, gliding had advanced sufficiently to be a real factor in the second World War.

Skilful use of up-currents enables the glider pilot to stay up, and if the air is rising faster than the glider is sinking, the glider will climb.

Gliders can now reach altitudes of over 40,000 feet, stay in the air for over 50 hours, and carry out flights of hundreds of miles. The flying of sailplanes apart from being an exhilarating sport has made important contributions to aeronautical and meteorological research.

## Golf.

Golf, a game of great antiquity, originated in Scotland, and is now widely popular in many countries. It consists of using a set of clubs with which to play a small white ball over a cross-country course of eighteen holes. Each hole will be several hundred yards long, and will have its fixed starting-point and its finish with an actual hole in the ground, the object being to complete the course, which will be several miles long, in as few strokes as possible.

The playing of each hole falls into three sections, driving, approaching, and putting. The starting-point will be a flat piece of ground on which the player will " tee up " his ball on a small rubber peg, or " tee," which he will carry round with him. He will then hit the ball towards the hole, concentrating on achieving distance. From the tee to near the hole is the " fairway," which will consist of fairly smooth ground, not entirely devoid of natural obstacles, and probably containing some sand traps, or " bunkers." On each side of the fairway is the " rough," which may consist of long grass, shrubs, woods, or even roads. The player will continue to play his ball towards the hole, concentrating now chiefly on direction. On the fairway or off it, he should always play his ball where it lies, but, should it be quite unplayable, or even lost, he may drop it or a new one, and pay a stroke penalty for the privilege. The actual hole will be on the " green," a rough circle of exceptionally well tended grass, and, once on it, the player will cover the last few yards by the more delicate art of " putting."

There are many different types of club, players being limited to fourteen. The shafts are generally steel, the striking surfaces being iron or, in the case of drivers, wood. The different " irons " have numbers, but golf clubs used to have special names, often descriptive of their functions, for instance, lofter, cleek, mashie, niblick, and even blaster. Originally, most golf courses were by the sea, and these were called " links," a term now loosely applied to any course.

There are two actual methods of competitive play, match play and medal play. Match play is by holes, a player completing any hole in fewer strokes than his opponent winning that hole. Once a player leads by more holes than there are still to play, the game finishes, the victory being by X and Y, where X is the number of holes he is " up," and Y the lesser number of unplayed holes. When a player leads by the same number of holes as there are still to play he is said to be " dormy " so many. Opponents level after eighteen holes proceed to the first hole, and play on until one is one hole up, when he is said to have won at the 19th, 20th, or whatever it may be. Some important match-play events are over 36 holes, or two complete rounds. Medal play is simply stroke play, the result depending on the number of strokes needed to complete the course. This demands a higher level of consistency, for one bad spell can ruin the total, whereas, in match play, it may cost only one hole. In play after the initial drive, the player farthest from the hole normally plays before his opponent.

In match-play championships and tournaments players are drawn against each other, the winners going on to the next round, and so on up to the final. In medal-play events players go round in pairs, but each is, of course, playing against the whole field. Team matches consist of singles and foursomes, in which the partners play shots in turn. Other, less-formal forms of golf are four-ball foursomes, in which each player plays his own ball; best-ball foursomes, in which both partners drive, but, thereafter, play in turn only

at the most successfully driven ball; and three-somes, in which each player plays for himself against the others. During a match, a player must not receive advice from anyone except his " caddie," if he has one, the caddie being an attendant who makes a profession of carrying golfers' clubs round.

Every course has its " bogey " and " par " figures, these being scores, with par representing the higher standard that a first-class player might achieve for the course. By assessing a member's own scores against these figures, clubs can allocate a handicap which indicates the player's standard. There are many minor competitions in which golfers play, not on level terms, but from their handicaps, which also serve as a perpetual incentive to players to improve their game, and therefore their handicaps. The possession of a handicap also makes it easier for players to arrange even matches with strangers. Handicaps are subject to alteration as a player's standard changes, and such alterations may be in either direction. The operation of the handicap in play takes the form of strokes deducted from the actual score at certain holes, in accordance with the arrangements in force at any particular club.

Golf offers a tremendous number of competitions of all standards, as well as championships and team matches. Probably the four most important individual championships are the British Open, the British Amateur, the American Open, and the American Amateur. These are long-established, but the two major international team events are quite new. They are the World Cup, open to teams of two professionals from any country, and the Eisenhower Cup, for teams of four amateurs, the three best scores counting, from any country. Other, much older international team events include the Ryder, Walker, and Curtis Cups, which are contests between Britain and the United States for professionals, amateurs, and women, respectively; though it is interesting to note that the actual inscription on the Curtis Cup indicates that this trophy is open to women golfers of any country.

Golf is ruled by the Royal and Ancient Club of St. Andrews, Scotland, which is recognised all over the world as the game's headquarters. There was an unusual illustration of this widespread recognition when the Eisenhower Cup competition was instituted by the United States in 1958, for, at the special request of the American organisers, the first meeting took place, not in the United States, but at St. Andrews. The Royal and Ancient Club makes the rules of golf, but these are generally supplemented by local rules in force at particular clubs.

The popular expression " rub of the green," used to describe an unexpected and unavoidable mischance, comes from golf, where it is used when a putt fails to take the expected line because of a slight flaw in the normally perfect turf of the green.

## Gymnastics.

Gymnastics is a system of exercising with apparatus, and also a competitive sport, the chief items of apparatus used being the horizontal bar, the parallel bars, rings, ropes, ladders, and the vaulting horse. The horizontal bar, the parallel bars, and the rings can all be used for similar exercises, some being fast swings and others slow movements requiring considerable strength. Strength and swinging also come into ladder exercises; and the rope, which can be climbed in several different ways, is a simple form of apparatus that demands, and will develop, strength. The horse can be used for a variety of vaults, in either the lengthways or sideways position, and still others are possible when pommels are fitted to it. In addition to those who specialise in gymnastics, many sportsmen of various kinds regularly attend gymnastic classes as part of their training for their own particular activities.

The Trampoline, which is something like a large and very springy mattress, and which has long been used by circus and stage acrobats, has now been accepted as a piece of gymnastic apparatus. Gymnasts, divers and other sportsmen use it in training; it is also used in the Services in the training of commandos and parachutists. There are trampoline competitions and championships, in which gymnasts perform many of the acrobatic feats normally performed on the floor.

**Head of the River Races.** *See* Boat Races.

**Henley Royal Regatta.** *See* Boat Races.

**Highland Games.** *See* Traditional Games and Customs.

**Hockey.**

Hockey originated about three-quarters of a century ago as a game confined to Britain, but with rules that varied in each of the home countries. However, in 1900, England, Ireland, and Wales combined to form the International Hockey Board, with a view to formulating rules that would apply wherever the game was played, and, two years later, Scotland joined the alliance. The game was also taken up with terrific enthusiasm in India, and Indian players became, and remain, the best players in the world. Their enthusiasm extended to what is now Pakistan, so

In play, the ball must be propelled only by the stick, and it must not be stopped with any part of the body except the hand, in which case it must only be stopped, and not caught or knocked forward. These prohibitions, however, do not apply to goalkeepers, who may stop the ball with any part of their body, and also kick it, when in their circle. No part of a player's stick must be raised above the shoulder either at the beginning or end of a stroke, or to stop the ball. Hitting the ball in the air and scooping it are allowed, but deliberate undercutting is not, and umpires can penalise any hit which they judge to be dangerous. Interfering with an opponent's stick, running between an opponent and the ball; and charging or other bodily contact are not allowed. Players must not tackle from the left unless they can play the ball without touching the opponent or his stick.

A player is " offside " if there are fewer than three opponents between him and the goal-line, unless he is in his own half, or unless a team-mate playing the ball is nearer to the goal-line than he is. A player who is offside is put onside if an opponent plays the ball, but not if the ball merely touches or glances off the opponent. Players who are offside are not penalised if they do not interfere with the play.

GROUND.—100 yards by 55 to 60 yards.   OPENING OF GOAL.—7 feet by 12 feet.
*Diagram of Ground as marked out for Hockey.*

the division that brought that country into existence also added one more to the list of hockey-playing countries, and without noticeably weakening India's own national team.

Hockey is now played in many other countries, but, for some time, it made little progress on the Continent. Eventually, though, it was tried, liked, and adopted in a number of European countries, and one of these, the Netherlands, has now established a right to a place alongside India, Pakistan, and Britain as the game's top layer. Hockey has, and has long had, Olympic Games status.

Hockey is played eleven-aside on a pitch marked out as in the accompanying diagram, the normal positions of the players being a goalkeeper, two full-backs, three half-backs, and five forwards, exactly as in Association Football (*q.v.*). The white ball can be either sewn, as is a cricket ball, or seamless, and it must weigh from 5½ to 5¾ ounces. Sticks must weigh from 12 to 28 ounces, and have a handle that can be passed through a ring with an inside diameter of 2 inches. They have a striking surface on the left side only, left-handed sticks not being permitted. A game consists of two 35-minute halves, unless the captains have agreed on a shorter period.

The game is started, and restarted after half-time and after a goal, by a bully at the centre of the ground. The players bullying stand facing the side-line, each with his own goal on his right. Each taps the ground between the ball and his own goal and his opponent's stick over the ball three times alternately, after which one of them must play the ball. At any bully, all the other players must be 5 yards from the ball, and between it and their own goal.

If the ball crosses the side-line it is rolled in by a player of the side that did not put it out. This player must have his hands, feet, and stick outside the field of play, and he must not play the ball again until someone else has done so. All the other players must have their feet and sticks inside the 7-yard line until the ball leaves the roller's hand.

If the ball is sent across the goal-line wide of the goal by an attacker, or, unintentionally, by a defender who is more than 25 yards from the goal-line, the restart is by a bully on the 25-yard line. If it is hit behind unintentionally by a defender who is within 25 yards of the goal-line, a corner is awarded to the attacking side. If it is hit behind intentionally by a defender from any part of the ground, a short, or penalty, corner is awarded to the attacking side. A corner is a hit from a point on either the goal-line or the side-line within 3 yards of the corner flag, while a short corner is a hit from a point on the goal-line 10 yards from the nearer goal-post. At a corner, all the defenders must be behind the goal-line, and all the attackers outside the circle. When the corner hit comes into the circle, attackers are not allowed to take a first-time shot, but must first stop the ball or slow it down. At no time during the game can a goal be scored unless it was hit from inside the circle.

Penalties for infringements outside the circles are generally free hits. Penalties for infringements inside the circle by defenders are short corners, unless they have been deliberately committed to prevent a goal, or have, in fact, prevented a goal, in which cases a penalty bully is awarded. In extreme cases, both short corners and penalty bullies can be awarded for offences anywhere behind the 25-yard line.

In 1963 the penalty stroke was introduced. This replaced the penalty bully, a duel between the offender and one opponent, with all the other players beyond the 25-yard line, that started with a bully 5 yards from the centre of the goal and continued until either a goal was scored or the ball was hit behind the attacker or out of the circle by the defender. If it was hit behind by the defender, the bully was restarted. This was a novel feature, but a not altogether satisfactory one, as the duel was sometimes protracted. The penalty stroke, if less spectacular, is also less complicated.

A game is controlled by two umpires, each of whom takes one half of the field and one complete side-line. Substitutes are not permitted in hockey.

Hockey is entirely an amateur game. Almost every match is a friendly, for, in Britain, there are no leagues and only a very few rather specialised cup competitions. There are, however, a great many representative games, from county matches up to internationals.

A major feature of the hockey season, which normally lasts from October until March, is the end-of-season Easter Hockey Festival. There are actually several festivals, most of them taking place at seaside resorts. Teams go to them from many different areas, including the Continent, and play three or four matches in four days against opponents whom they would not normally meet. Six-aside tournaments also take place occasionally during the season.

## Hurling.

Hurling, which might loosely be called the Irish brand of Hockey (q.v.), is played fifteen-aside, and has been described as the fastest game using a ball in the world. The ball, called the " slitter," and the sticks, called " hurleys," bear some resemblance to Hockey's ball and sticks, but nothing like Hockey's " sticks " rule applies. The slitter may be hit at any height, and with either side of the hurley, and it may be kicked or caught, though it must not be carried more than three steps, nor picked up off the ground. There is no offside, apart from the fact that attackers must not enter the parallelogram marked out near the goal ahead of the slitter. The goals have uprights that are extended above the cross-bar, and scoring is by goals, under the bar, and points, over the bar, a goal equalling three points. There is a good deal of bodily contact, and substitutes are permitted for injured players.

Hurling, rarely played by anyone who is not Irish, but often played by Irishmen outside Ireland, is of great antiquity, and the English authorities in Ireland first tried to suppress it six hundred years ago. It was kept alive, however, and it is very much alive to-day. To Irishmen, Hurling and Gaelic Football (q.v.) are symbols of nationalism and patriotism. They are governed by the Gaelic Athletic Association, which has a rule that states: " Any member who plays or encourages Rugby, Association Football, Hockey or Cricket by that very fact incurs immediate suspension from membership of the Association."

A form of Hurling with slightly different rules, called Shinty, is still preserved in another Celtic country, Scotland.

Ice-Hockey. *See* Skating.

Ice Skating. *See* Skating.

Ice Yachting. *See* Winter Sports.

Judo. *See* Wrestling.

Knur and Spell. *See* Old English Games and Customs.

## Korfball

Korfball is a team game with several unique features, the most striking being that it is a mixed game, a team consisting of twelve players—six men and six women. The game resembles Basketball (q.v.) in some ways, the goals, which are 11½ feet high, and the scoring of goals being similar. It can be played on any firm surface, the pitch measuring 300 feet by 133 feet, though a smaller pitch can be used, provided that length and width are reduced in proportion. The pitch is divided into three sections, and players do not move from one sector to another during actual play. They must, however, change to another zone after every two goals. This encourages all-round attacking and defensive ability, and ensures that, even in a one-sided match, every player gets a fair share of the game. Four players from each team play in each section, and players always mark opponents of their own sex. Players must not run with the ball, which is advanced purely by passing. There is no tackling, and the ball can only pass from one team to the other by interception. Players may not score if there is an opponent within arm's length. A game lasts for 90 minutes, divided into two halves.

Korfball originated in the Netherlands, where it was first played in 1902. It spread to Belgium in 1927, and reached England in 1947. There is an International Board, on which the Netherlands, Belgium, and England are represented. International inter-club matches are a regular feature of the game. Though really a winter game, Korfball is actually played all the year round, the international games between clubs from the three Korfball countries taking place during the summer.

## Lacrosse.

Lacrosse, which originated from a game played by the Red Indians, was introduced into England from Canada in 1867, and has been played here ever since.

Basically, it is, perhaps, the simplest of all field team games. The object is the propelling of a rubber ball through goals 6 feet wide and 6 feet high with a wooden " crosse " not more than a foot wide at its widest point, where there is a " mesh " of strings. The goals are from 90 to 110 yards apart, but play can take place behind them, for there are no boundaries to the pitch except the natural borders of the field, unless the captains have agreed otherwise. The only lines required are the centre circle, the goal-lines, and the goal-creases.

In England teams consist of twelve players, but in Canada and the United States the number was reduced to ten some years ago. Players line up right down the field, instead of only in their own half, and there is no offside, except that no attacker may enter the goal-crease before the ball. Should a player leave the field through injury, his opponents must also withdraw a man.

A game consists of four 20-minute periods, but the captains can agree to vary this, either to two 45-minute halves or otherwise. The game is started or re-started after a stoppage by one player from each side " facing " by placing the ball on the ground between the backs of the two crosses, and then drawing them apart, after which the ball is in play. It can then be advanced by running with it on the crosse, throwing it from the crosse, or kicking it, though no goal, except an " own goal," can be scored by a kick. Only the goalkeeper, who can deflect the ball with his hand, but not catch or throw it, may handle the ball. Players can shoulder opponents when trying to get the ball off the ground, and " body check " them by simply standing in front of them to impede them. A player can also check an opponent's crosse with his own crosse if the opponent has the ball. A foul is penalised by giving the non-offending player a " free position," which means that he is given the ball, and the game is then re-started.

Lacrosse demands speed and stamina, and a high level of skill demands practice, but it is not hard for a beginner to grasp the main objects or master the comparatively simple rules.

It is interesting to note that Lacrosse, which can be one of the roughest of all games, has been made a suitable game for women by very simple measures, such as the elimination of the body check; and that there are now more women playing than there are men.

## Lawn Tennis.

Originally called Sphairistike—or "Sticky" by those who disliked it—Lawn Tennis was invented in the seventies of the last century as a simplified, outdoor version of Real Tennis (q.v.), using a net, but no walls. It is now far more widely played than the parent game, being popular almost all over the world. As its name implies, it was originally intended to be played on grass, but it is now also played on hard courts of various surfaces, and indoors on wood.

The court is as shown in the accompanying diagram, the outer long boundary lines being the limitations for doubles, and those parallel to them being the boundaries for singles. Both server and receiver score, four points making a

## Modern Pentathlon.

Imagine a king's messenger riding with an important dispatch, and being hotly pursued. His horse is shot, and he has to escape his pursuers, first with his revolver, and then with the sword. Eventually, he breaks away, swims a river, and finishes his journey on foot and running.

That is the "plot" on which is based one of the most interesting, exciting, and testing of all sporting events, the Modern Pentathlon. Often wrongly thought to be a part of Athletics, the Pentathlon is a separate sport, but one that actually consists of five different sports: the five activities, in fact, of the king's messenger in the story, riding, revolver shooting, fencing, swimming, and running. True, the Pentathlon competitor does not have to carry them out one after the other, but he does have to take part in them in that order, one on each of five successive days, both riding and running being across country, the riding on a horse strange to him.

NET:—Height 3 ft. 6 in. at posts, 3 ft. at centre.
*Diagram of Ground as marked out for Lawn Tennis.*

game, six games won a set, and two out of three or three out of five sets won a match. Game points are scored "15," "30," "40," and "Game." The system of "vantage" games and sets is used. This means that, if 40-all—called "deuce"—is reached, a player must gain a clear lead of two points to win the game, the winner of the first point after deuce being said to have the "advantage." If the games reach 5-all, the set continues until one player has a clear lead of two games.

When the game began, there was considerable discussion before this scoring, which is taken from Tennis, was given preference over the straightforward one-two-three system of Rackets (q.v.). Much more recently, experiments have been made with the equally straightforward system of Table Tennis (q.v.), but the Tennis system survived these, and remains in force.

Service is almost invariably overhand, and the receiver plays the service after one bounce. Thereafter, strokes may be "ground" strokes, played after one bounce, or volleys, played before any bounce. In doubles, either partner may play the ball, but each must serve in turn.

In addition to being played by thousands of people, Lawn Tennis attracts large crowds of spectators. The big annual tournaments, such as Wimbledon, Forest Hills, and Paris, are amongst the major sporting events of the year; as are the Davis Cup competition, open to teams of men from every country in the world, and the Wightman Cup, a women's contest between Britain and the United States. All these events are amateur; but the game also has a top layer of professionals, whose annual world tours are a great attraction.

**Marbles.** *See* Old English Games and Customs.

The Pentathlon first appeared in the Olympic Games of 1912, but, in recent years, it has become so popular that, in addition to the Olympic event every four years, there are now annual world championships, as well as national championships in many countries, including Britain. The event was originally designed as one suitable for Army officers, and, though present-day Army training is rather different, most Pentathlon competitors are still servicemen, though they are not all officers. However, a civilian has won the Olympic event, and, in Britain, the Army authorities are willing to provide training facilities for civilian competitors who show signs of reaching a high standard. Many people believe that the "keys" to success in the Modern Pentathlon are swimming and running, and that competitors who are good at them can be taught the riding, shooting and fencing without too much difficulty.

## Mountaineering.

Among famous peaks, Mont Blanc was first conquered in 1786, the Jungfrau in 1811, and the Wetterhorn in 1854. By then, Mountaineering was becoming organised, and there were systematic assaults on the Alps; in Norway, the Caucasus, and Corsica; in the Rockies and the Andes; in Japan, New Zealand, and Kenya; and, of course, in the Himalayas, where over thirty years passed between the first assault on Everest and its conquest in 1953. There are still unconquered peaks in the Himalayas, but it is not only first ascents that interest the mountaineer; he can find exciting climbing in many parts of the world.

The way to master Mountaineering is to accompany and watch experts. Perfect physical and nervous fitness is essential, as is a detailed knowledge of snow, ice, avalanches, glaciers, crevasses, and cornices, and of the different techniques of ascending, descending, and traversing. Also to be learned is step-cutting, which is hard manual labour carried out under difficult conditions, conditions that may make perfect workmanship literally a matter of life or death. Clothing, properly nailed boots, ropes, ice axes, knives, maps, compasses, medical supplies, must be of the best, and yet, at the same time, light.

Mountaineering is generally taken to mean snow and ice climbing, but allied to it is Rock-climbing, which demands the same perfect physical and nervous condition, and, in place of knowledge of snow and ice, knowledge of several very different kinds of rock. Ascending, descending, and traversing all apply, and so do ropes, and the rock-climber should, in fact, be something of a knot expert. Light, rope-soled shoes replace the mountaineer's nailed boots. Skye is a favourite haunt of rock-climbers, and, in view of what might justifiably be called the antiquity of climbing, it is surprising to note that the highest peak in Skye, Sgurr Alasdair, was not conquered until 1873.

The Mountaineering Association, 102A Westbourne Grove, London, W.2, runs training schools for climbers at all stages in Britain and abroad; and also runs evening classes on rock climbing in conjunction with education authorities. The Holiday Fellowship organises climbing tours in the Highlands of Scotland, climbing many well-known mountains. In Scotland useful addresses are the Scottish Mountaineering Club, 406 Sauchiehall Street, Glasgow, C.2, and the Junior Mountaineering Club, 28 Croftmont Avenue, Croftfoot, Glasgow, S.4. At the White Hall Centre for Open Country Pursuits, Manchester Road, near Buxton, the Derbyshire County Council hold courses for those between 13 and 20 plus on hillcraft, rock climbing, camping, ski-ing, and canoeing. The Outward Bound Trust, 123 Victoria Street, London, S.W.1, runs schools in Wales and the Lake District to train boys—with a few courses for girls—how to face hazards and hardships of all kinds on mountains and sea.

## Music.

One of the most novel changes of the last generation or so has been the widespread diffusion of music not only in this country but all over the world. Twenty or thirty years ago it might have been necessary to travel a long way to hear the performance of a classical musical work; and the opportunity of doing so was only occasional. We can now have a constant flow of such music from wireless and record player. Several things follow from this change. Leisure has been transformed by " high fidelity " and the long-playing record. People listen more easily and frequently than they read; and it is music, rather than literature, which is at the centre of culture. Access to good music does not depend upon training and application to the same extent as access to good literature. It is easier for the timid person to enjoy music than a serious book. " Where the library shelves used to stand," says a commentator, " there are now the record albums, row upon proud and esoteric row." The listener may well be submerged, by the easy flow of music of vastly different kinds; but there is an opportunity for the discerning listener to compare and to select from the music of the different centuries, to study the difference between the classical and romantic masters, the emergence of modern orchestration, choral music, chamber music, opera, and oratorio. We may go on to study other aspects—the study of the personality of the composers; the relation between their work and the problems of the times; knowledge of the different instruments; and how to enjoy reading a musical score. By this means the listener can combine refreshment of spirit with the delights of exercising skills of various kinds.

All through the summer, all over the country there are opportunities for music lovers, whether active musicians or not, to spend a holiday together and pursue some aspect of music. The reader will probably be surprised to learn that there are nearly one hundred such summer schools each year, some for the week-end, others for a week or fortnight. The Rural Music Schools

Association at Hitchen, Herts. would help enquirers for particulars. A glance at the annual list shows how wide are the subjects offered: madrigal and other singing, recorder playing, orchestral and chamber music, Russian music, 18th-century music, discussion for wind teachers, the making of musical instruments. These summer schools are in addition to the Music Festivals held at Edinburgh, Bath, Cheltenham, and other places, not forgetting the Three Choirs Festival in the West (British Federation of Music Festivals, 106 Gloucester Place, London, W.1). Details of the various continental festivals can be obtained from the European Association of Music Festivals, 122 rue de Lausanne, Geneva, or 82 Beauchamp Place, London, S.W.3.

Your local public library probably has a music library. The National Operatic and Dramatic Association, 1 Crestfield Street, London, W.C.1, has a library of musical scores and dramatic works. The National Federation of Music Societies publishes a catalogue with practical details of some 500 choral works and assists music societies by advice, information, and in other ways; its address is 4 St. James's Square, London, W.C.1. The Workers Music Association provides opportunities for developing musical instincts and tastes, believing that genuine art moves people to work for the betterment of society. It organises classes, lectures, and week-end and summer schools; and offers correspondence courses in Harmony, Counterpoint, and Orchestration. Its address is 17 Bishops Bridge Road, London, W.2.

Many local authorities have record departments in their local libraries. The Central Gramophone Library (38 Russell Square, London W.C.1) has a circulating library of records which are available to adult education lecturers, music and gramophone societies and to hospitals and prisons. Those interested in forming a gramophone society should get into touch with the National Federation of Gramophone Societies. The British Institute of Recorded Sound, 38 Russell Square London W.C.1 contains the national archives of gramophone records and other sound-recordings and is the national centre for information and documents.

## Natural History and Field Studies.

There are nine Field Centres in England and Wales, at:

Juniper Hall, Dorking, Surrey.
Flatford Mill, East Bergholt, near Colchester, Essex.
Malham Tarn, near Settle, Yorkshire.
Dale Fort, Haverfordwest, Pembrokeshire (including Skokholm Bird Sanctuary).
Preston Montford, near Shrewsbury, Shropshire.
Slapton Ley, Slapton, Kingsbridge, Devonshire.
Orielton, near Pembroke, S. Wales.
Nettlecombe Court, Williton, Taunton, Somerset.
Rhyd-y-Creua, Betws-y-Coed, Caernarvonshire.

The nine centres have been set up by the Field Studies Council in localities selected for their ecological features and for their geological, geographical, archaeological, and artistic interest. Working facilities and expert guidance are available at the Field Centres to all who have a serious interest in the countryside—whether as amateur naturalists or as students or as research workers. They are not reserved for the academic student only. The Council want to encourage and help the beginner and the ordinary person who has an interest in some branch of natural history and wishes to learn of this or allied subjects. The Centres are staffed and suitably equipped to provide residential accommodation and working facilities for numbers ranging up to about sixty persons. Thus field workers enjoy the skilled guidance of the staff, local contacts and information, bench space, tools, maps and records, with something of the intellectual and social life of a small residential college. There are special courses for amateurs, and some of these are less formal than the word " course " suggests. The subjects vary widely, including bird study, land structure and scenery, and outdoor painting and sketching.

Juniper Hall, amidst the beautiful chalk hills of the North Downs, is well situated for almost every kind of field study. Flatford Mill is at the head of the Stour estuary, in the countryside of Constable and Gainsborough. The Stour, with its tributary streams, its mill pools and cattle ponds and dykes, provides excellent scope for water biology. Malham Tarn Centre is on the shore of the tarn on the limestone uplands at the head of Airedale in the Yorkshire Pennines. Here is the rich flora of well-drained pastures, screes, and limestone. The tarn itself supports an abundant fauna of invertebrates and fish. Dale Fort at the tip of a narrow peninsula guards the approach to Milford Haven. The flowers on the cliffs in May and June are the envy of the rock gardener. The opportunities for the marine biologist are unsurpassed. But there is no specialisation to the exclusion of any of the many subjects that can advantageously be studied. The Bird Observatory on Skokholm island is a part of Dale Fort Field Centre, and here work on birds has pride of place. Guillemots and razorbills breed on the rocks, and puffins and shearwaters burrow in the edges of the plateau. Preston Montford lies on the banks of the Severn four miles west of Shrewsbury, where geological formations are displayed conveniently for study. In the North Shropshire plain is scope for the study, too long neglected, of the ecology of ordinary English farming country that man has influenced for more than 2,000 years. There are numerous localities of archaeological interest, including the Roman town of Viroconium. The Slapton Ley the 300 acres of Slapton Nature Reserve offer ample scope for interest in most branches of Natural History. The Ley is separated from the sea by a shingle bank. There are moorland and bog: slate and limestone cliffs; lake shores and beaches; and woodlands. Enquiries can be made to the Field Studies Council, Ravensmead, Keston, Kent.

Everyone who *wants* to work in the field can find something useful to do, whatever his natural bent and his training, since the range of research is vast and the problems diverse, with such varying degrees of difficulty. This opportunity has been greatly extended by the increasing importance of ecology, which is a distinctive point of view in the approach to field biology. In its most general sense ecology may be defined as the study of plants and animals as they live *in their natural homes.* The growing popularity of the subject in this country represents a breakaway from the confinement of serious work in biology to the laboratory and museum. These are still, of course, absolutely necessary, but the primary place in which to work at ecology is the field.

*Bird-watching.* The pleasure of bird-song and the sight of their activities is a common one for most of us. From this point many are prompted to make a closer study of birds and their habits. To get the most pleasure it is a great advantage to turn for advice to those who have had a wide experience. The enthusiast will thus become equipped with some knowledge of methods of bird-watching, how to make field notes and keep records, hides, identification, tables of family likeness, migration, sanctuaries, bird photography, and the structure of the bird.

Bird-watching is not confined to those who live in the country. London has probably more bird-watchers than any other part of Britain. With the possible exception of the parish of Selborne in Hampshire, immortalised by Gilbert White, London, has the longest continuous history of ornithological observation in the British Isles. Groups of enthusiastic naturalists have collected a mass of detail about wild birds and their habits in London. The list of London birds is not only extraordinarily large but also contains many rarities and many birds of great scientific interest, like the black redstart and the little ringed plover. There are also special London problems, like the roosting of starlings in central London and the origin of this starling population. The reservoirs and the river, the commons and woods and parkland around London offer pleasant places for observation. The London Natural History Society (headquarters, the Natural History Museum, Cromwell Road, S.W.7) has, as its chief object, the study and enjoyment of natural history in the London area.

*Visiting Nature Reserves.* The Nature Conservancy welcome visitors to National Nature Reserves within the limits set by the Conservancy's own responsibilities towards these lands and their plants and wild life. The Reserves are maintained on behalf of the nation to conserve their natural fauna and flora, and so far as possible to enhance their interest and value to science. As far as possible the Reserves are accessible for the use and enjoyment of all who are prepared to respect the necessity for handing them on unimpaired to future generations and for avoiding interference with scientific work. Many Reserves are accessible without formality; elsewhere a permit is required. A list of the Reserves is obtainable from the Conservancy, 19 Belgrave Square, London, S.W.1, or in Scotland from 12 Hope Terrace, Edinburgh, 9. There are some eighty National Nature Reserves. Among the extremely small reserves is, for example, the North Fen Reserve, 4 miles S.S.W. of Ambleside showing a vegetational succession of open water rich in mineral salts to fen, carr, and bog. The largest in Britain is the Cairngorms in Scotland, of nearly 40,000 acres, with fauna rich in variety of species from wild cats to golden eagle and a diverse flora, which includes the arctic-alpine plants of the corries, screes, and exposed summits.

*The Council of Nature.* If you are interested in any aspect of natural history—for example in plants, birds, rocks, insects, trees, butterflies, or natural history photography—you will have no difficulty in finding the address of your local history society, of which there are a very large number. The local public library would doubtless give you the address you want, or you could enquire from the Council of Nature, 41 Queen's Gate, London, S.W.7, to which over two hundred organisations belong. These include the Royal Society for the Protection of Birds, which has upwards of 9,000 members and runs the Junior Bird Recorders' Club for young people interested in bird-watching. The Council links amateur and specialist in the study of natural history and the conservation of wild life. It has an Intelligence Unit which is ready to deal with requests for information on field natural history in the United Kingdom. The Film Officer of the Unit will advise amateur still and ciné photographers on all aspects of natural history photography. He will also be able to advise on what natural history films are available and on likely sources for photographs of any British wild animal or plant.

### Netball.

Netball, which is played exclusively by women, is similar to Basketball (*q.v.*), but it is played seven-aside, does not allow substitutes, and the goals have no backboards. It is almost always played outdoors on asphalt or grass.

### Nine Men's Morris. *See* Old English Games and Customs.

### Old English Games and Customs.

The story of England had its beginnings a very long time ago, and many of England's present-day customs, recreations, sports, and games can be traced far back in that story. Some, of course, have undergone very considerable changes, but the links with the past are still clear.

On 1 May, for instance, girls still awake in some villages to the realisation that they are to be May Queens, and to reign for a day, though they may not realise that they are preserving a custom that can point to origins in the days of the Druids, and that, in Tudor times, would have sent them and their fellow villagers out to spend the preceding night in the woods, gathering branches of trees and flowers with which to decorate their houses. Maypoles and morris dancers also belonged to May Day, and they can still be seen in England, and not only on that day.

More local, even quainter, but equally traditional is the trial for the Dunmow Flitch of Bacon in the village of Dunmow in Essex. The original conditions offer this award to any married couple who will go to the twelfth-century Augustinian priory, and there kneel on two sharp-pointed stones and swear that they have neither quarrelled nor repented of their marriage within a year and a day of its celebration. This award has lasted into modern times, not annually, it is true; but then it never was given annually, for it was instituted in 1244, and first claimed in 1445.

One annual event that is as traditional as it is strenuous in the Whit Monday cheese-chase at the village of Brockworth, near Gloucester. Records of this go back to the days of the Stuarts, for that was when they started to keep records of a custom that was already old then: so old that its origins are unknown, though they had to do with the villagers' cattle-grazing rights. A massive round cheese is rolled down nearby Coopers Hill, which has a gradient of one in four throughout its 150 yards; and, with a certain amount of risk to life and limb, the chasers tear down after it, the cheese being the prize for whoever catches it. Sometimes, the cheese hits a bump, and literally leaps out of reach over the hedge at the bottom of the hill, but the chase continues, the prize going to the first pursuer to reach the hedge, where "catchers" wait to halt the headlong rush of the runners. Despite the obvious dangers, the records to date mention nothing worse than a sprained ankle.

This brings us to sports and games; and, though today's most popular game, Football, is, in anything like its present form a comparatively recent growth, it can perhaps claim some relationship with Harpastum and Campball, which existed before the Norman Conquest; and it was one of the popular recreations banned in the interests of Archery. The football of those and later days, however, took the form of struggles between whole villages, the players battling *en masse* over a cross-country course of several miles. People past whose houses the battle was likely to rage prudently barred and shuttered all windows and doors, awaited the cessation of hostilities with anxiety, and probably helped to push this particular custom into oblivion.

The oldest English games are old indeed, and Cricket, too, has remote ancestors, from which the descent to today can be traced more directly. They included Bat and Trap, Creag, Cat and Dog, and Rounders. In Bat and Trap, the batsman hit a ball released from a trap between two posts. His opponent rolled it back underarm at the trap flap. If he knocked it down, the batsman was out: if not, the batsman scored one run and had another hit. This game is still played in Kent. Creag, which was played at the time of Edward II, used a curved stick, called a "cryc," as a bat, and a tree-stump as a wicket. Cat and Dog, which came later, was a game for three, two batsmen defending holes 13 yards apart, and trying to hit away the piece of wood that the third player aimed at the holes, the bats being the "dogs" and the piece of wood the "cat." It is worth noting that Baseball's accepted ancestors are games called One Old Cat and Two Old Cat, which clearly indicates a common origin for Cricket and Baseball. Some of the games in Cricket's ancestry remained popular after Cricket arrived, and Rounders is still a popular children's game.

The beginning of Athletics can also be found in old England. Putting the weight and casting the bar, a forerunner of throwing the hammer, were popular with the courtiers in Tudor days, while other events, including javelin throwing, were practised by ordinary people of the same period. Later, the early hammer throwing spread beyond the Court, and was even attempted by women, which modern hammer throwing is not.

Tournaments and jousts were popular from the Middle Ages until Tudor times. These were combats between mounted men, a joust being single combat, while a tournament involved many contestants. They were succeeded by dismounted combats, which still take place today in the sport of Fencing. Those taking part in tournaments and jousts were required to swear an oath to the effect that they were competing purely for sport; and those taking part in the Olympic Games and certain other big sports meetings to-day swear an almost identical oath. Somewhat similar to jousting, but not restricted, as jousting was, to the nobility, was Tilting at the Quintain, which was practised both mounted and on foot, and in which a lance was thrust at a wooden target, which, if not struck accurately, swung round and struck the tilter.

Other old games, clearly the ancestors of modern ones, included Handball, which became Fives, but which is still handball in the United States; Battledore and Shuttlecock, still a children's game, but now developed by adults into Badminton; and Shovelboard, an elaborate game, for the nobility, which consisted of sliding weights down a long table marked with lines, and which is certainly a forerunner of Shove-Ha'-penny. Another probable ancestor of Shove-Ha'penny was Squails, in which a coin was placed in the centre of a round table, and players tried to push their "squails," or discs, as close to the coin as possible, distances being measured by an instrument called a "swoggle." Also known as Skayles and Keels, this game appeared in the sixteenth century, lasted into the nineteenth century, and, under the name of Keels, achieved a poetic mention in Sidney's "Arcadia."

*Archery.* Archery goes back hundreds of years, to the days when the bow was the chief weapon of war, and, because of that, practice shooting and contests were officially encouraged: encouraged, in fact, to the extent that other popular recreations, like Football, Quoits, and Bowls, that might have interfered with it were banned, though the bans were always largely ignored. Eventually, the bow disappeared from the battle-fields, but, to this day, it has remained popular as a means of recreation and sport. Through the centuries, archery contests were generally of three kinds: shooting at a mark, or target; shooting purely for distance, though this was more popular abroad, in countries like Turkey, than in Britain; and shooting at "rovers," in which two or three archers would cover a cross-country course, taking it in turns to select a mark at which to shoot. To-day, archery, which retains enough of tradition in its terminology to remind the archer that he is following in a very long line, consists of shooting at a target containing rings coloured, going from the centre outwards, gold, red, blue, black, and white, the values being respectively, nine, seven, five, three, and one.

*Knur and Spell.* Knur and Spell belongs to Lancashire and Yorkshire, and originated in a children's game called Trap and Ball. The player uses a wooden club, the striking end of which, called the "pommel," is shaped something like a bottle, though it has a flat hitting surface, with which to hit a small ball, which he himself releases from a trap by means of a trigger. The ball, which is the "knur," weighs ½ ounce, measures 1 inch in diameter, and was originally wooden, though, later, porcelain was used. The trap is the "spell," and consists of a small brass cup with a strong spring, which is kept down by the trigger. The fixing of the spell is an elaborate process requiring the use of a spirit level, and, when it is in position, a player is allowed 10 minutes to adjust the tension of the spring. Players generally have their own spells. Each player has five consecutive hits, or "rises," and scores one point for every 20 yards covered.

*Marbles.* Marbles is supposed to have been played in ancient Egypt, but its popularity, with adults as well as children, in the England of the Middle Ages entitles it to count as an old English game. Marbles are often made of clay, but better ones are glass, and the best are pure marble. These are called "alleys," or "alley taws." There are several games of marbles, but they all involve the aiming of a marble at a target, which may be another marble or an opening, by bowling or "shooting" it along the ground. In shooting, the marble is held between the thumb and forefinger, with the knuckle of the forefinger on the ground, and is then flicked away.

Perhaps the best-known game is Ring Taw, in which players shoot from one circle at marbles placed in another about 6 feet away. Fortifications and Increase Pound use concentric circles, players shooting at marbles in each circle in turn. Three Holes and Handers involve shooting at holes in the ground; Arch Board or Bridge, at arches in an upright board; and Die Shot, at another marble on which a numbered die is balanced.

*Nine Men's Morris.* Nine Men's Morris is a fourteenth-century game for two, usually played outdoors on a diagram marked on the ground, but sometimes played indoors on a board. The diagram consists of three squares drawn inside each other. In addition to the outlines of each square, there are lines from the centre of each side of the inmost square, through the centre of the sides of the middle square, to the centre of the sides of the outermost square. The corner of each square and the centre of each side are the 24 points of importance in the game. Each player has nine men, often counters, and they play in turn, placing a man at an unoccupied point, and endeavouring to place three men in one row, continuing, when all the men are placed, to try to form rows by moving men along the lines. The completion of a row entitles a player to remove, or "pound," one of his opponent's men, the object of the game being either the capture of all the opposing men or blocking them so that they cannot move. The game has many variations, and many names, including ninepenny morris; fivepenny morris, for a version played with five men; and merils, marls, marrels, morals, morris and miracles, all for a version played with three men.

*Pall-Mall.* Two London thoroughfares, Pall Mall and the Mall, are reminders that Pall-Mall was once popular. Often described as a forerunner of Croquet, it was really more like a form of Golf, a game that arrived at about the same time, both having a common, if remote, ancestor in the Roman game, Paganica. In Paganica players walked across fields hitting a small, leather ball at trees with a curved stick, the object being to reach the target in the fewest possible strokes. It was played by country people, whereas pall-mall, which achieved rapid popularity in the seventeenth century, was a game for the nobility, though other people played simplified versions of it. Pall-Mall was played in special alleys, sometimes ½ mile long, and often surrounded by walls. A boxwood ball a foot in circumference had to be played down the alley, in which were a number of iron arches, in the fewest possible strokes. The player drove off as in golf. but, on reaching the arches, not only changed his club, but also substituted a small steel ball for the boxwood one.

*Quoits.* Dating back to the fifteenth century, Quoits is one of those ancient games that had the distinction of being banned because its popularity was such that it was believed to be keeping people from archery practice. The ban was not effective, and it continues to this day, though it is now less played than it used to be, Scotland, the North of England, and Suffolk being, perhaps, the last main strongholds. The pitch consists of two circles or squares of clay, 18 yards apart, and each having in its centre an iron pin, called the "hub," 1 inch of which remains above the surface. The quoits are iron rings with a diameter that must not exceed 8¼ inches. The weight is not fixed, but is often 3 lb. or more. The object of the game, which can be either "singles" or "doubles," is to throw the quoit over or near the hub from the opposite point, 18 yards away, one point being scored for each quoit nearer the hub than the opponent's quoits, and two being awarded for a quoit that drops over the hub, called a "ringer." No points are awarded if opposing quoits are the same distance from the hub, and none are awarded if each side has a ringer. A game is 11 points in "singles," and 15 points in "doubles." Quoits developed from pitching actual horseshoes, and, to this day, some players make their first practice attempts at it with horseshoes. It is, in fact, to the large-scale disappearance of horses, and, therefore, of horseshoes, from country life that some people attribute the drop in the popularity of quoits. It is interesting to note that, in the United States, horseshoe pitching itself is a game, and one that is still popular.

*Shove-Ha'penny.* Shove-Ha'penny, an old English game that is still popular, uses a cushioned wood or slate board, divided by parallel lines across it into nine "beds." The "halfpennies" may be actual halfpennies, but are generally round metal discs. The object of the game is to shove the halfpennies into one of the nine beds, the shoving usually being done with the ball of the thumb, though any part of the hand may be used. First turn is decided by shoving halfpennies at the number nine bed, the best attempt winning. A turn consists of five halfpennies, and the winner is the first player to shove three halfpennies into each bed, halfpennies that touch the cushion not counting. Should a player place more than three halfpennies in any bed, his opponent can claim the excess, if he needs them, but cannot win the final point of a game in this way. Push-Penny, a similar game using three coins is played in some parts of the country, mainly in Lincolnshire.

*Stoolball.* Yet another ancestor of Cricket, Stoolball is still a popular girls' game. The wicket is a board a foot square on a pole 4 feet 8 inches high, the bat has a round striking surface, and the ball is rubber. Wickets are 16 yards apart and eight balls constitute an over.

Oxford and Cambridge Boat Race. *See* Boat Races.

Pall-Mall. *See* Old English Games and Customs.

Parachute Jumping.

Parachute jumping is generally regarded as a last-resort safety measure, to be undertaken only in a supreme emergency, and with considerable anxiety; but it is now also a recreation and a competitive sport, practised entirely voluntarily, and for enjoyment. This form of jumping may be said to have grown out of the Second World War, in which jumping was used to a far greater extent than ever before, and not only for escape in an emergency. Now, international competitions take place, and the sport has an enthusiastic following in Britain.

Parachute jumping as a sport involves jumps of particular kinds, including landings in a certain area, marked by a circle, and demonstrating turns and body control in the air, the parachutist regulating his direction by pulling down the lines of the parachute. Jumps of this kind may be made from about 6000 feet.

The first point that occurs to many people when they think about Parachute Jumping is that it is extremely dangerous. However, those who jump as a recreation maintain that this is not so, and that it is about as dangerous as skiing. Injuries are few and slight, and, in three years, none of the hundred-odd members of the British Parachute Club, of Fairoaks, Surrey, suffered anything worse than a sprained ankle. The parachutes used are so reliable that they still work even if they have been badly packed. A parachute consists of twenty-eight sections, called "gores," each divided into four panels, so that, even if a hole should stretch right across one gore, which is rare, the remainder of the parachute remains intact, and will bring the jumper down safely. As an additional precaution, jumpers wear a small reserve parachute on the chest, but this is hardly ever needed.

Training, which generally takes place at weekends, starts with a period of learning how to fall, how to judge wind direction and speed, and how to pack a parachute. The first actual jumps are from 2,000 or 2,500 feet. Both men and women take part in Parachute Jumping.

Parachutists must be licensed by the Civil Aviation Department of the Board of Trade, and they must produce medical certificates of fitness. Third party insurance is also compulsory, but this is automatically covered by membership of the British Parachute Association. Leading centres of Parachute Jumping are at Blackbushe Airfield, Hampshire; Thruxton, Wiltshire; Manchester; and Gleneagles.

## Patience.

Patience is a card game for one person, and, though there are few different games for one, there are countless different forms of Patience. There are some using one pack, and others using two, almost all of them starting with the setting out of the cards on the table according to fixed rules, and having as their object the building up of the four suits on their aces.

The game that might almost be called the basic form of single-pack patience starts with a row of seven cards, only the left-hand one being exposed. Underneath this, and overlapping it, comes a row of six cards with the left-hand one exposed, and so on down to a " row " consisting of only a single exposed card, the exposed cards being left uncovered in each decreasing row. The object is to take out first the aces, and then the cards from two up to king, building each suit on its ace. From the " lay out," exposed cards can be moved when it is possible to put one on a card one pip higher in value of the opposite colour, when any card left uncovered by an exposed card can itself be exposed. The undealt cards can be played three at a time, the top one of each three being " playable," with the one underneath becoming " playable," if the top one is, in fact, played. The undealt cards can be played through three at a time in this manner as often as desired. A slight variation of this game allows the undealt cards to be played through one at a time, but this can be done only once.

Another single-pack game starts with a row of nine exposed cards, with, below it and overlapping, a row of eight, and so on down to one, all the cards being exposed, and the right-hand one being left uncovered in each decreasing row. The remaining seven cards form a separate row at the bottom. The object and the "move " are the same as in the previous game, only one card being moved at a time, and any card being eligible to fill any vacancy that might occur in the top row. Cards in the separate row can be played as required, but, once in the " lay out," they must remain there. This game is called King of the Belgians, and the last seven cards are referred to as the Belgian Reserve.

One to Six is a two-pack game. The player deals out a row of four cards, then discards two to a rubbish heap, and carries on like this until all the cards have been used. If, however, while doing it, he comes across any aces or kings, he takes them out, up to one of each from each suit, subsequently also taking out any that will fit on to these, building up from the aces and down from the kings. Then he goes through the rubbish heap, extracting any cards that will fit on the eight piles. The dealt-out cards, with the rubbish-heap cards, are then dealt again in the same way, the object being to complete the eight built-up suits in three rounds of dealing.

## Polo.

Polo, one of the oldest of all games, originated in Persia, then spread in one form or another to China, Japan, and India, eventually being brought from India to England by cavalry officers in the second half of the nineteenth century. Later, it was enthusiastically taken up in the United States and Argentina. Played four-aside, and mounted, on a pitch that should measure 300 yards by 160 yards, its object is to score goals by hitting a 5-ounce ball through goals 24 feet wide with a

stick consisting of a long cane fixed at a slight angle into a wooden or bamboo striking head. The game is divided into periods, called " chukkas," the number of periods varying slightly, as may be agreed for particular games.

Formerly, Polo was a game for the wealthy, for it entailed owning and maintaining a string of trained ponies. In recent years, however, certain stables and riding schools have provided facilities for playing and practising Polo, and these facilities include the hiring out of ponies. This apparently simple and obvious step is actually quite a revolutionary innovation that has brought Polo within the reach of almost anyone who wants to play, and thereby increased the popularity of an ancient and exciting game that might otherwise have died out because of the expense involved.

## Pony Trekking.

Pony Trekking as an organised recreation originated in Scotland in 1953, though something similar was known in India before that. The word *trekking* itself is Afrikaans. Chance and coincidence played a part in starting Pony Trekking, at least on a larger scale than might otherwise have been the case. The first trek was at Newtonmore, Inverness-shire, and was partly organised by officials of the Scottish Council of Physical Recreation. At about the same time, at Aberfoyle, Perthshire, *Rob Roy* was being filmed, and many townspeople who came to watch expressed great interest in the horses. This led to the planning of a trek in that area, the organisers of which knew nothing of the Newtonmore venture, though they subsequently heard of it, and received advice from its organisers. The first trek from this second centre took place in 1954. Now, there are about 70 approved centres, mainly in Scotland, Wales, the West Country, and the Lake District, though there are also some in Ireland and on the Continent. "Approved," incidentally, means that they are inspected every year by the Scottish Council of Physical Recreation or the Ponies of Britain Club and hold Certificates of Approval from one or other of those bodies.

Pony Trekking consists of riding over the hills and moors, through forests and along ancient tracks at a walking pace: for, if you ride faster than that, you cease to trek and begin to hack (*see* Riding). No experience whatever is needed, and the complete novice or child who has never ridden at all can enjoy Pony Trekking from the start. During the first two days of a trekking holiday, beginners will be given some elementary instruction in saddling, mounting, and starting and stopping the horse; and then they will start with short treks of from five to ten miles.

There are two forms of Pony Trekking, day trekking and post trekking. Most treks are day treks, consisting of circular, all-day tours starting and finishing at the centre. Post treks last for several days, and include stopping at a different post or centre each night. There are comparatively few post treks, partly because they are only suitable for experienced trekkers and partly because of the difficulty of obtaining accommodation for one night only during the height of the holiday season.

The Pony Trekking season is mainly from May until September, though some centres are open from March until December, and there is the occasional one that is open all the year round, weather permitting. Details of approved centres, including those especially suitable for children, can be obtained from the Scottish Council of Physical Recreation, 4 Queensferry Street, Edinburgh, 2, the Scottish Tourist Board, 2 Rutland Place, West End, Edinburgh, 1; or the Ponies of Britain Club, Brookside Farm, Ascot, Berks.

## Potholing.

Potholing might almost be described as mountaineering in reverse, for it consists in the exploration of underground passages, maybe to depths of several hundred feet. Besides being a challenging recreation, it offers opportunities for specialisation, e.g., diving, photography, surveying, and can yield useful information in connection with water supplies, water pollution and hydroelectric schemes.

The main potholing centres in Great Britain are in Yorkshire, Derbyshire, the Mendips, and South Wales, regions where rainwater, carrying dissolved carbon dioxide from the air, has attacked the massive limestone rocks and the drainage has passed underground. The nature of the passages varies with the geological area. A system containing many horizontal passages is known as a "cave", one with appreciable vertical drops as a "pothole". Drops or "pitches" are comparable to waterfalls in a surface stream and often carry an active stream themselves. A pitch may be over 200 ft. deep, and the system may reach a total depth of 600 ft. or extend for several miles. Potholers make their descents by means of flexible ladders constructed from steel wire and aluminium alloy. Recent developments include the adaptation of skin-diving techniques and equipment to enable the more arduous passages to be explored.

The underground world is far more varied than one would expect. The potholer's headlamp picks out beautiful shapes formed by dripping water containing dissolved limestone—stalactites hanging like icicles, stalagmites growing from the cave floor, curtain-like forms hanging in petrified folds, and smooth pebbles (known as cave pearls) in pure white, orange, green, and black, according to the metallic impurities.

The beginner is strongly urged to join a club, which organises trips and training and provides the proper equipment. Potholing could be dangerous to the novice exploring alone, but as a club member he (she) has the opportunity of taking part in an exciting and exhilarating sport, one of the few left that gives the thrill of original exploration.

### Public School Football.

All the forms of football popular to-day grew out of the games played at various English Public Schools a century and more ago. These games differed widely, the rules often depending on purely local considerations imposed by the available space. The Rugby game (q.v.) in its modern form is, of course, still played, both at that school and far beyond it; and other games that still survive at the schools that originated them are the Eton Field Game, the Eton Wall Game, the Harrow Base Game, and Winchester College Football.

### Punting.

Punting consists of propelling a long, narrow, flat-bottomed boat with a pole, the punter standing up; and it can be either a pleasant, leisurely recreation or a fairly strenuous competitive sport. The sporting side is governed by the Thames Punting Club, which has headquarters at the Thames at Staines in Middlesex. Women, as well as men, take part in competitive events.

Punting as a sport has the unique distinction of being confined, not only to one country, Britain, but to one river, the Thames; though in some parts of the world boats are poled from a standing position are used for various purposes. There have been rumours that Japan has, or had, a similar sport, but these have never been authenticated.

**Quoits.**   *See* Old English Games and Customs.

**Race Walking.**   *See* Athletics, Walking.

### Rackets.

Rackets is a fast, racket-and-ball game, played on a court measuring 62 feet by 31 feet, and using walls. A game consists of 15 points, unless 13-all is reached, when the non-server can set the game to 3 or 5, or 14-all is reached, when the non-server can set the game to 3, the game going to the first player to score the prescribed number of points.

Only the server scores, the receiver taking over service when he makes a winning shot. When served, the ball must strike the front wall above a line called the "cut" line before striking any other part of the court, but, in play, it may be played either on the volley or after one bounce. If a player impedes his opponent, it is a "let," and the point is re-started.

### Real Tennis.

Tennis, sometimes called "Real," "Royal," or "Court" Tennis, is a court game played with rackets and balls that has been called the King of Games, and that was once certainly the game of kings. Henry VIII played, and it is mentioned in Shakespeare's *Henry V*; but the first kings to play were of France, where the game originated.

It is a complicated game, and no description could give anyone who had never seen it an accurate idea of what it is like. Most racket-and-ball games use either a net, over which the ball is hit, or walls, against which it is hit, but Tennis uses both. Also, in most racket games, players change ends after so many games, but, in Tennis, they may do so during a game. Matches are in games and sets, a player winning six games completing a set towards the two out of three or three out of five that will make the match.

There are not many Tennis players in the country—there are only about a dozen courts—and very few women have ever played. People who do play, however, most of whom play other games as well, are almost unanimous in voting it the best of all games.

It is said that the term "love," used in so many games to indicate "nought," comes from Tennis, the original French term being "l'œuf," which, in that language, actually means "egg": an egg being, of course, something like the figure used for "nought." This derivation is not sufficiently well documented to be accepted as definite fact; but it is interesting to note that, in Cricket (q.v.), the term used for a score of "nought" is a "duck," or, in full, a "duck's egg."

**Revolver Shooting.**   *See* Rifle Shooting.

### Riding and Show-jumping.

The almost complete disappearance of the horse from everyday life has been followed by an increase of interest in Riding as a recreation. This is at least partly due to the great attention paid in recent years by both Press and television to one particular branch of horsemanship, Show-jumping. Before learning to jump, however, it is necessary to learn to ride, and many people never go, and have no wish to go, beyond the ordinary, unspectacular riding for pleasure that is called "hacking."

A great deal has been said and written about "correct" riding style, but, in actual fact, there are many different styles. The cavalryman, for instance, bends the leg to some extent; the Red Indian bends it to a much greater extent, more or less in the style that has been adopted by American jockeys; and the cowboy rides with an absolutely straight leg. Yet all these are expert horsemen. To assist in acquiring the normal English style, which is very close to that of the cavalryman, there is an old jingle that is now much less heard than it used to be, but is probably none the less helpful or accurate for that. It runs: "Your head and your heart keep up. Your hands and your heels keep down. Your knees keep close to your horse's sides, and your elbows close to your own." Old or not, anyone who learns it, and then builds up a certain amount of experience of putting it into actual practice is well on the way to becoming a rider.

Those who feel they would like to combine their Riding with something competitive might start with gymkhanas, which are sports meetings that generally include mounted equivalents of such novelty events as obstacle races and needle-threading races. For the more ambitious, gymkhanas could even be the first step towards the top-class competitive sport of Show-jumping.

*Show-jumping.* A Show-jumping contest is a mounted competition over a circuit of jumps, which the entrants attempt one at a time, each having the field to himself or herself, and being free to concentrate entirely on the jumps, without having to worry about other riders. The jumps, which have to be taken in a certain order, are of many kinds, including fences, double fences, walls, and water. Scoring is by points against, called "faults," so many being debited against an entrant for falling, knocking down an obstacle or displacing part of it, refusing, and other mistakes. Though the event is in no sense a race, there is normally a time limit that must not be exceeded, and, in some events, bonus points are awarded for fast rounds. Show-jumping is not restricted to riders who own their own horses, for some owners do not want to compete themselves, and are only too pleased to let good horsemen take their jumpers round for them. Incidentally, inexperienced riders taking up jumping for the first time will probably find it advisable to make some slight changes in their method of sitting in the saddle. Jumping needs a firm seat, and the novice rider may find it necessary to shorten the stirrups a little.

Allied to Show-jumping, and coupled with it in the difficult three-day competitions, is dressage. This is simply a mounted display revealing that the horse is obedient, balanced, supple, and, in a word, trained; and is a simplified form of the better-known " haute école," or highly-schooled riding. Good riders who seek absolute perfection can, if they are willing to pay for it, take an intensive course of haute école riding and all forms of horsemanship at the most famous of all riding schools, the Spanish Riding School in Vienna. Courses, which are conducted in German, consist of eight hours training a day for six months, and informality is not encouraged, the regulation dress for students being a bowler hat, black jacket, and white breeches. Riders who fall are immediately assisted by an attendant armed, not with a stretcher, but with a clothes brush. *See also* Pony Trekking.

## Rifle Shooting.

Considered as a sport, Rifle Shooting, which might almost be called the modern equivalent of archery, had its origins in virtually the same conditions and circumstances that had popularised the older weapon five hundred years previously; though, unlike archery, it did not enjoy legislation aimed at abolishing other recreations in its favour. Both were encouraged because, in their respective periods, efficiency at them meant, not only success in competitions, but also the most effective defence in time of war, the great period of the rifle's encouragement for this reason being the latter half of the nineteenth century. Archery as a sport survives to the present day, and Rifle Shooting as a sport continues, though it can no longer be regarded as the most effective weapon.

With a normal rifle, with a calibre of about ·300 inch, competitive shooting is at ranges from 200 yards to 1000 yards, and there are many competitions, the greatest of them being the annual contest at Bisley, Surrey, for the Queen's Prize. Almost equally popular, however, is small-bore shooting, with a calibre of ·22 inch, and this, too, offers many annual competitions.

*Revolver Shooting.* Revolver shooting, often called pistol shooting, is also a competitive sport, and a very difficult one. Impressions gained from cinema and television screens might lead anyone who has never fired one to think that the revolver is an easy weapon to fire without fuss and with devastating effect. It is the very reverse of this. It is fired, not from the hip, but with the extended arm raised, which is how, in real life, it was generally fired in the old West. It is extremely difficult to hit even a man-size target at 10 yards, and very few people can call themselves good revolver shots, just as few of the old Westerners were good revolver shots. The difficulty is caused by the tremendous " kick " of a weapon that is held, not by both hands and pressed into the shoulder, as a rifle is, but by one hand. Revolvers have sights, but the normal method of aiming is by using the " instinctive pointing sense," which is based on the fact that, if you point at an object in the ordinary way, you do, in fact, point accurately. This applies when pointing a revolver. As with rifles, small-bore target shooting, in which sights are used, is popular.

## Rink Hockey. *See* Skating.

## Rock Climbing. *See* Mountaineering.

## Roller Skating. *See* Skating.

## Rowing.

Rowing, meaning simply taking a boat out on the sea or a river for a short period, is a pleasant recreation and a healthy exercise, but competitive rowing is one of the most strenuous of all sports.

A racing oarsman either rows, which means that he uses one oar, or sculls, which means two oars. Races are of various kinds, the best-known being for crews of eight oarsmen with a cox. Then there are races for crews of four with cox, and for crews of four without cox. There are also events for pairs with cox, pairs without cox, double sculls, and single sculls. Eights, fours, and pairs row, while double and single scullers, of course, scull. In fours and pairs without cox, and in all sculling, the oarsmen steer themselves.

Race Rowing is mainly a river sport, but there are races on the sea. For these, crews are usually fours with cox, and they use heavier boats than the normal racing " shell." (*See also* Boat Races.)

## Rugby Fives. *See* Fives.

## Rugby Football.

As its name implies, Rugby Football is based on the game played at Rugby School in the days when football was not organised and various schools played to their own rules. The story of how the Rugby game originated is well known and widely accepted, but it is definitely not accurate and possibly almost entirely apocryphal.

The story is that, in 1823, a boy named William Webb Ellis disregarded the rules of that time by handling the ball, and that handling was subsequently made legal. In fact, handling the ball by catching it was allowed at Rugby before 1823, so, if Ellis was responsible for an innovation, it was not by handling the ball, but by running with it after catching it. Running with the ball certainly became, and remains, the leading feature of Rugby Football; but the story that Ellis was responsible, though commemorated by a plaque at the school, was first heard years after Ellis's death, and he never knew of the fame that became his. He was definitely at Rugby at the time, though, and, a few years later, he played in the first-ever Oxford and Cambridge cricket match.

The spread of the game beyond the school that originated it has led to, not one, but two games of Rugby Football, Rugby Union and Rugby League. About twenty-five years after the game had become organised, with the Rugby Union as its governing body, there was a dispute on the question of legalising payment for time lost from work by players. The Union would not agree to this, so twenty-two clubs, mainly in Yorkshire, seceded and formed the Northern Union, now the Rugby League. Both bodies originally played the same game, but now, after over sixty years of independent existence, during which each has made various rule changes, there are some important differences.

Rugby was originally played twenty-aside, but it is now fifteen-aside in R.U. and thirteen-aside in R.L., the positions being seven backs and eight forwards in R.U. and seven backs and six forwards in R.L. Played on a pitch marked out as in the diagram, and with an oval ball, Rugby is mainly a handling game, the chief object being the grounding of the ball behind the opponents' goal-line. This is a "try," which counts three points, and entitles the scoring side to an attempt to score a goal by kicking the ball over the cross-bar from a point measured in a straight line from where the ball was grounded. Other forms of goal are penalties, which may be awarded any-where, dropped goals during play, and goals from a "mark," after a player has signalled a "fair catch" of the ball during play by shouting, "Mark." In R.U. goals following tries, called "conversions," count two, and other goals three. In R.L. any goal counts two, but goals from a "mark" are not allowed.

The game is started, and restarted after a score, by a kick-off from the centre; and, there-after, the ball may be advanced by kicking or carrying. It may also be passed from hand, but not forward. Ball carriers may be tackled and thrown down, and they may "hand off" tacklers

though there is a top layer of clubs using part-time professionals.

### Sailing.

Mention of Sailing tends, perhaps, to conjure up visions of large, graceful yachts, beautiful to see, but clearly to be owned only by the wealthy. Sailing to-day, though, is very different from that. It is mainly sailing in small boats, many of them wholly or partly built by their owners. At first glance the building of a boat might seem a tre-mendous and highly skilled task, but, in actual fact, it can be as big and as hard or as small and as easy as the builder wishes. Some amateur builders start from the very beginning, acquiring the various materials needed bit by bit, and gradually bringing their boats into being. How-ever, those who either lack the time for this or

NOTES:—

Indicates Post with Flag.    Length and breadth of field to be as near to dimensions indicated as possible.

– – – These broken lines indicate 10 yards and 5 yards from half-way and touch lines respectively.

*Goal dimensions.*—10 feet is taken from the ground to the top edge of the crossbar and 18 feet 6 inches from inside to inside of the goal posts.

with the unclenched hand. A frequent method of restarting after a stoppage is the "scrum-mage," in which the forwards bend down and push against each other, three from each side constituting a front row, and the remainder two subsequent rows. The ball is then put into the tunnel between the front rows, the centre man of each, the "hooker," endeavouring to gain posses-sion by hooking it back into, and generally right through, his "scrum." In R.L. this method of restarting is used whenever the ball goes out over the touch-line; but in R.U. the ball is thrown in straight along a "line out" of both sets of forwards, unless the side whose throw it is demand a scrummage. In R.L. kicking the ball straight out over the touch-line is allowed only from a free-kick, the penalty being a scrummage at the point from which the ball was kicked. The effect of the differences between the two games is that R.L. is faster and more open, and the ball is more continuously in play. A game lasts for eighty minutes, divided into two halves.

In addition to Britain, both forms of Rugby are played in France, New Zealand, and Australia, and R.U. is played in South Africa. Both codes also have other, smaller "outposts" in various European countries, and there are minor R.U. centres in North and South America. R.U. is entirely an amateur game, and R.L. primarily so,

doubt their ability to construct a boat in which they would feel safe on the water can buy com-plete boat-building kits; and they can buy them at any stage of construction they choose from hardly started to complete except for a coat of paint. It is more economical to build a boat than to buy one complete and ready for launch-ing, and the earlier the stage of construction at which the owner takes over, the greater the saving. Some owners claim that they enjoy the building as much as the sailing, and it is probably true that the owner who has done some work on his boat, however little, takes more interest and pride in the finished article.

The fact that boat-building is now within the reach of practically everyone means, of course, that the end to which it is a means, Sailing, is also within the reach of practically everyone, for few people are far from some suitable stretch of water. Where there is sailing, there are clubs, which the boat owner can join for quite reasonable fees, and which provide either sheltered moorings or "dinghy parks" where the boat can be kept.

Eventually, the small-boat owner may want to try racing his craft, and there are many events for boats of all classes and sizes. Racing is an en-thralling pastime, for, though races are, of course, tests of speed, they are also very much more than

**U26**

that. There is tremendous scope for tactics, and the sport is in every sense a highly skilled one, as well, incidentally, as one with an interesting history behind it.

**Sculling.** *See* Rowing.

**Shove-Ha'penny.** *See* **Old English Games and Customs.**

**Show-Jumping.** *See* Riding and Show-Jumping.

**Skating.**

At first glance, ice-skating would not appear to be a normal activity for British people, for it is a part of Winter Sports (*q.v.*), which are possible in Britain only rarely and to a very small extent, and it was formerly restricted to brief periods when rivers, lakes, and ponds were frozen. Despite this, however, the people of this country have always appeared to possess a natural talent for it, and they have practised it whenever opportunity offered. The history of British Skating goes back a very long way, and includes occasions when Skating was possible, and took place, on the Thames, as well as many, more regular instances in the Fen district and other places. In recent years this wish to skate on ice has been catered for by the opening of many indoor rinks, which make the skater independent of weather and daylight, and enable Skating to be carried on throughout the year.

Many people ice-skate just for recreation, health, and amusement, but anyone keen to carry Skating a stage farther and acquire a higher level of skill can find a wide range of opportunities from which to choose. Figure-skating is very popular, and for those anxious to test their skill at it there is a series of medal tests, in which the skater is not in competition with anybody, but is attempting only to reach a fixed standard. Beyond these, there are many competitions and championships. Dancing on skates also attracts many people; and also offers those interested standard medal tests and competitions.

Another popular skating activity is speed-skating, which takes place indoors and, whenever possible, outdoors as well, though the methods and techniques of the two forms of racing differ widely. Outdoors, the skaters normally race in pairs, though each man is timed, and is actually racing against the whole field. Much of the racing is on long, straight stretches of ice. Indoors, skaters race perhaps four at a time, and are directly opposed to those on the ice with them. These races are on small tracks, a lap sometimes being no more than 130 yards. Standard outdoor distances range from 500 to 10,000 metres, while indoor races go from 440 yards to 2 miles. There are also indoor relays, generally of 3 miles, in which teams of four race on the "Madison" method, relieving each other, not at fixed points, but at will. In addition to competitions and championships, speed-skaters also have their standard medal tests.

Ice, however, is not the only surface on which Skating takes place, for, following an unusual history, roller-skating also maintains a large following. Roller-skating was originally introduced long before the arrival of the indoor ice rinks purely to provide ice-skaters with some kind of substitute when no natural ice was available. It progressed by fits and starts, varying from extraordinary "crazes" when it seemed that everybody was roller-skating, to periods when nobody appeared to be doing so. Eventually, it settled down to a steady existence as a popular recreation in its own right that has in no sense been pushed into the background by the increased facilities for ice-skating. The opportunities it offers are almost identical with those of ice-skating, for they include figure-skating, dancing, and speed-skating, with championships, competitions, and standard medal tests in all branches.

Both forms of Skating also offer a team game, and in both it is hockey. Ice-hockey, which is called simply hockey in Canada, where it originated, and, in the United States, is played six-aside, with substitutes permitted, and with a rubber disc, called a "puck," instead of a ball. It first began to win popularity in Britain soon after the First World War, and since then has had rather a chequered career, helped forward by the semi-professional players from Canada, who play in the National League teams, and held back by the lack of facilities for British youngsters to practise; for practice sessions mean closing rinks to all the other forms of Skating for certain periods. The game should, however, survive, for there is a definite demand for it.

Roller-hockey, generally known as rink-hockey, bears a closer resemblance to its parent game, outdoor field hockey, than does ice-hockey. It is played with a ball, and is five-aside, with one substitute permitted. Its popularity is such that it is now played throughout the year.

There is a form of hockey on ice that closely resembles outdoor hockey. This is Bandy, which originated in England, but is no longer played here, though it is popular in Sweden and the U.S.S.R. Some other games have been tried on skates from time to time. One is Badminton, which has been played on ice, but only as a stage exhibition. Basketball on roller-skates has been tried in several countries, and might well develop and spread.

Skating is not so much a recreation, sport, or game as a whole series of different recreations, sports, and games. Each has its following, and, while there are enthusiasts who are interested in both ice- and roller-skating, or in more than one branch of one or both of them, there are many ice-skaters who have no interest in or knowledge of roller-skating, and vice versa, and many keen supporters of just one branch of Skating who hardly know that the many other branches exist. It is, of course, quite possible to take part in both ice- and roller-skating, and in more than one branch of Skating, and greatly to increase one's enjoyment by doing so.

It is not particularly hard to learn to skate. It requires strong ankles, a good sense of balance, and plenty of confidence; and it is possible to start practising, at least to a limited extent, at home, for instance, by getting used to standing on skates. Skating is probably more easily mastered when young, but many adults have successfully taken it up.

**Skiing.** *See* Winter Sports.

**Ski-Joring.** *See* Winter Sports.

**Ski-Jumping.** *See* Winter Sports.

**Skittles.**

Skittles has been played in England since the 13th century and came from Germany where it was known as *Kegel.* There are several versions, but all consist in throwing a ball down a level alley at a set of pins.

In English Skittles, the ball is a flat-sided object called a *cheese*; in German and Dutch Skittles a round ball is used. Both types of ball weigh at least 10 lb. and sometimes as much as 16 lb. Over the years the number of pins has varied between 3 and 17, but the normal number is 9, hence the alternative name of Ninepins, though in some parts of England 10 are still preferred.

English Skittles, using nine pins, is played in an alley about 12 yards long and 3 or 4 yards wide. The pins are set up in diamond formation, and players throw the cheese at them from a distance of 6 or 8 yards, being allowed one step forward during the throw. There are several methods of scoring. In one, the object is to score 31 in as few throws as possible, each pin knocked down counting 1, and any throw in which more than the number still required are knocked down not counting. Another method is to knock down as many pins as possible in a fixed number of throws, the highest total winning. Yet another allows each player three throws in each of a fixed number of turns, scoring being 3 if all nine pins are knocked down in one throw, 2 if in two throws, 1 if in three throws, and 0 if any are still standing after the three throws. Pins must be hit by the cheese direct or by another falling pin. Pins knocked down by rebounds do not count.

The Dutch introduced Skittles, as played with a round ball and nine pins, to America in the 18th century. The game rapidly became popular but in 1841 it was made illegal because of the betting on it. However, the law specifically mentioned " nine pins ", so the organisers simply added a tenth, and the game survived. As Bowling, it became very popular in 1952 when a machine was invented for replacing the pins automatically and there are now over 30 million players in the United States.

In 1960 this form of the game reached Britain where it soon became easily the most popular version of Skittles, there now being well over half a million players. There is a British Tenpin Bowling Association and a Tenpin Bowling Proprietors' Association of Great Britain. The " bowls," some of them converted cinemas, offer many of the facilities of a social club. Competent instructors are available at them, and there are countless competitions and leagues.

**Snooker.** *See* Billiards.

**Snowshoe Running.** *See* Winter Sports.

**Softball.** *See* Baseball.

**Solo Whist.**

Solo Whist is a card game for four players, who normally act independently. Play is as at Whist (*q.v.*), but the cards are dealt in threes, the final round being dealt singly, and the dealer exposing his last card to indicate trumps.

Players then " declare " in turn, starting with the player on the dealer's left. The lowest call is " I propose," which entails making eight tricks with a partner, any one of the other players being eligible to " accept " in his turn. The next call is " Solo," which requires five tricks to be made unassisted. Next comes " Misère," in which every trick must be lost, and then comes " Abondance," in which nine tricks must be made. Higher still is " Misère Ouverte," in which every trick must be lost with the player's hand exposed, and highest of all is " Abondance Declarée," in which every trick must be made. Any player may " Pass," and, once a call has been made, later callers must make a higher call or pass.

Though calls are made with trumps already nominated, certain calls may alter the trumps; and, with regard to these, there are several views, all quite widely held, as to the rules that should apply. A player calling Abondance can choose his own trumps, though Abondance in the nominated trumps—called Royal Abondance—takes precedence over the same call in another suit. In Abondance one school of thought holds that the first round is played on the nominated trumps, while another takes the view that the first card only is played on the nominated trumps. In either of these circumstances a player making this call should not announce his trumps until the round or card has been played, unless it is necessary to announce Royal Abondance to overcall. There is, however, a third view, and it is the view of the majority of authorities who have actually written about the game, that the new trumps should be announced before the hand starts. Also the subject of differing views is Abondance Declarée, one view being that the caller can choose his own trumps, and another that, in this call, there are no trumps, though both views agree that this call confers the right to lead. A good player can easily adapt himself to any of these variations, the important thing being to check which versions are being used before starting to play. On the Misère calls there are no trumps,

and in Misère Ouverte the player need not expose his hand until the first round has been played.

**Speed-Skating.** *See* Skating.

**Squash Rackets.**

This game is played on the same principle as its forerunner Rackets (*q.v.*) but in a smaller court, with a shorter racket and a rubber ball. It is mainly a singles game, though doubles can be played.

The court has four walls with the rear part divided into two service courts, each having a small " service box " down the court by the side wall. The server must have one foot in the box and serve the ball on to the front wall above the " cut " line (6 ft. in singles) so that it comes back diagonally into the other service court. But it need not land direct, or land at all, but may strike the side wall or back wall or both and be volleyed by the receiver. The object of the game is to score points by striking the ball in such a way that the opponent is unable to return it or make a proper shot. Every shot played in a rally must hit the front wall (directly or via another wall) and must be played on the volley or after one bounce. The service ball must always hit the front wall first. Service proceeds from the two boxes alternately. It is important to note that unlike Lawn Tennis (*q.v.*) services that would be faults become good if taken by the receiver. A game is 9 points but if 8–8 is reached the winner is the next to score 2 consecutive points. Only the server scores points, winning shots by the receiver entitling him to take over the service. Players sometimes accidentally impede each other and when this happens it is a " let," and the point is replayed.

The game enjoys great and increasing popularity. The Central Council of Physical Recreation co-operates with the Squash Rackets Association (the game's governing body) in running courses and there are coaches at many clubs. Though many people play purely for exercise and enjoyment, there are many competitive events, both national and international. Internationally, Squash Rackets is largely dominated by the Egyptians and Pakistanis but a rapid rise in popularity, comparable with that in Britain, has brought Australia very close to the top. The game has developed along slightly different lines in the United States, but with the growth of international competition and the formation of an International Federation the differences from the standard game are likely to disappear.

**Stoolball.** *See* Old English Games and Customs.

**Strand-Pulling.** *See* Weight-lifting.

**Surf Riding.** *See* Swimming.

**Swimming.**

Swimming is an extremely popular pastime that also shares with walking the distinction of being a perfect exercise for health, as it exercises the whole body, and can be carried out as easily or as strenuously as the swimmer wishes. It is also a very useful accomplishment that may at any time put its possessor in a position to save a life.

There are several different swimming strokes, the basic stroke being the breast-stroke, now often seen in an alternative method, the butterfly. Faster strokes include the side-arm, the overarm, the trudgeon, and the crawl, but each of these attempts to speed up progress through the water has really superseded its predecessor, and the crawl is now almost universal. There are also two strokes used in swimming on the back, one being a back equivalent of the breast-stroke, and the other a back crawl. It is possible to swim under the water, using the breast-stroke, and to keep the eyes open while doing so. It is also possible to swim down through the water to retrieve objects that may have been dropped.

Ascending through the water is automatic, though it can be hastened by a kick. Remaining stationary in deep water can be achieved either by floating on the back or by treading water, which simply means moving the legs gently up and down.

It is not difficult to teach oneself to swim, and, like cycling, it is an accomplishment which, once learned, is never forgotten. The main thing is confidence, or an absence of any fear of the water. Such fears are quite unnecessary, for water is an element that always tends to keep a human being on the surface, and not to draw him under. Going underneath the water, and staying underneath, requires a definite physical effort, and, if that effort ceases, the swimmer is automatically brought to the surface again. Many non-swimmers who get into difficulties increase these by struggling wildly, for, by doing so, they may easily take and keep themselves under. If they would make only the gentle movements of treading water, they would both stay afloat much longer and present far fewer problems to any swimmer who might be trying to save them.

Saving life in the water is the object of the Royal Life-Saving Society, which teaches the best methods of bringing people who are in difficulties ashore, and also methods of artificial respiration for use in reviving the apparently drowned. Every swimmer should acquire some knowledge of life-saving, for even a strong swimmer may experience considerable difficulty in saving anyone unless he or she has some idea of the best way of setting about it. Many swimmers, for instance, normally use only the crawl and the back crawl, whereas, to save anyone, it is almost essential to use either the breast-stroke or its back equivalent.

Swimming has a well-organised competitive side, with many competitions and championships right up to the Olympic Games. Most races take place in baths, but there are some river and sea events, and the greatest competitive challenge to any swimmer is, of course, the English Channel. Although this has been conquered many times, the swimming of it remains, and will always remain, a wonderful achievement.

*Diving.* Generally accepted as being akin to Swimming, though actually it is quite a different sport, is Diving. Competition Diving means using boards of various heights, performing certain set dives, and choosing additional ones from an approved list. Diving requires a certain amount of nerve, and also gymnastic ability, including the ability to control the body in the air. Whereas strong swimmers are generally fairly big, divers are often much smaller and more compactly built.

*Water Polo.* In view of the popularity of Swimming, it is not surprising that there is a water team game, this being Water Polo, in which the object is the scoring of goals, the ball and the goals resembling those used in Soccer, though all shots and passes are, of course, thrown. Throughout a history of nearly eighty years, Water Polo has been beset by rule trouble, and has probably been the subject of more codes of rules than almost any other game. The difficulty is the detection of fouls under the water; the ideal, a game of the basketball type, free of bodily contact.

*Surf Riding.* Though straightforward Swimming, Diving, and Water Polo are the chief competitive water sports, there are other water activities with large and, in some cases, growing followings, some of them also having their competitive side. Fairly old-established is the Hawaiian sport of Surf Riding, which has been seen though generally in a rather milder form, in many parts of the world. It consists of placing a flat board on the water, and then lying, or, more rarely, kneeling or standing on it, and being carried ashore on the crest of a wave.

*Underwater Swimming.* Undoubtedly the fastest growing of all swimming activities is Underwater Swimming, which is a link between ordinary diving and swimming under water, with the swimmer, depending on his own lungs, able to remain below for only a few seconds, and fully-fledged deep-sea diving, with the diver weighed down with equipment and receiving assistance from the surface. The underwater swimmer receives no surface assistance, but he does use light equipment, consisting of an artificial " lung " and breathing tubes, and also a mask and flippers. This type of swimming developed during the Second World War, in which Naval underwater swimmers, called "frogmen," rendered great services. Frogmen can also render useful services in peacetime, in, for instance, the sometimes necessary searching of rivers and canals; in underwater photography; and in exploring wrecks, and even old, lost cities, now under water. There is also a vast amount of knowledge, excitement, and pleasure to be gained from a "close-up" study of the many fascinating aspects of the underwater world.

It might be thought that the first step towards becoming an underwater expert was to become an expert swimmer, but it is not essential for an underwater swimmer to be a surface swimmer of anything like championship class. There are, of course, dangers, and the newcomer to Underwater Swimming should not go down too deep until he has had a good deal of practice and gained a certain amount of experience. Preferably, the first descents to any depth should not be undertaken alone, and if the swimmer has gone at all deep he should come up slowly, otherwise he risks getting the "bends," which is caisson disease, and means that reduced air pressure has caused nitrogen bubbles to form in the tissues. There may also be danger from large fish, and underwater swimmers should not venture into undersea caverns without a light. It is always advisable to collect as much local information as possible before diving in a strange area. Though all kinds of equipment, including cameras, harpoons, knives, and torches, can be carried, the beginner will make a better start if he dives without encumbrances. Most of the dangers can be avoided or circumvented with care, and the reward for those who master Underwater Swimming is a whole new world to explore.

Table Tennis.

Originally simply an amusing parlour game known as "Ping-Pong," Table Tennis is now a serious, world-wide, competitive sport, with many championships and tournaments, and the ability to attract crowds of 10,000 spectators.

Resembling a miniature game of Lawn Tennis (*q.v.*), the net is set on a table 9 feet long by 5 feet wide, and the ball is a very light celluloid one. Players serve series of five balls in turn, both server and receiver scoring. The service has to bounce first on the server's side of the net, and then on the other, and, thereafter, all strokes are " ground " strokes, volleying not being allowed. A game is 21 points, and matches are usually the best two out of three or three out of five games. " Vantage " games are played, as, if the score reaches 20-all, each player serves once in turn until one has a clear lead of two points. Both singles and doubles are played.

Table Tennis requires perfect fitness and split-second reactions. Many Lawn Tennis players also play Table Tennis, and several of these have found it desirable to retire from the fast table game before giving up the outdoor game.

Tennis. *See* Lawn Tennis, Real Tennis.

Tobogganing. *See* Winter Sports.

Traditional Games and Customs.

Traditional and unusual sporting events are plentiful in many parts of the world, but few have a longer tradition behind them than the Calcio in Livrea that can still be seen, over 500 years after its inception, in the Italian city of Florence. It is a version of Football, based on an ancient Greek game called Episkuros and the old Roman game of Harpastum. Played twenty-seven-aside on a pitch rather smaller than an Association football pitch, it was originally restricted to the nobility, and in 1672 a game was cancelled when it was discovered that the selected teams included players who were only "gentlemen." The ordinary people did play, but the game as played by them was called Calcio Divisi, and was not regarded as the same thing. The playing of Calcio in Livrea faded out in 1739, but was revived in 1898, to stop again in 1902, only to be revived once more in 1930. To-day, there are generally two games a year between teams no longer restricted to the nobility and representing the four quarters of Florence. They are wonderful spectacles, for the players, and also numerous officials and attendants, wear fourteenth-century costume, and the games are preceded by ceremonial processions, and by a special address to the most distinguished person present. The trophy for the games is traditionally a white calf.

Another ancient Italian sporting event that still survives is found in Siena, and consists of horseracing in the city. It is a wild and fierce form of racing in which virtually anything that might further the cause of victory goes on between the riders. Riding events, many of them of great antiquity, figure prominently in countries in which great horsemanship is an age-old tradition. Russia offers Kop-Karri, a fifteen-aside mounted game that is a battle for possession of a sheep's pelt. Riders carry their reins in their teeth to leave their hands free for the fight, and anyone who gets the pelt is soon downed in what is one of the roughest and toughest games of all time. Played now by Kazakhs from the Steppes and Tadjiks from the Afghanistan border, this game originated in China, and was brought out of that country by the riders of the Golden Hordes of Genghis Khan. Also found in Russia is the mounted Kissing Game, in which a galloping male horseman seeks to snatch a kiss from a girl rider armed with a whip.

Horses are also prominent in North American Rodeos, which consist of competitions in cowboy skills, such as riding, roping, steer-wrestling, and chuck-wagon racing, which can still be seen annually in rodeos like the famous Stampede at Calgary in Alberta. Rather different are Chilean Rodeos, which consist mainly of displays involving horses and young bulls, and the Topeadura, in which two mounted teams push against a long log suspended horizontally between them. Chilean Rodeos carefully avoid anything that might harm the animals, which enter into things with excitement and enjoyment. This also applies to the bull races at Pamekasan in the Indonesian island of Madura. Based on the local method of ploughing, these consist of races in which a driver stands barefooted on a small wooden sled harnessed to a pair of bulls, though these need little driving. In India, elephant racing may be as much as a thousand years old, but it is now being allowed to decline because of reputed " feudal " associations. Recently, there was a not-very-serious attempt to introduce it into the United States, which is, however, more at home with events like Florida's Swamp Buggy Derby, in which vehicles carrying two hunters and their equipment must cover a figure-eight course of a mile within ten minutes.

Differing widely from these events in everything but speed is Pelota, or Jai Alai. Played in Spain, France, Portugal, North Africa, and South and Central America, pelota is a traditional Basque game that developed from a mediæval form of handball that was played against village church walls. To this day, many pelota courts, called " canchas," are next to churches, the wall, or " fronton," which is an integral part of the game being that of the church, and the priest very often being one of the best of the local players. The game, which is very fast and exhausting, can be between two players or between teams of two or three, and consists of playing a ball that is rather smaller than a tennis ball against a wall with either the hand or, in the case of the most popular form of the game, the Grand Chistera, with a long, narrow, wicker basket,

called a " chistera," that is strapped to the player's hand and arm.

Personal combat sports have always been popular, and Switzerland has a national sport of this type that had its first big tournament in 1905 in Das Schwingen, which means " The Swinging." It is a form of wrestling, in which the contestants, normally very powerful Alpine herdsmen, wear special belts and shorts by which holds are taken. The traditional prize for the winner of the annual Swiss championship is a two-year-old heifer. Iceland has a rather similar form of wrestling, called Glima. Much less similar is the Siamese form of boxing. Competitors in this wear, and use, ordinary boxing gloves, but they are also allowed to use their elbows, knees, and feet, which are bare.

Next, a group of recreations in which the feet are used lethally, starting with the Netherlands, and the Nijmegen Marches. Over half a century old, these are international long-distance walks that are not races, but reliability trials, in which complete teams must start and finish together within a certain time. The marches take four days, the distance to be covered each day varying between 25 and 30 miles according to the class. Classes catered for include men, women, and also police teams, walking in uniform, and military teams, carrying equipment. The walks, which attract over 10,000 competitors every July, are an unusual and colourful spectacle, and the opening ceremony is as well worth watching as that of the Olympic Games. British walkers, civilian, police, and military, regularly take part. Though called marches, they are really walks; and it is unlikely that many men would consider real precision marching as a recreation. However, women do in at least one country. This is New Zealand, where marching competitions are held between teams of twelve, with a leader, each team wearing a special uniform, and carrying out a three-minute routine to the music of a pipe band. Points are awarded, not only for the marching, but also for the costumes and the leading. Though the competitions are confined to women, teams are generally trained and drilled by men. This type of marching was seen in Britain a few years ago, when the Blair Atholl team toured the country giving demonstrations.

About fifty years old in its own country, Sweden, and quite likely to spread to other countries in the future is Orienteering, which consists of finding one's way about the country from one control point to another by using maps and compasses. Generally carried out on foot, and in wild country, it can also be done on horses, bicycles, motor-cycles, skis, and skates, and in cars and canoes, and in any kind of country, including urban areas. During the Second World War, in which Sweden, though not involved, had to be ready, Orienteering was extensively used in military and civil defence training; and it was then that night Orienteering began, with competitors wearing lamps strapped to their foreheads. Probably the most strenuous annual event in Orienteering is the Swedish three-day mountain race, in which contestants, working in teams of two, have to cover 60 miles of mountains, forests, and swamps on foot, carrying equipment that must include tents and food. Though mainly confined to Sweden, Orienteering has been successfully tried in Canada and the United States, where it acquired its English-language name.

Non-English recreations that English people do not have to travel very far to see are the many and various activities that go to make up Scotland's Highland Games. Highland Games meetings, or gatherings, are sports meetings, but sports meetings with their own definite and extremely colourful and spectacular characteristics. The chief sporting events at them are the " heavyweight " events, including tossing the caber, throwing the hammer in the Scots style, putting and throwing weights of various sizes, and wrestling. In addition, there are competitions in Highland dancing and piping, and often for pipe bands, all playing their parts in a spectacle that can hold its own with any of the many spectacular events that love of tradition and love of sport have combined to produce all over the world. (*See also* Old English Games and Customs.)

Trampoline. *See* Gymnastics.

## Tug-of-War.

A Tug-of-War is one of the least complicated and one of the most strenuous events in sport. It consists of eight men pulling on a rope against another set of eight pulling in the opposite direction, each team trying to pull the other forward across a line, and each helped by a coach, who instructs them when to "heave" and when to concentrate on resisting the opponents' heaves. A pull may be over in a few seconds, or it may take many minutes. Contests are generally the best two out of three pulls, and a competition may involve three such contests in one afternoon. Competitions may be at "catchweights," which means that there is no weight limit, or they may restrict the eight men to a total weight of, say, 104 stone or 100 stone. The Tug-of-War requires, and will help to develop, great strength.

A popular event that always arouses great enthusiasm amongst the spectators, the Tug-of-War fully merits this position, but it owes some of its success to the fact that it was introduced into the right place at the right time. In the nineteenth century, before athletic sports were really organised, most country sports meetings included events like obstacle races, sack races, and egg-and-spoon races. These, however, though they are found to this day in some children's and local sports, grew less popular, and began to give place to more "serious" ones, favourite replacement for them being the Tug-of-War. Then athletic sports became organised, and the Amateur Athletic Association was founded, and instituted its famous annual championships, including two Tug-of-War championships that still exist, where, a few years earlier, there might have been obstacle-race and sack-race championships.

For years, service units and police forces provided the leading Tug-of-War teams, but, more recently, they have been challenged by teams from big firms. A still later development has been the formation of clubs concentrating entirely on the Tug-of-War. Organisations and clubs with Tug-of-War teams now have their own association, and their own annual championship meeting.

## Underwater Swimming. *See* Swimming.

## Underwater Watching.

In recent years there has been a considerable increase of interest in the undersea world; and some participation in this has been brought within the reach of those who are unwilling or unable to take part in underwater swimming and diving by the use of glass-bottomed boats, often boats in which the viewer slides back a wooden panel at his feet to reveal the glass viewing panel. Such boats, of course, can only be of use where the water is exceptionally clear and transparent, but, where conditions are suitable, a surprising amount of the life and colour of the world beneath the seas can be seen, and without any of the strain or danger of diving.

Much of the Mediterranean Sea fulfils the necessary conditions of clarity and transparency, particularly, perhaps, the coasts of Corsica, Sardinia, Sicily, and Italy itself. Greek and Egyptian waters are also clear, as are the waters of the Spanish Costa Brava and the Balearic Islands. Going farther afield, there are very transparent waters off parts of the Australian coast, and, of course, in the West Indies.

## Volleyball.

Long-established in the United States, and played also in some other countries, Volleyball is a comparatively recent arrival in Britain, where it has been encouraged by leading personalities from the sport of Athletics, who saw in it an ideal game for maintaining fitness, and formed a governing body to organise and control it. A league started in London owed much of its early success to players of nationalities other than British, but the game took a big step forward when it was adopted by the London Fire Brigade as an effective method of physical training.

Volleyball might be compared with Basketball (*q.v.*) in that it is a team game that can be played indoors, though it can also be played on outdoor courts. The actual game, however, differs widely from Basketball. Played six-aside on a rectangular court that should not exceed 60 feet by 30 feet, it consists of "volleying" an inflated ball across a net 8 feet high with the hands, the object being to make it touch the ground in the opponents' court, while preventing it doing so in your own.

## Water Polo. *See* Swimming.

## Water Skiing.

Water Skiing originated in the United States in the early nineteen-twenties and actually descends from Surf Riding (*q.v.*). Surf Riding led to Aquaplaning, in which a board was towed by a motor-boat with the rider standing. A further development saw the board giving place to actual skis and Water Skiing was born. It eventually reached France, and then, in 1950, Britain.

In Britain, it rapidly became popular, partly through television, which demonstrated it when it was still in its infancy. This led directly to several new Water Skiing centres being opened up in various parts of the country. Britain now has over 75,000 water skiers and there are about a hundred clubs, most of them affiliated to the British Water Ski Federation. The Federation, which is second in size only to that of the United States, is in turn affiliated to the World Water Ski Union.

Water Skiing has been described as the ideal family recreation, for, though, at the highest level, it requires great skill and daring, almost anyone including children, can quite easily acquire sufficient skill to enjoy it as a recreation. The more ambitious can, if they wish, proceed to such variations as monoskiing, using only one ski; slalom, when the skier, generally on one ski, is towed through a staggered arrangement of buoys; jumping, from a ramp between three and six feet high; and tricks, which vary from the quite simple to the very difficult. There are Water Skiing championships, both national and international; these involve slalom, jumping, and tricks.

The Central Council of Physical Recreation holds Water Skiing courses and there are also coaches at many clubs. Water Skiing can be practised in a swimming suit, but many skiers wear special rubber suits, or at least jackets.

## Walking.

Walking comes so naturally that few people ever think about it. It is, however, worth thinking about, for it is the basis, not only of everyday life, but also of every physical, as opposed to purely mental, recreation, sport, and game, all of which involve, if not actual walking, then running, which is an equally natural step beyond walking. It is also the basis of training, either for health and fitness or for a strenuous sport. It has been said that it is impossible to walk too much; and, while those who have done little walking would, of course, have to increase the distance gradually, there is no doubt that a regular, daily two- or three-mile walk would in itself prove an effective method of maintaining health and fitness.

A great deal of pleasure can be added to walking about the countryside by taking an interest in those things which will help you to understand the history of this island. The countryside is rich in churches, historic buildings, ruins, wayside crosses, prehistoric camps, and dykes. Besides a good pair of shoes you need a pencil, a notebook, a 1-in. Ordnance Survey map, a good guide book, and a fund of optimism, imagination, and curiosity. During your rest intervals you can study the map and plan, and read one or more of the many background books to supplement what you have seen and stimulate you to further adventure. Not only is our countryside full of interest, it is remarkably varied. Among the organisations which provide rambling opportunities are the Ramblers' Association, the Holiday Fellowship, and the Co-operative Holidays Association. *See also* Long-distance Routes, Section L.

## Weight-lifting.

Weight-lifting is a method of exercising to maintain health and develop strength; a system of training that can usefully be at least a part of the preparation for almost any sport or game; and a highly organised and very popular competitive sport in its own right. Once, quite erroneously, thought to be an over-strenuous and "dangerous" activity, it has now, in more enlightened days, seen the pendulum swing completely in the opposite direction, with professional and amateur sportsmen of all kinds freely admitting how much they owe to it, and a large following of seekers after health and fitness, including women, many of them actresses, models, and others whose work demands a near-perfect figure.

When it is used as exercise and training, the strenuousness of it depends entirely on the wishes of the lifter or his or her adviser; for training with weights does not mean lifting as heavy a weight as possible, but carrying out a certain number of repetitions in various styles with weights well within the lifter's capacity. For those keen to develop the maximum strength of which, according to their build, they are capable, weight-lifting is certainly the quickest, and perhaps the only, way of achieving this. One of the charges levelled against it is that it makes one slow, but this is just another fallacy. It does not; and competitive weight-lifters actually make some of the fastest movements known in sport.

As a competitive sport, Weight-lifting is divided into weight classes, and there are many international and national championships and competitions. The sport is popular almost all over the world, and has been firmly established in Britain for many years.

*Strand-Pulling.* Akin to Weight-lifting in that it is a method of keeping fit and developing strength that is also a competitive sport is Strand-pulling, using a steel or rubber expander. Various different "pulls" are possible, and the strength and resistance of the expander can be altered at will. Many people use this old-established system of exercising for health and strength; and, for those interested, there are many strand-pulling championships and competitions.

## Whist.

Whist might be called the standard card game. It has never excited quite the furore of Bridge (*q.v.*), but it is long established and popular, both at home and at Whist Drives. It is probably the first card game, apart, perhaps, from a few simple games depending on luck, that most people learn, and it provides a sound foundation for the embryo card player.

It is played by four people, two partnerships of two opposing each other, and with a normal pack of cards. The partners sit opposite each other; and the pack is shuffled, cut for trumps, and dealt out singly. The cards are then played out in thirteen tricks of four each, the player on the dealer's left having first lead, and the winner of each trick leading in the next. Ace counts as the highest card—except in cutting, when it counts as the lowest—and it is followed by king, queen, knave, and then on from ten downwards. The higher card of any suit takes the lower, unless it is trumped by a player unable to follow suit, the tricks being gathered up by the winner as made.

It is necessary to concentrate, to watch the cards played, and to endeavour to "place" the unplayed cards. This comes with experience, as does an understanding of such unwritten rules as "Second in hand plays low" and "Third in hand plays high," and a knowledge of when to disregard these.

Three-handed Whist is possible, one suit being discarded.

## Winter Sports.

There are few fields of recreational or sporting activity to which, given the opportunity, British people take more eagerly than Winter Sports. Enthusiasts from Britain were going abroad to find, and in some cases start, them before the turn of the century; and to-day there are probably a hundred travellers for every one who went sixty years ago.

Switzerland is, of course, the traditional objective, but there is actually a wide choice, for facilities exist in Norway, Austria, Italy, France, Germany, and Czechoslovakia. There are opportunities to suit most purses, and to suit both those who want only sport and those who want sport combined with entertainment. If the object is simply Skiing, the most popular of the winter sports, there is really no need to travel further than Scotland, which provides excellent facilities, and is increasing these every year.

For those whose time and experience are both limited, skiing is normally of the downhill variety, rather than the lengthy journeys on the level as well as on hills, and up as well as down, at which many Continental, and particularly Scandinavian, skiers are adept. Greatly increased facilities in the way of ski-lifts enable the holiday skier to work in three times as many descents as the skier of only a few years ago. Almost every resort has a ski-school with an English-speaking instructor, and it is always advisable for a novice to join this. It is also advisable for novices to start training for a ski holiday some time in advance, both by ordinary physical training and by attending a dry ski-school. The air in winter sports resorts encourages more activity than is good for a completely untrained person, and the fitter the skier, the less his chance of being injured. Skiing accidents are plentiful, but many of them could be avoided by the exercise of a few simple precautions. Having lessons is one; being fit is another; short skis with safety bindings are still another; and refusing to ski late, which may be any time after four o'clock, is yet another, for, as the light fades, it is replaced by a bluish light that makes uneven patches difficult to see, and the snow tends to ice over. Most winter sports equipment can be hired, but hired or bought, and regardless of the extent to which fashionable skiing clothing may be advertised, the most important items are the boots. The winter sports season lasts from December until March, but the snow is sometimes late, and, while Christmas and New Year should be safe enough, February offers the certainty of snow, combined with longer days.

Ski-jumping is a separate sport, and one for experts. The jumper takes-off down a steep slope and over a platform, which he leaves at a speed of about 50 m.p.h., to land something like 150 feet below his take-off, and more than that distance out in front of it. Ski-Joring is really ski-racing behind unridden horses, but the term is also applied to quite gentle ski-trips behind ridden horses, horse-drawn vehicles, and mechanical vehicles.

The Biathlon is a combination of skiing over a 20-kilometre course and rifle-shooting. There is a World Championship, and Britain enters for this, but the leading exponents of this sport are the Scandinavians and the Russians. As with the Modern Penthathlon (*q.v.*), most British competitors are servicemen, but the sport is in no way barred to civilians.

Bobsleigh Riding and Tobogganing consist of riding and racing down ice runs at terrific speeds on sleighs, the bobsleigh being for two, four, or five riders, and the toboggan, which takes its name, not from anywhere in Europe, but from a Red Indian language, being for one rider. Bobsleigh crews sit, the first man steering by a wheel or ropes, and the last man operating the brake with which the sleigh is fitted. Toboggan riders lie face downwards, and brake through special spikes on their boots. Both sports are exceptionally thrilling, and both can be dangerous.

Even greater speeds, ranging from 50 to 100 m.p.h., and even greater danger, are to be found in Ice-Yachting. This sport, or something very like it, has actually been known for hundreds of years, but it is now rarely available in Europe because of the lack of frozen lakes large enough for the modern high-speed yachts. In the United States, however, there are over 3,000 such yachts to be seen during the season, which, as with European winter sports, lasts from December until March. One-man ice-yachts normally carry about 75 square feet of sail, but two-man yachts may carry as much as 650 square feet. Two-man yachts may be 56 feet long and weigh half-a-ton.

At the opposite extreme from the point of view of speed is the 400-year-old Scottish game of Curling, which is played on ice, but not on skates. It resembles Bowls (q.v.), but the implements used are curling stones weighing about 35 lb., and having handles. Slow, but still-moving stones are encouraged by sweeping the ice in front of them with brooms.

Not a European winter sport, but nevertheless a snow sport in Canada is Snowshoe Running. Like skiing, this is a useful method of travelling about on snow that has been made the subject of races. The Canadian side of the Atlantic is also the home of Snow Snakes, a Red Indian game that consists of throwing a polished wooden stick along an ice trough in the snow. These "snakes" have been known to go for over a mile and to travel at 120 m.p.h. (See also Skating.)

Wingfield Sculls. See Boat Races.

Wrestling.

Wrestling, an individual combat in which competitors, using only their bare hands, endeavour to throw each other, is one of the most natural sports, and also one of the oldest. It is practised in many countries, and in many different styles, in most of which the wrestlers are divided into classes by weight.

In Britain, probably the most popular style is Catch-As-Catch-Can, in which the wrestlers start apart, and may try to throw their opponents by grasping them with the hands or by various kinds of trip. During the bout, the competitors may be either on their feet or down on the mat, and the rules contain various provisions to prevent the bout lasting for an indefinite time. Wrestlers reaching a deadlock on the mat may be ordered to stand up and start again, and points decisions after a certain time are also possible. Certain dangerous holds are barred.

Another style is Cumberland and Westmorland Wrestling, which is extremely popular in those counties, and in Scotland. In this, the wrestler clasps his hands together behind his opponent's back, and all throwing is done by the legs, the breaking of the opponent's clasp constituting the fall. The initial hold is, therefore, of major importance, and the taking of it often takes longer than the actual bout.

A further form of British wrestling is Cornish Wrestling, in which the wrestlers wear canvas jackets, by which all holds are taken. A similar form of wrestling is found in Brittany.

In Græco-Roman Wrestling, which has always been very popular on the Continent, though less so in Britain, wrestlers start apart, and may take hold only above the waist. Bouts in this style may take a considerable time. At one time, there were many Græco-Roman handicap matches, in which a top-class wrestler undertook to win a fall, or a number of falls, in a fixed time.

Græco-Roman was formerly the style used in professional wrestling, but, in recent years, professionals have used the "Free" or "All-In" style. This has rules, but it is not always very clear just what they are, and this, combined with widespread suspicions that bouts are not really genuine contests, has led to the quite large following that it retains going to see it more as an amusing "stunt" than as a serious sporting event. In the United States efforts to widen interest in it have taken the form of staging bouts in a ring that has been turned into a sea of mud, or that has been filled with fish. All this has, of course, done considerable harm to the reputation of what is really a fine sport and a healthy exercise.

Judo. Wrestling has been popular for centuries in Oriental countries such as India, China, and Japan. Of the various styles, one from Japan has won popularity in many countries, including Britain.

This is Judo, which derives from the more elaborate Ju-Jitsu. Governed largely by rituals, and with wrestlers graded according to ability, Judo is now an international competitive sport; but it is still often taken up as an effective method of defence against a stronger or better-armed attacker. Requiring a knowledge of anatomy, it consists partly of defence by knowing how to fall, and partly of attack by locks which give the opponent a choice between capitulation and a broken bone, and by paralysing nerve centres. The various locks are potentially dangerous, and, when practising, should be released immediately the opponent requests this. Also developed in Japan, though it originated in China, is Karate, a combat system so potentially dangerous that, when practised as a sport, attacking moves must only be indicated, and never pressed home.

Yachting.

The first recorded sailing contest was a race from Greenwich to Gravesend on 1 October 1661, between Charles II, who won, and his brother, the Duke of York. In those days, such contests generally took the form of manoeuvring for positions of advantage, rather than straightforward racing, for the Royal Navy also relied on sailing, and every privately owned vessel was a potentially useful naval auxiliary: a fact that emphasises the appropriateness of the right of England's most famous yacht club, the Royal Yacht Squadron, to fly the White Ensign. The club was founded as the Yacht Club in 1815, becoming the Royal Yacht Club in 1817, when the Prince Regent joined, and taking its present name in 1832. In 1851 the club put up for competition a silver cup that has become the most famous trophy in yachting, and one of the most famous in sport. In that year a schooner of the then famous New York pilot-cutter type, called the America, sailed across the Atlantic to compete in a 53-mile race round the Isle of Wight for the new cup, capturing the trophy which now bears her name.

To date, there have been twenty challenges, sixteen by Great Britain, two by Canada, and two by Australia, but not one of them has succeeded. Britain's 1958 challenge, which was the seventeenth, pointed the present trend in yachting, which is towards smaller vessels. Previously, the America's Cup conditions stipulated that the races must be between very large yachts of the "J" or 21-metre type, and that, if the challenge was from across the Atlantic, the challenger must sail across. In 1958, the rule about sailing across the Atlantic was waived, and the event was between yachts of the 12-metre class.

Large vessels are still seen in the famous Bermuda Race, but the modern trend is very evident in the growing popularity of the annual Folkestone Dinghy Race across the Channel, which also has a class for catamarans, very fast and very popular boats that consist of two boats side by side joined by a kind of raft.

# ATHLETICS

## 1968 OLYMPIC GAMES WINNERS (HELD AT MEXICO CITY).

100 metres, J. Hines, U.S.A., 9·9 sec.
200 metres, T. Smith, U.S.A., 19·8 sec.
400 metres, L. Evans, U.S.A., 43·8 sec.
800 metres, R. Doubell, Australia, 1 min. 44·3 sec.
1500 metres, K. Keino, Kenya, 3 min. 34·9 sec.
5000 metres, M. Gammoudi, Tunisia, 14 min. 5 sec.
10,000 metres, N. Temu, Kenya, 29 min. 27·4 sec.
Marathon, M. Wolde, Ethiopia, 2 hr. 20 min. 26·4 sec.
4 × 100 metres Relay, U.S.A., 38·2 sec.
4 × 400 metres Relay, U.S.A., 2 min. 56·1 sec.
110 metres Hurdles, W. Davenport, U.S.A., 13·3 sec.
400 metres Hurdles, D. Hemery, U.K., 48·1 sec.
3000 metres Steeplechase, A. Biwott, Kenya, 8 min. 51 sec.
20,000 metres Walk, V. Golubnichiy, U.S.S.R., 1 hr. 33 min. 58·4 sec.
50,000 metres Walk, C. Hohne, East Germany, 4 hr. 20 min. 13·6 sec.
High Jump, R. Fosbury, U.S.A., 7 ft. 4¼ in.
Long Jump, R. Beamon, U.S.A., 29 ft. 2½ in.
Triple Jump, V. Saneyev, U.S.S.R., 57 ft. 0¾ in.
Pole Vault, R. Seagren, U.S.A., 17 ft. 8½ in.
Putting the Shot, R. Matson, U.S.A., 67 ft. 4¾ in.
Throwing the Discus, A. Oerter, U.S.A., 212 ft. 6½ in.

Throwing the Javelin, Y. Lusis, U.S.S.R., 295 ft. 7½ in.
Throwing the Hammer, G. Zsivotzky, Hungary, 240 ft. 8 in.
Decathlon, W. Toomey, U.S.A., 8193 pts.
100 metres (Women), W. Tyus, U.S.A., 11 sec.
200 metres (Women), I. Szewinska, Poland, 22·5 sec.
400 metres (Women), C. Besson, France, 52 sec.
800 metres (Women), M. Manning, U.S.A., 2 min. 0·9 sec.
4 × 100 metres Relay (Women), U.S.A., 42·8 sec.
80 metres Hurdles (Women), M. Caird, Australia, 10·3 sec.
High Jump (Women), M. Rezkova, Czechoslovakia, 5 ft. 11⅔ in.
Long Jump (Women), V. Viscopoleanu, Rumania, 22 ft. 4½ in.
Putting the Shot (Women), M. Gummel, East Germany, 64 ft. 4 in.
Throwing the Discus (Women), L. Manoliu, Rumania, 191 ft. 2½ in.
Throwing the Javelin (Women), A Nemeth, Hungary, 198 ft. 0½ in.
Pentathlon (Women), I. Becker, West Germany, 5098 pts.

## 1966 EUROPEAN CHAMPIONSHIPS WINNERS (HELD AT BUDAPEST).

100 metres, W. Maniak, Poland, 10·5 sec.
200 metres, R. Bambuck, France, 20·9 sec.
400 metres, S. Gredzinski, Poland, 46 sec.
800 metres, M. Matuschewski, East Germany, 1 min. 45·9 sec.
1500 metres, B. Tuemmler, West Germany, 3 min. 41·9 sec.
5000 metres, M. Jazy, France, 13 min. 42·8 sec.
10,000 metres, J. Haase, East Germany, 28 min. 26 sec.
Marathon, J. Hogan, Great Britain and Northern Ireland, 2 hr. 20 min. 4·6 sec.
4 × 100 metres Relay, France, 39·4 sec.
4 × 400 metres Relay, Poland, 3 min. 4·5 sec.
110 metres Hurdles, E. Ottoz, Italy, 13·7 sec.
400 metres Hurdles, R. Frinolli, Italy, [49·8 sec.
3000 metres Steeplechase, V. Kudinskiy, U.S.S.R., 8 min. 26·6 sec.
20,000 metres Walk, D. Lindner, East Germany, 1 hr. 29 min. 25 sec.
50,000 metres Walk, A. Pamich, Italy, 4 hr. 18 min. 42·2 sec.
High Jump, J. Madubost, France, 6 ft. 11½ in.
Long Jump, L. Davies, Great Britain and Northern Ireland, 26 ft. 2½ in.
Triple Jump, G. Stoykovski, Bulgaria, 54 ft. 8½ in.
Pole Vault, W. Nordwig, East Germany, 16 ft. 8¾ in.
Putting the Shot, V. Varju, Hungary, 63 ft. 9 in.

Throwing the Discus, D. Thorith, East Germany, 188 ft. 4½ in.
Throwing the Javelin, J. Lusis, U.S.S.R., 277 ft. 1½ in.
Throwing the Hammer, R. Klim, U.S.S.R., 229 ft. 8½ in.
Decathlon, W. von Moltke, West Germany, 7740 pts.
100 metres (Women), E. Klobukowska, Poland, 11·5 sec.
200 metres (Women), I. Kirszenstein, Poland, 23·1 sec.
400 metres (Women), A. Chmelkova, Czechoslovakia, 52·9 sec.
800 metres (Women), V. Nikolic, Yugoslavia, 2 min. 2·8 sec.
4 × 100 metres Relay (Women), Poland, 44·4 sec.
80 metres Hurdles (Women), K. Balzer, East Germany, 10·7 sec.
High Jump (Women), T. Chenchik, U.S.S.R., 5 ft. 8½ in.
Long Jump (Women), I Kirszenstein, Poland, 21 ft. 6 in.
Putting the Shot (Women), N. Chizhova, U.S.S.R., 56 ft. 5½ in.
Throwing the Discus (Women), C. Spielberg, East Germany, 189 ft. 6 in.
Throwing the Javelin (Women), M. Luettge, East Germany, 192 ft. 8½ in.
Pentathlon (Women), V. Tikhomirova, U.S.S.R., 4787 pts.

## 1966 EMPIRE AND COMMONWEALTH GAMES WINNERS (HELD AT KINGSTON, JAMAICA).

100 yards, H. Jerome, Canada, 9·4 sec.
220 yards, S. Allotey, Ghana, 20·7 sec.
440 yards, W. Mottley, Trinidad, 45·2 sec.
880 yards, N. Clough, Australia, 1 min. 46·9 sec.
1 mile, K. Keino, Kenya, 3 min. 55·3 sec.
3 miles, K. Keino, Kenya, 12 min. 57·4 sec.
6 miles, N. Temu, Kenya, 27 min. 14.6 sec.
Marathon, J. Alder, Scotland, 2 hr. 22 min. 7·8 sec.
4 × 110 yards Relay, Ghana, 39·8 sec.
4 × 440 yards Relay, Trinidad, 3 min. 2·9 sec.
120 yards Hurdles, D. Hemery, England, 14·1 sec.
440 yards Hurdles, K. Roche, Australia, 51 sec.
3000 metres Steeplechase, R. Welsh, New Zealand, 8 min. 29·6 sec.
20 miles Walk, R. Wallwork, England, 2 hr. 44 min. 42·8 sec.
High Jump, L. Peckham, Australia, 6 ft. 10 in.
Long Jump, L. Davies, Wales, 26 ft. 2½ in.
Triple Jump, S. Igun, Nigeria, 53 ft. 9½ in.
Pole Vault, T. Bickle, Australia, 15 ft. 9 in.
Putting the Shot, D. Steen, Canada, 61 ft. 8 in.

Throwing the Discus, L. Mills, New Zealand, 184 ft. 4 in.
Throwing the Javelin, J. Fitzsimmons, England, 261 ft. 9 in.
Throwing the Hammer, A. Payne, England, 203 ft. 4 in.
100 yards (Women), D. Burge, Australia, 10·6 sec.
220 yards (Women), D. Burge, Australia, 23·8 sec.
440 yards (Women), J. Pollock, Australia, 53 sec.
880 yards (Women), A. Hoffman, Canada, 2 min. 4·3 sec.
4 × 110 yards Relay (Women), Australia, 45·3 sec.
80 metres Hurdles (Women), P. Kilborn, Australia, 10·9 sec.
High Jump, M. Brown, Australia, 5 ft. 8 in.
Long Jump, M. Rand, England, 20 ft. 10¼ in.
Putting the Shot, V. Young, New Zealand, 54 ft. 1¾ in.
Throwing the Discus, V. Young, New Zealand, 163 ft. 4 in.
Throwing the Javelin, M. Parker, Australia, 168 ft. 7 in.

# THE DERBY

| | Horse. | Jockey. | Owner. |
|---|---|---|---|
| 1947 | Pearl Diver | G. Bridgland | Baron G. de Waldner. |
| 1948 | My Love | W. Johnstone | { The Aga Khan. M. L. Volterra. |
| 1949 | Nimbus | E. Elliott | Mrs. M. Glenister. |
| 1950 | Galcador | W. Johnstone | M. Boussac. |
| 1951 | Arctic Prince | C. Spares | Mr. J. McGrath. |
| 1952 | Tulyar | C. Smirke | The Aga Khan. |
| 1953 | Pinza | G. Richards | Sir V. Sassoon. |
| 1954 | Never Say Die | L. Piggott | Mr. R. S. Clark. |
| 1955 | Phil Drake | F. Palmer | Mme. Volterra. |
| 1956 | Lavandin | W. Johnstone | M. Wertheimer. |
| 1957 | Crepello | L. Piggott | Sir V. Sassoon. |

| | Horse. | Jockey. | Owner. |
|---|---|---|---|
| 1958 | Hard Ridden | C. Smirke | Sir V. Sassoon. |
| 1959 | Parthia | H. Carr | Sir H. de Trafford. |
| 1960 | St. Paddy | L. Piggott | Sir V. Sassoon. |
| 1961 | Psidium | R. Poincelet | Mrs. Arpad Plesch. |
| 1962 | Larkspur | N. Sellwood | Mr. R. Guest. |
| 1963 | Relko | Y. Saint-Martin | M. F. Dupré. |
| 1964 | Santa Claus | A. Breasley | Mr. J. Ismay. |
| 1965 | Sea Bird II | P. Glennon | M. J. Ternynck. |
| 1966 | Charlottown | A. Breasley | Lady Z. Wernher. |
| 1967 | Royal Palace | G. Moore | Mr. H. Joel. |
| 1968 | Sir Ivor | L. Piggott | Mr. R. Guest. |

# CRICKET

## TEST MATCHES

England v. Australia.
(first played 1876)
Won: England 66. Australia 80. Drawn: 57.

England v. South Africa.
(first played 1888)
Won: England 46. South Africa 18. Drawn: 28.

England v. West Indies.
(first played 1928)
(not including 1969 series)
Won: England 18. West Indies 16. Drawn: 21.

England v. New Zealand.
(first played 1929)
(not including 1969 series)
Won: England 17. New Zealand 0. Drawn: 20.

England v. India.
(first played 1932)
Won: England 18. India 3. Drawn: 16.

England v. Pakistan.
(first played 1954)
Won: England 8. Pakistan 1. Drawn: 9.

## COUNTY CHAMPIONSHIP

| 1949 | Middlesex and Yorkshire. |
| 1950 | Surrey and Lancashire. |
| 1951 | Warwickshire. |
| 1952 | Surrey. |
| 1953 | Surrey. |
| 1954 | Surrey. |
| 1955 | Surrey. |
| 1956 | Surrey. |
| 1957 | Surrey. |
| 1958 | Surrey. |
| 1959 | Yorkshire. |
| 1960 | Yorkshire. |
| 1961 | Hampshire. |
| 1962 | Yorkshire. |
| 1963 | Yorkshire. |
| 1964 | Worcestershire. |
| 1965 | Worcestershire. |
| 1966 | Yorkshire. |
| 1967 | Yorkshire. |
| 1968 | Yorkshire. |

# ASSOCIATION FOOTBALL

## WORLD CUP WINNERS

| 1934 | Italy. |
| 1938 | Italy. |
| 1950 | Uruguay. |
| 1954 | Western Germany. |
| 1958 | Brazil. |
| 1962 | Brazil. |
| 1966 | England. |

## EUROPEAN CHAMPION CLUBS CUP WINNERS

| 1958 | Real Madrid. |
| 1959 | Real Madrid. |
| 1960 | Real Madrid. |
| 1961 | Benfica. |
| 1962 | Benfica. |
| 1963 | Milano. |
| 1964 | Inter-Milan. |
| 1965 | Inter-Milan. |
| 1966 | Real Madrid. |
| 1967 | Glasgow Celtic. |
| 1968 | Manchester United. |

## EUROPEAN NATIONAL CUP HOLDERS CUP WINNERS

| 1963 | Tottenham Hotspur. |
| 1964 | S.C. Lisbon. |
| 1965 | West Ham United. |
| 1966 | Borussia Dortmund. |
| 1967 | Bayern Munich. |
| 1968 | A.C. Milan. |

## F.A. CUP WINNERS

| 1949 | Wolverhampton W. |
| 1950 | Arsenal. |
| 1951 | Newcastle United. |
| 1952 | Newcastle United. |
| 1953 | Blackpool. |
| 1954 | West Bromwich Albion. |
| 1955 | Newcastle United. |
| 1956 | Manchester City. |
| 1957 | Aston Villa. |
| 1958 | Bolton Wanderers. |
| 1959 | Nottingham Forest. |
| 1960 | Wolverhampton W. |
| 1961 | Tottenham Hotspur. |
| 1962 | Tottenham Hotspur. |
| 1963 | Manchester United. |
| 1964 | West Ham United. |
| 1965 | Liverpool. |
| 1966 | Everton. |
| 1967 | Tottenham Hotspur. |
| 1968 | West Bromwich Albion. |
| 1969 | Manchester City. |

## SCOTTISH CUP WINNERS

| 1949 | Rangers. |
| 1950 | Rangers. |
| 1951 | Celtic. |
| 1952 | Motherwell. |
| 1953 | Rangers. |
| 1954 | Celtic. |
| 1955 | Clyde. |
| 1956 | Heart of Midlothian. |
| 1957 | Falkirk. |
| 1958 | Clyde. |
| 1959 | St. Mirren. |
| 1960 | Rangers. |
| 1961 | Dunfermline Athletic. |
| 1962 | Rangers. |
| 1963 | Rangers. |
| 1964 | Rangers. |
| 1965 | Celtic. |
| 1936 | Rangers. |
| 1967 | Celtic. |
| 1968 | Dunfermline Athletic. |
| 1969 | Celtic. |

## OLYMPIC GAMES WINNERS

| 1908 | United Kingdom. |
| 1912 | United Kingdom. |
| 1920 | Belgium. |
| 1924 | Uruguay. |
| 1928 | Uruguay. |
| 1932 | No Competition. |
| 1936 | Italy. |
| 1948 | Sweden. |
| 1952 | Hungary. |
| 1956 | U.S.S.R. |
| 1960 | Yugoslavia. |
| 1964 | Hungary. |
| 1968 | Hungary. |

# RUGBY LEAGUE FOOTBALL

## WORLD CUP WINNERS

| 1954 | Great Britain. |
| 1957 | Australia. |
| 1960 | Great Britain. |
| 1968 | Australia. |

## R.L. CUP WINNERS

| 1949 | Bradford Northern. |
| 1950 | Warrington. |
| 1951 | Wigan. |
| 1952 | Workington Town. |
| 1953 | Huddersfield. |
| 1954 | Warrington. |
| 1955 | Barrow. |
| 1956 | St. Helens. |
| 1957 | Leeds. |
| 1958 | Wigan. |
| 1959 | Wigan. |
| 1960 | Wakefield Trinity. |
| 1961 | St. Helens. |
| 1962 | Wakefield Trinity. |
| 1963 | Wakefield Trinity. |
| 1964 | Widnes. |
| 1965 | Wigan. |
| 1966 | St. Helens. |
| 1967 | Featherstone Rovers. |
| 1968 | Leeds. |

# ROWING AND SCULLING

## THE UNIVERSITY BOAT RACE

| Year | Winner | | | | min. | sec. | Lengths. | | Year | Winner | | | | min. | sec. | Lengths. |
|---|---|---|---|---|---|---|---|---|---|---|---|---|---|---|---|---|
| 1950 | Cambridge | . | . | . | 20 | 15 | 3¼ | | 1960 | Oxford | . | . | . | 18 | 59 | 1¼ |
| 1951 | Cambridge | . | . | . | 20 | 50 | 12 | | 1961 | Cambridge | . | . | . | 19 | 22 | 4¼ |
| 1952 | Oxford | . | . | . | 20 | 23 | canvas | | 1962 | Cambridge | . | . | . | 19 | 46 | 5 |
| 1953 | Cambridge | . | . | . | 19 | 54 | 8 | | 1963 | Oxford | . | . | . | 20 | 47 | 5 |
| 1954 | Oxford | . | . | . | 20 | 23 | 4½ | | 1964 | Cambridge | . | . | . | 19 | 18 | 6½ |
| 1955 | Cambridge | . | . | . | 19 | 10 | 16 | | 1965 | Oxford | . | . | . | 18 | 7 | 4 |
| 1956 | Cambridge | . | . | . | 18 | 36 | 1½ | | 1966 | Oxford | . | . | . | 19 | 12 | 3¾ |
| 1957 | Cambridge | . | . | . | 19 | 1 | 2 | | 1967 | Oxford | . | . | . | 18 | 52 | 3½ |
| 1958 | Cambridge | . | . | . | 18 | 15 | 3½ | | 1968 | Cambridge | . | . | . | 18 | 22 | 3½ |
| 1959 | Oxford | . | . | . | 18 | 52 | 6 | | 1969 | Cambridge | . | . | . | 18 | 4 | 4 |

## DOGGETT'S COAT AND BADGE

| 1954 | K. Everest. | | 1958 | R. Crouch. | | 1962 | C. Dearsley. | | 1966 | D. Stent. |
|---|---|---|---|---|---|---|---|---|---|---|
| 1955 | J. Goulding. | | 1959 | G. Saunders. | | 1963 | D. Allen. | | 1967 | C. Briggs. |
| 1956 | C. Williams. | | 1960 | R. Easterling. | | 1964 | F. Walker. | | 1968 | J. Lupton. |
| 1957 | K. Collins. | | 1961 | K. Usher. | | 1965 | A. Collins. | | | |

## 1968 OLYMPIC GAMES WINNERS (HELD AT MEXICO CITY)

Single Sculls, J. Wienese, Netherlands.
Double Sculls, U.S.S.R.

Coxwainless Pairs, East Germany.
Coxed Pairs, Italy.
Coxwainless Fours, East Germany.

Coxed Fours, New Zealand.
Eights, West Germany.

# SWIMMING

## 1968 OLYMPIC GAMES WINNERS (HELD AT MEXICO CITY)

100 metres free-style, M. Wenden, Australia, 52·2 sec.
200 metres free-style, M. Wenden, Australia, 1 min. 55·2 sec.
400 metres free-style, M. Burton, U.S.A., 4 min. 9 sec.
1500 metres free-style, M. Burton, U.S.A., 16 min. 38·9 sec.
100 metres back-stroke, R. Matthes, East Germany, 58·7 sec.
200 metres back-stroke, R. Matthes, East Germany, 2 min. 9·6 sec.
100 metres breast-stroke, D. McKenzie, U.S.A., 1 min. 7·7 sec.
200 metres breast-stroke, F. Munoz, Mexico, 2 min. 28·7 sec.
100 metres butterfly, D. Russell, U.S.A., 55·9 sec.
200 metres butterfly, C. Robie, U.S.A., 2 min. 8·7 sec.
200 metres medley, C. Hickcox, U.S.A., 2 min. 12 sec.
400 metres medley, C. Hickcox, U.S.A., 4 min. 48·4 sec.
4 × 100 metres free-style Relay, U.S.A., 3 min. 31·7 sec.
4 × 200 metres free-style Relay, U.S.A., 7 min. 52·3 sec.
4 × 100 metres medley Relay, U.S.A., 3 min. 54·9 sec.
Highboard Diving, K. Dibiasi, Italy.
Springboard Diving, B. Wrightson, U.S.A.
Water Polo, Jugoslavia.

100 metres free-style (Women), J. Henne, U.S.A., 1 min.
200 metres free-style (Women), D. Meyer, U.S.A., 2 min. 10·5 sec.
400 metres free-style (Women), D. Meyer, U.S.A., 4 min. 31·8 sec.
800 metres free-style (Women), D. Meyer, U.S.A., 9 min. 24 sec.
100 metres back-stroke (Women), K. Hall, U.S.A., 1 min. 6·2 sec.
200 metres back-stroke (Women), P. Watson, U.S.A., 2 min. 24·8 sec.
100 metres breast-stroke (Women), D. Bjedov, Jugoslavia, 1 min. 15·8 sec.
200 metres breast-stroke (Women), S. Wichman, U.S.A., 2 min. 44·4 sec.
100 metres butterfly (Women), L. McClements, Australia, 1 min. 5·5 sec.
200 metres butterfly (Women), A. Kok, Netherlands, 2 min. 24·7 sec.
200 metres medley (Women), G. Kolb, U.S.A., 2 min. 24·7 sec.
400 metres medley (Women), G. Kolb, U.S.A., 5 min. 8·5 sec.
4 × 100 metres free-style Relay (Women), U.S.A., 4 min. 3·5 sec.
4 × 100 metres medley Relay (Women), U.S.A., 4 min. 28·3 sec.
Highboard Diving (Women), M. Duchkova, Czechoslovakia.
Springboard Diving (Women), S. Gossick, U.S.A.

# CROSS-COUNTRY

## THE INTERNATIONAL CHAMPIONSHIP

| 1948 | Belgium. | | 1954 | England. | | 1960 | England. | | 1965 | England. |
|---|---|---|---|---|---|---|---|---|---|---|
| 1949 | France. | | 1955 | England. | | 1961 | Belgium. | | 1966 | England. |
| 1950 | France. | | 1956 | France. | | 1962 | England. | | 1967 | England. |
| 1951 | England. | | 1957 | Belgium. | | 1963 | Belgium. | | 1968 | England. |
| 1952 | France. | | 1958 | England. | | 1964 | England. | | 1969 | England. |
| 1953 | England. | | 1959 | England. | | | | | | |

# HOCKEY

## OLYMPIC GAMES WINNERS

| 1920 | Great Britain. | | 1936 | India. | | 1956 | India. | | 1964 | India. |
|---|---|---|---|---|---|---|---|---|---|---|
| 1928 | India. | | 1948 | India. | | 1960 | Pakistan. | | 1968 | Pakistan. |
| 1932 | India. | | 1952 | India. | | | | | | |

# BASKETBALL

## OLYMPIC GAMES WINNERS

| 1936 | U.S.A. | | 1952 | U.S.A. | | 1960 | U.S.A. | | 1968 | U.S.A. |
|---|---|---|---|---|---|---|---|---|---|---|
| 1948 | U.S.A. | | 1956 | U.S.A. | | 1964 | U.S.A. | | | |

# GOLF

## WORLD CUP

| 1955 | U.S.A. | | 1958 | Ireland. | | 1961 | U.S.A. | | 1964 | U.S.A. | | 1967 | U.S.A. |
|---|---|---|---|---|---|---|---|---|---|---|---|---|---|
| 1956 | U.S.A. | | 1959 | Australia. | | 1962 | U.S.A. | | 1965 | South Africa. | | 1968 | Canada. |
| 1957 | Japan. | | 1960 | U.S.A. | | 1963 | U.S.A. | | 1966 | U.S.A. | | | |

# BASEBALL

## WORLD SERIES WINNERS

| 1957 | Milwaukee Braves. | | 1961 | New York Yankees. | | 1965 | Los Angeles Dodgers. |
|---|---|---|---|---|---|---|---|
| 1958 | New York Yankees. | | 1962 | New York Yankees. | | 1966 | Baltimore Orioles. |
| 1959 | Los Angeles Dodgers. | | 1963 | Los Angeles Dodgers. | | 1967 | St. Louis Cardinals. |
| 1960 | Pittsburgh Pirates. | | 1964 | St. Louis Cardinals. | | 1968 | Detroit Tigers. |

# LAWN TENNIS

### DAVIS CUP

| | | | | | | | |
|---|---|---|---|---|---|---|---|
| 1949 | U.S.A. | 1954 | U.S.A. | 1959 | Australia. | 1964 | Australia. |
| 1950 | Australia. | 1955 | Australia. | 1960 | Australia. | 1965 | Australia. |
| 1951 | Australia. | 1956 | Australia. | 1961 | Australia. | 1966 | Australia. |
| 1952 | Australia. | 1957 | Australia. | 1962 | Australia. | 1967 | Australia |
| 1953 | Australia. | 1958 | U.S.A. | 1963 | U.S.A. | 1968 | U.S.A. |

### WIMBLEDON CHAMPIONSHIP WINNERS

#### Men's Singles

| | | | | | |
|---|---|---|---|---|---|
| 1946 | Y. Petra (France). | 1954 | J. Drobny (Egypt). | 1962 | R. Laver (Australia). |
| 1947 | J. Kramer (U.S.A.). | 1955 | T. Trabert (U.S.A.). | 1963 | C. McKinley (U.S.A.). |
| 1948 | R. Falkenburg (U.S.A.). | 1956 | L. Hoad (Australia). | 1964 | R. Emerson (Australia). |
| 1949 | F. Schroeder (U.S.A.). | 1957 | L. Hoad (Australia). | 1965 | R. Emerson (Australia). |
| 1950 | B. Patty (U.S.A.). | 1958 | A. Cooper (Australia). | 1966 | M. Santana (Spain). |
| 1951 | R. Savitt (U.S.A.). | 1959 | A. Olmedo (Peru). | 1967 | J. Newcombe (Australia). |
| 1952 | F. Sedgman (Australia). | 1960 | N. Fraser (Australia). | 1968 | R. Laver (Australia). |
| 1953 | V. Seixas (U.S.A.). | 1961 | R. Laver (Australia). | | |

#### Women's Singles

| | | | | | |
|---|---|---|---|---|---|
| 1946 | P. Betz (U.S.A.). | 1954 | M. Connolly (U.S.A.). | 1962 | J. Susman (U.S.A.). |
| 1947 | M. Osborne (U.S.A.). | 1955 | L. Brough (U.S.A.). | 1963 | M. Smith (Australia). |
| 1948 | L. Brough (U.S.A.). | 1956 | S. Fry (U.S.A.). | 1964 | M. Bueno (Brazil). |
| 1949 | L. Brough (U.S.A.). | 1957 | A. Gibson (U.S.A.). | 1965 | M. Smith (Australia). |
| 1950 | L. Brough (U.S.A.). | 1958 | A. Gibson (U.S.A.). | 1966 | B-J. King (U.S.A.). |
| 1951 | D. Hart (U.S.A.). | 1959 | M. Bueno (Brazil). | 1967 | B-J. King (U.S.A.). |
| 1952 | M. Connolly (U.S.A.). | 1960 | M. Bueno (Brazil). | 1968 | B-J. King (U.S.A.). |
| 1953 | M. Connolly (U.S.A.). | 1961 | A. Mortimer (Gt. Britain). | | |

# RIFLE SHOOTING

### Queen's/King's Prize Winners

| | | | | | |
|---|---|---|---|---|---|
| 1946 | C. Willott. | 1954 | G. Twine. | 1962 | P. Hall. |
| 1947 | R. Bennett. | 1955 | L. Fenwick. | 1963 | K. Pilcher. |
| 1948 | P. Pavey. | 1956 | G. Twine. | 1964 | A. Harris. |
| 1949 | E. Brookes. | 1957 | J. Love. | 1965 | J. Allen. |
| 1950 | R. Greig. | 1958 | R. Fulton. | 1966 | R. Hampton. |
| 1951 | G. Boa. | 1959 | L. Mallabar. | 1967 | J. Powell. |
| 1952 | A. Kinnier-Wilson. | 1960 | G. Westling. | 1968 | A. Parks. |
| 1953 | N. McCaw. | 1961 | N. Beckett. | | |

# OLYMPIC ATHLETIC RECORDS

100 metres, 9·9 sec., J. Hines (U.S.A.), 1968, Mexico City.

200 metres, 19·8 sec., T. Smith (U.S.A.), 1968, Mexico City.

400 metres, 43·8 sec., L. Evans (U.S.A.), 1968, Mexico City.

800 metres, 1 min. 44·3 sec., R. Doubell (Australia), 1968, Mexico City.

1500 metres, 3 min. 34·9 sec., K. Keino (Kenya), 1968, Mexico City.

5000 metres, 13 min. 39·6 sec., V. Kuts (U.S.S.R.), 1956, Melbourne.

10,000 metres, 28 min. 24·4 sec., W. Mills (U.S.A.), 1964, Tokyo.

Marathon, 2 hr. 12 min. 11·2 sec., A. Bikele (Ethiopia), 1964, Tokyo.

4 × 100 metres Relay, 38·2 sec., U.S.A., 1968, Mexico City.

4 × 400 metres Relay, 2 min. 56·1 sec., U.S.A., 1968, Mexico City.

110 metres Hurdles, 13·3 sec.
W. Davenport (U.S.A.), 1968, Mexico City.
E. Hall (U.S.A.), 1968, Mexico City.

400 metres Hurdles, 48·1 sec., D. Hemery (U.K.), 1968, Mexico City.

3000 metres Steeplechase, 8 min. 30·8 sec., G. Roelants (Belgium), 1964, Tokyo.

20,000 metres Walk, 1 hr. 29 min. 34 sec., K. Matthews (U.K.), 1964, Tokyo.

50,000 metres Walk, 4 hr. 11 min. 12 sec., A. Pamich (Italy), 1964, Tokyo.

High Jump, 7 ft. 4¼ in., R. Fosbury (U.S.A.), 1968, Mexico City.

Long Jump, 29 ft. 2½ in., R. Beamon (U.S.A.), 1968, Mexico City.

Triple Jump, 57 ft. 0¾ in., V. Saneyev (U.S.S.R.), 1968, Mexico City.

Pole Vault, 17 ft. 8½ in.
R. Seagren (U.S.A.), 1968, Mexico City.
C. Schiprowski (West Germany), 1968, Mexico City.

W. Nordwig (East Germany), 1968, Mexico City.

Putting the Shot, 67 ft. 10½ in., R. Matson (U.S.A.), 1968, Mexico City.

Throwing the Discus, 212 ft. 6½ in., A. Oerter (U.S.A.), 1968, Mexico City.

Throwing the Javelin, 295 ft. 7¼ in., Y. Lusis (U.S.S.R.), 1968, Mexico City.

Throwing the Hammer, 240 ft. 8 in., G. Zsivotzky (Hungary), 1968, Mexico City.

Decathlon, 8193 pts, W. Toomey (U.S.A.), 1968, Mexico City.

100 metres (Women), 11 sec., W. Tyus (U.S.A.), 1968, Mexico City.

200 metres (Women), 22·5 sec., I. Szewinska (Poland), 1968, Mexico City.

400 metres (Women), 52 sec.
B. Cuthbert (Australia), 1964, Tokyo.
C. Besson (France), 1968, Mexico City.

800 metres (Women), 2 min. 0·9 sec., M. Manning (U.S.A.), 1968, Mexico City.

4 × 100 metres Relay (Women), 42·8 sec., U.S.A., 1968, Mexico City.

80 metres Hurdles (Women), 10·3 sec., M. Caird (Australia), 1968, Mexico City.

High Jump (Women), 6 ft. 2¾ in., I. Balas (Rumania), 1964, Tokyo.

Long Jump (Women), 22 ft. 4½ in., V. Viscopoleanu (Rumania), 1968, Mexico City.

Putting the Shot (Women), 64 ft. 4 in., M. Gummel (East Germany), 1968, Mexico City.

Throwing the Discus (Women), 191 ft. 2½ in., L. Manoliu (Rumania), 1968, Mexico City.

Throwing the Javelin (Women), 204 ft. 8 in., Y. Gorchakova (U.S.S.R.), 1964, Tokyo.

Pentathlon (Women), 5246 pts, I. Press (U.S.S.R.), 1964, Tokyo.

# DOMESTIC PETS

Feeding, management, and diseases
of: aquarium fish — cage-birds —
cats — cavies — dogs — ferrets —
golden hamsters — hedgehogs —
mice—rabbits—rats—tortoises

# DOMESTIC PETS

This section attempts to deal not with all the many hundreds of animals that may be kept as pets, but only with those that are best suited to average homes in Great Britain. The maintenance of monkeys, squirrels, bats, mongooses, and snakes, while quite feasible to those with experience and facilities, requires considerable time and—in some instances—expense. Those who contemplate such exotic pets should consult works of reference, study the methods adopted in zoological gardens, and discuss the matter with experts. Even in the case of the more common animals, the information provided in the following pages is to be regarded only as a beginning, to be supplemented so far as possible by practical experience, discussions with more knowledgeable owners, and the study of more detailed writings.

Certain considerations are basic. Never keep a pet unless you are really interested in it and are prepared to give it due—and regular—care and attention. Don't keep a pet you cannot afford to maintain in health and comfort. Scrupulous attention to cleanliness is essential, and wise feeding is one of the most important factors in avoiding illness and loss of condition.

Since the passing of the Veterinary Surgeons Act of 1948 it is illegal for anyone to practise the diagnosis and treatment of animal diseases unless he or she is: (1) a veterinary surgeon; or (2) a person whose name has been placed on the Supplementary Veterinary Register. (Certain employees of Animal Welfare Societies are specially licensed, but it is intended that in future all animal treatment shall be given by or under the direct supervision of members of the veterinary profession.) Not even a pharmacist may attempt to diagnose or treat an animal. Anyone may, of course, render " first aid," and an owner may—at his or her own risk—apply treatment. It is, of course, a wise precaution to seek veterinary advice for any ailing animal, and the sooner it is sought the more likely it is that good results will follow.

## BREEDS AND VARIETIES OF DOGS.

Of recent years, dog breeding and showing have become specialised occupations, which average people cannot be expected to take up without having adequate time or resources at their disposal. Any amateur who wishes to breed for profit from pedigree animals should seek expert advice before attempting to do so.

Dogs which are intended for shows or for pedigree breeding must be registered, in the name of the owner, with the Kennel Club, 1–4 Clarges Street, Piccadilly, London, W.1.

The following are the breeds of dogs recognised by the Kennel Club for the purpose of separate Registration and Stud Book entries:—

### SPORTING BREEDS

#### Hound Group

| | |
|---|---|
| Afghan Hounds | Dachshunds (Wire-haired) |
| Basenjis | Dachshunds Miniature |
| Basset Hounds | (Wire-haired) |
| Beagles | Deerhounds |
| Bloodhounds | Elkhounds |
| Borzois | Finnish Spitz |
| Dachshunds (Long-haired) | Foxhounds |
| Dachshunds Miniature | Irish Wolfhounds |
| (Long-haired) | Rhodesian Ridgebacks |
| Dachshunds (Smooth) | Salukis |
| Dachshunds Miniature (Smooth) | Whippets |

#### Gun-dog Group.

| | |
|---|---|
| English Setters | Retrievers (Labrador) |
| Gordon Setters | Spaniels (Clumber) |
| Irish Setters | Spaniels (Cocker) |
| Pointers | Spaniels (Field) |
| German Short-haired Pointers | Spaniels (Irish Water) |
| | Spaniels (Springer English) |
| Retrievers (Curly Coated) | Spaniels (Springer Welsh) |
| Retrievers (Flat Coated) | Spaniels (Sussex) |
| Retrievers (Golden) | Spaniels Weimaraners |

### Terrier Group.

| | |
|---|---|
| Airedale Terriers | Kerry Blue Terriers |
| Australian Terriers | Lakeland Terriers |
| Bedlington Terriers | Manchester Terriers |
| Border Terriers | Norwich Terriers |
| Bull Terriers | Scottish Terriers |
| Bull Terriers (Miniature) | Sealyham Terriers |
| | Skye Terriers |
| Cairn Terriers | Staffordshire Bull |
| Dandie Dinmont Terriers | Terriers |
| | Welsh Terriers |
| Fox Terriers (Smooth) | West Highland White |
| Fox Terriers (Wire) | Terriers |
| Irish Terriers | |

### NON-SPORTING BREEDS.

#### Non-sporting other than Toy.

| | |
|---|---|
| Alsatians (German Shepherd Dogs) | Poodles (Standard) |
| | Poodles (Miniature) |
| Bearded Collies | Poodles (Toy) |
| Boston Terriers | Pyrenean Mountain |
| Boxers | Dogs |
| Bulldogs | St. Bernards |
| Bullmastiffs | Samoyeds |
| Chow Chows | Schipperkes |
| Collies (Rough) | Schnauzers |
| Collies (Smooth) | Schnauzers (Miniature) |
| Dalmatians | Shetland Sheepdogs |
| Dobermanns | Shih Tzus |
| French Bulldogs | Tibetan Apsos |
| Great Danes | Tibetan Spaniels |
| Keeshonds | Tibetan Terriers |
| Mastiffs | Welsh Corgis (Cardigan) |
| Newfoundlands | |
| Old English Sheep Dogs | Welsh Corgis (Pembroke) |

#### Toy Group.

| | |
|---|---|
| Chihuahuas (Long-coat) | Cavalier King Charles Spaniels |
| Chihuahuas (Smooth-coat) | Maltese |
| | Miniature Pinschers |
| English Toy Terriers (Black and Tan) | Papillons |
| Griffons Bruxellois | Pomeranians |
| Italian Greyhounds | Pugs |
| King Charles Spaniels | Yorkshire Terriers |

A separate register, called a Breed Register, is kept by the Kennel Club for each of the above breeds or variety of breeds. A separate register is also kept for the following:—

| | |
|---|---|
| Setters (Crossbred) | Spaniels (Interbred) |
| Retrievers (Interbred) | Spaniels (Crossbred) |
| Retrievers (Crossbred) | |

A dog which is not eligible for entry in any of the above registers may be entered in one of the following registers kept by the Kennel Club:—

| | |
|---|---|
| Any Other Variety | Crossbred Dogs |
| Interbred Dogs | |

The following breeds, among others, are eligible for entry in the " Any Other Variety " register:—

| | |
|---|---|
| Alaskan Malamute | Maremma (Italian |
| Australian Kelpie | Sheepdogs) |
| Bovier Belge de | Mexican Hairless |
| Flanders | Norwegian Buhunds |
| Dachbracke | Pedengo Ibicenco |
| Groenendaels | Polish Sheepdogs |
| Hungarian Kavasz | Rottweilers |
| Hungarian Vislas | Soft-coated Wheaten |
| Husky | Terriers |
| Iceland Dog | Tibetan Mastiff |
| Japanese Akita | |

Any dog will be accepted for registration in the Obedience and Working Trials Record, irrespective of its ancestry, on condition that it competes only in Obedience Tests and/or Working Trials.

Challenge Certificates are issued by the Kennel Club to certain Championship Shows for each breed or variety of a breed of which a separate register is kept. A dog qualifies for the title of Champion when it has won three Challenge Certificates under three different Judges.

In the limited space available it is impossible to describe the special characteristics of the different breeds. The breeds recognised in Great Britain are subject to constant review by the Kennel Club, and it is probable that the number will continue to be added to from time to time.

The dog was probably the first animal to be domesticated in the true sense of the word, and the uses to which he has been put by man are almost legion. Throughout the world dogs are employed to help protect herds and flocks, and indeed the dog trained for shepherding plays an integral part in sheep management. The names Foxhound, Deerhound, and Otterhound all indicate the specific uses to which dogs have been put in the Chase. Greyhounds and Whippets are used in coursing, and work singly or in pairs, rather than in packs. As their names indicate, the various Setters and Pointers are employed to indicate the exact whereabouts of game, and Spaniels also are widely used as gun-dogs. The other uses to which dogs have been put in field sports include hunting over rough and difficult country by small terriers, and going to earth to kill or hold badgers, foxes, and otters. Fox Terriers, Dachshunds, Dandie Dinmonts, and Scottish Terriers are among the types which have been so employed. Dogs have played their part also in entertainment: thus there are performing dogs, notably the Poodle, and racing Whippets and Greyhounds, while in former times various types of fighting, including the baiting of bulls by Bull-dogs, were to be seen. The use of sledge-dogs is well known, while in Belgium and elsewhere dogs were at one time widely used as traction animals. In coaching days, the Dalmatian was a carriage dog, and modern scientists have recently suggested, as a result of experiments, that the position under or behind a coach which a Dalmatian automatically takes is determined by heredity! Perhaps the most exacting use to which man has ever put dog was in China, where the Chow-Chow was once maintained as a source of meat and fur! In Portugal, fishermen employ a race of dog to accompany their fleets. The dogs in question (Portuguese Water Dogs) will dive into the sea to retrieve a broken net or an escaped fish, and will even swim from one smack to another to convey messages! In New Guinea native dogs act as scavengers, while in various countries on the Continent of Europe " truffle dogs " are employed to locate the fungi known as truffles, relished as a table delicacy.

The above paragraph is far from exhaustive, and for those who wish to know more of the characteristics of the different varieties of dogs, reference should be made to such volumes as *Book of the Dog* by Brian Vesey-Fitzgerald (Nicholson and Watson, London: 2 guineas) or *Working Dogs of the World* by C. L. B. Hubbard (Sidgwick and Jackson Ltd., London: 16s.) For general guidance on dog management, see *The Right Way to Keep Dogs* by R. C. G. Hancock (Elliott, Kingswood, Surrey: 5s.)

For present purposes it is, however, as a pet or companion that we are considering the dog, and it must be agreed that many of the most successful animals for this purpose are cross-breeds or " mongrels." There are many fallacies or unsubstantiated generalisations regarding the relative merits of pure-breds and mongrels. This is in fact an intricate scientific problem, and probably the simplest way of summarising the true position would be to say that, from the point of view of health and temperament, there are good, bad, and indifferent specimens among pure-bred and cross-bred animals. It is true that within a breed (or within a local community of mongrels for that matter) certain weaknesses or undesirable traits may arise from hereditary defects.

It may be noted that the word " dog " is applied to the whole species, although it is used also to denote the male as opposed to the female, for which the correct term is " bitch." Young animals are referred to as " dog puppies " or " bitch puppies " respectively. A male animal employed regularly for breeding is known as a " stud dog," and the corresponding female as a " brood bitch." In hunting circles the Foxhound is referred to as a " hound," and the term dog and bitch are employed only as prefixes to denote the sex.

## CHOICE OF DOG.

However attractive the idea of keeping a dog may be, it is unwise and unkind to purchase or to accept one without very careful consideration. Dogs require regular feeding, grooming, and exercise and, if they are to be allowed to show their full capabilities, constant companionship and attention. Nothing is more pathetic than an unwanted dog, which may have been purchased because of a passing whim, and with which no one appears to have the courage to part. If, on the other hand, one is prepared to give all the necessary time and trouble to the proper care of the dog, the reward will be ample.

The size of the choice is important. Many people keep dogs which are far too large for their houses and for their purses. The smaller the dog, the less food, exercise, and house-room will he need, and the many varieties of terrier provide a range from which suitable choices for most households may be made. In any event, a very large dog should not be chosen unless expert advice has been taken about his feeding and other requirements.

Household dogs of six months of age or over must be licensed. Licences may be obtained from any post office (7s. 6d. at present).

## MANAGEMENT OF THE DOG.

**Accommodation.**—Up till comparatively recently most dogs were kennelled down out of doors. This practice has its advantages, but to-day the majority of pet dogs are allowed more or less the run of the house. A warm sleeping-place, such as a box or basket, should be provided, and should contain removable bedding. Newspaper is an excellent non-conductor of heat. It is a very useful material to place at the bottom of a dog's box; and on two or three thicknesses may be placed a rug or blanket on which the animal may lie. It is astonishing the amount of grit and dust a dog can bring into a house on his limbs and the lower part of his body. His bedding will require frequent shaking out and renewal, and paper is easily changed. The box or basket in which the dog lies should be allowed a place free from draughts, and requires airing daily when the dog leaves its bed in the morning. Wood-wool makes excellent bedding in outhouses or where a special structure is provided by way of dog-kennel, but is inclined to be messy about the house, as a dog will draw portions of it about the room as he leaves his bed. If straw is used, it is best stuffed into a sack and made into a kind of mattress. An odd piece of linoleum forms an excellent foundation to the dog's sleeping-box or kennel; it does not strike cold to the skin, is a slow conductor of heat, and has the advantage of being easily kept clean, particularly during illness, when there may be discharges and messes to be frequently cleaned up, until the animal can once more go out of doors.

**Exercise.**—Every dog should be exercised regularly, but there is no need to over-exercise, and the practice of allowing a dog (other than a large and athletic animal) to run behind a bicycle for mile after mile cannot be too strongly deprecated. Two or three fairly short walks a day are sufficient for a small terrier, always provided that there is a garden in which he can play on fine days and some open space where he can run freely for a short time. While still in the puppyhood stages, a dog should be trained to walk to heel and to beware of traffic. Even so, it is usually safer to put him on a lead in busy thoroughfares. One point which, to the annoyance of the public, many dog-owners fail to realise, is that their animals would show much less tendency to fight if allowed to investigate one another off the lead. A dog naturally feels aggressive if put on the lead immediately a rival hails in sight. There are, of course, certain dogs which attack others at sight; these are a public nuisance, and should never be allowed loose on the streets.

The practice of allowing a dog to take his own exercise is to be deprecated, especially in towns and suburbs. The animal will be tempted to sniff into dustbins, and, if a male, will tend to follow a bitch in season or to take part in the unsavoury " dog parties " which are so often to be seen. Furthermore, such an animal is usually responsible for the disgusting habit of fouling the pavements and gateways. In this connection, it should be emphasised that dogs may quite easily be trained to defecate in the gutter, or on the grass verge, and so avoid contamination of the pavement or carriage-way. In some districts owners are liable to a fine if their dogs foul the pavement.

**Training.**—Patience combined with the gift of putting yourself in the dog's place is the chief requisite for successful education. It is most important to encourage regularity of habit, as an animal will obviously learn very much more quickly if his daily walks, meals, and grooming take place at fairly constant times. A quiet firmness is the ideal method, and a puppy should learn early that a command *is* a command, and must be obeyed. There is no need to shout and make an exhibition of oneself, or to race in circles after a disobedient puppy; if these things are done, the animal will never become so well trained as it otherwise would. Again, it is rather ridiculous to chastise a puppy *after* he has somewhat belatedly decided to come to heel: quite obviously, he will then be liable to think that he has done wrong in actually coming to heel. Whatever happens, it must never be that the dog becomes master; there is no more unbecoming sight than that of a person with a frankly disobedient dog, and if the animal be large and powerful it may prove a menace to its owner and to the public.

Puppies should be house-trained at an early stage. If care and thought are given to the matter, the animal will soon learn not to make messes in the house. However, it is very stupid to forget all about a puppy or dog for many hours, and then, out of sheer vexation, chastise it for having made a mess. If puppies are let out every two hours or so at first, they will soon learn not to make a mess. Encourage them for performing in the right place rather than scold them for doing so in the wrong one. Physical punishment should be administered only where strictly necessary, and then in a sensible fashion. The most effective method is to grasp the dog or puppy by the skin of its neck and to shake it.

**Grooming and Washing.**—Whilst short-haired breeds need little or no attention to the coat, bar an occasional brisk rub down with a brush or rough towel (which incidentally puts a pleasant gloss on the smooth-haired breeds), yet with the long-haired breeds grooming should be carried out regularly, and if the habit is made a daily one it will not be forgotten so readily. Nearly all dogs love this procedure, and most dogs will actually ask for their daily groom by jumping on the table or bench on which it is carried out. Steel combs and brushes are sold by many shops, principally corn chandlers, though some store chemists also provide a suitable range of grooming kit for all breeds. There is a curious fetish current among many breeders that dogs should not be washed. There is no reason why, with a few simple precautions, a dog should not be washed whenever it is socially necessary. The first precaution is to use a soap that does not contain an excess of soda. The strong washing-up soaps, excellent as they are for certain purposes, are too irritant for a dog's skin. While some of the toilet soaps suitable for human use may be employed for dogs, the special dog soaps and shampoos are much better for the purpose. They are more suited to the dog's skin and coat, and have better detergent properties. It is important not to have water that is too hot—as with a baby's bath, it should be possible to dip the point of one's elbow into the water and find that it gives a pleasantly warm sensation but is easily bearable, *i.e.*, it should not be above 95–100 F. On emerging from a bath a dog will shake himself thoroughly, and then, if not curbed, will roll on the floor or ground and speedily cover himself with dust or dirt! It is therefore necessary to give him a brisk rub down with old (but clean) towelling, whereupon he may be allowed to dry off in a warm place free from draughts or, in good weather, put on a lead and taken for a brisk walk. In the case of many of the long-coated breeds it is customary to have them trimmed at the beginning of summer, and this is a sensible precaution that may avoid a good deal of distress during hot weather. The smaller long-haired dogs in particular, such as Scottish Terriers, suffer unduly from the heat if their coats are grown too long.

## FEEDING OF THE DOG.

Meat, usually beef, is generally regarded as the staple article of the dog's diet. It must be pointed out, however, that although the dog is naturally a carnivore (flesh-eater), ordinary meat (muscle or " flesh ") is not a completely adequate diet, and lacks certain factors which the wild dog would find in the blood, bones, liver, and other organs of his prey. Furthermore, it has been proved scientifically that dogs can thrive on a meatless diet. In spite of these reservations, however, meat must be regarded as an excellent article of food, and if properly supplemented will prove very satisfactory. In recommendations which have recently been made in America (Dr. S. R. Speelman, of the U.S. Department of Agriculture) it is suggested that meat (beef, lamb, mutton, or horseflesh, providing that the last is fed regularly and not spasmodically) or meat substitutes (fish, milk, eggs, etc.) should constitute one-half of the daily ration, and that the remainder should comprise approximately equal parts of cereal substances (bread, biscuits) and of vegetables (carrots, spinach, onion, beet, etc.). It is pointed out that many dogs do not accept the vegetable material readily. On this basis, the approximate quantities of food required by adult dogs have been calculated as follows:—

| Weight of dog. | Total food per day. |
|---|---|
| 1 lb. | 2 oz. |
| 10 lb. | 12 oz. |
| 25 lb. | 1½ lb. |
| 50 lb. | 2 lb. |
| 75 lb. | 3½ lb. |
| 100 lb. | 4½ lb. |
| 150 lb. | 5½ lb. |
| 225 lb. | 7 lb. |

(Weights of up to 10 lb. would include the toy breeds, 25 lb. would correspond to a Fox Terrier; Airedale Terriers and Retrievers would fall into the 50–75-lb. class, and the larger weights would be those of the very big breeds, such as the St. Bernard.) The quantities given are, of course, an *approximation* and no more. Dogs which lead a very active life will require more, while those which take little exercise, or which tend to put on fat easily, will require less. Common sense is necessary, and great care must be taken not to over-feed or to under-nourish.

*Meat* is probably best fed raw, or lightly cooked, but many animals appear to have a preference (probably through habit) for well-cooked meat. In any event, the meat should not be "over-done," as there is substantial evidence that prolonged heating destroys much of the food value of the meat protein. *Fish* is an excellent substitute. There need be no anxiety about the greed with which a dog swallows lumps of meat and also neglects to masticate them. The teeth of the dog are for tearing meat, he is not concerned with biting his food up small; indeed, his salivary glands contain no digestive ferments, as is the case with some other animals.

*Milk* is almost essential during pregnancy and lactation (see below), and may well be included in normal dietaries. Whether or not *bones* should be fed is a matter which has been hotly debated, but for mature household dogs the evidence suggests that they are unnecessary. (The teeth of racing greyhounds, which receive a "sloppy" diet, are quite as good as those of the average household dog.) Bone-feeding is responsible for much trouble, including constipation, actual impaction of the rectum, and lodgement of pieces of bone in the mouth or throat. The value of bones is, of course, that they contain large quantities of essential mineral substances, and for this reason the inclusion in the diet of bone-meal, or of steamed *bone-flour*, or, preferably, a mineral supplement, is recommended. Only very small quantities of these substances are required.

*Bread* is an article of food which is often overlooked in the case of the dog, but there is no doubt that wholemeal bread is very suitable indeed, provided it is not fed to excess.

The answer to the question whether a dog requires vegetables is, in the main, no. From the Vitamin C standpoint they are quite unnecessary, since it has been shown that a dog manufactures this vitamin for itself, but the fact remains that many dogs, particularly of the toy variety, enjoy a few slices of banana or apple, and there is no harm in letting them pander to their taste. Vegetables do help, however, to provide roughage, and cooked (*not raw*) *potatoes* may be used in place of bread or biscuits. The dog—like many other animals—cannot digest raw starch properly. *Flaked maize* and *oatmeal* are other substitutes, but it must be remembered that the energy value of maize is high and that the dogs must never be overfed. *Dog biscuits* are an item that were long in disfavour with some professional people on account of their often having been made from agenised white flour (see section on Canine Hysteria), but now that this factor has been overcome, and the biscuits themselves are being improved in other ways, their use for the non-meat portion of the diet may be recommended.

Clean fresh *water* must be provided at all times.

In addition to the diets recommended above, there are on the market several tinned dog foods which claim to be complete, or almost complete, diets for the dog. It must be said that many dogs (including those of the writer) have remained in excellent health when receiving one of these foods as a large part of the diet over long periods. There is, therefore, little that may be said against the widespread use of the better varieties of such products. Again, it is a matter for common sense: if an owner finds that his animal is thriving on such a diet, he is wise to continue to use it.

It is customary to give dogs two meals a day. There is no need to give more than two to healthy adults, for the dog's stomach is exceedingly capacious and adapted to long gaps between meals. Many dogs thrive on only one meal in twenty-four hours. Whatever plan is decided on, regularity should be adhered to, and a meal or meals given at the same times every day.

Dogs require vitamins A and D and B complex. There are several ways of administering these, but the special commercial preparations, including the modern form of condition-powder tablet, are the most convenient.

The *pregnant* and *lactating bitch* require special consideration. The food requirements are very much increased in a bitch which is carrying puppies, especially towards the end of the period. Normally, appetite is not a complete guide to a dog's food requirements, but in pregnancy and lactation the bitch must not be allowed to go hungry. It is quite normal for a heavily pregnant bitch to require over one and a half times her normal amount of food, and in lactation her requirements will increase still further. Milk is a most excellent article of diet at this time; indeed, there is no better way (apart from commercial preparations) of replacing the milk which the bitch is giving to her own puppies.

Up to the age of three weeks or so, *puppies* need have mother's milk only, but at any time after this it is a sound policy to give them additional food, and so spare the mother and also render weaning (at from six to eight weeks) a *gradual* process. At first a little cow's milk or one of the commercial "dog-milk" preparations may be given, and gradually the puppies should be encouraged to eat solid food. Eggs (if they can be spared), wholemeal bread in milk, or even finely minced meat may be given, at first in very small amounts but later in larger quantities. If this process is carefully carried out, there will be far less trouble at and after weaning time. After weaning, puppies should receive five or six meals a day, and this number may be cut down gradually until two or three only are given to the fully grown dog. (The smaller breeds are fully grown at about a year.) *More* meat or meat substitutes and milk, and *less* cereal or vegetable matter, should be fed to the growing dog as compared with the adult. This fact is important, as the substances present in meat and milk are required for laying down the growing tissues. Nevertheless, the energy portion of the ration is important, and the cereal or vegetable should be nutritious and not fibrous. It is possible to rear puppies by hand from birth if the bitch for any reason should die. It requires great patience for the first two or three weeks, as naturally the puppies will require feeding once or twice during the night. Special milks for puppies are to be recommended. Cow's milk requires enriching with fat and sugar to approximate to the composition of bitch's milk. Feeding will have to be done at every two or three hours, and a very useful gadget is a fountain-pen filler attached to cycle-valve tubing. Very small quantities are required for the first two or three days, and a level teaspoonful of milk is more than sufficient for the average terrier at first. Even with the best care in the world hand-fed puppies tend to be weaklings and do not grow as fast as those naturally fed. A foster bitch, if obtainable, is much to be preferred.

## BREEDING OF DOGS.

It is natural for adult dogs of both sexes to wish to breed, and in the case of the female especially it is an excellent thing if one can arrange for a suitable mating to take place. Bitches come "into season" or "on heat" (lay terms for œstrus) at approximately six-monthly intervals, but it is not advisable to breed from the first season which occurs usually at about eight to nine months of age, but over a wide range of age according to breed and other factors. The periods of season often occur between January and March and in early Autumn, but there is no fixed rule. Each season lasts for three weeks. For the first seven days, approximately (pro-œstrus), a bitch does not permit mating, though during this time she is a source of strong attraction to all males in the neighbourhood. At about the seventh to the tenth day the blood-stained discharge, which ushers in the heat, stops; this is usually taken by the breeder as an indication that the bitch will stand to service. If possible, it is always better when puppies are wanted to allow mating to occur more than once. Under natural conditions a dog and bitch are usually strictly monogamous and mate for life, and during the period of œstrus will mate many times. A dog and bitch that are kept together all the time will probably behave naturally, but under domestication both dogs and bitches usually become promiscuous. Many bitches will in fact accept service from different males on different days, and the phenomenon of superfecundation, i.e., the production of a litter that is fathered by two males, may occur. It is therefore wise to retain strict control of the bitch throughout the whole of the three weeks or so she is in season. At the end of season the bitch passes into a state of " metœstrus " if she has not conceived.

If a bitch conceives, she carries her puppies for a period of about nine weeks. There is, however, a normal variation of fifty-eight to seventy days, and puppies born before the fifty-eighth day sometimes live. The number of puppies born varies with breed; in the smaller terriers it is usually from four to six, but in Airedales and Alsatians the number may be eight to ten, and the larger breeds tend to have even more offspring at a time. Birth usually takes place fairly easily in the larger breeds, but there is often much difficulty in the case of the short-legged breeds, such as Scottish and Sealyham Terriers, Pekingese and Dachshunds. In some breeds, in fact, the problem is one that is giving serious concern to veterinary surgeons and breeders.

A short while before her puppies are due, a bitch will " make her bed." Owners are often amazed at the destruction of soft furnishings, or even of wall-paper, that a previously well-behaved bitch may carry out at this time; it is therefore by far the best to provide a suitable box (if the animal has not one already). A smooth flooring such as a strip of linoleum serves for the bitch to give birth to her puppies. Her instinct to tear up everything given to her for bedding may lead to suffocation of the puppies by pieces of bedding. Provided labour occurs in a warm room, it is sometimes better—according to the temperament of the bitch—to remove each puppy as it is born, placing a warm bottle underneath, and bring it back to the mother when the last birth has occurred. At this time the bitch should be watched carefully for any discharge from the vulva or for any evidence of straining. If either of these occurs without results, it is advisable to send for help as early as possible, especially in the case of the smaller breeds. Many hundreds of bitches are lost through neglect at this time, and usually because it was not suspected that anything was wrong. If the discharge becomes bloody, or green, help should be obtained at once if no puppy is delivered. Similarly, any great delay between births is a matter for concern. The afterbirth usually follows the puppy within a few minutes, but puppies are sometimes delivered in their fœtal membranes, and in this case the latter should be gently but quickly removed. It is quite normal for the umbilical cord to remain attached to the puppy, but the bitch will normally break it by biting through it.

The mother will wash and attend to the new born puppies, and after the last is born it is a good idea to burn all the mess and to provide clean newspaper, but do not worry or frighten the bitch more than is necessary. For the care and feeding of the bitch and her puppies see the sections on Management and Feeding. Puppies, like kittens, are born with their eyes closed, but open them after about nine days—there again being considerable variation.

The phenomenon of pseudopregnancy is common in bitches, and indeed to a minor degree it is probably present in most bitches following an œstrus without conception. In some bitches, however, presumably those with strong maternal drives, the changes in the ovary may be accompanied by external signs of " phantom " or " ghost " pregnancy. These may include not only enlargement but actual functioning of the mammary glands, and the making of a " nest " by the bitch just as if her puppies were really due. The average duration of pseudopregnancy is usually given as about two months, and although variable, it is often sufficiently near to the correct time after œstrus that everyone suspects the bitch to be truly pregnant. The condition may be suppressed with the aid of modern drugs, but in some instances it is not realised that the condition is not real. In many cases only professional advice can solve the mystery, and radiographical examinations have often proved necessary to ascertain the truth, particularly in fat bitches of the heavier breeds. It might be well to note, at this point, that there is another condition of the older bitch that is known as Pyometra. This condition usually reveals itself at the same time as the ghost pregnancy (and is sometimes a pathological extension of it) but is accompanied by considerable disturbance of health, coupled in many instances with purulent discharge from the vagina. A bitch which is off-colour in the weeks following pregnancy, or which develops a discharge from the vulva (especially one which is dark in colour), may well be a pyometra subject. The disease is most serious, and often requires surgical intervention. As the best chance of success is to operate or otherwise deal with early, a veterinary surgeon should be consulted immediately.

## DISEASES AND INJURIES OF THE DOG.

Canine Distemper and " Para-distemper " (Including so-called " Hard-pad ").—It has long been recognised that the commonest and most serious disease of dogs throughout the world is canine distemper. Dogs of all ages and breeds are susceptible, and no dog is free from the risk of infection unless it has recovered from the disease or has acquired an immunity for other reasons (see P8(2). The disease is caused primarily by a minute agent known as a filterable virus (see P7(2). which may be of varying type in that it will attack the body in different ways. Thus some strains of the virus are known as " neurotropic " because they show an affinity for the nervous system. Sometimes a dog will apparently recover from an attack of distemper, only to succumb later to " fits " or other nervous manifestations due to permanent damage to the central nervous system by the virus. Often, however, the virus is not fatal in itself, but will lower the dog's resistance and permit the entry or the activity of bacteria that may lead to pneumonia or other serious effects. These so-called " secondary invaders," as the bacteria are termed, may prove as harmful as the original virus. Indeed, once these bacteria have set to work it is too late to expect the best results from the use of serum, and whether or not the dog will live through will depend upon the severity of the attack, the dog's powers of resistance, and good nursing. It is therefore most important either to prevent the disease by vaccination or to be able to send for veterinary attention (and hence for an injection of serum) immediately an attack is suspected. Any puppy which is listless or off its food, or which may throw a fit, or which is obviously unwell with other symptoms (e.g., cough or diarrhœa) may well be in the early stages of distemper, and it is then (not the next day) that help should be sought. Many thousands of puppies (and older dogs) that have been injected with serum in the early stages of the disease have become perfectly normal within forty-eight hours. On the other hand, the number of dogs that die in Great Britain alone from distemper and distemper-like infections must assume enormous proportions. Distemper is a highly infectious disease, and it is important that the owner of an infected animal should do his best to avoid contact with other dogs, ferrets, or mink. Ferrets and mink are very susceptible to canine distemper. On the other hand, human beings and cats are not susceptible to canine distemper, and the so-called distemper of cats is quite a distinct disease.

A highly satisfactory means of vaccinating puppies against distemper was worked out about 1926-30, and this—named the " Laidlaw-Dunkin " after its two inventors—has since afforded protection to thousands of animals. Modern vaccines are based on a virus which has been modified by growth on developing egg embryos; or, more recently, in tissue culture. Puppies should be vaccinated when they are 10-12 weeks; prior to this age the immunity induced by the vaccine may not develop satisfactorily. After vaccination the puppy requires some time, possibly 2 weeks, before an immunity is established. Sometimes vaccinated dogs suffer distemper or distemper-like signs due to "secondary invaders" causing disease on their own account; or because they were already infected when vaccinated. Variants of distemper of which "hard pad" is an example may also overwhelm a vaccinated dog's immunity, alhough this is uncommon with modern vaccines, since several distemper strains are used in their production. Hyperimmune serum, which is collected from animals previously hyperimmunised against distemper, is available and can immediately aid the dog suffering from distemper but its effect is short-lived (7-10 days).

### Infectious Hepatitis or Rubarth's Disease.—

Another virus disease of dogs (and foxes) is known as Rubarth's disease, after one of its discoverers, now known as infectious hepatitis. This disease has been recognised in Sweden ever since the 1930s, but in Great Britain only since the end of the war. The condition is extremely sudden in onset, and an affected dog may be found dead. Many cases are, however, mild, and in some instances only one or two out of a large group of dogs have been affected. The changes seen after death vary, but the findings in the liver cells are usually character-istic. Specific treatment is not yet established as in the case of the distemper-like conditions, although the administration of antibiotics (see P9) may prevent the effects of secondary infection. An effective vaccine is now produced and often combined with the distemper chick embryo vaccine. A dog is thereby protected against both these diseases.

### Canine Hysteria

Canine Hysteria (called "fright disease" or "running fits" in the U.S.A.) is an alarming but not necessarily serious condition (in that it can often be cured very readily) which appears to arise from a variety of exciting causes. The affected animal rushes around wildly, often screaming and howling, and obviously loses all sense of whereabouts or ability to recognise people. After a more severe attack (and there are all degrees up to a full epileptiform fit) the dog may appear quite exhausted, but returns to normal. Sometimes there are many attacks in one day. The dog will not wilfully attack people during a bout of hysteria—at least, that has been the experience of the writer—but is very difficult to control. Apart from ensuring that the dog does itself no grievous bodily harm, there is little that can be done until the attack has subsided. Then the animal should be kept as quiet as possible and given a tranquilliser.

Hysteria may be an hereditary taint, derived from one or other parent. In certain circum-stances, however, it may arise in apparently normal animals. There are several possible causes (including parasites), but a definite one is the bleaching agent—nitrogen trichloride or "agene"—employed for some years in the manufacture of flour, and hence present in white bread and certain dog biscuits. Indeed, the clear demonstration that agene could set up hysteria in dogs, and subsequent scientific work, has led to the introduction of regulations that have led to its abandonment as a bleaching agent in favour of other methods which have been found not to cause hysteria. There has already been a marked decline in the incidence of hysteria due to dietary factors.

### Rabies

Rabies is a fatal disease of dogs, and is also due to a "filterable virus." It is transmissible to the human being and to many other species, but has fortunately been absent from Great Britain for many years. Stringent precautions are taken to prevent its entry, and dogs which are brought into Great Britain must spend a long period in quarantine. A vaccine is available and people taking dogs to countries where rabies occurs should have their animals protected. Many countries insist on this prodceure.

### Tonsilitis

Tonsilitis appears quite frequently in dogs, and seems in many cases to be part of a more general-ised infection. It demands expert treatment, but although it may persist for a long time, it usually yields to treatment.

### Nephritis.—

Nephritis.—Inflammation of the kidneys is unfortunately all too common in dogs, and in adult males in particular there is a high incidence of chronic kidney damage. One of the symptoms is a marked thirst. Sometimes this condition is a sequel to an infection known as leptospirosis, which calls for prompt veterinary treatment if death or permanent damage is not to follow. It is always worth while seeking professional advice for a dog that drinks excessively or has a some-what characteristic type of bad breath. A vaccine which gives a good immunity against the two common forms of leptospirosis is available.

### Anal Glands

Anal Glands, which are found in the dog and in other carnivora, often give rise to trouble. Ani-mals which "rub themselves along the ground" are not necessarily affected with "worms," but with impaction of these two little glands, which are situated one on each side of the anus. They secrete a peculiar dark-coloured, very offensive fluid, which sometimes is not discharged properly and causes the animal great discomfort. The glands in such cases should be relieved periodically. Those who do not mind this somewhat dirty task may perhaps learn how to do it themselves. Occasionally, segments of tapeworm are respon-sible for the impaction, but usually the trouble has nothing to do with worms. Whenever a dog pays considerable attention to his anus, this im-paction should be suspected. Actual infection of the glands is also fairly common, and demands expert attention.

### Diseases of the Ear

Diseases of the Ear, especially of the outer ear, are very common in dogs. The dog's outer ear is somewhat more complicated than is our own, and the drum is set more deeply. Hence it is easy for wax and dirt to accumulate, for various parasites to establish themselves, and for in-flammatory conditions to result. The word "canker" (which has no precise scientific mean-ing) is sometimes applied by lay people to the more serious or chronic forms of inflammation of the outer ear canal. It is not difficult to diagnose "ear trouble," as the affected animal usually shakes its head or worries or scratches its ear and rubs it along the ground. The ears should be inspected regularly to see that there is no great accumulation of wax or dirt. Cotton-wool twisted on to the end of a match-stick or orange-stick is quite satisfactory for cleaning out the ear, providing care is taken. A dog which is continually worrying its ear, or which has ears which are obviously diseased, should not be neg-lected, as the sooner expert treatment is begun the more readily will the condition be cured. Even if the lining of the ear is greatly thickened through inflammatory reaction, and the lumen nearly occluded, it is still possible for a plastic operation to be performed. Many hundreds of such cases have been successfully treated in this way. A percentage of inflammatory conditions of the outer ear is associated with ear mange mites. In such an event treatment with modern anti-mange preparations should be carried out.

### Deafness

Deafness in certain white dogs (e.g., in some Bull Terriers) appears to be hereditary, and is quite incurable. Old dogs often become deaf, and deafness has been produced experimentally in young puppies by feeding them on a deficient diet.

### Diseases of the Eye

Diseases of the Eye are very common in dogs, and are often the result of injury. Except for minor discharges from the corners of their eyes (and in younger dogs especially it must be ascer-tained that these are not a symptom of distemper) any eye disease is sufficiently serious to merit professional advice. Boracic lotion is not suitable for the eyes of dogs. It is slightly irritant, and dogs are apt to scratch and make the eyes raw after application. Colloidal silver eye lotions and ointments are far more suitable pending the advice of a veterinary surgeon. In eye inflammation avoid sunlight and wind. For some days in the early stages of inflamed eyes, the light in the room should be subdued. Pekingese seem to be especially prone to eye disease, but the remarkably unwholesome appearance of some affected eyes in this breed is not necessarily evidence that recovery is unlikely. Steps should be taken to ensure that the dog does not inflict further injury on an already diseased eye. Cat scratches are a frequent source of inflammatory conditions of the dog's eye. Eyes must never be neglected, for the consequences are serious.

**Skin Diseases** are common in dogs, and may be contagious. Among the common contagious causes of skin disease are lice, mange mites and fleas. Lice and mange mites (except for demodex) are killed by modern insecticides such as benzene hexachloride (gammexane) although two applications at a 10–14 day interval are required to destroy the young stages which are within the insecticide-resistant eggs at the first dressing. The flea actually on the dog, is only one of four stages in the life cycle of the flea; the others are in the house or dog's bedding. Insecticides used for flea control should therefore be applied every week or 10 days during the summer to kill the young fleas as they hatch and infest the dog. The dog's bedding should be discarded or cleaned. The dog also suffers from other skin diseases caused by systemic disorders for which expert attention is required.

**Diseases of the Teeth and Gums** are very common in household dogs. A serious systemic disease, such as distemper, may leave the enamel of the teeth permanently pitted, hence " distemper teeth." More serious than this, however, is a form of pyorrhœa, which is really a disease of the gums rather than a primary disease of the teeth themselves. The margins of the gums become red and swollen, and may bleed easily. As the condition progresses the teeth may become loosened. Particles of food become lodged between the teeth or between teeth and gums, and add to the inflammation and to the smell of the breath.

This disease may, if unchecked, become very serious. In many cases extraction of one or more teeth is indicated, but unfortunately it is not always possible to do this. The condition demands expert attention.

Another common condition of dogs' teeth is the deposition around them of " tartar." This should be removed by scaling or by special use of dental forceps. Some breeders and others may themselves have learnt how to carry out these operations with the requisite skill and care, but they are not easy to the amateur, and it is essential that no harm be done to the animal's soft tissues by injudicious use of the instruments. Ordinary dog-owners are strongly advised to take their dogs to a veterinary surgeon in order to have the " tartar " removed.

Most puppies lose their first or " milk " teeth quite regularly between the ages of three and five months, but sometimes there is difficulty and the primary teeth are not shed properly. These cases should be treated by a veterinary surgeon before the permanent teeth are thrown out of their proper alignment.

One hears very much about " teething fits " in puppies, and while these occur, owners should be *very* careful to ensure that a " teething fit " is not a sign of distemper, which often starts with a fit. As puppies of this age are so susceptible to distemper, it is advisable to seek professional advice should any form of fit occur. It may save much time, money, and trouble, and even the animal's life.

**Internal Parasites: " Worms."**—It is probable that more nonsense has been talked and written about " worms " in dogs than about any other canine subject. According to some people, " worms " are the root of nearly all doggy evil, and so long as a dog is regularly " wormed " all will go well with him. These beliefs are frankly absurd. The real facts are very different, and are stated in as brief a fashion as possible in the following sentences. In this country dogs are infested by a species of " roundworm " (a creature which is a dirty-white colour and in shape somewhat resembles the common earthworm) and by several species of " tapeworm," which are also whitish but which are flat and are made up of many small segments joined to a little " head " which is attached to the lining of the gut. In spite of all that is said, tapeworms as such are rarely responsible for much harm to the dog, although they can, of course, prove debilitating and should be removed. They are a nuisance, and attempts to remove them should be made by administration of the appropriate drug. Occasionally, segments of worm are responsible for impaction of the ducts of the *anal glands* (see above).

The roundworms may be extremely serious in young puppies, in which they cause stunting, " pot-belly," harshness of coat and dangerous or fatal illness. Fortunately, modern anti-roundworm preparations are available for animals of this age. Once over the age of 4–8 months, dogs rarely suffer serious illness from roundworms, although these may cause occasional vomiting, or even diarrhœa, and some loss of coat and bodily condition. It is now known that puppies are infected before birth from their mother. It is therefore desirable to keep down the incidence of roundworms in the mother—and in dogs generally—and fortunately the modern preparations are—unlike some of the old-fashioned ones—safe in use and unlikely to cause digestive disturbances. From all that has been said above owners will realise the necessity of taking professional advice about young dogs which are ill, and any signs of " worms " in young puppies—either in the stools or by some obvious intestinal upset or bloated appearance of the belly—should be acted upon. One last word about this aspect of worms—do not assume that your adult dog has " tapeworms " unless you see some evidence in his stools. There are so many " signs of worms " that veterinary surgeons must at times get a little tired of being assured that " My dog has worms " because of some trivial habit connected with appetite.

There is, however, another side to the study of tapeworms, and one which is not generally realised. The tapeworm which is found in the dog represents one stage in the life-cycle. The eggs, which are present in the ripe segment passed by the dog, develop, not in the outside world, but in another animal altogether. Thus one of the commonest tapeworms in this country has an intermediate stage, as it is called, in the flea, and it is when the flea is eaten by the dog that this intermediate stage develops further to become a tapeworm. Another tapeworm has an intermediate stage which develops in the sheep, and a third has one which develops in the ox. There is a fourth tapeworm which has an intermediate stage which *may* develop in man, to set up serious diseases in certain cases. Children may become infected through handling the dog, and so picking up the eggs, which may then be eaten through putting the hands in the mouth. The dogs which are most likely to be infested are those which have the opportunity to eat freshly killed sheep and other food-animals. An ordinary household dog is not likely to be infested, and people should not worry unduly in this connection, provided they do not allow their dogs to stray into the wrong places. It is illegal to allow dogs to enter a slaughter-house, but unfortunately one often sees dogs in such places. The routine worming of dogs is justified if evidence of infection exists, and certainly in country areas where opportunities of tapeworm re-infection may be plentiful.

**Tumours,** including malignant tumours (" cancers ") are relatively very common in the dog—probably as common as in the human subject. Space does not permit of a detailed account, but the following examples of growths may be mentioned: a proliferation of warts on the skin of puppies (usually disappear spontaneously); a true cancer of the tonsil in middle-aged and older dogs of both sexes; cancer of the mammary glands in bitches (both incurable); fatty growths of the vagina of bitches (amenable to operation). Space does not allow of the discussion of other diseases, but it should be pointed out that dogs are susceptible to human and bovine forms of *tuberculosis*, especially the former. In a household which contains a tubercular person, the dog should be watched for any signs of illness, and the thought entertained that he might be responsible for the further spread of the disease. For a discussion on ringworm see the appropriate heading in the section on the cat (Z12).

**Accidents and Injuries.**—In these days of swiftly moving motor transport, street accidents to dogs are extremely common. Many could be prevented by training the animal to walk to heel, by the use of a lead in busy thoroughfares, and by not allowing dogs to roam the streets unaccompanied—a thoroughly bad habit. Sometimes the victim escapes with a scare and a few bruises, and at others death is mercifully swift. In the vast majority of accidents, however, a more or less serious injury is incurred, and if the animal is unable to move, the police should be notified immediately. The dog is best left quiet, and it is not recommended that attempts be made to administer brandy or other supposed " stimulants " unless help is markedly delayed. Excessive hæmorrhage may in some instances be prevented by common-sense application of principles learnt in first-aid courses.

One of the commonest accidents to dogs, especially to young dogs, is a fracture involving the head of the femur, or thigh-bone. Inability to put one of the hind legs to the ground, or to bear any weight on this limb, is an indication of such an injury. (This injury may occur also from falling off a chair or wall.) Professional help is, of course, required in such cases.

**Cuts and Bruises,** if not serious, may be treated at home as in the case of human beings. The indiscriminate use of tincture of iodine is not to be recommended, and spirit alone makes a more satisfactory dressing in most cases. Simple washing and removal of dirt are usually sufficient, combined, perhaps, with modern antiseptic ointments or other preparations. The dog (and also the cat) are very liable to sepsis, and it is best in such cases to send for proper assistance early, or there may be grave trouble. It is probable that in nature many of the flesh-eating animals end their lives as victims of the sepsis following wounds.

Injuries from cat-scratches are exceedingly common, as are bites from other dogs. These are serious, as they more readily result in septic places. The scratch or bite sometimes penetrates quite deeply, leaving a pocket which fills up with pus. This pus may spread under the skin to form sinuses. Never neglect such places.

**Conclusion.**—There are a few concluding remarks on the treatment of the diseases of the dog:—

(1) It is not correct that " water should be withheld from a sick dog." It is true that an animal which is using water only to vomit, or which is drinking excessively, should have its water intake restricted, but it is wrong to deprive a dog altogether. It may be suffering from diabetes and should be taken to the vet for testing.

(2) There have been such wonderful advances in the field of veterinary anæsthetics that there is nowadays little to fear in this connection from operations to dogs and cats. The records over the past years at the Royal Veterinary College, London, and at other centres have been most encouraging, and the anæsthetic risk is now small indeed.

(3) When a dog's life is a burden to him, it is unfair to keep him alive, and he should be put to sleep. It must be realised, however, that putting a dog to sleep is a very skilled task. It is made much easier if an owner will allow his veterinary surgeon to administer an anæsthetic and not allow the animal " to come round," and shooting is also straightforward and painless if *skilfully* carried out. There are no " magical ways " of destroying human or animal life, and an owner must not expect his veterinary surgeon to be able to bring about death merely by holding a pad to the dog's face. It is far better that the task be carried out at a veterinary surgeon's own premises, where there is skilled assistance.

# CATS.

Many of the general remarks in the preceding section apply equally to cats, and will not be repeated unnecessarily in the following paragraphs.

## BREEDS AND VARIETIES OF CAT.

The following breeds and varieties are recognised for registration purposes by the Governing Council of the Cat Fancy:—

*Long-haired Cats.*

| | |
|---|---|
| Black | Tortoiseshell |
| White (Blue-eyed) | Tortoiseshell-and-White |
| White (Orange-eyed) | Blue Cream |
| Blue | Brown Tabby |
| Red Tabby | Chinchilla |
| Red Self | Smoke |
| Cream | Silver Tabby |

*Short-haired Cats.*

| | |
|---|---|
| Black | Spotted |
| White | Russian Blue |
| British Blue | Manx |
| Cream | Abyssinian |
| Tortoiseshell | Siamese (Seal-pointed) |
| Tortoiseshell-and-White | Siamese (Blue-pointed) |
| Silver Tabby | Siamese (Chocolate-pointed) |
| Brown Tabby | |
| Red Tabby | Burmese |
| Mackerel-striped Tabby | |

Pedigree breeding and showing are practised with a very small fraction of the total cat population of Great Britain, and the majority of these remarks will be concerned with the ordinary household cat. Nevertheless, in recent years there appears to have been a considerable increase in pedigree cat breeding. Registration—which is essential for showing and pedigree purposes—is controlled by the Governing Council of the Cat Fancy. Many of the breeds listed above have their own societies, which are affiliated to the Governing Council. The addresses and particulars of these and other cat societies and clubs may be had on application to the secretary of the Governing Council. The two most popular varieties of cat are the Blue Persian and the Siamese, and an exclusive show is held for each of them. In addition to these shows there are five big Championship Shows open to every variety of long- and short-haired cat, while there are classes for cats and kittens at some of the Agricultural Shows.

## CHOICE OF CAT.

Although there are, as noted above, many varieties of cat, most people are content to accept an ordinary kitten, and for them the chief points to consider will be: (a) whether to have a long-haired or a short-haired animal, (b) whether to have a male or female, (c) whether or not to have the kitten " doctored " (*i.e.*, castrated or spayed). As a general rule, short-haired cats are probably more suitable for the average household, since their fur does not become shed so noticeably and they probably suffer less from " fur-balling." Nevertheless, many long-haired cats are so attractive that they will obviously be preferred, and there is no reason why they should not be chosen. Sex is a rather more important question, although, as may be seen in the section on management, it is possible to have both males and females " doctored." Male cats which are kept as entires are often a nuisance in that they make abominable smells in the house and spend much of their time in fighting. These characteristics are by no means invariable; but they are so common as to justify the castration of the majority of males. Siamese males in particular may be a liability. Females are generally credited with a greater attachment to the home (although they wander when " in season ") and with being better mousers. The principal objection to females is that they seem to be bearing kittens almost continuously. In normal circumstances it is, of course, quite impossible to prevent cats from mating by keeping the female in confinement during her season, a practice which is frequently adopted in the case of the dog. For one thing, most people are never aware when their female cats are in season.

Whatever animal is chosen, it is essential to pick a healthy and preferably a fairly young—but *not* too young—kitten. It is best not to accept a kitten under about eight weeks of age.

For those who wish for something a little out of the ordinary, Siamese cats make excellent and highly intelligent pets. Siamese kittens are born white, but gradually develop their even pale fawn colour, with cream on belly and chest and with " seal brown " mask, ears, legs, feet, and tail. The coat is very short, and the eyes are blue. There has long been a popular belief that Siamese cats are delicate creatures, but the present writer has seen healthy specimens, kept under ordinary household conditions, living to a mature age. It is not wise to keep a male Siamese as a household pet. The male is a fierce fighter, and is generally a worse offender in the house than the males of other breeds, and should therefore be castrated if it is to be kept as a pet.

Many people find Manx cats attractive. Instead of the normal large number of tail bones, they have but three, and hence appear almost tailless. One should beware against fraudulent amputation of the tail of ordinary cats, which are then described as " Manx."

## MANAGEMENT OF THE CAT.

The cat is an independent creature, so much so that one may say that to a large extent it manages its own affairs. This, however, is not true of all cats, and every reasonable attempt should be made to provide the cat with a comfortable and friendly home. Cats are highly intelligent, and if sufficient patience is exercised they will respond to a very great degree to human attention. Kittens should not be neglected, but should be talked to and played with just as are puppies. Many cats, especially young cats, make excellent playmates for children.

In order to prevent to a large extent their nocturnal wanderings, many cats of both sexes are castrated or spayed (the popular lay expression for this is " doctored "). In the male cat the testicles are removed by an operation which is almost always safe and simple if carried out skilfully. From three to four months is a good age at which to have this done. Female cats may also be " doctored." As the female glands or ovaries lie within the body cavity, this operation is a major one, but it is nevertheless quite a straightforward, though a more expensive, procedure if conducted at the right age (about five months). Very many thousands of female cats have been so operated upon and the subsequent health of these cats has been excellent. Indeed, it has been said that a spayed female makes one of the best of all household cats.

Cats may choose to sleep in a variety of places, and will often lie on beds, chairs, mats, and other warm places. It is a sound policy to provide them with a box or basket, and to encourage them to use newspaper as a bedding. Most cats will take well to newspaper. The bed should be placed in a warm site—it is of little use putting it in a cold corner of a room and expecting the cat to lie in it.

Owing to the fact that, even in play, a cat's claws may inflict serious injury, dogs and cats do not always make the best of house companions. Nevertheless, the traditional enmity of cat and dog is often overcome, and if the two are brought up together they often make firm friends, sharing the same basket or hearth-rug and feeding together without serious consequences.

A cat normally attends to its own toilet, and everyone must be aware that a cat devotes long periods each day to cleaning and washing itself. Except in special cases, therefore, bathing is quite unnecessary, while in short-haired cats especially, grooming, too, is superfluous (this does not apply to show-cats). For some reason (and sometimes, apparently, because an owner attempts to assist in the daily grooming) an occasional cat may cease to wash or care for itself. Such an animal is a dejected sight, and should be taken to a veterinary surgeon to have its matted fur cut or combed, and

its dirt removed. Such animals (unless they completely re-acquire their self-respect) must be groomed regularly if they are to be kept at all.

All household cats are accustomed to take their own exercise, and it is advisable (except in any special circumstances) to allow them free access to and from the outer world. Do not shut your cat in the house for a long period and then blame it for making a mess. Cats are clean creatures; they normally dig small holes in which to defæcate or urinate, and subsequently cover the deposit with earth. If, therefore, they are for some reason debarred temporarily or permanently from access to a garden, they should be provided with a box or tray containing soil or cinders. Indeed, in many types of houses it is a good plan to encourage kittens to use such a device. (Note the corresponding remarks about puppies.)

It is generally stated that " cats never forget a blow," and for that reason it is recommended that cats are not chastised. It may be said that, if a cat (or dog) be brought up conscientiously and well, it should never, or very rarely, require such punishment. An animal which has been brought up properly seems to develop a fair sense of what is right and what is wrong.

For pedigree cats, or those kept in confinement for other reasons, see the relevent remarks in the section on breeding.

## FEEDING THE CAT.

Although most cats are capable of supplementing their diet by catching small rodents or birds, it is unwise to rely on this as a regular source of food. The idea that hungry cats make the best mousers is by no means always correct. Indeed, animals that are in poor condition are less likely to be successful hunters. Moreover, while the riddance of pests is an excellent matter from the human point of view—and one of the reasons why the keeping of cats is economically justified—the " cruel " fashion in which most cats tackle their prey is repulsive to most of us.

It is therefore necessary and desirable to provide regular daily feeding. Kittens should receive several meals a day, but by the time they are six months old the number of daily feeds should be reduced to one, or at most two. Most cats (many Siamese are exceptions) are extremely fond of *milk*, especially if it is creamy, and the cat's love of *fish* is well known. Many *meats*, especially *rabbit meat*, are relished, and a diet high in " animal protein " is indeed the aim, always provided that it contains sufficient " dietary energy." It is significant that cat's milk has a higher content of fat and sugar than cow's milk, *i.e.*, it is a richer source of energy. Some of the proprietary bitch-milk substitutes are nearer to cat's milk in composition than is cow's milk,

Many hundreds of cats have been reared and bred successfully in experimental laboratories on a diet consisting, in the main, of one part of fish or meat and two parts of *cooked potatoes*. This is relatively inexpensive, and may be supplemented by milk and by some of the proprietary cat foods.

Cats are also extremely fond of liver. Some of the proprietary cat foods—the better ones of which are excellent—and vitamin tablets contain liver, which is a rich source of the vitamin B complex.

Within reason a healthy kitten should be fed to appetite, always provided good-quality foods are available. The amount should be restricted when they are adult, however, except for pregnant and lactating cats, which are sometimes referred to as " queens " as opposed to the male " toms." An average daily allowance of solid food for a healthy non-pregnant adult cat should be of the order of $\frac{1}{2}$ oz. per 1 lb. body-weight.

Cats are fastidious eaters; they usually sniff and examine carefully any strange or doubtful food. At the same time they are often greedy, especially with relished food to which they are accustomed, but fortunately they can, like dogs, vomit very readily. Here, incidentally, is one very good tip—an excellent emetic for both cat and dog is a small crystal of washing-soda, given as a pill. People are usually amazed at the way this simple device results in a dog's or a cat's bringing up undesirable food.

It is important not to overfeed cats, and it is

almost equally important to prepare all food in a clean manner, and to make it as attractive as possible. Cats will greatly appreciate this care. While milk is an excellent food for kittens (see under breeding), and is relished by most adult cats, it must be supplemented by solid food.

Clean fresh water should be provided at all times, even if the cat appears to drink it but little.

## BREEDING OF CATS.

Pedigree animals are normally confined, and their breeding is strictly controlled. Ordinary household cats are at the opposite extreme, and there is little that can be done to prevent their mating. The length and scope of this article does not permit of a discussion of controlled mating.

Scientifically, there is as yet a good deal to learn about the reproductive behaviour of the cat. As an American physiologist has succinctly put it in a description of the reproductive cycle of the female cat, " no two authors agree." In Northern Europe there are two main heat periods a year, in spring and early autumn, but some animals may appear in heat at any time from January to July, and those who keep female cats in confinement describe their charges as " calling " quite frequently if not mated. A cat which is " in season " or " on heat " is often observed to be behaving in a quite characteristic fashion, rolling about on the floor and making peculiar sounds. The periods of heat, which commence usually at about eight months of age, may last for several days, and during this time the female will make every attempt to find a mate.

Gestation lasts about nine weeks, as in the case of the bitch, but here again there is a considerable variation. As most owners are quite unaware of the time at which their cats were mated, it is difficult to talk of " going overtime," but if there is any evidence of trouble during pregnancy, or at birth, veterinary advice should be obtained. As soon as a cat is obviously pregnant, her food allowance should be increased, and she should be allowed plenty of milk. It is highly important to increase her food and milk ration still further after the kittens are born, as lactation is a great drain on the mother.

Cats sometimes choose strange, out-of-the-way places in which to litter, and many healthy litters are born and reared out of doors. Rats are a source of danger, and will often destroy very young kittens during the mother's absence. For this and other reasons it is better in town and suburban areas to have the litter comfortably housed indoors. A wooden box containing news-paper is ideal, provided it is kept in a fairly warm place and out of the way of draughts. An average litter consists of three to six kittens, which are born blind, but which normally open their eyes after eight or nine days. There is no need to be alarmed if the eyes remain closed for a few days longer. Kittens which are born dead should be removed and buried or burnt. If the whole litter is born dead, the mother's food supply should be cut down considerably, and little milk given for a few days. If the mamary glands become inflamed, they may be bathed in a cold solution of alum. The glands normally return to their former size within a short space of time if they are not milked, but if there is persistent trouble veterinary advice should be sought.

While many pedigree owners wean kittens at four to five weeks of age, it is strongly advised that the household cat be allowed to continue to feed her family for a longer period, and eight weeks is not too long if the mother is still in good bodily condition. She *must*, however, be well fed and be allowed plenty of milk. As in the case of puppies, it is an excellent idea to provide the kittens with a little solid food as from a few weeks of age. It is very wrong to remove a kitten from its mother too early, and such an animal is often weakly, develops an intestinal infection, and dies as a miserable bedraggled creature. Moreover, during the period following weaning the mother educates her offspring in the art of living, particularly ratting and mousing.

As many litters are unwanted, some people get rid of all the kittens as soon as possible after birth. Drowning is frequently practised, but it is not recommended as a merciful death. Indeed, a hard blow on the back of the head is more humane if given accurately. It is much better to take the kittens to a veterinary surgeon or clinic.

## DISEASES AND INJURIES OF THE CAT.

The principal infectious diseases of cats are still in need of much scientific study. It is now clear, however, that there are at least two major cat plagues. Both have been given many names, and there is much confusion between them.

Feline Enteritis or Panleucopenia.—This is a highly infectious disease, due to a filterable virus. The symptoms include loss of appetite, sometimes accompanied by a rise in body temperature, followed by listlessness, usually vomiting, some-times diarrhoea, and a marked tendency to show tenderness or pain on being handled. This tenderness or pain is due to a developing peri-tonitis. The poor animal may become seriously ill, with loss of water from the tissues or dehydra-tion, prostrate and dead within 48 hours or less from the time of the first symptoms. The in-cubation period of the disease is believed to be from 4 to 8 days, or sometimes longer. There is a fall in the white-cell count of the blood, hence the term " panleucopenia." Some cats recover, the recovery rate in different outbreaks that have been studied ranging from 30 to 80 per cent., and recovered animals are probably immune to further attacks. Cats that are able to take a little food during the early stages of recovery have the best chance of recovery, but require careful nursing. There may be com-plications during the convalescent stage due to secondary bacterial infections or to vitamin deficiency, and a light nourishing diet, combined with vitamin preparations, is recommended. Fleas may transmit the disease to other cats, as may contact with infected materials. It has been shown that bedding and dirt trays from sick cats were infectious for other cats for up to 16 days. The disease is not transmissible to dogs or to human beings. There is nowadays a protective vaccine, and it is a wise precaution to have your pet vaccinated.

Feline Pneumonitis.—This disease is sometimes called " cat distemper "—as indeed is feline enteritis—but it has no connection with dog distemper, and is not transmissible to dogs or to human beings. Both mild and severe forms occur, and the incubation period varies from 5 to 8 days. The mild form may seem like a cold, and there is a weeping from the eyes and a varying degree of conjunctivitis. There is a thin, clear discharge from the nose, with a charac-teristic sneezing. Provided that the animals can be made to continue eating, and are kept in warm and dry but well ventilated conditions, recovery may be rapid and not entail serious loss of condition. The eyes should be treated with a suitable pre-paration, such as silver vitellin. There may be secondary bacterial infection in cases that are neglected.

The severe form of the disease has similar, although more severe, commencing symptoms, but the nasal discharge becomes purulent and there is often profuse salivation, with much spreading of the long ropes of saliva. The cat is listless, dislikes strong light, and seems to resent being disturbed. It loses its appetite, and rapidly becomes thinner over a period of from 2 to 5 days or so. Breathing becomes laboured, and a bronchopneumonia develops. There may be a high death rate in young kittens, and pregnant females may abort. Recovery tends to be slow, and is often complicated by bacterial infection. Some of the modern antibiotics appear to be highly effective in the treatment of many cases of this disease, but they must, of course, be given under veterinary supervision.

Tuberculosis.—The cat, like the dog, can con-tract tuberculosis, but so far as is known only the bovine form has been known to infect it. The infections usually comes, of course, from milk, and the elimination of bovine tuberculosis from this country will stop the incidence of the disease in cats. The disease commences in the abdomen, but may spread to the lungs. There is general wasting.

**Skin Diseases.**—As in the case of the dog, skin disease in the cat is usually of parasitic origin, and fleas and mange mites are again the chief source of trouble in Great Britain. Cats do so much of their own toilet that the average household cat has probably a cleaner skin than its canine counterpart. When skin disease does develop, it is strongly advised that the animal be taken to a veterinary surgeon for appropriate treatment. As a rule cats greatly resent the interference which must accompany any attempt to bathe or dress an affected place, and for this reason it is usually unwise for an owner to attempt to do other than make an inspection. Very small patches of skin eruption may clear satisfactorily if the surrounding hair is clipped away with curved scissors, but generally speaking skin disease calls for professional attention. The cat flea has a similar life cycle to the dog flea (*see* Z8).

**Diseases of the Ear.**—The outer ear of the cat is frequently affected, and in a great many cases a form of mange mite is responsible. The animal provides evidence of the trouble by scratching and shaking its ear and generally showing its discomfort. It will not always be possible for an owner to make a thorough examination, as in many cases the cat objects, but if it is possible to look inside the ear it will be seen that there is a dirty and usually brownish mess of tissue, sometimes mixed with dried blood or pus. Not all cases are as bad as this, of course, but if a cat persistently worries its ear it should be taken to a veterinary surgeon. There are satisfactory dressings for this condition, and owners will be able to dress their cats if the latter are docile. Otherwise it is necessary to have the ears dressed by a veterinary surgeon or by one of his staff.

A cat's ear is frequently the site of a blood blister, or hæmatoma. This is usually the sequel to a blow, such as a slamming door, and shows itself as a large, tense swelling, which when opened by the surgeon proves to be an accumulation of serum usually tinged with blood. Some cases become infected at the time of injury, some after with the patient's rubbing. With the greatest surgical skill in the world one must expect a slight deformity, and the cat develops a puckered ear, much the same as the human boxer.

**Disease of the Bladder.**—The bladder is a common seat of disease in cats, and is frequently affected through the blocking of the natural water-passage by small sand-like calculi. Naturally, male cats are more often affected, as the terminal end of the urinary tracts is wider and more dilatable in females. The urine is unable to escape, and the bladder becomes filled with a mixture of urine and the sandy calcular matter. The condition may be diagnosed quite readily, as the cat usually collapses, or partially collapses, and one may easily feel the distended bladder through the walls of the abdomen (belly). It is necessary to send for professional help immediately, and, while no relief can be guaranteed, it is often possible to relieve the condition by judicious manipulation. Owners should not attempt to do this themselves (unless help cannot be obtained), as they may easily burst the bladder. As the animal is usually in a state of collapse when the condition is discovered, it makes a bad risk for actual operation, and relief by *skilled* pressure is usually to be recommended.

**Ringworm.**—There are two common kinds of ringworm in the cat (a third, which may also infect the dog, is more rare; it is the trichophyton which is usually found on cattle). The first kind is acquired from rats and mice, and is most commonly to be found at the bases of the claws, from where it may spread to the ears and face. The individual lesions are circular and yellow in colour, and consist largely of a scabby material. This kind of ringworm is known as "favus."

The second type of ringworm (microsporon) is more important, because it is more readily transmissible to human beings. Whereas this form

usually sets up circular scaly lesions in the dog, it often infects cats without there being much naked-eye evidence of its presence. Indeed, in the cat the condition is often unsuspected until the owner himself becomes infected and consults his doctor.

Ringworm should be treated or dealt with by a veterinary surgeon, who will also confirm or refute by special methods the presence of microsporon in cats.

**Intestinal Parasites—" Worms."**—The cat also is subject to both roundworms and tapeworms. The roundworm which parasitises cats in this country is similar to that of the dog (although a different species) and is also much more harmful to the young than to the adult animal. In kittens the symptoms are a general unthriftiness, staring coat, and in some cases diarrhœa and a " pot-bellied " appearance.

The commonest cat tapeworm in this country is one which passes its intermediate stage in the rat or mouse, or sometimes in other rodents. The tapeworm, which, as mentioned under the section on dogs, is dangerous to man, is sometimes found in the cat also.

**Accidents and Injuries.**—Despite their sagacity and alertness in many ways, cats seem curiously unable, in many instances, to acquire road-sense. They are dazed by a car's head-lights, while if a motorist sounds his horn they tend to stop still in their tracks.

Injuries from traps, *e.g.*, gin-traps, are very common, and it is probable that many thousands of cats annually are maimed in this fashion. Cats suffer injury from shooting, from stoning, and from blows with sticks. Since they are predatory animals, they have often to pay the penalty inflicted on them by wrathful people. Needless to say, cats which survive to return home usually require expert treatment.

Poisoning may be included under this heading. Although there are doubtless many deliberate attempts to poison marauding cats, alleged " poisoning " is often no more than a case of feline enteritis, and owners should not claim glibly that their cats have been poisoned until they have expert evidence to back their judgment.

Fur-balling, as it has been termed, may be mentioned here. Cats, especially the long-haired varieties, must often ingest hair during their toilet, and occasionally serious trouble (a stoppage of the bowels) is brought about by a mass of such hair which has collected in a part of the bowel. There is constipation, loss of condition, and often evidence of considerable pain. Such cats should be taken to a veterinary surgeon.

Bites and scratches are even more common in the cat than they are in the dog, and subsequent sepsis is equally likely.

# FERRETS.

**Description.**—The ferret is probably a domesticated form of the pole-cat (*Mustela putorius*), and is known sometimes by that name and sometimes as *Mustela furo*. Most tame ferrets have pink eyes and yellowish-white fur, but there are darker forms believed to have resulted from crossing in previous generations with wild pole-cats. Indeed, these darker forms are popularly termed " pole-cat ferrets." They are of two main kinds, the first having creamy under fur and black guard hairs, and the second being a chocolate-brown colour, with brown upper parts and black under parts, and a few scattered light hairs on the face.

Ferrets are long creatures in relation to their body weight, and when fully-grown may have a body 14 in. long or more and a tail of 5 in. Some strains grow appreciably larger. The main use of the ferret is, of course, in rabbiting, for which purpose they have been employed for many centuries. Although they can become fierce if not accustomed to regular handling or kind treatment, and are capable of inflicting a nasty bite, they may nevertheless be made into docile and highly intelligent pets. It is most important to win their confidence from the beginning and to accustom them to regular handling from the time they are young " kittens."

**Accommodation.**—Ferrets must have dry, clean accommodation in a room free from draughts but well ventilated. Wood is warmer than metal, but more difficult to clean, and is best lined with hard asbestos sheeting, which is resistant to water. The most suitable accommodation comprises a sleeping compartment of similar proportions to a small kennel, leading by a small doorway or "pop-hole" to a wire-netting exercising run, which should be as large as possible compatible with cleanliness. It is a good idea to have a means of closing the doorway so that the ferret or ferrets may be confined within the sleeping-compartment if necessary. Wood-wool makes an excellent bedding, but if difficult to obtain newspaper may be provided for the ferret to lie on. The floor of the run may have a false bottom or may be sprinkled with sawdust. It is imperative to keep the whole of the accommodation clean and dry, not only to avoid smell but also to prevent the ferrets from developing a very serious necrotic infection of the feet known as "foot-rot."

**Feeding.**—Many ferrets are unfortunately not fed adequately. It must be appreciated that basically they are carnivorous animals, and that their food requirements are more similar to those of the dog and cat than those of rodents. Indeed, many of the general remarks made about the principles of feeding dogs and cats apply to ferrets also.

Most ferrets like bread-and-milk, and while this is an excellent article of diet, it is in itself inadequate. Up to about 4 oz. of raw meat (minced for younger animals) daily is an excellent basis, and this may be replaced by fish. Liver, especially raw liver, is an excellent source of many factors, and there is good reason to provide some at least weekly if it can be obtained. Failing this, it is advisable to add 1-2 per cent. of whole dry liver to the diet. Once ferrets are grown, one feeding daily—at a fixed time—is sufficient. The female (jill) should have ample supplies of milk just prior to the birth of her young and while she is suckling them.

**Breeding.**—In the northern hemisphere the female ferret usually comes into œstrus (season) in early March of the year following that in which it is born. If the jill does not conceive during this œstrus she will have a further œstral period in July or August. The desire of the jill to mate is very strong, and if not allowed to do so, some animals sometimes have been found to waste and pine. The act of mating is prefaced by very vigorous behaviour on the part of the male (hob), and anyone not appreciating the performance might think that he was out to kill his mate! The mating act itself is usually prolonged, and may take up to three hours. If left together the hob and jill will probably mate from two to four times during the course of a couple of days. As in the cat and rabbit, ovulation or the shedding of the egg from the ovary takes place as a result of mating, and not spontaneously. The period of gestation is forty-two days, and the numbers of young born usually varies from five to thirteen, the average litter being six to eight. Pseudo-pregnancy occurs if the jill is not mated, and may become outwardly obvious as in the case of certain bitches.

Males also have a seasonal rhythm, their capacity to fertilise being greatest from early March to August. Young hobs seem to be active about a month earlier than older ones. The length of daylight or, rather, the incrementation in light from day to day, has an important bearing on breeding capacity in both sexes, and by the use of artificial light it has proved possible to induce either œstrus or male activity at different times of the year.

The young are hairless and blind, and weigh on the average under ½ oz. at birth. Their eyes open at about four weeks, and they can then commence to eat small pieces of solid food to supplement their mother's milk. They may be weaned at from six to eight weeks.

**Diseases.**—The most serious disease of ferrets is *canine distemper*, and the variant known as "hard pad" (see under dog) is equally capable of infecting ferrets. Such infections can wipe out entire stocks, and every care should be taken to prevent their spread from dogs to ferrets—and vice versa. A veterinary surgeon should be consulted immediately when a ferret becomes ill or out of sorts. Ferrets are also susceptible to some strains of *human* influenza, and should not be tended by persons with colds or with any indications of "flu." The feeding of infected milk may give rise to *tuberculosis* (now entirely in Britain). *Foot-rot* has already been mentioned, and must on no account be neglected. *Mange* or "scabies" of the back and tail region should be dealt with promptly, employing modern preparations. Abscesses of the neck region are often encountered, and should receive professional treatment if they do not clear up rapidly, for they may spread with dire consequences.

## RATS.

**Description.**—Tame rats are domesticated varieties of the wild Norway or "brown" rat (*Rattus norvegicus*). Such rats are usually albinos or black-and-white, although other colours have been bred. The hooded varieties are those in which the head and foreparts are mainly black or chocolate and the remainder of the body, apart from small patches the same colours as the hood, is white. Tame rats differ materially from wild ones in disposition, and properly managed are extremely tractable. Healthy specimens accustomed to handling bite only when frightened, *e.g.*, when a sudden movement is made in front of them. Males appear to live longer than females, but three years is a good age.

"Black" rats, *i.e.*, the species (*Rattus rattus*) sometimes known as the ship or Alexandrine rat, have been bred in captivity, but tame strains are not generally available.

**Housing.**—Tame rats require a warm, even temperature—65-70° F. all the year round—and draughts or lowered temperature may precipitate lung disease or other disorders. It is best to have a complete spare set of boxes or cages, and to change to fresh quarters weekly except when the females have unweaned young with them. Empty cages should be cleaned and disinfected thoroughly before being used again. Provided the temperature conditions are suitable—and this is essential—metal cages of the types employed in scientific laboratories are best with wire-mesh false bottoms and trays containing sawdust to catch the droppings. Accommodation should be

SOLID TRAY TO CATCH DROPPINGS AND SPILLED FOOD, ETC.    CORNER LEDGES TO HOLD EDGES OF WIRE TRAY.

ample, and even for a pair of pet rats the cage should measure about 30 in. × 18 in. × 18 in. If wooden boxes are employed it may be desirable to line them with hard asbestos sheeting or galvanised metal to prevent damage from gnawing.

Small, dark "shelters" and exercising devices, *e.g.*, wheels or ladders, are appreciated by the rats, but must be kept clean. Wood-wool makes the best bedding.

**Feeding.**—Rats may take a wide variety of foods, including many of our own, and there are several successful ways of feeding them, including the provision of specially formulated " rat-cubes," of the same type as that described below for mice. A good daily diet is wholemeal bread, mixed cereals (e.g., oats, wheat, hempseed), with about

Opening→

WATER BULB SUITABLE FOR USE
WITH PET RODENTS

5 per cent. dried brewers yeast and milk either fed separately or mixed with the rest of the food. Twice weekly each rat should be given up to ½ oz. or more of meat, liver, fish, or other " animal protein." A little fresh greenfood (even grass) is appreciated, and in winter especially some supplement containing vitamins A and D is desirable. Expectant and nursing mothers should have as much milk as they require. Never overfeed or allow uneaten food residues to remain in the cage. Fresh water (preferably in bulbs or bottles) should be available at all times. Far cleaner than open dishes are the special but simple type of water bulbs suspended on or in front of the cage or box so that the rat can drink from the rounded end of the spout. A simple substitute is a medicine " flat " bottle—or even a ¼- or ½-pint milk-type bottle. This should be fitted with a cork—or, better, a rubber bung—pierced for a piece of bent glass tubing. Provided that the free end of the glass tubing is not sharp, and is chosen so that the aperture is considerably smaller than that of the tube itself, the water will not run out unless sucked out by the rat. The spout should, of course, be within easy access of the rat, which will soon learn to drink from it.

Breeding.—Rats can breed at quite a young age (usually being capable of mating when fifty to sixty days old), but it is better to separate the sexes within a fortnight or so of weaning (weaning being usually at twenty-one days of age) and to mate at about 100 to 120 days of age onwards. the female rat has an œstrous cycle lasting just over four days. One male (buck) may be mated to one female (doe)—this is probably best in the case of pet rats—or with two or three females if preferred, but it is unwise to keep more than one adult male in the presence of females. The gestation period is twenty-one to twenty-two days or occasionally a few days longer. The number born varies considerably, but often it is best to try to rear only six to eight young. The young have their ears open at 2½ to 3½ days, cut their incisor teeth at eight to ten days, can find their way to their mother at about the same time, open their eyes at fourteen to seventeen days, and may leave the nest at twenty-one days. In the case of pet rats it is probably best to leave the young with the mother for up to a week or so longer. Breeding can occur all the year round, but takes place less readily in winter.

Handling.—Rats should not be " tailed," or the skin may slough off. Regular handling after weaning is excellent and promotes docility. The weight of the body should be supported.

Diseases.—On the whole rats are much less liable to disease than mice, provided temperature conditions are suitable. The commonest infection is broncho-pneumonia, often precipitated through

draughts or cold. Mange (especially of the ear) and infestation with lice may occur, and should be dealt with promptly by means of modern insecticides. Avoid contact with wild rodents, or the use of food or bedding that may have been contaminated by wild rats and mice.

## MICE.

Description.—Tame mice are descended from the common house mouse (Mus musculus), and it is believed that mice have been domesticated for over 3,000 years. Apart from albino or " white mice," there are many varieties that have been bred by the extensive " mouse fancy," and there is a wide range of coat colour and also different types of coat, e.g., long-haired, short-haired, and rex. " Waltzing mice " have an abnormality of that part of the inner ear concerned with balance. Mice may live up to thirty months, and in exceptional cases attain the age of three years or more.

Housing.—Although strains vary, most tame mice require a warm even temperature and the same general remarks concerning temperature range, bedding, and wooden or metal cages apply as in the case of rats. If a solid floor is used, this should be covered with clean sawdust. It is a good plan to change to a clean cage regularly, except when the female (doe) is nursing her young. If the cage is large (as in the case of pet mice it should be, with a floor space of say 24 in. × 12 in. × 12 in. for a group of mice), inner nest-boxes should be provided—one for each doe if breeding is taking place, although two does will often share the same nest-box. (In changing to fresh cages the nest-box, with mother and young inside, may, of course, be moved over.) A " two-storey " cage, with a ladder or " staircase " to the upper part, is an attractive variation, although difficult to keep clean. Mice should be kept well out of reach of wild rodents, from which they may all too readily contract disease.

Feeding.—Mice have not quite such a wide dietary range as rats, but there are several different ways of feeding them, including the provision of special " mouse cubes." These mouse cubes are of varying composition. One of the most successful, devised by workers in the Medical Research Council's laboratories, is known as " Diet 41," and is made up of the following parts by weight: wholemeal flour, 45; Sussex ground oats, 40; fish meal, 8; dried yeast, 1; dried skimmed milk, 3; cod-liver oil, 1; and common salt, 1. Diet 41 has also been employed for rats and monkeys, although for the latter particularly it requires supplementing. It is perhaps worth emphasising that cod-liver oil must not be fed in excess (½% of the diet is quite sufficient, and should not be exceeded), or it may prevent breeding and possibly have other harmful effects. Cubed diets are best fed from a wire basket through which the mice enjoy gnawing and eventually pulling out the pieces. Wholemeal bread is excellent if not allowed to become stale, but it should not form the sole article of diet, and it is a good idea to feed it alternately with a grain mixture (made up of rolled oats, wheat and other cereal grains, or mixed bird seed). Up to about 5 per cent. dried brewers' yeast is excellent, and so is fresh or dried milk, especially for mothers that are carrying or nursing young. Cheese is relished, but may smell if not fed carefully. Mice sometimes like an occasional pinch of marmalade, and it is a good idea to provide lettuce or other greenfood every week or so. There should be a constant supply of fresh water, preferably from bulbs or bottles as described for rats.

Breeding.—Young mice may be weaned at twenty-one days, although it is usually preferable to leave them with their mother for a further week. The age at which mice are capable of mating varies considerably from one strain or individual to another, and while the average is six to eight weeks, it may be much younger. It is therefore desirable to separate the males from the females at or shortly after weaning.

Mice may be mated up at two to three months of age, and the best arrangements are one male (buck) to one or two females. A pair of mice or a "bigynous trio" makes a successful combination. The œstrus cycle is similar to that of the rat, but its length appears to vary with coat colour, being longest in the brown mice and shortest in blacks and albinos. The gestation period is usually from eighteen to twenty days, but may be prolonged if the female was still suckling her previous litter when she conceived. There may be up to twelve or more young in a litter, but the average litter size is from five to seven. The second litter is usually the largest, and subsequent litters tend to decrease in numbers, so that the sixth is usually smaller than the first. Breeding may take place all the year round, although, as with rats, fertility is higher during the summer months.

**Handling.**—Any rapid or rough movement may frighten mice and cause them to bite through fear. Mice should be lifted by the tail—not too near the tip—and may be held in the palm of the hand, where they may be suitably restrained by keeping the tail between two fingers.

**Diseases.**—Mice are unfortunately prone to many diseases, although the risks will be much lower if they are kept in suitable surroundings, great care is taken to avoid infection, scrupulous cleanliness is observed, and the standard of feeding is good. One common source of infection is the presence of the excreta of wild rodents on bedding or foodstuffs. A common disease is that sometimes called "mouse typhoid," caused by organisms of the Salmonella group. Although some mice recover, they may remain carriers of infection, and once this disease is diagnosed it is best to destroy the affected mice and those in contact with them, and not to employ any of the cages or utensils for fresh mice without adequate sterilisation. There are other septicæmia diseases of mice, and also virus diseases, including certain types of pneumonia and a condition known as infectious ectromelia. The accurate diagnosis of these calls for expert opinion and often for special bacteriological or other examinations. The mouse-owner should, however, be able to recognise signs of ill-health or departure from normal, one of the commonest being loss of appetite. In young mice the coat should be smooth and glossy. As mice get older there may be loss of pigmentation (in coloured mice) or even loss of fur. A sick mouse usually sits hunched up and has a ruffled coat, while the eyes may be partially closed or have some discharge. A healthy mouse will usually catch on to suitable objects when held by its tail and is capable of pulling quite hard, whereas the pull of a sick mouse is much weaker. If one or more mice die it is best to destroy at once any cage-mates that appear seedy. As in the case of rats, external parasites should be dealt with promptly with the aid of modern insecticidal preparations.

# GOLDEN HAMSTERS.

**Description.**—There are many species of hamsters in the world, and more than one kind can now be bred in captivity. The one referred to, however, is the Golden Hamster (Mesocricetus auratus), a delightful little creature of which a full-grown female (females are larger than males) rarely exceeds 7 in. in length. This history of the domestication of the golden hamster is quite remarkable, for prior to 1930 only museum specimens were known. In that year a mother and her twelve young were dug up in a field near Aleppo and were taken to the Hebrew University, Jerusalem, and from that one family have been bred the hundreds of thousands of golden hamsters now employed as pets or as laboratory animals in many parts of the world. The species has taken well to captivity and, although capable of inflicting a nasty little bite if frightened or handled roughly, becomes docile and friendly when properly cared for. Characteristic features are the soft, smooth fur, the large black eyes, the "cheek

pouches" in which food is stored and which may become enormously distended after a meal, the short, stumpy tail, and the extremely loose skin, inside which the hamster can turn round to a considerable degree.

**Housing.**—The same remarks about accommodation, environmental temperature, freedom from draughts, fittings, and other general considerations (including cleanliness) apply as in the case of rats and mice. For breeding purposes a dark inner chamber or nest-box is desirable. Several hamsters may be kept together, but the introduction of a stranger (or even the re-introduction of a former cage-mate that has been removed for some time) may lead to fighting.

**Feeding.**—Satisfactory diets include the following: (1) rat cubes (e.g., "Diet 41"), carrots, greenfood, and milk; (2) cereal grains and/or wholemeal bread, carrots, greenfood, and milk; (3) steamed Rangoon beans, wheat, maize meal bread, a little Marmite, and milk. Care must be taken not to allow storage of excess food, which will deteriorate and cause a smell. Grass is a suitable source of greenfood during its growing season. Apples and other fruits are often relished. Water, preferably in bulbs or bottles as described for rats, should always be available.

**Breeding.**—Golden Hamsters attain puberty at from ten to fifteen weeks of age, or even younger, males being usually earlier. Generally speaking, it is best to defer breeding until after fifteen weeks of age. There is an œstrus cycle of about four days, and the gestation period is very short, averaging sixteen days, although sometimes up to nineteen days. Mating not followed by conception results in phantom or pseudopregnancy. Litter size varies from one to fifteen, but the average is six to seven. Not many females have more than four litters and although both sexes may live up to two years, breeding by the female is rare after nine months. The young are naked and blind at birth. Hair first appears at five days, and covers the whole body at eight days. The eyes open at about eleven days, and soon after this the young begin to take food for themselves and may be weaned at three to four weeks. Care must be taken that the female does not injure the male, and for safety's sake it is probably better to keep only one female and one male together and to remove the male before the young are born.

**Handling.**—Gentleness is essential, and sudden movements should be avoided. The tail is much too short to use, and the easiest way is to lift them by the loose skin over the back and shoulders. As already noted, they can twist easily within their skins, unless a substantial amount is taken in the hand. After picking up they may be allowed to sit on the palm of the hand.

**Diseases.**—Several diseases of hamsters are now known, and, like most rodents, they are susceptible to Salmonellosis (see notes under "mouse typhoid" and "paratyphoid" in guinea-pigs). One of the most prevalent conditions is ear mange, in severe cases of which the condition spreads from the ears to other parts of the body. Modern anti-mange preparations are highly effective.

# CAVIES (GUINEA-PIGS).

**Description.**—Cavies or guinea-pigs (Cavia porcellus) are rodents, and are descended from one or more of the several kinds of wild cavy found in South America. They are believed to have been domesticated by the Incas long before Europeans "discovered" that part of the world. They make excellent pets, but are easily frightened, and should be treated gently and quietly. They usually behave quietly, although there may be fighting between adult males ("boars"), while the arrival of food—or the entry of a person into a room, which fact is obviously connected with feeding-time—usually sets up a chorus of chirruping squeaks. There is to-day a considerable cavy "fancy" in Great Britain and other countries, and many varieties are recognised, including rough-coated and smooth-coated types. Among recognised colours are the agouti (banded hairs), brindle, cinnamon, tortoiseshell (tricoloured), and Himalayan (white with attractive black points). The long-haired Peruvian and rosette-haired Abyssinian breeds are popular. Guinea-pigs may live up to two to three years. There is a small tail (composed of from five to seven caudal vertebræ), but usually this is so short that it does not project outside the body. There are four toes on each of the fore-feet and three on each hind foot. An adult guinea-pig may measure up to 10 in. or more in length, and sometimes its weight is well over 2 lb.

**Housing.**—Guinea-pigs may be kept outside or inside. If outside conditions are favoured, great care must be taken to protect them from dogs, cats, and rats. The last-named may be a danger also in conveying disease. The run should be in a sheltered position away from wind and direct summer sunlight. Tent-shaped waterproof shelters, with wooden floors covered by cleaning trays, have been found satisfactory. Another method is to keep them in hutches of the same type employed for rabbits and when conditions are suitable to let them out into a temporary run on the lawn surrounded by ½ in.-mesh wire-netting that is at least 12 in. high. (N.B. This will keep dogs or cats out.) Guinea-pigs will crop the grass and help to keep the lawn smooth. Great care should be taken not to allow the ground or floor to become so contaminated by guinea-pig excreta that it conveys disease from one animal to another.

If indoor methods are selected, an even, preferably warm temperature is desirable, and there should be freedom from draughts. Guinea-pigs have been found to thrive best at about 65° F. with a humidity range of 45-55 per cent. Provided warm conditions are available, metal cages are easier to keep clean than wooden ones, while a false bottom of wire mesh, above the cleaning tray, is helpful. Wood-wool is again the best bedding. Cages must not be too small, and a pair of pet guinea-pigs should have about 14 sq. ft. of floor space. It is a sound principle, as with rats and mice, to change frequently to a clean cage, the used one being cleaned and disinfected thoroughly before being used again.

**Feeding.**—Guinea-pigs, like human beings, apes, and monkeys, require a source of vitamin C (ascorbic acid). Normally they obtain this from greenfood, but in winter especially they may not secure enough in this way. The daily requirement of an adult guinea-pig is about 2 milligrammes, and supplies can be obtained from a chemist's shop.

There are many different methods of feeding guinea-pigs. Among cubed or pelleted diets is that known as "Diet 18," which is employed also for rabbits. It contains the following parts by weight: wheat feed, 15; grass meal, 30; decorticated groundnut meal, 15; linseed cake, 10; barley meal, 20; common salt, 1; and chalk, 1. This is fed together with fresh greenfood to supply vitamin C. For feeding without the use of compressed diets a good plan is to provide a daily "concentrate ration" of about 1 oz. per head of a mixture of 2 parts bran and 1 part crushed oats, and to feed in addition ample amounts of cabbage, lettuce or other greenfood, meadow hay of good quality, grass, and raw vegetables. Although guinea-pigs normally derive moisture from fresh greenfood, and may appear to take little or no water for long periods, it is a mistake not to provide a fresh supply, preferably from water bulbs, or from inverted bottles fitted with a stopper and drinking-spout. A little dried brewers' yeast makes an excellent addition to the diet, while for females ("sows") when pregnant or lactating, milk is excellent. Dead foliage should be removed from greenfood, and soil and dirt cleaned off. Frosted greenfood should be soaked in warm water before it is given to guinea-pigs. Unfortunately, hay may be contaminated by wild rodents, but it forms an excellent article of diet. Never allow food residues to remain in the cage.

**Breeding.**—The lactation period of the guinea-pig is a short one. The gestation period averages sixty-three to seventy-five days, although variations of fifty-eight to seventy-two days are known and the young are born in an advanced state with their eyes already open. They can run freely with their mother shortly after birth. They are able to nibble a little food as early as the second day, and by the time they are two to three weeks old they are completely independent and are neglected by their mother. A sow will often mate again the day the young are born, or shortly after, so that a rapid succession of litters often occurs.

Guinea-pigs are capable of mating from about fifty-five days of age, or even younger in certain circumstances, which include the provision of a high plane of nutrition. The œstrous cycle averages fifteen to seventeen days, although it may vary from thirteen to twenty-five days. The actual period during which mating may occur usually lasts only from about six to eleven hours. One boar may run with as many as twenty sows if so desired, but in the case of pets it is much more interesting to run a boar with only one sow, in which case she need not usually be removed to a separate cage before the young are born. The young guinea-pigs should be separated from the older ones shortly after weaning, and the sexes separated at four to five weeks of age if they are not to breed prematurely. It is better to wait until the animals are approaching six months of age or so before they are mated, for they do not become fully grown and "filled out" until they are between six and nine months.

**Handling.**—Guinea-pigs are timid creatures, and should be handled gently. They are best picked up with both hands. If a guinea-pig is to be held in order to examine it for any purpose, a good method is to place one hand over the animal's shoulders, with the fingers and thumb around its neck, and to extend its hind limbs with the other hand.

**Diseases.**—The most important infectious disease of guinea-pigs is, like "mouse typhoid," caused by organisms of the Salmonella group, and it may be contracted from wild rodents or from food or bedding contaminated by them. In guinea-pigs the disease is known usually as "paratyphoid" (or sometimes as "salmonellosis") and it may take an acute form, causing death within a few days, or a more chronic form in which many animals recover to become symptomless carriers of disease. Outwardly healthy, they may infect susceptible guinea-pigs with which they are placed. Cold or other environmental variations, and faulty feeding, can help to set off an outbreak, for there are few stocks in which the organisms are not lurking in some "latent carriers." Coccidiosis is common, but is a much less serious threat than in the case of rabbits. It has been set up in infected stocks by feeding inadequate diets, and provided that nutrition and hygiene are adequate there is rarely serious trouble from this disease. Infections of the respiratory tract may occur, but are uncommon except when there is overcrowding, high humidity, or damp bedding. Sometimes organisms of the Pneumococcus group cause not only disease of the respiratory tract but also a generalised infection of the serous membranes of the body. When this disease occurs it may produce death without much warning. It is possible that the infection sometimes comes from human beings. The disease known as pseudotuberculosis, and described under rabbits, occurs in guinea-pigs also. Again, environmental conditions and faulty feeding may predispose towards active infection.

With good fortune and sound management, trouble from these serious infections may never occur. External parasites should be dealt with promptly by insecticides. Sometimes non-parasitic skin disorders occur when the diet is faulty, e.g., too dry or lacking in sufficient fresh greenfood of good quality.

## RABBITS.

**Description.**—Domesticated varieties of the wild European rabbit (*Oryctolagus cuniculus*) are now kept in many countries. The wild rabbit is believed to have been introduced into Great Britain in the 12th cent. Tame rabbits have been bred for centuries, and the breeds and strains produced differ appreciably in size, colour, and habits from the common wild form. Some breeds have been specially bred for table purposes, while others (*e.g.*, the Angora, Sitka, and Argente de Champagne) have been developed for their fur. In addition, many varieties are produced for show purposes by the extensive rabbit "fancy." The small hardy Dutch rabbit (usually black and white) is one of the kinds suitable for beginners. Among well-known categories are the English, Japanese, Himalayan, Belgian Hare (really a rabbit), Flemish Giant, Beveren, Blue Imperial, Polish, Havana, Lop, Half-Lop, Chinchilla, and New Zealand White. The Copenhagen rabbit appears to be identical with the New Zealand White. The smaller breeds weigh only 4–6 lb. when fully grown, whereas some specimens of some of the giant breeds attain a weight of 20 lb. or more.

Rabbits and hares were formerly classified with the rodents, but are now placed in a separate Order of mammals, known as the Lagomorphs. Young rabbits (in contrast to leverets or young hares) are blind and helpless for some time after birth. Tame specimens may live for 4–5 years, and individuals have lived for up to 13 years.

**Housing.**—Since rabbits are kept for commercial purposes, various systems have been devised, including the use of movable ark-huts, with covered runs, that can be moved regularly to fresh ground. If kept indoors rabbits do not need special heating, but freedom from draughts, damp, excessive cold, and access by wild rodents is most desirable. A garage is regarded as an unsuitable place, owing to the susceptibility of rabbits to exhaust or engine fumes. One of the great difficulties of rabbit-keeping is coccidiosis, which is a serious disease in rabbits and hares. (European hares could never be bred successfully in captivity until means of overcoming coccidiosis were discovered.) With young rabbits especially (*i.e.*, those that have left the nest and are able to run about freely) it is a sound principle to move them to a clean floor or fresh ground every two days, so as to "break" the life-cycle of the coccidial parasite. One way of doing this is to have "back-to-back" cages or hutches, from one to the other of which the rabbits may be transferred easily. The empty cage or hutch may then be cleaned and disinfected thoroughly and allowed to dry out before the rabbits are returned to it. Wood-wool makes a suitable bedding material, although the female (doe) will pluck her own fur to line the nest when her litter is due to be born. Wire-mesh floors with a tray beneath are convenient, but if solid floors are used these should be sprinkled with fresh sawdust daily or every other day. Provided the standard of hygiene can be maintained, cages or hutches and their runs should be large. The absolute minimum is "1 sq. ft. of floor space for each 1 lb. weight of adult rabbit," *i.e.*, if there are two rabbits totalling 12 lb. in weight there must be at least 12 sq. ft. of floor space. If cages or hutches are stacked one on top of the other the lowest should be well clear of the ground, and if there is only one hutch this, for convenience and safety from wild rodents, should be 2–3 ft. off the floor.

**Feeding.**—The wild rabbit grazes at dusk and dawn, and it is preferable to feed tame rabbits twice daily, while pregnant or lactating does and young rabbits benefit from three meals a day. As in the case of guinea-pigs, the ration may be thought of as consisting of two parts, a concentrate portion and a portion consisting of greenfood and other succulent material. The concentrate portion consists usually of a mixture of cereal grains or of some other form of mash. Successful mashes, of which there are many, include: (1) a mixture of 4 parts cereal grains and 1 part dairy cake; (2) equal parts of bran, weatings, flaked maize—or barley meal—and fish meal. This

second is useful for breeding. If materials for the mash are in short supply they may in part be replaced by cooked potatoes. An average daily food allowance for a resting (non-breeding) adult of medium size would be: greenfood (grass, clover, weeds, lettuce, etc.) and/or roots, 12–16 oz.; hay (good quality), 2–3 oz.; and concentrates (cereal grain or meal mash), 2 oz. If cooked potatoes are used they should be fed at the rate of 4 parts to each 1 part of cereal that they replace. For a doe nursing her litter a suitable diet would comprise: greenfood to appetite, hay (good quality and preferably containing clover or other legume), 2–4 oz.; concentrates (preferably with fish meal or some other suitable source of "animal protein"), 4–6 oz.; and common salt at the level of up to 1 per cent. of the ration. A mineral mixture is preferable to salt alone. Excessive greenfood, especially in the form of cabbage and other Brassica plants, may cause polyuria, *i.e.*, the passage of excessive quantities of urine. No matter how much fresh greenfood rabbits may have available, a supply of fresh water should always be provided. The daily water requirement of the rabbit is quite high, and certain bad habits such as urine drinking or even cannibalism may result from an inadequate intake of water. Pots that cannot be overturned or, preferably, water bulbs or bottles as described for guinea-pigs, are the most suitable means of providing water. "Diet 18," described under guinea-pigs, is one of several types of compressed diet successfully employed for rabbits. Fresh greenfood is preferably fed in addition, while the water requirement with diets of this kind is considerable.

**Breeding.**—The age of puberty varies with the breed, and also with the time of year at which the individual rabbit was born. Rabbits born in spring are usually capable of breeding at a younger age than those born in the autumn. In Great Britain the wild rabbit has a fairly sharply defined main breeding season, lasting from January to June, but some degree of "out-of-season" breeding may take place at almost all other times. Tame rabbits may not breed freely during the winter months, especially if environmental conditions are cold. Mating may take place as early as four months of age, and although this does not often result in pregnancy, it is accompanied by competition and fighting between individuals of the same sex. Males (bucks) and females should therefore be separated at weaning or at least before they are four months old. Fertile matings may occur at from about 5½ months of age onwards, but it is wise to defer breeding until later—say seven to eight months for most breeds. The female does not ovulate or shed her eggs from the ovary spontaneously as do most domestic mammals, but, like the cat and ferret, does so in response to the act of mating or some other strong stimulus. Even playing between two does may precipitate ovulation, in which case a so-called "phantom pregnancy" (pseudopregnancy) may result, the doe that has ovulated appearing pregnant and even developing lactating mammary glands. There is not therefore an obvious regularly recurring œstrus cycle as in the domestic rat, mouse, and guinea-pig, and in summer at least the doe may be ready to mate at almost any time. Observation suggests, however, that there are fluctuations in the desire to mate. The act of mating in rabbits sometimes causes alarm that all is not well to those that have not hitherto witnessed it, for the buck usually emits a peculiar cry and loses his balance to fall over sideways. It is usually best to separate the buck from the doe before the young are born. The gestation period is usually thirty to thirty-two days. In wild rabbits a high percentage of embryos die and are "resorbed," and are therefore never born. In some populations it appears that about two-thirds of all rabbits conceived (including about 60 per cent. of total litters) are lost before birth in this way. Losses from this cause are probably much less common in domesticated rabbits, especially when the standards of feeding and management are high. Litter size is variable, and depends in part on the breed or strain. In some strains mean litter sizes up to eight or nine have been obtained, but a mean of four or so is more common. Does that do not prepare the nest or rear their young properly should not be selected for further breeding. The doe with her new-born litter should not be disturbed unduly, or she may desert her young, which are blind and helpless at birth and are entirely dependent on her for at least three weeks, after which they begin to nibble food to supplement the milk that they receive from her. The eyes open at about fourteen days. Weaning should be carried out at between six and eight weeks of age, by which time the young should be able to fend for themselves completely.

**Handling.**—Rabbits should never be lifted by the ears alone. One good way of lifting them is to grip the ears firmly but gently with one hand and to place the other hand under the rump to take the weight of the rabbit's body. Alternatively, one hand may be placed flat under the rabbit's belly, but this requires more care, and may be a risky procedure with pregnant does. Another convenient way to handle rabbits, especially young ones, is to lift them by the loose skin over the shoulders. Rabbits can inflict quite nasty scratches with the nails of the hind feet. It is incidentally a good plan to examine the nails of all four feet and to trim them if they are too long. A stout pair of scissors, or preferably a pair of clippers, is used, and care should be taken not to cut back as far as the "quick," *i.e.*, the bluish portion at the base of the nail that contains blood vessels and will bleed freely if damaged.

**Diseases.**—As already indicated, *coccidiosis* is a highly important disease of young rabbits. It may be either of the "hepatic type," affecting principally the liver, or the "intestinal type," affecting principally the gut. Even in the case of the hepatic type, however, the coccidial parasites are picked up by mouth and after penetrating the intestinal walls make their way via the blood-stream to the liver. Hygienic measures are the best means of preventing the disease (see under Housing), but should it break out, prompt treatment with certain sulphonamides or other anti-coccidial drugs may prove effective. In certain rabbitries in which coccidiosis is a constant problem, protection has been obtained by feeding a dilute solution of one of the soluble sulphonamides in place of drinking-water. There are certain types of digestive disturbance that may resemble coccidiosis, and one of these, the cause of which has not yet been established with certainty, is known as *mucoid enteritis*. Some such cases are probably variations of "*bloat*" ("the blows") a condition the cause of which is again not fully established, although there may in fact be several factors. A rabbit may, of course, "blow" after eating fermentative food, but cases of "bloat" can occur independently of this, and some may be due to a virus. "*Snuffles*" is characterised by a nasal discharge, and is not always associated with the same organism. In its milder forms it is not a severe disease, but with the more chronic forms the nasal discharge becomes marked and gives rise to a typical snuffing noise. Severe chronic cases become progressively worse and die of a terminal pneumonia. There is also a severe acute form, in which the rabbit dies so rapidly that the condition is sometimes not recognised. Acute cases that are treated in time with certain sulphonamides may respond well, but chronic mufflers are difficult to treat and go on spreading the infection, and hence are better destroyed. Correct environmental conditions are a great help in preventing this disease. A chronic type of infection is known as *pseudotuberculosis*, which is usually acquired from eating material contaminated by wild rodents or by other infected rabbits. It is caused by quite a different organism from that of true tuberculosis, which is much rarer in rabbits. Clinical cases should be killed, and prevention lies in hygienic measures. Infected wounds or skin abscesses may lead to a disease caused by the "necrosis bacillus" (*Fusiformis necrophorus*) and known sometimes as *necrobacillosis* It is usually characterised by subcutaneous swellings distributed irregularly over the head and body. Although in the early stages the affected rabbit may remain in appar-

ently good health, the spread of the disease is insidious and usually fatal, and in most instances it is kinder and safer to destroy a case before it progresses too far. There are unfortunately several other infectious conditions occurring in rabbits, but all call for expert help in diagnosis and treatment. Generally speaking, it is a bad policy not to cull an ailing rabbit immediately, and one that is ill should certainly be isolated at once and not fed or tended before the person looking after it touches the healthy rabbits.

Among non-infectious conditions *pregnancy toxæmia* is not uncommon in does during the very late pregnancy, and usually proves fatal within two to three days. It is a "metabolic disorder," *i.e.*, it is associated with some functional derangement of the endocrine or ductless glands or with the inability to control properly the utilisation of its food. Faulty feeding is probably a contributory cause. Diseases of the *heart and blood* may arise occasionally, and can be aggravated by faulty feeding.

Among external parasites, *ringworm* is not common, but may be acquired from rodents. Affected rabbits that are to be treated must be isolated. *Ear mange* (known usually as *ear canker*) is common, and may be treated by strict attention to hygiene, with thorough disinfection of the hut or cage, and by dressing with a modern anti-mange preparation. *Body mange* is much less common but far more difficult to treat.

Among internal parasites, so-called "*bladder worms*," *i.e.*, the larval stages of two dog tapeworms (*Taenia pisiformis* and *Taenia serialis*) are quite common, although rarely fatal. The feeding of grass or other greenstuff to which dogs have had access should be avoided, as well as the contamination of the drinking-water with dog faeces.

Domestic rabbits are susceptible to myxomatosis, and it is a wise precaution to have them vaccinated. The vaccine is inexpensive, and may be obtained through veterinary surgeons and pharmacists.

# HEDGEHOGS.

**Description.**—The European hedgehog (*Erinaceus europaeus*), found throughout Great Britain, belongs to the Order Insectivora, of which moles and shrews are also members. Its diet is, however, by no means restricted to insects, although in nature a considerable portion is probably made up of small invertebrates. There is a good deal of prejudice against them as pets, owing to the fact that freshly caught specimens are usually infested with fleas or other external parasites. The spines of the hedgehog, being well-spaced, make the presence of external parasites more obvious than is the case in animals with a coat of close fur. The hedgehog's spines form its defence, and its capacity to roll up into a prickly ball at the threat of danger is well known. This defence reaction is unfortunately of no avail to it when the danger is an oncoming car or lorry, and thousands of hedgehogs die every years as a result of being killed by vehicles on the roads. Many other species of mammals wander on to the roads, but most attempt to flee when they sense the approach of a vehicle. The capacity to roll up is not secure defence even against animal enemies. There are some foxes, dogs, and cats that have learned to "uncurl" a hedgehog, and subsequently eat it.

Provided that care is taken, a hedgehog makes an excellent pet, especially if given a suitable enclosure in the garden. For a variable time during winter hedgehogs hibernate, and during this time they must not be disturbed. Should they emerge at any time, however, food must be provided. Some specimens have lived for five years or more in captivity.

**Accommodation.**—The most satisfactory way to maintain a pet hedgehog is to provide it with a large "run" in part of the garden. If wire-netting is employed it should be sunk under the ground to a depth of several inches, or the hedgehog will burrow underneath and escape. The top of the run must be wired in, or alternatively there must be a " baffle board " or wire-frame (at least 9 in. wide) near the tope of the sides to prevent escape that way, for hedgehogs can scale wire-netting—and some other types of fence—with ease. There should be a warm, dry box for shelter, containing wood-wool or other bedding material. A simple but suitable shelter may be made out of a soap-box, preferably lined with asbestos sheeting or some other material impervious to water. A shallow sunken bath in the enclosure may be of interest, for hedgehogs take well to water, but the edges should be such that the hedgehog can get out easily.

If it is decided to keep a hedgehog indoors, then the best accommodation is probably similar to that described for ferrets.

**Feeding.**—The simplest diet consists of milk, some bread, and minced lean meat. Cooked meat is preferred to raw, but raw liver should be given occasionally. Another satisfactory diet comprises meat offals, " root " vegetables (e.g., carrot, potato, and swede), and wheaten wholemeal biscuit, steamed together until cooked, and then mixed and minced with a small proportion of raw liver. A small quantity (say 1–2 per cent.) of mineral mixture is also desirable, and milk should be given freely. Although hedgehogs appear to drink but little water, a fresh supply should always be provided.

**Breeding.**—During the breeding season marked changes occur in both males and females, and the structures associated with reproduction increase enormously in size from about March onwards. The female is capable of having two litters a year, the first in May or June and the second in August or September. The period of gestation has not been determined exactly, but is believed to be thirty-five days, possibly with variations of up to well over forty days. During the breeding season the males are very pugnacious towards each other if females are with them, and may do each other considerable damage. (The mixing of strange hedgehogs is often a difficult procedure anyway, for they often fight and inflict nasty bites on one another's feet.)

The litter size is usually four to six, and the young, which have " soft " spines, are suckled by their mother for nearly six weeks. The young can partake of some solid food at about three weeks, and there is some evidence that if left with their mother for longer than six weeks she may compete unfairly with them for food!

**Diseases.**—Hedgehogs in captivity are susceptible to respiratory infections, and can sometimes contract certain strains of human influenza. They are susceptible also to Salmonellosis (see under mice and guinea-pigs). Fleas and other external parasites have been mentioned; these often disappear spontaneously as the hedgehog begins to thrive in captivity, but if not they should be dealt with by modern methods. The nails of a hedgehog may need trimming. (See Rabbits.)

## LAND TORTOISES.

Tortoises are popular pets, but although many are kept with great success in Great Britain, the majority of those that are imported each year are never looked after adequately, or fail to thrive for other reasons.

Most land tortoises that are imported into Great Britain for sale through dealers are: (1) the Spur-thighed Mediterranean Land Tortoise (Testudo graeca), commonly known as the " Moroccan tortoise " and sometimes as the " Iberian " or " Algerian "; or (2) Hermann's Tortoise (Testudo hermanni). The second is distributed in Southern France, Southern Italy, the larger islands of the Western Mediterranean, and parts of Yugoslavia, Albania, and Greece. There is a species found in Greece, the Margined Tortoise (Testudo marginata), but while adaptable to life in Great Britain, it is more difficult to acquire. The two common species differ in several ways, the " Moroccan tortoise " having a small bony spur on the back of the thigh. (The upper part of the shell is termed the carapace and the ventral portion the plastron.)

In selecting a tortoise one should ensure that the animal appears healthy. It should be active and withdraw quickly into its shell on being disturbed. Its legs should be firm and not limp, and there should be no abnormal discharge from the eyes or nostrils. The shell and limbs should be uninjured. Females are generally larger and have a shorter tail than the male. The shield above the tail is flat in the former and curved in the male. It is a good idea to obtain a pair or more of tortoises, but not more than can be looked after with care. On being purchased they should be washed in tepid water.

Many tortoises are given free range in gardens, but this is not advised with all, as they eat a wide variety of vegetables and young plants, and being wandering animals are liable to get lost if the garden is not completely fenced or walled. They should be provided with as large a " pen " or " run " as possible, the walls or wire netting of which should be high enough to prevent their climbing over. The practice of tethering tortoises by a hole in the shell should be discouraged. They should always be provided with a box or shelter, the cheapest form being a wooden soap box turned on one side and with a sufficiently wide entrance, the wood being creosoted and covered with roofing felt. It can be lined with asbestos sheeting if desired, and have its floor covered with dry leaves or other bedding material. Some other shelter should also be provided in the run. The tortoises should be bathed during the hot weather. The occasional application of olive oil will keep the shell polished.

Land tortoises must be fed daily, and it is important to allow them to build up good reserves to enable them to hibernate through the winter successfully. Suitable foods include lettuce, young cabbage, peas, clover, dandelions, and a wide variety of green plants and ripe, sweet fruits. Generally bread and milk should be avoided. For young tortoises especially, it is recommended that once weekly or so the food should be sprinkled with powdered cuttlefish bone, or better still a small quantity of powered calcium gluconate or cod-liver oil. Fresh water in a shallow tray, or even a saucer, should always be provided.

One of the most difficult problems in tortoise keeping is hibernation. Some persons avoid allowing their pets to hibernate by transferring them to a warm place, such as a heated greenhouse; if this is done they must be kept well fed and their place maintained at a summer temperature. It is imperative to do one thing or the other—the half-torpid tortoise that is neither hibernating nor kept at summer temperature will die. Moreover, a tortoise that is allowed to hibernate must not be disturbed.

Signs of pending hibernation, including sluggishness and lowered appetite, are usually evident late in September or early in October. Tortoises living in the garden may commence to bury themselves. If this is allowed they must be well covered, else they may be killed by the ensuing frost. It is, though, more convenient and perhaps provides a greater chance of survival, due to the changeable winter conditions in Britain, to place the animal in a large box, which should be packed with straw, leaves, or hay. The box should be stored in a cool but frostproof place, such as out-building, cellar, or attic. It is important not to create conditions that will awaken the tortoise or tempt it to emerge before the following spring. Rats have been known to attack hibernating tortoises, and so due precautions should be taken.

On emerging from hibernation the eyes and nostrils are somewhat sealed, and should be released by bathing with a 4 per cent. boric acid solution and warm water.

Recently imported female tortoises frequently lay eggs, but it is not a common occurrence for pairs to breed freely in Britain. During the early part of the summer the male is sometimes seen butting the shell of the female, this being a courtship action. If eggs are laid it is unlikely that they will be fertile, and less likely that they can be hatched. They have been hatched by placing them on damp sand and storing them in a warm place—a heated greenhouse or airing cupboard. The eggs should not be disturbed or " turned " once incubation has commenced.

Tortoise ticks are often present on freshly imported specimens, and may best be removed by damping the tick with paraffin or methylated spirits and then removing it gently with tweezers. Round worms are very numerous in tortoises, and should they be seen in the faecal matter the remainder may be eliminated by sprinkling up to one grain of powdered santonin on the food once a week for six weeks. Possibly, some of the newer, safe anthelmintic preparations containing piperazine derivatives may be equally effective. Eye infections are common, and are usually remedied by bathing the eye well with a 4 per cent. boric acid solution or warm cod-liver oil. Continuous discharge from the nose indicates lung infection, and as a primary measure the animal should be kept warm. Bleeding can be stopped by using Friar's Balsam, and care should be taken to prevent insects settling on open wounds.

## WATER TORTOISES (TERRAPINS).

In Great Britain the tortoises that have become adapted to life in ponds and rivers are usually termed " terrapins," the name turtle being applied to marine forms. In the U.S.A. and Canada, however, not only the marine species but also terrapins and tortoises are all termed " turtles."

Several kinds of terrapin are available and capable of thriving in Great Britain. These include several American species, the European Pond Tortoise (*Emys orbicularis*), the Spanish Terrapin (*Clemmys leprosa*), the Caspian Terrapin (*Clemmys caspica*), and the Reeves' Terrapin (*Ohinemys reevesti*), which hails from China and Japan.

The ideal place in which to keep terrapins is a garden pond within an enclosure. The pond should contain an " island " of dry ground on to which the animals can climb easily. The water should vary in depth, and at one point be at least 2 ft. deep. Provided that there is a suitable " island " the boundary walls of the pond can be upright to prevent escape. The final coat of cement should be smooth and mixed with a waterproofing agent. Shade should be available, not only on the island but also in some parts of the water. This may be provided by suitable plants.

Terrapins are almost entirely carnivorous, although the young of some species may take a little lettuce or other vegetable food. Suitable foods include *small* pieces of raw meat, raw liver (this should certainly be given from time to time), fish, and earthworms. Terrapins prefer to take their food in the water, and it is best to feed them individually if there are several, to ensure that each receives his proper share.

Water tortoises also hibernate. Some bury themselves in mud or sand at the bottom of their ponds, others will dig themselves into the earth in the island or banks of their pond, while others again may go to sleep in the box that, as in the case of land tortoises, should preferably be provided for them on part of ther " land." Should they sleep at the bottom of the pond, it is as well to prevent freezing of the water. One means of doing this is to leave a log or logs floating on the surface. Moving these logs on cold mornings will help to break any ice formed and to prevent total freezing.

## AQUARIUM FISH.

There are two types of aquaria—the cold-water, for fish from this and other temperate countries, and the heated, for tropical varieties of fish. Apart from the fact that a suitable heating mechanism—usually electric, with thermostatic control—has to be maintained for tropical aquaria, the general principles governing the two types are much the same. There is a certain amount of additional initial expense in setting up a heated aquarium—the running costs are not high—but in some respects tropical fish are easier to maintain than many of the cold-water varieties.

It should be emphasised at the outset that those who want to keep fish should invest in a proper aquarium and not in a " goldfish bowl," unless the latter be very large in relation to the fish to be kept. Far too many fish suffer from overcrowding or from lack of sufficient water surface. In the case of cold freshwater fish such as carp and goldfish (which need quite different conditions from tropical fish) it has been calculated that every " 1 in. of body " requires 1 sq. ft. of water surface in order to obtain sufficient oxygen for respiration. Thus a fish the body of which (*i.e.*, the length minus the tail fins) is 4 in. will require at least 4 sq. ft. of water surface, *i.e.*, an area of 2 ft. × 2 ft. Two such fish will require twice this area, and so on. In *The Right Way to Keep Pet Fish* by R. Dutta (6s.), it is pointed out that a goldfish should normally live for twenty-five years in a suitable pond, and grow to its full length of over 14 in. There are few indoor aquaria capable of supporting many full-grown goldfish in adequate conditions, and indeed it is recommended that domestic varieties of goldfish such as shubunkins, fantails, veiltails, and orandas, which grow more slowly, are far better adapted to cold-water aquaria. Tropical fish of the varieties kept in aquaria are usually much smaller, differ in their oxygen requirements, and can be kept in more crowded conditions. Many have an average body length of only about 1¼ in., and eighteen such fish may be maintained in a suitably heated tank with an area of water surface of 18 in. × 12 in.

A beginner should not only read good books on the subject (including *Water Life* publications) but also consult experts and his local aquarist or dealer. Whatever aquarium is chosen, the conditions should be correct *before* any fish are introduced. Should fish be suddenly acquired, before a proper aquarium has been fitted up for them, they should be kept in some temporary (but sufficiently capacious) quarters until the aquarium is ready.

The instructions for installing and fitting up an aquarium are usually supplied, and should be followed carefully. The sand that is usually placed on the bottom should be thoroughly washed, and is best put in a little at a time. Make sure that the inside of the aquarium is thoroughly clean before anything at all is put into it. Ornamental rocks may next be introduced, and great care should be taken to ensure that these are of the correct type, unlikely to harm the fish physically or chemically. Water is then added very gently indeed, and suitable plants set. In the case of large tanks the planting is best done when the tank is only partly filled with water, but in any event the plants themselves should be kept wet all the time, or they may quickly shrivel up. In the case of cold-water aquaria everything may now be left for a few days—preferably a week or more—to ensure that all is well, and to allow certain micro-organisms that help form the food of the fish to develop. In the case of heated aquaria it is necessary also to ensure that the thermostat is working correctly and that the temperature is remaining constant or within very narrow limits. Here again it is advisable to wait at least a week before introducing any fish. Should conditions " go wrong " before or after the fish are introduced, it is best to start filling the tank all over again.

Fish should not be overfed, although regular feeding is essential. Attention must be paid to the feeding instructions issued with prepared fish foods, and to details given by the supplier of " live " foods. Provided fish are neither overcrowded not overfed, the amount of sediment that accumulates in the tank will not be excessive, but it should be siphoned away gently every month, or more often if necessary. Water lost by evaporation should be replaced, and in the case of heated tanks especially, it is most desirable that the added water be of the same temperature as that already in the tanks.

Certain species of water snail are often placed in aquaria to act as scavengers. It is necessary to ensure that, if snails are kept, they are of the right type, and it is important to consult experts on this matter.

Breeding is an interesting topic, there being both egg-laying and viviparous or " live-bearing " fish. The beginner is well advised to learn first how to keep fish in healthy condition in his aquarium before indulging in any planned breeding, and he should study the relevant information in books on the subject.

An aeration plant is often recommended on the grounds that it will increase the fish-carrying capacity of the aquarium. This is true up to a point, but overcrowding may bring other troubles besides those connected with lack of sufficient oxygen, and the golden rule is never to keep too many fish for the size of aquarium in question. Another factor to be remembered is that should the aerator break down it may leave the fish with less oxygen than their proper requirement. It has been recommended that an aerator is best thought of as a stand-by, to be employed only in emergencies, *e.g.*, when for some reason extra fish have to be added to a tank already holding all or almost all its proper capacity.

There are unfortunately many diseases of fish, and as yet scientific knowledge concerning many of them is far more detailed than it should be. It is clear, however, that environmental factors are responsible for many deaths or cases of unthriftiness, and among the factors concerned may be listed: overcrowding, overfeeding, the provision of a diet that is qualitatively inadequate, lack of "balance" in the aquarium leading to unsuitable conditions, dirt, too strong light, lead paint and noxious substances, that may somehow have come into contact with the water (*e.g.*, from the hands of the person tending them) or been absorbed from the atmosphere. One must be careful of such things as disinfectants, soaps, petrol, etc. In the case of tropical fish the temperature of the water may be incorrect. Should fish troubles occur, therefore, it is as well to consider these various possibilities, although one should not hesitate to seek professional advice where there appears to be a case of infectious disease. An ailing fish should certainly be removed from the tank (assuming that there are other fish present) and given separate quarters of its own if such a course is feasible.

It is not intended to provide a description of the separate diseases, although it may be mentioned that such signs as the appearance of material resembling cotton-wool (actual fungal growths) and "rotting" of the tail or fins, are among those that should lead the owner to isolate affected fish and to seek help immediately.

No attempt is made here to describe any of the many different species and varieties of fish suitable for private aquaria. Some of the " points "

LATERAL LINE — DORSAL FIN — CAUDAL OR TAIL FIN — ANAL FIN — PECTORAL FINS (PAIRED) — PELVIC OR VENTRAL FINS (PAIRED)

of a fish are shown in the accompanying illustration. Great care must be taken in mixing species, *e.g.*, " hard mouthed " and " soft mouthed " kinds should not be kept together. The temptation to put other species (*e.g.*, newts) with aquarium fish must likewise be avoided.

## CAGE BIRDS.

Very many species and varieties of birds are now maintained successfully in captivity, and there exists in Great Britain a large and expanding " cage-bird fancy," that caters for a considerable proportion of the smaller birds adapted to cage or aviary life. The increase in the numbers of budgerigars since the end of the Second World War has been phenomenal, and it was estimated during 1957 that the numbers of the species alone in the United Kingdom exceeded 6 millions, the corresponding figure for the U.S.A.—where the popular name is " parakeets "—being over 18 millions.

The different types and sizes of birds have different requirements, and in the space available it is not possible to do more than cover the general principles and to deal briefly with the special characteristics of the management of the more easily maintained species. The beginner is advised to restrict his attention to one of the better-

known species, *e.g.*, canaries or budgerigars, and not to attempt to maintain exotic varieties until he has acquired considerable experience.

Most species thrive best in aviaries, which may be indoor, outdoor, or of the combined " outdoor-indoor " type. An indoor aviary is usually all-wire and portable. The criticism of many such aviaries is that they tend to be high and narrow, whereas a fairly large floor-space is desirable. They should not be placed in cold or draughty places, nor too near a fire. If sited so as to receive much direct sunlight they must have adequate shelter. The wires must be close together, especially if smaller species are kept, a distance between them of about ⅜ in. being generally suitable. An outdoor aviary—suitable only for some species or at certain times in the case of others—should occupy a sunny position, although it too must include shade, and must be protected from winds. There ought in fact to be a sheltered portion, dry and well protected from the elements. The aviary must be strongly made and safe from all predators, including rats and mice. While it is often considered desirable to allow herbage to protrude through the wire-mesh floor, it is essential that the birds are never in close contact with wild rodents or their droppings. Most birds are highly susceptible to some forms of *salmonellosis* (see under mice and guinea-pigs), and can contract them in this way. It is advisable also that the roof of the aviary is solid: corrugated asbestos sheeting, projecting well clear of the edges of the uprights so as to prevent water and other matter from entering the interior, is excellent. The droppings of wild birds may be a potent source of bacterial infection or of internal parasites. To prevent close contact otherwise with wild birds, the wire or wire-netting " walls " of the aviary may be double. If an " outdoor-indoor " aviary is employed, there is usually an indoor flight cage, separated from the external portion either by a very light hanging door of suitable size, through which the birds can easily push their way, or by a sliding partition that the owner can operate as required.

3½" — 4½" — 5½"

SECTION THROUGH CAGE.

If an aviary is out of the question, then a suitable cage should be purchased or constructed. The cage need not be ornate—indeed simplicity of design usually facilitates the highly important task of keeping everything clean—but it must be large enough. A cross-section through a breeding-cage suitable for canaries, and for many other species, is shown in the accompanying illustration. Such a cage should measure about 40 in. in length × 12 in. wide × 18 in. high. It is constructed of wood or some suitable sheeting except for the front, which consists of vertical wires with horizontal stays, and can be divided into two parts by means of a suitable partition containing a removable section made of wire. By this means the cock and hen canaries can be introduced into the separate sections and develop a courtship before being allowed to be together for actual mating. The cross-section indicates the site and size of the removable portion of the partition, and it shows also the removable tray that is such an excellent fitting for almost any type of cage, and which greatly facilitates cleaning.

Whether an aviary or a cage is employed, it is essential to have proper fittings, including con-

PERCH.

veniently placed drinking-troughs, feeding-trays and bird-baths, and good perches. Much unnecessary discomfort is brought about through the use of unsuitable perches, or ones that are incorrectly situated or not sufficiently " firm."

NESTING-BOX WITH PLAIN WOOD BOTTOM.

A suitable type of perch, of which there should be several in the cage or aviary, is shown in the accompanying illustration, and it should be of the appropriate dimensions for the size of bird. In the case of the larger canaries (Norwich and

BIRD BATH.

Yorkshire), *e.g.*, the sectional measurements should be ½ in. × ½ in., whereas for a smaller canary (Border) they should be ⅜ in. × ⅜ in. The type of perch shown is easy to clean and does not possess awkward corners in which parasites may be harboured. The dimensions of a nesting box a bird-bath, and a feeding-tray suitable for

canaries are also given in the accompanying illustrations.

While wood is a convenient material for aviary and cage construction, it has, of course, several disadvantages. Out of doors it is best creosoted (lead paint must never be used for places in which birds or other small animals are kept), and indoors it is better lined with hard asbestos sheeting. Metal is suitable—provided that it does not rust or corrode and that the environmental conditions are warm enough.

In all cases a supply of clean, fresh water should be available. Strict cleanliness should be observed, and professional advice taken immediately if a bird is not thriving.

SEED TROUGH.

**CANARIES** (*Serinus canarius*).—These are domesticated forms of the race of wild serin found in the Canary Islands, and may live up to twenty-five years. Many varieties are known, and although most individuals are " canary yellow," other colours have been developed by fanciers. Many books have been written about the canary, although there is still much to be learned concerning its feeding and diseases—as is indeed the case with almost all cage-birds. The system of feeding generally recommended is based upon a mixture of 2 or 3 parts of canary seed (which is rich in energy, and which is sometimes mixed with a little millet seed) to 1 part of summer rape seed, which is high in fat and protein. There seems to have been some difficulty in obtaining suitable rape seed in some areas since the war. The best is German summer rape or Rübsen rape. Other seeds are employed as substitutes, or for special purposes, *e.g.*, niger is usually added at breeding time, and linseed if there is any indication of premature or soft (out-of-season) moult. Good proprietary seed mixtures are available. A little greenfood should be provided twice weekly, and a piece of cuttlefish bone placed between the wires is a suitable source of calcium. Soft-bill food (containing boiled egg, dried egg yolk, dried flies, and ants' pupæ) is also recommended by many breeders, while others give chopped egg alone. Others again favour milk, especially for young birds.

Breeding is usually started late in March or early in April, but not unless the daily shade temperature is at least 50° F. The pairs should be selected earlier than this and transferred to breeding-cages, with the partition in position. By the middle of February the wire partition may be installed so that the two birds can see one another. A little niger seed is usually added to the diet, while finely ground oystershell or eggshell may be sprinkled on the floor. (Otherwise the floor may be covered with washed sand that is not too fine and is free from dust.) When the birds begin to feed one another through the wire they are ready for mating, and the partition may be removed. The nest-box can then be inserted and suitable nesting materials, *e.g.*, cow hair and moss, placed in the cage. The incubation period is thirteen to fourteen days. After the eggs are laid some owners prefer to separate the cock and the hen, but allow him to rejoin her after the young are all about eight to nine days old and have opened their eyes. If it is desired that all the chicks be hatched together, then one can remove the first three eggs that are laid—usually one egg is laid daily—and keep them in a box at room temperature, substituting dummy eggs for them in the nest-box. On the afternoon of the third day of laying they are returned to the nest-box in place of the dummies.

When the young chicks are able to feed for themselves they should be provided with special food, such as egg and bread crumbs and a little cracked canary seed. If the cock bird interferes with them, or causes the hen to neglect them, he must be returned to his own section. Usually, however, all goes well, and the hen will go to the nest again when the first chicks are almost sixteen days old. Some three or four broods may be raised in a season.

### WAXBILLS, FINCHES, AND OTHER SEED-EATERS.

The canary is of course a finch, but most of the other " foreign finches " are considered by dealers and writers together with other types of seed-eating birds. Well over 30 species of *Avadavats, Buntings, Mannikins, Cardinals, Whydahs, Weavers,* and *Finches* of various descriptions have been maintained successfully in captivity in Great Britain. One of the most popular is the Zebra finch (*Taeniopygia castanotis*), from Australia, which has bred so successfully in this country that supplies no longer depend upon fresh importations, and which is already appearing in several varieties. The native bird, and many of its descendants, are grey and white, with red beaks. The male bird has orange cheek-patches, and orange flanks with white markings. The throat has black barring on a white background, and indeed the characteristic markings of the male have been the subject of interesting behaviour studies. The female lacks these special markings. The species is hardy, and is capable of living in outdoor aviaries all the year round, so long as it has shelter from draughts or strong winds and adequate facilities for roosting. If provided with nest-boxes, the birds will attempt—often successfully—to breed all the year round, so to avoid overbreeding it is better to remove these boxes in winter. A mixture of millet and canary seed forms the basis of their diet, which should be supplemented with fresh greenfood, millet sprays, fine grit, and cuttlebone—and, of course, fresh water should be available. Another bird suitable for the relatively uninitiated bird-keeper is the *Bengalese* (a domestic variety of *Munia striata*). It seems that these birds are the result of careful breeding by the Japanese, and may be regarded as fertile hybrids. Three main forms, the Chocolate-and-White, the Fawn-and-White, and the White, have been developed. These birds will thrive in cages or in aviaries. As in the case of Zebra Finches, they will attempt to breed all the year round if provided with nest-boxes. Bengalese are sociable birds, sometimes known in the U.S.A. as Society Finches. They appear to require less additional food than most species, thriving on a mixture of canary and millet seed, together with grit, cuttlebone, and an occasional millet spray or item of greenstuff.

For details of these birds, and of the many others from which a selection may be made, works of reference should be consulted. Three very useful books, all published by Cage Birds, London, are *Foreign Bird Keeping*, by Edward J. Boosey (63s.), *Foreign Birds for Beginners*, by D. H. S. Risdon (10s. 6d.), and *Foreign Birds for Garden Aviaries*, by Alec Brooksbank (10s. 6d.).

### BUDGERIGARS.

The increase in the popularity of this bird has been phenomenal, although to those who have experience of other birds as pets the reasons are soon fairly obvious. Apart from the capacity to talk, shown by many birds—especially males—kept alone and trained, there is a liveliness, almost a " cheekiness," and an apparent like of human companionship. The wild green budgerigar (*Melopsittacus undulatus*) exists in large numbers in the grassland and desert shrub regions of Australia. The usual colour is grass green—it is frequently known as the Grass Parakeet—with a yellow mask, with three black spots on either side. As a result of intensive breeding, a considerable number of colour varieties has been produced, and the genetics of colour are a constant source of interest to budgerigar breeders. A vast budgerigar " fancy " has been built up in the United Kingdom, the U.S.A., and other countries, and World Budgerigar Congresses are held every few years. Budgerigars will thrive in outdoor aviaries all the year round, but the vast majority are kept as indoor pets in cages or small aviaries. The cages can be similar to those used for canaries, and care should be taken that the perches are of the correct diameter. If nest-boxes are put up, and the environmental conditions are suitable, budgerigars suitably paired will breed at almost any time of the year. It is customary, however, to restrict breeding to the spring, summer, and early autumn. Overbreeding may lead to difficulties, including the production of " runners " or " French moult." The sexes may normally be distinguished, at any rate in mature individuals, by the colour of the cere at the base of the beak, which is blue in males and brown in females. Males may lose their colour if not in good condition and for other reasons.

There are now many proprietary seeds mixtures, but some owners prefer to make up their own mixtures of millet (usually mixing small yellow and large white varieties) and canary seed. Millet sprays, fresh greenfood, good grit, and cuttlebone are all desirable, and it is important that the correct size and consistency of grit be chosen. Variety in " extras " to the basal seeds diet is probably important, for the captive bird has not the same opportunities as its wild ancestors for ranging widely for, possibly, important trace items of food. Breeding birds secrete a " milk," comparable with the crop milk of pigeons and some other birds, and this is of importance in the early feeding of the young.

Most healthy budgerigars seem to live to the age of 5–7 years or more, and considerably greater ages have been attained in captivity.

Such is the development of the budgerigar fancy that most equipment as well as food can be obtained ready for use. The playful habits of budgerigars have led to their being given table-tennis balls or a variety of small toys to play with, while some forms of food are supplied as budgerigar bells or otherwise in special shapes that seem to amuse the birds as they take the constituent seed from them.

The study of budgerigar diseases is in its infancy, but already some important facts have become realised. *French moult* is certainly reproducible by overbreeding, and may be linked with deficiencies in the ability of the parent birds to feed their young—or to hand over to them at the time of laying sufficient nutritional reserves to carry them through hatching and parental feeding until the time that they can fend for themselves. A deficiency in the " milk " has been shown in some cases, and may be generally true. Large chic s can be produced by killing off or removing all but a single member of the clutch, and allowing the parents to deal with it alone.

A mite infestation, due to *Cnemidocoptes pilae*, may give rise to *Scaly face, Scaly beak,* or *Scaly leg,* for which veterinary treatment is now available. Another condition, known as *Brown hypertrophy of the cere,* is characterised by thickening and darkening of the surface of the cere. In the early stages it is sometimes thought that the bird is changing its sex. There is no known successful treatment at the time of writing, and if the overgrowth is cut away it will only reform. There are various disturbances of the *digestive tract,* and some of these may be associated with inability to stand properly.

There are many treatises on the budgerigar. A useful little work is *Budgerigar Guide,* by Cessa Feyerbrand (Fond du Lac, Wisconsin: All-Pets Magazine).

### LOVEBIRDS AND PARROTLETS

are also members of the parrot family, and while they are unlikely to equal the budgerigar in popularity, they are nevertheless interesting birds that are being kept in increasing numbers as pets. Lovebirds, of the genus *Agapornis*, are African in origin, and some six species are commonly kept in captivity. Parrotlets derive from South America, the commonest species being the Guiana Parrotlet, *Forpus passerinus.* Both types of bird are relatively simple to maintain in aviaries or large cages, and their basal diet (which should be supplemented widely) is a mixture of millet and canary seed. They are hardy and vigorous creatures, many details of which are to be found in condensed form in *Lovebirds and Parrotlets,* by C. P. Luke (London: Cage Birds, 8s. 6d.).

# CALENDAR FOR 1969.

**January**

| S | M | T | W | T | F | S |
|---|---|---|---|---|---|---|
| | | | 1 | 2 | 3 | 4 |
| 5 | 6 | 7 | 8 | 9 | 10 | 11 |
| 12 | 13 | 14 | 15 | 16 | 17 | 18 |
| 19 | 20 | 21 | 22 | 23 | 24 | 25 |
| 26 | 27 | 28 | 29 | 30 | 31 | |

**February**

| S | M | T | W | T | F | S |
|---|---|---|---|---|---|---|
| | | | | | | 1 |
| 2 | 3 | 4 | 5 | 6 | 7 | 8 |
| 9 | 10 | 11 | 12 | 13 | 14 | 15 |
| 16 | 17 | 18 | 19 | 20 | 21 | 22 |
| 23 | 24 | 25 | 26 | 27 | 28 | |

**March**

| S | M | T | W | T | F | S |
|---|---|---|---|---|---|---|
| | | | | | | 1 |
| 2 | 3 | 4 | 5 | 6 | 7 | 8 |
| 9 | 10 | 11 | 12 | 13 | 14 | 15 |
| 16 | 17 | 18 | 19 | 20 | 21 | 22 |
| 23 | 24 | 25 | 26 | 27 | 28 | 29 |
| 30 | 31 | | | | | |

**April**

| S | M | T | W | T | F | S |
|---|---|---|---|---|---|---|
| | | 1 | 2 | 3 | 4 | 5 |
| 6 | 7 | 8 | 9 | 10 | 11 | 12 |
| 13 | 14 | 15 | 16 | 17 | 18 | 19 |
| 20 | 21 | 22 | 23 | 24 | 25 | 26 |
| 27 | 28 | 29 | 30 | | | |

**May**

| S | M | T | W | T | F | S |
|---|---|---|---|---|---|---|
| | | | | 1 | 2 | 3 |
| 4 | 5 | 6 | 7 | 8 | 9 | 10 |
| 11 | 12 | 13 | 14 | 15 | 16 | 17 |
| 18 | 19 | 20 | 21 | 22 | 23 | 24 |
| 25 | 26 | 27 | 28 | 29 | 30 | 31 |

**June**

| S | M | T | W | T | F | S |
|---|---|---|---|---|---|---|
| 1 | 2 | 3 | 4 | 5 | 6 | 7 |
| 8 | 9 | 10 | 11 | 12 | 13 | 14 |
| 15 | 16 | 17 | 18 | 19 | 20 | 21 |
| 22 | 23 | 24 | 25 | 26 | 27 | 28 |
| 29 | 30 | | | | | |

**July**

| S | M | T | W | T | F | S |
|---|---|---|---|---|---|---|
| | | 1 | 2 | 3 | 4 | 5 |
| 6 | 7 | 8 | 9 | 10 | 11 | 12 |
| 13 | 14 | 15 | 16 | 17 | 18 | 19 |
| 20 | 21 | 22 | 23 | 24 | 25 | 26 |
| 27 | 28 | 29 | 30 | 31 | | |

**August**

| S | M | T | W | T | F | S |
|---|---|---|---|---|---|---|
| | | | | | 1 | 2 |
| 3 | 4 | 5 | 6 | 7 | 8 | 9 |
| 10 | 11 | 12 | 13 | 14 | 15 | 16 |
| 17 | 18 | 19 | 20 | 21 | 22 | 23 |
| 24 | 25 | 26 | 27 | 28 | 29 | 30 |
| 31 | | | | | | |

**September**

| S | M | T | W | T | F | S |
|---|---|---|---|---|---|---|
| | 1 | 2 | 3 | 4 | 5 | 6 |
| 7 | 8 | 9 | 10 | 11 | 12 | 13 |
| 14 | 15 | 16 | 17 | 18 | 19 | 20 |
| 21 | 22 | 23 | 24 | 25 | 26 | 27 |
| 28 | 29 | 30 | | | | |

**October**

| S | M | T | W | T | F | S |
|---|---|---|---|---|---|---|
| | | | 1 | 2 | 3 | 4 |
| 5 | 6 | 7 | 8 | 9 | 10 | 11 |
| 12 | 13 | 14 | 15 | 16 | 17 | 18 |
| 19 | 20 | 21 | 22 | 23 | 24 | 25 |
| 26 | 27 | 28 | 29 | 30 | 31 | |

**November**

| S | M | T | W | T | F | S |
|---|---|---|---|---|---|---|
| | | | | | | 1 |
| 2 | 3 | 4 | 5 | 6 | 7 | 8 |
| 9 | 10 | 11 | 12 | 13 | 14 | 15 |
| 16 | 17 | 18 | 19 | 20 | 21 | 22 |
| 23 | 24 | 25 | 26 | 27 | 28 | 29 |
| 30 | | | | | | |

**December**

| S | M | T | W | T | F | S |
|---|---|---|---|---|---|---|
| | 1 | 2 | 3 | 4 | 5 | 6 |
| 7 | 8 | 9 | 10 | 11 | 12 | 13 |
| 14 | 15 | 16 | 17 | 18 | 19 | 20 |
| 21 | 22 | 23 | 24 | 25 | 26 | 27 |
| 28 | 29 | 30 | 31 | | | |

# CALENDAR FOR 1970.

**January**

| S | M | T | W | T | F | S |
|---|---|---|---|---|---|---|
| | | | | 1 | 2 | 3 |
| 4 | 5 | 6 | 7 | 8 | 9 | 10 |
| 11 | 12 | 13 | 14 | 15 | 16 | 17 |
| 18 | 19 | 20 | 21 | 22 | 23 | 24 |
| 25 | 26 | 27 | 28 | 29 | 30 | 31 |

**February**

| S | M | T | W | T | F | S |
|---|---|---|---|---|---|---|
| 1 | 2 | 3 | 4 | 5 | 6 | 7 |
| 8 | 9 | 10 | 11 | 12 | 13 | 14 |
| 15 | 16 | 17 | 18 | 19 | 20 | 21 |
| 22 | 23 | 24 | 25 | 26 | 27 | 28 |

**March**

| S | M | T | W | T | F | S |
|---|---|---|---|---|---|---|
| 1 | 2 | 3 | 4 | 5 | 6 | 7 |
| 8 | 9 | 10 | 11 | 12 | 13 | 14 |
| 15 | 16 | 17 | 18 | 19 | 20 | 21 |
| 22 | 23 | 24 | 25 | 26 | 27 | 28 |
| 29 | 30 | 31 | | | | |

**April**

| S | M | T | W | T | F | S |
|---|---|---|---|---|---|---|
| | | | 1 | 2 | 3 | 4 |
| 5 | 6 | 7 | 8 | 9 | 10 | 11 |
| 12 | 13 | 14 | 15 | 16 | 17 | 18 |
| 19 | 20 | 21 | 22 | 23 | 24 | 25 |
| 26 | 27 | 28 | 29 | 30 | | |

**May**

| S | M | T | W | T | F | S |
|---|---|---|---|---|---|---|
| | | | | | 1 | 2 |
| 3 | 4 | 5 | 6 | 7 | 8 | 9 |
| 10 | 11 | 12 | 13 | 14 | 15 | 16 |
| 17 | 18 | 19 | 20 | 21 | 22 | 23 |
| 24 | 25 | 26 | 27 | 28 | 29 | 30 |
| 31 | | | | | | |

**June**

| S | M | T | W | T | F | S |
|---|---|---|---|---|---|---|
| | 1 | 2 | 3 | 4 | 5 | 6 |
| 7 | 8 | 9 | 10 | 11 | 12 | 13 |
| 14 | 15 | 16 | 17 | 18 | 19 | 20 |
| 21 | 22 | 23 | 24 | 25 | 26 | 27 |
| 28 | 29 | 30 | | | | |

**July**

| S | M | T | W | T | F | S |
|---|---|---|---|---|---|---|
| | | | 1 | 2 | 3 | 4 |
| 5 | 6 | 7 | 8 | 9 | 10 | 11 |
| 12 | 13 | 14 | 15 | 16 | 17 | 18 |
| 19 | 20 | 21 | 22 | 23 | 24 | 25 |
| 26 | 27 | 28 | 29 | 30 | 31 | |

**August**

| S | M | T | W | T | F | S |
|---|---|---|---|---|---|---|
| | | | | | | 1 |
| 2 | 3 | 4 | 5 | 6 | 7 | 8 |
| 9 | 10 | 11 | 12 | 13 | 14 | 15 |
| 16 | 17 | 18 | 19 | 20 | 21 | 22 |
| 23 | 24 | 25 | 26 | 27 | 28 | 29 |
| 30 | 31 | | | | | |

**September**

| S | M | T | W | T | F | S |
|---|---|---|---|---|---|---|
| | | 1 | 2 | 3 | 4 | 5 |
| 6 | 7 | 8 | 9 | 10 | 11 | 12 |
| 13 | 14 | 15 | 16 | 17 | 18 | 19 |
| 20 | 21 | 22 | 23 | 24 | 25 | 26 |
| 27 | 28 | 29 | 30 | | | |

**October**

| S | M | T | W | T | F | S |
|---|---|---|---|---|---|---|
| | | | | 1 | 2 | 3 |
| 4 | 5 | 6 | 7 | 8 | 9 | 10 |
| 11 | 12 | 13 | 14 | 15 | 16 | 17 |
| 18 | 19 | 20 | 21 | 22 | 23 | 24 |
| 25 | 26 | 27 | 28 | 29 | 30 | 31 |

**November**

| S | M | T | W | T | F | S |
|---|---|---|---|---|---|---|
| 1 | 2 | 3 | 4 | 5 | 6 | 7 |
| 8 | 9 | 10 | 11 | 12 | 13 | 14 |
| 15 | 16 | 17 | 18 | 19 | 20 | 21 |
| 22 | 23 | 24 | 25 | 26 | 27 | 28 |
| 29 | 30 | | | | | |

**December**

| S | M | T | W | T | F | S |
|---|---|---|---|---|---|---|
| | | 1 | 2 | 3 | 4 | 5 |
| 6 | 7 | 8 | 9 | 10 | 11 | 12 |
| 13 | 14 | 15 | 16 | 17 | 18 | 19 |
| 20 | 21 | 22 | 23 | 24 | 25 | 26 |
| 27 | 28 | 29 | 30 | 31 | | |

# CALENDAR FOR 1971.

**January**

| S | M | T | W | T | F | S |
|---|---|---|---|---|---|---|
| | | | | | 1 | 2 |
| 3 | 4 | 5 | 6 | 7 | 8 | 9 |
| 10 | 11 | 12 | 13 | 14 | 15 | 16 |
| 17 | 18 | 19 | 20 | 21 | 22 | 23 |
| 24 | 25 | 26 | 27 | 28 | 29 | 30 |
| 31 | | | | | | |

**February**

| S | M | T | W | T | F | S |
|---|---|---|---|---|---|---|
| | 1 | 2 | 3 | 4 | 5 | 6 |
| 7 | 8 | 9 | 10 | 11 | 12 | 13 |
| 14 | 15 | 16 | 17 | 18 | 19 | 20 |
| 21 | 22 | 23 | 24 | 25 | 26 | 27 |
| 28 | | | | | | |

**March**

| S | M | T | W | T | F | S |
|---|---|---|---|---|---|---|
| | 1 | 2 | 3 | 4 | 5 | 6 |
| 7 | 8 | 9 | 10 | 11 | 12 | 13 |
| 14 | 15 | 16 | 17 | 18 | 19 | 20 |
| 21 | 22 | 23 | 24 | 25 | 26 | 27 |
| 28 | 29 | 30 | 31 | | | |

**April**

| S | M | T | W | T | F | S |
|---|---|---|---|---|---|---|
| | | | | 1 | 2 | 3 |
| 4 | 5 | 6 | 7 | 8 | 9 | 10 |
| 11 | 12 | 13 | 14 | 15 | 16 | 17 |
| 18 | 19 | 20 | 21 | 22 | 23 | 24 |
| 25 | 26 | 27 | 28 | 29 | 30 | |

**May**

| S | M | T | W | T | F | S |
|---|---|---|---|---|---|---|
| | | | | | | 1 |
| 2 | 3 | 4 | 5 | 6 | 7 | 8 |
| 9 | 10 | 11 | 12 | 13 | 14 | 15 |
| 16 | 17 | 18 | 19 | 20 | 21 | 22 |
| 23 | 24 | 25 | 26 | 27 | 28 | 29 |
| 30 | 31 | | | | | |

**June**

| S | M | T | W | T | F | S |
|---|---|---|---|---|---|---|
| | | 1 | 2 | 3 | 4 | 5 |
| 6 | 7 | 8 | 9 | 10 | 11 | 12 |
| 13 | 14 | 15 | 16 | 17 | 18 | 19 |
| 20 | 21 | 22 | 23 | 24 | 25 | 26 |
| 27 | 28 | 29 | 30 | | | |

**July**

| S | M | T | W | T | F | S |
|---|---|---|---|---|---|---|
| | | | | 1 | 2 | 3 |
| 4 | 5 | 6 | 7 | 8 | 9 | 10 |
| 11 | 12 | 13 | 14 | 15 | 16 | 17 |
| 18 | 19 | 20 | 21 | 22 | 23 | 24 |
| 25 | 26 | 27 | 28 | 29 | 30 | 31 |

**August**

| S | M | T | W | T | F | S |
|---|---|---|---|---|---|---|
| 1 | 2 | 3 | 4 | 5 | 6 | 7 |
| 8 | 9 | 10 | 11 | 12 | 13 | 14 |
| 15 | 16 | 17 | 18 | 19 | 20 | 21 |
| 22 | 23 | 24 | 25 | 26 | 27 | 28 |
| 29 | 30 | 31 | | | | |

**September**

| S | M | T | W | T | F | S |
|---|---|---|---|---|---|---|
| | | | 1 | 2 | 3 | 4 |
| 5 | 6 | 7 | 8 | 9 | 10 | 11 |
| 12 | 13 | 14 | 15 | 16 | 17 | 18 |
| 19 | 20 | 21 | 22 | 23 | 24 | 25 |
| 26 | 27 | 28 | 29 | 30 | | |

**October**

| S | M | T | W | T | F | S |
|---|---|---|---|---|---|---|
| | | | | | 1 | 2 |
| 3 | 4 | 5 | 6 | 7 | 8 | 9 |
| 10 | 11 | 12 | 13 | 14 | 15 | 16 |
| 17 | 18 | 19 | 20 | 21 | 22 | 23 |
| 24 | 25 | 26 | 27 | 28 | 29 | 30 |
| 31 | | | | | | |

**November**

| S | M | T | W | T | F | S |
|---|---|---|---|---|---|---|
| | 1 | 2 | 3 | 4 | 5 | 6 |
| 7 | 8 | 9 | 10 | 11 | 12 | 13 |
| 14 | 15 | 16 | 17 | 18 | 19 | 20 |
| 21 | 22 | 23 | 24 | 25 | 26 | 27 |
| 28 | 29 | 30 | | | | |

**December**

| S | M | T | W | T | F | S |
|---|---|---|---|---|---|---|
| | | | 1 | 2 | 3 | 4 |
| 5 | 6 | 7 | 8 | 9 | 10 | 11 |
| 12 | 13 | 14 | 15 | 16 | 17 | 18 |
| 19 | 20 | 21 | 22 | 23 | 24 | 25 |
| 26 | 27 | 28 | 29 | 30 | 31 | |

# CALENDAR FOR 1972.

**January**

| S | M | T | W | T | F | S |
|---|---|---|---|---|---|---|
| | | | | | | 1 |
| 2 | 3 | 4 | 5 | 6 | 7 | 8 |
| 9 | 10 | 11 | 12 | 13 | 14 | 15 |
| 16 | 17 | 18 | 19 | 20 | 21 | 22 |
| 23 | 24 | 25 | 26 | 27 | 28 | 29 |
| 30 | 31 | | | | | |

**February**

| S | M | T | W | T | F | S |
|---|---|---|---|---|---|---|
| | | 1 | 2 | 3 | 4 | 5 |
| 6 | 7 | 8 | 9 | 10 | 11 | 12 |
| 13 | 14 | 15 | 16 | 17 | 18 | 19 |
| 20 | 21 | 22 | 23 | 24 | 25 | 26 |
| 27 | 28 | 29 | | | | |

**March**

| S | M | T | W | T | F | S |
|---|---|---|---|---|---|---|
| | | | 1 | 2 | 3 | 4 |
| 5 | 6 | 7 | 8 | 9 | 10 | 11 |
| 12 | 13 | 14 | 15 | 16 | 17 | 18 |
| 19 | 20 | 21 | 22 | 23 | 24 | 25 |
| 26 | 27 | 28 | 29 | 30 | 31 | |

**April**

| S | M | T | W | T | F | S |
|---|---|---|---|---|---|---|
| | | | | | | 1 |
| 2 | 3 | 4 | 5 | 6 | 7 | 8 |
| 9 | 10 | 11 | 12 | 13 | 14 | 15 |
| 16 | 17 | 18 | 19 | 20 | 21 | 22 |
| 23 | 24 | 25 | 26 | 27 | 28 | 29 |
| 30 | | | | | | |

**May**

| S | M | T | W | T | F | S |
|---|---|---|---|---|---|---|
| | 1 | 2 | 3 | 4 | 5 | 6 |
| 7 | 8 | 9 | 10 | 11 | 12 | 13 |
| 14 | 15 | 16 | 17 | 18 | 19 | 20 |
| 21 | 22 | 23 | 24 | 25 | 26 | 27 |
| 28 | 29 | 30 | 31 | | | |

**June**

| S | M | T | W | T | F | S |
|---|---|---|---|---|---|---|
| | | | | 1 | 2 | 3 |
| 4 | 5 | 6 | 7 | 8 | 9 | 10 |
| 11 | 12 | 13 | 14 | 15 | 16 | 17 |
| 18 | 19 | 20 | 21 | 22 | 23 | 24 |
| 25 | 26 | 27 | 28 | 29 | 30 | |

**July**

| S | M | T | W | T | F | S |
|---|---|---|---|---|---|---|
| | | | | | | 1 |
| 2 | 3 | 4 | 5 | 6 | 7 | 8 |
| 9 | 10 | 11 | 12 | 13 | 14 | 15 |
| 16 | 17 | 18 | 19 | 20 | 21 | 22 |
| 23 | 24 | 25 | 26 | 27 | 28 | 29 |
| 30 | 31 | | | | | |

**August**

| S | M | T | W | T | F | S |
|---|---|---|---|---|---|---|
| | | 1 | 2 | 3 | 4 | 5 |
| 6 | 7 | 8 | 9 | 10 | 11 | 12 |
| 13 | 14 | 15 | 16 | 17 | 18 | 19 |
| 20 | 21 | 22 | 23 | 24 | 25 | 26 |
| 27 | 28 | 29 | 30 | 31 | | |

**September**

| S | M | T | W | T | F | S |
|---|---|---|---|---|---|---|
| | | | | | 1 | 2 |
| 3 | 4 | 5 | 6 | 7 | 8 | 9 |
| 10 | 11 | 12 | 13 | 14 | 15 | 16 |
| 17 | 18 | 19 | 20 | 21 | 22 | 23 |
| 24 | 25 | 26 | 27 | 28 | 29 | 30 |

**October**

| S | M | T | W | T | F | S |
|---|---|---|---|---|---|---|
| 1 | 2 | 3 | 4 | 5 | 6 | 7 |
| 8 | 9 | 10 | 11 | 12 | 13 | 14 |
| 15 | 16 | 17 | 18 | 19 | 20 | 21 |
| 22 | 23 | 24 | 25 | 26 | 27 | 28 |
| 29 | 30 | 31 | | | | |

**November**

| S | M | T | W | T | F | S |
|---|---|---|---|---|---|---|
| | | | 1 | 2 | 3 | 4 |
| 5 | 6 | 7 | 8 | 9 | 10 | 11 |
| 12 | 13 | 14 | 15 | 16 | 17 | 18 |
| 19 | 20 | 21 | 22 | 23 | 24 | 25 |
| 26 | 27 | 28 | 29 | 30 | | |

**December**

| S | M | T | W | T | F | S |
|---|---|---|---|---|---|---|
| | | | | | 1 | 2 |
| 3 | 4 | 5 | 6 | 7 | 8 | 9 |
| 10 | 11 | 12 | 13 | 14 | 15 | 16 |
| 17 | 18 | 19 | 20 | 21 | 22 | 23 |
| 24 | 25 | 26 | 27 | 28 | 29 | 30 |
| 31 | | | | | | |